British National Bibliography

1977

The British National Bibliography has been published since 1950. The BNB Weekly Lists give in subject order the new publications of the week together with an author and title list. Full indexes under authors and titles, and subjects for the month appear in the last issue of each month. Interim cumulations are published at four-monthly intervals, providing an up-to-date reference service to books published in Great Britain. Cumulations for the periods 1950–54, 1955–59, 1960–64, 1965–67 and 1968–70 are available. A Cumulated Index for 1971–73 is also available.

British National Bibliography

A Subject Catalogue of new British books received by the Copyright Receipt Office of the British Library, arranged according to the Dewey Decimal Classification and catalogued according to the British Text of the Anglo-American Cataloguing Rules, with a full Author & Title Index, a Subject Index, and a List of Publishers

1977

Volume 1: Subject Catalogue

The British Library BIBLIOGRAPHIC SERVICES DIVISION

The British National Bibliography is compiled within
The British Library
BIBLIOGRAPHIC SERVICES DIVISION
Store Street, London WC1E 7DG
Telephone 01–636 1544
Telex 22787

ISBN 0-900220-69-4

ISSN 0007-1544

Annual subscription: Full service including cumulations and annual volume £110 (£140 overseas)

British Library Cataloguing in Publication data:
British national bibliography
1977
1. Great Britain—Imprints
I British Library. Bibliographic Services Division
015'.41 Z2001

ISBN 0-900220-69-4 Set of 2 vols.
ISSN 0007-1544

Computer-controlled phototypesetting by Computaprint Ltd London
Printed in Great Britain at the University Press, Oxford

Preface

The objects of the British National Bibliography are to list every new work published in the British Isles, to describe each work in detail and to give the subject matter of each work as precisely as possible. These operations are undertaken by a staff of qualified librarians. The material catalogued is based upon the items received, under the Copyright Act, 1911, by the Copyright Receipt Office of the British Library. Every endeavour is made to ensure the accuracy of the information given.

A few classes of publications are intentionally excluded, they are:

a) Periodicals (except the first issue of a new periodical and the first issue of a periodical under a new title, a complete list of which will be found in the Author & Title Index under the heading Periodicals)
b) Music (listed separately in the *British Catalogue of Music*)
c) Maps
d) Certain Government publications*
e) Publications without a British imprint, except those published in the Republic of Ireland†.

Hints for tracing information

This bibliography is in three sections: in the first, or Classified Subject Catalogue, the entries are arranged according to the Dewey Decimal system of subject classification; in the second the entries are arranged alphabetically by authors, titles, editors, series, etc.; the third section, the Subject Index, is an alphabetical index of subjects appearing in the Classified Subject Catalogue. The fullest information about a book is given in the Classified Subject Catalogue, including the fullest form of name used by the author in his books, the full title, the number of pages, the kind of illustrations, the size and the series as well as the edition, publisher, price and date of publication. A shorter entry is given in the Author & Title Index under the name of the author, including the short title, edition, publisher and price, the International Standard Book Number, Dewey Decimal Classification Number and BNB Serial Number.

Authors

When the author of a book is known look under his name in the Author & Title Index. The information given there will be adequate for many purposes. If the fullest information about a book is required, refer to the entry in the Classified Subject Catalogue. This is easily found by means of the first reference number (the Dewey Decimal Classification Number) at the end of any entry in the Author & Title Index. The number is read as a decimal number. Thus, for example, the number 621 will be found after the number 598.2942 and before the number 621.384.

The second reference number—the number in round brackets beginning (B77-   )—is the book's serial number in the British National Bibliography.

Sometimes entries are made under the names of countries and cities which are considered to be the authors of their official publications. Transactions, reports and journals of societies are entered under the name of the society, and anonymous works, periodicals and some year-books under the first word of the title which is not an article.

Titles, series, editors, translators, illustrators, etc.

Entries are made in the Author & Title Index under the titles of works, so that if the author is not known a work can be found by looking up its title in this Index.

If neither the author nor the title are known, it may still be possible to trace the work by means of the editor, translator, illustrator, series, etc.

Subjects

One of the most important aspects of this bibliography is its exhaustive index to the subject matter of books. The Classified Subject Catalogue itself displays the works on a subject in such a way that the whole field of literature on that subject can be easily perused. The Subject Index lists all the subjects found in the Classified Subject Catalogue and shows by means of the code number (i.e. the Dewey Decimal Classification Number) where books on those subjects are listed in the Classified Subject Catalogue. For example, in the Subject Index under the word Africa is a full list of the places in the Classified Subject Catalogue where books in any way concerned with Africa may be found, thus:

---

*Many titles published by Her Majesty's Stationery Office and included in its Selected Subscription Service to libraries are recorded in the British National Bibliography.

The following categories of very specialised material are ***not*** included in B.N.B.:

Parliamentary Papers
House of Lords Papers and Bills, House of Lords Parliamentary Debates; House of Commons Papers relating solely to the business of the House, House of Commons Parliamentary Debates, House of Commons Bills; Local Acts, Private Acts, Church Assembly Measures.

Non-Parliamentary Papers
Such routine administrative publications as:
Amendments, Appeals, Awards; Circulars; Defence Guides, Lists and Specifications; Examination Papers; Forms, Licences; Memoranda; Notices; Orders; Regulations; Returns; Tax Cases; Warrants.

†Government publications of the Republic of Ireland are not included.

Africa	Colonial administration	325.6
	East Africa. Geography	916.7
	Foreign relations with South Africa	327.6068
	Iron Age antiquities	960
	Kingship. Religious aspects	299.6
	Negro miniature wood carvings	732.2
	Southern Africa. *Guidebooks*	916.8046
	Tales and legends	398.2096
	Tropical regions. Economic development	338.967
	West Africa. Lepidoptera.	595.780966

Classification numbers

Entries in the British National Bibliography are classified by 18th edition of the Dewey Decimal Classification.

International Standard Bibliographic Description for Monographs

Entries in the Classified Subject Catalogue are prepared according to the requirements of the International Standard Bibliographic Description for Monographs (ISBD(M)). Certain abbreviations and conventions have been used. The chief of these are given in the next column. It will be found that a very precise picture of a work can be formulated and its suitability to a special need satisfactorily assessed.

Publisher and place of publication

The place of publication is always given before the name of the publisher thus:

London: Harrap.

Where there are two publishers they are shown thus:

New York: Columbia U.P.; London: Oxford U.P.

The address of a publisher is given in full in an entry if his name does not appear in the List of Publishers at the end of this volume.

Date of Publication

The year of publication is given after the publisher. 1976 [i.e. 1977] means that the book bears the date 1976 in its imprint but was actually published in 1977.

Prices

Prices given are those current at the time of appearance of an entry in the Weekly List.

Cataloguing in Publication (CIP)

When "CIP entry" appears in an annotation it indicates that the entry has been prepared from advance information supplied by the publisher and not from the book itself. CIP entries are expanded as titles are published and deposited at the Copyright Receipt Office.

International Standard Book Number

The International Standard Book Number (ISBN) relating to an individual book is given in the entry for that book in the Classified Subject Catalogue and in all related entries in the Author and Title Index. The International Standard Book Number consists of five parts: the initials ISBN; a country code; a publisher code; a title code and, finally, a 'check digit'. For example ISBN 0 406 5550 1 means:

ISBN - International Standard Book Number
0 - UK/US group of publishers
406 - Butterworths
55500 - specific title: An introduction to English legal history, by J. H. Baker
1 - the check digit (a device preventing incorrectly quoted numbers from being processed).

Collation

The collation is that part of the entry which describes the physical make-up of the book. The abbreviations used are:

v.	volumes.
p	pages. The preliminary pages, if they are separately numbered, are shown separately. For example, vii,222p. means seven preliminary pages are numbered with roman numerals and two hundred and twenty-two pages of text.
plates	pages not forming part of the main and preliminary sequences of pagination, generally containing illustrative matter, frequently numbered and sometimes on different paper.
ill	illustrations in the text or on plates.
col ill	coloured illustrations.
facsims	facsimile reproductions.
geneal table	genealogical table.
port	portrait.
cm	centimetres—used to give the height of a book.
Lp	limp cloth cover.
Ls	loose-leaf binder.
Pbd	paper board cover.
Pbk	paperback book (*i.e.* a book normally over 48 pages, sewn or perfect bound, with a drawn-on heavy-paper cover, known in the book trade as a 'Paperback').
s.l.	sine loco—no place of publication.
s.n.	sine nomine—no publisher's name.
Sd	a publication normally of not more than 48 pages, sewn, wire-stitched, or consisting of separate leaves stapled or glued together with or without a cover and requiring special storage conditions.
Sp	spiral binding.
Bibl	list of books or references used by the author or recommended by him for further study. When a bibliography occupies a distinct part of a book its pagination is given after the abbreviation.
Index	the presence of an index in a book is indicated at the end of the collation statement.

Where no indication is given as to the kind of binding it is taken to be cloth boards.

An entry fully explained will be found on the opposite page.

J. C. Downing
Director of Copyright and English Language Services.

Fürer-Haimendorf, Christoph von

Return to the naked Nagas: an anthropologist's view of Nagaland, 1936–1970 / [by] Christoph von Fürer-Haimendorf. — New ed. — London: J. Murray, 1976. — vii, 268p, [12]p of plates: ill, ports; 23cm.
Previous ed.: published as 'The naked Nagas'. London: Methuen, 1939. — Index
ISBN 0–7195–3417–8: £4.95

(B77–09512)

means

Return to the naked Nagas: an anthropologist's view of Nagaland, 1936–70, by Christoph von Fürer-Haimendorf. Published in London by John Murray in 1976, this is a new edition of the title, first published in 1939 by Methuen as 'The naked Nagas'. This present edition contains a total of 275 pages, numbered in two sequences, and 12 unnumbered pages of plates (cf note above at 'plates'), and contains also illustrations and portraits.
The book is 23cm high: i.e. demy octavo and contains an index. The International Standard Book Number is 0–7195–3417–8. The BNB number of the entry is (B77–09512).

Outline of the Dewey Decimal Classification

000 Generalities
001 Knowledge
010 Bibliographies & Catalogues
016 Bibliographies of Specific Subjects
020 Library & Information Sciences
028 Reading & Reading Aids
029 Documentation Sciences
030 Encyclopaedias
050 General Periodicals
060 General Organisations
069 Museums
070 Journalism, Publishing, Newspapers
080 General Collections
090 Rare Books

100 Philosophy & Related Disciplines
110 Metaphysics
130 Popular Psychology, Parapsychology, Occultism
150 Psychology
160 Logic
170 Ethics
180 Ancient, Medieval & Oriental Philosophy
190 Modern Western Philosophy

200 Religion
210 Natural Religion
220 Bible
230 Christian Doctrine
270 Christian Church. Historical & Geographical Treatment
280 Christian Church, Denominations & Sects
290 Non-Christian Religions

300 Social Sciences
301 Sociology
301.1 Social Psychology
309 Social Conditions
310 Statistics
320 Political Science
327 International Relations
330 Economics
340 Law
350 Public Administration
355 Military Forces
358.4 Air Forces
359 Naval Forces
360 Social Services
364 Criminology
368 Insurance
370 Education
380 Commerce
390 Custom & Folklore

400 Languages
410 Linguistics
420 English Language
430 Germanic Languages
440 Romance Languages
470 Italic Languages
480 Classical Languages & Modern Greek
490 Other Languages

500 Science
510 Mathematics
520 Astronomy
526 Geodesy
527 Celestial Navigation
530 Physics
540 Chemistry
548 Crystallography
549 Mineralogy
550 Earth Sciences
551.5 Meteorology
560 Palaeontology
570 Life Sciences
572 Ethnology
573 Physical Anthropology
574 Biology
580 Botanical Sciences
590 Zoological Sciences

600 Technology
610 Medical Sciences
620 Engineering
630 Agriculture
634.9 Forestry
635 Gardening
636 Livestock, Domestic Animals
639 Hunting, Trapping, Fishing
640 Household Management
647 Institutional Management
650 Business Practices
657 Accounting
658 Management
660 Chemical Technology
664 Food Manufactures
669 Metallurgy
670 Manufactures
690 Building

700 Fine Arts
710 Civic & Landscape Art
711 Town and Country Planning
720 Architecture
730 Sculpture & Plastic Arts
737 Numismatics
740 Drawing & Decorative Arts
750 Painting
760 Graphic Arts
770 Photography
780 Music
790 Recreation
791 Public Entertainment
793 Indoor Games & Amusements
796 Sports & Games

800 Literature
810 American Literature
820 English Literature
830 Germanic Literatures
840 Romance Literatures
870 Italic Literatures
880 Classical & Modern Greek Literatures
890 Other Literatures

900 Geography, History & their Auxiliaries
910 Geography & Travel
920 Biography
929 Genealogy & Heraldry
930 Ancient History
940 History. Europe
950 History. Asia
960 History. Africa
970 History. North America
980 History. South America
990 History. Oceania, etc.
999 History. Extraterrestial Worlds

Classified subject catalogue

001.2 — SCHOLARSHIP AND LEARNING
001.2 — Scholarship. *Festschriften*
From Parnassus : essays in honor of Jacques Barzun / edited by Dora B. Weiner and William R. Keylor. — New York [etc.] ; London : Harper and Row, [1977]. — xxii, 386p : music, ports ; 24cm.
Published in the United States: 1976. — Bibl.: p.353-376.
ISBN 0-06-014549-8 : £9.75
(B77-12807)

001.2′092′4 — Scholarship. Powell, Lawrence Fitzroy. *Oxfordshire. Oxford. Biographies*
Simmons, John Simon Gabriel. Lawrence Fitzroy Powell, 1881-1975 : a tribute / [by J.S.G. Simmons]. — Oxford (All Souls College, Oxford) : The author, 1977. — 10p : port ; 21cm.
Limited ed. of 154 numbered copies. — 'Reprinted ... from "The New Rambler", Journal of the Johnson Society of London, 1976' - title page verso.
ISBN 0-9504373-1-x Sd : Unpriced
(B77-23043)

001.3 — HUMANITIES
001.3′01 — Humanities. *Philosophical perspectives*
Bird, Otto. Cultures in conflict : an essay in the philosophy of the humanities / [by] Otto A. Bird. — Notre Dame ; London : University of Notre Dame Press, 1976. — xii,220p ; 24cm.
Bibl.: p.207-214. — Index.
ISBN 0-268-00713-6 : £11.20
(B77-05160)

001.3′07′2 — Humanities. Research organisations: Overseas institutes sponsored by British Academy
British Academy. A handbook to the British schools and institutes abroad / [British Academy]. — [London] : The Academy, 1977. — 46p ; 25cm.
ISBN 0-85672-146-8 Sd : £1.25
(B77-14505)

001.3′07′2 — Humanities. Research projects using digital computer systems. *Directories*
Computer-assisted research in the humanities : a directory of scholars active / edited by Joseph Raben. — New York [etc.] ; Oxford : Pergamon, 1977. — [7],251p ; 29cm.
Index.
ISBN 0-08-019870-8 : £27.50
(B77-27625)

001.4 — METHODOLOGY AND RESEARCH
001.4′2 — Problem solving. *Manuals*
Jackson, Keith Frederic. The art of solving problems / [by] K.F. Jackson. — London : Teach Yourself Books, 1977. — xi,244p : ill ; 18cm. — (Teach yourself books)
Originally published: London : Heinemann, 1975. — Bibl.: p.235-236. Index.
ISBN 0-340-21256-x Pbk : £1.25
(B77-00559)

001.4′22 — Statistics. *Secondary school texts*
Moss, Peter, *b.1921.* Statistics alive / [by] Peter Moss & Owen Perry ; [illustrated by Michael White]. — Cambridge : Hobson's Press [for] Careers Research and Advisory Centre, 1976. — 64p : ill, maps ; 30cm.
Cover title. — Bibl.: p.64. — Index.
ISBN 0-86021-058-8 Pbk : £1.25
(B77-01958)

001.4′24 — Continuous systems. Simulations. Applications of computer systems
Smith, Jon Michael. Mathematical modeling and digital simulation for engineers and scientists / [by] Jon M. Smith. — New York ; London [etc.] : Wiley, 1977. — xv,332p : ill ; 24cm.
'A Wiley-Interscience publication'. — Index.
ISBN 0-471-80344-8 : Unpriced
(B77-24640)

001.4′24 — Mathematical models. Applications of digital computer systems. Programming languages: GPSS language
Bobillier, P A. Simulation with GPSS and GPSS V / [by] P.A. Bobillier, B.C. Kahan, A.R. Probst. — Englewood Cliffs ; London [etc.] : Prentice-Hall, 1976. — xvi,495p : ill ; 24cm.
Index..
ISBN 0-13-810549-9 : £13.50
(B77-03860)

001.4′24 — Operations research
Gillett, Billy E. Introduction to operations research : a computer-oriented algorithmic approach / [by] Billy E. Gillett. — New York ; London [etc.] : McGraw-Hill, 1976. — xv, 617p : ill ; 25cm. — (McGraw-Hill series in industrial engineering and management science)
Bibl. — Index.
ISBN 0-07-023245-8 : £15.35
(B77-04513)

001.4′24 — Operations research. Mathematical models
Cooper, Leon. Introduction to operations research models / by Leon Cooper, U. Narayan Bhat, Larry J. LeBlanc. — Philadelphia ; London [etc.] : Saunders, 1977. — ix,404p : ill, map, plan ; 26cm.
Index.
ISBN 0-7216-2688-2 : £12.25
(B77-22301)

001.4′24 — Operations research. Techniques: PERT. Time estimates. Reliability. Mathematical models
Davies, Emily Mary. The effects of uncertainty in the time estimates for PERT / [by] E.M. Davies. — [Birmingham] ([P.O. Box 363, Birmingham B15 2TT]) : University of Birmingham, Environmental Modelling and Survey Unit, 1977. — [2],5 leaves ; 30cm.
ISBN 0-7044-0272-6 Sd : £0.25
(B77-26726)

001.4′24 — Problem solving. Applications of digital computer systems. Programming languages: Fortran language
Spencer, Donald Dean. Problem solving with FORTRAN / [by] Donald D. Spencer. — Englewood Cliffs ; London [etc.] : Prentice-Hall, 1977. — xiv,320p : ill ; 24cm.
Bibl.: p.310-311. — Index.
ISBN 0-13-720094-3 Pbk : £7.95
(B77-23044)

001.4′24 — Problem solving. Applications of digital computer systems. Programming languages: PL/1 language
Kieburtz, Richard B. Structural programming and problem-solving with PL-1 / [by] Richard B. Kieburtz. — Englewood Cliffs ; London [etc.] : Prentice-Hall, 1977. — xv,348p : ill ; 24cm.
Index.
ISBN 0-13-854943-5 Pbk : £7.95
(B77-23045)

001.4′24 — Problem solving. Mathematical models
Haberman, Richard. Mathematical models : mechanical vibrations, population dynamics and traffic flow : (an introduction to applied mathematics) / [by] Richard Haberman. — Englewood Cliffs ; London [etc.] : Prentice-Hall, 1977. — xiii,402p : ill, chart ; 24cm.
Bibl. — Index.
ISBN 0-13-561738-3 : £15.15
(B77-23046)

001.4′24 — Problem solving. Simulations. Applications of digital computer systems
Poole, T G. Using simulation to solve problems / [by] T.G. Poole, J.Z. Szymankiewicz. — London [etc.] : McGraw-Hill, 1977. — x,333p : ill, facsims ; 26cm.
With solutions to exercises. — Bibl.: p.327. — Index.
ISBN 0-07-084472-0 : £10.00
(B77-23047)

001.4′3′02541 — Research institutions. *Great Britain. Directories*
United Kingdom research establishments / [Data Research Group]. — Amersham (Hill House, [Hill Ave.], Amersham, Bucks.) : The Group. 1976. — 1976. — 61 leaves in various pagings ; 30cm.
ISBN 0-905570-73-1 Sp : Unpriced
(B77-07757)

001.4′3′0941 — Research by Great Britain. Department of the Environment. *Directories*
Great Britain. *Department of the Environment.* Register of research / Department of the Environment. — London (2 Marsham St., SW1P 3EB) : Headquarters Library, Department of the Environment.
1976. Part 1 : Building and construction. — 1976. — [2],iv,227p ; 30cm.
Index.
ISBN 0-7184-0038-0 Pbk : Unpriced
(B77-12254)

1976. Part 2 : Environmental planning. — 1976. — [2],viii,390p ; 30cm.
Index.
ISBN 0-7184-0039-9 Pbk : Unpriced
(B77-12255)

1976. Part 3 : Roads and transport. — Crowthorne (Crowthorne, Berks. [RG11 6AU] : Technical Information and Library Services, Transport and Road Research Laboratory, 1976. — vi,416p ; 30cm.
Index.
ISBN 0-7184-0040-2 Pbk : Unpriced
(B77-12256)

1976. Part 4 : Environmental pollution. — 1976. — [2],vii,255p ; 30cm.
Index.
ISBN 0-7184-0041-0 Pbk : Unpriced
(B77-12257)

001.4'3'0942498 — Research by Lanchester Polytechnic. *Reports, surveys. Serials*
Lanchester Polytechnic. Research report / Lanchester Polytechnic. — Coventry [etc.] (Priory St., Coventry CV1 5FB) : [The Polytechnic].
1973-1975. — [1975]. — 175p ; 22cm.
Pbk : Unpriced
(B77-16691)

001.4'34'0182 — Experiments. Design. Statistical methods
Montgomery, Douglas C. Design and analysis of experiments / [by] Douglas C. Montgomery. — New York ; London [etc.] : Wiley, 1976. — xiv,418p : ill ; 24cm.
Bibl.: p.387-391. — Index.
ISBN 0-471-61421-1 : £13.50
(B77-06404)

001.5 — INFORMATION AND COMMUNICATION
001.5 — Communication. *Juvenile literature*
Ramsbottom, Edward. News / [by] Edward Ramsbottom and Joan Redmayne ; illustrated by Mark Peppé. — London [etc.] : Macmillan, 1977. — 16p : col ill ; 30cm. — (Bright ideas)
ISBN 0-333-19639-2 Sd : £0.48
(B77-19953)

001.5'01'4 — Man. Communication. Linguistic aspects
Greene, Judith. Communication / prepared for the [Open University Social Psychology] Course Team by Judith Greene ; preface by Richard Stevens. — Milton Keynes : Open University Press, 1976. — 68p : ill ; 30cm. — (Social sciences, a third level course : social psychology ; block 11) (D305 ; block 11 (22-23))
Bibl.: p.65-68.
ISBN 0-335-07110-4 Pbk : £0.90
(B77-26059)

001.5'028 — Communication equipment. *Juvenile literature*
Milsome, John. Machines and communication / [by] John Milsome ; illustrated by Harry Sheldon. — London [etc.] : Burke, 1977. — 32p : col ill ; 22cm. — (The world of machines)
ISBN 0-222-00508-4 : £1.60
ISBN 0-222-00509-2 Pbk : £1.00
(B77-31647)

001.5'08 — Communication. *Lectures, speeches*
The **art** and business of communication / by James Cameron ... et al. — Edinburgh ([Chambers St., Edinburgh EH1 1HX]) : Heriot-Watt University, 1976. — [8],72p ; 21cm. — (Heriot-Watt University. Lectures ; 1976)
Cover title.
ISBN 0-901658-37-5 Pbk : £1.75
(B77-11013)

001.5'0999 — Man. Communication with extraterrestrial life. Data banks installed by man on extrasolar planets
Saunders, Michael William. Databank for an inhabited extrasolar planet : purpose, indication and installation / [by M.W. Saunders]. — Caterham (Caterham, Surrey) : Downs Books, 1976. — 18 columns : ill ; 21x30cm.
ISBN 0-9502260-7-6 Sd : £0.40
(B77-04514)

001.53 — Cybernetics
George, Frank Honywill. The foundations of cybernetics / [by] F.H. George. — London [etc.] : Gordon and Breach, 1977. — xiv,286p : ill ; 24cm.
Bibl.: p.267-275. — Index.
ISBN 0-677-05340-1 : £13.70
(B77-05807)

001.53 — Cybernetics. *Conference proceedings*
Progress in cybernetics and systems research. — Washington, D.C. : Hemisphere Publishing Corporation ; New York ; London [etc.] : Wiley.
'This Symposium was organized by the Austrian Society for Cybernetic Studies in cooperation with [the] Society for General Systems Research [and the] International Association of Cybernetics' - note. — In 2 vols.

Vol.2 : Socio-economic systems, cybernetics of cognition and learning, systems education, cybernetics in organization and management, special aspects / edited by Robert Trappl and F. de P. Hanika ; with introduction by Stafford Beer. — 1975. — x,442p : ill ; 29cm.
'A Halsted Press book'. — Includes papers in German. — Bibl. — Index.
ISBN 0-470-88476-2 : £17.45
Also classified at 003
(B77-10083)

001.53 — Cybernetics. Environmental aspects
George, Frank Honywill. Cybernetics and the environment / [by] F.H. George. — London : Elek, 1977. — vi,71p ; 22cm. — (Environmental studies)
Bibl.: p.70. — Index.
ISBN 0-236-40021-5 Pbk : £2.95
(B77-28323)

001.53'3 — Pattern recognition. *Conference proceedings*
Joint Workshop on Pattern Recognition and Artificial Intelligence, *Hyannis, 1976.* Pattern recognition and artificial intelligence / edited by C.H. Chen. — New York [etc.] ; London : Academic Press, 1976 [i.e. 1977]. — ix,621p : ill ; 24cm.
'The Joint Workshop on Pattern Recognition and Artificial Intelligence ... held June 1-3, 1976, at Hyannis, Massachusetts' - Preface. — Published in the United States: 1976. — Bibl. — Index.
ISBN 0-12-170950-7 : £20.25
Also classified at 001.53'5
(B77-14506)

001.53'3 — Self-organising systems
Nicolis, G. Self-organization in nonequilibrium systems : from dissipative structures to order through fluctuations / [by] G. Nicolis, I. Prigogine. — New York ; London [etc.] : Wiley, 1977. — xiii,491p : ill ; 24cm.
'A Wiley-Interscience publication'. — Bibl.: p.475-486. — Index.
ISBN 0-471-02401-5 : £20.00
(B77-26727)

001.53'5 — Artificial intelligence
Boden, Margaret A. Artificial intelligence and natural man / [by] Margaret A. Boden. — Hassocks : Harvester Press, 1977. — xv,537p : ill ; 25cm.
Bibl.: p.475-494. — Index.
ISBN 0-85527-435-2 : £13.50 : CIP rev.
(B77-08160)

Machine intelligence. — Chichester : Ellis Horwood ; New York ; London [etc.] : [Distributed by] Wiley.
8 / edited by E.W. Elcock and Donald Michie. — 1977. — 630p : ill ; 26cm.
Bibl. — Index.
ISBN 0-85312-058-7 : £24.00
(B77-29861)

001.53'5 — Artificial intelligence. *Conference proceedings*
Joint Workshop on Pattern Recognition and Artificial Intelligence, *Hyannis, 1976.* Pattern recognition and artificial intelligence / edited by C.H. Chen. — New York [etc.] ; London : Academic Press, 1976 [i.e. 1977]. — ix,621p : ill ; 24cm.
'The Joint Workshop on Pattern Recognition and Artificial Intelligence ... held June 1-3, 1976, at Hyannis, Massachusetts' - Preface. — Published in the United States: 1976. — Bibl. — Index.
ISBN 0-12-170950-7 : £20.25
Primary classification 001.53'3
(B77-14506)

001.54'2 — Speech
Jeffrey, Robert C. Speech : a text with adapted readings / [by] Robert C. Jeffrey, Owen Peterson. — 2nd ed. — New York [etc.] ; London : Harper and Row, [1976]. — xiii, 473p : col ill ; 24cm.
Published in the United States: 1975. — Previous ed.: 1971. — Bibl. — Index.
ISBN 0-06-043277-2 : £9.50
(B77-08161)

001.54'36 — Codes & ciphers. *Juvenile literature*
Lamb, Geoffrey. Your book of secret writing / [by] Geoffrey Lamb. — London : Faber, 1976. — 80p : ill ; 16x22cm.
Index.
ISBN 0-571-10777-x : £2.30
(B77-01109)

Travis, Falcon. Knight book of secret codes / [by] Falcon Travis. — Leicester : Knight Books, 1977. — 96p : ill ; 18cm.
Cover title: Secret codes.
ISBN 0-340-19778-1 Pbk : £0.50
(B77-06405)

001.54'36'09 — Cryptology, to 1972
Kahn, David. The codebreakers / [by] David Kahn. — Abridged [ed.]. — London : Sphere, 1977. — xvi,476p : ill, facsims ; 18cm.
Abridged ed. originally published: 1973. — Bibl.: p.458-459. — Index.
ISBN 0-7221-5149-7 Pbk : £1.25
(B77-32346)

001.54'36'09 — Cryptology, to 1976
Way, Peter. Codes and ciphers / [by] Peter Way. — London : Aldus Books, 1977. — 144p : ill(some col), facsims, ports(some col) ; 27cm. — (Undercover)
Index.
ISBN 0-490-00372-9 : £3.95
(B77-11014)

001.55 — Limestone mines. Graffiti. *Wiltshire. Box. Reports, surveys*
Cotham Spelaeological Society. Scripta legenda : (Box quarries - Wiltshire) / surveyed and produced by members of the Cotham Spelaeological Society ; edited by R.J. Tucker. — [S.l.] (c/o R.J. Tucker, 18 Springfield Grove, Westbury Park, Bristol 6) : Free Troglophile Association.
Vol.1 : Lower Hill series. — 1976. — [1],40p, fold plate : maps ; 26cm.
ISBN 0-9505630-0-5 Sd : £0.90
(B77-11015)

001.55'2 — Information sources: Theses
Davinson, Donald Edward. Theses and dissertations as information sources / [by] Donald Davinson. — London : Bingley [etc.], 1977. — 88p ; 23cm.
Bibl. — Index.
ISBN 0-85157-227-8 : £3.00
(B77-15054)

001.55'2'0937 — Books. *Ancient Rome*
Dilke, Oswald Ashton Wentworth. Roman books and their impact / by O.A.W. Dilke. — Leeds (10 Elmete Ave., Leeds LS8 2JX) : Elmete Press, 1977. — ix,95p,[24]p of plates : ill(some col), facsims ; 26cm.
'... an adapted and enlarged version of the Sir D. Owen Evans Memorial Lectures, given at the University College of Wales, Aberystwyth ...' - Acknowledgements. — Limited ed. of 460 numbered copies. — Bibl.: p.87-88. — Index.
£41.00
(B77-28324)

001.56 — Diagrams
Albarn, Keith. Diagram : the instrument of thought / [by] Keith Albarn, Jenny Miall Smith. — London : Thames and Hudson, 1977. — 144p : ill(some col) ; 29cm.
Bibl.: p.139-140. — Index.
ISBN 0-500-01186-9 : £6.50
(B77-26060)

001.56 — Pictographs. *Illustrations*
Handbook of pictorial symbols : 3,250 examples from international sources / [compiled by] Rudolf Modley, with the assistance of William R. Myers. — New York : Dover Publications [etc.] ; London : Constable, 1976. — iii-xiv, 143p : chiefly ill, map ; 28cm. — (Dover pictorial archive series)
Bibl.: p.xi. — Index.
ISBN 0-486-23357-x Pbk : £2.50
(B77-25337)

001.56 — Signs & symbols. *Primary school texts*
Ramsbottom, Edward. Looking for signs / [by] Edward Ramsbottom and Joan Redmayne ; illustrated by Desmond Knight. — London [etc.] : Macmillan, 1977. — 16p : col ill ; 30cm. — (Bright ideas)
ISBN 0-333-19642-2 Sd : £0.48
(B77-23941)

001.6 — DATA PROCESSING

001.6'02'4658 — Data processing. *For management*

Oliver, E C. Data processing : an instructional manual for business and accountancy students / [by] E.C. Oliver, R.J. Chapman. — Winchester (4 Amport Close, Harestock, Winchester, Hants.) : D.P. Publications, 1975. — vii,200p : ill, form ; 25cm.
Previous ed.: 1973. — Index.
ISBN 0-905435-00-1 Pbk : Unpriced
(B77-04515)

Oliver, E C. Data processing : an instructional manual for business and accountancy students / [by] E.C. Oliver, R.J. Chapman. — Winchester (4 Amport Close, [Harestock], Winchester, Hants. SO22 6LP) : D.P. Publications.
Progress test supplement : comprising answers to 45 questions from examinations of the major accountancy bodies up to and including 1976. — 1976. — [2],24,[1]p : ill, form ; 21cm.
ISBN 0-905435-02-8 Sd : Unpriced
(B77-04516)

001.6'03 — Data processing. *Glossaries*

British Standards Institution. Glossary of terms used in data processing = Lexique des termes utilisés dans le traitement de l'information = Lexikon der Begriffe der Datenverarbeitung / British Standards Institution. — London : B.S.I.
ISO title: Data processing vocabulary.
Part 2 = Partie 2 = Teil 2 : Arithmetic and logic operations = Opérations arithmétiques et logiques = Arithmetische und logische Operationen. — 1st revision. — 1976. — [2], 18p ; 30cm. — (BS3527 : Part 2 : 1976) (ISO 2382/11-1976)
Pierced for binder. — Index.
ISBN 0-580-09238-0 Sd : £4.00
(B77-00560)

British Standards Institution. Glossary of terms used in data processing = Lexique des term[e]s utilisés dans le traitement de l'information = Lexikon der Begriffe der Datenverarbeitung / British Standards Institution. — London : B.S.I.
ISO title: Data processing vocabulary.
Part 3 = Partie 3 = Teil 3 : Equipment technology (selected terms) = Matériels et technologie (sélection des termes) = Einrichtungstechnik (ausgewählte Begriffe). — 1st revision. — 1976. — [2],6p ; 30cm. — (BS3527 : Part 3 : 1976) (ISO2382/111-1976)
Pierced for binder. — Index.
ISBN 0-580-09088-4 Sd : £1.50
(B77-00561)

British Standards Institution. Glossary of terms used in data processing = Lexique des termes utilisés dans le traitement de l'information = Lexikon der Begriffe der Datenverarbeitung / British Standards Institution. — London : B.S.I.
Part 7 = Partie 7 = Teil 7 : Digital computer programming = Programmation des calculateurs numériques = Programmierung von Digitalrechnern. — 1st revision. — 1977. — [2],19,[2]p ; 30cm. — (BS3527 : Part 7 : 1977) (ISO 2382/VII-1977)
'ISO title: Data processing - Vocabulary - Section 07 : Digital computer programming'. — Pierced for binder. — Index.
ISBN 0-580-09526-6 Sd : £4.70
(B77-33005)

001.6'3'024658 — Automatic data processing systems. *Manuals. For management*

Automatic data processing handbook / edited by the Diebold Group, Inc. — New York ; London [etc.] : McGraw-Hill, 1977. — 988p in various pagings : ill, forms, map, plan ; 24cm.
Bibl. — Index.
ISBN 0-07-016807-5 : £22.15
(B77-26728)

001.6'4 — Computer sciences

Brady, J M. The theory of computer science : a programming approach / [by] J.M. Brady. — London : Chapman and Hall [etc.], 1977. — xiii,287p : ill ; 24cm.
'A Halsted Press book'. — Bibl.: p.272-280. — Index.
ISBN 0-412-14930-3 : £7.50
ISBN 0-412-15040-9 Pbk : £3.95
(B77-21649)

001.6'4 — Computer systems

Bartee, Thomas Creson. Introduction to computer science / [by] Thomas Bartee. — Tokyo ; London [etc.] : McGraw-Hill Kogakusha, 1975 [i.e. 1977]. — xi,404p : ill ; 21cm.
Originally published: New York ; London : McGraw-Hill, 1975. — Bibl.: p.393-399. — Index.
ISBN 0-07-085033-x Pbk : £5.50
(B77-23048)

Davis, Gordon Bitter. Computer data processing / [by] Gordon B. Davis. — 2nd ed. — New York ; London [etc.] : McGraw-Hill, 1973. — x,662p : ill(chiefly col), forms(some col) ; 25cm.
Previous ed.: 1969. — Bibl.: p.645-656. — Index.
ISBN 0-07-015785-5 : Unpriced
(B77-19151)

Emery, Glyn. Elements of computer science / [by] Glyn Emery with additional material by David Bale. — London : Pitman, 1977. — vi, 2-153p : ill ; 25cm.
Bibl.: p.150. — Index.
ISBN 0-273-00246-5 Pbk : £2.95 : CIP rev.
(B77-07006)

Laver, Frederick John Murray. Introducing computers / by Murray Laver ; [for the] Civil Service Department. — 3rd ed. — London : H.M.S.O., 1976. — [4],65p,12p of plates : ill ; 25cm.
Previous ed.: 1973. — Bibl.: p.61. — Index.
ISBN 0-11-630333-6 Pbk : £1.50
(B77-14507)

Piper, Roger. The story of computers / [by] Roger Piper. — Revised ed. — London [etc.] : Hodder and Stoughton, 1977. — 95p : ill, map ; 21cm.
Previous ed.: i.e. 2nd revised ed. London : Brockhampton Press, 1970. — Index.
£2.95
ISBN 0-340-03863-2
(B77-06406)

Race, John. Computer-based systems / [by] John Race. — Sevenoaks : Teach Yourself Books, 1977 [i.e. 1976]. — vii,216p : ill, forms ; 18cm. — (Teach yourself books)
Bibl.: p.211-. — Index.
ISBN 0-340-20772-8 Pbk : £1.50
(B77-00562)

001.6'4 — Computer systems. *Conference proceedings*

Computer Systems and Technology *(Conference), University of Sussex, 1977.* Proceedings of the conference on Computer Systems and Technology, [held] Tuesday 29th to Thursday 31st March 1977 [at the] University of Sussex : organized by the Institution of Electronic and Radio Engineers with the association of ... [others]. — London (8 Bedford Sq., WC1B 8RG) : I.E.R.E., 1977. — viii,283p : ill ; 30cm. — (Institution of Electronic and Radio Engineers. Conference proceedings ; no.36)
Cover title: Conference on computer systems and technology.
ISBN 0-903748-31-2 Pbk : £15.00
(B77-17848)

International Computing Symposium, *5th, Liège, 1977.* International Computing Symposium 1977 : proceedings of the International Computing Symposium 1977, Liège, Belgium, 4-7 April 1977, organized by the European Chapters of the Association for Computing Machinery (ACM) with the support of the European Cooperation in Informatics (ECI) / edited by E. Morlet and D. Ribbens. — Amsterdam [etc.] ; Oxford : North-Holland Publishing Co., 1977. — iii-xi,613p : ill ; 27cm.
'... the fifth [symposium] of its kind ...' - Foreword. — Bibl.
ISBN 0-7204-0741-9 : £28.10
(B77-26729)

001.6'4 — Computer systems. *Juvenile literature*

Law, Felicia. Computers / written by Felicia Law ; illustrated by Stephen Cartwright. — London [etc.] : Collins, 1977. — 32p : col ill ; 22cm. — (Dandelions)
ISBN 0-00-651307-7 Sd : £0.50
(B77-29862)

001.6'4 — Computer systems. *Reviews of research*

Advances in computers. — New York [etc.] ; London : Academic Press.
Vol.15 / edited by Morris Rubinoff and Marshall C. Yovits. — 1976. — xiii,301p ; 24cm.
Bibl. — Index.
ISBN 0-12-012115-8 : £17.40
(B77-03861)

001.6'4 — Computer systems. *Secondary school texts*

Scottish Computers in Schools Project. The computer, yours obediently / Scottish Computers in Schools Project. — Edinburgh [etc.] : W. and R. Chambers.
Book 2 : Man uses the computer. — Revised ed. — 1977. — 119p : ill, forms(some col), map ; 19x24cm.
Previous ed.: 1973.
ISBN 0-550-77121-2 Pbk : £1.60
(B77-33552)

001.6'4 — Computer systems. Design. *Conference proceedings*

International Workshop on Modelling and Performance Evaluation of Computer Systems, *2nd, Stresa, 1976.* Modelling and performange [i.e. performance] evaluation of computer systems : proceedings of the international workshop organized by the Commission of the European Communities Joint Research Centre, Ispra Establishment, Department A, Ispra (Varese), Italy, October 4-6, 1976 / edited by H. Beilner and E. Gelenbe. — Amsterdam [etc.] ; Oxford : North-Holland Publishing Co., 1977. — x,515p : ill ; 23cm.
'... the Second International Workshop on Modelling and Performance Evaluation of Computer Systems which took place in Stresa on October 4-6, 1976 ...' - Foreword. — Bibl. — Index.
ISBN 0-7204-0554-8 : £19.00
(B77-19954)

001.6'4 — Computer systems. Evaluation

Svobodova, Liba. Computer performance measurement and evaluation methods : analysis and applications / [by] Liba Svobodova. — New York ; Oxford [etc.] : Elsevier, 1976. — xiii,146p : ill ; 24cm. — (Elsevier computer science library : computer design and architecture series ; 2)
Bibl. — Index.
ISBN 0-444-00192-1 : £8.67
ISBN 0-444-00197-2 Pbk : £4.00
(B77-07007)

001.6'4'03 — Computer systems. *Dictionaries*

Chandor, Anthony. A dictionary of computers / [by] Anthony Chandor with John Graham, Robin Williamson. — 2nd ed. — Harmondsworth [etc.] : Penguin, 1977. — 440p ; 19cm.
Previous ed.: 1970.
Pbk : £1.00
ISBN 0-14-051039-7
(B77-07008)

001.6'4'03 — Computer systems. *Glossaries*

A **glossary** of computing terms for introductory courses / [produced by a Working Party of the Schools Committee of the British Computer Society]. — London : The Society. 1977. — [1977]. — [2],27p ; 21cm.
Index.
ISBN 0-901865-19-2 Sd : £0.50
(B77-29108)

001.6'4044 — Digital computer systems

Bohl, Marilyn. Information processing / [by] Marilyn Bohl. — 2nd ed. — Chicago ; Henley-on-Thames [etc.] : Science Research Associates, 1976. — x,438p : ill(some col) ; 24cm.
Previous ed.: 1971. — Bibl. — Index.
ISBN 0-574-21040-7 Pbk : £6.25
(B77-00563)

Bohl, Marilyn. Information processing / [by] Marilyn Bohl. — 2nd ed. — Chicago ; Henley-on-Thames [etc.] : Science Research Associates.
Previous ed.: 1971.
Instructor's guide. — 1976. — [2],79,126p : ill ; 28cm.
ISBN 0-574-21041-5 Pbk : £2.05
(B77-00564)

Study guide. — 1976. — [5],160p : ill, forms ; 24cm.
Fill in book. — With answers.
ISBN 0-574-21042-3 Pbk : £3.45
(B77-00565)

Davis, Gordon Bitter. Introduction to computers / [by] Gordon B. Davis. — 3rd ed. — New York ; London [etc.] : McGraw-Hill, 1977. — xi,781p : ill, facsims ; 25cm.
With answers to self-testing quizzes. — Previous ed.: published as 'Introduction to electronic computers'. 1971. — Bibl.: p.755-762. — Index.
ISBN 0-07-015825-8 : £12.70
(B77-33006)

Fry, Thomas Frederick. Further computer appreciation / [by] T.F. Fry. — London [etc.] : Newnes-Butterworths, 1977. — [6],202p : ill ; 22cm.
Index.
ISBN 0-408-00239-5 Pbk : £3.75
(B77-16138)

Fuori, William Michael. Introduction to computer operations / [by] William M. Fuori, Anthony D'Arco, Lawrence Orilia. — New York ; London [etc.] : McGraw-Hill, 1973. — xvii,644[i.e.654]p : ill, facsims, forms ; 25cm.
Bibl. — Index.
ISBN 0-07-022619-9 : Unpriced
(B77-19152)

Hellerman, Herbert. Digital computer system principles / [by] Herbert Hellerman. — 2nd ed. — New York ; London [etc.] : McGraw-Hill, 1973. — xiii,466p : ill ; 24cm. — (McGraw-Hill computer science series)
Text on lining papers. — Previous ed.: 1967. — Bibl. — Index.
ISBN 0-07-028073-8 : Unpriced
(B77-19153)

Lynch, Robert Emmett. Computers, their impact and use : structured programming in FORTRAN / [by] Robert E. Lynch, John R. Rice. — New York ; London [etc.] : Holt, Rinehart and Winston, 1977. — ix,455p : ill, facsims, maps ; 24cm.
Bibl. — Index.
ISBN 0-03-088525-6 Pbk : £8.00
(B77-23049)

Meek, Brian Lawrence. Using computers / [by] Brian Meek, Simon Fairthorne. — Chichester : Ellis Horwood [etc.], 1977. — 208p : ill ; 24cm. — (Mathematics & its applications)
Bibl.: p.199-202. — Index.
ISBN 0-85312-045-5 : £7.50
ISBN 0-85312-046-3 Pbk : £2.75
(B77-29109)

001.6'4'044 — Digital computer systems. Evaluation. Bench marking. *Conference proceedings*
Benchmarking *'74 (Conference), Churchill College, Cambridge, 1974.* Benchmarking : computer evaluation and measurement / edited by Nicholas Benwell. — Washington, D.C. ; London : Hemisphere ; New York ; London [etc.] : Wiley, [1977]. — xviii,190p : ill ; 24cm.
'A Halsted Press book'. — 'Benchmarking '74 was a conference ... [held] at Churchill College, Cambridge, in October '74' - Preface. — Published in the United States: 1975. — Bibl.: p.183-185. — Index.
ISBN 0-470-06595-8 : £15.55
(B77-11512)

001.6'4044 — Digital computer systems: IBM system 370
Katzan, Harry. Computer organization and the system-370 / [by] Harry Katzan, Jr. — New York ; London [etc.] : Van Nostrand Reinhold, 1971. — ix,308p : ill ; 24cm. — (Computer science series)
Index.
ISBN 0-442-24250-6 : £11.15
(B77-19955)

001.6'4044 — Digital computer systems. Multiprocessors
Infotech International Limited. Multiprocessor systems / [Infotech International Limited] ; [C.H. White, editor]. — Maidenhead : Infotech International, 1976. — vii,555[i.e.561]p : ill ; 31cm. — (Infotech state of the art report)
Bibl.: p.475-511. — Index.
ISBN 0-85539-290-8 : £95.00
(B77-28325)

001.6'4044 — Distributed digital computer systems. *Reports, surveys*
Down, Peter John. Why distributed computing? : an NCC review of potential and experience in the UK / by P.J. Down and F.E. Taylor. — Manchester : NCC Publications, 1976. — viii, 168p : ill, map ; 21cm.
ISBN 0-85012-170-1 Pbk : £7.00
(B77-01111)

001.6'4044 — Distributed digital computer systems. *Reviews of research*
Infotech International Limited. Distributed systems / [Infotech International Limited] ; [editor J.P. Spencer]. — Maidenhead : Infotech International, 1976. — viii,488p : ill, ports ; 31cm. — (Infotech state of the art report)
Bibl.: p.419-454. — Index.
ISBN 0-85539-310-6 : Unpriced
(B77-01112)

001.6'4044 — Laboratories. Minicomputer systems. *Study examples: DEC PDP-11 minicomputer systems*
Cooper, James W. The minicomputer in the laboratory : with examples using the PDP-11 / [by] James W. Cooper. — New York ; London [etc.] : Wiley, 1977. — xvii,365p : ill ; 24cm.
'A Wiley-Interscience publication'. — With answers. — Index.
ISBN 0-471-01883-x : £13.00
(B77-23050)

001.6'4044 — Microcomputer systems
Introduction to microprocessors / edited by D. Aspinall and E.L. Dagless. — London : Pitman [etc.], 1977. — vii,162p : ill ; 23cm.
Bibl.: p.138. — Index.
ISBN 0-273-01060-3 Pbk : £4.95
Primary classification 621.3819'58'35
(B77-21935)

001.6'4044 — Microcomputer systems. *Manuals*
Motorola Semiconductor Products Inc.
Microprocessor applications manual / Motorola Semiconductor Products Inc. ; contributors Alvin W. Moore ... [et al.]. — New York ; London [etc.] : McGraw-Hill, [1977]. — 720p in various pagings : ill ; 29cm. — (Motorola series in solid-state electronics)
Published in the United States: 1975. — Index.
ISBN 0-07-043527-8 : £20.75
(B77-12808)

001.6'4044 — Microcomputer systems. *Periodicals*
Microcomputer analysis : the authority on microcomputing : a monthly information service. — Luton (Victoria House, Victoria St., Luton LU1 5DH) : Macintosh Publications Ltd.
Vol.1, no.1- ; June 1976-. — 1976-. — 30cm.
16p. in 1st issue. — Bibl.
Sd : £180.00 yearly
ISSN 0309-5444
(B77-14006)

001.6'4044 — Microcomputer systems. Design
Peatman, John Burling. Microcomputer-based design / [by] John B. Peatman. — New York ; London [etc.] : McGraw-Hill, 1977. — xv, 540p : ill ; 25cm.
Index.
ISBN 0-07-049138-0 : £15.75
(B77-22302)

001.6'4044 — Microprocessor systems
Ward, Brice. Microprocessor-microprogramming handbook / [by] Brice Ward ; with a specially written chapter for the guidance of the English reader by W. Oliver. — Slough : Foulsham-Tab, 1977. — vii,5-293p : ill ; 21cm.
Originally published: Blue Ridge Summit, Pa. : Tab Books, 1975. — Index.
ISBN 0-7042-0175-5 Pbk : £3.50
(B77-19956)

001.6'4044 — Microprocessor systems. *Conference proceedings*
Second Euromicro symposium on microprocessing and microprogramming, October 12-14, 1976, Venice, organized by Euromicro / edited by Jan Wilmink, Mariagiovanna Sami, Rodnay Zaks. — Amsterdam [etc.] : North-Holland Publishing Co., 1977. — xix,335p : ill ; 27cm.
Bibl.
ISBN 0-7204-0557-2 : £15.00
(B77-19957)

001.6'4044 — Minicomputer systems. *Periodicals. For marketing*
Mini-market micro-market monitor : news and analysis of minicomputer and microprocessor market directions. — London (140 Camden St., NW1 9PF) : IDC Europa Ltd.
Vol.1, no.1- ; Aug. 24, 1976-. — 1976-. — 30cm.
Twenty issues a year. — 12p. in 1st issue.
Sd : £1.75(£30.00 yearly)
ISSN 0308-9371
Also classified at 621.3819'58'35
(B77-03310)

001.6'4044 — Minicomputer systems: IBM system 5100
Katzan, Harry. The IBM 5100 portable computer : a comprehensive guide for users and programmers / [by] Harry Katzan, Jr. — New York ; London [etc.] : Van Nostrand Reinhold, 1977. — xii,576p : ill ; 24cm. — (Computer science series)
Bibl. — Index.
ISBN 0-442-24270-0 : £16.15
(B77-23051)

001.6'4044 — Small digital computer systems. *For engineering & science*
Korn, Granino Arthur. Microprocessors and small digital computer systems for engineers and scientists / [by] Granino A. Korn. — [2nd ed.]. — New York ; London [etc.] : McGraw-Hill, 1977. — xix,390p : ill ; 24cm.
Previous ed.: published as 'Minicomputers for engineers and scientists'. New York : McGraw-Hill, 1973. — Index.
ISBN 0-07-035367-0 : £18.40
(B77-31648)

001.6'4044'05 — Digital computer systems. *Periodicals*
Systems international. — London (106 Church Rd, Upper Norwood, SE19 2UB) : Gershire Ltd.
Continues: Systems.
[No.1]- ; May 1976-. — [1976]-. — ill ; 29cm.
Monthly. — 82p. in Mar. 1977 issue. — Cover title: International systems.
Pbk : £2.50
ISSN 0309-5177
(B77-12258)

001.6'4'07 — Computer systems. Information sources. *Great Britain. Lists. For secondary school teaching*
British Computer Society. *Schools Committee. Resources Working Party.* Computer educational aids and resources for teachers / prepared by the Resources Working Party of the British Computer Society Schools Committee. — London (33 Queen Anne St., W1M 0AL) : National Committee for Audio-Visual Aids in Education, [1977]. — [1], 30,[1]p ; 30cm.
Sd : £0.95
(B77-33554)

001.6'4'0904 — Computer systems, to 1975
Hollingdale, Stuart Havelock. Mathematics and man / prepared by S.H. Hollingdale, R.L. Wilder and Graham Flegg ; for the [Open University] Course Team. — Milton Keynes : Open University Press, 1976. — 47p : ill, facsims ; 30cm. — (Arts/mathematics, an interfaculty second level course : history of mathematics ; unit 11) (AM 289 ; 11)
Bibl.
ISBN 0-335-05014-x Sd : £1.25
Also classified at 519.5'09
(B77-03862)

001.6'4'0941 — Computer services. *Great Britain. Yearbooks*
The **computer** users' year book. — Brighton [etc.] (18 Queen's Rd, Brighton BN1 3XA) : The Computer Users' Year Book.
1976. — [1976]. — [2],866p : ill, port ; 29cm.
ISBN 0-902908-06-5 : £16.95
(B77-05161)

001.64'096 — Computer systems. Applications. *Africa*
The **computer** and Africa : applications, problems and potential / edited by D.R.F. Taylor, R.A. Obudho. — New York ; London : Praeger, 1977. — xxiii,341p : ill, maps ; 25cm. — (Praeger special studies in international economics and development)
Bibl.: p.309-332. — Index.
ISBN 0-275-56820-2 : £18.40
(B77-26061)

001.6'42 — Digital computer systems. Programming
Maisel, Herbert. Computers : programming and applications / [by] Herbert Maisel. — Chicago ; Henley-on-Thames [etc.] : Science Research Associates.
Instructor's guide. — 1976. — [3],100p : ill ; 22cm.
ISBN 0-574-21071-7 Pbk : £1.35
(B77-00566)

Maurer, Herman Adolf. Data structures and programming techniques / [by] Herman A. Maurer ; translated [from the German] by Camille C. Price. — Englewood Cliffs ; London [etc.] : Prentice-Hall, 1977. — ix,228p : ill ; 24cm.
Translation of: 'Datenstrukturen und Programmierverfahren'. Stuttgart : Teubner, 1974. — Bibl.: p.217-220. — Index.
ISBN 0-13-197038-0 : £10.85
Also classified at 001.6'442
(B77-28326)

Tausworthe, Robert C. Standardized development of computer software / [by] Robert C. Tausworthe. — Englewood Cliffs ; London [etc.] : Prentice-Hall, 1977. — iii-xv,379p : ill, form ; 24cm.
Index.
ISBN 0-13-842195-1 : £15.95
(B77-21650)

001.6'42 — Digital computer systems. Programming. *Reviews of research*
Current trends in programming methodology. — Englewood Cliffs ; London [etc.] : Prentice-Hall.
Vol.1 : Software specification and design / Raymond T. Yeh, editor. — 1977. — xi,275p : ill ; 25cm.
Bibl.: p.243-271. — Index.
ISBN 0-13-195701-5 : £13.55
(B77-23942)

001.6'42 — Digital computer systems. Programming. Algorithms. Design
Guttmann, Anthony J. Programming and algorithms : an introduction / [by] Anthony J. Guttmann. — London : Heinemann Educational, 1977. — x,214p : ill ; 23cm.
With solutions to selected problems. — Bibl.: p.206-209. — Index.
ISBN 0-435-77541-3 Pbk : £3.50
(B77-23052)

001.6'42 — Digital computer systems. Programs. Optimisation. *Reviews of research*
Infotech International Limited. Program optimization / [Infotech International Limited] ; [D. Bates, editor]. — Maidenhead : Infotech International, 1976. — viii,448p : ill ; 30cm. — (Infotech state of the art report)
Bibl.: p.383-407. — Index.
ISBN 0-85539-300-9 : Unpriced
(B77-06407)

001.6'42 — Digital computer systems. Programs written in Cobol language. Abends. Debugging
Boar, B H. Abend debugging for COBOL programmers / [by] B.H. Boar. — New York ; London [etc.] : Wiley, 1976. — xiii,321p : ill ; 26cm.
'A Wiley-Interscience Publication'. — Bibl.: p.314-315. — Index.
ISBN 0-471-08413-1 : £13.50
(B77-11513)

001.6'42 — Digital computer systems. Structured programming
Hughes, Joan Kirkby. A structured approach to programming / [by] Joan K. Hughes, Jay I. Michtom. — Englewood Cliffs ; London [etc.] : Prentice-Hall, 1977. — viii,264p : ill ; 25cm.
Bibl.: p.257-260. — Index.
ISBN 0-13-854356-9 : £12.75
(B77-29110)

001.6'42'0184 — Digital computer systems. Programs. Mathematical models
Spirn, Jeffrey R. Program behavior : models and measurements / [by] Jeffrey R. Spirn. — New York ; Oxford [etc.] : Elsevier, 1977. — x, 277p : ill ; 24cm. — (Elsevier computer science library : operating and programming systems series)
Bibl.: p.264-271. — Index.
ISBN 0-444-00219-7 : Unpriced
ISBN 0-444-00220-0 Pbk : Unpriced
(B77-26730)

001.6'424 — Digital computer systems. Programming languages
Barron, David William. An introduction to the study of programming languages / [by] D.W. Barron. — Cambridge [etc.] : Cambridge University Press, 1977. — viii,165p : ill ; 24cm. — (Cambridge computer science texts ; 7)
Bibl.: p.150-152. — Index.
ISBN 0-521-21317-7 : £4.95
ISBN 0-521-29101-1 Pbk : £2.50
(B77-15644)

Open University. Operating systems / prepared by the [Open University] Course Team ; in consultation with I.H. Witten. Computer languages and microprogramming / prepared by the Course Team. — Milton Keynes : Open University Press, 1975. — 35,47p : ill ; 30cm. — (TM221 ; 13 and 14) (A second level course : the digital computer ; units 13 and 14)
With answers to SAQs. — Index.
ISBN 0-335-02756-3 Pbk : £1.85
Primary classification 001.6'425
(B77-25340)

Tucker, Allen B. Programming languages / [by] Allen B. Tucker, Jr. — New York ; London [etc.] : McGraw-Hill, 1977. — xvii,439p : ill, forms ; 25cm. — (McGraw-Hill computer science series)
Index. — Includes facsimile reprints.
ISBN 0-07-065415-8 : £13.15
(B77-26062)

001.6'424 — Digital computer systems. Programming languages: Algol 60 language
Vowels, R A. ALGOL 60 and FORTRAN IV / [by] R.A. Vowels. — Sydney ; London [etc.] : Wiley, [1977]. — x,173p : ill ; 23cm.
Published in Australia: 1974. — Bibl.: p.166-168. — Index.
ISBN 0-471-91192-5 Pbk : £6.20
Also classified at 001.6'424
(B77-10084)

001.6'424 — Digital computer systems. Programming languages: Algol 68 language
Lindsey, Charles Hodgson. Informal introduction to ALGOL 68 / [by] C.H. Lindsey, S.G. van der Meulen. — Revised ed. — London [etc.] : North-Holland Publishing Co., 1977. — [8], 361p : ill ; 23cm.
Text on lining papers. — Previous ed.: 1971. — Index.
ISBN 0-7204-0726-5 : £14.00
(B77-24642)

001.6'424 — Digital computer systems. Programming languages: ANS 74 Cobol language. *Manuals*
Robinson, P B. Advanced COBOL : ANS 74 / [by] P.B. Robinson. — London : Macdonald and Jane's [etc.], 1976. — xvi,215p : ill ; 23cm. — (Computer monographs ; 24)
Index.
ISBN 0-356-08427-2 : £4.50
(B77-05808)

001.6'424 — Digital computer systems. Programming languages: ANS Cobol language. *Manuals*
Stern, Nancy Beth. COBOL programming / [by] Nancy B. Stern, Robert A. Stern. — 2nd ed. — New York ; London [etc.] : Wiley, 1975 [i.e. 1977]. — xiv,482p : ill ; 28cm.
Published in the United States: 1975. — Previous ed.: 1970. — Index.
ISBN 0-471-82329-5 Pbk : £8.35
(B77-09456)

001.6'424 — Digital computer systems. Programming languages: APL 360 language
Grey, Louis David. A course in APL with applications / [by] Louis D. Grey. — 2nd ed. — Reading, Mass. ; London [etc.] : Addison-Wesley, [1977]. — xii,358p : ill ; 24cm.

This ed. published in the United States: 1976. — Previous ed.: published as 'A course in APL360 with applications'. 1973. — Bibl.: p.298-300. — Index.
ISBN 0-201-02563-9 Pbk : £8.00
(B77-10085)

Hellerman, Herbert. APL/360 programming and applications / [by] Herbert Hellerman, Ira A. Smith. — New York ; London [etc.] : McGraw-Hill, 1976. — xi,203p : ill, forms ; 24cm.
Bibl.: p.169. — Index.
ISBN 0-07-027950-0 Pbk : £7.90
(B77-04517)

001.6'424 — Digital computer systems. Programming languages: APL language
Harms, Edward. Introduction to APL and computer programming / [by] Edward Harms, Michael P. Zabinski. — New York ; London [etc.] : Wiley, 1977. — xvi,400p : ill, ports ; 28cm.
With answers. — Bibl.: p.369-372. — Index.
ISBN 0-471-35201-2 Pbk : £7.00
(B77-18503)

001.6'424 — Digital computer systems. Programming languages: APL language. *Manuals*
Gilman, Leonard. APL : an interactive approach / [by] Leonard Gilman, Allen J. Rose. — 2nd ed., revised reprinting. — New York ; London [etc.] : Wiley, 1976. — [16], 378p : ill ; 28cm.
With answers. — Previous ed.: i.e. 2nd ed. 1974. — Index.
ISBN 0-471-30022-5 Pbk : £7.95
(B77-25338)

001.6'424 — Digital computer systems. Programming languages: Basic language
Gosling, P E. Beginning BASIC / [by] P.E. Gosling. — London [etc.] : Macmillan, 1977. — vi,105p : ill ; 24cm. — (Macmillan basis books in electronics)
Index.
ISBN 0-333-22304-7 Pbk : £2.95 : CIP rev.
(B77-21651)

Mullish, Henry. A basic approach to BASIC / [by] Henry Mullish. — New York ; London [etc.] : Wiley, 1976. — xv,303p ; 26cm.
Index.
ISBN 0-471-62375-x Pbk : £6.10
(B77-20854)

001.6'424 — Digital computer systems. Programming languages: Basic language. *Manuals*
Hartley, P J. Introduction to BASIC : a case study approach / [by] P.J. Hartley. — London [etc.] : Macmillan, 1976. — viii,119p : ill ; 24cm.
With solutions to selected exercises. — Bibl.: p.115.
ISBN 0-333-19620-1 Pbk : £1.95
(B77-07009)

001.6'424 — Digital computer systems. Programming languages: Cobol language
Philippakis, Andreas S. Structured COBOL / [by] Andreas S. Philippakis, Leonard J. Kazmier. — [Revised ed.]. — New York ; London [etc.] : McGraw-Hill, 1977. — xv, 446p : ill, forms ; 24cm.
Previous ed.: published as 'COBOL for business applications'. New York : McGraw-Hill, 1973. — Index.
ISBN 0-07-049797-4 Pbk : £7.45
(B77-26063)

001.6'424 — Digital computer systems. Programming languages: Cobol language. *Manuals*
Worth, Thomas. COBOL for beginners / [by] Thomas Worth. — Englewood Cliffs ; London [etc.] : Prentice-Hall, 1977. — [11],369p : ill ; 28cm.
Index.
ISBN 0-13-139378-2 Pbk : £7.80
(B77-29863)

001.6'424 — Digital computer systems. Programming languages: Cobol language. *Serials*
Conference on Data Systems Language. CODASYL COBOL journal of development / [prepared by the Programming Language Committee of the Conference on Data Systems Languages (CODASYL)]. — [London] ([29 Portland Place, W.1]) : British Computer Society.
1976. — [1976]. — 2v.(604p) in various pagings : ill ; 30cm.
Previous control number ISBN 0-901865-16-8. Pbk : £9.00
ISBN 0-901865-16-8 (Part 1)
ISBN 0-901865-17-6 (Part 2)
(B77-01959)

001.6'424 — Digital computer systems. Programming languages: Coral 66 language. *Manuals*
National Computing Centre. A course in standard CORAL 66 / [text by] J.D. Halliwell & T.A. Edwards. — Manchester : NCC Publications, 1977. — 385p in various pagings : ill, form ; 30cm.
'This volume contains the notes issued as part of NCC's package of standard CORAL 66 training material' - half title page.
ISBN 0-85012-187-6 Pbk : £3.00 : CIP rev.
(B77-06408)

001.6'424 — Digital computer systems. Programming languages: Fortran language
Monro, Donald Martin. Computing with FORTRAN : a practical course / [by] Donald M. Monro. — London : Edward Arnold, 1977. — vi,242p : ill, map ; 25cm.
Index.
ISBN 0-7131-2546-2 Pbk : £3.95
(B77-17849)

Vowels, R A. ALGOL 60 and FORTRAN IV / [by] R.A. Vowels. — Sydney ; London [etc.] : Wiley, [1977]. — x,173p : ill ; 23cm.
Published in Australia: 1974. — Bibl.: p.166-168. — Index.
ISBN 0-471-91192-5 Pbk : £6.20
Primary classification 001.6'424
(B77-10084)

001.6'424 — Digital computer systems. Programming languages. Grammar
Cleaveland, J Craig. Grammars for programming languages / [by] J. Craig Cleaveland, Robert C. Uzgalis. — New York ; Oxford [etc.] : Elsevier, 1977. — xiii,154p : ill ; 24cm. — (Elsevier computer science library : programming languages series ; 4)
Bibl.: p.149-151. — Index.
ISBN 0-444-00187-5 : £55.00
ISBN 0-444-00199-9 Pbk : Unpriced
(B77-24643)

001.6'424 — Digital computer systems. Programming languages: MPL II language. *Manuals*
Computer Management System (CMS), Message Processing Language (MPL II) reference manual. — Hounslow ([International Technical Information Organisation, Wardpark, Cumbernauld, Glasgow]) : Burroughs Machines Limited [etc.], 1976. — 1v. ; 28cm.
One hundred and fifty nine p. in various pagings on publication.
ISBN 0-905811-01-1 Ls : Unpriced
(B77-03863)

001.6'424 — Digital computer systems. Programming languages: Pascal language
Webster, C A G. Introduction to Pascal / [by] C.A.G. Webster. — London [etc.] : Heyden, 1976. — xi,129p : ill ; 25cm. — (Heyden international topics in science)
With solutions to selected exercises. — Index.
ISBN 0-85501-225-0 : £5.50
(B77-07010)

001.6'424 — Digital computer systems. Programming languages: PL/1 language
Pollack, Seymour Victor. A guide to PL/1 / [by] Seymour V. Pollack, Theodor D. Sterling. — 2nd ed. — New York ; London [etc.] : Holt, Rinehart and Winston, 1976. — xxvi,630p : ill, facsims ; 24cm.
Previous ed.: 1974. — Bibl. — Index.
ISBN 0-03-089467-0 : £12.50
(B77-00567)

001.6'424 — Digital computer systems. Programming languages: RTL/2 language
Barnes, J G P. RTL/2 : design and philosophy / [by] J.G.P. Barnes. — London [etc.] : Heyden, 1976. — xi,164p : ill ; 25cm. — (Heyden international topics in science)
Index.
ISBN 0-85501-224-2 : £5.50
(B77-07011)

001.6'424 — Digital computer systems. Structured programming. *Study examples: PL/1 language*
Marcotty, Michael. Structured programming with PL-1 : an introduction / [by] Michael Marcotty. — Englewood Cliffs ; London [etc.] : Prentice-Hall, 1977. — xii,452p : ill, forms ; 24cm.
Index.
ISBN 0-13-854885-4 Pbk : £9.45
(B77-25339)

001.6'425 — Computer systems. Software. *Conference proceedings*
Proceedings of the symposium on computer software engineering, New York, N.Y., April 20-22, 1976 / Jerome Fox, editor. — New York : Polytechnic Press ; New York ; London [etc.] : Distributed by Wiley, 1976. — [1],xx, 583p : ill, forms ; 23cm. — (Microwave Research Institute. Symposia series ; vol.24)
Spine title: Computer software engineering. — Index.
ISBN 0-470-98948-3 : £24.00
(B77-27626)

001.6'425 — Digital computer systems. Compilers. Design
Lewis, Philip M. Compiler design theory / [by] Philip M. Lewis II, Daniel J. Rosenkrantz, Richard E. Stearns. — Reading, Mass. ; London [etc.] : Addison-Wesley, 1976. — iii-xx, 647p : ill ; 25cm. — (The systems programming series)
Ill. on lining papers. — Bibl.: p.619-633. — Index.
ISBN 0-201-14455-7 : £16.15
(B77-16139)

001.6'425 — Digital computer systems: IBM system 370. Assembly programming
Burian, Barbara J. A simplified approach to S-370 assembly language programming / [by] Barbara J. Burian. — Englewood Cliffs ; London [etc.] : Prentice-Hall, 1977. — xviii, 558p : ill, facsims, forms ; 25cm.
Index.
ISBN 0-13-810119-1 : £11.95
(B77-26064)

001.6'425 — Digital computer systems. Operating systems
Davis, William S. Operating systems : a systematic view / [by] William S. Davis. — Reading, Mass. ; London [etc.] : Addison-Wesley, 1977. — [1],xviii,395p : ill ; 24cm.
Index.
ISBN 0-201-01118-2 : £11.20
(B77-29111)

Open University. Operating systems / prepared by the [Open University] Course Team ; in consultation with I.H. Witten. Computer languages and microprogramming / prepared by the Course Team. — Milton Keynes : Open University Press, 1975. — 35,47p : ill ; 30cm. — (TM221 ; 13 and 14) (A second level course : the digital computer ; units 13 and 14)
With answers to SAQs. — Index.
ISBN 0-335-02756-3 Pbk : £1.85
Also classified at 001.6'424
(B77-25340)

001.6'425 — Digital computer systems. Software
Halstead, Maurice Howard. Elements of software science / [by] Maurice H. Halstead. — New York ; Oxford [etc.] : Elsevier, 1977. — xiv, 127p : ill ; 24cm. — (Operating and programming systems series ; 2) (Elsevier computer science library)
Bibl.: p.120-124. — Index.
ISBN 0-444-00205-7 : Unpriced
ISBN 0-444-00215-4 Pbk : Unpriced
(B77-25341)

001.6'425 — Digital computer systems. Software. Portability
Software portability : an advanced course / editor P.J. Brown ... — Cambridge [etc.] : Cambridge University Press, 1977. — xiv,328p : ill ; 24cm.
' ... based on an Advanced Course on Software Portability from March 26th to April 9th, 1976' - Preface. — Bibl. — Index.
ISBN 0-521-21485-8 : £7.00
(B77-14508)

001.6'425 — Digital computer systems. Software. Reliability
Myers, Glenford J. Software reliability : principles and practices / [by] Glenford J. Myers. — New York ; London [etc.] : Wiley, 1976. — xvii,360p : ill, form ; 24cm. — (Business data processing)
Text on lining paper. — 'A Wiley-Interscience publication'. — Index.
ISBN 0-471-62765-8 : £15.85
(B77-03864)

001.6'425 — Information retrieval. Digital computer systems. Software packages: FIND. *Secondary school texts*
Computer Education in Schools. Information retrieval in schools / Computer Education in Schools. — London (322 Euston Rd, NW1 3BD) : C.E.S.
In 2 vols.
Teachers' guide / [written by Colin Monson]. — 1976. — [5],T161p : ill(incl 2 col), forms, 2 maps ; 30cm. — (Publication ; 3444)
Index.
ISBN 0-903885-16-6 Pbk : £5.00
(B77-16140)

001.6'4404 — Digital computer systems. Networks. Data transmission. Design & analysis
Schwartz, Mischa. Computer-communication network design and analysis / [by] Mischa Schwartz. — Englewood Cliffs ; London [etc.] : Prentice-Hall, 1977. — xi,372p : ill, maps ; 24cm.
Bibl.: p.348-357. — Index.
ISBN 0-13-165134-x : £15.15
(B77-25342)

001.6'4404 — On-line computer systems. Design. Applications of quantitative methods
Pritchard, John Arthur Thomas. Quantitative methods in on-line systems / by J.A.T. Pritchard. — Manchester : NCC Publications [etc.] ; [Letchworth] : [Distributed by Dent], 1976. — xii,312,[4]p : ill ; 22cm.
With solutions. — Bibl.: p.237-241. — Index.
ISBN 0-85012-129-9 : £9.00
(B77-13456)

001.6'4404 — Real time computer systems. Design
Tebbs, David. Real time systems : management and design / [by] David Tebbs and Garfield Collins. — London [etc.] : McGraw-Hill, 1977. — ix,357p : ill, forms ; 24cm.
Index.
ISBN 0-07-084482-8 : £7.25
(B77-26731)

001.6'442 — Computer systems. Machine-readable files. Management
Martin, James, *b.1933.* Computer data-base organization / [by] James Martin. — 2nd ed. — Englewood Cliffs ; London [etc.] : Prentice-Hall, 1977. — xviii,713p : ill(some col), geneal tables(some col) ; 25cm. — (Prentice-Hall series in automatic computation)
Col. ill. on lining papers. — Previous ed.: 1975. — Index.
ISBN 0-13-165423-3 : £21.20
(B77-33555)

001.6'442 — Data processing systems. Magnetic disc packs: Eleven disc packs. *Standards*
British Standards Institution. Specification for magnetic eleven-disk packs for data processing, mechanical and magnetic properties = Chargeurs à onze disques magnétiques pour le traitement de l'information, caractéristiques mécaniques et magnétiques = Magnetische elfscheibige Büchsen zur Datenverarbeitung, mechanische und magnetische Eigenschaften / British Standards Institution. — London : B.S.I, 1976. — [2],22,[2]p : ill ; 30cm. — (BS5359 : 1976)
Pierced for binder.
ISBN 0-580-09034-5 Sd : £4.00
(B77-01961)

001.6'442 — Digital computer systems. Data. Input. Structure
Horowitz, Ellis. Fundamentals of data structures / [by] Ellis Horowitz, Sartaj Sahni. — London [etc.] : Pitman, 1977. — xii,564p : ill ; 23cm. — (Computer software engineering series) (A Pitman international text)
Originally published: Woodland Hills, Calif. : Computer Science Press, 1976. — Index.
ISBN 0-273-01062-x Pbk : £5.95 : CIP rev.
(B77-06409)

001.6'442 — Digital computer systems. Data. Structure
Flores, Ivan. Data structure and management / [by] Ivan Flores. — 2nd ed. — Englewood Cliffs ; London [etc.] : Prentice-Hall, 1977. — ix,390p : ill ; 24cm.
Previous ed.: Englewood Cliffs ; Hemel Hempstead : Prentice-Hall, 1970. — Index.
ISBN 0-13-197335-5 : £15.15
(B77-22303)

Maurer, Herman Adolf. Data structures and programming techniques / [by] Herman A. Maurer ; translated [from the German] by Camille C. Price. — Englewood Cliffs ; London [etc.] : Prentice-Hall, 1977. — ix,228p : ill ; 24cm.
Translation of: 'Datenstrukturen und Programmierverfahren'. Stuttgart : Teubner, 1974. — Bibl.: p.217-220. — Index.
ISBN 0-13-197038-0 : £10.85
Primary classification 001.6'42
(B77-28326)

Pfaltz, John L. Computer data structures / [by] John L. Pfaltz. — New York ; London [etc.] : McGraw-Hill, 1977. — xiii,446p : ill ; 25cm.
Bibl.: p.434-436. — Index.
ISBN 0-07-049743-5 : £13.45
(B77-21652)

Tremblay, Jean Paul. An introduction to data structures with applications / [by] J.P. Tremblay, P.G. Sorenson. — New York ; London [etc.] : McGraw-Hill, 1976. — xvi, 704p : ill ; 24cm. — (McGraw-Hill computer science series)
Bibl. — Index.
ISBN 0-07-065150-7 : £12.20
(B77-01962)

001.6'442 — Digital computer systems. Machine-readable files. Design. *For management*
IFIP Working Conference on Modelling in Data Base Management Systems, *Nice, 1977.* Architecture and models in data base management systems : proceedings of the IFIP Working Conference on Modelling in Data Base Management Systems / edited by G.M. Nijssen. — Amsterdam [etc.] ; Oxford : North-Holland Publishing Co., 1977. — viii,326p : ill ; 23cm.
'IFIP Working Conference on Modelling in Data Base Management Systems, Nice, France, 3-7 January 1977 organized by IFIP Technical Committee 2, Programming, International Federation for Information Processing' - half title page verso. — Bibl.
Unpriced
(B77-28327)

001.6'442 — Digital computer systems. Machine-readable files. Management
Wiederhold, Gio. Database design / [by] Gio Wiederhold. — New York ; London [etc.] : McGraw-Hill, 1977. — xiii,658p : ill ; 24cm. — (McGraw-Hill computer science series)
Bibl.: p.617-645. — Index.
ISBN 0-07-070130-x : £16.50
(B77-25343)

001.6'442 — Digital computer systems. Machine-readable files. Management. Applications of software packages. *Reports, surveys*

Davis, Brian, *b.1934.* The selection of database software / by B. Davis. — Manchester : NCC Publications, 1977. — xxiii,315p : ill ; 31cm.
Bibl.: p.311-314.
ISBN 0-85012-173-6 : Unpriced : CIP rev.
(B77-06410)

001.6'442 — Digital computer systems. Very large machine-readable files. *Conference proceedings*

International Conference on Very Large Data Bases, *2nd, Brussels, 1976.* Systems for large data bases : proceedings of the 2nd International Conference on Very Large Data Bases / edited by P.C. Lockemann and E.J. Neuhold. — Amsterdam [etc.] ; Oxford : North-Holland Publishing Co., 1977. — ix, 224p : ill ; 23cm.
Bibl. — Index. — Previous control number ISBN 0-7204-0463-0.
ISBN 0-7204-0546-7 : £14.05
(B77-14509)

001.6'442 — Information systems: Digital computer systems. Machine readable files. Design & operation

Ghosh, Sakti P. Data base organization for data management / [by] Sakti P. Ghosh. — New York [etc.] ; London : Academic Press, 1977. — xi,376p : ill ; 24cm. — (Computer science and applied mathematics)
Bibl. — Index.
ISBN 0-12-281850-4 : £20.95
(B77-21653)

Judd, Denis Onan. Use of files / [by] D.R. [i.e. D.O.] Judd. — 2nd ed. — London : Macdonald and Jane's [etc.], 1975. — ix,154p : ill ; 23cm. — (Computer monographs)
Previous ed.: London : Macdonald and Co., 1973. — Bibl.: p.143-151. — Index.
ISBN 0-356-08443-4 : £3.25
(B77-21654)

Tsichritzis, Dionysios C. Data base management systems / [by] Dionysios C. Tsichritzis, Frederick H. Lochovsky. — New York [etc.] ; London : Academic Press, 1977. — xvi,388p : ill ; 24cm. — (Computer science and applied mathematics)
Bibl.: p.364-374. — Index.
ISBN 0-12-701740-2 : £12.05
(B77-21655)

001.6'442 — Machine readable files. Design. *Conference proceedings. For management*

IFIP Working Conference on Modelling in Data Base Management Systems, *Freudenstadt, 1976.* Modelling in data base management systems : proceedings of the IFIP Working Conference on Modelling in Data Base Management Systems, Freudenstadt, Germany, 5-8 January 1976, organized by IFIP Technical Committee 2, Programming / edited by G.M. Nijssen. — Amsterdam [etc.] ; Oxford : North-Holland Publishing Co., 1976. — vii,418p ; 23cm.
Index.
ISBN 0-7204-0459-2 : Unpriced
(B77-33007)

001.9 — CONTROVERSIAL AND SPURIOUS KNOWLEDGE

001.9'3 — Curiosities

Baumann, Elwood David. They came from space / by Elwood D. Baumann. — New York ; London : F. Watts, 1977. — [9],109,[1] p : ill ; 25cm.
Bibl.: p.101-102. — Index.
ISBN 0-531-00388-4 : £2.50
(B77-28328)

Däniken, Erich von. According to the evidence : my proof of man's extraterrestrial origins / [by] Erich von Däniken ; translated [from the German] by Michael Heron. — London : Souvenir Press, 1977. — xi,348p : ill, facsim, maps, ports ; 23cm.
Map on lining papers. — Translation of: 'Beweise'. Düsseldorf : Econ Verlag, 1977. — Bibl.: p.337-348.
ISBN 0-285-62301-x : £4.50
(B77-30905)

Dem, Marc. The lost tribes from outer space / by Marc Dem ; translated [from the French] by Lowell Bail. — London : Corgi, 1977. — [9], 212p ; 18cm.
This translation originally published: New York : Bantam, 1977. — Translation of: 'Les juifs de l'espace'. Paris : Albin Michel, 1977. — Index.
ISBN 0-552-10540-6 Pbk : £0.75
(B77-29112)

Landsburg, Alan. In search of strange phenomena / [by] Alan Landsburg ; foreword by Leonard Nimoy. — London : Corgi, 1977. — xii,192,[1]p,[32]p of plates : ill, ports ; 18cm.
Bibl.: p.191-192.
ISBN 0-552-10516-3 Pbk : £0.85
(B77-29864)

Michell, John. Phenomena : a book of wonders / [by] John Michell, Robert J.M. Rickard. — London : Thames and Hudson, 1977. — 128p : ill(some col), coats of arms, facsims, map, ports ; 29cm.
£3.95
Also classified at 001.9'4
(B77-28329)

Sitchin, Zecharia. The twelfth planet / [by] Zecharia Sitchin. — London [etc.] : Allen and Unwin, 1977. — 384p : ill, maps ; 25cm.
Originally published: New York : Stein and Day, 1976. — Bibl.: p.374-377. — Index.
ISBN 0-04-113001-4 : £5.50
(B77-30906)

Tomas, Andrew. We are not the first : riddles of ancient science / [by] Andrew Tomas. — London : Sphere, 1976. — 224p,[12]p of plates : ill, maps, ports ; 18cm.
Originally published: London : Souvenir Press, 1971. — Bibl.: p.223-224.
Pbk : £0.75
ISBN 0-7221-8541-3
(B77-00568)

001.9'3 — Curiosities: Great Siberian Explosion. *Russia (RSFSR). Siberia, 1908*

Furneaux, Rupert. The Tungus event : the great Siberian catastrophe of 1908 / [by] Rupert Furneaux. — St Albans : Panther, 1977. — 128p,[8]p of plates : ill, maps, ports ; 18cm.
Bibl.: p.124-125.
ISBN 0-586-04423-x Pbk : £0.60
(B77-24644)

001.9'3 — Man. Spontaneous combustion

Harrison, Michael. Fire from heaven : a study of spontaneous combustion in human beings / [by] Michael Harrison. — Revised ed. — London [etc.] : Pan Books, 1977. — 287p,[4]p of plates : ill, facsim, port ; 18cm.
Previous ed.: London : Sidgwick and Jackson, 1976. — Bibl.: p.277-281. — Index.
ISBN 0-330-25146-5 Pbk : £0.80
(B77-25344)

001.9'3 — Scientific curiosities. *Juvenile literature*

Knight, David Carpenter. Bees can't fly, but they do : things that are still a mystery to science / by David C. Knight ; illustrated by Barbara Wolff. — New York : Macmillan ; London : Collier Macmillan, 1976. — 48p : ill ; 22cm.
ISBN 0-02-750860-9 : £5.25
(B77-11016)

001.9'3'0924 — Curiosities. Theories of Däniken, Erich von. *Critical studies*

Story, Ronald. The space-gods revealed : a close look at the theories of Erich von Däniken / [by] Ronald Story. — [London] : New English Library, 1976. — xix,139p : ill, maps ; 22cm.
Also published: New York : Harper and Row, 1976. — Index.
ISBN 0-450-03199-3 : £4.50
(B77-21656)

001.9'4 — Mysteries

Furneaux, Rupert. Ancient mysteries / [by] Rupert Furneaux. — London [etc.] : White Lion Publishers, 1977. — 234p,[16]p of plates : ill, plan ; 21cm.
Originally published: London : Futura Publications, 1976. — Bibl.: p.231-234.
ISBN 0-7274-0385-0 : £4.50
(B77-26065)

Furneaux, Rupert. Ancient mysteries / [by] Rupert Furneaux. — London : Futura Publications, 1976. — 234p,[16]p of plates : ill, facsim ; 18cm. — (Mysteries of time and space)
Bibl.: p.231-234.
ISBN 0-86007-104-9 Pbk : £0.85
(B77-09457)

Haining, Peter. Ancient mysteries / [by] Peter Haining. — London : Sidgwick and Jackson, 1977. — 178p : ill, facsims, maps, plans, ports ; 26cm.
Bibl.: p.174. — Index.
ISBN 0-283-98321-3 : £5.50
(B77-15645)

Jenkins, Stephen. The undiscovered country : adventures into other dimensions / [by] Stephen Jenkins. — Sudbury : Spearman, 1977. — 240p, [8]p of plates : ill, map ; 23cm.
Index.
ISBN 0-85435-073-x : £3.95
(B77-19154)

Kolosimo, Peter. Not of this world / [by] Peter Kolosimo ; translated [from the Italian] by A.D. Hills. — London : Sphere, 1977. — 245p, 12p of plates : ill ; 18cm.
This translation originally published: London : Souvenir Press, 1970. — Translation of: 'Non è terrestre'. Milano : Sugar Editore, 1969.
ISBN 0-7221-5327-9 Pbk : £0.95
(B77-30907)

Kolosimo, Peter. Timeless earth / [by] Peter Kolosimo ; translated [from the Italian] by Paul Stevenson. — London : Sphere, 1977. — 255p, [40]p of plates : ill, maps, ports ; 18cm.
This translation originally published: London : Garnstone Press, 1973. — Translation of: 'Terra senza tempo'. Milano : Sugar, 1964. — Bibl.: p.237-239. — Index.
ISBN 0-7221-5329-5 Pbk : £0.95
(B77-30908)

Michell, John. Phenomena : a book of wonders / [by] John Michell, Robert J.M. Rickard. — London : Thames and Hudson, 1977. — 128p : ill(some col), coats of arms, facsims, map, ports ; 29cm.
£3.95
Primary classification 001.9'3
(B77-28329)

Mooney, Richard Edwin. Gods of air and darkness : the possibility of a nuclear war in the past / [by] Richard E. Mooney. — St Albans : Panther, 1977. — 190p ; 18cm.
Originally published: London : Souvenir Press, 1975.
ISBN 0-586-04345-4 Pbk : £0.75
(B77-07758)

Steiger, Brad. Mysteries of time and space / [by] Brad Steiger ; special archaeological research by Ron Calais. — London : Sphere, 1977. — 283p, [16]p of plates : ill, ports ; 18cm.
Originally published: Englewood Cliffs : Prentice-Hall, 1974. — Bibl.: p.259-272. — Index.
ISBN 0-7221-8131-0 Pbk : £0.95
(B77-19958)

The **unexplained** : a sourcebook of strange phenomena / [compiled by] William R. Corliss. — Toronto [etc.] ; London : Bantam, 1976. — viii,338,[1]p : ill, maps ; 18cm.
Index.
ISBN 0-553-02812-x Pbk : £0.75
(B77-05162)

The **world's** last mysteries. — London [etc.] : Reader's Digest Association, 1977. — 320p : ill(chiefly col), col maps, ports(1 col), col plans ; 31cm.
Ill. on lining papers. — Index.
£8.95
(B77-29865)

001.9'4'08 — Mysteries. *Collections. Juvenile literature*

Haining, Peter. The monster trap, and other true mysteries / [by] Peter Haining. — London : Armada Paperbacks, 1976. — 127p ; 18cm.
ISBN 0-00-691163-3 Pbk : £0.40
(B77-03865)

001.9'4'09162 — Mysteries. *Oceans*

Winer, Richard. From the Devil's Triangle to the Devil's Jaw / [by] Richard Winer. — Toronto [etc.] ; London : Bantam, 1977. — xii,242,[1]p, [16]p of plates : ill, ports ; 18cm.
Bibl.: p.240-242.
ISBN 0-553-10860-3 Pbk : £0.85
(B77-33008)

001.9'4'094276 — Mysteries. *Lancashire*

Rickman, Philip. Mysterious Lancashire : legends and by-lines of Lancelot's Shire / by Philip Rickman and Graham Nown. — Clapham, N. Yorkshire : Dalesman, 1977. — 64p : ill, map ; 21cm.
Bibl.: p.64.
ISBN 0-85206-374-1 Pbk : £0.65
(B77-16692)

001.9'4'0977 — Mysteries. *North America. Great Lakes*

Gourley, Jay. The Great Lakes triangle / [by] Jay Gourley. — [London] : Fontana, 1977. — 192p : map ; 18cm.
Also published: Greenwich, Conn. : Fawcett, 1977. — Index.
ISBN 0-00-635081-x Pbk : £0.75
(B77-29113)

001.9'4'09991 — Mysteries. *Moon*
Leonard, George H. Someone else is on our moon / [by] George H. Leonard. — London : W.H. Allen, 1977. — xxi,232p,[32]p of plates : ill ; 22cm.
Originally published: as 'Somebody else is on the moon'. New York : McKay, 1976. — Bibl.: p.215-221. — Index.
ISBN 0-679-50606-3 : £4.95
(B77-19959)

001.9'42 — Unidentified flying objects
Collyns, Robin. Ancient astronauts : a time reversal? / [by] Robin Collyns. — London : Pelham, 1976. — 110p,[8]p of plates : ill, ports ; 23cm.
Bibl.: p.109-110.
ISBN 0-7207-0935-0 : £4.25
(B77-01113)

Constable, Trevor James. The cosmic pulse of life : the revolutionary biological power behind UFOs / by Trevor James Constable. — Sudbury : Spearman, 1977. — [1],xiii,410p,[32]p of plates : ill ; 23cm.
Originally published: United States : Merlin Press, 1976. — Index.
ISBN 0-85435-194-9 : £4.75
(B77-23053)

Keel, John A. Operation Trojan Horse : an exhaustive study of unidentified flying objects, revealing their source and the forces that control them / [by] John A. Keel. — London : Abacus, 1976. — 320p : ill ; 20cm.
Originally published: as 'UFO'S : Operation Trojan Horse', New York : Putnam, 1970 ; and as 'Operation Trojan Horse', London : Souvenir Press, 1971. — Bibl.: p.308-312. — Index.
ISBN 0-349-12085-4 Pbk : £1.50
(B77-02712)

Le Poer Trench, Brinsley. Mysterious visitors : the UFO story / [by] Brinsley Le Poer Trench. — Revised ed. — London [etc.] : Pan Books, 1977. — xiv,175p,[16]p of plates : ill ; 18cm.
This ed. originally published: 1975. — Index.
Pbk : £0.70
ISBN 0-330-24252-0
(B77-26066)

Ortzen, Len. Strange stories of UFOs / [by] Len Ortzen. — London : A. Barker, 1977. — [5], 152p ; 23cm.
Bibl.: p.151-152.
ISBN 0-213-16634-8 : £3.95
(B77-19155)

Smith, Warren. UFO trek / [by] Warren Smith. — London : Sphere, 1977. — 189p ; 18cm.
Originally published: United States : s.n., 1976.
ISBN 0-7221-7950-2 Pbk : £0.85
(B77-29866)

Vallee, Jacques. Anatomy of a phenomenon / [by] Jacques Vallee. — London : Tandem, 1974. — xi,210p,[8]p of plates : ill, chart, facsims, maps ; 18cm.
Originally published: Chicago : Regnery, 1965 ; London : Spearman, 1966. — Index.
ISBN 0-426-13071-5 Pbk : £0.35
(B77-18504)

Vallee, Jacques. UFOs, the psychic solution / [by] Jacques Vallee. — St Albans : Panther, 1977. — 221p : ill ; 18cm.
Originally published: as 'The invisible college'. New York : Dutton, 1975. — Bibl.: p.213. — Index.
ISBN 0-586-04653-4 Pbk : £0.85
(B77-20855)

001.9'42 — Unidentified flying objects. *Juvenile literature*
Blumberg, Rhoda. UFO / by Rhoda Blumberg. — New York ; London : F. Watts, 1977. — [7] ,64p : ill ; 23cm. — (A first book)
Bibl.: p.60-61. — Index.
ISBN 0-531-00397-3 : £2.25
(B77-29867)

001.9'42 — Unidentified flying objects. Engineering aspects
Cramp, Leonard. An engineer looks at UFOs : presented by Leonard Cramp at the first National Research and Investigations Conference, Stoke-on-Trent, England - May 1975. — London (c/o The Secretary, 6 Cairn Ave., W5 5HX) : British UFO Research Association, 1976. — [1],7p ; 22cm. — (British Unidentified Flying Object Research Association. Science papers ; 3 ISSN 0309-7331)
Sd : £0.50(£0.30 to members of BUFORA)
(B77-33009)

001.9'42 — Unidentified flying objects. Sources of evidence: Ancient Eastern myths
Drake, Walter Raymond. Gods and spacemen in the ancient East / [by] W. Raymond Drake. — London : Sphere, 1976. — 240p ; 18cm.
Originally published: as 'Spacemen in the ancient East'. London : Spearman, 1968. — Index.
ISBN 0-7221-3057-0 Pbk : £0.75
(B77-24645)

001.9'42'05 — Unidentified flying objects. *Periodicals*
The **Fountain** journal : (Warminster UFO sightings). — Warminster (Star House, 78 Portway, Warminster, Wilts.) : ['Fountain journal'].
No.1- ; [1976]-. — [1976]-. — 21cm.
28p. in 1st issue.
Sd : £0.35
(B77-10706)

001.9'42'072 — Unidentified flying objects. Investigation. *Manuals*
British Unidentified Flying Object Research Association. UFO investigation : a field investigator's handbook / [British UFO Research Association] ; [Roger H. Stanway editor, Jenny Randles, assistant editor]. — [London] (c/o The Secretary, 6 Cairn Ave., W5 5HX]) : BUFORA, 1976. — [141]p : ill, forms, map ; 30cm.
Pierced for binder.
ISBN 0-903649-01-2 Ls : £3.00
(B77-13458)

Whitaker, Trevor. Investigation procedures : presented by Trevor Whitaker at the first National Research and Investigations Conference, Stoke on Trent, England, May 1975. — Stoke on Trent (Newchapel Observatory, Stoke on Trent, Staffs.) : British Unidentified Flying Object Research Association, 1976. — [1],6p ; 21cm. — (British Unidentified Flying Object Research Association. Science papers ; 2)
Sd : £0.50(£0.30 to members of the Association)
(B77-19156)

001.9'42'09 — Unidentified flying objects, to 1975
Drake, Walter Raymond. Gods and spacemen throughout history / [by] W. Raymond Drake. — London : Sphere, 1977. — 253p ; 18cm.
Originally published: London : Spearman, 1975. — Bibl.: p.238-246. — Index.
ISBN 0-7221-3038-4 Pbk : £0.75
(B77-15646)

Landsburg, Alan. In search of extraterrestrials / [by] Alan Landsburg ; foreword by Leonard Nimoy. — London : Corgi, 1977. — x,164,[1]p, [32]p of plates : ill, ports ; 18cm.
Originally published: New York : Bantam Books, 1976. — Bibl.: p.163-164.
ISBN 0-552-10449-3 Pbk : £0.85
(B77-20856)

Shuttlewood, Arthur. The flying saucerers / [by] Arthur Shuttlewood. — London : Sphere, 1977. — 159p,[8]p of plates : ill ; 18cm.
Originally published: 1976.
ISBN 0-7221-7809-3 Pbk : £0.75
(B77-28330)

Shuttlewood, Arthur. The flying saucerers / [by] Arthur Shuttlewood. — London : Sphere, 1976. — 159p,[8]p of plates : ill ; 18cm.
ISBN 0-7221-7810-7 Pbk : £0.65
(B77-01963)

Tansley, David. Omens of awareness : startling parallels between UFO phenomena and the expanding consciousness of man / [by] David Tansley. — Sudbury : Spearman, 1977. — 318p : ill ; 23cm.
Bibl.: p.317-318.
ISBN 0-85435-134-5 : £5.35
(B77-22304)

001.9'42'09 — Unidentified flying objects, to 1976
Drake, Walter Raymond. Messengers from the stars / [by] W. Raymond Drake. — [New ed.]. — London : Sphere, 1977. — 238p ; 18cm.
Previous ed.: published as 'Gods or spacemen?'. Amherst, Wis. : Amherst Press, 1964. — Index.
ISBN 0-7221-3032-5 Pbk : £0.85
(B77-23943)

001.9'42'09754 — Unidentified flying objects. Claimed observations. *West Virginia, 1965-1975*
Keel, John A. Visitors from space : the astonishing true story of the Mothman prophecies / [by] John A. Keel. — St Albans : Panther, 1976. — 237,[1]p ; 18cm.
Originally published: as 'The Mothman prophecies'. New York : Saturday Review Press, 1975.
ISBN 0-586-04402-7 Pbk : £0.75
(B77-00569)

001.9'44 — Aquatic monsters. Claimed observations, ca 1870-1975
Dinsdale, Tim. The leviathans / [by] Tim Dinsdale. — Revised ed. — London : Futura Publications, 1976. — 247p,[16]p of plates : ill, maps ; 18cm.
Previous ed.: London : Routledge and Kegan Paul, 1966.
ISBN 0-86007-365-3 Pbk : £0.75
(B77-13459)

001.9'44 — Bigfoot. Claimed observations, to 1975
Slate, B Ann. Bigfoot / by B. Ann Slate and Alan Berry. — Toronto [etc.] ; London : Bantam, 1976. — xv,171,[1]p,[8]p of plates : ill, ports ; 18cm.
ISBN 0-552-62968-5 Pbk : £0.60
(B77-01114)

001.9'44 — Loch Ness monster
Grimshaw, Roger. The meaning of the Loch Ness monster / by Roger Grimshaw and Paul Lester. — Birmingham (Birmingham B15 2TT) : Centre for Contemporary Cultural Studies, University of Birmingham, 1976. — [1],42p ; 30cm.
Bibl.: p.41-42.
Sd : Unpriced
(B77-29114)

001.9'44 — Monsters. *Juvenile literature*
Miller, Carey. All about monsters / [written by Carey Miller] ; [illustrators John Francis et al.]. — London : Usborne, 1977. — 32p : ill(chiefly col), maps(chiefly col) ; 28cm. — (The world of the unknown)
Spine-title: Monsters. — Bibl.: p.32. — Index.
ISBN 0-86020-146-5 Pbk : £0.95
(B77-28331)

001.9'44 — Yetis
Grumley, Michael. There are giants in the earth / [by] Michael Grumley ; illustrations by the author. — St Albans : Panther, 1976. — 155p,[4]p of plates : ill, maps, port ; 18cm.
Originally published: Garden City, N.Y. : Doubleday, 1974 ; London : Sidgwick and Jackson, 1975. — Bibl.: p.147-149. — Index.
ISBN 0-586-04399-3 Pbk : £0.60
(B77-00570)

Napier, John Russell. Bigfoot : the Yeti and Sasquatch in myth and reality / [by] John Napier. — [2nd ed.]. — London : Abacus, 1976. — 204p,[12]p of plates : ill, ports ; 20cm.

Previous ed.: London : Cape, 1972. — Index.
ISBN 0-349-12496-5 Pbk : £1.25
(B77-07012)

001.9'5'09 — Deceptions & hoaxes, to 1976
Moss, Norman. The pleasures of deception / by Norman Moss. — London : Chatto and Windus, 1977. — 208p ; 23cm.
Index.
ISBN 0-7011-2204-8 : £4.95 : CIP rev.
(B77-05809)

003 — SYSTEMS
003 — Complex systems
Waddington, Conrad Hal. Tools for thought / [by] C.H. Waddington. — London : Cape, 1977. — 250p : ill ; 21cm.
Bibl.: p.234-239. — Index.
ISBN 0-224-01077-8 : £5.95
(B77-15056)

Waddington, Conrad Hal. Tools for thought / [by] C.H. Waddington. — St Albans : Paladin, 1977. — 250p : ill ; 20cm.
Also published: London : Cape, 1977. — Bibl.: p.234-239. — Index.
ISBN 0-586-08254-9 Pbk : £1.95
(B77-25345)

003 — Dynamical systems
Goodman, Michael R. Study notes in system dynamics / [by] Michael R. Goodman. — Cambridge, Mass. : Wright-Allen Press ; Chichester : [Distributed by] Wiley, 1974. — xiv,388p : ill ; 26cm.
With answers.
ISBN 0-914700-00-6 Pbk : Unpriced
(B77-11514)

003 — General systems theory. *Conference proceedings*
Progress in cybernetics and systems research. — Washington, D.C. : Hemisphere Publishing Corporation ; New York ; London [etc.] : Wiley.
'This Symposium was organized by the Austrian Society for Cybernetic Studies in cooperation with [the] Society for General Systems Research [and the] International Association of Cybernetics' - note. — In 2 vols.

Vol.2 : Socio-economic systems, cybernetics of cognition and learning, systems education, cybernetics in organization and management, special aspects / edited by Robert Trappl and F. de P. Hanika ; with introduction by Stafford Beer. — 1975. — x,442p : ill ; 29cm.
'A Halsted Press book'. — Includes papers in German. — Bibl. — Index.
ISBN 0-470-88476-2 : £17.45
Primary classification 001.53
(B77-10083)

003 — Large scale systems theory. *Conference proceedings*
Conference on Directions in Decentralized Control, Many Person Optimization, and Large-Scale Systems, *Wakefield, Mass., 1975.* Directions in large-scale systems : many-person optimization and decentralized control / edited by Y.C. Ho and S.K. Mitter. — New York ; London : Plenum Press, 1976. — xii,434p : ill ; 26cm.
'... papers presented at the Conference on Directions in Decentralized Control, Many-Person Optimization, and Large-Scale Systems held at the Colonial Hilton Inn, Wakefield, Massachusetts from September 1-3, 1975' - Introduction. — Bibl. — Index.
ISBN 0-306-30937-8 : £24.89
(B77-16693)

003 — System identification. *Reviews of research*
System identification : advances and case studies / edited by Raman K. Mehra, Dimitri G. Lainiotis. — New York [etc.] ; London : Academic Press, 1976. — xi,593p : ill ; 24cm. — (Mathematics in science and engineering ; vol.126)
ISBN 0-12-487950-0 : £13.50
(B77-17850)

003 — Systems analysis
Semprevivo, Philip Carmine. Systems analysis : definition, process, and design / [by] Philip C. Semprevivo. — Chicago [etc.] ; Henley-on-Thames : Science Research Associates.
Instructor's manuals. — 1976. — [3],140p : ill ; 28cm.
ISBN 0-574-21046-6 Pbk : £2.05
(B77-01110)

003 — Systems analysis. HIPO method
Katzan, Harry. Systems design and documentation : an introduction to the HIPO method / [by] Harry Katzan, Jr. — New York ; London [etc.] : Van Nostrand Reinhold, 1976. — ix,157p : ill, forms ; 24cm. — (Computer science series)
Bibl. — Index.
ISBN 0-442-24267-0 : £9.85
(B77-16141)

003 — Systems. Failure. Role of man
Study guide. — [Milton Keynes] ([Walton Hall, Milton Keynes MK7 6AA]) : [Open University], 1977. — 31p : ill ; 30cm. — (Technology, a third level course : systems performance, human factors and systems failures) (TD342 ; SG)
Sd : Unpriced
(B77-14510)

003 — Systems. Synergism
Fuller, Richard Buckminster. Synergetics : explorations in the geometry of thinking / [by] R. Buckminster Fuller in collaboration with E.J. Applewhite ; preface and contribution by Arthur L. Loeb. — New York : Macmillan ; London : Collier Macmillan, 1975 [i.e. 1976]. — ii-xxxii,877p : ill, facsims ; 24cm.
Text, ill. on lining papers. — Published in the United States: 1975. — Bibl.: p.875-876.
ISBN 0-02-541870-x : £18.75
(B77-05163)

003 — Systems theory
Berlinski, David. On systems analysis : an essay concerning the limitations of some mathematical methods in the social, political, and biological sciences / [by] David Berlinski. — Cambridge, Mass. ; London : M.I.T. Press, 1976. — xi,186p : ill ; 24cm.
Index.
ISBN 0-262-02120-x : £11.25
(B77-05810)

003 — Universities. *Great Britain. Open University. Curriculum subjects: Analysis of systems failure. Projects. Manuals*
Spear, Roger. Systems performance, human factors and systems failures, project guide / prepared for the [Open University] Course Team by Roger Spear. — [Milton Keynes] : Open University Press, [1976]. — 52p : ill ; 30cm. — (A third level course : systems performance, human factors and systems failures ; units 11 and 12) (TD342 ; unit11/12) (TMA ; 03)
Pbk : Unpriced
(B77-03866)

003'.01'84 — Systems. Reliability. Mathematical models
Singh, Chanan. System reliability, modelling and evaluation / [by] Chanan Singh and Roy Billinton. — London : Hutchinson, 1977. — viii,248p : ill ; 24cm.
Index.
ISBN 0-09-126500-2 : £14.00
(B77-15057)

003'.02'462 — General systems theory. *For engineering*
Faurre, Pierre. Elements of system theory / by Pierre Faurre, Michel Depeyrot ; translated [from the French] by Norbert Cot, Michael Cotton, John T. Gill. — Amsterdam [etc.] ; Oxford : North-Holland Publishing Co., 1977. — xii,281p : ill ; 23.
Translation of: 'Éléments d'automatique'. Paris : Dunod, 1974. — Bibl.: p.275-278. — Index.
ISBN 0-7204-0440-1 : Unpriced
(B77-03867)

003'.08 — General systems theory. *Readings*
Systems behaviour / edited by John Beishon and Geoff Peters. — 2nd ed. — London [etc.] : Harper and Row for the Open University Press, 1976. — 327p : ill ; 25cm. — (Open University. Set books)
Previous ed.: 1972. — Bibl. — Index.
ISBN 0-06-318056-1 : £7.50
ISBN 0-06-318057-x Pbk : £3.95
(B77-06411)

011 — GENERAL BIBLIOGRAPHIES

011 — Books: Bestsellers. *United States, 1895-1975. Bibliographies*
Hackett, Alice Payne. 80 years of best sellers, 1895-1975. — [New ed.] / [compiled by] Alice Payne Hackett and James Henry Burke. — New York ; London : Bowker, 1977. — xiii, 265p ; 24cm.
Previous ed.: published as '70 years of best sellers, 1895-1965' / by Alice Payne Hackett. 1967. — Bibl.: p.227-232. — Index.
ISBN 0-8352-0908-3 : £10.75
(B77-12809)

011 — Books. Sequels. *Bibliographies*
Gardner, Frank Matthias. Sequels. — [6th] ed. / compiled by Frank M. Gardner and Lisa-Christina Persson. — [Harrogate] : Association of Assistant Librarians.
In 2 vols.
Vol.2 : Junior books. — 1976. — 112p ; 24cm.
Spine title: Junior sequels. — ' ... first edition of "Junior sequels" to appear as a separate volume' - Preface. — 'Previous editions included in "Sequels"' - title page verso.
ISBN 0-900092-27-0 : £6.50(£4.50 to members of the Library Association)
(B77-12260)

011 — Cinema films: Educational films. Organisations. *Great Britain. British Film Institute. Higher Education Film Library. Catalogues*
Higher Education Film Library. Higher Education Film Library [catalogue] / [compiled by the British Universities Film Council]. — London (72 Dean St., W1V 5HB) : British Universities Film Council.
Supplement and price list. — 1975. — 20p ; 21cm.
Index.
ISBN 0-901299-13-8 Sd : £1.00
(B77-19960)

011 — Cinema films. Organisations. *London. Hounslow (London Borough). Rank Film Library. Stock: Cinema films available for hire. Catalogues*
Rank Film Library. Rank Film Library 16mm entertainment film catalogue. — Brentford (P.O. Box 20, Great West Rd, Brentford, Middx TW8 9HR) : The Library.
1976-77. — [1977]. — 176p,[8]leaves : ill(some col), forms ; 28cm.
Cover title. — Previously published: as '16mm entertainment film catalogue'. — Index.
Pbk : £1.00
(B77-29868)

011 — Great Britain. Welsh Office. Film Library. Stock. *Catalogues*
Great Britain. *Welsh Office. Film Library.* Catalog = Catalogue / y Swyddfa Gymreig Llyfrgell Ffilmiau = Welsh Office Film Library. — [Cardiff] ([Oxford House, Hills St., Cardiff CF1 2XG]) : [The Library].
1976-77 / [prepared by the Welsh Office and the Central Office of Information]. — 1976. — [1],56p ; 21cm.
Index.
Sd : Unpriced
(B77-24646)

011 — Microforms. *Abstracts. Serials*
National Reprographic Centre for documentation. NRCd micrographics abstracts. — Hatfield (Hatfield Polytechnic, Endymion Road Annexe, Hatfield, Herts. AL10 8AU) : NRCd.
2001-3000 / edited by Gordon Harris. — 1976. — [3],168p ; 30cm.
'... cumulates abstracts published in "NRCd bulletin" and "Reprographics quarterly" between Autumn 1972 and Winter 1975/1976' - Introduction. — Index.
ISBN 0-85267-100-8 Sp : £6.75(£4.50 to subscribers)
(B77-07013)

011 — Microforms in print. *Lists. Serials*
Guide to microforms in print : incorporating 'International microforms in print'. — London : Mansell Information Publishing.
1977 / edited by John J. Walsh. — 1977. — xxi,410p ; 29cm.
English text, English, French, German and Spanish introductions.
ISBN 0-7201-0711-3 : £20.00
ISSN 0017-5293
(B77-27627)

011 — Microforms in print. *Subject indexes. Serials*
Subject guide to microforms in print. — London : Mansell Information Publishing.
1976. — 1976. — xiii,247p ; 28cm.
ISBN 0-7201-0631-1 Pbk : £10.50
ISSN 0090-290x
(B77-08162)

Subject guide to microforms in print : incorporating 'International microforms in print'. — London : Mansell Information Publishing.
1977 / edited by John J. Walsh. — 1977. — xxvii,495p ; 29cm.
English, French, German, Spanish introductions. — Index.
ISBN 0-7201-0727-x : Unpriced
ISSN 0090-290x
(B77-26733)

011 — Public libraries. *Northern Ireland. Southern Education and Library Board. Library Service. Stock: Cassette tape recordings. Lists*
Southern Education and Library Board. *Library Service.* Cassettes / S.E.L.B. Library Service. — [Craigavon] ([Library Headquarters, Brownlow Rd, Legahory, Craigavon, County Armagh]) : [S.E.L.B. Library Service].
1. — [1976]. — [5],32,[4]p : 1 ill ; 21cm.
Sd : Unpriced
(B77-04518)

011'.02 — Reference books. *Bibliographies*
Ziskind, Sylvia. Reference readiness : a manual for librarians and students. — 2nd ed., revised and enlarged / [by] Sylvia Ziskind and Agnes Ann Hede. — Hamden, Conn. : Linnet Books ; London : Bingley, 1977. — xv,341p ; 24cm.
Previous ed.: / by Sylvia Ziskind. 1971. — Index.
ISBN 0-85157-246-4 : £12.00
(B77-30910)

011'.02 — Universities. Libraries. *Scotland. Strathclyde Region. Glasgow. University of Glasgow. Library. Stock: Reference books. Catalogues*
University of Glasgow. *Library.* KWIC index to general reference books in Glasgow University Library. — Revised [ed.]. — Glasgow (Glasgow G12 8QE) : The Library, 1976. — [127]p ; 30cm.
ISBN 0-85261-141-2 Sd : Unpriced
(B77-09459)

013 — BIBLIOGRAPHIES OF SPECIFIC CLASSES OF WRITERS

013'.375'0941 — Theses accepted by British universities, 1716-1950. *Bibliographies*

Retrospective index to theses of Great Britain and Ireland, 1716-1950 / Roger R. Bilboul, editor, Francis L. Kent, associate editor. — Santa Barbara : ABC-Clio ; Oxford : EBC-Clio.

In 5 vols.
Vol.1 : Social sciences and humanities. — [1976]. — [7],x,393p : facsim ; 31cm.
Published in the United States: 1975.
ISBN 0-903450-03-8 : £58.00
ISBN 0-903450-02-x Set of 5 vols : unpriced
(B77-01964)

Vol.2 : Applied sciences and technology. — 1976. — [7],xii,159p : facsim ; 31cm.
ISBN 0-903450-04-6 : £28.00
ISBN 0-903450-02-x Set of 5 vols : Unpriced
(B77-30911)

Vol.4 : Physical sciences. — 1976. — [7],xii, 99p ; 31cm.
ISBN 0-903450-06-2 : £23.00
ISBN 0-903450-02-x Set of 5 vols : Unpriced
(B77-30912)

Vol.5 : Chemical sciences. — 1976. — [7],xii, 251p : facsim ; 31cm.
ISBN 0-903450-07-0 : £34.00
ISBN 0-903450-02-x Set of 5 vols : Unpriced
(B77-30913)

013'.375'0942821 — Universities. Libraries. *South Yorkshire (Metropolitan County). Sheffield. University of Sheffield. Library. Stock: Theses accepted by University of Sheffield, 1920-1970. Catalogues*

University of Sheffield. Index to theses, 1920-1970 / [Sheffield University] ; compiled by J. Pandya. — Sheffield ([Sheffield S10 2TN]) : University of Sheffield Library.
2nd supplement : 1974-1975 / compiled by Sue Pandya. — 1976. — [4],i,45p ; 30cm.
Index.
ISBN 0-903284-11-1 Pbk : £2.00
(B77-01965)

013'.375'0942982 — Theses accepted by University College of Swansea, 1920-. *Bibliographies*

University College of Swansea. Higher degree theses, 1920-1970 / University College of Swansea. — [Swansea] ([Singleton Park, Swansea]) : University College of Swansea, Library.
Supplement no.5. 1975. — [1976]. — [2],9,2 leaves ; 30cm.
Index.
Sp : Unpriced
(B77-17243)

015 — BIBLIOGRAPHIES OF WORKS FROM SPECIFIC PLACES

015'.41 — Books for persons with dyslexia: Books with British imprints. *Lists*

Hardwick, Paula. Books for the dyslexic / compiled and reviewed by Paula Hardwick. — London [etc.] (14 Crondace Rd, SW6 4BB) : Helen Arkell Dyslexia Centre, [1977?]. — [22] p ; 30cm.
Sd : Unpriced
(B77-32347)

015'.41 — Books published by Richard Bentley and Son (Firm), 1829-1898. *Lists*

Turner, Michael Lawrence. Index and guide to the lists of the publications of Richard Bentley & Son, 1829-1898 / [by] Michael L. Turner. — Bishops Stortford (45 South St., Bishops Stortford, Herts. CM34 3AG) : Chadwyck-Healey Ltd [etc.], 1975. — [5],337p ; 23cm.
ISBN 0-85964-012-4 : £10.50
(B77-03868)

015'.41 — Books with British imprints. *Bibliographies. Serials*

British national bibliography : a subject catalogue of new British books received by the Copyright Receipt Office of the British Library, arranged according to the Dewey Decimal Classification and catalogued according to the British Text of the Anglo-American Cataloguing Rules [1967], with a full author & title index, a subject index and a list of publishers. — London : British Library, Bibliographic Services Division.
1976. — 1977. — 2v.(viii,2907p) ; 31cm.
Index.
ISBN 0-900220-61-9 : £40.00 : CIP rev
ISBN 0-900220-62-7 (Vol.1)
ISBN 0-900220-63-5 (Vol.2)
ISSN 0007-1544
(B77-21657)

015'.41 — Books with British imprints. National bibliographies: British National Bibliography. *Proposals*

Chaplin, Arthur Hugh. New patterns of national published bibliographies / by A.H. Chaplin. — London : British Library, Bibliographic Services Division, [1977]. — 10p ; 30cm.
ISBN 0-900220-65-1 Sd : Unpriced
(B77-09460)

015'.41 — British government publications. *Bibliographies*

Catalogue of government publications. — London : H.M.S.O.
1975 supplement : International organisations and overseas agencies publications. — 1976. — [5],87,xxxi p ; 22cm.
Index.
ISBN 0-11-700319-0 Pbk : £0.65
(B77-07014)

015'.41 — British government publications: Reports. *Indexes. Serials*

Kite, Vernon John. British government reports, indexes of chairmen and subjects / [compiled by John Kite]. — Bristol (P.O. Box 11, Avon House, The Haymarket, Bristol BS99 7DE) : Avon County Director of Public Relations and Publicity for Avon County Library.
1971-1975. — 1977. — [2],40p ; 21cm.
ISBN 0-86063-015-3 Sd : £1.50
(B77-31650)

015'.41 — British government serial publications. *Bibliographies. Serials*

Check list of British official serial publications. — London (Great Russell St., WC1B 3DG) : British Library Official Publications Library.
1976 : 8th ed. / editor Eve Johansson. — 1976. — 67p ; 30cm.
ISBN 0-904654-06-0 Sd : £3.50
ISSN 0084-8085
(B77-00001)

Check list of British official serial publications. — London (Great Russell St., WC1B 3DG) : British Library, Official Publications Library.
1977 : 9th ed. / edited by Eve Johansson and Gwyneth Morgan. — 1977. — 83p ; 30cm.
ISBN 0-904654-08-7 Sd : £3.50 : CIP rev.
ISSN 0084-8085
(B77-19961)

015'.41 — Commercial television services. *Great Britain. Granada Television. Television programmes. Indexes*

Granada Television. Granada Television programme index. — London [etc.] (36 Golden Sq., W1R 4AH) : Granada Television Ltd.
Year 21 : 3 May 1956 to 2 May 1977. — 1977. — 132p ; 22cm.
Pbk : Unpriced
(B77-26734)

015'.41 — Documents published by Great Britain. Her Majesty's Stationery Office, 1910-1919. *Lists*

Annual catalogues of British official and parliamentary publications, 1910-1919. — Bishops Stortford (45 South St., Bishops Stortford, Herts.) : Chadwyck-Healey [etc.], 1975. — c 530p ; 23cm.
Facsimile reprints. — Originally published: in 19 vols. London : H.M.S.O., 1911-1920. — Index.
ISBN 0-85964-017-5 : £22.00
(B77-03869)

015'.41 — Documents published by Great Britain. Her Majesty's Stationery Office, 1922-1972. *Indexes*

Blackmore, Ruth Matteson. Cumulative index to the annual catalogues of Her Majesty's Stationery Office publications, 1922-1972 / compiled by Ruth Matteson Blackmore ; with an introduction by James Gordon Ollé. — Washington [D.C.] ; Inverness ([c/o Historical Documents Institute, 64 Eastgate, Inverness]) : Carrollton Press.
Vol.1 : A-K. — 1976. — xxi,567p ; 29cm.
Text on lining papers.
ISBN 0-8408-0140-8 : Unpriced
(B77-05811)

Vol.2 : L-Z. — 1976. — xxi,583p ; 29cm.
Text on lining papers.
ISBN 0-8408-0141-6 : Unpriced
(B77-05812)

015'.418'35 — Books published by Dolmen Press, 1951-1976. *Bibliographies*

Dolmen Press. Dolmen XXV : an illustrated bibliography of the Dolmen Press, 1951-1976 / compiled by Liam Miller. — Dublin : Dolmen Press, 1976. — 96p,[4]p of plates : ill(some col), ports ; 28cm.
Limited ed. of 650 copies, of which fifty, numbered 1-50, are signed by the compiler and specially bound. — Index.
ISBN 0-85105-309-2 : £15.00
Signed ed. : Unpriced
(B77-05813)

015'.42 — Public libraries. *West Midlands (Metropolitan County). Birmingham. Birmingham Public Libraries. Exhibits: Books printed between 1476 & 1976: Books with English imprints. Catalogues*

Birmingham Public Libraries. 500 years of British printing, Caxton 1476-1976 : an exhibition in the Reference Library, Language and Literature Department [Birmingham Public Libraries], 30 September-30 October 1976. — [Birmingham] ([Ratcliff Place, Birmingham B1 2AR]) : [Birmingham Public Libraries], [1976]. — [1],17[i.e. 21]p : facsims ; 30cm.
ISBN 0-901011-14-2 Sd : £0.30
(B77-03870)

015'.42 — Universities. Libraries. *Scotland. Strathclyde Region. Glasgow. University of Glasgow. Library. Exhibits: Books with English imprints, 1479-1600. Catalogues*

University of Glasgow. *Library.* Printing in England from William Caxton to Christopher Barker : [catalogue of an exhibition held at] Glasgow University Library, Exhibition Room, November 1976-April 1977. — [Glasgow] : [The Library], [1976]. — [1],68p ; 30cm.
ISBN 0-85261-140-4 Sd : £0.50
(B77-13460)

015'.73 — American government publications. *Bibliographies*

Leidy, William Philip. A popular guide to government publications / compiled by W. Philip Leidy. — 4th ed. — New York ; Guildford : Columbia University Press, 1976. — xxi,440p ; 21cm.
Previous ed.: 1968. — Index.
ISBN 0-231-04019-9 : £17.34
(B77-02713)

015'.73 — Books in English: Books with American imprints. *Lists. Serials*

'**American** book publishing record' cumulative. — New York ; London : Bowker.
1970-1974 : a record of American book production ... as cataloged by the Library of Congress and recorded both in 'Weekly record' and in the monthly issues of the 'American book publishing record', arranged by subject according to the Dewey Decimal Classification and indexed by author and title. — 1976 [i.e. 1977]. — 4v. ; 29cm.
Published in the United States: 1976. — Index.
ISBN 0-8352-0911-3 : £71.00
ISSN 0002-7707
(B77-11017)

015'.73 — Books in English: Books with American imprints: Books in print. *Lists. Serials*

Books in print. — New York ; London : Bowker.

1975 : [28th ed.]. — [1976]. — 4v. ; 28cm.
Published in the United States: 1975.
ISBN 0-8352-0825-7 : £41.50
ISSN 0068-0214
(B77-00571)

Books in print supplement : authors, titles, subjects. — New York ; London : Bowker.
1976-1977. — 1977. — xi,2002p ; 29cm.
ISBN 0-8352-0957-1 : £26.00
ISSN 0000-0310
(B77-26735)

The **reader's** adviser : a layman's guide to literature. — 12th ed. — New York ; London : Bowker.
In 3 vols. — Previous ed.: published in 2 vols, 1968-9.
Vol.2 : The best in American and British drama and world literature in English translation / edited by F.J. Sypher. — 1977. — xv,774p ; 27cm.
Index.
ISBN 0-8352-0852-4 : £18.00
ISSN 0094-5943
(B77-14511)

Vol.3 : The best in the reference literature of the world / edited by Jack A. Clarke. — 1977. — xiii,1034p ; 27cm.
Index.
ISBN 0-8352-0853-2 : £18.00
ISSN 0094-5943
(B77-14512)

015'.73 — Books with American imprints: Books in print. *Subject indexes. Serials*
Subject guide to books in print. — New York ; London : Bowker.
1976. — 1976. — 2v.([83],4316)p ; 29cm.
ISBN 0-8352-0907-5 : £41.00
ISSN 0000-0159
(B77-07015)

015'.73 — Books with American imprints: Books published in series. *Lists. Serials*
Books in series in the United States : original, reprinted, in-print, and out-of-print books, published or distributed in the US in popular, scholarly and professional series. — New York ; London : Bowker.
1966-1975. — 1977. — xi,2486,[18]p ; 28cm.
ISBN 0-8352-0902-4 : £35.75
(B77-12810)

016 — BIBLIOGRAPHIES OF SPECIFIC SUBJECTS

016.0016'4'05 — Periodicals on computer systems. *Bibliographies*
Aslib. *Computer Information Group.* World list of computer periodicals. — 2nd ed. / Aslib Computer Information Group. — London : United Trade Press, [1977]. — [2],ii,140p ; 30cm.
Previous ed.: Manchester : National Computing Centre, 1970.
ISBN 0-85471-028-0 Pbk : Unpriced
(B77-28332)

016.016 — Libraries. Cooperation. Organisations. *Humberside. Humberside Libraries Technical Interloan Scheme. Members. Stock: Abstracts & indexes. Catalogues*
Humberside Libraries. *Technical Interloan Scheme.* A guide to abstracts and indexes in HULTIS members libraries. — Hull (Central Library, Albion St., Hull HU1 3TF) : Library of Science, Technology and Commerce, 1977. — [7],40p ; 30cm.
Index.
ISBN 0-904451-06-2 Sp : £0.50
(B77-06414)

016.0163091'94 — Australia. Society, to 1974. *Bibliographies of bibliographies*
Mayer, Henry. ARGAP : a research guide to Australian politics and cognate subjects / [by] Henry Mayer with Margaret Bettison and Judy Keene. — Melbourne [etc.] ; London : Cheshire Publishing ; [Aylesbury] : [Distributed by Ginn], 1976. — xxxi,329p ; 27cm.
Index.
ISBN 0-7015-1786-7 : £8.50
(B77-12261)

016.016355 — Bibliographies prepared in Imperial War Museum. Department of Printed Books. *Lists*
Imperial War Museum. *Department of Printed Books.* Subject guide to booklists corrected to June 1976 / Imperial War Museum, Department of Printed Books. — London (Lambeth Rd, SE1 6HZ) : The Museum, [1976]. — [1],ii,27p ; 21cm.
Sd : Unpriced
(B77-21658)

016.01682 — English literature, to 1975. *Bibliographies of bibliographies*
Doyle, Paul Aloysius. Guide to basic information sources in English literature / by Paul A. Doyle ; with a foreword by Harrison T. Meserole. — New York ; London [etc.] : Wiley, 1976. — xi,143p ; 22cm. — (Information resources series)
Spine title: Guide to English literature. — 'A Halsted Press book'. — Index.
ISBN 0-470-15011-4 : £7.70
(B77-23054)

016.02 — Librarianship & information science. *Bibliographies*
MacCafferty, Maxine. Library-information science : bibliographies, guides, reviews, surveys / compiled by Maxine MacCafferty. — London : Aslib, 1976. — ix,104p ; 30cm. — (Aslib. Bibliographies ; no.3 ISSN 0308-7522)
Index.
ISBN 0-85142-087-7 Pbk : £4.50(£3.75 to members of Aslib)
(B77-11515)

016.02 — Theses on librarianship & information science: Theses accepted by British universities & schools of librarianship, 1950-1974. *Bibliographies*
Library and information studies in the United Kingdom and Ireland, 1950-1974 : an index to theses / edited by Peter J. Taylor. — London : Aslib, 1976. — viii,69p ; 30cm.
Bibl.: p.vi. — Index.
ISBN 0-85142-085-0 Pbk : £4.50(£3.50 to members of Aslib)
(B77-07016)

016.0276'6 — Welfare services. Libraries. *Bibliographies*
Cumming, Eileen Elizabeth. Hospital and welfare library services : an international bibliography / compiled and edited by Eileen E. Cumming. — London : Library Association, 1977. — ix, 174p ; 25cm.
English, French and German foreword and introduction. — 'Based on work begun by Mona E. Goring for the International Federation of Library Associations, Sub-Section of Libraries in Hospitals'.
ISBN 0-85365-139-6 : £8.50(£6.80 to members of the Library Association) : CIP rev.
(B77-05164)

016.028'9 — Adults. Reading habits, ca 1930-1975. *Bibliographies*
Mann, Margaret Gwendoline. The reading habits of adults : a select annotated bibliography / by Margaret Mann. — London (Publications Officer, British Library Research and Development Department, Sheraton House, Great Chapel St., W1V 4BH) : British Library, 1977. — 72p ; 20x21cm. — (British National Bibliography Research Fund. Reports ; no.1)
Index.
ISBN 0-85350-143-2 Pbk : £5.95
(B77-12811)

016.05 — Directories with British imprints. *Lists. Serials*
'British rate & data' directories & annuals. — London (76 Oxford St., W1N 0HH) : Maclean-Hunter Ltd.
1976 / editor Angela Hoad. — [1976]. — [2], 60,vi p : ill ; 28cm.
Index.
Sd : £2.50
(B77-31652)

1977 / editor Angela Hoad. — [1977]. — [2], 56,vi p : ill ; 28cm.
Index.
Sd : £3.00
(B77-31653)

016.05 — Directories with Commonwealth imprints. *Bibliographies*
Current British directories : a guide to the directories published in Great Britain, Ireland, the British Commonwealth and South Africa. — Beckenham (154 High St., Beckenham, Kent BR3 1EA) : CBD Research Ltd.
Edition 8 / edited by I.G. Anderson. — 1977. — xvi,430p : ill ; 31cm.
Text on lining papers. — Previously published: as 'G.P. Henderson's current British directories'. — Index.
ISBN 0-900246-21-9 : Unpriced
ISSN 0070-1858
(B77-16142)

016.05 — Libraries. Cooperation. Organisations. *Humberside. Humberside Libraries Technical Interloan Scheme. Members. Stock: Periodicals. Catalogues*
Humberside Libraries. *Technical Interloan Scheme.* A checklist of members' periodicals / Humberside County Libraries, HULTIS. — Hull (Central Library, Albion St., Hull HU1 3TF) : Library of Science, Technology and Commerce.
1977. — [1977]. — [11],275p ; 30cm.
ISBN 0-904451-05-4 Sp : £2.50
ISSN 0305-8948
(B77-06415)

016.05 — Libraries. Stock: Periodicals. *East Sussex. Brighton region. Catalogues*
Union list of periodicals in libraries of the Brighton area / Brighton Polytechnic Learning Resources. — [Brighton] ([Moulsecoomb, Brighton BN2 4GJ]) : [Brighton Polytechnic Learning Resources].
[1976]. — 1976. — [3]leaves,137p ; 30cm.
Sd : £2.50
(B77-11516)

016.05 — Libraries. Stock: Periodicals. *Staffordshire. Catalogues*
Mid and South Staffordshire Libraries in Co-operation. Union list of periodicals / compiled with the assistance of six member libraries on behalf of MISLIC ; and edited by Staffordshire County Library. — 5th ed. — Stafford (County Library Headquarters, Friars Terrace, Stafford ST17 4AY) : [Staffordshire County Library], 1976. — [1],vii,255p ; 30cm.
Section H ([7]p.) as insert. — Previous ed.: 1972.
ISBN 0-903363-03-8 Pbk : £3.00(£2.50 to members of MISLIC)
(B77-11018)

016.05 — National libraries. *Great Britain. British Library. Lending Division. Stock: Periodicals: Translations into English language. Lists*
British Library. *Lending Division.* Journals in translation / [British Library, Lending Division] ; edited by B. Smith. — Boston Spa : The Division, 1976. — [2],83p : ill, facsim ; 30cm.
Index.
ISBN 0-85350-159-9 Sd : £2.00
(B77-03871)

016.05 — Universities. Libraries. *Cambridgeshire. Cambridge. University of Cambridge. Library. Stock: Serial publications. Catalogues. Serials*
University of Cambridge. *Library.* Current serials available in the [Cambridge] University Library and in other libraries connected with the University. — Cambridge (West Rd, Cambridge CB3 9DR) : The Library.
1976. — 1976. — 2v.([24],1492p,[2]fold leaves of plates) : 3 maps ; 22cm.
ISBN 0-902205-21-8 : £17.50
ISSN 0306-4174
(B77-05814)

016.052 — Literary periodicals: Little magazines: Periodicals with British imprints, 1930-1939. *Indexes*
Bloomfield, Barry Cambray. An author index to selected British 'little magazines', 1930-1939 / [by] B.C. Bloomfield. — London : Mansell Information Publishing, 1976. — xiii,153p ; 26cm.
Bibl.: p.xi-xii.
ISBN 0-7201-0542-0 : £15.00
(B77-01966)

016.052 — Periodical articles in English. *Bibliographies*
British humanities index. — London : Library Association.
1976 / Betty M. King (editor) [with] Joyce Asbury-Williams, Rosemary Heath. — 1977. — [4],538,216p ; 31cm.
ISBN 0-85365-369-0 : £37.00
ISSN 0007-0815
(B77-19158)

016.059'956 — Libraries. Stock: Periodicals with Japanese imprints: Periodicals in Japanese. *Great Britain. Catalogues*
Carnell, Peter W. Check-list of Japanese periodicals held in British university and research libraries. — 2nd ed. / by Peter W. Carnell. — [Sheffield] ([Sheffield S10 2TN]) : Sheffield University [Library].
Previous ed.: [i.e. revised ed.] in 1 vol. 1971.
Part 1 : Japanese titles. — 1976. — [2],v,305p ; 30cm.
At head of title: Japan Library Group.
ISBN 0-903284-12-x Pbk : £3.00
(B77-06416)

016.06 — National libraries. *Great Britain. British Library. Lending Division. Stock: Conference proceedings. Catalogues. Serials*
British Library. *Lending Division.* Index of conference proceedings received, annual cumulation / [British Library, Lending Division]. — Boston Spa : B.L.L.D.
1976. — 1977. — [2],840p ; 30cm.
'... a cumulated publication containing details of all conferences, which have been listed in the "Index of conference proceedings received" during 1976, i.e. numbers 100-111 inclusive' - Preface.
Pbk : £8.00
ISSN 0305-5183
(B77-23944)

016.07 — Libraries. Stock: National newspapers. *Great Britain. Catalogues*
Webber, Rosemary. World list of national newspapers : a union list of national newspapers in libraries in the British Isles / compiled by Rosemary Webber under the auspices of the Standing Conference of National and University Libraries in contract with the Social Science Research Council. — London [etc.] : Butterworth, 1976. — [8],95p ; 28cm.
Bibl.: p.89-90. — Index.
ISBN 0-408-70817-4 : £9.50
(B77-03872)

016.071'47'1 — Newspapers for negroes: Newspapers with New York imprints, 1827-1841. *Indexes*
Jacobs, Donald M. Antebellum black newspapers : indices to New York 'Freedom's journal' (1827-1829), 'The Rights of all' (1829), 'The Weekly advocate' (1837), and 'The Colored American' (1837-1841) / edited [i.e. compiled] by Donald M. Jacobs assisted by ... [others]. — Westport, Conn. ; London : Greenwood Press, 1976. — xii,587p ; 25cm.
ISBN 0-8371-8824-5 : £25.30
(B77-16694)

016.072'8'2 — Newspapers with South Yorkshire (Metropolitan County) imprints, 1754-1975. *Lists*
Munford, Anthony Peter. South Yorkshire newspapers, 1754-1976 / compiled by Anthony P. Munford. — Barnsley (70 Vernon Rd, Worsbrough Bridge, Barnsley [S. Yorkshire] S70 5LM) : South Yorkshire County Council, Recreation, Culture and Health Department, 1976. — [2],19p ; 21cm. — (South Yorkshire County Archive Service. Archive handlists ; no.1 ISSN 0309-7919)
Sd : £0.30
(B77-23945)

016.079'51 — Provincial & regional newspapers with Chinese imprints, 1949-1969. *Catalogues*
Goodman, David S G. Research guide to Chinese provincial and regional newspapers / [by] David S.G. Goodman. — London (Malet St., WC1E 7HP) : Contemporary China Institute, School of Oriental and African Studies, University of London, 1976. — [4],v,140p ; 24cm. — (Contemporary China Institute. Research notes and studies ; no.2 ISSN 0308-6119)
Catalogue of the holdings of the Library of Congress, the Union Research Institute, Hong Kong and the East Asian Library of the Hoover Institution on War, Revolution and Peace.
ISBN 0-7286-0036-6 Sd : Unpriced
(B77-07018)

016.079'54 — Great Britain. Foreign and Commonwealth Office. Libraries: India Office Library. Stock: Newspapers with South Asian imprints: Newspapers in English. *Catalogues*
India Office Library. Catalogue of the newspaper collection in the India Office Library / [compiled by] Dorothy Walker. — London ([197 Blackfriars Rd, S.E.1]) : [The Library], 1977. — ix,19p ; 30cm. — (India Office Library. Occasional publications ; no.2)
Sd : £0.75
(B77-19962)

016.09 — Universities. Libraries. *West Midlands (Metropolitan County). Birmingham. University of Birmingham. Library. Exhibits: Documents collected by Birmingham Bibliographic Society. Catalogues*
Birmingham Bibliographical Society. Members' exhibition held in Birmingham University Library October-December 1974, [organized by the] Birmingham Bibliographical Society / [catalogue edited by Christine L. Penney]. — [Birmingham] ([P.O. Box 363, Birmingham B15 2TT]) : The Library, 1974. — 16 leaves ; 30cm.
ISBN 0-904474-00-3 Sd : £0.40
(B77-16143)

016.091 — Libraries. Stock: Manuscripts. *Great Britain, to 1500. Catalogues*
Ker, Neil Ripley. Medieval manuscripts in British libraries / by N.R. Ker. — Oxford : Clarendon Press.
2 : Abbotsford-Keele. — 1977. — xliii,999p ; 24cm.
Bibl.: p.xxxvii-xliii.
ISBN 0-19-818162-0 : £30.00
(B77-14007)

016.091 — Libraries. Stock: Manuscripts in Indonesian languages. *Great Britain. Catalogues*
Ricklefs, Merle Calvin. Indonesian manuscripts in Great Britain : a catalogue of manuscripts in Indonesian languages in British public collections / by M.C. Ricklefs and P. Voorhoeve. — Oxford [etc.] : Oxford University Press, 1977. — xxix,237p ; 24cm. — (London Oriental bibliographies ; vol.5)
Bibl.: p.188-202. — Index.
ISBN 0-19-713592-7 : £16.00
(B77-20857)

016.091 — Museums. Libraries. *London. Kensington & Chelsea (London Borough). Victoria and Albert Museum. Library. Stock: English non-illuminated manuscripts. Catalogues*
Victoria and Albert Museum. *Library.* Catalogue of English non-illuminated manuscripts in the National Art Library up to December 1973 / Victoria and Albert Museum. — London : [Victoria and Albert Museum].
Supplement. 1975 : accessions and re-catalogued items. — 1975. — [1],12p ; 30cm.
Index.
Sd : Unpriced
(B77-11020)

Victoria and Albert Museum. *Library.* Catalogue of English non-illuminated manuscripts in the National Art Library up to December 1973 / Victoria and Albert Museum ; compiled by Joyce Irene Whalley with the assistance of Alan T. Richmond. — [London] : [Victoria and Albert Museum], 1975. — [1],iii,130p : 1 ill, facsims ; 30cm.
Index.
Sd : £1.50
(B77-11019)

Victoria and Albert Museum. *Library.* Catalogue of English non-illuminated manuscripts in the National Art Library up to December 1973 / Victoria and Albert Museum. — London : [Victoria and Albert Museum].
Supplement. 1974 : accessions and re-catalogued items. — 1975. — [1],7p ; 30cm.
Index.
Sd : £0.25
(B77-11021)

016.091 — National libraries. *Great Britain. British Library. Department of Manuscripts. Stock: Acquisitions, 1756-1782. Catalogues*
British Library. Catalogue of additions to the manuscripts, 1756-1782, additional manuscripts 4101-5017 / the British Library [Department of Manuscripts]. — London : British Museum Publications Ltd for the British Library, 1977. — ix,706p ; 27cm.
ISBN 0-7141-0490-6 : £45.00
(B77-26067)

016.091 — National libraries. *Great Britain. British Library. Department of Manuscripts. Stock: Acquisitions, 1961- . Catalogues*
British Library. *Department of Manuscripts.* 'Rough register' of acquisitions of the Department of Manuscripts, British Library. — London : Swift.
1971-1975. — 1977. — [2],xviii,246[i.e.247]p ; 33cm. — (List and Index Society. Special series ; vol.10)
ISBN 0-902573-59-4 Pbd : £6.30(£5.05 to members of the List and Index Society)
(B77-08163)

016.091 — National libraries. *Great Britain. British Library. Department of Manuscripts. Stock: Manuscripts in Spanish. Catalogues*
British Library. Catalogue of the manuscripts in the Spanish language in the British Library / [compiled by] Don Pascual de Gayangos. — London : British Museum Publications Ltd for the British Library, 1976. — 4v. ; 26cm.
ISBN 0-7141-0491-4 : £60.00
(B77-26068)

016.091 — Records. Repositories. Stock. Acquisitions: Manuscripts. *Great Britain. Lists. Serials*
Historical Manuscripts Commission. Accessions to repositories and reports added to the National Register of Archives / the Royal Commission on Historical Manuscripts. — London : H.M.S.O.
1975. — 1976. — vii,93p ; 25cm.
Index.
ISBN 0-11-440090-3 Pbk : £2.25
ISSN 0308-0986
(B77-08712)

016.091 — Universities. Colleges. Libraries. *London. Camden (London Borough). University College, London. Library. Stock: Manuscripts. Collections. Catalogues*
University College, London. *Library.* Manuscript collections in the library of University College, London : a handlist. — London ([Gower St., WC1E 6BT]) : The Library, 1975. — [3],18p ; 30cm. — (Occasional publications ; no.1 ISSN 0309-3352)
ISBN 0-905937-00-7 Sd : Unpriced
(B77-12262)

016.091 — Universities. Libraries. *Oxfordshire. Oxford. Bodleian Library. Stock: European illuminated manuscripts, ca 800-ca 1540. Catalogues*
Bodleian Library. Treasures from the Bodleian Library / [by] A.G. and W.O. Hassall ; introduction by R.W. Hunt. — London : Gordon Fraser Gallery, 1976. — 160p : col ill, col facsims ; 37cm.
In slip case. — Bibl. — Index.
ISBN 0-900406-52-6 : £26.00
(B77-07019)

016.094 — Art galleries. *London. Waltham Forest (London Borough). William Morris Gallery. Exhibits: Books designed by Morris, William, b.1834. Catalogues*
William Morris Gallery. In fine print : William Morris as book designer : [catalogue of an exhibition held at the] William Morris Gallery & Brangwyn Gift, Lloyd Park, Forest Road, London E17 4PP ... , 18 December 1976-19 March 1977. — London ([c/o Central Library, High St., Walthamstow, E17 7JN]) : London Borough of Waltham Forest, Libraries and Arts Department, 1976. — [3],ii,75p ; 30cm.
Bibl.: p.71-74.
ISBN 0-901974-05-6 Pbk : £1.00
(B77-11517)

016.094 — Books. Organisations. *Great Britain. National Book League. Exhibits: Books notable for design & production. Catalogues. Serials*
British book design and production / National Book League. — [London] : National Book League.
1976 : Catalogue of an exhibition of books published in 1975 [held at the] Frankfurt International Book Fair 16-21 September 1976 [and at the] National Book League ... 23 September-9 October 1976 / the books selected by Peter Guy, John Mercer, Jeffrey Tabberner. — 1976. — 64p : ill, facsims ; 22cm.
Index.
ISBN 0-85353-250-8 Pbk : £2.00
ISSN 0302-2846
(B77-02714)

016.094 — Books. Organisations. *Great Britain. National Book League. Exhibits: Documents printed by private presses, 1916-1968. Catalogues*
Jerome, Joseph. An exhibition of the work of three private presses : Saint Dominic's Press, Ditchling, Edward Walters, Primrose Hill, Saint Albert's Press, Aylesford, devised and presented by Brocard Sewell ... at the National Book League ... from 14 July-4 August 1976 : catalogue / [by Joseph Jerome]. — Faversham (Whitefriars, Faversham, Kent) : St Albert's Press, 1976. — [1],15[i.e. 16]p : 1 ill ; 22cm.
Cover title: St Dominic's Press and two other private presses.
ISBN 0-904849-20-1 Sd : £0.75
(B77-14008)

016.094 — National libraries. *Great Britain. British Library. Reference Division. Stock: Books in English: Books published by private presses between ca 1850 & 1965. Catalogues*
British Library. Modern British and American private presses (1850-1965) : [catalogue of the] holdings of the British Library / [compiled by P.A.H. Brown]. — London : British Museum Publications Ltd for the Library, 1976. — [3], 211p ; 26cm.
Index.
ISBN 0-7141-0367-5 : £20.00
(B77-01967)

016.094 — Public libraries. *London. Camden (London Borough). Camden (London Borough). Libraries and Arts Department. Swiss Cottage Library. Exhibits: Documents published by English private presses. Catalogues*
Camden *(London Borough). Libraries and Arts Department.* Catalogue of an exhibition of books and printed ephemera from twenty-eight contemporary private presses, [held] 3 December 1976 to 12 January 1977 [at] Swiss Cottage Library : [organised by the London Borough of Camden, Libraries and Arts Department]. — London (St Pancras Library, 100 Euston Rd, NW1 2AJ) : [The Department], 1976. — [24]p : ill ; 30cm.
Cover title: Private presses.
ISBN 0-901389-25-0 Sd : £0.80
(B77-08713)

016.128'2 — Mind. Philosophical perspectives. *Bibliographies*
Lindley, R C. The philosophy of mind : a bibliography / by R.C. Lindley and J.M. Shorter. — Oxford (10 Merton St., Oxford) : [University of Oxford, Sub-faculty of Philosophy]. — (University of Oxford. Sub-faculty of Philosophy. Study aids ; vol.6)
In 2 vols.
Part 1 : The self. — 1977. — [3] leaves,76[i.e.87]p ; 30cm.
Cover title.
Pbk : £0.65
(B77-29115)

016.133'092'4 — Occultism. Crowley, Aleister. Texts. *Bibliographies*
Parfitt, Will. A Crowley cross-index / [by Will Parfitt & A. Drylie]. — Bath (c/o Agapé Magazine, 7 Turner's Tower, Faulkland, Nr Bath, Avon) : ZRO, 1976. — [4],36p ; 21cm.
ISBN 0-905896-00-9 Sd : Unpriced
(B77-11022)

016.2 — Religion. *Bibliographies*
A **reader's** guide to the great religions / edited by Charles J. Adams. — 2nd ed. — New York : Free Press ; London : Collier Macmillan, 1977. — xvii,521p ; 24cm.
Previous ed.: 1965. — Index.
ISBN 0-02-900240-0 : £13.50
(B77-28334)

016.207'3'2 — Christianity. Historiology. *Bibliographies*
Bauckham, Richard. History & Christianity : a bibliography / prepared for the Historians Study Group of the UCCF Associates by Richard Bauckham and David Bebbington. — [Leeds] ([c/c Department of Theology, University of Leeds, Leeds LS2 9JT]) : [The author], [1977]. — [47]p ; 20cm.
Sd : £0.40
(B77-33556)

016.236 — Christian doctrine. Eschatology. Gerardus de Vliederhoven. Cordiale de IV novissimis. Versions in High German. Manuscripts. *Lists*
Byrn, R F M. Cordiale manuscript lists / [by R.F.M. Byrn]. — Leeds : University of Leeds, Department of German, [1976]. — [1],15,[1]p ; 22cm.
'from: R.F.M. Byrn['s] "The Cordiale-Auszug. A study of Gerard van Vliederhoven's 'Cordiale de IV novissimis' with particular reference to the High German versions" Leeds University Ph.D. thesis, 1976'.
ISBN 0-905938-00-3 Sd : Private circulation
(B77-11518)

016.3 — Great Britain. Departments of the Environment and Transport Library Services. Stock. *Abstracts. Periodicals*
Great Britain. *Departments of the Environment and Transport Library Services.* Departments of the Environment and Transport Library bulletin. — London (2 Marsham St., SW1P 3EB) : The Library Services.
No.1- ; 1977-. — 1977-. — 21cm.
Annual. — [4],ii,94p. in 1st issue. — Index.
Sd : £24.90 yearly
(B77-14513)

016.3 — Social sciences. *Bibliographies*
British Library of Political and Economic Science. A London bibliography of the social sciences / British Library of Political and Economic Science. — London : Mansell Information Publishing.
Vol.33 : 1975 : 10th supplement. — 1976. — [9],408[i.e.410]p ; 29cm.
Index.
ISBN 0-7201-0634-6 : £24.25
ISSN 0076-051x
(B77-05165)

Vol.34 : 1977 : 11th supplement. — 1977. — [9],447p ; 29cm.
ISBN 0-7201-0721-0 : £24.25 : CIP rev.
ISSN 0076-051x
(B77-24647)

016.3'00994 — Australia. Government. Social policies, 1950-1975. *Bibliographies*
Monie, Joanna. Social policy and its administration : a survey of the Australian literature, 1950-1975 / [compiled by] Joanna Monie and Adrienne Wise ; introduction by D.H. Borchardt. — Rushcutters Bay ; Exeter [etc.] : Pergamon, 1977. — xvi,594p ; 27cm.
Index.
ISBN 0-08-021943-8 : £15.75
(B77-29116)

016.301 — Sociology. *Bibliographies*
International bibliography of sociology = Bibliographie internationale de sociologie / prepared by the International Committee for Social Science Information and Documentation = établie par le Comité international pour l'information et la documentation en sciences sociales. — London : Tavistock Publications [etc.].
1975 : Vol.25 / [managing editor Jean Viet]. — 1977. — lx[i.e. lviii],390p ; 24cm. — (International bibliography of the social sciences = Bibliographie internationale des sciences sociales)
English and French text. — Index.
ISBN 0-422-76230-x : £25.00
ISSN 0085-2066
(B77-16144)

016.3012'2 — Documents for subcultures. *Indexes*
Index to the alternative and underground press / edited by John L. Noyce. — Brighton : Noyce, 1977. — 2v.([106]p;[49],74p) ; 30cm.
ISBN 0-903612-44-5 Sd : £7.00
(B77-11023)

016.3012'2'05 — Periodicals for subcultures: Periodicals with British imprints. *Lists*
The **underground** and alternative press in Britain. — Hassocks : Harvester Press.
Previous control number ISBN 0-85527-224-4.
1974 : a bibliographical guide : a title and chronological index to the underground-alternative press microform collection / compiled by Ruth Sandys and Brenda Harris. — 1976. — 28p ; 23cm. — (Harvester Primary Social Sources)
'... issued with the Harvester-Primary Social Sources silver-halide microfiche and 35mm roll-film collection "The underground and alternative press in Britain during 1914"' - title page verso.
ISBN 0-85527-359-3 : £6.50 : CIP rev
(B77-05166)

016.30129'181'20519 — Western world. Relations with Korea, 1898-1975. *Bibliographies*
Lee, Helen F MacRae Parker. The Helen F. MacRae collection : a bibliography of Korean relations with Canadians and other Western peoples which includes a checklist of documents and reports, 1898-1975 / compiled by Helen F. MacRae Parker Lee ; edited by M. Doreen E. Fraser. — London (21 Gwendolen Ave., [SW15 6ET]) : Vine Press, [1976]. — 212 leaves in various pagings ; 28cm. — (Dalhousie University. Dalhousie University Libraries and Dalhousie University School of Library Service occasional papers ; no.12)
ISBN 0-905305-03-5 Sp : £2.50
Primary classification 016.30129'519'01812
(B77-11519)

016.30129'519'01812 — Korea. Relations with Western world, 1898-1975. *Bibliographies*
Lee, Helen F MacRae Parker. The Helen F. MacRae collection : a bibliography of Korean relations with Canadians and other Western peoples which includes a checklist of documents and reports, 1898-1975 / compiled by Helen F. MacRae Parker Lee ; edited by M. Doreen E. Fraser. — London (21 Gwendolen Ave., [SW15 6ET]) : Vine Press, [1976]. — 212 leaves in various pagings ; 28cm. — (Dalhousie University. Dalhousie University Libraries and Dalhousie University School of Library Service occasional papers ; no.12)
ISBN 0-905305-03-5 Sp : £2.50
Also classified at 016.30129'181'20519
(B77-11519)

016.30131 — Environment. Economic aspects. *Bibliographies*
Growth and resources : bibliography of environmental economics / edited by R. Kerry Turner, D.W. Pearce, Barrie O. Pettman. — Bradford : MCB [for] the International Institute of Social Economics.
In 2 vols.
Vol.1. — 1976. — viii,79p ; 24cm.
Index.
ISBN 0-905440-11-0 Pbk : £12.95
(B77-31654)

Pollution : bibliography of environmental economics. — Bradford : MCB [for] the International Institute of Social Economics.
Vol.2 / edited by R. Kerry Turner, D.W. Pearce, Barrie O. Pettman. — 1977. — viii, 72p ; 25cm.
Index.
ISBN 0-905440-12-9 Pbk : Unpriced
(B77-33557)

016.30141 — Sexual liberation movements. *Great Britain. Bibliographies*
Lipshitz, Susan. Sexual politics in Britain : a bibliographical guide with historical notes / by Susan Lipshitz ; published with a title and chronological index as a companion to the 'Sexual politics in Britain' collection prepared for microform publication by Brenda Harris. — Hassocks : Harvester Press, 1977. — 41p ; 23cm. — (Harvester Primary Social Sources)
ISBN 0-85527-610-x : £5.50
(B77-16145)

016.30143'14 — Documentary films on children. *Lists*
National Children's Bureau. *Information Service.* An index of documentary films about children / [National Children's Bureau, Information Service]. — [Revised ed.]. — London (8 Wakley St., EC1V 7QE) : The Information Service, 1976. — 53p ; 30cm.
Previous ed.: 1973. — Index.
Sd : Unpriced
(B77-11024)

National Children's Bureau. *Information Service.* An index of documentary films about children / [National Children's Bureau Information Service]. — [Revised ed. reprinted] with 1977 supplement. — London (8 Wakley St., EC1V 7QE) : The Information Service, 1977. — 60p ; 30cm.
This ed. originally published: 1976. — Index.
Sd : £2.50
(B77-29117)

016.30143'15 — Young persons. *Bibliographies*
Derrick, Deborah. Selected and annotated bibliography of youth, youth work, and provision for youth / compiled by Deborah Derrick. — Leicester : National Youth Bureau, 1976. — [1],x,411p ; 21cm.
Index.
ISBN 0-902095-26-9 Pbk : £3.50
(B77-27629)

016.30145'11'13 — White persons. Attitudes of negroes. *United States. Bibliographies*
Obudho, Constance E. Black-white racial attitudes : an annotated bibliography / by Constance E. Obudho. — Westport, Conn. ; London : Greenwood Press, 1976. — xii,180p ; 22cm.
Bibl.: p.xi-xii. — Index.
ISBN 0-8371-8582-3 : £8.50
Primary classification 016.30145'19'6073
(B77-20858)

016.30145'19'6073 — Negroes. Attitudes of white persons. *United States. Bibliographies*
Obudho, Constance E. Black-white racial attitudes : an annotated bibliography / by Constance E. Obudho. — Westport, Conn. ; London : Greenwood Press, 1976. — xii,180p ; 22cm.
Bibl.: p.xi-xii. — Index.
ISBN 0-8371-8582-3 : £8.50
Also classified at 016.30145'11'13
(B77-20858)

016.3015'4 — Housing. Improvement. *Great Britain. Bibliographies*
Great Britain. *Department of the Environment. Housing Improvement Group/H6.* Research related to the renewal of older housing areas : a list of current research projects and a bibliography / [Department of the Environment] Housing Improvement Group H6. — London : Department of the Environment, 1976. — [5],22p ; 30cm. — (Area improvement occasional papers ; 6-76)
'... a supplement to "Research into the renewal of older housing areas", Area Improvement Occasional Paper 3-75' - Introduction. — Bibl.: p.16-22.
Sd : Unpriced
Primary classification 301.5'4
(B77-17934)

016.3015'4 — Housing schemes. Government circulars. *England. Indexes*
Great Britain. *Department of the Environment.* Housing schemes : new-build, improvement and conversion projects : index to current departmental circulars and other publications as at 30th June, 1976 / Department of the Environment [and] Welsh Office. — London : H.M.S.O., 1976. — [30]p ; 30cm.
Pierced for binder.
ISBN 0-11-751121-8 Sd : £0.70
(B77-22306)

016.3015'4 — Squatting. *Great Britain. Bibliographies*
Fawkes, S. Squatting / compiled by S. Fawkes and J. Hargreaves ; [for the] Greater London Council Research Library. — London : G.L.C., 1976. — [3],9p ; 30cm. — (Greater London Council. Intelligence Unit. Research Library. Research bibliographies ; no.77 ISSN 0306-8587)
ISBN 0-7168-0869-2 Sd : £1.40
(B77-14514)

016.3015'4 — Universities. Libraries. *Lancashire. Lancaster. University of Lancaster. Library. Stock: Documents on housing. Catalogues*
Stewart, John Michael. Housing bibliography : subject classification / [by] J.M. Stewart. — [Lancaster] ([Bailrigg, Lancaster]) : University of Lancaster, Department of Social Administration, 1976. — [4],39[i.e. 40]leaves ; 30cm.
ISBN 0-901699-41-1 Sd : £0.75
(B77-01968)

016.3016'32 — Non-violence. *Bibliographies*
Blumberg, Herbert H. Nonviolent liberation : a bibliography / [compiled and edited by Herbert H. Blumberg]. — Brighton : Noyce, 1977. — 122p ; 22x30cm.
Index.
Sd : £3.50
(B77-23946)

016.3016'333'0903 — Revolution, 1555-1975. *Bibliographies*
Blackey, Robert. Modern revolutions and revolutionists : a bibliography / [by] Robert Blackey. — Santa Barbara : ABC-Clio ; Oxford : EBC-Clio, 1976. — xxvii,257p ; 24cm. — (War-peace bibliography series)
Index.
ISBN 0-87436-223-7 : £9.65
(B77-05167)

016.3091'034 — Social conditions. Documents on social conditions: Documents published by Independent Labour Party, to 1932. *Lists*
Woolven, Gillian B. Publications of the Independent Labour Party, 1893-1932 / by Gillian B. Woolven. — Coventry : Society for the Study of Labour History ; Stanmore (103 Stanmore Hill, Stanmore, Middx) : Distributed by Michael Katanka (Books) Ltd, 1977. — xiv, 38p ; 25cm. — (Society for the Study of Labour History. 'Bulletin' supplements : aids to research ; no.2)
Index.
ISBN 0-904260-02-x Sd : £3.00(£1.75 to members)
(B77-15058)

016.3091'4'055 — Universities. Libraries. *Leicestershire. Leicester. University of Leicester. Library. Stock: Documents published by European Community. Catalogues*
University of Leicester. *Library.* The European Documentation Centre : a guide to European Community publications in Leicester University Library / [compiled] by Michael Hopkins. — Leicester ([University Rd, Leicester LE1 7RH]) : The Library, 1976. — 20p ; 22cm.
Index.
Sd : Unpriced
(B77-17244)

016.3091'41'0857 — Great Britain. Social conditions. Research projects, 1976. *Lists*
Science Policy Foundation. Research and surveys, 1976 / [compiled by the Science Policy Foundation] ; [for the Headquarters Library, Department of the Environment]. — London : Headquarters Library, Department of the Environment, 1977. — [2],v,348p ; 30cm. — (Great Britain. Department of the Environment. Library. Information series ; no.24)
'The projects have been collected as part of the 1976 DOE Register of research ... ' - Introduction. — Index.
ISBN 0-7184-0072-0 Pbk : Unpriced
(B77-14009)

016.3091'429'4 — South Wales. Valleys. Social conditions, to 1974. *Bibliographies*
Baggs, Teresa. The South Wales valleys : a contemporary socio-economic bibliography / [compiled by] Teresa Baggs, Paul H. Ballard, Paul Vining. — Aberfan ([55 Aberfan Rd., Merthyr Tydfil, CF48 4QJ]) : Ty Toronto, 1974. — [3],122p ; 29cm.
'Compiled for the Valleys '74 [:Towards a Socio-Economic Strategy for the Valleys] Conference held at Glamorgan Polytechnic on Saturday, 2nd November 1974'. — Index.
Sd : £0.75
(B77-18505)

016.3091'47 — Eastern Europe & Soviet Union. Social conditions, to 1975. *Bibliographies*
Whetten, Lawrence Lester. Current research in comparative communism : an analysis and bibliographic guide to the Soviet system / [by] Lawrence L. Whetten. — New York [etc.] ; London : Praeger, [1977]. — vii,163p ; 25cm. — (Praeger special studies in international politics and government)
Published in the United States: 1976.
ISBN 0-275-23550-5 : £11.20
Also classified at 301.29'47
(B77-14010)

016.31 — Public reference libraries. *Derbyshire. Derby. Derby Central Library. Reference Library. Stock: Statistical publications. Catalogues*
Derby Central Library. *Reference Library.* An index of statistical sources / compiled in Derby Reference Library. — 2nd ed. — Matlock (County Offices, Matlock, Derbyshire) : Derbyshire County Library, 1976. — [104]p ; 30cm.
Previous ed.: / compiled by Cheryl Stell. Derbyshire : s.n., 197-.
ISBN 0-903463-02-4 Pbk : £0.30
(B77-09461)

016.3141 — Great Britain. Official statistics. *Bibliographies. Serials*
Great Britain. *Central Statistical Office.* Guide to official statistics / Central Statistical Office. — London : H.M.S.O.
No.1. — 1976. — vi,391p ; 30cm.
'... first post-war edition ...' - Foreword. — 'The present plan is to update continuously the file of information and to publish subsequent editions at approximately annual intervals ...' p.iv. — Index.
ISBN 0-11-630132-5 Pbk : £7.50
(B77-01969)

016.3153'8 — Saudi Arabia. Statistics. *For marketing. Bibliographies*
Great Britain. *Department of Industry. Statistics and Market Intelligence Library.* Saudi Arabia / Department of Industry [Statistics and Market Intelligence Library] ; [prepared by Margaret Aitchison]. — London (50 Ludgate Hill, EC4M 7HU) : The Library, 1976. — [2], 12p ; 21cm. — (Sources of statistics and market information ; 7)
ISBN 0-904913-04-x Sd : Unpriced
(B77-15648)

016.32 — Theses on politics: Theses accepted by British universities. *Bibliographies. Serials*
Political science theses register : a register of research theses, supported from all sources, and being prepared for higher degrees in the United Kingdom on topics of interest to scholars of political science. — London : Social Science Research Council.
1977 : 2nd complete ed. / compiled and edited by Anthony Barker. — 1977. — 84p ; 30cm.
Index.
ISBN 0-900296-62-3 Pbk : £1.50
ISSN 0140-4601
(B77-30914)

016.3209'41'082 — Left-wing political movements. *Great Britain, 1904-1972. Bibliographies*
Spiers, John, *b.1941.* The Left in Britain : a checklist and guide : with historical notes to 37 Left-wing political movements and groupings active in Britain between 1904-1972 whose publications comprise the Harvester-Primary Social Sources Microform Collection / [by] John Spiers, Ann Sexsmith, Alastair Everitt. — Hassocks : Harvester Press, 1976. — 168p ; 23cm. — (Harvester Primary Social Sources)
'... issued with the Harvester Primary Social Sources silver-halide microform collection "The Left in Britain - Parts One, Two, Three and Four"' - title page verso. — Index.
ISBN 0-85527-234-1 : £12.50
(B77-05815)

016.3209'56 — Middle East. Politics, to 1975. *Bibliographies*
Gordon Drabek, Anne. The politics of African and Middle Eastern states : an annotated bibliography / compiled by Anne Gordon Drabek and Wilfrid Knapp. — Oxford [etc.] : Pergamon, 1976. — x,192p ; 22cm. — (Pergamon international library)
ISBN 0-08-020584-4 : £7.75
ISBN 0-08-020583-6 Pbk : £3.85
Primary classification 016.3209'6
(B77-11025)

016.3209'6 — Africa. Politics, to 1975. *Bibliographies*
Gordon Drabek, Anne. The politics of African and Middle Eastern states : an annotated bibliography / compiled by Anne Gordon Drabek and Wilfrid Knapp. — Oxford [etc.] : Pergamon, 1976. — x,192p ; 22cm. — (Pergamon international library)
ISBN 0-08-020584-4 : £7.75
ISBN 0-08-020583-6 Pbk : £3.85
Also classified at 016.3209'56
(B77-11025)

016.3224'2'09411 — Nationalist movements. *Scotland, 1844-1973. Bibliographies*
Fraser, Kenneth C. A bibliography of the Scottish national movement (1844-1973) / by Kenneth C. Fraser. — Dollar (31 Craiginnan Gardens, Dollar FK14 7JA) : Douglas S. Mack, 1976. — 40p ; 30cm.
Index.
ISBN 0-9505416-0-5 Sd : £0.75
(B77-08714)

016.3231'19'6073 — Negroes. Nationalism. *United States, to 1975. Bibliographies*
Jenkins, Betty Lanier. Black separatism : a bibliography / [by] Betty Lanier Jenkins & Susan Phillis. — Westport, Conn. ; London : Greenwood Press, 1976. — xxv,163p ; 22cm.
'Under the auspices of Metropolitan Applied Research Center, Inc.'. — Index.
ISBN 0-8371-8378-2 : £8.95
(B77-17852)

016.32344 — Personal freedom. Right-wing writers. *Bibliographies*
Centre for Policy Studies. Bibliography of freedom / Centre for Policy Studies. — London (8 Wilfred St., S.W.1) : The Centre, 1976. — [2],28p ; 14cm.
ISBN 0-9504392-6-6 Sd : £0.20
(B77-31655)

016.32747'0497 — Soviet Union. Foreign relations with Yugoslavia, 1948-1972. *Bibliographies*
Hunter, Brian. Soviet-Yugoslav relations, 1948-1972 : a bibliography of Soviet, Western and Yugoslav comment and analysis / [compiled by] Brian Hunter. — New York ; London : Garland, 1976. — 223p ; 23cm. — (Garland reference library in social science ; vol.18)
Index.
ISBN 0-8240-9971-0 : Unpriced
Also classified at 016.327497'047
(B77-17853)

016.327497'047 — Yugoslavia. Foreign relations with Soviet Union, 1948-1972. *Bibliographies*
Hunter, Brian. Soviet-Yugoslav relations, 1948-1972 : a bibliography of Soviet, Western and Yugoslav comment and analysis / [compiled by] Brian Hunter. — New York ; London : Garland, 1976. — 223p ; 23cm. — (Garland reference library in social science ; vol.18)
Index.
ISBN 0-8240-9971-0 : Unpriced
Primary classification 016.32747'0497
(B77-17853)

016.32768'073 — Southern Africa. Foreign relations with United States. *Bibliographies*
American-Southern African relations : bibliographic essays / edited by Mohamed A. El-Khawas, Francis A. Kornegay, Jr. — Westport, Conn. ; London : Greenwood Press, 1975. — xix,188p ; 22cm. — (African Bibliographic Center. Special bibliographic series : new series ; no.1)
ISBN 0-8371-8398-7 : £8.75
Primary classification 016.32773'068
(B77-17854)

016.32773'068 — United States. Foreign relations with Southern Africa. *Bibliographies*
American-Southern African relations : bibliographic essays / edited by Mohamed A. El-Khawas, Francis A. Kornegay, Jr. — Westport, Conn. ; London : Greenwood Press, 1975. — xix,188p ; 22cm. — (African Bibliographic Center. Special bibliographic series : new series ; no.1)
ISBN 0-8371-8398-7 : £8.75
Also classified at 016.32768'073
(B77-17854)

016.329'023'17241 — Elections. *Commonwealth countries, 1945-1970. Bibliographies*
Bloomfield, Valerie. Commonwealth elections, 1945-1970 : a bibliography / [by] Valerie Bloomfield. — London : Mansell Information Publishing, 1976. — xvi,306p ; 26cm.
Index.
ISBN 0-7201-0543-9 : £16.00
(B77-05816)

016.33 — Economics. *Bibliographies*
International bibliography of economics = Bibliographie internationale de science économique / prepared by the International Committee for Social Science Documentation = établie par le comité international pour l'information et la documentation en sciences sociales. — London : Tavistock Publications [etc.]. — (International bibliography of the social sciences = Bibliographie internationale des sciences sociales)
1974 : Vol.23 / [managing editor Jean Viet]. — 1976. — lxiii,476p ; 25cm.
English and French text. — Index.
ISBN 0-422-80790-7 : £25.00
ISSN 0085-204x
(B77-27630)

International bibliography of economics = Bibliographie internationale de science économique / prepared by the International Committee for Social Science Information and Documentation = établie par le Comité international pour l'information et la documentation en sciences sociales. — London : Tavistock Publications [etc.]. — (International bibliography of the social sciences = Bibliographie internationale des sciences sociales)
1975 : Vol.24 / [managing editor Jean Viet]. — 1977. — lxix,513p ; 25cm.
English and French text. — Index.
ISBN 0-422-76220-2 : £29.50
ISSN 0085-204x
(B77-27631)

016.3309 — Colleges of further education. Libraries. *Derbyshire. Chesterfield. Chesterfield Colleges of Art and Technology. Library. Stock: Periodicals published by banks. Periodical articles on economic conditions. Indexes*
Chesterfield Colleges of Art and Technology. *Library and Resources Centre.* Bank reviews index : a subject index of articles from bank reviews published 1946-1975 [and a supplement for 1976] / Derbyshire Education Committee, Chesterfield Colleges of Art and Technology, Library and Resources Centre. — [Chesterfield] ([Infirmary Centre, Chesterfield, S41 7NG]) : [Chesterfield Colleges of Art and Technology, Library and Resources Centre], [1977]. — [5], 77p ; 30cm. — (Library booklist ; no.6)
Sd : £1.00
(B77-17855)

016.3309'41'0857 — Great Britain. Economic conditions. *Bibliographies. For marketing*
Hull, Christine. Principal sources of marketing information / compiled by Christine Hull. — [New ed.]. — London : Times Newspapers, 1976. — [2],43,[1]p ; 23cm.
Previous ed.: 1974.
ISBN 0-7230-0157-x Sd : £2.50 •
(B77-14011)

016.331'09427'32 — Industrial relations. *Greater Manchester (Metropolitan County). Salford (District), to 1976. Bibliographies*
Labour history of Manchester and Salford : a bibliography / compiled by Eddie Conway ... [et al.]. — [Manchester] ([c/o The Secretary, 9 Evelyn St., Fallowfield, Manchester M14 6WG]) : [Manchester Centre for Marxist Education], [1977]. — 34p : ill ; 21cm. — (Manchester Centre for Marxist Education. Pamphlets)
ISBN 0-9505655-0-4 Sd : £0.30
Also classified at 016.331'09427'33
(B77-13461)

016.331'09427'33 — Industrial relations. *Greater Manchester (Metropolitan County). Manchester, to 1976. Bibliographies*
Labour history of Manchester and Salford : a bibliography / compiled by Eddie Conway ... [et al.]. — [Manchester] ([c/o The Secretary, 9 Evelyn St., Fallowfield, Manchester M14 6WG]) : [Manchester Centre for Marxist Education], [1977]. — 34p : ill ; 21cm. — (Manchester Centre for Marxist Education. Pamphlets)
ISBN 0-9505655-0-4 Sd : £0.30
Primary classification 016.331'09427'32
(B77-13461)

016.3311'09421 — Employment. Research projects. *London. Lists*
Greater London Council. *Intelligence Unit. Research Library.* Research projects on employment within the London boroughs, 1966-November 1976 / Greater London Council [Intelligence Unit] Research Library ; compiled from the register of research in the London boroughs by Ian Crockett. — 2nd ed. — London : G.L.C., 1976. — [1],iv,13p ; 30cm. — (Greater London Council. Intelligence Unit. Research Library. Research bibliographies ; no.76 ISSN 0306-8587)
Previous ed.: 1976. — Index.
ISBN 0-7168-0825-0 Sd : £1.40
(B77-16146)

016.3312'592 — Industrial training. *Bibliographies*
British Association for Commercial and Industrial Education. The BACIE bibliography of publications in the field of education and training in commerce and industry / devised and edited by P.J.C. Perry. — London : BACIE.
Reprinted and cumulated from the 'BACIE journal'.
Vols, 1, 2, 3 and 4, March 1960 to November 1973. — 1977. — 408p in various pagings ; 24cm.
Includes original pagination. — Vols 1, 2 and 3 originally published together, 1971. — Index.
ISBN 0-85171-065-4 : £20.00
(B77-17856)

016.33187'2 — Trade unions. State federations. Proceedings. *United States, to 1974. Bibliographies*
American Federation of Labor and Congress of Industrial Organizations. *Library.* State labor proceedings : a bibliography of the AFL, CIO, and AFL-CIO proceedings, 1885-1974, held in the AFL-CIO Library / Gary M. Fink editor, Mary Mills compiler. — Westport, Conn. ; London : Greenwood Press, 1975. — xviii, 291p ; 23cm.
ISBN 0-8371-8278-6 : Unpriced
(B77-09462)

016.3321'09421'2 — Financial institutions. *London (City). Bibliographies*
Smith, Gerry Michael. The financial activities of the City of London : a select bibliography / by Gerry M. Smith. — London (P.O. Box 261, N4 4EN) : Business School Press, 1976. — 27p ; 21cm. — (Business school bibliography ; no.1 ISSN 0309-1694)
ISBN 0-905704-00-2 Sd : £3.20
(B77-03873)

016.3324'1 — Finance. Inflation. *Great Britain. Bibliographies*
MacCafferty, Maxine. Inflation in the United Kingdom / compiled by Maxine MacCafferty. — London : Aslib, 1977. — ix,75p ; 30cm. — (Aslib. Bibliographies ; no.6 ISSN 0308-7522)
Index.
ISBN 0-85142-097-4 Pbk : £4.50(£3.50 to members of Aslib)
(B77-23947)

016.3326'44 — Futures commodity markets. *Bibliographies*
Woy, James Bayly. Commodity futures trading : a bibliographic guide / [by] James B. Woy. — New York ; London : Bowker, 1976. — x, 206p ; 24cm.
ISBN 0-8352-0899-0 : £12.50
(B77-01970)

016.3333'23'0942 — Estates. *England. Howard estates. Archives. Catalogues*
Arundel Castle. Arundel Castle archives / edited by Francis W. Steer. — Chichester (County Hall, Chichester [Sussex PO19 1RN]) : West Sussex County Council.
Vol.3 : A catalogue. — 1976. — ix,108p ; 25cm.
Index.
£7.00
(B77-19964)

016.3337 — Energy resources. Use. *Abstracts. Periodicals*
Electricity utilisation and energy abstracts. — London : Electricity Council, Intelligence Section.
Vol.1, no.1- ; [Jan. 1977]-. — 1977-. — 30cm.
Monthly. — [2],21p. in 1st issue. — Pierced for binder.
Sd : Unpriced
ISSN 0309-1856
(B77-10708)

016.3337'8'091734 — Recreation facilities. *Rural regions. Abstracts. Periodicals*
Rural recreation and tourism abstracts. — Farnham Royal : Commonwealth Agricultural Bureaux.
Vol.1, no.1- ; Jan. 1976-. — 1976-. — 30cm.
Quarterly. — [4],36,[5]p. in Vol.1, no.1. — Index.
Sd : £10.00 a year
ISSN 0308-0137
(B77-25346)

016.335'009 — Labour movements, to 1976. *Bibliographies*
International Association of Labour History Institutions. Basic reading list / International Association of Labour History Institutions. — [London] ([c/o Labour Party Library, Transport House, Smith Sq., SW1P 3JA]) : [The Association], [1977]. — 49 leaves in various pagings ; 28cm.
Cover title.
Pbk : £2.00
(B77-29870)

016.335'1'0941 — Periodicals on British labour movements, 1790-1970. *Lists*
Harrison, Royden. The Warwick guide to British labour periodicals, 1790-1970 : a check list / arranged and compiled by Royden Harrison, Gillian B. Woolven, Robert Duncan. — Hassocks : Harvester Press [etc.], 1977. — xxiii, 685p ; 23cm.
Index.
ISBN 0-901759-76-7 : Unpriced : CIP rev.
(B77-06417)

016.3354'05 — Periodicals on Marxism: Periodicals in English. *Bibliographies*
Shaffer, Harry George. Periodicals on the socialist countries and on Marxism : a new annotated index of English-language publications / [by] Harry G. Shaffer. — [New] ed. — New York [etc.] ; London : Praeger, 1977. — xv,135p ; 25cm. — (Praeger special studies in international politics and government)

Previous ed.: i.e. 1st ed. published as 'English language periodic publications on communism'. Columbia : Research Institute on Communist Affairs, Columbia University, 1971. — Index.
ISBN 0-275-24010-x : £12.20
Primary classification 016.909'09'717
(B77-15655)

016.3354'092'4 — Marxism. Gramsci, Antonio. *Italy. Bibliographies*
Cozens, Phil. Twenty years of Antonio Gramsci : a bibliography of Gramsci and Gramsci studies published in English, 1957-1977 / [by] Phil Cozens. — London : Lawrence and Wishart, 1977. — [3],12p ; 21cm.
ISBN 0-85315-404-x Sd : £0.35
(B77-27632)

016.33543'09597 — Communism. *Vietnam. Bibliographies*
Phan Thien Chau. Vietnamese communism : a research bibliography / [by] Phan Thien Chau. — Westport, Conn. ; London : Greenwood Press, 1975. — xix,359p ; 25cm.
Index.
ISBN 0-8371-7950-5 : £14.55
(B77-16695)

016.33543'3 — Trotskyism. *Current awareness bulletins*
Bonner, R A. Trotskyist current awareness and abstracts bulletin / compiled ... by R.A. Bonner. — London (21 Kinnoull Mansions, Rowhill Rd, E5 8EB) : The author.
No.1- ; July 1977-. — [1977]-. — 30cm.
Monthly. — 13p. in 1st issue.
Sd : £0.20
ISSN 0140-3303
(B77-26736)

016.335'83 — Universities. Libraries. *Scotland. Central Region. Stirling. University of Stirling. Library. Stock: Documents on anarchism. Lists*
University of Stirling. *Library.* A handlist of anarchist material in the library of the University of Stirling / compiled by Nick Sherington. — Brighton : Smoothie Publications, 1976. — 9p ; 30cm. — (Smoothie's alternative indexing series)
ISBN 0-903612-36-4 Sd : £0.80
(B77-01115)

016.3381 — Documents published by personnel of University of Reading. Department of Agricultural Economics and Management. *Lists. Serials*
University of Reading. *Department of Agricultural Economics and Management.* Chronological list of publications / University of Reading, Department of Agricultural Economics & Management. — [Reading] : [The Department].
10th : academic years 1971-72-1975-76. — 1977. — [2],12 leaves ; 30cm.
ISBN 0-7049-0675-9 Sd : Unpriced
(B77-29871)

016.3383'72'7 — Fishing industries. *Abstracts. Periodicals*
Fisheries economics newsletter. — Edinburgh (10 Young St., Edinburgh EH2 4JQ) : Fishery Economics Research Unit.
No.1- : Apr. 1976-. — 1976-. — 30cm.
Two issues a year. — Cover title. — [1],8 leaves in 1st issue.
Sp : Unpriced
ISSN 0309-4294
(B77-08715)

016.3384'7'628 — Water industries. *England. Bibliographies*
Ellender, Pat. Water industry in England and Wales / compiled by Pat Ellender. — London (1 Queen Anne's Gate, SW1H 9BT) : National Water Council, 1976. — [19]p ; 30cm. — (Water Information Centre (Great Britain). Bibliographies ; no.1 ISSN 0309-8443)
ISBN 0-904561-07-0 Pbk : £0.50
(B77-17245)

016.3388'8 — International business enterprise. *Bibliographies*
International business bibliography / [edited by] Michael Z. Brooke, Mary Black and Paul Neville ; [for the] International Business Unit, University of Manchester Institute of Science and Technology. — London [etc.] : Macmillan, 1977. — xv,481p ; 23cm.
Index.
ISBN 0-333-21625-3 : £15.00
(B77-23948)

016.3389 — Great Britain. Department of Industry. Statistics and Market Intelligence Library. Stock: Documents on economic planning. *Lists*
Great Britain. *Department of Industry. Statistics and Market Intelligence Library.* Development plans available in the Statistics & Market Intelligence Library [Department of Industry] / [prepared by Margaret Aitchison]. — London (50 Ludgate Hill, EC4M 7HU) : The Library, 1976. — [23]p ; 21cm. — (Sources of statistics and market information ; 6)
ISBN 0-904913-05-8 Sd : Unpriced
(B77-15649)

016.34 — Great Britain. Treasury Solicitor's Department. Library. Stock. *Catalogues*
Great Britain. *Treasury Solicitor's Department. Library.* Catalogue of the Legal Library of the Treasury Solicitor / compiled by R. Toole Stott. — 6th ed. — [London] ([Matthew Parker St., S.W.1]) : [The Department], 1977. — 171p ; 30cm.
Previous ed.: 1975.
ISBN 0-9501916-2-0 Pbk : Unpriced
(B77-15650)

016.34 — Law. *Bibliographies. Periodicals*
Where to look for your law : a bi-monthly bulletin containing comprehensive details of newly published legal books. — [Alton] ([16 Newman La., Alton, Hants. GU34 2PJ]) : Hammick, Sweet and Maxwell.
Bulletin 1- ; Jan.-Feb. 1977-. — [1977]-. — 21cm.
Six issues a year. — [2],37p. in 1st issue.
Sd : £16.00 yearly
ISSN 0309-4537
(B77-18506)

016.34'005 — Periodicals on law: Periodicals with non-common law country imprints. *Indexes. Serials*
Index to foreign legal periodicals. — London (17 Russell Sq., W.C.1) : Institute of Advanced Legal Studies, University of London [etc.].
1975 : annual volume / American Association of Law Libraries ; [general editor W.A. Steiner ; assistant editor T.N. March Hunnings]. — 1976. — xv,439p ; 26cm.
ISBN 0-901190-18-7 : Unpriced
(B77-03311)

016.34'00947 — Universities. Colleges. Libraries. *London. Camden (London Borough). University College, London. Library. Exhibits: Books on Soviet law, ca 1650-ca 1940. Catalogues*
Butler, William Elliott. Russian and Soviet legal history : a catalogue of an exhibition of books from London collections on the occasion of the Russian-Soviet Legal History Conference, 10-12 December 1976 / [text W.E. Butler]. — [London] ([Malet St., W.C.1]) : Faculty of Laws, University College, London, [1976]. — [2],24,[2]p : 1 ill, facsim ; 21cm.
Limited ed. of 100 numbered copies.
ISBN 0-905955-00-5 Sd : Unpriced
(B77-10709)

016.341'0263'2 — European Community. Law. Secondary legislation. *Indexes. Serials*
Secondary legislation of the European Communities, subject list and table of effects. — London : H.M.S.O.
1976 / prepared for the Statutory Publications Office by the Department of Industry Library Services. — 1977. — [2],122p ; 30cm.
Index.
ISBN 0-11-330510-9 Pbk : £3.75
(B77-19965)

016.341'0264'41 — Great Britain. Treaties. *Indexes*
Index to 'Treaty series' / presented to Parliament by the Secretary of State for Foreign and Commonwealth Affairs ... — London : H.M.S.O.
1976. — [1977]. — 30p ; 25cm. — (Treaty series ; no.114(1976)) (Cmnd.6788)
ISBN 0-10-167880-0 Sd : £0.80
(B77-15059)

016.341'0264'41 — Great Britain. Treaties. Ratifications, accessions & withdrawals. *Lists*
Supplementary list of ratifications, accessions, withdrawals, etc. for 1976 ... — London : H.M.S.O.
3rd. — [1977]. — 28p ; 25cm. — (Treaty series ; no.112(1976)) (Cmnd.6718)
ISBN 0-10-167180-6 Sd : £0.50
(B77-08164)

4th. — [1977]. — 29p ; 25cm. — (Treaty series ; no.113(1976)) (Cmnd.6747)
ISBN 0-10-167470-8 Sd : £0.60
(B77-14013)

Supplementary list of ratifications, accessions, withdrawals, etc. for 1977 ... — London : H.M.S.O.
1st. — [1977]. — 30p ; 25cm. — (Treaty series ; no.60(1977)) (Cmnd.6933)
ISBN 0-10-169330-3 Sd : £0.90
(B77-28335)

016.342'73'024 — Constitutional conventions. *United States. States, 1959-1975. Bibliographies*
Yarger, Susan Rice. State constitutional conventions, 1959-1975 : a bibliography / compiled by Susan Rice Yarger ; introduction by Richard H. Leech. — Westport, Conn. ; London : Greenwood Press, 1976. — xxxiii, 50p ; 25cm.
ISBN 0-8371-8683-8 : £7.95
(B77-18507)

016.342'73'087 — Sex discrimination. Law. *United States, to 1976. Bibliographies*
Equal Rights Amendment Project. The Equal Rights Amendment : a bibliographic study / compiled by the Equal Rights Amendment Project ; Anita Miller, project director, Hazel Greenberg, editor and compiler. — Westport, Conn. ; London : Greenwood Press, 1976. — xxvii,367p ; 25cm.
Index.
ISBN 0-8371-9058-4 : Unpriced
(B77-23949)

016.346'42'0438 — Public records. Repositories. *Great Britain. Public Record Office. Stock: Legal instruments: Deeds in archives of England and Wales. Augmentation Office, to 1603. Collections: Ancient Deeds. Lists*
England. *Augmentation Office.* Ancient Deeds series BB (E.328) calendar and index / Exchequer, Augmentation Office ; [compiled by J. Conway Davies]. — London : Swift, 1977. — [2],254p ; 33cm. — (List and Index Society. Publications ; vol.137)
Records deposited in the Public Record Office.
ISBN 0-902573-58-6 Pbd : Unpriced
(B77-08165)

016.347'42'035 — Public records. Repositories. *Great Britain. Public Record Office. Stock: Chancery patent rolls. Lists. Latin texts. Manuscripts. Facsimiles*
England and Wales. *Court of Chancery.* Chancery patent rolls 8 James I, calendar. — London : Swift, 1976. — [2],229p ; 33cm. — (List and Index Society. Publications ; vol.122)
Records deposited in the Public Record Office. — Facsimile of MSS.
Pbd : Unpriced
(B77-01116)

England and Wales. *Court of Chancery.* Chancery patent rolls 9 James I calendar. — London : Swift, 1977. — [2],184p ; 33cm. — (List and Index Society. Publications ; vol.133)
Records deposited in the Public Record Office. — Facsimile of MSS.
ISBN 0-902573-54-3 Pbd : £4.30
(B77-07020)

England and Wales. *Court of Chancery.* Chancery patent rolls 10, 11 James I calendar. — London : Swift, 1977. — [2],314p ; 33cm. — (List and Index Society. Publications ; vol.134)
Records deposited in the Public Record Office. — Facsimile of MSS.
ISBN 0-902573-55-1 Pbd : £5.05
(B77-07021)

016.354'41'05 — Public records. Repositories. *Great Britain. Public Record Office. Stock: Memoranda of Great Britain. Cabinet Office, 1939-1945. Lists*
Great Britain. *Cabinet Office.* Cabinet Office list of War Cabinet memoranda (CAB 66) (WP & CP series), 1939 Sept.-1945 July. — London : Swift Printers, 1977. — [2],211p ; 33cm. — (List and Index Society. Publications ; vol.136)
ISBN 0-902573-57-8 Pbd : Unpriced
(B77-10087)

016.354'42'062 — England. Exchequer. Accounts, 1163-1214. Pipe rolls published by Pipe Roll Society. Introductions. *Indexes*
Liber memorialis : Doris Mary Stenton, honorary secretary to the Pipe Roll Society, 1923-1961. — London ([c/o Hon. Secretary, Department of History, University of Reading, Whiteknights, Reading RG6 2AA]) : Pipe Roll Society, 1976. — x,220p,plate : port ; 26cm. — (Pipe Roll Society. Publications : new series ; vol.41)
Bibl.: p.33-34. — Includes indexes by Margaret Walker to introductions of all the volumes published by the Society which concern royal finance.
Unpriced
(B77-24649)

016.361 — Documents published by Great Britain. Department of Health and Social Security. *Lists. Serials*
Great Britain. *Department of Health and Social Security.* Annual list of publications / Department of Health and Social Security. — London (Alexander Fleming House, Elephant and Castle, SE1 6BY) : D.H.S.S. Library.
1975. — [1976]. — [3],iv,45p ; 30cm.
Index.
ISBN 0-902650-10-6 Sd : Free
(B77-07022)

016.361 — Social services. *Abstracts. Periodicals*
Social service abstracts. — London (Alexander Fleming House, Elephant and Castle, SE1 6BY) : Department of Health and Social Security Library.
1- ; Jan. 1977-. — [1977]-. — 30cm.
Monthly. — [4],25p. in 1st issue. — Index.
Sd : Unpriced
ISSN 0309-4693
(B77-30915)

Wiltshire social services abstracts. — [Trowbridge] ([Library and Museum Headquarters, Bythesea Rd, Trowbridge, Wilts.]) : Wiltshire Library and Museum Service.
[No.1]- ; Dec. 1974-. — [1974]-. — 30cm.
Monthly. — [6]p. in 10th issue.
Sd : £10.00 yearly
ISSN 0308-2911
(B77-03874)

016.3621'0951 — Health services. *China. Bibliographies*
Health care in China. — London (152 Camden High St., N.W.1) : Anglo-Chinese Educational Institute, 1976. — [4],ii,62p ; 21cm. — (Modern China series ; no.8 ISSN 0309-0639)
Contents: The mass line / by Joshua Horn - Annotated bibliography.
ISBN 0-903193-10-8 Sd : £0.60
(B77-01971)

016.3622 — Medicine. Psychiatry. Anthropological perspectives, 1925-1974. *Bibliographies*
Favazza, Armando R. Anthropological and cross-cultural themes in mental health : an annotated bibliography, 1925-1974 / [by] Armando R. Favazza and Mary Oman. — Columbia ; London : University of Missouri Press, 1977. — [5],386p ; 26cm. — (University of Missouri. Studies ; 65)
Index.
ISBN 0-8262-0215-2 : £22.50
(B77-33559)

016.3627'1 — Battered children. *Bibliographies*
Jobling, Megan. The abused child : an annotated bibliography / [by] Megan Jobling. — London (8 Wakley St., EC1V 7QE) : National Children's Bureau, 1976. — 37p ; 15x21cm.
ISBN 0-902817-09-4 Sd : £0.84
(B77-12264)

016.3627'32 — Children. Residential care. *Bibliographies*
Prosser, Hilary. Perspectives on residential child care : an annotated bibliography : research and other literature in the United States, Canada and Great Britain, 1966-74 / [by] Hilary Prosser. — Windsor : NFER, 1976. — 109,[2] p ; 22cm. — (National Children's Bureau. Reports)
Index.
ISBN 0-85633-113-9 Pbk : Unpriced
(B77-06418)

016.364 — Crime & punishment. *Bibliographies*
Radzinowicz, *Sir* Leon. Criminology and the administration of criminal justice : a bibliography / [by] Leon Radzinowicz and Roger Hood. — London : Mansell Information Publishing, 1976. — xiii,400p ; 24cm.
Index.
ISBN 0-7201-0522-6 : £15.75
(B77-05817)

016.3646 — Juvenile delinquency. Intermediate treatment. *Great Britain, 1968-1976. Bibliographies*
Thomas, Jim. A bibliography of intermediate treatment, 1968-1976 / compiled by Jim Thomas and Trevor Locke. — Leicester : National Youth Bureau, 1977. — 48p ; 30cm.
Index.
ISBN 0-902095-37-4 Sd : £1.50
(B77-29118)

016.365'45 — Universities. Libraries. *West Midlands (Metropolitan County). Coventry. University of Warwick. Library. Modern Records Centre. Stock: Documents published by Amnesty International. Catalogues*
Amnesty International. Modern Records Centre, University of Warwick Library, Coventry CV4 7AL, MSS. 34 Amnesty International / [catalogue compiled] by Janet Druker. — [New ed.]. — Coventry (Coventry CV4 7AL) : [The Centre], 1976. — 13 leaves ; 30cm.
'... in April 1974 the Modern Records Centre, Warwick University Library, was designated an official repository for all Amnesty [International] publications ... this catalogue includes items received prior to April 1976' - note. — Previous ed.: 1975.
Sd : Private circulation
(B77-02715)

016.37 — Education. Documents on education: Documents written by personnel of Open University. Institute of Educational Technology. *Bibliographies*
Open University. *Institute of Educational Technology.* A bibliography of published and unpublished work by members of the Institute / the Open University Institute of Educational Technology ; [compiled] by Adrian Kirkwood. — [2nd ed.]. — Milton Keynes : [The Institute], [1976]. — [3],78p ; 30cm. — (Open University. Institute of Educational Technology. Monographs ; no.2)
'... the entries are those selected for inclusion by the authors themselves' - Introduction.
Sp : Unpriced
(B77-11520)

016.37 — Periodical articles on education. *Bibliographies. Serials*
British education index. — London : British Library, Bibliographic Services Division.
Vol.12 : Jan.-Dec. 1976. — 1977. — viii,281p ; 31cm.
ISBN 0-900220-59-7 : £11.00 : CIP rev.
ISSN 0007-0637
(B77-06419)

016.37 — Research papers on education: Research papers with Northern Irish imprints. *Lists*
Register of research in education, Northern Ireland. — [Belfast] ([52 Malone Rd, Belfast BT9 5BS]) : Northern Ireland Council for Educational Research.
Vol.1 : 1945-70. — [1977?]. — iii-vii leaves,73p ; 30cm. — (Northern Ireland Council for Educational Research. Publications)
Sp : Unpriced
(B77-26737)

016.37 — Technical colleges of education. Libraries. *Greater Manchester (Metropolitan County). Bolton College of Education (Technical). Library. Stock: Theses on education: Theses accepted by University of Manchester. Abstracts*
Bolton College of Education (Technical). *Library.* Research abstracts / Bolton College of Education (Technical) [Library] ; [editor A.R. Hembrough]. — [Bolton] ([Chadwick St., Bolton BL2 1JW]) : [Bolton College of Education (Technical) Library], [1976]. — [1], 42p ; 21cm.
Index.
ISBN 0-9504588-1-3 Sd : £1.00
(B77-06420)

016.37 — Theses on education: Theses accepted by British higher education institutions. *Lists*
Register of advanced studies in further and higher education originating in the colleges of education (technical). — [Bolton] ([Chadwick St., Bolton BL2 1JW]) : [Bolton College of Education (Technical)].
1976. — [1976]. — [5]p,35 leaves ; 30cm.
Cover title.
ISBN 0-9504588-3-x Pbk : Unpriced
(B77-16147)

016.37 — Universities. Libraries. *Hampshire. Southampton. University of Southampton. Library. Stock: Reference books on education. Catalogues*
University of Southampton. *Library.* Bibliographical aids and reference tools for the literature of education : a guide to works in the Education Library, with some reference to works in other parts of the University Library / [University of Southampton, Library] ; by Joan V. Marder. — 3rd ed. — Southampton ([Southampton SO9 5NH]) : The Library, 1976. — iv,30p ; 30cm. — (A user's guide)
Index.
ISBN 0-85432-163-2 Sd : £1.00
(B77-03312)

016.37011'4 — Moral education. *Bibliographies*
Doeser, W M. Moral education. — [New ed.] / compiled by W.M. Doeser and H.J. Blackham ; for the Social Morality Council's Moral Education Centre. — London : National Book League, 1976. — 42p ; 21cm.
Previous ed.: / selected by Harold J. Blackham. 1971.
ISBN 0-85353-258-3 Sd : £0.50(£0.40 to members of the NBL)
(B77-14515)

016.37'0942 — Education. Local history. *England, to 1974. Bibliographies*
Cunningham, Peter, *b.1948.* Local history of education in England and Wales : a bibliography / [compiled] by Peter Cunningham. — [Leeds] ([Leeds LS2 9JT]) : Museum of the History of Education, University of Leeds, 1976. — [2],188p ; 22cm. — (Educational administration and history monographs ; no.4)
Pbk : £2.20
(B77-27633)

016.3711'46 — Schools. Professional tutors. *Great Britain. Bibliographies*
Hill, Barry. The professional tutor : a bibliography on inservice training, probation and school practice, supervision, and staff development / compiled by B. Hill, K. Dobson and C. Riches. — Hatfield (The Library, Hatfield Polytechnic, P.O. Box 110, Hatfield AL10 9AD) : Hatfield Polytechnic, 1977. — [3] ,51p ; 21cm.
ISBN 0-85267-101-6 Sd : £2.00
(B77-14516)

016.3712 — Schools. Administration. *Bibliographies*
Coulson, Alan Arthur. School administration and management : a select annotated bibliography / compiled by Alan A. Coulson. — [1st ed.] reprinted with additions. — Hull : Flag Publications ; Driffield (31 Driffield Rd, Nafferton, Driffield, N. Humberside YO25 0JL) : Distributed by 'Studies in Education', 1977. — [1],36p ; 21cm.
Originally published: 1975.
Sd : £0.75
ISBN 0-9503827-0-1
(B77-31656)

016.3724'145 — Primary schools. Curriculum subjects: Reading. Teaching. Use of phonics. Audio-visual aids. *Lists*
Herbert, Doris. A classroom index of phonic resources / [by] Doris Herbert, Gareth Davies-Jones. — [2nd ed.]. — [Stafford] ([4 Old Croft Rd, Walton-on-the-Hill, Stafford ST17 0LF]) : [National Association for Remedial Education], [1976]. — 32,[2]p(2 fold),[62]leaves : 1 ill, forms ; 30cm.
Fold. leaf as insert. — Bibl.
ISBN 0-9502507-3-2 Sd : £1.65
(B77-03313)

016.3726'5 — Primary schools. Non-English speaking students. Curriculum subjects: English language. Teaching. *Bibliographies*
English-Teaching Information Centre. English for young beginners / the British Council, English Teaching Information Centre. — [New ed.]. — London (10 Spring Gardens, SW1A 2BN) : [The Centre], 1976. — [3],45,[1]p ; 30cm. — (Information guide ; 1)
Previous ed.: published as 'English as a foreign language for young beginners'. 1971. — Index.
ISBN 0-901618-14-4 Sd : £1.00
(B77-12812)

016.3781'66'2 — Higher education. Examinations. *Bibliographies*
Quiney, Lynn. Examinations : a select bibliography with special reference to higher education / by Lynn Quiney. — London (Borough Rd, S.E.1) : Polytechnic of the South Bank, Library, 1976. — [2],22p ; 21cm.
Sp : £0.50
ISBN 0-905267-02-9
(B77-04519)

016.37873 — Higher education institutions. *United States. Bibliographies*
Beach, Mark. A bibliographic guide to American colleges and universities : from colonial times to the present / [compiled by] Mark Beach. — Westport, Conn. ; London : Greenwood Press, 1975. — vi,314p ; 25cm.
Index.
ISBN 0-8371-7690-5 : £12.90
(B77-17246)

016.3805'097 — Transport. *North America. Bibliographies*
Davis, Bob J. Information sources in transportation, material management and physical distribution : an annotated bibliography and guide / edited and compiled by Bob J. Davis. — Westport, Conn. ; London : Greenwood Press, 1976. — xv,715,[1] p ; 29cm.
Index.
ISBN 0-8371-8379-0 : £23.00
Also classified at 016.6587'8'097
(B77-26738)

016.381 — Hypermarkets & shopping centres. *Bibliographies*
Unit for Retail Planning Information. Hypermarkets & superstores : bibliography & research / [the Unit for Retail Planning Information Limited]. — 2nd ed. — Reading (229 King's Rd, Reading RG1 4LS) : U.R.P.I., 1976. — [2],i,18p ; 30cm.
ISBN 0-905912-00-4 Sd : Unpriced
(B77-07759)

016.381 — Small shops. *Bibliographies*
Unit for Retail Planning Information. Small shops & local shopping : bibliography & research / [the Unit for Retail Planning Information Limited]. — 3rd ed. — Reading (229 King's Rd, Reading RG1 4LS) : U.R.P.I., 1976. — [3],20p ; 30cm.
ISBN 0-905912-02-0 Sd : Unpriced
(B77-07023)

016.382 — Foreign trade. Prices. Variation. *Bibliographies*
Stern, Robert Mitchell. Price elasticities in international trade : an annotated bibliography / by Robert M. Stern, Jonathan Francis and Bruce Schumacher. — London [etc.] : Macmillan for the Trade Policy Research Centre, 1976. — xvi,363p ; 23cm.
Index.
ISBN 0-333-21270-3 : £15.00
(B77-07760)

016.38454 — Broadcasting services. *Abstracts. Periodicals*
Broadcasting abstracts / [Radio Telefís Eireann, Central Library]. — Dublin (Donnybrook, Dublin 4) : R.T.E. Central Library.
Vol.1, 1- ; Mar.-Apr. 1976-. — [1976]-. — 21cm.
Six issues a year. — [1],iv,19p. in 1st issue. — Includes some abstracts in Irish. — Index.
Sd : Unpriced
(B77-19966)

016.3884'1 — Pedestrians. *Great Britain. Urban regions. Bibliographies*
Elkington, John. The pedestrian : planning of research : a literature review and annotated bibliography / [by] John Elkington, Roger McGlynn & John Roberts. — London (24 Floral St., WC2E 9DS) : Transport and Environment Studies, 1976. — [4],235p,[10] leaves ; 21cm.
Index.
ISBN 0-905545-01-x Pbk : £4.95
(B77-00572)

016.3942'68282 — Christmas. *Bibliographies*
Smiles, Julie A. Christmas : a select bibliography / compiled by Julie A. Smiles. — Stevenage (14 Wisden Rd, Stevenage, Herts. SG1 5HZ) : Clover Publications, 1977. — 73p ; 30cm.
Index.
Sp : £4.25
(B77-22307)

016.398 — Theses on folklore: Theses accepted by American higher education institutions. *Lists*
Dundes, Alan. Folklore theses and dissertations in the United States / compiled by Alan Dundes. — Austin ; London : University of Texas Press for the American Folklore Society, 1976. — xix,610p ; 24cm. — (American Folklore Society. Bibliographical and special series ; vol.27)
Index.
ISBN 0-292-72413-6 : Unpriced
(B77-01117)

016.3988 — Books. Organisations. *Great Britain. National Book League. Exhibits: Books of nursery rhymes in English: Books with British imprints. Catalogues*
Opie, Iona. Three centuries of nursery rhymes and poetry for children / presented by Iona and Peter Opie. — 2nd ed., revised and expanded. — Oxford [etc.] : Oxford University Press [etc.], 1977. — xvi,116p,leaf of plate,xxiv p of plates : ill, facsims ; 26cm.
Catalogue of an exhibition held at the National Book League in May 1973. — Limited ed. of 500 copies numbered and signed. — Previous ed.: 1973. — Index.
ISBN 0-19-211566-9 : £15.00
(B77-31657)

016.401'9 — Children. Language skills. Acquisition. *Bibliographies*
Abrahamsen, Adele A. Child language : an interdisciplinary guide to theory and research / by Adele A. Abrahamsen. — Baltimore ; London [etc.] : University Park Press, 1977. — xxv,381p ; 23cm.
Index.
ISBN 0-8391-1128-2 Pbk : £8.95
(B77-29119)

016.407'2'041 — Languages. Research in British institutions. *Lists. Serials*
Language and language teaching, current research in Britain : a register compiled at the Centre for Information on Language Teaching and Research. — London : Longman.
1972-75 / edited by Helen N. Lunt. — 1976. — xi,259p ; 23cm.
Bibl.: p.257-259. — Index.
ISBN 0-582-55536-1 : £6.25
(B77-05818)

016.42 — English language. *Bibliographies. Serials*
Annual bibliography of English language and literature / [Modern Humanities Research Association]. — London (c/o Hon. Treasurer, King's College, Strand, WC2R 2LS) : The Association.
Vol.48 : 1973 / editor John Horden ; American editor James B. Misenheimer, Jr. — 1976. — xl,859p ; 22cm.
Index.
ISBN 0-900547-46-4 : £13.00
ISSN 0066-3786
Also classified at 016.82
(B77-09463)

016.42'07'1041 — Schools. Curriculum subjects: English language. Teaching. *Great Britain. Bibliographies*
Adams, Anthony. Teaching English / selected and annotated by Anthony Adams. — 3rd ed. — London : National Book League, 1976. — 45p ; 21cm.
'Produced in conjunction with a travelling exhibition ...'. — Previous ed.: 1974.
ISBN 0-85353-249-4 Sd : £0.60(£0.45 to members)
(B77-08716)

016.428'2'4 — English language. *Bibliographies. For teaching of English language to non-English speaking students*
English-Teaching Information Centre. English for speakers of other languages : a bibliography / the British Council [English-Teaching Information Centre]. — [London] ([10 Spring Gardens, SW1A 2BN]) : The Centre, 1974. — [3],52,[2]p ; 30cm.
Index.
Sd : £0.50
(B77-06422)

016.428'2'4 — Non-English speaking students. Education. Curriculum subjects: English language. Teaching. Visual aids. *Lists*
English-Teaching Information Centre. Aids to English language / the British Council [English-Teaching Information Centre]. — [London] ([10 Spring Gardens, SW1A 2BN]) : The Centre, 1975. — [3],39p ; 30cm. — (Information guide ; no.4)
Sd : £1.00
(B77-06421)

English-Teaching Information Centre. Aids to English language teaching / the British Council, English Teaching Information Centre. — [New ed.]. — [London] ([10 Spring Gardens, SW1A 2BN]) : [The Centre], 1976. — [3],31p ; 30cm. — (Information guide ; 4)
Previous ed.: published as 'Aids to English language'. 1975.
Sd : £1.00
(B77-13462)

016.428'2'4 — Non-English speaking students. Education. Curriculum subjects: English language. Texts. *Bibliographies*
English-Teaching Information Centre. English for specific purposes / the British Council, English Teaching Information Centre. — [New ed.]. — [London] ([10 Spring Gardens, SW1A 2BN]) : [The Centre], 1976. — [3],64p ; 30cm. — (Information guide ; 2)
Previous ed.: published as 'English for special purposes'. 1973.
ISBN 0-901618-13-6 Sd : £1.00
(B77-12813)

016.428'4'071 — Schools. Curriculum subjects: Reading. Teaching. *Bibliographies*
Moyle, Donald. Teaching reading / selected and annotated by Donald Moyle. — [New ed.]. — London : National Book League : United Kingdom Reading Association, [1977]. — 29p ; 21cm.
'Produced in conjunction with a travelling exhibition ...'. — Previous ed.: 1974.
ISBN 0-85353-248-6 Sd : £0.60(£0.45 to members)
(B77-08166)

016.428'6'2 — Books for illiterate adults & books for reluctant readers: Books in English. *Bibliographies*
Root, Betty. Starting point / selected and annotated by Betty Root and Sue Brownhill. — London : National Book League, 1977. — 48p ; 21cm.
Originally published: 1975.
ISBN 0-85353-252-4 Sd : £0.60(£0.45 to members)
(B77-11026)

016.428'6'2 — English language. Reading books for illiterate adults. *Bibliographies*
New readers start here : a critical evaluation of reading schemes used by tutors of adult new readers together with an annotated list of other materials found to be useful. — 2nd ed. / edited by Jean Bell. — London : Library Association, 1976. — 73p ; 21cm.
Previous ed.: / edited by Margaret Redfern. 1975. — Index.
ISBN 0-85365-059-4 Sd : £0.70
(B77-07761)

016.428'6'2 — Public libraries. *London. Southwark (London Borough). London Borough of Southwark Library Services. Stock: English language. Reading books for slow readers. Catalogues*
London Borough of Southwark Library Services. Literacy scheme collection / London Borough of Southwark Library Services. — 5th ed. — London ([Administration Dept., 20 Lordship La., SE22 8HN]) : [London Borough of Southwark Library Services], 1976. — [1],19p ; 30cm.
Previous ed.: 1975.
ISBN 0-905849-00-0 Sd : Unpriced
(B77-04520)

016.443 — French language. Dictionaries. *Bibliographies*
Klaar, R M. French dictionaries / compiled by R.M. Klaar. — [London] ([20 Carlton House Terrace, SW1Y 5AP]) : [Centre for Information on Language Teaching and Research], 1976. — 71p ; 21cm. — (Centre for Information on Language Teaching and Research. Specialised bibliographies)
Index.
ISBN 0-903466-11-2 Pbk : £2.00
(B77-09464)

016.4918 — Periodical articles in English, 1920-1975: Periodical articles on Slavonic languages. *Indexes*
Terry, Garth Michael. A subject and name index to articles on the Slavonic and East European languages and literatures, music and theatre, libraries and the press, contained in English-language journals, 1920-1975 / by Garth M. Terry. — Nottingham (Nottingham NG7 2RD) : University Library, University of Nottingham, 1976. — [1],v,198p ; 30cm.
ISBN 0-9505359-0-7 Pbk : £3.25
Primary classification 016.947
(B77-01978)

016.5 — Science. *Bibliographies*
Grogan, Denis. Science and technology : an introduction to the literature / [by] Denis Grogan. — 3rd ed. revised. — London : Bingley [etc.], 1976. — 343p : ill ; 23cm.
Previous ed. i.e. 2nd ed. revised.: 1973. — Index.
ISBN 0-85157-223-5 : £6.25
Also classified at 016.6
(B77-00573)

016.5 — Science. Documents on science: Documents published by scientific societies: Documents in print. *Bibliographies. Serials*
Scientific, engineering and medical societies publications in print. — New York ; London : Bowker.
1976-1977 / [compiled by] James M. Kyed, James M. Matarazzo. — 1976. — xiii,509p ; 29cm.
Index.
ISBN 0-8352-0898-2 : £15.00
Also classified at 016.61; 016.62
(B77-04521)

016.5009'2'4 — Museums. *Scotland. Grampian Region. Forres. Falconer Museum. Stock: Documents associated with Falconer, Hugh. Catalogues*
Falconer Museum. The Falconer papers, Forres / [catalogue by] Patrick J. Boylan. — Leicester (96 New Walk, Leicester LE1 6TD) : Leicestershire Museums, Art Galleries and Records Service, 1977. — vi,63p ; 30cm.
Papers from the collection of the Falconer Museum, Forres, now held by Moray Archive Office.
Sp : Unpriced
(B77-29120)

016.501 — Philosophy of science. *Bibliographies*
Harré, Romano. A selective bibliography of philosophy of science / by R. Harré and John Hawthorn. — 2nd ed. / revised by J.D. Greenwood, R. Harré and W. Newton-Smith. — Oxford (10 Merton St., Oxford) : Sub-faculty of Philosophy [University of Oxford], 1977. — [7],69[i.e.77]p ; 30cm. — (University of Oxford. Sub-faculty of Philosophy. Study aids ; vol.2)
Previous ed.: 1974.
Pbk : Unpriced
(B77-23950)

016.509 — Science, to 1965. *Bibliographies*
Isis cumulative bibliography : a bibliography of the history of science formed from Isis critical bibliographies 1-90, 1913-65 / edited by Magda Whitrow. — London : Mansell Information Publishing [for] the History of Science Society. Vol.3 : Subjects. — 1976. — xciv,678p ; 29cm.
Index.
ISBN 0-7201-0296-0 : £30.00
(B77-05819)

016.509 — Science, to 1977. *Bibliographies*
Lorch, R P. Aids to research in the history of science / compiled by R.P. Lorch. — Manchester ([Department of History of Science and Technology, University of Manchester Institute of Science and Technology, P.O. Box 88, Manchester M60 1QD]) : [The author], 1977. — [3],13p ; 21cm.
Sd : £0.25
(B77-33010)

016.51 — Mathematics. *Bibliographies*
Use of mathematical literature / editor A.R. Dorling. — London [etc.] : Butterworth, 1977. — xii,260p ; 23cm. — (Information sources for research and development)
Index.
ISBN 0-408-70913-8 : Unpriced
(B77-27634)

016.516'2 — Geometry. Euclid. Elements. Editions, 1482-1600. *Bibliographies*
Thomas-Stanford, Charles. Early editions of Euclid's 'Elements' / by Charles Thomas-Stanford. — New ed. — San Francisco : Alan Wofsy Fine Arts ; Folkestone : Distributed by Dawson, 1977. — iii-ix,67p,[8]p of plates,[4],xii[i.e.xiii]leaves of plates : ill, facsims(some col) ; 29cm.
Limited ed. of 450 copies, of which 134 contain an original leaf from the first ed. of Euclid's 'Elements'. Venice : E. Ratdott, 1482. — Previous ed.: published as Vol.20 in the 'Illustrated Monographs' series. London : Bibliographical Society, 1926. — Index.
ISBN 0-7129-0805-6 : £17.50
(B77-32349)

016.52'05 — National libraries. *Great Britain. British Library. Science Reference Library. Stock: Periodicals on astronomy. Catalogues*
British Library. *Science Reference Library.* Periodicals on astronomy held by the SRL / British Library, Science Reference Library ; [compiled by George Jackson and Olive Bradley]. — London (10 Porchester Gardens, Queensway, W2 4DE) : S.R.L., [1976]. — [2], vi,26p ; 30cm.
ISBN 0-902914-34-0 Sd : Unpriced
(B77-08717)

016.5268'092'4 — National libraries. *Great Britain. British Library. Map Library. Exhibits: Documents associated with Roy, William. Catalogues*
O'Donoghue, Yolande. William Roy, 1726-1790 : pioneer of the Ordnance Survey / [by] Yolande O'Donoghue. — London : British Museum Publications Ltd for the British Library, 1977. — [8],56p : ill, facsims, maps, ports ; 25cm.
Catalogue of an exhibition mounted by the British Library Map Library in 1976. — Bibl.: p.56.
ISBN 0-7141-0387-x Sd : £1.50 : CIP rev.
(B77-07763)

016.5269'9 — Hydrographic surveying. *Bibliographies*
Hydrographic Society. Reading list / the Hydrographic Society. — [London] ([c/o The Hon. Secretary, c/o Department of Land Surveying, North East London Polytechnic, E17 4JB]) : [The Society], [1977]. — [48]p ; 21x30cm. — (Special publication ; 1 ISSN 0309-8303)
Cover title.
Pbk : £0.50
(B77-19967)

016.5269'9'0941 — British hydrographic surveys, 1776-1820. *Bibliographies*
David, A C F. The surveyors of the 'Bounty' : a preliminary study of the hydrographic surveys of William Bligh, Thomas Hayward and Peter Heywood and the charts published from them / by A.C.F. David. — [Taunton] (['Oak End', West Monkton, Taunton, Somerset TA2 8QZ]) : The author, 1976. — iii,48 leaves ; 31cm.
Bibl.: leaves 47-48.
Sd : Unpriced
(B77-14014)

016.53'0092'4 — Physics. Newton, Sir Isaac. *Bibliographies*
Wallis, Peter John. Newton and Newtoniana, 1672-1975 : a bibliography / [by] Peter & Ruth Wallis. — Folkestone : Dawson [for the] Project for Historical Bibliography, 1977. — xxiv,362p ; 28cm.
Index.
ISBN 0-7129-0769-6 : £30.00 : CIP rev.
(B77-19968)

016.535 — Optics. *Abstracts. Periodicals*
Optics abstracts. — London (The Old Mill, Dorset Place, E15 1DJ) : Multi Science Publishing Company Ltd.
Vol.1, no.1- ; Sept.-Oct. 1976-. — 1976-. — 25cm.
Six issues a year. — [3],77,[1]p. in 1st issue.
Sd : £39.00 yearly
ISSN 0309-5150
(B77-10710)

016.535'84 — National libraries. *Great Britain. British Library. Science Reference Library. Stock: Documents on spectra. Bibliographies*
British Library. *Science Reference Library.* A guide to the published collections of spectral data held by the SRL / [compiled by] Ruth Coman. — [3rd ed.]. — London (25 Southampton Buildings, Chancery La., WC2A 1AW) : Science Reference Library, 1977. — [2], iii,43p ; 30cm. — (British Library. Science Reference Library. Occasional publications)
Previous ed.: published as 'A guide to the literature on spectral data' / by Ann Clarke. London : National Reference Library of Science and Invention, 1972.
ISBN 0-902914-35-9 Sd : Unpriced
(B77-15651)

016.536 — Heat. *Bibliographies. Serials*
Heat bibliography. — Guildford : IPC Science and Technology Press.
1974 / editors L.B. Cousins, W.J. Ramsay ; [for the] Heat Transfer and Flow Service, Harwell and National Engineering Laboratory. — 1976. — ix,227p ; 31cm.
ISBN 0-902852-70-1 : Unpriced
ISSN 0073-151x
(B77-19969)

016.5375'352 — Spectroscopy. Mössbauer effect. *Bibliographies*
Mössbauer effect data index. — New York [etc.] : IFI/Plenum Data Co ; London : Plenum Press.
[1973] : Covering the 1973 literature / edited by John G. Stevens and Virginia E. Stevens. — [1976]. — x,495p : ill ; 29cm.
Published in the United States: 1975.
ISBN 0-306-65144-0 : £31.19
(B77-01972)

016.541'28 — Periodical articles on vibration spectra of inorganic compounds. *Indexes*
Greenwood, Norman Neill. Index of vibrational spectra of inorganic and organometallic compounds / [by] N.N. Greenwood, E.J.F. Ross, B.P. Straughan. — London : Butterworth.
In 3 vols.
Vol.3 : 1964-1966 / [by] N.N. Greenwood, E.J.F. Ross. — 1977. — [7],1600p ; 23cm.
ISBN 0-408-70791-7 : £55.00
(B77-26739)

016.541'36 — Fluid mixtures. Low temperature properties. *Bibliographies*
Hiza, M J. Equilibrium properties of fluid mixtures : a bibliography of data on fluids of cryogenic interest / [compiled] by M.J. Hiza, A.J. Kidnay and R.C. Miller. — New York [etc.] : IFI/Plenum Data Co. ; London : Plenum Press, [1976]. — vi,160p ; 29cm. — (National Standard Reference Data System. Bibliographic series)
Published in the United States: 1975.
ISBN 0-306-66001-6 : £18.59
(B77-01973)

016.541'395 — Catalysts. *Abstracts. Periodicals*
Catalysts in chemistry : collected notes on catalysts used in chemical reactions. — Braintree (P.O. Box 55, Braintree, Essex CM7 6HD) : R.H. Chandler Ltd.
Vol.1, no.1- ; Jan. 1977-. — 1977-. — 28cm.
Monthly. — 65p. in 1st issue.
Sd : £80.00 yearly
ISSN 0309-5770
(B77-12265)

016.544'92 — Periodical articles on column chromatography. *Bibliographies. Serials*
Bibliography of liquid column chromatography, and survey applications. — Amsterdam ; Oxford [etc.] : Elsevier.
1971-1973 / [edited by] Zdeněk Deyl, Jan Kopecký. — 1976[i.e.1977]. — xix,1135p ; 24cm. — ('Journal of chromatography' supplementary volume ; no.6)
Published in the Netherlands: 1976. — Index.
ISBN 0-444-41469-x Pbk : £60.66
(B77-11521)

016.544'926 — Gas chromatography. *Bibliographies*
Signeur, Austin V. Guide to gas chromatography literature / by Austin V. Signeur. — New York [etc.] : IFI/Plenum ; London : Plenum Press.
Vol.3. — [1976]. — ix,1089p ; 28cm.
Published in the United States: 1974. — Index.
ISBN 0-306-68203-6 : £40.95
(B77-05820)

016.546'22 — Water. Properties. *Bibliographies*
Hawkins, Donald T. Physical and chemical properties of water : a bibliography, 1957-1974 / [by] Donald T. Hawkins ; with a foreword by Frank H. Stillinger. — New York [etc.] : IFI/Plenum ; London : Plenum Press, 1976. — xiv,556p : 1 ill ; 28cm.
'... composed of two bibliographies prepared ... by the Libraries and Information Systems Center of Bell Laboratories ... Part 1 [was] compiled by the late E.S. Turner ...' - Preface. — Index.
ISBN 0-306-65164-5 : £42.53
(B77-17858)

016.546'662 — Cadmium. *Abstracts. Periodicals*
Cadmium abstracts. — London (34 Berkeley Sq., W1X 6AJ) : Cadmium Association [etc.].
Vol.1, no.1- ; Jan. 1977-. — 1977-. — 21cm.
Six issues a year. — [2],16p. in 1st issue.
Sd : Unpriced
ISSN 0309-1139
(B77-10088)

016.551 — Geophysics. *Abstracts. Periodicals*
Geophysical abstracts. — Norwich (University of East Anglia, Norwich NR4 7TJ) : Geo Abstracts Ltd.
1977/1-. — 1977-. — 25cm.
Six issues a year. — [1],78p. in 1st issues.
Sd : £15.00 yearly
ISSN 0309-4332
(B77-17859)

016.5514'609 — Great Britain. Estuaries. *Bibliographies. Serials*
Estuaries of the British Isles : a bibliography of recent scientific papers. — Plymouth (Citadel Hill, Plymouth, Devon) : Library and Information Services, Marine Biological Association of the United Kingdom.
No.1 : 1977 / edited by Elizabeth Roberts and Allen Varley. — 1977. — iv,32 leaves : map ; 30cm.
'Supplementing and updating "Bibliography of estuarine research", edited by P. Head. (Natural Environment Research Council Publications, Series C, No.17, 1976)'. — Index.
Pbk : £2.00
ISSN 0309-3964
(B77-08167)

016.5514'8 — Theses on hydrology: Theses accepted by North American universities, 1962-1976. *Lists*
University Microfilms International. Doctoral dissertations on hydrology & desalination / compiled by University Microfilms International. — London (18 Bedford Row, WC1R 4EJ) : University Microfilms International, [1977]. — 24p ; 28cm.
Sd : Unpriced
Also classified at 016.6281'67
(B77-32350)

016.5541 — Theses on geological features of Great Britain: Theses accepted by British higher education institutions, 1960-1975. *Bibliographies*
Hodgson, A V. The Herrington list : titles of research theses, 1960-1975 on the geology of the British Isles and offshore areas, with classified subdiscipline-regional list / compiled by A.V. Hodgson and D.J.C. Laming ; in co-operation with the Computer Centre, Sunderland Polytechnic. — 2nd ed. — Worthing (52 Little Paddocks, Ferring, Worthing, Sussex BN12 5NH) : Bibliographic Press Ltd, 1976. — [2],128,[2]p : map ; 22cm.
Previous ed.: 1975 (Limited circulation). — Index.
ISBN 0-9505568-0-7 Sd : £3.50
(B77-10089)

016.5741'92'05 — National libraries. *Great Britain. British Library. Science Reference Library. Stock: Periodicals on biochemistry. Catalogues*
British Library. *Science Reference Library.* Periodicals on biochemistry held by the SRL / [compiled by George Jackson, Olive Bradley and Jane Gaworska]. — London (10 Porchester Gardens, Queensway, W2 4DE) : S.R.L., 1977. — [2],vi,27p ; 30cm.
ISBN 0-902914-37-5 Sd : Unpriced : CIP rev.
(B77-07762)

016.5745 — Natural environment. Research projects supported by Natural Environment Research Council. *Lists. Serials*
Natural Environment Research Council. Research grants in the natural environmental sciences : NERC research grants / [Natural Environment Research Council]. — [London] : [The Council].
1976 : current on 1st October. — 1977. — [1], v,60p ; 30cm. — (Natural Environment Research Council. Publications : series D ; no.9)
Index.
Sd : Unpriced
(B77-26069)

Natural Environment Research Council. Research training in the natural environmental sciences : NERC research students and fellows / [Natural Environment Research Council]. — [London] ([27 Charing Cross Rd, WC2H 0AX]) : The Council.
[1975-76] / [compiled by L.I. Edwins, A. Harris]. — 1975. — [7],90[i.e.103]p ; 30cm. — (Natural Environment Research Council. Publications : series D ; no.7)
Index.
ISBN 0-901875-45-7 Sp : Unpriced
(B77-05821)

Natural Environment Research Council. Research training in the natural environmental sciences : NERC research students and fellows / [Natural Environment Research Council]. — London : [The Council].
1976-[77] : as at 1st October / [compiled by L.I. Edwins]. — 1976. — [7],77[i.e.91]p ; 30cm. — (Natural Environment Research Council. Publications : series D ; no.8)
Index.
Sp : Unpriced
(B77-26070)

016.575'0092'4 — Evolution. Darwin, Charles. *Bibliographies*
Freeman, Richard Broke. The works of Charles Darwin : an annotated bibliographical handlist / by R.B. Freeman. — 2nd ed., revised and enlarged. — Folkestone : Dawson [etc.], 1977. — 235p,plate : 1 ill ; 23cm.
Previous ed.: London : Dawsons, 1965. — Index.
ISBN 0-7129-0740-8 : £10.00
(B77-10711)

016.581 — Vascular plants. *Bibliographies. Serials*
The **Kew** record of taxonomic literature relating to vascular plants / Royal Botanic Gardens, Kew. — London : H.M.S.O.
1974. — 1976. — xv,384p : map ; 30cm.
Index.
ISBN 0-11-241111-8 Pbk : £34.00
ISSN 0307-2835
(B77-06423)

016.581'05 — National libraries. *Great Britain. British Library. Science Reference Library. Stock: Periodicals on botany. Catalogues*
British Library. *Science Reference Library.* Periodicals on botany held by the SRL / [compiled by Beryl Leigh and Peter Walsh]. — London (10 Porchester Gardens, W2 4DE) : British Library, Science Reference Library, 1977. — [2],v,49p ; 30cm.
ISBN 0-902914-36-7 Sd : Unpriced : CIP rev.
(B77-07024)

016.582'13 — Universities. Libraries. *Scotland. Strathclyde Region. Glasgow. University of Glasgow. Library. Exhibits: Books on flowering plants. Catalogues*
University of Glasgow. *Library.* Great flower books : [catalogue of] an exhibition [held] 15 March-22 April 1977 [at] Glasgow University Library. — [Glasgow] ([The University, Glasgow G12 8QG]) : [The Library], [1977]. — [1],15p ; 30cm.
ISBN 0-85261-142-0 Sd : £0.50
(B77-19159)

016.5911'05 — National libraries. *Great Britain. British Library. Science Reference Library. Stock: Periodicals on animal physiology. Catalogues*
British Library. *Science Reference Library.* Periodicals on animal physiology held by the SRL / [British Library, Science Reference Library] ; [compiled by George Jackson, Olive Bradley and Jane Gaworska]. — London (10 Porchester Gardens, Queensway, W2 4DE) : S.R.L., [1976]. — [2],vi,49p ; 30cm.
ISBN 0-902914-31-6 Sd : Unpriced
(B77-01118)

016.593'1'04524 — Animals. Cells. Parasites: Protozoa. *Abstracts. Periodicals*
Protozoological abstracts. — Slough : Commonwealth Agricultural Bureaux.
Vol.1, no.1- ; Jan. 1977-. — 1977-. — 21cm.
Monthly. — 144p. in various pagings in 1st issue. — Index.
Sd : Unpriced
ISSN 0309-1287
(B77-10712)

016.597'5'041858 — Teleostei. Integumentary system. *Bibliographies*
Hatton, J P. The dermatology of teleost fishes : a bibliography / [compiled and edited by] J.P. Hatton, assisted by R.J. Roberts & A.M. Bullock. — Stirling ([Stirling FK9 4LA]) : University of Stirling, 1976. — [2],vi,264p ; 30cm.
Index.
ISBN 0-901636-11-8 Pbk : £4.25
(B77-01119)

016.5982'05 — National libraries. *Great Britain. British Library. Science Reference Library. Stock: Periodicals on ornithology. Catalogues*
British Library. *Science Reference Library.* Periodicals on ornithology held by the SRL / [compiled by George Jackson]. — London (10 Porchester Gardens, W2 4DE) : S.R.L., [1976]. — [2],iv,13,[1]p ; 30cm.
ISBN 0-902914-33-2 Sd : Unpriced
(B77-01120)

016.6 — Subscription libraries. *London. Camden (London Borough). Lewis (H.K.) and Company. Library. Stock. Catalogues*
Lewis (H.K.) and Company. *Library.* Catalogue of Lewis's medical, scientific and technical lending library. — New ed., revised to Dec. 31, 1972. — [London] : [H.K. Lewis].
Previous ed.: 1965-66.
Supplement. 1973-1975. — [1976]. — iii,337p ; 22cm.
Cover title. — Index.
ISBN 0-7186-0424-5 Pbk : £3.00(£2.50 to members of the Library)
(B77-16696)

016.6 — Technology. *Bibliographies*
Grogan, Denis. Science and technology : an introduction to the literature / [by] Denis Grogan. — 3rd ed. revised. — London : Bingley [etc.], 1976. — 343p : ill ; 23cm.
Previous ed. i.e. 2nd ed. revised.: 1973. — Index.
ISBN 0-85157-223-5 : £6.25
Primary classification 016.5
(B77-00573)

016.602'1'2 — Technology. British standards. *Lists. Serials*
British Standards yearbook. — London : British Standards Institution.
1977 : complete to 30 September 1976. — [1977]. — xxxii,980p ; 21cm.
Index.
ISBN 0-580-09499-5 Pbk : £6.60
ISSN 0068-2578
(B77-10090)

016.604'6 — Industrial waste materials. *Abstracts. Periodicals*
Waste management information bulletin. — Oxfordshire (Bldg 151, Harwell Laboratory, Oxon. OX11 0RA) : Waste Research Unit [Harwell Laboratory].
Continues: Industrial wastes information bulletin.
Vol.8, no.1- ; Jan. 1977-. — [1977]-. — 29cm.
Monthly. — 37,[4],xix p. in Jan. 1977 issue. — Index.
Sd : £35.00 yearly
ISSN 0309-5398
(B77-11522)

016.61 — Books on medicine: Books in print. *Lists. Serials*
Bowker's medical books in print : subject index, author index, title index. — New York ; London : Bowker.
1977. — 1977. — [9],1039p ; 29cm.
Index.
ISBN 0-8352-0964-4 : £26.75
ISSN 0076-5929
(B77-24650)

016.61 — Medicine. Documents on medicine: Documents published by medical societies: Documents in print. *Bibliographies. Serials*
Scientific, engineering and medical societies publications in print. — New York ; London : Bowker.
1976-1977 / [compiled by] James M. Kyed, James M. Matarazzo. — 1976. — xiii,509p ; 29cm.
Index.
ISBN 0-8352-0898-2 : £15.00
Primary classification 016.5
(B77-04521)

016.61073 — Medicine. Nursing. *Current awareness bulletins*
LEGS update. — New York ; London [etc.] : Wiley.
1976 / [compiled by] Anne K. Roe, Mary C. Sherwood. — 1976. — iv,40p ; 28cm.
Leaves perforated at inside edge. — Pierced for binder.
ISBN 0-471-01935-6 Sd : £0.25
(B77-08168)

016.612'397 — Man. Lipids. Metabolism. *Abstracts. Periodicals*
Lipid abstracts : a quarterly selection from the current English language literature on human lipid metabolism, diet and atherosclerosis. — London (1 Wimpole St., W1M 8AE) : Royal Society of Medicine.
Vol.1, no.1- ; 1977-. — 1977-. — 25cm.
[1],16p. in vol.1, no.1.
Sd : Free to fellows of the Society
ISSN 0309-5797
(B77-19970)

016.6132 — Dietetics. *Abstracts. Periodicals*
Feeding-weight & obesity abstracts. — London [etc.] (1 Falconberg Court, W1V 5FG) : Information Retrieval Ltd.
Vol.1, no.1- ; July 1976-. — 1976-. — 23cm.
Quarterly. — [6],97,[27]p. in 1st issue. — Index.
Pbk : £18.00 yearly
ISSN 0308-2997
(B77-08169)

016.6136'2 — Industrial health. Conferences. *Abstracts*
International Congress on Occupational Health, *18th, Brighton, 1975.* Abstracts [of the] XVIII International Congress on Occupational Health, Brighton, England, 14-19 September 1975. — [London] ([c/o Dr R. Murray, Quality House (4th floor), Quality Court, Chancery La., WC2A 1HP]) : [Permanent Commission and International Association on Occupational Health], 1975. — 495p : ill ; 21cm.
Includes abstracts in French, German and Spanish. — Bibl.
Pbk : Unpriced
(B77-19160)

016.6139'4'0924 — Man. Contraception. Stopes, Marie. *Bibliographies*
Eaton, Peter. Marie Stopes : a checklist of her writings / [compiled by] Peter Eaton and Marilyn Warwick. — London : Croom Helm, 1977. — 59p ; 23cm.
Bibl.: p.53-54. — Index.
ISBN 0-85664-397-1 : £5.95
(B77-04522)

016.6148'52 — Plastics industries & rubber industries. Industrial safety. *Great Britain. Abstracts. Periodicals*
Recent literature on hazardous environments in industry. — Shrewsbury (Shawbury, Shrewsbury SY4 4NR) : Rubber and Plastics Research Association of Great Britain.
Continues: RAPRA communication.
Vol.2, no.4- ; Apr. 1977-. — [1977]-. — 30cm.
Monthly. — [5],25p. in 1st issue. — Versos of leaves blank.
Sd : £100.00 yearly
ISSN 0140-4156
(B77-29872)

016.616'043 — Periodical articles on teratogens of man. *Abstracts*
Shepard, Thomas H. Catalog of teratogenic agents / [by] Thomas H. Shepard. — 2nd ed. — Baltimore ; London : Johns Hopkins University Press, 1976. — xxiii,291,[1]p : ill(on lining papers) ; 24cm.
Text on lining papers. — Previous ed.: 1973. — Bibl. — Index.
ISBN 0-8018-1881-8 : £13.25
(B77-17247)

016.6169'63 — Periodical articles on schistosomiasis, 1963-1974. *Abstracts*
Warren, Kenneth S. Schistosomiasis III : abstracts of the complete literature, 1963-1974 / [by] Kenneth S. Warren, Donald B. Hoffman, Jr, with the assistance of Kate W. Sanders. — Washington, D.C. ; London : Hemisphere Publishing ; New York ; London [etc.] : Distributed by Wiley, 1976. — 2v.(vi,730p) : ill ; 29cm.
'A Halsted Press book'. — Includes abstracts in French, German and Spanish. — Index.
ISBN 0-470-15204-4 : £67.00
(B77-19161)

016.6169'92 — Oncology. *Abstracts*
Oncology abstracts : experimental & clinical studies. — London [etc.] (1 Falconberg Court, W1V 5FG) : Information Retrieval Ltd.
Vol.1, no.1- ; Jan. 1977-. — 1977-. — 23cm.
Monthly. — [6],226[i.e. 227]p. in Vol.1, no.1. — Index.
Pbk : £75.00 yearly
ISSN 0308-7980
(B77-08718)

016.6189'28'5 — Children. Hyperactivity. *Bibliographies*
Winchell, Carol Ann. The hyperkinetic child : a bibliography of medical, educational and behavioral studies / [by] Carol Ann Winchell. — Westport, Conn. ; London : Greenwood Press, 1976. — xiv,182,[1]p ; 25cm.
Originally published: Westport : Greenwood Press, 1975. — Index.
ISBN 0-8371-7813-4 : £9.75
(B77-15060)

016.62 — Engineering. Documents on engineering: Documents published by engineering societies: Documents in print. *Bibliographies. Serials*
Scientific, engineering and medical societies publications in print. — New York ; London : Bowker.
1976-1977 / [compiled by] James M. Kyed, James M. Matarazzo. — 1976. — xiii,509p ; 29cm.
Index.
ISBN 0-8352-0898-2 : £15.00
Primary classification 016.5
(B77-04521)

016.621 — Mechanical engineering. *Abstracts*
Engineering synopses. — London : Institution of Mechanical Engineers.
Vol.1, no.1- ; Jan. 1977-. — 1977-. — ill ; 29cm.
Six issues a year. — [1],18p. in 1st issue. — Bibl.
Sd : £10.00 yearly
ISSN 0309-2186
(B77-08170)

016.621385 — Facsimile transmission. *Bibliographies*
MacCafferty, Maxine. Fax & Teletext / compiled by Maxine MacCafferty. — London : Aslib, 1977. — ix,77p ; 30cm. — (Aslib. Bibliographies ; no.5 ISSN 0308-7522)
Index.
ISBN 0-85142-093-1 Pbk : £4.25(£3.25 to members of Aslib)
Primary classification 016.621388
(B77-17250)

016.621388 — Television equipment: Teletext systems. *Bibliographies*
MacCafferty, Maxine. Fax & Teletext / compiled by Maxine MacCafferty. — London : Aslib, 1977. — ix,77p ; 30cm. — (Aslib. Bibliographies ; no.5 ISSN 0308-7522)
Index.
ISBN 0-85142-093-1 Pbk : £4.25(£3.25 to members of Aslib)
Also classified at 016.621385
(B77-17250)

016.6214 — Energy engineering. *Bibliographies*
Metz, Karen S. Information sources in power engineering : a guide to energy resources and technology / [by] Karen S. Metz. — Westport, Conn. ; London : Greenwood Press, 1975. — xiii,114p ; 22cm.
Bibl.: p.107-109. — Index.
ISBN 0-8371-8538-6 : £8.25
(B77-16697)

016.62143'3 — Gas turbines. High temperature alloys. *Bibliographies*
English Electric Company. *Library.* High temperature materials for gas turbines / [English Electric Company Library]. — Leicester (Whetstone, Leicester LE8 3LH) : GEC Power Engineering Ltd, Library.
Supplement 3 / compiled by Tom Crawshaw. — 1976. — 73[i.e.75]p ; 30cm. — (Bibliography ; Bib 132 Suppl. 3)
Cumulated subject index to BIB 132 and Supplements 1, 2 and 3.
ISBN 0-901664-28-6 Sp : £5.00
(B77-08171)

016.62146'2 — Stepping motors. *Bibliographies*
Biscoe, G I. A bibliography of published works on stepping motors / [by] G.I. Biscoe, A.S. Mills, D. Crook. — [Leatherhead] : Electrical Research Association, 1977. — 188p in various pagings ; 30cm.
Sp : Unpriced
(B77-15652)

016.62147 — Solar energy. *Bibliographies*
Loyd, Stephen. Heat and power from the sun : an annotated bibliography with a survey of available products and their suppliers / by Stephen Loyd and Colin Starling. — 3rd ed. — Bracknell : Building Services Research and Information Association, 1977. — [2],70p ; 30cm. — (Building Services Research and Information Association. Bibliographies ; LB 101/77 ISSN 0307-6059)
Previous ed.: 1975.
ISBN 0-86022-052-4 Pbk : Unpriced
(B77-31659)

016.62148'1 — Steam generating heavy water reactors. *Bibliographies*
English Electric Company. *Library.* Steam generating heavy water reactors / [English Electric Company Library] ; [compiled] by S. Spriggs. — Revised [ed.]. — Leicester (Whetstone, Leicester LE8 3LH) : GEC Power Engineering Ltd, Library, 1976. — [1],19p ; 30cm. — (EE bib ; 137 (Rev 2)) (Bibliography ; Bib 137 (Rev 2))
Index. — '... incorporates Reading List 931, Sept. 1969'.
ISBN 0-901664-29-4 Sd : £2.00
(B77-08172)

016.6216'91 — Jet ejectors. *Bibliographies*
Bonnington, Sidney Thorpe. Jet pumps and ejectors : a state of the art review and bibliography / [by] S.T. Bonnington, A.L. King. — 2nd revised ed. / J.A.G. Hemmings, additional bibliography and editing ... — Cranfield (Cranfield, Bedford MK43 0AJ) : BHRA Fluid Engineering, 1976. — vi,110,[4]p : ill ; 30cm. — (British Hydromechanics Research Association. Fluid Engineering. Series ; vol.1)
Previous ed.: 1972. — Index.
ISBN 0-900983-63-9 Pbk : Unpriced
(B77-12814)

016.621'8'6 — Films on materials handling: Films available for hire. *Lists*
National Materials Handling Centre. Materials handling film catalogue / National Materials Handling Centre. — [Cranfield] ([Cranfield Institute of Technology, Cranfield, Beds. MK43 0AL]) : [The Centre], [1976]. — iv,105 leaves ; 30cm.
Cover title. — Index.
ISBN 0-905823-00-1 Sp : £2.50
(B77-08173)

016.6281'67 — Theses on desalination of water: Theses accepted by North American universities, 1962-1976. *Lists*
University Microfilms International. Doctoral dissertations on hydrology & desalination / compiled by University Microfilms International. — London (18 Bedford Row, WC1R 4EJ) : University Microfilms International, [1977]. — 24p ; 28cm.
Sd : Unpriced
Primary classification 016.5514'8
(B77-32350)

016.628'3 — Sewage. Treatment. Applications of automation. *Bibliographies*
Water Research Centre. Automation in sewage works, sewerage systems, water treatment and supply, and the treatment of trade waste waters : an annotated bibliography covering the period 1960-1977 / Water Research Centre. — Marlow [etc.] (Medmenham Laboratory, Medmenham, PO Box 16, Marlow, Bucks. SL7 2HD) : [The Centre], [1977]. — [7],84p ; 30cm. — (Occasional report ; 9)
'... prepared on the occasion of the International Association of Water Pollution Research Workshop on "Instrumentation and Control for Water and Waste-Water Treatment and Transport Systems", London and Stockholm, May 16-21, 1977. — ... an updated version of Water Pollution report no.446R ...' - p.[5]. — Index.
Sp : Unpriced
(B77-21659)

016.6292 — Motor vehicles. *Abstracts. Periodicals*
Automobile abstracts / the Motor Industry Research Association. — [Nuneaton] : [M.I.R.A.].
Supersedes: MIRA abstracts.
[No.1]- ; 1975-. — [1975]-. — 21cm.
[2],40p. in Aug. 1977 issue.
Sd : £40.00 yearly
ISSN 0309-0817
(B77-30916)

016.6292 — Public libraries. *Bedfordshire. Luton. Luton Central Library. Stock: Documents on motor vehicle engineering. Lists*
Luton Central Library. Automobile engineering : additions to the special collections of the Luton Central Library, July 1971 to December 1976 / [compiled by Jane Tasker]. — Luton (Central Library, Bridge St., Luton LU1 2NG) : Bedfordshire County Library Luton District, [1977]. — [4],37p ; 21cm.
Index.
Sd : £0.50
(B77-18509)

016.63 — Theses on agriculture: Theses accepted by North American universities, 1973-1976. *Lists*
University Microfilms International. Doctoral dissertations on agriculture & agronomy / compiled by University Microfilms International. — [London] ([18 Bedford Row, WC1R 4EJ]) : [University Microfilms International], [1977]. — [3],51p ; 28cm.
'The Dissertations ... have been submitted to North American Universities during the years 1973-1976'.
Sd : Unpriced
(B77-32351)

016.63 — Universities. Agricultural colleges. Libraries. *Kent. Wye. Wye College. Library. Stock: Books printed between 1543 & 1918. Catalogues*
Wye College. *Library.* A catalogue of agricultural & horticultural books, 1543-1918, in Wye College Library. — Ashford, Kent : The Library, [1977]. — [1],ii,100p ; 30cm.
ISBN 0-901859-63-x Sd : £1.50
(B77-19971)

016.633'171 — Crops: Millets. *Abstracts. Serials*
Sorghum and millets abstracts. — Farnham Royal : Commonwealth Agricultural Bureaux [etc.].
Vol.1, no.1- ; Jan. 1976-. — 1976-. — 30cm.
Monthly. — [4],15,4p. in 1st issue. — English text, English, French and Spanish subject indexes. — Index.
Sd : £20.00 yearly
ISSN 0308-2970
Primary classification 016.633'174
(B77-06424)

016.633'174 — Crops: Sorghum. *Abstracts. Serials*
Sorghum and millets abstracts. — Farnham Royal : Commonwealth Agricultural Bureaux [etc.].
Vol.1, no.1- ; Jan. 1976-. — 1976-. — 30cm.
Monthly. — [4],15,4p. in 1st issue. — English text, English, French and Spanish subject indexes. — Index.
Sd : £20.00 yearly
ISSN 0308-2970
Also classified at 016.633'171
(B77-06424)

016.633'5 — Crops: Fibres. *Abstracts. Serials*
Cotton and tropical fibres abstracts. — Farnham Royal : Commonwealth Agricultural Bureaux [etc.].
Vol.1, no.1- ; Jan. 1976-. — 1976-. — 30cm.
Monthly. — [6],28,9p. in 1st issue. — English text, English, French and Spanish subject indexes. — Index.
Sd : £20.00 yearly
ISSN 0308-6577
(B77-06425)

016.633'85 — Tropical oilseeds. *Abstracts. Periodicals*
Tropical oil seeds abstracts. — Slough : Commonwealth Agricultural Bureaux.
Vol.1, no.1- ; Jan. 1976-. — [1976]-. — 30cm.
Monthly. — [32]p. in July 1976 issue. — English text, English, French and Spanish index.
Sd : £20.00 yearly
ISSN 0308-2962
(B77-12266)

016.6367'08'96042 — Livestock: Dogs. Genetic disorders. *Bibliographies*
Robinson, Roy. Catalogue & bibliography of canine genetic anomalies / [compiled by] Roy Robinson. — 2nd ed. — Exeter (1 Old Park Rd, Longbrook St., Exeter EX4 4EZ) : Co-operative Hereditary Abnormalities Research Team, 1972. — [3],52p ; 27cm.
Previous ed.: West Wickham : Co-operative Hereditary Abnormalities Research Team, 1969.
ISBN 0-9500144-1-9 Sd : £0.50
(B77-03875)

016.6'4404 — Real time computer systems
Freedman, A L. Real-time computer systems / [by] A.L. Freedman, R.A. Lees. — New York : Crane Russak ; London : Edward Arnold, 1977. — ii-x,277p : ill ; 24cm. — (Computer systems engineering series)
Bibl.: p.263-269. — Index.
ISBN 0-7131-2634-5 : £14.00
(B77-30917)

016.658 — Management. *Abstracts*
Anbar yearbook. — [Wembley] : Anbar Publications.
5 : (to August 76) / [managing editor H.P. Cemach, editors J.W. Goodman, C.K. Vernon]. — 1976. — 267p in various pagings ; 31cm.
Cover title: The compleat Anbar. — Bibl.: p.222-263. — List of films: p.263-265. — Index.
£35.00
ISSN 0307-0409
(B77-07025)

016.658 — Management. *Bibliographies*
Sandeau, Georges. Selective management bibliography / [by] Georges Sandeau. — London [etc.] : Bowker, [1976]. — 402p ; 31cm.
Published in the United States: 1975. — Index.
ISBN 0-85935-037-1 : Unpriced
(B77-01121)

016.658 — Theses accepted by University of Bradford. Management Centre, to 1976. *Lists*
University of Bradford. *Management Centre.* List of theses and dissertations / [University of Bradford Management Centre]. — [Bradford] ([The Administrative Assistant, Management Centre, University of Bradford, Emm La., Bradford, W. Yorkshire BD9 4JL]) : The Centre, [1977]. — [4],34p ; 21cm.
ISBN 0-904401-01-4 Sd : £0.50
(B77-12815)

016.6581'54 — Libraries. Budgeting. Planning, programming, budgeting systems. *Bibliographies*
Noyce, John Leonard. PPBS and MbO in libraries / [compiled by] John L. Noyce. — 5th ed. — Brighton : Smoothie Publications, 1976. — [9]p ; 30cm.
Previous ed.: 1974.
ISBN 0-903612-37-2 Sd : £0.80
Also classified at 016.6584
(B77-00574)

016.6584 — Libraries. Management by objectives. *Bibliographies*
Noyce, John Leonard. PPBS and MbO in libraries / [compiled by] John L. Noyce. — 5th ed. — Brighton : Smoothie Publications, 1976. — [9]p ; 30cm.
Previous ed.: 1974.
ISBN 0-903612-37-2 Sd : £0.80
Primary classification 016.6581'54
(B77-00574)

016.6584'7 — Digital computer systems. Security measures. *Bibliographies*
MacCafferty, Maxine. Computer security / compiled by Maxine MacCafferty. — London : Aslib, 1976. — [2],vii,91p ; 30cm. — (Aslib. Bibliographies ; no.4 ISSN 0308-7522)
Index.
ISBN 0-85142-088-5 Pbk : £4.25(£3.50 to members of Aslib)
(B77-11523)

016.6587'8'097 — Goods. Physical distribution. *North America. Bibliographies*
Davis, Bob J. Information sources in transportation, material management and physical distribution : an annotated bibliography and guide / edited and compiled by Bob J. Davis. — Westport, Conn. ; London : Greenwood Press, 1976. — xv,715,[1] p ; 29cm.
Index.
ISBN 0-8371-8379-0 : £23.00
Primary classification 016.3805'097
(B77-26738)

016.6602'8425 — Vapour-liquid equilibria. Technical data. *Bibliographies*
Wichterle, Ivan. Vapor-liquid equilibrium data bibliography / [by] Ivan Wichterle, Jan Linek, Eduard Hála. — Amsterdam ; Oxford [etc.] : Elsevier.
Supplement 1. — 1976. — vii,333p ; 25cm.
£21.00
(B77-02716)

016.665'77 — Fuels: Methane. Production. Use of sewage. Use of anaerobic digesters. *Bibliographies*
Freeman, Christina. Methane generation by anaerobic fermentation : an annotated bibliography : a critical review of the literature with particular reference to small-scale and rural applications / compiled by Christina Freeman and Leo Pyle. — London : Intermediate Technology Publications, 1977. — [4],64p : ill ; 26cm.
Index.
ISBN 0-903031-41-8 Sd : £1.50
(B77-23951)

016.666'88 — Synthetic gemstones. Materials. *Bibliographies*
O'Donoghue, Michael. Synthetic gem materials / [by] Michael O'Donoghue. — London ([Central House, Whitechapel High St., E1 7PF]) : The Worshipful Company of Goldsmiths, 1976. — [2],215p ; 30cm.
Bibl.: p.4-17.
ISBN 0-9501079-1-3 Pbk : £12.00
(B77-01974)

016.667'9 — Powder coatings. *Abstracts*
Chandler, J I. Powder coating, 1976 / collected and edited by J.I. Chandler from references in 'Continental paint & resin news' and 'Paint and resin patents'. — Braintree (PO Box 55, Braintree, Essex) : R.H. Chandler Ltd, 1977. — 66p : ill ; 28cm. — (Bibliographies in paint technology ; no.28)
Index.
Pbk : £3.00
(B77-17861)

016.669'3 — Copper. *Abstracts. Periodicals*
International copper information bulletin : recent reports, publications and abstracts on copper, its alloys and compounds. — Potters Bar : Copper Development Association.
Supersedes: Copper abstracts.
[No.]1- ; [Sept. 1976]-. — [1976]-. — 30cm.
Quarterly. — [1],20p. in 1st issue. — Bibl.
Sd : Unpriced
ISSN 0309-2216
(B77-20859)

016.67 — Periodical articles on consumer durables. *Bibliographies*
Clover information index. — Stevenage (14 Wisden Rd, Stevenage, Herts. SG1 5HZ) : Clover Publications.
[Vol.1, no.1]- ; July 1975-. — [1975]-. — 30cm.
Quarterly. — 49p. in Vol.3, no.1. — Also includes topics covered by popular periodicals.
Sp : Unpriced
ISSN 0140-1939
(B77-26071)

016.6717'3 — Metal coils. Coating, 1970-1976. *Bibliographies*
Chandler, R H. Coil coating review, 1970-76 / by R.H. Chandler. — Braintree (P.O. Box 25, Braintree, Essex) : R.H. Chandler Ltd, 1977. — [1],55p : ill ; 28cm. — (Bibliographies in paint technology ; no.27)
Index.
ISBN 0-85462-039-7 Pbk : £5.00
(B77-15653)

016.681'11 — Clockmakers. Guilds. Libraries. *London (City). Worshipful Company of Clockmakers. Library. Stock. Catalogues*
Worshipful Company of Clockmakers. *Library.* The clockmakers' library : the catalogue of the books and manuscripts in the library of the Worshipful Company of Clockmakers / compiled by John Bromley. — London (Russell Chambers, Covent Garden, W.C.2) : Sotheby Parke Bernet Publications, 1977. — xii,136p : ill, facsims, ports ; 29cm.
Index.
ISBN 0-85667-033-2 : £15.00
(B77-24651)

016.681'11 — Patents on time measuring instruments, to 1853. *Lists*
Aked, Charles Kenneth. Complete list of English horological patents up to 1853 / compiled by Charles K. Aked. — Ashford, Kent (P.O. Box 22, Ashford, Kent) : Brant Wright Associates Ltd, 1975. — [2],33p ; 22cm.
£3.75
(B77-03314)

016.6862'092'4 — Libraries. *London (City). St Bride Printing Library. Exhibits: Documents associated with Caxton, William. Catalogues*
St Bride Printing Library. Caxtoniana, or, The progress of Caxton studies from the earliest times to 1976 : [catalogue of] an exhibition at the St Bride Printing Library ... 20 September-29 October 1976 ... — London (St Bride Institute, Bride La., EC4Y 8EE) : The Library, 1976. — 16p : ill ; 25cm.
ISBN 0-9504161-2-6 Sd : £0.75
(B77-02445)

016.6862'092'4 — National libraries. *Great Britain. British Library. Reference Division. Exhibits: Documents associated with Caxton, William. Catalogues*
British Library. *Reference Division.* William Caxton : an exhibition to commemorate the quincentenary of the introduction of printing into England [held in the] British Library Reference Division, 24 September 1976-31 January 1977 / [catalogue compiled by Janet Backhouse, Mirjam Foot and John Barr]. — London : British Museum Publications Ltd for the British Library [Reference Division], 1976. — 94p : ill, facsims ; 25cm.
ISBN 0-7141-0388-8 Pbk : £2.00
(B77-27635)

016.6862'092'4 — Universities. Libraries. *Cambridgeshire. Cambridge. University of Cambridge. Library. Exhibits: Documents associated with Caxton, William. Catalogues*
Cook, Jayne. William Caxton : catalogue of an exhibition held in the University Library, Cambridge, 24 September 1976-31 January 1977 in celebration of the quincentenary of the introduction of printing into England / [compiled by Jayne Cook and Brian Jenkins]. — [Cambridge] ([West Rd, Cambridge CB3 9DR]) : Cambridge University Library, 1976. — [64]p : facsims ; 25cm.
ISBN 0-902205-20-x Sd : £1.25
(B77-05822)

016.69 — Buildings. Construction. Documents on building construction: Documents published by Great Britain. Department of the Environment. Property Services Agency. *Lists*
Great Britain. *Department of the Environment. Property Services Agency. Library Service.* Building design and construction : an annotated list / [Property Services Agency Library Service] ; [compiled by Mavis Parry and Henry Field ; edited by Nola Pressey]. — Croydon (Whitgift Centre, Croydon CR9 3LY) : The Service, [1976]. — v,66p ; 30cm. — (PSA publications 1976)
Index.
ISBN 0-7184-0023-2 Sd : Unpriced
(B77-01975)

016.7 — Universities. Libraries. *Essex. Colchester. University of Essex. Library. Stock: Reference books on visual arts. Catalogues*
University of Essex. *Library.* Fine arts : a guide to the bibliographical and reference materials held by the [University of Essex] Library / [compiled] by W.R.C. Longley. — [Colchester] ([Wivenhoe Park, Colchester, Essex]) : The Library, 1976. — [5],68p ; 21cm.
Index.
Pbk : £0.45
(B77-32352)

016.7'0098 — Libraries. Stock: Serial publications on Latin American arts. *Great Britain. Catalogues*
Committee on Latin America. Literature with language, art and music / the Committee on Latin America ; edited on behalf of the Committee by L. Hallewell ; with a preface by Lord Eccles ; and a note on periodical indexes by A.J. Walford and the editor. — London (c/o Hispanic and Luso-Brazilian Council, 2 Belgrave Sq., SW1X 8PJ) : C.O.L.A., 1977. — 2-253p ; 23cm. — (Latin American serials ; vol.3)
ISBN 0-9505324-0-1 : £8.00
(B77-17862)

016.711'74 — Pedestrianisation. *Bibliographies*
Unit for Retail Planning Information.
Pedestrianisation : bibliography & research / [the Unit for Retail Planning Information Limited]. — 2nd ed. — Reading (229 King's Rd, Reading RG1 4LS) : U.R.P.I., 1975. — [2], 28p ; 30cm.
ISBN 0-905912-03-9 Sd : Unpriced
(B77-07764)

016.725'56 — Residential institutions for old persons. Architectural design. Social aspects. *Bibliographies*
Harris, Howard. An annotated bibliography on the architectural design implications of residential homes for old people / prepared by Howard Harris and Anne Griffiths ... — Cardiff (28 Park Place, Cardiff) : Welsh School of Architecture, Research and Development, UWIST, [1976]. — [1],63p ; 30cm.
Sd : £1.00
(B77-04523)

016.725'822'09046 — Theatres. Architectural design, 1960-1970. *Bibliographies*
Cheshire, David Frederick. Bibliography of theatre and stage design : a select list of books and articles published 1960-1970 / compiled by D.F. Cheshire. — London (9 Fitzroy Sq.,W1P 6AE) : Commission for a British Theatre Institute, 1974. — [2],ii,20p ; 22cm. — (Bibliographic series ; 2)
ISBN 0-904512-01-0 Sd : Unpriced
Also classified at 016.792'025'09046
(B77-19162)

016.7452 — Industrial design. Organisations. Libraries. *Great Britain. Design Council. Slide Library. Stock: Transparencies. Catalogues*
Design Council. *Slide Library.* Design Council Slide Library catalogue : a comprehensive and classified list of 35mm mounted transparencies in colour and black and white. — [London] : [The Library], 1973. — [4],150p ; 30cm.
ISBN 0-85072-077-x Sp : £1.00
(B77-10091)

016.7454 — Design. *Abstracts. Periodicals*
Design abstracts international / elaborated by Amt für Industrielle Formgestaltung, Centre de création industrielle. — Oxford [etc.] : Pergamon [for ICSID].
[Vol.1, no.1]- ; Jan. 1977-. — 1977-. — 25cm.
Quarterly. — 84p. in 1st issue. — Index.
Pbk : Unpriced
ISSN 0145-2118
(B77-10713)

016.78 — Music & musical scores. *Bibliographies. Serials*
British catalogue of music. — London : British Library, Bibliographic Services Division.
1976. — 1977. — [6],114p ; 31cm.
ISBN 0-900220-60-0 : £10.00 : CIP rev.
ISSN 0068-1407
(B77-06426)

016.78'042'0904 — Popular music, 1900-1965. *Lists*
Lowe, Leslie. Directory of popular music, 1900-1965 / by Leslie Lowe. — Droitwich (Peterson House, Droitwich, Worcs.) : Peterson Publishing Co. Ltd, 1975. — 1034p ; 22cm.
Index.
ISBN 0-904702-00-6 : £10.00
(B77-07765)

016.78'092'4 — Austrian music. Mozart, Wolfgang Amadeus. Criticism. *Bibliographies. German texts*
Zentralinstitut für Mozartforschung.
Mozart-Jahrbuch des Zentralinstitutes für Mozartforschung der Internationalen Stiftung Mozarteum Salzburg. — Kassel [etc.] ; London ([32 Great Titchfield St., W1P 7AD]) : Bärenreiter.
1975 : [Mozart-Bibliographie (bis 1970)] / [zusammengestellt von Rudolph Angermüller und Otto Schneider]. — 1976. — vii,363p ; 25cm.
Index.
£16.80
(B77-07026)

016.78'092'4 — English music. Walton, Sir William. *Thematic catalogues*
Craggs, Stewart R. William Walton : a thematic catalogue of his musical works / [compiled by] Stewart R. Craggs, with a critical appreciation by Michael Kennedy. — London [etc.] : Oxford University Press, 1977. — [5],273p : music ; 24cm.
Bibl.: p.255-259. — List of works: p.260-262. — Index.
ISBN 0-19-315433-1 : £12.50
(B77-26072)

016.78'092'4 — English music. Warlock, Peter. *Lists*
Tomlinson, Fred. A Peter Warlock handbook / compiled by Fred Tomlinson. — Rickmansworth (22 Pheasants Way, Rickmansworth, Herts.) : Triad Press.
Vol.2. — 1977. — p55-112,fold leaf,[2]p of plates : facsim, port ; 30cm.
Limited ed. of 300 numbered copies.
ISBN 0-902070-20-7 Pbk : £4.95
(B77-14517)

016.78'092'4 — Italian music. Sammartini, Giovanni Battista. *Thematic catalogues*
Jenkins, Newell. Thematic catalogue of the works of Giovanni Battista Sammartini : orchestral and vocal music / by Newell Jenkins and Bathia Churgin. — Cambridge, Mass. ; London : Harvard University Press for the American Musicological Society, 1976. — [12], 315p,leaf of plate,[6]p of plates : ill, facsims, music, col port ; 24cm.
Bibl.: p.295-302. — Index.
ISBN 0-674-87735-7 : £26.25
(B77-24652)

016.7817'429 — Welsh music. Musical scores. *Bibliographies*
Guild for the Promotion of Welsh Music.
Catalogue of contemporary Welsh music / the Guild for the Promotion of Welsh Music = Yr Urdd er Hyrwyddo Cerddoriaeth Cymru. — [Swansea] ([Huw Rhys Rogers, Angel Chambers, 94 Walter Rd, Swansea SA1 5QA]) : [The Guild].
6th / compiled by Robert Smith. — [1977]. — 63p ; 30cm.
No.5 published as: 'A complete catalogue of contemporary Welsh music'. — Index.
ISBN 0-901248-02-9 Sd : £2.50
(B77-16149)

016.7828'5 — Cinema films. Jazz, to 1977. *Filmographies*
Meeker, David. Jazz in the movies : a guide to jazz musicians, 1917-1977 / by David Meeker. — London (27 Sumatra Rd, NW6 1PS) : Talisman Books, 1977. — [287]p : ill, ports ; 22cm.
Not the same as B72-15718. — Index.
ISBN 0-905983-00-9 : £6.95
ISBN 0-905983-01-7 Pbk : £4.95
(B77-30918)

016.784 — Vocal music in European languages. *Thematic catalogues*
Barlow, Harold. A dictionary of opera and song themes : including cantatas, oratorios, Lieder, and art songs / compiled by Harold Barlow and Sam Morgenstern. — Revised ed. — London [etc.] : E. Benn, 1976. — [9],547p : music ; 25cm.
Previous ed.: published as 'A dictionary of vocal themes'. New York : Crown, 1950 ; London : Benn, 1956. — Index.
ISBN 0-510-35500-5 : £8.50
(B77-06427)

016.7844'92'4 — Folk songs in English. Baez, Joan. *Bibliographies*
Swan, Peter. Joan Baez, a bio-disco-bibliography : being a selected guide to material in print, on record, on cassette and on film, with a biographical introduction / by Peter Swan. — Brighton : Noyce, 1977. — 23p ; 30cm.
Index.
Sd : Unpriced
Also classified at 016.7899'12
(B77-23055)

016.7844'94174 — Universities. Colleges. *Dublin. University College, Dublin. Department of Folklore. Stock: Folk songs in Irish: Galway (County) folk songs. Indexes. Irish texts*
Ní Dhorchaí, Proinnsias. Clár amhrán an achréiḍh / [le] Proinnsias Ní Dhorchaí. — Baile Atha Cliath [i.e. Dublin] ([15 Bóthar Ġhráinseach an Déin, An Charraig Dhubh, Co. Átha Cliath]) : An Clóchomhar Tta, 1974. — xxi,242p,plate : map ; 23cm. — (Leabhair thaighde ; 22)
Index.
ISBN 0-7171-0599-7 : £2.00
(B77-05168)

016.7899'12 — Folk songs in English. Baez, Joan. *Discographies*
Swan, Peter. Joan Baez, a bio-disco-bibliography : being a selected guide to material in print, on record, on cassette and on film, with a biographical introduction / by Peter Swan. — Brighton : Noyce, 1977. — 23p ; 30cm.
Index.
Sd : Unpriced
Primary classification 016.7844'92'4
(B77-23055)

016.7899'12 — Music. American disc records, 1895-1925. *Discographies*
Moses, Julian Morton. Collectors' guide to American recordings, 1895-1925 / by Julian Morton Moses ; foreword by Giuseppe de Luca. — New York : Dover Publications [etc.] ; London : Constable, 1977. — [2],200p ; 22cm.
Originally published: New York : American Record Collectors' Exchange, 1949. — Index.
ISBN 0-486-23448-7 Pbk : £2.50
(B77-25347)

016.7899'12 — Music. Columbia Broadcasting System recordings. *Discographies*
Columbia Broadcasting System. Main alphabetical & numerical catalogue including Blue Sky, Caribou, CBS, CBS Harmony Series, Embassy, Epic, Invictus, Monument, Mums, Neighborhood, Philadelphia International / [Columbia Broadcasting System]. — London (17 Soho Sq., W1V 6HE) : CBS Records.
1976-77. — 1976. — [5] leaves,174p : ill, facsims, ports ; 28cm.
'This catalogue incorporates all LP discs and tapes which at the time of going to press had been announced for release up to and including 24th September 1976'.
Pbk : Unpriced
(B77-00575)

016.7899'12 — Music. Disc records. *Discographies*
The **art** of record buying : a list of recommended microgroove recordings. — London : E.M.G.
1977. — [1977]. — [2],290p : map ; 23cm.
ISBN 0-900982-08-x : £5.25
(B77-05169)

016.7899'12 — Music. Dominion disc records, to 1937. *Discographies*
Badrock, Arthur. Dominion Records : a catalogue and history / by Arthur Badrock. — Bournemouth (19 Glendale Rd, Bournemouth BH6 4JA) : Talking Machine Review, 1976. — [1],31p,plate : facsims ; 26cm.
ISBN 0-902338-27-7 Sd : £0.60
(B77-01122)

016.7899'12 — Negro traditional jazz. Disc records. *Louisiana. New Orleans, 1937-1972. Discographies*
Stagg, Tom. New Orleans, the revival : a tape and discography of Negro traditional jazz recorded in New Orleans or by New Orleans bands 1937-1972 / compiled by Tom Stagg & Charlie Crump. — Dublin ([65 Dublin Industrial Estate, Glasnevin, Dublin 11]) : Bashall Eaves, 1973. — [5],vi,307,[11]p,[14]p of plates : ports ; 22cm.
Index.
ISBN 0-902638-01-7 : £5.25
(B77-11524)

016.7899'12 — Pop music. Disc records: British top fifty singles, 1954-1976. *Discographies*
Solomon, Clive. Record hits : the British top 50 charts, 1954-1976 / compiled by Clive Solomon. — London [etc.] : Omnibus Press, 1977. — 263p ; 22cm.
Index.
ISBN 0-86001-314-6 Pbk : Unpriced
(B77-29121)

016.7899'12 — Popular music. Disc records available in Great Britain. *Discographies. Serials*
Music master. — London (25 Exmouth Market, EC1R 4QL) : John Humphries.
Includes lists of cassettes and cartridges.
1977 / [compiled by Michael Preston]. — 1977. — 11-970p ; 22cm.
English text, preliminaries in English, French, German, Finnish and Swedish.
ISBN 0-904520-04-8 : £30.00
ISSN 0308-9347
(B77-16150)

016.7899'12 — Vocal music. Russian singers. Gramophone Company recordings, 1899-1915. *Discographies*
Gramophone Company. A catalogue of vocal recordings from the Russian catalogues of the Gramophone Company Limited (Obshchestvo Grammofon c [i.e. s] ogr. otv.) 1899-1915 / [compiled] by John R. Bennett. — [Blandford] : Oakwood Press, 1977. — [1],xi,220p ; 21cm. — (Voices of the past ; vol.11)
Spine title: The HMV Russian catalogue. — Index.
ISBN 0-85361-206-4 : £6.60
(B77-12816)

016.7902'05 — Universities. Libraries. *Lancashire. Lancaster. University of Lancaster. Library. Stock: Serial publications on performing arts. Catalogues*
University of Lancaster. *Library.* Performing arts serials / University of Lancaster Library. — [Lancaster] ([Bailrigg, Lancaster LA1 4YH]) : The Library, 1976. — viii,27p : 1 ill ; 21cm. — (Miscellaneous publications)
Index.
ISBN 0-901699-40-3 Sd : £0.25
(B77-10092)

016.79143 — 8mm cinema films & 16mm cinema films: Feature films. *United States. Lists*
Limbacher, James Louis. Feature films on 8mm and 16mm : a directory of feature films available for rental, sale, and lease in the United States and Canada, with serials and directors' indexes / compiled and edited by James L. Limbacher. — 5th ed. — New York ; London : Bowker, 1977. — ix,422p ; 29cm.
Previous ed.: 1974. — Bibl.: p.411. — Index.
ISBN 0-8352-0919-9 : £14.50
(B77-17863)

016.79143 — Periodical articles on cinema films. *Indexes*
International index to film periodicals : an annotated guide. — London : St James Press [etc.].
1975 / edited by Frances Thorpe ; [for the] International Federation of Film Archives (FIAF). — 1976. — xvi,511p ; 29cm.
Index.
ISBN 0-900997-34-6 : £12.50
(B77-14518)

016.792'025'09046 — Stage design, 1960-1970. *Bibliographies*
Cheshire, David Frederick. Bibliography of theatre and stage design : a select list of books and articles published 1960-1970 / compiled by D.F. Cheshire. — London (9 Fitzroy Sq.,W1P 6AE) : Commission for a British Theatre Institute, 1974. — [2],ii,20p ; 22cm. — (Bibliographic series ; 2)
ISBN 0-904512-01-0 Sd : Unpriced
Primary classification 016.725'822'09046
(B77-19162)

016.792'025'0924 — Libraries & private collections. Stock: Stage design. Craig, Edward Gordon. Texts. *Catalogues*
Newman, Lindsay Mary. Gordon Craig archives : international survey / by L.M. Newman. — London (145c Devonshire Rd, SE23 3LZ) : The Malkin Press, 1976. — xi,79p ; 25cm.
Limited ed. of 500 copies of which nos.1-25 are signed by the author. — Bibl.: p.43-52. — Index. — Includes: Resources for the future study of Edward Gordon Craig : the seventh annual Gordon Craig Memorial Lecture delivered in Venice on 14 September 1974.
ISBN 0-9504928-0-9 Pbk : £6.15
(B77-08174)

016.7938 — Conjuring. *Bibliographies*
Gill, Robert. Magic as a performing art : a bibliography of conjuring / [by] Robert Gill. — London [etc.] : Bowker, 1976. — xxii,252p ; 23cm. — (College of librarianship, Wales. Bibliographies)
Index.
ISBN 0-85935-038-x : £7.50
(B77-11028)

016.7938'09'03 — Conjuring, 1581-1876. *Bibliographies*
Toole Stott, Raymond. A bibliography of English conjuring, 1581-1876 / by Raymond Toole Stott. — Derby ([Rowditch Printing Works, Derby]) : Harper and Sons, 1976. — 2-288p,leaf of plate,[16]p of plates : ill, facsims, ports ; 23cm.
£13.50
(B77-01123)

016.7941'8 — Universities. Libraries. *Cambridgeshire. Cambridge. University of Cambridge. Library. Stock: Books on fairy chess. Catalogues*
University of Cambridge. *Library.* A catalogue of fairy chess books and opuscules donated to Cambridge University Library, 1972-1973 / by Anthony Dickins. — 2nd ed. — Kew Gardens (6a Royal Parade, Kew Gardens, Surrey [TW9 3QD]) : The Q Press, 1976. — [6]p ; 21cm.
Limited ed. of 50 copies. — Previous ed.: 1973.
ISBN 0-901911-12-7 Sd : £1.00
(B77-01976)

016.796 — Cinema films on sports: Cinema films available for hire. *Lists*
Sports Council. *Information Centre.* A catalogue of sports films / compiled by the Information Centre of the Sports Council. — London : The Council.
1977. — 1977. — [2],66p ; 30cm.
Index.
ISBN 0-900979-54-2 Pbk : £2.75
(B77-21660)

016.796358 — Cricket. *Bibliographies*
Padwick, Eric William. A bibliography of cricket / compiled by E.W. Padwick. — London : Library Association for the Cricket Society, 1977. — xxi,649p ; 24cm.
Index.
ISBN 0-85365-129-9 : £32.00(£25.60 to members of the Library Association) : CIP rev.
(B77-08175)

016.7964 — Libraries. *West Midlands (Metropolitan County). Birmingham. National Centre for Athletics Literature. Stock: Dave Roberts Papers. Catalogues*
National Centre for Athletics Literature. A complete list of the ... Dave Roberts papers in the National Centre for Athletics Literature, the Library, the University of Birmingham / compiled by John Bromhead. — Birmingham ([The Library, University of Birmingham, P.O. Box 363, Birmingham B15 2TT]) : N.C.A.L., 1976. — [3],ii,17 leaves ; 30cm.
Notebook format.
ISBN 0-7044-0233-5 Sd : Free
(B77-08719)

016.80882 — Public libraries. *Devon. Devon Library Services. Stock: Drama. Play sets. Lists*
Devon Library Services. Playset catalogue / Devon Library Services. — [Exeter] ([Barley House, Administrative Centre, Isleworth Rd, Exeter, Devon]) : [Devon Library Services], [1976]. — [1],iv leaves,267[i.e.273]p ; 30cm.
Index.
ISBN 0-905053-01-x Pbk : £1.00
(B77-05170)

016.80882 — Public libraries. *Dorset. Dorset County Library. Stock: Drama in European languages, to 1976. Play sets. Catalogues*
Dorset County Library. Play sets : catalogue / Dorset County Library. — [Dorchester] ([Colliton Park, Dorchester, Dorset]) : [The Library].
1976. — [1976]. — [3]leaves,55p ; 30cm.
ISBN 0-85216-165-4 Sd : £0.30
(B77-02717)

016.80882 — Public libraries. Cooperation. Organisations. *Yorkshire. Yorkshire Libraries Joint Music and Drama Collection. Stock: Drama in European languages, to 1975. Play sets. Lists*
Yorkshire Libraries Joint Music and Drama Collection. Full length plays in sets / Yorkshire Libraries Joint Music and Drama Collection. — [Wakefield] ([Wakefield Metropolitan District Library Headquarters, Balne Lane, Wakefield, W. Yorkshire WF2 0DQ]) : [Yorkshire and Humberside Joint Library Services], 1976. — iv, 72p ; 21cm.
Index.
ISBN 0-900297-05-0 Pbk : £0.50
(B77-07027)

016.813'5'4 — Fiction in English. American writers. Burroughs, William, b.1914. *Bibliographies*
Goodman, Michael B. William S. Burroughs : an annotated bibliography of his works and criticism / [by] Michael B. Goodman. — New York ; London : Garland, 1975 [i.e. 1976]. — 96p ; 23cm. — (Garland reference library of the humanities ; vol.24)
Published in the United States: 1975. — Index.
ISBN 0-8240-9989-3 : £7.00
(B77-03876)

016.813'5'4 — Fiction in English. American writers. Nabokov, Vladimir. *Bibliographies*
Field, Andrew. Nabokov, a bibliography / [by] Andrew Field. — New York ; London [etc.] : McGraw-Hill, 1973. — xxvi,249p ; 24cm.
Index.
ISBN 0-07-020680-5 : £10.13
(B77-22308)

016.82 — English literature. *Bibliographies*
The **new** Cambridge bibliography of English literature. — [New ed.] / [edited by George Watson and I.R. Willison].
In 5 vols. — Previous ed. in 4 vols, published as 'The Cambridge bibliography of English literature'. 1940.
Vol.5 : Index / compiled by J.D. Pickles. — Cambridge : Cambridge University Press, 1977. — xiv p,542 columns ; 26cm.
ISBN 0-521-21310-x : £10.00
(B77-28336)

016.82 — English literature. *Bibliographies. Serials*
Annual bibliography of English language and literature / [Modern Humanities Research Association]. — London (c/o Hon. Treasurer, King's College, Strand, WC2R 2LS) : The Association.
Vol.48 : 1973 / editor John Horden ; American editor James B. Misenheimer, Jr. — 1976. — xl,859p ; 22cm.
Index.
ISBN 0-900547-46-4 : £13.00
ISSN 0066-3786
Primary classification 016.42
(B77-09463)

016.82 — English literature, 1475-1950. *Bibliographies. Chronologies*
Annals of English literature, 1475-1950 : the principal publications of each year together with an alphabetical index of authors with their works. — 2nd ed. — Oxford : Clarendon Press, [1976]. — [1],vi,380p ; 19cm.
This ed. originally published: 1961. — Index.
ISBN 0-19-866129-0 Pbk : £1.95
(B77-00576)

016.82 — English literature, to 1975. *Bibliographies*
Bateson, Frederick Wilse. A guide to English and American literature. — 3rd ed. / [by] F.W. Bateson and Harrison T. Meserole assisted by ... [others]. — London [etc.] : Longman, 1976. — [4],viii,334p ; 23cm.
Previous ed.: published as 'A guide to English literature' / by F.W. Bateson. London : Longmans, 1967. — Index.
ISBN 0-582-48414-6 : £7.50
ISBN 0-582-48417-0 Pbk : Unpriced
(B77-29122)

016.82'08'09415 — English literature. Irish writers, to 1976. *Bibliographies*
Harmon, Maurice. Select bibliography for the study of Anglo-Irish literature and its backgrounds : an Irish studies handbook / [by] Maurice Harmon. — Portmarnock : Wolfhound Press, 1977. — 187p : maps ; 22cm.
ISBN 0-905473-04-3 : £7.50
ISBN 0-905473-05-1 Pbk : Unpriced
(B77-26073)

016.82'08'0994 — English literature. Australian writers, to 1976. *Bibliographies*
Lock, Fred. Australian literature : a reference guide / [by] Fred Lock and Alan Lawson. — Melbourne ; London [etc.] : Oxford University Press, 1977. — xi,84p ; 22cm. — (Australian bibliographies)
Index.
ISBN 0-19-550538-7 Pbk : £2.75
(B77-25348)

016.821'4 — Poetry in English. Cowley, Abraham. Texts. *Bibliographies*
Perkin, M R. Abraham Cowley : a bibliography / by M.R. Perkin. — Folkestone : Dawson, 1977. — 130p,plate : port ; 23cm. — (Pall Mall bibliographies ; no.5)
Microfiche in pocket. — Index.
ISBN 0-7129-0697-5 : £12.50 : CIP rev.
(B77-05823)

016.821'7 — Poetry in English. Blake, William. *Bibliographies*
Bentley, Gerald Eades. Blake books : annotated catalogues of William Blake's writings in illuminated printing, in conventional typography and in manuscript, and reprints thereof, reproductions of his designs, books with his engravings, catalogues, books he owned and scholarly and critical works about him / [by] G.E. Bentley, Jr. — Revised ed. — Oxford [etc.] : Clarendon Press, 1977. — xii,1079p, plate : port ; 24cm.
Previous ed.: i.e. 1st ed. published as 'A Blake bibliography' / by G.E. Bentley, Jr and M.K. Nurmi. London : Oxford University Press, 1964. — Index.
ISBN 0-19-818151-5 : £40.00
(B77-14015)

016.821'7 — Public libraries. London. Westminster *(London Borough). Westminster City Libraries. Stock: Documents associated with Blake, William. Collections: Preston Blake Library. Catalogues*
Westminster City Libraries. William Blake : catalogue of the Preston Blake Library presented by Kerrison Preston in 1967 / [compiled by Phyllis Goff]. — London (Marylebone Library, Marylebone Rd, NW1 5PS) : Westminster City Libraries.
Cumulative supplement to the printed catalogue of 1969 / compiled by Phyllis Goff. — 1976. — [52]leaves ; 27cm.
ISBN 0-900802-02-2 Pbk : £0.50
(B77-04524)

016.821'9'12 — Poetry in English. Aldington, Richard. *Correspondence. Lists*
Gates, Norman Timmins. A checklist of the letters of Richard Aldington / compiled with an introduction by Norman Timmins Gates. — Carbondale [etc.] : Southern Illinois University Press ; London [etc.] : Feffer and Simons, 1977. — xv,171p ; 24cm.
Index.
ISBN 0-8093-0781-2 : £7.40
(B77-16151)

016.821'9'1408 — Poetry in English, 1945-1977. *Bibliographies*
Mackenzie, Michael. British poetry since 1970 / selected by Michael Mackenzie. — London : National Book League, 1977. — 15p ; 21cm.
Produced in conjunction with an exhibition.
ISBN 0-85353-282-6 Sd : £0.35
(B77-33560)

016.822'9'1408 — Drama in English, 1945-1976. *Bibliographies*
Mikhail, Edward Halim. Contemporary British drama, 1950-1976 : an annotated critical bibliography / [by] E.H. Mikhail ; with a foreword by William A. Armstrong. — London [etc.] : Macmillan, 1976. — ix,147p ; 23cm.
ISBN 0-333-19913-8 : £7.95
(B77-06428)

016.823'9'12 — Fiction in English. Doyle, Sir Arthur Conan. *Bibliographies*
Goldscheider, Gaby. Conan Doyle bibliography : a bibliography of the works of Sir Arthur Conan Doyle MD, LLD, (1859-1930) / by Gaby Goldscheider. — Windsor (29 Temple Rd, Windsor [Berks.]) : The author, 1977. — 40p : ill, ports ; 22cm.
ISBN 0-9505725-0-0 Pbk : £3.00
(B77-25349)

016.823'9'12 — Physicians. Organisations. *England. Royal College of Physicians of London. Exhibits: Documents associated with Joyce, James, b.1882. Catalogues*
Royal College of Physicians of London. My impossible health, or, The case of James Joyce : catalogue of an exhibition, January 1977, [organised by the Royal College of Physicians of London]. — London : The College, [1977]. — [1],vii,35p ; 26cm.
Bibl.: p.31-32.
ISBN 0-900596-41-4 Pbk : Unpriced
(B77-15654)

016.828'8'08 — Prose in English. Hudson, William Henry, b.1841. Texts. *Bibliographies*
Payne, John R. W.H. Hudson : a bibliography / [by] John R. Payne ; foreword by Alfred A. Knopf. — Folkestone : Dawson [etc.], 1977. — xv,248p,plate : port ; 23cm.
Index.
ISBN 0-7129-0750-5 : £10.00 : CIP rev.
(B77-04525)

016.828'9'1409 — Universities. Libraries. *Berkshire. Reading. University of Reading. Library. Exhibits: Documents associated with Wain, John. Catalogues*
University of Reading. *Library.* John Wain : poet, novelist, critic : catalogue of an exhibition held in the Library, University of Reading, 16 May-30 June 1977. — [Reading] ([Whiteknights Park, Reading RG6 2AH]) : University of Reading, 1977. — 19p ; 22cm.
ISBN 0-7049-0481-0 Sd : Unpriced
(B77-29123)

016.833'9'12 — Fiction in German. Hesse, Hermann. *Bibliographies*
Mileck, Joseph. Hermann Hesse : biography and bibliography / by Joseph Mileck. — Berkeley [etc.] ; London : University of California Press, 1977. — 2v.(xxiv,1402p) : ill, facsims, ports ; 27cm.
Index.
ISBN 0-520-02756-6 : £43.00
(B77-23056)

016.84'09 — French literature. Research in British institutions. *Lists. Serials*
Current research in French studies at universities and university colleges in the United Kingdom. — Sheffield (c/o Dr M. Shaw, Department of French, The University, Sheffield S10 2TN) : Society for French Studies.
1976-1977 : Vol.9 / compiled for the Society for French Studies by Marjorie Shaw. — [1977] . — vii,89p ; 30cm.
Index.
Sd : £3.00
(B77-26074)

016.841'9'12 — Poetry in French. Reverdy, Pierre. *Bibliographies*
Bishop, Michael. Pierre Reverdy : a bibliography / [compiled by] Michael Bishop. — London : Grant and Cutler, 1976. — 88p ; 23cm. — (Research bibliographies and checklists)
Index.
ISBN 0-7293-0016-1 Pbk : £3.80
(B77-29873)

016.841'9'12 — Poetry in French. Saint-John Perse. *Bibliographies*
Little, Roger. Saint-John Perse : a bibliography for students of his poetry / [by] Roger Little. — London : Grant and Cutler. — (Research bibliographies and checklists ; 1)
Supplement no.1. — 1976. — 88p ; 21cm.
Index.
ISBN 0-7293-0026-9 Pbk : £3.00
(B77-29124)

016.843'5'08 — Fiction in French, 1715-1815. *Bibliographies. French texts*
Martin, Angus. Bibliographie du genre romanesque français, 1751-1800 / [by] Angus Martin, Vivienne G. Mylne, Richard Frautschi. — London : Mansell Information Publishing [etc.], 1977. — lxxii,529p : ill, facsims ; 29cm.
Index.
ISBN 0-7201-0379-7 : £50.00 : CIP rev.
(B77-07028)

016.861'3 — Poetry in Spanish. Quevedo y Villegas, Francisco Gómez de. *Bibliographies. Spanish texts*
Crosby, James O. Guía bibliográfica para el estudio crítico de Quevedo / por James O. Crosby. — London : Grant and Cutler, 1976. — 140p ; 23cm. — (Research bibliographies & checklists ; 13)
Index.
ISBN 0-7293-0012-9 Pbk : £5.40
(B77-29125)

016.862 — Universities. Libraries. *Cambridgeshire. Cambridge. University of Cambridge. Library. Stock: Comedias sueltas. Catalogues*
University of Cambridge. *Library.* 'Comedias sueltas' in Cambridge University Library : a descriptive catalogue / compiled by A.J.C. Bainton. — Cambridge ([West Rd, Cambridge CB3 9DR]) : The Library, 1977. — xvi,281p ; 22cm. — (University of Cambridge. Library. Historical bibliography series ; 2)
Index.
ISBN 0-902205-23-4 : £6.50
(B77-26075)

016.863'6'2 — Fiction in Spanish. Blasco Ibáñez, Vicente. *Bibliographies*
Smith, Paul, *b.1934.* Vicente Blasco Ibáñez : an annotated bibliography / by Paul Smith. — London : Grant and Cutler, 1976. — 127p ; 23cm. — (Research bibliographies & checklists ; 14)
Index.
ISBN 0-7293-0015-3 Pbk : £5.40
(B77-28337)

016.8916'6 — Welsh literature, to 1975. *Bibliographies*
Llyfryddiaeth llenyddiaeth Gymraeg / golygwyd gan Thomas Parry a Merfyn Morgan. — Caerdydd [i.e. Cardiff] : Gwasg Prifysgol Cymru, 1976. — xxiii,313p ; 24cm.
Compiled for the Language and Literature Committee of the Board of Celtic Studies. — Index.
ISBN 0-7083-0631-4 : £8.50
(B77-04526)

016.9 — Books on world, to 1974: Books with British imprints, 1971-1975. *Lists*
Taylor, Rosemary, *b.1932.* Bibliography of historical works issued in the United Kingdom, 1971-1975 / compiled for the Tenth Anglo-American Conference of Historians by Rosemary Taylor. — London ([Senate House, Malet St., W.C.1]) : University of London, Institute of Historical Research, 1977. — xiii, 272p ; 23cm.
Index.
ISBN 0-901179-45-0 Pbk : £6.00
(B77-29874)

016.9 — History. *Bibliographies*
Day, Alan Edwin. History : a reference handbook / [by] Alan Edwin Day. — London : Bingley [etc.], 1977. — 3-354p ; 23cm.
Index.
ISBN 0-85157-225-1 : £5.50
(B77-05824)

016.909'04'924 — Jewish studies. Parkes, James. Texts. *Bibliographies*
Sugarman, Sidney. A bibliography of the printed works of James Parkes : with selected quotations / compiled, with biographical notes by Sidney Sugarman and Diana Bailey ; edited, with additions and amendments by David A. Pennie. — [Southampton] ([Southampton University Library, Southampton SO9 5NH]) : University of Southampton, 1977. — xvi,132p ; 24cm.
Index.
ISBN 0-85432-167-5 : £4.50
(B77-33561)

016.909'04'927 — Arab Islamic civilization. *Bibliographies*
Arab Islamic bibliography : the Middle East Library Committee guide : based on Giuseppe Gabrieli's 'Manuale di bibliografia musulmana' / edited by Diana Grimwood-Jones, Derek Hopwood, J.D. Pearson with ... [others]. — Hassocks : Harvester Press [etc.], 1977. — xvii,292p ; 24cm.
Index.
ISBN 0-85527-384-4 : £28.50 : CIP rev.
(B77-05171)

016.909'09'717 — Periodicals on communist countries, to 1976: Periodicals in English. *Bibliographies*
Shaffer, Harry George. Periodicals on the socialist countries and on Marxism : a new annotated index of English-language publications / [by] Harry G. Shaffer. — [New] ed. — New York [etc.] ; London : Praeger, 1977. — xv,135p ; 25cm. — (Praeger special studies in international politics and government)

Previous ed.: i.e. 1st ed. published as 'English language periodic publications on communism'. Columbia : Research Institute on Communist Affairs, Columbia University, 1971. — Index.
ISBN 0-275-24010-x : £12.20
Also classified at 016.3354'05
(B77-15655)

016.909'09'7671 — Islamic studies. *Bibliographies. Periodicals*
The **Quarterly** index Islamicus : current books, articles and papers on Islamic studies. — London : Mansell Information Publishing.
Vol.1, no.1- ; Jan. 1977-. — 1977-. — 24cm.
[3],33,[1]p. in 1st issue. — Also available on microfiche.
Sd : £3.00(£9.50 yearly)
ISSN 0308-7395
(B77-15061)

016.91'0202 — Guidebooks compiled by Baedeker, Karl, to 1938. *Lists*
Baedeker's handbook(s) for travellers : a bibliography of English editions published prior to World War II. — Westport, Conn. ; London : Greenwood Press, 1975. — [5],38p ; 22cm.
ISBN 0-8371-8209-3 : £5.75
(B77-18511)

016.911'73 — Illustrations for books, to 1976: Maps of War of American Independence. *Indexes*

Clark, David Sanders. Index to maps of the American Revolution in books and periodicals : illustrating the revolutionary war and other events of the period 1763-1789 / [compiled] by David Sanders Clark. — Westport, Conn. ; London : Greenwood Press, 1974. — xiv,301,[1] p ; 25cm.
'A T.N. Dupuy Associates book'. — Bibl.: p.235-301.
ISBN 0-8371-7582-8 : £13.25
(B77-15062)

016.912 — Maps. *Bibliographies*

International Cartographic Association. *Commission V : Communication in Geography.* Bibliography of works on cartographic communication = Bibliographie des oeuvres sur la communication cartographique / International Cartographic Association, Commission V, Communication in Cartography = Association cartographique internationale, [Commission V], Communication en cartographie ; edited by = rédaction par Christopher Board. — Provisional ed. = Edition provisoire. — London (c/o Dr C. Board, Geography Department, London School of Economics and Political Science, Houghton St., WC2A 2AE) : [International Cartographic Association], 1976. — xiv,147p ; 21cm.
'... the 1975 meeting of Commission V ...' - Introduction. — English text, English and French introduction, dictionary, key word index. — Index.
ISBN 0-85328-052-5 Sd : Unpriced
(B77-07029)

016.912'429'54 — National libraries. *Wales. National Library of Wales. Stock: Printed maps of Radnor (District), 1578-1900. Lists*

National Library of Wales. The printed maps of Radnorshire, 1578-1900 / [National Library of Wales] ; by M. Gwyneth Lewis. — Aberystwyth : The Library, 1977. — [2],30p,4p of plates : maps ; 25cm.
Cover title. — Index.
ISBN 0-901833-81-9 Pbk : £0.75
(B77-20860)

016.9141'04'857 — Trails. Walkers' guides. *Great Britain. Urban regions. Lists. Serials*

Britain, town trails / [British Tourist Authority]. — London : B.T.A.
[1976] / [edited by Michael H. Glen]. — [1976] . — [2],50p : ill, map ; 21cm. — (British Tourist Authority. Information sheets ; no.356/76/14)
Bibl.: p.50. — Index.
ISBN 0-85630-410-7 Sd : £0.30
(B77-01977)

016.92'0042 — Theses: Biographies of English persons, 1000-1485. *Indexes*

Reel, Jerome V. Index to biographies of Englishmen 1000-1485 found in dissertations and theses / [compiled by] Jerome V. Reel, Jr. — Westport, Conn. ; London : Greenwood Press, 1975. — xiii,689p ; 25cm.
Bibl.: p.679-688.
ISBN 0-8371-7846-0 : £27.75
(B77-15063)

016.929'1 — Public libraries. *West Midlands (Metropolitan County). Birmingham. Birmingham Public Libraries. Central Libraries. Stock: Periodical articles on genealogy. Indexes*

Genealogy index. — Birmingham (c/o The Honorary Secretary, 48 Howard Rd, Kings Heath, Birmingham B14 7PQ) : Birmingham and Midland Society for Genealogy and Heraldry.
1975 / compiled by D. Wright. — 1976. — [1], vi leaves, 29p ; 30cm.
Sd : £0.50
ISSN 0309-5827
(B77-16152)

016.929'341 — Parish registers. *Great Britain. Bibliographies*

Steel, Donald John. National index of parish registers / by D.J. Steel, assisted by A.E.F. Steel. — London [etc.] : Phillimore for the Society of Genealogists.
Vol.1 : General sources of births, marriages and deaths before 1837 / by D.J. Steel, with additional articles by E. Gillett ... [et al.]. — 1976. — xxiv p,p3-439 ; 24cm.
Bibl.: p.383-439.
ISBN 0-900592-41-9 : £6.00
(B77-29875)

Vol.5 : South Midlands and Welsh Border counties, comprising the counties of Gloucestershire, Herefordshire, Oxfordshire, Shropshire, Warwickshire and Worcestershire / compiled by D.J. Steel, assisted by A.E.F. Steel and C.W. Field. — 1976. — xxv,300p ; 24cm.
ISBN 0-900592-45-1 : £6.00
(B77-29876)

016.929'34174 — Church of Ireland. Killaloe (Diocese). Consistory Court. Probate records, to 1838. *Indexes*

Index to Clonfert and Kilmacduagh wills / edited by Patrick Smythe-Wood. — [Ballycastle] ([Clare Park, Ballycastle, Co. Antrim]) : [The editor], 1977. — [3],19p ; 21cm.
Sd : £1.20
(B77-33011)

016.929'342 — Records. Repositories. Stock: Parish registers. *England. Lists*

Tallis, J A. Original parish registers in record offices and libraries / [compiled by J.A. Tallis]. — Matlock (Tawney House, Matlock, Derbyshire) : 'Local Population Studies' [for] the Cambridge Group for the History of Population and Social Structure.
1st supplement / [compiled by E.O. Peach]. — 1976. — 60p ; 22cm.
ISBN 0-9503951-1-0 Sd : £1.80(£1.20 to members of Local Population Studies Society)
(B77-12817)

016.929'3421 — Parish registers. *Inner London, 1538-1837. Lists*

Graham, Norman Henry. The genealogist's consolidated guide to parish registers in the inner London area, 1538 to 1837 / compiled and arranged by Norman H. Graham. — [Revised ed.]. — Orpington (40 Beaumont Rd, Petts Wood, Orpington, Kent BR5 1JJ) : The compiler, 1976. — a-e,88p,fold plate : map ; 15x22cm.
Previous ed.: 1976. — Index.
Pbk : £2.00
(B77-04527)

016.929'3422'5 — Genealogical societies. *East Sussex. Brighton. Sussex Family History Group. Library. Stock: East & West Sussex parish registers. Lists*

Sussex Family History Group. *Library.* Handlist of Sussex parish register copies in the library of the Sussex Family History Group. — Brighton (4/33 Sussex Sq., Brighton, Sussex BN2 5AB) : The Group, 1977. — [13] leaves ; 26cm.
ISBN 0-9504657-3-9 Sd : £0.20
(B77-15656)

016.932 — Ancient Egypt. *Bibliographies. Periodicals*

University of Cambridge. *Faculty of Oriental Studies.* Egyptology titles / Faculty of Oriental Studies, University of Cambridge [and] Wilbour Library of Egyptology, the Brooklyn Museum. — Warminster (c/o B.J. Kemp, Faculty of Oriental Studies, University of Cambridge, Sidgwick Ave., Cambridge CB3 9DA) : Aris and Phillips.
Nos. 1 & 2- ; 1976-. — [1976]-. — 22cm.
Four issues a year. — [2], 46p. in 1st issue. — 'Incorporating "Wilbour Library Acquisitions List"'.
Sd : £2.00 yearly
(B77-00002)

016.94053 — World War 2. *Bibliographies*

Enser, Alfred George Sidney. A subject bibliography of the Second World War : books in English, 1939-1974 / [by] A.G.S. Enser. — London : Deutsch, 1977. — 592p ; 23cm. — (A Grafton book)
Index.
ISBN 0-233-96742-7 : £11.95
(B77-15657)

016.94054'886'41 — British black propaganda: Leaflets. *Germany, 1941-1945. Lists*

Auckland, Reginald George. Catalogue of British 'black' propaganda to Germany, 1941-1945 / compiled by R.G. Auckland. — St Albans (60 High St., Sandridge, St Albans, Herts. AL4 9BZ) : R.G. Auckland for the Psywar Society, 1977. — 32p : facsims ; 21cm. — (Blatter catalogue ; no.13)
Bibl.: p.25.
ISBN 0-9502151-2-0 Sd : £1.50
(B77-14519)

016.941 — Great Britain. *History. Bibliographies. Serials*

Annual bibliography of British and Irish history / Royal Historical Society. — Hassocks : Harvester Press [etc.] for the Society.
Publications of 1976 / general editor G.R. Elton. — 1977. — ix,193p ; 23cm.
Index.
ISBN 0-85527-819-6 : £10.95
ISSN 0308-4558
(B77-32353)

016.941 — Great Britain, ca 450-. *Bibliographies*

Writings on British history. — Folkestone : Dawson for the Royal Historical Society and the Institute of Historical Research.
1939 : A bibliography of books and articles on the history of Great Britain from about 450 A.D. to 1914, published during the year 1939, with an appendix containing a select list of publications in 1939 on British history since 1914 / compiled by Alexander Taylor Milne. — 1977. — 310p ; 23cm.
Originally published: London : Cape, 1953. — Index.
ISBN 0-7129-0801-3 : £10.00 : CIP rev.
(B77-19972)

1940-1945 : A bibliography of books and articles on the history of Great Britain from about 400 A.D. to 1914, published during the years 1940-45 inclusive, with and appendix containing a select list of publications in these years on British history since 1914 / compiled by Alexander Taylor Milne. — 1977. — 2v. (1021p) ; 23cm.
Index.
ISBN 0-7129-0802-1 : £35.00 : CIP rev.
ISBN 0-7129-0813-7 Part 1. - ISBN 0-7129-0814-5 Part 2
(B77-18512)

Writings on British history. — [London] ([Senate House, Malet St., WC1E 7HU]) : University of London, Institute of Historical Research.
1955-1957 : a bibliography of books and articles on the history of Great Britain from about 450 AD to 1939, published during the years 1955-57 inclusive with an appendix containing a select list of publications in these years on British history since 1939 / edited by John Merriman Sims and Phyllis M. Jacobs. — 1977. — xx,362p ; 24cm.
Index.
ISBN 0-901179-44-2 : Unpriced
ISSN 0084-2753
(B77-23952)

016.94107 — Great Britain, 1714-1789. *Bibliographies*

Bibliography of British history, the eighteenth century, 1714-1789 / issued under the direction of the American Historical Association and the Royal Historical Society of Great Britain ; edited by Stanley Pargellis and D.J. Medley. — Hassocks : Harvester Press [etc.], 1977. — xxvi, 642p ; 25cm.
Originally published: Oxford : Clarendon Press, 1951. — Index.
ISBN 0-85527-136-1 : £12.50 : CIP rev.
(B77-10714)

016.94107 — Great Britain, 1789-1851. *Bibliographies*

Bibliography of British history, 1789-1851 / issued under the direction of the American Historical Association and the Royal Historical Society of Great Britain ; edited by Lucy M. Brown and Ian R. Christie. — Oxford : Clarendon Press, 1977. — xxxi,759p ; 24cm.
Index.
ISBN 0-19-822390-0 : £20.00
(B77-13463)

016.942082'092'4 — Great Britain. Parliament. House of Lords. Record Office. Stock: Documents of Benn, William Wedgwood, Viscount Stansgate. *Catalogues*

Great Britain. *Parliament. House of Lords. Records Office.* Handlist of the papers of William Wedgwood Benn, MP, First Viscount Stansgate / compiled by S.K. Ellison, assistant in the House of Lords Record Office. — [London] ([Westminster, SW1A 0PW]) : The Record Office, 1976. — [3],v,57p ; 30cm. — (Memorandum ; no.56)
ISBN 0-902614-03-7 Sd : Unpriced
(B77-12818)

016.9421'89 — London. Enfield (London Borough), to 1975. *Bibliographies*

Pam, David Owen. Enfield, Edmonton, Southgate : a local history book list / compiled by D.O. Pam and G. Dalling. — [Enfield] : Edmonton Hundred Historical Society, 1976. — [3],18p : 1 ill ; 30cm.
Sd : Unpriced
(B77-23057)

016.9422'5'07 — East & West Sussex, 1700-1900. *Bibliographies*
Farrant, John Howard. Sussex in the 18th and 19th centuries : a bibliography / by John H. Farrant. — 2nd ed. — Brighton (Education Development Building, Brighton BN1 9RG) : Centre for Continuing Education, University of Sussex, 1977. — [1],44p ; 21cm. — (University of Sussex. Centre for Continuing Education. Occasional papers ; no.1 ISSN 0306-1108)
Previous ed.: 1973. — Index.
ISBN 0-904242-07-2 Sd : £0.30
(B77-29126)

016.9422'56 — East Sussex. Brighton, to 1976. *Bibliographies*
Farrant, Sue. A guide to printed sources for the study of the history and geography of the Borough of Brighton / by Sue Farrant. — [Brighton] ([Falmer, Brighton BN1 9PH]) : [Brighton Polytechnic, Humanities Department], [1977]. — [3],33p ; 30cm.
Sd : £0.20
(B77-23953)

016.9422'76 — Hampshire. Southampton, to 1976. *Bibliographies*
Southampton District Library. Southampton's history : a guide to the printed sources / Hampshire County Library, Southampton District Library ; [compiled by G. Forrest]. — 2nd ed. — Southampton ([Central Library, Southampton, Hants.]) : [The Library], 1977. — 24p ; 22cm.
Previous ed.: issued by Southampton Public Libraries. 1968.
Sd : £0.45
(B77-31660)

016.9423'5 — Libraries. Stock: Books on Devon. *Devon. Catalogues*
Brockett, Allan. The Devon union list (DUL) : a collection of written material relating to the county of Devon / gathered and arranged by Allan Brockett. — Exeter ([Prince of Wales Rd, Exeter EX4 4PT]) : University of Exeter Library, 1977. — [2],iii,571p ; 22cm.
Index.
ISBN 0-902746-06-5 : £8.00
(B77-27636)

016.9425'74 — Oxfordshire. Oxford, to 1975. *Bibliographies*
Cordeaux, Edward Harold. A bibliography of printed works relating to the city of Oxford / by E.H. Cordeaux and D.H. Merry. — Oxford : Clarendon Press for the Oxford Historical Society, 1976. — xiv,377p ; 23cm. — (Oxford Historical Society. Publications: new series ; vol.25)
Index.
ISBN 0-19-951325-2 : Unpriced
(B77-10093)

016.9427'14 — Cheshire. Chester, 1800-1900. *Bibliographies*
Cheshire County Libraries and Museums. The gentle reader's guide to 19th century Chester / [Cheshire County] Libraries and Museums. — [Chester] ([91 Hoole Rd, Chester CH2 3NG]) : [Cheshire] Libraries and Museums.
2 : Architecture, guides and illustrations / [compiled by Barry Mills]. — [1976]. — [1],iii, 16p ; 30cm.
'... a selective guide to the material available [in Chester Library]' - p.ii.
ISBN 0-904532-20-8 Sd : Unpriced
(B77-04528)

016.9429 — National libraries. *Wales. National Library of Wales. Stock: Books associated with Wales: Books with American imprints, to 1928. Lists*
Blackwell, Henry. A bibliography of Welsh Americana / by Henry Blackwell. — 2nd ed. — Aberystwyth : [National Library of Wales], 1977. — x,126p ; 25cm.
Previous ed.: 1972. — '... includes a reprint of Blackwell's "Bibliography", with a substantial Appendix of additional items compiled by Mr Gareth Watts ... [et al.]' - Foreword.
ISBN 0-901833-82-7 Pbk : £2.00
(B77-20861)

016.947 — Periodical articles in English, 1920-1975: Periodical articles on Eastern European culture, to 1975. *Indexes*
Terry, Garth Michael. A subject and name index to articles on the Slavonic and East European languages and literatures, music and theatre, libraries and the press, contained in English-language journals, 1920-1975 / by Garth M. Terry. — Nottingham (Nottingham NG7 2RD) : University Library, University of Nottingham, 1976. — [1],v,198p ; 30cm.
ISBN 0-9505359-0-7 Pbk : £3.25
Also classified at 016.4918
(B77-01978)

016.9497 — Yugoslavia, to 1976. *Bibliographies*
Terry, Garth Michael. Yugoslav studies : an annotated list of basic bibliographies and reference works / by Garth M. Terry. — Twickenham (30 Staines Rd, Twickenham, Middx) : Anthony C. Hall, 1977. — xi,89p ; 21cm.
Index.
ISBN 0-901997-05-6 : £4.25
(B77-32354)

016.95 — Repositories. Stock: Documents on Far East: Documents in European languages. *Great Britain. Lists*
Matthews, Noel. A guide to manuscripts and documents in the British Isles relating to the Far East / compiled by Noel Matthews and M. Doreen Wainwright ; edited by J.D. Pearson. — Oxford [etc.] : Oxford University Press [for the] School of Oriental and African Studies, 1977. — xiv,182p ; 26cm.
Index.
ISBN 0-19-713591-9 : £17.50 : CIP rev.
(B77-05825)

016.95'005 — Educational institutions. Libraries. *Oxfordshire. Oxford. Oriental Institute Library. Stock: Serial publications. Catalogues*
Oriental Institute Library. List of serial titles / Oriental Institute Library. — [Oxford] ([Pusey La., Oxford OX1 2LE]) : University of Oxford, 1975. — [2],10p ; 30cm.
ISBN 0-905833-00-7 Sd : Unpriced
(B77-03877)

016.953'32 — Yemen (Arab Republic), to 1976. *Bibliographies*
Mondesir, Simoné L. A select bibliography of Yemen Arab Republic and People's Democratic Republic of Yemen / compiled by Simoné L. Mondesir. — [Durham] ([Elvet Hill, Durham DH1 3TR]) : University of Durham, Centre for Middle Eastern and Islamic Studies, [1977]. — iii[i.e.iv],59p ; 25cm. — (University of Durham. Centre for Middle Eastern and Islamic Studies. Occasional papers series ; no.5)
Cover title.
Pbk : £3.00
Also classified at 016.953'35
(B77-29877)

016.953'35 — Yemen (People's Democratic Republic), to 1976. *Bibliographies*
Mondesir, Simoné L. A select bibliography of Yemen Arab Republic and People's Democratic Republic of Yemen / compiled by Simoné L. Mondesir. — [Durham] ([Elvet Hill, Durham DH1 3TR]) : University of Durham, Centre for Middle Eastern and Islamic Studies, [1977]. — iii[i.e.iv],59p ; 25cm. — (University of Durham. Centre for Middle Eastern and Islamic Studies. Occasional papers series ; no.5)
Cover title.
Pbk : £3.00
Primary classification 016.953'32
(B77-29877)

016.954 — Information services on Commonwealth. *London. Kensington and Chelsea (London Borough). Commonwealth Institute. Stock: Records on India. Lists. For teaching*
Commonwealth Institute. India : a teacher's guide to study resources / Commonwealth Institute. — London : The Institute, [1976]. — [2],15,[1] p : 2 ill, col map, plan ; 30cm.
Bibl.
Sd : £0.25
(B77-26740)

016.9549'3 — Sri Lanka, to 1973. *Bibliographies*
Goonetileke, H A I. A bibliography of Ceylon : a systematic guide to the literature on the land, people, history and culture published in western languages from the sixteenth century to the present day / [by] H.A.I. Goonetileke. — Zug : Inter Documentation Company AG ; London : Inter Documentation Company UK Ltd.
Vol.3 : supplementing volumes I and II and containing additional materials up to June 1973. — 1976. — [5],xxxvii,507p ; 21cm. — (Bibliotheca Asiatica ; 14)
Also available on microfiche. — Index.
Unpriced
ISBN 3-85750-015-8
(B77-11029)

016.96 — Africa, to 1974. *Bibliographies*
Panofsky, Hans E. A bibliography of Africana / [by] Hans E. Panofsky. — Westport, Conn. ; London : Greenwood Press, 1975. — xi,350p : map ; 22cm. — (Contributions in librarianship and information science ; no.11)
Index.
ISBN 0-8371-6391-9 : £10.95
(B77-17865)

016.963 — Ethiopia, to 1972. *Bibliographies*
Hidaru, Alula. A short guide to the study of Ethiopia : a general bibliography / edited [i.e. compiled] by Alula Hidaru and Dessalegn Rahmato. — Westport, Conn. ; London : Greenwood Press, 1976. — xiii,176,[1]p ; 25cm. — (African Bibliographic Center. Special bibliographic series : new series ; no.2)
Index.
ISBN 0-8371-9284-6 : £9.65
(B77-16698)

016.967'7305 — Somalia. *Bibliographies*
Salad, Mohamed Khalief. Somalia : a bibliographical survey / compiled by Mohamed Khalief Salad. — Westport, Conn. ; London : Greenwood Press, 1977. — xvi,468,[1]p ; 25cm. — (African Bibliographic Center. Special bibliographic series : new series ; no.4)
ISBN 0-8371-9480-6 : £17.75
(B77-33562)

016.971 — Information services on Commonwealth. *London. Kensington and Chelsea (London Borough). Commonwealth Institute. Stock : Records on Canada. Lists. For teaching*
Commonwealth Institute. Canada : a teacher's guide to study resources / Commonwealth Institute. — London : The Institute, [1976]. — [2],18,[1]p : col map, plan ; 31cm.
Bibl.
Sd : £0.25
(B77-26741)

016.97282 — Information services on Commonwealth. *London. Kensington and Chelsea (London Borough). Commonwealth Institute. Stock: Records on Belize. Lists. For teaching*
Commonwealth Institute. Guyana and Belize : a teacher's guide to study resources, Commonwealth Institute. — London : The Institute, [1976]. — [2],11,[1]p : col map, 2 plans ; 30cm.
Bibl.
Sd : £0.25
Primary classification 016.988'1
(B77-26742)

016.9729 — Repositories. Stock: Manuscripts associated with Commonwealth Caribbean countries. *North America. Lists*
Ingram, Kenneth Everard. Manuscripts relating to Commonwealth Caribbean countries in United States and Canadian repositories / [by] K.E. Ingram. — St Lawrence, Barbados : Caribbean Universities Press ; Epping : Bowker, 1975. — xxix,422p ; 23cm.
Index.
ISBN 0-85474-029-5 : Unpriced
ISBN 0-85474-029-5 Pbk : Unpriced
(B77-19164)

016.97292 — Jamaica, 1655-1838. *Bibliographies*
Ingram, K E. Sources of Jamaican history, 1655-1838 : a bibliographical survey with particular reference to manuscript sources / [by] K.E. Ingram. — Zug ; London : Inter Documentation Co., 1976. — 2v.([38],1310p) ; 21cm.
Index.
Unpriced
ISBN 3-85750-017-4
(B77-15659)

016.973 — Higher education institutions. Libraries. *Buckinghamshire. Buckingham. University College at Buckingham. Library. Stock: Documents on United States, 1705-1825. Catalogues*
University College at Buckingham. *Library.* These United States : the American Revolution and the making of the constitution : a select bibliography of material available in the Library of the University College at Buckingham / compiled by Alex Noel-Tod. — [Buckingham] ([Buckingham MK18 1EG]) : [The Library], 1976. — [2],9p ; 30cm.
Sd : Unpriced
(B77-19973)

016.973 — Libraries. Stock: Books on history of United States. *Scotland. Catalogues*
Cross, David S. A bibliography of research aids, bibliographies, periodicals and government documents relating to the history of the United States and held by the university and major reference libraries of Scotland / compiled by David S. Cross ; under the direction of W.R. Brock [for the Sir Denis Brogan Centre for Research in American History]. — [Glasgow] ([Glasgow G12 8QQ]) : University of Glasgow, 1977. — 96[i.e.98]p,[4]leaves : 2 ill, map ; 22cm.
Cover title: American history in Scottish universities : a list of research aids and printed source material.
ISBN 0-85261-144-7 Sd : £1.25
(B77-33563)

016.973 — United States, 1812-1970. Documents on United States, 1812-1970: Documents with Russian imprints, 1945-1970. *Lists*
Okinshevich, Leo. United States history & historiography in postwar Soviet writings, 1945-70 / compiled by Leo Okinshevich. — Santa Barbara : ABC-Clio ; Oxford : EBC-Clio, [1977]. — xvi,432p ; 24cm.
Published in the United States: 1976. — Bibl.: p.377-388. — Index.
ISBN 0-87436-208-3 : £17.90
(B77-11527)

016.973922'092'4 — United States. Kennedy, John Fitzgerald. *Bibliographies*
Newcomb, Joan I. John F. Kennedy : an annotated bibliography / by Joan I. Newcomb. — Metuchen ; London : Scarecrow Press ; [Folkestone] : [Distributed by Bailey and Swinfen], 1977. — 143p ; 23cm.
Index.
ISBN 0-8108-1042-5 : £5.10
(B77-33564)

016.988'1 — Information services on Commonwealth. *London. Kensington and Chelsea (London Borough). Commonwealth Institute. Stock: Records on Guyana. Lists. For teaching*
Commonwealth Institute. Guyana and Belize : a teacher's guide to study resources, Commonwealth Institute. — London : The Institute, [1976]. — [2],11,[1]p : col map, 2 plans ; 30cm.
Bibl.
Sd : £0.25
Also classified at 016.97282
(B77-26742)

016.994 — Australia, to 1975. *Bibliographies*
Borchardt, Dietrich Hans. Australian bibliography : a guide to printed sources of information / [by] D.H. Borchardt. — [New ed.]. — Rushcutters Bay ; Oxford [etc.] : Pergamon, 1976. — xvi,270p : 1 ill, facsims, port ; 22cm.
Previous ed.: i.e. 2nd ed., revised and enlarged. Melbourne : F.W. Cheshire, 1966. — Bibl.: p.201-264. — Index.
ISBN 0-08-020551-8 : £9.00
ISBN 0-08-020550-x Pbk : £5.50
(B77-05172)

017 — SUBJECT CATALOGUES
017 — Museums. Libraries. *London. Greenwich (London Borough). National Maritime Museum. Library. Stock. Catalogues*
National Maritime Museum. *Library.* Catalogue of the library / National Maritime Museum. — London : H.M.S.O.
Vol.5 : Naval history. Part 1 : The Middle Ages to 1815. — 1976. — xi,209p,xii p of plates : ill, facsims, maps, ports ; 25cm.
Index.
ISBN 0-11-880760-9 : £12.00
(B77-08720)

017'.1 — Libraries. *London. Lambeth (London Borough). National Audio-Visual Aids Library. Stock: 16mm films. Subject catalogues*
National Audio-Visual Aids Library. 16mm films in the National Audio-Visual Aids Library. — [London] : Educational Foundation for Visual Aids, 1976. — x,288p ; 22cm.
Index.
Pbk : £2.20
(B77-29127)

018 — AUTHOR CATALOGUES
018'.2 — Museums. *Kent. Tenterden. Ellen Terry Memorial Museum. Exhibits: Books owned by Terry, Ellen. Author catalogues*
Ellen Terry Memorial Museum. Catalogue of the working library of Ellen Terry at Smallhythe Place, Tenterden, Kent / [compiled by F.T. Bowyer]. — [London] : National Trust [for] the Museum, 1977. — 63p ; 22cm.
Sd : Unpriced
(B77-19974)

020 — LIBRARY AND INFORMATION SCIENCES
020 — Comparative librarianship. *Reviews of research*
Comparative & international library science / edited by John F. Harvey. — Metuchen ; London : Scarecrow Press ; [Folkestone] : [Distributed by Bailey and Swinfen], 1977. — ix,286p ; 23cm.
Bibl. — Index.
ISBN 0-8108-1060-3 : £12.45
(B77-33565)

020 — Information services & libraries. Organisation. *Manuals*
National library and information services : a handbook for planners / edited by C.V. Penna, D.J. Foskett, P.H. Sewell. — London [etc.] : Butterworth, 1977. — xxiv,231p : ill ; 23cm.
Bibl.: p.214-215. — Index.
ISBN 0-408-70818-2 : £8.00
(B77-14016)

020 — Librarianship
Manual of library economy : a conspectus of professional librarianship for students and practitioners / edited by R. Northwood Lock. — London : Bingley [etc.], 1977. — 447p,16p of plates : ill, facsims, forms, plans ; 23cm.
Bibl. — Index.
ISBN 0-85157-226-x : £9.50
(B77-20862)

020 — Librarianship. *Conference proceedings*
Library Association. *National Conference, Scarborough, 1976.* Proceedings, papers and summaries of discussions at the National Conference [of] the Library Association held at Scarborough, 6th September to 9th September, 1976. — London : Library Association, 1976. — 72,[1]p ; 30cm.
Cover title: Proceedings of the National Conference.
ISBN 0-85365-199-x Sd : £1.50
(B77-03315)

020 — Librarianship & information science. *State-of-the-art reviews*
British librarianship and information science. — London : Library Association.
1971-1975 / edited by H.A. Whatley. — 1977. — xiii,379p,plate : 1 ill ; 26cm.
Bibl. — Index.
ISBN 0-85365-099-3 : £12.50(£10.00 to members of the Library Association) : CIP rev.
(B77-08176)

020'.21'2 — Serial publications on librarianship: Statistical publications. Provision. *Research reports*
Moore, Nick. Statistical series relevant to libraries / [by] Nick Moore. — [London] : British Library ; Wetherby : Distributed by the British Library Lending Division, 1976. — [2], ii,34p ; 30cm. — (British Library. Research and Development Department. Reports ; no.5300)
ISBN 0-85350-142-4 Sp : £2.50
(B77-03316)

020'.3 — Librarianship. *Encyclopaedias*
Harrod, Leonard Montague. The librarians' glossary of terms used in librarianship, documentation and the book crafts, and reference book / [by] Leonard Montague Harrod. — 4th revised ed. — London : Deutsch, 1977. — 903p ; 23cm.
'A Grafton book'. — Previous ed.: 1971.
ISBN 0-233-96744-3 : £15.00 : CIP rev.
(B77-19975)

020'.622'41 — Librarianship. Christian organisations. *Great Britain. Librarians' Christian Fellowship. Periodicals*
Christian librarian : the journal and yearbook of the Librarians' Christian Fellowship. — [Southport] ([c/o Hon. Secretary, 4 Salford Rd, Southport, Merseyside PR8 3JN]) : [The Fellowship].
1976. — [1976]. — [3],32[i.e.33]p ; 30cm.
Pbk : £0.25(free to members)
ISSN 0309-4170
(B77-11030)

020'.622'41 — Librarianship. Organisations. *Great Britain. Library Association, to 1977*
Munford, William Arthur. A history of the Library Association, 1877-1977 / [by] W.A. Munford. — London : Library Association, 1976. — xii,360p,leaf of plate, 24p of plates : ill, ports ; 23cm.
'A Library Association centenary volume'. — Bibl.: p.342-343. — Index.
ISBN 0-85365-488-3 : £8.50(£6.80 to members of the Library Association)
(B77-05826)

020'.622'41 — Librarianship. Organisations. *Great Britain. Library Association, to 1977. Illustrations*
Plumb, Philip Walter. Libraries by association : the Library Association's first centenary / compiled by Philip Plumb. — London : Library Association, 1977. — 48p : ill ; 21cm.
ISBN 0-85365-359-3 Sd : £0.10(free to members) : CIP rev.
(B77-13464)

020'.622'41 — Librarianship. Organisations. *Great Britain. Library Association. Yearbooks*
Library Association. Year book / the Library Association. — London : Library Association.
'76. — 1976. — 107,288p,plate : port ; 25cm.
Bibl.: p.95-107.
ISBN 0-85365-398-4 Pbk : £6.25(£5.00 to members)
ISSN 0075-9066
(B77-03878)

020'.622'417 — Librarianship. Organisations. *Ireland (Republic). Library Council. Periodicals*
Irish library news. — Dublin (c/o Editor, 53 Upper Mount St., Dublin 2) : Library Council.
No.1- ; Sept. 1977-. — [1977]-. — 30cm.
Monthly. — Sheet ([2] sides) as 1st issue.
Unpriced
ISSN 0332-0049
(B77-33566)

020'.7 — Librarians. Professional education. *Great Britain. Serials*
Library Association. Students' handbook / the Library Association. — London : The Association.
1977-78. — 1977. — 56p : map(on inside front cover) ; 21cm.
ISBN 0-85365-710-6 Pbk : £0.75 : CIP rev.
ISSN 0305-1072
(B77-19976)

020'.71 — Librarians & information scientists. Professional education. Short courses. *Great Britain. Reports, surveys*
Slater, Margaret. Assessing the need for short courses in library/information work / [by] Margaret Slater. — London : Aslib, 1976. — iv,88p : forms ; 30cm ; 30cm. — (Aslib. Occasional publications ; no.19 ISSN 0066-8532)
ISBN 0-85142-090-7 Pbk : £6.75(£5.75 to members)
(B77-11528)

020.75 — BOOK COLLECTING
020'.75 — Book collectors. *Directories*
International directory of book collectors : a directory of book collectors in Britain, America and the rest of the world. — Beckenham ([117 Kent House Rd, Beckenham, Kent BR3 1JJ]) : Trigon Press.
1976-77 / compiled by Roger and Judith Sheppard. — 1976. — viii,271p ; 20cm.
ISBN 0-904929-00-0 : £10.00
(B77-03317)

020'.75 — Books. Collecting. Morris, William, b.1834
Needham, Paul. William Morris and the art of the book / with essays on William Morris as book collector / by Paul Needham ; as calligrapher / by Joseph Dunlap ; and, as typographer / by John Dreyfus ; [edited by Paul Needham]. — New York : Pierpont Morgan Library ; London [etc.] : Oxford University Press, 1976. — 3-140,[1]p,cxiv[i.e. cxviii]p of plates : ill, facsims(some col), port ; 31cm.
Ill. on lining papers. — Includes a catalogue based on the Pierpont Morgan Library's exhibition "William Morris and the Art of the Book", September-November 1976.
ISBN 0-19-519910-3 : £30.00
Primary classification 686.2'2'0924
(B77-04948)

020.8 — LIBRARY AND INFORMATION SCIENCES. COLLECTIONS
020'.8 — Librarianship. *Readings*
The **information** explosion : articles on practical librarianship, contributed to the Librarians for Social Change conference on information handling, London, May 8-9, 1976. — Brighton : Librarians for Social Change, [1976]. — [11]p : ill ; 30cm.
ISBN 0-903612-41-0 : £0.60
(B77-01124)

020.9 — LIBRARY AND INFORMATION SCIENCES. HISTORICAL AND GEOGRAPHICAL TREATMENT

020'.9 — Librarianship, to 1974

Thompson, James, *b.1932.* A history of the principles of librarianship / by James Thompson. — London : Bingley [etc.], 1977. — 236p ; 23cm.
Bibl.: p.226-227. — Index.
ISBN 0-85157-241-3 : £4.75
(B77-23954)

020'.92'4 — Librarianship. Savage, Ernest Albert. *Great Britain. Biographies*

Ollé, James Gordon. Ernest A. Savage : librarian extraordinary / [by] James G. Ollé. — London : Library Association, 1977. — xiii, 225p,leaf of plate,[8]p of plates : ill, facsim, ports ; 23cm.
'A Library Association centenary volume'. — Bibl.: p.201-207. — Index.
ISBN 0-85365-459-x : £8.00(£6.40 to members of the Library Association) : CIP rev.
(B77-17866)

020'.941 — Librarianship. *Great Britain*

British librarianship today / edited by W.L. Saunders. — London : Library Association, 1976. — xxi,378p ; 22cm.
'A Library Association centenary volume'. — Bibl. — Index.
ISBN 0-85365-498-0 : £8.25(£6.60 to members of the Library Association)
(B77-05827)

020'.941 — Librarianship. *Great Britain. Documents. Collections*

A **librarian's** handbook / compiled by L.J. Taylor. — London : Library Association, 1976. — x,882p : ill, forms ; 25cm.
Bibl.: p.795-852. — Index.
ISBN 0-85365-079-9 Pbk : £15.00(£12.00 to members)
(B77-11031)

020'.941 — Librarianship. *Great Britain. Festschriften*

Of one accord : essays in honour of W.B. Paton / edited by Frank McAdams. — Glasgow (18 Crosslees Park, Glasgow G46 7DX) : Scottish Library Association, 1977. — ix,126p,plate : port ; 23cm. — (Scottish library studies ; 4)
Bibl.: p.110-122. — Index.
ISBN 0-900649-13-5 : £5.00 : CIP rev. (£4.00 to members of the Scottish Library Association)
(B77-12819)

020'.941 — Librarianship. *Great Britain. Forecasts*

Prospects for British librarianship / edited by K.C. Harrison. — London : Library Association, 1976. — xiii,299p ; 22cm.
'A Library Association centenary volume'. — Index.
ISBN 0-85365-009-8 : £6.50(£5.20 to members of the Library Association)
(B77-05828)

020'.973 — Librarianship. *United States*

Gates, Jean Key. Introduction to librarianship / [by] Jean Key Gates. — 2nd ed. — New York ; London [etc.] : McGraw-Hill, 1976. — xiii, 288p ; 24cm. — (McGraw-Hill series in library education)
Previous ed.: New York : McGraw-Hill, 1968. — Bibl.: p.259-277. — Index.
ISBN 0-07-022977-5 : £8.45
(B77-01125)

020'.973 — Librarianship. *United States. Reviews of research*

Advances in librarianship. — New York [etc.] ; London : Academic Press.
Vol.7 / edited by Melvin J. Voight and Michael H. Harris. — 1977. — xv,348p : ill ; 24cm.
Bibl. — Index.
ISBN 0-12-785007-4 : £15.95
(B77-17867)

021 — LIBRARIES

021 — Libraries. Size. *United States. Conference proceedings*

Touching Bottom in the Bottomless Pit *(Conference), Chicago, 1975.* Farewell to Alexandria : solutions to space, growth and performance problems of libraries / edited by Daniel Gore. — Westport, Conn. ; London : Greenwood Press, 1976. — vi,184p : ill, forms ; 22cm.
'All of the contributions ... , except the last, were presented at a conference sponsored by The Associated Colleges of the Midwest, held in Chicago, April 17-18, 1975. Entitled "Touching Bottom in the Bottomless Pit"...' - Introduction. — Bibl.: p.104.
ISBN 0-8371-8587-4 : £10.25
(B77-17251)

021'.0025'41 — Libraries. *Great Britain. Directories*

The **libraries,** museums and art galleries year book. — Cambridge : J. Clarke.
1976 / editors Adrian Brink & Derry Watkins. — 1976. — [2],254p ; 31cm.
Index.
ISBN 0-227-67824-9 : £15.00
Also classified at 069'.025'41; 708'.941
(B77-00003)

Library Association. Libraries in the United Kingdom and the Republic of Ireland : a complete list of public library services and a select list of academic and other library addresses / [Library Association]. — 7th ed. — London : Library Association, 1977. — 166p : 1 ill ; 21cm.
Previous ed.: 1975. — Index.
ISBN 0-85365-289-9 Pbk : £2.50(£2.00 to members) : CIP rev.
(B77-05173)

021'.0025'411 — Libraries. Services. *Scotland. Directories*

Library resources in Scotland. — Glasgow (Department of Librarianship, University of Strathclyde, Glasgow G1 1XH) : Scottish Library Association.
1976-1977 / [edited by] James A. Tait, Heather F.C. Tait. — 1976. — viii,111p ; 24cm.
Index.
ISBN 0-900649-12-7 Pbk : £6.00(£5.00 to members of the Library Association)
(B77-05829)

021'.0025'6 — Libraries. *Africa. Directories*

The **African** book world & press, a directory = Répertoire du livre et de la presse en Afrique / compiled by the 'African book publishing record' ; Hans M. Zell, editor. — Oxford (P.O. Box 56, Oxford OX1 3EL) : Hans Zell (Publishers) Ltd, 1977. — xxvi,[1],296,[1]p ; 31cm.
English and French text.
ISBN 0-905450-00-0 : £25.00
Also classified at 338.4'7'6860256
(B77-23058)

021'.00941 — Libraries. *Great Britain*

Harrison, Kenneth Cecil. The library and the community / [by] K.C. Harrison. — 3rd revised ed. — London : Deutsch, 1977. — 125p ; 23cm. — (A Grafton book)
Previous ed.: 1966. — Bibl.: p.119-121. — Index.
ISBN 0-233-96875-x : £3.50
(B77-20863)

021'.00941 — Libraries. Services. *Great Britain. Conference proceedings*

Library Association. *London and Home Counties Branch. Conference, London, 1976.* Survival '76 : papers read at the one-day Conference of the London and Home Counties Branch of the Library Association, held at the Library Association, 12th May, 1976, under the chairmanship of Miss E. McNeill / edited by Vaughan Whibley. — Orpington (c/o V. Whibley, 14 Chestnut Close, Green Street Green, Orpington, Kent BR6 6LP) : Library Association, London and Home Counties Branch, 1976. — 47p : ill ; 19cm.
ISBN 0-902119-19-2 Sd : £2.50
(B77-12820)

021'.00952 — Libraries. *Japan. Reports, surveys*

Welch, Theodore Franklyn. Toshokan : libraries in Japanese society / by Theodore F. Welch. — London : Bingley [etc.], 1976. — x,306p,[16]p of plates : ill, map(on lining papers) ; 23cm.
Bibl.: p.278-296. — Index.
ISBN 0-85157-220-0 : £8.00
(B77-00577)

021.4 — LIBRARIES AS SOCIAL FORCES

021'.4'0973 — United States. Society. Role of libraries. *Readings*

Social responsibilities and libraries : a 'Library journal', 'School library journal' selection / compiled and edited by Patricia Glass Schuman. — New York ; London : Bowker, 1976. — x,402p ; 24cm.
Bibl. — Index.
ISBN 0-8352-0952-0 : £9.50
(B77-03318)

021.6 — LIBRARY EXTENSION AND COOPERATION

021.6'4 — Librarianship. Cooperation

Jefferson, George. Library co-operation / [by] George Jefferson. — 2nd revised ed. — London : Deutsch, 1977. — 189p ; 23cm. — (A Grafton book)
Previous ed.: 1966. — Bibl.: p.169-182. — Index.
ISBN 0-233-96851-2 : £4.95
(B77-21663)

021.6'4 — Libraries holding stock for inter-library loans through British Library. Lending Division. Codes. *Directories*

British Library. *Lending Division.* Directory of library codes / [British Library Lending Division]. — Interim ed. — Boston Spa : B.L.L.D., 1976. — [4],42p ; 30cm.
Previous ed.: / issued by the National Central Library. London : N.C.L., 1972.
Sd : Unpriced
(B77-02718)

021.6'4'02541 — Libraries. Cooperation. Organisations. *Great Britain. Standing Conference of Co-operative Library and Information Services. Directories*

Standing Conference of Co-operative Library and Information Services. Directory of members / Standing Conference of Co-operative Library & Information Services. — [Birmingham] ([c/o Susan Fleetwood, Quick Reference and Commercial Information Library, Birmingham Public Library, Birmingham B3 3HQ]) : S.C.O.C.L.I.S.
1976. — [1976]. — 32[i.e. 33]p ; 30cm.
Cover title.
ISBN 0-905657-00-4 Pbk : £1.00(free to members)
ISSN 0309-1767
(B77-03879)

021.8 — LIBRARIES AND GOVERNMENT

021.8'0973 — Libraries. Relations with government. *United States*

Molz, Kathleen. Federal policy and library support / [by] Redmond Kathleen Molz. — Cambridge, Mass. ; London : M.I.T. Press, [1977]. — xiii,118p : 1 ill ; 21cm.
Published in the United States: 1976. — Bibl. — Index.
ISBN 0-262-13120-x : £9.40
Primary classification 353.008'52
(B77-12942)

022.9 — LIBRARIES. EQUIPMENT, FURNITURE, FURNISHINGS

022'.9 — Libraries. Applications of digital computer systems

Tedd, L A. An introduction to computer-based library systems / [by] L.A. Tedd. — London [etc.] : Heyden, 1977. — xiv,208p : ill, facsims, forms ; 25cm. — (Heyden international topics in science)
Bibl. — Index.
ISBN 0-85501-221-8 : £8.50
(B77-20864)

022'.9 — Libraries using computer systems. *Great Britain. Directories*

Aslib. *Computer Applications Group. Acquisitions, Cataloguing and Circulation Working Party.* Directory of operational computer applications in United Kingdom libraries and information units / [Aslib Computer Applications Group, Acquisitions, Cataloguing and Circulation Working Party] ; edited by C.W.J. Wilson. — 2nd ed. — London : Aslib, 1977. — [4],196p ; 30cm.
Previous ed.: 1973. — Index.
ISBN 0-85142-092-3 Pbk : £9.00(£7.50 to members of Aslib)
(B77-17252)

023.5 — LIBRARY STAFF. PROFESSIONAL

023.5 — Libraries. Personnel. Training. *Great Britain. Reports, surveys*

Working Party on Training. Training in libraries : report of the Library Association Working Party on Training. — London : Library Association, 1977. — 26p ; 21cm.
ISBN 0-85365-339-9 Sd : £0.75 : CIP rev.
(B77-05830)

024 — LIBRARY REGULATIONS

024 — Universities. *London. University of London. Libraries. Users. Admission. Regulations*

University of London. *Library Resources Co-ordinating Committee.* Guide to admission to libraries in the University of London / [Library Resources Co-ordinating Committee]. — [3rd revised ed.]. — [London] ([c/o University of London Library, Senate House, Malet St., WC1E 7HU]) : The Committee, 1976. — [1],v,31p : forms ; 22cm.
Previous ed.: published as 'Guide to the admission of academic staff, students and other visitors to libraries within the University of London' / Standing Conference of Librarians of the Libraries of the University of London. London : Standing Conference of Librarians, 1970- ?.
Sd : Unpriced
(B77-33567)

025 — LIBRARY OPERATIONS

025'.02 — Great Britain. Parliament. House of Lords. Record Office. Technical services

Great Britain. *Parliament. House of Lords. Record Office.* The House of Lords Record Office technical services / [compiled by H.S. Cobb, Deputy Clerk of the Records]. — [London] ([Houses of Parliament, S.W.1]) : The Record Office, 1975. — [3],12p : ill ; 30cm.
Sd : Unpriced
(B77-01126)

025'.02'02854044 — Public libraries. Processing systems. Applications of digital computer systems. *West Sussex*

West Sussex *(County). Data Processing Division.* Library data processing system description / West Sussex County Council, Data Processing Division. — [Chichester] ([County Hall, Tower St., Chichester, W. Sussex]) : [The Division], 1976. — [5],47p,[153] leaves : forms ; 30cm. — (Report ; no.DP-LDP-0025)
Some leaves printed on both sides. — Page height varies. — Originally published: 1974.
ISBN 0-900800-17-8 Sp : £10.00
(B77-11032)

025.1 — LIBRARY ADMINISTRATION

025.17 — Libraries. Stock: Non-book materials. Collections. Administration

Hicks, Warren Braukman. Managing multimedia libraries / by Warren B. Hicks and Alma M. Tillin. — New York ; London : Bowker, 1977. — xv,264p : ill, 2 forms ; 26cm.
Bibl.: p.223-243. — Index.
ISBN 0-8352-0628-9 : £9.50
(B77-11529)

025.17 — Non-book materials. Collections. *Great Britain. Lists*

Line, Joyce. Archival collections of non-book materials : a preliminary list indicating policies for preservation and access / [by] Joyce Line. — London : British Library, 1977. — [2],ii, 60p ; 30cm. — (British Library. Research and development reports ; no. 5330 HC ISSN 0308-2385)
Bibl.: p.47-51. — Index.
ISBN 0-905984-00-5 Sp : £2.50 : CIP rev.
(B77-10715)

025.17'1 — Archives. Administration. *Manuals*

Cook, Michael. Archives administration : a manual for intermediate and smaller organizations and for local government / [by] Michael Cook. — Folkestone : Dawson, 1977. — x,258p : ill, forms, plans ; 23cm.
Bibl.: p.228-247. — Index.
ISBN 0-7129-0749-1 : £10.00 : CIP rev.
(B77-14018)

025.17'1 — Archives. Administration. Planning. *Developing countries. Conference proceedings*

General Conference on the Planning of Archival Development in the Third World, *Dakar, 1975.* Proceedings of the General Conference on the Planning of Archival Development in the Third World (Dakar, 28-31 January 1975) = Actes de la Conférence generale sur la planification du développement des Archives dans le Tiers-Monde (Dakar, 28-31 janvier 1975) / [editor = rédacteur Wilhelm Lenz] ; [for the] International Council on Archives = [pour le] Conseil international des archives. — München [i.e. Munich] : Verlag Dokumentation ; [London] : [Distributed by Mansell Information Publishing], 1976. — 117p ; 24cm. — ('Archivum' special volume = 'Archivum' cahier hors série ; no.1)
Chiefly English and French text, some contributions in Spanish.
Pbk : £7.50
ISBN 3-7940-3750-2
(B77-11033)

025.17'3 — Electrical engineering. Institute of Electrical and Electronics Engineers. Serial publications. Codes: Alphabets. Letters. *Lists*

Pottage, Michael York. IEEE letter code guide / compiled by M.Y. Pottage. — London : Aslib, 1975. — iv,16p ; 21cm. — (Aslib. Electronics Group. Publications)
Index.
ISBN 0-85142-306-x Sd : £1.50
(B77-01127)

025.17'3 — Information services. Stock: Unpublished reports

Information work with unpublished reports ... / by A.H. Holloway ... [et al.]. — London : Deutsch [for] the Institute of Information Scientists, 1976. — 302p,[4]p of plates : ill, facsims, forms ; 23cm. — (Institute of Information Scientists. Monograph series) (A Grafton book)
Bibl. — Index.
ISBN 0-233-96824-5 : £6.95
(B77-02719)

025.17'73'0257 — Resource centres. Film services. *North America. Directories*

North American film and video directory : a guide to media collections and services / compiled by Olga S. Weber with the assistance of Deirdre Boyle, consultant. — New York ; London : Bowker, 1976. — xi,284p ; 29cm.
Index.
ISBN 0-8352-0883-4 : £16.50
ISSN 0362-7802
Also classified at 025.17'8
(B77-10094)

025.17'8 — Resource centres. Videotape services. *North America. Directories*

North American film and video directory : a guide to media collections and services / compiled by Olga S. Weber with the assistance of Deirdre Boyle, consultant. — New York ; London : Bowker, 1976. — xi,284p ; 29cm.
Index.
ISBN 0-8352-0883-4 : £16.50
ISSN 0362-7802
Primary classification 025.17'73'0257
(B77-10094)

025.17'9 — Libraries. Stock: Microforms

Teague, Sydney John. Microform librarianship / [by] S.J. Teague. — London [etc.] : Butterworth, 1977. — viii,117p : ill ; 22cm.
Index.
ISBN 0-408-70799-2 : £4.00
(B77-09465)

025.17'9 — Libraries. Stock: Microforms. *Readings*

Studies in micropublishing, 1853-1976 : documentary sources / edited by Allen B. Veaner. — London : Mansell Information Publishing, [1977]. — xxi,489p : ill ; 24cm. — (Microform Review series in library micrographics management ; 2)
Also published: Westport, Conn. : Microform Review, 1977. — Bibl. — Index.
ISBN 0-7201-0726-1 : £13.75 : CIP rev.
(B77-25457)

025.2 — LIBRARY ACQUISITIONS

025.2'05 — Libraries. Stock. Acquisition. *Periodicals*

Library acquisitions : practice and theory. — New York ; Oxford : Pergamon.
Vol.1, no.1- ; Jan. 1977-. — 1977-. — ill ; 26cm.
Quarterly. — Cover title. — [2],79p. in 1st issue. — Bibl.
Pbk : Unpriced
ISSN 0364-6408
(B77-23059)

025.2'0941 — Libraries. Stock. *Great Britain. Conference proceedings*

The **future** of library collections : proceedings of a seminar held by the Library Management Research Unit, University of Technology, Loughborough, 21-23 March 1977 / edited by J.W. Blackwood. — [Loughborough] ([Loughborough, Leics. LE11 3TU]) : The Unit, 1977. — iv leaves,80p ; 30cm. — (Loughborough University of Technology. Library Management Research Unit. Reports ; no.7 ISSN 0309-4804)
ISBN 0-904924-11-4 Sd : £3.00
(B77-29878)

025.2'1 — Circulating subscription libraries. Stock: Fiction in English. Censorship. *Great Britain, ca 1880. Early works*

Moore, George. Literature at nurse, or, Circulating morals : a polemic on Victorian censorship / [by] George Moore. — [1st ed. reprinted] / edited with an introduction by Pierre Coustillas. — Hassocks : Harvester Press [etc.], 1976. — 53,[1],22p ; 20cm. — (Society and the Victorians)
Facsimile reprint of: 1st ed. London : Vizetelly, 1885. — Includes the text of 'A new censorship of literature' / by George Moore and the ensuing correspondence in the 'Pall Mall gazette'.
ISBN 0-85527-164-7 : £2.95
(B77-12267)

025.2'1 — Public libraries. Stock. Censorship, to 1976

Noyce, John Leonard. Censorship in public libraries / by John Noyce. — Brighton : Noyce, 1977. — 14,[9]p : ill ; 30cm.
Sd : £1.20
(B77-31661)

025.3 — CATALOGUING

025.3 — Libraries. Catalogues. Use. *Great Britain. Reports, surveys*

Scott, Aldyth D. UK catalogue use survey : physical form and guiding : a report / by Aldyth D. Scott. — Revised [ed.]. — Brighton ([Moulsecoomb, Brighton BN2 4GJ]) : Brighton Polytechnic, Department of Communication and European Studies, School of Librarianship, 1976. — vii,92p : forms ; 30cm.
Previous ed.: 1973.
ISBN 0-904167-02-x Sp : £1.00
(B77-05831)

025.3'028'54 — Libraries. Stock: Documents. Cataloguing. Applications of digital computer systems. Projects: Scottish Libraries Co-operative Automation Project. *Periodicals*

Scottish Libraries Co-operative Automation Project. Newsletter / Scottish Libraries Co-operative Automation Project. — Edinburgh (National Library of Scotland, George IV Bridge, Edinburgh EH1 1EW) : SCOLCAP.
No.1- ; Aug. 1976-. — [1976]-. — 30cm.
Published at irregular intervals. — Cover title: SCOLCAP. — [1],2,6 leaves in 1st issue.
Sd : £0.50
ISSN 0309-0086
(B77-03319)

025.3'028'54 — National libraries. *Great Britain. British Library. MARC services. Use by British libraries. Conference proceedings*

Proceedings of a conference held in Plymouth on 16 and 17 April 1975 / Marc Users' Group ; edited by F.A. Clements. — Exeter (c/o F.A. Clements, Devon Library Services, Barley House, Isleworth Rd, St Thomas, Exeter, Devon) : Marc Users' Group, [1975]. — 35p : 1 ill ; 22cm.
ISBN 0-905463-00-5 Sd : £1.00
(B77-06430)

025.3'028'5442 — Documents. Cataloguing. Machine-readable files: UK MARC records. *Periodicals*

MARC news / British Library Bibliographic Services Division. — London (c/o BLAISE, 7 Rathbone St., W1P 2AL) : The British Library.

No.1- ; Aug. 1977-. — [1977]-. — 30cm.
Published at irregular intervals. — 12p. in 1st issue.
Sd : Free to subscribers to British Library Bibliographic Services Division publications
ISSN 0140-217x
(B77-32355)

025.3'3 — Documents. Subject indexing

Foskett, Antony Charles. The subject approach to information / by A.C. Foskett. — 3rd ed. — London : Bingley [etc.], 1977. — xvi,476p : ill ; 23cm.
Previous ed.: 1971. — Index.
ISBN 0-85157-238-3 : £9.90
Primary classification 025.4
(B77-30922)

025.3'3 — Subject indexing. Multilingual thesauri. *Europe. Conference proceedings*

Workshop on Multilingual Systems, *Dunchurch Industrial Staff College, 1975.* Report of a Workshop on Multilingual Systems / [by] Verina Horsnell ; [for the Polytechnic of North London, School of Librarianship]. — London : British Library, 1976. — iii,35p ; 30cm. — (British Library. Research and Development Department. Reports ; 5265 HC)
'... held at Dunchurch Industrial Staff College on 6-7 October 1975' - title page verso.
ISBN 0-85350-137-8 Sp : £2.50
(B77-00578)

025.3'3001'64 — Computer systems. *Thesauri*

National Computing Centre. NCC thesaurus of computing terms / [National Computing Centre]. — 8th ed. — Manchester : NCC Publications ; [Letchworth] : [Distributed by Dent], 1976. — [17],147,147p ; 30cm.
Cover title: Thesaurus of computing terms. — Previous ed.: 1974. — Index.
ISBN 0-85012-169-8 Pbk : £19.00
(B77-10095)

025.3'353 — Physics. *Thesauri*
INSPEC. Inspec thesaurus. — [3rd ed.]. — [London] : Institution of Electrical Engineers, 1977. — viii,372,[1],h45p ; 30cm.
Previous ed.: i.e. revised ed. 1975.
ISBN 0-85296-437-4 Pbk : £25.00
Also classified at 025.3'3621'3
(B77-09466)

025.3'3621'3 — Electrical engineering. *Thesauri*
INSPEC. Inspec thesaurus. — [3rd ed.]. — [London] : Institution of Electrical Engineers, 1977. — viii,372,[1],h45p ; 30cm.
Previous ed.: i.e. revised ed. 1975.
ISBN 0-85296-437-4 Pbk : £25.00
Primary classification 025.3'353
(B77-09466)

025.3'3624 — Construction. *Thesauri*
CIT Agency. Construction industry thesaurus. — 2nd ed. / [compiled by the CIT Agency at the Polytechnic of the South Bank ; under the direction of Michael J. Roberts]. Abridged version / selected by Caroline Kenward and Michael J. Roberts at the Polytechnic of the South Bank. — London ([2 Marsham St., S.W.1]) : Property Services Agency, 1976. — 119p ; 30cm.
Second ed. originally published: 1976.
£9.00
Pbk : £7.00
(B77-27637)

CIT Agency. Construction industry thesaurus. — 2nd ed. / compiled by the CIT Agency at the Polytechnic of the South Bank ; under the direction of Michael J. Roberts. — London ([2 Marsham St., S.W.1]) : Property Services Agency, 1976. — 419p ; 31cm.
Previous ed.: i.e. Development ed. / compiled under the direction of the Polytechnic of the South Bank and the Polytechnic of North London, School of Librarianship. 1972.
Unpriced
(B77-27638)

025.3'3686'43 — Micrography. *Thesauri*
National Reprographic Centre for documentation. Thesaurus of micrographic terms / National Reprographic Centre for documentation ; by B.J.S. Williams. — 3rd ed. / revised by Gordon Harris. — Hatfield (Hatfield Polytechnic, Endymion Rd Annexe, Hatfield, Herts. AL10 8AU) : The Centre, 1976. — 35 leaves : ill ; 30cm.
Previous ed. / by B.J.S. Williams. 1972.
ISBN 0-85267-090-7 Sp : £2.00(£1.25 to members)
(B77-08178)

025.3'4 — Non-book materials. Descriptive cataloguing. *Rules*
International Federation of Library Associations and Institutions. *Working Group on the International Standard Bibliographic Description for Non-Book Materials.* ISBD (NBM) : International Standard Bibliographic Description for Non-Book Materials / recommended by the Working Group on the International Standard Bibliographic Description for Non-Book Materials set up by the IFLA Committee on Cataloguing. — London (c/o British Library, Reference Division, Great Russell St., WC1B 3DG) : IFLA International Office for UBC, 1977. — iii-viii,60p ; 30cm.
ISBN 0-903043-12-2 Sd : £5.00 : CIP rev.
(B77-10096)

025.3'4'3 — Serial publications. Descriptive cataloguing. *Rules*
International Federation of Library Associations and Institutions. *Joint Working Group on the International Standard Bibliographic Description for Serials.* ISBD(S) : International Standard Bibliographic Description for Serials / prepared by the Joint Working Group on the International Standard Bibliographic Description for Serials set up by the IFLA Committee on Cataloguing and the IFLA Committee on Serial Publications. — 1st standard ed. — London (c/o British Library, Reference Division, Great Russell St., WC1B 3DG) : IFLA International Office for UBC, 1977. — iii-viii,61p ; 30cm.
Previous ed.: London : IFLA Committee on Cataloguing, 1974.
ISBN 0-903043-13-0 Sd : £5.00 : CIP rev.
(B77-14520)

025.3'4'6 — Maps. Descriptive cataloguing. *Standards*
British Standards Institution. Recommendations for bibliographical references to maps and charts = Recommandations pour les références bibliographiques aux plans et cartes = Empfehlungen für bibliographische Verweisungen auf Pläne und Karten / British Standards Institution. — London : B.S.I.
Part 2 = Partie 2 = Teil 2 : References in books and articles = Références dans les livres et articles = Verweisungen in Büchen und Artiken. — 1977. — [2],5,[1]p ; 30cm. — (BS5195 : Part 2 : 1977)
Pierced for binder.
ISBN 0-580-09950-4 Sd : £1.60
(B77-14521)

025.3'4'73 — Museums. *London. Southwark (London Borough). Imperial War Museum. Stock: Films. Descriptive cataloguing. Manuals*
Imperial War Museum. *Department of Information Retrieval.* Film cataloguing handbook / [Imperial War Museum], Department of Information Retrieval ; [compiled by] Roger B.N. Smither with David J. Penn. — London (Lambeth Rd, SE1 6HZ) : The Museum, 1976. — [1],iv,58p : ill ; 30cm.
Sp : £2.75
(B77-26077)

025.4 — CLASSIFICATION
Classification in the 1970s : a second look / edited by Arthur Maltby. — Revised ed. — London : Bingley [etc.], 1976. — 262p ; 23cm.
Previous ed.: 1972. — Bibl. — Index.
ISBN 0-85157-221-9 : £5.50
(B77-05175)

Foskett, Antony Charles. The subject approach to information / by A.C. Foskett. — 3rd ed. — London : Bingley [etc.], 1977. — xvi,476p : ill ; 23cm.
Previous ed.: 1971. — Index.
ISBN 0-85157-238-3 : £9.90
Also classified at 025.3'3
(B77-30922)

025.4'3 — Documents. *Classification schedules*
Bliss, Henry Evelyn. Bliss bibliographic classification. — 2nd ed. — London [etc.] : Butterworth.
Previous ed.: published as 'A bibliographic classification'. New York : H.W. Wilson Co., 1940-1953.
Class J : Education / [by] J. Mills and Vanda Broughton ; with the assistance of Valerie Lang. — 1977. — xvii,21p ; 28cm.
Index.
ISBN 0-408-70829-8 Pbk : £6.00
(B77-13465)

Class P : Religion, the occult, morals and ethics / [by] J. Mills and Vanda Broughton ; with the assistance of Valerie Lang. — 1977. — xx,43p ; 29cm.
Index.
ISBN 0-408-70832-8 : £6.00
(B77-17253)

Class Q : Social welfare / [by] J. Mills and Vanda Broughton ; with the assistance of Valerie Lang. — 1977. — xxiii,36p ; 29cm.
Index.
ISBN 0-408-70833-6 : £6.00
(B77-13466)

Introduction and auxiliary schedules / [by] J. Mills and Vanda Broughton ; with the assistance of Valerie Lang. — 1977. — xiv, 209p : port ; 29cm.
Index.
ISBN 0-408-70821-2 : £15.00
(B77-13467)

Universal Decimal Classification = Classification Décimale Universelle = Dezimalklassification. — English full ed. (4th international ed.). — London : British Standards Institution. — (Fédération internationale de documentation. Publications ; no.179)
UDC 626/627 = DK 626/627 : Hydraulic (water) construction works = Wasserbau = Construction hydraulique. — 1977. — [2],25,[2] p ; 30cm. — (BS 1000[626/627] : 1977)
Pierced for binder. — Index.
ISBN 0-580-09666-1 Sd : £4.70
(B77-32356)

Universal Decimal Classification = Classification Décimale Universelle = Dezimalklassifikation. — English full ed. (4th international ed.). — London : British Standards Institution. — (BS1000 [681.5] : 1976)
UDC 681.5 = CDU 681.5 = DK 681.5 : Automatic control engineering = L'automatique = Regelungstechnik. — 1976. — [2],12,[2]p ; 30cm. — (Fédération internationale de documentation. Publications ; no.179)
Pierced for binder. — Index.
ISBN 0-580-09289-5 Sd : £3.60
(B77-10097)

025.4'3 — Documents. *Classification schedules. For school libraries*
Winslade, Brian Anthony John. Introduction to the Dewey Decimal Classification for British schools. — 3rd ed. / compiled by B.A.J. Winslade. — Albany, N.Y. : Forest Press for the School Library Association ; Oxford : [Distributed by the Association], 1977. — 176p : maps(on lining papers) ; 24cm.
Previous ed. / by Marjorie Chambers. London : Gresswell, 1968. — 'Based on Abridged Dewey Decimal Classification, Edition 10 ... [Lake Placid Club : Forest Press, 1971]' - title page verso. — Index.
ISBN 0-910608-18-0 : £3.00
(B77-30923)

025.4'3 — Documents. Subject classification schemes: Dewey Decimal Classification. 10th abridged edition. *Indexes. For school libraries in Buckinghamshire*
Buckinghamshire County Library. *School Library Service.* Subject index, secondary school edition : based on the 10th abridged edition of Dewey / Buckinghamshire County Library School Library Service. — [Aylesbury] ([Aylesbury, Bucks.]) : The Library, [1976]. — [1],30p ; 21cm.
ISBN 0-902805-54-1 Sd : Unpriced
(B77-01979)

025.4'6'616 — Man. Diseases. *Classification schedules*
World Organisation of National Colleges, Academies and Academic Associations of General Practitioners/Family Physicians. An international classification of the health problems of primary care / [World Organisation of National Colleges, Academies and Academic Associations of General Practitioners/Family Physicians]. — London (14 Princes Gate, Hyde Park, SW1 7PU) : 'Journal of the Royal College of General Practitioners', 1976. — [3],41,[2]p ; 25cm. — (Royal College of General Practitioners. 'Journal of the Royal College of General Practitioners' occasional papers ; 1 ISSN 0309-6300)
'[At] the fifth World Conference on General Practice/Family Medicine, in Melbourne, Australia in October 1972 ... The World Organisation of National Colleges, Academies and Academic Associations of General Practitioners/Family Physicians (WONCA) formed a working party ... [to develop the classification]. On 7 November 1974, the General Assembly of WONCA (at the sixth World Conference) unanimously accepted this classification' - p.11.
ISBN 0-85084-058-9 Sd : £2.25
(B77-14020)

025.4'6'616992 — Man. Tumours. *Classification schedules*
International classification of diseases for oncology : ICD-O. — Geneva : World Health Organization ; [London] : [H.M.S.O.], 1976. — [2],xxiii,131p ; 28cm.
'A number of working parties constituted by WHO and IARC [International Agency for Research on Cancer] contributed to the preparation of ICD-O' - Preface. — '... ICD-O represents an extension of Chaper II (Neoplasms) of the Ninth Revision of the "International Classification of Diseases" (ICD-9)' - Preface.
Pbk : Unpriced
ISBN 92-4154056-7
(B77-06431)

025.4'6'624 — Construction. Documents on construction. Classification. *Manuals*
CI/SFB construction indexing manual / [edited by] Alan Ray-Jones and David Clegg ; [for the] SFB Agency UK. — 3rd revised ed. — London : RIBA Publications, 1976. — 215p : ill, forms, plans ; 30cm.
Previous ed. published: as 'Construction indexing manual'. 1968. — Index.
ISBN 0-900630-51-5 Pbk : £8.00
(B77-01980)

025.4'6'65 — Business practices. Documents on business practices. Subject classification schemes: London Classification of Business Studies. Users. *Directories*
Bakewell, Kenneth Graham Bartlett. The London Classification of Business Studies : an introduction and directory of users / compiled by K.G.B. Bakewell and D.A. Cotton. — [Liverpool] (Tithebarn St., Liverpool L2 2ER) : Liverpool Polytechnic, Department of Library and Information Studies, 1976. — 17p ; 30cm. — (Liverpool Polytechnic. Department of Library and Information Studies. Occasional papers ; 76)
ISBN 0-901537-06-3 Pbk : £1.00
(B77-10098)

025.5 — LIBRARY SERVICES TO PATRONS
025.5 — Higher education institutions. Libraries. Guidance for users. *Great Britain. Reports, surveys*
Stevenson, M B. User education programmes : a study of their development, organization, methods and assessment / [by] M.B. Stevenson. — [London] : British Library ; Wetherby : Distributed by the British Library Lending Division, 1977. — [4],44p ; 30cm. — (British Library. Research and development reports ; no.5320 HC ISSN 0308-2385)
Bibl.: p.35.
ISBN 0-85350-140-8 Sp : £3.00
(B77-11530)

025.5 — Public libraries. Use. Surveys. *Great Britain, 1900-1976. Reports, surveys*
Ward, Martin L. Readers and library users : a study of reading habits and library use / [by] Martin L. Ward ; with an introduction by Bryan Luckham. — London : Library Association, 1977. — 96p ; 21cm.
Bibl.: p.91-95. — Index.
ISBN 0-85365-479-4 Pbk : £3.75(£3.00 to members of th5 Library Association) : CIP rev.
(B77-12269)

025.6 — LIBRARY CIRCULATION SERVICES
025.6 — Public libraries. Stock: Books. Postal lending. *United States. Manuals*
Kim, Choong H. Books by mail : a handbook for libraries / [by] Choong H. Kim. — Westport, Conn. ; London : Greenwood Press, 1977. — xiv,416,[1]p : ill, facsims, forms ; 25cm.
Index.
ISBN 0-8371-9029-0 : £15.75
(B77-33012)

025.6 — Universities. Libraries. Charging systems. Applications of digital computer systems. *Great Britain*
Tso, Pak Suet. Computer-based charging systems in British university libraries / by Pak Suet Tso. — [Loughborough] ([Loughborough, Leics. LE11 3TU]) : Loughborough University, 1977. — [5],98p : 1 ill ; 30cm. — (Loughborough University of Technology. Department of Library and Information Studies. Dissertation series ; no.1 ISSN 0309-6602)
ISBN 0-905867-00-9 Pbk : £3.00
(B77-17254)

025.8 — LIBRARIES. MAINTENANCE AND PRESERVATION OF COLLECTIONS
025.8 — Libraries. Stock. Relegation. *Great Britain. Reports, surveys*
Urquhart, J A. Relegation and stock control in libraries / by J.A. Urquhart and N.C. Urquhart. — Stocksfield [etc.] : Oriel Press, 1976. — [6],154p : ill ; 31cm.
Bibl.: p.146-153.
ISBN 0-85362-162-4 : £9.60
(B77-03320)

025.8'4'05 — Documents. Conservation. *Periodicals*
The **paper** conservator : journal of the IIC United Kingdom Group Paper Group. — London (The Editor, P.O. Box 17, WC1N 2PE) : Paper Group.
Vol.1- ; 1976-. — 1976. — ill, ports ; 30cm.
Annual. — [2],38p. in 1st issue. — English text, French abstracts.
Pbk : Free to members
ISSN 0309-4227
(B77-17868)

026 — SPECIAL LIBRARIES
026'.3 — Universities. Colleges. Libraries. *London. Westminster (London Borough). British Library of Political and Economic Science. Guidebooks*
British Library of Political and Economic Science. Outline of the resources of the library / British Library of Political and Economic Science. — 3rd ed. — London (Houghton St., WC2A 2AE) : The Library, 1976. — 43p : plans ; 22cm.
Previous ed.: 1972.
ISBN 0-903338-07-6 Sd : Unpriced
(B77-03321)

026'.3 — Universities. Libraries. *West Midlands (Metropolitan County). Coventry. University of Warwick (Library). Modern Records Centre. Stock*
University of Warwick. *Library. Modern Records Centre.* Guide to the Modern Records Centre, University of Warwick Library / compiled by Richard Storey & Janet Druker. — [Coventry] ([Gibbet Hill Rd, Coventry CV4 7AL]) : The Library, 1977. — 152p ; 21cm. — (University of Warwick. Library. Occasional publications ; no.2)
Index.
ISBN 0-903220-01-6 Pbk : £1.50
(B77-32357)

026'.30131 — Environmental records. Repositories. *Great Britain. Conference proceedings*
Conference on Centres for Environmental Records, *Leicester?, 1973.* Conference on Centres for Environmental Records, 30-31 March 1973 : papers presented at a conference organised by the Department of Adult Education at the University of Leicester in collaboration with the University Department of Museum Studies and the Biological Records Centre of the Nature Conservancy / edited by G. Stansfield. — [Leicester] ([The University, Leicester LE1 7RH]) : University of Leicester, Department of Adult Education, 1973. — [3], 78p,[2]leaves of plates(1 fold) : 1 ill, col map ; 30cm. — (Vaughan papers in adult education ; no.18 ISSN 0308-9258)
Cover title: Centres for environmental records. — Map (fold. leaf; [1] side) as insert.
ISBN 0-901507-05-9 Sd : £0.45
(B77-26743)

026'.34 — Law libraries. *Great Britain. Directories*
Directory of law libraries in the British Isles / [compiled and] edited by Barbara Mangles. — [Birmingham] ([c/o Harding Law Library, University of Birmingham, Birmingham B15 2TT]) : British and Irish Association of Law Librarians, 1976. — ix,150p ; 21cm.
Index.
ISBN 0-9502081-2-4 Pbk : £3.00
(B77-03322)

026'.34 — Law libraries. *Manuals*
Manual of law librarianship : the use and organization of legal literature / edited by Elizabeth M. Moys. — London : Deutsch for the British and Irish Association of Law Librarians, 1976. — 733p : ill, facsims, forms ; 23cm. — (A Grafton book)
Bibl. — Index.
ISBN 0-233-96735-4 : £15.00
(B77-01128)

026'.5 — National libraries. *Great Britain. British Library. Science Reference Library*
British Library. *Science Reference Library.* Guide to the Science Reference Library. — [New ed.]. — [London] ([25 Southampton Buildings, WC2A 1AW]) : [S.R.L.], [1976]. — 12p : 1 ill, 2 col maps ; 21cm.
Previous ed.: 1975.
ISBN 0-902914-32-4 Sd : Unpriced
(B77-05176)

026'.5 — Universities. Scientific libraries. *United States*
Mount, Ellis. University science and engineering libraries : their operation, collections, and facilities / [by] Ellis Mount. — Westport, Conn. ; London : Greenwood Press, 1975. — ix,214p ; 22cm. — (Contributions in librarianship and information science ; no.15)
Index.
ISBN 0-8371-7955-6 : £11.95
Also classified at 026'.62
(B77-18513)

026'.61 — Medical libraries. Cooperation. *Great Britain. Conference proceedings*
Library Association. *Medical Section. Annual Conference, University of Liverpool, 1976.* Regional medical library systems : papers given at the Annual Conference of the Medical Section of the Library Association, held at the University of Liverpool, 10th-13th September 1976. — London : Library Association, 1977. — v,78p : form ; 21cm.
ISBN 0-85365-399-2 Sd : £2.00(£1.60 to members of the Association)
(B77-26744)

026'.61 — Universities. Medical libraries. *West Midlands (Metropolitan County). Birmingham. Barnes Library, University of Birmingham. Guidebooks*
Barnes Library, *University of Birmingham.* Guide to the Barnes Medical Library. — Birmingham (P.O. Box 353, Birmingham B15 2TJ) : University of Birmingham Library, 1976. — [1],26p ; 21cm. — (Special guide ; no.B3)
ISBN 0-7044-0219-x Sd : £0.40
(B77-01981)

026'.62 — Universities. Engineering libraries. *United States*
Mount, Ellis. University science and engineering libraries : their operation, collections, and facilities / [by] Ellis Mount. — Westport, Conn. ; London : Greenwood Press, 1975. — ix,214p ; 22cm. — (Contributions in librarianship and information science ; no.15)
Index.
ISBN 0-8371-7955-6 : £11.95
Primary classification 026'.5
(B77-18513)

026'.9411 — Libraries. Local history collections. *Scotland*
Armstrong, Norma E S. Local collections in Scotland / by Norma E.S. Armstrong. — Glasgow (18 Crosslees Park, Thornliebank, Glasgow G46 7DX) : Scottish Library Association, 1977. — ix,174p : map ; 23cm. — (Scottish library studies ; no.5)
ISBN 0-900649-15-1 : £8.50 : CIP rev. (£7.50 to members of the Scottish Library Association)
(B77-30924)

026'.947 — Libraries. Stock: Documents on Eastern Europe. *North America. Directories*
East Central and Southeast Europe : a handbook of library and archival resources in North America / Paul L. Horechy chief editor, David H. Kraus associate editor. — Santa Barbara ; Oxford : Clio Press, [1975]. — xi,468p ; 26cm. — (Joint Committee on Eastern Europe. Publication series ; no.3)
Index.
ISBN 0-87436-214-8 : £21.00
(B77-25350)

026'.947 — Universities. *West Midlands (Metropolitan County). Birmingham. University of Birmingham. Libraries. Stock: Documents on Eastern Europe & Soviet Union*
University of Birmingham. Russian and East European holdings of the University of Birmingham : a reader's guide / University of Birmingham. — 2nd ed. / by J.J. Brine and T. Hnik ; edited by T. Hnik. — [Birmingham] ([Superintendent of Reader Services, P.O. Box 363, Birmingham B15 2TT]) : University of Birmingham [Library], 1976. — [4],81p : forms, plan ; 21cm. — (University of Birmingham. Library. Special guides ; no.13 ISSN 0306-2031)

Previous ed.: published as 'Russian and East European library materials at the University of Birmingham' / University of Birmingham Library. 1972.
ISBN 0-7044-0221-1 Sp : £1.20
(B77-24654)

026'.95 — Libraries. Stock: Documents associated with oriental countries. *Great Britain. Conference proceedings*
Standing Conference of National and University Libraries. *Group of Orientalist Libraries. Annual Conference, Durham, 1977.* Report of the Annual Conference held at the University of Durham, 6th-7th January 1977 [of the] SCONUL Group of Orientalist Libraries. — [Hull] ([c/o Miss B.E. Moon, The Brynmor Jones Library, University of Hull, Hull]) : The Group, 1977. — [2],43p ; 30cm.
ISBN 0-85958-505-0 Sd : Unpriced
ISSN 0309-3727
(B77-19978)

026'.95 — National libraries. *Great Britain. British Library. Department of Oriental Manuscripts and Printed Books. Guidebooks*
British Library. *Department of Oriental Manuscripts and Printed Books.* Guide to the Department of Oriental Manuscripts and Printed Books / compiled by H.J. Goodacre and A.P. Pritchard. — London : British Museum Publications Ltd for the British Library, 1977. — 3-72p : ill, facsims ; 24cm.
Bibl.: p.15-16.
ISBN 0-7141-0658-5 Pbk : £1.50
(B77-26745)

026'.954 — Great Britain. Foreign and Commonwealth Office. Libraries: India Office Library. *Reports, surveys. Serials*
India Office Library. India Office Library and Records : report for the year. — London ([197 Blackfriars Rd, SE1 8NG]) : Foreign and Commonwealth Office.
1974. — 1976. — [5],103p,plate : ill(incl 1 col), facsim, port ; 25cm.
ISBN 0-903359-13-8 Pbk : Unpriced
Also classified at 026'.954
(B77-00579)

026'.954 — Great Britain. Foreign and Commonwealth Office. Public records. Repositories: India Office Record Office. *Reports, surveys. Serials*
India Office Library. India Office Library and Records : report for the year. — London ([197 Blackfriars Rd, SE1 8NG]) : Foreign and Commonwealth Office.
1974. — 1976. — [5],103p,plate : ill(incl 1 col), facsim, port ; 25cm.
ISBN 0-903359-13-8 Pbk : Unpriced
Primary classification 026'.954
(B77-00579)

026'.954 — Libraries. Stock: Documents on South Asia. *North America. Conference proceedings*
Boston Conference on South Asian Library Resources in North America, *1974.* South Asian library resources in North America : papers from the Boston Conference, 1974 [organized by the] Committee on South Asian Libraries and Documentation of the Association for Asian Studies / edited by Maureen L.P. Patterson and Martin Yanuck. — Zug : Inter Documentation Company AG ; London : Inter Documentation Company UK Ltd, 1975. — [10],362p : map ; 21cm. — (Bibliotheca Asiatica ; 11)
'... a product of the proceedings of the Boston Conference on South Asian Library Resources in North America held from April 4th to 6th, 1974' - Preface. — Also available on microfiche. — Bibl.
Unpriced
ISBN 3-85750-010-7
(B77-11525)

026'.954 — Libraries. Stock: Documents on South Asia. *North America. Reports, surveys*
South Asian library resources in North America : a survey / prepared for the Boston Conference, 1974 ; edited by Maureen L.P. Patterson ; [for the] Committee on South Asian Libraries and Documentation of the Association for Asian Studies. — Zug : Inter Documentation Company AG ; London : Inter Documentation Company UK Ltd, 1975. — [5],223p : maps ; 21cm. — (Bibliotheca Asiatica ; 12)
Also available on microfiche.
Unpriced
ISBN 3-85750-011-5
(B77-11526)

026'.96 — Documents with African imprints. Bibliographic control. *Conference proceedings*
Progress in African bibliography : SCOLMA conference [held at the] Commonwealth Institute, London, 17-18 March 1977, proceedings. — [London] : SCOLMA, 1977. — 318p in various pagings ; 21cm.
Bibl.
ISBN 0-904090-02-7 Pbk : £5.00
(B77-28338)

027 — GENERAL LIBRARIES
027'.047'31 — Archives & manuscripts. Repositories. *Russia (RSFSR). Moscow. Guidebooks*
Grimsted, Patricia Kennedy. Archives and manuscript repositories in the USSR : Moscow and Leningrad / [by] Patricia Kennedy Grimsted. — Princeton : Princeton University Press, 1973.
Supplement 1 : Bibliographical addenda. — Zug : Inter Documentation Company ; London (c/o Inter Documentation Company BV The Netherlands, Uiterstegracht 45, Leiden, The Netherlands) : Inter Documentation Company UK Ltd, 1976. — [4],xiv,203p ; 25cm. — (Bibliotheca slavica ; 9)
Index.
Unpriced
Also classified at 027'.047'45
(B77-05832)

027'.047'45 — Archives & manuscripts. Repositories. *Russia (RSFSR). Leningrad. Guidebooks*
Grimsted, Patricia Kennedy. Archives and manuscript repositories in the USSR : Moscow and Leningrad / [by] Patricia Kennedy Grimsted. — Princeton : Princeton University Press, 1973.
Supplement 1 : Bibliographical addenda. — Zug : Inter Documentation Company ; London (c/o Inter Documentation Company BV The Netherlands, Uiterstegracht 45, Leiden, The Netherlands) : Inter Documentation Company UK Ltd, 1976. — [4],xiv,203p ; 25cm. — (Bibliotheca slavica ; 9)
Index.
Unpriced
Primary classification 027'.047'31
(B77-05832)

027.2 — PROPRIETARY LIBRARIES
027'.2'0942 — Independent libraries. *England. Reports, surveys*
Francis, *Sir* **Frank Chalton.** Independent libraries in England : a survey of selected institutional, proprietary and endowed libraries, October 1973-December 1975 : report presented to the Council on Library Resources, Washington / project director Sir Frank Francis ; research associate Valerie Bloomfield. — London ([c/o The Vine, Nether Winchendon, Aylesbury, Bucks. HP18 0DY]) : [The author], 1976. — [2],143p,[2] leaves ; 30cm.
Bibl.: p.92-94.
Sp : Unpriced
(B77-09467)

027.4 — PUBLIC LIBRARIES
027.4'025'411 — Library authorities. *Scotland. Directories*
Directory of public library authorities and school library services in Scotland / [the National Library of Scotland]. — Edinburgh ([George IV Bridge, Edinburgh, EH1 1EW]) : National Library of Scotland, Lending Services.
1976. — 1976. — [1],16p ; 30cm.
ISBN 0-902474-02-2 Sd : Unpriced
(B77-03323)

027.4'09173 — Public libraries. *Sparsely populated regions. Conference proceedings*
Anglo-Scandinavian Public Library Conference, *8th, Brighton, 1976.* Service points in sparsely populated areas : papers and discussions of the conference held at Brighton, England, 7-11 May 1976, with a report on the study tour / edited by Colston Hartley. — London : Library Association, 1976. — 47p ; 21cm.
'Eighth Anglo-Scandinavian Public Library Conference'.
ISBN 0-85365-189-2 Sd : £1.00
(B77-03880)

027.4'41 — Public libraries. *Great Britain. Statistics*
Public library statistics. Actuals / the Chartered Institute of Public Finance and Accountancy [and] the Society of County Treasurers. — London : C.I.P.F.A. ; Reading : The Society.
1974-75. — 1976. — iv,35p ; 21x26cm.
At head of title: Statistical Information Service. — Page width varies.
Sd : £2.50
(B77-05833)

027.4'41 — Public libraries. *Great Britain, to 1975*
Kelly, Thomas, *b.1909.* Books for the people : an illustrated history of the British public library / [by] Thomas Kelly ; illustrations selected by Edith Kelly. — London : Deutsch, 1977. — 271p : ill, facsims, maps, plan, ports ; 29cm.
Bibl. — Index.
ISBN 0-233-96795-8 : £15.00
(B77-19979)

Kelly, Thomas, *b.1909.* A history of public libraries in Great Britain, 1845-1975 / by Thomas Kelly. — 2nd ed. (revised). — London : Library Association, 1977. — xiii, 582p,xvi p of plates : ill, map, plans, ports ; 26cm.
Previous ed.: 1973. — Bibl.: p.533-553. — Index.
ISBN 0-85365-239-2 : £13.75(£11.00 to members of the Library Association) : CIP rev.
(B77-07030)

027.4'41 — Public libraries. Political aspects. *Great Britain. Socialist viewpoints*
O'Kelly, Joss. The political role of public libraries / [by] Joss O'Kelly. — Brighton : Smoothie Publications, 1975. — [2],14,[2]p ; 30cm.
Bibl.
ISBN 0-903612-38-0 Sd : £1.00
(B77-00005)

O'Kelly, Joss. The political role of public libraries / [by] Joss O'Kelly. — Revised ed. — Brighton : Noyce, 1977. — [3],16p ; 30cm.
Previous ed.: Brighton : Smoothie Publications, 1975. — Bibl.: p.15-16.
Sd : £1.20
(B77-29129)

027.4'421 — Public libraries. *London, to 1914*
Ball, Alan William. The public libraries of Greater London : a pictorial history, 1856-1914 / [by] Alan W. Ball. — London ([c/o Vaughan Whibley, 65 Glentrammon Rd, Green Street Green, Orpington, Kent]) : Library Association, London and Home Counties Branch, 1977. — 108p : ill, facsims, map, plans, ports ; 31cm.
Bibl.: p.107-108. — Index.
ISBN 0-902119-17-6 : £5.50
ISBN 0-902119-18-4 Pbk : £3.00
(B77-23955)

027.4'714'281 — Public libraries. *Quebec (Province). Montreal. Fraser-Hickson Institute, to 1976*
Moodey, Edgar C. The Fraser-Hickson library : an informal history / by Edgar C. Moodey ; with a foreword by Edgar Andrew Collard. — London : Bingley, 1977. — viii,224p,[16]p of plates : ill, map, ports ; 23cm.
Map on lining papers. — Bibl.: p.216-218. — Index.
ISBN 0-85157-233-2 : £6.00
(B77-14522)

027.5 — GOVERNMENT LIBRARIES
027.541 — Great Britain. Parliament. House of Lords. Record Office. *Reports, surveys. Serials*
Great Britain. *Parliament. House of Lords. Record Office.* Report / [House of Lords Record Office]. — [London] ([Westminster, SW1A 0PW]) : The Record Office.
1976. — 1977. — [1],22p ; 30cm. — (Memorandum ; no.57)
ISBN 0-902614-04-5 Sd : Unpriced
(B77-12268)

027.541 — National libraries. *Great Britain. British Library. Lending Division. Use. Manuals*
British Library. *Lending Division.* Users' handbook / the British Library, Lending Division. — 2nd ed. — [Boston Spa] : [B.L.L.D.], 1977. — [1],v,26,[1]p : ill, forms ; 21x30cm.
Previous ed.: 1974. — Index.
Sd : Unpriced
(B77-23060)

027.541 — National libraries. *Great Britain. British Library. Reports, surveys. Serials*
British Library. Annual report / British Library. — London (Store St., WC1E 7DG) : British Library Board.
1975-76 : 3rd. — [1976]. — 48p : 3 ill(incl 1 col) ; 24cm.
Bibl.: p.42-45. — Index.
ISBN 0-904654-07-9 Sd : Unpriced
ISSN 0305-7887
(B77-00580)

027.541 — National libraries. *Great Britain. National Central Library, to 1973*
Filon, S P L. The National Central Library : an experiment in library co-operation / [by] S.P.L. Filon. — London : Library Association, 1977. — xv,300p,[8]p of plates : ill, ports ; 22cm.
'A Library Association centenary volume'. — Bibl.: p.273-288. — Index.
ISBN 0-85365-249-x : £7.50(£6.00 to members of the L.A.) : CIP rev.
(B77-07766)

027.541 — Public records. Repositories. *Great Britain. Public Record Office. Reports, surveys. Serials*
Public Record Office. Annual report of the Keeper of Public Records on the work of the Public Record Office ; and, the report of the Advisory Council on Public Records [for the] Lord Chancellor's Office. — London : H.M.S.O.
18th : 1976. — [1977]. — iii,32p ; 25cm. — ([1976-77 H.C.]323)
ISBN 0-10-232377-1 Sd : £0.60
(B77-15661)

027.5411 — National libraries. *Scotland. National Library of Scotland. Reports, surveys. Serials*
National Library of Scotland. Annual report / National Library of Scotland. — Edinburgh ([George IV Bridge, Edinburgh 1]) : [The Library].
1975-76. — 1976. — vi,70p ; 21cm.
ISBN 0-902220-17-9 Sd : £1.50
(B77-01129)

027.5421 — Records. Repositories. *London. Greater London Record Office. Reports, surveys. Serials*
Greater London Record Office. Greater London Record Office and Library report. — [London] : Greater London Council.
1975. — [1976]. — [1],28p ; 21cm.
ISBN 0-7168-0834-x Sd : £0.30
ISSN 0308-0811
(B77-15064)

027.5422'792 — Records. Repositories. *Hampshire. Portsmouth. Portsmouth City Record Office. Periodicals*
Portsmouth archives review. — Portsmouth (3 Museum Rd, Portsmouth) : Portsmouth City Record Office.
Vol.1- ; 1976-. — [1977]-. — 21cm.
Annual. — [2],72p. in 1st issue.
Sd : £0.75
ISSN 0309-2828
(B77-10099)

027.5423'15 — Records. Repositories. *Wiltshire. Trowbridge. Wiltshire County Record Office. Reports, surveys. Serials*
Wiltshire records : annual report of the Records Sub-committee of Wiltshire County Council. — [Trowbridge] ([County Record Office, County Hall, Trowbridge, Wilts.]) : [The Sub-committee].
1975. — [1976]. — [2],16p : facsims, map ; 21cm.
Bibl.: p.15-16.
ISBN 0-901562-03-3 Sd : Unpriced
(B77-01982)

027.6 — LIBRARIES FOR SPECIAL GROUPS AND SPECIFIC ORGANISATIONS
027.6'62'094271 — Hospitals. Libraries. *Cheshire. Reports, surveys*
Pattinson, Michael. Library and information services to the Cheshire Area Health Authority : a report / by Michael Pattinson. — [Chester] ([91 Hoole Rd, Chester OH2 3NG]) : Cheshire County Libraries ; [Chester] : Cheshire Area Health Authority, [1976]. — [5], 57[i.e.59]p,[2]leaves : col map(fold) ; 30cm.
ISBN 0-904532-30-5 Pbk : £2.00
Also classified at 029'.9'61
(B77-00581)

027.6'63 — Libraries for blind persons. *State-of-the-art reviews*
Schauder, Donald E. Libraries for the blind : an international study of policies and practices / [by] Donald E. Schauder and Malcolm D. Cram. — Stevenage : Peregrinus, 1977. — vi, 152p ; 24cm. — (Librarianship and information studies ; vol.4)
Bibl.: p.119-142. — Index.
ISBN 0-901223-91-3 : £7.90
(B77-23061)

027.6'7'0942446 — Cathedrals. Libraries. *Hereford and Worcester. Hereford. Hereford Cathedral. Chained Library*
Morgan, Frederick Charles. Hereford Cathedral Chained Library : a short account / by F.C. and Penelope E. Morgan. — 2nd revised ed. — [Hereford] ([Hereford Cathedral, Hereford]) : Hereford Cathedral Library, 1977. — [8]p : ill ; 22cm.
Previous ed.: published as 'Hereford Cathedral - a short account of the Chained Library'. Hereford : Hereford Cathedral, 1973. — Bibl.: p.[8].
Sd : Unpriced
(B77-32358)

027.7 — COLLEGE AND UNIVERSITY LIBRARIES
027.7 — Community colleges. Libraries. *United States*
Veit, Fritz. The community college library / [by] Fritz Veit. — Westport, Conn. ; London : Greenwood Press, 1975. — xiv,223p : ill, plans ; 22cm. — (Contributions in librarianship and information science ; no.14)
Index.
ISBN 0-8371-6412-5 : £10.45
(B77-15662)

027.7'05 — Universities. Libraries. *Periodicals*
International Association of Technological University Libraries. Proceedings / International Association of Technological University Libraries. — [Loughborough] (c/o Library, University of Technology, Loughborough, Leics.) : [I.A.T.U.L.].
[Vol.1, no.1]-. — [196- ?]-. — 30cm.
Cover title. — 49p. in vol. 8, 1976. — Bibl.: p.46-49.
Pbk : £1.20
ISSN 0018-8476
(B77-08722)

027.7412'92 — Universities. Libraries. *Scotland. Fife Region. St Andrews. University of St Andrews. Library. Guidebooks*
University of St Andrews. *Library.* University of St Andrews Library, 1976 / [prepared by the project architects and the staff of the University Library]. — [St Andrews] ([St Andrews, Fife]) : The Library, 1977. — [23]p : ill, plans ; 15x18cm.
ISBN 0-900897-02-3 Sd : £0.50
(B77-14523)

027.7414'57 — Colleges. Libraries. *Scotland. Strathclyde Region. Hamilton. Bell College. Library. Periodicals*
Bell College. *Library.* Bulletin / Bell College of Technology Library. — [Hamilton] ([Hamilton, Lanarkshire]) : [The Library].
No.1- ; 1977-. — [1977]-. — ill ; 30cm.
Three issues a year. — [3],34p. in 1st issue.
Sd : £1.50 yearly
ISSN 0309-6033
(B77-18514)

027.7429'61 — Universities. Colleges. Libraries. *Dyfed. Aberystwyth. University College of Wales. Library, to 1976*
Lloyd, T G. The College Library, 1872-1976 / [by T.G. Lloyd]. — Aberystwyth : University College of Wales, 1977. — [2],18p : ill ; 21cm.
ISBN 0-904222-08-x Sd : £0.50
(B77-26079)

027.7429'61 — Universities. Colleges. Libraries. *Dyfed. Aberystwyth. University College of Wales. Library, to 1976. Welsh texts*
Lloyd, T G. Llyfrgell y Coleg, 1872-1976 / [gan T.G. Lloyd]. — Aberystwyth : University College of Wales, 1977. — [2],18p : ill ; 21cm.
ISBN 0-904222-09-8 Sd : £0.50
(B77-26080)

028.5 — READING OF YOUNG PEOPLE
028.5 — Children's books. *Critical studies*
Smith, Lillian H. The unreluctant years : a critical approach to children's literature / by Lillian H. Smith. — Harmondsworth [etc.] : Penguin, 1976. — 3-193p ; 20cm.
Originally published: Chicago : American Library Association, 1953. — Bibl. — Index.
ISBN 0-14-004456-6 Pbk : Unpriced
(B77-24655)

028.5 — Children's books, 1900-1975. *Readings*
The **cool** web : the pattern of children's reading / [edited by] Margaret Meek, Aidan Warlow, Griselda Barton. — London [etc.] : Bodley Head, 1977. — [4],427p ; 23cm.
Bibl.: p.399-418. — Index.
ISBN 0-370-10863-9 : £7.50
(B77-09468)

028.52 — Books for multiracial school students. *Lists*
Elkin, Judith. Books for the multi-racial classroom : a select list of children's books, showing the backgrounds of the Indian sub-continent and the West Indies. — 2nd (revised) ed. / compiled by Judith Elkin. — London : National Book League ; Birmingham (c/o Miss L. Hopkins, Central Children's Library, Paradise, Birmingham B3 3HQ) : Library Association Youth Libraries Group, 1976. — [1],112,[1]p : ill ; 22cm. — (Library Association. Youth Libraries Group. Pamphlets ; no.17)
Previous ed.: / compiled by Judith Elkin in collaboration with Birmingham Public Libraries. Birmingham : Library Association, Youth Libraries Group, 1971. — Index.
ISBN 0-85365-069-1 Sd : £1.00
(B77-26081)

028.52 — Books for partially sighted children: Books with British imprints. *Lists*
Marshall, Margaret Richardson. Seeing clear : books suitable for the partially sighted child / selected and annotated by Margaret R. Marshall. — [Oxford] : School Library Association, 1977. — vi,24p ; 21cm. — (School Library Association. Lists)
Index.
ISBN 0-900641-31-2 Sd : £1.40(£1.00 to members of the School Library Association)
(B77-26082)

028.52 — Children's books. *Bibliographies. Serials*
Children's books of the year. — London : Hamilton [for] the National Book League and the British Council.
1976 / selected and annotated by Elaine Moss. — 1977. — 144p : ill ; 22cm.
Index.
ISBN 0-241-89620-7 Pbk : £2.00
(B77-22309)

028.52 — Children's books: Books for children, 6-9 years: Books with British imprints. *Bibliographies*
Sherrard-Smith, Barbara. Read & find out, information books, 6-9 / chosen and annotated by Barbara Sherrard-Smith. — Revised ed. — London : National Book League, 1976. — 26p ; 21cm.
Previous ed.: 1975.
ISBN 0-85353-257-5 Sd : £0.40(£0.30 to members)
(B77-11035)

028.52 — Children's stories in English. Australian writers. to 1972. *Bibliographies*
Muir, Marcie. A bibliography of Australian children's books / [by] Marcie Muir. — London : Deutsch.
Vol. 2. — 1976. — 554p,[20]p of plates : ill(some col), facsims(some col) ; 24cm. — (A Grafton book)
Index.
ISBN 0-233-96743-5 : £17.50
(B77-01130)

028.52 — English language. Reading books for primary school students. *Bibliographies*
Moon, Cliff. Individualised reading : comparative lists of selected books for young readers / [by] Cliff Moon. — [6th ed. completely revised]. — [Reading] ([29 Eastern Ave., Reading RG1 5RU]) : Centre for the Teaching of Reading, School of Education, University of Reading, [1976]. — [2],22p ; 30cm.
Previous ed.: 1975 or 6. — Index.
ISBN 0-7049-0398-9 Sd : Unpriced
(B77-07767)

028.7 — USE OF BOOKS AND OTHER RECORDS AS SOURCES OF INFORMATION
028.7 — Reference books. Use. *Secondary school texts*
Fergus, Andrew. Finding out from books / [by] Andrew Fergus. — Amersham : Hulton, 1977. — 96p : ill(some col), chart, facsims, maps(some col), ports ; 26cm.
ISBN 0-7175-0751-3 Pbk : £1.70
(B77-16153)

028.9 — READING INTERESTS AND HABITS
028'.9 — Librarianship. Morgan, Frederick Charles. Reading habits, 1882-1900
Morgan, Frederick Charles. Stratford-upon-Avon, a 19th century library and my reading from the age of 4 to 20 years / by Frederick Charles Morgan. — Hereford (1A The Cloisters, Hereford HR1 2NG) : The author, 1977. — 22, [1]p,leaf of plate,[4]p of plates : ill, facsims, port ; 22cm.
Sd : £0.50
(B77-32359)

029 — DOCUMENTATION
029 — Information. Dissemination. *Forecasts*
Harvey, Peter, *b.1919.* The future of professional information services / [by] Peter Harvey. — [Bradford] ([200 Keighley Rd, Bradford, W. Yorkshire BD9 4JZ]) : MCB, [1976]. — [4],42, ii p,plate : 1 ill ; 30cm. — (Library research occasional paper ; no.2 ISSN 0309-2232)
Bibl.: p.ii.
ISBN 0-903763-97-4 Sd : £4.50
(B77-07768)

029 — Information services. *Manuals*
Arnold, Denis Victor. The management of the information department / [by] Denis V. Arnold. — London : Deutsch [for] the Institute of Information Scientists, 1976. — 143p : plans ; 23cm. — (Institute of Information Scientists. Monograph series) (A Grafton book)
Bibl.: p.131-137. — Index.
ISBN 0-233-96652-8 : £3.95
(B77-01983)

029'.03 — Documentation. *Glossaries*
British Standards Institution. Glossary of documentation terms = Glossaire de termes relatifs à la documentation = Glossar von Dokumentationsbegriffen / British Standards Institution. — London : B.S.I., 1976. — [2], 81p ; 30cm. — (BS5408 : 1976)
Pierced for binder.
ISBN 0-580-09407-3 Sd : £7.50
(B77-05834)

029'.05 — Information science. *Periodicals*
Journal of informatics. — London (Gower St., WC1E 6BT) : School of Library, Archive and Information Studies, University College London.
Vol.1, no.1- ; Apr. 1977-. — 1977. — ill ; 30cm.
Three issues a year. — [2],53p. in 1st issue. — Bibl.
Sd : £3.50 yearly(£7.00 to libraries)
ISSN 0309-5657
(B77-25352)

029'.07 — Information services. Users. Training. *Great Britain. Reports, surveys*
Review Committee on Education for Information Use. Review Committee on Education for Information Use - final report. — [London] : British Library ; London (Sheraton House, Great Chapel St., W1V 4BH) : Distributed by British Library Research and Development Department, 1977. — [4],26p ; 30cm. — (British Library. Research and development reports ; no.5325 HC ISSN 0308-2385)
Bibl.: p.21.
ISBN 0-85350-147-5 Sp : £2.00 : CIP rev.
(B77-07031)

029.5 — INDEXING
029.5 — Documents. Indexes. *Standards*
British Standards Institution. Recommendations, the preparation of indexes to books, periodicals and other publications = Récommandations pour la préparation des indexes des livres, périodiques et d'autres publications = Empfehlungen für die Aufstellung von Inhaltsverzeichnissen für Bücher, Zeitschriften und sonstige Veröffentlichungen / British Standards Institution. — 1st revision. — London : B.S.I., 1976. — [2],10,[2]p ; 30cm. — (BS3700 : 1976)
Pierced for binder. — Index.
ISBN 0-580-09271-2 Sd : £3.60
(B77-17255)

029.5 — Information retrieval. Use of edge-coded cards
Day, Arthur Colin. Getting the edge on card files / by A.C. Day. — High Wycombe (Horsleys Green, Stokenchurch, High Wycombe, Bucks. HP14 3XL) : Summer Institute of Linguistics, 1976. — 61p : ill ; 26cm. — (Introduction to practical linguistics)
Sp : £0.80
(B77-07032)

029.7 — MECHANISED STORAGE, SEARCH, AND RETRIEVAL OF INFORMATION
029.7 — Automated bibliographic data processing systems. *Conference proceedings*
Information systems and networks : eleventh annual symposium, March 27-29, 1974 / edited by John Sherrod. — Westport, Conn. ; London : Greenwood Press [for] Informatics Incorporated, 1975. — x,200,[1]p : ill ; 24cm.
'The papers in this volume constitute the Proceedings of a symposium co-sponsored by Informatics Inc., and the University of California at Los Angeles and held on the Westwood campus, March 27-29, 1974' - Foreword. — Bibl.
ISBN 0-8371-7717-0 : £10.25
(B77-15663)

029.7 — Bibliographic data. Information retrieval. Applications of minicomputer systems. *Feasibility studies*
Hyman, Mike. Mini-computers and bibliographic information retrieval / [by] Mike Hyman and Eleanor Wallis. — [London] : British Library ; Boston Spa : Distributed by Publications Dept, British Library Lending Division, 1976. — [9], 122p : ill ; 30cm. — (British Library. Research and development reports ; no.5305 HC ISSN 0308-2385)
ISBN 0-85350-144-0 Sp : £5.00
(B77-07033)

029.7 — Information retrieval. Applications of digital computer systems
Paice, C D. Information retrieval and the computer / [by] C.D. Paice. — London : Macdonald and Jane's, 1977. — [10],206p : ill, 2 forms ; 23cm. — (Computer monographs)
Bibl.: p.201-202. — Index.
ISBN 0-354-04095-2 : £5.95
(B77-33013)

029.7 — Information retrieval systems using digital computer systems
Wessel, Andrew E. The social use of information : ownership and access / [by] Andrew E. Wessel. — New York ; London [etc.] : Wiley, 1976. — xix,244p : ill ; 24cm. — (Information sciences series)
'A Wiley-Interscience publication'. — Index.
ISBN 0-471-93377-5 : £12.30
(B77-01984)

029.7 — National libraries. *Great Britain. British Library. On-line information processing systems: BLAISE. Manuals*
British Library. *Bibliographic Services Division.* BLAISE user manual / [British Library, Bibliographic Services Division]. — London (The British Library, BLAISE, 7 Rathbone St., W1P 2AL) : The Division, 1977. — 1v. ; 32cm.
In binder. — At head of title: British Library Automated Information Service. — 115p. in various pagings on publication.
ISBN 0-900220-66-x Ls : £10.00 : CIP rev.
(B77-08723)

029.7 — National libraries. *Great Britain. British Library. On-line information processing systems: BLAISE. Periodicals*
British Library. The British Library BLAISE newsletter. — London (7 Rathbone St., W1P 2AL) : British Library, BLAISE.
No.1- ; June 1977-. — [1977]. — 30cm.
[1],13p. in 1st issue.
Sd : Free to registered BLAISE subscribers
ISSN 0309-796x
(B77-19980)

029.7 — On-line bibliographic information retrieval systems. Use. *Research reports*
Baker, C A. An investigation of man-computer interaction in an online bibliographic information retrieval system / by C.A. Baker. — [Loughborough] ([Loughborough, Leics.]) : Loughborough University of Technology Library, 1977. — [10],112p,fold leaf : ill ; 30cm.
Bibl.: p.111-112.
Pbk : Unpriced
(B77-31664)

029.7 — On-line information retrieval services. *For management*
Akeroyd, John. Online information services : a managers guide / [by] John Akeroyd. — Hatfield : Hertis, 1977. — [3],29p : 1 ill ; 21cm. — (Hertis. Occasional papers ; no.8)
Bibl.: p.22-24.
ISBN 0-85267-115-6 Sd : £1.00
(B77-29130)

029.7 — On-line information retrieval services: DIALOG. *Manuals*
Vickery, A. How to use Dialog (Lockheed Research Laboratory) : users' manual / compiled by A. Vickery. — [London] ([Senate House, Malet St., WC1E 7HU]) : Central Information Services, Library Resources Co-ordinating Committee, University of London, 1976. — [1],10p : ill ; 30cm.
ISBN 0-7187-0433-9 Sp : £0.50
(B77-12822)

029.7 — Universities. Libraries. *Leicestershire. Loughborough. Loughborough University of Technology. Library. Information services on interdisciplinary subjects. Applications of automated information processing systems. Reports, surveys*
Loughborough University of Technology. *Library.* Automated library processes and interdisciplinary information studies / Loughborough University of Technology Library. — [Loughborough] ([Loughborough, Leics. LE11 3TU]) : [The Library].
Part 1 : Automated library processes : general / [by] M.E. Robinson and R.A. Wall. — 1975. — [3],92[i.e. 106]p : ill, facsims, form ; 30cm. — (LUT/LIB/R9)
Pbk : £2.50
(B77-01133)

Part 3 : Interdisciplinary information studies / [by] P.M. Linn. — 1975. — [4],43[i.e. 48]p : ill, facsims ; 30cm. — (LUT/LIB/R11)
Pbk : £1.50
(B77-01131)

Part 2 : Automated library processes : applications of the Plessey Data Capture Unit / [by] R.A. Wall and M.E. Robinson. — 1975. — [3],114[i.e. 143]p : ill, facsims ; 30cm. — (LUT/LIB/R10)
Pbk : £3.50
(B77-01132)

029.9 — DOCUMENTATION OF SPECIFIC SUBJECTS
029'.9'3 — Social sciences: Documents on social sciences. Citations. Collection & coding. *Reports, surveys*
Ritchie, Maureen. The collection and construction of a file of citation data / by Maureen Ritchie and David Nicholas. — [London] : Polytechnic of North London ; [Bath] : Bath University [Library], 1976. — [1], vi,83p : form ; 30cm. — (Design of Information Systems in the Social Sciences. Research reports : series B ; no.5 ISSN 0305-8379)
ISBN 0-900843-49-7 Sd : £3.00
(B77-16154)

029'.9'32841 — Great Britain. Parliament. House of Commons. Library. Stock. Indexing. Applications of digital computer systems. *Proposals*
Great Britain. *Parliament. House of Commons. Select Committee on House of Commons (Services).* Computer-based indexing for the Library : fifth report from the Select Committee on House of Commons (Services), session 1976-77, together with the minutes of evidence taken before the Library Sub-committee on 30 March and 5 April and an appendix. — London : H.M.S.O., [1977]. — xv,33p ; 25cm. — ([1976-77 H.C.]377)
ISBN 0-10-237777-4 Sd : £0.85
(B77-22310)

029'.9'33 — Information on economics. Information retrieval & dissemination. *Conference proceedings*
Organization and Retrieval of Economic Knowledge *(Conference), Kiel, 1975.* The organization and retrieval of economic knowledge : proceedings of a conference held by the International Economic Association at Kiel, West Germany / edited by Mark Perlman. — London [etc.] : Macmillan, 1977. — xiii,520p : ill ; 23cm.
'... the International Economics Association Kiel Symposium on "The Organization and Retrieval of Economic Knowledge"...' - Introduction. — Bibl. — Index.
ISBN 0-333-21707-1 : £20.00
(B77-25354)

029'.9'3326202541 — Information services on stockbroking. *Great Britain. Directories*
Hilton, K Patience. Stockbrokers' research and information services available to non-investor clients / compiled by K. Patience Hilton, John G. Watson. — [Oxford] ([Kennington, Oxford OX1 5NY]) : Oxford Centre for Management Studies, 1977. — xvi p ; 21cm.
Bibl. — Index.
Sd : £1.50
(B77-29131)

029'.9'338 — Information services for industries. *Forecasts for 1980. Conference proceedings*
Information in the 1980's : proceedings of an Aslib seminar for information planners and industry, held 13-14 May 1976 at the Bell House Hotel, Beaconsfield / edited by L.J. Anthony. — London : Aslib, 1976. — [4],98p : ill, map ; 30cm.
Bibl.: p.38-39.
ISBN 0-85142-086-9 Pbk : £5.00(£4.00 to Aslib members)
(B77-07769)

029'.9'352041 — Local authorities. Information services. Requirements. *Great Britain. Reports, surveys*
Local Authorities Management Services and Computer Committee. *Working Party on Information Requirements.* Information, what local governors need to know / [Local Authorities Management Services and Computer Committee Working Party on Information Requirements]. — London : L.A.M.S.A.C., 1976. — [1],24,[1]p ; 30cm.
'Interim report of the General Management Panel of LAMSAC' - note.
ISBN 0-85497-092-4 Sd : £2.00
(B77-12271)

029'.9'37 — Education. Documents on education. Information retrieval services using digital computer systems. Machine-readable files: ERIC data base. Searching. Use of DIALOG. *Manuals*
Wiseman, Devra. Searching ERIC on-line using Dialog : users' manual / by D. Wiseman. — [London] ([Senate House, Malet St., WC1E 7HU]) : Central Information Services, Library Resources Co-ordinating Committee, University of London, 1976. — [1],19p : facsims ; 30cm.
Bibl.: p.19.
ISBN 0-7187-0434-7 Sp : £0.50
(B77-12823)

029'.9'5 — Information on science. Information retrieval & dissemination
Maltha, D J. Technical literature search and the written report / [by] D.J. Maltha ; [translated from the Dutch by J.C. Rigg]. — [Revised ed.]. — London [etc.] : Pitman, 1976. — viii,175p : ill ; 22cm.
Previous ed.: published as: 'Literatuuronderzoek en schriftelijk rapporteren'. Wageningen : Pudoc, 1972. — Bibl. — Index.
ISBN 0-273-00399-2 Pbk : £5.00
Also classified at 029'.9'6
(B77-03881)

029'.9'50943 — Information services on science. *West Germany. Reports, surveys*
Organisation for Economic Co-operation and Development. Review of national scientific and technical information policy, Germany / Organisation for Economic Co-operation and Development. — Paris : O.E.C.D. ; [London] : [H.M.S.O.], 1977. — [2],iii,122p ; 24cm.
'... undertaken by the OECD Information Policy Group' - Introductory note.
Pbk : £3.00
ISBN 92-64-11645-1
Also classified at 029'.9'60943
(B77-17256)

029'.9'53 — Physics. Documentation services: INSPEC. *Manuals*
INSPEC. Inspec database users' guide. — London : Institution of Electrical Engineers, [1976]. — 98p in various pagings ; 30cm.
ISBN 0-85296-436-6 Sp : £7.50
Primary classification 029'.9'6213
(B77-11531)

029'.9'53 — Physics. Documents on physics. Information retrieval services using digital computer systems. Machine-readable files: INSPEC records. Format. Conversion of abstracts & bibliographic descriptions of GRA records. *Reports, surveys*
Evans, Lynn. Merging of databases for the production of secondary information publications, phase 1 / [by] L. Evans, B.J. Field and A.M. Gould. — London (Savoy Place, WC2R 0BL) : INSPEC, 1976. — [1],iv,47 leaves : 1 ill ; 30cm. — (INSPEC. Reports ; no.76-26)
Bibl.: leaf 19.
ISBN 0-85296-435-8 Sd : £3.00
Primary classification 029'.9'6213
(B77-04529)

029'.9'6 — Information on technology. Information retrieval & dissemination
Maltha, D J. Technical literature search and the written report / [by] D.J. Maltha ; [translated from the Dutch by J.C. Rigg]. — [Revised ed.]. — London [etc.] : Pitman, 1976. — viii,175p : ill ; 22cm.
Previous ed.: published as: 'Literatuuronderzoek en schriftelijk rapporteren'. Wageningen : Pudoc, 1972. — Bibl. — Index.
ISBN 0-273-00399-2 Pbk : £5.00
Primary classification 029'.9'5
(B77-03881)

029'.9'60871812 — Information on patents. Management. *Western world. Reports, surveys*
Japan Patent Association. Patent information study team in Europe and America : report / by Japan Patent Association ; [translated from the Japanese by Derwent Publications Ltd]. — London (128 Theobalds Rd, WC1X 8RP) : Derwent Publications Ltd, 1976. — xii,204p : ill, facsims, ports ; 25cm.
ISBN 0-901157-04-x : £7.50
(B77-03324)

029'.9'60943 — Information services on technology. *West Germany. Reports, surveys*
Organisation for Economic Co-operation and Development. Review of national scientific and technical information policy, Germany / Organisation for Economic Co-operation and Development. — Paris : O.E.C.D. ; [London] : [H.M.S.O.], 1977. — [2],iii,122p ; 24cm.
'... undertaken by the OECD Information Policy Group' - Introductory note.
Pbk : £3.00
ISBN 92-64-11645-1
Primary classification 029'.9'50943
(B77-17256)

029'.9'61 — Hospitals. Information services. *Cheshire. Reports, surveys*
Pattinson, Michael. Library and information services to the Cheshire Area Health Authority : a report / by Michael Pattinson. — [Chester] ([91 Hoole Rd, Chester OH2 3NG]) : Cheshire County Libraries ; [Chester] : Cheshire Area Health Authority, [1976]. — [5], 57[i.e.59]p,[2]leaves : col map(fold) ; 30cm.
ISBN 0-904532-30-5 Pbk : £2.00
Primary classification 027.6'62'094271
(B77-00581)

029'.9'6213 — Electrical engineering. Documentation services: INSPEC. *Manuals*
INSPEC. Inspec database users' guide. — London : Institution of Electrical Engineers, [1976]. — 98p in various pagings ; 30cm.
ISBN 0-85296-436-6 Sp : £7.50
Also classified at 029'.9'53
(B77-11531)

029'.9'6213 — Electrical engineering. Documents on electrical engineering. Information retrieval services using digital computer systems. Machine-readable files: INSPEC records. Format. Conversion of abstracts & bibliographic descriptions of GRA records. *Reports, surveys*
Evans, Lynn. Merging of databases for the production of secondary information publications, phase 1 / [by] L. Evans, B.J. Field and A.M. Gould. — London (Savoy Place, WC2R 0BL) : INSPEC, 1976. — [1],iv,47 leaves : 1 ill ; 30cm. — (INSPEC. Reports ; no.76-26)
Bibl.: leaf 19.
ISBN 0-85296-435-8 Sd : £3.00
Also classified at 029'.9'53
(B77-04529)

029'.9'6240941 — Construction industries. Information services. *Great Britain. Periodicals*
Construction Industry Information Group. CIIG review. — London (26 Store St., W.C.1) : Construction Industry Information Group.
Supersedes: CIIG bulletin.
No.1- ; Winter 1976-77-. — [1976]-. — ill ; 30cm.
Published at irregular intervals. — 27p. in 1st issue.
Sd : £2.50 (free to members)
ISSN 0309-5347
(B77-17869)

Construction Industry Information Group. Newsletter / Construction Industry Information Group. — London (26 Store St., WC1E 7BT) : C.I.I.G.
[No.1]- ; Mar. 1976-. — [1976]-. — 30cm.
Published at irregular intervals. — [3] leaves in 1st issue.
Sd : Unpriced
(B77-26746)

029'.9'9090971241 — Information services on Commonwealth. *London. Kensington and Chelsea (London Borough). Commonwealth Institute. Reports, surveys*
Commonwealth Institute. Annual report of the Director to the Board of Governors / Commonwealth Institute. — London : The Institute.
1976. — [1977]. — 55,[1]p : ill(some col), map, ports(some col) ; 30cm.
Sd : Unpriced
(B77-27639)

032 — ENGLISH ENCYCLOPAEDIAS
032 — English encyclopaedias. *Texts*
Collins concise encyclopedia / [general editor James Mallory]. — London [etc.] : Collins, 1977. — vii,624,[5]p : ill, maps, ports ; 26cm.
ISBN 0-00-434317-4 : £5.95
(B77-29132)

The **Fontana** dictionary of modern thought / edited by Alan Bullock and Oliver Stallybrass. — London : Collins, 1977. — xix,684p ; 23cm.
ISBN 0-00-216149-4 : £8.50
(B77-31665)

The **Fontana** dictionary of modern thought / edited by Alan Bullock and Oliver Stallybrass. — London : Fontana, 1977. — xix,684p ; 20cm.
ISBN 0-00-634884-x Pbk : £2.95
(B77-31666)

The **Mitchell** Beazley joy of knowledge library / [general editor James Mitchell]. — London : Mitchell Beazley.
Man and machines / [edited by John Clark] ; introduced by Sir Jack Collard. — 1977. — 264p : ill(chiefly col), facsims(1 col), col maps, music, ports(some col) ; 30cm.
Index.
ISBN 0-85533-106-2 : £12.50
(B77-15664)

The natural world / [edited by Ruth Binney] ; introduced by Gwynne Vevers. — 1977. — 271p : ill(chiefly col), col maps, ports ; 30cm.
Index.
ISBN 0-85533-105-4 : £12.50
(B77-15665)

The **new** Caxton encyclopedia / [editor Bernard A. Workman]. — [New ed.]. — London : Caxton Publishing Co., 1977. — 20v. : ill(chiefly col), col charts, facsims(chiefly col), col maps, plans(some col), ports(chiefly col) ; 31cm.
Previous ed.: in 18 vols. 1966-. — Index.
ISBN 0-7014-0039-0 : £320.00
(B77-18515)

The **new** Hutchinson 20th century encyclopedia / edited by E.M. Horsley. — [Revised and enlarged ed.]. — London : Hutchinson, 1977. — [6],1326,[8]p,leaf of plate,32p of plates : ill, charts, geneal tables, maps(some col), plans, ports ; 26cm.
Previous ed.: i.e. 5th revised ed., published as 'Hutchinson's new 20th century encyclopedia'. 1970.
ISBN 0-09-120030-x : £9.95
(B77-30926)

032 — English encyclopaedias for children. *Texts*
Junior colour encyclopaedia / [compiled and edited by Gerald E. Speck]. — Revised ed. — London : Ward Lock, 1976. — 192p : ill(chiefly col), col charts, col maps, port ; 28cm.
Cover-title: Ward Lock's junior colour encyclopedia. — Previous ed.: 1972.
£2.95
ISBN 0-7063-1146-9
(B77-01985)

Junior Pears encyclopaedia. — 17th ed. / edited by Edward Blishen ; illustrated by E. Brooks ... [et al.]. — London : Pelham, 1977. — 688p in various pagings : ill, chart, coats of arms, geneal table, maps, music, port ; 19cm.
Previous ed.: 1976. — Bibl.
ISBN 0-7207-1005-7 : £3.25
(B77-27640)

Ward Lock's world of wonder encyclopedia / [editor, Jane Olliver]. — London : Ward Lock, 1977. — 5-189p : ill(chiefly col), col facsim, col maps, ports(chiefly col) ; 30cm.
Spine title: World of wonder encyclopedia. — 'A Kingfisher Book'. — Index.
ISBN 0-7063-5350-1 : £3.95
(B77-30927)

World of knowledge encyclopedia / [editor Norman Barrett]. — London [etc.] : Hamlyn, 1977. — 256p : ill(some col), charts(some col), facsims, maps(some col), music, ports(some col) ; 31cm.
Index.
ISBN 0-600-33619-0 : £3.95
(B77-23062)

032'.02 — English encyclopaedias. Books of miscellaneous facts. *Texts*
Cartland, Barbara. Barbara Cartland's book of useless information ... / with a foreword by Earl Mountbatten of Burma. — London : Corgi, 1977. — 128p : ill ; 18cm.
ISBN 0-552-10559-7 Pbk : £0.70
(B77-32360)

032'.02 — English encyclopaedias for children. Books of miscellaneous facts. *Texts*
Andrew, Cliff. The biggest, smallest, fastest, strangest, book / written by Cliff Andrew. — London : Cassell, 1976. — 4-94p : ill(chiefly col), col maps, ports ; 29cm.
Col. ill. on lining papers. — Index.
ISBN 0-304-29739-9 : £1.95
(B77-08179)

Clements, Jonathan. More crazy, but true! / [by] Jonathan Clements ; with drawings by Roger Smith. — London : Armada Paperbacks, 1976. — 95p : ill ; 18cm.
With answers.
ISBN 0-00-691129-3 Pbk : £0.40
(B77-09469)

032'.02 — General knowledge. *Yearbooks*
'**Daily** mail' year book. — London : Associated Newspapers Group.
1977 : [77th year of publication] / edited by G.B. Newman. — 1976. — 384p : ill, coats of arms, geneal table ; 18cm.
Index.
ISBN 0-85144-139-4 Pbk : £1.15
ISSN 0301-7761
(B77-03325)

Pears cyclopaedia : a book of background information and reference. — London : Pelham.
1977-78 : 86th ed. Anniversary edition, 1897-1977 / edited by L. Mary Barker and Christopher Cook. — 1977. — 1055p in various pagings : ill, col maps ; 21cm.
Index.
ISBN 0-7207-1004-9 : £4.25
(B77-27641)

032'.02 — Records of achievement. *Collections*
Guinness book of records. — Enfield : Guinness Superlatives.
[23rd ed.] / editors and compilers Norris McWhirter (Ross McWhirter 1955-1975) ; sports editor Stan Greenberg. — 1976. — 3-350p : ill(some col), ports(some col) ; 31cm.
Index.
ISBN 0-900424-37-0 : £2.95
ISSN 0300-1679
(B77-11036)

[24th ed.] / editor and compiler Norris McWhirter ; sports editor Stan Greenberg. — 1977. — 3-350p : ill(some col), col coat of arms, facsim, 2 maps(1 col), ports(some col) ; 31cm.
Text on lining paper. — Index.
ISBN 0-900424-80-x : £3.50
ISSN 0300-1679
(B77-29880)

037 — ENCYCLOPAEDIAS IN SLAVIC LANGUAGES
037'.1 — Russian encyclopaedias. *English texts*
Great Soviet encyclopedia / [A.M. Prokhorov editor in chief]. — New York : Macmillan ; London : Collier Macmillan.
Vol.10. — 1976. — xviii,649p : ill ; 29cm.
Translation of: 'Bol'shaia sovetskaia entsiklopediia'. 3-e izd. T.10. Moscow : Sovetskaia Entsiklopediia Publishing House, 1970. — Bibl.
ISBN 0-02-880110-5 : £31.25
(B77-17870)

Vol.11. — 1976. — xxii,663p : ill, maps ; 29cm.
Translation of: 'Bol'shaia sovetskaia entsiklopediia'. 3-e izd. T.11. Moscow : Sovetskaia Entsiklopediia Publishing House, 1973. — Bibl.
ISBN 0-02-880120-2 : £31.25
(B77-17871)

Vol.12. — 1976. — xxii,714p : ill ; 29cm.
Translation of: 'Bol'shaia sovetskaia entsiklopediia'. 3-e izd. T.12. Moscow : Sovetskaia Entsiklopediia Publishing House, 1973. — Bibl.
ISBN 0-02-880150-4 : £31.25
(B77-17872)

Vol.13. — 1976. — xxii,618p : ill ; 29cm.
Translation of: 'Bol'shaia sovetskaia entsiklopediia'. 3-e izd. T.13. Moscow : Sovetskaia Entsiklopediia Publishing House, 1973. — Bibl.
ISBN 0-02-880160-1 : £31.25
(B77-17873)

039 — ENCYCLOPAEDIAS IN MINOR EUROPEAN AND NON-EUROPEAN LANGUAGES
039'.9166 — English encyclopaedias. Books of miscellaneous facts. *Welsh texts*
'Choelia ti byth! / [gan] Deidre Sanders ... [et al.] ; [cyfieithiwyd o'r Saesneg]. — Penygroes, Gwynedd ([Bryn Mair, Dolydd Y Groeslon, Caernarfon, Gwynedd]) : Cyhoeddiadau Mei, 1977. — 112p : ill ; 19cm.
Translation of: 'Would you believe it?'. London : Talmy Franklin, 1973.
ISBN 0-905775-02-3 Pbk : £0.90
(B77-29133)

050 — GENERAL PERIODICALS AND THEIR INDEXES
050'.25 — Periodicals. *Directories*
Willing's press guide : a guide to the press of the United Kingdom and to the principal publications of Europe and USA. — Haywards Heath [etc.] : T. Skinner.
1977 : 103rd annual ed. — 1977. — [7],766p : ill ; 22cm.
Index.
ISBN 0-611-00624-3 : £8.00
Also classified at 070'.025
(B77-14525)

050'.25'41 — Periodicals. *Great Britain. Directories. Periodicals*
EMA : editorial media analysis. — London (13 Curtain Rd, EC2A 3LT) : Bill Gibbs-PNA Group.
Vol.1, issue 1- ; Apr. '77-. — [1977]-. — 21x30cm.
Monthly. — Cover title. — [197]p. in 1st issue. — Index.
Pbk : £29.00 yearly
ISSN 0309-779x
Also classified at 070'.025'41
(B77-28339)

051 — AMERICAN PERIODICALS
051 — Periodicals for women: Periodicals with American imprints, 1883-1976. *Texts. Facsimiles*
The **journal** of the century / compiled by Bryan Holme with the editors of the Viking Press and the 'Ladies' home journal'. — London : Secker and Warburg, 1976. — 352p : ill(some col), facsims, music, plans, ports(some col) ; 31cm.
Also published: New York : Viking Press, 1976. — Index.
ISBN 0-436-24060-2 : £8.50
(B77-01986)

051 — Periodicals with American imprints: 'Life', to 1976
Hamblin, Dora Jane. That was the 'Life' / by Dora Jane Hamblin. — London : Deutsch, 1977. — 2-320p : ill, facsims, ports ; 24cm.
Index.
ISBN 0-233-96930-6 : £5.50 : CIP rev.
(B77-21665)

052 — ENGLISH PERIODICALS
052 — Children's periodicals: Periodicals published by Band of Hope. *Texts*
Hotshot. — London (45 Great Peter St., SW1P 3LT) : UK Band of Hope Union.
[No.1]- ; [Oct. 1976]-. — [1976]-. — ill(some col) ; 48x39cm fold to 24x20cm.
Six issues a year. — Sheet ([4]p.) as 1st issue.
£0.90 yearly
(B77-03882)

052 — Literary periodicals: Little magazines: Periodicals in English. *Directories*
International directory of little magazines & small presses. — [Paradise, Calif.] : [Dustbooks] ; [New Malden] ([56 Blakes La., New Malden, Surrey KT3 6NX]) : [Distributed by Gerald England].
1973-74 : 9th ed. / [editors Len Fulton, James Boyer May]. — [1973]. — [2],iv,160p : ill ; 21cm.
ISBN 0-913218-08-1 Sd : £1.50
ISSN 0084-9979
Also classified at 338.4'7'070593025
(B77-09470)

052 — Periodicals for adolescent girls: Periodicals with British imprints. *Texts*
Oh boy!. — London : IPC Magazines.
No.1- ; 23rd Oct. 1976-. — 1976-. — ill(some col), ports(some col) ; 30cm.
Weekly. — [40]p. in 1st issue.
Sd : £0.12
(B77-01987)

052 — Periodicals for boys: Periodicals with British imprints. *Texts. Facsimiles*
The **best** of British pluck : 'The boy's own paper' revisited / [compiled] by Philip Warner. — London : Macdonald and Jane's, 1976. — [6], 202p : ill, facsims, ports ; 29cm.
ISBN 0-354-04017-0 : £5.95
(B77-02720)

052 — Periodicals for University College, Dublin: Periodicals with Dublin imprints. *Texts*
Third degree. — Dublin (c/o Room G303, Arts Building, UCD, Belfield, Dublin 4) : [University College, Dublin].
Vol.1, no.1- ; Spring 1977-. — [1977]-. — 22cm.
[2],36p. in 1st issue.
Sd : £0.50
(B77-27642)

052 — Periodicals for women: Periodicals with British imprints. *Texts*
'Woman's weekly' good life. — London : IPC Magazines.
No.1- ; Oct. 1977-. — [1977]-. — ill(some col), ports ; 22cm.
Monthly. — 98p. in 1st issue.
Sd : £0.20
ISSN 0140-5462
(B77-29881)

Woman's world. — [London] : IPC Magazines].
No.1- ; Apr. 1977-. — [1977]-. — ill(some col), ports(some col) ; 31cm.
Monthly. — 164p. in 1st issue.
Sd : £0.30
ISSN 0309-6084
(B77-15065)

052 — Periodicals for women: Periodicals with British imprints, 1946-1976. *Reports, surveys*
White, Cynthia Leslie. The women's periodical press in Britain, 1946-1976 / by Cynthia L. White. — London : H.M.S.O., 1977. — 85p : form ; 25cm. — (Great Britain. Royal Commission on the Press. Working papers ; no.4)
Bibl.: p.83-85.
ISBN 0-11-730076-4 Sd : £1.50
(B77-28340)

052 — Periodicals with British imprints. *Reports, surveys*
Great Britain. *Royal Commission on the Press.* Periodicals and the alternative press / Royal Commission on the Press ; chairman O.R. McGregor. — London : H.M.S.O., 1977. — x, 73p ; 25cm. — (Great Britain. Royal Commission on the Press. Research series ; 6) (Cmnd.6810-6)
ISBN 0-10-168106-2 Sd : £1.35
Also classified at 301.2'2'05
(B77-28341)

052 — Periodicals with British imprints. *Texts*
Wells, David. Acid rain / written by David Wells. — London (194 Goldhurst Terrace, N.W.6) : The author.
Issue 1- ; July 1977-. — 1977-. — 21cm.
Quarterly. — 21p. in 1st issue.
Sd : £0.30
ISSN 0140-6485
(B77-32361)

052 — Periodicals with English imprints. *Texts*
The **once** and future worm. — Helston (21 Trenethick Parc, Helston, Cornwall TR13 8LH) : Archie and Beryl Mercer.
No.1- ; Oct. 1976-. — 1976-. — 30cm.
Four issues a year. — 16p. in 1st issue. — Supersedes: Middle earthworm.
Sd : Unpriced
ISSN 0309-0973
(B77-03326)

052 — Serial publications for University of Oxford: Serial publications with Oxford imprints. *Texts*
The **'Cherwell'** guide to Oxford. — Oxford (9a Saint Michael's St., Oxford OX1 2ED) : Oxford Student Press for Oxford Student Publications Ltd and the Oxford University Student Union.
[1976] : (incorporating the 'Oxford University What's What' and 'Univoxon') / [editor Bridget Townsend]. — 1976. — 57p : ill ; 28cm.
ISBN 0-9503661-3-7 Sd : £0.50
(B77-01988)

060 — GENERAL ORGANISATIONS
060 — Conferences & exhibitions. *Europe. Calendars*
Exhibitions & conferences year book. — [London] ([12 York Way, King's Cross, N1 9AA]) : [York Publishing Co.].
1977 / [compiled by Owen Spence and Jane Nightingale]. — [1977]. — 416p : ill ; 30cm.
Cover title.
ISBN 0-903383-06-3 Pbk : £8.50 yearly with 'Exhibitions & conferences gazette'
ISSN 0307-6601
(B77-16699)

060 — Learned institutions. *Directories*
The **world** of learning. — London : Europa.
1976-77 : twenty-seventh ed. — 1976. — 2v. ([30],1992p) ; 26cm.
Index.
ISBN 0-900362-97-9 : £24.00
(B77-12824)

060.4'2 — Organisations. Procedure. *United States*
Deschler, Lewis. Deschler's rules of order / by Lewis Deschler. — Englewood Cliffs ; London [etc.] : Prentice-Hall, 1976. — xii,228p : forms ; 24cm.
Text on lining papers. — Index.
ISBN 0-13-219543-7 : £7.30
(B77-03883)

061'.47'95 — Cultural activities. Organisations. *New York (State). Chautauqua. Chautauqua Institution, to 1973*
Morrison, Theodore. Chautauqua : a center for education, religion, and the arts in America / [by] Theodore Morrison ; drawings by Jane E. Nelson. — Chicago ; London : University of Chicago Press, 1974. — viii,351p : ill, ports ; 22cm.
Bibl.: p.339-341. — Index.
ISBN 0-226-54062-6 : Unpriced
(B77-19165)

062'.1 — German organisations. *London. Guidebooks*
German sites in London : a pictorial guide / edited by Rolf Breitenstein and Angelika Hommerich. — London : Wolff [for] the Embassy of the Federal Republic of Germany, London, 1976. — vi,78p : chiefly ill, facsim, ports ; 19cm.
ISBN 0-85496-207-7 Pbk : £1.75
(B77-05177)

062'.1 — Organisations. *London. Directories*
Taylor, Elisabeth Russell. London lifelines / [by] Elisabeth Russell Taylor. — London : Wildwood House, 1977. — [9],256,[22]p ; 23cm.
Index.
ISBN 0-7045-0258-5 : £4.95
ISBN 0-7045-0259-3 Pbk : Unpriced
(B77-23063)

068'.181'2 — International organisations. *Western world*
European-Atlantic Movement. The all-in-one guide to European-Atlantic organisations (intergovernmental and supporting voluntary bodies) : what they are, what they do, and where to get further information. Plus a specially prepared chronology 1945-1976 / [European-Atlantic Movement]. — 9th ed., revised. — Exeter (7 Cathedral Close, Exeter, Devon) : European-Atlantic Movement (TEAM), 1976. — [2],24,[2]p ; 11x14cm.
Previous ed.: i.e. 8th ed., 1972.
ISBN 0-85450-005-7 Sd : £0.25
(B77-12825)

068'.41 — British culture. Dissemination. Organisations: British Council. *Reports, surveys. Serials*
British Council. Annual report / the British Council. — London : The Council.
1975-76. — [1977]. — 72p : ill(incl 1 col), col maps, ports ; 30cm.
Bibl.: p.71-72.
ISBN 0-900229-25-x Pbk : £0.50
(B77-07034)

068'.41 — Organisations. *Great Britain. Directories*
Councils, committees, & boards : a handbook of advisory, consultative, executive & similar bodies in British public life / edited by I.G. Anderson. — 3rd ed. — Beckenham (154 High St., Beckenham, Kent BR3 1EA) : C.B.D. Research Ltd, 1977. — ii-xiv,402p ; 31cm.
Text on lining paper. — Previous ed.: 1973. — Index.
ISBN 0-900246-22-7 : £22.50
ISSN 0070-1211
(B77-33014)

068'.41 — Organisations. *Great Britain. Directories. For foreign visitors*
Britain, meet the British / [British Tourist Authority]. — London : B.T.A.
[1977]. — 1977. — [2],27p : map ; 21cm. — (British Tourist Authority. Information sheets ; no. 322/77/14)
English text, French, German, Dutch, Italian and Spanish introduction.
ISBN 0-85630-387-9 Sd : Unpriced
(B77-31667)

069 — MUSEUMS

069'.025'41 — Museums. *Great Britain. Directories*
The **libraries,** museums and art galleries year book. — Cambridge : J. Clarke.
1976 / editors Adrian Brink & Derry Watkins. — 1976. — [2],254p ; 31cm.
Index.
ISBN 0-227-67824-9 : £15.00
Primary classification 021'.0025'41
(B77-00003)

Museums and art galleries in Great Britain and Ireland. — Dunstable (Oldhill, London Rd, Dunstable, Beds.) : ABC Historic Publications. 1977. — [1976]. — 93p : ill ; 28cm.
Index.
ISBN 0-900486-19-8 Sd : £0.55
(B77-03327)

Museums yearbook : including a directory of museums and galleries of the British Isles and an index to their administering authorities / [Museums Association]. — London : The Association.
1977 / editor Pauline J. Maliphant. — [1977]. — 135p : ill, forms ; 30cm.
Pbk : Unpriced
ISBN 0-902102-38-9
ISSN 0307-7675
(B77-26083)

A **travel** guide to bygones. — Hayfield (Fox Hall Barn, Kinder Rd, Hayfield, Derbyshire) : Pro-Motion, 1977. — 95p : ill, 2 maps ; 21cm.
ISBN 0-905960-00-9 Pbk : £0.95
(B77-18516)

069'.025'41 — National museums. *Great Britain. Directories*
Britain, what's where in national museums / [British Tourist Authority]. — London : B.T.A. — (British Tourist Authority. Information sheets ; no.339)
1977. — 1976. — [2],34p : ill, map, ports ; 21cm.
English text, English, French, German, Dutch, Italian and Spanish introductions. — Bibl.
ISBN 0-85630-103-5 Sd : £0.20
(B77-04530)

069'.0941 — Museums. *Great Britain*
Finlay, Ian. Priceless heritage : the future of museums / [by] Ian Finlay. — London : Faber, 1977. — 183p ; 23cm.
Bibl.: p.177. — Index.
ISBN 0-571-09107-5 : £4.95
(B77-13468)

069'.0941 — Museums. *Great Britain. Conference proceedings*
Museums Association. *Annual Conference, Bristol, 1976.* Annual conference [of the Museums Association] Bristol, 1976 / editor Patrick J. Boylan. — London : Museums Association, [1977]. — 53p : map ; 30cm.
Cover title: Conference proceedings 1976. — Previous control number ISBN 0-902102-38-9.
ISBN 0-902102-39-7 Sd : £1.50
(B77-12826)

069'.09421'42 — Museums. *London. Camden (London Borough). British Museum. Guidebooks*
British Museum. British Museum guide. — London : British Museum Publications Ltd, 1976. — 295[i.e.315]p : ill(some col), maps(some col), plans(some col), ports(some col) ; 26cm.
Col. plans on lining papers. — Index.
ISBN 0-7141-0047-1 : £5.95
ISBN 0-7141-0048-x Pbk : £1.95 (available only from the British Museum)
(B77-07035)

069'.09427'642 — Museums. *Lancashire. Burnley. Towneley Hall Art Gallery and Museums, to 1975*
Towneley Hall Art Gallery and Museums. Towneley Hall Art Gallery and Museums. — [Burnley] ([Town Hall, Burnley, Lancs.]) : Burnley Borough Council, [1976]. — 43p : ill, coat of arms, ports ; 22cm.
Sd : £0.20
(B77-06432)

069'.09429'87 — Museums. *Cardiff. National Museum of Wales, to 1977*
National Museum of Wales. National Museum of Wales, 1927-77. — [Cardiff] : The Museum, 1977. — 63p : ill(some col), plan, ports ; 21cm.

Bibl.: p.60-63.
ISBN 0-7200-0203-6 Pbk : £0.65
(B77-32362)

069'.095694 — Museums. *Israel*
Rahmani, L Y. The museums of Israel / [by] L.Y. Rahmani ; photographs by Peter Larsen. — London : Secker and Warburg, 1976. — 239p : ill(some col) ; 30cm.
ISBN 0-436-24238-9 : £12.50
(B77-01134)

069'.1 — Museums. Services for handicapped persons. *Conference proceedings*
Museums and the Handicapped *(Conference), Leicester, 1975.* Museums and the handicapped : seminar [held at] College Hall, Leicester, 12-14 September 1975, [organised by the] Group for Educational Services in Museums, [and] Departments of Museum Studies and Adult Education, University of Leicester / [edited and additional material added by D.S. Sorrell]. — Leicester (96 New Walk, Leicester LE1 6TD) : Leicestershire Museums, Art Galleries and Records Service, 1976. — [10],68[i.e. 88]p : ill ; 30cm.
Bibl.: p.66-68.
ISBN 0-85022-008-4 Sp : £0.80
(B77-10716)

069'.52 — Museums. *Cambridgeshire. Cambridge. Sedgwick Museum. Stock. Cataloguing. Applications of digital computer systems. Reports, surveys*
Porter, M F. A unified approach to the computerization of museum catalogues / [by] M.F. Porter, R.B. Light, D.A. Roberts. — London (Research and Development Department, Sheraton House, Great Chapel St., W1V 4BH) : British Library, 1977. — v,72p : ill ; 30cm. — (British Library. Research and development reports ; 5338 HC ISSN 0308-2385)
ISBN 0-905984-01-3 Sp : £2.50 : CIP rev.
(B77-14526)

069'.52 — Museums. Documentation services. *Great Britain. Periodicals*
Museum Documentation Association. MDA information. — Duxford (Museum Documentation Advisory Unit, Imperial War Museum, Duxford Airdield [i.e. Airfield], Duxford, Cambs. CB2 4QR) : The Association.
No.1- ; Apr. 1977-. — 1977-. — 30cm.
Monthly. — 9p. in 1st issue.
Sd : Unpriced
ISSN 0309-6653
(B77-29882)

069'.53 — Art objects. Restoration. *Encyclopaedias*
Savage, George. The art and antique restorers' handbook : a dictionary of materials and processes used in the restoration & preservation of all kinds of works of art / by George Savage. — Revised ed. — London : Barrie and Jenkins, 1976. — [6],142p ; 23cm.
This ed. originally published: London : Barrie and Rockliff, 1967. — Bibl.: p.133. — Index.
ISBN 0-214-20268-2 : £2.50
Also classified at 745.1'028
(B77-01135)

069'.53'0941 — Art objects. Conservation. *Great Britain. Periodicals*
Conservation news / United Kingdom Group of the International Institute for Conservation of Historic and Artistic Works. — [London] ([c/o The Editor, Department of Conservation and Technical Services (M.L.A.), British Museum, Great Russell St., WC1B 3DG]) : The Group.
No.1- ; Nov. 1976-. — [1976]-. — 30cm.
Three issues a year. — 4p. in 1st issue. — Pierced for binder.
Sd : Unpriced
ISSN 0309-2224
(B77-07036)

070 — JOURNALISM, PUBLISHING, NEWSPAPERS

070 — Magazines. Production. *Amateurs' manuals*
Jeeves, Terry. Duplicating notes / by Terry Jeeves. — Sheffield (230 Bannerdale Rd, Sheffield S11 9FE) : The author, 1977. — [63] p : ill(some col) ; 26cm.
'An ERG publication'.
ISBN 0-9501698-1-1 Sd : £1.00
(B77-12827)

070'.025 — Newspapers. *Directories*
Willing's press guide : a guide to the press of the United Kingdom and to the principal publications of Europe and USA. — Haywards Heath [etc.] : T. Skinner.
1977 : 103rd annual ed. — 1977. — [7],766p : ill ; 22cm.
Index.
ISBN 0-611-00624-3 : £8.00
Primary classification 050'.25
(B77-14525)

070'.025'41 — Newspapers. *Great Britain. Directories. Periodicals*
EMA : editorial media analysis. — London (13 Curtain Rd, EC2A 3LT) : Bill Gibbs-PNA Group.
Vol.1, issue 1- ; Apr. '77-. — [1977]-. — 21x30cm.
Monthly. — Cover title. — [197]p. in 1st issue. — Index.
Pbk : £29.00 yearly
ISSN 0309-779x
Primary classification 050'.25'41
(B77-28339)

070'.05 — Journalism. *Periodicals*
Journalism studies review. — Cardiff ([34 Cathedral Rd, Cardiff]) : University College, Cardiff.
Vol.1, no.1- ; June 1976-. — 1976-. — ill, facsims, ports ; 28cm.
Annual. — 'Published ... under the auspices of ... the Centre for Journalism Studies, University College, Cardiff'. — 54p. in 1st issue.
Sd : £1.50
ISSN 0309-1724
(B77-04531)

070.1 — NEWS MEDIA

070.1'72 — Newspapers. *Juvenile literature*
Law, Felicia. Newspapers / written by Felicia Law ; illustrated by Tony Morris. — London [etc.] : Collins, 1976. — 32p : ill(chiefly col) ; 22cm. — (Dandelions)
ISBN 0-00-651185-6 Sd : £0.50
(B77-01989)

070.1'9 — Radio programmes: News programmes. Journalism. *Great Britain. Manuals*
Herbert, John. The techniques of radio journalism / [by] John Herbert. — London : A. and C. Black, 1976. — 123p ; 23cm.
Bibl.: p.117-118. — Index.
ISBN 0-7136-1650-4 : £4.50
(B77-00582)

070.4 — JOURNALISM. TECHNIQUES AND TYPES

070.4'092'4 — Journalism. Cudlipp, Hugh, Baron Cudlipp. *Autobiographies*
Cudlipp, Hugh, *Baron Cudlipp.* Walking on the water / [by] Hugh Cudlipp. — London [etc.] : Bodley Head, 1976. — 428p,[16]p of plates : ill, facsims, ports ; 23cm.
Index.
ISBN 0-370-11313-6 : £5.95
(B77-00006)

070.4'092'4 — Journalism. Hobson, Joshua. *West Yorkshire (Metropolitan County). Huddersfield. Biographies*
Chadwick, Stanley. A bold and faithful journalist : Joshua Hobson, 1810-1876 / [by] Stanley Chadwick. — Huddersfield (c/o Directorate of Educational Services, Kirklees Metropolitan Council Headquarters, Princess Alexandra Walk, Huddersfield HD1 2SU) : Kirklees Libraries and Museums Service, 1976. — 82p : ill, facsims, map, ports ; 24cm.
At head of title: Centenary memorial. — Bibl.: p.79. — Index.
ISBN 0-9502568-3-8 Pbk : £1.00
(B77-07770)

070.4'092'4 — Journalism. Hough, Henry Beetle. *United States. Autobiographies*
Hough, Henry Beetle. To the harbor light / [by] Henry Beetle Hough. — Large print [ed.]. — London : Prior [etc.], 1977. — [3],347p ; 24cm.
Originally published: Boston, Mass. : Houghton Mifflin, 1976.
ISBN 0-86043-052-9 : £4.95
(B77-23064)

070.4'1 — Newspapers. Copy-editing. *Manuals*
Baskette, Floyd K. The art of editing / [by] Floyd K. Baskette, Jack Z. Sissors. — 2nd ed. — New York : Macmillan ; London : Collier Macmillan, 1977. — ix,468p : ill, facsims ; 26cm.
Previous ed.: New York : Macmillan, 1971. — Index.
ISBN 0-02-306270-3 : £10.50
(B77-23065)

070.4'3 — Journalism. Investigative reporting. *United States. Manuals*
Anderson, David, *b.1942.* Investigative reporting / [by] David Anderson & Peter Benjaminson. — Bloomington ; London : Indiana University Press, 1976. — xi,307p ; 25cm.
Index.
ISBN 0-253-33164-1 : Unpriced
ISBN 0-253-20196-9 Pbk : £2.80
(B77-00007)

070.4'49'301451914041 — South Asian immigrants. Attitudes of newspapers. *Great Britain, 1976. Reports, surveys*
Evans, Peter, *b.1932.* Publish and be damned? / by Peter Evans ; with a foreword by E.J.B. Rose. — [London] : Runnymede Trust, 1976. — 37p : 1 ill, facsims ; 21cm.
Sd : £1.30
(B77-23066)

070.4'49'364941 — Crime. Reporting by newspapers. *Great Britain*
Chibnall, Steve. Law-and-order news : an analysis of crime reporting in the British press / [by] Steve Chibnall. — London : Tavistock Publications, 1977. — xiv,288p : ill, facsim ; 21cm.
Bibl.: p.262-267. — Index.
ISBN 0-422-74960-5 : £8.00
ISBN 0-422-74970-2 Pbk : £3.50
(B77-23067)

070.4'49'63 — Agriculture. Journalism. Organisations. *Great Britain. Guild of Agricultural Journalists. Directories*
Guild of Agricultural Journalists. Year book / Guild of Agricultural Journalists. — London (151 Great Portland St., W1N 5FB) : Graham Cherry Organisation.
1977 : 20th ed. / edited by Graham Cherry. — 1977. — 112p : ill, port ; 22cm.
Pbk : £3.00
(B77-17874)

070.4'49'7960924 — Sports. Reporting. Wilson, Peter, b.1913 (Aug). *Great Britain. Autobiographies*
Wilson, Peter, *b.1913 (Aug.).* The man they couldn't gag / [by] Peter Wilson. — London : Hutchinson, 1977. — 387p,[32]p of plates : ill, ports ; 24cm.
Index.
ISBN 0-09-128930-0 : £5.95
(B77-28342)

070.4'8327'0924 — Periodicals for girls: Periodicals with British imprints: Girl's Own Paper. Klickmann, Flora. *Biographies*
Lazell, David. Flora Klickmann and her Flower Patch : the story of 'The Girl's own paper' and the Flower Patch among the hills / by David Lazell. — Bristol (127 Tower Rd South, Warmley, Bristol BS15 5BT) : 'Flower patch magazine', [1976]. — 36p : ill ; 21cm.
Limited ed.
ISBN 0-9505397-0-8 Sd : £0.40
(B77-02721)

070.4'86 — Company newspapers & house journals. Editing. Organisations. *Europe. Federation of European Industrial Editors Associations. Periodicals*
Federation of European Industrial Editors Associations. FEIEA news. — London (c/o E. Towers, RHM Centre, 152 Grosvenor Rd, SW1V 3JL) : F.E.I.E.A.
[No.1]- ; 1977-. — [197-]-. — ports ; 29cm.
Folder (4p.) as Spring 1977 issue.
Unpriced
(B77-15666)

070.5 — PUBLISHING

070.5 — Conjuring. Documents on conjuring. Printing & publishing. *England, 1800-1850*
Hall, Trevor Henry. Some printers & publishers of conjuring books and other ephemera, 1800-1850 / by Trevor H. Hall and Percy H. Muir. — Leeds (10 Elmete Ave., Leeds LS8 2JX) : Elmete Press, 1976. — x,97p : ill, facsims(some col) ; 30cm.
Ill. on lining papers. — Limited ed. of 465 numbered copies. — Index.
ISBN 0-9503367-3-4 : £39.00
(B77-04532)

070.5'092'4 — Children's books. Publishing. Cundall, Joseph. *Great Britain*
McLean, Ruari. Joseph Cundall, a Victorian publisher : notes on his life and a check-list of his books / by Ruari McLean. — Pinner (['Ravelston', South View Rd, Pinner, Middx]) : Private Libraries Association, 1976. — viii,96p : ill(some col), facsims, geneal table, ports ; 28cm.
Index.
ISBN 0-900002-13-1 : £8.00
(B77-07037)

070.5'092'4 — Publishing. Athill, Diana. *Great Britain. Autobiographies*
Athill, Diana. Instead of a letter / [by] Diana Athill. — London : Deutsch, 1976. — 224p ; 21cm.
Originally published: London : Chatto and Windus, 1963.
ISBN 0-233-96838-5 : £3.50
(B77-01990)

070.5'092'4 — Publishing. Hefner, Hugh. *United States. Biographies*
Brady, Frank, *b.1934.* Hefner / [by] Frank Brady. — London : Sphere, 1976. — 3-223p, [16]p of plates : ill, ports ; 18cm.
Originally published: New York : Macmillan, 1974 ; London : Weidenfeld and Nicolson, 1975.
ISBN 0-7221-1845-7 Pbk : £0.95
(B77-00583)

070.5'092'4 — Publishing. Johnson, Joseph. *Great Britain*
Haywood, Peter. Joseph Johnson, publisher, 1738-1809 / [by] Peter Haywood. — [Aberystwyth] ([Aberystwyth, Dyfed SY23 3AS]) : College of Librarianship, Wales, 1976. — [5],62[i.e. 63]p : facsims ; 30cm. — (College of Librarianship, Wales. Students projects ; no.6)
ISBN 0-904020-01-0 Sd : £0.75
(B77-05835)

070.5'092'4 — Publishing. Woolf, Leonard. *Great Britain. Biographies*
Spater, George. A marriage of true minds : an intimate portrait of Leonard and Virginia Woolf / [by] George Spater and Ian Parsons. — London : Cape : Hogarth Press, 1977. — xiv,210p : ill, facsims, ports ; 25cm.
Index.
ISBN 0-224-01407-2 : £5.95 : CIP rev.
ISBN 0-7012-0436-2 (Hogarth) : £5.95 CIP rev.
Primary classification 823'.9'12
(B77-18425)

070.5'1 — Periodicals on science. Editing
DeBakey, Lois. The scientific journal : editorial policies and practices, guidelines for editors, reviewers, and authors / [by] Lois DeBakey ; in collaboration with Paul F. Cranefield ... [et al.]. — St Louis : Mosby ; London : Distributed by Kimpton, 1976. — xiii,129p : ill, facsims, form ; 24cm.
Index.
ISBN 0-8016-1223-3 : £8.05
(B77-20865)

070.5'72'0212 — Serial publications. Statistics, 1955-1976. *Reports, surveys*
Wootton, Christopher B. Trends in size, growth and cost of the literature since 1955 / [by] Christopher B. Wootton. — London : British Library, 1977. — viii,90p : ill ; 30cm. — (British Library. Research and development reports ; no.5323 HC ISSN 0308-2385)
ISBN 0-85350-146-7 Sp : £3.50 : CIP rev.
Primary classification 070.5'73'0212
(B77-07038)

070.5'73 — School texts. Publishing. *Great Britain*
Educational Publishers Council. Publishing for schools : a short guide to educational publishing / Educational Publishers Council. — London (19 Bedford Sq., WC1B 3HJ) : The Council, 1977. — viii,56p : ill ; 18x22cm.
ISBN 0-85386-041-6 Pbk : £0.95
(B77-28343)

070.5'73'0212 — Monographs. Statistics, 1955-1976. *Reports, surveys*
Wootton, Christopher B. Trends in size, growth and cost of the literature since 1955 / [by] Christopher B. Wootton. — London : British Library, 1977. — viii,90p : ill ; 30cm. — (British Library. Research and development reports ; no.5323 HC ISSN 0308-2385)
ISBN 0-85350-146-7 Sp : £3.50 : CIP rev.
Also classified at 070.5'72'0212
(B77-07038)

070.5'73'0942921 — Books. Printing & publishing. *Gwynedd. Ynys Môn, to ca 1900. Welsh texts*
Jones, Bedwyr Lewis. Argraffu a chyhoeddi ym Môn / [gan] Bedwyr Lewis Jones. — [Llangefni] ([Area Library Headquarters, Lon y Felin, Llangefni, Gwynedd LL77 7RT]) : Gwasanaeth Llyfrgell Gwynedd, Rhanbarth Môn, 1976. — [2],18p ; 21cm. — (Cyfres darlithoedd Môn ; 1 ISSN 0309-2267)
'Darlith a draddodwyd yng Nghanolfan Athrawon Môn, 20 Hydref 1976 dan nawdd y Gwasanaeth Llyfrgell'. — Bibl.: p.18.
ISBN 0-9501551-1-x Sd : £0.20
(B77-10100)

070.5'73'0973 — Books. Publishing. *United States. Readings*
The **business** of publishing : a PW anthology / with an introduction by Arnold W. Ehrlich. — New York ; London : Bowker, 1976 [i.e. 1977]. — ix,303p ; 24cm.
'... contains 45 of the most provocative and important articles that appeared in "Publishers Weekly" over the past five years' - jacket. — Published in the United States: 1976. — Index.
ISBN 0-8352-0893-1 : £7.00
(B77-10101)

070.9 — NEWSPAPERS AND JOURNALISM. HISTORICAL TREATMENT

070'.92'4 — Journalism. Barber, Noel. *Autobiographies*
Barber, Noel. The natives were friendly - so we stayed the night / [by] Noel Barber. — London [etc.] : Macmillan, 1977. — 3-226p,[16]p of plates : ill, ports ; 23cm.
Ill. on lining papers. — Index.
ISBN 0-333-22558-9 : £4.95 : CIP rev.
(B77-17257)

070'.92'4 — Journalism. Hemingway, Mary Welsh. *United States. Autobiographies*
Hemingway, Mary Welsh. How it was / [by] Mary Welsh Hemingway. — London : Weidenfeld and Nicolson, 1977. — vi,537,xi p,[24]p of plates : ill, facsims, ports ; 24cm.
Ill. on lining papers. — Originally published: New York : Knopf, 1976. — Index.
ISBN 0-297-77265-1 : £6.95
Primary classification 813'.5'2
(B77-12041)

070'.92'4 — Journalism. Leitch, David. *Great Britain. Autobiographies*
Leitch, David. God stand up for bastards / [by] David Leitch. — London [etc.] : Pan Books, 1977. — 224p ; 18cm.
Originally published: London : Deutsch, 1973.
ISBN 0-330-25008-6 Pbk : £0.75
(B77-11037)

070'.92'4 — Journalism. McWhirter, Alan Ross. *Great Britain. Biographies*
McWhirter, Norris Dewar. Ross : the story of a shared life / [by] Norris McWhirter. — London (2 Lord North St., S.W.1) : Churchill Press Limited, 1976. — ix,240p : ill, ports ; 23cm.
Index.
ISBN 0-902782-23-1 : £4.50
(B77-19981)

070'.92'4 — Journalism. Muggeridge, Malcolm. Interpersonal relationships with Kingsmill, Hugh & Pearson, Hesketh
Ingrams, Richard. God's apology : a chronicle of three friends / [by] Richard Ingrams. — London : Deutsch, 1977. — 256p,[4]p of plates : ill, ports ; 23cm.
Bibl.: p.253. — Index.
ISBN 0-233-96888-1 : £5.50
Primary classification 823'.9'12
(B77-25248)

070'.92'4 — Journalism. Redwood, Hugh. *Biographies*
Clark, William, *b.1925.* Hugh Redwood : with God in Fleet Street / by William Clark. — London [etc.] : Hodder and Stoughton, 1976. — 126p ; 18cm. — (Hodder Christian paperbacks)
ISBN 0-340-20437-0 Pbk : £0.70
(B77-08180)

070'.92'4 — Journalism. Terkel, Studs. *United States. Autobiographies*
Terkel, Studs. Talking to myself : a memoir of my times / [by] Studs Terkel. — London : Wildwood House, 1977. — xiv,316,[1]p : ports(on lining papers) ; 25cm.
Also published: New York : Pantheon Books, 1977.
ISBN 0-7045-0294-1 : £7.50
(B77-22311)

070'.92'4 — Journalism. Whyte, Don. *Scotland. Autobiographies*
Whyte, Don, *b.1926.* On the lonely shore : an autobiography / [by] Don Whyte ; foreword by Hugh MacDiarmid. — London : Hutchinson, 1977. — 192p,[8]p of plates : ill, ports ; 23cm.
Index.
ISBN 0-09-128800-2 : £3.95
(B77-29883)

071/079 — NEWSPAPERS AND JOURNALISM. GEOGRAPHICAL TREATMENT
072 — Provincial newspapers published by Northcliffe Newspapers Group Limited. *England. Reports, surveys*
Scanning the provinces. — London (Carmelite House, EC4Y 0JA) : Northcliffe Newspapers Group Limited.
1977. — 1977. — [3],55p : facsims, maps ; 30cm.
Pbk : Unpriced
(B77-22312)

072'.1 — Newspapers with London imprints: Times, The, 1800-1900. *Juvenile literature*
James, Alan, *b.1943.* Newspapers and 'The Times' in the 19th century / [by] Alan James ; illustrated from contemporary sources. — London : Longman, 1976. — 96p : ill, facsims, ports ; 19cm. — (Then and there series)
ISBN 0-582-22121-8 Pbk : £0.50
(B77-06433)

072'.422'19 — Newspapers for Americans: Newspapers with Surrey imprints: Newspapers with Farnham imprints. *Texts*
The **American.** — Farnham (114 West St., Farnham, Surrey GU9 7HL) : Princes Weekly Newspapers Ltd.
No.1-. — [1976]-. — ill, facsims, maps, ports ; 46cm.
Fortnightly. — 32p. in 18th issue.
Sd : £0.15
(B77-25355)

072'.5'25 — Newspapers for ethnic minorities: Newspapers with Nottinghamshire imprints: Newspapers with Sutton-in-Ashfield imprints. *Texts*
News focus. — Sutton-in-Ashfield (The Croft, Church St., Sutton-in-Ashfield, Notts.) : R. Chandran.
No.1- ; Feb. 1977-. — [1977]-. — ill, ports ; 42cm.
Published at irregular intervals. — 8p. in 1st issue.
Sd : £0.10
ISSN 0140-2463
(B77-32363)

072'.6'59 — Newspapers with Cambridge imprints. Influence, 1780-1850
Murphy, Michael Joseph. Cambridge newspapers and opinion, 1780-1850 / [by] Michael J. Murphy. — Cambridge : Oleander Press, 1977. — 143p : ill, facsims, map, ports ; 22cm. — (Cambridge town, gown and county ; vol.12)
Bibl.: p.123-135. — Index.
ISBN 0-900891-15-7 : £4.50 : CIP rev.
(B77-19982)

072'.9'98 — Newspapers with Chepstow imprints, 1855-1976. *Critical studies*
Waters, Ivor. Chepstow printers and newspapers / [by] Ivor Waters. — Revised [ed.]. — Chepstow ([c/o Hon. Sec. Mervyn Prothero, 1 Wyebank Close, Tutshill, Chepstow, Gwent NP6 7ET]) : The Chepstow Society, 1977. — iii,40p : ill, facsim, map, ports ; 21cm. — (Chepstow Society. Pamphlet series ; no.9)
Previous ed.: 1970.
ISBN 0-900278-38-2 Sd : Unpriced
Primary classification 686.2'09429'98
(B77-24365)

079.41 — Press. *Great Britain*
Boyd-Barrett, Oliver. Studies on the press / by Oliver Boyd-Barrett, Colin Seymour-Ure, Jeremy Tunstall. — London : H.M.S.O., 1977. — 397p : ill ; 25cm. — (Great Britain. Royal Commission on the Press. Working papers ; no.3)
ISBN 0-11-730075-6 Pbk : £5.50
(B77-28344)

079'.41 — Press. *Great Britain. Inquiry reports*
Great Britain. *Royal Commission on the Press.* Final report ... / Royal Commission on the Press ; chairman O.R. McGregor. — London : H.M.S.O., [1977]. — [2],xix,298p ; 25cm. — (Cmnd.6810)
Index.
ISBN 0-10-168100-3 Pbk : £4.25
(B77-23068)

Great Britain. *Royal Commission on the Press.* Final report ... / Royal Commission on the Press ; chairman O.R. McGregor. — London : H.M.S.O.
Appendices. — [1977]. — [2],ii,166p ; 25cm. — (Cmnd.6810-I)
ISBN 0-10-168101-1 Pbk : £2.60
(B77-23069)

079'.414'43 — Newspapers with Glasgow imprints: Scottish daily news, 1975
McKay, Ron. The story of the 'Scottish daily news' / [by] Ron McKay and Brian Barr. — Edinburgh : Canongate Publishing, 1976. — vi, 170p,[8]p of plates : ill, ports ; 23cm.
Index.
ISBN 0-903937-24-7 : £3.95
ISBN 0-903937-25-5 Pbk : £1.60
(B77-16155)

080 — GENERAL COLLECTIONS
081 — General essays in English. American writers. *Texts*
Prance, Claude Annett. The laughing philosopher : a further miscellany on books, booksellers and book collecting / by Claude A. Prance. — London : Villiers Publications, 1976. — 282p ; 23cm.
Bibl. — Index.
ISBN 0-900777-07-9 : £4.50
(B77-00584)

082 — Anthologies in English. *For adolescent girls. Serials*
'**Mates**' annual. — London : IPC Magazines.
1978. — [1977]. — 127p : ill(some col), ports(some col) ; 28cm. — (A Fleetway annual)
Cover title.
ISBN 0-85037-340-9 : £1.45
(B77-32364)

Oh boy! annual. — London : IPC Magazines.
1978. — 1977. — 95p : ill(some col), ports(some col) ; 28cm. — (A Fleetway annual)
Cover title.
ISBN 0-85037-370-0 : £1.45
ISSN 0140-7112
(B77-33015)

'**Pink**' annual. — London : IPC Magazines.
1978. — [1977]. — 127p : ill(some col), ports(some col) ; 28cm. — (A Fleetway annual)
Cover title.
ISBN 0-85037-344-1 : £1.45
(B77-32365)

082 — Anthologies in English, 1800-1900. *Texts. Facsimiles*
Print and the people, 1819-1851 / edited, with an introduction and commentary, by Louis James. — London : Allen Lane, 1976. — 368p : ill, facsims, map ; 25cm.
Bibl.: p.355-363. — Index.
ISBN 0-7139-0778-9 : £7.50
(B77-10102)

082 — General essays in English. *Extracts from newspapers*
The **bedside** 'Guardian' : a selection from 'The Guardian'. — London : Collins.
26 : 1976-77 / edited by W.L. Webb ; with an introduction by J.K. Galbraith ; cartoons by Gibbard and Bryan McAllister. — 1977. — 252p : ill, map ; 21cm.
Index.
ISBN 0-00-211394-5 : £4.00
(B77-29884)

082 — General essays in English. *Texts*
Morris, William, *b.1834.* [Selections]. Selected writings and designs [of] William Morris / edited with an introduction by Asa Briggs ; with a supplement by Graeme Shankland on William Morris, designer. — Harmondsworth [etc.] : Penguin, 1977. — 312,[32]p : ill, facsims ; 18cm. — (Pelican books)
Originally published: 1963.
Pbk : £1.10
ISBN 0-14-020521-7
(B77-25356)

Rothschild, Nathaniel Mayer Victor, *Baron Rothschild.* Meditations of a broomstick / [by] Lord Rothschild. — London : Collins, 1977. — 187p,[4]p of plates,[2]leaves of plates : ill(incl 1 col) ; 24cm.
Index.
ISBN 0-00-216512-0 : £6.50
(B77-26084)

Russell, Bertrand, *Earl Russell.* Sceptical essays / [by] Bertrand Russell. — London : Allen and Unwin, 1977. — 3-189p ; 20cm.
Originally published: 1928.
ISBN 0-04-104003-1 Pbk : £1.50
(B77-19983)

082 — General essays in English: Essays from British boys' public school magazines. *Anthologies*
The **bedside** book of boys public schools / compiled and edited by Nigel Hadow ; illustrations by John Grant. — Lewes (Sandhill, Halland, Lewes, Sussex BN8 6PP) : Nigel Hadow Publications, 1976. — 146p : ill ; 22cm.

ISBN 0-905698-00-2 Pbk : £1.50
Also classified at 373.2'22'02541
(B77-01991)

082 — General knowledge
The **Guinness** book of answers / general editor Norris McWhirter, associate editors ... [others]. — Enfield : Guinness Superlatives, 1976. — 3-251p : ill, coats of arms, col maps, ports ; 31cm.
Text on lining papers. — Index.
ISBN 0-900424-35-4 : £4.95
(B77-12272)

082 — General knowledge. *Exercises, worked examples. Primary school texts*
Marshall, Isobel. Junior progress tests / [by] Isobel Marshall. — London : Heinemann Educational.
Book 1. — 1977. — [120]p : ill ; 25cm.
Cover title. — Fill-in book.
ISBN 0-435-01473-0 Pbk : £0.95
(B77-26747)

Book 1. Teachers' book. — 1977. — [124]p : ill ; 25cm.
With answers.
ISBN 0-435-01474-9 Pbk : £2.50
(B77-26748)

082 — General knowledge. *Juvenile literature*
Amazing but true / illustrated by Peter Dennis, John Glover and Krystyna Turska. — London [etc.] : Beaver Books, 1977. — 126p : ill ; 20cm.
'The articles in this collection were originally published in the magazine "Look and learn" between 1963 and 1975 ...' - title page verso.
ISBN 0-600-30332-2 Pbk : £0.50
(B77-30928)

Ardley, Neil. Purnell's find out about wonders of the world / [by Neil Ardley] ; [editorial Trisha Pike et al. ; artists Eric Jewell Associates et al.]. — [Maidenhead] : [Purnell], [1976]. — 2-224p : ill(some col), maps(1 col), col plan, ports ; 27cm.
Index.
ISBN 0-361-03500-4 : £2.75
(B77-11532)

Brandreth, Gyles. Hotchpotch / [by] Gyles Brandreth ; illustrated by Ann Axworthy. — London : Carousel Books, 1976. — 128p : ill ; 20cm. — (Carousel books)
With answers.
ISBN 0-552-54112-5 Pbk : £0.45
(B77-02722)

Brandreth, Gyles. The second how and why bumper wonder book / [text by Gyles Brandreth]. — London : Transworld, 1977. — 96p : ill(chiefly col), col map ; 28cm.
Cover title: How and why bumper wonder book, 2. — With answers.
ISBN 0-552-86593-1 : £1.95
(B77-26749)

The **children's** book of questions & answers / edited by Anthony Addison. — [London] : Octopus Books for W.H. Smith, 1977. — 480p : ill(chiefly col), facsims(some col), col maps, music, ports(some col) ; 29cm.
Index.
ISBN 0-7064-0620-6 : £2.25
(B77-30929)

Dyer, Sue. How funtastic / [by] Sue Dyer ; cover and text illustrations by John Hamon and Terry Russell. — London : Independent Television Books : Arrow Books, 1977. — 94p : ill ; 20cm. — (Look-in books)
With answers.
ISBN 0-09-915480-3 Pbk : £0.65
(B77-23956)

Every boy's handbook. — 8th revised ed. — London [etc.] : Hamlyn, 1976. — 256p : ill, maps ; 18cm.
Previous ed.: 1974.
ISBN 0-600-33126-1 : £0.95
(B77-06434)

I-spy holiday special. — London (382 Edgware Rd, W2 1EP) : Polystyle Publications Ltd, 1977. — 47p : ill(some col), facsims ; 28cm.
Sd : £0.35
(B77-31668)

Pollard, Michael. How, why, where / [by] Michael Pollard. — London : Ward Lock, 1976. — 92p : chiefly ill(some col), maps(some col), ports ; 29cm.
With answers. — Index.
ISBN 0-7063-1861-7 : £1.95
(B77-02723)

Stroud, Jean. Piccolo encyclopedia of useful facts / [by] Jean Stroud ; cover illustration by Brian Webb, text illustrations by Robin Lawrie. — Revised ed. — London [etc.] : Pan Books, 1975 [i.e. 1976]. — viii,216p : ill, map ; 20cm. — (A piccolo original)
Previous ed.: 1974.
ISBN 0-330-24267-9 Pbk : £0.50
(B77-04533)

Stroud, Jean. Piccolo encyclopedia of useful facts / [by] Jean Stroud ; cover illustration by Brian Webb ; text illustrations by Robin Lawrie. — Revised ed., with a new sports section. — London [etc.] : Pan Books, 1977. — [6],218p : ill, chart ; 20cm. — (A piccolo original)
Previous ed.: 1976.
ISBN 0-330-25207-0 Pbk : £0.60
(B77-12273)

082 — General knowledge. *Juvenile literature. Illustrations*

Maclean, Moira. It's fun finding out - / edited by Deborah Manley ; illustrated by Moira and Colin Maclean and Kailer-Lowndes. — Maidenhead : Purnell, 1977. — 4-62p : chiefly col ill ; 33cm.
Col. ill. on lining papers. — With answers.
ISBN 0-361-03875-5 : £1.75
(B77-23957)

Roberts, David, *b.1926.* First book of knowledge / [by] David Roberts. — [London] ([59 Grosvenor St., W.1]) : Sundial Books Ltd, [1977]. — 5-156p : col ill ; 29cm.
Spine title: The St Michael first book of knowledge. — Col. ill. on lining papers.
ISBN 0-904230-38-4 : £1.99
(B77-33568)

082 — General knowledge. *Juvenile literature. Serials*

The '**Look** and learn' book. — London : IPC Magazines.
1978. — 1977. — 2-127p : ill(some col), col map, ports(some col) ; 28cm. — (A Fleetway annual)
With answers.
ISBN 0-85037-337-9 : £1.45
(B77-32366)

'**Tell** me why' annual. — [London] : [IPC Magazines].
1978. — [1977]. — 3-78p : ill(chiefly col), col ports ; 28cm. — (A Fleetway annual)
Cover title. — Text, col. ill. on lining papers.
ISBN 0-85037-359-x : £1.65
(B77-32367)

082 — General knowledge. *Secondary school texts*

Dobinson, Humphrey Mark. Basic skills you need / [by] H.M. Dobinson. — Sunbury-on-Thames [etc.] : Nelson, 1976. — 144p : ill(some col), facsim, forms, maps ; 25cm.
Index.
ISBN 0-17-433386-2 Pbk : £1.25
(B77-00585)

082 — General knowledge. *Topics for discussion groups*

National Adult School Union. The lines are open : studies in communication: a book of current knowledge and interests for group study, 1977 / [National Adult School Union]. — London : N.A.S.U., [1976]. — [5],234p : 1 ill, music ; 19cm. — (A study handbook) (Handbooks ; 67th)
Bibl.
Pbk : £1.00
(B77-01136)

083'.1 — General essays in German. *English texts*

Hesse, Hermann. Reflections / [by] Hermann Hesse ; selected from his books and letters by Volker Michels ; translated [from the German] by Ralph Manheim. — London : Cape, 1977. — [7],197p ; 23cm.
This translated selection originally published: New York : Farrar, Straus and Giroux, 1974. — Translation of: 'Lektüre für Minuten'. Frankfurt am Main : Suhrkamp Verlag, 1971.
ISBN 0-224-01257-6 : £4.95
(B77-11038)

085'.1 — General essays in Italian. Texts: Leonardo da Vinci. 'Literary works of Leonardo da Vinci'

Pedretti, Carlo. The literary works of Leonardo da Vinci, compiled and edited from the original manuscripts by Jean Paul Richter / commentary by Carlo Pedretti. — Oxford : Phaidon, 1977. — 2v.(xxi,403p,[30]p of plates;[7],442p,[14]p of plates) : ill, facsims, ports ; 26cm. — (Kress Foundation. Studies in the history of European art ; no.5)
English text, Italian manuscripts with English translation. — Bibl.: p.xv-xxi. — Index.
ISBN 0-7148-1489-x : £29.50
(B77-19167)

089'.9166 — General essays in Welsh. *Texts*

Roberts, Selyf. Mesur byr : ysgrifau / [gan] Selyf Roberts. — Llandysul : Gwasg Gomer, 1977. — 110p ; 19cm.
ISBN 0-85088-426-8 Pbk : £1.00
(B77-29134)

Williams, John Roberts. Annwyl gyfeillion / [gan] John Roberts Williams (John Aelod Jones). — Llandysul : Gwasg Gomer, 1975. — 79p ; 19cm.
ISBN 0-85088-335-0 Pbk : £0.50
(B77-00586)

091 — MANUSCRIPTS

091 — English manuscripts: Manuscripts copied by Thornton, Robert. *Texts. Facsimiles*

The **Thornton** manuscript (Lincoln Cathedral MS. 91) / introductions by D.S. Brewer & A.E.B. Owen. — [Facsimile ed.] reprinted with introductions revised. — London : Scolar Press, 1977. — xxii,[642]p ; 36cm.
'[A facsimile reprint of] the Lincoln manuscript, now Lincoln Cathedral MS. 91 (formerly A.S.2.) ... [probably written c.1430-50]' - Introduction. — Facsimile ed. originally published: 1975. — Bibl.: p.xxi-xxii.
ISBN 0-85967-352-9 : £50.00
Also classified at 821'.1'08
(B77-28345)

091 — Illuminated manuscripts: Books of hours, 1300-1500

Harthan, John. Books of hours and their owners / [by] John Harthan. — [London] : Thames and Hudson, 1977. — 192p : ill(chiefly col), coats of arms, facsims(some col), geneal tables ; 32cm.
Bibl.: p.185. — Index.
ISBN 0-500-23217-2 : £10.50
(B77-29135)

091 — Tebtunis papyri in Greek. *Texts with commentaries*

The **Tebtunis** papyri. — London : Egypt Exploration Society for the British Academy. — (Graeco-Roman memoirs ; no.64 ISSN 0306-9222)
Vol.4 / edited with translations [from the Greek] and notes by James G. Keenan and John C. Shelton. — 1976. — xv,293p ; 27cm.
Greek texts, English introduction, translations and notes. — Index.
ISBN 0-85698-073-0 : £21.00
(B77-17875)

095 — BOOKS NOTABLE FOR BINDINGS

095'.09415 — Irish bookbindings, 1639-1815

Craig, Maurice James. Irish bookbindings / by Maurice Craig. — Dublin ([65 Middle Abbey St., Dublin 1]) : Eason and Son, 1976. — [28] p(2 fold) : ill(some col) ; 25cm. — (The Irish heritage series ; 6)
Bibl.: p.[27].
Sd : £0.70
(B77-17258)

100 — PHILOSOPHY AND RELATED DISCIPLINES

100 — Philosophy

Brody, Baruch Alter. Beginning philosophy / [by] Baruch A. Brody. — Englewood Cliffs ; London [etc.] : Prentice-Hall, 1977. — x,244p ; 23cm.
ISBN 0-13-073882-4 Pbk : £5.55
(B77-29136)

Goddard, Leonard. Philosophical problems / [by] Leonard Goddard. — Edinburgh : Scottish Academic Press, 1977. — x,90p ; 22cm.
Bibl.: p.88-90.
ISBN 0-7073-0136-x Pbk : £2.25
(B77-26750)

The **owl** of Minerva : philosophers on philosophy / edited and with an introduction by Charles J. Bontempo and S. Jack Gdell. — New York ; London [etc.] : McGraw-Hill, [1976]. — xvi,264p ; 21cm.
Published in the United States: 1975. — Bibl.: p.259-260. — Index.
ISBN 0-07-006480-6 : £8.30
ISBN 0-07-006481-4 Pbk : £3.30
(B77-03328)

Piaget, Jean. Insights and illusions of philosophy / [by] Jean Piaget ; translated from the French by Wolfe Mays. — London [etc.] : Routledge and Kegan Paul, 1977. — xvii,237p ; 23cm.
This translation originally published: New York : World Publishing, 1971 ; London : Routledge and Kegan Paul, 1972. — Translation of: 'Sagesse et illusions de la philosophie'. 2e édition augmentée d'une postface. Paris : Presses universitaires de France, 1968. — Index.
Unpriced
ISBN 0-7100-8659-8 Pbk : £2.40
(B77-29137)

Titus, Harold Hopper. Living issues in philosophy. — 6th ed. / [by] Harold H. Titus, Marilyn S. Smith. — New York ; London [etc.] : D. Van Nostrand, [1977]. — xiii,561p : ill, ports ; 24cm.
Text on lining papers. — This ed. published in the United States: 1974. — Previous ed.: / by Harold H. Titus, 1970. — Bibl. — Index.
ISBN 0-442-25820-8 : £7.70
(B77-07039)

100 — Philosophy. *Secondary school texts*

Mullen, Peter. Beginning philosophy / [by] Peter Mullen. — London : Edward Arnold, 1977. — viii,69p ; 22cm.
Bibl.: p.68-69.
ISBN 0-7131-0129-6 Pbk : £1.50
(B77-21666)

105 — Philosophy. *Periodicals*

Seminar : journal of the Philosophical Seminar, University College, Cork. — Cork (c/o G. Barden, Philosophy Department, University College, Cork) : The Philosophical Seminar.
1- ; 1977-. — 1977-. — 22cm.
[3],48p. in 1st issue.
Sd : Unpriced
(B77-29885)

109 — Thought, to 1976. *Secondary school texts*
Sauvain, Philip Arthur. Man the thinker / by Philip A. Sauvain. — Amersham : Hulton, 1977. — 64p : ill(some col), facsim, 2 maps(1 col), ports ; 19x25cm. — (Exploring the world of man)
ISBN 0-7175-0673-8 Pbk : £1.15
(B77-18517)

110 — METAPHYSICS
Aristotle. [Metaphysics. English]. Aristotle's metaphysics. — Oxford : Clarendon Press. — (Clarendon Aristotle series)
Books M and N / translated [from the Greek] with introduction and notes by Julia Annas. — 1976. — [8],227p ; 21cm.
Bibl.: p.220-222. — Index.
ISBN 0-19-872085-8 : £6.25
(B77-02724)

Bennett, John Godolphin. The dramatic universe / [by] J.G. Bennett. — Sherborne, Glos. : Coombe Springs Press.
In 4 vols.
Vol.1 : The foundations of natural philosophy. — 1976. — xlii,534p : ill ; 22cm.
Originally published: London : Hodder and Stoughton, 1957. — Index.
ISBN 0-900306-39-4 Pbk : £4.25
(B77-10103)

Vol.2 : The foundations of moral philosophy. — 1976. — iii-xxviii,356p : ill ; 22cm.
Originally published: London : Hodder and Stoughton, 1961. — Index.
ISBN 0-900306-42-4 Pbk : £4.25
(B77-10104)

Vol.3 : Man and his nature. — 1976. — xxxvi, 315p : ill ; 22cm.
Originally published: London : Hodder and Stoughton, 1966. — Index.
ISBN 0-900306-43-2 Pbk : £4.25
(B77-10105)

Vol.4 : History. — 1977. — l,462p : ill ; 21cm.
Originally published: London : Hodder and Stoughton, 1967. — Index.
ISBN 0-900306-44-0 Pbk : £4.50
(B77-28346)

Hegel, Georg Wilhelm Friedrich. [Phänomenologie des Geistes. English]. Phenomenology of spirit / by G.W.F. Hegel ; translated [from the German] by A.V. Miller ; with analysis of the text and foreword by J.N. Findlay. — Oxford : Clarendon Press, 1977. — xxxv,595p ; 23cm.
Cover title: Hegel's phenomenology of spirit. — Translation of: 'Phänomenologie des Geistes'. 5th ed. / edited by J. Hoffmeister. Hamburg : Felix Meiner, 1952. — Index.
ISBN 0-19-824530-0 : £16.50 : CIP rev.
(B77-10106)

Sire, James W. The universe next door : a guide to world views / [by] James W. Sire. — Leicester : Inter-Varsity Press, 1977. — 239p ; 20cm.
Originally published: Downers Grove, Ill. : Inter Varsity Press, 1976. — Index.
ISBN 0-85110-582-3 Pbk : £1.95
(B77-14527)

Whiteley, Charles Henry. An introduction to metaphysics / [by] C.H. Whiteley. — Hassocks : Harvester Press [etc.], 1977. — xv, 174p ; 23cm.
Originally published: London : Methuen, 1950. — Bibl. — Index.
ISBN 0-85527-126-4 : Unpriced : CIP rev.
(B77-11533)

110'.8 — Metaphysics. *Lectures, speeches*
Quine, Willard Van Orman. Ontological relativity, and other essays / by W.V. Quine. — New York ; London : Columbia University Press, [1977]. — ix,165p ; 21cm. — (The John Dewey essays in philosophy ; vol.1)
'The title essay ... was presented as a pair of lectures of the same title at Columbia University, March 26 and 28, 1968 ... the first of the John Dewey Lectures ...' - Preface. — Originally published: 1969. — Index.
ISBN 0-231-08357-2 Pbk : £2.60
(B77-29886)

111 — ONTOLOGY
111 — Identity. *Philosophical perspectives*
Griffin, Nicholas. Relative identity / [by] Nicholas Griffin. — Oxford : Clarendon Press, 1977. — xii,234p : ill ; 23cm. — (Clarendon library of logic and philosophy)
Bibl.: p.220-227. — Index.
ISBN 0-19-824409-6 : £8.50
(B77-26751)

111 — Universals & particulars. *Readings*
Universals and particulars : readings in ontology / edited by Michael J. Loux. — [Revised ed.]. — Notre Dame ; London : University of Notre Dame Press, 1976. — [4], 396p ; 21cm.
Previous ed.: Garden City, N.Y. : Anchor Books, 1970. — Bibl.: p.387-396.
ISBN 0-268-01908-8 : £12.75
ISBN 0-268-01909-6 Pbk : £4.50
(B77-10107)

111.1 — Non-existence. *Philosophical perspectives*
Gale, Richard Milton. Negation and non-being / [by] Richard M. Gale. — Oxford : Blackwell, 1976. — [8],117p ; 22cm. — ('American philosophical quarterly' monograph series ; no.10 ISSN 0084-6422)
Index.
ISBN 0-631-11540-4 Pbk : £4.00
(B77-01137)

113 — COSMOLOGY
113'.092'4 — Cosmology. Donnolo, Shabbetai. *Critical studies*
Sharf, Andrew. The universe of Shabbetai Donnolo / [by] A. Sharf. — Warminster : Aris and Phillips, 1976. — viii,214p ; 22cm.
Bibl.: p.194-206. — Index. — Includes original Hebrew texts.
ISBN 0-85668-052-4 : £7.50
ISBN 0-85668-053-2 Pbk : £4.95
(B77-03329)

115 — TIME, DURATION, ETERNITY
115 — Time. *Philosophical perspectives*
Newman, Laurence Frederick. Time / [by L.F. Newman]. — [High Wycombe] ([1 The Pastures, Downley, High Wycombe, Bucks.]) : The author, [1977]. — [3]leaves : 1 ill ; 30cm.
ISBN 0-905825-00-4 Sd : Unpriced
(B77-14021)

Nicoll, Maurice. Living time and the integration of the life / [by] Maurice Nicoll. — London : Watkins, 1976. — viii,252p : ill ; 20cm.
Originally published: London : Stuart, 1952. — Bibl.: p.247. — Index.
ISBN 0-7224-0146-9 Pbk : £2.85
(B77-08724)

116 — MOTION, CHANGE, EVOLUTION
116 — Change
Crickmay, Christopher Lindsey. Boundary shifting / prepared for the [Open University, Art and Environment] Course Team by Christopher Crickmay. — Milton Keynes : Open University Press, 1976. — 56p : ill ; 30cm. — ([Technology/arts/social sciences], a second level interdisciplinary course : art and environment ; unit 13) (TAD292 ; 13)
Bibl.: p.53-55.
ISBN 0-335-06212-1 Pbk : Unpriced
(B77-14528)

120 — KNOWLEDGE, CAUSE, PURPOSE, MAN
120 — Intention. *Philosophical perspectives*
Aquila, Richard E. Intentionality : a study of mental acts / [by] Richard E. Aquila. — University Park [Pa] ; London : Pennsylvania State University Press, 1977. — xi,168p ; 24cm.
Index.
ISBN 0-271-01228-5 : £10.00
(B77-23070)

121 — EPISTEMOLOGY
Chisholm, Roderick Milton. Theory of knowledge / [by] Roderick M. Chisholm. — 2nd ed. — Englewood Cliffs ; London [etc.] : Prentice-Hall, 1977. — xi,144p ; 24cm. — (Prentice-Hall foundations of philosophy series)
Previous ed.: 1966. — Index.
ISBN 0-13-914168-5 : £7.95
ISBN 0-13-914150-2 Pbk : £3.95
(B77-15066)

121 — Epistemology. Kant, Immanuel. Kritik der reinen Vernunft. Teil 1. *Critical studies*
Paton, Herbert James. Kant's metaphysic of experience : a commentary on the first half of the 'Kritik der reinen Vernunft' / by H.J. Paton. — [Hassocks] : Harvester Press [etc.], 1976. — 2v.(3-585p ; 3-510p) ; 23cm. — (Muirhead library of philosophy)
Originally published: London : Allen and Unwin, 1936. — Index.
ISBN 0-85527-550-2 : £20.00
(B77-07040)

121 — Knowledge. *Philosophical perspectives*
Hampshire, Stuart. Knowledge and the future / by Stuart Hampshire. — [Southampton] : University of Southampton, 1976. — 17p ; 21cm. — (Fawley Foundation. Lectures ; 22nd)
'... delivered ... on November 25th, 1976, in the Nuffield Theatre of the University ...' - title page verso.
ISBN 0-85432-166-7 Sd : £0.50
(B77-13469)

Locke, John. An essay concerning human understanding / [by] John Locke. — New ed., abridged / abridged and edited with an introduction by John W. Yolton. — London : Dent [etc.], 1976. — xlvi,398p : 1 facsim ; 19cm. — (Everyman's university library)
Previous ed.: i.e. Revised ed., 1965. — Bibl.: p.xxxv-xxxvi. — Index.
ISBN 0-460-11332-1 Pbk : £1.00
(B77-01138)

Plato. [Theaetetus. English]. The 'Theaetetus' of Plato / translated [from the Greek] by M.J. Levett. — [Glasgow] : University of Glasgow Press, 1977. — xi,132p ; 18cm.
This translation originally published: Glasgow : Jackson, Wylie and Co., 1928. — Bibl.: p.xi.
ISBN 0-85261-138-2 Pbk : £1.50
(B77-06435)

121 — Knowledge. Justification
Rescher, Nicholas. Methodological pragmatism : a systems-theoretic approach to the theory of knowledge / [by] Nicholas Rescher. — Oxford : Blackwell, 1977. — xv,315p : ill ; 23cm.
Index.
ISBN 0-631-17030-8 : £10.50 : CIP rev.
(B77-05836)

Williams, Michael. Groundless belief : an essay on the possibility of epistemology / [by] Michael Williams. — Oxford : Blackwell, 1977. — viii,181,[2]p ; 23cm. — (Library of philosophy and logic)
Index.
ISBN 0-631-17610-1 : £5.50 : CIP rev.
(B77-05837)

121 — Knowledge. Philosophical perspectives. Theories of Marxists
Ruben, David-Hillel. Marxism and materialism : a study in Marxist theory of knowledge / [by] David-Hillel Ruben. — Hassocks : Harvester Press [etc.], 1977. — x,199p ; 23cm. — (Marxist theory and contemporary capitalism)
ISBN 0-85527-570-7 : £10.50 : CIP rev.
(B77-15667)

121 — Man. Perception. *Philosophical perspectives*
Jackson, Frank. Perception : a representative theory / [by] Frank Jackson. — Cambridge [etc.] : Cambridge University Press, 1977. — [9] ,180p ; 23cm.
Bibl.: p.173-177. — Index.
ISBN 0-521-21550-1 : £6.50
(B77-19168)

121'.02'4092 — Knowledge. *For librarianship*
Kemp, David Alasdair. The nature of knowledge : an introduction for librarians / by D.A. Kemp. — London : Bingley [etc.], 1976. — 199p : ill ; 23cm.
Bibl.: p.175-189. — Index.
ISBN 0-85157-216-2 : £4.25
(B77-01992)

121'.076 — Secondary schools. Curriculum studies: Epistemology. Examinations: International Baccalaureate. Syllabuses
International Baccalaureate theory of knowledge course : syllabus and teachers' notes / edited by Richard Whitfield. — Revised interim ed. — Birmingham (Gosta Green, Birmingham B4 7ET) : Department of Education, University of Aston in Birmingham [for] the International Baccalaureate Office, 1976. — [2],64p : ill ; 21cm. — (Aston educational enquiry monograph ; no.2)
Bibl.
Sd : £0.75
(B77-27644)

121'.092'4 — Epistemology. Theories of Locke, John. *Critical studies. Readings*
Locke on human understanding : selected essays / edited by I.C. Tipton. — Oxford [etc.] : Oxford University Press, 1977. — [8], 170p ; 21cm. — (Oxford readings in philosophy)
Bibl.: p.164-167. — Index.
ISBN 0-19-875039-0 Pbk : £1.95 : CIP rev.
(B77-08725)

121'.6 — Uncertainty
Bennett, John Godolphin. Hazard / compiled by A.G.E. Blake from the unpublished writings and talks of John G. Bennett. — Sherborne, Glos. : Coombe Springs Press, 1976. — [5], 147p : 2 ill ; 20cm. — (The dramatic universe series ; 1)
ISBN 0-900306-33-5 Pbk : £1.45
(B77-11039)

121'.6'0924 — Knowledge. Certainty. Theories of Wittgenstein, Ludwig
Wilde, Carolyn. Certainty : a discussion of Wittgenstein's notes 'On certainty' / prepared by Carolyn Wilde ; for the [Open University] Course Team. — Milton Keynes : Open University Press, 1976. — 89p ; 30cm. — (Arts, a fourth level course : thought and reality, central themes in Wittgenstein's philosophy ; units 29-31) (A402 ; 29-31)
Bibl.: p.89.
ISBN 0-335-05211-8 Pbk : £2.15
(B77-03330)

122 — CAUSATION
122'.08 — Causation. *Readings*
The **nature** of causation / edited and with an introduction by Myles Brand. — Urbana [etc.] ; London : University of Illinois Press, 1976. — [9],387p ; 25cm.
Facsimile reprints. — Bibl.: p.369-387.
ISBN 0-252-00407-8 : £9.05
(B77-01139)

123 — FREEDOM AND NECESSITY
123 — Determinism & free will. *Philosophical perspectives*
Boyle, Joseph M. Free choice : a self-referential argument / [by] Joseph M. Boyle, Jr, Germain Grisez, Olaf Tollefsen. — Notre Dame, Ind. ; London : University of Notre Dame Press, 1976. — xi,207p ; 24cm.
Index.
ISBN 0-268-00940-6 : £12.00
(B77-18518)

126 — CONSCIOUSNESS AND PERSONALITY
126 — Man. Identity. *Philosophical perspectives*
The **identities** of persons / edited by Amélie Oksenberg Rorty. — Berkeley [etc.] ; London : University of California Press, 1976. — [5], 333p : ill ; 23cm. — (Topics in philosophy)
Bibl.: p.325-333.
ISBN 0-520-03030-3 : £11.60
(B77-13470)

126 — Self
The **self** : psychological and philosophical issues / edited by Theodore Mischel. — Oxford : Blackwell, 1977. — xiii,359p ; 23cm.
'The ... volume results from a closed working conference ... held December 19 through 21, 1975, at the Center for Psychosocial Studies in Chicago' - Preface. — Bibl. — Index.
ISBN 0-631-17860-0 : £9.00 : CIP rev.
(B77-05178)

128 — MAN
Cherjo. A cosmic joke / [by] Cherjo. — Edwardstown, S. Australia : The author ; Ilfracombe : [Distributed by] Stockwell, 1976. — 14p ; 18cm.
ISBN 0-7223-1008-0 Pbk : Unpriced
(B77-11040)

Kustra, B. The message of truth : rational theory of a true man / [by] B. Kustra. — Ilfracombe : Stockwell, 1976. — 60p ; 18cm.
ISBN 0-7223-0952-x Pbk : £1.25
(B77-12274)

Moriarty, Theodore William Cart. The mystery of man / [by] Theodore W.C. Moriarty ; [editor Eleanor E. Whittall]. — Southall (15 The Green, Southall, Middx) : Blackburn Business Services Ltd.
Vol.1. — 1976. — [7],277p : 2 ports ; 30cm.
'Lectures given in England in 1921-23'.
ISBN 0-9504728-0-8 Pbk : £6.50
(B77-00587)

Chattopadhyaya, D P. Individuals and worlds : essays in anthropological rationalism / [by] D.P. Chattopadhyaya. — Delhi ; London [etc.] : Oxford University Press, 1976. — x, 227p ; 23cm.
Index.
ISBN 0-19-560715-5 : £5.75
(B77-21667)

128 — Man. Behaviour. Evolution. *Philosophical perspectives*
Evolution and consciousness : human systems in transition / edited by Erich Jantsch and Conrad H. Waddington. — Reading, Mass. ; London [etc.] : Addison-Wesley, 1976 [i.e. 1977]. — xii, 259p ; 24cm.
Published in the United States: 1976. — Bibl. — Index.
ISBN 0-201-03438-7 : £16.60
ISBN 0-201-03439-5 Pbk : £7.60
(B77-12275)

128 — Man. Behaviour. Explanation. *Philosophical perspectives*
Walker, Nigel, *b.1917.* Behaviour and misbehaviour : explanations and non-explanations / [by] Nigel Walker. — Oxford : Blackwell, 1977. — x,154p ; 23cm.
Bibl.: p.145-150. — Index.
ISBN 0-631-17810-4 : £5.00 : CIP rev.
(B77-12276)

128 — Western thought. Symbols: Man, to 1968
Durand, Gilbert. On the disfiguration of the image of man in the West / [by] Gilbert Durand ; [translated from the French by Jane A. Pratt ; adapted by Chantal Robin and James Hillman assisted by others]. — Ipswich (3 Cambridge Drive, Ipswich IP2 9EP) : Golgonooza Press, 1977. — 25p : ill ; 23cm.
'This article, which first appeared in "Spring 76" (Zürich), is a condensed version of the central portion of a lecture entitled "Défiguration philosophique et figure traditionnelle de l'homme en Occident" given at the Eranos Conference, August 1969, and published in French in "Eranos". 38 (1969) p.45-93' - title page verso.
ISBN 0-903880-14-8 Sd : £0.90
(B77-11041)

128'.2 — Mind. *Philosophical perspectives*
Abelson, Raziel. Persons : a study in philosophical psychology / [by] Raziel Abelson. — London [etc.] : Macmillan, 1977. — xiv, 137p ; 23cm.
Bibl.: p.127-130. — Index.
ISBN 0-333-21415-3 : £8.95
(B77-20867)

128'.2'08 — Mind. *Philosophical perspectives. Essays*
Malcolm, Norman. Thought and knowledge : essays / by Norman Malcolm. — Ithaca ; London : Cornell University Press, 1977. — 218p ; 23cm.
Index.
ISBN 0-8014-1074-6 : Unpriced
(B77-17260)

128'.2'08 — Mind. *Philosophical perspectives. Readings*
The **philosophy** of mind / edited by Jonathan Glover. — Oxford : Oxford University Press, 1976. — [5],170p : ill ; 21cm. — (Oxford readings in philosophy)
Bibl.: p.164-168. — Index.
ISBN 0-19-875038-2 Pbk : £1.50
(B77-08726)

128'.3 — Imagination. *Phenomenological viewpoints*
Casey, Edward S. Imagining : a phenomenological study / [by] Edward S. Casey. — Bloomington ; London : Indiana University Press, 1976. — xvi,240p : 2 ill ; 24cm. — (Studies in phenomenology and existential philosophy)
Index.
ISBN 0-253-32912-4 : £9.35
(B77-23071)

128'.3 — Man. Actions. *Philosophical perspectives*
Goldman, Alvin Ira. A theory of human action / [by] Alvin I. Goldman. — Princeton ; Guildford : Princeton University Press, 1976. — [1],xi,230p : ill ; 22cm.
Originally published: Englewood Cliffs : Hemel Hempstead : Prentice-Hall, 1970. — Index.
ISBN 0-691-07216-7 : £10.10
ISBN 0-691-01974-6 Pbk : £3.15
(B77-13471)

Hollis, Martin. Models of man : philosophical thoughts on social action / [by] Martin Hollis. — Cambridge [etc.] : Cambridge University Press, 1977. — vii,198p : ill ; 23cm.
Bibl.: p.191-195. — Index.
ISBN 0-521-21546-3 : £7.00
ISBN 0-521-29181-x Pbk : £2.50
(B77-33569)

Thalberg, Irving. Perception, emotion and action : a component approach / [by] Irving Thalberg. — Oxford : Blackwell, 1977. — [8], 142p ; 23cm. — (Library of philosophy and logic)
Bibl.: p.131-137. — Index.
ISBN 0-631-17600-4 : £3.75 : CIP rev.
(B77-05838)

128'.3 — Man. Nature. *Anthroposophical viewpoints*
Trevelyan, *Sir* **George,** *bart.* A vision of the aquarian age / [by] George Trevelyan. — London : Coventure, [1977]. — vii,162p ; 23cm.
ISBN 0-904576-31-0 : £4.95
(B77-26752)

128'.3 — Man. Sensations. *Philosophical perspectives*
Matson, Wallace I. Sentience / by Wallace I. Matson. — Berkeley [etc.] ; London : University of California Press, 1976. — [9], 190p : 1 ill ; 21cm.
Index.
ISBN 0-520-09538-3 : £7.15
(B77-13472)

128.5 — NATURE OF LIFE AND DEATH
128'.5 — Death
Koestenbaum, Peter. Is there an answer to death? / [by] Peter Koestenbaum. — Englewood Cliffs ; London : Prentice-Hall, 1976. — xii,212p : ill ; 21cm. — (Spectrum books in humanistic psychology)
Index.
ISBN 0-13-506105-9 Pbk : £7.95
0-13-506097-4 Pbk : £2.70
(B77-01993)

Malraux, André. Lazarus / [by] André Malraux ; translated [from the French] by Terence Kilmartin. — London : Macdonald and Jane's, 1977. — [5],149p ; 22cm.
'... part of the second volume of 'The Mirror of Limbo" - title page verso. — Translation of: 'Lazare'. Paris : Editions Gallimard, 1974.
ISBN 0-354-04165-7 : £6.25
(B77-30931)

Neale, Robert E. The art of dying / [by] Robert E. Neale. — New York [etc.] : Harper and Row, 1976. — xiii,158p : forms ; 21cm.
Originally published: New York : Harper and Row, 1973. — Bibl.: p.151-158.
ISBN 0-06-066085-6 Pbk : £2.55
(B77-15668)

New meanings of death / [edited by] Herman Feifel. — [New ed.]. — New York ; London [etc.] : McGraw-Hill, 1977. — xvi,367p : ill ; 24cm.
'A Blakiston Publication'. — Previous ed.: published as 'The meaning of death'. 1959. — Bibl. — Index.
ISBN 0-07-020350-4 : £8.95
ISBN 0-07-020349-0 Pbk : £5.95
(B77-19984)

128'.5 — Life & death
Chiari, Joseph. Reflections on life and death / [by] Joseph Chiari. — London : Elek, 1977. — 141p ; 23cm.
ISBN 0-236-40099-1 : £4.95
(B77-29887)

129 — ORIGIN AND DESTINY OF INDIVIDUAL SOULS
129'.4 — Reincarnation. *Christian viewpoints*
Frieling, Rudolf. Christianity and reincarnation / [by] Rudolf Frieling ; [translated from the German by Rudolf and Margaret Koehler]. — Edinburgh (21 Napier Rd, Edinburgh EH10 5AZ) : Floris Books, 1977. — [2],117p ; 22cm.
Translation of: 'Christentum und Wiederverkörperung'. Stuttgart : Verlag Urachaus, 1974.
ISBN 0-903540-05-3 Pbk : £3.50
(B77-29888)

131 — POPULAR PSYCHOLOGY
131'.3 — Self-development
Mandus, *Brother.* All about you / [by] Brother Mandus. — London : Turnstone Books, 1976. — 197p ; 23cm.
ISBN 0-85500-068-6 : £2.95
ISBN 0-85500-070-8 Pbk : £1.95
(B77-05839)

131'.3 — Self-development. *Manuals*
Harris, Anthony B. Overdrive : a human maintenance manual / [by] Anthony B. Harris. — Newton Abbot [etc.] : David and Charles, 1977. — 175p : ill ; 23cm.
Bibl.: p.174-175.
ISBN 0-7153-7399-4 : £3.95
(B77-26753)

Schwartz, David Joseph. The magic of psychic power / by David J. Schwartz. — Wellingborough : Aquarian Press, 1976. — vii-225p ; 22cm.
Originally published: West Nyack, N.Y. : Parker Publishing, 1965 ; London : Aquarian Press, 1967.
ISBN 0-85030-136-x Pbk : £2.50
(B77-13473)

131'.3 — Self-development. Applications of transactional analysis. *Manuals*
James, Muriel. A new self : self-therapy with transactional analysis / [by] Muriel James and Louis Savary. — Reading, Mass. ; London [etc.] : Addison-Wesley, 1977. — xvii,331p : ill, forms ; 24cm.
Index.
ISBN 0-201-03464-6 : £7.70
ISBN 0-201-03463-8 Pbk : £4.80
(B77-26085)

131'.32 — Meditation
Baker, Douglas. The seven pillars of ancient wisdom : (the synthesis of yoga, esoteric science and psychology) / by Douglas Baker. — Essendon ('Little Elephant', High Rd, Essendon, Herts.) : The author.
Vol.2 : The theory and practice of meditation. — 1975. — 297,[26]p : ill(chiefly col), ports ; 30cm.
Cover title : Meditation. — Index.
Pbk : £7.50
(B77-03884)

Kampf, Harold. In search of serenity : a guide to successful meditation / by Harold Kampf. — Wellingborough : Thorsons, 1976. — 63p ; 22cm.
Originally published: 1974. — Bibl.: p.63.
ISBN 0-7225-0346-6 Pbk : Unpriced
(B77-14022)

131'.32 — Meditation. *Manuals*
LeShan, Lawrence. How to meditate : a guide to self-discovery / [by] Lawrence LeShan ; afterword by Edgar N. Jackson. — London : Wildwood House, 1976. — [8],210p ; 21cm.
Originally published: Boston, Mass. : Little, Brown, 1974.
ISBN 0-7045-0271-2 : £3.95
(B77-01140)

131'.35 — Scientology
Church of Scientology of California. The Scientology religion / [Church of Scientology World Wide]. — East Grinstead (Saint Hill Manor, East Grinstead, Sussex) : Church of Scientology, 1974. — [9],129p ; 24cm.
Pbk : Unpriced
(B77-06436)

133 — PARANORMAL PHENOMENA AND OCCULTISM
133 — Atlanteans. Meditation. *Manuals*
Atlanteans. Atlantean meditation course. — Cheltenham (42 St George's St., Cheltenham GL50 4AF) : Atlanteans.
3rd. — 1976. — 21[i.e.23]p ; 30cm.
ISBN 0-900112-09-3 Sp : £2.85(£1.25 to members)
(B77-00588)

133 — Colour. Occult aspects
Sturzaker, James. The twelve rays : colour and its esoteric significance / by James Sturzaker. — Wellingborough : Aquarian Press, 1976. — 64p ; 18cm.
ISBN 0-85030-131-9 Pbk : £0.60
(B77-07041)

133 — Hermetism. Bruno, Giordano
Yates, Frances Amelia. Giordano Bruno and the Hermetic tradition / by Frances A. Yates. — London [etc.] : Routledge and Kegan Paul [etc.], 1977. — xiv,466p,leaf of plate,[16]p of plates : ill ; 23cm.
Originally published: 1964. — Index.
ISBN 0-7100-2337-5 : £8.95
(B77-13474)

133 — Man. Body. Occult aspects. *Encyclopaedias*
Walker, Benjamin. Encyclopedia of esoteric man / [by] Benjamin Walker. — London [etc.] : Routledge and Kegan Paul, 1977. — x, 343p ; 24cm.
Bibl. — Index.
ISBN 0-7100-8479-x : £5.95
(B77-09471)

133 — Man. Occult aspects
Tansley, David V. Subtle body : essence and shadow / [by] David V. Tansley. — London : Thames and Hudson, 1977. — 96p : ill(some col), facsims, ports ; 28cm. — (Art and imagination)
Bibl.: p.96.
ISBN 0-500-81014-1 Pbk : £2.50
(B77-19985)

133 — Man. Third eye. *Theosophical viewpoints*
Baker, Douglas. The opening of the third eye / by Douglas Baker. — Wellingborough : Aquarian Press, 1977. — 127p : ill ; 22cm.
Originally published: Essenden : The author, 1976.
ISBN 0-85030-140-8 Pbk : £1.80
(B77-13475)

Baker, Douglas. The opening of the third eye / by Douglas Baker. — [Essenden] (['Little Elephant', High Rd, Essenden, Herts.]) : [The author], [1976?]. — 128p : ill(some col) ; 21cm.
ISBN 0-9505502-0-5 Pbk : Unpriced
(B77-07771)

133 — Material objects. *Occult viewpoints*
Bennett, John Godolphin. Material objects / [by] John G. Bennett. — Sherborne, Glos. : Coombe Springs Press, 1977. — [7],59p ; 19cm. — (The Sherborne theme talks series ; 3)
ISBN 0-900306-35-1 Pbk : £0.75
(B77-32369)

133 — Occult practices. Priestesses. Ordination. *Rites*
Robertson, Olivia. Ordination of a priestess / [by] Olivia Robertson. — Enniscorthy (Huntington Castle, Clonegal, Enniscorthy, Eire) : Cesara Publications, [1977]. — [16]p : ports ; 23cm.
Sd : £0.40
(B77-19986)

133 — Occultism
Alder, Vera Stanley. The finding of the 'third eye' / [by] Vera Stanley Alder ; illustrated by the author. — Revised ed. — London : Rider, 1977. — 187p : ill ; 20cm.
Revised ed. originally published: 1968. — Bibl.: p.187.
ISBN 0-09-027343-5 Pbk : £2.25
(B77-17876)

Ashe, Geoffrey. The ancient wisdom / by Geoffrey Ashe. — London [etc.] : Macmillan, 1977. — 232p,[8]p of plates : ill, facsim, map, 2 ports ; 25cm.
Bibl.: p.222-226. — Index.
ISBN 0-333-19867-0 : £4.95 : CIP rev.
(B77-16156)

Baker, Douglas. The seven rays : key to the mysteries / by Douglas Baker. — Wellingborough : Aquarian Press, 1977. — 126p : ill ; 22cm.
ISBN 0-85030-145-9 Pbk : £1.80
(B77-30932)

Bennett, John Godolphin. The image of God in work / [by] John G. Bennett. — Sherborne, Glos. : Coombe Springs Press, 1976. — [6], 74p : 1 ill ; 20cm. — (The transformation of man series ; 5)
ISBN 0-900306-27-0 Pbk : £0.75
(B77-10108)

Bennett, John Godolphin. Needs of a new age community / [compiled by A.G.E. Blake from the unpublished writings and talks of] J.G. Bennett. — Sherbourne, Glos. : Coombe Springs Press, 1977. — [7],99p : 1 ill, port ; 20cm. — (The transformation of man series ; no.7)
ISBN 0-900306-47-5 Pbk : £1.00
(B77-28347)

Bennett, John Godolphin. The sevenfold work / [by] John G. Bennett. — Sherborne, Glos. : Coombe Springs Press, 1975. — [2],vi,116p ; 20cm. — (Transformation of man series ; no.4)
Index.
ISBN 0-900306-23-8 Pbk : £1.00
(B77-10109)

Bennett, John Godolphin. A spiritual psychology / [by] J.G. Bennett. — Revised ed. — Sherborne, Glos. : Coombe Springs Press, 1974. — 3-268p : ill ; 22cm.
This ed. also published: Lakemont : CSA Press, 1974. — Previous ed.: London : Hodder and Stoughton, 1964. — Index.
ISBN 0-900306-14-9 Pbk : £2.00
(B77-10110)

Blair, Lawrence. Rhythms of vision / [by] Lawrence Blair. — St Albans : Paladin, 1976. — 255p : ill, chart, map, port ; 20cm.
Originally published: London : Croom Helm, 1975. — Bibl.: p.247. — Index.
ISBN 0-586-08264-6 Pbk : £1.95
(B77-08181)

Caddy, Eileen. The spirit of Findhorn / [by] Eileen Caddy ; preface, introduction and biography of the author by Roy McVicar. — Romford : L.N. Fowler, 1977. — xii,127p : ill ; 23cm.
ISBN 0-85243-337-9 : Unpriced
(B77-33016)

Cavendish, Richard, *b.1930.* The black arts / [by] Richard Cavendish. — London : Pan Books, 1977. — 414p : ill ; 20cm. — (Picador)
Originally published: London : Routledge and Kegan Paul, 1967. — Bibl.: p.390-399. — Index.
ISBN 0-330-25140-6 Pbk : £1.25
(B77-15067)

Collin, Rodney. The mirror of light : from the notebooks of Rodney Collin. — London : Watkins, 1976. — 89p ; 20cm.
Originally published: London : Stuart, 1959.
ISBN 0-7224-0159-0 Pbk : £2.00
(B77-06437)

The **complete** book of fate & fortune. — London : Marshall Cavendish, 1974. — 128, 128,128p : ill(some col), ports(some col) ; 30cm. — (A 'Golden hands' book)
Originally published: in the part work 'Fate and fortune'. 1974-.
ISBN 0-85685-084-5 : Unpriced
(B77-19987)

Crowley, Aleister. 777 : vel prolegomena symbolica ad systemam sceptico-mysticae viae explicandae, fundamentum hieroglyphicum sanctissimorum scientiae summae / by Aleister Crowley. — [Enlarged ed.]. — Hastings (Archer's Court, Hastings, Sussex) : Metaphysical Research Group, 1977. — xxviii, 155p : ill ; 21cm.
First ed. originally published: s.l. : The author, 1909.
ISBN 0-900684-24-0 Pbk : £2.50
(B77-17877)

Fortune, Dion. The cosmic doctrine / [by] Dion Fortune. — [New ed.] ; revised and with additional matter from the same sources. — Wellingborough : Aquarian Press, 1976. — 157p ; 23cm.
Previous ed.: i.e. Revised and enlarged ed. 1957.
ISBN 0-85030-135-1 : £2.75
(B77-15669)

Grant, Kenneth, *b.1924.* Nightside of Eden / [by] Kenneth Grant. — London : Muller, 1977. — xv,304p,leaf of plate,[16]p of plates : ill ; 23cm.
Bibl.: p.286-289. — Index.
ISBN 0-584-10206-2 : £7.95 : CIP rev.
(B77-06438)

His pupil. The initiate : some impressions of a great soul / by His pupil. — London [etc.] : Routledge and Kegan Paul, 1977. — xv,381p ; 20cm.
Facsimile reprint of: 1st ed. London : G. Routledge and Sons, 1920.
ISBN 0-7100-1588-7 : £5.50
ISBN 0-7100-8570-2 Pbk : £2.75
(B77-12277)

His pupil. The initiate in the dark cycle : a sequel to "The initiate" and to "The initiate in the new world" / by His pupil. — London [etc.] : Routledge and Kegan Paul, 1977. — xvii,215p ; 19cm.
Facsimile reprint of: 1st ed. London : G. Routledge and Sons, 1932.
ISBN 0-7100-1587-9 : £4.25
ISBN 0-7100-8572-9 Pbk : £2.10
(B77-12278)

His pupil. The initiate in the new world : a sequel to "The initiate" / by His pupil. — London [etc.] : Routledge and Kegan Paul, 1977. — x,302p ; 19cm.
Facsimile reprint of: 1st ed. London : G. Routledge and Sons, 1927.
ISBN 0-7100-7077-2 : £4.50
ISBN 0-7100-8571-0 Pbk : £2.25
(B77-12279)

Randall-Stevens, Hugh Clayton. The wisdom of the soul / inspirationally received by H.C. Randall-Stevens (El Eros). — 3rd ed. — London [etc.] (La Maison de Leoville, St Ouen, Jersey, Channel Islands) : Order of the Knights Templars of Aquarius, 1962 [i.e. 1974]. — 135p,leaf of plate,4p of plates : ill(incl 1 col) ; 23cm.
Previous ed.: 1962. — Index.
ISBN 0-904361-05-5 : £3.50
(B77-05840)

Scott, Mary, *b.1906.* Science & subtle bodies : towards a clarification of issues / [by] Mary Scott. — London (16 Queensberry Place, S.W.7) : College of Psychic Studies, 1975. — 49p ; 22cm. — (College of Psychic Studies. Papers ; no.8)
'The Oliver Lodge Research Thesis, 1973-74'.
ISBN 0-903336-07-3 Sd : £0.75
(B77-17878)

133 — Occultism. *Atlantean viewpoints*
Helio-Arcanophus. Spirit evolution : the teachings and lectures of Helio-Arcanophus, founder of the Atlanteans. — [Cheltenham] ([42 St George's St., Cheltenham, [Glos.] GL50 4AF) : [The Atlanteans], 1976. — 60p ; 21cm. — (Third series)
ISBN 0-900112-11-5 Sd : £0.60
(B77-04534)

133 — Occultism. *Christian viewpoints*
Gillett, David. The occult / [by] David Gillett. — 2nd ed. — London : Falcon Books, 1976. — 31p ; 18cm. — (A falcon booklet)
Previous ed.: 1974. — Bibl.: p.29-31.
ISBN 0-85491-148-0 Sd : £0.30
(B77-02725)

133 — Occultism. Superconsciousness
Sadhu, Mouni. Samadhi : the superconsciousness of the future / [by] Mouni Sadhu. — London : Unwin Books, 1976. — 3-182p ; 20cm. — (Mandala books)
Originally published: London : Allen and Unwin, 1962. — Bibl.: p.182.
ISBN 0-04-149039-8 Pbk : £1.95
(B77-08182)

133 — Paranormal phenomena
Buttlar, Johannes von. Journey to infinity : travels in time / [by] Johannes von Buttlar ; translated from the German by Olga Sieveking. — [London] : Fontana, 1976. — 192p,[4]p of plates : ill, port ; 18cm.
This translation originally published: as 'Journey into infinity'. London : Spearman, 1975. — Translation of: 'Reisen in die Ewigkeit'. Vienna : Econ, 1973. — Bibl.: p.182-187. — Index.
ISBN 0-00-634247-7 Pbk : £0.70
(B77-01994)

Däniken, Erich von. Miracles of the gods : a hard look at the supernatural / [by] Erich von Däniken ; translated from the German by Michael Heron. — London : Corgi, 1977. — 237p,[24]p of plates : ill, ports ; 18cm.
This translation originally published: London : Souvenir Press, 1975. — Translation of 'Erscheinungen'. Düsseldorf : Econ-Verlag, 1974. — Bibl.: p.221-230.
ISBN 0-552-10371-3 Pbk : £0.85
(B77-11042)

Oscott, F L. The secret of the sphinx / by Pharaoh Amigdar assisted by ... others ; [reported by] F.L. Oscott ; translated from the Italian by Gavin Gibbons. — Sudbury : Spearman, 1977. — xi,173p,[12]p of plates : ill, facsims, maps, plans ; 23cm.
Originally published: in Italian. Rome : Edizioni Mediterranee, 1975.
ISBN 0-85435-083-7 : £3.95
(B77-10717)

The **supernatural**. — London : Aldus Books : [Distributed by] Jupiter Books.
Guide and index / [biographical research Margaret Fishley ; editor Sally Burningham]. — 1976. — 128p : ill(some col), col facsim, ports(some col) ; 27cm.
Index.
£3.25
(B77-26086)

133 — Paranormal phenomena. *Christian viewpoints*
Moore, Evelyn Garth. Believe it or not : Christianity and psychical research / by E. Garth Moore. — London [etc.] : Mowbrays, 1977. — x,131p ; 22cm.
Bibl.: p.123-126. — Index.
ISBN 0-264-66010-2 Pbk : £2.50
(B77-17261)

133 — Parapsychology
Hammond, David. The search for psychic power / [by] David Hammond. — London : Corgi, 1976. — [9],292p ; 18cm.
Originally published: London : Hodder and Stoughton, 1975. — Bibl. — Index.
ISBN 0-552-10308-x Pbk : £0.75
(B77-02726)

133 — Personality. Occult aspects
De Jongh, Tammo. The magic circle of the soul, the 12 aspects of the mind : an astonishing revelation about human types / [by] Tammo de Jongh. — London (21 Cloncurry St., SW6 6OR) : Rigel Press Ltd, 1974. — [4],26p : ill ; 25cm.
Originally published: 1971.
ISBN 0-85528-011-5 Pbk : Unpriced
(B77-19169)

133 — Time. Occult aspects
Tomas, Andrew. Beyond the time barrier / [by] Andrew Tomas. — London : Sphere, 1977. — 160p,[8]p of plates : ill, ports ; 18cm.
Originally published: Salisbury : Compton Russell Ltd ; London : Sphere, 1974.
ISBN 0-7221-8555-3 Pbk : £0.85
(B77-30933)

133 — World. Occult aspects. *History*
Brennan, James Herbert. An occult history of the world / [by] J.H. Brennan. — London : Futura Publications.
Vol.1. — 1976. — 320p : 1 ill ; 18cm.
Bibl.: p.312-315. — Index.
ISBN 0-86007-338-6 Pbk : £0.90
(B77-08727)

133'.03 — Occultism. *Encyclopaedias*
Lamb, Geoffrey. Magic, witchcraft and the occult / [by] Geoffrey Lamb. — Newton Abbot [etc.] : David and Charles [etc.], 1977. — 176p : ill ; 23cm.
ISBN 0-7153-7356-0 : £4.50
(B77-15670)

Weaver, Graham, *b.1949.* A-Z of the occult / [by] Graham Weaver. — London : Everest, 1975. — 175p : ill ; 18cm.
Cover title: A to Z of the occult.
ISBN 0-903925-27-3 Pbk : £0.50
(B77-18519)

133'.07 — Occultism. Organisations: Order of the Golden Star. Members. Training
Order of the Golden Star. The training for magic / Order of the Golden Star. — Cardiff (47 Forrest Rd, Cardiff CF5 1HQ) : Elliott, Pollak & Warren, 1976. — 41 leaves ; 26cm.
Bibl.: leaf 41.
ISBN 0-905814-00-2 Sp : £1.65
(B77-03331)

133'.07'2 — Parapsychology. Research
Moss, Thelma. The probability of the impossible : scientific discoveries and explorations in the psychic world / by Thelma Moss. — London [etc.] : Routledge and Kegan Paul, 1976 [i.e. 1977]. — [5],410p : ill ; 24cm.
Originally published: Los Angeles : J.P. Torcher, 1974. — Bibl.: p.402-404. — Index.
ISBN 0-7100-8520-6 : £5.95
(B77-10111)

133'.08 — Paranormal phenomena. *Readings*
Peachment, Brian. Judge for yourself : more writings on the strange and supernatural / [by] Brian Peachment. — London : Edward Arnold, 1977. — v,103p : ill, facsims, map, port ; 22cm.

Bibl.: p.101-103. — Previous control number B7716158.
ISBN 0-7131-0086-9 Pbk : £1.25
(B77-16158)

133'.09'044 — Occultism, 1944-1956. *Correspondence*
Collin, Rodney. The theory of conscious harmony : from the letters of Rodney Collin. — London : Watkins, 1976. — xii,212p ; 22cm.
Originally published: London : V. Stuart, 1958.
ISBN 0-7224-0019-5 Pbk : £3.25
(B77-08728)

133'.092'4 — Occultism. *Personal observations*
Holroyd, Stuart. Prelude to the landing on planet earth / [by] Stuart Holroyd. — London : W.H. Allen, 1977. — [9],337p ; 23cm.
Bibl.: p.330-332. — Index.
ISBN 0-491-02321-9 : £6.95
(B77-28348)

133'.092'4 — Occultism. Crowley, Aleister. *Biographies*
King, Francis, *b.1904.* The magical world of Aleister Crowley / [by] Francis King. — London : Weidenfeld and Nicolson, 1977. — ix, 210p,[8]p of plates : ill, ports ; 23cm.
Bibl.: p.199-201. — Index.
ISBN 0-297-77423-9 : £6.50
(B77-33570)

133'.0941 — Occultism. Organisations. *Great Britain. Reports, surveys*
The **many** ways of being / edited by Stephen Annett. — London : Abacus, 1976. — 286p : map ; 20cm.
Also published: London : Turnstone Books, 1976. — Index. — Includes sections on Christian organisations & groups connected with alternative medicine.
ISBN 0-349-10071-3 Pbk : £1.25
(B77-05179)

133'.0981 — Paranormal phenomena. *Brazil*
Playfair, Guy Lyon. The unknown power : research into paranormal phenomena in the world's most psychic country / [by] Guy Lyon Playfair. — St Albans : Panther, 1977. — 332p, [16]p of plates : ill, facsims, ports ; 18cm.
Originally published: as 'The flying cow'. London : Souvenir Press, 1975. — Index.
ISBN 0-586-04235-0 Pbk : £0.95
(B77-20868)

133.1 — GHOSTS
133.1 — Ghosts. *Juvenile literature*
A **shiver** of spooks : true ghost stories / compiled by Christine Bernard. — London : Armada Books, 1976. — 125p ; 18cm. — (Armada's spinechiller series)
ISBN 0-00-691030-0 Pbk : £0.40
(B77-01141)

133.1'07'2 — Ghosts. Investigation. *Manuals*
Green, Andrew. Ghost hunting : a practical guide / [by] Andrew Green. — St Albans : Mayflower, 1976. — 159p : ill, 2 plans ; 18cm.
Originally published: London : Garnstone Press, 1973. — Bibl.: p.145-149.
ISBN 0-583-12500-x Pbk : £0.60
(B77-03885)

133.1'08 — Ghosts. *Readings*
'Weekend' book of ghosts / edited by Richard Whittington-Egan. — [London] : Associated Newspapers Group, 1975. — 127p : ill, ports ; 22cm.
'... stories ... first appeared in "Weekend"' - p.6.

ISBN 0-85144-127-0 Pbk : £0.60
(B77-00008)

133.1'29'41 — Ghosts. *Great Britain*
Moss, Peter, *b.1921.* Ghosts over Britain / [by] Peter Moss ; illustrated by Angela Lewer. — London : Elm Tree Books, 1977. — 173p : ill, ports ; 25cm.
ISBN 0-241-89743-2 : £3.95
(B77-29889)

133.1'29'41 — Ghosts. *Great Britain, 1850-1975. Stories, anecdotes*
MacManus, Diarmuid Arthur. Between two worlds : true ghost stories of the British Isles / by Diarmuid MacManus. — Gerrard Cross : Smythe, 1977. — 154p,plate : 2 ill ; 23cm.
ISBN 0-900675-83-7 : £3.75
(B77-17262)

133.1'29'41 — Haunted buildings. *Great Britain*
Braddock, Joseph. Haunted houses / [by] Joseph Braddock ; illustrated by Felix Kelly. — Large print ed. — Bath : Chivers, 1977. — xiv,321p : ill ; 23cm.
Originally published: London : Batsford, 1956.
ISBN 0-85997-202-x : £5.60(£4.20 to members of the Library Association)
(B77-10112)

133.1'29'41 — Women ghosts. *Great Britain, 1950-1975. Directories*
Green, Andrew. Phantom ladies / [by] Andrew Green. — Folkestone : Bailey and Swinfen, 1977. — [8],151p,[16]p of plates : ill ; 23cm. — (Ghost hunters' library)
Bibl.: p.151.
ISBN 0-561-00295-9 : £3.85 : CIP rev.
(B77-04535)

133.1'29'42 — Ghosts. *England, to 1976. Stories, anecdotes*
Chambers, Aidan. Ghost carnival : stories of ghosts in their haunts / [by] Aidan Chambers ; illustrated by Peter Wingham. — London : Heinemann, 1977. — 152p : ill ; 24cm.
ISBN 0-434-93162-4 : £3.90
(B77-30934)

133.1'29'422 — Ghosts. *Central Southern England*
Poole, Keith Baddeley. Ghosts of Wessex / [by] Keith B. Poole. — Newton Abbot [etc.] : David and Charles, 1976. — 127p ; 23cm. — (Regional ghost series)
Bibl.: p.127.
ISBN 0-7153-7287-4 : £3.50
(B77-16159)

133.1'29'4237 — Ghosts. *Cornwall*
Alexander, Marc. Ghostly Cornwall / by Marc Alexander ; photographs by the author. — [Gilsland] ([Crooks Cottage, Gilsland, Cumbria]) : Pacific Press, 1977. — 2-47p : ill, map ; 21cm.
Sd : Unpriced
(B77-29139)

133.1'29'42584 — Ghosts. *Hertfordshire. Tring region*
Richards, Sheila. Ghosts of Tring / [by Sheila Richards]. — [Tring] ([West Leith, Tring, Herts.]) : The author, 1976. — [13]p ; 21cm.
ISBN 0-9505538-0-8 Sd : Unpriced
(B77-08184)

133.1'29'426 — Ghosts. *East Anglia*
Forman, Joan. Haunted East Anglia / [by] Joan Forman. — [London] : Fontana, 1976. — 224p, [8]p of plates : ill, port ; 18cm.
Originally published: London : Hale, 1974. — Index.
ISBN 0-00-634009-1 Pbk : £0.80
(B77-06439)

Forman, Joan. Haunted East Anglia / [by] Joan Forman. — [London] : Fontana, 1977. — 224p, [8]p of plates : ill, port ; 18cm.
Originally published: London : Hale, 1974. — Index.
Pbk : £0.80
ISBN 0-00-634009-1
(B77-15671)

133.1'29'427 — Ghosts. *Northern England*
Hallam, Jack. Ghosts of the North / [by] Jack Hallam. — Newton Abbot [etc.] : David and Charles, 1976. — 135p : map ; 23cm.
Bibl.: p.133-134.
ISBN 0-7153-7320-x : £3.25
(B77-05180)

133.1'29'4288 — Haunted castles. *England. Border country*
Alexander, Marc. Legendary castles of the border / by Marc Alexander ; photographs by the author. — Gilsland (Crooks Cottage, Gilsland, Cumbria) : Pacific Press, [1977]. — 2-51p : ill, map ; 21cm.
Sd : £0.45
(B77-29140)

133.1'4 — Poltergeists, ca 1700-1970. *Juvenile literature*
Knight, David Carpenter. Poltergeists : hauntings and the haunted / [by] David C. Knight. — London [etc.] : Dent, 1977. — 159p : ill, facsim, ports ; 22cm. — (The weird and horrible library)
Originally published: Philadelphia : Lippincott, 1972. — Index.
ISBN 0-460-06810-5 : £2.50 : CIP rev.
(B77-22313)

133.3 — DIVINATORY ARTS
133.3 — Psychic phenomena: Divination. *Manuals*
Gibson, Walter Brown. The encyclopaedia of prophecy / [by] Walter B. Gibson and Litzka R. Gibson ; drawings by Murray Keshner. — London [etc.] : Mayflower, 1977. — xi,336p : ill ; 20cm.
Originally published: as 'The complete illustrated book of divination and prophecy'. Garden City, N.Y. : Doubleday, 1973 ; London : Souvenir Press, 1974. — Index.
ISBN 0-583-12512-3 Pbk : £1.25
(B77-33017)

133.3'092'4 — Psychic phenomena: Divination. Leftwich, Robert
Wilson, Colin. Strange powers / [by] Colin Wilson. — London : Abacus, 1975. — 126p ; 20cm.
Originally published: London : Latimer New Dimensions, 1973.
ISBN 0-349-13733-1 Pbk : £0.65
Primary classification 133.9
(B77-18522)

133.3'0969'1 — Psychic phenomena: Divination. *Malagasy Republic, ca 1890*
Pennick, Nigel. Madagascar divination / by Nigel Pennick. — Cambridge (142 Pheasant Rise, Bar Hill, Cambridge CB3 8SD) : Fenris-Wolf, 1975. — [1],8p : ill ; 30cm. — (Megalithic visions antiquarian papers ; no.8)
ISBN 0-9505403-5-8 Sd : £0.20
(B77-14023)

133.3'2 — Prophecies. Coinneach Ódhar
Mackenzie, Alexander, *b.1838.* The prophecies of the Brahan Seer = Coinneach Odhar Fiosaiche / [by] Alexander Mackenzie. — [New ed.] / with a foreword, commentary and conclusion by Elizabeth Sutherland. — London : Constable, 1977. — 152p,[16]p of plates : ill, maps(on lining papers), ports ; 23cm.
Previous ed.: i.e. New ed. Golspie : Sutherland Press, 1970. — Bibl.: p.143-144. — Index.
ISBN 0-09-461720-1 : £3.50
(B77-27645)

133.3'23 — Dowsing. *Manuals*
Elliot, J Scott. Dowsing one man's way / [by] J. Scott Elliott. — Jersey : Neville Spearman (Jersey) Ltd ; Sudbury : Distributed by Spearman, 1977. — 159p,leaf of plate,[8]p of plates : ill, maps, port ; 23cm.
ISBN 0-85978-025-2 : £3.50
(B77-11043)

133.3'24 — Fortune-telling
Cheiro. The Cheiro book of fate and fortune : palmistry, numerology, astrology. — London : Barrie and Jenkins, 1977. — [12],339p : ill ; 22cm.
Originally published: 1971.
ISBN 0-214-20401-4 Pbk : £2.95
(B77-29890)

133.3'24 — Fortune-telling. Techniques. *Manuals*
Pelton, Robert Wayne. Ancient secrets of fortune-telling / [by] Robert W. Pelton. — South Brunswick ; New York : Barnes ; London : Yoseloff, 1976. — 281p : ill, port ; 26cm.
Bibl.: p.275-281.
ISBN 0-498-01487-8 : £6.00
(B77-29891)

133.3'2424 — Tarot cards
Gardner, Richard. Fortune telling by Tarot cards / [by] Richard Gardner. — London (21 Cloncurry St., SW6 6OR) : Rigel Press Limited, 1974. — 38,[1]p : ill ; 11cm.
'... a short extract from "The Tarot Speaks" by Richard Gardner. [London : Rigel Press, 1971]' - p.36.
ISBN 0-85528-009-3 Sd : Unpriced
(B77-18520)

Ouspensky, P.D. The symbolism of the Tarot : philosophy of occultism in pictures and numbers / [by] P.D. Ouspensky ; translated [from the Russian] by A.L. Pogossky. — New York : Dover Publications [etc.] ; London : Constable, 1976. — [2],63,[2]p(2 fold) : col ill ; 22cm.
Facsimile reprint. — This translation originally published: New York : Dover Publications, 1913.
ISBN 0-486-23291-3 Pbk : £1.15
(B77-03332)

133.3'33 — Abbeys. *Somerset. Glastonbury. Glastonbury Abbey. Geomantic aspects*
Pennick, Nigel. The geomancy of Glastonbury Abbey / by Nigel Pennick. — [Cambridge] ([142 Pheasant Rise,] Bar Hill [Cambridge CB3 8SD]) : Fenris-Wolf Publications, 1976. — [1], 8p : ill, map, plans ; 20cm. — (Megalithic visions antiquarian papers ; no.11)
ISBN 0-9505403-7-4 Sd : £0.25
(B77-13476)

133.3'33 — Antiquities. Geomantic aspects. *Great Britain*
Pennick, Nigel. Leys & zodiacs / by Nigel Pennick. — Revised ed. — Cambridge (142 Pheasant Rise, Bar Hill, Cambridge CB3 8SD) : Fenris-Wolf, 1976. — [17]p : ill, maps ; 30cm. — (Megalithic visions antiquarian papers ; no.5)
Previous ed.: 1975.
Sd : £0.20
(B77-14024)

133.3'33 — Geomancy
Pennick, Nigel. Sacred geometry : an introduction / by Nigel Pennick. — Cambridge (142 Pheasant Rise, Bar Hill, Cambridge CB3 8SD) : Fenris-Wolf, [1977]. — [1],8p,plate : ill, plan ; 30cm. — (Megalithic visions antiquarian papers ; no.14)
Bibl.: p.8.
Sd : Unpriced
(B77-23959)

133.3'33 — Mazes. Geomantic aspects. *England*
Pennick, Nigel. Caerdroia : ancient turf, stone & pavement mazes / by Nigel Pennick. — Cambridge (113 Shelford Rd, Trumpington, Cambridge CB2 2NB) : Megalithic Visions Etcetera, [1974]. — 13p : ill, plans ; 29cm. — ([Megalithic visions antiquarian papers ; no.2])
Limited ed. of 200 numbered copies.
Sd : £0.20
(B77-14025)

133.3'33 — Measurement. Geomantic aspects
Pennick, Nigel. European metrology / by Nigel Pennick ; foreword by Rupert Pennick. — Cambridge (142 Pheasant Rise, Bar Hill, Cambridge CB3 8SD) : Fenris-Wolf, 1975. — [1],12p : 1 ill ; 30cm. — (Megalithic visions antiquarian papers ; no.4)
Bibl.: p.11.
ISBN 0-9505403-8-2 Sd : £0.20
(B77-14026)

133.3'33 — Royal parks. *London. Westminster (London Borough). Regent's Park. Design. Geomantic aspects*
Pennick, Rupert. Regent's Park : town planning - or geomancy? / by Rupert Pennick & Nigel Pennick. — Cambridge (142 Pheasant Rise, Bar Hill, Cambridge CB3 8SD) : Fenris-Wolf, 1977. — [1],8p : ill, map, plans ; 30cm. — (Megalithic visions antiquarian papers ; no.13)
Sd : Unpriced
(B77-23960)

133.3'33 — Structures. Siting & construction. Geomantic aspects. *East Anglia, to ca 1500*
Pennick, Nigel. East Anglian geomancy / by Nigel Pennick. — Cambridge (142 Pheasant Rise, Bar Hill, Cambridge CB3 8SD) : Fenris-Wolf, 1975. — [1],14p : ill, plans ; 30cm. — (Megalithic visions antiquarian papers ; no.7)
Bibl.: p.13.
Sd : £0.30
(B77-14529)

133.3'33 — Templar churches. *Scotland. Orkney. Orphir Church, Orkney. Geomantic aspects*
Worden, Ian P. The round church of Orphir, Orkney / by Ian P. Worden. — Cambridge (142 Pheasant Rise, Bar Hill, Cambridge CB3 8SD) : Institute of Geomantic Research, 1976. — 5p,plate : ill, plan ; 30cm. — (Institute of Geomantic Research. Occasional papers ; no.6 ISSN 0308-1966)
ISBN 0-905376-04-8 Sd : Unpriced
(B77-11534)

133.3'33 — Templar churches. Geomantic aspects. *Great Britain*
Pennick, Nigel. Holy sepulchre : the round churches of Britain / by Nigel Pennick. — Cambridge (113 Shelford Rd, Trumpington, Cambridge [CB2 2NB]) : Megalithic Visions Etcetera, [1974]. — 9p : ill, plan ; 30cm. — (Megalithic visions antiquarian papers ; no.3)
ISBN 0-9505403-1-5 Sd : £0.20
(B77-14027)

133.3'33'05 — Geomancy. *Periodicals*
Journal of geomancy. — [Cambridge] ([142 Pheasant Rise, Bar Hill, Cambridge CB3 8SD]) : Institute of Geomantic Research. Vol.1, no.1- ; 1976-. — 1976-. — ill, ports ; 30cm.
Quarterly. — [2]leaves, p.24-44,[5]leaves of plates (1 fold) in 2nd issue.
Sd : £0.60(free to members)
ISSN 0308-5406
(B77-12828)

133.3'33'08 — Geomancy. *Essays*
Mann, Ludovic McLellan. A forgotten researcher, Ludovic McLellan Mann / introduction by Michael Behrend. — Cambridge (142 Pheasant Rise, Bar Hill, Cambridge CB3 8SD) : Institute of Geomantic Research, 1977. — 22p,[2]leaves of plates : ill, plans ; 30cm. — (Institute of Geomantic Research. Occasional papers ; no.7 ISSN 0308-1966)
Consists chiefly of the texts of unpublished articles by Ludovic McLellan Mann. — Bibl.: p.22.
ISBN 0-905376-05-6 Sd : £0.75
(B77-13477)

133.3'34 — Swastikas
Pennick, Nigel. The swastika / by Nigel Pennick ; introduction by Rupert Pennick. — Cambridge (142 Pheasant Rise, Bar Hill, Cambridge CB3 8SD) : Fenris-Wolf, 1975. — [1],10p : ill ; 30cm. — (Megalithic visions antiquarian papers ; no.10)
Sd : Unpriced
(B77-23961)

133.3'35 — Numerology
Ellis, Keith, *b.1927.* Numberpower : in nature, art, and everyday life / [by] Keith Ellis. — London : Heinemann, 1977. — xv,236p : ill, plans ; 22cm.
Cover title: Number power. — Index.
ISBN 0-434-90526-7 Pbk : £2.50
(B77-22314)

133.3'35 — Pyramidology
Lemesurier, Peter. The Great Pyramid decoded / [by] Peter Lemesurier. — Tisbury : Compton Russell, 1977. — [10],350p : ill, maps ; 24cm.
Bibl.: p.341-343. — Index.
ISBN 0-85955-015-x : £6.95
(B77-21668)

Schul, Bill. The psychic power of pyramids / [by] Bill Schul and Ed Pettit. — London : Coronet, 1977. — 224p : ill, plans, ports ; 18cm.
Originally published: New York : Fawcett, 1976. — Bibl.: p.218-219. — Index.
ISBN 0-340-21815-0 Pbk : £0.95
(B77-19988)

133.4 — MAGIC, WITCHCRAFT, DEMONOLOGY

133.4 — Magic & witchcraft. *Juvenile literature*
Law, Felicia. Magic / written by Felicia Law ; illustrated by Gillian Were. — London [etc.] : Collins, 1977. — 32p : col ill ; 22cm. — (Dandelions)
ISBN 0-00-651260-7 Sd : £0.50
(B77-32370)

133.4 — Spiritism. *Brazil*
McGregor, Pedro. Brazilian magic : is it the answer? / [by] Pedro McGregor ; in association with T. Stratton Smith. — London : Sphere, 1976. — 206p,[4]p of plates : ill, ports ; 18cm. — (The Dennis Wheatley library of the occult ; 42)
Originally published: as 'The moon and two mountains'. London : Souvenir Press, 1966.
ISBN 0-7221-5941-2 Pbk : £0.60
(B77-16160)

133.4'07 — Witchcraft. Literary sources
The **damned** art : essays in the literature of witchcraft / edited by Sydney Anglo. — London [etc.] : Routledge and Kegan Paul, 1977. — viii,258p ; 23cm.
Index.
ISBN 0-7100-8589-3 : £8.50 : CIP rev.
(B77-11044)

133.4'09 — Witchcraft, to 1965. *Collections. Juvenile literature*
Covens & cauldrons / [edited by] Jacynth Hope-Simpson ; illustrated by Krystyna Turska. — London [etc.] : Beaver Books, 1977. — 175p : ill ; 20cm.
This collection originally published: as 'The Hamish Hamilton book of witches'. London : Hamilton, 1966.
ISBN 0-600-39385-2 Pbk : £0.55
(B77-33571)

133.4'09 — Witchcraft, to 1974. *Juvenile literature*
Garden, Nancy. Witches / [by] Nancy Garden. — London [etc.] : Dent, 1977. — 160p : ill, facsim, music, ports ; 22cm. — (The weird and horrible library)
Originally published: Philadelphia : Lippincott, 1975. — Index.
ISBN 0-460-06811-3 : £2.50 : CIP rev.
(B77-19170)

133.4'09181'2 — Magic. *Western world, to 1975*
Cavendish, Richard, *b.1930.* A history of magic / [by] Richard Cavendish. — London : Weidenfeld and Nicolson, 1977. — [5],180p,[16] p of plates : ill, facsims, ports ; 26cm.
Bibl.: p.168-172. — Index.
ISBN 0-297-77252-x : £4.95
(B77-13478)

133.4'092'2 — Magicians, to 1972. *Juvenile literature*
Cohen, Daniel. Magicians, wizards, & sorcerers / by Daniel Cohen. — London : Dent, 1977. — 159p : ill, ports ; 22cm. — (The weird and horrible library)
Originally published: Philadelphia : Lippincott, 1973. — Index.
ISBN 0-460-06813-x : £2.50 : CIP rev.
(B77-19171)

133.4'092'4 — Magic. Crowley, Aleister. Works. *Critical studies*
Fuller, John Frederick Charles. The star in the west : a critical essay upon the works of Aleister Crowley / by J.F.C. Fuller. — 2nd ed. [i.e. 1st ed. reprinted]. — London (49a Museum St., W.C.1) : Neptune Press, 1976. — [7],327p : 1 ill ; 20cm.
Limited ed. of 500 numbered copies. — Facsimile reprint of: 1st ed. London : Walter Scott Publishing Co., 1907.
ISBN 0-9505001-1-9 : £7.50
(B77-12280)

133.4'0932 — Ancient Egyptian magic
Vandenberg, Philipp. The curse of the pharaohs / [by] Philipp Vandenberg ; translated [from the German] by Thomas Weyr. — Sevenoaks : Coronet, 1977. — 235p : ill, geneal table, maps, plan ; 18cm.
This translation originally published: Philadelphia : Lippincott ; London : Hodder and Stoughton, 1975. — Translation of: 'Der Fluch der Pharaonen'. Bern : Scherz, 1973. — Bibl.: p.221-226. — Index.
ISBN 0-340-21310-8 Pbk : £0.70
Also classified at 932
(B77-16161)

133.4'09427'645 — Witches. *Lancashire. Pendle (District), ca 1600-ca 1640*
Bennett, Walter. The Pendle witches / by Walter Bennett. — [Lancaster] ([Town Hall, Lancaster LA1 1HT]) : Lancashire County Council Library and Leisure Committee, 1976. — 32p ; 22cm.
Originally published: Burnley : County Borough of Burnley Libraries and Arts Committee, 1957.
ISBN 0-902228-27-7 Sd : £0.40
(B77-10113)

Towneley Hall Art Gallery and Museums. The Pendle witches : a trial in 17th century Lancashire : exhibition at Towneley Hall Art Gallery and Museum[s], Burnley, 19th May-30th September 1972, arranged by John D. Blundell, curator. — [Burnley] ([c/o Towneley Hall Art Gallery and Museum, Burnley, Lancs.]) : County Borough of Burnley, Art Gallery and Museum Sub-committee, 1972. — 23p : ill, facsim ; 21cm.
'Hand list of Exhibits' (6p.) as insert. — Bibl.: p.23.
Sd : £0.12
(B77-07042)

133.4'09429 — Witchcraft. *Wales, to ca 1900. Welsh texts*
Bosse-Griffiths, Kate. Byd y dyn hysbys : swyngyfaredd yng Nghymru / [gan] Kate Bosse Griffiths. — Talybont, Dyfed (Talybont, Dyfed SY24 5ER) : Y Lolfa, 1977. — 144p : ill, facsims, port ; 19cm. — ([Pocedlyfrau'r Lolfa])
Bibl.: p.135-138. — Index.
ISBN 0-904864-25-1 : £2.75
ISBN 0-904864-24-3 Pbk : Unpriced
(B77-30935)

133.4'09744'5 — Witchcraft. *Massachusetts. Salem, 1688-1692*
Pennick, Rupert. Witchcraft in New England : an investigation / by Rupert Pennick. — Cambridge (142 Pheasant Rise, Bar Hill, Cambridge CB3 8SD) : Fenris-Wolf, 1976. — [1],11p ; 30cm. — (Megalithic visions antiquarian papers ; no.12)
ISBN 0-9505403-9-0 Sd : £0.30
(B77-14028)

133.4'23 — Vampires. *Anthologies*
The **Dracula** scrapbook : articles, essays, letters, newspaper cuttings, anecdotes, illustrations, photographs and memorabilia about the vampire legend / edited by Peter Haining ; foreword by Christopher Lee. — London : New English Library, 1976. — 176p : ill, facsims, map, ports ; 31cm.
Ill. on lining papers. — Bibl.: p.37.
ISBN 0-450-03047-4 : £6.50
(B77-09472)

The **Dracula** scrapbook : articles, essays, letters, newspaper cuttings, anecdotes, illustrations, photographs and memorabilia about the vampire legend / edited by Peter Haining ; foreword by Christopher Lee. — London : New English Library, 1976 [i.e. 1977]. — 176p : ill, facsims, maps, ports ; 30cm.
This collection originally published: 1976. — Bibl.: p.37.
ISBN 0-450-03525-5 Pbk : £4.50
(B77-28349)

133.4'23 — Vampires, to 1974
Underwood, Peter. The vampire's bedside companion : the amazing world of vampires in fact and fiction / written and edited by Peter Underwood ; with contributions by ... [others]. — London : Coronet, 1976. — 189p,[8]p of plates : ill, ports ; 20cm.
Originally published: London : Frewin, 1975. — Bibl.: p.189.
ISBN 0-340-20813-9 Pbk : £1.00
(B77-03333)

133.4'26'094463 — Man. Demonic possession. *France. Loudun, ca 1634*
Huxley, Aldous. The devils of Loudun / [by] Aldous Huxley. — St Albans : Triad, 1977. — 316p : ill, 2 facsims, 2 ports ; 18cm.
Originally published: London : Chatto and Windus, 1952. — Bibl.: p.315-316.
ISBN 0-586-04442-6 Pbk : £0.95
(B77-22315)

133.4'3 — Curses & spells. *Juvenile literature*
Cohen, Daniel. Curses, hexes, & spells / by Daniel Cohen. — London [etc.] : Dent, 1977. — 125p : ill, ports ; 22cm. — (The weird and horrible library)
Originally published: Philadelphia : Lippincott, 1974. — Index.
ISBN 0-460-06814-8 : £2.50 : CIP rev.
(B77-19172)

133.4'7 — Voodoo
Gilfond, Henry. Voodoo : its origins and practices / by Henry Gilfond. — New York ; London : F. Watts, 1976. — x,114,[1]p : ill, facsim, map ; 25cm.
Bibl.: p.101-102. — Index.
ISBN 0-531-00347-7 : £2.75
(B77-16700)

133.5 — ASTROLOGY
Hickey, Isabel M. Astrology : a cosmic science / [by] Isabel M. Hickey. — London (4 Holland St., W.8) : The Equinox (Booksellers and Publishers) Ltd, 1975. — [1],280p : ill ; 26cm.
Originally published: Watertown : Fellowship House Bookshop, 1974.
ISBN 0-905841-01-8 : £5.00
(B77-04536)

Sadalah, Mustafa L. Astrology and you / [by] Mustafa L. Sadalah. — Ilfracombe : Stockwell, 1977. — 42p ; 18cm.
ISBN 0-7223-0911-2 Pbk : £0.45
(B77-25357)

Vogh, James. Arachne rising : the thirteenth sign of the zodiac / [by] James Vogh. — London [etc.] : Hart-Davis MacGibbon, 1977. — [6], 202p : ill, plan ; 23cm.
Bibl.: p.196-198. — Index.
ISBN 0-246-10931-9 : £3.95
(B77-23072)

133.5 — Astrology. Book of fate. *Critical studies*
Deacon, Richard. 'The Book of fate', its origins and uses / [by] Richard Deacon. — London : Muller, 1976. — 238p,[10]p of plates,(2 fold) : ill, facsims, ports ; 23cm.
Ill. on lining papers. — Bibl.: p.233-234. — Index. — Includes a simplified and modernised version of 'The Book of fate'.
ISBN 0-584-10216-x : £4.95
(B77-01142)

133.5'01'515785 — Astrology. Applications of analysis of harmonic oscillations
Addey, John Michael. Harmonics in astrology : an introductory text-book to the new understanding of an old science / by John M. Addey. — Romford : L.N. Fowler, 1976. — 263p : ill ; 22cm.
Index.
ISBN 0-85243-334-4 Pbk : £2.95
(B77-07043)

133.5'05 — Astrological predictions. *Serials*
Raphael, Edwin. Raphael's astrological almanac / edited by Edwin Raphael. — Slough : Foulsham.
1978. — 1977. — 114p : ill, ports ; 18cm.
ISBN 0-572-00972-0 Pbk : £0.75
(B77-29141)

133.5'05 — Irish astrological almanacs, 1587-1844. *Critical studies. Early works*

Evans, Edward, *b. ca1830.* Historical and bibliographical account of almanacks, directories, etc., etc. published in Ireland from the sixteenth century : their rise, progress and decay : with jottings of their compilers and printers / by Edward Evans. — Facsimile ed. ; with an introduction by Thomas Wall. — Blackrock (25 Newtown Ave., Blackrock, Co. Dublin) : Carraig Books, 1976. — xiv,149p : col facsim ; 19cm.
Originally published: Dublin : 'The Irish Builder', 1897.
ISBN 0-902512-15-3 Pbk : £2.50
(B77-04537)

133.5'0951 — Chinese astrology

White, Suzanne. Suzanne White's book of Chinese chance : what the oriental Zodiac can tell you about yourself and your future. — London : Souvenir Press, 1977. — [7],359p ; 24cm.
Originally published: New York : M. Evans, 1976.
ISBN 0-285-62258-7 : £4.50
(B77-10114)

133.5'2 — Signs of the zodiac

Trevelyan, *Sir* **George,** *bart.* Twelve seats at the round table / [by] Sir George Trevelyan & Edward Matchett. — St Helier : Neville Spearman (Jersey) Ltd ; Sudbury (57 Friars St., Sudbury, Suffolk) : Distributed by Spearman, 1976. — 104p,[12]p of plates : ill ; 24cm.
ISBN 0-85978-027-9 Pbk : £2.95
(B77-08729)

133.5'2 — Signs of the zodiac. Related to English forenames

Parker, Derek. Derek & Julia Parker's compleat zodiac name book : the guide to your name and naming your child. — London : Luscombe, 1976. — 96p : ill ; 5cm.
Index on lining papers.
ISBN 0-86002-079-7 : £2.95
Primary classification 929.4'0942
(B77-01060)

133.5'3 — Astrology. Aspects

Lee, Jason. Planets in signs / by Jason Lee. — Grimsby (42 Worlaby Rd, Grimsby, S. Humberside) : The author, 1977. — 99[i.e.101] p : ill ; 30cm.
Sd : £0.50
(B77-25358)

133.5'3 — Saturn. Astrological aspects

Greene, Liz. Saturn : a new look at an old devil / [by] Liz Greene. — Wellingborough : Aquarian Press, 1977. — 196p : 1 ill ; 21cm.
Originally published: New York : Samuel Weiser, 1976.
ISBN 0-85030-148-3 Pbk : £2.75
(B77-33018)

133.5'4 — Astrological predictions. Horoscopes

Jones, Marc Edmund. Astrology : how and why it works : an introduction to basic horoscopy / [by] Marc Edmund Jones. — London [etc.] : Routledge and Kegan Paul, 1977. — x,437p : ill ; 19cm.
Originally published: Philadelphia : D. McKay, 1945. — Index.
ISBN 0-7100-8578-8 : £5.25
(B77-16162)

133.5'4 — Astrological predictions. Horoscopes. *Texts*

Sheridan, Jo. Your horoscope / by ... Jo Sheridan. — [St Albans] : Mayflower.
1976. Aquarius, January 20-February 18. — [1975]. — 47p : ill ; 18cm.
Cover title.
ISBN 0-583-12685-5 Pbk : £0.30
(B77-19173)

1976. Aries, March 21-April 19. — [1975]. — 47p : ill ; 18cm.
Cover title.
ISBN 0-583-12687-1 Pbk : £0.30
(B77-19174)

1976. Cancer, June 21-July 22. — [1975]. — 47p : ill ; 18cm.
Cover title.
ISBN 0-583-12690-1 Pbk : £0.30
(B77-19175)

1976. Capricorn, December 22-January 19. — [1975]. — 47p : ill ; 18cm.
Cover title.
ISBN 0-583-12696-0 Pbk : £0.30
(B77-19176)

1976. Gemini, May 22-June 20. — [1975]. — 47p : ill ; 18cm.
Cover title.
ISBN 0-583-12689-8 Pbk : £0.30
(B77-19177)

1976. Leo, July 23-August 22. — [1975]. — 47p : ill ; 18cm.
Cover title.
ISBN 0-583-12691-x Pbk : £0.30
(B77-19178)

1976. Libra, September 23-October 22. — [1975]. — 47p : ill ; 18cm.
Cover title.
ISBN 0-583-12693-6 Pbk : £0.30
(B77-19179)

1976. Pisces, February 19-March 20. — [1975]. — 47p : ill ; 18cm.
Cover title.
ISBN 0-583-12686-3 Pbk : £0.30
(B77-19180)

1976. Sagittarius, November 22-December 21. — [1975]. — 47p : ill ; 18cm.
Cover title.
ISBN 0-583-12695-2 Pbk : £0.30
(B77-19181)

1976. Scorpio, October 23-November 21. — [1975]. — 47p : ill ; 18cm.
Cover title.
ISBN 0-583-12694-4 Pbk : £0.30
(B77-19182)

1976. Taurus, April 20-May 21. — [1975]. — 47p : ill ; 18cm.
Cover title.
ISBN 0-583-12688-x Pbk : £0.30
(B77-19183)

1976. Virgo, August 23-September 22. — [1975]. — 47p : ill ; 18cm.
Cover title.
ISBN 0-583-12692-8 Pbk : £0.30
(B77-19184)

1978. Aquarius, January 20-February 18. — 1977. — 47p : ill ; 18cm.
Cover title.
ISBN 0-583-12623-5 Pbk : £0.35
(B77-24656)

1978. Aries, March 21-April 19. — 1977. — 47p : ill ; 18cm.
Cover title.
ISBN 0-583-12625-1 Pbk : £0.35
(B77-24657)

1978. Cancer, June 21-July 22. — 1977. — 47p : ill ; 18cm.
Cover title.
ISBN 0-583-12628-6 Pbk : £0.35
(B77-24658)

1978. Capricorn, December 22-January 19. — 1977. — 47p : ill ; 18cm.
Cover title.
ISBN 0-583-12634-0 Pbk : £0.35
(B77-24659)

1978. Gemini, May 22-June 20. — 1977. — 47p : ill ; 18cm.
Cover title.
ISBN 0-583-12627-8 Pbk : £0.35
(B77-24660)

1978. Leo, July 23-August 22. — 1977. — 47p : ill ; 18cm.
Cover title.
ISBN 0-583-12629-4 Pbk : £0.35
(B77-24661)

1978. Libra, September 23-October 22. — 1977. — 47p : ill ; 18cm.
Cover title.
ISBN 0-583-12631-6 Pbk : £0.35
(B77-24662)

1978. Pisces, February 19-March 20. — 1977. — 47p : ill ; 18cm.
Cover title.
ISBN 0-583-12624-3 Pbk : £0.35
(B77-24663)

1978. Sagittarius, November 22-December 21. — 1977. — 47p : ill ; 18cm.
Cover title.
ISBN 0-583-12633-2 Pbk : £0.35
(B77-24664)

1978. Scorpio, October 23-November 21. — 1977. — 47p : ill ; 18cm.
Cover title. — Previous control number ISBN 0-583-12211-6.
Pbk : £0.35
ISBN 0-583-12211-6
(B77-24665)

1978. Taurus, April 20-May 21. — 1977. — 47p : ill ; 18cm.
Cover title.
ISBN 0-583-12626-x Pbk : £0.35
(B77-24666)

1978. Virgo, August 23-September 22. — 1977. — 47p : ill ; 18cm.
Cover title.
ISBN 0-583-12630-8 Pbk : £0.35
(B77-24667)

133.5'4 — Astrological predictions. Horoscopes. Interpretation. *Manuals*

Innes, Brian. Horoscopes : how to draw and interpret them / [by] Brian Innes. — London : Orbis Books, 1976. — [1],89p : ill(some col), charts, ports(some col) ; 30cm.
Ill. on lining papers.
ISBN 0-85613-208-x : £2.50
Also classified at 133.5'42
(B77-21669)

Jones, Marc Edmund. How to learn astrology : a beginner's manual / [by] Marc Edmund Jones. — [Revised ed.]. — London [etc.] : Routledge and Kegan Paul, 1977. — x,197p : ill ; 19cm.
This ed. originally published: Stanwood : Sabian Pub. Society, 1969. — Index.
ISBN 0-7100-8579-6 : £4.50
(B77-14029)

133.5'4 — Pop music. Stars. *Horoscopes*

Leach, Robert, *b.1917.* How the planets rule the superstars / [by] Robert Leach. — London : Everest, 1975. — 3-173p : ill ; 18cm.
ISBN 0-903925-39-7 Pbk : £0.45
(B77-01995)

133.5'42 — Astrological predictions. Horoscopes. Casting. *Manuals*

Innes, Brian. Horoscopes : how to draw and interpret them / [by] Brian Innes. — London : Orbis Books, 1976. — [1],89p : ill(some col), charts, ports(some col) ; 30cm.
Ill. on lining papers.
ISBN 0-85613-208-x : £2.50
Primary classification 133.5'4
(B77-21669)

Mayo, Jeff. How to cast a natal chart / by Jeff Mayo ; illustrations by the author. — 4th revised ed. — Romford : L.N. Fowler, 1976. — 194p : ill ; 19cm. — (The astrologer's handbook series ; no.3)
With answers. — Previous ed.: 1973. — Index.
ISBN 0-85243-056-6 Pbk : £1.80
(B77-03334)

133.5'8'6132 — Man. Diet. Astrological aspects

King, Teri. The astrologer's diet book / [by] Teri King ; drawings by Maggie Ragner. — London : Allison and Busby, 1977. — 168p : ill ; 23cm.
ISBN 0-85031-193-4 : £3.25
(B77-29892)

133.5'8'641357 — Herbs. *Astrological viewpoints*

Petulengro, Leon. Herbs and astrology / [by] Leon Petulengro ; illustrated by Linda Diggins. — London : Darton, Longman and Todd, 1977. — 95p,[4]p of plates : ill(some col), port ; 18cm. — (Herbwise ; 1)
ISBN 0-232-51346-5 Pbk : £0.95
(B77-11045)

133.5'8'92972 — Great Britain. Royal families. Astrological aspects

Elliot, Roger. Astrology and the Royal Family / [by] Roger Elliot. — London [etc.] : Pan Books, 1977. — 191p ; 18cm.
ISBN 0-330-24710-7 Pbk : £0.60
(B77-08185)

133.6 — PALMISTRY

133.6 — Palmistry. *Manuals*

Cheiro. You and your hand / [by] Cheiro. — [New] ed. / revised by Louise Owen. — London : Sphere, 1977. — xix,187p,[16]p of plates : ill, port ; 18cm.
This ed. originally published: London : Jarrolds, 1969. — Index.
ISBN 0-7221-2263-2 Pbk : £0.85
(B77-29142)

133.8 — EXTRASENSORY PERCEPTION AND PSYCHOKINESIS

133.8 — Extrasensory perception

Tart, Charles T. Learning to use extrasensory perception / [by] Charles T. Tart. — Chicago ; London : University of Chicago Press, 1976. — xi,170p : ill, plan ; 21cm.
Bibl.: p.157-161. — Index.
ISBN 0-226-78991-8 : £9.40
(B77-05181)

133.8 — Extrasensory perception. *Manuals*

Huson, Paul. How to test and develop your ESP / [by] Paul Huson. — London : Abacus, 1977. — 155p : ill, forms ; 20cm.
Originally published: New York : Stein and Day, 1975. — Bibl.: p.144-146. — Index.
ISBN 0-349-11802-7 Pbk : £1.25
(B77-18521)

133.8 — Psychic phenomena: Sensitivity

Copen, Bruce. Are you a sensitive? / by Bruce Copen. — Haywards Heath : Academic Publications, 1977. — [2],84p ; 20cm.
Pbk : £2.10
(B77-16701)

133.8 — Psychic powers. Development. *Manuals*

Carrington, Hereward. Your psychic powers and how to develop them / by Hereward Carrington. — Wellingborough : Aquarian Press, 1976. — [13],358p ; 22cm.
Facsimile reprint of: 1st ed. New York : American Universities Publishing Co. ; London : Kegan Paul, 1920.
ISBN 0-85030-137-8 Pbk : Unpriced
(B77-30936)

Powell, Ivor. How to be more psychic / [by] Ivor Powell. — Sudbury : Spearman, 1977. — 173p : ill ; 23cm.
ISBN 0-85435-143-4 : £2.95
(B77-30937)

133.8 — Psychic powers. Development & exploitation

Dubin, Reese P. Telecult power : the amazing new way to psychic and occult wonders / by Reese P. Dubin. — Wellingborough : A. Thomas, 1977. — 3-225p : ill ; 22cm.
Originally published: West Nyack : Parker, 1970.
ISBN 0-85454-035-0 Pbk : £1.75
(B77-13479)

133.8′092′4 — Extrasensory perception & psychokinesis. Geller, Uri

Newman, Laurence Frederick. Thesis on Uri Geller phenomena / [by L.F. Newman]. — [High Wycombe] ([1 The Pastures, Downley, High Wycombe, Bucks.]) : The author, [1977]. — [3]leaves ; 30cm.
ISBN 0-905825-01-2 Sd : Unpriced
(B77-14530)

Wilson, Colin. The Geller phenomenon / by Colin Wilson. — London : Aldus Books, 1976. — 144p : ill(some col), ports(some col) ; 27cm.
Index.
ISBN 0-490-00329-x : £3.25
(B77-08186)

133.8′092′4 — Extrasensory perception & psychokinesis. Geller, Uri. *Autobiographies*

Geller, Uri. My story / [by] Uri Geller. — London : Corgi, 1977. — 284p,[8]p of plates : ill, ports ; 18cm.
Originally published: London : Robson Books, 1975. — Index.
ISBN 0-552-10391-8 Pbk : £0.85
(B77-12829)

133.9 — PSYCHIC PHENOMENA

Hamilton, T Glen. Intention and survival : psychical research studies and the bearing of intentional actions by trance personalities on the problem of human survival / by T. Glen Hamilton ; edited by James D. Hamilton. — 2nd ed. / edited by Margaret Lillian Hamilton. — London : Regency Press, 1977. — xxxix, 216p : ill, facsims, plan, ports ; 23cm.
Previous ed.: Toronto : Macmillan Co. of Canada, 1942.
ISBN 0-7212-0490-2 : £3.50
(B77-21670)

Holroyd, Stuart. PSI and the consciousness explosion / [by] Stuart Holroyd. — London [etc.] : Bodley Head, 1977. — 235p ; 23cm.
Index.
ISBN 0-370-10503-6 : £4.95
(B77-05841)

LeShan, Lawrence. Alternate realities : the search for the full human being / [by] Lawrence LeShan. — London : Sheldon Press, 1976. — xv,232p ; 22cm.
Also published: New York : M. Evans, 1976.
ISBN 0-85969-074-1 : £3.95
(B77-09473)

Wilson, Colin. Strange powers / [by] Colin Wilson. — London : Abacus, 1975. — 126p ; 20cm.
Originally published: London : Latimer New Dimensions, 1973.
ISBN 0-349-13733-1 Pbk : £0.65
Also classified at 133.3′092′4; 133.9′3; 133.9
(B77-18522)

133.9 — Psychic phenomena: Reincarnation. *Case studies*

Iverson, Jeffrey. More lives than one? : the evidence of the remarkable Bloxham tapes / [by] Jeffrey Iverson ; foreword by Magnus Magnusson. — London : Souvenir Press, 1976. — 192p,[8]p of plates : ill, ports ; 23cm.
Bibl.: p.191-192.
ISBN 0-285-62239-0 : £3.50
(B77-03886)

Iverson, Jeffrey. More lives than one? : the evidence of the remarkable Bloxham tapes / [by] Jeffrey Iverson ; foreword by Magnus Magnusson. — London [etc.] : Pan Books, 1977. — 156p,[4]p of plates : ill, ports ; 18cm.
Originally published: London : Souvenir Press, 1976. — Bibl.: p.156.
ISBN 0-330-25256-9 Pbk : £0.75
(B77-28350)

133.9 — Psychic phenomena: Reincarnation. Guirdham, Arthur

Wilson, Colin. Strange powers / [by] Colin Wilson. — London : Abacus, 1975. — 126p ; 20cm.
Originally published: London : Latimer New Dimensions, 1973.
ISBN 0-349-13733-1 Pbk : £0.65
Primary classification 133.9
(B77-18522)

133.9 — Spiritualism

Baker, Douglas. The powers latent in man / by Douglas Baker. — Wellingborough : Aquarian Press, 1977. — 95p : ill ; 22cm.
ISBN 0-85030-144-0 Pbk : £1.80
(B77-30938)

Edwards, Harry, *b.1893.* Life in spirit : with a guide for the development of mediumship / by Harry Edwards. — Guildford (Burrows Lea, Shere, Guildford, Surrey) : Healer Publishing Co. Ltd, 1976. — 238p,leaf of plate,[8]p of plates : ill, ports ; 23cm.
Index.
£3.00
(B77-25359)

Jefferson, Laura. Spiritualism : yesterday - today and tomorrow / [by] Laura Jefferson. — [Brighton] ([6 Powis Sq., Brighton BN1 3DS]) : [The author], [1976]. — [1],19p ; 20cm.
Sd : £0.30
(B77-29893)

133.9′013 — Future life. *Spiritualist viewpoints*

Death, an interesting journey : from teachings by The Messenger / compiled by Stanley Bedford. — St Helier : Neville Spearman (Jersey) ; Sudbury : Distributed by Spearman, 1977. — 151p,plate : facsim ; 23cm.
Originally published: Welwyn Garden City : Alcuin Press, 1954.
ISBN 0-85978-030-9 : £2.75
(B77-29143)

Hinz, Walther. The corner stone / [by] Walter Hinz ; [translated from the German by Ernst Rose and Sheila Willson]. — Sudbury : Spearman, 1977. — [5],182p ; 23cm.
Translation of: 'Geborgenheit'. Zürich : Brunner, 1972.
ISBN 0-85435-124-8 : £2.40
(B77-19989)

Miller, Paul. The invisible presence / by Paul Miller. — London : Psychic Press, 1976[i.e.1977]. — 208p ; 20cm.
ISBN 0-85384-046-6 : £2.50
(B77-08187)

133.9′07′2047 — Psychic phenomena. Research. *Eastern Europe*

Ostrander, Sheila. PSI : psychic discoveries behind the Iron Curtain / [by] Sheila Ostrander and Lynn Schroeder ; introduction by Ivan T. Sanderson. — London : Abacus, 1976. — 446p, [16]p of plates : ill, facsim, ports ; 20cm.
Originally published: as 'Psychic discoveries behind the Iron Curtain', Englewood Cliffs : Prentice-Hall, 1970 ; and as 'PSI : psychic discoveries behind the Iron Curtain', London : Abacus, 1973. — Bibl.: p.415-435. — Index.
ISBN 0-349-12668-2 Pbk : £1.50
(B77-07044)

133.9′08 — Spiritualism. *Essays*

John, *Brother.* Truth has no label / by Brother John. — London : Psychic Press, 1977. — 238p ; 19cm.
ISBN 0-85384-050-4 Pbk : £3.25
(B77-33572)

133.9′092′4 — Psychic phenomena. *Personal observations*

Manning, Matthew. In the minds of millions / [by] Matthew Manning. — London : W.H. Allen, 1977. — v,169p,[6]p of plates : ill, facsims, ports ; 23cm.
ISBN 0-491-02340-5 : £3.95
(B77-23073)

Wellman, J Dover. A priest's psychic diary / [by] J. Dover Wellman ; foreword by Richard Baker. — London : SPCK, 1977. — xiii,156p ; 20cm.
ISBN 0-281-03561-x Pbk : £1.95
(B77-27646)

133.9′092′4 — Spiritualism. *Personal observations*

Cecil, *Lord* **Martin.** On eagle's wings / [by] Lord Martin Cecil. — London : Mitre Press, 1977. — 186p ; 20cm.
ISBN 0-7051-0257-2 : £2.70
ISBN 0-7051-0258-0 Pbk : £0.90
(B77-33019)

Pilgrim, A. Stepping stones : from orthodoxy to a new understanding / by A. Pilgrim (J. Sykes Rymer). — [Onchan] ([York Lodge, 1 Bay View Rd, Onchan, Isle of Man]) : [Barbara M. Rymer], [1976]. — 152p : ports ; 21cm.
ISBN 0-9505509-0-6 Pbk : £1.30
(B77-04538)

Von Harten, Marjorie. A way of living / [by] Marjorie von Harten. — Sherborne, Glos. : Coombe Springs Press, 1974. — [4],v,83p ; 20cm.
ISBN 0-900306-08-4 Pbk : £1.00
(B77-08188)

133.9′092′4 — Spiritualism. Corbett, Percy Ernest. *Great Britain. Autobiographies*

Corbett, Percy Ernest. On wings of spirit : an autobiography / [by] Percy E. Corbett. — London : Research Publishing Co., 1977. — 181p ; 22cm.
ISBN 0-7050-0044-3 : £3.00
(B77-26087)

133.9′2 — Astral projection

Baker, Douglas. Practical techniques of astral projection / by Douglas Baker ; drawings by Patricia D. Ludlow. — Wellingborough : Aquarian Press, 1977. — 96p : ill ; 22cm.
Bibl.: p.94.
ISBN 0-85030-141-6 Pbk : £1.80
(B77-11535)

Holroyd, Stuart. Psychic voyages / by Stuart Holroyd. — London : Aldus Books, 1976. — 144p : ill(some col), facsims, ports(some col) ; 27cm.
Previous control number B7707772.
ISBN 0-490-00347-8 : £3.25
(B77-07772)

Society of Metaphysicians. An introduction to the study of astral projection with a syllabus of instruction for the course 'Practical astral projection' by Oliver Fox / [Society of Metaphysicians]. — Hastings (Archers' Court, Hastings, E. Sussex) : Society of Metaphysicians Ltd, 1977. — [3],14p ; 20cm.
Bibl.: p.11-14.
ISBN 0-900684-25-9 Sd : £0.30
(B77-33020)

Walker, Benjamin. Beyond the body : the human double and the astral planes / [by] Benjamin Walker. — London [etc.] : Routledge and Kegan Paul, 1977. — viii,224p ; 22cm.
Originally published: 1974. — Bibl.: p.195-207. — Index.
ISBN 0-7100-8581-8 Pbk : £1.95
(B77-29894)

133.9'3 — Spiritualism. Automatic writing. *Texts*
The **book** of Matan : automatic writing from the brink of eternity / compiled by Nik Douglas ; with foreword by Lyall Watson and collage illustrations by Penny Slinger. — Sudbury : Spearman, 1977. — xxii,178p,[5]leaves of plates : ill(chiefly col), facsims ; 24cm.
ISBN 0-85435-214-7 : £5.25
(B77-30939)

Spare, Austin Osman. Anathema of Zos : the sermon to the hypocrites : an automatic writing / by Austin Osman Spare. — London (49a Museum St., W.C.1) : Neptune Press, 1976. — 2-21p ; 30cm.
Limited ed. of 500 numbered copies. — Facsimile reprint of: 1st ed., originally published in a limited ed. of 100 copies. s.l. : s.n., 1927.
ISBN 0-9505001-0-0 Sd : £7.50
(B77-12830)

133.9'3 — Spiritualism. Automatic writing. Beattie, Eunice
Wilson, Colin. Strange powers / [by] Colin Wilson. — London : Abacus, 1975. — 126p ; 20cm.
Originally published: London : Latimer New Dimensions, 1973.
ISBN 0-349-13733-1 Pbk : £0.65
Primary classification 133.9
(B77-18522)

133.9'3 — Spiritualism. Communication. *Texts*
Banwell, Kathleen M D. Heaven to earth / by Kathleen M.D. Banwell. — Swindon (50 Kent Rd, Swindon SN1 3NG) : The author, 1976. — 26,[1]p ; 16cm.
ISBN 0-9505449-0-6 : £1.00
(B77-03335)

Hand, Ione. The teachings of White Lily : through the mediumship of Mrs Ione Hand / transcribed from the tapes by Hazel Cox. — London [etc.] : Regency Press, 1977. — 63p ; 23cm.
£2.00
(B77-26088)

Twigg, Ena. Scripts from a naturalist / [received through the mediumship of Ena Twigg]. — London (16 Queenberry Place, S.W.7) : College of Psychic Studies, 1976. — 19p ; 21cm. — (College of Psychic Studies. Papers ; no.9)
ISBN 0-903336-08-1 Sd : £0.40
(B77-18523)

135 — DREAMS AND THE MYSTIC TRADITIONS
135.3 — Dreams. Interpretation. Parapsychological aspects
Leek, Sybil. The night voyagers : you and your dreams / [by] Sybil Leek. — Large print [ed.]. — London : Prior [etc.], 1977. — [7],325p ; 25cm.
Originally published: as 'The night voyagers', New York : Mason-Charter, 1975 ; and as 'Dreams', London : W.H. Allen, 1976.
ISBN 0-86043-048-0 : £4.95
(B77-21671)

Zolar. The interpretation of dreams / [by] Zolar. — London : Sphere, 1977. — 191p ; 18cm.
Originally published: as 'Numerology dreambook', New York : Fawcett, 1971 ; and as 'The interpretation of dreams', London : Sphere, 1974.
ISBN 0-7221-9429-3 Pbk : £0.85
(B77-30940)

135.4 — Cabala
Love, Jeff. The quantum gods : the origin and nature of matter and consciousness / [by] Jeff Love. — Tisbury : Compton Russell, 1976. — x,245p : ill ; 24cm.
ISBN 0-85955-030-3 : £3.95
(B77-03887)

135.4 — Cabala. Sepher Yetsira. *Critical studies*
Suarès, Carlo. The 'Sepher Yetsira', including the original astrology according to the Qabala and its Zodiac / [by] Carlo Suarès ; translated from the French by Micheline & Vincent Stuart. — Boulder, Colo. ; London : Shambhala Publications ; London : Distributed by Routledge and Kegan Paul, 1976. — 173p : ill ; 22cm.
Translation of: 'Le "Sepher Yetsira"'. Geneva : Editions du Mont-Blanc, 1968. — Includes the text of the 'Sepher Yetsira' in Hebrew with English translation.
ISBN 0-87773-093-8 Pbk : £3.00
(B77-12831)

135.4'3 — Hermetic Order of the Golden Dawn. Rituals. *Texts*
Torrens, Robert George. The secret rituals of the Golden Dawn / by R.G. Torrens. — Wellingborough : Aquarian Press, 1973 [i.e. 1977]. — 304p : ill ; 22cm.
Originally published: 1973. — Bibl.: p.227-230. — Index. — Includes texts of some of the rituals, edited from original manuscripts.
ISBN 0-85030-124-6 Pbk : £2.25
(B77-13480)

137 — PERSONALITY ANALYSIS AND IMPROVEMENT
137'.7 — Graphology. *Manuals*
Aylesworth, Thomas G. Graphology : a guide to handwriting analysis / by Thomas G. Aylesworth. — New York ; London : F. Watts, 1976. — [12],60p : ill, facsims ; 25cm. — (A concise guide)
Bibl.: p.51. — Index.
ISBN 0-531-00323-x : £1.95
(B77-16163)

White, Fraser. Key to graphology : a complete guide to graphology / by Fraser White. — London : W.H. Allen, 1977. — viii,213p : facsims ; 23cm.
ISBN 0-491-02410-x : £3.95
(B77-23074)

140 — PHILOSOPHICAL VIEWPOINTS
141'.4'05 — Individualism. *Periodicals*
Ego : an individualist review : (incorporating 'Minus one'). — London (186 Gloucester Terrace, W.2) : S.E. Parker.
No.1- ; 1977-. — 1977-. — 30cm.
Published at irregular intervals. — 12p. in 1st issue.
Sd : £1.00 for 6 issues
ISSN 0309-5010
(B77-14531)

142'.7 — Existentialism. Theories of French writers. Related to theories of French writers of dialectical materialism, 1945-1968
Poster, Mark. Existential Marxism in postwar France : from Sartre to Althusser / [by] Mark Poster. — Princeton ; Guildford : Princeton University Press, 1977. — xii,415p ; 22cm.
Originally published: Princeton : Princeton University Press, 1975. — Bibl.: p.399-415. — Index.
ISBN 0-691-01994-0 Pbk : £3.80
Also classified at 146'.3
(B77-23075)

144'.094 — Humanism. *Europe, 1050-1500*
Ullmann, Walter. Medieval foundations of Renaissance humanism / [by] Walter Ullmann. — London : Elek, 1977. — xii,212p ; 25cm.
Index.
ISBN 0-236-40081-9 : £6.95
(B77-23076)

145 — Ideology. Theories, 1605-1945
Barth, Hans. Truth and ideology / by Hans Barth ; translated [from the German] by Frederic Lilge ; foreword by Reinhard Bendix. — Berkeley [etc.] ; London : University of California Press, 1976. — xvii,201p ; 23cm.
Translation of: 'Wahrheit und Ideologie'. 2., erw. Aufl. Erlenback : Rentsch, 1961. — Index.
ISBN 0-520-02820-1 : £8.90
(B77-20869)

146'.3 — Marxism. Dialectical materialism. *Philosophical perspectives*
Sartre, Jean Paul. Critique of dialectical reason / [by] Jean Paul Sartre. — London : NLB.
1 : Theory of practical ensembles / translated [from the French] by Alan Sheridan-Smith ; edited by Jonathan Rée. — 1976. — 836p ; 22cm.
Translation of: 'Critique de la raison dialectique, précédé questions de méthode. T.1 Théorie des ensembles pratiques'. Paris : Gallimard, 1960. — Index.
ISBN 0-902308-01-7 : £15.00
(B77-17879)

146'.3 — Marxism. Dialectical materialism. Philosophical perspectives. Theories of French writers. Related to theories of French writers of existentialism, 1945-1968
Poster, Mark. Existential Marxism in postwar France : from Sartre to Althusser / [by] Mark Poster. — Princeton ; Guildford : Princeton University Press, 1977. — xii,415p ; 22cm.
Originally published: Princeton : Princeton University Press, 1975. — Bibl.: p.399-415. — Index.
ISBN 0-691-01994-0 Pbk : £3.80
Primary classification 142'.7
(B77-23075)

146'.3 — Materialism
Witzenmann, Herbert. The origin and overcoming of the materialistic world-outlook : the natural-scientific attitude of consciousness as world danger and hope for the future / [by] Herbert Witzenmann ; [translated from the German by E. Bunzl, O. Fynes-Clinton, C. Lawrie]. — [Forest Row] ([3 Medway Cottages, Forest Row, E. Sussex]) : Living Art Publishing, 1976. — [1],12p ; 21cm.
'... the resumé of a lecture ... at the Conference "World Dangers and Hopes of our time", held at the Gottlieb Duttweiler-Institut, Rüschlikon, Zurichsee, Switzerland on 21.6.1975 ...' - postscript. — '... appeared in the periodical "Aus der Arbeitsgemeinschaft für angewandte Sozialökonomie. Beitraege zur Loesung sozialer Gegenwarts aufgaben", Nr.3 1975' - postscript.
Sd : Unpriced
(B77-15068)

149'.3 — Enneagrams
Bennett, John Godolphin. The enneagram / [by] J.G. Bennett. — Sherborne, Glos. : Coombe Springs Press, 1974. — [8],64p,[5]leaves of plates : ill ; 20cm. — (Transformation of man series ; 2)
ISBN 0-900306-17-3 Pbk : £0.75
(B77-11536)

149'.3 — Mysticism. *Transcripts of discussions*
Bennett, John Godolphin. Intimations : talks with J.G. Bennett at Beshara / with introduction by Rashid Hornsby. — Aldsworth (Swyre Farm, Aldsworth, Glos.) : Beshara Publications, 1975. — xi,100p ; 24cm.
ISBN 0-904975-03-7 : Unpriced
ISBN 0-904975-02-9 Pbk : £1.90
(B77-33021)

149'.7 — Rationalism. *Conference proceedings*
Rationalist Press Association. *Annual Conference, Oxford, 1971.* Rationalism in the 1970s : proceedings of the 1971 Conference of the RPA, held at St Peter's College, Oxford, entitled 'Rationalism : an Answer to the Problems of the 1970s'. — London : Pemberton, 1973. — 112p ; 19cm.
Bibl.: p.42.
ISBN 0-301-72043-6 : £1.25
ISBN 0-301-73070-3 Pbk : Unpriced
(B77-19990)

149'.94 — Meaning. *Philosophical perspectives*
Lewy, Casimir. Meaning and modality / [by] Casimir Lewy. — Cambridge [etc.] : Cambridge University Press, 1976. — xi,157,[1]p ; 23cm.
Index.
ISBN 0-521-21314-2 : £6.50
(B77-08730)

149'.94 — Statements. Reference. *Philosophical perspectives. Readings*
Naming, necessity, and natural kinds / edited by Stephen P. Schwartz. — Ithaca ; London : Cornell University Press, 1977. — 277,[1]p : 1 ill ; 22cm.
Bibl.: p.267-272. — Index.
ISBN 0-8014-1049-5 : £11.25
ISBN 0-8014-9861-9 Pbk : £3.95
(B77-22316)

149'.94 — Utterances. *Philosophical perspectives*
Austin, John Langshaw. How to do things with words / [by] J.L. Austin. — 2nd ed. / edited by J.O. Urmson and Marina Sbisà. — London [etc.] : Oxford University Press, 1976. — ix, 169p ; 20cm. — (William James lectures ; 1955)
This ed. originally published: Oxford : Clarendon Press, 1975. — Index.
ISBN 0-19-281205-x Pbk : £1.50
(B77-05842)

150 — PSYCHOLOGY
Bourne, Lyle Eugene. Psychology, its principles and meanings / [by] Lyle E. Bourne, Jr, Bruce R. Ekstrand. — 2nd ed. — New York ; London [etc.] : Holt, Rinehart and Winston, 1976. — xviii,540p,[4]p of plates : ill(some col), forms, ports ; 29cm.
Previous ed.: Hinsdale, Ill. : Dryden Press, 1973. — Bibl.: p.519-523. — Index.
ISBN 0-03-089628-2 : £10.00
(B77-01143)

Davidoff, Linda L. Introduction to psychology / [by] Linda L. Davidoff. — New York ; London [etc.] : McGraw-Hill, 1976. — xiv,560p : ill(some col), ports ; 25cm.
With answers. — Bibl. — Index.
ISBN 0-07-015459-7 : £11.60
(B77-03336)

Desiderato, Otello. Investigating behavior : principles of psychology / [by] Otello Desiderato, Diane Black Howieson, Joseph H. Jackson. — New York [etc.] ; London : Harper and Row, 1976. — xxiii,606p : ill(chiefly col), port ; 25cm.
Bibl.: p.573-591. — Index.
ISBN 0-06-041614-9 : £9.70
(B77-05843)

Essential psychology / general editor Peter Herriot. — London : Methuen.
F5 : Psychology and the environment / [by Terence Lee]. — 1976. — 143p : ill, plan ; 19cm.
Bibl.: p.139-143. — Index.
ISBN 0-416-81910-9 : £2.50
ISBN 0-416-81920-6 Pbk : £0.80
(B77-03337)

F6 : How do we choose? : a study in consumer behaviour / [by Mary Tuck]. — 1976. — 144p : ill ; 19cm.
Bibl.: p.137-142. — Index.
ISBN 0-416-81990-7 : £2.50
ISBN 0-416-82000-x Pbk : £0.80
(B77-03888)

Eysenck, Hans Jürgen. Psychology is about people / [by] H.J. Eysenck. — Harmondsworth [etc.] : Penguin, 1977. — xvii,331p ; 19cm.
Originally published: London : Allen Lane, 1972. — Bibl.: p.325-326. — Index.
ISBN 0-14-021980-3 Pbk : £0.90
(B77-23962)

Liebert, Robert Mandel. Psychology / [by] Robert M. Liebert, John M. Neale. — New York ; London [etc.] : Wiley, 1977. — xii,492p, [8]p of plates : ill(some col), facsim, ports(some col) ; 25cm.
Bibl.: p.445-467. — Index.
ISBN 0-471-53431-5 : £9.40
(B77-17880)

Liebert, Robert Mandel. Psychology / [by] Robert M. Liebert, John M. Neale. — New York ; London [etc.] : Wiley.
Instructor's resource manual / [by] Susan Franzblau and R.A. Vachon. — [1977]. — vi, 142p ; 24cm.
Bibl. — Lists of films.
ISBN 0-471-01777-9 Pbk : Unpriced
(B77-23963)

Student study guide / [by] R.A. Vachon, Judith Doran. — 1977. — [9],273p ; 24cm.
With answers.
ISBN 0-471-01776-0 Pbk : £1.50
(B77-23964)

Test items / [by] Susan Franzblau and R.A. Vachon. — [1977]. — [5],89p ; 24cm.
ISBN 0-471-01775-2 Sd : £1.00
(B77-23965)

Lindsay, Peter H. Human information processing : an introduction to psychology / [by] Peter H. Lindsay, Donald A. Norman. — 2nd ed. — New York [etc.] ; London : Academic Press, 1977. — xxiii,777[i.e.779]p,[4]p of plates : ill(some col) ; 24cm.
Previous ed.: 1972. — Bibl.: p.735-762. — Index.
ISBN 0-12-450960-6 : £9.95
(B77-29895)

Statt, David A. Psychology : making sense / [by] David A. Statt. — New York [etc.] ; London : Harper and Row, 1977. — xii,227p : ill ; 24cm.
Bibl.: p.217-221. — Index.
ISBN 0-06-046412-7 Pbk : Unpriced
(B77-19991)

Whittaker, James Oliver. Introduction to psychology / [by] James O. Whittaker. — 3rd ed. / contributors S.M. Luria ; statistical appendix written by Darrell Huff. — Philadelphia ; London [etc.] : Saunders, 1976. — xvi,823p : ill(some col), facsims, maps, ports ; 27cm.
Ill on lining papers. — Previous ed.: / by James O. Whittaker ; contributing authors S.M. Luria and Russell Sergeant. — Bibl.: p.765-790. — Index.
ISBN 0-7216-9307-5 : £11.00
(B77-00589)

150 — Man. Behaviour

Baron, Robert A. Psychology : understanding behavior / [by] Robert A. Baron, Donn Byrne, Barry H. Kantowitz. — Philadelphia ; London [etc.] : Saunders, 1977. — xviii,652p,[4]p of plates : ill(some col), maps, ports ; 28cm.
Col. ill. on lining papers. — Bibl.: p.597-618. — Index.
ISBN 0-7216-1568-6 : £6.50
(B77-23077)

Gauld, Alan. Human action and its psychological investigation / [by] Alan Gauld and John Shotter. — London [etc.] : Routledge and Kegan Paul, 1977. — ix,237p : 1 ill ; 23cm.
Bibl.: p.222-229. — Index.
ISBN 0-7100-8568-0 : £5.50 : CIP rev.
(B77-08731)

Kendler, Howard Harvard. Basic psychology / [by] Howard H. Kendler. — Brief [ed.]. — Menlo Park ; London [etc.] : Benjamin, 1977. — xii,483p,[4]p of plates,leaf of plate : ill(some col), ports ; 24cm.
Previous ed.: 1974. — Bibl. — Index.
ISBN 0-8053-5195-7 Pbk : £8.80
(B77-26754)

McConnell, James Vernon. Understanding human behavior : an introduction to psychology / [by] James V. McConnell. — 2nd ed. — New York ; London [etc.] : Holt, Rinehart and Winston, 1977. — xv,736p,[8]p of plates : ill(some col), maps, ports ; 29cm.
Previous ed.: 1974. — Bibl.: p.710-729. — Index.
ISBN 0-03-089715-7 : £8.50
(B77-20870)

McNeil, Elton Burbank. The psychology of being human / [by] Elton B. McNeil. — 2nd ed. / [revised by] Zick Rubin. — San Francisco : Canfield Press ; New York [etc.] ; London : Harper and Row, 1977. — xviii,646p : ill(some col), form, ports ; 29cm.
Col. ill. on lining papers. — Previous ed.: 1974. — Bibl.: p.623-634. — Index.
ISBN 0-06-385434-1 : £11.20
(B77-20871)

Paulus, Paul B. Psychology : understanding behaviour / [by] Paul B. Paulus and Robert A. Baron. — Philadelphia ; London [etc.] : Saunders.
Student manual. — 1977. — xvi,260p : ill ; 27cm.
With answers to questions.
ISBN 0-7216-7108-x Pbk : £5.00
(B77-27648)

150 — Man. Behaviour. *Occult viewpoints*

Bennett, John Godolphin. How we do things / [by] J.G. Bennett. — Sherborne, Glos. : Coombe Springs Press, 1974. — [6],69p ; 20cm.
ISBN 0-900306-04-1 Pbk : £0.85
(B77-11537)

150 — Psychology. *Conference proceedings*

Nebraska Symposium on Motivation, *1975.* Nebraska Symposium on Motivation, 1975 : conceptual foundations of psychology / volume editor William J. Arnold ; [contributors] Joseph R. Royce ... [et al.]. — Lincoln [Neb.] ; London : University of Nebraska Press, 1976 [i.e. 1977]. — xxvii,586p : ill ; 24cm. — (Current theory and research in motivation ; vol.23)
Published in the United States: 1976. — Bibl. — Index.
ISBN 0-8032-0618-6 : £16.90
ISBN 0-8032-5624-8 Pbk : £8.95
(B77-09474)

150 — Psychology. *Secondary school texts*

Human psychology ... / [by] Deanna Kuhn ... [et al.]. — New York [etc.] ; London : Harcourt Brace Jovanovich, [1976]. — xvi,574p : ill, forms, ports ; 24cm.
With answers to selected questions. — Published in the United States: 1975. — Bibl. — Index.
ISBN 0-15-372150-2 : Unpriced
(B77-05844)

Human psychology. — New York [etc.] ; London : Harcourt Brace Jovanovich.
Development : becoming who we are. Teacher's manual / [by] Deanna Kuhn. — [1976]. — iii, 43p ; 23cm.
Published in the United States: 1975. — Bibl. — Lists of films.
ISBN 0-15-372155-3 Sd : £0.60
(B77-08189)

Development ; Learning ; Social interaction. Teacher's manual / [by] Deanna Kuhn ... [et al.]. — [1976]. — v,132p : ill ; 24cm.
Published in the United States: 1975. — Bibl. — Lists of films.
ISBN 0-15-372154-5 Pbk : £1.35
(B77-08190)

Development : becoming who we are / [by] Deanna Kuhn. — [1976]. — viii,175p : ill, ports ; 24cm.
Published in the United States: 1975. — Bibl. — Index.
ISBN 0-15-372151-0 Pbk : £2.25
(B77-08191)

Learning : one way we change. Teacher's manual / [by] Albert Kingston, William White. — [1976]. — iii,44p : ill ; 24cm.
Published in the United States: 1975. — Bibl. — Lists of films.
ISBN 0-15-372156-1 Sd : £0.70
(B77-08192)

Learning : one way we change / [by] Albert Kingston, William White. — [1976]. — x, 179p : ill, ports ; 24cm.
Published in the United States: 1975. — Bibl. — Index.
ISBN 0-15-372152-9 Pbk : £2.25
(B77-08193)

Social interaction : shaping each other's lives / [by] Michele Toomey. — [1976]. — viii,224p : ill ; 24cm.
Published in the United States: 1975. — Bibl. — Index.
ISBN 0-15-372153-7 Pbk : £2.20
(B77-08194)

150 — Psychology. *Transcripts of interviews*

Cohen, David, *b.1946.* Psychologists on psychology / [by] David Cohen. — London [etc.] : Routledge and Kegan Paul, 1977. — [7], 360p ; 24cm.
Bibl.: p.357-360.
ISBN 0-7100-8502-8 : £6.95
(B77-24668)

150'.1 — Psychology. Theories

Neel, Ann. Theories of psychology : a handbook / [by] Ann Neel. — Revised and enlarged ed. — Cambridge, Mass. : Schenkman ; London : Distributed by Wiley, 1977. — [4],699p ; 24cm.
'A Halsted Press Book'. — Previous ed.: Cambridge, Mass. : Schenkman, 1969 ; London : University of London Press, 1971. — Bibl. — Index.
ISBN 0-470-98968-8 : £17.50
ISBN 0-470-98969-6 Pbk : £6.95
(B77-31670)

150'.19'2 — Humanistic psychology

Humanistic psychology : new frontiers / edited by Dorothy D. Nevill. — New York : Gardner Press ; New York ; London [etc.] : Distributed by Wiley, 1977. — xii,230p : 1 ill ; 24cm.
Bibl. — Index.
ISBN 0-470-99165-8 : £13.00
(B77-26089)

150'.19'2 — Humanistic psychology. *Readings*

The **healthy** personality : readings / edited by Hung-Min Chiang, Abraham H. Maslow. — 2nd ed. — New York ; London [etc.] : D. Van Nostrand, 1977. — ix,261p : ill ; 23cm.
Previous ed.: New York ; London : Van Nostrand Reinhold, 1970. — Bibl.
ISBN 0-442-21546-0 Pbk : £2.80
(B77-30941)

150'.19'2 — Humanistic psychology. Methodology

Rychlak, Joseph Frank. The psychology of rigorous humanism / [by] Joseph F. Rychlak. — New York ; London [etc.] : Wiley, 1977. — xiii,547p : ill ; 24cm.
'A Wiley-Interscience Publication'. — Bibl.: p.509-525. — Index.
ISBN 0-471-74796-3 : £14.00
(B77-23966)

150'.19'2 — Psychology. Theories of May, Rollo

Reeves, Clement. The psychology of Rollo May / [by] Clement Reeves ; reflections and commentary by Rollo May. — San Francisco [etc.] ; London : Jossey-Bass, 1977. — xvi, 336p ; 24cm. — (The Jossey-Bass behavioural science series)
Bibl.: p.311-329. — Index.
ISBN 0-87589-303-1 : £12.35
(B77-29144)

150'.19'43 — Behaviourism

Mackenzie, Brian D. Behaviourism and the limits of scientific method / [by] Brian D. Mackenzie. — London [etc.] : Routledge and Kegan Paul [etc.], 1977. — xiv,193p ; 23cm. — (International library of philosophy and scientific method)
Index.
ISBN 0-7100-8543-5 : £4.95
(B77-19992)

150'.19'5 — Psychoanalysis
Lacan, Jacques. The four fundamental concepts of psycho-analysis / by Jacques Lacan ; edited by Jacques-Alain Miller ; translated from the French by Alan Sheridan. — London : Hogarth Press : Institute of Psycho-analysis, 1977. — xi, 290p : ill ; 23cm. — (The international psycho-analytical library ; no.106)
Translation of: 'Les quatre concepts fondamentaux de la psychanalyse'. Paris : Seuil, 1973. — Index.
ISBN 0-7012-0433-8 : £8.50 : CIP rev.
(B77-16704)

150'.19'5 — Psychoanalysis. *Festschriften*
New directions in psycho-analysis : the significance of infant conflict in the pattern of adult behaviour / edited by Melanie Klein, Paula Heimann, R.E. Money-Kyrle ; with a preface by Ernest Jones. — London (H. Karnac (Books) Ltd, 58 Gloucester Rd, S.W.7) : Maresfield Reprints, 1977. — xiii,534p : port ; 22cm.
Originally published: London : Tavistock Publications, 1955. — Bibl. — Index.
ISBN 0-9501647-5-5 : £9.60
(B77-22317)

150'.19'5 — Psychoanalysis. Applications of language. Theories of Lacan, Jacques
Lemaire, A. Jacques Lacan / [by] Anika Lemaire ; translated [from the French] by David Macey. — London [etc.] : Routledge and Kegan Paul, 1977. — xxix,266p ; 23cm.
Translation and revision of: 'Jacques Lacan'. Brussels : C. Denart, 1970. — Bibl.: p.254-260. — Index.
ISBN 0-7100-8621-0 : £7.25 : CIP rev
(B77-19185)

150'.19'5 — Psychoanalysis. Theories
Schafer, Roy. The psychoanalytic life history / [by] Roy Schafer. — London : H.K. Lewis for University College, London, 1976. — 20p ; 21cm. — (University College, London. Freud memorial inaugural lectures)
'delivered 30 October 1975'.
Sd : £1.00
(B77-16164)

150'.19'5 — Psychoanalysis. Theories of Kraus, Karl
Szasz, Thomas Stephen. Karl Kraus and the soul-doctors : a pioneer critic and his criticism of psychiatry and psychoanalysis / [by] Thomas Szasz. — London [etc.] : Routledge and Kegan Paul, 1977. — [1],xviii,180p : port ; 23cm.
Originally published: Baton Rouge : Louisiana State University Press, 1976. — Index.
ISBN 0-7100-8555-9 : £6.95
(B77-22318)

150'.19'503 — Psychoanalysis. *Dictionaries*
Rycroft, Charles. A critical dictionary of psychoanalysis / [by] Charles Rycroft. — Harmondsworth [etc.] : Penguin, 1977. — xxvi, 189p ; 18cm. — (Penguin reference books)
Originally published: London : Nelson, 1968. — Bibl.: p.181-189.
Pbk : £0.80
ISBN 0-14-051052-4
(B77-16165)

150'.19'508 — Psychoanalysis. *Essays*
Lacan, Jacques. Écrits : a selection / [by] Jacques Lacan ; translated from the French by Alan Sheridan. — London : Tavistock Publications, 1977. — xiv,338p : ill ; 24cm.
Translation of: nine essays from 'Ecrits'. Paris : Éditions du Seuil, 1966. — Index.
ISBN 0-422-74140-x : £12.00
(B77-21672)

150'.19'52 — Psychoanalysis. Freud, Sigmund. *Biographies. Juvenile literature*
Neimark, Anne E. Sigmund Freud, the world within / [by] Anne E. Neimark. — New York ; London : Harcourt Brace Jovanovich, 1976. — [7],120p : ports ; 22cm.
Bibl.: p.115-116. — Index.
ISBN 0-15-274164-x : £4.65
(B77-24669)

150'.19'52 — Psychoanalysis. Freud, Sigmund. *Personal observations*
Wortis, Joseph. Fragments of an analysis with Freud / by Joseph Wortis. — New York ; London [etc.] : McGraw-Hill, [1976]. — xi,208, [1]p : facsims ; 22cm.
Originally published: New York : Simon and Schuster, 1954. — Index.
ISBN 0-07-071903-9 : £5.75
ISBN 0-07-071904-7 Pbk : £2.90
(B77-07045)

150'.19'52 — Psychoanalysis. Freudian system
Guntrip, Harry. Psychoanalytic theory, therapy and the self / [by] Harry Guntrip. — London ([c/o] H. Karnac (Books) Ltd, 58 Gloucester Rd, S.W.7) : Maresfield Reprints, 1977. — xii, 204p ; 22cm.
Originally published: New York : Basic Books ; London : Hogarth Press, 1971. — Index.
ISBN 0-9501647-4-7 : £5.50
(B77-17881)

Jahoda, Marie. Freud and the dilemmas of psychology / by Marie Jahoda. — London : Hogarth Press, 1977. — vi,186p : ill ; 23cm.
Index.
ISBN 0-7012-0425-7 : £5.95 : CIP rev.
ISBN 0-7012-0437-0 Pbk : £2.50
(B77-06441)

150'.19'52 — Psychoanalysis. Freudian system. *Essays*
Jones, Ernest, *b.1879.* Papers on psycho-analysis / by Ernest Jones. — 5th ed. — London (H. Karnac (Books) Ltd, 58 Gloucester Rd, S.W.7) : Maresfield Reprints, 1977. — vii,504p ; 22cm.
This ed. originally published: London : Baillière, Tindall and Cox, 1948. — Index.
ISBN 0-9501647-6-3 : £9.60
(B77-22319)

150'.19'52 — Psychoanalysis. Freudian system. *Marxist viewpoints*
Voloshinov, Valentin Nikolaevich. Freudianism : a Marxist critique / [by] V.N. Voloshinov ; translated [from the Russian] by I.R. Titunik ; and edited in collaboration with Neal H. Bruss. — New York [etc.] ; London : Academic Press, 1976. — xix,153p ; 24cm.
Translation of: 'Freĭdizm : kriticheskiĭ ocherk'. Moscow ; Leningrad : State Publishing House, 1927. — Index.
ISBN 0-12-723250-8 : £6.70
(B77-00590)

150'.19'52 — Psychoanalysis. Freudian system. Testing
Fisher, Seymour. The scientific credibility of Freud's theories and therapy / [by] Seymour Fisher & Roger P. Greenberg. — Hassocks : Harvester Press, 1977. — x,502p ; 24cm.
Bibl.: p.417-492. — Index.
ISBN 0-85527-989-3 : £12.50
(B77-18524)

150'.19'52 — Psychoanalysis. Theories of Freud, Sigmund
Nagera, Humberto. Basic psychoanalytic concepts on metapsychology, conflicts, anxiety and other subjects / by Humberto Nagera and ... [others]. — London : Allen and Unwin, 1970 [i.e. 1977]. — 3-233p ; 22cm. — (Hampstead Clinic. Psychoanalytic library ; vol.4)
Originally published: 1970. — Index.
ISBN 0-04-150062-8 Pbk : £1.95
(B77-08732)

150'.19'52 — Psychoanalysis. Theories of Freud, Sigmund. Attitudes of existentialists, to 1975
Izenberg, Gerald N. The existentialist critique of Freud : the crisis of autonomy / by Gerald N. Izenberg. — Princeton ; Guildford : Princeton University Press, 1976. — xii,354,[1]p ; 23cm.
Bibl.: p.336-346. — Index.
ISBN 0-691-07214-0 : £12.70
(B77-05845)

150'.19'52 — Psychoanalysis. Theories of Freud, Sigmund. Influence of Jewish thought
Robert, Marthe. From Oedipus to Moses : Freud's Jewish identity / [by] Marthe Robert ; translated [from the French] by Ralph Manheim. — London [etc.] : Routledge and Kegan Paul, 1977. — [7],229p ; 23cm. — (The Littman library of Jewish civilization)
This translation originally published: Garden City, N.Y. : Anchor Books, 1976. — Translation of: 'D'OEdipe à Moïse'. Paris : Calmann-Lévy, 1974. — Bibl.: p.217-218. — Index.
ISBN 0-7100-8710-1 : £5.00 : CIP rev.
(B77-23078)

150'.19'53 — Psychology. Adlerian system
Rom, Paul. Alfred Adler's individual psychology and its history / by Paul Rom. — London (11 Osborne House, 414 Wimbledon Park Rd, SW19 6PW) : Adlerian Society of Great Britain, 1976. — [14]p ; 21cm. — (Individual psychology pamphlets ; no.1 ISSN 0309-1988)
ISBN 0-905860-00-4 Sd : £0.25
(B77-05846)

150'.19'54 — Man. Behaviour. Theories of Jung, Carl Gustav. *Texts*
Jung, Carl Gustav. The collected works of C.G. Jung / editors Sir Herbert Read ... [et al.]. — London [etc.] : Routledge and Kegan Paul.
[Vol.18] : The symbolic life : miscellaneous writings / translated [from the German] by R.F.C. Hull. — 1977. — xix,913p ; 24cm.
Bibl.: p.833-852. — Index. — Includes: Analytical psychology, its theory and practice. Originally published: London : Routledge and Kegan Paul, 1968 - Symbolic life. Originally published: London : Guild of Pastoral Psychology, 1954.
ISBN 0-7100-8291-6 : £14.50
(B77-14030)

Jung, Carl Gustav. The portable Jung / edited, with an introduction, by Joseph Campbell ; translated [from the German] by R.F.C. Hull. — Harmondsworth [etc.] : Penguin, 1976. — xlii,659p ; 19cm. — (Viking portable library)
This collection of translations originally published: New York : Viking Press, 1971. — Bibl.: p.651-659.
ISBN 0-14-015070-6 Pbk : £1.95
(B77-10115)

150'.19'54 — Psychoanalysis. Jung, Carl Gustav. *Biographies*
Hannah, Barbara. Jung, his life and work : a biographical memoir / by Barbara Hannah. — London : Joseph, 1977. — 376p ; 24cm.
Originally published: New York : Putnam, 1976. — Bibl.: p.361-365. — Index.
ISBN 0-7181-1613-5 : £6.95
(B77-22320)

150'.19'54 — Psychoanalysis. Jung, Carl Gustav. *Critical studies*
Franz, Marie-Louise von. C.G. Jung, his myth in our time / [by] Marie-Louise von Franz ; translated from the German by William H. Kennedy. — London [etc.] : Hodder and Stoughton, 1975. — x,355,[1]p,plate : port ; 23cm.
This translation also published: New York : Putnam for the C.G. Jung Foundation for Analytical Psychology, 1975. — Translation of: 'C.G. Jung : sein Mythos in unserer Zeit'. Frauenfeld ; Stuttgart : Huber, 1972. — Bibl.: p.288-319. — Index.
ISBN 0-340-17370-x : £4.95
(B77-03889)

150'.19'54 — Psychoanalysis. Jungian system
Jung, Carl Gustav. Analytical psychology, its theory and practice : the Tavistock lectures / [by] C.G. Jung ; foreword by E.A. Bennett. — London [etc.] : Routledge and Kegan Paul, 1976. — xvi,224p : ill ; 22cm.
Transcript of five lectures delivered in English, Sept. 30 to Oct. 4 1935, edited by Mary Barker and Margaret Game ; with minor stylistic revisions by R.F.C. Hull. — Originally published: 1968. — Bibl.: p.211-213. — Index.
ISBN 0-7100-8414-5 Pbk : £1.95
(B77-01144)

150'.19'54 — Psychoanalysis. Jungian system. Related to yoga
Mooney, Lucindi Frances. Storming Eastern temples : a psychological exploration of yoga / by Lucindi Frances Mooney. — Wheaton [etc.] ; London : Theosophical Publishing House, 1976. — [8],212p ; 21cm. — (A quest book)
Bibl.: p.205-207. — Index.
ISBN 0-8356-0479-9 Pbk : £3.90
Also classified at 181'.45
(B77-05182)

150'.19'54 — Psychoanalysis. Theories of Jung, Carl Gustav. Religious aspects
Meier, Carl Alfred. Jung's analytical psychology and religion / by Carl Alfred Meier. — Carbondale [etc.] : Southern Illinois University Press ; London [etc.] : Feffer and Simons, 1977. — [4],81p ; 20cm. — (Arcturus paperbacks ; AB137)
Originally published: as 'Jung and analytical psychology', Newton Centre, Mass. : Dept of Psychology, Andover Newton Theological School, 1959.
ISBN 0-8093-0807-x Pbk : £2.20
(B77-12832)

150'.19'57 — Psychoanalysis. Theories of Sullivan, Harry Stack
Chrzanowski, Gerard. Interpersonal approach to psychoanalysis : contemporary view of Harry Stack Sullivan / by Gerard Chrzanowski. — New York : Gardner Press ; New York ; London [etc.] : Distributed by Wiley, 1977. — xv,242p ; 24cm.
Bibl.: p.219-239. — Index.
ISBN 0-470-99071-6 : Unpriced
(B77-22321)

150'.19'8 — Double bind theory
Double bind : the foundation of the communicational approach to the family / edited by Carlos E. Sluzki, Donald C. Ransom. — New York ; London [etc.] : Grune and Stratton, [1977]. — xix,359p : 1 ill ; 24cm.
Published in the United States: 1976. — Bibl.: p.333-347. — Index.
ISBN 0-8089-0950-9 : £12.05
(B77-14532)

150'.2'461 — Psychology. *For medicine*
Introductory psychology : a text book for health students / edited by John C. Coleman. — London [etc.] : Routledge and Kegan Paul, 1977. — x,350p : ill ; 23cm.
Bibl. — Index.
ISBN 0-7100-8442-0 : £6.95
ISBN 0-7100-8443-9 Pbk : £3.50
(B77-16705)

150'.7'2 — Psychology. Research. Statistical methods
Novick, Melvin Robert. Statistical methods for educational and psychological research / [by] Melvin R. Novick, Paul H. Jackson. — New York ; London [etc.] : McGraw-Hill, 1974. — xviii,456p : ill ; 24cm. — (McGraw-Hill series in psychology)
Text on lining paper. — Lining paper perforated at inside edge. — Bibl.: p.xvii-xviii. — Index.
ISBN 0-07-047550-4 : Unpriced
Primary classification 370'.78
(B77-18673)

150'.7'24 — Psychology. Experimental techniques
Christensen, Larry B. Experimental methodology / [by] Larry B. Christensen. — Boston, Mass. ; London [etc.] : Allyn and Bacon, 1977. — x,372p : ill, forms ; 24cm.
Bibl.: p.345-365. — Index.
ISBN 0-205-05721-7 Pbk : £5.95
(B77-30942)

150'.72'4 — Psychology. Experiments
Sheridan, Charles Lawrence. Fundamentals of experimental psychology / [by] Charles L. Sheridan. — 2nd ed. — New York ; London [etc.] : Holt, Rinehart and Winston, 1976. — xx,475p : ill, ports ; 25cm.
Previous ed.: 1971. — Bibl.: p.435-451. — Index.
ISBN 0-03-089538-3 : £10.75
(B77-01996)

150'.7'24 — Psychology. Experiments. Techniques
Barber, Theodore Xenophon. Pitfalls in human research : ten pivotal points / [by] Theodore Xenophon Barber. — New York ; Oxford [etc.] : Pergamon, 1976. — vii,117p ; 24cm. — (Pergamon international library) (Pergamon general psychology series ; vol.67)
Bibl.: p.92-111. — Index.
ISBN 0-08-020935-1 : £3.50
(B77-05183)

150'.7'24 — Psychology. Experiments. Volunteer subjects. Behaviour. Effects of laboratory techniques
Silverman, Irwin. The human subject in the psychological laboratory / [by] Irwin Silverman. — New York ; Oxford [etc.] : Pergamon, 1977. — xii,151p : ill ; 24cm. — (Pergamon international library) (Pergamon general psychology series ; 68)
Bibl.: p.123-143. — Index.
ISBN 0-08-021080-5 : £6.25
ISBN 0-08-021079-1 Pbk : £2.75
(B77-23079)

150'.8 — Psychology. *Readings*
Being human today : psychological perspectives / [edited by] Phillip Whitten. — San Francisco : Canfield Press ; New York [etc.] ; London : Harper and Row, 1977. — [11],177p : ill, ports ; 28cm.
Facsimile reprints. — Bibl.
ISBN 0-06-389340-1 Pbk : £4.15
(B77-21673)

150'.9'04 — Psychology. Theories, 1900-1976. Related to fiction in European languages, 1900-1976
May, Keith M. Out of the maelstrom : psychology and the novel in the twentieth century / [by] Keith M. May. — London : Elek, 1977. — xvi,135p ; 23cm.
Bibl.: p.127-132. — Index.
ISBN 0-236-40095-9 : £5.50
Primary classification 809.3'04
(B77-23650)

150'.92'4 — Psychology. Theories of Piaget, Jean
Rotman, Brian. Jean Piaget : psychologist of the real / [by] Brian Rotman. — Hassocks : Harvester Press, 1977. — 200p : 1 ill ; 23cm.
Bibl.: p.194-196. — Index.
ISBN 0-85527-670-3 : £7.95 : CIP rev.
(B77-17264)

150'.994 — Psychology. *Australia, to 1977*
Psychology in Australia : achievements & prospects / edited by Mary Nixon and Ronald Taft. — Rushcutters Bay ; Oxford [etc.] : Pergamon, 1977. — xi,318p ; 22cm.
Bibl. — Index.
ISBN 0-08-021043-0 Pbk : Unpriced
ISBN 0-08-020561-5 Pbk : £5.25
(B77-26090)

152 — PHYSIOLOGICAL AND EXPERIMENTAL PSYCHOLOGY

152 — Experimental psychology
Dunham, Philip J. Experimental psychology : theory and practice / [by] Philip J. Dunham. — New York [etc.] ; London : Harper and Row, 1977. — xvii,487p : ill ; 24cm. — (Harper's experimental psychology series)
Bibl.: p.433-467. — Index.
ISBN 0-06-041805-2 : £10.45
(B77-29145)

152 — Man. Behaviour. Physiological aspects
Carlson, Neil R. Physiology of behavior / [by] Neil R. Carlson. — Boston [Mass.] ; London [etc.] : Allyn and Bacon, 1977. — xiv,650, I24p : ill ; 24cm.
Bibl.: p.625-650. — Index.
ISBN 0-205-05706-3 Pbk : £6.95
(B77-24670)

Leukel, Francis. Introduction to physiological psychology / [by] Francis Leukel. — 3rd ed. — Saint Louis : Mosby ; London : Distributed by Kimpton, 1976. — xii,514p : ill ; 27cm.
Previous ed.: 1972. — Bibl.: p.467-481. — Index.
ISBN 0-8016-2974-8 : £12.00
(B77-03338)

152 — Man. Body perception. Development. *For nursing*
Brown, Marie Scott. Normal development of body image / author and consultant Marie Scott Brown. — New York ; London [etc.] : Wiley, 1977. — ix,106p : ill, forms ; 28cm. — (Wiley nursing concept modules)
With answers. — Pages perforated at inside edge and pierced for binder. — 'A Wiley medical publication'. — Bibl.: p.106.
ISBN 0-471-02170-9 Pbk : Unpriced
(B77-28351)

152 — Man. Posture. Psychological factors
Kurtz, Ron. The body reveals : an illustrated guide to the psychology of the body / [by] Ron Kurtz and Hector Prestera ; photography Frank Descisciolo ; illustrations Mick Brady and Lynda Braun ; foreword John C. Lilly. — New York [etc.] ; London : Harper and Row [etc.], 1976. — x,148,[1]p : ill ; 24cm.
Bibl.: p.147-148.
ISBN 0-06-066680-3 Pbk : £3.70
(B77-14533)

152 — Neuropsychology. Freud, Sigmund. Entwurf einer Psychologie. *Critical studies*
Pribram, Karl Harry. Freud's 'Project' reassessed / [by] Karl H. Pribram, Merton M. Gill. — London : Hutchinson, 1976. — 192p : ill ; 24cm.
Bibl.: p.173-181. — Index.
ISBN 0-09-124980-5 : £6.75
(B77-00009)

152 — Patients. Body perception. *For nursing*
Distortions in body image in illness and disability / consultant Marie Scott Brown. — New York ; London [etc.] : Wiley, 1977. — xi, 116p : 1 ill ; 28cm. — (Wiley nursing concept modules)
'A Wiley medical publication'. — With answers. — Pages perforated at inside edge. — Pierced for binder. — Fill in book. — Bibl.
ISBN 0-471-02169-5 Pbk : £4.45
(B77-23080)

152 — Physiological psychology
Bruce, Richard Loren. Fundamentals of physiological psychology / [by] Richard L. Bruce. — New York ; London [etc.] : Holt, Rinehart and Winston, 1977. — xii,416p : ill, map ; 25cm.
Bibl.: p.387-396. — Index.
ISBN 0-03-002841-8 : £7.50
(B77-21674)

152.1 — PSYCHOLOGY. SENSORY PERCEPTION
McBurney, Donald. Introduction to sensation - perception / [by] Donald McBurney, Virginia Collings. — Englewood Cliffs ; London [etc.] : Prentice-Hall, 1977. — vii,296p : ill ; 24cm. — (Prentice-Hall series in experimental psychology)
Bibl.: p.271-285. — Index.
ISBN 0-13-496000-9 : £10.35
(B77-27649)

152.1'01 — Man. Sensory perception. *Philosophical perspectives*
Hayek, Friedrich August. The sensory order : an inquiry into the foundations of theoretical psychology / [by] F.A. Hayek ; with an introduction by Heinrich Klüver. — London [etc.] : Routledge and Kegan Paul, 1976. — xxii,209p ; 23cm.
Originally published: 1952. — Bibl.: p.195-203. — Index.
ISBN 0-7100-1504-6 : £4.95
(B77-03890)

152.1'4 — Man. Visual perception. *Conference proceedings*
Light and Sight *(Conference), Amsterdam, 1973.* Light and Sight : an Anglo-Netherlands symposium, 2 and 3 May 1973, Trippenhuis, Amsterdam : under the auspices of the Royal Netherlands Academy of Arts and Sciences in association with the Royal Society and the British Academy. — Amsterdam ; London : North-Holland Publishing Co., 1974. — 62p : ill, facsim ; 25cm.
'... the Symposium "Light and Sight"' - p.7.
ISBN 0-7204-8277-1 Pbk : Unpriced
(B77-19186)

152.1'4 — Man. Visual perception. Constancies
Stability and constancy in visual perception / William Epstein, editor. — New York ; London [etc.] : Wiley, 1977. — xiii,463p : ill ; 24cm. — (Wiley series in behavior)
'A Wiley-Interscience publication'. — Bibl. — Index.
ISBN 0-471-24355-8 : £16.90
(B77-19187)

152.1'48 — Optical illusions. *Juvenile literature*
Paraquin, Charles H. Eye teasers : optical illusion puzzles / by Charles H. Paraquin ; [translated from the German by Paul Kuttner]. — New York : Sterling [etc.] ; London : Distributed by Ward Lock, 1976. — 96p : ill ; 21cm.
With answers. — Translation of: 'Schummelbilder'. Ravensburg : Otto Maier, 1975. — Index.
ISBN 0-7061-2515-0 : £2.50
(B77-12281)

152.1'5 — Man. Auditory perception
Moore, Brian C J. Introduction to the psychology of hearing / [by] Brian C.J. Moore. — London [etc.] : Macmillan, 1977. — 311p : ill ; 23cm.
Bibl.: p.277-300. — Index.
ISBN 0-333-19700-3 : £10.00
ISBN 0-333-19701-1 Pbk : £4.95
(B77-20872)

152.1'5 — Speech. Perception by man
Contemporary issues in experimental phonetics / edited by Norman J. Lass. — New York [etc.] ; London : Academic Press, 1976. — xiii,498p : ill ; 25cm. — (Perspectives in neurolinguistics and psycholinguistics)
Bibl. — Index.
ISBN 0-12-437150-7 : £10.70
Primary classification 612'.78
(B77-00780)

Sanders, Derek Alan. Auditory perception of speech : an introduction to principles and problems / [by] Derek A. Sanders. — Englewood Cliffs ; London [etc.] : Prentice-Hall, 1977. — x,246p : ill ; 24cm.
Bibl. — Index.
ISBN 0-13-052787-4 : £8.80
(B77-10718)

152.1'57 — Sounds. Tones. Perception by man
Plomp, Reinier. Aspects of tone sensation : a psychophysical study / [by] Reinier Plomp. — London [etc.] : Academic Press, 1976. — ix, 167p : ill ; 24cm. — (Academic Press series in cognition and perception)
Bibl.: p.147-160. — Index.
ISBN 0-12-558350-8 : £6.50
(B77-09475)

152.3 — PSYCHOLOGY. MOVEMENTS AND MOTOR FUNCTIONS

152.3 — Man. Motor skills. Development. *For physical education*

Schmidt, Richard A. Motor skills / [by] Richard A. Schmidt. — New York [etc.] ; London : Harper and Row, 1975. — xvii,158p : ill ; 20cm. — (Harper's series on scientific perspectives of physical education)
Bibl.: p.147-153. — Index.
ISBN 0-06-045784-8 Pbk : £3.70
(B77-02727)

152.3'224 — Man. Operant behaviour

Handbook of operant behavior / edited by Werner K. Honig, J.E.R. Staddon. — Englewood Cliffs ; London [etc.] : Prentice-Hall, 1977. — xiv,689p : ill ; 29cm. — (Century psychology series)
Bibl. — Index.
ISBN 0-13-380535-2 : £31.95
(B77-17882)

152.3'24 — Man. Instincts. Theories of Freud, Sigmund

Nagera, Humberto. Basic psychoanalytic concepts on the theory of instincts / by Humberto Nagera and ... [others]. — London : Allen and Unwin, 1970[i.e.1977]. — 3-136p ; 22cm. — (Hampstead Clinic. Psychoanalytic library ; vol.3)
Originally published: 1970. — Index.
ISBN 0-04-150061-x Pbk : £1.95
(B77-09476)

152.3'3 — Man. Habits

Nicholson, John, *b.1945.* Habits : why do you do what you do? / [by] John Nicholson. — London [etc.] : Macmillan, 1977. — 192p : ill ; 23cm.
Bibl.: p.187-188. — Index.
ISBN 0-333-22343-8 : £3.95 : CIP rev.
(B77-18525)

152.3'34 — Motor activities. Learning by man

Lawther, John Dobson. The learning and performance of physical skills / [by] John D. Lawther. — 2nd ed. — Englewood Cliffs ; London [etc.] : Prentice-Hall, 1977. — xi,240p : ill ; 24cm. — (The Prentice-Hall foundations of physical education and sport series)
Previous ed.: published as 'The learning of physical skills'. 1968. — Index.
ISBN 0-13-527325-0 : £7.20
(B77-11538)

152.3'34 — Motor activities. Learning by man. *Information processing perspectives*

Marteniuk, Ronald G. Information processing in motor skills / [by] Ronald G. Marteniuk. — New York ; London [etc.] : Holt, Rinehart and Winston, 1976. — xi,244p : ill ; 24cm.
Bibl.: p.232-240. — Index.
ISBN 0-03-006091-5 : £9.50
(B77-06442)

152.4 — PSYCHOLOGY. EMOTIONS AND FEELINGS

152.4 — Love

Arieti, Silvano. Love can be found : a guide to the most desired and most elusive emotion / [by] Silvano Arieti and James A. Arieti. — New York ; London : Harcourt Brace Jovanovich, 1977. — [10],230p ; 22cm.
Bibl.: p.218-223. — Index.
ISBN 0-15-154722-x : £5.80
(B77-30943)

152.4 — Love. Psychosocial aspects

Peele, Stanton. Love and addiction / [by] Stanton Peele, with Archie Brodsky. — London : Abacus, 1977. — 284p ; 20cm.
Originally published: New York : Taplinger, 1975. — Bibl.: p.269-275. — Index.
ISBN 0-349-12703-4 Pbk : £1.50
(B77-22322)

152.4'2 — Man. Aggression

Fromm, Erich. The anatomy of human destructiveness / [by] Erich Fromm. — Harmondsworth [etc.] : Penguin, 1977. — 679p ; 18cm.
Originally published: New York : Holt, Rinehart and Winston, 1973 ; London : Cape, 1974. — Bibl.: p.633-660. — Index.
ISBN 0-14-004258-x Pbk : £1.50
(B77-26755)

152.4'2 — Man. Aggression. Physiological aspects

Moyer, K E. The psychobiology of aggression / [by] K.E. Moyer. — New York [etc.] ; London : Harper and Row, 1976. — xix,402p : ill ; 24cm. — (Harper's physiological psychology series)
Bibl.: p.301-371. — Index.
ISBN 0-06-044641-2 : £8.95
(B77-08195)

152.4'2 — Man. Humour. *Conference proceedings*

International Conference on Humour and Laughter, *Cardiff, 1976.* It's a funny thing, humour / edited by Antony J. Chapman and Hugh C. Foot ; illustrated by Roy R. Behrens. — Oxford [etc.] : Pergamon, 1977. — xvii, 507p : ill ; 26cm.
Proceedings of the International Conference on Humour and Laughter held in Cardiff, 13-17th July 1976. — Bibl.
ISBN 0-08-021376-6 : £12.50
(B77-24671)

152.4'32 — Man. Fear. *Theosophical viewpoints*

Challoner, H.K. What of tomorrow? : the problem of fear / by H.K. Challoner. — London : Theosophical Publishing House, 1976. — [7],178p ; 19cm.
ISBN 0-7229-5079-9 Pbk : £1.95
(B77-23081)

152.4'32 — Man. Fear. Self-help

Rosen, Gerald M. Don't be afraid : a program for overcoming your fears and phobias / [by] Gerald M. Rosen. — Englewood Cliffs ; London [etc.] : Prentice-Hall, [1977]. — [12] 128p : forms ; 22cm.
'A spectrum book'. — Published in the United States: 1976. — Bibl.: p.125-128.
ISBN 0-13-218412-5 : £7.20
ISBN 0-13-218404-4 Pbk : £2.35
(B77-12833)

152.4'34 — Jealousy. *Readings*

Jealousy / edited by Gordon Clanton, Lynn G. Smith. — Englewood Cliffs ; London [etc.] : Prentice-Hall, 1977. — xii,244p ; 21cm.
Bibl.: p.238-244.
ISBN 0-13-509364-3 : £7.20
ISBN 0-13-509356-2 Pbk : £3.15
(B77-15673)

152.4'34 — Man. Shyness

Zimbardo, Philip. Shyness : what it is, what to do about it / [by] Philip G. Zimbardo ; research in collaboration with Paul A. Pilkonis ; therapy in collaboration with Margaret E. Marnell. — Reading, Mass. ; London [etc.] : Addison-Wesley, 1977. — viii, 263p : ill ; 24cm.
Bibl.: p.235-250. — Index.
ISBN 0-201-08793-6 : £5.95
ISBN 0-201-08794-4 Pbk : £3.30
(B77-24672)

152.4'43 — Man. Likes & dislikes. *Occult viewpoints*

Bennett, John Godolphin. The first liberation : freedom from like and dislike / [by] John G. Bennett. — Sherborne, Glos. : Coombe Springs Press, 1976. — [8],35p ; 19cm. — (The Sherborne theme talks series ; 1)
'The Sherborne Theme Talks Series are taken from tape recordings of meetings at Sherborne House between 1972 and 1975' - cover. — Booklet (8p.), 'The thematic technique' as insert.
ISBN 0-900306-32-7 Pbk : £0.75
(B77-11047)

152.5 — PSYCHOLOGY. MOTIVATION

Cattell, Raymond Bernard. Motivation and dynamic structure / by Raymond B. Cattell and Dennis Child. — London [etc.] : Holt, Rinehart and Winston, 1975. — xi,287p : ill ; 24cm.
Text on lining paper. — Bibl.: p.262-278. — Index.
ISBN 0-03-910164-9 : £6.50
(B77-03891)

Ferguson, Eva Dreikurs. Motivation : an experimental approach / [by] Eva Dreikurs Ferguson ; with a chapter contribution by Richard E. Musty. — New York ; London [etc.] : Holt, Rinehart and Winston, 1976. — xvii,453p : ill ; 24cm.
Bibl.: p.397-437. — Index.
ISBN 0-03-012726-2 : £10.00
(B77-01145)

152.5 — Man. Motivation. *Reviews of research*

The **psychology** of learning and motivation : advances in research and theory. — New York [etc.] ; London : Academic Press.
Vol.10 / edited by Gordon H. Bower. — 1976. — xiii,247p : ill ; 24cm.
Bibl. — Index.
ISBN 0-12-543310-7 : £11.95
ISSN 0079-7421
Primary classification 153.1'5
(B77-06443)

152.5'2 — Achievement motivation. Related to economic development

McClelland, David Clarence. The achieving society / by David C. McClelland. — [1st ed. reprinted] ; with a new introduction. — New York : Irvington ; New York ; London [etc.] : Distributed by Wiley, 1976. — xv,512,A-G p : ill ; 24cm.
Originally published: Princeton : Van Nostrand, 1961. — Bibl.: p.439-449. — Index.
ISBN 0-470-01397-4 : £12.75
Primary classification 330.9
(B77-24751)

152.5'2 — Man. Achievement motivation. Measurement

The **achievement** motive / by David C. McClelland ... [et al.]. — [1st ed. reprinted] ; with a new preface with hindsight by John W. Atkinson. — New York : Irvington ; New York ; London [etc.] : Distributed by Wiley, 1976. — [12],xxiii,386p,[2]p plates : ill ; 22cm. — (The century psychology series)
Originally published: New York : Appleton-Century-Crofts, 1953. — Bibl.: p.377-384. — Index.
ISBN 0-470-01390-7 : £11.90
(B77-08196)

152.5'2 — Man. Achievement motivation. Persistence

Nygard, Roald. Personality, situation, and persistence : a study with emphasis on achievement motivation / [by] Roald Nygard. — Oslo [etc.] : Universitetsforlaget ; Henley on Thames (37 Queen St., Henley on Thames, Oxon. RG9 1AJ) : [Distributed by] Global Book Resources [etc.], 1977. — 282p : ill ; 22cm. — (Norwegian studies in education ; no.6)
Bibl.: p.255-266. — Index.
Pbk : £10.40
(B77-28352)

153 — PSYCHOLOGY. INTELLIGENCE, INTELLECTUAL AND CONSCIOUS MENTAL PROCESSES

153 — Man. Mental processes

Rumelhart, David E. Introduction to human information processing / [by] David E. Rumelhart. — New York ; London [etc.] : Wiley, 1977. — ix,306p : ill ; 24cm.
Bibl.: p.266-275. — Index.
ISBN 0-471-74500-6 : £6.95
(B77-29146)

153 — Man. Reading behaviour & speech behaviour. Psychological aspects

Winokur, Stephen. A primer of verbal behavior : an operant view / [by] Stephen Winokur. — Englewood Cliffs ; London [etc.] : Prentice-Hall, 1976. — xi,164p : ill ; 24cm. — (Prentice-Hall series in experimental psychology)
Bibl.: p.155-159. — Index.
ISBN 0-13-700609-8 : £6.20
(B77-08197)

153'.01'84 — Man. Mental processes. Mathematical models. Applications of digital computer systems

Anderson, John Robert, *b.1947.* Language, memory and thought / [by] John R. Anderson. — Hillsdale : Erlbaum ; New York [etc.] ; London : Distributed by Wiley, 1976. — xiv, 546p : ill ; 24cm. — (The experimental psychology series)
Bibl. — Index.
ISBN 0-470-15187-0 : £15.40
(B77-01997)

153.1 — PSYCHOLOGY. MEMORY AND LEARNING

153.1 — Man. Learning & memory

Kintsch, Walter. Memory and cognition / [by] Walter Kintsch. — 2nd ed. — New York ; London [etc.] : Wiley, 1977. — vi,490p : ill ; 24cm.
Previous ed.: published as 'Learning, memory, and conceptual processes'. New York : Chichester : Wiley, 1970. — Bibl.: p.445-474. — Index.
ISBN 0-471-48072-x : £9.40
(B77-19189)

Wickelgren, Wayne A. Learning and memory / [by] Wayne A. Wickelgren. — Englewood Cliffs ; London [etc.] : Prentice-Hall, 1977. — xv,448p : ill ; 24cm. — (Prentice-Hall series in experimental psychology)
Bibl.: p.431-433. — Index.
ISBN 0-13-527663-2 : £11.15
Also classified at 156'.3'1
(B77-20873)

153.1′2 — Man. Memory
Brown, Mark. Memory matters / [by] Mark Brown. — Newton Abbot [etc.] : David and Charles, 1977. — 159p : ill ; 23cm.
Bibl.: p.156-158.
ISBN 0-7153-7379-x : £4.50
(B77-23967)

Eysenck, Michael W. Human memory : theory, research and individual differences / by Michael W. Eysenck. — Oxford [etc.] : Pergamon, 1977. — x,366p : ill ; 22cm. — (International series in experimental psychology ; vol.22)
Bibl.: p.295-347. — Index.
ISBN 0-08-020405-8 : £8.00
(B77-25360)

Underwood, Geoffrey. Attention and memory / by Geoffrey Underwood. — Oxford [etc.] : Pergamon, 1976. — viii,280p : ill ; 22cm. — (Pergamon international library)
Bibl.: p.253-269. — Index.
ISBN 0-08-019615-2 : £6.00
ISBN 0-08-018754-4 Pbk : £4.45
Also classified at 153.7′33
(B77-05847)

153.1′2 — Man. Memory. *Philosophical perspectives*
Malcolm, Norman. Memory and mind / [by] Norman Malcolm. — Ithaca ; London : Cornell University Press, 1977. — 277,[3]p ; 22cm.
Index.
ISBN 0-8014-1018-5 : £9.75
(B77-13481)

153.1′4 — Man. Memory. Training
Lorayne, Harry. Remembering people / [by] Harry Lorayne ; [photographs by Robert B. Bell]. — London : W.H. Allen, 1976. — 3-220p : ill, ports ; 24cm.
Originally published: New York : Stein and Day, 1975.
ISBN 0-491-01528-3 : £3.95
(B77-00010)

153.1′4 — Man. Memory. Training. *Manuals*
Buzan, Tony. Speed memory / [by] Tony Buzan. — Revised and updated [ed.]. — Newton Abbot [etc.] : David and Charles, 1977. — 158p : ill ; 23cm.
Previous ed.: i.e. 1st ed., London : Sphere, 1971.
ISBN 0-7153-7365-x : £1.95
(B77-12834)

Halacy, Daniel Stephen. How to improve your memory / by Dan Halacy ; illustrated by George MacClain. — New York ; London : F. Watts, 1977. — [8],64p : ill ; 25cm. — (A concise guide)
Index.
ISBN 0-531-00094-x : £1.95
(B77-28353)

Higbee, Kenneth L. Your memory : how it works and how to improve it / [by] Kenneth L. Higbee. — Englewood Cliffs ; London [etc.] : Prentice-Hall, 1977. — xiii,208p : ill ; 21cm.
Index.
ISBN 0-13-980144-8 : £7.95
ISBN 0-13-980136-7 Pbk : £3.20
(B77-28354)

Lorayne, Harry. How to develop a super-power memory / [by] Harry Lorayne. — Revised ed. — London [etc.] : Pan Books, 1977. — 188p : ill ; 18cm.
This ed. originally published: as 'Develop a super-power memory'. London : New English Library, 1963.
ISBN 0-330-25104-x Pbk : £0.75
(B77-21675)

153.1′5 — Learning by adults. *Reviews of research*
Adult learning : psychological research and applications / edited by Michael J.A. Howe. — London [etc.] : Wiley, 1977. — xvii,291p : ill, forms ; 24cm.
Bibl. — Index.
ISBN 0-471-99458-8 : £9.50
(B77-20874)

153.1′5 — Learning by man. *Reviews of research*
Handbook of learning and cognitive processes. — Hillsdale : Erlbaum ; New York ; London [etc.] : Distributed by Wiley.
In 6 vols.
Vol.4 : Attention and memory / edited by W.K. Estes. — 1976. — x,436p : ill ; 24cm.
Bibl. — Index.
ISBN 0-470-98908-4 : £15.90
(B77-05848)

The **psychology** of learning and motivation : advances in research and theory. — New York [etc.] ; London : Academic Press.
Vol.10 / edited by Gordon H. Bower. — 1976. — xiii,247p : ill ; 24cm.
Bibl. — Index.
ISBN 0-12-543310-7 : £11.95
ISSN 0079-7421
Also classified at 152.5
(B77-06443)

153.1′5 — Learning by man. *Secondary school texts*
Hanson, William John. Learning / [by] W.J. Hanson. — London : Longman, 1977. — 2-47p : ill(some col), facsim, maps, ports ; 27cm. — (Enquiries)
Bibl.: p.47.
ISBN 0-582-21999-x Sd : £0.75
(B77-19190)

153.1′5 — Learning by man. Behavioural factors
Argyris, Chris. Increasing leadership effectiveness / [by] Chris Argyris. — New York ; London [etc.] : Wiley, 1976. — xvii, 286p : ill ; 24cm. — (Wiley series in behavior)
'A Wiley-Interscience publication'. — Bibl.: p.280-281. — Index.
ISBN 0-471-01668-3 : £11.90
(B77-08198)

153.1′5 — Learning by man. Social factors
Bandura, Albert. Social learning theory / [by] Albert Bandura. — Englewood Cliffs ; London [etc.] : Prentice-Hall, 1977. — viii,247p : ill ; 24cm. — (Prentice-Hall series in social learning theory)
Bibl.: p.216-233. — Index.
ISBN 0-13-816751-6 : £7.60
ISBN 0-13-816744-3 Pbk : £4.75
(B77-32371)

153.1′5 — Man. Biofeedback training
Biofeedback : theory and research / edited by Gary E. Schwartz, Jackson Beatty. — New York [etc.] ; London : Academic Press, 1977. — x,467p : ill ; 24cm.
Bibl. — Index.
ISBN 0-12-632450-6 : £17.60
(B77-25661)

Karlins, Marvin. Biofeedback : turning on the power of your mind / [by] Marvin Karlins and Lewis M. Andrews. — London : Abacus, 1975. — 140p ; 20cm.
Originally published: Philadelphia : Lippincott, 1972 ; London : Garnstone Press, 1973. — Bibl.: p.115-136. — Index.
ISBN 0-349-12072-2 Pbk : £0.75
(B77-09723)

153.1′5 — Man. Biofeedback training. *Manuals*
Heisel, Dorelle Markley. The biofeedback guide : affiliating with excellence / by Dorelle Markley Heisel ; photographs by Connie Sullivan. — New York ; London [etc.] : Gordon and Breach, 1977. — [ii],269p : ill, port ; 24cm.
ISBN 0-677-00020-0 : £8.30
(B77-29896)

153.2 — PSYCHOLOGY. IDEATION
153.2′3 — Man. Concept formation
Bolton, Neil. Concept formation / by Neil Bolton. — Oxford [etc.] : Pergamon, 1977. — viii,163p : ill ; 22cm. — (Pergamon international library)
Bibl.: p.148-155. — Index.
ISBN 0-08-021493-2 : £4.50
ISBN 0-08-021494-0 Pbk : £2.95
(B77-29147)

153.3 — PSYCHOLOGY. IMAGINATION AND IMAGERY
153.3 — Geographical features. Mental images
Downs, Roger M. Maps in minds : reflections on cognitive mapping / [by] Roger M. Downs, David Stea. — New York [etc.] ; London : Harper and Row, 1977. — xx,284p : ill, facsim, maps ; 24cm. — (Harper and Row series in geography)
Bibl.: p.264-272. — Index.
ISBN 0-06-041733-1 Pbk : £3.95
(B77-25361)

153.3′5 — Creativity
Koestler, Arthur. The act of creation / [by] Arthur Koestler. — 2nd Danube ed. [i.e. 1st ed. reprinted] ; with a new preface by the author. — London : Hutchinson, 1976. — 4-751p : ill ; 21cm.
This ed. originally published: 1964. — Bibl.: p.717-728. — Index. — Includes both parts of the original edition.
ISBN 0-09-128270-5 : £6.95
(B77-08733)

Storr, Anthony. The dynamics of creation / [by] Anthony Storr. — Harmondsworth [etc.] : Penguin, 1976. — 304p ; 18cm. — (Pelican books)
Originally published: London : Secker and Warburg, 1972. — Index.
ISBN 0-14-021932-3 Pbk : £0.90
(B77-11048)

153.3′5 — Creativity. *State-of-the-art reviews*
Arasteh, A Reza. Creativity in human development : an interpretive and annotated bibliography / [by] A. Reza Arasteh, Josephine D. Arasteh. — [Revised ed.]. — Cambridge, Mass. : Schenkman ; New York ; London [etc.] : Distributed by Wiley, 1976. — [5],154p : 1 ill ; 24cm.
Previous ed.: published in 2 vols as 'Creativity in the life cycle'. Leiden : E.J. Brill, 1968.
ISBN 0-470-98933-5 : £9.50
(B77-08199)

153.3′5 — Creativity. Theories
May, Rollo. The courage to create / [by] Rollo May. — London : Collins, 1976. — 142p ; 22cm.
Originally published: New York : Norton, 1975.
ISBN 0-00-215114-6 : £2.95
(B77-05185)

153.3′5′05 — Creativity. *Periodicals*
Creativity network. — [Manchester] ([c/o The Editor, Manchester Business School, Booth Street West, Manchester M15 6PB]) : ['Creativity Network'].
Vol.1, [no.1]-. — [1974]-. — ill ; 26cm.
Quarterly. — [12]p. in 1st issue. — Size varies.
Sd : Unpriced
ISSN 0140-0673
(B77-25362)

153.4 — PSYCHOLOGY. COGNITION
153.4 — Man. Cognition
Blumenthal, Arthur L. The process of cognition / [by] Arthur L. Blumenthal. — Englewood Cliffs ; London [etc.] : Prentice-Hall, 1977. — x,230p : ill ; 24cm. — (Experimental psychology series)
Bibl.: p.199-221. — Index.
ISBN 0-13-722983-6 : £7.95
(B77-20875)

153.4 — Man. Cognition. *Conference proceedings*
Cognitive theory. — Hillsdale : Erlbaum ; New York ; London [etc.] : Distributed by Wiley.
Bibl. — Index.
Vol.2 / edited by N. John Castellan, Jr, David B. Pisoni, George R. Potts. — 1977. — ix, 342p : ill ; 24cm.
'... contains chapters based on papers presented as part of the Eighth Annual Indiana Cognitive/Mathematical Psychology Conference held at Indiana University in April, 1975' - Preface.
ISBN 0-470-99025-2 : Unpriced
(B77-23968)

Perceiving, Acting and Knowing *(Conference), University of Minnesota, 1973.* Perceiving, acting and knowing : toward an ecological psychology / edited by Robert Shaw, John Bransford. — Hillsdale : Erlbaum ; New York ; London [etc.] : Distributed by Wiley, 1977. — xi,492p : ill ; 24cm.
'The chapters in this volume derive from a conference on Perceiving, Acting and Knowing held by the Center for Research in Human Learning at the University of Minnesota, July 23-August 17, 1973' - Preface. — Bibl. — Index.
ISBN 0-470-99014-7 : £15.00
Also classified at 153.7
(B77-24673)

153.4 — Man. Cognition. *Philosophical perspectives*
Fodor, Jerry Alan. The language of thought / [by] Jerry A. Fodor. — Hassocks : Harvester Press, 1976. — x,214p : ill ; 25cm. — (The language and thought series)
Originally published: New York : Crowell, 1975. — Bibl.: p.206-212. — Index.
ISBN 0-85527-309-7 : £8.95
(B77-00591)

153.4 — Man. Cognition. Neuropsychological aspects
Brown, Jason. Mind, brain and consciousness : the neuropsychology of cognition / [by] Jason Brown. — New York [etc.] ; London : Academic Press, 1977. — x,190p : ill ; 24cm. — (Perspectives in neurolinguistics and psycholinguistics)
Bibl.: p.177-184. — Index.
ISBN 0-12-137550-1 : £8.85
(B77-19191)

153.4 — Man. Cognition. Related to social behaviour. *Conference proceedings*
Symposium on Cognition, *11th, Carnegie-Mellon University, 1975.* Cognition and social behavior / edited by John S. Carroll, John W. Payne. — Hillsdale : Erlbaum ; New York ; London [etc.] : Distributed by Wiley, 1976. — xiii,290p : ill ; 24cm.
'... the collected papers of the Eleventh Annual Symposium on Cognition, held at Carnegie-Mellon University in April 1975' - Preface. — Bibl.: p.269-286. — Index.
ISBN 0-470-99007-4 : £12.40
Also classified at 301.1
(B77-23082)

153.4 — Man. Cognitive development. Cultural factors. *Soviet Central Asia. Case studies*
Luriia, Aleksandr Romanovich. Cognitive development : its cultural and social foundations / [by] A.R. Luria ; translated [from the Russian] by Martin Lopez-Morillas and Lynn Solotaroff ; edited by Michael Cole. — Cambridge, Mass. ; London : Harvard University Press, 1976 [i.e. 1977]. — xvi,175p : ill ; 24cm.
This translation published in the United States: 1976. — Translation of: 'Ob istoricheskom razvitii poznavatel'nykh protsessov'. Moskva : Nauka, 1974. — Bibl.: p.167-169. — Index.
ISBN 0-674-13731-0 : £9.35
(B77-13482)

153.4 — Man. Cognitive styles. Related to adaptation. *Study examples: Nomadic communities*
Berry, John Widdup. Human ecology and cognitive style : comparative studies in cultural and psychological adaptation / [by] John W. Berry. — [Beverly Hills] : Sage Publications ; New York ; London [etc.] : Distributed by Wiley, 1976. — xiii,242p : ill, map ; 24cm. — (Cross-cultural research and methodology series ; [vol.3])
Bibl.: p.229-242.
ISBN 0-470-15103-x : £12.50
Primary classification 301.2'1
(B77-03938)

153.4'3 — Analogical reasoning. Psychological aspects
Sternberg, Robert J. Intelligence, information processing, and analogical reasoning : the componential analysis of human abilities / [by] Robert J. Sternberg. — Hillsdale : Erlbaum ; New York [etc.] ; London : Distributed by Wiley, 1977. — xiii,348p : ill ; 24cm. — (The experimental psychology series)
Bibl.: p.326-333. — Index.
ISBN 0-470-99137-2 : £15.00
(B77-25363)

153.7 — PSYCHOLOGY. PERCEPTUAL PROCESSES
153.7 — Man. Attribution. *Reviews of research*
New directions in attribution research. — Hillsdale : Erlbaum ; New York ; London [etc.] : Distributed by Wiley.
Vol.1 / edited by John H. Harvey, William John Ickes, Robert F. Kidd. — 1976. — xi, 467p ; 24cm.
Bibl. — Index.
ISBN 0-470-98910-6 : £15.40
(B77-06444)

153.7 — Man. Perception
Bennett, John Godolphin. Noticing / [by] John G. Bennett. — Sherborne, Glos. : Coombe Springs Press, 1976. — [6],48p ; 19cm. — (The Sherborne theme talks series ; 2)
'The Sherborne Theme Talks Series are taken from tape recordings of meetings at Sherborne House between 1972 and 1975' - cover.
ISBN 0-900306-34-3 Pbk : £0.75
(B77-10116)

Handbook of perception / edited by Edward C. Carterette and Morton P. Friedman. — New York [etc.] ; London : Academic Press.
Vol.7 : Language and speech. — 1976. — xviii, 501p : ill ; 24cm.
Bibl. — Index.
ISBN 0-12-161907-9 : £16.25
(B77-03892)

Rock, Irvin. An introduction to perception / [by] Irvin Rock. — New York ; Macmillan ; London : Collier Macmillan, [1976]. — xii, 580p,4p of plates : ill(some col) ; 24cm.
Published in the United States: 1975. — Index.
ISBN 0-02-402490-2 Pbk : £10.00
(B77-01998)

153.7 — Man. Perception. *Conference proceedings*
Perceiving, Acting and Knowing *(Conference), University of Minnesota, 1973.* Perceiving, acting and knowing : toward an ecological psychology / edited by Robert Shaw, John Bransford. — Hillsdale : Erlbaum ; New York ; London [etc.] : Distributed by Wiley, 1977. — xi,492p : ill ; 24cm.
'The chapters in this volume derive from a conference on Perceiving, Acting and Knowing held by the Center for Research in Human Learning at the University of Minnesota, July 23-August 17, 1973' - Preface. — Bibl. — Index.
ISBN 0-470-99014-7 : £15.00
Primary classification 153.4
(B77-24673)

153.7'33 — Man. Attention
Underwood, Geoffrey. Attention and memory / by Geoffrey Underwood. — Oxford [etc.] : Pergamon, 1976. — viii,280p : ill ; 22cm. — (Pergamon international library)
Bibl.: p.253-269. — Index.
ISBN 0-08-019615-2 : £6.00
ISBN 0-08-018754-4 Pbk : £4.45
Primary classification 153.1'2
(B77-05847)

153.7'53 — Time. Perception by man. Sex differences
Cottle, Thomas J. Perceiving time : a psychological investigation with men and women / [by] Thomas J. Cottle. — New York ; London [etc.] : Wiley, 1976. — xv,267p : ill ; 24cm.
'A Wiley-Interscience publication'. — Bibl.: p.195-214. — Index.
ISBN 0-471-17530-7 : £10.60
(B77-08200)

153.8 — PSYCHOLOGY. VOLITION
153.8'3 — Decision making. Psychological aspects
Janis, Irving Lester. Decision making : a psychological analysis of conflict, choice, and commitment / [by] Irving L. Janis, Leon Mann. — New York : Free Press ; London : Collier Macmillan, 1977. — xx,488,[1]p : ill ; 24cm.
Bibl.: p.445-473. — Index.
ISBN 0-02-916160-6 : £12.00
(B77-23083)

153.8'3'0184 — Decision making. Use of mathematical models
Open University. *Systems Modelling Course Team.* Models and the decision maker / prepared by the [Open University, Systems Modelling] Course Team. — Milton Keynes : Open University Press, 1975. — 66p : ill ; 30cm. — (Technology, a third level course : systems modelling ; unit 11) (T341 ; 11)
With answers. — Bibl.: p.62.
ISBN 0-335-06054-4 Pbk : £2.85
(B77-26756)

153.8'5 — Man. Behaviour modification. *For welfare work*
Nay, W Robert. Behavioral intervention : contemporary strategies / [by] W. Robert Nay. — New York : Gardner Press ; New York ; London [etc.] : Distributed by Wiley, 1976. — xiv,384p : ill, facsims, forms ; 24cm.
Bibl.: p.341-370. — Index.
ISBN 0-470-15088-2 : £15.00
(B77-13483)

153.8'5 — Man. Behaviour modification. *Reviews of research*
Progress in behavior modification / edited by Michel Hersen, Richard M. Eisler, Peter M. Miller. — New York [etc.] ; London : Academic Press.
Vol.3. — 1976. — xiii,362p : ill ; 24cm.
Bibl. — Index.
ISBN 0-12-535603-x : £11.00
(B77-05849)

Progress in behavior modification / edited by Michael Hersen, Richard M. Eisler, Peter M. Miller. — New York [etc.] ; London : Academic Press.
Vol.4. — 1977. — xv,380p ; 24cm.
Bibl. — Index.
ISBN 0-12-535604-8 : £13.85
(B77-29148)

153.9 — PSYCHOLOGY. INTELLIGENCE AND APTITUDES
153.9 — Man. Intelligence. *State-of-the-art reviews*
Brody, Erness Bright. Intelligence : nature, determinants, and consequences / [by] Erness Bright Brody, Nathan Brody. — New York [etc.] ; London : Academic Press, 1976 [i.e. 1977]. — x,241p : ill ; 24cm. — (Educational psychology)
Published in the United States: 1976. — Bibl.: p.227-237. — Index.
ISBN 0-12-134250-6 : £8.85
(B77-13484)

153.9 — Man. Intelligence. Theories
Blake, Anthony George Edward. Intelligence now / [by] A.G.E. Blake. — Revised ed. — Sherborne, Glos. : Coombe Springs Press, 1975. — [8],59p,[4]p of plates : ill ; 20cm.
Previous ed.: 1973.
ISBN 0-900306-09-2 Pbk : £0.75
(B77-10117)

153.9'2 — Man. Intelligence. Environmental factors. Compared with genetic factors
Kamin, Leon J. The science and politics of I.Q. / [by] Leon J. Kamin. — Harmondsworth [etc.] : Penguin, 1977. — 252p : ill ; 19cm. — (Penguin education)
Originally published: Potomac : Erlbaum, 1974. — Index.
ISBN 0-14-080932-5 Pbk : £0.95
(B77-26757)

153.9'3 — Children. Intelligence tests. *Collections*
Wilson, Glenn Daniel. Know your child's IQ / [by] Glenn Wilson & Diana Grylls. — London : Futura Publications, 1977. — 144p : ill ; 18cm. — (Pocket guides)
Bibl.: p.144.
ISBN 0-7088-0982-0 Pbk : £0.65
(B77-29897)

153.9'3 — Man. Intelligence. Measurement
The **IQ** controversy : critical readings / edited by Ned Block & Gerald Dworkin. — London : Quartet Books, 1977. — xiii,559p : ill ; 23cm.
Originally published: New York : Pantheon Books, 1976. — Bibl. — Index.
ISBN 0-7043-2130-0 : £8.95
ISBN 0-7043-3133-0 Pbk : £4.95
(B77-07046)

154 — PSYCHOLOGY. SUBCONSCIOUS STATES AND PROCESSES
154 — Man. Unconscious mind. *Philosophical perspectives*
MacIntyre, Alasdair Chalmers. The unconscious : a conceptual analysis / by A.C. MacIntyre. — London [etc.] : Routledge and Kegan Paul [etc.], 1976. — ix,100p ; 20cm. — (Studies in philosophical psychology)
Originally published: 1958. — Bibl.: p.vii-ix. — Index.
ISBN 0-7100-3834-8 : £2.50
ISBN 0-7100-7800-5 Pbk : £1.25
(B77-00592)

154.2 — PSYCHOLOGY. THE SUBCONSCIOUS
154.2'2 — Ego functions
Haan, Norma. Coping and defending : processes of self-environment organization / [by] Norma Haan with contributions by ... [others]. — New York [etc.] ; London : Academic Press, 1977. — xiv,346p : ill ; 24cm. — (Personality and psychopathology)
Bibl.: p.333-342. — Index.
ISBN 0-12-312350-x : £12.40
(B77-26758)

154.3 — PSYCHOLOGY. SECONDARY CONSCIOUSNESS
154.3 — Daydreaming
Singer, Jerome Leonard. Daydreaming and fantasy / [by] Jerome L. Singer. — London : Allen and Unwin, 1976. — xi,281p ; 23cm.
Originally published: New York : Harper and Row, 1975. — Bibl.: p.263-269. — Index.
ISBN 0-04-154003-4 : £4.50
(B77-07773)

154.3 — Sexual fantasies
Dally, Peter. The fantasy game / [by] Peter Dally. — London [etc.] : Quartet Books, 1977. — xii,218p ; 20cm.
Originally published: as 'The fantasy factor'. London : Weidenfeld and Nicolson, 1975. — Index.
ISBN 0-7043-3129-2 Pbk : £1.95
(B77-20876)

154.6 — PSYCHOLOGY. SLEEP PHENOMENA
154.6 — Man. Posture during sleep. Psychological aspects
Dunkell, Samuel. Sleep positions : the night language of the body / by Samuel Dunkell. — London : Heinemann, 1977. — 191p : ill ; 22cm.
ISBN 0-434-21666-6 : £4.50
(B77-17883)

154.6'3'0924 — Dreams. Theories of Freud, Sigmund
Nagera, Humberto. Basic psychoanalytic concepts on the theory of dreams / by Humberto Nagera and ... [others]. — London : Allen and Unwin, 1969 [i.e. 1977]. — 121p ; 22cm. — (Hampstead Clinic. Psychoanalytic library ; vol.2)
Originally published: 1969. — Index.
ISBN 0-04-150060-1 Pbk : £1.95
(B77-09477)

154.6'34'03 — Dreams. Interpretation. *Encyclopaedias*
Chetwynd, Tom. Dictionary for dreamers / [by] Tom Chetwynd. — St Albans : Paladin, 1974. — 208p ; 20cm.
Originally published: London : Allen and Unwin, 1972. — Bibl.: p.193-194. — Index.
ISBN 0-586-08159-3 Pbk : £0.60
(B77-19993)

Chetwynd, Tom. Dictionary for dreamers / [by] Tom Chetwynd. — St Albans : Paladin, 1977. — 208p : ill ; 20cm.
Originally published: London : Allen and Unwin, 1972. — Bibl.: p.193-194. — Index.
Pbk : £0.95
ISBN 0-586-08159-3
(B77-29898)

Miller, Gustavus Hindman. Ten thousand dreams interpreted, or, What's in a dream : a scientific and practical exposition / by Gustavus Hindman Miller. — [1st ed. reprinted]. — London [etc.] : E. Benn, 1977. — 3-617,xvii p ; 20cm.
Spine title: 10,000 dreams interpreted. — Facsimile reprint of: 1st ed. reprinted. Chicago : M.A. Donohue, 1931. — Originally published: as 'What's in a dream'. New York : G.W. Dillingham Co., 1901. — Index.
ISBN 0-510-41002-2 Pbk : £2.95
(B77-23969)

154.7 — HYPNOTISM
154.7 — Hypnotism. Methodology
Sheehan, Peter Winston. Methodologies of hypnosis : a critical appraisal of contemporary paradigms of hypnosis / [by] Peter W. Sheehan, Campbell W. Perry. — Hillsdale : Erlbaum ; New York ; London [etc.] : Distributed by Wiley, 1976. — xv,329p : ill ; 24cm.
Bibl.: p.299-316. — Index.
ISBN 0-470-15028-9 : £13.50
(B77-01146)

154.7'09'03 — Hypnotism, to 1975
Thornton, E M. Hypnotism, hysteria and epilepsy : an historical synthesis / [by] E.M. Thornton. — London : Heinemann Medical, 1976. — vii,205p : ill, facsims ; 23cm.
Bibl.: p.193-205. — Index.
ISBN 0-433-32321-3 : £5.95
(B77-07774)

154.7'72'0924 — Hypnotism. Trances. Special subjects: Historical events, B.C.1500-A.D.1975. *Personal observations*
Stuart-Knill, Eve, *Lady.* Experiences as seen under hypnosis / by Eve, Lady Knill. — London (Crawford House, Willow St., E4 7EQ) : E.G. Ellis and Sons, 1977. — 18p ; 21cm.
Sd : £1.00
(B77-19192)

155 — DIFFERENTIAL AND GENETIC PSYCHOLOGY
155 — Developmental psychology
Contemporary issues in developmental psychology / edited and with commentary by Norman S. Endler, Lawrence R. Boulter, Harry Osser ; foreword by J. McV. Hunt. — 2nd ed. — New York ; London [etc.] : Holt, Rinehart and Winston, 1976. — xiii,689p : ill, form ; 25cm.
Previous ed.: 1968. — Bibl. — Index.
ISBN 0-03-008421-0 : £11.00
(B77-01147)

Liebert, Robert Mandel. Developmental psychology / [by] Robert M. Liebert, Rita Wicks Poulos, Gloria Strauss Marmor. — 2nd ed. — Englewood Cliffs ; London [etc.] : Prentice-Hall, 1977. — xvii,572p,plate : ill(some col), ports ; 24cm.
Previous ed.: 1974. — Bibl.: p.521-552. — Index.
ISBN 0-13-208231-4 : £11.95
(B77-19994)

155 — Exceptional persons
Telford, Charles Witt. The exceptional individual / [by] Charles W. Telford, James M. Sawrey. — 3rd ed. — Englewood Cliffs ; London [etc.] : Prentice-Hall, 1977. — viii, 535p : ill ; 24cm.
Previous ed.: 1972. — Bibl. — Index.
ISBN 0-13-293837-5 : £11.15
(B77-32372)

155 — Man. Development. *Readings*
Readings in human development : contemporary perspectives / edited by David Elkind and Donna C. Hetzel. — New York [etc.] ; London : Harper and Row, 1977. — xi,272p : ill, ports ; 28cm. — (Contemporary perspectives reader series)
Includes facsimile reprints.
ISBN 0-06-047055-0 Pbk : £5.20
(B77-26759)

155.2 — PERSONALITY
155.2 — Individuality
Buss, Allan R. Individual differences : traits and factors / [by] Allan R. Buss and Wayne Poley. — New York : Gardner Press ; New York ; London [etc.] : Distributed by Wiley, [1977]. — ix,275p : ill ; 24cm.
Published in the United States: 1976. — Bibl.: p.258-269. — Index.
ISBN 0-470-15099-8 : £11.25
(B77-15069)

155.2 — Man. Behaviour. Personal construct theory
New perspectives in personal construct theory / edited by D. Bannister. — London [etc.] : Academic Press, 1977. — x,355p : ill ; 24cm.
Bibl. — Index.
ISBN 0-12-077940-4 : £10.80
(B77-29149)

155.2 — Man. Behaviour. Personal construct theory. Repertory grid technique
Fransella, Fay. A manual for repertory grid technique / [by] Fay Fransella and Don Bannister. — London [etc.] : Academic Press, 1977. — xiii,193p : ill ; 24cm.
Bibl.: p.149-171, 175-184. — Index.
ISBN 0-12-265450-1 : £7.50
ISBN 0-12-265456-0 Pbk : £3.80
(B77-29150)

155.2 — Man. Identity. Psychological aspects
Strauss, Anselm Leonard. Mirrors and masks : the search for identity / by Anselm L. Strauss. — London : Martin Robertson, 1977. — [4], 186p ; 23cm. — (Medicine in society series)
Originally published: Glencoe, Ill. : Free Press, 1959.
ISBN 0-85520-218-1 : £6.95
(B77-29899)

155.2 — Persona. *Christian viewpoints*
Jacobi, Jolande. Masks of the soul / by Jolande Jacobi ; translated [from the German] by Ean Begg. — London : Darton, Longman and Todd, 1976. — 94p ; 21cm.
Translation of: 'Die Seelenmaske'. Olten : Walter, 1971.
ISBN 0-232-51203-5 Pbk : £2.25
(B77-12835)

155.2 — Personality. *Middle school texts*
Bull, Norman John. Persons / [by] Norman J. Bull. — London : Longman, 1976. — 112p : ill, facsims, forms, ports ; 25cm. — (The way of wisdom series ; book 5)
Index.
ISBN 0-582-21425-4 Pbk : £1.50
Primary classification 301.11
(B77-00029)

155.2 — Personality. Perception by man. Role of language
Bromley, Dennis Basil. Personality description in ordinary language / [by] D.B. Bromley. — London [etc.] : Wiley, 1977. — x,278p ; 24cm.
Bibl.: p.257-263. — Index.
ISBN 0-471-99443-x : £9.00
(B77-20877)

155.2 — Personality. Theories
DiCaprio, Nicholas S. The good life : models for a healthy personality / [by] Nicholas S. DiCaprio. — Englewood Cliffs ; London [etc.] : Prentice-Hall, [1977]. — xiii,210p ; 22cm.
Published in the United States: 1976. — Bibl.: p.198-200. — Index.
ISBN 0-13-360396-2 : £7.15
ISBN 0-13-360388-1 Pbk : £3.20
(B77-10118)

Handbook of modern personality theory / edited by Raymond B. Cattell, Ralph Mason Dreger. — Washington, D.C. ; London : Hemisphere Publishing ; New York ; London [etc.] : Distributed by Wiley, 1977. — xi,804p : ill ; 25cm. — (The series in clinical and community psychology)
'A Halsted Press book'. — Bibl.: p.744-790. — Index.
ISBN 0-470-15201-x : £28.00
(B77-17884)

Hjelle, Larry A. Personality theories : basic assumptions, research and applications / [by] Larry A. Hjelle, Daniel J. Ziegler. — New York ; London [etc.] : McGraw-Hill, 1976. — xix,362p : ill, ports ; 25cm. — (McGraw-Hill series in psychology)
Bibl. — Index.
ISBN 0-07-029061-x : £9.90
(B77-04539)

Schultz, Duane Philip. Growth psychology : models of the healthy personality / [by] Duane Schultz. — New York ; London [etc.] : D. Van Nostrand, 1977. — vii,151p ; 23cm.
Bibl. — Index.
ISBN 0-442-27434-3 Pbk : £4.00
(B77-19995)

155.2 — Psychology. Interactionism. *Conference proceedings*
Personality at the crossroads : current issues in international psychology / edited by David Magnusson, Norman S. Endler. — Hillsdale : Erlbaum ; New York ; London [etc.] : Distributed by Wiley, 1977. — x,454p : ill ; 24cm.
'... a symposium, on International Psychology ... took place in Stockholm, Sweden, June 22-27, 1975' - Preface. — Bibl.: p.409-437. — Index.
ISBN 0-470-99135-6 : £18.70
(B77-22323)

155.2 — Self-actualisation
Bruno, Frank Joe. Human adjustment and personal growth : seven pathways / [by] Frank J. Bruno. — New York ; London [etc.] : Wiley, 1977. — xii,499p : ill, ports ; 25cm.
With answers. — Bibl. — Index.
ISBN 0-471-11435-9 : £9.35
(B77-21677)

Dawson, Peter, *b.1920.* The brain game / [by] Peter Dawson. — [Hove] ([P.O. Box 422, Valance Rd, Hove BN3 2DU]) : Valldaro Books, 1976. — 108p : ill ; 20cm.
ISBN 0-86077-002-8 Pbk : £1.50
(B77-00011)

Moustakas, Clark Edward. Creative life / [by] Clark E. Moustakas. — New York ; London [etc.] : Van Nostrand Reinhold, 1977. — xi, 114p ; 24cm.
ISBN 0-442-25588-8 : £6.00
(B77-24674)

Rosenblatt, Daniel. Your life is a mess, and what to do about it / [by] Daniel Rosenblatt ; illustrations by Charles Morris Mount. — New York [etc.] ; London : Harper and Row, 1976. — [8],149p : ill ; 18cm. — (Perennial library)
ISBN 0-06-080374-6 Pbk : £1.10
(B77-06445)

155.2'01 — Optimal personality. Theories
Coan, Richard Welton. Hero, artist, sage, or saint? : a survey of views on what is variously called mental health, normality, maturity, self-actualization, and human fulfillment / [by] Richard W. Coan. — New York ; Guildford : Columbia University Press, 1977. — xiii,322p ; 24cm.
Index.
ISBN 0-231-03806-2 : £14.70
ISBN 0-231-08355-6 Pbk : £4.75
(B77-23084)

155.2'08 — Personality. *Essays*
Maslow, Abraham Harold. The farther reaches of human nature / [by] Abraham H. Maslow. — Harmondsworth [etc.] : Penguin, 1976. — xxi, 407p ; 19cm. — (Esalen books)
Originally published: New York : Viking Press, 1972. — Bibl.: p.376-400. — Index.
ISBN 0-14-004265-2 Pbk : Unpriced
(B77-01148)

155.2'08 — Personality. *Readings*
Personality / edited by Rom Harré. — Oxford : Blackwell, [1977]. — viii,255p : ill ; 23cm.
Bibl. — Index.
ISBN 0-631-17360-9 : £7.50
(B77-07775)

155.2'32 — Anti-authoritarianism. Psychological aspects. Theories
Kreml, William P. The anti-authoritarian personality / by William P. Kreml. — Oxford [etc.] : Pergamon, 1977. — xi,118p ; 26cm. — (International series of monographs in experimental psychology ; vol.21)
Bibl.: p.110-115. — Index.
ISBN 0-08-021063-5 : £7.25
(B77-18526)

155.2'34 — Moral development
Moral development and behavior : theory, research, and social issues / editor Thomas Lickona. — New York ; London [etc.] : Holt, Rinehart and Winston, 1976. — xvii,430p : ill ; 24cm.
Bibl.: p.364-402. — Index.
ISBN 0-03-002811-6 : £10.25
(B77-02729)

155.2'4 — Man. Transitions. Psychological aspects
Adams, John. Transition : understanding & managing personal change / [by] John Adams, John Hayes, Barrie Hopson. — London : Martin Robertson, 1976. — xiii,241p : ill ; 23cm.
Bibl.: p.225-233. — Index.
ISBN 0-85520-129-0 : £7.85
(B77-10119)

Moustakas, Clark Edward. Turning points / [by] Clark E. Moustakas. — Englewood Cliffs ; London [etc.] : Prentice-Hall, 1977. — xiv, 129p : music ; 21cm.
ISBN 0-13-933168-9 : Unpriced
ISBN 0-13-933150-6 Pbk : £2.75
(B77-33573)

155.2'4 — Social adjustment. Psychological aspects. *Readings*
The **psychology** of adjustment : current concepts and applications. — 3rd ed. / edited by Walter Katkovsky, Leon Gorlow. — New York ; London [etc.] : McGraw-Hill, 1976. — xiii, 539p : ill ; 24cm.
Previous ed.: published as 'Readings in the psychology of adjustment' / edited by Leon Gorlow & Walter Katkovsky. 1968. — Bibl. — Index.
ISBN 0-07-033345-9 Pbk : £7.05
(B77-06446)

155.2'4 — Social adjustment. Role of problem solving. Psychological aspects
Spivack, George. The problem-solving approach to adjustment / [by] George Spivack, Jerome J. Platt, Myrna B. Shure. — San Francisco [etc.] ; London : Jossey-Bass, 1976 [i.e. 1977]. — xvii, 318p : forms ; 24cm. — ([The Jossey-Bass behavioral science series])
Published in the United States: 1976. — Bibl.: p.298-312. — Index.
ISBN 0-87589-290-6 : £8.65
(B77-10120)

155.2'5 — Ego. Development
Loevinger, Jane. Ego development / [by] Jane Loevinger, with the assistance of Augusto Blasi. — San Francisco [etc.] ; London : Jossey-Bass, 1976. — xxi,504p : ill ; 24cm. — (The Jossey-Bass behavioral science series)
Bibl.: p.459-482. — Index.
ISBN 0-87589-275-2 : £14.40
(B77-20878)

155.2'5 — Personality. Development
White, Robert Winthrop. The enterprise of living : a view of personal growth / [by] Robert W. White. — 2nd ed. — New York ; London [etc.] : Holt, Rinehart and Winston, 1976. — xi,563p : ill, facsims, ports ; 25cm.
Previous ed.: 1972. — Bibl.: p.527-548. — Index.
ISBN 0-03-089522-7 : £10.75
(B77-01999)

155.2'5 — Personality. Development. Influence of social class
Lundberg, Margaret J. The incomplete adult : social class constraints on personality development / [by] Margaret J. Lundberg. — Westport, Conn. ; London : Greenwood Press, 1974. — xv,245p : ill ; 22cm. — (Contributions in sociology ; no.15)
Bibl.: p.215-228. — Index.
ISBN 0-8371-7362-0 : £10.25
(B77-15070)

155.2'5 — Personality. Development. Role of family life
L'Abate, Luciano. Understanding and helping the individual in the family / [by] Luciano L'Abate. — New York [etc.] ; London : Grune and Stratton, [1977]. — ix,261p : ill ; 24cm.
Published in the United States: 1976. — Bibl.: p.229-244. — Index.
ISBN 0-8089-0969-x : £11.70
(B77-14534)

155.2'5 — Self-evaluation. Measurement
Wells, L Edward. Self-esteem : its conceptualization and measurement / [by] L. Edward Wells, Gerald Marwell. — Beverly Hills ; London : Sage Publications, 1976. — [5], 290p ; 22cm. — (Sage library of social research ; vol.20)
Bibl.: p.255-278. — Index.
ISBN 0-8039-0383-9 : £9.20
ISBN 0-8039-0394-4 Pbk : £4.50
(B77-03339)

155.2'8 — Personality. Assessment
Cattell, Raymond Bernard. The scientific analysis of personality and motivation / by R.B. Cattell and P. Kline. — New York [etc.] ; London : Academic Press, 1977. — xii,385p ; 24cm. — (Personality and psychopathology ; 17)
Bibl.: p.355-371. — Index.
ISBN 0-12-164250-x : £11.50
(B77-23085)

Sundberg, Norman Dale. Assessment of persons / [by] Norman D. Sundberg. — Englewood Cliffs ; London [etc.] : Prentice-Hall, 1977. — xiii,353p : ill ; 24cm. — (The Prentice-Hall series in personality)
Bibl.: p.305-344. — Index.
ISBN 0-13-049585-9 : £9.55
(B77-16166)

155.2'8 — Personality. Measurement. *Readings*
The **measurement** of personality / readings selected and comments written by H.J. Eysenck. — Lancaster : M.T.P. Press, 1976. — xviii,511p : ill ; 26cm.
Bibl.
ISBN 0-85200-148-7 : £12.50
(B77-08201)

155.2'83 — Intrapersonal space. Perception by man. Measurement. Grid techniques. *Research reports*
The **measurement** of intrapersonal space by grid technique / edited by Patrick Slater. — London [etc.] : Wiley.
Vol.2 : Dimensions of intrapersonal space / [by] Patrick Slater ; with contributions from Jane Chetwynd ... [et al.]. — 1977. — xii,270p : ill ; 24cm.
Bibl. — Index.
ISBN 0-471-99450-2 : £12.00
(B77-26091)

155.2'84 — Personality. Projective tests: Bender Gestalt Test
Hutt, Max Lewis. The Hutt adaptation of the Bender-Gestalt test / [by] Max L. Hutt. — 3rd ed. — New York [etc.] ; London : Grune and Stratton, 1977. — viii,279p : ill ; 24cm.
Previous ed.: New York : Grune and Stratton, 1969. — Bibl.: p.258-268. — Index.
ISBN 0-8089-0990-8 : £10.30
(B77-26760)

155.2'842 — Personality. Projective tests: Rorschach Inkblot Test. Interpretation
Aronow, Edward. Rorschach content interpretation / [by] Edward Aronow, Marvin Reznikoff. — New York [etc.] ; London : Grune and Stratton, 1976. — xv,362p ; 24cm.
Bibl.: p.317-340. — Index.
ISBN 0-8089-0961-4 : £11.90
(B77-08202)

155.3 — SEX PSYCHOLOGY
155.3 — Man. Sexual attraction
Wilson, Glenn Daniel. Love's mysteries : the secrets of sexual attraction / [by] Glenn Wilson and David Nias. — [London] : Fontana, 1977. — 192p ; 18cm.
Originally published: as 'Love's mysteries : the psychology of sexual attraction'. London : Open Books, 1976. — Bibl.: p.179-187. — Index.
ISBN 0-00-634575-1 Pbk : £0.80
(B77-12836)

155.3 — Man. Sexual behaviour
Bennett, John Godolphin. Sex / [by] John G. Bennett. — Sherborne, Glos. : Coombe Springs Press, 1975. — [4],85p : 1 ill ; 20cm. — (Transformation of man series ; 3)
ISBN 0-900306-16-5 Pbk : £1.10
(B77-10121)

Lowen, Alexander. Love and orgasm : a revolutionary guide to sexual fulfillment / [by] Alexander Lowen. — New York : Collier ; London : Collier Macmillan, 1976. — 319p : ill ; 18cm.
Originally published: New York : Macmillan, 1965 ; London : Staples Press, 1966.
ISBN 0-02-077320-x Pbk : £1.35
(B77-06447)

155.3'1'0924 — Libido. Theories of Freud, Sigmund
Nagera, Humberto. Basic psychoanalytic concepts on the libido theory / by Humberto Nagera and ... [others]. — London : Allen and Unwin, 1969 [i.e. 1977]. — 3-194p ; 22cm. — (Hampstead Clinic. Psychoanalytic library ; vol.1)
Originally published: 1969. — Index.
ISBN 0-04-150059-8 Pbk : £1.95
(B77-08734)

155.3'4'01 — Sex relations. Psychological aspects. Theories of Taoism
Watts, Alan, *b.1915.* Nature, man and woman / [by] Alan Watts. — London : Abacus, 1976. — 159p ; 20cm.
Originally published: New York : Pantheon ; London : Thames and Hudson, 1958. — Bibl.: p.158-159.
ISBN 0-349-13617-3 Pbk : £0.75
(B77-11539)

155.4 — CHILD PSYCHOLOGY
Erikson, Erik Homburger. Childhood and society / [by] Erik H. Erikson. — Revised ed. — St Albans : Triad, 1977. — 397p : ill ; 20cm.
This ed. originally published: New York : Norton, 1964 ; Harmondsworth : Penguin, 1965. — Index.
ISBN 0-586-08356-1 Pbk : £1.95
(B77-09478)

Helms, Donald B. Exploring child behavior / [by] Donald B. Helms, Jeffrey S. Turner. — Philadelphia ; London [etc.] : Saunders, 1976. — xvii,726p : ill(some col), facsim, form, ports ; 27cm.
Bibl.: p.661-696. — Index.
ISBN 0-7216-4635-2 : £16.50
(B77-01149)

155.4 — Children. Development
Bee, Helen Lucille. The developing child / [by] Helen Bee. — Harper international ed. — New York [etc.] ; London : Harper and Row, 1975 [i.e. 1976]. — xvii,413p : ill ; 23cm.
Previous ed.: 1975. — Bibl. — Index.
ISBN 0-06-350133-3 Pbk : £5.00
(B77-03893)

Brown, Geoffrey, *b.1935.* Child development / [by] Geoffrey Brown. — London : Open Books, 1977. — viii,167p : ill ; 21cm. — (Psychology and education)
Bibl.: p.156-165. — Index.
ISBN 0-7291-0048-0 : £4.50
ISBN 0-7291-0043-x Pbk : £1.95
(B77-14031)

Smart, Mollie Stevens. Children, development and relationships / [by] Mollie S. Smart and Russell C. Smart. — 3rd ed. — New York : Macmillan ; London : Collier Macmillan, 1977. — x,705p : ill ; 26cm.
Ill. on lining papers. — Previous ed.: 1972. — Bibl. — Index.
ISBN 0-02-411950-4 : £11.25
(B77-21678)

Travers, John F. The growing child : introduction to child development / [by] John F. Travers. — New York ; London [etc.] : Wiley, 1977. — xi,531p : ill(some col), 2 ports ; 24cm.
Bibl.: p.503-518. — Index.
ISBN 0-471-88500-2 Pbk : £8.00
(B77-12282)

155.4 — Children. Development. Effects of psychological deprivation
Langmeier, J. Psychological deprivation in childhood / [by] J. Langmeier and Z. Matějček ; [translated from the Czech by Peter Anger]. — 3rd ed. (English) / edited by G.L. Mangan. — St Lucia : University of Queensland Press [etc.] ; Hemel Hempstead : Distributed by Prentice-Hall, 1975. — xiv,496p, leaf of plate,[48]p of plates : ill ; 23cm.
Translation of: 'Psychická deprivace v dětství'. 3. ed. Praha [i.e. Prague] : Avicenum, 1974. — Bibl.: p.417-481. — Index.
ISBN 0-7022-0893-0 : £10.90
(B77-16167)

155.4 — Children. Development. Role of interpersonal relationships with fathers
The **role** of the father in child development / edited by Michael E. Lamb. — New York ; London [etc.] : Wiley, 1976. — xiii,407p : ill ; 24cm. — (Wiley series in personality processes)

'A Wiley-Interscience publication'. — Bibl. — Index.
ISBN 0-471-51172-2 : £14.50
(B77-07047)

155.4 — Children. Psychological development
Cobb, Edith. The ecology of imagination in childhood / [by] Edith Cobb ; with an introduction by Margaret Mead. — London [etc.] : Routledge and Kegan Paul, 1977. — [9], 139p ; 23cm.
Also published: New York : Columbia University Press, 1977. — Bibl.: p.119-136. — Index.
ISBN 0-7100-8793-4 : £5.75 : CIP rev.
(B77-23970)

McCandless, Boyd Rowden. Children : behavior and development. — 3rd ed. / [by] Boyd R. McCandless, Robert J. Trotter, contributors [others]. — New York ; London [etc.] : Holt, Rinehart and Winston, 1977. — xiv,562p : ill, ports ; 25cm.
Text on lining papers. — Previous ed.: / by Boyd R. McCandless. 1967. — Bibl. — Index.
ISBN 0-03-089750-5 : £9.50
(B77-23971)

155.4 — Children. Psychological development. Evaluation
Johnson, Orval G. Tests and measurements in child development, handbook II / [by] Orval G. Johnson. — San Francisco [etc.] ; London : Jossey-Bass. — (Jossey-Bass behavioral science series)
In 2 vols. — ' ... an extension, supplementary and not overlapping, of "Handbook I". [1971]' - jacket.
Vol.1. — 1976. — xiii,674p : ill ; 27cm.
Bibl.
ISBN 0-87589-278-7 : £21.30
(B77-14535)

Vol.2. — 1976. — xiii,p675-1327 ; 27cm.
Bibl. — Index.
ISBN 0-87589-279-5 : £21.30
(B77-14536)

155.4 — Children, to 11 years. Development
Lee, Catherine. The growth and development of children / [by] Catherine Lee. — 2nd ed. — London [etc.] : Longman, 1977. — vii,191p ; 20cm.
Previous ed.: 1969. — Bibl. — Index.
ISBN 0-582-48828-1 Pbk : £2.50
(B77-17885)

155.4'08 — Children. Development. ***Readings***
Readings in child development and relationships / [compiled by] Russell C. Smart and Mollie S. Smart. — 2nd ed. — New York : Macmillan ; London : Collier Macmillan, 1977. — xviii,477p : ill ; 24cm.
Previous ed.: 1972. — Bibl. — Index.
ISBN 0-02-412110-x Pbk : £5.25
(B77-23086)

155.4'08 — Children. Psychological development. ***Readings***
Understanding a child's world : readings in infancy through adolescence / [compiled by] Pamela Cantor. — New York ; London [etc.] : McGraw-Hill, 1977. — xii,500p : ill ; 24cm.
Bibl.
ISBN 0-07-009766-6 Pbk : £6.70
(B77-22324)

155.4'09 — Children. Development. Theories, to ca 1970
Cleverley, John Farquhar. From Locke to Spock : influential models of the child in modern Western thought / [by] John Cleverley, D.C. Phillips. — Melbourne : Melbourne University Press ; Hemel Hempstead : Distributed by Prentice-Hall, 1976. — ix,120p ; 22cm. — (The second century in Australian education ; 14)
Bibl.: p.115-117. — Index.
ISBN 0-522-84104-x Pbk : £3.15
(B77-33022)

155.4'12 — Children, 4-12 years. Motor skills. Acquisition. Related to cognitive development
Piaget, Jean. The grasp of consciousness : action and concept in the young child / [by] Jean Piaget, collaborators ... [others] ; translated [from the French] by Susan Wedgwood. — London [etc.] : Routledge and Kegan Paul, 1977. — viii,360p : ill ; 23cm.
This translation originally published: Cambridge, Mass. : Harvard University Press, 1976. — Translation of: 'La prise de conscience'. Paris : Presses universitaires de France, 1974. — Index.
ISBN 0-7100-8400-5 : £8.50
Also classified at 155.4'13
(B77-17886)

155.4'12 — Normal children. Motor skills. Development. Compared with motor development in mentally retarded children
Holle, Britta. Motor development in children, normal and retarded : a practical guide for sensory-motor stimulation / [by] Britta Holle ; preface by Annalise Dupont. — Copenhagen : Munksgaard ; Oxford [etc.] : Distributed by Blackwell Scientific, 1976. — [9],218p : ill, forms ; 25cm.
Fold. sheet in pocket. — Bibl.: p.211-214. — Index.
ISBN 0-632-00065-1 Pbk : £8.50
Primary classification 155.4'5'28
(B77-22327)

155.4'13 — Children, 4-12 years. Cognitive development. Related to acquisition of motor skills
Piaget, Jean. The grasp of consciousness : action and concept in the young child / [by] Jean Piaget, collaborators ... [others] ; translated [from the French] by Susan Wedgwood. — London [etc.] : Routledge and Kegan Paul, 1977. — viii,360p : ill ; 23cm.
This translation originally published: Cambridge, Mass. : Harvard University Press, 1976. — Translation of: 'La prise de conscience'. Paris : Presses universitaires de France, 1974. — Index.
ISBN 0-7100-8400-5 : £8.50
Primary classification 155.4'12
(B77-17886)

155.4'13 — Children. Attention
Pick, Anne Danielson. Children's attention : the development of selectivity / [by] Anne D. Pick, Daniel G. Frankel and Valerie L. Hess. — Chicago ; London : University of Chicago Press, 1975 [i.e. 1976]. — [5],58p ; 23cm.
Published in the United States: 1975. — '... originally appeared as Chapter 6 of "Review of Child Development Research", Volume 5 (1975)' - title page verso. — Bibl.: p.46-58.
ISBN 0-226-33162-8 Pbk : £1.70
(B77-02000)

155.4'13 — Children. Cognitive development
The **development** of cognitive processes / edited by Vernon Hamilton and Magdalen D. Vernon. — London [etc.] : Academic Press, 1976. — x, 772p : ill ; 24cm.
Bibl. — Index.
ISBN 0-12-321750-4 : £21.00
(B77-11049)

Flavell, John Hurley. Cognitive development / [by] John H. Flavell. — Englewood Cliffs ; London [etc.] : Prentice-Hall, 1977. — xi,286p : 4 ill ; 24cm. — (The Prentice-Hall series in experimental psychology)
Bibl.: p.257-273. — Index.
ISBN 0-13-139774-5 : £8.80
ISBN 0-13-139766-4 Pbk : £5.55
(B77-14537)

Modgil, Sohan. Piagetian research : compilation and commentary / [by] Sohan Modgil and Celia Modgil ; foreword by Bärbel Inhelder. — Windsor : NFER.
In 8 vols.
Vol.7 : Training techniques. — 1976. — 190p : ill ; 22cm.
Bibl.: p.168-186. — Index.
ISBN 0-85633-107-4 Pbk : £4.50
ISBN 0-85633-112-0 Set of 8 vols : £47.00
(B77-03340)

Vol.8 : Cross-cultural studies. — 1976. — 238p : ill ; 22cm.
Bibl.: p.208-234. — Index.
ISBN 0-85633-108-2 Pbk : £4.50
ISBN 0-85633-112-0 Set of 8 vols: £47.00
(B77-05850)

Piaget, Jean. The principles of genetic epistemology / [by] Jean Piaget ; translated from the French by Wolfe Mays. — London [etc.] : Routledge and Kegan Paul, 1977. — v, 98p ; 22cm.
This translation originally published: 1972. — Translation of: 'L'epistémologie génétique'. Paris : Presses universitaires de France, 1970. — Index.
ISBN 0-7100-8660-1 Pbk : £1.25
(B77-33023)

155.4'13 — Children. Cognitive development. Theories of Piaget, Jean
Piaget and knowing : studies in genetic epistemology / edited by Beryl A. Geber. — London [etc.] : Routledge and Kegan Paul, 1977. — x,258p : ill ; 23cm.
Bibl. — Index.
ISBN 0-7100-8500-1 : £5.75
(B77-16706)

Sigel, Irving Edward. Cognitive development from childhood to adolescence : a constructivist perspective / [by] Irving E. Sigel, Rodney R. Cocking. — New York ; London [etc.] : Holt, Rinehart and Winston, 1977. — xv,256p : ill ; 21cm. — (Principles of educational psychology series)
Bibl.: p.235-246. — Index.
ISBN 0-03-015636-x Pbk : £3.25
(B77-22325)

155.4'13 — Children. Cognitive development. Theories of Piaget, Jean. Research. ***Reports, surveys***
Modgil, Sohan. Piagetian research : compilation and commentary / [by] Sohan Modgil and Celia Modgil ; foreword by Bärbel Inhelder. — Windsor : NFER.
In 8 vols.
Vol.5 : Personality, socialization and emotionality, Reasoning among handicapped children. — 1976. — 380p : ill ; 22cm.
Bibl.: p.336-374. — Index.
ISBN 0-85633-105-8 Pbk : £8.00
(B77-00593)

Vol.6 : The cognitive-developmental approach to morality. — 1976. — 224p ; 22cm.
Bibl.: p.199-220. — Index.
ISBN 0-85633-106-6 Pbk : £5.00
(B77-02001)

155.4'13 — Children. Intellectual development. Effects of malnutrition
Malnutrition and intellectual development / edited by John D. Lloyd-Still. — Lancaster : M.T.P. Press, 1976. — vii,194p : ill, map ; 24cm.
Index.
ISBN 0-85200-140-1 : £8.95
(B77-02002)

155.4'13 — Children. Intelligence. Measurement
Sattler, Jerome M. Assessment of children's intelligence / [by] Jerome M. Sattler. — Revised [ed.]. — Philadelphia ; London [etc.] : Saunders, [1977]. — ii-xxii,591p : ill, forms ; 27cm. — (Saunders books in psychology)
Published in the United States: 1974. — Previous ed.: 1974. — Bibl.: p.459-501. — Index.
ISBN 0-7216-7944-7 : £13.50
(B77-10122)

155.4'13 — Children. Logical thought. Development
Osherson, Daniel N. Logical abilities in children / by Daniel N. Osherson. — Hillsdale : Lawrence Erlbaum ; New York ; London [etc.] : Distributed by Wiley.
Vol.4 : Reasoning and concepts. — 1976. — viii,248p ; 24cm. — ([Child psychology])
Bibl.: p.245-246. — Index.
ISBN 0-470-99009-0 : £11.20
(B77-18527)

155.4'13 — Children. Mental development. Effects of diet. ***Conference proceedings***
Nutrition and mental functions / edited by George Serban ; foreword by Jean Mayer. — New York ; London : Plenum Press, [1976]. — xiii,281p : ill ; 26cm. — (Advances in behavioral biology ; vol.14)
'Proceedings of a symposium of the Kittay Scientific Foundation held March 29-30, 1973' - title page verso. — Published in the United States: 1975. — Bibl. — Index.
ISBN 0-306-37914-7 : Unpriced
(B77-03894)

155.4'13 — Games for children: Games to foster development of imagination
De Mille, Richard. Put your mother on the ceiling : children's imagination games / [by] Richard de Mille. — [1st ed. reprinted] ; [with new preface]. — Harmondsworth [etc.] : Penguin, 1976. — xvi,175p ; 18cm.
This ed. originally published: New York : Walker, 1967.
ISBN 0-14-004379-9 Pbk : Unpriced
(B77-05851)

155.4'13 — Learning by children
Reese, Hayne Waring. Basic learning processes in childhood / [by] Hayne W. Reese. — New York ; London [etc.] : Holt, Rinehart and Winston, 1976. — xv,174p : ill ; 21cm. — (Principles of educational psychology series)
Bibl.: p.161-165. — Index.
ISBN 0-03-013216-9 Pbk : £3.25
(B77-03895)

155.4'18 — Children. Cooperative behaviour
Bryan, James H. Children's cooperation and helping behaviors / [by] James H. Bryan. — Chicago ; London : University of Chicago Press, 1975 [i.e. 1976]. — [5],53p ; 23cm.
Published in the United States: 1975. — '... originally appeared as Chapter 3 of "Review of Child Development Research", Volume 5 (1975)' - title page verso. — Bibl.: p.47-53.
ISBN 0-226-33157-1 Pbk : £1.70
(B77-02003)

155.4'18 — Children. Development. Role of play
Garvey, Catherine. Play / [by] Catherine Garvey. — [London] : Fontana, 1977. — 128p ; 18cm. — (The developing child)
Also published: London : Open Books, 1977. — Bibl.: p.123-124. — Index.
ISBN 0-00-634854-8 Pbk : £1.00
(B77-17265)

Garvey, Catherine. Play / [by] Catherine Garvey. — London : Open Books, 1977. — 128p ; 23cm. — (The developing child)
Also published: London : Fontana, 1977. — Bibl.: p.123-124. — Index.
ISBN 0-7291-0029-4 : £3.50
(B77-19996)

Lieberman, J Nina. Playfulness : its relationship to imagination and creativity / [by] J. Nina Lieberman. — New York [etc.] ; London : Academic Press, 1977. — xv,179p ; 24cm. — (Educational psychology)
Bibl.: p.163-175. — Index.
ISBN 0-12-449450-1 : £8.50
(B77-29900)

155.4'18 — Children. Interpersonal relationships with mothers. Psychological aspects
Schaffer, Heinz Rudolph. Mothering / [by] Rudolph Schaffer. — [London] : Fontana, 1977. — 127p ; 18cm. — (The developing child)
Also published: London : Open Books, 1977. — Bibl.: p.122-123. — Index.
ISBN 0-00-634856-4 Pbk : £1.00
(B77-17887)

Schaffer, Heinz Rudolph. Mothering / [by] Rudolph Schaffer. — London : Open Books, 1977. — 127p ; 23cm. — (The developing child)
Also published: London : Fontana, 1977. — Bibl.: p.122-123. — Index.
ISBN 0-7291-0016-2 : £3.50
(B77-20879)

155.4'18 — Children. Moral development
Piaget, Jean. The moral judgement of the child / by Jean Piaget, with the assistance of seven collaborators ; translated [from the French] by Marjorie Gabian. — Harmondsworth [etc.] : Penguin, 1977. — 399p ; 18cm. — (Penguin education)
This translation originally published: London : Routledge and Kegan Paul, 1932. — Translation of: 'Le jugement moral chez l'enfant'. Paris : s.n., 1932. — Index.
ISBN 0-14-080927-9 Pbk : £1.95
(B77-18528)

Symposium on Moral Development, *Chicago, 1973.* Moral development : current theory and research / edited by David J. DePalma, Jeanne M. Foley. — Hillsdale, N.J. : Lawrence Erlbaum Associates ; New York ; London [etc.] : Distributed by Wiley, 1975 [i.e. 1977]. — viii,206p : ill ; 24cm. — (Child psychology)
'... first presented at the Symposium on Moral Development at Loyola, University of Chicago in December, 1973' - Introduction. — Published in the United States: 1975. — Bibl. — Index.
ISBN 0-470-20950-x : £10.15
(B77-10123)

155.4'18 — Children. Personality. Development. *Reviews of research*
Advances in child development and behavior. — New York [etc.] ; London : Academic Press.
Vol.11 / edited by Hayne W. Reese. — 1976[i.e. 1977]. — xi,282p : ill ; 24cm.
Published in the United States: 1976. — Bibl. — Index.
ISBN 0-12-009711-7 : £12.80
(B77-07776)

155.4'18 — Children. Personality. Projective tests: Bender Gestalt Test
Koppitz, Elizabeth Munsterberg. The Bender Gestalt Test for young children / [by] Elizabeth Munsterberg Koppitz. — New York ; London : Grune and Stratton, [1976]. — [11],195p : ill ; 26cm.
Originally published: New York : Grune and Stratton, 1964. — Bibl.: p.190-192. — Index.
ISBN 0-8089-0239-3 : £8.15
(B77-04540)

155.4'18 — Young persons, 9 & 19 years. Aggression. *United States. Longitudinal studies*
Growing up to be violent : a longitudinal study of the development of aggression / [by] Monroe M. Lefkowitz ... [et al.]. — New York ; Oxford [etc.] : Pergamon, 1977. — ix,236p : ill, forms ; 23cm. — (Pergamon international library) (Pergamon general psychology series ; vol.66)
Bibl.: p.212-224. — Index.
ISBN 0-08-019515-6 : £7.00
ISBN 0-08-019514-8 Pbk : £4.00
(B77-25364)

155.4'2 — Children born prematurely, to 7 years. Development. *Study regions: Tyne and Wear (Metropolitan County). Newcastle upon Tyne. Research reports*
Born too soon or born too small : a follow-up study to seven years of age / [by] G.A. Neligan ... [et al.]. — London : Heinemann Medical [etc. for] Spastics International Medical Publications, 1976. — xx,101p : ill ; 25cm. — (Clinics in developmental medicine ; no.61)
Bibl.: p.94-98. — Index.
ISBN 0-433-18826-x : £4.50
(B77-11540)

155.4'22 — Babies. Interpersonal relationships with mothers. Psychological aspects. *Conference proceedings*
Studies in mother-infant interaction : proceedings of the Loch Lomond symposium, Ross Priory, University of Strathclyde, September 1975 / edited by H.R. Schaffer. — London [etc.] : Academic Press, 1977. — x,478p : ill ; 24cm.
Bibl. — Index.
ISBN 0-12-622560-5 : £14.80
(B77-22326)

155.4'22 — Babies. Psychological development. Physiological aspects
Developmental Psychobiology *(Conference), San Francisco, 1974.* Developmental psychobiology : the significance of infancy / edited by Lewis P. Lipsitt. — Hillsdale : Erlbaum ; New York ; London [etc.] : Distributed by Wiley, 1976. — x,143p : ill ; 24cm.
' ... based on a symposium of the same title held in San Francisco at the 1974 meetings of the American Association for the Advancement of Science' - Preface. — Bibl. — Index.
ISBN 0-470-15127-7 : £7.65
(B77-02004)

Dunn, Judy. Distress and comfort / [by] Judy Dunn. — [London] : Fontana, 1977. — 126p ; 18cm. — (The developing child)
Also published: London : Open Books, 1977. — Bibl.: p.122. — Index.
ISBN 0-00-634855-6 Pbk : £1.00
(B77-17888)

Dunn, Judy. Distress and comfort / [by] Judy Dunn. — London : Open Books, 1977. — 126p ; 23cm. — (The developing child)
Also published: London : Fontana, 1977. — Bibl.: p.122. — Index.
ISBN 0-7291-0008-1 : £3.50
(B77-19997)

155.4'22 — Babies, to 18 months. Intelligence. Development
Piaget, Jean. The origin of intelligence in the child / [by] Jean Piaget ; translated [from the French] by Margaret Cook. — Harmondsworth [etc.] : Penguin, 1977. — 464p ; 18cm. — (Penguin education)
This translation originally published: London : Routledge and Kegan Paul, 1953. — Translation of: 'La naissance de l'intelligence chez l'enfant'. Paris : Neuchâtel, 1936. — Index.
ISBN 0-14-080928-7 Pbk : £1.95
(B77-20880)

155.4'22 — Children, to 4 years. Cognitive styles. *State-of-the-art reviews*
Kogan, Nathan. Cognitive styles in infancy and early childhood / [by] Nathan Kogan. — Hillsdale : Erlbaum ; New York ; London [etc.] : Distributed by Wiley, 1976. — xiii, 146p : ill ; 24cm.
Bibl.: p.128-138. — Index.
ISBN 0-470-15149-8 : £9.75
(B77-02728)

155.4'22 — Children, to 5 years. Development. *For parents*
Rayner, Claire. Family feelings : understanding your child from 0 to 5 / written and devised by Claire Rayner ; illustrations by Kathy Wyatt and David English. — London : Arrow Books, 1977. — 96p : ill ; 21cm.
'In association with the Health Education Council'. — Index.
ISBN 0-09-915420-x Pbk : £1.25
(B77-29901)

155.4'22 — Children, to 5 years. Development. *Secondary school texts*
Foster, John Louis. From 0 to 5 : the pre-school years / [by] John L. Foster. — London : Edward Arnold, 1976. — 16p : ill, plan ; 30cm. — (Checkpoint ; 8)
ISBN 0-7131-0052-4 Sd : £2.50(set of 5 copies)
(B77-10124)

155.4'22 — Children, to 5 years. Development. Assessment
Erickson, Marcene L. Assessment and management of developmental changes in children / [by] Marcene L. Erickson ; chapter 9 contributed by Peggy L. Pipes ; original photographs by Janis K. Smith ; original drawings by Mary K. Shrader ; original cover art by Greg Owen. — Saint Louis : Mosby ; London : Distributed by Kimpton, 1976. — xi, 268p : ill, forms ; 26cm.
Bibl. — Index.
ISBN 0-8016-1526-7 Pbk : £6.95
Also classified at 649'.1'019
(B77-05852)

155.4'22 — Children, to 5 years. Development. Assessment. *Manuals*
National Children's Bureau. Development guide handbook / National Children's Bureau. — London (8 Wakley St., EC1V 7QE) : N.C.B.
0-5 years. — Experimental version. — 1977. — [1],36p : ill ; 21cm.
Summary chart (folder ([8]p.)) as insert.
ISBN 0-902817-12-4 Pbk : £1.70
(B77-27650)

155.4'22 — Children, to 5 years. Development. Teaching aids: Games. *For parents*
Jeffree, Dorothy Maud. Let me play / by Dorothy M. Jeffree, Roy McConkey, Simon Hewson. — London : Souvenir Press, 1977. — 252p : ill ; 23cm. — (Human horizons series) (A condor book)
Index.
ISBN 0-285-64834-9 : £4.00
ISBN 0-285-64835-7 Pbk : £2.50
Primary classification 155.4'5'1
(B77-29902)

155.4'22 — Newborn babies. Interpersonal relationships with parents. Psychological aspects
Klaus, Marshall H. Maternal-infant bonding : the impact of early separation or loss on family development / [by] Marshall H. Klaus, John H. Kennell. — Saint Louis : Mosby ; London : Distributed by Kimpton, 1976. — xvii,257p : ill ; 24cm.
Bibl.: p.242-250. — Index.
£7.25
(B77-05186)

155.4'22 — Reality. Perception by babies. Development
Piaget, Jean. The child's construction of reality / [by] Jean Piaget ; translated [from the French] by Margaret Cook. — London [etc.] : Routledge and Kegan Paul, 1976. — xiii,386p : 1 ill ; 23cm.
This translation originally published: New York : Basic Books, 1954 ; London : Routledge and Kegan Paul, 1955. — Translation of 'La construction du réel chez l'enfant'. Neuchâtel ; Paris : Delachaux and Niestle, 1937.
ISBN 0-7100-1952-1 : £7.50
(B77-02730)

155.4'44 — Twins. Personality. Influence of heredity & environmental factors. *United States. Reports, surveys*
Loehlin, John C. Heredity, environment & personality : a study of 850 sets of twins / [by] John C. Loehlin & Robert C. Nichols. — Austin ; London : University of Texas Press, 1976. — xii,202p : ill, forms ; 29cm.
Bibl.: p.193-197. — Index.
ISBN 0-292-73003-9 : £7.20
(B77-06448)

155.4'5'1 — Handicapped children. Development. Teaching aids: Games. *For parents*
Jeffree, Dorothy Maud. Let me play / by Dorothy M. Jeffree, Roy McConkey, Simon Hewson. — London : Souvenir Press, 1977. — 252p : ill ; 23cm. — (Human horizons series) (A condor book)
Index.
ISBN 0-285-64834-9 : £4.00
ISBN 0-285-64835-7 Pbk : £2.50
Also classified at 155.4'22
(B77-29902)

155.4'5'1 — Physically handicapped children. Hands. Use. Development. Role of toys
Richardson, Anne. I can use my hands / [by Anne Richardson, Alison Wisbeach]. — London (10 Gunthorpe St., E1 7RW) : Toy Libraries Association, 1976. — [2],20p : ill ; 21cm. — (Noah's Ark publications)
Bibl.: p.19.
Sd : £0.40
(B77-04541)

155.4'5'28 — Mentally retarded children. Motor skills. Development. Compared with motor development in normal children
Holle, Britta. Motor development in children, normal and retarded : a practical guide for sensory-motor stimulation / [by] Britta Holle ; preface by Annalise Dupont. — Copenhagen : Munksgaard ; Oxford [etc.] : Distributed by Blackwell Scientific, 1976. — [9],218p : ill, forms ; 25cm.
Fold. sheet in pocket. — Bibl.: p.211-214. — Index.
ISBN 0-632-00065-1 Pbk : £8.50
Also classified at 155.4'12
(B77-22327)

155.4'5'5 — Gifted children. Psychology
Vernon, Philip Ewart. The psychology and education of gifted children / [by] Philip E. Vernon, Georgina Adamson and Dorothy F. Vernon. — London : Methuen, 1977. — viii, 216p : ill ; 23cm.
Bibl.: p.197-208. — Index.
ISBN 0-416-84390-5 : £5.95
ISBN 0-416-84400-6 Pbk : £2.95
Primary classification 371.9'5
(B77-18046)

155.4'5'508 — Gifted children. *Readings*
The **intellectually** gifted : an overview / edited by Wayne Dennis and Margaret W. Dennis. — New York [etc.] ; London : Grune and Stratton, [1977]. — xiii,336p : port ; 24cm.
Published in the United States: 1976. — Bibl. — Index.
ISBN 0-8089-0962-2 : £15.85
(B77-13485)

155.4'5'67 — Children raised by wolves. *India (Republic). Midnapore, ca 1920-ca 1930*
Maclean, Charles. The wolf children / [by] Charles Maclean. — London : Allen Lane, 1977. — xii,324p,[16]p of plates : ill, map, ports ; 23cm.
Bibl.: p.305-312. — Index.
ISBN 0-7139-1016-x : £4.95
(B77-30944)

155.4'5'67 — Feral children
Malson, Lucien. Wolf children / [by] Lucien Malson. The wild boy of Aveyron / [by] Jean Itard / [translated from the French by Edmund Fawcett, Peter Ayrton and Joan White]. — London : NLB, 1972[i.e.1976]. — 179p ; 21cm.
This translation originally published: 1972. — 'Wolf children' translation of: 'Les enfants sauvages'. Paris : Union générale d'editions, 1964. — 'The wild boy of Aveyron' translation of: 'Mémoire et rapport sur Victor de l'Aveyron'. Paris : Union générale d'editions, 1964.
ISBN 0-902308-24-6 Pbk : £2.00
(B77-14538)

155.5 — PSYCHOLOGY OF ADOLESCENTS
Manaster, Guy J. Adolescent development and the life tasks / [by] Guy J. Manaster ; [illustrations by Michael Crawford]. — Boston [Mass.] ; London [etc.] : Allyn and Bacon, 1977. — xiii,337p : ill ; 24cm.
Bibl.: p.301-325. — Index.
ISBN 0-205-05547-8 : Unpriced
(B77-10125)

155.5 — Adolescents. Psychological development. Social factors
Conger, John Janeway. Adolescence and youth : psychological development in a changing world / [by] John Janeway Conger. — 2nd ed. — New York [etc.] ; London : Harper and Row, 1977. — xvii,670p : ill ; 24cm.
Previous ed.: 1973. — Bibl. — Index.
ISBN 0-06-041362-x Pbk : £4.95
(B77-16168)

155.5 — Undergraduates. Personality. Assessment. Cattell's 16 Personality Factor Inventory & Eysenck Personality Inventory. *Great Britain. Reports, surveys*
Saville, Peter. Undergraduate personality by factored scales : a large scale study on Cattell's 16 PF and the Eysenck personality inventory / [by] Peter Saville, Steve Blinkhorn. — Windsor : NFER, 1976. — 176p : ill, map ; 22cm.
Bibl.: p.169-176.
ISBN 0-85633-104-x Pbk : £6.50
(B77-02005)

155.5'08 — Adolescents. Psychology. *Readings*
Readings in adolescent psychology : contemporary perspectives / edited by Thomas J. Cottle. — New York [etc.] ; London : Harper and Row, 1977. — [10],338p : ill, ports ; 28cm. — (Contemporary perspectives reader series)
Bibl.
ISBN 0-06-047057-7 Pbk : £5.45
(B77-27651)

155.5'33 — Adolescent girls. Moral development. *United States. Research reports*
O'Byrne, Simon. Moral development and logical reasoning of adolescents : an experimental research study with adolescent girls comparing different techniques / by Simon O'Byrne. — Dublin : Frederick Press, 1976. — [1],xii,166p ; 22cm.
Bibl.: p.111-120.
Unpriced
(B77-20881)

155.6 — PSYCHOLOGY OF ADULTS
155.6 — Adults. Developmental psychology
Elias, Merrill F. Basic processes in adult developmental psychology / [by] Merrill F. Elias, Penelope Kelly Elias, Jeffrey W. Elias. — Saint Louis : Mosby ; London : Distributed by Kimpton, 1977. — xi,336p : ill, ports ; 27cm.
Bibl.: p.304-327. — Index.
ISBN 0-8016-1519-4 : Unpriced
(B77-26761)

155.6'08 — Adults. Developmental psychology. *Readings*
Readings in adult psychology : contemporary perspectives / edited by Lawrence R. Allman and Dennis T. Jaffe. — New York [etc.] ; London : Harper and Row, 1977. — [13],388p : ill, port ; 28cm. — (Contemporary perspectives reader series)
Bibl. — Includes facsimile reprints.
ISBN 0-06-047054-2 Pbk : £5.45
(B77-29903)

155.6'32 — Men. Psychology
Bishop, Beata. Below the belt : an irreverent analysis of the male ego / by Beata Bishop, with Pat McNeill. — London : Coventure, 1977. — [7],143p ; 23cm.
ISBN 0-904576-27-2 : £3.75
(B77-33024)

Johnson, Robert A. He : understanding masculine psychology : based on the legend of Parsifal and his search for the Grail, using Jungian psychological concepts / [by] Robert A. Johnson ; foreword by Ruth Tiffany Barnhouse ; introductory essay by John A. Sanford. — New York [etc.] ; London : Harper and Row, 1977. — vii,83p ; 18cm. — (Perennial library)
Originally published: King of Prussia : Religious Publishing Co., 1974. — Bibl.: p.82-83.
ISBN 0-06-080415-7 Pbk : £1.25
(B77-33025)

155.6'33 — Women. Psychology
Johnson, Robert A. She : understanding feminine psychology : an interpretation based on the myth of Amor and Psyche and using Jungian psychological concepts / [by] Robert A. Johnson. — New York [etc.] ; London : Harper and Row, 1977. — [5],72p ; 18cm. — (Perennial library)
Originally published: King of Prussia : Religious Publishing Co., 1976. — Bibl.: p.72.
ISBN 0-06-080416-5 Pbk : £1.25
(B77-33026)

Women : a psychological perspective / [compiled by] Elaine Donelson, Jeanne E. Gullahorn. — New York ; London [etc.] : Wiley, 1977. — x, 342p : ill ; 24cm.
Bibl.: p.291-313. — Index.
ISBN 0-471-21779-4 : £10.45
ISBN 0-471-21781-6 Pbk : £6.75
(B77-20882)

155.6'33 — Women. Self-awareness. Stimulation. Role of discussion groups
Bruley, Sue. Women awake : the experience of consciousness raising / [by Sue Bruley]. — London (38d Clapham Rd, S.W.9) : The author, 1976. — 25p ; 21cm.
Sd : £0.25
(B77-23087)

155.6'33 — Women. Self-realisation. Transactional analysis. *Manuals*
Jongeward, Dorothy. Women as winners : transactional analysis for personal growth / [by] Dorothy Jongeward, Dru Scott. — Reading, Mass. ; London [etc.] : Addison-Wesley, 1976. — xviii,318p : ill, ports ; 25cm.
Index.
ISBN 0-201-03386-0 : £6.95
ISBN 0-201-03435-2 Pbk : £3.25
(B77-14032)

155.7 — HEREDITARY PSYCHOLOGY
155.7 — Man. Behaviour. Evolutionary aspects
Harrison, Charles. The neurotic primate : a matter of instinct / [by] Charles Harrison. — London : Wildwood House, 1977. — [6],314p : ill, port ; 21cm.
Bibl.: p.299-304. — Index.
ISBN 0-7045-0246-1 : £4.95
(B77-29904)

155.8 — ETHNOPSYCHOLOGY AND NATIONAL PSYCHOLOGY
155.8 — Cross-cultural psychology. *Reviews of research*
Studies in cross-cultural psychology. — London [etc.] : Academic Press.
Vol.1 / edited by Neil Warren. — 1977. — xvii,212p : ill ; 24cm.
Bibl. — Index.
ISBN 0-12-609201-x : £8.50
(B77-29905)

155.9 — PSYCHOLOGY OF INFLUENCE, PATTERN, EXAMPLE
155.9 — Environmental psychology
An **introduction** to environmental psychology / [by] William H. Ittelson ... [et al.] ; David Dempsey, editorial associate. — New York ; London [etc.] : Holt, Rinehart and Winston, [1976]. — x,406p : ill, plans ; 25cm.
Published in the United States: 1974. — Bibl. — Index.
ISBN 0-03-001346-1 : £8.75
(B77-02731)

155.9 — Man. Stress
Selye, Hans. Stress without distress : how to survive in a stressful society / [by] Hans Selye. — Sevenoaks : Teach Yourself Books, 1977. — viii,131p,[4]p of plates : ill, port ; 18cm. — (Teach yourself books)
Originally published: Philadelphia : Lippincott ; London [etc.] : Hodder and Stoughton, 1974. — Bibl.: p.109-126. — Index.
ISBN 0-340-21387-6 Pbk : £1.25
(B77-29906)

155.9 — Man. Stress. *Readings*
Stress and coping : an anthology / edited by Alan Monat and Richard S. Lazarus. — New York ; Guildford : Columbia University Press, 1977. — xvii,426p : ill ; 24cm.
Bibl.: p.389-418. — Index.
ISBN 0-231-04013-x : £14.30
(B77-23972)

155.9 — Man. Stress. *Reviews of research*
Stress and anxiety. — Washington, D.C. : Hemisphere Publishing Corporation ; New York ; London [etc.] : Wiley.
Vol.2 / edited by Irwin G. Sarason, Charles D. Spielberger. — [1977]. — xiv,397p : ill ; 24cm. — (The series in clinical psychology)
'A Halsted Press book'. — Published in the United States: 1975. — Bibl. — Index.
ISBN 0-470-75412-5 : £13.80
(B77-09479)

Vol.4 / edited by Charles D. Spielberger, Irwin G. Sarason. — 1977. — xvi,336p : ill ; 24cm.
'... based on papers ... presented at a conference on "Dimensions of Anxiety and Stress" held in Oslo, Norway, June 29-July 3 1975' - Preface. — 'A Halsted Press book'. — Bibl. — Index.
ISBN 0-470-99016-3 : £14.00
(B77-17266)

155.9 — Physical environment. Psychological aspects
Canter, David Victor. The psychology of place / [by] David Canter. — London : Architectural Press, 1977. — x,198p : ill, maps, plans ; 22cm.
Bibl.: p.186-192. — Index.
ISBN 0-85139-532-5 : £5.95
ISBN 0-85139-535-x Pbk : £3.95
(B77-22328)

155.9'08 — Environmental psychology. *Readings*
Environmental psychology : people and their physical settings / edited by Harold M. Proshansky, William H. Ittelson, Leanne G. Rivlin. — 2nd ed. — New York ; London [etc.] : Holt, Rinehart and Winston, 1976. — xiii,632p : ill, facsims, maps, plans ; 25cm.
Previous ed.: 1970. — Bibl.: p.574-612. — Index.
ISBN 0-03-089679-7 : £10.00
(B77-02732)

155.9'16 — Patients. Behaviour modification. *For nursing*
Berni, Rosemarian. Behavior modification and the nursing process / [by] Rosemarian Berni, Wilbert E. Fordyce. — 2nd ed. — Saint Louis : Mosby ; London : Distributed by Kimpton, 1977. — xv,160p : ill ; 22cm.
Previous ed.: 1973. — Bibl.: p.158-160.
ISBN 0-8016-0656-x Pbk : Unpriced
(B77-28355)

155.9'37 — Death. Psychological aspects
Kastenbaum, Robert. Death, society & the human experience / [by] Robert J. Kastenbaum. — Saint Louis : Mosby ; London : Distributed by Kimpton, 1977. — xi, 328p : forms ; 24cm.
Bibl.: p.320-321. — Index.
ISBN 0-8016-2617-x Pbk : £6.45
(B77-19998)

155.9'37 — Man. Dying. Psychological aspects
Pattison, E Mansell. The experience of dying / [by] E. Mansell Pattison [et al.]. — Englewood Cliffs ; London [etc.] : Prentice-Hall, 1977. — xiv,335p : ill ; 22cm.
Bibl.: p.329-335.
ISBN 0-13-294629-7 : £9.55
ISBN 0-13-294611-4 Pbk : £3.95
(B77-30945)

156 — COMPARATIVE PSYCHOLOGY

156 — Man. Behaviour. Compared with animal behaviour
Fox, Michael Wilson. Between animal and man / [by] Michael W. Fox. — London [etc.] : Blond and Briggs, 1977. — 223p : ill, maps ; 23cm.
Originally published: New York : Coward, McCann and Geoghegan, 1976.
ISBN 0-85634-056-1 : £5.75
(B77-23088)

156 — Man. Behaviour. Compared with behaviour of primates
Morris, Desmond. The naked ape / [by] Desmond Morris. — St Albans : Triad, 1977. — [2],219p ; 18cm.
Originally published: London : Cape, 1967. — Bibl.: p.215-219.
ISBN 0-583-12822-x Pbk : £0.65
(B77-09480)

156.2 — ANIMAL PSYCHOLOGY. PHYSIOLOGICAL PSYCHOLOGY

156'.2'33 — Man. Habituation. Compared with animal habituation. *Conference proceedings*
Habituation : perspectives from child development, animal behavior and neurophysiology / edited by Thomas J. Tighe, Robert N. Leaton. — Hillsdale : Erlbaum ; New York ; London [etc.] : Distributed by Wiley, 1976. — xi,356p : ill ; 24cm.
'... based on a conference ... held at Dartmouth College's Minary Conference Center in Holderness, New Hampshire, September 12-17, 1974' - Preface. — Bibl. — Index.
ISBN 0-470-99008-2 : £15.00
(B77-22329)

156'.2'42 — Mammals. Aggression. Nonverbal communication. *Conference proceedings*
Symposium on Communication and Affect, *4th, University of Toronto, 1974.* Nonverbal communication of aggression / edited by Patricia Pliner, Lester Krames and Thomas Alloway. — New York ; London : Plenum Press, 1975 [i.e. 1976]. — ix,196p : ill ; 24cm. — (Advances in the study of communication and affect ; vol.2)
'Proceedings of the Fourth Annual Symposium on Communication and Affect held at Erindale College, University of Toronto, March 28-30, 1974' - title page verso. — Published in the United States: 1975. — Bibl. — Index.
ISBN 0-306-35902-2 : £11.03
(B77-02006)

156.3 — ANIMAL PSYCHOLOGY. INTELLIGENCE AND INTELLECTUAL PROCESSES

156'.3'1 — Mammals. Learning & memory
Wickelgren, Wayne A. Learning and memory / [by] Wayne A. Wickelgren. — Englewood Cliffs ; London [etc.] : Prentice-Hall, 1977. — xv,448p : ill ; 24cm. — (Prentice-Hall series in experimental psychology)
Bibl.: p.431-433. — Index.
ISBN 0-13-527663-2 : £11.15
Primary classification 153.1
(B77-20873)

156.3'1'2 — Animals. Memory
Processes of animal memory / edited by Douglas L. Medin, William A. Roberts, Roger T. Davis. — Hillsdale : Erlbaum ; New York ; London [etc.] : Distributed by Wiley, 1976. — xiii, 267p : ill ; 24cm.
Bibl.: p.229-243. — Index.
ISBN 0-470-15189-7 : £11.50
(B77-02007)

156'.3'15 — Languages. Learning by chimpanzees. Applications of computer systems. *Study examples: Language Analogue Project*
Language learning by a chimpanzee : the Lana project / edited by Duane M. Rumbaugh. — New York [etc.] ; London : Academic Press, 1977. — xxii,312p : ill ; 24cm. — (Communication and behavior ; 1)
Bibl.
ISBN 0-12-601850-2 : £12.40
(B77-23973)

156'.3'15 — Learning by invertebrates
Invertebrate learning / edited by W.C. Corning and J.A. Dyal and A.O.D. Willows. — New York ; London : Plenum Press.
In 3 vols.
Vol.1 : Protozoans through annelids. — [1976]. — xvii,296p : ill ; 24cm.
Published in the United States: 1973. — Bibl. — Index.
ISBN 0-306-37671-7 : £11.66
(B77-03341)

Vol.2 : Arthropods and gastropod mollusks. — [1976]. — xiii,284p : ill ; 24cm.
Published in the United States: 1973. — Bibl. — Index.
ISBN 0-306-37672-5 : £11.66
(B77-03342)

156'.3'4 — Man. Cognition. *Ethological perspectives*
Lorenz, Konrad. Behind the mirror : a search for a natural history of human knowledge / [by] Konrad Lorenz ; translated [from the German] by Ronald Taylor. — London : Methuen, 1977. — [6],261p : ill ; 23cm.
Translation of: 'Die Rückseite des Spiegels'. München : Piper, 1973. — Bibl.: p.251-257. — Index.
ISBN 0-416-94270-9 : £4.90
ISBN 0-416-94280-6 Pbk : £3.00
(B77-17267)

156'.3'9 — Man. Intelligence. Compared with intelligence of chimpanzees
Premack, David. Intelligence in ape and man / [by] David Premack. — Hillsdale : Lawrence Erlbaum Associates ; New York ; London [etc.] : Distributed by Wiley, 1976. — xiii, 370p : ill ; 24cm.
Bibl.: p.356-361. — Index.
ISBN 0-470-98909-2 : £12.50
(B77-18529)

156.7 — ANIMAL PSYCHOLOGY. ABNORMAL BEHAVIOUR

156'.7 — Medicine. Psychopathology. *Ethological perspectives*
Ethological psychiatry : psychopathology in the context of evolutionary biology / edited by Michael T. McGuire, Lynn A. Fairbanks. — New York [etc.] ; London : Grune and Stratton, 1977. — x,230p : ill ; 24cm. — (Seminars in psychiatry)
Index.
ISBN 0-8089-0988-6 : £10.65
(B77-33027)

157 — ABNORMAL PSYCHOLOGY

Martin, Barclay. Abnormal psychology : clinical and scientific perspectives / by Barclay Martin ... [et al.]. — New York ; London [etc.] : Holt, Rinehart and Winston, 1977. — xiv,2-642p,[4]p of plates : ill(some col), facsim, ports ; 26cm.
Bibl.: p.601-630. — Index.
ISBN 0-03-014896-0 : £10.00
(B77-19194)

Rimm, David C. Abnormal psychology / [by] David C. Rimm, John W. Somervill. — New York [etc.] ; London : Academic Press, 1977. — xvi,696p : ill, ports ; 24cm.
Bibl.: p.615-662. — Index.
ISBN 0-12-588840-6 : £10.65
(B77-29907)

Zax, Melvin. Abnormal psychology : changing conceptions / [by] Melvin Zax and Emory L. Cowen. — 2nd ed. — New York ; London [etc.] : Holt, Rinehart and Winston, 1976. — xii,643p : ill, ports ; 25cm.
Previous ed.: 1972. — Bibl.: p.577-611. — Index.
ISBN 0-03-089517-0 : £11.00
(B77-01150)

157 — Psychoticism. Theories
Eysenck, Hans Jürgen. Psychoticism as a dimension of personality / [by] Hans J. Eysenck and Sybil B.G. Eysenck. — London [etc.] : Hodder and Stoughton, 1976. — xi, 232p : ill ; 24cm.
Bibl.: p.204-224. — Index.
ISBN 0-340-20919-4 : £6.50
(B77-07777)

157.2 — FUNCTIONAL PSYCHOSES

157'.2'83 — Man. Dementia. Psychological aspects
Miller, Edgar. Abnormal ageing : the psychology of senile and presenile dementia / [by] Edgar Miller. — London [etc.] : Wiley, 1977. — x, 166p : ill ; 24cm.
Bibl.: p.145-160. — Index.
ISBN 0-471-99439-1 : £5.75
(B77-14033)

157.3 — PSYCHONEUROSES. HYSTERIA AND RELATED DISORDERS

157'.3'2 — Man. Neuroses: Anxiety. Ethnopsychological aspects. *Conference proceedings*
Cross-cultural anxiety / edited by Charles D. Spielberger, Rogelio Diaz-Guerrero. — Washington [D.C.] ; London : Hemisphere Publishing Corporation ; New York ; London [etc.] : [Distributed by] Wiley, 1976. — xii, 195p : ill ; 24cm. — (The series in clinical and community psychology)
'A Halsted Press book'. — ' ... grows out of a Symposium on Cross-Cultural Research on State and Trait Anxiety that was held in Bogota, Columbia, in December 1974, at the XVth Interamerican Congress of Psychology ... Following the Symposium the papers were revised ... and additional contributions were invited ... ' - Preface. — Bibl. — Index.
ISBN 0-470-98940-8 : £14.30
(B77-08735)

157'.3'2 — Man. Neuroses: Insecurity. Psychological aspects
Shapiro, Stephen. Feeling safe : making space for the self / [by] Stephen Shapiro, Hilary Ryglewicz. — Englewood Cliffs ; London [etc.] : Prentice-Hall, 1976. — ix,148p ; 22cm.
Bibl.: p.147-148.
ISBN 0-13-314005-9 : £7.15
ISBN 0-13-313999-9 Pbk : £2.15
(B77-05187)

157.6 — PSYCHONEUROTIC ADDICTIONS AND INTOXICATIONS

157'.6'3 — Man. Behaviour. Effects of cannabis. *Reports, surveys*
Berke, Joseph. The cannabis experience : an interpretative study of the effects of marijuana and hashish / [by] Joseph Berke and Calvin Hernton. — London : Quartet Books, 1977. — 288p : forms ; 20cm.
Originally published: London : Owen, 1974. — Index.
ISBN 0-7043-3100-4 Pbk : £1.95
(B77-07778)

157.7 — PSYCHONEUROSES. DISORDERS OF CHARACTER AND PERSONALITY

157'.7 — Gambling. Psychological aspects. *Readings*
The **psychology** of gambling / edited by Jon Halliday and Peter Fuller. — Harmondsworth [etc.] : Penguin, 1977. — x,310p ; 18cm. — (Pelican books)
Originally published: London : Allen Lane, 1974. — Bibl.: p.297-301. — Index.
ISBN 0-14-022004-6 Pbk : £0.95
(B77-23974)

158 — APPLIED PSYCHOLOGY

Harari, Herbert. Psychology : personal and social adjustment / [by] Herbert Harari and Robert M. Kaplan. — New York [etc.] ; London : Harper and Row, 1977. — xv,390p : ill, facsims ; 24cm.
Index.
ISBN 0-06-042639-x : £8.65
(B77-15674)

158'.1 — Happiness. Achievement. *Manuals*
De Bono, Edward. The happiness purpose / [by] Edward de Bono. — London : Temple Smith, 1977. — 232,[1]p : ill ; 23cm.
ISBN 0-85117-125-7 : £6.00
(B77-27652)

158'.1 — Man. Personal problems. Solutions
The **personal** problem solver / edited by Charles Zastrow, Dae H. Chang. — Englewood Cliffs ; London [etc.] : Prentice-Hall, 1977. — xv, 383p : ill ; 21cm.
Bibl. — Index.
ISBN 0-13-657312-6 : £8.80
ISBN 0-13-657304-5 Pbk : £3.95
(B77-19195)

158'.1 — Man. Personal problems. Solutions. *Proposals*
Calhoun, Lawrence G. Dealing with crisis : a guide to critical life problems / [by] Lawrence G. Calhoun, James W. Selby, H. Elizabeth King. — Englewood Cliffs ; London [etc.] : Prentice-Hall, [1977]. — xii,275p ; 21cm.
'A Spectrum book'. — Published in the United States: 1976. — Bibl. — Index.
ISBN 0-13-197723-7 : £7.95
ISBN 0-13-197715-6 Pbk : £3.95
(B77-11541)

Proops, Marjorie. Dear Marje / [by] Marjorie Proops. — London : Coronet, 1977. — 203p ; 18cm.
Originally published: London : Deutsch, 1976.
ISBN 0-340-21819-3 Pbk : £0.75
(B77-21679)

Williams, Robert L. Toward a self-managed life style / [by] Robert L. Williams, James D. Long. — Boston [Mass.] [etc.] ; London : Houghton Mifflin, 1975. — xii,235p : ill, forms ; 21cm.
Bibl. — Index.
ISBN 0-395-18922-5 Pbk : Unpriced
(B77-29908)

158'.1 — Personal success. *Manuals*
Copen, Bruce. Be a millionaire / by Bruce Copen. — Revised ed. — Haywards Heath : Academic Publications, 1977. — [3],67p : ill ; 21cm.
Previous ed.: 1960.
Pbk : Unpriced
(B77-21680)

158'.1 — Self-realisation. *Manuals*
Baker, Samm Sinclair. Conscious happiness : how to get the most out of living / by Samm Sinclair Baker. — Toronto [etc.] ; London : Bantam, 1976. — ix,337,[1]p ; 18cm.
Originally published: New York : Grosset and Dunlap, 1975.
ISBN 0-553-02356-x Pbk : £0.75
(B77-09481)

Brent, Kurt. You / by Kurt Brent and Kay Batchelor. — Great Missenden (67 High St., Great Missenden, Bucks.) : Topaz Publications Ltd, 1977. — [8],349p : ill ; 19cm.
ISBN 0-905553-02-0 Pbk : £0.95
(B77-26092)

Dyer, Wayne W. Your erroneous zones / [by] Wayne W. Dyer. — London : Joseph, 1977. — ix,241p ; 23cm.
Also published: London : Sphere, 1977. — Originally published: New York : Funk and Wagnalls, 1976. — Index.
ISBN 0-7181-1654-2 : £4.50
(B77-32373)

Dyer, Wayne W. Your erroneous zones / [by] Wayne W. Dyer. — London : Sphere, 1977. — [9],241p ; 18cm.
Also published: London : Joseph, 1977. — Originally published: New York : Funk and Wagnalls, 1976. — Index.
ISBN 0-7221-3151-8 Pbk : £0.95
(B77-31671)

Lowen, Alexander. Pleasure : a creative approach to life / [by] Alexander Lowen. — Harmondsworth [etc.] : Penguin, 1976. — 251p : ill ; 18cm.
Originally published: New York : Coward-McCann, 1970.
ISBN 0-14-004033-1 Pbk : Unpriced
(B77-00594)

Maltz, Maxwell. The search for self-respect / [by] Maxwell Maltz. — Toronto [etc.] ; London : Bantam, 1976. — [7],214p ; 18cm.
Originally published: New York : Grosset and Dunlap, 1973.
ISBN 0-552-68527-5 Pbk : £0.60
(B77-14539)

Sharpe, Robert. The success factor : how to be who you want to be / [by] Robert Sharpe and David Lewis. — London [etc.] : Pan Books, 1977. — 253p : ill ; 18cm.
Originally published: London : Souvenir Press, 1976.
ISBN 0-330-25179-1 Pbk : £0.80
(B77-33028)

158'.1 — Self-realisation. *Readings*
Glad to be me : building self-esteem in yourself and others / edited by Dov Peretz Elkins. — Englewood Cliffs ; London [etc.] : Prentice-Hall, [1977]. — [6],138p : ill ; 24cm.
'A Spectrum book' - title page verso. — Published in the United States: 1976. — Bibl.: p.136-137.
ISBN 0-13-357327-3 : £7.20
ISBN 0-13-357319-2 Pbk : £3.20
(B77-11542)

158'.1 — Self-realisation. Use of stress. *Manuals*
Sharpe, Robert. Thrive on stress : how to make it work to your advantage / by Robert Sharpe and David Lewis. — London : Souvenir Press, 1977. — 339p : ill ; 23cm.
ISBN 0-285-62252-8 : £4.95 : CIP rev.
(B77-16169)

158'.2 — Dyadic interpersonal relationships. Psychological aspects
Theory and practice in interpersonal attraction / edited by Steve Duck. — London [etc.] : Academic Press, 1977. — x,438p : ill ; 24cm.
Bibl.: p.405-429. — Index.
ISBN 0-12-222850-2 : £9.80
(B77-22330)

158'.2 — Games using prescribed epigrams. *Manuals*
Lowenstein, Tom. Booster : a game of divination / by Tom Lowenstein. — London (40 Walford Rd, N16 8ED) : The Many Press, 1976. — [23]p : ill ; 21cm.
Limited ed. of 200 copies.
Sd : £0.40
(B77-17889)

158'.2 — Interpersonal relationships. Psychological aspects. Games. *Collections*
Awareness games : personal growth through group interaction / [by] Claus-Jürgen Höper ... [et al.] ; translated [from the German] by Hilary Davies. — New York : St Martin's Press ; London : St James Press, 1975. — 159p ; 21cm.
'Griffin books' - cover. — Translation of: 'Die spielende Gruppe'. 2. Aufl. Wuppertal : Jugenddienst-Verlag, 1975. — Bibl.: p.159.
ISBN 0-900997-83-4 Pbk : £1.95
(B77-23089)

158'.2 — Nonverbal communication. Interpretation. *Manuals*
Morris, Desmond. Manwatching : a field guide to human behaviour / [by] Desmond Morris. — London : Cape, 1977. — 320p : ill(some col), ports(some col) ; 29cm.
Bibl.: p.316-317. — Index.
ISBN 0-224-01533-8 : £7.95 : CIP rev.
(B77-21681)

158'.2'02436 — Interpersonal relationships. Psychological aspects. *For community work. Readings*
The **helping** relationship sourcebook / edited by Donald Avila, Arthur W. Combs, William W. Purkey. — 2nd ed. — Boston, Mass. ; London [etc.] : Allyn and Bacon, 1977. — xvii,253p ; 24cm.
Previous ed.: Boston, Mass. : Allyn and Bacon, 1971. — Bibl.
ISBN 0-205-05843-4 Pbk : £7.95
(B77-29909)

158'.26 — Personnel. Interpersonal relationships. *United States. Manuals. For school leavers*
Fruehling, Rosemary T. Working at human relations / [by] Rosemary T. Fruehling. — New York ; London [etc.] : McGraw-Hill, 1977. — [8],136p : ill, forms ; 28cm. — (Career core competencies, a cooperative work-experience program)
Pages perforated at inside edge.
ISBN 0-07-028331-1 Pbk : £2.95
(B77-26093)

158.7 — Industries. Personnel. Stress. *Great Britain*
Goodwin, Rowland. Stress at work : a study of a growing problem in industry / [by] Rowland Goodwin. — London : Chester House Publications, 1976. — 142p : ill, form ; 22cm.
Bibl.: p.135-136. — Index.
ISBN 0-7150-0063-2 Pbk : £2.00
(B77-33574)

158.7 — Man. Organisational behaviour
Korman, Abraham K. Organizational behavior / [by] Abraham K. Korman. — Revised ed. — Englewood Cliffs ; London [etc.] : Prentice-Hall, 1977. — x,438p : ill ; 24cm.
Previous ed.: published as 'Industrial and organizational psychology'. Englewood Cliffs ; Hemel Hempstead : Prentice-Hall, 1971. — Bibl.: p.398-432. — Index.
ISBN 0-13-640938-5 : £10.35
(B77-17268)

160 — LOGIC
Berger, Fred R. Studying deductive logic / [by] Fred R. Berger. — Englewood Cliffs ; London [etc.] : Prentice-Hall, 1977. — xiii,156p : ill ; 23cm.
Bibl.: p.147-149. — Index.
ISBN 0-13-858811-2 Pbk : £4.75
(B77-14540)

Frege, Gottlob. Logical investigations / [by] Gottlob Frege ; edited with a preface by P.T. Geach ; translated [from the German] by P.T. Geach and R.H. Stoothoff. — Oxford : Blackwell, 1977. — ix,82p ; 23cm. — (Library of philosophy and logic)
Bibl.: p.79-82.
ISBN 0-631-17190-8 : £2.75 : CIP rev.
(B77-06449)

George, Frank Honywill. Precision, language and logic / by F.H. George. — Oxford [etc.] : Pergamon, 1977. — xi,216p : ill ; 26cm. — (Pergamon international library)
Bibl. — Index.
ISBN 0-08-019650-0 : £9.75
(B77-25365)

Manicas, Peter Theodore. Logic : the essentials / [by] Peter T. Manicas, Arthur N. Kruger. — [Revised ed.]. — New York ; London [etc.] : McGraw-Hill, 1976. — xiv,498p : ill ; 25cm.
Text on lining papers. — With answers. — Previous ed.: published as 'Essentials of logic'. New York : American Book Co., 1968. — Index.
ISBN 0-07-039893-3 : £10.40
(B77-03896)

160 — Lateral thought
De Bono, Edward. Lateral thinking : a textbook of creativity / [by] Edward de Bono. — Harmondsworth : Penguin, 1977. — 260p : ill ; 18cm. — (Pelican books)
Originally published: London : Ward Lock, 1970.
ISBN 0-14-021978-1 Pbk : £0.80
(B77-25366)

160 — Logical thought
Geach, Peter Thomas. Reason and argument / [by] P.T. Geach. — Oxford : Blackwell, 1976. — xi,99p : ill ; 23cm.
ISBN 0-631-17680-2 : £4.00
ISBN 0-631-17280-7 Pbk : £2.75
(B77-07779)

160 — Tense logic
Prior, Arthur Norman. Worlds, times and selves / [by] A.N. Prior and Kit Fine. — London : Duckworth, 1977. — 175p ; 23cm.
Index.
ISBN 0-7156-0822-3 : £7.95
(B77-16170)

170 — ETHICS
Donagan, Alan. The theory of morality / [by] Alan Donagan. — Chicago ; London : University of Chicago Press, 1977. — xvi,278p ; 23cm.
Bibl.: p.263-274. — Index.
ISBN 0-226-15566-8 : £10.80
(B77-26094)

Kaplan, Morton A. Justice, human nature and political obligation / [by] Morton A. Kaplan. — New York : Free Press ; London : Collier Macmillan, 1976. — xix,283p ; 22cm.
Index.
ISBN 0-02-916890-2 : £9.00
(B77-12837)

Mackie, John Leslie. Ethics : inventing right and wrong / [by] J.L. Mackie. — Harmondsworth [etc.] : Penguin, 1977. — 249p ; 18cm. — (A Pelican original)
Index.
ISBN 0-14-021957-9 Pbk : £1.00
(B77-23975)

170 — Ethics. *Latin texts*
Seneca, Lucius Annaeus, *b. 5 B.C.?.* Dialogorum libri duodecim / L. Annaei Senecae ; recognovit brevique adnotatione critica instruxit L.D. Reynolds. — Oxonii [Oxford] : E. Typographeo Clarendoniano [Clarendon Press], 1977. — xx, 327p ; 19cm. — ([Oxford classical texts])
Index.
ISBN 0-19-814659-0 : £5.50
(B77-33575)

170 — Ethics. *Lectures, speeches*
Dewey, John. Lectures on psychological and political ethics, 1898 / [by] John Dewey ; edited and with an introduction by Donald F. Koch. — New York : Hafner ; London : Collier Macmillan, 1976. — l,462p ; 25cm.
'The following text is based on notes taken by an unknown stenographer (or stenographers) which were then typed and duplicated' - Prefatory notes. — Bibl.: p.451-452. — Index.
ISBN 0-02-847930-0 : Unpriced
(B77-12838)

170 — Ethics. Theories of Marxists. *Philosophical perspectives*
Ash, William. Morals and politics : the ethics of revolution / [by] William Ash. — London [etc.] : Routledge and Kegan Paul, 1977. — ix, 170p ; 24cm.
'Routledge direct editions'. — '... a considerably expanded and completely re-worked version of an earlier book, "Marxism and Moral Concepts", published by Monthly Review Press, New York, in 1964' - Acknowledgments. — Bibl.: p.164-166. — Index.
ISBN 0-7100-8558-3 Pbk : £2.95
(B77-33029)

170 — Man. Self-discipline. Ethical aspects
Partridge, David. Make break make / by David Partridge ; foreword by the Bishop of Portsmouth ; illustrated by Clive Yeomans. — [s.l.] : [The author] ; Havant ([19 West St., The Pelham, Havant, Hants.]) : Distributed by Ian Harrap, 1976. — 86p : ill ; 21cm.
ISBN 0-9505402-0-x Pbk : £1.60
(B77-02008)

170 — Moral judgment. *Philosophical perspectives*
Brennan, J M. The open-texture of moral concepts / [by] J.M. Brennan. — London [etc.] : Macmillan, 1977. — 171p ; 23cm. — (New studies in practical philosophy)
ISBN 0-333-18603-6 : £6.95
(B77-21682)

170'.8 — Ethics. *Essays*
Kolnai, Aurel. Ethics, value, and reality : selected papers of Aurel Kolnai. — London : Athlone Press, 1977. — xxv,251p ; 23cm.
Bibl.: p.226-237. — Index.
ISBN 0-485-11169-1 : £9.00 : CIP rev.
(B77-25367)

170'.8 — Ethics. *Readings*
Moral philosophy : an introduction / edited by Jack Glickman. — New York : St Martin's Press ; London : St James Press, 1976. — ix, 692p ; 24cm.
Index.
ISBN 0-900997-76-1 : £5.95
(B77-18530)

170'.92'4 — Ethics. Theories of Plato
Irwin, Terence. Plato's moral theory : the early and middle dialogues / [by] Terence Irwin. — Oxford : Clarendon Press, 1977. — xvii,376p ; 23cm.
Bibl.: p.346-357. — Index.
ISBN 0-19-824567-x : £9.50 : CIP rev.
(B77-10126)

170'.92'4 — Ethics. Theories of Sidgwick, Henry
Schneewind, Jerome B. Sidgwick's ethics and Victorian moral philosophy / by J.B. Schneewind. — Oxford : Clarendon Press, 1977. — xvi,465p ; 23cm.
Bibl.: p.423-456. — Index.
ISBN 0-19-824552-1 : £17.50 : CIP rev.
(B77-10127)

171 — ETHICS. SYSTEMS AND DOCTRINES
171'.9 — Ethics. Eudaimonism. *Philosophical perspectives*
Norton, David L. Personal destinies : a philosophy of ethical individualism / by David L. Norton. — Princeton ; Guildford : Princeton University Press, [1977]. — xiv,398p ; 23cm.
Published in the United States: 1976. — Index.
ISBN 0-691-07215-9 : £18.20
(B77-15071)

172 — ETHICS OF POLITICAL RELATIONSHIPS
172'.1 — Politics. Violence. Ethical aspects
Honderich, Ted. Three essays on political violence / [by] Ted Honderich. — Oxford : Blackwell, 1976. — x,118p ; 23cm.
Index.
ISBN 0-631-17040-5 : £4.50
(B77-08736)

173 — ETHICS OF FAMILY RELATIONSHIPS
173 — Children. Family life. Ethical aspects. *Juvenile literature*
Bradburne, Elizabeth Sutton. Happy families / by E. Bradburne and K. Voller. — London : Grosvenor Books, 1976. — 64p : chiefly ill(chiefly col) ; 20cm.
Originally published: London : Blandford Press, 1950.
ISBN 0-901269-20-4 : £0.75
(B77-07784)

174 — PROFESSIONAL AND OCCUPATIONAL ETHICS
174'.2 — Death. Ethical aspects
Veatch, Robert M. Death, dying and the biological revolution : our last quest for responsibility / [by] Robert M. Veatch. — New Haven ; London : Yale University Press, 1976. — ix,323p ; 24cm.
Bibl.: p.307-318. — Index.
ISBN 0-300-01949-1 : £8.55
(B77-08203)

174'.2 — Medicine. Ethics
Biomedical ethics and the law / edited by James M. Humber and Robert F. Almeder. — New York ; London : Plenum Press, 1976. — xiii, 541p : ill ; 24cm.
Bibl. — Index.
ISBN 0-306-30902-5 : £12.29
(B77-26095)

Ethics in medicine : historical perspectives and contemporary concerns / edited by Stanley Joel Reiser, Arthur J. Dyck and William J. Curran. — Cambridge, Mass. ; London : M.I.T. Press, 1977. — xiii,679p : ill, form ; 29cm.
Bibl.: p.667. — Index.
ISBN 0-262-18081-2 : £28.00
(B77-25368)

Restak, Richard M. Premeditated man : bioethics and the control of future human life / [by] Richard M. Restak. — Harmondsworth [etc.] : Penguin, 1977. — xviii,202p ; 18cm.
Originally published: New York : Viking Press, 1975. — Index.
ISBN 0-14-004411-6 Pbk : Unpriced
(B77-33576)

174'.2 — Medicine. Nursing. Research. Ethical aspects
Royal College of Nursing. Ethics related to research into nursing : guidance for nurses involved in research or any study-project concerning human subjects / [Royal College of Nursing of the United Kingdom]. — London (Henrietta Place, W1M 0AB) : The College, 1977. — [3],8p ; 21cm.
Bibl.: p.8.
ISBN 0-902606-52-2 Sd : £0.25
(B77-11050)

174'.2 — Medicine. Psychotherapy. Ethical aspects. *United States*
Van Hoose, William H. Ethical and legal issues in counseling and psychotherapy / [by] William H. Van Hoose, Jeffrey A. Kottler. — San Francisco [etc.] ; London : Jossey-Bass, 1977. — xv,224p : 1 ill ; 24cm. — (Jossey-Bass behavioral science series)
Bibl.: p.195-217. — Index.
ISBN 0-87589-317-1 : £10.00
Also classified at 344'.73'044
(B77-23976)

174'.2'03 — Medicine. Ethics. *Encyclopaedias*
Thomson, William Archibald Robson. A dictionary of medical ethics and practice / by William A.R. Thomson. — Bristol : J. Wright, 1977. — [8],264p ; 23cm.
Bibl.
ISBN 0-7236-0454-1 : £10.00 : CIP rev.
(B77-11543)

174'.2'071141 — Doctors. Professional education. Curriculum subjects: Ethics. *Great Britain. Christian viewpoints*
Crouch, Muriel. Imparting ethics to medical students / by Muriel Crouch. — London : Christian Medical Fellowship, 1977. — 23p ; 22cm. — (Rendle Short lectures)
'The 1977 Rendle Short Lecture given at a Conference of the Christian Medical Fellowship at Bournemouth on Saturday, May 7th, 1977 ...' - title page verso.
ISBN 0-85111-960-3 Sd : £0.25
(B77-33577)

174'.9'309 — Anthropology. Ethical aspects
Ethics and anthropology : dilemmas in fieldwork / [edited by] Michael A. Rynkiewich and James P. Spradley. — New York ; London [etc.] : Wiley, 1976. — xi,186p : ill, form, maps ; 24cm.
Bibl.
ISBN 0-471-81766-x : £7.25
ISBN 0-471-81767-8 Pbk : £4.65
(B77-24678)

176 — SEXUAL ETHICS
176 — Family planning. Ethical aspects
Sai, Fred T. Some ethical issues in family planning / by Fred T. Sai. — London : International Planned Parenthood Federation, 1976. — 35p ; 21cm. — (Sai, Fred T. Occasional essays ; no.1)
ISBN 0-900924-88-8 Sd : £0.85
(B77-16171)

179.3 — ETHICS. CRUELTY TO ANIMALS
179'.3 — Animals. Treatment by man. Ethics
Clark, Stephen Richard Lyster. The moral status of animals / [by] Stephen R.L. Clark. — Oxford : Clarendon Press, 1977. — [9],221p ; 23cm.
Bibl.: p.200-212. — Index.
ISBN 0-19-824578-5 : £5.95 : CIP rev.
(B77-10128)

179.7 — ETHICS. RESPECT AND DISRESPECT FOR HUMAN LIFE
179'.7 — Killing. Ethical aspects
Glover, Jonathan. Causing death and saving lives / [by] Jonathan Glover. — Harmondsworth [etc.] : Penguin, 1977. — 328p ; 18cm. — (A pelican original)
Bibl.: p.299-324. — Index.
ISBN 0-14-022003-8 Pbk : £1.25
(B77-27653)

179'.7 — Life. Ethical aspects
Temkin, Owsei. Respect for life in medicine, philosophy and the law / [by] Owsei Temkin, William K. Frankena, Sanford H. Kadish. — Baltimore ; London : Johns Hopkins University Press, 1977. — xi,107,[1]p ; 21cm. — (The Alvin and Fanny Blaustein Thalheimer lectures ; 1975)
Index.
ISBN 0-8018-1942-3 : £5.95
(B77-33578)

179'.7 — Torture. Attitudes of professional personnel. Ethical aspects. *Amnesty International viewpoints*
Heijder, Alfred. Professional codes of ethics / [by] Alfred Heijder, Herman van Geuns. — London (53 Theobald's Rd, WC1X 8SP) : Amnesty International Publications, 1976. — 32p ; 21cm.
Bibl.: p.22.
ISBN 0-900058-32-3 Sd : £0.40
(B77-03343)

180 — ANCIENT, MEDIEVAL, ORIENTAL PHILOSOPHY
180 — Ancient Greek thought. Related to Christian doctrine
Weil, Simone. Intimations of Christianity among the ancient Greeks / [by] Simone Weil ; edited and translated [from the French] by Elisabeth Chase Geissbuhler. — London [etc.] : Routledge and Kegan Paul, 1976. — vii,208p ; 23cm.
This translation originally published: 1957. — Translation of: chapters from 'La source grècque', Paris : Gallimard, 1952 and 'Les intuitions pré-chrétiennes', Paris : La Colombe, 1951.
ISBN 0-7100-8524-9 : £4.00
Also classified at 230
(B77-03897)

181 — ORIENTAL PHILOSOPHY
181 — Ancient Middle Eastern thought
The intellectual adventure of ancient man : an essay on speculative thought in the Ancient Near East / by H. and H.A. Frankfort ... [et al.]. — [1st ed. reprinted] ; with revised bibliographies. — Chicago ; London : University of Chicago Press, 1977. — vii,401p : 1 ill ; 23cm. — (University of Chicago. Oriental Institute. Essays) (A phoenix book)
Originally published: Chicago : University of Chicago Press, 1946. — Bibl. — Index.
ISBN 0-226-26008-9 Pbk : £4.10
(B77-33030)

181'.04'3 — Buddhist philosophy
Guenther, Herbert V. Buddhist philosophy in theory and practice / [by] Herbert V. Guenther. — Boulder ; London : Shambhala ; London [etc.] : Distributed by Routledge and Kegan Paul, 1976. — 3-240p : ill, ports ; 19cm.
Originally published: Berkeley : Shambhala, 1971 ; Harmondsworth : Penguin, 1972. — Bibl.: p.210-212. — Index.
ISBN 0-87773-091-1 Pbk : £2.50
(B77-07785)

181'.09'514 — Chinese philosophy. Lao Tzu. *Texts*
Lao Tze, philosopher. — London ([4 Stradella Rd, SE24 9HA]) : Narbulla Agency, 1977. — [1],25[i.e.2]p ; 57mm.
Cover title. — Limited ed. of 100 copies. — Concertina folded.
£1.00
(B77-21683)

181'.11 — Chinese philosophy. I Ching. *Critical studies*
Melyan, Gary G. I-Ching, the hexagrams revealed / by Gary G. Melyan & Wen-Kuang Chu. — Rutland, Vt. [etc.] : Tuttle ; London : [Distributed by] Prentice-Hall, 1977. — 182p : ill ; 19cm.
Bibl.: p.179-182.
ISBN 0-8048-1182-2 : Unpriced
(B77-25369)

Richmond, Nigel. Language of the lines : 'The I Ching Oracle' / [by] Nigel Richmond. — London : Wildwood House, 1977. — [5],178p : ill ; 21cm.
ISBN 0-7045-0299-2 : £5.95
ISBN 0-7045-0298-4 Pbk : £2.95
(B77-28356)

181'.11 — Chinese philosophy. Wang Yang-ming, to 1509. *Critical studies*
Tu, Wei-ming. Neo-Confucian thought in action : Wang Yang-ming's youth, (1472-1509) / [by] Tu Wei-ming. — Berkeley [etc.] ; London : University of California Press, 1976. — xvi, 222p ; 25cm.
Bibl.: p.199-209. — Index.
ISBN 0-520-02968-2 : £8.00
(B77-14034)

181'.4 — Indian philosophy. *Texts. Collections*
The **mind** of India / edited with an introduction, notes & bibliography by William Gerber. — Carbondale [etc.] : Southern Illinois University Press ; London [etc.] : Feffer and Simons, 1977. — xxxi,256p ; 20cm.
Originally published: New York : Macmillan, 1967. — Bibl.: p.239-256.
ISBN 0-8093-0804-5 Pbk : £2.95
(B77-15675)

181'.45 — Hatha-yoga
Louis Frédéric. Yoga asanas : a natural method of physical and mental training / by Louis Frédéric ; introduction and poses by Swami-Vishnoudevananda ; photographs by Louis Frédéric ; translated from the French by Geoffrey A. Dudley. — Wellingborough : Thorsons, 1973. — 159p : chiefly ill, port ; 23cm.
This translation originally published: 1959. — Translation of: 'Yoga Asanas'. Paris : Éditions J. Oliven, 1956. — Index.
ISBN 0-7225-0347-4 Pbk : Unpriced
(B77-15676)

181'.45 — Hatha-yoga. *Manuals. Sanskrit-English parallel texts*
The **Ghersanda** Samhita : a treatise on Hatha Yoga / translated [from the Sanskrit] by Sris Chandra Vasu. — 3rd ed. — London [etc.] : Theosophical Publishing House, 1976. — xviii, 132p ; 20cm.
Sanskrit text, English translation. — Previous ed.: Adyar : Theosophical Publishing House, 1933.
ISBN 0-7229-5066-7 : £3.00
ISBN 0-7229-5068-3 Pbk : £2.25
(B77-33031)

181'.45 — Raja-yoga
Johns, Edgar. Yoga power / by Edgar Johns ; postures by Iain Rodney. — Hove ([PO B 422, Valance Rd, Hove, E. Sussex BN3 2DU]) : Valldaro Publications, 1975. — 52p,xii p of plates : ill ; 21cm.
ISBN 0-86077-003-6 Pbk : Unpriced
(B77-00595)

181'.45 — Transcendental meditation
Russell, Peter, *b.1946.* The TM technique : an introduction to transcendental meditation and the teachings of Maharishi Mahesh Yogi / [by] Peter Russell. — London [etc.] : Routledge and Kegan Paul, 1977. — 195p : ill ; 22cm.
Originally published: 1976. — Index.
ISBN 0-7100-8539-7 Pbk : £1.75
(B77-14035)

181'.45 — Transcendental meditation. *Periodicals*
Creative intelligence : an international publication devoted to the science of creative intelligence. — London (32 Cranbourn St., WC2H 7EY) : Spiritual Regeneration Movement Foundation of Great Britain.
No.1-. — 1972-. — 25cm.
Published at irregular intervals. — [2],56p. in 1st issue. — Bibl.
Sd : Unpriced
ISSN 0309-538x
(B77-15072)

181'.45 — Yoga
Gent, John. Yoga seeker / by John Gent. — Mansfield (136 Oak Tree La., Mansfield, Notts.) : The author.
Part 6 : Jnana yoga and the eternal wisdom. — 1976. — [2],14p : 1 ill ; 21cm.
ISBN 0-905408-04-7 Sd : £0.30
(B77-03898)

Part 7 : Health, healing and bhakti yoga. — 1977. — [2],26p ; 21cm.
Sd : £0.40
(B77-17269)

Part 9 : Mantra yoga, the music of the mind. — 1977. — [12]p ; 21cm.
Sd : £0.30
(B77-32374)

Hittleman, Richard Lowell. Yoga : the 8 steps to health and peace / [by] Richard Hittleman. — Toronto [etc.] ; London : Bantam, 1976. — [6], 217,[1]p : ill ; 18cm.
Originally published: New York : Deerfield Communications, 1975. — Bibl.: p.217.
ISBN 0-552-62116-1 Pbk : £0.75
(B77-13486)

Satchidananda, *Swami.* Living Yoga : the value of Yoga in today's life / [by] Swami Satchidananda and ... [others]. — New York ; London : Gordon and Breach, 1977. — xi,323p, [8]p of plates : ill, ports ; 24cm. — (Psychic studies)
'An interface book'.
ISBN 0-677-05230-8 : Unpriced
(B77-24679)

181'.45 — Yoga. Related to Jungian system of psychoanalysis
Mooney, Lucindi Frances. Storming Eastern temples : a psychological exploration of yoga / by Lucindi Frances Mooney. — Wheaton [etc.] ; London : Theosophical Publishing House, 1976. — [8],212p ; 21cm. — (A quest book)
Bibl.: p.205-207. — Index.
ISBN 0-8356-0479-9 Pbk : £3.90
Primary classification 150'.19'54
(B77-05182)

181'.45'05 — Yoga. *Periodicals*
Yoga and life. — London (9 Old Bond St., W1X 3TA) : Yoga for Health Clubs.
No.1- ; Spring 1977-. — [1977]-. — ill ; 30cm.
Quarterly. — 34p. in 1st issue.
Sd : £0.40
ISSN 0309-5568
(B77-15677)

181'.5 — Sufi philosophy. Shah, Idries. *Reviews. Facsimiles. Collections*
Books by Idries Shah : reviews and comments, etc. / compiled and edited by C. Robert Ferguson. — London (10 Dryden Chambers, 119 Oxford St., W.1) : Key Press Service.
Vol.1. — 1973. — 2-52p : ports ; 30cm.
Bibl.: p.43-52. — Facsimile reprints. — Includes 2 original texts with English translations.
Pbk : Unpriced
(B77-17270)

184 — PLATONIC PHILOSOPHY
184 — Ancient Greek philosophy. Plato. *Texts*
Plato. Phaedrus ; and, The seventh and eighth letters / [by] Plato ; translated [from the Greek] with introductions by Walter Hamilton. — Harmondsworth [etc.] : Penguin, 1977. — 160p ; 18cm. — (The Penguin classics)
These translations originally published: 1973. — Bibl.: p.159-160. — Previous control number ISBN 0-14-044275-8.
Pbk : £0.50
ISBN 0-14-044275-8
(B77-26762)

Plato. The portable Plato : 'Protagoras', 'Symposium', 'Phaedo', and 'The Republic', complete, in the English translation [from the Greek] of Benjamin Jowett / edited, with an introduction, by Scott Buchanan. — Harmondsworth [etc.] : Penguin, 1977. — [7], 696p ; 19cm. — (Viking portable library)
This edition originally published: New York : Viking Press, 1948. — Bibl.: p.41-2.
ISBN 0-14-015040-4 Pbk : £1.95
(B77-26096)

184 — Ancient Greek philosophy. Plato. Criticism. *State-of-the-art reviews*
Skemp, Joseph Bright. Plato / by J.B. Skemp. — Oxford : Clarendon Press, 1976. — 63p ; 24cm. — ('Greece & Rome' new surveys in the classics ; no.10)
Sd : £0.85
(B77-06450)

184 — Ancient Greek philosophy. Plato. Phaedo. Commentaries, 400-600. *Collections. Greek-English parallel texts*
The **Greek** commentaries on Plato's 'Phaedo' / [edited by] L.G. Westerink. — Amsterdam ; Oxford [etc.] : North-Holland Publishing Co.
In 2 vols. — Parallel Greek text and English translation, English introduction and notes.
Vol.1 : Olympiodorus. — 1976. — 204p ; 26cm. — (Nederlandse Akademie van Wetenschappen. Afdeling Letterkunde. Verhandelingen : nieuwe reeks ; deel 92)
Index.
Pbk : Unpriced
(B77-19196)

184 — Platonism, B.C.80-A.D.220
Dillon, John, *b.1939.* The middle Platonists : a study of Platonism, 80 BC to AD 220 / [by] John Dillon. — London : Duckworth, 1977. — xvii,429p ; 23cm.
Bibl.: p.416-421. — Index.
ISBN 0-7156-1091-0 : £12.00
(B77-10719)

185 — ARISTOTELIAN PHILOSOPHY
185 — Dialectics. Theories of Aristotle
Evans, J D G. Aristotle's concept of dialectic / [by] J.D.G. Evans. — Cambridge [etc.] : Cambridge University Press, 1977. — x,150p ; 23cm.
Bibl.: p.136-140. — Index.
ISBN 0-521-21425-4 : £5.90
(B77-14541)

185'.08 — Ancient Greek philosophy. Aristotle. *Critical studies. Readings*
Articles on Aristotle. — London : Duckworth.
In 4 vols.
2 : Ethics and politics / edited by Jonathan Barnes, Malcolm Schofield, Richard Sorabji. — 1977. — xiv,254p,plate : 2 ports ; 23cm.
Bibl.: p.219-233. — Index. — '... contains 17 articles. Three of them are translated from French and one from German. One is newly written' - jacket.
ISBN 0-7156-0929-7 : £12.00
ISBN 0-7156-0930-0 Pbk : £3.95
(B77-27654)

186 — SCEPTIC AND NEOPLATONIC PHILOSOPHY
186'.4 — Ancient Greek philosophy. Neoplatonism. *Greek texts*
Plotinus. Plotini opera / ediderunt Paul Henry et Hans-Rudolf Schwyzer. — Oxonii [i.e. Oxford] : E. Typographeo Clarendoniano [Clarendon Press]. — ([Oxford classical texts])
Tomus 2 : Enneades 4-5. — 1977. — xxxvi, 302p ; 19cm.
Greek text, Latin preface and notes. — Bibl.: p.xxv-xxxi.
ISBN 0-19-814582-9 : £7.50
(B77-17890)

189 — MEDIAEVAL WESTERN PHILOSOPHY
189 — European thought, ca 1300-ca 1400
Leff, Gordon. The dissolution of the medieval outlook : an essay on intellectual and spiritual change in the fourteenth century / [by] Gordon Leff. — New York [etc.] ; London : Harper and Row, 1976. — [6],154p ; 21cm. — (Torchbooks)
Index.
ISBN 0-06-131897-3 Pbk : £5.70
(B77-08205)

189'.4 — Scholastic philosophy. Abélard, Pierre. *Correspondence with Héloïse, Abbess of the Paraclete*
Abélard, Pierre. [Historia calamitatum. English]. The story of his misfortunes ; and, The personal letters / [by] Abélard & Héloïse ; translated [from the Latin] with an introduction and notes by Betty Radice ; wood-engravings by Raymond Hawthorn. — London : Folio Society, 1977. — 130p : ill, map(on lining paper) ; 26cm.
In slip case. — This translation originally published: as 'The letters of Abélard and Héloise'. Harmondsworth : Penguin, 1974.
£4.95
Primary classification 271'.979
(B77-28376)

189'.4 — Scholastic philosophy. Abélard, Pierre. Correspondence with Héloïse, Abbess of the Paraclete. Authenticity. *Sources of data: European literatures, to 1500*
Dronke, Peter. Abelard and Heloise in medieval testimonies / by Peter Dronke. — [Glasgow] : University of Glasgow Press, 1976. — 61p ; 21cm. — (W.P. Ker memorial lecture ; 26th)
'... delivered in the University of Glasgow 29th October, 1976'. — Includes Latin and Middle French texts.
ISBN 0-85261-136-6 Sd : £1.25
Primary classification 271'.979
(B77-10159)

189'.4 — Scholastic philosophy. Thomas Aquinas, Saint. *Critical studies*
Copleston, Frederick Charles. Thomas Aquinas / by Frederick Copleston. — London : Search Press [etc.], 1976. — 272p ; 23cm.
Originally published: as 'Aquinas'. Harmondsworth : Penguin, 1955. — Bibl.: p.265-267. — Index.
ISBN 0-85532-369-8 : £5.95
(B77-19999)

189'.4 — Scholastic philosophy. Thomas Aquinas, Saint. *Critical studies. Readings*
Aquinas : a collection of critical essays / edited by Anthony Kenny. — Notre Dame, Ind. ; London : University of Notre Dame Press, 1976 [i.e. 1977]. — vi,389p ; 21cm. — (Modern studies in philosophy)
This collection originally published: New York : Doubleday, 1969 ; London : Macmillan, 1970. — Bibl.: p.384-389.
ISBN 0-268-00579-6 : £9.00
ISBN 0-268-00580-x Pbk : £3.75
(B77-10129)

190 — MODERN WESTERN PHILOSOPHY

190 — Western philosophy. *Conference proceedings*
Contemporary aspects of philosophy / edited by Gilbert Ryle. — Stocksfield [etc.] : Oriel Press, 1976 [i.e. 1977]. — x,300p ; 22cm.
'Contributions to the Oxford International Symposium held at Christ Church College in 1975' - jacket. — Bibl.
ISBN 0-85362-161-6 : £8.00
(B77-06451)

190 — Western philosophy. *Critical studies*
Geach, Kenneth. Brainwashing / by Ken Geach. — Walton on Thames (53 Winchester Rd, Walton on Thames, Surrey KT12 2RH) : Ken Geach Publications, 1977. — [1],11 leaves ; 21cm.
Sd : £0.50
(B77-33579)

Machan, Tibor R. Introduction to philosophical inquiries / [by] Tibor R. Machan. — Boston, Mass. ; London [etc.] : Allyn and Bacon, 1977. — xviii,365p ; 24cm.
Bibl.: p.353-358. — Index.
ISBN 0-205-05536-2 Pbk : Unpriced
(B77-13487)

190 — Western philosophy, to ca 1975. *Texts. Collections*
Philosophy : paradox and discovery / [edited by] Arthur J. Minton with editorial assistance from ... [others]. — New York ; London [etc.] : McGraw-Hill, 1976. — xxvii,452p ; 24cm.
Bibl.
ISBN 0-07-042412-8 Pbk : £6.25
(B77-12839)

190'.8 — European philosophy. *Critical studies. Essays*
Grene, Marjorie. Philosophy in and out of Europe / [by] Marjorie Grene. — Berkeley [etc.] ; London : University of California Press, 1976. — xi,169p ; 23cm.
Index.
ISBN 0-520-03121-0 : £6.35
(B77-14036)

190'.8 — Western philosophy. *Readings*
The **problems** of philosophy : classical and contemporary sources / edited with introductions by C.F. Delaney ... [et al.]. — Notre Dame, Ind. ; London : University of Notre Dame Press, 1976. — ix422p ; 26cm.
Bibl.
ISBN 0-268-01521-x : £10.40
(B77-05188)

190'.8 — Western philosophy, 1600-1800. *Readings*
Dialogues of modern philosophy / [edited by] Philip E. Davis. — Boston, Mass. ; London [etc.] : Allyn and Bacon, 1977. — xxxv,419p : ports ; 24cm.
Bibl.: p.400-406. — Index.
ISBN 0-205-05511-7 Pbk : Unpriced
(B77-02733)

190'.9 — Western philosophy, to ca 1964
Stumpf, Samuel Enoch. Socrates to Sartre : a history of philosophy / [by] Samuel Enoch Stumpf. — 2nd ed. — New York ; London [etc.] : McGraw-Hill, [1976]. — xvi,527p ; 24cm.
This ed. published in the United States: 1975. — Previous ed.: 1965. — Bibl.: p.486-502. — Index.
ISBN 0-07-062326-0 : £5.85
(B77-00596)

190'.9 — Western thought, ca 1100-1940
Randall, John Herman. The making of the modern mind : a survey of the intellectual background of the present age / [by] John Herman Randall, Jr. — 50th anniversary ed. [i.e. Revised ed.] ; with a foreword by Jacques Barzun. — New York ; Guildford : Columbia University Press, 1976. — xxi,696p ; 21cm.
Revised ed. originally published: Boston, Mass. : Houghton Mifflin, 1940. — Bibl. — Index.
ISBN 0-231-04142-x : £13.88
ISBN 0-231-04143-8 Pbk : £5.55
(B77-03899)

190'.9 — Western thought, to 1975
De Bono, Edward. The greatest thinkers / [by] Edward de Bono [et al.] ; diagrams by Edward de Bono with George Daulby. — London : Weidenfeld and Nicolson, 1976. — 215p : ill, chart, facsims, maps, ports ; 25cm.
Index.
ISBN 0-297-77198-1 : £5.95
(B77-00012)

190'.9'033 — European thought, 1715-1793
Hampson, Norman. The Enlightenment / [by] Norman Hampson. — Harmondsworth [etc.] : Penguin, 1976. — 304p ; 18cm. — (Pelican books)
Originally published: 1968. — Bibl.: p.291-297. — Index.
ISBN 0-14-021004-0 Pbk : £0.90
(B77-03344)

190'.9'034 — European thought, 1859-1960
Neville, Tony. The challenge of modern thought / [by] Tony Neville. — London : University Tutorial Press, 1977. — 158p,[16]p of plates : ill, ports ; 25cm.
Bibl.
ISBN 0-7231-0739-4 : £2.90
ISBN 0-7231-0710-6 Pbk : £1.85
(B77-32375)

190'.9'034 — Western philosophy, 1860-1960
Randall, John Herman. Philosophy after Darwin : chapters for 'The career of philosophy' volume III, and other essays / [by] John Herman Randall, Jr ; edited by Beth J. Singer. — New York ; Guildford : Columbia University Press, 1977. — x,352p ; 24cm.
Index.
ISBN 0-231-04114-4 : £12.85
(B77-33580)

190'.9'04 — European thought, 1870-1976
Biddiss, Michael Denis. The age of the masses : ideas and society in Europe since 1870 / [by] Michael D. Biddiss. — Harmondsworth [etc.] : Penguin, 1977. — 3-379p ; 18cm. — (The pelican history of European thought ; vol.6) (A pelican original)
Bibl.: p.357-362. — Index.
ISBN 0-14-021987-0 Pbk : £1.50
(B77-26097)

191 — American philosophy. *Texts*
Dewey, John. The middle works, 1899-1924 / [by] John Dewey ; edited by Jo Ann Boydston. — Carbondale [etc.] : Southern Illinois University Press ; London [etc.] : Feffer and Simons.
In 15 vols.
Vol.1 : 1899-1901 / with an introduction by Joe R. Burnett. — 1976. — xxiii,456p : ill ; 22cm.
Bibl.: p.442-446. — Index.
ISBN 0-8093-0753-7 : Unpriced
(B77-17891)

Vol.2 : 1902-1903 / with an introduction by Sidney Hook. — 1976. — xxi,449p ; 23cm.
Bibl.: p.432-435. — Index.
ISBN 0-8093-0754-5 : Unpriced
(B77-17892)

James, William, *b.1842.* The work of William James / editors Frederick H. Burkhardt, general editor ; Fredson Bowers, textual editor ; Ignas K. Skrupskelis, associate editor ... — [Cambridge, Mass.] ; [London] : [Harvard University Press].
[Vol.4] : [A pluralistic universe] / ... Fredson Bowers, textual editor ; Ignas K. Skrupskelis, associate editor ; introduction by Richard J. Bernstein. — [1977]. — xxix,488p : port ; 24cm.
Index.
ISBN 0-674-67391-3 : £15.75
(B77-26763)

James, William, *b.1842.* The works of William James / editors Frederick H. Burkhardt, general editor, Fredson Bowers, textual editor, Ignas K. Skrupskelis, associate editor ... — [Cambridge, Mass.] ; [London] : [Harvard University Press].
[Vol.3] : [Essays in radical empiricism] / ... Fredson Bowers, textual editor ; Ignas K. Skrupskelis, associate editor ; introduction by John J. McDermott. — [1977]. — xlviii,318p : facsim, port ; 24cm.
Published in the United States: 1976. — Index.
ISBN 0-674-26717-6 : £10.20
(B77-11051)

Weiss, Paul. First considerations : an examination of philosophical evidence / [by] Paul Weiss ; with comments by Abner Shimony ... [et al.]. — Carbondale [etc.] : Southern Illinois University Press ; London [etc.] : Feffer and Simons, 1977. — xii,273p ; 24cm.
Index.
ISBN 0-8093-0797-9 : £10.85
(B77-20883)

191 — American philosophy. Adler, Mortimer Jerome. *Autobiographies*
Adler, Mortimer Jerome. Philosopher at large : an intellectual autobiography / by Mortimer J. Adler. — London : Weidenfeld and Nicolson, 1977. — xiii,349p,[32]p of plates : ill, ports ; 24cm.
Also published: New York : Macmillan, 1977. — Bibl.: p.330-337. — Index.
ISBN 0-297-77281-3 : £12.50
(B77-29910)

191 — American philosophy. Dewey, John. *Lectures, speeches*
John Dewey reconsidered / edited by R.S. Peters. — London [etc.] : Routledge and Kegan Paul, 1977. — viii,128p ; 23cm. — (International library of the philosophy of education)
Bibl. — Index.
ISBN 0-7100-8623-7 : £4.50 : CIP rev.
(B77-15678)

191 — American thought. Influence of theories of origins of solar system of Laplace, Pierre Simon, marquis de, to 1900
Numbers, Ronald L. Creation by natural law : Laplace's nebular hypothesis in American thought / by Ronald L. Numbers. — Seattle ; London : University of Washington Press, 1977. — xi,184p : 1 ill ; 23cm.
Bibl.: p.171-178. — Index.
ISBN 0-295-95439-6 : £11.25
(B77-33032)

192 — British philosophy, ca 1930-1970. *Critical studies. Transcripts of interviews*
Modern British philosophy / [edited by] Bryan Magee. — St Albans : Paladin, 1973. — 287p ; 20cm.
Originally published: London : Secker and Warburg, 1971. — Bibl.: p.268-274. — Index.
ISBN 0-586-08153-4 Pbk : £0.75
(B77-19197)

192 — English philosophy. *Texts*
Cartwright, *Sir* Fairfax L. The mystic rose from the garden of the king : a fragment of the vision of Sheikh Haji Ibrahim of Kerbela / by Sir Fairfax L. Cartwright. — London : Watkins, 1976. — xx,196p ; 20cm.
Originally published: s.l. : s.n., 1898.
ISBN 0-7224-0155-8 Pbk : £2.50
(B77-07048)

Locke, John. The Locke reader : selections from the works of John Locke / with a general introduction and commentary [by] John W. Yolton. — Cambridge [etc.] : Cambridge University Press, 1977. — xv,335p : facsim ; 24cm.
Bibl.: p.330-331. — Index.
ISBN 0-521-21282-0 : £13.50
ISBN 0-521-29084-8 Pbk : £3.50
(B77-12840)

192 — English philosophy. Austin, John Langshaw. *Critical studies*
Graham, Keith. J.L. Austin : a critique of ordinary language philosophy / by Keith Graham. — Hassocks : Harvester Press, 1977. — x,281p ; 22cm. — (Harvester studies in philosophy)
Bibl.: p.274-276. — Index.
ISBN 0-85527-650-9 : £8.50 : CIP rev.
(B77-21685)

192 — English philosophy. Ayer, Sir Alfred Jules, to 1946. *Autobiographies*
Ayer, *Sir* Alfred Jules. Part of my life / [by] A.J. Ayer. — London : Collins, 1977. — 318p,[8]p of plates : ill, ports ; 24cm.
Index.
ISBN 0-00-216017-x : £6.95
(B77-30947)

192 — English philosophy. Herbert, Edward, Baron Herbert, b.1583. *Autobiographies*
Herbert, Edward, *Baron Herbert, b.1583.* The life of Edward, first Lord Herbert of Cherbury / written by himself ; edited with an introduction by J.M. Shuttleworth. — London [etc.] : Oxford University Press, 1976. — xxvii,156p, [12]p of plates : ill, facsim, ports ; 24cm. — (Oxford English memoirs and travels)
'This text is based on the original manuscripts ... now deposited in the National Library of Wales under the general heading of Powis MSS' - Note on the text. — Bibl.: p.xxiv-xxv. — Index.
ISBN 0-19-255411-5 : £8.00
(B77-03345)

192 — English philosophy. Mill, John Stuart. Influence of women
Kamm, Josephine. John Stuart Mill in love / [by] Josephine Kamm. — London : Gordon and Cremonesi, 1977. — 253p,plate : ports ; 23cm.
Bibl.: p.242-246. — Index.
ISBN 0-86033-020-6 : £6.90 : CIP rev.
(B77-13488)

192 — English philosophy. Popper, Sir Karl Raimund. *Autobiographies*
Popper, *Sir* Karl Raimund. Unended quest : an intellectual autobiography / [by] Karl Popper. — [Revised ed.]. — [London] : Fontana, 1976. — 255p ; 18cm.
Previous ed.: published as 'Autobiography of Karl Popper' in 'The philosophy of Karl Popper'. La Salle, Ill. : Open Court, 1974. — Bibl.: p.240-247. — Index.
ISBN 0-00-634116-0 Pbk : £1.00
(B77-07786)

192 — English philosophy. Wittgenstein, Ludwig. *Biographies*
Bartley, William Warren. Wittgenstein / [by] William Warren Bartley III. — London [etc.] : Quartet Books, 1977. — [12],145p,[4]p of plates : facsims, ports ; 20cm.
Originally published: Philadelphia : Lippincott, 1973 ; London : Quartet Books, 1974. — Bibl.: p.138-139. — Index.
ISBN 0-7043-3093-8 Pbk : £2.25
(B77-29911)

192 — English philosophy. Wittgenstein, Ludwig. *Critical studies*
Pears, David Francis. Ludwig Wittgenstein / [by] David Pears. — Harmondsworth [etc.] : Penguin, 1977. — [13],208p ; 18cm. — (Penguin modern masters)
Originally published: as 'Wittgenstein'. New York : Viking Press, 1970 ; London : Fontana, 1971. — Bibl.: p.203-205. — Index.
ISBN 0-14-004497-3 Pbk : Unpriced
(B77-33033)

192 — English philosophy. Wittgenstein, Ludwig. Theories. Related to theories of Madhyamika school of Mahayana Buddhism
Gudmunsen, Chris. Wittgenstein and Buddhism / [by] Chris Gudmunsen. — London [etc.] : Macmillan, 1977. — ix,128p ; 23cm.
Bibl.: p.121-124. — Index.
ISBN 0-333-21244-4 : £8.95
Also classified at 294.3'92
(B77-28357)

192 — Ideology. Theories of Walsby, Harold
Walford, George W. An outline sketch of systematic ideology / by George W. Walford. — London (The Bookshop, 186 Upper St., N1 1RH) : Walsby Society, 1977. — [1],33p ; 19cm.
Bibl.: p.32-33.
ISBN 0-9505445-0-7 Sd : £0.40
(B77-11046)

192 — Irish philosophy. Browne, Peter. *Critical studies*
Winnett, Arthur Robert. Peter Browne : provost, bishop, metaphysician / [by] Arthur Robert Winnett. — London : S.P.C.K., 1974. — x, 260p,plate : port ; 22cm. — (Church historical series ; no.95)
Bibl.: p.247-256. — Index.
ISBN 0-281-02754-4 : £4.95
(B77-18532)

192 — Scottish philosophy. *Texts*
Hume, David. A treatise of human nature / by David Hume ; reprinted from the original edition in three volumes, and edited, with an analytical index, by L.A. Selby-Bigge. — Oxford : Clarendon Press, 1975. — xix,709[i.e. 713]p ; 19cm.
Facsimile reprint of: 1888 ed. — 'A treatise of human nature' originally published: London : s.n., 1739. — Index.
ISBN 0-19-824321-9 Pbk : £1.95
(B77-05189)

Hume, David. A treatise of human nature / [by] David Hume ; introduction by A.D. Lindsay. — London [etc.] : Dent [etc.], 1977. — iii-xxix, 2-320p ; 19cm. — (Everyman's library)
This ed. originally published: in 2 vols. 1911. — 'Treatise of human nature' originally published: London : s.n., 1739-40. — Bibl.: p.xxvi.
ISBN 0-460-00548-0 : £4.50
(B77-29152)

192 — Scottish philosophy. Hume, David. *Biographies. Early works*
Home, John, *b.1722.* A sketch of the character of Mr Hume ; and, Diary of a journey from Morpeth to Bath, 23 April-1 May 1776 / by John Home ; edited by David Fate Norton. — Edinburgh ([137 Warrender Park Rd, Edinburgh EH9 1DS]) : Tragara Press, 1976. — 28,[1]p ; 23cm.
Limited ed. of 250 copies. — 'Diary of a journey from Morpeth to Bath ...' originally published: in 'An account of the life and writings of John Home, esq. / by Henry Mackenzie. Edinburgh : Printed for A. Constable, 1822.
ISBN 0-902616-33-1 Pbk : £6.00
(B77-26764)

192 — Scottish philosophy. Hume, David. *Critical studies*
Stroud, Barry. Hume / [by] Barry Stroud. — London [etc.] : Routledge and Kegan Paul, 1977. — xii,280p ; 25cm. — (The arguments of the philosophers)
Bibl.: p.271-276. — Index.
ISBN 0-7100-8601-6 : £7.50 : CIP rev.
(B77-13489)

192 — Scottish philosophy. Hume, David. *Critical studies. Festschriften*
David Hume : bicentenary papers / edited by G.P. Morice. — Edinburgh : Edinburgh University Press, 1977. — [8],232p : ill ; 23cm.
'From the 9th to the 14th August, 1976, the University of Edinburgh, in conjunction with its Institute for Advanced Studies in the Humanities, sponsored a conference in Edinburgh to commemorate the bicentenary of the death of David Hume' - Preface. — Index. — Includes a paper in French.
ISBN 0-85224-316-2 : £6.50
(B77-32376)

192 — Scottish philosophy. Hume, David. Treatise of human nature. Editions. *Textual criticisms*
Nidditch, Peter Harold. An apparatus of variant readings for Hume's 'Treatise of human nature' : including a catalogue of Hume's manuscript amendments / by P.H. Nidditch. — [Sheffield] ([Sheffield S10 2TN]) : Department of Philosophy, University of Sheffield, 1976. — 55p ; 22cm.
ISBN 0-902737-02-3 Sd : £0.60
(B77-03900)

192 — Welsh philosophy. Price, Richard, b.1723. *Critical studies*
Thomas, David Oswald. The honest mind : the thought and work of Richard Price / [by] D.O. Thomas. — Oxford : Clarendon Press, 1977. — xvi,366p ; 22cm.
Bibl.: p.343-357. — Index.
ISBN 0-19-824571-8 : £12.50 : CIP rev.
(B77-10130)

192'.08 — English philosophy. *Essays*
Berlin, *Sir* Isaiah. Selected writings / [by] Isaiah Berlin ; edited by Henry Hardy. — London : Hogarth Press.
[Vol.1] : Russian thinkers / [edited by Henry Hardy and Aileen Kelly] ; [with an introduction by Aileen Kelly]. — 1978. — xxiv, 312p ; 23cm.
Index.
ISBN 0-7012-0438-9 : £6.95 : CIP rev.
(B77-20884)

193 — Anthroposophy. Theories of Steiner, Rudolf
Harwood, Alfred Cecil. Rudolf Steiner / [by A.C. Harwood]. — London (35 Park Rd, NW1 6XT) : Anthroposophical Society, [1976]. — Folder([6]p) : ill, port ; 21cm.
Bibl.: p.[6].
Unpriced
(B77-16702)

Rudolf Steiner and the modern age : a brief introduction to his mind and work. — London : Rudolf Steiner Press, [1976]. — 16p ; 19cm.
Sd : £0.075
(B77-16703)

193 — German philosophy. *Extracts, selections*
Nietzsche, Friedrich. A Nietzsche reader / selected and translated [from the German] with an introduction by R.J. Hollingdale. — Harmondsworth [etc.] : Penguin, 1977. — 286p ; 18cm. — (Penguin classics)
Bibl.: p.285-286.
ISBN 0-14-044329-0 Pbk : £1.00
(B77-26098)

193 — German philosophy. *Texts*
Nietzsche, Friedrich. The portable Nietzsche / selected and translated [from the German], with an introduction, prefaces, and notes, by Walter Kaufmann. — Harmondsworth [etc.] : Penguin, 1976. — x,692p ; 18cm. — (The Viking portable library)
These translations originally published: New York : Viking Press, 1954. — Bibl.: p.24-26. — Includes: Thus spoke Zarathustra - Twilight of the idols - The antichrist - Nietzsche contra Wagner.
ISBN 0-14-015062-5 Pbk : Unpriced
(B77-10131)

193 — German philosophy. Hegel, Georg Wilhelm Friedrich. *Critical studies. Readings*
Hegel : a collection of critical essays / edited by Alasdair MacIntyre. — Notre Dame ; London : University of Notre Dame Press, 1976. — ix, 350p ; 22cm. — (Modern studies in philosophy)

This collection originally published: Garden City, N.Y. : Anchor Books, 1972. — Bibl.: p.349-350.
ISBN 0-268-01066-8 : £11.25
ISBN 0-268-01067-6 Pbk : £3.75
(B77-26765)

193 — German philosophy. Leibniz, Gottfried Wilhelm von. *Critical studies. Readings*
Leibniz : a collection of critical essays / edited by Harry G. Frankfurt. — Notre Dame ; London : University of Notre Dame Press, 1976. — ix,425p ; 21cm. — (Modern studies in philosophy)
Originally published: Garden City, N.Y. : Anchor Books, 1972. — Bibl.: p.421-425.
ISBN 0-268-01258-x : £12.75
ISBN 0-268-01259-8 Pbk : £4.50
(B77-33581)

193 — German philosophy. Marx, Karl. *Critical studies*
McBride, William Leon. The philosophy of Marx / [by] William Leon McBride. — London [etc.] : Hutchinson, 1977. — 175p ; 23cm. — ([Hutchinson university library])
Bibl.: p.167-169. — Index.
ISBN 0-09-127980-1 : £5.50
ISBN 0-09-127981-x Pbk : £2.75
(B77-10132)

194 — French philosophy. *Texts*
Descartes, René. The essential writings [of] René Descartes / translated [from the Latin and French] and with introductions and a conceptual index by John J. Blom ; foreword by Paul Oskar Kristeller. — New York [etc.] ; London : Harper and Row, 1977. — xv,271p ; 21cm. — (Harper torchbooks)
Contents include: Rules for the direction of native talents. Translation of: 'Regulae ad directionem ingenii'. Originally published: in 'Opuscula posthuma, physica et mathematica'. Amstelodami : Ex typographia P. & J. Blau, 1701 - Discourse concerning method. Translation of: 'Discours de la méthode'. A Leyde : I. Maire, 1637 - Meditations concerning first philosophy. Translation of: 'Meditationes de prima philosophia'. Paris : M. Soly, 1641.
ISBN 0-06-131909-0 Pbk : £3.70
(B77-28358)

194 — French philosophy. Descartes, René. *Critical studies*
Grayeff, Felix. Descartes / [by] Felix Grayeff. — London (92 Linden Way, Southgate) : Philip Goodall, 1977. — 3-126p ; 22cm.
Index.
ISBN 0-905678-01-x : £2.50
ISBN 0-905678-00-1 Pbk : £1.20
(B77-12841)

194 — French philosophy. La Rochefoucauld, François, duc de. *Critical studies*
Lewis, Philip E. La Rochefoucauld : the art of abstraction / [by] Philip E. Lewis. — Ithaca ; London : Cornell University Press, 1977. — 201,[1]p ; 23cm.
Bibl.: p.193-195. — Index.
ISBN 0-8014-0848-2 : £8.00
(B77-25370)

194 — French philosophy. Pascal, Blaise. Pensées, Les. *Concordances*
Pascal, Blaise. Pensées sur la réligion, et sur quelques autres sujets / [by] Pascal ; edited by Louis Lafuma. — Paris : Éditions du Luxembourg, 1952.
Concordance / edited by Hugh M. Davidson and Pierre H. Dubé. — Ithaca ; London : Cornell University Press, 1975 [i.e. 1976]. — xi, 1476p ; 25cm. — (The Cornell concordances)
Published in the United States: 1975.
ISBN 0-8014-0972-1 : £22.25
(B77-06452)

194 — French philosophy. Rousseau, Jean Jacques. *Correspondence. French texts*
Rousseau, Jean Jacques. Correspondance complète de Jean Jacques Rousseau. — Ed. critique / établie et annotée par R.A. Leigh. — Oxford (Taylor Institution, [St Giles], Oxford) : Voltaire Foundation.
T.27 : Septembre-novembre 1765. — 1976. — iii-xxvii,371p,[3]leaves of plates : facsims ; 24cm.
Bibl.: p.xiii-xxiv. — Index.
ISBN 0-7294-0050-6 : £16.25
(B77-02009)

T.28 : Décembre 1765-février 1766. — 1977. — iii-xxvi,379p,[4]leaves of plates : facsims ; 24cm.
Bibl.: p.xiii-xxiv. — Index.
£18.25
(B77-16708)

T.29 : Mars-juin 1766. — 1977. — iii-xxxiii, 329p,[2]leaves of plates : 2 facsims, col port ; 24cm.
Bibl.: p.xiii-xxiv. — Index.
Unpriced
(B77-26766)

194 — French philosophy. Sartre, Jean Paul. *Critical studies*
Murdoch, Iris. Sartre : romantic rationalist / [by] Iris Murdoch. — [London] : Fontana, 1977. — 126p ; 18cm.
Originally published: Cambridge : Bowes and Bowes, 1953. — Bibl.: p.125-126.
ISBN 0-00-635046-1 Pbk : £0.95
(B77-27655)

194 — French philosophy. Weil, Simone. *Biographies*
Pétrement, Simone. Simone Weil : a life / [by] Simone Pétrement ; translated from the French by Raymond Rosenthal. — London [etc.] : Mowbrays, 1977. — xiv,577p,[24]p of plates : ill, facsims, ports ; 24cm.
This translation also published: New York : Pantheon Books, 1977. — Translation of: 'La vie de Simone Weil'. Paris : Fayard, 1973. — Index.
ISBN 0-264-66239-3 : £10.00
(B77-20885)

194 — French philosophy. Weil, Simone. *Notebooks*
Weil, Simone. The notebooks of Simone Weil / translated from the French by Arthur Wills. — London [etc.] : Routledge and Kegan Paul.
In 2 vols. — This translation originally published: 1956. — Translation of: 'Les cahiers de Simone Weil'. 3 vols. Paris : Plon, 1952-1955.
Vol.1. — 1976. — [4],331p,plate : facsim ; 23cm.
ISBN 0-7100-8522-2 : £6.50
(B77-03901)

Vol.2. — 1976. — [4]p,p333-648 ; 23cm.
Index.
ISBN 0-7100-8523-0 : £6.50
(B77-03902)

195 — Italian philosophy. Della Volpe, Galvano. *Critical studies*
Fraser, John, *b.1939.* An introduction to the thought of Galvano della Volpe / by John Fraser. — London : Lawrence and Wishart, 1977. — 320p ; 22cm.
Index.
ISBN 0-85315-389-2 Pbk : £3.00
(B77-17271)

197'.2 — Russian philosophy. Gurdjieff, George. *Critical studies*
Bennett, John Godolphin. Gurdjieff, a very great enigma : three lectures / by J.G. Bennett. — Sherborne, Glos. : Coombe Springs Press, 1975. — [5],100p : 1 ill, maps ; 21cm.
'Given at Denison House, Summer 1963'. — Originally published: 1969. — Previous control number ISBN 0-900306-06-8.
Pbk : £1.00
ISBN 0-900306-06-8
(B77-11052)

Bennett, John Godolphin. Gurdjieff today / [by] J.G. Bennett. — Sherborne, Glos. : Coombe Springs Press, 1974. — [6],47p ; 20cm. — (Transformation of man series ; no.1)
'... based on a lecture given at Caxton Hall, London in December 1973' - jacket.
ISBN 0-900306-13-0 Pbk : £0.75
(B77-11053)

197'.2 — Russian philosophy. Gurdjieff, George. All and everything. 1st series. *Critical studies*
Bennett, John Godolphin. John G. Bennett's talks on 'Beelzebub's tales' / compiled by A.G.E. Blake from the unpublished writings and talks of John G. Bennett. — Sherborne, Glos. : Coombe Springs Press, 1977. — [6],147p,[5] leaves ; 20cm. — (Transformation of man series ; 6)
ISBN 0-900306-36-x Pbk : £1.75
(B77-29912)

197'.2 — Theosophy. Blavatsky, Helena Petrovna. *Biographies*
Leonard, Maurice. Madame Blavatsky - medium, mystic and magician / by Maurice Leonard. — London [etc.] : Regency Press, 1977. — 115p ; 23cm.
£2.00
(B77-11054)

199'.439 — Hungarian philosophy. Lukács, György. *Critical studies*
Goldmann, Lucien. Lukács and Heidegger : towards a new philosophy / [by] Lucien Goldmann ; translated [from the French] by William Q. Boelhower. — London [etc.] : Routledge and Kegan Paul, 1977. — xxiii, 112p ; 23cm.
Translation and revision of: 'Lukács et Heidegger'. Paris : Denoël, 1973.
ISBN 0-7100-8625-3 : £3.50 : CIP rev
(B77-20886)

Parkinson, George Henry Radcliffe. Georg Lukács / by G.H.R. Parkinson. — London [etc.] : Routledge and Kegan Paul, 1977. — viii,205p ; 23cm.
Bibl.: p.196-200. — Index.
ISBN 0-7100-8678-4 : £4.95 : CIP rev.
(B77-18533)

199'.492 — Dutch philosophy. Spinoza, Benedictus de. *Critical studies*
Hampshire, Stuart. Spinoza / [by] Stuart Hampshire. — Harmondsworth [etc.] : Penguin, 1976. — 237p ; 18cm. — (A pelican original)
Originally published: 1951. — Index.
ISBN 0-14-020253-6 Pbk : £1.00
(B77-25371)

199'.492 — Dutch philosophy. Spinoza, Benedictus de. *Critical studies. Esperanto texts*
Goodheir, Albert. Fondita sur roko : la filozofio de Spinoza post tri jarcentoj / Albert Goodheir. — Coatbridge (16 Woodlands Drive, Coatbridge ML5 1LE) : Eldonejo Kardo, 1977. — iii-x,37p,[2]leaves of plates : 1 ill, port ; 21cm.
Bibl.: p.37.
ISBN 0-905149-04-1 Pbk : Unpriced
(B77-32377)

199'.72 — Mexican philosophy, 1900-1975
Weinstein, Michael A. The polarity of Mexican thought : instrumentalism and finalism / [by] Michael A. Weinstein. — University Park [Pa] ; London : Pennsylvania State University Press, 1976. — xi,128p ; 24cm.
Index.
ISBN 0-271-01232-3 : £9.00
(B77-21686)

200 — RELIGION, CHRISTIANITY

200 — Christianity
James, Derek C. Just in time! / [by] Derek C. James. — Leicester (38 De Montfort St., Leicester LE1 7GP) : Inter-Varsity Press, 1977. — 123p : ill ; 18cm.
ISBN 0-85110-455-x Pbk : £0.75
(B77-12284)

Küng, Hans. On being a Christian / [by] Hans Küng ; translated [from the German] by Edward Quinn. — London : Collins, 1977. — 720p ; 24cm.
Translation of: 'Christ sein'. München : R. Piper, 1974. — Bibl.: p.603-606. — Index.
ISBN 0-00-215610-5 : £7.95
(B77-02734)

Leonard, Graham. The Gospel is for everyone / by Graham Leonard. — [2nd ed.]. — London : Church Literature Association, 1977. — 86p ; 19cm.
Previous ed.: London : Faith Press, 1971.
ISBN 0-85191-117-x Pbk : £1.50
(B77-30948)

Obeying Christ in a changing world / general editor John Stott. — [London] ([14 St James's Place, S.W.1]) : [Fountain Books].
In 3 vols.
Vol.1 : The Lord Christ / edited by John Stott. — [1977]. — 158p ; 18cm.
ISBN 0-00-624639-7 Pbk : £0.65
(B77-10720)

Vol.2 : The people of God / edited by Ian Cundy. — [1977]. — 159p ; 18cm.
ISBN 0-00-624640-0 Pbk : £0.65
(B77-10721)

Vol.3 : The changing world / edited by Bruce Kaye. — [1977]. — 156p ; 18cm.
ISBN 0-00-624641-9 Pbk : £0.65
(B77-10722)

Rees-Mogg, William. An humbler heaven : the beginnings of hope / [by] William Rees-Mogg. — London : Hamilton, 1977. — [7],99p ; 23cm.
ISBN 0-241-89692-4 : £3.50
(B77-20887)

200 — Christianity. *Church Union viewpoints*
Smith, Charles, *b.1915.* What is Catholic? / [by] Charles Smith. — London : Church Literature Association, 1977. — [2],10p ; 17cm.
Sd : £0.15
(B77-18534)

200 — Christianity. *Feminist viewpoints*
For the banished children of Eve : an introduction to feminist theology / [editor Mary Condren]. — Bristol (c/o S.C.M. Publications, 14 Prince Arthur Terrace, Rathmines, Dublin 6) : Student Christian Movement of Britain and Ireland, [1976?]. — 24p ; 30cm. — ('Movement' pamphlet ; no.24)
Sd : £0.30
(B77-26767)

200 — Christianity. Related to Zen Buddhism
Callaway, Tucker N. Zen way, Jesus way / [by] Tucker N. Callaway. — Rutland [Vt] [etc.] : Tuttle ; London : [Distributed by] Prentice-Hall, 1976. — 263p ; 19cm.
Index.
ISBN 0-8048-1190-3 : Unpriced
Primary classification 294.3'927
(B77-11570)

200 — Religion
Reyner, John Hereward. A philosophy of delight / by J.H. Reyner. — London : Watkins, 1976. — vii,66p ; 21cm.
ISBN 0-7224-0144-2 Pbk : £2.00
(B77-05853)

200 — Religion. *Secondary school texts*
Religious Education in Secondary Schools Project. Journeys into religion / Religious Education in Secondary Schools Project. — [St Albans] : Hart-Davis Educational for the Schools Council.
How others see life. — 1976. — 40p : ill(some col), col maps, ports ; 30cm.
ISBN 0-247-12758-2 Sd : £0.75
(B77-08737)

Religion in Britain today. — 1976. — 16p : ill(incl 1 col), col plan, port ; 30cm.
ISBN 0-247-12755-8 Sd : £0.32
(B77-08738)

Religion through culture : Judaism. — 1976. — 24p : ill(some col), facsim, col plan ; 30cm.
ISBN 0-247-12759-0 Sd : £0.48
(B77-08739)

Signs and symbols : the language of religion. — 1976. — 32p : ill(some col), music, ports ; 30cm.
ISBN 0-247-12756-6 Sd : £0.64
(B77-08740)

Teacher's handbook A. — [1977]. — 169p : ill ; 24cm.
Bibl.
ISBN 0-247-12777-9 Pbk : £3.50
(B77-19198)

The life of man : the family. — 1976. — 24p : ill, col map ; 30cm.
ISBN 0-247-12757-4 Sd : £0.48
(B77-08741)

The man from Nazareth as they saw Him. — 1976. — 32p : ill(some col), facsims, col maps, ports ; 30cm.
ISBN 0-247-12754-x Sd : £0.64
(B77-08742)

200 — Religion. Evolutionary aspects
Allegro, John Marco. Lost gods / [by] John Allegro. — London : Joseph, 1977. — 191p ; 23cm.
Index.
ISBN 0-7181-1633-x : £4.95
(B77-22331)

Roszak, Theodore. Unfinished animal : the aquarian frontier and the evolution of consciousness / [by] Theodore Roszak. — London : Faber, 1976. — xi,271p : ill ; 22cm.
Originally published: New York : Harper and Row, 1975. — Index.
ISBN 0-571-11014-2 Pbk : £2.95
(B77-03346)

200 — Religions
The **concise** encyclopedia of living faiths / edited by R.C. Zaehner. — [3rd ed.]. — London : Hutchinson, 1977. — xxi,436p : map ; 22cm. — (Open University. Set books)
Previous ed.: 1971. — Bibl.: p.415-422. — Index.
ISBN 0-09-107521-1 Pbk : £4.00
(B77-28360)

Holm, Jean Lydia. The study of religions / [by] Jean Holm. — London : Sheldon Press, 1977. — x,118p ; 20cm. — (Issues in religious studies)
Index.
ISBN 0-85969-111-x Pbk : £1.60
(B77-20000)

Parrinder, Geoffrey. The world's living religions / [by] Geoffrey Parrinder. — London [etc.] : Pan Books, 1977. — 208p ; 18cm.
Originally published: 1964. — Index.
ISBN 0-330-23877-9 Pbk : £0.75
(B77-26099)

Rice, Edward. The five great religions / [by] Edward Rice ; photographs by the author. — Toronto [etc.] ; London : Bantam, 1977. — [5], 248,[1]p : ill, port ; 18cm.
Originally published: New York : Four Winds Press, 1973. — Index.
ISBN 0-553-10106-4 Pbk : £0.75
(B77-18535)

Ringgren, Helmer. Religions of mankind : today & yesterday / by Helmer Ringgren and Ake V. Ström ; edited by J.C.G. Greig ; translated [from the Swedish] by Niels L. Jensen. — English ed. — Philadelphia : Fortress Press ; [London] : [Distributed by Sheldon Press], 1967 [i.e. 1977]. — xlii,426p ; 21cm.
This ed. originally published: Edinburgh : Oliver and Boyd, 1967. — 'Translation and restructuring of: 'Religionerna i historia och nutid'. [3 ed. Stockholm : Diakonistyrelses, 1964]' - title page verso. — Bibl.: p.422-426.
ISBN 0-85969-102-0 Pbk : £3.75
(B77-09482)

200 — Religions. Symbolism. *Secondary school texts*
Roadley, K P. Questing : symbol in world religions / [by] K.P. Roadley ; drawings by Trevor Stubley. — London : Edward Arnold, 1977. — [6],81p : ill ; 21cm.
Bibl.
ISBN 0-7131-0143-1 Sd : £1.20
(B77-26768)

200'.1 — Religion. Belief. *Philosophical perspectives*
Phillips, Dewi Zephaniah. Religion without explanation / [by] D.Z. Phillips. — Oxford : Blackwell, 1976. — xiii,200p ; 23cm.
Bibl.: p.192-195. — Index.
ISBN 0-631-17100-2 : £7.00
(B77-10133)

200'.19 — Religious experiences. Expounded by Jungian system of psychoanalysis. *Periodicals*
Meanings : an occasional paper of the Guild of Pastoral Psychology. — [London] (c/o The Secretary, 9 Phoenix House, 5 Waverley Rd, N8 9QU) : ['Meanings'].
No.1- ; 1976-. — [1976]-. — 21cm.
Three issues a year. — [16]p. in 1st issue.
Sd : Free to members
(B77-20001)

200'.7'1041 — Schools. Curriculum subjects: Religion. Teaching. *Great Britain. Periodicals*
RS today. — Leicester (38 De Montfort St., Leicester LE1 7GP) : Universities and Colleges Christian Fellowship.
Supersedes: RE bulletin.
Vol.1, no.1- ; [Autumn '75?]-. — 1975-. — 30cm.
Three issues a year. — 12p. in Vol.2, no.2.
Sd : £0.10
ISSN 0308-843x
(B77-16709)

200'.7'1041 — Schools. Religious education. *Great Britain. Proposals*
Professional Association of Teachers. Religious education in state schools / [Professional Association of Teachers]. — Derby (24 The Strand, Derby DE1 1BE) : The Association, 1976. — 16p ; 22cm.
ISBN 0-9504050-3-5 Sd : £0.25
(B77-14037)

200'.7'1041 — Schools. Religious education. Objectives. *Great Britain*
Aims in religious education / edited by Norman Richards. — London (47 Marylebone La., W1M 6AX) : Association of Christian Teachers, 1976. — 31p ; 21cm. — (RE booklet series ; no.1)
Bibl.: p.31.
ISBN 0-9505501-0-8 Sd : £0.50
(B77-05190)

200'.7'1042 — Schools. Religious education. *England. Free Church Federal Council viewpoints*
Free Church Federal Council. *Education Committee.* Religious education in county schools : a discussion document / prepared by the Free Church Federal Council Education Committee. — London : The Council, [1976]. — 16p ; 21cm.
ISBN 0-901152-03-x Sd : £0.06
(B77-02010)

200'.7'12429 — Secondary schools. Religious education. *Wales. Reports, surveys. Welsh-English parallel texts*
Great Britain. *Welsh Education Office.* Religious education in the secondary schools of Wales = Addysg grefyddol yn ysgolion uwchradd Cymru / [prepared by the Welsh Education Office]. — [Cardiff] : H.M.S.O., 1976. — 43p ; 22cm. — (Welsh education survey ; no.3)
Parallel Welsh text and English translation.
ISBN 0-903702-03-7 Sd : Unpriced
(B77-15679)

200'.76 — Religions. *Exercises, worked examples. Secondary school texts*
Greenwood, William Nicoll. New objective tests in religious studies / [by] W.N. Greenwood, H.W. Marratt. — London [etc.] : Hodder and Stoughton, 1977. — 154p : maps ; 22cm.
With answers.
ISBN 0-340-19466-9 Pbk : £1.50
(B77-23977)

200'.8 — Religions. *Readings*
Man's religious quest : a reader / edited by Whitfield Foy. — London : Croom Helm ; [Milton Keynes] : Open University Press, 1978. — [16],725p : ill ; 23cm.
Index.
ISBN 0-85664-548-6 : £9.95 : CIP rev.
ISBN 0-85664-599-0 Pbk : £4.95
(B77-27656)

200'.92'4 — Philosophy of religion. Theories of Hegel, Georg Wilhelm Friedrich. *Critical studies*
Reardon, Bernard Morris Garvin. Hegel's philosophy of religion / [by] Bernard M.G. Reardon. — London [etc.] : Macmillan, 1977. — xvii,147p ; 23cm. — (Library of philosophy and religion)
Bibl.: p.142-143. — Index.
ISBN 0-333-18659-1 : £8.95
(B77-22332)

200'.92'4 — Philosophy of religion. Theories of Wittgenstein, Ludwig. *Critical studies*
Sherry, Patrick. Religion, truth and language-games / [by] Patrick Sherry. — London [etc.] : Macmillan, 1977. — x,234p : 1 ill ; 23cm. — (Library of philosophy and religion)
Bibl.: p.214-228. — Index.
ISBN 0-333-19710-0 : £8.95
(B77-21687)

200'.92'4 — Religion. Historiography. Eliade, Mircea, 1957-1969. *Autobiographies*
Eliade, Mircea. No souvenirs : journal, 1957-1969 / [by] Mircea Eliade ; translated from the French by Fred H. Johnson, Jr. — London [etc.] : Routledge and Kegan Paul, 1978. — xvii,343p ; 23cm.
This translation originally published: New York : Harper and Row, 1977. — Translation of: 'Fragments d'un journal', p.229-571. Paris : Gallimard, 1973. — Index.
ISBN 0-7100-8752-7 : £7.95 : CIP rev.
(B77-30949)

200'.9362 — Religions. Historical sources: Antiquities. *England, 43-410*
Green, Miranda Jane. A corpus of religious material from the civilian areas of Roman Britain / [by] Miranda J. Green. — Oxford : British Archaeological Reports, 1976. — [21], 321p : ill, maps ; 30cm. — (British archaeological reports ; 24 ISSN 0306-1205)
Cover title: The religions of civilian Roman Britain.
ISBN 0-904531-27-9 Pbk : £5.90
(B77-00597)

200'.973 — Religion. *United States, 1945-1976*
Religious movements in contemporary America / edited by Irving I. Zaretsky and Mark P. Leone. — Princeton ; Guildford : Princeton University Press, 1977. — xxxvi,837p : ill, music ; 24cm.
Originally published: Princeton : Princeton University Press, 1974. — Bibl.: p.771-813. — Index.
ISBN 0-691-01993-2 Pbk : £5.20
(B77-29153)

200'.973 — Religions. Social aspects. *United States*
Marty, Martin Emil. A nation of behavers / [by] Martin E. Marty. — Chicago ; London : University of Chicago Press, 1976. — xi,239p ; 21cm.
Index.
ISBN 0-226-50891-9 : £6.15
(B77-04542)

201 — CHRISTIANITY. PHILOSOPHY AND THEORY
201 — Christianity. Belief
Loysen, Jacobus A St Morilyon. True to life : genuine Christian belief for Western and Eastern modern man / by Jacobus A. St Morilyon Loysen. — London [etc.] : Regency Press, 1977. — 126p ; 23cm.
ISBN 0-7212-0487-2 : £2.50
(B77-16710)

201'.1 — Christian theology
Jennings, Theodore W. Introduction to theology : an invitation to reflection upon the Christian mythos / [by] Theodore W. Jennings, Jr. — London : S.P.C.K., 1977. — viii,184p ; 22cm.
Originally published: Philadelphia : Fortress Press, 1976. — Index.
ISBN 0-281-02985-7 Pbk : £3.95
(B77-23092)

Macquarrie, John. Principles of Christian theology / [by] John Macquarrie. — Revised ed. — London : S.C.M. Press, 1977. — xv, 544p ; 23cm.
Previous ed.: New York : Scribner, 1966 ; London : S.C.M. Press, 1967. — Index.
ISBN 0-334-01301-1 : £9.50
(B77-23093)

Schmaus, Michael. Dogma / by Michael Schmaus. — Kansas City ; London : Sheed and Ward.
6 : Justification and the last things. — 1977. — xii,276p ; 21cm.
'A project of John XXIII Institute, Saint Xavier College, Chicago' - half title page verso. — Index.
ISBN 0-7220-7716-5 Pbk : £3.00
(B77-24680)

Wiles, Maurice. What is theology? / [by] Maurice Wiles. — London [etc.] : Oxford University Press, 1976. — viii,117p ; 21cm.
Bibl.: p.112-114. — Index.
ISBN 0-19-213525-2 : £2.50
ISBN 0-19-289066-2 Pbk : £1.10
(B77-08206)

201'.1 — Christian theology. *Essays*
Troeltsch, Ernst. Writings on theology and religion / [by] Ernst Troeltsch ; translated [from the German] and edited by Robert Morgan and Michael Pye. — London : Duckworth, 1977. — xi,260p : 1 ill ; 24cm.
'The first three essays ... are from ... "Gesammelte Schriften II" ... The fourth ["The significance of historical Jesus for faith"] was published separately, [as "Die Bedeutung der Geschichtlichkeit Jesu für den Glauben"] Tübingen [: Mohr], 1911 ...' - Sources and Acknowledgments. — Bibl. — Index.
ISBN 0-7156-0955-6 : £12.50
(B77-33582)

201'.1 — Christian theology. *Philosophical perspectives*
Pannenberg, Wolfhart. Theology and the philosophy of science / [by] Wolfhart Pannenberg ; translated [from the German] by Francis McDonagh. — London : Darton, Longman and Todd, 1976. — [6],458p ; 23cm.
Translation of: 'Wissenschaftstheorie und Theologie'. Frankfurt am Main : Suhrkamp, 1973. — Index.
ISBN 0-232-51290-6 : £9.00
(B77-03347)

205 — CHRISTIANITY. PERIODICALS
205 — Christianity. *Periodicals*
Impact : the Avon quarterly for Christian leaders. — Bristol (23 Brynland Ave., Bristol BS7 9DS) : Impact.
Vol.1, no.1- ; Easter 1974-. — 1974-. — ill, ports ; 28cm.
16p. in 1st issue. — Supersedes: Contact.
Sd : £0.10
(B77-15680)

Third way : towards a biblical world view. — London (19 Draycott Place, SW3 2SJ) : Thirty Press.
Vol.1, no.1- ; 13 Jan. 1977-. — [1977]-. — ill, facsims, ports ; 30cm.
Fortnightly - 24p. in 1st issue.
Sd : £0.30
ISSN 0309-3492
(B77-08743)

207 — CHRISTIANITY. STUDY AND TEACHING
207 — Christian religious education. *Periodicals*
Link : house journal of the National Christian Education Council. — Redhill (Robert Denholm House, Nutfield, Redhill, Surrey RH1 4HW) : The Council.
No.1- ; 1971-. — [1971]-. — ill, facsims, ports ; 29cm.
Three issues a year. — [8]p. in 21st issue.
Sd : Unpriced
ISSN 0309-6076
(B77-18536)

207'.12 — Adolescents. Christian religious education. Projects
Blueprint : a series of reference books for use in secondary school assemblies, religious education and liberal studies classes, project work, church worship and Sunday school, adult education / general editor John Bailey. — London : Galliard.
In 4 vols.
Book 3. — 1976. — xii p,p645-1000,vii p : music ; 30cm.
In binder. — Index.
ISBN 0-85249-353-3 Ls : £12.50
(B77-12285)

Book 4. — 1976. — xii p,p1001-1334,xxxviii p : music ; 30cm.
In binder. — Index.
ISBN 0-85249-354-1 Ls : £12.50
(B77-12286)

207'.3'8 — Children. Christian religious education. Teaching. Story-telling. Visual aids: Drawings. Techniques. *Manuals*
Thompson, Keith, *b.1931.* Sketching & telling stories to children : 18 wonderful easy-to-draw stories / written and illustrated by Keith Thompson. — Eastbourne : Victory Press, 1977. — 57p : ill(some col) ; 22cm.
Originally published: Sydney : Anzea, 1973.
ISBN 0-85476-270-1 Sd : £0.95
(B77-28362)

207'.41 — Secondary schools. Christian religious education. *Great Britain. Order of Christian Unity viewpoints*
Order of Christian Unity. *Education Committee.* Ways whereby Christian education in state schools should be saved : a submission to the Secretary of State for Education and Science, including a survey of head teachers' views [and] an appeal to local education authorities from the Education Committee, Order of Christian Unity. — Revised ed. — London (39 Victoria St., S.W.1) : The Order, 1976. — [2],33,[1]p : form ; 21cm.
Previous ed.: 1973.
Sd : £0.20
(B77-26769)

207'.421'42 — Theological colleges. *London. Camden (London Borough). Hampstead. New College, London, to 1977*
Nuttall, Geoffrey Fillingham. New College, London and its library : two lectures / by Geoffrey F. Nuttall. — London : Dr Williams's Trust, 1977. — 61p ; 22cm. — (Dr Williams's Library. Friends of Dr Williams's Library. Lectures ISSN 0305-3962)
'Delivered on 19 May 1977 at Dr Williams's Library ... and on 16 June 1977 at St Andrew's Church, Frognal'. — Index.
Sd : £0.75
(B77-26770)

207'.426'59 — Theological colleges. *Cambridgeshire. Cambridge. Romsey House Theological Training College, to 1974*
Habermann, M D. Persistent whisper : an account of the establishing of Romsey House Theological Training College, Cambridge / [by] M.D. Habermann. — Cambridge (Romsey House, 274 Mill Rd, Cambridge) : [The author], 1975. — 111p : ill ; 19cm.
Pbk : £0.80
(B77-24681)

207'.429'61 — Theological colleges. *Dyfed. Lampeter. Saint David's University College. History*
Price, D T W. A history of Saint David's University College Lampeter / by D.T.W. Price. — Cardiff : University of Wales Press.
Vol.1 : To 1898. — 1977. — xv,222p,leaf of plate,8p of plates : ill(incl 1 col), ports ; 24cm.
Bibl.: p.211-212. — Index.
ISBN 0-7083-0606-3 : £8.00
(B77-20888)

208 — CHRISTIANITY. COLLECTIONS
208 — Christianity. *Essays*
Murray, John, *b.1898.* Collected writings of John Murray, Professor of Systematic Theology, Westminster Theological Seminary, Philadelphia, Pennsylvania, 1937-1966. — Edinburgh : Banner of Truth Trust.
Vol.1 : The claims of truth. — 1976. — xiv, 374p ; 24cm.
ISBN 0-85151-241-0 : £3.50
(B77-06453)

208 — Christianity. *Readings*
Heart of the saints : the Christian ideal in the lives and ecumenical teaching of the saints / [compiled by] Francis W. Johnston. — London (221 Golders Green Rd, N.W.11) : T. Shand Publications, 1975. — 331p ; 22cm.
ISBN 0-904210-01-4 Pbk : £3.25
(B77-02736)

209 — CHRISTIANITY. HISTORICAL AND GEOGRAPHICAL TREATMENT
209'.2'2 — Christian women, to 1941. *Biographies*
Deen, Edith. Great women of the Christian faith / [by] Edith Deen. — New York [etc.] ; London : Harper and Row, 1976. — xix,410p ; 21cm.
Originally published: New York : Harper and Row, 1959 ; and as 'Great women of faith', London : Independent Press, 1960. — Bibl.: p.393-397. — Index.
ISBN 0-06-061849-3 Pbk : £3.70
(B77-28363)

209'.2'2 — Christians. *Wales, 1580-1920. Lectures, speeches. Welsh texts*
Cwmwl o dystion / golygydd E. Wyn James. — Abertawe [i.e. Swansea] : C. Davies, 1977. — 129p ; 21cm.
ISBN 0-7154-0431-8 Pbk : £1.75
(B77-32378)

209'.2'2 — Christians, 1880-1976. *Biographies*
Mason, Phil. This is our life / by Phil Mason. — Kettering (1 Whitney Rd, Burton Latimer, Kettering, Northants. NN15 5SL) : The author, [1977]. — 43p ; 19cm.
ISBN 0-9500388-4-9 Sd : £0.40
(B77-15073)

209'.2'2 — Christians, 354-1945. *Biographies*
Muggeridge, Malcolm. A third testament / [by] Malcolm Muggeridge. — London : Collins : British Broadcasting Corporation, 1977. — 207p : ill(some col), facsims(some col), ports ; 25cm.
'A Time-Life Television Book'. — Based on the Canadian television series 'A third testament', produced by Nielsen-Ferns Limited, Toronto. — Originally published: Toronto : Little, Brown and Co. (Canada) Ltd, 1976.
ISBN 0-00-216783-2 : £4.95
ISBN 0-563-17201-0 (B.B.C.) : £4.95
(B77-11056)

209'.2'2 — Christians, ca 1830-1975. *Biographies*
Kenneth, *Brother, CGA.* Saints of the twentieth century / by Brother Kenneth. — Guildford [etc.] : Lutterworth Press, 1976. — xvii,206p ; 20cm.
Originally published: London, etc. : Mowbrays, 1976. — Bibl.: p.190-195. — Index.
ISBN 0-7188-2294-3 Pbk : £2.25
(B77-02737)

209'.2'2 — Christians, ca 1895-1976. *Biographies*
Cooper, Brian G. Meeting famous Christians / by Brian G. Cooper. — Great Wakering : Mayhew-McCrimmon, 1977. — 111p : ports ; 21cm.
ISBN 0-85597-205-x Pbk : £1.90
(B77-33034)

209'.2'2 — Christians, ca 480-1892. *Biographies*
Rupp, Ernest Gordon. Just men : historical pieces / [by] Gordon Rupp. — London : Epworth Press, 1977. — ix,181p ; 22cm.
ISBN 0-7162-0267-0 Pbk : £2.75
(B77-16172)

209'.47 — Christianity. *Soviet Union, to 1976*
Bourdeaux, Michael. Opium of the people : the Christian religion in the USSR / by Michael Bourdeaux. — [2nd ed.]. — London [etc.] : Mowbrays, 1977. — 248p,[8]leaves of plates : ill, map, port ; 22cm. — (Keston book ; no.9)
Previous ed.: London : Faber, 1965. — Bibl.: p.240-243. — Index.
ISBN 0-264-66420-5 Pbk : £2.95
(B77-32379)

210 — NATURAL THEOLOGY
210 — Natural religion. *Early works*
Hume, David. The natural history of religion / by David Hume ; edited by A. Wayne Colver ; and, Dialogues concerning natural religion / by David Hume ; edited by John Valdimir Price. — Oxford : Clarendon Press, 1976. — viii,299p, plate : facsim ; 23cm.
'The natural history of religion' originally published: in 'Four dissertations'. London : A. Millar, 1757. — 'Dialogues concerning natural religion' originally published: London : s.n., 1779. — Bibl.: p.287-295. — Index.
ISBN 0-19-824379-0 : £10.00
(B77-03348)

211 — God. Attributes. Self-consistency
Swinburne, Richard. The coherence of theism / [by] Richard Swinburne. — Oxford : Clarendon Press, 1977. — [7],302p ; 23cm. — (Clarendon library of logic and philosophy)
Index.
ISBN 0-19-824410-x : £9.00 : CIP rev.
(B77-12842)

211'.01 — God. Theories
Lilly, John Cunningham. Simulations of God : the science of belief / by John C. Lilly. — Toronto [etc.] ; London : Bantam, 1976. — xvii,284,[1]p ; 18cm.
Originally published: New York : Simon and Schuster, 1975. — Bibl.: p.273-275.
ISBN 0-552-62442-x Pbk : £0.75
(B77-02738)

211'.6'0942 — Secularism. *England, 1850-1960*
Budd, Susan. Varieties of unbelief : atheists and agnostics in English society, 1850-1960 / [by] Susan Budd. — London : Heinemann, 1977. — viii,307p ; 23cm.
Bibl.: p.282-299. — Index.
ISBN 0-435-82100-8 : £9.50
(B77-12287)

212 — God. Substance. Theories, to ca 400
Stead, George Christopher. Divine substance / by Christopher Stead. — Oxford : Clarendon Press, 1977. — xiii,315p ; 23cm.
Bibl.: p.281-296. — Index.
ISBN 0-19-826630-8 : £12.50 : CIP rev.
(B77-10134)

212'.5 — Subud
Sawrey-Cookson, Roseanna. A first introduction to Subud / [by] Roseanna Sawrey-Cookson. — Didcot (North Moreton House, Nr Didcot, Berks. OX11 9AY) : Subud Publications International, [1976]. — [8]p ; 21cm.
Sd : Unpriced
(B77-16173)

213'.5 — Evolution. Theories. *Christian viewpoints*
Andrews, Edgar Harold. Is evolution scientific? / [by] E.H. Andrews. — Welwyn : Evangelical Press, 1977. — [1],21p : ill ; 26cm.
ISBN 0-85234-077-x Sd : £0.45
(B77-17272)

215 — Christian doctrine. Implications of science. *Welsh texts*
Morris-Jones, H V. Y meddwl gwyddonol a'r efengyl / gan H.V. Morris-Jones. — Caernarfon : Llyfrfa'r Methodistiaid Calfinaidd, 1975. — 80p ; 19cm. — (Davies lectures ; 1964)
Bibl.: p.80.
Pbk : £0.40
(B77-03349)

220 — BIBLE
220 — Bible. *Critical studies*
Hayward, Alan. God's truth! : a scientist shows why it makes sense to believe the Bible / [by] Alan Hayward. — Revised ed. — London : Marshall, Morgan and Scott, 1977. — [10], 302p,[2]p of plates : ill ; 18cm.
Previous ed.: 1973. — Index.
Pbk : £0.95
ISBN 0-551-00761-3
(B77-13490)

Hendriksen, William. Survey of the Bible : a treasury of Bible information / [by] William Hedriksen. — 4th revised ed. — Welwyn [etc.] : Evangelical Press, 1977. — 497p : ill, geneal table, map, plan ; 23cm.
This ed. originally published: Grand Rapids : Baker Book House, 1976. — Index.
ISBN 0-85234-076-1 : £5.95
(B77-17273)

220 — Bible. *Critical studies. Welsh texts*
Efrydiau Beiblaidd Bangor. — Abertawe [i.e. Swansea] ([11 St Helen's Rd, Swansea, W. Glam.]) : Gwasg John Penry.
[1] : Cyfrol deyrnged i'r Athro Bleddyn Jones Roberts / golygwyd gan D.R. Ap-Thomas. — 1973. — xxiv,202p,plate : port ; 22cm.
Bibl.: p.xvii-xx.
Unpriced
(B77-33035)

2 : Cyfrol deyrnged i Dafydd R. Ap-Thomas / golygwyd gan Gwilym H. Jones. — 1977. — xvi,178p,plate : port ; 22cm.
Bibl.: p.xi-xiii.
£2.95
(B77-25372)

220 — Bible. *Middle school texts. Welsh texts*
Darganfod yn yr Eglwys : llawlyfr ar gyfer dosbarthiadau o 11-14 oed / golygydd Rheinallt A. Thomas. — Caernarfon : Llyfrfa'r Methodistiaid Calfinaidd, 1976. — 99p,[12]p of plates : facsims ; 22cm.
Adaptation of 'Exploring in the Church' / prepared by Church of Scotland, Committee on Parish Education. Edinburgh : St Andrew Press, 1975.
ISBN 0-901330-63-9 Pbk : £0.60
(B77-03350)

220'.07 — Bible study by small groups
Metcalf, William. By all means : new approaches to group Bible study / [by] William Metcalf. — London : Oliphants, 1977. — 96p ; 19cm. — (Oliphants outlook books)
ISBN 0-551-00772-9 : £0.95
(B77-33036)

220'.076 — Bible. *Questions & answers*
Barber, Fred. What do you know? : Bible quiz book / by Fred Barber. — London [etc.] : Pickering and Inglis, 1977. — 96p ; 19cm.
With answers. — Originally published: as 'Know your Bible'. London : Epworth Press, 1963.
ISBN 0-7208-0395-0 Pbk : £0.65
(B77-25373)

Gleaner, A. Numbers of the Bible quiz / [by] 'A gleaner'. — Ilkeston : Moorley's Bible and Bookshop, [1977?]. — [2],20,[1]p ; 21cm.
ISBN 0-86071-003-3 Sd : £0.20
(B77-27657)

Gleaner, A. Quizzical gleanings / [by] 'A gleaner'. — Ilkeston : Moorley's Bible and Bookshop, [1977?]. — [2],10,[1]p ; 21cm.
ISBN 0-86071-002-5 Sd : £0.14
(B77-27658)

220'.07'8 — Christian religious education. Curriculum subjects: Bible. Visual aids. Making. *Manuals*
Pigrem, Sheila. Help, I can't draw! : a pictorial workbook of the Bible / [by] Sheila Pigrem. — London : Falcon Books.
In 3 vols.
1. — 1977. — [50]p : chiefly ill ; 21x30cm.
Index.
ISBN 0-85491-851-5 Sd : £1.25
(B77-20002)

2. — 1977. — [50]p : of ill ; 21x30cm.
ISBN 0-85491-852-3 Sd : £1.25
(B77-20003)

3. — 1977. — [50]p : of ill ; 21x30cm.
ISBN 0-85491-853-1 Sd : £1.25
(B77-20004)

220.1'2 — Bible. Canon
Noakes, Kenneth. The making of the Bible / [by] Kenneth Noakes. — London : Church Literature Association, 1975. — [1],7p ; 21cm. — (Hillingdon papers ; 6)
Sd : £0.18
(B77-23978)

220.2 — Bible. Topics. *Concordances*
Joy, Charles Rhind. Harper's topical concordance / compiled by Charles R. Joy. — Revised and enlarged ed. — New York [etc.] ; London : Harper and Row, 1976. — xi,628p ; 24cm.
This ed. originally published: 1962.
ISBN 0-06-064229-7 Pbk : £6.70
(B77-01151)

220.5'2 — Bible. English. Taylor. Selections. *Texts*
Let the Living Bible help you / [edited by] Alice Zillman Chapin. — [London] (14 St James's Place, S.W.1) : Fountain Books, 1977. — vi, 185p : ill ; 19cm.
Originally published: New York : Harper and Row, 1975.
ISBN 0-00-215472-2 : £1.95
ISBN 0-00-624310-x Pbk : £0.70
(B77-20889)

220.5'2 — Bible. English. Today's English. *Critical studies*
Nida, Eugene Albert. Good news for everyone : how to use the Good News Bible (Today's English version) / [by] Eugene A. Nida. — London ([14 St James's Place, S.W.1]) : Fount Paperbacks, 1977. — 124p : ill ; 18cm.
Also published: Waco : Word Books, 1977.
ISBN 0-00-625005-x Pbk : £0.75
(B77-27659)

220.5'201 — Bible. English. Geneva. *Critical studies*
Lupton, Lewis. A history of the Geneva Bible / [by] Lewis Lupton. — London : Olive Tree.
[Vol.8] : Faith : supplementary volume containing a study of a poetic agent, Henry Lok. — 1976. — 223p : ill, chart, coats of arms, facsims, maps, plans, ports ; 23cm.
Map on lining papers.
ISBN 0-902093-11-8 : £7.20(£5.30 to subscribers)
(B77-01152)

220.5'204 — Bible. English. Revised standard. Selections. *Texts*
[Bible. *English. Revised standard. Selections. 1977].* The book of I am : sayings from the scriptures / [compiled by] Peter Dunstan. — Berkhamsted : Lion Publishing, 1977. — 63p : ill ; 20cm.
ISBN 0-85648-075-4 : £1.25
(B77-12288)

220.5'206 — Bible. English. New English. *Texts*
[Bible. *English. New English. 1975].* The New English Bible. — Pocket ed. — [London] : Oxford University Press : Cambridge University Press, 1975. — xxi,1071,ix,315p ; 18cm.
With zip fastener. — In slip case. — Originally published: 1970.
£8.50
(B77-30950)

[Bible. *English. New English. 1977].* The New English Bible. — [London] : Collins [etc.], [1977]. — xvi,1035,64p,leaf of plate,[30]p of plates : col ill, col maps, col plans ; 20cm.
Originally published: London : Oxford University Press : Cambridge University Press, 1970. — Includes: 'Bible study aids' / by William Barclay.
ISBN 0-00-512612-6 : £2.75
ISBN 0-00-512613-4 Imitation leather ed. : £3.95
(B77-12843)

220.6 — Bible. *Expositions*
Dale, Alan Taylor. Living in our world : a guide to reading the Bible / by Alan T. Dale. — Nutfield : Denholm House Press [for] the International Bible Reading Association, 1977. — 63p ; 18cm.
ISBN 0-85213-157-7 Pbk : Unpriced
(B77-26771)

Goldingay, John. How to read the Bible / [by] John Goldingay. — London : Oliphants, 1977. — 160p : ill, geneal table, map ; 19cm. — (Oliphants outlook books)
Bibl.: p.11.
ISBN 0-551-00602-1 Pbk : £1.50
(B77-28364)

Schneidau, Herbert N. Sacred discontent : the Bible and Western tradition / [by] Herbert N. Schneidau. — Berkeley [etc.] ; London : University of California Press, 1977. — xiii,331, [2]p,[20]p of plates : ill ; 23cm.
Originally published: Baton Rouge : Louisiana State University Press, 1976. — Bibl.: p.307-320. — Index.
ISBN 0-520-03165-2 Pbk : £4.45
(B77-22333)

220.6 — Bible. *Expositions. Transcripts of discussions*
Symington, J H. And I will turn my hand upon the little ones : [readings, meetings held in] Chicago and Vancouver, May 1976 / [by] J.H. Symington [et al.] ; [editors Wilbert J. Seed, Russell J. Langrell]. — Kingston-upon-Thames (2 Upper Teddington Rd, Kingston-upon-Thames KT1 4DX) : Bible and Gospel Trust, 1977. — [4],272p ; 16cm.
'Volume 37'.
Pbk : Unpriced
(B77-33583)

Symington, J H. I called him when he was alone : [readings, meetings held in] Detroit and Philadelphia, November 1975 / [by] J.H. Symington [et al.] ; editor Henry Magahy. — Kingston-upon-Thames (2 Upper Teddington Rd, Kingston-upon-Thames KT1 4DX) : Bible and Gospel Trust, 1977. — [4],278p ; 16cm.
'Volume 35'.
Pbk : Unpriced
(B77-16711)

220.6 — Bible. Interpretation
Nineham, Dennis Eric. The use and abuse of the Bible : a study of the Bible in an age of rapid cultural change / [by] Dennis Nineham. — London [etc.] : Macmillan, 1976. — xi,295p : ill ; 23cm. — (Library of philosophy and religion)
Index.
ISBN 0-333-10489-7 : £10.00
(B77-02739)

220.6'3 — Bible. Hermeneutics
Stacey, David. Interpreting the Bible / [by] David Stacey. — London : Sheldon Press, 1976. — vii,120p ; 20cm. — (Issues in religious studies)
Bibl.: p.117-118. — Index.
ISBN 0-85969-091-1 Pbk : £1.60
(B77-09483)

220.6'6 — Bible. *Exegetical studies*
Rattenbury, H Morley. Lively oracles : clues to the reading of the Bible / [by] H. Morley Rattenbury. — London : Epworth Press, 1976. — 96p ; 19cm. — (Cell books ; 5)
ISBN 0-7162-0257-3 Pbk : £0.50
(B77-05854)

Torrey, Reuben Archer. What the Bible teaches : a thorough and comprehensive study of what the Bible has to say concerning the great doctrines of which it treats / [by] R.A. Torrey. — London : Marshall, Morgan and Scott, 1977. — [4],539p ; 22cm. — (Marshalls study library)

Facsimile reprint of: 1st ed. London : Nisbet, 1898. — Index.
ISBN 0-551-05558-8 Pbk : £3.95
(B77-29154)

220.6'7 — Bible. Historical criticism
History, criticism & faith : four exploratory studies / [by] Gordon J. Wenham ... [et al.] ; edited by Colin Brown. — Leicester [etc.] : Inter-Varsity Press, 1976. — 3-224,[9]p ; 21cm.
Bibl. — Index.
ISBN 0-85111-315-x Pbk : £2.95
(B77-17274)

220.6'8 — Bible. *Occult viewpoints*
Wells, G Weston. The best kept secret in the world / by G. Weston Wells ; [line diagrams in the text by the author]. — London [etc.] : Regency Press, [1977]. — 130p : ill ; 23cm.
Bibl.: p.130.
ISBN 0-7212-0484-8 : £2.40
(B77-11057)

220.7 — Bible. *Commentaries*
Meyer, Frederick Brotherton. Great verses through the Bible : a devotional commentary on key verses / by F.B. Meyer. — London : Marshall, Morgan and Scott, 1974. — 269p ; 24cm.
Originally published as: 'Our daily homily'. 1966.
ISBN 0-551-05442-5 : £3.50
(B77-18537)

The **new** Bible commentary. — 3rd ed. completely revised and reset / edited by D. Guthrie, J.A. Motyer ... — London : Inter-Varsity Press, 1975. — xv,1310p : maps, plans ; 25cm.
This ed. originally published: 1970.
£6.50
ISBN 0-85110-615-3
(B77-03903)

220.7'7 — Bible. English. New international. *Texts with commentaries*
The **expositor's** Bible commentary : with the New International Version of the Holy Bible / general editor Frank E. Gaebelein. — London : Pickering and Inglis.
In 12 vols.
Vol.10 : (Romans-Galatians). — 1976. — xvi, 508p : 1 ill, 2 maps, plan ; 25cm.
Bibl.
ISBN 0-7208-0389-6 : £9.50
(B77-16712)

220.7'7 — Bible. Selections. *Texts with commentaries*
[**Bible**. *English. Selections. 1976*]. The basic Bible : 160 key readings with notes / edited by John Rogers. — London : Hutchinson, 1977. — [355]p : geneal table, maps, plan ; 23cm.
Originally published: as 'A silhouette of the Bible'. Petersfield : John Penrose Rogers, 1976. — Index.
ISBN 0-09-131710-x : £4.95
ISBN 0-09-131711-8 Pbk : £2.50
(B77-33037)

[**Bible**. *English. Selections. 1976*]. A silhouette of the Bible : being 160 key passages with notes / [compiled by John Penrose Rogers]. — Petersfield (c/o Bedales School, Petersfield, Hants.) : The compiler, 1976. — [352]p : geneal table, maps, plan ; 21cm.
Spine title: Biblos, a silhouette of the Bible. — Index.
ISBN 0-9505297-0-2 Pbk : £2.00
(B77-02011)

220.8'581 — Bible. Special subjects: Plants
King, Eleanor Anthony. Bible plants for American gardens / by Eleanor Anthony King. — New York : Dover Publications [etc.] ; London : Constable, 1975 [i.e. 1976]. — iii-xii, 204p,leaf of plate,[8]p of plates : ill ; 21cm.
Originally published: New York : Macmillan, 1941. — Index.
ISBN 0-486-23188-7 Pbk : £1.95
Also classified at 635'.0973
(B77-02012)

220.8'635 — Bible. Special subjects: Horticulture
Shewell-Cooper, Wilfred Edward. God planted a garden : (horticulture in the Bible) / by W.E. Shewell-Cooper. — Evesham : James, 1977. — 3-221p : ill ; 21cm.
ISBN 0-85305-193-3 : £5.25
(B77-29155)

220.9 — BIBLICAL GEOGRAPHY AND HISTORY
220.9'3 — Biblical antiquities. Archaeological investigation
Kitchen, Kenneth Anderson. The Bible and its world : the Bible and archaeology today / by K.A. Kitchen. — Exeter : Paternoster Press, 1977. — 168p : 3 maps ; 22cm.
Bibl.: p.154-158. — Index.
ISBN 0-85364-211-7 Pbk : £2.20 : CIP rev.
(B77-31672)

220.9'5 — Ancient Palestine. Historical sources: Bible. *School texts*
Sutcliffe, John, *b.1933*. Getting to know about people in the lands of the Bible / [by] John and Ann Sutcliffe ; artist Anne Farncombe. — Redhill : Denholm House Press, 1977. — 32p : col ill, col maps ; 25cm. — (Getting to know about ; book 10)
Index.
ISBN 0-85213-161-5 Sd : £0.75
(B77-29914)

220.9'505 — Bible. *Stories for children*
Dowman, Pamela. Story time one / [by] Pamela Dowman ; illustrated by Gwen Gibson. — London : Scripture Union, 1977. — 89p : ill ; 20cm.
Cover title: Storytime one. — This collection originally published: 1967.
ISBN 0-85421-165-9 Pbk : £0.95
(B77-32380)

The **greatest** Bible stories / [edited by Diana Bremer]. — London : Octopus Books, 1977. — 128p : col ill ; 31cm.
Title page has author statement: edited by Howard Jennings.
ISBN 0-7064-0633-8 : £1.99
(B77-30951)

Sibley, Jacqueline. Story time four / [by] Jacqueline Sibley ; illustrated by Sheila Bewley. — London : Scripture Union, 1977. — 95p : ill ; 20cm.
Cover title: Storytime four. — This collection originally published: 1970.
Pbk : £0.95
ISBN 0-85421-265-5
(B77-32381)

Sibley, Jacqueline. Story time two / [by] Jacqueline Sibley ; illustrated by Jennifer Kisler. — London : Scripture Union, 1977. — 89p : ill ; 20cm.
Cover title: Storytime two. — This collection originally published: 1968.
ISBN 0-85421-177-2 Pbk : £0.95
(B77-32382)

Simon and Sarah. — London : Scripture Union.
Book 2 / by Jennifer Chadwick ; illustrated by Gwen Gibson. — 1972. — [64]p : ill(some col) ; 16x22cm.
Originally published: 1970.
ISBN 0-85421-222-1 Pbk : £0.20
(B77-08744)

Book 3 / by Doreen Bairstow ; illustrated by Gwen Gibson. — 1972. — [64]p : ill(some col) ; 15x22cm.
Originally published: 1970.
ISBN 0-85421-223-x Pbk : £0.20
(B77-08745)

Wesson, Jeanne. Story time three / [by] Jeanne Wesson ; illustrated by Donald Grey. — London : Scripture Union, 1977. — 89p : ill ; 20cm.
Cover title: Storytime three. — This collection originally published: 1968.
ISBN 0-85421-183-7 Pbk : £0.95
(B77-32383)

220.9'505'0222 — Bible. *Stories, anecdotes. Illustrations*
Bond, Bob, *b.1940*. Here come the giraffes : Bible droodles / by Bob Bond. — Exeter : Paternoster Press, 1976. — [95]p : ill ; 18cm. — (Paternoster pocket books ; no.23)
ISBN 0-85364-206-0 Pbk : £0.85
(B77-06454)

221 — OLD TESTAMENT
221 — Bible. Old Testament. *Critical studies*
Blanch, Stuart Yarworth. For all mankind : a new approach to the Old Testament / [by] Stuart Blanch. — 2nd ed. revised and enlarged. — London : Bible Reading Fellowship : J. Murray, 1977. — viii,120p : map ; 19cm.
Previous ed.: London : Bible Reading Fellowship, 1976. — Bibl.: p.116-117. — Index.

ISBN 0-900164-38-7 : £1.95
ISBN 0-7195-3363-5 (J. Murray) £1.95
ISBN 0-900164-37-9 (B.R.F.) Pbk : £0.95
ISBN 0-7195-3362-7 (J. Murray) Pbk : £0.95
(B77-10135)

Rhymer, Joseph. Companion to the 'Good news Old Testament' / [by] Joseph Rhymer and Anthony Bullen. — [London] : Fontana, 1976. — 223p : maps, plan ; 18cm. — (Fontana theology and philosophy series)
ISBN 0-00-623354-6 Pbk : £0.95
(B77-17275)

Traditions and theology in the Old Testament / edited by Douglas A. Knight ; with contributions by Walter Harrelson ... [et al.]. — London : S.P.C.K., 1977. — xv,336p ; 24cm.
Index.
ISBN 0-281-02986-5 : £10.50
(B77-26100)

221 — Bible. Old Testament. *Secondary school texts*
Edwards, James, *b.1910*. The Old Testament and its background / by James Edwards, Maureen Payne ; illustrated by Mary Camidge. — London : Blandford Press.
In 3 vols.
Book 2 : They were God's messengers : Solomon to the Exile. — 2nd ed. — 1974. — 96p : ill, maps ; 22cm.
Cover title: They were God's messengers. — Previous ed.: 1970. — Index.
ISBN 0-7137-3323-3 Pbk : £0.55
(B77-10136)

Edwards, James, *b.1910*. The Old Testament and its background / by James Edwards, Maureen Payne ; illustrated by Mary Camidge. — London : Blandford Press.
In 3 vols.
Book 1 : They heard God's voice : Abraham to Solomon. — Revised ed. — 1974. — 96p : ill, maps ; 22cm.
Cover title: They heard God's voice. — Previous ed.: 1969. — Index.
ISBN 0-7137-3322-5 Pbk : £0.55
(B77-10137)

221 — Bible. Old Testament. Theology
Phillips, Anthony. God B.C. / [by] Anthony Phillips ; with a foreword by The Bishop of London. — Oxford [etc.] : Oxford University Press, 1977. — xiii,96p ; 21cm.
Index.
ISBN 0-19-213959-2 : £2.50
ISBN 0-19-281211-4 Pbk : £0.95
(B77-14038)

221 — Bible. Old Testament. Theology. Related to New Testament theology. Theories, to 1975
Baker, D L. Two Testaments, one Bible : a study of some modern solutions to the theological problem of the relationship between the Old and New Testaments / by D.L. Baker. — Leicester : Inter-Varsity Press, 1976. — 554p ; 22cm.
Bibl.: p.391-535. — Index.
ISBN 0-85111-500-4 Pbk : £4.95
Also classified at 225
(B77-05191)

221'.076 — Bible. Old Testament. *Questions & answers. Secondary school texts. Cards*
Horton, Robert Harold. Beginnings ; and, Servants of God / [by] Robert H. Horton. — [London] : Edward Arnold, 1976. — Case : ill, map ; 22cm.
Thirty six cards ([72] sides).
ISBN 0-7131-0075-3 : £2.95
(B77-10138)

221.4 — Bible. Old Testament. *Textual criticisms. Readings*
Qumran and the history of the Biblical text / edited by Frank Moore Cross and Shemaryahu Talmon. — Cambridge, Mass. ; London : Harvard University Press, 1976. — [9],415p : 1 ill, facsims ; 24cm.
English, French and German text. — Originally published: Cambridge, Mass. : Harvard University Press, 1975. — Bibl.
ISBN 0-674-74360-1 : £12.40
ISBN 0-674-74362-8 Pbk : £4.50
(B77-11544)

221.6 — Bible. Old Testament. *Expositions*
Sawyer, John Frederick Adam. From Moses to Patmos : new perspectives in Old Testament study / [by] John F.A. Sawyer. — London : S.P.C.K., 1977. — ix,150p ; 22cm.
Bibl.: p.142-145. — Index.
ISBN 0-281-03564-4 Pbk : £3.50
(B77-33584)

221.7 — Bible. Old Testament. *Commentaries. Irish texts*
Paodhar, Muiris. Teagasc ar an Sean-Tiomna / Muiris Paodhar a scríobh ; Breandán Ó Madagáin a chuir in eagar. — Baile Átha Cliath [i.e. Dublin] ([15 Bóthar Ghráinseach an Déin, An Charraig Dhubh, Co. Átha Cliath]) : An Clóchomhar Tta, 1974. — xxvii,466p,[2] leaves of plates : facsim, port ; 22cm. — (Leabhair thaighde ; 23)
Bibl.: p.461-463. — Index.
ISBN 0-7171-0601-2 : £3.50
(B77-03904)

221.9'3 — Bible. Old Testament. Historicity. Archaeological sources
Barnett, Richard David. Illustrations of Old Testament history / [by] R.D. Barnett. — 2nd ed. revised and enlarged. — London : British Museum Publications Ltd for the Trustees, 1977. — 112p : ill, facsims, map ; 24cm.
Previous ed.: 1966. — Bibl.: p.103-108. — Index.
ISBN 0-7141-1092-2 : £4.00
ISBN 0-7141-1088-4 Pbk : £1.95
(B77-27661)

Millard, Alan Ralph. The Bible BC : what can archaeology prove? / [by] A.R. Millard. — Leicester : Inter-Varsity Press, 1977. — 48p : ill, map ; 18cm.
Bibl.: p.45.
ISBN 0-85110-230-1 Sd : £0.50
(B77-26772)

221.9'505 — Bible. Old Testament. *Stories for children*
De la Mare, Walter. Stories from the Bible / [retold] by Walter de la Mare. — [1st ed. reprinted] / illustrated by Edward Ardizzone. — London : Faber, 1977. — 3-418p : ill ; 20cm.
Originally published: / with decorations by C. Guercio. London : Faber and Gwyer, 1929. — '... versions of but a few of the narratives related in the first nine books of the Old Testament ...' - Introduction.
ISBN 0-571-11086-x Pbk : £2.75
(B77-13491)

Ralph, Margaret. God's special people / stories from the Old Testament retold by Margaret Ralph ; illustrated by Gordon King. — London : Scripture Union ; Maidenhead : Purnell, 1977. — [30]p : col ill ; 26cm. — (A giraffe book)
ISBN 0-85421-507-7 : £0.75
ISBN 0-361-03970-0 (Purnell) : £0.75
(B77-29915)

Spencer, Chris. Great adventures of the Bible / stories [retold] by Chris Spencer ; illustrations by Victor Mitchell ; [maps and diagrams Tony Cantale]. — Berkhamsted : Lion Publishing, 1976. — 3-61p : ill(chiefly col), col maps ; 28cm.
ISBN 0-85648-048-7 : £1.25
(B77-00598)

Spencer, Chris. Great champions of the Bible / stories [retold] by Chris Spencer ; illustrations by Victor Marshall ; [maps and diagrams Tony Cantale]. — Berkhamsted : Lion Publishing, 1976. — 2-61p : ill(chiefly col), col maps ; 28cm.
ISBN 0-85648-047-9 : £1.25
(B77-00599)

222'.11 — Bible. Old Testament. Genesis. *Critical studies*
Wiseman, P J. Clues to creation in Genesis / [by] P.J. Wiseman ; [edited] with a foreword by D.J. Wiseman. — London : Marshall, Morgan and Scott, 1977. — viii,232p ; 20cm.
'A revised version, originally published in two volumes entitled "New Discoveries in Babylonia About Genesis" (1936) and "Creation Revealed in Six Days" (1948) ...' - title page verso. — Bibl.: p.232.
ISBN 0-551-05567-7 Pbk : £2.95
(B77-31673)

222'.11 — Bible. Old Testament. Genesis. Creation. Projects. *For Christian religious education*
Perridge, Brenda. Make & tell, the story of Creation / written by Brenda Perridge ; designed and illustrated by Philip and Betty Miles. — Berkhamsted : Lion Publishing, 1977. — 32p : chiefly ill(some col) ; 30cm.
Index.
ISBN 0-85648-063-0 Sd : £0.50
(B77-13492)

222'.11 — Bible. Old Testament. Genesis I-XI. *Commentaries*
Watson, David Charles Cuningham. Myths and miracles : a new approach to Genesis 1-11 / [by] David C.C. Watson. — Worthing : Walter, 1976. — viii,119p : ill, map ; 24cm.
Bibl.: p.117-119.
ISBN 0-85479-601-0 Pbk : £1.50
(B77-07787)

222'.11 — Bible. Old Testament. Genesis. Noah's ark. *Stories for children*
Bull, Geoffrey Taylor. I wish I lived when Noah did / by Geoffrey T. Bull ; illustrated by Chris Higham. — London : Pickering and Inglis, 1977. — [20]p : col ill ; 21cm. — (Far-away books)
Text, col. ill. on lining papers.
ISBN 0-7208-2244-0 : £0.60
(B77-27662)

222'.11'0924 — Bible. Old Testament. Genesis. Joseph. *Stories for children*
Bull, Geoffrey Taylor. I wish I lived when Joseph did / by Geoffrey T. Bull ; illustrated by Chris Higham. — London [etc.] : Pickering and Inglis, 1977. — [20]p : col ill ; 21cm. — (Far-away books)
Text, col. ill. on lining papers.
ISBN 0-7208-2245-9 : £0.60
(B77-27663)

222'.12'07 — Bible. Old Testament. Exodus. *Commentaries*
Dobson, John H. A guide to Exodus / [by] John H. Dobson. — London : S.P.C.K., 1977. — xiv,201p : ill, map, plan, ports ; 22cm. — (Theological Education Fund. Study guides ; 13)
'Published in association with the United Society for Christian Literature ...'. — Bibl.: p.xiii. — Index.
ISBN 0-281-02951-2 Pbk : £2.95
(B77-20005)

Knight, George Angus Fulton. Theology as narration : a commentary on the Book of Exodus / [by] George A.F. Knight. — Edinburgh (33 Montgomery St., Edinburgh) : Handsel Press Ltd, 1976. — xiv,209p ; 23cm.
ISBN 0-905312-01-5 : £5.00
(B77-12844)

222'.14'077 — Bible. Old Testament. Numbers. English. New English. *Texts with commentaries*
[**Bible**. Old Testament. Numbers. *English. New English. 1976].* Numbers / commentary by John Sturdy. — Cambridge [etc.] : Cambridge University Press, 1976. — x,252p : maps ; 21cm. — (The Cambridge Bible commentary, New English Bible)
Index.
ISBN 0-521-08632-9 : £7.50
ISBN 0-521-09776-2 Pbk : £2.95
(B77-02740)

222'.15'077 — Bible. Old Testament. Deuteronomy. *Texts with commentaries*
Craigie, Peter C. The book of Deuteronomy / by Peter C. Craigie. — London [etc.] : Hodder and Stoughton, 1976. — 424p ; 23cm. — (The new international commentary on the Old Testament)
Also published: Grand Rapids : Eerdmans, 1976. — Index. — Includes the text of Deuteronomy.
ISBN 0-340-21509-7 : £5.75
(B77-14542)

222'.16'06 — Ten Commandmants. *Expositions*
Packer, James Innell. The Ten Commandments / [by] J.I. Packer. — Basingstoke (The Vyne, Sherborne St John, Basingstoke, Hants.) : Chandos Press ; Abingdon : Marcham Books, [1977]. — [20]p ; 22cm.
ISBN 0-905681-01-0 Sd : £0.30
(B77-14039)

222'.32'0924 — Bible. Old Testament. Judges. Gideon. *Stories for children*
Bull, Geoffrey Taylor. I wish I lived when Gideon did / by Geoffrey T. Bull ; illustrated by Chris Higham. — London [etc.] : Pickering and Inglis, 1977. — [20]p : col ill ; 21cm. — (Far-away books)
Text, col. ill. on lining papers.
ISBN 0-7208-2246-7 : £0.60
(B77-27664)

222'.4'06 — Bible. Old Testament. Samuel. *Topics for discussion groups*
Pogue, Victor Charles. Who measures the ruler? / [by] V.C. Pogue. — Edinburgh : Church of Scotland, Department of Education, 1976. — 42p : ill, map ; 21cm.
ISBN 0-7152-0338-x Pbk : £0.40
Also classified at 222'.5'06
(B77-09484)

222'.43'0922 — Bible. Old Testament. Samuel 1. David & Goliath. *Stories for children*
Bull, Geoffrey Taylor. I wish I lived when David did / by Geoffrey T. Bull ; illustrated by Chris Higham. — London [etc.] : Pickering and Inglis, 1977. — [20]p : col ill ; 21cm. — (Far-away books)
Text, col. ill. on lining papers.
ISBN 0-7208-2247-5 : £0.60
(B77-27665)

222'.5'06 — Bible. Old Testament. Kings. *Topics for discussion groups*
Pogue, Victor Charles. Who measures the ruler? / [by] V.C. Pogue. — Edinburgh : Church of Scotland, Department of Education, 1976. — 42p : ill, map ; 21cm.
ISBN 0-7152-0338-x Pbk : £0.40
Primary classification 222'.4'06
(B77-09484)

222'.54'077 — Bible. Old Testament. Kings 2. English. New English. *Texts with commentaries*
[**Bible**. Old Testament. Kings 2. *English. New English. 1976].* The second book of Kings / commentary by J. Robinson. — Cambridge [etc.] : Cambridge University Press, 1976. — xii,256p : maps ; 21cm. — (The Cambridge Bible commentary, New English Bible)
Index.
ISBN 0-521-08646-9 : £8.25
ISBN 0-521-09774-6 Pbk : £3.50
(B77-02741)

222'.6'0895694 — Bible. Old Testament. Chronicles. Special subjects: Israel
Williamson, H G M. Israel in the books of Chronicles / [by] H.G.M. Williamson. — Cambridge [etc.] : Cambridge University Press, 1977. — xi,170p ; 23cm.
Bibl.: p.141-154. — Index.
ISBN 0-521-21305-3 : £7.50
(B77-29156)

222'.9'09505 — Bible. Old Testament. Esther. *Stories for children*
Bull, Geoffrey Taylor. I wish I lived when Esther did / by Geoffrey T. Bull ; illustrated by Chris Higham. — London [etc.] : Pickering and Inglis, 1977. — [20]p : col ill ; 21cm. — (Far-away books)
Text, col. ill. on lining papers.
ISBN 0-7208-2248-3 : £0.60
(B77-26773)

223'.05'9162 — Bible. Old Testament. Poetical books. Irish. *Texts*
[**Bible**. Old Testament. Hagiographa. *Irish. Selections. 1976].* Leabhair na hEagna / arna aistriú ón Eabhrais agus ón nGréigis faoi threoir ó easpaig na hEireann. — Má Nuad [i.e. Maynooth] ([Maynooth, Co. Kildare]) : [Maynooth College], 1976. — 241p ; 22cm. — (Bíobla Mhá Nuad)
Contents: Job - Proverbs - Ecclesiastes - Wisdom of Solomon - Ecclesiasticus.
£2.00
Pbk : £1.50
(B77-08746)

223'.1'06 — Bible. Old Testament. Job. *Expositions*
Job, John B. Where is my father? : studies in the book of Job / [by] John Job. — London : Epworth Press, 1977. — 128p ; 22cm.
Index.
ISBN 0-7162-0291-3 Pbk : £1.50
(B77-33038)

223'.2 — Bible. Old Testament. Psalms CI-CL. English. New English. *Texts with commentaries*
[Bible. Old Testament. Psalms CI-CL. *English. New English. 1977].* Psalms 101-150 / commentary by J.W. Rogerson and J.W. McKay. — Cambridge [etc.] : Cambridge University Press, 1977. — xi,193p ; 21cm. — (The Cambridge Bible commentary, New English Bible)
Bibl.: p.190. — Index.
ISBN 0-521-21465-3 : £7.90
ISBN 0-521-29162-3 Pbk : £2.95
(B77-22334)

223'.2 — Bible. Old Testament. Psalms I-L. English. New English. *Texts with commentaries*
[Bible. Old Testament. Psalms I-L. *English. New English. 1977].* Psalms 1-50 / commentary by J.W. Rogerson and J.W. McKay. — Cambridge [etc.] : Cambridge University Press, 1977. — xi, 243p ; 21cm. — (The Cambridge Bible commentary, New English Bible)
Bibl.: p.240. — Index.
ISBN 0-521-21463-7 : £8.50
ISBN 0-521-29160-7 Pbk : £3.20
(B77-22335)

223'.2 — Bible. Old Testament. Psalms LI-C. English. New English. *Texts with commentaries*
[Bible. Old Testament. Psalms LI-C. *English. New English. 1977].* Psalms 51-100 / commentary by J.W. Rogerson and J.W. McKay. — Cambridge [etc.] : Cambridge University Press, 1977. — xi,236p ; 21cm. — (The Cambridge Bible commentary, New English Bible)
Bibl.: p.231. — Index.
ISBN 0-521-21464-5 : £8.50
ISBN 0-521-29161-5 Pbk : £3.20
(B77-22336)

223'.2'052 — Bible. Old Testament. Psalms. English. Frost and others. *Texts*
[Bible. Old Testament. Psalms. *English. Frost and others. 1977].* The Psalms / a new translation for worship [prepared by David L. Frost and a panel of Hebrew and Biblical scholars]. — London : Collins Liturgical, 1977. — 254p ; 19cm.
'Published in cooperation with the Church Information Office'.
ISBN 0-00-599550-7 : £1.95
ISBN 0-00-599585-x Pbk : £1.25
(B77-24682)

[Bible. Old Testament. Psalms. *English. Frost and others. 1977].* The Psalms / a new translation for worship [prepared by David L. Frost and a panel of Hebrew and Biblical scholars]. — [Pointed ed.]. — London : Collins Liturgical, 1977. — 269p ; 19cm.
'Pointed for singing to Anglican chant'. — 'Published in cooperation with the Church Information Office'.
ISBN 0-00-599546-9 : £1.99
ISBN 0-00-599584-1 Pbk : £1.35
(B77-24683)

223'.2'052 — Bible. Old Testament. Psalms. English. Levi. *Texts*
[Bible. Old Testament. Psalms. *English. Levi. 1977].* The psalms / translated [from the Hebrew] by Peter Levi ; with an introduction by Nicholas de Lange. — Harmondsworth [etc.] : Penguin, 1976[i.e.1977]. — xxvii,239p ; 19cm. — (The Penguin classics)
Bibl.: p.xxvii.
ISBN 0-14-044319-3 Pbk : £0.95
(B77-14543)

223'.2'05201 — Bible. Old Testament. Psalms. English. Coverdale. *Texts*
[Bible. Old Testament. Psalms. *English. Coverdale. 1977].* The psalms of David. — Folkestone : Dawson, 1977. — 152p ; 35cm.
'A Deighton Bell Edition' - p.4. — Limited ed. of 315 numbered copies, of which 20 are numbered I-XX and are bound in full vellum. — '... the translation ... is the work of Miles Coverdale, taken not from the Coverdale Bible of 1535, but his revision for the Great Bible of 1539' - p.5.
£150.00
(B77-32384)

223'.2'06 — Bible. Old Testament. Psalms. *Expositions*
Stradling, Leslie Edward. Praying the Psalms / [by] Leslie E. Stradling. — London : S.P.C.K., 1977. — vii,119p ; 19cm.
Bibl.: p.119.
ISBN 0-281-02960-1 Pbk : £1.50
(B77-23979)

223'.2'07 — Bible. Old Testament. Psalms. *Commentaries*
Blaiklock, Edward Musgrave. Commentary on the Psalms / [by] E.M. Blaiklock. — London : Scripture Union.
In 2 vols.
Vol.1 : Psalms for living, Psalms 1-72. — 1977. — 156p ; 21cm.
ISBN 0-85421-520-4 Pbk : Unpriced
(B77-29916)

Vol.2 : Psalms for worship, Psalms 73-150. — 1977. — 144p ; 21cm.
ISBN 0-85421-521-2 Pbk : Unpriced
(B77-29917)

224'.06 — Bible. Old Testament. Prophets. *Expositions*
Heaton, Eric William. The Old Testament prophets / [by] E.W. Heaton. — [New and revised ed.]. — London : Darton, Longman and Todd, 1977. — ix,178p ; 22cm.
Previous ed.: Harmondsworth : Penguin, 1958. — Bibl.: p.151-158. — Index.
ISBN 0-232-51361-9 Pbk : £2.95
(B77-23094)

224'.5'077 — Bible. Old Testament. Daniel. English. New English. *Texts with commentaries*
[Bible. Old Testament. Daniel. *English. New English. 1976].* The book of Daniel / commentary by Raymond Hammer. — Cambridge [etc.] : Cambridge University Press, 1976. — xii,127p : map ; 21cm. — (The Cambridge Bible commentary, New English Bible)
Index.
ISBN 0-521-08654-x : £4.95
ISBN 0-521-09765-7 Pbk : £2.20
(B77-02742)

224'.5'09505 — Bible. Old Testament. Daniel. *Stories for children*
Bull, Geoffrey Taylor. I wish I lived when Daniel did / by Geoffrey T. Bull ; illustrated by Chris Higham. — London [etc.] : Pickering and Inglis, 1977. — [20]p : col ill ; 21cm. — (Far-away books)
Text, col. ill. on lining papers.
ISBN 0-7208-2249-1 : £0.60
(B77-27666)

225 — NEW TESTAMENT
225 — Bible. New Testament. *Critical studies*
Machen, John Gresham. The New Testament : an introduction to its literature and history / [by] J. Gresham Machen ; edited by W. John Cook. — Edinburgh [etc.] : Banner of Truth Trust, 1976. — [1],386p,plate : col map ; 23cm.

Originally published in periodical form as 'The literature and history of New Testament times. Student's text book, and, Teacher's manual'.
ISBN 0-85151-240-2 : £2.75
(B77-02743)

225 — Bible. New Testament. *Jewish viewpoints*
Sandmel, Samuel. A Jewish understanding of the New Testament / by Samuel Sandmel. — Augmented ed. — London : S.P.C.K., 1977. — iii-xxxiv,336p ; 22cm.
This ed. originally published: New York : Ktav Pub. House, 1974. — Bibl.: p.322-325. — Index.
ISBN 0-281-02987-3 Pbk : £4.75
(B77-26101)

225 — Bible. New Testament. *Secondary school texts*
Edwards, James, *b.1910.* The New Testament and its background / by James Edwards ; illustrated by Mary Camidge and Mary Sims. — Poole : Blandford Press.
In 3 vols.
Book 1 : Jesus of Palestine : people, work and customs. — 1977. — 96p : ill, maps, plan ; 22cm.
Index.
ISBN 0-7137-3023-4 Pbk : £1.20(non-net)
(B77-10140)

Book 2 : Jesus, Son of God : the Messiah and His message. — 1977. — 96p : ill, map ; 22cm.

Index.
ISBN 0-7137-3024-2 Pbk : £1.20(non-net)
(B77-10141)

Book 3 : Jesus Victor! : the Acts of the Apostles. — 1977. — 96p : ill, maps ; 22cm.
Index.
ISBN 0-7137-3025-0 Pbk : £1.20(non-net)
(B77-10142)

225 — Bible. New Testament. Theology. Related to Old Testament theology. Theories, to 1975
Baker, D L. Two Testaments, one Bible : a study of some modern solutions to the theological problem of the relationship between the Old and New Testaments / by D.L. Baker. — Leicester : Inter-Varsity Press, 1976. — 554p ; 22cm.
Bibl.: p.391-535. — Index.
ISBN 0-85111-500-4 Pbk : £4.95
Primary classification 221
(B77-05191)

225'.01'4 — Bible. New Testament. Words
Moulton, Harold Keeling. The challenge of the concordance : some New Testament words studied in depth / [by] Harold K. Moulton. — London : Bagster, 1977. — xv,288p ; 22cm.
Originally published: Madras : Christian Literature Society for the Senate of Serampore College, 1967. — Index.
ISBN 0-85150-124-9 Pbk : £3.75
(B77-16713)

225'.076 — Bible. New Testament. *Questions & answers. Secondary school texts. Cards*
Horton, Robert Harold. Birth of the Christian Church / [by] Robert H. Horton. — [London] : Edward Arnold, [1976]. — Case : ill, maps ; 22cm.
Thirty six workcards ([72]sides ; 17x21cm). — With answers to crossword puzzles.
ISBN 0-7131-0094-x : £3.20
(B77-27667)

225.2 — Bible. New Testament. *Concordances*
Modern concordance to the New Testament / edited and revised following all current English translations of the New Testament by Michael Darton. — London : Darton, Longman and Todd, 1976. — xxi,788p ; 29cm.
In slip case. — Key to signs, symbols and abbreviations (sheet, 22x15cm) as insert. — 'Based on the French "Concordance de la Bible, Nouveau Testament" produced under the aegis of the Association de la Concordance française de la Bible'. Paris : Éditions du Cerf-Desclée De Brouwer, 1970. — Index (English and Greek).
ISBN 0-232-51330-9 : £25.00
(B77-02744)

225.4 — Bible. New Testament. Versions, to 1000. *Textual criticisms*
Metzger, Bruce Manning. The early versions of the New Testament : their origin, transmission and limitations / by Bruce M. Metzger. — Oxford : Clarendon Press, 1977. — xix,498p ; 22cm.
Index.
ISBN 0-19-826170-5 : £10.00 : CIP rev.
(B77-10143)

225.4'8 — Bible. New Testament. Greek. Words: Pneuma
Isaacs, Marie E. The concept of spirit : a study of pneuma in Hellenistic Judaism and its bearing on the New Testament / by Marie E. Isaacs. — London (11 Cavendish Sq., W1M 0AN) : Heythrop College, 1976. — [4],xi,186p ; 21cm. — (Heythrop monographs ; 1 ISSN 0309-4723)
Bibl.: p.159-169. — Index.
ISBN 0-905764-00-5 Pbk : £3.50
Also classified at 229'.04'8
(B77-13493)

225.4'8'014 — Bible. New Testament. Greek. Linguistic aspects
Rienecker, Fritz. A linguistic key to the Greek New Testament / [by] Fritz Rienecker ; translated, with additions and revisions, from the German ... ; edited by Cleon L. Rogers, Jr. — London : Bagster.
Translation and revision of: 'Sprachlicher Schlüssel zum griechischen Neuen Testament'. Bearb. 13.Aufl. Giessen, etc. : Brunne, 1970.
Vol.1 : Matthew through Acts. — 1977. — [5], xiv,345p ; 23cm.
Bibl.: p.v-xiii.
ISBN 0-85150-117-6 : £10.95
(B77-17893)

225.5'2 — Bible. New Testament. English. Barclay. *Texts*
[Bible. New Testament. *English. Barclay. 1976].* The New Testament / a new translation by William Barclay. — [London] : Fontana, 1976. — 576p ; 18cm.
This translation originally published: in 2 vols. London : Collins, 1968-69.
ISBN 0-00-624269-3 Pbk : £0.95
(B77-13494)

225.6 — Bible. New Testament. Interpretation
New Testament interpretation : essays on principles and methods / edited by I. Howard Marshall. — Exeter : Paternoster Press, 1977. — 406p ; 23cm.
Bibl.: p.369-388. — Index.
ISBN 0-85364-196-x : Unpriced : CIP rev.
ISBN 0-85364-204-4 Pbk : £6.00
(B77-07049)

225.7 — Bible. New Testament. *Commentaries*
Barclay, William, *b.1907.* The men, the meaning, the message of the books : a series of New Testament studies / [by] William Barclay. — Edinburgh : St Andrew Press, 1976. — vii, 149p ; 19cm.
'These studies were first published as a series of monthly articles in the Church of Scotland magazine, "Life and Work"' - cover.
ISBN 0-7152-0254-5 Pbk : £1.25
(B77-03351)

225.7'7 — Bible. New Testament. English. Barclay. *Texts with commentaries*
Barclay, William, *b.1907.* The daily study Bible / [by William Barclay]. — Revised ed. — Edinburgh : St Andrew Press.
In 17 vols.
The Acts of the Apostles. — 1976. — x,195p ; 18cm.
Previous ed.: i.e. 2nd ed., 1955. — Bibl.: p.195. — Includes the text of The Acts of the Apostles.
ISBN 0-7152-0293-6 : £4.00
ISBN 0-7152-0276-6 Pbk : £1.30
(B77-00013)

Barclay, William, *b.1907.* The daily study Bible / [by William Barclay]. — Revised ed. — Edinburgh : St Andrew Press.
In 17 vols.
The letters to the Galatians and Ephesians. — 1976. — xv,187p ; 18cm.
Previous ed.: i.e. Combined ed., 1958. — Bibl.: p.187. — Includes the text of the Epistles.
ISBN 0-7152-0296-0 : £4.00
ISBN 0-7152-0279-0 Pbk : £1.30
(B77-00600)

225.8 — Bible. New Testament. Special subjects: Testimony
Trites, Allison A. The New Testament concept of witness / [by] Allison A. Trites. — Cambridge [etc.] : Cambridge University Press, 1977. — x, 294p ; 23cm. — (Society for New Testament Studies. Monograph series ; 31)
Bibl.: p.240-254. — Index.
ISBN 0-521-21015-1 : £12.00
(B77-14544)

225.9'24 — Bible. New Testament. Paul, Saint
Bruce, Frederick Fyvie. Paul : apostle of the free spirit / [by] F.F. Bruce. — Exeter : Paternoster Press, 1977. — 491p,[16]p of plates : ill, col map(on lining papers) ; 24cm.
Bibl.: p.476-479. — Index.
ISBN 0-85364-209-5 : £9.60 : CIP rev.
(B77-24684)

225.9'5 — Bible. New Testament. Historicity
Robinson, John Arthur Thomas. Can we trust the New Testament? / [by] John A.T. Robinson. — London [etc.] : Mowbrays, 1977. — 142p ; 18cm.
Bibl.: p.135-137. — Index.
ISBN 0-264-66081-1 Pbk : £0.75
(B77-06455)

226'.04'7 — Bible. New Testament. Gospels. Latin. Lindisfarne Gospels. Glosses in Old English. *Texts with commentaries*
Boyd, W J P. Aldred's marginalia : explanatory comments in the Lindisfarne Gospels / by W.J.P. Boyd. — [Exeter] : University of Exeter, 1975. — x,62p ; 22cm. — (Exeter medieval English texts and studies)
Index.
ISBN 0-85989-036-8 Pbk : £5.00
(B77-29157)

226'.05'2 — Bible. New Testament. Gospels. English. Marrow. *Texts*
[Bible. New Testament. Gospels. *English. Marrow. 1977].* The four Gospels / newly translated from the Greek by Norman Marrow. — Luton ([Crescent Rd, Luton LU2 0AG]) : White Crescent Press Ltd, 1977. — 196p ; 21cm.
'For the most part ... [the translator has] followed the Greek text of the British and Foreign Bible Society's Centenary Edition ...' - Acknowledgements.
ISBN 0-9505565-0-5 Pbk : £1.80
(B77-23095)

226'.05'2 — Bible. New Testament. Gospels. Scouse. Williams-Shaw. *Texts*
[Bible. New Testament. Gospels. *Scouse. Williams-Shaw. 1977].* The Gospels in Scouse / [by] Dick Williams and Frank Shaw ; illustrated by Derek Alder ; with an introduction by David Sheppard. — Revised ed. — London [etc.] : White Lion Publishers, 1977. — 125p : ill ; 23cm. — ([Gospels in dialect])
Previous ed.: Liverpool : Gear Press, 1967.
ISBN 0-7285-0007-8 : £2.75
(B77-17276)

226'.07 — Bible. New Testament. Gospels. *Commentaries*
Cardenal, Ernesto. Love in practice : the Gospel in Solentiname / [by] Ernesto Cardenal ; translated [from the Spanish] by Donald D. Walsh. — London : Search Press, 1977. — x, 265p ; 23cm.
This translation originally published: Maryknoll, N.Y. : Orbis Books, 1976. — Translation of: 'El Evangelio en Solentiname'. Salamanca : Ediciones Sígueme, 1975.
ISBN 0-85532-368-x : £4.95
(B77-17277)

226'.09'22 — Bible. New Testament. Gospels. *Biographies*
Griffith, Leonard. Gospel characters : the personalities around Jesus / by Leonard Griffith. — London [etc.] : Hodder and Stoughton, 1976. — 192p ; 22cm. — (Ecclesia books)
Also published: Grand Rapids, Mich. : Eerdmans, 1976.
ISBN 0-340-20555-5 Pbk : £2.75
(B77-08747)

226'.09'22 — Bible. New Testament. Gospels. Characters. *Stories, anecdotes*
Patrick, Sam. Jesus loved them / by Sam Patrick and Omar Garrison. — London : Oliphants, 1977. — [8],87p : ill ; 24cm.
Originally published: Englewood Cliffs : Prentice-Hall ; London : Bailey and Swinfen, 1957.
ISBN 0-551-00765-6 Pbk : £1.75
(B77-16174)

226'.09'5050222 — Bible. New Testament. Gospels. *Stories, anecdotes. Illustrations*
Hoth, Iva. The real Jesus. — London : Scripture Union, 1976. — 135p : col ill ; 23cm.
Author: Iva Hoth. — Illustrator: Andre Le Blanc. — Originally published: as 'Jesus : Matthew-John', vol.5 of 'The picture Bible for all ages'. Guildford : Lutterworth Press ; London : Scripture Union, 1974.
ISBN 0-85421-441-0 Pbk : £1.25
(B77-11545)

Thivollier, P. Jesus and his message of liberation : the Gospel told in picture strips / text and lay-out P. Thivollier ; illustrations P. Rousseau ; translation [from the French] J. Selby-Lowndes. — London : Bible Reading Fellowship, 1976. — [2],119p : chiefly col ill, col maps ; 29cm.
Originally published: in French. Paris : Editions Chemineinents, 1976.
ISBN 0-900164-39-5 Pbk : £1.50
(B77-30953)

226'.2 — Bible. New Testament. Matthew V, 14-16. *Stories for children*
Farncombe, Anne. Reuben and the olive harvest / written and illustrated by Anne Farncombe. — Guildford [etc.] : Lutterworth Press, 1977. — [24]p : ill(some col) ; 25cm. — (Farncombe, Anne. Stories of Bible times)
ISBN 0-7188-2209-9 Sd : £0.50
(B77-32385)

226'.2 — Bible. New Testament. Matthew XIII. Parables. *Commentaries*
Kingsbury, Jack Dean. The parables of Jesus in Matthew 13 : a study in redaction-criticism / [by] J.D. Kingsbury. — London : S.P.C.K., 1977. — xii,180p ; 22cm.
Originally published: 1969. — Bibl.: p.167-170. — Index. — Includes the text of the chapter.
ISBN 0-281-02974-1 Pbk : £2.95
(B77-10144)

226'.2'07 — Bible. New Testament. Matthew. *Commentaries*
Morgan, George Campbell. The Gospel according to Matthew / by G. Campbell Morgan. — London : Marshall, Morgan and Scott, 1976. — 3-321p ; 22cm. — (Marshall's study library)
Facsimile reprint of: 1st ed. New York : Revell, 1929 ; London : Oliphants, 1946.
ISBN 0-551-05548-0 Pbk : £2.95
(B77-15074)

226'.2'077 — Bible. New Testament. Matthew. English. Today's English. *Texts with commentaries*
[Bible. New Testament. Matthew. *English. Today's English. 1976].* Good news in Matthew : Matthew in Today's English Version / introduced [with commentary] by Pierson Parker. — [London] : Fontana [for] the Bible Reading Fellowship, 1976. — 285p : ill, maps ; 18cm.
ISBN 0-00-623927-7 Pbk : £0.95
(B77-06456)

226'.3'06 — Bible. New Testament. Mark. *Expositions*
Richards, John Richards. Jesus, son of God and son of man : a Marcan study / [by] J.R. Richards. — Penarth (Education and Communications Centre, Woodland Place, Penarth, [S. Glam.] CF6 2EX) : Church in Wales Publications, [1973]. — 147p ; 21cm. — (Pantyfedwen Trust lectures ; 1972)
Pbk : £0.90
(B77-17278)

226'.3'07 — Bible. New Testament. Mark. *Commentaries*
Morgan, George Campbell. The Gospel according to Mark / by G. Campbell Morgan. — London : Marshall, Morgan and Scott, 1976. — [1],350p ; 22cm.
Facsimile reprint of: 1st ed., New York : Fleming H. Revell, 1927 ; London : Oliphants, 1947.
ISBN 0-551-05549-9 Pbk : £2.95
(B77-14040)

226'.4 — Bible. New Testament. Luke. Widow's mite. *Stories for children*
Farncombe, Anne. Philip visits the temple / written and illustrated by Anne Farncombe. — Guildford [etc.] : Lutterworth Press, 1977. — [24]p : ill(some col) ; 25cm. — (Farncombe, Anne. Stories of Bible times)
ISBN 0-7188-2207-2 Sd : £0.50
(B77-32386)

226'.4 — Bible. New Testament. Luke XV, 8-10. *Stories for children*
Farncombe, Anne. Sarah and the search / written and illustrated by Anne Farncombe. — Guildford [etc.] : Lutterworth Press, 1977. — [24]p : ill(some col) ; 25cm. — (Farncombe, Anne. Stories of Bible times)
ISBN 0-7188-2208-0 Sd : £0.50
(B77-33585)

226'.4'066 — Bible. New Testament. Luke. *Exegetical studies. Festschriften*
Studies in Luke-Acts : essays presented in honor of Paul Schubert, Buckingham Professor of New Testament Criticism and Interpretation at Yale University / edited by Leander E. Keck, J. Louis Martyn. — London : S.P.C.K., 1976. — 316p ; 22cm.
Originally published: Nashville : Abingdon Press, 1966 ; London : S.P.C.K., 1968.
ISBN 0-281-02969-5 Pbk : £3.50
Also classified at 226'.6'066
(B77-10145)

226'.4'07 — Bible. New Testament. Luke. *Commentaries*
Morgan, George Campbell. The Gospel according to Luke / by G. Campbell Morgan. — London : Marshall, Morgan and Scott, 1976. — 284p ; 22cm. — (Marshall's study library)
Facsimile reprint of: 1st ed. New York : Revell, 1931 ; London : Oliphants, 1947.
ISBN 0-551-05550-2 Pbk : £2.95
(B77-15075)

226'.5 — Bible. New Testament. John XIII-XVII. *Commentaries*
Bowen, George. Love revealed : meditations on chapters 13-17 of the Gospel by John / [by] George Bowen. — New British ed. [i.e. 1st ed. reprinted]. — Stoke-on-Trent (247 Newcastle St., Burslem, Stoke-on-Trent) : M.O.V.E. Press, 1977. — 263p ; 19cm.
Originally published: Edinburgh : David Douglas, 1885. — Includes the text of the chapters.
Pbk : £1.50
(B77-28365)

226'.5'07 — Bible. New Testament. John. *Commentaries*
Morgan, George Campbell. The Gospel according to John / by G. Campbell Morgan. — London : Marshall, Morgan and Scott, 1976. — 333p ; 22cm. — (Marshall's study library)
Facsimile reprint of: 1st ed. New York : Revell ; London : Marshall, Morgan and Scott, 1933.
ISBN 0-551-05551-0 Pbk : £2.95
(B77-15076)

226'.6'066 — Bible. New Testament. Acts. *Exegetical studies. Festschriften*
Studies in Luke-Acts : essays presented in honor of Paul Schubert, Buckingham Professor of New Testament Criticism and Interpretation at Yale University / edited by Leander E. Keck, J. Louis Martyn. — London : S.P.C.K., 1976. — 316p ; 22cm.
Originally published: Nashville : Abingdon Press, 1966 ; London : S.P.C.K., 1968.
ISBN 0-281-02969-5 Pbk : £3.50
Primary classification 226'.4'066
(B77-10145)

226'.6'07 — Bible. New Testament. Acts. *Commentaries*
Morgan, George Campbell. The Acts of the Apostles / [by] G. Campbell Morgan. — London : Pickering and Inglis, 1976. — 429p ; 18cm.
Originally published: New York : F.H. Revell Co., 1924 ; London : Pickering and Inglis, 1946.
ISBN 0-7208-0387-x Pbk : £1.80
(B77-07050)

226'.7 — Christ. Miracles: Feeding of the five thousand. *Stories for children*
Blyton, Enid. The boy with the loaves and fishes. [New ed.] ; [and, The man who stopped to help] / [by] Enid Blyton ; illustrated by Susan Hunter. — Leicester : Knight Books, 1976. — 96p ; 18cm.
This ed. of 'The boy with the loaves and fishes' originally published: London : Lutterworth Press, 1955 - 'The man who stopped to help' originally published: London : Lutterworth Press, 1965.
ISBN 0-340-18734-4 Pbk : £0.45
Also classified at 226'.8
(B77-06457)

Farncombe, Anne. Danny's picnic / written and illustrated by Anne Farncombe. — Guildford [etc.] : Lutterworth Press, 1977. — [24]p : ill(some col) ; 25cm. — (Farncombe, Anne. Stories of Bible times)
ISBN 0-7188-2206-4 Sd : £0.50
(B77-32387)

226'.7 — Christ. Miracles: Raising of Jairus' daughter. *Stories for children*
Blyton, Enid. The little girl at Capernaum. [New ed.] ; [and, The boy who came back] / [by] Enid Blyton ; illustrated by Susan Hunter. — Leicester : Knight Books, 1976. — 93p : ill ; 18cm.
This ed. of 'The little girl at Capernaum' originally published: London : Lutterworth Press, 1955 - 'The boy who came back' originally published: London : Lutterworth Press, 1966.
ISBN 0-340-18733-6 Pbk : £0.45
Also classified at 226'.8
(B77-06458)

226'.8 — Bible. New Testament. Parables: Good Samaritan. *Stories for children*
Blyton, Enid. The boy with the loaves and fishes. [New ed.] ; [and, The man who stopped to help] / [by] Enid Blyton ; illustrated by Susan Hunter. — Leicester : Knight Books, 1976. — 96p ; 18cm.
This ed. of 'The boy with the loaves and fishes' originally published: London : Lutterworth Press, 1955 - 'The man who stopped to help' originally published: London : Lutterworth Press, 1965.
ISBN 0-340-18734-4 Pbk : £0.45
Primary classification 226'.7
(B77-06457)

226'.8 — Bible. New Testament. Parables: Prodigal son. *Stories for children*
Blyton, Enid. The little girl at Capernaum. [New ed.] ; [and, The boy who came back] / [by] Enid Blyton ; illustrated by Susan Hunter. — Leicester : Knight Books, 1976. — 93p : ill ; 18cm.
This ed. of 'The little girl at Capernaum' originally published: London : Lutterworth Press, 1955 - 'The boy who came back' originally published: London : Lutterworth Press, 1966.
ISBN 0-340-18733-6 Pbk : £0.45
Primary classification 226'.7
(B77-06458)

226'.8'06 — Bible. New Testament. Parables. *Expositions*
Capel, Evelyn Francis. The timeless storyteller / by Evelyn Francis Capel. — London (51 Queen Caroline St., Hammersmith, W6 9OL) : Temple Lodge Press, 1975. — 152p ; 22cm.
ISBN 0-904693-00-7 Pbk : £1.00
(B77-03905)

226'.8'063 — Bible. New Testament. Parables. Hermeneutics
Evans, Christopher Francis. Parable and dogma / by C.F. Evans. — London : Athlone Press, 1977. — 21p ; 22cm. — (The Ethel M. Wood lecture ; 1976)
'... delivered before the University of London on 24 February 1976'.
ISBN 0-485-14320-8 Sd : £0.75
(B77-15077)

226'.8'09505 — Bible. New Testament. Parables. *Stories for children*
Ralph, Margaret. Stories Jesus told / stories from the New Testament retold by Margaret Ralph ; illustrated by Gordon King. — London : Scripture Union ; Maidenhead : Purnell, 1977. — [28]p : col ill ; 27x13cm. — (A giraffe book)
Col. ill., text on lining papers.
ISBN 0-85421-508-5 : £0.75
ISBN 0-361-03971-9 (Purnell) : £0.75
(B77-33586)

226'.9'06 — Sermon on the Mount. *Expositions*
Pink, Arthur Walkington. An exposition of the Sermon on the mount / by Arthur W. Pink. — Welwyn : Evangelical Press, 1977. — 453p ; 21cm.
Cover title: The Sermon on the mount. — Originally published: Swengel, Pa : Bible Truth Depot, 1950. — Index.
ISBN 0-85234-083-4 Pbk : £2.95
(B77-28366)

227'.06'6 — Bible. New Testament. Epistles of Paul. *Exegetical studies*
Bruce, Frederick Fyvie. Paul and Jesus / [by] F.F. Bruce. — London : S.P.C.K., 1977. — 87p ; 22cm.
'... contains a revised version of the six lectures delivered at Ontario Bible College's annual Thomas F. Staley Academic Lecture Series' - Preface.
ISBN 0-281-02966-0 Pbk : £1.50
Primary classification 232.9'54
(B77-09487)

Ridderbos, Herman Nicolaas. Paul, an outline of his theology / [by] Herman Ridderbos ; translated [from the Dutch] by John Richard de Witt. — London : S.P.C.K., 1977. — 3-587p ; 24cm.
This translation originally published: Grand Rapids : Eerdmans, 1975. — Translation of: 'Paulus, ontwerp van zijn theologie'. Kampen : J. Kok, 1966. — Bibl.: p.10. — Index.
ISBN 0-281-02999-7 : £8.95
(B77-22337)

227'.07'7 — Bible. New Testament. Epistles. English. Today's English. *Texts with commentaries*
[**Bible**. New Testament. Epistles. *English. Today's English. 1976].* Good news in the early Church : 1 & 2 Timothy, Titus, James, 1 & 2 Peter, 1,2, & 3 John and Jude in Today's English Version / introduced [with commentary] by Martin E. Marty. — [London] : Fontana [for] the Bible Reading Fellowship, 1976. — 221p : ill, maps ; 18cm.
ISBN 0-00-624437-8 Pbk : £0.95
(B77-06459)

227'.2'077 — Bible. New Testament. Corinthians. English. Today's English. *Texts with commentaries*
[**Bible**. New Testament. Corinthians. *English. Today's English. 1977].* Good news in Corinthians I & II : Paul's first and second letters to the Corinthians in Today's English version / introduced [with commentary] by William Neil. — [London] : Fontana [for] the Bible Reading Fellowship, 1977. — 126p : ill, map ; 18cm.
ISBN 0-00-624031-3 Pbk : £0.95
(B77-32388)

227'.5 — Bible. New Testament. Ephesians VI. *Expositions*
Lloyd-Jones, David Martyn. The Christian warfare : an exposition of Ephesians 6, 10 to 13 / [by] D.M. Lloyd-Jones. — Edinburgh [etc.] : Banner of Truth Trust, 1976. — 373p ; 23cm.
ISBN 0-85151-243-7 : £3.00
(B77-03352)

227'.87'06 — Bible. New Testament. Hebrews. *Expositions*
Thomas, J J A. The letter to the Hebrews, and other addresses / by J.J.A. Thomas. — Penarth (Education and Communications Centre, Woodlands Rd, Penarth, S. Glam. CF6 2EX) : Church in Wales Publications, 1976. — 48p ; 21cm.
Pbk : £1.00
Also classified at 252'.03
(B77-17894)

227'.87'077 — Bible. New Testament. Hebrews. English. Today's English. *Texts with commentaries*
[**Bible**. New Testament. Hebrews. *English. Today's English. 1976].* Good news in Hebrews : the Letter to the Hebrews in Today's English Version / introduced [with commentary] by Thomas Corbishley. — [London] : Fontana [for] the Bible Reading Fellowship, 1976. — 124,[2]p : ill, map ; 18cm.
Bibl. ; p.8.
ISBN 0-00-623747-9 Pbk : £0.65
(B77-06460)

227'.91'077 — Bible. New Testament. James. *Texts with commentaries*
Johnstone, Robert. [Lectures exegetical and practical on the Epistle of James]. A commentary on James / [by] Robert Johnstone. — 2nd ed. — Edinburgh [etc.] : Banner of Truth Trust, 1977. — viii,444p : ill(on lining papers) ; 23cm. — (A Geneva series commentary)
Spine title: The epistle of James. — Facsimile reprint. — 'Lectures exegetical and practical on the Epistle of James'. 2nd ed., originally published: Edinburgh : Oliphant Anderson, 1889.
ISBN 0-85151-257-7 : £3.50
(B77-33040)

227'.94'06 — Bible. New Testament. Epistles of John. *Expositions. Welsh texts*
Lloyd, J Trefor. Epistolau Ioan : esboniad / gan J. Trefor Lloyd. — Caernarfon : Llyfrfa'r Methodistiaid Calfinaidd, 1976. — 150p ; 19cm.
ISBN 0-901330-62-0 : £1.20
(B77-03353)

228 — Bible. New Testament. Revelation I-XI. *Expositions*
Ramsey, James B. [The spiritual kingdom]. The Book of Revelation : an exposition of the first eleven chapters / [by] James B. Ramsey ; with an introduction by Charles Hodge. — Edinburgh [etc.] : Banner of Truth Trust, 1977. — 556p in various pagings : ill(on lining papers) ; 23cm. — (A Geneva series commentary)
Facsimile reprint. — 'The spiritual kingdom' originally published: Richmond, Va : Presbyterian Committee of Publication, 1873.
ISBN 0-85151-256-9 : £4.00
(B77-32389)

228'.05'203 — Bible. New Testament. Revelation. English. Authorized. *Texts*
[**Bible**. New Testament. Revelation. *English. Authorized. 1973].* The book of Revelation : from King James version of the Holy Bible. — New York [etc.] ; London : Harper and Row, 1973. — xxi,70p ; 18cm. — (Perennial library)
ISBN 0-06-080284-7 Pbk : Unpriced
(B77-20006)

228'.06 — Bible. New Testament. Revelation. *Expositions*
Heidenreich, Alfred. The Book of Revelation / by Alfred Heidenreich. — Edinburgh (21 Napier Rd, Edinburgh EH10 5AZ) : Floris Books, 1977. — 192p ; 23cm.
'Includes an edited version by Margaret Roberts of a text taken from tapes made at seven lectures given by Alfred Heidenreich in Rudolf Steiner Hall, London, from January to March, 1968' - title page verso. — Includes the author's own rendering of the Book.
ISBN 0-903540-03-7 : £5.75
ISBN 0-903540-04-5 Pbk : £2.95
(B77-17279)

228'.07'7 — Bible. New Testament. Revelation. English. Today's English. *Texts with commentaries*
[**Bible**. New Testament. Revelation. *English. Todays English. 1977].* Good news in Revelation : the Revelation to John in Todays English version / introduced [with commentary] by Vernon Sproxton. — [London] : Collins [for] the Bible Reading Fellowship, 1977. — 143p : ill, map ; 18cm.
Bibl.: p.140-141.
ISBN 0-00-624259-6 Pbk : £0.95
(B77-31674)

229 — BIBLE. APOCRYPHA, PSEUDEPIGRAPHA, DEUTEROCANONICAL WORKS

229'.04'8 — Bible. Old Testament. Apocryphal books. Greek. Words: Pneuma

Isaacs, Marie E. The concept of spirit : a study of pneuma in Hellenistic Judaism and its bearing on the New Testament / by Marie E. Isaacs. — London (11 Cavendish Sq., W1M 0AN) : Heythrop College, 1976. — [4],xi,186p ; 21cm. — (Heythrop monographs ; 1 ISSN 0309-4723)
Bibl.: p.159-169. — Index.
ISBN 0-905764-00-5 Pbk : £3.50
Primary classification 225.4'8
(B77-13493)

229'.9 — Bible. New Testament. Apocryphal books. *Texts*

The **apocryphal** New Testament : being the apocryphal Gospels, Acts, Epistles, and Apocalypses, with other narratives and fragments / newly translated by Montague Rhodes James. — Oxford : Clarendon Press, 1975. — xxxi,594p ; 19cm.
Originally published: 1924. — Index.
ISBN 0-19-826121-7 : £5.50
(B77-06461)

230 — CHRISTIAN DOCTRINE

Benton, John, *b.1949.* Coming to faith in Christ / [by] John Benton. — Edinburgh [etc.] : Banner of Truth Trust, 1977. — [1],16, [1]p ; 19cm.
Sd : £0.15
(B77-29158)

Christian theology : a case method approach / editors Robert A. Evans, Thomas D. Parker, consulting editors ... [others]. — London : S.P.C.K., 1977. — xv,272p ; 22cm.
Originally published: New York : Harper and Row, 1976. — Bibl.: p.271-272.
ISBN 0-281-02980-6 Pbk : £3.95
(B77-22338)

Hard questions : ... a discussion of thirty-eight basic Christian problems / edited by Frank Colquhoun. — London : Falcon Books, 1976. — 140p ; 20cm.
At head of title-page: Now when the Queen of Sheba heard of the fame of Solomon she came to Jerusalem to test him with - . — Not the same as B72-13707.
ISBN 0-85491-849-3 Pbk : £1.25
(B77-02745)

Joint Commission between the Roman Catholic Church and the World Methodist Council. Growth in understanding : report of the Joint Commission between the Roman Catholic Church and the World Methodist Council. — Abbots Langley (74 Gallows Hill La., Abbots Langley, Herts. WD5 0BZ) : Catholic Information Services ; London (19 Thayer St., W1M 5LJ) : The Methodist Ecumenical Committee, [1977]. — [4],30p ; 21cm.
Sd : £0.20
(B77-08207)

Knight, Trevor F. Blood bought / by Trevor F. Knight. — [Batley] ([14 Huddersfield Rd, Birstall, Batley, W. Yorkshire WF17 9AD]) : National Young Life Campaign, 1977. — [2], 28,[1]p ; 18cm.
Sd : Unpriced
(B77-30954)

Morrice, William G. We joy in God / [by] William G. Morrice ; foreword by William Barclay. — London : S.P.C.K., 1977. — viii, 88p ; 19cm.
Index.
ISBN 0-281-02967-9 Pbk : £1.95
(B77-25374)

Osborne, Denis. Way out : some parables of science and faith / [by] Denis Osborne. — Leicester : Inter-Varsity Press, 1977. — 95p : ill ; 18cm.
Bibl.: p.86-88.
ISBN 0-85110-398-7 Pbk : £1.00
(B77-30955)

Packer, James Innell. I want to be a Christian / [by] J.I. Packer. — Eastbourne : Kingsway, 1977. — 240p ; 18cm.
ISBN 0-86065-002-2 Pbk : £0.95
(B77-29918)

Warren, Norman. Directions : fourteen Bible study outlines on basic Christianity / [by] Norman Warren. — 2nd ed. — London : Church Pastoral Aid Society, 1976. — [1],14p : ill ; 18cm. — (A falcon booklet)
Previous ed.: 1969.
ISBN 0-85491-138-3 Sd : £0.12
(B77-02746)

230 — Christian doctrine. *Arabic texts*

Lewis, Gordon R. As-Sab¯il al-am¯in li-Ktiš¯af al-yaq¯in / Kard¯un R. Luw¯is ; [translated from the English]. — Loughborough (P.O. Box 31, Loughborough, Leics. LE11 1SP) : North Africa Mission, 1976. — 140p in various pagings ; 21cm.
Arabic text. — Translation of: 'Decide for yourself'. Downers Grove, Ill. : Inter-Varsity Press, 1970. — Contains translations into Arabic of chapters 6,7,14,15 and 16 from 'A summary of Christian doctrine' / by Louis Berkhof. Originally published: Grand Rapids, Mich. : W.B. Eerdmans, 1938 ; London : Banner of Truth Trust, 1960.
Pbk : Unpriced
(B77-08748)

230 — Christian doctrine. Related to Ancient Greek thought

Weil, Simone. Intimations of Christianity among the ancient Greeks / [by] Simone Weil ; edited and translated [from the French] by Elisabeth Chase Geissbuhler. — London [etc.] : Routledge and Kegan Paul, 1976. — vii,208p ; 23cm.
This translation originally published: 1957. — Translation of: chapters from 'La source grècque', Paris : Gallimard, 1952 and 'Les intuitions pré-chrétiennes', Paris : La Colombe, 1951.
ISBN 0-7100-8524-9 : £4.00
Primary classification 180
(B77-03897)

230 — Process theology

Cobb, John Boswell. Process theology : an introductory exposition / [by] John B. Cobb, Jnr, David Ray Griffin. — Belfast : Christian Journals, 1977. — 195p ; 22cm.
Originally published: Philadelphia : Westminster Press, 1976. — Index.
ISBN 0-904302-24-5 Pbk : £3.60
(B77-08749)

230'.076 — Christian doctrine. *Questions & answers*

Forster, Roger Thomas. That's a good question / [by] Roger T. Forster and V. Paul Marston. — Completely revised and enlarged ed. — Eastbourne : Coverdale House, 1977. — [158] p ; 18cm.
Previous ed. i.e. Revised and enlarged ed.: published as 'Yes, but'. Eastbourne : Victory Press, 1972. — Bibl.
ISBN 0-902088-96-3 Pbk : £0.95
(B77-29159)

Prime, Derek. Questions on the Christian faith answered from the Bible / by Derek Prime. — Eastbourne : Victory Press, 1976. — 128p ; 18cm.
Originally published: London : Hodder and Stoughton, 1967.
ISBN 0-85476-260-4 Pbk : £0.75
(B77-07788)

230'.08 — Christian doctrine. *Essays*

Pannenberg, Wolfhart. Faith and reality / [by] Wolfhart Pannenberg ; translated [from the German] by John Maxwell. — London : Search Press [etc.], 1977. — ix,138p ; 23cm.
Translation of: 'Glaube und Wirklichkeit'. Munich : Kaiser Verlag, 1975.
ISBN 0-85532-378-7 : £4.95
(B77-23096)

230'.09'015 — Christian doctrine, ca 90-451

Kelly, John Norman Davidson. Early Christian doctrines / by J.N.D. Kelly. — 5th revised ed. — London : A. and C. Black, 1977. — xii, 511p ; 23cm.
Previous ed.: 1968. — Bibl. — Index.
ISBN 0-7136-1756-x : £6.75 : CIP rev.
(B77-11058)

230'.09'015 — Christian doctrine, to 325

Daniélou, Jean. A history of early Christian doctrine before the Council of Nicaea / [by] Jean Daniélou. — London : Darton, Longman and Todd [etc.].
Translation of: 'Histoire des doctrines chrétiennes avant Nicée. 3 : Les origines du christianisme Latin'. Paris : Desclée, 197-?. — Bibl.: p.478-486. — Index.
Vol.3 : The origins of Latin Christianity / translated [from the French] by David Smith and John Austin Baker ; edited and with a postscript by John Austin Baker. — 1977. — xvi,511p ; 23cm.
ISBN 0-232-48197-0 : £8.00
(B77-31675)

230'.092'4 — Christian doctrine. Theories of Bultmann, Rudolf

Roberts, Robert Campbell. Rudolf Bultmann's theology : a critical interpretation / by Robert Campbell Roberts. — London : S.P.C.K., 1977. — 333p ; 21cm.
Originally published: Grand Rapids : Eerdmans, 1976. — Bibl.: p.327-329. — Index.
ISBN 0-281-02981-4 Pbk : £4.95
(B77-23097)

230'.092'4 — Christian doctrine. Theories of Tillich, Paul

Pauck, Wilhelm. Paul Tillich : his life & thought / [by] Wilhelm & Marion Pauck. — London : Collins.
In 2 vols.
Vol.1 : Life. — 1977. — xii,340p,[8]p of plates : ill, ports ; 22cm.
Index.
ISBN 0-00-216650-x : £5.95
(B77-11546)

230'.2 — Roman Catholic Church. Apologetics

Thomas Aquinas, *Saint.* [Summa contra gentiles. English]. Summa contra gentiles / Saint Thomas Aquinas ; translated [from the Latin] ... by Anton C. Pegis ... [et al.]. — Notre Dame, Ind. ; London : University of Notre Dame Press, 1975. — 5v. ; 21cm.
This translation originally published: as 'On the truth of the Catholic faith'. Garden City, N.Y. : Hanover House, 1955-1957. — Index.
ISBN 0-268-01675-5 : £44.00 the set
ISBN 0-268-01676-3 Pbk : £15.20 the set
(B77-02747)

230'.2 — Roman Catholic Church. Apologetics. *Early works. Facsimiles*

Fonseca, Jeronimo Osorio da. An epistle / [by] Osorio da Fonseca ; [translated from the Latin by Richard Shacklock]. The rosarie of our ladie / [by] Thomas Worthington. — Ilkley [etc.] : Scolar Press, 1977. — 321p in various pagings : ill ; 20cm. — (English recusant literature, 1558-1640 ; vol.329)
Facsimile reports. — 'An epistle' originally published: in English. Antwerp : Aegidius Diest, 1565. — 'Rosarie of our ladie' originally published: Antverpiae : Apud Ioannem Keerbergium, 1600.
ISBN 0-85967-345-6 : Unpriced
Also classified at 242'.742
(B77-16175)

Smith, Richard, *b.1566.* A conference of the Catholike and Protestante doctrine / [by] Richard Smith ; [translated from the Latin]. — Ilkley [etc.] : Scolar Press, 1977. — [36],798, [10]p ; 24cm. — (English recusant literature, 1558-1640 ; vol.334)
Facsimile reprint of: 1st ed. of this translation of part 2 of 'The prudentiall ballance of religion'. Doway : Printed by the widdowe of Mark Wyon, 1631. — Translation and revision: of 'Collatio dottrinae Catholicorum ac Protestantium cum expressis S. Scripturae verbis'. Parisiis : Ex typographia J. Laquehay, 1622.
ISBN 0-85967-369-3 : Unpriced
(B77-15681)

230'.2 — Roman Catholic Church. Apologetics. Knott, Edward. Mercy and truth. Criticism. Chillingworth, William. Religion of Protestants. *Critical studies. Facsimiles*

Floyd, John. The Church conquerant over humane wit / [by] John Floyd. — Ilkley [etc.] : Scolar Press, 1976. — [4],143,[3]p ; 21cm. — (English recusant literature, 1558-1640 ; vol.320)
Facsimile reprint of: 1st ed. s.l. : s.n., 1639?.
ISBN 0-85967-335-9 : £10.00
(B77-10146)

230'.2 — Roman Catholic Church. Christian doctrine

Duff, Frank. The woman of Genesis / [by] Frank Duff. — Dublin (De Montfort House, North Brunswick St., Dublin 7) : Praedicanda Publications, 1976. — 3-527p ; 19cm.
Pbk : £1.06
(B77-18538)

Hardon, John Anthony. The Catholic catechism / [by] John A. Hardon. — London [etc.] : G. Chapman, 1977. — 623p ; 23cm.
Originally published: Garden City, N.Y. : Doubleday, 1975. — Index.
ISBN 0-225-66136-5 : £5.95
(B77-12845)

Your faith. — Alton : Redemptorist Publications, 1976. — 60,[1]p : ill, ports ; 28cm.
'A Redemptorist publication' - cover. — '... first published as a series of four-page pull-out supplements in "Novena magazine"...' - Introduction.
ISBN 0-85231-027-7 Sd : £0.65
(B77-17280)

230'.2 — Roman Catholic Church. Christian doctrine. *Early works. Facsimiles*
Arias, Francisco. The judge / [by] Francisco Arias ; [translated into English from the Spanish by G.M. i.e. Sir Tobias Matthew]. The gagge of the reformed gospell / [by] John Heigham. — Ilkley [etc.] : Scolar Press, 1977. — 429p in various pagings ; 20cm. — (English recusant literature, 1558-1640 ; vol.336)
Facsimile reprints. — 'The judge' originally published: St Omer : s.n., 1621. — 'The gagge of the reformed gospell'. 2nd ed. originally published: s.l. : s.n., 1623.
ISBN 0-85967-372-3 : Unpriced
Primary classification 236'.9
(B77-15081)

Avila, Juan de. Certain selected spirituall epistles / [by] Juan de Avila ; [translated from the Spanish]. — Ilkley [etc.] : Scolar Press, 1977. — [10],441p ; 21cm. — (English recusant literature, 1558-1640 ; vol.331)
Facsimile reprint of: 1st ed. of this translation, Roüen : Iohn le Cousturier, 1631.
ISBN 0-85967-347-2 : £10.00
(B77-14545)

230'.2 — Roman Catholic Church. Christian doctrine. *For Southern African students. Sunday school texts*
Nadal, Paul. You are my witnesses / text by Paul Nadal and Sister Theodula. — London : G. Chapman, 1974. — 127p : ill, map, ports ; 20cm. — (The people of God series ; book 5)
ISBN 0-225-65989-1 Pbk : £0.75
(B77-09485)

230'.2 — Roman Catholic Church. Christian doctrine. *Latin texts*
Abélard, Pierre. Sic et non / [by] Peter Abailard ; a critical edition [by] Blanche B. Boyer and Richard McKeon. — Chicago ; London : University of Chicago Press.
Latin text, English introduction.
Fasc.5. — 1977. — p385-480 ; 31cm.
ISBN 0-226-00062-1 Pbk : £9.80
(B77-32390)

Fasc.6. — 1977. — p481-575 ; 31cm.
ISBN 0-226-00064-8 Pbk : £9.80
(B77-32391)

230'.2 — Roman Catholic Church. Christian doctrine. *Latin-English parallel texts*
Thomas Aquinas, *Saint.* [Summa theologiae. English & Latin]. Summa theologiae / [by] St Thomas Aquinas ; Latin text and English translation, introductions, notes, appendices and glossaries. — London : Blackfriars : Eyre and Spottiswoode [etc.].
[Vol.24] : [The gifts of the Spirit (1a2ae.68-70)] / [edited and translated by Edward D. O'Connor]. — [1974]. — xix, 2-164p ; 23cm.
Parallel Latin text and English translation. — Bibl.: p.151-152. — Index.
ISBN 0-413-35240-4 : £3.75
(B77-19199)

[Vol.48] : [The incarnate word (3a. 1-6)] / [edited and translated by R.J. Hennessey]. — 1976. — xx,204p ; 23cm.
Parallel Latin text and English translation. — Index.
ISBN 0-413-35480-6 : £4.60
(B77-03906)

230'.2 — Roman Catholic Church. Christian doctrine. *Polish texts*
Maciocha, Waclaw. Dlaczego jestem wierzącym Katolikiem / W. Maciocha. — London : Veritas Foundation Publication Centre, 1976. — 279p ; 20cm. — (Bibloteka polska : seria niebieska ; tom 27)
Bibl.: p.267-275.
ISBN 0-901215-65-1 : £2.50
(B77-05855)

230'.2 — Roman Catholic Church. Christian doctrine. *Secondary school texts*
Conran, Una Mary. New life in Christ Jesus : a two-year course in religious education of pupils in the fourth and fifth forms of Catholic secondary schools / by Una Mary Conran. — Slough : St Paul Publications, 1977. — Portfolio : ill, music ; 31cm.
Eleven booklets. — Text on portfolio. — Index.
ISBN 0-85439-131-2 : £8.50
(B77-11059)

230'.2'05 — Roman Catholic Church. Christian doctrine. *Periodicals*
Faith today. — Dublin (St Saviour's, Upper Dorset St., Dublin 1) : Dominican Publications.
1- ; 1975-. — 1975-. — 23cm.
Ten issues a year. — Folder (8p.) as 12th issue. — Bibl.: p.8.
£0.06
(B77-20007)

230'.2'0924 — Roman Catholic Church. Christian doctrine. Theories of Joachim, Abbot of Fiore
Reeves, Marjorie. Joachim of Fiore and the prophetic future / [by] Marjorie Reeves. — London : S.P.C.K., 1976. — ix,212p,[4]p of plates : ill, facsims ; 22cm.
Bibl.: p.198-202. — Index.
ISBN 0-281-02887-7 Pbk : £3.95
(B77-15078)

230'.3 — Church of England. Apologetics. Jewel, John. Apologia Ecclesiae Anglicanae. *Critical studies*
Dorman, Thomas. A proufe of certeyne articles / [by] Thomas Dorman ; [and, The totall summe]. — Ilkley [etc.] : Scolar Press, 1976. — [4],194,[2],104p ; 21cm. — (English recusant literature, 1558-1640 ; vol.321)
Author of 'The totall summe' : John Floyd. — Facsimile reprints. — 'A proufe of certeyne articles' originally published: Antwerp : Printed by John Latius, 1564. — 'The totall summe' originally published: St Omer : s.n., 1639.
ISBN 0-85967-336-7 : £10.00
(B77-08208)

Rastell, John. The third booke / [by] John Rastell. — Ilkley [etc.] : Scolar Press, 1977. — [29]p,239 leaves ; 20cm. — (English recusant literature, 1558-1640 ; vol.332)
Leaves printed on both sides. — Facsimile reprint of: 1st ed., Antverpiae : ex officina Ioannis Fouleri, 1566.
ISBN 0-85967-348-0 : Unpriced
(B77-15079)

230'.3 — Church of England. Christian doctrine
Cleobury, Frank Harold. From clerk to cleric / [by] F.H. Cleobury ; with a foreword by Edward Carpenter. — Cambridge : J. Clarke, 1976. — [4],44p ; 20cm.
ISBN 0-227-67825-7 Pbk : £1.50
(B77-02013)

Dyson, Anthony Oakley. We believe / [by] A.O. Dyson. — London [etc.] : Mowbrays, 1977. — xvi,128p ; 23cm. — (Mowbrays library of theology)
Index.
ISBN 0-264-66451-5 : £6.00
ISBN 0-264-66251-2 Pbk : £3.25
(B77-33587)

230'.5'2 — Presbyterian Church of Wales. Christian doctrine. *Essays. Welsh texts*
Williams, Harri. Oni threngodd Duw? / [gan] Harri Williams. — [Caernarfon] : Llyfrafa'r Methodistiaid Calfinaidd, 1975. — 168p ; 19cm.
ISBN 0-901330-67-1 : £1.20
(B77-03907)

230'.5'2 — Presbyterian Church of Wales. Christian doctrine. *Welsh texts*
Williams, Harri. Ein ffydd heddiw : llawlyfr ar gyfer lleygwyr / [gan] Harri Williams. — Caernarfon : Argraffty'r Methodistaid Calfinaidd, 1976. — 60p ; 19cm.
Bibl.: p.59-60.
Pbk : £0.60
(B77-26102)

230'.5'908 — Puritanism. Christian doctrine. *Quotations*
The **golden** treasury of Puritan quotations / compiled by I.D.E. Thomas. — Edinburgh [etc.] : Banner of Truth Trust, 1977. — 3-321p ; 18cm. — (Puritan paperbacks)
Originally published: Chicago : Moody, 1975. — Index.
ISBN 0-85151-249-6 Pbk : £1.50
(B77-33588)

230'.6 — Baptist churches. Christian doctrine
Pawson, David. Truth to tell / [by] David Pawson. — London [etc.] : Hodder and Stoughton, 1977. — 160p ; 18cm. — (Hodder Christian paperbacks)
ISBN 0-340-21291-8 Pbk : £0.80
(B77-17895)

230'.8 — Unitarian churches. Christian doctrine. *Welsh texts*
Jones, J Eric. Egwyddorion Undodiaeth / gan J. Eric Jones. — Aberdâr [i.e. Aberdare] (22 Stuart St., Aberdare, M. Glam. CF44 7LY) : Gwasg y Fflam, [1974]. — [18]p : ill ; 21cm.
Bibl.: p.[17]-[18].
ISBN 0-906032-01-6 Sd : £0.10
(B77-16176)

230'.9'5 — Church of Christ, Scientist. Christian doctrine
Buchan-Sydserff, Rose Margaret. Fundamentally speaking / [by] R.M. Buchan-Sydserff. — Woking (P.O. Box 29, Woking, Surrey) : The Society for Spreading the Knowledge of True Prayer, 1976. — viii,171p ; 24cm.
ISBN 0-900678-10-0 Pbk : £2.75
(B77-03354)

Rawson, Frederick Lawrence. Life understood : from a scientific and religious point of view, and the practical method of destroying sin, disease and death / by F.L. Rawson. — 7th ed. — [Woking] ([c/o P.O. Box 29, Woking, Surrey GU21 4AU]) : Society for Spreading the Knowledge of True Prayer, 1974. — xx,436p, plate : port ; 23cm.
This ed. originally published: 1947. — Index.
£3.00
(B77-03355)

230'.9'9 — Brethren. Christian doctrine. *Correspondence*
Taylor, James. Letters of James Taylor Jr / editor J. Taylor III. — Kingston upon Thames (2 Upper Teddington Rd, Kingston-upon-Thames KT1 4DX) : Bible and Gospel Trust.
Vol.1. — 1976. — [3],364p ; 16cm.
ISBN 0-9504309-4-3 Pbk : Unpriced
(B77-10723)

230'.9'9 — Brethren. Christian doctrine. *Transcripts of discussions*
Brown, George William. The spirit of God : meetings in Toronto, November 1975 / [by] G.W. Brown [et al.]. — London (50 Red Post Hill, SE24 9JQ) : E.C. Burr, [1976]. — [4], 124p ; 16cm.
Contains transcripts of discussions and two addresses.
ISBN 0-9503958-8-9 Pbk : £0.50
(B77-07789)

Parker, A B. 'My assembly' : meetings in Buckie, May 1974 / A.B. Parker [et al.]. — London (50 Red Post Hill, SE24 9JQ) : E.C. Burr, [1976]. — [4],134p ; 16cm.
ISBN 0-9503958-7-0 Pbk : £0.50
(B77-07790)

Symington, J H. Pass the time of your sojourn in fear : [readings, addresses held at] Stamford, September 1975 / [by] J.H. Symington [et al.] ; edited by Henry Magahy. — Kingston-upon-Thames (2 Upper Teddington Rd, Kingston-upon-Thames [Surrey] KT1 4DX) : Bible and Gospel Trust, 1977. — [4], 147p ; 16cm.
'Volume 33'.
ISBN 0-9504309-5-1 Pbk : Unpriced
(B77-12846)

Symington, J H. The truth answered to in the new generation : [meetings held at] Bristol, Coventry and Endbach, June 1976 / [with] J.H. Symington [et al.] ; editor Wilbert J. Seed. — Kingston upon Thames (2 Upper Teddington Rd, Kingston-upon-Thames, [Surrey] KT1 4DX) : Bible and Gospel Trust, 1977. — [6], 328p ; 16cm.
'Volume 38'.
Pbk : £0.70
(B77-26774)

Symington, J H. Uninterrupted pain in the heart of Paul : [meetings held at] Guildford, Bristol and Lyon October 1975 / [by] J.H. Symington ; editor Henry Magahy. — Kingston-upon-Thames (2 Upper Teddington Rd, Kingston-upon-Thames KT1 4DX) : Bible and Gospel Trust, 1977. — [5],217,[1]p ; 16cm.
'Volume 34'.
ISBN 0-9504309-6-x Pbk : Unpriced
(B77-15080)

Welch, Archibald John Edmund. Resources of power : meetings in Plainfield, April 1976 / [by] A.J.E. Welch [et al.]. — London (50 Red Post Hill, SE24 9JQ) : E.C. Burr, [1977]. — [5] ,148p ; 16cm.
Spine title: Meetings in Plainfield. — Contains transcripts of discussions and 5 addresses.
Pbk : £0.50
(B77-17896)

230'.9'9 — Christian Community (Founded 1922). Christian doctrine
Capel, Evelyn Francis. The tenth hierarchy / by Evelyn Francis Capel. — London (Temple Lodge Press, 51 Queen Caroline St., Hammersmith, W6 9QL) : Christian Community, 1976. — [6],95p ; 22cm.
ISBN 0-904693-01-5 Pbk : £1.00
(B77-06462)

230'.9'9 — Elim Pentecostal Church. Christian doctrine. *Essays*
Canty, George. What's going on? : the George Canty viewpoint. — [Cheltenham] ([P.O. Box 38, Cheltenham, Glos.]) : [Greenhurst Press], 1977. — iv,116p ; 19cm.
ISBN 0-905857-02-x Pbk : Unpriced
(B77-31676)

231 — CHRISTIAN DOCTRINE. GOD, TRINITY, GODHEAD
231 — Christian doctrine. God
Barclay, William, *b.1907.* The character of God / [by] William Barclay. — Redhill : Denholm House Press, 1977. — 64p ; 18cm.
ISBN 0-85213-155-0 Pbk : Unpriced
(B77-27669)

Lampe, Geoffrey William Hugo. God as spirit / by G.W.H. Lampe. — Oxford : Clarendon Press, 1977. — [8],239p ; 23cm. — (The Bampton lectures ; 1976)
Index.
ISBN 0-19-826644-8 : £6.50 : CIP rev.
(B77-28367)

Robinson, John Arthur Thomas. Exploration into God / [by] John A.T. Robinson. — London [etc.] : Mowbrays, 1977. — 158p ; 22cm.
Originally published: London : S.C.M. Press, 1967. — Bibl.: p.146-152. — Index.
Pbk : £3.25
(B77-28368)

Ward, Keith, *b.1938.* The concept of God / [by] Keith Ward. — [London] ([14 St James's Place, S.W.1]) : Fount Paperbacks, 1977. — iv,236p ; 18cm.
Originally published: Oxford : Blackwell, 1974. — Index.
ISBN 0-00-624816-0 Pbk : £1.25
(B77-29919)

231 — Christian doctrine. God. *Transcripts of discussions*
Burr, Eric Cyril. The mystery of God : meetings in London, October 1976 / [by] E.C. Burr. — London (50 Red Post Hill, SE24 9JQ) : The author, [1977]. — [7],172p ; 16cm.
Pbk : £0.50
(B77-23980)

231 — Christian doctrine. Trinity
Jüngel, Eberhard. The doctrine of the Trinity : God's being is in becoming / [by] Eberhard Jüngel ; translated [from the German] by Horton Harris. — Edinburgh [etc.] : Scottish Academic Press, 1976. — xxi,110p ; 23cm. — (Monograph supplements to the Scottish journal of theology)
Translation of: 'Gottes Sein ist im Werden'. 2., verb. Aufl. Tübingen : Mohr, 1967. — Index.
ISBN 0-7073-0115-7 : £3.25
(B77-08209)

231 — Christian doctrine. Trinity, to 325
Lonergan, Bernard Joseph Francis. The way to Nicea : the dialectical development of trinitarian theology : a translation [from the Latin] by Conn O'Donovan from the first part of 'De Deo trino' / by Bernard Lonergan. — London : Darton, Longman and Todd, 1976. — xxxi,143p ; 23cm.
Translation of: Pars dogmatica of 'De Deo trino'. Rome : Gregorian University Press, 1964. — Index.
ISBN 0-232-51354-6 : £5.50
(B77-03908)

231'.3 — Christian church. Sermons. Special subjects: Holy Spirit
Ramsey, Arthur Michael. Come Holy Spirit / [by] Michael Ramsey, Leon-Joseph Cardinal Suenens ; with sermons by John Maury Allin ... [et al.]. — London : Darton, Longman and Todd, 1977. — 105p ; 20cm.
Originally published: New York : Morehouse-Barlow, 1976.
ISBN 0-232-51385-6 Pbk : £1.60
(B77-23981)

231'.3 — Christian doctrine. Holy Spirit
Duncan, George Baillie. The person and work of the Holy Spirit in the life of the believer / [by] George B. Duncan. — London : Lakeland, 1973. — viii,87p ; 18cm.
ISBN 0-551-00487-8 Pbk : £0.50
(B77-19200)

Gih, Andrew. Twice born - and then? : the autobiography and messages of Andrew Gih / foreword by J. Edwin Orr. — 2nd ed. / edited by Ruth J. Corbin. — London : Lakeland, 1976. — 128p ; 18cm.
This ed. originally published: London : Marshall, Morgan and Scott, 1954.
ISBN 0-551-00597-1 Pbk : £0.90
(B77-02014)

Suenens, Léon Joseph. A new Pentecost? / [by] Léon Joseph, Cardinal Suenens ; translated [from the French] by Francis Martin. — [London] ([14 St James's Place, S.W.1]) : Fountain Books, 1977. — xii,239p ; 19cm.
'Revision in the text made by the author after the English translation' - title page verso. — This translation originally published: New York : Seabury Press ; London : Darton, Longman and Todd, 1975. — Translation of: 'Une nouvelle Pentecôte?'. Paris : Desclée de Brouwer, 1974.
ISBN 0-00-624340-1 Pbk : £0.95
(B77-10724)

231'.7 — Christian doctrine. Covenant
Most, William G. Covenant and redemption / [by] William G. Most. — [Slough] : St Paul Publications, [1975]. — 3-122p ; 19cm.
Pbk : £1.50
(B77-20890)

231'.73 — Mary, Mother of Jesus. Manifestations. *Portugal. Fátima, 1916-1917*
Johnston, Francis. Have you forgotten Fatima? / by Francis Johnston. — London : Catholic Truth Society, [1976]. — [16]p : col ill, col ports ; 19cm.
ISBN 0-85183-185-0 Sd : £0.20
(B77-07051)

Walne, Damien. Oh, what a beautiful lady! : the message of Fatima / by Damien Walne & Joan Flory. — Chulmleigh : Augustine, 1976. — 139p : ill, facsims, ports ; 19cm.
ISBN 0-85172-760-3 Pbk : £1.75
(B77-12847)

231'.74 — Christian doctrine. Prophecy
Atkinson, David. Prophecy / by David Atkinson. — Bramcote : Grove Books, 1977. — 24p ; 22cm. — (Grove booklet on ministry and worship ; no.49 ISSN 0305-3067)
Bibl.: p.24.
ISBN 0-905422-06-6 Sd : £0.30
(B77-15682)

Baker, John Austin. Prophecy in the Church / [by] John Austin Baker. — London : Church Literature Association, 1976. — [2],9p ; 21cm.
'This essay was first given as a talk to the Westminster Deanery Chapter on 3 February 1976' - title page verso.
ISBN 0-85191-086-6 Sd : £0.25
(B77-18539)

231'.8 — Christian doctrine. Theodicy
Elphinstone, Andrew. Freedom, suffering and love / [by] Andrew Elphinstone. — London : S.C.M. Press, 1976. — xii,147p ; 23cm.
ISBN 0-334-00502-7 : £4.50
(B77-00601)

Geach, Peter Thomas. Providence and evil / [by] Peter Geach. — Cambridge [etc.] : Cambridge University Press, 1977. — xxii,153p ; 21cm. — (The Stanton lectures ; 1971-2)
This volume contains all but one of the eight Stanton Lectures delivered in 1971-2' - Preface. — Index.
ISBN 0-521-21477-7 : £4.50
(B77-17897)

Hick, John. Evil and the God of love / [by] John Hick. — 2nd ed. — London [etc.] : Macmillan, 1977. — xiii,389p ; 23cm.
Previous ed.: 1966. — Index.
ISBN 0-333-19672-4 : £8.95
(B77-17281)

231'.8 — Suffering. *Christian viewpoints*
Scott, John E. 'Lord, how long?' / by John E. Scott. — Ellistown (Ellistown Vicarage, Ellistown, Leics.) : J.E. and B.M. Scott, 1977. — 111p ; 22cm.
ISBN 0-9505746-0-0 : £2.50
(B77-30956)

232 — CHRIST
De Rosa, Peter. Jesus who became Christ / [by] Peter de Rosa. — Revised ed. — [London] ([14 St James's Place, S.W.1]) : Fountain Books, 1977. — 287p ; 19cm.
This ed. originally published: London : Collins, 1975. — Index.
ISBN 0-00-624682-6 Pbk : £0.95
(B77-16714)

Martin, Malachi. Jesus now / [by] Malachi Martin. — Revised and shortened [ed.]. — [London] ([14 St James's Place, S.W.1]) : Fount Paperbacks, 1977. — 3-349p ; 18cm.
This ed. originally published: London : Collins, 1975.
ISBN 0-00-624564-1 Pbk : £1.25
(B77-29920)

Nolan, Albert. Jesus before Christianity : the gospel of liberation / [by] Albert Nolan. — London : Darton, Longman and Todd, 1977. — vii,159p ; 22cm.
Originally published: Cape Town : Philip, 1976. — Bibl.: p.153-155. — Index.
ISBN 0-232-51373-2 Pbk : £2.40
(B77-17282)

232 — Bible. New Testament. Gospels. Special subjects: Christian doctrine. Christ
Baker, John Austin. Jesus of Nazareth / [by] John Austin Baker. — London : Church Literature Association.
In 2 vols.
1. — 1975. — [1],12p ; 21cm. — (Hillingdon papers ; 8)
Sd : £0.22
(B77-24685)

2. — 1975. — [1],13p ; 21cm. — (Hillingdon papers ; 9)
Sd : £0.22
(B77-24686)

232 — Bible. New Testament. Special subjects: Christian doctrine. Christ
Marshall, Ian Howard. The origins of New Testament christology / [by] I. Howard Marshall. — Downers Grove ; Leicester : Inter-Varsity Press, 1976. — 132p ; 21cm. — (Issues in contemporary theology)
Index.
ISBN 0-85111-400-8 Pbk : £1.95
(B77-19201)

Moule, Charles Francis Digby. The origin of Christology / [by] C.F.D. Moule. — Cambridge [etc.] : Cambridge University Press, 1977. — x, 187p ; 23cm.
Bibl.: p.ix-x. — Index.
ISBN 0-521-21290-1 : £7.50
(B77-27670)

232 — Christ. *Meditations*
Bessiere, Gérard. Jesus ahead / [by] Gérard Bessiere ; translated from the French by Barbara Lucas. — London : Burns and Oates, [1977]. — [7],129p ; 22cm.
Translation of: 'Jésus est devant'. Paris : Editions du Cerf, 1973.
ISBN 0-86012-019-8 Pbk : £1.95
(B77-10147)

232'.1 — Christ. Incarnation
Carey, G L. God incarnate / [by] G.L. Carey. — Leicester : Inter-Varsity Press, 1977. — 63p ; 18cm. — (Arena)
Bibl.: p.63.
ISBN 0-85110-231-x Sd : £0.60
(B77-30957)

232'.1 — Christ. Incarnation. *Welsh texts*
Athanasius, *Saint, Patriarch of Alexandria.* [De Incarnatione Verbi Dei. Welsh]. De incarnatione = Ymgnawdolied y Gair / [gan] Athanasios ; cyfieithiad [o'r Lladin] gan Euros Bowen. — Caernarfon : Llyfrfa'r Methodistiaid Calfinaidd, 1976. — 151p ; 19cm.
Index.
£1.50
(B77-15683)

232'.1'0902 — Christ. Incarnation. Theories, ca 450-1975
Leech, Kenneth, *b.1939.* Believing in the Incarnation and its consequences / [by] Kenneth Leech. — London : Church Literature Association for the Jubilee Group, 1976. — 12p ; 21cm. — (Jubilee Group. Papers)
'This essay has also appeared as an article in "Theology" (March 1976)' - p.12.
ISBN 0-85191-089-0 Sd : £0.15
(B77-10148)

232'.3 — Christ. Mediation. *Welsh texts*
Pritchard, T Arthur. Heddiw mae'n eiriol / [gan] T. Arthur Pritchard. — [Bridgend] ([Bryntirion, Bridgend, M. Glam.]) : Mudiad Efengylaidd Cymru, 1977. — 40p ; 19cm.
'Sylwedd anerchiadau ar Iesu Grist yr Eiriolwr a draddodwyd yng Nghynhadledd Gymraeg y Mudiad Efengylaidd yn Aberystwyth, Awst 1976'.
Sd : £0.40
(B77-32392)

232'.5 — Christ. Resurrection
Torrance, Thomas Forsyth. Space, time and resurrection / [by] Thomas F. Torrance. — Edinburgh (33 Montgomery St., Edinburgh) : Handsel Press, 1976. — xiii,196p ; 23cm.
Index.
ISBN 0-905312-00-7 : £5.00
(B77-11060)

232'.6 — Christ. Second coming
David, Alexander. Jesus the Christ : His Second Coming : prophecies, visions, visitations / [by] Brother Alexander David. — London : Watkins, 1977. — xvi,211p : 1 ill ; 22cm.
ISBN 0-7224-0154-x Pbk : £3.00
(B77-33041)

232'.6 — Christ. Second coming. *Polish texts*
Richaud, Paul. Pan blisko jest : rozmyslania / P. Richaud ; tlumaczenie [z polskiego jazyka] Siostr F ... — London : Veritas Foundation Publication Centre, 1977. — 32p ; 18cm.
Translation of: 'Le Seigneur est proche'.
Sd : £0.40
(B77-29160)

232.9'01 — Christ. Life. *Secondary school texts*
Stewart, James Stuart. The life and teaching of Jesus Christ / [by] James S. Stewart. — 2nd ed. ; [reprinted] with minor amendments. — Edinburgh : St Andrew Press, 1977. — vii, 209p ; 19cm.
Second ed. originally published: New York : Abingdon Press ; Scotland : Church of Scotland Committee on the Religious Instruction of Youth, 1957.
ISBN 0-7152-0352-5 Pbk : £1.50
(B77-23982)

232.9'01 — Christ. Life
Barclay, William, *b.1907.* A life of Christ / text by William Barclay ; scripted by Iain Reid ; cartoons by Eric Fraser. — London : Darton, Longman and Todd, 1977. — 95p : ill ; 18x22cm.
ISBN 0-232-51342-2 Pbk : £1.50
(B77-20891)

Faber-Kaiser, A. Jesus died in Kashmir : Jesus, Moses and the ten lost tribes of Israel / [by] A. Faber-Kaiser ; [translated from the Spanish]. — London : Gordon and Cremonesi, 1977. — viii, 184p,[16]p of plates : ill, facsims, maps, plan, ports ; 24cm.
Translation of: 'Jesus vivio y murio en Cachemira'. Barcelona : Editorial A.T.E., 1976. — Bibl.: p.170-180. — Index.
ISBN 0-86033-041-9 : £4.90
(B77-25375)

Transcriptor. A modern man's view on the story of Jesus : with an appendix on prophecy up to the year 2000 / by Transcriptor. — London [etc.] : Regency Press, 1977. — 97p ; 23cm.
£3.00
(B77-26103)

Who is this man Jesus? : the complete life of Jesus from the Living Bible. — Toronto [etc.] ; London : Bantam, 1976. — viii,215p : maps ; 18cm.
'The text ... is taken from "Living gospels" by Kenneth N. Taylor, ... [Wheaton, Ill.:] Tyndale House, 1966' - Preface. — Index.
ISBN 0-553-07911-5 Pbk : £0.60
(B77-10149)

232.9'01 — Christ. Life. *Juvenile literature*
Boros, Ladislaus. The book of Jesus : telling the story of his life and its meaning for children today / [by] Ladislaus Boros ; illustrated by Marlene Reidel ; translated [from the German] by Rosaleen Ockenden. — [London] : Collins, 1977. — 5-107p,[1]p : col ill ; 28cm.
Col. ill. on lining papers. — Translation of: 'Das Buch von unserem Herrn Jesus'. Düsseldorf : Patmos-Verlag, 1977.
ISBN 0-00-107187-4 : £4.95
(B77-29161)

Brandon, Leonard George. What do we know about Jesus? / [by] L.G. Brandon. — London : Edward Arnold, 1977. — vi,104p : ill, 2 maps, plan ; 22cm.
ISBN 0-7131-0095-8 Sd : £1.40
(B77-20892)

Ralph, Margaret. The life of Jesus / stories from the New Testament retold by Margaret Ralph ; illustrated by Gordon King. — London : Scripture Union ; Maidenhead : Purnell, 1977. — [30]p : col ill ; 27x13cm. — (A giraffe book)
ISBN 0-85421-509-3 : £0.75
ISBN 0-361-03972-7 (Purnell) : £0.75
(B77-29921)

232.9'01 — Christ. Life. *State-of-the-art reviews*
Aulén, Gustaf. Jesus in contemporary historical research / by Gustaf Aulén ; translated [from the Swedish] by Ingalill H. Hjelm. — London : S.P.C.K., 1976. — viii,167p ; 24cm.
Translation of: 'Jesus i nutida historisk forskning'. 2.ed., Stockholm : Verbum, 1974.
ISBN 0-281-02968-7 : £8.50
(B77-10150)

232.9'01 — Christ. Life. *Stories, anecdotes*
Barclay, William, *b.1907.* Jesus of Nazareth / [by] William Barclay ; based on the film directed by Franco Zeffirelli from the script by Anthony Burgess, Suso Cecchi d'Amico and Franco Zeffirelli ; photographs by Paul Ronald. — London : Collins, 1977. — 287p : col ill, map ; 26cm.
ISBN 0-00-216467-1 : £4.95
(B77-13495)

Barclay, William, *b.1907.* Jesus of Nazareth / [by] William Barclay ; based on the film directed by Franco Zeffirelli from the script by Anthony Burgess, Suso Cecchi d'Amico and Franco Zeffirelli. — [London] ([14 St James's Place, S.W.1]) : Fountain Books, 1977. — 128p, [16]p of plates : col ill ; 18cm.
Cover title: Franco Zeffirelli's Jesus of Nazareth.
ISBN 0-00-624875-6 Pbk : £0.75
(B77-13496)

232.9'01 — Christ. Life. *Welsh texts*
Thomas, Thomas Glyn. Dyddiadur Iesu o Nasareth / [gan] T. Glyn Thomas. — Abertawe [i.e. Swansea] ([11 St Helen's Rd, Swansea, W. Glam.]) : Tŷ John Penry, 1976. — 167p ; 19cm.
ISBN 0-903701-06-5 : £2.35
(B77-11061)

232.9'08 — Christ. Life. Historicity
Grant, Michael, *b.1914.* Jesus / [by] Michael Grant. — London : Weidenfeld and Nicolson, 1977. — [6],261p : maps ; 25cm.
Bibl.: p.251. — Index.
ISBN 0-297-77134-5 : £6.50
(B77-12848)

Marshall, Ian Howard. I believe in the historical Jesus / by I. Howard Marshall. — London [etc.] : Hodder and Stoughton, 1977. — 253p ; 22cm.
Bibl.: p.251-253.
ISBN 0-340-18855-3 Pbk : £2.95
(B77-29922)

The **truth** of God incarnate / edited by Michael Green. — London [etc.] : Hodder and Stoughton, 1977. — 144p ; 18cm. — (Hodder Christian paperbacks)
ISBN 0-340-22575-0 Pbk : £0.80
(B77-26104)

232.91'092'4 — Christian doctrine. Mary, Mother of Jesus. Theories of Barth, Karl
Louth, Andrew. Mary and the mystery of the incarnation : an essay on the Mother of God in the theology of Karl Barth / by Andrew Louth ; with an introduction. — Oxford : S.L.G. Press, 1977. — [2],19p ; 21cm. — (Fairacres publications ; no.67 ISSN 0307-1413)

'A paper given to the Ecumenical Society of the Blessed Virgin Mary in Oxford on 25 October 1976 under the title "Karl Barth and the problem of Mariology"'.
ISBN 0-7283-0073-7 Sd : £0.30
(B77-31677)

232.9'21 — Christ. Nativity
Schmitt, Ernest. The Son of God : birth and trial of Jesus : in its historical, political and religious aspect / [by] Ernest Schmitt ; [translated from the German]. — Stuttgart : Grail Message Foundation ; London ([10 Dryden Chambers, 119 Oxford St., W1R 1PA]) : Grail Foundation, 1974. — [2],38p ; 24cm. — (Stiftung Gralsbotschaft. Publications ; 2)
Translation of: 'Der Gottessohn'. Stuttgart : Stiftung Gralsbotschaft, 1973.
Sd : Unpriced
ISBN 3-87860-072-0
Also classified at 232.9'62
(B77-19202)

232.9'21 — Christ. Nativity. *Stories for children*
Robertson, Jenny. King in a stable / text by Jenny Robertson ; illustrations by Sheila Bewley. — London : Scripture Union, 1977. — [42]p : col ill ; 22x27cm.
ISBN 0-85421-463-1 : £1.95
(B77-30958)

232.9'21 — Christ. Nativity. *Stories for children. Welsh texts*
Bruna, Dick. Stori'r Nadolig / [gan] Dick Bruna. — Abertawe [i.e. Swansea] : C. Davies, 1976. — [28]p : col ill ; 14x27cm.
Originally published: in Dutch, as 'Kerstmis'. Utrecht : Bruna and Zoom, 1963. — Translation of: 'The Christmas book'. London : Methuen, 1964.
ISBN 0-7154-0342-7 : £1.25
(B77-02015)

232.9'54 — Christ. Language. Poetic aspects. *Welsh texts*
Morris, William, *b.1889.* Crist y bardd / gan William Morris. — Caernarfon : Llyfrfa'r Methodistiaid Calfinaidd, 1975. — 192p ; 22cm. — (Davies lectures)
Index.
£1.50
(B77-03356)

232.9'54 — Christ. Questions. *For discussion groups*
Pogue, Victor Charles. Questions Jesus asked / edited [i.e. written] by V.C. Pogue. — Edinburgh : Church of Scotland, Department of Education, 1976. — 37p ; 21cm.
Index.
ISBN 0-7152-0348-7 Sd : £0.40
(B77-09486)

232.9'54 — Christ. Teachings
Bruce, Frederick Fyvie. Paul and Jesus / [by] F.F. Bruce. — London : S.P.C.K., 1977. — 87p ; 22cm.
'... contains a revised version of the six lectures delivered at Ontario Bible College's annual Thomas F. Staley Academic Lecture Series' - Preface.
ISBN 0-281-02966-0 Pbk : £1.50
Also classified at 227'.06'6
(B77-09487)

Lockyer, Herbert. What Jesus taught about - / [by] Herbert Lockyer. — Eastbourne : Victory Press.
In 5 vols. — Originally published: as 'Everything Jesus taught'. New York : Harper and Row, 1976.
Book 1 : Himself, God, the Holy Spirit, the Scriptures. — 1977. — 124p ; 18cm.
Bibl.: p.122-124.
ISBN 0-85476-263-9 Pbk : £0.80
(B77-33589)

Book 2 : Man, sin, repentance, forgiveness, salvation, righteousness. — 1977. — 125p ; 18cm.
Bibl.: p.123-125.
ISBN 0-85476-264-7 Pbk : £0.80
(B77-33590)

Book 3 : Faith, humility, money, prayer, the Sabbath, sickness and death. — 1977. — 125p ; 18cm.
Bibl.: p.123-125.
ISBN 0-85476-265-5 Pbk : £0.80
(B77-33591)

Book 4 : Love, marriage and divorce, women, children. — 1977. — 128p ; 18cm.
Bibl.: p.126-128.
ISBN 0-85476-266-3 Pbk : £0.80
(B77-33592)

Book 5 : Angels, heaven, Satan, hell, the Kingdom, the Second Coming. — 1977. — 126p ; 18cm.
Bibl.: p.124-126.
ISBN 0-85476-267-1 Pbk : £0.80
(B77-33593)

232.9'6 — Anglicans. Christian life. Prayer. Stations of the Cross. *Meditations*
Shaw, Gilbert. The face of love : meditations on the Way of the Cross / by Gilbert Shaw. — Revised ed. — Oxford : S.L.G. Press, 1977. — xxi,125p : 1 ill ; 20cm. — (Fairacres publication ISSN 0307-1405)
Previous ed.: i.e. 1st ed., Oxford : Mowbray, 1959.
ISBN 0-7283-0060-5 Pbk : £1.75
(B77-16715)

232.9'62 — Christ. Trial
Schmitt, Ernest. The Son of God : birth and trial of Jesus : in its historical, political and religious aspect / [by] Ernest Schmitt ; [translated from the German]. — Stuttgart : Grail Message Foundation ; London ([10 Dryden Chambers, 119 Oxford St., W1R 1PA]) : Grail Foundation, 1974. — [2],38p ; 24cm. — (Stiftung Gralsbotschaft. Publications ; 2)
Translation of: 'Der Gottessohn'. Stuttgart : Stiftung Gralsbotschaft, 1973.
Sd : Unpriced
ISBN 3-87860-072-0
Primary classification 232.9'21
(B77-19202)

232.9'63 — Christ. Crucifixion
Moore, Sebastian. The crucified is no stranger / [by] Sebastian Moore. — London : Darton, Longman and Todd, 1977. — xii,116p ; 22cm.
ISBN 0-232-51375-9 Pbk : £1.95
(B77-20008)

232.9'635 — Christian life. Prayer. Seven Words from the Cross. *Meditations*
Ward, Joseph Neville. Friday afternoon / [by] J. Neville Ward. — London : Epworth Press, 1976. — 140p ; 22cm.
ISBN 0-7162-0259-x Pbk : £1.25
(B77-08210)

232.9'66 — Christ. Relics: Holy Shroud of Turin
Billon, B M. Man of the Turin Shroud / [by] B.M. Billon. — Ilfracombe : Stockwell, 1977. — 54p : ill, map ; 19cm.
ISBN 0-7223-1033-1 Pbk : £0.75
(B77-27671)

233 — CHRISTIAN DOCTRINE. MAN
Peacocke, A H. From cosmos to love : the meaning of human life / [by] A.H. Peacocke and J. Dominian. — London : Darton, Longman and Todd, 1976. — 77p ; 22cm.
ISBN 0-232-51363-5 Pbk : £1.30
(B77-09488)

Williams, Derek, *b.1945.* About people : what the Bible says / [by] Derek Williams. — Leicester (38 De Montfort St., Leicester LE1 7GP) : Inter-Varsity Press, 1977. — 151p ; 18cm.
Bibl.: p.149-151.
ISBN 0-85110-399-5 Pbk : £1.30
(B77-29162)

233'.1 — Christian doctrine. Creation
Lambert, James. Why creation? / [by] James Lambert. — London : Church Literature Association, 1975. — [2],12,[1]p ; 21cm. — (Hillingdon papers ; no.2)
ISBN 0-85191-098-x Sd : £0.20
(B77-09489)

234 — CHRISTIAN DOCTRINE. SALVATION
234'.1 — Christian doctrine. Gifts of the Holy Spirit
Bittlinger, Arnold. Gifts and ministries / by Arnold Bittlinger ; [translated from the German MS.] ; introduction by Kilian McDonnell. — London [etc.] : Hodder and Stoughton, 1974. — 127p ; 18cm. — (Hodder Christian paperbacks)
Translator: Clara K. Dyck. — This translation originally published: Grand Rapids : Eerdmans, 1973.
ISBN 0-340-18954-1 Pbk : £0.45
(B77-18540)

Chantry, Walter John. Signs of the Apostles : observations on Pentecostalism old and new / [by] Walter J. Chantry. — 2nd ed. revised. — Edinburgh [etc.] : Banner of Truth Trust, 1976. — viii,147p ; 18cm.
Previous ed.: 1973. — Bibl.: p.147.
Pbk : £0.60
ISBN 0-85151-175-9
(B77-05192)

234'.1 — Christian doctrine. Grace
Birkin, John Leonard. This is the true grace of God / [by John L. Birkin]. — Caerphilly (40 Alexander Court, Lansbury Park, Caerphilly, Mid Glamorgan CF8 1RJ) : The author.
In 2 vols.
[Part 1]. — 1977. — [3],ii,34p ; 30cm.
ISBN 0-9503978-3-0 Pbk : £0.25
(B77-14546)

234'.16 — Christian doctrine. Sacraments
Gelpi, Donald L. Charism and sacrament : a theology of Christian conversion / [by] Donald L. Gelpi. — London : S.P.C.K., 1977. — x, 258p : 2 ill ; 20cm.
Originally published: New York : Paulist Press, 1976.
ISBN 0-281-02977-6 Pbk : £3.95
(B77-28369)

Rahner, Karl. Meditations on the sacraments / [by] Karl Rahner ; [translated from the German by James M. Quigley, Dorothy White and Salvator Attanasio]. — London : Burns and Oates [etc.], 1977. — xix,105p ; 22cm.
This translation also published: New York : Seabury Press, 1977. — Translation of: 'Die siebenfältige Gabe'. München : Verlag Ars Sacra, 1974.
ISBN 0-86012-053-8 Pbk : £1.95
(B77-32393)

234'.163 — Christian doctrine. Eucharist
Sykes, Colin. Commentary on an agreed statement on Eucharistic doctrine, 1971 / [by] Colin Sykes. — Enfield : Catholic League ; London : Distributed by the Church Literature Association, 1977. — [2],24p ; 21cm.
Includes the text of the agreed statement, by the Anglican-Roman Catholic International Commission.
Sd : £0.35
(B77-32394)

234'.163'0924 — Christian doctrine. Eucharist. Theories of Cranmer, Thomas
Buchanan, Colin Ogilvie. What did Cranmer think he was doing? / by Colin Buchanan. — Bramcote : Grove Books, 1976. — 32p : ill ; 22cm. — (Grove liturgical studies ; no.7 ISSN 0306-0608)
ISBN 0-901710-98-9 Sd : £0.65
(B77-01153)

234'.164 — Christian doctrine. Ministry
Louth, Andrew. Commentary on an agreed statement on ministry and ordination, 1973 / [by] Andrew Louth. — Enfield : Catholic League ; London : Distributed by Church Literature Association, 1977. — [2],25p ; 21cm.

Includes the text of the agreed statement, by the Anglican-Roman Catholic International Commission.
Sd : £0.35
(B77-32395)

235 — CHRISTIAN DOCTRINE. SPIRITUAL BEINGS
235'.3 — Christian doctrine. Angels
Boros, Ladislaus. Angels and men / [by] Ladislaus Boros ; illustrated by Max von Moors ; translated [from the German] by John Maxwell. — London : Search Press, 1976. — 128p : ill ; 22cm.
Translation of: 'Engel und Menschen'. Olten : Walter, 1974.
ISBN 0-85532-375-2 Pbk : £2.25
(B77-03357)

Graham, Billy. Angels : God's secret agents / [by] Billy Graham. — London [etc.] : Hodder and Stoughton, 1977. — 160p ; 18cm. — (Hodder Christian paperbacks)
Originally published: Garden City, N.Y. : Doubleday, 1975 ; London : Hodder and Stoughton, 1976.
ISBN 0-340-21670-0 Pbk : £0.75
(B77-23983)

235'.4 — Christian doctrine. Devils
Leech, Kenneth, *b.1939.* The charismatic movement and the demons / [by] Kenneth Leech. — London : Church Literature Association for the Jubilee Group, 1976. — 8p ; 21cm. — (Jubilee Group. Papers)
Sd : £0.12
(B77-20893)

236 — CHRISTIAN DOCTRINE. ESCHATOLOGY
236'.2 — Christian doctrine. Eternal punishment
Devas, Dominic. The doctrine of eternal punishment / by Dominic Devas. — London : Catholic Truth Society, 1977. — 3-12p ; 18cm.
ISBN 0-85183-192-3 Sd : £0.15
(B77-15684)

236'.2 — Christian doctrine. Future life
Badham, Paul. Christian beliefs about life after death / [by] Paul Badham. — London [etc.] : Macmillan, 1976. — viii,174p ; 23cm. — (Library of philosophy and religion)
Index.
ISBN 0-333-19769-0 : £8.95
(B77-02748)

236'.2 — Christian doctrine. Future life. *Secondary school texts*
Parrinder, Geoffrey. Something after death? / [by] Geoffrey Parrinder. — Nutfield : Denholm House Press, 1974. — 64p : ill(some col) ; 20cm. — (Search for meaning ; 2)
ISBN 0-85213-127-5 Pbk : £1.10
(B77-20009)

236'.9 — Christian doctrine. Last Judgment. *Early works. Facsimiles*
Arias, Francisco. The judge / [by] Francisco Arias ; [translated into English from the Spanish by G.M. i.e. Sir Tobias Matthew]. The gagge of the reformed gospell / [by] John Heigham. — Ilkley [etc.] : Scolar Press, 1977. — 429p in various pagings ; 20cm. — (English recusant literature, 1558-1640 ; vol.336)
Facsimile reprints. — 'The judge' originally published: St Omer : s.n., 1621. — 'The gagge of the reformed gospell'. 2nd ed. originally published: s.l. : s.n., 1623.
ISBN 0-85967-372-3 : Unpriced
Also classified at 230'.2
(B77-15081)

239 — CHRISTIAN DOCTRINE. APOLOGETICS
239'.1 — Christian church. Apologetics, to ca 100
Bruce, Frederick Fyvie. First-century faith : Christian witness in the New Testament / [by] F.F. Bruce. — Revised ed. — Leicester : Inter-Varsity Press, 1977. — ix,107p ; 18cm.
Previous ed.: published as 'The apostolic defence of the Gospel'. London : Inter-Varsity Fellowship, 1960. — Index.
ISBN 0-85110-393-6 Pbk : £0.95
(B77-33594)

240 — CHRISTIANITY. MORAL AND DEVOTIONAL THEOLOGY
241 — Christian ethics
Baelz, Peter Richard. Ethics and belief / [by] Peter Baelz. — London : Sheldon Press, 1977. — ix,118p ; 20cm. — (Issues in religious studies)
Bibl.: p.114-115. — Index.
ISBN 0-85969-110-1 Pbk : £1.60
(B77-20010)

Lehmann, Paul Louis. Ethics in a Christian context / [by] Paul L. Lehmann. — New York [etc.] ; London : Harper and Row, 1976. — 384p ; 21cm.
Originally published: New York : Harper and Row ; London : S.C.M. Press, 1963. — Bibl.: p.367-370. — Index.
ISBN 0-06-065231-4 Pbk : £3.70
(B77-29923)

Moral questions : a discussion of Christian attitudes to some thirty-five social issues / edited by Frank Colquhoun. — London : Falcon Books, 1977. — 159p ; 20cm.
Bibl.
ISBN 0-85491-854-x Pbk : £1.50
(B77-31678)

241 — Salvation Army ethics
Clifton, Shaw. What does the Salvationist say - ? : (about divorce, abortion, race relations, euthanasia, war) / by Shaw Clifton. — London : Salvationist Publishing and Supplies, 1977. — [5],30p ; 22cm.
'Most of the material in this book first appeared in 1975 as a series of articles in "The Officer" magazine' - Introduction. — Bibl.
ISBN 0-85412-287-7 Sd : £0.55
(B77-16716)

241'.04'2 — Roman Catholic ethics
Curran, Charles Edward. Catholic moral theology in dialogue / [by] Charles E. Curran. — Notre Dame [Ind.] ; London : University of Notre Dame Press, 1976. — [6],270p ; 22cm.
Originally published: Notre Dame, Ind. : Fides Publishers, 1972. — Index.
ISBN 0-268-00716-0 : £8.80
ISBN 0-268-00717-9 Pbk : £3.20
(B77-03358)

Curran, Charles Edward. New perspectives in moral theology / [by] Charles E. Curran. — Notre Dame [Ind.] ; London : University of Notre Dame Press, 1976. — ix,284p ; 22cm.
Originally published: Notre Dame, Ind. : Fides Publishers, 1974. — Index.
ISBN 0-268-01449-3 : £8.80
ISBN 0-268-10450-7 Pbk : £3.20
(B77-03359)

241'.1 — Conscience. *Christian viewpoints*
Gladwin, John. Conscience / by John Gladwin. — Bramcote : Grove Books, 1977. — 24p ; 22cm. — (Grove booklets on ethics ; no.18 ISSN 0305-4241)
ISBN 0-905422-17-1 Sd : £0.35
(B77-24687)

241'.4 — Christian ethics. Agape
Outka, Gene Harold. Agape : an ethical analysis / by Gene Outka. — New Haven ; London : Yale University Press, 1976. — ix, 321p ; 21cm. — (Yale publications in religion ; 17)
Originally published: 1972. — Index.
ISBN 0-300-02122-4 Pbk : £3.75
(B77-26775)

241'.4 — Christian ethics. Virtues
Geach, Peter Thomas. The virtues / [by] Peter Geach. — Cambridge [etc.] : Cambridge University Press, 1977. — xxxv,173p ; 21cm. — (The Stanton lectures ; 1973-4)
'... delivered at Cambridge in 1973-4 ...' - Preface. — Index.
ISBN 0-521-21350-9 : £4.95
(B77-17899)

241'.4 — Roman Catholics. Christian life. Charity. Ethics. *Early works. Facsimiles*
Arias, Francisco. A treatise of benignity / [by] Francisco Arias ; [translated from the Spanish by Sir Tobias Matthew]. A direction to be observed by N.N. / [by] Matthew Wilson. — Ilkley [etc.] : Scolar Press, 1977. — [16],297, 42p ; 19cm. — (English recusant literature, 1558-1640 ; vol.339)
Facsimile reprints. — 'A treatise of benignity' originally published: St Omer : s.n., 1630. — 'A direction to be observed by N.N.' originally published: s.l. : s.n., 1636.
ISBN 0-85967-375-8 : Unpriced
(B77-15685)

241.6'4'24 — Euthanasia. *Christian viewpoints*
Searle, John Derek. Kill or care? / [by] John Searle. — Exeter : Paternoster Press, 1977. — 35p ; 18cm. — (Paternoster punchline ; no.8)
ISBN 0-85364-213-3 Sd : £0.45 : CIP rev.
(B77-27672)

241'.6'6 — Sex relations. Ethics. *Roman Catholic viewpoints*
Dominian, Jacob. Proposals for a new sexual ethic / [by] Jack Dominian. — London : Darton, Longman and Todd, 1977. — 90p ; 22cm.
Index.
ISBN 0-232-51379-1 : £1.50
(B77-21688)

Martinez de Toledo, Alfonso. [Corvacho, ó Reprobación del amor mundano. English]. Little sermons on sin : the Archpriest of Talavera / by Alfonso Martinez de Toledo ; translated [from the Spanish] by Lesley Byrd Simpson. — Berkeley [etc.] ; London : University of California Press, 1977. — viii, 200p ; 19cm.
This translation originally published: Berkeley : California University Press ; London : Cambridge University Press, 1959. — Translation of: 'Corvacho, ó Reprobación del amor mundano'. — Bibl.: p.200.
ISBN 0-520-03281-0 Pbk : £2.25
(B77-31679)

241'.6'98 — Sins: Pride. *Christian viewpoints*
Sparrow, John. The sin of pride : the University sermon : preached in the University Church of St Mary the Virgin, Oxford on 23 November 1975 / by John Sparrow. — Burford : Cygnet Press ; [London] : [Distributed by Bodley Head], 1977. — 11,[1]p ; 21cm.
Limited ed. of 100 copies.
Sd : Unpriced
(B77-30959)

242 — CHRISTIANITY. DEVOTIONAL LITERATURE
242 — Anglicans. Christian life. *Meditations. For Lent*
Richards, John Richards. Under His banner / [by] J.R. Richards. — Penarth ([Education and Communications Centre, Woodland Place], Penarth [S. Glam.]) : Church in Wales Publications, 1973. — 48p ; 21cm.
'Church in Wales book for Lent' - cover.
ISBN 0-85326-017-6 Pbk : £0.55
(B77-16177)

242 — Catholic Apostolic Church (Founded 1944). Families. Christian life. Devotions. *Rites*
A manual of family devotions / compiled by Georgius I, Metropolitan of Glastonbury ; [for] the Catholic Apostolic Church (Metropolis of Glastonbury) ... — Glastonbury ([7 Glebe Court, Blackheath, SE3 9TH]) : Metropolitical Press, 1973. — [7],iii,41p : 1 ill ; 26cm.
ISBN 0-905146-05-0 : £1.50
(B77-05193)

242 — Christian life. *Devotional works*
Grigor Narekatsi. [Narek. English. *Selections].* Lamentations of Narek : mystic soliloquies with God / [by] Grigor Narekatsi ; translated from the classical Armenian by Mischa Kudian. — London (BCM-Mashtots, W.C.1) : Mashtots Press, 1977. — 96p ; 23cm.
ISBN 0-903039-04-4 : £3.60
(B77-33595)

Hughes, Bill. The world in my prayers : devotions and epilogues / by Bill Hughes. — Ilkeston : Moorley's Bible and Bookshop, [1977]. — [2],2-79p : ill ; 21cm.
Index.
ISBN 0-86071-006-8 Pbk : £0.70
(B77-33042)

Snowden, Rita Frances. It's a pleasure : devotional openings for meetings / [by] Rita F. Snowden. — London : Epworth Press, 1977. — 92p ; 20cm.
ISBN 0-7162-0290-5 Pbk : £1.00
(B77-33596)

242 — Christian life. *Meditations*
Falconer, Ronald Hugh Wilson. The seeing eye, the understanding heart : pictorial meditations / by Ronald Falconer. — Edinburgh : St Andrew Press, 1977. — [5],44, [3]p,[44]p of plates : chiefly ill, ports ; 10x16cm.
ISBN 0-7152-0350-9 Pbk : £0.95
(B77-29924)

Gillet, Lev. In Thy presence / by Lev Gillet ; [translated from the French]. — London [etc.] : Mowbrays, 1977. — 144p ; 18cm. — (Popular Christian paperbacks)
Contents: Limitless love. Translation of: 'Amour sans limites'. Paris? : Editions et Librarie de Chevetogne, 1973 - Thy presence today. Translation of: 'Présence du Christ'. Paris : Desclée, 1961.
ISBN 0-264-66361-6 Pbk : £0.75
(B77-17283)

242 — Christian life. *Meditations. Welsh texts*
Davies, Thomas James. Munud o edrych / [gan] T.J. Davies. — Llandysul : Gwasg Gomer, 1976. — 92p : ill ; 19cm. — (Llyfrau poced Gomer)
ISBN 0-85088-352-0 Pbk : £0.75
Also classified at 891.6'6'12
(B77-10151)

242 — Christian life. Meditations. Ignatius of Loyola, Saint. Exercitia spiritualia
Woodgate, Michael J. Ignatian spirituality / [by] Michael J. Woodgate. — Ilfracombe : Stockwell, 1977. — 22p ; 18cm.
'Being a paper read at a conference on "Spirituality" held at St Edward's House, [London] on Thursday, 9th September, 1976' - p.3.
ISBN 0-7223-1020-x Pbk : Private circulation
(B77-31680)

242 — Roman Catholics. Christian life. *Meditations*
Carretto, Carlo. Summoned by love / [by] Carlo Carretto ; translated [from the Italian] by Alan Neame. — London : Darton, Longman and Todd, 1977. — 143p ; 20cm.
Translation of: 'Padre mio, mi abbandono a te'. Rome : Citta Nuova Editrice, 197-.
ISBN 0-232-51365-1 Pbk : £1.50
(B77-21689)

LeBuffe, Francis. Friends aren't kept waiting / [by] Francis LeBuffe. — Revised ed. [i.e. 1st ed.]. — London : Sheed and Ward, 1977. — vi, 119p ; 20cm. — (The Hart library)
These meditations originally published: in 'My changeless friend'. New York : Apostleship of Prayer, 1949.
ISBN 0-7220-7706-8 Pbk : £1.00
(B77-26105)

LeBuffe, Francis. My changeless friend / [by] Francis LeBuffe. — Revised ed. — London : Sheed and Ward, 1976. — ix,116p ; 20cm.
This ed. originally published: New York : Arena Lettres, 1974.
ISBN 0-7220-7675-4 Pbk : £1.35
(B77-02749)

Rahner, Karl. Meditations on hope and love / [by] Karl Rahner ; [translated from the German by V. Green]. — London : Burns and Oates, 1976. — 85p ; 22cm.
Translation of: 'Was sollen wir jetzt tun?', Freiburg im Breisgau : Herder, 1974 ; and, 'Gott ist Mensch geworden', Freiburg im Breisgau : Herder, 1975.
ISBN 0-86012-027-9 Pbk : £1.95
(B77-02750)

242 — Roman Catholics. Christian life. *Meditations. Facsimiles*
Hill, Thomas. A plaine path-way to heaven / [by] Thomas Hill. — Ilkley [etc.] : Scolar Press, 1976. — [45],878p ; 19cm. — (English recusant literature, 1558-1640 ; vol.324)
The first part. — Facsimile reprint of: 1634 ed. Douay : M. Bogart, 1634.
ISBN 0-85967-339-1 : £20.00
(B77-14547)

Hill, Thomas. A plaine path-way to heaven - the second part / [by] Thomas Hill. — Ilkley [etc.] : Scolar Press, 1976. — [4],1269p ; 20cm. — (English recusant literature, 1558-1640 ; vol.325)
Facsimile reprint of: 1637 ed. St Omer ; s.n., 1637.
ISBN 0-85967-341-3 : £20.00
(B77-14548)

Perin, William. Spirituall exercyses and goostly meditations / [by] William Peryn. [A copy of the decree / by Thomas Preston]. — Ilkley [etc.] : Scolar Press, 1977. — [4]p,136 leaves,[1],67p ; 20cm. — (English recusant literature, 1558-1640 ; vol.337)
Leaves printed on both sides. — Facsimile reprints. — This ed. of 'Spirituall exercyses and goostly meditations' originally published: Caen : Peter le Chandelier, 1598. — Translation and adaptation of the 'Exercitia' of N. van Ess. — 'A copy of the decree' originally published under the name Roger Widdrington. s.l. : s.n., 1614.
ISBN 0-85967-373-1 : Unpriced
(B77-15082)

Villacastin, Tomas de. A manuall of devout meditations / [by] Tomas de Villacastin ; [translated from the Spanish]. — Ilkley [etc.] : Scolar Press, 1976. — [17],558,[6]p ; 20cm. — (English recusant literature, 1558-1640 ; vol.326)
'Drawne for the most part, out of the spiritual Exercises of B.F. Ignatious' - p.[6]. — Facsimile reprint of: 1618 ed. of this translation. St Omer : s.n., 1618.
ISBN 0-85967-342-1 : Unpriced
(B77-15083)

242 — Unitarians. Christian life. *Devotional works. Welsh texts*
Myfyrdod mudiad. — Aberdâr [i.e. Aberdare] ([22 Stuart St., Aberdare, M. Glam. CF44 7LY]) : Gwasg y Fflam, [1977?]. — [1],19p ; 17cm.
Sd : £0.20
(B77-17284)

242 — Unitarians. Christian life. *Meditations*
Helverson, Ralph Norman. Living in the questions / by Ralph Norman Helverson. — London : Lindsey Press, 1977. — 322p in various pagings ; 22cm.
Also published: United States : s.n., 1977?. — Index.
Pbk : £2.00
(B77-30960)

242'.08 — Christian life. *Devotional works. Anthologies*
With heart and soul and strength / [compiled by] Dorothy B. King ; with foreword by Patience Strong. — Nutfield : Denholm House Press, 1976. — [128]p ; 18cm. — (Day by day with the love of God ; vol.2)
ISBN 0-85213-150-x Pbk : £1.00
(B77-07791)

242'.1 — Christian life. Mysticism. Juliana of Norwich, Mother. Revelations of divine love. *Texts*
Juliana of Norwich, *Mother.* [Revelations of divine love]. A revelation of love / [by] Julian of Norwich ; edited by Marion Glasscoe. — [Exeter] : University of Exeter, 1976. — xviii, 111p ; 21cm. — (Exeter medieval English texts)

Text of the revelations as found in British Museum Sloane manuscript No.2499. — Middle English text, modern English introduction and notes. — Bibl.: p.xviii.
ISBN 0-85989-061-9 Sd : £1.00
(B77-16717)

242'.2 — Christian life. *Daily readings*
Barclay, William, *b.1907.* Through the year with William Barclay : devotional readings for every day / edited by Denis Duncan. — London [etc.] : Hodder and Stoughton, 1977. — 381p ; 18cm.
Originally published: 1971.
ISBN 0-340-21329-9 Pbk : £1.00
(B77-10152)

Gay, Francis. The friendship book of Francis Gay. — London [etc.] : D.C. Thomson. [1978]. — 1977. — [192]p : ill(some col) ; 19cm.
£0.70
(B77-30961)

Neill, Stephen. Seeing the Bible whole / by Stephen Neill. — London : Bible Reading Fellowship, 1977. — v,162p ; 19cm.
Originally published: 1957. — Index.
ISBN 0-900164-40-9 Pbk : £1.00
(B77-31681)

Notes on Bible readings. — Redhill : International Bible Reading Association.
1978 / [Aubrey G. Smith, general editor Joy R. Standen, editor]. — 1977. — 256p ; 18cm.
ISBN 0-7197-0164-3 Pbk : Unpriced
(B77-27673)

Tucker, John, *b.1934.* Start here : a book for those who want to read the Bible / [by] John Tucker. — Redhill : International Bible Reading Association, 1977. — 64p ; 19cm.
ISBN 0-7197-0168-6 Pbk : Unpriced
(B77-31682)

242'.2'05 — Christian life. Family worship. *Daily readings. Serials*

Family prayers / Scripture Union. — London : Scripture Union.
[1978] / by Mary Batchelor ... [et al.]. — 1977. — 185p ; 20cm.
ISBN 0-85421-526-3 Pbk : £1.25
(B77-33597)

242'.33 — Christian life. *Meditations. For Advent*

Terra, Russell G. The coming God : daily homily-meditation themes for Advent / [by] Russell G. Terra. — Slough : St Paul Publications, 1977. — xii,123p ; 22cm.
Originally published: New York : Alba House, 1976.
ISBN 0-85439-135-5 Pbk : £1.50
(B77-33598)

242'.34 — Christian life. *Meditations. For Lent*

Martineau, Robert. Truths that endure / [by] Robert Martineau. — London : S.P.C.K., 1977. — 48p ; 21cm.
ISBN 0-281-02976-8 Sd : £0.60
(B77-11062)

242'.726 — Catholic Apostolic Church (Founded 1944). Christian life. Prayer. Jesus Prayer. *Manuals*

Paulus, *Father.* Living vessels / by Father Paulus. — Glastonbury ([7 Glebe Court, London SE3 9TH]) : Metropolitical Press, 1976. — [4],2,iv,91p : ill ; 30cm.
Index.
ISBN 0-905146-06-9 : £0.95
(B77-16718)

242'.742 — Roman Catholics. Christian life. Prayer. Rosary. *Prayer books*

Fonseca, Jeronimo Osorio da. An epistle / [by] Osorio da Fonseca ; [translated from the Latin by Richard Shacklock]. The rosarie of our ladie / [by] Thomas Worthington. — Ilkley [etc.] : Scolar Press, 1977. — 321p in various pagings : ill ; 20cm. — (English recusant literature, 1558-1640 ; vol.329)
Facsimile reports. — 'An epistle' originally published: in English. Antwerp : Aegidius Diest, 1565. — 'Rosarie of our ladie' originally published: Antverpiae : Apud Ioannem Keerbergium, 1600.
ISBN 0-85967-345-6 : Unpriced
Primary classification 230'.2
(B77-16175)

242'.8 — Christian life. Prayer. *Prayer books*

Appleton, George. One man's prayers / [by] George Appleton. — 2nd ed. — London : S.P.C.K., 1977. — vi,89p ; 19cm.
Previous ed.: 1967.
ISBN 0-281-02215-1 Pbk : £1.25
(B77-08211)

A **book** of praise and prayer / edited by Frank S. Mead. — Berkhamsted : Lion Publishing, 1977. — 96p ; 20cm.
This collection originally published: as 'Talking with God'. Philadelphia : A.J. Holman Co., 1976. — Index.
ISBN 0-85648-076-2 : £1.50
(B77-11547)

A **book** of short prayers / [compiled by] Graham Smith. — Dublin : Veritas Publications, 1977. — 87p ; 18cm.
ISBN 0-905092-17-1 Sd : £0.50
(B77-17900)

De Rosa, Peter. Prayers for pagans and hypocrites / [by] Peter De Rosa ; illustrations by Haro. — London : Collins, 1977. — 128p : ill ; 21cm.
ISBN 0-00-216657-7 : £2.50
(B77-27674)

Geres, Paul. Prayers for impossible days / [by] Paul Geres ; translated [from the French] by Ingalill H. Hjelm. — London : S.P.C.K., 1976. — viii,51p ; 19cm.
This translation also published: Philadelphia : Fortress Press, 1976. — Translation of selections from: 'Prières pour les jours intenables'. Paris : Les Éditions Oeuvrières, 1971.
ISBN 0-281-02954-7 Pbk : £0.95
(B77-12849)

Hollings, Michael. You must be joking, Lord : more prayers / by Michael Hollings and Etta Gullick. — Great Wakering : Mayhew-McCrimmon, 1975. — 159p ; 15cm.
Index.
ISBN 0-85597-089-8 Pbk : £0.60
(B77-19203)

Kossoff, David. 'You have a minute, Lord?' : a sort of prayer book / by David Kossoff ; illustrated by the author. — London : Robson Books, 1977. — 96p : ill ; 21cm.
'Including the three pieces "Words for Paul"'.
ISBN 0-86051-009-3 : £1.95 : CIP rev.
(B77-17901)

Niebuhr, Reinhold. Justice and mercy / [by] Reinhold Niebuhr ; edited by Ursula M. Niebuhr. — New York [etc.] ; London : Harper and Row, 1976. — xi,139,[1]p ; 21cm.
Originally published: 1974. — Bibl.: p.139. — Index.
ISBN 0-06-066172-0 Pbk : £2.20
Primary classification 252
(B77-02758)

Redford, Pauline. Positive prayers for negative people like me - ! / [by] Pauline Redford. — Lincs. : Pilgrim Press, 1976. — 35p ; 15cm.
ISBN 0-9505405-0-1 Sd : £0.25
(B77-02751)

Weatherhead, Leslie Dixon. A private house of prayer / [by] Leslie D. Weatherhead. — London [etc.] : Hodder and Stoughton, 1977. — xiv,338p ; 18cm. — (Hodder Christian paperbacks)
Originally published: 1958. — Index.
ISBN 0-340-21674-3 Pbk : £1.25
(B77-33043)

242'.802 — Roman Catholics. Christian life. Prayer. *Prayer books*

Personal prayers / [compiled by] Helen Thomas. — London : Sheed and Ward, 1977. — [7], 85p : ill ; 20cm.
ISBN 0-7220-7713-0 Pbk : £1.75
(B77-17902)

242'.82 — Children. Christian life. Prayer. *Prayer books*

Bullen, Anthony. Fifty prayers for young people / [by] Anthony Bullen. — Slough : St Paul Publications, 1977. — 112p : col ill ; 12x19cm.
ISBN 0-85439-132-0 Sd : £0.75
(B77-33044)

The **Lion** book of children's prayers / [prayers compiled by Mary Batchelor ; photographs by Jean-Luc Ray ; illustrations by Gillian Gaze]. — Berkhamsted : Lion Publishing, 1977. — 3-94p : ill(some col) ; 25cm.
Col. ill. on lining papers. — Index.
ISBN 0-85648-070-3 : £1.95
(B77-11548)

242'.8'3 — Adolescents. Christian life. Prayer. *Prayer books*

More prayers for young people / [compiled by] William Barclay. — [London] ([14 St James's Place, S.W.1]) : Fountain Books, 1977. — 127p ; 18cm.
ISBN 0-00-624668-0 Pbk : £0.75
(B77-18541)

242'.843 — Mothers. Christian life. Prayer. *Prayer books*

Mattison, Judith. Prayers from a mother's heart / [by] Judith Mattison ; illustrations by Audrey Teeple. — Great Wakering : Mayhew-McCrimmon, 1975. — 95p : ill ; 20cm.
Also published: Minneapolis : Augsburg, 1975.
ISBN 0-85597-090-1 Pbk : £0.80
(B77-10153)

245 — CHRISTIANITY. HYMNS WITHOUT MUSIC

245'.092'2 — Hymns. Words. British writers, to 1975. *Lists*

Hayden, Andrew J. British hymn writers and composers : a check-list giving their dates & places of birth & death / by Andrew J. Hayden and Robert F. Newton. — Croydon (c/o Addington Palace, Croydon CR9 5AD) : Hymn Society of Great Britain and Ireland, 1977. — [94]p ; 21cm.
Bibl.: p.[4].
ISBN 0-9505589-0-7 Pbk : £2.40
Primary classification 783.9'092'2
(B77-08494)

246 — CHRISTIAN SYMBOLISM

246'.53 — Iconoclasm. *Byzantine Empire, 726-843. Conference proceedings*

Spring Symposium of Byzantine Studies, *9th, University of Birmingham, 1975.* Iconoclasm : papers given at the Ninth Spring Symposium of Byzantine Studies, University of Birmingham, March 1975 / edited by Anthony Bryer and Judith Herrin. — Birmingham : University of Birmingham, Centre for Byzantine Studies, 1977. — xi[i.e.x],195p : ill, facsims, geneal tables ; 31cm.
Bibl.: p.x-xi. — Index.
ISBN 0-7044-0226-2 : £15.00
(B77-26776)

246'.9 — Churches. Architectural features. Liturgical aspects. *Conference proceedings*

Looking to the future : papers read at an international symposium on prospects for worship, religious architecture and socio-religious studies, 1976 / editor J.G. Davies. — [Birmingham] : University of Birmingham, Institute for the Study of Worship and Religious Architecture, [1976]. — [6], 171p : map ; 30cm. — (University of Birmingham. Institute for the Study of Worship and Religious Architecture. Publications ; 24)
ISBN 0-7044-0234-3 Sp : £1.35
(B77-04543)

246'.9 — Shrines. *Mayo (County). Knock. Shrine of Our Lady of Knock*

Neary, Tom. Knock : the pilgrim's hope / by Tom Neary. — Dublin (37 Lower Leeson St., Dublin 2) : Irish Messenger Office, [1976]. — 35p ; 16cm.
Sd : £0.12
(B77-19204)

Robertson, James V. The holy ground, Mary's Knock / author James V. Robertson ; editor Tom Neary ; design & photography Seamus Mallee. — Knock, Co. Mayo (Secretary, Inquiry Office, Knock Shrine, Claremorris, Co. Mayo) : Custodians of Knock Shrine, 1975. — 63p : ill, facsim, map, ports, plan ; 25cm.
Sd : £0.60
(B77-19205)

246'.9 — Shrines. *Mayo (County). Knock. Shrine of Our Lady of Knock, to 1974*

Neary, Tom. The cross & the glory : a chronicle of the Shrine of Our Lady of Knock, Co. Mayo, Ireland / [author and editor Tom Neary]. — Knock ([The Shrine, Knock, Co. Mayo, Ireland]) : The Custodians of Knock Shrine, 1975. — 40p : ill ; 19cm.
'This pamphlet contains the text of the commentary which accompanies the major set of Knock slides'. — Also available on cassette tape.
Sd : £0.25
(B77-31683)

248 — CHRISTIAN LIFE

Bye, Beryl. What about life-style? / [by] Beryl Bye. — Exeter : Paternoster Press, 1977. — 36p ; 18cm. — (Pater noster punchline ; no.6)
ISBN 0-85364-210-9 Sd : £0.45 : CIP rev.
(B77-26777)

Copley, Derek Bryan. Shock wave : how today's Christian prepares for tomorrow / [by] Derek and Nancy Copley. — Ilkeston : Moorley's Bible and Bookshop, 1976. — v,89p : ill ; 21cm.
Bibl.: p.88-89.
ISBN 0-901495-87-5 Pbk : £0.75
(B77-02752)

Daily, Starr. Four ways to God / [by] Starr Daily. — Evesham : James, 1964 [i.e. 1977]. — 126p ; 21cm.
Originally published: 1964.
ISBN 0-85305-081-3 : £1.25
(B77-27675)

Darnall, Jean. Life in the overlap / [by] Jean Darnall. — London : Lakeland, 1977. — 144p : ill ; 18cm.
ISBN 0-551-00786-9 Pbk : £0.95
(B77-30962)

Duncan, George Baillie. It could be your problem / [by] George B. Duncan. — London [etc.] : Pickering and Inglis, 1977. — 112p ; 18cm.
ISBN 0-7208-0396-9 Pbk : £1.00
(B77-26106)

Fletcher, Peter, *b.1935.* God with us / [by] Peter Fletcher. — London : Epworth Press, 1977. — 96p ; 19cm.
ISBN 0-7162-0284-0 Pbk : £1.00
(B77-17285)

Frith, Christopher. 'I belong' : being a Christian today / by Christopher Frith. — London : Scripture Union, 1977. — 64p : ill ; 21cm.
ISBN 0-85421-465-8 Pbk : £0.70
(B77-33599)

Gardner, Geoffrey. The key of life : without which life has no meaning and no purpose / [by] Geoffrey Gardner. — Esher (8 Tellisford, The Green, Esher, Surrey KT10 8AE) : Geoffrey Gardner Publications, 1977. — vii, 119p ; 22cm.
ISBN 0-9505543-0-8 Pbk : £1.95
(B77-30964)

Green, Michael, *b.1930.* You must be joking : popular excuses for avoiding Jesus Christ / by Michael Green. — London [etc.] : Hodder and Stoughton, 1976. — 159p : ill ; 18cm.
Bibl.: p.157-159.
ISBN 0-340-21126-1 Pbk : £0.70
(B77-18542)

Hurnard, Hannah. Simply by faith / [by] Hannah Hurnard. — Eastbourne : Victory Press, 1977. — 128p ; 18cm.
Also published: Wheaton, Ill. : Tyndale House, 1977.
ISBN 0-85476-271-x Pbk : £0.95
(B77-29163)

Little, Paul Eagleson. Day by day guidance / [by] Paul Little. — London : Falcon Books, 1976. — 24p ; 18cm. — (A falcon booklet)
Originally published: Downers Grove : Inter Varsity Press, 1971.
ISBN 0-85491-139-1 Sd : £0.25
(B77-02753)

Pilkinton, Ross. The Master says 'Come' / by Ross Pilkinton ; illustrated by John Pickering. — London : Scripture Union, 1977. — 16p ; 22cm.
Bibl.: p.16.
ISBN 0-85421-524-7 Sd : Unpriced
(B77-33045)

Pink, Arthur Walkington. Spiritual growth : growth in grace, or Christian progress / by Arthur W. Pink. — Welwyn : Evangelical Press, 1977. — 3-200p ; 21cm.
Originally published: Grand Rapids : Baker Book House, 1971. — Index.
ISBN 0-85234-084-2 Pbk : £1.65
(B77-29164)

Rahner, Karl. Christian at the crossroads / [by] Karl Rahner ; [this translation was made from the German by V. Green]. — London : Burns and Oates, 1975. — 95p ; 22cm.
Translation of: 'Wagnis des Christen'. Freiburg im Breisgau : Herder, 1974.
ISBN 0-86012-020-1 Pbk : £1.50
(B77-09490)

Taylor, James, *b.1930.* Grow in the faith / [by] James Taylor. — Glasgow (280 St Vincent St., Glasgow G2 5RT) : Tell Publishing, Scripture Union, 1976. — 32p : ill ; 18cm.
ISBN 0-904974-03-0 Sd : £0.25
(B77-02016)

Warren, Norman. Journey into life : a practical guide to Christian faith / [by] Norman Warren. — 2nd ed. — London : Falcon Books, 1976. — 15p : ill ; 18cm. — (A falcon booklet)
Previous ed.: London : Church Pastoral-Aid Society, 1964. — Bibl.: p.15.
ISBN 0-85491-143-x Sd : £0.12
(B77-02754)

Warren, Norman. The way ahead : a practical guide to Christian living / [by] Norman Warren. — 2nd ed. — London : Church Pastoral Aid Society, 1976. — 16p : ill ; 18cm. — (A falcon booklet)
Previous ed.: 1966.
ISBN 0-85491-145-6 Sd : £0.12
(B77-02755)

White, John. The fight : a practical handbook for Christian living / [by] John White. — Leicester : Inter-Varsity Press, 1977. — 230p ; 18cm.
ISBN 0-85110-394-4 Pbk : £1.20
(B77-32396)

White, Paul. Get moving! : motivation for living / [by] Paul White. — Exeter : Paternoster Press, 1976. — 128p ; 18cm.
Bibl.: p.126-128.
ISBN 0-85364-202-8 Pbk : £0.90
(B77-05856)

Wright, Michael. Call to action / [by] Michael Wright. — London [etc.] : Mowbrays, 1976 [i.e. 1977]. — 141p ; 18cm.
ISBN 0-264-66378-0 Pbk : £0.75
(B77-10154)

248 — Christian life. *Juvenile literature*
Gorrie, Richard Bingham. One life to live : a young person's guide to vocation / [by] Richard Gorrie. — London : Falcon Books, 1976. — 60p ; 18cm.
Bibl.
ISBN 0-85491-531-1 Pbk : £0.55
(B77-03360)

248 — Christian life. *Personal observations*
Lubich, Chiara. Yes yes, no no / [by] Chiara Lubich ; [translated from the Italian]. — London : New City ; London (57 Twyford Ave., W3 9PZ) : [Distributed by] Mariapolis Ltd, 1977. — [7],152p ; 16cm.
Translation of: 'Sí, sí. No, no'. Roma : Città Nuova, 1973.
ISBN 0-904287-07-6 Pbk : £1.60
(B77-33600)

Marshall, Catherine. Something more / [by] Catherine Marshall. — London [etc.] : Hodder and Stoughton, 1977. — 317p ; 18cm. — (Hodder Christian paperbacks)
Originally published: 1974.
ISBN 0-340-21328-0 Pbk : £0.95
(B77-25376)

Neve, Rosemary. At the name of Jesus / by Rosemary Neve. — Evesham : James, 1976. — 110p ; 19cm.
ISBN 0-85305-189-5 Pbk : £2.25
(B77-05194)

Steele, Gordon. One in all and all in one / [by] Gordon Steele. — Ilfracombe : Stockwell, 1977. — 40p ; 18cm.
ISBN 0-7223-1023-4 Pbk : £0.75
(B77-25377)

Wilkerson, David. Beyond 'The cross and the switchblade' / by David Wilkerson ; with a foreword by John and Elizabeth Sherrill. — London [etc.] : Hodder and Stoughton, 1977. — 190p ; 18cm. — (Hodder Christian paperbacks)
Originally published: Old Tappan : Chosen Books, 1974 ; London : Hodder and Stoughton, 1975.
ISBN 0-340-21260-8 Pbk : £0.80
(B77-13497)

248 — Christian life. *Secondary school texts. Welsh texts*
Datblygu yn yr Eglwys : llawlyfr ar gyfer dosbarthiadau o 14 i 18 oed / golygydd Rheinallt A. Thomas. — Caernarfon : Llyfrfa'r Methodistiaid Calfinaidd, 1976. — 98p : ill, map ; 22cm.
Adaptation of: 'Advancing in the Church' / prepared by Church of Scotland, Committee on Parish Education, Edinburgh : St Andrew Press, 1974.
ISBN 0-901330-61-2 Pbk : £0.60
(B77-03361)

248 — Christian life. *Stories for children. For teaching*
Mathews, Horace Frederick. Talks to children / [by] H.F. Mathews. — Redhill : Denholm House Press, 1977. — 92p ; 18cm.
This material first appeared in 'The expository times'. — Index.
ISBN 0-85213-164-x Pbk : Unpriced
(B77-33046)

248 — Christian life. *Welsh texts*
Dewi Maelog. Tystion i mi : rhai agweddau ar genhadu Cristnogol / [gan] Dewi Maelog. — Aberystwyth ('Bethesda', Penparcau, Aberystwyth, Dyfed SY23 1RY) : Undeb Cristnogol, [1975]. — 50p ; 22cm.
ISBN 0-904372-04-9 Sd : £0.25
(B77-08212)

Roberts, Emyr. Dyfod yn Gristion / [gan] Emyr Roberts. — Ail argraffiad. — Aberystwyth (['Bethesda', Penparcau, Aberystwyth, Dyfed SY23 1RY]) : Undeb Cristnogol Cymraeg, 1974. — [2],29p ; 12cm.
Previous ed.: s.l. : IUF, 1955.
ISBN 0-904372-03-0 Sd : £0.10
(B77-08213)

Stott, John Robert Walmsley. Os wyt Gristion - / [gan] John R.W. Stott. — Aberystwyth ('Bethesda', Penparcau, Aberystwyth, Dyfed SY23 1RY) : Undeb Cristnogol Cymraeg, [1976]. — 15p ; 18cm.
ISBN 0-904372-02-2 Sd : £0.10
(B77-08214)

248 — Man. Identity. *Christian viewpoints*
Carey, George. I believe in man / by George Carey. — London [etc.] : Hodder and Stoughton, 1977. — 190p ; 22cm.
Index.
ISBN 0-340-18100-1 Pbk : £2.95
(B77-32397)

248'.01'9 — Christian life. Psychological aspects
Rowe, Trevor Taylor. Wholeness : body, mind and spirit - one man / [by] Trevor Rowe. — London : Epworth Press, 1976. — 79p ; 19cm. — (Cell books ; 6)
Bibl.
ISBN 0-7162-0258-1 Pbk : £0.50
(B77-07792)

248'.02'4055 — Christian life. *For young persons. Extracts from periodicals*
Little fat 'Buzz' / compiled and edited by Chris Spencer ; executive editor Peter Meadows. — London [etc.] : Hodder and Stoughton, 1977. — 189p : ill, facsims ; 18cm.
ISBN 0-340-21484-8 Pbk : £0.90
(B77-11549)

248'.05 — Christian life. *For graduates. Periodicals*
Universities and Colleges Christian Fellowship. *Colleges' Department.* Broadsheet / UCCF Colleges' Dept. — Leicester (38 De Montfort St., Leicester LE1 7GP) : Universities and Colleges Christian Fellowship.
[No.1]-. — [197-?]-. — ill, ports ; 42cm.
Three issues a year. — [6]p. in Summer 1976 issue.
Sd : £0.06
ISSN 0308-9606
(B77-03909)

248'.08 — Christian life. *Collections. Juvenile literature*
Free Presbyterian Church of Scotland. Gospel gleanings for young people / [Free Presbyterian Church of Scotland]. — Glasgow (133 Woodlands Rd, Glasgow G.3) : Free Presbyterian Publications, 1976. — 127p ; 20cm.
Cover title. — Originally published: Inverness : Free Presbyterian Church of Scotland, 1961.
ISBN 0-902506-07-2 Pbk : £0.90
(B77-13498)

248'.2 — Christian life. Religious experiences
Leech, Kenneth, *b.1939.* Soul friend : a study of spirituality / [by] Kenneth Leech. — London : Sheldon Press, 1977. — [5],250p ; 22cm.
Bibl.: p.246-248. — Index.
ISBN 0-85969-113-6 Pbk : £3.95
(B77-20894)

Tissington, Eric Milford. Living light : an awakening to spiritual identity in Christ experienced by Eric Milford Tissington. — Woking (P.O. Box 29, Woking, Surrey, GU21 4AR) : Society for Spreading the Knowledge of True Prayer, 1974. — [2],15p ; 16cm.
Sd : £0.20
(B77-25378)

248'.2 — Roman Catholics. Christian life. Religious experiences
Doherty, Catherine de Hueck. Poustinia : Christian spirituality of the East for Western man / [by] Catherine de Hueck Doherty. — [London] ([14 St James's Place, S.W.1]) : Fountain Books, 1977. — 216p ; 18cm.
Originally published: Notre Dame, Ind. : Ave Maria Press, 1975.
ISBN 0-00-624806-3 Pbk : £0.75
(B77-10725)

248'.22 — Christian life. Mysticism
Goldsmith, Joel Solomon. Consciousness is what I am / [by] Joel S. Goldsmith ; edited by Lorraine Sinkler. — Romford : L.N. Fowler, [1977]. — xi,142p ; 22cm.
Originally published: New York : Harper and Row, 1976.
ISBN 0-85243-336-0 Pbk : £2.25
(B77-16719)

248'.22'08 — Christian life. Mysticism. *Readings*
An anthology of mysticism / edited with biographical notes by Paul de Jaegher and translated by Donald Attwater and others. — Abridged ed. — London : Burns and Oates, 1977. — vii,2-185p ; 22cm.
Full ed. originally published: 1935.
ISBN 0-86012-051-1 Pbk : £2.25
(B77-20011)

248'.22'0924 — Christian life. Mysticism. Francis of Assisi, Saint
Moorman, John Richard Humpidge. Richest of poor men : the spirituality of St Francis of Assisi / [by] John R.H. Moorman. — London : Darton, Longman and Todd, 1977. — 110p ; 19cm.
Bibl.: p.110.
ISBN 0-232-51371-6 Pbk : £1.25
(B77-22339)

248'.22'0924 — Christian life. Mysticism. Underhill, Evelyn
Ramsey, Arthur Michael. Evelyn Underhill : two centenary essays / by Michael Ramsey and A.M. Allchin. — Oxford : S.L.G. Press, 1977. — [4],23p ; 21cm. — (Fairacres publications ; no.63 ISSN 0307-1405)
ISBN 0-7283-0068-0 Sd : £0.35
(B77-17286)

248'.22'0946 — Christian life. Mysticism. *Spain. Collections*
The **wisdom** of the Spanish mystics / compiled by Stephen Clissold. — London : Sheldon Press, 1977. — [5],88p ; 20cm.
ISBN 0-85969-106-3 Pbk : £1.50
(B77-23098)

248'.22'0947 — Russkaia Pravoslavnaia Tserkov'. Monks. Christian life. Mysticism. *Soviet Union, to 1962*
Bolshakoff, Sergius. Russian mystics / by Sergius Bolshakoff ; introduction by Thomas Merton ; [translated from the Italian by the author]. — Kalamazoo : Cistercian Publications ; London : Mowbrays, 1977. — xxx,303p ; 22cm. — (Cistercian studies series ; no.26)
Translation and revision of: 'I mistici russi'. Torino : Società editrice internazionale, 1962. — Bibl.: p.285-303.
ISBN 0-264-66294-6 : £10.50
ISBN 0-264-66394-2 Pbk : £3.75
(B77-23984)

248'.246 — Christianity. Conversion of non-Christians
Godwin, J C. What it means to be born again / [by] J.C. Godwin. — Eastbourne : Coverdale House, 1977. — 95p ; 18cm.
ISBN 0-902088-97-1 Pbk : £0.85
(B77-33047)

248'.246 — Christianity. Conversion of non-Christians. *Collections*
Turner, Graham. More than conquerors / by Graham Turner. — London [etc.] : Hodder and Stoughton, 1976. — 224p ; 22cm.
ISBN 0-340-18478-7 : £4.50
(B77-11063)

248'.246 — Christianity. Conversion of non-Christians. *Japan. Personal observations*
Abrahams, Olga. Seiko : the story of a Japanese girl / [by] Olga Abrahams ; illustrations by John Rawding. — [Revised ed.]. — London : Overseas Missionary Fellowship, [1976]. — [1], 43p : ill ; 18cm.
Previous ed.: published as 'The spider's thread'. 1973.
ISBN 0-85363-112-3 Pbk : £0.35
(B77-07052)

248'.246 — Christianity. Conversion of non-Christians. *Personal observations*
Lemon, Fred. Breakout / by Fred Lemon ; with Gladys Knowlton. — London : Lakeland, 1977. — 190p ; 18cm.
ISBN 0-551-00598-x Pbk : £0.95
(B77-15686)

248'.246'0924 — Christianity. Conversion of drug addicts. *Great Britain. Personal observations*
Wilson, Frank, *b.1940.* House of new beginnings / [by] Frank W. Wilson with Linda Ball. — London : Lakeland, 1977. — 139p ; 18cm.
ISBN 0-551-00776-1 Pbk : £0.95
(B77-28370)

248'.25'0924 — Moral Re-Armament. Buchman, Frank Nathan Daniel. *Biographies*
Spoerri, Theophil. Dynamic out of silence : Frank Buchman's relevance today / [by] Theophil Spoerri ; [translated from the German by John Morrison and Peter Thwaites]. — London : Grosvenor Books, 1976. — 219p ; 18cm.
Translation of: 'Dynamik aus der Stille'. Luzern : Caux, 1971.
ISBN 0-901269-19-0 Pbk : £1.30
(B77-07793)

248'.29 — Christian life. Speaking in tongues
Parnell, Chris W. Understanding tongues-speaking / [by] Chris W. Parnell. — London : Lakeland, 1974. — 121p ; 18cm.
Originally published: Cape Town : National Commercial Printers Ltd, 1972.
ISBN 0-551-00512-2 Pbk : £0.50
(B77-20012)

248'.29 — Christian pilgrimages to miraculous shrines, to ca 1550
Finucane, Ronald C. Miracles and pilgrims : popular beliefs in medieval England / [by] Ronald C. Finucane. — London [etc.] : Dent, 1977. — 3-248p,16p of plates : ill, facsims, maps ; 24cm.
Bibl.: p.242-244. — Index.
ISBN 0-460-12019-0 : £6.95 : CIP rev.
(B77-19206)

248'.3 — Anglicans. Christian life. Contemplation
Paternoster, Michael. Study to be quiet / [by] Michael Paternoster. — Oxford : S.L.G. Press, 1976. — [1],12p ; 21cm. — (Fairacres publications ; no.59 ISSN 0307-1405)
ISBN 0-7283-0062-1 Sd : £0.15
(B77-05857)

248'.3 — Baptists. Christian life. Prayer
Dixon, Francis Willmore. Great and mighty things / [by] Francis W. Dixon. — London : Lakeland, 1976. — 96p ; 18cm. — (Words of life paperbacks ; 3)
ISBN 0-551-00584-x Pbk : £0.60
(B77-01154)

248'.3 — Christian life. Contemplation
Baker, Eve. The mystical journey : a western alternative / [by] Eve Baker. — London : Wildwood House, 1977. — [6],121p : ill ; 22cm.
Bibl.: p.117-121.
ISBN 0-7045-0249-6 : £4.50
ISBN 0-7045-0250-x Pbk : £1.95
(B77-14549)

Slade, Herbert Edwin William. Contemplative intimacy / [by] Herbert Slade. — London : Darton, Longman and Todd, 1977. — 218p : ill ; 22cm.
Bibl.: p.217-218.
ISBN 0-232-51367-8 : £2.95
(B77-17903)

248'.3 — Christian life. Meditation
Goldsmith, Joel Solomon. Practising the presence / by Joel S. Goldsmith. — 9th ed. — Romford : L.N. Fowler, 1976. — 200p ; 19cm.
Previous ed.: 1971.
ISBN 0-85243-021-3 Pbk : Unpriced
(B77-23985)

248'.3 — Christian life. Meditation. *Manuals*
Kelsey, Morton Trippe. The other side of silence : a guide to Christian meditation / [by] Morton T. Kelsey. — London : S.P.C.K., 1977. — viii,314p : ill ; 23cm.
Originally published: New York : Paulist Press, 1976.
ISBN 0-281-02984-9 Pbk : £3.50
(B77-22340)

Tilmann, Klemens. The practice of meditation / by Klemens Tilmann ; [translated from the German by David Smith]. — London : Search Press, 1977. — [4],139p : ill ; 22cm.
Translation of: 'Übungsbuch zur Meditation'. Zürich : Benziger Verlag, 1973.
ISBN 0-85532-374-4 Pbk : £2.50
(B77-10726)

248'.3 — Christian life. Prayer
Boros, Ladislaus. Prayer / [by] Ladislaus Boros ; translated [from the German] by David Smith. — London : Search Press, 1976. — [6],121p ; 22cm.
Translation of: 'Über das christliche Beten'. Mainz : Grünewald, 1973.
ISBN 0-85532-357-4 Pbk : £1.95
(B77-09491)

Bryant, Christopher, *b.1905.* Why prayer? / [by] Christopher Bryant. — London : Church Literature Association, [1977]. — [1],15,[1]p ; 22cm. — (Hillingdon papers ; 5)
'... condensed and thoroughly revised version of two lectures given in the Hillingdon Deanery in 1974 ...' - p.15.
Sd : £0.25
(B77-33601)

Christians at prayer / edited by John Gallen. — Notre Dame, Ind. ; London : University of Notre Dame Press, 1977. — xiii,160p ; 24cm. — (Liturgical studies)
Index.
ISBN 0-268-00718-7 : £7.50
(B77-21690)

Clark, Glenn. The soul's sincere desire / by Glenn Clark. — Evesham : James, 1976. — 105p ; 20cm.
Originally published: Boston, Mass. : Atlantic Monthly Press, 1925 ; Evesham : James, 1954.
ISBN 0-85305-012-0 Pbk : £1.50
(B77-16178)

Ecclestone, Alan. A staircase for silence / [by] Alan Ecclestone. — London : Darton, Longman and Todd, 1977. — [8],152p ; 22cm.
Bibl.: p.151-152.
ISBN 0-232-51364-3 Pbk : £2.00
(B77-08750)

Gullick, Etta. Getting to know you : prayer and God / by Etta Gullick. — Great Wakering : Mayhew-McCrimmon, 1976. — 192p ; 15cm.
ISBN 0-85597-100-2 Pbk : £0.85
(B77-05858)

Lane, Denis. God's powerful weapon / [by] Denis Lane. — London : OMF Books, 1977. — 42p ; 18cm.
ISBN 0-85363-117-4 Pbk : £0.30
(B77-20013)

Loew, Jacques. Face to face with God : the Bible's way to prayer / [by] Jacques Loew ; translated [from the French] by Alan Neame. — London : Darton, Longman and Todd, 1977. — xii,121p ; 22cm.
Translation of: 'La prière à l'école des grands priants'. Paris : Fayard, 1975.
ISBN 0-232-51360-0 Pbk : £1.95
(B77-17287)

Williams, Harry Abbott. Becoming what I am : a discussion of the methods and results of Christian prayer / [by] H.A. Williams. — London : Darton, Longman and Todd, 1977. — xii,77p ; 20cm.
ISBN 0-232-51362-7 Pbk : £1.50
(B77-11064)

248'.3 — Christian Scientists. Christian life. Prayer
Rawson, Frederick Lawrence. Right thinking, the basis of true prayer / by F.L. Rawson. — Woking (c/o P.O. Box 29, Woking, Surrey GU21 4AU) : Society for Spreading the Knowledge of True Prayer, 1976. — 32p ; 15cm.
Originally published: 1918.
Sd : £0.50
(B77-04544)

248'.3 — Roman Catholics. Christian life. Prayer. *Manuals. Facsimiles*
Peter of Alcantara, *Saint.* A golden treatise of mentall praier / [by] St Peter of Alcantara ; [translated from the Latin by G.W. i.e. Giles Willoughby]. Ordo baptizandi. — Ilkley [etc.] : Scolar Press, 1977. — [81],176,[5],135p ; 20cm. — (English recusant literature, 1558-1640 ; vol.338)
Facsimile reprints. — 'A golden treatise of mentall praier' originally published: Brussels : the Widow of Hubert Antony, 1632. — 'Ordo baptizandi' originally published: Paris : s.n., 1636.
ISBN 0-85967-374-x : Unpriced
Also classified at 264'.025
(B77-17288)

248'.3 — Roman Catholics. Christian life. Prayer. *Personal observations*
Torkington, Rayner. Peter Calvey, hermit : a personal rediscovery of prayer / by Rayner Torkington. — London : Shand, 1977. — 107p ; 21cm.
ISBN 0-904210-07-3 Pbk : £1.75
(B77-29165)

248'.3 — Russian Orthodox Church. Christian life. Prayer
Sofrony, *Archimandrite.* His life is mine / by Archimandrite Sophrony ; translated from the Russian [MS?] by Rosemary Edmonds. — London [etc.] : Mowbrays, 1977. — 128p ; 23cm.
ISBN 0-264-66311-x : £2.95
(B77-16720)

248'.4 — Christian life. Commitment
White, John. The cost of commitment / [by] John White. — Leicester : Inter-Varsity Press, 1976. — 91p ; 18cm.
ISBN 0-85110-392-8 Pbk : £0.60
(B77-05195)

248'.4 — Christian life. Solitude
Solitude and communion : papers on the hermit life given at St David's, Wales in the autumn of 1975 / edited by A.M. Allchin. — Oxford : S.L.G. Press, 1977. — vi,84p : facsim ; 21cm. — (Fairacres publications ; no.66 ISSN 0307-1413)
ISBN 0-7283-0072-9 Pbk : £1.50
(B77-29166)

248'.4 — Death. *Christian viewpoints*
Smith, JoAnn Kelley. Free fall / [by] JoAnn Kelley Smith ; foreword by Elizabeth Kübler-Ross. — London : S.P.C.K., 1977. — 138p : ill, port ; 22cm.
Originally published: Valley Forge : Judson Press, 1975.
ISBN 0-281-02978-4 Pbk : £2.50
(B77-23986)

248'.4 — Lonely persons. Christian life. *Personal observations*
Wiebe, Katie F. Alone : a search for joy / [by] Katie F. Wiebe. — London : Lakeland, 1977. — 286p ; 18cm.
Originally published: Wheaton, Ill. : Tyndale House, 1976.
ISBN 0-551-00774-5 Pbk : £1.25
(B77-30965)

248'.4 — Love. *Christian viewpoints*
Curle, Adam. Peace and love : the violin and the oboe / by Adam Curle. — London : Lindsey Press, 1977. — 13p ; 21cm. — (Essex Hall lectures)
'The Essex Hall lecture for 1977 ... delivered in London on April 13, 1977'.
Sd : £0.50
Also classified at 261.8'73
(B77-29925)

248'.4 — Sick persons. Christian life
Autton, Norman. When sickness comes : a simple guide / [by] Norman Autton. — [Penarth, S. Glam.] ([8 Hickman Rd, Penarth, S. Glam.]) : [Church in Wales Publications], 1973. — 67p ; 21cm.
Pbk : £0.85
(B77-20014)

248'.5 — Christian church. Children, 9-14 years. Personal evangelism
Prince, John. Early harvest - : leading a child to Christ / [by] John Prince. — London : Falcon Books, 1976. — [1],48p ; 20cm.
Bibl.: p.47-48.
ISBN 0-85491-147-2 Pbk : £0.60
(B77-04545)

248'.82 — Children. Christian life. *Juvenile literature*
Warren, Norman. Road clear / [by] Norman Warren. — 2nd ed. — London : Church Pastoral Aid Society, 1976. — 15p : ill ; 18cm. — (A falcon booklet)
Previous ed.: 1972.
ISBN 0-85491-144-8 Sd : £0.12
(B77-02756)

248'.83'0947 — Young persons. Christian life. *Soviet Union*
Bourdeaux, Michael. Young Christians in Russia / [by] Michael Bourdeaux and Katharine Murray. — London : Lakeland, 1976. — 156p ; 18cm. — (Keston books ; no.5)
ISBN 0-551-00752-4 Pbk : £0.75
(B77-02757)

248'.86 — Bereavement. *Christian viewpoints*
Snowden, Rita Frances. When sorrow comes / [by] Rita F. Snowden. — [London] ([14 St James's Place, S.W.1]) : Fountain Books, 1977. — 95p ; 18cm.
ISBN 0-00-624594-3 Pbk : £0.75
(B77-18543)

248'.892 — Roman Catholic Church. Clergy. Vocation. *Poland. Personal observations. Polish texts*
Makowski, Jerzy. Wspomnienia kaplana / Jerzy Makowski. — London : Veritas Foundation Publication Centre, 1975. — 332p ; 19cm. — (Biblioteka polska : seria czerwona ; tom 79)
ISBN 0-901215-64-3 : £3.30
(B77-08215)

248'.8943'8 — Anchoresses. Christian life. *Manuals. Early works*
[Ancren Riwle]. The English text of the 'Ancrene Riwle' / edited from Magdalene College, Cambridge MS. Pepys 2498 by A. Zettersten. — London [etc.] : Oxford University Press for the Early English Text Society, 1976. — xxiii, 184p,[2]fold leaves of plates(tipped in) : 2 facsims ; 23cm. — (Early English Text Society. Original series ; no.274)
Middle English text, English introduction and notes.
ISBN 0-19-722276-5 : £3.75
(B77-03910)

248'.9 — Salvation Army. Christian life. *For teaching*
Salvation Army. Preparation for soldiership : a handbook of lessons for the use of officers and others who conduct young people's recruits' preparatory classes / [Salvation Army]. — 2nd ed. — London : Salvationist Publishing and Supplies, 1977. — v,36p ; 19cm.
Previous ed.: 1956.
ISBN 0-85412-304-0 Pbk : Unpriced
(B77-25379)

248'.9'2 — Roman Catholics. Christian life
Entwistle, Harry. Sin, guilt and freedom / [by] Harry Entwistle. — London : Church Literature Association, 1976. — [2],18p ; 21cm.
ISBN 0-85191-083-1 Sd : £0.30
(B77-08751)

Martin, Ralph, *b.1942.* Hungry for God : practical help in personal prayer / [by] Ralph Martin ; with an introduction by David Winter. — Shortened and revised ed. — [London] : Fontana, 1976. — 157p ; 19cm.
This ed. originally published: London : Collins, 1975.
ISBN 0-00-624456-4 Pbk : £0.75
(B77-11550)

National Conference of Catholic Bishops *(United States).* To live in Christ Jesus : a pastoral reflection on the moral life / National Conference of Catholic Bishops of the United States. — London : Catholic Truth Society, 1976. — 40p ; 19cm.
Sd : £0.30
(B77-33602)

Suenens, Léon Joseph. Ways of the spirit : the spirituality of Cardinal Suenens / drawn from the writings of Cardinal Suenens and edited with an introduction by Elizabeth Hamilton. — London : Darton, Longman and Todd, 1976. — 124p ; 19cm.
Bibl.: p.123-124.
ISBN 0-232-51359-7 Pbk : £1.20
(B77-02017)

Teresa, *Saint, of Avila.* [Camino de perfección. English]. Way of perfection / [by] St Teresa of Avila ; translated [from the Spanish by] E. Allison Peers. — London : Sheed and Ward, 1977. — vi,186p ; 20cm. — (Spiritual masters)
This translation originally published: in 'The complete works of Saint Teresa of Jesus'. 1946.
ISBN 0-7220-7717-3 Pbk : £1.50
(B77-18544)

248'.9'2 — Roman Catholics. Christian life. *Secondary school texts*
McGurk, Thomas. Growing faith / [by] Thomas McGurk, A.P. Purnell, Dolores Dodgson ; art and design by John Dugan. — Edinburgh : Holmes-McDougall.
Book 3. — [1976]. — 96p : ill(some col), ports ; 21x28cm.
ISBN 0-7157-1014-1 Pbk : £1.80
(B77-10727)

McGurk, Thomas. Growing faith / [by] Thomas McGurk, A.P. Purnell, Dolores Dodgson ; art and design by John Dugan. — Edinburgh : Holmes McDougall.
Book 3. [Teacher's book]. — [1976]. — 122p : ill(chiefly col), ports ; 21x28cm.
ISBN 0-7157-1015-x Pbk : Unpriced
(B77-28371)

248'.9'3 — Anglicans. Christian life
Silvester, Hugh. The Christian difference / [by] Hugh Silvester ; foreword by the Bishop of Rochester. — London : Falcon Books, 1977. — 112p ; 20cm.
ISBN 0-85491-535-4 Pbk : £0.95
(B77-17289)

248'.9'3 — Anglicans. Christian life. *Personal observations*
Israel, Martin. Precarious living : the path to life / by Martin Israel. — London [etc.] : Hodder and Stoughton, 1976. — 190p ; 23cm.
ISBN 0-340-20690-x : £3.75
(B77-16721)

248'.9'52 — Church of Scotland. Christian life. *Personal observations*
Barclay, William, *b.1907.* Testament of faith / by William Barclay. — New ed. — London [etc.] : Mowbrays, 1977. — xii,124p ; 18cm. — (Mowbray popular Christian paperback)
Bibl.: p.123-124.
ISBN 0-264-66377-2 Pbk : £0.75
(B77-31684)

248'.9'708 — Methodists. Christian life. *Anthologies*
BM's Jubilee soapbox / general editor Eric A. Thorn. — Basildon (Trinity Methodist Church, Clay Hill Rd, Basildon, Essex) : 'Basildon Methodist', 1977. — [16]p : ill ; 21cm.
'An anthology of articles reprinted from the "Basildon Methodist" - a monthly publication from the Basildon Circuit of the Methodist Church' - cover.
Sd : Unpriced
(B77-33603)

248'.9'99 — Christian spiritualists. Christian life. *Welsh texts*
Collins, Irene, *b.1916.* Sicrwydd / gan Irene Collins. — Llandysul : Gwasg Gomer, 1976. — 132p ; 22cm.
ISBN 0-85088-410-1 Pbk : £1.00
(B77-05859)

249 — CHRISTIAN WORSHIP IN FAMILY LIFE

249 — Activities for Roman Catholic families: Activities connected with Christmas & activities connected with Easter. *Collections*
Pratt, Oliver. The Christmas and Easter ideas book / [by] Oliver and Ianthe Pratt ; illustrated by Ianthe and Clare Pratt. — London : Sheed and Ward, 1977. — ix,85p : ill ; 20cm.
Bibl.: p.70-72.
ISBN 0-7220-7714-9 Pbk : £1.95
(B77-23099)

251 — CHRISTIAN CHURCH. PREACHING

251 — Christian church. Preaching. *Lectures, speeches*
Pitt-Watson, Ian. A kind of folly : toward a practical theology of preaching / [by] Ian Pitt-Watson. — Edinburgh : St Andrew Press, 1976. — ix,109p ; 23cm. — (The Warrack lectures ; 1972-1975)
ISBN 0-7152-0344-4 : £3.75
(B77-22341)

251'.0092'4 — Nonconformist churches. Preaching. Morgan, M P. *Personal observations. Welsh texts*
Evans, Daniel John. M.P. Morgan, Blaenannerch, 1876-1964 / gan D.J. Evans. — Caernarfon : [Llyfrfa'r Methodistiaid Calfinaidd], 1976. — 88p,[2]p of plates : 1 ill, ports ; 19cm.
ISBN 0-901330-66-3 Pbk : £0.60
(B77-03362)

251'.02'05 — Christian church. Sermons. *Sermon outlines. Serials*
The **ministers** manual (Doran's). — New York [etc.] ; London : Harper and Row.
1977 ed. : fifty-second annual issue / edited by Charles L. Wallis. — [1977]. — viii,276p ; 21cm.
Published in the United States: 1976. — Index.
ISBN 0-06-069022-4 : £4.85
(B77-09492)

252 — CHRISTIAN CHURCH. SERMONS

252 — Christian church. Sermons. *Texts*
Dixon, Francis Willmore. Some names worth having / [by] Francis W. Dixon. — London : Lakeland, 1977. — 94p ; 18cm. — (Words of life paperbacks ; 4)
ISBN 0-551-00767-2 Pbk : £0.75
(B77-23100)

Kershaw, John, *b.1792.* Grace alone : ten sermons / by John Kershaw ; [edited and with a] foreword by K.W.H. Howard. — Ossett : Zoar Publications, 1976. — [8],170p ; 19cm.
ISBN 0-904435-09-1 : £3.75
(B77-19207)

Niebuhr, Reinhold. Justice and mercy / [by] Reinhold Niebuhr ; edited by Ursula M. Niebuhr. — New York [etc.] ; London : Harper and Row, 1976. — xi,139,[1]p ; 21cm.
Originally published: 1974. — Bibl.: p.139. — Index.
ISBN 0-06-066172-0 Pbk : £2.20
Also classified at 242'.8
(B77-02758)

Thomas, Isaac David Ellis. The hidden hand / [by] I.D.E. Thomas. — Swansea : C. Davies, 1976. — 166p ; 22cm.
ISBN 0-7154-0116-5 : £3.25
(B77-14550)

252'.00947 — Christian church. Sermons. *Eastern Europe. Anthologies*
Here they stand : biblical sermons from Eastern Europe / compiled and edited by Lewis A. Drummond. — London : Marshall, Morgan and Scott, 1976. — v,186p : maps ; 22cm.
ISBN 0-551-05539-1 Pbk : £2.95
(B77-16722)

252'.02 — Roman Catholic Church. Sermons. *Texts*
Carroll, John. The John Carroll papers / Thomas O'Brien Hanley, editor ; under the auspices of the American Catholic Historical Association ; endorsed by the National Historical Publications and Records Commission. — Notre Dame ; London : University of Notre Dame Press, 1976. — 3v.(li,551p,[4]p of plates;liv,543p,[2]p of plates;liii,517p,[4]p of plates) : ill, geneal table, ports ; 25cm.
In 3 vols. — Bibl. — Index. — Includes some papers in French and Latin.
ISBN 0-268-01186-9 : £60.00
Primary classification 282'.092'4
(B77-04549)

252'.02 — Roman Catholic Church. Sermons. *Texts. For church year*
Nassan, Maurice. In the Name of the Father : topics and reflections for Sundays and feast days, year C / [by] Maurice Nassan. — London (221 Golders Green Rd, N.W.11) : T. Shand Publications, 1976. — 67p ; 22cm.
Cover title.
ISBN 0-904210-05-7 Pbk : £1.00
(B77-02759)

Redemptorists. *English Province.* The living word / [Redemptorists, English Province]. — Alton : Redemptorist Publications.
Cycle A. Part 1 / written and edited by the Redemptorists of the London Province. — 1977. — [64]p ; 21cm.
'1st Sunday of Advent 1977 to 5th Sunday of the year 1978, homilies for baptisms and funerals' - cover.
ISBN 0-85231-034-x Pbk : Unpriced
(B77-33604)

Cycle C. Part 2 / written and edited by the Redemptorists of the London Province. — 1977. — [64]p ; 21cm.
'1st Sunday of Lent to Pentecost 1977' - cover.
ISBN 0-85231-017-x Pbk : £1.25
(B77-09493)

Cycle C. Part 3 / written and edited by the Redemptorists of the London Province. — 1977. — [64]p ; 21cm.
'Trinity Sunday to 21st Sunday of the year 1977' - Cover.
ISBN 0-85231-032-3 Pbk : £1.25
(B77-25380)

Cycle C. Part 4 / written and edited by the Redemptorists of the London Province. — 1977. — [64]p ; 21cm.
'22nd Sunday of the year to Christ the King 1977, homilies for weddings' - cover.
ISBN 0-85231-033-1 Pbk : £1.25
(B77-25381)

252'.02'0902 — Roman Catholic Church. Sermons, ca 400-ca 1500. *Periodicals*
Medieval sermon studies newsletter. — Coventry (Coventry CV4 7AL) : English Department, University of Warwick.
No.1- ; Summer 1977-. — 1977-. — 21cm.
Published at irregular intervals. — 6 leaves in 1st issue.
Sd : £0.25
ISSN 0140-1211
(B77-30966)

252'.03 — Church in Wales. Sermons. *Texts*
Thomas, J J A. The letter to the Hebrews, and other addresses / by J.J.A. Thomas. — Penarth (Education and Communications Centre, Woodlands Rd, Penarth, S. Glam. CF6 2EX) : Church in Wales Publications, 1976. — 48p ; 21cm.
Pbk : £1.00
Primary classification 227'.87'06
(B77-17894)

252'.05'2 — Church of Scotland. Sermons. *Texts*
Wright, Ronald Selby. Seven sevens : a miscellany / [by] Ronald Selby Wright. — Edinburgh : Scottish Academic Press, 1977. — ix,167p,plate : ill, port ; 23cm.
Index.
ISBN 0-7073-0139-4 : £2.50
(B77-27676)

252'.07 — Methodist churches. Sermons. *Texts*
Morris, Colin, *b.1928.* Bugles in the afternoon / [by] Colin Morris. — London : Epworth Press, 1977. — 190p ; 19cm.
ISBN 0-7162-0300-6 Pbk : £1.00
(B77-33605)

252'.53 — Christian church. Children's sermons. *Texts*
Morrison, Edith. Holidays abroad : story-object lessons for children / by Edith Morrison ; illustrations by Elizabeth M. Reeve. — Ilkeston : Moorley's Bible and Bookshop, 1976. — 74p : ill ; 21cm.
ISBN 0-901495-92-1 Pbk : £0.55
(B77-06464)

253 — CHRISTIAN CHURCH. CLERGY AND PASTORAL WORK

253 — Christian church. Pastoral work. *Manuals*
Hocking, Michael. A handbook of pastoral work / by Michael Hocking. — London [etc.] : Mowbrays, 1977. — xiv,117p ; 19cm.
Index.
ISBN 0-264-66312-8 Pbk : £1.95
(B77-32398)

White, Reginald Ernest Oscar. A guide to pastoral care : a practical primer of pastoral theology / [by] R.E.O. White. — London : Pickering and Inglis, 1976. — ix,325p ; 21cm.
Bibl.: p.321-322.
ISBN 0-7208-0377-2 : £7.50
(B77-05196)

253 — Pastoral work. *Meditations*
Newbigin, Lesslie. 'The Good Shepherd' : meditations on Christian ministry in today's world / [by] Lesslie Newbigin ; foreword by the Archbishop of Canterbury. — Revised ed. — Leighton Buzzard : Faith Press, 1977. — 158p ; 19cm.
'... talks ... originally given to the clergy of the Church of South India working in ... Madras' - Preface. — Previous ed.: Madras : Christian Literature Society, 197-.
ISBN 0-7164-0445-1 Pbk : £1.50
(B77-08752)

253 — Roman Catholic Church. Clergy. Pastoral role. *London. Personal observations*
Boyd, Neil. Bless me, Father / [by] Neil Boyd. — London : Hale, 1977. — 172p ; 23cm.
ISBN 0-7091-5860-2 : £3.75
(B77-14551)

253 — Roman Catholic Church. Parish work. *Great Britain*
The **caring** parish : some approaches / [Social Welfare Commission]. — Abingdon (1a Stert St., Abingdon, Oxon. OX14 3JF) : Social Welfare Commission, [1977]. — [2],25,[1]p : ill, ports ; 30cm.
ISBN 0-9502393-3-x Sd : £0.50
(B77-15084)

254 — CHRISTIAN CHURCH. PARISH WORK. ORGANISATION

254'.02'42 — Roman Catholic Church. Parish work. Organisation. *Great Britain. For Roman Catholic religious communities*
Gaine, Michael. Pastoral policies / by Michael Gaine. — [Liverpool] ([Christ's College, Woolton Rd, Liverpool L16 8ND]) : Liverpool Institute of Socio-Religious Studies [for] the Conference of Major Religious Superiors of England and Wales, 1977. — [3],25p ; 21cm. — (Pastoral investigation of social trends ; working paper no.8)
'... basically the text of a lecture delivered at Los Angeles Conference on "Religion and the Humanising of Man" in September 1972' - Preface.
ISBN 0-905052-08-0 Sd : £0.60
(B77-25382)

254'.7 — Church of England. Redundant churches. St Edmundsbury and Ipswich (Diocese). Bishop, 1966- (Brown). Bishop's Commission on Reorganization in the Ipswich Deanery. Report. *Critical studies*
Fitch, John, *b.1922.* A curate's egg : the Ipswich Deanery reorganization report considered / by John Fitch. — Brandon ([The Rectory, Brandon, Suffolk IP27 0HZ]) : The author, 1972. — [1],12p ; 26cm.
Sd : £0.25
(B77-29926)

254'.7 — Redundant churches. *Great Britain*
Binney, Marcus. Change & decay : the future of our churches / [by Marcus Binney and John Physick]. — [London] : Victoria and Albert Museum, 1977. — [2],12,[2]p : ill ; 21cm.
Published to accompany the exhibition at the Victoria and Albert Museum.
ISBN 0-905209-08-7 Sd : £0.15
(B77-20895)

Change & decay : the future of our churches / [edited by] Marcus Binney and Peter Burman. — London : Studio Vista, 1977. — 192p : ill, coat of arms, plans, ports ; 26cm.
ISBN 0-289-70774-9 : £8.25
ISBN 0-289-70775-7 Pbk : £3.75
(B77-28372)

254'.7'06242821 — Parish churches. Maintenance. Organisations. *South Yorkshire (Metropolitan County). Sheffield. Sheffield Church Burgesses Trust, to 1977*
Pye-Smith, Brian C. An historical note on the Sheffield Church Burgesses Trust, 1554-1977 / by Brian C. Pye-Smith. — [Sheffield] ([Somerleyton, 1 Stratford Rd, Sheffield S10 3LR]) : [The author], 1977. — 20p : ill(tipped in), port(tipped in) ; 24cm.
Sd : Unpriced
(B77-26778)

255 — CHRISTIANITY. RELIGIOUS CONGREGATIONS AND ORDERS

255 — Roman Catholic Church. Religious orders. Community life. *Lectures, speeches*
Hume, George Basil. Searching for God / by George Basil Hume. — London [etc.] : Hodder and Stoughton, 1977. — 192p ; 23cm.
ISBN 0-340-22278-6 : £4.25
ISBN 0-340-22277-8 Pbk : £2.95
(B77-32399)

255'.1'00941 — Benedictines. *Great Britain. Yearbooks*
Benedictines. *English Congregation.* The Benedictine yearbook : a guide to the abbeys, priories, parishes, and schools of the monks and nuns of the Order of Saint Benedict in the British Isles and their foundations abroad. — Warrington (c/o St Alban's Priory, Bewsey St., Warrington WA2 7JQ) : [English Congregation of the Order of St Benedict].
1977 / edited by Gordon Beattie. — [1976]. — 162p : ill, map, ports(some col) ; 18cm.
Pbk : £0.25
ISSN 0522-8883
(B77-03911)

255'.9 — Christian church. Nuns
Bernstein, Marcelle. Nuns / [by] Marcelle Bernstein. — London : Collins, 1976. — 361p ; 22cm.
Index.
ISBN 0-00-215579-6 : £4.95
(B77-00014)

255'.979 — Bernardine Cistercians. *Great Britain*
Bernardine Cistercians. *English Province.* Freely - in faith / [Bernardine Cistercians, English Province]. — [Slough] ([1 Langley Rd, Slough, Berks. SL3 7AF]) : [St Bernard's Convent], [1977]. — [35]p : ill ; 16cm.
Sd : £0.20
(B77-33048)

260 — CHRISTIAN CHURCH. THEOLOGY AND PRACTICES

260 — Christian church
Robinson, John Arthur Thomas. On being the Church in the world / [by] John A.T. Robinson. — [3rd ed.]. — London [etc.] : Mowbrays, 1977. — 3-199p ; 22cm.
Previous ed.: i.e. 1st ed. London : S.C.M. Press, 1960.
ISBN 0-264-66459-0 Pbk : £3.25
(B77-29167)

Sharp, David G. No stained-glass-window saints : the Church in the New Testament and today / [by] David G. Sharp. — London : Epworth Press, 1976. — 128p ; 19cm.
Bibl.
ISBN 0-7162-0268-9 Pbk : £1.50
(B77-03363)

Snyder, Howard A. New wineskins : changing the man-made structures of the church / [by] Howard A. Snyder. — London : Marshall, Morgan and Scott, 1977. — 3-192p : 1 ill ; 20cm.
Originally published: as 'The problem of wine skins'. Downers Grove, Ill. : Intervarsity Press, 1975.
ISBN 0-551-05562-6 Pbk : £1.95
(B77-19208)

260 — Christian church. *Roman Catholic viewpoints*
Bühlmann, Walbert. Forward, Church! : essays in ecclesiastical spirituality / [by] Walbert Bühlmann ; [translated from the Italian by Mary Smith]. — Slough : St Paul Publications, 1977. — 149p ; 21cm.
Translation of: 'Coraggio, Chiesa!'. Rome : Edizioni Paoline, 1977.
ISBN 0-85439-134-7 Pbk : £2.00
(B77-25383)

261 — CHRISTIANITY. SOCIAL THEOLOGY

261 — Authority. *Christian viewpoints*
Dominian, Jacob. Authority : a Christian interpretation of the psychological evolution of authority / [by] Jack Dominian. — London : Burns and Oates, 1976. — [5],iii,107p ; 22cm.
ISBN 0-86012-022-8 Pbk : £2.50
(B77-11551)

261 — Society. *Christian viewpoints*
Ferguson, John, *b.1921.* O my people : God's call to society / [by] John Ferguson. — London : Oliphants, 1977. — 144p ; 19cm. — (Oliphant outlook books)
Bibl.: p.137-138. — Index.
ISBN 0-551-00773-7 Pbk : £1.25
(B77-32400)

261.1 — Education. *Christian viewpoints*
Christian Education Movement. Christians asking questions about education / [Christian Education Movement]. — London : C.E.M., 1977. — [2],25p : ill ; 22cm.
ISBN 0-905022-21-1 Sd : £0.35
(B77-23987)

261.1 — Education. *Ireland (Republic). Roman Catholic viewpoints*
Have the snakes come back? : education and the Irish child / by a group of Catholic parents. — Dublin (55 Lower Gardiner St., Dublin 1) : Vera Verba Publications, [1975]. — [2],72,[2]p ; 19cm.
Bibl.: p.61.
Sd : £0.40
(B77-20896)

261.1 — Environment. *Church of England viewpoints*
Paternoster, Michael. Man : the world's high priest : an ecological approach / [by] Michael Paternoster. — Oxford : S.L.G. Press, 1976. — [1],12p ; 21cm. — (Fairacres publications ; no.58 ISSN 0307-1405)
ISBN 0-7283-0063-x Sd : £0.15
(B77-07053)

261.1 — Further education & higher education. Role of Christian church. *Great Britain*
The **language** of the church in higher and further education : an account of the Bradwell Consultation / [edited] by Michael Pye ; with papers by Charles Carter ... [et al.]. — [London] ([General Synod, Board of Education, Church House, Dean's Yard, SW1 3NZ]) : The Bradwell Consultation, 1977. — [3],iii,73p ; 21cm.
ISBN 0-9505459-0-2 Sd : £1.00
(B77-12289)

261.1 — Ireland (Republic). Social planning. *Council for Social Welfare viewpoints*
Council for Social Welfare. Planning for social development : what needs to be done / Council for Social Welfare (a committee of the Catholic Bishops' Conference). — Dublin ([169 Booterstown Ave., Blackrock, Co. Dublin]) : The Council, 1976. — [3],29p ; 30cm.
ISBN 0-9503413-3-9 Sp : £0.50
(B77-05860)

261.1 — Medicine. *Christian viewpoints*
Burkitt, Denis Parsons. Our priorities / [by] D.P. Burkitt. — London : Christian Medical Fellowship, 1976. — 20p ; 18cm.
'An Address given at the Annual Breakfast of the Christian Medical Fellowship (held during the Conjoint Annual General Meeting of the British, Irish and Canadian Medical Associations in Dublin, June 1976) ...' - title page verso.
ISBN 0-85111-957-3 Sd : £0.20
(B77-03364)

Gardner, Reginald Frank Robert. By what standard? / [by] R.F.R. Gardner. — London : Christian Medical Fellowship, 1977. — 16p ; 18cm.
'An address given at the Annual Breakfast of the Christian Medical Fellowship (held during the Annual Conference of the British Medical Association in Glasgow, July 1977) ...' - title page verso.
ISBN 0-85111-959-x Sd : £0.20
(B77-30967)

261.1 — Political events. Role of World Council of Churches, 1948-1976. *Christian Affirmation Campaign viewpoints*
Smith, Bernard, *b.1925 (Dec.).* The fraudulent gospel : politics and the World Council of Churches / by Bernard Smith. — Richmond, Surrey : Foreign Affairs Publishing Co., 1977. — 99p ; 21cm.
ISBN 0-900380-20-9 Sd : £1.00
(B77-27677)

261.1 — Society. Role of Christian church. Related to Marxism
Hebblethwaite, Peter. The Christian-Marxist dialogue : beginnings, present status, and beyond / by Peter Hebblethwaite. — London : Darton, Longman and Todd, 1977. — [3], 122p ; 22cm.
Index.
ISBN 0-232-51390-2 Pbk : £2.50
Also classified at 335.4
(B77-29927)

Vree, Dale. On synthesizing Marxism and Christianity / [by] Dale Vree. — New York ; London [etc.] : Wiley, 1976. — xxiii,206p ; 22cm.
'A Wiley-Interscience publication'. — Bibl.: p.183-201. — Index.
ISBN 0-471-01603-9 : £11.20
Also classified at 335.4
(B77-14041)

261.1'09689'7 — Malawi. Northern Province. Society. Role of Livingstonia Mission, 1875-1940
McCracken, John Leslie. Politics and Christianity in Malawi, 1875-1940 : the impact of the Livingstonia Mission in the Northern Province / [by] John McCracken. — Cambridge [etc.] : Cambridge University Press, 1977. — xv,324p : maps ; 24cm. — (Cambridge Commonwealth series)
Bibl.: p.295-310. — Index.
ISBN 0-521-21444-0 : £12.00
(B77-29168)

261.2 — Christian church. Relations with Judaism. Theories of Origen
De Lange, Nicholas. Origen and the Jews : studies in Jewish-Christian relations in third-century Palestine / [by] N.R.M. de Lange. — Cambridge [etc.] : Cambridge University Press, 1976. — x,240p ; 23cm. — (University of Cambridge. Oriental publications ; no.25)
Bibl.: p.209-215. — Index.
ISBN 0-521-20542-5 : £8.00
Also classified at 296.3'87'2
(B77-06465)

261.2 — Non-Christian religions. Attitudes of Christianity
Cragg, Kenneth. The Christian and other religion : the measure of Christ / [by] Kenneth Cragg. — London [etc.] : Mowbrays, 1977. — xiv,138p ; 23cm. — (Mowbrays library of theology)
Index.
ISBN 0-264-66413-2 : £6.00
ISBN 0-264-66256-3 Pbk : £2.95
(B77-14552)

261.7 — Elected assemblies. Devolution of powers of British government. *Scotland & Wales. British Council of Churches viewpoints*
Johnston, W B. Devolution and the British churches / [by] W.B. Johnston, W.D. Pattinson, the Archbishop of Wales. — London : British Council of Churches, 1977. — iv,55p ; 21cm.
'Report to the Spring 1977 Assembly of the British Council of Churches'.
Sd : £1.00
(B77-26107)

261.7 — Human rights. *Roman Catholic viewpoints*
Bogan, Robert. This is right / [by Robert Bogan]. — London : Catholic Truth Society, [1976]. — [6],51p ; 21cm.
'A summary ... of the working paper "The Church and human rights" published in 1975 by the Pontifical Commission "Justitia et Pax"' - cover.
ISBN 0-85183-175-3 Sd : £0.40
(B77-02018)

261.7 — Natural justice. *Roman Catholic viewpoints*
Bogan, R V. Our world and you / [prepared by R.V. Bogan]. — London : Catholic Truth Society, [1972]. — [2],14p ; 19cm.
ISBN 0-85183-182-6 Sd : £0.15
(B77-05197)

261.8 — Social services. Policies of government. Attitudes of Roman Catholics. *Great Britain, 1940-1965*
Coman, Peter. Catholics and the welfare state / [by] Peter Coman. — London [etc.] : Longman, 1977. — ix,118p ; 23cm.
Bibl.: p.111-114. — Index.
ISBN 0-582-48543-6 : £5.25
(B77-27678)

261.8'3 — Social conditions. *United Reformed Church viewpoints. Periodicals*
GOAD. — London (87 Tavistock Place, WC1H 9RT) : Fellowship of United Reformed Youth. No.1- ; Autumn 1975-. — [1975]-. — ill ; 26cm.
Three issues a year. — Folder ([4]p.) as 1st issue.
£0.02(£0.25 yearly)
ISSN 0308-7913
(B77-00602)

261.8'3 — Violence. *Ireland. Christian viewpoints. Reports, surveys*
Violence in Ireland : a report to the churches. — Belfast (2 Bristow Park, Belfast BT9 6TH) : Christian Journals Ltd [etc.], 1976. — 128p ; 18cm.
'This report comes from the fifth Working Party appointed by the Irish Council of Churches/Roman Catholic Church Joint Group on Social Questions' - Foreword. — Bibl.: p.127.
ISBN 0-904302-27-x Pbk : £0.90
(B77-01155)

261.8'32 — Welfare services for pregnant women. *Great Britain. Roman Catholic viewpoints*
Barrell, Dilys. You don't need to have an abortion / by Dilys Barrell. — London : Catholic Truth Society, 1976. — 12p ; 19cm.
ISBN 0-85183-186-9 Sd : £0.15
(B77-05861)

261.8'32'1 — Health services. *Christian viewpoints. Secondary school texts*
Billington, Roy. Health / by Roy Billington ; edited by Harry Undy. — London (2 Chester House, Pages La., N10 1PR) : Christian Education Movement, 1977. — 34p : ill ; 26cm. — (Probe ISSN 0305-3776)
ISBN 0-905022-14-9 Sd : £0.70
(B77-11552)

261.8'32'20941 — Mental health services. *England. Roman Catholic viewpoints*
Wertheimer, Alison. Out of mind : mental illness / by Alison Wertheimer. — Liverpool ([Christ's College, Woolton Rd, Liverpool L16 8ND]) : Liverpool Institute of Socio-Religious Studies [for] the Conference of Major Religious Superiors of England and Wales, 1977. — [3], 40p ; 21cm. — (Pastoral investigation of social trends ; working paper no.9)
Bibl.: p.40. — List of films: p.39-40.
ISBN 0-905052-09-9 Sd : £0.60
(B77-30968)

261.8'32'292 — Alcoholic drinks. *Band of Hope viewpoints*
A **short** straight look at alcohol / edited and compiled by A. Candler Page ; art work and design by John Pickering. — London (45 Great Peter St., SW1P 3LT) : Hope Press, [1976]. — 52p : ill ; 20cm.
ISBN 0-9505333-0-0 Sd : £0.50
(B77-00015)

261.8'33'66 — Capital punishment. *Christian viewpoints*
O'Donovan, Oliver. Measure for measure : justice in punishment and the sentence of death / by Oliver O'Donovan. — Bramcote : Grove Books, 1977. — 24,[1]p ; 22cm. — (Grove booklets on ethics ; 19 ISSN 0305-4241)
ISBN 0-905422-22-8 Sd : £0.35
(B77-32401)

261.8'34'157 — Homosexuality. *Christian viewpoints*
Moss, Roger. Christians and homosexuality / [by] Roger Moss. — Exeter : Paternoster Press, 1977. — 48p ; 18cm. — ([Paternoster punchline ; no.7])
Bibl.: p.48.
ISBN 0-85364-212-5 Sd : £0.55 : CIP rev.
(B77-30969)

Oraison, Marc. The homosexual question / by Marc Oraison ; translated from the French by Jane Zeni Flinn. — London : Search Press, 1977. — [7],132p ; 21cm.
Translation of: 'La question homosexuelle'. Paris : Seuil, 1975.
ISBN 0-85532-377-9 Pbk : £2.95
(B77-23988)

261.8'34'157 — Homosexuality. *Gay Christian Movement viewpoints*
Cotter, Jim. Freedom and framework : the study of gay relationships / by Jim Cotter. — [Cambridge] ([15 Bermuda Rd, Cambridge]) : Gay Christian Movement, 1977. — [15]p ; 21cm.
'A paper given to a GCM conference held in Birmingham on 18 September 1976' - p.[2].
Sd : £0.15
(B77-32402)

261.8'34'157 — Homosexuality. Attitudes of Roman Catholic Church, to 1976
McNeill, John J. The Church and the homosexual / [by] John J. McNeill. — London : Darton, Longman and Todd, 1977. — xi,211p ; 22cm.
Originally published: Kansas City : Sheed and Ward, 1976.
ISBN 0-232-51370-8 Pbk : £2.60
(B77-12290)

261.8'34'17 — Sex relations. *Gay Christian Movement viewpoints*
Coggin, Sara. Sexual expression and moral chaos / by Sara Coggin. — [Cambridge] ([15 Bermuda Rd, Cambridge]) : Gay Christian Movement, 1976. — [11]p ; 21cm.
'A paper given to a GCM conference held in Birmingham on 18th September 1976 ...' - p.[2].
Sd : £0.12
(B77-33049)

261.8'34'17 — Sex relations. *Roman Catholic viewpoints*
Suenens, Léon Joseph. Christian love and human sexuality / [by] Cardinal Suenens. — London : Catholic Truth Society, 1976. — [2],32p ; 19cm.
ISBN 0-85183-181-8 Sd : £0.20
(B77-04546)

261.8'34'2 — Marriage. *Christian viewpoints*
Autton, Norman. Getting married / [by] Norman Autton. — Penarth (Education and Communications Centre, Woodland Place, Penarth, S. Glam. [CF6 2EX]) : Church in Wales Publications, 1976. — 28p ; 18cm.
Sd : £0.25
(B77-16723)

Lee, Helen. Christian marriage / [by] Helen Lee. — Oxford : Mowbrays, 1977. — 126p ; 18cm.
ISBN 0-264-66205-9 Pbk : £0.75
(B77-27679)

261.8'34'2 — Marriage. *Church of England viewpoints*
Stevens, David, *b.1916.* Marriage : towards a Christian understanding and consensus / [by] David Stevens. — London : Church Literature Association, 1976. — [2],5p ; 21cm. — (Dolphin papers ; 6)
Sd : £0.15
(B77-18545)

261.8'34'2 — Marriage. *Roman Catholic viewpoints*
Schillebeeckx, Edward. Marriage : human reality and saving mystery / [by] Edward Schillebeeckx ; translated [from the Dutch] by N.D. Smith. — London : Sheed and Ward, 1976. — xxxii,416p ; 22cm. — (Stagbooks)
This translation originally published: in 2 vols. 1965. — Translation of: 'Het huwelijk, aardse werkelijkheid en heilsmysterie'. Bilthoven : Nelissen, 1964. — Bibl. — Index.
ISBN 0-7220-7664-9 Pbk : £4.25
(B77-01156)

261.8'34'2096 — Marriage. *Africa. Christian viewpoints. Reports, surveys*
Kisembo, Benezeri. African Christian marriage / [by] Benezeri Kisembo, Laurenti Magesa and Aylward Shorter. — London [etc.] : G. Chapman, 1977. — xvii,242p ; 22cm.
'This book is the final report of a five-year programme of research into the sociology and theology of marriage with special reference to East, Central and Southern Africa ... The programme was known as The Churches' Research on Marriage in Africa (CROMIA) ...' - Introduction. — Bibl.: p.217-225. — Index.
ISBN 0-225-66181-0 Pbk : £2.75
(B77-27680)

261.8'34'27 — Family life. Role of husbands. *Christian viewpoints*
Merrill, Dean. The husband book / [by] Dean Merrill. — Exeter : Paternoster Press, 1977. — 122p ; 22cm.
Also published: Grand Rapids : Zondervan, 1977.
ISBN 0-85364-197-8 Pbk : £1.40 : CIP rev.
(B77-31685)

261.8'34'510941 — Race relations. Role of Roman Catholic Church. *Great Britain*
Kentish, Barbara. Chaos or community? / [by] Barbara Kentish. — London : Catholic Truth Society, 1977. — [2],13p ; 19cm.
Bibl.: p.12.
Sd : £0.15
(B77-25384)

261.8'34'51096891 — Race relations. *Rhodesia. Christian viewpoints*
Lamont, Donal. Speech from the dock / by Donal Lamont. — Leigh-on-Sea (55 Leigh Rd, Leigh-on-Sea, Essex) : Kevin Mayhew Ltd [for the] Catholic Institute for International Relations, 1977. — 143p : maps ; 19cm.
ISBN 0-905725-29-8 Pbk : £0.90
(B77-29169)

261.8'34'5196073 — Negroes. Liberation. Role of Christianity. *United States*
Cone, James H. God of the oppressed / [by] James H. Cone. — London : S.P.C.K., 1977. — viii,280p ; 22cm.
Originally published: New York : Seabury Press, 1975. — Index.
ISBN 0-281-03566-0 Pbk : £3.95
(B77-25385)

261.8'5 — Capitalism. Development. Role of Protestant ethics
Weber, Max. The Protestant ethic and the spirit of capitalism / [by] Max Weber ; translated [from the German] by Talcott Parsons. — 2nd ed. ; introduction by Anthony Giddens. — London : Allen and Unwin, 1976. — [2],292p ; 23cm.
Previous ed. of this translation: 1930. — Translation of: 'Die protestantische Ethik und der "Geist" des Kapitalismus'. — Index.
ISBN 0-04-331068-0 : £6.50
ISBN 0-04-331069-9 Pbk : £2.95
(B77-08753)

261.8'5 — Developed countries. Foreign trade with developing countries. *Church of England viewpoints*
Munro, Duncan. Trade, justice and the wealth of nations / by Duncan Munro. — Bramcote : Grove Books, 1976. — 24p ; 22cm. — (Grove booklets on ethics ; no.14 ISSN 0305-4241)
ISBN 0-905422-00-7 Sd : £0.30
(B77-07794)

261.8'7 — United States. Foreign relations. Policies of government, 1937-1945. Attitudes of Roman Catholic Church
Flynn, George Q. Roosevelt and Romanism : Catholics and American diplomacy, 1937-1945 / [by] George Q. Flynn. — Westport, Conn. ; London : Greenwood Press, 1976. — xx,268p ; 22cm. — (Contributions in American history ; no.47)
Bibl.: p.235-243. — Index.
ISBN 0-8371-8581-5 : £10.95
(B77-18546)

261.8'73 — Nuclear weapons. Proliferation. *Christian viewpoints*
Kent, Bruce. Christians and nuclear disarmament / [by] Bruce Kent, Frank Williams, Roger Gray. — [London] ([Eastbourne House, Bullards Place, E2 0PT]) : Campaign for Nuclear Disarmament, 1977. — [2],18p ; 21cm. — (Campaign for Nuclear Disarmament. Christian CND pamphlets)
Sd : £0.20
(B77-33606)

261.8'73 — Pacifism. *Anglican viewpoints*
Wilson, Gordon. Faith and power : from ruin to rebirth : address by Gordon Wilson, Chairman of the Anglican Pacifist Fellowship, at its Annual Summer Conference at the Abbey House, Glastonbury, July 1976. — Oxford (St Mary's Church House, Bayswater Rd, Oxford OX3 9EY) : The Fellowship, [1976]. — 8p ; 21cm.
ISBN 0-9505500-0-0 Sd : £0.05
(B77-06466)

261.8'73 — Peace. *Christian viewpoints*
Curle, Adam. Peace and love : the violin and the oboe / by Adam Curle. — London : Lindsey Press, 1977. — 13p ; 21cm. — (Essex Hall lectures)
'The Essex Hall lecture for 1977 ... delivered in London on April 13, 1977'.
Sd : £0.50
Primary classification 248'.4
(B77-29925)

261.8'73 — War. *Christian viewpoints*
O'Donovan, Oliver. In pursuit of a Christian view of war / by Oliver O'Donovan. — Bramcote : Grove Books, 1977. — 24p ; 22cm. — (Grove booklets on ethics ; 15 ISSN 0305-4241)
ISBN 0-905422-04-x Sd : £0.30
(B77-11553)

262 — CHRISTIAN CHURCH. GOVERNMENT AND ORGANISATION

262 — Christian church, ca 250. *Regulations*
Hippolytus, *Saint.* [Apostolic tradition. English]. Hippolytus, a text for students / with introduction, translation, commentary and notes by Geoffrey J. Cuming. — Bramcote : Grove Books, 1976. — 32p ; 22cm. — (Grove liturgical studies ; 8 ISSN 0306-0608)
'... each section is translated as it stands from the oldest source, be it Greek, Latin, Coptic, or Ethiopic' - Preface. — Bibl.: p.32.
ISBN 0-905422-02-3 Sd : £0.65
(B77-11554)

262'.001 — Alternative churches
Vincent, John James. Alternative church / by John J. Vincent. — Belfast (Bristow Park, Belfast BT9 6TH) : Christian Journals Ltd, 1976. — 149p ; 18cm.
ISBN 0-904302-22-9 Pbk : £0.90
(B77-00016)

262'.0094 — Christian church. Reform. *Frankish Empire, 789-895*
McKitterick, Rosamond. The Frankish church and the Carolingian reforms, 789-895 / [by] Rosamond McKitterick. — London : Royal Historical Society, 1977. — xxi,236p,[2]leaves of plates : 1 ill, facsim, 2 maps ; 23cm. — (Royal Historical Society. Studies in history)
List of MSS.: p.219-222. — Index.
ISBN 0-901050-32-6 : £6.25
(B77-21692)

262'.009411 — Christian church. Benedict XIII, Antipope. Official correspondence to Christian church in Scotland, 1394-1419. *Collections*
Roman Catholic Church. *Antipope, 1394-1419 (Benedict XIII).* Calendar of Papal letters to Scotland of Benedict XIII of Avignon, 1394-1419 / edited [and translated from the Latin] by Francis McGurk. — Edinburgh ([c/o T. and A. Constable, Hopetown St., Edinburgh EH7 4NF]) : Scottish History Society, 1976. — xxv,456,6p ; 23cm. — (Scottish History Society. Publications : fourth series ; vol.13)
Bibl.: p.xxxiv-xxxv. — Index. — Includes the annual report of the Society.
ISBN 0-9500260-9-3 : £5.00
(B77-26779)

262'.009411 — Christian church. Clement VII, Antipope. Official correspondence to Christian church in Scotland, 1378-1394. *Collections*
Roman Catholic Church. *Antipope, 1378-1394 (Clement VII).* Calendar of Papal letters to Scotland of Clement VII of Avignon, 1378-1394 / edited [and translated from the Latin] by Charles Burns. Annie I. Dunlop (1897-1973) : a memoir / by Ian B. Cowan. — Edinburgh (c/o T. & A. Constable Ltd, Hopetown St., Edinburgh EH7 4NF]) : Scottish History Society, 1976. — lxii,240,6,33p,plate : port ; 23cm. — (Scottish History Society. Publications : fourth series ; vol.12)
Bibl. — Index. — Includes the annual report of the Society.
ISBN 0-9500260-8-5 : £5.00
(B77-26780)

262'.00942 — Christian church. Administration. *England, to 1534*
Rodes, Robert E. This house I have built : a study of the legal history of establishment in England / [by] Robert E. Rodes, Jr. — Notre Dame ; London ([70 Great Russell St., WC1B 3BY]) : University of Notre Dame Press.
In 3 vols.
Ecclesiastical administration in medieval England : the Anglo-Saxons to the Reformation. — 1977. — xvi,287p ; 24cm.
Bibl.: p.205-211. — Index.
ISBN 0-268-00903-1 : £15.00
(B77-29170)

262'.03'415 — Church of Ireland. Administration. *Reports, surveys*
Church of Ireland. *General Synod.* Journal of the first ordinary session of the thirty-sixth General Synod of the Church of Ireland holden in Dublin, Anno Domini MDCCCCLXXVI : with an appendix containing statutes passed, reports of committees etc. etc. / edited by J.L.B. Deane. — Dublin (36 Dawson St., Dublin) : Association for Promoting Christian Knowledge, 1976. — clxxxvii,3-279p ; 22cm.
Cover title: Journal of the General Synod 1976. — Index.
Unpriced
(B77-17904)

262'.03'42 — Church of England. Administration
Adair, John, *b.1934.* The becoming Church / [by] John Adair ; foreword by the Archbishop of Canterbury. — London : S.P.C.K., 1977. — x,244p : ill ; 23cm.
Bibl.: p.237-238. — Index.
ISBN 0-281-02964-4 : £5.50
(B77-10155)

262'.05'2411 — Church of Scotland. Administration. *Reports, surveys. Serials*
Church of Scotland. Reports to the General Assembly [of] the Church of Scotland with the legislative acts. — [Edinburgh] : [St Andrew Press].
1976. — [1976]. — xv,672,45p ; 22cm.
ISBN 0-7152-0342-8 : £5.00
(B77-07054)

262'.11 — Roman Catholic Church. Apostolic Succession. *Early works. Facsimiles*
Sander, Nicholas. The rocke of the Churche / [by] Nicholas Sander. — Ilkley [etc.] : Scolar Press, 1977. — [69],570,[2]p ; 20cm. — (English recusant literature, 1558-1640 ; vol.328)
Facsimile reprint of: 1567 ed. Lovanii : Apud Joannem Foulerum, 1567.
ISBN 0-85967-344-8 : Unpriced
(B77-15687)

262'.13 — Christian church. Role of papacy
A **Pope** for all Christians? : an inquiry into the role of Peter in the modern Church / edited by Peter J. McCord. — London : S.P.C.K., 1977. — ix,212p ; 22cm.
Originally published: New York : Paulist Press, 1976.
ISBN 0-281-03567-9 Pbk : £3.25
(B77-26108)

262'.13'0924 — Roman Catholic Church. Pius X, Pope. *Biographies*
O'Brien, Felicity. St Pius X / by Felicity O'Brien. — London : Catholic Truth Society, 1976. — 20p ; 19cm.
ISBN 0-85183-183-4 Sd : £0.15
(B77-05198)

262'.131 — Papacy. Infallibility
Chirico, Peter. Infallibility : the crossroads of doctrine / by Peter Chirico. — London : Sheed and Ward, 1977. — xxi,349,[1]p ; 24cm.
Index.
ISBN 0-7220-7740-8 : £9.50
(B77-30970)

262'.135'0924 — Roman Catholic Church. Newman, John Henry. *England. Correspondence & diaries*
Newman, John Henry. The letters and diaries of John Henry Newman. — Oxford : Clarendon Press.
Vol.31 : The last years, January 1885 to August 1890 : with a supplement of addenda to volumes XI-XXX / edited at the Birmingham Oratory with notes and an introduction by Charles Stephen Dessain and Thomas Gornall. — 1977. — xviii,328,111p ; 24cm.
Bibl.: p.xi-xii. — Index.
ISBN 0-19-920083-1 : £18.50 : CIP rev.
(B77-04547)

262'.135'0924 — Roman Catholic Church. Wiseman, Nicholas Patrick Stephen. *England. Biographies*
Jackman, Sydney Wayne. Nicholas Cardinal Wiseman : a Victorian prelate and his writings / [by] S.W. Jackman. — [Dublin] : Five Lamps Press ; Gerrards Cross : [Distributed by] Smythe, 1977. — 143p : port ; 23cm.
Index.
ISBN 0-901072-70-2 : £5.50
(B77-23101)

262'.14 — Christian church. Ministry
Harper, Michael. Let my people grow! : ministry and leadership in the Church / by Michael Harper. — London [etc.] : Hodder and Stoughton, 1977. — 254p ; 22cm. — (Ecclesia books)
Bibl.: p.247-248. — Index.
ISBN 0-340-21573-9 Pbk : £2.95
(B77-19209)

262'.14 — Church of England. Women's ministry
Demant, Vigo Auguste. Why the Christian priesthood is male / [by] V.A. Demant. — 2nd ed. — London : Church Literature Association, 1977. — [2],21p ; 21cm. — (The ordination of women)
Previous ed.: 1972.
ISBN 0-85191-116-1 Sd : £10.20
(B77-30971)

Saward, John. Christ and his bride / [by] John Saward. — London : Church Literature Association, 1977. — [2],16,[1]p ; 21cm. — (The ordination of women)
Sd : £0.20
(B77-30972)

262'.14 — Church of England. Women's ministry. *Correspondence*
The **replies** of the leaders of certain churches to letters from the Archbishop of Canterbury concerning the ordination of women to the priesthood : with extracts from the Archbishop's letters. — London : Church Literature Association for the Church Union, [1977]. — [1],6p ; 22cm.
Sd : £0.05
(B77-22342)

262'.14 — Nonconformist churches. Ministry. *South Wales. Valleys. Proposals*
Birkin, John Leonard. Vision for the Valleys. — Caerphilly (40 Alexander Court, Lansbury Park, Caerphilly, M. Glam. CF8 1RJ) : The author, 1976. — [1],7p ; 22cm.
Author: John Leonard Birkin.
ISBN 0-9503978-2-2 Sd : £0.05
(B77-11555)

262'.14 — Roman Catholic Church. Clergy
Rahner, Karl. The priest of today / [by] Karl Rahner ; [translated from the German]. — Dublin : Veritas Publications, 1977. — 16p ; 19cm.
'From the edition published by Sheed & Ward Ltd, London [1973] entitled "Meditations on Priestly Life" [Translation of "Einübung priestlicher Existenz". Freiburg im Breisgau : Herder, 1970]' - title page verso.
ISBN 0-905092-30-9 Sd : £0.20
(B77-09494)

262'.14 — Roman Catholic Church. Women's ministry
Roman Catholic Church. *Congregatio pro Doctrina Fide.* The ordination of women : official commentary from the Sacred Congregation for the Doctrine of the Faith on its declaration (inter insigniores) 'Women and the priesthood' of 15th October 1976 together with the exchange of correspondence in 1975 and 1976 between His Grace the Most Reverend Dr Frederick Donald Coggan, Archbishop of Canterbury and His Holiness Pope Paul VI. — London : Catholic Truth Society, [1977]. — [2],32p ; 19cm.
Sd : £0.30
(B77-17905)

Roman Catholic Church. *Congregatio pro Doctrina Fide.* Women and the priesthood : declaration (inter insigniores) on the question of the admission of women to the ministerial priesthood / Sacred Congregation for the Doctrine of the Faith ; [translated from the Latin]. — Vatican City : Vatican Polyglot Press ; London : Catholic Truth Society, 1976. — [3],18p ; 19cm.
ISBN 0-85183-190-7 Sd : £0.20
(B77-11556)

262'.15 — Lutheran Church. Missouri Synod. Role of laity, 1900-1970
Graebner, Alan. Uncertain saints : the laity in the Lutheran Church - Missouri Synod, 1900-1970 / [by] Alan Graebner. — Westport, Conn. ; London : Greenwood Press, 1975. — xiii,284,[1]p ; 22cm. — (Contributions in American history ; no.42)
Bibl.: p.273-278. — Index.
ISBN 0-8371-7963-7 : £11.95
(B77-17906)

262'.15 — Roman Catholic Church. Laity Commission. *Reports, surveys*
Barnes, Eleanor. Together in the Church : the chairman's review of the Laity Commission's work, May 1972-June 1976 / [by] Eleanor Barnes. — Abbots Langley (74 Gallows Hill La., Abbots Langley, Herts. WD5 0BZ) : Catholic Information Services, [1977]. — [3],15,[1]p ; 21cm.
Sd : Unpriced
(B77-19210)

262'.17 — Ukrainian Catholic Church. Patriarchate
Muzyczka, Ivan. Why this unnecessary clamour : an open letter to Ukrainian and foreign journalists / [by] I. Muzyczka ; footnotes by I. Dmytriw. — London ([200 Liverpool Rd, N1 1LF]) : Ukrainian Information Service, 1977. — 15p : port ; 24cm.
'This article appeared for the first time in the Ukrainian weekly newspaper "The Ukrainian Thought", and subsequently in the quarterly magazine "The Ukrainian Review", Vol.XXIII, No.4., 1976' - p.15.
£0.25
(B77-23102)

262'.17 — Ukrainian Catholic Church. Patriarchate. *Proposals. Readings*
Documents & comments related to the struggle for the patriarchal rights of the Ukrainian Catholic Church / collected & edited by I. Dmytriw ; translated [from the Ukrainian] by W. Slez. — London ([49 Linden Gardens, W2 4HG]) : Central Committee for a Ukrainian Catholic Patriarchate (Great Britain), 1976. — 72p : ill, port ; 23cm.
ISBN 0-9505349-0-0 Sd : £0.50
(B77-01157)

262'.5 — Christian church. Ecumenical councils, 1378-1460. *Documents*
Crowder, C M D. Unity, heresy and reform, 1378-1460 : the conciliar response to the Great Schism / [by] C.M.D. Crowder. — London : Edward Arnold, 1977. — x,212p ; 24cm. — (Documents of medieval history ; 3)
Bibl.: p.190-205. — Index.
ISBN 0-7131-5941-3 : £9.95
ISBN 0-7131-5942-1 Pbk : £4.95
(B77-23103)

262'.8 — Christian church. Authority
Anglican-Roman Catholic International Commission. Agreement on authority : the Anglican-Roman Catholic statement / [Anglican-Roman Catholic International Commission] ; with commentary by Julian W. Charley. — Bramcote : Grove Books, 1977. — 26p ; 21cm. — (Grove booklets on ministry and worship ; 48 ISSN 0305-3067)
ISBN 0-905422-03-1 Sd : £0.30
(B77-11557)

Anglican-Roman Catholic International Commission. Authority in the Church : a statement on the question of authority, its nature, exercise, and implications agreed by the Anglican-Roman Catholic International Commission, Venice, 1976. — London : S.P.C.K. : Catholic Truth Society, 1977. — 24p ; 19cm.
ISBN 0-281-03560-1 Sd : £0.20
ISBN 0-85183-180-x (Catholic Truth Society) : £0.20
(B77-10156)

Anglican-Roman Catholic International Commission. Authority in the Church : text of the agreed statement [of the Anglican-Roman Catholic International Commission]. Together with a guide : Rev. David Miles Board presents a Catholic viewpoint derived from conversations with Bishop Alan Clark, Catholic co-chairman of the International Commission. — Abbots Langley (74 Gallows Hill La., Abbots Langley, Herts. WD5 0BZ) : Infoform, [1977]. — [2],42,[1]p ; 22cm.
ISBN 0-905241-06-1 Sd : £0.40
(B77-10157)

Goldingay, John. Authority and ministry / by John Goldingay. — Bramcote : Grove Books, 1976. — 24p ; 21cm. — (Grove booklets on ministry and worship ; 46 ISSN 0305-3067)
ISBN 0-901710-99-7 Sd : £0.30
(B77-01158)

Lash, Nicholas. Voices of authority / [by] Nicholas Lash. — London : Sheed and Ward, 1976. — viii,119p ; 20cm.
ISBN 0-7220-7662-2 Pbk : £2.50
(B77-01159)

262'.8 — Roman Catholic Church. Authority. Related to freedom of communication of Roman Catholic theologians
Daly, Cahal Brendan. Theologians and the magisterium / [by] Cahal B. Daly. — Dublin : Veritas Publications, 1977. — 34p ; 19cm.
'First published in 1977 in "The Irish theological quarterly"' - title page verso.
ISBN 0-905092-41-4 Sd : £0.50
(B77-29928)

262.9 — Christian church. Synod of St Patrick, 1st. *Texts with commentaries. Latin-English parallel texts*
The **bishop's** synod : (the first synod of St Patrick) : a symposium with text, translation and commentary / edited by M.J. Faris. — Liverpool (School of Classics, Abercromby Sq., University of Liverpool, P.O. Box 147, Liverpool L69 3BX) : Francis Cairns, 1976. — [5],63,[11]p : facsims ; 21cm. — (Arca, classical and medieval texts papers and monographs ; 1)
Parallel Latin text and English translation of MS.279 of Corpus Christi College, Cambridge ; together with a facsimile reprint of the MS., and the papers of a symposium held at Queen's University, Belfast, organised by the Ulster Society for Medieval Latin Studies. — Bibl.: p.61-63.
ISBN 0-905205-01-4 Pbk : £2.50
(B77-16724)

262.9'8'3 — Church of England. Canterbury (Diocese). Ecclesiastical courts, 1559-1565. *Cases*
Canterbury *(Diocese).* Church life in Kent : being Church court records of the Canterbury Diocese, 1559-1563 / [compiled] by Arthur J. Willis. — London [etc.] : Phillimore, 1975. — viii,97p,[2]p of plates : 2 facsims ; 23cm.
Index.
ISBN 0-85033-202-8 : £5.00
(B77-02019)

262.9'8'3 — Church of England. Law. *Commentaries*
Church of England. *Legal Board.* Opinions of the Legal Board [of the Church of England]. — 5th ed. reprinted with two supplements. — London : Church Information Office for the Legal Advisory Commission of the General Synod of the Church of England, 1976. — 1v. ; 23cm.
In binder. — 198p. in various pagings on publication. — Fifth ed. originally published: 1973.
ISBN 0-7151-9513-1 Ls : £4.50
(B77-13499)

262.9'8'52411 — Church of Scotland. Law. *Cases. Serials*
Church of Scotland. *General Assembly.* Assembly papers : cases with deliverances / the Church of Scotland [General Assembly]. — Edinburgh : Blackwood for the General Assembly of the Church of Scotland.
1975. — [1975]. — v,129p ; 22cm.
£2.00
(B77-16179)

1976. — [1976]. — v,80p ; 21cm.
£2.00
(B77-16180)

263 — CHRISTIANITY. DAYS, TIMES, PLACES OF RELIGIOUS OBSERVANCE
263'.4'0973 — Sunday. Observance. Influence of Puritanism. *United States, to 1740*
Solberg, Winton Udell. Redeem the time : the Puritan Sabbath in early America / [by] Winton U. Solberg. — Cambridge, Mass. ; London : Harvard University Press, 1977. — xv,406p : ill ; 24cm. — (Harvard University. Center for the Study of the History of Liberty in America. Publications)
Bibl.: p.367-383. — Index.
ISBN 0-674-75130-2 : Unpriced
(B77-29171)

263'.91 — Christian church. Christmas. *Secondary school texts*
Shepherd, Robin. Christmas / [text by Robin Shepherd]. — London : S.C.M. Press, 1973. — 32p : ill, facsims, music, port ; 23cm. — (Probe ; 16 ISSN 0305-3776)
Bibl.: p.32.
ISBN 0-334-00203-6 Sd : £0.25
(B77-11065)

264 — CHRISTIAN CHURCH. PUBLIC WORSHIP
Perry, Michael. The paradox of worship / [by] Michael Perry. — London : S.P.C.K., 1977. — x,118p ; 20cm.
'... expanded version of the Selwyn Lectures for 1976, delivered at St John's College Auckland ...' - Preface. — Index.
ISBN 0-281-02973-3 Pbk : £2.50
(B77-23104)

264 — Christian church. Public worship. Drama & dancing. *Manuals*
Long, Anne. Praise Him in the dance / by Anne Long. — London [etc.] : Hodder and Stoughton, 1976. — 192p,[8]p of plates : ill, music ; 22cm. — (Ecclesia books)
Bibl.: p.192.
ISBN 0-340-20976-3 Pbk : £3.75
(B77-03365)

264 — Christian church. Worship
Lee, Edwin Kenneth. Worship and society / [by] E.K. Lee. — London : Church Literature Association, 1977. — [4],26p ; 21cm.
ISBN 0-85191-092-0 Sd : £0.35
(B77-18547)

264'.02 — Roman Catholic Church. Public worship. Liturgical aspects
Merton, Thomas. Meditations on liturgy / [by] Thomas Merton. — London [etc.] : Mowbrays, 1976. — 171p ; 23cm.
Originally published: as 'Seasons of celebration'. New York : Farrar, Straus and Giroux, 1965.
ISBN 0-264-66363-2 : £5.00
ISBN 0-264-66353-5 Pbk : £2.50
(B77-00017)

264'.02 — Roman Catholic Church. Public worship. Reform, 1962-
Davies, Michael, *b.1936.* Liturgical revolution / by Michael Davies. — Chulmleigh : Augustine. In 3 vols.
Part 1 : Cranmer's godly order : the destruction of Catholicism through liturgical change. — 1976. — xiv,162p : ill, facsims, ports ; 19cm.
Bibl.: p.151-152. — Index.
ISBN 0-85172-771-9 : £2.50
ISBN 0-85172-770-0 Pbk : £1.00
(B77-14553)

Part 2 : Pope John's council. — 1977. — xvi, 336p ; 20cm.
Bibl.: p.325-328. — Index.
ISBN 0-85172-774-3 : £3.50
ISBN 0-851272-773-5 Pbk : £2.50
(B77-20897)

264'.02 — Roman Catholic Church. Public worship. Saints' days. *Daily readings*
Saints in season : a companion to the lectionary / edited by Austin Flannery. — Dublin (St Saviour's, Dublin 1) : Dominican Publications, 1976. — vii,225p ; 21cm.
Index.
ISBN 0-9504797-1-3 Pbk : £2.95
(B77-04548)

264'.02'005 — Roman Catholic Church. Public worship. *Periodicals*
Liturgy. — London (39 Eccleston Sq., SW1V 1PL) : Liturgy Commission.
No.1, vol.1- ; [Oct.-Nov. 1976]-. — 1976-. — ill ; 21cm.
Six issues a year. — [3],34p. in 1st issue.
Sd : £0.50
ISSN 0309-4308
(B77-14554)

264'.02'00924 — Roman Catholic Church. Liturgy and ritual. Reform. Opposition of Lefebvre, Marcel, 1974-1976
Congar, Yves Marie Joseph. Challenge to the church : the case of Archbishop Lefebvre / [by] Yves Congar ; [translated from the French by Paul Inwood] ; preface by George Patrick Dwyer. — London : Collins Liturgical, 1977. — 96p ; 18cm.
Translation of: 'La crise dans l'église et Mgr Lefebvre'. Paris : Les Editions du Cerf, 1976.
ISBN 0-00-599583-3 Pbk : £1.50
(B77-23989)

Davies, Michael, *b.1936.* Archbishop Lefebvre : the truth / by Michael Davies. — Chumleigh : Augustine, 1977. — [2],32p : port ; 19cm.
ISBN 0-85172-778-6 Sd : £0.15
(B77-21693)

Leonard, George. Light on Archbishop Lefebvre / by George Leonard. — London : Catholic Truth Society, 1976. — 24p ; 19cm.
ISBN 0-85183-178-8 Sd : £0.20
(B77-02760)

264'.02'009411 — Roman Catholic Church. Public worship. *Scotland. Yearbooks*
Roman Catholic Church. *Liturgy and ritual.* Liturgical calendar for Scotland / issued by the authority of their lordships the archbishops and bishops of Scotland. — Glasgow : J. Burns.
1976-7. — 1976. — xxviii,76p ; 19cm.
ISBN 0-900243-59-7 Pbk : £0.80
ISBN 0-900243-60-0. Interleaved ed. : £1.40
(B77-03366)

264'.0203 — Roman Catholic Church. Paschaltide services
Ryan, Vincent. Pasch to Pentecost : the liturgy of Paschaltide / [by] Vincent Ryan. — Dublin : Veritas Publications, 1977. — 80p ; 19cm.
Bibl.: p.79-80.
ISBN 0-905092-32-5 Pbk : £1.00
(B77-20016)

264'.023 — Roman Catholic Church. Eucharist. *Rites. Juvenile literature*
Roman Catholic Church. *Liturgy and ritual.* [Missal]. Let's receive Our Lord / [text by Audrey Bilski]. — London : Catholic Truth Society, [1977]. — [23]p : col ill ; 14cm.
ISBN 0-85183-188-5 Sd : £0.15
(B77-07795)

264'.023 — Roman Catholic Church. Eucharist. *Rites. Latin-English parallel texts*
Roman Catholic Church. *Liturgy and ritual.* [Missal]. The order of Mass in Latin and English. — London : Catholic Truth Society, 1977. — [1],57,[1]p ; 15cm.
Parallel Latin text and English translation.
Sd : £0.25
(B77-17907)

264'.023 — Roman Catholic Church. Eucharist. Adolescents' services. *Rites*
A liturgy of life : Mass themes for young people / [by] David Konstant in collaboration with ... [others]. — Great Wakering : Mayhew-McCrimmon, 1975. — 133p ; 21cm.
Bibl.: p.133.
ISBN 0-85597-086-3 Pbk : £1.50
(B77-05199)

264'.024 — Roman Catholic Church. Liturgy and ritual. Liturgy of the hours. Matins & Vespers. *Rites*
Roman Catholic Church. *Liturgy and ritual.* [Liturgy of the hours. *Selections].* Morning and evening prayer, with night prayer / from the Divine Office. — London [etc.] : Collins [etc.], 1976. — lix,1214p ; 18cm.
'Taken from "The Divine Office", a translation of "Liturgia Horarum" ...' - title page verso.
ISBN 0-00-599564-7 : £3.00
ISBN 0-00-599565-5 Deluxe ed. : £4.00
(B77-02020)

264'.025 — Roman Catholic Church. Admission of baptised non-Catholics. *Rites*
Roman Catholic Church. *Liturgy and ritual.* Rite of reception of baptized Christians into full communion with the Catholic Church : approved for use in the dioceses of England, Wales and Scotland : the Roman ritual / revised by decree of the Second Vatican Ecumenical Council and published by authority of Pope Paul VI ; English translation prepared by the International Commission on English in the Liturgy. — London : Catholic Truth Society, 1977. — 40p ; 21cm.
Pbk : £0.75
(B77-33607)

264'.025 — Roman Catholic Church. Baptism. *Rites. Facsimiles*
Peter of Alcantara, *Saint.* A golden treatise of mentall praier / [by] St Peter of Alcantara ; [translated from the Latin by G.W. i.e. Giles Willoughby]. Ordo baptizandi. — Ilkley [etc.] : Scolar Press, 1977. — [81],176,[5],135p ; 20cm. — (English recusant literature, 1558-1640 ; vol.338)
Facsimile reprints. — 'A golden treatise of mentall praier' originally published: Brussels : the Widow of Hubert Antony, 1632. — 'Ordo baptizandi' originally published: Paris : s.n., 1636.
ISBN 0-85967-374-x : Unpriced
Primary classification 248'.3
(B77-17288)

264'.025 — Roman Catholic Church. Sacraments: Penance. *Ireland. Rites. Irish & English texts*
Roman Catholic Church. *Liturgy and ritual.* Rite of penance, approved for use in the dioceses of Ireland = Gńas na haithrí, ceadaithe chun úsáide i ndeoisí uile na hEireann : The Roman ritual revised by decree of the Second Vatican Ecumenical Council ... — [Dublin] : Veritas Publications, 1976. — [4],331,48p : music ; 23cm.
Includes Irish introduction and text of the rite.
Unpriced
(B77-03367)

264'.025 — Roman Catholic Church. Sacraments: Penance. *Rites*
Roman Catholic Church. *Liturgy and ritual.* A simple penance book. — London : Catholic Truth Society, 1976. — [2],29p ; 15cm.
Sd : £0.15
(B77-08754)

264'.03 — Church of England. Holy Week services
Brecknell, David. This is Holy Week / by David Brecknell. — London : Church Literature Association, 1976. — 16,[1]p ; 16cm.
Sd : £0.12
(B77-20017)

264'.03 — Church of England. Liturgy and ritual. Book of Common Prayer. 3rd edition. *Periodicals*
Faith and worship : the magazine of the Lincoln Branch of the Prayer Book Society. — Grimsby [etc.] (c/o I.R. Thompson, 259 Ashby Rd, Scunthorpe, S. Humberside DN16 2AB) : The Branch.
[No.1]- ; Autumn 1976-. — 1976-. — 21cm.
Two issues a year. — 18p. in 1st issue.
Sd : Unpriced
ISSN 0309-1627
(B77-03912)

264'.03 — Church of England. Public worship
Perry, Michael. A handbook of parish worship / [by] Michael Perry. — London [etc.] : Mowbrays, 1977. — xiii,137p ; 19cm. — (Mowbrays parish handbooks)
Bibl.: p.xiii. — Index.
ISBN 0-264-66274-1 Pbk : £1.95
(B77-18548)

264'.0303 — Church of England. Public worship. Use of English versions of the Bible, 1900-1976

Gresswell, G Gilbert. Words and worship : some thoughts on the use of modern translations of the Bible in public worship / by G. Gilbert Gresswell. — Carlisle (Burgh By Sands, Carlisle) : Fort House, 1977. — 24p ; 19cm.
ISBN 0-9505901-0-x Sd : £0.20
(B77-33050)

264'.031 — Church of England. Eucharist. *Calendars*

Order for celebrating Mass. — Wantage ([The Convent, Wantage, Oxon OX12 9DJ]) : St Mary's Press.
1977. — [1976]. — 54p ; 20cm.
ISBN 0-85438-029-9 Sp : £0.50
(B77-01160)

264'.031 — Church of England. Public worship. Proposed calendars. Church of England. Liturgical Commission. Calendar, lectionary and rules to order the service. *Critical studies*

Birch, Elizabeth. The calendar : a lay comment / [by] Elizabeth Birch. — London : Church Literature Association, 1976. — 8p ; 16cm.
ISBN 0-85191-088-2 Sd : £0.10
(B77-11558)

Moreton, Michael. Theological principle in the calendar & lectionary / [by] Michael Moreton. — London : Church Literature Association, 1976. — [2],10p ; 21cm.
'A letter to the members of the Anglican Communion from the Orthodox Church in America, convened at its Fourth all-American Council, Cleveland, Ohio, 10th-13th November 1975' (Folder ([4]p.)) as insert. — ' ... revision of an article that first appeared in "Theology" in July 1973 ... ' - title page verso.
ISBN 0-85191-084-x Sd : £0.20
(B77-11559)

264'.032 — Church in Wales. Divine office. *Lectionaries. Welsh-English parallel texts*

Church in Wales. *Liturgy and Ritual.* Cyflwyniadur llithoedd y Sul = Introducing Sunday lessons. — [Penarth] ([Education and Communications Centre, Woodland Place, Penarth, S. Glam.]) : Church in Wales Publications for the Liturgical Commission of the Church in Wales, 1971. — 2-33[i.e.2-66]p ; 22cm.
Parallel Welsh and English texts.
ISBN 0-85326-020-6 Sd : £0.30
(B77-15688)

264'.035 — Church in Wales. Lay readers. Licensing. *Rites. Welsh-English parallel texts*

Church in Wales. *Liturgy and ritual.* Gwasanaeth derbyn a thrwyddedu darllenwyr = Office for the admission and licensing of readers. — [Penarth] ([Education and Communications Centre, Woodland Place, Penarth, S. Glam.]) : Church in Wales Publications, 1973. — 4[i.e.7] p ; 21cm.
Parallel Welsh and English texts.
Sd : £0.15
(B77-16725)

264'.035 — Church of England. Eucharist. *Rites*

Church of England. *Liturgy and ritual.* [Holy Communion]. Holy Communion. — London : Cambridge University Press [etc.], 1976. — [3], 46p ; 15cm. — (Alternative services : series 1 & 2 revised)
Parallel texts of revised versions of Holy Communion 1 & 2.
Sd : Unpriced
(B77-10728)

264'.035 — Church of England. Eucharist. Children's prayers. *Prayer books*

With joy and gladness : Holy Communion prayers for young people / arranged from well-known sources by Enid Chadwick. — London : Church Literature Association, [1977]. — [3],8,[1]p ; 17cm.
ISBN 0-85191-093-9 Sd : £0.12
(B77-20018)

264'.035 — Church of England. Liturgy and ritual. Order for Marriage, series 3. *Commentaries*

Hutchins, Charles Henry. Liturgy for marriage : some guidelines with reference to the Series 3 service / by Charles H. Hutchins. — Bramcote : Grove Books, 1976. — 24p ; 22cm. — (Grove booklets on ministry and worship ; no.47 ISSN 0305-3067)
ISBN 0-905422-01-5 Sd : £0.30
(B77-07796)

264'.035 — Church of England. Ordination. *Rites*

Church of England. *Liturgical Commission.* Ordination services : a report / by the Liturgical Commission of the General Synod of the Church of England. — London : S.P.C.K., 1977. — 45p ; 24cm. — (Alternative services : series 3) (GS ; 327)
'... not authorized for liturgical use'.
ISBN 0-281-02971-7 Sd : £1.25
(B77-24688)

264'.035 — Church of England. Public worship. Jubilee thanksgiving services. *Rites*

A form of prayer & of thanksgiving to Almighty God on the occasion of the silver jubilee of the accession of Our Sovereign Lady Queen Elizabeth the Second. — London : Cambridge University Press : Eyre and Spottiswoode : Oxford University Press, [1977]. — 14p ; 21cm.

'This service is published with the approval of The Archbishops of Canterbury & York, The Cardinal Archbishop of Westminster and the Moderator of the Free Church Federal Council'.
Sd : £0.08
(B77-20019)

264'.036 — Church of England. Public worship. Collects. *Texts*

Church of England. *Liturgy and ritual.* Collects. — Cambridge : Cambridge University Press [etc. for] the Registrars of the Provinces of Canterbury and York, [1977]. — [2],54p ; 15cm. — (Alternative services : series 3)
ISBN 0-521-50515-1 Sd : £0.35
(B77-11560)

264'.05'8 — Union of Welsh Independents. Public worship. Hymns. *Welsh texts*

Y caniedydd. — Ail argraffiad. — Abertawe [i.e. Swansea] : Undeb yr Annibynwyr Cymraeg, 1970. — lvi,333p ; 19cm.
Includes some hymns in English. — Previous ed.: 1960. — Index.
Unpriced
(B77-07055)

Caniedydd newydd : ar gyfer yr ysgol Sul ac ysglion dydd (yn cynnwys detholiad newydd o weddïau ac emynau Saesneg) / [golygyddion Elfed et al.]. — Abertawe [i.e. Swansea] ([11 St Helen's Rd, Swansea, West Glamorgan]) : Gwasg John Penry, 1969. — ix,102p ; 19cm.
Index.
ISBN 0-903701-04-9 Pbk : £0.65
(B77-07056)

Detholiad o emynau o'r caniedydd : at wasanaeth cyfarfodydd blynyddol ac achlysuron neilltnol. — Abertawe [i.e. Swansea] ([11 St Helen's Rd, Swansea SA1 4AL]) : Tŷ John Penry [ar ran] Undeb yr Annibynwyr Cymraeg, 1974. — 40p ; 16cm.
Includes some hymns in English. — Index.
Sd : Unpriced
(B77-32403)

264'.07'1 — Methodist Church. Liturgy and ritual. Methodist service book. *Commentaries*

Dixon, Neil. At your service : a commentary on 'The Methodist service book' / [by] Neil Dixon. — London : Epworth Press, 1976. — 94p ; 19cm. — (Cell books ; 4)
ISBN 0-7162-0256-5 Pbk : £0.50
(B77-08755)

264'.07'101 — Methodist Church. Public worship. Vestry prayer. *Prayer books*

A book of vestry prayers / compiled by C.N.R. Wallwork. — London : Epworth Press, 1976. — 117p ; 22cm.
ISBN 0-7162-0277-8 Pbk : £1.50
(B77-03913)

264'.09'9 — Catholic Apostolic Church (Founded 1944). Public worship. *Rites*

Catholic Apostolic Church *(Founded 1944).* The sacred liturgy according to the Glastonbury rite / [the Catholic Apostolic Church, (Metropolis of Glastonbury)]. — Glastonbury ([31 Hatcliffe Close, London SE3 9UE]) : Metropolitical Press.
Liber VI. Propria : Part 2. The Christmas cycle. — 1975. — [5]p,p131-446 ; 26cm.
Spine title: Glastonbury rite. Liber VI. Propria.
£5.00
(B77-17290)

264'.1 — Anglican churches. Prayers of intercession. Intentions. *Calendars*

Cycle of prayer for Anglican use. — London : Church Information Office.
1977 / edited by Austin Masters. — [1976]. — 31p ; 16cm.
'The "Cycle of Prayer" is reported on at each meeting of the Anglican Consultative Council' - p.7. — Previous control number ISBN 0-7151-5516-4.
Sd : £0.25
ISBN 0-7151-5516-4
ISSN 0307-5176
(B77-05862)

264'.13 — Christian church. Public worship. Prayer. *Prayer books*

Toobe, H G B. Prayers before service / by H.G.B. Toobe. — [Bebington] (['Heathfield', Stanley Ave., Bebington, Wirral, Merseyside L63 5QE]) : [The author], [1976]. — [2],27 leaves ; 24cm.
Index.
ISBN 0-9505584-0-0 Pbk : £0.50
(B77-08216)

264'.13 — Young persons' organisations. *Wales. Urdd Gobaith Cymru. Meetings. Epilogues. Prayers & readings. Welsh texts*

Roberts, Elfed ap Nefydd. Epilogau byr ar gyfer adran ac aelwyd / [gan] Elfed ap Nefydd Roberts. — [Aberystwyth] : Urdd Gobaith Cymru, [1977]. — [2],15p ; 30cm.
Sd : £0.30
(B77-20898)

264'.2 — Hymns. *Anthologies*

Hymns and spiritual songs for the little flock. — Amended ed. — Kingston-on-Thames (2 Upper Teddington Rd, Kingston-on-Thames [Surrey]) : Bible and Gospel Trust, 1974. — [362]p ; 16cm.
This ed. originally published: 1973. — Index.
Pbk : Unpriced
(B77-02021)

Hymns and spiritual songs for the little flock. — Amended ed. — Kingston-on-Thames (2 Upper Teddington Rd, Kingston-on-Thames [Surrey]) : Bible and Gospel Trust, 1973. — [364]p ; 16cm.
Previous ed.: 1962. — Index.
ISBN 0-9504309-3-5 Pbk : Unpriced
(B77-02022)

Praise the Lord. — Words ed. / edited by John Ainslie, Stephen Dean, Paul Inwood. — London [etc.] : G. Chapman, 1977. — [138]p ; 21cm.
Previous ed.: 1972. — Index.
ISBN 0-225-66116-0 Pbk : £0.65
(B77-14042)

264.2 — Hymns. *Anthologies. Juvenile literature*

Children's Service hymns and songs for use at Chelsea Old Church. — [London] ([c/o Rev. C.E. Leighton Thomson, Old Church House, 4 Old Church St., SW3 5DQ]) : [Chelsea Old Church], 1977. — [107]p ; 16cm.
Sd : Unpriced
(B77-33051)

264'.2 — Salvation Army. Public worship. Hymnals: Keep singing. *Critical studies*

Taylor, Gordon. A short companion to 'Keep singing' / by Gordon Taylor. — [Addington] ([44 Crossways, Addington, South Croydon, Surrey]) : [The author], 1976. — [1],54p ; 21cm.
Index.
ISBN 0-9505694-0-2 Sd : £0.50
(B77-17291)

264'.3 — Christian church. Worship. Use of Bible

Using the Bible in worship / edited by Christopher Byworth. — Bramcote : Grove Books, 1977. — 33p ; 22cm. — (Grove liturgical studies ; 11 ISSN 0306-0608)
ISBN 0-905422-21-x Sd : £0.75
(B77-32404)

264'.7 — Christian church. Prayer groups. Contemplation. *Manuals*

Dodson, Peter, *b.1932.* Towards contemplation : a practical introduction for prayer groups / by Peter Dodson. — Oxford : S.L.G., 1977. — [2], 12p ; 21cm. — (Fairacres publication ; no.64 ISSN 0307-1405)
Bibl.: p.12.
ISBN 0-7283-0069-9 Sd : £0.20
(B77-17908)

265 — CHRISTIAN RITES, CEREMONIES, ORDINANCES

265 — Roman Catholic Church. Sacraments. *Juvenile literature*
Meeting Christ now : prayer and the sacraments for young people / [compiled by] David Konstant and Winifred Wilson ; photographs by Noeline Kelly ; illustrations by Anne-Marie Stuart. — London (187 Piccadilly, W1V 9DA) : Collins Liturgical Publications, 1976. — 96p : ill ; 18cm.
ISBN 0-00-599563-9 Pbk : £0.95
(B77-05863)

265 — Roman Catholic Church. Sacraments. Administration. *Manuals*
Roman Catholic Church. *Episcopal Conference of Ireland.* The sacraments : pastoral directory of the Irish Episcopal Conference / Seán Swayne (ed.). — Dublin : Veritas Publications, 1976. — 173p ; 19cm.
Bibl.: p.170-173.
ISBN 0-905092-13-9 Pbk : £1.10
(B77-14555)

265'.12 — Christian church. Infant baptism. *Church of England viewpoints*
Pratt, Edward. Thinking about - baptism / [author Edward Pratt]. — Bramcote : Grove Books, 1977. — Folder([8]p) : ill ; 22cm.
ISBN 0-905422-07-4 : £0.07
(B77-26781)

265'.12 — Church of Scotland. Infant baptism
Stein, Jock. Twenty questions about infant baptism / by Jock Stein. — Dundee (128 Arbroath Rd, Dundee DD4 7HR) : The author, 1976. — [1],23p ; 21cm. — (A handsel booklet)
Bibl.: p.23.
ISBN 0-9505510-0-7 Sd : £0.15
(B77-05200)

265'.2 — Roman Catholic Church. Confirmation
Brentwood Religious Education Service.
Confirmed in love : the Holy Spirit and the sacrament of confirmation / prepared by the Brentwood Religious Education Service ; illustrations Maggie Gould ; cover Sister Eileen Carroll. — Slough : St Paul Publications, 1977. — [5],28,[8]p : ill, music ; 22cm.
Includes extracts from the rite of baptism for children, the rite of confirmation and the Order of Mass.
ISBN 0-85439-125-8 Sd : £0.70
(B77-11561)

265'.3 — Church of England. Eucharist. Celebration by laity
Lay presidency at the Eucharist? / edited by Trevor Lloyd. — Bramcote : Grove Books, 1977. — 32p ; 22cm. — (Grove liturgical studies ; 9 ISSN 0306-0608)
ISBN 0-905422-09-0 Sd : £0.75
(B77-23105)

265'.3 — Roman Catholic Church. Eucharist. Transubstantiation. *Early works. Facsimiles*
Pointz, Robert. Testimonies for the Real Presence / [by] Robert Pointz. — Ilkley [etc.] : Scolar Press, 1977. — [21]p, 200 leaves ; 20cm. — (English recusant literature, 1558-1640 ; vol.327)
Leaves printed on both sides. — Facsimile reprint of: 1st ed. Lovanii : Apud Ioannem Foulerum, 1566.
ISBN 0-85967-343-x : £10.00
(B77-15085)

265'.6 — Church of England. Sacraments: Penance. *Manuals. For confessors*
Ross, Kenneth. Hearing confessions / [by] Kenneth Ross. — London : S.P.C.K., 1974. — ix,117p ; 23cm.
Bibl.: p.111-113. — Index.
ISBN 0-281-02770-6 : £1.95
(B77-18549)

265'.6 — Roman Catholic Church. Sacraments: Penance. *Early works. Facsimiles*
A **treatise** of auricular confession. The fore-runner of Bels downefall / [by] Philip Woodward. — Ilkley [etc.] : Scolar Press, 1976. — 429p in various pagings ; 20cm. — (English recusant literature, 1558-1640 ; vol.322)
Facsimile reprints. — 'A treatise of auricular confession' originally published: s.l. : John Heigham, 1622. — 'The fore-runner of Bels downefall' originally published: s.l. : s.n., 1605.
ISBN 0-85967-338-3 : Unpriced
Also classified at 282
(B77-06467)

265'.6'09024 — Christian church. Sacraments: Penance, ca 1400-ca 1520
Tentler, Thomas N. Sin and confession on the eve of the Reformation / [by] Thomas N. Tentler. — Princeton ; Guildford : Princeton University Press, 1977. — xxiv,395p : 1 ill ; 25cm.
Bibl.: p.371-389. — Index.
ISBN 0-691-07219-1 : £18.80
(B77-29172)

265'.82 — Christian church. Ministry of healing
East, Reginald. Heal the sick / [by] Reginald East. — London [etc.] : Hodder and Stoughton, 1977. — 154p ; 18cm. — (Hodder Christian paperbacks)
Bibl.: p.153-154.
ISBN 0-340-21669-7 Pbk : £0.80
(B77-32405)

265'.82 — Christian church. Prayers for the sick. *Anthologies*
Watch with the sick / compiled by Norman Autton. — Revised and enlarged ed. — London : S.P.C.K., 1976. — xii,116p ; 20cm.
Previous ed.: published as 'A manual of prayers and readings with the sick'. 1970. — Bibl.: p.109-110. — Index.
ISBN 0-281-02924-5 Pbk : £1.95
(B77-11066)

265'.9 — Church of England. Exorcism. *Personal observations*
Petitpierre, Robert. Exorcising devils / [by] Robert Petitpierre. — London : Hale, 1976. — 172p ; 23cm.
ISBN 0-7091-5843-2 : £3.95
(B77-00018)

266 — CHRISTIAN MISSIONS

Warren, Max Alexander Cunningham. I believe in the great commission / by Max Warren. — London [etc.] : Hodder and Stoughton, 1976. — 190p ; 22cm.
Bibl.: p.186-190.
ISBN 0-340-21220-9 Pbk : £2.60
(B77-17292)

266'.022'09421 — Christian missions. *London. London City Mission, to 1976*
Wrintmore, Frederick Henry. Twentieth century miracles : a review of the ministry of the London City Mission / by F.H. Wrintmore. — London : London City Mission, [1977]. — 98p, [2]leaves of plates,[10]p of plates : ill, ports ; 19cm.
Pbk : £0.75
(B77-22343)

266'.023'0922 — Christian missions. Crawford, Tarleton Perry; Moon, Charlotte & Mateer, Calvin Wilson. *China. Eastern Shantung. Biographies*
Hyatt, Irwin T. Our ordered lives confess : three nineteenth-century American missionaries in East Shantung / [by] Irwin T. Hyatt, Jr. — Cambridge, Mass. ; London : Harvard University Press, 1976 [i.e. 1977]. — xv,323p : map, ports ; 24cm. — (Harvard studies in American-East Asian relations ; 8)
Published in the United States: 1976. — Bibl.: p.297-313. — Index.
ISBN 0-674-64735-1 : £13.85
(B77-13500)

266'.023'0924 — Christian missions. *Burma, 1965-1972. Personal observations*
Morse, Eugene. Exodus to a hidden valley / [by] Eugene Morse. — [London] ([14 St James's Place, S.W.1]) : Fount Paperbacks, 1977. — 224p : map ; 18cm.
Originally published: New York : Reader's Digest Press, 1974 ; London : Collins, 1975.
ISBN 0-00-625004-1 Pbk : £0.75
(B77-33052)

266'.023'0924 — Christian missions. *Philippines. Mindoro. Personal observations. Juvenile literature*
Linden, Elly van der. The village on stilts / by Elly van der Linden ; translated from the Dutch by Sonja van den Bergh ; illustrated by Alice Bush. — Revised ed. — London : Overseas Missionary Fellowship, 1976. — 31p : ill, map ; 19cm.
'An OMF oriole book'. — Previous ed.: published as 'The boy from Mindoro'. London : China Inland Mission, 1963.
ISBN 0-85363-110-7 Sd : £0.25
(B77-06468)

266'.023'0924 — Christian missions. Cowie, Vera. *China. Autobiographies*
Cowie, Vera. Girl Friday to Gladys Aylward / [by] Vera Cowie. — London : Lakeland, 1976. — 156p,[4]p of plates : ports ; 18cm.
ISBN 0-551-00763-x Pbk : £0.95
(B77-08756)

266'.023'0924 — Christian missions. Moffat, Mary. *Africa south of the Sahara. Biographies*
Dickson, Mora. Beloved partner : Mary Moffat of Kuruman / by Mora Dickson. — London : Dobson, 1976. — [8],244,[2]p : ill, maps, ports ; 23cm.
Originally published: London : Gollancz, 1974. — Bibl.: p.225 - Index.
ISBN 0-234-72015-8 : £4.50
ISBN 0-234-72017-4 Pbk : £2.50
(B77-03368)

266'.023'095 — Christian missions. *Far East. Overseas Missionary Fellowship, to 1975*
Lyall, Leslie Theodore. A passion for the impossible : the continuing story of the mission Hudson Taylor began / by Leslie T. Lyall. — London : OMF Books, 1976. — 227p : map ; 19cm.
Originally published: London : Hodder and Stoughton, 1965. — Bibl.: p.217. — Index.
ISBN 0-85363-116-6 : £1.50
ISBN 0-85363-115-8 Pbk : £0.80
(B77-09495)

266'.023'09593 — Christian missions to Miao. *Northern Thailand*
Scheuzger, Otto. The new trail / by Otto Scheuzger ; translated [from the German] by Joyce Baldwin. — New ed. — London : OMF Books, 1976. — 63p ; 19cm.
Previous ed., i.e. 1st ed., of this translation: London : China Inland Mission, 1963. — Translation of: 'Der neue Pfad'. Giesen : Brunnen, 1961.
ISBN 0-85363-114-x Pbk : £0.45
(B77-08757)

266'.023'095982 — Christian missions. *Indonesia. East Java, to 1966*
Bentley-Taylor, David. Java saga : Christian progress in Muslim Java / [by] David Bentley-Taylor. — London : OMF Books, 1976. — xi,148p : maps ; 19cm.
Originally published: as 'The weathercock's reward'. London : Overseas Missionary Fellowship, 1967. — Bibl.: p.147-148.
ISBN 0-85363-100-x Pbk : £0.75
(B77-02761)

266'.025'0924 — Christian medical missions. Roseveare, Helen. *Zaire. Biographies*
Burgess, Alan. Daylight must come : the story of Dr Helen Roseveare / [by] Alan Burgess. — London [etc.] : Pan Books, 1977. — 286p,[8]p of plates : ill, 3 maps, ports ; 18cm.
Originally published: London : Joseph, 1975.
ISBN 0-330-25063-9 Pbk : £0.75
(B77-15086)

266'.025'0924 — Salvation Army medical missions. Hartog, Eva den. *Bangladesh. Biographies*
Maule, Henry. Moved with compassion : Eva den Hartog's world of hope in the midst of despair / by Henry Maule. — London : Souvenir Press, 1977. — 238p,[12]p of plates : ill, ports ; 23cm.
ISBN 0-285-62272-2 : £3.95
(B77-26782)

266'.025'095 — Christian medical missions. *Asia. Bible and Medical Missionary Fellowship, to 1976*
Fleming, Guy. Asian advance - there shall be no end / compiled by Guy Fleming in collaboration with Moonyeen Littleton and Allan Baird. — London (352 Kennington Rd, SE11 4LF) : Bible and Medical Missionary Fellowship, 1977. — [65]p(1 fold) : ill(some col), maps, ports ; 30cm.
Spine title: - there shall be no end.
Pbk : £1.25
(B77-19211)

266'.1'951156 — Russian Orthodox missions. *China. Peking, ca 1700-ca 1800*
Widmer, Eric. The Russian ecclesiastical mission in Peking during the eighteenth century / by Eric Widmer. — [Cambridge, Mass.] : East Asian Research Center, Harvard University ; Cambridge, Mass. ; London : Distributed by Harvard University Press, 1976. — xii,262p : map ; 24cm. — (Harvard East Asian monographs ; 69)
Bibl.: p.233-250. — Index.
ISBN 0-674-78129-5 : £11.25
(B77-03914)

266'.3 — Anglican missions: Church Missionary Society, 1910-1942
Hewitt, Gordon, *b.1912.* The problems of success : a history of the Church Missionary Society, 1910-1942 / [by] Gordon Hewitt. — London : S.C.M. Press for the C.M.S.
In 2 vols.
Vol.2 : Asia ; [and], Overseas partners. — 1977. — xii,424p ; 25cm.
Index.
ISBN 0-334-01313-5 : £10.00
(B77-27681)

266'.7'6795 — Methodist missions to Indians of North America. *Oregon, 1834-1843*
Loewenberg, Robert J. Equality on the Oregon frontier : Jason Lee and the Methodist mission, 1834-43 / [by] Robert J. Loewenberg. — Seattle ; London : University of Washington Press, 1976. — xi,287p ; 24cm.
Bibl.: p.242-275. — Index.
ISBN 0-295-95491-4 : £14.00
(B77-08217)

267 — CHRISTIAN ASSOCIATIONS FOR RELIGIOUS WORK

267 — Christian religious communities
Clark, David, *b.1934.* Basic communities : towards an alternative society / [by] David Clark. — London : S.P.C.K., 1977. — x,329p ; 22cm.
ISBN 0-281-03568-7 : £8.95
ISBN 0-281-02965-2 Pbk : £5.50
(B77-26783)

267'.13'0924 — Businessmen's Christian organisations: Full Gospel Business Men's Fellowship International. Shakarian, Demos. *Autobiographies*
Shakarian, Demos. The happiest people on earth : the long-awaited personal story of Demos Shakarian / as told to John and Elizabeth Sherrill. — London [etc.] : Hodder and Stoughton, 1977. — 205p ; 18cm. — (Hodder Christian paperbacks)
Originally published: Chappaqua : Chosen Books, 1975.
ISBN 0-340-21599-2 Pbk : £0.95
(B77-26784)

267'.15 — Salvation Army. *Regulations*
Salvation Army. Chosen to be a soldier : orders and regulations for soldiers of the Salvation Army / originally prepared by The Founder. — [New ed.]. — London (International Headquarters, 101 Queen Victoria St., EC4P 4EP) : Salvation Army, 1977. — [8],91p ; 19cm.
Previous ed.: i.e. Revised ed., published as 'Orders and regulations for soldiers of the Salvation Army'. 1927.
ISBN 0-902430-01-7 Pbk : £0.35
(B77-16181)

267'.15 — Salvation Army. *Secondary school texts*
Kew, Clifford W. The Salvation Army / by Clifford W. Kew ; foreword by Clarence Wiseman. — Exeter [etc.] : Religious Education Press, 1977. — 55p : ill, coat of arms, ports ; 19cm. — (The Christian denominations series)
Bibl.: p.54.
ISBN 0-08-021184-4 Pbk : £0.90
ISBN 0-08-021183-7 Pbk : £0.60(non-net)
(B77-16726)

267'.15'05 — Salvation Army. *Yearbooks*
Salvation Army. The Salvation Army year book ... — London : Salvationist Publishing and Supplies.
1977. — 1976. — [6],250p : ill, maps ; 19cm.
Index.
ISBN 0-85412-295-8 : £1.50
ISSN 0080-567x
(B77-00019)

1978. — 1977. — [6],255p : ill, maps ; 20cm.
Index.
ISBN 0-85412-309-1 : Unpriced
ISSN 0080-567x
ISBN 0-85412-308-3 Pbk : £0.95
(B77-33608)

267'.15'0924 — Salvation Army. Field, Martha. *Biographies*
Endersbee, Mary. A thoroughly modern Martha : the life of Brigadier Martha Field / by Mary Endersbee. — London [etc.] : Hodder and Stoughton, 1977. — 189p ; 18cm. — (Hodder Christian paperbacks)
ISBN 0-340-20124-x Pbk : £0.90
(B77-16182)

267'.15'0924 — Salvation Army. Schmidtke, Ernst. *Biographies*
Linnett, Arthur. Radiant rebel : the story of Ernst Schmidtke / by Arthur Linnett. — London : Salvationist Publishing and Supplies, 1976. — [5],97p ; 19cm.
ISBN 0-85412-292-3 Pbk : £0.85
(B77-10729)

267'.18'34215 — Church of England religious communities. *London. Tower Hamlets (London Borough). Stepney. Royal Foundation of Saint Katharine, to 1975*
Royal Foundation of Saint Katharine. The Royal Foundation of Saint Katharine. — [London] ([Butcher Row, E14 8DS]) : The Foundation, [1976?]. — [12]p : ill, map, plan ; 14x23cm.
Sd : Unpriced
(B77-16183)

267'.18'342332 — Church of England religious communities. *Dorset. Whatcombe. Barnabas Fellowship, to 1975*
Gunstone, John. The beginnings at Whatcombe : an experience of community / by John Gunstone ; drawings by Sylvia Lawton. — London [etc.] : Hodder and Stoughton, 1976. — 125p : ill ; 18cm. — (Hodder Christian paperbacks)
ISBN 0-340-20994-1 Pbk : £0.70
(B77-17909)

267'.18'5241423 — Church of Scotland religious communities. *Scotland. Strathclyde Region. Iona. Iona Community, to 1967*
Morton, Thomas Ralph. The Iona Community : personal impressions of the early years / [by] T. Ralph Morton. — Edinburgh : St Andrew Press, 1977. — v,142p ; 19cm.
ISBN 0-7152-0357-6 Pbk : £2.00
(B77-29929)

267'.44'3 — Women's Church of England organisations: Spearhead, to 1964
Cropper, Margaret. The Girls' Diocesan Association, 1901-1961 and Spearhead, 1961-1964 / by Margaret Cropper. — [London] ([c/o Miss Priscilla Lethbridge, Flat 5, 7 Embankment Gardens, SW3 4LJ]) : [Girls' Diocesan Association, Trustees], [1976]. — [5], 58p ; 22cm.
ISBN 0-9505366-0-1 Pbk : £0.60
(B77-00603)

267'.6'0941 — Christian youth work. *Great Britain*
Inside out : a handbook for youth leaders / edited by Michael Eastman ; preface by David Sheppard. — London : Falcon Books, 1976. — 128p ; 20cm.
Bibl.: p.128.
ISBN 0-85491-829-9 Pbk : £1.15
(B77-03915)

267'.61'0942659 — Universities. *Cambridgeshire. Cambridge. University of Cambridge. Christian organisations: Cambridge Inter-Collegiate Christian Union, to 1977*
Barclay, Oliver Rainsford. Whatever happened to the Jesus Lane lot? / [by] Oliver R. Barclay. — Leicester : Inter-Varsity Press, 1977. — 176p ; 19cm.
Bibl.: p.169-170. — Index.
ISBN 0-85110-624-2 : £2.25
ISBN 0-85110-396-0 Pbk : £0.95
(B77-25386)

267'.7'0941 — Boys' Christian organisations. *Great Britain. Covenanter Union. Leadership. Manuals*
Covenanter Union. The Covenanter leader's handbook / [Covenanter Union]. — London (Nasmith House, 175 Tower Bridge Rd, SE1 2AG) : The Union, 1976. — 148p in various pagings : ill, facsims, forms, music, plan, ports ; 23cm.
Tab indexed. — In binder. — Includes sound disc (2s. 7in. 33 1/3 rpm.) in pierced pocket. — Index.
ISBN 0-9503896-1-7 : £2.70
(B77-02762)

267'.7'0941 — Boys' Christian organisations. *Great Britain. Covenanter Union. Periodicals*
The **Covenanter** : the official magazine of the Covenanter Union. — London (175 Tower Bridge Rd, SE1 2AG) : Covenanter Union. [No.1]- ; Jan.-Feb. 1976-. — [1976]-. — ill(some col), port ; 20x22cm.
Six issues a year. — 12p. in 1st issue. — Supersedes: The Bridge.
Sd : £0.10
ISSN 0308-9096
(B77-01161)

268 — CHRISTIANITY. RELIGIOUS TRAINING AND INSTRUCTION

268'.432 — Religious education. *For Sunday school teaching*
The **new** programme plus / [edited by V.C. Pogue and I.J.M. Kelly]. — [Edinburgh] : Church of Scotland, Department of Education.
4. — [1976]. — [3],47p : ill(incl 2 col) ; 21cm.
Cover title.
ISBN 0-7152-0345-2 Pbk : £0.45
(B77-08218)

Resources. — [1976]. — [1],28p ; 22cm.
Cover title.
ISBN 0-7152-0347-9 Sd : £0.35
(B77-08219)

268'.6 — Roman Catholic Church. Christian doctrine. Catechetics
Roman Catholic Church. *Congregatio pro Clericis.* [Directorium catechisticum generale. English]. General catechetical directory / Sacred Congregation for the Clergy ; [translated from the Latin]. — London : Catholic Truth Society, 1973. — 104p ; 19cm.
Originally published: 1972.
Pbk : £0.25
(B77-33053)

268'.6 — Roman Catholic Church. Christian doctrine. Catechetics. *Great Britain*
Catechetics : the future in focus : some responses to 'Catechetics in our time', the preparatory documents to the Synod of Bishops, Rome, September-October 1977. — Abbots Langley (74 Gallows Hill La., Abbots Langley, Herts. WD5 0BZ) : Catholic Information Services, [1977]. — [3],27,[1]p ; 21cm.
'... responses from England and Wales, Scotland and Ireland ... also a statement drawn up at a meeting in Birmingham ... of representatives working in Religious Education in all four countries' - Introduction.
Sd : Unpriced
(B77-16727)

Pastoral catechetics in action : 70 humble experiments / [compiled and introduced by Kevin Nichols]. — Slough : St Paul Publications, 1977. — 111p ; 22cm.
ISBN 0-85439-144-4 Sd : £1.25
(B77-33054)

269 — CHRISTIANITY. ORGANISED SPIRITUAL RENEWAL

269'.2 — Christian church. Evangelism
Neill, Stephen. Salvation tomorrow / by Stephen Neill. — Guildford [etc.] : Lutterworth Press, 1976. — x,150p ; 22cm.
ISBN 0-7188-2272-2 Pbk : £1.75
(B77-02763)

Sider, Ronald J. Evangelism, salvation and social justice / by Ronald J. Sider ; with a response by John R.W. Stott. — Bramcote : Grove Books, 1977. — 24p ; 22cm. — (Grove booklets on ethics ; 16 ISSN 0305-4241)
'Ronald J. Sider's original article ... was published in the "International Review of Mission" for July 1975 ...' - title page verso.
ISBN 0-905422-08-2 Sd : £0.30
(B77-19212)

Watson, David Christopher Knight. I believe in evangelism / by David Watson. — London [etc.] : Hodder and Stoughton, 1976. — 190p ; 22cm.
ISBN 0-340-18103-6 Pbk : £2.75
(B77-29930)

269'.2'0924 — Christian church. Evangelism. Graham, Billy
Strober, Gerald S. Graham : a day in Billy's life / [by] Gerald S. Strober. — London [etc.] : Hodder and Stoughton, 1977. — 160p ; 18cm. — (Hodder Christian paperbacks)
Originally published: Garden City, N.Y. : Doubleday, 1976.
ISBN 0-340-21672-7 Pbk : £0.85
(B77-22344)

269'.2'0924 — Christian church. Evangelism. Ten Boom, Corrie, to 1939. *Autobiographies*
Ten Boom, Corrie. In my father's house : the years before 'The hiding place' / [by] Corrie ten Boom with C.C. Carlson. — London [etc.] : Hodder and Stoughton ; London : Christian Literature Crusade, 1977. — 160p ; 18cm. — (Hodder Christian paperbacks)
Originally published: Old Tappan, N.J. : F.H. Revell, 1976.
ISBN 0-340-21593-3 Pbk : £0.75
(B77-26785)

269'.2'0924 — Christian church. Revivals. *Cornwall, 1841-1860. Personal observations*
Haslam, W. From death into life / by W. Haslam. — St Austell (31a Fore St., St Austell, Cornwall PL25 5EP) : Good News Crusade Publications, 1976. — 315p ; 18cm.
Originally published: London : Morgan and Scott, 1880.
ISBN 0-903437-07-4 Pbk : £1.25
(B77-03369)

269'.2'0941612 — Christian church. Revivals. *Antrim (County). Six Mile Water, 1625*
Bailie, W D. The Six Mile Water Revival of 1625 / [by] W.D. Bailie. — [Newcastle, Co. Down] ([Main St., Newcastle, Co. Down]) : ['Mourne Observer'], 1976. — iv,28p ; 22cm.
Bibl.: p.28.
Sd : £0.50
(B77-17910)

270 — CHRISTIAN CHURCH. HISTORICAL AND GEOGRAPHICAL TREATMENT

270 — Christian church, to 1933. *Conference proceedings*
Renaissance and Renewal in Christian History *(Conference), University of Exeter, 197-.* Renaissance and renewal in Christian history : papers read at the Fifteenth Summer Meeting and the Sixteenth Winter Meeting of the Ecclesiastical History Society / edited by Derek Baker. — Oxford : Blackwell for the Society, 1977. — xv,428p,8p of plates : ill, facsims ; 23cm. — (Studies in church history ; 14)
'... "Renaissance and Renewal in Christian History" was the theme of the Fifteenth Summer Meeting of the Society, held at the University of Exeter and of the Sixteenth Winter Meeting' - Preface. — Bibl.: p.419-428.
ISBN 0-631-17780-9 : £12.00
(B77-26786)

270 — Christian church, to 1975
Forristal, Desmond. The Christian heritage / [by] Desmond Forristal. — Dublin : Veritas Publications, 1976. — 192p,[8]p of plates : ill(some col), ports(some col) ; 25cm.
ISBN 0-905092-20-1 : £6.00(£6.60 including VAT in Rep. of Ireland)
(B77-07797)

Foster, John, *b.1898.* Church history / [by] John Foster [and Alan Thomson]. — London : S.P.C.K.
In 3 vols. — With keys to study suggestions. — 'Published in association with the United Society for Christian Literature for the Theological Education Fund'.
3 : New movements : reform, rationalism, revolution, 1500-1800 / [by] Alan Thomson. — 1976. — xiii,161p : ill, maps, ports ; 22cm. — (Theological Education Fund. Study guides ; 14)
Bibl.: p.xiii. — Index.
ISBN 0-281-02930-x Pbk : £1.50(non-net)
ISBN 0-281-02929-6 : £2.50(net)
(B77-00604)

270 — Christian church, to 1976
Gascoigne, Bamber. The Christians / [by] Bamber Gascoigne ; with photographs by Christina Gascoigne. — London : Cape, 1977. — 304p,[48]p of plates : ill(some col), facsims, map, ports ; 26cm.
'... this book [was] written while preparing thirteen programmes on "The Christians" for television' - Preface. — Index.
ISBN 0-224-01355-6 : £7.50 : CIP rev.
(B77-12291)

The **history** of Christianity / organizing editor Tim Dowley ; consulting editors ... [others]. — Berkhamsted : Lion Publishing, 1977. — xxiv, 658p : ill(chiefly col), facsims(1 col), col maps, plans, ports(some col) ; 23cm. — (A Lion handbook)
Col. ill. on lining papers. — Index.
ISBN 0-85648-073-8 : £7.50(£6.95 until 31 December 1977)
(B77-26787)

270 — Men saints. *Biographies. Juvenile literature*
Windham, Joan. Seven saints for boys / [by] Joan Windham ; illustrated by Mona Doneux. — London : Sheed and Ward, 1975. — 64p : ill ; 19cm.
ISBN 0-7220-7561-8 Sd : £0.40
(B77-08758)

270 — Saints. *Biographies. Juvenile literature*
Windham, Joan. Seven saints of all sorts / [by] Joan Windham ; illustrated by Elizabeth Andrewes. — London : Sheed and Ward, 1975. — 64p : ill ; 19cm.
ISBN 0-7220-7563-4 Sd : £0.40
(B77-08759)

Windham, Joan. Seven six o'clock saints / [by] Joan Windham ; illustrated by Mona Doneux. — London : Sheed and Ward, 1975. — 64p : ill ; 19cm.
ISBN 0-7220-7564-2 Sd : £0.40
(B77-08760)

270 — Women saints. *Biographies. Juvenile literature*
Windham, Joan. Seven saints for girls / [by] Joan Windham ; illustrated by Renée George. — London : Sheed and Ward, 1975. — 64p : ill ; 19cm.
ISBN 0-7220-7562-6 Pbk : £0.40
(B77-08761)

270'.08 — Christian church, to 1971. *Readings from contemporary sources*
Records of Christianity. — Oxford : Blackwell.
Vol.2 : Christendom / [edited by] David Ayerst & A.S.T. Fisher. — 1977. — xvi,329p,[8]p of plates : ill, facsims, maps, plans ; 23cm.
Index.
ISBN 0-631-17170-3 : £10.00
(B77-28374)

270.1 — Christian church, to 70
Maier, Paul Luther. First Christians : Pentecost and the spread of Christianity / [by] Paul L. Maier. — London [etc.] : Mowbrays, 1976. — 160p,[4]p of plates : ill(some col), map ; 22cm.
Also published: New York : Harper and Row, 1976.
ISBN 0-264-66402-7 : £3.50
(B77-13501)

270.2 — Christian church, 235-ca 500
Smith, John Holland. The death of classical paganism / [by] John Holland Smith. — London [etc.] : G. Chapman, 1976. — viii, 280p ; 24cm.
Bibl.: p.269-274. — Index.
ISBN 0-225-66097-0 : £7.50
(B77-16184)

270.2'092'2 — Christian church. Brigid, Saint; Columba, Saint & Patrick, Saint. *Biographies. Juvenile literature*
Donnelly, Maureen. Patrick, Brigid and Colmcille / by Maureen Donnelly. — Bangor, Co. Down (18 Fairview Gardens, Bangor, County Down, N. Ireland) : Donard Publishing Company, 1977. — 31p : ill ; 22cm.
Sd : £0.60
(B77-20020)

270.2'092'4 — Christian church. Bede, Saint. *Conference proceedings*
Bedan Conference, *Durham, 1973.* Famulus Christi : essays in commemoration of the thirteenth centenary of the birth of the Venerable Bede / edited by Gerald Bonner. — London : S.P.C.K., 1976. — xii,404p : geneal tables, plans ; 23cm.
' ... papers ... prepared for ... the Bedan Conference, held at Hatfield College, Durham, from 10 to 14 September 1973 ... ' - Introduction. — Index.
ISBN 0-281-02949-0 : £12.50
(B77-10158)

270.2'092'4 — Christian church. Nicholas, Saint. *Biographies. Juvenile literature*
Ebon, Martin. Saint Nicholas : life and legend / [by] Martin Ebon. — New York [etc.] ; London : Harper and Row, [1976]. — [8], 120p : ill, facsims, ports ; 24cm.
Published in the United States: 1975. — Bibl.: p.119.
ISBN 0-06-062113-3 : £6.70
Also classified at 398'.352
(B77-00020)

270.2'092'4 — Christian church. Winifred, Saint. *Biographies. Facsimiles*
Robert, *Prior of Shrewsbury.* [Gaude Wenefrida pura virgo. English]. The admirable life of Saint Wenefride / [by] Robert, Prior of Shrewsbury ; [translated from the Latin by I.F.]. — Ilkley [etc.] : Scolar Press, 1976. — [39],275,[11]p : port ; 20cm. — (English recusant literature ; vol.319)
Facsimile reprint of: 1635 ed. of this translation. St Omer : s.n., 1635. — 'Gaude Wenefrida pura virgo, etc.' originally published: Westminster : William Caxton, 1485?.
ISBN 0-85967-333-2 : Unpriced
(B77-05201)

270.6'092'4 — Christian church. Luther, Martin. *Biographies*
Marius, Richard. Luther / [by] Richard Marius. — London : Quartet Books, 1975 [i.e. 1977]. — 269p ; 22cm.
Originally published: Philadelphia : Lippincott, 1974 ; London : Quartet Books, 1975. — Bibl.: p.257-264. — Index.
ISBN 0-7043-3192-6 Pbk : £1.95
(B77-31686)

270.6'092'4 — Christian church. Luther, Martin. *Biographies. Secondary school texts*
Cubitt, Heather. Luther and the Reformation / [by] Heather Cubitt ; illustrated from contemporary sources. — London : Longman, 1976. — 96p : ill, facsims, map, ports ; 20cm. — (Then and there series)
ISBN 0-582-20542-5 Pbk : £0.50
(B77-05202)

270.6'092'4 — Christian church. Reformation. Zwingli, Ulrich. *Biographies*
Potter, George Richard. Zwingli / [by] G.R. Potter. — Cambridge [etc.] : Cambridge University Press, 1976. — xix,432p : 2 maps, plan ; 24cm.
Bibl.: p.viii-xvii. — Index.
ISBN 0-521-20939-0 : £18.50
(B77-03370)

270.6'092'4 — Christian church. Tyndale, William. *Biographies*
Edwards, Brian Herbert. God's outlaw / [by] Brian H. Edwards. — Welwyn [etc.] : Evangelical Press, 1976. — 180p : ill, facsims, port ; 22cm.
Bibl.: p.171-174. — Index.
ISBN 0-85234-067-2 : £2.70
ISBN 0-85234-066-4 Pbk : £1.80
(B77-05203)

270.8'2 — Christian church. Ecumenical movement
Huxtable, John. A new hope for Christian unity / [by] John Huxtable. — [London] ([14 St James's Place, S.W.1]) : Fount Paperbacks, 1977. — 127p ; 18cm.
ISBN 0-00-625127-7 Pbk : £0.95
(B77-31687)

270.8'2 — Christian church. Ecumenical movement. *Church Union viewpoints*
Kemp, Eric Waldram. Inaugural address to the General Council of the Church Union / by Eric Kemp. — London : Church Literature Association for the Church Union, 1976. — [2], viii,[1]p ; 20cm.
'[Given] 6 December 1976'. — '... issued as a supplement to the February 1977 issue of "Church Observer"' - title page verso.
Sd : £0.10
(B77-11562)

270.8'2 — Christian church. Ecumenical movement. *Methodist viewpoints*
Voice of Methodism Association. Ten points of Christian unity : an alternative statement. — Southport (111 Windsor Rd, Southport, Merseyside PR9 9BX) : Aldersgate Press, [1976]. — Folder ([4]p) ; 19cm.
Author: Voice of Methodism Association.
ISBN 0-9505517-0-8 : Free
(B77-08762)

270.8'2 — World Council of Churches. Assembly, 5th, Nairobi, 1975. *Reports, surveys*
World Council of Churches. *Assembly, 5th, Nairobi, 1975.* Breaking barriers, Nairobi 1975 : the official report of the fifth Assembly of the World Council of Churches, Nairobi, 23 November-10 December, 1975 / edited by David M. Paton. — London : S.P.C.K. [etc.], 1976. — xii,411p,[8]p of plates : ill, music, ports ; 22cm.
Index.
ISBN 0-281-02922-9 Pbk : £3.50
(B77-05864)

271 — CHRISTIAN CHURCH HISTORY. RELIGIOUS CONGREGATIONS AND ORDERS

271'.008 — Monasticism. *Essays*
Merton, Thomas. The monastic journey / [by] Thomas Merton ; edited by Patrick Hart. — London : Sheldon Press, 1977. — xii,185p : ill ; 23cm.
Originally published: Kansas : Sheed Andrews and McMeel, 1977. — Bibl.: p.185.
ISBN 0-85969-108-x : £4.95
(B77-20899)

271'.0094 — Religious communities. Geographical aspects. *Celtic countries, to ca 900*
Bowen, Emrys George. Saints, seaways and settlements in the Celtic lands / by E.G. Bowen. — 1st ed., reprinted ; with revised plates and second preface. — Cardiff : University of Wales Press, 1977. — xvii,245p, 15p of plates : ill, maps, plans ; 22cm.
First ed. originally published: 1969. — Bibl.: p.226-233. — Index.
Pbk : £3.90
ISBN 0-900768-30-4
(B77-33609)

271'.1'024 — Benedictines. Anselm, Saint
Ward, Benedicta. Anselm of Canterbury, a monastic scholar : an expanded version of a paper given to the Anselm Society, St Augustine's College, Canterbury, in May 1973 / by Benedicta Ward. — Revised and enlarged [ed.]. — Oxford : S.L.G. Press, 1977. — 23p ; 21cm. — (Fairacres publication ; no.62 ISSN 0307-1405)
Previous ed.: 1973?.
ISBN 0-7283-0067-2 Sd : £0.30
(B77-23990)

271'.12'024 — Cistercians. Bernard, Saint, of Clairvaux
The **influence** of Saint Bernard : Anglican essays / with an introduction by Jean Leclercq ; edited by Benedicta Ward. — Oxford : S.L.G. Press, 1976. — xviii,144p : ill, facsim ; 21cm. — (Fairacres publications ; no.60 ISSN 0307-1405)
Bibl.: p.22.
ISBN 0-7283-0061-3 Pbk : £1.75
(B77-07057)

271'.12'042219 — Abbeys. *Surrey. Waverley (District). Waverley Abbey. Community life, to 1536*
Ware, Gwen. The White Monks of Waverley / by Gwen Ware. — Farnham (38 West St., Farnham, Surrey) : Farnham and District Museum Society, 1976. — [4],44,[1]p,plate : 2 ill, map, plan ; 18cm.
Bibl.: p.42.
ISBN 0-901638-06-4 Pbk : £1.10
(B77-06469)

271'.125'024 — Trappists. Merton, Thomas, 1939-1941. *Diaries*
Merton, Thomas. The secular journal of Thomas Merton. — London : Sheldon Press, 1977. — xv,270p : ill ; 21cm.
Originally published: as 'A secular journal'. London : Hollis and Carter, 1959.
ISBN 0-85969-119-5 Pbk : £3.25
(B77-31688)

271'.3'024 — Franciscans. Francis of Assisi, Saint. *Biographies. Early works. Collections*
[Fioretti. *English].* The little flowers of St Francis / [translated from the Italian by Thomas Okey]. The mirror of perfection / [translated from the Latin by Robert Steele]. St Bonaventure's life of St Francis / [translated from the Latin by E. Gurney Salter]. — [1st ed. reprinted] ; introduction by Hugh McKay ; with a postscript on 'The mirror of perfection' and 'The life of St Francis' by Eric Doyle. — London : Dent, 1976. — xiv,397p ; 19cm. — (Everyman's library)
This collection originally published: 1910. — Bibl.: p.xii-xiii.
ISBN 0-460-04296-3 : £3.30
(B77-07058)

271'.62'024 — Passionists. Paul of the Cross, Saint. *Correspondence*
Paul of the Cross, *Saint.* Words from the heart : a selection from the personal letters of Saint Paul of the Cross / translated [from the Italian] and annotated by Edmund Burke ; [edited by] Roger Mercurio, Silvan Rouse. — Dublin : Gill and Macmillan, 1976. — viii,168p ; 23cm.
Index.
ISBN 0-7171-0806-6 : £7.00
(B77-06470)

271'.79 — Brothers Hospitallers of St John of God. John of God, Saint. *Biographies*
Cross, Walter. St John of God : patron saint of hospitals, the sick, nurses and all who look after the sick / [by] Walter Cross. — London : Catholic Truth Society, [1977]. — [2],18p ; 19cm.
Sd : £0.25
(B77-30973)

271'.91'024 — Sisters of Charity. Bernadette of Lourdes, Saint. *Biographies*
Trouncer, Margaret. A grain of wheat : the story of Saint Bernadette of Lourdes, 1844-1879 / [by] Margaret Trouncer. — Large print ed. — Bath : Chivers, 1976. — xiv,396p ; 23cm.
Originally published: London : Hutchinson, 1958. — Bibl.: p.391-393.
ISBN 0-85997-194-5 : £5.60(£4.20 to members of the Library Association)
(B77-03371)

271'.93 — Handmaids of the Sacred Heart of Jesus. Porras, Raphaela Mary, Saint. *Biographies*
Birch, Norah. Saint Raphaela Mary Porras / by Norah Birch. — London : Catholic Truth Society, [1977]. — [1],16p ; 19cm.
Sd : £0.20
(B77-11563)

271'.973'024 — Franciscans. Third Order. Nuns: Joan of the Cross, Sister. *Biographies*
Daca, Antonio. [Historia, vida, y milagros. English]. The historie -- of the Blessed Virgin, Sister Joane / [by] Antonio Daca ; [translated from the Spanish by Francis Bell]. — Ilkley [etc.] : Scolar Press, 1977. — [23],3-302p ; 19cm. — (English recusant literature, 1558-1640 ; vol.335)
Facsimile reprint of: 1st ed. of this translation, S. Omers : Charles Bascard for John Heigham, 1625. — Translation of: 'Historia, vida, y milagros'. Caragoça : Lucas Sanchez, 1611.
ISBN 0-85967-371-5 : Unpriced
(B77-17293)

271'.973'024 — Poor Clares. Clare of Assisi, Saint. *Biographies*
Devas, Dominic. Saint Clare of Assisi / [by] Dominic Devas. — London : Catholic Truth Society, [1977?]. — [23]p : ill, port ; 19cm.
Sd : £0.20
(B77-28375)

271'.979 — Christian church. Nuns: Héloïse, Abbess of the Paraclete. *Correspondence with Abélard, Pierre*
Abélard, Pierre. [Historia calamitatum. English]. The story of his misfortunes ; and, The personal letters / [by] Abélard & Héloïse ; translated [from the Latin] with an introduction and notes by Betty Radice ; wood-engravings by Raymond Hawthorn. — London : Folio Society, 1977. — 130p : ill, map(on lining paper) ; 26cm.
In slip case. — This translation originally published: as 'The letters of Abélard and Héloïse'. Harmondsworth : Penguin, 1974.
£4.95
Also classified at 189'.4
(B77-28376)

271'.979 — Christian church. Nuns: Héloïse, Abbess of the Paraclete. Correspondence with Abélard, Pierre. Authenticity. *Sources of data: European literatures, to 1500*
Dronke, Peter. Abelard and Heloise in medieval testimonies / by Peter Dronke. — [Glasgow] : University of Glasgow Press, 1976. — 61p ; 21cm. — (W.P. Ker memorial lecture ; 26th)
'... delivered in the University of Glasgow 29th October, 1976'. — Includes Latin and Middle French texts.
ISBN 0-85261-136-6 Sd : £1.25
Also classified at 189'.4
(B77-10159)

272 — CHRISTIAN CHURCH HISTORY. PERSECUTIONS

272 — Methodist churches. Persecution. *West Midlands (Metropolitan County). Wednesbury, 1743-1744*
Waddy, J Leonard. The bitter sacred cup : the Wednesbury riots, 1743-44 / [by] J. Leonard Waddy. — London : Pinhorns for the World Methodist Historical Society (British Section), 1976. — viii[i.e. ix],46p : map ; 21cm. — (Wesley Historical Society. Lectures ; no.36)
'[Lecture delivered to the] Methodist Conference 1970, a synopsis of which was delivered at Levenshulme Methodist Church Manchester 1st July 1970' - p.iv. — Index. — Previous control number ISBN 0-901262-18-8.
ISBN 0-901262-20-x Sd : £0.60
(B77-10160)

272'.8 — Witches. Persecution. Historiology. *Europe, to ca 1700*
Cohn, Norman. Europe's inner demons / [by] Norman Cohn. — St Albans : Paladin, 1976. — xvi,302p,8p of plates ; 20cm.
Originally published: London : Chatto : Heinemann for Sussex University Press, 1975. — Index.
ISBN 0-586-08235-2 Pbk : £1.75
(B77-01162)

273 — CHRISTIAN CHURCH HISTORY. DOCTRINAL CONTROVERSIES AND HERESIES

273'.1 — Gnosticism
Lacarrière, Jacques. The Gnostics / [by] Jacques Lacarrière ; foreword by Lawrence Durrell ; translated from the French by Nina Rootes. — London : Owen, 1977. — 136p ; 23cm.
Translation of: 'Les gnostiques'. Paris : Gallimard, 1973.
ISBN 0-7206-0364-1 : £4.95
(B77-14043)

273'.6 — Catharism. *Occult viewpoints*
Guirdham, Arthur. The great heresy / [by] Arthur Guirdham. — St Helier : Neville Spearman (Jersey) ; Sudbury : Distributed by Spearman, 1977. — [5],183p ; 23cm.
ISBN 0-85978-023-6 : £2.95
(B77-09496)

273'.6 — Christian church. Heretical movements, 1000- ca 1500
Lambert, Malcolm David. Medieval heresy : popular movements from Bogomil to Hus / [by] M.D. Lambert. — London : Edward Arnold, 1977. — xvi,430p : ill, facsims, maps ; 24cm.
Ill. on lining papers. — Bibl.: p.388-391. — Index.
ISBN 0-7131-5894-8 : £15.00
(B77-15087)

274 — CHRISTIAN CHURCH. EUROPE

274 — Europe. Christian church, 1000-1300. *Festschriften*
Church and government in the Middle Ages : essays presented to C.R. Cheney on his 70th birthday and edited by C.N.L. Brooke ... [et al.]. — Cambridge [etc.] : Cambridge University Press, 1976. — xv,312p,[2] leaves of plates : facsim, port ; 24cm.
Bibl.: p.275-284. — Index.
ISBN 0-521-21172-7 : £15.00
Also classified at 354'.4
(B77-07798)

274.1 — Christian church. Ecumenical movement. Churches' Unity Commission. Visible unity. *Great Britain. Roman Catholic viewpoints*
Roman Catholic Church. *Ecumenical Commission for England and Wales.* The Roman Catholic Church in England and the Ten Propositions of the Churches' Unity Commission : a paper / by the Ecumenical Commission of England & Wales. — Abbots Langley (74 Gallows Hill La., Abbots Langley, Herts. WD5 0BZ) : Catholic Information Office, 1976. — [1],8p ; 21cm.
ISBN 0-905241-04-5 Ls : £0.15
(B77-02023)

274'.11 — Christian church. *Scotland, 500-1930. Encyclopaedias*
Towill, Edwin Sprott. People and places in the story of the Scottish Church / [by] Edwin Sprott Towill ; illustrated by Colin Gibson. — Edinburgh : St Andrew Press, 1976. — xix, 99p : ill, ports ; 24cm.
ISBN 0-7152-0322-3 : £3.25
ISBN 0-7152-0252-9 Pbk : £2.00
(B77-11564)

274.2 — Christian church. *England, 1450-1660*
Cross, Claire. Church and people, 1450-1660 : the triumph of the laity in the English Church / [by] Claire Cross. — Hassocks : Harvester Press, 1976. — 272p ; 23cm. — (Fontana library of English history ; vol.2)
Bibl.: p.250-262. — Index.
ISBN 0-85527-129-9 : £7.00
(B77-02024)

274.28 — Christian church. *North-east England, to 800*
Gallyon, Margaret. The early church in Northumbria / by Margaret Gallyon. — Lavenham : T. Dalton, 1977. — 120p,[16]p of plates : ill, facsim, map(on lining papers), ports ; 23cm.
Bibl.: p.117-118. — Index.
ISBN 0-900963-74-3 : £3.80
(B77-21694)

274.29 — Christian church. *Wales, 1282-1536*
Williams, Glanmor. The Welsh Church from Conquest to Reformation / by Glanmor Williams. — Revised ed. — Cardiff : University of Wales Press, 1976. — xiv,612p,fold leaf ; 23cm.
Previous ed.: 1962. — Bibl.: p.569-591. — Index.
ISBN 0-7083-0084-7 : £12.00
(B77-01163)

274.29 — Christian church. *Wales, to ca 900*
Victory, Siân. The Celtic church in Wales / [by] Siân Victory. — London : S.P.C.K., 1977. — xii,146p,iv p of plates : ill ; 22cm.
Bibl.: p.139-140. — Index.
ISBN 0-281-02945-8 Pbk : £2.95
(B77-10161)

274.3 — Christian church. Reformation. *Germany, to 1530*
Dickens, Arthur Geoffrey. The German nation and Martin Luther / [by] A.G. Dickens. — [London] : Fontana, 1976. — xi,254p : map ; 19cm.
Originally published: London : Edward Arnold, 1974. — Bibl.: p.227-243. — Index.
ISBN 0-00-634383-x Pbk : £1.00
(B77-12292)

274.965 — Christian church. *Albania. Personal observations*
Peterson, Reona. Tomorrow you die / [by] Reona Peterson. — London : Lakeland, 1977. — [7],132p ; 18cm.
Originally published: United States : Bible Voice, 1976.
ISBN 0-551-00766-4 Pbk : £0.95
(B77-26788)

275 — CHRISTIAN CHURCH. ASIA
275 — Christian church. *East & South-east Asia*
Griffiths, Michael, *b.1928.* Changing Asia / by Michael Griffiths ; photographs by Fritz Fankhauser. — Berkhamsted : Lion Publishing, 1977. — 120p : ill(some col) ; 25cm.
Col. ill. on lining papers.
ISBN 0-85648-064-9 : £3.95
(B77-28377)

275.4 — Christian church. *India (Republic). Stories, anecdotes*
Cleator, Margaret. The God who answers by fire / by Margaret Cleator. — Eastbourne : Victory Press, 1976. — 127p ; 18cm.
Originally published: London : Bible and Medical Missionary Fellowship, 1966.
ISBN 0-85476-259-0 Pbk : £0.70
(B77-08220)

275.9 — Christian church. *South-east Asia, ca 1935-1960*
Gih, Andrew. The Church behind the bamboo curtain / [by] Andrew Gih ; foreword by J. Edwin Orr. — London : Lakeland, 1976. — 128p ; 18cm.
Originally published: London : Marshall, Morgan and Scott, 1961.
ISBN 0-551-00753-2 Pbk : £0.90
(B77-02764)

275.91 — Christian church. Nyein Tha, Daw. *Burma. Biographies*
Procter, Marjorie. The world my country : the story of Daw Nyein Tha of Burma / by Marjorie Procter. — London : Grosvenor Books, 1976. — 142p,[8]p of plates : ill, ports ; 19cm. — (A Grosvenor biography)
ISBN 0-901269-22-0 Pbk : £1.25
(B77-01164)

277 — CHRISTIAN CHURCH. NORTH AMERICA
277 — Christian church. *North America, to 1975*
Handy, Robert Theodore. A history of the churches in the United States and Canada / [by] Robert T. Handy. — Oxford : Clarendon Press, 1976 [i.e. 1977]. — xiii,471p : maps ; 24cm. — (Oxford history of the Christian Church)
Bibl.: p.428-449. — Index.
ISBN 0-19-826910-2 : £9.50
(B77-09497)

280 — CHRISTIAN CHURCH. DENOMINATIONS AND SECTS
280'.4 — Nonconformist churches. *Great Britain, 1800-1900*
Sellers, Ian. Nineteenth-century Nonconformity / [by] Ian Sellers. — London : Edward Arnold, 1977. — ix,102p ; 22cm. — (Foundations of modern history)
Bibl.: p.99-100. — Index.
ISBN 0-7131-5909-x : £5.95
ISBN 0-7131-5910-3 Pbk : £2.95
(B77-23106)

280'.4 — Nonconformist churches. *Gwynedd, ca 1915-1975. Personal observations. Welsh texts*
Thomas, William John. Ffiolau Cwm-yr-Haf / [gan] W.J. Thomas. — Caernarfon : Llyfrfa'r Methodistiaid Calfinaidd, 1976. — 127p,[4]p of plates : ill, port ; 19cm.
£1.25
(B77-06471)

280'.4 — Nonconformist churches. *London, 1616-1649*
Tolmie, Murray. The triumph of the saints : the separate churches of London, 1616-1649 / [by] Murray Tolmie. — Cambridge [etc.] : Cambridge University Press, 1977. — xii,251p ; 24cm.
Bibl.: p.237-244. — Index.
ISBN 0-521-21507-2 : £9.00
(B77-31689)

280'.4 — Nonconformist churches. *London. Waltham Forest (London Borough). Walthamstow, to 1976*
Batsford, M E. Non-conformity in Walthamstow / by M.E. Batsford. — London : Walthamstow Antiquarian Society.
Vol.1 : Congregationalists & Baptists. — 1977. — [2],30p,iv p of plates : ill ; 21cm. — (Walthamstow Antiquarian Society. Monographs : new series ; no.19)
ISBN 0-85480-034-4 Sd : £0.70
(B77-18550)

280'.4 — Nonconformist churches. Ambrose, Isaac. *Biographies*
Goreham, Norman J. Isaac Ambrose, Lancashire nonconformist / by Norman J. Goreham. — Preston (42 Fylde St., Preston, Lancs.) : Henry L. Kirby, 1977. — [1],9p ; 21cm.
Bibl.: p.9.
ISBN 0-9505653-0-x Sd : £0.15
(B77-14044)

280'.4 — Nonconformist churches. Organisations. *England. Free Church Federal Council. Reports, surveys. Serials*
Free Church Federal Council. Annual report / Free Church Federal Council. — London : The Council.
1976 ; and, Directory for 1977. — 1977. — [2], 60p : port ; 22cm.
ISBN 0-901152-04-8 Sd : £0.20
(B77-11565)

280'.4 — Protestant churches. *Roman Catholic viewpoints. Early works. Facsimiles*
Kellison, Matthew. A survey of the new religion / [by] Matthew Kellison. — Ilkley [etc.] : Scolar Press, 1977. — 473p in various pagings ; 21cm. — (English recusant literature, 1558-1640 ; vol.333)
Facsimile reprint of: 1605 ed. Doway : L. Kellam, 1605. — Index.
ISBN 0-85967-362-6 : £10.00
(B77-15088)

280'.4 — Protestant churches. Kellison, Matthew. Survey of the new religion. Criticism. Sutcliffe, Matthew. Abridgement or survey of poperie. *Critical studies. Facsimiles*
Kellison, Matthew. A reply to Sotcliffes answer / [by] Matthew Kellison. — Ilkley [etc.] : Scolar Press, 1977. — [57],439,[31]p ; 20cm. — (English recusant literature, 1558-1640 ; vol.330)
Facsimile reprint of: 1st ed. Rhemes : Simon Foigny, 1608. — Index.
ISBN 0-85967-346-4 : Unpriced
(B77-16728)

280'.4'0924 — Protestant churches. Nettleton, Asahel. *United States. Biographies*
Thornbury, John F. God sent revival : the story of Asahel Nettleton and the second great awakening / [by] John F. Thornbury. — Welwyn [etc.] : Evangelical Press, 1977. — 238p,[4]p of plates,[3]leaves of plates : ill, facsims, ports ; 22cm.
Index.
ISBN 0-85234-100-8 : £3.50
ISBN 0-85234-099-0 Pbk : £2.80
(B77-30974)

280'.4'0947 — Protestant churches. *Soviet Union, to 1975*
Brandenburg, Hans. The meek and the mighty : the emergence of the evangelical movement in Russia / [by] Hans Brandenburg ; [translated from the German]. — London [etc.] : Mowbrays, 1976. — xii,210p ; 22cm. — (Keston book ; no.7)
Translation of: 'Christen im Schatten der Macht'. Wuppertal : R. Brockhaus, 1974. — Bibl.: p.206. — Index.
ISBN 0-264-66349-7 Pbk : £3.25
(B77-03916)

281 — CHRISTIAN CHURCH. PRIMITIVE AND ORIENTAL CHURCHES
281'.4 — Latin Church Fathers, 325-636
Rusch, William G. The later Latin Fathers / [by] William G. Rusch. — London : Duckworth, 1977. — ix,214p ; 23cm. — (Studies in theology)
Index.
ISBN 0-7156-0817-7 : £8.95
(B77-15089)

281.9'092'4 — Russian Orthodox Church. Zachariah, Starets. *Biographies*
An **early** Soviet saint : the life of Father Zachariah / translated [from the Russian MS.] by Jane Ellis ; and with an introduction by Sir John Lawrence. — London [etc.] : Mowbrays, 1976. — xiv,111p ; 23cm. — (Keston books ; no.6) (Modern Russian spirituality series)
ISBN 0-264-66334-9 : £4.25
(B77-05204)

282 — ROMAN CATHOLIC CHURCH
Worlock, Derek. Give me your hand / [by] Derek Worlock. — Slough : St Paul Publications, 1977. — [7],196p ; 21cm.
ISBN 0-85439-133-9 Pbk : £3.00
(B77-15689)

282 — Roman Catholic Church. *Secondary school texts*
Murphy, Martin. The Roman Catholic Church / by Martin Murphy ; foreword by Bishop Butler. — Exeter [etc.] : Religious Education Press, 1977. — 56p : ill, 2 maps, ports ; 19cm. — (The Christian denominations series)
Bibl.: p.54-55.
ISBN 0-08-020913-0 Pbk : £0.90
ISBN 0-08-020912-2 Pbk : £0.60(non-net)
(B77-16729)

282 — Roman Catholic Church. Bell, Thomas, fl.1593-1610. Downfall of Poperie. *Critical studies. Facsimiles*
A **treatise** of auricular confession. The fore-runner of Bels downefall / [by] Philip Woodward. — Ilkley [etc.] : Scolar Press, 1976. — 429p in various pagings ; 20cm. — (English recusant literature, 1558-1640 ; vol.322)
Facsimile reprints. — 'A treatise of auricular confession' originally published: s.l. : John Heigham, 1622. — 'The fore-runner of Bels downefall' originally published: s.l. : s.n., 1605.
ISBN 0-85967-338-3 : Unpriced
Primary classification 265'.6
(B77-06467)

282 — Roman Catholic Church. Relations with Church of England, 1966-1977
Stewart, Richard Louis. Anglicans and Roman Catholics / by Richard L. Stewart. — London : Catholic Truth Society, 1977. — v,26p ; 19cm.
Bibl.: p.21-24.
Sd : £0.20
Also classified at 283'.42
(B77-26109)

282'.08 — Roman Catholic Church. *Lectures, speeches*
Newman, John Henry. Sayings of Cardinal Newman. — Blackrock (25 Newtown Ave., Blackrock, Co. Dublin) : Carraig Books, 1976. — [4],80p,plate : port ; 21cm. — (Carraig Books reprints ; 3)
Facsimile reprint of: 1st ed. London : Burns and Oates, 1890. — Bibl.: p.77-80.
ISBN 0-902512-14-5 Pbk : £1.00
(B77-14045)

282'.09'03 — Roman Catholic Church, 1500-1800
Delumeau, Jean. Catholicism between Luther and Voltaire : a new view of the Counter-Reformation / [by] Jean Delumeau ; with an introduction by John Bossy ; [translated from the French by Jeremy Moiser]. — London : Burns and Oates [etc.], 1977. — [19]294p ; 23cm.
Translation of: 'Le catholicisme entre Luther et Voltaire'. Paris : Presses universitaires de France, 1971. — Bibl.: p.262-284. — Index.
ISBN 0-86012-043-0 : £9.50
(B77-29173)

282'.09'047 — Roman Catholic Church, 1969-1974
Pycroft, Frank. Catholic facts and figures / compiled [by] Frank Pycroft. — London : Sheed and Ward, 1977. — vii,87p ; 20cm.
ISBN 0-7220-7715-7 Pbk : £1.95
(B77-24689)

282'.092'4 — Roman Catholic Church. Carroll, John. *United States. Correspondence*
Carroll, John. The John Carroll papers / Thomas O'Brien Hanley, editor ; under the auspices of the American Catholic Historical Association ; endorsed by the National Historical Publications and Records Commission. — Notre Dame ; London : University of Notre Dame Press, 1976. — 3v.(li,551p,[4]p of plates;liv,543p,[2]p of plates;liii,517p,[4]p of plates) : ill, geneal table, ports ; 25cm.
In 3 vols. — Bibl. — Index. — Includes some papers in French and Latin.
ISBN 0-268-01186-9 : £60.00
Also classified at 252'.02
(B77-04549)

282'.092'4 — Roman Catholic Church. Croke, Thomas William. *Ireland. Biographies*
Tierney, Mark. Croke of Cashel : the life of Archbishop Thomas William Croke, 1823-1902 / [by] Mark Tierney. — Dublin : Gill and Macmillan, 1976. — xvi,293p : 1 ill, maps ; 23cm.
Index.
ISBN 0-7171-0804-x : £8.50
(B77-06472)

282'.092'4 — Roman Catholic Church. Maklhouf, Charbal, Saint. *Biographies*
Johnston, Francis. Charbal Maklhouf : saint of the Mass / [by] Francis Johnston. — London : Catholic Truth Society, [1977]. — [2],10p ; 19cm.
Cover title: Saint Charbal Maklhouf.
Sd : £0.20
(B77-29931)

282'.092'4 — Roman Catholic Church. Malachy, Saint. *Biographies*
Scott, A Brian. Malachy / [by] A. Brian Scott. — Dublin : Veritas Publications, 1976. — 119p ; 19cm.
Bibl.: p.118-119.
ISBN 0-905092-10-4 Pbk : £1.00
(B77-04550)

282'.092'4 — Roman Catholic Church. Mayne, Cuthbert, Saint. *Biographies*
Caraman, Philip. Saint Cuthbert Mayne / [by Philip Caraman]. — London : Catholic Truth Society, [1977?]. — [14]p : col ill, col port ; 19cm.
Sd : £0.20
(B77-28378)

282'.092'4 — Roman Catholic Church. Neumann, John, Saint. *Biographies*
Dwan, Peter. Saint John Neumann / by Peter Dwan. — London : Catholic Truth Society, [1977]. — 13,[1]p ; 17cm.
Sd : £0.15
(B77-28379)

282'.092'4 — Roman Catholic Church. Ogilvie, John, Saint. *Biographies*
Richardson, M K. Father John Ogilvie, S.J. / [by] M.K. Richardson. — London (221 Golders Green Rd, N.W.11) : T. Shand Publications, 1976. — [2],40p ; 22cm.
ISBN 0-904210-06-5 Sd : £0.65
(B77-03917)

282'.092'4 — Roman Catholic Church. Quoist, Michel. *Biographies*
Cryer, Neville Barker. Michel Quoist : a biography / by Neville Cryer. — London [etc.] : Hodder and Stoughton, 1977. — 122p ; 22cm. — (Ecclesia books)
Bibl.: p.119-120. — Index.
ISBN 0-340-20096-0 Pbk : £2.50
(B77-23991)

282'.411 — Roman Catholic Church. *Scotland. Directories*
The **Catholic** directory for Scotland. — Glasgow : J. Burns.
1977. — 1977. — iii-lii,440p : ill, coats of arms, col port ; 19cm.
Index.
ISBN 0-900243-56-2 : Unpriced
ISSN 0306-5677
(B77-29174)

282'.42 — Roman Catholic Church. *England. Directories*
The **Catholic** directory of England and Wales. — London (21 Fleet St., EC4Y 1AP) : 'The Universe' for the Hierarchy.
1977 : one hundred and thirty-eighth year of issue. — 1977. — x,677,94p : ill, coats of arms ; 23cm.
Index.
ISBN 0-904359-03-4 : £6.75
(B77-07059)

282'.42 — Roman Catholic Church. *England. Reports, surveys*
Roman Catholic Church. *Joint Working Party on Pastoral Strategy.* A time for building : report of the Joint Working Party on Pastoral Strategy. — Abbots Langley (74 Gallows Hill La., Abbots Langley, Herts. WD5 0BZ) : Catholic Information Services of the Bishops' Conference of England and Wales, [1976]. — 48p ; 22cm.
ISBN 0-905241-05-3 Sd : £0.45
(B77-03918)

282'.42 — Roman Catholic Church. Recusants. *England, 1534-1830*
Aveling, John Cedric H. The handle and the axe : the Catholic recusants in England from Reformation to emancipation / [by] J.C.H. Aveling. — London : Blond and Briggs, 1976. — 384p ; 23cm.
Bibl.: p.361-375. — Index.
ISBN 0-85634-047-2 : £9.50
(B77-04551)

282'.42 — Roman Catholic Church. Relations with Church of England. *England, 1967-1976*
Keeton, Barry. Some observations on Anglican-Roman Catholic relations / [by] Barry Keeton. — London : Church Literature Association, 1976. — [2],6p ; 21cm. — (Dolphin papers ; 5)
ISBN 0-85191-099-8 Sd : £0.15
Primary classification 283'.42
(B77-11567)

282'.423'98 — Roman Catholic Church. *Avon. Bath, 1559-1850. Documents*
Post-Reformation Catholicism in Bath. — [London] ([Flat 5, 24 Lennox Gardens, SW1X 0DG]) : Catholic Record Society.
'Printed here are the first two registers of the Bath Catholic mission' - Introduction.
Vol.2 : Registers, 1780-1825 / edited by J. Anthony Williams. — 1976. — xiv,244p,fold plate : map ; 23cm. — (Catholic Record Society. Publications : records series ; vol.66)
Spine title: Catholicism in Bath. — Bibl.: p.xi. — Index.
Unpriced
(B77-11067)

282'.427'87 — Roman Catholic Church. Our Lady and St Michael, Workington. *Cumbria. Workington, to 1976*
Our Lady & St Michael, Workington : centenary, 1876-1976. — [Workington] ([Workington, Cumbria]) : [The Priory], [1976]. — [2],20,[1] p : ill, ports ; 25cm.
ISBN 0-9505428-0-6 Sd : £0.30
(B77-03372)

282'.428'19 — Roman Catholic Church. Diocese of Leeds. *Directories*
Roman Catholic Church. *Diocese of Leeds.* The Leeds diocesan directory. — Doncaster (c/o The Presbytery, 54 High St., Bentley, Doncaster, S. Yorkshire DN5 0AT) : 'Leeds Diocesan Directory'.
1977 / edited by Kevin J. Martin. — [1977]. — 194p : ill(some col), map, ports(some col) ; 22cm.
ISBN 0-905737-01-6 Pbk : £0.40
ISSN 0309-1589
(B77-08221)

282'.429 — Roman Catholic Church. Relations with Church in Wales. *Wales. Reports, surveys*
Church in Wales-Roman Catholic Joint Working Group. An interim report / Church in Wales-Roman Catholic Joint Working Group. — [Penarth] ([Education and Communications Centre, Woodland Place, Penarth, S. Glam.]) : [Church in Wales Publications], [1974?]. — [1], 8p ; 21cm.
ISBN 0-85326-018-4 Sd : £0.20
Also classified at 283'.429
(B77-16185)

282'.429'87 — Roman Catholic Church. Archdiocese of Cardiff. *Yearbooks*
Roman Catholic Church. *Archdiocese of Cardiff.* Cardiff archdiocesan year book. — Shoreham-by-Sea (Caxton House, Shoreham-by-Sea, Sussex BN4 6QD) : Service Publications Ltd.
1974 : [forty-eighth ed.]. — [1974]. — 128p : ports ; 19cm.
ISBN 0-901614-19-x Sd : £0.15
(B77-00022)

Roman Catholic Church. *Archdiocese of Cardiff.* Directory and year book / Archdiocese of Cardiff. — [Cardiff] ([c/o The editor, 106 Clive Rd, Pencisely, Cardiff CF5 1GN]) : [Archdiocese of Cardiff].
1975 : [forty-ninth annual publication]. — [1975]. — 144p : ill, ports ; 19cm.
Previously published: as 'Cardiff archdiocesan yearbook'.
ISBN 0-905750-00-4 Pbk : £0.15
(B77-00023)

1976 : fiftieth annual publication. — [1976]. — 175p : ill, ports ; 19cm.
ISBN 0-905750-01-2 Pbk : £0.20
(B77-00024)

282'.45 — Roman Catholic Church. *Italy, 1400-1500*
Hay, Denys. The Church in Italy in the fifteenth century / [by] Denys Hay. — Cambridge [etc.] : Cambridge University Press, 1977. — x, 184p : 1 ill ; 23cm. — (Birkbeck lectures in ecclesiastical history ; 1971)
Bibl.: p.159-176. — Index.
ISBN 0-521-21532-3 : £7.95
(B77-29932)

282'.47'71 — Periodicals for Ukrainian Catholics: Periodicals with British imprints. *Ukrainian texts*
TSerkovni visti = Church news : neperiodychniĭ dodatok do zhurnalu 'Nasha tserkva'. — London (St Olga's House, 14 Newburgh Rd, W3 6DQ) : Apostol's'kyĭ Ekzarkhat Ukraïns'koï Katolyts'koï TSerkvy u Velykiĭ Brytaniï.
R.1, ch.1- ; 1977-. — 1977-. — 34cm.
Published at irregular intervals. — Ukrainian title transliterated, Ukrainian text. — 16p. in 1st issue.
Sd : Unpriced
ISSN 0309-7129
(B77-23992)

282'.669 — Roman Catholic Church. *Nigeria. Directories*
Official Nigeria Catholic directory / [Catholic Secretariat of Nigeria]. — Ibadan ; London : Evans Bros.
1976-7. — 1976 [i.e. 1977]. — [2],139p : port ; 22cm.
Published in Nigeria: 1976.
ISBN 0-237-50106-6 Pbk : £2.90
(B77-11566)

283 — ANGLICAN CHURCHES
McAdoo, Henry Robert. Being an Anglican / [by] Henry R. McAdoo. — Dublin : A.P.C.K. ; London : S.P.C.K., 1977. — 64p ; 19cm.
'These lectures were given to, and the subject chosen by, the Christian Study Centre at St. Bartholomew's Church, Dublin'.
ISBN 0-900010-15-0 Pbk : £1.00
ISBN 0-281-03587-3 (S.P.C.K.) : £1.00
(B77-23993)

283'.025 — Anglican churches. *Directories*
Crockford's clerical directory : a reference book of the clergy of the provinces of Canterbury and York and of other Anglican provinces and dioceses. — London [etc.] : Oxford University Press.
1975-76 : eighty-sixth issue. — 1976. — 40,xl, 1504p,fold leaf of plate : ill, coats of arms, maps(1 col) ; 26cm.
Index.
ISBN 0-19-200008-x : £25.00
(B77-02765)

283'.092'2 — Church of England. *England. Rural regions, 1837-1901. Biographies*
Colloms, Brenda. Victorian country parsons / [by] Brenda Colloms. — London : Constable, 1977. — 288p,[12]p of plates : ill, ports ; 23cm.
Bibl.: p.275-276. — Index.
ISBN 0-09-461280-3 : £6.50
(B77-28380)

283'.092'4 — Church of England. Buckler, William. *Biographies*
Cox, James Stevens. Rev. William Buckler : Rector of St Mary Major, Ilchester, 1837-1876 / by J. Stevens Cox. — St Peter Port : Toucan Press, 1977. — p137-144 : ill, port ; 26cm. — (Ilchester and district occasional papers ; no.7)
Sd : Unpriced
(B77-21695)

283'.092'4 — Church of England. De Blank, Joost. *Biographies*
De Blank, Bartha. Joost de Blank : a personal memoir / [by] Bartha de Blank. — Ipswich : Boydell Press, 1977. — [9],209p,[8]p of plates : ill, ports ; 23cm.
Index.
ISBN 0-85115-082-9 : £6.50
(B77-32406)

283'.092'4 — Church of England. Essex, Rosamund. *Autobiographies*
Essex, Rosamund. Woman in a man's world / [by] Rosamund Essex. — London : Sheldon Press, 1977. — x,178p,[4]p of plates : ill, ports ; 23cm.
ISBN 0-85969-129-2 : £4.95
(B77-28381)

283'.092'4 — Church of England. Hunkin, Joseph Wellington. *Biographies*
Dunstan, Alan. Cornish bishop / [by] Alan Dunstan and John S. Peart-Binns. — London : Epworth Press, 1977. — 174p ; 22cm.
Bibl.: p.166-169. — Index.
ISBN 0-7162-0282-4 Pbk : £2.50
(B77-24690)

283'.092'4 — Church of England. King, Edward, b.1829. *Biographies*
Newton, John Anthony. Search for a saint : Edward King / [by] John A. Newton. — London : Epworth Press, 1977. — 128p,plate : port ; 22cm.
Bibl.: p.127. — Index.
ISBN 0-7162-0281-6 Pbk : £2.00
(B77-17911)

283'.092'4 — Church of England. Newton, John, b.1725. *Biographies*
Edward, Brian Herbert. Through many dangers / [by] Brian H. Edwards. — Welwyn [etc.] : Evangelical Press, 1976. — 270p : ill, ports ; 21cm.
Originally published: 1975. — Bibl.: p.267-269. — Index.
ISBN 0-85234-075-3 : Unpriced
ISBN 0-85234-069-9 Pbk : £1.95
(B77-28382)

283'.092'4 — Church of England. Otter, Anthony. *Autobiographies*
Otter, Anthony. From atoms to infinity / by Anthony Otter. — [Revised ed.]. — Evesham : James, 1977. — 92p ; 20cm.
Previous ed.: published as 'Beginning with atoms'. 1971.
ISBN 0-85305-195-x Pbk : £1.95
(B77-23107)

283'.092'4 — Church of England. Oxford Movement. Keble, John. *Biographies*
Martin, Brian W. John Keble : priest, professor and poet / [by] Brian W. Martin. — London : Croom Helm, 1976. — 191p ; 23cm.
Bibl.: p.183-187. — Index.
ISBN 0-85664-381-5 : £6.50
(B77-02026)

283'.092'4 — Church of England. Pusey, Edward Bouverie. *Biographies*
Liddon, Henry Parry. Dr Pusey and the Pusey House : a sermon / by H.P. Liddon. — Oxford (Pusey House, Oxford OX1 3LZ) : The Friends of Pusey House, [1974]. — [16]p ; 21cm.
'Originally delivered in St Margaret's Church, Prince's Road, Liverpool, on January 20th, 1884' - title page verso.
Sd : £0.25
(B77-17294)

283'.092'4 — Church of England. Ryle, John Charles. *Biographies*
Toon, Peter. John Charles Ryle, evangelical bishop / by Peter Toon and Michael Smout. — Cambridge : J. Clarke, 1976. — 123p,plate : port ; 24cm.
Bibl.: p.123.
ISBN 0-227-67826-5 : £3.75
(B77-02027)

283'.092'4 — Church of England. Sheppard, Dick, b.1880. *Biographies*
Scott, Carolyn. Dick Sheppard : a biography / by Carolyn Scott. — London [etc.] : Hodder and Stoughton, 1977. — 253p ; 23cm.
Index.
ISBN 0-340-19429-4 : £4.95
(B77-14556)

283'.092'4 — Church of England. Simeon, Charles. *Biographies*
Hopkins, Hugh Evan. Charles Simeon of Cambridge / [by] Hugh Evan Hopkins. — London : Hodder and Stoughton, 1977. — 240p : ill(on lining papers) ; 24cm.
Bibl.: p.236. — Index.
ISBN 0-340-22071-6 : £5.95
(B77-26110)

283'.092'4 — Episcopal Church in Scotland. Forbes, Alexander Penrose
Allchin, Arthur Macdonald. Alexander Penrose Forbes : the search for integrity / by A.M. Allchin. — [Dundee] ([Dundee DD1 4HN]) : [The University, Dundee], [1977]. — [1],19p ; 21cm.
'A lecture given in the University of Dundee ... on 19 November 1975'.
ISBN 0-901396-12-5 Sd : £0.27
(B77-09498)

283'.418'35 — Church of Ireland. St Ann's Church, Dublin. *Dublin, to 1976*
Poyntz, Samuel Greenfield. St Ann's : the church in the heart of the city / [by] S.G. Poyntz. — [Dublin] ([c/o St Ann's Church, Dublin]) : [The author], [1977]. — 106p : ill, ports ; 23cm.
Unpriced
(B77-19213)

283'.42 — Church of England
Taylor, Denis Erskine. In His presence : a prayer book and guide to Confirmation, Communion and Church teaching / by Denis E. Taylor. — [New ed.] / with the Holy Communion Alternative Service One and Two revised. — [Exeter] : Religious Education Press, 1977. — 113p : ill ; 23cm.
Previous ed.: i.e. Series 2 and 3 ed. 1973.
ISBN 0-08-021767-2 : Unpriced
ISBN 0-08-021766-4 Pbk : Unpriced
(B77-33056)

283'.42 — Church of England. *Yearbooks*
Church of England. *General Synod.* The Church of England year book : the official year book of the General Synod of the Church of England. — London : Church Information Office.
1977 : [93rd ed.]. — 1977. — xxxii,432p : ill ; 22cm.
ISBN 0-7151-4556-8 Pbk : £4.50
ISSN 0069-3987
(B77-32407)

283'.42 — Church of England. Central records. *Reports, surveys*
The **central** records of the Church of England : a report and survey presented to the Pilgrim and Radcliffe Trustees. — London ([Church House, Dean's Yard, SW1P 3NZ]) : CIO Publishing, 1976. — iv,100p ; 22cm.
Report by a special committee, survey carried out by C.J. Kitching.
ISBN 0-7151-3678-x Pbk : £3.00
(B77-05865)

283'.42 — Church of England. Relations with Roman Catholic Church, 1966-1977
Stewart, Richard Louis. Anglicans and Roman Catholics / by Richard L. Stewart. — London : Catholic Truth Society, 1977. — v,26p ; 19cm.
Bibl.: p.21-24.
Sd : £0.20
Primary classification 282
(B77-26109)

283'.42 — Church of England. Relations with Roman Catholic Church in England, 1967-1976
Keeton, Barry. Some observations on Anglican-Roman Catholic relations / [by] Barry Keeton. — London : Church Literature Association, 1976. — [2],6p ; 21cm. — (Dolphin papers ; 5)
ISBN 0-85191-099-8 Sd : £0.15
Also classified at 282'.42
(B77-11567)

283'.42 — Church of England, to 1974. *Case studies*
Balleine, George Reginald. A popular history of the Church of England / by G.R. Balleine. — Revised ed. / brought up to date by G.C.B. Davies. — London : Vine Books, 1976. — 206p : ill, map, plan, port ; 19cm.
Previous ed.: s.l. : s.n., 1913.
ISBN 0-85190-071-2 Pbk : £1.95
(B77-13502)

283'.421 — Church of England. London (Diocese). *Directories*
London *(Diocese).* London Diocese book. — London (33 Bedford Sq., WC1B 3ER) : London Diocesan House.
1977. — [1977]. — xi,[1],210p : ill, coat of arms ; 19cm.
Index.
ISBN 0-901338-07-9 Pbk : £1.00
ISSN 0306-1515
(B77-11068)

283'.422'323 — Church of England. Rochester (Diocese). *Directories*
Rochester *(Diocese).* Rochester diocesan directory. — Ramsgate : Corbett and Dixon.
1976-77 : ninety-sixth year of issue / editor N. Radford. — [1976]. — 140p,fold leaf : ill, coat of arms, map ; 19cm.
Pbk : Unpriced
ISSN 0305-1994
(B77-33057)

283'.422'62 — Church of England. Chichester (Diocese). *Directories*
Chichester *(Diocese).* Chichester diocesan directory. — [Hove] ([9 Brunswick Sq., Hove, BN3 1EN]) : [Diocesan Fund and Board of Finance (Incorporated)].
[1977]. Part 2 : List of clergy and lay workers. — [1977]. — [1],2-56p ; 30cm.
Index.
Sp : £1.00
ISSN 0305-7003
(B77-32408)

283'.423'19 — Church of England. Salisbury (Diocese). *Directories*
Salisbury *(Diocese).* The Sarum diocesan directory. — Salisbury (Church House, Salisbury, Wilts.) : The Board of Finance.
1977-8. — [1977]. — 180p : ill, map ; 21cm.
Index.
ISBN 0-901358-06-1 Pbk : £1.75
(B77-12850)

283'.423'8 — Church of England. Bath and Wells (Diocese). *Directories*
Bath and Wells *(Diocese).* Bath and Wells diocesan directory. — Wells (The Old Deanery, Wells, Somerset) : The Diocesan Board of Finance.
[1977]. — [1977]. — 213p ; 19cm.
Index.
ISBN 0-902504-04-5 Pbk : £0.50
ISSN 0305-5485
(B77-11568)

283'.423'93 — Church of England. Bristol (Diocese). *Directories*
Bristol *(Diocese).* The Bristol diocesan directory. — Bristol (23 Great George St., Bristol) : Bristol Diocesan Board of Finance.
1976-7 ed. / [edited by Richard C. Titball]. — [1976]. — 126p : ill ; 22cm.
Index.
ISBN 0-901921-03-3 Pbk : £1.00
(B77-02028)

283'.424'14 — Church of England. Gloucester (Diocese), 1603. *Reports, surveys*
An **ecclesiastical** miscellany. — Bristol (c/o 9A Pembroke Rd, Clifton, Bristol) : Bristol and Gloucestershire Archaeological Society, 1976. — ix,159p : map ; 23cm. — (Bristol and Gloucestershire Archaeological Society. Records Section. Publications ; vol.11)
Index. — Contents: A register of the churches of the monastery of St Peter's, Gloucester / by David Walker - A survey of the Diocese of Gloucester, 1603 / transcribed by Alicia C. Percival ; edited by W.J. Sheils - Wesleyan membership in Bristol, 1783 / by John Kent.
ISBN 0-900197-11-0 : £4.50(£2.50 to members of the Society)
Primary classification 333.3'22'0942414
(B77-12349)

283'.424'46 — Church of England. Hereford (Diocese). *Yearbooks*
Hereford *(Diocese).* The Hereford diocesan church year book and clergy list. — Hereford : Adams and Sons (Printers) Ltd ; Hereford (Diocesan Office, The Palace, Hereford) : [Diocese of Hereford].
[1976-77] / edited by J.C. Wilding. — [1976]. — xvi,119p : 2 coats of arms ; 19cm.
Index.
Pbk : £0.95
ISSN 0305-3415
(B77-01165)

283'.424'68 — Church of England. Lichfield (Diocese). *Directories*
Lichfield *(Diocese).* Lichfield diocesan directory. — Lichfield (St Mary's House, Lichfield WS13 7LD) : Lichfield Diocesan Board of Finance.
1977 : one-hundred-and-fourteenth issue / joint editors G.N. Strong, P. Hughes. — [1977]. — xx,256p : ill ; 19cm.
Index.
ISBN 0-904807-02-9 Pbk : £1.25
ISSN 0306-1507
(B77-12293)

283'.424'96 — Church of England. *West Midlands (Metropolitan County). Rednal. St Stephen the Martyr, Rednal, to 1976*
St Stephen the Martyr, *Rednal.* Our heritage : St Stephen the Martyr, Rednal, silver jubilee, 1951-1976 / [early research by Horace M. Long ; edited with additional material by Howard Mumford]. — Rednal (Rednal, Birmingham [B45]) : Church of St Stephen the Martyr, 1976. — 28p : ill, ports ; 21cm.
Cover title: St Stephen the Martyr, Rednal, silver jubilee, 1951-1976. — Limited ed. of 1,000 copies.
Sd : £0.40
(B77-06473)

283'.424'96 — Church of England. Birmingham (Diocese). *Periodicals*
Lookout. — Birmingham (c/o Revd A. Priestley, 316 Vicarage Rd, King's Heath, Birmingham) : Diocese of Birmingham.
Supersedes: Diocesan leaflet.
[No.1]- ; Spring 77-. — [1977]-. — ill, ports ; 30cm.
Three issues a year. — 8p. in 1st issue.
Sd : £0.03
(B77-23108)

283'.425'42 — Church of England. Leicester (Diocese). *Yearbooks*
Leicester *(Diocese).* Leicester Diocesan calendar, clergy list and year book. — Leicester (19 Wellington St., Leicester LE1 6HH) : Barker and Co. (Leicester) Ltd.
1977 : forty-ninth year of publication / editor P. Etchells. — [1977]. — 192,viii p : ill ; 20cm.
Index.
ISBN 0-901046-08-6 Pbk : £2.00
(B77-09499)

283'.425'42 — Church of England. Leicester (Diocese), to 1976
Lloyd, Philip. Fifty years, thirteen centuries : a history of the Church and some churchmen in Leicestershire to mark the golden jubilee of the refounding of the Diocese of Leicester, 1926-1976 / ... historical notes Philip Lloyd, historical biographies Terence Y. Cocks. — [Leicester] ([5 St Martin's East, Leicester]) : [The Diocese of Leicester], [1976]. — 88p : ill, ports ; 21cm.
Bibl.: p.88.
ISBN 0-901046-07-8 Sd : £0.80
(B77-03373)

283'.425'74 — Church of England. Oxford (Diocese). *Directories*
Oxford *(Diocese).* The Oxford diocesan year book. — Oxford (Diocesan Church House, North Hinksey, Oxford) : [Diocese of Oxford]. 1977 : One hundred and twentieth year of issue / edited by J.T.M. Hine. — 1976. — 147, x p : ill ; 21cm.
Index.
ISBN 0-904923-02-9 Pbk : £2.00
(B77-12294)

283'.425'85 — Church of England. St Albans (Diocese). *Directories*
St Albans *(Diocese).* The Diocese of St Albans. — [St Albans] ([Diocesan House, St Albans, Herts.]) : [Diocese of St Albans].
1977-78 / editor D.W. Yates. — [1977]. — 171, xv p : ill ; 19cm.
'Incorporating the 99th edition of the St Albans diocesan year book'.
Pbk : Unpriced
(B77-32409)

283'.427'34 — Church of England. S. Paul's Church, Heaton Moor. *Greater Manchester (Metropolitan County). Heaton Moor, to 1976*
Openshaw, Eunice M. The story of S. Paul's Church, Heaton Moor / written by Eunice M. Openshaw. — [Stockport] ([17 Highfield Park, Heaton Mersey, Stockport, Cheshire]) : [The author], 1976. — 55p,[8]p of plates : ill, facsim, ports ; 21cm.
Cover title: S. Paul's Church Heaton Moor, 1877-1976.
ISBN 0-9505582-0-6 Sd : £0.90
(B77-10162)

283'.427'623 — Church of England. Blackburn (Diocese). *Directories*
Blackburn *(Diocese).* The Diocese of Blackburn. — [Blackburn] ([Diocesan Church House, Cathedral Close, Blackburn BB1 5AA]) : Blackburn Diocesan Board of Finance Ltd.
1977. — 1976. — 264p : 2 maps ; 21cm.
Index.
ISBN 0-902640-01-1 Pbk : £0.75
(B77-13503)

283'.428'13 — Church of England. Church of St John the Evangelist, Dewsbury Moor. *West Yorkshire (Metropolitan County). Dewsbury, to 1977*
Brooksbank, I M. The church and its people, 1827-1977 / [by] I.M. Brooksbank. — [Dewsbury] ([50 Staincliffe Rd, Dewsbury, W. Yorkshire WF13 4EF]) : [The author], [1977]. — 40p : ill ; 22cm.
Cover title: The Church of S. John the Evangelist, Dewsbury Moor.
Sd : Unpriced
(B77-32410)

283'.428'42 — Church of England. Ripon (Diocese). Influence of Oxford Movement, 1836-1934
Yates, Nigel. Leeds and the Oxford Movement : a study of 'High Church' activity in the Rural Deaneries of Allerton, Armley, Headingley and Whitkirk in the Diocese of Ripon, 1836-1934 / [by] Nigel Yates. — Leeds (23 Clarendon Rd, Leeds LS2 9NZ) : Thoresby Society, 1975. — ix,92p,4p of plates : ill, port ; 23cm. — (Thoresby Society. Publications ; vol.55, no.121)

Bibl.: p.86-88. — Index.
ISBN 0-900741-11-2 Pbk : £2.50
(B77-00025)

283'.429 — Church in Wales. Relations with Roman Catholic Church in Wales. *Reports, surveys*
Church in Wales-Roman Catholic Joint Working Group. An interim report / Church in Wales-Roman Catholic Joint Working Group. — [Penarth] ([Education and Communications Centre, Woodland Place, Penarth, S. Glam.]) : [Church in Wales Publications], [1974?]. — [1], 8p ; 21cm.
ISBN 0-85326-018-4 Sd : £0.20
Primary classification 282'.429
(B77-16185)

283'.429 — Church in Wales, to 1975
A **history** of the Church in Wales / edited by David Walker ; foreword by the Archbishop of Wales. — Penarth (Education and Communications Centre, Woodland Place, Penarth, S. Glam.) : Church in Wales Publications for the Historical Society of the Church in Wales, 1976. — xv,221p,8p of plates : ill, facsim, ports ; 23cm.
Bibl.: p.191-200. — Index.
ISBN 0-85326-010-9 : £2.75
ISBN 0-85326-011-7 Pbk : £1.75
(B77-09500)

283'.429'25 — Church in Wales. Bangor (Diocese). *Directories*
Bangor *(Diocese).* Blwyddlyfr = Year book / Esgobaeth Bangor = Diocese of Bangor. — Bangor (Diocesan Office, Ffordd Gwynedd, Bangor, Gwynedd) : Bangor Diocese.
1976-77 / edited by = golygwyd gan Trevor O. Evans and Ifor Thomas. — [1976]. — 96p ; 19cm.
Index.
Sd : £0.30
ISSN 0308-9878
(B77-00605)

283'.429'98 — Church in Wales. Monmouth (Diocese). *Yearbooks*
Monmouth *(Diocese).* The Monmouth diocesan year book : together with the list of parishes, clergy list etc. — Newport, Gwent : R.H. Johns.
1976-77 / editor A.V. Blake. — 1976. — 140p, [2]p of plates : ill, coat of arms, port ; 19cm.
Index.
ISBN 0-900499-27-3 Pbk : £0.45
(B77-09501)

284 — PROTESTANT DENOMINATIONS OF CONTINENTAL ORIGIN

284'.092'4 — Continental Protestant churches. Barth, Karl. *Biographies*
Busch, Eberhard. Karl Barth : his life from letters and autobiographical texts / [by] Eberhard Busch ; [translated from the German by John Bowden]. — London : S.C.M. Press, 1976. — xvii,569p,plate : ill, facsims, geneal table, maps, ports ; 23cm.
Translation of: 'Karl Barths Lebenslauf, nach seinen Briefen und autobiographischen Texten'. 2nd revised ed. München : Kaiser, 1976. — Bibl.: p.509-512. — Index.
ISBN 0-334-00077-7 : £10.00
(B77-05205)

284'.1'0924 — Jansonists. Jansson, Erik. *Biographies*
Elmen, Paul. Wheat flour messiah : Eric Jansson of Bishop Hill / [by] Paul Elmen. — Carbondale [etc.] : Southern Illinois University Press ; London [etc.] : Feffer and Simons for the Swedish Pioneer Historical Society, 1976. — xvii,222p : ill, ports ; 23cm.
Bibl.: p.208-214. — Index.
ISBN 0-8093-0787-1 : £6.36
(B77-08222)

284'.1'0924 — Lutheran churches. Bonhoeffer, Dietrich. *Biographies*
Bethge, Eberhard. Dietrich Bonhoeffer : theologian, Christian, contemporary / [by] Eberhard Bethge ; translated from the German by Eric Mosbacher ... [et al.] ; under the editorship of Edwin Robertson. — London ([14 St James's Place, S.W.1]) : Fountain Books, 1977. — xx,867p ; 20cm.
This translation originally published: London : Collins, 1970. — Translation of: 'Dietrich Bonhoeffer'. München : Kaiser, 1967. — Index.

ISBN 0-00-624631-1 Pbk : £3.00
(B77-10730)

285.1 — PRESBYTERIAN CHURCHES OF UNITED STATES ORIGIN

285'.1'0924 — Presbyterian Church in the United States. Dabney, Robert Lewis. *Biographies*
Johnson, Thomas Cary. The life and letters of Robert Lewis Dabney / [by] Thomas Cary Johnson. — Edinburgh [etc.] : Banner of Truth Trust, 1977. — [1],xvi,585p,[10]leaves of plates(2 fold) : ill, 2 geneal tables, 2 ports ; 23cm.
Originally published: Richmond, Va: Presbyterian Committee of Publication, 1903. — Index.
ISBN 0-85151-253-4 : £4.00
(B77-33610)

285.2 — PRESBYTERIAN CHURCHES OF BRITISH COMMONWEALTH ORIGIN

285'.2 — United Reformed Church. *Yearbooks*
United Reformed Church. The United Reformed Church year book : containing the lists of churches and ministers. — London : United Reformed Church.
1977 / editor Percy W. Bush. — [1976]. — iv, 289p : ill, map, port ; 21cm.
Index.
ISBN 0-902256-19-x Pbk : £3.50
ISSN 0069-8849
(B77-05866)

285'.2 — United Reformed Church. Castle Gate United Reformed Church. *Nottinghamshire. Nottingham, 1905-1975*
Duce, Robert. Castle Gate Church in the twentieth century : being a continuation of the 'History of Castle Gate Church, Nottingham, 1655-1905' by A.R. Henderson (published on the Church's 250th anniversary in 1905) / by Robert Duce ; with a final chapter by W.E. Round ; and a foreword by Hamish Baillie. — [Nottingham] ([Mrs F.C. Dossor, 34 Riverdale Rd, Attenborough, Nottingham]) : St Andrew's-with-Castle Gate United Reformed Church, 1977. — [6],ii,134p : ill, ports ; 21cm.
Sd : £1.00
(B77-23994)

285'.2 — United Reformed Church. Gatley United Reformed Church. *Greater Manchester (Metropolitan County). Gatley, to 1977*
Shercliff, William Henry. Gatley United Reformed Church : a short history, 1777-1977 / by W.H. Shercliff. — Manchester ([c/o Dr G. Jessup, 462 Palatine Rd, Manchester 22]) : The Church, 1976 [i.e. 1977]. — 64p : ill, facsim, map, 2 plans, ports ; 22cm.
Bibl.: p.63. — Index.
ISBN 0-9505183-0-1 Sd : £0.50
(B77-24691)

285'.2 — United Reformed Church. Liscard United Reformed Church. *Merseyside (Metropolitan County). Liscard, to 1851*
Moxey, E W. The Independent Chapel in Liscard : foundation and early years, a paper read to the Wallasey & District Historical Society, 3rd September 1976 / by E.W. Moxey. — Wallasey ([Mr B.W. Morgan, 181 Mount Pleasant Rd, Wallasey, Merseyside]) : [Liscard United Reformed Church], 1976. — [3],12p ; 33cm.
Sd : £0.30
(B77-24692)

285'.2'0924 — Presbyterian Church of Wales. Elias, John. *Biographies*
Jones, Robert Tudur. John Elias : prince among preachers / [by] R. Tudur Jones. — Bridgend (Bryntirion, Bridgend, Mid-Glamorgan) : Evangelical Library of Wales, 1975. — 33p ; 19cm. — (Evangelical Library of Wales. Annual lectures ; 1974)
ISBN 0-9502686-2-3 Sd : £0.35
(B77-08763)

285'.2'0924 — Presbyterian Church of Wales. Griffiths, Ann. *Biographies. Welsh texts*
Jones, Bobi. Ann Griffiths : y cyfrinydd sylweddol / [gan] Bobi Jones ; ynghyd â braslun o fywyd yr emynyddes gan E. Wyn James. — Pen-y-Bont ar Ogwr [i.e. Bridgend] (Bryntirion, Bridgend, M. Glam.) : Llyfrgell Efengylaidd Cymru, 1977. — 48p ; 19cm. — (Evangelical Library of Wales. Annual lectures)

Sd : £0.55
(B77-31691)

285'.2'0924 — Presbyterian Church of Wales. Roberts, Robert, b.1762. *Wales. Biographies. Welsh texts*
Roberts, Emyr. Robert Roberts : y seraff bregethwr : portread / gan Emyr Roberts. Y seraff annwyl : llythyrau Robert Roberts, Clynnog ; golygwyd, gyda rhagymadrodd a nodiadau, gan E. Wyn James. — Pen-y-bont ar Ogwr [i.e Bridgend] : Llyfrgell Efengylaidd Cymru, 1976. — 55p ; 19cm.
Sd : £0.45
(B77-09502)

285'.2411 — Church of Scotland. *Secondary school texts*
Bulloch, James. The Church of Scotland / by James Bulloch ; foreword by Thomas F. Torrance. — Exeter [etc.] : Religious Education Press, 1977. — 56p : ill ; 19cm. — (The Christian denominations series)
Bibl.: p.55-56.
ISBN 0-08-021188-7 Pbk : £0.90
ISBN 0-08-021187-9 Pbk : £0.60(non-net)
(B77-16730)

285'.2411 — United Free Church of Scotland. *Directories*
United Free Church of Scotland. The handbook of the United Free Church of Scotland. — Glasgow (11 Newton Place, Glasgow G3 7PR) : United Free Church of Scotland.
1977. — [1977]. — 53p ; 18cm.
Index.
Sd : £0.50
(B77-32411)

285'.2429 — Presbyterian Church of Wales. *Regulations. Welsh texts*
Presbyterian Church of Wales. Llawlyfr trefn a rheolau / Eglwys Bresbyteraidd Cymru. — Caernarfon : Llyfrfa'r Methodistiaid Calfinaidd, [1976]. — 129p ; 19cm.
ISBN 0-901330-64-7 Pbk : £1.00
(B77-03374)

285'.2429 — Presbyterian Church of Wales. *Yearbooks*
Presbyterian Church of Wales. Y blwyddiadur = The year book / Eglwys Methodistiaid Calfinaidd Cymru = The Presbyterian Church of Wales. — Caernarfon : Llyfrfa'r Cyfundeb.
1976 : Cyfrol 79 / golygydd J. Alwyn Parry. — [1976]. — 323p ; 22cm.
Welsh and English text. — Index.
ISBN 0-9500366-1-7 Pbk : £1.80
(B77-01166)

285'.2429'21 — Presbyterian Church of Wales. Capel Mawr, Amlwch. *Gwynedd. Ynys Môn. Amlwch, to 1977. Welsh texts*
Llyn y fendith : hanes y Capel Mawr, Amlwch. — Amlwch : Pwyllgor Dathlu Daucanmlwyddiant y Capel Mawr ; Dinbych [i.e. Denbigh] : [Distributed by] Gwasg Gee, 1977. — 133p,leaf of plate,[20]p of plates : ill, ports ; 23cm.
£2.00
(B77-32412)

285.8 — CONGREGATIONAL CHURCHES
285'.8'0924 — Congregational churches. Edwards, Jonathan. *United States*
Jonathan Edwards : his life and influence : papers and discussions / by Conrad Cherry ... [et al.] ; edited by Charles Angoff. — Rutherford [etc.] : Fairleigh Dickinson University Press ; London (108 New Bond St., W1Y 0QX) : Associated University Presses, 1975. — 3-65p ; 22cm. — (The Leverton lecture series)
ISBN 0-8386-1571-6 : £2.00
(B77-25387)

285'.8'0924 — Congregational churches. Hooker, Thomas. *New England. Biographies*
Shuffelton, Frank. Thomas Hooker, 1586-1647 / [by] Frank Shuffelton. — Princeton ; Guildford : Princeton University Press, 1977. — xii,324,[1]p ; 23cm.
Bibl.: p.309-317. — Index.
ISBN 0-691-05249-2 : £13.40
(B77-29175)

285.9 — PURITANISM
285'.9'09429 — Puritanism. *Wales, ca 1580-ca 1670*
Gruffydd, Robert Geraint. 'In that gentle country - ' : the beginnings of Puritan nonconformity in Wales / [by] R. Geraint Gruffydd. — Bridgend (Bryntirion, Bridgend, M. Glam.) : Evangelical Library of Wales, 1976. — 31p ; 19cm. — (Evangelical Library of Wales. Annual lectures ; 1975)
ISBN 0-9502686-1-5 Sd : £0.45
(B77-10163)

286 — BAPTIST CHURCHES
286'.1 — Baptist churches. *Secondary school texts*
Wood, John, *b.1932.* The Baptists / by John Wood ; foreword by Raymond Brown. — Exeter [etc.] : Religious Education Press, 1977. — 62p : ill, facsim, map, plans, ports ; 19cm. — (The Christian denominations series)
Bibl.: p.59-61.
ISBN 0-08-020911-4 Pbk : £0.90
ISBN 0-08-020910-6 Pbk : £0.60(non-net)
(B77-16731)

286'.1'0922 — Baptist churches. Thomas, James & Thomas, John, b.1886. *Wales. Biographies. Welsh texts*
Gruffydd, William John, *b.1916.* James a John : dau Frawd, dau broffwyd : cofiant i'r Parchedigion James Thomas, B.A., Y Tabernacl, Caerfyrddin, a John Thomas, Blaenywaun / gan W.J. Gruffydd. — Llandysul : Gwasg Gomer, 1976. — 121p ; 19cm.
ISBN 0-85088-359-8 Pbk : £0.75
(B77-10731)

286'.141 — Baptist Union of Great Britain and Ireland. *Directories*
Baptist Union of Great Britain and Ireland. The Baptist Union directory / edited and published under the direction of the Council of the Baptist Union of Great Britain and Ireland. — London : The Union.
1977-8 : one hundred and sixteenth year of issue. — [1977]. — 298p,plate : port ; 21cm.
Index.
Pbk : £2.75
ISSN 0302-3184
(B77-28383)

286'.1426'795 — Baptist churches. Avenue Baptist Church, Southend-on-Sea. *Essex. Southend-on-Sea, to 1975*
Jeremy, David J. A century of grace / by David J. Jeremy, John Barfield, Kenneth S. Newman. — [Southend-on-Sea] ([Southend-on-Sea, Essex]) : Avenue Baptist Church, 1976. — [5], 50p,[8]p of plates : ill, facsim, map, ports ; 25cm.
Bibl.: p.47-48.
ISBN 0-9505620-0-9 Pbk : £1.25
(B77-11569)

286.7 — ADVENTIST CHURCHES
286'.741 — Seventh-Day Adventists. *Great Britain. Periodicals*
Messenger : church paper for Seventh-Day Adventists in the British Isles. — [Watford] ([Stanborough Park, Watford, Herts. WD2 6JP]) : [British Union Conference of Seventh-Day Adventists].
Continues: British advent messenger.
Vol.82, no.1- ; Jan. 7 1977-. — [1977]-. — ill, ports ; 28cm.
Fortnightly. — 8p. in 1st issue.
Sd : Unpriced
ISSN 0309-3654
(B77-11069)

287 — METHODIST CHURCHES
287'.09 — Methodist churches, to 1976
Davies, Rupert Eric. Methodism / [by] Rupert E. Davies. — New and revised ed. — London : Epworth Press, 1976. — 196p ; 22cm.
Previous ed.: 1963. — Bibl.: p.187-188. — Index.
ISBN 0-7162-0280-8 Pbk : £1.75
(B77-05867)

287'.092'4 — Methodist churches. Coke, Thomas
Vickers, John Ashley. Thomas Coke and world Methodism / [by] John A. Vickers. — Bognor Regis (87 Marshall Ave., Bognor Regis, W. Sussex) : World Methodist Historical Society (British Section), 1976. — 20p ; 21cm. — (Wesley Historical Society. Lectures ; 1964)
'... delivered at the Methodist Conference in Sheffield, 1964' - Preface.
ISBN 0-9505559-0-8 Sd : £0.40
(B77-08764)

287'.092'4 — Methodist churches. Wesley, John. *Biographies. Juvenile literature*
Vickers, John Ashley. John Wesley : founder of Methodism / by John A. Vickers ; with illustrations by Ronald Jackson. — Loughborough : Ladybird Books, 1977. — 52p : ill(chiefly col) ; 18cm. — (Ladybird history series ; 44)
Text, ill. on lining papers. — Index.
ISBN 0-7214-0466-9 : £0.24
(B77-17912)

287'.09429 — Methodist churches. *Wales, 1762. Welsh texts*
Morgan, Derec Llwyd. Taith i Langeitho, 1762 / [gan] Derec Llwyd Morgan. — [Llangefni] ([Shire Hall, Llangefni, Gwynedd]) : Gwasanaeth Llyfrgell Gwynedd, Rhanbarth Môn, 1976. — [2],21p ; 21cm. — (Cyfres darlithoedd Môn ; 2)
'Darlith a draddodwyd ym Mrynsiencyn, 17 Tachwedd 1976'.
ISBN 0-9501551-2-8 Sd : £0.20
(B77-07799)

287'.1'0924 — Methodist Church. Whitefield, George, 1734-1742. *Correspondence. Facsimiles*
Whitefield, George. Letters of George Whitefield, for the period 1734-1742. — Edinburgh [etc.] : Banner of Truth Trust, 1976. — xiii,570p : port ; 23cm.
Spine title: George Whitefield's letters, 1734-1742. — 'This reprint includes 34 letters omitted from [the 1st] edition ... ' - jacket. — Facsimile reprint of: 1st ed. of vol.1 of 'George Whitefield's works'. London : Edward and Charles Dilly ; Edinburgh : Kincaid and Bell, 1771. — Index.
ISBN 0-85151-239-9 : £3.50
(B77-03919)

287'.1421'73 — Methodist Church. Woodford Methodist Church. *London. Redbridge (London Borough). Woodford, to 1976*
Fulcher, Ernest A. The Methodist Chapel, Derby Road, Woodford, 1876-1976 / by Ernest A. Fulcher. — London (Derby Rd, E.18) : Woodford Methodist Church, 1976. — [4],55p, [4]p of plates : ill, 2 facsims, port ; 23cm.
ISBN 0-9504893-0-1 Sd : £1.00
(B77-11070)

287'.1423'17 — Methodist Church. Seend Methodist Chapel. *Wiltshire. Seend, to 1975*
Griffiths, Harold J. Seend Methodist Chapel, 1775 to 1975 : bi-centenary, March 1975 : notes and observations / compiled by Harold J. Griffiths. — [Seend] ([Seend, Wilts.]) : Seend Methodist Chapel, 1974. — 18 : ill ; 23cm.
Bibl.: p.18.
ISBN 0-85966-020-6 Sd : £0.25
(B77-19214)

287'.1423'93 — Wesleyan Methodist Connexion. *Avon. Bristol, 1783. Registers*
An **ecclesiastical** miscellany. — Bristol (c/o 9A Pembroke Rd, Clifton, Bristol) : Bristol and Gloucestershire Archaeological Society, 1976. — ix,159p : map ; 23cm. — (Bristol and Gloucestershire Archaeological Society. Records Section. Publications ; vol.11)
Index. — Contents: A register of the churches of the monastery of St Peter's, Gloucester / by David Walker - A survey of the Diocese of Gloucester, 1603 / transcribed by Alicia C. Percival ; edited by W.J. Sheils - Wesleyan membership in Bristol, 1783 / by John Kent.
ISBN 0-900197-11-0 : £4.50(£2.50 to members of the Society)
Primary classification 333.3'22'0942414
(B77-12349)

287'.1424'91 — Methodist Church. Beckminster Methodist Church. *West Midlands (Metropolitan County). Wolverhampton, to 1976*
Beckminster Methodist Church, Wolverhampton, 1926-1976 / [edited by] Nigel Collinson. — Wolverhampton (9 Tudor Cres., Penn Fields, Wolverhampton) : [The editor], [1976]. — 20p : 2 ill ; 25cm.
ISBN 0-9505440-0-0 Sd : £0.20
(B77-01167)

287'.1425'21 — Methodist Church. *Nottinghamshire. Everton, to 1975*
Biggs, Barry John. Everton Methodism past and present / by B.J. Biggs. — Retford ([Retford, Notts.]) : History Department, Eaton Hall College, 1976. — 7 leaves ; 30cm.
Cover title. — Bibl.: leaf 7.
ISBN 0-901343-05-6 Pbk : £0.10
(B77-00026)

287'.1425'56 — Methodist Church. Hinton Methodist Church. *Northamptonshire. Hinton, 1820-1977*
Anscomb, J W. History of Hinton Methodist Church, 1820-1977 / [by J.W. Anscomb]. — Daventry (18 Nelson Ave., Woodford Halse, Daventry, Northants.) : The author, [1977]. — 18p ; 21cm.
Sd : £0.35
(B77-26789)

288 — UNITARIAN CHURCHES
288'.092'4 — Unitarian churches. Davies, Jacob. *Wales. Personal observations. Collections. Welsh & English texts*
Cofio Jacob / J. Eric Jones, golygydd. — Abedâr [i.e. Aberdare] (22 Stuart St., Aberdare [M. Glam. CF44 7LY]) : Gwasg y Fflam, [1974]. — [4],30p : port ; 22cm.
Includes 3 contributions in English.
ISBN 0-906032-00-8 Sd : Unpriced
(B77-16186)

289.6 — SOCIETY OF FRIENDS
289.6'092'4 — Society of Friends. Penn, William. Local associations: Southern Buckinghamshire & South-west Hertfordshire
Parrott, Edmund Vaughan. William Penn's connections with South-West Hertfordshire & South Buckinghamshire : a guide book / by E.V. Parrott. — [Rickmansworth] ([66 The Queens Drive, Rickmansworth, Herts.]) : [EP Publications], [1977]. — [14]p : ill, map, port ; 19cm.
Sd : £0.25
(B77-23109)

289.6′42 — Society of Friends. *England. Humorous texts*
Donne-Smith, Basil. Much madder : the chronicles of a Quaker meeting / [by Basil Donne-Smith]. — Crewkerne ([The Abbey], Crewkerne, Somerset) : Countryside Libraries Ltd, 1975. — 2-112p : map ; 21cm.
ISBN 0-9504025-0-8 Pbk : £0.80
(B77-19215)

289.9 — ASSEMBLIES OF GOD, BRETHREN, PENTECOSTAL CHURCHES, ETC.
289.9 — British-Israel movement
Gresty, L. Buxton. Christ or the Kremlin? : alerting the English-speaking and kindred peoples to their imminent peril / [by] L. Buxton Gresty. — Revised, abridged, updated [ed.]. — London : Covenant Publishing Co., 1976. — [7],71,[1]p : 2 ill, facsim, maps ; 20cm.
Map, ill., text on lining papers. — Previous ed.: published as 'Satan fights for Muscovy'. 1952.
£1.40
(B77-28384)

289.9 — Catholic Apostolic Church (Founded 1944)
Newman-Norton, Seraphim. Fitly framed together : a summary of the history, beliefs and mission of the Orthodox Church of the British Isles / by Seraphim Newman-Norton. — Glastonbury (31 Hatcliffe Close, London SE3 9UE) : Metropolitical Press, 1976. — 20p : ill, port ; 22cm.
Bibl.: p.19-20.
ISBN 0-905146-02-6 : £0.50
(B77-01168)

289.9 — Catholic Apostolic Church (Founded 1944). *Regulations*
Catholic Apostolic Church *(Founded 1944).* The book of regulations / the Orthodox Church of the British Isles. — Glastonbury ([7 Glebe Court, Blackheath, SE3 9TH]) : Metropolitical Press, 1971 [i.e. 1973?]. — [3],33p ; 26cm.
ISBN 0-905146-04-2 : £1.85
(B77-05206)

289.9 — Christadelphians. *West Indies. Stories, anecdotes*
Eyre, Alan. At last, true Christianity / [by] Alan Eyre. — Birmingham (Dept 153C, 3 Regent St., Birmingham B1 3HG) : Christadelphians Worldwide, 1976. — 155p ; 19cm.
ISBN 0-9504436-2-x : Unpriced
ISBN 0-9504436-3-8 Pbk : Unpriced
(B77-10164)

289.9 — Pentecostal churches. *Secondary school texts*
Ottosson, Krister. The Pentecostal churches / by Krister Ottosson. — Exeter [etc.] : Religious Education Press, 1977. — 55p : ill, facsim ; 19cm. — (The Christian denominations series)
Bibl.: p.53.
ISBN 0-08-021186-0 Pbk : £0.90
ISBN 0-08-021185-2 Pbk : £0.60(non-net)
(B77-16732)

289.9 — Rastafarians. *Jamaica, to 1975*
Dalrymple, Henderson. Bob Marley : music, myth & the Rastas / [by] Henderson Dalrymple. — Sudbury (37 Priory Ave., Sudbury, Middx) : Carib-Arawak Publishers, 1976. — 77,[1]p : ill, ports ; 21cm.
ISBN 0-9505688-0-5 Sd : £1.00
Primary classification 784′.092′4
(B77-16534)

290 — NON-CHRISTIAN RELIGIONS
290 — Oriental religions
McGill, Ormond. Religious mysteries of the Orient / [by] Ormond McGill and Ron Ormond ; photography by Ron Ormond. — South Brunswick ; New York : Barnes ; London : Yoseloff, 1976. — 3-274p : ill, map, ports ; 26cm.
Index.
ISBN 0-498-01496-7 : £5.50
(B77-29176)

291 — COMPARATIVE RELIGION
Parrinder, Geoffrey. Comparative religion / [by] Geoffrey Parrinder. — 2nd ed. — London : Sheldon Press, 1977. — 3-130p ; 20cm.
Previous ed.: London : Allen and Unwin, 1962. — Index.
ISBN 0-85969-101-2 Pbk : £1.95
(B77-09503)

291′.0966 — Non-Christian religions. Attitudes of Crowther, Samuel. *West Africa*
McKenzie, Peter Rutherford. Inter-religious encounters in West Africa : Samuel Ajayi Crowther's attitude to African traditional religion and Islam / by P.R. McKenzie. — [Leicester] ([2 University Rd, Leicester LE1 7RB]) : Study of Religion Sub-department, University of Leicester, 1976. — 115p,4p of plates : ill, maps, ports ; 24cm. — (Leicester studies in religion ; 1)
Bibl.: p.107-110. — Index.
ISBN 0-905510-00-3 Pbk : £3.00
(B77-07061)

291.1′3 — Mythology
Campbell, Joseph. The hero with a thousand faces / [by] Joseph Campbell. — London : Abacus, 1975. — 350p,[24]p of plates : ill ; 20cm.
Originally published: New York : Pantheon Books, 1949. — Index.
ISBN 0-349-10480-8 Pbk : £1.70
(B77-20021)

Campbell, Joseph. The masks of God / [by] Joseph Campbell. — Harmondsworth [etc.] : Penguin.
In 4 vols.
[Vol.1] : Primitive mythology. — Revised ed. — 1976. — xv,504p : ill, 2 maps ; 20cm.
This ed. originally published: New York : Viking Press, 1969 ; London : Souvenir Press, 1973. — Index.
ISBN 0-14-004304-7 Pbk : Unpriced
(B77-03375)

Campbell, Joseph. The masks of God / [by] Joseph Campbell. — Harmondsworth [etc.] : Penguin.
In 4 vols.
[Vol.3] : Occidental mythology. — 1976. — xii, 564p : ill ; 20cm.
Originally published: New York : Viking Press, 1964 ; London : Secker and Warburg, 1965. — Index.
ISBN 0-14-004306-3 Pbk : Unpriced
(B77-03376)

291.1′3 — Myths. Special subjects: Creation
Maclagan, David. Creation myths : man's introduction to the world / [by] David Maclagan. — London : Thames and Hudson, 1977. — 96p : ill(some col), facsim ; 28cm. — (Art and imagination)
Bibl.: p.96.
ISBN 0-500-81010-9 Pbk : £2.50
(B77-33611)

291.1′3 — Myths. Symbolism. *Secondary school texts*
Roadley, K P. Travellers : symbol in story / [by] K.P. Roadley ; drawings by Trevor Stubley. — London : Edward Arnold, 1976. — iv,75p : ill ; 21cm.
Bibl.
ISBN 0-7131-0082-6 Sd : £1.20
(B77-10165)

291.1′3′03 — Myths. *Encyclopaedias*
Pears encyclopaedia of myths and legends. — London : Pelham.
In 4 vols.
[Book 2] : Northern Europe, Southern and Central Africa / by Sheila Savill ; advisory editor Geoffrey Parrinder, general editors Mary Barker and Christopher Cook. — 1977. — 191p,[8]p of plates : ill (some col), facsims(1 col) ; 26cm.
Bibl. — Index.
ISBN 0-7207-0931-8 : £5.50
Also classified at 398.2′2′03
(B77-12851)

[Book 3] : The Orient / by Sheila Savill ; advisory editor Geoffrey Parrinder ; general editors Mary Barker and Christopher Cook. — 1977. — 247p,[8]p of plates : ill(some col), facsims, ports ; 26cm.
Bibl. — Index.
ISBN 0-7207-1001-4 : £7.50
Also classified at 398.2′2′03
(B77-30975)

291.2′11 — Goddesses. Worship, to ca 400. *Feminist viewpoints*
Stone, Merlin. The paradise papers : the suppression of women's rites / [by] Merlin Stone. — [London] : Virago, 1977. — [15],275, [9]p,[16]p of plates : ill, maps ; 20cm.
Originally published: 1976. — Bibl.: p.261-275. — Index.
ISBN 0-7043-3807-6 Pbk : £2.50
(B77-14046)

291.2′11 — Isis. Worship. *Manuals*
Durdin-Robertson, Lawrence. Communion with the goddess : the manual of Fellowship of Isis / by Lawrence Durdin-Robertson. — Clonegal (Huntington Castle, Clonegal, Enniscorthy, [Co. Wexford]) : Cesara Publications.
Part 1 : The vital elements. — Anno Deae Cesara, Hiberniae Dominae, MMMMCCCXXIV [i.e. 1976]. — 40p ; 24cm.
ISBN 0-9503871-5-0 Sd : £0.75
(B77-04552)

Durdin-Robertson, Lawrence. Communion with the goddess : the manual of the Fellowship of Isis / by Lawrence Durdin-Robertson. — Clonegal (Huntington Castle, Clonegal, Enniscorthy, Eire) : Cesara Publications.
Part 2 : Initiation and the mysteries. — 1976. — 40p ; 24cm.
ISBN 0-9503871-6-9 Sd : £0.75
(B77-06474)

Part 3 : The occasional rites. — 1976. — 47p ; 25cm.
ISBN 0-9503871-8-5 Sd : £0.75
(B77-12295)

Priestesses. — 1976. — 46p ; 24cm.
Sd : £1.00
(B77-20022)

Temples of the Near and Far East. — Anno Deae Cesarae, Hiberniae Dominal, MMMMCCCXXV [i.e. 1977]. — [1],46p ; 25cm.
Sd : £1.00
(B77-33612)

291.2′3 — Future life
Lobsang Rampa, Tuesday. I believe / [by] T. Lobsang Rampa. — London : Corgi, 1977. — 175p ; 18cm.
ISBN 0-552-10416-7 Pbk : £0.65
(B77-17913)

Moody, Raymond A. Life after life : the investigation of a phenomenon, survival of bodily death / [by] Raymond A. Moody, Jr ; with a foreword by Elisabeth Kubler-Ross. — Toronto [etc.] ; London : Bantam, 1976 [i.e. 1977]. — xiii,187,[1]p ; 18cm.
Originally published: Covington : Mockingbird Books, 1975. — Bibl.: p.187.
ISBN 0-553-10080-7 Pbk : £0.65
(B77-09504)

291.3 — Inter-faith public worship. *Christian viewpoints*
Akehurst, Peter Russell. Inter-faith worship? / by Peter R. Akehurst and R.W.F. Wootton. — Bramcote : Grove Books, 1977. — 22p ; 21cm. — (Grove booklet on ministry and worship ; no.52 ISSN 0305-3067)
ISBN 0-905422-16-3 Sd : £0.35
(B77-29177)

291.3′6 — Religious festivals. *Calendars*
Calendar of religious festivals. — London : Community Relations Commission.
July 1976-July 1977 / edited by Religious Education Centre, Borough Road College, Isleworth ; on behalf of the Shap Working Party. — 1976. — [2],iv,7p ; 30cm.
Index.
ISBN 0-902355-68-6 Sd : Free
(B77-08765)

291.4′2 — Man. Religious feelings. *Christian viewpoints*
Davis, Charles. Body as spirit : the nature of religious feeling / by Charles Davis. — London [etc.] : Hodder and Stoughton, 1976. — [7], 181p ; 23cm.
Originally published: New York : Seabury Press, 1976. — Index.
ISBN 0-340-21339-6 : £4.25
(B77-12852)

291.4′2 — Religious life. Mysticism, to 1900
Smith, Margaret. An introduction to mysticism / [by] Margaret Smith. — London : Sheldon Press, 1977. — vi,121p ; 20cm.
Originally published: as 'An introduction to the history of mysticism'. London : S.P.C.K., 1930. — Bibl.: p.117-118. — Index.
ISBN 0-85969-104-7 Pbk : £1.75
(B77-23110)

291.4′2 — Spirit possession. *Case studies*
Case studies in spirit possession / edited by Vincent Crapanzano, Vivian Garrison. — New York ; London [etc.] : Wiley, 1977. — xxiii, 457p : ill ; 24cm. — (Contemporary religious movements)
'A Wiley-Interscience publication'. — Bibl. — Index.
ISBN 0-471-18460-8 : £16.00
(B77-17914)

291.4′3 — Meditation. Psychological aspects
Naranjo, Claudio. On the psychology of meditation / [by] Claudio Naranjo and Robert E. Ornstein. — Harmondsworth [etc.] : Penguin, 1976. — [7],248p : ill ; 20cm. — (Esalen books)
Originally published: New York : Viking Press, 1971 ; London : Allen and Unwin, 1972. — Bibl.: p.247-248.
ISBN 0-14-004420-5 Pbk : Unpriced
(B77-11071)

291.6 — Religious leaders. *Occult viewpoints*
Bennett, John Godolphin. The masters of wisdom / [by] John G. Bennett. — London : Turnstone Books, 1977. — 224p : ill, geneal table, maps ; 23cm.
Index.
ISBN 0-85500-052-x : £3.95
ISBN 0-85500-069-4 Pbk : Unpriced
(B77-14557)

291.6′2 — Shamanism
Drury, Nevill. Don Juan, Mescalito and modern magic : the mythology of inner space / [by] Nevill Drury. — London [etc.] : Routledge and Kegan Paul, 1978. — x,229p : ill ; 22cm.
Bibl.: p.222-225. — Index.
ISBN 0-7100-8582-6 Pbk : £2.95 : CIP rev.
(B77-29178)

291.8′2 — Sacred works. *Extracts, selections*
Values : an anthology for seekers / compiled by J.G. Bennett. — Sherborne, Glos. : Coombe Springs Press, 1977. — 168p ; 20cm.
Originally published: s.l. : s.n., 1951.
ISBN 0-900306-02-5 Pbk : £1.75
(B77-30976)

291.8′2 — Scriptures. *Extracts, selections*
The **portable** world bible / edited by Robert O. Ballou. — Condensed [ed.]. — Harmondsworth [etc.] : Penguin, 1976. — xviii,605p : ill ; 18cm. — (The Viking portable library)
Spine title: World bible. — This ed. originally published: New York : Viking Press, 1944. — Index.
ISBN 0-14-015005-6 Pbk : £1.95
(B77-14558)

292 — CLASSICAL RELIGIONS
292′.1′3 — Ancient Greek mythology. *Secondary school texts*
Discovering Greek mythology / [by] P. Kenneth Corsar ... [et al.] ; drawings by D.B. Lewis. — London : Edward Arnold, 1977. — iv,116p : ill, maps, 2 ports ; 24cm. — (Classical studies)
ISBN 0-7131-0078-8 Pbk : £2.50
(B77-21696)

292′.1′3 — Ancient Greek myths. *Juvenile literature*
Garfield, Leon. The god beneath the sea / [by] Leon Garfield and Edward Blishen ; illustrated by Charles Keeping. — London : Carousel Books, 1977. — [8],168p : ill ; 20cm.
Originally published: Harlow : Longman, 1970.
ISBN 0-552-98012-9 Pbk : £0.65
(B77-18551)

292′.1′3 — Ancient Greek myths. Special subjects: Spices
Detienne, Marcel. The gardens of Adonis : spices in Greek mythology / [by] Marcel Detienne ; translated from the French by Janet Lloyd ; with an introduction by J.-P. Vernant. — Hassocks : Harvester Press, 1977. — [4],xxxv, 184p,[4]p of plates : ill ; 23cm. — (European philosophy and the human sciences)
Translation of: 'Les jardins d'Adonis'. Paris : Gallimard, 1972. — Index.
ISBN 0-901759-26-0 : £10.650
(B77-26790)

292′.1′3 — Classical myths
Field, D M. Greek and Roman mythology / [by] D.M. Field. — London [etc.] : Hamlyn, 1977. — 192p : ill(some col), ports ; 31cm.
Col. ill. on lining papers. — Index.
ISBN 0-600-36247-7 : £3.95
(B77-20900)

292′.1′308 — Ancient Greek myths. *Anthologies. Juvenile literature*
Caselli, Giovanni. Gods, men & monsters from the Greek Myths / illustrations by Giovanni Caselli ; text by Michael Gibson. — London (2 Queens Drive, W3 0HA) : Peter Lowe, 1977. — 5-156p : ill(chiefly col), 2 maps(1 col) ; 28cm.
Index.
ISBN 0-85654-027-7 : £3.50
(B77-23112)

292′.2′11 — Ancient Greek religion. Aphrodite
Grigson, Geoffrey. The goddess of love : the birth, triumph, death and return of Aphrodite / [by] Geoffrey Grigson. — London : Constable, 1976. — 256p : ill(incl 1 col), geneal table ; 24cm.
Bibl.: p.243-246. — Index.
ISBN 0-09-460170-4 : £6.50
(B77-03920)

292′.2′11 — Ancient Greek religion. Dionysos, to A.D.400
Kerényi, Carl. Dionysos : archetypal image of indestructible life / [by] C. Kerényi ; translated from the German [MS.] by Ralph Manheim. — London : Routledge and Kegan Paul, 1976. — xxxvii,474p,[88]p of plates : ill ; 26cm. — (Archetypal images in Greek religion ; vol.2)
Bibl. — Index.
ISBN 0-7100-7975-3 : £20.00
(B77-14047)

293 — GERMANIC NON-CHRISTIAN RELIGIONS
293 — Norse religion
Magnusson, Magnus. Hammer of the North / [by] Magnus Magnusson ; photographs by Werner Forman. — London : Orbis Books, 1976. — 128p : col ill, col facsims, 2 maps(1 col) ; 31cm. — (Echoes of the ancient world)
Col. ill. on lining papers. — Bibl.: p.126. — Index.
ISBN 0-85613-301-9 : £5.95
(B77-07800)

293′.1′3 — Teutonic myths. Compared with fiction in English of Tolkien, John Ronald Reuel
Noel, Ruth S. The mythology of Middle-earth / [by] Ruth S. Noel. — London : Thames and Hudson, 1977. — x,198p ; 22cm.
Bibl.: p.192-193. — Index.
ISBN 0-500-01187-7 : £4.50
Primary classification 823′.9′12
(B77-27490)

294 — RELIGIONS OF INDIC ORIGIN
294 — Asian religions. Goddesses
Durdin-Robertson, Lawrence. The goddesses of India, Tibet, China and Japan / by Lawrence Durdin-Robertson ; with illustrations by Anna Durdin-Robertson. — Clonegal (Huntington Castle, Clonegal, Enniscorthy, Eire) : Cesara Publications, 1976. — [9],532p,[8]leaves of plates : ill ; 19cm.
Bibl.: p.469-472. — Index.
Pbk : £2.00
(B77-17295)

294 — Tantrism
Mookerjee, Ajitcoomar. The tantric way : art, science, ritual / [by] Ajit Mookerjee and Madhu Khanna. — London : Thames and Hudson, 1977. — 208p : ill(some col), facsims(some col) ; 26cm.
Bibl.: p.201-204. — Index.
ISBN 0-500-01172-9 : £8.50
(B77-12296)

294.1 — THE VEDAS
294′.1 — Hinduism. Vedas. *Extracts, selections with commentaries*
Coomaraswamy, Ananda Kentish. The Vedas : essays in translation and exegesis / by Ananda K. Coomaraswamy. — Beckenham (68 Birkbeck Rd, Beckenham, Kent BR3 4SP) : Prologos Books, 1976. — xv,159p : ill ; 21cm.
Facsimile reprints. — Contents: A new approach to the Vedas. Originally published: London : Luzac, 1933 - The Rg Veda as Land-Náma-Bók. Originally published: London : Luzac, 1935.
ISBN 0-9505218-1-7 Pbk : £4.75
(B77-13504)

294′.1 — Hinduism. Vedas. Special subjects: Triads. *Critical studies*
Gonda, Jan. Triads in the Veda / by J. Gonda. — Amsterdam ; Oxford [etc.] : North-Holland Publishing Co., 1976. — 246p ; 26cm. — (Nederlandse Akademie van Wetenschappen. Afdeling Letterkunde. Verhandelingen : nieuwe reeks ; deel 91)
Index.
ISBN 0-7204-8310-7 Pbk : Unpriced
(B77-02766)

294.3 — BUDDHISM
Buddhism in the modern world / Heinrich Dumoulin editor, John C. Maraldo associate editor ; [contributions in German translated by John C. Maraldo]. — New York : Collier ; London : Collier Macmillan, 1976. — xii,368p ; 24cm.
Cover title: The cultural, political and religious significance of Buddhism in the modern world. — Translation and revision of: 'Buddhismus der Gegenwart'. Freiburg im Breisgau : Herder, 1970. — Bibl.: p.323-349. — Index.
ISBN 0-02-084790-4 Pbk : £5.25
(B77-10166)

Matsunami, Kodo. Introducing Buddhism / by Kodo Matsunami. — [Revised ed., 4th ed.]. — Rutland, Vt [etc.] : Tuttle ; London : Prentice-Hall [etc.], 1976. — 304p,[4]leaves of plates : ill ; 19cm.
This ed. originally published: Honolulu : Jodo Mission of Hawaii, 1973. — Bibl.: p.273-287. — Index.
ISBN 0-8048-1192-x Pbk : £2.80
(B77-05207)

294.3′3′3 — Buddhist myths. *Texts*
[Vessantara jataka. *English].* The perfect generosity of Prince Vessantara : a Buddhist epic / translated from the Pali and illustrated by unpublished paintings from Sinhalese temples [by] Margaret Cone and Richard F. Gombrich. — Oxford : Clarendon Press, 1977. — xlvii,111p,leaf of plate,A-D,40p of plates : ill(some col) ; 24cm.
Bibl.: p.109-111.
ISBN 0-19-826530-1 : £11.00 : CIP rev.
(B77-10167)

294.3′4′22 — Buddhist doctrine. Grace. Theories
Pallis, Marco. Is there room for 'grace' in Buddhism? / by Marco Pallis. — Bedfont (Pates Manor, Bedfont, Middx) : 'Studies in Comparative Religion', [1976]. — 18p ; 22cm.
Sd : Unpriced
(B77-16187)

294.3′4′4 — Buddhist life
Humphreys, Christmas. The Buddhist way of action : a working philosophy for daily life / [by] Christmas Humphreys. — London : Mandala Books, 1977. — 3-195p,8p of plates : ill ; 20cm.
Originally published: as 'The way of action'. London : Allen and Unwin, 1960. — Bibl.: p.193-195.
ISBN 0-04-294100-8 Pbk : £1.95
(B77-33059)

294.3′4′4 — Zen Buddhist life
The **blue** cliff record / translated from the Chinese 'Pi yen lu' by Thomas and J.C. Cleary ; foreword by Taizan Maezumi Roshi. — Boulder ; London : Shambhala ; London [etc.] : Distributed by Routledge and Kegan Paul.
Vol.1. — 1977. — xxv,268p ; 22cm.
Bibl.: p.267-268.
ISBN 0-87773-094-6 Pbk : £3.00
(B77-14048)

Humphreys, Christmas. Zen comes West : the present and future of Zen Buddhism in Western society / [by] Christmas Humphreys. — 2nd ed. — London : Curzon Press [etc.], 1977. — [2],218p,plate : 3 ports ; 23cm.
Previous ed.: London : Allen and Unwin, 1960. — Bibl.: p.211-213. — Index.
ISBN 0-7007-0075-7 : £3.50 : CIP rev.
(B77-07062)

Schloegl, Irmgard. The Zen way / [by] Irmgard Schloegl. — London : Sheldon Press, 1977. — viii,117p ; 20cm.
Bibl.: p.117.
ISBN 0-85969-098-9 Pbk : £2.95
(B77-08223)

294.3′4′43 — Buddhist life. Meditation. Mantras
Blofeld, John. Mantras : sacred words of power / [by] John Blofeld. — London : Allen and Unwin, 1977. — iii-xiv,106p,[8]p of plates : ill(chiefly col) ; 21cm.
ISBN 0-04-294096-6 : £4.50
ISBN 0-04-294097-4 Pbk : £1.95
(B77-06475)

294.3′4′43 — Zen Buddhist life. *Meditations*
The **grace** of Zen : parables, prayers and meditations / by Karlfried Dürckheim ... [et al.] ; [selected and translated by John Griffiths]. — London : Search Press, 1977. — [10],107p : ill ; 22cm.
ISBN 0-85532-373-6 Pbk : £1.95
(B77-19216)

294.3'82 — Mahayana Buddhism. Scriptures. *Texts*
Aśvaghosha. The awakening of faith / attributed to Aśvaghosha ; translated [from the Chinese], with commentary by Yoshito S. Hakeda. — New York ; London : Columbia University Press, [1974]. — xi,128p ; 21cm. — (Columbia College. Program of translations from the oriental classics)
This translation originally published: 1967. — Bibl.: p.119-122. — Index.
ISBN 0-231-08336-x Pbk : Unpriced
(B77-18552)

[Saddharma-Pandar̄ika. *English].* Scripture of the lotus blossom of the fine dharma / translated from the Chinese of Kum̄araj̄iva by Leon Hurvitz. — New York ; Guildford : Columbia University Press, 1976. — xxix,421p ; 24cm. — (Columbia College. Program of translations from the oriental classics, publications) (Buddhist studies and translations) (Records of civilization, sources and studies ; no.94)
Index.
ISBN 0-231-03789-9 : £10.41
ISBN 0-231-03920-4 Pbk : Unpriced
(B77-02767)

294.3'82 — Theravada Buddhism. Scriptures. *Anthologies*
The **wisdom** of the early Buddhists / compiled by Geoffrey Parrinder. — London : Sheldon Press, 1977. — [5],86p ; 20cm.
ISBN 0-85969-105-5 Pbk : £1.50
(B77-23113)

294.3'823 — Mahayana Buddhism. Sutras. *Texts*
[Vimalak̄irti Nirdeśa S̄utra. *English].* The holy teaching of Vimalak̄irti : a Mah̄aȳana scripture / translated [from the Tibetan] by Robert A.F. Thurman. — University Park [Pa] ; London : Pennsylvania State University Press, 1976. — x,166p : 1 ill ; 24cm.
ISBN 0-271-01209-9 : £11.60
(B77-05868)

294.3'823 — Theravada Buddhism. Sutras. *Texts*
[Dhammapada. *English].* The Dhammapada : the sayings of the Buddha / a new rendering by Thomas Byrom ; photography by Sandra Weiner ; with a preface by Ram Dass. — London : Wildwood House, 1976. — xiii,165p, [2] leaves : ill ; 28cm.
ISBN 0-7045-0274-7 Pbk : £3.95
(B77-03377)

294.3'91 — Theravada Buddhism
David-Néel, Alexandra. Buddhism : its doctrines and its methods / [by] Alexandra David-Néel ; [translated from the French by H.N.M. Hardy and Bernard Miall]. — [1st ed. reprinted] ; with a foreword by Christmas Humphreys. — London [etc.] : Bodley Head, 1977. — 299p ; 21cm.
Translation of: 'Le Bouddhisme, ses doctrines et ses méthodes'. Paris : Plon, 1936. — This translation originally published: London : John Lane, 1939. — Index.
ISBN 0-370-30047-5 : £3.95
(B77-26791)

294.3'91'095493 — Theravada Buddhism. *Sri Lanka, 1750-1900*
Malalgoda, Kitsiri. Buddhism in Sinhalese society, 1750-1900 : a study of religious revival and change / [by] Kitsiri Malalgoda. — Berkeley [etc.] ; London : University of California Press, 1976. — xiii,300p,fold plate : map ; 25cm.
Bibl.: p.269-284. — Index.
ISBN 0-520-02873-2 : £13.20
(B77-13505)

294.3'92 — Mahayana Buddhism. Madhyamika school. Theories. Related to theories of Wittgenstein, Ludwig
Gudmunsen, Chris. Wittgenstein and Buddhism / [by] Chris Gudmunsen. — London [etc.] : Macmillan, 1977. — ix,128p ; 23cm.
Bibl.: p.121-124. — Index.
ISBN 0-333-21244-4 : £8.95
Primary classification 192
(B77-28357)

294.3'923 — Tibetan Buddhism
Kongtrul, Jamgon. The torch of certainty / [by] Jamgon Kongtrul ; translated from the Tibetan by Judith Hanson ; foreword by Chögyam Trungpa. — Boulder ; London : Shambhala ; London [etc.] : Distributed by Routledge and Kegan Paul, 1977. — xix,161p : ill ; 22cm. — (Clear light series)
Originally published: in Tibetan. s.l. : s.n., 1844?. — Bibl.: p.141-144. — Index.
ISBN 0-87773-100-4 : Unpriced
ISBN 0-87773-101-2 Pbk : £3.95
(B77-30977)

294.3'927 — Zen Buddhism
Dürckheim-Montmartin, Karlfried, *Graf von.* Hara : the vital centre of man / [by] Karlfried, Graf von Dürckheim ; translated from the German by Sylvia-Monica von Kospoth in collaboration with Estelle R. Healey. — London : Unwin Books, 1977. — [6],208p : ill, ports ; 20cm. — (Mandala books)
This translation originally published: London : Allen and Unwin, 1962. — Translation of: 'Hara : die Erdmitte des Menschen'. Munich : Barth, 1956.
ISBN 0-04-290011-5 Pbk : £1.95
(B77-06476)

294.3'927 — Zen Buddhism. Related to Christianity
Callaway, Tucker N. Zen way, Jesus way / [by] Tucker N. Callaway. — Rutland [Vt] [etc.] : Tuttle ; London : [Distributed by] Prentice-Hall, 1976. — 263p ; 19cm.
Index.
ISBN 0-8048-1190-3 : Unpriced
Also classified at 200
(B77-11570)

294.3'927'03 — Zen Buddhism. *Dictionaries*
Wood, Ernest Egerton. Zen dictionary / [by] Ernest Wood. — Harmondsworth [etc.] : Penguin, 1977. — 128p ; 19cm. — (Pelican books)
Originally published: New York : Philosophical Library, 1956 ; London : Owen, 1963. — Bibl.: p.128.
ISBN 0-14-021998-6 Pbk : £0.50
(B77-12853)

294.3'927'08 — Zen Buddhism. *Essays*
Rajneesh, *Bhagwan Shree.* No water, no moon : reflections on Zen / [by] Bhagwan Shree Rajneesh ; compiled by Ma Yoga Gautami ; edited by Ma Yoga Anurag. — London : Sheldon Press, 1977. — [7],246p : ill ; 22cm.
Originally published: Poona : Rajneesh Foundation, 1975.
ISBN 0-85969-103-9 Pbk : £2.95
(B77-08766)

294.3'927'08 — Zen Buddhism. *Readings*
The **tiger's** cave : translations of Japanese Zen texts / [by] Trevor Leggett. — London [etc.] : Routledge and Kegan Paul, 1977. — 192p,[4]p of plates : ill ; 22cm.
These translations originally published: London : Rider, 1964.
ISBN 0-7100-8636-9 Pbk : £2.50 : CIP rev.
(B77-09505)

294.5 — HINDUISM
294.5 — Hinduism. *Middle school texts*
Ewan, John. Understanding your Hindu neighbour / [by] John Ewan. — Guildford [etc.] : Lutterworth, 1977. — 56p : ill, facsim ; 22cm. — (World religions)
Bibl.: p.10.
ISBN 0-7188-1800-8 : £1.95
(B77-33060)

294.5'03 — Hinduism, to 1500. *Encyclopaedias*
Stutley, Margaret. A dictionary of Hinduism : its mythology, folklore and development, 1500 BC-AD 1500 / [by] Margaret and James Stutley. — London [etc.] : Routledge and Kegan Paul, 1977. — xx,372p : map ; 26cm.
Bibl.: p.353-368.
ISBN 0-7100-8398-x : £12.50 : CIP rev.
(B77-07063)

294.5'1'3 — Hindu myths. Krishna. *Anthologies*
Frith, Nigel. The legend of Krishna / [by] Nigel Frith. — London : Abacus, 1976. — 238p ; 20cm.
Originally published: London : Sheldon Press, 1975.
ISBN 0-349-11342-4 Pbk : £0.95
(B77-07064)

294.5'1'3 — Hindu myths. Special themes: Evil
O'Flaherty, Wendy Doniger. The origins of evil in Hindu mythology / [by] Wendy Doniger O'Flaherty. — Berkeley [etc.] ; London : University of California Press, 1976. — xi, 411p ; 25cm. — (Hermeneutics : studies in the history of religions ; 6)
Bibl.: p.381-396. — Index.
ISBN 0-520-03163-6 : £11.25
(B77-20901)

294.5'42 — Hindu life. Mysticism. Kab̄ir
Rosemary, *Sister.* Kab̄ir, the way of love and paradox / by Sister Rosemary ; with a foreword by Bishop Appleton. — Oxford : S.L.G. Press, 1977. — [4],20p : ill ; 21cm. — (Fairacres publications ; no.61 ISSN 0307-1413)
ISBN 0-7283-0064-8 Sd : £0.30
(B77-11571)

294.5'6'1 — Hinduism. Ramana, Maharshi. *Biographies*
Mahadevan, T M P. Ramana Maharshi : the sage of Arun̄acala / [by] T.M.P. Mahadevan. — London : Allen and Unwin, 1977. — 3-186p ; 21cm.
Index.
ISBN 0-04-149040-1 : £4.50
ISBN 0-04-149041-x Pbk : Unpriced
(B77-07801)

294.5'61'0924 — Swamis. *India (Republic). Personal observations*
Boyd, Doug. Swami / [by] Doug Boyd. — London : Rider, 1977. — iii-xx,331p ; 22cm.
Originally published: New York : Random House, 1976.
ISBN 0-09-129961-6 Pbk : £3.50
(B77-29934)

294.5'92 — Hinduism. Vishnusahasranama stotra. *Extracts, selections. Sanskrit & English texts*
[Vishnusahasranama stotra. *English & Sanskrit. Selections].* The song of a thousand names / [selected and translated from the Sanskrit, with drawings by Raksha Mehta]. — London : Watkins, 1976. — [111]p : ill(some col) ; 20cm.
ISBN 0-7224-0145-0 Pbk : £2.00
(B77-09506)

294.5'923'0924 — Hinduism. Mah̄abh̄arata. Characters: Bhrgus
Goldman, Robert P. Gods, priests, and warriors : the Bhrgus of the 'Mah̄abh̄arata' / [by] Robert P. Goldman. — New York ; Guildford : Columbia University Press, 1977. — xii,195p ; 22cm. — (Studies in oriental culture ; no.12)
Bibl.: p.175-184. — Index.
ISBN 0-231-03941-7 : £8.85
(B77-28385)

294.6 — SIKHISM
294.6'8'2 — Sikhism. Ādi-Granth. Characters
Dhillon, N S. Pillars of divine philosophy : they speak in the Holy Granth / by N.S. Dhillon. — London (36 Rosebery Ave., E12 6PZ) : The author, 1977. — [4],xiv,100p ; 18cm.
Sd : £1.95
(B77-21697)

296 — JUDAISM
Jessup, Gordon. No strange God : an outline of Jewish life and faith / [by] Gordon Jessup. — London : Olive Press, 1976. — 125p : ill ; 18cm.
Index.
ISBN 0-904054-11-x Pbk : £0.90
(B77-16733)

296 — Judaism. Religious buildings. *Ancient Palestine. School texts*
Sutcliffe, John, *b.1933.* Getting to know about places of worship in lands of the Bible / [by] John and Ann Sutcliffe ; artist Anne Farncombe ; editor Joy R. Standen. — Redhill : Denholm House Press, 1977. — 32p : ill(chiefly col), col maps, col plans ; 25cm. — (Getting to know about ; book 9)
Index.
ISBN 0-85213-160-7 Sd : Unpriced
(B77-29179)

296'.09'01 — Judaism, to ca 100
Lohse, Eduard. The New Testament environment / [by] Eduard Lohse ; [translated from the German by John E. Steely]. — London : S.C.M. Press, 1976. — 300p : geneal tables, maps ; 23cm. — (New Testament library)
This translation also published: Nashville : Abingdon Press, 1976. — Translation of: 'Umwelt des Neuen Testaments'. 2., durchges. u. erg. Aufl. Gottingen : Vandenhoeck und Ruprecht, 1974. — Bibl.: p.281-285. — Index.
ISBN 0-334-02213-4 : £6.00
Also classified at 938'.09
(B77-01169)

296'.0973 — Judaism. *United States, to 1975*
Blau, Joseph Leon. Judaism in America : from curiosity to third faith / [by] Joseph L. Blau. — Chicago ; London : University of Chicago Press, 1976. — xiv,156p ; 21cm. — (Chicago history of American religion)
Index.
ISBN 0-226-05727-5 : Unpriced
(B77-15090)

296.1'405'21 — Judaism. Midrashim. *Texts*
Schwartz, Howard. Midrashim : collected Jewish parables / [by] Howard Schwartz ; drawings by John Swanson ; foreword by Raphael Patai ; introduction by James S. Diamond. — London (23 Fitzwarren Gardens, N19 3TR) : The Menard Press, 1976. — 63p : ill ; 22cm.
ISBN 0-903400-18-9 Pbk : £1.20
(B77-11072)

296.1′6 — Judaism. Cabala. Gematria
Bond, Frederick Bligh. Gematria : a preliminary investigation of the Cabala contained in the Coptic Gnostic books, and of a similar Gematria in the Greek text of the New Testament : showing the presence of a system of teaching by means of the doctrinal significance of numbers, by which the holy names are clearly seen to represent aeonial relationships which can be conceived in a geometric sense and are capable of a typical expression of that order / by Frederick Bligh Bond and Thomas Simcox Lea. — [1st ed. reprinted] ; [with new notes by Anne Macauley and new foreword by Keith Critchlow]. — London : Research into Lost Knowledge Organization ; Wellingborough : Distributed by Thorsons, 1977. — xv,3-113p : ill, plan ; 22cm.
Facsimile reprint of: 1st ed. Oxford : Blackwell, 1917.
ISBN 0-7225-0355-5 Pbk : £2.75
(B77-12854)

296.3′87′2 — Judaism. Relations with Christian church. Theories of Origen
De Lange, Nicholas. Origen and the Jews : studies in Jewish-Christian relations in third-century Palestine / [by] N.R.M. de Lange. — Cambridge [etc.] : Cambridge University Press, 1976. — x,240p ; 23cm. — (University of Cambridge. Oriental publications ; no.25)
Bibl.: p.209-215. — Index.
ISBN 0-521-20542-5 : £8.00
Primary classification 261.2
(B77-06465)

296.4′37 — Judaism. Passover services. *Rites. Hebrew-English parallel texts*
Jews. *Liturgy and ritual.* [Haggadah]. The Haggadah of Passover / illustrations by Parenzo ; text edited by David and Tamar De Sola Pool. — South Brunswick [etc.] ; London : Yoseloff, 1975. — [7],138p : ill(some col) ; 25cm. — (Sara F. Yoseloff memorial publications in Judaism and Jewish affairs)
Ill. on lining papers. — Parallel Hebrew text and English translation. — Originally published: New York : Jewish Welfare Board, 1944.
ISBN 0-498-06401-8 : £4.50
(B77-05208)

296.6′5′09421 — Synagogues. *London. United Synagogue, to 1970*
Newman, Aubrey. The United Synagogue, 1870-1970 / [by] Aubrey Newman. — London [etc.] : Routledge and Kegan Paul, 1977. — xv, 239p,8p of plates : ill, facsim, maps, ports ; 22cm.
Index.
ISBN 0-7100-8456-0 : £5.50
(B77-08767)

296.6′5′0942187 — Synagogues. *London. Barnet (London Borough). Finchley Synagogue, to 1976*
Levin, Hilary S. Jubilee at Finchley, 1926-1976 : the story of a congregation / by Hilary S. Levin & Salmond S. Levin. — [London] ([Kinloss Gardens, N.3]) : Finchley Synagogue, [1977]. — 29p : 2 ill ; 22cm.
Bibl.: p.29.
ISBN 0-9505629-0-4 Sd : £0.50
(B77-11572)

296.6′5′0973 — Orthodox Jews. Synagogue life. *United States. Case studies*
Heilman, Samuel C. Synagogue life : a study in symbolic interaction / [by] Samuel C. Heilman. — Chicago ; London : University of Chicago Press, 1976. — xiii,306p : plans ; 23cm.
Bibl.: p.291-296. — Index.
ISBN 0-226-32488-5 : £8.85
(B77-05869)

297 — ISLAM
Ahsan, M M. Islam : faith and practice / [by] M.M. Ahsan. — Leicester [etc.] (223 London Rd, Leicester LE2 1ZE) : Islamic Foundation, 1977. — 48p,fold plate : ill, facsim, col map ; 21cm.
Bibl.: p.47-48.
ISBN 0-86037-001-1 Pbk : Unpriced
(B77-20024)

297′.09 — Islam. Origins. Influence of Judaism
Crone, Patricia. Hagarism : the making of the Islamic world / by Patricia Crone, Michael Cook. — Cambridge [etc.] : Cambridge University Press, 1977. — ix,268p ; 23cm.
Bibl.: p.237-258. — Index.
ISBN 0-521-21133-6 : £7.50
(B77-21698)

297′.09′03 — Islam, 1700-1956
Smith, Wilfred Cantwell. Islam in modern history / by Wilfred Cantwell Smith. — Princeton ; Guildford : Princeton University Press, 1977. — xi,317p ; 24cm.
Originally published: Princeton : Princeton University Press ; Oxford : Oxford University Press, 1957. — Index.
ISBN 0-691-03030-8 : £10.80
ISBN 0-691-01991-6 Pbk : £2.60
(B77-29180)

297′.1221 — Islam. Koran. Compilation
Burton, John, *b.1929.* The collection of the Qur′ān / [by] John Burton. — Cambridge [etc.] : Cambridge University Press, 1977. — vii,273p ; 24cm.
Bibl.: p.241-244. — Index.
ISBN 0-521-21439-4 : £8.50
(B77-29181)

297′.1226 — Islam. Koran. Interpretation
Wansbrough, John. Quranic studies : sources and methods of scriptural interpretation / by John Wansbrough. — Oxford [etc.] : Oxford University Press, 1977. — xxvi,256p ; 24cm. — (London Oriental series ; vol.31)
Bibl.: p.xiii-xxvi. — Index.
ISBN 0-19-713588-9 : £16.00
(B77-26111)

297′.1226′6 — Islam. Koran. *Exegetical studies*
Gätje, Helmut. The Qur′ān and its exegesis : selected texts with classical and modern Muslim interpretations / by Helmut Gätje ; translated [from the German] and edited by Alford T. Welch. — London [etc.] : Routledge and Kegan Paul, 1976. — xiv,313p ; 23cm. — (The Islamic world series)
Translation of: 'Koran und Koranexegese'. Zurich : Artemis, 1971. — Bibl.: p.286-295. — Index.
ISBN 0-7100-8327-0 : £8.50
(B77-03921)

297′.12405′21 — Islam. Hadith. *Texts*
40 hadith / collected by Imam an-Nawawi. — Norwich (Wood Dalling Hall, Norwich NR11 6SG) : Diwan Press for Darqawi Institute, [1977]. — [28]p ; 22cm.
Sd : £0.50
(B77-33613)

297′.2 — Sufi doctrine
Farid al-Din Attar. [Ilāhī-nāma. English]. The 'Ilāhī-nāma, or, Book of God of Farīd al-Din 'Attār / translated from the Persian by John Andrew Boyle ; with a foreword by Annemarie Schimmel. — Manchester : Manchester University Press, 1976. — xxii,392p ; 24cm. — (Unesco. Collection of representative works : Persian heritage series)
Bibl.: p.385-387. — Index.
ISBN 0-7190-0663-5 : £9.95
(B77-20025)

297′.4′0924 — Sufism. Al-Muhāsibī, Hārith B. Asad. *Baghdad. Biographies*
Smith, Margaret. An early mystic of Baghdad : a study of the life and teaching of Hārith B. Asad al-Muhāsibī, A.D. 781-857 / [by] Margaret Smith. — London : Sheldon Press, 1977. — v-xi,311p ; 22cm.
Originally published: 1935. — Bibl.: p.292-297. — Index.
ISBN 0-85969-131-4 Pbk : £6.50
(B77-24695)

297′.4′0924 — Sufism. Zarrūq, Ahmad ibn Ahmad
Khushaim, Ali Fahmi. Zarrūq the Sūfī : a guide in the way and a leader to the truth : a biographical and critical study of a mystic from North Africa / by Ali Fahmi Khushaim. — Tripoli : General Company for Publication ; London : Distributed by Hale, 1976. — vi, 218p : ill, facsims, maps ; 24cm.
Bibl.
ISBN 0-904604-01-2 : £5.00
(B77-19218)

297′.4′096 — Sufism. *Africa, 1800-1900*
Martin, B G. Muslim brotherhoods in nineteenth-century Africa / [by] B.G. Martin. — Cambridge [etc.] : Cambridge University Press, 1976 [i.e. 1977]. — xiii,267p : maps ; 24cm. — (African studies series ; 18 ISSN 0065-406x)
Bibl.: p. 238-246. — Index.
ISBN 0-521-21062-3 : £10.00
(B77-07065)

297′.89′0922 — Bahais. *Western world, 1894-1957. Biographies*
Whitehead, O Z. Some early Bahá'is of the West / by O.Z. Whitehead. — Oxford : Ronald, 1976. — xii,227p,[24]p of plates : ports ; 23cm.
ISBN 0-85398-065-9 : £3.25
ISBN 0-85398-067-5 Pbk : £2.00
(B77-11573)

299 — NON-CHRISTIAN RELIGIONS OF TRIBAL AND OTHER SOCIETIES
299 — Religions. Gods. *Ancient Middle East, B.C.1000-ca A.D.300*
Teixidor, Javier. The pagan god : popular religion in the Greco-Roman Near East / by Javier Teixidor. — Princeton ; Guildford : Princeton University Press, 1977. — xii,192p : maps ; 23cm.
Bibl.: p.165-174. — Index.
ISBN 0-691-07220-5 : £7.80
(B77-33614)

299.5 — NON-CHRISTIAN RELIGIONS OF EAST AND SOUTHEAST ASIAN ORIGIN
299′.514 — Taoism
Creel, Herrlee Glessner. What is Taoism? and other stories in Chinese cultural history / [by] Herrlee G. Creel. — Chicago ; London : University of Chicago Press, 1977. — viii,192p ; 23cm.
Originally published: 1970. — Index.
ISBN 0-226-12042-2 Pbk : £2.75
Also classified at 354′.31
(B77-31692)

299′.5148′2 — Taoism. Scriptures. *Texts*
Lao Tzu. Tao tê ching / [by Lao Tzu] ; translated from the Chinese by Ch'u Ta-Kao. — [New ed.]. — London (Ruskin House, Museum St., WC1A 1LU) : Mandala Books, 1976. — 96p ; 20cm.
This ed. originally published: 1972.
ISBN 0-04-299007-6 Pbk : £1.25
(B77-07066)

299.6 — NON-CHRISTIAN RELIGIONS OF BLACK AFRICAN AND NEGRO ORIGIN
299′.6 — Dogon religion
Griaule, Marcel. Conversations with Ogotemmêli : an introduction to Dogon religious ideas / by Marcel Griaule ; with an introduction by Germaine Dieterlin ; [translated from the French]. — London [etc.] : Oxford University Press for the International African Institute, 1975 [i.e. 1976]. — 230p : ill, map, plans ; 21cm. — (A galaxy book ; 446)
This translation originally published: 1965. — Translation of 'Dieu d'eau'. Paris : Editions du Chêne, 1948. — Bibl.: p.224-226. — Index.
ISBN 0-19-519821-2 Pbk : £2.00
(B77-04554)

299.7 — NON-CHRISTIAN RELIGIONS OF NORTH AMERICAN INDIAN ORIGIN
299′.7 — Mandans. Religious ceremonies: O-kee-pa. *North Dakota, 1832. Early works*
Catlin, George, *b.1796.* O-kee-pa : a religious ceremony and other customs of the Mandans / by George Catlin. — [New ed.] / edited and with an introduction by John C. Ewers ... — Lincoln [Neb.] ; London : University of Nebraska Press, 1976. — ix,106p,[12]p of plates : col ill ; 23cm.
This ed. originally published: New Haven, Conn. ; London : Yale University Press, 1967. — Bibl.: p.101-103. — Index.
ISBN 0-8032-5845-3 Pbk : £6.40
(B77-07802)

299′.7 — Toltec myths. Special subjects: Quetzalcoatl. *Anthologies*
López-Portillo, José. Quetzalcoatl : a myth / [by] José Lopez Portillo ; translated from the Spanish by Eliot Weinberger & Diana S. Goodrich. — Cambridge : J. Clarke, 1977. — [6],151p ; 23cm.
This translation originally published: New York : Seabury Press, 1976. — Translation of: 'Quetzalcóatl'. Mexico : Librería de M. Porrúa, 1965.
ISBN 0-227-67827-3 : £3.95
(B77-10732)

299′.7 — Yamana myths. *Anthologies*
Gusinde, Martin. Folk literature of the Yamana indians : Martin Gusinde's collection of Yamana narratives / [translated from the German] ; Johannes Wilbert editor. — Berkeley [etc.] ; London : University of California Press, 1977. — xi,308p : maps, ports ; 24cm. — (Latin American studies series ; vol.40)
Translations selected from 'Die Feuerland-Indianer'. Wien-Modling : 'Anthropos', 1931-1974. — Bibl.: p.306-308.
ISBN 0-520-03299-3 : £9.70
(B77-23995)

299.9 — NON-CHRISTIAN RELIGIONS OF AUSTRONESIAN, OCEANIC, MISCELLANEOUS ORIGIN

299'.9 — Religions. *Ancient Mesopotamia, to ca B.C. 500*

Jacobsen, Thorkild. The treasures of darkness : a history of Mesopotamian religion / [by] Thorkild Jacobsen. — New Haven ; London : Yale University Press, 1976. — ix,273p : ill ; 24cm.
Index.
ISBN 0-300-01844-4 : £8.25
(B77-08768)

300 — SOCIAL SCIENCES

300 — Governments. Social policies

What government does / Matthew Holden, Jr and Dennis L. Dresang, editors. — Beverly Hills ; London : Sage Publications, [1976]. — 320p ; 24cm. — (Sage yearbooks in politics and public policy ; vol.1)
Published in the United States: 1975. — Bibl.
ISBN 0-8039-0243-3 : £9.00
ISBN 0-8039-0491-6 Pbk : £4.00
(B77-00027)

300 — Governments. Social policies. Evaluation

Public policy evaluation / Kenneth M. Dolbeare, editor ; with a section on crime control evaluation edited by John A. Gardiner. — Beverly Hills ; London : Sage Publications, [1976]. — 286p : ill ; 24cm. — (Sage yearbooks in politics and public policy ; vol.2)
Published in the United States: 1975. — Bibl.
ISBN 0-8039-0268-9 : £12.65
ISBN 0-8039-0312-x Pbk : £5.00
(B77-02768)

300 — Modern studies. *Secondary school texts*

Sources for modern studies / edited by B.J. Elliott, D.A. Osler ; designed and illustrated by Lewis Eadie. — Edinburgh : Holmes-McDougall.
In 2 vols.
Vol.1 : Economy and society. — [1977]. — 207p : ill, maps(chiefly col) ; 25cm.
Bibl.: p.204-205. — Index.
ISBN 0-7157-1348-5 Pbk : £2.75
(B77-12297)

300 — Organisation for Economic Co-operation and Development countries. Governments. Social policies. Reports, surveys

Organisation for Economic Co-operation and Development. Social sciences policy / [Organisation for Economic Co-operation and Development]. — Paris : O.E.C.D. ; [London] : [H.M.S.O.].
Norway. — 1976. — 187p ; 24cm.
Pbk : £3.60
ISBN 92-64-11576-5
(B77-00606)

300 — Social controversies. *Topics for discussion groups*

Pros & cons : a debater's handbook. — 16th ed. / [revised] by Michael D. Jacobson. — London [etc.] : Routledge and Kegan Paul, 1977. — x,236p ; 21cm.
Previous ed.: / revised by Anne Robinson. 1965. — Index.
ISBN 0-7100-8525-7 : £2.50 : CIP rev.
ISBN 0-7100-8526-5 Pbk : £1.95
(B77-08769)

300 — Social sciences. *For Australian students. Primary school texts. Cards*

Miller, Don. At home on earth / [by] Don Miller ; illustrated by Geoff Hocking. — Melbourne ; London [etc.] : Macmillan, 1976. — 1v. : ill(incl 1 col) ; 26cm.
Teacher's guide(15p.), 51 cards ([101]sides) in polythene bag.
ISBN 0-333-21023-9 : £4.95
(B77-26112)

300 — Social sciences. Measurement. Use of scaling

Gorden, Raymond L. Unidimensional scaling of social variables : concepts and procedures / [by] Raymond L. Gorden. — New York : Free Press ; London : Collier Macmillan, 1977. — xiii,175p : ill, forms ; 25cm.
Bibl.: p.169-171. — Index.
ISBN 0-02-912580-4 : £8.25
(B77-30978)

300 — Social sciences. Related to historiology

Bullock, Alan, *Baron Bullock.* Is history becoming a social science? : the case of contemporary history / [by] Alan Bullock. — Cambridge [etc.] : Cambridge University Press, 1977. — [1],23,[1]p ; 19cm. — (The Leslie Stephen lecture ; 1976)
'... delivered in the University of Cambridge on 5 March 1976' - p.23.
ISBN 0-521-29222-0 Sd : £0.60
Primary classification 907'.2
(B77-34271)

300 — Society. *Secondary school texts*

Connexions : a series of topic books for students in schools and colleges of further education. — 2nd ed. — Harmondsworth [etc.] : Penguin.
Out of your mind? : the impact of drugs on medicine and everyday life / [by] Peter Newmark. — 1977. — 64p : ill, facsims, map, ports ; 23cm. — (Penguin education)
Previous ed.: i.e. Revised ed. 1972.
Sd : £0.70
ISBN 0-14-080023-9
(B77-24696)

The lawbreakers / [by] Ray Jenkins. — 1977. — 64p : ill, facsims, ports ; 23cm.
Previous ed.: i.e. Revised ed. 1971.
Sd : £0.70
ISBN 0-14-080089-1
(B77-24697)

Learning for change in world society : reflections, activities and resources / [compiled by the World Studies Project ; edited by Robin Richardson]. — London (c/o One World Trust, 24 Palace Chambers, Bridge St., S.W.1) : World Studies Project, 1976. — 120p : ill, facsims ; 30cm.
Bibl. — Index.
ISBN 0-900581-03-4 Sp : £1.75
(B77-03922)

O'Donnell, Gerard. The human web / [by] Gerard O'Donnell. — 2nd ed. — London : J. Murray, 1977. — vi,249p : ill, map ; 22cm.
Previous ed.: 1975. — Bibl. — Index.
ISBN 0-7195-3389-9 Pbk : £1.95
(B77-31693)

300 — Society. Economic aspects. *Essays*

Becker, Gary Stanley. The economic approach to human behavior / [by] Gary S. Becker. — Chicago ; London : University of Chicago Press, 1976 [i.e. 1977]. — [6],314p : ill ; 24cm.
Published in the United States: 1976. — Bibl.: p.295-309. — Index.
ISBN 0-226-04111-5 : £7.50
(B77-12856)

300'.1 — Social sciences. Holism

Phillips, Denis Charles. Holistic thought in social science / [by] D.C. Phillips. — London [etc.] : Macmillan, 1977. — x,149p ; 22cm.
Originally published: Stanford, Calif. : Stanford University Press, 1976. — Bibl.: p.135-144. — Index.
ISBN 0-333-21662-8 : £6.95
(B77-11073)

300'.1 — Social sciences. Related to social policies. *Philosophical perspectives. Essays*

Rein, Martin. Social science and public policy / [by] Martin Rein. — Harmondsworth [etc.] : Penguin Education, 1976. — 272p ; 18cm. — (Penguin education)
Index.
ISBN 0-14-080367-x Pbk : £1.00
(B77-03923)

300'.1 — Social sciences. Structuralism

Gardner, Howard. The quest for mind : Piaget, Lévi-Strauss and the structuralist movement / [by] Howard Gardner. — London : Quartet Books, 1976. — iii-xiii,276,vii,[1]p ; 20cm.
Originally published: New York : Knopf, 1973 ; London : Coventure, 1975.
ISBN 0-7043-3056-3 Pbk : £2.50
(B77-03378)

300'.1 — Social sciences. Theories

Bernstein, Richard Jacob. The restructuring of social and political theory / [by] Richard J. Bernstein. — Oxford : Blackwell, 1976. — [1], xxiv,286p ; 24cm.
Also published: New York : Harcourt Brace Jovanovich, 1976. — Bibl.: p.265-275. — Index.

ISBN 0-631-17590-3 : £9.50
(B77-02769)

Veblen, Thorstein. The portable Veblen / edited, and with an introduction, by Max Lerner. — Harmondsworth [etc.] : Penguin, 1976. — vii, 632p ; 18cm. — (The Viking portable library)
Originally published: New York : Viking Press, 1948. — Bibl.:p.629-632.
ISBN 0-14-015036-6 Pbk : Unpriced
(B77-00607)

300'.1'8 — Social sciences. Methodology

Hindess, Barry. Philosophy and methodology in the social sciences / [by] Barry Hindess. — Hassocks : Harvester Press, 1977. — [6],258p : ill ; 23cm.
Bibl.: p.246-252. — Index.
ISBN 0-85527-344-5 : £9.95 : CIP rev.
(B77-10733)

Warfield, John Nelson. Societal systems : planning, policy and complexity / [by] John N. Warfield. — New York ; London [etc.] : Wiley, 1976. — xxix,490p : ill ; 24cm. — (Wiley series on systems engineering and analysis)
'A Wiley-Interscience publication'. — Bibl.: p.470-473. — Index.
ISBN 0-471-01569-5 : £22.20
(B77-10734)

300'.1'82 — Social policies. Formulation. Use of statistical mathematics

Statistics and public policy / William B. Fairley, Frederick Mosteller, editors. — Reading, Mass. ; London [etc.] : Addison-Wesley, 1977. — xiv,397p : ill, map ; 25cm. — (Addison-Wesley series in behavioral science : quantitative methods)
Bibl.
ISBN 0-201-02185-4 : £12.00
(B77-29937)

300'.1'82 — Social sciences. Statistical methods

Pine, Vanderlyn R. Introduction to social statistics / [by] Vanderlyn R. Pine. — Englewood Cliffs ; London [etc.] : Prentice-Hall, 1977. — xiv,415p : ill ; 24cm. — (Prentice-Hall methods of social science series)
Index.
ISBN 0-13-496844-1 : £11.15
(B77-23996)

300'.1'84 — Social sciences. Causal models

Asher, Herbert B. Causal modeling / [by] Herbert B. Asher. — Beverly Hills ; London : Sage Publications, 1976. — 80p : ill ; 22cm. — (Quantitative applications in the social sciences ; no.07-003) (Sage university papers)
Bibl.: p.72-75.
ISBN 0-8039-0654-4 Pbk : £1.95
(B77-32413)

300'.1'84 — Social sciences. Mathematical models. Applications of digital computer systems

Coats, R B. Computer models in the social sciences / [by] R.B. Coats and A. Parkin. — London : Edward Arnold, 1977. — vii,184p : ill ; 25cm.
Bibl.: p.80-92. — Index.
ISBN 0-7131-2630-2 Pbk : £3.75
(B77-30979)

300'.28'5425 — Social sciences. Software packages: SPSS. *Manuals*

Klecka, William R. SPSS primer : Statistical Package for the Social Sciences primer / [by] William R. Klecka, Norman H. Nie, C. Hadlai Hull. — New York ; London [etc.] : McGraw-Hill, [1977]. — x,134p : ill, facsims ; 28cm.
Published in the United States: 1975. — Bibl. — Index.
ISBN 0-07-035023-x Pbk : £4.95
(B77-13506)

SPSS : statistical package for the social sciences / [by] Norman H. Nie ... [et al.]. — 2nd ed. — New York ; London [etc.] : McGraw-Hill, [1976]. — xxiv,675p : ill, facsims ; 28cm.
This ed. published in the United States: 1975. — Previous ed.: 1970. — Bibl. — Index.
ISBN 0-07-046531-2 Pbk : £9.90
(B77-05870)

300'.3 — Social sciences. *Dictionaries*

Reading, Hugo F. A dictionary of the social sciences. — London : Routledge and Kegan Paul, 1977. — 1v.
Originally published: London : Sociologia Publications, 1976. — Previous control number ISBN 0-7100-8650-4.
ISBN 0-7100-8642-3 : CIP entry
(B77-08770)

Reading, Hugo F. A dictionary of the social sciences / [by] Hugo F. Reading. — London [etc.] ([77 Manor Park Rd, N.W.10]) : Sociologia Publications Ltd, 1976. — 231p ; 22cm.
ISBN 0-9504831-0-9 : £3.50
ISBN 0-9504831-1-7 Pbk : £1.80
(B77-03924)

300'.7 — Social sciences. Information sources

Smith, Paul, *b.1944.* The use of libraries and the literature of the social sciences / prepared for the [Open University] course team by Paul Smith. — [Milton Keynes] : [Open University Press], 1976. — 15p ; 30cm. — (Social sciences, a foundation course : making sense of society) (D101 ; LG)
Bibl.: p.8-13.
Sd : Unpriced
(B77-03379)

Use of social sciences literature / editor N. Roberts. — London [etc.] : Butterworth, 1977. — [10],326p ; 23cm. — (Information sources for research and development)
Bibl. — Index.
ISBN 0-408-10602-6 : £10.00
(B77-12857)

300'.7'1042 — Schools. Curriculum subjects: Social sciences. Integrated studies. *England. Proposals*
Reeves, Frank. Integrated social science : a distinct possibility / [by] Frank Reeves. — [Walsall] ([c/o The Secretary, 19 Mandeville Gardens, Walsall WS1 3AT]) : [Association for the Teaching of the Social Sciences], [1976]. — [1],24,[1]p ; 21cm. — (Association for the Teaching of the Social Sciences. Monographs ; no.3)
ISBN 0-904344-03-7 Sd : Unpriced
(B77-14049)

300'.7'1073 — Schools. Curriculum subjects: Social sciences. Teaching. Individualised instruction. *United States*
Bechtol, William M. Individually guided social studies / [by] William M. Bechtol, Anthony E. Conte. — Reading, Mass. ; London [etc.] : Addison-Wesley, [1977]. — xiii,290p : ill, forms ; 24cm. — (Leadership series in individually guided education)
Sound film and 2 sound filmstrips also available. — Published in the United States: 1976. — Bibl. — Index.
ISBN 0-201-19611-5 Pbk : £4.80
(B77-12298)

300'.7'1073 — Schools. Curriculum subjects: Social studies. Teaching. *United States. For trainee teachers*
Jarolimek, John. Social studies competencies and skills : learning to teach as an intern / [by] John Jarolimek. — New York : Macmillan ; London : Collier Macmillan, 1977. — xii,272p : ill, forms, map ; 26cm.
Bibl.: p.267-268. — Index.
ISBN 0-02-360380-1 Pbk : £5.45
(B77-26792)

300'.7'1241 — Middle schools & secondary schools. Curriculum subjects: Social studies. Teaching. *Great Britain*
Gleeson, Denis. Developments in social studies teaching / [by] Denis Gleeson and Geoff Whitty. — London : Open Books, 1976. — viii, 119p ; 21cm. — (The changing classroom)
Bibl.: p.113-116. — Index.
ISBN 0-7291-0099-5 : £3.90
ISBN 0-7291-0094-4 Pbk : £1.75
(B77-00608)

300'.7'1241 — Middle schools. Curriculum subjects: Social studies. Projects. *Great Britain*
History, Geography and Social Science 8-13 *(Project).* Place, time and society, 8-13 / [History, Geography and Social Science 8-13]. — [London] : Collins ; Bristol : Educational Systems for the Schools Council.
An introduction / [by] Alan Blyth ... [et al.]. — 1975. — 32p ; 21cm.
ISBN 0-00-380001-6 Sd : £0.50
ISBN 0-00-380023-7 Set of 4 booklets, wallcharts, spirit masters: £6.25
(B77-02029)

[Clues, clues, clues : detective work in history]. Clues / [by] Allan Waplington. — 1975. — 29p : ill ; 26cm.
ISBN 0-00-380024-5 Sd : £0.90
ISBN 0-00-380023-7 Set of 4 booklets, wallcharts, spirit masters : £6.25
(B77-02030)

Clues, clues, clues : detective work in history. Spirit masters / [by] Allan Waplington. — 1975. — 1v. : ill, map, plan ; 29cm.
Eight spirit-duplicator master sheets in envelope.
ISBN 0-00-381001-1 : Unpriced
ISBN 0-00-380023-7 Set of 4 booklets, wall charts, spirit masters : £6.25
(B77-02031)

Clues, clues, clues : detective work in history. [Wallcharts]. — 1975. — 1v. : ill, port ; 59x43cm.
Two fold. sheets ([2] sides).
ISBN 0-00-381002-x : £1.20
ISBN 0-00-380023-7 Set of 4 booklets, wallcharts, spirit masters : £6.25
(B77-02032)

300'.7'12411 — Secondary schools. Curriculum subjects: Modern studies. *Scotland. For teaching*
Modern studies : origins, aims and development / edited by Oliver J. Dunlop. — Basingstoke [etc.] : Macmillan, 1977. — xiii,170p : ill, facsims ; 24cm.
Bibl.
ISBN 0-333-17444-5 Pbk : £2.50 : CIP rev
(B77-04555)

300'.7'1273 — Secondary schools. Curriculum subjects: Social studies. Teaching. *United States*
Phillips, Richard C. Teaching for thinking in high school social studies / [by] Richard C. Phillips. — Reading, Mass. ; London [etc.] : Addison-Wesley, 1974. — xiii,338p : ill, 2 forms ; 24cm.
Bibl.: p.329-332. — Index.
ISBN 0-201-05822-7 : Unpriced
(B77-19219)

Phillips, Richard C. Teaching for thinking in high school social studies / [by] Richard C. Phillips. — Reading, Mass. ; London [etc.] : Addison-Wesley, 1974. — xiii,338p : ill, form ; 24cm.
Bibl.: p.329-332. — Index.
£9.80
(B77-27682)

300'.7'2 — Social indicators. *Organisation for Economic Co-operation and Development countries. Reports, surveys*
Organisation for Economic Co-operation and Development. Measuring social well-being : a progress report on the development of social indicators / [Organisation for Economic Co-operation and Development]. — Paris : O.E.C.D. ; [London] : [H.M.S.O.], 1976. — 213p : ill ; 24cm.
'The OECD Social Indicator Development Programme ; 3' - cover.
Pbk : £4.20
ISBN 92-64-11590-0
(B77-05871)

300'.7'2 — Social sciences. Research. Field studies
Douglas, Jack Daniell. Investigative social research : individual and team field research / [by] Jack D. Douglas. — Beverly Hills ; London : Sage Publications, 1976. — xv,229p : 2 ill ; 22cm. — (Sage library of social research ; vol.29)
Bibl.: p.227-229.
ISBN 0-8039-0675-7 : £8.00
ISBN 0-8039-0676-5 Pbk : £4.55
(B77-02033)

300'.7'2 — Social sciences. Research. Methodology
Labovitz, Sanford. Introduction to social research / [by] Sanford Labovitz, Robert Hagedorn. — 2nd ed. — New York ; London [etc.] : McGraw-Hill, 1976. — xii,147p ; 21cm.
Previous ed.: New York : McGraw-Hill, 1971. — Bibl. — Index.
ISBN 0-07-035776-5 : £6.60
ISBN 0-07-035775-7 Pbk : £4.55
(B77-03925)

Nachmias, David. Research methods in the social sciences / [by] David Nachmias, Chava Nachmias. — London : Edward Arnold, 1976. — x,335p : ill, forms ; 24cm.
Originally published: New York : St Martin's Press, 1976. — Bibl. — Index.
ISBN 0-7131-5901-4 : £9.95
ISBN 0-7131-5902-2 Pbk : £4.95
(B77-00609)

300'.7'2041 — Social sciences. Research organisations. *Great Britain. Social Science Research Council (Great Britain). Reports, surveys. Serials*
Social Science Research Council *(Great Britain).* Report of the Social Science Research Council, April-March ... — London : H.M.S.O.
1976-1977. — [1977]. — 61p ; 25cm. — ([1976-77 H.C.]481)
Bibl.: p.48-59. — Index.
ISBN 0-10-248177-6 Sd : £1.15
(B77-27683)

300'.7'2041 — Social sciences. Research projects supported by Social Science Research Council (Great Britain). *Directories*
Social Science Research Council *(Great Britain).* Research supported by the Social Science Research Council. — London : S.S.R.C.
1976. — 1976. — [5],493p ; 21cm.
Index.
ISBN 0-900296-52-6 Pbk : £2.00
(B77-00610)

1977. — 1977. — vi,456p ; 21cm.
Index.
ISBN 0-900296-63-1 Pbk : £2.50
(B77-31694)

300'.8 — Society. *Essays*
Hand, Learned. The spirit of liberty : papers and addresses of Learned Hand / collected, and with an introduction and notes, by Irving Dilliard. — 3rd ed., enlarged. — Chicago ; London : University of Chicago Press, 1977. — [2],xxxi,311p : port ; 21cm. — (A phoenix book)
This ed. originally published: New York : Knopf, 1960.
ISBN 0-226-31544-4 Pbk : £3.40
(B77-30980)

Lukes, Steven. Essays in social theory / [by] Steven Lukes. — London [etc.] : Macmillan, 1977. — x,227p ; 22cm.
ISBN 0-333-19662-7 : £8.95
ISBN 0-333-19693-7 Pbk : Unpriced
(B77-26113)

Philosophy, politics and society. — Oxford : Blackwell.
4th series : a collection / edited by Peter Laslett, W.G. Runciman and Quentin Skinner. — 1972 [i.e. 1976]. — [6],219p ; 22cm.
This collection originally published: 1972.
ISBN 0-631-17740-x Pbk : £2.95
(B77-02034)

300'.92'4 — Social sciences. Applications of theories of phenomenology of Merleau-Ponty, Maurice
Spurling, Laurie. Phenomenology and the social world : the philosophy of Merleau-Ponty and its relation to the social sciences / [by] Laurie Spurling. — London [etc.] : Routledge and Kegan Paul, 1977. — xiii,208p ; 23cm. — (International library of sociology)
Bibl.: p.197-202. — Index.
ISBN 0-7100-8712-8 : £6.95 : CIP rev.
(B77-24699)

300'.92'4 — Social sciences. Theories of Schutz, Alfred
Gorman, Robert A. The dual vision : Alfred Schutz and the myth of phenomenological social science / [by] Robert A. Gorman. — London [etc.] : Routledge and Kegan Paul, 1977. — [6],234p ; 23cm. — (International library of sociology)
Bibl.: p.215-228. — Index.
ISBN 0-7100-8450-1 : £4.95
(B77-05872)

300'.92'4 — Society. Theories of Godwin, William
Clark, John Philip. The philosophical anarchism of William Godwin / by John P. Clark. — Princeton ; Guildford : Princeton University Press, 1977. — ix,343,[1]p ; 23cm.
Bibl.: p.321-333. — Index.
ISBN 0-691-07217-5 : £12.40
(B77-23997)

300'.941 — Great Britain. Government. Social policies, 1977-1980. *Proposals*
TUC-Labour Party Liaison Committee. The next three years, and into the eighties / TUC-Labour Party Liaison Committee. — London : Labour Party, 1977. — 16p ; 22cm.
Sd : £0.20
(B77-32414)

300'.942 — England. Government. Social policies, 1830-1870
MacDonagh, Oliver. Early Victorian government, 1830-1870 / [by] Oliver MacDonagh. — London : Weidenfeld and Nicolson, 1977. — xi, 242p ; 22cm.
Bibl.: p.230-233. — Index.
ISBN 0-297-77250-3 : £6.95
ISBN 0-297-77301-1 Pbk : £3.75
(B77-12299)

300'.973 — Social sciences. *United States, 1776-1976*
Social science in America : the first two hundred years / edited by Charles M. Bonjean, Louis Schneider, Robert L. Lineberry. — Austin ; London : University of Texas Press, 1976. — [7],221p ; 24cm.
'Previously published as the special Bicentennial issue of "Social Science Quarterly" 57, no.1 (June 1976)' - title page verso. — Bibl.
ISBN 0-292-77530-x : £7.50
ISBN 0-292-77531-8 Pbk : £3.00
(B77-15690)

300'.973 — United States. Government. Social policies. Evaluation. *Conference proceedings*
Social Programs Evaluation *(Conference), Cambridge, Mass., 1974.* The evaluation of social programs / edited by Clark C. Abt. — Beverly Hills ; London : Sage Publications, 1976. — 503p : ill, form ; 23cm.
'... consists of the formal and informal discussions at a conference on Social Programs Evaluation sponsored by and held at Abt Associates Inc. in Cambridge, Massachusetts on September 23 and 24 of 1974' - Preface. — Bibl. — Index.
ISBN 0-8039-0735-4 : £16.00
(B77-19220)

301 — SOCIOLOGY
Bierstedt, Robert. The social order / [by] Robert Bierstedt. — 4th ed. — New York ; London [etc.] : McGraw-Hill, 1974. — xi,579p ; 24cm.
Previous ed.: 1970. — Index.
ISBN 0-07-005253-0 : Unpriced
(B77-18553)

Broom, Leonard. Sociology : a text with adapted readings / [by] Leonard Broom, Philip Selznick. — 6th ed. — New York [etc.] ; London : Harper and Row, 1977. — xvii,619p : ill(some col), facsims, forms, col map, plan, ports ; 24cm.
Previous ed.: 1973. — Bibl. — Index.
ISBN 0-06-350226-7 Pbk : £5.95
(B77-18554)

Collins, Randall. Conflict sociology : toward an explanatory science / [by] Randall Collins, with a contribution by Joan Annett. — New York [etc.] ; London : Academic Press, 1975 [i.e. 1977]. — xi,584p ; 23cm.
Originally published: 1975. — Bibl.: p.550-574. — Index.
ISBN 0-12-181352-5 Pbk : £5.70
(B77-24000)

Congalton, A A. The individual in the making : an introduction to sociology / [by] A.A. Congalton, A.E. Daniel. — Sydney ; London [etc.] : Wiley, 1976. — x,285p : ill ; 25cm.
Bibl. — Index.
ISBN 0-471-16836-x Pbk : £8.20
(B77-17916)

Horton, Paul Burleigh. Sociology / [by] Paul B. Horton & Chester L. Hunt. — 4th ed. — New York ; London [etc.] : McGraw-Hill, 1976. — xi,562p : ill(some col) ; 25cm.
Previous ed.: New York : McGraw-Hill, 1972. — Bibl.: p.492-533. — Index.
ISBN 0-07-030426-2 : £11.60
(B77-03926)

The **new** social sciences / edited by Baidya Nath Varma. — Westport, Conn. ; London : Greenwood Press, 1976. — xii,276p ; 22cm. — (Contributions in sociology ; no.18)
Bibl. — Index.
ISBN 0-8371-8591-2 : £12.95
(B77-16734)

Pilkington, Andrew. What is sociology? / by Andrew Pilkington. — Gloucester : Thornhill Press, 1976. — 32p ; 22cm.
Bibl.: p.32.
ISBN 0-904110-48-6 Sd : £0.75
(B77-09507)

Schneider, Louis. The sociological way of looking at the world / [by] Louis Schneider. — New York ; London [etc.] : McGraw-Hill, [1976]. — xv,343p : ill ; 24cm.
Published in the United States: 1975. — Bibl.: p.333-335. — Index.
ISBN 0-07-055463-3 : £6.95
(B77-03927)

Worsley, Peter. Introducing sociology / [by] Peter Worsley ... [et al.]. — 2nd ed. — Harmondsworth [etc.] : Penguin, 1977. — 605p : ill, maps ; 20cm. — (Open University. Set books) (Penguin education)
Previous ed.: 1970. — Bibl.: p.567-591. — Index.
Pbk : £1.50
ISBN 0-14-080187-1
(B77-23114)

301 — Social processes. Geographical aspects
Jones, Emrys, *b.1920.* An introduction to social geography / [by] Emrys Jones and John Eyles. — Oxford [etc.] : Oxford University Press, 1977. — xiv,273p : ill, facsims, maps, form ; 23cm.
Bibl.: p.265. — Index.
ISBN 0-19-874062-x : £6.50 : CIP rev.
ISBN 0-19-874063-8 Pbk : £2.95
(B77-04556)

301 — Sociology. Concepts
Labovitz, Sanford. An introduction to sociological concepts / [by] Sanford Labovitz. — New York ; London [etc.] : Wiley, 1977. — xii,244p : ill ; 23cm.
Two chapters in collaboration with Robert Hagedorn. — Bibl. — Index.
ISBN 0-471-51148-x Pbk : £4.65
(B77-22345)

301 — Sociology. Related to welfare work
Brewster, Bob. Sociology and social work : new perspectives for practitioners / [by] Bob Brewster and John Whiteford. — Hatfield (c/o G. Newfield, School of Social Sciences, The Hatfield Polytechnic, P.O. Box 109, Hatfield, Herts. AL10 9AB) : Organisation of Sociologists in Polytechnics and Cognate Institutions, 1976. — [2],16p ; 21cm. — (Organisation of Sociologists in Polytechnics and Cognate Institutions. SIP papers ; no.2)
' ... revised version of a paper given to the Annual Conference of SIP at Lanchester Polytechnic in June 1976' - note.
ISBN 0-905509-01-3 Sd : £0.50(free to members)
Also classified at 361
(B77-10168)

301'.01 — Sociology. Critical theory
Slater, Phil. Origin and significance of the Frankfurt School : a Marxist perspective / [by] Phil Slater. — London [etc.] : Routledge and Kegan Paul, 1977. — xvi,185p ; 23cm. — (International library of sociology)
Bibl.: p.175-182. — Index.
ISBN 0-7100-8438-2 : £5.95
(B77-05209)

301'.01 — Sociology. Critical theory. *Readings*
On critical theory / editor John O'Neill. — London : Heinemann Educational, 1977. — vi, 265p ; 22cm.
Originally published: New York : Seabury Press, 1976.
ISBN 0-435-82668-9 : £5.50
(B77-05210)

301'.01 — Sociology. Expounded by arts
Nisbet, Robert. Sociology as an art form / [by] Robert Nisbet. — London : Heinemann Educational, 1976. — [9],145p ; 21cm.
Index.
ISBN 0-435-82654-9 Pbk : £1.80
(B77-02035)

301'.01 — Sociology. Functionalism
Sztompka, Piotr. System and function : toward a theory of society / [by] Piotr Sztompka. — New York [etc.] ; London : Academic Press, 1974. — xvii,213p : 1 ill ; 24cm. — (Studies in anthropology)
Bibl.: p.183-201. — Index.
ISBN 0-12-681850-9 : Unpriced
(B77-18555)

301'.01 — Sociology. Theories
Goudsblom, Johan. Sociology in the balance : a critical essay / [by] Johan Goudsblom ; [translated from the Dutch]. — Oxford : Blackwell, 1977. — viii,232p ; 23cm.
Translation and revision of: 'Balans van de sociologie'. Utrecht : Spectrum, 1974. — Bibl.: p.205-222. — Index.
ISBN 0-631-17320-x : £7.00 : CIP rev.
ISBN 0-631-17330-7 Pbk : £3.25
(B77-05873)

Morris, Monica B. An excursion into creative sociology / [by] Monica B. Morris. — Oxford : Blackwell, 1977. — xi,212p ; 24cm.
Bibl.: p.191-206. — Index.
ISBN 0-631-17850-3 : £6.25
(B77-18556)

301'.01 — Sociology. Theories. *Essays*
Giddens, Anthony. Studies in social and political theory / [by] Anthony Giddens. — London : Hutchinson, 1977. — 416p : ill ; 23cm. — ([Hutchinson university library])
Index.
ISBN 0-09-129200-x : £8.95
(B77-29183)

301'.01 — Sociology. Theories. *Festschriften*
Explorations in general theory in social science : essays in honor of Talcott Parsons / edited by Jan J. Loubser ... [et al.]. — New York : Free Press ; London : Collier Macmillan, 1976. — 2v.(xvi,909,xv p) : ill ; 24cm.
Index.
ISBN 0-02-919370-2 : £45.00
(B77-11574)

301'.01 — Sociology. Theories of Frankfurt school. *Collections*
Critical sociology : selected readings / edited by Paul Connerton. — Harmondsworth [etc.] : Penguin, 1976. — 520p ; 18cm. — (Penguin education) (Penguin modern sociology readings)
Bibl.: p.498-509. — Index.
ISBN 0-14-080966-x Pbk : £1.50
(B77-05211)

301'.01'5 — Sociology. Applications of science
Laborit, Henri. Decoding the human message / [by] Henri Laborit ; translated [from the French] by Stephen Bodington & Alison Wilson. — London : Allison and Busby, 1977. — 239p : ill ; 23cm. — (Motive)
Translation of: 'La nouvelle grille'. Paris : Laffont, 1974.
ISBN 0-85031-186-1 : £6.50
ISBN 0-85031-187-x Pbk : £2.95
(B77-31695)

301'.01'8 — Sociology. Methodology
Lin, Nan. Foundations of social research / [by] Nan Lin. — New York ; London [etc.] : McGraw-Hill, 1976. — xix,458p : ill ; 25cm.
Index.
ISBN 0-07-037867-3 : £10.40
(B77-04557)

301'.01'8 — Sociology. Methodology. *Serials*
Sociological methodology. — San Francisco [etc.] ; London : Jossey-Bass. — (American Sociological Association. Official publications) (The Jossey-Bass behavioral science series)
1975 / David R. Heise, editor. — 1974. — xv, 221p : ill ; 24cm.
Bibl. — Index.
ISBN 0-87589-241-8 : Unpriced
(B77-19221)

1977 / David R. Heise, editor. — 1977. — xvi, 320p : ill ; 24cm.
Bibl. — Index.
ISBN 0-87589-286-8 : £13.25
(B77-13507)

301'.01'8 — Sociology. Methodology. Aesthetic aspects
Brown, Richard Harvey. A poetic for sociology : toward a logic of discovery for the human sciences / [by] Richard H. Brown. — Cambridge [etc.] : Cambridge University Press, 1977. — x,302p : ill ; 24cm.
Bibl.: p.266-294. — Index.
ISBN 0-521-21121-2 : £10.50
(B77-23115)

301'.05 — Sociology. *Periodicals*
Writing sociology. — London (New Cross, SE14 6NW) : Department of Sociology, University of London Goldsmiths' College.
No.1- ; [Oct. 1976]-. — 1976-. — ill ; 21cm.
Published at irregular intervals. — [2],112p. in 1st issue.
Sd : £0.65
ISSN 0308-8715
(B77-14050)

301'.07'2 — Sociology. Research. Methodology
Sociological research methods : an introduction / edited by Martin Bulmer. — London [etc.] : Macmillan, 1977. — xii,363p : ill ; 23cm.
Bibl.: p.338-363.
ISBN 0-333-21252-5 : £12.00
ISBN 0-333-21273-8 Pbk : £4.95
(B77-20026)

301'.07'20931 — Sociology. Research. *New Zealand*
Baldock, Cora V. Sociology in Australia and New Zealand : theory and methods / [by] Cora V. Baldock and Jim Lally. — Westport, Conn. ; London : Greenwood Press, 1974. — xii,329p ; 22cm. — (Contributions in sociology ; no.16)
Bibl.: p.291-314. — Index.
ISBN 0-8371-6126-6 : £12.75
Primary classification 301'.07'2094
(B77-15091)

301'.07'2094 — Sociology. Research. *Australia*
Baldock, Cora V. Sociology in Australia and New Zealand : theory and methods / [by] Cora V. Baldock and Jim Lally. — Westport, Conn. ; London : Greenwood Press, 1974. — xii,329p ; 22cm. — (Contributions in sociology ; no.16)
Bibl.: p.291-314. — Index.
ISBN 0-8371-6126-6 : £12.75
Also classified at 301'.07'20931
(B77-15091)

301'.07'6 — Secondary schools. Curriculum subjects: Sociology. G.C.E. A-level examinations. Syllabuses. *England. Conference proceedings*

Sociology in the Social Sciences, 16-19 *(Conference), University of Keele, 1975.* Sociology : the choice at A Level / edited by Geoff Whitty and Denis Gleeson ; for the Association for the Teaching of the Social Sciences. — Driffield (Nafferton, Driffield [Humberside] YO25 0JL) : Studies in Education Ltd, 1976. — [6],132p : ill ; 22cm. — (Issues in sociology, politics and education)
'... papers ... presented at a weekend conference ... held at the University of Keele in September 1975 ... [entitled] "Sociology in the Social Sciences, 16-19" ...' - Introduction. — 'Nafferton Books'. — Bibl.
ISBN 0-905484-07-x Pbk : £1.80
(B77-28386)

301'.08 — Sociology. *Essays*

Bierstedt, Robert. Power and progress : essays on sociological theory / [by] Robert Bierstedt. — New York ; London [etc.] : McGraw-Hill, 1975. — ix,330p ; 21cm.
Originally published: New York : McGraw-Hill, 1974. — Bibl.: p.322-323. — Index.
ISBN 0-07-005231-x Pbk : £2.90
(B77-02036)

Wrong, Dennis Hume. Skeptical sociology / [by] Dennis H. Wrong. — London : Heinemann Educational, 1977. — ix,322p ; 24cm.
Originally published: New York : Columbia University Press, 1976. — Index.
ISBN 0-435-82968-8 : £6.90
(B77-08225)

301'.09 — Sociology, to 1975

Eisenstadt, Samuel Noah. The form of sociology : paradigms and crises / [by] S.N. Eisenstadt with M. Curelaru. — New York ; London [etc.] : Wiley-Interscience, 1976. — xix,386p ; 24cm.
Index.
ISBN 0-471-23472-9 : £12.75
(B77-00611)

Handbook of contemporary developments in world sociology / edited by Raj P. Mohan and Don Martindale. — Westport, Conn. ; London : Greenwood Press, 1975. — xviii, 493p ; 22cm. — (Contributions in sociology ; no.17)
Bibl. — Index.
ISBN 0-8371-7961-0 : £19.95
(B77-16189)

301'.09'03 — Sociology. *Western world, 1700-1975*

Hawthorn, Geoffrey. Enlightenment and despair : a history of sociology / [by] Geoffrey Hawthorn. — Cambridge [etc.] : Cambridge University Press, 1976. — [7],295p ; 23cm.
Bibl.: p.261-286. — Index.
ISBN 0-521-21308-8 : £7.75
ISBN 0-521-29093-7 Pbk : £2.75
(B77-01170)

301'.09'034 — Sociology. Theories, ca 1830-ca 1930

De Coppens, Peter Roche. Ideal man in classical sociology : the views of Comte, Durkheim, Pareto and Weber / [by] Peter Roche de Coppens. — University Park ; London : Pennsylvania State University Press, 1976. — vii,174p : 1 ill ; 24cm.
Bibl.: p.161-164. — Index.
ISBN 0-271-01206-4 : £11.60
(B77-14051)

301'.092'4 — Sociology. Eichthal, Gustave d'. *Biographies*

Eichthal, Gustave d'. A French sociologist looks at Britain : Gustave d'Eichthal and British society in 1828 / translated [from the French] and edited by Barrie M. Ratcliffe and W.H. Chaloner. — Manchester : Manchester University Press [etc.], 1977. — vi,169p ; 23cm. — (University of Manchester. Faculty of Arts. Publications ; no.22)
Index. — Includes a memoir of Gustave d'Eichthal / by Barrie M. Ratcliffe.
ISBN 0-7190-1283-x : £7.50
Primary classification 309.1'41'074
(B77-24725)

301'.092'4 — Sociology. Theories of Parsons, Talcott

Menzies, Ken. Talcott Parsons and the social image of man / [by] Ken Menzies. — London [etc.] : Routledge and Kegan Paul, 1976 [i.e.1977]. — viii,197p : ill ; 23cm. — (International library of sociology)
Bibl.: p.177-185. — Index.
ISBN 0-7100-8369-6 : £4.95
(B77-05874)

301.1 — SOCIAL PSYCHOLOGY

Harvey, John H. Social psychology : an attributional approach / [by] John H. Harvey, William P. Smith ; Yvette Harvey editorial assistant. — Saint Louis : Mosby ; London : Distributed by Kimpton, 1977. — xvii,426p : ill ; 26cm.
Bibl.: p.382-408. — Index.
ISBN 0-8016-2079-1 Pbk : £8.05
(B77-17917)

Kando, Thomas Matyas. Social interaction / [by] Thomas M. Kando. — Saint Louis : Mosby ; London : Distributed by Kimpton, 1977. — xv, 349p : ill ; 26cm.
Bibl. — Index.
ISBN 0-8016-2614-5 Pbk : £7.50
(B77-20902)

Secord, Paul Frank. Understanding social life : an introduction to social psychology / [by] Paul F. Secord, Carl W. Backman, David R. Slavitt. — New York ; London [etc.] : McGraw-Hill, 1976. — xii,394p : ill ; 25cm.
Bibl.: p.367-380. — Index.
ISBN 0-07-055917-1 : £9.90
(B77-04558)

Segall, Marshall H. Human behavior and public policy : a political psychology / [by] Marshall H. Segall. — New York ; Oxford [etc.] : Pergamon, [1977]. — xiv,321p : ill ; 24cm. — (Pergamon international library) (Pergamon general psychology series ; 41)
Published in the United States: 1976. — Bibl.: p.285-305. — Index.
ISBN 0-08-017087-0 : £9.00
ISBN 0-08-017853-7 Pbk : £4.65
(B77-09508)

Social psychology / [editors Ruth Zaslavsky, Daniel Liberatore] ; consulting editor Kurt W. Back. — New York ; London [etc.] : Wiley, 1977. — xiv,498p : ill ; 25cm.
Bibl. — Index.
ISBN 0-471-03983-7 : £8.70
(B77-20027)

301.1 — Man. Social behaviour

Barash, David P. Sociobiology and behavior / [by] David P. Barash ; foreword by Edward O. Wilson. — New York ; Oxford [etc.] : Elsevier, 1977. — xvii,378p : ill ; 24cm.
Bibl.: p.333-365. — Index.
ISBN 0-444-99029-1 : £7.14
ISBN 0-444-99036-4 Pbk : Unpriced
Also classified at 591.5
(B77-22346)

Rowan, John. Psychological aspects of society / [by] John Rowan. — London : Davis-Poynter.
In 4 vols.
Book 3 : The power of the group. — 1976. — 5-212p : ill ; 23cm.
Index.
ISBN 0-7067-0149-6 : £5.00
(B77-00028)

301.1 — Man. Social behaviour. *Anthropological perspectives. Reviews of research*

Knowledge and behaviour / edited by Ladislav Holy. — [Belfast] : [Queen's University of Belfast, Department of Social Anthropology], [1976]. — xii,123p ; 21cm. — (Queen's University of Belfast. Papers in social anthropology ; vol.1 ISSN 0308-8170)
'All the papers ... were first read and discussed at a research seminar for staff and students ... at the Queen's University in Belfast in 1974-1975' - Introduction. — Bibl.
ISBN 0-85389-107-9 Pbk : £1.75
(B77-03928)

301.1 — Man. Social behaviour. *Topics for discussion groups. Secondary school texts. Cards*

Parfit, Cliff. Pros and cons / [by] Cliff Parfit. — London [etc.] : Hodder and Stoughton, 1976. — 1v. : ill ; 20cm.
'Notes for teachers' ([2],8p),48 cards ([59] sides).
ISBN 0-340-20832-5 : £3.50
(B77-08226)

301.1 — Man. Social behaviour. Related to cognition. *Conference proceedings*

Symposium on Cognition, *11th, Carnegie-Mellon University, 1975.* Cognition and social behavior / edited by John S. Carroll, John W. Payne. — Hillsdale : Erlbaum ; New York ; London [etc.] : Distributed by Wiley, 1976. — xiii,290p : ill ; 24cm.
'... the collected papers of the Eleventh Annual Symposium on Cognition, held at Carnegie-Mellon University in April 1975' - Preface. — Bibl.: p.269-286. — Index.
ISBN 0-470-99007-4 : £12.40
Primary classification 153.4
(B77-23082)

301.1 — Man. Social behaviour. Role of personality

Personality variables in social behavior / edited by Thomas Blass. — Hillsdale : Erlbaum ; New York ; London [etc.] : Distributed by Wiley, 1977. — x,405p : ill ; 24cm.
Bibl. — Index.
ISBN 0-470-99133-x : £15.00
(B77-24001)

301.1 — Man. Social behaviour. Rules. *Conference proceedings*

Social Rules and Social Behaviour *(Conference), Oxford, 197-?.* Social rules and social behaviour / edited by Peter Collett. — Oxford : Blackwell, 1977. — vi,185p ; 23cm.
'... papers ... presented in a seminar of the same title that was held in the Department of Experimental Psychology at Oxford' - Preface. — Bibl.: p.174-185.
ISBN 0-631-17340-4 : £7.00 : CIP rev.
(B77-05875)

301.1 — Social psychology. *Reviews of research*

Advances in experimental social psychology. — New York [etc.] ; London : Academic Press.
Vol.10 / edited by Leonard Berkowitz. — 1977. — x,338p : ill ; 24cm.
Bibl. — Index.
ISBN 0-12-015210-x : £13.50
(B77-24002)

301.1'07 — Social psychology. Information sources

Smith, Paul, *b.1944.* The use of libraries and the literature of social psychology / [prepared for the Open University, Social Psychology Course Team by Paul Smith]. — [Milton Keynes] : [Open University Press], 1976. — 20p ; 30cm. — (Social sciences, a third level course : social psychology) (D305 ; UL)
Sd : Unpriced
(B77-03929)

301.1'07'1141 — Universities. *Great Britain. Open University. Curriculum subjects: Social psychology. Courses: 'Social psychology'*

Brown, Hedy. Social psychology in retrospect : a review of the course / prepared for the [Open University, Social Psychology] Course Team by Hedy Brown and Richard Stevens. — Milton Keynes : Open University Press, 1976. — 43p : col ill ; 30cm. — (Social sciences, a third level course : social psychology ; block 15) (D305 ; block 15 (32))
Bibl.: p.42-43.
ISBN 0-335-07114-7 Pbk : Unpriced
(B77-03930)

Open University. *Social Psychology Course Team.* Introduction and guide to the course / [prepared for the Open University, Social Psychology Course Team by Jeff Harvey]. — [Milton Keynes] : [Open University Press], 1976. — 15p ; 30cm. — (Social sciences, a third level course : social psychology) (D305 ; CG)
Bibl.: p.15.
Sd : Unpriced
(B77-03931)

301.1'07'24 — Social psychology. Experiments. Methodology

Carlsmith, James Merrill. Methods of research in social psychology / [by] J. Merrill Carlsmith, Phoebe C. Ellsworth, Elliot Aronson. — Reading, Mass. ; London [etc.] : Addison-Wesley, [1977]. — x,326p : ill ; 25cm.
Published in the United States: 1976. — Bibl.: p.310-320. — Index.
ISBN 0-201-00346-5 : £6.95
(B77-11575)

301.1'08 — Man. Social behaviour. *Anthropological perspectives. Essays*

Radcliffe-Brown, Alfred Reginald. The social anthropology of Radcliffe-Brown / edited by Adam Kuper. — London [etc.] : Routledge and Kegan Paul, 1977. — viii,296p : ill, map ; 23cm.
Bibl.: p.287-292. — Index.
ISBN 0-7100-8556-7 : £6.95 : CIP rev.
ISBN 0-7100-8557-5 Pbk : £3.50
(B77-06477)

301.11 — Interpersonal relationships

Lofland, John. Doing social life : the qualitative study of human interaction in natural settings / [by] John Lofland. — New York ; London [etc.] : Wiley, 1976. — xxi,328p : ill ; 24cm.
'A Wiley-Interscience publication'. — Bibl.: p.314-315. — Index.
ISBN 0-471-01563-6 : £10.60
(B77-06478)

301.11 — Interpersonal relationships. *Middle school texts*
Bull, Norman John. Persons / [by] Norman J. Bull. — London : Longman, 1976. — 112p : ill, facsims, forms, ports ; 25cm. — (The way of wisdom series ; book 5)
Index.
ISBN 0-582-21425-4 Pbk : £1.50
Also classified at 155.2
(B77-00029)

301.11 — Interpersonal relationships. *Secondary school texts*
Conflict / [by Geoffrey Hacker, James Learmonth, Rony Robinson]. — Sunbury-on-Thames [etc.] : Nelson.
3 / [compiled] by James Learmonth, Rony Robinson. — 1976. — 157p : ill, facsims ; 22cm.
ISBN 0-17-433014-6 Pbk : £1.00
(B77-04559)

Juniper, Dean Francis. Human relationships for schools and colleges / [by] Dean F. Juniper. — Peppard Common (Kestrels House, Peppard Common, Oxon.) : Cressrelles Publishing Co., 1977. — [9],413p : ill, forms, map ; 23cm.
Bibl.
ISBN 0-85956-032-5 : £6.00
(B77-20028)

301.11 — Interpersonal relationships. Nonverbal communication
Rosenfeld, Lawrence B. With words unspoken : the nonverbal experience / [by] Lawrence B. Rosenfeld, Jean M. Civikly. — New York ; London [etc.] : Holt, Rinehart and Winston, 1976. — xiii,254p,plate : ill, plan, ports ; 26cm.
Bibl.: p.237-247. — Index.
ISBN 0-03-015671-8 Pbk : £6.75
(B77-02037)

301.11 — Man. Social development. Role of interpersonal relationships
Gubrium, Jaber F. Toward maturity / [by] Jaber F. Gubrium, David R. Buckholdt. — San Francisco [etc.] ; London : Jossey-Bass, 1977. — xv,224p ; 24cm. — (The Jossey-Bass behavioral science series)
Bibl.: p.205-218. — Index.
ISBN 0-87589-311-2 : £10.00
(B77-20903)

301.11 — Social influence
Moscovici, Serge. Social influence and social change / [by] Serge Moscovici ; translated [from the French MS.] by Carol Sherrard and Greta Heinz. — London [etc.] : Academic Press [for the] European Association of Experimental Social Psychology, 1976. — ix, 239p ; 24cm. — (European monographs in social psychology ; 10)
Bibl.: p.225-231. — Index.
ISBN 0-12-508450-1 : £7.00
(B77-12858)

301.11'01 — Personality. Social aspects. Theories
Holland, Ray. Self and social context / [by] Ray Holland. — London [etc.] : Macmillan, 1977. — 303p ; 23cm.
Bibl.: p.289-291. — Index.
ISBN 0-333-19811-5 : £10.00 : CIP rev.
ISBN 0-333-19812-3 Pbk : £4.95
(B77-21699)

301.11'01'2 — Interpersonal relationships. Taxonomic aspects
Shantock Systematics Group. A systematics handbook / prepared by Shantock Systematics Group. — Sherborne, Glos. : Coombe Springs Press, 1975. — [9],35p : ill ; 21cm.
Bibl.: p.33-34.
ISBN 0-900306-12-2 Pbk : £0.50
(B77-10169)

301.11'072 — Man. Social behaviour. Research methods: Observation. *Teaching kits*
Rossan, Sheila. Observation / prepared for the [Open University, Social Psychology] Course Team by Sheila Rossan. — [Milton Keynes] : [Open University Press], 1976. — Portfolio ; 22x31cm. — (Social sciences, a third level course : social psychology ; project 1) (D305)
Six booklets. — Bibl.
£0.90
(B77-08771)

301.11'2 — Friendship
Brain, Robert. Friends and lovers / [by] Robert Brain. — St Albans : Paladin, 1977. — 287p : ill ; 20cm.
Originally published: St Albans : Hart-Davis MacGibbon, 1976. — Bibl.: p.273-278. — Index.
ISBN 0-586-08162-3 Pbk : £1.25
(B77-12859)

301.11'2 — Interpersonal relationships: Acquaintance
Duck, Steven Weatherill. The study of acquaintance / [by] Steve Duck. — Farnborough, Hants. : Saxon House, 1977. — ix,236p ; 23cm.
Bibl.: p.200-229. — Index.
ISBN 0-566-00160-8 : £8.50 : CIP rev.
(B77-16190)

301.11'2 — Interpersonal relationships. Face-to-face communication. Role of perception of social status
Status characteristics and social interactions : an expectation-states approach / [by] Joseph Berger ... [et al.]. — New York ; Oxford [etc.] : Elsevier, 1977. — xi,196p : ill ; 24cm.
Bibl.: p.173-183. — Index.
ISBN 0-444-99032-1 : £15.48
(B77-26115)

301.11'2 — Man. Interpersonal attraction
Foundations of interpersonal attraction / [edited by] Ted L. Huston. — New York ; London : Academic Press, 1974. — xvi,422p : ill ; 24cm.
Bibl. — Index.
ISBN 0-12-362950-0 : Unpriced
(B77-20029)

301.11'3 — Loneliness
Bowskill, Derek. People need people : a journey through the landscape of loneliness / [by] Derek Bowskill. — London : Wildwood House, 1977. — [12],243p ; 23cm.
ISBN 0-7045-0235-6 : £5.50
ISBN 0-7045-0236-4 Pbk : £2.95
(B77-20904)

301.11'3 — Society. Role of individuals
Russell, Bertrand, *Earl Russell.* Authority and the individual / [by] Bertrand Russell. — London : Allen and Unwin, 1977. — 3-95p ; 20cm.
Originally published: 1949.
ISBN 0-04-170030-9 Pbk : £1.25
(B77-22347)

301.11'3'091812 — Western world. Society. Role of individuals, ca 1700-1976
Sennett, Richard. The fall of public man / by Richard Sennett. — Cambridge [etc.] : Cambridge University Press, 1977. — xii,386p ; 24cm.
Also published: New York : Knopf, 1977. — Index.
ISBN 0-521-21642-7 : £10.50
ISBN 0-521-29215-8 Pbk : £3.95
(B77-11576)

301.14 — Communication. Social aspects
Myers, Gail E. The dynamics of human communication : a laboratory approach / [by] Gail E. Myers, Michele Tolela Myers. — 2nd ed. — New York ; London [etc.] : McGraw-Hill, 1976. — xix,424p : ill, forms ; 24cm.
Previous ed.: New York : McGraw-Hill, 1973. — Bibl. — Index.
ISBN 0-07-044212-6 Pbk : £7.15
(B77-27684)

301.14 — Hearsay. Psychosocial aspects
Rosnow, Ralph Leon. Rumor and gossip : the social psychology of hearsay / [by] Ralph L. Rosnow, Gary Alan Fine. — New York ; Oxford [etc.] : Elsevier, 1976. — xi,166p : ill ; 24cm.
Bibl.: p.143-156. — Index.
ISBN 0-444-99031-3 : £9.15
ISBN 0-444-99035-6 Pbk : Unpriced
(B77-07804)

301.14 — Interpersonal relationships. Communication
Explorations in interpersonal communication / Gerald R. Miller, editor. — Beverly Hills ; London : Sage Publications, [1977]. — 278p : ill ; 24cm. — (Sage annual reviews of communication research ; vol.5)
Published in the United States: 1976. — Bibl.
ISBN 0-8039-0665-x : £12.50
ISBN 0-8039-0666-8 Pbk : £6.35
(B77-09509)

301.14 — Interpersonal relationships. Face to face communication
Duncan, Starkey. Face-to-face interaction : research, methods, and theory / [by] Starkey Duncan, Jr, Donald W. Fiske. — Hillsdale : Erlbaum ; New York ; London [etc.] : Distributed by Wiley, 1977. — xv,361p : ill ; 24cm.
Bibl.: p.345-351. — Index.
ISBN 0-470-99113-5 : Unpriced
(B77-22348)

301.14 — Interpersonal relationships. Face to face communication. *For management*
Honey, Peter. Face to face : a practical guide to interactive skills / [by] Peter Honey. — London : Institute of Personnel Management, 1976. — 149p : 1 ill ; 23cm. — ([Management in perspective])
ISBN 0-85292-142-x : £4.95
(B77-00612)

Williams, Beryl, *b.1938.* Communicating effectively : a manager's guide to getting through to people / by Beryl Williams. — Wellingborough : Thorsons, 1977. — 125p : ill ; 23cm. — ([Business success series])
Bibl.: p.119. — Index.
ISBN 0-7225-0391-1 : £2.95
(B77-22349)

301.14'08 — Interpersonal relationships. Communication. *Readings*
Patton, Bobby R. Interpersonal communication in action : basic text and readings / [by] Bobby R. Patton, Kim Giffin ... [et al.]. — 2nd ed. — New York [etc.] ; London : Harper and Row, 1977. — xi,452p : ill ; 24cm.
Previous ed.: published as 'Interpersonal communication'. New York : Harper and Row, 1974. — Bibl. — Index.
ISBN 0-06-042316-1 Pbk : £7.45
(B77-15691)

301.15 — Social groups. Social control
Power and control : social structures and their transformation / edited by Tom R. Burns and Walter Buckley. — London [etc.] : Sage Publications [for] the International Sociological Association, 1976. — [5],290p ; 23cm. — (Sage studies in international sociology ; 6)
Bibl.
ISBN 0-8039-9959-3 : £6.00
ISBN 0-8039-9978-x Pbk : £3.00
Also classified at 301.18
(B77-10170)

301.15'4 — American people. Attitudes, 1960-1975
Wuthnow, Robert. The consciousness reformation / [by] Robert Wuthnow. — Berkeley [etc.] ; London : University of California Press, [1977]. — x,309p : 1 ill, form ; 25cm.
Published in the United States: 1976. — Index.
ISBN 0-520-03138-5 : £10.00
(B77-14559)

301.15'4 — Attitudes. Change. Theories
Zimbardo, Philip. Influencing attitudes and changing behavior : an introduction to method, theory, and applications of social control and personal power / [by] Philip G. Zimbardo, Ebbe B. Ebbesen, Christina Maslach. — 2nd ed. — Reading, Mass. ; London [etc.] : Addison-Wesley, 1977. — xv,271p : ill, facsims, forms, ports ; 24cm. — (Topics in social psychology)
Previous ed.: 1969. — Bibl.: p.243-252. — Index.
ISBN 0-201-08796-0 Pbk : £4.80
(B77-22350)

301.15'4 — Electorate. Attitudes. Theories. *United States, 1972. Reports, surveys*
Raine, Alden S. Change in the political agenda : social and cultural conflict in the American electorate / [by] Alden S. Raine. — Beverly Hills ; London : Sage Publications, 1977. — 60, [1]p : ill ; 22cm. — (Sage professional papers in American policies ; vol.3, no.04-035)
Bibl.: p.58-60.
ISBN 0-8039-0634-x Pbk : £1.75
(B77-30981)

301.15'4 — Printed royal propaganda. *France, 1643-1715*
Klaits, Joseph. Printed propaganda under Louis XIV : absolute monarchy and public opinion / by Joseph Klaits. — Princeton ; Guildford : Princeton University Press, [1977]. — xiii, 342p ; 23cm.
Published in the United States: 1976. — Bibl.: p.307-330. — Index.
ISBN 0-691-05238-7 : £16.40
(B77-13508)

301.15'4 — Propaganda, to 1976
Thomson, Oliver. Mass persuasion in history : an historical analysis of the development of propaganda techniques / [by] Oliver Thomson. — Edinburgh : P. Harris, 1977. — [10],142p, leaf of plate,[12]p of plates : ill, facsims ; 23cm.
Bibl.: p.133-137. — Index.
ISBN 0-904505-16-2 : £6.00
(B77-26116)

301.15'4 — Utterances. Persuasiveness. Influence of style
Sandell, Rolf. Linguistic style and persuasion / [by] Rolf Sandell. — London [etc.] : Academic Press [for the] European Association of Experimental Social Psychology, 1977. — xiv, 329p : ill ; 24cm. — (European monographs in social psychology ; 11)
Bibl.: p.306-318. — Index.
ISBN 0-12-618150-0 : £10.50
(B77-15092)

301.15'4'0973 — Attitudes & public opinion. *United States*
Oskamp, Stuart. Attitudes and opinions / [by] Stuart Oskamp, in collaboration with ... [others]. — Englewood Cliffs ; London [etc.] : Prentice-Hall, 1977. — xiii,466p : ill, ports ; 24cm. — (Clinical and social psychology series)
Bibl.: p.405-448. — Index.
ISBN 0-13-050393-2 : £11.95
(B77-25388)

301.15'43'07941 — Press. Attitudes of society. *Great Britain. Reports, surveys*
Social and Community Planning Research. Attitudes to the press : a report ... / by Social and Community Planning Research. — London : H.M.S.O., 1977. — xvii,380p : forms ; 25cm. — (Great Britain. Royal Commission on the Press. Research series ; 3) (Cmnd.6810-3)
ISBN 0-10-168103-8 Pbk : £5.50
(B77-28387)

301.15'43'301540941 — Housing. Policies of government. Attitudes of public. *Great Britain. Reports, surveys*
British Market Research Bureau. BMRB housing consumer survey : a survey of attitudes towards current and alternative housing policies / [for the Building EDC]. — London : H.M.S.O. [for the] National Economic Development Office, 1977. — iv,71p ; 30cm.
ISBN 0-11-700854-0 Pbk : £2.25
(B77-33062)

301.15'43'32773 — United States. Foreign relations. Policies of government. Public opinion, 1937-1947
Leigh, Michael, *b.1948.* Mobilizing consent : public opinion and American foreign policy, 1937-1947 / [by] Michael Leigh. — Westport, Conn. ; London : Greenwood Press, 1976. — xvi,187,[1]p ; 22cm.
Bibl.: p.172-178. — Index.
ISBN 0-8371-8772-9 : £11.95
(B77-20905)

301.15'43'371 — Community schools. *Nottinghamshire. Sutton-in-Ashfield. Sutton Centre School. Attitudes of parents. Reports, surveys*
Elsey, Barry. The school in the community : a case study in community education / [by] Barry Elsey and Ken Thomas. — [Nottingham] : [University of Nottingham], 1976. — [5],i,67,[8] p : forms ; 30cm. — (Occasional paper in social and environmental studies ; no.3)
ISBN 0-85359-041-9 Pbk : £1.00
(B77-03932)

301.15'43'61304244 — Women. Health. Attitudes of society, ca 1860-1973. *Feminist viewpoints*
Ehrenreich, Barbara. Complaints and disorders : the sexual politics of sickness / [by] Barbara Ehrenreich and Deirdre English. — London (14 Talacre Rd, NW5 3PE) : Writers and Readers Publishing Cooperative, 1976. — 95p : ill, facsims, port ; 20cm.
Originally published: Old Westbury, N.Y. : Feminist Press, 1973 ; London : Compendium, 1974. — Bibl.: p.94-95.
ISBN 0-904613-25-9 Pbk : £0.85
(B77-12860)

301.15'43'65910941 — Advertising. Attitudes of society. *Great Britain, 1963-1972. Reports, surveys. Collections*
Attitudes towards advertising : a collection of published studies from October 1963 to July 1972. — London : Institute of Practitioners in Advertising, 1975. — [5],80[i.e.81]p ; 30cm.
Contents: The goldfish bowl - As others see us / by John Treasure and Timothy Joyce - Advertising and the public / by John Treasure - Attitudes to advertising / British Market Research Bureau for the Advertising Association - Advertisers opinions of advertising / prepared for the Institute of Practitioners in Advertising by the British Market Research Bureau.
Sp : £1.50
(B77-24701)

301.15'52 — Organisations. Power
Swingle, Paul George. The management of power / [by] Paul G. Swingle. — Hillsdale : Erlbaum ; New York ; London [etc.] : Distributed by Wiley, 1976. — xiii,178p : ill ; 24cm.
Bibl.: p.171-172. — Index.
ISBN 0-470-15030-0 : £10.50
(B77-05212)

301.15'52 — Power. *Sociological perspectives*
Martin, Roderick. The sociology of power / [by] Roderick Martin. — London [etc.] : Routledge and Kegan Paul, 1977. — ix,203p : 2 ill ; 23cm. — (International library of sociology)
Index.
ISBN 0-7100-8563-x : £6.75
(B77-17918)

301.15'52 — Power. Social aspects. *Anthropological perspectives. Conference proceedings*
The **anthropology** of power : ethnographic studies from Asia, Oceania and the New World / edited by Raymond D. Fogelson, Richard N. Adams. — New York [etc.] ; London : Academic Press, 1977. — xiv,429p : ill ; 24cm. — (Studies in anthropology)
'[Proceedings of a]... 3 1/2 day conference ... held under the auspices of the American Association for the Advancement of Science in San Francisco in February of 1974 ...' - Preface. — Bibl. — Index.
ISBN 0-12-261550-6 : £13.85
(B77-22351)

301.15'52'019 — Power. Psychological aspects
Kipnis, David. The powerholders / [by] David Kipnis. — Chicago ; London : University of Chicago Press, 1976. — x,230p ; 23cm.
Bibl.: p.217-227. — Index.
ISBN 0-226-43731-0 : £8.50
(B77-02038)

301.15'54 — Universities. Decision making. *Sociological perspectives*
The **supernatural** omnibus : being a collection of stories of apparitions, witchcraft, werewolves, diabolism, necromancy, satanism, divination, sorcery, goety, voodoo, possession, occult, doom and destiny / edited, with an introduction, by Montague Summers. — Harmondsworth [etc.] : Penguin.
In 2 vols. — This collection originally published: in 1 vol. London : Gollancz, 1931.
Vol.2 : Diabolism, witchcraft and evil lore. — 1976. — 298p ; 18cm.
ISBN 0-14-004185-0 Pbk : £0.90
(B77-04394)

301.15'54'015193 — Man. Social behaviour. Decision making. Applications of game theory
Harsanyi, John C. Rational behavior and bargaining equilibrium in games and social situations / [by] John C. Harsanyi. — Cambridge [etc.] : Cambridge University Press, 1977. — xi,314p : ill ; 24cm.
Bibl.: p.305-307. — Index.
ISBN 0-521-20886-6 : £15.00
(B77-30982)

301.15'7 — Socialisation. *Anthropological perspectives. Festschriften*
Socialization as cultural communication : development of a theme in the work of Margaret Mead / Theodore Schwartz, editor. — Berkeley [etc.] ; London : University of California Press, 1976. — xviii,251p,[5]leaves of plates,[12]p of plates : ill(some col), maps, ports ; 25cm.
Bibl.
ISBN 0-520-03061-3 : £12.00
(B77-14052)

301.15'7 — Socialisation. Role of educational institutions
Bourdieu, Pierre. Reproduction in education, society and culture / [by] Pierre Bourdieu and Jean-Claude Passeron ; translated from the French by Richard Nice ; with a foreword by Tom Bottomore. — London [etc.] : Sage Publications, 1977. — [1],xx,254p,fold plate : ill ; 23cm. — (Sage studies in social and educational change ; vol.5)
Translation of 'La reproduction'. Paris : Éditions de Minuit, 1970. — Bibl.: p.237-241. — Index.
ISBN 0-8039-9994-1 : £8.05
ISBN 0-8039-9995-x Pbk : £4.05
(B77-22352)

301.15'73 — German prisoners of war. Re-education. *Great Britain, 1945-1948*
Faulk, Henry. Group captives : the re-education of German prisoners of war in Britain, 1945-1948 / by Henry Faulk. — London : Chatto and Windus, 1977. — 233p ; 23cm.
Index.
ISBN 0-7011-2196-3 : £7.50 : CIP rev..
(B77-08772)

301.16'1 — American documentaries, 1930-1945. *Critical studies*
Stott, William. Documentary expression and thirties America / [by] William Stott. — London [etc.] : Oxford University Press, 1976. — xvi,361p,[64]p of plates : ill, facsims, ports ; 21cm.
'A Galaxy Book' - cover. — Originally published: New York : Oxford University Press, 1973. — Bibl.: p.348-353. — Index.
ISBN 0-19-502099-5 Pbk : £3.25
(B77-05876)

301.16'1 — Book industries & trades. *Western world. Sociological perspectives*
Gedin, Per. Literature in the marketplace / [by] Per Gedin ; translated [from the Swedish] by George Bisset. — London : Faber, 1977. — 3-211p : 1 ill ; 23cm.
Translation of: 'Litteraturen i verkligheten'. Stockholm : Prisma, 1975. — Index.
ISBN 0-571-11053-3 : £5.95 : CIP rev.
(B77-10171)

301.16'1 — Broadcasting services. *Great Britain. British Broadcasting Corporation. Sociological perspectives*
Burns, Tom, *b.1913.* The BBC : public institution and private world / [by] Tom Burns. — London [etc.] : Macmillan, 1977. — xviii,313p : ill ; 23cm. — (Edinburgh studies in sociology)
Index.
ISBN 0-333-19720-8 : £8.95
(B77-21700)

301.16'1 — Mass media. Influence of American media & British media
Tunstall, Jeremy. The media are American : Anglo-American media in the world / [by] Jeremy Tunstall. — London : Constable, 1977. — 352p,leaf of plate,[12]p of plates : ill, facsims, ports ; 23cm. — (Communication and society)
Bibl.: p.315-342. — Index.
ISBN 0-09-460260-3 : £6.00
ISBN 0-09-461510-1 Pbk : £2.95
(B77-33615)

301.16'1 — Mass media. Social aspects
Gurevitch, Michael. The media : contexts of study / [prepared for the Open University, Mass Communication and Society Course Team by Michael Gurevitch, Carrie Roberts and James Curran]. — [Milton Keynes] : Open University Press, [1977]. — 46,68p : ill, facsims ; 21x30cm. — (Social sciences, a third level course : mass communication and society ; block 1, units 1-2) (DE353 ; 1-2)
With answers. — Bibl.
ISBN 0-335-07240-2 Pbk : Unpriced
(B77-29184)

301.16'1 — Newspapers with British imprints. Contents. *Research reports*
McQuail, Denis. Analysis of newspaper content : a report ... / by Denis McQuail. — London : H.M.S.O., [1977]. — xi,364p : form ; 24cm. — (Great Britain. Royal Commission on the Press. Research series ; 4)
ISBN 0-10-168104-6 Pbk : £5.25
(B77-23117)

301.16'1 — Popular arts. Influence of mass media. *United States. Readings*
Mass media and the popular arts / [compiled by] Fredric Rissover, David C. Birch. — 2nd ed. — New York ; London [etc.] : McGraw-Hill, 1977. — xviii,494p : ill, facsims ; 23cm.
Previous ed.: New York : McGraw-Hill, 1971. — Bibl.: p.458-473. — Index.
ISBN 0-07-052950-7 Pbk : £5.95
(B77-26793)

301.16'1 — Readers. Influence of printed media
Zimet, Sara Goodman. Print and prejudice / [by] Sara Goodman Zimet ; with an additional chapter by Mary Hoffman. — London : Hodder and Stoughton [for] the United Kingdom Reading Association, 1976. — 144p ; 22cm. — (Open University. Set books) (Teaching of reading monographs)
Bibl.: p.122-136. — Index.
ISBN 0-340-21026-5 Pbk : £1.45
(B77-06479)

301.16'1 — Society. Effects of telephones
The **social** impact of the telephone / Ithiel de Sola Pool, editor. — Cambridge, Mass. ; London : M.I.T. Press, 1977. — x,502p : ill, facsims, maps ; 24cm. — (Massachusetts Institute of Technology. MIT bicentennial studies ; 1)
Bibl. — Index.
ISBN 0-262-16066-8 : £11.20
(B77-26794)

301.16'1 — Society. Role of mass media. Political aspects
Open University. *Mass Communication and Society Course Team.* The study of culture / Open University [Mass Communication and Society Course Team]. — [Milton Keynes] : Open University Press.
1. — [1977]. — 72,77p : ill, ports ; 21x30cm. — (Social sciences, a third level course : mass communication and society ; block 2, units 3-4) (DE353 ; 3-4)
With answers. — Bibl.
ISBN 0-335-07241-0 Pbk : Unpriced
(B77-26795)

2. — [1977]. — 75,61p : ill, facsims ; 21x30cm. — (Social sciences, a third level course : mass communication and society ; block 2, units 5-6) (DE353 ; 5-6)
With answers. — Bibl.
ISBN 0-335-07242-9 Pbk : Unpriced
(B77-26796)

301.16'1 — Television services. Social aspects. *Great Britain*
Baggaley, Jon. Dynamics of television / [by] Jon Baggaley, Steve Duck. — Farnborough, Hants. : Saxon House, 1976. — xv,180,[1]p : ill ; 24cm.
Bibl. — Index.
ISBN 0-566-00124-1 : £6.50
(B77-00030)

301.16'1 — Television services. Social aspects. *United States*
Aspen Program on Communications and Society. *Workshop on Television.* Television as a cultural force / [the Aspen Program's Workshop on Television] ; [edited by Richard Adler, Douglass Cater]. — New York [etc.] ; London : Praeger [for] the Aspen Institute Program on Communications and Society, 1976. — [7],199p ; 24cm. — (Praeger special studies in US economic, social and political issues)
'This volume is the second collection of essays to come from the Aspen Program's Workshop on Television' - p.1. — Bibl.: p.175-184. — Index.
ISBN 0-275-23180-1 : £12.75
ISBN 0-915436-19-1 Pbk : Unpriced
(B77-12300)

301.16'1 — United States. Politics. Attitudes of society. Influence of television programmes: News programmes
Diamond, Edwin. The tin kazoo : television, politics and the news / [by] Edwin Diamond. — Cambridge, Mass. ; London : M.I.T. Press, 1977. — xvi,271p : ill ; 21cm.
Originally published: 1975. — Index.
ISBN 0-262-54032-0 Pbk : £3.40
(B77-26797)

301.16'1 — Women. Portrayal by mass media. *Feminist viewpoints*
Is this your life? : images of women in the media / edited by Josephine King and Mary Stott ; illustrated by Liz Mackie. — London : Quartet Books [for] Virago, 1977. — [8],199p : ill ; 20cm.
Index.
ISBN 0-7043-3804-1 Pbk : £1.95
(B77-10172)

301.16'1'071141 — Universities. *Great Britain. Open University. Curriculum subjects: Social aspects of mass media. Courses: Mass communication and society*
Course guide / prepared for the [Open University] Course Team by Michael Gurevitch. — [Milton Keynes] ([Walton Hall, Milton Keynes MK7 6AA]) : [Open University], 1977. — 15p ; 30cm. — (Social sciences, a third level course : mass communication and society) (DE353 ; G)
Sd : Unpriced
(B77-14053)

301.16'1'072041 — Mass media. Research in higher education institutions in Great Britain. *Directories*
Current British research on mass media and mass communication : register of ongoing and recently completed research. — Leicester (Leicester Documentation Centre for Mass Communication Research, Centre for Mass Communication Research, University of Leicester, 104 Regent Rd, Leicester) : C. Ellis. 1976, June / [compiled by Connie Ellis]. — [1976]. — [5],74p ; 30cm.
Pierced for binder.
Ls : £1.50
(B77-32416)

301.16'1'08 — Society. Role of mass media. *Readings*
Mass communication and society / edited by James Curran, Michael Gurevitch, Janet Woollacott, assistant editors ... [others]. — London : Edward Arnold [for] the Open University Press, 1977. — ix,479p : 1 ill ; 22cm. — (Open University. Set books)
Bibl. — Index.
ISBN 0-7131-5940-5 Pbk : £3.50
(B77-20030)

301.16'1'0941 — Mass media. *Great Britain. Lists. For advertising*
Bill Gibbs-PNA Group. Editorial media analysis : EMA : a data bank of editorial contacts on trade, consumer, broadcasting and general news media for the United Kingdom ... : the media selection system of the Bill Gibbs-PNA Group press distribution services. — London (13 Curtain Rd, EC2A 3LT) : The Group, [1976]. — 1v. ; 35cm.
Tab indexed. — In binder. — 297 leaves on publication (50 leaves printed on both sides). — Updated every calendar month.
ISBN 0-905873-00-9 Ls : £29.00
(B77-05877)

301.16'1'0941 — Mass media. *Great Britain. Periodicals*
The **media** reporter. — Sale (39 Legh Rd, Sale, Cheshire M33 2SU) : Brennan Publications. Vol.1, no.1- ; Autumn 1976-. — 1976-. — ill, facsims, ports ; 26cm.
Quarterly. — 52p. in 1st issue.
Sd : £1.00
ISSN 0309-0256
(B77-03933)

301.16'1'0941 — Mass media. Political aspects. *Great Britain*
Whale, John. The politics of the media / [by] John Whale. — [London] : Fontana, 1977. — 176p ; 18cm. — (Political issues of modern Britain)
Also published: Manchester : Manchester University Press, 1977. — Bibl.: p.169-170. — Index.
ISBN 0-00-634881-5 Pbk : £1.00
(B77-30983)

301.16'1'0943 — Mass media. *German speaking countries, to 1975*
Sandford, John. The mass media of the German-speaking countries / by John Sandford. — London : Wolff, 1976. — xii,235p ; 23cm.
Bibl.: p.222-224. — Index.
ISBN 0-85496-203-4 : £5.25
(B77-03934)

301.16'1'0944 — Mass media. *France. Secondary school texts*
Bate, Michèle. The media in France / [by] Michèle Bate. — London : Harrap, 1977. — [1],16,[1]p : ill, facsims, map, ports ; 14x22cm. — ([Destination France] : life French style)
ISBN 0-245-53052-5 Sd : £0.35
(B77-15093)

301.16'1'0973 — Mass media. *United States*
Agee, Warren Kendall. Introduction to mass communications. — 5th ed. / [by] Warren K. Agee, Phillip H. Ault, Edwin Emery. — New York [etc.] ; London : Harper and Row, 1976. — xiv,469p : ill, facsims, ports ; 23cm.
Previous ed. / by Edwin Emery, Phillip H. Ault and Warren K. Agee. New York : Dodd, Mead, 1973. — Bibl.: p.418-453. — Index.
ISBN 0-06-041909-1 Pbk : Unpriced
(B77-08227)

301.16'1'0973 — Mass media. *United States, to 1975*
Read, William H. America's mass media merchants / [by] William H. Read. — Baltimore ; London : Johns Hopkins University Press, 1976. — xi,209p ; 24cm.
Index.
ISBN 0-8018-1851-6 : £8.75
(B77-23118)

301.16'1'0994 — Mass media. *Australia. Secondary school texts*
Dwyer, Barry. Meeting the media : a trip around the mighty modern mass media of entertainment, information, advertisement in order to discover what on earth they are up to / [by] Barry Dwyer, Bruce Thomson ; design and illustration by Daphne Howie, project editor R.D. Washe. — Revised ed. — Sydney ; London [etc.] : Reed Education, 1976. — [3], 61p : ill, forms ; 25cm.
This ed. originally published: 1974.
ISBN 0-589-09134-4 Pbk : £2.15
(B77-20906)

301.16'2 — Children. Influence of television programmes
Howe, Michael John Anthony. Television and children / [by] Michael J.A. Howe. — London : New University Education, 1977. — 157p ; 23cm.
Index.
ISBN 0-85157-517-x : £3.75
(B77-12301)

301.16'2 — Children. Influence of television programmes. *Readings*
Children and television / edited by Ray Brown. — London : Collier Macmillan, 1976. — 368p : ill ; 23cm.
Bibl. — Index.
ISBN 0-02-977290-7 : £7.50
(B77-02039)

301.16'2 — Pre-school children. Influence of television programmes
Dunn, Gwen. The box in the corner : television and the under-fives : a study / by Gwen Dunn. — London [etc.] : Macmillan, 1977. — x,160p ; 23cm.
Bibl.: p.158-160.
ISBN 0-333-19222-2 : £7.95
ISBN 0-333-19223-0 Pbk : £2.95
(B77-20907)

301.16'2 — Society. Effects of violence in cinema films & television programmes. *Reviews of research*
Brody, Stephen Robert. Screen violence and film censorship : a review of research / by Stephen Brody. — London : H.M.S.O., 1977. — vii, 176p ; 25cm. — (Great Britain. Home Office. Research studies ; no.40) (Great Britain. Home Office. Research Unit. Reports)
Bibl.: p.147-169. — Index.
ISBN 0-11-340680-0 Pbk : £2.75
(B77-28388)

301.18 — Social groups
Gaskell, George. Groups / prepared for the [Open University, Social Psychology] Course Team by George Gaskell and Philip Sealy. — Milton Keynes : Open University Press, 1976. — 81p : ill(some col) ; 30cm. — (Social sciences, a third level course : social psychology ; block 13) (D305 ; block 13(26-29))
Bibl.: p.78-81.
ISBN 0-335-07113-9 Pbk : Unpriced
(B77-02770)

301.18 — Social groups. Power
Power and control : social structures and their transformation / edited by Tom R. Burns and Walter Buckley. — London [etc.] : Sage Publications [for] the International Sociological Association, 1976. — [5],290p ; 23cm. — (Sage studies in international sociology ; 6)
Bibl.
ISBN 0-8039-9959-3 : £6.00
ISBN 0-8039-9978-x Pbk : £3.00
Primary classification 301.15
(B77-10170)

301.18'31'09 — Voluntary associations, to 1900. *Sociological perspectives*
Ross, Jack C. An assembly of good fellows : voluntary associations in history / [by] Jack C. Ross. — Westport, Conn. ; London : Greenwood Press, 1976. — xiii,325,[1]p ; 22cm.
Bibl.: p.283-295. — Index.
ISBN 0-8371-8586-6 : £12.75
(B77-17919)

301.18'32 — Industries. Personnel. Behaviour. Regulation. *Sociological perspectives*
Loveridge, Ray. Socio-cultural effects on regulation / prepared for the [Open University, Industrial Relations] Course Team by Ray Loveridge. — Milton Keynes : Open University Press, 1976. — 61p : ill(incl 1 col) ; 30cm. — (A post-experience course : industrial relations ; unit 11) (P881 ; unit 11)
With answers to self-assessment questions. — Bibl.: p.60-61.
ISBN 0-335-00061-4 Sd : £1.80
(B77-03935)

301.18'32 — Interorganisational relations. *Readings*
Interorganizational relations : selected readings / edited by William M. Evan. — Harmondsworth [etc.] : Penguin, 1976. — 442p : ill ; 19cm. — (Penguin education) (Penguin modern management readings)
Bibl.: p.423-427. — Index.
ISBN 0-14-080924-4 Pbk : £1.75
(B77-00613)

301.18'32 — Man. Organisational behaviour. *Sociological perspectives*
Herbert, Theodore T. Dimensions of organizational behavior / [by] Theodore T. Herbert. — New York : Macmillan ; London : Collier Macmillan, 1976. — xiii,530p : ill ; 24cm.
Index.
ISBN 0-02-979960-0 Pbk : £5.95
(B77-23119)

Perspectives on behavior in organizations / edited by J. Richard Hackman, Edward E. Lawler III, Lyman W. Porter. — New York ; London [etc.] : McGraw-Hill, 1977. — x,486p : ill ; 24cm.
Bibl.
ISBN 0-07-025413-3 Pbk : £7.45
(B77-22353)

Porter, Lyman W. Behavior in organisations / [by] Lyman W. Porter, Edward E. Lawler III, J. Richard Hackman. — Tokyo ; London [etc.] : McGraw-Hill Kogakusha, [1977]. — xiv, 561p : ill, form ; 21cm. — (McGraw-Hill series in psychology) (McGraw-Hill series in management)
Originally published: New York ; London : McGraw-Hill, 1975. — Bibl.: p.525-547. — Index.
ISBN 0-07-085564-1 Pbk : £6.25
(B77-23120)

301.18'32 — Organisations
Critical issues in organizations / edited by Stewart Clegg and David Dunkerley. — London [etc.] : Routledge and Kegan Paul, 1977. — vii,109p ; 24cm.
'Routledge direct editions'. — Bibl.: p.99-106. — Index.
ISBN 0-7100-8506-0 Pbk : £3.25
(B77-20031)

Evan, William Martin. Organization theory : structures, systems, and environments / [by] William M. Evan. — New York ; London [etc.] : Wiley, [1977]. — xv,312p : ill ; 24cm.
'A Wiley-Interscience publication'. — Published in the United States: 1976. — Index.
ISBN 0-471-01512-1 : £10.30
(B77-10173)

301.18'32 — Organisations. *Sociological perspectives*
Hall, Richard Hammond. Organizations : structure and process / [by] Richard H. Hall. — 2nd ed. — Englewood Cliffs ; London [etc.] : Prentice-Hall, 1977. — xi,356p : ill ; 24cm.
Previous ed.: 1972. — Index.
ISBN 0-13-642025-7 : £10.35
(B77-33063)

Kilmann, Ralph H. Social systems design : normative theory and the MAPS design technology / [by] Ralph H. Kilmann. — New York ; Oxford [etc.] : North-Holland Publishing Co., 1977. — xv,327p : ill, 2 forms ; 24cm.
Bibl.: p.295-317. — Index.
ISBN 0-7204-8607-6 : £15.48
(B77-24702)

301.18'32 — Organisations. Analysis. Methodology
Rowbottom, Ralph. Social analysis : a collaborative method of gaining usable scientific knowledge of social institutions / [by] Ralph Rowbottom. — London : Heinemann Educational, 1977. — xii,178p : ill ; 24cm.
Bibl.: p.169-174. — Index.
ISBN 0-435-82772-3 : £6.50
ISBN 0-435-82773-1 Pbk : £2.80
(B77-31696)

301.18'32 — Organisations. Effectiveness. Analysis
Levinson, Harry. Organizational diagnosis / [by] Harry Levinson, with Janice Molinari and Andrew G. Spohn. — Cambridge, Mass. ; London : Harvard University Press, 1976 [i.e.1977]. — xviii,557p : forms ; 22cm.
Originally published: Cambridge, Mass. : Harvard University Press, 1972. — Bibl.: p.544-557.
ISBN 0-674-64345-3 : £16.35
ISBN 0-674-64346-1 Pbk : £6.00
(B77-12861)

301.18'32 — Organisations. Key factors. Analysis. *Conference proceedings*
A **conference** on key factor analysis : a logic leading to social accountability : papers presented at a conference jointly sponsored by the Illinois Regional Medical Program and the Southern Illinois University School of Medicine / edited by Irwin M. Jarett and Patricia A. Brady. — Carbondale [etc.] : Southern Illinois University Press ; London [etc.] : Feffer and Simons for the Program and the School, 1976. — xii,438p : ill, map ; 24cm.
Bibl.
ISBN 0-8093-0793-6 : Unpriced
ISBN 0-8093-0795-2 Pbk : Unpriced
(B77-11577)

301.18'32 — Organisations. Organisation climate
Steele, Fritz. The feel of the work place : understanding and improving organization climate / [by] Fritz Steele, Stephen Jenks. — Reading, Mass. ; London [etc.] : Addison-Wesley, 1977. — x,194p : ill ; 21cm.
Bibl.: p.191-194.
ISBN 0-201-07213-0 Pbk : £6.40
(B77-33064)

301.18'32 — Organisations. Personnel. Behaviour. *Case studies*
Silverman, David. Organizational work : the language of grading, the grading of language / [by] David Silverman, Jill Jones. — London : Collier Macmillan, 1976. — [8],197p ; 23cm.
Bibl.: p.183-185. — Index.
ISBN 0-02-977280-x : £8.30
(B77-03380)

301.18'32 — Organisations. Personnel. Behaviour. *Case studies. For management*
DuBrin, Andrew J. Casebook of organizational behavior / by Andrew J. DuBrin. — New York ; Oxford [etc.] : Pergamon, 1977. — xi, 326p ; 24cm. — (Pergamon international library)
Bibl.: p.287-326.
ISBN 0-08-020503-8 : £7.00
ISBN 0-08-020502-x Pbk : £4.00
(B77-25390)

301.18'32 — Organisations. Structure
Organizational behaviour in its context : the Aston programme III / edited by D.S. Pugh, R.L. Payne. — Farnborough, Hants. : Saxon House, 1977. — xv,189p : ill ; 24cm.
Bibl.: p.176-184. — Index.
ISBN 0-566-00159-4 : £8.50
(B77-23121)

301.18'32 — Organisations. Theories
Hicks, Herbert Gosa. Organizations : theory and behavior / [by] Herbert G. Hicks, C. Ray Gullett, in collaboration with ... [others]. — Tokyo ; London [etc.] : McGraw-Hill, 1975. — xvii,446p : ill ; 21cm. — (McGraw-Hill series in management)
Bibl. — Index.
ISBN 0-07-085314-2 Pbk : £5.20
(B77-21702)

301.18'5 — Group discussions
Harnack, R Victor. Group discussion : theory and technique. — 2nd ed. / by R. Victor Harnack, Thorrel B. Fest, Barbara Schindler Jones. — Englewood Cliffs ; London [etc.] : Prentice-Hall, 1977. — xv,299p : ill, forms ; 24cm.
Previous ed.: / by R. Victor Harnack and Thorrel B. Fest. New York : Appleton-Century-Crofts, 1964. — Bibl.: - Index.
ISBN 0-13-365247-5 : £10.35
(B77-33616)

301.18'5 — Group dynamics
Shaw, Marvin Evert. Group dynamics : the psychology of small group behavior / [by] Marvin E. Shaw. — 2nd ed. — New York ; London [etc.] : McGraw-Hill, 1976. — xv, 464p : ill ; 24cm. — (McGraw-Hill series in psychology)
Previous ed.: 1971. — Bibl.: p.409-443. — Index.
ISBN 0-07-056501-5 : £10.45
(B77-17296)

301.18'5 — Group dynamics. Theories. *For welfare workers*
Heap, Ken. Group theory for social workers : an introduction / by Ken Heap ; [translated from the Norwegian by the author]. — Oxford [etc.] : Pergamon, 1977. — xiv,252p : 1 ill ; 22cm. — (Pergamon international library : social work series)
Translation of: 'Gruppeteori for sosialairbeidere'. Oslo : Universitetsforlaget, 1977?. — Bibl.: p.236-246. — Index.
ISBN 0-08-018956-3 : £7.50
ISBN 0-08-018955-5
(B77-29185)

301.18'5 — Small groups. Communication & decision making
Fisher, B Aubrey. Small group decision making : communication and the group process / [by] B. Aubrey Fisher. — New York [etc.] ; London : McGraw-Hill, [1976]. — xiii,264p : ill ; 24cm. — (McGraw-Hill series in speech)
Published in the United States: 1974. — Bibl.: p.251-258. — Index.
ISBN 0-07-021090-x : £7.65
(B77-01171)

301.2 — CULTURAL PROCESSES
Keesing, Roger Martin. Cultural anthropology : a contemporary perspective / [by] Roger M. Keesing. — New York ; London [etc.] : Holt, Rinehart and Winston, 1976. — xiii,637p : ill, geneal tables, maps, plan ; 25cm.
Bibl.: p.573-618. — Index.
ISBN 0-03-089424-7 : £10.25
(B77-02771)

301.2 — Anthropology
Beals, Ralph Leon. An introduction to anthropology. — 5th ed. / [by] Ralph L. Beals, Harry Hoijer, Alan R. Beals. — New York : Macmillan ; London : Collier Macmillan, 1977. — xviii,749p,[4]leaves of plates : ill(some col), forms, maps(chiefly col), col plan ; 26cm.
Maps on lining papers. — Previous ed.: / by Ralph L. Beals, Harry Hoijer. 1971. — Bibl. — Index.
ISBN 0-02-307450-7 : £10.50
ISBN 0-02-979310-6 Pbk : £5.85
(B77-20908)

Benderly, Beryl Lieff. Discovering culture : an introduction to anthropology / [by] Beryl Lieff Benderly, Mary F. Gallagher, John M. Young. — New York ; London [etc.] : D. Van Nostrand, 1977. — vii,290p : ill, ports ; 24cm.
Bibl.: p.271-275. — Index.
ISBN 0-442-20694-1 Pbk : Unpriced
(B77-21703)

Friedl, John. Anthropology, the study of people / [by] John Friedl, John E. Pfeiffer. — New York [etc.] ; London : Harper's College Press, 1977. — xvi,558p : ill, facsim, maps, plan, ports ; 25cm.
Bibl. — Index.
ISBN 0-06-167412-5 : £11.20
(B77-29938)

Sahlins, Marshall David. Culture and practical reason / [by] Marshall Sahlins. — Chicago ; London : University of Chicago Press, [1977]. — xi,252p : ill ; 23cm.
Published in the United States: 1976. — Bibl.: p.223-240. — Index.
ISBN 0-226-73359-9 : £7.35
(B77-12862)

301.2 — Anthropology. Related to archaeology
Archaeology and anthropology : areas of mutual interest / edited by Matthew Spriggs. — Oxford : British Archaeological Reports, 1977. — [8],176p : ill, plans ; 30cm. — (British archaeological reports : supplementary series ; 19)
Bibl.
ISBN 0-904531-63-5 Pbk : £3.30
Also classified at 930'.1
(B77-20909)

301.2 — Culture
Approaches to popular culture / edited by C.W.E. Bigsby. — London : Edward Arnold, 1976. — viii,280p : ill ; 23cm.
Bibl. — Index.
ISBN 0-7131-5834-4 : £5.95
ISBN 0-7131-5835-2 Pbk : £2.95
(B77-02772)

301.2 — International relations
Home, Alec Douglas-Home, *Baron.* Diplomacy, détente and the democracies : lectures to mark the Bicentenary of the American Revolution, and in honour of David K.E. Bruce, given in the University of Keele / by the Lord Home of the Hirsel, Roy Jenkins, George W. Ball ; edited with a foreword and a memoir on David Bruce by D.K. Adams. — Keele ([University of Keele, Newcastle, Staffs. ST5 5BG]) : David Bruce Centre for American Studies, 1976. — 48p ; 21cm. — (University of Keele. David Bruce Centre for American Studies. Lectures ; 1976)
ISBN 0-9505646-0-5 Sd : £1.25
(B77-13509)

301.2 — International relations, 1900-1976. Racial aspects
Tinker, Hugh. Race, conflict and the international order : from empire to United Nations / [by] Hugh Tinker. — London [etc.] : Macmillan, 1977. — [7],157p : maps ; 23cm. — (The making of the 20th century)
Bibl.: p.140-145. — Index.
ISBN 0-333-19664-3 : £5.95
ISBN 0-333-19665-1 Pbk : £2.50
(B77-29186)

301.2 — Man. Sociobiological aspects. *Anthropological perspectives*
Sahlins, Marshall David. The use and abuse of biology : an anthropological critique of sociobiology / [by] Marshall Sahlins. — London : Tavistock Publications, 1977. — xv, 120p ; 19cm.
Originally published: Ann Arbor : University of Michigan Press, 1976. — Bibl.: p.115-120.
ISBN 0-422-76270-9 Pbk : £1.95
(B77-23123)

301.2 — Primitive peoples. Relations with Western world, to 1976
Sinclair, Andrew. The savage : a history of misunderstanding / [by] Andrew Sinclair. — London : Weidenfeld and Nicolson, 1977. — [7],168p ; 24cm.
Index.
ISBN 0-297-77226-0 : £5.00
Also classified at 301.29'181'2
(B77-14560)

301.2 — Social anthropology
Ember, Carol R. Cultural anthropology / [by] Carol R. Ember, Melvin Ember. — 2nd ed. — Englewood Cliffs ; London [etc.] : Prentice-Hall, 1977. — xviii,361p : ill(some col), facsim, col maps, ports ; 24cm.
Previous ed.: New York : Appleton-Century-Crofts, 1973. — Bibl. — Index.
ISBN 0-13-195198-x Pbk : £7.95
(B77-16736)

Hoebel, Edward Adamson. Cultural and social anthropology / [by] E. Adamson Hoebel, Everett L. Frost. — New York ; London [etc.] : McGraw-Hill, 1976. — v,442p : ill, maps ; 24cm.
... 'built on pertinent chapters of Hoebel's "Anthropology" [4th ed. New York : McGraw-Hill, 1972] with appropriate updating, reorganization, and newly written sections ...' - Preface. — Bibl. — Index.
ISBN 0-07-029145-4 Pbk : £8.25
(B77-03936)

Lisitzky, Gene. Four ways of being human : an introduction to anthropology / by Gene Lisitzky ; illustrated by C.B. Falls. — Harmondsworth [etc.] : Penguin, 1976. — 303p : ill ; 20cm.
Originally published: New York : Viking Press, 1956. — Index.
ISBN 0-14-004391-8 Pbk : Unpriced
(B77-08773)

301.2 — Social anthropology. *Marxist viewpoints*
Godelier, Maurice. Perspectives in Marxist anthropology / [by] Maurice Godelier ; translated [from the French] by Robert Brain. — Cambridge [etc.] : Cambridge University Press, 1977. — v,243p ; 24cm. — (Cambridge studies in social anthropology ; 18 ISSN 0068-6794)
'Translation of some of the essays from the author's "Horizon, trajets marxistes en anthropologie"' - Library of Congress Cataloging in Publication Data.
ISBN 0-521-21311-8 : £9.20
ISBN 0-521-29098-8 Pbk : £3.00
(B77-16191)

301.2'01 — Social anthropology. Theories
Bourdieu, Pierre. Outline of a theory of practice / [by] Pierre Bourdieu ; translated [from the French] by Richard Nice. — Cambridge [etc.] : Cambridge University Press, 1977. — viii,248p : ill ; 24cm. — (Cambridge studies in social anthropology ; 16)
Translation of: 'Esquisse d'une théorie de la pratique, précédé de trois études d'ethnologie kabyle'. Geneva : Librairie Droz, 1972. — Index.
ISBN 0-521-21178-6 : £9.00
ISBN 0-521-29164-x Pbk : £2.95
Also classified at 301.29'65'3
(B77-26798)

301.2'01'8 — Anthropology. Methodology. *Exercises, worked examples*
Hunter, David Emanuel. Doing anthropology : a student-centered approach to cultural anthropology / [by] David E. Hunter, MaryAnn B. Foley. — New York [etc.] ; London : Harper and Row, 1976. — xiii,267p : ill ; 28cm.
Pierced for binder. — Bibl.
ISBN 0-06-043011-7 Pbk : £4.45
(B77-07805)

301.2'01'82 — Anthropology. Statistical methods
Thomas, David Hurst. Figuring anthropology : first principles of probability and statistics / [by] David Hurst Thomas. — New York ; London [etc.] : Holt, Rinehart and Winston, 1976. — xi,532p : ill ; 24cm.
With answers to odd-numbered exercises. — Bibl.: p.515-524. — Index.
ISBN 0-03-002856-6 : £8.00
(B77-03381)

301.2'07 — Anthropology. Information sources. *For teaching. Serials*
Royal Anthropological Institute. Teachers' resource guide / Royal Anthropological Institute. — [London] : [The Institute]. 1976-7. — [1976]. — [3],74p ; 30cm.
Bibl.: p.56-74. — List of films: p.24-35.
Sp : £1.50
(B77-29939)

301.2'08 — Anthropology. *Essays*
Hallowell, Alfred Irving. Contributions to anthropology : selected papers of A. Irving Hallowell / [edited by Raymond D. Fogelson] ; with introductions by Raymond D. Fogelson ... [et al.]. — Chicago ; London : University of Chicago Press, 1976. — xvii,534p : port ; 24cm.
Facsimile reprints. — Bibl.
ISBN 0-226-31414-6 : £16.35
(B77-01172)

301.2'08 — Cultural processes. *Readings*
Exploring the ways of mankind : a text-casebook / [edited by] Walter Goldschmidt. — 3rd ed. — New York ; London [etc.] : Holt, Rinehart and Winston, 1977. — x,566p : ill ; 24cm.
Previous ed.: 1971. — Index.
ISBN 0-03-089948-6 Pbk : £6.50
(B77-24004)

The **production** of culture / edited by Richard A. Peterson. — Beverly Hills ; London : Sage Publications, 1976. — 144p ; 22cm. — (Sage contemporary social science issues ; 33)
Bibl.
ISBN 0-8039-0734-6 Pbk : £3.45
(B77-14561)

301.2'08 — Culture. *Anthropological perspectives. Readings*
Ideas of culture : sources and uses / edited by Frederick C. Gamst, Edward Norbeck. — New York [etc.] ; London : Holt, Rinehart and Winston, 1976. — x,353p : ill ; 24cm.
Bibl. — Index.
ISBN 0-03-015866-4 : £9.00
(B77-03937)

301.2'08 — Culture. *Sociological perspectives. Essays*
Goldmann, Lucien. Cultural creation in modern society / [by] Lucien Goldmann ; introduction by William Mayrl ; translated [from the French] by Bart Grahl ; bibliography and appendices compiled by Ileana Rodriguez and Marc Zimmerman. — Oxford : Blackwell, 1977. — [2],173p ; 23cm.
Translation of: 'La création culturelle dans la société moderne'. Paris : Denoël-Gonthier, 1971. — Bibl.: p.146-173.
ISBN 0-631-18220-9 : £7.00 : CIP rev.
(B77-17297)

301.2'08 — Culture, to 1926. *Marxist viewpoints. Extracts from periodicals. Early works*
Trotsky, Leon. Culture & socialism / [by] Leon Trotsky ; [translated from the Russian by Brian Pearce]. Manifesto, Towards a free revolutionary art / [by André Breton and Diego Rivera in collaboration with Leon Trotsky ; translated by Dwight Macdonald]. — London : New Park Publications, 1975. — 36p : facsim, ports ; 21cm.
Cover title: Culture & socialism ; and, A manifesto, Art and revolution. — '[This collection] reprinted from "Labour Review", Autumn 1962' - title page verso. — '["Culture and socialism" translated] from the version printed in Vol.XXI of Leon Trotsky's "Works", published [in Moscow] in 1927' - note. — '["Manifesto, Towards a free revolutionary art"] appeared [in English] in the New York "Partisan Review" for Autumn 1938' - note.
ISBN 0-902030-67-1 Sd : £0.35
(B77-01944)

301.2'08 — Social anthropology. *Readings*
Man's many ways / [edited by] Richard A. Gould. — New York [etc.] ; London : Harper and Row, 1973. — xiii,379p : ill, maps ; 24cm.
Consists mostly of articles which have appeared in 'Natural history' magazine.
ISBN 0-06-042435-4 Pbk : Unpriced
(B77-20910)

301.2'08 — Social anthropology. Structuralism. *Essays*
Lévi-Strauss, Claude. Structural anthropology / [by] Claude Lévi-Strauss ; translated from the French by Claire Jacobson and Brooke Grundfest Schoepf. — Harmondsworth [etc.] : Penguin, 1977. — xxi,410p,[12]p of plates : ill ; 21cm. — (Peregrine books)
This translation originally published: New York : Basic Books, 1963 ; London : Allen Lane, 1968. — Translation of: 'Anthropologie structurale'. Paris : Plon, 1958. — Bibl.: p.385-398. — Index.
ISBN 0-14-055110-7 Pbk : £2.80
(B77-30984)

Lévi-Strauss, Claude. Structural anthropology / [by] Claude Lévi-Strauss. — London : Allen Lane.
Vol.2 / translated from the French by Monique Layton. — 1977. — xv,383p ; 24cm.
Translation of: 'Anthropologie structurale'. 2. Paris : Plon, 1973. — Bibl.: p.363-372. — Index.
ISBN 0-7139-1021-6 : £6.50
(B77-09510)

301.2'09 — Social anthropology. Theories, to 1976
Garbarino, Merwyn Stephens. Sociocultural theory in anthropology : a short history / [by] Merwyn S. Garbarino. — New York ; London [etc.] : Holt, Rinehart and Winston, 1977. — xiii,114p : ports ; 24cm. — (Basic anthropology units)
Bibl.: p.105-110. — Index.
ISBN 0-03-013021-2 Pbk : £3.25
(B77-22354)

301.2'1 — Age-group systems. *Anthropological perspectives*
Stewart, Frank Henderson. Fundamentals of age-group systems / [by] Frank Henderson Stewart. — New York [etc.] ; London : Academic Press, 1977. — xv,381p : ill, maps ; 24cm. — (Studies in anthropology)
Text on lining papers. — Bibl.: p.347-369. — Index.
ISBN 0-12-670150-4 : £18.45
(B77-23124)

301.2'1 — Bilingualism. Social aspects. *Conference proceedings*
Bilingualism : psychological, social, and educational implications / edited by Peter A. Hornby. — New York [etc.] ; London : Academic Press, 1977. — xi,167p ; 24cm.
'... [proceedings] of a Canadian-American conference ... that was held on the Plattsburgh Campus of the State University of New York, March 12-13, 1976' - Preface. — Bibl. — Index.
ISBN 0-12-356350-x : £6.75
(B77-23125)

301.2'1 — Children. Language skills. Social aspects. *Conference proceedings*
American Anthropological Association. *Annual Meeting, Mexico City, 1974.* Child discourse / edited by Susan Ervin-Tripp, Claudia Mitchell-Kernan. — New York [etc.] ; London : Academic Press, 1977. — xii,266p : ill ; 24cm. — (Language, thought and culture : advances in the study of cognition)
'... a symposium on child discourse at the Annual Meeting of the American Anthropological Association in Mexico City in November 1974' - Preface. — Bibl.: p.245-258. — Index.
ISBN 0-12-241950-2 : £6.75
(B77-26799)

301.2'1 — Cults, to 1975
The **supernatural**. — [United States] : Danbury Press ; London : Aldus Books.
Previous control number ISBN 0-490-00347-8.
Strange cults / by Angus Hall. — 1976. — 144p : ill(some col), facsims, ports(some col) ; 27cm.
ISBN 0-490-00342-7 : £3.25
(B77-00614)

301.2'1 — Culture. Symbols. *New Mexico. Santa Fe. Anthropological perspectives*
Grimes, Ronald L. Symbol and conquest : public ritual and drama in Santa Fe, New Mexico / [by] Ronald L. Grimes. — Ithaca ; London : Cornell University Press, 1976 [i.e. 1977]. — 281,[1]p : ill, coat of arms, map ; 22cm. — (Symbol, myth and ritual series)
Published in the United States: 1976. — Bibl.: p.271-276. — Index.
ISBN 0-8014-1037-1 : £14.00
(B77-15094)

301.2'1 — Customs. *Anthropological perspectives*
Harris, Marvin. Cows, pigs, wars & witches : the riddles of culture / [by] Marvin Harris. — [London] : Fontana, 1977. — 192p ; 18cm.
Originally published: New York : Random House, 1974 ; London : Hutchinson, 1975. — Bibl.: p.186-192.
ISBN 0-00-634111-x Pbk : £0.80
(B77-09511)

301.2'1 — Ethnocentrism. *Developed countries*
Sachs, Ignacy. The discovery of the Third World / [by] Ignacy Sachs ; [translated from the French by Michael Fineberg]. — Cambridge, Mass. ; London : M.I.T. Press, [1977]. — xiii,287p : ill ; 21cm.
This translation published in the United States: 1976. — Translation of: 'La découverte du tiers monde'. Paris : Flammarion, 1971.
ISBN 0-262-19145-8 : £11.25
(B77-14054)

301.2'1 — Evil eye. *Anthropological perspectives*
The **evil** eye / Clarence Maloney, editor. — New York ; Guildford : Columbia University Press, 1976. — xxi,335p : ill, map ; 24cm.
Bibl. — Index.
ISBN 0-231-04006-7 : £10.41
(B77-08228)

301.2'1 — Food supply. *Anthropological perspectives*
Oswalt, Wendell Hillman. An anthropological analysis of food-getting technology / [by] Wendell H. Oswalt ; with the assistance of Gloria Mann and Leonn Satterthwait ; illustrated by Patrick Finnerty. — New York ; London [etc.] : Wiley, 1976. — xvii,310p : ill, port ; 24cm.
'A Wiley-Interscience publication'. — Bibl.: p.295-303. — Index.
ISBN 0-471-65729-8 : £13.50
(B77-08229)

301.2'1 — Gaelic language. Isle of Harris usage. *Sociological perspectives*
MacKinnon, Kenneth. Language, education and social processes in a Gaelic community / [by] Kenneth MacKinnon. — London [etc.] : Routledge and Kegan Paul, 1977. — xii,222p : ill, map ; 24cm.
'Routledge direct editions'. — Bibl.: p.208-215. — Index.
ISBN 0-7100-8466-8 Pbk : £4.75
(B77-19222)

301.2'1 — Hallucinogenic drugs. Use by primitive peoples. *Anthropological perspectives*
Dobkin De Rios, Marlene. The wilderness of mind : sacred plants in cross-cultural perspective / [by] Marlene Dobkin de Rios. — Beverly Hills ; London : Sage Publications, 1976. — 79p ; 22cm. — (Sage research papers in the social sciences : cross-cultural studies series ; vol.5, no.90-039)
Bibl.: p.73-78.
ISBN 0-8039-0752-4 Pbk : Unpriced
(B77-20911)

301.2'1 — Honour. *Mediterranean region. Anthropological perspectives. Study regions: Spain. Andalusia*
Pitt-Rivers, Julian Alfred. The fate of Shechem, or, The politics of sex : essays in the anthropology of the Mediterranean / [by] Julian Pitt-Rivers. — Cambridge [etc.] : Cambridge University Press, 1977. — xiv,193p : geneal table ; 24cm. — (Cambridge studies in social anthropology ; no.19)
Index.
ISBN 0-521-21427-0 : £6.95
(B77-17298)

301.2'1 — Indians of Brazil. Archery. *Anthropological perspectives*
Heath, Ernest Gerald. Brazilian Indian archery : a preliminary ethno-toxological study of the archery of the Brazilian Indians / [by] E.G. Heath and Vilma Chiara. — Manchester (Manchester Museum, The University, Manchester M13 9PL) : Simon Archery Foundation, 1977. — xx,188p,xvi p of plates : ill, maps ; 25cm.
Bibl.: p.171-180. — List of films: p.180-181. — Index.
ISBN 0-9503199-1-0 Pbk : Unpriced
(B77-29940)

301.2'1 — Knowledge. *Sociological perspectives*
Barnes, Barry. Interests and the growth of knowledge / [by] Barry Barnes. — London [etc.] : Routledge and Kegan Paul, 1977. — x, 109p ; 24cm.
'Routledge direct editions'. — Bibl.: p.104-106. — Index.
ISBN 0-7100-8669-5 Pbk : £2.95 : CIP rev.
(B77-16737)

301.2'1 — Literacy. Political aspects
The **politics** of literacy / edited by Martin Hoyles. — London : Writers and Readers Publishing Cooperative, 1977. — 21,[1]p ; 21cm.
Bibl.: p.199.
ISBN 0-904613-47-x : £3.95
ISBN 0-904613-28-3 Pbk : £1.50
(B77-28389)

301.2'1 — Man. Adaptation. Related to cognitive styles. *Study examples: Nomadic communities*
Berry, John Widdup. Human ecology and cognitive style : comparative studies in cultural and psychological adaptation / [by] John W. Berry. — [Beverly Hills] : Sage Publications ; New York ; London [etc.] : Distributed by Wiley, 1976. — xiii,242p : ill, map ; 24cm. — (Cross-cultural research and methodology series ; [vol.3])
Bibl.: p.229-242.
ISBN 0-470-15103-x : £12.50
Also classified at 153.4
(B77-03938)

301.2'1 — Maya festivals. *Guatemala. Anthropological perspectives*
Smith, Waldemar R. The fiesta system and economic change / [by] Waldemar R. Smith. — New York ; Guildford : Columbia University Press, 1977. — xi,194p,[12]p of plates : ill, maps ; 24cm.
Bibl.: p.183-190. — Index.
ISBN 0-231-04180-2 : £10.70
(B77-24703)

301.2'1 — Mexicans. National identity, 1531-1813. Religious aspects
Lafaye, Jacques. Quetzalcóatl and Guadalupe : the formation of Mexican national consciousness, 1531-1813 / [by] Jacques Lafaye ; with a foreword by Octavio Paz ; translated [from the French] by Benjamin Keen. — Chicago ; London : University of Chicago Press, 1976. — xxx,336p ; 24cm.
Translation of: 'Quetzalcóatl et Guadalupe'. Paris : Gallimard, 1974. — Index.
ISBN 0-226-46794-5 : £16.50
(B77-08774)

301.2'1 — Nigerian decorative arts: Adamawa decorative arts. *Anthropological perspectives. Study examples: Decorated gourds*
Chappel, T J H. Decorated gourds in north-eastern Nigeria / [by] T.J.H. Chappel. — London (14 West Central St., WC1A 1JH) : Ethnographica [etc.], 1977. — vii,222p,[14]p of plates : ill(some col), map ; 30cm.
Bibl.: p.216-218. — Index.
ISBN 0-905788-02-8 : £20.00
(B77-23126)

301.2'1 — Primitive societies. Folk medicine. *Anthropological perspectives. Conference proceedings*
Social anthropology and medicine / edited by J.B. Loudon. — London [etc.] : Academic Press, 1976. — xxv,600p ; 24cm. — (Association of Social Anthropologists of the Commonwealth. Monographs ; 13)
'... derives mainly from material presented at a conference on social anthropology and medicine ... held at the University of Kent at Canterbury, 5-8 April 1972' - title page verso. — Bibl. — Index.
ISBN 0-12-456350-3 : £7.00
(B77-02040)

301.2'1 — Primitive visual arts. *Anthropological perspectives*
Ethnic and tourist arts : cultural expressions from the Fourth World / Nelson H.H. Graburn, editor. — Berkeley [etc.] ; London : University of California Press, 1976. — xv, 412p,8p of plates : ill(some col), maps, ports ; 23cm.
Bibl.: p.371-393. — Index.
ISBN 0-520-02949-6 : £14.95
(B77-26117)

301.2'1 — Primitive visual arts. Social aspects
Attenborough, David. The tribal eye / [by] David Attenborough. — London : British Broadcasting Corporation, 1976. — 144p,[24]p of plates : chiefly ill(some col), maps, ports(some col) ; 27cm.
Based on the BBC Television series 'The tribal eye'. — Bibl.: p.142. — Index.
ISBN 0-563-17005-0 : £7.00
(B77-00031)

301.2'1 — Social anthropology. Role of linguistics, ca 1850-1976
Crick, Malcolm. Explorations in language and meaning : towards a semantic anthropology / [by] Malcolm Crick. — London : Malaby Press, 1976. — vii,212p ; 23cm.
Bibl.: p.177-195. — Index.
ISBN 0-460-14012-4 : £6.95
(B77-08775)

301.2'1 — Sociolinguistics
Hymes, Dell. Foundations in sociolinguistics : an ethnographic approach / [by] Dell Hymes. — London : Tavistock Publications, 1977. — iii-x, 248p : 2 ill ; 23cm.
Originally published: Philadelphia : University of Pennsylvania Press, 1974. — Bibl.: p.211-233. — Index.
ISBN 0-422-74810-2 : £7.50
(B77-24704)

301.2'1 — Symbolism. *Psychological perspectives*
Symbols and sentiments : cross-cultural studies in symbolism / edited by Ioan Lewis. — London [etc.] : Academic Press, 1977. — x,300p ; 24cm.

'Most of the papers included were originally presented at an inter-collegiate seminar held at the London School of Economics in the Michaelmas term, 1973' - Preface. — Bibl. — Index.
ISBN 0-12-446650-8 : £8.50
(B77-27685)

301.2'1 — Tzotzil myths. Symbolism. *Mexico. Zinacantan. Anthropological perspectives. Study examples: Hummingbird, The*
Hunt, Eva. The transformation of 'The hummingbird' : cultural roots of a Zinacantecan mythical poem / [by] Eva Hunt. — Ithaca ; London : Cornell University Press, 1977. — 312p : ill ; 22cm. — (Symbol, myth and ritual series)
Bibl.: p.290-303. — Index.
ISBN 0-8014-1022-3 : £13.90
(B77-30986)

301.2'1 — Witchcraft. Social aspects. *Massachusetts. Salem, ca 1640-ca 1700*
Boyer, Paul. Salem possessed : the social origins of witchcraft / [by] Paul Boyer and Stephen Nissenbaum. — Cambridge, Mass. ; London : Harvard University Press, 1976. — xxi,231p : ill, facsim, geneal tables, maps ; 22cm.
Originally published: Cambridge, Mass. : Harvard University Press, 1974. — Index.
ISBN 0-674-78525-8 : £9.40
ISBN 0-674-78526-6 Pbk £2.25
(B77-03382)

301.2'2'05 — Newspapers for subcultures: Newspapers with London imprints. *Texts*
International times. — London : 'International times', 1966-.
A not very detailed index to nos 1-23 / compiled by John Noyce. — Brighton : Smoothie Publications, 1975. — [8]p ; 30cm. — (Alternative press indexing)
ISBN 0-903612-40-2 Sd : £0.80
(B77-01173)

301.2'2'05 — Periodicals for subcultures: Periodicals with British imprints. *Reports, surveys*
Great Britain. *Royal Commission on the Press.* Periodicals and the alternative press / Royal Commission on the Press ; chairman O.R. McGregor. — London : H.M.S.O., 1977. — x, 73p ; 25cm. — (Great Britain. Royal Commission on the Press. Research series ; 6) (Cmnd.6810-6)
ISBN 0-10-168106-2 Sd : £1.35
Primary classification 052
(B77-28341)

301.2'2'0924 — Alternative society. Beam, Alan. *England. Autobiographies*
Beam, Alan. Rehearsal for the year 2000 : (drugs, religions, madness, crime, communes, love, visions, festivals and lunar energy) : the rebirth of Albion Free State (known in the Dark Ages as England) : memoirs of a male midwife (1966-1976) / by Alan Beam (assisted by Pete Morrison). — London (65 Edith Grove, S.W.10) : Revelaction Press, 1976. — 220p,[14] leaves ; 33cm.
ISBN 0-9505244-0-9 Sd : £1.95
ISBN 0-9505244-1-7 Library ed. : £4.95
(B77-17299)

301.2'4 — Futurology. Organisations. *Directories*
McHale, John. The 'Futures' directory : an international listing and description of organizations and individuals active in future studies and long-range planning / compiled by John McHale and Magda Cordell McHale with ... [others]. — Guildford : IPC Science and Technology Press [etc.], 1977. — xii,394p ; 22cm.
'A "Futures" special publication'. — Index.
ISBN 0-902852-64-7 : £12.00
(B77-26118)

301.24 — Prehistoric man. Social change. Theories. *Conference proceedings*
Research Seminar in Archaeology and Related Subjects. *International Meeting, University of Sheffield, 1971.* The explanation of culture change : models in prehistory : proceedings of a meeting of the Research Seminar in Archaeology and Related Subjects held at the University of Sheffield / edited by Colin Renfrew. — London : Duckworth, 1973 [i.e. 1976]. — xv,788p : ill, maps ; 25cm.
Originally published: 1973. — Bibl. — Index.
ISBN 0-7156-1141-0 Pbk : £7.50
(B77-05213)

301.24 — Social change
Lauer, Robert H. Perspectives on social change / [by] Robert H. Lauer. — 2nd ed. — Boston, Mass. ; London [etc.] : Allyn and Bacon, 1977. — xii,384p : ill ; 25cm.
Previous ed.: Boston, Mass. : Allyn and Bacon, 1973. — Index.
ISBN 0-205-05846-9 : £10.35
(B77-23127)

Smith, Anthony David. Social change : social theory and historical processes / [by] Anthony D. Smith. — London [etc.] : Longman, 1976. — viii,184p ; 21cm. — (Aspects of modern sociology : social processes)
Bibl.: p.162-175. — Index.
ISBN 0-582-48010-8 : £3.75
ISBN 0-582-48011-6 Pbk : £1.95
(B77-02041)

301.24 — Social change. *Anthropological perspectives. Case studies*
Spindler, Louise S. Culture change and modernization : mini-models and case studies / [by] Louise S. Spindler. — New York ; London [etc.] : Holt, Rinehart and Winston, 1977. — xiii,177p : ill ; 24cm. — (Basic anthropology units)
Bibl.: p.165-171. — Index.
ISBN 0-03-091290-3 Pbk : £4.95
(B77-28391)

301.24 — Social change. *Anthropological perspectives. Conference proceedings*
Rethinking modernization : anthropological perspectives / edited by John J. Poggie, Jr and Robert N. Lynch. — Westport, Conn. ; London : Greenwood Press, 1974. — iii-xii, 405p : ill, maps, ports ; 22cm.
'... a symposium held at the University of Rhode Island on May 27-29, 1971' - Acknowledgements. — Bibl.: p.377-394. — Index.
ISBN 0-8371-6394-3 : £13.75
(B77-15692)

301.24 — Social change. *Islamic viewpoints*
Rosser-Owen, Dawud G. Social change in Islam : the progressive dimension / [by] Dawud G. Rosser-Owen. The quest for a new science / [by] Ziauddin Sardar. — Slough (32 Warrington Ave., Slough, Berks.) : Open Press, 1976. — 38p ; 30cm. — (Muslim Institute for Research and Planning. Papers ; 1)
ISBN 0-905081-01-3 Pbk : £1.00
(B77-10174)

301.24 — Social change. *Marxist viewpoints*
The **humanisation** of socialism : writings of the Budapest school / [by] Andras Hegedus ... [et al.]. — London : Allison and Busby, 1976. — 177p : ill ; 23cm.
Index.
ISBN 0-85031-184-5 : £5.25
ISBN 0-85031-185-3 Pbk : £2.95
(B77-05214)

301.24 — Social change. Related to organisational change
Zaltman, Gerald. Strategies for planned change / [by] Gerald Zaltman, Robert Duncan. — New York ; London [etc.] : Wiley, 1977. — xi,404p : ill ; 24cm.
'A Wiley-Interscience publication'. — Bibl.: p.359-377. — Index.
ISBN 0-471-98131-1 : £13.35
Also classified at 301.24'8
(B77-29941)

301.24 — Society. Evolution
Parsons, Talcott. The evolution of societies / [by] Talcott Parsons ; edited and with an introduction by Jackson Toby. — Englewood Cliffs ; London [etc.] : Prentice-Hall, 1977. — xiii,269p : ill ; 24cm. — (Prentice-Hall foundations of modern sociology series)
Bibl. — Index. — Contents: 'Societies'. Originally published: London : Prentice-Hall, 1966 - 'The system of modern societies'. Originally published: London : Prentice-Hall, 1971.
ISBN 0-13-293647-x : £9.55
ISBN 0-13-293639-9 Pbk : £5.55
(B77-24705)

Stonier, Tom Ted. The natural history of humanity : past, present and future / by T.T. Stonier. — [Bradford] ([Bradford, W. Yorkshire BD7 1DP]) : [University of Bradford], [1976]. — [1],48p : 1 ill ; 21cm. — (University of Bradford. Inaugural lectures)
'... delivered at the University of Bradford on 17 February 1976'.
ISBN 0-901945-22-6 Sd : Unpriced
(B77-00032)

301.24 — Society. Evolution. *Essays*
Steward, Julian Haynes. Evolution and ecology : essays on social transformation / by Julian H. Steward ; edited by Jane C. Steward and Robert F. Murphy. — Urbana [etc.] ; London : University of Illinois Press, 1977. — ix,406p : 3 ill, 3 maps ; 24cm.
Bibl.
ISBN 0-252-00612-7 : £9.75
(B77-24005)

301.24'07'2 — Social change. Research
Galt, Anthony H. Models and the study of social change / [by] Anthony H. Galt and Larry J. Smith. — Cambridge, Mass. : Schenkman ; New York ; London [etc.] : Distributed by Wiley, 1976. — ix,180p : ill ; 21cm.
'A Halsted Press Book'. — Bibl.: p.169-174. — Index.
ISBN 0-470-15156-0 : £7.70
ISBN 0-470-15163-3 Pbk : £4.25
(B77-06480)

301.24'08 — Social change. *Essays*
Responses to change : society, culture and personality / edited by George A. DeVos. — New York ; London [etc.] : D. Van Nostrand, 1976. — vi,375p : ill ; 23cm.
'... [based on] a conference and subsequent colloquium held in [Hakone], Japan [1968] ... in conjunction with the VIIIth International Congress of Anthropological and Ethnological Sciences' - Preface. — Bibl. — Index.
ISBN 0-442-22094-4 Pbk : £5.30
(B77-02042)

301.24'08 — Social change. *Readings*
The **planning** of change. — 3rd ed. / edited by Warren G. Bennis ... [et al.]. — New York ; London [etc.] : Holt, Rinehart and Winston, 1976. — ix,517p : ill ; 25cm.
Previous ed.: / edited by Warren G. Bennis, Kenneth D. Benne, Robert Chin. 1969. — Bibl. — Index.
ISBN 0-03-089518-9 : £8.00
(B77-04560)

301.24'1'097984 — Aleuts. Social change. Influence of American culture. *Alaska. Aleutian Islands. Case studies*
Jones, Dorothy M. Aleuts in transition : a comparison of two villages / by Dorothy M. Jones. — Seattle ; London : University of Washington Press for the Institute of Social, Economic and Government Research, University of Alaska, [1977]. — vii,125p ; 22cm.
Published in the United States: 1976. — Bibl.: p.117-122. — Index.
ISBN 0-295-95519-8 : £7.30
(B77-11578)

301.24'2 — Innovation
Kingston, William. Innovation : the creative impulse in human progress : industry-art-science / [by] William Kingston. — London : J. Calder : [Distributed by Calder and Boyars], 1977. — 160p : ill ; 23cm. — (Platform books)
Bibl.: p.155-157. — Index.
ISBN 0-7145-3540-0 : £5.95
ISBN 0-7145-3611-3 Pbk : £2.25
(B77-20032)

301.24'2 — Social change. Role of social movements
Social movements and social change / edited by Robert H. Lauer. — Carbondale [etc.] : Southern Illinois University Press ; London [etc.] : Feffer and Simons, 1976. — xxviii,292p ; 24cm.
Bibl.: p.265-285. — Index.
ISBN 0-8093-0771-5 : £7.50
(B77-11074)

301.24'2 — Social reform
Gane, Michael. The reformist perspective / prepared for the [Open University] Course Team by Michael Gane. The politics of reform ; [and], Consensus or conflict : a case study in planning / prepared by Andrew Blowers ; for the [Open University] Course Team. — Milton Keynes : Open University Press, 1976. — [2],iv, 3-104p : ill ; 30cm. — (Social science, a third level course : patterns of inequality ; section 4 : reform or revolution? ; unit 29, unit 30) (D302 ; 29-30)
Bibl.
ISBN 0-335-07160-0 Pbk : £1.35
Also classified at 309.2'62'0941
(B77-03939)

301.24'2'0962 — Egypt. Social reform, ca 1870-ca 1950. *Muslim viewpoints*
Badawi, Zaki. The reformers of Egypt : a critique of Al-Afghani, 'Abduh and Ridha / [by] Zaki Badawi. — Slough (32 Warrington Ave., Slough, Berks.) : Open Press, 1976. — xiii,95p ; 30cm. — (Muslim Institute. Papers ; 2 ISSN 0309-3212)
Bibl.: p.xiii.
ISBN 0-905081-02-1 Pbk : £2.00
(B77-08230)

301.24'3 — Biology. Research. Social aspects. *Conference proceedings*
Biology and the Future of Man *(Conference), Sorbonne, 1974.* Biology and the Future of Man : proceedings of the international conference, [held at the Sorbonne from the 18th to 24th September 1974] / [edited by Charles Galpérine]. — [Paris] : Universities of Paris ; Paris ; London [etc.] : Distributed by McGraw-Hill, 1976. — xv,610p ; 24cm.
English and French text. — Bibl. — Index.
Pbk : £14.00
ISBN 2-7042-0093-9
(B77-02043)

301.24'3 — Biology. Social aspects
Butler, John Alfred Valentine. Modern biology and its human implications / [by] J.A.V. Butler. — London [etc.] : Hodder and Stoughton, 1976. — viii,120p : ill ; 23cm. — (Biological science texts)
Bibl.: p.114-117. — Index.
ISBN 0-340-20043-x : £3.95
ISBN 0-340-20055-3 Pbk : £2.45
(B77-02773)

301.24'3 — Computer systems. Social aspects
Adams, J. Mack. Social effects of computer use and misuse / [by] J. Mack Adams, Douglas H. Haden. — New York ; London [etc.] : Wiley, 1976. — x,326p : ill, map, port ; 26cm.
Bibl. — Index.
ISBN 0-471-00463-4 Pbk : £7.95
(B77-01174)

301.24'3 — Computer-telecommunication systems. Applications. Social aspects. *Organisation for Economic Co-operation and Development countries. Conference proceedings*
Conference on Computer/Telecommunications Policy, *Paris, 1975.* Conference on Computer/Telecommunications Policy : proceedings of the OECD conference, February 4-6, 1975. — Paris : Organisation for Economic Co-operation and Development ; [London] : [H.M.S.O.], 1976. — 336p : ill ; 24cm. — (Organisation for Economic Co-operation and Development. Informatics studies ; 11)
'... organised by a Steering Group set up by the OECD's Computer Utilisation Group under the auspices of the Committee for Scientific and Technological Policy' - Preface.
Pbk : £6.40
ISBN 92-64-11547-1
(B77-01175)

301.24'3 — Digital computer systems. Applications. Social aspects
Arbib, Michael Anthony. Computers and the cybernetic society / [by] Michael A. Arbib ; with many exercises supplied by Jonathan V. Post. — New York [etc.] ; London : Academic Press, 1977. — xxi,494p : ill ; 25cm.
Bibl. — Index.
ISBN 0-12-059040-9 : £9.25
(B77-29942)

Rothman, Stanley. Computers and society : the technology and its social implications / [by] Stanley Rothman, Charles Mosmann. — 2nd ed. — Chicago ; Henley-on-Thames [etc.] : Science Research Associates.
Previous ed.: 1972.
Instructor's guide. — [1976]. — [4],78p : 1 ill ; 28cm.
ISBN 0-574-21056-3 Sd : £1.40
(B77-00615)

301.24'3 — Firearms. Social aspects. *United States, to 1974*
Kennett, Lee. The gun in America : the origins of a national dilemma / [by] Lee Kennett and James LaVerne Anderson. — Westport, Conn. ; London : Greenwood Press, 1975. — x,339p : ill, facsims, port ; 22cm. — (Contributions in American history ; no.37)
Bibl.: p.315-323. — Index.
ISBN 0-8371-7530-5 : £10.95
(B77-15693)

301.24'3 — Genetic engineering. Social aspects
Goodfield, June. Playing God : genetic engineering and the manipulation of life / [by] June Goodfield. — London : Hutchinson, 1977. — iii-xv,218,[1]p ; 23cm.
ISBN 0-09-131890-4 : £5.95
(B77-32418)

301.24'3 — Information science. Social aspects
McHale, John. The changing information environment / [by] John McHale. — London : Elek, 1976. — ix,117p : ill, map ; 22cm. — (Environmental studies)
Index.
ISBN 0-236-40052-5 Pbk : £2.95
(B77-01176)

301.24'3 — Materials. Social aspects. *Periodicals*
Materials and society. — [Oxford] : Pergamon.
Vol.1, no.1- ; May 1977-. — 1977-. — 28cm.
Cover title. — Six issues a year. — [5],71,[1]p. in 1st issue.
Pbk : £49.54 yearly
ISSN 0146-6399
(B77-23128)

301.24'3 — Nuclear power. Social aspects. *Great Britain*
Flood, Michael. Nuclear prospects : a comment on the individual, the state and nuclear power / by Michael Flood and Robin Grove-White. — London (9 Poland St., W1V 3DG) : Friends of the Earth Ltd ; London : Council for the Protection of Rural England ; London : National Council for Civil Liberties, 1976. — vi,64p ; 21cm.
Bibl.: p.62-64.
Sd : £1.20
(B77-25391)

301.24'3 — Science. Social aspects. *Conference proceedings*
Future of Science *(Conference), Gustavus Adolphus College, Minnesota, 1975.* The future of science : 1975 Nobel conference, organized by Gustavus Adolphus College, St Peter, Minnesota / edited by Timothy C.L. Robinson. — New York ; London [etc.] : Wiley, 1977. — xxiii,145p ; 24cm.
'A Wiley-Interscience publication'. — '... the talks given during the eleventh annual Nobel Conference held at Gustavus Adolphus College in 1975. The theme of the Conference was "The Future of Science" ...' - jacket.
ISBN 0-471-01524-5 : £9.75
(B77-21704)

301.24'3 — Science. Social aspects. *Marxist viewpoints*
The **political** economy of science : ideology of/in the natural sciences / edited by Hilary Rose and Steven Rose. — London [etc.] : Macmillan, 1976. — xxvi,218p ; 23cm. — (Critical social studies)
Index.
ISBN 0-333-21138-3 : £10.00
ISBN 0-333-21139-1 Pbk : £3.95
(B77-08776)

The **radicalisation** of science : ideology of/in the natural sciences / edited by Hilary Rose and Steven Rose. — London [etc.] : Macmillan, 1976. — xxvi,205p ; 23cm. — (Critical social studies)
Index.
ISBN 0-333-21140-5 : £10.00
ISBN 0-333-21141-3 Pbk : £3.95
(B77-08777)

301.24'3 — Social change. Effects of technological development. *Study regions: United States*
Brzezinski, Zbigniew Kazimierz. Between two ages : America's role in the technetronic era / [by] Zbigniew Brzezinski. — Harmondsworth [etc.] : Penguin, 1976. — xvii,334p ; 20cm.
Originally published: New York : Viking Press, 1970. — Index.
ISBN 0-14-004314-4 Pbk : Unpriced
(B77-02044)

301.24'3 — Society. Effects of technological development
Winner, Langdon. Autonomous technology : technics-out-of-control as a theme in political thought / [by] Langdon Winner. — Cambridge, Mass. ; London : M.I.T. Press, 1977. — x, 386p ; 21cm.
Index.
ISBN 0-262-23078-x : £11.95
(B77-33065)

301.24'3 — Technological development. Social aspects
Hidden factors in technological change / editors Edward Semper ... [et al.]. — Oxford [etc.] : Pergamon [for the] Standing Conference on Schools' Science and Technology, 1976. — xiii, 252p : map ; 21cm.
Bibl.
ISBN 0-08-021007-4 Pbk : £5.00
Also classified at 370
(B77-10175)

Scorer, Richard Segar. The clever moron / [by] R.S. Scorer. — London [etc.] : Routledge and Kegan Paul, 1977. — xii,171p ; 23cm.
Index.
ISBN 0-7100-8552-4 : £3.95
(B77-17920)

301.24'3 — Technology. Environmental aspects
Braun, Ernest, *b.1925.* Technology and survival / [by] Ernest Braun and David Collingridge ; [for] Science in a Social Context. — London [etc.] : Butterworth, 1977. — v,71p : ill ; 22cm.
Bibl.
ISBN 0-408-71301-1 Pbk : £1.00
(B77-17300)

301.24'3 — Telecommunication systems. Social aspects. *Readings*
Open University. *Telecommunication Systems Course Team.* Telecommunications and society / prepared by the [Open University Telecommunication Systems] Course Team. — Milton Keynes : Open University Press, 1976. — [55]p : ill, ports ; 30cm. — (Technology, a third level course : telecommunication systems ; unit 16) (T321 ; 16)
Pierced for binder. — Bibl.: p.[47]-[48].
ISBN 0-335-06108-7 Pbk : £2.95
(B77-04561)

301.24'3 — Universities. *Great Britain. Open University. Curriculum subjects: Technological development. Social aspects. Courses: Man-made futures, design and technology*
Cross, Nigel. Course guide / prepared for the [Open University] course team by Nigel Cross. — New ed. — Milton Keynes : Open University [Press], 1976. — 25p ; 30cm. — ([Technology second level course] : man-made futures, design and technology) (T262 ; CG)
Previous ed.: i.e. 1st ed., 1975. — Index.
Sd : Unpriced
(B77-03940)

301.24'3 — Western world. Society. Role of technology
Open University. *Technology for Teachers Course Team.* Technology and man / the Open University [Technology for Teachers Course Team]. — Milton Keynes : Open University Press.
3 : Industry. — 1975. — 62p : ill(some col) ; 30cm. — (Educational studies/technology, a post-experience and second level course : technology for teachers ; block 4, unit 13) (PET271 ; block 4 (13))
With answers. — Bibl.: p.61.
ISBN 0-335-02808-x Pbk : £1.80
(B77-28392)

301.24'3'05 — Science. Social aspects. *Periodicals*
Science in a Social Context. SISCON newsletter. — Stirling (c/o Newsletter Editor, Department of Management Science and Technology Studies, University of Stirling, Stirling FK9 4LA) : 'Siscon newsletter'.
No.1- ; Mar. 1976-. — [1976]-. — 21cm.
Six issues a year. — 24p. in issue no.4. — Bibl.
Sd : Unpriced
ISSN 0309-555x
(B77-15694)

301.24'3'08 — Technology. Social aspects. *Readings*
Technology as a social and political phenomenon / [edited by] Philip L. Bereano. — New York ; London [etc.] : Wiley, [1977]. — ix,544p : ill ; 26cm.
Published in the United States: 1976.
ISBN 0-471-06875-6 : £10.40
(B77-12302)

301.24'3'0917671 — Islamic countries. Technological development. Social aspects
Sardar, Ziauddin. Science, technology and development in the Muslim world / [by] Ziauddin Sardar. — London : Croom Helm for the Muslim Institute, 1977. — 215p ; 23cm.
Bibl.: p.189-210. — Index.
ISBN 0-85664-554-0 : £7.95 : CIP rev.
(B77-23129)

301.24'3'0952 — Industrialisation. Social aspects. *Japan, 1868-1975. Conference proceedings*
Conference on Japanese Industrialization and Its Social Consequences, *Seattle, 1973.* Japanese industrialization and its social consequences / edited by Hugh Patrick ; with the assistance of Larry Meissner. — Berkeley [etc.] ; London : University of California Press, 1976. — x,505p : ill ; 25cm.
'The Conference on Japanese Industrialization and Its Social Consequences [held 20-24 August at Seattle] was one of a series of five international conferences planned under the auspices of the Joint Committee on Japanese Studies of the American Council of Learned Societies and the Social Science Research Council' - Preface. — Bibl. — Index.
ISBN 0-520-03000-1 : £20.00
(B77-13510)

301.24'3'0973 — Technocratic movements. *United States, 1900-1941*
Akin, William Elmus. Technocracy and the American dream : the technocrat movement, 1900-1941 / [by] William E. Akin. — Berkeley [etc.] ; London : University of California Press, 1977. — xv,227p ; 23cm.
Bibl.: p.205-221. — Index.
ISBN 0-520-03110-5 : £7.10
(B77-22355)

301.24'8 — Organisational change. Related to social change
Zaltman, Gerald. Strategies for planned change / [by] Gerald Zaltman, Robert Duncan. — New York ; London [etc.] : Wiley, 1977. — xi,404p : ill ; 24cm.
'A Wiley-Interscience publication'. — Bibl.: p.359-377. — Index.
ISBN 0-471-98131-1 : £13.35
Primary classification 301.24
(B77-29941)

301.29'172'4 — Social change. Theories. *Developing countries. Rural regions*
Long, Norman. An introduction to the sociology of rural development / [by] Norman Long. — London : Tavistock Publications, 1977. — ix, 221p ; 23cm.
Bibl.: p.202-215. — Index.
ISBN 0-422-74480-8 : £5.75
ISBN 0-422-74490-5 Pbk : £3.00
(B77-26800)

301.29'181'2 — Western world. Relations with primitive peoples, to 1976
Sinclair, Andrew. The savage : a history of misunderstanding / [by] Andrew Sinclair. — London : Weidenfeld and Nicolson, 1977. — [7],168p ; 24cm.
Index.
ISBN 0-297-77226-0 : £5.00
Primary classification 301.2
(B77-14560)

301.29'181'2051 — Western world. Relations with China, to 1949
Cameron, Nigel. Barbarians and mandarins : thirteen centuries of Western travelers in China / [by] Nigel Cameron. — Chicago ; London : University of Chicago Press, 1976. — 443p : ill, facsims, maps, plans, ports ; 24cm. — (A phoenix book)
Originally published: New York : Walker/Weatherhill, 1970. — Bibl.: p.421-428. — Index.
ISBN 0-226-09229-1 Pbk : £6.00
Primary classification 301.29'51'01812
(B77-02046)

301.29'182'2 — Mediterranean region. Cultural processes
Davis, John. People of the Mediterranean : an essay in comparative social anthropology / [by] J. Davis. — London [etc.] : Routledge and Kegan Paul, 1977. — xi,288p ; 23cm. — (Library of man)
Bibl.: p.261-279. — Index.
ISBN 0-7100-8412-9 : £5.50
(B77-05215)

301.29'4'06 — Europe. Relations with Africa, to 1960
Bennett, Norman Robert. Africa and Europe : from Roman times to the present / [by] Norman R. Bennett. — New York ; London : Africana Publishing Co. ; London : Holmes and Meier, 1975. — [6],246p : maps ; 21cm.
Bibl.: p.225-234. — Index.
ISBN 0-8419-0172-4 : Unpriced
ISBN 0-8419-01730-2 Pbk : Unpriced
Also classified at 301.29'6'04
(B77-18558)

301.29'41 — Local communities. Twinning with local communities overseas. *Great Britain. Reports, surveys*
Joint Twinning Committee of the Local Authority Associations of Great Britain. Places in partnership, a twinning handbook / Joint Twinning Committee [of the Local Authority Associations of Great Britain]. — London (65 Davies St., W1Y 2AA) : The Committee, 1976. — 36p : ill ; 21cm.
Sd : Unpriced
(B77-00616)

301.29'41 — Local communities. Twinning with local communities overseas. *Great Britain, to 1975. Lists*
Joint Twinning Committee of the Local Authority Associations of Great Britain. Places in partnership, list of twinnings / Joint Twinning Committee [of the Local Authority Associations of Great Britain]. — London (65 Davies St., W1Y 2AA) : The Committee, 1976. — 36p ; 21cm.
Index.
ISBN 0-900229-26-8 Sd : Unpriced
(B77-02045)

301.29'41'043 — Great Britain. Relations with West Germany. Role of British non-governmental organisations, 1945-1975. *Personal observations. Collections*
Total war to total trust : personal accounts of 30 years of Anglo-German relations : the vital role of non-governmental organisations / edited by Rolf Breitenstein ; introduced by Lothar Kettenacker. — London : Wolff [for] the Embassy of the Federal Republic of Germany, 1976. — [4],92p ; 19cm.
Index.
ISBN 0-85496-208-5 Pbk : £2.75
Also classified at 301.29'43'041
(B77-07067)

301.29'41'06694 — Great Britain. Relations with Igbo in Eastern states of Nigeria, 1860-1960
Nwabara, Samuel N. Iboland : a century of contact with Britain, 1860-1960 / [by] S.N. Nwabara. — London [etc.] : Hodder and Stoughton, 1977. — 251p : maps ; 22cm.
Bibl.: p.239-251.
ISBN 0-340-18794-8 Pbk : £5.50 : CIP rev.
Also classified at 301.29'669'4041
(B77-26119)

301.29'427'84 — Cumbria. Whitehaven. Relations with Virginia, to 1913
Lawrence-Dow, Elizabeth. Whitehaven to Washington / [by] Elizabeth Lawrence-Dow and Daniel Hay. — [Cleator] ([The Council Chambers, Cleator, Cumbria CA23 3DS]) : Copeland Borough Council, 1974. — 48p : ill, ports ; 21cm.
Index.
ISBN 0-904667-00-6 Sd : £0.60
Also classified at 301.29'755'042784
(B77-20033)

301.29'43'041 — West Germany. Relations with Great Britain. Role of British non-governmental organisations, 1945-1975. *Personal observations. Collections*
Total war to total trust : personal accounts of 30 years of Anglo-German relations : the vital role of non-governmental organisations / edited by Rolf Breitenstein ; introduced by Lothar Kettenacker. — London : Wolff [for] the Embassy of the Federal Republic of Germany, 1976. — [4],92p ; 19cm.
Index.
ISBN 0-85496-208-5 Pbk : £2.75
Primary classification 301.29'41'043
(B77-07067)

301.29'44 — France. Rural regions. Social change, 1870-1914
Weber, Eugen. Peasants into Frenchmen : the modernization of rural France, 1870-1914 / [by] Eugen Weber. — London : Chatto and Windus, 1977. — xv,615p : maps ; 25cm.
Maps on lining papers. — Bibl.: p.573-596. — Index.
ISBN 0-7011-2210-2 : £12.00
(B77-10176)

301.29'458'2 — Italy. Western Sicily. Cultural processes, to 1975
Schneider, Jane. Culture and political economy in western Sicily / [by] Jane Schneider, Peter Schneider. — New York [etc.] ; London : Academic Press, 1976. — xv,256p : ill, maps ; 24cm. — (Studies in social discontinuity)
Bibl.: p.239-250. — Index.
ISBN 0-12-627850-4 : £9.60
(B77-01177)

301.29'47 — Eastern Europe & Soviet Union. Social change, to 1975. Political aspects
Whetten, Lawrence Lester. Current research in comparative communism : an analysis and bibliographic guide to the Soviet system / [by] Lawrence L. Whetten. — New York [etc.] ; London : Praeger, [1977]. — vii,163p ; 25cm. — (Praeger special studies in international politics and government)
Published in the United States: 1976.
ISBN 0-275-23550-5 : £11.20
Primary classification 016.3091'47
(B77-14010)

301.29'481'073 — Norway. Relations with United States, to 1975
Skard, Sigmund. The United States in Norwegian history / [by] Sigmund Skard. — Westport, Conn. ; London : Greenwood Press [etc.], 1976. — xii,216p ; 22cm. — (Contributions in American studies ; no.26)
Bibl.: p.205-209. — Index.
ISBN 0-8371-8909-8 : £10.50
Also classified at 301.29'73'0481
(B77-17301)

301.29'498'2 — Romania. Wallachia. Social change, 1250-1970
Chirot, Daniel. Social change in a peripheral society : the creation of a Balkan colony / [by] Daniel Chirot. — New York [etc.] ; London : Academic Press, 1976. — xix,179p : maps, ports ; 24cm. — (Studies in social discontinuity)
Bibl.: p.165-172. — Index.
ISBN 0-12-173150-2 : £7.25
(B77-02774)

301.29'51'01812 — China. Relations with Western world, to 1949
Cameron, Nigel. Barbarians and mandarins : thirteen centuries of Western travelers in China / [by] Nigel Cameron. — Chicago ; London : University of Chicago Press, 1976. — 443p : ill, facsims, maps, plans, ports ; 24cm. — (A phoenix book)
Originally published: New York : Walker/Weatherhill, 1970. — Bibl.: p.421-428. — Index.
ISBN 0-226-09229-1 Pbk : £6.00
Also classified at 301.29'181'2051
(B77-02046)

301.29'54'165 — Nagas. *India (Republic), 1939-1970. Anthropological perspectives*
Fürer-Haimendorf, Christoph von. Return to the naked Nagas : an anthropologist's view of Nagaland, 1936-1970 / [by] Christoph von Fürer-Haimendorf. — New ed. — London : J. Murray, 1976. — vii,268p,[12]p of plates : ill, ports ; 23cm.
Previous ed.: published as 'The naked Nagas'. London : Methuen, 1939. — Index.
ISBN 0-7195-3417-8 : £4.95
(B77-09512)

301.29'54'87 — India (Republic). Karnataka (State). Rampura. Cultural processes
Srinivas, M N. The remembered village / [by] M.N. Srinivas. — Berkeley [etc.] ; London : University of California Press, 1976. — iii-xviii, 356p,[2]leaves of plates,[12]p of plates : ill, maps, plans, port ; 23cm.
Index.
ISBN 0-520-02997-6 : £8.75
(B77-21705)

301.29'59 — South-east Asia. Cultural processes
Keyes, Charles F. The golden peninsula : culture and adaptation in mainland Southeast Asia / [by] Charles F. Keyes. — New York : Macmillan ; London : Collier Macmillan, 1977. — xiv,370p : ill, maps ; 24cm.
Index.
ISBN 0-02-364430-3 Pbk : £5.25
(B77-23130)

301.29'6 — Africa. Cultural processes
Turnbull, Colin Macmillan. Man in Africa / [by] Colin M. Turnbull ; drawings by John Morris. — Newton Abbot [etc.] : David and Charles, 1976. — ii-xxi,313p,[8]p of plates : ill, map ; 23cm.
Index.
ISBN 0-7153-7348-x : £4.95
(B77-04562)

301.29'6'04 — Africa. Relations with Europe, to 1960
Bennett, Norman Robert. Africa and Europe : from Roman times to the present / [by] Norman R. Bennett. — New York ; London : Africana Publishing Co. ; London : Holmes and Meier, 1975. — [6],246p : maps ; 21cm.
Bibl.: p.225-234. — Index.
ISBN 0-8419-0172-4 : Unpriced
ISBN 0-8419-01730-2 Pbk : Unpriced
Primary classification 301.29'4'06
(B77-18558)

301.29'65'3 — Kabyles. *Algeria. Anthropological perspectives*
Bourdieu, Pierre. Outline of a theory of practice / [by] Pierre Bourdieu ; translated [from the French] by Richard Nice. — Cambridge [etc.] : Cambridge University Press, 1977. — viii,248p : ill ; 24cm. — (Cambridge studies in social anthropology ; 16)
Translation of: 'Esquisse d'une théorie de la pratique, précédé de trois études d'ethnologie kabyle'. Geneva : Librairie Droz, 1972. — Index.
ISBN 0-521-21178-6 : £9.00
ISBN 0-521-29164-x Pbk : £2.95
Primary classification 301.2'01
(B77-26798)

301.29'664 — Kurankos. *Sierra Leone. Anthropological perspectives*
Jackson, Michael. The Kuranko : dimensions of social reality in a West African society / [by] Michael Jackson. — London : C. Hurst, 1977. — xviii,256p,[8]p of plates : ill, maps, ports, plans ; 23cm.
Bibl.: p.247-252. — Index.
ISBN 0-903983-69-9 : £13.00 : CIP rev.
(B77-14562)

301.29'669'3 — Itsekiri. Relations with Urhobo. Political aspects. *Nigeria. Bendel (State), 1884-1936*
Ikime, Obaro. Niger Delta rivalry : Itsekiri-Urhobo relations and the European presence, 1884-1936 / [by] Obaro Ikime. — London : Longman, 1977. — xxi,301p,[3]fold leaves of plates : maps ; 22cm. — (Ibadan history series)
Originally published: Harlow : Longman, 1969. — Bibl.: p.285-290. — Index.
ISBN 0-582-64638-3 Pbk : £2.75
(B77-18559)

301.29'669'4041 — Igbo. Relations with Great Britain. *Nigeria. Eastern states, 1860-1960*
Nwabara, Samuel N. Iboland : a century of contact with Britain, 1860-1960 / [by] S.N. Nwabara. — London [etc.] : Hodder and Stoughton, 1977. — 251p : maps ; 22cm.
Bibl.: p.239-251.
ISBN 0-340-18794-8 Pbk : £5.50 : CIP rev.
Primary classification 301.29'41'06694
(B77-26119)

301.29'67 — Africa south of the Sahara. Cultural processes. *Festschriften*
Studies in African social anthropology / edited by Meyer Fortes and Sheila Patterson. — London [etc.] : Academic Press, 1975. — x, 267p,plate : geneal table, 2 maps, port ; 24cm.
'Essays presented to Professor Isaac Schapera' - p.vi. — Bibl. — Index.
ISBN 0-12-262250-2 : £7.50
(B77-19223)

301.29'676'1 — Sebei. Cultural processes. *Eastern Uganda*
Goldschmidt, Walter. Culture and behavior of the Sebei : a study in continuity and adaptation / by Walter Goldschmidt with the assistance of Gale Goldschmidt. — Berkeley [etc.] ; London : University of California Press, 1976. — xvi,395,[8]p,[40]p of plates : ill, geneal table, maps, plans, ports ; 26cm. — (Studies in culture and ecology)
Bibl.: p.379-384. — Index.
ISBN 0-520-02828-7 : £17.45
(B77-00033)

301.29'68'1 — !Kung. Cultural processes. *Botswana. Kalahari Desert*
Kalahari hunter-gatherers : studies of the !Kung San and their neighbors / edited by Richard B. Lee and Irven DeVore. — Cambridge, Mass. ; London : Harvard University Press, 1976. — xix,408p : ill, maps ; 25cm.
Bibl.: p.377-394. — Index.
ISBN 0-674-49980-8 : £13.90
(B77-08231)

301.29'68'8 — !Kung. Cultural processes. *Namibia. Kalahari Desert*
Marshall, Lorna. The !Kung of Nyae Nyae / [by] Lorna Marshall. — Cambridge, Mass. ; London : Harvard University Press, 1976. — xxvi,433p : ill, maps, ports ; 24cm.
Index.
ISBN 0-674-50569-7 : £15.00
(B77-04563)

301.29'7 — Indians of North America. Cultural processes. *Case studies*
Native North American cultures : four cases, the Hano Tewa, the Kwakiutl, the Blackfeet, the Menominee / edited by George and Louise Spindler. — New York ; London [etc.] : Holt, Rinehart and Winston, 1977. — [3],508p : ill, maps, plan ; 24cm.
Bibl. — Index. — Contents: Hano / by Edward P. Dozier. Originally published: 1966 - The Kwakiutl / by Ronald P. Rohner and Evelyn C. Rohner. Originally published: 1970 - Modern Blackfeet / by Malcolm McFee. Originally published: 1972 - Dreamers without power / by George Spindler and Louise Spindler. Originally published: 1971.
ISBN 0-03-018401-0 Pbk : £4.75
(B77-31698)

301.29'7 — Museums. *East Sussex. Brighton. Royal Pavilion, Art Gallery and Museums, Brighton. Exhibits: Artefacts of Eskimos and Indians of North America. Catalogues*
Bankes, George. Eskimos and Indians : the North American collections in Brighton Museum / by George Bankes. — Brighton ([North Gate House, Church St., Brighton BN1 1UE]) : Royal Pavilion, Art Gallery and Museums, Brighton, [1977?]. — [8]p : ill ; 30cm. — (Royal Pavilion, Art Gallery and Museums, Brighton. Information sheets ; 2)
Bibl.: p.[8].
Sd : Unpriced
(B77-26801)

301.29'71'073 — Canada. Relations with United States
Canada-United States relations / edited by H. Edward English. — New York [etc.] ; London : Praeger for the Academy of Political Science, 1976. — xii,180p ; 24cm. — (Praeger special studies in international politics and government)

'Most of the essays in the volume were discussed at a conference ... in Washington, D.C., on October 23 and 24, 1975' - Foreword. — Index.
ISBN 0-275-23300-6 : £10.95
Primary classification 301.29'73'071
(B77-05216)

301.29'72'6 — Maya. *Mexico. Yucatan region, to 1976. Anthropological perspectives*
Anthropology and history in Yucatán / edited by Grant D. Jones. — Austin ; London : University of Texas Press, 1977. — xxiv,344p, leaf of plate,[14]p of plates : ill, maps ; 25cm. — (The Texas pan American series)
Bibl.: p.293-316. — Index.
ISBN 0-292-70314-7 : £12.75
(B77-23131)

301.29'726 — Mexico. Yucatan (State). Pustunich. Cultural processes
Press, Irwin. Tradition and adaptation : life in a modern Yucatan Maya village / [by] Irwin Press. — Westport, Conn. ; London : Greenwood Press, 1975. — xi,224p : ill, map ; 22cm.
Index.
ISBN 0-8371-7954-8 : £11.95
(B77-17921)

301.29'73 — United States. Cultural processes, ca 1780-1860
Bush, Clive. The dream of reason : American consciousness and cultural achievement from Independence to the Civil War / [by] Clive Bush. — London : Edward Arnold, 1977. — xi, 397p : ill, facsim, ports ; 24cm.
Bibl.: p.361-371. — Index.
ISBN 0-7131-5926-x : £14.95
(B77-21706)

301.29'73 — United States. Social change. Forecasting. Use of surveys of advertisements
Fowles, Jib. Mass advertising as social forecast : a method for futures research / [by] Jib Fowles. — Westport, Conn. ; London : Greenwood Press, 1976. — xi,153,[1]p : 1 ill, facsims ; 22cm.
Bibl.: p.127-149. — Index.
ISBN 0-8371-8595-5 : £8.95
(B77-17922)

301.29'73'0481 — United States. Relations with Norway, to 1975
Skard, Sigmund. The United States in Norwegian history / [by] Sigmund Skard. — Westport, Conn. ; London : Greenwood Press [etc.], 1976. — xii,216p ; 22cm. — (Contributions in American studies ; no.26)
Bibl.: p.205-209. — Index.
ISBN 0-8371-8909-8 : £10.50
Primary classification 301.29'481'073
(B77-17301)

301.29'73'071 — United States. Relations with Canada
Canada-United States relations / edited by H. Edward English. — New York [etc.] ; London : Praeger for the Academy of Political Science, 1976. — xii,180p ; 24cm. — (Praeger special studies in international politics and government)

'Most of the essays in the volume were discussed at a conference ... in Washington, D.C., on October 23 and 24, 1975' - Foreword. — Index.
ISBN 0-275-23300-6 : £10.95
Also classified at 301.29'71'073
(B77-05216)

301.29'755'042784 — Virginia. Relations with Whitehaven, Cumbria, to 1913
Lawrence-Dow, Elizabeth. Whitehaven to Washington / [by] Elizabeth Lawrence-Dow and Daniel Hay. — [Cleator] ([The Council Chambers, Cleator, Cumbria CA23 3DS]) : Copeland Borough Council, 1974. — 48p : ill, ports ; 21cm.
Index.
ISBN 0-904667-00-6 Sd : £0.60
Primary classification 301.29'427'84
(B77-20033)

301.29'756'8 — North Carolina. Little Laurel Valley. Cultural processes
Hicks, George Leon. Appalachian valley / by George L. Hicks. — New York ; London [etc.] : Holt, Rinehart and Winston, 1976. — xiv,112p : ill, map ; 24cm. — (Case studies in cultural anthropology)
Bibl.: p.109-112.
ISBN 0-03-077305-9 Pbk : £2.25
(B77-03383)

301.29'794'66 — Persons born 1920-1921. Social change. Effects of economic depressions, 1929-1933. *California. Oakland, 1932-1964. Longitudinal studies*
Elder, Glen H. Children of the Great Depression : social change in life experience / [by] Glen H. Elder, Jr. — Chicago ; London : University of Chicago Press, 1977. — xxiii, 400p : ill ; 22cm. — (A phoenix book)
Originally published: 1974. — Bibl.: p.377-388. — Index.
ISBN 0-226-20263-1 Pbk : £4.80
(B77-29943)

301.29'798'7 — Eskimos. Cultural processes. *North Alaska*
Spencer, Robert Francis. The North Alaskan Eskimo : a study in ecology and society / [by] Robert F. Spencer. — New York : Dover Publications [etc.] ; London : Constable, 1976. — vi,490p,[3]leaves of plates,9p of plates : ill, 5 maps, plan ; 22cm.
Originally published: Washington, D.C. : U.S. Government Printing Office, 1959 ; Newton Abbot : Distributed by David and Charles, 1969. — Bibl.: p.455-461. — Index.
ISBN 0-486-23369-3 Pbk : £4.25
(B77-25392)

301.29'8 — Latin America. Social change. Political aspects
Ideology & social change in Latin America / edited by June Nash, Juan Corradi, Hobart Spalding, Jr. — New York ; London [etc.] : Gordon and Breach, 1977. — vi,305[i.e.307]p, plate : 1 ill ; 24cm.
Bibl. — Index.
ISBN 0-677-04170-5 : £9.70
(B77-25393)

301.29'81'073 — Brazil. Influence of United States, 1960-1973
Black, Jan Knippers. United States penetration of Brazil / [by] Jan Knippers Black. — Manchester : Manchester University Press, 1977. — xx,313p ; 24cm.
Also published: Philadelphia : University of Pennsylvania Press, 1977. — Bibl.: p.268-296. — Index.
ISBN 0-7190-0699-6 : £11.50
(B77-29944)

301.29'81'1 — Y̧anomamö. Cultural processes. *Brazil*
Chagnon, Napoleon Alphonseau. Y̧anomamö : the fierce people / by Napoleon A. Chagnon. — 2nd ed. — New York [etc.] ; London : Holt, Rinehart and Winston, 1977. — xvi,174p,[2]p of plates : ill, 2 maps, ports ; 24cm. — (Case studies in cultural anthropology)
Previous ed.: 1968. — Bibl.: p.167-169. — List of films: p.170-172. — Index.
ISBN 0-03-089978-8 Pbk : £3.05
Primary classification 301.29'87'6
(B77-24006)

301.29'85 — Peru. Social change, 1890-1975. *Essays*
Social and economic change in modern Peru / edited by Rory Miller, Clifford T. Smith and John Fisher. — [Liverpool] ([P.O. Box 147, Liverpool L69 3BX]) : Centre for Latin-American Studies, University of Liverpool, [1976]. — [5],197p : ill, maps ; 30cm. — (University of Liverpool. Centre for Latin-American Studies. Monograph series ; no.6)
'The papers ... originated in a conference at the Centre for Latin-American Studies in Liverpool University in February 1974' - Introduction. — Bibl.: p.194-197.
ISBN 0-902806-05-x Sp : £2.75
Primary classification 330.9'85
(B77-03990)

301.29'866'4 — Canelos Quechuas. Cultural processes. *Ecuador*
Whitten, Norman Earl. Sacha Runa : ethnicity and adaptation of Ecuadorian jungle Quichua / [by] Norman E. Whitten, Jr with the assistance of ... [others]. — Urbana [etc.] ; London : University of Illinois Press, 1976. — xviii,348p, fold leaf : ill, maps ; 24cm.
Bibl.: p.313-323. — Index.
ISBN 0-252-00553-8 : £10.00
(B77-04564)

301.29'87'6 — Yąnomamö. Cultural processes. *Venezuela*
Chagnon, Napoleon Alphonseau. Yąnomamö : the fierce people / by Napoleon A. Chagnon. — 2nd ed. — New York [etc.] ; London : Holt, Rinehart and Winston, 1977. — xvi,174p,[2]p of plates : ill, 2 maps, ports ; 24cm. — (Case studies in cultural anthropology)
Previous ed.: 1968. — Bibl.: p.167-169. — List of films: p.170-172. — Index.
ISBN 0-03-089978-8 Pbk : £3.05
Also classified at 301.29'81'1
(B77-24006)

301.29'942 — Australian aborigines. Cultural processes. *Central Australia*
Róheim, Géza. Children of the desert : the western tribes of Central Australia / [by] Géza Róheim ; edited and with an introduction by Werner [i.e. Warner] Muensterberger. — New York [etc.] ; London : Harper and Row.
Vol.1. — 1976. — xix,262p : ill ; 21cm.
Originally published: New York : Basic Books, 1974. — Index.
ISBN 0-06-131906-6 Pbk : Unpriced
(B77-08778)

301.29'953 — Papua New Guinea. Trobriand Islands. Cultural processes
Weiner, Annette B. Women of value, men of renown : new perspectives in Trobriand exchange / [by] Annette B. Weiner. — Austin ; London : University of Texas Press, 1976. — xxi,299p : ill, maps, plan, ports ; 24cm.
Bibl.: p.261-273. — Index.
ISBN 0-292-79004-x : £11.25
(B77-16738)

301.29'95'3 — Primitive societies. *Papua New Guinea. Anthropological perspectives. Essays*
Williams, Francis Edgar. The Vailala Madness, and other essays / [by] Francis Edgar Williams ; edited, with an introduction by Erik Schwimmer. — London : C. Hurst, 1976. — 432p : ill, maps, port ; 23cm.
Bibl.: p.422-427. — Index.
ISBN 0-903983-46-x : £11.00
(B77-11075)

301.29'96'6 — Caroline Islands. Yap. Cultural processes
Labby, David. The demystification of Yap : dialectics of culture on a Micronesian island / [by] David Labby. — Chicago ; London : University of Chicago Press, 1976. — xiv,144p, [8]p of plates : ill, maps ; 23cm.
Bibl.: p.139-141. — Index.
ISBN 0-226-46711-2 : £8.85
(B77-02775)

301.3 — HUMAN ECOLOGY AND COMMUNITY

301.31 — Australia. Environment. Conservation, 1788-1914
Powell, Joseph Michael. Environmental management in Australia, 1788-1914 : guardians, improvers and profit : an introductory survey / [by] J.M. Powell. — Melbourne ; London [etc.] : Oxford University Press, 1976. — xi,191p : ill, facsim, maps, plan, ports ; 25cm.
Bibl.: p.175-184. — Index.
ISBN 0-19-550478-x : £15.00
ISBN 0-19-550479-8 Pbk : Unpriced
(B77-26802)

301.31 — Climate. Changes. Social aspects
Schneider, Stephen H. The genesis strategy : climate and global survival / [by] Stephen H. Schneider with Lynne E. Mesirow. — New York ; London : Plenum Press, 1976. — xxi, 419p : ill, charts ; 24cm.
Bibl.: p.373-376. — Index.
ISBN 0-306-30904-1 : £9.45
(B77-08779)

301.31 — England. Environment. Conservation by local community action groups. *Manuals*
Hampshire Council of Community Service. *Rural Committee.* Making your voice heard : an aid to amenity groups in the protection of their interests / compiled by the Rural Committee of the Hampshire Council of Community Service ... — London : Bedford Square Press : Distributed by Research Publications Services, 1977. — iv,26p ; 22cm.
Bibl.: p.26.
ISBN 0-7199-0927-9 Sd : £0.65
(B77-25394)

301.31 — England. Environment. Conservation. Organisations. *Manuals*
Civic Trust for the North West. ASK : amenity, society, know-how / Civic Trust for the North West ; edited by David E. Fletcher. — Manchester (56 Oxford St., Manchester M1 6EU) : The Trust, 1976. — 108p : ill, forms ; 31cm.
Bibl. — Index.
ISBN 0-901347-31-0 Sp : £2.50
(B77-09513)

301.31 — Environment
Harvey, Brian, *b.1939.* Environment and society : an introductory analysis / [by] Brian Harvey and John D. Hallett. — London [etc.] : Macmillan, 1977. — ix,163p : ill ; 23cm.
Bibl.: p.158-159. — Index.
ISBN 0-333-18415-7 : £6.95
ISBN 0-333-18416-5 Pbk : Unpriced
(B77-20912)

Managing the commons / edited by Garrett Hardin and John Baden. — San Francisco ; Reading : W.H. Freeman, 1977. — xiii,294p : ill ; 24cm.
ISBN 0-7167-0476-5 Pbk : £5.10
(B77-23132)

Santos, Miguel A. Ecology, natural resources and pollution / by Miguel A. Santos. — Anglo-American ed. — London : Living Books [etc.], 1975. — 106p : ill, map ; 21cm.
Bibl.: p.100-102. — Index.
ISBN 0-8210-0082-9 : Unpriced
ISBN 0-8210-0083-7 Pbk : Unpriced
(B77-19224)

Watt, Kenneth Edmund Ferguson. Principles of environmental science / [by] Kenneth E.F. Watt. — New York ; London [etc.] : McGraw-Hill, 1973. — xiv,319p,[8]p of plates : ill(some col) ; 25cm.
Col. ill. on lining papers. — Bibl. — Index.
ISBN 0-07-068575-4 : Unpriced
(B77-19225)

301.31 — Environment. *Juvenile literature*
Davies, Geoffrey. Round the year / by Geoffrey Davies ; illustrations by Ultra Art Ltd. — Edinburgh : Holmes-McDougall, [1974]. — 48p : col ill ; 21cm. — (Exploring your world : man ; section D : our surroundings ; book 3D)
Index.
ISBN 0-7157-1188-1 Pbk : Unpriced
ISBN 0-7157-1072-9 Pbk : Unpriced(non-net)
Primary classification 574.5'43
(B77-19375)

301.31 — Environment. *Secondary school texts*
Holme, Reginald. Quality of life / [by] Reginald Holme and Gordon Perry. — Poole : Blandford Press, 1977. — 72p : ill(some col), ports ; 25cm. — (Blandford social studies series ; 6)
Bibl.: p.70. — Index.
ISBN 0-7137-3357-8 Pbk : £1.30
(B77-26120)

301.31 — Environment. *Teaching kits*
Undy, Harry. Our world / [by Harry Undy]. — London (2 Chester House, Pages La., N10 1PR) : Christian Education Movement, [1976]. — Portfolio : ill, maps ; 25cm. — (Topic folder ; no.3)
Eight folders ([32]p.). — Text on portfolio. — Bibl.: p.[4](of portfolio).
ISBN 0-905022-12-2 : £0.70
(B77-00617)

301.31 — Environment. Conservation. *Proposals*
Ehrlich, Paul Ralph. How to be a survivor / [by] Paul R. Ehrlich and Richard L. Harriman. — London : Pan Books, 1972. — [11],177p ; 18cm.
Originally published: New York ; London : Ballantine Books, 1971. — Bibl.: p.170-173.
Pbk : £0.40
ISBN 0-345-02125-8
(B77-23133)

301.31 — Environment. Conservation. Information sources. *Lists*
Herring, Horace. Guide to environmental resources / compiled by Horace Herring. — Brighton : Smoothie Publications, 1975. — 32p ; 30cm.
Bibl.: p.6-10.
ISBN 0-903612-32-1 Sd : £1.20
(B77-01178)

301.31 — Environment. Influence of man
Design and nature? / edited for the [Open University, Art and Environment] Course Team by Barry Cunliffe and Christopher Crickmay. — Milton Keynes : Open University Press, 1976. — 63p : ill(some col), charts, facsim, maps, plans, ports ; 30cm. — ([Technology/ arts/social sciences], a second level interdisciplinary course : art and environment ; unit 15) (TAD292 ; 15)
Bibl.: p.61.
ISBN 0-335-06214-8 Pbk : Unpriced
(B77-14563)

301.31 — Environment. Perception by man
Stea, David. Environmental mapping / prepared for the [Open University Art and Environment] Course Team by David Stea. — Milton Keynes : Open University Press, 1976. — 48,[1] p,[4]p of plates : ill(some col), facsim, maps ; 30cm. — (A second level interdisciplinary course : art and environment ; unit 14) (TAD292 ; 14)
Bibl.: p.47-48.
ISBN 0-335-06213-x Pbk : £1.20
(B77-04565)

301.31 — Environment. Policies. Economic aspects
Hjalte, Krister. Environmental policy and welfare economics / [by] Krister Hjalte, Karl Lidgren, Ingemar Stahl ; translated [from the Swedish MS.] by Curt Wells. — Cambridge [etc.] : Cambridge University Press, 1977. — vii,111p : ill ; 23cm.
Bibl.: p.109-111.
ISBN 0-521-21549-8 : £5.50
ISBN 0-521-29182-8 Pbk : £2.50
(B77-30987)

301.31 — Environment. Pollution. *Juvenile literature*
Lyth, Mike. The war on pollution / [by] Mike Lyth. — Hove : Priory Press, 1977. — 89p : ill ; 24cm. — (Science in action)
Bibl.: p.86-87. — Index.
ISBN 0-85078-219-8 : £3.25
(B77-05878)

301.31 — Environment. Pollution. Research organisations. *Directories*
Pollution research index : a guide to world research in air, land, marine and freshwater pollution. — [St Peter Port] : Hodgson, 1975. — 431p ; 26cm.
Index. — Previous control number ISBN 0-85280-131-9.
Unpriced
ISBN 0-85280-131-9
(B77-24706)

301.31 — Environmental impact analysis
Jain, Ravindra K. Environmental impact analysis : a new dimension in decision making / [by] R.K. Jain, L.V. Urban, G.S. Stacey. — New York ; London [etc.] : Van Nostrand Reinhold, 1977. — [2],xiii,330p : ill ; 24cm. — (Van Nostrand Reinhold environmental engineering series)
Index.
ISBN 0-442-28807-7 : £18.25
(B77-29188)

301.31 — Great Britain. Environment. Conservation
Christian, Roy. Vanishing Britain / [by] Roy Christian ; foreword by Christopher Hall. — Newton Abbot [etc.] : David and Charles, 1977. — 144p : ill ; 26cm.
Bibl.: p.138-140. — Index.
ISBN 0-7153-7346-3 : £4.95
(B77-20034)

Conservation planning in town and country / papers by Robin Bloxsidge ... [et al.] ; edited by Josephine Reynolds. — Liverpool : Liverpool University Press, 1976. — 136p,[16]p of plates : ill, maps, plans ; 25cm.
Papers originally published as a special issue of 'Town planning review', issued in 1975 to commemorate European Architectural Heritage Year. — Bibl.: p.121-136.
ISBN 0-85323-393-4 Pbk : £4.50
(B77-09514)

301.31 — Great Britain. Environment. Conservation. *For education. Periodicals*
Heritage education news. — London (17 Carlton House Terrace, SW1Y 5AW) : Heritage Education Group.
Summer 1976-. — 1976-. — ill, facsims, ports ; 42cm.
Two issues a year. — Sheet (2 sides) as 1st issue.
Sd : Unpriced
ISSN 0140-0487
(B77-32419)

301.31 — Great Britain. Environment. Conservation. *Proposals*
Cormack, Patrick. Heritage in danger / [by] Patrick Cormack. — London : New English Library, 1976. — 268p,[24]p of plates : ill, map, ports ; 22cm.
Bibl.: p.263-264. — Index.
ISBN 0-450-03060-1 : £5.50
(B77-02776)

301.31 — Great Britain. Environment. Conservation & pollution. *Secondary school texts*
Hanson, William John. Pollution and conservation / [by] W.J. Hanson. — London : Longman, 1977. — 46p : ill, maps ; 27cm. — (Enquiries)
Adaptation of: 'Wat Heet? - Vuil' / edited by Gerard Groen, Han van der Meer and Jan de Werd ; translated by Olive Ordish. 's-Hertogenbosch : L.C.G. Malmberg, 1970. — Bibl.: p.46.
ISBN 0-582-22003-3 Sd : £0.75
(B77-17302)

301.31 — Great Britain. Environment. Conservation. Organisations. Organisation. *Manuals*
British Trust for Conservation Volunteers. Organising a local conservation corps / [British Trust for Conservation Volunteers]. — 2nd ed. — London (Zoological Gardens, Regents Park, NW1 4RY) : The Trust, 1977. — 60p : ill, facsims, form ; 30cm.
Previous ed.: 1972. — Bibl.: p.58-60.
ISBN 0-9501643-3-x Sd : £1.50
(B77-16192)

301.31 — Great Britain. Environment. Pollution. Implications of policies of government on nuclear power. Great Britain. Royal Commission on Environmental Pollution. Report. 6th: Nuclear power and the environment. *Critical studies*
Great Britain. *Department of the Environment.* Nuclear power and the environment : the Government's response to the sixth report of the Royal Commission on Environmental Pollution (Cmnd.6618) / prepared to Parliament by the Secretary of State for the Environment ... — London : H.M.S.O., [1977]. — 21p ; 25cm. — (Cmnd.6820)
ISBN 0-10-168200-x Sd : £0.45
(B77-17923)

301.31 — Kent. Environment. Conservation. Organisations. *Directories*
Kent Council of Social Service. An environmental directory for Kent : statutory and voluntary organisations in Kent of interest to those concerned with amenity and the environment / [Kent Council of Social Service]. — Folkestone (1 Holmesdale Terrace, Folkestone, Kent CT20 2AH) : Kent Council of Social Service, 1975. — [5],87p ; 30cm.
Index.
ISBN 0-900947-84-5 Pbk : Unpriced
(B77-08780)

301.31 — Man. Ecology
Doxiadis, Constantinos Apostolou. Ecology and ekistics / [by] C.A. Doxiadis ; edited by Gerald Dix. — London : Elek, 1977. — xxvii,91p : ill, maps ; 22cm. — (Environmental studies)
Index.
ISBN 0-236-40045-2 Pbk : £3.75
(B77-31699)

Treshow, Michael. The human environment / [by] Michael Treshow. — New York [etc.] ; London : McGraw-Hill, 1976. — xix,396p : ill ; 23cm. — (McGraw-Hill series in population biology)
Index.
ISBN 0-07-065136-1 Pbk : £6.60
(B77-04566)

301.31 — Man. Ecology. *Anthropological perspectives*
Hardesty, Donald L. Ecological anthropology / [by] Donald L. Hardesty. — New York ; London [etc.] : Wiley, 1977. — ix,310p : ill, maps ; 23cm.
Bibl.: p.261-283. — Index.
ISBN 0-471-35144-x : £9.35
(B77-14055)

301.31 — Norfolk Broads. Environment. Conservation. *Proposals*
Nature Conservancy Council. The future of Broadland : a statement / by the Nature Conservancy Council. — London [etc.] : The Council, 1977. — [20]p : ill ; 26cm.
ISBN 0-901204-47-1 Sd : Unpriced
(B77-25395)

301.31 — Organisation for Economic Co-operation and Development countries. Environment. Effects of government policies on exploitation of energy resources. *Reports, surveys*
Organisation for Economic Co-operation and Development. Energy production and environment / Organisation for Economic Co-operation and Development. — Paris : O.E.C.D. ; [London] : [H.M.S.O.], 1977. — 107p ; 24cm.
Bibl.: p.103-107.
Pbk : £2.60
ISBN 92-64-11585-4
(B77-17924)

301.31 — United States. Environment. Conservation. Attitudes of negroes
Ostheimer, John M. Environment, energy, and black Americans / [by] John M. Ostheimer, Leonard G. Ritt. — Beverly Hills ; London : Sage Publications, 1976. — 38,[1]p ; 22cm. — (Sage research papers in the social sciences : human ecology ; vol.4, no.90-025)
Bibl.: p.33-35.
ISBN 0-8039-0545-9 Pbk : £1.50
(B77-14564)

301.31 — United States. Environment. Conservation. Participation of public
Caldwell, Lynton K. Citizens and the environment : case studies in popular action / [by] Lynton K. Caldwell, Lynton R. Hayes, Isabel M. MacWhirter. — Bloomington ; London : Indiana University Press, 1976. — xxx,449p ; 24cm.
Bibl. — Index.
ISBN 0-253-31355-4 : £14.00
(B77-03941)

301.31 — United States. Environment. Conservation. Participation of public. Political aspects
Haefele, Edwin Theodore. Representative government and environmental management / by Edwin T. Haefele. — Baltimore ; London : Johns Hopkins University Press for Resources for the Future, 1973. — xiii,188p : ill, 2 maps ; 24cm.
ISBN 0-8018-1571-1 : Unpriced
(B77-20035)

301.31 — Urban regions. Climate. Changes. Social aspects
The **urban** costs of climate modification / edited by Terry A. Ferrar. — New York ; London [etc.] : Wiley, [1977]. — xviii,284p : ill, charts, maps ; 24cm. — (Environmental science & technology)
'A Wiley-Interscience publication'. — Published in the United States: 1976. — Bibl. — Index.
ISBN 0-471-25767-2 : £14.25
(B77-14056)

301.31'01'8 — Environmental studies. Applications of remote sensing. *Conference proceedings*
Environmental remote sensing. — London : Edward Arnold.
2 : Practices and problems : papers presented at the Second Bristol Symposium on Remote Sensing, Department of Geography, University of Bristol / edited by Eric C. Barrett and Leonard F. Curtis. — 1977. — vi,314p,[4] leaves of plates : ill(some col), maps ; 24cm.
Bibl. — Index.
ISBN 0-7131-5866-2 : £16.00
(B77-14565)

Remote Sensing Applied to Energy-Related Problems Symposium, *Miami, 1974.* Symposium proceedings : Remote Sensing Applied to Energy-Related Problems, Symposium Course, [held] 2-4 December 1974 [at] Miami, Florida, presented [i.e. organized] by Clean Energy Research Institute, School of Engineering and Environmental Design, University of Miami, Coral Gables, Florida, sponsored by School of Continuing Studies, University of Miami / edited by T. Nejat Veziroglu. — Coral Gables : University of Miami ; Oxford [etc.] : Distributed by Pergamon, [1977]. — 426p in various pagings : ill, charts, form, maps ; 29cm.
Bibl.
ISBN 0-08-021563-7 Pbk : £25.00
(B77-11076)

301.31'01'84 — United States. Environment. Policies of government. Decision making. Applications of mathematical models. *Reports, surveys*
Holcomb Research Institute. Environmental modeling and decision making : the United States experience : a report / by the Holcomb Research Institute, Butler University ; for the Scientific Committee on Problems of the Environment. — New York [etc.] ; London : Praeger, [1977]. — xxiv,152p : 1 ill ; 24cm. — (Praeger special studies in US economic, social and political issues)
Published in the United States: 1976. — Bibl.: p.123-137. — Index.
ISBN 0-275-24190-4 : £12.20
(B77-08781)

301.31'022'2 — Environment. *Illustrations. Secondary school texts*
Olphert, Derek. Response to vision / [text by] Derek Olphert ; photography and design by the author. — [London etc.] : Reed Education. 5. — [1975]. — [64]p : chiefly ill ; 21x30cm.
Pbk : Unpriced
(B77-17303)

301.31'07 — Environmental studies facilities. *Scotland. Rural regions. Conference proceedings*
Countryside Facilities for Environmental Education *(Conference), Battleby, 1976.* Countryside facilities for environmental education : report on a conference [held] 1 December 1976 : [organised by the] Countryside Commission for Scotland. — Redgorton : The Commission, [1977]. — [3], 60p,4p of plates : ill(some col) ; 20cm.
'... our meeting about Countryside Facilities for Environmental Education ...' - p.1. — Bibl.: p.45.
ISBN 0-902226-37-1 Sd : £1.00
(B77-29189)

301.31'07 — Teachers. Professional education. Curriculum subjects: Environmental studies. Courses. *Great Britain. Directories*
National Association for Environmental Education. Teaching environmental studies / National Association for Environmental Education. — [Great Britain] : [The Association], [1974?]. — [8]p ; 21cm. — (Information leaflet ; 74/1)
Sd : £0.10
(B77-33617)

301.31'07'2041 — Great Britain. Environment. Research organisations: Centre for Environmental Studies. *Reports, surveys. Serials*
Centre for Environmental Studies. Annual report / Centre for Environmental Studies. — London : [The Centre].
9th : Spring 1975-Spring 1976. — [1976]. — [2],v,85p : 1 ill ; 24cm.
Bibl.: p.71-76.
Sd : Unpriced
ISSN 0305-8573
(B77-29945)

301.31'07'2042 — Field studies. Organisations. *England. Field Studies Council. Reports, surveys. Serials*
Field Studies Council. Annual report / Field Studies Council. — London (9 Devereux Court, Strand, WC2R 3JR) : [The Council].
1975-1976. — [1977]. — [2],40p : ill, 2 ports ; 25cm.
Sd : Free to members
(B77-26803)

301.31'08 — Man. Ecology. Biosocial aspects. *Readings. Serials*
Readings in ecology, energy and human society : contemporary perspectives / edited by William R. Burch, Jr. — New York [etc.] ; London : Harper and Row. — (Contemporary perspectives reader series)
1977-1978 ed. — 1977. — xiv,308p : ill, maps, plans, ports ; 29cm.
Bibl. — Includes facsimile reprints.
ISBN 0-06-047058-5 Pbk : £5.20
(B77-26804)

301.31'094113'5 — Scotland. Shetland. Sullom Voe region. Environment. Effects of oil terminals. *Reports, surveys*
Sullom Voe Environmental Advisory Group. Oil terminal at Sullom Voe : environmental impact assessment / the Sullom Voe Environmental Advisory Group. — Sandwick (Sandwick, Shetland) : Thuleprint Ltd, 1976. — 133p, plate : 1 ill, col maps ; 29cm.
Bibl.: p.130-133.
Pbk : £1.00
(B77-17304)

301.31'09425'3 — Lincolnshire. Environment. *Reports, surveys. For structure plan making*
Lincolnshire *(County). Planning Department.* Leisure, landscape and buildings : a background paper to the Lincolnshire structure plan / [Lincolnshire County Planning Department]. — [Lincoln] ([County Offices, Lincoln LN1 1YJ]) : [The Department], 1976. — 41[i.e.43]p : maps(some col) ; 30cm.
Cover title: Lincolnshire structure plan, background paper, leisure, landscape & buildings. — Summary (2p.) as insert.
Sp : £0.55
(B77-22356)

301.31'09426'7 — Essex. Coastal regions. Environment. *Reports, surveys. For structure plan making*
Essex *(County). Planning Department.* The Essex coast, technical report / Essex County Council [Planning Department]. — [Chelmsford] ([County Hall, Chelmsford CM1 1LF]) : [The Department], 1977. — [9],105p,19 leaves of plates : maps, plans ; 30cm.
Cover title: Essex structure plan, Essex coast, technical report. — Bibl.: p.103-104.
Sp : £1.00
(B77-26805)

301.31'09485 — Sweden. Environment. Policies of government. *Reports, surveys*
Organisation for Economic Co-operation and Development. Environmental policy in Sweden / [Organisation for Economic Co-operation and Development]. — Paris : O.E.C.D. ; [London] : [H.M.S.O.], 1977. — 144p : ill, maps ; 24cm.
Pbk : £3.00
ISBN 92-64-11610-9
(B77-26121)

301.32 — Historical demography
Hollingsworth, Thomas Henry. Historical demography / by T.H. Hollingsworth. — Cambridge [etc.] : Cambridge University Press [for] The Sources of History Ltd, 1976. — 448p : ill ; 22cm. — (Sources of history, studies in the uses of historical evidence)
Originally published: London : Hodder and Stoughton, 1969. — Bibl.: p.391-421. — Index.
ISBN 0-521-21454-8 : £7.50
ISBN 0-521-29154-2 Pbk : £2.95
(B77-12863)

301.32 — Population
Henry, Louis. Population : analysis and models / [by] Louis Henry ; translated [from the French] by Etienne van de Walle and Elise F. Jones. — London : Edward Arnold, 1976. — xiii,301p : ill ; 24cm.
Translation of: 'Démographie - analyse et modèles'. Paris : Larousse, 1972. — Bibl.: p.291. — Index.
ISBN 0-7131-5868-9 : £9.95
ISBN 0-7131-5869-7 Pbk : £4.95
(B77-09515)

Matras, Judah. Introduction to population : a sociological approach / [by] Judah Matras. — Englewood Cliffs ; London [etc.] : Prentice-Hall, 1977. — x,452p : ill, forms, maps ; 24cm.
Text on lining papers. — Bibl.: p.427-441. — Index.
ISBN 0-13-493122-x : £11.95
(B77-27686)

301.32 — Population. *Secondary school texts*
Richards, Michael, *b.1941.* Population / [by] Michael Richards. — London : Longman, 1977. — [2],38p : ill, maps, ports ; 24cm. — (Longman social science studies : series two)
Bibl.: p.38.
ISBN 0-582-22153-6 Sd : £0.80
(B77-20913)

301.32 — Population. Conferences: World Population Conference, Bucharest, 1974
Carillo-Flores, Antonio. The World Population Conference 1974 / by Antonio Carillo-Flores. — Cardiff ([P.O. Box 78, Cardiff CF1 1XL]) : University College, [1975]. — 11p ; 21cm. — (Sir David Owen memorial lecture ; 4th)
ISBN 0-901426-16-4 Sd : £0.35
(B77-00034)

301.32 — Population. Growth
Overbeek, Johannes. The population challenge : a handbook for nonspecialists / [by] Johannes Overbeek. — Westport, Conn. ; London : Greenwood Press, 1976. — xiv,214,[1]p : ill ; 22cm. — (Contributions in sociology ; no.19)
Bibl.: p.200-204. — Index.
ISBN 0-8371-8896-2 : £11.50
(B77-17305)

301.32 — Population. Growth. *Reports, surveys*
Population Concern. World population report. — Revised [ed.] / Population Concern ; [edited by E.J. McGraw]. — London (27 Mortimer St., W1N 7RJ) : Population Concern, 1977. — [8] p : ill ; 30cm.
Previous ed.: / Population CountDown. 1976. — Bibl.: p.[8]. — List of films: p.[8].
Sd : £0.15
(B77-32421)

Population CountDown. World population report / Population CountDown. — London (27 Mortimer St., W1A 4QW) : Population CountDown, 1976. — [8]p : ill ; 30cm.
Bibl.: p.[8]. — List of films: p.[8].
Sd : £0.15
(B77-32422)

301.32 — Population. Growth. *Secondary school texts*
Hay, David. Human populations / [by] David Hay. — Harmondsworth : Kestrel Books, 1976. — 96p : ill, facsims, maps, ports ; 23cm.
Originally published: Harmondsworth : Penguin, 1972. — Bibl.: p.90-92. — List of films : p.93. — Index.
ISBN 0-7226-5290-9 : £2.75
(B77-03942)

301.32 — Population. Growth. Economic aspects
Clark, Colin, *b.1905.* Population growth and land use / [by] Colin Clark. — 2nd ed. — London [etc.] : Macmillan, 1977. — ix,415p,fold leaf : ill, maps ; 23cm.
This ed. originally published: New York : St Martin's Press, 1977. — Previous ed.: 1967. — Index.
ISBN 0-333-22753-0 : £10.00
ISBN 0-333-22754-9 Pbk : £4.95
(B77-28393)

301.32'01'8 — Demography. Methodology
Shryock, Henry S. The methods and materials of demography / [by] Henry S. Shryock, Jacob S. Siegel and associates. — Condensed ed. / by Edward G. Stockwell. — New York [etc.] ; London : Academic Press, 1976. — ix,577p : ill, forms, maps ; 29cm. — (Studies in population)
Previous ed.: in 2 vols. Washington : US Bureau of the Census, 1971. — Bibl. — Index.
ISBN 0-12-641150-6 : £9.55
(B77-05217)

301.32'01'8 — Population. Spatial analysis
Rees, P H. Spatial population analysis / [by] P.H. Rees and A.G. Wilson. — London : Edward Arnold, 1977. — x,356p : ill, map ; 26cm.
Bibl.: p.346-350. — Index.
ISBN 0-7131-5848-4 : £27.50
(B77-14566)

301.32'09 — Population. Growth. Theories, to 1976
Parsons, Jack. Population fallacies / [by] Jack Parsons. — London : Elek : Pemberton, 1977. — xv,286p : ill ; 23cm.
Bibl.: p.263-271. — Index.
ISBN 0-301-74031-3 : £8.00
ISBN 0-301-74032-1 Pbk : £4.00
(B77-12303)

301.32'1 — Birth control. *Illustrations*
Family Planning Association. *SW London Branch.* Too great a risk / [written by Gillian Crampton Smith ; for FPA SW London Branch]. — London : Family Planning Association, [1976]. — Folder ([5]p) : ill ; 21cm.
ISBN 0-903289-09-1 : £0.025
(B77-03943)

301.32'1 — Birth control. Attitudes of doctors. *Scotland. Reports, surveys*
Aitken-Swan, Jean. Fertility control and the medical profession / [by] Jean Aitken-Swan. — London : Croom Helm, 1977. — 238p ; 23cm.
Index.
ISBN 0-85664-463-3 : £7.25
(B77-23134)

301.32'1 — Negroes. Birth control. United States. Related to racial discrimination by society
Weisbord, Robert G. Genocide? : birth control and the black American / [by] Robert G. Weisbord. — Westport, Conn. ; London : Greenwood Press [etc.], 1975. — ix,219p ; 22cm.
Bibl.: p.189-207. — Index.
ISBN 0-8371-8084-8 : £6.75
Also classified at 301.45'19'6073
(B77-17306)

301.32'1 — Population. Control. *Secondary school texts*
Jay, Eric. Population and family planning / [text by Eric Jay]. — London : S.C.M. Press [for] the Christian Education Movement, 1971. — 32p : ill ; 23cm. — (Probe ; 1 ISSN 0305-3776)
Originally published: 1969. — Bibl.: p.32.
Sd : £0.15
ISBN 0-334-01268-6
(B77-11579)

301.32'1 — United Nations Fund for Population Activities, to 1975
Salas, Rafael M. People : an international choice : the multilateral approach to population / by Rafael M. Salas. — Oxford [etc.] : Pergamon, 1976. — xv,154p,[3]leaves of plates,[10]p of plates : ill, ports ; 21cm. — (Pergamon international library)
Fold. cover. — Index.
ISBN 0-08-021029-5 : £3.00
(B77-09516)

301.32'1'091724 — Birth control. *Developing countries. Reports, surveys*
The **feasibility** of fertility planning : micro perspectives / edited by T. Scarlett Epstein and Darrell Jackson. — Oxford [etc.] : Pergamon, 1977. — viii,244p,[10]p of plates : ill, ports ; 26cm.
Bibl.: p.239-244.
ISBN 0-08-021452-5 : £12.50
ISBN 0-08-021837-7 Pbk : £4.00
(B77-33618)

301.32'1'0941 — Married persons. Birth control. *Great Britain, 1967-1968. Reports, surveys*
Langford, C M. Birth control practice and marital fertility in Great Britain : a report on a survey carried out in 1967-68 / [by] C.M. Langford. — London (Houghton St., Aldwych, WC2A 2AE) : Population Investigation Committee, London School of Economics, 1976. — xi,141p ; 25cm.
ISBN 0-905804-00-7 Pbk : £5.00
(B77-11580)

301.32'1'0945 — Italy. Population. Fertility, ca 1800-1971
Livi-Bacci, Massimo. A history of Italian fertility during the last two centuries / by Massimo Livi-Bacci. — Princeton ; Guildford : Princeton University Press for the Office of Population Research, Princeton University, 1977. — xxii, 311,[1]p : ill, maps ; 25cm.
Index.
ISBN 0-691-09369-5 : £12.70
(B77-24007)

301.32'1'0973 — Birth control. *United States, 1945-1970. Reports, surveys*
Westoff, Charles F. The contraceptive revolution / [by] Charles F. Westoff and Norman B. Ryder. — Princeton ; Guildford : Princeton University Press for the Office of Population Research, Princeton University, 1977. — vii,388,[1]p : ill ; 25cm.
Bibl.: p.383-384. — Index.
ISBN 0-691-09371-7 : £14.20
(B77-22357)

301.32'1'0973 — Women. Fertility. Effects of family planning services. *United States, 1965-1975*
Cutright, Phillips. Impact of family planning programs on fertility : the US experience / [by] Phillips Cutright, Frederick S. Jaffe. — New York [etc.] ; London : Praeger, 1977. — xix, 151p : ill ; 25cm. — (Praeger special studies in US economic, social and political issues)
ISBN 0-275-23350-2 : £11.10
(B77-15695)

301.32'2 — Deaths due to diseases associated with cigarette smoking. *England. Cohort studies*
Todd, George Frederick. Cohort analysis of cigarette smoking and of mortality from four associated diseases / by G.F. Todd, P.N. Lee and M.J. Wilson. — London (Glen House, Stag Place, SW1E 5AG) : Tobacco Research Council, 1976. — 55p : 1 ill ; 30cm. — (Tobacco Research Council. Occasional papers ; 3 ISSN 0306-8196)
Bibl.: p.55.
ISBN 0-901026-13-1 Sd : Unpriced
(B77-14567)

301.32'2 — Deaths due to diseases associated with cigarette smoking. Great Britain. Related to social class. *Reports, surveys*
Todd, George Frederick. Social class variations in cigarette smoking and in mortality from associated diseases / by G.F. Todd. — London (Glen House, Stag Place, SW1E 5AG) : Tobacco Research Council, 1976. — 31p ; 30cm. — (Tobacco Research Council. Occasional papers ; 2 ISSN 0306-8196)
Bibl.: p.31.
ISBN 0-901026-12-3 Sd : Unpriced
Primary classification 301.5'7
(B77-14576)

301.32'2 — Man. Mortality rate
Preston, Samuel H. Mortality patterns in national populations : with special reference to recorded causes of death / [by] Samuel H. Preston. — New York [etc.] ; London : Academic Press, 1976. — xi,201p : ill ; 24cm. — (Studies in population)
Bibl.: p.187-193. — Index.
ISBN 0-12-564450-7 : £10.05
(B77-08232)

301.32'2 — Man. Mortality rate. Sex differences, 1910-1965
Retherford, Robert D. The changing sex differential in mortality / [by] Robert D. Retherford. — Westport, Conn. ; London : Greenwood Press, 1975. — xi,139p ; 22cm. — (Studies in population and urban demography ; no.1)
Bibl.: p.127-134. — Index.
ISBN 0-8371-7848-7 : £8.95
(B77-17925)

301.32'3 — Indians of North America. Demographic aspects. *California, 1769-1970*
Cook, Sherburne Friend. The population of the California Indians, 1769-1970 / [by] Sherburne F. Cook ; with a foreword by Woodrow Borah and Robert F. Heizer. — Berkeley [etc.] ; London : University of California Press, 1976. — xvii,222p : ill, maps ; 24cm.
Bibl.: p.203-204. — Index.
ISBN 0-520-02923-2 : £10.20
(B77-14057)

301.32'3 — West Indian immigrants. Distribution. *London, 1961-1976. Reports, surveys*
Lee, Trevor. Race and residence : the concentration and dispersal of immigrants in London / by Trevor R. Lee. — Oxford : Clarendon Press, 1977. — xi,193p : ill, form, maps ; 25cm. — (Oxford research studies in geography)
Bibl.: p.182-188. — Index.
ISBN 0-19-823215-2 : £6.95
(B77-15095)

301.32'4'0941 — Immigration to Great Britain. *Labour Party viewpoints*
Labour Party. Immigration & racialism / [Labour Party] ; [researched by Liz Atkins]. — London : Labour Party, 1977. — Folder([4]p) : ill ; 30cm. — (Labour Party. Political education discussion papers ; no.4)
Unpriced
Also classified at 301.45'1'0941
(B77-16193)

301.32'6 — Internal migration
Internal migration : a comparative perspective / edited by Alan A. Brown, Egon Neuberger. — New York [etc.] ; London : Academic Press, 1977. — xiv,508p : ill, maps ; 24cm.
'This book is the third in a series of publications sponsored by the Committee on Comparative Urban Economics' - Preface. — Bibl. — Index.
ISBN 0-12-137350-9 : £20.95
(B77-28394)

301.32'6'09421 — Internal migration. Stochastic models. *London*
Bonnar, Desmond M. Stochastic models for migration analysis : applications to Greater London / [by] Desmond M. Bonnar. — Reading (Whiteknights, Reading [RG6 2AB]) : Department of Geography, University of Reading, 1976. — [2],ii,43p : ill, maps ; 21cm. — (Geographical papers ; no.51 ISSN 0305-5914)
Bibl.: p.32-35.
ISBN 0-7049-0461-6 Sd : £0.70
(B77-17307)

301.32'6'0944 — Internal migration. *France, 1891-1968*
Winchester, H P M. Changing patterns of French internal migration, 1891-1968 / [by] H.P.M. Winchester. — Oxford (Mansfield Rd, Oxford OX1 3TB) : University of Oxford, School of Geography, 1977. — 37p : maps ; 22cm. — (University of Oxford. School of Geography. Research papers ; no.17 ISSN 0305-8190)
Bibl.: p.33-37.
Sd : Unpriced
(B77-26122)

301.32'6'09598 — Internal migration. *Indonesia*
Hardjono, J M. Transmigration in Indonesia / [by] J.M. Hardjono. — Kuala Lumpur ; London [etc.] : Oxford University Press, 1977. — xv,116p : maps ; 26cm. — (Oxford in Asia current affairs)
Bibl.: p.103-111. — Index.
ISBN 0-19-580344-2 Pbk : £6.00
(B77-26806)

301.32'8'4073 — Europe. Emigration to United States, 1815-1914
Jones, Maldwyn Allen. Destination America / [by] Maldwyn A. Jones. — [London] : Fontana, 1977. — 224p,[16]p of plates : ill, facsims, 2 maps ; 20cm.
'... written to accompany the Thames Television series of the same name ...' - cover. — Originally published: London : Weidenfeld and Nicolson, 1976. — Bibl.: p.213-215. — Index.
ISBN 0-00-634435-6 Pbk : £1.50
(B77-27687)

301.32'8'429073 — Wales. Emigration to United States, 1776-1914
Williams, Glanmor. A prospect of paradise? / [by] Glanmor Williams ; [translated from the Welsh]. — [Cardiff] : B.B.C. Wales, 1976. — 30p ; 18cm. — (British Broadcasting Corporation. Welsh Region. Annual radio lectures ; 1976)
'Broadcast [in Welsh] on BBC Wales Radio 4 15 November, 1976 at 8 p.m.'. — Translation of: 'Y baradwys bell?'. 1976.
ISBN 0-563-17264-9 Sd : £0.25
(B77-05879)

301.32'8'65044 — International migration. *Study examples: Emigration from Algeria to France, 1870-1976*
Adler, Stephen. International migration and dependence / [by] Stephen Adler. — Farnborough, Hants. : Saxon House, 1977. — xv,235p : ill ; 23cm.
Bibl.: p.220-230. — Index.
ISBN 0-566-00202-7 : £8.50 : CIP rev.
(B77-25396)

301.32'9'171241 — Commonwealth countries. Population, to 1945. *Reports, surveys*
Kuczynski, Robert René. Demographic survey of the British Colonial Empire / by R.R. Kuczynski ; [completed by Brigitte Long]. — Fairfield : Augustus M. Kelley ; Hassocks : Harvester Press, 1977. — 3v.(xiii,821; x,983; xiii,497p) ; 26cm.
Originally published: / issued by Royal Institute of International Affairs. London : Oxford University Press, 1948. — Bibl. — Index.
ISBN 0-85527-769-6 : £75.00
(B77-14568)

301.32'9'1724 — Developing countries. Population. Growth. Socioeconomic aspects
Sai, Fred T. Population and national development : the dilemma of developing countries / by Fred T. Sai ; with editorial assistance from Penny Kane. — London : International Planned Parenthood Federation, 1977. — 30p : ill ; 21cm. — (Sai, Fred T. Occasional essays ; no.2)
ISBN 0-900924-91-8 Sd : £0.85
(B77-26807)

301.32'9'4 — Migration. *Europe, 1945-1975*
Migration in post-war Europe : geographical essays / edited by John Salt and Hugh Clout. — London [etc.] : Oxford University Press, 1976. — x,228p : ill, maps ; 24cm.
Bibl. — Index.
ISBN 0-19-874027-1 : £6.00
ISBN 0-19-874028-x Pbk : £2.95
(B77-04567)

301.32'9'41 — Great Britain. Population. Growth. *Conservation Society viewpoints*
Guillebaud, John. The twilight of parenthood / [by] John Guillebaud. The elderly in a stationary or declining population / [based on a longer article by Jane Pink]. — Chertsey (12 London St., Chertsey, Surrey KT16 8AA) : Conservation Society, [1976]. — Folder([4]p) : ill ; 25cm.
'Two population studies by the Conservation Society reprinted from ... "Conservation News". No.56, dated June, 1975'. — Bibl.: p.[2].
ISBN 0-903127-10-5 : £0.15
(B77-00035)

301.32'9'41 — Great Britain. Population. Growth. *Forecasts. Serials*
Population projections : population projections by sex, age and marital status for United Kingdom and constituent counties, from mid-1975 / prepared by the Government Actuary ; [for the] Office of Population Censuses and Surveys. — London : H.M.S.O.
[1975-2015] : from mid-1975. — 1977. — [5], 74p : ill ; 30cm. — (PP2 ; no.7)
ISBN 0-11-690642-1 Pbk : £2.00
(B77-28395)

301.32'9'42 — England. Population. Effects of plague, 1348-1530. Economic aspects
Hatcher, John. Plague, population and the English economy, 1348-1530 / prepared for the Economic History Society by John Hatcher. — London [etc.] : Macmillan, 1977. — 95p ; 21cm. — (Studies in economic and social history)
Bibl.: p.81-91. — Index.
ISBN 0-333-21293-2 Pbk : £1.75
(B77-26808)

301.32'9'421 — England. Population. Mid-year estimates. *Study regions: London*
Hollis, John. Mid-year population estimates : a commentary / by John Hollis and A. Miryam Field ; [for the Greater London Council] Director-General's Department, Policy Studies and Intelligence Branch. — London : G.L.C., 1976. — [3],18[i.e.22]p : ill ; 30cm. — (Greater London Council. Intelligence Unit. Research memoranda ; RM494 ISSN 0306-7203)
ISBN 0-7168-0847-1 Sd : £2.30
(B77-15696)

301.32'9'423 — South-west England. Population, to 1975. *Essays*
Population and marketing : two studies in the history of the South-west / edited by Walter Minchinton. — [Exeter] : University of Exeter, 1976. — 139p : ill, maps ; 30cm. — (Exeter papers in economic history ; no.11)
Papers from two seminars held at Dartington.
ISBN 0-85989-035-x Pbk : £1.75
Also classified at 338.1'09423
(B77-20914)

301.32'9423'3 — South-east Dorset. Population. *Reports, surveys. For structure plan making*
Dorset *(County). Council.* Study report, population : Dorset County Council, South East Dorset structure plan. — [Dorchester] ([County Hall, Dorchester, Dorset]) : [The Council], 1976. — [6],33,v p,[5] leaves of plates : ill(some col), 2 col maps ; 30cm. — (SP ; 18)
Cover title: Structure plan, SE Dorset, study report, population.
ISBN 0-85216-146-8 Pbk : £0.70
(B77-12864)

301.32'9'42341 — Jersey. Population, 1976. *Census tables*
Jersey. *States. Etat Civil Committee.* Report of the Census for 1976 / presented to the States [of Jersey] on the 15th January 1977 by the Etat Civil Committee. — Jersey : States of Jersey, 1977. — [2] leaves,62p : ill ; 30cm. — (R.C. (Series II))
Sd : £2.50
(B77-29190)

301.32'9'42342 — Guernsey. Population, 1976. *Census tables*
Guernsey. *States. States Economist.* Guernsey Census 1976 / [prepared by the States Economist of Guernsey as Census Supervisor]. — Guernsey : States Office, Guernsey, [1977]. — [3],58p(2 fold) : form, maps ; 30cm.
'The Census ... was conducted by officers of the States Advisory and Finance Committee ...' - Foreword.
Sd : Unpriced
(B77-29191)

301.32'9'42838 — Humberside. Holderness. Population, 1538-1731. Historical sources: Parish registers
Smith, M H. Parish registers and population in South Holderness : some researches into the parish registers of Keyingham, Patrington and Winestead / by M.H. Smith. — Beverley (24 Wylies Rd, Beverley, N. Humberside) : Hedon and District Local History Society, 1976. — [2],27p : facsim ; 22cm. — (Hedon local history series ; no.3 ISSN 0305-1056)
ISBN 0-9501697-3-0 Sd : £0.50
(B77-11581)

301.32'9'47 — Eastern Europe & Soviet Union. Population. *Conference proceedings*
International Slavic Conference, *1st, Banff, Alta, 1974.* Demographic developments in Eastern Europe / edited by Leszek A. Kosinski. — New York ; London : Praeger, 1977. — xx, 346p : ill, maps ; 25cm. — (Praeger special studies in international politics and government)

'The papers ... are selected from among those presented at the First International Slavic Conference held in Banff, Alberta, Canada, September 4-7, 1974' - General Editor's Foreword. — Bibl. — Index.
ISBN 0-275-56180-1 : £16.25
(B77-26123)

301.32'9'47 — Soviet Union. Population. *Reports, surveys*
Chinn, Jeff. Manipulating Soviet population resources / [by] Jeff Chinn. — London [etc.] : Macmillan, 1977. — vii,163p ; 23cm.
Bibl.: p.146-158. — Index.
ISBN 0-333-22564-3 : £10.00 : CIP rev.
(B77-17308)

301.32'9'7 — America. Population, 1492
The **native** population of the Americas in 1492 / edited by William M. Denevan. — Madison ; London : University of Wisconsin Press, 1976. — xxii,353,[1]p : ill, maps ; 24cm.
Bibl.: p.299-331. — Index.
ISBN 0-299-07050-6 : £11.25
(B77-22358)

301.32'9'87 — Venezuela. Population, 1750-1850
Lombardi, John V. People and places in colonial Venezuela / [by] John V. Lombardi ; maps and figures by Cathryn L. Lombardi. — Bloomington ; London : Indiana University Press, [1977]. — xv,484p : ill, facsims, maps ; 28cm.
Published in the United States: 1976. — Index.
ISBN 0-253-34330-5 : £18.75
(B77-11077)

301.34 — Communities
Power, paradigms and community research / edited by Roland J. Liebert and Allen W. Imershein. — London [etc.] : Sage Publications [for] the International Sociological Association, 1977. — [5],343p : ill ; 22cm. — (Sage studies in international sociology ; 9)
Bibl. — Index.
ISBN 0-8039-9999-2 : £8.00
ISBN 0-8039-9850-3 Pbk : £3.95
(B77-33066)

301.34'06'141 — Community relations. Organisations. *Great Britain. Community Relations Commission. Reports, surveys. Serials*
Community relations : the report of the Community Relations Commission ... — London : H.M.S.O.
1975, July-76, November. — [1976]. — vi, 103p ; 25cm. — ([1976-77 H.C.] 51)
Bibl.: p.85-87.
ISBN 0-10-205177-1 Sd : £1.75
(B77-07069)

301.34'094 — Human settlements. *Europe. Conference proceedings*
Medieval settlement : continuity and change / edited by P.H. Sawyer. — London : Edward Arnold, 1976. — ix,357p : ill, maps, plans ; 26cm.
'The colloquium on which this volume is based was held at the University of Leeds in July 1974' - Preface. — Bibl.: p.327-340. — Index.
ISBN 0-7131-5864-6 : £19.50
(B77-10736)

301.34'09471 — Human settlements. Effects of uplift of land. *Finland, to 1971*
Jones, Michael, *b.1944.* Finland : daughter of the sea / [by] Michael Jones. — Folkestone : Dawson [etc.], 1977. — 247p : ill, maps ; 23cm. — (Studies on historical geography ISSN 0308-6607)
Ill. on lining papers. — Index.
ISBN 0-7129-0695-9 : £9.00
(B77-10177)

301.35 — Depopulation. *Great Britain. Rural regions. Reports, surveys*
Rural depopulation : report / by an interdepartmental group ... ; with the assistance of Office of Population Censuses and Surveys, General Register Office (Scotland). — [London] ([Parliament St., SW1P 3AG]) : H.M. Treasury, 1976. — [7],43[i.e.45],[1]p : 2 col maps ; 30cm.
Sp : Private circulation
(B77-14569)

Rural depopulation : report / by an interdepartmental group ... ; with the assistance of Office of Population Censuses and Surveys, General Register Office (Scotland). — [London] ([Parliament St., SW1P 3AG]) : H.M. Treasury.

Appendices. — 1976. — [125]p ; 30cm.
Versos of many leaves blank.
Pbk : Private circulation
(B77-14570)

301.35 — Rural communities
Sanders, Irwin T. Rural society / [by] Irwin T. Sanders. — Englewood Cliffs ; London [etc.] : Prentice-Hall, 1977. — xv,170p : map ; 24cm. — (Prentice-Hall foundations of modern sociology series)
Bibl.: p.159-162. — Index.
ISBN 0-13-784447-6 : £7.15
ISBN 0-13-784439-5 Pbk : £3.95
(B77-26809)

301.35 — Rural communities. Cooperation. *Conference proceedings*
Rural Communities - Inter-Cooperation and Development *(Conference), Haifa and Rehovot, 1973.* Rural communities - inter-cooperation and development / edited by Yehuda H. Landau ... [et al.]. — New York [etc.] ; London : Praeger ; [London] : [Distributed by Martin Robertson], 1976. — xxi,169p : ill ; 24cm. — (Praeger special studies in international economics and development)
'... based on the proceedings of the French-Israeli Conference on "Rural Communities - Inter-Cooperation and Development", which convened in Israel, Haifa and Rehovot, in the week of 13-18 May 1973 ...' - Preface.
ISBN 0-275-55700-6 : £10.95
(B77-08782)

301.35'0941 — Human settlements. *Great Britain. Rural regions, to ca 1800*
Roberts, Brian K. Rural settlement in Britain / [by] Brian K. Roberts. — Folkestone : Dawson [etc.], 1977. — 221p : ill, maps, plans ; 23cm. — (Studies in historical geography ISSN 0308-6607)
Ill. on lining papers. — Bibl.: p.212-215. — Index.
ISBN 0-7129-0701-7 : £6.00
(B77-10178)

301.35'09428'6 — Human settlements. Geographical aspects. *Durham (County). Rural regions, to 1975*
Roberts, Brian K. The green villages of County Durham : a study in historical geography / by Brian K. Roberts. — Durham ([County Librarian, County Hall, Durham DH1 5TY]) : Durham County Council, 1977. — [2],iv,56[i.e. 68]p : ill, maps ; 30cm. — (Durham County Library. Local history publications ; no.12 ISSN 0306-0330)
Bibl.: p.53-56.
ISBN 0-903268-09-4 Sd : £1.00
(B77-24008)

301.35'0995'3 — Human settlements. Size. Related to social structure. *Study regions: Papua New Guinea. East Sepik (District). Ilahita*
Tuzin, Donald F. The Ilahita Arapesh : dimensions of unity / [by] Donald F. Tuzin ; with a foreword by Margaret Mead. — Berkeley [etc.] ; London : University of California Press, [1977]. — xxxv,376p : ill, maps, ports ; 24cm.
Published in the United States: 1976. — Bibl.: p.357-365. — Index.
ISBN 0-520-02860-0 : £13.25
Primary classification 301.4'00995'3
(B77-14061)

301.35'2'0901 — Prehistoric agricultural settlements
Hunters, gatherers and first farmers beyond Europe : an archaeological survey / edited by J.V.S. Megaw. — [Leicester] : Leicester University Press, 1977. — 256p : ill, maps ; 25cm.
Bibl. — Index.
ISBN 0-7185-1136-0 Pbk : £5.95
(B77-28396)

301.35'2'09591 — Agricultural communities. Socioeconomic aspects. *South-east Asia. Study regions: Burma, 1920-1965*
Scott, James Cameron. The moral economy of the peasant : rebellion and subsistence in Southeast Asia / [by] James C. Scott. — New Haven ; London : Yale University Press, 1976 [i.e. 1977]. — ix,246p : ill, maps ; 24cm.
Published in the United States: 1976. — Index.
ISBN 0-300-01862-2 : £10.90
Also classified at 301.35'2'09597
(B77-16194)

301.35'2'09597 — Agricultural communities. Socioeconomic aspects. *South-east Asia. Study regions: Vietnam, 1920-1965*
Scott, James Cameron. The moral economy of the peasant : rebellion and subsistence in Southeast Asia / [by] James C. Scott. — New Haven ; London : Yale University Press, 1976 [i.e. 1977]. — ix,246p : ill, maps ; 24cm.
Published in the United States: 1976. — Index.
ISBN 0-300-01862-2 : £10.90
Primary classification 301.35'2'09591
(B77-16194)

301.35'2'0985 — Agricultural communities. Social change. *Peru, ca 1950-ca 1970. Reports, surveys*
Whyte, William Foote. Power, politics and progress : social change in rural Peru / [by] William Foote Whyte and Giorgio Alberti. — New York ; Oxford [etc.] : Elsevier, 1976. — xiii,307p : ill, maps ; 24cm.
Bibl.: p.301-307.
ISBN 0-444-99028-3 : £12.19
(B77-07070)

301.36 — Man. Behaviour. Effects of crowding. *United States. Urban regions. Sociological perspectives*
Booth, Alan, *b.1935.* Urban crowding and its consequences / [by] Alan Booth. — New York [etc.] ; London : Praeger, 1976 [i.e. 1977]. — xiii,141p : form ; 25cm. — (Praeger special studies in US economic, social and political issues)
Published in the United States: 1976. — Bibl.: p.127-135. — Index.
ISBN 0-275-23650-1 : £10.20
(B77-14058)

301.36 — Man. Effects of urban environment. *Sociological perspectives*
Morgan, Elaine. Falling apart : the rise and decline of urban civilisation / by Elaine Morgan. — London : Souvenir Press [etc.], 1976. — 272p : ill ; 23cm.
Bibl.: p.265-266. — Index.
ISBN 0-285-62234-x : £3.60
(B77-00618)

Porteous, John Douglas. Environment & behavior : planning and everyday urban life / [by] J. Douglas Porteous. — Reading, Mass. ; London [etc.] : Addison-Wesley, 1977. — xiv, 446p : ill, maps, plans ; 24cm.
Bibl.: p.369-425. — Index.
ISBN 0-201-05867-7 : £10.40
(B77-16739)

301.36 — Urban regions. *Anthropological perspectives*
Eames, Edwin. Anthropology of the city : an introduction to urban anthropology / [by] Edwin Eames, Judith Granich Goode. — Englewood Cliffs ; London [etc.] : Prentice-Hall, 1977. — viii,344p ; 23cm. — (Prentice-Hall series in anthropology)
Bibl.: p.325-327. — Index.
ISBN 0-13-038414-3 Pbk : £7.20
(B77-25397)

301.36 — Urban regions. *Sociological perspectives. Marxist viewpoints*
Castells, Manuel. The urban question : a Marxist approach / [by] Manuel Castells ; translated [from the French] by Alan Sheridan. — [English-language ed.]. — London : Edward Arnold, 1977. — x,502p,fold leaf : ill ; 24cm. — (Social structure and social change ; 1)
Previous ed.: published as 'La question urbaine'. 2. éd. Paris : Maspero, 1976. — Bibl.: p.472-492. — Index.
ISBN 0-7131-5917-0 : £12.00
ISBN 0-7131-5918-9 Pbk : £5.95
(B77-23135)

301.36 — Urban regions. Ecology
Berry, Brian Joe Lobley. Contemporary urban ecology / [by] Brian J.L. Berry, John D. Kasarda. — New York : Macmillan ; London : Collier Macmillan, 1977. — xiii,497p : ill, maps ; 24cm.
Bibl.: p.430-475. — Index.
ISBN 0-02-309050-2 : £9.75
(B77-23136)

301.36 — Urban regions. Growth. *Conference proceedings*
Growth and change in the future city region / edited by Tom Hancock ; contributors John Boynton ... [et al.]. — [Glasgow] : L. Hill, 1976. — xxii,262p : ill, maps ; 24cm.
'The symposium on which this book is based was held under the auspices of The British Council in the late spring of 1975' - Preface. — Index.
ISBN 0-249-44148-9 : £6.95
(B77-06481)

301.36'01'84 — Urban regions. Spatial models. Effects of zoning systems
Sammons, Roger. Zoning systems for spatial models / [by] Roger Sammons. — Reading (Whiteknights, Reading RG6 2AB) : Department of Geography, University of Reading, 1976. — [2],ii,54p : ill, facsim, maps ; 20cm. — (Geographical papers ; no.52 ISSN 0305-5914)
Bibl.: p.41-42.
ISBN 0-7049-0462-4 Pbk : £0.70
(B77-08783)

301.36'05 — Urban regions. *Periodicals*
Urban. — London (77A College Rd, NW10 5ES) : Urban Publishing Co.
[No.1]- ; Feb. 1977-. — [1977]-. — ill, maps, ports ; 30cm.
Monthly. — 32p. in 1st issue.
Sd : £1.00
ISSN 0309-4731
(B77-14059)

301.36'08 — Urban regions. *Readings*
The **many** facets of human settlements : science and society : papers prepared for AAAS activities in connection with HABITAT : the UN Conference on Human Settlements / editors Irene Tinker and Mayra Buvinic. — Oxford [etc.] : Pergamon, 1977. — vi,405p : ill, maps ; 26cm.
Bibl.: p.403-405.
ISBN 0-08-021994-2 : £41.50
(B77-30988)

301.36'08 — Urban regions. *Sociological perspectives. Readings*
Captive cities : studies in the political economy of cities and regions / edited by Michael Harloe. — London [etc.] : Wiley, 1977. — [9],218p : 1 ill, 2 maps ; 24cm.
'Sponsored by the International Sociological Association Research Committee on the Sociology of Regional and Urban Development'. — Index.
ISBN 0-471-99436-7 : £7.95
(B77-20915)

Cities in change : studies on the urban condition / [edited by] John Walton, Donald E. Carns. — 2nd ed. — Boston, Mass. ; London [etc.] : Allyn and Bacon, 1977. — xiv,586p : ill, map ; 24cm.
Previous ed.: Boston, Mass. : Allyn and Bacon, 1973. — Bibl.
ISBN 0-205-05579-6 Pbk : Unpriced
(B77-09517)

301.36'0941 — Urban sociology. *Study regions: Great Britain*
Mellor, J R. Urban sociology in an urbanized society / [by] J.R. Mellor. — London [etc.] : Routledge and Kegan Paul, 1977. — xvi,309p ; 23cm. — (International library of sociology)
Index.
ISBN 0-7100-8683-0 : £6.95 : CIP rev.
(B77-16195)

301.36'09415 — Ireland. Urban regions, to 1900
The **development** of the Irish town / edited by R.A. Butlin. — London : Croom Helm [etc.], 1977. — 144p : facsims, maps ; 23cm. — (Croom Helm historical geography series)
Index.
ISBN 0-85664-489-7 : £6.95
(B77-22359)

301.36'0942 — England. Urban regions, 1450-ca 1800. *Readings*
The **early** modern town : a reader / edited with an introduction by Peter Clark. — London : Longman [for] the Open University Press, 1976. — viii,382p : maps ; 23cm. — (Open University. Set books)
Index.
ISBN 0-582-48404-9 : £6.50
ISBN 0-582-48405-7 Pbk : £3.10
(B77-02777)

301.36'0942 — Towns. Social aspects. *England, 1500-1700*
Clark, Peter, *b.1944.* English towns in transition, 1500-1700 / [by] Peter Clark and Paul Slack. — London [etc.] : Oxford University Press, 1976. — vii,176p : maps ; 21cm.
Bibl.: p.163-167. — Index.
ISBN 0-19-215816-3 : £3.50
ISBN 0-19-289060-3 Pbk : £1.75
(B77-02047)

301.36'097 — North America. Urban regions. Environmental aspects. *Secondary school texts*
A **guide** to urban studies / contributing authors John K. Wallace ... [et al.] ; editor William A. Andrews. — Scarborough, Ont. ; London [etc.] : Prentice-Hall, 1976. — x,293p : ill(some col), col forms, maps(chiefly col), col plans ; 23cm. — (Contours, studies of the environment)
Cover title: Urban studies. — Bibl. — Index.
ISBN 0-13-939280-7 : £5.95
(B77-22360)

301.36'0973 — United States. Urban regions. Social aspects. *Readings*
Urban studies : an introductory reader / edited by Louis K. Loewenstein. — 2nd ed. — New York : Free Press ; London : Collier Macmillan, 1977. — xxiii,488p : ill, maps ; 24cm.
Previous ed.: 1971. — Index.
ISBN 0-02-919470-9 : £11.25
ISBN 0-02-919440-7 Pbk : £6.25
(B77-27688)

301.36'0973 — Urban sociology. *United States*
Butler, Edgar W. Urban sociology : a systematic approach / [by] Edgar W. Butler. — New York [etc.] ; London : Harper and Row, 1976. — xviii,526p : ill, facsims, maps, ports ; 24cm.
Bibl. — Index.
ISBN 0-06-041106-6 : £10.45
(B77-08233)

301.36'09773'11 — Local communities. *Illinois. Chicago. Near North Side, 1929*
Zorbaugh, Harvey Warren. The Gold Coast and the slum : a sociological study of Chicago's Near North Side / by Harvey Warren Zorbaugh. — Chicago ; London : University of Chicago Press, 1976. — xxii,287p,[15]leaves of plates : 1 ill, maps ; 21cm. — (A phoenix book)

Facsimile reprint of: 1st ed. Chicago : University of Chicago Press, 1929. — Index.
ISBN 0-226-98944-5 Pbk : £3.40
(B77-32423)

301.36'1 — Migrants from Tzintzuntzan. Social conditions. *Mexico. Mexico City*
Kemper, Robert V. Migration and adaptation : Tzintzuntzan peasants in Mexico City / [by] Robert V. Kemper. — Beverly Hills ; London : Sage Publications, 1977. — 223p : ill, maps ; 23cm. — (Sage library of social research ; vol.43)
Bibl.: p.213-221.
ISBN 0-8039-0687-0 : £8.50
ISBN 0-8039-0688-9 Pbk : £4.40
(B77-30989)

301.36'1 — Migration from rural regions. *Developing countries. Urban regions. Reports, surveys*
Institute of Development Studies. *Village Studies Programme.* Migration from rural areas : the evidence from village studies / Institute of Development Studies, Village Studies Programme ; by John Connell ... [et al.]. — Delhi ; Oxford [etc.] : Oxford University Press, 1976. — vii,228p ; 23cm.
'A study prepared for the International Labour Office ...'. — Bibl.: p.219-221. — Index.
ISBN 0-19-560789-9 : £4.50
(B77-31700)

301.36'1 — Migration from rural regions. Developing countries. Urban regions. Related to unemployment in urban regions. *Study regions: Tanzania. Reports, surveys*
Barnum, H N. Migration, education and urban surplus labour : the case of Tanzania / by H.N. Barnum and R.H. Sabot. — Paris : Development Centre of the Organisation for Economic Co-operation and Development ; [London] : [H.M.S.O.], 1976. — 115p : ill ; 24cm. — (Organisation for Economic Co-operation and Development. Development Centre. Studies : employment series ; no.13)
Bibl.: p.111-115.
Pbk : £2.40
ISBN 92-64-11531-5
Primary classification 331.1'379678
(B77-05246)

301.36'1 — Migration from rural regions. Role of education. *Urban regions. Study regions: Tanzania. Reports, surveys*
Barnum, H N. Migration, education and urban surplus labour : the case of Tanzania / by H.N. Barnum and R.H. Sabot. — Paris : Development Centre of the Organisation for Economic Co-operation and Development ; [London] : [H.M.S.O.], 1976. — 115p : ill ; 24cm. — (Organisation for Economic Co-operation and Development. Development Centre. Studies : employment series ; no.13)
Bibl.: p.111-115.
Pbk : £2.40
ISBN 92-64-11531-5
Primary classification 331.1'379678
(B77-05246)

301.36'1 — Squatter settlements. *Turkey*
Karpat, Kemal H. The gecekondu : rural migration and urbanization / [by] Kemal H. Karpat. — Cambridge [etc.] : Cambridge University Press, 1976. — vii,291p : maps ; 22cm.
Bibl.: p.272-284. — Index.
ISBN 0-521-20954-4 : £14.00
(B77-05880)

301.36'1 — Urbanisation. *Reviews of research*
Urbanization and counter-urbanization / edited by Brian J.L. Berry. — Beverly Hills ; London : Sage Publications, [1977]. — 334p : ill, maps ; 24cm. — (Urban affairs annual reviews ; vol.11)
Published in the United States: 1976. — Bibl.
ISBN 0-8039-0499-1 : £14.40
ISBN 0-8039-0682-x Pbk : £6.35
(B77-10737)

301.36'1 — Urbanisation. Influence of marketing. Quantitative analysis. Applications of linear programming. *Developing countries*
Gore, C G. Measuring some costs of unbalanced urbanization : a linear programming approach / [by] C.G. Gore. — Swansea (The Secretary, Editorial Board, Occasional Papers and Monographs Series, Singleton Park, Swansea SA2 8PP) : Centre for Development Studies, University College of Swansea, 1977. — [3],31,[1] leaves : ill, maps ; 30cm. — (University College of Swansea. Centre for Development Studies. Occasional papers ; no.2)
Bibl.: leaves 30-31.
Sd : £0.50
(B77-25398)

301.36'1'0936 — Urbanisation. *Europe, to 100. Conference proceedings*
Origins of Urbanization in Barbarian Europe *(Conference), Oxford, 1975.* Oppida, the beginnings of urbanisation in barbarian Europe : papers presented to a conference at Oxford, October 1975 / edited by Barry Cunliffe & Trevor Rowley. — Oxford : British Archaeological Reports, 1976. — [12],367p : ill, maps, plans ; 30cm. — (British archaeological reports : supplementary series ; 11)
'... the Oxford University Department of External Studies decided to organise an international weekend conference devoted to the theme of "The Origins of Urbanization in Barbarian Europe" ... from 10-12 October 1975' - Preface. — Cover title: Oppida in barbarian Europe. — Bibl.
ISBN 0-904531-46-5 Pbk : £6.75
(B77-00036)

301.36'1'0942 — Urbanisation. Role of canals. *England. Study examples : Canal ports*
Porteous, John Douglas. Canal ports : the urban achievement of the canal age / [by] J. Douglas Porteous. — London [etc.] : Academic Press, 1977. — xvii,249p : ill, maps, plans ; 24cm.
Index.
ISBN 0-12-561950-2 : £7.50
(B77-17926)

301.36'1'09437 — Communist countries. Urbanisation. *Study regions: Czechoslovakia*
Kansky, Karel Joseph. Urbanization under socialism : the case of Czechoslovakia / [by] Karel Joseph Kansky. — New York [etc.] ; London : Praeger ; [London] : [Distributed by Martin Robertson], 1976. — xvii,313,[1]p : ill, maps ; 24cm. — (Praeger special studies in international economics and development)
Bibl.: p.294-305. — Index.
ISBN 0-275-56770-2 : £16.45
(B77-07071)

301.36'1'0956 — Urbanisation. Social aspects. *Middle East*
Costello, Vincent Francis. Urbanization in the Middle East / [by] V.F. Costello. — Cambridge [etc.] : Cambridge University Press, 1977. — ix, 121p : ill ; 24cm. — (Urbanization in developing countries)
Bibl.: p.114-118. — Index.
ISBN 0-521-21324-x : £4.95
ISBN 0-521-29110-0 Pbk : £1.95
(B77-15697)

301.36'1'0959 — Urbanisation. *South-east Asia*
Changing South-East Asian cities : readings on urbanization / edited by Y.M. Yeung & C.P. Lo. — Singapore ; London [etc.] : Oxford University Press, 1976. — xxiv,245p,[8]p of plates : ill, maps ; 26cm. — (Oxford in Asia university readings)
Bibl.: p.234-245.
ISBN 0-19-580316-7 : £15.00
(B77-18560)

301.36'3 — Cities. *Anthropological perspectives*
Fox, Richard Gabriel. Urban anthropology : cities in their cultural settings / [by] Richard G. Fox. — Englewood Cliffs ; London [etc.] : Prentice-Hall, 1977. — xiii,176p ; 23cm.
Bibl.: p.163-169. — Index.
ISBN 0-13-939462-1 Pbk : £4.80
(B77-16196)

301.36'3 — Cities. Inner areas. Social aspects. *England. Reports, surveys*
Bartles-Smith, Douglas. Urban ghetto / [by] Douglas Bartles-Smith and David Gerrard. — Guildford [etc.] : Lutterworth Press, 1976. — ix,115p ; 22cm.
ISBN 0-7188-2293-5 Pbk : £1.95
(B77-04568)

301.36'3 — Cities. Social aspects
Social areas in cities / edited by D.T. Herbert and R.J. Johnston. — London [etc.] : Wiley.
In 2 vols.
Vol.1 : Spatial processes and form. — 1976. — xiii,281p : ill, maps ; 24cm.
Bibl. — Index.
ISBN 0-471-99417-0 : £8.00
(B77-03384)

Vol.2 : Spatial perspectives on problems and policies. — 1976. — xvii,243p : ill, maps ; 24cm.
Bibl. — Index.
ISBN 0-471-37305-2 : £7.75
(B77-03385)

301.36'3'018 — Cities. Spatial analysis
Bird, James. Centrality and cities / [by] James Bird. — London [etc.] : Routledge and Kegan Paul, 1977. — xvi,203p,plate : ill, maps, plan ; 24cm.
'Routledge direct editions'. — 1 ill. tipped in. — Bibl.: p.158-184. — Index.
ISBN 0-7100-8445-5 Pbk : £3.95
(B77-06482)

301.36'3'0722 — Cities. *Case studies*
Hall, Peter, *b.1932.* The world cities / [by] Peter Hall. — 2nd ed. — London : Weidenfeld and Nicolson, 1977. — [7],271p : ill, maps ; 23cm.
Previous ed.: 1966. — Bibl.: p.257-267. — Index.
ISBN 0-297-77310-0 : £6.50
ISBN 0-297-77311-9 Pbk : £3.95
(B77-31701)

301.36'3'0941835 — Community relations. *Ireland (Republic). Study regions: Dublin. Reports, surveys*
Mac Gréil, Mícheál. Prejudice and tolerance in Ireland : based on a survey of intergroup attitudes of Dublin adults and other sources / [by] Mícheál Mac Gréil. — Dublin (Sandford Rd, Ranelagh, Dublin 6) : College of Industrial Relations, Research Section, 1977. — xxiv, 634p : ill, forms, map ; 26cm.
Bibl.: p.533-542. — Index.
ISBN 0-905957-00-8 : £9.90
(B77-33067)

301.36'3'095482 — Slum communities. Social aspects. *India (Republic). Madras. Chennanagar. Reports, surveys*
Wiebe, Paul D. Social life in an Indian slum / [by] Paul D. Wiebe. — Delhi [etc.] : Vikas ; Hemel Hempstead (66 Wood End La., Hemel Hempstead, Herts.) : Distributed by International Book Distributors, 1975. — vii, 179p : 2 maps ; 23cm.
Bibl.: p.169-175. — Index.
ISBN 0-7069-0357-9 : Unpriced
(B77-12304)

301.36'3'0979491 — California. Santa Barbara. Growth. Effects. *Forecasts*
The **effects** of urban growth : a population impact analysis / [by] Richard P. Appelbaum ... [et al.]. — New York [etc.] ; London : Praeger, 1976. — xx,331p : ill, maps ; 25cm. — (Praeger special studies in US economic, social and political issues)
Bibl.: p.319-330.
ISBN 0-275-55980-7 : £16.75
(B77-06483)

301.36'4'091722 — Metropolitan regions. Development. *Developed countries*
Pred, Allan Richard. City-systems in advanced economics : past growth, present processes and future development options / [by] Allan Pred. — London : Hutchinson, 1977. — 256p : ill, maps ; 23cm.
Bibl.: p.231-247. — Index.
ISBN 0-09-129160-7 : £6.95
ISBN 0-09-129161-5 Pbk : £3.50
(B77-29947)

301.36'4'0977866 — United States. Urban regions. Social aspects. *Study regions: Missouri. St Louis*
Neighborhood change : lessons in the dynamics of urban decay / [by] Charles L. Leven ... [et al.]. — New York [etc.] ; London : Praeger, [1977]. — xvi,206p : ill, maps ; 25cm. — (Praeger special studies in US economic, social and political issues)
Published in the United States: 1976.
ISBN 0-275-56600-5 : £11.90
(B77-14060)

301.4 — SOCIAL STRUCTURE
Wilhelmsen, Jens J. Man and structures / [by] Jens J. Wilhelmsen. — London : Grosvenor Books, 1977. — ix,76p ; 19cm.
ISBN 0-901269-25-5 Pbk : £0.75
(B77-11582)

301.4 — United States. Society. Role of single persons
Stein, Peter J. Single / [by] Peter J. Stein. — Englewood Cliffs, N.J. ; London [etc.] : Prentice-Hall, 1976. — x,134p ; 21cm.
Bibl.: p.125-131. — Index.
ISBN 0-13-810572-3 : £5.80
ISBN 0-13-810564-2 Pbk : £2.15
(B77-02048)

301.4'00932 — Social structure. Influence of ideology. *Study examples: Ancient Egypt*
Carlton, Eric. Ideology and social order / [by] Eric Carlton. — London [etc.] : Routledge and Kegan Paul, 1977. — [5],320p ; 23cm. — (International library of sociology)
Bibl.: p.302-312. — Index.
ISBN 0-7100-8474-9 : £7.75
Also classified at 301.4'00938'5
(B77-09518)

301.4'00938'5 — Social structure. Influence of ideology. *Study examples: Ancient Greece. Athens*
Carlton, Eric. Ideology and social order / [by] Eric Carlton. — London [etc.] : Routledge and Kegan Paul, 1977. — [5],320p ; 23cm. — (International library of sociology)
Bibl.: p.302-312. — Index.
ISBN 0-7100-8474-9 : £7.75
Primary classification 301.4'00932
(B77-09518)

301.4'009439 — Hungary. Social structure. *Marxist viewpoints*
Hegedüs, András. The structure of socialist society / [by] András Hegedüs ; [translated from the Hungarian by Rudolf Fisher and revised by Peter Szente]. — London : Constable, 1977. — iii-viii,230p ; 23cm. — ([Sociology & social welfare series ; 12])
Translation and revision of: 'A szocialista társadalom struktúrájáról', Budapest : Akadémiai Kiadó, 1966 ; and 'Változó világ', Budapest : Akadémiai Kiadó, 1970. — Index.
ISBN 0-09-459400-7 : £3.50
(B77-13511)

301.4'00944 — France. Social structure. Effects of economic growth, 1945-1975
Marceau, Jane. Class and status in France : economic change and social immobility 1945-1975 / [by] Jane Marceau. — Oxford : Clarendon Press, 1977. — xii,217p ; 23cm.
Bibl.: p.196-214. — Index.
ISBN 0-19-827217-0 : £6.00 : CIP rev.
(B77-12305)

301.4'00959 — South-east Asia. Social structure
Brown, D E. Principles of social structure, Southeast Asia / [by] D.E. Brown. — London : Duckworth, 1976. — 248p : ill ; 23cm.
Bibl.: p.227-239. — Index.
ISBN 0-7156-0917-3 : £8.95
(B77-03386)

301.4'00995'3 — Human settlements. Social structure. Related to size. *Study regions: Papua New Guinea. East Sepik (District). Ilahita*
Tuzin, Donald F. The Ilahita Arapesh : dimensions of unity / [by] Donald F. Tuzin ; with a foreword by Margaret Mead. — Berkeley [etc.] ; London : University of California Press, [1977]. — xxxv,376p : ill, maps, ports ; 24cm.
Published in the United States: 1976. — Bibl.: p.357-365. — Index.
ISBN 0-520-02860-0 : £13.25
Also classified at 301.35'0995'3
(B77-14061)

301.41 — Men. Interpersonal relationships with women
The **love** game / [editor Nicolas Wright ; compiled by Anne Maclean]. — London [etc.] : Hamlyn : Phoebus, 1977. — 256p : ill(some col), facsim, ports(chiefly col) ; 31cm.
'This material first appeared in "Understanding human behavior"' - title page verso.
ISBN 0-600-35532-2 : £4.95
(B77-29192)

301.41 — Men. Interpersonal relationships with women. *Conference proceedings*
Aspen Workshop on Women and Men, *1975.* Women and men : changing roles, relationships and perceptions / [edited by] Libby A. Cater, Anne Firor Scott with Wendy Martyna. — New York ; London : Praeger [for] the Aspen Institute for Humanistic Studies, 1977. — xvi, 277,[1]p : 1 ill ; 24cm. — (Praeger special studies in US economic, social and political issues)
'... Aspen Workshop on Women and Men August 1-10, 1975' - p.ix. — Bibl. — Index.
ISBN 0-03-021476-9 : £11.70
(B77-29948)

301.41 — Sex differences
Exploring sex differences / edited by Barbara Lloyd, John Archer. — London [etc.] : Academic Press, 1976. — xi,280p : ill ; 24cm.
Bibl. — Index.
ISBN 0-12-453550-x : £5.00
(B77-01179)

301.41 — Sex roles
Safilios-Rothschild, Constantina. Love, sex and sex roles / [by] Constantina Safilios-Rothschild. — Englewood Cliffs ; London [etc.] : Prentice-Hall, 1977. — x,150p ; 21cm.
Bibl.: p.139-147. — Index.
ISBN 0-13-540948-9 : £7.20
ISBN 0-13-540930-6 Pbk : £3.15
(B77-32424)

301.41 — Sex roles. Social aspects. *Feminist viewpoints*
Brogger, Suzanne. Deliver us from love / [by] Suzanne Brogger ; translated from the Danish by Thomas Teal. — London : Quartet Books, 1977. — xi,298p ; 23cm.
This translation originally published: New York : Delacorte Press, 1976. — Translation of: 'Fri os fra kaerligheden'. Kobenhavn : Rhodos, 1973.
ISBN 0-7043-2132-7 : £4.50
(B77-11583)

301.41'0942 — Sex roles. Social aspects. *England. Feminist viewpoints*
Nicholson, Joyce. What society does to girls / [by] Joyce Nicholson ; illustrated by Mary Leunig. — London : Virago, 1977. — 3-80p : ill ; 21cm.
Originally published: Carlton : Pitman (Australia), 1975. — Bibl.: p.77-80.
ISBN 0-86068-021-5 Pbk : £1.35
(B77-26811)

301.41'0995'3 — Primitive societies. Sex roles. *Papua New Guinea. Anthropological perspectives. Case studies*
Mead, Margaret. Sex and temperament in three primitive societies / [by] Margaret Mead. — London [etc.] : Routledge and Kegan Paul, 1977. — xxii,335p ; 23cm.
Originally published: New York : Morrow ; London : Routledge, 1935.
ISBN 0-7100-8665-2 : £5.75 : CIP rev.
(B77-07068)

301.41'2 — Married women. *United States. Feminist viewpoints*
McBride, Angela Barron. A married feminist / [by] Angela Barron McBride. — New York [etc.] ; London : Harper and Row, 1976. — [9], 244p ; 22cm.
ISBN 0-06-012881-x : £4.95
(B77-29949)

301.41'2 — Social change. Influence of women
Boulding, Elise. Women in the twentieth century world / [by] Elise Boulding. — [Beverly Hills] : Sage Publications ; New York ; London [etc.] : Distributed by Wiley, 1977. — 264p : ill, maps ; 23cm.
'A Halsted Press book' - jacket. — Bibl.: p.245-252. — Index.
ISBN 0-470-98947-5 : £10.50
(B77-28397)

301.41'2 — Society. Role of women
Janeway, Elizabeth. Man's world, woman's place : a study in social mythology / [by] Elizabeth Janeway. — Harmondsworth [etc.] : Penguin, 1977. — 350p ; 18cm.
Originally published: New York : Morrow, 1971 ; London : Joseph, 1972. — Index.
ISBN 0-14-003940-6 Pbk : £1.00
(B77-24708)

Women in the community / edited by Marjorie Mayo. — London [etc.] : Routledge and Kegan Paul [for] the Association of Community Workers, 1977. — xiii,141p ; 24cm.
Bibl.: p.24.
ISBN 0-7100-8384-x Pbk : £3.75
(B77-13512)

301.41'2 — Society. Role of women. *Anthropological perspectives. Comparative studies*
Martin, M Kay. Female of the species / [by] M. Kay Martin, Barbara Voorhies. — New York ; London : Columbia University Press, 1975. — xiii,432p : ill ; 24cm.
Bibl.: p.411-425. — Index.
ISBN 0-231-03875-5 : Unpriced
ISBN 0-231-03876-3 Pbk : Unpriced
(B77-17927)

301.41'2 — Society. Role of women. Attitudes of women
Fransella, Fay. On being a woman : a review of research on how women see themselves / [by] Fay Fransella and Kay Frost. — London : Tavistock Publications, 1977. — 237p : ill ; 20cm. — (Tavistock women's studies)
Bibl.: p.206-228. — Index.
ISBN 0-422-76070-6 : £6.00
ISBN 0-422-76080-3 Pbk : £2.60
(B77-24009)

301.41'2 — Society. Role of women. Effects of economic development
Seminar on Women in Development, *Mexico, 1975.* Women and world development : with an annotated bibliography / edited by Irene Tinker, Michèle Bo Bramsen, Mayra Buvinić. — New York [etc.] ; London : Praeger [for] the Overseas Development Council, 1976. — xi, 382p : ill ; 25cm. — (Praeger special studies in international economics and development)
'... the American Association for the Advancement of Science ... [assumed] a leading role in the convening of a Seminar on Women in Development ... which took place in Mexico City, June 15-18, 1975 ...' - Introduction. — Bibl.: p.244-375. — Index.
ISBN 0-275-56520-3 : £14.80
(B77-08234)

301.41'2 — United States. Society. Role of married women. *Sociological perspectives*
Women into wives : the legal and economic impact of marriage / edited by Jane Roberts Chapman and Margaret Gates. — Beverly Hills ; London : Sage Publications, 1977. — 320p : ill ; 24cm. — (Sage yearbooks in women's policy studies ; vol.2)
Bibl.
ISBN 0-8039-0700-1 : £9.00
ISBN 0-8039-0701-x Pbk : £4.50
(B77-14571)

301.41'2 — Women. *Anthropological perspectives*
Kessler, Evelyn S. Women : an anthropological view / [by] Evelyn S. Kessler. — New York ; London [etc.] : Holt, Rinehart and Winston, 1976. — xiii,267p ; 24cm.
Bibl.: p.249-253. — Index.
ISBN 0-03-014876-6 : £6.00
(B77-02049)

301.41'2 — Women. Social status. *Comparative studies*
Women : roles and status in eight countries / edited by Janet Zollinger Giele, Audrey Chapman Smock. — New York ; London [etc.] : Wiley, 1977. — xv,443p : 2 ill ; 24cm.
'A Wiley-Interscience publication'. — Bibl. — Index.
ISBN 0-471-01504-0 : £12.50
(B77-22361)

301.41'2'014 — Society. Role of women. Linguistic aspects
Miller, Casey. Words and women / by Casey Miller and Kate Swift. — London : Gollancz, 1977. — xvii,197p ; 21cm.
Originally published: Garden City, N.Y. : Anchor Press, 1976. — Index.
ISBN 0-575-02350-3 : £4.50
(B77-26812)

301.41'2'0212 — Women. Social conditions. *Statistics*
Handbook of international data on women / [by] Elise Boulding ... [et al.]. — [Beverly Hills] : Sage Publications ; New York ; London [etc.] : Wiley, 1976. — [11],468p : map ; 24cm.
Bibl.: p.467-468.
ISBN 0-470-15183-8 : £16.00
(B77-17928)

301.41'2'06241 — Women's institutes. *Great Britain, to 1976*
Goodenough, Simon. Jam and Jerusalem / by Simon Goodenough. — Glasgow [etc.] : Collins, 1977. — 124p : ill(some col), ports(some col) ; 26cm.
ISBN 0-00-411806-5 : £3.95
ISBN 0-00-411807-3 Pbk : £1.90
(B77-29193)

301.41'2'062429 — Women's organisations. *Wales. Merched y Wawr, to 1977. Welsh texts*
Bowen, Zonia. Y dyddiau cynnar / [gan] Zonia Bowen. — [Bala] : Llyfrau'r Faner [ar ran] Merched y Wawr, [1977]. — [18]p : ill, ports ; 32cm.
Sd : Unpriced
(B77-33068)

301.41'2'072 — Women. Historiography, to 1975. *Feminist viewpoints. Readings*
Liberating women's history : theoretical and critical essays / edited by Berenice A. Carroll. — Urbana [etc.] ; London : University of Illinois Press, 1976. — xiv,434p ; 24cm.
ISBN 0-252-00441-8 : £12.00
ISBN 0-252-00569-4 Pbk : £4.80
Primary classification 301.41'2'09
(B77-02050)

301.41'2'08 — Society. Role of women. *Readings*
Women in a changing world / edited by Uta West. — New York ; London [etc.] : McGraw-Hill, [1976]. — xxii,170p ; 21cm.
Published in the United States: 1975.
ISBN 0-07-069465-6 Pbk : £3.30
(B77-04569)

301.41'2'08 — Women. Attitudes of society. *Essays*
Women and folklore / edited by Claire R. Farrer. — Austin ; London : University of Texas Press, [1976]. — xvii,100p : ill, music, ports ; 26cm.
Published in the United States: 1975. — 'Previously published in "Journal of American Folklore". 88, no.347 (January-March 1975)' - title page verso.
ISBN 0-292-79005-8 : £8.00
ISBN 0-292-79006-6 Pbk : £2.80
(B77-06484)

301.41'2'09 — Women, to 1975. *Feminist viewpoints. Readings*
Liberating women's history : theoretical and critical essays / edited by Berenice A. Carroll. — Urbana [etc.] ; London : University of Illinois Press, 1976. — xiv,434p ; 24cm.
ISBN 0-252-00441-8 : £12.00
ISBN 0-252-00569-4 Pbk : £4.80
Also classified at 301.41'2'072
(B77-02050)

301.41'2'09034 — Women. Emancipation, to 1975
Gane, Michael. Responses to inequality / prepared for the [Open University] Course Team by Michael Gane. A case study in social change : women in society / prepared for the [Open University] Course Team by Jean Gardiner. — Milton Keynes : Open University Press, 1976. — [2],78p ; 30cm. — (Social science, a third level course : patterns of inequality ; section 4 : reform or revolution? ; unit 31, unit 32) (D302 ; 31-32)
Bibl.
ISBN 0-335-07161-9 Pbk : £1.35
Primary classification 301.44'01
(B77-03948)

301.41'2'091746 — Hispanic culture. Role of women
Pescatello, Ann. Power and pawn : the female in Iberian families, societies and cultures / [by] Ann M. Pescatello. — Westport, Conn. ; London : Greenwood Press, 1976. — xix,281p ; 22cm. — (Contributions in intercultural and comparative studies ; no.1)
Bibl.: p.235-273. — Index.
ISBN 0-8371-8583-1 : £12.95
(B77-20916)

301.41'2'0917671 — Islamic countries. Society. Role of women
Lemu, B Aisha. Woman in Islam / [by] B. Aisha Lemu, Fatima Heeren. — [London] : Islamic Council of Europe ; Leicester (233 London Rd, Leicester LE2 1ZE) : [Distributed by] the Islamic Foundation, 1976. — 51p ; 21cm.
Papers delivered at the International Islamic Conference, held in London from 3rd to 12th April, 1976.
ISBN 0-86037-004-6 Pbk : £0.80
(B77-02051)

301.41'2'091812 — Feminism. *Western world, to 1920*
Evans, Richard John. The feminists : women's emancipation movements in Europe, America and Australasia, 1840-1920 / [by] Richard J. Evans. — London : Croom Helm [etc.], 1977. — 266p ; 23cm.
Bibl.: p.254-255. — Index.
ISBN 0-85664-212-6 : £8.95 : CIP rev.
(B77-18561)

301.41'2'0924 — Feminism. Wollstonecraft, Mary. *Biographies*
Tomalin, Claire. The life and death of Mary Wollstonecraft / [by] Claire Tomalin. — Harmondsworth [etc.] : Penguin, 1977. — 398p : geneal table ; 19cm. — (Pelican biographies)
Originally published: London : Weidenfeld and Nicolson, 1974. — Bibl.: p.366-376. — Index.
ISBN 0-14-021972-2 Pbk : £1.50
(B77-08235)

301.41'2'0924 — Feminism. Wollstonecraft, Mary. *Correspondence with Godwin, William*
Godwin, William. Godwin & Mary : letters of William Godwin and Mary Wollstonecraft / edited by Ralph M. Wardle. — Lincoln, Neb. ; London : University of Nebraska Press, 1977. — x,125p : ill, ports ; 21cm.
'A Bison book'. — This collection originally published: Lawrence, Kan. : University of Kansas Press, 1966 ; London : Constable, 1967. — Index.
ISBN 0-8032-0901-0 : £6.00
ISBN 0-8032-5852-6 Pbk : Unpriced
Primary classification 828'.6'09
(B77-31577)

301.41'2'0924 — Women's liberation movements. *United States, 1963-1975. Personal observations*
Friedan, Betty. It changed my life : writings on the women's movement / by Betty Friedan ; with a foreword by Mary Stott. — London : Gollancz, 1977. — iii-xix,3-240p ; 24cm.
Originally published: New York : Random House, 1976.
ISBN 0-575-02312-0 : £5.95
(B77-26813)

301.41'2'0941 — Great Britain. Society. Role of women, 1714-1830
Calder-Marshall, Arthur. The grand century of the lady / [by] Arthur Calder-Marshall. — London (34 Seymour Rd, N8 0BE) : Gordon and Cremonesi, 1976. — 184p,[40]p of plates : ill(some col), ports ; 27cm.
In slip case. — Bibl.: p.175-176. — Index.
ISBN 0-86033-011-7 : £15.00
(B77-02778)

301.41'2'0941 — Great Britain. Society. Role of women, ca 1938
Woolf, Virginia. Three guineas / [by] Virginia Woolf. — London : Hogarth Press, 1977. — 3-329p ; 21cm.
Originally published: 1938.
ISBN 0-7012-0276-9 : £4.95
(B77-23137)

301.41'2'0942 — England. Society. Role of women writers of literature, to 1929
Woolf, Virginia. A room of one's own / [by] Virginia Woolf. — St Albans : Triad, 1977. — 108p ; 18cm.
Originally published: London : L. & V. Woolf, 1929.
ISBN 0-586-04449-3 Pbk : £0.60
(B77-17309)

301.41'2'0942184 — England. Society. Role of girls. *Study regions: London. Ealing (London Borough)*
Sharpe, Sue. 'Just like a girl' : how girls learn to be women / [by] Sue Sharpe. — Harmondsworth [etc.] : Penguin, 1976. — 328p ; 19cm. — (A pelican original)
Index.
ISBN 0-14-021953-6 Pbk : £0.95
(B77-07072)

301.41'2'0943 — Feminism. *Germany, 1894-1933*
Evans, Richard John. The feminist movement in Germany, 1894-1933 / [by] Richard J. Evans. — London [etc.] : Sage Publications, 1976. — [1],xiv,310,[1]p ; 23cm. — (Sage studies in 20th century history ; vol.6)
Bibl.: p.282-297. — Index.
ISBN 0-8039-9951-8 : £7.00
ISBN 0-8039-9996-8 Pbk : £3.50
(B77-02052)

301.41'2'09437 — Eastern Europe & Soviet Union. Society. Role of women, 1945-1973. *Study regions: Czechoslovakia*
Scott, Hilda. Women and socialism : experiences from Eastern Europe / [by] Hilda Scott. — London : Allison and Busby, 1976. — iii-xi, 240p ; 23cm. — (Motive)
Originally published: as 'Does socialism liberate women?'. Boston, Mass. : Beacon Press, 1975. — Index.
ISBN 0-85031-210-8 : £5.25
ISBN 0-85031-211-6 Pbk : £2.95
(B77-29951)

301.41'2'0944 — France. Society. Role of women, 1610-1652. Expounded by French arts
Maclean, Ian, *b.1945.* Woman triumphant : feminism in French literature, 1610-1652 / [by] Ian Maclean. — Oxford : Clarendon Press, 1977. — xv,314p,[16]p of plates : ill, 2 facsims, ports ; 23cm.
Bibl.: p.271-305. — Index.
ISBN 0-19-815741-x : £12.50 : CIP rev.
(B77-08236)

301.41'2'0944 — Women. Attitudes of society. *France, 1600-1700*
Lougee, Carolyn C. Le Paradis des femmes : women, salons, and social stratification in seventeenth-century France / by Carolyn C. Lougee. — Princeton ; Guildford : Princeton University Press, 1976 [i.e. 1977]. — ix,252p ; 24cm.
Published in the United States: 1976. — Bibl.: p.229-249. — Index.
ISBN 0-691-05239-5 : £11.50
(B77-10179)

301.41'2'0951 — China. Society. Role of women, to 1974
Kristeva, Julia. About Chinese women / [by] Julia Kristeva ; translated from the French by Anita Barrows. — London : Boyars : Distributed by Calder and Boyars, 1977. — 203p,[8]p of plates : ill, ports ; 23cm. — ([Open forum])
Translation of: 'Des Chinoises'. Paris : Éditions des Femmes, 1974. — Bibl.: p.202-203.
ISBN 0-7145-2521-9 : £5.95
ISBN 0-7145-2522-7 Pbk : £2.50
(B77-11584)

301.41'2'0956 — Middle East. Society. Role of Muslim women. *Readings*
Middle Eastern Muslim women speak / edited by Elizabeth Warnock Fernea and Basima Qattan Bezirgan. — Austin ; London : University of Texas Press, 1977. — xxvi,402,[2]p,[18] leaves of plates,[20]p of plates : ill, map, ports ; 24cm. — (The Dan Danciger publication series)
'Many of the selections have been translated by the editors from Arabic, Persian, or French' - jacket. — Bibl.
ISBN 0-292-75033-1 : £12.75
Also classified at 301.41'2'0961
(B77-32425)

301.41'2'095694 — Kibbutzim. Women. *Israel. Sociological perspectives*
Tiger, Lionel. Women in the kibbutz / [by] Lionel Tiger and Joseph Shepher. — Harmondsworth [etc.] : Penguin, 1977. — ix, 334p : ill ; 20cm. — (Peregrine books)
Originally published: New York : Harcourt Brace Jovanovich, 1975. — Bibl.: p.311-326. — Index.
ISBN 0-14-055123-9 Pbk : £1.95
(B77-22362)

301.41'2'0961 — North Africa. Society. Role of Muslim women. *Readings*
Middle Eastern Muslim women speak / edited by Elizabeth Warnock Fernea and Basima Qattan Bezirgan. — Austin ; London : University of Texas Press, 1977. — xxvi,402,[2]p,[18] leaves of plates,[20]p of plates : ill, map, ports ; 24cm. — (The Dan Danciger publication series)
'Many of the selections have been translated by the editors from Arabic, Persian, or French' - jacket. — Bibl.
ISBN 0-292-75033-1 : £12.75
Primary classification 301.41'2'0956
(B77-32425)

301.41'2'09726 — Maya. Society. Role of women. *Mexico. Chan Kom*
Elmendorf, Mary. Nine Mayan women : a village faces change / [by] Mary Elmendorf. — Cambridge, Mass. : Schenkman ; New York ; London [etc.] : Wiley, 1976. — xxv,159p : ill ; 24cm.
'... an expanded and enlarged version of a previous work, "La mujer Maya y el cambio", published in Spanish by the Mexican Ministry of Education and of a limited multilith version by CIDOC [Centro Intercultural de Documentación]' - Preface. — Bibl.: p.156-159.
ISBN 0-470-23862-3 : £9.40
ISBN 0-470-23864-x Pbk : £4.00
(B77-23138)

301.41'2'0973 — Feminism. *United States, ca 1820-ca 1920*
Flexner, Eleanor. Century of struggle : the woman's rights movement in the United States / [by] Eleanor Flexner. — Revised ed. — Cambridge, Mass. ; London ([126 Buckingham Palace Rd, SW1W 9SD]) : Belknap Press of Harvard University Press, 1976. — xviii,405p, [4]p of plates,[4]leaves of plates : ill, ports ; 21cm.
This ed. originally published: 1976. — Index.
ISBN 0-674-10652-0 Pbk : £3.05
(B77-15698)

301.41'2'0973 — United States. Society. Role of women
Ephron, Nora. Crazy salad : some things about women / by Nora Ephron. — Toronto [etc.] ; London : Bantam, 1976. — xiii,208,[1]p ; 18cm.
Originally published: New York : Knopf, 1975.
ISBN 0-553-02815-4 Pbk : £0.60
(B77-05881)

301.41'2'0973 — United States. Society. Role of women, to 1973. *Teaching kits*
Women's rights in the United States / compiled by Mary Stetson Clarke. — New York : Grossman ; London : Jackdaw [etc.], 1974. — Portfolio : ill, facsims, music, ports ; 24x35cm. — ([American] jackdaw ; no.A20)
Introductory folder ([6]p.) and 23 items. — Bibl.
ISBN 0-305-62094-0 : £1.95
(B77-02053)

301.41'2'0974 — New England. Society. Role of women, 1780-1835
Cott, Nancy F. The bonds of womanhood : 'woman's sphere' in New England, 1780-1835 / [by] Nancy F. Cott. — New Haven ; London : Yale University Press, 1977. — xii,225p ; 22cm.
Bibl.: p.207-220. — Index.
ISBN 0-300-02023-6 : £9.00
(B77-24709)

301.41'2'098 — Women. Discrimination by society. *Latin America*
Sex and class in Latin America / edited by June Nash, Helen Icken Safa. — New York [etc.] ; London : Praeger ; [London] : [Distributed by Martin Robertson], 1976. — xv,332p ; 24cm. — (Praeger special studies in international politics and government)
'... essays ... first presented at a conference organized by the editors ... , held at the Torcuato di Tella Institute in Buenos Aires on March 18-23, 1974' - Introduction. — Bibl. — Index.
ISBN 0-275-55720-0 : £17.15
(B77-05218)

301.41'2'09931 — New Zealand. Society. Role of women, 1871-1974
Aitken, Judith. A woman's place? : a study of the changing role of women in New Zealand / by Judith Aitken. — London [etc.] : Heinemann Educational, 1975. — vi,90p : ill, facsims, ports ; 19x23cm.
Bibl.: p.89.
Pbk : Unpriced
(B77-26814)

301.41'5 — Deviant sex relations. *Periodicals*
Bizarre review. — East Molesey (11a Creek Rd, East Molesey, Surrey KT8 9BE) : Beau Reynolds for S.R.A. Publications.
Vol.1, no.1- ; [?July 1976]-. — [1976]-. — ill ; 24cm.
Monthly. — 66p. in first issue.
Sd : £1.00
(B77-00037)

301.41'53 — Wife swapping
Bowskill, Derek. Swingers & swappers / [by] Derek Bowskill. — London : Star Books, 1975. — 157p ; 18cm.
ISBN 0-352-39831-0 Pbk : £0.60
(B77-11078)

301.41'54 — Boys. Prostitution. *United States*
Lloyd, Robin. Playland : a study of boy prostitution / [by] Robin Lloyd. — Revised and expanded ed. — London : Blond and Briggs, 1977. — 208p ; 23cm.
Previous ed.: published as 'For money or love'. New York : Vanguard Press, 1976. — Includes sections on Great Britain.
ISBN 0-85634-066-9 : £5.50
(B77-33621)

301.41'54 — Brothels. *France. Paris. No.122 rue de Provence, 1946. Personal observations*
Jamet, Fabienne. Palace of sweet sin / [by] Fabienne Jamet ; translated [from the French] by Derek Coltman. — London : W.H. Allen, 1977. — 221p,[8]p of plates : ill, ports ; 23cm.
Translation of: 'One two two'. Paris : Orban, 1975.
ISBN 0-491-01898-3 : £4.95
(B77-22363)

301.41'54'0941 — Prostitution. *Great Britain*
Sandford, Jeremy. Prostitutes / [by] Jeremy Sandford. — Revised ed. — London : Abacus, 1977. — 212p ; 20cm.
Previous ed.: London : Secker and Warburg, 1975. — Bibl.: p.210-211.
ISBN 0-349-13122-8 Pbk : £1.95
(B77-32426)

301.41'54'0954 — Courtesans. *India, to ca A.D.1500*
Chandra, Moti. The world of courtesans / [by] Moti Chandra. — Delhi [etc.] ; London : Vikas ; [Hemel Hempstead] ([66 Wood Lane End, Hemel Hempstead, Herts.]) : [Distributed by International Book Distributors Ltd], [1976]. — viii,245p,[8]p of plates : ill ; 24cm.
Published in India: 1973. — Index.
ISBN 0-7069-0082-0 : £5.00
(B77-03944)

301.41'57 — Homosexuality
Understanding homosexuality : its biological and psychological bases / edited by J.A. Loraine. — Lancaster : M.T.P. Press, 1974. — [7],217p : ill ; 23cm.
Index.
ISBN 0-85200-088-x : Unpriced
(B77-18562)

301.41'57 — Homosexuality. *State-of-the-art reviews*
West, Donald James. Homosexuality re-examined / [by] D.J. West. — 4th ed. — London : Duckworth, 1977. — viii,359p ; 26cm.
Previous ed.: published as 'Homosexuality'. 1968. — Bibl.: p.323-348. — Index.
ISBN 0-7156-0935-1 : £12.00
(B77-20917)

301.41'57'02436 — Homosexuality. *For counselling*
Babuscio, Jack. We speak for ourselves : experiences in homosexual counselling / [by] Jack Babuscio. — London : S.P.C.K., 1976. — xiv,151p ; 22cm.
Bibl.: p.144-151.
ISBN 0-281-02963-6 Pbk : £2.95
(B77-09519)

301.41'57'05 — Periodicals for homosexuals: Periodicals with British imprints. *Texts*
Out : for and about gay women and men. — Manchester (P.O. Box 427, 33 King St., Manchester M60 2EL) : Campaign for Homosexual Equality.
No.1- ; Oct.-Nov. 1976-. — 1976-. — ill ; 30cm.
Six issues a year. — 12p. in 1st issue.
Sd : £0.20
ISSN 0308-8332
(B77-03945)

301.41'57'05 — Periodicals for male homosexuals: Periodicals with British imprints. *Texts*
Q international : an international magazine for men. — [London] ([289 Kings Rd, S.W.3]) : [Q Centaur Ltd].
Vol.1, no.1- ; [1976]-. — [1976]-. — ill, ports(some col) ; 30cm.
Ten issues a year. — 54p. in 1st issue.
Sd : £1.00
(B77-02779)

301.41'57'09 — Male homosexuality, to 1976
Rowse, Alfred Leslie. Homosexuals in history : a study of ambivalence in society, literature and the arts / [by] A.L. Rowse. — London : Weidenfeld and Nicolson, 1977. — xiii,346p, [16]p of plates : ports ; 24cm.
Index.
ISBN 0-297-77299-6 : £7.95
(B77-16197)

301.41'57'0922 — Lesbianism. *Great Britain. Personal observations. Transcripts of interviews*
Cassidy, Jules. We're here : conversations with lesbian women / Jules Cassidy and Angela Stewart-Park ; photographs by Angela Stewart-Park and J.P. Goodchild. — London [etc.] : Quartet Books, 1977. — [7],152p : ports ; 20cm.
ISBN 0-7043-3117-9 Pbk : £1.95
(B77-26124)

301.41'57'0924 — Lesbianism. *United States. Personal observations*
Millett, Kate. Sita / [by] Kate Millett. — London : Virago, 1977. — [7],322p ; 22cm.
Originally published: New York : Farrar, Straus and Giroux, 1977.
ISBN 0-86068-023-1 : £6.95
ISBN 0-86068-024-x Pbk : £1.95
(B77-28398)

301.41'57'0924 — Male homosexuality. Crisp, Quentin. *Great Britain. Autobiographies*
Crisp, Quentin. The naked civil servant / [by] Quentin Crisp. — [London] : Fontana, 1977. — 3-217p ; 18cm.
Originally published: London : Cape, 1968.
ISBN 0-00-634746-0 Pbk : £0.85
(B77-13513)

Crisp, Quentin. The naked civil servant / [by] Quentin Crisp. — London : Duckworth, 1977. — 217p ; 23cm.
Originally published: London : Cape, 1968.
ISBN 0-7156-1187-9 : £4.95
(B77-10180)

301.41'57'0924 — Male homosexuals. Interpersonal relationships. *United States. Personal observations*
Brown, Howard, *b.1924.* Familiar faces, hidden lives : the story of homosexual men in America today / [by] Howard Brown. — New York ; London : Harcourt Brace Jovanovich, 1976. — [5],246p ; 22cm.
ISBN 0-15-130149-2 : £5.95
(B77-12865)

301.41'57'0941 — Homosexuality. Social aspects. *Great Britain, ca 1850-1976*
Weeks, Jeffrey. Coming out : homosexual politics in Britain from the nineteenth century to the present / [by] Jeffrey Weeks. — London [etc.] : Quartet Books, 1977. — x,278p ; 23cm.
Bibl.: p.239-246. — Index.
ISBN 0-7043-2146-7 : £8.50
ISBN 0-7043-3175-6 Pbk : £3.95
(B77-33069)

301.41'57'09421 — Male homosexuality. Cleveland Street scandal. *London*
Simpson, Colin, *b.1931.* The Cleveland Street affair / [by] Lewis Chester, David Leitch, Colin Simpson. — London : Weidenfeld and Nicolson, 1977. — [8],236p,[8]p of plates : ill, ports ; 23cm.
Originally published: / by Colin Simpson, Lewis Chester, Davie Leitch. Boston, Mass. : Little, Brown, 1976. — Bibl.: p.233-236.
ISBN 0-297-77113-2 : £5.95
(B77-30991)

301.41'57'0973 — Lesbianism. *United States*
Simpson, Ruth, *b.1926.* From the closet to the courts : the lesbian transition / [by] Ruth Simpson. — Harmondsworth [etc.] : Penguin, 1977. — xi,180p ; 18cm.
Originally published: New York : Viking Press, 1976.
ISBN 0-14-004353-5 Pbk : Unpriced
(B77-13514)

301.41'58 — Paedophilia. *Periodicals*
Understanding paedophilia. — London (c/o 'Release', 1 Elgin Ave., W.9) : Paedophile Information Exchange.
Vol.1, no.1- ; Apr.-May 1976-. — 1976-. — ill, ports ; 29cm.
Six issues a year. — 8p. in 2nd issue.
Sd : £0.40
(B77-02780)

301.41'58 — Paedophilia. Expounded by English literature, ca 1860-ca 1940
Fraser, Morris. The death of Narcissus / [by] Morris Fraser. — London : Secker and Warburg, 1976. — xi,244p ; 24cm.
Bibl.: p.237-240. — Index.
ISBN 0-436-16466-3 : £4.90
(B77-04570)

301.41'7 — Man. Feet & shoes. Sexual aspects
Rossi, William A. The sex life of the foot and shoe / [by] William A. Rossi. — London [etc.] : Routledge and Kegan Paul, 1977. — [5], 265p : ill, facsims ; 24cm.
Originally published: New York : Saturday Review Press, 1976. — Bibl.: p.254-258. — Index.
ISBN 0-7100-8508-7 : £4.75
(B77-18563)

301.41'7 — Sex relations
Understanding sex / [editor Nicolas Wright, deputy editor Susan Joiner ; compiled by Anne Maclean]. — London [etc.] : Hamlyn, 1977. — 256p : ill(some col), ports ; 31cm.
'This material first appeared in "Understanding human behavior"' - title page verso. — Index.
ISBN 0-600-39018-7 : £4.95
(B77-18564)

West, Uta. If love is the answer, what is the question? / [by] Uta West. — London : Weidenfeld and Nicolson, 1977. — xix,227p ; 23cm.
Bibl.: p.225-227.
ISBN 0-297-77413-1 : £4.95
(B77-28399)

Whitehouse, Mary. Whatever happened to sex? / [by] Mary Whitehouse. — Hove : Wayland, 1977. — 224p : ill ; 23cm.
Bibl.: p.215-217. — Index.
ISBN 0-85340-460-7 : £4.95
(B77-20036)

301.41'7 — Sex relations. *Correspondence*
More sex life letters / edited by Anne Hooper. — St Albans : Mayflower, 1977. — 352p ; 18cm.
'... from the pages of "Forum" magazine' - cover. — Index.
ISBN 0-583-12762-2 Pbk : £0.95
(B77-26125)

301.41'7'024055 — Sex relations. *For adolescents*
Claxton, Ernest. Tomorrow's parents : life, sex and purpose : missing factors in sex education / [by] Ernest Claxton, James Fry. — London : Grosvenor Books, 1977. — [1],40,[1]p : ill ; 15x21cm.
Bibl.: p.40.
ISBN 0-901269-26-3 Sd : £0.25
(B77-18565)

301.41'7'05 — Sex relations. *Periodicals*
Silk. — London (3 Valentine Place, S.E.1) : Tabor Publications.
Vol.1, no.1- ; [Oct. 1976]-. — 1976-. — ill(chiefly col) ; 30cm.
Monthly. — 114p. in first issue.
Sd : £0.90
(B77-00038)

301.41'74'51042 — Interracial sex relations. Attitudes of society. *United States*
Stember, Charles Herbert. Sexual racism : the emotional barrier to an integrated society / [by] Charles Herbert Stember. — New York ; Oxford [etc.] : Elsevier, 1976. — xviii,234p : 1 ill ; 24cm.
Bibl.: p.222-229. — Index.
ISBN 0-444-99034-8 : £9.51
(B77-06485)

301.41'76'320924 — Men. Sex relations. *Personal observations*
The **autobiography** of an Englishman / [by] Y. — London : Futura Publications, 1976. — 176p ; 18cm.
Originally published: London : Elek, 1975.
ISBN 0-86007-199-5 Pbk : £0.60
(B77-12306)

301.41'76'33 — Women. Sex relations
Male, X. Eve in wonderland : a crime story for adult neuters / by X. Male. — London : Poets' and Painters' Press, 1976. — 101p ; 22cm.
ISBN 0-902571-91-5 Pbk : £3.50
(B77-08784)

301.41'7'6330924 — Middle aged women. Sex relations. *Personal observations*
Cumming, Anne. The love habit / [by] Anne Cumming. — Tiptree : Blond and Briggs, 1977. — 316p ; 23cm.
ISBN 0-85634-059-6 : £4.95
(B77-26126)

301.41'76'330924 — Women. Sex relations. *Personal observations*
Richmond, Fiona. Fiona / [by] Fiona Richmond. — London : Star Books, 1977. — 188p ; 18cm.
Originally published: 1976.
ISBN 0-352-39877-9 Pbk : £0.50
(B77-24710)

301.41'76'330924 — Women. Sex relations. Caron, Sue. *Autobiographies*
Caron, Sue. A screw loose : my story so far / [by] Sue Caron. — London (45 Calthorpe St., WC1X 0HH) : B and T Publishers, 1977. — 272p ; 23cm.
ISBN 0-905934-00-8 : £4.75
(B77-27689)

301.41'76'330973 — Women. Sex relations. *United States. Reports, surveys*
Hite, Shere. The Hite report : a nationwide study on female sexuality / [by] Shere Hite. — New York : Macmillan ; London : Collier Macmillan, 1976 [i.e. 1977]. — xl,438p : form ; 25cm.
Published in the United States: 1976.
ISBN 0-02-551851-8 : £9.40
(B77-12866)

301.41'76'7 — Old persons. Sex relations. *Manuals*
Butler, Robert Neil. Sex after sixty : a guide for men and women for their later years / [by] Robert N. Butler and Myrna I. Lewis. — New York [etc.] ; London : Harper and Row, 1976. — ix,165,[1]p : ill ; 22cm.
Bibl.: p.157-159. — Index.
ISBN 0-06-010593-3 : £5.20
(B77-07073)

301.41'792'2 — Sex relations. Theories of Carpenter, Edward, b.1844 & Ellis, Havelock
Rowbotham, Sheila. Socialism and the new life : the personal and sexual politics of Edward Carpenter and Havelock Ellis / [by] Sheila Rowbotham, Jeffrey Weeks. — London : Pluto Press, 1977. — 198p : 2 ports ; 21cm.
Bibl.: p.187-192. — Index.
ISBN 0-904383-53-9 : £4.50
ISBN 0-904383-52-0 Pbk : £1.80
(B77-30992)

301.41'7943 — Sex relations. Influence of Christianity. *West Germany, ca 1800-ca 1860*
Phayer, J Michael. Sexual liberation and religion in nineteenth century Europe / [by] J. Michael Phayer. — London : Croom Helm [etc.], 1977. — 176p : ill, maps ; 23cm.
Bibl.: p.165-173. — Index.
ISBN 0-85664-230-4 : £7.50
Also classified at 301.41'7944
(B77-15096)

301.41'7944 — Sex relations. Influence of Christianity. *France, ca 1800-ca 1860*
Phayer, J Michael. Sexual liberation and religion in nineteenth century Europe / [by] J. Michael Phayer. — London : Croom Helm [etc.], 1977. — 176p : ill, maps ; 23cm.
Bibl.: p.165-173. — Index.
ISBN 0-85664-230-4 : £7.50
Primary classification 301.41'7943
(B77-15096)

301.41'795 — Sex relations. *Orient, to 1975*
Edwardes, Allen. The jewel in the lotus : a historical survey of the sexual culture of the East / [by] Allen Edwardes ; introduction by Albert Ellis. — Toronto [etc.] ; London : Bantam, 1976. — xviii,268p ; 18cm.
Originally published: New York : Julian Press, 1959 ; London : Blond, 1961. — Bibl.: p.256-267.
ISBN 0-552-60289-2 Pbk : £0.75
(B77-14063)

301.41'8 — Sex relations. Kissing. *Manuals*
Morris, Hugh. The art of kissing / [by] Hugh Morris. — [1st ed. reprinted] / afterword by Dave Wagner ; illustrated by Emanuel Schongut. — London [etc.] : Pan Books, 1977. — 119p : ill ; 18cm.
Originally published: New York : Padell Book Co., 1936.
ISBN 0-330-25352-2 Pbk : £0.50
(B77-33070)

301.42 — Adolescents. Marriage. *United States. Study regions: California. Reports, surveys*
Weeks, John R. Teenage marriages : a demographic analysis / [by] John R. Weeks. — Westport, Conn. ; London : Greenwood Press, 1976. — xxi,3-171,[1]p : ill ; 22cm. — (Studies in population and urban demography ; no.2)
Bibl.: p.149-166. — Index.
ISBN 0-8371-8898-9 : £9.50
(B77-24010)

301.42 — Agricultural communities. Marriage
Goody, Jack. Production and reproduction : a comparative study of the domestic domain / [by] Jack Goody. — Cambridge [etc.] : Cambridge University Press, 1976. — xiii,157p : ill ; 24cm. — (Cambridge studies in social anthropology ; 17 ISSN 0068-6794)
Bibl.: p.145-152. — Index.
ISBN 0-521-21294-4 : £6.00
ISBN 0-521-29088-0 Pbk : £2.80
(B77-16198)

301.42 — Marriage
Leslie, Gerald Ronnell. Marriage in a changing world / [by] Gerald R. Leslie, Elizabeth McLaughlin Leslie. — New York ; London [etc.] : Wiley, 1977. — xii,452p : ill(some col), col map ; 25cm.
Bibl.: p.403-423. — Index.
ISBN 0-471-52801-3 : £8.95
(B77-17310)

Scanzoni, Letha. Men, women and change : a sociology of marriage and family / [by] Letha Scanzoni, John Scanzoni. — New York ; London [etc.] : McGraw-Hill, 1976. — viii, 504p : ill, ports ; 25cm.
Bibl.: p.484-498. — Index.
ISBN 0-07-055040-9 : £10.75
(B77-04571)

301.42 — Marriage. *Anthropological perspectives*
Mair, Lucy. Marriage / [by] Lucy Mair. — London : Scolar Press, 1977. — 223p ; 21cm.
Originally published: Harmondsworth : Penguin, 1971. — Bibl.: p.213-217. — Index.
ISBN 0-85967-363-4 : £5.00
ISBN 0-85967-360-x Pbk : £2.50
(B77-33071)

301.42'092'4 — Marriage. *England, 1930-1940. Personal observations*
Powell, Margaret. My children and I / [by] Margaret Powell. — London : Joseph, 1977. — 190p ; 23cm.
ISBN 0-7181-1639-9 : £4.50
(B77-25399)

301.42'094 — Marriage. *Europe, ca 1400-ca 1500. Juvenile literature*
Lasker, Joe. Merry ever after : the story of two medieval weddings / written and illustrated by Joe Lasker. — London : Hamilton, 1977. — [48]p : col ill ; 26cm.
Originally published: New York : Viking Press, 1976.
ISBN 0-241-89469-7 : £3.50
(B77-28400)

301.42'0973 — Marriage. *United States. Secondary school texts*
Landis, Paul Henry. Your marriage and family living / [by] Paul H. Landis. — 4th ed. — New York ; London [etc.] : McGraw-Hill, 1977. — viii,472p : ill ; 25cm.
Previous ed.: St Louis : McGraw-Hill, 1969. — Index.
ISBN 0-07-036187-8 : £8.10
(B77-20918)

301.42'1 — Families
Leslie, Gerald Ronnell. The family in social context / [by] Gerald R. Leslie. — 3rd ed. — New York ; London [etc.] : Oxford University Press, 1976. — viii,815p : ill ; 24cm.
Previous ed.: 1973. — Bibl. — Lists of films. — Index.
Unpriced
(B77-01180)

301.42'1 — Families. *Secondary school texts*
Jones, Anne. Living choices : home and family in modern society / [by] Anne Jones, Jan Marsh and A.G. Watts. — Cambridge : Hobsons Press [for the Careers Research and Advisory Centre], 1976. — [2],32p : ill ; 30cm. — (Life style series)
ISBN 0-86021-063-4 Sd : £0.95
(B77-10738)

301.42'1 — Families. Decision making
Paolucci, Beatrice. Family decision making : an ecosystem approach / [by] Beatrice Paolucci, Olive A. Hall, Nancy W. Axinn. — New York ; London [etc.] : Wiley, 1977. — xiii, 190p : ill ; 23cm.
Bibl. — Index.
ISBN 0-471-65838-3 Pbk : £4.25
(B77-20919)

301.42'1 — Family life. *Secondary school texts*
Families & friends / [compiled by] John Foster & Rod Hunt. — Basingstoke [etc.] : Macmillan, 1977. — [1],32p : ill, coat of arms, geneal table ; 20x21cm. — (Investigations)
Bibl.
ISBN 0-333-19832-8 Sd : £0.55
(B77-27690)

301.42'1 — Ga. Social change. Role of family life. *Ghana. Accra*
Azu, Diana Gladys. The Ga family and social change / by Diana Gladys Azu. — Leiden : Afrika-Studiecentrum ; Cambridge ([University of Cambridge, Sidgwick Ave., Cambridge]) : African Studies Centre, 1974. — vii,137,fold plate : ill, geneal table, maps, plans ; 23cm. — (African social research documents ; vol.5)
Bibl.: p.117-119.
Pbk : Unpriced
(B77-25401)

301.42'1'0917496073 — Negroes. Family life. *United States*
Scanzoni, John Henry. The black family in modern society : patterns of stability and security / [by] John H. Scanzoni. — [New ed.]. — Chicago ; London : University of Chicago Press, 1977. — xv,365p : ill ; 21cm. — (A phoenix book)
Previous ed.: Boston, Mass. : Allyn and Bacon, 1971. — Bibl.: p.345-357. — Index.
ISBN 0-226-73341-6 Pbk : £4.10
(B77-29952)

301.42'1'094 — Family life. *Western Europe, to 1976*
Laslett, Peter. Family life and illicit love in earlier generations : essays in historical sociology / [by] Peter Laslett. — Cambridge [etc.] : Cambridge University Press, 1977. — vii,270p : ill, facsims, map ; 24cm.
Bibl.: p.261-264. — Index.
ISBN 0-521-21408-4 : £15.00
ISBN 0-521-29221-2 Pbk : £4.95
(B77-22364)

301.42'1'0942 — Families. *England, 1500-1800*
Stone, Lawrence. The family, sex and marriage in England, 1500-1800 / [by] Lawrence Stone. — London : Weidenfeld and Nicolson, 1977. — xxxi,800p,24p of plates : ill, facsims, ports ; 24cm.
Ports. on lining papers. — Bibl.: p.759-781. — Index.
ISBN 0-297-77133-7 : £16.00
(B77-25400)

301.42'1'0942 — Families. Demographic aspects. *England, 1550-1850*
Levine, David. Family formation in an age of nascent capitalism / [by] David Levine. — New York [etc.] ; London : Academic Press, 1977. — xiv,194p : ill ; 24cm. — (Studies in social discontinuity)
Bibl.: p.175-191. — Index.
ISBN 0-12-445050-4 : £10.30
(B77-31702)

301.42'1'0942264 — Households. Demographic aspects. *West Sussex. Horsham, 1851-1871*
Constable, Derek. Household structure in three English market towns, 1851-1871 / [by] Derek Constable. — Reading (Whiteknights, Reading RG6 2AB) : Department of Geography, University of Reading, 1977. — [2],iii,63p : ill ; 21cm. — (Geographical papers ; no.55 ISSN 0305-5914)
ISBN 0-7049-0465-9 Sd : £0.70
Also classified at 301.42'1'0942313; 301.42'1'0942319
(B77-31703)

301.42'1'0942313 — Households. Demographic aspects. *Wiltshire. Swindon, 1851-1871*
Constable, Derek. Household structure in three English market towns, 1851-1871 / [by] Derek Constable. — Reading (Whiteknights, Reading RG6 2AB) : Department of Geography, University of Reading, 1977. — [2],iii,63p : ill ; 21cm. — (Geographical papers ; no.55 ISSN 0305-5914)
ISBN 0-7049-0465-9 Sd : £0.70
Primary classification 301.42'1'0942264
(B77-31703)

301.42'1'0942319 — Households. Demographic aspects. *Wiltshire. Salisbury, 1851-1871*
Constable, Derek. Household structure in three English market towns, 1851-1871 / [by] Derek Constable. — Reading (Whiteknights, Reading RG6 2AB) : Department of Geography, University of Reading, 1977. — [2],iii,63p : ill ; 21cm. — (Geographical papers ; no.55 ISSN 0305-5914)
ISBN 0-7049-0465-9 Sd : £0.70
Primary classification 301.42'1'0942264
(B77-31703)

301.42'1'0954 — Indian families. Structure
Parekh, Bhikhu. The Indian family / by B.C. Parekh. — Southall (46 High St., Southall, Middx) : Scope Communication, [1977]. — [1], 13p ; 30cm.
ISBN 0-9505709-0-7 Sd : £0.15
(B77-15699)

301.42'1'0967112 — Family life. *Southern Cameroun Republic. Reports, surveys*
Weekes-Vagliani, Winifred. Family life and structure in southern Cameroon / by Winifred Weekes-Vagliani in collaboration with Manga Bekombo and with the assistance of Lynn Wallisch. — Paris : Organisation for Economic Co-operation and Development, Development Centre ; [London] : [H.M.S.O.], 1976. — 87p : ill, maps, port ; 24cm. — (Organisation for Economic Co-operation and Development. Development Centre. Technical papers)
Bibl.: p.63-66.
Pbk : £1.80
ISBN 92-64-11477-7
(B77-01181)

301.42'1'0972 — Kinship. *Mexico. Anthropological perspectives*
Essays on Mexican kinship / Hugo G. Nutini, Pedro Carrasco, James M. Taggart, editors. — [Pittsburgh] : University of Pittsburgh Press ; London : Feffer and Simons : [Distributed by Transatlantic Book Service], 1976. — xii,256p : ill, map ; 24cm. — (Pitt Latin American series)
Bibl.: p.241-249. — Index.
ISBN 0-8229-3307-1 : £11.21
(B77-05882)

301.42'1'0973 — Families. *United States. Sociological perspectives. Readings*
The **family** : functions, conflicts, and symbols / [compiled by] Peter J. Stein, Judith Richman, Natalie Hannon. — Reading, Mass. ; London [etc.] : Addison-Wesley, 1977. — x,452p ; 24cm.
Bibl.
ISBN 0-201-07362-5 Pbk : £7.20
(B77-22365)

301.42'1'0973 — Negro families. Social conditions. *United States, 1750-1925*
Gutman, Herbert George. The black family in slavery and freedom, 1750-1925 / [by] Herbert G. Gutman. — Oxford : Blackwell, 1976. — xxviii,664p : ill, facsims, geneal tables ; 25cm.
Facsims on lining papers. — Also published: New York : Pantheon Books, 1976. — Index.
ISBN 0-631-17650-0 : £10.50
(B77-09520)

301.42'12 — Fathers. *Children's viewpoints. Collections*
To dad : a gift book written by children for fathers everywhere / edited by Richard & Helen Exley. — Watford (63 Kingsfield Rd, Watford, Herts. WD1 4PP) : Exley Publications Ltd, 1976. — 63p : ill(some col) ; 22cm.
ISBN 0-905521-01-3 : £1.95
(B77-19226)

301.42'12 — Mothers. *Children's viewpoints. Collections*
To mum : a gift book written by children for mothers everywhere / edited by Richard & Helen Exley. — Watford (63 Kingsfield Rd, Watford, Herts. WD1 4PP) : Exley Publications Ltd, 1976. — 63p : ill(some col) ; 22cm.
ISBN 0-905521-00-5 : £1.95
(B77-20037)

301.42'6 — Children. Sexes. Preferences of parents. *Comparative studies*
Williamson, Nancy E. Sons or daughters : a cross-cultural survey of parental preferences / [by] Nancy E. Williamson ; preface by David M. Heer ; series editor's preface by Jetse Sprey. — Beverly Hills ; London : Sage Publications [for] the National Council on Family Relations, 1976. — 207p ; 22cm. — (Sage library of social research ; vol.31)
Bibl.: p.171-194. — Index.
ISBN 0-8039-0673-0 : £7.50
ISBN 0-8039-0674-9 Pbk : £4.00
(B77-15700)

301.42'6 — Families. Size. Social factors. *England, 1945-1976*
Busfield, Joan. Thinking about children : sociology and fertility in post-war England / [by] Joan Busfield, Michael Paddon. — Cambridge [etc.] : Cambridge University Press, 1977. — xii,312p ; 24cm.
Bibl.: p.298-305. — Index.
ISBN 0-521-21402-5 : £6.50
(B77-26128)

301.42'6 — Family planning. *Reports, surveys. French texts*
International Planned Parenthood Federation. Le planning familial dans cinq continents / [International Planned Parenthood Federation]. — London : The Federation, 1973. — [2],41p ; 21x30cm.
ISBN 0-900924-53-5 Sd : £0.25
(B77-18566)

301.42'6 — Voluntarily childless married couples. *United States. Sociological perspectives*
Nason, Ellen Mara. Voluntarily childless couples : the emergence of a variant lifestyle / [by] Ellen Mara Nason, Margaret M. Poloma. — Beverly Hills ; London : Sage Publications, 1976. — 54,[1]p ; 22cm. — (Sage research papers in the social sciences : studies of marriage and the family series ; vol.5, no.90-040)
Bibl.: p.49-50.
ISBN 0-8039-0755-9 Pbk : Unpriced
(B77-20920)

301.42'6'05 — Family planning. *Periodicals*
Family planning today : bi-monthly bulletin on fertility control, human relationships, population and related topics. — London : Family Planning Association.
Previously published: as 'Family planning' and 'FP news'.
[Vol.1, no.1]- ; Sept. 1976-. — [1976]-. — ill, ports ; 30cm.
Folder (4p.) as 1st issue.
Unpriced
ISSN 0309-1112
(B77-29194)

301.42'6'0723 — Family planning. Surveys. *Nigeria. Reports, surveys*
McWilliam, John, *b.1945.* Nigeria : selected studies : social science research for population and family planning policies and programme / by John McWilliam and Chukwudum Uche. — London : Evaluation and Social Sciences Department, International Planned Parenthood Federation, 1976. — [4],50[i.e. 55]p ; 22cm. — (Research for action ; no.1 ISSN 0309-2615)
Bibl.: p.40-50.
ISBN 0-900924-79-9 Sd : £0.50
(B77-10181)

301.42'6'09713541 — Family planning. *Canada, 1946-1970. Study regions: Ontario. Toronto*
Balakrishnan, T R. Fertility and family planning in a Canadian metropolis / [by] T.R. Balakrishnan, J.F. Kantner, J.D. Allingham. — Montreal ; London : McGill-Queen's University Press, 1975. — xvi,217p : ill, forms ; 24cm.
Bibl.: p.209-213. — Index.
ISBN 0-7735-0204-1 : Unpriced
(B77-17929)

301.42'7 — Adolescent girls. Interpersonal relationships with parents. Conflict. *Great Britain. Case studies*
Willans, Angela. Breakaway : family conflict and the teenage girl / [by] Angela Willans. — London : Temple Smith, 1977. — 201p ; 23cm.

ISBN 0-85117-129-x : £6.25
ISBN 0-85117-134-6 Pbk : £2.65
(B77-25402)

301.42'7 — Children. Violence of parents. *Great Britain. Inquiry reports*
Great Britain. *Parliament. House of Commons. Select Committee on Violence in the Family.* Violence to children : first report from the Select Committee on Violence in the Family, session 1976-77. — London : H.M.S.O.
In 3 vols.
Vol.1 : Report : (together with the proceedings of the Committee). — [1977]. — lxxxii p ; 25cm. — ([1976-77 H.C.]329-i)
ISBN 0-10-288477-3 Sd : £1.35
(B77-17930)

Vol.2 : Evidence. — [1977]. — vi,440[i.e.442] p(2 fold) ; 25cm. — ([1976-77] H.C.329-II)
Bibl.: p.121-125.
ISBN 0-10-286677-5 Pbk : £8.35
(B77-17931)

Vol.3 : Appendices. — [1977]. — iv p,p441-689 : ill, form ; 25cm. — ([1976-77 H.C.]329-III)
Bibl.
ISBN 0-10-288577-x Pbk : £3.10
(B77-17932)

301.42'7 — Dual-career families. *Great Britain. Case studies*
Rapoport, Rhona. Dual-career families re-examined : new integrations of work & family / [by] Rhona & Robert N. Rapoport. — [2nd ed.]. — London : Martin Robertson, 1976. — 382p ; 21cm.
Previous ed.: published as 'Dual-career families'. Harmondsworth : Penguin, 1971. — Bibl.: p.373-382.
ISBN 0-85520-125-8 : £6.50
ISBN 0-85520-124-x Pbk : £2.95
(B77-04572)

301.42'7 — Families. Interpersonal relationships. *Case studies*
Institute of Family Development. *Research Department.* Case histories and notes / [prepared by the Research Department of Institute of Family Development]. — Camberley ([41 Park Rd, Camberley, Surrey]) : [The Institute], [1976]. — 274p in various pagings ; 32cm.
Title supplied by cataloguer. — In binder.
Ls : Unpriced
(B77-19227)

301.42'7 — Families. Violence. Inquiry reports. *Great Britain. Great Britain. Parliament. House of Commons. Select Committee on Violence in Marriage. Report from the Select Committee on Violence in Marriage, session 1974-1975. Critical studies*
Observations on the report from the Select Committee on Violence in Marriage / Department of Health and Social Security ... [et al.]. — London : H.M.S.O., 1976. — 37p ; 25cm. — (Cmnd.6690)
ISBN 0-10-166900-3 Sd : £0.60
(B77-05883)

301.42'7 — Marriage. Interpersonal relationships
Makins, Peggy. Evelyn Home's new handbook of marriage / [by] Peggy Makins. — London : Hutchinson, 1977. — 128p ; 23cm.
ISBN 0-09-128600-x : £2.95
ISBN 0-09-914140-x Pbk : £0.50
(B77-09521)

O'Neill, Nena. Open marriage : a new life style for couples / [by] Nena O'Neill and George O'Neill. — London : Abacus, 1975. — 237p : 1 ill ; 20cm.
Originally published: New York : M. Evans, 1972 ; London : Owen, 1973. — Bibl.: p.231-237.
ISBN 0-349-12641-0 Pbk : £0.90
(B77-08237)

Scoresby, A Lynn. The marriage dialogue / [by] A. Lynn Scoresby. — Reading, Mass. ; London [etc.] : Addison-Wesley, 1977. — xii,189p : ill ; 21cm. — (Addison-Wesley series in sociology)
Bibl.: p.187-189.
ISBN 0-201-06789-7 Pbk : £4.00
(B77-23139)

301.42'7 — Marriage. Interpersonal relationships. *For women*
Morgan, Marabel. Total joy / [by] Marabel Morgan. — London [etc.] : Hodder and Stoughton, 1977. — 157p ; 21cm.
Originally published: Old Tappan, N.J. : Revell, 1976. — Bibl.: p.156.
ISBN 0-340-22085-6 : £2.50
(B77-20921)

301.42'7 — Marriage. Interpersonal relationships. Communication
Thomas, Edwin John. Marital communication and decision making : analysis, assessment and change / [by] Edwin J. Thomas. — New York : Free Press ; London : Collier Macmillan, 1977. — xiii,239p ; 24cm.
Bibl.: p.220-227. — Index.
ISBN 0-02-932570-6 : £9.75
(B77-29196)

301.42'7 — Marriage. Interpersonal relationships. Conflict. *United States, 1700-1800*
Lantz, Herman R. Marital incompatibility and social change in early America / [by] Herman R. Lantz. — Beverly Hills ; London : Sage Publications, 1976. — 48p ; 22cm. — (Sage research papers in the social sciences : studies of marriage and the family series ; vol.4, no.90-026)
Bibl.: p.46-48.
ISBN 0-8039-0546-7 Pbk : £1.50
(B77-15097)

301.42'7 — Motherhood
Barber, Virginia. The mother person / by Virginia Barber and Merrill Maguire Skaggs. — London : Severn House : [Distributed by Hutchinson], 1977. — [6],218p ; 23cm.
Originally published: Indianapolis : Bobbs-Merrill, 1975. — Bibl.: p.[6].
ISBN 0-7278-0224-0 : £4.25
(B77-14064)

Rich, Adrienne Cecile. Of woman born : motherhood as experience and institution / [by] Adrienne Rich. — London : Virago, 1977. — [2],318p ; 21cm.
Originally published: New York : Norton, 1976. — Index.
ISBN 0-86068-030-4 : £7.50
ISBN 0-86068-031-2 Pbk : £2.50
(B77-27691)

301.42'7 — Parenthood, to 1976
Rapoport, Rhona. Fathers, mothers and others : towards new alliances / [by] Rhona Rapoport and Robert N. Rapoport and Ziona Strelitz with Stephen Kew. — London [etc.] : Routledge and Kegan Paul, 1977. — ix,421p ; 23cm.
Bibl.: p.366-405. — Index.
ISBN 0-7100-8577-x : £6.95 : CIP rev.
(B77-07074)

301.42'7'0922 — Married couples. Interpersonal relationships. *Ireland. (Republic). Personal observations. Collections*
McElhone, Patricia. When the honeymoon is over : seven true accounts of the experience of marriage / [compiled by] Patricia McElhone. — Dublin : Veritas Publications, 1977. — 112p ; 19cm.
ISBN 0-905092-27-9 Pbk : Unpriced
(B77-28401)

301.42'86 — Death. Social aspects. *Secondary school texts*
Milne, Katharine. A time to die / [by] Katharine Milne. — Hove : Wayland, 1977. — 80p : ill, form ; 25cm. — (A new citizen book)
Bibl.: p.78. — Index.
ISBN 0-85340-228-0 : £2.95
(B77-15701)

301.43'14 — Adopted children. Social development. Great Britain. Compared with social development of children in care subsequently restored to natural parents. *Reports, surveys*
Tizard, Barbara. Adoption : a second chance / [by] Barbara Tizard. — London : Open Books, 1977. — xii,251p : ill ; 23cm.
Index.
ISBN 0-7291-0191-6 : £7.50
ISBN 0-7291-0196-7 Pbk : £3.95
(B77-29953)

301.43'14 — Childhood
Tucker, Nicholas. What is a child? / [by] Nicholas Tucker. — [London] : Fontana, 1977. — 128p ; 18cm.
Also published: London : Open Books, 1977. — Index.
ISBN 0-00-634877-7 Pbk : £1.00
(B77-33072)

301.43'14 — Communes. Children. *United States*
Constantine, Larry L. Treasures of the island : children in alternative families / [by] Larry L. Constantine, Joan M. Constantine. — Beverly Hills ; London : Sage Publications, 1976. — 37,[1]p : ill ; 22cm. — (Sage research papers in the social sciences : studies of marriage and the family series ; vol.5, no.90-038)
Bibl.: p.35-37.
ISBN 0-8039-0751-6 Pbk : £1.75
(B77-15702)

301.43'14 — Poor children. Social conditions. *Italy. Naples. Personal observations*
West, Morris. Children of the sun / [by] Morris West. — [London] : Fontana, 1977. — 188,[4] p,[4]p of plates : ill, ports ; 18cm.
Originally published: London : Heinemann, 1957.
ISBN 0-00-634306-6 Pbk : £0.70
(B77-13515)

301.43'14'09411 — Art galleries. *Edinburgh. Scottish National Portrait Gallery. Exhibits: Items associated with children in Scotland, 1600-1700. Catalogues*

Marshall, Rosalind Kay. Childhood in seventeenth century Scotland : the Scottish National Portrait Gallery, 19 August-19 September 1976 / [by] Rosalind K. Marshall. — Edinburgh (c/o [Portrait Gallery Buildings, 1 Queen St., Edinburgh 2]) : Trustees of the National Galleries of Scotland, 1976. — 67p : ill, ports ; 30cm.
' ... the latest in [the] series of Edinburgh Festival Exhibitions' - Foreword. — Col. poster (60x42cm.) as insert.
ISBN 0-903148-06-4 Sd : £1.25
(B77-01683)

301.43'15 — Adolescent girls. *Samoa. Anthropological perspectives*

Mead, Margaret. Coming of age in Samoa : a study of adolescence and sex in primitive societies / [by] Margaret Mead. — Harmondsworth [etc.] : Penguin, 1977. — 240p ; 19cm. — (Pelican books)
Originally published: New York : Morrow, 1928 ; London : Cape, 1929. — Index.
ISBN 0-14-020127-0 Pbk : £0.80
(B77-33073)

301.43'15 — Adolescents, 16 years. *Great Britain. Reports, surveys*

Britain's sixteen year olds : preliminary findings of the third follow-up of the National Child Development Study (1958 cohort) / edited by Ken Fogelman ; appendix by Harvey Goldstein. — London (8 Wakley St., EC1V 9QE) : National Children's Bureau, 1976. — 82p ; 21cm. — (National Children's Bureau. Reports)
Bibl.: p.8-9.
ISBN 0-902817-10-8 Sd : £2.00
(B77-14572)

301.43'15 — Society. Role of adolescents. *Conference proceedings*

International Colloquium on Adolescence in the Year 2000, *Amsterdam, 1975.* Adolescence and youth in prospect / edited by John P. Hill and Franz J. Mönks. — Guildford : IPC Science and Technology Press, 1977. — viii,217p : ill ; 22cm.
'... the proceedings, conclusions, and recommendations of ... the International Colloquium on Adolescence in the Year 2000, held in Amsterdam from 15-19 September 1975 under the sponsorship of [i.e. organised by] the Jeugdprofiel 2000 Foundation' - Overview and outcomes. — Bibl.
ISBN 0-902852-66-3 : £6.80
(B77-15098)

301.43'15'05 — Newspapers for adolescents: Newspapers with Leicester imprints. *Texts*

Scene : the newpaper for young adults. — Leicester (17 Albion St., Leicester LE1 6GD) : National Youth Bureau.
No.1- ; Sept. 1975-. — 1975-. — ill, ports ; 42cm.
Monthly. — Folder ([4]p.) as 1st issue. — 'Ads' (sheet ([1]p.)) as insert.
Sd : £0.05
(B77-33622)

301.43'15'0722 — Adolescents. Social development. *United States. Case studies*

Moriarty, Alice Ewell. Adolescent coping / [by] Alice E. Moriarty, Povl W. Toussieng ; with a foreword by Gardner Murphy and Lois Barclay Murphy. — New York [etc.] ; London : Grune and Stratton, 1976. — xv,220p ; 24cm.
Index.
ISBN 0-8089-0942-8 : £8.85
(B77-02781)

301.43'15'0941 — Adolescents. Social values. *Great Britain. Reports, surveys*

Frontier Youth Trust. Searching for values : the report of a study into youth and values / by Frontier Youth Trust ; [written by Roger Mitchell]. — [London] : [The Trust], [1976]. — [1],43p ; 22cm.
Sd : £0.80
(B77-26129)

301.43'15'0973 — Adolescents. Psychosocial aspects. *United States*

Sebald, Hans. Adolescence : a social psychological analysis / [by] Hans Sebald. — 2nd ed. — Englewood Cliffs ; London [etc.] : Prentice-Hall, 1977. — xiv,530p ; 23cm.
Previous ed.: published as 'Adolescence : a sociological analysis'. New York : Appleton-Century-Crofts, 1968. — Index.
ISBN 0-13-008599-5 Pbk : £9.55
(B77-22366)

301.43'4 — Adults. Ageing. Social aspects. *Reports, surveys*

Maas, Henry Sigmund. From thirty to seventy / [by] Henry S. Maas, Joseph A. Kuypers. — San Francisco [etc.] ; London : Jossey-Bass, 1974. — xv,240p ; 24cm. — (The Jossey-Bass behavioral science series)
Bibl.: p.229-231. — Index.
ISBN 0-87589-234-5 : Unpriced
(B77-18567)

301.43'4'0973 — Middle aged persons. *United States. Case studies*

Sheehy, Gail. Passages : predictable crises of adult life / [by] Gail Sheehy. — New York : Dutton ; [Leicester] ([Euston St., Freemen's Common, Aylestone Rd, Leicester LE2 7SS]) : Distributed by WHS Distributors, 1976. — xv, 393p ; 24cm.
'Portions of this book previously appeared in "New York" magazine' - title page verso. — Bibl.: p.375-381. — Index.
ISBN 0-525-17613-6 : £4.95
(B77-12867)

Sheehy, Gail. Passages : predictable crises of adult life / by Gail Sheehy. — Toronto [etc.] ; London : Bantam, 1977. — xiv,561p : ill ; 18cm.
Originally published: New York : Dutton, 1976. — Bibl.: p.541-548. — Index.
ISBN 0-552-10466-3 Pbk : £0.95
(B77-33074)

301.43'5 — Old age. *Sociological perspectives*

Beauvoir, Simone de. Old age / [by] Simone de Beauvoir ; translated [from the French] by Patrick O'Brian. — Harmondsworth [etc.] : Penguin, 1977. — 654p ; 18cm.
This translation originally published: London : Deutsch : Weidenfeld and Nicolson, 1972. — Translation of 'La Vieillesse'. Paris : Gallimard, 1970. — Index.
ISBN 0-14-004058-7 Pbk : £1.95
(B77-08785)

301.43'5 — Old persons. Economic status. Assessment. *United States*

Moon, Marilyn. The measurement of economic welfare : its application to the aged poor / [by] Marilyn Moon. — New York [etc.] ; London : Academic Press, 1977. — xiv,146p : 2 ill ; 24cm. — (University of Wisconsin. Institute for Research on Poverty. Monograph series)
Bibl.: p.137-140. — Index.
ISBN 0-12-504650-2 : £9.60
(B77-25403)

301.43'5 — Old persons. Social aspects

Elder, Gladys. The alienated : growing old today / by Gladys Elder ; edited by Christine Bernard ; photographs by Mike Abrahams ; introduction by J.B. Priestley. — London : Writers and Readers Publishing Cooperative, 1977. — 144p : ill, ports ; 21cm.
Bibl.: p.142.
ISBN 0-904613-63-1 : £3.95
ISBN 0-904613-64-x Pbk : £1.50
(B77-29197)

Fontana, Andrea. The last frontier : the social meaning of growing old / [by] Andrea Fontana ; preface by Fred Davis. — Beverly Hills ; London : Sage Publications, 1977. — 215p ; 22cm. — (Sage library of social research ; vol.42)
Bibl.: p.201-208. — Index.
ISBN 0-8039-0832-6 : £8.50
ISBN 0-8039-0833-4 Pbk : £4.50
(B77-26130)

301.43'5 — Personal adjustment to retirement

Hubbard, Lorna MacIntosh. What next? : a basic booklet about the problems of retirement / by Lorna M. Hubbard in association with Ernie J. Hewitt ; illustrations by Liz Bayts. — Tiverton ([1 Magnolia Villas, Briton St., Bampton, Tiverton, Devon EX16 9LL]) : [The author], 1977. — [1],34p : ill ; 15x22cm.
Bibl.
ISBN 0-9505904-0-1 Sd : £0.75
(B77-33623)

301.43'5 — Residential homes for old persons. Community life. *France. Paris. Sociological perspectives. Study examples: Floralies, Les. Reports, surveys*

Ross, Jennie-Keith. Old people, new lives : community creation in a retirement residence / [by] Jennie-Keith Ross. — Chicago ; London : University of Chicago Press, 1977. — xi,227p : 1 ill ; 23cm.
Bibl.: p.215-223. — Index.
ISBN 0-226-72825-0 : £6.50
(B77-33624)

301.43'5 — Retirement. *Great Britain*

Loughton, Arch. Retirement the new beginning / [by] Arch Loughton ; foreword by Jack Jones. — London : Bachman and Turner, 1976. — [9] ,134p : ill, facsim ; 23cm.
Bibl.: p.128-130. — Index.
ISBN 0-85974-060-9 : £3.25
(B77-06486)

301.43'5 — Retirement. Personal adjustment of manual personnel. *London. Camden (London Borough). Case studies*

Spiers, Peter. Transition in retirement : an account of some conversations with recently retired manual workers / by Peter and Barbara Spiers ; [for] Camden Council of Social Service. — London (c/o Camden Council of Social Service, 11 Tavistock Place, WC1H 9QH) : The authors, 1975. — [1],22p ; 21cm.
ISBN 0-904634-02-7 Sd : Unpriced
(B77-03387)

301.43'5 — Retirement. Planning. *Manuals*

Dewhurst, Robin. Approaching retirement / [by] Robin Dewhurst ... — Cambridge : Woodhead-Faulkner [for Stewart Wrightson Assurance Consultants], 1976. — viii,117p ; 22cm.
Bibl. — Index.
ISBN 0-85941-058-7 : £3.25
ISBN 0-85941-048-x Pbk : £1.95
(B77-03946)

Felstein, Ivor. Looking at retirement / by Ivor Felstein. — London : British Medical Association, [1977]. — 31p : ill ; 19cm. — (A 'Family doctor' booklet)
Bibl.: p.31.
Sd : £0.30
(B77-33075)

301.43'5 — Seaside resorts. Retirement of retired persons. *England. Reports, surveys*

Karn, Valerie Ann. Retiring to the seaside / [by] Valerie A. Karn. — London [etc.] : Routledge and Kegan Paul, 1977. — xii,388p : form, 2 maps ; 23cm. — (International library of social policy)
Not the same as B76-11178. — Bibl.: p.374-377. — Index.
ISBN 0-7100-8418-8 : £7.50
(B77-13516)

301.43'5 — Slums. Hotels. Residents: Old persons. *United States. Sociological perspectives*

Stephens, Joyce. Loners, losers and lovers : elderly tenants in a slum hotel / [by] Joyce Stephens. — Seattle ; London : University of Washington Press, 1976. — xix,118p ; 23cm.
Bibl.: p.113-118.
ISBN 0-295-95494-9 : £7.20
(B77-04573)

301.43'5'08 — Old age. *Readings*

Let's learn about aging : a book of readings / edited by John R. Barry and C. Ray Wingrove. — Cambridge, Mass. : Schenkman ; New York ; London [etc.] : Wiley, 1977. — iii-xv, 528p : ill ; 24cm.
Bibl.
ISBN 0-470-98965-3 : £13.90
ISBN 0-470-98967-x Pbk : £7.15
(B77-31704)

301.43'5'08 — Old age. *Readings. Serials*

Readings in aging and death : contemporary perspectives / edited by Steven H. Zarit. — New York [etc.] ; London : Harper and Row. — (Contemporary perspectives reader series)
1977-1978 ed. — 1977. — xiv,307p : ill, facsims, map, ports ; 29cm.
Bibl. — Includes facsimile reprints.
ISBN 0-06-047056-9 Pbk : £5.20
(B77-28403)

301.43'5'0941 — Old persons. Social aspects. *Great Britain. Secondary school texts*

Leigh, Francis. Growing old / [by] Francis Leigh. — London : Edward Arnold, 1976. — 16p : ill ; 30cm. — (Checkpoint ; 7)
ISBN 0-7131-0051-6 Sd : £2.50(set of 5 copies)
(B77-10182)

301.43'5'094215 — Old persons. Family life. *Great Britain. Study regions: London. Tower Hamlets (London Borough). Bethnal Green*

Townsend, Peter, *b.1928.* The family life of old people : an inquiry in East London / [by] Peter Townsend. — Abridged ed. ; with a new postscript. — Harmondsworth [etc.] : Penguin, 1977. — 331p : ill, geneal table ; 18cm. — (Pelican books)
This ed. originally published: 1963. — Bibl.: p.314-321. — Index.
ISBN 0-14-020634-5 Pbk : £0.95
(B77-32427)

301.43'5'0944 — Old persons. Attitudes of society, ca 1800-1975. *Study regions: France*
Stearns, Peter Nathaniel. Old age in European society : the case of France / [by] Peter N. Stearns. — London : Croom Helm, 1977. — [4],163p ; 23cm.
Index.
ISBN 0-85664-307-6 : £6.95
(B77-06487)

301.43'5'0973 — Old persons. Social aspects. *United States*
Age in society / edited by Anne Foner. — Beverly Hills ; London : Sage Publications, 1976. — 126p ; 22cm. — (Sage contemporary social science issues ; 30)
'... originally appeared as a special issue of "American behavioral scientist" (Volume 19, Number 2, November/December 1975)' - title page verso. — Bibl.
ISBN 0-8039-0731-1 Pbk : £2.50
(B77-15099)

Jones, Rochelle. The other generation : the new power of older people / [by] Rochelle Jones. — Englewood Cliffs ; London [etc.] : Prentice-Hall, 1977. — x,264p ; 21cm.
'A spectrum book'. — Index.
ISBN 0-13-643064-3 : Unpriced
ISBN 0-13-643056-2 Pbk : £3.95
(B77-33625)

Sarason, Seymour Bernard. Work, aging and social change : professionals and the one life-one career imperative / [by] Seymour B. Sarason ; with a chapter 'The Santa Fe experience' by David Krantz. — New York : Free Press ; London : Collier Macmillan, 1977. — xv,298p ; 24cm.
Bibl.: p.289-293. — Index.
ISBN 0-02-927860-0 : £11.25
Primary classification 301.5'5
(B77-29205)

301.44 — Children, 5-7 years. Social class. Related to language skills
Adlam, Diana S. Code in context / [by] Diana S. Adlam ; with the assistance of Geoffrey Turner and Lesley Lineker. — London [etc.] : Routledge and Kegan Paul, 1977. — xvii,253p : ill ; 23cm. — (Primary socialization, language and education)
Bibl.: p.245-247. — Index.
ISBN 0-7100-8481-1 : £6.25
Primary classification 401'.9
(B77-16331)

301.44 — Industrialised societies. Social stratification
Offe, Claus. Industry and inequality : the achievement principle in work and social status / [by] Claus Offe ; translated [from the German] by James Wickham. — London : Edward Arnold, 1976. — [5],158p : ill ; 22cm.
Translation of: 'Leistungsprinzip und industrielle Arbeit'. Frankfurt am Main : Europäische Verlagsanstalt, 1970. — Bibl.: p.147-153. — Index.
ISBN 0-7131-5892-1 : £5.95
ISBN 0-7131-5893-x Pbk : £2.95
(B77-03947)

301.44 — Social classes. Economic aspects. *Capitalist countries. Marxist viewpoints*
Carchedi, Guglielmo. On the economic identification of social classes / [by] Guglielmo Carchedi. — London [etc.] : Routledge and Kegan Paul, 1977. — vii,224p : ill ; 24cm.
Bibl.: p.214-219. — Index.
ISBN 0-7100-8648-2 Pbk : £4.95 : CIP rev.
(B77-21707)

301.44 — Social equality. Related to social policies. Political aspects
Weale, Albert. Equality and social policy / [by] Albert Weale. — London [etc.] : Routledge and Kegan Paul, 1978. — xi,149p ; 23cm. — (The international library of welfare and philosophy)
Bill.: p.138-145. — Index.
ISBN 0-7100-8770-5 : £4.95 : CIP rev.
ISBN 0-7100-8771-3 Pbk : £2.50
(B77-29954)

301.44 — Social inequality
Béteille, André. Inequality among men / [by] André Béteille. — Oxford : Blackwell, 1977. — x,178p ; 23cm. — (Pavilion series, social anthropology)
Index.
ISBN 0-631-17410-9 : £6.50 : CIP rev.
ISBN 0-631-17420-6 Pbk : £3.25
(B77-05884)

Inequalities, conflict & change / edited by Andrew Blowers and Grahame Thompson at the Open University with Stephanie Goodenough. — Milton Keynes ([c/o Open University Educational Enterprises Ltd, 12 Cofferidge Close, Stony Stratford, Milton Keynes MK11 1BY]) : Open University Press, 1976. — 300p : 2 ill ; 21cm. — (Open University. Set books)
Bibl. — Index.
ISBN 0-335-01961-7 Pbk : £3.50
(B77-12868)

301.44 — Social inequality. Geographical aspects
Coates, Bryan Ellis. Geography and inequality / [by] B.E. Coates, R.J. Johnston and P.L. Knox. — Oxford [etc.] : Oxford University Press, 1977. — [8],292p : ill, maps ; 23cm.
Bibl.: p.258-279. — Index.
ISBN 0-19-874069-7 : £6.50 : CIP rev.
ISBN 0-19-874070-0 Pbk : £2.95
(B77-04574)

301.44'01 — Social inequality. Theories
Gane, Michael. Responses to inequality / prepared for the [Open University] Course Team by Michael Gane. A case study in social change : women in society / prepared for the [Open University] Course Team by Jean Gardiner. — Milton Keynes : Open University Press, 1976. — [2],78p ; 30cm. — (Social science, a third level course : patterns of inequality ; section 4 : reform or revolution? ; unit 31, unit 32) (D302 ; 31-32)
Bibl.
ISBN 0-335-07161-9 Pbk : £1.35
Also classified at 301.41'2'09034
(B77-03948)

301.44'044'0941 — Middle classes & working classes. Social change. *Great Britain, 1945-1975*
Zweig, Ferdynand. The new acquisitive society / by Ferdynand Zweig. — Chichester [etc.] : Rose [for] the Centre for Policy Studies, 1976. — 144p ; 22cm.
ISBN 0-85992-078-x : £4.00
ISBN 0-85992-083-6 Pbk : £2.00
(B77-11079)

301.44'07'1141 — Universities. *Great Britain. Open University. Curriculum subjects: Social inequality. Courses: 'Patterns of inequality'*
Blowers, Andrew. Patterns of inequality, course guide / [by] Andrew Blowers, Judith Riley and Paul Gunnion. — Milton Keynes : Open University Press, 1976. — 30p ; 30cm. — (Social science, a third level course : patterns of inequality) (D302 ; CG)
Bibl.: p.19-25.
Sd : Unpriced
(B77-03949)

301.44'0941 — Social class. *Great Britain*
The **fragmentary** class structure / [by] K. Roberts ... [et al.]. — London : Heinemann Educational, 1977. — viii,200p ; 23cm.
Bibl.: p.186-194. — Index.
ISBN 0-435-82765-0 : £5.50
ISBN 0-435-82766-9 Pbk : £2.75
(B77-20922)

Reid, Ivan. Social class differences in Britain : a sourcebook / [by] Ivan Reid. — London : Open Books, 1977. — xv,266p : ill, 2 maps ; 21cm.
Bibl.: p.246-258. — Index.
ISBN 0-7291-0165-7 : £5.75
ISBN 0-7291-0160-6 Pbk : £2.95
(B77-16199)

301.44'0941 — Social classes. Influence of social democratic parties. *Capitalist countries. Study regions: Great Britain*
Scase, Richard. Social democracy in capitalist society : working-class politics in Britain and Sweden / [by] Richard Scase. — London : Croom Helm [etc.], 1977. — 184p ; 23cm.
Bibl.: p.172-180. — Index.
ISBN 0-85664-372-6 : £7.95
Primary classification 301.44'09485
(B77-15100)

301.44'0941 — Social classes. Segregation. Great Britain. Urban regions. Compared with segregation of social classes in urban regions in United States
Morgan, Barrie S. Social status segregation in comparative perspective : the case of the United Kingdom and United States / [by] Barrie S. Morgan. — London ([Strand, WC2R 2LS]) : University of London, King's College, Department of Geography, 1976. — [1],28p : map ; 30cm. — (King's College, London. Geography Department. Occasional papers ; no.3 ISSN 0309-2178)
Bibl.: p.26-28.
Sp : £0.50
Also classified at 301.44'0973
(B77-07806)

301.44'0941 — Social inequality. *Capitalist countries. Marxist viewpoints. Study regions: Great Britain*
Westergaard, John. Class in a capitalist society : a study of contemporary Britain / [by] John Westergaard, Henrietta Resler. — Harmondsworth [etc.] : Penguin, 1976. — xv,432p : ill ; 19cm. — (Pelican books)
Originally published: London : Heinemann Educational, 1975. — Index.
ISBN 0-14-021974-9 Pbk : £1.50
(B77-03950)

301.44'0944'331 — Feudalism. Social aspects. *France. Troyes region, 1152-1284*
Evergates, Theodore. Feudal society in the bailliage of Troyes under the Counts of Champagne, 1152-1284 / [by] Theodore Evergates. — Baltimore ; London : Johns Hopkins University Press, [1967]. — xiv,273p : geneal tables, maps ; 24cm.
Published in the United States: 1975. — Bibl.: p.252-258. — Index.
ISBN 0-8018-1663-7 : £11.20
(B77-06488)

301.44'09485 — Social classes. Influence of social democratic parties. *Capitalist countries. Study regions: Sweden*
Scase, Richard. Social democracy in capitalist society : working-class politics in Britain and Sweden / [by] Richard Scase. — London : Croom Helm [etc.], 1977. — 184p ; 23cm.
Bibl.: p.172-180. — Index.
ISBN 0-85664-372-6 : £7.95
Also classified at 301.44'0941
(B77-15100)

301.44'0967 — Social inequality. *East Africa. Rural regions. Reports, surveys*
Kitching, G N. Economic and social inequality in rural East Africa : the present as a clue to the past / [by] G.N. Kitching. — Swansea (The Secretary, Editorial Board, Occasional Papers and Monographs Series, Singleton Park, Swansea SA2 8PP) : Centre for Development Studies, University of Swansea, 1977. — [1],ii,65,[1] leaves : 1 ill ; 30cm. — (University College of Swansea. Centre for Development Studies. Monographs ; no.1)
Sd : £1.29
(B77-23140)

301.44'0973 — Social classes. Segregation. United States. Urban regions. Compared with segregation of social classes in urban regions in Great Britain
Morgan, Barrie S. Social status segregation in comparative perspective : the case of the United Kingdom and United States / [by] Barrie S. Morgan. — London ([Strand, WC2R 2LS]) : University of London, King's College, Department of Geography, 1976. — [1],28p : map ; 30cm. — (King's College, London. Geography Department. Occasional papers ; no.3 ISSN 0309-2178)
Bibl.: p.26-28.
Sp : £0.50
Primary classification 301.44'0941
(B77-07806)

301.44'0973 — Social stratification. *United States*
Curtis, Richard Farnsworth. Inequality in American communities / [by] Richard F. Curtis, Elton F. Jackson. — New York [etc.] ; London : Academic Press, 1977. — xii,354p : ill ; 24cm. — (Quantitive studies in social relations)
Bibl.: p.343-350. — Index.
ISBN 0-12-200250-4 : £13.85
(B77-22367)

301.44'0985'3 — Social inequality. *Peru. Cuzco region*
Van den Berghe, Pierre Louis. Inequality in the Peruvian Andes : class and ethnicity in Cuzco / [by] Pierre L. van den Berghe, George P. Primov, with the assistance of ... [others]. — Columbia ; London : University of Missouri Press, 1977. — ix,324p,[8]p of plates : ill, map ; 24cm.
Bibl.: p.297-320. — Index.
ISBN 0-8262-0213-6 : £11.85
(B77-26815)

301.44'1 — Gentry. *England, to ca 1930*
Mingay, Gordon Edmund. The gentry : the rise and fall of a ruling class / [by] G.E. Mingay. — London [etc.] : Longman, 1976. — xii,216p : map ; 22cm. — (Themes in British social history)
Index.
ISBN 0-582-48402-2 : £6.50
ISBN 0-582-48403-0 Pbk : £3.50
(B77-00039)

301.44'1 — Gentry. *Yorkshire, 1370-1480*
Vale, Malcolm Graham Allan. Piety, charity and literacy among the Yorkshire gentry, 1370-1480 / by M.G.A. Vale. — [York] : [St Anthony's Press], 1976. — [5],32p : 1 ill ; 21cm. — (Borthwick papers ; no.50 ISSN 0524-0913)
ISBN 0-900701-43-9 Sd : £0.60
(B77-05219)

301.44'1 — Knights. *Juvenile literature*
Gascoyne, David, *b.1939.* Knights / by David Gascoyne ; illustrations by David C. Wray. — Oxford : Blackwell, 1977. — 59p,[4]leaves of plates : ill(some col) ; 21cm. — (Blackwell's learning library ; no.97)
Ill. on lining paper. — Index.
ISBN 0-631-13420-4 : £0.95
(B77-17933)

301.44'1 — Lower middle classes. Social conditions. *Great Britain, 1870-1914*
The **lower** middle class in Britain, 1870-1914 / edited by Geoffrey Crossick. — London : Croom Helm, 1977. — 213p ; 23cm.
Index.
ISBN 0-85664-348-3 : £7.95
(B77-05220)

301.44'1 — Middle classes. *Great Britain*
Hutber, Patrick. The decline and fall of the middle class, and how it can fight back / [by] Patrick Hutber. — [Revised ed.]. — Harmondsworth [etc.] : Penguin, 1977. — 172p : ill ; 18cm.
Previous ed.: London : Associated Business Programmes, 1976.
ISBN 0-14-004492-2 Pbk : £0.75
(B77-29955)

301.44'1 — Middle classes. Soviet Union, ca 1945-ca 1955. Expounded by fiction in Russian, 1917-
Dunham, Vera Sandomirsky. In Stalin's time : middleclass values in Soviet fiction / [by] Vera S. Dunham ; introduction by Jerry F. Hough. — Cambridge [etc.] : Cambridge University Press, 1976. — xv,283p ; 24cm.
Bibl.: p.275-278. — Index.
ISBN 0-521-20949-8 : £10.00
(B77-02782)

301.44'1 — Poor persons. Social conditions. *Senegal. Dakar*
Gerry, C. Urban poverty, underdevelopment and 'recuperative' production in Dakar, Senegal / [by] C. Gerry. — Swansea : The Secretary, Editorial Board, Occasional Papers and Monographs Series, Singleton Park, Swansea SA2 8PP : Centre for Development Studies, University College of Swansea, 1977. — [1],9, [1] leaves ; 30cm. — (University College of Swansea. Centre for Development Studies. Occasional papers ; no.1)
Sd : £0.50
(B77-23141)

301.44'1 — Poverty. *Great Britain. For Roman Catholic religious communities*
Winyard, Steve. No fault of their own : poverty in Britain / by Stephen Winyard. — [Liverpool] ([Christ's College, Woolton Rd, Liverpool L16 8ND]) : Liverpool Institute of Socio-Religious Studies [for] the Conference of Major Religious Superiors of England and Wales, 1977. — [3], 32p ; 21cm. — (Pastoral investigation of social trends ; working paper no.10)
Bibl.: p.29.
ISBN 0-905052-10-2 Sd : £0.60
(B77-26965)

301.44'1 — Poverty. *Scotland*
Norris, Geoff. Poverty : the facts in Scotland / [by] Geoff Norris. — London : Child Poverty Action Group, 1977. — [7],65p : 1 ill, map ; 21cm. — (Poverty pamphlet ; 30 ISSN 0306-1868)
Sd : £0.70
(B77-32428)

301.44'1 — Samurai. *Japan, to 1877*
Turnbull, S R. The Samurai : a military history / [by] S.R. Turnbull. — London : Osprey Publishing, 1977. — xvi,304p,[16]p of plates : ill(some col), geneal tables, maps, plans, ports(some col) ; 26cm.
Bibl.: p.296-298. — Index.
ISBN 0-85045-097-7 : £8.00
(B77-27692)

301.44'1 — Socially disadvantaged persons. Social conditions. *Great Britain*
Rutter, Michael. Cycles of disadvantage : a review of research / [by] Michael Rutter, Nicola Madge. — London : Heinemann, 1976. — vii,413p ; 23cm.
Bibl.: p.328-396. — Index.
ISBN 0-435-82851-7 : £6.50
ISBN 0-435-82852-5 Pbk : £2.50
(B77-07807)

301.44'1 — Socially disadvantaged persons. Social conditions. *Great Britain. Reports, surveys*
Berthoud, Richard. The disadvantages of inequality : a study of social deprivation / [by] Richard Berthoud. — London : Macdonald and Jane's, 1976. — 207p : ill ; 23cm. — (Political and Economic Planning. Reports)
Index.
ISBN 0-354-04047-2 : £4.95
(B77-01182)

301.44'2 — Aristocracy. *Ancient Greece, to ca B.C.320*
Arnheim, M T W. Aristocracy in Greek society / [by] M.T.W. Arnheim. — London : Thames and Hudson, 1977. — 221p : geneal table, map ; 23cm. — (Aspects of Greek and Roman life)
Bibl.: p.209-215. — Index.
ISBN 0-500-40031-8 : £7.00
(B77-26816)

301.44'2 — Fulani. Aristocracy. Effects of social change. *Northern Cameroun Republic, ca 1880-1975*
Azarya, Victor. Dominance and change in North Cameroon : the Fulbe aristocracy / [by] Victor Azarya. — Beverly Hills ; London : Sage Publications, [1977]. — 71p : maps ; 22cm. — (Sage research papers in the social sciences : studies in comparative modernization series ; vol.4, no.90-030)
Published in the United States: 1976. — Bibl.: p.68-70.
ISBN 0-8039-0547-5 Pbk : £1.75
(B77-12869)

301.44'2'094551 — Upper class households. Social structure. *Italy. Florence, 1400-1500*
Kent, Francis William. Household and lineage in Renaissance Florence : the family life of the Capponi, Ginori and Rucellai / [by] Francis William Kent. — Princeton ; Guildford : Princeton University Press, 1977. — xiii,325p : geneal tables ; 23cm.
Index.
ISBN 0-691-05237-9 : £13.40
(B77-16200)

301.44'42 — Coal mining communities. Cultural processes. *North-east England, ca 1800-ca 1915*
Colls, Robert. The collier's rant : song and culture in the industrial village / [by] Robert Colls. — London : Croom Helm [etc.], 1977. — [4],216p ; 23cm. — (Croom Helm social history series)
Index.
ISBN 0-85664-253-3 : £6.50
(B77-16740)

301.44'42'0922 — Working class communities. *Greater Manchester (Metropolitan County). Partington. Autobiographies*
Half-way home / by [and about] Ron and Hazel ; edited by Greg. — Manchester (Hilton House, Hilton St., Manchester M1 2FE) : Manchester Polytechnic, [1976]. — [1],84p ; 21cm. — (Lifetimes, a group autobiography ; 7)
ISBN 0-905252-06-3 Sd : Unpriced
(B77-01183)

301.44'42'0922 — Working classes. *England, ca 1820- ca 1930. Autobiographies. Extracts, selections. Collections*
Useful toil : autobiographies of working people from the 1820s to the 1920s / edited by John Burnett. — Harmondsworth [etc.] : Penguin, 1977. — 365p : ill ; 20cm. — (Pelican books)
'... assembles twenty-seven extracts from autobiographies and diaries of working people' - cover. — Originally published: London : Allen Lane, 1974.
ISBN 0-14-021994-3 Pbk : £1.00
(B77-25427)

301.44'42'094 — Working classes. *Europe, to 1971*
Abendroth, Wolfgang. A short history of the European working class / [by] Wolfgang Abendroth ; [translated from the German by Nicholas Jacobs and Brian Trench ; postscript translated by Joris de Bres]. — London : NLB, 1972 [i.e. 1976]. — 204p ; 21cm.
This translation originally published: 1972. — Translation of: 'Sozialgeschichte der europäischen Arbeiterbewegung'. 2 Aufl. Frankfurt : Suhrkamp, 1965. — Bibl.: p.198-204.
ISBN 0-902308-47-5 Pbk : £2.00
(B77-03951)

301.44'42'0941 — Working classes. *Great Britain. History. Periodicals*
Studies in labour history. — [Brighton] ([P.O. Box 450, Brighton BN1 8GR]) : [The editor]. No.1 : 1976 / edited by John L. Noyce. — [1976]. — [1],31,[4]p(2 fold) : facsims ; 30cm.
Bibl.
ISBN 0-903612-42-9 Sd : £1.20
(B77-00040)

301.44'42'0942 — Working classes. *England, 1890-1914*
Meacham, Standish. A life apart : the English working class, 1890-1914 / [by] Standish Meacham. — London : Thames and Hudson, 1977. — 272p,[16]p of plates : ill, port ; 25cm.
Bibl.: p.264-268. — Index.
ISBN 0-500-25055-3 : £6.95
(B77-20923)

301.44'42'0942 — Working classes. Social conditions. *England, 1866-1913. Readings from contemporary sources*
Into unknown England, 1866-1913 : selections from the social explorers / edited by Peter Keating. — [London] : Fontana, 1976. — 320p ; 18cm.
'A hardback edition of this book is published by Manchester University Press' - title-page verso. — Bibl.: p.318-320.
ISBN 0-00-633629-9 Pbk : £1.50
(B77-00619)

301.44'42'0942 — Working classes. Social control. *England, 1800-1900*
Social control in nineteenth century Britain / edited by A.P. Donajgrodzki. — London : Croom Helm [etc.], 1977. — 3-258p ; 23cm.
Bibl.: p.132-137. — Index.
ISBN 0-85664-589-3 : £8.50 : CIP rev.
(B77-15703)

301.44'42'09427393 — Working classes. Class consciousness. *England. Urban regions. Study regions: Greater Manchester (Metropolitan County). Oldham, ca 1780-1870*
Foster, John, *b.1940.* Class struggle and the Industrial Revolution : early industrial capitalism in three English towns / [by] John Foster ; with a foreword by E.J. Hobsbawm. — London : Methuen, 1977. — xiii,346p : ill, maps ; 22cm. — (University paperbacks ; 600)
Originally published: London : Weidenfeld and Nicolson, 1974. — Bibl.: p.337-338. — Index.
ISBN 0-416-84100-7 Pbk : £2.75
(B77-14573)

301.44'42'09438 — Working classes. Social conditions. Political aspects. *Poland. Russian texts*
Rabochie volneniia v pol'she prodolzhaiutsia : materialy o sobytiiakh 25-go iiunia 1976 g. komitet zashchity rabochikh / sostavitel' Vladimir Malyshev. — London : Overseas Publications Interchange, 1977. — 19cm.
Russian title transliterated. — Russian text. — 2nd title page has English title 'Workers' revolt in Poland continues'.
ISBN 0-903868-10-5 Pbk : £5.00
(B77-29956)

301.44'42'095487 — Working classes. *India. Sociological perspectives. Study examples: Factories. Personnel. Study regions: Bangalore*
Holmström, Mark. South Indian factory workers : their life and their world / [by] Mark Holmström. — Cambridge [etc.] : Cambridge University Press, 1976. — xi,158p ; 23cm. — (Cambridge South Asian studies ; 20)
Bibl.: p.148-150. — Index.
ISBN 0-521-21134-4 : £5.95
(B77-05885)

301.44'42'0973 — Working classes. Class consciousness. *United States. Case studies*
Sennett, Richard. The hidden injuries of class / by Richard Sennett and Jonathan Cobb. — Cambridge [etc.] : Cambridge University Press, 1977. — xi,275,[1]p ; 23cm.
Originally published: New York : Knopf, 1972. — Bibl.: p.272-275.
ISBN 0-521-21641-9 : £7.00
ISBN 0-521-29214-x Pbk : £3.00
(B77-11080)

301.44'43 — Peasants. *Spain. Toledo (Province), to 1971*
Weisser, Michael R. The peasants of the Montes : the roots of rural rebellion in Spain / [by] Michael R. Weisser. — Chicago ; London : University of Chicago Press, 1976 [i.e. 1977]. — xi,143p : ill, map ; 22cm.
Published in the United States: 1976. — Index.
ISBN 0-226-89158-5 : £8.65
(B77-12307)

301.44'43 — Peasants. Social change. *Developing countries*
Migdal, Joel Samuel. Peasants, politics, and revolution : pressures toward political and social change in the Third World / [by] Joel S. Migdal. — Princeton ; Guildford : Princeton University Press, 1977. — x,300,[1]p : 1 ill ; 22cm.
Originally published: Princeton ; London : Princeton University Press, 1974. — Bibl.: p.275-296. — Index.
ISBN 0-691-02177-5 Pbk : £3.80
(B77-23142)

301.44'43 — Peasants. Social conditions. *Soviet Union, ca 1920. Readings*
The **Russian** peasant 1920 and 1984 / edited by R.E.F. Smith. — London [etc.] : Cass, 1977. — vii,120p ; 24cm. — (Library of peasant studies ; no.4)
Bibl.: p.119-120.
ISBN 0-7146-3078-0 : £8.50
(B77-11081)

301.44'43'09426 — Agricultural industries. Personnel. Social conditions. *East Anglia, 1850-1976*
Newby, Howard. The deferential worker : a study of farm workers in East Anglia / [by] Howard Newby. — London : Allen Lane, 1977. — 462p ; 23cm.
ISBN 0-7139-0892-0 : £9.00
(B77-28405)

301.44'46 — Scientists: Nobel prizewinners. Social status. *United States*
Zuckerman, Harriet. Scientific elite : Nobel laureates in the United States / [by] Harriet Zuckerman. — New York : Free Press ; London : Collier Macmillan, 1977. — xv,335p : ill ; 24cm.
Bibl.: p.304-325. — Index.
ISBN 0-02-935760-8 : £11.25
(B77-22368)

301.44'5 — Developing countries. Society. Role of intellectuals
Alatas, Syed Hussein. Intellectuals in developing societies / [by] Syed Hussein Alatas. — London : Cass, 1977. — xvi,130p ; 23cm.
Bibl.: p.119-125. — Index.
ISBN 0-7146-3004-7 : £8.50
(B77-11585)

301.44'5 — Intellectuals. *Sociological perspectives. Conference proceedings*
World Congress of Sociology, *8th, Toronto, 1974.* The intelligentsia and the intellectuals : theory, method and case study / edited by Aleksander Gella. — London [etc.] : Sage Publications [for] the International Sociological Association, [1977]. — 235p ; 22cm. — (Sage studies in international sociology ; 5)
'... a Round Table entitled "Toward the Sociology of the Intelligentsia" for the VIIIth World Congress of Sociology, Toronto, August 1974' - Preface. — Published in the United States: 1976. — Bibl.
ISBN 0-8039-9958-5 : £8.05
ISBN 0-8039-9972-0 Pbk : £3.50
(B77-10183)

301.44'92'0944 — Elites. *France, 1500-1600*
Huppert, George. Les bourgeois gentilshommes : an essay on the definition of elites in Renaissance France / [by] George Huppert. — Chicago ; London : University of Chicago Press, 1977. — xii,237p ; 24cm.
Index.
ISBN 0-226-36099-7 : £12.95
(B77-23143)

301.44'92'09489 — Political elites. *Denmark, 1848-1975. Sociological perspectives*
Pedersen, Mogens N. Political development and elite transformation in Denmark / [by] Mogens N. Pedersen. — London [etc.] : Sage Publications, 1976. — 61,[1]p : ill ; 22cm. — (Sage professional papers in contemporary political sociology ; vol.2, no.06-018 ISSN 0305-3482)
Bibl.: p.60-61.
ISBN 0-8039-9861-9 Pbk : £1.75
(B77-08786)

301.44'93'09171241 — Slavery. *Commonwealth countries, to 1838. Readings from contemporary sources*
Slavery, abolition and emancipation : black slaves and the British Empire : a thematic documentary / [compiled] by Michael Craton, James Walvin and David Wright. — London [etc.] : Longman, 1976. — xiv,347p : ill, map ; 23cm.
Bibl.
ISBN 0-582-48092-2 : £6.80
ISBN 0-582-48093-0 Pbk : £3.75
(B77-02054)

301.44'93'0967 — Slavery. *East Africa, 1800-1890*
Cooper, Frederick. Plantation slavery on the east coast of Africa / [by] Frederick Cooper. — New Haven ; London : Yale University Press, 1977. — xviii,314p : 4 maps ; 25cm. — (Yale historical publications : miscellany ; 113)
Bibl.: p.283-304. — Index.
ISBN 0-300-02041-4 : £9.00
(B77-24712)

301.44'93'097 — Slavery. *America, to 1972*
Hoetink, Hermannus. Slavery and race relations in the Americas : comparative notes on their nature and nexus / [by] H. Hoetink. — New York [etc.] ; London : Harper and Row, 1973. — viii,232p ; 21cm. — (Crosscurrents in Latin America) (Harper torchbooks)
Bibl.: p.211-223. — Index.
ISBN 0-06-131710-1 Pbk : Unpriced
Primary classification 301.45'1'097
(B77-20038)

301.44'93'0973 — Slavery. *United States, to 1863. Teaching kits*
Slavery in the United States / compiled by William C. Hine. — New York : Grossman ; London : Jackdaw [etc.], 1975. — Portfolio : ill, facsims ; 23x35cm. — ([American] jackdaw ; no. A30)
Introductory leaflet ([4]p.), 20 items. — Bibl.
ISBN 0-305-62117-3 : £1.95
(B77-01184)

301.44'94 — Child tramps. Social aspects. *United States, 1929-1933. Early works*
Minehan, Thomas. Boy and girl tramps of America / by Thomas Minehan ; illustrated with photographs by the author. — [1st ed. reprinted] ; introduction to the Americana library edition by Donald W. Whisenhunt. — Seattle ; London : University of Washington Press, 1976. — xxviii,267p : ill ; 23cm. — (Americana library)
Facsimile reprint of: 1st ed. New York : Farrar and Rinehart, 1934.
ISBN 0-295-95450-7 : £11.25
(B77-27693)

301.44'94'0904 — Hell's Angels, to 1976. *Readings*
Barbarians on wheels / edited by Sam Wilde. — [London] : New English Library, [1977]. — 160p : ill(chiefly col), ports(1 col) ; 35cm.
ISBN 0-450-03222-1 : £5.95
(B77-29957)

301.44'94'0924 — Hippy communities. *United States. Personal observations*
Vonnegut, Mark. The Eden Express / [by] Mark Vonnegut. — Toronto [etc.] ; London : Bantam, 1976. — [11],274,[1]p ; 18cm.
Originally published: New York : Praeger, 1975 ; London : Cape, 1976.
ISBN 0-552-10419-1 Pbk : £0.85
Primary classification 362.2
(B77-17385)

301.45 — Cultural pluralism. *United States. Conference proceedings*
Pluralism in a Democratic Society *(Conference), New York, 1975.* Pluralism in a democratic society / edited by Melvin M. Tumin, Walter Plotch. — New York [etc.] ; London : Praeger [for] the Anti-Defamation League of B'nai B'rith, 1977. — xx,250p : ill ; 25cm. — (Praeger special studies in US economic, social and political issues)
'A conference, which was called "Pluralism in a Democratic Society : An Interdisciplinary Inquiry into Its Meaning and Educational Uses", was held in April 1975 in New York ... convened by the Anti-Defamation League of B'nai B'rith ...' - Foreword. — Bibl.
ISBN 0-275-23310-3 : £11.10
(B77-15101)

301.45 — Nomadic tribes. Social conditions. *West Africa. Sahel, 1973-1976. Reports, surveys*
Marnham, Patrick. Nomads of the Sahel / by Patrick Marnham. — London (36 Craven St., WC2N 5NG) : Minority Rights Group, 1977. — [1],19,[1]p : 1 ill, map ; 30cm. — (Minority Rights Group. Reports ; no.33 ISSN 0305-6252)

Bibl.: p.19. — List of films: p.19.
Sd : £0.75
(B77-28406)

301.45'07 — Ethnic minorities. Information sources. *United States. Lists*
Ethnic American minorities : a guide to media and materials / edited and compiled by Harry A. Johnson. — New York ; London : Bowker, 1976. — xi,304p ; 24cm.
Index.
ISBN 0-8352-0766-8 : Unpriced
(B77-08787)

301.45'1 — Ethnic groups
Huxley, Francis. Peoples of the world in colour / [by] Francis Huxley ; illustrated by Mary Sims and Mary Camidge. — London : Blandford Press, 1975. — 182p : ill(chiefly col), maps(chiefly col) ; 19cm. — ([Blandford colour series])
Originally published: 1964. — Index.
ISBN 0-7137-0726-7 : £1.50
(B77-10184)

301.45'1 — Ethnic groups. *Conference proceedings*
Ethnicity : theory and experience / edited by Nathan Glazer and Daniel P. Moynihan, with the assistance of Corrine Saposs Schelling. — Cambridge, Mass. ; London : Harvard University Press, 1975. — xi,531p ; 22cm.
'This book is the product of a conference, convened with the support of the Ford Foundation at the American Academy of Arts and Sciences in Brookline, Massachusetts, in October 1972' - Acknowledgements. — Bibl. — Index.
ISBN 0-674-26855-5 : £12.40
ISBN 0-674-26856-3 Pbk : £4.50
(B77-04575)

301.45'1 — Interethnic relations
Francis, Emerich K. Interethnic relations : an essay in sociological theory / [by] E.K. Francis. — New York ; Oxford [etc.] : Elsevier, 1976. — xxi,432p ; 27cm.
Bibl. — Index.
ISBN 0-444-99011-9 : £17.44
(B77-00041)

301.45'1 — Race relations
Thomson, Grant. Race relations / [by] Grant Thomson. — Glasgow [etc.] : Blackie, 1977. — [5],66p : ill, maps ; 21cm. — (Crossroads)
Bibl.: p.66.
ISBN 0-216-90367-x Pbk : £1.10
(B77-30994)

301.45'1042 — Race relations. Influence of mass media. *Great Britain*
White media and black Britain : a critical look at the role of the media in race relations today / edited by Charles Husband. — London : Arrow Books, 1975. — 222p ; 18cm.
Bibl.
ISBN 0-09-912220-0 Pbk : £0.95
(B77-25404)

301.45'1042'05 — Coloured persons. Racial discrimination by society. *Periodicals. For coloured persons*
Samaj. — [London] ([98 Gifford St., N.1]) : ['Samaj'].
No.1- ; Sept. 1976-. — [1976]-. — ill, facsims, ports ; 41cm.
Published at irregular intervals. — [10]p. in 1st issue.
Sd : £0.10
ISSN 0309-0795
(B77-05221)

301.45'1042'0941 — Coloured persons. Social conditions. *Great Britain. Urban regions. Reports, surveys*
Community Relations Commission. Urban deprivation, racial inequality and social policy : a report / by the Community Relations Commission. — London : H.M.S.O., 1977. — xii,100p ; 21cm.
At head of title: Home Office.
ISBN 0-11-340756-4 Pbk : £1.75
(B77-12870)

301.45'1042'0941 — Racial discrimination. *Great Britain. Reports, surveys*
Smith, David John, *b.1941.* Racial disadvantage in Britain : the PEP report / [by] David J. Smith. — Harmondsworth [etc.] : Penguin, 1977. — 349p : facsims ; 18cm. — (A pelican original)
Index.
ISBN 0-14-021979-x Pbk : £1.25
(B77-26131)

301.45'1042'0941 — Racial discrimination. *Great Britain. Secondary school texts*
Jay, Eric. Racial discrimination / [text by Eric Jay]. — London : S.C.M. Press [for] the Christian Education Movement, 1971. — 32p : ill, ports ; 23cm. — (Probe ; 3 ISSN 0305-3776)
Originally published: 1969. — Bibl.: p.32.
Sd : £0.15
ISBN 0-334-01374-7
(B77-11082)

301.45'1042'0942 — Ethnic minorities. Social conditions. Policies of local authorities. *England. For councillors*
Community Relations Commission. The multi-racial community : a guide for local councillors / [Community Relations Commission] ; [written by Vivien Stern and Cathy Carmichael]. — London : The Commission, 1977. — 34p : 1 ill ; 21cm.
Bibl.: p.32-34.
Sd : Unpriced
(B77-32429)

301.45'1042'0968 — Apartheid. Social aspects
Separation in South Africa / edited by David M. Smith. — London ([Mile End Rd, E1 4NS]) : Department of Geography, Queen Mary College, University of London.
In 2 vols.
2 : Homelands and cities. — 1976. — [7],v,97[i.e.107]p : ill, maps ; 30cm. — (Queen Mary College. Department of Geography. Occasional papers ; no.7 ISSN 0306-2740)
Bibl.
ISBN 0-904791-06-8 Pbk : £1.00
(B77-00042)

301.45'1042'0973 — Ethnic groups. Social behaviour. Influence of their attitudes to Old World. *United States, 1860-1970*
Jones, Maldwyn Allen. The Old World ties of American ethnic groups / by Maldwyn A. Jones. — London : H.K. Lewis, 1976. — 31p ; 26cm. — (University College, London. Inaugural lectures)
'... delivered at University College London 17 January 1974'.
ISBN 0-7186-0430-x Sd : £0.65
(B77-04576)

301.45'1042'0973 — Ethnic groups. Social conditions. Effects of religious denomination. *United States*
Greeley, Andrew Moran. Ethnicity, denomination, and inequality / [by] Andrew M. Greeley. — Beverly Hills ; London : Sage Publications, 1976. — 85,[1]p : ill ; 22cm. — (Sage research papers in the social sciences : studies in religion and ethnicity ; vol.4, no.90-029)
Bibl.: p.78-79.
ISBN 0-8039-0641-2 Pbk : £1.75
(B77-14574)

301.45'1042'0973 — Racial integration. Attitudes of white persons. *United States*
Caditz, Judith. White liberals in transition : current dilemmas of ethnic integration / [by] Judith Caditz. — New York : Spectrum Publications ; New York [etc.] ; London : Distributed by Wiley, 1976. — [9],187p ; 24cm.
Bibl.: p.173-180. — Index.
ISBN 0-470-15182-x : £9.35
(B77-14065)

301.45'1'06141 — Race relations. Organisations. *Great Britain. Race Relations Board. Reports, surveys. Serials*
Race Relations Board. Report of the Race Relations Board ... — London : H.M.S.O. 1975-1976 : January 1975-June 1976. — [1976]. — iii,72p ; 25cm. — ([1976-77 H.C.] 3)
Bibl.: p.72.
ISBN 0-10-200377-7 Sd : £1.40
(B77-07075)

301.45'1'094 — Linguistic minorities. Social conditions. *Western Europe*
Stephens, Meic. Linguistic minorities in Western Europe / [by] Meic Stephens. — Llandysul : Gomer Press, 1976. — iii-xxxv,796p : maps ; 22cm.
Bibl.: p.739-767. — Index.
ISBN 0-85088-362-8 : £9.50
(B77-08238)

301.45'1'0941 — Ethnic minorities. Social conditions. *Great Britain*
Between two cultures : migrants and minorities in Britain / edited by James L. Watson. — Oxford : Blackwell, 1977. — viii,338p ; 22cm.
Bibl. — Index.
ISBN 0-631-18300-0 : Unpriced : CIP rev.
ISBN 0-631-18710-3 Pbk : £3.95
(B77-24713)

301.45'1'0941 — Immigrant children, to 5 years. *Great Britain. Reports, surveys*
Fisher, Thelma. All our children / research by Thelma and Frank Fisher ; edited by Rachel Jenkins. — London (137 Clapham Rd, SW9 0PT) : Save the Children Fund, [1976]. — 24p : ill, map ; 15x21cm.
Bibl.: p.20-23.
ISBN 0-9500262-2-0 Sd : Unpriced
(B77-02055)

301.45'1'0941 — Race relations. *Great Britain*
Bidwell, Sydney. Red, white & black : race relations in Britain / [by] Sidney [i.e. Sydney] Bidwell ; foreword by Michael Foot. — London : Gordon and Cremonesi, 1976. — vii, 213p,[8]p of plates : ill, facsim, port ; 22cm.
Bibl.: p.205. — Index.
ISBN 0-86033-022-2 : £5.90
(B77-04577)

301.45'1'0941 — Race relations. *Great Britain. Labour Party viewpoints*
Labour Party. Immigration & racialism / [Labour Party] ; [researched by Liz Atkins]. — London : Labour Party, 1977. — Folder([4]p : ill ; 30cm. — (Labour Party. Political education discussion papers ; no.4)
Unpriced
Primary classification 301.32'4'0941
(B77-16193)

301.45'1'097 — Race relations. *America, to 1972*
Hoetink, Hermannus. Slavery and race relations in the Americas : comparative notes on their nature and nexus / [by] H. Hoetink. — New York [etc.] ; London : Harper and Row, 1973. — viii,232p ; 21cm. — (Crosscurrents in Latin America) (Harper torchbooks)
Bibl.: p.211-223. — Index.
ISBN 0-06-131710-1 Pbk : Unpriced
Also classified at 301.44'93'097
(B77-20038)

301.45'1'097671 — European immigrants. Social conditions. *Missouri. Ozark Highlands*
Gerlach, Russel L. Immigrants in the Ozarks : a study in ethnic geography / [by] Russel L. Gerlach. — Columbia [Miss.] ; London : University of Missouri Press ; [London] : [Distributed by American University Publishers], [1977]. — xiii,206p : ill, maps ; 24cm. — (University of Missouri. Studies ; 64)
Published in the United States: 1976. — Bibl.: p.184-196. — Index.
ISBN 0-8262-0201-2 : £12.00
(B77-11586)

301.45'1'0977434 — Race relations. *Michigan. Detroit, 1915-1926*
Levine, David Allan. Internal combustion : the races in Detroit, 1915-1926 / [by] David Allan Levine. — Westport, Conn. ; London : Greenwood Press, 1976 [i.e. 1977]. — xi,3-221, [1]p : map ; 22cm. — (Contributions in Afro-American and African studies ; no.24)
Published in the United States: 1976. — Index.
ISBN 0-8371-8588-2 : Unpriced
(B77-09522)

301.45'12'8 — South Africa. Society. Role of English-speaking South Africans. *Conference proceedings*
English-Speaking South Africa : an Assessment *(Conference), Grahamstown, 1974.* English-speaking South Africa today : proceedings of the National Conference July 1974 / edited by André de Villiers. — Cape Town ; Oxford [etc.] : Oxford University Press for 1820 Settlers National Monument Foundation, 1976 [i.e. 1977]. — vi,387p : ill ; 22cm.
' ... papers delivered at the conference, "English-speaking South Africa : an Assessment", held in Grahamstown from 15th to 19th July, 1974 ... ' - Introduction. — Published in South Africa: 1976. — Bibl.
ISBN 0-19-570072-4 : £15.00
(B77-12308)

301.45'15'1074797 — Italian immigrant families. Social conditions. *New York (State). Buffalo, 1880-1930*
Yans-McLaughlin, Virginia. Family and community : Italian immigrants in Buffalo, 1880-1930 / [by] Virginia Yans-McLaughlin. — Ithaca ; London : Cornell University Press, 1977. — 286p : map, plan ; 23cm.
Bibl.: p.267-279. — Index.
ISBN 0-8014-1036-3 : £9.35
(B77-30995)

301.45'15'9041 — Romanians. Organisations. *Great Britain. Asociaţiei Culturale a Românilor din Anglia. Lectures, speeches. Romanian texts*
Asociaţiei Culturale a Românilor din Anglia. ACARDA şi organizarea exilului : extrase dın cuvântari, comentarii şi intervenţii scrise. — London (54 Regent St., W.1) : Free Romanian Press, 1976. — [1],12 leaves ; 30cm.
ISBN 0-905460-01-4 Sd : Unpriced
(B77-12871)

301.45'19'14041 — South Asians. Cultural identity. *Great Britain. Conference proceedings*
Cultural Conflict and the Asian Family *(Conference), University of Leicester, 1975.* Cultural conflict & the Asian family : report of a conference organized by the National Association of Indian Youth / edited by Pramila Parekh and Bhikhu Parekh. — [Southall] ([46 High St., Southall, Middx]) : Scope Communication, 1976. — [1],13,[1]p ; 30cm.
'The National Association of Indian Youth organized its third annual conference on the general theme of "Cultural Conflict and the Asian Family" ... held in Beaumont Hall of the University of Leicester from 26th to 28th September 1975 ...' - Introduction.
Sd : £0.15
(B77-17311)

301.45'19'1411 — Divorced Hindu women & separated Hindu women. Social conditions. *India (Republic). Reports, surveys*
Mehta, Rama. Divorced Hindu woman / [by] Rama Mehta. — Delhi [etc.] : Vikas ; Hemel Hempstead (66 Wood Lane End, Hemel Hempstead, Herts.) : Distributed by International Book Distributors Ltd, 1975. — vii,173p ; 23cm.
Index.
ISBN 0-7069-0385-4 : Unpriced
(B77-10185)

301.45'19'14110682 — Indians. Racial discrimination by society. *South Africa. Transvaal, 1885-1906*
Pillay, Bala. British Indians in the Transvaal : trade, politics and imperial relations, 1885-1906 / [by] Bala Pillay. — London : Longman, 1976. — xvii,259p,[4]p of plates : ill, ports ; 23cm.
Bibl.: p.243-251. — Index.
ISBN 0-582-64201-9 : £3.75
(B77-11587)

301.45'19'141106982 — Indians. Social conditions. *Mauritius, to 1974*
Hazareesingh, Kissoonsingh. History of Indians in Mauritius / [by] K. Hazareesingh. — London [etc.] : Macmillan, 1976. — x,150p : ill, ports ; 22cm.
Originally published: 1975. — Bibl.: p.138-140. — Index.
ISBN 0-333-21979-1 Pbk : £1.95
(B77-23144)

301.45'19'1497041 — Gypsies. Social aspects. *Great Britain. Secondary school texts*
Love, John R. Gypsies / by John R. Love and Carey Edwards. — London : Harrap, 1977. — 24p : ill, facsims, 2 maps ; 28cm. — (Issues)
Bibl.: p.3.
ISBN 0-245-52961-6 Pbk : £0.70
(B77-33626)

301.45'19'1497041 — Gypsies. Social conditions. *Great Britain*
Sandford, Jeremy. Gypsies / [by] Jeremy Sandford. — London : Abacus, 1975. — 252p, [8]p of plates : ill, ports ; 20cm.
Originally published: London : Secker and Warburg, 1973. — Bibl.: p.247-248.
ISBN 0-349-13120-1 Pbk : £1.10
(B77-08788)

301.45'19'162 — Anglo-Irish communities. *Ireland, to 1921*
Beckett, James Camlin. The Anglo-Irish tradition / [by] J.C. Beckett. — London : Faber, 1976. — 159p ; 23cm.
Index.
ISBN 0-571-10908-x : £5.50
(B77-02056)

301.45'19'185041 — Poles. Organisations. *Great Britain. Polski Ośrodek Spoleczno-Kulturalny. Periodicals. Polish texts*
Polski Ośrodek Spoleczno-Kulturalny. Biuletyn informacyjny / Polski Ośrodek Spoleczno-Kulturalny. — London (238 King St., W.6) : Polish Social and Cultural Association.
R.1, nr 1- ; Stycz. 1977-. — [1977]-. — 25cm.
Six issues a year. — 8p. in 1st issue.
Sd : £0.10
ISSN 0309-5967
(B77-18568)

301.45'19'185041 — Poles. Organisations. *Great Britain. Zjednoczenie Polskie w Wielkiej Brytanii. Periodicals*
Zjednoczenie Polskie w Wielkiej Brytanii. Biuletyn Miedzypolonijny / [Zjednoczenie Polskie w Wielkiej Brytanii]. — London (9 Charleville Rd, W14 9JL) : [Z.P.W.B.].
Nr 1, 1- ; Grudz. 1976-. — 1976-. — 33cm.
Published at irregular intervals. — 28p. in 1st issue. — Bibl.: p.26-27.
Sd : Private circulation
ISSN 0309-6785
(B77-12872)

301.45'19'1992056 — Armenians. Social conditions. *Middle East. Reports, surveys*
Lang, David Marshall. The Armenians / by David Marshall Lang and Christopher Walker. — London (36 Craven St., WC2N 5NG) : Minority Rights Group, [1976]. — [1],24,[1]p : 1 ill, 2 maps ; 30cm. — (Minority Rights Group. Reports ; no.32 ISSN 0305-6252)
Bibl.: p.23-24. — List of films: p.24.
ISBN 0-903114-34-8 Sd : £0.45
(B77-06489)

301.45'19'19920566 — Ottoman Empire. Society. Role of Armenians, 1860-1908. *Study regions: Eastern Turkey*
Krikorian, Mesrob K. Armenians in the service of the Ottoman Empire, 1860-1908 / [by] Mesrob K. Krikorian. — London : Routledge and Kegan Paul, 1977 [i.e. 1978]. — xii,149p : map ; 24cm.
'Routledge direct editions'. — Bibl.: p.124-133. — Index.
ISBN 0-7100-8564-8 Pbk : £3.00 : CIP rev.
Also classified at 301.45'19'199205691
(B77-19228)

301.45'19'199205691 — Ottoman Empire. Society. Role of Armenians, 1860-1908. *Study regions: Syria*
Krikorian, Mesrob K. Armenians in the service of the Ottoman Empire, 1860-1908 / [by] Mesrob K. Krikorian. — London : Routledge and Kegan Paul, 1977 [i.e. 1978]. — xii,149p : map ; 24cm.
'Routledge direct editions'. — Bibl.: p.124-133. — Index.
ISBN 0-7100-8564-8 Pbk : £3.00 : CIP rev.
Primary classification 301.45'19'19920566
(B77-19228)

301.45'19'24041 — Jews. Organisations. *Great Britain. World Jewish Congress. British Section, to 1976*
Fraenkel, Josef. The history of the British Section of the World Jewish Congress / by Josef Fraenkel. — London ([55 New Cavendish St., W.1]) : World Jewish Congress European Branch, [1977]. — 11p : ports ; 22cm.
'Published on the occasion of the 40th Anniversary of the World Jewish Congress 1936-1976'.
Sd : £0.25
(B77-24011)

301.45'19'240438 — Jews. Social conditions. *Poland, 1918-1939*
Heller, Celia Stopnicka. On the edge of destruction : Jews of Poland between the two world wars / [by] Celia S. Heller. — New York ; Guildford : Columbia University Press, 1977. — xiii,369p : ill, map, ports ; 24cm.
Index.
ISBN 0-231-03819-4 : £8.80
(B77-15102)

301.45'19'2404675 — Xuetas. *Spain. Majorca, to 1975. Anthropological perspectives*
Moore, Kenneth, *b.1930.* Those of the street : the Catholic-Jews of Mallorca : a study in urban cultural change / [by] Kenneth Moore. — Notre Dame [Ind.] ; London : University of Notre Dame Press, 1976. — viii,218p,[2]p of plates : ill, map(on lining papers) ; 24cm.
Bibl.: p.211-214. — Index.
ISBN 0-268-01830-8 : £7.50
(B77-20924)

301.45'19'24047 — Jews. Social conditions. *Soviet Union, to 1975*
Baron, Salo Wittmayer. The Russian Jew under tsars and Soviets / [by] Salo W. Baron. — 2nd ed. revised and enlarged. — New York : Macmillan ; London : Collier Macmillan, 1976. — xvii,468p ; 24cm.
Previous ed.: 1964. — Index.
ISBN 0-02-507300-1 : £11.25
(B77-11588)

301.45'19'24073 — Jews. Organisations. *United States. Jewish Defense League, to 1976*
Dolgin, Janet L. Jewish identity and the JDL / by Janet L. Dolgin. — Princeton ; Guildford : Princeton University Press, 1977. — xi,189,[1] p ; 23cm.
Bibl.: p.179-184. — Index.
ISBN 0-691-09368-7 : £10.10
(B77-14066)

301.45'19'2407471 — Jewish immigrants. Social aspects. *New York (City), 1870-1914*
Rischin, Moses. The promised city : New York's Jews 1870-1914 / by Moses Rischin. — Cambridge, Mass. ; London : Harvard University Press, 1977. — xx,342p,[12]p of plates : ill, ports ; 22cm.
Originally published: Cambridge, Mass. : Harvard University Press ; London : Oxford University Press, 1962. — Bibl.: p.275-282. — Index.
ISBN 0-674-71502-0 : Unpriced
ISBN 0-674-71501-2 Pbk : £3.50
(B77-24714)

301.45'19'2705694 — Arabs. Racial discrimination by society. *Israel, 1948-1973*
Jiryis, Sabri. The Arabs in Israel / [by] Sabri Jiryis ; translated from the Arabic by Inea Bushnaq. — [2nd ed.]. — New York ; London : Monthly Review Press, 1976. — xix, 314p ; 21cm.
ISBN 0-85345-377-2 : £6.75
(B77-03952)

301.45'19'451104984 — Hungarians. Social aspects. *Romania. Transylvania*
Michael-Titus, Constantin. In search of 'cultural genocide' / [by] C. Michael-Titus. — [Upminster] ([44 Howard Rd, Upminster, Essex RM14 2UF]) : Panopticum Press, 1976. — 36p : ill, facsims, port ; 21cm.
ISBN 0-9504138-3-6 Sd : Free
(B77-07808)

301.45'19'4805483 — Nayars. Social conditions. *India. Kerala*
Fuller, C J. The Nayars today / [by] C.J. Fuller. — Cambridge [etc.] : Cambridge University Press, 1976. — xii,173p : ill, map ; 23cm. — (Changing cultures)
Bibl.: p.163-171. — Index.
ISBN 0-521-21301-0 : £4.95
ISBN 0-521-29091-0 Pbk : £2.40
(B77-05222)

301.45'19'56079461 — Japanese. Cultural processes. *United States. Study regions: California. San Francisco. Reports, surveys*
Kiefer, Christie W. Changing cultures, changing lives / [by] Christie W. Kiefer. — San Francisco [etc.] ; London : Jossey-Bass, 1974. — xxvii,260p ; 24cm. — (The Jossey-Bass behavioral science series)
Bibl.: p.239-250. — Index.
ISBN 0-87589-232-9 : Unpriced
(B77-18569)

301.45'19'6008 — Negroes. Race relations. *Essays*
Garvey, Marcus. The philosophy and opinions of Marcus Garvey / edited by Amy Jacques Garvey. — London : Cass.
Vol.3 : More philosophy and opinions of Marcus Garvey / selected and edited from previously unpublished material by E.U. Essien-Udom and Amy Jacques Garvey. — 1977. — xiii,248p,plate : port ; 23cm. — (Cass library of African studies : Africana modern library ; no.20)
ISBN 0-7146-1751-2 : £9.50
ISBN 0-7146-4027-1 Pbk : £3.95
(B77-28407)

301.45'19'6024 — Universal Negro Improvement Association of the World. Garvey, Marcus
Martin, Tony, *b.1942.* Race first : the ideological and organizational struggles of Marcus Garvey and the Universal Negro Improvement Association / [by] Tony Martin. — Westport, Conn. ; London : Greenwood Press, 1976. — x, 421,[1]p : ill, port ; 22cm. — (Contributions in Afro-American and African studies ; no.19)
Bibl.: p.375-395. — Index.
ISBN 0-8371-8280-8 : Unpriced
(B77-02783)

301.45'19'6041 — Negroes. Social conditions. *Great Britain, 1555-1833*
Shyllon, Folarin Olawale. Black people in Britain, 1555-1833 / [by] Folarin Shyllon. — London [etc.] : Oxford University Press for the Institute of Race Relations, 1977. — xi,290p,[8] leaves of plates : ill, facsim, ports ; 22cm.
Index.
ISBN 0-19-218413-x : £8.50 : CIP rev.
(B77-10186)

301.45'19'6041 — Negroes. Social conditions. *Great Britain. Conference proceedings*
Black People in Britain, the Way Forward *(Conference), London, 1975.* Black People in Britain, the Way Forward : a report of a conference held [in Bloomsbury Hotel, London] 17-19 January 1975 / written up and edited by Rajeev Dhavan on behalf of the Post Conference Constituent Committee. — London (98 Portland Place, W1N 4ET) : [The Committee], 1976. — 227p ; 21cm.
ISBN 0-9505659-0-3 Pbk : £1.00
(B77-12873)

301.45'19'6073 — Negro communities. *United States. Sociological perspectives*
Staples, Robert. Introduction to black sociology / [by] Robert Staples. — New York ; London [etc.] : McGraw-Hill, 1976. — xi, 338p ; 21cm.
Bibl. — Index.
ISBN 0-07-060840-7 Pbk : £6.25
(B77-06490)

301.45'19'6073 — Negroes. Attitudes. *United States. Northern states. Urban regions, 1890-1930*
Nielson, David Gordon. Black ethos : northern urban negro life and thought, 1890-1930 / [by] David Gordon Nielson. — Westport, Conn. ; London : Greenwood Press, 1977. — xxi,248,[1] p ; 22cm. — (Contributions in Afro-American and African studies ; no.29)
Bibl.: p.221-238. — Index.
ISBN 0-8371-9402-4 : £11.75
(B77-33627)

301.45'19'6073 — Negroes. Race awareness. Influence of African negro culture. *United States, 1816-1970*
Weisbord, Robert G. Ebony kinship : Africa, Africans and the Afro-American / [by] Robert G. Weisbord ; foreword by Floyd B. McKissick. — Westport, Conn. ; London : Greenwood Press, 1974. — xi,256p ; 21cm. — (Contributions in Afro-American and African studies ; no.14)
Originally published: 1973. — Bibl.: p.227-240. — Index.
ISBN 0-8371-7340-x Pbk : £3.25
(B77-20039)

301.45'19'6073 — Negroes. Race relations. *United States, to 1976*
Franklin, John Hope. Racial equality in America / [by] John Hope Franklin. — Chicago ; London : University of Chicago Press, 1976. — xi,113p ; 22cm. — (Jefferson lecture in the humanities ; 1976)
ISBN 0-226-26073-9 : £6.00
(B77-07076)

301.45'19'6073 — Negroes. Racial discrimination by society. United States. Related to birth control
Weisbord, Robert G. Genocide? : birth control and the black American / [by] Robert G. Weisbord. — Westport, Conn. ; London : Greenwood Press [etc.], 1975. — ix,219p ; 22cm.
Bibl.: p.189-207. — Index.
ISBN 0-8371-8084-8 : £6.75
Primary classification 301.32'1
(B77-17306)

301.45'19'6073 — Negroes. Social conditions. Effects of 'The Messenger'. *United States, 1917-1928*
Kornweibel, Theodore. No crystal stair : black life and the 'Messenger', 1917-1928 / [by] Theodore Kornweibel, Jr. — Westport, Conn. ; London : Greenwood Press, 1975. — xvi, 3-306p ; 22cm. — (Contributions in Afro-American and African studies ; no.20)
Bibl.: p.277-289. — Index.
ISBN 0-8371-8284-0 : £10.95
(B77-02784)

301.45'19'6073075 — Negroes. Social conditions. *United States. Southern states, 1865-1975*
Taylor, Arnold H. Travail and triumph : black life and culture in the South since the Civil War / [by] Arnold H. Taylor. — Westport, Conn. ; London : Greenwood Press, 1976. — viii,326p,[18]p of plates : ill, ports ; 25cm. — (Contributions in Afro-American and African studies ; no.26)
Index.
ISBN 0-8371-8912-8 : £10.75
(B77-22369)

301.45'19'6073076335 — Negro communities. *Louisiana. New Orleans, 1860-1880*
Blassingame, John W. Black New Orleans, 1860-1880 / [by] John W. Blassingame. — Chicago ; London : University of Chicago Press, 1976. — xviii,301p : ill, ports ; 22cm.
Originally published: 1973. — Bibl.: p.275-292. — Index.
ISBN 0-226-05708-9 Pbk : £3.05
(B77-00620)

301.45'19'60730771 — Negroes. Social conditions. *Ohio, 1860-1915*
Gerber, David A. Black Ohio and the color line, 1860-1915 / [by] David A. Gerber. — Urbana [etc.] ; London : University of Illinois Press, 1976. — xii,500p : map ; 24cm. — (Blacks in the New World)
Index.
ISBN 0-252-00534-1 : £11.25
(B77-15103)

301.45'19'608 — Negroes. Social conditions. *Latin America, to 1973*
Slavery and race relations in Latin America / edited with an introduction by Robert Brent Toplin. — Westport, Conn. ; London : Greenwood Press, 1974. — xiv,450p : maps ; 22cm. — (Contributions in Afro-American and African studies ; no.17)
Index.
ISBN 0-8371-7374-4 : £14.50
(B77-16201)

301.45'19'6695 — Ethnic groups. *Nigeria. Northern states*
Kirk-Greene, Anthony Hamilton Millard. Faces north : some peoples of Nigeria / text by Anthony Kirk-Greene and Pauline Ryan ; illustrations by Martin Archdale and Leslie Gibb. — Knaphill (Knaphill, Woking, Surrey) : Pikin Publications Ltd, 1975. — 5-62p : ill(some col), maps ; 31cm.
Map on lining papers.
ISBN 0-905010-00-0 : £3.95
(B77-08789)

301.45'19'68 — Negroes. Racial discrimination by society. *South Africa. Personal observations*
Braithwaite, E R. 'Honorary white' : a visit to South Africa / [by] E.R. Braithwaite. — London : New English Library, 1977. — 142p ; 18cm.
Originally published: London : Bodley Head, 1975.
ISBN 0-450-03116-0 Pbk : £0.60
(B77-09523)

301.45'19'68 — Social stratification. *Southern Africa. Study examples: Griquas, to ca 1880*
Ross, Robert, *b.1949.* Adam Kok's Griquas : a study in the development of stratification in South Africa / [by] Robert Ross. — Cambridge [etc.] : Cambridge University Press, 1976. — xiv,194p : geneal table, maps ; 24cm. — (African studies series ; 21 ISSN 0065-406x)
Bibl.: p.175-189. — Index.
ISBN 0-521-21199-9 : £5.75
(B77-07077)

301.45'19'69729041 — West Indians. Social aspects. *Great Britain. Inquiry reports*
Great Britain. *Parliament. House of Commons. Select Committee on Race Relations and Immigration.* The West Indian community : [report from the] Select Committee on Race Relations and Immigration, session 1976-7[7]. — London : H.M.S.O.
In 2 vols.
Vol.1 : Report : with minutes of proceedings and appendices to the report. — [1977]. — lxxxii p ; 24cm. — ([1976-77]H.C.180-I)
ISBN 0-10-279477-4 Sd : £1.35
(B77-12309)

Vol.2 : Evidence. — [1977]. — vi,425p ; 25cm. — ([1976-77]H.C.180-II)
ISBN 0-10-280777-9 Pbk : £8.10
(B77-12310)

301.45'19'7073 — Indians of North America. Social conditions. *United States*
Levitan, Sar A. Indian giving : federal programs for native Americans / [by] Sar A. Levitan and William B. Johnston. — Baltimore ; London : Johns Hopkins University Press, [1976]. — x, 83,[1]p : ill ; 22cm. — (Policy studies in employment and welfare ; no.20)
Published in the United States: 1975.
ISBN 0-8018-1739-0 : £6.10
ISBN 0-8018-1740-4 Pbk : £1.75
(B77-07809)

301.45'19'996 — Circassians. Social conditions. *Israel*
Wasserstein, David. The Druzes and Circassians of Israel / by David Wasserstein. — London : Anglo-Israel Association, 1976. — [1],21p ; 23cm. — (Anglo-Israel Association. Pamphlets ; no.55)
Bibl.: p.21.
Sd : £0.40
Also classified at 301.45'29'71
(B77-31705)

301.45'28 — Nonconformists. Social aspects. *England, 1780-1920*
Binfield, Clyde. So down to prayers : studies in English Nonconformity, 1780-1920 / [by] Clyde Binfield. — London : Dent [etc.], 1977. — xiv, 296p ; 23cm.
Bibl.: p.249-251. — Index.
ISBN 0-460-10366-0 : £8.50 : CIP rev.
(B77-07078)

301.45'28'2042 — England. Population, ca 1860-ca 1970. *Study examples: Roman Catholics. Reports, surveys*
Mufti, Rashid. Demographic trends / by Rashid Mufti. — [Liverpool] ([Christ's College, Woolton Rd, Liverpool L16 8ND]) : Liverpool Institute of Socio-Religious Studies [for] the Conferences of Major Religious Superiors of England and Wales, 1976. — [3],67p : ill ; 22cm. — (Pastoral investigation of social trends ; working paper no.3)
Bibl.: p.65-67.
ISBN 0-905052-03-x Sd : £0.50
(B77-09524)

301.45'29'45054 — Hindus. Relations with Muslims. *India (Republic)*
Harman, S. Plight of Muslims in India / [by] S. Harman. — 2nd ed. — London (89 Polesworth House, Alfred Rd, W2 5EU) : DL Publications, 1977. — [5],207p : form ; 23cm.
Previous ed.: 1976.
£6.50
ISBN 0-9502818-1-6
ISBN 0-9502818-2-4 Pbk : £4.50
Primary classification 301.45'29'71054
(B77-29198)

301.45'29'71 — Druzes. Social conditions. *Israel*
Wasserstein, David. The Druzes and Circassians of Israel / by David Wasserstein. — London : Anglo-Israel Association, 1976. — [1],21p ; 23cm. — (Anglo-Israel Association. Pamphlets ; no.55)
Bibl.: p.21.
Sd : £0.40
Primary classification 301.45'19'996
(B77-31705)

301.45'29'71054 — Muslims. Relations with Hindus. *India (Republic)*
Harman, S. Plight of Muslims in India / [by] S. Harman. — 2nd ed. — London (89 Polesworth House, Alfred Rd, W2 5EU) : DL Publications, 1977. — [5],207p : form ; 23cm.
Previous ed.: 1976.
£6.50
ISBN 0-9502818-1-6
ISBN 0-9502818-2-4 Pbk : £4.50
Also classified at 301.45'29'45054
(B77-29198)

301.5 — SOCIAL INSTITUTIONS

301.5 — Abortion. *Great Britain. Reports, surveys*
Great Britain. *Parliament. House of Commons. Select Committee on Abortion.* Report from the Select Committee on Abortion, session 1975-76. — London : H.M.S.O.
1st. Vol.2 : Minutes of evidence and appendices. — [1976]. — iv,322p : ill ; 25cm. — ([1975-76] H.C.573-II)
ISBN 0-10-267176-1 Pbk : £5.05
(B77-00043)

2nd : together with the proceedings of the Committee, minutes of evidence and appendices. — [1976]. — xix,27p ; 25cm. — ([1975-76 H.C.]737)
ISBN 0-10-009676-x Sd : £0.85
(B77-05886)

301.5 — Abortion. *Secondary school texts*
Finnis, J M. What do you know about abortion? / by J.M. Finnis and C.W.A. Flynn ; drawings by Cherry Denman. — [Oxford] ([c/o Bocardo and Church Army Press Ltd, Cowley, Oxford]) : Oxford School Publications, 1976. — iii,37p : ill, facsims ; 21x30cm.
Bibl.: p.37.
ISBN 0-905697-00-6 Pbk : £1.65(non-net)
(B77-08239)

301.5 — Abortion, to 1976
Potts, Malcolm. Abortion / [by] Malcolm Potts, Peter Diggory, John Peel. — Cambridge [etc.] : Cambridge University Press, 1977. — x,575p : ill, maps ; 24cm.
Index.
ISBN 0-521-21442-4 : £17.50
ISBN 0-521-29150-x Pbk : £5.95
(B77-29199)

301.5 — Astronautics, to 1975. Social aspects
Bainbridge, William Sims. The spaceflight revolution : a sociological study / [by] William Sims Bainbridge. — New York ; London [etc.] : Wiley, [1977]. — x,294p : ill ; 24cm. — (Science, culture and society)
'A Wiley-Interscience publication'. — Published in the United States: 1976. — Bibl.: p.282-289. — Index.
ISBN 0-471-04306-0 : £12.55
Also classified at 813'.0876
(B77-12311)

301.5 — Families. Health. Effects of family structure. *Asia. Developing countries. Reports, surveys*
Family formation patterns and health : an international collaborative study in India, Iran, Lebanon, Philippines and Turkey / study coordinators and editors A.R. Omran, C.C. Standley ; principal investigators J.E. Azar ... [et al.]. — Geneva : World Health Organization ; [London] : [H.M.S.O.], 1976. — 562p : ill, form ; 24cm.
Pbk : £14.00
ISBN 92-4-156053-3
(B77-11589)

301.5 — Legal abortion. *England. Statistics*
Abortion statistics : legal abortions carried out under the 1967 Abortion Act in England and Wales / Office of Population Censuses and Surveys. — London : H.M.S.O.
1974. — 1977. — vi,56p ; 30cm. — (Series AB ; no.1)
ISBN 0-11-690635-9 Sd : £1.75
ISSN 0140-5314
(B77-31706)

301.5 — Man. Sickness. Social aspects
Dingwall, Robert. Aspects of illness / [by] Robert Dingwall. — London : Martin Robertson, 1976. — x,166p : ill ; 23cm. — (Medicine in society series)
Bibl.: p.161-166.
ISBN 0-85520-148-7 : £5.95
(B77-15104)

301.5 — Medicine. *Anthropological perspectives*
Culture, disease, and healing : studies in medical anthropology / edited by David Landy. — New York : Macmillan ; London : Collier Macmillan, 1977. — xv,559p : ill, map ; 26cm.
Bibl.: p.519-559.
ISBN 0-02-367390-7 : £10.50
(B77-22370)

301.5 — Medicine. *Sociological perspectives*
Health care and health knowledge / edited by Robert Dingwall ... [et al.]. — London : Croom Helm [etc.], 1977. — 3-209p : ill ; 22cm. — (Explorations in sociology)
Bibl.
ISBN 0-85664-482-x : £6.95
(B77-22371)

301.5 — Medicine. *United States. Sociological perspectives*
Twaddle, Andrew C. A sociology of health / [by] Andrew C. Twaddle and Richard M. Hessler ; with foreword by Talcott Parsons. — Saint Louis : Mosby ; London : Distributed by Kimpton, 1977. — xvii,349p : ill, ports ; 26cm.
Bibl.: p.318-334. — Index.
ISBN 0-8016-5153-0 Pbk : £7.25
(B77-22372)

301.5 — Medicine. Nursing. Social aspects
Current perspectives in nursing : social issues and trends. — St Louis : Mosby ; London : Distributed by Kimpton. — (Mosby's current practice and perspectives in nursing series)
Vol.1 / [edited by] Michael H. Miller, Beverly C. Flynn. — 1977. — xiii,174p : ill ; 25cm.
Bibl.
ISBN 0-8016-3464-4 Pbk : Unpriced
(B77-26817)

301.5 — Medicine. Social aspects
Illich, Ivan. Limits to medicine : medical nemesis : the expropriation of health / [by] Ivan Illich. — [New ed.]. — Harmondsworth [etc.] : Penguin, 1977. — 296p ; 19cm. — (Pelican books)
This ed. originally published: London : Boyars, 1976. — Index.
ISBN 0-14-022009-7 Pbk : £0.90
(B77-24715)

Rhodes, Philip. The value of medicine / [by] Philip Rhodes. — London : Allen and Unwin, 1976. — 3-159p ; 23cm.
Bibl.: p.159.
ISBN 0-04-610004-0 : £4.95
(B77-05223)

Studies in everyday medical life / edited by Michael Wadsworth and David Robinson. — London : Martin Robertson, 1976. — xiv,218p : ill ; 23cm. — (Medicine in society series)
Bibl.: p.212-218.
ISBN 0-85520-147-9 : £7.85
(B77-04578)

301.5 — Medicine. Social aspects. *Great Britain, to 1976*
Cartwright, Frederick Fox. A social history of medicine / [by] Frederick F. Cartwright. — London [etc.] : Longman, 1977. — [1],209p ; 23cm. — (Themes in British social history)
Bibl.: p.189-199. — Index.
ISBN 0-582-48393-x : £5.50
ISBN 0-582-48394-8 Pbk : £2.95
(B77-12312)

301.5 — Nyuswa. Medicine. *South Africa. Natal. Anthropological perspectives*
Ngubane, Harriet. Body and mind in Zulu medicine : an ethnography of health and disease in Nyuswa-Zulu thought and practice / [by] Harriet Ngubane. — London [etc.] : Academic Press, 1977. — xvi,184p : ill ; 24cm. — (Studies in anthropology)
Bibl.: p.167-169. — Index.
ISBN 0-12-518250-3 : £6.80
(B77-25405)

301.5 — Patients. Care. *Great Britain. Sociological perspectives. Personal observations. Collections*
Medical encounters : the experience of illness and treatment / edited by Alan Davis and Gordon Horobin. — London : Croom Helm, 1977. — 223p ; 23cm.
ISBN 0-85664-328-9 : £7.95
(B77-09525)

301.5 — Persons. Time. Allocation. *United States. Reports, surveys*
Robinson, John P. How Americans use time : a social-psychological analysis of everyday behavior / [by] John P. Robinson. — New York ; London : Praeger, 1977. — xii,210p : ill, form ; 25cm. — (Praeger special studies in US economic, social and political issues)
Bibl.: p.202-207. — Index.
ISBN 0-275-24200-5 : £11.70
(B77-27694)

301.5 — Puerto Ricans. Psychotherapy. Role of spiritism. *New York (City). Sociological perspectives*
Harwood, Alan. PX : spiritist as needed : a study of a Puerto Rican community mental health resource / [by] Alan Harwood. — New York ; London [etc.] : Wiley, 1977. — xix,251p ; 24cm. — (Contemporary religious movements)
'A Wiley-Interscience publication'. — Bibl.: p.227-241. — Index.
ISBN 0-471-35828-2 : £14.25
(B77-26132)

301.5′1 — Consumer goods. Consumption. Social aspects
The **consumer** society / edited by I.R.C. Hirst and W. Duncan Reekie. — London : Tavistock Publications, 1977. — xv,198p : 2 ill ; 23cm. — (Social issues in the seventies ; 5)
'... the principal contributions to a seminar organized by the Faculty of Social Sciences of Edinburgh University in May 1973' - Editors' preface. — Bibl. — Index.
ISBN 0-422-76260-1 : £7.25
(B77-18570)

301.5′1 — Economic inequality. *Sociological perspectives*
Equity, income and policy : comparative studies in three worlds of development / edited by Irving Louis Horowitz. — New York ; London : Praeger, 1977. — xviii,298p : 2 ill ; 25cm. — (Praeger special studies in international politics and government)
Bibl. — Index.
ISBN 0-275-56570-x : £16.75
(B77-23145)

301.5′1 — Industries. Large companies. Social aspects. *United States. Case studies*
Sethi, S Prakash. Up against the corporate wall : modern corporations and social issues of the seventies / [by] S. Prakash Sethi. — 3rd ed. — Englewood Cliffs ; London [etc.] : Prentice-Hall, 1977. — xxi,482p : 2 ill ; 23cm.
Previous ed.: Englewood Cliffs : Prentice-Hall, 1974. — Bibl.
ISBN 0-13-938217-8 Pbk : £6.35
(B77-16741)

301.5′1 — Man. Social behaviour. Economic aspects. *Anthropological perspectives. Conference proceedings*
Themes in economic anthropology / edited by Raymond Firth. — London [etc.] : Tavistock Publications, 1975. — x,292p : ill ; 22cm. — (Association of Social Anthropologists of the Commonwealth. Monographs ; 6)
'... derives mainly from material presented at a Conference on Economic Anthropology sponsored by the Association of Social Anthropologists of the Commonwealth and held at St Antony's College, University of Oxford, 28-30 June 1965' - title page verso. — Originally published: 1967. — Bibl. — Index.
ISBN 0-422-72540-4 Pbk : £3.20
(B77-02785)

301.5′1 — Markets. *Philippines. Luzon. Baguio. Sociological perspectives*
Davis, William G. Social relations in a Philippine market : self-interest and subjectivity / [by] William G. Davis. — Berkeley [etc.] ; London : University of California Press, 1973. — [1],xiii, 315p : maps ; 23cm. — (University of California. Center for South and South-east Asia Studies. Publications)
Bibl.: p.293-308. — Index.
ISBN 0-520-01904-0 : Unpriced
(B77-19229)

301.5′1′091722 — Developed countries. Economic conditions. *Sociological perspectives. Conference proceedings*
British Sociological Association. *Annual Conference, 1975.* Industrial society : class, cleavage and control / edited by Richard Scase. — London : Allen and Unwin, 1977. — 3-221p : ill ; 23cm. — (Explorations in sociology ; 8)
'The papers in this volume were all given at the 1975 Annual Conference of the British Sociological Association' - Preface. — Bibl.: p.203-216. — Index.
ISBN 0-04-300067-3 : £6.50
ISBN 0-04-30068-1 Pbk : £2.95
(B77-14575)

301.5′4 — Agricultural industries. Tied cottages. *Great Britain. Proposals*
Shelter. Agricultural tied cottages : Shelter's reply to the Government Consultative Document on the allocation of agricultural tied cottages / [written by] Bob Widdowson. — London (86 Strand, WC2R 0ER) : Shelter, 1975. — 11 leaves in various pagings ; 30cm.
ISBN 0-9503981-1-x Sd : £0.40
(B77-04579)

301.5′4 — Agricultural industries. Tied cottages. *Great Britain. Research reports*
Irving, Barrie Leslie. Tied cottages in British agriculture / [by] Barrie Irving and Linden Hilgendorf. — London : Tavistock Institute of Human Relations ; London (Victoria Hall, East Greenwich, SE10 0RF) : Distributed by Research Publications Services Ltd.
Working paper no.1 : Basic statistics. — 1975. — [6],104p : ill ; 21cm.
Sd : £2.50
(B77-00621)

301.5′4 — Homes. Social aspects. *Secondary school texts*
Moore, Wilfred George. Homes / [by] W.G. Moore ; [maps and diagrams by A.G. Hodgkiss]. — Amersham : Hulton. — (Man and his world)
Work book. — 1976. — [32]p ; 21cm.
Index.
ISBN 0-7175-0768-8 Sd : £0.25
(B77-03953)

301.5′4 — Housing. Discrimination. *United States. Suburbs*
Danielson, Michael Nils. The politics of exclusion / [by] Michael N. Danielson. — New York ; Guildford : Columbia University Press, 1976. — xiii,443p : ill, facsim ; 24cm.
Index.
ISBN 0-231-03697-3 : Unpriced
ISBN 0-231-08342-4 Pbk : Unpriced
(B77-03388)

301.5′4 — Housing. Improvement. *Great Britain. Proposals*
National Home Improvement Council.
Improvement of United Kingdom housing : a reappraisal : a discussion document / prepared by the National Home Improvement Council. — London (26 Store St., WC1E 7BT) : The Council, 1976. — 99p in various pagings : ill ; 30cm.
ISBN 0-9505049-1-2 Sp : £8.00
(B77-08790)

301.5′4 — Housing. Improvement. Research projects. *Great Britain. Lists*
Great Britain. *Department of the Environment. Housing Improvement Group/H6.* Research related to the renewal of older housing areas : a list of current research projects and a bibliography / [Department of the Environment] Housing Improvement Group H6. — London : Department of the Environment, 1976. — [5],22p ; 30cm. — (Area improvement occasional papers ; 6-76)
'... a supplement to "Research into the renewal of older housing areas", Area Improvement Occasional Paper 3-75' - Introduction. — Bibl.: p.16-22.
Sd : Unpriced
Also classified at 016.3015′4
(B77-17934)

301.5′4 — Housing. Policies
Burns, Leland S. The housing of nations : analysis and policy in a comparative framework / [by] Leland S. Burns and Leo Grebler. — London [etc.] : Macmillan, 1977. — xv,255p : ill ; 23cm.
Index.
ISBN 0-333-19810-7 : £10.00
(B77-21708)

301.5′4 — Housing. Racial discrimination. Policies of government. Great Britain. Compared with government policies of United States
McKay, David H. Housing and race in industrial society : civil rights and urban policy in Britain and the United States / [by] David H. McKay. — London : Croom Helm [etc.], 1977. — 3-193p ; 23cm.
Index.
ISBN 0-85664-485-4 : £7.50
(B77-24012)

301.5′4 — Housing. Shortages. Assessment. Use of census data. *Great Britain. Study regions: London. Hammersmith (London Borough). Research reports*
O'Dell, A. The use of census data to identify and describe housing stress / [by] A. O'Dell and J. Parker. — Watford : Building Research Establishment, 1977. — [3],33p : ill, col maps ; 30cm. — (Building Research Establishment. Current papers ; 6/77)
Sd : Unpriced
(B77-19230)

301.5'4 — Immigrants. Housing. Segregation. *France. Paris, 1851-1975*
Ogden, Philip Ernest. Foreigners in Paris : residential segregation in the nineteenth and twentieth centuries / [by] Philip E. Ogden. — London (c/o The Editor, Mile End Rd, E1 4NS) : Department of Geography, Queen Mary College, University of London, 1977. — [11], 71p : ill, maps ; 30cm. — (Queen Mary College. Department of Geography. Occasional papers ; no.11 ISSN 0306-2740)
Bibl.: p.57-66.
ISBN 0-904791-11-4 Pbk : £1.00
(B77-33628)

301.5'4 — Low-income families. Housing. *New York (City). Manhattan, to 1976*
Jackson, Anthony, *b.1926.* A place called home : a history of low-cost housing in Manhattan / [by] Anthony Jackson. — Cambridge, Mass. ; London : M.I.T. Press, [1977]. — xi,359p : ill, maps, plans ; 21cm.
Published in the United States: 1976. — Bibl. — Index.
ISBN 0-262-10017-7 : £13.10
(B77-13517)

301.5'4 — Mobile homes. *Great Britain. Reports, surveys*
Great Britain. *Department of the Environment.* Report of the mobile homes review : a study carried out within the Department of the Environment / [for the] Department of the Environment [and the] Welsh Office. — London : H.M.S.O., 1977. — v,38p,4p of plates : ill ; 30cm.
ISBN 0-11-751231-1 Sd : £1.25
(B77-28408)

301.5'4 — Old persons. Housing. *Great Britain. Age Concern viewpoints*
Age Concern. Home truths on housing for the elderly / Age Concern ; [photographs Will Green]. — Mitcham : Age Concern, [1976]. — 20p : ill ; 21cm.
ISBN 0-904502-68-6 Sd : £0.25
(B77-02786)

301.5'4 — Second homes
Second homes : curse or blessing? / edited by J.T. Coppock. — Oxford [etc.] : Pergamon, 1977. — xii,228p : ill, maps ; 26cm. — (Pergamon Oxford geographies) (Pergamon international library)
Bibl. — Index.
ISBN 0-08-021371-5 : £7.50
ISBN 0-08-021370-7 Pbk : £3.00
(B77-29200)

301.5'4 — Social minorities. Housing. *Europe. Conference proceedings*
Housing for special groups : proceedings of an international seminar organized by the Committee on Housing, Building and Planning of the United Nations Economic Commission for Europe, and held in The Hague at the invitation of the Government of the Netherlands, 8-23 November 1976. — Oxford [etc.] : Pergamon for the United Nations, 1977. — vi,182p : 2 ill ; 26cm.
'A supplement to the international journal "Habitat"' - title page verso.
ISBN 0-08-021985-3 Pbk : £11.00
(B77-30997)

301.5'4 — Squatting. *London. Sociological perspectives*
Cant, D H. Squatting and private property rights : an analysis of the effects of squatting seen in the context of a theory about how increased activity by the state affects the way change comes about in our society / by D.H. Cant. — London (22 Gordon Sq., W.C.1) : [University College London], School of Environmental Studies, 1976. — v leaves,71p : ill ; 30cm. — (Town planning discussion paper ; no.24)
Bibl.: p.70-71.
Sd : £1.00
(B77-33076)

301.5'4'05 — Housing. *Periodicals*
International journal for housing science and its applications. — Oxford [etc.] : Pergamon. Vol.1, no.1- ; Aug. 1977-. — 1977-. — ill, ports ; 26cm.
Cover title. — Six issues a year. — [4],115p. in 1st issue.
Pbk : £50.00 yearly
ISSN 0146-6518
(B77-29958)

301.5'4'0941 — Homelessness. *Great Britain. Reports, surveys*
Bailey, Ron. The homeless and the empty houses / [by] Ron Bailey. — Harmondsworth [etc.] : Penguin, 1977. — 287p ; 18cm. — (A Penguin special)
ISBN 0-14-052324-3 Pbk : £0.95
(B77-29201)

301.5'4'0941 — Housing. *Great Britain. Reports, surveys*
Royal Institution of Chartered Surveyors. Housing : the chartered surveyors' report / [Royal Institution of Chartered Surveyors]. — [London] : R.I.C.S., 1976. — 47p : 1 ill ; 30cm.
ISBN 0-85406-076-6 Sd : £1.85
(B77-03954)

Shelter. The housing crisis nationwide / [Shelter] ; written by Frances Kelly and Jim Wintour. — London (157 Waterloo Rd, SE1 8UU) : Shelter, 1977. — [4],xxv,55p : ill ; 30cm.
Sd : £1.00
(B77-29959)

301.5'4'0941 — Housing. *Great Britain. Secondary school texts*
Leigh, Francis. Housing / [by] Francis Leigh. — London : Edward Arnold, 1976. — 16p : ill, facsims, map, port ; 30cm. — (Checkpoint ; 6)
ISBN 0-7131-0050-8 Sd : £2.50(set of 5 copies)
(B77-09526)

Sutcliffe, Ann. Housing / [text by Ann Sutcliffe] ; [edited by Ian Birnie]. — London : S.C.M. Press [for] the Christian Education Movement, 1972. — 32p : ill ; 23cm. — (Probe ; 7 ISSN 0305-3776)
Originally published: 1971. — Bibl.: p.32.
Sd : £0.20
ISBN 0-334-00651-1
(B77-10187)

301.5'4'0941 — Housing. Policies. *Great Britain*
Economic Development Committee for Building. Housing for all : a document for discussion / [Building EDC]. — London : H.M.S.O. [for the] National Economic Development Office, 1977. — viii,50p : 1 ill ; 30cm.
ISBN 0-11-700853-2 Sd : £1.75
(B77-33077)

301.5'4'0941 — Middle classes. Housing. *Great Britain. Urban regions, 1750-1914*
Middle class housing in Britain / edited by M.A. Simpson and T.H. Lloyd. — Newton Abbot [etc.] : David and Charles [etc.], 1977. — 217p, [8]p of plates : ill, maps, plans ; 23cm.
Index.
ISBN 0-7153-7273-4 : £6.50
(B77-11590)

301.5'4'09411 — Housing. *Scotland. Periodicals. For tenants*
Housing action notes. — Edinburgh (6 Castle St., Edinburgh EH2 3AT) : Shelter.
No.1- ; Jan. 1976-. — [1976]-. — 30cm.
Published at irregular intervals. — 10p. in 1st issue.
Sd : Unpriced
ISSN 0140-5152
(B77-32431)

301.5'4'09411 — Housing. Policies of local authorities. Formulation. *Scotland. Manuals*
Great Britain. *Scottish Development Department.* Scottish housing handbook / Scottish Development Department. — [Edinburgh] : H.M.S.O.
1 : Assessing housing need : a manual of guidance. — 1977. — [2],106p,fold leaf : ill, forms, maps ; 30cm.
Bibl.: p.100-101. — Index.
ISBN 0-11-491482-6 Pbk : £2.25
(B77-29202)

3 : Housing development, layout, roads and services. — 1977. — [117]p : ill, plans ; 30cm.
Pierced for binder. — Bibl.
ISBN 0-11-491457-5 Sd : £5.50
(B77-18285)

301.5'4'0942 — Homelessness. *England. Reports, surveys*
Great Britain. *Department of the Environment.* Homelessness : a consultation paper / [Department of the Environment, Department of Health & Social Security, Welsh Office]. — [London] : Department of the Environment : Department of Health and Social Security : Welsh Office, 1975. — [1],9,2p ; 30cm.
Sd : Unpriced
(B77-23146)

301.5'4'0942 — Housing. *England*
Great Britain. *Department of the Environment.* Housing policy, technical volume / Department of the Environment. — London : H.M.S.O. In 3 vols. — '... descriptive and analytical material prepared in connection with the Housing Policy Review for England and Wales' - Introduction to the technical volume.
Part 3. — 1977. — iv,210p ; 25cm.
ISBN 0-11-751228-1 Pbk : £3.25
(B77-29203)

301.5'4'0942 — Housing. *England. Statistics*
Housing statistics (England and Wales) / the Chartered Institute of Public Finance and Accounting. — London : [C.I.P.F.A.].
1975-76. Part 2 : Housing revenue account. — 1976. — 31p ; 21x26cm.
ISBN 0-85299-182-7 Sd : £3.00
ISSN 0309-6238
(B77-08791)

301.5'4'0942 — Housing. Policies. *England*
Great Britain. *Department of the Environment.* Housing policy : a consultative document / presented to Parliament by the Secretary of State for the Environment and the Secretary of State for Wales ... — London : H.M.S.O., [1977]. — vi,154p : ill ; 25cm. — (Cmnd.6851)
ISBN 0-10-168510-6 Pbk : £2.50
(B77-20925)

301.5'4'09421 — Housing. Policies. *London, 1837-1901*
Wohl, Anthony Stephen. The eternal slum : housing and social policy in Victorian London / [by] Anthony S. Wohl. — London : Edward Arnold, 1977. — xxv,386p,[16]p of plates : ill, maps, plans ; 24cm. — (Studies in urban history ; 5)
Ill., ports on lining papers. — Bibl.: p.341-355. — Index.
ISBN 0-7131-5945-6 : £15.50
(B77-32432)

301.5'4'0942256 — Housing. Effects of structure plans. *East Sussex. Brighton region*
Ambrose, Peter John. Who plans Brighton's housing crisis? / by Peter Ambrose. — London (86 Strand, WC2R 0EP) : Shelter, 1976. — [4], 19p : 1 ill ; 30cm. — (Shelter. Shelter local reports ; no.1 ISSN 0309-216x)
ISBN 0-901242-37-3 Sd : £0.40
(B77-06491)

301.5'4'094253 — Housing. *Lincolnshire. Reports, surveys. For structure plan making*
Lincolnshire (County). *Planning Department.* Housing : a background paper to the Lincolnshire structure plan / [Lincolnshire County Planning Department]. — [Lincoln] ([County Offices, Lincoln LN1 1Y]) : The Department, 1976. — 39p : ill, col map ; 30cm.
Cover title: Lincolnshire structure plan, background paper, housing. — Summary (sheet;[2]p. : 2 maps) as insert. — 'Report of Survey Part III' - inside front cover.
Sp : £0.40
(B77-21709)

301.5'4'0942659 — Housing. *Cambridgeshire. Cambridge. Reports, surveys*
Cambridge *(District). Department of Architecture and Planning.* City housing study / City of Cambridge [Department of Architecture and Planning]. — [Cambridge] ([The Guildhall, Cambridge CB2 3QL]) : [The Department], 1977. — [3],68[i.e.69],16p,[39] leaves of plates : ill, forms, maps ; 30cm.
Sd : £2.00
(B77-29204)

301.5'4'0945 — Housing. Policies. *Italy, 1968-1976*
Angotti, Thomas. Housing in Italy : urban development and political change / [by] Thomas Angotti. — New York ; London : Praeger, 1977. — xx,107p : ill, 2 maps ; 25cm. — (Praeger special studies in international politics and government)
Bibl. — Index.
ISBN 0-275-23660-9 : £10.05
(B77-32433)

301.5'4'095456 — Housing. *Developing countries. Urban regions. Study regions: India (Republic). Delhi*
Payne, Geoffrey K. Urban housing in the Third World / [by] Geoffrey K. Payne. — London : L. Hill [etc.], 1977. — xiv,242p : ill, forms, maps, plans, port ; 24cm.
Index.
ISBN 0-249-44149-7 : £8.00
(B77-11591)

301.5'4'0973 — Housing. *United States. Conference proceedings*
Decent Housing, a Promise to Keep *(Conference), Washington, D.C., 1975.* Housing costs and housing needs / edited by Alexander Greendale, Stanley F. Knock, Jr. — New York [etc.] ; London : Praeger ; [London] : [Distributed by Martin Robertson], 1976. — xxiii,180,[2]p ; 25cm. — (Praeger special studies in US economic, social and political issues)
'Papers delivered at a conference entitled "Decent Housing, a Promise to Keep" (April 22-24, 1975, Washington D.C.). Sponsored [i.e. organized] by the Interreligious Coalition for Housing. Included is a follow-up "Action guide" based on the papers and proceedings' - title-page verso.
ISBN 0-275-56220-4 : £9.75
(B77-02057)

301.5'5 — Adolescents. Occupations. *Great Britain. Sociological perspectives*
Ashton, D N. Young workers / [by] D.N. Ashton and David Field. — London : Hutchinson, 1976. — 192p : ill ; 23cm. — (Industry in action)
Bibl.: p.175-184. — Index.
ISBN 0-09-127370-6 : £4.95
(B77-06492)

301.5'5 — Agricultural industries. Organisations. *United States. Southern states. Southern Farmers' Alliance, 1880-1890. Sociological perspectives*
Schwartz, Michael. Radical protest and social structure : the Southern Farmers' Alliance and cotton tenancy, 1880-1890 / [by] Michael Schwartz. — New York [etc.] ; London : Academic Press, 1976. — xi,302p : ill ; 24cm. — (Studies in social discontinuity)
Index.
ISBN 0-12-632850-1 : £12.40
(B77-15105)

301.5'5 — Agricultural industries. Social aspects. *Great Britain. Conference proceedings*
Reading University Agricultural Club. *Annual Conference, 11th, University of Reading, 1977.* Agriculture and its social responsibilities : proceedings of the Eleventh Annual Conference of the Reading University Agricultural Club, 1977 / edited by S.F.L. Ball. — [Reading] (Department of Agriculture and Horticulture, University of Reading, [Reading] RG6 2AT) : Reading University Agricultural Club, 1977. — [6],61p ; 30cm.
Text on back cover. — Bibl.
ISBN 0-7049-0305-9 Pbk : Unpriced
ISSN 0305-201x
(B77-26818)

301.5'5 — Business firms. *Sociological perspectives. Case studies*
Business in the international environment : a casebook / [edited by] Yair Aharoni with Clifford Baden. — London [etc.] : Macmillan, 1977. — x,245p : ill, maps ; 23cm.
ISBN 0-333-16780-5 : £10.00 : CIP rev.
(B77-07079)

301.5'5 — Capitalist countries. Society. Role of trade unions, to 1976. *Readings*
Trade unions under capitalism / edited by Tom Clarke and Laurie Clements. — [London] : Fontana, 1977. — 413p ; 18cm.
Index.
ISBN 0-00-634883-1 Pbk : £1.95
(B77-29960)

301.5'5 — Chemical industries. *Great Britain. Sociological perspectives*
Nichols, Theo. Living with capitalism : class relations and the modern factory / [by] Theo Nichols and Huw Beynon. — London [etc.] : Routledge and Kegan Paul, 1977. — xvi,204p ; 23cm.
ISBN 0-7100-8594-x : £5.75 : CIP rev.
ISBN 0-7100-8595-8 Pbk : £2.75
(B77-08792)

301.5'5 — Health services. Personnel. Division of labour. *Sociological perspectives. Conference proceedings*
Sociology, Health and Illness *(Conference), 1976.* Health and the division of labour / edited by Margaret Stacey ... [et al.]. — London : Croom Helm [etc.], 1977. — 3-237p : ill, map ; 23cm. — (Explorations in sociology ; 10)
'... assembled from papers given at the 1976 British Sociological Association Conference on "Sociology, Health and Illness"' - jacket. — Bibl.
ISBN 0-85664-487-0 : £7.50 : CIP rev.
(B77-12313)

301.5'5 — Hops. Picking. Social aspects. *Kent, to 1976*
Bignell, Alan. Hopping down in Kent / [by] Alan Bignell. — London : Hale, 1977. — 176p, [12]p of plates : ill ; 23cm.
Index.
ISBN 0-7091-6257-x : £4.25
(B77-24716)

301.5'5 — Industrial relations. *Great Britain. Sociological perspectives*
Aldridge, Alan, *b.1947.* Power, authority and restrictive practices : a sociological essay on industrial relations / [by] Alan Aldridge. — Oxford : Blackwell, 1976. — xviii,135p ; 23cm.
Bibl.: p.127-133. — Index.
ISBN 0-631-17230-0 : £5.00
(B77-04580)

301.5'5 — Industrial relations. Organisations. Social aspects. *Great Britain*
Loveridge, Ray. Institutions and the socio-cultural environment / prepared for the [Open University, Industrial Relations] Course Team by Ray Loveridge and Pat Morrish. — Milton Keynes : Open University Press, 1976. — 45p : ill(some col) ; 30cm. — (A post-experience course : industrial relations ; unit 10) (P881 ; unit 10)
With answers to self-assessment questions. — Bibl.: p.44-45.
ISBN 0-335-00060-6 Sd : £1.70
(B77-03955)

301.5'5 — Industries. Supervisors. Role perception. *Reports, surveys*
Scholefield, Jock. Lack of clarity in the foreman's role with regard to delegated authority / by Jock Scholefield and J.R.C. Smith. — London (Gresham College, Basinghall St., EC2V 5AH) : City University Business School, 1977. — 5,24p ; 30cm. — (City University, London. Business School. Working paper series ; no.1 ISSN 0140-1041)
Sd : Unpriced
(B77-26819)

301.5'5 — Journalists. *United States. Sociological perspectives*
Johnstone, John Wallace Claire. The news people : a sociological portrait of American journalists and their work / [by] John W.C. Johnstone, Edward J. Slawski, William W. Bowman. — Urbana [etc.] ; London : University of Illinois Press, 1976. — ix,257p : ill ; 24cm.
Bibl.: p.245-250. — Index.
ISBN 0-252-00310-1 : £7.50
(B77-17935)

301.5'5 — Medicine. Nursing. *Sociological perspectives*
Smith, James Patrick. Sociology and nursing / [by] James P. Smith. — Edinburgh [etc.] : Churchill Livingstone, 1976. — [7],179p : ill ; 22cm. — (Livingstone nursing texts)
Bibl. — Index.
ISBN 0-443-01473-6 Pbk : £2.95
(B77-04581)

301.5'5 — Migrant personnel from Southern states of United States. Social aspects. *Ohio. Cleveland. Cohort studies*
Petersen, Gene B. Southern newcomers to northern cities : work and social adjustment in Cleveland / [by] Gene B. Petersen, Laure M. Sharp, Thomas F. Drury. — New York ; London : Praeger [for] the Bureau of Social Science Research, 1977. — xli,273p : ill, maps ; 25cm. — (Praeger special studies in US economic, social and political issues)
ISBN 0-275-24000-2 : £13.40
(B77-26133)

301.5'5 — Occupational attainment. Cameroun Republic. Related to qualifications of personnel, 1945-1975
Clignet, Remi. The Africanization of the labor market : educational and occupational segmentation in the Cameroun / [by] Remi Clignet. — Berkeley [etc.] ; London : University of California Press, 1976. — xvi, 230p : 1 ill, map ; 25cm.
Index.
ISBN 0-520-03019-2 : £10.20
Primary classification 331.1'142'096711
(B77-15129)

301.5'5 — Organisations. Personnel. Careers. *Sociological perspectives*
Organizational careers : some new perspectives / edited by John Van Maanen. — London [etc.] : Wiley, 1977. — xii,199p : ill ; 24cm. — (Wiley series on individuals, groups and organizations)
Bibl.: p.181-189. — Index.
ISBN 0-471-99409-x : £5.95
(B77-14067)

301.5'5 — Personnel management. *Sociological perspectives*
Watson, Tony J. The personnel managers : a study in the sociology of work and employment / [by] Tony J. Watson. — London [etc.] : Routledge and Kegan Paul, 1977. — xvi,246p : ill ; 23cm. — (International library of sociology)
Bibl.: p.224-238. — Index.
ISBN 0-7100-8743-8 : £5.95 : CIP rev.
(B77-24717)

301.5'5 — Physics. Conferences. Attendance by physicists
Hensman, Sandy. Conference attendance patterns among physicists / [by] Sandy Hensman. — London : Aslib, 1977. — iv,52p : forms ; 30cm. — (Aslib. Occasional publications ; no.20 ISSN 0066-8532)
ISBN 0-85142-098-2 Pbk : £6.00(£5.00 to members of Aslib)
(B77-24014)

301.5'5 — Trade unions. Portrayal by mass media. *Great Britain. Sociological perspectives*
Trade unions and the media / edited by Peter Beharrell and Greg Philo. — London [etc.] : Macmillan, 1977. — xi,150p ; 22cm. — (Critical social studies)
Bibl.: p.149-150.
ISBN 0-333-22055-2 Pbk : £2.50 : CIP rev.
(B77-13518)

301.5'5 — Women. Employment. *United States. Sociological perspectives*
Class, sex and the woman worker / edited by Milton Cantor and Bruce Laurie ; introduction by Caroline F. Ware. — Westport, Conn. ; London : Greenwood Press, 1977. — ix,253,[1] p ; 22cm. — (Contributions in labor history ; no.1)
Index.
ISBN 0-8371-9032-0 : £11.75
(B77-30998)

301.5'5 — Work. *Juvenile literature*
Scarry, Richard. Richard Scarry's at work. — London [etc.] : Hamlyn, 1977. — [24]p : col ill ; 21cm. — (A golden look-look book)
Originally published: New York : Golden Press, 1976.
ISBN 0-600-39387-9 Sd : £0.40
(B77-29962)

301.5'5 — Work. *Sociological perspectives*
Open University. *People and Work Course Team.* Work and society / prepared by the [Open University, People and Work] Course Team. — Milton Keynes : Open University Press, 1976. — 119p : ill ; 30cm. — (Social sciences, a third level course : people and work ; block 1, units 1-3) (DE351 ; 1-3)
Bibl.
ISBN 0-335-07000-0 Pbk : £2.80
(B77-13519)

People and work. — [Milton Keynes] : [Open University Press].
Media booklet 1 / [by Graeme Salaman et al.]. — 1976. — [1],106p : map, port ; 30cm. — (Social sciences, a third level course : people and work) (DE351 ; MB)
Prepared for the Open University, People and Work Course Team. — Bibl. — Includes facsimile reprints.
Sd : Unpriced
(B77-02058)

Media booklet 3 / [compiled by Peter Hamilton and David Thompson]. — [1976]. — [1],44p ; 30cm. — (Social sciences, a third level course : people and work) (DE351 ; MB)
Prepared for the Open University, People and Work Course Team.
Sd : Unpriced
(B77-02059)

Media booklet 4 / [by Graeme Salaman, Geoff Esland, Eric Willis]. — 1976. — [1],44p : ill ; 30cm. — (Social sciences, a third level course : people and work) (DE351 ; MB)
Prepared for the Open University, People and Work Course Team. — Bibl.
Sd : Unpriced
(B77-02060)

301.5'5 — Work. Attitudes of personnel. *United States. Transcripts of interviews*
Garson, Barbara. All the livelong day : the meaning and demeaning of routine work / [by] Barbara Garson. — Harmondsworth [etc.] : Penguin, 1977. — xvii,221p ; 18cm.
Originally published: Garden City, N.Y. : Doubleday, 1975.
ISBN 0-14-004381-0 Pbk : Unpriced
(B77-14068)

Working : people talk about what they do all day and how they feel about what they do / [compiled by] Studs Terkel. — Revised ed. — Harmondsworth [etc.] : Penguin, 1977. — [13], 479p ; 21cm. — (Peregrine books)
This ed. originally published: London : Wildwood House, 1975.
ISBN 0-14-055124-7 Pbk : £3.00
(B77-25406)

301.5'5 — Work. Psychosocial aspects
Anthony, Peter. The ideology of work / [by] P.D. Anthony. — London : Tavistock Publications, 1977. — viii,340p ; 23cm.
Bibl.: p.322-330. — Index.
ISBN 0-422-74310-0 : £8.00
(B77-26820)

301.5'5 — Work. Social aspects. *United States*
Sarason, Seymour Bernard. Work, aging and social change : professionals and the one life-one career imperative / [by] Seymour B. Sarason ; with a chapter 'The Santa Fe experience' by David Krantz. — New York : Free Press ; London : Collier Macmillan, 1977. — xv,298p ; 24cm.
Bibl.: p.289-293. — Index.
ISBN 0-02-927860-0 : £11.25
Also classified at 301.43'5'0973
(B77-29205)

301.5'5 — Working class school leavers. First employment. Choice. *Great Britain. Sociological perspectives. Case studies*
Willis, Paul E. Learning to labour : how working class kids get working class jobs / [by] Paul E. Willis. — Farnborough, Hants. : Saxon House, 1977. — x,204p ; 23cm.
Index.
ISBN 0-566-00150-0 : £7.50 : CIP rev.
(B77-21710)

301.5'5 — Working mothers. *United States. Sociological perspectives*
Hoffman, Lois Wladis. Working mothers / [by] Lois Wladis Hoffman, F. Ivan Nye, with ... [others]. — San Francisco [etc.] ; London : Jossey-Bass, 1974. — xv,272p : 4 ill ; 24cm. — (The Jossey-Bass behavioral science series)
Bibl.: p.233-263. — Index.
ISBN 0-87589-243-4 : Unpriced
(B77-19231)

301.5'5'0973 — Occupations. *United States. Sociological perspectives*
Montagna, Paul D. Occupations and society : toward a sociology of the labor market / [by] Paul D. Montagna. — New York ; London [etc.] : Wiley, 1977. — xix,456p : ill ; 24cm.
Index.
ISBN 0-471-61383-5 : £8.75
(B77-22374)

301.5'5'0973 — Professions. *United States. Sociological perspectives*
Professions for the people : the politics of skill / edited by Joel Gerstl and Glenn Jacobs. — Cambridge, Mass. : Schenkman ; New York ; London [etc.] : Distributed by Wiley, 1976. — [5],230p ; 24cm.
Bibl.
ISBN 0-470-29702-6 : £7.50
ISBN 0;470-29703-4 Pbk : £3.50
(B77-03389)

301.5'5'0973 — Work. Attitudes of society. *United States, 1700-1780*
Crowley, J E. This Sheba, self : the conceptualization of economic life in eighteenth-century America / [by] J.E. Crowley. — Baltimore ; London : Johns Hopkins University Press, [1976]. — xiv,161,[1] p ; 24cm. — (Johns Hopkins University. Studies in historical and political science : 92nd series (1974) ; 2)
Published in the United States: 1974. — Index.
ISBN 0-8018-1579-7 : £5.90
(B77-01185)

301.5'5'0973 — Work. Theories. *United States*
O'Toole, James. Work, learning, and the American future / [by] James O'Toole. — San Francisco [etc.] ; London : Jossey-Bass, 1977. — xvii,238p ; 24cm.
Bibl.: p.223-232. — Index.
ISBN 0-87589-304-x : £8.00
(B77-29206)

301.5'6 — Comprehensive education. *England. Sociological perspectives*
Bellaby, Paul. The sociology of comprehensive schooling / [by] Paul Bellaby. — London : Methuen, 1977. — 127p : 1 ill ; 20cm. — (Contemporary sociology of the school)
Bibl.: p.119-123. — Index.
ISBN 0-416-55880-1 : £3.80
ISBN 0-416-55890-9 Pbk : £1.60
(B77-24015)

301.5'6 — Education. *Sociological perspectives*
Educability, schools and ideology / edited by Michael Flude and John Ahier. — London : Croom Helm, 1974. — [7],220p ; 23cm.
Bibl. — Index.
ISBN 0-85664-126-x : £4.75
(B77-19232)

The **process** of schooling : a sociological reader / edited by Martyn Hammersley and Peter Woods ; for the Schooling and Society Course at the Open University. — London [etc.] : Routledge and Kegan Paul [for] the Open University Press, 1976. — vii,232p : ill, plans ; 26cm. — (Open University. Set books)
Bibl. — Index.
ISBN 0-7100-8495-1 : £3.75
ISBN 0-7100-8496-x Pbk : £1.90
(B77-04582)

Rationality, education and the social organization of knowledge : papers for a reflexive sociology of education / edited by Chris Jenks. — London [etc.] : Routledge and Kegan Paul, 1977. — viii,96p : 2 ill ; 24cm.
'Routledge direct editions'. — Bibl.
ISBN 0-7100-8513-3 Pbk : £2.50 : CIP rev.
(B77-11083)

School experience : explorations in the sociology of education / edited by Peter Woods and Martyn Hammersley. — London : Croom Helm, 1977. — 297,[1]p : ill ; 23cm.
Bibl. — Index.
ISBN 0-85664-324-6 : £7.50
(B77-05887)

301.5'6 — Education. Equality of opportunity. *Great Britain. Sociological perspectives. Reviews of research*
Tyler, William. The sociology of educational inequality / [by] William Tyler. — London : Methuen, 1977. — 143p : 1 ill ; 20cm. — (Contemporary sociology of the school)
Bibl.: p.133-140. — Index.
ISBN 0-416-55840-2 : £4.00
ISBN 0-416-55850-x Pbk : £1.80
(B77-23147)

301.5'6 — Health visitors. Professional education. *Great Britain. Sociological perspectives*
Dingwall, Robert. The social organisation of health visitor training / [by] Robert Dingwall. — London : Croom Helm, 1977. — 249p : forms ; 23cm.
Bibl.: p.243-246. — Index.
ISBN 0-85664-432-3 : £8.50
(B77-12314)

301.5'6 — Independent progressive schools. *Devon. Dartington. Dartington Hall School, 1926-1957. Sociological perspectives*
Punch, Maurice. Progressive retreat : a sociological study of Dartington Hall School 1926-1957 and some of its former pupils / [by] Maurice Punch. — Cambridge [etc.] : Cambridge University Press, 1977. — x,185p ; 24cm.
Bibl.: p.176-179. — Index.
ISBN 0-521-21182-4 : £4.90
(B77-23148)

301.5'6 — Middle schools. *England. Sociological perspectives*
Blyth, William Alan Lansdell. The social significance of middle schools / [by] W.A.L. Blyth, R. Derricott. — London : Batsford, 1977. — [6],246p : ill, maps ; 23cm.
Bibl.: p.228-239. — Index.
ISBN 0-7134-0487-6 : £6.95
ISBN 0-7134-0488-4 Pbk : £3.75
(B77-24718)

301.5'6 — Primary & secondary education. Ecological aspects. *England*
Eggleston, John. The ecology of the school / [by] John Eggleston. — London : Methuen, 1977. — 127p : 2 ill ; 20cm. — (Contemporary sociology of the school)
Bibl.: p.117-123. — Index.
ISBN 0-416-82900-7 : £3.80
ISBN 0-416-82910-4 Pbk : £1.80
(B77-26134)

301.5'6 — Schools. Curriculum. *Great Britain. Sociological perspectives*
Eggleston, John. The sociology of the school curriculum / [by] John Eggleston. — London [etc.] : Routledge and Kegan Paul, 1977. — ix, 171p : 1 ill ; 23cm.
Bibl.: p.154-163. — Index.
ISBN 0-7100-8565-6 : £4.95 : CIP rev.
ISBN 0-7100-8566-4 Pbk : £2.25
(B77-07874)

301.5'6 — Schools. Trainee teachers. Socialisation. *Case studies*
Lacey, Colin. The socialization of teachers / [by] Colin Lacey. — London : Methuen, 1977. — 160p : ill ; 20cm. — (Contemporary sociology of the school)
Bibl.: p.154-158. — Index.
ISBN 0-416-56230-2 : £4.00
ISBN 0-416-56240-x Pbk : £1.90
(B77-24719)

301.5'6 — Sociology of education. *State-of-the-art reviews*
Bernbaum, Gerald. Knowledge and ideology in the sociology of education / [by] Gerald Bernbaum. — London [etc.] : Macmillan, 1977. — 78p ; 21cm. — (Studies in sociology)
Bibl.: p.71-72.
ISBN 0-333-15762-1 Pbk : £1.50
(B77-14069)

301.5'6'08 — Education. *Sociological perspectives. Readings*
Worlds apart : readings for a sociology of education / edited by John Beck ... [et al.]. — London : Collier Macmillan, 1976. — [6],568p : ill ; 23cm.
Bibl.: p.561-568.
ISBN 0-02-977260-5 : £7.50
ISBN 0-02-977270-2 Pbk : £4.75
(B77-00622)

301.5'6'0941 — Education. *Great Britain. Sociological perspectives*
King, Ronald, *b.1934.* Education / [by] Ronald King. — 2nd ed. — London [etc.] : Longman, 1977. — vii,176p ; 20cm. — (Aspects of modern sociology : the social structure of modern Britain)
Previous ed.: 1969. — Bibl.: p.146-169. — Index.
ISBN 0-582-48550-9 Pbk : £2.25
(B77-31707)

301.5'6'0941 — Education. *Great Britain. Sociological perspectives. Readings*
Schooling and capitalism : a sociological reader / edited by Roger Dale, Geoff Esland and Madeleine MacDonald ; for the Schooling and Society course at the Open University. — London [etc.] : Routledge and Kegan Paul [for] the Open University Press, 1976. — vii,232p : ill ; 26cm. — (Open University. Set books)
Bibl. — Index.
ISBN 0-7100-8493-5 : £3.75
ISBN 0-7100-8494-3 Pbk : £1.90
(B77-05224)

301.5'6'09729 — Education. *Caribbean region. Sociological perspectives. Readings*
Sociology of education : a Caribbean reader / edited by Peter M.E. Figueroa and Ganga Persaud. — Oxford [etc.] : Oxford University Press, 1976. — [14],284p : ill ; 22cm.
Bibl.: p.268-284.
ISBN 0-19-878001-x Pbk : £2.50
(B77-05888)

301.5'7 — Alcoholic drinks. Consumption by young persons. Social aspects. *For parents*
Teachers' Advisory Council on Alcohol and Drug Education. Teaching your child about alcohol : guidelines for parents / [script by TACADE staff]. — Manchester (2 Mount St., Manchester M2 5NG) : Teachers' Advisory Council on Alcohol and Drug Education, [1977]. — [1], 2-14,[1]p : ill ; 21cm.
ISBN 0-905954-00-9 Sd : Unpriced
(B77-11592)

301.5'7 — Association football supporters. Crowds. Anti-social behaviour. *Scotland. Inquiry reports*
Great Britain. *Working Group on Football Crowd Behaviour.* Report of the Working Group on Football Crowd Behaviour. — Edinburgh : H.M.S.O., 1977. — xviii,41p ; 25cm.
Chairman: Frank McElhone.
ISBN 0-11-491514-8 Sd : £1.00
(B77-33078)

301.5'7 — Casinos. Social aspects
Hughes, Barrie. The educated gambler : a guide to casino games / [by] Barrie Hughes. — London : Paul, 1976. — 222p : ill ; 24cm.
Bibl.: p.217-218. — Index.
ISBN 0-09-127700-0 : £4.95
Primary classification 795
(B77-02523)

301.5'7 — Cigarette smoking behaviour. Great Britain. Related to social class. *Reports, surveys*
Todd, George Frederick. Social class variations in cigarette smoking and in mortality from associated diseases / by G.F. Todd. — London (Glen House, Stag Place, SW1E 5AG) : Tobacco Research Council, 1976. — 31p ; 30cm. — (Tobacco Research Council. Occasional papers ; 2 ISSN 0306-8196)
Bibl.: p.31.
ISBN 0-901026-12-3 Sd : Unpriced
Also classified at 301.32'2
(B77-14576)

301.5'7 — Communities. Role of leisure. *Great Britain. Conference proceedings*
Leisure and the community : conference proceedings : papers from a conference held by the Leisure Studies Association at Birmingham University on Friday 10th and Saturday 11th December, 1976 / edited by J.T. Haworth and A.J. Veal. — Birmingham : Centre for Urban and Regional Studies, University of Birmingham for the Association, [1976]. — 153p in various pagings : ill ; 30cm.
ISBN 0-7044-0244-0 Sd : £1.50
(B77-29963)

301.5'7 — Excursions. Social aspects. *Great Britain, ca 1840-1975*
Delgado, Alan. The annual outing and other excursions / [by] Alan Delgado. — London : Allen and Unwin, 1977. — 3-173p,[16]p of plates : ill, facsims, port ; 23cm.
Bibl.: p.165-167. — Index.
ISBN 0-04-942148-4 : £4.95
(B77-11593)

301.5'7 — Holiday resorts. Visitors. *Wales. Reports, surveys*
Wales Tourist Board. Surveys of summer visitors to Welsh resorts / Bwrdd Croeso Cymru = Wales Tourist Board. — Cardiff : The Board. — (Wales Tourist Board. Research studies)
Report 8 : Aberaeron, summary report. — 1976. — [11],16[i.e.21]p ; 30cm.
Sp : £1.00
(B77-21711)

Report 10 : Bala. — 1976. — [9],39[i.e.61]p,[8] p of plates,leaf of plate : form ; 30cm.
Sp : £1.50
(B77-21712)

Wales Tourist Board. Surveys of summer visitors to Welsh resorts / Wales Tourist Board. — Cardiff : The Board. — (Wales Tourist Board. Research studies)
Report 11 : Barry. — 1976. — [2],ii leaves,41[i.e.67]p : forms ; 30cm.
Sp : Unpriced
(B77-24720)

Wales Tourist Board. Surveys of summer visitors to Welsh resorts / Bwrdd Croeso Cymru = Wales Tourist Board. — Cardiff : The Board. — (Wales Tourist Board. Research studies)
Report 11 : Barry. — 1976. — ii,41[i.e.72]p : forms ; 30cm.
ISBN 0-900784-58-x Sp : £1.00
(B77-12315)

301.5'7 — Inland waterways controlled by British Waterways Board. Freshwater angling. *Great Britain. Reports, surveys*
Inland Waterways Amenity Advisory Council. Angling on the British Waterways Board system / [Inland Waterways Amenity Advisory Council]. — [London] ([122 Cleveland St., W1P 2DN]) : The Council, [1975]. — [3],24 leaves ; 30cm.
Text on verso of leaf [1].
Sp : £1.00
(B77-26821)

301.5'7 — Irish immigrants. Drinking habits. *United States, 1850-1950. Sociological perspectives*
Stivers, Richard. A hair of the dog : Irish drinking and American stereotype / [by] Richard Stivers. — University Park ; London : Pennsylvania State University Press, [1977]. — [10],197p : ill ; 24cm.
Published in the United States: 1975. — Index.
ISBN 0-271-01219-6 : £10.10
(B77-11084)

301.5'7 — Leisure. *Sociological perspectives*
Cheek, Neil H. The social organization of leisure in human society / [by] Neil H. Cheek, Jr, William R. Burch, Jr. — New York [etc.] ; London : Harper and Row, 1976. — xx,283p ; 25cm.
Bibl.: p.249-275. — Index.
ISBN 0-06-041037-x : £8.20
(B77-07810)

301.5'7 — Leisure. Adjustment by society. Role of education
Brightbill, Charles Kestner. Educating for leisure-centered living. — 2nd ed. / [by] Charles K. Brightbill, Tony A. Mobley. — New York ; London [etc.] : Wiley, 1977. — xii, 128p ; 23cm.
Previous ed.: / by Charles K. Brightbill. Harrisburg, Pa : Stackpole Books, 1966.
ISBN 0-471-94914-0 Pbk : £4.50
(B77-20040)

301.5'7 — Local authority indoor swimming pools. Use. *Great Britain, 1968-1969. Reports, surveys*
Collins, Michael Frank. Indoor swimming pools in Britain : summary results of a national survey of attendance and public use / by M.F. Collins. — London : Sports Council, 1977. — 6p : ill ; 30cm. — (Sports Council. Research working papers ; 1 ISSN 0308-9754)
ISBN 0-900979-42-9 Sd : £0.30
(B77-13520)

301.5'7 — Parks & public gardens. Use. *Leicestershire. Leicester. Reports, surveys*
Bowler, I R. Parks and gardens in Leicester : a survey / [by] I.R. Bowler and A.J. Strachan. — [Leicester] ([52 Charles St., Leicester]) : Recreational and Cultural Services [Department], Leicester City Council, 1976. — [7],73[i.e. 78]p : 1 ill, maps ; 30cm.
ISBN 0-901675-19-9 Sp : £2.00
(B77-11085)

301.5'7 — Secondary schools. Curriculum subjects: Alcoholic drinks. Consumption. Social aspects. *Great Britain. For teaching*
Teachers' Advisory Council on Alcohol and Drug Education. Alcohol education / Teachers' Advisory Council on Alcohol and Drug Education. — [Manchester] ([2 Mount St., Manchester M2 5NG]) : [The Council], 1976. — [1],11 leaves ; 30cm. — (TACADE advice leaflet ; no.1)
Bibl.: leaves 10-11. — List of films: leaf 10. — List of tapes: leaf 11.
ISBN 0-905954-03-3 Sp : £0.15
(B77-11594)

301.5'7 — Sports centres. *Warwickshire. Rugby. Rugby Sports Centre. Squash facilities. Use. Reports, surveys*
Jenkins, Charles. Squash at Rugby Sports Centre : an exploratory study / by C. Jenkins, B. Knapp & K. Bonser. — London : Sports Council, 1977. — 6p : 2 ill ; 30cm. — (Sports Council. Research working papers ; 2 ISSN 0308-9754)
ISBN 0-900979-44-5 Sd : £0.30
(B77-14070)

301.5'7 — Sports centres. *West Midlands (Metropolitan County). Birmingham. Sutton Coldfield. Wyndley Leisure Centre. Squash facilities. Use. Reports, surveys*
Jenkins, Charles. Squash at Wyndley Leisure Centre : an exploratory study / by C. Jenkins, B. Knapp & K. Bonser. — London : Sports Council, 1977. — 6p : 2 maps ; 30cm. — (Sports Council. Research working papers ; 3 ISSN 0308-9754)
ISBN 0-900979-43-7 Sd : £0.30
(B77-14071)

301.5'7 — Summer visitors. *Dyfed. Aberystwyth, 1972. Reports, surveys*
Wales Tourist Board. Survey of summer visitors to Aberystwyth / [Wales Tourist Board]. — Cardiff : The Board. — (Wales Tourist Board. Research studies)
1972. — [1973]. — 15,[5]leaves ; 30cm.
Pbk : £0.50
(B77-24016)

301.5'7 — Summer visitors. *Gwynedd. Llandudno, 1972. Reports, surveys*
Wales Tourist Board. Survey of summer visitors to Llandudno / [Wales Tourist Board]. — Cardiff : The Board. — (Wales Tourist Board. Research studies)
1972. — [1973]. — 15,[6]leaves ; 30cm.
Pbk : £0.50
(B77-24017)

301.5'7 — Summer visitors. *Mid Glamorgan. Porthcawl, 1972. Reports, surveys*
Wales Tourist Board. Survey of summer visitors to Porthcawl / [Wales Tourist Board]. — Cardiff : The Board. — (Wales Tourist Board. Research studies)
1972. — [1973]. — 14,[6]leaves ; 30cm.
Pbk : £0.50
(B77-24018)

301.5'7 — Theatre. *Sociological perspectives*
Burns, Elizabeth. Theatricality : a study of convention in the theatre and in social life / [by] Elizabeth Burns. — New York [etc.] ; London : Harper and Row, [1973?]. — vii, 246p ; 22cm.
Originally published: Harlow : Longman, 1972. — Index.
ISBN 0-06-136127-5 : £5.91
(B77-33079)

301.5'7 — Vacation activities. *Directories. For Irish young persons. Serials*
Summer opportunities / [National Youth Council of Ireland]. — Dublin (6 Waterloo Rd, Dublin 4) : National Youth Council of Ireland.
76 / [edited by Brigid Coyle]. — [1976]. — 12p : ill ; 30cm.
Sd : Unpriced
(B77-20926)

77. — [1977]. — [16]p : ill ; 29cm.
Bibl.: p.[15].
Sd : £0.10
(B77-20927)

301.5'7 — Vacations. *Juvenile literature*
Scarry, Richard. Richard Scarry's on holiday. — London [etc.] : Hamlyn, 1977. — [24]p : col ill ; 21cm. — (A golden look-look book)
Originally published: as 'Richard Scarry's on vacation'. New York : Golden Press, 1976.
ISBN 0-600-34539-4 Sd : £0.40
(B77-29964)

301.5'7 — Vacations by Britons. *Secondary school texts*
McIver, Nick. Holidays / by Nick McIver. — [Harlow] : Longman, 1977. — 12p : ill, form, maps ; 30cm. — (Young Britain)
ISBN 0-582-74069-x Sd : £0.33
(B77-28409)

301.5'7 — Vacations by Britons. Social aspects. *Scotland & Wales. Reports, surveys*
Morton-Williams, Jean. Holiday motivations / [by] Jean Morton-Williams. — London (16 Duncan Terrace, N1 8BZ) : Social and Community Planning Research : Centre for Sample Surveys, 1973. — [3],viii,100[i.e.102] leaves,20p : ill, form ; 30cm.
ISBN 0-904607-09-7 Sp : Private circulation
(B77-05890)

301.5'7'0941 — Leisure activities. *Great Britain, 1100-1976*
Armitage, John. Man at play : nine centuries of pleasure making / [by] John Armitage. — London [etc.] : F. Warne, 1977. — 192p : ill, map, ports ; 24cm.
Index.
ISBN 0-7232-2018-2 : £4.95
(B77-31708)

301.5'7'0941 — Leisure facilities. Projects. *Great Britain, 1973-1976. Reports, surveys*
Leisure and the quality of life : the report of a central steering group of officials on four local experiments. — London : H.M.S.O.
In 2 vols.
Vol.1. — 1977. — x,142p,[8]p of plates : ill, maps ; 25cm.
ISBN 0-11-751233-8 Pbk : £2.75
(B77-29207)

301.5'7'0941 — Leisure services. *Great Britain. Urban regions. Periodicals*
Leisure and entertainment review / Civic Entertainment Officers Association. — London (2 Victoria Way, Charlton, SE7 7RT) : Civic Entertainment Officers Association.
Continues: Civic leisure and entertainment review.
Vol.1, no.1- ; Summer 1973-. — 1973-. — ill, plan, ports ; 30cm.
Quarterly. — 32p. in 1st issue.
Sd : Unpriced
ISSN 0309-4502
(B77-12874)

301.5′7′09411 — Leisure activities. Surveys. *Scotland, 1972-1973. Reports, surveys*
Owen, Michael Leonard. Survey description / written and compiled by M.L. Owen and Brian S. Duffield ; edited by J.T. Coppock. — Edinburgh (High School Yards, Edinburgh EH1 1NR) : Tourism and Recreation Research Unit, University of Edinburgh, 1975. — 108p in various pagings : ill, forms, maps(some col) ; 30cm. — (University of Edinburgh. Tourism and Recreation Research Unit. Research reports ; no.14 ISSN 0305-487x) (STARS series ; no.1)
Commissioned by the Countryside Commission for Scotland, Scottish Tourist Board, Highlands and Islands Development Board, Forestry Commission and the Scottish Arts Council.
ISBN 0-904828-03-4 Pbk : £2.50
(B77-04583)

301.5′7′0942 — Leisure activities. *England. Illustrations*
Ward, Patrick. Wish you were here : the English at play / photographs by Patrick Ward ; introduction & commentary by James Cameron. — London : Gordon Fraser Gallery, 1977. — [104]p : of ill ; 25cm.
ISBN 0-900406-70-4 Pbk : £4.95 : CIP rev.
(B77-16203)

301.5′7′094225 — Leisure activities. *England, 1800-1910. Study regions: East & West Sussex*
Lowerson, John. Time to spare in Victorian England / [by] John Lowerson and John Myerscough. — Hassocks : Harvester Press, 1977. — viii,151p,[16]p of plates : ill, facsims, map, ports ; 23cm.
Bibl.: p.135-139. — Index.
ISBN 0-901759-56-2 : £5.95 : CIP rev.
(B77-07081)

301.5′7′09429 — Leisure facilities. Visitors. *Wales. Reports, surveys*
Wales Tourist Board. Surveys of visitors to tourist attractions, 1973 / [Wales Tourist Board]. — Cardiff : The Board. — (Wales Tourist Board. Research studies)
Report 3 : Caernarfon Castle. — 1975. — [6],ii leaves,37[i.e.40]p,[6]p of plates : form ; 30cm.
Sp : £1.00
(B77-20928)

Report 4 : The Talyllyn Railway. — 1974. — [6],ii leaves,33[i.e.35]p,[6]p of plates,[2]leaves of plates : form, maps ; 30cm.
Sp : £1.00
(B77-20929)

Report 5 : Welsh Folk Museum, St Fagans. — 1975. — [8],ii leaves,39[i.e.44]p,[6]p of plates,leaf of plate : form, map ; 30cm.
Sp : £1.00
(B77-20930)

Wales Tourist Board. Surveys of visitors to tourist attractions, 1974 / [Wales Tourist Board]. — Cardiff : The Board. — (Wales Tourist Board. Research studies)
Report 6 : Chepstow Castle. — 1976. — [7], 32[i.e.46]p : form ; 30cm.
ISBN 0-900784-61-x Sp : £1.00
(B77-12316)

Report 7 : Dan yr Ogof Caves. — 1976. — [7], 31[i.e.45]p : form ; 30cm.
ISBN 0-900784-60-1 Sp : £1.00
(B77-12317)

Report 8 : Penscynor Bird Gardens. — 1976. — [7],29[i.e.43]p : form ; 30cm.
ISBN 0-900784-59-8 Sp : £1.00
(B77-12318)

Report 9 : Welshpool and Llanfair Light Railway. — 1976. — [9]leaves,30[i.e.35]p,[6]p of plates : form ; 30cm.
Sp : £1.00
(B77-20931)

301.5′7′097 — Leisure. Social aspects. *Study regions: North America. Reports, surveys*
Godbey, Geoffrey. Leisure studies and services : an overview / [by] Geoffrey Godbey, Stanley Parker. — Philadelphia ; London [etc.] : Saunders, 1976. — xi,194p ; 25cm.
Index.
ISBN 0-7216-4141-5 : £3.75
(B77-04584)

301.5′8 — Buddhist sects. *China, to ca 1970. Sociological perspectives*
Overmyer, Daniel L. Folk Buddhist religion : dissenting sects in late traditional China / [by] Daniel L. Overmyer. — Cambridge, Mass. ; London : Harvard University Press, 1976. — xi, 295p ; 24cm. — (Harvard East Asian series ; 83)
Bibl.: p.261-280. — Index.
ISBN 0-674-30705-4 : £9.55
(B77-03390)

301.5′8 — Christian church. *France. Champagne, 1500-1600. Sociological perspectives*
Galpern, A N. The religions of the people in sixteenth-century Champagne / [by] A.N. Galpern. — Cambridge, Mass. ; London : Harvard University Press, 1976. — [9],240[i.e. 242]p,[2]p of plates : ill, maps, plan ; 24cm. — (Harvard historical studies ; 92)
Bibl.: p.215-233. — Index.
ISBN 0-674-75836-6 : £14.60
(B77-08240)

301.5′8 — Christian church. Clergy. *Great Britain. Sociological perspectives*
Ranson, Stewart. Clergy, ministers and priests / [by] Stewart Ranson, Alan Bryman and Bob Hinings. — London [etc.] : Routledge and Kegan Paul, 1977. — xii,204p : forms ; 23cm. — (International library of sociology)
Bibl.: p.194-198. — Index.
ISBN 0-7100-8713-6 : £5.95 : CIP rev.
(B77-19233)

301.5′8 — Christian church. Social aspects. *England, 1525-1625*
Church and society in England, Henry VIII to James I / edited by Felicity Heal and Rosemary O'Day. — London [etc.] : Macmillan, 1977. — vi,206p ; 23cm. — (Problems in focus series)
Bibl.: p.180-187. — Index.
ISBN 0-333-18524-2 : £5.95
ISBN 0-333-18525-0 Pbk : £2.95
(B77-23150)

301.5′8 — Christian church. Social aspects. *Lincolnshire. East Lindsey (District) & West Lindsey (District), 1825-1875*
Obelkevich, James. Religion and rural society, South Lindsey, 1825-1875 / [by] James Obelkevich. — Oxford : Clarendon Press, 1976. — xiii,353p : 2 maps ; 23cm.
Bibl.: p.337-346. — Index.
ISBN 0-19-822426-5 : £12.00
(B77-03392)

301.5′8 — Churches. Attendance. *Wales, 1851. Statistics*
Great Britain. *General Register Office.* The Religious Census of 1851, a calendar of the returns relating to Wales. — Cardiff : University of Wales Press.
'The returns ... have been transcribed and ... presented in a standardized form' - jacket. — 'The Religious Census was taken as ... part of the decennial Census of Population, and was thus the responsibility of the Registrar-General ...' - Introduction. — Index.
Vol.1 : South Wales / edited by Ieuan Gwynedd Jones and David Williams ; with an introduction by Ieuan Gwynedd Jones. — 1976. — xxxv,698p : facsims ; 26cm. — (University of Wales. Board of Celtic Studies. History and law series ; no.30)
ISBN 0-7083-0619-5 : £8.00
(B77-11595)

301.5′8 — France. Society. Role of Roman Catholic clergy, 1750-1791. *Study examples: Clergy of Roman Catholic Church. Diocese of Gap*
Tackett, Timothy. Priest & parish in eighteenth-century France : a social and political study of the curés in a diocese of Dauphiné, 1750-1791 / by Timothy Tackett. — Princeton ; Guildford : Princeton University Press, 1977. — xiii,350p : ill, maps, ports ; 23cm.
Bibl.: p.307-331. — Index.
ISBN 0-691-05243-3 : £14.60
(B77-26822)

301.5′8 — Hare Krishna Movement. *United States. Anthropological perspectives*
Daner, Francine Jeanne. The American children of Krsna : a study of the Hare Krsna movement / by Francine Jeanne Daner. — New York ; London [etc.] : Holt, Rinehart and Winston, 1976. — x,118p : ill, port ; 24cm. — (Case studies in cultural anthropology)
Bibl.: p.116-118.
ISBN 0-03-013546-x Pbk : £2.25
(B77-03391)

301.5′8 — Islam. Social aspects. *Morocco. Study regions: Boujad*
Eickelman, Dale F. Moroccan Islam : tradition and society in a pilgrimage center / by Dale F. Eickelman. — Austin ; London : University of Texas Press, 1976. — xx,303p : ill, geneal tables, maps ; 24cm. — (Modern Middle East series ; no.1)
Bibl.: p.287-296. — Index.
ISBN 0-292-75025-0 : £12.00
(B77-02061)

301.5′8 — Primitive religions. Philosophy of religion. *Anthropological perspectives*
Skorupski, John. Symbol and theory : a philosophical study of theories of religion in social anthropology / [by] John Skorupski. — Cambridge [etc.] : Cambridge University Press, 1976. — xv,265p ; 23cm.
Bibl.: p.256-261. — Index.
ISBN 0-521-21200-6 : £7.50
(B77-00623)

301.5′8 — Religious cults. *United States. Sociological perspectives*
Enroth, Ronald M. Youth, brainwashing, and the extremist cults / [by] Ronald Enroth. — Exeter : Paternoster Press, 1977. — 221p ; 22cm.
Also published: Grand Rapids : Zondervan, 1977. — Bibl.: p.219. — Index.
ISBN 0-85364-215-x Pbk : £2.40 : CIP rev.
(B77-31709)

301.5′8 — Roman Catholic Church. Jamaa. *Zaire. Sociological perspectives*
De Craemer, Willy. The Jamaa and the Church : a Bantu Catholic movement in Zaïre / by Willy De Craemer. — Oxford : Clarendon Press, 1977. — ix,192p ; 22cm. — (Oxford studies in African affairs)
Bibl.: p.186-189. — Index.
ISBN 0-19-822708-6 : £8.00 : CIP rev.
(B77-08793)

301.5′8 — Scientology. *Sociological perspectives*
Wallis, Roy. The road to total freedom : a sociological analysis of Scientology / [by] Roy Wallis. — London : Heinemann Educational, 1976. — xiv,282p : 1 ill ; 25cm.
Bibl.: p.270-279. — Index.
ISBN 0-435-82916-5 : £6.50
(B77-03956)

301.5′8 — Secularisation. *Sociological perspectives*
Glasner, Peter E. The sociology of secularisation : a critique of a concept / [by] Peter E. Glasner. — London [etc.] : Routledge and Kegan Paul, 1977. — viii,137p ; 23cm. — (International library of sociology)
Bibl.: p.123-134. — Index.
ISBN 0-7100-8455-2 : £4.75
(B77-20041)

301.5′92 — China. Politics. Group discussions by small groups, 1949-1973
Whyte, Martin King. Small groups and political rituals in China / [by] Martin King Whyte. — Berkeley [etc.] ; London : University of California Press, 1974. — viii,271p ; 24cm. — (Michigan studies on China)
Index.
ISBN 0-520-02499-0 : Unpriced
(B77-03393)

301.5′92 — Fiji. Politics. Leadership
Nayacakalou, R R. Leadership in Fiji / [by] R.R. Nayacakalou ; with a foreword by Ratu Sir Kamisese Mara. — Melbourne ; London [etc.] : Oxford University Press, 1975. — xiii,170p ; 23cm.
Bibl.: p.161-163. — Index.
ISBN 0-19-550462-3 : £11.25
(B77-02062)

301.5′92 — Foreign relations. *Sociological perspectives*
Luard, Evan. Types of international society / [by] Evan Luard. — New York : Free Press ; London : Collier Macmillan, 1976. — ix,389p ; 24cm.
Index.
ISBN 0-02-919450-4 : £11.25
(B77-20932)

301.5′92 — India (Republic). Politics. Participation of public. *Research reports*
Goel, Madan Lal. Political participation in a developing nation : India / [by] Madan Lal Goel. — London : Asia Publishing House, 1975. — xvii,234p : 3 ill ; 23cm.
Bibl.: p.225-230. — Index.
ISBN 0-210-22354-5 : £8.00
(B77-11086)

301.5'92 — Kingdoms. *Africa south of the Sahara, to ca 1970. Anthropological perspectives*
Mair, Lucy. African kingdoms / [by] Lucy Mair. — Oxford : Clarendon Press, 1977. — [6], 151p : map ; 23cm.
Bibl.: p.141-143. — Index.
ISBN 0-19-821698-x : £3.95 : CIP rev.
ISBN 0-19-874075-1 Pbk : £1.95
(B77-08241)

301.5'92 — Korea. Politics. Leadership. *Conference proceedings*
Political leadership in Korea / edited by Dae-Sook Suh and Chae-Jin Lee. — Seattle ; London : University of Washington Press, 1976. — xvi,272,[2]p : ill ; 24cm. — (University of Washington. Institute for Comparative and Foreign Area Studies. Publications on Asia ; no.27)
'... selected papers presented at two symposia on Korean leadership held in Seoul during the summers of 1971 and 1972 ... under the auspices of the University of Washington, Seattle ...' - Acknowledgments. — Index.
ISBN 0-295-95437-x : £7.00
(B77-04585)

301.5'92 — Legislatures. New members. Political socialisation. *Study examples: California. Assembly*
Bell, Charles G. The first term : a study of legislative socialization / [by] Charles G. Bell, Charles M. Price ; preface by Heinz Eulau. — Beverly Hills ; London : Sage Publications, [1976]. — 215p : ill, forms ; 22cm. — (Sage library of social research ; vol. 18)
Published in the United States : 1975.
ISBN 0-8039-0500-9 : £8.05
ISBN 0-8039-0501-7 Pbk : £3.95
(B77-03957)

301.5'92 — Mass society. Political behaviour. Theories
Halebsky, Sandor. Mass society and political conflict : toward a reconstruction of theory / [by] Sandor Halebsky. — Cambridge [etc.] : Cambridge University Press, 1976. — ix,309p ; 22cm.
Index.
ISBN 0-521-20541-7 : £9.50
ISBN 0-521-09884-x Pbk : £3.25
(B77-07811)

301.5'92 — Norway. Politics. Participation of public. Equality of opportunity. *Sociological perspectives*
Martinussen, Willy. The distant democracy : social inequality, political resources and political influence in Norway / [by] Willy Martinussen. — London [etc.] : Wiley, 1977. — viii,246p : ill ; 24cm.
Bibl.: p.238-242. — Index.
ISBN 0-471-99413-8 : £7.50
(B77-12319)

301.5'92 — Political elites. Social aspects. *China*
Wong, Paul. China's higher leadership in the socialist transition / [by] Paul Wong. — New York : Free Press ; London : Collier Macmillan, 1976. — ix,310p : ill ; 24cm.
Bibl.: p.287-298. — Index.
ISBN 0-02-935600-8 : £12.75
(B77-11596)

301.5'92 — Political groups. *Sociological perspectives. Readings*
Friends, followers and factions : a reader in political clientelism / edited by Steffen W. Schmidt ... [et al.]. — Berkeley [etc.] ; London : University of California Press, 1977. — xxxvii, 512p : ill ; 25cm.
Bibl.
ISBN 0-520-02696-9 : £15.00
(B77-26135)

301.5'92 — Political issues. Formulation. Participation of public. *United States*
Cobb, Roger W. Participation in American politics : the dynamics of agenda-building / [by] Roger W. Cobb, Charles D. Elder. — Baltimore ; London : Johns Hopkins University Press, 1972. — ix,182p ; 21cm.
Bibl.: p.171-178. — Index.
ISBN 0-8018-1716-1 Pbk : Unpriced
(B77-19234)

301.5'92 — Political parties. Identification of electorate. Social aspects. *United States*
Knoke, David. Change and continuity in American politics : the social bases of political parties / [by] David Knoke. — Baltimore ; London : Johns Hopkins University Press, 1976. — xv,192p : ill ; 24cm.
Bibl.: p.174-187. — Index.
ISBN 0-8018-1790-0 : £9.20
(B77-14577)

301.5'92 — Political parties. Identification of electorate. United States. Related to voting behaviour
Trilling, Richard J. Party image and electoral behavior / [by] Richard J. Trilling. — New York ; London [etc.] : Wiley, 1976. — xv, 234p ; 24cm.
'A Wiley-Interscience publication'. — Index.
ISBN 0-471-88935-0 : £11.90
(B77-08794)

301.5'92 — Political systems. Effects of urbanisation. *Latin America. Sociological perspectives*
Peeler, John A. Urbanization and politics / [by] John A. Peeler. — Beverly Hills ; London : Sage Publications, 1977. — 56p : ill ; 22cm. — (Sage professional papers in comparative politics ; vol.6, no.01-062 ISSN 0080-5343)
Bibl.: p.53-56.
ISBN 0-8039-0757-5 Pbk : £1.95
(B77-32434)

301.5'92 — Politics. *Sociological perspectives*
Lasswell, Harold Dwight. Harold D. Lasswell on political sociology / edited and with an introduction by Dwaine Marvick. — Chicago ; London : University of Chicago Press, 1977. — vi,456p ; 21cm. — (The heritage of sociology)
Bibl.: p.425-443. — Index.
ISBN 0-226-46920-4 : £15.40
(B77-33629)

301.5'92 — Politics. Leadership. Psychology. *Readings*
A **psychological** examination of political leaders / edited by Margaret G. Hermann with Thomas W. Milburn. — New York : Free Press ; London : Collier Macmillan, 1977. — xii,516p : ill ; 24cm.
Bibl.: p.474-505. — Index.
ISBN 0-02-914590-2 : £14.00
(B77-24019)

301.5'92 — Quebec (Province). Politics. Role of Social Credit Party, 1962. *Sociological perspectives*
Pinard, Maurice. The rise of a third party : a study in crisis politics / [by] Maurice Pinard ; with a foreword by Neil J. Smelser. — Enlarged ed. — Montreal ; London : McGill-Queen's University Press, 1975. — xxv, 307p : 1 ill ; 23cm.
Previous ed.: Englewood Cliffs : Prentice-Hall, 1971. — Index.
ISBN 0-7735-0231-9 Pbk : Unpriced
(B77-17312)

301.5'92 — Sierra Leone. Politics. Leadership, 1951-1967. *Case studies*
Cartwright, John R. Political leadership in Sierra Leone / [by] John R. Cartwright. — London : Croom Helm, 1978. — [2],308p : 2 maps ; 23cm.
Index.
ISBN 0-85664-625-3 : £12.95 : CIP rev.
(B77-31710)

301.5'92 — Turkey. Politics. Participation of public. Influence of social change
Özbudun, Ergun. Social change and political participation in Turkey / [by] Ergun Özbudun. — Princeton ; Guildford : Princeton University Press, [1977]. — xiii,254p ; 23cm.
'Written under the auspices of the Center for International Affairs, Harvard University' - p.ii. — Published in the United States: 1976. — Bibl.: p.231-247. — Index.
ISBN 0-691-07580-8 : £9.40
(B77-09527)

301.5'92 — United States. Politics. Attitudes of negro children. *Reports, surveys*
Abramson, Paul Robert. The political socialization of black Americans : a critical evaluation of research on efficacy and trust / [by] Paul R. Abramson. — New York : Free Press ; London : Collier Macmillan, 1977. — xi,195p : map ; 24cm.
Bibl.: p.176-189. — Index.
ISBN 0-02-900170-6 : £9.75
(B77-22375)

301.5'92 — United States. Politics. Participation of public
Citizen preferences and urban public policy : models, measures, uses / edited by Terry Nichols Clark. — Beverly Hills ; London : Sage Publications, 1976 [i.e. 1977]. — 142p : ill, form ; 22cm. — (Sage contemporary social science issues ; 34)
Published in the United States: 1976. — '... originally appeared as a special issue of "Policy and politics" (Volume 4, Number 4, June 1976)' - title page verso.
ISBN 0-8039-0749-4 Pbk : £2.90
(B77-11087)

301.5'92 — United States. Politics. Participation of working class women. *Study regions: Illinois. Chicago*
McCourt, Kathleen. Working-class women and grass-roots politics / [by] Kathleen McCourt. — Bloomington ; London : Indiana University Press, 1977. — v,256p ; 24cm.
Bibl.: p.251-256.
ISBN 0-253-36650-x : £7.50
(B77-29965)

301.5'92'0941 — Great Britain. Politics. *Sociological perspectives. Readings*
Studies in British politics : a reader in political sociology / edited by Richard Rose. — 3rd ed. — London [etc.] : Macmillan, 1976. — xi, 547p : ill ; 23cm.
Previous ed.: 1969. — Bibl.: p.512-547.
ISBN 0-333-19796-8 : £10.00
ISBN 0-333-19797-6 Pbk : £4.95
(B77-06493)

301.5'92'0941 — Great Britain. Politics. *Sociological perspectives. Serials*
British political sociology yearbook. — London : Croom Helm.
Vol.3 : Participation in politics / edited by Colin Crouch. — 1977. — [6],282p : ill ; 23cm.

Bibl.: p.270-272. — Index.
ISBN 0-85664-242-8 : £12.95
ISSN 0307-0328
(B77-21713)

301.5'92'09481 — Norway. Political development. Compared with political development in Sweden, 1875-1965. *Sociological perspectives*
Klingman, David. Social change, political change and public policy : Norway and Sweden, 1875-1965 / [by] David Klingman. — London [etc.] : Sage Publications, 1976. — 54,[1]p : ill ; 22cm. — (Sage papers in contemporary political sociology ; vol.2, no.06-019 ISSN 0305-3482)
Bibl.: p.51-54.
ISBN 0-8039-9862-7 Pbk : £1.75
Also classified at 301.5'92'09485
(B77-09528)

301.5'92'09485 — Sweden. Political development. Compared with political development in Norway, 1875-1965. *Sociological perspectives*
Klingman, David. Social change, political change and public policy : Norway and Sweden, 1875-1965 / [by] David Klingman. — London [etc.] : Sage Publications, 1976. — 54,[1]p : ill ; 22cm. — (Sage papers in contemporary political sociology ; vol.2, no.06-019 ISSN 0305-3482)
Bibl.: p.51-54.
ISBN 0-8039-9862-7 Pbk : £1.75
Primary classification 301.5'92'09481
(B77-09528)

301.5'92'09492 — Netherlands. Politics, 1917-1974. Expounded by pluralism. *Sociological perspectives*
Lijphart, Arend. The politics of accommodation : pluralism and democracy in the Netherlands / by Arend Lijphart. — 2nd ed., revised. — Berkeley [etc.] ; London : University of California Press, 1975. — [1],xiv,231p ; 23cm.
Previous ed.: Berkeley : University of California Press ; London : Cambridge University Press, 1968. — Index.
ISBN 0-520-02900-3 : £9.60
ISBN 0-520-02918-6 Pbk : £2.70
(B77-14072)

301.5'92'095 — Politicians. *Asia, to 1974. Sociological perspectives. Conference proceedings*
The **making** of politicians : studies from Africa and Asia / edited by W.H. Morris-Jones. — London : Athlone Press for the Institute of Commonwealth Studies, 1976. — x,249p ; 22cm. — (Commonwealth papers ; 20 ISSN 0076-0765)
'The papers ... presented during 1972-74 to a seminar on comparative politics at the Institute of Commonwealth studies ... ' - Preface. — Index.
ISBN 0-485-17620-3 Pbk : £5.50
Also classified at 301.5'92'096
(B77-05891)

301.5'92'095694 — Israel. Politics, to 1975. *Sociological perspectives*
Etzioni-Halevy, Eva. Political culture in Israel : cleavage and integration among Israeli Jews / [by] Eva Etzioni-Halevy, with Rina Shapira. — New York ; London : Praeger, 1977. — xxiv, 251p : ill ; 25cm. — (Praeger special studies in international politics and government)
Bibl.: p.229-243. — Index.
ISBN 0-275-23790-7 : £13.40
(B77-26136)

301.5'92'096 — Africa. Politics. *Sociological perspectives*

Markovitz, Irving Leonard. Power and class in Africa : an introduction to change and conflict in African politics / [by] Irving Leonard Markovitz. — Englewood Cliffs ; London [etc.] : Prentice-Hall, 1977. — xiv,398p : map ; 24cm.
Bibl.: p.350-377. — Index.
ISBN 0-13-686691-3 : £10.35
ISBN 0-13-686642-5 Pbk : £7.15
(B77-17936)

301.5'92'096 — Politicians. *Africa, to 1974. Sociological perspectives. Conference proceedings*

The **making** of politicians : studies from Africa and Asia / edited by W.H. Morris-Jones. — London : Athlone Press for the Institute of Commonwealth Studies, 1976. — x,249p ; 22cm. — (Commonwealth papers ; 20 ISSN 0076-0765)
'The papers ... presented during 1972-74 to a seminar on comparative politics at the Institute of Commonwealth studies ... ' - Preface. — Index.
ISBN 0-485-17620-3 Pbk : £5.50
Primary classification 301.5'92'095
(B77-05891)

301.5'92'096761 — Social classes. Political development. *Uganda, to 1972. Marxist viewpoints*

Mamdani, Mahmood. Politics and class formation in Uganda / by Mahmood Mamdani. — London [etc.] : Heinemann Educational, 1976. — viii,339p : map ; 21cm.
Bibl.: p.319-328. — Index.
ISBN 0-435-96500-x : £8.00
ISBN 0-435-96501-8 Pbk : £2.50
(B77-10739)

301.5'92'0994 — Australia. Politics. *Sociological perspectives*

Connell, Robert William. Ruling class, ruling culture : studies of conflict, power and hegemony in Australian life / [by] R.W. Connell. — Cambridge [etc.] : Cambridge University Press, 1977. — xii,250p : ill ; 23cm.
Index.
ISBN 0-521-21392-4 : £9.50
ISBN 0-521-29133-x Pbk : £2.95
(B77-11088)

301.5'93 — Military power. *Sociological perspectives*

Cortese, Charles F. Modernization, threat and the power of the military / [by] Charles F. Cortese. — Beverly Hills ; London : Sage Publications, 1976. — 64p : ill ; 22cm. — (Sage professional papers in international studies ; vol.4, no.02-045)
Bibl.: p.60-64.
ISBN 0-8039-0624-2 Pbk : £1.75
(B77-15704)

301.5'93 — United States. Army. Social control

Radine, Lawrence B. The taming of the troops : social control in the United States Army / [by] Lawrence B. Radine. — Westport, Conn. ; London : Greenwood Press, 1977. — xiii,276, [1]p ; 22cm. — (Contributions in sociology ; no.22)
Index.
ISBN 0-8371-8911-x : £14.50
(B77-20933)

301.5'93'0903 — Military forces, ca 1500-1975. *Sociological perspectives*

Feld, Maury D. The structure of violence : armed forces as social systems / [by] Maury D. Feld ; preface by Charles C. Moskos Jnr. — Beverly Hills ; London : Sage Publications [for the] Inter-University Seminar on Armed Forces and Society, 1977. — 204p ; 23cm. — (Sage series on armed forces and society ; vol.10)
ISBN 0-8039-0729-x : £11.00
(B77-21714)

301.5'93'0941 — Great Britain. Army, 1800-1900. *Sociological perspectives*

Harries-Jenkins, Gwyn. The Army in Victorian society / [by] Gwyn Harries-Jenkins. — London : Routledge and Kegan Paul [etc.], 1977. — xi,320p ; 23cm. — (Studies in social history)
Index.
ISBN 0-7100-8447-1 : £5.50
(B77-20042)

301.5'93'0973 — Military service. Psychosocial aspects. *United States*

The **social** psychology of military service / edited by Nancy L. Goldman and David R. Segal. — Beverly Hills ; London : Sage Publications, 1976. — 303p : ill ; 24cm. — (Sage research progress series on war, revolution and peacekeeping ; vol.6)
'... a two-day research conference ... was held on April 23-25, 1975, at the Center for Continuing Education, University of Chicago ...' - Introduction. — Bibl.: p.281-299.
ISBN 0-8039-0598-x : £10.00
ISBN 0-8039-0599-8 Pbk : £4.95
(B77-00624)

301.6 — SOCIAL CONFLICT AND ACCOMMODATION

301.6'2 — Alienation

Alienation in contemporary society : a multidisciplinary examination / edited by Roy S. Bryce-Laporte, Claudewell S. Thomas. — New York [etc.] ; London : Praeger ; [London] : [Distributed by Martin Robertson], 1976. — xxxv,394p ; 24cm. — (Praeger special studies in US economic, social and political issues)
ISBN 0-275-09800-1 : £20.35
(B77-03958)

301.6'2 — Deviance. Cultural aspects. *Comparative studies*

Newman, Graeme. Comparative deviance : perception and law in six cultures / [by] Graeme Newman ; preface by Marvin E. Wolfgang. — New York ; Oxford [etc.] : Elsevier, 1976. — xiii,332p : ill, form ; 24cm.
Bibl.: p.299-316. — Index.
ISBN 0-444-99026-7 : £11.42
(B77-07082)

301.6'2'01 — Alienation. *Philosophical perspectives*

Kaplan, Morton A. Alienation and identification / [by] Morton A. Kaplan. — New York : Free Press ; London : Collier Macmillan, 1976. — xv,206p ; 22cm.
Index.
ISBN 0-02-916790-6 : £7.50
(B77-12876)

301.6'2'0973 — Deviance. Theories. *United States*

McCaghy, Charles H. Deviant behavior : crime, conflict and interest groups / [by] Charles H. McCaghy. — New York : Macmillan ; London : Collier Macmillan, 1976. — xiii, 400p ; 24cm.
Index.
ISBN 0-02-378400-8 Pbk : £6.00
(B77-12877)

301.6'3 — Conflict

Richardson, Robin. World in conflict / [by Robin Richardson]. — Sunbury-on-Thames [etc.] : Nelson, 1977. — 48,[1]p : ill, ports ; 19x25cm. — (World studies)
Bibl.: p.48.
ISBN 0-17-438171-9 Sd : Unpriced
(B77-31711)

301.6'3 — Social conflict

Rummel, Rudolph Joseph. Understanding conflict and war / [by] R.J. Rummel. — [Beverly Hills] ; [London] : Sage Publications ; New York ; London [etc.] : Distributed by Wiley.
Vol.2 : The conflict helix. — 1976. — [12], 400p : ill ; 24cm.
Bibl.: p.377-390. — Index.
ISBN 0-470-15123-4 : £12.45
(B77-02787)

301.6'3'09 — Social conflict. Political aspects, 1750-1976

Gurr, Ted Robert. The politics of crime and conflict : a comparative history of four cities / [by] Ted Robert Gurr, Peter N. Grabosky, Richard C. Hula ; with contributions by ... [others]. — Beverly Hills ; London : Sage Publications, 1977. — xii,792,[1]p : ill ; 24cm.
Index.
ISBN 0-8039-0677-3 : £20.00
Primary classification 364'.903
(B77-19290)

301.6'3'091732 — Urban regions. Social conflict

McCord, Arline. Urban social conflict / [by] Arline McCord, William McCord. — Saint Louis : Mosby ; London : Distributed by Kimpton, 1977. — xiii,201p ; 26cm.
Bibl. — Index.
ISBN 0-8016-3220-x Pbk : £5.60
(B77-18571)

301.6'3'09953 — Tauade. Social conflict. *Papua New Guinea*

Hallpike, Christopher Robert. Bloodshed and vengeance in the Papuan mountains : the generation of conflict in Tauade society / [by] C.R. Hallpike. — Oxford : Clarendon Press, 1977. — xx,317p,leaf of plate,[8]p of plates : ill, geneal table, maps, ports ; 23cm.
Bibl.: p.300-306. — Index.
ISBN 0-19-823192-x : £12.50
(B77-08795)

301.6'33'0973 — Violence. *United States*

Toplin, Robert Brent. Unchallenged violence : an American ordeal / [by] Robert Brent Toplin. — Westport, Conn. ; London : Greenwood Press, 1975. — xx,332p ; 22cm.
Index.
ISBN 0-8371-7748-0 : £11.95
(B77-17313)

301.6'34 — Strikes. *Sociological perspectives*

Suffolk *(County). Council.* The work of the County Council / Suffolk County Council. — [Ipswich] ([County Hall, Ipswich IP4 2JS]) : [The Council], 1976. — 519p in various pagings,[11]fold leaves of plates : ill, maps ; 30cm.
Cover title. — Index.
ISBN 0-86055-001-x Sp : £3.00
(B77-05973)

301.6'37'0947 — Social classes. Conflict. *Soviet Union, 1917-*

Bettelheim, Charles. Class struggles in the USSR / by Charles Bettelheim ; translated [from the French] by Brian Pearce. — Hassocks : Harvester Press. — ([Marxist theory and contemporary capitalism ; 6])
[Vol.1] : First period, 1917-1923. — 1977. — 567p ; 21cm.
This translation originally published: New York : Monthly Review Press, 1976. — Translation of: 'Les luttes de classes en URSS'. Paris : Maspero/Seuil, 1974. — Bibl.: p.531-537. — Index.
ISBN 0-85527-620-7 : £12.50 : CIP rev.
(B77-03959)

301.6'4 — Negotiation. Psychosocial aspects

Morley, Ian E. The social psychology of bargaining / [by] Ian E. Morley, Geoffrey M. Stephenson. — London : Allen and Unwin, 1977. — 3-317p : ill ; 24cm.
Bibl.: p.294-310. — Index.
ISBN 0-04-301081-4 : £11.50
(B77-23151)

301.6'4 — Vigilantes. *United States, to 1975*

Burrows, William E. Vigilante! / [by] William E. Burrows. — New York ; London : Harcourt Brace Jovanovich, [1977]. — xix,311p,[8]p of plates : ill, facsims, ports ; 22cm.
Published in the United States: 1976. — Bibl.: p.297-301. — Index.
ISBN 0-15-193655-2 : £7.90
(B77-10188)

301.6'4'09416 — Peace. Peace movements. *Northern Ireland. Peace People*

Peace in Northern Ireland : the story of the Peace People. — London : Catholic Truth Society, [1977]. — [15]p : col ill, col ports ; 19cm.
ISBN 0-85183-179-6 Sd : £0.20
(B77-08251)

309 — SOCIAL CONDITIONS

309'.07'23 — Social surveys by market research industries. Commissioning by social scientists. *Manuals*

Marsh, Cathie. Some guidelines for commissioning an interview survey from a research company / [by] Cathie Marsh. — [London] ([89 Kingsway, WC2 6RH]) : [Social Science Research Council, Survey Unit], 1976. — [3],20,[1]p ; 30cm.
Cover title: Guidelines for commissioning an interview survey from a research company. — Bibl.: p.[1].
ISBN 0-900296-53-4 Pbk : £0.30
(B77-10189)

309'.07'23 — Social surveys. Cohort analysis

Glenn, Norval D. Cohort analysis / [by] Norval D. Glenn. — Beverly Hills ; London : Sage Publications, 1977. — 72p ; 22cm. — (Quantitative applications in the social sciences ; no.07-005) (Sage university papers)
Bibl.: p.70-72.
ISBN 0-8039-0794-x Pbk : £1.95
(B77-25407)

309'.07'23 — Social surveys. Data. Analysis. Applications of digital computer systems
Sonquist, John A. Survey and opinion research : procedures for processing and analysis / [by] John A. Sonquist, William C. Dunkelberg. — Englewood Cliffs ; London [etc.] : Prentice-Hall, 1977. — ix,502p : ill, forms ; 25cm.
Bibl.: p.471-498. — Index.
ISBN 0-13-878264-4 : £15.95
(B77-31000)

309'.07'23 — Social surveys. Data. Analysis. Applications of digital computer systems. Software packages. *Technical data*
Rowe, Beverley Charles. Computer software for social science data / [by] Beverley Rowe and Marianne Scheer (for the Study Group on Computers and Survey Analysis). — London : Social Science Research Council, 1976. — [3], 246p : form ; 21x30cm.
Bibl.: p.237-246.
ISBN 0-900296-55-0 Pbk : £1.00
(B77-08796)

309'.07'23 — Social surveys. Data. Multivariate analysis
The **analysis** of survey data / edited by Colm A. O'Muircheartaigh and Clive Payne. — London [etc.] : Wiley, 1977. — 2v.(xv,273p;[15],255p) : ill ; 24cm.
Bibl. — Index.
ISBN 0-471-99466-9 : £20.50
(B77-15106)

309.1 — SOCIAL CONDITIONS. HISTORICAL AND GEOGRAPHICAL TREATMENT

309.1 — Social conditions. Geographical aspects
Smith, David Marshall. Human geography : a welfare approach / [by] David M. Smith. — London : Edward Arnold, 1977. — xiv,402p : ill, maps ; 24cm.
Bibl.: p.376-395. — Index.
ISBN 0-7131-5924-3 : £9.95
ISBN 0-7131-5925-1 Pbk : £4.50
(B77-16204)

309.1'03 — Social conditions, ca 1700-1963
Moore, Barrington. Social origins of dictatorship and democracy : lord and peasant in the making of the modern world / [by] Barrington Moore, Jr. — Harmondsworth [etc.] : Penguin, 1977. — xvi,559p ; 20cm. — (Peregrine books)
Originally published: Boston, Mass. : Beacon Press, 1966 ; London : Allen Lane, 1967. — Bibl.: p.524-546. — Index.
Pbk : £2.25
ISBN 0-14-055086-0
(B77-14073)

309.1'04 — Social conditions, 1891-1975. *Secondary school texts. For New Zealand students*
Perspectives in modern history / general editor J.H. Jensen. — Wellington [N.Z.] ; London [etc.] : Reed Education.
2 : [cultural interaction] : Black and white in South Africa, 1919-61 : a study in cultural interaction / [by] Geoffrey Rice. — 1976. — vi, 50p : ill, maps, ports ; 20x22cm.
Originally published: 1975. — Bibl.: p.48.
ISBN 0-589-04570-9 Pbk : £1.65
Also classified at 909.82
(B77-24020)

Perspectives in modern history / general editor, J.H. Jensen. — London [etc.] : Reed Educational.
5 : Government. — 1976. — vi,87p : ill, maps, ports ; 20x22cm.
Bibl. — Contents: British government, 1931-51 / by David Keen - The government of the Soviet Union, 1924-57 / by J.H. Jensen.
ISBN 0-589-04565-2 Pbk : £3.00
(B77-24722)

Perspectives in modern history / general editor J.H. Jensen. — London [etc.] : Reed Educational.
6 : Leadership. — 1976. — vi,98p : ill, coat of arms, maps, music, ports ; 20x22cm.
Bibl. — Contents: China, 1921-49 / by W. Rushbrook - Leadership in Indonesia since 1945 / by J.S. Hoadley.
ISBN 0-589-04566-0 Pbk : £3.05
Also classified at 909.82
(B77-02063)

309.1'046 — Social conditions, 1962-1973. *Essays*
Enzensberger, Hans Magnus. Raids and reconstructions : essays on politics, crime and culture / [by] Hans Magnus Enzensberger ; translations [from the German] by Michael Roloff, Stuart Hood, Richard Woolley and the author. — London : Pluto Press, 1976. — 312p ; 21cm.
Nine essays, 5 of which were originally published in these translations as: 'Politics and crime', New York : Seabury Press, 1974. — Index.
ISBN 0-904383-21-0 : £7.50
ISBN 0-904383-16-4 Pbk : £3.30
(B77-03960)

309.1'04'7 — Social conditions. *Lectures, speeches. Welsh texts*
Trafodion economaidd a chymdeithasol 1964-1973 / golygwyd gan W. Huw R. Davies ac R.O. Roberts. — Caerdydd [i.e. Cardiff] : Gwasg Prifysgol Cymru, 1977. — 101p ; 22cm.
'... detholiad o ddarlithiau a draddodwyd i'r Adran o Urdd Graddedigion Prifysgol Cymru ...' - Rhagair.
ISBN 0-7083-0644-6 Pbk : £2.75
(B77-24021)

309.1'047 — Social conditions. *Secondary school texts*
Dalgleish, Neil. World survey / [by] Neil Dalgleish. — Amersham : Hulton, 1976. — [4], 120p : ill, facsims, maps, ports ; 25cm.
ISBN 0-7175-0750-5 Pbk : £1.60
(B77-00046)

309.1'047 — Social conditions. *Yearbooks*
The **book** of the world. — London : W.H. Allen.
1977-78 : Fully revised ed. / editor John Eppstein, assisted by Richard Rossiter and Carolyn Vernon. — 1977. — x,288p : ill, maps, ports ; 19cm.
ISBN 0-491-01738-3 : £4.50
(B77-16743)

The **international** year book and statesmen's who's who. — Kingston upon Thames : Kelly's Directories.
1977 : [25th ed.] / compiled by Robert M. Bradfield ; research Jean-Pierre Keillor (biographies section) ; Mervyn O. Pragnell (countries section). — 1977. — ciii,821p : ill ; 26cm.
Previously published: as 'International yearbook and statesman's who's who'. — Index.
ISBN 0-610-00505-7 : £25.00
(B77-24723)

The **statesman's** year-book : statistical and historical annual of the states of the world for year. — London [etc.] : Macmillan.
1977-1978 / edited by John Paxton. — 1977. — xxviii,1572p,[2]fold leaves of plates : 2 col maps ; 21cm.
Bibl. — Index.
ISBN 0-333-19449-7 : £8.95
(B77-26823)

309.1'171'7 — Communist countries. Society. Effects of modernisation, 1945-1975
Social consequences of modernization in communist societies / edited by Mark G. Field. — Baltimore ; London : Johns Hopkins University Press, 1976. — ix,277p : ill ; 27cm.
'Based on a selection of papers presented at a symposium in Salzburg, Austria, in Sept. 1972, sponsored by the American Council of Learned Societies under the general auspices of its Planning Group on Comparative Communist Studies' - Library of Congress Cataloging in Publication Data. — Index.
ISBN 0-8018-1786-2 : £10.15
(B77-00047)

309.1'173'2 — Urban regions. Social conditions. Spatial models
Batty, Michael. Dynamic urban models based on information-minimising / [by] Michael Batty, Lionel March. — Reading (Whiteknights, Reading RG6 2AB) : Department of Geography, University of Reading, 1976. — [2], ii,41p : ill, map ; 21cm. — (Geographical papers ; no.48 ISSN 0305-5914)
Bibl.: p.37-39.
ISBN 0-7049-0457-8 Sd : £0.70
(B77-03394)

Rodriguez-Bachiller, Agustin. Gravity models in a dynamic framework / [by] Agustin Rodriguez-Bachiller. — Reading (Whiteknights, Reading [RG6 2AB]) : Department of Geography, University of Reading, 1976. — [2], ii,54p : ill ; 21cm. — (Geographical papers ; no.40 ISSN 0305-5914)
Bibl.: p.44-49.
ISBN 0-7049-0347-4 Sd : £0.60
(B77-07083)

309.1'181'2 — Western world. Social conditions. Influence of theories of providence of God, to ca 1800
Viner, Jacob. The role of providence in the social order : an essay in intellectual history / [by] Jacob Viner. — Princeton ; Guildford : Princeton University Press, 1976. — ix,113p ; 22cm. — (Jayne lectures ; 1966)
Originally published: Philadelphia : American Philosophical Society, 1972.
ISBN 0-691-01990-8 Pbk : £2.40
(B77-14074)

309.1'181'2 — Western world. Social conditions. Policies of governments. *Comparative studies*
Heidenheimer, Arnold Joseph. Comparative public policy : the politics of social choice in Europe and America / [by] Arnold J. Heidenheimer, Hugh Heclo, Carolyn Teich Adams. — London [etc.] : Macmillan, 1976. — [11],296p : ill ; 24cm.
Originally published: New York : St Martin's Press, 1975. — Index.
ISBN 0-333-19980-4 : £7.95
ISBN 0-333-19981-2 Pbk : £2.95
(B77-03395)

309.1'181'2 — Western world. Society. Cultural aspects, ca 1900-ca 1975
Carroll, John, *b.1944.* Puritan, paranoid, remissive : a sociology of modern culture / [by] John Carroll. — London [etc.] : Routledge and Kegan Paul, 1977. — xi,148p ; 23cm.
Bibl.: p.137-138. — Index.
ISBN 0-7100-8622-9 : £3.95 : CIP rev.
(B77-15705)

309.1'38'5 — Greece. Athens. Society, ca B.C. 400-ca B.C.300. *Readings from contemporary sources*
Social values in classical Athens / [translated from the Greek and] edited with an introduction by N.R.E. Fisher. — London : Dent [etc.], 1976. — iii-xiv,177p : 2 geneal tables ; 20cm. — (The ancient world, source books)
Bibl.: p.xiii-xiv. — Index.
ISBN 0-460-10630-9 : £3.95
ISBN 0-460-11630-4 Pbk : £2.25
(B77-02064)

309.1'4'01 — Western Europe. Social conditions, ca 900-ca 1350. *Essays*
Duby, Georges. The chivalrous society / [by] Georges Duby ; translated [from the French] by Cynthia Postan. — London : Edward Arnold, 1977. — viii,246p : ill, maps ; 24cm.
Index.
ISBN 0-7131-5943-x : £15.00 : CIP rev.
(B77-24724)

309.1'4'055 — Europe. Social conditions. *Secondary school texts*
Europe today and tomorrow / edited by Peggotty Freeman. — London : Longman [for] the Centre for Contemporary European Studies, 1977. — [10],181p : ill, facsim, maps, ports ; 24cm.
Bibl. — Index.
ISBN 0-582-35170-7 Pbk : £3.95
(B77-33631)

309.1'41'07 — Great Britain. Social conditions, 1700-1970. *Secondary school texts*
Titley, David Paul. Machines, money and men : an economic and social history of Great Britain from 1700 to the 1970's / [by] D.P. Titley. — 2nd ed. — St Albans : Hart-Davis Educational, 1977. — [8],278p : ill, facsims, maps, ports ; 22cm.
Previous ed.: i.e. New ed. Oadby : Blond Educational, 1973. — Bibl.: p.271-274. — Index.
ISBN 0-247-12768-x Pbk : £1.95
(B77-26137)

309.1'41'07 — Great Britain. Social conditions, 1700-1975
Hill, Charles Peter. British economic and social history, 1700-1975 / [by] C.P. Hill. — 4th ed. — London : Edward Arnold, 1977. — xi,322p, [16]p of plates : ill, maps, ports ; 22cm.
Previous ed.: published as 'British economic and social history, 1700-1964'. 1970. — Bibl.: p.308-310. — Index.
ISBN 0-7131-0099-0 Pbk : £2.25
(B77-24022)

309.1'41'07 — Great Britain. Social conditions, 1700-1976. *Secondary school texts*
Case, Stephen Leslie. A social and economic history of Britain, 1700-1976 / [by] S.L. Case and D.J. Hall. — 2nd ed. — London : Edward Arnold, 1977. — [5],154p : ill, facsims, form, maps, ports ; 25cm.
Previous ed.: 1971. — Index.
ISBN 0-7131-0158-x Sd : £1.95 : CIP rev.
(B77-08676)

309.1'41'07 — Great Britain. Social conditions, 1750-1850
Thomis, Malcolm Ian. Responses to industrialisation : the British experience, 1780-1850 / [by] Malcolm I. Thomis. — Newton Abbot [etc.] : David and Charles [etc.], 1976. — 3-194p ; 23cm.
Index.
ISBN 0-7153-6762-5 : £5.50
(B77-10740)

309.1'41'074 — Great Britain. Social conditions, 1828
Eichthal, Gustave d'. A French sociologist looks at Britain : Gustave d'Eichthal and British society in 1828 / translated [from the French] and edited by Barrie M. Ratcliffe and W.H. Chaloner. — Manchester : Manchester University Press [etc.], 1977. — vi,169p ; 23cm. — (University of Manchester. Faculty of Arts. Publications ; no.22)
Index. — Includes a memoir of Gustave d'Eichthal / by Barrie M. Ratcliffe.
ISBN 0-7190-1283-x : £7.50
Also classified at 301'.092'4
(B77-24725)

309.1'41'083 — Great Britain. Social conditions, 1920-1940
Stevenson, John. Social conditions in Britain between the wars / [by] John Stevenson. — Harmondsworth [etc.] : Penguin, 1977. — 295p ; 18cm. — (Penguin education)
Index.
ISBN 0-14-080969-4 Pbk : £1.75
(B77-09529)

309.1'41'083 — Great Britain. Social conditions, ca 1905-ca 1940. *Marxist viewpoints. Essays*
Trotsky, Leon. Collected writings and speeches on Britain / [by] Leon Trotsky. — London : New Park Publications.
In 3 vols.
Vol.1 / [translated from the Russian] ; edited by R. Chappell and Alan Clinton. — 1974. — iii-xxiii,236p ; 21cm.
Cover title: Trotsky's writings on Britain. — Index. — Contents: History and culture - The decline of British imperialism, 1908-1926 - The labour movement, 1906-1924.
ISBN 0-902030-60-4 Pbk : £1.65
(B77-03396)

309.1'41'085 — Great Britain. Social conditions, 1952-1977
Colville, John Rupert. The new Elizabethans, 1952-1977 / [by] John Colville. — London : Collins, 1977. — 319p ; 24cm.
Index.
ISBN 0-00-216241-5 : £6.50
(B77-14578)

309.1'41'0856 — Great Britain. Social conditions, ca 1965-ca 1975. Compared with social conditions in Northern Ireland, ca 1965-ca 1975
Evason, Eileen. Poverty : the facts in Northern Ireland / [by] Eileen Evason. — London : Child Poverty Action Group, 1976. — 48p : maps ; 21cm. — (Poverty pamphlet ; 27 ISSN 0308-647x)
ISBN 0-903963-33-7 Sd : £0.70
Primary classification 309.1'416'0823
(B77-00625)

309.1'41'0857 — Great Britain. Social conditions
Irwin, John, *b.1942.* Modern Britain : an introduction / [by] John Irwin. — London : Allen and Unwin, 1976. — 173p ; 23cm.
Bibl.: p.167-170. — Index.
ISBN 0-04-301079-2 : £4.25
ISBN 0-04-301080-6 Pbk : £2.75
(B77-00048)

Roberts, Joe. Up the middle / by Joe Roberts. — [Daventry etc.] ([Braunston, Daventry, Northants.]) : [Merryhill Publishing], [1977]. — [5],181,[2]p ; 19cm.
Index.
ISBN 0-9505464-0-2 Pbk : £0.95
(B77-15107)

Walker, Peter, *b.1932.* The ascent of Britain / [by] Peter Walker. — London : Sidgwick and Jackson, 1977. — 224p,[8]p of plates : ports ; 23cm.
Index.
ISBN 0-283-98338-8 : £5.50
(B77-18572)

309.1'41'0857 — Great Britain. Social conditions. *Conservative and Unionist Party viewpoints*
Conservative and Unionist Party. The right approach : a statement of Conservative aims / [Conservative and Unionist Party]. — London : Conservative Central Office, 1976. — 71p ; 21cm.
ISBN 0-85071-028-6 Sd : £0.25
(B77-08797)

309.1'41'0857 — Great Britain. Social conditions. *Serials*
Britain : an official handbook / prepared by the Central Office of Information. — London : H.M.S.O.
1977. — 1977. — ix,509p,[24]p of plates : ill(chiefly col), geneal table, maps, col ports ; 25cm.
Fold. plate (col. map) attached to back lining paper. — Bibl.: p.452-473. — Index.
ISBN 0-11-700793-5 : £6.00
(B77-10741)

309.1'41'0857 — Great Britain. Social conditions, 1975-1977. *Lectures, speeches*
Thatcher, Margaret. Let our children grow tall : selected speeches, 1975-1977 / [by] Margaret Thatcher. — London (Wilfred St., S.W.1) : Centre for Policy Studies, 1977. — viii,114p, plate : ports ; 22cm.
ISBN 0-905880-06-4 : £4.95
ISBN 0-905880-05-6 Pbk : £2.95
(B77-31712)

309.1'41'0857 — Great Britain. Social conditions. Mathematical models. *Case studies*
Projects in economic and social statistics / edited by David G. Mayes. — [Exeter] : University of Exeter, 1976. — [5],141p : ill ; 21cm.
Bibl.
ISBN 0-85989-046-5 Pbk : £1.00
(B77-21715)

309.1'41'0857 — Great Britain. Social conditions. Projects. *Secondary school texts*
Nixon, Brian. Focus on the community / [by] Brian Nixon ; illustrated by John Light. — London : University Tutorial Press.
In 2 vols.
Book 1. — 1977. — [4],92p,fold plate : ill(some col), forms, col maps, plans ; 25cm.
ISBN 0-7231-0720-3 Pbk : £1.10
(B77-24023)

Book 2. — 1977. — [4],108p : ill(some col), chart, forms, maps(chiefly col), plans ; 25cm.
ISBN 0-7231-0721-1 Pbk : £1.20
(B77-24024)

309.1'41'0857 — Great Britain. Society. *Secondary school texts*
Hebden, Ralph. The world we live in / [by] Ralph Hebden and Kenneth Wilkinson. — London : Muller.
In 3 vols.
Book 2 : The world of today. — 1976. — 62p : ill(chiefly col), col maps, col plans ; 23cm.
Index.
ISBN 0-584-64412-4 : £2.25
(B77-08798)

Book 3 : The world of the past. — 1976. — 62p : ill(some col), maps, col plan ; 23cm.
Index.
ISBN 0-584-64413-2 : £2.25
(B77-08799)

Individual and society / editorial Margaret Jarvie ... [et al.]. — London : Heinemann Educational [for] Inner London Education Authority, Learning Materials Service, 1977. — 1v. : ill(some col), facsims, col map, port ; 22x31cm. — (You in the seventies)
Teacher's notes ([2]p.), 8 worksheets (16p.), 10 discussion sheets ([39]p.) in folder.
ISBN 0-435-46561-9 : £2.00
(B77-14075)

309.1'41'0857 — Great Britain. Society, 1970-1976. Theories
Briggs, Harold William. Building a society fit for drop-outs to live in / by Harold W. Briggs. — Reading (118 Dee Rd, Tilehurst, Reading RG3 4BL) : RORETT Press, 1977. — [2],63p ; 20cm.
Sd : £0.35
(B77-28410)

309.1'41'0857 — Great Britain. Urban regions. Social conditions. Surveys: Quality of Life survey: (urban Britain, 1973). Use. *Manuals*
Research Services Limited. Quality of life survey : (urban Britain, 1973) / [prepared by Research Services Ltd for the] SSRC Survey Unit. — London (Fifth Floor, 83 Kingsway, W.C.1) : S.S.R.C. Survey Unit.
Vol.1 : Distribution of responses and questionnaire / [by] John Hall ... [et al.]. — [1976]. — [5]p,50 leaves,[28]p : forms ; 30cm. — (Users manual)
Cover title.
ISBN 0-900296-54-2 Pbk : £1.50
(B77-11597)

309.1'411 — Scotland. Social conditions, 1600-1900
Comparative aspects of Scottish and Irish economic and social history, 1600-1900 / edited by L.M. Cullen & T.C. Smout. — Edinburgh : Donald, [1977]. — viii,252p : ill, map ; 24cm.
Proceedings of a seminar held in Dublin in September 1976. — Index.
ISBN 0-85976-017-0 : £10.00
Also classified at 309.1'415
(B77-22376)

309.1'411 — Scotland. Social conditions, 1652-1914. *Festschriften*
Scottish themes : essays in honour of Professor S.G.E. Lythe / edited by John Butt & J.T. Ward. — Edinburgh (33 Montgomery St., Edinburgh EH7 5JX) : Scottish Academic Press, 1976. — xvi,189p,leaf of plate,[16]p of plates : ill, port ; 26cm.
Bibl.: p.xv-xvi. — Index.
ISBN 0-7073-0125-4 : £5.00
(B77-02065)

309.1'411'073 — Scotland. Social conditions, 1760-1820. *Secondary school texts. Teaching kits*
Changing life in Scotland, 1760-1820 / [edited by] Andrew Forrester, Michael Moss ; [contributors] Ian Adams ... [et al.]. — London : Heinemann Educational, 1977. — 1v. : ill(some col), facsims, maps, ports ; 25cm. — (History broadsheets)
Fifteen folders ([60]p.), 8 sheets ([16]sides) in plastic envelope.
ISBN 0-435-31641-9 : £1.80
(B77-26138)

309.1'411'0857 — Scotland. Social conditions
The **future** of Scotland / edited by Robert Underwood. — London : Croom Helm [for] the Nevis Institute, 1977. — 181p : ill, map ; 23cm.

Index.
ISBN 0-85664-476-5 : £5.95 : CIP rev.
ISBN 0-85664-695-4 Pbk : £2.95
(B77-11598)

309.1'411'0857 — Scotland. Social conditions. *Secondary school texts*
Ness, Tom. Scotland's people : where they live and work / by Tom Ness. — 3rd ed. — London : Heinemann Educational, 1976. — [4], 43p : ill, maps ; 19x22cm. — (Contemporary Scotland ; 6)
Previous ed.: 1974. — Bibl.: p.43.
ISBN 0-435-34198-7 Sd : £0.75
(B77-03961)

309.1'4111'0857 — Northern Scotland. Social conditions. Research. *Directories*
North of Scotland register of research in the social sciences / [edited by R.S. Moore, R.J. Ardern]. — 2nd ed. — [Aberdeen] : Department of Sociology, University of Aberdeen ; [Inverness] : Highlands and Islands Development Board, 1976 [i.e. 1977]. — [6], 41p : map ; 30cm.
Limited ed. of 400 copies. — Previous ed.: 1974. — Index.
Sd : Unpriced
(B77-13521)

309.1'4113'50857 — Scotland. Shetland. Social conditions. Effects of exploitation of petroleum deposits in North Sea
The **Shetland** way of oil : reactions of a small community to big business / edited by John Button. — Sandwick (Sandwick, Shetland) : Thuleprint Ltd, 1976. — 134p : ill, maps ; 21cm.
Bibl.: p.131-134. — Index.
Pbk : £2.40
(B77-16205)

309.1'4116'5 — Estates. *Scotland. Highland Region. Sutherland (District). Sutherland Estates. Social conditions, 1780-1830*
The **Sutherland** clearances, 1806-1820 : a documentary survey / editor David Forbes. — Ayr ([Ayr KA8 0SR]) : Craigie College of Education, 1976. — [2],52,[1]p : ill, maps ; 30cm.
Bibl.: p.51-52.
ISBN 0-903369-03-6 Sp : £0.30
(B77-11599)

309.1'414'43081 — Scotland. Strathclyde Region. Glasgow. Social conditions, 1875-1975
Checkland, Sydney George. The upas tree : Glasgow 1875-1975 : a study in growth and contraction / [by] S.G. Checkland ; with eight illustrations by Muirhead Bone. — [Glasgow] : University of Glasgow Press, 1976. — xi,124p, 8p of plates : ill, maps ; 21cm.
Bibl.: p.103-109. — Index.
ISBN 0-85261-133-1 Pbk : £2.75
(B77-03962)

309.1'415 — Ireland. Social conditions, 1600-1900
Comparative aspects of Scottish and Irish economic and social history, 1600-1900 / edited by L.M. Cullen & T.C. Smout. — Edinburgh : Donald, [1977]. — viii,252p : ill, map ; 24cm.
Proceedings of a seminar held in Dublin in September 1976. — Index.
ISBN 0-85976-017-0 : £10.00
Primary classification 309.1'411
(B77-22376)

309.1'415'081 — Ireland. Social conditions, 1845-1848. *Secondary school texts*
Speed, Peter Frederick. The potato famine and the Irish emigrants / [by] P.F. Speed ; illustrated from contemporary sources. — London : Longman, 1976. — 96p : ill, facsim, map, ports ; 20cm. — (Then and there series)
ISBN 0-582-21721-0 Pbk : £0.50
(B77-07084)

309.1'416'0823 — Northern Ireland. Social conditions, ca 1965-ca 1975. Compared with social conditions in Great Britain, ca 1965-ca 1975
Evason, Eileen. Poverty : the facts in Northern Ireland / [by] Eileen Evason. — London : Child Poverty Action Group, 1976. — 48p : maps ; 21cm. — (Poverty pamphlet ; 27 ISSN 0308-647x)
ISBN 0-903963-33-7 Sd : £0.70
Also classified at 309.1'41'0856
(B77-00625)

309.1'416'0824 — Northern Ireland. Social conditions. *Serials*
The **Ulster** year book : the official handbook of Northern Ireland. — Belfast : H.M.S.O.
1976. — 1976. — xiv,314p,[12]p of plates, fold leaf of plate : ill, col map ; 25cm.
Bibl.: p.290-304. — Index.
ISBN 0-337-01026-9 Pbk : £2.50
(B77-07085)

309.1'416'7081 — Belfast. Social conditions, 1780-1870. *Readings from contemporary sources*
Problems of a growing city : Belfast, 1780-1870. — [Belfast] ([66 Balmoral Ave., Belfast BT9 6NY]) : Public Record Office of Northern Ireland, [1973]. — xxi,245,[13]p : maps, plan ; 30cm.
Cover title. — Index. — Includes facsimile reprints.
Pbk : £1.50
(B77-17314)

309.1'417'0824 — Ireland (Republic). Society. *Primary school texts*
Ó Loingsigh, Colm. Illustrated civics / [by] Colm Ó Loingsigh. — Dublin : Educational Company of Ireland.
2. — 1977. — [6],102p : ill, maps, music, ports ; 19x21cm.
Sd : £0.99
(B77-20043)

309.1'42 — Cities. Inner areas. Social conditions. *England. Reports, surveys*
Liverpool, Birmingham and Lambeth : summaries of consultants' final reports / [for the] Department of the Environment. — London : H.M.S.O., 1977. — [5],49p : maps ; 25cm. — (Inner area studies)
ISBN 0-11-751135-8 Sd : £1.50
(B77-12320)

309.1'42 — England. Metropolitan regions. Inner areas. Social conditions. *Reports,surveys*
Great Britain. *Department of the Environment.* Study of the inner areas of conurbations / [Department of the Environment]. — [London] ([Room 638, Church House, Great Smith St., SW1P 3BL]) : [Department of the Environment, Eastern Regional Directorate, Strategic Planning Division].
Supplement. Analysis of 1971 census indicators. — 1975. — [1],4,72[i.e.80]p : maps, plans ; 30cm.
Cover title.
Pbk : Unpriced (private circulation)
(B77-31713)

309.1'42'03 — England. Social conditions, 1100-1450. *Readings*
Peasants, knights and heretics : studies in medieval English social history / edited by R.H. Hilton. — Cambridge [etc.] : Cambridge University Press, 1976. — vi,330p ; 22cm. — ('Past and present' publications)
Index.
ISBN 0-521-21276-6 : £5.00
(B77-02788)

309.1'42'07 — England. Social conditions, 1780-1835
Clarke, John, *b.1947.* The price of progress : Cobbett's England, 1780-1835 / [by] John Clarke. — London [etc.] : Hart-Davis MacGibbon, 1977. — vii,200p,[16]p of plates : ill, facsim, map, ports ; 23cm.
Bibl.: p.194-195. — Index.
ISBN 0-246-10604-2 : £6.95
(B77-29968)

309.1'42'07 — England. Social conditions, 1800-1976
Ryder, Judith. Modern English society / [by] Judith Ryder & Harold Silver. — 2nd ed., revised and with additions. — London : Methuen, 1977. — xvii,390p : ill, ports ; 21cm.
Previous ed.: 1970. — Bibl.: p.361-376. — Index.
ISBN 0-416-55490-3 : £6.75
ISBN 0-416-55500-4 Pbk : £3.95
(B77-28411)

309.1'42'081 — England. Rural regions. Social conditions, 1837-1901
Mingay, Gordon Edmund. Rural life in Victorian England / by G.E. Mingay. — London : Heinemann, 1977. — 212p : ill, facsims ; 23cm.
Bibl.: p.200-204. — Index.
ISBN 0-434-46750-2 : £5.95
(B77-03963)

309.1'42'0857 — England. Urban regions. Social conditions. Effects of industrial development. *Case studies*
Community Development Project *(Great Britain).* The costs of industrial change / CDP. — London (5 Tavistock Place, WC1H 9SS) : CDP Inter-Project Editorial Team, 1977. — 96p : ill, facsims, maps, ports ; 26cm.
Sd : £0.80
(B77-13522)

309.1'421'0857 — London. Social conditions
Hall, John Martin. London, metropolis and region / [by] John M. Hall. — Oxford [etc.] : Oxford University Press, 1976. — 48p : ill(some col), col maps ; 25cm. — (Problem regions of Europe)
Bibl.: p.48.
ISBN 0-19-913194-5 Pbk : £1.50
(B77-00049)

309.1'421'420857 — London. Camden (London Borough). Social conditions. *Reports, surveys. Serials*
Camden *(London Borough). Town Clerk's Department. Policy Analysis Unit.* Community profile / London Borough of Camden, Town Clerk's Department, Policy Analysis Unit. — [London] ([The Town Hall, Euston Rd, NW1 2RU]) : [The Unit].
1976. — 1976. — [1],v,78p : ill ; 30cm.
ISBN 0-905819-00-4 Sd : Unpriced
(B77-03964)

309.1'422 — Southern England. Social conditions, 800-1500
Hinton, David Alban. Alfred's kingdom : Wessex and the South 800-1500 / [by] David A. Hinton. — London : Dent, 1977. — xii,228p, [16]p of plates : ill, maps, plans ; 24cm. — (History in the landscape series)
Bibl.: p.211-219. — Index.
ISBN 0-460-04289-0 : £5.95 : CIP rev.
(B77-11600)

309.1'422'5607 — East Sussex. Brighton. Social conditions, 1789-1854
Dale, Antony. Brighton town and Brighton people / by Antony Dale. — London [etc.] : Phillimore, 1976. — viii,254p,[12]p of plates : ill, ports ; 23cm.
Index.
ISBN 0-85033-219-2 : £4.95
(B77-00626)

309.1'422'60857 — West Sussex. Social conditions. *Reports, surveys. For structure plan making*
West Sussex *(County). Planning Department.* County structure plan / West Sussex [County Planning Department]. — Chichester ([County Hall, Tower St., Chichester, W. Sussex PO19 1RL]) : [The Department].
General aviation : topic report. — 1976. — [2], iv,49p,[9]fold plates : maps, plans ; 30cm.
ISBN 0-900800-16-x Sp : £0.50
(B77-08242)

Mobility. — 1976. — 100p(4 fold) in various pagings,[8]leaves of plates(8 fold) : ill, maps ; 30cm. — (Topic reports)
ISBN 0-900800-14-3 Sp : £1.00
(B77-03397)

People, homes and jobs : topic report. — 1977. — [1],iv,127[i.e.137]p,fold plate : ill, map ; 31cm.
Sp : Unpriced
(B77-31714)

Recreation and tourism. — 1976. — 84p in various pagings, 6 leaves of plates (6 fold) : maps ; 30cm. — (Topic reports)
Bibl.: p.67-68.
ISBN 0-900800-15-1 Sp : £0.75
(B77-03398)

Resources : topic report. — 1977. — [1],iii,51p, [3]fold leaves of plates : ill, maps ; 31cm.
ISBN 0-900800-20-8 Sp : £0.75
(B77-33632)

The countryside. — 1976. — 86p in various pagings,[7]leaves of plates(7 fold) : ill, maps ; 31cm. — (Topic reports)
Bibl.: p.71-73.
ISBN 0-900800-13-5 Sp : £1.00
(B77-03399)

309.1'423'50857 — Devon. Social conditions. *Reports, surveys. For structure plan making*
Devon *(County). Planning Department.* County structure plan, report of the survey / Planning Department, Devon County Council. — Exeter (County Hall, Topsham Rd, Exeter EX2 4QH) : The Council, 1977. — 3-183p,fold plate : col ill, maps(chiefly col) ; 30cm.
Pbk : £2.00
(B77-20934)

309.1'423'70857 — Cornwall. Social conditions. *Reports, surveys. For structure plan making*
Cornwall *(County). Planning Department.* County structure plan, policy choice consultation document / Cornwall County Council [Planning Department]. — [Truro] ([County Hall, Truro, Cornwall TR1 3AY]) : [The Department], 1976. — [5],157[i.e.167]p : ill, maps ; 30cm.
ISBN 0-902319-12-4 Sp : Unpriced
(B77-04586)

309.1'423'70857 — Cornwall. Social conditions, 1971-1976. *Essays*
Whetter, James. Cornish essays, 1971-76 = Scryvow Kernewek, 1971-76 / by James Whetter. — [St Austell] ([Trelispen, Gorran, St Austell, Cornwall]) : [C.N.P. Publications], [1977]. — [8],148p : ill, map ; 21cm.
ISBN 0-906009-00-6 Sd : £1.80
(B77-26824)

309.1'423'91 — Avon. Frome Valley. Social conditions, to 1973. *Secondary school texts*
Morris, George Reginald. The mid Frome Valley : an environmental study of the areas of Mangotsfield, Soundwell, Staple Hill, Downend, Frenchay, Winterbourne, Hambrook, Frampton Cotterell / by George R. Morris with contributions by ... [others]. — Bristol (82 Bromley Heath Rd, Downend, Bristol BS16 6JT) : The author.
A supplement concerning contrasts, space relations, topography and place names, coal mining and land utilization. — 1976. — [4], 17p : ill ; 30cm.
ISBN 0-9503251-1-2 Sd : £0.20
(B77-03400)

309.1'424'10857 — Gloucestershire. Social conditions. *For structure plan making*

Gloucestershire *(County). Planning Department.* Gloucestershire county structure plan, the problems? : a background report presenting for public consideration the problems suggested for investigation by the structure plan / [Gloucestershire County Planning Department]. — [Gloucester] ([Shire Hall, Gloucester GL1 2TN]) : [The Department], 1976. — [3],59p : ill ; 30cm.
Sd : Unpriced
(B77-28412)

309.1'425'30857 — Lincolnshire. Social conditions. *Reports, surveys. For structure plan making*

Lincolnshire *(County). Planning Department.* Settlement : a background paper to the Lincolnshire structure plan / [Lincolnshire County Planning Department]. — [Lincoln] ([County Offices, Lincoln LN1 1YJ]) : [The Department], 1976. — 68p : maps, plans ; 30cm.
Cover title: Lincolnshire Structure Plan : background paper, settlement.
ISBN 0-906001-00-5 Sp : £0.90
(B77-14579)

309.1'425'450857 — Leicestershire. Rutland (District). Social conditions. *Reports, surveys. For structure plan making*

Leicestershire *(County). Planning Department.* Structure plan for Rutland, report of survey / [Leicestershire County Planning Department]. — Leicester (County Hall, Glenfield, Leicester [LE3 8RA]) : [The Department], 1977. — [5], 144p,plate : ill, maps, plans ; 31cm.
Sp : £2.50
(B77-31002)

309.1'425'820857 — Households. Social conditions. *Hertfordshire. Stevenage, 1976. Reports, surveys*

Stevenage Development Corporation. Stevenage Household Survey, March 1976 / [Stevenage Development Corporation]. — [Stevenage] ([Daneshill House, Danestrete, Stevenage, Herts. SG1 1XD]) : The Corporation, [1976]. — 79 leaves(9 fold) in various pagings,[9]fold leaves of plates : ill, maps ; 30cm.
Sd : £2.00
(B77-29208)

309.1'425'90857 — Buckinghamshire. Social conditions. *Reports, surveys. For structure plan making*

Buckinghamshire *(County). Council.* Buckinghamshire county structure plan 1976, report of survey / [Buckinghamshire County Council]. — [Aylesbury] ([County Hall, Aylesbury, Bucks.]) : County Planning Department, [1976]. — [13],312,xi p,fold plate : ill, maps, plans ; 30cm.
ISBN 0-902805-84-3 Sp : £4.50
(B77-15706)

309.1'426'50857 — Cambridgeshire. Social conditions. *Reports, surveys. For structure plan making*

Cambridgeshire *(County). Planning Department.* Cambridgeshire structure plan, report of survey, consultation draft / [Cambridgeshire County Planning Department]. — Cambridge (Shire Hall, Cambridge) : [Cambridgeshire County Council], 1976. — [7],160p,[5]leaves : ill(some col), maps(chiefly col) ; 30cm.
ISBN 0-902436-15-5 Sp : £1.50
(B77-11089)

309.1'426'756 — Essex. Althorne. Social conditions. *Reports, surveys. For structure plan making*

Maldon *(District). Council.* Althorne plan, consultation / Maldon District Council. — [Maldon] ([Council Offices, Maldon, Essex]) : [The Council], [1977]. — [6]leaves,30[i.e.42]p,7 leaves of plates : ill, maps ; 21x30cm.
ISBN 0-901084-06-9 Sp : £0.50
(B77-12321)

309.1'426'756 — Essex. Cold Norton. Social conditions. *Reports, surveys. For structure plan making*

Maldon *(District). Council.* Cold Norton village plan, consultation / Maldon District Council. — Maldon (Council Offices, Maldon, Essex) : The Council, [1976]. — [7],52p : ill, maps ; 21x30cm.
ISBN 0-901084-07-7 Sp : £0.50
(B77-12322)

309.1'426'756 — Essex. Mayland region. Social conditions. *Reports, surveys. For structure plan making*

Maldon *(District). Council.* Mayland and Maylandsea district plan / Maldon District Council. — [Maldon] ([Council Offices, Maldon, Essex]) : [The Council], [1977]. — [6], 20p : col plan ; 21x30cm.
Plan on fold leaf in pocket.
ISBN 0-901084-09-3 Sp : £1.50
(B77-12323)

Maldon *(District). Council.* Mayland and Maylandsea village plan, consultation / Maldon District Council. — [Maldon] ([Council Offices, Maldon, Essex]) : [The Council], [1977]. — [49] leaves,7[i.e.6]leaves of plates : ill, maps, plan ; 22x30cm.
ISBN 0-901084-08-5 Sp : £0.50
(B77-12324)

309.1'426'756 — Essex. Tollesbury. Social conditions. *Reports, surveys. For structure plan making*

Maldon *(District). Council.* Tollesbury plan, consultation / Maldon District Council. — [Maldon] ([Council Offices, Maldon, Essex]) : [The Council], [1977]. — [6],52[i.e. 73]leaves : ill, maps, plans ; 21x30cm.
ISBN 0-901084-10-7 Sp : £0.50
(B77-14076)

309.1'426'7560857 — Essex. Maldon (District). Social conditions. *Reports, surveys. For structure plan making*

Maldon *(District). Council.* Maldon District study / Maldon District Council. — [Maldon] ([Council Offices, Maldon, Essex]) : [The Council].
[1] : [Population]. — [1977]. — [5],31[i.e.33]p, [12]leaves of plates : ill, maps ; 21x30cm.
ISBN 0-901084-01-8 Sp : £0.75
(B77-12325)

[2] : [Housing]. — [1977]. — [54]p : ill, 2 maps ; 21x30cm.
Versos of some leaves blank.
ISBN 0-901084-02-6 Sp : £0.75
(B77-12326)

[3] : [Public utilities and services]. — [1977]. — [5],19p,[2]leaves of plates : 2 maps ; 21x30cm.
ISBN 0-901084-03-4 Sp : £0.50
(B77-12327)

[4] : [Agriculture]. — [1977]. — [6],23[i.e.25]p, 4 leaves of plates : maps ; 21x30cm.
ISBN 0-901084-04-2 Sp : £0.50
(B77-12328)

[5] : [Employment and industry]. — [1977]. — [2],ii leaves,45,[1]p,[17]leaves of plates : maps, plans ; 21x30cm.
Bibl.: p.45.
ISBN 0-901084-05-0 Sp : £0.85
(B77-12329)

309.1'427'0857 — North-west England. Social conditions. *For industrial development*

North West Industrial Development Association. North West England - the facts / North West Industrial Development Association. — Manchester (Brazennose House, Brazennose St., Manchester M2 5AZ) : The Association, [1977]. — [2],20,[2]p(2 fold) : ill(some col), col maps ; 30cm.
Sd : Unpriced
(B77-17315)

309.1'427'84 — Cumbria. Cleator Moor. Social conditions, 1840-1960

Barber, Ross. Iron ore and after : boom time, depression and survival in a West Cumbrian town, Cleator Moor, 1840-1960 / researched and written by Ross Barber ; photographs prepared by Joseph Campbell ; drawings by Joanna Pearce. — York ([c/o The Public Library, Cleator Moor, Cumbria]) : York University [for] Cleator Moor Local Studies Group, 1976. — [4],71p : ill, facsims, maps, ports ; 21x30cm.
Bibl.: p.70-71.
Pbk : £1.50
(B77-17316)

309.1'428'0857 — England. Pennines. Social conditions. *Reports, surveys*

The **Pennine** uplands : socio-economic interactions and opportunities in the Yorkshire Pennines. — London : H.M.S.O. for the Department of the Environment, 1976. — vi, 139p : ill, col maps ; 30cm.
This volume is the result of a study carried out on behalf of a number of government departments and local authorities, based on the Research Group of the Yorkshire and Humberside Economic Planning Board. — Bibl. : p.119-120.
ISBN 0-11-751006-8 Pbk : £8.00
(B77-01186)

309.1'428'1082 — West Yorkshire (Metropolitan County). Social conditions, 1890-1930

Hartley, Marie. Life & tradition in West Yorkshire / by Marie Hartley and Joan Ingilby. — London : Dent, 1976. — 160p,[48]p of plates : ill, maps, ports ; 25cm.
Index.
ISBN 0-460-04239-4 : £7.50
(B77-00050)

309.1'428'207 — South Yorkshire (Metropolitan County). Social conditions, 1700-1975

Essays in the economic and social history of South Yorkshire / edited by Sidney Pollard and Colin Holmes ; with an introduction by Sidney Pollard. — [Barnsley] ([County Council Offices, 70 Vernon Rd, Worsbrough Bridge, Barnsley, S. Yorkshire]) : South Yorkshire County Council, Recreation, Culture and Health Department, 1976. — 308p : map ; 21cm.
Index.
ISBN 0-86046-000-2 Pbk : £2.50
(B77-13523)

309.1'428'70857 — Tyne and Wear (Metropolitan County). Social conditions. *Reports, surveys. For structure plan making*

Tyne and Wear *(Metropolitan County). Planning Department.* Structure plan, summary report of survey / [Tyne and Wear County Council, Planning Department]. — [Newcastle upon Tyne] ([Sandyford House, Newcastle upon Tyne NE2 1ED]) : The Council, 1976. — [1],36p : ill, maps ; 30cm.
Sd : Unpriced
(B77-00627)

Tyne and Wear *(Metropolitan County). Planning Department.* Tyne and Wear County Council structure plan, report of survey / [Tyne and Wear County Council, Planning Department]. — [Newcastle upon Tyne] ([Sandyford House, Newcastle upon Tyne NE2 1ED]) : The Council, 1976. — [12],293[i.e.300]p,[4]leaves, [59]leaves of plates (10 fold) : col ill, maps(chiefly col) ; 30cm.
'Tyne and Wear County Council structure plan, what's in it for us?' (8p.: col. ill., form. Sd) as insert.
Sp : £4.50
(B77-00628)

309.1'428'760857 — Households. Social conditions. *Tyne and Wear (Metropolitan County). Newcastle upon Tyne, 1975. Reports, surveys*

Urban trends : a report on the Newcastle upon Tyne Household Survey. — [Newcastle upon Tyne] ([Civic Centre, Barras Bridge, Newcastle upon Tyne NE99 2BM]) : [Newcastle upon Tyne Metropolitan District Council].
1975. — [1977]. — [10],85p : ill, forms, maps ; 30cm.
Bibl.: p.[10].
ISBN 0-902653-02-4 Sd : £2.50
(B77-16206)

309.1'429'0857 — Wales. Social conditions. *Reports, surveys*

Wilding, Paul. Poverty : the facts in Wales / [by] Paul Wilding. — London : Child Poverty Action Group, 1977. — [4],62p : map ; 21cm. — (Poverty pamphlet ; 29 ISSN 0306-1868)
Sd : £0.70
(B77-33633)

309.1'429'0857 — Wales. Social conditions. Research sponsored by Great Britain. Welsh Office. *Reports, surveys. Serials*

Great Britain. *Welsh Office.* Ymchwil, Cymru = Research, Wales / Y Swyddfa Gymreig = Welsh Office. — Cardiff : H.M.S.O.
1976-77 : Pedwerydd adroddiad = Fourth report. — 1977. — 24p ; 30cm.
English text, English and Welsh introductory material.
ISBN 0-11-790097-4 Sd : £1.25
(B77-31715)

309.1'43 — Social systems. Analysis. Methodology. *Study regions: West Germany*
Laumann, Edward Otto. Networks of collective action : a perspective on community influence systems / [by] Edward O. Laumann, Franz U. Pappi. — New York [etc.] ; London : Academic Press, 1976. — xx,329p : ill ; 24cm. — (Quantitative studies in social relations)
Bibl.: p.299-318. — Index.
ISBN 0-12-437850-1 : £10.45
(B77-00051)

309.1'43'1087 — East Germany. Social conditions, 1945-1976
Steele, Jonathan. Socialism with a German face : the state that came in from the cold / [by] Jonathan Steele. — London : Cape, 1977. — xiv,256p ; 23cm.
Index.
ISBN 0-224-01348-3 : £6.95
(B77-24026)

309.1'44 — France. Rural regions. Social conditions, to 1974. *Readings*
Rural society in France : selections from the 'Annales, économies, sociétés, civilisations' / edited by Robert Forster and Orest Ranum ; translated [from the French] by Elborg Forster and Patricia M. Ranum. — Baltimore ; London : Johns Hopkins University Press, 1977. — xv,180p ; 24cm.
ISBN 0-8018-1916-4 : £9.35
ISBN 0-8018-1917-2 Pbk : £2.80
(B77-28413)

309.1'45'32 — Italy. Veneto. Arqua. Social conditions, to 1970
Evans, Robert H. Life and politics in a Venetian community / [by] Robert H. Evans. — Notre Dame, Ind. ; London : University of Notre Dame Press, 1976. — ii-xxi,228p,[18]p of plates : ill, map, plan, port ; 21cm. — (University of Notre Dame. Committee on International Relations. International studies)
Bibl.: p.217-222. — Index.
ISBN 0-268-01256-3 : £12.00
(B77-25408)

309.1'46'7082 — Spain. Catalonia. Rural regions. Social conditions, 1939-1970
Hansen, Edward Charles. Rural Catalonia under the Franco regime : the fate of regional culture since the Spanish Civil War / [by] Edward C. Hansen. — Cambridge [etc.] : Cambridge University Press, 1977. — x,182p : ill, maps ; 24cm.
Bibl.: p.176-178. — Index.
ISBN 0-521-21457-2 : £8.00
(B77-31003)

309.1'47 — Eastern Europe. Social conditions. *Polish texts*
Brzeziński, Zbigniew Kazimierz. System międzynarodowy napięcia i przemiany / Zbigniew Brzeziński. — Londyn [i.e. London] ([27 Hamilton Rd, Bedford Park, W4 1AL]) : Odnowa, 1976. — 20p ; 22cm. — (Polska w świecie współczesnym ; zesz.3)
ISBN 0-903705-13-3 Sd : £1.00
(B77-09530)

309.1'47'0842 — Soviet Union. Social conditions, 1926-1929
Carr, Edward Hallett. Foundations of a planned economy, 1926-1929 / by Edward Hallett Carr and R.W. Davies. — London [etc.] : Macmillan. — (Carr, Edward Hallett. History of Soviet Russia)
Vol.3. [Part] 1 / by Edward Hallett Carr. — 1976. — x,313p ; 23cm.
ISBN 0-333-13204-1 : £15.00
(B77-02067)

Vol.3. [Part] 2 / by Edward Hallett Carr. — 1976. — [4]p,p315-644 ; 23cm.
ISBN 0-333-19270-2 : £15.00
(B77-02066)

309.1'47'085 — Soviet Union. Social conditions. *Extracts from periodicals. Russian texts*
Dvadtsatyĭ vek : obshchestvenno-politicheskiĭ i literaturnyĭ al'manakh : izbrannye materialy iz samizdatnogo zhurnala 'XX-ĭ vek'. — London : T.C.D. Publications ; London : Distributed by Orbis Books.
No.1-. — 1976-. — 19cm.
Published at irregular intervals. — Second title page has English title 'The twentieth century'. — 237p. in 1st issue. — Selected material from the 'Samizdat' magazine 'XX-ĭ vek'. Moskva, 1975-.
Pbk : £3.00
ISSN 0308-1486
(B77-06494)

309.1'471 — Finland. Social conditions, 1967-1972. *Case studies*
Lander, Patricia Slade. In the shadow of the factory : social change in a Finnish community / [by] Patricia Slade Lander. — Cambridge, Mass. : Schenkman ; New York ; London [etc.] : Distributed by Wiley, 1976. — xii,191p : ill, maps ; 24cm.
'A Halsted Press Book'. — Bibl.: p.183-186. — Index.
ISBN 0-470-01379-6 : £9.95
ISBN 0-470-01380-x Pbk : £4.20
(B77-06495)

309.1'5 — Asia. Society. Theories of Marx, Karl
Melotti, Umberto. Marx and the Third World / [by] Umberto Melotti ; translated [from the Italian] by Pat Ransford ; edited with a foreword by Malcolm Caldwell. — London [etc.] : Macmillan, 1977. — x,222p ; 23cm.
Translation of: 'Marx e il Terzo mondo'. Milano : Centro studi Terzo mondo, 1931. — Bibl.: p.213-218. — Index.
ISBN 0-333-18981-7 : £8.95
ISBN 0-333-19817-4 Pbk : £3.95
(B77-26114)

309.1'51'05 — China. Social conditions
Ascher, Isaac. China's social policy / [by] Isaac Ascher. — [2nd ed.]. — London (152 Camden High St., NW1 0NE) : Anglo-Chinese Educational Institute, 1976. — [5],iii,79,[1]p : map ; 21cm. — (Modern China series ; no.3 ISSN 0309-0639)
Previous ed.: 1972. — Bibl.: p.71-73. — Index.
ISBN 0-903193-08-6 Sd : £0.60
(B77-02068)

309.1'51'25 — Hong Kong. Social conditions. *Reports, surveys. Serials*
Hong Kong, report for the year. — Hong Kong : Hong Kong Government Press ; London : H.M.S.O. for the Foreign and Commonwealth Office.
1975. — 1976. — iii-vi,256p,[82]p of plates : col ill, col coat of arms, col facsims, col maps(on lining papers), col ports ; 25cm.
Spine title: Hong Kong 1976. — Index.
Unpriced
(B77-16207)

309.1'51'7305 — Mongolia (People's Republic). Social conditions
Mongolia. — London (40 Kensington Place, W8 7PR) : Diplomatist Publications, 1976. — [2], 26p : ill(some col), col coat of arms, col map, ports(1 col) ; 22cm.
ISBN 0-900026-02-2 Sd : Unpriced
(B77-00052)

309.1'52'04 — Japan. Social conditions, 1945-1975
Norbeck, Edward. Changing Japan / by Edward Norbeck. — 2nd ed. — New York ; London [etc.] : Holt, Rinehart and Winston, 1976. — xiv,108p,[2]p of plates : ill, map ; 24cm. — (Case studies in cultural anthropology)
Previous ed.: 1965. — Bibl.: p.107-108.
ISBN 0-03-017546-1 Pbk : £2.50
(B77-03965)

309.1'52'135 — Japan. Tokyo. Shitayama-cho. Social conditions, 1951
Dore, Ronald. City life in Japan : a study of a Tokyo ward / by R.P. Dore. — Berkeley [etc.] ; London : University of California Press, 1973. — viii,472p,[8]p of plates : ill, plans ; 21cm.
Originally published: London : Routledge and Kegan Paul, 1958. — Index.
ISBN 0-520-00341-1 : £7.20
ISBN 0-520-00344-6 Pbk : £3.10
(B77-17317)

309.1'53'5 — United Arab Emirates. Social conditions, to 1975
Fenelon, Kevin Gerard. The United Arab Emirates : an economic and social survey / [by] K.G. Fenelon. — 2nd ed. — London [etc.] : Longman, 1976. — [6],164p : maps ; 24cm.
Map on lining papers. — Previous ed.: 1973. — Bibl.: p.157. — Index.
ISBN 0-582-78066-7 : £4.75
(B77-03966)

309.1'53'605 — Arabia. Gulf States. Social conditions. Effects of petroleum industries
Osborne, Christine. The Gulf States and Oman / text and photographs [by] Christine Osborne. — London : Croom Helm, 1977. — 208p,24p of plates : ill(some col), maps, ports(some col) ; 23cm.
Bibl.: p.205-206. — Index.
ISBN 0-85664-515-x : £7.95 : CIP rev.
(B77-19235)

309.1'54'05 — India (Republic). Social conditions. *Essays*
Mitra, Ashok. Calcutta diary / [by] Ashok Mitra. — London [etc.] : Cass, 1977. — xiii, 206p ; 23cm.
'Many of [these] pieces ... have appeared as "Calcutta Diary" [in the "Economic and Political Weekly"]' - Introduction.
ISBN 0-7146-3082-9 : £8.50
(B77-23152)

309.1'595'2 — Singapore. Social conditions, to 1975
Singapore, society in transition / edited by Riaz Hassan. — Kuala Lumpur ; London [etc.] : Oxford University Press, 1976. — xix,371p : ill ; 26cm. — (East Asian social science monographs)
Bibl.: p.348-358. — Index.
ISBN 0-19-580352-3 : £14.95
(B77-22377)

309.1'6'03 — Africa. Social conditions
Contemporary Africa : geography and change / edited by C. Gregory Knight, James L. Newman. — Englewood Cliffs ; London : Prentice-Hall, 1976. — xiv,546p : ill, maps ; 24cm.
Bibl.: p.507-530. — Index.
ISBN 0-13-170035-9 : £10.90
(B77-01187)

Kanza, Thomas. Evolution & revolution in Africa / [by] Thomas R. Kanza ; [translated from the French MS. by the author]. — London : Collings, 1971. — 141p ; 19cm.
£1.50
ISBN 0-901720-18-0 Pbk : £0.65
(B77-03967)

309.1'66 — West Africa. Social conditions. *Secondary school texts*
Phillips, Howard. Progress and change in West Africa / [by Howard and Jenifer Phillips]. — London : Longman, 1976. — 49p : ill(chiefly col), col maps, col plan ; 23cm. — (Longman revised colour geographies)
Bibl.: p.49. — Lists of filmstrips: p.49.
ISBN 0-582-20126-8 Sd : £0.85
(B77-09531)

309.1'669'5 — Nigeria. Batagarawa & Dorayi. Social conditions, 1900-1972
Hill, Polly. Population, prosperity and poverty : rural Kano, 1900 and 1970 / [by] Polly Hill. — Cambridge [etc.] : Cambridge University Press, 1977. — xviii,240p : ill, maps, plan ; 24cm.
Bibl.: p.223-228. — Index.
ISBN 0-521-21511-0 : £8.50
(B77-31004)

309.1'67 — Sociology. *Study regions: Africa south of the Sahara. For African students*
Peil, Margaret. Consensus and conflict in African societies : an introduction to sociology / [by] Margaret Peil. — London : Longman, 1977. — xv,396p : ill, maps ; 23cm.
Bibl.: p.362-387. — Index.
ISBN 0-582-64173-x : Unpriced
ISBN 0-582-64174-8 Pbk : £3.50
(B77-29969)

309.1'676'2504 — Kenya. Nairobi. Social conditions
Hake, Andrew. African metropolis : Nairobi's self-help city / by Andrew Hake. — London : Chatto and Windus for Sussex University Press, 1977. — 284p,4p of plates : ill, maps ; 23cm.
Index.
ISBN 0-85621-066-8 : £10.00 : CIP rev.
(B77-08706)

309.1'68'06 — South Africa. Social conditions
Hitchcock, Bob. Flashpoint South Africa / [by] Bob Hitchcock. — London : Hale, 1977. — [4], 212p,[16]p of plates : ill, ports ; 25cm.
ISBN 0-7091-6286-3 : £5.95
(B77-26825)

309.1'68'06 — South Africa. Social conditions. *Reports, surveys*
Caird, George Bradford. South Africa : reflections on a visit / by George B. Caird, John Johansen-Berg. — London : United Reformed Church, 1976. — [2],29p ; 21cm.
ISBN 0-902256-25-4 Sd : £0.50
(B77-02789)

309.1'68'06 — South Africa. Social conditions. Role of British Petroleum Company subsidiaries & Shell UK Oil (Firm) subsidiaries. *Anti-Apartheid Movement viewpoints & Haslemere Group viewpoints*
Bailey, Martin. Shell and BP in South Africa / by Martin Bailey. — London ([c/o] Third World Publications, 151 Stratford Rd, Birmingham) : Haslemere Group ; London : Anti-Apartheid Movement, 1977. — [3],44,[1] p : ill, facsims ; 21cm.
Bibl.: p.44.
Sd : £0.35
(B77-28415)

309.1'689'404 — Zambia. Social conditions. *Marxist viewpoints*
Zambia, humanist rhetoric, capitalist reality. — [London] ([97 Caledonian Rd, N1 9BT]) : International Marxist Group, 1975. — [1],23p : ill, map, ports ; 31cm. — ('Africa in struggle' occasional publication ; no.1)
'... written by a supporter of the Fourth International in Zambia'. — 'An International Marxist Group, Africa Commission publication' - cover.
Sd : £0.35
(B77-02069)

309.1'69'6 — Seychelles Islands. Social conditions
Commonwealth Institute. Seychelles / [Commonwealth Institute]. — London : The Institute, 1977. — [1],7p : col map ; 30cm. — (Commonwealth fact sheet ISSN 0306-3801)
Bibl.: p.7.
Sd : £0.30
(B77-28416)

309.1'71'0644 — Canada. Social conditions
Marchak, M Patricia. Ideological perspectives on Canada / [by] M. Patricia Marchak. — Toronto ; London [etc.] ([McGraw-Hill House, Shoppenhangers Rd, Maidenhead, Berks. SL6 2LQ]) : McGraw-Hill Ryerson Ltd, [1976]. — ix,146p : 2 ill ; 23cm. — (McGraw-Hill Ryerson series in Canadian sociology)
Published in Canada: 1975. — Bibl.: p.121-139. — Index.
ISBN 0-07-082197-6 Pbk : Unpriced
(B77-07086)

309.1'71'0644 — Canada. Society
Issues in Canadian society : an introduction to sociology / [edited by] Dennis Forcese, Stephen Richer. — Scarborough, Ont. ; London [etc.] : Prentice-Hall, 1975[i.e.1976]. — x,517p : ill, maps ; 24cm.
Published in Canada: 1975. — Bibl. — Index.
ISBN 0-13-506360-4 : Unpriced
ISBN 0-13-506352-3 Pbk : Unpriced
(B77-09532)

309.1'7127'402 — Manitoba. Winnipeg. Social conditions, to 1914
Artibise, Alan F J. Winnipeg : a social history of urban growth, 1874-1914 / [by] Alan F.J. Artibise. — Montreal ; London : McGill-Queen's University Press, 1975. — xiv, 382p,[18]p of plates(2 fold) : ill, facsim, maps, plans, ports ; 24cm.
Bibl.: p.361-372. — Index.
ISBN 0-7735-0202-5 : Unpriced
(B77-16744)

309.1'7282 — Belize. Social conditions, to 1871
Bolland, O Nigel. The formation of a colonial society : Belize, from conquest to Crown Colony / [by] O. Nigel Bolland. — Baltimore ; London : Johns Hopkins University Press, 1977. — xvi,240p : geneal tables, map ; 24cm. — (Johns Hopkins studies in Atlantic history and culture)
Bibl.: p.225-234. — Index.
ISBN 0-8018-1887-7 : £13.60
(B77-26139)

309.1'7292'1 — Cayman Islands. Social conditions. *Reports, surveys. Serials*
Cayman Islands : report. — London : H.M.S.O. [for the Foreign and Commonwealth Office]. 1975. — 1976. — [2],97p,fold plate(tipped in) : ill, col map ; 21cm.
Bibl.: p.94-95.
ISBN 0-11-580190-1 Sd : £1.50
(B77-02790)

309.1'73 — United States. Society, to 1975
Fairlie, Henry. The spoiled child of the Western world : the miscarriage of the American idea in our time / [by] Henry Fairlie. — London : Sheldon Press, 1976. — x,350p ; 22cm.
Originally published: New York : Doubleday, 1975. — Index.
ISBN 0-85969-093-8 : £4.95
(B77-10190)

309.1'73'09 — Muckraking. *United States, 1900-1975*
Filler, Louis. The muckrakers / [by] Louis Filler. — New and enlarged ed. — University Park [Pa] ; London : Pennsylvania State University Press, 1976. — xvi,456p : ill, facsims, ports ; 23cm.
Previous ed.: published as 'Crusaders for American liberalism'. Yellow Springs : Antioch Press, 1950. — Index.
ISBN 0-271-01212-9 : £9.40
ISBN 0-271-01213-7 Pbk : £4.50
(B77-06496)

309.1'73'092 — United States. Social conditions, 1940-1973
Hodgson, Godfrey. In our time : America from World War II to Nixon / [by] Godfrey Hodgson. — London [etc.] : Macmillan, 1977. — x,564p ; 23cm.
Originally published: Garden City, N.Y. : Doubleday, 1976. — Index.
ISBN 0-333-14167-9 : £7.95
(B77-11601)

309.1'73'092 — United States. Social conditions, 1960-1975
Stewart, Elbert Wilton. The troubled land : social problems in modern America / [by] Elbert W. Stewart. — 2nd ed. — New York ; London [etc.] : McGraw-Hill, 1976. — xiii, 369p : ill, port ; 24cm.
Previous ed.: New York : McGraw-Hill, 1972. — Bibl. — Index.
ISBN 0-07-061417-2 : £9.90
ISBN 0-07-061418-0 Pbk : £7.45
(B77-04587)

309.1'73'092 — United States. Social conditions, ca 1960-1976
McCord, William Maxwell. American social problems : challenges to existence / [by] William McCord, Arline McCord. — Saint Louis : Mosby ; London : Distributed by Kimpton, 1977. — xi,291p ; 26cm.
Bibl.: p.271-281. — Index.
ISBN 0-8016-3221-8 Pbk : £6.45
(B77-18573)

309.1'73'0925 — United States. Social conditions, 1976
Bromhead, Peter. Life in modern America / [by] Peter Bromhead. — 2nd ed. — London : Longman, 1977. — [14],224p : ill, map, ports ; 20cm.
Previous ed.: 1970. — Index.
ISBN 0-582-55352-0 Pbk : £2.10
(B77-21716)

309.1'73'0925 — United States. Social conditions. Policies of government, 1975. *Conference proceedings*
Measurement of Social and Economic Data and Public Policy *(Conference), University of Texas at Austin, 1975.* Current issues in social policy / edited by W. Boyd Littrell, Gideon Sjoberg. — Beverly Hills ; London : Sage Publications, 1976. — [6],248p : ill ; 22cm.
'The chapters in this volume were originally prepared ... for an interdisciplinary conference, "The Measurement of Social and Economic Data and Public Policy" ... held on April 10 and 11, 1975, at the University of Texas at Austin' - Acknowledgements. — Bibl.
ISBN 0-8039-0609-9 : £8.00
ISBN 0-8039-0610-2 Pbk : £3.95
(B77-02070)

309.1'73'0925 — United States. Social conditions. Policies of government. Implementation, 1975. *Readings*
Social program implementation / edited by Walter Williams, Richard F. Elmore. — New York [etc.] ; London : Academic Press, 1976. — xv,299p : 2 ill ; 24cm. — (Quantitative studies in social relations)
Bibl. — Index.
ISBN 0-12-756850-6 : £8.40
(B77-02071)

309.1'73'0926 — United States. Social conditions. *Readings. Serials*
Readings in social problems : contemporary perspectives / edited by Peter Wickman. — New York [etc.] ; London : Harper and Row. — (Contemporary perspectives reader series) 1977-1978 ed. — 1977. — xiv,279p : ill, map, ports ; 28cm.
Bibl. — Includes facsimile reprints.
ISBN 0-06-047053-4 Pbk : £5.20
(B77-26826)

309.1'73'0926 — United States. Society. *Sociological perspectives*
Wilson, H T. The American ideology : science, technology and organization as modes of rationality in advanced industrial societies / [by] H.T. Wilson. — London [etc.] : Routledge and Kegan Paul, 1977. — viii,355p ; 23cm. — (International library of sociology)
Bibl.: p.315-348. — Index.
ISBN 0-7100-8501-x : £6.50 : CIP rev.
(B77-20935)

309.1'748'11 — Pennsylvania. Germantown. Social conditions, 1683-1800
Wolf, Stephanie Grauman. Urban village : population, community and family structure in Germantown, Pennsylvania, 1683-1800 / [by] Stephanie Grauman Wolf. — Princeton ; Guildford : Princeton University Press, [1977]. — xi,361,[1]p : ill, map ; 23cm.
Published in the United States: 1976. — Bibl.: p.339-347. — Index.
ISBN 0-691-04632-8 : £15.80
(B77-12878)

309.1'752'02 — Maryland. Social conditions, ca 1630-1880
Conference on Maryland History, *1st, Annapolis, 1974.* Law, society and politics in early Maryland : proceedings of the First Conference on Maryland History, June 14-15, 1974 / edited by Aubrey C. Land, Lois Green Carr and Edward C. Papenfuse. — Baltimore ; London : Johns Hopkins University Press, 1977. — xvi, 350,[2]p : ill, maps, port ; 24cm. — (Studies in Maryland history and culture)
Bibl.: p.333-335. — Index.
ISBN 0-8018-1872-9 : £13.15
(B77-33634)

309.1'8 — Andean Group countries. Social conditions. Influence of United States, 1800-1976
Pike, Frederick Braun. The United States and the Andean Republics : Peru, Bolivia and Ecuador / [by] Frederick B. Pike. — Cambridge, Mass. ; London : Harvard University Press, 1977. — xxi,493p : maps ; 25cm. — (The American foreign policy library)
Index.
ISBN 0-674-92300-6 : £13.65
(B77-24726)

309.1'82'06 — Chile. Social conditions. Influence of military governments, 1973-1976. *World University Service (UK) viewpoints*
World University Service (UK). The present situation in Chile and Argentina / [World University Service (UK)]. — London (260 High Rd, N.15) : W.U.S. (U.K.), 1976. — [2],21p ; 22cm.
Bibl.: p.21.
Sd : £0.20
Also classified at 309.1'83'064
(B77-16745)

309.1'83'064 — Argentina. Social conditions. Influence of military governments, 1973-1976. *World University Service (UK) viewpoints*
World University Service (UK). The present situation in Chile and Argentina / [World University Service (UK)]. — London (260 High Rd, N.15) : W.U.S. (U.K.), 1976. — [2],21p ; 22cm.
Bibl.: p.21.
Sd : £0.20
Primary classification 309.1'82'06
(B77-16745)

309.1'895'06 — Uruguay. Social conditions, ca 1850-1974
Weinstein, Martin. Uruguay : the politics of failure / [by] Martin Weinstein. — Westport, Conn. ; London : Greenwood Press, 1975. — xviii,190p ; 22cm.
Bibl.: p.162-185. — Index.
ISBN 0-8371-7845-2 : £10.95
(B77-16746)

309.1'9 — Pacific islands. Social conditions, 1945-1975
Oceania and beyond : essays on the Pacific since 1945 / F.P. King, editor. — Westport, Conn. ; London : Greenwood Press, 1976. — xxviii,265, [1]p : maps ; 25cm.
Bibl. — Index.
ISBN 0-8371-8904-7 : £14.95
(B77-24027)

309.1'931'03 — New Zealand. Social conditions. *Festschriften*
Spirit of an age : New Zealand in the seventies : essays in honour of W.B. Sutch / edited by John L. Robson and Jack Shallcrass. — Wellington [N.Z.] [etc.] ; London : A.H. and A.W. Reed, 1975. — vii,259p : port ; 26cm.
Bibl.: p.239-258.
ISBN 0-589-00892-7 : £6.50
(B77-27695)

309.1'95'5 — Papua New Guinea. Karkar Island. Social conditions, to 1972
McSwain, Romola. The past and future people : tradition and change on a New Guinea island / [by] Romola McSwain. — Melbourne ; London [etc.] : Oxford University Press, 1977. — xx, 213p : maps ; 23cm.
Bibl.: p.198-207. — Index.
ISBN 0-19-550521-2 : £15.25
(B77-31005)

309.1'96'81 — Gilbert and Ellice Islands. Social conditions. *Reports, surveys. Serials*
Gilbert and Ellice Islands Colony and the Central and Southern Line Islands : report for the year. — London : H.M.S.O. [for the] Foreign and Commonwealth Office.
1974. — 1976. — iv,81p,[4]p of plates,fold leaf of plate : ill, map ; 22cm.
ISBN 0-11-580187-1 Pbk : £1.35
(B77-07087)

309.2 — SOCIAL PLANNING AND ASSISTANCE
309.2 — Social development
Towards a re-definition of development : essays and discussion on the nature of development in an international perspective / [edited by] Alain Birou and Paul-Marc Henry. — [English ed.] / edited by John P. Schlegel. — Oxford [etc.] : Pergamon for the Development Centre of the Organisation for Economic Co-operation and Development, Paris, 1977. — xi,353p ; 22cm.
Contains extended essays and replies to a questionnaire, some of which have been translated into English.
ISBN 0-08-020580-1 : £5.50
(B77-16747)

309.2 — Social planning
Holliday, John. Design for environment : social change and the need for new approaches in planning / [by] John C. Holliday. — London [etc.] : C. Knight, 1977. — 192p : ill, maps ; 23cm.
Index.
ISBN 0-85314-259-9 : £7.50
(B77-11602)

Turner, R Kerry. The economics of planning / [by] R. Kerry Turner and Clive Collis. — London [etc.] : Macmillan, 1977. — 103p ; 21cm. — (Macmillan studies in economics)
ISBN 0-333-19657-0 Pbk : £1.95
(B77-20936)

309.2 — Social planning. Cost-benefit analysis
Edwards, Michael, *b.1942.* The ideological function of cost-benefit analysis in planning / [by] Michael Edwards. — London (22 Gordon St., WC1H 0QB) : School of Environmental Studies, University College, London, 1977. — [1],13p ; 30cm. — (Town planning discussion papers ; no.25)
Bibl.: p.12-13.
Sd : £1.00
(B77-28417)

309.2'01'84 — Social planning. Decision making. Political aspects. Mathematical models
Batty, Michael. A political theory of planning and design : incorporating concepts of collective decision-making and social power / [by] Michael Batty. — Reading (Whiteknights, Reading [RG6 2AB]) : Department of Geography, University of Reading, 1976. — [2], ii,64p : ill ; 21cm. — (Geographical papers ; no.45 ISSN 0305-5914)
Bibl.: p.42-43.
ISBN 0-7049-0454-3 Sd : £0.70
(B77-02791)

309.2'01'84 — Social planning. Mathematical models
Thomas, Alan, *b.1948.* Modelling and community decisions / prepared for the [Open University, Systems Modelling] Course Team by Alan Thomas. — Milton Keynes : Open University Press, 1975. — 80p : ill ; 30cm. — (Technology, a third level course : systems modelling ; units 12 and 13) (T341 ; 12 and 13)
With answers.
ISBN 0-335-06057-9 Pbk : £2.95
(B77-31006)

309.2'01'84 — Social planning. Simulations
Friedmann, John. Innovation, flexible response and social learning : a problem in the theory of meta-planning / [by] John Friedmann. — Reading : Whiteknights, Reading RG6 2AB : Department of Geography, University of Reading, 1976. — [1],ii,18p ; 21cm. — (Geographical papers ; no.49 ISSN 0305-5914)
Bibl.: p.17-18.
ISBN 0-7049-0459-4 Sd : £0.45
(B77-08800)

309.2'03 — Social planning. *Polyglot glossaries*
International planning glossary ... / [general editor Gordon Logie]. — [Hemel Hempstead] ([23 Connaught Close, Hemel Hempstead, Herts. HP2 7AB]) : [G. Logie].
In 20 parts.
Vol.3 : Transport 1. [3,1] : [Transport = Transport = Trasporto]. — [1977]. — [5], 136p : ill ; 26cm.
Bibl.: p.133-134. — Index.
Sp : £4.00
(B77-07088)

Vol.3 : Transport 1. [3,2] : [Transport = Transport = Transport]. — [1977]. — [5], 134p : ill ; 26cm.
Bibl.: p.131-132. — Index.
ISBN 0-9504753-7-8 Sp : £4.00
(B77-07089)

International planning glossary ... / [general editor Gordon Logie]. — [Hemel Hempstead] ([23 Connaught Close, Hemel Hempstead, Herts. HP2 7AB]) : [G.Logie].
In 20 parts.
Vol.3 : Transport 1. [3,3] : [Transport = Transport = Kuljetus]. — [1977]. — [5],128p : ill ; 26cm.
Bibl.: p.125-126. — Index.
ISBN 0-9504753-8-6 Sp : £4.00
(B77-07090)

International planning glossary ... / [general editor Gordon Logie]. — [Hemel Hempstead] ([23 Connaught Close, Hemel Hempstead, Herts. HP2 7AB]) : [G. Logie].
In 20 parts.
Vol.3 : Transport 1. [3,5] : Transport = Transport = Transport. — [1977]. — [5],134p : ill ; 26cm.
Index.
Sp : £4.00
(B77-07091)

309.2'23'09171241 — Commonwealth countries. Foreign assistance. *Reports, surveys*
Commonwealth Fund for Technical Co-operation. Commonwealth skills for Commonwealth needs / Commonwealth Fund for Technical Co-operation. — London : Commonwealth Secretariat, [1977]. — [3],24,[1]p : ill(some col) ; 25cm.
Sd : Unpriced
(B77-26827)

309.22'32'4 — European Community countries. Social conditions. Policies of European Economic Community
Shanks, Michael. European social policy, today and tomorrow / by Michael Shanks. — Oxford [etc.] : Pergamon, 1977. — xi,105p ; 22cm. — (Pergamon international library)
Bibl.: p.x-xi. — Index.
ISBN 0-08-021444-4 : Unpriced
ISBN 0-08-021443-6 Pbk : £2.75
(B77-23153)

309.2'233'4101823 — Pacific region. Developing countries. Foreign assistance by Great Britain. Policies of British government, to 1976
Great Britain. *Central Office of Information. Reference Division.* Asia and the Pacific / [prepared by Reference Division, Central Office of Information]. — London : H.M.S.O., 1977. — [3],52p,[4]p of plates : ill ; 24cm. — (Britain and the developing countries) (Central Office of Information reference pamphlet ; 147)
Bibl.: p.52.
ISBN 0-11-700804-4 Sd : £1.40
Primary classification 309.2'233'4105
(B77-12330)

309.2'233'4105 — Asia. Developing countries. Foreign assistance by Great Britain. Policies of British government, to 1976
Great Britain. *Central Office of Information. Reference Division.* Asia and the Pacific / [prepared by Reference Division, Central Office of Information]. — London : H.M.S.O., 1977. — [3],52p,[4]p of plates : ill ; 24cm. — (Britain and the developing countries) (Central Office of Information reference pamphlet ; 147)
Bibl.: p.52.
ISBN 0-11-700804-4 Sd : £1.40
Also classified at 309.2'233'4101823
(B77-12330)

309.2'233'4106 — Africa. Commonwealth developing countries. Foreign assistance by Great Britain
Great Britain. *Central Office of Information. Reference Division.* Africa / [prepared by Reference Division, Central Office of Information]. — 2nd ed. — London : H.M.S.O., 1977. — [4],82p,[4]p of plates,fold leaf of plate : ill, map ; 24cm. — (Britain and the developing countries) (Central Office of Information reference pamphlet ; 94)
Previous ed.: 1970. — Bibl.: p.82.
ISBN 0-11-700924-5 Pbk : £1.65
(B77-26829)

309.22'33'41068 — Southern Africa. Developing countries. Foreign assistance by Great Britain
Jones, David, *b.1942.* Aid and development in Southern Africa : British aid to Botswana, Lesotho and Swaziland / [by] David Jones. — London : Croom Helm [for] the Overseas Development Institute, 1977. — 313p ; 23cm.
Index.
ISBN 0-85664-511-7 : £11.95 : CIP rev.
(B77-12879)

309.2'233'73 — Technology transfer. Policies of government. *United States*
Nau, Henry R. Technology transfer and US foreign policy / [by] Henry R. Nau [et al.]. — New York [etc.] ; London : Praeger, 1976. — xvii,325,[2]p : ill ; 25cm. — (Praeger special studies in US economic, social and political issues)
Index.
ISBN 0-275-56790-7 : £16.65
(B77-07092)

309.2'3 — Social planning. Participation of public
Fagence, Michael. Citizen participation in planning / by Michael Fagence. — Oxford [etc.] : Pergamon, 1977. — v,379p : ill ; 22cm. — (Urban and regional planning series ; vol.19) (Pergamon international library)
Bibl. — Index.
ISBN 0-08-020397-3 : £8.50
ISBN 0-08-020398-1 Pbk : £5.25
(B77-26140)

309.2'3'072 — Social development. Research. Information sources. Evaluation. *Organisation for Economic Co-operation and Development countries. Reports, surveys*
Batscha, Robert M. The effectiveness of dissemination methods for social and economic development research / by Robert Batscha. — Paris : Development Centre of the Organisation for Economic Co-operation and Development ; [London] : [H.M.S.O.], 1976. — 201p ; 24cm. — (Organisation for Economic Co-operation and Development. Development Centre. Technical papers)
Bibl.: p.200-201.
Pbk : £3.70
ISBN 92-64-11490-4
(B77-05892)

309.2'3'091724 — Developing countries. Social development. Role of communication
Communication and development : critical perspectives / edited by Everett M. Rogers. — Beverly Hills ; London : Sage Publications, 1976 [i.e. 1977]. — 148p ; 22cm. — (Sage contemporary social science issues ; 32)
Published in the United States: 1976. — ' ... originally appeared as a special issue of "Communication research" (volume 3, number 2 ; April 1976)' - title page verso. — Bibl.
ISBN 0-8039-0733-8 Pbk : £2.50
(B77-11091)

309.2'3'0941 — Great Britain. Social planning. *Proposals*
Carter, Charles Frederick. The problem of social priorities / by Charles F. Carter. — Stockport : Manchester Statistical Society, [1977]. — [1], 11p ; 20cm.
Text of a paper read before the Society 18th February 1976.
ISBN 0-85336-032-4 Sd : £1.20
(B77-14077)

309.2'3'09415 — Ireland. Social planning. *Conference proceedings*
Irish Congress of Trade Unions. *Summer Course, Johnstown Castle, Co. Wexford, 1976.* Economic and social planning : ICTU Summer Course '76, Johnstown Castle, Co. Wexford, 18-23 July 1976. — [Dublin] ([1 Grand Parade, Dublin 6]) : [Irish Congress of Trade Unions, Advisory Education and Training Services], [1977]. — 175p ; 21cm.
Bibl.
Pbk : Unpriced
(B77-20937)

309.2'3'096 — Africa. Social development. Policies of political leaders, ca 1950-1975
Damachi, Ukandi Godwin. Leadership ideology in Africa : attitudes toward socioeconomic development / [by] Ukandi G. Damachi. — New York [etc.] ; London : Praeger ; [London] : [Distributed by Martin Robertson], 1976. — xiii,113p ; 24cm. — (Praeger special studies in international economics and development)
Bibl.: p.107-112.
ISBN 0-275-56760-5 : £9.15
(B77-08801)

309.2'3'096762 — Kenya. Social development, 1968-1970. *Lectures, speeches. Extracts, selections*
Kenyatta, Jomo. The challenge of Uhuru : the progress of Kenya 1968 to 1970 : selected and prefaced extracts from the public speeches of His Excellency Mzee Jomo Kenyatta, President of the Republic of Kenya. — [Nairobi] : East African Publishing House ; Birmingham (151 Stratford Rd, Birmingham B11 1RD) : [Distributed by] Third World Publications, 1971. — 52,[1]p : ill, ports ; 19x24cm.
Sd : Unpriced
(B77-20044)

309.2'3'0973 — United States. Social planning, 1929-1975
Graham, Otis L. Toward a planned society : from Roosevelt to Nixon / [by] Otis L. Graham, Jr. — London [etc.] : Oxford University Press, 1977. — xvii,357p ; 21cm. — (A galaxy book)
Originally published: New York : Oxford University Press for the Center of Technology Assessment and Resource Policy, Stanford University, 1976. — Bibl.: p.333-351. — Index.
ISBN 0-19-502181-9 Pbk : £2.75
(B77-16208)

309.2'3'09866 — Ecuador. Social planning
Bromley, R J. Development and planning in Ecuador / [by] R.J. Bromley. — [London] ([31 Tavistock Sq., W.C.1]) : Latin American Publications Fund, 1977. — ix,116p : 1 ill, maps ; 21cm.
Bibl.: p.108-116.
ISBN 0-9500787-5-1 Pbk : £2.80
(B77-29209)

309.2'5 — Organisation for Economic Co-operation and Development countries. Regional development. Policies of governments. *Reports, surveys*
Organisation for Economic Co-operation and Development. Regional problems and policies in OECD countries / [Organisation for Economic Co-operation and Development]. — Paris : O.E.C.D. ; [London] : [H.M.S.O.].
In 2 vols.
Vol.2 : United Kingdom, Belgium, Netherlands, Norway, Finland, Spain, Austria, Germany, Canada, Switzerland. — 1976. — 213p : ill, maps(1 col) ; 24cm.
Pbk : £4.40
ISBN 92-64-11572-2
(B77-05893)

309.2'5 — Regional analysis. *Conference proceedings*
Alternative frameworks for analysis / edited by Doreen B. Massey, P.W.J. Batey. — London : Pion ; London [etc.] : Distributed by Academic Press, 1977. — [5],167p : ill, maps ; 23cm. — (London papers in regional science ; 7)
'... contains selections from two separate Regional Science Conferences [the Third Annual Meeting of the North West European Multilingual Regional Science Association and the Eighth Meeting of the British Section of the Regional Science Association] both of which were held in London during 1975' - Introduction. — Bibl.
ISBN 0-85086-061-x Pbk : £4.50
(B77-19236)

309.2'5 — Regional development. *Periodicals*
International journal of urban and regional research = Revue internationale de recherche urbaine et régionale. — London : Edward Arnold.
Vol.1, no.1- ; Mar. 1977-. — 1977-. — maps ; 24cm.
Three issues a year. — [2],192p. in 1st issue. — English and French text. — Bibl.
Pbk : £12.50 yearly
ISSN 0309-1317
Also classified at 309.2'62
(B77-31007)

309.2'5 — Regional planning. Role of geography. *Conference proceedings*
Spatial dimensions of public policy / edited by J.T. Coppock and W.R.D. Sewell. — Oxford [etc.] : Pergamon, 1976. — xv,271p : ill, form, maps ; 24cm. — (Pergamon Oxford geographies) (Pergamon international library)
'The inspiration for this volume came from the annual meeting of the Institute of British Geographers, held at the University of East Anglia in Norwich, in January, 1974 ... Some of the chapters ... are based upon papers presented at the I.B.G. meeting and a number of others were invited from geographers in the United Kingdom and elsewhere' - Acknowledgements. — Bibl. — Index.
ISBN 0-08-020629-8 : £5.85
(B77-07093)

309.2'5'0941 — Great Britain. Regional development
Great Britain. *Central Office of Information. Reference Division.* Regional development in Britain / [prepared by Reference Division Central Office of Information]. — 3rd ed. — London : H.M.S.O., 1976. — [4],68p : maps ; 24cm. — (Reference pamphlet ; 80)
Previous ed.: 1974. — Bibl.: p.67-68.
ISBN 0-11-700800-1 Sd : £1.20
(B77-02792)

309.2'5'094141 — Scotland. Strathclyde Region. Social planning. *Proposals*
West Central Scotland Plan *(Group).* West Central Scotland Plan. — Glasgow (21 Gordon St., Glasgow G1 3PL) : The Plan.
Supplementary report 4 : Social issues. — 1974. — [1],xx[i.e.xxi],328[i.e.336]p : ill, maps ; 30cm.

ISBN 0-9505558-0-0 Pbk : Unpriced
(B77-05894)

309.2'5'0941693 — Donegal (County). Glenties region. Social planning. *Proposals*
University College, *Dublin. School of Architecture.* A development study in West Donegal / University College, Dublin, School of Architecture. — [Dublin] ([Belfield, Dublin 4]) : [The School], [1977?]. — 168 leaves in various pagings : ill, maps ; 21x30cm.
Sp : Unpriced
(B77-33635)

309.2'5'09419 — Clare (County), Limerick (County) & Tipperary (County). Regional development. *Reports, surveys*
Katsiaouni, Olympios. A pilot study of regional and community development in the Mid-West / [by] Olympios Katsiaouni. — Dublin : Institute of Public Administration, 1975. — 232 leaves in various pagings : ill, maps(chiefly col) ; 30cm.
Bibl.(2 leaves).
Pbk : Unpriced
(B77-21717)

309.2'5'09424 — England. West Midlands. Social development, 1950-1977
Metropolitan development and change : the West Midlands : a policy review / edited by Frank Joyce. — Birmingham : University of Aston in Birmingham ; Farnborough, Hants. (1 Westmead, Farnborough, Hants. GU14 7RU) : Teakfield Ltd for the British Society for the Advancement of Science, 1977. — [2],xiii,446p : ill, maps ; 26cm.
'This collected volume of papers is published on behalf of the local organising committee of the British Association for the Advancement of Science to coincide with the 139th annual meeting of the Association at the University of Aston in Birmingham in 1977' - p.v. — Bibl.
ISBN 0-566-00193-4 : £10.50 : CIP rev.
(B77-22378)

309.2'5'094251 — Derbyshire. High Peak (District). Social planning
High Peak *(District). Planning Department.* Planning information handbook / Borough of High Peak [Planning Department]. — London : Pyramid Press, [1977]. — 36p : ill, ports ; 21cm.
Sd : Unpriced
(B77-32435)

309.2'5'094253 — Lincolnshire. Social planning. Policies. *Reports, surveys. For structure plan making*
Lincolnshire *(County). Planning Department.* Existing policies : a background paper to the Lincolnshire structure plan / [Lincolnshire County Planning Department]. — [Lincoln] ([County Offices, Lincoln LN1 1YJ]) : [The Department], 1976. — 50p : maps ; 30cm.
Cover title: Lincolnshire structure plan, background paper, existing policies. — Summary (2p.) as insert.
Sp : £0.85
(B77-22379)

309.2'5'09427 — Northern England. Regional planning. *Proposals*
Northern Region Strategy Team. Strategic plan for the Northern Region / Northern Region Strategy Team. — [Newcastle upon Tyne] : The Team ; [London] : Distributed by H.M.S.O.
In 5 vols.
Vol.1 : Main report. — 1977. — [1],iv,87p, plate : maps(1 col) ; 30cm.
ISBN 0-905771-01-x Pbk : £3.50(£17.00 the set)
(B77-17937)

Vol.2 : Economic development policies. — 1977. — [1],vii,178p,plate : col map ; 30cm.
ISBN 0-905771-02-8 Pbk : £4.25(£17.00 the set)
(B77-17938)

Vol.3. Part A : Social policies. Part B : Environmental policies. — 1977. — [1],vi,149[i.e.150]p,[2]leaves,plate : ill, maps(some col) ; 30cm.
ISBN 0-905771-03-6 Pbk : £4.25(£17.00 the set)
(B77-17939)

Vol.4. Part A : Settlement pattern. Part B : Transport policies. — 1977. — [1],vi,167[i.e. 168]p,[2]leaves,plate : maps(2 col) ; 30cm.
ISBN 0-905771-04-4 Pbk : £4.00(£17.00 the set)
(B77-17940)

Vol.5 : Public expenditure priorities. — 1977. — [1],iv,77p,plate : col map ; 30cm.
ISBN 0-905771-05-2 Pbk : £2.25(£17.00 the set)
(B77-17941)

309.2'5'094275 — Merseyside (Metropolitan County). Social planning. *Proposals*
Merseyside *(Metropolitan County). Planning Department.* Targets for Merseyside for the 1980's / [Merseyside County Planning Department]. — Liverpool (Metropolitan House, P.O. Box 95, Old Hall St., Liverpool L69 3EL) : [The Department], 1977. — [5],26[i.e. 28]p ; 31cm.
ISBN 0-905161-02-5 Sd : Unpriced
(B77-15707)

309.2'5'0942751 — Merseyside (Metropolitan County). Wirral (District). Social planning
Wirral *(Metropolitan District). Department of Development.* Wirral planning handbook / [compiled], designed and illustrated by the Department of Development, Metropolitan Borough of Wirral. — Carshalton : Home Publishing Co., [1977]. — 72,[1]p : ill, maps, plans ; 21cm.
Sd : Unpriced
(B77-32436)

309.2'5'0942983 — West Glamorgan. Lliw Valley (District). Social planning
Lliw Valley *(District). Council.* Planning information handbook, 1977 / Lliw Valley Borough Council. — London : Pyramid Press, [1977]. — 24p : ill ; 21cm.
Sd : Unpriced
(B77-32437)

309.2'5'096762 — Western Kenya. Regional planning
Obudho, Robert. Periodic markets, urbanization, and regional planning : a case study from Western Kenya / [by] Robert A. Obudho, Peter P. Waller. — Westport, Conn. ; London : Greenwood Press, 1976. — xviii,289,[3]p : ill, maps ; 22cm. — (Contributions in Afro-American and African studies ; no.22)
Bibl.: p.259-278. — Index.
ISBN 0-8371-8375-8 : £19.95
(B77-17942)

309.2'5'0973 — United States. Regional planning
Lynch, Kevin. Managing the sense of a region / [by] Kevin Lynch. — Cambridge, Mass. ; London : M.I.T. Press, [1977]. — xii,221p : ill, maps ; 21cm.
Published in the United States: 1976. — Bibl.: p.199-212. — Index.
ISBN 0-262-12072-0 : £9.05
(B77-13524)

309.2'5'0973 — United States. Regional planning, 1925-1932. *Regional Planning Association of America viewpoints*
Regional Planning Association of America. Planning the fourth migration : the neglected vision of the Regional Planning Association of America / edited by Carl Sussman. — Cambridge, Mass. ; London : M.I.T. Press, [1977]. — xiii,277p : ill, maps ; 21cm.
Published in the United States: 1976. — Index.
ISBN 0-262-19148-2 : £11.25
(B77-14078)

309.2'5'0974725 — New York (State). Long Island. Suffolk (County). Regional planning
Gottdiener, Mark. Planned sprawl : private and public interests in suburbia / [by] Mark Gottdiener ; preface by Gerald D. Suttles. — Beverly Hills ; London : Sage Publications, 1977. — 189p : ill ; 22cm. — (Sage library of social research ; vol.38)
Bibl.: p.185-188.
ISBN 0-8039-0593-9 : £8.00
ISBN 0-8039-0594-7 Pbk : £4.50
(B77-29210)

309.2'6'0941135 — Scotland. Shetland. Unst. Social planning. *Proposals*
Shetland *(Islands). Council.* Unst District plan / [Shetland Islands Council]. — [Lerwick] ([Town Hall, Lerwick, Shetland ZE1 0HD]) : The Council, 1975. — [7],61[i.e.64],[21]p,[2] leaves of plates,[2]p of plates : maps(some col) ; 30cm.
ISBN 0-905924-01-0 Sp : £3.00
(B77-05895)

309.2'6'0941135 — Scotland. Shetland. Yell. Social planning. *Proposals*
Shetland *(Islands). Council.* Yell District plan / [Shetland Islands Council]. — [Lerwick] ([Town Hall, Lerwick, Shetland ZE1 0HD]) : The Council, 1975. — [7],59[i.e.63],17p,leaf of plate,[6]p of plates : maps(1 col) ; 30cm.
ISBN 0-905924-00-2 Sp : £3.00
(B77-05896)

309.2'6'09426723 — Essex. Colchester (District). Social planning
Colchester *(District). Department of Planning and Building Control.* Planning handbook / Colchester Borough Council [Department of Planning and Building Control]. — New ed. — [Colchester] ([Lexden Grange, 127 Lexden Rd, Colchester CO3 3RT]) : [The Department], [1977]. — 68p : ill, maps ; 22cm.
Previous ed.: issued by Colchester Borough Planning Department. London : Pyramid Press, 1975.
Sd : Unpriced
(B77-29971)

309.2'62 — Cities. Inner areas. Social planning. Policies of government. *Great Britain*
Great Britain. *Department of the Environment.* Policy for the inner cities / presented to Parliament by the Secretary of State for the Environment, the Secretary of State for Scotland and the Secretary of State for Wales ... — London : H.M.S.O., [1977]. — [3],33p ; 25cm. — (Cmnd.6845)
ISBN 0-10-168450-9 Sd : £0.60
(B77-23154)

309.2'62 — Cities. Social planning
Needham, Barrie. How cities work : an introduction / by Barrie Needham. — Oxford [etc.] : Pergamon, 1977. — x,185p : ill, maps ; 22cm. — (Urban and regional planning series ; vol.17 ISSN 0305-5582) (Pergamon international library)
Bibl. — Index.
ISBN 0-08-020529-1 Pbk : £8.00
ISBN 0-08-020528-3 Pbk : £4.75
(B77-24028)

309.2'62 — Colonies. Urban development
King, Anthony Douglas. Colonial urban development : culture, social power and environment / [by] Anthony D. King. — London [etc.] : Routledge and Kegan Paul, 1976. — xvi,328p : ill, facsim, maps, plans ; 24cm.
Bibl.: p.300-315. — Index.
ISBN 0-7100-8404-8 : £7.50
(B77-01188)

309.2'62 — New towns. Social planning
Golany, Gideon. New-town planning : principles and practice / [by] Gideon Golany. — New York ; London [etc.] : Wiley, 1976. — xxiii, 389p : ill, maps, plans ; 29cm.
'A Wiley-Interscience publication'. — Bibl.: p.351-380. — Index.
ISBN 0-471-31038-7 : £19.25
(B77-00629)

309.2'62 — Urban development. *Periodicals*
International journal of urban and regional research = Revue internationale de recherche urbaine et régionale. — London : Edward Arnold.
Vol.1, no.1- ; Mar. 1977-. — 1977-. — maps ; 24cm.
Three issues a year. — [2],192p. in 1st issue. — English and French text. — Bibl.
Pbk : £12.50 yearly
ISSN 0309-1317
Primary classification 309.2'5
(B77-31007)

309.2'62 — Urban regions. Social planning. Economic aspects
Broadbent, Thomas Andrew. Planning and profit in the urban economy / [by] T.A. Broadbent. — London : Methuen, 1977. — xiv,274p : ill, map ; 24cm.
Bibl.: p.251-265. — Index.
ISBN 0-416-56320-1 : £6.50
ISBN 0-416-56330-9 Pbk : £3.95
(B77-17318)

309.2'62 — Urban regions. Social planning. Environmental factors
Grandjean, Etienne. Environmental factors in urban planning : air pollution, noise, urban open spaces, sunlight and natural lighting indoors / [by] E. Grandjean and A. Gilgen ; [translated from the German by Harold Oldroyd]. — London : Taylor and Francis, 1976. — xiii,206p : ill ; 25cm.
Translation of: 'Umwelthygiene in der Raumplanung'. Thun : Ott Verlag, 1973. — Index.
ISBN 0-85066-084-x : £9.75
(B77-00053)

309.2'62 — Urban regions. Social planning. Influence of planners' theories of social justice. Assessment. Criteria: Accessibility of urban amenities. *Research reports*
Loodmer, Tisha. Social justice and planning : the use of the accessibility matrix / [by] Tisha Loodmer. — [London] : London School of Economics and Political Science, Graduated Geography Department, 1976. — [1],16[i.e. 17]p : ill ; 30cm. — (London School of Economics and Political Science. Graduate School of Geography. Discussion papers ; no.57 ISSN 0307-1960)
Bibl.: p.15-16.
ISBN 0-85328-054-1 Sd : Unpriced
(B77-01189)

309.2'62'02854 — Urban regions. Social planning. Applications of computer systems. *Periodicals*
Urban systems : an international journal. — New York ; Oxford [etc.] : Pergamon.
Continues: Computers & urban society.
Vol.2, no.1- ; 1977-. — 1977-. — ill, forms ; 28cm.
Quarterly. — [2],61p. in 1st issue.
Pbk : £27.00 yearly
ISSN 0147-8001
(B77-29972)

309.2'62'0720417 — Ireland (Republic). Urban regions. Social planning. Research projects. *Directories*
National Institute for Physical Planning and Construction Research *(Republic of Ireland).* Urban and regional research projects in Ireland, 1975 : an annotated list / prepared by An Foras Forbartha, Dublin ; [for the United Nations Economic Commission for Europe, Committee on Housing, Building and Planning, Group of Experts on Urban and Regional Research]. — Dublin : The Institute, 1976. — [2],67 leaves ; 30cm.
Cover title.
Pbk : Unpriced
(B77-33636)

309.2'62'0941 — Great Britain. Town planning. Social aspects
Stenhouse, David, *b.1938.* Understanding towns / [by] David Stenhouse. — Hove : Wayland, 1977. — 120p : ill, maps, plans ; 26cm.
Bibl. — Index.
ISBN 0-85340-440-2 : £4.50
(B77-19237)

309.2'62'0941 — Great Britain. Urban regions. Social planning
Gane, Michael. The reformist perspective / prepared for the [Open University] Course Team by Michael Gane. The politics of reform ; [and], Consensus or conflict : a case study in planning / prepared by Andrew Blowers ; for the [Open University] Course Team. — Milton Keynes : Open University Press, 1976. — [2],iv, 3-104p : ill ; 30cm. — (Social science, a third level course : patterns of inequality ; section 4 : reform or revolution? ; unit 29, unit 30) (D302 ; 29-30)
Bibl.
ISBN 0-335-07160-0 Pbk : £1.35
Primary classification 301.24'2
(B77-03939)

309.2'62'0941 — Great Britain. Urban regions. Social planning. *Conservative and Unionist Party viewpoints*
Eyre, Reginald. Hope for our towns & cities : the right approach to urban affairs / by Reginald Eyre. — London : Conservative Political Centre, 1977. — 24p ; 21cm. — (Conservative Political Centre. Publications ; no.606)
ISBN 0-85070-600-9 Sd : £0.40
(B77-25409)

309.2'62'09411 — New towns. *Scotland. Reports, surveys. Serials*
Reports of the Cumbernauld, East Kilbride and Stonehouse, Glenrothes, Irvine and Livingston Development Corporations for the year ended 31st March ... — Edinburgh : H.M.S.O.
[1976]-1977. — [1977]. — 176p,[4]fold leaves of plates,[20]p of plates : ill, plans, ports ; 25cm. — ([1976-77 H.C.]473)
ISBN 0-10-247377-3 Pbk : £3.50
(B77-28418)

309.2'62'094167 — Belfast. Shankill Road. Development. Role of social planning, ca 1930-1970. *Personal observations*
Wiener, Ron. The rape and plunder of the Shankill in Belfast : people and planning / by Ron Wiener. — [Belfast] ([76 Shankill Rd, Belfast]) : [Nothems Press], [1976]. — 167p,[8]p of plate : ill, maps ; 21cm.
ISBN 0-9504292-0-1 Pbk : £1.00
(B77-00054)

309.2'62'0942 — England. Urban regions. Social planning, 1945-1972
The **containment** of urban England / by Peter Hall ... [et al.]. — London : Allen and Unwin [etc. for] P.E.P., [1977]. — 3-648,3-464p : ill, maps ; 24cm.
Originally published: in 2 vols. 1973. — Indexes. — Contents: Vol.1 : Urban and metropolitan growth processes, or, Megalopolis denied - Vol.2 : The planning system.
ISBN 0-04-352066-9 Pbk : £12.50
(B77-10191)

309.2'62'0942 — New towns. *England. Reports, surveys. Serials*
Reports of the Development Corporations [for the year ended] 31st March ... — London : H.M.S.O.
[1976]-1977. Aycliffe ... [et al.]. — [1977]. — v, 481p,[32]p of plates,[2]leaves of plates : ill, map, ports ; 25cm. — ([1976-77 H.C.]539)
ISBN 0-10-253977-4 Pbk : £7.85
(B77-31008)

[1976]-1977. Cwmbran [and] Newton (Mid-Wales). — [1977]. — iii,46p,[4]p of plates : ill ; 25cm. — ([1976-77 H.C.]533)
ISBN 0-10-253377-6 Sd : £1.35
(B77-31009)

Reports of the Development Corporations [for the year ended] 31st March. — London : H.M.S.O.
[1975]-1976. Aycliffe ... [et al.]. — [1976]. — v, 496p,[36]p of plates : ill, map, plan, port ; 25cm. — ([1975-76 H.C.]630)
ISBN 0-10-263076-3 Pbk : £6.70
(B77-05897)

[1975]-1976. Cwmbran [and] Newtown (Mid-Wales). — [1976]. — iii,46p,[4]p of plates : ill ; 25cm. — ([1975-76 H.C.]633)
ISBN 0-10-263376-2 Sd : £0.85
(B77-05898)

309.2'62'09421 — Central London. Social planning. *Proposals*

Central London Planning Conference. Advisory plan for Central London, policy document / Central London Planning Conference. — London (G.L.C. Bookshop, County Hall, SE1 7PB) : The Conference, 1976. — [1],26p,[6] leaves of plates(5 fold) : col maps ; 30cm.
ISBN 0-7168-0863-3 Sp : £1.00
(B77-08802)

309.2'62'09421 — Central London. Social planning. *Reports, surveys*

Central London Planning Conference. Advisory plan for Central London, technical document / Central London Planning Conference. — London (G.L.C. Bookshop, County Hall, SE1 7PB) : The Conference, 1976. — [1],54p,7 leaves of plates(5 fold) : col maps ; 30cm.
ISBN 0-7168-0864-1 Sp : £2.50
(B77-08803)

309.2'62'0942164 — London. Southwark (London Borough). Bermondsey. Social planning. Role of government, 1850-1975

Dimoldenberg, Paul. The evolving role of the State and its impact on the development of Bermondsey, 1850-1975 / [by] Paul Dimoldenberg. — [Oxford] ([Headington, Oxford OX3 0BP]) : Oxford Polytechnic, Department of Town Planning, [1977]. — [1], vii leaves,107[i.e.112],[1]p ; 30cm. — (Oxford working papers in planning education and research ; no.24)
Bibl.
ISBN 0-9504310-6-0 Sd : Unpriced
(B77-13525)

309.2'62'0942165 — London. Lambeth (London Borough). Social planning. *Proposals*

Shankland, Cox Partnership. Inner London, policies for dispersal and balance : final report of the Lambeth Inner Area Study / Shankland Cox Partnership [and the] Institute of Community Studies ; [for the] Department of the Environment ; [written by] Graeme Shankland, Peter Willmott and David Jordan. — London : H.M.S.O., 1977. — x,243p : ill, maps ; 25cm.
Bibl.: p.235-238. — Index.
ISBN 0-11-751141-2 Pbk : £6.00
(B77-20938)

Shankland, Cox Partnership. Lambeth, inner area study / by the consultants Shankland, Cox Partnership in association with the Institute of Community Studies. — London : Department of the Environment.
Housing management and design : report. — 1977. — [2],ii,99p : ill, form, maps, plan ; 30cm. — (Inner area studies ; LA/18)
Sd : £2.20
(B77-23155)

Shankland Cox Partnership. Lambeth, inner area study / Shankland Cox Partnership in association with the Institute of Community Studies. — London : Department of the Environment.
Local employers' study : report / by the consultants. — [1977]. — [2],ii,[3],88p ; 30cm. — (Inner area studies ; LA/16)
Sd : £1.30
(B77-17943)

Shankland, Cox Partnership. Lambeth, inner area study / by the consultants Shankland, Cox Partnership in association with the Institute of Community Studies. — London : Department of the Environment.
Multi-service project : report. — [1976]. — ii, 30[i.e.33],[7]p : map ; 30cm. — (Inner area studies ; LA/14)
Sd : £0.40
(B77-23156)

Schools project : report. — [1976]. — [2],iii,28, A3(a)-(v)p : ill ; 30cm. — (Inner area studies ; LA/13)
Sd : £1.05
(B77-23157)

Shankland Cox Partnership. Lambeth, inner area study / Shankland Cox Partnership in association with the Institute of Community Studies. — London : Department of the Environment.
Second report on multiple deprivation : report / by the consultants. — [1977]. — [2],ii,[1],70p, plate : ill ; 30cm. — (Inner area studies ; LA/15)
Sd : £1.10
(B77-17944)

The Groveway project : an experiment in salaried childminding : report / by the consultants ; [written by Phyllis Willmott, Linda Challis]. — [1977]. — [2],ii,[4],85p : map ; 30cm. — (Inner area studies ; LA/17)
Sd : £1.60
(B77-17945)

Shankland, Cox Partnership. Lambeth, inner area study / by the consultants Shankland, Cox Partnership in association with the Institute of Community Studies. — London : Department of the Environment.
The implications of social ownership : report. — [1976]. — [2],iii,69p : map ; 30cm. — (Inner area studies ; LA/12)
Sd : £1.00
(B77-23158)

309.2'62'0942176 — London. Newham (London Borough). Social planning

Newham *(London Borough). Department of Planning and Architecture.* Planning tomorrow's Newham : a guide to the work of Newham Council's Department of Planning and Architecture / [Newham Department of Planning and Architecture]. — London : Pyramid Press, [1977]. — 48p : ill, coats of arms, facsims, map ; 21cm.
Bibl.: p.36-37.
Sd : Unpriced
(B77-29211)

309.2'62'094225 — East & West Sussex. Urban development, to 1975

Aldsworth, Fred. Historic towns in Sussex : an archaeological survey / [by] Fred Aldsworth and David Freke. — [London] ([c/o Institute of Archaeology, 31 Gordon Sq., WC1H 0PY]) : [Sussex Archaeological Field Unit], 1976. — [6] ,66p : maps ; 30cm.
Bibl.
Pbk : £1.00
(B77-06497)

309.2'62'0942496 — West Midlands (Metropolitan County). Birmingham. Social planning. *Proposals*

Llewelyn-Davies, Weeks, Forestier-Walker and Bor *(Firm).* Birmingham inner area study / by the consultants Llewelyn-Davies, Weeks, Forestier-Walker & Bor. — London : Department of the Environment.
Housing policies for the inner city : report. — [1976]. — [2],v,159p : ill, maps ; 30cm. — (Inner area studies ; B/11)
Bibl.: p.157-159.
Sd : £2.00
(B77-23159)

Industrial employment and property availability : report. — [1976]. — [2],iv,85p : ill, maps ; 30cm. — (Inner area studies ; B/9)
Bibl.: p.81-85.
Sd : £1.10
(B77-23160)

The management of urban renewal : report. — [1976]. — [2],v,85p : ill, form, maps, plans ; 30cm. — (Inner area studies ; B/10)
Sd : £1.00
(B77-23161)

Llewelyn-Davies, Weeks, Forestier-Walker and Bor *(Firm).* Unequal city : final report of the Birmingham Inner Area Study / Llewelyn-Davies Weeks Forestier-Walker & Bor ; [for the] Department of the Environment. — London : H.M.S.O., 1977. — xii,339p : ill, maps ; 25cm.
Bibl.: p.329-337.
ISBN 0-11-751142-0 Pbk : £9.00
(B77-20939)

309.2'62'094258 — New towns. *Hertfordshire. Reports, surveys. Serials*

Commission for the New Towns. Report of the Commission for the New Towns for the period ended 31st March : Crawley, Hatfield, Hemel Hempstead, Welwyn Garden City ... — London : H.M.S.O.
[1976]-1977. — [1977]. — ix,50p,[4]p of plates : ill, map ; 25cm. — ([1976-77 H.C.]538)
ISBN 0-10-253877-8 Sd : £1.35
(B77-31010)

309.2'62'0942753 — Merseyside (Metropolitan County). Liverpool. Social planning

Liverpool *(Metropolitan District). Planning Department.* Planning handbook / City of Liverpool [Planning Department]. — London : Pyramid Press.
1977. — [1977]. — 136p : ill(some col), maps(2 col), plans(2 col) ; 25cm.
Cover title: Liverpool planning handbook.
Pbk : Unpriced
(B77-33081)

309.2'62'0942753 — Merseyside (Metropolitan County). Liverpool. Social planning. *Proposals*

Hugh Wilson and Lewis Womersley *(Firm).* Liverpool inner area study / [by Hugh Wilson & Lewis Womersley and others]. — London : Department of the Environment.
Adult education : report / by the consultants Hugh Wilson & Lewis Womersley. — 1977. — [2],iii,iii,29p : ill ; 30cm. — (Inner area studies ; LI/15)
Sd : £0.50
(B77-24727)

Area resource analysis, District D tables, 1973-74 : report / by the consultants Hugh Wilson & Lewis Womersley in association with Roger Tym & Associates. — [1976]. — [2],viii, 125p ; 30cm. — (Inner area studies ; LI/9)
Chiefly notebook format. — Versos of some leaves blank.
Sd : £1.55
(B77-23162)

Change or decay : final report / Hugh Wilson & Lewis Womersley, Roger Tym and Associates, Jamieson Mackay and Partners. — London : H.M.S.O, 1977. — xiv,240p : ill, maps ; 25cm.
ISBN 0-11-751143-9 Pbk : £6.00
(B77-20940)

Community care of the elderly : report / by the consultants Hugh Wilson & Lewis Womersley. — 1977. — 61,[10]p,plate : form, map ; 30cm. — (Inner area studies ; LI/17)
Sd : £1.00
(B77-23163)

Environmental care project : report / by the consultants Hugh Wilson & Lewis Womersley [and] Jamieson, Mackay and Partners. — [1977]. — 60,[10]p,[4]leaves of plates : ill, 2 maps, 2 plans ; 30cm. — (Inner area studies ; LI/19)
Sd : £1.30
(B77-23164)

Housing maintenance project : report / by the consultants Hugh Wilson & Lewis Womersley. — [1976]. — 32[i.e.36],[9]p,plate : ill, maps, plans ; 30cm. — (Inner area studies ; LI/10)
Sd : £0.65
(B77-23165)

Housing management : report / by the consultants Hugh Wilson & Lewis Womersley. — 1977. — [2],iii,iii,27p,plate : map ; 30cm. — (Inner area studies ; LI/16)
Sd : £0.50
(B77-24728)

Inner area play : report / by the consultants Hugh Wilson & Lewis Womersley [in association with Roger Tym and Associates and Jamieson, Mackay and Partners]. — 1977. — [1],iii,v,67p,6 leaves of plates : ill, maps ; 30cm. — (Inner area studies ; LI/14)
Sd : £1.15
(B77-16748)

Single and homeless : report / by the consultants Hugh Wilson & Lewis Womersley. — 1977. — [2],iii,vi,73p : ill ; 30cm. — (Inner area studies ; LI/13)
Sd : £1.10
(B77-24729)

Single parent families : report / by the consultants Hugh Wilson & Lewis Womersley. — 1977. — 31,[9]p,[2]leaves of plates : 2 maps ; 30cm. — (Inner area studies ; LI/18)
Sd : £0.60
(B77-23166)

In our Liverpool home : a collective response by community organisations to the publication of the Inner Areas Study summary report. — Liverpool (14 Castle St., Liverpool L2 0NJ) : Liverpool Council for Voluntary Service ; Liverpool : Community Development Section [of the Liverpool City Council], 1977. — [1],9, [14]p : ill ; 30cm.
'This exercise was organised by the Community Development Section of the [Liverpool] City Council ... [and others]'.
Sd : Unpriced
(B77-17319)

309.2'62'0973 — Local authorities. Policies. Decision making. Role of professional personnel. *United States. Urban regions. Study examples: Social planning*
Buck, J Vincent. Politics and professionalism in municipal planning / [by] J. Vincent Buck. — Beverly Hills ; London : Sage Publications, 1976. — 55,[1]p ; 22cm. — (Sage professional papers in administrative and policy studies ; vol.3, no.03-033)
Bibl.: p.53-55.
ISBN 0-8039-0627-7 Pbk : £1.75
(B77-14079)

309.2'62'0973 — New towns. Social planning. Innovation. *United States*
Innovations for future cities / edited by Gideon Golany. — New York [etc.] ; London : Praeger ; [London] : [Distributed by Martin Robertson], 1976. — xix,268p : ill, maps, plans ; 24cm. — (Praeger special studies in US economic, social and political issues)
Bibl. — Index.
ISBN 0-275-22860-6 : £13.50
(B77-07094)

309.2'62'0973 — United States. Urban regions. Social planning
Finkler, Earl. Urban nongrowth : city planning for people / [by] Earl Finkler, William J. Toner, Frank J. Popper. — New York [etc.] ; London : Praeger ; [London] : [Distributed by Martin Robertson], 1976. — ix,229p ; 24cm. — (Praeger special studies in US economic, social and political issues)
Bibl.: p.217-220. — Index.
ISBN 0-275-02230-7 : £12.05
(B77-04588)

309.2'62'0973 — United States. Urban regions. Social planning. Applications of systems analysis
Gibson, John Egan. Designing the new city : a systemic approach / [by] J.E. Gibson. — New York ; London [etc.] : Wiley, 1977. — xiii, 288p : ill, maps ; 24cm. — (Wiley series on systems engineering and analysis)
'A Wiley-Interscience publication'. — Index.
ISBN 0-471-29752-6 : £15.00
(B77-28419)

309.2'62'098 — Latin America. Urban regions. Social planning
Latin American urban research. — Beverly Hills ; London : Sage Publications.
Vol.4 : Anthropological perspectives on Latin American urbanization / Wayne A. Cornelius and Felicity M. Trueblood, editors. — [1977]. — 296p : ill ; 22cm.
Spine title: Anthropological perspectives on Latin American urbanization. — Originally published: 1974. — Bibl.: p.263-296.
ISBN 0-8039-0852-0 Pbk : £4.95
(B77-22380)

309.2'62'098 — Latin America. Urban regions. Social planning. *Reports, surveys*
Gall, Pirie M. Municipal development programs in Latin America : an intercountry evaluation / [by] Pirie M. Gall assisted by ... [others]. — New York [etc.] ; London : Praeger, 1976. — xv,124,[1]p : ill, map ; 25cm. — (Praeger special studies in international economics and development)
Bibl. — Index.
ISBN 0-275-23280-8 : £11.25
(B77-09533)

309.2'62'09816 — Brazil. São Paulo. Urban development, to 1976. Social aspects
Kowarick, Lucio. The logic of disorder : capitalist expansion in the metropolitan area of Greater São Paulo / by Lucio Kowarick. — Brighton : Institute of Development Studies, 1977. — [3], 29p ; 30cm. — (Institute of Development Studies. Discussion papers ; 102 ISSN 0308-5864)
Sd : £1.30
(B77-23167)

309.2'62'09817 — Brazil. Brasília. Social planning
Epstein, David G. Brasília, plan and reality : a study of planned and spontaneous urban development / [by] David G. Epstein. — Berkeley [etc.] ; London : University of California Press, 1973. — xiii,206p,[8]p of plates : ill, maps ; 24cm.
Bibl.: p.187-197. — Index.
ISBN 0-520-02203-3 : Unpriced
(B77-20045)

309.2'63 — Rural regions. Social planning
Lassey, William R. Planning in rural environments / [by] William R. Lassey. — New York ; London [etc.] : McGraw-Hill, 1977. — xiii,257p : ill, 2 ports ; 24cm. — (McGraw-Hill publications in the agricultural sciences)
Bibl.: p.239-247. — Index.
ISBN 0-07-036580-6 : £10.45
(B77-26141)

309.2'63'0941 — Great Britain. Rural regions. Social planning
Davidson, Joan. Planning and the rural environment / by Joan Davidson and Gerald Wibberley. — Oxford [etc.] : Pergamon, 1977. — xii,225p,[2]fold leaves of plates,[14]p of plates : ill, maps, port ; 26cm. — (Urban and regional planning series ; vol.18 ISSN 0305-5582) (Pergamon international library)
Index.
ISBN 0-08-020527-5 : £7.50
ISBN 0-08-020526-7 Pbk : £4.50
(B77-22381)

Rural planning problems / edited by Gordon E. Cherry ; contributors Gordon E. Cherry ... [et al.]. — [London] : L. Hill, [1976]. — x,286p : ill ; 24cm.
Bibl. — Index.
ISBN 0-249-44150-0 : £6.95
(B77-03968)

Woodruffe, Brian J. Rural settlement policies and plans / [by] Brian J. Woodruffe. — London [etc.] : Oxford University Press, 1976. — 64p : maps ; 21cm. — (Theory and practice in geography)
Bibl. — Index.
ISBN 0-19-874043-3 Pbk : £1.25
(B77-03969)

309.2'63'094252 — Villages. Social planning. *Nottinghamshire. Conference proceedings*
Living Village *(Conference), Newark, 1976.* Report on a one-day conference on 'The Living Village' [organized by the] Community Council for Nottinghamshire. — Nottingham (Shire Hall, High Pavement, Nottingham NG1 1HR) : The Council, 1976. — [1],18p ; 30cm.
'... held at Kelham Hall, Newark, Nottinghamshire, on Saturday, 25th September, 1976' - Introduction.
ISBN 0-905618-01-7 Sd : £0.15
(B77-02793)

310 — STATISTICS
310 — World. *Statistics. For marketing*
International marketing data and statistics. — London (P.O. Box 115, 41 Russell Sq., WC1B 5DL) : Euromonitor Publications Ltd.
2nd ed. — 1977. — [5],310p ; 26cm.
Index.
ISBN 0-903706-11-3 : £30.00
ISSN 0308-2938
(B77-10192)

312 — POPULATION STATISTICS
312 — Population. *Statistics. Spanish texts*
International Planned Parenthood Federation. La planificación familiar en cinco continentes / [Federation International de Planificacion de la Familia]. — Londres [i.e. London] : The Federation, 1974. — [2],41p ; 21x30cm.
ISBN 0-900924-60-8 Sd : £0.25
Primary classification 362.8'2
(B77-21044)

312'.09411 — Scotland. Population. *Estimates*
Annual estimates of the population of Scotland / the Registrar General, Scotland. — Edinburgh : H.M.S.O.
1976. — 1977. — 21,[1]p ; 21cm.
ISBN 0-11-491479-6 Sd : £0.60
(B77-15708)

312'.09411 — Scotland. Population. *Statistics*
Great Britain. *General Register Office, Scotland.* Annual report ... / Registrar General, Scotland. — Edinburgh : H.M.S.O.
1975 : [No.121]. Part 1 : Mortality statistics. — 1977. — 414p : ill, maps ; 30cm.
ISBN 0-11-491445-1 Pbk : £10.00
(B77-12331)

1975 : [No.121]. Part 2 : Population and vital statistics. — 1977. — 230p : ill, maps ; 30cm.
ISBN 0-11-491446-x Pbk : £6.00
(B77-12332)

312'.09416 — Northern Ireland. Population. *Statistics*
Northern Ireland. *General Register Office.* Annual report of the Registrar General ... — Belfast : H.M.S.O.
53rd : 1974. — 1976. — vi,264p : ill ; 25cm.
ISBN 0-337-23200-8 Pbk : £4.00
(B77-03970)

54th : 1975. — 1977. — vi,270p : ill ; 24cm.
ISBN 0-337-23248-2 Pbk : £5.00
(B77-31716)

312'.0942 — England. Population. *Statistics*
Local authority vital statistics : vital statistics for administrative and health areas of England and Wales / Office of Population Censuses and Surveys. — London : H.M.S.O. — (VS ; no.1)
1974. — 1976. — viii,2-14p ; 30cm.
ISBN 0-11-690620-0 Sd : £0.65
(B77-07095)

312'.0942 — England. Population, 1971. *Census tables*
Great Britain. *Office of Population Censuses and Surveys.* Census 1971, England and Wales, ... report for the county / Office of Population Censuses and Surveys. — London : H.M.S.O.
Hereford and Worcester, as constituted on 1st April 1974. — 1977. — viii,113p : map ; 32cm.
ISBN 0-11-690482-8 Pbk : £4.50
(B77-11092)

Great Britain. *Office of Population Censuses and Surveys.* Census 1971, England and Wales, report for the county / Office of Population Censuses and Surveys. — London : H.M.S.O.
Cleveland, as constituted on 1st April 1974. — 1976. — viii,62p : map ; 32cm.
ISBN 0-11-690477-1 Pbk : £2.30
(B77-02072)

Dorset, as constituted on 1st April 1974. — 1977. — viii,103p : map ; 32cm.
ISBN 0-11-690480-1 Pbk : £3.30
(B77-08804)

Gloucestershire, as constituted on 1st April 1974. — 1976. — viii,83p : map ; 32cm.
ISBN 0-11-690479-8 Pbk : £2.90
(B77-05225)

Nottinghamshire, as constituted on 1st April 1974. — 1977. — viii,103p : map ; 32cm.
ISBN 0-11-690481-x Pbk : £3.30
(B77-08805)

Somerset, as constituted on 1st April 1974. — 1976. — viii,68p : map ; 32cm.
ISBN 0-11-690478-x Pbk : £2.30
(B77-05226)

312'.09421 — London. Population, 1971. *Census tables*
Morrey, C R. 1971 census, demographic, social and economic indices for wards in Greater London / [by] C.R. Morrey. — London : Greater London Council, 1976. — 2v.([1],ii, 60(26 fold);i,210p) ; 30cm. — (Greater London Council. Research reports ; 20)
Bibl.: p.12-13 (Vol.1).
ISBN 0-7168-0843-9 : £8.00
(B77-15108)

312'.09425'61 — Bedfordshire. Cardington. Population, 1782. *Lists*
The **inhabitants** of Cardington in 1782 / [edited by] David Baker. — [Ampthill] ([c/o A.G. Underwood, 39 Church St., Ampthill, Beds.]) : Bedfordshire Historical Record Society, 1973. — viii,242p,plate : facsim ; 22cm. — (Bedfordshire Historical Record Society. Publications ; vol.52)
Bibl.: p.232-233. — Index.
ISBN 0-85155-034-7 Pbk : £2.50
(B77-03401)

312'.0971 — Canada. Population, 1851-1973. *Statistics*
Kubat, Daniel. A statistical profile of Canadian society / [by] Daniel Kubat, David Thornton. — Toronto ; London [etc.] ([McGraw Hill House, Shoppenhangers Rd, Maidenhead, Berks. SL6 2QL]) : McGraw-Hill Ryerson Ltd, [1977]. — xvi,200p : ill, map ; 23cm. — (McGraw-Hill Ryerson series in Canadian sociology)
Published in Canada: 1974. — Bibl.
ISBN 0-07-077799-3 Pbk : Unpriced
(B77-09534)

312'.1'411 — Married women. Fertility. *Scotland, 1971. Census tables*
Great Britain. *General Register Office, Scotland.* Census 1971, Scotland, fertility tables / General Register Office, Edinburgh. — Edinburgh : H.M.S.O.
Part 2 : (10% sample). — 1976. — xxi,230p ; 34cm.
ISBN 0-11-491441-9 Pbk : £7.70
(B77-12333)

312'.1'416 — Married women. Fertility. *Northern Ireland, 1971. Census tables*
Northern Ireland. *General Register Office.* Census of population 1971, fertility tables, Northern Ireland / Northern Ireland General Register Office. — Belfast : H.M.S.O., 1976. — ix,89p,leaf of plate,[6]fold p of plates : forms, map ; 30cm.
ISBN 0-337-23208-3 Sd : £2.25
(B77-20046)

312'.1'42 — Births. *England. Statistics*
Birth statistics : review of the Registrar General on births and patterns of family building in England and Wales. — London : H.M.S.O.
1974. — 1977. — vii,104p ; 30cm. — (FMI ; no.1)
ISBN 0-11-690636-7 Pbk : £2.25
ISSN 0140-2587
(B77-29212)

312'.2'0942 — Deaths. *England. Statistics*
Mortality statistics, area : review of the Registrar General on deaths by area of usual residence, in England and Wales / Office of Population Censuses and Surveys. — London : H.M.S.O.
1974. — 1976. — vi,2-97p ; 30cm. — (Series DH5 ; no.1)
ISBN 0-11-690556-5 Pbk : £1.70
(B77-11603)

312'.2'0942 — Deaths. Causes. *England, 1968-1974. Statistics*
Great Britain. *Office of Population Censuses and Surveys. Medical Statistics Division.* Mortality surveillance, 1968-1974, England and Wales : deaths and death rates by A-list cause, sex and age group / Office of Population Censuses and Surveys, Medical Statistics Division. — [London] ([10 Kingsway, WC2B 6JP]) : [The Division], 1976. — [154] leaves ; 21x30cm.
Sp : £14.50
(B77-20047)

312'.2'0942 — Deaths. Causes. *England. Statistics*
Mortality statistics, cause : review of the Registrar General on deaths by cause, sex and age, in England and Wales / Office of Population Censuses and Surveys. — London : H.M.S.O.
1974. — 1977. — iii,82p ; 30cm. — (Series DH2 ; no.1)
ISBN 0-11-690628-6 Pbk : £2.00
(B77-11093)

312'.23'42 — Babies, to 1 year. Deaths. *England. Statistics*
Mortality statistics, childhood : review of the Registrar General on deaths in England and Wales / Office of Population Censuses and Surveys. — London : H.M.S.O.
1974. — 1977. — viii,76p ; 30cm. — (DH3 : no.1)
ISBN 0-11-690629-4 Pbk : £2.00
(B77-14080)

312'.269'9400941 — Deaths due to cancer. *Great Britain, 1911-1970. Statistics*
Serial mortality tables : neoplastic diseases / [by] R.A.M. Case ... [et al.]. — London ([34 Sumner Place, S.W.7]) : Division of Epidemiology, Institute of Cancer Research.
In 4 vols.
Vol.1 : England and Wales, 1911-70 : deaths and death rates by sex, age, site and calendar period. — 1976. — [1],iii,141 leaves ; 35cm.
Leaves printed on both sides. — Bibl.: p.10.
ISBN 0-905986-00-8 Sd : Unpriced
(B77-13526)

Vol.2 : Ireland (Republic), 1922-70 : deaths and death rates by sex, age, site and calendar period. — 1976. — [1],iii[i.e. v],142[i.e. 144]p ; 33cm.
Bibl.: p.10.
ISBN 0-905986-01-6 Sd : Unpriced
(B77-13527)

Vol.3 : Northern Ireland, 1922-70 : deaths and death rates by sex, age, site and calendar period. — 1976. — [1],iii[i.e. v],142[i.e.143]p ; 33cm.
Bibl.: p.10.
ISBN 0-905986-02-4 Sd : Unpriced
(B77-13528)

Vol.4 : Scotland, 1911-70 : deaths and death rates by sex, age, site and calendar period. — 1976. — [1],iv,140[i.e.142]p ; 31cm.
Bibl.: p.10.
ISBN 0-905986-03-2 Sd : Unpriced
(B77-13529)

312'.27'0942 — Deaths due to accidents & deaths due to violence. *England. Statistics*
Mortality statistics, accidents and violence : review of the Registrar General on deaths attributed to accidental and violent causes in England and Wales / Office of Population Censuses and Surveys. — London : H.M.S.O.
1974. — 1976. — viii,35p ; 30cm. — (DH4 ; no.1)
ISBN 0-11-690555-7 Sd : £0.95
(B77-01190)

312'.32'4400941 — Man. Lungs. Pneumoconiosis. *Great Britain. Statistics*
Digest of pneumoconiosis statistics / Health and Safety Executive. — London : H.M.S.O.
1974. — 1976. — ii,17p ; 30cm.
Previously issued by the Department of Energy.
ISBN 0-11-880487-1 Sd : £1.00
ISSN 0308-5015
(B77-02794)

1975. — 1977. — ii,17,[1]p ; 30cm.
ISBN 0-11-882006-0 Sd : £2.00
ISSN 0308-5015
(B77-25410)

312'.38'9009417 — Mentally handicapped persons. *Ireland (Republic). Census tables. Serials*
Census of the mentally handicapped in the Republic of Ireland / the Medico-Social Research Board. — Dublin (73 Lower Baggot St., Dublin 2) : The Board.
1974. Non-residential / by Michael Mulcahy. — [1977]. — [1],25p : 1 ill ; 25cm.
Bibl.: p.17.
Sd : £0.60
(B77-20941)

312'.39'0942 — Man. Communicable diseases. *England. Statistics*
Statistics of infectious diseases : notifications of infectious diseases in England and Wales / Office of Population Censuses and Surveys. — London : H.M.S.O.
1975 : No.2. — 1976. — iv,37p ; 24cm. — (Morbidity ; 2)
ISBN 0-11-690621-9 Sd : £0.95
(B77-07096)

312'.8 — Great Britain. Population. Journeys. *Census tables*
Great Britain. *Office of Population Censuses and Surveys. Social Survey Division.* National travel survey, 1972-3 : number of journeys per week by different types of households, individuals and vehicles / [Social Survey Division of the Office of Population Censuses and Surveys ; for the] Department of the Environment. — London : H.M.S.O., 1976. — viii,23p : ill ; 30cm.
ISBN 0-11-550404-4 Sd : £1.25
(B77-08806)

312'.8'0941 — Migration. *Great Britain, 1971. Census tables*
Great Britain. *Office of Population Censuses and Surveys.* Census 1971, Great Britain, migration tables (10% sample) / Office of Population Censuses and Surveys, London [and] General Register Office, Edinburgh. — London : H.M.S.O.
Part 3(A). — 1977. — xxiii,229p : facsim, map ; 32cm.
ISBN 0-11-690625-1 Pbk : £9.25
(B77-15109)

Part 3(B). — 1977. — xxiii,174p : facsim, map ; 32cm.
ISBN 0-11-690626-x Pbk : £8.25
(B77-15110)

Part 3(C). — 1977. — xxiii,228p : facsim, map ; 32cm.
ISBN 0-11-690627-8 Pbk : £9.25
(B77-15111)

312'.8'09411 — Migration. *Scotland, 1971. Census tables*
Great Britain. *General Register Office, Scotland.* Census 1971, Scotland, migration tables ... / General Register Office, Edinburgh. — Edinburgh : H.M.S.O.
Part 3 : (10% sample). — 1976. — xxi,183p : map ; 34cm.
ISBN 0-11-491448-6 Pbk : £6.80
(B77-12880)

Part 4 : (10% sample). — 1977. — xxv,286p : map ; 33cm.
ISBN 0-11-491474-5 Pbk : £11.00
(B77-20942)

Part 5 : (10% sample). — 1977. — xviii,139p : map ; 34cm.
ISBN 0-11-491500-8 Pbk : £6.00
(B77-26830)

312'.8'09416 — Migration. *Northern Ireland, 1971. Census tables*
Northern Ireland. *General Register Office.* Census of population 1971, migration tables, Northern Ireland / Northern Ireland General Register Office. — Belfast : H.M.S.O., 1976. — x,49p,leaf of plate,[6]fold p of plates : forms, map ; 30cm.
ISBN 0-337-23160-5 Sd : £0.85
(B77-20048)

312'.8'0942 — Migration. *England, 1971. Census tables*
Great Britain. *Office of Population Censuses and Surveys.* Census 1971, England and Wales, migration regional report (10% sample) / Office of Population Censuses and Surveys. — London : H.M.S.O.
East Midlands Region. Part 3. — 1977. — xxxviii,257p : map ; 32cm.
ISBN 0-11-690505-0 Pbk : £11.25
(B77-27696)

North Region. Part 3. — 1977. — xxxviii, 281p : map ; 32cm.
ISBN 0-11-690529-8 Pbk : £11.25
(B77-24030)

Yorkshire & Humberside Region. Part 3. — 1977. — xxxviii,364p : map ; 32cm.
ISBN 0-11-690508-5 Pbk : £14.75
(B77-27697)

312'.9 — Households. Social conditions. *Great Britain, 1974. Statistics*
Great Britain. *Office of Population Censuses and Surveys. Social Survey Division.* The General Household Survey, 1974 : an inter-departmental survey sponsored by the Central Statistical Office / Office of Population Censuses and Surveys, Social Survey Division. — London : H.M.S.O., 1977. — v,243p : ill, form ; 30cm.
ISBN 0-11-700820-6 Pbk : £7.00
(B77-29213)

312'.9 — Qualified manpower. *Northern Ireland, 1971. Census tables*
Northern Ireland. *General Register Office.* Census of population 1971, education tables, Northern Ireland / Northern Ireland General Register Office. — Belfast : H.M.S.O., 1975. — xii,78p,[6]fold p of plates : forms, map ; 30cm.
ISBN 0-337-23170-2 Sd : £2.00
(B77-20049)

312'.94'09416 — Population. Economic activity. *Northern Ireland, 1971. Census tables*
Northern Ireland. *General Register Office.* Census of population 1971, economic activity tables, Northern Ireland / Northern Ireland General Register Office. — Belfast : H.M.S.O., 1977. — xiii,2-303p,[6]fold p of plates : forms, map ; 30cm.
ISBN 0-337-23236-9 Pbk : £7.50
(B77-20050)

314 — GENERAL STATISTICS OF EUROPE
314.1 — Great Britain. *Statistics*
Annual abstract of statistics / Central Statistical Office. — London : H.M.S.O.
[No.113] : 1976. — 1976. — xvi,488p ; 28cm.
Index.
ISBN 0-11-630155-4 Pbk : £7.50
(B77-05899)

Regional statistics / Central Statistical Office. — London : H.M.S.O.
No.12 : 1976. — 1976. — viii,214p : ill, maps ; 28cm.
Index.
ISBN 0-11-630152-x Pbk : £6.50
ISSN 0308-146x
(B77-05900)

Social trends. — London : H.M.S.O.
No.7 : 1976 / edited by Eric J. Thompson, associate editor Chris Lewis ; [for the] Central Statistical Office. — 1976. — [2],269p : ill(chiefly col), 2 col maps tipped in ; 28cm.
Bibl.: p.258-262. — Index.
ISBN 0-11-630156-2 Pbk : £6.90
ISSN 0306-7742
(B77-07097)

314.1 — Great Britain. *Statistics. For marketing*
International Publishing Corporation. IPC marketing manual of the United Kingdom. — [London] ([Fleetway House, Farringdon St., EC4A 4AD]) : I.P.C.
1976 / editor : R.A. Critchley. — 1976. — 1v. : maps ; 28cm.
Ca 700p. (5 fold) on publication. — In binder. — Tab indexed. — Bibl. — Index.
ISBN 0-901640-13-1 Ls : £21.00
(B77-02795)

314.11 — Scotland. *Statistics*
Scottish abstract of statistics / Scottish Office. — [Edinburgh] : H.M.S.O.
No.6 : 1976. — 1977. — [2],vii,211p : maps ; 30cm.
Index.
ISBN 0-11-491439-7 Pbk : £5.75
(B77-11604)

314.15 — Ireland. Statistics. Information sources
McGilvray, James William. Social statistics in Ireland : a guide to their sources and uses / [by] James McGilvray. — Dublin : Institute of Public Administration, 1977. — iii-x,204p : ill ; 22cm.
Bibl. — Index.
ISBN 0-902173-74-x Pbk : £3.50
(B77-13530)

314.21 — London, 1971. *Census tables*
Cole, Brian, *b.1950.* Social and economic indices for London constituencies (1971 census) / by B. Cole ; [for the Greater London Council] Director-General's Department Policy Studies and Intelligence Branch. — London : G.L.C., 1976. — [4],xi,46p : map ; 30cm. — (Greater London Council. Intelligence Unit. Research memoranda ; RM502 ISSN 0306-7203)
Bibl.: p.xi.
ISBN 0-7168-0865-x Sd : £2.30
(B77-16209)

314.27 — North-west England. *Statistics*
North West economic & social trends. — [Manchester] ([Sunley Building, Piccadilly Plaza, Manchester M1 4BE]) : North West Economic Planning Council.
1975 ed. / [prepared by the Economic Planning Research Section of the North West Regional Office of the Department of the Environment ; with contributions from others]. — [1975]. — [1],v p,57 leaves,plate : ill(chiefly col), maps(chiefly col) ; 30cm.
Leaves printed on both sides. — Previously published: as 'Economic and social trends'. — Bibl.: p.55(a)-(b).
ISBN 0-903377-02-0 Sd : Unpriced
(B77-08243)

1976 ed. / [prepared by the Economic Planning Research Section of the North West Regional Office of the Department of the Environment ; with contributions from others]. — [1977]. — [1],v p,50 leaves : ill(chiefly col), maps(some col) ; 30cm.
Leaves printed on both sides. — Bibl.: p.48(a)-(b).
Sd : Unpriced
(B77-20051)

314.27'53 — Merseyside (Metropolitan County). Liverpool. *Statistics*
Hart, J F. Some statistics of social contrast in Liverpool from the 1971 census / [by] J.F. Hart. — Liverpool (14 Castle St., Liverpool L2 0NJ) : Liverpool Council for Voluntary Service, [1976]. — [3],49[i.e.51]p,[8]leaves of plates : maps(chiefly col) ; 30cm.
'Prepared from the 1971 census for Liverpool'.
ISBN 0-9501260-5-5 Sd : £0.40
(B77-03971)

314.28'2 — South Yorkshire (Metropolitan County). *Statistics*
South Yorkshire statistics / [compiled by South Yorkshire County Council]. — Barnsley (County Hall, Barnsley, S. Yorkshire S70 2TN) : The Council.
1976. — 1976. — [1],156,[2]p,14p of plates : maps(chiefly col) ; 30cm.
Index.
ISBN 0-86046-002-9 Pbk : £1.00
ISSN 0309-4685
(B77-11094)

320 — POLITICAL SCIENCE
Ball, Alan R. Modern politics and government / [by] Alan R. Ball. — 2nd ed. — London [etc.] : Macmillan, 1977. — xi,276p ; 23cm.
Previous ed.: 1971. — Bibl.: p.257-267. — Index.
ISBN 0-333-22611-9 : £5.95
ISBN 0-333-22612-7 Pbk : £2.95
(B77-33637)

Introduction to political science. — 3rd ed. / [by] Carlton Clymer Rodee ... [et al.]. — New York ; London [etc.] : McGraw-Hill, 1976. — xi,466p : ill ; 25cm.
Previous ed.: / by Carlton Clymer Rodee, Totton James Anderson, Carl Quimby Christol. 1967. — Bibl. — Index.
ISBN 0-07-053376-8 : £10.75
(B77-04589)

320 — Politics
Ellsworth, John W. Politics and political systems : an introduction to political science / [by] John W. Ellsworth, Arthur A. Stahnke. — New York ; London [etc.] : McGraw-Hill, 1976. — x,350p : ill ; 24cm.
Bibl. — Index.
ISBN 0-07-019250-2 Pbk : £7.45
(B77-04590)

Van Dalen, Hendrik. Introduction to political science : people, politics and perception / [by] Hendrik Van Dalen, L. Harmon Zeigler. — Englewood Cliffs ; London [etc.] : Prentice-Hall, 1977. — ix,275p : ill ; 23cm.
Bibl. — Index.
ISBN 0-13-493205-6 Pbk : £5.55
(B77-19238)

Winter, Herbert R. People and politics : an introduction to political science / [by] Herbert R. Winter, Thomas J. Bellows, in collaboration with ... [others]. — New York ; London [etc.] : Wiley, 1977. — xiv,514p : ill, form, map, ports ; 24cm.
Bibl. — Index.
ISBN 0-471-95485-3 : £9.00
(B77-17320)

320 — Politics. *Early works*
Harrington, James. The political works of James Harrington / edited with an introduction by J.G.A. Pocock. — Cambridge [etc.] : Cambridge University Press, 1977. — xviii, 878p,plate : 1 ill ; 24cm. — (Cambridge studies in the history and theory of politics)
Index.
ISBN 0-521-21161-1 : £30.00
(B77-26831)

320 — Politics. *Marxist viewpoints. Essays*
Coates, Ken. Beyond wage slavery / [by] Ken Coates. — Nottingham : Bertrand Russell Peace Foundation for Spokesman Books, 1977. — xi,170p ; 20cm.
Index.
ISBN 0-85124-176-x : £4.50
ISBN 0-85124-177-8 Pbk : Unpriced
(B77-25411)

320 — Politics. *Socialist Union (Internationalist) viewpoints*
Socialist Union (Internationalist). Manifesto of the Socialist Union (Internationalist). — [2nd ed.]. — Doncaster (c/o 16 Abbeyfield Rd, Dunscroft, Doncaster, S. Yorkshire) : Socialist Union (Internationalist).
Previous ed.: 1974.
Part 2 : The revolutionary road to socialism. — [1977]. — [3],66p : ill ; 30cm.
ISBN 0-9504115-5-8 Sd : £0.25
(B77-15112)

320 — Politics. Aristotle. 'Politics'. *Critical studies*
Mulgan, R G. Aristotle's political theory : an introduction for students of political theory / by R.G. Mulgan. — Oxford : Clarendon Press, 1977. — vii,156p ; 23cm.
Bibl.: p.151-152. — Index.
ISBN 0-19-827415-7 : £4.50 : CIP rev.
ISBN 0-19-827416-5 Pbk : £1.85
(B77-24031)

320'.01 — Politics. *Philosophical perspectives*
Raphael, David Daiches. Problems of political philosophy / [by] D.D. Raphael. — Revised ed. — London [etc.] : Macmillan, 1976. — viii, 207p ; 22cm.
Previous ed.: London : Pall Mall Press, 1970. — Index.
ISBN 0-333-21164-2 Pbk : £2.95
(B77-04591)

320'.01 — Politics. Theories
Bowie, Norman E. The individual and the political order : an introduction to social and political philosophy / [by] Norman E. Bowie, Robert L. Simon. — Englewood Cliffs ; London [etc.] : Prentice-Hall, 1977. — viii,280p ; 23cm.
Bibl. — Index.
ISBN 0-13-457143-6 Pbk : £6.35
(B77-15709)

Christie, David, *b.1942.* Economics in action / [by] David Christie, Alex Scott. — London [etc.] : Heinemann Educational, 1977. — [4], 140p : ill ; 25cm.
Includes facsimile reprints. — Index.
ISBN 0-435-84796-1 Pbk : £1.95
(B77-19239)

Montesquieu, Charles Louis de Secondat, *baron de.* The political theory of Montesquieu / [selected and translated from the French by] Melvin Richter. — Cambridge [etc.] : Cambridge University Press, 1977. — xi,355p ; 24cm.
Index. — Contents: Selections from 'Persian letters', 'Considerations on the causes of the Romans' greatness and decline' and 'The spirit of the laws'.
ISBN 0-521-21156-5 : £10.50
ISBN 0-521-29061-9 Pbk : £3.95
(B77-20052)

Russell, Bertrand, *Earl Russell.* Political ideals / [by] Bertrand Russell. — London : Allen and Unwin, 1977. — 80p ; 20cm.
Originally published: New York : Century, 1917 ; London : Allen and Unwin, 1963. — Index.
ISBN 0-04-320120-2 Pbk : £1.25
(B77-20053)

320'.01 — Politics. Theories. Concepts: Need
Human needs and politics / edited by Ross Fitzgerald. — Rushcutters Bay, N.S.W. ; Oxford [etc.] : Pergamon, 1977. — xvi,278p : ill ; 23cm.
Bibl.: p.261-271. — Index.
ISBN 0-08-021402-9 : £8.50
(B77-29974)

320'.01 — Politics. Theories of Aristotle
Morrall, John Brimyard. Aristotle / [by] John B. Morrall. — London [etc.] : Allen and Unwin, 1977. — 3-120p ; 23cm. — (Political thinkers ; 7)
Bibl.: p.113-116. — Index.
ISBN 0-04-320121-0 : £6.50
ISBN 0-04-320122-9 Pbk : £2.95
(B77-31718)

320'.01 — Politics. Theories of Bentham, Jeremy
Steintrager, James. Bentham / [by] James Steintrager. — London : Allen and Unwin, 1977. — 3-133p ; 23cm. — (Political thinkers ; 5)
Bibl.: p.126-129. — Index.
ISBN 0-04-320115-6 : £6.50
ISBN 0-04-320116-4 Pbk : £2.95
(B77-18574)

320'.01 — Politics. Theories of Hobbes, Thomas
Raphael, David Daiches. Hobbes : morals and politics / [by] D.D. Raphael. — London : Allen and Unwin, 1977. — 3-104p ; 23cm. — (Political thinkers ; no.6)
Index.
ISBN 0-04-320118-0 : £6.50
ISBN 0-04-320119-9 Pbk : £2.95
(B77-26832)

320'.01 — Politics. Theories of Jung, Carl Gustav
Odajnyk, Volodymyr Walter. Jung and politics : the political and social ideas of C.G. Jung / [by] Volodymyr Walter Odajnyk ; foreword by Marie-Louise von Franz. — New York [etc.] ; London : Harper and Row, 1976. — xv,190,[1] p ; 21cm. — (Harper colophon books)
Index.
ISBN 0-06-090448-8 Pbk : £3.70
(B77-14081)

320'.01 — Politics. Theories of Machiavelli, Niccolò
Bonadeo, Alfredo. Corruption, conflict, and power in the works and times of Niccolò Machiavelli / by Alfredo Bonadeo. — Berkeley [etc.] ; London : University of California Press, 1973. — ix,127p ; 24cm. — (University of California. Publications in modern philology ; vol.108)
ISBN 0-520-09464-6 Pbk : £2.15
(B77-01191)

320'.03 — Politics. *English-Welsh glossaries*
Termau gwleidyddiaeth / [trefnwyd gan John Davies et al.]. — Caerdydd [i.e. Cardiff] : Gwasg Prifysgol Cymru ar ran Bwrdd Gwybodau Celtaidd Prifysgol Cymru, 1976. — 57p ; 18cm.
ISBN 0-7083-0625-x Sd : £0.45
(B77-03402)

320'.05 — Politics. *Revolutionary Communist Tendency viewpoints. Periodicals*

Revolutionary communist papers. — London (RCT Association, BM RCT, WC1V 6XX) : Revolutionary Communist Tendency.
No.1- ; Mar. 1977-. — [1977]-. — 30cm.
Quarterly? - [1],56p. in 1st issue.
Sd : £0.50
ISSN 0309-4634
(B77-20944)

320'.08 — Political science. *Lectures, speeches*

The **study** of politics : a collection of inaugural lectures / edited by Preston King. — London [etc.] : Cass, 1977. — xiv,322p : ill ; 23cm.
ISBN 0-7146-3084-5 : £12.50
(B77-33638)

320'.08 — Politics. *Essays*

Gandhi, Rajmohan. A writer's duty : extracts from his articles in 'Himmat' (Courage), the Bombay weekly of which he is chief editor / [by] Rajmohan Gandhi ; with a foreword by Graham Turner. — London : Grosvenor Books, 1977. — viii,47p ; 20cm.
ISBN 0-901269-24-7 Sd : £0.40
(B77-06498)

Mill, John Stuart. Essays on politics and society / by John Stuart Mill ; editor of the last text J.M. Robson ; introduction by Alexander Brady. — Toronto [etc.] : University of Toronto Press ; London : Routledge and Kegan Paul, 1977. — 2v.(xcv,vii,780p) ; 25cm. — (Collected works of John Stuart Mill ; vols 18-19)
Bibl.: p.659-753. — Index.
ISBN 0-7100-8451-x : Unpriced
(B77-25412)

320'.0946 — Politics. Theories of Spanish writers, 1516-1559

Fernández-Santamaria, J A. The state, war and peace : Spanish political thought in the Renaissance, 1516-1559 / [by] J.A. Fernández-Santamaria. — Cambridge [etc.] : Cambridge University Press, 1977. — xv,316p ; 24cm. — (Cambridge studies in early modern history)
Bibl.: p.295-308. — Index.
ISBN 0-521-21438-6 : £11.50
(B77-24731)

320.1 — POLITICS. THE STATE

320.1'09 — State systems, to 1969. *Essays*

Wight, Martin. Systems of state / [by] Martin Wight ; edited with an introduction by Hedley Bull. — Leicester : Leicester University Press [for] the London School of Economics and Political Science, 1977. — [5],232p ; 23cm.
Bibl.: p.201-202. — Index.
ISBN 0-7185-1153-0 : £7.00
(B77-11605)

320.1'09 — State, to 1976. *Secondary school texts*

Yapp, Malcolm. The growth of the state / by Malcolm Yapp. — London : Harrap, 1976. — [1],32p : ill, facsims, form, map ; 24cm. — (Harrap world history programme : set 14)
ISBN 0-245-52546-7 Sd : £0.60
(B77-07812)

320.3 — COMPARATIVE POLITICS

320.3 — Industrialised societies. Politics, to 1976. *Comparative studies*

Mayer, Lawrence C. Politics in industrial societies : a comparative perspective / [by] Lawrence C. Mayer with John H. Burnett. — New York ; London [etc.] : Wiley, 1977. — xi, 388p : ill ; 24cm.
Index.
ISBN 0-471-57986-6 : £7.75
(B77-23168)

320.3'01'8 — Comparative politics. Methodology

Czudnowski, Moshe M. Comparing political behavior / [by] Moshe M. Czudnowski ; preface by Heinz Eulau ; foreword by Sidney Verba. — Beverly Hills ; London : Sage Publications, 1976. — [5],178p : ill ; 22cm. — (Sage library of social research ; vol.28)
Bibl.: p.167-178.
ISBN 0-8039-0691-9 : £8.00
ISBN 0-8039-0692-7 Pbk : £4.55
(B77-02073)

320.3'094 — European countries. Politics. *Comparative studies*

Roskin, Michael. Other governments of Europe : Sweden, Spain, Italy, Yugoslavia and East Germany / [by] Michael Roskin. — Englewood Cliffs ; London [etc.] : Prentice-Hall, 1977. — x,182p : 1 ill ; 23cm. — (Prentice-Hall contemporary comparative politics series)
Bibl.: p.177-180. — Index.
ISBN 0-13-642959-9 Pbk : £4.80
(B77-31012)

320.4 — CIVICS

320.4'07'10417 — Schools. Curriculum subjects: Civics. Teaching. *Ireland (Republic). Periodicals*

Blueprint : a source magazine for teachers of civics and allied subjects. — [Dublin] : [Institute of Public Administration].
Supersedes: Civics teachers' newsletter.
Vol.1, no.1- ; Oct. 1975-. — 1975-. — ill, maps, ports ; 44cm.
Published at irregular intervals. — Folder ([4]p.) as 1st issue.
Unpriced
(B77-19240)

320.4'41 — Great Britain. Civics

Harvey, Jack, *b.1917.* The British constitution / by J. Harvey and L. Bather. — 4th ed. — Basingstoke [etc.] : Macmillan, 1977. — xiv, 648p : ill, 2 maps ; 22cm.
Previous ed.: 1972. — Bibl. — Index.
ISBN 0-333-21470-6 Lp : £3.95 : CIP rev.
(B77-04592)

Madgwick, Peter James. Introduction to British politics / [by] P.J. Madgwick. — 2nd ed. — London : Hutchinson, 1976. — 390p : ill ; 24cm.
Previous ed.: 1970. — Bibl.: p.373-378. — Index.
ISBN 0-09-127501-6 Pbk : £2.95
(B77-17321)

Padfield, Colin Frank. British constitution made simple / [by] Colin F. Padfield. — 3rd ed. — London : W.H. Allen, 1976. — xii,355p : ill, facsim, maps ; 22cm. — (Made simple books ISSN 0464-2902)
Previous ed.: 1975. — Index.
Pbk : £1.50
ISBN 0-491-01862-2
(B77-22382)

320.4'41 — Great Britain. Civics. *Secondary school texts*

Mosley, Richard Kenneth. Westminster workshop : a student's guide to the British Constitution / [by] R.K. Mosley. — 3rd ed. — Oxford [etc.] : Pergamon, 1976. — ix,222p ; 21cm. — (Pergamon international library)
This ed. originally published: 1972. — Bibl. — Index.
£2.50
ISBN 0-08-016953-8
ISBN 0-08-016954-6 Pbk : £1.75
(B77-05901)

320.4'41 — Great Britain. Civics. *Serials*

Mosley, Richard Kenneth. British government and politics : a survey for students / [by] R.K. Mosley. — Southampton (8 Cedar Ave., Shirley, Southampton SO1 5GW) : The author.
1977. — 1977. — 48p ; 21cm.
Bibl.: p.47-48.
Sd : £0.60
(B77-17322)

320.4'41 — Great Britain. Civics, 1931-1951. *Secondary school texts*

Penney, Sarah E W. Government : Britain, 1931-51, USSR, 1924-57 / [by] Sarah E.W. Penney and Graeme G. Ash. — Christchurch, N.Z. [etc.] ; London : Whitcoulls, 1976. — 71p : ill, facsims, maps, ports ; 25cm. — (School Certificate history theme ; 5)
ISBN 0-7233-0462-9 Sd : Unpriced
Also classified at 320.4'47
(B77-00055)

320.4'47 — Soviet Union. Civics, 1924-1957. *Secondary school texts*

Penney, Sarah E W. Government : Britain, 1931-51, USSR, 1924-57 / [by] Sarah E.W. Penney and Graeme G. Ash. — Christchurch, N.Z. [etc.] ; London : Whitcoulls, 1976. — 71p : ill, facsims, maps, ports ; 25cm. — (School Certificate history theme ; 5)
ISBN 0-7233-0462-9 Sd : Unpriced
Primary classification 320.4'41
(B77-00055)

320.4'66 — West Africa. Civics. *For Nigerian students. Secondary school texts*

Keay, Elliot Alexander. West African government for Nigerian students / [by] E.A. Keay and H. Thomas. — 3rd ed. — London [etc.] : Hutchinson, 1977. — 271p,[4]p of plates : ill, maps, port ; 19cm.
Previous ed.: 1969. — Index.
ISBN 0-09-129181-x Pbk : £1.45
(B77-25414)

320.4'73 — United States. Civics

Adrian, Charles Raymond. State and local governments / [by] Charles R. Adrian. — 4th ed. — New York ; London [etc.] : McGraw-Hill, 1976. — ix,416p : ill ; 25cm.
Previous ed.: 1972. — Bibl. — Index.
ISBN 0-07-000450-1 : £10.75
(B77-04593)

Ferguson, John Henry. The American system of government / [by] John H. Ferguson, Dean E. McHenry. — 13th ed. — New York ; London [etc.] : McGraw-Hill, 1977. — ix,644p : ill, maps ; 25cm.
Previous ed.: New York : McGraw-Hill, 1973. — Bibl. — Index. — Includes the text of the United States Constitution.
ISBN 0-07-020525-6 : £11.20
(B77-26833)

Manley, John F. American government and public policy / [by] John F. Manley. — New York : Macmillan ; London : Collier Macmillan, 1976. — x,515p : ill ; 24cm.
Index. — Includes the text of the Constitution of the United States of America.
ISBN 0-02-375700-0 Pbk : £6.00
(B77-12334)

320.4'73 — United States. Civics, to 1976

Denenberg, R V. Understanding American politics / [by] R.V. Denenberg. — [London] : Fontana, 1976. — 218p ; 18cm.
Bibl.: p.213. — Index.
ISBN 0-00-633736-8 Pbk : £0.85
(B77-09535)

320.5 — POLITICAL THEORIES AND IDEOLOGIES

320.5 — Political ideologies. Comparative studies

Schubert, Glendon. Political attitudes and ideologies / [by] Glendon Schubert. — Beverly Hills ; London : Sage Publications, 1977. — 72p : ill ; 22cm. — (Sage professional papers in comparative politics ; vol.6, no.01-061 ISSN 0080-5343)
Bibl.: p.69-72.
ISBN 0-8039-0756-7 Pbk : £1.95
(B77-31719)

320.5 — Political ideologies. Theories of Marxists

Laclau, Ernesto. Politics and ideology in Marxist theory : capitalism, fascism, populism / [by] Ernesto Laclau. — London : NLB, 1977. — 203p ; 22cm.
Index.
ISBN 0-902308-74-2 : £6.00
(B77-26834)

320.5'01'9 — Political ideologies. Psychological aspects

Loye, David. The leadership passion / [by] David Loye. — San Francisco [etc.] ; London : Jossey-Bass, 1977. — xxi,249p : ill ; 24cm. — (Jossey-Bass behavioral science series)
Bibl.: p.225-237. — Index.
ISBN 0-87589-302-3 : £10.60
(B77-15113)

320.5'09 — Politics. Theories, to ca 1970

Berki, Robert Nandor. The history of political thought : a short introduction / [by] R.N. Berki. — London [etc.] : Dent [etc.], 1977. — viii,216p ; 24cm. — (Everyman's university library)
Bibl.: p.208-213. — Index.
ISBN 0-460-10177-3 : £5.95 : CIP rev.
ISBN 0-460-11177-9 Pbk : £2.95
(B77-07098)

320.5'1 — Political ideologies: Liberalism

Nott, Kathleen. The good want power : an essay in the psychological possibilities of liberalism / [by] Kathleen Nott. — London : Cape, 1977. — xii,319p ; 23cm.
Bibl.: p.309-311. — Index.
ISBN 0-224-01382-3 : £6.50 : CIP rev.
(B77-09536)

320.5'1'091812 — Political ideologies: Liberalism. Theories. *Western world, ca 1830-1975*

Smith, Neil Allan. The new enlightenment : an essay in political and social realism / by N.A. Smith. — London : J. Calder, 1976. — 256p ; 22cm. — (A platform book)
ISBN 0-7145-3603-2 : £6.50
ISBN 0-7145-3604-0 Pbk : £3.50
(B77-05902)

320.5'1'0924 — Politics. Paine, Thomas. *Biographies*
Foner, Eric. Tom Paine and Revolutionary America / [by] Eric Foner. — London [etc.] : Oxford University Press, 1977. — xxi,326p : ill, facsims, map, port ; 21cm. — (A galaxy book)
Originally published: New York : Oxford University Press, 1976. — Index.
ISBN 0-19-502182-7 Pbk : £2.50
(B77-14580)

320.5'1'0941 — Political ideologies: Liberalism. *Great Britain, 1914-1929*
Bentley, Michael. The liberal mind, 1914-1929 / [by] Michael Bentley. — Cambridge [etc.] : Cambridge University Press, 1977. — viii,279p ; 23cm. — (Cambridge studies in the history and theory of politics)
Bibl.: p.266-270. — Index.
ISBN 0-521-21243-x : £9.50
(B77-16749)

320.5'1'0942 — Universities. Teachers. Political ideologies: Liberalism. *England, 1860-1886*
Harvie, Christopher. The lights of liberalism : university liberals and the challenge of democracy, 1860-86 / [by] Christopher Harvie. — London : Allen Lane, 1976. — 343p : ill ; 23cm.
Index.
ISBN 0-7139-0718-5 : £9.50
(B77-12881)

320.5'1'0973 — Political ideologies: Liberalism. *United States, 1914-1920*
Rochester, Stuart I. American liberal disillusionment in the wake of World War 1 / [by] Stuart I. Rochester. — University Park ; London : Pennsylvania State University Press, 1977. — xi,172p ; 24cm.
Index.
ISBN 0-271-01233-1 : £10.00
(B77-23169)

320.5'1'0973 — Political ideologies: Liberalism. *United States, to 1976*
Goldstene, Paul N. The collapse of liberal empire : science and revolution in the twentieth century / [by] Paul N. Goldstene. — New Haven ; London : Yale University Press, 1977. — xv,139p ; 22cm.
Index.
ISBN 0-300-02029-5 : £7.50
(B77-24732)

320.5'12 — Politics. Theories of Montesquieu, Charles Louis de Secondat, baron de
Hulliung, Mark. Montesquieu and the old regime / [by] Mark Hulliung. — Berkeley [etc.] ; London : University of California Press, 1976. — xi,258p ; 23cm.
Index.
ISBN 0-520-03108-3 : £7.70
(B77-20945)

320.5'12'05 — Libertarianism. *Periodicals*
The **journal** of libertarian studies : an interdisciplinary review. — Oxford [etc.] : Pergamon.
Vol.1, no.1- ; Winter 1977-. — 1977-. — 25cm.

Quarterly. — Cover title. — 79p. in 1st issue.
Pbk : Unpriced
ISSN 0363-2873
(B77-20054)

320.5'2'094 — Conservatism. *Europe, 1770-1945*
Weiss, John. Conservatism in Europe, 1770-1945 : traditionalism, reaction and counter-revolution / [by] John Weiss. — London : Thames and Hudson, 1977. — 180p : ill, facsim ; 22cm. — ([Library of European civilization])
Bibl.: p.174-177. — Index.
ISBN 0-500-32035-7 : £4.00
(B77-16210)

320.5'2'0941 — Conservatism. *Great Britain, ca 1680-1976*
Gilmour, Ian. Inside right : a study of Conservatism / [by] Ian Gilmour. — London : Hutchinson, 1977. — 294p ; 23cm.
Bibl.: p.261-272. — Index.
ISBN 0-09-131760-6 : £5.95
(B77-29214)

320.5'3'091812 — New Left movement. Political ideologies. *Western world, 1953-1974*
Young, Nigel. An infantile disorder? : the crisis and decline of the New Left / [by] Nigel Young. — London [etc.] : Routledge and Kegan Paul, 1977. — xxii,490p ; 23cm.
Bibl.: p.477-479. — Index.
ISBN 0-7100-8467-6 : £9.95 : CIP rev.
(B77-19241)

320.5'3'0943 — Left-wing political movements. Political ideologies. *West Germany, 1945-1973*
Graf, William David. The German Left since 1945 : socialism and social democracy in the German Federal Republic / [by] William David Graf, with an epilogue by Ossip K. Flechtheim. — Cambridge [etc.] : Oleander Press, 1976 [i.e. 1977]. — 318p ; 22cm.
Bibl.: p.292-309. — Index.
ISBN 0-902675-54-0 : £8.95
ISBN 0-902675-68-0 Pbk : £4.50
(B77-10193)

320.5'315 — Marxism. Political aspects
Miliband, Ralph. Marxism and politics / [by] Ralph Miliband. — Oxford [etc.] : Oxford University Press, 1977. — viii,199p ; 21cm. — (Marxist introductions)
Bibl.: p.191-194. — Index.
ISBN 0-19-876059-0 : £3.50 : CIP rev.
ISBN 0-19-876062-0 Pbk : Unpriced
(B77-05227)

320.5'315 — Proletarian dictatorship. Theories of Marxists. *Parti Communiste Français viewpoints*
Balibar, Etienne. On the dictatorship of the proletariat / [by] Etienne Balibar ; introduction by Grahame Lock ; afterword by Louis Althusser ; translated [from the French] by Grahame Lock. — London : NLB, 1977. — 237p ; 22cm.
Translation of: 'Sur la dictature du Prolétariat'. Paris : Maspero, 1976. — Index.
ISBN 0-902308-59-9 : £6.50
(B77-28420)

320.5'32 — Communism. Political aspects. Related to state communism
Revel, Jean François. The totalitarian temptation / [by] Jean-François Revel ; translated from the French by David Hapgood. — London : Secker and Warburg, 1977. — 311p ; 23cm.
This translation also published: Garden City, N.Y. : Doubleday, 1977. — Translation of: 'La tentation totalitaire'. Paris : R. Laffont, 1976.
ISBN 0-436-41140-7 : £4.90
Primary classification 321.9'2
(B77-31013)

320.5'322'0924 — Politics. Theories of Lenin, Vladimir Il'ich
Harding, Neil. Lenin's political thought / [by] Neil Harding. — London [etc.] : Macmillan.
Vol.1 : Theory and practice in the democratic revolution. — 1977. — ix,360p ; 23cm.
Bibl.: p.333-339. — Index.
ISBN 0-333-21287-8 : £12.50 : CIP rev.
ISBN 0-333-21288-6 Pbk : Unpriced
(B77-24734)

320.5'33 — Fascism. Political aspects
De Felice, Renzo. Interpretations of fascism / [by] Renzo de Felice ; translated [from the Italian] by Brenda Huff Everett. — Cambridge, Mass. ; London : Harvard University Press, 1977. — xvi,248p ; 25cm.
Translation of: 'Le interpretazioni del fascismo'. 4.ed. Bari : Laterza, 1972. — Bibl.: p.243-244. — Index.
ISBN 0-674-45962-8 : £10.25
(B77-28421)

320.5'33'09436 — Fascism. Political aspects. *Austria, 1875-1938*
Carsten, Francis Ludwig. Fascist movements in Austria : from Schönerer to Hitler / [by] F.L. Carsten. — London [etc.] : Sage Publications, 1977. — 356p ; 23cm. — (Sage studies in 20th century history ; vol.7)
Bibl.: p.337-344. — Index.
ISBN 0-8039-9992-5 : £9.20
ISBN 0-8039-9857-0 Pbk : £4.60
(B77-18575)

320.5'4 — Nationalism. *Anarchist viewpoints*
Bonanno, Alfredo M. Anarchism and the national liberation struggle / [by] Alfred M. Bonnano ; [translated from the Italian]. — Port Glasgow (c/o A. and V. McGowan, 83 Langside Terrace, Port Glasgow [Renfrewshire]) : Bratach Dubh Publications, 1976. — [2],18p ; 22cm. — (Bratach Dubh (Collective). Anarchist pamphlets ; no.1)
'... translated from "Anarchismo" No.7 ...' - title page verso.
Sd : £0.15
(B77-33640)

320.5'4'08 — Nationalism. *Marxist viewpoints. Essays*
Luxemburg, Rosa. The national question : selected writings / by Rosa Luxemburg ; [translated from the Polish and the German] ; edited with an introduction by Horace B. Davis. — New York ; London : Monthly Review Press, 1976. — 320p ; 21cm.
ISBN 0-85345-355-1 : £9.25
(B77-04594)

320.5'4'09 — Nationalism, to ca 1970. *Secondary school texts*
Yapp, Malcolm. Nationalism / by Malcolm Yapp. — London : Harrap, 1976. — [1],32p : ill, facsim, maps, ports ; 24cm. — (Harrap world history programme : set 14)
ISBN 0-245-52547-5 Sd : £0.60
(B77-07099)

320.5'4'0924 — Pan-Africanism. Williams, Henry Sylvester. *Biographies*
Mathurin, Owen Charles. Henry Sylvester Williams and the origins of the pan-African movement, 1869-1911 / [by] Owen Charles Mathurin. — Westport, Conn. ; London : Greenwood Press, 1976 [i.e. 1977]. — xvi,183, [1]p ; 22cm. — (Contributions in Afro-American and African studies ; no.21)
Published in the United States: 1976. — Bibl.: p.170-178. — Index.
ISBN 0-8371-8594-7 : Unpriced
(B77-10194)

320.5'4'0941 — Nationalism. *Great Britain, 1640-1975. Marxist viewpoints*
Nairn, Tom. The break-up of Britain : crisis and neo-nationalism / [by] Tom Nairn. — London : NLB, 1977. — 368p ; 22cm.
'Most of the contents of this book appeared previously in "New Left Review" ...' - Acknowledgements. — Index.
ISBN 0-902308-57-2 : £7.50
(B77-23170)

320.5'4'09415 — Nationalism. *Ireland, 1900-1976*
Rumpf, E. Nationalism and socialism in twentieth-century Ireland / [by] E. Rumpf and A.C. Hepburn. — Liverpool : Liverpool University Press, 1977. — xvii,275p : maps(1 col) ; 24cm.
Bibl.: p.250-260. — Index.
ISBN 0-85323-343-8 : £10.00
(B77-10195)

320.5'4'09429 — Nationalism. *Wales*
Hearne, Derrick. The joy of freedom / [by] Derrick Hearne. — Talybont, Dyfed (Talybont Dyfed SY24 5ER) : Y Lolfa, 1977. — 2-111p ; 19cm. — (Pocedlyfrau'r Lolfa)
ISBN 0-904864-38-3 : Unpriced
ISBN 0-904864-37-5 Pbk : £1.85
(B77-24735)

320.5'4'09437 — Neo-Slavism. *Czechoslovakia, to 1914*
Vyšný, Paul. Neo-Slavism and the Czechs, 1898-1914 / [by] Paul Vyšný. — Cambridge [etc.] : Cambridge University Press, 1977. — xiv,287p : map ; 23cm. — (Soviet and East European studies)
Bibl.: p.258-273. — Index.
ISBN 0-521-21230-8 : £9.50
(B77-09537)

320.5'4'09471 — Nationalism. Role of Finnish folklore. *Finland, to 1972*
Wilson, William A. Folklore and nationalism in modern Finland / [by] William A. Wilson. — Bloomington ; London : Indiana University Press, 1976. — xii,272p : ill, maps ; 25cm.
Bibl.: p.209-230. — Index.
ISBN 0-253-32327-4 : £10.15
(B77-14082)

320.5'4'09561 — Nationalism. *Turkey, 1876-1908*
Kushner, David, *b.1938.* The rise of Turkish nationalism, 1876-1908 / [by] David Kushner. — London : Cass, 1977. — xi,126p ; 23cm.
Bibl.: p.118-120. — Index.
ISBN 0-7146-3075-6 : Unpriced
(B77-23171)

320.5'4'096 — Nationalism. Role of military forces. *Africa*
Ogueri, Eze. African nationalism and military ascendancy / [by] Eze Ogueri, II. — Owerri [etc.] ; London : Conch Magazine Limited (Publishers), 1976. — vi,85p ; 22cm. — (Contemporary African politics series)
Index.
ISBN 0-914970-13-5 : £8.07
ISBN 0-914970-14-3 Pbk : Unpriced
(B77-06499)

320.5'4'0973 — Nationalism. *United States, 1815-1861*
Wilson, Major L. Space, time and freedom : the quest for nationality and the irrepressible conflict, 1815-1861 / [by] Major L. Wilson. — Westport, Conn. ; London : Greenwood Press, 1974. — x,309p ; 22cm. — (Contributions in American history ; no.35)
Index.
ISBN 0-8371-7373-6 : £11.95
(B77-16211)

320.9 — POLITICS. HISTORICAL AND GEOGRAPHICAL TREATMENT

320.9'04'7 — Anti-fascist movements. *Periodicals*
Searchlight on the struggle against racism and fascism. — Birmingham (21 Great Western Buildings, 6 Livery St., Birmingham 3) : A.F. and R. Publications.
No.1- ; [1975?]-. — [1975?]-. — ill, facsims, ports ; 30cm.
Monthly. — 19p. in 21st issue.
Sd : £0.30
(B77-15710)

320.9'04'7 — Politics. *Yearbooks*
Political handbook of the world : governments and intergovernmental organizations as of January 1. — New York ; London [etc.] : McGraw-Hill for the Center for Comparative Political Research of the State University of New York at Binghamton and for the Council on Foreign Relations.
1975 / edited by Arthur S. Banks ... [et al.]. — [1976]. — xv,491p : map(on lining papers) ; 29cm.
Published in the United States: 1975.
ISBN 0-07-003713-2 : £14.75
Also classified at 341.2'05
(B77-02074)

1976 / edited by Arthur S. Banks ... [et al.]. — 1976. — xi,545p : map(on lining papers) ; 29cm.
ISBN 0-07-003640-3 : £14.75
Also classified at 341.2'05
(B77-02075)

Political handbook of the world : governments, regional issues, and intergovernmental organizations as of January 1. — New York [etc.] ; London : McGraw-Hill for the Center for Social Analysis of the State University of New York at Binghamton and for the Council on Foreign Relations.
1977 / edited by Arthur S. Banks ... [et al.]. — 1977. — xii,604p : map(on lining papers) ; 29cm.
Index.
ISBN 0-07-003641-1 : Unpriced
Also classified at 341.2'05
(B77-29975)

320.9'171'7 — Communist countries. Political development, to 1976
Political culture and political change in communist states / edited by Archie Brown and Jack Gray. — London [etc.] : Macmillan, 1977. — xiii,286p : ill ; 23cm.
Index.
ISBN 0-333-21429-3 : £10.00
(B77-26142)

320.9'172'4 — Developing countries. Politics. Role of religion. *Conference proceedings*
Religion and political modernization / edited by Donald Eugene Smith. — New Haven ; London : Yale University Press, 1974. — x, 340p : 1 ill ; 24cm.
'... papers prepared for a conference held in Honolulu in March 1971 ... sponsored by the Institute of Religion and Social Change' - Foreword. — Index.
ISBN 0-300-01730-8 : £12.60
(B77-19242)

320.9'4'055 — Left-wing political movements. *Western Europe. Periodicals*
Euro-red / West-European Sub-committee of the International Department of the Communist Party of Great Britain. — London (16 King St., W.C.2) : [West-European Sub-Committee, International Department, Communist Party of Great Britain].
No.1- ; [1976]-. — [1976]-. — 30cm.
Published at irregular intervals. — 16p. in 1st issue.
Sd : £0.15
ISSN 0309-5975
(B77-17323)

320.9'4'055 — Western Europe. Politics
Crozier, Michel. The governability of West European societies / [by] Michel Crozier. — [Colchester] ([Wivenhoe Park, Colchester CO4 3SQ]) : University of Essex, 1977. — 15p ; 21cm. — (Noel Buxton lectures ; 1977)
'The twelfth Noel Buxton Lecture at the University of Essex, 18th May 1977' - title page verso.
Sd : Unpriced
(B77-32440)

320.9'41'075 — Great Britain. Politics, 1830-1850
Prest, John. Politics in the age of Cobden / [by] John Prest. — London [etc.] : Macmillan, 1977. — vii,165p ; 23cm.
Index.
ISBN 0-333-22349-7 : £7.95 : CIP rev.
(B77-24032)

320.9'41'081 — Great Britain. Politics, 1841-1846
Crosby, Travis L. Sir Robert Peel's administration, 1841-1846 / [by] Travis L. Crosby. — Newton Abbot [etc.] : David and Charles [etc.], 1976. — 190p : ill ; 23cm. — ([Elections and administrations series])
Bibl.: p.175-184. — Index.
ISBN 0-7153-7159-2 : £5.50
(B77-08245)

320.9'41'081 — Great Britain. Politics, 1893-1898 & 1904-1915. *Diaries*
Hobhouse, Charles. Inside Asquith's Cabinet : from the diaries of Charles Hobhouse / edited by Edward David. — London : J. Murray, 1977. — x,295p,[12]p of plates : ill, ports ; 23cm.
Index.
ISBN 0-7195-3387-2 : £6.25
(B77-25415)

320.9'41'081 — Great Britain. Politics. Role of Irish Parliamentary Party, 1880-1886
O'Day, Alan. The English face of Irish nationalism : Parnellite involvement in British politics, 1880-86 / [by] Alan O'Day. — Dublin : Gill and Macmillan [etc.], 1977. — x, 210p ; 23cm.
Index.
ISBN 0-7171-0816-3 : £7.00
(B77-14083)

320.9'41'085 — Great Britain. Politics, 1945-1975
Johnson, Nevil. In search of the constitution : reflections on state and society in Britain / by Nevil Johnson. — Oxford [etc.] : Pergamon, 1977. — ix,239p ; 22cm.
Index.
ISBN 0-08-021379-0 : £6.50
(B77-22383)

320.9'41'085 — Great Britain. Politics, ca 1940-ca 1960. *Socialist viewpoints*
Bevan, Aneurin. In place of fear / [by] Aneurin Bevan. — [New] ed. ; with a foreword by Jennie Lee. — Wakefield : EP Publishing, 1976. — 203p,leaf of plate,[8]p of plates : ports ; 23cm.
This ed. originally published: London : MacGibbon and Kee, 1961.
ISBN 0-7158-1168-1 : £4.75
(B77-08246)

320.9'41'0856 — Great Britain. Politics. Influence of Powell, Enoch, 1963-1975
Schoen, Douglas E. Enoch Powell and the Powellites / [by] Douglas E. Schoen. — London [etc.] : Macmillan, 1977. — xviii,317p : ill ; 23cm.
Bibl.: p.280-287. — Index.
ISBN 0-333-19866-2 : £10.00
(B77-26030)

320.9'41'0857 — Great Britain. Politics
Punnett, Robert Malcolm. British government and politics / [by] R.M. Punnett. — 3rd ed. — London : Heinemann, 1976. — xiii,522p ; 23cm.
Previous ed.: 1971. — Bibl.: p.423-299. — Index.
ISBN 0-435-83736-2 : £6.00
ISBN 0-435-83737-0 Pbk : £3.25
(B77-00056)

320.9'411'069 — Scotland. Politics, 1700-1707
Daiches, David. Scotland and the Union / [by] David Daiches. — London : J. Murray, 1977. — viii,212p,plate : 1 ill ; 23cm.
Bibl.: p.205-207. — Index.
ISBN 0-7195-3391-0 : £5.50
(B77-22384)

320.9'411'0857 — Scotland. Self government. *Radical viewpoints*
The **radical** approach : papers on an independent Scotland / [edited by Gavin Kennedy]. — Edinburgh (56 Dean St., Edinburgh EH4 1LQ) : Palingenesis Press Ltd, 1976. — vi, 109p : map ; 22cm.
ISBN 0-905470-01-x : £3.95
ISBN 0-905470-00-1 Pbk : £1.75
(B77-26835)

320.9'4113'50857 — Scotland. Shetland. Self government. Proposals. Implications of self government of self governing islands in Great Britain & Scandinavia
Gronneberg, Roy. Island governments : the experience of autonomous island groups in northern Europe in relation to Shetland's political future / [by] Roy Gronneberg. — Sandwick (Sandwick, Shetland) : Thuleprint Ltd, 1976. — 30,[1]p ; 21cm.
Bibl.: p.29-30.
Sd : £0.45
(B77-17324)

320.9'415'0821 — Ireland. Unionism, 1885-1921. *Teaching kits*
Steps to partition : Irish Unionism, 1885-1921 / [with commentary] by C.W. Breen, P. Buckland, S. Kelly. — Belfast [etc.] : H.M.S.O. for the Public Record Office of Northern Ireland, 1976. — Portfolio : ill, facsims, maps, ports ; 31cm. — (Education facsimiles ; 201-220)
Booklet (12p.), 20 sheets (some fold.), 13 worksheets in folder, all in plastic envelope. — Bibl.: p.11-12.
ISBN 0-337-23176-1 : £1.00
(B77-05228)

320.9'417'082 — Ireland (Republic). Politics. Theories of O'Brien, Conor Cruise
Lysaght, D R O'Connor. End of a liberal : the literary politics of Conor Cruise O'Brien / [by] D.R. O'Connor Lysaght. — Dublin (38 Clanawley Rd, Dublin 5) : Plough Books, [1977]. — [1],56,[1]p ; 21cm.
Sd : £0.30
(B77-28422)

320.9'42'04 — England. Politics, 1450-1509. *Essays*
Lander, Jack Robert. [Crown and nobility, 1450-1509. Ch.1]. Politics and power in England, 1450-1509 / [by] J.R. Lander. — London : Edward Arnold, 1976. — iv,68p ; 24cm.
'Crown and nobility, 1450-1509' originally published: 1976. — Bibl.: p.iv. — Index.
ISBN 0-7131-5905-7 Pbk : £1.95
(B77-02796)

320.9'42'05 — England. Politics, 1450-1660
Loades, David Michael. Politics and the nation, 1450-1660 : obedience, resistance and public order / [by] D.M. Loades. — [London] : Fontana, 1977. — 5-484p ; 20cm. — (Fontana library of English history)
Originally published: London : Fontana ; Brighton : Harvester Press, 1974. — Bibl.: p.462-472. — Index.
Pbk : £2.25
ISBN 0-00-633339-7
(B77-16750)

320.9'42'06 — England. Politics, 1675-1725
Plumb, John Harold. The growth of political stability in England, 1675-1725 / [by] J.H. Plumb. — London [etc.] : Macmillan, 1977. — xviii,206p ; 23cm.
Originally published: 1967. — Index.
ISBN 0-333-02331-5 : £7.95
ISBN 0-333-23061-2 Pbk : Unpriced
(B77-29216)

320.9'42'068 — England. Politics, 1688-1702
Horwitz, Henry. Parliament, policy and politics in the reign of William III / [by] Henry Horwitz. — Manchester : Manchester University Press, 1977. — xiii,385p ; 24cm.
Index.
ISBN 0-7190-0661-9 : £8.50
(B77-10196)

320.9'42'081 — England. Urban regions. Politics, 1837-1901
Fraser, Derek. Urban politics in Victorian England : the structure of politics in Victorian cities / [by] Derek Fraser. — [Leicester] : Leicester University Press, 1976. — 324p : maps ; 25cm.
Index.
ISBN 0-7185-1145-x : £12.00
(B77-00057)

320.9'42'0857 — England. Politics. *English National Party viewpoints. Periodicals*
England : the journal of the English National Party. — [London] (76 Lock Chase, S.E.3) : E.N.P.
[1]- ; Oct. 1, 1976-. — 1976-. — 30cm.
Weekly. — Sheet ([1]p.) as 1st issue.
Unpriced
ISSN 0309-0515
(B77-01192)

England : an independent journal : new series. — London (76 Lock Chase, Blackheath, SE3 9HA) : 'England'.
Supersedes : England [first series].
No.1- ; Oct. 27, 1976-. — 1976-. — 30cm.
Weekly. — 2 leaves in 1st issue.
Sd : £0.10
ISSN 0309-0515
(B77-03972)

320.9'423'39 — Dorset. Christchurch. Politics, 1572-1900
Lavender, Ruth. From pocket borough to parliamentary democracy / by Ruth Lavender. — [Dorchester, Dorset] ([County Hall, Dorchester, Dorset DT1 1XJ]) : Dorset County Council Education Committee, 1976. — [1], 31p ; 21cm.
'No.627'. — Bibl.: p.31.
ISBN 0-85216-153-0 Sd : Unpriced
(B77-09538)

320.9'425'807 — Museums. *Hertfordshire. Hertford. Hertford Museum. Exhibits: Items associated with politics in Hertfordshire, 1700-1800. Catalogues*
Hertford Museum. The hart and the eagle : a guide [and catalogue] to the exhibition held at the Hertford Museum July-November 1976. — [Hertford] ([Hertford, Herts.]) : Hertford Museum, 1976. — 391 leaves : 1 ill, geneal tables ; 30cm.
Bibl.: leaf 39.
Sp : £0.50
(B77-20946)

320.9'427'32 — Greater Manchester (Metropolitan County). Salford. Politics, 1830-1900
Garrard, John. Leaders and politics in nineteenth century Salford : a historical analysis of urban political power / [by] John Garrard. — [Salford] ([Salford M5 4WT]) : [University of Salford, Department of Sociological and Political Studies], [1977]. — [3],91[i.e.96]p,[2] leaves of plates : ill ; 30cm. — (Salford city politics research series)
Sp : Unpriced
(B77-26836)

320.9'429'081 — Radical movements. *Wales, 1800-1900. Essays. Welsh texts*
Jones, Frank Price. Radicaliaeth a'r werin Gymreig yn y bedwaredd ganrif ar bymtheg : casgliad o ysgrifau / gan Frank Price Jones ; golygwyd gan Alun Llywelyn-Williams ac Elfed ap Nefydd Roberts. — Caerdydd [i.e. Cardiff] : Gwasg Prifysgol Cymru, 1977. — 211p ; 22cm.
Index.
ISBN 0-7083-0673-x Pbk : £3.95
(B77-33082)

320.9'43'084 — Germany. Politics, 1894-1897
Wilke, Ekkehard-Teja P W. Political decadence in imperial Germany : personnel-political aspects of the German government crisis, 1894-97 / [by] Ekkehard-Teja P.W. Wilke. — Urbana [etc.] ; London : University of Illinois Press, 1976. — xv,311p ; 24cm. — (Illinois studies in the social sciences ; 59)
Bibl.: p.294-302. — Index.
ISBN 0-252-00571-6 : £7.70
(B77-17325)

320.9'438 — Poland. Politics, 1900-1976. *Polish texts*
Wasiutyński, Wojciech. Zródla niepodleglości / Wojciech Wasiutyński. — Londyn [i.e. London] (8 Alma Terrace, Allen St., W8 6QY) : Instytut Romana Dmowskiego, 1977. — 178p ; 21cm.
ISBN 0-9505705-0-8 Pbk : £3.75
(B77-15114)

320.9'438'05 — Poland. Politics, 1948-1975. *Polish texts*
Drewnowski, Jan. O myśl polityczną / Jan Drewnowski. — Londyn [i.e. London] (27 Hamilton Rd, Bedford Park, W4 1AL) : Odnowa, 1976. — 100p ; 22cm.
ISBN 0-903705-12-5 Pbk : £2.70
(B77-09539)

320.9'44'083 — France. Politics
Giscard d'Estaing, Valéry. Towards a new democracy / [by] V. Giscard d'Estaing ; translated [from the French] by Vincent Cronin. — London : Collins, 1977. — 150p ; 22cm.
Translation of: 'Démocratie française'. Paris : Fayard, 1976.
ISBN 0-00-216156-7 : £2.95
(B77-29976)

320.9'45 — Italy. Politics, 1400-1945. *Essays*
Gilbert, Felix. History : choice and commitment / [by] Felix Gilbert. — Cambridge, Mass. ; London : Belknap Press of Harvard University Press, 1977. — ix,549p ; 24cm.
Index.
ISBN 0-674-39656-1 : £12.65
Also classified at 907'.2
(B77-33083)

320.9'45'09 — Italy. Politics, 1910-1926. *Marxist viewpoints. Essays*
Gramsci, Antonio. Selections from political writings [of] Antonio Gramsci / selected and edited by Quintin Hoare ; translated [from the Italian] by John Mathews. — London : Lawrence and Wishart.
In 2 vols.
[Vol.1] : 1910-1920 / with additional texts by Bordiga and Tasca. — 1977. — xxi,393p ; 23cm.
'The great majority of the texts translated here ... have been taken from the collections entitled "Scritti giovanili 1914-18" (Turin [: Einaudi], 1958) and "L'Ordine nuovo 1919-20" (Turin [: Einaudi], 1955) - Introduction. — Index.
ISBN 0-85315-387-6 : £6.00
ISBN 0-85315-386-8 Pbk : £3.00
(B77-11606)

320.9'45'091 — Italy. Politics, 1919-1930
Salvemini, Gaetano. The origins of fascism in Italy / [by] Gaetano Salvemini ; edited and with an introduction by Roberto Vivarelli. — New York [etc.] ; London : Harper and Row, 1973. — iii-xx,445p ; 21cm. — (Harper torch books)
Bibl.: p.xiv-xx. — Index.
ISBN 0-06-131646-6 Pbk : Unpriced
(B77-18576)

320.9'45'091 — Italy. Politics. Role of Roman Catholics, 1919-1926
Molony, John N. The emergence of political catholicism in Italy : Partito popolare 1919-1926 / [by] John N. Molony. — London : Croom Helm [etc.], 1977. — 3-225p ; 23cm.
Bibl.: p.200-215. — Index.
ISBN 0-85664-412-9 : £7.95
(B77-20055)

320.9'46'082 — Spain. Politics, 1938-1976
Amodia, José. Franco's political legacy : from dictatorship to façade democracy / [by] José Amodia. — London : Allen Lane, 1977. — 348p ; 23cm.
Bibl.: p.320-337. — Index.
ISBN 0-7139-0488-7 : £9.00
(B77-10197)

320.9'47'08 — Soviet Union. Politics, 1861-1976
McAuley, Mary. Politics and the Soviet Union / [by] Mary McAuley. — Harmondsworth [etc.] : Penguin, 1977. — 352p ; 18cm. — (Penguin education)
Bibl.: p.338-345. — Index.
ISBN 0-14-080929-5 Pbk : £1.50
(B77-10198)

320.9'47'085 — Soviet Union. Politics
The **dynamics** of Soviet politics / edited by Paul Cocks, Robert V. Daniels, Nancy Whittier Heer. — Cambridge, Mass. ; London : Harvard University Press, 1976. — [9],427p : 1 ill ; 24cm. — (Harvard University. Russian Research Center. Studies ; 76)
Index.
ISBN 0-674-21881-7 : £13.15
(B77-17326)

Medvedev, Roĭ Aleksandrovich. On socialist democracy / [by] Roy A. Medvedev ; translated from the Russian and edited by Ellen de Kadt. — Nottingham : Spokesman Books for the Bertrand Russell Peace Foundation, 1977. — [1],xxii,405,xv p ; 22cm. — (European socialist thought series ; no.9)
This translation originally published: New York : Knopf ; London : Macmillan, 1975. — Translation of: 'Kniga o sotsialisticheskoĭ demokratii'. Amsterdam : Herzen Foundation, 1972. — Index.
ISBN 0-85124-161-1 Pbk : £3.95
(B77-24033)

320.9'497'02 — Yugoslavia. Politics, 1948-1974
Rusinow, Dennison Ivan. The Yugoslav experiment, 1948-1974 / by Dennison Rusinow. — London : C. Hurst for the Royal Institute of International Affairs, 1977. — xxi,410p : map ; 23cm.
Bibl.: p.395-400. — Index.
ISBN 0-903983-65-6 : £9.50
(B77-15115)

320.9'5'042 — Asia. Politics
Kim, Chong-Iik Eugene. An introduction to Asian politics / [by] C.I. Eugene Kim, Lawrence Ziring. — Englewood Cliffs ; London [etc.] : Prentice-Hall, 1977. — xi,400p : ill, maps ; 24cm.
Bibl. — Index.
ISBN 0-13-478081-7 : £9.55
(B77-29977)

320.9'51'04 — China. Politics, 1921-1976. *British and Irish Communist Organisation viewpoints*
The **politics** of revolutionary China. — Belfast : British and Irish Communist Organisation, 1977. — [1],45p ; 24cm.
Includes the three part series by P. McMorrow entitled 'The politics of revolutionary China', and other articles originally published in issues of 'The Irish communist' and 'The communist' during 1976.
Sd : Unpriced
(B77-32441)

320.9'51'04 — China. Politics. Role of Yenching University, 1916-1952
West, Philip. Yenching University and Sino-Western relations, 1916-1952 / [by] Philip West. — Cambridge, Mass. ; London : Harvard University Press, 1976. — xiii,327p,[4]p of plates : ill, ports ; 25cm. — (Harvard East Asian series ; 85)
Bibl.: p.303-310. — Index.
ISBN 0-674-96569-8 : £12.00
(B77-08807)

320.9'51'05 — China. Politics, 1949-1972
Starr, John Bryan. Ideology and culture : an introduction to the dialectic of contemporary Chinese politics / [by] John Bryan Starr. — New York [etc.] ; London : Harper and Row, [1977]. — xvii,300p : ill, maps ; 21cm. — (Harper's comparative government series)
Published in the United States: 1973. — Index.
ISBN 0-06-046413-5 Pbk : £4.45
(B77-12882)

320.9'51'05 — China. Politics, 1949-1976
Guillermaz, Jacques. The Chinese Communist Party in power, 1949-1976 / [by] Jacques Guillermaz ; translated [from the French] by Anne Destenay. — Folkestone : Dawson, 1976. — xxiii,614p : maps ; 25cm.
Translation and updated revision of: 'Le parti communiste chinois au pouvoir'. Paris : Payot, 1972. — Bibl.: p.581-599. — Index.
ISBN 0-7129-0752-1 : £18.00 : CIP rev.
(B77-07750)

Wang Gungwu. China and the world since 1949 : the impact of independence, modernity and revolution / [by] Wang Gungwu. — London [etc.] : Macmillan, 1977. — xi,190p : map ; 23cm. — (The making of the 20th century)
Bibl.: p.179-183. — Index.
ISBN 0-333-15592-0 : £5.95
ISBN 0-333-15593-9 Pbk : £2.95
(B77-25416)

320.9'51'05 — China. Politics, 1969-1973
Domes, Jürgen. China after the Cultural Revolution : politics between two party congresses / [by] Jürgen Domes ; with a contribution by Marie-Luise Näth ; translated from the German by Annette Berg and David Goodman. — London : C. Hurst, [1977]. — xii, 283p : map ; 23cm.
Translation of: 'China nach der Kulturrevolution'. München : W. Fink, 1975. — Index.
ISBN 0-903983-43-5 : £6.50 : CIP rev.
(B77-07100)

320.9'54'035 — India. Politics, 1857-1964. *Readings from contemporary sources*
Documents on political thought in modern India / [compiled by] A. Appadorai. — Bombay ; London [etc.] : Oxford University Press.
Vol.2. — 1976. — vii,892p : 1 ill ; 23cm.
Index.
ISBN 0-19-560384-2 : £14.00
(B77-29978)

320.9'54'035 — India. Politics, 1916-1921
Robb, P G. The government of India and reform : policies towards politics and the constitution, 1916-1921 / by P.G. Robb. — Oxford [etc.] : Oxford University Press, 1976. — xiv,379p,plate : ports ; 23cm. — (London Oriental series ; vol.32)
Bibl.: p.361-370. — Index.
ISBN 0-19-713590-0 : £10.50
(B77-11607)

320.9'549'303 — Sri Lanka. Politics
Kearney, Robert Norman. The politics of Ceylon (Sri Lanka) / [by] Robert N. Kearney. — Ithaca ; London : Cornell University Press, 1973. — xix,249p : ill, maps ; 22cm. — (South Asian political systems)
Bibl.: p.229-243. — Index.
ISBN 0-8014-0798-2 : Unpriced
(B77-18577)

320.9'549'8 — Bhutan. Politics, 1947-1975
Rose, Leo Eugene. The politics of Bhutan / [by] Leo E. Rose. — Ithaca ; London : Cornell University Press, 1977. — 237p : 1 ill, map ; 23cm. — (South Asian political systems)
Bibl.: p.228-233. — Index.
ISBN 0-8014-0909-8 : £14.65
(B77-28423)

320.9'56'04 — Middle East. Politics, 1968-1976
Price, David Lynn. Oil and Middle East security / [by] David Lynn Price. — Beverly Hills ; London : Sage Publications [for] the Center for Strategic and International Studies, Georgetown University, 1976. — 84p : 2 maps ; 22cm. — (The Washington papers ; 41) (A Sage policy paper)
Bibl.: p.84.
ISBN 0-8039-0791-5 Pbk : £1.95
(B77-20056)

320.9'561'03 — Turkey. Politics
Mango, Andrew. Turkey : a delicately poised ally / [by] Andrew Mango. — Beverly Hills ; London : Sage Publications for the Center for Strategic and International Studies, 1975 [i.e. 1977]. — [5],73p : map ; 21cm. — (The Washington papers ; 28) (A Sage policy paper)
Published in the United States: 1975. — Bibl.: p.72-73.
ISBN 0-8039-0578-5 Pbk : £1.50
(B77-11095)

320.9'561'03 — Turkey. Politics, 1950-1975
Ahmad, Feroz. The Turkish experiment in democracy, 1950-1975 / [by] Feroz Ahmad. — London : C. Hurst for the Royal Institute of International Affairs, 1977. — xii,474p ; 23cm.
Bibl.: p.435-455. — Index.
ISBN 0-903983-54-0 : £12.00
(B77-12883)

320.9'5694 — Israel. Politics, to 1976
Weidenfeld, George, *Baron Weidenfeld.* The seven deadly clichés : address to the Anglo-Israel Association annual general meeting on Tuesday 14 December 1976 / by Lord Weidenfeld. — London : The Association, 1977. — 14p ; 23cm.
ISBN 0-900063-49-1 Sd : Unpriced
(B77-15116)

320.9'597'04 — Vietnam. Politics, 1976. ***Trotskyist viewpoints***
Posadas, J. The draft resolution for the Congress of the Communist Party and the function of Posadism / [by] J. Posadas. — London (24 Cranbourn St., W.C.2) : Revolutionary Workers Party (Trotskyist), 1977. — [1],12,[1]p ; 21cm. — (A 'European Marxist review' publication)
At head of title: Workers of the world, unite!. — Includes 'Extracts from the thesis for the Congress of the Workers Party of Vietnam', reproduced from 'Unita', 17-11-76.
Sd : £0.15
(B77-29979)

320.9'66 — West Africa. English speaking countries. Politics, ca 1900-1971
Price, Joseph Henry. Political institutions of West Africa / [by] J.H. Price. — 3rd ed. — London : Hutchinson, 1977. — 297p : ill, map ; 22cm.
Previous ed.: 1975. — Bibl.: p.287-289. — Index.
ISBN 0-09-131461-5 Pbk : £2.25
(B77-29980)

320.9'66'303 — Senegal. Political development, 1885-1945
Gellar, Sheldon. Structural changes and colonial dependency : Senegal, 1885-1945 / [by] Sheldon Gellar. — Beverly Hills ; London : Sage Publications, [1977]. — 80p : map ; 22cm. — (Sage research papers in the social sciences : studies in comparative modernization series ; vol.5, no.90-036)
Published in the United States: 1976. — Bibl.: p.76-80.
ISBN 0-8039-0636-6 Pbk : £1.75
(B77-11096)

320.9'66'52 — Guinea. Politics, to 1976
Rivière, Claude. Guinea : the mobilization of a people / [by] Claude Rivière ; translated from the French [MS.] by Virginia Thompson and Richard Adloff. — Ithaca ; London : Cornell University Press, 1977. — 262p : maps ; 21cm. — (Africa in the modern world)
Bibl.: p.247-252. — Index.
ISBN 0-8014-0904-7 : £12.40
(B77-26837)

320.9'676'203 — Kenya. Politics, 1918-1926. ***Correspondence***
Leys, Norman. By Kenya possessed : the correspondence of Norman Leys and J.H. Oldham, 1918-1926 / edited and with an introduction by John W. Cell. — Chicago ; London : University of Chicago Press, 1976. — x,382p : port ; 23cm. — (Studies in imperialism)
Index.
ISBN 0-226-09971-7 : £14.25
(B77-03403)

320.9'68'05 — South Africa. Politics, 1910-1976
Brotz, Howard Merwin. The politics of South Africa : democracy and racial diversity / [by] Howard Brotz. — Oxford [etc.] : Oxford University Press, 1977. — xii,164p,plate : ill, maps, port ; 23cm.
Index.
ISBN 0-19-215671-3 : £5.00 : CIP rev.
(B77-03973)

320.9'68'06 — Southern Africa. Politics, 1960-1975
Stockholm International Peace Research Institute. Southern Africa : the escalation of a conflict : a politico-military study / Stockholm International Peace Research Institute ; [written by Signe Landgren-Bäckström]. — New York [etc.] ; London : Praeger, 1976. — x,235p,2p of plates : ill, maps(on lining papers), ports ; 24cm. — (Praeger special studies in international politics and government)
Originally published: Stockholm : Almqvist and Wiksell, 1976. — Bibl.: p.224-228. — Index.
ISBN 0-275-56840-7 : £18.50
(B77-05903)

320.9'7282 — Belize. Politics, to 1974
Grant, Cedric Hilburn. The making of modern Belize : politics, society & British colonialism in Central America / [by] C.H. Grant. — Cambridge [etc.] : Cambridge University Press, 1976. — xvi,400p : map ; 24cm. — (Cambridge Commonwealth series)
Bibl.: p.385-389. — Index.
ISBN 0-521-20731-2 : £14.00
(B77-00630)

320.9'7286 — Costa Rica. Politics. Influence of Inter-American Development Bank, to 1976
DeWitt, R Peter. The Inter-American Development Bank and political influence : with special reference to Costa Rica / [by] R. Peter DeWitt, Jr. — New York ; London : Praeger, 1977. — xix,199p : ill ; 25cm. — (Praeger special studies in international economics and development)
Bibl.: p.182-194. — Index.
ISBN 0-275-24460-1 : Unpriced
(B77-26838)

320.9'73'04 — Democratic societies & republican societies. ***United States, 1790-1800. Documents***
The **Democratic-Republican** societies, 1790-1800 : a documentary sourcebook of constitutions, declarations, addresses, resolutions and toasts / edited, with an introduction, by Philip S. Foner ; foreword by Richard B. Morris. — Westport, Conn. ; London : Greenwood Press, 1976. — xiii,484,[1]p ; 25cm.
Bibl.: p.447-459. — Index.
ISBN 0-8371-8907-1 : £19.75
(B77-29981)

320.9'73'091 — United States. Politics. Role of Niebuhr, Reinhold, 1916-1950
Merkley, Paul. Reinhold Niebuhr : a political account / [by] Paul Merkley. — Montreal ; London : McGill-Queen's University Press, 1975. — xii,289p ; 24cm.
Bibl.: p.273-277. — Index.
ISBN 0-7735-0216-5 : Unpriced
(B77-17947)

320.9'73'0913 — United States. Politics. Role of Hoover, Herbert, 1918-1921
Best, Gary Dean. The politics of American individualism : Herbert Hoover in transition, 1918-1921 / [by] Gary Dean Best. — Westport, Conn. ; London : Greenwood Press, 1975. — vi,202p ; 22cm.
Bibl.: p.181-193. — Index.
ISBN 0-8371-8160-7 : £10.95
(B77-17327)

320.9'73'092 — Political movements. Influence of United States. Federal Bureau of Investigation. ***United States, 1946-1975***
Cointelpro : the FBI's secret war on political freedom / edited by Cathy Perkus ; introduction by Noam Chomsky. — New York : Monad Press ; New York ; London (47 The Cut, SE1 8LL) : Distributed by Pathfinder Press, 1975 [i.e. 1976]. — 3-190p : facsims ; 22cm.
Published in the United States: 1975.
ISBN 0-913460-41-9 : £4.50
ISBN 0-913460-42-7 Pbk : £1.15
(B77-03974)

320.9'73'0924 — United States. Politics, ca 1970-1975. ***Readings***
American political institutions in the 1970s : a 'Political science quarterly' reader / edited by Demetrios Caraley. — New York ; Guildford : Columbia University Press, 1976. — xvi,407p : ill ; 24cm.
'The articles have been reprinted exactly as they first appeared in "Political Science Quarterly"' - Acknowledgements.
ISBN 0-231-04106-3 : Unpriced
ISBN 0-231-04107-1 Pbk : Unpriced
(B77-01193)

320.9'73'0925 — United States. Politics
Bullitt, Stimson. To be a politician / [by] Stimson Bullitt ; foreword by David Riesman. — [New] revised ed. — New Haven ; London : Yale University Press, 1977. — xviii,294p : 1 ill ; 22cm.
Previous ed.: i.e. Revised ed. Garden City, N.Y. : Doubleday, 1961. — Index.
ISBN 0-300-02009-0 : £10.80
(B77-24736)

320.9'73'0925 — United States. Politics, 1975
McKenna, George. American politics : ideals and realities / [by] George McKenna. — New York [etc.] ; London : McGraw-Hill, 1976. — xiv, 345p : ill ; 24cm.
Index.
ISBN 0-07-045355-1 Pbk : £5.35
(B77-01194)

320.9'8'003 — Latin America. Politics
Needler, Martin Cyril. An introduction to Latin American politics : the structure of conflict / [by] Martin C. Needler. — Englewood Cliffs ; London [etc.] : Prentice-Hall, 1977. — ix,358p : maps ; 24cm.
Bibl.: p.347-353. — Index.
ISBN 0-13-486043-8 : £7.95
(B77-11608)

320.9'8'003 — Latin America. Politics. ***Periodicals***
Latin America political report. — London (90 Cowcross St., EC1M 6BL) : Latin American Newsletters Ltd.
Continues : Latin America.
Vol.11, no.1- ; 7 Jan. 1977-. — 1977-. — ill ; 28cm.
Weekly (fifty issues a year). — 8p. in 1st issue.
Sd : £55.00 yearly
ISSN 0309-2992
(B77-08247)

321 — POLITICS. FORMS OF STATES

321'.02'09034 — Federalism, to 1975
Sawer, Geoffrey. Modern federalism / [by] Geoffrey Sawer. — New ed. — Carlton ; London [etc.] : Pitman, 1976. — vii,170p ; 22cm.
Previous ed.: London : Watts, 1969. — Index.
ISBN 0-85896-448-1 Pbk : £4.50
(B77-24737)

321'.02'09669 — Nigeria. Federalism, 1954-1964
Eleazu, Uma O. Federalism and nation-building : the Nigerian experience, 1954-1964 / [by] Uma O. Eleazu. — Ilfracombe : Stockwell, 1977. — 280p : ill, maps ; 23cm.
Index.
ISBN 0-7223-0987-2 : £3.75
(B77-24034)

321'.02'0971 — Canada. Federalism. Theories
Black, Edwin R. Divided loyalties : Canadian concepts of federalism / [by] Edwin R. Black. — Montreal ; London : McGill-Queen's University Press, 1975. — xiii,272p ; 24cm.
Index.
ISBN 0-7735-0230-0 : Unpriced
ISBN 0-7735-0238-6 Pbk : Unpriced
(B77-16751)

321'.03'08 — Imperialism. *British and Irish Communist Organisation viewpoints. Lectures, speeches*
Warren, Bill. Imperialism & neo-colonialism / by Bill Warren. — [Belfast] : British and Irish Communist Organisation, [1977]. — [1],32p ; 24cm.
Sd : Unpriced
(B77-32442)

321'.03'09 — Imperialism, to ca 1965. *Secondary school texts*
Amey, Peter. Imperialism / by Peter Amey. — London : Harrap, 1976. — [1],32p : ill, maps, ports ; 24cm. — (Harrap world history programme : set 14)
ISBN 0-245-52548-3 Sd : £0.60
(B77-07101)

321'.04 — Europe. Political integration, 1945-1975. *Documents*
Post-war integration in Europe / [compiled by] Richard Vaughan. — London : Edward Arnold, 1976. — x,211p ; 21cm. — (Documents of modern history)
Bibl.: p.205-206. — Index.
ISBN 0-7131-5881-6 : £5.95
ISBN 0-7131-5882-4 Pbk : £2.95
(B77-02797)

321'.04 — Europe. Political integration, 1945-1976
Blacksell, Mark. Post-war Europe : a political geography / [by] Mark Blacksell. — Folkestone : Dawson, 1977. — 205p : ill, maps ; 23cm.
Bibl.: p.191-193. — Index.
ISBN 0-7129-0789-0 : £6.00 : CIP rev.
(B77-11610)

321'.05 — Internal political integration
The **politics** of divison, partition, and unification / edited by Ray Edward Johnston. — New York [etc.] ; London : Praeger ; [London] : [Distributed by Martin Robertson], 1976. — xxv,100p ; 25cm. — (Praeger special studies in international politics and government)
Bibl.
ISBN 0-275-55660-3 : £12.25
(B77-07813)

321'.05'0722 — Internal political integration. *Case studies*
Small states and segmented societies : national political integration in a global environment / edited by Stephanie G. Neuman. — New York [etc.] ; London : Praeger ; [London] : [Distributed by Martin Robertson], 1976. — xiv,240p ; 24cm. — (Praeger special studies in international politics and government)
Index.
ISBN 0-275-55730-8 : £12.05
(B77-07814)

321'.05'09513 — Internal political integration. Role of regional governments. *China, 1949-1954. Study regions: South-western China*
Solinger, Dorothy J. Regional government and political integration in Southwest China, 1949-1954 : a case study / [by] Dorothy J. Solinger. — Berkeley [etc.] ; London : University of California Press, 1977. — ix, 291p : maps ; 24cm.
Bibl.: p.269-283. — Index.
ISBN 0-520-03104-0 : £13.15
(B77-23172)

321'.07 — Utopianism, to 1975
Lasky, Melvin J. Utopia and revolution : on the origins of a metaphor, or some illustrations of the problem of political temperament and intellectual climate and how ideas, ideals, and ideologies have been historically related / [by] Melvin J. Lasky. — London [etc.] : Macmillan, 1977. — xiii,726p ; 24cm.
Originally published: Chicago : University of Chicago Press, 1976. — Index.
ISBN 0-333-21333-5 : £15.00
(B77-12335)

321'.07 — Utopias. *Greek texts. Early works*
Plato. [Republic. Book 1]. Republic. Book 1 / [by] Plato ; edited by D.J. Allan. — 2nd ed. reprinted ; with a new preface. — Letchworth : Bradda Books, 1977. — iii-xi,130p ; 21cm.
Greek text, English preface, introduction and notes. — This ed. originally published: London : Methuen, 1944.
ISBN 0-904679-11-x Pbk : £1.50
(B77-12884)

321.1'2 — Patriarchy. Theories
Goldberg, Steven. The inevitability of patriarchy / [by] Steven Goldberg. — [New ed.]. — London : Temple Smith, 1977. — 224p ; 23cm.
Previous ed.: New York : Morrow, 1973. — Index.
ISBN 0-85117-126-5 : £6.95
(B77-20947)

321.4'0938 — Classical antiquity. Representative government
Larsen, J A O. Representative government in Greek and Roman history / [by] J.A.O. Larsen. — Berkeley [etc.] ; London : University of California Press, 1976. — vii,247p ; 22cm.
Originally published: Berkeley : University of California Press, 1955. — Index.
ISBN 0-520-03240-3 : £9.20
(B77-29982)

321.8 — Democracy
Macpherson, Crawford Brough. The life and times of liberal democracy / [by] C.B. Macpherson. — Oxford [etc.] : Oxford University Press, 1977. — [8],120p ; 21cm.
Bibl.: p.116-117. — Index.
ISBN 0-19-219120-9 : £2.95 : CIP rev.
ISBN 0-19-289106-5 Pbk : £1.25
(B77-20057)

Moss, Robert, *b.1946.* The collapse of democracy / [by] Robert Moss. — [New] ed. updated. — London : Abacus, 1977. — 256p ; 20cm.
Previous ed.: i.e. 1st ed. London : Temple Smith, 1975. — Index.
ISBN 0-349-12395-0 Pbk : £1.50
(B77-12885)

321.8'0973 — Democracy. Cultural aspects. *United States, to 1973*
Warren, Robert Penn. Democracy and poetry / [by] Robert Penn Warren. — Cambridge, Mass. ; London : Harvard University Press, 1976. — xvi,102p ; 22cm. — (Jefferson lecture in the humanities ; 1974)
Originally published: 1975.
£4.50
ISBN 0-674-19625-2
Primary classification 810'.9'38
(B77-04376)

321.9 — Corporatism. *Great Britain. Conference proceedings*
Corporate State, Reality or Myth? *(Conference), London, 1976.* The corporate state, reality or myth? : a symposium. — London : Centre for Studies in Social Policy, [1977]. — [3],160p : 1 ill ; 30cm.
'On Friday 24th September 1976 the Centre for Studies in Social Policy held a symposium ... on the theme of "The Corporate State - Reality or Myth?"' - Preface.
Sp : £2.50
(B77-20948)

321.9'2 — Proletarian dictatorship. *Trotskyist viewpoints. Essays*
Posadas, J. On the dictatorship of the proletariat : selection of articles / [by] J. Posadas. — London (24 Cranbourn St., W.C.2) : Fourth International Publications [for the Revolutionary Workers Party (Trotskyist)], 1976. — [1],11,[1]p ; 22cm. — (A 'European Marxist review' publication)
At head of title: Workers of the world, unite!.
Sd : £0.15
(B77-29983)

321.9'2 — State communism. Related to political aspects of communism
Revel, Jean François. The totalitarian temptation / [by] Jean-François Revel ; translated from the French by David Hapgood. — London : Secker and Warburg, 1977. — 311p ; 23cm.
This translation also published: Garden City, N.Y. : Doubleday, 1977. — Translation of: 'La tentation totalitaire'. Paris : R. Laffont, 1976.
ISBN 0-436-41140-7 : £4.90
Also classified at 320.5'32
(B77-31013)

322 — POLITICS. RELATION OF STATE TO ORGANISED GROUPS

322.1'09171'7 — Christian church. Relations with state. *Communist countries. Periodicals*
Religion & communism. — [Keston] ([Keston, Kent BR2 6BA]) : [Keston College, Centre for the Study of Religion and Communism]. [No.1]- ; 1976-. — [1976]. — ports ; 43cm.
Monthly. — 8p. in October 1976 issue.
Sd : £0.25
(B77-15711)

322'.1'0941 — Christian church. Relations with state. *Great Britain, 1832-1868*
Machin, G I T. Politics and the churches in Britain, 1832 to 1868 / [by] G.I.T. Machin. — Oxford : Clarendon Press, 1977. — ix,438p ; 25cm.
Bibl.: p.387-418. — Index.
ISBN 0-19-826436-4 : £15.00 : CIP rev.
(B77-26839)

322'.1'0941 — Roman Catholics. Emancipation, 1793-1829. *Great Britain. Teaching kits*
Catholic emancipation, 1793-1829 / [with commentary] by Anthony Malcomson. — Belfast [etc.] : H.M.S.O. for the Public Record Office of Northern Ireland, 1976. — Portfolio : ill, facsims, ports ; 31cm. — (Education facsimiles ; 241-260)
Booklet (52p.), 20 sheets(chiefly fold.) in folder, all in plastic envelope. — Bibl.: p.50.
ISBN 0-337-23194-x : £1.50
(B77-05229)

322'.1'0942 — Christian church. Relations with state. *England. Early works*
Coleridge, Samuel Taylor. On the constitution of the church and state / [by Samuel Taylor Coleridge] ; edited by John Colmer. — London : Routledge and Kegan Paul [etc.], 1976. — lxviii,303p,4 leaves of plates : facsims, port ; 23cm. — (Bollingen series ; 75) (The collected works of Samuel Taylor Coleridge ; 10)
'The text ... follows Coleridge's second edition ... [with] ... corrections of Coleridge's Greek quotations ...' - p.xiii. — Second ed. originally published: London : Hurst, Chance, 1830. — Index.
ISBN 0-7100-8107-3 : £10.00
(B77-13531)

322'.1'09593 — Thailand. Politics. Role of Sangha, 1965-1976
Suksamran, Somboon. Political Buddhism in Southeast Asia : the role of the Sangha in the modernization of Thailand / by Somboon Suksamran ; edited, with an introduction by Trevor O. Ling. — London : C. Hurst, 1977. — xxi,154p : ill, map ; 23cm.
Bibl.: p.138-148. — Index.
ISBN 0-903983-58-3 : £8.00 : CIP rev.
(B77-15712)

322'.1'0973 — Christian church. Relations with state. *United States*
Mead, Sidney E. The old religion in the brave new world : reflections on the relation between Christendom and the Republic / [by] Sidney E. Mead. — Berkeley [etc.] ; London : University of California Press, 1977. — xii,189p ; 21cm. — (The Jefferson memorial lectures)
Index.
ISBN 0-520-03322-1 : £7.50
(B77-26143)

322'.2'0941 — Trade unions. Political power. *Great Britain. Conservative and Unionist Party viewpoints*
Martin, Peter, *b.1941.* No foundation - : the truth about union power / by Peter Martin. — London : Bow Publications, 1976. — [2],13p ; 21cm.
ISBN 0-900182-76-8 Sd : £0.40
(B77-03975)

322'.3 — Great Britain. Politics. Role of Confederation of British Industry, to 1976
Grant, Wyn. The Confederation of British Industry / [by] Wyn Grant and David Marsh. — London [etc.] : Hodder and Stoughton, 1977. — ix,226p ; 25cm.
Spine title : The CBI. — Index.
ISBN 0-340-17613-x : £6.50
ISBN 0-340-21472-4 Pbk : £3.95
(B77-14084)

322'.3'0973 — United States. Politics. Role of business firms
Miller, Arthur Selwyn. The modern corporate state : private governments and the American constitution / [by] Arthur Selwyn Miller. — Westport, Conn. ; London : Greenwood Press, 1976. — xvi,269,[1]p ; 22cm. — (Contributions in American studies ; no.23)
Index.
ISBN 0-8371-8589-0 : £9.95
(B77-23173)

322.4 — Declarations of independence by social minorities. *United States, 1829-1975*
We, the other people : alternative declarations of independence by labor groups, farmers, woman's rights advocates, socialists, and blacks, 1829-1975 / edited, with introduction and notes, by Philip S. Foner. — Urbana [etc.] ; London : University of Illinois Press, 1976. — [6],205p ; 21cm.
ISBN 0-252-00623-2 : £5.60
ISBN 0-252-00624-0 Pbk : £2.06
(B77-02076)

322.4 — Great Britain. Government. Opposition
Ponton, Geoffrey. Political opposition / [by] Geoffrey Ponton. — London (12 Gower St., WC1E 6DP) : Politics Association, 1976. — 35p ; 22cm. — (Politics Association. Occasional publications ; 4)
ISBN 0-9503394-3-1 Sd : £0.74
(B77-09540)

322.4'2 — Jamaica. Politics. Violence, 1960-1970
Lacey, Terry. Violence and politics in Jamaica, 1960-70 : internal security in a developing country / [by] Terry Lacey. — Manchester : Manchester University Press, 1977. — viii, 184p ; 23cm.
Index.
ISBN 0-7190-0633-3 : £8.50
(B77-22385)

322.4'2 — Middle East. Politics. Violence, 1882-1976
Hirst, David, *b.1936.* The gun and the olive branch : the roots of violence in the Middle East / [by] David Hirst. — London : Faber, 1977. — 3-367p ; 23cm.
Index.
ISBN 0-571-11136-x : £6.50 : CIP rev.
(B77-22386)

322.4'2 — Nationalist movements
Nationalist movements / edited by Anthony D. Smith. — London [etc.] : Macmillan, 1976. — vi,185p ; 23cm.
Index.
ISBN 0-333-18185-9 : £7.95
ISBN 0-333-18186-7 Pbk : £3.50
(B77-04595)

322.4'2 — Politics. Violence. *Serials*
Annual of power and conflict : a survey of political violence and international influence. — London : Institute for the Study of Conflict. 1976-77 / editor Brian Crozier. — 1977. — [8], 356p ; 22cm.
Bibl.: p.354-356.
£7.50
ISSN 0307-031x
(B77-29984)

322.4'2 — Terrorism
Clutterbuck, Richard. Guerrillas and terrorists / [by] Richard Clutterbuck. — London : Faber, 1977. — 3-125p ; 23cm.
Bibl.: p.117-119. — Index.
ISBN 0-571-11027-4 : £4.25 : CIP rev.
(B77-07102)

Wilkinson, Paul. Terrorism and the liberal state / [by] Paul Wilkinson. — London [etc.] : Macmillan, 1977. — xiv,257p ; 23cm.
Index.
ISBN 0-333-19123-4 : £7.95
ISBN 0-333-22770-0 Pbk : £3.95
(B77-33084)

322.4'2 — Underground National Socialist movements. *South Africa. Ossewabrandwag, 1938-1948*
Visser, George Cloete. OB, traitors or patriots? / [by] George Cloete Visser. — Johannesburg : Macmillan South Africa ; London : [Macmillan], 1976. — 216p,[12]p of plates : ill, ports ; 23cm.
Index.
ISBN 0-86954-030-0 : £4.95
(B77-11611)

322.4'2 — United States. Politics. Violence
Stohl, Michael. War and domestic political violence : the American capacity for repression and reaction / [by] Michael Stohl ; preface by Ted Robert Gurr. — Beverly Hills ; London : Sage Publications, [1977]. — [6],153p : ill, form ; 22cm. — (Sage library of social research ; vol.30)
Published in the United States: 1976. — Bibl.: p.145-151.
ISBN 0-8039-0575-0 : £7.00
ISBN 0-8039-0576-9 Pbk : £4.00
(B77-11612)

322.4'2'0722 — Revolutionary movements, 1945-1975. *Case studies*
Bell, John Bowyer. On revolt : strategies of national liberation / [by] J. Bowyer Bell. — Cambridge, Mass. ; London : Harvard University Press, 1976. — xv,272p,[12]p of plates : ill, ports ; 25cm.
Bibl.: p.241-247. — Index.
ISBN 0-674-63655-4 : £10.20
(B77-02077)

322.4'2'0904 — Revolutionary movements, 1900-ca 1970. *Essays*
Hobsbawm, Eric John. Revolutionaries : contemporary essays / [by] E.J. Hobsbawm. — London : Quartet Books, 1977. — viii,278p ; 20cm.
This collection originally published: London : Weidenfeld and Nicolson, 1973. — Index.
ISBN 0-7043-3098-9 Pbk : £2.50
(B77-08248)

322.4'2'091724 — Revolutionary movements. *Developing countries, 1945-1976*
Chaliand, Gérard. Revolution in the Third World : myths and prospects / [by] Gérard Chaliand ; [translated from the French by Diana Johnstone] ; foreword by Immanuel Wallerstein. — Hassocks : Harvester Press, 1977. — xxiii,195p ; 22cm.
Translation of: 'Mythes révolutionnaires du tiers monde'. Paris : Éditions du Seuil, 1976.
ISBN 0-85527-339-9 : £6.95 : CIP rev.
(B77-12886)

322.4'2'0924 — Black power movements. *Great Britain. Black Liberation Army. Malik, Michael Abdul. Biographies*
Humphry, Derek. False Messiah : the story of Michael X / [by] Derek Humphry, David Tindall. — London : Hart-Davis MacGibbon, 1977. — 221p,[8]p of plates : 1 ill, ports ; 23cm.
Index.
ISBN 0-246-10884-3 : £6.95
(B77-21718)

322.4'2'0924 — Black power movements. *United States. Black Panthers. Cleaver, Eldridge, 1968-1976. Biographies*
Otis, George. Eldridge Cleaver : ice and fire! / [by] George Otis. — London : Lakeland, 1977. — [9],144p : ill, ports ; 18cm.
Originally published: Van Nuys, Calif. : Bible Voice, 1977. — Bibl.: p.143-144.
ISBN 0-551-00789-3 Pbk : £0.95
(B77-29985)

322.4'2'0924 — Palestinian Arab resistance movements: Palestine Liberation Organisation. Arafat, Yasir. *Biographies*
Kiernan, Thomas. Yasir Arafat : the man and the myth / [by] Thomas Kiernan. — London : Abacus, 1976. — 223p ; 20cm.
Also published: New York : Norton, 1976.
ISBN 0-349-12089-7 Pbk : £0.95
(B77-14581)

322.4'2'0924 — Racial discrimination. Organisations. *United States. Ku Klux Klan, 1959-1965. Personal observations*
Rowe, Gary Thomas. My undercover years with the Ku Klux Klan / by Gary Thomas Rowe, Jr. — Toronto [etc.] ; London : Bantam, 1976. — [8],216p ; 18cm.
ISBN 0-552-66476-6 Pbk : £0.65
(B77-02078)

322.4'2'0924 — Revolutionary movements. *United States. Symbionese Liberation Army. Remiro, Joe. Biographies*
Bryan, John, *b.1934.* This soldier still at war / [by] John Bryan. — London : Quartet Books, 1976. — [9],341p,[8]p of plates : ill, facsims, map, ports ; 23cm.
Originally published: New York : Harcourt Brace Jovanovich, 1975. — Index.
ISBN 0-7043-2104-1 : £4.95
(B77-03976)

322.4'2'0924 — Terrorism. Martinez-Torres, Carlos
Dobson, Christopher. The Carlos complex : a pattern of violence / by Christopher Dobson and Ronald Payne. — London [etc.] : Hodder and Stoughton, 1977. — 254p ; 24cm.
Index.
ISBN 0-340-21361-2 : £5.50
(B77-29217)

322.4'2'094 — Peasant revolutionary movements. *Europe, ca 800-ca 1400*
Hilton, Rodney. Bond men made free : medieval peasant movements and the English rising of 1381 / [by] Rodney Hilton. — London : Methuen, 1977. — 240p ; 22cm. — (University paperbacks)
Originally published: London : Temple Smith, 1973. — Index.
ISBN 0-416-82520-6 Pbk : £2.40
Also classified at 942.03'8
(B77-16212)

322.4'2'094 — Revolutionary movements. *Europe, 1815-1848*
Collins, Irene, *b.1925.* Revolutionaries in Europe, 1815-1848 / [by] Irene Collins. — London : Historical Association, 1974. — [2],30p : 1 ill, ports ; 22cm. — (Appreciations in history ; no.4)
Bibl.: p.29-30.
Sd : £0.30
(B77-24738)

322.4'2'0941 — Revolutionary left-wing political movements. *Great Britain, 1900-1922*
Challinor, Raymond. The origins of British bolshevism / [by] Raymond Challinor. — London : Croom Helm [etc.], 1977. — 5-291p ; 23cm.
Index.
ISBN 0-85664-448-x : £8.50 : CIP rev.
(B77-17328)

322.4'2'0941 — Revolutionary movements. *Great Britain, 1789-1848*
Thomis, Malcolm Ian. Threats of revolution in Britain, 1789-1848 / [by] Malcolm I. Thomis and Peter Holt. — London [etc.] : Macmillan, 1977. — [8],147p ; 22cm.
Bibl.: p.135-139. — Index.
ISBN 0-333-21374-2 : £6.95
ISBN 0-333-21375-0 Pbk : £2.50
(B77-32443)

322.4'2'09415 — Nationalist movements. Role of labour movements. *Ireland, 1911-1912*
Gilmore, George. Labour & the Republican Movement / [by] George Gilmore. — [Dublin] ([30 Gardiner Place, Dublin 1]) : Repsol, [1977]. — [4],15p : port ; 21cm. — (A Repsol pamphlet)
Originally published: 1966.
ISBN 0-86064-010-8 Sd : £0.20
(B77-12336)

322.4'2'09415 — Revolutionary movements. *Ireland. Irish Republican Brotherhood, to 1924*
Ó Broin, Leon. Revolutionary underground : the story of the Irish Republican Brotherhood, 1858-1924 / [by] Leon Ó Broin. — Dublin : Gill and Macmillan, 1976. — x,245p ; 23cm.
Bibl.: p.234-238. — Index.
ISBN 0-7171-0778-7 : £6.95
(B77-03977)

322.4'2'0943 — Resistance movements. *Germany, 1933-1945*
Hoffmann, Peter. The history of the German resistance 1933-1945 / [by] Peter Hoffmann ; translated from the German by Richard Barry. — 3rd ed. (1st English ed.) / revised and expanded by the author. — London : Macdonald and Jane's, 1977. — xii,847p : ill, maps, plans ; 24cm.
Translation and revision of: 'Widerstand, Staatsstreich, Attentat'. 2. expanded and revised ed. Munich : Piper, 1970. — Bibl.: p.773-813. — Index.
ISBN 0-356-08393-4 : £15.00
(B77-17948)

322.4'2'0943 — Revolutionary movements. *West Germany. Rote Armee Fraktion, to 1976*
Becker, Jillian. Hitler's children : the story of the Baader-Meinhof terrorist gang / [by] Jillian Becker. — London : Joseph, 1977. — 322[i.e. 320]p : ill, map, ports ; 23cm.
Also published: Philadelphia : Lippincott, 1977. — Bibl.: p.307-313. — Index.
ISBN 0-7181-1582-1 : £6.50
(B77-22387)

322.4'2'0947 — Soviet Union. Politics. Opposition movements, 1917-1922
Schapiro, Leonard. The origin of the Communist autocracy : political opposition in the Soviet State, first phase, 1917-1922 / by Leonard Schapiro. — 2nd ed. — London [etc.] : Macmillan [for] the London School of Economics and Political Science, 1977. — xxiii, 397p ; 23cm.
Previous ed.: London : Bell, 1955. — Bibl.: p.369-387. — Index.
ISBN 0-333-21163-4 : £10.00
(B77-09541)

322.4'2'0951 — Revolutionary movements. Role of Chinese communities in Malaysia & Singapore. *China, 1900-1911*
Yen Ching Hwang. The overseas Chinese and the 1911 revolution : with special reference to Singapore and Malaya / [by] Yen Ching Hwang. — Kuala Lumpur ; London [etc.] : Oxford University Press, 1976. — xxvii,439p, [16]p of plates : ill, facsims, ports ; 23cm. — (East Asian historical monographs) (Oxford in Asia series)
Bibl.: p.356-414. — Index.
ISBN 0-19-580311-6 : £18.00
(B77-22388)

322.4'2'095115 — Revolutionary movements. *China, 1911. Study regions: Hopeh (Province)*
Esherick, Joseph W. Reform and revolution in China : the 1911 Revolution in Hunan and Hubei / [by] Joseph W. Esherick. — Berkeley [etc.] ; London : University of California Press, 1976. — xi,324p : map ; 25cm. — (Michigan studies on China)
Bibl.: p.301-308. — Index.
ISBN 0-520-03084-2 : £12.00
Also classified at 322.4'2'095118
(B77-14085)

322.4'2'095118 — Revolutionary movements. *China, 1911. Study regions: Honan (Province)*
Esherick, Joseph W. Reform and revolution in China : the 1911 Revolution in Hunan and Hubei / [by] Joseph W. Esherick. — Berkeley [etc.] ; London : University of California Press, 1976. — xi,324p : map ; 25cm. — (Michigan studies on China)
Bibl.: p.301-308. — Index.
ISBN 0-520-03084-2 : £12.00
Primary classification 322.4'2'095115
(B77-14085)

322.4'2'095482 — Nationalist movements. *India (Republic). Tamil Nadu (State). Dravida Munnetra Kazhagam, to 1975*
Barnett, Marguerite Ross. The politics of cultural nationalism in South India / [by] Marguerite Ross Barnett. — Princeton ; Guildford : Princeton University Press, 1976. — xii,368p : 3 ill, map ; 24cm.
Bibl.: p.345-358. — Index.
ISBN 0-691-07577-8 : £15.70
(B77-09542)

322.4'2'096 — Revolutionary movements. Role of communist countries. *Africa. Trotskyist viewpoints*
Posadas, J. The tour of Fidel Castro and Podgorny in Africa, the Permanent Revolution and the world objective necessity of socialism / [by] J. Posadas. — London (24 Cranbourn St., W.C.2) : Revolutionary Workers Party (Trotskyist), 1977. — [1],17,[1]p ; 21cm. — (A 'European Marxist review' publication)
At head of title: Workers of the world, unite!.
Sd : £0.15
(B77-29986)

322.4'2'096711 — Nationalist movements. *Cameroun Republic. Union des Populations du Cameroun, 1938-1956*
Joseph, Richard A. Radical nationalism in Cameroun : social origins of the UPC rebellion / by Richard A. Joseph. — Oxford : Clarendon Press, 1977. — xiii,383p : maps ; 23cm. — (Oxford studies in African affairs)
Includes 2 appendices in French. — Bibl.: p.362-376. — Index.
ISBN 0-19-822706-x : £15.00 : CIP rev.
(B77-08808)

322.4'2'09688 — Nationalist movements. *Namibia. South West Africa People's Organisation (SWAPO) of Namibia. Periodicals*
Namibia : organ of the South West Africa People's Organisation (SWAPO) of Namibia. — London (21 Tabernacle St., EC2A 4DE) : SWAPO Department of Information and Publicity.
[Vol.1, no.1]- ; 1977-. — [1977]-. — ill, maps, ports ; 30cm.
Six issues a year. — 16p. in 1st issue.
Sd : £0.30
ISSN 0140-5330
(B77-33642)

322.4'2'0972 — Revolutionary movements. Role of intellectuals. *Mexico, 1900-1913*
Cockcroft, James Donald. Intellectual precursors of the Mexican Revolution, 1900-1913 / [by] James D. Cockcroft. — Austin ; London : University of Texas Press, 1976. — iii-xxi, 329p : ill, maps ; 23cm. — (Latin American monographs ; no.14)
Originally published: 1968. — Bibl.: p.259-293. — Index.
ISBN 0-292-73808-0 Pbk : £4.50
(B77-19243)

322.4'2'0973 — Trotskyist movements. *United States, 1917-1976*
Myers, Constance Ashton. The prophet's army : Trotskyists in America, 1928-1941 / [by] Constance Ashton Myers. — Westport, Conn. ; London : Greenwood Press, 1977. — xiii,282p ; 22cm. — (Contributions in American history ; no.56)
Bibl.: p.257-272. — Index.
ISBN 0-8371-9030-4 : £13.25
(B77-32444)

322.4'2'098 — Latin America. Politics. Opposition movements. Suppression by government. *Inquiry reports*
Russell Tribunal 2 on Repression in Brazil, Chile and Latin America. Found guilty : the verdict of the Russell Tribunal session in Brussels. — Nottingham : Bertrand Russell Peace Foundation for 'The Spokesman', [1976]. — [2], 36p ; 22cm. — ('Spokesman' pamphlet ; no.51)
'The work of this Second Session of the Second Russell Tribunal, on repression in Brazil, Chile and Latin America ...' p.3.
Sd : £0.40
(B77-00058)

322.4'2'098 — Revolutionary movements. Guerilla warfare. Theories. *Latin America, 1960-1973. Marxist viewpoints*
Debray, Régis. A critique of arms / [by] Régis Debray. — Harmondsworth [etc.] : Penguin.
Vol.1 / translated [from the French] by Rosemary Sheed. — 1977. — 315p ; 20cm. — (Peregrine books)
Translation of: 'La critique des armes'. Tome 1. Paris : Éditions du Seuil, 1974.
ISBN 0-14-055120-4 Pbk : £2.95
(B77-24739)

322.4'3'02541 — Pressure groups. *Great Britain. Directories*
The **'Guardian'** directory of pressure groups & representative associations / research by Chris Bazlinton and Anne Cowen ; edited and with an introduction by Peter Shipley. — London (16 Regency St., S.W.1) : Wilton House Publications, 1976. — vi,265p ; 24cm.
Index.
ISBN 0-904655-00-8 : £7.50
(B77-08809)

322.4'4 — Secularism. Political aspects. *Great Britain, ca 1790-ca 1890. Documents*
The **infidel** tradition : from Paine to Bradlaugh / edited by Edward Royle. — London [etc.] : Macmillan, 1976. — xvii,228p ; 23cm. — (History in depth)
Bibl.: p.221-224. — Index.
ISBN 0-333-17434-8 : £10.00
(B77-09543)

322.4'4 — Social protest: Non-violent action, 1930-1975. *Case studies*
Liberation without violence : a third-party approach / edited by A. Paul Hare and Herbert H. Blumberg. — London : Collings, 1977. — x, 368p ; 24cm.
Bibl.: p.288-341. — Index.
ISBN 0-86036-023-7 : £8.50
(B77-26840)

322.4'4 — Students. Protest movements. Members. Victimisation. *Great Britain*
Lanning, Hugh. Victimisation handbook / by Hugh Lanning. — London : NUS Publications, 1975. — 96p : ill, port ; 21cm.
Bibl.: p.96. — Includes facsimile reprints.
ISBN 0-900554-97-5 Sd : £0.95
(B77-26144)

322.4'4'0924 — Slavery. British abolitionist movements. Ramsay, James. *Biographies*
Shyllon, Folarin Olawale. James Ramsay : the unknown abolitionist / [by] Folarin Shyllon. — Edinburgh : Canongate Publishing, 1977. — viii,144p,plate : port ; 23cm.
Bibl.: p.134-139. — Index.
ISBN 0-903937-11-5 : £4.75
(B77-22389)

322.4'4'0924 — Slavery. British abolitionist movements. Smith, John, b.1790. *Guyana. Demerara. Biographies*
Northcott, Cecil. Slavery's martyr : John Smith of Demerara and the emancipation movement, 1817-24 / [by] Cecil Northcott. — London : Epworth Press, 1976. — 136p : facsims, maps ; 22cm.
Bibl.: p.131-133. — Index.
ISBN 0-7162-0269-7 Pbk : £1.50
(B77-03978)

322.4'4'0924 — Slavery. British abolitionist movements. Wilberforce, William. *Biographies*
Pollock, John. Wilberforce / [by] John Pollock. — London : Constable, 1977. — xvi,368p,[2] leaves of plates(1 fold),[8]p of plates : ill, facsims, geneal table, ports(1 col) ; 24cm.
Bibl.: p.355-359. — Index.
ISBN 0-09-460780-x : £8.00
(B77-18580)

322.4'4'0947 — Eastern Europe. Politics. Dissent
Michael-Titus, Constantin. A testimony for Europe / [by] C. Michael-Titus. — Upminster (44 Howard Rd, Upminster RM14 2UF) : Panopticum Press, 1977. — 15p ; 21cm.
Cover title: Yalta, Helsinki, Belgrade?.
Sd : Unpriced
(B77-33643)

322.4'4'0947 — Soviet Union. Society. Dissent. Political aspects. Related to foreign relations, ca 1960-1976
Barghoorn, Frederick Charles. Détente and the democratic movement in the USSR / [by] Frederick C. Barghoorn. — New York : Free Press ; London : Collier Macmillan, 1976. — x, 229p ; 24cm.
Index.
ISBN 0-02-901850-1 : £9.00
Primary classification 327.47
(B77-12890)

322.4'4'0973 — Alcoholic drinks. Prohibition movements. Political aspects. *United States, 1890-1913*
Blocker, Jack S. Retreat from reform : the prohibition movement in the United States, 1890-1913 / [by] Jack S. Blocker, Jr. — Westport, Conn. ; London : Greenwood Press, 1976. — xii,261,[1]p ; 22cm. — (Contributions in American history ; no.51)
Bibl.: p.247-252. — Index.
ISBN 0-8371-8899-7 : £11.95
(B77-19244)

322.4'4'0973 — Negroes. Protest movements. *United States. Northern states, 1827-1861*
Dick, Robert C. Black protest : issues and tactics / [by] Robert C. Dick. — Westport, Conn. ; London : Greenwood Press, 1974. — xiii,338p : ports ; 22cm. — (Contributions in American studies ; no.14)
Bibl.: p.311-331. — Index.
ISBN 0-8371-6366-8 : £12.75
(B77-16752)

322.4'4'0973 — Progressivism. *United States, to 1948*
Filler, Louis. Appointment at Armageddon : muckracking and progressivism in the American tradition / [by] Louis Filler. — Westport, Conn. ; London : Greenwood Press, 1976. — xiii,476p : ill, facsim, ports ; 22cm. — (Contributions in American studies ; no.20)
Bibl.: p.437-446. — Index.
ISBN 0-8371-8261-1 : £12.95
(B77-18581)

Salmon, John. The Suffolk-Essex border / [by] John Salmon ; illustrated by Michael Norman. — Ipswich : Boydell Press, 1977. — [8]p,120p : ill, map ; 23cm.
Index.
ISBN 0-85115-074-8 : £3.50
Also classified at 914.26'7
(B77-12203)

322.4'4'0973 — Slavery. American abolitionist movements, 1830-1865
Walters, Ronald G. The antislavery appeal : American abolitionism after 1830 / [by] Ronald G. Walters. — Baltimore ; London : Johns Hopkins University Press, 1976. — xvii,196,[2] p : ill ; 24cm.
Index.
ISBN 0-8018-1861-3 : £7.70
(B77-21719)

322.4'942 — Money. *England, 1279-1344. Conference proceedings*
Edwardian monetary affairs (1279-1344) : [proceedings of] a symposium held in Oxford, August 1976 / edited by N.J. Mayhew. — Oxford : British Archaeological Reports, 1977. — [10],186p : ill, map ; 30cm. — (British archaeological reports ; 36 ISSN 0306-1206)
Bibl.: p.20-25.
ISBN 0-904531-64-3 Sd : £3.50
(B77-20949)

322'.5 — Military governments
Nordlinger, Eric Allen. Soldiers in politics : military coups and governments / [by] Eric A. Nordlinger. — Englewood Cliffs ; London [etc.] : Prentice-Hall, 1977. — xiii,224p ; 23cm. — (Prentice-Hall contemporary comparative politics series)
Bibl.: p.212-219. — Index.
ISBN 0-13-822163-4 Pbk : £7.20
(B77-32445)

322'.5'091724 — Politics. Role of military forces. *Developing countries*
Janowitz, Morris. Military institutions and coercion in the developing nations / [by] Morris Janowitz. — Expanded ed. — Chicago ; London : University of Chicago Press, 1977. — xiii,211p ; 21cm.
Previous ed.: published as 'The military in the political development of new nations'. 1964. — Index.
ISBN 0-226-39309-7 : £8.75
ISBN 0-226-39310-0 Pbk : £2.80
(B77-26841)

322'.5'094 — Military governments. Overthrow. *Southern Europe, 1972-1974*
Poulantzas, Nicos. The crisis of the dictatorships : Portugal, Greece, Spain / [by] Nicos Poulantzas ; translated [from the French] by David Fernbach. — London : NLB, 1976. — 166p ; 22cm.
Translation of: 'La crise des dictatures'. Paris : Maspero, 1975. — Index.
ISBN 0-902308-77-7 : £5.25
(B77-20058)

322'.5'097291 — Cuba. Politics. Role of Cuba. Ejército, 1898-1958
Pérez, Louis A. Army politics in Cuba, 1898-1958 / [by] Louis A. Pérez, Jr. — [Pittsburgh] : University of Pittsburgh Press ; London : Feffer and Simons : [Distributed by Transatlantic Book Service], 1976. — xvi,240p ; 24cm.
Bibl.: p.211-233. — Index.
ISBN 0-8229-3303-9 : £7.46
(B77-06500)

323 — POLITICS. RELATION OF STATE TO INDIVIDUALS AND SOCIAL CLASSES

323.1'19'24043 — Jews. Racial discrimination by society. Political aspects. *Germany, 1933-1939*
Dawidowicz, Lucy S. The war against the Jews, 1933-45 / [by] Lucy Dawidowicz. — Harmondsworth [etc.] : Penguin, 1977. — 550p : 2 maps ; 18cm. — (Pelican books)
Originally published: London : Weidenfeld and Nicolson, 1975. — Bibl.: p.523-536. — Index.
ISBN 0-14-022007-0 Pbk : £1.95
Primary classification 940.53'1503'924
(B77-27565)

323.1'19'43 — Ethnic minorities. Policies of government. *Soviet Union, 1917-1971. Study examples: Tatars. Study regions: Uzbekistan. Russian texts*
Davletshin, Tamurbek. Sovetskiĭ Tatarstan : teoriia i praktika leninskoĭ natsional'noĭ politiki / Tamurbek Davletshin. — London (35 Notting Hill Gate, W.11) : 'Our Word' Publishers, 1974. — 392p,[4]p of plates,[2] leaves of plates : maps, ports ; 24cm.
Second title page in English. — Bibl.: p.363-385. — Index.
ISBN 0-85016-002-2 Pbk : £5.60
(B77-01195)

323.1'196 — Negroes. Separatism. Theories
Black separatism and social reality : rhetoric and reason / editor Raymond L. Hall. — New York ; Oxford [etc.] : Pergamon, 1977. — xvii, 280p : ill ; 31cm.
Bibl. — Index.
ISBN 0-08-019510-5 : £12.50
ISBN 0-08-019509-1 Pbk : £6.00
(B77-25417)

323.1'19'6073 — Negroes. Political movements. *United States, ca 1960-1976*
Blair, Thomas Lucien. Retreat to the ghetto : the end of a dream? / [by] Thomas L. Blair. — London : Wildwood House, 1977. — xxiii, 263p ; 21cm.
Bibl.: p.244-253. — Index.
ISBN 0-7045-0318-2 : £8.95
(B77-32446)

323.1'19'6073075 — Negroes. Race relations. Political aspects. Role of Kennedy, John Fitzgerald. *United States. Southern states, 1960-1963*
Brauer, Carl M. John F. Kennedy and the second reconstruction / by Carl M. Brauer. — New York ; Guildford : Columbia University Press, 1977. — xv,396p ; 24cm. — (Contemporary American history series)
Bibl.: p.367-379. — Index.
ISBN 0-231-03862-3 : £11.00
(B77-28424)

323.1'19'70881 — Indians of South America. Policies of government. *Guyana, 1803-1873*
Menezes, Mary Noel. British policy towards the Amerindians in British Guiana, 1803-1873 / by Mary Noel Menezes. — Oxford : Clarendon Press, 1977. — xiii,326p : 3 maps ; 23cm.
Bibl.: p.298-314. — Index.
ISBN 0-19-821567-3 : £8.50 : CIP rev.
(B77-08249)

323.1'41 — Coloured persons. Social conditions. Political aspects. *Great Britain. Periodicals*
Black struggle : a journal against racism and capitalism. — London (15 Portland Rd, N.15) : 'Black struggle'.
[No.1]- ; [Aug. 1976]-. — 1976-. — ill, facsims, ports ; 30cm.
Quarterly. — 31p. in 1st issue.
Sd : £1.50 yearly
ISSN 0309-0523
(B77-03979)

323.1'51 — Minorities. Policies of government. *China, 1949-1975*
Dreyer, June Teufel. China's forty millions : minority nationalities and national integration in the People's Republic of China / [by] June Teufel Dreyer. — Cambridge, Mass. ; London : Harvard University Press, 1976. — [10],333p : ill, map ; 25cm. — (Harvard East Asian series ; 87)
Bibl.: p.317-326. — Index.
ISBN 0-674-11964-9 : £10.50
(B77-20059)

323.1'68 — Apartheid
International Defence and Aid Fund. South Africa, apartheid quiz / [International Defence and Aid Fund]. — Revised ed. — London : The Fund, 1975. — [1],54p ; 18cm.
Cover title: Apartheid quiz. — Previous ed.: London : Christian Action Publications, 1972. — Index.
ISBN 0-904759-01-6 Sd : £0.20
(B77-19245)

323.3 — Educated classes. Political aspects. *Russia, 1801-1855*
Riasanovsky, Nicholas Valentine. A parting of ways : government and the educated public in Russia, 1801-1855 / [by] Nicholas V. Riasanovsky. — Oxford : Clarendon Press, 1976. — ix,323p ; 23cm.
Bibl.: p.298-311. — Index.
ISBN 0-19-822533-4 : £12.00
(B77-07815)

323.3 — Working classes. Radicalism. *England, 1840-1870*
Tholfsen, Trygve Rainone. Working class radicalism in mid-Victorian England / [by] Trygve R. Tholfsen. — London : Croom Helm, 1976. — 332p ; 23cm. — (Croom Helm social history series)
Index.
ISBN 0-85664-249-5 : £9.95
(B77-06501)

323.4 — CIVIL RIGHTS
323.4 — Children. Rights. *Great Britain. Paedophiliac viewpoints. Periodicals*
Childhood rights. — London (c/o Release, 1 Elgin Ave., W.9) : Paedophile Information Exchange, Children's Rights Section.
Vol.1, no.1- ; [1977?]-. — [1977?]-. — 35cm.
Folder ([4]p.) as 1st issue.
Sd : Unpriced
ISSN 0309-8974
(B77-33644)

323.4 — Civil rights movements. Resources. Allocation. Applications of linear programming. *United States*
Nagel, Stuart Samuel. The application of mixed strategies : civil rights and other multiple-activity policies / [by] Stuart Nagel, Marian Neef. — Beverly Hills ; London : Sage Publications, [1977]. — 60,[1]p : ill ; 22cm. — (Sage professional papers in American politics ; vol.3, no.04-029)
Published in the United States: 1976. — Bibl.: p.49.
ISBN 0-8039-0541-6 Pbk : £1.75
(B77-11097)

323.4 — Equality. Theories of Americans, ca 1776
Greene, Jack Phillip. All men are created equal : some reflections on the character of the American Revolution / by Jack P. Greene. — Oxford : Clarendon Press, 1976. — 41p ; 22cm. — (University of Oxford. Inaugural lectures)
'... delivered before the University of Oxford on 10 February 1976'.
ISBN 0-19-951509-3 Sd : £1.25
(B77-00632)

323.4 — Human rights. *Comparative studies*
Comparative human rights / edited by Richard P. Claude. — Baltimore ; London : Johns Hopkins University Press, 1976. — xvi,410p ; 24cm.
ISBN 0-8018-1784-6 : £11.55
(B77-00059)

Duchacek, Ivo Duka. Rights & liberties in the world today : constitutional promise & reality / [by] Ivo D. Duchacek. — Santa Barbara : ABC-Clio ; Oxford : EBC-Clio, [1976]. — xiii, 269p : ill ; 24cm. — (Studies in comparative politics)
Published in the United States: 1973. — Bibl.: p.259-266. — Index.
ISBN 0-87436-112-5 : £9.50
ISBN 0-87436-113-3 Pbk : £4.80
(B77-00060)

323.4 — Human rights. *Muslim viewpoints*
Mawdudi, Abul A'la. Human rights in Islam / [by] Abul A'la Mawdudi ; [translated from the Urdu by Kurshid Ahmad and Ahmed Said Khan]. — Leicester [etc.] (223 London Rd, Leicester LE2 1ZE) : Islamic Foundation, 1976. — 43p ; 21cm.
'... an English translation of a talk given ... at the invitation of Civic Rights and Liberties Forum, at Flatties Hotel, Lahore, Pakistan on 16th November, 1975' - Preface.
ISBN 0-9503954-9-8 Sd : Unpriced
(B77-11613)

323.4 — Human rights. *Secondary school texts*
Birnie, Ian Howard. Human rights / [text by Ian Birnie and Sheila M. Hobden]. — London : S.C.M. Press [for] the Christian Education Movement, 1971. — 32p : ill ; 23cm. — (Probe ; 4 ISSN 0305-3776)
Originally published: 1969. — Bibl.: p.32.
Sd : £0.15
ISBN 0-334-00654-6
(B77-10199)

323.4 — Human rights. Implications of oppression of scientists. *Reports, surveys*
Study Group on Scholarly Freedom and Human Rights. Scholarly freedom and human rights : the problem of persecution and oppression of science and scientists : [report of a Study Group on Scholarly Freedom and Human Rights]. — [Chichester] : Rose for the Council for Science and Society [and] the British Institute of Human Rights, 1977. — 63p ; 21cm.
'... Council for Science and Society ... [established] a Study Group on Scholarly Freedom and Human Rights' - Preface.
ISBN 0-85992-099-2 Pbk : £2.25
(B77-14582)

323.4 — Social justice
Robbins, Lionel, *Baron Robbins.* Liberty and equality / [by] Lord Robbins. — London : Institute of Economic Affairs, 1977. — 24p ; 21cm. — (Institute of Economic Affairs. Occasional papers ; 52 ISSN 0073-909x)
Bibl.: p.24.
ISBN 0-255-36099-1 Sd : £0.60
(B77-24740)

323.4 — Women. Civil rights. *Great Britain. Practical information*
Coote, Anna. Women's rights, a practical guide / [by] Anna Coote and Tess Gill ; drawings by Posy Simmonds. — 2nd ed. — Harmondsworth [etc.] : Penguin, 1977. — 499p : ill ; 19cm. — (Penguin handbooks)
Previous ed.: 1974. — Index.
ISBN 0-14-046283-x Pbk : £1.25
(B77-26145)

323.4 — Women. Rights. *United States, 1848-1888. Essays*
Douglass, Frederick. Frederick Douglass on women's rights / Philip S. Foner, editor. — Westport, Conn. ; London : Greenwood Press, 1976. — x,190p ; 22cm. — (Contributions in Afro-American and African studies ; no. 25)
Index.
ISBN 0-8371-8895-4 : £10.95
(B77-32447)

323.4'01 — Human rights. Philosophical perspectives
Flathman, Richard Earl. The practice of rights / [by] Richard E. Flathman. — Cambridge [etc.] : Cambridge University Press, 1976. — vi, 250p ; 22cm.
Index.
ISBN 0-521-21170-0 : £8.50
(B77-11614)

323.4'0973 — Civil rights. *United States*
Way, Howard Frank. Liberty in the balance : current issues in civil liberties / [by] H. Frank Way, Jr. — 4th ed. — New York ; London [etc.] : McGraw-Hill, [1977]. — ix,128p : 1 ill ; 21cm. — (Foundations of American government and political science)
This ed. published in the United States: 1976. — Previous ed.: New York : McGraw-Hill, 1971. — Bibl.: p.120-121. — Index.
ISBN 0-07-068659-9 Pbk : £3.75
(B77-12337)

323.4'0973 — Civil rights. *United States, to 1976*
Freedom in America : a 200-year perspective / edited with an introduction by Norman A. Graebner. — University Park ; London : Pennsylvania State University Press, 1977. — viii,269p ; 24cm.
Index.
ISBN 0-271-01234-x : £9.35
(B77-24035)

323.4'0973 — Civil rights. Policies of government. *United States*
Civil liberties : policy and policy making / edited by Stephen L. Wasby. — Carbondale [etc.] : Southern Illinois University Press ; London [etc.] : Feffer and Simons, 1977. — xiv,241p : 1 ill ; 21cm.
Originally published: Lexington, Mass. ; London : D.C. Heath, 1976. — Bibl. — Index.
ISBN 0-8093-0817-7 Pbk : £3.70
(B77-16213)

323.4'0973 — Negroes. Civil rights. Effects of negro military service in American Civil War. *United States, 1861-1868*
Berry, Mary Frances. Military necessity and civil rights policy : black citizenship and the Constitution, 1861-1868 / [by] Mary Frances Berry. — Port Washington ; London : Kennikat Press, 1977. — xii,132p ; 23cm. — (Kennikat Press national university publications : series in American studies)
Bibl.: p.125-129. — Index.
ISBN 0-8046-9166-5 : £7.60
(B77-24741)

323.44 — Liberty. *Great Britain*
The **individual,** the enterprise and the state : a collection of ideas and insights from a series of seminars held at the Oxford Centre for Management Studies, England / edited by R.I. Tricker ; with contributions from Lord Armstrong ... [et al.]. — London : Associated Business Programmes, 1977. — [5],169p : ill ; 23cm.
'A Halsted Press book'.
ISBN 0-85227-077-1 : £5.95
(B77-24742)

323.44 — Liberty. *Western world*
Hayek, Friedrich August. The constitution of liberty / [by] F.A. Hayek. — London [etc.] : Routledge and Kegan Paul, 1976. — x,570p ; 24cm.
Originally published: 1960. — Index.
ISBN 0-7100-1503-8 : £7.59
ISBN 0-7100-8518-4 Pbk : £3.95
(B77-03404)

323.44 — Liberty. Implications of theories of justice
Hayek, Friedrich August. Law, legislation and liberty : a new statement of the liberal principles of justice and political economy / [by] F.A. Hayek. — London [etc.] : Routledge and Kegan Paul.
Vol.2 : The mirage of social justice. — 1976. — xiv,195p ; 23cm.
Index.
ISBN 0-7100-8403-x : £4.95
(B77-03405)

323.44 — Privacy. Encroachment by computer systems. *Great Britain*
Sieghart, Paul. Privacy and computers / [by] Paul Sieghart ; foreword by Sir Leslie Scarman. — London : Latimer New Dimensions, 1976. — viii,228p : ill ; 23cm.
Bibl.: p.142-146.
ISBN 0-901539-56-2 : £6.50
(B77-00061)

323.44 — Privacy. Encroachment by computer systems. Control. *Great Britain. Proposals*
British Computer Society. Submission of evidence to the Data Protection Committee / [British Computer Society]. — London : The Society, [1977]. — [1],31,37 leaves ; 30cm.
ISBN 0-901865-21-4 Pbk : £6.00
(B77-16214)

323.44 — Privacy. Encroachment by data banks. Control. *Great Britain. Proposals*
National Council for Civil Liberties. Individual privacy : evidence to the Data Protection Committee / [National Council for Civil Liberties]. — London : N.C.C.L., [1977]. — [3],13p ; 30cm. — (National Council for Civil Liberties. Reports ; no.18 ISSN 0306-8994)
ISBN 0-901108-64-2 Sd : £0.25
(B77-15713)

323.44'0941 — Personal freedom. *Great Britain. Conservative and Unionist Party viewpoints*
Griffiths, Eldon. Fighting for the life of freedom / [by] Eldon Griffiths. — London : Conservative Political Centre, 1977. — 23,[1]p ; 21cm. — (Conservative Political Centre. Publications ; no.601)
ISBN 0-85070-595-9 Sd : £0.40
(B77-20060)

323.44'5 — Freedom of press. *Great Britain & United States*
The **freedom** of the press / with an introduction by Sir William Haley. — London : Hart-Davis MacGibbon, 1974. — 91p ; 18cm. — (The Granada Guildhall lectures ; 1974)
Contents: The half-free press / by Harold Evans - Government and the media / by Lord Windlesham - The freedom of the American press / by Katharine Graham.
ISBN 0-246-10827-4 Pbk : £0.75
(B77-18582)

323.44'5 — Official documents. Access. Rights of public. *Great Britain*
Wraith, Ronald Edward. Open government : the British interpretation / [by] Ronald Wraith. — London : Royal Institute of Public Administration, 1977. — 74p ; 22cm. — (Royal Institute of Public Administration. Research booklets)
ISBN 0-900628-15-4 Pbk : £1.90
(B77-24743)

323.4'6'01 — Property rights. *Philosophical perspectives*
Becker, Lawrence Carlyle. Property rights : philosophic foundations / [by] Lawrence C. Becker. — London [etc.] : Routledge and Kegan Paul, 1977. — xi,135p ; 23cm.
Index.
ISBN 0-7100-8679-2 : £4.95 : CIP rev.
(B77-18583)

323.6 — CITIZENSHIP
323.6'2'0941 — British citizenship. Acquisition. *Statistics*
Statistics of persons acquiring citizenship of the United Kingdom and colonies ... / Home Office. — London : H.M.S.O.
1976. — [1977]. — 11p ; 25cm. — (Cmnd.6899)
ISBN 0-10-168990-x Sd : £0.35
(B77-27698)

324 — ELECTIONS
324 — Electorate. *England. Statistics*
Electoral statistics : parliamentary and local government electors in constituencies and local government areas of England and Wales / Office of Population Censuses and Surveys. — London : H.M.S.O.
1976. — 1977. — iv,20p : form ; 30cm. — (Series EL ; no.3)
ISBN 0-11-690622-7 Sd : £0.85
(B77-15117)

324'.15 — Negroes. Voting rights. *United States. Southern states, 1944-1969*
Lawson, Steven F. Black ballots : voting rights in the South, 1944-1969 / [by] Steven F. Lawson. — New York ; Guildford : Columbia University Press, 1976 [i.e. 1977]. — xv,474p : 1 ill ; 24cm. — (Contemporary American history series)
Published in the United States: 1976. — Bibl.: p.429-449. — Index.
ISBN 0-231-03978-6 : £13.88
ISBN 0-231-08352-1 Pbk : £4.82
(B77-09544)

324'.21 — European Parliament. British members. Direct election
Great Britain. *Home Office.* Direct elections to the European Assembly ... / Home Office, Foreign and Commonwealth Office. — London : H.M.S.O., [1977]. — 28p ; 25cm. — (Cmnd.6768)
ISBN 0-10-167680-8 Sd : £0.60
(B77-12338)

324'.21 — European Parliament. British members. Direct election. *Proposals*
Great Britain. *Parliament. House of Commons. Select Committee on Direct Elections to the European Assembly.* Report from the Select Committee on Direct Elections to the European Assembly, session 1975-76. — London : H.M.S.O.
3rd : together with the proceedings of the Committee and the minutes of evidence taken before the Committee on 14th October 1976. — [1976]. — xxi,22p ; 25cm. — ([1975-76 H.C.] 715) ([1975-76 H.C.] 462-XII)
ISBN 0-10-009366-3 Sd : £0.85
(B77-03980)

324'.21 — European Parliament. Members. Direct election. *Periodicals*
European elections briefing. — London (20 Kensington Palace Gardens, W.8) : European Parliament.
1- ; Jan. 1977-. — 1977-. — ill, ports ; 30cm.
Folder ([4]p.) as 1st issue.
Unpriced
(B77-31014)

324'.21 — United States. Presidents. Elections. Electoral college system. Biases, 1960-1980
Yunker, John H. The electoral college : its biases newly measured for the 1960s and 1970s / [by] John H. Yunker, Lawrence D. Longley. — Beverly Hills ; London : Sage Publications, 1976. — 56p : ill ; 22cm. — (Sage professional papers in American politics ; vol.3, no.04-031)
Bibl.
ISBN 0-8039-0556-4 Pbk : £1.75
(B77-15118)

324'.21'0941 — Electoral systems. Reform. *Great Britain*
Mayhew, Christopher. The disillusioned voter's guide to electoral reform / [by] Christopher Mayhew. — London [etc.] : Arrow Books, 1976. — 64p : ill, facsims, port ; 23cm. — (An Arrow special)
ISBN 0-09-913410-1 Sd : £0.60
(B77-04596)

324'.21'0941 — Electoral systems. Reform. *Great Britain. Proposals*
Bradbury, Farel. Electoral reform : V2P : voting for policies as well as for politicians : a political essay / by Farel Bradbury. — [2nd ed.]. — Ross-on-Wye ([P.O. Box 4, Ross-on-Wye] HR9 6EB) : Hydatum, 1975. — [3],14,[2]p : forms ; 25cm.
Previous ed.: 1975?.
ISBN 0-905682-04-1 Sd : £0.75
(B77-02079)

Electoral Reform Society of Great Britain and Ireland. Evidence to the Hansard Society Commission on Electoral Reform, 1976 / the Electoral Reform Society. — London (6 Chancel St., SE1 0UX) : The Society, [1976]. — [12]p ; 21cm.
Sd : £0.15
(B77-11615)

Newland, Robert Arthur. Electing the United Kingdom Parliament / [by Robert A. Newland]. — London (6 Chancel St., SE1 0UX) : Electoral Reform Society, 1976. — [2], 17p ; 21cm.
Bibl.: p.17.
ISBN 0-903291-06-1 Sd : £0.20
(B77-11616)

Newland, Robert Arthur. Electoral systems / [by] Robert A. Newland. — London (6 Chancel St., SE1 0UX) : Electoral Reform Society, [1976]. — [2],25p ; 21cm.
'... based on a lecture given at the Conservative Action for Electoral Reform Course held during the weekend of 7-9 November 1975 at Swinton Conservative College, North Yorkshire' - title page verso.
ISBN 0-903291-05-3 Sd : £0.25
(B77-11617)

324'.242'0941 — Electorate. Voting behaviour. *Great Britain, 1679-1722*
Holmes, Geoffrey. The electorate and the national will in the first age of party / by Geoffrey Holmes. — [Lancaster] ([Bailrigg, Lancaster LA1 4YH]) : University of Lancaster, 1976. — [4],33p ; 22cm. — (University of Lancaster. Inaugural lectures)
'... delivered on 26 November 1975'.
Sd : Unpriced
(B77-11618)

324'.242'09417 — Electorate. Voting behaviour. *Ireland (Republic), 1927-1973*
Gallagher, Michael. Electoral support for Irish political parties, 1927-1973 / [by] Michael Gallagher. — London [etc.] : Sage Publications, 1976. — 75,[1]p ; 22cm. — (Sage professional papers in contemporary political sociology ; vol.2, no.06-017 ISSN 0305-3482)
Bibl.: p.73-75.
ISBN 0-8039-9860-0 Pbk : £1.75
(B77-08810)

324'.242'0973 — Electorate. Voting behaviour. *United States, 1952-1975. Cohort studies*
Converse, Philip E. The dynamics of party support : cohort-analyzing party identification / [by] Philip E. Converse. — Beverly Hills ; London : Sage Publications, 1976. — 175p : ill ; 22cm. — (Sage library of social research ; vol.35)
Bibl.: p.169-171. — Index.
ISBN 0-8039-0727-3 : £8.65
ISBN 0-8039-0728-1 Pbk : £4.60
(B77-15119)

324'.3'0924 — Women's suffrage movements. Lytton, Lady Constance. *Great Britain, 1908-1911. Autobiographies*
Lytton, *Lady* **Constance.** Prisons and prisoners : experiences of a suffragette / [by] Lady Constance Lytton. — Wakefield : EP Publishing, 1976. — xi,337p,[2]leaves of plates : 2 ports ; 20cm.
Facsimile reprint of: 1st ed. originally published: / under the names Constance Lytton and Jane Wharton as 'Prisons & prisoners, some personal experiences'. London : Heinemann, 1914.
ISBN 0-7158-1154-1 : £5.00
(B77-33645)

324'.3'0924 — Women's suffrage movements. Pankhurst, Dame Christabel. *Great Britain. Biographies*
Mitchell, David, *b.1924.* Queen Christabel : a biography of Christabel Pankhurst / [by] David Mitchell. — London : Macdonald and Jane's, 1977. — x,397p,[24]p of plates : ill, facsims, ports ; 24cm.
Bibl.: p.372-379. — Index.
ISBN 0-354-04152-5 : £8.95
(B77-27699)

324'.3'0941 — Women's suffrage movements. *Great Britain, to 1918*
Ramelson, Marian. The petticoat rebellion : a century of struggle for women's rights / [by] Marian Ramelson. — 3rd ed. — London : Lawrence and Wishart, 1976. — 208p : 2 ill ; 22cm.
Previous ed.: 1972. — Bibl.: p.199-205. — Index.
ISBN 0-85315-272-1 Pbk : £1.50
(B77-06502)

324'.41 — Electoral processes. *England, ca 1825-ca 1870*
Moore, David Cresap. The politics of deference : a study of the mid-nineteenth century English political system / [by] David Cresap Moore. — Hassocks : Harvester Press [etc.], 1976. — ix, 529p : ill, maps ; 24cm.
Bibl.: p.505-515. — Index.
ISBN 0-901759-07-4 : £15.50
(B77-05230)

324'.41 — Electoral processes. *Great Britain*
McLean, Iain. Elections / [by] Iain McLean. — London : Longman, 1976. — ix,102p ; 21cm. — (Political realities)
Bibl.: p.97-99. — Index.
ISBN 0-582-36615-1 : £3.50
ISBN 0-582-36626-7 Pbk : £1.75
(B77-08250)

324'.73 — Electoral processes. *United States*
The **impact** of the electoral process / edited by Louis Maisel and Joseph Cooper. — Beverly Hills ; London : Sage Publications, 1977. — 304p : ill, facsims ; 24cm. — (Sage electoral studies yearbooks ; vol.3)
Bibl.
ISBN 0-8039-0709-5 : Unpriced
ISBN 0-8039-0710-9 Pbk : Unpriced
(B77-31015)

324'.73 — Electoral processes. *United States, 1948-1975*
Bone, Hugh Alvin. Politics and voters / [by] Hugh A. Bone, Austin Ranney. — 4th ed. — New York ; London [etc.] : McGraw-Hill, [1977]. — vii,135p : ill ; 21cm. — (Foundations of American government and political science)
This ed. published in the United States: 1976. — Previous ed.: New York : McGraw-Hill, 1971. — Bibl.: p.125-127. — Index.
ISBN 0-07-006491-1 Pbk : £3.75
(B77-11619)

324'.73 — United States. Presidents. Elections. *Juvenile literature*
Gray, Lee Learner. How we choose a president : the election year / by Lee Learner Gray. — 4th ed. — New York : St Martin's Press ; London : St James Press, 1976. — [7],167p ; 22cm.
Previous ed.: New York : St Martin's Press, 1972. — Bibl.: p.159-162. — Index.
ISBN 0-900997-50-8 : £3.25
(B77-22390)

325.2 — EMIGRATION

325'.247'0943 — Germans. Transfer from Eastern Europe. *West Germany, 1944-1947*
De Zayas, Alfred M. Nemesis at Potsdam : the Anglo-Americans and the expulsion of the Germans : background, execution, consequences / [by] Alfred M. de Zayas ; foreword by Robert Murphy. — London [etc.] : Routledge and Kegan Paul, 1977. — xxvii, 268p,[32]p of plates : ill, facsims, maps, ports ; 23cm.
Bibl.: p.242-259. — Index.
ISBN 0-7100-8468-4 : £5.95
(B77-07816)

325.3 — COLONIAL ADMINISTRATION

325'.341'0954 — India. Colonial administration by Great Britain, 1942-1947. State papers. *Collections*
The **transfer** of power, 1942-7 / editor-in-chief Nicholas Mansergh. — London : H.M.S.O. — (Constitutional relations between Britain and India)
Vol.7 : The Cabinet Mission, 23 March-29 June 1946 / assistant editor Penderel Moon. — 1977. — lxxxiii,1130p,plate : ports ; 28cm.
Spine title: India, the transfer of power, 1942-7. — Index.
ISBN 0-11-580082-4 : £35.00
(B77-26146)

325'.341'0954 — India. Colonial administration by Great Britain. Bentinck, Lord William, 1828-1835. *Correspondence*
Bentinck, *Lord* **William.** The correspondence of Lord William Cavendish Bentinck, Governor-General of India 1828-1835 / edited with an introduction by C.H. Philips. — Oxford [etc.] : Oxford University Press [for the School of Oriental and African Studies], 1977. — 2v.(xlix,[4],1483p) ; 24cm.
Index.
ISBN 0-19-713571-4 : £55.00
(B77-32448)

325'.341'0973 — United States. Colonial administration by Great Britain, 1770-1783. State papers. *Collections*
Great Britain. *Colonial Office.* Documents of the American Revolution, 1770-1783. Colonial Office series. — Dublin : Irish University Press.

Vol.12 : Transcripts, 1776 / edited by K.G. Davies. — 1976. — vi,301p ; 25cm.
Records held at the Public Record Office. — Index.
ISBN 0-7165-2097-4 : £20.00
ISBN 0-7165-2085-0 Set : Unpriced
(B77-07103)

Vol.13 : Calendar, 1777-1778 / edited by K.G. Davies. — 1976. — vi,481p ; 25cm.
Records held at the Public Record Office. — Index.
ISBN 0-7165-2098-2 : £25.00
ISBN 0-7165-2085-0 Set : Unpriced
(B77-07104)

Vol.14 : Transcripts, 1777 / edited by K.G. Davies. — 1976. — vi,299p ; 25cm.
Records held at the Public Record Office. — Index.
ISBN 0-7165-2099-0 : £21.00
ISBN 0-7165-2085-0 Set : Unpriced
(B77-10742)

Vol.15 : Transcripts, 1778 / edited by K.G. Davies. — 1976. — vi,320p ; 25cm.
Records held at the Public Record Office. — Index.
ISBN 0-7165-2100-8 : £21.00
ISBN 0-7165-2085-0 Set : Unpriced
(B77-10743)

Vol.16 : Calendar, 1779-1780 / edited by K.G. Davies. — 1977. — vi,550p ; 25cm.
Title page has title statement: Documents of the American Revolution, 1779-1780. — Records held at the Public Record Office. — Index.
ISBN 0-7165-2101-6 : Unpriced
ISBN 0-7165-2085-0 Set : Unpriced
(B77-32449)

Vol.17 : Transcripts, 1779 / edited by K.G. Davies. — 1977. — vi,291p ; 25cm.
Records held at the Public Record Office. — Index.
ISBN 0-7165-2102-4 : Unpriced
ISBN 0-7165-2085-0 Set : Unpriced
(B77-32450)

325'.368'709686 — Lesotho. Administration by South Africa. Cape Province, 1871-1884
Burman, S B. The justice of the Queen's government : the Cape's administration of Basutoland, 1871-1884 / [by] S.B. Burman. — Leiden : Afrika-Studiecentrum ; Cambridge (Sidgwick Ave., Cambridge) : African Studies Centre, 1976. — viii,131p : maps ; 23cm. — (African social research documents ; vol.9)
Bibl.: p.122-125. — Index.
Pbk : £2.75
(B77-33085)

325.4/9 — POLITICS. MIGRATION. GEOGRAPHICAL TREATMENT

325.41 — Immigration to Great Britain. *Statistics*
Control of immigration statistics / Home Office ... — London : H.M.S.O.
1976. — [1977]. — 23p ; 25cm. — (Cmnd.6883)
ISBN 0-10-168830-x Sd : £0.60
(B77-26147)

325.41 — Immigration to Great Britain. Policies of government, 1800-1971
Jones, Catherine. Immigration and social policy in Britain / [by] Catherine Jones. — London : Tavistock Publications, 1977. — ix,291p ; 23cm.
Bibl.: p.266-271. — Index.
ISBN 0-422-74670-3 : £7.85
(B77-18584)

325.41 — India. Emigration to Great Britain. Entry controls. *Reports, surveys*
Akram, Mohammed. Firm but unfair? : immigration control in the Indian sub-continent : a preliminary report / by Mohammed Akram and Jan Elliot. — London : Runnymede Trust, 1976. — [2],iii,11 leaves ; 30cm.
Sp : £0.50
(B77-17329)

327 — FOREIGN RELATIONS

Bull, Hedley. The anarchical society : a study of order in world politics / [by] Hedley Bull. — London [etc.] : Macmillan, 1977. — xv,335p ; 23cm.
Index.
ISBN 0-333-19914-6 : £12.00
ISBN 0-333-19915-4 Pbk : £4.95
(B77-14086)

Wendzel, Robert L. International relations : a policymaker focus / [by] Robert L. Wendzel. — New York ; London [etc.] : Wiley, 1977. — xiii,286p ; 23cm.
Bibl. — Index.
ISBN 0-471-93361-9 Pbk : £5.50
(B77-09545)

327 — Foreign relations. Effects of technological development
Basiuk, Victor. Technology, world politics & American policy / [by] Victor Basiuk. — New York ; Guildford : Columbia University Press, 1977. — xvii,409p : ill ; 24cm.
Index.
£12.90
ISBN 0-231-04154-1
(B77-24036)

327 — Foreign relations. Policies. Formulation
Cottam, Richard W. Foreign policy motivation : a general theory and a case study / [by] Richard W. Cottam. — [Pittsburgh] : University of Pittsburgh Press ; London : Feffer and Simons, 1977. — vii,374p : ill ; 24cm.
Bibl.: p.357-363. — Index.
ISBN 0-8229-3323-3 : £9.38
(B77-33086)

327 — Foreign relations. Role of military power. *Conference proceedings*
Beyond nuclear deterrence : new aims, new arms / edited by Johan J. Holst, Uwe Nerlich. — London : Macdonald and Jane's, 1977. — xv,314p : ill ; 24cm.
'The chapters in the book have been discussed in two workshops devoted to a reexamination of Western security problems : the first was held in Ebenhausen near Munich in March, 1975 ... the second took place in Copenhagen in September, 1975 ...' - Editors' Preface. — Bibl.: p.299-301. — Index.
ISBN 0-354-01093-x : £10.50
(B77-20950)

327 — Foreign relations. Role of nonstate nations
Nonstate nations in international politics : comparative system analyses / edited by Judy Bertelsen. — New York [etc.] ; London : Praeger, 1977. — vi,265p ; 25cm. — (Praeger special studies in international politics and government)
Bibl. — Index.
ISBN 0-275-56320-0 : £14.80
(B77-15714)

327'.01 — Foreign relations. Theories
Holsti, Kalevi Jaque. International politics : a framework for analysis / [by] K.J. Holsti. — 3rd ed. — Englewood Cliffs ; London [etc.] : Prentice-Hall, 1977. — xi,548p : ill ; 24cm.
Previous ed.: 1972. — Bibl. — Index.
ISBN 0-13-473371-1 : £10.00
(B77-15715)

327'.01'84 — Foreign relations. Mathematical models
Mathematical models in international relations / edited by Dina A. Zinnes, John V. Gillespie. — New York [etc.] ; London : Praeger, 1976. — xviii,399p : ill ; 25cm. — (Praeger special studies in international politics and government)
ISBN 0-275-55870-3 : £21.85
(B77-05231)

327'.01'84 — Foreign relations. Mathematical models. Applications of digital computer systems
Bremer, Stuart A. Simulated worlds : a computer model of national decision-making / [by] Stuart A. Bremer. — Princeton ; Guildford : Princeton University Press, 1977. — xvi,249,[1] p : ill ; 23cm.
Bibl.: p.231-244. — Index.
ISBN 0-691-05661-7 : £12.50
(B77-20951)

327'.01'84 — Foreign relations. Mathematical models. Research. *Conference proceedings*
Mathematical systems in international relations research / edited by John V. Gillespie, Dina A. Zinnes. — New York [etc.] ; London : Praeger, 1977. — xxiv,432p : ill ; 25cm. — (Praeger special studies in international politics and government)
'This volume is based on a conference held in Bloomington, Indiana in April 1975' - Preface.
ISBN 0-275-55620-4 : £22.20
(B77-16215)

327'.01'9 — Foreign relations. Psychological aspects
Jervis, Robert. Perception and misperception in international politics / [by] Robert Jervis. — Princeton, N.J. ; Guildford : Princeton University Press, 1976. — xii,445p ; 25cm.
Bibl.: p.425-431. — Index.
ISBN 0-691-05656-0 : £15.70
ISBN 0-691-10049-7 Pbk : £8.00
(B77-03981)

327'.05 — Foreign relations. *Serials*
Survey of international affairs. — Oxford [etc.] : Oxford University Press [for] the Royal Institute of International Affairs.
1963 / by D.C. Watt. — 1977. — xi,351p ; 25cm.
Index.
ISBN 0-19-214733-1 : £25.00
ISSN 0308-6798
(B77-19246)

The **year** book of world affairs. — London : Stevens [for] the London Institute of World Affairs.
1977 : [Vol.31] / editors George W. Keeton and Georg Schwarzenberger. — 1977. — vii, 364p : 5 ill ; 26cm.
Bibl.: p.1-7. — Index.
ISBN 0-420-45240-0 : £8.75
ISSN 0084-408x
(B77-09546)

327'.07'2 — Foreign relations. Research. Methodology
In search of global patterns / edited by James N. Rosenau. — New York : Free Press ; London : Collier Macmillan, 1976. — ix,389p : ill ; 24cm.
Bibl. — Index.
ISBN 0-02-927050-2 : £11.25
(B77-22391)

Reynolds, Charles. Theory and explanation in international politics / [by] Charles Reynolds. — London : Martin Robertson, 1975. — viii, 367p ; 24cm.
Originally published: 1973. — Bibl.: p.257-261. — Index.
ISBN 0-85520-101-0 Pbk : £3.25
(B77-00062)

327'.08 — Foreign relations. British state papers. *Collections*
British and foreign state papers. — London : H.M.S.O.
Vol.169 : 1967-68 / compiled and edited in the Library and Records Department of the Foreign and Commonwealth Office. — 1976. — xxiv,1218p ; 22cm.
Index.
ISBN 0-11-591569-9 : £40.00
(B77-03406)

327'.09'04 — Foreign relations, 1945-1975
Bown, Colin. Cold war to détente / [by] Colin Bown, Peter J. Mooney. — London : Heinemann Educational, 1976. — ix,198p : maps ; 23cm. — (Studies in modern history)
Index.
ISBN 0-435-32133-1 : £5.00
ISBN 0-435-32134-x Pbk : £2.25
(B77-05232)

327'.09'04 — Foreign relations. Role of Western Europe, 1945-1975. *Polish texts*
Kisielewski, Stefan. Czy istnieje walka o świat? / Stefan Kisielewski. — Londyn [i.e. London] : Odnowa, 1976. — 24p ; 22cm. — (Polska w świecie współczesnym ; zesz.2)
ISBN 0-903705-11-7 Sd : £1.00
(B77-09547)

327'.09'044 — Foreign relations. Effects of foreign relations between Soviet Union & United States, 1947-1953
The **impact** of the cold war : reconsiderations / edited by Joseph M. Siracusa and Glen St John Barclay. — Port Washington ; London : Kennikat Press, 1977. — viii,208p ; 23cm. — (Kennikat Press national university publications : series in American studies)
Index.
ISBN 0-8046-9158-4 : £10.60
ISBN 0-8046-9182-7 Pbk : Unpriced
(B77-28425)

327'.091712'4 — Developing countries. Foreign relations. Policies of governments. Formulation
Foreign policy making in developing states : a comparative approach / edited by Christopher Clapham. — Farnborough, Hants. : Saxon House, 1977. — x,184p : maps ; 23cm.
Bibl. — Index.
ISBN 0-566-00173-x : £8.50 : CIP rev.
(B77-17330)

327'.09171'241 — Commonwealth Heads of Government Meeting. London, 1977. Decisions. *Reports, surveys*
Commonwealth heads of government, meeting in London, 8-15 June 1977, final communiqué. — London : Commonwealth Secretariat, [1977]. — 23,[1]p ; 21cm.
Cover title: Commonwealth heads of government, the London communiqué, June 1977.
Sd : Unpriced
(B77-20061)

Commonwealth heads of government meeting, London, 8 June-15 June 1977 : communiqué / presented to Parliament by the Prime Minister ... — London : H.M.S.O., [1977]. — 18p ; 25cm. — (Cmnd.6889)
ISBN 0-10-168890-3 Sd : £0.35
(B77-33087)

327'.09171'3 — Western bloc countries. Foreign relations with communist countries, 1945-1972
Lister, Ian. The cold war / [by] Ian Lister. — London [etc.] : Methuen, 1974. — 90p : 1 ill, map ; 20cm. — (General studies)
With answers. — Bibl.: p.86-89.
ISBN 0-423-46890-1 Pbk : £1.50
Also classified at 327'.09171'7
(B77-33088)

327'.09171'7 — Communist countries. Détente with United States. Role of Kissinger, Henry Alfred, 1969-1977
Bell, Coral. The diplomacy of detente : the Kissinger era / [by] Coral Bell. — London : Martin Robertson, 1977. — viii,278p ; 23cm.
Bibl.: p.269-270. — Index.
ISBN 0-85520-191-6 : £8.50 : CIP rev.
Primary classification 327'.73'01717
(B77-16216)

327'.09171'7 — Communist countries. Foreign relations with Western bloc countries, 1945-1972
Lister, Ian. The cold war / [by] Ian Lister. — London [etc.] : Methuen, 1974. — 90p : 1 ill, map ; 20cm. — (General studies)
With answers. — Bibl.: p.86-89.
ISBN 0-423-46890-1 Pbk : £1.50
Primary classification 327'.09171'3
(B77-33088)

327'.09172'4 — Developing countries. Foreign relations
Rothstein, Robert Lewis. The weak in the world of the strong : the developing countries in the international system / [by] Robert L. Rothstein. — New York ; Guildford : Columbia University Press [for the Institute of War and Peace Studies, Columbia University], 1977. — xiii,384p ; 24cm.
Index.
ISBN 0-231-04338-4 : £11.20
Primary classification 382.1'09172'4
(B77-31811)

327'.09172'4 — Developing countries. Foreign relations with European Community countries. *Reports, surveys*
Sutton, Mary. The EEC and the developing world : a changing relationship / by Mary Sutton. — Dublin (169 Booterstown Ave., [Blackrock], Co. Dublin) : Trócaire : Irish Commission for Justice and Peace, 1976. — [2], vii,59p ; 30cm. — (Joint Development Education Programme)
Bibl.: p.58-59.
Sd : £0.60
Primary classification 327.4'0172'4
(B77-09548)

327'.09172'4 — Developing countries. Foreign relations with Soviet Union, 1953-1973
The **Soviet** Union and the developing nations / edited by Roger E. Kanet. — Baltimore ; London : Johns Hopkins University Press, 1974. — xiii,302,[2]p ; 24cm.
Index.
ISBN 0-8018-1501-0 : Unpriced
Primary classification 327.47'0172'4
(B77-18587)

327'.0917'4927 — Arab countries. Foreign relations with Israel, 1967-1974. *Transcripts of discussions*
Friedländer, Saul. Arabs & Israelis : a dialogue [between] Saul Friedländer [and] Mahmoud Hussein / moderated by Jean Lacouture ; translated [from the French] by Paul Auster and Lydia Davis. — New York ; London (1 Hallswelle Parade, Finchley Rd, NW11 0DL) : Holmes and Meier, 1975. — xiii,221,[2]p : maps ; 23cm.
Translation of: 'Arabes & Israéliens'. Paris : Seuil, 1974.
ISBN 0-8419-0208-9 : Unpriced
Primary classification 327.5694'017'4927
(B77-02082)

327'.09181'2 — Western world. Foreign relations. Role of information services
Deibel, Terry L. Culture and information : two foreign policy functions / [by] Terry L. Deibel, Walter R. Roberts. — Beverly Hills ; London : Sage Publications [for] the Center for Strategic and International Studies, Georgetown University, 1976. — 62p ; 22cm. — (The Washington papers ; 40) (A Sage policy paper)
Bibl.: p.62.
ISBN 0-8039-0789-3 Pbk : £1.95
(B77-15120)

327'.11 — Foreign relations. Implications of inequalities in power & wealth of states
Tucker, Robert Warren. The inequality of nations / [by] Robert W. Tucker. — London : Martin Robertson, 1977. — x,214p ; 22cm.
Also published: New York : Basic Books, 1977. — Index.
ISBN 0-85520-222-x : £7.50
(B77-31016)

327'.11 — Foreign relations. Role of Palestinian Arabs, ca 1900-1975
Bertelsen, Judy. The Palestinian Arabs : a non-state nation systems analysis / [by] Judy Bertelsen. — Beverly Hills ; London : Sage Publications, 1976. — 81,[1]p ; 22cm. — (Sage professional papers in international studies ; vol.4, no.02-043)
Bibl.: p.79-81.
ISBN 0-8039-0622-6 Pbk : £1.75
(B77-15716)

327'.112'09 — Balance of power, to 1976
Quester, George Herman. Offense and defense in the international system / [by] George H. Quester. — New York ; London [etc.] : Wiley, 1977. — xiii,219p : ill ; 22cm. — (International relations series)
Index.
ISBN 0-471-70255-2 : £8.20
ISBN 0-471-70256-0 Pbk : £4.65
(B77-21721)

327'.116'094 — Europe. International security, 1954-1977. State papers. *Collections*
Selected documents relating to problems of security and cooperation in Europe, 1954-77 / presented to Parliament by the Secretary of State for Foreign and Commonwealth Affairs ... — London : H.M.S.O., [1977]. — x,362p : 2 ill ; 25cm. — (Miscellaneous ; no.17(1977)) (Cmnd.6932)
ISBN 0-10-169320-6 Pbk : £5.10
(B77-29987)

327'.116'095694 — Israel. International security. Policies of United States government
Pelcovits, N A. Security guarantees in a Middle East settlement / [by] N.A. Pelcovits ; [for the] Foreign Policy Research Institute. — Beverly Hills ; London : Sage Publications, 1976. — [5], 69p ; 22cm. — (The foreign policy papers ; vol.2, 5) (A Sage policy paper)
ISBN 0-8039-0644-7 Pbk : £1.75
(B77-16753)

327'.12 — Espionage
Palmer, Raymond. The making of a spy / [by] Raymond Palmer. — London : Aldus Books, 1977. — 144p : ill(some col), facsims, col maps, ports(some col) ; 27cm. — (Undercover)
Index.
ISBN 0-490-00371-0 : £3.95
(B77-08811)

327'.12'09 — Espionage, to 1945. *Juvenile literature*
Finlay, Winifred. Spies and secret agents / [by] Winifred Finlay and Gillian Hancock ; illustrated by Gavin Rowe. — London : Kaye and Ward, 1977. — 128p : ill ; 23cm.
ISBN 0-7182-1149-9 : £2.75
(B77-15717)

327'.12'09 — Espionage, to 1976
Haswell, Jock. Spies and spymasters : a concise history of intelligence / [by] Jock Haswell. — London : Thames and Hudson, 1977. — 176p : ill, facsims, maps, ports ; 25cm.
Bibl.: p.167-168. — Index.
ISBN 0-500-01178-8 : £4.95
(B77-22392)

327'.12'0904 — Secret services, ca 1900-1975
FitzGibbon, Constantine. Secret intelligence in the twentieth century / by Constantine FitzGibbon. — London : Hart-Davis MacGibbon, 1976. — 350p ; 25cm.
Index.
ISBN 0-246-10817-7 : £6.95
(B77-02080)

327'.12'0924 — Secret services. *Soviet Union. Komitet gosudarstvennoĭ bezopasnosti, 1965-1974. Personal observations*
Myagkov, Alekseĭ. Inside the KGB : an exposé by an officer of the Third Directorate / by Alekseĭ Myagkov. — Richmond, Surrey : Foreign Affairs Publishing Co., 1976. — [3], 131p ; 23cm.
ISBN 0-900380-19-5 : £3.00
(B77-05233)

327'.12'0973 — American intelligence services. Alleged illegal methods, ca 1935-1975
The **lawless** state : the crimes of the US intelligence agencies / by Morton H. Halperin ... [et al.]. — Harmondsworth [etc.] : Penguin, 1976. — [8],328p : ill ; 18cm.
Bibl.: p.315-318. — Index.
ISBN 0-14-004386-1 Pbk : Unpriced
(B77-05234)

327'.12'0973 — United States. Central Intelligence Agency. Role, 1960-1975. *Inquiry reports*
United States. *Congress. House. Select Committee on Intelligence.* CIA : the Pike report / with an introduction by Philip Agee. — Nottingham : Spokesman Books for the Bertrand Russell Peace Foundation, 1977. — 284p ; 20cm.
'... findings of the US House of Representatives Select Committee [on Intelligence], chaired by Congressman Otis Pike' - jacket.
ISBN 0-85124-172-7 : £6.50
ISBN 0-85124-173-5 Pbk : Unpriced
(B77-26148)

327'.12'0973 — United States. Central Intelligence Agency, to 1976
Paine, Lauran. The CIA at work / by Lauran Paine. — London : Hale, 1977. — 192p,[8]p of plates : ill, ports ; 23cm.
Bibl.: p.186-187. — Index.
ISBN 0-7091-6413-0 : £4.95
(B77-31720)

327'.17'094 — International cooperation. Conferences. *Europe. Conference on Security and Co-operation in Europe, Helsinki, 1975. Implementation. Inquiry reports*
Great Britain. *Parliament. House of Commons. Expenditure Committee.* Progress towards implementation of the final act of the Conference on Security and Co-operation in Europe : fifth report from the Expenditure Committee, session 1976-77, together with part of the minutes of the evidence taken before the Defence and External Affairs Sub-committee on 16th March, 23rd Marcb, 5th April, 6th April, and 19th April 1977, and appendices. — London : H.M.S.O., [1977]. — xlvi,98p ; 25cm. — ([1976-77 H.C.] 392)
ISBN 0-10-239277-3 Pbk : £2.60
(B77-29218)

327'.172 — Peace. Definition
Johnson, L Gunnar. Conflicting concepts of peace in contemporary peace studies / [by] L. Gunnar Johnson. — Beverly Hills ; London : Sage Publications, 1976. — 63,[1]p ; 22cm. — (Sage professional papers in international studies ; vol.4, no.02-046)
Bibl.: p.60-63.
ISBN 0-8039-0625-0 Pbk : £1.75
(B77-15121)

327'.172 — Peace movements
Somerville, John. The peace revolution : ethos and social process / [by] John Somerville. — Westport, Conn. ; London : Greenwood Press, 1975. — xiv,237p ; 22cm. — (Contributions in philosophy ; no.7)
Index.
ISBN 0-8371-7532-1 : £10.50
(B77-17949)

327'.172'0922 — Nobel Peace Prize winners, to 1975. *Biographies*
Gray, Tony. Champions of peace : the story of Alfred Nobel, the Peace Prize and the Laureates / [by] Tony Gray. — [London] : Paddington Press, 1976. — 320p : ill, ports ; 25cm.
Bibl.: p.315. — Index.
ISBN 0-8467-0143-x : £5.95
(B77-29988)

327'.172'0973 — Peace movements. *United States, 1887-1914*
Patterson, David S. Toward a warless world : the travail of the American peace movement, 1887-1914 / by David S. Patterson. — Bloomington ; London : Indiana University Press, 1976. — xi,339p ; 25cm.
Index.
ISBN 0-253-36019-6 : £11.25
(B77-10744)

327'.174 — Nuclear weapons. Arms control
Epstein, William, *b.1912.* The last chance : nuclear proliferation and arms control / [by] William Epstein. — New York : Free Press ; London : Collier Macmillan, 1976. — xxiv, 341p ; 24cm.
Index.
ISBN 0-02-909661-8 : £11.25
(B77-12887)

327'.174 — Nuclear weapons. Arms control. *Conference proceedings*
Arms control and technological innovation / edited by David Carlton and Carlo Schaerf. — London : Croom Helm, 1977. — 366p : ill ; 23cm.
'... papers ... presented to the Sixth Course of the International School on Disarmament and Research on Conflicts, held in Nemi, Italy, from 21 June to 5th July 1976' - Preface. — Also published: New York : Wiley, 1977.
ISBN 0-85664-443-9 : £8.95 : CIP rev.
(B77-24037)

327'.174 — Nuclear weapons. Proliferation. Control measures. *Proposals*
Greenwood, Ted, *b.1944.* Nuclear proliferation : motivations, capabilities, and strategies for control / by Ted Greenwood, Harold A. Feiveson, Theodore B. Taylor ; introduction by David C. Gompert. — New York [etc.] ; London : McGraw-Hill [for] the 1980s Project, 1977. — xii,210,[1]p : ill ; 24cm. — (1980s Project. Studies)
Bibl.: p.195-196. — Index.
ISBN 0-07-024344-1 : £6.70
ISBN 0-07-024345-x Pbk : £3.70
(B77-29219)

327'.174'0904 — Disarmament, ca 1945-1975
Myrdal, Alva. The game of disarmament : how the United States and Russia run the arms race / [by] Alva Myrdal. — Manchester : Manchester University Press, 1977. — xxvi, 399p ; 25cm.
Originally published: New York : Pantheon Books, 1976. — Index.
ISBN 0-7190-0693-7 : £9.95
(B77-23175)

327'.174'094 — Arms control. International cooperation. *Europe*
Coffey, Joseph Irving. Arms control and European security : a guide to East-West negotiations / [by] J.I. Coffey. — London : Chatto and Windus for the International Institute for Strategic Studies, 1977. — 271p ; 23cm. — (Studies in international security ; 19)
Bibl.: p.236-246. — Index.
ISBN 0-7011-2118-1 : £10.00 : CIP rev.
(B77-10200)

327'.2'0924 — British diplomatic service. Parrott, Sir Cecil. *Autobiographies*
Parrott, *Sir* **Cecil.** The serpent and the nightingale / [by] Cecil Parrott. — London : Faber, 1977. — 3-224p,[12]p of plates : ill, maps, ports ; 23cm.
Index.
ISBN 0-571-10869-5 : £7.50 : CIP rev.
(B77-22394)

327'.2'0924 — British diplomatic service. Stepney, George. *Biographies*
Hollaender, Albert Edwin Johannes. Mr Resident George Stepney and the 'Pietas Austriaca', 1693 / [by] Albert Hollaender. — [London] ([69 Aldwych, W.C.2]) : [Leopard's Head Press], [1976]. — [1]p,p217-227 ; 25cm.
'Reprinted from "Tribute to an antiquary : essays presented to Marc Fitch by some of his friends"'.
ISBN 0-904920-02-x Sd : £10.00
(B77-04597)

327'.2'0924 — Chilean diplomatic service. *Cuba, 1970-1971. Personal observations*
Edwards, Jorge. Persona non grata : an envoy in Castro's Cuba / [by] Jorge Edwards ; translated from the Spanish by Colin Harding. — London [etc.] : Bodley Head, 1977. — [6],275p ; 23cm.
Translation of: 'Persona non grata'. Barcelona : Barral, 1973.
ISBN 0-370-10375-0 : £6.95
(B77-06503)

327'.2'0924 — United States. Foreign relations. Diplomacy. Hill, David Jayne. *Biographies*
Parkman, Aubrey. David Jayne Hill and the problem of world peace / [by] Aubrey Parkman. — Lewisbury [Pa] : Bucknell University Press ; London (108 New Bond St., W1Y 0QX) : Associated University Presses, [1976]. — 293p,leaf of plate,[2]p of plates : ill, ports ; 22cm.
Published in the United States: 1975. — Bibl.: p.255-282. — Index.
ISBN 0-8387-1259-2 : £6.50
(B77-02081)

327'.2'0924 — United States. Foreign relations. Diplomacy. Kissinger, Henry Alfred
Liska, George. Beyond Kissinger : ways of conservative statecraft / [by] George Liska. — Baltimore ; London : Johns Hopkins University Press, [1976]. — ix,159,[1]p ; 21cm. — (Studies in international affairs ; no.26)
Published in the United States: 1975.
ISBN 0-8018-1763-3 : £9.60
ISBN 0-8018-1764-1 Pbk : £6.80
(B77-07105)

327'.2'0943 — German diplomatic service, 1871-1914
Cecil, Lamar. The German diplomatic service, 1871-1914 / [by] Lamar Cecil. — Princeton, N.J. ; Guildford : Princeton University Press, 1976. — xiv,352p ; 23cm.
Bibl.: p.329-336. — Index.
ISBN 0-691-05235-2 : £13.90
(B77-03407)

327'.2'0947 — Soviet Union. International negotiations. Methods
Samelson, Louis J. Soviet and Chinese negotiating behavior : the Western view / [by] Louis J. Samelson. — Beverly Hills ; London : Sage Publications, 1976. — 62,[1]p ; 22cm. — (Sage professional papers in international studies ; 02-048)
Bibl.: p.59-62.
ISBN 0-8039-0762-1 Pbk : £1.95
Also classified at 327'.2'0951
(B77-15718)

327'.2'0951 — China. International negotiations. Methods
Samelson, Louis J. Soviet and Chinese negotiating behavior : the Western view / [by] Louis J. Samelson. — Beverly Hills ; London : Sage Publications, 1976. — 62,[1]p ; 22cm. — (Sage professional papers in international studies ; 02-048)
Bibl.: p.59-62.
ISBN 0-8039-0762-1 Pbk : £1.95
Primary classification 327'.2'0947
(B77-15718)

327'.2'0966 — West Africa. Foreign relations. Diplomacy, to ca 1900
Smith, Robert S. Warfare and diplomacy in pre-colonial West Africa / [by] Robert S. Smith. — [London] : Methuen, 1976. — vii, 240p ; 19cm. — (Studies in African history ; 15)
Bibl.: p.225-235. — Index.
ISBN 0-416-55060-6 : £5.50
ISBN 0-416-55070-3 Pbk : £2.90
Primary classification 355.02'0966
(B77-04041)

327.3/9 — FOREIGN RELATIONS OF SPECIAL COUNTRIES

327.4 — European countries. Foreign relations with other European countries, 1918-1933
Marks, Sally. The illusion of peace : international relations in Europe, 1918-1933 / [by] Sally Marks. — London [etc.] : Macmillan, 1976. — vi,184p ; 21cm. — (The making of the 20th century)
Bibl.: p.152-161. — Index.
ISBN 0-333-15031-7 : £5.95
ISBN 0-333-15032-5 Pbk : £2.95
(B77-08812)

327.4'0172'4 — European Community countries. Foreign relations with developing countries. *Reports, surveys*
Sutton, Mary. The EEC and the developing world : a changing relationship / by Mary Sutton. — Dublin (169 Booterstown Ave., [Blackrock], Co. Dublin) : Trócaire : Irish Commission for Justice and Peace, 1976. — [2], vii,59p ; 30cm. — (Joint Development Education Programme)
Bibl.: p.58-59.
Sd : £0.60
Also classified at 327'.09172'4
(B77-09548)

327.4'0411 — Europe. Foreign relations with Scotland, to 1975
Squair, Olive Maud. Scotland in Europe : a study in race relations / by Olive M. Squair. — Inverness (31 Braeside Park, Balloch, Inverness IV1 2HJ) : Graphis Publications.
In 3 vols.
Vol.1 / introduction by Hugh MacDiarmid. — 1976. — viii,86p,fold plate : geneal tables ; 21cm.
ISBN 0-903570-03-3 Pbk : £2.75
Primary classification 327.411'04
(B77-07106)

Vol.2 / introduction by Hugh MacDiarmid. — 1976. — x p,p87-180,fold plate : geneal tables ; 21cm.
ISBN 0-903570-04-1 Pbk : £2.75
Primary classification 327.411'04
(B77-07107)

Vol.3. — 1976. — xi p,p181-246 : ill, ports ; 21cm.
ISBN 0-903570-05-x Pbk : £1.50
Primary classification 327.411'04
(B77-12889)

327.4'063 — Europe. Foreign relations with Ethiopia, 1800-1900
Rubenson, Sven. The survival of Ethiopian independence / [by] Sven Rubenson ; [maps drawn by Peter McClure]. — London [etc.] : Heinemann [etc.], 1976. — xiii,437p,[8]p of plates,fold leaf of plate : ill, facsims, maps, ports ; 23cm. — (Lund studies in international history ; 7)
Bibl.: p.417-427. — Index.
ISBN 0-435-94240-9 : £15.00
ISBN 0-435-94241-7 Pbk : £4.50
Primary classification 327.63'04
(B77-01196)

327.41 — Great Britain. Foreign relations, 1919-1939. *Documents*
Great Britain. *Foreign Office.* Documents on British foreign policy, 1919-1939. 1st series / [Foreign Office]. — London : H.M.S.O.
Vol.20 : [German reparation and Allied military control 1922, Russia March 1921-December 1922] / edited by W.N. Medlicott, Douglas Dakin and M.E. Lambert. — 1976. — lxx, 970p ; 25cm.
Includes some documents in French.
ISBN 0-11-591553-2 : £23.00
(B77-11620)

Great Britain. *Foreign Office.* Documents on British foreign policy, 1919-1939. Second series / [Foreign Office]. — London : H.M.S.O.

Vol.15 : [The Italo-Ethiopian War and German affairs, October 3, 1935-February 29, 1936] / edited by W.N. Medlicott, Douglas Dakin and M.E. Lambert. — 1976. — lxiv,791p ; 25cm.
ISBN 0-11-590190-6 : £16.50
(B77-10201)

327.41 — Great Britain. Foreign relations. Decision making
Barbar, James. Who makes British foreign policy? / [by] James Barber. — Milton Keynes : Open University Press, 1976. — vii, 132p ; 21cm. — (Open University. Set books)
Bibl.: p.129-132.
ISBN 0-335-01962-5 Pbk : £1.85
(B77-04598)

Wallace, William, *b.1941.* The foreign policy process in Britain / [by] William Wallace. — London : Allen and Unwin [for] the Royal Institute of International Affairs, 1977. — x, 320p ; 22cm.
Originally published: 1976. — Bibl.: p.282-284. — Index.
ISBN 0-04-327057-3 Pbk : £3.95
(B77-26149)

327.41 — Great Britain. Foreign relations. Policies of government, 1905-1916
British foreign policy under Sir Edward Grey / edited by F.H. Hinsley. — Cambridge [etc.] : Cambridge University Press, 1977. — viii,702p ; 24cm.
Bibl.: p.662-691. — Index.
ISBN 0-521-21347-9 : £27.50
(B77-28426)

327.41'0415 — Great Britain. Foreign relations with Ireland, 1800-1921
Dangerfield, George. The damnable question : a study in Anglo-Irish relations / by George Dangerfield. — London : Constable, 1977. — xvi,400p,leaf of plate,[12]p of plates : ill, map, ports ; 25cm.
Originally published: Boston, Mass. : Little, Brown, 1976. — Bibl.: p.370-376. — Index.
ISBN 0-09-461620-5 : £6.95
Primary classification 327.415'041
(B77-31017)

327.41'043 — Great Britain. Foreign relations with Germany. Policies of British government, 1930-1939
Rock, William R. British appeasement in the 1930s / [by] William R. Rock. — London : Edward Arnold, 1977. — viii,111p ; 22cm. — (Foundations of modern history)
Bibl.: p.102-105. — Index.
ISBN 0-7131-5913-8 : £5.95
ISBN 0-7131-5914-6 Pbk : £2.50
Also classified at 327.41'045; 327.43'041; 327.45'041
(B77-23176)

327.41'045 — Great Britain. Foreign relations with Italy. Policies of British government, 1930-1939
Rock, William R. British appeasement in the 1930s / [by] William R. Rock. — London : Edward Arnold, 1977. — viii,111p ; 22cm. — (Foundations of modern history)
Bibl.: p.102-105. — Index.
ISBN 0-7131-5913-8 : £5.95
ISBN 0-7131-5914-6 Pbk : £2.50
Primary classification 327.41'043
(B77-23176)

327.41'047 — Great Britain. Foreign relations with Russia, 1828-1914: Foreign relations concerning political events in South-west Asia
Gillard, David. The struggle for Asia, 1828-1914 : a study in British and Russian imperialism / [by] David Gillard. — London : Methuen, 1977. — x,214p : maps ; 24cm.
Bibl.: p.186-197. — Index.
ISBN 0-416-13250-2 : £8.95
Primary classification 950
(B77-31639)

327.41'047 — Great Britain. Foreign relations with Soviet Union, 1924-1927
Gorodetsky, Gabriel. The precarious truce : Anglo-Soviet relations 1924-27 / [by] Gabriel Gorodetsky. — Cambridge [etc.] : Cambridge University Press, 1977. — xiii,289p ; 23cm. — (Soviet and East European studies)
Bibl.: p.267-275. — Index.
ISBN 0-521-21226-x : £9.00
Also classified at 327.47'041
(B77-12888)

327.41'05 — Great Britain. Foreign relations with East Asia, 1937-1941
Lowe, Peter. Great Britain and the origins of the Pacific War : a study of British policy in East Asia, 1937-1941 / by Peter Lowe. — Oxford : Clarendon Press, 1977. — xii,318p : 2 maps ; 23cm.
Bibl.: p.298-310. — Index.
ISBN 0-19-822427-3 : £8.50 : CIP rev.
Also classified at 327.5'041
(B77-18585)

327.41'051 — Great Britain. Foreign relations with China. Policies of British government, 1937-1939
Shai, Aron. Origins of the war in the East : Britain, China and Japan, 1937-39 / [by] Aron Shai. — London : Croom Helm, 1976. — 267p : maps ; 23cm.
Bibl.: p.249-259. — Index.
ISBN 0-85664-333-5 : £9.50
Also classified at 327.51'041
(B77-05904)

327.41'055 — Great Britain. Foreign relations with Iran, 1787-1921
Wright, *Sir* **Denis,** *b.1911.* The English amongst the Persians during the Qajat period, 1787-1921 / [by] Denis Wright. — London : Heinemann, 1977. — xvii,218p,[16]p of plates : ill(incl 1 col tipped in), map, ports ; 25cm.
Bibl.: p.201-210. — Index.
ISBN 0-434-87820-0 : £6.50
Also classified at 327.55'041
(B77-11098)

327.41'0561 — Great Britain. Foreign relations with Turkey, 1933-1939
Zhivkova, Ludmila. Anglo-Turkish relations, 1933-1939 / [by] Ludmila Zhivkova ; [translated from the Bulgarian]. — London : Secker and Warburg, 1976. — xv,132p ; 24cm.
Translation of: 'Anglo-turskite otnosheniia, 1933-1939'. Sofiia : Nauka i izkustvo, 1971. — Bibl.: p.127-129. — Index.
ISBN 0-436-59255-x : £5.00
Also classified at 327.561'041
(B77-04599)

327.41'071 — Great Britain. Foreign relations with Canada, 1917-1926
Wigley, Philip G. Canada and the transition to Commonwealth : British-Canadian relations, 1917-1926 / [by] Philip G. Wigley. — Cambridge [etc.] : Cambridge University Press, 1977. — x,294p ; 24cm. — (Cambridge Commonwealth series)
Bibl.: p.284-291. — Index.
ISBN 0-521-21157-3 : £12.50
Also classified at 327.71'041
(B77-33089)

327.41'073 — Great Britain. Foreign relations with United States. Influence of George III, King of Great Britain, 1760-1776
Andrews, Allen. The king who lost America : George III and independence / by Allen Andrews. — London : Jupiter Books, 1976. — 184p : ill, coat of arms, facsims, map, ports(some col) ; 26cm.
Bibl.: p.179-182.
ISBN 0-904041-54-9 : £5.50
Also classified at 327.73'041
(B77-17950)

327.411'04 — Scotland. Foreign relations with Europe, to 1975
Squair, Olive Maud. Scotland in Europe : a study in race relations / by Olive M. Squair. — Inverness (31 Braeside Park, Balloch, Inverness IV1 2HJ) : Graphis Publications.
In 3 vols.
Vol.1 / introduction by Hugh MacDiarmid. — 1976. — viii,86p,fold plate : geneal tables ; 21cm.
ISBN 0-903570-03-3 Pbk : £2.75
Also classified at 327.4'0411
(B77-07106)

Vol.2 / introduction by Hugh MacDiarmid. — 1976. — x p,p87-180,fold plate : geneal tables ; 21cm.
ISBN 0-903570-04-1 Pbk : £2.75
Also classified at 327.4'0411
(B77-07107)

Vol.3. — 1976. — xi p,p181-246 : ill, ports ; 21cm.
ISBN 0-903570-05-x Pbk : £1.50
Also classified at 327.4'0411
(B77-12889)

327.411'042 — Scotland. Foreign relations with England, to 1707
Ferguson, William. Scotland's relations with England : a survey to 1707 / [by] William Ferguson. — Edinburgh : Donald, 1977. — vii, 319p ; 24cm.
Bibl.: p.304-308. — Index.
ISBN 0-85976-022-7 : £12.00
Also classified at 327.42'0411
(B77-15122)

327.415'041 — Ireland. Foreign relations with Great Britain, 1800-1921
Dangerfield, George. The damnable question : a study in Anglo-Irish relations / by George Dangerfield. — London : Constable, 1977. — xvi,400p,leaf of plate,[12]p of plates : ill, map, ports ; 25cm.
Originally published: Boston, Mass. : Little, Brown, 1976. — Bibl.: p.370-376. — Index.
ISBN 0-09-461620-5 : £6.95
Also classified at 327.41'0415
(B77-31017)

327.42'0411 — England. Foreign relations with Scotland, to 1707
Ferguson, William. Scotland's relations with England : a survey to 1707 / [by] William Ferguson. — Edinburgh : Donald, 1977. — vii, 319p ; 24cm.
Bibl.: p.304-308. — Index.
ISBN 0-85976-022-7 : £12.00
Primary classification 327.411'042
(B77-15122)

327.43'041 — Germany. Foreign relations with Great Britain. Policies of British government, 1930-1939
Rock, William R. British appeasement in the 1930s / [by] William R. Rock. — London : Edward Arnold, 1977. — viii,111p ; 22cm. — (Foundations of modern history)
Bibl.: p.102-105. — Index.
ISBN 0-7131-5913-8 : £5.95
ISBN 0-7131-5914-6 Pbk : £2.50
Primary classification 327.41'043
(B77-23176)

327.43'1'047 — East Germany. Foreign relations with Soviet Union, 1961-1976
Croan, Melvin. East Germany : the Soviet connection / [by] Melvin Croan. — Beverly Hills ; London : Sage Publications [for] the Center for Strategic and International Studies, [1977]. — 71p : 2 maps ; 22cm. — (The Washington papers ; 36) (A Sage policy paper)
Published in the United States: 1976. — Bibl.: p.67-69.
ISBN 0-8039-0656-0 Pbk : £1.75
Also classified at 327.47'043'1
(B77-13532)

327.436'045 — Austria. Foreign relations with Italy, ca 1915-1969: Foreign relations concerning Trentino-Alto Adige
Toscano, Mario. Alto Adige, South Tyrol : Italy's frontier with the German world / by Mario Toscano ; edited by George A. Carbone. — Baltimore ; London : Johns Hopkins University Press, [1976]. — xiv,283,[1]p : map ; 24cm.
Published in the United States: 1975. — Translation and revision of: 'Storia diplomatica della questione dell'Alto Adige'. 2.ed. Bari : Laterza, 1968. — Index.
ISBN 0-8018-1567-3 : £12.00
Primary classification 945'.38'09
(B77-06998)

327.45 — Italy. Foreign relations, 1922-1943
Mack Smith, Denis. Mussolini's Roman empire / [by] Denis Mack Smith. — Harmondsworth : Penguin, 1977. — xiii,322p : map ; 20cm.
Originally published: London : Longman, 1976. — Bibl.: p.289-310. — Index.
ISBN 0-14-003849-3 Pbk : £1.80
(B77-31721)

Mack Smith, Denis. Mussolini's Roman empire / [by] Denis Mack Smith. — London [etc.] : Longman, 1976. — xiii,322p : maps ; 24cm.
Bibl.: p.289-310. — Index.
ISBN 0-582-50266-7 : £1.50
(B77-00063)

327.45'041 — Italy. Foreign relations with Great Britain. Policies of British government, 1930-1939
Rock, William R. British appeasement in the 1930s / [by] William R. Rock. — London : Edward Arnold, 1977. — viii,111p ; 22cm. — (Foundations of modern history)
Bibl.: p.102-105. — Index.
ISBN 0-7131-5913-8 : £5.95
ISBN 0-7131-5914-6 Pbk : £2.50
Primary classification 327.41'043
(B77-23176)

327.45'0436 — Italy. Foreign relations with Austria, ca 1915-1969: Foreign relations concerning Trentino-Alto Adige
Toscano, Mario. Alto Adige, South Tyrol : Italy's frontier with the German world / by Mario Toscano ; edited by George A. Carbone. — Baltimore ; London : Johns Hopkins University Press, [1976]. — xiv,283,[1]p : map ; 24cm.
Published in the United States: 1975. — Translation and revision of: 'Storia diplomatica della questione dell'Alto Adige'. 2.ed. Bari : Laterza, 1968. — Index.
ISBN 0-8018-1567-3 : £12.00
Primary classification 945'.38'09
(B77-06998)

327.47 — Eastern Europe. Foreign relations. *Conference proceedings*
The **international** politics of Eastern Europe / edited by Charles Gati. — New York [etc.] ; London : Praeger, [1977]. — xii,313p ; 25cm. — (Praeger special studies in international politics and government)
'Studies of the Institute on East Central Europe and the Research Institute on International Change, Columbia University'. — '... based on papers presented at the March 1975 Columbia University conference on the international politics of Eastern Europe' - Preface. — Published in the United States: 1976. — Bibl.: p.292-296. — Index.
ISBN 0-275-55960-2 : £16.65
ISBN 0-275-89500-9 Pbk : £4.60
(B77-08813)

327.47 — Soviet Union. Foreign relations. Policies of government, 1962-1974
Edmonds, Robin. Soviet foreign policy 1962-1973 : the paradox of super power / [by] Robin Edmonds. — London [etc.] : Oxford University Press, 1977. — xv,197p : maps ; 21cm. — (A Galaxy book)
Originally published: 1975. — Bibl.: p.182-184. — Index.
ISBN 0-19-519908-1 Pbk : £1.95
(B77-18586)

327.47 — Soviet Union. Foreign relations. Related to dissent in Soviet Union, ca 1960-1976
Barghoorn, Frederick Charles. Détente and the democratic movement in the USSR / [by] Frederick C. Barghoorn. — New York : Free Press ; London : Collier Macmillan, 1976. — x, 229p ; 24cm.
Index.
ISBN 0-02-901850-1 : £9.00
Also classified at 322.4'4'0947
(B77-12890)

327.47'0172'4 — Soviet Union. Foreign relations with developing countries, 1953-1973
The **Soviet** Union and the developing nations / edited by Roger E. Kanet. — Baltimore ; London : Johns Hopkins University Press, 1974. — xiii,302,[2]p ; 24cm.
Index.
ISBN 0-8018-1501-0 : Unpriced
Also classified at 327'.09172'4
(B77-18587)

327.47'041 — Russia. Foreign relations with Great Britain, 1828-1914: Foreign relations concerning political events in South-west Asia
Gillard, David. The struggle for Asia, 1828-1914 : a study in British and Russian imperialism / [by] David Gillard. — London : Methuen, 1977. — x,214p : maps ; 24cm.
Bibl.: p.186-197. — Index.
ISBN 0-416-13250-2 : £8.95
Primary classification 950
(B77-31639)

327.47'041 — Soviet Union. Foreign relations with Great Britain, 1924-1927
Gorodetsky, Gabriel. The precarious truce : Anglo-Soviet relations 1924-27 / [by] Gabriel Gorodetsky. — Cambridge [etc.] : Cambridge University Press, 1977. — xiii,289p ; 23cm. — (Soviet and East European studies)
Bibl.: p.267-275. — Index.
ISBN 0-521-21226-x : £9.00
Primary classification 327.41'047
(B77-12888)

327.47'043'1 — Soviet Union. Foreign relations with East Germany, 1961-1976
Croan, Melvin. East Germany : the Soviet connection / [by] Melvin Croan. — Beverly Hills ; London : Sage Publications [for] the Center for Strategic and International Studies, [1977]. — 71p : 2 maps ; 22cm. — (The Washington papers ; 36) (A Sage policy paper)
Published in the United States: 1976. — Bibl.: p.67-69.
ISBN 0-8039-0656-0 Pbk : £1.75
Primary classification 327.43'1'047
(B77-13532)

327.47'05 — Soviet Union. Foreign relations with Asia, 1970-1976
Sen Gupta, Bhabani. Soviet-Asian relations in the 1970s and beyond : an interperceptional study / [by] Bhabani Sen Gupta. — New York [etc.] ; London : Praeger, [1977]. — xiii,369p ; 25cm. — (Praeger special studies in international politics and government)
Published in the United States: 1976. — Index.
ISBN 0-275-23740-0 : £17.00
Also classified at 327.5'047
(B77-12891)

327.47'054 — Soviet Union. Foreign relations with India, to 1971
Kaushik, Devendra. Soviet relations with India and Pakistan / [by] Devendra Kaushik. — 2nd revised and enlarged ed. — Delhi [etc.] ; London : Vikas ; [Hemel Hempstead] ([66 Wood Lane End, Hemel Hempstead, Herts.]) : [Distributed by International Book Distributors Limited], 1974 [i.e.1976]. — xi,155p ; 23cm.
This ed. published in India: 1974. — Previous ed.: 1971. — Index.
ISBN 0-7069-0293-9 : £2.20
Also classified at 327.54'047
(B77-05235)

327.47'056 — Soviet Union. Foreign relations with Middle East, 1972-1974
Golan, Galia. Yom Kippur and after : the Soviet Union and the Middle East crisis / [by] Galia Golan. — Cambridge [etc.] : Cambridge University Press, 1977. — x,350p ; 23cm. — (Soviet and East European studies)
Bibl.: p.317-329. — Index.
ISBN 0-521-21090-9 : £9.00
Also classified at 327.56'047
(B77-10745)

327.47'062 — Soviet Union. Foreign relations with Egypt, 1967-1975
Rubinstein, Alvin Zachery. Red star on the Nile : the Soviet-Egyptian influence relationship since the June War / by Alvin Z. Rubinstein. — Princeton ; Guildford : Princeton University Press, 1977. — xxiv,384p ; 24cm. — (Foreign Policy Research Institute. Books)
Bibl.: p.367-374. — Index.
ISBN 0-691-07581-6 : £20.10
ISBN 0-691-10048-9 Pbk : £8.10
Primary classification 327.62'047
(B77-15124)

327.47'073 — Soviet Union. Foreign relations with United States, 1941-1947. *Readings from contemporary sources*
The **American** diplomatic revolution : a documentary history of the Cold War, 1941-1947 / edited by Joseph M. Siracusa. — Port Washington, N.Y. ; London : Kennikat Press, 1977. — [6],263,[3]p : 2 maps ; 24cm. — (Kennikat Press national university publications : series in American studies)
Originally published: Sydney : Holt, Rinehart and Winston, 1976. — Bibl.: p.260-263.
ISBN 0-8046-9174-6 : £11.00
ISBN 0-8046-9180-0 Pbk : Unpriced
Primary classification 327.73'047
(B77-20952)

327.47'073 — Soviet Union. Foreign relations with United States, 1945-1975: Foreign relations concerning political events in Eastern Europe & Latin America
Kaufman, Edy. The superpowers and their spheres of influence / [by] Edy Kaufman. — London : Croom Helm, 1976. — 208p : ill ; 23cm.
Index.
ISBN 0-85664-389-0 : £7.95
Primary classification 980'.03
(B77-07754)

327.47'073 — Soviet Union. Foreign relations with United States. Crises. Management, ca 1945-1975
Williams, Phil. Crisis management : confrontation and diplomacy in the nuclear age / [by] Phil Williams. — London : Martin Robertson, 1976. — ix,230p ; 23cm.
Index.
ISBN 0-85520-098-7 : £7.85
Primary classification 327.73'047
(B77-07108)

327.47'073 — Soviet Union. Foreign relations with United States. Policies of Soviet government, to 1976
Gilbert, Stephen P. Soviet images of America / [by] Stephen P. Gilbert, contributing authors ... [others]. — London : Macdonald and Jane's, 1977. — [5],viii,167p ; 24cm.
Also published: New York : Crane, Russak, 1977. — Bibl.: p.155-159. — Index.
ISBN 0-354-01120-0 : £10.50
Also classified at 327.73'047
(B77-22395)

327.5 — Asia. Foreign relations, 1940-1955
International Environment in Postwar Asia *(Conference), Kyoto, 1975.* The origins of the cold war in Asia / edited by Yōnosuke Nagai, Akira Iriye. — New York ; Guildford : Columbia University Press [etc.], 1977. — ix, 448p ; 24cm.
'The essays ... (with the exception of four ...) were originally presented at an international symposium on "The International Environment in Postwar Asia", held in Kyoto from November 27 to 30, 1975' - Preface. — Index.
ISBN 0-231-04390-2 : £14.70
(B77-33090)

327.5'041 — East Asia. Foreign relations with Great Britain, 1937-1941
Lowe, Peter. Great Britain and the origins of the Pacific War : a study of British policy in East Asia, 1937-1941 / by Peter Lowe. — Oxford : Clarendon Press, 1977. — xii,318p : 2 maps ; 23cm.
Bibl.: p.298-310. — Index.
ISBN 0-19-822427-3 : £8.50 : CIP rev.
Primary classification 327.41'05
(B77-18585)

327.5'047 — Asia. Foreign relations with Soviet Union, 1970-1976
Sen Gupta, Bhabani. Soviet-Asian relations in the 1970s and beyond : an interperceptional study / [by] Bhabani Sen Gupta. — New York [etc.] ; London : Praeger, [1977]. — xiii,369p ; 25cm. — (Praeger special studies in international politics and government)
Published in the United States: 1976. — Index.
ISBN 0-275-23740-0 : £17.00
Primary classification 327.47'05
(B77-12891)

327.51 — China. Foreign relations, 1949-1976
Dimensions of China's foreign relations / edited by Chün-tu Hsüeh. — New York [etc.] ; London : Praeger, 1977. — xv,297p : 1 ill ; 25cm. — (Praeger special studies in international politics and government)
Index.
ISBN 0-275-56780-x : £14.80
(B77-15123)

327.51'041 — China. Foreign relations with Great Britain. Policies of British government, 1937-1939
Shai, Aron. Origins of the war in the East : Britain, China and Japan, 1937-39 / [by] Aron Shai. — London : Croom Helm, 1976. — 267p : maps ; 23cm.
Bibl.: p.249-259. — Index.
ISBN 0-85664-333-5 : £9.50
Primary classification 327.41'051
(B77-05904)

327.51'052 — China. Foreign relations with Japan, 1945-1975
Lee, Chae-Jin. Japan faces China : political and economic relations in the postwar era / [by] Chae-Jin Lee. — Baltimore ; London : Johns Hopkins University Press, 1976. — xiv,242p : ill, map ; 24cm.
Index.
ISBN 0-8018-1738-2 : £8.75
Primary classification 327.52'051
(B77-00064)

327.51'073 — China. Foreign relations with United States, ca 1935-1973
Kahn, Ely Jacques. The China hands : America's foreign service officers and what befell them / [by] E.J. Kahn, Jr. — Harmondsworth [etc.] : Penguin, 1976. — xiii,337p : map ; 20cm.
Originally published: New York : Viking Press, 1975. — Bibl.: p.324-327. — Index.
ISBN 0-14-004301-2 Pbk : Unpriced
Primary classification 327.73'051
(B77-02083)

327.51'073 — China. Foreign relations with United States. Crises. Management, ca 1945-ca 1975
Williams, Phil. Crisis management : confrontation and diplomacy in the nuclear age / [by] Phil Williams. — London : Martin Robertson, 1976. — ix,230p ; 23cm.
Index.
ISBN 0-85520-098-7 : £7.85
Primary classification 327.73'047
(B77-07108)

327.51'073 — China. Foreign relations with United States. Policies of Chinese government, 1945-1975
Hinton, Harold Clendenin. Peking-Washington : Chinese foreign policy and the United States / [by] Harold C. Hinton. — Beverly Hills ; London : Sage Publications [for] the Center for Strategic and International Studies, [1977]. — 96p ; 22cm. — (The Washington papers ; 34) (A Sage policy paper)
Published in the United States: 1976. — Bibl.: p.92-96.
ISBN 0-8039-0649-8 Pbk : £1.75
Also classified at 327.73'051
(B77-14087)

327.51'073 — China. Foreign relations with United States. Policies of United States government. Influence of pressure groups, 1953-1971
Bachrack, Stanley D. The Committee of One Million : 'China lobby' politics, 1953-1971 / [by] Stanley D. Bachrack. — New York ; Guildford : Columbia University Press, 1976. — xi,371p ; 24cm.
Bibl.: p.349-356. — Index.
ISBN 0-231-03933-6 : £10.37
Primary classification 327.73'051
(B77-03408)

327.519'3 — North Korea. Foreign relations, 1945-1975
Kiyosaki, Wayne S. North Korea's foreign relations : the politics of accommodation, 1945-75 / [by] Wayne S. Kiyosaki. — New York [etc.] ; London : Praeger ; [London] : [Distributed by Martin Robertson], 1976. — xv, 135p ; 25cm. — (Praeger special studies in international politics and government)
Bibl.: p.115-129. — Index.
ISBN 0-275-23490-8 : £12.25
(B77-05236)

327.52 — Japan. Foreign relations. Policies of government, 1869-1942
Nish, Ian Hill. Japanese foreign policy, 1869-1942 : Kasumigaseki to Miyakezaka / [by] Ian Nish. — London [etc.] : Routledge and Kegan Paul, 1977. — xii,346p : 2 maps ; 23cm. — (Foreign policies of the great powers)
Bibl.: p.329-337. — Index.
ISBN 0-7100-8421-8 : £6.25
(B77-08814)

327.52'051 — Japan. Foreign relations with China, 1945-1975
Lee, Chae-Jin. Japan faces China : political and economic relations in the postwar era / [by] Chae-Jin Lee. — Baltimore ; London : Johns Hopkins University Press, 1976. — xiv,242p : ill, map ; 24cm.
Index.
ISBN 0-8018-1738-2 : £8.75
Also classified at 327.51'052
(B77-00064)

327.54 — India (Republic). Foreign relations, 1947-1962
India's foreign relations during the Nehru era : some studies / edited by M.S. Rajan. — Bombay ; London [etc.] : Asia Publishing House, [1977]. — xxiii,351p ; 25cm.
Published in India: 1976. — Bibl. — Index.
ISBN 0-210-22289-1 : £10.00
(B77-10202)

327.54 — India (Republic). Foreign relations, 1947-1964
Indian foreign policy : the Nehru years / edited by B.R. Nanda. — Delhi [etc.] : Vikas [for the] Nehru Memorial Museum and Library ; Hemel Hempstead (66 Wood Lane End, Hemel Hempstead, Herts.) : International Book Distributors Limited, 1976. — ix,279p ; 23cm.
'Based on a series of lectures delivered in the Nehru Memorial Museum & Library in 1973-74 ...' - jacket. — Index.
ISBN 0-7069-0393-5 : Unpriced
(B77-26842)

327.54 — India (Republic). Foreign relations, 1947-1974
Singh, Baljit. Indian foreign policy : an analysis / [by] Baljit Singh. — London : Asia Publishing House, 1976. — ix,111p ; 23cm.
Bibl.: p.93-105. — Index.
ISBN 0-210-40570-8 : £6.00
(B77-10203)

327.54'047 — India. Foreign relations with Soviet Union, to 1971
Kaushik, Devendra. Soviet relations with India and Pakistan / [by] Devendra Kaushik. — 2nd revised and enlarged ed. — Delhi [etc.] ; London : Vikas ; [Hemel Hempstead] ([66 Wood Lane End, Hemel Hempstead, Herts.]) : [Distributed by International Book Distributors Limited], 1974 [i.e.1976]. — xi,155p ; 23cm.
This ed. published in India: 1974. — Previous ed.: 1971. — Index.
ISBN 0-7069-0293-9 : £2.20
Primary classification 327.47'054
(B77-05235)

327.549'1 — Developing countries. Foreign relations. *Study regions: Pakistan. Essays*
Bhutto, Zulfikar Ali. The Third World, new directions / [by] Zulfikar Ali Bhutto. — London : Quartet Books, 1977. — 144p ; 23cm.
Index.
ISBN 0-7043-2145-9 : £3.95
(B77-12339)

327.55'041 — Iran. Foreign relations with Great Britain, 1787-1921
Wright, *Sir* **Denis,** *b.1911.* The English amongst the Persians during the Qajat period, 1787-1921 / [by] Denis Wright. — London : Heinemann, 1977. — xvii,218p,[16]p of plates : ill(incl 1 col tipped in), map, ports ; 25cm.
Bibl.: p.201-210. — Index.
ISBN 0-434-87820-0 : £6.50
Primary classification 327.41'055
(B77-11098)

327.56 — Middle East. Foreign relations. Policies of governments. Formulation, 1945-1976
McLaurin, Ronald De. Foreign policy making in the Middle East : domestic influences on policy in Egypt, Iraq, Israel and Syria / [by] R.D. McLaurin, Mohammed Mughisuddin, Abraham R. Wagner. — New York ; London : Praeger, 1977. — xi,315p : 3 ill ; 25cm. — (Praeger special studies in international politics and government)
Bibl.: p.289-304. — Index.
ISBN 0-275-23870-9 : Unpriced
ISBN 0-275-65010-3 Pbk : £5.15
(B77-32451)

327.56'047 — Middle East. Foreign relations with Soviet Union, 1972-1974
Golan, Galia. Yom Kippur and after : the Soviet Union and the Middle East crisis / [by] Galia Golan. — Cambridge [etc.] : Cambridge University Press, 1977. — x,350p ; 23cm. — (Soviet and East European studies)
Bibl.: p.317-329. — Index.
ISBN 0-521-21090-9 : £9.00
Primary classification 327.47'056
(B77-10745)

327.561'041 — Turkey. Foreign relations with Great Britain, 1933-1939
Zhivkova, Ludmila. Anglo-Turkish relations, 1933-1939 / [by] Ludmila Zhivkova ; [translated from the Bulgarian]. — London : Secker and Warburg, 1976. — xv,132p ; 24cm.
Translation of: 'Anglo-turskite otnosheniia, 1933-1939'. Sofiia : Nauka i izkustvo, 1971. — Bibl.: p.127-129. — Index.
ISBN 0-436-59255-x : £5.00
Primary classification 327.41'0561
(B77-04599)

327.5694'017'4927 — Israel. Foreign relations with Arab countries, 1967-1974. *Transcripts of discussions*
Friedländer, Saul. Arabs & Israelis : a dialogue [between] Saul Friedländer [and] Mahmoud Hussein / moderated by Jean Lacouture ; translated [from the French] by Paul Auster and Lydia Davis. — New York ; London (1 Hallswelle Parade, Finchley Rd, NW11 0DL) : Holmes and Meier, 1975. — xiii,221,[2]p : maps ; 23cm.
Translation of: 'Arabes & Israéliens'. Paris : Seuil, 1974.
ISBN 0-8419-0208-9 : Unpriced
Also classified at 327'.0917'4927
(B77-02082)

327.6 — Africa. Foreign relations, to 1976
The **foreign** policies of African states / edited by Olajide Aluko. — London [etc.] : Hodder and Stoughton, 1977. — vi,243p ; 24cm.
ISBN 0-340-21030-3 Pbk : £4.50
(B77-23177)

327.62'047 — Egypt. Foreign relations with Soviet Union, 1967-1975
Rubinstein, Alvin Zachery. Red star on the Nile : the Soviet-Egyptian influence relationship since the June War / by Alvin Z. Rubinstein. — Princeton ; Guildford : Princeton University Press, 1977. — xxiv,384p ; 24cm. — (Foreign Policy Research Institute. Books)
Bibl.: p.367-374. — Index.
ISBN 0-691-07581-6 : £20.10
ISBN 0-691-10048-9 Pbk : £8.10
Also classified at 327.47'062
(B77-15124)

327.63'04 — Ethiopia. Foreign relations with Europe, 1800-1900
Rubenson, Sven. The survival of Ethiopian independence / [by] Sven Rubenson ; [maps drawn by Peter McClure]. — London [etc.] : Heinemann [etc.], 1976. — xiii,437p,[8]p of plates,fold leaf of plate : ill, facsims, maps, ports ; 23cm. — (Lund studies in international history ; 7)
Bibl.: p.417-427. — Index.
ISBN 0-435-94240-9 : £15.00
ISBN 0-435-94241-7 Pbk : £4.50
Also classified at 327.4'063
(B77-01196)

327.71'041 — Canada. Foreign relations with Great Britain, 1917-1926
Wigley, Philip G. Canada and the transition to Commonwealth : British-Canadian relations, 1917-1926 / [by] Philip G. Wigley. — Cambridge [etc.] : Cambridge University Press, 1977. — x,294p ; 24cm. — (Cambridge Commonwealth series)
Bibl.: p.284-291. — Index.
ISBN 0-521-21157-3 : £12.50
Primary classification 327.41'071
(B77-33089)

327.73 — United States. Foreign relations, 1939-1976
Fox, Annette Baker. The politics of attraction : four middle powers and the United States / [by] Annette Baker Fox. — New York ; Guildford : Columbia University Press, 1977. — xi,371p ; 24cm.
Index. — Concerns foreign relations with Australia, Brazil, Canada, and Mexico.
ISBN 0-231-04116-0 : £11.35
(B77-10746)

327.73 — United States. Foreign relations, 1945-1969
Steel, Ronald. Pax Americana / [by] Ronald Steel. — Revised ed. — Harmondsworth [etc.] : Penguin, 1977. — xi,365p ; 19cm.
This ed. originally published: New York : Viking Press, 1970. — Index.
ISBN 0-14-004664-x Pbk : £1.95
(B77-28427)

327.73 — United States. Foreign relations, 1945-1975
Graebner, Norman Arthur. Cold War diplomacy : American foreign policy, 1945-1975 / [by] Norman A. Graebner. — [2nd ed.]. — New York ; London [etc.] : D. Van Nostrand, 1977. — viii,248p ; 23cm.
Previous ed.: 1962. — Bibl.: p.237-243. — Index.
ISBN 0-442-22788-4 Pbk : £4.80
(B77-21722)

327.73 — United States. Foreign relations. Policies of government. Implications of international security
Foreign policy and US national security : major postelection issues / edited by William W. Whitson. — New York [etc.] ; London : Praeger ; [London] : [Distributed by Martin Robertson], 1976. — x,373p : ill ; 24cm. — (Praeger special studies in international politics and government)
Bibl.: p.341-358. — Index.
ISBN 0-275-56540-8 : £16.25(£5.85 paperback)
ISBN 0-275-85700-x Student ed. : Unpriced
(B77-00065)

327.73 — United States. Foreign relations. Policies of government. Influence of interest groups. Expounded by policies of government on conflict between Arab countries & Israel, 1966-1974
Trice, Robert H. Interest groups and the foreign policy process : US policy in the Middle East / [by] Robert H. Trice. — Beverly Hills ; London : Sage Publications, 1976. — 80p : 1 ill ; 22cm. — (Sage professional papers in international studies ; vol.4, no.02-047)
Bibl.: p.75-80.
ISBN 0-8039-0761-3 Pbk : Unpriced
(B77-24038)

327.73 — United States. Foreign relations. Policies of government. Influence of Republican Party (United States), 1941-1945
Darilek, Richard E. A loyal opposition in time of war : the Republican party and the politics of foreign policy from Pearl Harbor to Yalta / [by] Richard E. Darilek. — Westport, Conn. ; London : Greenwood Press, 1976 [i.e. 1977]. — x,239,[1]p ; 22cm. — (Contributions in American history ; no.49)
Published in the United States: 1976. — Bibl.: p.223-231. — Index.
ISBN 0-8371-8773-7 : £11.95
(B77-25418)

327.73 — United States. Foreign relations. Policies of government. Influence of Wallace, Henry A, 1933-1950
Walker, J Samuel. Henry A. Wallace and American foreign policy / [by] J. Samuel Walker. — Westport, Conn. ; London : Greenwood Press, 1976. — x,224,[1]p ; 22cm. — (Contributions in American history ; no.50)
Index.
ISBN 0-8371-8774-5 : £11.50
(B77-17951)

327.73 — United States. Foreign relations, to 1914
Iriye, Akira. From nationalism to internationalism : US foreign policy to 1914 / [by] Akira Iriye. — London [etc.] : Routledge and Kegan Paul, 1977. — viii,368p ; 23cm. — (Foreign policies of the great powers)
Index.
ISBN 0-7100-8444-7 : £6.50
(B77-22396)

327'.73'01717 — United States. Détente with Communist countries. Role of Kissinger, Henry Alfred, 1969-1977
Bell, Coral. The diplomacy of detente : the Kissinger era / [by] Coral Bell. — London : Martin Robertson, 1977. — viii,278p ; 23cm.
Bibl.: p.269-270. — Index.
ISBN 0-85520-191-6 : £8.50 : CIP rev.
Also classified at 327'.09171'7
(B77-16216)

327.73'041 — United States. Foreign relations with Great Britain. Influence of George III, King of Great Britain, 1760-1776
Andrews, Allen. The king who lost America : George III and independence / by Allen Andrews. — London : Jupiter Books, 1976. — 184p : ill, coat of arms, facsims, map, ports(some col) ; 26cm.
Bibl.: p.179-182.
ISBN 0-904041-54-9 : £5.50
Primary classification 327.41'073
(B77-17950)

327.73'047 — United States. Foreign relations with Soviet Union, 1941-1947. *Readings from contemporary sources*
The **American** diplomatic revolution : a documentary history of the Cold War, 1941-1947 / edited by Joseph M. Siracusa. — Port Washington, N.Y. ; London : Kennikat Press, 1977. — [6],263,[3]p : 2 maps ; 24cm. — (Kennikat Press national university publications : series in American studies)
Originally published: Sydney : Holt, Rinehart and Winston, 1976. — Bibl.: p.260-263.
ISBN 0-8046-9174-6 : £11.00
ISBN 0-8046-9180-0 Pbk : Unpriced
Also classified at 327.47'073
(B77-20952)

327.73'047 — United States. Foreign relations with Soviet Union, 1945-1975: Foreign relations concerning political events in Eastern Europe & Latin America
Kaufman, Edy. The superpowers and their spheres of influence / [by] Edy Kaufman. — London : Croom Helm, 1976. — 208p : ill ; 23cm.
Index.
ISBN 0-85664-389-0 : £7.95
Primary classification 980'.03
(B77-07754)

327.73'047 — United States. Foreign relations with Soviet Union. Crises. Management, ca 1945-1975
Williams, Phil. Crisis management : confrontation and diplomacy in the nuclear age / [by] Phil Williams. — London : Martin Robertson, 1976. — ix,230p ; 23cm.
Index.
ISBN 0-85520-098-7 : £7.85
Also classified at 327.47'073; 327.73'051; 327.51'073
(B77-07108)

327.73'047 — United States. Foreign relations with Soviet Union. Policies of Soviet government, to 1976
Gilbert, Stephen P. Soviet images of America / [by] Stephen P. Gilbert, contributing authors ... [others]. — London : Macdonald and Jane's, 1977. — [5],viii,167p ; 24cm.
Also published: New York : Crane, Russak, 1977. — Bibl.: p.155-159. — Index.
ISBN 0-354-01120-0 : £10.50
Primary classification 327.47'073
(B77-22395)

327.73'051 — United States. Foreign relations with China, ca 1935-1973
Kahn, Ely Jacques. The China hands : America's foreign service officers and what befell them / [by] E.J. Kahn, Jr. — Harmondsworth [etc.] : Penguin, 1976. — xiii,337p : map ; 20cm.
Originally published: New York : Viking Press, 1975. — Bibl.: p.324-327. — Index.
ISBN 0-14-004301-2 Pbk : Unpriced
Also classified at 327.51'073
(B77-02083)

327.73'051 — United States. Foreign relations with China. Crises. Management, ca 1945-ca 1975
Williams, Phil. Crisis management : confrontation and diplomacy in the nuclear age / [by] Phil Williams. — London : Martin Robertson, 1976. — ix,230p ; 23cm.
Index.
ISBN 0-85520-098-7 : £7.85
Primary classification 327.73'047
(B77-07108)

327.73'051 — United States. Foreign relations with China. Policies of Chinese government, 1945-1975
Hinton, Harold Clendenin. Peking-Washington : Chinese foreign policy and the United States / [by] Harold C. Hinton. — Beverly Hills ; London : Sage Publications [for] the Center for Strategic and International Studies, [1977]. — 96p ; 22cm. — (The Washington papers ; 34) (A Sage policy paper)
Published in the United States: 1976. — Bibl.: p.92-96.
ISBN 0-8039-0649-8 Pbk : £1.75
Primary classification 327.51'073
(B77-14087)

327.73'051 — United States. Foreign relations with China. Policies of United States government. Influence of pressure groups, 1953-1971
Bachrack, Stanley D. The Committee of One Million : 'China lobby' politics, 1953-1971 / [by] Stanley D. Bachrack. — New York ; Guildford : Columbia University Press, 1976. — xi,371p ; 24cm.
Bibl.: p.349-356. — Index.
ISBN 0-231-03933-6 : £10.37
Also classified at 327.51'073
(B77-03408)

327.73'08 — United States. Foreign relations with Spanish America, 1910-1975. Policies of United States government
Blasier, Cole. The hovering giant : US responses to revolutionary change in Latin America / [by] Cole Blasier. — [Pittsburgh] : University of Pittsburgh Press ; London : Feffer and Simons : [Distributed by Transatlantic Book Service], 1976. — xix,315p,[16]p of plates : ill, ports ; 25cm. — (Pitt Latin American series)
Index.
ISBN 0-8229-3304-7 : £11.96
ISBN 0-8229-5264-5 Pbk : Unpriced
Also classified at 327.8'073; 980'.03
(B77-07109)

327.8 — Latin America. Foreign relations, to 1976. International political aspects
Atkins, G Pope. Latin America in the international political system / [by] G. Pope Atkins. — New York : Free Press ; London : Collier Macmillan, 1977. — xv,448p : maps ; 24cm.
Bibl.: p.384-435. — Index.
ISBN 0-02-901060-8 : £9.00
(B77-26843)

327.8'073 — Spanish America. Foreign relations with United States, 1910-1975. Policies of United States government
Blasier, Cole. The hovering giant : US responses to revolutionary change in Latin America / [by] Cole Blasier. — [Pittsburgh] : University of Pittsburgh Press ; London : Feffer and Simons : [Distributed by Transatlantic Book Service], 1976. — xix,315p,[16]p of plates : ill, ports ; 25cm. — (Pitt Latin American series)
Index.
ISBN 0-8229-3304-7 : £11.96
ISBN 0-8229-5264-5 Pbk : Unpriced
Primary classification 327.73'08
(B77-07109)

327.81 — Brazil. Foreign relations
Perry, William. Contemporary Brazilian foreign policy : the international strategy of an emerging power / [by] William Perry ; [for the] Foreign Policy Research Institute. — Beverly Hills ; London : Sage Publications, 1976. — [5], 89p ; 22cm. — (The foreign policy papers ; vol.2,6) (A Sage policy paper)
ISBN 0-8039-0645-5 Pbk : £1.75
(B77-16754)

328 — LEGISLATURES, PARLIAMENTS

328'.3'0973 — Legislatures. Decision making. *United States. States. Reports, surveys*
Uslaner, Eric M. Patterns of decision making in state legislatures / [by] Eric M. Uslaner, Ronald E. Weber. — New York ; London : Praeger, 1977. — xix,211p : forms ; 25cm. — (Praeger special studies in US economic, social and political issues)
Bibl.: p.195-206. — Index.
ISBN 0-275-23230-1 : £12.40
(B77-32452)

328'.33455'01 — Gerrymandering. Theories
Musgrove, Philip. The general theory of gerrymandering / [by] Philip Musgrove. — Beverly Hills ; London : Sage Publications, 1977. — 78,[1]p : ill ; 22cm. — (Sage professional papers in American politics ; vol.3, no.04-034)
Bibl.: p.66.
ISBN 0-8039-0633-1 Pbk : £1.95
(B77-25419)

328.41 — Great Britain. Parliament. House of Commons. Information services for public. *Reports, surveys*
Great Britain. *Parliament. House of Commons. Select Committee on House of Commons (Services).* Services for the public : eighth report from the Select Committee on House of Commons (Services), session 1976-77, together with the minutes of evidence taken before the Accommodation and Administration Sub-committee between 16 February and 23 March, and appendices. — London : H.M.S.O., [1977]. — xviii,105p ; 25cm. — ([1976-77 H.C.] 509)
ISBN 0-10-250977-8 Pbk : £2.35
(B77-27700)

328.41'0028'54 — Great Britain. Parliament. Applications of computer systems. *Inquiry reports*
Great Britain. *Parliament. Joint Committee on Computers.* Report of the informal Joint Committee on Computers to the Leaders of both Houses. — London : H.M.S.O., [1977]. — iv,36p ; 25cm. — ([1976-77]H.L.35) ([1976-77] H.C.78)
ISBN 0-10-207877-7 Sd : £0.70
(B77-13533)

328.41'005 — Great Britain. Parliament. *Periodicals*
The House magazine. — [London] ([191 Wardour St., W1V 3FA]) : [Parliamentary Communications Ltd].
No.1, vol.1- ; Oct.11-17 1976-. — 1976-. — ill, ports ; 30cm.
Weekly while Parliament is sitting. — 20p. in 1st issue.
Sd : Unpriced(free to members and peers)
ISSN 0309-0426
(B77-04600)

328.41'005 — Great Britain. Parliament. *Yearbooks*
Dod's parliamentary companion. — Hailsham (Elm Cottage, Chilsham La., Herstmonceux, Hailsham, E. Sussex BN27 4QQ) : Dod's Parliamentary Companion Ltd.
1977 : one hundred and forty fifth year : one hundred and fifty seventh issue. — [1977]. — ix,886p ; 13cm.
Index.
ISBN 0-905702-00-x : £9.00
ISSN 0070-7007
(B77-07818)

328.41'04 — Great Britain. Government. Policies. Queen's Speech. *Texts*
Great Britain. *Sovereign, 1952- (Elizabeth II).* Her Majesty's most gracious speech to both Houses of Parliament, delivered on Wednesday, 24th November 1976. — London : H.M.S.O., [1976]. — 6p ; 25cm.
ISBN 0-10-499977-2 Sd : £0.25
(B77-04601)

328.41'05 — Great Britain. Parliament. House of Commons. Questions. Tabling. *Inquiry reports*
Great Britain. *Parliament. House of Commons. Select Committee on Procedure.* Tabling of questions and access to the Table Office : third report from the Select Committee on Procedure (Sessional Committee), session 1975-76, together with the proceedings of the Committee. — London : H.M.S.O., [1976]. — 6p ; 25cm. — ([1975-76 H.C.]719)
ISBN 0-10-009326-4 Sd : £0.20
(B77-05237)

328.41'05 — Great Britain. Parliament. House of Commons. Sittings. Division between two items of business. Business of the house motions. *Inquiry reports*
Great Britain. *Parliament. House of Commons. Select Committee on Procedure.* Business of the House motions : fourth report from the Select Committee on Procedure (Sessional Committee), session 1976-77, together with the proceedings of the Committee. — London : H.M.S.O., 1977. — viii p ; 25cm. — ([1976-77 H.C.] 247)
ISBN 0-10-224777-3 Sd : £0.25
(B77-22397)

328.41'05 — Great Britain. Parliament. Proceedings. Radio broadcasting. *Reports, surveys. Serials*
Great Britain. *Parliament. Joint Committee on Sound Broadcasting.* Special report from the Joint Committee on Sound Broadcasting, session 1975-76. — London : H.M.S.O.
2nd : together with the minutes of proceedings of the Committee. — [1976]. — 11p ; 25cm. — ([1975-76] H.L.387) ([1975-76] H.C.723)
ISBN 0-10-009396-5 Sd : £0.25
(B77-04602)

328.41'07'209 — Great Britain. Parliament. House of Commons, 1970-1976
Study of Parliament Group. The Commons in the seventies / edited by S.A. Walkland and Michael Ryle ; for the Study of Parliament Group. — [2nd ed.]. — [London] : Fontana, 1977. — 285p ; 18cm.
This ed. also published: London : Martin Robertson, 1977. — Previous ed.: published as 'The Commons in transition'. 1970. — Index.
ISBN 0-00-634497-6 Pbk : £1.50
(B77-23178)

Study of Parliament Group. The Commons in the seventies / edited by S.A. Walkland and Michael Ryle ; for the Study of Parliament Group. — [2nd ed.]. — London : Martin Robertson [etc.], 1977. — 285p ; 23cm.
This ed. also published: London : Fontana, 1977. — Previous ed.: published as 'The Commons in transition'. London : Fontana, 1970. — Index.
ISBN 0-85520-189-4 : £8.50
(B77-25420)

328.41'07'3 — Great Britain. Parliament. House of Commons. Members sponsored by trade unions, 1874-1975
Muller, William D. The 'kept men'? : the first century of trade union representation in the British House of Commons, 1874-1975 / [by] William D. Muller. — Hassocks : Harvester Press [etc.], 1977. — xx,283p : 2 ill ; 23cm.
Bibl.: p.247-266. — Index.
ISBN 0-85527-184-1 : £10.95 : CIP rev.
(B77-05238)

328.41'07'30922 — Great Britain. Parliament. House of Commons. Members, 1832-1975. *Biographical dictionaries*
Who's who of British Members of Parliament : a biographical dictionary of the House of Commons based on annual volumes of 'Dod's parliamentary companion' and other sources. — Hassocks : Harvester Press [etc.].
Vol.1 : 1832-1885 / [compiled by] Michael Stenton. — 1976. — xvi,444p ; 24cm.
Index.
ISBN 0-85527-219-8 : £25.95
(B77-04603)

328.41'07'33 — Great Britain. Parliament. Members. Expense allowances & remuneration. *Proposals*
Review Body on Top Salaries. Ministers of the Crown and Members of Parliament and the Peers' expenses allowance / Review Body on Top Salaries. — London : H.M.S.O.
Part 3. — [1977]. — v,46p ; 25cm. — (Report ; no.9) (Cmnd.6749)
ISBN 0-10-167490-2 Sd : £0.75
(B77-16755)

328.41'07'34 — Parliamentary representation. *Great Britain, 1830-1850*
Gash, Norman. Politics in the age of Peel : a study in the technique of Parliamentary representation, 1830-1850 / [by] Norman Gash. — 2nd ed. ; with a new introduction [by the author]. — Hassocks : Harvester Press [etc.], 1977. — xxxiii,496p ; 23cm.
Previous ed.: London : Longmans, Green, 1953. — Bibl. — Index.
ISBN 0-85527-139-6 : £10.95
(B77-06504)

328.41'07'47 — Great Britain. Parliament. House of Commons. Alleged breach of privilege by attempted control of sponsored members by National Union of Public Employees. *Inquiry reports*
Great Britain. *Parliament. House of Commons. Committee of Privileges.* Complaint of actions by the National Union of Public Employees : fourth report from the Committee of Privileges, session 1976-77, together with the proceedings of the Committee. — London : H.M.S.O., [1977]. — viii p ; 25cm. — ([1976-77 H.C.]512)

ISBN 0-10-251277-9 Sd : £0.25
(B77-29989)

328.41'07'47 — Great Britain. Parliament. Privileges. *Proposals*
Great Britain. *Parliament. House of Commons. Committee of Privileges.* Recommendations of the Select Committee on Parliamentary Privilege : third report from the Committee of Privileges, session 1976-77, together with the proceedings of the Committee. — London : H.M.S.O., [1977]. — lx p ; 25cm. — ([1976-77 H.C.]417)
ISBN 0-10-241777-6 Sd : £1.10
(B77-21723)

328.41'07'62 — Great Britain. Parliament. House of Commons. Speakers, to 1976
Lloyd, Selwyn, *Baron Selwyn-Lloyd.* Mr Speaker, sir / [by] Selwyn Lloyd. — Large print ed. — Bath : Firecrest, 1977. — xix,290p,[4]p of plates : ill, ports ; 22cm.
Originally published: London : Cape, 1976. — Index.
ISBN 0-85119-013-8 : £4.65
(B77-20953)

328.41'07'75 — Great Britain. Parliament. House of Lords. Proceedings: Divisions, 1685-1857. *Lists*
Great Britain. *Parliament. House of Lords.* Divisions in the House of Lords : an analytical list 1685 to 1857 / compiled by J.C. Sainty and D. Dewar. — London : H.M.S.O., 1976. — ix, 41p,4p of plates : ill ; 25cm. — (Great Britain. Parliament. House of Lords. Record Office. Occasional publications ; no.2)
'The detailed list of divisions ... is contained in eight microfiches inserted in a pocket on the inside back cover' - note.
ISBN 0-11-700365-4 Pbk : £15.64
(B77-16217)

328.416'07'33 — Northern Ireland. Parliament. Members. Superannuation schemes: Members' Contributory Pension (Northern Ireland) Fund. *Accounts*
Northern Ireland. *Parliament.* Members' Contributory Pension (Northern Ireland) Fund accounts : together with the report of the Comptroller and Auditor-General thereon. — Belfast : H.M.S.O.
1974-1975. — [1976]. — 7p ; 25cm.
Issued by the Northern Ireland Exchequer and Audit Department.
ISBN 0-337-23203-2 Sd : £0.27
(B77-03409)

328.42'07'78 — England. Criminal law: Black Act 1723. Enactment. Social aspects
Thompson, Edward Palmer. Whigs and hunters : the origin of the Black Act / [by] E.P. Thompson. — [1st ed.] ; [reprinted with a new postscript]. — Harmondsworth [etc.] : Penguin, 1977. — 328p,[12]p of plates : ill, 2 maps, plan, ports ; 21cm. — (Peregrine books)
Originally published: London : Allen Lane, 1975. — Index. — Includes the text of the Act.

ISBN 0-14-055129-8 Pbk : £3.25
(B77-29990)

328.42'09 — England and Wales. Parliament, 1536-1547
Lehmberg, Stanford Eugene. The later parliaments of Henry VIII, 1536-1547 / [by] Stanford E. Lehmberg. — Cambridge [etc.] : Cambridge University Press, 1977. — ix,379p ; 23cm.
Bibl.: p.352-362. — Index.
ISBN 0-521-21256-1 : £12.50
(B77-16218)

328.73 — Legislatures. *United States*
Keefe, William Joseph. The American legislative process : Congress and the states / [by] William J. Keefe, Morris S. Ogul. — 4th ed. — Englewood Cliffs ; London [etc.] : Prentice-Hall, 1977. — xiii,497p : ill, map ; 24cm.
Previous ed.: 1973. — Index.
ISBN 0-13-028100-x : £10.35
(B77-22398)

328.73 — United States. Congress
Fiorina, Morris Paul. Congress : keystone of the Washington establishment / [by] Morris P. Fiorina. — New Haven ; London : Yale University Press, 1977. — xiii,105p : ill, facsim ; 21cm.
Index.
ISBN 0-300-02132-1 : £6.40
ISBN 0-300-02125-9 Pbk : £2.25
(B77-24746)

328.73'04 — United States. 1st Congress, 1789-1791. House. *Documents*
United States. *1st Congress, 1789-1791. House.* House of Representatives journal / Linda Grant De Pauw, editor, Charlene Bangs Bickford, associate editor, LaVonne Siegel Hauptman, associate editor. — Baltimore ; London : Johns Hopkins University Press, 1977. — xxix,900p ; 24cm. — (Documentary history of the first Federal Congress of the United States of America, March 4, 1789-March 3, 1791 ; vol.3)

Index.
ISBN 0-8018-1819-2 : £21.35
(B77-31723)

328.73'07'456 — United States. Government. Executive branches. Supervision by United States. Congress
Ogul, Morris Samuel. Congress oversees the bureaucracy : studies in legislative supervision / [by] Morris S. Ogul. — [Pittsburgh] : University of Pittsburgh Press ; London : Feffer and Simons : [Distributed by Transatlantic Book Service], 1976. — xii,237p ; 21cm.
Bibl.: p.219-231. — Index.
ISBN 0-8229-3313-6 : £7.46
(B77-07110)

328.73'07'65 — United States. Congress. House. Committee on Rules
Matsunaga, Spark M. Rulemakers of the House / [by] Spark M. Matsunaga and Ping Chen. — Urbana [etc.] ; London : University of Illinois Press, 1976. — xv,208p ; 24cm.
Bibl.: p.198-202. — Index.
ISBN 0-252-00626-7 : £6.35
(B77-07111)

328.73'07'65 — United States. Congress. House. Committees. Reform, 1973-1974
Davidson, Roger Harry. Congress against itself / [by] Roger H. Davidson and Walter J. Oleszek. — Bloomington ; London : Indiana University Press, 1977. — xiii,306p : ill ; 24cm.
Bibl.: p.275-282. — Index.
ISBN 0-253-31405-4 : £11.25
(B77-23179)

328.73'07'75 — United States. Congress. Voting by members: Voting on legislation on emancipation of negroes, 1838-1869. *Statistics*
Linden, Glenn M. Politics or principle : congressional voting on the Civil War amendments and pro-Negro measures, 1838-69 / by Glenn M. Linden. — Seattle ; London : University of Washington Press, [1977]. — xvii,88p,2 fold leaves ; 29cm.
Published in the United States: 1976. — Bibl.: p.87-88.
ISBN 0-295-95434-5 : £8.45
(B77-11621)

328.773 — Illinois. General Assembly
Gove, Samuel K. The Illinois legislature : structure and process / [by] Samuel K. Gove, Richard W. Carlson, Richard J. Carlson. — Urbana [etc.] ; London : University of Illinois Press for the Institute of Government and Public Affairs, [University of Illinois], 1976. — xi,189p : 1 ill ; 23cm.
Bibl.: p.171-181. — Index.
ISBN 0-252-00621-6 Pbk : £4.80
(B77-07112)

329 — POLITICAL PARTIES AND RELATED TOPICS

329'.01'08 — Elections. Campaigns. *Democracies. Readings*
Changing campaign techniques : elections and values in contemporary democracies / edited by Louis Maisel. — Beverly Hills ; London : Sage Publications, 1976. — 274p : ill, maps ; 24cm. — (Sage electoral studies yearbook ; vol.2)
Bibl.
ISBN 0-8039-0683-8 : £9.00
ISBN 0-8039-0684-6 Pbk : £4.00
(B77-05239)

329'.02 — Political parties
Sartori, Giovanni. Parties and party systems : a framework for analysis / [by] Giovanni Sartori. — Cambridge [etc.] : Cambridge University Press.
In 2 vols.
Vol.1. — 1976. — xiii,370p : ill ; 24cm.
Index.
ISBN 0-521-21238-3 : £15.00
0-521-29106-2 Pbk : £4.50
(B77-01197)

329'.02'094 — Communist parties. *Western Europe*
McInnes, Neil. Euro-communism / [by] Neil McInnes. — Beverly Hills ; London : Sage Publications [for] the Center for Strategic and International Studies, 1976. — 80p ; 22cm. — (The Washington papers ; 37) (A Sage policy paper)
Bibl.: p.80.
ISBN 0-8039-0658-7 Pbk : £1.75
(B77-10204)

329'.02'094 — Liberal parties. *European Community countries*
Steed, Michael. Who's a Liberal in Europe / by Michael Steed. — Manchester (2nd Floor, 121 Princess St., Manchester 1) : North West Community Newspapers Ltd, [1975]. — [2], 26p ; 21cm.
Bibl.: p.26.
Sd : £0.25
(B77-31724)

329'.02'094 — Social democratic parties. *Western Europe*
Social democratic parties in Western Europe / edited by William E. Patterson and Alastair H. Thomas. — London : Croom Helm, 1977. — 444p : ill ; 23cm.
Bibl. — Index.
ISBN 0-85664-366-1 : £9.95 : CIP rev.
(B77-08815)

329'.02'0973 — Political parties. *United States, 1789-1800*
Zvesper, John. Political philosophy and rhetoric : a study of the origins of American party politics / [by] John Zvesper. — Cambridge [etc.] : Cambridge University Press, 1977. — viii,237p ; 22cm. — (Cambridge studies in the history and theory of politics)
Index.
ISBN 0-521-21323-1 : £7.90
(B77-23180)

329'.0221'0973 — Political parties. Presidential nominating conventions. *United States. Democratic Party (United States). National Convention, New York (City), 1976*
Reeves, Richard. Convention / [by] Richard Reeves. — London : Hutchinson, 1977. — ix, 246p ; 23cm.
Also published: New York : Harcourt Brace Jovanovich, 1977. — Index.
ISBN 0-09-129530-0 : £4.50
(B77-27701)

329'.023'4108 — Great Britain. Parliament. House of Commons. Members. Elections, 1832-1970. *Statistics*
Craig, Frederick Walter Scott. British parliamentary election results / compiled and edited by F.W.S. Craig. — London [etc.] : Macmillan.
1832-1885. — 1977. — xvii,692p ; 26cm.
Bibl.: p.645-647. — Index.
ISBN 0-333-17153-5 : £17.50
(B77-31018)

329'.023'41082 — Great Britain. Parliament. House of Commons. Members. Elections, 1885-1975. *Statistics*
Craig, Frederick Walter Scott. British electoral facts, 1885-1975 / compiled & edited by F.W.S. Craig. — 3rd ed. — London [etc.] : Macmillan, 1976. — xv,182p ; 26cm.
Previous ed.: published as 'British parliamentary election statistics, 1918-1970'. Chichester : Political Reference Publications, 1971. — Index.
ISBN 0-333-19734-8 : £8.50
ISBN 0-333-21624-5 Pbk : £4.95
(B77-08252)

329'.023'41082 — Great Britain. Parliament. House of Commons. Members. Elections, 1918-1949. *Statistics*
Craig, Frederick Walter Scott. British parliamentary election results, 1918-1949 / compiled and edited by F.W.S. Craig. — Revised ed. — London [etc.] : Macmillan, 1977. — xviii,785p ; 26cm.
Previous ed.: Glasgow : Political Reference Publications, 1969. — Index.
ISBN 0-333-23048-5 : £15.00
(B77-24747)

329'.023'4160824 — Elections. *Northern Ireland, 1973. Reports, surveys*
Knight, James. Northern Ireland, the elections of 1973 / by James Knight. — London (2 Greycoat Place, SW1P 1SD) : Arthur McDougall Fund, 1974. — 78p(24 fold) : 1 ill, maps ; 30cm.
Sheet as insert. — Bibl.: p.51.
ISBN 0-903278-03-0 Pbk : Unpriced
(B77-19247)

329'.023'420857 — County councils. Councillors. Elections. *England, 1977*
Clark, David Michael. Battle for the counties : guide to the county council elections May 1977 / [by] David M. Clark. — Newcastle upon Tyne (284 Wingrove Rd, Newcastle upon Tyne [NE4 9EE]) : Redrose Publications, 1977. — 100p : facsims, maps ; 30cm.
Bibl.: p.3.
Sd : £2.95
(B77-17953)

329'.023'4210823 — Elections. *Inner London, 1900-1914*
Knott, Simon. The electoral crucible : the politics of London, 1900-1914 / [by Simon Knott]. — London (22 Blomfield St., E.C.2) : Greene & Co., [1977]. — iii,194p ; 21cm.
Bibl.: p.193-194.
Pbk : Unpriced
(B77-15125)

329'.023'429082 — Great Britain. Parliament. House of Commons. Members. Elections in Wales, 1900-1975. *Statistics. Welsh-English parallel texts*
Jones, Beti. Etholiadau seneddol yng Nghymru, 1900-1975 = Parliamentary elections in Wales, 1900-1975 / [compiled by] Beti Jones. — Talybont, Dyfed (Talybont, Dyfed SY24 5ER) : Y Lolfa, 1977. — 191p : maps, ports ; 19cm.
Parallel English and Welsh text. — Index.
ISBN 0-904864-33-2 : £2.85
(B77-33647)

329'.023'7303 — Federal elections. *United States, 1788-1790. Readings from contemporary sources*
The **documentary** history of the first federal elections, 1788-1790 / edited by Merrill Jensen, Robert A. Becker. — Madison ; London : University of Wisconsin Press.
In 3 vols.
Vol.1. — 1976. — xxxi,896p ; 25cm.
Bibl.: p.xix-xxi. — Index.
ISBN 0-299-06690-8 : £22.50
(B77-04604)

329'.023'730918 — United States. Presidents. Elections. Role of Progressive Party (United States), 1948
Yarnell, Allen. Democrats and Progressives : the 1948 Presidential election as a test of postwar liberalism / by Allen Yarnell. — Berkeley [etc.] ; London : University of California Press, 1974. — xiii,155p ; 22cm.
Bibl.: p.137-148. — Index.
ISBN 0-520-02539-3 : Unpriced
(B77-20062)

329'.024'091822 — Mediterranean countries. Politics. Role of patronage. *Conference proceedings*
Patrons and clients : in Mediterranean societies / edited by Ernest Gellner and John Waterbury. — London : Duckworth [for] the Center for Mediterranean Studies of the American Universities Field Staff, 1977. — xii,348p : 3 ill ; 26cm.
'... papers at a Conference held under the patronage of the Center for Mediterranean Studies of the American Universities Field Staff in Rome ...' - Preface. — Bibl. — Index.
ISBN 0-7156-0941-6 : £12.00
(B77-22399)

329'.025'0943 — Political parties. Financial assistance by government. *West Germany*
Watson, Alan, *b.1941.* The political foundations in West Germany / by Alan Watson. — London [etc.] (St Stephen's House, Victoria Embankment, SW1A 2LA) : Anglo-German Foundation for the Study of Industrial Society, [1976]. — [3],23p ; 21cm. — (Anglo-German Foundation for the Study of Industrial Society. Series A ; 0176)
ISBN 0-905492-01-3 Sd : £1.00
(B77-14088)

329'.025'0943 — Political parties. Financial assistance by government. *West Germany. German texts*
Watson, Alan, *b.1941.* Die politischen Stiftungen in Westdeutschland / von Alan Watson ; [aus den Englischen übersetzt]. — London [etc.] (St Stephen's House, Victoria Embankment, SW1A 2LA) : Anglo-German Foundation for the Study of Industrial Society, [1976]. — [3],25p ; 21cm. — (Anglo-German Foundation for the Study of Industrial Society. Series A ; 0276)
ISBN 0-905492-02-1 Sd : Unpriced
(B77-14089)

329'.03'0941 — Great Britain. Parliament. House of Commons. Members. Elections. Role of pressure groups, 1837-1901
Hamer, David Allan. The politics of electoral pressure : a study in the history of Victorian reform agitations / [by] D.R. Hamer. — Hassocks : Harvester Press [etc.], 1977. — x, 386p ; 23cm.
Index.
ISBN 0-85527-839-0 : £10.95 : CIP rev.
(B77-05240)

329.3 — Negroes. Attitudes of Democratic Party (United States). *United States, 1868-1892*
Grossman, Lawrence, *b.1945.* The Democratic Party and the negro : northern and national politics, 1868-92 / [by] Lawrence Grossman. — Urbana [etc.] ; London : University of Illinois Press, 1976. — xv,212p ; 24cm. — (Blacks in the New World)
Bibl.: p.173-203. — Index.
ISBN 0-252-00575-9 : £7.00
(B77-10205)

329'.3'009044 — Political parties. *United States. Democratic Party (United States), 1941-1948*
Garson, Robert A. The Democratic Party and the politics of sectionalism, 1941-1948 / [by] Robert A. Garson. — Baton Rouge : Louisiana State University Press ; [London] : London School of Economics and Political Science, 1974. — xiii,353p ; 24cm.
Bibl.: p.323-342. — Index.
ISBN 0-8071-0070-6 : Unpriced
(B77-26844)

329'.81'009044 — Political parties. *United States. Socialist Workers Party, 1940-1943. Essays*
Cannon, James Patrick. The Socialist Workers Party in World War II : writings and speeches, 1940-43 / [by] James P. Cannon ; [edited by Les Evans]. — New York ; [London] ([47 The Cut, SE1 8LL]) : Pathfinder Press, 1975. — 3-446p : ill, ports ; 22cm.
Index.
ISBN 0-87348-457-6 Pbk : £2.35
(B77-02084)

329.9'41 — Political parties. *Great Britain, 1689-1720*
Kenyon, John Philipps. Revolution principles : the politics of party, 1689-1720 / [by] J.P. Kenyon. — Cambridge [etc.] : Cambridge University Press, 1977. — viii,248p ; 23cm. — (Cambridge studies in the history and theory of politics) (The Ford lectures ; 1975)
Bibl.: p.242. — Index.
ISBN 0-521-21542-0 : £9.50
(B77-31725)

329.9'41 — Political parties. *Great Britain, 1689-1742*
Hill, Brian William. The growth of Parliamentary parties, 1689-1742 / [by] B.W. Hill. — London : Allen and Unwin, 1976. — 3-265p ; 23cm.
Bibl.: p.248-254. — Index.
ISBN 0-04-942149-2 : £7.95
(B77-00633)

329.9'41 — Political parties. *Great Britain. Communist Organisation in the British Isles. Policies*
Communist Organisation in the British Isles. Platform of the Communist Organisation in the British Isles. — Edinburgh (c/o J. Maisels, 3 May Court, Edinburgh EH4 4SD) : C.O.B.I., 1976. — [1],24p ; 22cm.
ISBN 0-9505624-0-8 Sd : £0.30
(B77-11622)

329.9'41 — Political parties. *Great Britain. Communist Party of Great Britain. Communist viewpoints*
Communist Party of Great Britain. *Education Department.* The revolutionary party / Education Department of the Communist Party [of Great Britain]. — London : The Department, 1977. — [2],16p ; 29cm.
Bibl.: p.16.
ISBN 0-900302-73-9 Sd : £0.25
(B77-29991)

329.9'41 — Political parties. *Great Britain. Communist Party of Great Britain. Policies. Proposals*
Communist Party of Great Britain. The British road to socialism : draft for discussion : Communist Party programme / [Communist Party of Great Britain]. — [New ed.]. — London : Communist Party of Great Britain, [1977]. — [37]p ; 30cm.
Previous ed.: i.e. 3rd revised ed. 1968.
ISBN 0-900302-72-0 Sd : £0.30
(B77-11623)

329.9'41 — Political parties. *Great Britain. Conservative and Unionist Party, 1945-1975*
Blake, Robert, *Baron Blake, b.1916.* Conservatism in an age of revolution / by Robert Blake ; with a foreword by Margaret Thatcher. — London (2 Lord North St., [SW1P 3LB]) : Churchill Press Ltd, 1976. — 24p ; 19cm.
'Paper presented to the Conservative Philosophy Group'.
ISBN 0-902782-22-3 Pbk : £0.50
(B77-03410)

329.9'41 — Political parties. *Great Britain. Conservative and Unionist Party. Leaders, 1940-1976*
Fisher, Nigel. The Tory leaders : their struggle for power / [by] Nigel Fisher. — London : Weidenfeld and Nicolson, 1977. — ix,209p,[8]p of plates : ill, ports ; 23cm.
Index.
ISBN 0-297-77342-9 : £5.95
(B77-28428)

329.9'41 — Political parties. *Great Britain. Conservative and Unionist Party. Policies*
Conservative and Unionist Party. *Conservative Research Department.* The campaign guide, 1977 / [Conservative Research Department]. — [London] : Conservative Central Office, 1977. — iii,789p ; 25x11cm.
Previous ed.: 1974. — Index.
Pbk : £4.75
(B77-31019)

329.9'41 — Political parties. *Great Britain. Conservative and Unionist Party. Policies. Proposals*
Parlett, R J. Conservatism : the standpoint of a rank & file Tory / by R.J. Parlett. — Cobham ([Joynings, Seven Hills Rd, Cobham, Surrey]) : The author, 1976. — [1],16,[1]p ; 21cm.
ISBN 0-9505580-0-1 Sd : £0.30
(B77-08816)

329.9'41 — Political parties. *Great Britain. Conservative and Unionist Party, to 1965*
The **Conservatives** : a history from their origins to 1965 / by Norman Gash ... [et al.] ; edited with an introduction and epilogue by Lord Butler. — London [etc.] : Allen and Unwin, 1977. — 3-492p ; 23cm.
Index.
ISBN 0-04-942157-3 : £7.50
(B77-27702)

329.9'41 — Political parties. *Great Britain. Labour Party, 1931-1940*
Pimlott, Ben. Labour and the Left in the 1930s / [by] Ben Pimlott. — Cambridge [etc.] : Cambridge University Press, 1977. — xi,259p ; 24cm.
Bibl.: p.245-250. — Index.
ISBN 0-521-21448-3 : £6.50
Also classified at 335'.00941
(B77-24748)

329.9'41 — Political parties. *Great Britain. Labour Party, 1945-1977*
Wyatt, Woodrow. What's left of the Labour Party? / [by] Woodrow Wyatt. — London : Sidgwick and Jackson, 1977. — 183p ; 23cm.
Index.
ISBN 0-283-98427-9 : £4.95
(B77-27703)

329.9'41 — Political parties. *Great Britain. Labour Party. Conference proceedings*
Labour Party. *Annual Conference, 75th, Blackpool, 1976.* Report of the seventyfifth annual conference of the Labour Party, Blackpool, 1976, September 27-October 1. — London : The Party, [1977]. — [2],401,[1]p ; 21cm.
Index.
ISBN 0-900507-95-0 Pbk : £1.50
(B77-15719)

329.9'41 — Political parties. *Great Britain. Labour Party. Democracy*
Cole, H B. The British Labour Party : a functioning participatory democracy / by H.B. Cole. — Oxford [etc.] : Pergamon, 1977. — xi, 90p : ill ; 21cm. — (Pergamon international library)
Bibl.: p.74-75. — Index.
ISBN 0-08-021811-3 Pbk : £1.50
(B77-31020)

329.9'41 — Political parties. *Great Britain. Labour Party. Directories*
Labour Party. Directory / [Labour Party]. — London : Labour Party.
1977. — [1977]. — 48p ; 16cm.
ISBN 0-900507-92-6 Sd : Unpriced
(B77-12340)

329.9'41 — Political parties. *Great Britain. Labour Party. Leaders. Election. Procedure. Proposals*
Coates, Ken. Democracy in the Labour Party / by Ken Coates. — Nottingham : Spokesman Books, 1977. — 116p ; 19cm.
Bibl.: p.111. — Index.
ISBN 0-85124-205-7 : Unpriced
ISBN 0-85124-206-5 Pbk : £0.95
(B77-31021)

329.9'41 — Political parties. *Great Britain. Labour Party. Women's organisations*
Labour Party. Women's organisation in the Labour Party : a guide. — [Revised ed.] / by Joyce Gould. — London : The Party, [1977]. — [1],40p : forms ; 21cm.
Previous ed.: published as 'Women's sections : their constitution and activities'. 1950.
ISBN 0-900507-87-x Sd : £0.30
(B77-16219)

329.9'41 — Political parties. *Great Britain. Liberal Party, 1857-1868*
Vincent, John, *b.1937.* The formation of the British Liberal Party, 1857-1868 / [by] J.R. Vincent. — 2nd ed. — Hassocks : Harvester Press [etc.], 1976. — li,300p ; 23cm.
Previous ed.: published as 'The formation of the Liberal Party, 1857-1868'. London : Constable, 1966. — Bibl.: p.275-291. — Index.
ISBN 0-901759-18-x : £7.50
(B77-03982)

329.9'41 — Political parties. *Great Britain. Liberal Party. Strategy. Proposals*
Mayhew, Christopher. Blueprint for a breakthrough : 1-2-3-x / [by] Christopher Mayhew. — London (9 Poland St., W1V 3DG) : Liberal Publication Department, 1976. — [1],15p : ill ; 21cm.
ISBN 0-900520-51-5 Sd : £0.30
(B77-02798)

329.9'41 — Political parties. *Great Britain. Liberal Party, to 1976*
Cyr, Arthur. Liberal Party politics in Britain / by Arthur Cyr ; with a foreword by Michael Steed. — London : J. Calder : [Distributed by Calder and Boyars], 1977. — 318p : 1 ill ; 23cm. — (Platform books)
Bibl.: p.303-310. — Index.
ISBN 0-7145-3546-x : £9.95
(B77-22400)

329.9'41 — Political parties. *Great Britain. National Front. Socialist Workers' Party viewpoints*
The **fight** against the racists : the Nazional Front and how to smash it. — [New ed.]. — London (Corbridge Works, Corbridge Cres., E2 9DS) : 'Socialist worker', [1977]. — 15p : ill, ports ; 30cm. — (A 'Socialist worker' pamphlet)
Previous ed.: published as 'The new Nazis : organize against them'. 1975.
ISBN 0-905998-09-x Sd : £0.10
(B77-16220)

329'.9'41 — Political parties. *Great Britain. National Front, to 1976*
Walker, Martin. The National Front / [by] Martin Walker. — [London] : Fontana, 1977. — 224p ; 18cm.
ISBN 0-00-634824-6 Pbk : £1.00
(B77-23181)

329.9'41 — Political parties. *Great Britain. New Communist Party*
New Communist Party. The case for the New Communist Party. — London (118 High St., Colliers Wood) : The Party, [1977]. — 14,[1]p ; 21cm.
'A New Communist Party Pamphlet'.
Sd : £0.15
(B77-26845)

329.9'41 — Political parties. Great Britain. Leftwing Liberal Party. Compared with Plaid Cymru
Cavendish, Rupert. Differences and similarities between radical liberalism and Plaid Cymru / by Rupert Cavendish. — Manchester (2nd Floor, 121 Princess St., Manchester M1 7AG) : North West Community Newspapers Ltd, 1977. — 16p ; 31cm.
Sd : £0.25
(B77-31022)

329.9'41 — Right-wing political parties. *Great Britain, 1957-1976*
The **British** right : Conservative and right wing politics in Britain / edited by Neill Nugent, Roger King. — Farnborough, Hants. : Saxon House, 1977. — vi,231p ; 23cm.
Bibl.: p.222-230.
ISBN 0-566-00156-x : £7.50 : CIP rev.
(B77-16221)

329.9'411 — Political parties. *Scotland. Scottish National Party & Scottish Labour Party. Socialist Workers' Party viewpoints*
Armstrong, Allan. Nationalism or socialism : the SNP and SLP exposed / by Allan Armstrong. — London (6 Cottons Gardens, E2 8DN) : Socialist Worker Printers and Publishers, [1977]. — 8p : ill ; 30cm. — (A 'Socialist worker' pamphlet)
ISBN 0-905998-06-5 Sd : £0.10
(B77-16222)

329.9'416 — Political parties. *Northern Ireland. Social Democratic and Labour Party, to 1976*
McAllister, Ian. The Northern Ireland Social Democratic and Labour Party : political opposition in a divided society / [by] Ian McAllister ; foreword by Richard Rose. — London : Macmillan, 1977. — xxi,200p : ill ; 23cm.
Bibl.: p.191-194. — Index.
ISBN 0-333-22347-0 : £10.00 : CIP rev.
(B77-24039)

329.9'417 — Political parties. *Ireland (Republic). Fianna Fáil. Periodicals*
Fianna Fáil. Iris Fianna Fáil : Party journal. — Dublin (13 Upper Mount St., Dublin 2) : Fianna Fáil.
No.1- ; Winter 1974-. — [1974]-. — ill, ports ; 30cm.
Quarterly. — Subtitle varies. — 16p. in 1st issue. — Size varies. — Includes articles in Irish.
Sd : £1.00 yearly
ISSN 0332-0596
(B77-32453)

329.9'428 — Political parties. *North-east England. Labour Party. Corruption. Exposure. Personal observations*
Milne, Edward. Not shining armour / [by] Edward Milne. — London : J. Calder : [Distributed by Calder and Boyars], 1976. — 263p : facsim ; 22cm. — (A platform book)
Index.
ISBN 0-7145-3501-x : £4.95
ISBN 0-7145-3514-1 Pbk : £1.95
(B77-15720)

329.9'43 — Political parties. *Germany. Kommunistische Partei Deutschlands, 1918-1931. Personal observations*
Leviné-Meyer, Rosa. Inside German communism : memoirs of party life in the Weimar Republic / [by] Rosa Leviné-Meyer ; edited and introduced by David Zane Mairowitz. — London : Pluto Press, 1977. — [5],222p,[16]p of plates : ill, ports ; 23cm.
Index.
ISBN 0-904383-34-2 : £4.80
(B77-20954)

329.9'43 — Political parties. *Germany. Nationalsozialistische Deutsche Arbeiter-Partei, 1923-1933. Personal observations*
Krebs, Albert. The infancy of Nazism : the memoirs of ex-Gauleiter Albert Krebs, 1923-1933 / edited and translated [from the German] by William Sheridan Allen. — New York ; London : New Viewpoints ; [London] : [Distributed by] F. Watts, 1976. — xv,328p ; 22cm.
Translation of: 'Tendenzen und Gestalten der NSDAP : Erinnenungen an die Frühzeit der Partei von Albert Krebs'. Stuttgart : Deutsche Verlags-Anstalt, 1959. — Bibl.: p.316-320. — Index.
ISBN 0-531-05376-8 : £7.50
ISBN 0-531-05583-3 Pbk : Unpriced
(B77-00066)

329.9'43 — Political parties. *West Germany. Christlich-Demokratische Union, to 1976*
Pridham, Geoffrey. Christian democracy in Western Germany : the CDU/CSU in government and opposition, 1945-1976 / [by] Geoffrey Pridham. — London : Croom Helm, 1977. — 5-371p ; 23cm.
Also published: New York : St Martin's Press, 1977. — Bibl.: p.359-363. — Index.
ISBN 0-85664-508-7 : £9.95 : CIP rev.
(B77-24040)

329.9'44 — Political parties. *France. Parti Communiste Français, 1945-1972. Conference proceedings*
Communism in Italy and France / edited by Donald L.M. Blackmer and Sidney Tarrow. — [1st ed. reprinted] ; with new preface. — Princeton ; Guildford : Princeton University Press, 1977. — xviii,651p ; 24cm.
Originally published: 1975. — Index.
ISBN 0-691-10054-3 Pbk : £7.25
Primary classification 329.9'45
(B77-23182)

329.9'45 — Political parties. *Italy. Partito Comunista Italiano, 1945-1972. Conference proceedings*
Communism in Italy and France / edited by Donald L.M. Blackmer and Sidney Tarrow. — [1st ed. reprinted] ; with new preface. — Princeton ; Guildford : Princeton University Press, 1977. — xviii,651p ; 24cm.
Originally published: 1975. — Index.
ISBN 0-691-10054-3 Pbk : £7.25
Also classified at 329.9'44
(B77-23182)

329.9'51 — Political parties. *China. Chinese Community Party. Leadership. Training, 1920-1945*
Price, Jane L. Cadres, commanders and commissars : the training of the Chinese Communist leadership, 1920-45 / [by] Jane L. Price. — Folkestone : Dawson, 1976. — viii, 226p ; 24cm. — (Columbia University. East Asian Institute. Studies)
Originally published: Boulder, Colo. : Westview Press, 1975. — Bibl.: p.199-216. — Index.
ISBN 0-7129-0739-4 : £12.00
(B77-09550)

329.9'52 — Political parties. *Japan, 1931-1941*
Berger, Gordon Mark. Parties out of power in Japan, 1931-1941 / [by] Gordon Mark Berger. — Princeton ; Guildford : Princeton University Press, 1977. — xvii,413,[1]p : ill, ports ; 23cm.
Bibl.: p.360-394. — Index.
ISBN 0-691-03106-1 : £16.10
(B77-22401)

329.9'54 — Political parties. *India, to 1947*
Misra, Bankey Bihari. The Indian political parties : an historical analysis of political behaviour up to 1947 / [by] B.B. Misra. — Delhi ; Oxford [etc.] : Oxford University Press, 1976. — xv,665p ; 22cm.
Bibl.: p.645-649. — Index.
ISBN 0-19-560598-5 : £11.50
(B77-33091)

329.9'63 — Political parties. *Ethiopia. Ethiopian Democratic Union. Policies*
Ethiopian Democratic Union. EDU : what does it stand for? : who is behind it? : what after the Dergue? / Ethiopian Democratic Union. — London (WC1V 6XX) : BM-EDU, 1976. — [1] ,7p ; 26cm.
Sd : Unpriced
(B77-22402)

329.9'71 — Political parties. *Canada, to 1974*
Engelmann, Frederick C. Canadian political parties : origin, character, impact / [by] Frederick C. Engelmann, Mildred A. Schwartz. — Scarborough, Ont. ; London [etc.] : Prentice-Hall, [1976]. — ix,358p ; 26cm.
Published in Canada : 1975. — Bibl.: p.330-351. — Index.
ISBN 0-13-113308-x : Unpriced
ISBN 0-13-113241-5 Pbk : Unpriced
(B77-08817)

330 — ECONOMICS

Attiyeh, Richard. Basic economics : theory and cases / [by] Richard Attiyeh, George Leland Bach, Keith Lumsden. — 2nd ed. — Englewood Cliffs ; London [etc.] : Prentice-Hall, 1977. — viii,456p : ill ; 24cm.
With answers. — Previous ed.: Englewood Cliffs : Prentice-Hall, 1973. — Index.
ISBN 0-13-059030-4 Pbk : £6.35
(B77-15126)

Bach, George Leland. Economics : an introduction to analysis and policy / [by] George Leland Bach. — 9th ed. — Englewood Cliffs ; London [etc.] : Prentice-Hall, 1977. — ii-xxii,712p : ill(some col) ; 24cm.
Col. ill. on lining papers. — Previous ed.: 1974. — Bibl. — Index.
ISBN 0-13-227348-9 : £11.15
(B77-16223)

Hanson, John Lloyd. A textbook of economics / [by] J.L. Hanson. — 7th ed. — Plymouth : Macdonald and Evans, 1977. — xxxii,604p : ill ; 21cm.
Previous ed.: 1972. — Bibl. — Index.
ISBN 0-7121-2020-3 Pbk : £2.50
(B77-16224)

Harvey, Jack, *b.1917.* Elementary economics / [by] J. Harvey. — 4th ed. — Basingstoke [etc.] : Macmillan, 1977. — xiii,514p : ill, maps ; 22cm.
This ed. originally published: 1976. — Index.
ISBN 0-333-22412-4 Pbk : £1.50
(B77-24041)

Heyne, Paul T. Toward economic understanding / [by] Paul Heyne, Thomas Johnson. — Chicago [etc.] ; Henley-on-Thames : Science Research Associates.
Instructor's manual. — 1976. — [6],250p ; 22cm.
Bibl.
ISBN 0-574-19256-5 Pbk : £1.40
(B77-01198)

Student's guide / [by] Thomas Johnson. — 1976. — vi,185p : ill ; 22x28cm.
With answers.
ISBN 0-574-19257-3 Pbk : £3.45
(B77-00634)

Introducing economics / [by] B.J. McCormick ... [et al.]. — 2nd ed. — Harmondsworth [etc.] : Penguin, 1977. — 826p : ill ; 20cm. — (Penguin modern economics) (Penguin education)
Previous ed.: 1974. — Bibl.: p.803-808. — Index.
Pbk : £3.75
ISBN 0-14-080911-2
(B77-22403)

Manchester Economics Project. Understanding economics / the Manchester Economics Project ; project head C. Giles. — Revised ed. — Aylesbury : Ginn, 1976. — vii,336p : ill, map ; 25cm.
With answers. — Previous ed.: London : Ginn, 1972. — Index.
ISBN 0-602-22328-8 Pbk : £4.25
(B77-19298)

Miller, Roger LeRoy. Economics today / [by] Roger LeRoy Miller. — Brief ed. — San Francisco : Canfield Press ; New York [etc.] ; London : Harper and Row, 1976. — xii,466p : ill(chiefly col), ports ; 25cm.
Full ed. i.e. 2nd ed. originally published: 1976. — Bibl. — Index.
ISBN 0-06-385457-0 : £8.95
(B77-06505)

Norris, Keith. Economics for everyone / [by] Keith Norris and John Vaizey. — London : Hodder and Stoughton, 1977. — vi,202p : ill ; 18cm. — (Teach yourself books)
Bibl. — Index.
ISBN 0-340-21905-x Pbk : £1.50
(B77-24042)

Perrow, John Arthur. Economics / [by] John A. Perrow. — 3rd ed. — London : University Tutorial Press, 1977. — vi,642p : ill ; 22cm.
Previous ed.: 1975. — Index.
ISBN 0-7231-0751-3 Pbk : £3.60
(B77-29992)

Samuelson, Paul Anthony. Economics / [by] Paul A. Samuelson. — 10th ed. / with the assistance in statistical updating of Peter Temin. — Tokyo : McGraw-Hill Kogakusha ; Auckland ; London [etc.] : [McGraw-Hill], 1976. — xxix, 917p : col ill ; 24cm.
Previous ed.: New York ; London [etc.] : McGraw-Hill, 1973. — Index.
Pbk : £6.95
(B77-03983)

Schumacher, Ernst Friedrich. Small is beautiful : a study of economics as if people mattered / [by] E.F. Schumacher. — London : Abacus, 1976. — 255p : ill ; 20cm.
Originally published: London : Blond and Briggs, 1973.
ISBN 0-349-13141-4 Pbk : £1.50
(B77-13534)

Simmons, David Alan. Economic power / [by] D.A. Simmons. — Northolt (5 Russell Rd, Northolt, Middx) : Gemini Books, 1976. — [5], 192p : forms ; 22cm.
Bibl.: p.190.
£3.50
ISBN 0-905071-01-1 Pbk : £1.40
(B77-18589)

Thirkettle, George Leslie. Advanced economics / [by] G.L. Thirkettle. — 2nd ed. — Plymouth : Macdonald and Evans, 1976. — xiv,138p : ill ; 19cm. — (The M. & E. handbook series)
Previous ed.: 1968. — Bibl.: p.125. — Index.
ISBN 0-7121-0164-0 Pbk : £1.00
(B77-06506)

Toch, Henry. Economics for professional studies / [by] Henry Toch. — 2nd ed. — Plymouth : Macdonald and Evans, 1977. — xvi,224p : ill, map ; 18cm. — (The M. & E. handbook series)
Previous ed.: 1974. — Index.
ISBN 0-7121-0568-9 Pbk : £1.25
(B77-31727)

Whitehead, Geoffrey. Economics made simple / [by] Geoffrey Whitehead. — 7th (revised) ed. — London : W.H. Allen, 1977. — xv,384p : ill, maps ; 22cm. — (Made simple books ISSN 0464-2902)
Previous ed.: 1976. — Bibl. — Index.
Pbk : £1.75
ISBN 0-491-01751-0
(B77-20063)

330 — Applied economics
Hartley, Keith. Problems of economic policy / by Keith Hartley. — London : Allen and Unwin, 1977. — 3-233p : ill ; 23cm. — (Economics and society series ; no.3)
Bibl.: p.223-227. — Index.
ISBN 0-04-339008-0 : £5.50
ISBN 0-04-339009-9 Pbk : £2.95
(B77-28429)

330 — Economics. *Conference proceedings*
Association of University Teachers of Economics. *Annual conference, Edinburgh, 1976.* Studies in modern economic analysis : the proceedings of the Association of University Teachers of Economics, Edinburgh, 1976 / edited by M.J. Artis, A.R. Nobay. — Oxford : Blackwell, 1977. — xiv,350p : ill ; 24cm.
Bibl.
ISBN 0-631-17970-4 : £10.00
(B77-17331)

Resource allocation and economic policy / edited by Michael Allingham and M.L. Burstein. — London [etc.] : Macmillan, 1976. — xiii,251p : ill ; 23cm.
'... the proceedings of a conference sponsored by the University College at Buckingham and the Institute of Economic Affairs, and held in London in June 1975' - Preface. — Bibl. — Index.
ISBN 0-333-18617-6 : £14.00
(B77-02085)

330 — Economics. *Festschriften*
Economic progress, private values, and public policy : essays in honor of William Fellner / edited by Bela Balassa and Richard Nelson. — Amsterdam [etc.] ; Oxford : North-Holland Publishing Co., 1977. — viii,339p : ill ; 23cm.
Bibl. — Index. — Includes a selected list of the writings of William John Fellner.
ISBN 0-7204-0515-7 : £25.76
(B77-15721)

The **market** and the state : essays in honour of Adam Smith / edited by Thomas Wilson and Andrew S. Skinner. — Oxford : Clarendon Press, 1976. — xi,359p ; 22cm.
'... papers ... presented at a conference ... at the University of Glasgow in April 1976 ...' - Preface. — Index.
ISBN 0-19-828406-3 : £8.00
(B77-07819)

Relevance and precision : from quantitative analysis to economic policy : essays in honour of Pieter de Wolff / editors J.S. Cramer, A. Heertje, P. Venekamp. — Alphen aan den Rijn : Samsom ; Amsterdam [etc.] ; Oxford : North-Holland Publishing Co., 1976. — 318p : ill, port ; 26cm.
Bibl.
ISBN 0-7204-0534-3 : Unpriced
(B77-24043)

330 — Economics. *For African students. Secondary school texts*
Obone, A E. Economics : its principles and practice in developing Africa / [by] A.E. Obone. — London [etc.] : Evans Bros, 1977. — x,290p : ill ; 22cm.
Bibl.: p.281-282. — Index.
ISBN 0-237-49912-6 Pbk : Unpriced
(B77-11624)

330 — Economics. *For West African students*
Nwankwo, G O. Basic economics : an introduction for West African students / [by] G.O. Nwankwo. — Cambridge [etc.] : Cambridge University Press, 1977. — vii,263p : ill ; 23cm.
ISBN 0-521-21122-0 Pbk : £2.70
(B77-29220)

330 — Economics. *For West African students. Secondary school texts*
Benemy, Frank William Georgeson. Economics : a revision scheme for students preparing for the West African School Certificate ('O' Level) and the Cambridge Overseas School Certificate / [by] F.W.G. Benemy. — London [etc.] : Evans Bros, 1977. — 64p : ill ; 19cm. — (Evans pocket facts)
ISBN 0-237-50072-8 Sd : £3.90
(B77-14583)

Teriba, O. Certificate economics for West Africa / [by] O. Teriba. — London : Longman, 1976. — [6],250p : ill ; 24cm.
Index.
ISBN 0-582-60931-3 Pbk : £1.50
(B77-11099)

330 — Economics. *Juvenile literature*
Armstrong, Louise. How to turn lemons into money : a child's guide to economics / by Louise Armstrong ; illustrated by Bill Basso. — New York ; London : Harcourt Brace Jovanovich, [1977]. — [32]p : ill(chiefly col) ; 22cm.
Published in the United States: 1976.
ISBN 0-15-237250-4 : £3.00
ISBN 0-15-237251-2 Pbk : £1.05
(B77-08254)

330 — Economics. *Secondary school texts*
Harvey, Jack, *b.1917.* Intermediate economics / by J. Harvey. — 3rd ed. — Basingstoke [etc.] : Macmillan, 1976. — xviii,494p : ill ; 22cm.
With answers. — Bibl. — Index.
ISBN 0-333-19605-8 Pbk : £3.75
(B77-31023)

Powicke, John Colyer. An introduction to economics / [by] John C. Powicke, Peter H. May. — 3rd ed. — London : Edward Arnold, 1977. — vi,254p : ill, map ; 22cm.
Previous ed.: 1969. — Index.
ISBN 0-7131-0088-5 Pbk : £2.50
(B77-14584)

Stanlake, George Frederick. Introductory economics / [by] G.F. Stanlake. — 3rd ed. — London : Longman, 1976. — ix,463p : ill, forms, maps ; 22cm.
Previous ed.: 1971. — Index.
ISBN 0-582-33050-5 Pbk : £1.75
(B77-00067)

330 — Economics. *Transcripts of discussions*
Friedman, Milton. Milton Friedman in Australia, 1975. — [Sydney] : Constable and Bain [etc.] ; Caterham (c/o 26 Manor Ave., Caterham, Surrey) : [Distributed by] Australiana Publications, [1977]. — 80,[1]p : ill, port ; 22cm.
'... contains transcripts of the two Sydney gatherings, ... a seminar conducted by the Graduate Business School Club and a public dinner hosted by Constable & Bain' - Preface. — Published in Australia: 1975.
ISBN 0-909162-02-6 Pbk : £3.25
(B77-09551)

330 — Economics. Externalities. *Conference proceedings*
Conference on Externalities, *Southern Illinois University, 1974.* Theory and measurement of economic externalities / edited by Steven A.Y. Lin. — New York [etc.] ; London : Academic Press, 1976. — xiv,265p : ill ; 24cm. — (Economic theory and mathematical economics)

'Proceedings of the Conference on Externalities held at Southern Illinois University at Edwardsville, April 19-20, 1974' - jacket. — Bibl. — Index.
ISBN 0-12-450450-7 : £11.90
(B77-07113)

330 — Economics. Samuelson, Paul Anthony. 'Economics'. *Critical studies*
Linder, Marc. The anti-Samuelson / by Marc Linder [in collaboration with Julius Sensat, Jr]. — New York : Urizen Books ; London : [Distributed by] Pluto Press [etc.].
In 2 vols.
Vol.1 : Macroeconomics : basic problems of the capitalist economy. — 1977. — xvii,395p : ill ; 23cm.
ISBN 0-916354-14-8 : £8.70
ISBN 0-916354-25-6 Pbk : £3.90
(B77-29993)

Vol.2 : Microeconomics : basic problems of the capitalist economy. — 1977. — [5],472p : ill ; 23cm.
Bibl.: p.443-472.
ISBN 0-916354-16-4 : £8.70
ISBN 0-916354-17-2 Pbk : £3.90
(B77-29994)

330'.01 — Economics. Implications of political individualism. *Essays*
Hayek, Friedrich August. Individualism and economic order / [by] F.A. Hayek. — London [etc.] : Routledge and Kegan Paul, 1976. — vii, 272p ; 23cm.
This collection originally published: 1949.
ISBN 0-7100-8521-4 : £5.50
(B77-03411)

330'.01'51 — Economics. Applications of control theory mathematics
Applications of control theory to economic analysis / edited by John D. Pitchford, Stephen J. Turnovsky. — Amsterdam [etc.] ; Oxford : North-Holland Publishing Co., 1977. — xii, 363p : ill ; 23cm. — (Contributions to economic analysis ; 101)
Bibl.
ISBN 0-7204-0455-x : £28.10
(B77-14090)

330'.01'51 — Economics. Mathematics
Archibald, George Christopher. An introduction to a mathematical treatment of economics / [by] G.C. Archibald and Richard G. Lipsey. — 3rd ed. — London : Weidenfeld and Nicolson, 1977. — viii,523p : ill ; 24cm.
With answers. — Previous ed.: 1973. — Index.
ISBN 0-297-77313-5 : £12.50
ISBN 0-297-77314-3 Pbk : £4.00
(B77-24044)

330'.01'5193 — Economics. Game theory
Bacharach, Michael. Economics and the theory of games / [by] Michael Bacharach. — London [etc.] : Macmillan, 1976. — ix,163p : ill ; 23cm.
Bibl.: p.157-158. — Index.
ISBN 0-333-19592-2 : £7.95
ISBN 0-333-19593-0 Pbk : £3.95
(B77-17332)

330'.01'82 — Econometric models
Naughton, John. Modelling for understanding : a case study in econometrics / prepared for the [Open University Systems Modelling] Course Team by John Naughton. — Milton Keynes : Open University Press, 1976. — 99p : col ill ; 30cm. — (Technology, a third level course : systems modelling ; units 14 and 15) (T341 ; 14-15)
With answers to self-assessment questions. — Bibl.: p.95-97.
ISBN 0-335-06055-2 Pbk : Unpriced
(B77-02799)

330'.01'82 — Econometrics
Maddala, G S. Econometrics / [by] G.S. Maddala. — New York ; London [etc.] : McGraw-Hill, 1977. — xii,516p : ill ; 25cm. — (Economics handbook series)
Index.
ISBN 0-07-039412-1 : £13.85
(B77-20956)

Phillips, P C B. Econometrics : a view from the toolroom / [by] P.C.B. Phillips. — [Birmingham] : University of Birmingham, 1977. — [2],20p ; 21cm. — (University of Birmingham. Inaugural lectures)
'... delivered in the University of Birmingham on 18 January 1977' - title page verso. — Bibl.: p.18-20.
ISBN 0-7044-0253-x Sd : Unpriced
(B77-33092)

330'.01'82 — General equilibrium theory. Equilibria. Computation. *Conference proceedings*
Computing Equilibria : How and Why *(Conference), Nicholas Copernicus University of Toruń, 1974.* Computing equilibria : how and why / editors Jerzy Łoś and Maria W. Łoś ; contributors A.E. Anderson ... [et al.]. — Amsterdam ; Oxford [etc.] : North-Holland Publishing Co., 1976. — xv,332p : ill ; 24cm.
'... proceedings of the conference "Computing Equilibria : How and Why?" held in Toruń, Poland, July 8-13, 1974. The Computing Centre of the Polish Academy of Sciences organized the conference ...' - Preface. — Bibl.
ISBN 0-7204-2837-8 : £24.39
(B77-08818)

330'.01'84 — Economic conditions. Mathematical models. Applications of digital computer systems: LINK system
The **models** of Project LINK / edited by J. Waelbroeck. — Amsterdam [etc.] ; Oxford : North-Holland Publishing Co., 1976. — x, 409p : ill ; 23cm. — (Contributions to economic analysis ; 102)
ISBN 0-7204-0514-9 : £20.93
(B77-00635)

330'.01'84 — Economics. Mathematical models
Cole, Sam. Global models and the international economic order : a paper for the United Nations Institute for Training and Research project on the future / [by] Sam Cole. — Oxford [etc.] : Pergamon, 1977. — [11],80p : ill ; 25cm.
Bibl.: p.79-80.
ISBN 0-08-022025-8 Sd : £3.75 : CIP rev.
(B77-24045)

330'.01'84 — Economics. Mathematical models. Hamiltonian functions
The **Hamiltonian** approach to dynamic economics / edited by David Cass and Karl Shell. — New York [etc.] ; London : Academic Press, 1976 [i.e. 1977]. — x,201p ; 24cm. — (Economic theory and mathematical economics)
Published in the United States: 1976. — '... originally appeared as papers in the "Journal of economic theory", Vol.12, no.1 (February 1976)' - Acknowledgments. — Bibl. — Index.
ISBN 0-12-163650-x : £7.10
(B77-12341)

330'.02'4658 — Economics. *for marketing*
Livesey, Frank. A modern approach to economics / [by] Frank Livesey. — London : Heinemann [for] the Institute of Marketing, 1977. — x,271p : ill, map ; 23cm.
With answers to objective test questions. — Bibl. — Index.
ISBN 0-434-91149-6 Pbk : £3.90
(B77-10747)

330'.03 — Economics. *Dictionaries*
Dowling, Noel. Dictionary of economic definitions for the Leaving Certificate / [by] Noel Dowling. — Dublin : Helicon, 1977. — [2],45p : ill ; 21cm.
Sd : £0.55
(B77-22404)

330'.03 — Economics. *Encyclopaedias*
Bannock, Graham. The Penguin dictionary of economics / [by] G. Bannock, R.E. Baxter and R. Rees. — London : Allen Lane [etc.], 1977. — 3-427p : ill ; 23cm.
Originally published: Harmondsworth : Penguin, 1972.
ISBN 0-7139-1038-0 : £3.95
(B77-29995)

Becket, Michael Ivan H. Economic alphabet : an irreverent guide to finance for the layman / by Michael Becket. — [London] ([11 South Sq., Gray's Inn, W.C.1]) : Flame Books, 1976. — 3-95p : ill ; 18cm. — (A Money-go-round guide)
ISBN 0-905340-00-0 Pbk : £0.90
(B77-03984)

Hanson, John Lloyd. A dictionary of economics and commerce / [by] J.L. Hanson. — 5th ed. — Plymouth : Macdonald and Evans, 1977. — vi,472p : ill ; 22cm.
Previous ed.: 1974.
ISBN 0-7121-0426-7 : Unpriced
ISBN 0-7121-0424-0 Pbk : £3.00
(B77-33093)

330'.05 — Economics. *Periodicals*
Cambridge journal of economics. — London [etc.] : Academic Press for the Cambridge Political Economy Society.
Vol.1, no.1- ; Mar. 1977-. — 1977-. — ill, ports ; 25cm.
Quarterly. — Cover title. — 112p., plate in 1st issue. — Bibl.
Pbk : £10.00 yearly
ISSN 0309-166x
(B77-18590)

330'.07'1142132 — Universities. Colleges. *London. Westminster (London Borough). London School of Economics and Political Science, 1929-1976. Personal observations. Collections*
My LSE / [by] Chaim Bermant ... [et al.] ; edited and introduced by Joan Abse. — London : Robson, 1977. — 223p,[4]p of plates : 1 ill, ports ; 23cm.
ISBN 0-86051-014-x : £5.25 : CIP rev.
(B77-23183)

330'.07'1142132 — Universities. Colleges. *London. Westminster (London Borough). London School of Economics and Political Science. Calendars*
London School of Economics and Political Science. Calendar / the London School of Economics and Political Science. — [London] : [L.S.E.].
1977-78. — [1977]. — [2],500p : coat of arms, 2 maps ; 22cm.
Index.
ISBN 0-85328-057-6 Pbk : £3.50
ISSN 0308-9681
(B77-29996)

330'.07'1241 — Secondary schools. Curriculum subjects: Economics. *Great Britain. Conference proceedings*
Extending Economics Within the Curriculum *(Conference), Worcester College of Education, 1975.* Extending economics within the curriculum / edited by Keith Robinson and Robert Wilson ; on behalf of the Economics Association. — London [etc.] : Routledge and Kegan Paul, 1977. — xiii,201p : ill ; 24cm.
'... the title "Extending Economics Within the Curriculum" ... [was] chosen for the papers presented at the second curriculum development seminar held by the Economics Association in September 1975 at Worcester College of Education' - Introduction. — 'Routledge direct editions'. — Bibl. — Index.
ISBN 0-7100-8629-6 Pbk : £3.75 : CIP rev.
(B77-20957)

330'.076 — Economics. *Exercises, worked examples*
Burke, Edmund, *b.1929.* Economics : multiple choice for advanced students / [by] Edmund Burke and Philip Selby. — London : Harrap, 1977. — 143p : ill ; 23cm.
With key and answers.
ISBN 0-245-52985-3 Pbk : £1.85
(B77-31024)

Curzon, Leslie Basil. An introduction to economics : a workbook and study guide / [by] L.B. Curzon. — Plymouth : Macdonald and Evans, 1977. — ix,190p : ill ; 21cm.
With answers. — Bibl.: p.vii-viii.
ISBN 0-7121-0949-8 Pbk : £1.50
(B77-33094)

330'.076 — Economics. *Exercises, worked examples. Secondary school texts*
Thomas, David John. Objective tests in economics / [by] D.J. Thomas. — London [etc.] : Pitman, 1976. — v,81p : 1 ill ; 22cm.
ISBN 0-273-00733-5 Pbk : £0.95
(B77-17333)

Watts, Michael, *b.1943.* Worked examples in data response questions for A Level economics / [by] Michael Watts and Matthew Glew. — London : Heinemann Educational, 1977. — [4],108p : ill ; 22cm.
ISBN 0-435-84892-5 Pbk : £1.25
(B77-31728)

330'.076 — Economics. *Questions & answers*
Curzon, Leslie Basil. Objective tests in economics / [by] L.B. Curzon. — Plymouth : Macdonald and Evans, 1977. — vii,184p : ill ; 19cm.
With answers.
ISBN 0-7121-1517-x Pbk : £1.25
(B77-26150)

330'.07'7 — Economics. *Programmed texts*
Kapoor, S S. Dynamic approach to economics / by S.S. Kapoor, Barry Finlayson. — Edinburgh : Holmes-McDougall, 1976. — 199p : ill ; 21x29cm.
ISBN 0-7157-0489-3 Pbk : £3.80
(B77-08819)

330'.07'8 — Universities. Curriculum subjects: Economics. Teaching. Applications of computer systems. *Study examples: University of Notre Dame. Department of Economics*
Davisson, William I. Computer-assisted instruction in economic education : a case study / [by] William I. Davisson and Frank J. Bonello. — Notre Dame [Ind.] ; London : University of Notre Dame Press, 1976. — ix, 269p : ill, form ; 24cm.
ISBN 0-268-00715-2 : £7.50
(B77-15127)

330'.08 — Economics. *Essays*
Georgescu-Roegen, Nicholas. Energy and economic myths : institutional and analytical economic essays / [by] Nicholas Georgescu-Roegen. — New York ; Oxford [etc.] : Pergamon, [1977]. — xxviii,380p : ill ; 26cm. — (Pergamon international library)
Facsimile reprints. — This collection published in the United States: 1976. — Bibl. — Index.
ISBN 0-08-021027-9 : £8.85
ISBN 0-08-021056-2 Pbk : £5.00
(B77-09552)

Hicks, *Sir* **John Richard.** Economic perspectives : further essays on money and growth / by John Hicks. — Oxford : Clarendon Press, 1977. — xix,199p : ill ; 20cm.
Index.
ISBN 0-19-828407-1 : £5.00 : CIP rev.
(B77-09553)

Hutt, William Harold. Individual freedom : selected works of William H. Hutt / edited by Svetozar Pejovich and David Klingaman. — Westport, Conn. ; London : Greenwood Press, 1975. — vi,250p ; 22cm. — (Contributions in economics and economic history ; no.14)
Bibl.: p.241-243. — Index.
ISBN 0-8371-8283-2 : £12.95
(B77-17954)

330'.092'4 — Economics. Beveridge, William Henry, Baron Beveridge. *Great Britain. Biographies*
Harris, José. William Beveridge : a biography / [by] José Harris. — Oxford : Clarendon Press, 1977. — [8],488p,2 leaves of plates : ports ; 25cm.
Bibl.: p.477-479. — Index.
ISBN 0-19-822459-1 : £9.50 : CIP rev.
(B77-17334)

330'.092'4 — Economics. Jevons, William Stanley. *Documents*
Jevons, William Stanley. Papers and correspondence of William Stanley Jevons. — London [etc.] : Macmillan [for] the Royal Economic Society.
In 7 vols.
Vol.3 : Correspondence, 1863-1872 / edited by R.D. Collison Black. — 1977. — xxi,257p : ill ; 24cm.
ISBN 0-333-10253-3 : £10.00
(B77-22405)

Vol.4 : Correspondence, 1873-1878 / edited by R.D. Collison Black. — 1977. — xxv,306p : ill ; 25cm.
ISBN 0-333-19977-4 : £10.00
(B77-32454)

Vol.5 : Correspondence, 1879-1882 / edited by R.D. Collison Black. — 1977. — xix,202p ; 25cm.
Includes some letters in French.
ISBN 0-333-19978-2 : £10.00
(B77-33649)

Vol.6 : Lectures on political economy, 1875-1876 / edited by R.D. Collison Black. — 1977. — xi,140p : ill ; 24cm.
ISBN 0-333-10258-4 : £10.00
(B77-31729)

330'.092'4 — Economics. Smith, Adam, b.1723. *Correspondence*
Smith, Adam, *b.1723.* The correspondence of Adam Smith / edited by Ernest Campbell Mossner and Ian Simpson Ross. — Glasgow ed. — Oxford : Clarendon Press, 1977. — xxx, 441p ; 24cm.
Bibl. — Index.
ISBN 0-19-828185-4 : £15.00
(B77-27704)

330.1 — ECONOMICS. SYSTEMS AND THEORIES

330.1 — Economics. Liberalist theories
O'Neill, Gerard K. The high frontier : human colonies in space / by Gerard K. O'Neill. — London : Cape, 1977. — 288p : ill ; 23cm.
Also published: New York : Morrow, 1977. — Index.
ISBN 0-224-01406-4 : £5.95 : CIP rev.
(B77-07952)

Peacock, Alan. The credibility of liberal economics / [by] Alan Peacock. — London : Institute of Economic Affairs for the Wincott Foundation, 1977. — [1],29p ; 22cm. — (Institute of Economic Affairs. Occasional papers ; 50 ISSN 0073-909x) (Wincott memorial lectures ; 7)
'... delivered at the London School of Economics ... 9 December, 1976'.
ISBN 0-255-36092-4 Sd : £0.60
(B77-26846)

330.1 — Economics. Theories
Economics, an anti-text / edited by Francis Green and Petter Nore. — London [etc.] : Macmillan, 1977. — xii,215p : ill ; 23cm.
Bibl. — Index.
ISBN 0-333-21201-0 : £7.95
ISBN 0-333-21202-9 Pbk : £2.95
(B77-14091)

Hutchison, Terence Wilmot. Knowledge and ignorance in economics / [by] T.W. Hutchison. — Oxford : Blackwell, 1977. — ix,186p ; 23cm.
Index.
ISBN 0-631-17560-1 : £7.00 : CIP rev.
(B77-07114)

Levine, David P. Economic studies : contributions to the critique of economic theory / [by] David P. Levine. — London [etc.] : Routledge and Kegan Paul, 1977. — xiii,318p : ill ; 24cm.
Index.
ISBN 0-7100-8573-7 : £9.50
(B77-29997)

330.1 — Economics. Theories. *Essays*
Leontief, Wassily W. Essays in economics : theories and theorizing / [by] Wassily Leontief. — Oxford : Blackwell.
In 2 vols.
Vol.1. — 1977. — xii,252p : ill ; 24cm.
Originally published: New York : Oxford University Press, 1966. — Index.
ISBN 0-631-17830-9 : £8.00
(B77-14092)

330.1 — Economics. Theories, 1918. *Early works*
Douglas, Clifford Hugh. Economic democracy / by C.H. Douglas. — 5th (authorised) ed. ; with an introductory chapter by Geoffrey Dobbs. — Epsom ([The Old Priory, Priory Walk, Sudbury, Suffolk]) : Bloomfield Books, 1974. — 166p : 1 ill ; 19cm.
Previous ed.: London : Stanley Nott, 1934. — Index. — Includes: 'The delusion of super-production'. Originally published: in 'The English review', Dec. 1918.
ISBN 0-904656-00-4 : £2.20
(B77-24046)

330.1 — Economics. Theories, ca 1776-1946
Barber, William Joseph. A history of economic thought / [by] William J. Barber. — Harmondsworth [etc.] : Penguin, 1977. — 266p ; 18cm. — (A pelican original)
Originally published: 1967. — Index.
ISBN 0-14-020890-9 Pbk : £1.00
(B77-21724)

330.1 — Economics. Theories of Galbraith, John Kenneth
McGadzean, *Sir* **Frank Scott.** The economics of John Kenneth Galbraith : a study in fantasy / [by] Sir Frank McGadzean. — London (Wilfred St., S.W.1) : Centre for Policy Studies, 1977. — vii,51p ; 21cm.
ISBN 0-905880-00-5 Pbk : £1.50
(B77-18591)

330.1 — Economics. Theories of Hayek, Friedrich August. *Critical studies*
Essays on Hayek / edited by Fritz Machlup ; foreword by Milton Friedman ; [contributors] William F. Buckley, Jr ... [et al.]. — London [etc.] : Routledge and Kegan Paul, 1977. — xxiv,182p : port ; 23cm.
'... [delivered at] a special regional meeting of the Mont Pelerin Society, held from August 24 to 28, 1975, at Hillsdale College in Hillsdale, Michigan' - Notes from the editor. — Originally published: New York : New York University Press, 1976. — Bibl.: p.51-59. — List of works: p.177. — Index.
ISBN 0-7100-8561-3 : £4.25
(B77-13535)

330.1 — Economics. Theories of Walras, Leon
Morishima, Michio. Walras' economics : a pure theory of capital and money / [by] Michio Morishima. — Cambridge [etc.] : Cambridge University Press, 1977. — viii,212p : ill ; 22cm.
Index.
ISBN 0-521-21487-4 : £7.50
(B77-24750)

330.12 — Economic systems. *Comparative studies*
Holesovsky, Vaclav. Economic systems : analysis and comparison / [by] Vaclav Holesovsky. — New York ; London [etc.] : McGraw-Hill, 1977. — xiv,495p : ill ; 25cm.
Bibl. — Index.
ISBN 0-07-029557-3 : £11.95
(B77-23184)

Montias, John Michael. The structure of economic systems / [by] John Michael Montias. — New Haven ; London : Yale University Press, 1976. — xii,323p : ill ; 24cm.
Index.
ISBN 0-300-01833-9 : £13.20
(B77-08820)

Wiles, Peter John de la Fosse. Economic institutions compared / [by] P.J.D. Wiles. — Oxford : Blackwell, 1977. — xi,608p : ill ; 25cm.
Index.
ISBN 0-631-16990-3 : £10.00 : CIP rev.
(B77-05905)

330.12'2 — Capitalism
Davis, William, *b.1933.* It's no sin to be rich / [by] William Davis. — London : Osprey Publishing, 1976. — 254p ; 23cm.
Index.
ISBN 0-85045-278-3 : £3.95
(B77-00636)

330.12'2 — Capitalism. *Forecasts*
Heilbroner, Robert Louis. Business civilization in decline / [by] Robert L. Heilbroner. — Harmondsworth [etc.] : Penguin, 1977. — 103p ; 19cm. — (Pelican books)
Originally published: New York : Norton ; London : Boyars, 1976. — Index.
ISBN 0-14-022015-1 Pbk : £0.80
(B77-31026)

330.12'2'09 — Capitalism, 1400-1976
Braudel, Fernand. Afterthoughts on material civilization and capitalism / [by] Fernand Braudel ; translated [from the French] by Patricia M. Ranum. — Baltimore ; London : Johns Hopkins University Press, 1977. — xiii, 122p : ill, facsims ; 21cm. — (The Johns Hopkins symposia in comparative history)
ISBN 0-8018-1901-6 : £5.95
(B77-31730)

330.12'2'09033 — Capitalism. Theories, ca 1700-ca 1900
Hirschman, Albert Otto. The passions and the interests : political arguments for capitalism before its triumph / by Albert O. Hirschman. — Princeton ; Guildford : Princeton University Press, 1977. — x,153,[1]p : 1 ill ; 23cm.
Index.
ISBN 0-691-04214-4 : £8.10
ISBN 0-691-00357-2 Pbk : £2.40
(B77-15722)

330.12'2'0904 — Capitalism, ca 1900-1940
Schumpeter, Joseph Alois. Capitalism, socialism and democracy / [by] Joseph A. Schumpeter. — 5th ed. ; with a new introduction by Tom Bottomore. — London : Allen and Unwin, 1976. — xiv,437p ; 23cm.
Previous ed.: London : Allen and Unwin, 1954. — Index.
ISBN 0-04-335031-3 : £8.00
ISBN 0-04-5032-1 Pbk : £3.95
Primary classification 335'.009'04
(B77-08842)

330.12'2'091713 — Capitalism. *Western bloc countries*
Institute for the Study of Conflict. The survival of the 'capitalist system' : challenge to the pluralist societies of the West : report of a study group of the Institute for the Study of Conflict / [written] by Russell Lewis. — London : The Institute, 1977. — [2],56p ; 30cm. — (Institute for the Study of Conflict. Special reports)
Summary (sheet ([2]p.)) as insert.
ISBN 0-903366-53-3 Sd : £5.00
(B77-12892)

330.12'2'094 — Capitalism. *Europe, 1945-1976. Conference proceedings*
University Association for Contemporary European Studies. *Annual Conference, 7th, University of Sussex, 1977.* Government, business and labour in European capitalism : papers presented at the January 1977 Conference of the University Association for Contemporary European Studies / edited by Richard T. Griffiths. — London (77 New Bond St., W1Y 9DB) : Europotentials Press, 1977. — 229p : ill ; 23cm.
'... Seventh Annual Conference of the University Association for Contemporary European Studies (UACES) held at Sussex University ...' - Acknowledgements. — Index.
ISBN 0-906039-00-2 : £9.50 : CIP rev.
(B77-14093)

330.12'2'0944 — Capitalism. *France. Socialist viewpoints. Extracts from newspapers*
Bosquest, Michel. Capitalism in crisis and everyday life / [by] Michel Bosquet ; translated from the French by John Howe. — Hassocks : Harvester Press, 1977. — [7],199p ; 23cm. — (Marxist theory and contemporary capitalism)
Translation of: 'Critique du capitalisme quotidien'. Paris : Editions Galilée, 1973.
ISBN 0-901759-08-2 : £8.95 : CIP rev.
ISBN 0-85527-590-1 Pbk : £2.95
(B77-07115)

330.15'5 — Institutional economics. Theories of Ayres, Clarence Edwin. *Critical studies*
Science and ceremony : the institutional economics of C.E. Ayres / edited by William Patton Culbertson, Jr ; foreword by John Kenneth Galbraith. — Austin ; London : University of Texas Press, 1976. — xviii,210p : ill, port ; 24cm. — (The Dan Danciger publication series)
Bibl.: p.191-201. — Index.
ISBN 0-292-77523-7 : £12.00
(B77-06507)

330.15'5 — Welfare economics
Bowen, Howard R. Toward social economy / [by] Howard R. Bowen. — [1st ed. reprinted] ; with a foreword by C. Addison Hickman and an afterword by the author. — Carbondale [etc.] : Southern Illinois University Press ; London [etc.] : Feffer and Simons, 1977. — xiv, 354p : ill ; 22cm. — (Political & social economy)
Originally published: New York : Rinehart, 1948. — Index.
ISBN 0-8093-0813-4 : Unpriced
(B77-14585)

Nath, Shiv Kumar. A reappraisal of welfare economics / [by] S.K. Nath. — London [etc.] : Routledge and Kegan Paul [etc.], 1976. — viii, 247 : ill ; 23cm.
Originally published: 1969. — Bibl. — Index.
£5.95
(B77-02800)

Price, Catherine M. Welfare economics in theory and practice / [by] Catherine M. Price. — London [etc.] : Macmillan, 1977. — viii,175p : ill ; 23cm.
Bibl.: p.169-172. — Index.
ISBN 0-333-19122-6 : £7.95
ISBN 0-333-19838-7 Pbk : £3.95
Also classified at 330.9'41'085
(B77-17335)

330.15'6 — Economics. Theories of Keynes, John Maynard, Baron Keynes. *Critical studies*
Hutchison, Terence Wilmot. Keynes versus the 'Keynesians' - ? : an essay in the thinking of J.M. Keynes and the accuracy of its interpretation by his followers / [by] T.W. Hutchison. — London : Institute of Economic Affairs, 1977. — xii,83p ; 22cm. — (Hobart paperback ; no.11 ISSN 0309-1783)
Index.
ISBN 0-255-36101-7 Pbk : £2.00
(B77-24047)

Moggridge, Donald Edward. John Maynard Keynes / [by] D.E. Moggridge. — Harmondsworth [etc.] : Penguin, 1976. — xiii, 190p : ill ; 19cm. — (Penguin modern masters)
Originally published: as 'Keynes'. London : Fontana, 1976. — Bibl.: p.175-182. — Index.
ISBN 0-14-004319-5 Pbk : Unpriced
(B77-03412)

330.9 — ECONOMIC CONDITIONS
330.9 — Economic conditions. *Records of achievement*
Button, Henry George. The Guinness book of the business world / by Henry G. Button and Andrew P. Lampert. — Enfield : Guinness Superlatives, 1976. — 256p : ill(some col), facsims, ports ; 25cm.
Bibl.: p.188-190. — Index.
ISBN 0-900424-32-x : £6.50
(B77-00637)

330.9 — Economic conditions. Geographical aspects
Conkling, Edgar Clark. Man's economic environment / [by] Edgar C. Conkling, Maurice Yeates. — New York ; London [etc.] : McGraw-Hill, 1976. — xi,308p : ill, maps ; 25cm. — (McGraw-Hill series in geography)
Bibl.: p.287-294. — Index.
ISBN 0-07-012408-6 : £11.60
(B77-04605)

Lloyd, Peter E. Location in space : a theoretical approach to economic geography / [by] Peter E. Lloyd & Peter Dicken. — 2nd ed. — London [etc.] : Harper and Row, 1977. — xii, 474p : ill, maps ; 25cm.
Previous ed.: 1972. — Bibl.: p.450-464. — Index.
ISBN 0-06-318058-8 : £8.95
ISBN 0-06-318059-6 Pbk : £5.95
(B77-31027)

Paterson, John Harris. Land, work and resources : an introduction to economic geography / [by] J.H. Paterson. — 2nd ed. — London : Edward Arnold, 1976. — xiv,265p : ill, maps ; 23cm.
Previous ed.: 1972. — Bibl.: p.254-258. — Index.
ISBN 0-7131-5879-4 Pbk : £2.95
(B77-01199)

Thoman, Richard Samuel. The geography of economic activity. — 3rd ed. / [by] Richard S. Thoman, Peter B. Corbin. — New York ; London [etc.] : McGraw-Hill, 1974. — viii, 420p : ill(chiefly col), col maps ; 24cm. — (McGraw-Hill series in geography)
Col. maps on lining papers. — Previous ed.: / by Richard S. Thoman, Edgar C. Conkling, Maurice H. Yeates. 1968. — Bibl.: p.403-408. — Index.
ISBN 0-07-064207-9 : Unpriced
(B77-19248)

330.9 — Economic conditions. Geographical aspects. *Secondary school texts*
Robinson, Harry, *b.1915.* Economic geography / [by] H. Robinson. — 2nd ed. — Plymouth : Macdonald and Evans, 1976. — xiii,299p : ill, maps, plan ; 19cm. — (The M. & E. handbook series)
Previous ed.: 1968. — Lists of films. — Index.
ISBN 0-7121-0558-1 Pbk : £1.35
(B77-15723)

330.9 — Economic conditions, to ca 1970. *Secondary school texts*
Killingray, David. A world economy / by David Killingray. — London : Harrap, 1976. — [1], 32p : ill, maps ; 24cm. — (Harrap world history programme : set 14)
ISBN 0-245-52549-1 Sd : £0.60
(B77-07820)

330.9 — Economic development
Kindleberger, Charles Poor. Economic development. — 3rd ed. / [by] Charles P. Kindleberger, Bruce Herrick. — New York ; London [etc.] : McGraw-Hill, 1977. — xv, 397p : ill ; 25cm. — (Economics handbook series)
Previous ed.: / by Charles P. Kindleberger. 1965. — Bibl. — Index.
ISBN 0-07-034583-x : £11.95
(B77-21725)

330.9 — Economic development. *Marxist viewpoints*
Amin, Samir. [Le développement inégal. English]. Unequal development : an essay on the social formations of peripheral capitalism / by Samir Amin ; translated [from the French] by Brian Pearce. — Hassocks : Harvester Press, 1976. — 440p ; 21cm. — (Marxist theory and contemporary capitalism)
This translation also published: New York : Monthly Review Press, 1976. — Translation of: 'Le développement inégal'. Paris : Les Éditions de Minuit, 1973. — Bibl.: p.387-417. — Index.
ISBN 0-901759-46-5 : £10.50
(B77-07821)

330.9 — Economic development. Ecological aspects
Singh, Narindar. Economics and the crisis of ecology / [by] Narindar Singh. — Delhi [etc.] ; Oxford : Oxford University Press, 1976. — xiv, 154p ; 22cm.
Bibl.: p.151. — Index.
ISBN 0-19-560749-x : £4.75
(B77-26847)

330.9 — Economic development. Related to achievement motivation
McClelland, David Clarence. The achieving society / by David C. McClelland. — [1st ed. reprinted] ; with a new introduction. — New York : Irvington ; New York ; London [etc.] : Distributed by Wiley, 1976. — xv,512,A-G p : ill ; 24cm.
Originally published: Princeton : Van Nostrand, 1961. — Bibl.: p.439-449. — Index.
ISBN 0-470-01397-4 : £12.75
Also classified at 152.5'2
(B77-24751)

330.9 — Economic development. Role of governments & international organisations. *Conference proceedings*
International organization, national policies and economic development / editors Karl Brunner, Allan H. Meltzer. — Amsterdam [etc.] ; Oxford : North-Holland Publishing Co., 1977. — viii,240p : ill ; 24cm. — (Carnegie-Rochester conference series on public policy ; vol.6)
'This ... volume ... offered as a supplement to the Journal of Monetary Economics, contains papers presented at the April 1976 Conference' - Introduction to the Series. — Bibl.
ISBN 0-7204-0744-3 Pbk : £8.00
(B77-29222)

330.9 — Economic development. Social aspects
The sustainable society : implications for limited growth / edited by Dennis Clark Pirages. — New York ; London : Praeger, 1977. — xv, 342p : ill ; 24cm. — (Praeger special studies in US economic, social and political issues)
ISBN 0-275-23890-3 : £14.40
ISBN 0-275-64760-9 Pbk : £5.30
(B77-25422)

330.9 — Economic policies. *Conference proceedings*
British Association for the Advancement of Science. *Meeting, Section F (Economics), University of Lancaster, 1976.* Structure, system and economic policy : proceedings of Section F of the British Association for the Advancement of Science [annual meeting] held at the University of Lancaster, 1-8 September 1976 / edited by Wassily Leontief. — Cambridge [etc.] : Cambridge University Press, 1977. — xii,223p : ill, maps ; 24cm.
Bibl.
ISBN 0-521-21724-5 : £9.00
(B77-29998)

330.9 — Industrialised societies. Economic conditions. *Marxist viewpoints*
Šik, Ota. The third way : Marxist-Leninist theory and modern industrial society / [by] Ota Šik ; translated [from the German] by Marian Sling. — London : Wildwood House [etc.], 1976. — 431p ; 23cm.
Translation of: 'Der dritte Weg'. Hamburg : Hoffmann und Campe, 1972. — Bibl.: p.416-427. — Index.
ISBN 0-7045-0180-5 : £10.00
(B77-01200)

330.9 — Organisation for Economic Co-operation and Development countries. Economic conditions, 1960-1976. *Reports, surveys*
Towards full employment and price stability, a report to the OECD / by a group of independent experts, Paul McCracken ... [et al.]. — Paris : Organisation for Economic Co-operation and Development ; [London] : [H.M.S.O.], 1977. — 341p : ill ; 24cm.
Bibl.
Pbk : £7.80
ISBN 92-64-11644-3
(B77-20064)

330.9 — Regional economic conditions
Brown, Arthur Joseph. Regional economic problems : comparative experiences of some market economies / by A.J. Brown and E.M. Burrows. — London : Allen and Unwin, 1977. — 3-209p : maps ; 23cm. — (Studies in economics ; 13)
Bibl.: p.200-250. — Index.
ISBN 0-04-339010-2 : £7.50
ISBN 0-04-339011-0 Pbk : £3.50
(B77-29223)

330.9'01 — Prehistoric man. Economic conditions. Mathematical models. *Sources of data: Primitive societies*
Jochim, Michael A. Hunter-gatherer subsistence and settlement : a predictive model / [by] Michael A. Jochim. — New York [etc.] ; London : Academic Press, 1976. — xvii,206p : ill, maps ; 24cm. — (Studies in archeology)
Bibl.: p.189-202. — Index.
ISBN 0-12-385450-4 : £7.85
(B77-00068)

330.9'03 — Economic conditions. Influence of economic theories, 1750-1976
Galbraith, John Kenneth. The age of uncertainty / [by] John Kenneth Galbraith. — London : British Broadcasting Corporation : Deutsch, 1977. — 366p : ill(some col), facsims, ports(some col) ; 26cm.
Index.
ISBN 0-563-12887-9 : £7.25
ISBN 0-233-96847-4 (Deutsch) : £7.25
(B77-13536)

330.9'04 — Economic conditions. Political aspects, 1900-1975. *Readings*
The end of the Keynesian era : essays on the disintegration of the Keynesian political economy / edited by Robert Skidelsky ; contributors Robert Skidelsky ... [et al.]. — London [etc.] : Macmillan, 1977. — xiv,114p ; 23cm.
'These essays appeared in the "Spectator" between May 1976 and January 1977, most of them in shortened form' - Preface. — Index.
ISBN 0-333-21298-3 : £6.95 : CIP rev.
ISBN 0-333-21306-8 Pbk : £2.95
(B77-21726)

330.9'041 — Economic conditions, 1914-1918
Hardach, Gerd. The First World War, 1914-1918 / [by] Gerd Hardach ; [translated from the German by Peter and Betty Ross]. — London : Allen Lane, 1977. — xvi,328p ; 23cm. — (History of the world economy in the twentieth century ; 2)
Translation of: 'Der erste Weltkrieg, 1914-1918'. München : Deutscher Taschenbuch-Verlag, 1973. — Bibl.: p.295-323. — Index.
ISBN 0-7139-1024-0 : £7.00
(B77-22406)

330.9'04'2 — Economic conditions, 1919-1929
Aldcroft, Derek Howard. From Versailles to Wall Street, 1919-1929 / [by] Derek H. Aldcroft. — London : Allen Lane, 1977. — xi, 372p : map ; 23cm. — (History of the world economy in the twentieth century ; 3)
Bibl.: p.314-359. — Index.
ISBN 0-7139-1023-2 : £7.00
(B77-21727)

330.9'04'7 — Economic conditions. *Reviews of research*
Royal Economic Society. Surveys of applied economics / the Royal Economic Society, the Social Science Research Council. — London : Macmillan.
Vol.2 : Surveys 1-5. — 1977. — vi,282p : ill ; 24cm.
Bibl.
ISBN 0-333-14762-6 : £10.00
(B77-11625)

330.9'04'7 — Economic conditions. *Statistics*
World tables : from the data files of the World Bank. — Baltimore ; London : Johns Hopkins University Press for the World Bank.
1976. — 1976. — vii,552p ; 29cm.
Index.
ISBN 0-8018-1886-9 : £18.00
ISBN 0-8018-1898-2 Pbk : £6.75
(B77-12893)

330.9'04'7 — Economic conditions. *Yearbooks*
The '**Financial** times' international business year book. — London (Bracken House, Cannon St., EC4P 4BY) : Financial Times Limited.
1977-78 / managing editor Pamela Jenkins. — 1977. — 2-767p : ill ; 22cm.
Index.
ISBN 0-900671-80-7 : £12.50
ISSN 0309-7528
(B77-32455)

330.9'04'7 — Economic development. *Liberal Party viewpoints*
Liberal Party. World development / [Liberal Party]. — London : Liberal Publication Department, [1977]. — [1],8p ; 30cm. — (Liberal Party. Study papers ; no.4 ISSN 0308-9657)
ISBN 0-900520-56-6 Sd : £0.20
(B77-14094)

330.9'04'7 — Economic policies. *Conference proceedings*
Optimal policies, control theory and technology exports / editors Karl Brunner, Allan H. Meltzer. — Amsterdam [etc.] ; Oxford : North-Holland Publishing Co., 1977. — viii, 238p : ill ; 24cm. — (Carnegie-Rochester conference series on public policy ; vol.7)
'... contains papers presented at the November 1976 conference' - Introduction to the series. — Bibl.
ISBN 0-444-85027-9 Pbk : £8.24
(B77-33650)

330.9'13 — Economic activity. Effects of climate. *Tropical regions*
Kamarck, Andrew Martin. The tropics and economic development : a provocative inquiry into the poverty of nations / [by] Andrew M. Kamarck ; with a foreword by Paul Streeten. — Baltimore ; London : Johns Hopkins University Press for the World Bank, 1976. — xiv,113p : maps ; 24cm.
Bibl.: p.93-102. — Index.
ISBN 0-8018-1891-5 : £6.00
ISBN 0-8018-1903-2 Pbk : £2.40
(B77-14095)

330.9'171'241 — Commonwealth developing countries. Economic development. *Conference proceedings*
Commonwealth and Development *(Conference), Windsor, 1976.* The Commonwealth and Development : the report of the Conference jointly sponsored by ODI and St Catharine's, Cumberland Lodge, at Cumberland Lodge, 13-15 February 1976. — London : Overseas Development Institute, 1976. — [3],59p ; 21cm.

'The conference explored three main themes under the rubric of "The Commonwealth and Development" ...' - Report of the Conference.
ISBN 0-85003-058-7 Sd : £1.50
(B77-00069)

330.9'172'2 — Developed countries. Economic conditions. Related to size
Kohr, Leopold. The overdeveloped nations : the diseconomies of scale / [by] Leopold Kohr. — Swansea : C. Davies, 1977. — [8],x,185p : ill ; 22cm.
Translation of: 'Die Überentwickelten, oder, Die Gefahr der Grösse'. Düsseldorf : EconVerlag, 1962. — Bibl.: p.175-178. — Index.
ISBN 0-7154-0343-5 : £6.75
(B77-20065)

330.9'172'4 — Developing countries. Economic conditions. Effects of technology transfer from developed countries
Stewart, Frances. Technology and underdevelopment / [by] Frances Stewart. — London [etc.] : Macmillan, 1977. — xiv,303p : ill ; 23cm.
Bibl.: p.280-294. — Index.
ISBN 0-333-19510-8 : £12.00
(B77-26151)

330.9'172'4 — Developing countries. Economic conditions. Theories
Todaro, Michael P. Economics for a developing world : an introduction to principles, problems and policies for development / [by] Michael P. Todaro. — London : Longman, 1977. — xxiii, 444p : ill ; 25cm.
Bibl. — Index.
ISBN 0-582-64200-0 : £7.00
ISBN 0-582-64199-3 Pbk : £3.50
(B77-15724)

330.9'172'4 — Developing countries. Economic development
Todaro, Michael P. Economic development in the Third World : an introduction to problems and policies in a global perspective / [by] Michael P. Todaro. — London [etc.] : Longman, 1977. — xxvi,445p : ill ; 26cm.
Text, ill, on lining papers. — Bibl. — Index.
ISBN 0-582-44628-7 : £9.95
(B77-26848)

330.9'172'4 — Developing countries. Economic development. Projects. Evaluation. Applications of shadow prices
Squire, Lyn. Economic analysis of projects / [by] Lyn Squire, Herman G. van der Tak. — Baltimore ; London : Johns Hopkins University Press for the World Bank, [1976]. — xi,153p ; 24cm. — (International Bank for Reconstruction and Development. World Bank research publications)
Published in the United States: 1975. — Bibl.: p.151-153.
ISBN 0-8018-1817-6 : £8.00
ISBN 0-8018-1818-4 Pbk : £3.20
(B77-07116)

330.9'172'4 — Developing countries. Economic development. Research by Institute of Development Studies, 1966-1976. *Reports, surveys*
Institute of Development Studies. Development studies, 1966-1976 : a select list of the writings in Third World development / by members of the Institute of Development Studies at the University of Sussex. — Revised ed. / by Claire M. Lambert. — Brighton : I.D.S., 1976. — [1] p,ii leaves,88p ; 21cm.
Index.
ISBN 0-903354-16-0 Sd : Unpriced
(B77-17336)

330.9'172'4 — Developing countries. Economic development. Research organisations: Institute of Development Studies, to 1976. *Reports, surveys*
Institute of Development Studies. 1966-76, ten year review and annual report 1976 / Institute of Development Studies. — Brighton : The Institute, 1977. — [4],110p,[4]p of plates : ill, map ; 21cm.
English text, English, French and Spanish preface.
ISBN 0-903354-42-x Pbk : Unpriced
(B77-17955)

330.9'172'4 — Developing countries. Economic development. Social aspects. *Conference proceedings*
Recession or Revival, Co-operation to Restructure the World Economy *(Conference), London, 1976.* Third World, change or chaos? : documents from the Conference "Recession or Revival" called by Liberation and the World Development Movement at TUC Congress House, London, in March 1976 ; and, The speech of President Baumedienne of Algeria on the New International Economic Order at the United Nations in April, 1974 / [edited by Stan Newens]. — Nottingham : Bertrand Russell Peace Foundation for Spokesman Books, 1977. — 96p ; 19cm.
'... conference ... entitled "Recession or Revival, Co-operation to Restructure the World Economy"' - Introduction.
ISBN 0-85124-178-6 Pbk : £0.95
(B77-28430)

330.9'172'4 — Developing countries. Economic policies. *Essays*
Balassa, Bela. Policy reform in developing countries / by Bela Balassa. — Oxford [etc.] : Pergamon, 1977. — ix,175p ; 25cm. — (Pergamon international library)
Index.
ISBN 0-08-021477-0 : Unpriced
ISBN 0-08-021478-9 Pbk : £5.95
(B77-33095)

330.9'173'2 — Urban regions. Economic aspects. Theories. *State-of-the-art reviews*
Richardson, Harry Ward. The new urban economics : and alternatives / [by] H.W. Richardson. — London : Pion, 1977. — [9], 266p : ill ; 24cm. — (Research in planning and design)
Bibl.: p.245-259. — Index.
ISBN 0-85086-058-x : £8.50
(B77-16757)

330.9'17'4927 — Arab countries. Economic conditions. *Periodicals*
Arab business report. — London (20 Foubert's Place, Regent St., W1V 1HH) : Gt Arab Publishing Co.
No.1- ; 21 May 1976-. — [1976]-. — 30cm.
Fortnightly. — 12p. in issue no.1.
Sd : £50.00 yearly
ISSN 0309-7080
(B77-13537)

330.9'17'671 — Islamic countries. Economic conditions. Influence of Islam
Rodinson, Maxime. Islam and capitalism / [by] Maxime Rodinson ; translated [from the French] by Brian Pearce. — Harmondsworth [etc.] : Penguin, 1977. — xviii,306p ; 18cm. — (Pelican books)
This translation originally published: London : Allen Lane, 1974. — Translation of: 'Islam et capitalisme'. Paris : Editions du Seuil, 1966. — Index.
ISBN 0-14-021769-x Pbk : £1.20
(B77-25423)

330.9'181'2 — Western world. Economic conditions, to 1973
Clough, Shepard Bancroft. European economic history : the economic development of western civilization. — 3rd ed. / [by] Shepard B. Clough, Richard T. Rapp. — New York ; London [etc.] : McGraw-Hill, [1976]. — xix, 571p : ill, maps ; 24cm.
This ed. published in the United States: 1975. — Previous ed.: / by Shepard B. Clough. 1968. — Bibl.: p.527-551. — Index.
ISBN 0-07-011393-9 : £11.30
(B77-01201)

330.9'181'2 — Western world. Economic conditions, to 1976
Roll, *Sir* **Eric.** Economics, government and business / by Sir Eric Roll. — London : Athlone Press, 1976. — 27p ; 22cm. — (Stamp memorial lecture ; 1976 ISSN 0307-8167)
'... delivered before the University of London on 11 November 1976'.
ISBN 0-485-16431-0 Sd : £1.00
(B77-04606)

330.9'361'01 — Human settlements. Economic aspects. *Great Britain, B.C.3000-B.C.1000. Conference proceedings*
Settlement and economy in the third and second millenia BC : papers delivered at a conference organised by the Department of Adult Education, University of Newcastle upon Tyne, January 1976 / edited by Colin Burgess and Roger Miket ; contributors John Barrett ... [et al.]. — Oxford : British Archaeological Reports, 1976. — [13],iii,331p,fold plate : ill, maps, plans ; 30cm. — (British archaeological reports ; 33 ISSN 0306-1205)
Bibl.
ISBN 0-904531-52-x Pbk : £5.90
(B77-22407)

330.9'4 — Europe. Economic conditions, 500-
The **Cambridge** economic history of Europe. — Cambridge [etc.] : Cambridge University Press.
In 8 vols.
Vol.5 : The economic organization of early modern Europe / edited by E.E. Rich and C.H. Wilson. — 1977. — xi,749p : ill, maps ; 24cm.
Bibl.: p.623-680. — Index.
ISBN 0-521-08710-4 : £18.50
(B77-28431)

330.9'4'01 — Europe. Economic conditions, 500-1500
The **Middle** Ages / editor Carlo M. Cipolla. — Hassocks : Harvester Press [etc.], 1976. — 389p : maps, plans ; 23cm. — (The Fontana economic history of Europe ; vol.1)
Originally published: London : Fontana, 1972. — Bibl. — Index.
ISBN 0-85527-159-0 : £8.00
(B77-07117)

330.9'4'01 — Europe. Economic development, 500-1500
Gimpel, Jean. The medieval machine : the industrial revolution of the Middle Ages / [by] Jean Gimpel. — London : Gollancz, 1977. — xiii,274p : ill, facsims, maps, plan ; 24cm.
Originally published: in French translation as 'La révolution industrielle du Moyen Age'. Paris : Editions du Seuil, 1975. — Index.
ISBN 0-575-02135-7 : £7.50
(B77-11626)

330.9'4'02 — Europe. Economic conditions, 1500-1750
The **sixteenth** and seventeenth centuries / editor Carlo M. Cipolla. — Hassocks : Harvester Press [etc.], 1977. — 640p : 1 ill, maps ; 23cm. — (The Fontana economic history of Europe ; 2)
Originally published: London : Fontana, 1974. — Bibl. — Index.
ISBN 0-85527-175-2 : £10.50
(B77-24051)

330.9'4'021 — Europe. Economic conditions, 1450-1640
Wallerstein, Immanuel. The modern world-system : capitalist agriculture and the origins of the European world-economy in the sixteenth century / [by] Immanuel Wallerstein. — New York [etc] ; London : Academic Press, [1976]. — xv,410p : ill ; 24cm. — (Studies in social discontinuity)
Published in the United States: 1974. — Bibl.: p.359-386. — Index.
ISBN 0-12-785920-9 : £10.70
ISBN 0-12-785921-7 Pbk : £3.00
(B77-02086)

330.9'4'0252 — Europe. Economic conditions, 1600-1750
De Vries, Jan, *b.1943.* Economy of Europe in an age of crisis, 1600-1750 / [by] Jan de Vries. — Cambridge [etc.] : Cambridge University Press, 1976. — xi,284p : ill, maps ; 21cm.
Index.
ISBN 0-521-21123-9 : £8.00
ISBN 0-521-29050-3 Pbk : £2.95
(B77-00070)

330.9'4'028 — European countries. Economic development, 1850-1914
Milward, Alan Steele. The development of the economies of continental Europe, 1850-1914 / by Alan S. Milward and S.B. Saul. — London : Allen and Unwin, 1977. — 3-555p : 1 ill, maps ; 22cm.
Bibl. — Index.
ISBN 0-04-330277-7 : £12.50
ISBN 0-04-330278-5 Pbk : £6.95
(B77-26849)

330.9'4'05 — Europe. Economic conditions, 1913-1970
The **twentieth** century / editor Carlo M. Cipolla. — Hassocks : Harvester Press [etc.]. — (The Fontana economic history of Europe ; vol.5)
In 2 vols. — This collection originally published: London : Fontana, 1976.
1. — 1977. — xi,402p : ill, maps ; 23cm.
Bibl. — Contents: Population in Europe, 1920-1970 / by Milos Macura - The structure of demand, 1920-1970 / by A.S. Deaton - The labour force and labour problems, 1920-1970 / by Walter Galenson - Management, 1920-1970 / by Giorgio Pellicelli - The sources of energy, 1920-1970 / by Georges Brondel - The social relations of science and technology, 1914-1939 / by Roy and Kay MacLeod - The Keynesian revolution, 1920-1970 / by Robert Campbell.
ISBN 0-85527-185-x : £9.50
(B77-24753)

2. — 1977. — [6]p,p403-810 : ill ; 23cm.
Bibl. — Index. — Contents: The changing role of agriculture, 1920-1970 / by Hermann Priebe - Economic policy and performance in Europe, 1913-1970 / by Angus Maddison - International trade and capital movements, 1920-1970 / by Carlo Zacchia - The trial of managed money : currency, credit and prices, 1920-1970 / by Fred Hirchand, Peter Oppenheimer - National economic planning and policies in twentieth century Europe, 1920-1970 / by Benjamin Ward - Economy, society and environment, 1920-1970 / by Max Nicholson.
ISBN 0-85527-809-9 : £9.50
(B77-24754)

The **twentieth** century / editor Carlo M. Cipolla. — [London] : Fontana. — (The Fontana economic history of Europe ; 5)
In 2 vols.
Part 1. — 1976. — xi,402p : ill, maps ; 18cm.
Originally published: as 7 separate pamphlets, 1974. — Bibl. — Contents: Population in Europe, 1920-1970 / by Miloš Macura - The structure of demand, 1920-1970 / by A.S. Deaton - The labour force and labour problems, 1920-1970 / by Walter Galenson - Management, 1920-1970 / by Giorgio Pellicelli - The sources of energy, 1920-1970 / by Georges Brondel - The social relations of science and technology, 1914-1939 / by Roy and Kay MacLeod - The Keynesian revolution, 1920-1970 / by Robert Campbell.
ISBN 0-00-634228-0 Pbk : £1.95
(B77-01202)

Part 2. — 1976. — [6]p,p403-810 : ill ; 18cm.
Originally published: as 6 separate pamphlets, 1974-1976. — Bibl. — Index. — Contents: The changing role of agriculture, 1920-1970 / by Hermann Priebe - Economic policy and performance in Europe, 1913-1970 / by Angus Maddison - International trade and capital movements, 1920-1970 / by Carlo Zacchia - The trial of managed money : currency, credit and prices, 1920-1970 / by Peter Oppenheimer - National economic planning and policies in twentieth century Europe, 1920-1970 / by Benjamin Ward - Economy, society and environment, 1920-1970 / by Max Nicholson.
ISBN 0-00-634260-4 Pbk : £1.95
(B77-01203)

330.9'4'05 — Europe. Economic conditions, 1914-1970
Aldcroft, Derek Howard. The European economy, 1914-1970 / [by] Derek H. Aldcroft. — London : Croom Helm, 1978. — 251p ; 23cm.
Originally published: New York : St Martin's Press, 1977. — Bibl.: p.232-242. — Index.
ISBN 0-85664-380-7 : £6.95 : CIP rev.
ISBN 0-85664-379-3 Pbk : £3.50
(B77-24052)

Contemporary economies / editor Carlo M. Cipolla. — Hassocks : Harvester Press [etc.]. — (The Fontana economic history of Europe ; vol.6)
In 2 vols.
1. — 1977. — vii,376p : ill, maps ; 23cm.
This collection originally published: London : Fontana, 1976. — Bibl. — Contents: Benelux, 1920-1970 / by Johan de Vries - France, 1920-1970 / by Claude Fohlen - Great Britain, 1920-1970 / by A.J. Youngson - Germany, 1914-1970 / by Karl Hardach - Italy, 1920-1970 / by Sergio Ricossa - Europe in the world economy, 1920-1970 / by John Pinder.
ISBN 0-85527-155-8 : £9.00
(B77-26152)

2. — 1977. — [6]p,p377-779 : ill ; 23cm.
This collection originally published: London : Fontana, 1976. — Bibl. — Index. — Contents: Scandinavia, 1914-1970 / by Lennart Jörberg and Olle Krantz - Spain, 1914-1970 / by Josep Fontana and Jordi Nadal - Switzerland, 1920-1970 / by Hansjörg Siegenthaler - Russia and Eastern Europe, 1920-1970 / by Alfred Zauberman - Statistical appendix / by B.R. Mitchell.
ISBN 0-85527-165-5 : £9.50
(B77-26153)

Contemporary economies / editor Carlo M. Cipolla. — [London] : Fontana. — (The Fontana economic history of Europe ; 6)
In 2 vols.
Part 1. — 1976. — vii,376p : ill, maps ; 18cm.
Originally published: as 6 separate pamphlets, 1972-1976. — Bibl. — Contents: Benelux, 1920-1970 / by Johan de Vries - France, 1920-1970 / by Claude Fohlen - Great Britain, 1920-1970 / by A.J. Youngson - Germany, 1914-1970 / by Karl Hardach - Italy, 1920-1970 / by Sergio Ricossa - Europe in the world economy, 1920-1970 / by John Pinder.
ISBN 0-00-634261-2 Pbk : £1.95
(B77-01204)

Part 2. — 1976. — [6]p,p377-779 : ill ; 18cm.
Originally published: as 5 separate pamphlets, 1974-1976. — Bibl. — Index. — Contents: Scandinavia, 1914-1970 / by Lennart Jörberg and Olle Krantz - Spain, 1914-1970 / by Josep Fontana and Jordi Nadal - Switzerland, 1920-1970 / by Hansjörg Siegenthaler - Russia and Eastern Europe, 1920-1970 / by Alfred Zauberman - Contemporary economies, statistical appendix / by B.R. Mitchell.
ISBN 0-00-634577-8 Pbk : £1.95
(B77-01205)

330.9'4'055 — Europe. Economic conditions, 1945-1976
European economic issues : agriculture, economic security, industrial democracy, the OECD / [by] John S. Marsh ... [et al.]. — New York ; London : Praeger for the Atlantic Institute for International Affairs, 1977. — xv,267p ; 25cm. — (Atlantic Institute for International Affairs. Atlantic Institute studies ; 3) (Praeger special studies in international economics and development)
ISBN 0-275-24410-5 : £13.40
(B77-32456)

330.9'4'055 — European Community countries. Regional economic conditions
Clout, Hugh Donald. The regional problem in Western Europe / [by] Hugh Clout. — Cambridge [etc.] : Cambridge University Press, 1976. — [4],59p : ill, maps ; 26cm. — (Cambridge topics in geography series)
Bibl.: p.58. — Index.
ISBN 0-521-20909-9 : £3.30
ISBN 0-521-09997-8 Pbk : £1.60
(B77-02801)

330.9'41'074 — Great Britain. Economic policies, 1815-1830
Hilton, Boyd. Corn, cash, commerce : the economic policies of the Tory governments, 1815-1830 / by Boyd Hilton. — Oxford [etc.] : Oxford University Press, 1977. — xii,338p ; 23cm. — (Oxford historical monographs)
Bibl.: p.315-326. — Index.
ISBN 0-19-821864-8 : £8.50 : CIP rev.
(B77-17956)

330.9'41'074 — Great Britain. Economic policies, 1819-1823. *Sources of data: 'Parliamentary debates'*
Gordon, Barry. Political economy in Parliament, 1819-1823 / [by] Barry Gordon. — London [etc.] : Macmillan, 1976. — x,246p ; 23cm.
Index.
ISBN 0-333-15571-8 : £10.00
(B77-10206)

330.9'41'081 — Great Britain. Economic conditions. Compared with economic conditions in United States, 1850-1939
Holmes, Graeme Molyneux. Britain and America : a comparative economic history, 1850-1939 / [by] Graeme M. Holmes. — Newton Abbot [etc.] : David and Charles [etc.], 1976. — 224p ; 23cm.
Bibl.: p.208-220. — Index.
ISBN 0-7153-7256-4 : £5.95
Also classified at 330.9'73'08
(B77-05241)

330.9'41'083 — Great Britain. Economic conditions, 1928. *Liberal Party viewpoints. Early works*
Liberal Industrial Inquiry. Britain's industrial future : being the report of the Liberal Industrial Inquiry of 1928. — [1st ed. reprinted] ; with a foreword by David Steel. — London [etc.] : E. Benn, 1977. — xxiv,503p, fold plate : 1 ill ; 23cm.
'... formal titles were academic ; "The Yellow Book" is the name by which it will always be known' - Foreword. — Facsimile reprint of: 1st ed. 1928. — Index.
ISBN 0-510-02300-2 : £7.00
ISBN 0-510-02301-0 Pbk : Unpriced
(B77-14096)

330.9'41'085 — Great Britain. Economic conditions, 1945-1975
Pollard, Sidney. The British economic miracle : paper given to a joint meeting of the Loughborough Branch of the Historical Association and the East Midlands Branch of the Economic [i.e. Economics] Association on 6 November, 1975 / by Sidney Pollard. — London (Room 340, Hamilton House, Mabledon Place, WC1H 9BH) : Economics Association, 1976. — [2],19p ; 21cm.
Sd : £0.45
(B77-16758)

330.9'41'085 — Great Britain. Economic conditions, 1945-1976
The **UK** space : resources, environment and the future / edited by J.W. House. — 2nd ed. — London : Weidenfeld and Nicolson, 1977. — xxiii,528p : maps, plan ; 24cm.
Previous ed.: 1973. — Bibl. — Index.
ISBN 0-297-77356-9 : £7.95
ISBN 0-297-77357-7 Pbk : £4.25
(B77-29224)

330.9'41'085 — Great Britain. Economic conditions. Organisations: Institute of Economic Affairs, 1957-1977
Harris, Ralph, *b.1924.* Not from benevolence- : 20 years of economic dissent / [by] Ralph Harris, Arthur Seldon. — London : Institute of Economic Affairs, 1977. — xv,159p ; 22cm. — (Hobart paperback ; no.10 ISSN 0309-1783)
ISBN 0-255-36090-8 Pbk : £2.00
(B77-08821)

330.9'41'085 — Great Britain. Economic policies, 1945-1976. Social aspects
Price, Catherine M. Welfare economics in theory and practice / [by] Catherine M. Price. — London [etc.] : Macmillan, 1977. — viii,175p : ill ; 23cm.
Bibl.: p.169-172. — Index.
ISBN 0-333-19122-6 : £7.95
ISBN 0-333-19838-7 Pbk : £3.95
Primary classification 330.15'5
(B77-17335)

330.9'41'0856 — Great Britain. Economic policies, 1964-1976
Stewart, Michael, *b.1933.* The Jekyll and Hyde years : politics and economic policy since 1964 / [by] Michael Stewart. — London : Dent [etc.], 1977. — vii,272p ; 24cm.
Bibl.: p.248-258. — Index.
ISBN 0-460-12005-0 : £8.50 : CIP rev.
(B77-04607)

330.9'41'0857 — Ethnic minorities. Economic conditions. *Great Britain. Reports, surveys*
Community Relations Commission. CRC evidence to the Royal Commission on the Distribution of Income & Wealth / Community Relations Commission. — London : [The Commission], [1976]. — [1],17p ; 30cm.
Bibl.: p.17.
ISBN 0-902355-71-6 Sd : Unpriced
(B77-12342)

330.9'41'0857 — Great Britain. Economic conditions
The **economic** system in the UK / edited by Derek Morris. — Oxford [etc.] : Oxford University Press, 1977. — xiii,490p : ill ; 24cm.

Bibl. — Index.
ISBN 0-19-877077-4 : £10.00
ISBN 0-19-877078-2 Pbk : £4.95
(B77-12894)

330.9'41'0857 — Great Britain. Economic conditions. *Case studies*
Case studies in macroeconomics / edited by Peter Maunder ; [contributors] John Day ... [et al.]. — London [etc.] : Heinemann Educational [for] the Economics Association, 1977. — [5],86p : ill ; 20cm. — (Case studies in economic analysis ; 5)
Bibl.: p.34-35.
ISBN 0-435-84473-3 Pbk : £1.30
(B77-21728)

Case studies in macroeconomics / edited by Peter Maunder ; [contributors] John Day ... [et al.]. — London [etc.] : Heinemann Educational [for] the Economics Association. — (Case studies in economic analysis ; 5)
[Teacher's guide]. — 1977. — [5],138p : ill ; 20cm.
Bibl.
ISBN 0-435-84474-1 Pbk : £2.25
(B77-21729)

330.9'41'0857 — Great Britain. Economic conditions. *Essays. Serials*
New contributions to economic statistics / Central Statistical Office. — London : H.M.S.O.
8th series : reprinted from 'Economic trends', January 1974-February 1975. — 1977. — iii, 146p : ill ; 28cm. — (Studies in official statistics ; no.28)
ISBN 0-11-630149-x Pbk : £4.75
(B77-11627)

330.9'41'0857 — Great Britain. Economic conditions. *Reports, surveys*
National Institute of Economic and Social Research. The United Kingdom economy / National Institute of Economic and Social Research ; contributors R.I.G. Allen ... [et al.]. — 2nd ed. — London : Heinemann Educational, 1976. — ix,132p ; 20cm. — (Studies in the British economy ; [26])
A report commissioned by the Commission of the European Communities following the accession of the United Kingdom to the Community in 1973. — Previous ed.: s.l. : Commission of the European Communities, 1975. — Bibl.: p.121-132.
ISBN 0-435-84567-5 Pbk : £1.25
(B77-03985)

University of Cambridge. *Department of Applied Economics.* A programme for growth / University of Cambridge, Department of Applied Economics. — [London] : Chapman and Hall.
12 : Structural change in the British economy, 1948-1968. — 1974. — xii,169p ; 28cm.
Bibl.: p.163-169.
ISBN 0-412-12600-1 Pbk : £3.90
(B77-18592)

330.9'41'0857 — Great Britain. Economic conditions. *Trades Union Congress viewpoints. Serials*
Economic review / Trades Union Congress. — London : T.U.C.
1977. — 1977. — 94,[1]p ; 21cm.
ISBN 0-900878-51-7 Sd : £0.40
(B77-14586)

330.9'41'0857 — Great Britain. Economic conditions. Effects of exploitation of petroleum deposits in North Sea. *Forecasts for 1977-1985*
Robinson, Colin, *b.1932.* North Sea oil and the British economy, 1977-1985 / [by] Colin Robinson and Jon Morgan. — London (42 Colebrooke Row, N1 8AF) : Staniland Hall Associates Ltd, 1977. — viii,82p,fold plate : ill, col map ; 21x30cm. — (Economic, industrial and market forecasts)
Sp : £45.00
(B77-26850)

330.9'41'0857 — Great Britain. Economic conditions. Mathematical models
Economic structure and policy : with applications to the British economy / editor Terence S. Barker. — London : Chapman and Hall [etc.] for the Department of Applied Economics, University of Cambridge, 1976. — xix,421p : ill ; 24cm. — (Cambridge studies in applied econometrics ; 2)
Bibl.: p.404-412. — Index.
ISBN 0-412-14390-9 : £11.00
(B77-03413)

330.9'41'0857 — Great Britain. Economic conditions. Related to economic conditions in South Africa. *Anti-apartheid viewpoints*
Good, Dorcas. South Africa, the crisis in Britain and the apartheid economy / [by] Dorcas Good & Michael Williams. — London : Anti-Apartheid Movement, 1976. — [2],23p : 1 ill ; 30cm. — (Foreign investment in South Africa ; no.1 ISSN 0309-0752)
Bibl.: p.23.
ISBN 0-900065-00-1 Sd : £0.50
Primary classification 330.9'68'06
(B77-05244)

330.9'41'0857 — Great Britain. Economic conditions. Theories
Goyder, George. The end of economic man / by George Goyder. — Wellingborough (Wollaston, Wellingborough, Northants. NN9 7RL) : Scott Bader Commonwealth Ltd, 1977. — 28,[1]p ; 21cm. — (Scott Bader Commonwealth. Monographs ; no.7) (Ernest Bader common ownership lecture ; 1976)
ISBN 0-9505684-0-6 Sd : Unpriced
(B77-14587)

330.9'41'0857 — Great Britain. Economic development. *Forecasts for 1977-1980*
Budd, Alan. Economic outlook, 1977-1980 / by Alan Budd and Terry Burns ; [for] London Business School, Centre for Economic Forecasting. — London (Sussex Place, Regent's Park, NW1 4SA) : London Graduate School of Business Studies, 1977. — [2],60,[31]leaves : ill, facsim ; 31cm.
ISBN 0-902583-04-2 Ls : £2.50
(B77-11100)

330.9'41'0857 — Great Britain. Economic policies. *Confederation of British Industry viewpoints*
Confederation of British Industry. The road to recovery / [Confederation of British Industry]. — London : C.B.I., 1976. — 72p : ill ; 30cm.
ISBN 0-85201-123-7 Pbk : £3.50
(B77-01206)

Confederation of British Industry. The road to recovery, [a report] for presentation to the council of the CBI, 20 October 1976 / [Confederation of British Industry]. — [London] : C.B.I., [1976]. — 142p in various pagings : ill ; 30cm.
Cover title.
ISBN 0-85201-124-5 Pbk : Unpriced
(B77-01207)

330.9'41'0857 — Great Britain. Economic policies. *Fabian viewpoints*
Bosanquet, Nicholas. Economic strategy : a new social contract / [by] Nicholas Bosanquet. — London : Fabian Society, 1977. — [2],44p ; 22cm. — (Fabian research series ; 333 ISSN 0305-3555)
ISBN 0-7163-1333-2 Sd : £0.75
(B77-32457)

330.9'41'0857 — Great Britain. Economic policies. *Liberal Party viewpoints*
Martin-Kaye, Niel. Democratic enterprise / [by] Niel Martin-Kaye. — London : Liberal Publication Department, 1976. — 38p ; 21cm. — (Strategy 2,000 : 1st series ; no.8)
ISBN 0-900520-49-3 Sd : £0.40
(B77-00071)

330.9'41'0857 — Great Britain. Economic policies. *Proposals*
Young Liberals. *Economics and Industry Commission.* Industry and the community : a Young Liberal approach to industry, economics and the community / produced by the Economics and Industry Commission of the National League of Young Liberals. — Loughborough (13 Piper Drive, Long Whatton, Loughborough, Leics.) : The Commission, 1976. — 39,[1]p ; 26cm.
Bibl.: p.39.
ISBN 0-9505508-0-9 Sd : £0.30
(B77-05906)

330.9'41'0857 — Great Britain. Economic policies. *Socialist viewpoints*
Sedgemore, Brian. The how and why of socialism / [by] Brian Sedgemore. — Nottingham : Bertrand Russell Peace Foundation for Spokesman Books, 1977. — 88p ; 19cm.
Contents: 'How? Strategy and alternative strategy' - 'Why? The moral basis of socialism'.
ISBN 0-85124-196-4 Pbk : £0.95
(B77-27705)

330.9'41'0857 — Great Britain. Economic policies. *Trades Union Congress viewpoints*
Murray, Lionel. 'A trade union view of Britain's economic prospects' / by Lionel (Len) Murray. — Stockport : Manchester Statistical Society, [1977]. — [1],16p ; 20cm.
'[Paper] read on 18th March, 1976'.
Sd : £1.50
(B77-32458)

330.9'41'0857 — Great Britain. Economic policies, 1975-1976. *Conservative and Unionist Party viewpoints*
Joseph, *Sir* **Keith,** *bart.* Stranded on the middle ground? : reflections on circumstances and policies / [by] Sir Keith Joseph. — London (Wilfred St., London S.W.1) : Centre for Policy Studies, 1976. — 80p ; 21cm.
ISBN 0-9504392-5-8 Pbk : £2.00
(B77-03986)

330.9'41'0857 — Great Britain. Economic policies. Decision making. *Secondary school texts*
Donaldson, Peter. The economy and decision making / [by] Peter Donaldson and Jim Clifford. — London : Longman, 1977. — x, 187p : ill ; 24cm. — (Understanding business)
Index.
ISBN 0-582-35546-x Pbk : £2.25
(B77-24756)

Donaldson, Peter. The economy and decision making / [by] Peter Donaldson and Jim Clifford. — London : Longman. — (Understanding business)
Bibl.
Teachers guide. — 1977. — [2],57,[1]p : ill ; 30cm.
ISBN 0-582-35553-2 Sp : £1.15
(B77-31731)

330.9'41'0857 — Great Britain. Regional economic development. Policies of government. *Case studies*
Button, Kenneth John. Case studies in regional economics / [by] Kenneth J. Button and David Gillingwater. — London [etc.] : Heinemann Educational [for] the Economics Association, 1976. — [5],88p : maps ; 20cm. — (Case studies in economic analysis ; 3)
ISBN 0-435-84090-8 Pbk : £1.20
(B77-05242)

Button, Kenneth John. Case studies in regional economics / [by] Kenneth J. Button and David Gillingwater. — London [etc.] : Heinemann Educational [for] the Economics Association. — (Case studies in economic analysis ; 3)
[Teachers' guide]. — 1976. — [5],144p : ill, maps ; 20cm.
Bibl.
ISBN 0-435-84091-6 Pbk : £1.90
(B77-05243)

330.9'411'0857 — Scotland. Economic conditions. Effects of exploitation of petroleum deposits in North Sea
Gaskin, Maxwell. North Sea oil and Scotland, the changing prospect / [by] Maxwell Gaskin. — Edinburgh (The Economist, 42 St Andrew Sq., Edinburgh EH2 2YE) : Royal Bank of Scotland Ltd, 1977. — 22p : 2 col ill ; 21cm.
Sd : Unpriced
(B77-18594)

Gaskin, Maxwell. North Sea oil and Scotland, the developing impact / by Maxwell Gaskin. — Edinburgh (42 St Andrews Sq., Edinburgh EH2 2YE) : Royal Bank of Scotland, [1977]. — 25p, [2]leaves of plates : col ill, col map ; 21cm.
ISBN 0-9504676-1-8 Sd : Unpriced
(B77-12895)

330.9'411'0857 — Scotland. Economic development. Organisations: Scottish Development Agency
Scottish Development Agency. Finance and development aid for industry / Scottish Development Agency. — Glasgow (120 Bothwell St., Glasgow G2) : The Agency, [1977]. — [6]p ; 30cm.
ISBN 0-905574-01-x Sd : Free
(B77-08822)

330.9'411'0857 — Scotland. Economic development. Organisations: Scottish Development Agency. *Reports, surveys. Serials*
Scottish Development Agency. Report of the Scottish Development Agency. — Glasgow (450 Sauchiehall St., Glasgow G2 3LA) : The Agency.
1st : 1975-1976 : 15 December 1975-31st March 1976. — 1976. — [12]p ; 30cm.
Sd : Unpriced
ISSN 0309-2844
(B77-10207)

330.9'411'0857 — Scotland. Economic policies. Effects of self government. *Forecasts for 1980*
Scotland 1980 : the economics of self-government / edited by Donald MacKay. — Edinburgh (58 Queen St., Edinburgh EH2 3NS) : Q Press, 1977. — viii,211p : 1 ill ; 22cm.
Bibl.
ISBN 0-905470-03-6 : £5.95
ISBN 0-905470-02-8 Pbk : £2.40
(B77-27706)

330.9'4111'0857 — Scotland. Highlands & Islands. Economic development. Organisations: Highlands and Islands Development Board. *Accounts*
Highlands and Islands Development Board. Accounts of the Highlands and Islands Development Board showing the income and expenditure for the year ended 31st March and balance sheet as at 31st March, together with the report of the Comptroller and Auditor General thereon ... — London : H.M.S.O.
1975-76. — [1977]. — 7p ; 25cm. — ([1976-77 H.C.] 147)
ISBN 0-10-214777-9 Sd : £0.25
(B77-08823)

330.9'4111'0857 — Scotland. Highlands & Islands. Economic development. Organisations: Highlands and Islands Development Board. *Reports, surveys. Serials*
Highlands and Islands Development Board. Report ... / Highlands and Islands Development Board. — Inverness : The Board.
11th : 1976. — 1977. — [1],3-139p : ill(some col), col maps ; 24cm.
Col. map on inside covers.
ISBN 0-902347-53-5 Pbk : £1.75
(B77-26154)

Highlands and Islands Development Board. Report / Highlands and Islands Development Board. — Inverness : The Board.
10th : 1975. — 1976. — 119p : ill(some col), col maps ; 25cm.
ISBN 0-902347-43-8 Pbk : £0.90
(B77-04608)

330.9'412'5 — Scotland. Tayside Region. Economic conditions. Effects of tourism. *Reports, surveys*
Henderson, David M. The economic impact of tourism : a case study in Greater Tayside / written by David M. Henderson, assisted by R. Lee Cousins ; edited by J.T. Coppock, Brian S. Duffield and M.L. Owen ; computation and analysis by Steve Dowers ; for the Scottish Tourist Board. — Edinburgh ([High School Yards, Edinburgh EH1 1NR]) : Tourism and Recreation Research Unit, University of Edinburgh, 1975. — xxiv,216p : ill, forms, maps ; 30cm. — (University of Edinburgh. Tourism and Recreation Research Unit. Research reports ; no.13 ISSN 0305-487x)
Bibl.: p.211-213.
ISBN 0-904828-02-6 Pbk : £5.00
(B77-03414)

330.9'415'08 — Ireland. Economic development, 1770-1976. *Sinn Fein viewpoints*
Sinn Fein. *Department of Economic Affairs. Research Section.* The Irish industrial revolution / Research Section, Department of Economic Affairs, Sinn Fein-The Workers' Party. — Dublin (30 Gardiner Place, Dublin 1) : Repsol Publications, 1977. — [4],iii,3-151p : ill ; 26cm. — (Studies in political economy)
ISBN 0-86064-009-4 Pbk : £1.30
Primary classification 338'.09417
(B77-12915)

330.9'415'0824 — Ireland. Economic conditions
Economic activity in Ireland : a study of two open economies / editors Norman J. Gibson and John E. Spencer ; contributors W. Black ... [et al.]. — Dublin : Gill and Macmillan [etc.], 1977. — xxii,272p : ill ; 23cm.
Bibl. — Index.
ISBN 0-7171-0779-5 : £10.00
(B77-08824)

330.9'417'0824 — Ireland (Republic). Economic conditions. *Forecasts for 1976-1981*
Fforde, Adam. The republic of Ireland : forecasts for the economy, 1976-1981 / by Adam Fforde. — London (9 Orchard Ave., N3 3NL) : Staniland Hall Associates, 1976. — [2],28 leaves : ill ; 21x30cm. — (Economic, industrial and market forecasts)
ISBN 0-9504055-4-x Sp : Unpriced
(B77-06508)

330.9'417'0824 — Ireland (Republic). Economic conditions. *Radical Economists Group viewpoints*
The **Irish** economy, the workers and the economic crisis. — Dublin (c/o A. Coughlan, Convenor, T.C.D., Dublin 2) : Radical Economists Group, 1976. — 10,[1]p ; 22cm. — (Radical Economists Group. Pamphlets ; no.2)
Sd : £0.25
(B77-20958)

330.9'417'0824 — Ireland (Republic). Economic conditions. *Reports, surveys. Serials*
Organisation for Economic Co-operation and Development. Ireland / Organisation for Economic Co-operation and Development. — Paris : O.E.C.D. ; [London] : [H.M.S.O.]. — (Economic surveys ISSN 0474-5183)
[1976]. — 1976. — 62p(4 fold) : ill ; 24cm.
Pbk : £1.10
ISBN 92-64-11582-x
(B77-05907)

330.9'42 — England. Economic conditions, 1000-. *Readings from contemporary sources*
Documents in English economic history / edited by B.W. Clapp, H.E.S. Fisher and A.R.J. Juřica. — London : G. Bell.
In 2 vols.
England from 1000 to 1760 / edited by H.E.S. Fisher and A.R.J. Juřica. — 1977. — xxiii, 547p ; 23cm.
Index.
ISBN 0-7135-1985-1 : £16.00
(B77-28433)

330.9'42 — England. Economic conditions, 1450-1750
Coleman, Donald Cuthbert. The economy of England, 1450-1750 / [by] D.C. Coleman. — London [etc.] : Oxford University Press, 1977. — xi,223p : ill ; 21cm.
Bibl.: p.206-215. — Index.
ISBN 0-19-215355-2 : £3.75
ISBN 0-19-289070-0 Pbk : £1.75
(B77-08825)

330.9'42 — England. Economic conditions, 1500-1750
Holderness, B A. Pre-industrial England : economy and society, 1500-1750 / [by] B.A. Holderness. — London : Dent [etc.], 1976. — x,244p : 2 ill, maps ; 24cm.
Bibl. — Index.
ISBN 0-460-10157-9 : £6.50
ISBN 0-460-1157-3 Pbk : £2.95
(B77-01208)

330.9'42'05 — England. Economic conditions, 1500-1700
Jack, Sybil Milliner. Trade and industry in Tudor and Stuart England / [by] Sybil M. Jack. — London : Allen and Unwin, 1977. — 3-200p ; 23cm. — (Historical problems, studies and documents ; 27)
Index.
ISBN 0-04-942155-7 : £10.50
ISBN 0-04-942156-5 Pbk : £4.95
(B77-23185)

330.9'42'07 — England. Economic conditions, 1760-1972. *Documents*
Documents in English economic history / edited by B.W. Clapp, H.E.S. Fisher and A.R.J. Juřica. — London : Bell.
In 2 vols. — Index.
England since 1760 / edited by B.W. Clapp. — 1976. — xix,544p ; 23cm.
ISBN 0-7135-1871-5 : £16.00
(B77-03987)

330.9'426'0857 — East Anglia. Economic conditions. *Reports, surveys*
East Anglia Economic Planning Council. Regional economic review / East Anglia Economic Planning Council. — [London] ([Room 429A, Charles House, 375 Kensington High St., W14 8QH]) : [The Council], 1976. — [7],92p,plate : 2 ill, map ; 30cm.
Sd : Unpriced
(B77-29999)

330.9'429'0857 — Wales. Economic conditions. *Statistics*
Welsh economic trends = Tueddiadau'r economi / Welsh Office = Y Swyddfa Gymreig. — Cardiff : H.M.S.O.
No.3 : 1976. — 1976. — vi,68p : ill(chiefly col), col maps ; 21x30cm.
ISBN 0-11-790067-2 Sd : £2.70
(B77-14097)

330.9'429'0857 — Wales. Economic development. *Periodicals*
Wales ahead : the newspaper of the Welsh Development Agency. — Pontypridd (Treforest Industrial Estate, Pontypridd, M. Glam. CF37 5UT) : Welsh Development Agency, Information Department.
No.1- ; June 1977-. — [1977]-. — ill(some col), maps, ports(some col) ; 42cm.
8p. in 1st issue.
Sd : Unpriced
ISSN 0140-3354
(B77-23186)

330.9'429'0857 — Wales. Economic development. Organisations: Welsh Development Agency. Policies. *Proposals*
Welsh Development Agency. A statement of policies and programmes / Welsh Development Agency. — Pontypridd (Treforest Industrial Estate, Pontypridd, M. Glam. CF37 5UT) : The Agency, 1977. — [2],12p ; 30cm.
Sd : Unpriced
(B77-28434)

330.9'43'087 — West Germany. Economic policies, 1973-1976

Zweig, Konrad. Germany through inflation and recession : an object lesson in economic management, 1973-1976 / [by] Konrad Zweig. — London (Wilfred St., S.W.1) : Centre for Policy Studies, 1976. — viii,52p ; 22cm.
Bibl.: p.52.
ISBN 0-9504392-2-3 Pbk : £1.85
(B77-02802)

330.9'436'04 — Austria. Economic policies, 1900-1904

Gerschenkron, Alexander. An economic spurt that failed : four lectures in Austrian history / by Alexander Gerschenkron. — Princeton ; Guildford : Princeton University Press, 1977. — x,172p : facsims, 2 maps, port ; 23cm. — (Eliot Janeway lectures on historical economics in honor of Joseph Schumpeter)
Index.
ISBN 0-691-04216-0 : £9.40
(B77-26851)

330.9'436'05 — Austria. Economic conditions. *Reports, surveys. Serials*

Organisation for Economic Co-operation and Development. Austria / Organisation for Economic Co-operation and Development. — Paris : O.E.C.D. ; [London] : [H.M.S.O.]. — (Economic surveys ISSN 0474-5183)
[1976]. — 1976. — 54,[4]p(4 fold) : ill ; 24cm.
Pbk : £1.10
ISBN 92-64-11541-2
(B77-01209)

330.9'44'083 — France. Economic conditions. *Reports, surveys. Serials*

Organisation for Economic Co-operation and Development. France / [Organisation for Economic Co-operation and Development]. — Paris : O.E.C.D. ; [London] : [H.M.S.O.]. — (Economic surveys ISSN 0474-5183)
[1977]. — 1977. — 66,[4]p(4 fold) : ill ; 24cm.
Pbk : £1.10
ISBN 92-64-11617-6
ISSN 0376-6438
(B77-08255)

330.9'45'7092 — Southern Italy. Economic development. Theories

Chapman, Graham, *b.1951.* Development and underdevelopment in Southern Italy / [by] Graham Chapman. — Reading (Whiteknights, Reading [RG6 2AB]) : Department of Geography, University of Reading, 1976. — [2], ii,32p ; 21cm. — (Geographical papers ; no.41 ISSN 0305-5914)
Bibl.: p.31-32.
ISBN 0-7049-0453-5 Sd : £0.60
(B77-06509)

330.9'46'082 — Spain. Economic conditions, 1959-1976

Wright, Alison. The Spanish economy, 1959-1976 / [by] Alison Wright. — London [etc.] : Macmillan, 1977. — xii,195p : map ; 23cm.
Index.
ISBN 0-333-21491-9 : £8.95 : CIP rev.
(B77-08826)

330.9'469'042 — Portugal. Economic conditions. *Reports, surveys. Serials*

Organisation for Economic Co-operation and Development. Portugal / Organisation for Economic Cooperation and Development. — Paris : O.E.C.D. ; [London] : [H.M.S.O.]. — (Economic surveys ISSN 0474-5183)
[1976]. — 1976. — 60,[4]p(4 fold) : ill ; 24cm.
Pbk : £1.10
ISBN 92-64-11584-6
(B77-08256)

330.9'47'085 — Soviet Union. Economic conditions

Nove, Alec. The Soviet economic system / by Alec Nove. — London : Allen and Unwin, 1977. — 3-399p ; 23cm.
Bibl.: p.380-390. — Index.
ISBN 0-04-335035-6 : £10.50
ISBN 0-04-335036-4 Pbk : £4.95
(B77-26852)

330.9'47'085 — Soviet Union. Economic conditions. Effects of economic relations between Soviet Union & Western world, 1955-1973

Hanson, Philip. External influences on the Soviet economy since the mid-1950s : the import of Western technology / by Philip Hanson. — Birmingham (P.O. Box 363, Birmingham B15 2TT) : Centre for Russian and East European Studies, University of Birmingham, [1975?]. — [2],36p ; 30cm. — (University of Birmingham. Centre for Russian and East European Studies. Discussion papers ; no.7 ISSN 0307-3467)
ISBN 0-7044-0115-0 Sd : Unpriced
(B77-20067)

330.9'471'03 — Finland. Economic conditions. *Reports, surveys. Serials*

Organisation for Economic Co-operation and Development. Finland / Organisation for Economic Co-operation and Development. — Paris : O.E.C.D. ; [London] : [H.M.S.O.]. — (Economic surveys)
[1977]. — 1977. — 62,[4]p(4 fold) : ill ; 24cm.
Pbk : £1.10
ISBN 92-64-11594-3
ISSN 0376-6438
(B77-07118)

330.9'489'05 — Denmark. Economic conditions. *Reports, surveys. Serials*

Organisation for Economic Co-operation and Development. Denmark / [Organisation for Economic Co-operation and Development]. — Paris : O.E.C.D. ; [London] : [H.M.S.O.].
[1977] / [by the OECD Economic and Development Review Committee]. — 1977. — 68,[4]p(4 fold) : ill ; 25cm. — (Economic surveys ISSN 0376-6438)
Pbk : £1.10
ISBN 92-64-11626-5
(B77-14588)

330.9'491'204 — Iceland. Economic conditions. *Reports, surveys. Serials*

Organisation for Economic Co-operation and Development. Iceland / [Organisation for Economic Co-operation and Development]. — Paris : O.E.C.D. ; [London] : [H.M.S.O.]. — (Economic surveys ISSN 0376-6438)
[1976]. — 1976. — 59,[4]p(4 fold) : ill ; 24cm.
Pbk : £1.10
ISBN 92-64-11583-8
(B77-05908)

330.9'492 — Netherlands. Rural regions. Economic conditions, 1500-1700

De Vries, Jan, *b.1943.* The Dutch rural economy in the golden age, 1500-1700 / [by] Jan de Vries. — New Haven ; London : Yale University Press, 1974. — xx,316p : ill, maps ; 24cm. — (Yale series in economic history)
Bibl.: p.285-305. — Index.
ISBN 0-300-01608-5 : Unpriced
(B77-20068)

330.9'493'04 — Belgium. Economic conditions. *Reports, surveys. Serials*

Organisation for Economic Co-operation and Development. Belgium-Luxembourg / Organisation for Economic Co-operation and Development. — Paris : O.E.C.D. ; [London] : [H.M.S.O.]. — (Economic surveys ISSN 0376-6438)
[1977]. — 1977. — 60,[4]p(4 fold) : ill ; 24cm.
Pbk : £1.10
ISBN 92-64-11662-1
Also classified at 330.9'493'504
(B77-20069)

330.9'493'504 — Luxembourg. Economic conditions. *Reports, surveys. Serials*

Organisation for Economic Co-operation and Development. Belgium-Luxembourg / Organisation for Economic Co-operation and Development. — Paris : O.E.C.D. ; [London] : [H.M.S.O.]. — (Economic surveys ISSN 0376-6438)
[1977]. — 1977. — 60,[4]p(4 fold) : ill ; 24cm.
Pbk : £1.10
ISBN 92-64-11662-1
Primary classification 330.9'493'04
(B77-20069)

330.9'494'07 — Switzerland. Economic conditions. *Reports, surveys. Serials*

Organisation for Economic Co-operation and Development. Switzerland / Organisation for Economic Co-operation and Development. — Paris : O.E.C.D. ; [London] : [H.M.S.O.]. — (Economic surveys ISSN 0376-6438)
[1977]. — 1977. — 62,[4]p(4 fold) : ill ; 24cm.
Pbk : £1.10
ISBN 92-64-11622-2
(B77-11101)

330.9'495'07 — Greece. Economic conditions. *Reports, surveys. Serials*

Organisation for Economic Co-operation and Development. Greece / Organisation for Economic Co-operation and Development. — Paris : O.E.C.D. ; [London] : [H.M.S.O.]. — (Economic surveys ISSN 0376-6438)
[1976]. — 1976. — 64,[4]p(4 fold) : ill ; 24cm.
Pbk : £1.10
ISBN 92-64-11512-9
(B77-01210)

[1977]. — 1977. — 50,[4]p(4 fold) : ill ; 24cm.
Pbk : £1.10
ISBN 92-64-11667-2
(B77-20070)

330.9'497'02 — Yugoslavia. Economic conditions. *For British businessmen*

Weisskopf, Kurt. Trading with Yugoslavia / [by] Kurt Weisskopf. — [London] ([69 Cannon St., London EC4N 5AB]) : London Chamber of Commerce and Industry, 1976. — ix,70p : map ; 24cm.
ISBN 0-901902-46-2 Pbk : £6.00
(B77-25425)

330.9'497'02 — Yugoslavia. Economic conditions. *Reports, surveys. Serials*

Organisation for Economic Co-operation and Development. Yugoslavia / Organisation for Economic Co-operation and Development. — Paris : O.E.C.D. ; [London] : [H.M.S.O.]. — (Economic surveys ISSN 0376-6438)
[1977]. — 1977. — 66,[4]p(4 fold) : ill ; 24cm.
Pbk : £1.10
ISBN 92-64-11649-4
(B77-20071)

330.9'4977'03 — Eastern European countries. Economic conditions. *Study examples: Bulgaria*

Feiwel, George Richard. Growth and reforms in centrally planned economies : the lessons of the Bulgarian experience / [by] George R. Feiwel. — New York [etc.] ; London : Praeger, 1977. — xxxi,347p ; 25cm. — (Praeger special studies in international economics and development)
Bibl.: p.338-345.
ISBN 0-275-23330-8 : £18.50
(B77-16225)

330.9'51'03 — China. Economic conditions, 1600-1918

Moulder, Frances V. Japan, China and the modern world economy : toward a reinterpretation of East Asian development ca 1600 to ca 1918 / [by] Frances V. Moulder. — Cambridge [etc.] : Cambridge University Press, 1977. — x,255p ; 22cm.
Bibl.: p.235-246. — Index.
ISBN 0-521-21174-3 : £9.00
Also classified at 330.9'52'025
(B77-24053)

330.9'51'05 — China. Economic conditions. *For British businessmen*

Metra Consulting Group. China, business opportunities : a business study / by Metra Consulting ; [written by Geoffrey Hemy]. — London : 'Financial times', 1976. — [10],277p : ill, maps ; 30cm.
Bibl.: p.275-277.
ISBN 0-900671-66-1 Sp : £60.00
(B77-03988)

330.9'51'05 — China. Economic conditions. Compared with economic conditions in India (Republic), 1950-1975

Lateef, Sarwar. China and India, economic performance and prospects / [by] K. Sarwar Lateef. — [Falmer] ([Andrew Cohen Building, University of Sussex, Falmer, Brighton BN1 9RE]) : Institute of Development Studies, [1976]. — [4],42p ; 30cm. — (Institute of Development Studies. Communications ; 118 ISSN 0308-5856)
Bibl.: p.41-42.
ISBN 0-903354-34-9 Sd : £2.00
Also classified at 330.9'54'04
(B77-03415)

330.9'51'05 — China. Economic conditions. Political aspects, 1949-1975. *Essays*

Gurley, John G. China's economy and the Maoist strategy / [by] John G. Gurley. — New York ; London : Monthly Review Press, 1976. — ix,325p : 1 ill ; 21cm.
ISBN 0-85345-395-0 : £8.45
(B77-12896)

330.9'51'05 — China. Economic development. *Forecasts for 1950-1980*

Lateef, Sarwar. Economic growth in China & India, 1950-1980 / by Sarwar Lateef. — London : Economist Intelligence Unit, 1976. — 2v.([4],95p,[10]p of plates; [4],64p) : ill, col maps ; 30cm. — (Economist Intelligence Unit. Special reports ; no.30)
Bibl.: p.61-64 (vol.2).
ISBN 0-900351-66-7 Sd : Unpriced
Also classified at 330.9'54'04
(B77-02803)

330.9'51'05 — China. Economic development, 1949-1976

Eckstein, Alexander. China's economic revolution / [by] Alexander Eckstein. — Cambridge [etc.] : Cambridge University Press, 1977. — xii,340p ; 24cm.
ISBN 0-521-29189-5 Pbk : £4.95
ISBN 0-521-21283-9 : £12.50
(B77-22408)

330.9'51'05 — Economic conditions. Comparative studies. Methodology. *Study examples: Economic conditions in China compared with economic conditions in India (Republic)*
Potter, David, *b.1931.* India & China / prepared by David Potter ; for the [Open University] Course Team. — Milton Keynes : Open University Press, 1976. — 18p : col maps ; 30cm. — (Social science, a third level course : patterns of inequality ; section 3 : inequalities between nations ; units 25-28, part 1) (D302 ; 25-28, part 1)
Bibl.: p.18.
ISBN 0-335-07159-7 Sd : Unpriced
Also classified at 330.9'54'05
(B77-00072)

330.9'51'24905 — Taiwan. Economic conditions, 1945-1975
Lumley, F A. The Republic of China under Chiang Kai-shek : Taiwan today / [by] F.A. Lumley. — London : Barrie and Jenkins, 1976. — 168p ; 21cm. — (World realities series)
Bibl.: p.160-161. — Index.
ISBN 0-214-20351-4 Pbk : £5.50
(B77-11102)

330.9'519'304 — North Korea. Economic development, 1945-1975
Brun, Ellen. Socialist Korea : a case study in the strategy of economic development / [by] Ellen Brun and Jacques Hersh. — New York ; London : Monthly Review Press, 1976. — 3-423p,viii p of plates : ill, map ; 21cm.
ISBN 0-85345-386-1 : £9.25
(B77-13538)

330.9'519'5043 — South Korea. Economic conditions. *Reports, surveys. For British businessmen*
Confederation of British Industry. Republic of Korea / [Confederation of British Industry]. — London : C.B.I., 1977. — 20p ; 30cm. — (CBI market study)
Bibl.: p.20.
ISBN 0-85201-130-x Sd : £6.00
(B77-15128)

330.9'519'5043 — South Korea. Economic conditions, 1960-1975
Hasan, Parvez. Korea : problems and issues in a rapidly growing economy / [by] Parvez Hasan. — Baltimore ; London : Johns Hopkins University Press for the World Bank, 1976. — xv,277p : ill(on lining papers), map ; 24cm. — (International Bank for Reconstruction and Development. Country economic reports)
Index.
ISBN 0-8018-1864-8 : £12.00
(B77-13539)

330.9'519'5043 — South Korea. Economic development, 1953-1976
Kuznets, Paul W. Economic growth and structure in the Republic of Korea / [by] Paul W. Kuznets. — New Haven ; London : Yale University Press, 1977. — xv,238p : 1 ill ; 22cm.
'A publication of the Economic Growth Center, Yale University'. — Bibl.: p.221-232. — Index.
ISBN 0-300-02019-8 : £11.90
(B77-24758)

330.9'519'5043 — South Korea. Economic policies, 1960-1969
Brown, Gilbert T. Korean pricing policies and economic development in the 1960's / [by] Gilbert T. Brown. — Baltimore ; London : Johns Hopkins University Press, 1973. — xvii, 317p : 2 ill ; 24cm.
Index.
ISBN 0-8018-1479-0 : Unpriced
(B77-20072)

330.9'52'025 — Japan. Economic conditions, 1600-1918
Moulder, Frances V. Japan, China and the modern world economy : toward a reinterpretation of East Asian development ca 1600 to ca 1918 / [by] Frances V. Moulder. — Cambridge [etc.] : Cambridge University Press, 1977. — x,255p ; 22cm.
Bibl.: p.235-246. — Index.
ISBN 0-521-21174-3 : £9.00
Primary classification 330.9'51'03
(B77-24053)

330.9'52'04 — Economic conditions, 1971-1976. *Study regions: Japan*
Kojima, Kiyoshi. Japan and a new world economic order / [by] Kiyoshi Kojima. — London : Croom Helm, 1977. — [1],190p : ill ; 23cm.
Index.
ISBN 0-85664-248-7 : £7.95
(B77-08827)

330.9'52'04 — Japan. Economic conditions. *Forecasts to 1980*
Boston Consulting Group. Japan in 1980 : the economic system and its prospects : an economic report / by the Boston Consulting Group ; with a foreword by Peter Shore. — London : 'Financial times', 1974. — [10],245[i. e.249]p ; 30cm.
'... commissioned by the Department of Trade in cooperation with the Central Policy Review Staff and other governmental departments' - preliminaries.
ISBN 0-900671-11-4 Sp : Unpriced
(B77-18595)

330.9'53'5 — Sharjah. Economic conditions, 1970
Sharjah 1970 / prepared ... by the 'Middle East economic digest' to commemorate the fifth anniversary of the Accession of His Highness Shaikh Khalid bin Mohammad Al-Qasimi, Ruler of Sharjah and Dependencies ; editor Jonathan Wallace. — London (84 Chancery La., W.C.2) : Economic Features Limited, [1971]. — 80p : ill(some col), maps(chiefly col), ports(1 col) ; 27cm.
Sd : Unpriced
(B77-29225)

330.9'53'805 — Saudi Arabia. Economic conditions, 1960-1970. Econometric models
Al-Bashir, Faisal Safooq. A structural econometric model of the Saudi Arabian economy, 1960-1970 / [by] Faisal Safooq al-Bashir. — New York ; London [etc.] : Wiley, 1977. — x,134p ; 24cm.
'A Wiley-Interscience publication'. — Bibl.: p.122-125. — Index.
ISBN 0-471-02177-6 : £12.70
(B77-26155)

330.9'54'04 — India (Republic). Economic conditions. Compared with economic conditions in China, 1950-1975
Lateef, Sarwar. China and India, economic performance and prospects / [by] K. Sarwar Lateef. — [Falmer] ([Andrew Cohen Building, University of Sussex, Falmer, Brighton BN1 9RE]) : Institute of Development Studies, [1976]. — [4],42p ; 30cm. — (Institute of Development Studies. Communications ; 118 ISSN 0308-5856)
Bibl.: p.41-42.
ISBN 0-903354-34-9 Sd : £2.00
Primary classification 330.9'51'05
(B77-03415)

330.9'54'04 — India (Republic). Economic development. *Forecasts for 1950-1980*
Lateef, Sarwar. Economic growth in China & India, 1950-1980 / by Sarwar Lateef. — London : Economist Intelligence Unit, 1976. — 2v.([4],95p,[10]p of plates; [4],64p) : ill, col maps ; 30cm. — (Economist Intelligence Unit. Special reports ; no.30)
Bibl.: p.61-64 (vol.2).
ISBN 0-900351-66-7 Sd : Unpriced
Primary classification 330.9'51'05
(B77-02803)

330.9'54'05 — Economic conditions. Comparative studies. Methodology. *Study examples: Economic conditions in India (Republic) compared with economic conditions in China*
Potter, David, *b.1931.* India & China / prepared by David Potter ; for the [Open University] Course Team. — Milton Keynes : Open University Press, 1976. — 18p : col maps ; 30cm. — (Social science, a third level course : patterns of inequality ; section 3 : inequalities between nations ; units 25-28, part 1) (D302 ; 25-28, part 1)
Bibl.: p.18.
ISBN 0-335-07159-7 Sd : Unpriced
Primary classification 330.9'51'05
(B77-00072)

330.9'54'05 — South & South-east Asia. Economic development
Myrdal, Gunnar. Asian drama : an inquiry into the poverty of nations / [by] Gunnar Myrdal ; an abridgement of the Twentieth Century Fund study by Seth King. — Harmondsworth [etc.] : Penguin, 1977. — x,388p ; 18cm. — (Pelican books)
This abridgement originally published: New York : Pantheon Books ; London : Allen Lane, 1972. — Index.
ISBN 0-14-021517-4 Pbk : £1.75
(B77-20959)

330.9'55'05 — Iran. Economic development. *Forecasts for 1978-1990*
Looney, Robert E. A development strategy for Iran through the 1980s / [by] Robert E. Looney. — New York ; London : Praeger, 1977. — xiv,208p ; 25cm. — (Praeger special studies in international economics and development)
Bibl.: p.191-202. — Index.
ISBN 0-03-021956-6 : £14.40
(B77-32459)

330.9'56 — Middle East. Economic conditions, 1800-1976
The **Middle** Eastern economy : studies in economics and economic history / edited by Elie Kedourie. — London [etc.] : Cass, 1977. — [5],185p : 2 ill ; 23cm.
'This group of studies first appeared in a Special Issue on The Middle Eastern Economy of "Middle Eastern Studies", Vol.12, no.3., published by Frank Cass and Company Limited' - title page verso.
ISBN 0-7146-3074-8 : £8.50
(B77-20960)

330.9'56'04 — Middle East. Economic conditions. *Yearbooks*
Middle East annual review. — Saffron Walden : Middle East Review Co. Ltd ; Basingstoke : Distributed by Macmillan.
[1977] : incorporating material prepared by the Economist Intelligence Unit / editor Michael Field. — 1976. — 400p : ill, maps ; 27cm.
ISBN 0-333-21475-7 Pbk : £6.95
ISSN 0305-3210
(B77-24054)

330.9'56'04 — Middle East. Economic conditions, 1945-1976
Askari, Hossein. Middle East economies in the 1970s : a comparative approach / [by] Hossein Askari, John Thomas Cummings. — New York [etc.] ; London : Praeger, [1977]. — xxxiii, 583p ; 25cm. — (Praeger special studies in international economics and development)
Published in the United States: 1976. — Bibl.: p.519-570. — Index.
ISBN 0-275-23130-5 : £25.50
(B77-12897)

330.9'561'03 — Turkey. Economic conditions. *Reports, surveys. Serials*
Organisation for Economic Co-operation and Development. Turkey / Organisation for Economic Co-operation and Development. — Paris : O.E.C.D. ; [London] : [H.M.S.O.]. — (Economic surveys ISSN 0474-5183)
[1976]. — 1976. — 63,[4]p(4 fold) : ill ; 24cm.
Pbk : £1.10
ISBN 92-64-11573-0
(B77-00638)

330.9'595'05 — Developing countries. Economic development. Related to exporting of primary commodities. *Study regions: Malaysia*
Thoburn, John T. Primary commodity exports and economic development : theory, evidence and a study of Malaysia / [by] John T. Thoburn. — London [etc.] : Wiley, 1977. — xvi,310p : map ; 24cm.
Bibl.: p.287-302. — Index.
ISBN 0-471-99441-3 : £9.00
Also classified at 382'.4'09595
(B77-24055)

330.9'598'03 — Indonesia. Economic conditions. *For businessmen*
Metra Consulting Group. Indonesia, business opportunities / by Metra Consulting. — London (23 Lower Belgrave St., SW1W 0NS) : Metra Consulting Group Ltd, 1977. — [12], 202p : maps ; 30cm.
ISBN 0-902231-08-1 Sp : £62.00
(B77-28435)

330.9'598'6 — Indonesia. Lesser Sunda Islands. Economic conditions, to ca 1970. *Study regions: Roti & Savu*
Fox, James J. Harvest of the palm : ecological change in Eastern Indonesia / [by] James J. Fox. — Cambridge, Mass. ; London : Harvard University Press, 1977. — xxi,290p : ill, maps, ports ; 24cm.
Bibl.: p.277-284. — Index.
ISBN 0-674-38111-4 : £10.25
(B77-30000)

330.9'6'03 — Africa. Economic development. Political aspects. *Marxist viewpoints*
The **political** economy of contemporary Africa / Peter C.W. Gutkind and Immanuel Wallerstein, editors. — Beverly Hills ; London : Sage Publications, [1977]. — 318p : map ; 24cm. — (Sage series on African modernization and development ; vol.1)
Published in the United States: 1976. — Bibl.
ISBN 0-8039-0506-8 : £11.00
ISBN 0-8039-0592-0 Pbk : £4.95
(B77-10748)

330.9'624'04 — Sudan. Economic development, ca 1950-1976
Lees, Francis A. The economic and political development of the Sudan / [by] Francis A. Lees and Hugh C. Brooks. — London [etc.] : Macmillan, 1977. — xii,172p : 1 ill, maps ; 23cm.
Bibl.: p.158-163. — Index.
ISBN 0-333-21654-7 : £8.95
(B77-30001)

330.9'66 — West Africa. Economic conditions. *For West African students. Secondary school texts*
Anderson, David John. Economics of West Africa / [by] David J. Anderson. — London [etc.] : Macmillan, 1977. — ix,342p : ill, 2 forms ; 22cm.
Index.
ISBN 0-333-21575-3 Pbk : £0.80
(B77-20961)

330.9'662'305 — Mali. Rural regions. Economic conditions, 1960-1968. *Marxist viewpoints*
Ernst, Klaus. Tradition and progress in the African village : the non-capitalist transformation of rural communities in Mali / [by] Klaus Ernst ; [translated from the German by Salomea Genen]. — London : C. Hurst, 1976. — 262p : 2 maps ; 23cm.
Translation of: 'Tradition und Fortschritt im afrikanischen Dorf'. Berlin : Akademie, 1973. — Bibl.: p.245-262.
ISBN 0-903983-44-3 : £9.50
(B77-07119)

330.9'669'05 — Nigeria. Economic conditions. *For British businessmen*
Metra Consulting Group. Nigeria, business opportunities / by Metra Consulting ; [report written by Geoffrey Tewson in consultation with David Cotton]. — London (23 Lower Belgrave St., SW1W 0NS) : The Group, 1977. — [11],144p : maps ; 30cm.
ISBN 0-902231-07-3 Sp : Unpriced
(B77-33651)

330.9'669'05 — Nigeria. Economic development. *Periodicals. For British businessmen*
Nigerian & West African business monitor. — London (c/o 7 Bell Yard, Fleet St., WC2 2JR) : West African Business Monitor.
No.1- ; Aug. 1976-. — 1976-. — 30cm.
Monthly. — 8p. in 1st issue.
Sd : £40.00 yearly
ISSN 0308-6704
(B77-02804)

330.9'67 — Africa. Tropical regions. Economic conditions. *History. Readings*
An **economic** history of tropical Africa / selected and edited by Z.A. Konczacki and J.M. Konczacki. — London [etc.] : Cass.
In 3 vols.
Vol.1 : The pre-colonial period. — 1977. — xii, 310p : maps ; 23cm.
Bibl. — Index.
ISBN 0-7146-2919-7 : £9.95
(B77-25426)

Vol.2 : The colonial period. — 1977. — xv, 260p : ill, map ; 23cm.
Index.
ISBN 0-7146-2915-4 : £11.00
(B77-27707)

330.9'678'2 — East Africa. Economic development. *Study regions: Tanzania. Tanganyika, 1850-1950*
Kjekshus, Helge. Ecology control and economic development in East African history : the case of Tanganyika, 1850-1950 / [by] Helge Kjekshus. — London [etc.] : Heinemann Educational, 1977. — viii,215p : ill, maps ; 23cm.
Bibl.: p.190-209. — Index.
ISBN 0-435-94526-2 : £7.50
ISBN 0-435-94527-0 Pbk : £2.80
(B77-14098)

330.9'68'05 — South Africa. Economic conditions, 1900-1975
Houghton, Desmond Hobart. The South African economy / [by] D. Hobart Houghton. — 4th ed. — Cape Town ; London [etc.] : Oxford University Press, 1976. — [1],xiii,310p : ill, map ; 22cm.
Previous ed.: 1973. — Bibl.: p.295-304. — Index.
ISBN 0-19-570080-5 : £9.50
ISBN 0-19-570081-3 Pbk : £5.25
(B77-00639)

330.9'68'05 — South Africa. Economic conditions, 1900-1976. *Festschriften*
Public policy and the South African economy : essays in memory of Desmond Hobart Houghton / edited by M.L. Truu. — Cape Town ; Oxford [etc.] : Oxford University Press, 1976. — xiv,206p,plate : ill, port ; 22cm.
Bibl.: p.xiii-xiv.
ISBN 0-19-570079-1 : £10.00
(B77-19249)

330.9'68'06 — South Africa. Economic conditions. Related to economic conditions in Great Britain. *Anti-apartheid viewpoints*
Good, Dorcas. South Africa, the crisis in Britain and the apartheid economy / [by] Dorcas Good & Michael Williams. — London : Anti-Apartheid Movement, 1976. — [2],23p : 1 ill ; 30cm. — (Foreign investment in South Africa ; no.1 ISSN 0309-0752)
Bibl.: p.23.
ISBN 0-900065-00-1 Sd : £0.50
Also classified at 330.9'41'0857
(B77-05244)

330.9'71'0644 — Canada. Economic conditions. *Reports, surveys. Serials*
Organisation for Economic Co-operation and Development. Canada / Organisation for Economic Co-operation and Development. — Paris : O.E.C.D. ; [London] : [H.M.S.O.]. — (Economic surveys ISSN 0474-5183)
[1976]. — 1976. — 60,[4]p(4 fold) : ill ; 24cm.
Pbk : £1.10
ISBN 92-64-11526-9
(B77-00640)

330.9'7287'05 — Panama. Economic conditions, ca 1920-1975
Looney, Robert E. The economic development of Panama : the impact of world inflation on an open economy / [by] Robert E. Looney. — New York [etc.] ; London : Praeger, 1976. — xv,249p : map ; 25cm. — (Praeger special studies in international economics and development)
Bibl.: p.225-236. — Index.
ISBN 0-275-05390-3 : £12.20
(B77-08828)

330.9'73 — United States. Economic conditions, 1860-1914
Vatter, Harold G. The drive to industrial maturity : the US economy, 1860-1914 / [by] Harold G. Vatter. — Westport, Conn. ; London : Greenwood Press, 1975. — ix,368,[1] p : ill, maps ; 22cm. — (Contributions in economics and economic history ; no.13)
Bibl.: p.339-357. — Index.
ISBN 0-8371-8180-1 : £11.95
(B77-17337)

330.9'73 — United States. Economic conditions, to 1975
Gunderson, Gerald. A new economic history of America / [by] Gerald Gunderson. — New York ; London [etc.] : McGraw-Hill, [1977]. — xi,530p : ill, maps ; 25cm.
Published in the United States: 1976. — Bibl. — Index.
ISBN 0-07-025180-0 : £10.30
(B77-12898)

Scheiber, Harry N. American economic history. — [9th ed.] / [by] Harry N. Scheiber, Harold G. Vatter, Harold Underwood Faulkner. — New York [etc.] ; London : Harper and Row, 1976. — xi,514p : ill, maps ; 27cm.
Previous ed.: / by Harold Underwood Faulkner. New York : Harper and Row ; London : Hamilton, 1960. — Bibl. — Index.
ISBN 0-06-042001-4 : £14.20
(B77-08829)

330.9'73 — United States. Economic conditions, to 1975. *Marxist viewpoints*
Harrington, Michael. The twilight of capitalism / by Michael Harrington. — London [etc.] : Macmillan, 1977. — 446p ; 23cm.
Originally published: New York : Simon and Schuster, 1976. — Bibl.: p.421-431. — Index.
ISBN 0-333-21749-7 : £8.95
(B77-12343)

330.9'73 — United States. Economic development, to 1975. *Readings*
Growth in America / edited by Chester L. Cooper. — Westport, Conn. ; London : Greenwood Press, 1976. — ix,262p : ill, ports ; 22cm. — (Contributions in American studies ; no.21)
'... essays selected from among those prepared for a set of conferences sponsored [i.e. organised] by the Woodrow Wilson International Center for Scholars' - Library of Congress Cataloging in Publication Data. — Index.
ISBN 0-8371-8596-3 : £11.95
(B77-18596)

330.9'73'08 — Negroes. Economic conditions. *United States, 1865-1914*
Higgs, Robert. Competition and coercion : blacks in the American economy, 1865-1914 / [by] Robert Higgs. — Cambridge [etc.] : Cambridge University Press, 1977. — x,208p ; 24cm. — (Hoover Institution on War, Revolution and Peace. Publications ; P163)
Bibl.: p.175-203. — Index.
ISBN 0-521-21120-4 : £8.00
(B77-14589)

330.9'73'08 — United States. Economic conditions. Compared with economic conditions in Great Britain, 1850-1939
Holmes, Graeme Molyneux. Britain and America : a comparative economic history, 1850-1939 / [by] Graeme M. Holmes. — Newton Abbot [etc.] : David and Charles [etc.], 1976. — 224p ; 23cm.
Bibl.: p.208-220. — Index.
ISBN 0-7153-7256-4 : £5.95
Primary classification 330.9'41'081
(B77-05241)

330.9'73'09 — United States. Economic policies, 1936-1975. Influence of theories of economics of Keynes, John Maynard, Baron Keynes
Buchanan, James McGill. Democracy in deficit : the political legacy of Lord Keynes / [by] James M. Buchanan, Richard E. Wagner. — New York [etc.] ; London : Academic Press, 1977. — xii,195p ; 24cm.
Index.
ISBN 0-12-138850-6 : £8.15
(B77-17957)

330.9'73'092 — United States. Economic conditions. *Reports, surveys. Serials*
Organisation for Economic Co-operation and Development. United States / Organisation for Economic Co-operation and Development. — Paris : O.E.C.D. ; [London] : [H.M.S.O.]. — (Economic surveys ISSN 0474-5183)
[1976]. — 1976. — 58,[4]p(4 fold) : ill ; 24cm.
Pbk : £1.10
ISBN 92-64-11542-0
(B77-01211)

330.9'73'092 — United States. Economic conditions, 1945-1976
Galbraith, John Kenneth. The affluent society / [by] John Kenneth Galbraith. — 3rd ed., revised. — London : Deutsch, 1977. — xxxi, 287p ; 23cm.
This ed. originally published: Boston, Mass. : Houghton Mifflin, 1976. — Index.
ISBN 0-233-96874-1 : £4.95
(B77-13541)

330.9'73'092 — United States. Economic conditions, 1973-2000
Tuve, George Lewis. Energy, environment, populations and food : our four interdependent crises / [by] George L. Tuve. — New York ; London [etc.] : Wiley, 1976. — xiii,264p ; 24cm.
'A Wiley Interscience Publication'. — Index.
ISBN 0-471-02091-5 : £11.00
ISBN 0-471-02090-7 Pbk : £5.75
(B77-20962)

330.9'73'092 — United States. Economic development, 1945-1975. Geographical factors
Estall, Robert Charles. A modern geography of the United States : aspects of life and economy / [by] Robert Estall. — 2nd ed. — Harmondsworth [etc.] : Penguin, 1976. — 3-466p : ill, maps ; 20cm. — (Pelican geography and environmental studies)
Previous ed.: 1972. — Bibl.: p.452-459. — Index.
Pbk : £2.50
ISBN 0-14-021365-1
(B77-12899)

330.9'73'0924 — United States. Economic policies, 1970-1975. *Conference proceedings*
Conference on Individual Liberty and Governmental Policies in the 1970's, *Ohio University, 1975.* Governmental controls and the free market : the US economy in the 1970's / edited by Svetozar Pejovich. — College Station ; London ([c/o 70 Great Russell St., WC1B 3BY]) : Texas A & M University Press, 1976. — [10],225p : ill ; 24cm.
'... papers presented at the Conference on Individual Liberty and Governmental Policies in the 1970's held under the auspices of the Department of Economics, Ohio University, 1975' - Preface.
ISBN 0-89096-020-8 : £9.40
(B77-26853)

330.9'73'0924 — United States. Economic policies, 1971-1974. *Conference proceedings*
Institutions, policies and economic performance / editors Karl Brunner, Allan H. Meltzer. — Amsterdam [etc.] ; Oxford : North-Holland Publishing Co., 1976. — viii,353p : ill ; 24cm. — (Carnegie-Rochester conference series on public policy ; vol.4)
'This ... volume ... offered as a supplement to the Journal of Monetary Economics, contains papers presented at the November 1974 and April 1975 conferences' - Introduction. — Bibl.
ISBN 0-7204-0564-5 Pbk : £9.61
(B77-07120)

330.9'73'0925 — United States. Economic conditions. Related to education, 1976
Bowles, Samuel. Schooling in capitalist America : educational reform and the contradictions of economic life / [by] Samuel Bowles and Herbert Gintis. — London [etc.] : Routledge and Kegan Paul, 1977. — ix,340p : ill ; 22cm.
Originally published: New York : Basic Books ; London : Routledge and Kegan Paul, 1976. — Bibl.: p.297. — Index.
ISBN 0-7100-8486-2 Pbk : £2.95
Primary classification 370'.973
(B77-02891)

330.9'73'0926 — United States. Economic conditions. *Radical viewpoints*
Sherman, Howard. Stagflation : a radical theory of unemployment and inflation / [by] Howard J. Sherman. — New York [etc.] ; London : Harper and Row, 1976. — xv,252p : ill ; 24cm.
Bibl.: p.244. — Index.
ISBN 0-06-046106-3 Pbk : £2.95
(B77-16759)

330.9'8 — Latin America. Economic development, 1492-1975
Furtado, Celso. Economic development of Latin America : historical background and contemporary problems / [by] Celso Furtado ; translated [from the Portuguese] by Suzette Macedo. — 2nd ed. — Cambridge [etc.] : Cambridge University Press, 1976. — xviii, 317p : maps ; 23cm. — (Cambridge Latin American studies ; 8)
Translation of: 'Formação econômica da América Latina'. 2.ed. Rio de Janeiro : Lia, 1970. — Previous English ed.: 1970. — Bibl.: p.305-312. — Index.
ISBN 0-521-21197-2 : £8.80
ISBN 0-521-29070-8 Pbk : £2.95
(B77-20963)

330.9'8'003 — Latin America. Economic development. International political aspects
Silva Michelena, José A. Politics and power blocs : crisis in the international system / by José A. Silva-Michelena. — Brighton : Institute of Development Studies, 1976. — [3],44p ; 30cm. — (Institute of Development Studies. Discussion papers ; no.99 ISSN 0308-5864)
Sd : £1.25
(B77-18597)

330.9'8'003 — Latin America. Economic development. Role of governments. *Conference proceedings*
The **state** and economic development in Latin America : proceedings of a conference held at Cambridge in December, 1976 / edited by E.V.K. Fitzgerald, E. Floto, A.D. Lehmann. — Cambridge ([History Faculty Building, West Rd, Cambridge CB3 9EF]) : Centre of Latin American Studies, University of Cambridge, 1977. — [4],vi[i.e.vii],342p : ill ; 30cm. — (University of Cambridge. Centre of Latin American Studies. Occasional papers ; 1 ISSN 0309-9164)
'... held at Cambridge between the 15th and the 18th of December 1976' - Preface. — Includes 3 papers in Spanish.
ISBN 0-904927-18-0 Pbk : £2.50
(B77-33097)

330.9'83'064 — Chile. Economic policies, 1971-1975
Letelier, Orlando. Chile, economic 'freedom' and political repression / by Orlando Letelier. — Nottingham : Bertrand Russell Peace Foundation ; London : Institute of Race Relations [etc.], [1976]. — 17p : port ; 21cm. — (Transnational Institute. Pamphlets ; no.1) ('Spokesman' pamphlet ; no.56) ('Race and class' pamphlet ; no.2)
Sd : £0.30
(B77-06510)

330.9'83'064 — Chile. Rural regions. Economic conditions, 1919-1973
Loveman, Brian. Struggle in the countryside : politics and rural labor in Chile, 1919-1973 / by Brian Loveman. — Bloomington ; London : Indiana University Press, 1976. — xxxvi,439,[1] p : ill, maps ; 24cm. — (Indiana University. International Development Research Center. Studies in development ; no.10)
Bibl.: p.393-423. — Index.
ISBN 0-253-35565-6 : £10.50
(B77-03989)

330.9'85 — Peru. Economic development, 1776-1940. *Essays*
Social and economic change in modern Peru / edited by Rory Miller, Clifford T. Smith and John Fisher. — [Liverpool] ([P.O. Box 147, Liverpool L69 3BX]) : Centre for Latin-American Studies, University of Liverpool, [1976]. — [5],197p : ill, maps ; 30cm. — (University of Liverpool. Centre for Latin-American Studies. Monograph series ; no.6)
'The papers ... originated in a conference at the Centre for Latin-American Studies in Liverpool University in February 1974' - Introduction. — Bibl.: p.194-197.
ISBN 0-902806-05-x Sp : £2.75
Also classified at 301.29'85
(B77-03990)

330.9'931'03 — New Zealand. Economic conditions. *Reports, surveys. Serials*
Organisation for Economic Co-operation and Development. New Zealand / Organisation for Economic Co-operation and Development. — Paris : O.E.C.D. ; [London] : [H.M.S.O.]. — (Economic surveys ISSN 0474-5183)
[1976]. — 1976. — 46,[4]p(4 fold) : ill ; 24cm.
Pbk : £1.10
ISBN 92-64-11544-7
(B77-01212)

330.9'94 — Australia. Economic conditions, to 1975
Carroll, Brian. Earning a crust : an illustrated economic history of Australia / [by] Brian Carroll. — Sydney [etc.] ; London : A.H. and A.W. Reed, 1977. — 176p : ill, facsims, ports ; 27cm.
Ill. on lining papers. — Bibl.: p.172. — Index.
ISBN 0-589-07196-3 : £8.25
(B77-30002)

331 — LABOUR ECONOMICS

331'.041'0705720941 — Periodical publishing industries. Industrial relations. *Great Britain. Inquiry reports*
Great Britain. *Advisory, Conciliation and Arbitration Service.* Industrial relations in the provincial newspaper and periodical industries : a report / by the Advisory, Conciliation and Arbitration Service. — London : H.M.S.O., [1977]. — x,158p : 1 ill ; 25cm. — (Great Britain. Royal Commission on the Press. Research series ; 2) (Cmnd.6810-2)
Index.
ISBN 0-10-168102-x Pbk : £2.60
Primary classification 331'.041'07941
(B77-22409)

331'.041'07941 — National newspaper publishing industries. Industrial relations. *Great Britain. Inquiry reports*
Great Britain. *Advisory, Conciliation and Arbitration Service.* Industrial relations in the national newspaper industry : a report / by the Advisory, Conciliation and Arbitration Service. — London : H.M.S.O., [1976]. — xiv,342p : ill ; 25cm. — (Great Britain. Royal Commission on the Press. Research series ; 1) (Cmnd. 6680)
Index.
ISBN 0-10-166800-7 Pbk : £5.00
(B77-05909)

331'.041'07941 — Provincial newspaper publishing industries. Industrial relations. *Great Britain. Inquiry reports*
Great Britain. *Advisory, Conciliation and Arbitration Service.* Industrial relations in the provincial newspaper and periodical industries : a report / by the Advisory, Conciliation and Arbitration Service. — London : H.M.S.O., [1977]. — x,158p : 1 ill ; 25cm. — (Great Britain. Royal Commission on the Press. Research series ; 2) (Cmnd.6810-2)
Index.
ISBN 0-10-168102-x Pbk : £2.60
Also classified at 331'.041'0705720941
(B77-22409)

331'.041'353 — Public sector. Industrial relations. *United States, 1960-1975. Comparative studies*
Chauhan, D S. Public labor relations : a comparative state study / [by] D.S. Chauhan with Mark Rounsavall. — Beverly Hills ; London : Sage Publications, [1977]. — 70,[1]p : 2 ill ; 22cm. — (Sage professional papers in administrative and policy studies ; vol.3, no.03-035)
Published in the United States: 1976. — Bibl.: p.63-66.
ISBN 0-8039-0629-3 Pbk : £1.75
(B77-11628)

331'.041'35441001 — Civil service. Industrial relations. *Great Britain*
Great Britain. *Civil Service Department.* Staff relations in the Civil Service / Civil Service Department. — 4th ed. — London : H.M.S.O., 1976. — [3],68p ; 21cm.
This ed. originally published: 1965.
ISBN 0-11-630209-7 Sd : £1.00
(B77-26157)

331'.041'36210941 — National health services. Industrial relations. *Great Britain*
Berridge, John. A suitable case for treatment : a case study of industrial relations in the National Health Service / prepared for the [Open University, Industrial Relations] Course Team by John Berridge. — Milton Keynes : Open University Press, 1976. — 74p : ill(incl 1 col) ; 30cm. — (A post-experience course : industrial relations ; unit 9) (P881 ; unit 9)
With answers. — Bibl.: p.65.
ISBN 0-335-00059-2 Sd : £1.70
(B77-04609)

331'.041'387109421 — Dockers. Industrial relations. *Port of London. Inquiry reports*
Report of a panel of investigation into current difficulties affecting the Transport and General Workers Union, the Dagenham Cold Store and associated companies at Ripple Road, Dagenham, and F.J. Robertson Limited and also the effect on employers of registered dock labour in the London area. — London (Cleland House, Page St., SW1P 4ND) : Advisory, Conciliation and Arbitration Service, [1975]. — v,34p ; 21cm. — (Great Britain. Advisory, Conciliation and Arbitration Service. ACAS reports ; no.2 ISSN 0309-717x)
ISBN 0-906073-01-4 Sd : Unpriced
(B77-15725)

331'.046'91420973 — Steel industries. Industrial relations. *United States, to 1975*
Abel, I W. Collective bargaining : labor relations in steel : then and now / [by] I.W. Abel. — [Pittsburgh] : [Carnegie-Mellon University Press] ; New York ; Guildford : Distributed by Columbia University Press, 1976. — 62p : 2 ports ; 23cm. — (Benjamin F. Fairless memorial lectures ; 1975)
ISBN 0-915604-05-1 : £5.30
(B77-02805)

331'.048'531097445 — Shoemaking industries. Labour movements. *Massachusetts. Lynn, ca 1830-ca 1900*
Dawley, Alan. Class and community : the Industrial Revolution in Lynn / [by] Alan Dawley. — Cambridge, Mass. ; London : Harvard University Press, 1976. — xi,301p : ill ; 24cm. — (Harvard studies in urban history)
Bibl.: p.255-266. — Index.
ISBN 0-674-13390-0 : £13.15
(B77-04610)

331'.07'1141 — Universities. *Great Britain. Open University. Curriculum subjects: Industrial relations. Courses: 'Industrial relations'*

Open University. *Industrial Relations Course Team.* Introduction and guide to the course / prepared for the [Open University, Industrial Relations] Course Team by John Beishon. — Milton Keynes : Open University Press, 1976. — 20p,[3]leaves of plates : ill ; 30cm. — (A post-experience course : industrial relations) (P881 ; CG)
Sp : Unpriced
(B77-03991)

Open University. *Industrial Relations Course Team.* Introduction and study guide / prepared by Ed Rhodes and the [Open University, Industrial Relations] Course Team. — Revised [ed.]. — Milton Keynes : Open University Press, 1977. — 28p,iii leaves of plates : ill(incl 1 col) ; 30cm. — (A post-experience course : industrial relations) (P881 ; CG)
'Course plan 1977' (Sheet ([1]p.) as insert. — Previous ed.: / prepared for the Open University Industrial Relations Course Team by John Brishon. 1976.
Sp : Unpriced
(B77-26158)

331'.07'201724 — Villages. Personnel. Research. *Developing countries. Reports, surveys*

Connell, John, *b.1946.* Assessing village labour situations in developing countries : a study prepared for the International Labour Office, within the framework of the World Employment Programme, at the Institute of Development Studies, University of Sussex, Brighton / by John Connell, Michael Lipton. — Delhi ; Oxford [etc.] : Oxford University Press, 1977. — [9],180p ; 22cm.
At head of title: Institute of Development Studies, Village Studies Programme. — Bibl.: p.158-171. — Index.
ISBN 0-19-560794-5 : £3.95
(B77-33652)

331'.0941 — Employment. Labour. *Great Britain, 1918-1939*

Essays in labour history, 1918-1939 / edited by Asa Briggs, John Saville. — London : Croom Helm [etc.], 1977. — 292p ; 23cm.
Index.
ISBN 0-85664-239-8 : £7.95
(B77-12900)

331'.0941 — Industrial relations. *Europe. Periodicals*

European industrial relations review. — London (170 Finchley Rd, N.W.3) : Eclipse Publications.
No.1- ; Jan. 1974-. — 1974-. — 30cm.
Monthly. — 32p. in no.37.
Sd : £45.00 yearly
ISSN 0309-7234
(B77-19250)

331'.0941 — Industrial relations. *Great Britain*

Clegg, Hugh Armstrong. The system of industrial relations in Great Britain / [by] Hugh Armstrong Clegg. — 3rd ed. — Oxford : Blackwell, 1976. — xiii,522p ; 23cm. — ([Warwick studies in industrial relations])
Previous ed.: 1972. — Index.
ISBN 0-631-17160-6 : £5.75
(B77-16226)

Great Britain. *Central Office of Information. Reference Division.* Industrial relations / [prepared by Reference Division, Central Office of Information]. — London : H.M.S.O., 1977. — [4],37p ; 24cm. — (Manpower and employment in Britain) (Central Office of Information reference pamphlet ; 148)
Bibl.: p.36-37.
ISBN 0-11-700921-0 Sd : £0.90
(B77-16227)

Jackson, Michael Peart. Industrial relations : a textbook / [by] Michael P. Jackson. — London : Croom Helm, 1977. — 281p ; 23cm.
Bibl.: p.250-275. — Index.
ISBN 0-85664-194-4 : £8.50 : CIP rev.
ISBN 0-85664-199-5 Pbk : £3.00
(B77-11103)

Whitehead, Ken. Industrial relations / [by] Ken Whitehead. — Sevenoaks : Teach Yourself Books, 1977. — viii,223p : 1 ill ; 18cm. — (Teach yourself books) (Business & management studies)
Index.
ISBN 0-340-22082-1 Pbk : £1.50
(B77-27708)

331'.0941 — Industrial relations. Policies of government. *Great Britain, 1956-1975*

Crouch, Colin. Class conflict and the industrial relations crisis : compromise and corporatism in the policies of the British state / [by] Colin Crouch. — [New York] : Humanities Press ; London [etc.] : Heinemann Educational, 1977. — xvii,302p ; 23cm.
Bibl.: p.273-289. — Index.
ISBN 0-435-82250-0 : £7.50
(B77-29226)

331'.0941 — Industrial relations. Role of government. *Great Britain*

Hillard, John. Institutions and political and legal environments / prepared for the [Open University, Industrial Relations] Course Team by John Hillard. — Milton Keynes : Open University Press, 1976. — 67p : 1 col ill ; 30cm. — (A post-experience course : industrial relations ; unit 13) (P881 ; unit 13)
With answers. — Bibl.: p.65-67.
ISBN 0-335-00063-0 Sd : Unpriced
(B77-14590)

Hillard, John. Political and legal factors and regulation / prepared for the [Open University, Industrial Relations] Course Team by John Hillard. — Emergency ed. — Milton Keynes : Open University Press, 1976. — 51p ; 30cm. — (A post-experience course : industrial relations ; unit 14) ([P881 ; unit 14])
With answers. — Bibl.: p.50-51.
ISBN 0-335-00064-9 Sd : Unpriced
(B77-14591)

331'.0941 — Personnel. *Great Britain. Statistics*

British labour statistics year book / Department of Employment. — London : H.M.S.O.
1975. — 1977. — 370p : ill ; 30cm.
Index.
ISBN 0-11-361097-1 Pbk : £20.00
(B77-27709)

331.1 — LABOUR FORCE AND MARKET

331.1 — Employment. *Organisation for Economic Co-operation and Development countries. Conference proceedings*

Structural determinants of employment and unemployment : experts' meeting, Paris, 7th-11th March 1977. — Paris : Organisation for Economic Co-operation and Development ; [London] : [H.M.S.O.].
In 2 vols.
Vol.1. — 1977. — [2],i,107p : ill ; 24cm.
Pbk : £2.50
ISBN 92-64-11668-0
(B77-17958)

331.1 — Employment. Policies of governments. *Organisation for Economic Co-operation and Development countries. Conference proceedings*

Organisation for Economic Co-operation and Development. *Manpower and Social Affairs Committee.* Ministers of labour and the problems of employment : papers and introductory and concluding statements at the first meeting of the Manpower and Social Affairs Committee [Organisation for Economic Co-operation and Development] at ministerial level, Paris, 4th and 5th March, 1976. — Paris : O.E.C.D. ; [London] : [H.M.S.O.].
Vol.2. — 1977. — 46p ; 24cm.
Pbk : £1.70
ISBN 92-64-11664-8
(B77-20073)

331.1 — Overseas employment. *Practical information. For British personnel*

The **directory** of jobs & careers abroad / edited by Roger Brown. — 3rd ed. — Oxford (9 Park End St., Oxford) : Vacation Work, 1977. — xiv,282p ; 23cm.
Previous ed.: published as 'Jobs & careers abroad'. 1975.
ISBN 0-901205-37-0 : £4.95
(B77-10208)

Golzen, Godfrey. Working abroad : the 'Daily telegraph' guide to working and living overseas / [by] Godfrey Golzen & Margaret Stewart. — London : Kogan Page, 1977. — 239p : ill ; 22cm.
ISBN 0-85038-053-7 : £4.95
ISBN 0-85038-054-5 Pbk : £2.95
(B77-29227)

331.1'01'82 — Employment. Statistics. Information sources. *Great Britain*

Buxton, Neil Keith. British employment statistics : a guide to sources and methods / [by] N.K. Buxton, D.I. MacKay ; assisted by C.L. Wood. — Oxford : Blackwell, 1977. — xv, 197p ; 23cm. — (Warwick studies in industrial relations)
Index.
ISBN 0-631-17240-8 : £10.00 : CIP rev.
(B77-05245)

331.1'07'2041 — Employment. Research sponsored by Great Britain. Department of Employment. *Great Britain. Reports, surveys. Serials*

Great Britain. *Department of Employment.* Research / Department of Employment [and] Manpower Services Commission ... [et al.]. — London : H.M.S.O.
1975-76. — 1977. — v,72p ; 21cm.
ISBN 0-11-361088-2 Sd : £1.40
(B77-11629)

331.1'09424'51 — Employment. *Salop. Oswestry (District). Reports, surveys*

Oswestry *(District). Council.* Employment and population in Oswestry Borough : the problems & potential : a report to the Development Commission / [Oswestry District Council]. — [Oswestry] ([Council Offices, Castle View, Oswestry, Shropshire SY11 1JR]) : The Council, 1977. — [4],14[i.e.17]p : maps ; 26cm.
'Minutes of the Development Committee of the Borough of Oswestry held ... Tuesday, April 5 1977' ([3]p.;sd) as insert.
Sp : Unpriced
(B77-17959)

331.1'09424'68 — Employment. *Staffordshire. Lichfield (District). Reports, surveys*

Smith, Barbara Mary Dimond. Employment opportunities in the Lichfield area of South Staffordshire / by Barbara M.D. Smith. — [Birmingham] : Centre for Urban and Regional Studies, University of Birmingham. — (University of Birmingham. Centre for Urban and Regional Studies. Research memoranda ; no.29 ISSN 0306-4034)
Technical appendix. Part 1. The study area : population, migration, employers and jobs in the study area : a technical appendix to the main report. — 1974. — [6],211,[5]leaves,[2] leaves of plates : 2 maps ; 30cm.
Ls : £2.00
(B77-19251)

331.1'09425'3 — Employment. *Lincolnshire. Reports, surveys. For structure plan making*

Lincolnshire *(County). Planning Department.* Employment and industry : a background paper to the Lincolnshire structure plan / Lincolnshire County Council [Planning Department]. — [Lincoln] ([County Offices, Lincoln LN1 1YJ]) : [The Department], 1976. — 52p : ill, form, maps ; 30cm. — (Report of survey ; part 8)
Cover title: Lincolnshire structure plan, background paper, employment & industry . — 'Summary' (sheet ([2]p.) as insert.
Sp : £0.70
(B77-31732)

331.1'09426'752 — Employment. *Essex. Chelmsford (District). Rural regions. Reports, surveys*

Chelmsford *(District). Council.* Rural areas study, employment / Chelmsford District Council. — Chelmsford (Planning Department, Burgess Well Rd, Chelmsford CM1 1TR) : [The Council], [1977]. — [3],11[i.e.13]p ; 30cm. — (Subject report ; 6)
Sd : £0.20
(B77-11630)

331.1'098 — Employment. Effects of technological choice. Role of multinational companies. *Latin America*

Hellinger, Douglas A. Unemployment and the multinationals : a strategy for technological change in Latin America / [by] Douglas A. Hellinger, Stephen H. Hellinger ; foreword by Barbara Ward. — Port Washington ; London : Kennikat Press, 1976. — [1],viii,158p ; 23cm. — (Kennikat Press national university publications)
Bibl.: p.146-153. — Index.
ISBN 0-8046-9126-6 : £8.25
(B77-00641)

331.1'1 — Air services. Manpower. *Great Britain. Reports, surveys. Serials*

Manpower in air transport / [Air Transport and Travel Industry Training Board]. — Staines (Staines House, High St., Staines, Middx TW18 4AS) : The Board.
1975. — [1976]. — 42,[1]p : ill(chiefly col) ; 30cm.
Sd : £2.00
(B77-02806)

331.1'1 — Church of England. Manpower. Clergy. *Reports, surveys*

Buchanan, Colin Ogilvie. Inflation deployment and the job prospects of the clergy / by Colin Buchanan. — Bramcote : Grove Books, 1976. — 16p ; 22cm.
ISBN 0-901710-84-9 Sd : £0.30
(B77-03416)

331.1'1 — Civil service. Manpower planning. *Great Britain. Reports, surveys*
Manpower planning in the Civil Service / [by] A.R. Smith ... [et al.] ; edited by A.R. Smith. — London : H.M.S.O., 1976. — vii,292p : ill, form ; 25cm. — (Civil Service studies ; no.3)
Bibl.: p.290-292.
ISBN 0-11-630233-x Pbk : £10.00
(B77-11631)

331.1'1 — Great Britain. Royal Navy. Manpower, 1693-1873. *Readings from contemporary sources*
The **manning** of the Royal Navy : selected public pamphlets, 1693-1873 / edited by J.S. Bromley. — [London] : Navy Records Society, 1974 [i.e. 1976]. — [4],l,409p,[4]p of plates : 1 ill, facsims ; 23cm. — (Navy Records Society. Publications ; vol.119)
Spine title: Manning pamphlets, 1693-1873. — Bibl.: p.vii-viii. — Index.
ISBN 0-85354-079-9 : £9.00
(B77-07121)

331.1'1 — Health services. Auxiliary personnel. Employment. *United States*
Goldstein, Harold M. Entry-level health occupations : development and future / [by] Harold M. Goldstein and Morris A. Horowitz. — Baltimore ; London : Johns Hopkins University Press, 1977. — xi,100p : 1 ill ; 21cm. — (Policy studies in employment and welfare ; no.27)
Bibl.: p.93-95. — Index.
ISBN 0-8018-1911-3 : £6.80
ISBN 0-8018-1912-1 Pbk : £2.60
(B77-23187)

331.1'1 — Information services & libraries. Manpower planning. *Great Britain. Research reports*
Sergean, Robert. Librarianship and information work : job characteristics and staffing needs / [by] R. Sergean. — London (Publications, British Library Research and Development Department, Sheraton House, Great Chapel St., W1V 4BH) : British Library, 1977. — vi,60p : ill ; 30cm. — (British Library. Research and development reports ; no.5321HC ISSN 0308-2385)
ISBN 0-85350-145-9 Sp : £2.50
(B77-16228)

331.1'1 — Manpower. *Organisation for Economic Co-operation and Development countries. Statistics*
Labour force statistics = Statistiques de la population. — Paris : Organisation for Economic Co-operation and Development ; [London] : [H.M.S.O.].
[No.1]- ; Feb. = Fév. 1977-. — 1977-. — ill ; 27cm.
Quarterly. — 37p. in 1st issue. — Parallel English and French text. — 'Quarterly supplement to the yearbook' - cover.
Sd : £3.60 yearly
ISSN 0304-3312
(B77-11104)

331.1'1 — Manpower planning. Mathematical models
Grinold, Richard C. Manpower planning models / [by] Richard C. Grinold, Kneale T. Marshall. — New York ; Oxford [etc.] : North-Holland Publishing Co., 1977. — xxix, 267p : ill ; 24cm. — (Publications in operations research series)
Bibl.: p.259-264. — Index.
ISBN 0-7204-8606-8 : £15.48
(B77-24759)

331.1'1 — Manpower services. Organisations. *Great Britain. Manpower Services Commission. Reports, surveys. Serials*
Manpower Services Commission. Annual report / Manpower Services Commission. — [London] ([c/o R.L. Polk and Co. Ltd, Gun Wharf, 128 Wapping High St., E1 9NE]) : [The Commission].
1976-77. — [1977]. — [2],36p : ill(chiefly col), port ; 30cm.
ISBN 0-905932-02-1 Sd : £1.50
(B77-26159)

331.1'1 — Road transport services. Manpower planning. *Great Britain. Case studies*
Road Transport Industry Training Board. Local manpower studies, 1976-1977 : six micro-economic studies in manpower planning in the road transport industry / [Road Transport Industry Training Board]. — Wembley (Capitol House, Empire Way, Wembley, Middx) : The Training Board, 1977. — [3],121p : ill, maps ; 30cm.
Pbk : Unpriced
(B77-20074)

331.1'1 — Social services. Manpower requirements. *Great Britain. Reports, surveys*
Working Party on Manpower and Training for the Social Services. Manpower and training for the social services : report of the Working Party [on Manpower and Training for the Social Services ; for the] Department of Health and Social Security. — London : H.M.S.O., 1976. — iv,178p : ill ; 25cm.
ISBN 0-11-320221-0 Pbk : £2.00
Primary classification 361'.007'1141
(B77-06567)

331.1'1'0941 — Manpower. Policies. *Great Britain*
Manpower Services Commission. Towards a comprehensive manpower policy / [Manpower Services Commission]. — London (166 High Holborn, WC1V 6PF) : M.S.C., [1976]. — 43p : col ill ; 30cm.
ISBN 0-905932-00-5 Sd : Free
(B77-08258)

331.1'142 — Graduates. Employment. *Great Britain*
Prentice, William R. The employment of graduates / by William R. Prentice. — New Malden (46 Coombe Rd, New Malden, Surrey KT3 4QL) : Croner Publications Ltd, 1976. — xvi,205p ; 22cm.
Bibl.: p.194-197. — Index.
ISBN 0-900319-19-4 : £4.95
(B77-24760)

331.1'142 — Graduates. Employment. Role of higher education. *United States. Reports, surveys*
Solmon, Lewis Calvin. College as a training ground for jobs / [by] Lewis C. Solmon, Ann S. Bisconti, Nancy L. Ochsner. — New York ; London : Praeger [for] the Higher Education Research Institute, 1977. — xv,185p : forms ; 25cm. — (Praeger special studies in US economic, social and political issues)
Bibl.: p.175-179. — Index.
ISBN 0-275-24450-4 : £11.70
(B77-33098)

331.1'142 — Graduates. First employment. *Great Britain. Reports, surveys. Serials*
First destination of university graduates / University Grants Committee. — London : H.M.S.O.
1974-75. — 1976. — 78p : ill ; 28cm.
ISBN 0-11-700320-4 Sd : £1.85
ISSN 0302-3311
(B77-07122)

331.1'142 — Polytechnic leavers. First employment. *Great Britain. Statistics*
Polytechnic first degree and HND students : some details of first destination and employment. — Manchester : Central Services Unit for Careers and Appointments Services, 1976.
1975. Statistical supplement / [prepared by the] Polytechnic Careers Advisers Statistics Working Party. — London (c/o Polytechnic of Central London, 104 Bolsover St., W1P 7HF) : Polytechnic Careers Advisers Statistics Working Party, [1977]. — [1],74p ; 30cm.
ISBN 0-905526-02-3 Sp : £2.85
(B77-13542)

331.1'142 — Universities. *Nottinghamshire. Nottingham. University of Nottingham. School of Education. Students. First employment. Reports, surveys*
Shipstone, David Michael. Obtaining an initial teaching post : a report on teaching posts obtained by Post Graduate Certificate of Education students from Nottingham University 1976 / by D.M. Shipstone and K.E. Selkirk. — [Nottingham] ([University Park, Nottingham NG7 2RD]) : University of Nottingham, School of Education, 1977. — [1],ii,28p : form, map ; 30cm.
ISBN 0-85359-047-8 Sp : £0.50
(B77-14099)

331.1'142'096711 — Personnel. Qualifications. Cameroun Republic. Related to occupational attainment, 1945-1975
Clignet, Remi. The Africanization of the labor market : educational and occupational segmentation in the Cameroun / [by] Remi Clignet. — Berkeley [etc.] ; London : University of California Press, 1976. — xvi, 230p : 1 ill, map ; 25cm.
Index.
ISBN 0-520-03019-2 : £10.20
Also classified at 301.5'5
(B77-15129)

331.1'1734'097292 — Slavery. Economic aspects. *Jamaica, 1807-1834*
Higman, B W. Slave population and economy in Jamaica, 1807-1834 / [by] B.W. Higman. — Cambridge [etc.] : Cambridge University Press, 1976 [i.e. 1977]. — viii,327p : ill, maps ; 24cm.
Bibl.: p.311-323. — Index.
ISBN 0-521-21053-4 : £14.00
(B77-11632)

331.1'2 — Labour market. Effects of taxation. *Conference proceedings*
Fiscal policy and labour supply. — [London] : Institute for Fiscal Studies, 1977. — 108p : ill ; 30cm. — (Institute for Fiscal Studies. Conference series ; no.4 ISSN 0140-2633)
'This volume contains the papers presented at a two day conference organised jointly by the University of Stirling and the Institute for Fiscal Studies and held at the University of Stirling in September 1976' - Preface.
ISBN 0-902992-24-4 Pbk : £4.00(£2.67 to members)
(B77-32460)

331.1'2 — Low-income personnel. Labour market. *United States, 1960-1970. Reports, surveys*
Wool, Harold. The labor supply for lower-level occupations / [by] Harold Wool assisted by Bruce Dana Phillips. — New York [etc.] ; London : Praeger ; [London] : [Distributed by Martin Robertson], 1976. — xxi,383p : ill ; 25cm. — (Praeger special studies in US economic, social and political issues)
Bibl.: p.372-382.
ISBN 0-275-23160-7 : £17.45
(B77-07822)

331.1'2'0184 — Labour market. Mathematical models
Pissarides, Christopher A. Labour market adjustment : microeconomic foundations of short-run neoclassical and Keynesian dynamics / [by] Christopher A. Pissarides. — Cambridge [etc.] : Cambridge University Press, 1976. — xi,258p : ill ; 23cm.
Bibl.: p.249-254. — Index.
ISBN 0-521-21064-x : £8.50
(B77-02087)

331.1'2'094 — Labour market. Policies of governments. *European Community countries. Comparative studies*
Mukherjee, Santosh. Governments and labour markets : aspects of policies in Britain, France, Germany, Netherlands and Italy / [by] Santosh Mukherjee. — [London] : P.E.P.], [1976]. — viii,77p ; 21cm. — (Political and Economic Planning. Broadsheets ; no.566)
ISBN 0-85374-153-0 Pbk : £3.20
(B77-01213)

331.1'2'0973 — Labour market. United States. Related to foreign trade
Mitchell, Daniel Jesse Brody. Labor issues of American international trade and investments / [by] Daniel J.B. Mitchell. — Baltimore ; London : Johns Hopkins University Press, 1976. — xiii,112p ; 22cm. — (Policy studies in employment and welfare ; no.24)
ISBN 0-8018-1848-6 : £5.95
ISBN 0-8018-1849-4 Pbk : £2.05
Primary classification 382'.0973
(B77-01322)

331.1'26 — Engineering industries. Manpower. Supply & demand. *Great Britain. Reports, surveys*
Committee on the Supply and Utilisation of Skilled Engineering Manpower. Engineering craftsmen : shortages and related problems : a report / by the Manpower Services Commission - National Economic Development Office Committee on the Supply and Utilisation of Skilled Engineering Manpower. — London : National Economic Development Office, 1977. — v,51p : ill ; 30cm.
ISBN 0-7292-0175-9 Sd : £1.10
(B77-17960)

331.1'26 — Higher education institutions. Places. Demand. *United States*
Radner, Roy. Demand and supply in US higher education / by Roy Radner and Leonard S. Miller ; with the collaboration of ... [others] ; ... prepared for the Carnegie Commission on Higher Education. — New York ; London [etc.] : McGraw-Hill, [1976]. — xxxi,468p : ill ; 24cm.
Published in the United States: 1975. — Bibl.: p.453-459. — Index.
ISBN 0-07-010113-2 : Unpriced
(B77-09554)

331.1'26 — Higher education institutions. Teachers: Doctors of philosophy. Supply & demand. Forecasting. *United States*
Cartter, Allan Murray. Ph D's and the academic labor market / by Allan M. Cartter ; ... prepared for the Carnegie Commission on Higher Education. — New York ; London [etc.] : McGraw-Hill, 1976. — xix,260p : ill ; 24cm.
Bibl.: p.251-256. — Index.
ISBN 0-07-010132-9 : Unpriced
(B77-07123)

331.1'26'091724 — Manpower. Supply & demand. Developing countries. Urban regions. Related to industrial development
Bienefeld, Manfred A. Capital accumulation and employment in the periphery : a programme of research / by Manfred Bienefeld and Hubert Schmitz. — Brighton : Institute of Development Studies, 1976. — [5],29p ; 30cm. — (Institute of Development Studies. Discussion papers ; no.98 ISSN 0308-5864)
Bibl.: p.27-29.
Sd : £1.00
Also classified at 338'.09172'4
(B77-18598)

331.1'27 — Librarians. Mobility. *Western Europe, 1975-1976. Reports, surveys*
Thompson, Anthony. MEILLEUR : Mobility of Employment International, for Librarians in Europe : professional staff exchanges and secondments between libraries in Western Europe : a survey of opportunities and difficulties / by Anthony Thompson. — London : Library Association, 1977. — 68p ; 30cm. — (Library Association. Research publications ; 20)
At head of title: College of Librarianship, Wales and the Library Association.
ISBN 0-85365-660-6 Pbk : £5.00(£4.00 to members of the Library Association) : CIP rev.
(B77-16229)

331.1'27 — Personnel. Migration. Effects. *Organisation for Economic Co-operation and Development countries*
Bourguignon, François. International labour migrations and economic choices : the European case / by François Bourguignon and Georges Gallais-Hamonno, with Bernard Fernet. — Paris : Development Centre of the Organisation for Economic Co-operation and Development ; [London] : [H.M.S.O.], 1977. — 294p : ill ; 24cm. — (Organisation for Economic Co-operation and Development. Development Centre. Studies)
Pbk : £7.00
ISBN 92-64-11632-x
(B77-17961)

331.1'28 — Employment services. *Great Britain. Periodicals*
Recruitment : the monthly review of the employment industry. — [St Leonards-on-Sea] ([20 Saxon St., St Leonards-on-Sea, E. Sussex TN37 6AG]) : [Monk Personnel Enterprises Ltd].
Jan. 1977-. — [1977]-. — ill, ports ; 42cm.
Sixteen p. in 1st issue.
Sd : £3.95 yearly
ISSN 0140-1025
(B77-29228)

331.1'28 — Job hunting. *Manuals*
Bostwick, Burdette E. Finding the job you've always wanted / [by] Burdette E. Bostwick. — New York ; London [etc.] : Wiley, 1977. — xi, 243p : ill ; 24cm.
'A Wiley-Interscience publication'. — Index.
ISBN 0-471-09059-x : £10.00
(B77-10749)

331.1'28 — State employment services. *Great Britain, to 1975*
Showler, Brian. The public employment service / [by] Brian Showler. — London [etc.] : Longman, 1976. — ix,101p : ill ; 22cm.
Index.
ISBN 0-582-48541-x : £4.50
ISBN 0-582-48542-8 Pbk : £2.50
(B77-02088)

331.1'28'0973 — Job hunting. *United States. Manuals. For school leavers*
Lynch, Richard L. Getting the job / [by] Richard L. Lynch. — New York ; London [etc.] : McGraw-Hill, 1977. — [8],136p : ill, facsims, forms ; 28cm. — (Career core competencies, a cooperative work-experience program)
Pages perforated at inside edge.
ISBN 0-07-028335-4 Pbk : £2.95
(B77-26160)

331.1'37'01 — Unemployment. Theories
Malinvaud, Edmond. The theory of unemployment reconsidered / [by] E. Malinvaud. — Oxford : Blackwell, 1977. — ix, 128p : ill ; 21cm. — (Yrjö Jahnsson lectures)
ISBN 0-631-17350-1 : £5.00 : CIP rev.
(B77-05910)

331.1'377 — Job creation programmes. *Great Britain. Inquiry reports*
Great Britain. *Parliament. House of Commons. Expenditure Committee.* The Job Creation Programme : seventh report from the Expenditure Committee, session 1976-77, together with the minutes of evidence taken before the Social Services and Employment Sub-committee in session 1976-77, appendices and index. — London : H.M.S.O.
Vol.1. — [1977]. — xxxix p ; 25cm. — ([1976-77 H.C.]394-I)
Vol.1 has title: The Jobs Creation Programme.
ISBN 0-10-292477-5 Sd : £0.70
(B77-21730)

Great Britain. *Parliament. House of Commons. Expenditure Committee.* The Job Creation Programme : seventh report from the Expenditure Committee, session 1976-77, together with the minutes of evidence taken before the Social Services and Employment Sub-committee in session 1976-77 and appendices. — London : H.M.S.O.
Vol.2. — [1977]. — xi,407p : ill, form ; 25cm. — ([1976-77 H.C.] 394-II)
ISBN 0-10-299677-6 Pbk : £7.85
(B77-33099)

331.1'37941 — Unemployment. *Great Britain*
The **conscript** army : a study of Britain's unemployed / edited by Frank Field. — London [etc.] : Routledge and Kegan Paul, 1977. — xii,160p : ill ; 22cm. — (Inequality in society)
Bibl.: p.153-157. — Index.
ISBN 0-7100-8779-9 Pbk : £3.25 : CIP rev.
(B77-24057)

Cox, Sarah. Down the road : unemployment and the fight for the right to work / text Sarah Cox ; photography and design Robert Golden. — London : Writers and Readers Publishing Cooperative, 1977. — 127p : ill, facsims, ports ; 21cm.
Bibl.: p.126-127.
ISBN 0-904613-43-7 : £3.50
ISBN 0-904613-35-6 Pbk : £1.50
(B77-20075)

331.1'37941 — Unemployment. Related to government expenditure. *Great Britain*
Burgess, Ronald. Full employment and public spending / [by] Ronald Burgess. — London : Aims for Freedom and Enterprise, [1977]. — [3],19p : ill.
ISBN 0-7281-0073-8 Sd : £0.50
Also classified at 336.3'9'0941
(B77-28436)

331.1'379415 — Unemployment. Policies of government. *Ireland (Republic). Reports, surveys*
Geary, Robert Charles. A study of schemes for the relief of unemployment in Ireland / by R.C. Geary and M. Dempsey with appendix [by] E. Costa. — Dublin : Economic and Social Research Institute, 1977. — vi,147p,2 fold leaves : 1 ill ; 21cm. — (Economic and Social Research Institute. Broadsheets ; no.14)
Bibl.: p.141-147.
ISBN 0-7070-0084-x Pbk : £2.00
(B77-26161)

331.1'379421 — Unemployment. *London, 1971-1975. Reports, surveys*
Oakeshott, J J. Unemployment in London / by J.J. Oakeshott ; [for the Greater London Council] Director-General's Department Policy Studies and Intelligence Branch. — London : G.L.C., 1975. — [1],iv,48p : 2 forms, 2 maps ; 30cm. — (Greater London Council. Intelligence Unit. Research memoranda ; RM499 ISSN 0306-7203)
ISBN 0-7168-0854-4 Sd : £2.30
(B77-15130)

331.1'379678 — Unemployment. Developing countries. Urban regions. Related to migration from rural regions to urban regions. *Study regions: Tanzania. Reports, surveys*
Barnum, H N. Migration, education and urban surplus labour : the case of Tanzania / by H.N. Barnum and R.H. Sabot. — Paris : Development Centre of the Organisation for Economic Co-operation and Development ; [London] : [H.M.S.O.], 1976. — 115p : ill ; 24cm. — (Organisation for Economic Co-operation and Development. Development Centre. Studies : employment series ; no.13)
Bibl.: p.111-115.
Pbk : £2.40
ISBN 92-64-11531-5
Also classified at 301.36'1; 301.36'1
(B77-05246)

331.2 — WORKERS. CONDITIONS OF EMPLOYMENT

331.2'041'374 — Further education institutions. Teachers. Conditions of service. *England. Periodicals*
National Association of Teachers in Further and Higher Education. NATFHE information series. — [London] : [National Association of Teachers in Further and Higher Education].
No.1- ; Mar. 1976-. — [1976]-. — 21cm.
Published at irregular intervals. — Folder (6p.) as 1st issue.
Sd : Unpriced
Also classified at 331.2'041'378120942
(B77-04611)

331.2'041'378120942 — Higher education institutions. Teachers. Conditions of service. *England. Periodicals*
National Association of Teachers in Further and Higher Education. NATFHE information series. — [London] : [National Association of Teachers in Further and Higher Education].
No.1- ; Mar. 1976-. — [1976]-. — 21cm.
Published at irregular intervals. — Folder (6p.) as 1st issue.
Sd : Unpriced
Primary classification 331.2'041'374
(B77-04611)

331.2'042'20942 — Minerals industries. Working conditions. *England, 1800-1900*
Miners, quarrymen and saltworkers / edited by Raphael Samuel. — London [etc.] : Routledge and Kegan Paul, 1977. — xvi,363p,[24]p of plates : ill, facsim, map, ports ; 23cm. — (History Workshop. Series)
Index.
ISBN 0-7100-8353-x : £6.50
ISBN 0-7100-8354-8 Pbk : £3.75
(B77-18599)

331.2'042'92065485 — Motor vehicle industries. *Sweden. Volvo. Working conditions*
Gyllenhammar, Pehr G. People at work / [by] Pehr G. Gyllenhammar. — Reading, Mass. ; London [etc.] : Addison-Wesley, 1977. — xi, 164p : ill ; 22cm.
ISBN 0-201-02499-3 : £5.95
(B77-30004)

331.2'042'920924 — Motor vehicle industries. *Hungary. Budapest. V or os Csillag Traktorgy ar. Working conditions, 1970-1972. Personal observations*
Haraszti, Miklós. A worker in a worker's state : piece-rates in Hungary / [by] Miklós Haraszti ; translated [from the Hungarian MS.] by Michael Wright ; with a foreword by Heinrich Böll ; a note about the author and a transcript of the author's trial. — Harmondsworth [etc.] : Penguin, 1977. — 175p ; 19cm. — (A pelican original)
ISBN 0-14-021988-9 Pbk : £0.85
(B77-30005)

331.2'043'0942 — Agricultural industries. Working conditions. *England. Reports, surveys. Serials*
Report on safety, health, welfare and wages in agriculture : (including the reports of proceedings required by section 13 of the Agricultural Wages Act 1948, section 21 of the Agriculture (Safety, Health and Welfare Provisions) Act 1956, and section 29 of the Health and Safety at Work etc. Act 1974) / Ministry of Agriculture, Fisheries and Food. — London : H.M.S.O.
1975 : (extended to 29 February 1976 for health and safety). — 1977. — 29p : ill ; 25cm.
ISBN 0-11-241133-9 Sd : £0.70
(B77-22410)

331.2′0968 — American companies. Personnel. Working conditions. *South Africa, to 1976. Reports, surveys*
Myers, Desaix. Labor practices of US corporations in South Africa / [by] Desaix Myers III ; introduction by Dick Clark. — New York ; London : Praeger [for] the Investor Responsibility Research Center, 1977. — xvi, 123p : map ; 25cm. — (Praeger special studies in international business, finance and trade)
ISBN 0-275-24520-9 : £11.05
(B77-26854)

331.2′15 — Road freight transport services. Personnel. Remuneration. Determination. Wages councils. *Great Britain. Road Haulage Wages Council. Abolition. Proposals. Inquiry reports*
Great Britain. *Advisory, Conciliation and Arbitration Service.* Road Haulage Wages Council : report of an inquiry into questions referred to ACAS by the Secretary of State for Employment as to whether the Road Haulage Wages Council should be abolished or whether it should become a statutory joint industrial council / Advisory, Conciliation and Arbitration Service. — [London] ([Cleland House, Page St., SW1P 4ND]) : [The Service], [1977]. — 64p ; 21cm. — (Great Britain. Advisory, Conciliation and Arbitration Service. ACAS reports ; no.6 ISSN 0309-717x)
ISBN 0-906073-04-9 Sd : Unpriced
(B77-15727)

331.2′15′06141 — Personnel. Remuneration. Arbitration. Organisations. *Great Britain. Central Arbitration Committee. Cases*
Incomes Data Services. Central Arbitration Committee awards, 1976 / [Incomes Data Services]. — London (140 Great Portland St., W.1) : I.D.S., 1977. — [4],168,[3]p ; 21cm. — (Incomes Data Services. Handbook series ; no.5 ISSN 0308-7085)
Index.
Pbk : £2.50
(B77-16760)

331.2′164′0941 — Personnel. Remuneration. Incentive schemes. *Great Britain. Reports, surveys*
Lloyd, Penelope Anne. Incentive payment schemes : a review of current practice in 245 organisations / [by] Penelope A. Lloyd. — London : British Institute of Management, 1976. — 51,[2]p : ill ; 30cm. — (Management survey report ; no.34 ISSN 0305-8352)
Bibl.: p.50-51.
ISBN 0-85946-073-8 Sd : £20.00
(B77-00074)

331.2′166 — Music. Recordings. Copyright fees. *Great Britain. Inquiry reports*
Francis, Hugh Elvet. Public inquiry into music royalties payable under section 8 of the Copyright Act 1956 : report / by Hugh E. Francis ; presented to Parliament by the Secretary of State for Trade ... — London : H.M.S.O., [1977]. — [1],39p : ill ; 25cm. — (Cmnd.6903)
ISBN 0-10-169030-4 Sd : £0.75
(B77-28437)

331.2′2 — Personnel. Remuneration. London. Compared with remuneration of South-east England personnel. *Reports, surveys*
Jaroszek, J. Earnings in relation to employment changes / by J. Jaroszek ; [for the Greater London Council] Director General's Department Policy Studies and Intelligence Branch. — London : G.L.C., 1975. — [1],ii, 42p : ill ; 30cm. — (Greater London Council. Intelligence Unit. Research memoranda ; RM500 ISSN 0306-7203)
ISBN 0-7168-0861-7 Sd : £2.30
(B77-15728)

331.2′52 — Local authorities. Personnel. Superannuation schemes. *Great Britain*
The **local** government superannuation scheme : an explanation. — [New ed.]. — London : Shaw and Sons, 1976. — ii,32p ; 22cm.
Previous ed.: 1975. — Index.
ISBN 0-7219-0354-1 Sd : £0.43
(B77-14100)

331.2′52 — Superannuation schemes. *Organisation for Economic Co-operation and Development countries. Reports, surveys*
Old age pension schemes. — Paris : Organisation for Economic Co-operation and Development ; [London] : [H.M.S.O.], 1977. — 206p : 3 ill ; 24cm.
'... Lucienne Cahen, principal administrator in the Directorate of Social Affairs, Manpower and Education, prepared a report ... as a basic working document for the Working Group [on Social Aspects of Income Transfer Policy] which met on 28th, 29th and 30th April, 1975. This document ... was brought up to date on the basis of comments from the Member countries ...' - Preface.
Pbk : Unpriced
(B77-11633)

331.2′52′0941 — Companies. Superannuation schemes. *Great Britain*
Labour Research Department. Guide to company pension schemes and the Social Security Pensions Act 1975 / Labour Research Department. — London : L.R.D., 1977. — 29p ; 19cm.
ISBN 0-900508-33-7 Sd : £0.25
(B77-11634)

331.2′52′0941 — Companies. Superannuation schemes. *Great Britain. For personnel*
Company Pensions Information Centre. How a pension fund works / [Company Pensions Information Centre]. — London (7 Old Park La., W1Y 2LJ) : The Centre, 1976. — [1],12p : col ill ; 15x21cm.
ISBN 0-9504274-2-x Sd : Free
(B77-07124)

331.2′52′0941 — Occupational superannuation schemes. *Great Britain. For trade unionism*
Lucas, Harry. Pensions and industrial relations : a practical guide for all involved in pensions / by Harry Lucas. — Oxford [etc.] : Pergamon, 1977. — xiv,191p ; 22cm.
Index.
ISBN 0-08-021947-0 : £8.50 : CIP rev.
ISBN 0-08-021946-2 Pbk : £3.75
(B77-17962)

331.2′52′0941 — Occupational superannuation schemes. *Great Britain. Reports, surveys. Serials*
National Association of Pension Funds. Survey of occupational pension schemes / the National Association of Pension Funds. — Croydon (Prudential House, Wellesley Rd, Croydon CR0 2A) : The Association.
1975. — 1975. — [2],70p ; 30cm.
ISBN 0-905796-00-4 Sd : £2.00(£1.00 to members)
ISSN 0309-0078
(B77-02089)

331.2′52′0941 — Occupational superannuation schemes. Great Britain. Related to state superannuation schemes
National Association of Pension Funds. State and occupational pension schemes / [National Association of Pension Funds]. — [Croydon] ([Prudential House, Wellesley Rd, Croydon CR0 2A5) : [The Association], [1976]. — [1], 15p ; 21cm. — (Notes on pensions ; no.1 ISSN 0309-006x)
ISBN 0-905796-03-9 Sd : Unpriced
Also classified at 368.4′3′00941
(B77-01214)

331.2′52′0941 — Superannuation schemes. *Great Britain*
Hosking, Gordon Albert. Hosking's pension schemes and retirement benefits. — 4th ed. / by K. Muir McKelvey, A.E.G. Round, T.G. Arthur. — London : Sweet and Maxwell, 1977. — ix,372p : forms ; 22cm.
Previous ed.: published as 'Pension schemes and retirement benefits'. 1968. — Index.
ISBN 0-421-19290-9 Pbk : £8.50
(B77-26162)

331.2′52′0941 — Superannuation schemes. *Great Britain. Reports, surveys*
Economist Intelligence Unit. A study of pensions in the United Kingdom / [Economist Intelligence Unit]. — London : E.I.U., 1977. — [8],i,215p,[7]leaves of plates : ill ; 30cm. — (An EIU multi-client project)
Sp : £500.00
(B77-31029)

331.2′52′09417 — Occupational superannuation schemes. *Ireland (Republic)*
Pension and Investment Consultants Limited. Guide to employee benefits in Ireland / prepared by Pension & Investment Consultants Ltd, Willis Faber (Ireland) Ltd. — [New ed.]. — Dublin (6 Harcourt Rd, Dublin 2) : [Pension and Investment Consultants Ltd] ; Dublin : [Willis Faber (Ireland) Ltd], 1975. — 22p ; 31cm.
One sheet as insert. — Previous ed.: 1974.
Sd : Unpriced
(B77-18600)

331.2′52′0973 — Superannuation schemes. Policies of government. *United States*
Greenough, William Croan. Pension plans and public policy / [by] William C. Greenough & Francis P. King. — New York ; Guildford : Columbia University Press, 1976. — xiii,311p : ill ; 24cm.
Index.
ISBN 0-231-04070-9 : Unpriced
(B77-02090)

331.2′55 — Redundancy payments. Rebates. Redundancy Fund. *Great Britain. Accounts*
Redundancy Fund account : account of the Redundancy Fund for the year ended 31st March, together with the report of the Comptroller and Auditor General thereon ... — London : H.M.S.O.
1975-76. — [1976]. — 9p ; 25cm. — ([1976-77 H.C.] 85)
ISBN 0-10-208577-3 Sd : £0.25
(B77-07125)

331.2′57 — Personnel. Time. Allocation. *Conference proceedings*
Chalendar, J de. Lifelong allocation of time / report prepared by J. de Chalendar in co-operation with a group of experts. — Paris : Organisation for Economic Co-operation and Development ; [London] : [H.M.S.O.], 1976. — 84p ; 24cm.
'In November 1974 a meeting of experts was organised ... The present report describes the essential features of the written and oral statements' - Introduction. — Bibl.: p.75-84.
Pbk : £2.20
(B77-06511)

331.2′576 — Personnel. Adult education. Provision of paid leave. *Europe. Reports, surveys*
Von Moltke, Konrad. Educational leaves for employees : European experience for American consideration / [by] Konrad von Moltke, Norbert Schneevoigt. — San Francisco [etc.] ; London : Jossey-Bass, 1977. — xvii,269p ; 24cm. — (Carnegie Council on Policy Studies in Higher Education. Series)
Bibl.: p.251-60. — Index.
ISBN 0-87589-316-3 : £10.00
(B77-26855)

331.2′576 — Psychiatric hospitals. Nurses. Sickness & unauthorised absence from work. *Great Britain. Study examples: Dundee Northern Hospital Group. Reports, surveys*
Cormack, Desmond. Sickness and absence amongst nursing staffs in a psychiatric, mental deficiency hospital group / [by] D. Cormack. — Dundee : Royal Dundee Liff Hospital ; [Dundee] ([c/o Dundee College of Technology, Bell St., Dundee DD1 1HG]) : [Distributed by the author], 1973. — [3],27p ; 23cm.
Bibl.: p.25-26.
ISBN 0-9505369-0-3 Sd : Unpriced
(B77-02807)

331.2′592 — Air services. Industrial training. Organisations. *Great Britain. Air Transport and Travel Industry Training Board. Reports, surveys. Serials*
Air Transport and Travel Industry Training Board. Report and statement of accounts for the year ended 31 March / Air Transport and Travel Industry Training Board. — Staines (158 High St., Staines, Middx TW18 4AS) : The Board.
[1975]-1976. — [1976]. — [5],39p : 2 ill ; 30cm.
Sd : Unpriced
(B77-06512)

331.2'592 — Catering industries. Industrial training. Organisations. *Northern Ireland. Northern Ireland Catering Industry Training Board. Reports, surveys. Serials*

Northern Ireland Catering Industry Training Board. Report and statement of accounts for the period 1 April to 31 March ... / Northern Ireland Catering Industry Training Board. — Belfast : H.M.S.O.
1974-1975. — [1976]. — 24p ; 24cm.
ISBN 0-337-07125-x Sd : £0.40
(B77-20077)

331.2'592 — Ceramics industries. Industrial training. Organisations. *Great Britain. Ceramics, Glass and Mineral Products Industry Training Board. Reports, surveys. Serials*

Ceramics, Glass and Mineral Products Industry Training Board. Report and statement of accounts for the year ended 31 March / Ceramics, Glass and Mineral Products Industry Training Board. — [Harrow] ([Bovis House, Northolt Rd, Harrow, Middx HA2 0EF]) : [The Board].
1976. — [1976]. — [2],31p : ill ; 21x30cm.
Sd : £0.85
ISSN 0307-7047
(B77-02091)

331.2'592 — Distributive trades. Industrial training. Organisations. *Great Britain. Distributive Industry Training Board. Reports, surveys. Serials*

Distributive Industry Training Board. Report and statement of accounts for the year ended 31st March / Distributive Industry Training Board. — Manchester (Information Service Division, MacLaren House, Talbot Rd, Stretford, Manchester M32 0FP) : D.I.T.B.
1976. — [1977]. — [1],40,[1]p : ill, map, ports ; 21cm.
Sd : Unpriced
ISSN 0309-8427
(B77-19252)

331.2'592 — Distributive trades. Industrial training. Organisations. *Northern Ireland. Northern Ireland Distributive Industry Training Board. Reports, surveys. Serials*

Northern Ireland Distributive Industry Training Board. Report and statement of accounts for the period 1 April to 31 March ... / Northern Ireland Distributive Industry Training Board. — Belfast : H.M.S.O.
1974-1975. — [1976]. — 16p ; 24cm.
ISBN 0-337-07126-8 Sd : £0.30
(B77-02808)

331.2'592 — Engineering industries. Industrial training. Grants from Engineering Industry Training Board. *Great Britain. Serials*

Engineering Industry Training Board. Guide to levy, exemption and grant scheme / Engineering Industry Training Board. — [Watford] : E.I.T.B.
1977-78. — 1977. — [1],56p ; 30cm.
Two sheets, 2 leaflets ([3]sides, 8p.,8p. : chiefly forms) in pocket. — Thumb indexed. — Index.
Sd : Unpriced
ISSN 0140-153x
(B77-25428)

331.2'592 — Engineering industries. Industrial training. Organisations. *Great Britain. Engineering Industry Training Board. Reports, surveys. Serials*

Engineering Industry Training Board. Annual report and accounts / Engineering Industry Training Board. — [Watford] : [The Board].
1975/76. — [1976]. — 131[i.e. 133]p(2 fold) : ill, map ; 30cm.
Previously published: as 'Report and statement of accounts'. — Includes 'Annual report and accounts 1975/76' of the Foundry Industry Training Committee.
Pbk : £1.00
ISSN 0309-2879
(B77-04612)

331.2'592 — Engineering industries. Industrial training. Organisations. *Northern Ireland. Northern Ireland Engineering Industry Training Board. Reports, surveys. Serials*

Northern Ireland Engineering Industry Training Board. Report and statement of accounts for the period 1 April to 31 March ... / Northern Ireland Engineering Industry Training Board. — Belfast : H.M.S.O.
1974-1975. — [1976]. — 19p ; 25cm.
ISBN 0-337-07128-4 Sd : £0.30
(B77-02809)

331.2'592 — Food & drinks industries. Industrial training. Organisations. *Northern Ireland. Northern Ireland Food and Drink Industry Training Board. Reports, surveys. Serials*

Northern Ireland Food and Drink Industry Training Board. Report and statement of accounts for the period 1 April to 31 March ... / Northern Ireland Food and Drink Industry Training Board. — Belfast : H.M.S.O.
1974-1975. — [1976]. — 23p ; 25cm.
ISBN 0-337-07122-5 Sd : £0.35
(B77-02810)

331.2'592 — Footwear, leather working & fur skin working industries. Industrial training. Grants from Footwear, Leather and Fur Skin Industry Training Board. *Great Britain. Serials*

Footwear, Leather and Fur Skin Industry Training Board. Grant scheme / Footwear, Leather and Fur Skin Industry Training Board. — Sutton Coldfield (29 Birmingham Rd, Sutton Coldfield, W. Midlands B72 1QE) : [The Board].
Training year 8 : 1st August 1976 to 31st July 1977. — [1976]. — [1],19p : facsim ; 30cm.
ISBN 0-905892-00-3 Sd : Unpriced
(B77-07126)

331.2'592 — Footwear, leather working & fur skin working industries. Industrial training. Organisations. *Great Britain. Footwear, Leather and Fur Skin Industry Training Board. Reports, surveys. Serials*

Footwear, Leather and Fur Skin Industry Training Board. Report and statement of accounts for the year ended 31st March / Footwear, Leather and Fur Skin Industry Training Board. — [Sutton Coldfield] ([29 Birmingham Rd, Sutton Coldfield, W. Midlands B72 1QE]) : [The Training Board].
[1975]-1976. — [1976]. — [1],16p ; 21cm.
Sd : Unpriced
ISSN 0140-0738
(B77-27710)

[1976]-1977. — [1977]. — [1],19p ; 21cm.
Sd : Unpriced
ISSN 0140-0738
(B77-33653)

331.2'592 — Iron & steel industries. Industrial training. Organisations. *Great Britain. Iron and Steel Industry Training Board. Reports, surveys. Serials*

Iron and Steel Industry Training Board. Annual report / Iron and Steel Industry Training Board. — London (4 Little Essex St., WC2R 3LH) : The Board.
1976-77. — [1977]. — [2],35,[1]p : ill, form, map ; 30cm.
Sd : £1.00
ISSN 0305-2265
(B77-31733)

331.2'592 — Knitting, lace & net industries. Industrial training. Levies. Exemption. *Great Britain. Regulations*

Knitting, Lace and Net Industry Training Board. Employers' guide to levy exemption and special grants / Knitting, Lace and Net Industry Training Board. — Nottingham (4 Hamilton Rd, Nottingham NG5 1AU) : [The Board].
1976-77. — [1976]. — [2],29,[2]p : 1 ill ; 15x21cm.
Summary (Folder ([4]p.)) as insert.
ISBN 0-7037-0034-0 Sd : Unpriced
(B77-01215)

331.2'592 — Local authorities. Personnel. Industrial training. Organisations. *England. Local Government Training Board. Reports, surveys. Serials*

Local Government Training Board. Report and accounts / Local Government Training Board. — Luton (8 The Arndale Centre, Luton LU1 2TS) : [The Board].
1975-76. — [1977]. — [1],32,[1]p : ill, port ; 30cm.
Bibl.: p.29-32.
ISBN 0-903994-04-6 Sd : Unpriced
(B77-10750)

331.2'592 — Paper manufacturing industries & paper products industries. Industrial training. *Great Britain. Reports, surveys*

Paper and Paper Products Industry Training Board. Report on the Paper and Paper Products Industry Training Board Manpower Survey 1975. — Potters Bar (Star House, Potters Bar, Herts. EN6 2PG) : The Board.
The industry. — 1976. — [3],9p ; 30cm.
ISBN 0-902929-16-x Sd : Unpriced
(B77-14101)

The waste paper processing sector. — 1976. — [1],iii,9p ; 30cm.
Sd : £0.35
(B77-28442)

The paper and pulp agents sector. — 1976. — [1],iii,6p ; 30cm.
Sd : £0.25
(B77-28440)

The wallcoverings sector. — 1976. — [1],iii, 15p ; 30cm.
Sd : £0.25
(B77-28439)

The paper merchants sector. — 1976. — [1],iii, 15p ; 30cm.
Sd : £0.25
(B77-28438)

The converting sector. — 1976. — [1],iii,26p ; 30cm.
Sd : £0.25
(B77-28441)

331.2'592 — Paper manufacturing industries & paper products industries. Industrial training. Levies. Exemption. *Great Britain. Regulations*

Paper and Paper Products Industry Training Board. Levy abatement and exemption scheme 1st April-31st March / Paper and Paper Products Industry Training Board. — [Potters Bar] ([Star House, Potters Bar, Herts. EN6 2PG]) : [The Training Board].
1977-1978. — [1977]. — [2],8p ; 30cm.
Sheet ([2] sides : form) as insert.
ISBN 0-902929-15-1 Sd : Unpriced
(B77-10209)

331.2'592 — Paper manufacturing industries & paper products industries. Industrial training. Organisations. *Great Britain. Paper and Paper Products Industry Training Board. Reports, surveys. Serials*

Paper and Paper Products Industry Training Board. Annual report and statement of accounts for the year ended 31st March / [Paper and Paper Products Industry Training Board]. — [Potters Bar] ([Star House, Potters Bar, Herts. EN6 2PG]) : [The Board].
1976. — [1976]. — 48p : ill(some col), col map, ports ; 30cm.
ISBN 0-902929-14-3 Sd : Unpriced
(B77-06513)

Paper and Paper Products Industry Training Board. Annual report and statement of accounts for the year ended 31st March / [Paper and Paper Products Industry Training Board]. — Potters Bar (Star House, Potters Bar, Herts. EN6 2PG) : The Board.
[1976]-1977. — [1977]. — [2],41p : col ill, facsim ; 30cm.
Sd : Unpriced
(B77-26856)

331.2'592 — Plastics & rubber industries. Industrial training. Organisations. *Great Britain. Rubber and Plastics Processing Industry Training Board. Reports, surveys. Serials*

Rubber and Plastics Processing Industry Training Board. Report and statement of accounts for the year ended 31 March / Rubber and Plastics Processing Industry Training Board. — Brentford (950 Great West Rd, Brentford, Middx) : The Board.
[1975]-1976. — [1977?]. — [2],28p : ill(some col), ports ; 30cm.
Bibl.: p.28.
Sd : £0.75
(B77-31734)

331.2'592 — Printing & publishing industries. Industrial training. Organisations. *Great Britain. Printing and Publishing Industry Training Board. Reports, surveys. Serials*

Printing and Publishing Industry Training Board. Report and statement of accounts [for the year ended 31st March] / Printing and Publishing Industry Training Board. — London (Merit House, Edgware Rd, NW9 5AG) : The Board.
1976-77. — [1977]. — [2],32,[2]p : ill(chiefly col), ports ; 28cm.
Sd : Unpriced
ISSN 0308-9746
(B77-31735)

331.2'592 — Road transport services. Industrial training. Organisations. *Great Britain. Road Transport Industry Training Board. Reports, surveys. Serials*
Road Transport Industry Training Board. Report and statement of accounts for the year ended 31st March / Road Transport Industry Training Board. — Wembley (Capital House, Empire Way, Wembley, Middx HA9 0NG) : The Board.
[1975]-1976. — 1976. — [4],110p : ill, map ; 30cm.
Pbk : £3.50
ISSN 0308-8707
(B77-32463)

[1976]-1977. — 1977. — [4],127p : ill, map ; 30cm.
Pbk : £3.50
ISSN 0308-8707
(B77-32462)

331.2'592 — Road transport services. Industrial training. Organisations. *Northern Ireland. Northern Ireland Road Transport Industry Training Board. Reports, surveys. Serials*
Northern Ireland Road Transport Industry Training Board. Report and statement of accounts for the period 1 April to 31 March ... / Northern Ireland Road Transport Industry Training Board. — Belfast : H.M.S.O.
1974-1975. — [1976]. — 19p ; 25cm.
ISBN 0-337-07123-3 Sd : £0.30
(B77-03417)

331.2'592 — Shipbuilding industries. Industrial training. Organisations. *Great Britain. Shipbuilding Industry Training Board. Reports, surveys. Serials*
Shipbuilding Industry Training Board. Annual report and statement of accounts for year ended 31 March / [Shipbuilding Industry Training Board]. — South Harrow (Raebarn House, Northolt Rd, South Harrow, Middx HA2 0DR) : The Board.
[1975]-1976. — [1977]. — [1],71p : ill, map, ports ; 30cm.
Sd : Unpriced
ISSN 0140-1459
(B77-24762)

331.2'592 — Synthetic fibre industries. Industrial training. Organisations. *Great Britain. Man-made Fibres Producing Industry Training Board. Reports, surveys. Serials*
Man-Made Fibres Producing Industry Training Board. Report and statement of accounts for the year ended 31st March / Man-Made Fibres Producing Industry Training Board. — London (3 Pond Place, SW3 6QR) : M.M.F.P.I.T.B.
1976. — 1976. — 36,[1]p : ill(some col) ; 21cm.

Sd : Free
(B77-10210)

331.2'592 — Synthetic fibre industries. Industrial training. Organisations. *Northern Ireland. Northern Ireland Man-made Fibres Producing Industry Training Board. Reports, surveys. Serials*
Northern Ireland Man-made Fibres Producing Industry Training Board. Report and statement of accounts for the period 1 April to 31 March ... / Northern Ireland Man-made Fibres Producing Industry Training Board. — Belfast : H.M.S.O.
1974-1975. — [1976]. — 11p ; 24cm.
ISBN 0-337-07127-6 Sd : £0.22
(B77-03992)

331.2'592 — Textile industries. Industrial training. Organisations. *Northern Ireland. Northern Ireland Textiles Industry Training Board. Reports, surveys. Serials*
Northern Ireland Textiles Industry Training Board. Report and statement of accounts for the period 1 April to 31 March ... / Northern Ireland Textile Industry Training Board. — Belfast : H.M.S.O.
1974-1974. — [1976]. — 21p ; 25cm.
ISBN 0-337-07120-9 Sd : £0.35
(B77-03993)

331.2'592'05 — Industrial training. *Periodicals*
Journal of European industrial training. — Bradford (200 Keighley Rd, Bradford, W. Yorkshire BD9 4JQ) : MCB Journals.
Vol.1, no.1- ; 1977-. — 1977-. — ill, ports ; 30cm.
Six issues a year. — [2],viii,[8],32p. in 1st issue. — Supersedes: Industrial training international ; and, Journal of European training.
Sd : £19.70 yearly
ISSN 0309-0590
(B77-15729)

331.2'592'061416 — Industrial training. Organisations. *Northern Ireland. Northern Ireland Training Council. Reports, surveys. Serials*
Northern Ireland Training Council. Report / Northern Ireland Training Council ... — Belfast : H.M.S.O.
[1975]. — [1975]. — 35p : map ; 25cm.
At head of title: Northern Ireland Assembly.
ISBN 0-337-07103-9 Sd : £0.34
ISSN 0140-2013
(B77-25429)

331.2'592'061416 — Industrial training. Organisations. *Northern Ireland. Northern Ireland Training Executive. Reports, surveys. Serials*
Northern Ireland Training Executive. Report and statement of accounts for the period 1 April to 31 March / Northern Ireland Training Executive. — Belfast : H.M.S.O.
1974-1975. — [1976]. — 16p ; 25cm.
At head of title: Department of Manpower Services.
ISBN 0-337-07117-9 Sd : £0.30
(B77-02811)

331.2'592'0941 — Industrial training. Policies of government. *Great Britain, to 1976*
Perry, Peter John Charles. The evolution of British manpower policy : from the Statute of Artificers 1563 to the Industrial Training Act 1964 / by P.J.C. Perry. — [Chichester] : The author ; London : Distributed by the British Association for Commercial and Industrial Education, 1976. — xx,329p : ill ; 25cm.
Index.
ISBN 0-905675-01-0 : £16.00
ISBN 0-905675-00-2 Pbk : £14.00
(B77-15730)

331.2'81'35500941 — British military forces. Personnel. Remuneration. *Reports, surveys. Serials*
Review Body on Armed Forces Pay. Report / Review Body on Armed Forces Pay. — London : H.M.S.O.
1977 : 6th. — [1977]. — iii,17p ; 25cm. — (Cmnd.6801)
ISBN 0-10-168010-4 Sd : £0.45
(B77-15202)

331.2'81'371100942 — Schools. Teachers. Remuneration. Burnham Scale. *England. Proposals. Serials*
Scales of salaries for teachers in primary and secondary schools, England and Wales ... / Department of Education and Science. — London : H.M.S.O.
1977. — 1977. — v,54p ; 25cm.
ISBN 0-11-270453-0 Sd : £1.75
(B77-17963)

331.2'81'610941 — Doctors. Remuneration. *Great Britain. Proposals*
Review Body on Doctors' and Dentists' Remuneration. Report [of the] Review Body on Doctors' and Dentists' Remuneration. — London : H.M.S.O.
1977 : 7th. — 1977. — v,73p ; 24cm. — (Cmnd.6800)
ISBN 0-10-168000-7 Sd : £1.35
ISSN 0301-3877
Also classified at 331.2'81'617600941
(B77-20964)

331.2'81'617600941 — Dentists. Remuneration. *Great Britain. Proposals*
Review Body on Doctors' and Dentists' Remuneration. Report [of the] Review Body on Doctors' and Dentists' Remuneration. — London : H.M.S.O.
1977 : 7th. — 1977. — v,73p ; 24cm. — (Cmnd.6800)
ISBN 0-10-168000-7 Sd : £1.35
ISSN 0301-3877
Primary classification 331.2'81'610941
(B77-20964)

331.2'941 — Personnel. Low pay. *Great Britain, ca 1950-1975*
Are low wages inevitable? / edited by Frank Field. — Nottingham : Bertrand Russell Peace Foundation for Spokesman Books, 1977. — 144p ; 23cm.
'Most of the contributions ... were prepared for a Low Pay Unit seminar ... organised by Jackie Lebe and Pauline Wingate of the Acton Society Trust' - Preface. — Bibl.: p.142-144.
ISBN 0-85124-164-6 : £4.75
ISBN 0-85124-165-4 Pbk : Unpriced
(B77-24763)

331.2'941 — Personnel. Remuneration. *Great Britain. Reports, surveys. Periodicals*
Reward : employment market survey. — Hitchin (Bancroft Court, Hitchin, Herts. SG5 1LW) : Synergy Publishing Ltd.
[July 1975]-. — 1975-. — 30cm.
Three issues a year. — 52p. in 1st issue.
Sd : £37.80 yearly (£32.40 to members or clients of the sponsoring bodies)
ISSN 0140-0770
(B77-32464)

331.2'941 — Personnel. Remuneration. *Great Britain. Statistics*
New earnings survey / Department of Employment. — London : H.M.S.O.
1976. Part A : Report, general and selected key results. — 1976. — 64p : form ; 28cm.
ISBN 0-11-723803-1 Sd : £1.50
(B77-02812)

1976. Part C : Analyses by industry. — 1976. — 55p ; 28cm.
ISBN 0-11-723804-x Sd : £1.50
(B77-07127)

1976. Part D : Analyses by occupation. — 1977. — 55p ; 28cm.
ISBN 0-11-723805-8 Sd : £1.50
(B77-11635)

1976. Part E : Analyses by region and age-group. — 1976. — [1],63p ; 28cm.
ISBN 0-11-723806-6 Sd : £1.50
(B77-10211)

1976. Part F : Hours, earnings by length of service, earnings of part-time workers. — 1977. — 59p ; 28cm.
ISBN 0-11-723807-4 Sd : £1.50
(B77-11105)

331.2'954 — Personnel. Remuneration. Control. Policies of government. *India (Republic)*
Dasgupta, Ajit Kumar. A theory of wage policy / by A.K. Das Gupta. — Delhi ; London [etc.] : Oxford University Press, 1976. — xii,78p : 3 ill ; 22cm.
Index.
ISBN 0-19-560699-x Pbk : £1.95
(B77-16230)

331.2'982 — Personnel. Remuneration. *Argentina, 1880-1910*
Cortés Condé, Roberto. Trends of real wages in Argentina (1880-1910) / by R. Cortés Condé. — Cambridge (History Faculty Building, West Rd, Cambridge CB3 9EF) : Centre of Latin American Studies, University of Cambridge, 1976. — [3],46p ; 30cm. — (University of Cambridge. Centre of Latin American Studies. Working papers ; no.26 ISSN 0306-6290)
ISBN 0-904927-17-2 Sd : £0.50
(B77-14102)

331.3 — WORKERS. SPECIAL AGE GROUPS

331.3'4 — Adolescents. Vacation employment. Organisations. *Great Britain. Directories*
The **directory** of summer jobs in Britain. — Oxford (9 Park End St., Oxford) : Vacation-Work.
1977 ed. / editor Carole Moor. — 1977. — 155p : ill, map ; 22cm.
Cover title: Summer jobs in Britain.
ISBN 0-901205-34-6 Pbk : £1.75
(B77-10212)

331.3'4 — British adolescents. Overseas vacation employment. Organisations. *Directories*
The **directory** of summer jobs abroad. — Oxford (9 Park End St., Oxford) : Vacation-Work.
1977 ed. / editor David Stevens. — 1977. — 156p : ill ; 22cm.
Cover title: Summer jobs abroad.
ISBN 0-901205-39-7 Pbk : £1.75
ISSN 0308-7123
(B77-10213)

331.3'4 — Employment. Personal adjustment of male school leavers. *Scotland. Reports, surveys*
Weir, Alexander Douglas. Glad to be out? : (a study of school leavers) / [by] A.D. Weir and F.J. Nolan. — Edinburgh (16 Moray Place, Edinburgh EH3 6DR) : Scottish Council for Research in Education, 1977. — [2],iv,134p ; 21cm.
Bibl.: p.131-134.
ISBN 0-901116-12-2 Pbk : £2.00
(B77-25430)

331.3'4 — Factories. Working conditions. Attitudes of young personnel. *Great Britain. Case studies*

Simon, Martin. Youth into industry : a study of young people's attitudes to work at a large Midlands factory / [by] Martin Simon. — Leicester : National Youth Bureau, 1977. — 69p ; 21cm.
ISBN 0-902095-77-3 Sd : £2.50
(B77-33654)

331.3'4 — First employment. Personal adjustment of young persons. *Organisation for Economic Co-operation and Development countries. Reports, surveys*

Organisation for Economic Co-operation and Development. Entry of young people into working life : general report / [Organisation for Economic Co-operation and Development]. — Paris : O.E.C.D. ; [London] : [H.M.S.O.], 1977. — 106p : ill ; 24cm.
Bibl.: p.103-106.
Pbk : £3.00
ISBN 92-64-11641-9
Also classified at 331.3'4
(B77-14592)

331.3'4 — School leavers. First employment. *Tyne and Wear (Metropolitan County). Newcastle upon Tyne. Research reports*

Moor, Christine H. From school to work : effective counselling and guidance / [by] Christine H. Moor. — London [etc.] : Sage Publications, 1976. — 191,[1]p : 1 ill ; 23cm. — (Sage studies in social and educational change ; vol.3)
ISBN 0-8039-9947-x : £6.00
ISBN 0-8039-9856-2 Pbk : £3.00
(B77-00073)

331.3'4 — Young persons. Unemployment. *Organisation for Economic Co-operation and Development countries. Reports, surveys*

Organisation for Economic Co-operation and Development. Entry of young people into working life : general report / [Organisation for Economic Co-operation and Development]. — Paris : O.E.C.D. ; [London] : [H.M.S.O.], 1977. — 106p : ill ; 24cm.
Bibl.: p.103-106.
Pbk : £3.00
ISBN 92-64-11641-9
Primary classification 331.3'4
(B77-14592)

331.3'4'061416 — Young persons. Employment. Organisations. *Northern Ireland. Northern Ireland Youth Employment Service Board. Reports, surveys. Serials*

Northern Ireland Youth Employment Service Board. Annual report of the Northern Ireland Youth Employment Service Board for the period ended 31 December .... — Belfast : H.M.S.O.
1974 : 11th : and accounts for the period 1 April 1974 to 31 December 1974, together with the report of the Comptroller and Auditor-General thereon. — [1975]. — 45p ; 24cm.
At head of title: Department of Manpower Services.
ISBN 0-337-07137-3 Sd : £0.75
(B77-08830)

331.3'4'0941 — School leavers. First employment. *Great Britain. Illustrations. Secondary school texts*

Smith, Gillian Crampton. It's only fair / [by Gillian Crampton Smith and Sarah Curtis]. — [London] : [Longman], [1977]. — 1v. : ill ; 30cm. — (Longman thinkstrips)
Teachers' booklet (3 leaves), 10 copies of folder ([4]p.) in envelope. — Bibl.: leaf[3] of teachers' booklet.
ISBN 0-582-22261-3 : £0.85
Also classified at 331.4'0941
(B77-16761)

331.3'4'0941 — School leavers. First employment. *Great Britain. Secondary school texts*

Schools Council Careers Education and Guidance Project. Work out : the job market / [Schools Council Careers Education and Guidance Project]. — [London] ([160 Great Portland St., W.1]) : Schools Council, 1977. — 16p : ill(some col), ports ; 19x24cm.
Sd : Unpriced
(B77-20965)

331.3'4'0941 — Young persons. Employment. *Great Britain. Proposals*

Manpower Services Commission. Young people and work : report on the feasibility of a new programme of opportunities for unemployed young people / [Manpower Services Commission]. — London (166 High Holborn, WC1V 6PF) : The Commission, 1977. — 63p : ill(some col) ; 30cm.
Sd : Unpriced
(B77-26857)

331.3'4'09729 — Young persons. Employment. *Caribbean region. Conference proceedings*

The **young** unemployed : a Caribbean development problem : report of a Caribbean symposium on employment strategies and programmes [organized through the] Commonwealth Youth Programme. — London : Commonwealth Secretariat, 1976. — [1],iv,112p ; 29cm.
'... held in Barbados from September 29 to October 10, 1975' - Introduction. — Bibl.: p.53-55.
ISBN 0-85092-107-4 Pbk : £0.75
(B77-02813)

331.3'86'9141094249 — Iron industries. Personnel: Children. Working conditions. *West Midlands (Metropolitan County). Black Country, 1841. Inquiry reports. Facsimiles. Secondary school texts*

Great Britain. *Commission for Inquiry into the Employment and Condition of Children in Mines and Manufactories.* [Children's Employment Commission : second report of the Commissioners on Trades and Manufactures. Reports by R.H. Home, Esq., on the Employment of Children and Young Persons in the Iron Trades and other Manufactures of South Staffordshire, and the neighbouring parts of Worcestershire and Shropshire ..]. Black Country children of iron. — [Stafford] ([Tipping St., Stafford]) : [Staffordshire County Council Education Committee], [1977]. — [1], 78p ; 30cm. — (Staffordshire study book ; 7)
'Reports on Wolverhampton and Sedgley' - p.1. — Facsimile reprints. — Bibl.: p.4.
Sd : £0.50
(B77-33100)

331.4 — WOMEN WORKERS

331.4 — Women. Employment. Discrimination by society. *Conference proceedings*

Women and the workplace : the implications of occupational segregation / edited by Martha Blaxall and Barbara Reagan. — Chicago ; London : University of Chicago Press, 1976. — x,326p : ill ; 24cm.
'... an expanded version of the proceedings of a workshop conference on occupational segregation held in May 1975' - Preface. — '... originally appeared as a supplement to the Spring 1976 issue of "Signs : Journal of Women in Culture and Society" (Volume 1, Number 3, Part 2)' - title page verso. — Index.
ISBN 0-226-05821-2 : £9.40
ISBN 0-226-05822-0 Pbk : £3.00
(B77-02092)

331.4 — Women. Home employment. *Practical information*

Franklin, Olga. A practical guide to making money at home / [by] Olga Franklin. — London : Macdonald and Jane's, 1977. — [5], 136p ; 23cm.
Index.
ISBN 0-354-04129-0 : £4.95
ISBN 0-354-04106-1 Pbk : £2.95
(B77-31030)

331.4 — Women personnel. Industrial training. *Great Britain. Reports, surveys*

Training Services Agency. Training opportunities for women / [Training Services Agency]. — London (162 Regent St., W1R 6DE) : The Agency, [1976]. — [6],40p : ill(chiefly col) ; 30cm.
ISBN 0-9504011-5-3 Sd : Unpriced
(B77-16231)

331.4 — Women. Trade unionism. *Great Britain, to 1976*

Lewenhak, Sheila. Women and trade unions : an outline history of women in the British trade union movement / [by] Sheila Lewenhak. — London [etc.] : E. Benn, 1977. — xii,308p : ill, facsims, ports ; 23cm.
Bibl.: p.296-301. — Index.
ISBN 0-510-00007-x : £7.50
(B77-26858)

331.4'0941 — Women. Employment. *Great Britain*

Mackie, Lindsay. Women at work / [by] Lindsay Mackie & Polly Pattullo. — London : Tavistock Publications, 1977. — 192p ; 20cm. — (Tavistock women's studies)
Bibl.: p.180-186. — Index.
ISBN 0-422-75980-5 : £5.50
ISBN 0-422-75990-2 Pbk : £2.50
(B77-22411)

331.4'0941 — Women. Employment. Discrimination by society. *Great Britain*

Counter Information Services. Women under attack / [Counter Information Services]. — London (9 Poland St., W.1) : Counter Information Services, [1976]. — [2],33p : ill, ports ; 27cm. — (Counter Information Services. Anti-reports ; no.15 ISSN 0305-1242) (Crisis)
Bibl.: p.33.
Sd : £0.45
(B77-16232)

331.4'0941 — Women. Employment. Discrimination by society. *Great Britain. Periodicals*

Women's charter : paper of the Working Women's Charter Campaign. — London (36 Bradmore House, Jamaica St., E.1) : The Campaign.
[No.1- ; 1976-]. — 1976-. — ill ; 45cm.
Six issues a year. — 8p. in Autumn 1976 issue.
Sd : £0.10(£1.00 yearly)
ISSN 0309-2860
(B77-08259)

331.4'0941 — Women. Employment. Equality of opportunity. *Great Britain. Illustrations. Secondary school texts*

Smith, Gillian Crampton. It's only fair / [by Gillian Crampton Smith and Sarah Curtis]. — [London] : [Longman], [1977]. — 1v. : ill ; 30cm. — (Longman thinkstrips)
Teachers' booklet (3 leaves), 10 copies of folder ([4]p.) in envelope. — Bibl.: leaf[3] of teachers' booklet.
ISBN 0-582-22261-3 : £0.85
Primary classification 331.3'4'0941
(B77-16761)

331.4'09411 — Women personnel. Effects of Equal Pay Act 1970 & Sex Discrimination Act 1975. *Scotland. Reports, surveys*

Marshall, Margaret. The Equal Pay and Sex Discrimination Acts : report from Scotland / by Margaret Marshall & Chris Aldred. — Aberdeen (163 King St., Aberdeen) : Aberdeen People's Press, [1977]. — [2],25p : ill ; 30cm. — (An Aberdeen People's Press special report)
Sd : £0.46
(B77-30006)

331.4'81'610974461 — Women doctors. Employment. Equality of opportunity. *United States, 1835-1975. Study regions: Massachusetts. Boston*

Walsh, Mary Roth. 'Doctors wanted, no women need apply' : sexual barriers in the medical profession, 1835-1975 / [by] Mary Roth Walsh. — New Haven ; London : Yale University Press, 1977. — xxiii,303p : ill, ports ; 22cm.
Bibl.: p.285-287. — Index.
ISBN 0-300-02024-4 : £10.80
(B77-24764)

331.5 — WORKERS. CATEGORIES BY SOCIAL AND ECONOMIC STATUS

331.5 — Socially disadvantaged persons. Employment. United States. Related to vocational education. *Forecasts for 1976-1985*

Lecht, Leonard Abe. Occupational choices and training needs : prospects for the 1980s / [by] Leonard A. Lecht. — New York ; London : Praeger [for] the Conference Board, 1977. — xv,205p ; 25cm. — (Praeger special studies in US economic, social and political issues)
Index.
ISBN 0-275-23960-8 : £12.40
Also classified at 371.9'67
(B77-24765)

331.5'9 — Occupational superannuation schemes. Membership of physically handicapped persons. *Great Britain. Inquiry reports*

Great Britain. *Occupational Pensions Board.* Occupational pension scheme cover for disabled people : report of the Occupational Pensions Board ... — London : H.M.S.O., [1977]. — v, 38p ; 25cm. — (Cmnd.6849)
ISBN 0-10-168490-8 Sd : £0.75
(B77-22412)

331.5'9 — Physically handicapped professional personnel. Employment. *Great Britain. Reports, surveys*

Kettle, Melvyn. The Tennant survey : an independent analysis / by Melvyn Kettle. — [Banstead] ([c/o General Secretary, The Stables, 73 Pound Rd, Banstead, Surrey SM7 2HU]) : Association of Disabled Professionals, 1976. — [20] leaves ; 21x30cm.
ISBN 0-9505457-0-8 Sd : £0.50
(B77-09555)

331.5'9'094253 — Mentally handicapped persons. Employment. *Lincolnshire. Reports, surveys*

Callaghan, G Geoffrey. Employing the mentally handicapped : a look at the work and wealth producing potential of the mentally handicapped, which will assist those who might employ them / by G. Geoffrey Callaghan. — Rugby (St Mark's House, Lincoln LN5 7AE) : Mantec Publications [for] Lincolnshire North Community Health Council, 1976. — [3],37p : ill, port ; 22cm.
Bibl.: p.32.
ISBN 0-902540-15-7 Sd : £0.50
(B77-07128)

331.6 — WORKERS. CATEGORIES BY RACIAL, ETHNIC, NATIONAL ORIGIN

331.6'0941 — Ethnic minorities. Employment. Equality of opportunity. *Great Britain. For management*

Carby, Keith. No problems here? : management and the multi-racial workforce, including a guide to the Race Relations Act 1976 / [by] Keith Carby, Manab Thakur. — London : Institute of Personnel Management, 1977. — 156p ; 19cm. — (Management paperbacks)
Bibl.: p.153-154.
ISBN 0-85292-151-9 Pbk : Unpriced
(B77-25431)

331.6'2 — Professional immigrant personnel: Scientists. Discrimination by organisations. *United States*

Parlin, Bradley W. Immigrant professionals in the United States : discrimination in the scientific labor market / [by] Bradley W. Parlin. — New York [etc.] ; London : Praeger ; [London] : [Distributed by Martin Robertson], 1976. — xi,98p : forms ; 24cm. — (Praeger special studies in US economic, social and political issues)
Bibl.: p.90-95. — Index.
ISBN 0-275-01050-3 : £8.15
(B77-05911)

331.6'2'410892 — Paraguay. Economic development. Role of British personnel, 1850-1870

Plá, Josefina. The British in Paraguay, 1850-1870 / [by] Josefina Plá ; translated from the Spanish [MS.] by Brian Charles MacDermot. — Richmond, Surrey (Orchard Rd, Richmond, Surrey) : Richmond Publishing Co. [for] St Antony's College, Oxford, 1976. — [6],xxix,277p,fold plate : map ; 23cm.
Bibl.: p.215-217. — Index.
ISBN 0-85546-196-9 : £8.95
(B77-05912)

331.6'2'72073 — Mexican immigrant personnel. Employment. *United States, 1900-1940*

Reisler, Mark. By the sweat of their brow : Mexican immigrant labor in the United States, 1900-1940 / [by] Mark Reisler. — Westport, Conn. ; London : Greenwood Press, 1976. — xiii,298p ; 22cm.
Bibl.: p.275-288. — Index.
ISBN 0-8371-8894-6 : £9.75
(B77-23188)

331.6'3'6872073 — Chicanos. Employment. *United States*

Briggs, Vernon M. The Chicano worker / [by] Vernon M. Briggs, Jr, Walter Fogel, and Fred H. Schmidt. — Austin ; London : University of Texas Press, 1977. — xv,3-129p ; 24cm.
Bibl.: p.117-124. — Index.
ISBN 0-292-71040-2 : £7.00
(B77-23189)

331.6'3'951073 — Chinese. Employment. *United States. Reports, surveys*

Sung, Betty Lee. A survey of Chinese-American manpower and employment / [by] Betty Lee Sung. — New York [etc.] ; London : Praeger ; [London] : [Distributed by Martin Robertson], 1976. — xxii,249p : maps ; 25cm. — (Praeger special studies in US economic, social and political issues)
Bibl.: p.235-243. — Index.
ISBN 0-275-23090-2 : £14.80
(B77-05913)

331.7 — LABOUR ECONOMICS OF SPECIAL OCCUPATIONS

331.7 — Occupations. *Juvenile literature*

What people do. — Maidenhead : Purnell, 1977. — [12]p : chiefly col ill ; 22cm.
Pbd : £0.45
(B77-16762)

331.7'02 — Careers. Choice. *Secondary school texts*

Schools Council Careers Education and Guidance Project. Work / Schools Council Careers Education and Guidance Project. — London : Longman for the Schools Council.
Part 1. Framework 1. — 1976. — 8p : ill(some col), plan, ports ; 42cm.
ISBN 0-582-22401-2 Sd : £1.00(for 10 copies)
(B77-03418)

Part 1. Framework 1-8. Teachers' guide. — 1977. — [3],79p : ill, forms, plans ; 28cm.
ISBN 0-582-22409-8 Sd : £2.95
(B77-24766)

Part 1. Framework 2. — 1976. — 8p : ill, plan, ports ; 42cm.
ISBN 0-582-22402-0 Sd : £1.00(for 10 copies)
(B77-03419)

331.7'02 — First employment. *Great Britain. For school leavers*

Adamson, Hilary. Starting work / [by] Hilary Adamson. — Revised [ed]. / revised by Mazzie Lewis. — London : Industrial Society, 1976. — [1],v,30p ; 20cm.
Previous ed.: 1972.
ISBN 0-85290-138-0 Sd : £0.45
(B77-11636)

331.7'02 — First employment. *United States. For school leavers*

Wilson, Maurice E. Growing on the job / [by] Maurice E. Wilson. — New York ; London [etc.] : McGraw-Hill, 1977. — [8],136p : ill, facsims, forms ; 28cm. — (Career core competencies, a cooperative work-experience program)
Pages perforated at inside edge.
ISBN 0-07-028337-0 Pbk : £2.95
(B77-28443)

331.7'02 — Spare-time occupations. *Manuals. Juvenile literature*

Archard, Merry. Extra money / [by] Merry Archard ; illustrated by Mik Brown. — London [etc.] : Beaver Books, 1977. — 107p : ill ; 18cm.
Cover title: The Beaver book of extra money.
ISBN 0-600-36259-0 Pbk : £0.45
(B77-27711)

331.7'02'0941 — Careers. Change. *Great Britain. Manuals*

Lancashire, Ruth. Career change / [by] Ruth Lancashire, Roger Holdsworth. — Cambridge : Hobsons Press [for the] Careers Research and Advisory Centre, 1976. — [3],108p : ill, forms, ports ; 22cm.
ISBN 0-86021-064-2 : £4.40
ISBN 0-86021-062-6 Pbk : £1.40
(B77-02814)

331.7'02'0941 — Careers. Choice. *Great Britain. For school leavers*

March, Peter. Your choice at 17+ : a guide to choices after 'A'-Level / [by] Peter March and Michael Smith. — Cambridge : Hobsons Press [for the] Careers Research and Advisory Centre, 1976. — [3],160p : ill, forms ; 18cm.
Bibl.: p.158-160.
ISBN 0-86021-057-x Pbk : £0.95
(B77-01216)

331.7'02'0941 — Careers. Choice. *Great Britain. For school leavers. Serials*

Rethink / [Careers Research and Advisory Centre]. — Cambridge : Hobsons Press.
1976. — 1976. — 111p : ill, form ; 30cm.
Bibl.: p.78. — Index.
ISBN 0-86021-098-7 Sd : £1.00
(B77-03994)

331.7'02'0941 — Occupations. *Great Britain. Career guides*

'Daily telegraph' careers A-Z : careers information service. — New revised ed. — London [etc.] : Collins, 1977. — 192p ; 21cm.
Previous ed.: 1975.
ISBN 0-00-412081-7 : £2.75
ISBN 0-00-412079-5 Pbk : £0.95
(B77-31736)

Employment Service Agency. *Careers and Occupational Information Centre.* Choosing your career. — 3rd ed. / [prepared by the] Careers and Occupational Information Centre of the Employment Service Agency [in association with the Careers Service Branch of the Department of Employment, and by the Central Office of Information]. — [London] : H.M.S.O., 1977. — [2],36,[1]p : ill ; 22cm. — (Choice of careers : new series ; 1)
Previous ed.: / prepared by the Central Youth Employment Executive. 1971.
ISBN 0-11-880909-1 Sd : £0.30
(B77-18601)

Synopsis : the annual guide to employment opportunities. — [London] ([76 St James's La., N10 3RD]) : New Opportunity Press Ltd ; [London] : Sunday Times.
76 / [editor Pamela Pocock]. — [1976]. — 223p : ill, facsims, ports ; 22x26cm.
Index.
Pbk : £2.20
ISSN 0309-3751
(B77-08831)

Synopsis : the good job guide. — [London] ([76 St James' La., N10 3RD]) : New Opportunity Press Ltd ; [London] : 'Sunday times'.
77-78 / [editor Pamela Pocock]. — [1977]. — 302p : ill(some col), facsims, forms, maps(1 col), ports ; 21x25cm.
Previously published: as Synopsis : the annual guide to employment opportunities. — Index.
ISBN 0-903578-27-1 Pbk : £2.95
ISSN 0309-3751
(B77-33656)

331.7'02'0941 — Occupations. *Great Britain. Career guides. For graduates. Serials*

Graduate employment and training / [Careers Research and Advisory Centre]. — Cambridge : Hobsons Press.
1976-77. — 1976. — 400p : ill, forms ; 22cm.
Previously published: as 'Careers beyond a degree'.
ISBN 0-86021-097-9 : Unpriced
ISSN 0309-894x
ISBN 0-86021-096-0 Pbk : Unpriced
(B77-27712)

331.7'02'0941 — Occupations. *Great Britain. Career guides. For school leavers in Southern England*

Opportunities : the New Opportunity Press book for school leavers in the South. — [London] ([2 All Saints St., N1 9RL]) : [New Opportunity Press].
1975. — [1976]. — [2],509p : ill(some col), coats of arms, maps, ports ; 28cm.
Cover title. — Previously published: as 'Opportunities for school leavers in the South'. — Index.
ISBN 0-903578-25-5 Pbk : Unpriced
(B77-05247)

Opportunities for school leavers in the South. — London ([2 All Saints St., N1 9RL]) : New Opportunity Press Ltd.
1974 / with a message from the Parliamentary Under Secretary for Education and Science, Lord Sandford. — [1974]. — 479p : ill(some col), maps, ports ; 28cm.
Index.
Pbk : £0.80
(B77-03995)

331.7'02'0941 — Occupations. *Great Britain. Career guides. Serials*

Annual careers guide : opportunities in the professions, industry, commerce and the public service / [Employment Service Agency] Careers and Occupational Information Centre. — London : H.M.S.O.
[1977 : 15th ed.]. — 1977. — 516p in various pagings ; 24cm.
Index.
ISBN 0-11-885302-3 Pbk : £2.80
(B77-30007)

331.7'02'0941 — Occupations. *Great Britain. Rural regions. Career guides*

Crow, Ivan P. Directory of countryside opportunities / compiled and edited by Ivan P. Crow. — [1977 ed.]. — [Aldridge] ([White Cottage, 63 Longwood Rd, Aldridge, W. Midlands WS9 0TA]) : [The compiler], [1977]. — [17]leaves ; 30cm.
Sd : Unpriced
(B77-33657)

331.7'02'0973 — Careers. Choice. *United States. For school leavers*
Healy, Charles C. Discovering you / [by] Charles C. Healy ; educational consultant Edwin L. Herr ; consulting editor Charles S. Winn. — New York ; London [etc.] : Gregg Division, McGraw-Hill, 1976. — [7],120p : ill(some col), port ; 28cm. — (Careers in focus)
ISBN 0-07-071051-1 Pbk : £3.45
(B77-07129)

331.7'02'0973 — Careers. Choice. *United States. Manuals. For school leavers*
Herr, Edwin L. Schools and careers / [by] Edwin L. Herr. — New York ; London [etc.] : McGraw-Hill, 1977. — [8],136p : ill, forms ; 28cm. — (Career core competencies, a cooperative work-experience program)
Pages perforated at inside edge.
ISBN 0-07-028325-7 Pbk : £2.95
(B77-26859)

331.7'12'0621 — Professions. Organisations. *Commonwealth countries. Commonwealth Foundation. Reports, surveys. Serials*
Commonwealth Foundation. The Commonwealth Foundation. — [London] (Marlborough House [Pall Mall, SW1Y 5HU]) : [The Foundation].
5th report : The first ten years, 1966-1976. — 1976. — 3-97p ; 25cm.
ISBN 0-903850-14-1 Pbk : Free
ISSN 0302-3222
(B77-08260)

331.7'61 — Nationalised industries. Boards of directors. *Great Britain. Lists. Serials*
Public boards : list of members of public boards of a commercial character : with salaries, together with a list of those holding more than one appointment / presented to Parliament by the Minister for the Civil Service. — London : H.M.S.O.
1977, 1st April. — [1977]. — 27p ; 25cm. — (Cmnd.6803)
ISBN 0-10-168030-9 Sd : £0.75
(B77-16233)

331.7'61'3400942 — Solicitors. *England, to 1975*
Kirk, Harry. Portrait of a profession : a history of the solicitor's profession, 1100 to the present day / by Harry Kirk. — London : Oyez Publishing, 1976. — ix,218p ; 24cm.
Index.
ISBN 0-85120-289-6 : £8.75
(B77-10214)

331.7'61'352041 — Great Britain. Local government. Personnel. *Periodicals*
Local government manpower : journal of the Local Authorities' Conditions of Service Advisory Board. — London (41 Belgrave Sq., SW1X 8NZ) : L.A.C.S.A.B.
Continues: News summary.
Vol.21, no.3- ; July 1977-. — [1977]-. — ill ; 30cm.
Six issues a year. — 24p. in 1st issue.
Sd : £2.00 yearly
ISSN 0140-1017
(B77-26860)

331.7'61'36170941 — Voluntary social services. Personnel. *Great Britain. Reports, surveys*
Webb, Adrian Leonard. Voluntary social service manpower resources / [by] Adrian Webb, Lesley Day, Douglas Weller. — London (2 Torrington Place, WC1E 7HN) : Personal Social Services Council, [1976]. — [4],49,[1]p ; 30cm.
ISBN 0-905250-02-8 Sd : £1.20
(B77-09556)

331.7'61'361973 — Welfare services. Paraprofessional personnel. Employment. *United States, 1965-1975. Reports, surveys*
Cohen, Robert, *b.1941.* 'New careers' grows older : a perspective on the paraprofessional experience, 1965-1975 / [by] Robert Cohen. — Baltimore ; London : Johns Hopkins University Press, 1976. — ix,132,[1]p ; 24cm. — (Policy studies in employment and welfare ; no.26)
Bibl.: p.125-132.
ISBN 0-8018-1909-1 : £9.50
ISBN 0-8018-1910-5 Pbk : £3.00
(B77-29229)

331.7'61'3622209421 — Day care centres for mentally ill persons. Personnel. *London, 1966-1973. Statistics*
Thompson, Richard. Staff of local authority residential and day care establishments for the mentally disordered in the London boroughs, 1966-1973 / by Richard Thompson ; [for the Greater London Council] Director-General's Department, Policy Studies and Intelligence Branch. — London : G.L.C., 1975. — [1],ii,27,[52]p ; 30cm. — (Greater London Council. Intelligence Unit. Research memoranda ; RM492 ISSN 0306-7203)
ISBN 0-7168-0852-8 Sd : £2.30
Primary classification 331.7'61'3623
(B77-15731)

331.7'61'3622309421 — Residential institutions for mentally ill persons. Personnel. *London, 1966-1973. Statistics*
Thompson, Richard. Staff of local authority residential and day care establishments for the mentally disordered in the London boroughs, 1966-1973 / by Richard Thompson ; [for the Greater London Council] Director-General's Department, Policy Studies and Intelligence Branch. — London : G.L.C., 1975. — [1],ii,27,[52]p ; 30cm. — (Greater London Council. Intelligence Unit. Research memoranda ; RM492 ISSN 0306-7203)
ISBN 0-7168-0852-8 Sd : £2.30
Primary classification 331.7'61'3623
(B77-15731)

331.7'61'3623 — Day care centres for mentally handicapped persons & residential institutions for mentally handicapped persons. Personnel. *London, 1966-1973. Statistics*
Thompson, Richard. Staff of local authority residential and day care establishments for the mentally disordered in the London boroughs, 1966-1973 / by Richard Thompson ; [for the Greater London Council] Director-General's Department, Policy Studies and Intelligence Branch. — London : G.L.C., 1975. — [1],ii,27,[52]p ; 30cm. — (Greater London Council. Intelligence Unit. Research memoranda ; RM492 ISSN 0306-7203)
ISBN 0-7168-0852-8 Sd : £2.30
Also classified at 331.7'61'3622209421; 331.7'61'3622309421
(B77-15731)

331.7'61'370941 — Education. Personnel. *Great Britain. Reports, surveys*
British Library Project on Experimental Information Services in Education. Personnel in education and training : a survey of the potential market for educational information services / British Library Project on Experimental Information Services in Education ; [prepared] by Dai Hounsell, Philip Payne, Irene Willett. — [Lancaster] ([Lancaster LA1 4YL]) : University of Lancaster, Centre for Educational Research and Development, 1977. — xiii,155[i.e.159]p(8 fold) : ill ; 30cm. — (British Library. Research and development reports ; no.5326 ISSN 0308-2385)
Cover title. — Bibl.: p.141-144. — Index.
ISBN 0-901699-90-x Pbk : £3.00
(B77-24058)

331.7'61'38715 — Docks. Personnel. Employment. Organisations. *Great Britain. National Dock Labour Board. Reports, surveys. Serials*
National Dock Labour Board. Annual report with statement of accounts / National Dock Labour Board. — London (22 Albert Embankment, SE1 7TE) : The Board.
30th : at 25 December, 1976. — [1977]. — [1], ii,30,[1]p(4 fold) : map ; 25cm.
Sd : £0.20
(B77-20966)

331.7'61'38750942393 — Merchant shipping. Personnel: Sailors. *Avon. Bristol, 1747-1789*
Press, Jonathan. The merchant seamen of Bristol, 1747-1789 / by Jonathan Press. — Bristol (c/o Peter Harris, 74 Bell Barn Rd, Stoke Bishop, Bristol [BS9 2DG]) : Bristol Branch of the Historical Association, 1976. — [2],23p,[4]p of plates : 2 ill, 2 facsims ; 22cm. — (Historical Association. Bristol Branch. Local history pamphlets ; 38)
Bibl.: p.22-23.
ISBN 0-901388-16-5 Sd : £0.50
(B77-02093)

331.7'61'38773609411 — Airports. Personnel. *Scotland. Reports, surveys*
British Airports Authority. 1976 survey on airport workers - Aberdeen, Edinburgh, Glasgow and Prestwick / British Airports Authority. — [London] ([2 Buckingham Gate, SW1E 6JL]) : [B.A.A.], 1976. — [3],23 leaves,[8]p : forms, maps ; 30cm.
ISBN 0-903460-11-4 Sp : £3.00
(B77-01217)

331.7'61'38773609421 — Airports. Personnel. *London. Reports, surveys*
British Airports Authority. 1975 survey on airport workers - Heathrow, Gatwick and Stansted : summary of results / British Airports Authority. — [London] ([2 Buckingham Gate, SW1E 6JL]) : [B.A.A.], 1976. — [33],22 leaves,[19]p : forms, maps ; 30cm.
ISBN 0-903460-07-6 Sp : £3.00
(B77-01218)

331.7'61'607241 — Research & development. Personnel. *Great Britain. Statistics*
Great Britain. *Central Statistical Office.* Research and development, expenditure and employment / Central Statistical Office. — [New ed.]. — London : H.M.S.O., 1976. — iii, 54p ; 30cm. — (Studies in official statistics ; no.27)
Previous ed.: published as 'Research and development expenditure'. 1973.
ISBN 0-11-630139-2 Sd : £2.00
Primary classification 338.4'3
(B77-07170)

331.7'61'61 — Universities. *Netherlands. Leiden. Rijksuniversiteit te Leiden. British graduates with medical degrees. Careers, 1701-1800*
Underwood, Edgar Ashworth. Boerhaave's men : at Leyden and after / [by] E. Ashworth Underwood. — Edinburgh : Edinburgh University Press, 1977. — vii,227p,[16]p of plates : ill, ports ; 24cm.
Index.
ISBN 0-85224-304-9 : £10.00
(B77-19253)

331.7'61'6107309411 — Women nurses. Employment. *Scotland. Reports, surveys*
Hockey, Lisbeth. Women in nursing : a descriptive study / directed by Lisbeth Hockey. — London [etc.] : Hodder and Stoughton, 1976. — 253p,fold plate : ill ; 23cm.
'... the first Report produced by a team of research workers in the Nursing Research Unit under the leadership of the Director, Miss Lisbeth Hockey' - Foreword. — Bibl.
ISBN 0-340-20425-7 : £5.95
(B77-07130)

331.7'61'61754 — Hospitals. Thoracic medicine departments. Personnel: Registrars. *Great Britain*
Royal College of Physicians of London. *Standing Committee on Thoracic Medicine.* [Memoranda] / Royal College of Physicians of London, Standing Committee on Thoracic Medicine. — [London] : [The Committee], 1976. — [3],4,2p ; 21cm.
Title taken from content of work.
Sd : Unpriced
(B77-20967)

331.7'62'92220973 — Car industries. Personnel. *United States*
Auto work and its discontents / edited by B.J. Widick ; foreword by Eli Ginzberg. — Baltimore ; London : Johns Hopkins University Press, 1976. — ix,112p ; 21cm. — (Policy studies in employment and welfare ; no.25)
Bibl.: p.109-112.
ISBN 0-8018-1856-7 : £5.60
ISBN 0-8018-1857-5 Pbk : £2.05
(B77-04613)

331.7'63'095 — Agricultural industries. Employment. Effects of technological development. *Asia*
Bartsch, William H. Employment and technology choice in Asian agriculture / [by] William H. Bartsch. — New York ; London : Praeger, 1977. — xxi,127,[1]p ; 25cm. — (Praeger special studies in international economics and development)
'A study prepared for the International Labour Office within the framework of the World Employment Programme'. — Bibl.: p.108-122. — Index.
ISBN 0-275-24280-3 : £11.05
(B77-33658)

331.7'98'095 — Unskilled personnel. Opportunity costs. *Asia. Developing countries*
McDiarmid, Orville John. Unskilled labor for development : its economic cost / [by] Orville John McDiarmid. — Baltimore ; London : Johns Hopkins University Press for the World Bank, 1977. — xii,206p : ill ; 24cm. — (International Bank for Reconstruction and Development. World Bank research publications)
Bibl.: p.203-206.
ISBN 0-8018-1938-5 : £10.00
ISBN 0-8018-1949-0 Pbk : £3.60
(B77-25432)

331.8 — TRADE UNIONS AND COLLECTIVE BARGAINING

331.87'09181'2 — Trade unions. Organisation structure. Social aspects. Western world. Related to collective bargaining. *Comparative studies*
Clegg, Hugh Armstrong. Trade unionism under collective bargaining : a theory based on comparisons of six countries / [by] Hugh Armstrong Clegg. — Oxford : Blackwell, 1976. — xi,121p ; 23cm. — (Warwick studies in industrial relations)
Index.
ISBN 0-631-17210-6 : £5.50
ISBN 0-631-17220-3 Pbk : 2.25
Also classified at 331.89'09181'2
(B77-02815)

331.87'2 — Trades councils. *Great Britain, 1900-1940*
Clinton, Alan. The trade union rank and file : trades councils in Britain, 1900-40 / [by] Alan Clinton. — Manchester : Manchester University Press [etc.], 1977. — x,262p : 1 ill ; 23cm.
Bibl.: p.239-254. — Index.
ISBN 0-7190-0655-4 : £11.50 : CIP rev.
(B77-08261)

331.87'3 — Engineering industries. Industrial relations. Role of shop stewards. Political aspects. *Great Britain, 1920-1921*
Hinton, James. The first shop stewards' movement / [by] James Hinton. — London : Allen and Unwin, 1973 [i.e. 1977]. — 3-352p : 1 ill, map ; 22cm. — (Studies in social history)
Originally published: 1973. — Bibl.: p.341-343. — Index.
ISBN 0-04-331070-2 Pbk : £3.50
(B77-26861)

331.88 — TRADE UNIONS

331.88 — Trade unions. Growth. Related to trade cycles
Bain, George Sayers. Union growth and the business cycle : an econometric analysis / [by] George Sayers Bain, Farouk Elsheikh. — Oxford : Blackwell, 1976. — xv,155p : ill ; 23cm. — (Warwick studies in industrial relations)
Index.
ISBN 0-631-16650-5 : £10.00
Also classified at 338.5'4
(B77-02816)

331.88'06'2415 — Trade unions. Organisations. *Ireland. Irish Congress of Trade Unions. Reports, surveys. Serials*
Irish Congress of Trade Unions. Annual report / Irish Congress of Trade Unions. — Dublin (19 Raglan Rd, Dublin 4) : Executive Council of the Irish Congress of Trade Unions.
18th : [1976, Galway]. — [1977]. — 736,[2]p(2 fold) : ill ; 22cm.
Index.
Pbk : Unpriced
(B77-17338)

331.88'092'2 — Trade unionism. *United States. Biographical dictionaries*
Biographical dictionary of American labor leaders / editor-in-chief Gary M. Fink, advisory editor Milton Cantor, contributing editors John Hevener ... [et al.]. — Westport, Conn. ; London : Greenwood Press, 1974. — xiv,561p ; 25cm.
Index.
ISBN 0-8371-7643-3 : £19.95
(B77-16234)

331.88'0941 — Trade unionism. *Great Britain, to 1976*
Pelling, Henry. A history of British trade unionism / by Henry Pelling. — 3rd ed. — London [etc.] : Macmillan, 1976. — xiii,326p, 8leaves of plates : ill, facsims ; 23cm.
Also published: Harmondsworth : Penguin, 1976. — Previous ed.: 1972. — Bibl.: p.306-316. — Index.
ISBN 0-333-21330-0 : £8.95
(B77-03420)

331.88'0941 — Trade unions. *Great Britain*
Great Britain. *Central Office of Information. Reference Division.* Trade unions / [prepared by Reference Division, Central Office of Information]. — 2nd ed. — London : H.M.S.O., 1977. — [3],30p ; 24cm. — (Manpower and employment in Britain) (Central Office of Information reference pamphlet ; 128)
Previous ed.: 1975.
ISBN 0-11-700926-1 Sd : £0.75
(B77-26863)

331.88'0941 — Trade unions. *Great Britain, 1875-1933*
Lovell, John. British trade unions, 1875-1933 / prepared for the Economic History Society by John Lovell. — London [etc.] : Macmillan, 1977. — 75p ; 21cm. — (Studies in economic and social history)
Bibl.: p.65-71. — Index.
ISBN 0-333-17926-9 Pbk : £1.50
(B77-12344)

331.88'0941 — Trade unions. *Great Britain. Conference proceedings*
Trades Union Congress. *Annual Congress, 108th, Brighton, 1976.* Report of the 108th annual Trades Union Congress, held in the Dome, Brighton, September 6th to 10th, 1976, president Mr Cyril Plant, OBE / reported by McIntosh and Ireland. — London : T.U.C., [1977]. — vii,764p ; 24cm.
Index.
Pbk : Unpriced
(B77-33101)

331.88'0941 — Trade unions. Policies of government. *Great Britain, to 1976*
Macdonald, Donald Farquhar. The state and the trade unions / by D.F. Macdonald. — 2nd ed. — London [etc.] : Macmillan, 1976. — iii-viii, 217p ; 23cm.
Previous ed.: 1960. — Index.
ISBN 0-333-21196-0 : £7.95
ISBN 0-333-21197-9 Pbk : £2.95
(B77-06514)

331.88'0941 — Trade unions. Recognition. *Great Britain. For personnel management*
Institute of Personnel Management. *National Committee on Employee Relations.* Trade union recognition / ... prepared by the Institute of Personnel Management's National Committee on Employee Relations. — London : I.P.M., 1977. — [3],68p ; 30cm.
ISBN 0-85292-148-9 Pbk : £5.00
(B77-17964)

331.88'0968 — Trade unions. *South Africa, to 1975*
Du Toit, M A. South African trade unions : history, legislation, policy / [by] M.A. du Toit. — Johannesburg ; London [etc.] : McGraw-Hill, 1976. — [9],198p : 1 ill ; 24cm.
ISBN 0-07-091311-0 : Unpriced
(B77-23190)

331.88'0973 — Trade unions. *United States, to 1976*
Labor unions / editor-in-chief Gary M. Fink. — Westport, Conn. ; London : Greenwood Press, 1977. — xiii,520,[1]p ; 25cm. — (The Greenwood encyclopedia of American institutions ; [1])
Index.
ISBN 0-8371-8938-1 : £21.50
(B77-31738)

331.88'11'371100973 — Teachers. Trade unions. *United States, to 1975*
Donley, Marshall Owen. Power to the teacher : how America's educators became militant / [by] Marshall O. Donley, Jr. — Bloomington ; London : Indiana University Press, 1976. — xii, 242p : ill, ports ; 25cm. — (A Midland giant)
'Published in association with Phi Delta Kappa' - half title page verso. — Bibl.: p.225-236. — Index.
ISBN 0-253-34562-6 : £8.25
ISBN 0-253-20194-2 Pbk : £3.00
(B77-00075)

331.88'12'1380941 — Telecommunication services: Post Office. Trade unions. *Great Britain. Post Office Engineering Union, to 1970*
Bealey, Frank. The Post Office Engineering Union : the history of the Post Office Engineers, 1870-1970 / [by] Frank Bealey ; foreword by Bryan Stanley. — London : Bachman and Turner, 1976. — 432p : ill, ports ; 23cm.
Index.
ISBN 0-85974-049-8 : £6.90
(B77-05914)

331.88'18'620973 — Printing industries. Trade unions. *United States. International Typographical Union, to 1955*
Lipset, Seymour Martin. Union democracy : the internal politics of the International Typographical Union / [by] Seymour Martin Lipset, Martin A. Trow, James S. Coleman ; with a foreword by Clark Kerr. — New York : Free Press ; London : Collier Macmillan, 1977. — xxiv,455p : ill ; 21cm.
Originally published: Glencoe, N.Y. : Free Press, 1956. — Index.
ISBN 0-02-919210-2 Pbk : £4.50
(B77-31739)

331.88'6'0945 — Factory Councils. *Italy, 1918-1921*
Clark, Martin. Antonio Gramsci and the revolution that failed / [by] Martin Clark. — New Haven ; London : Yale University Press, 1977. — xii,255p ; 23cm.
Bibl.: p.237-241. — Index.
ISBN 0-300-02077-5 : £8.00
(B77-27713)

331.88'92 — Business firms. Closed shops. Recognition. Agreements. *Great Britain. For management*
Sweeney, Shelagh. Closed shop agreements : a practical guide / [prepared under the auspices of the Institute's National Committee on Employee Relations by Shelagh Sweeney and Deirdre Gill]. — London : Institute of Personnel Management, 1976. — [6],41p ; 30cm.
ISBN 0-85292-147-0 Sp : £9.50
(B77-08832)

331.88'92 — Journalism. Closed shops. Effects of enactment of Trade Union and Labour Relations (Amendment) Act 1976. Protest movements. *Great Britain, 1974-1976. Personal observations*
Beloff, Nora. Freedom under Foot : the battle over the closed shop in British journalism / [by] Nora Beloff. — London : Temple Smith, 1976. — 143p ; 23cm.
Index.
ISBN 0-85117-118-4 : £4.00
ISBN 0-85117-119-2 Pbk : £1.95
(B77-03996)

331.89 — COLLECTIVE BARGAINING AND DISPUTES

331.89 — Industries. Management. Control by personnel. Economic aspects. *Portugal, 1975-1976. Reports, surveys*
Goodey, Chris. Workers' control in Portugal : a report / by the British members [Chris Goodey, Ray Ellis, Joe Burke] of the Second Russell Commission of Enquiry organised by the Russell Committee for Portugal. — Nottingham : Institute for Workers' Control, [1977]. — 16p ; 21cm. — (Institute for Workers' Control. Pamphlet series ; no.52 ISSN 0579-5125)
ISBN 0-901740-50-0 Sd : £0.20
(B77-13544)

331.89'041'37873 — Higher education institutions. Collective bargaining by teachers. *United States. For administrators*
Angell, George W. Handbook of faculty bargaining / [by] George W. Angell, Edward P. Kelley, Jr and associates. — San Francisco [etc.] ; London : Jossey-Bass, 1977. — iii-xxix, 593p ; 24cm. — (The Jossey-Bass series in higher education)
Bibl. — Index.
ISBN 0-87589-320-1 : £15.00
(B77-25434)

331.89'041'37873 — Higher education institutions. Collective bargaining by teachers. *United States. Reports, surveys*
Garbarino, Joseph William. Faculty bargaining : change and conflict / by Joseph W. Garbarino in association with Bill Aussieker ; ... prepared for the Carnegie Commission on Higher Education and the Ford Foundation. — New York ; London [etc.] : McGraw-Hill, [1976]. — ix,278p ; 24cm.
Published in the United States: 1975. — Bibl.: p.261-268. — Index.
ISBN 0-07-010111-6 : £8.30
(B77-05248)

331.89'041'3877360941235 — Airports. *Scotland. Grampian Region. Aberdeen. Dyce Airport. Industrial relations. Disputes between Bristow Helicopters Limited & British Air Line Pilots Association. Inquiry reports*
McDonald, Robert Howat, *Lord McDonald.* Report of a court of inquiry into a trade dispute at Dyce Airport, Aberdeen, between Bristow Helicopters Limited and members of the British Air Line Pilots Association, conducted by the Hon. Lord McDonald MC ... — London : H.M.S.O., [1977]. — [1],54p ; 25cm. — (Cmnd.6951)
ISBN 0-10-169510-1 Sd : £0.75
(B77-33102)

331.89'041'77028 — Photographic processing industries. *London. Brent (London Borough). Grunwick Processing Laboratories Limited. Industrial relations. Disputes with Association of Professional, Executive, Clerical and Computer Staff*
Rogaly, Joe. Grunwick / [by] Joe Rogaly. — Harmondsworth [etc.] : Penguin, 1977. — 199p ; 18cm. — (A Penguin special)
ISBN 0-14-052325-1 Pbk : £0.80
(B77-31031)

331.89'041'77028 — Photographic processing industries. *London. Brent (London Borough). Grunwick Processing Laboratories Limited. Industrial relations. Disputes with Association of Professional, Executive, Clerical and Computer Staff. Inquiry reports*
Scarman, *Sir* **Leslie.** Report of a court of inquiry under the Rt Hon. Lord Justice Scarman, OBE into a dispute between Grunwick Processing Laboratories Limited and members of the Association of Professional, Executive, Clerical and Computer Staff / [by L.G. Scarman, J.P. Lowry, T. Parry] ; presented to Parliament by the Secretary of State for Employment ... — London : H.M.S.O., [1977]. — [1],25p ; 25cm. — (Cmnd.6922)
ISBN 0-10-169220-x Sd : £0.50
(B77-26864)

331.89'042'1310941 — Electricity supply industries. Collective bargaining by managers. *Great Britain. Inquiry reports*
Great Britain. *Advisory, Conciliation and Arbitration Service.* Electricity supply industry : report of an inquiry into the negotiating and representative arrangements for managerial and higher executive grades / [Advisory, Conciliation and Arbitration Service]. — London (Cleland House, Page St., SW1P 4ND) : The Service, [1976]. — iv,26,[1]p ; 21cm. — (Great Britain. Advisory, Conciliation and Arbitration Service. ACAS reports ; no.4 ISSN 0309-717x)
ISBN 0-906073-03-0 Sd : Unpriced
(B77-15732)

331.89'042'920942574 — Motor vehicle industries. *Oxfordshire. Cowley. British Leyland Motor Corporation. Industrial relations. Disputes. Inquiry reports*
Report of a panel of investigation into the dispute between British Leyland, Cowley and the Amalgamated Union of Engineering Workers and Transport and General Workers Union concerning mechanical rectifiers (tuners) in the Cowley assembly plant. — London (Cleland House, Page St., SW1P 4ND) : Advisory, Conciliation and Arbitration Service, [1975]. — iv,40p ; 21cm. — (Great Britain. Advisory, Conciliation and Arbitration Service. ACAS reports ; no.1 ISSN 0309-717x)
ISBN 0-906073-00-6 Sd : Unpriced
(B77-15733)

331.89'046'910941 — Iron & steel industries. *Great Britain. British Steel Corporation. Industrial relations. Disputes with National Union of Blastfurnacemen. Inquiry reports*
Report of a court of inquiry into a dispute between the National Union of Blastfurnacemen and the British Steel Corporation. — London (Cleland House, Page St., SW1P 4ND) : Advisory, Conciliation and Arbitration Service, [1976]. — 52,[1]p ; 21cm. — (Great Britain. Advisory, Conciliation and Arbitration Service. ACAS reports ; no.3 ISSN 0309-717x)
ISBN 0-906073-02-2 Sd : Unpriced
(B77-16235)

331.89'09181'2 — Collective bargaining. Western world. Related to social aspects of organisation structure of trade unions
Clegg, Hugh Armstrong. Trade unionism under collective bargaining : a theory based on comparisons of six countries / [by] Hugh Armstrong Clegg. — Oxford : Blackwell, 1976. — xi,121p ; 23cm. — (Warwick studies in industrial relations)
Index.
ISBN 0-631-17210-6 : £5.50
ISBN 0-631-17220-3 Pbk : 2.25
Primary classification 331.87'09181'2
(B77-02815)

331.89'0941 — Collective bargaining. *Great Britain*
Jenkins, Clive. Collective bargaining : what you always wanted to know about trade unions and never dared to ask / [by] Clive Jenkins and Barrie Sherman. — London [etc.] : Routledge and Kegan Paul, 1977. — [3],156p ; 23cm.
Index.
ISBN 0-7100-8690-3 : £5.50 : CIP rev.
ISBN 0-7100-8691-1 Pbk : Unpriced
(B77-18602)

331.89'0941 — Collective bargaining. *Great Britain. For trade unionism*
Industrial studies. — London : Arrow Books [for] the Society of Industrial Tutors. — (Trade union industrial studies)
2 : The bargaining context / edited by Ed Coker & Geoffrey Stuttard. — 1976. — 282p : ill ; 21cm.
Bibl.: p.261-282.
ISBN 0-09-912250-2 Pbk : £3.95
(B77-29230)

331.89'0973 — Collective bargaining. *United States*
Richardson, Reed C. Collective bargaining by objectives : a positive approach / [by] Reed C. Richardson. — Englewood Cliffs ; London [etc.] : Prentice-Hall, 1977. — xii,387p : ill, forms ; 24cm.
Bibl. — Index.
ISBN 0-13-140517-9 : £12.75
ISBN 0-13-140509-8 Pbk : £7.15
(B77-33659)

331.89'1'0941 — Industrial relations. Agreements. *Great Britain. Forms & precedents*
Industrial Society. Model procedural agreements / [Industrial Society]. — Revised [ed.]. — London : The Society, 1976. — v,37p : forms ; 21cm.
Previous ed.: 1972.
ISBN 0-85290-139-9 Sd : £2.50
(B77-06515)

331.89'14 — Industrial democracy. *Europe. Reports, surveys*
Institute of Personnel Management. Industrial democracy : evidence from the Institute of Personnel Management to the Committee of Inquiry. — London : The Institute, 1976. — [2],ii,63p ; 30cm.
ISBN 0-85292-131-4 Sp : £1.50
(B77-07131)

331.89'14 — Industrial democracy. *Great Britain*
Drinkwater, A. Industrial democracy : company views & the Bullock Committee / [by] A. Drinkwater. — Henley-on-Thames (Greenlands, Henley-on-Thames, Oxon. RG9 3AU) : Administrative Staff College, [1976]. — 3 leaves,129[i.e.137]p ; 31cm.
ISBN 0-900839-26-0 Sp : £2.00
(B77-03997)

Fatchett, Derek John. Industrial democracy : prospects after Bullock / [by] Derek Fatchett. — [Leeds] : University of Leeds ; [Nottingham] : University of Nottingham [for] the Institute of Personnel Management, 1977. — v,38p ; 21cm. — (Occasional papers in industrial relations ; 2)
Bibl.: p.38.
ISBN 0-85292-149-7 Sd : £1.50
(B77-26865)

Gordon-Brown, Ian. Industrial democracy 1976 : the state of play / [by Ian Gordon-Brown in association with Nigel Vinson and D. Wallace Bell]. — London (25 Buckingham Gate, SW1E 6LP) : Industrial Participation Association, 1976. — [1],45 leaves ; 26cm. — (Industrial Participation Association. IPA study papers ; no.4)
Sd : £2.00
(B77-33103)

331.89'14 — Industrial democracy. *Great Britain. Conference proceedings*
The **great** debate : report of the conference on industrial democracy held 18-19 May 1976 / [edited by] Elizabeth B. Sharp. — London : Industrial Society, 1976. — [5],24p ; 30cm.
ISBN 0-85290-140-2 Sd : £2.50
(B77-12901)

331.89'14 — Industrial democracy. *Great Britain. Inquiry reports*
Committee of Inquiry on Industrial Democracy. Report of the Committee of Inquiry on Industrial Democracy / chairman Lord Bullock ; presented to Parliament by the Secretary of State for Trade ... — London : H.M.S.O., [1977]. — ix,205p ; 25cm. — (Cmnd. 6706)
ISBN 0-10-167060-5 Pbk : £3.00
(B77-07132)

331.89'14 — Industrial democracy. *Great Britain. Institute for Workers' Control viewpoints*
Institute for Workers' Control. Accountability and industrial democracy / [by Michael Barratt Brown and Ken Coates for the Institute for Workers' Control]. — Nottingham : I.W.C., [1977]. — [2],14p ; 21cm. — (Institute for Workers' Control. Pamphlet series ; no.50 ISSN 0579-5125)
ISBN 0-901740-48-9 Sd : £0.20
(B77-13545)

331.89'14 — Industrial democracy. *Great Britain. Liberal Party viewpoints*
Abel, Stephen. Industrial democracy / [by] Stephen Abel. — London : Liberal Publication Department, [1977]. — [5],14p ; 21cm. — (Towards a new political agenda ; 3 ISSN 0140-377x)
'... one of a series of papers commissioned by the Standing Committee of the Liberal Party'.
Sd : £0.50
(B77-32465)

331.89'14 — Industrial democracy. *Great Britain. Trades Union Congress viewpoints*
Trades Union Congress. Industrial democracy : a statement of policy endorsed by the 1974 Trades Union Congress together with the supplementary note of evidence submitted by the TUC to the Bullock Committee of Inquiry on Industrial Democracy endorsed by the 1976 Trades Union Congress. — New ed. — London : T.U.C., 1977. — 49p ; 24cm.
Previous ed.: 1974.
ISBN 0-900878-49-5 Sd : £0.50
(B77-14103)

331.89'14 — Industrial democracy. *Western Europe. Reports, surveys*
Industrial democracy : European experience : two research reports / [prepared for the] Industrial Democracy Committee ; with a preface by Lord Bullock. — London : H.M.S.O., 1976. — 88p ; 25cm.
Bibl. — Contents: Industrial democracy and worker representation at board level : a review of the European experience / by Eric Batstone - European experience with worker representation on the board / by P.L. Davies.
ISBN 0-11-511767-9 Sd : £1.05
(B77-01219)

331.89'14 — Industrial democracy. Committee of Inquiry on Industrial Democracy. Report. *Great Britain. Critical studies*
Trades Union Congress. TUC guide to the Bullock report on industrial democracy. — London : T.U.C., 1977. — 26p ; 24cm.
ISBN 0-900878-50-9 Sd : £0.35
(B77-14593)

331.89'14 — Industrial democracy. Committee of Inquiry on Industrial Democracy. Report. *Great Britain. Critical studies. For shop stewards*
Coates, Ken. The shop steward's guide to the Bullock Report / by Ken Coates and Tony Topham. — [Nottingham] : Spokesman Books, 1977. — 127p ; 19cm. — ([Practical guides to industrial relations ; no.3])
Bibl.: p.127.
ISBN 0-85124-188-3 : £3.95
ISBN 0-85124-185-9 Pbk : Unpriced
(B77-25435)

331.89'14 — Industrial democracy. Economic aspects. *Great Britain*
Denton, Geoffrey. Beyond Bullock : economic implications of worker participation in control and ownership of industry / [by] Geoffrey Denton. — London (12A Maddox St., W1R 9PL) : Federal Trust for Education and Research, 1977. — vi,25p ; 30cm. — (Federal Trust for Education and Research. Reports)
ISBN 0-901573-21-3 Sd : £2.00
(B77-22413)

331.89'14'06141 — Industrial relations. Disputes. Conciliation. Organisations. *Great Britain. Advisory, Conciliation and Arbitration Service. Accounts*
Accounts for the period ended 31 March / Advisory, Conciliation and Arbitration Service [and] Certification Officer [and] Central Arbitration Committee. — London : H.M.S.O. [1975]-1976. — [1976]. — Folder (4p) ; 25cm. — ([1975-76 H.C.] 694)
ISBN 0-10-009156-3 : £0.12
(B77-06516)

331.89'14'06141 — Industrial relations. Disputes. Conciliation. Organisations. *Great Britain. Advisory, Conciliation and Arbitration Service. Reports, surveys. Serials*
Great Britain. *Advisory, Conciliation and Arbitration Service.* Annual report / Advisory, Conciliation and Arbitration Service. — London (Cleland House, Page St., SW1P 4ND) : [A.C.A.S.].
1976 / [prepared by the Advisory Conciliation and Arbitration Service and the Central Office of Information]. — 1977. — 80p : 1 ill ; 21cm.
Sd : Unpriced
(B77-27714)

331.89'25'0941235 — Political strikes. *Scotland. Grampian Region. Aberdeen. General Strike, 1926*
Kibblewhite, Liz. Aberdeen in the General Strike / [by] Liz Kibblewhite and Andy Rigby. — Aberdeen : Aberdeen People's Press ; London (27 Clerkenwell Close, EC1R 0AT) : [Distributed by] Publications Distribution Co-op, 1977. — 33p : ill ; 23cm.
Bibl.: p.32.
Sd : £0.40
(B77-29231)

331.89'282'148072044365 — Nuclear engineering. Research organisations. *France. Saclay. Centre d'Etudes Nucléaires de Saclay. Industrial relations. Strikes. Role of workers' councils, 1968*
Pesquet, Jacques. Soviets at Saclay? : the first assessment of an experiment in setting up Workers' Councils at the Atomic Energy Commission Centre for Nuclear Research, Saclay / compiled by Jacques Pesquet ; translated [from the French] by Robert Biel. — London : Stage 1, 1976. — 71p ; 19cm.
Translation of: 'Des Soviets à Saclay?'. Paris : F. Maspéro, 1968.
ISBN 0-85035-005-0 Pbk : £0.90
(B77-05915)

331.89'2941 — Industrial relations. Strikes. *Great Britain*
Hyman, Richard. Strikes / [by] Richard Hyman. — 2nd (revised) ed. — [London] : Fontana, 1977. — 218p ; 18cm.
Previous ed.: 1972. — Bibl.: p.205-216. — Index.
ISBN 0-00-635098-4 Pbk : £1.25
(B77-31740)

331.89'3 — Industrial sabotage, 1890-1976
Brown, Geoff, *b.1946.* Sabotage : a study in industrial conflict / [by] Geoff Brown. — Nottingham : Bertrand Russell Peace Foundation for Spokesman Books, 1977. — xiii, 396p ; 23cm.
Index.
ISBN 0-85124-158-1 : £8.50
(B77-25436)

331.89'3 — Ports. Blockades by inshore fishermen. *Great Britain, 1975*
Cargill, Gavin. Blockade '75 : the story of the fishermen's blockade of the ports / [by] Gavin Cargill. — Glasgow : Molendinar Press, 1976. — [4],52p : ill, maps, ports ; 20cm.
'A Molendinar special'.
ISBN 0-904002-15-2 Pbk : £1.50
(B77-02817)

332 — FINANCE
Chandler, Lester Vernon. The economics of money and banking. — 7th ed. / [by] Lester V. Chandler, Stephen M. Goldfeld. — New York [etc.] ; London : Harper and Row, 1977. — viii,630p : col ill, col map ; 23cm.
Previous ed.: / by Lester V. Chandler. 1973. — Bibl. — Index.
ISBN 0-06-041234-8 Pbk : £5.95
(B77-17339)

332 — Capital markets. *Great Britain*
Midgley, Kenneth, *b.1926.* The capital market : its nature and significance / [by] Kenneth Midgley and Ronald Burns. — London [etc.] : Macmillan, 1977. — viii,148p : 3 ill ; 23cm. — (Studies in finance and accounting)
Bibl. — Index.
ISBN 0-333-17437-2 : £8.95
ISBN 0-333-21486-2 Pbk : £3.95
(B77-20968)

Rose, Harold Bertram. The British capital market and the economy : villain or scapegoat? / [by] Harold Rose. — [London] : [Head Office, 54 Lombard St., E.C.3] : [Barclays Bank Ltd], [1977]. — [2],11p ; 21cm.
'One of the 1976 series of Stockton Lectures, given on February 12 ... at the London Graduate School of Business Studies' - title page verso.
Sd : Unpriced
(B77-20078)

332 — Finance. *For banking*
Forrest, George Viner. Understanding money : a practical reader for the practitioners and the students of banking / by George Forrest. — 2nd ed. — Oxford (11 Bardwell Rd, Oxford OX2 6SU) : Oxford Educational Systems, 1976. — 113p : ill, forms ; 21cm.
Previous ed.: 1974. — Index.
Pbk : £2.00
(B77-31741)

332 — Finance. Crises. *United States. Conference proceedings*
Financial crises : institutions and markets in a fragile environment / edited by Edward I. Altman and Arnold W. Sametz. — New York ; London [etc.] : Wiley, 1977. — xv,288p : ill ; 24cm.
'Conference ... held on May 20-21, 1976, at New York University' - Preface. — 'A Wiley-Interscience publication'. — Index.
ISBN 0-471-02685-9 : £13.45
(B77-25437)

332'.024 — England. Mildmay, Benjamin, Earl Fitzwalter. Accounts, 1724-1754. *Extracts, selections*
Edwards, Arthur Charles. The account books of Benjamin Mildmay, Earl Fitzwalter / by A.C. Edwards. — London [etc.] : Regency Press, 1977. — [4],213,[11]p,plate : ill, facsims ; 23cm.
Spine title: Benjamin Mildmay, Earl Fitzwalter. — '... extracts arranged under subjects ... each subject [prefaced] with a short explanatory narrative' - Introduction. — Index.
ISBN 0-7212-0480-5 : £3.00
(B77-11637)

332'.024 — Personal finance
Hastings, Paul Guiler. Personal finance / [by] Paul Hastings, Norbert Mietus. — 2nd ed. — New York ; London [etc.] : McGraw-Hill, 1977. — ix,612p : ill, facsims, forms ; 25cm. — (McGraw-Hill series in finance)
Previous ed.: New York : McGraw-Hill, 1972. — Index.
ISBN 0-07-027013-9 : £11.20
(B77-24059)

332'.024 — Personal finance. *Manuals*
Hallman, G Victor. Personal financial planning : how to plan for your financial freedom / [by] G. Victor Hallman, Jerry S. Rosenbloom. — New York ; London [etc.] : McGraw-Hill, 1975. — xv,397p : forms ; 25cm.
Index.
ISBN 0-07-025639-x : £7.45
(B77-17965)

Richards, Kenneth, *b.1943.* Managing your money : a guide to personal financial planning / [by] Kenneth Richards. — Sevenoaks : Teach Yourself Books, 1977. — x, 254p : 1 ill ; 18cm. — (Teach yourself books)
Index.
ISBN 0-340-21257-8 Pbk : £1.25
(B77-13546)

332'.024'0941 — Personal finance. *Great Britain. Practical information*
Allen, Margaret, *b.1933.* The money book : your money and your life / [by] Margaret Allen. — London : Sidgwick and Jackson, 1977. — xx, 442p : ill, forms ; 24cm.
Index.
ISBN 0-283-98387-6 : £6.50
(B77-32466)

332'.024'0941 — Personal finance. Effects of inflation. Control. *Great Britain. Manuals*
Toch, Henry. How to survive inflation / [by] Henry Toch. — London : Pitman, 1977. — iv, 124p ; 22cm.
Index.
ISBN 0-273-00198-1 Pbk : £1.95 : CIP rev.
(B77-10215)

332'.024'09417 — Personal finance. *Ireland (Republic). Manuals*
Pension and Investment Consultants Limited. A guide to personal finance and saving / [Pension & Investment Consultants Ltd, Willis Faber (Ireland) Limited]. — Dublin (6 Harcourt Rd, Dublin 2) : [Pension and Investment Consultants Ltd] ; Dublin : [Willis Faber (Ireland) Ltd], [1977]. — [1],41p ; 15x21cm.
Sd : Unpriced
(B77-20079)

332'.024'0973 — Personal finance. *United States. Manuals*
De Salvo, Louis J. Consumer finance / [by] Louis J. De Salvo ; Marie F. Baker, editorial consultant. — New York ; London [etc.] : Wiley, 1977. — xiii,337p : ill, facsims, forms ; 26cm.
Bibl. — Index.
ISBN 0-471-04391-5 Pbk : £6.95
(B77-23191)

Rosenberg, Reuben Robert. Schaum's outline of theory and problems of personal finance and consumer economics / by R. Robert Rosenberg and Ralph V. Naples. — New York ; London [etc.] : McGraw-Hill, 1976. — [7],199p : ill, forms ; 28cm. — (Schaum's outline series)
Spine title: Personal finance & consumer economics. — Cover title: Theory and problems of personal finance and consumer economics. — With answers. — Index.
ISBN 0-07-053834-4 Pbk : £2.95
(B77-20080)

332'.024'09931 — Personal finance. *New Zealand. Secondary school texts*
Smyth, W M. Commerce and the consumer / [by] W.M. Smyth. — Christchurch, N.Z. [etc.] ; London : Whitcoulls, 1976. — 79p : ill(some col), facsims ; 25cm.
ISBN 0-7233-0481-5 : Unpriced
(B77-16236)

332'.041 — Capital. Estimation. Methodology. *Organisation for Economic Co-operation and Development countries. Reports, surveys*
Ward, Michael. The measurement of capital : the methodology of capital stock estimates in OECD countries / by Michael Ward. — Paris : Organisation for Economic Co-operation and Development ; [London] : [H.M.S.O.], 1976. — 148p : ill ; 24cm.
Bibl.: p.142-148.
Pbk : £3.20
ISBN 92-64-11596-x
(B77-05916)

332'.041 — Capital. Theories
Hayek, Friedrich August. The pure theory of capital / [by] F.A. Hayek. — London [etc.] : Routledge and Kegan Paul, 1976. — xxxi, 454p : ill ; 23cm.
Originally published: London : Macmillan, 1941. — Bibl.: p.441-449. — Index.
ISBN 0-7100-1508-9 : £8.75
(B77-00076)

332'.09172'4 — Finance. *Developing countries. Readings*
Finance in developing countries / edited by P.C.I. Ayre. — London [etc.] : Cass, 1977. — [5],174p : ill ; 24cm.
'This collection of essays first appeared in a Special Issue ... of the "Journal of Development Studies", Volume 13 no.2 ...' - title page verso. — Bibl.
ISBN 0-7146-3077-2 : £9.50
(B77-23192)

332'.092'4 — Finance. Rasmussen, Anne-Marie. *United States. Autobiographies*
Rasmussen, Anne-Marie. There was once a time / [by] Anne-Marie Rasmussen. — New York ; London : Harcourt Brace Jovanovich, [1977]. — xiii,237p,[32]p of plates : ill, ports ; 23cm.
Published in the United States: 1975. — Index.
ISBN 0-15-189481-7 : Unpriced
(B77-11638)

332'.0941 — Finance. *Great Britain, 1970-1975. Statistics*
Johnson, Christopher, *b.1931.* Anatomy of UK finance, 1970-75 / by Christopher Johnson. — London : 'Financial times' [etc.], [1976]. — [2], xiv,275p : ill ; 30cm.
Bibl.: p.273-275.
ISBN 0-900671-61-0 Sp : £25.00
(B77-00642)

332'.09426'7 — Finance. *Essex. Reports, surveys. For structure plan making*
Essex *(County). Planning Department.* Financial resources / Essex County Council [Planning Department]. — [Chelmsford] ([County Hall, Chelmsford CM1 1LF]) : [The Department], 1977. — [5],43p : ill ; 30cm.
Cover title: Essex structure plan, financial resources.
Sd : £0.55
(B77-25451)

332.1 — BANKS AND BANKING
332.1 — Banking. *Capitalist countries, 1970-1976*
Heller, Robert. Can you trust your bank? / [by] Robert Heller and Norris Willatt. — London : Weidenfeld and Nicolson, 1977. — vi,298p ; 23cm.
Index.
ISBN 0-297-77318-6 : £5.50
(B77-29232)

332.1 — Banking. *Reports, surveys*
World banking : 'Statist' annual survey. — London : 'Investors chronicle'.
1976-77 : 66th. — 1977. — xxiv,259p : ill, ports ; 30cm.
Index.
ISBN 0-901369-27-6 Pbk : £11.50
(B77-09557)

332.1 — Banks. Capital. *United States*
Orgler, Yair E. Bank capital / [by] Yair E. Orgler, Benjamin Wolkowitz. — New York ; London [etc.] : Van Nostrand Reinhold, 1976. — xiii,139p : ill ; 24cm.
Bibl. — Index.
ISBN 0-442-26302-3 : £12.15
(B77-20969)

332.1'025 — Banks. *Directories*
The **bankers'** almanac and year book. — Haywards Heath : T. Skinner.
1976-77 : 132nd year of publication. — 1977. — v-xlviii,985,G1317p,[16]p of plates,[4]leaves of plates : ill ; 26cm.
Tab indexed. — English text, French, German and Spanish introductions. — Index.
ISBN 0-611-00620-0 : £22.50
(B77-13547)

332.1'025'4212 — Financial institutions. *London (City). Directories*
The **city** directory : an 'Investors chronicle' guide to financial and professional services allied to the City of London. — Cambridge : Woodhead-Faulkner.
1976-77 / compiled by David W. Pygott. — 1976. — 337p : ill ; 26cm.
Index.
ISBN 0-85941-046-3 : £8.50
ISBN 0-85941-031-5 Pbk : £5.95
ISSN 0308-9088
(B77-02094)

332.1'0941 — Banking. *Great Britain*
Valentine, S P. Basics of banking / [by] S.P. Valentine and S. Mason. — [Sevenoaks] : Teach Yourself Books, 1976. — x,292p : ill, form ; 18cm. — (Teach yourself books)
Bibl.: p.284. — Index.
ISBN 0-340-21021-4 Pbk : £1.50
(B77-13548)

332.1'0941 — Banking. *Great Britain, 1960-1975*
Channon, Derek French. British banking strategy and the international challenge / [by] Derek F. Channon. — London [etc.] : Macmillan, 1977. — xii,207p : ill ; 23cm.
Index.
ISBN 0-333-19808-5 : £15.00
(B77-25438)

332.1'0941 — Financial institutions. Role. *Great Britain. Association of British Chambers of Commerce viewpoints*
Association of British Chambers of Commerce. At whose expense? : first submission from the ABCC [i.e. Association of British Chambers of Commerce] to the committee of enquiry into the role and functioning of the financial institutions [i.e. Committee to Review the Functioning of Financial Institutions]. — London : A.B.C.C., 1977. — 25p : ill ; 30cm.
Sd : £1.75
(B77-28445)

332.1'09425'37 — Banking. *Lincolnshire. Boston, to 1970*
Davis, S N. Banking in Boston / by S.N. Davis. — Boston, Lincs. (80 Sleaford Rd, Boston, Lincs. PE21 8EU) : Richard Kay for the History of Boston Project, 1976. — 44p : ill, facsims ; 22cm. — (History of Boston series ; no.14 ISSN 0305-2079)
ISBN 0-902662-64-3 Sd : £1.20
(B77-08262)

332.1'0973 — Banking. *United States*
Luckett, Dudley G. Money and banking / [by] Dudley G. Luckett. — New York ; London [etc.] : McGraw-Hill, 1976. — xvii,585p : ill ; 25cm.
Index.
ISBN 0-07-038954-3 : £11.60
Primary classification 332.4'973
(B77-03998)

Ranlett, John Grant. Money and banking : an introduction to analysis and policy / [by] John G. Ranlett. — 3rd ed. — Santa Barbara ; London [etc.] : Wiley, 1977. — x,614p : ill ; 24cm.
'A Wiley/Hamilton Publication'. — Previous ed.: 1969. — Bibl. — Index.
ISBN 0-471-70815-1 : £10.50
Primary classification 332.4'973
(B77-22416)

332.1'0973 — Banking. *United States, 1933-1935*
Burns, Helen M. The American banking community and New Deal banking reforms, 1933-1935 / [by] Helen M. Burns. — Westport, Conn. ; London : Greenwood Press, 1974. — xiii,203,[1]p ; 22cm. — (Contributions in economics and economic history ; no.11)
Bibl.: p.189-195. — Index.
ISBN 0-8371-6362-5 : £10.95
(B77-17966)

332.1'1'094212 — Central banks. *London (City). Bank of England. Inquiry reports*
Great Britain. *Parliament. House of Commons. Select Committee on Nationalised Industries.* The Bank of England : seventh report from the Select Committee on Nationalised Industries, session 1975-76, report, together with minutes of proceedings of the Committee, minutes of evidence and appendices. — London : H.M.S.O., [1976]. — xl[i.e.xc],182p ; 25cm. — ([1975-76 H.C.]672)
ISBN 0-10-009336-1 Pbk : £3.60
(B77-05917)

332.1'1'094212 — Central banks. *London (City). Bank of England. Reports, surveys. Serials*
Bank of England. Report and accounts / Bank of England. — [London] ([Threadneedle St., E.C.2]) : [The Bank].
1977 : for the year ended 28th February. — [1977]. — 36p ; 30cm.
Sd : Unpriced
ISSN 0308-5279
(B77-31032)

332.1'1'0973 — Central banking. Reform. *United States, 1863-1923*
West, Robert Craig. Banking reform and the Federal Reserve, 1863-1923 / [by] Robert Craig West. — Ithaca ; London : Cornell University Press, 1977. — 243,[3]p : ill ; 23cm.
Bibl.: p.231-239. — Index.
ISBN 0-8014-1035-5 : £10.90
(B77-22414)

332.1'2'025 — Commercial banks. Affiliates & subsidiaries. *Directories*
Who owns what in world banking : a guide to the subsidiary and affiliated interests of the world's major banks. — London (Bracken House, Cannon St., EC4P 4BY) : Banker Research Unit.
1975-6 / editors Philip Thorn, Dorothy Shearman. — [1975]. — [284]p ; 30cm.
Index.
ISBN 0-902998-06-4 Sp : £19.00
ISSN 0305-3954
(B77-01220)

1976-7 / editors Philip Thorn, Jean Lack. — 1976. — [268]p ; 30cm.
Index.
ISBN 0-902998-08-0 Sp : £19.00
ISSN 0305-3954
(B77-01221)

332.1'2'0941 — Commercial banks. *Great Britain. Juvenile literature*
Peacock, Frank. Let's go to the bank / [by] Frank Peacock ; ... colour photographs by G.W. Hales. — London [etc.] : F. Watts, 1977. — 32p : col ill, forms(some col) ; 22cm.
ISBN 0-85166-631-0 : £1.75
(B77-20970)

332.1'5 — Commercial banks. International services: Lloyds Bank International. *Directories*
Lloyds Bank International. LBI guide. — London ([P.O. Box 241, 40 Queen Victoria St., EC4P 4EL]) : Lloyds Bank International Ltd. 1977. — [1977]. — iv,70p ; 21cm.
Cover title.
ISBN 0-903332-01-9 Pbk : Unpriced
ISSN 0306-7637
(B77-10216)

332.1'5 — International banking. Role of offshore capital markets
Chown, John Francis. Offshore investment centres / by John F. Chown and Thomas F. Kelen ; edited by Farida Mazhar. — London (Bracken House, Cannon St., EC4P 4BY) : Banker Research Unit, [1976]. — [5],261p ; 30cm.
ISBN 0-902998-04-8 Pbk : Unpriced
(B77-00643)

332.1'5'025 — Commercial banks. Foreign representation. *Directories*
Who is where in world banking : a guide to the overseas representation of the world's major banks classified by financial centre. — London (Bracken House, Cannon St., EC4P 4BY) : Banker Research Unit.
1975-6 / editor Philip Thorn. — [1975]. — [1], x,210p : ill ; 30cm.
ISBN 0-902998-07-2 Sp : £9.00
ISSN 0305-3822
(B77-02818)

1976-7 / editors Philip Thorn, Jean Lack. — [1976]. — [1],viii,229p ; 30cm.
ISBN 0-902998-05-6 Sp : £9.00
ISSN 0305-3822
(B77-02819)

332.1'52 — International Monetary Fund. Members. Subscriptions. Increases. *Proposals*
International Monetary Fund. Proposals for increasing the resources of the International Monetary Fund / presented to Parliament by the Chancellor of the Exchequer ... — London : H.M.S.O., [1977]. — 15p ; 25cm. — (Cmnd. 6704)
ISBN 0-10-167040-0 Sd : £0.35
(B77-11106)

332.1'53 — International Development Association. Finance. *Proposals*
International Development Association. Bridging arrangements for advance contributions to the fifth replenishment : memorandum of the President of the Association dated 2nd March 1977 ... / International Development Association. — London : H.M.S.O., [1977]. — 8p ; 25cm. — (Cmnd.6854)
At head of title: Ministry of Overseas Development.
ISBN 0-10-168540-8 Sd : £0.25
(B77-23193)

International Development Association. Fifth replenishment of IDA resources : report of the Executive Directors to the Board of Governors dated 29th March 1977 ... / International Development Association. — London : H.M.S.O., [1977]. — 28p(6 fold) ; 25cm. — (Cmnd.6838)
ISBN 0-10-168380-4 Sd : £0.60
(B77-23194)

332.1'7 — Banking services for industry. *Great Britain. Conference proceedings*
The **banks** and industry : based on the seminar held at Christ's College, Cambridge, 5-10 September, 1976, [organized by] the Institute of Bankers. — London : [The Institute], 1976. — [3],106p ; 21cm.
Bibl.: p.100-101.
ISBN 0-85297-041-2 Pbk : Unpriced
(B77-00077)

332.1'75 — Commercial banks. Funds. Management
Roussakis, Emmanuel N. Managing commercial bank funds / [by] Emmanuel N. Roussakis. — New York ; London : Praeger, 1977. — xvii, 181p : ill, forms ; 25cm. — (Praeger special studies in US economic, social and political issues)
Bibl.: p.172-176. — Index.
ISBN 0-03-021966-3 : £12.40
(B77-33104)

332.2 — SPECIALISED BANKING INSTITUTIONS

332.2'1 — Personal finance. Savings. Organisations. *Great Britain. National Savings Committee. Reports, surveys. Serials*

National Savings Committee. Annual report for the year ending 31st March / National Savings Committee. — London : H.M.S.O.
1977. — 1977. — 55p : ill, ports ; 22cm.
ISBN 0-11-700875-3 Sd : £1.00
(B77-27715)

332.2'6'0941 — Trustee savings banks. *Great Britain. Reports, surveys. Serials*

Trustee savings banks : report of the Inspection Committee of Trustee Savings Banks for the year ended 20th November. — London : H.M.S.O.
85th and final annual report : 1976. — 1977. — 20,[1]p ; 25cm.
ISBN 0-11-630257-7 Sd : £0.60
(B77-27716)

332.3 — CREDIT AND LOAN INSTITUTIONS

332.3'2'0922 — Building societies. *Biographical dictionaries. Serials*

Building societies who's who : a biographical directory of the home-owning and savings movement throughout the world / compiled and edited by Franey and Co. Ltd. — London : Franey.
1977-78. — [1977]. — 320p : ill ; 22cm.
£9.90
(B77-26866)

332.3'2'0941 — Building societies. *Great Britain. Yearbooks*

Building societies year book : official handbook of the Building Societies Association / compiled and edited by Franey & Co. Ltd. — London : [Franey].
1976. — [1976]. — 960p : ill, port ; 22cm.
£9.60
(B77-30008)

332.4 — MONEY

Frankel, Sally Herbert. Money : two philosophies : the conflict of trust and authority / [by] S. Herbert Frankel. — Oxford : Blackwell, 1977. — x,163p ; 23cm.
Bibl.: p.139-153. — Index.
ISBN 0-631-17960-7 : £6.50 : CIP rev.
(B77-26163)

332.4 — Monetary systems

Goodhart, Charles Albert Eric. Money, information and uncertainty / [by] C.A.E. Goodhart. — London [etc.] : Macmillan, 1976. — ix,331p : ill ; 24cm.
Originally published: 1975. — Bibl.: p.311-323. — Index.
ISBN 0-333-21841-8 Pbk : £4.95
(B77-11639)

332.4 — Monetary systems. Related to balance of payments

The **monetary** approach to the balance of payments / edited by Jacob A. Frenkel, Harry G. Johnson. — London : Allen and Unwin, 1977. — 5-388p : ill ; 22cm.
Originally published: 1976. — Bibl. — Index.
ISBN 0-04-330276-9 Pbk : £6.95
Primary classification 382.1'7
(B77-13609)

332.4 — Money. *Juvenile literature*

Maynard, Christopher. The amazing world of money / [author Christopher Maynard] ; [editor Deborah Manley ; illustrators Bill Fallover, George Thompson]. — London [etc.] : Angus and Robertson, 1977. — 32p : ill(chiefly col), facsims(some col), col map, ports(1 col) ; 33cm.
Index.
ISBN 0-207-95757-6 : £1.95
(B77-32467)

332.4 — Money. Origins

Grierson, Philip. The origins of money / [by] Philip Grierson. — London : Athlone Press, 1977. — 44p ; 22cm. — (Creighton lectures in history ; 1970)
'... some of the original references have become out-of-date. They have therefore been revised ... The text itself has undergone only minor changes' - Preface.
ISBN 0-485-14115-9 Sd : £1.40
(B77-14104)

332.4'01 — Monetary systems. Theories

Makinen, Gail E. Money, the price level and interest rates : an introduction to monetary theory / [by] Gail E. Makinen. — Englewood Cliffs ; London [etc.] : Prentice-Hall, 1977. — xv,446p : ill ; 24cm.
Bibl. — Index.
ISBN 0-13-600486-5 : £12.75
(B77-25439)

332.4'01 — Money supply. Theories, to 1976

Rees-Mogg, William. Democracy and the value of money : the theory of money from Locke to Keynes / [by] William Rees-Mogg. — London : Institute of Economic Affairs, 1977. — [1],32p ; 22cm. — (Institute of Economic Affairs. Occasional papers ; 53 ISSN 0073-909x)
ISBN 0-255-36100-9 Sd : £0.60
(B77-26164)

332.4'022'2 — Money, to 1976. *Illustrations. Juvenile literature*

Picture reference book of money / general editor Boswell Taylor ; design and illustrations Leslie Marshall. — Leicester : Hodder and Stoughton Children's Books, 1977. — [1],33p : chiefly ill, coat of arms, facsims, map, ports ; 25cm. — (Picture reference)
Cover title: Money. — Ill. on lining papers.
ISBN 0-340-10445-7 : £1.75
(B77-24768)

332.4'042 — Ancient Roman silver coins. Quantitative analysis. *Research reports*

Walker, David Richard. The metrology of the Roman silver coinage / [by] D.R. Walker. — Oxford : British Archaeological Reports.
Part 1 : From Augustus to Domitian. — 1976. — [8],159p : ill ; 30cm. — (British archaeological reports : supplementary series ; 5)
Bibl.: p.[8].
ISBN 0-904531-37-6 Pbk : £2.50
(B77-00078)

Part 2 : From Nerva to Commodus. — 1977. — [8],120p : ill ; 30cm. — (British archaeological reports : supplementary series ; 22)
Spine title: Roman silver coinage II. — Bibl.: p.[8].
ISBN 0-904531-68-6 Pbk : £2.30
(B77-20971)

332.4'042'0937 — Coinage. *Ancient Rome, ca B.C.45-ca A.D.260*

Sutherland, Carol Humphrey Vivian. The emperor and the coinage : Julio-Claudian studies / by C.H.V. Sutherland. — London : Spink, 1976. — [6],146p,x p of plates : ill ; 25cm.
Index.
ISBN 0-900696-73-7 : £10.00
(B77-10217)

332.4'1 — Finance. Inflation

Hagger, Alfred James. Inflation : theory and policy / [by] A.J. Hagger. — London [etc.] : Macmillan, 1977. — x,290p : ill ; 24cm.
Index.
ISBN 0-333-16939-5 : £12.00
ISBN 0-333-21246-0 Pbk : £5.95
(B77-11107)

Trevithick, James Anthony. Inflation : a guide to the crisis in economics / [by] J.A. Trevithick. — Harmondsworth [etc.] : Penguin, 1977. — 132p : ill ; 19cm. — (A pelican original)
Bibl.: p.129-130. — Index.
ISBN 0-14-021950-1 Pbk : £0.70
(B77-18603)

332.4'1 — Finance. Inflation. *Conference proceedings*

Inflation theory and anti-inflation policy : proceedings of a conference held by the International Economic Association at Saltsjöbaden, Sweden, [1975] / edited by Erik Lundberg. — London [etc.] : Macmillan, 1977. — xiv,545p : ill ; 23cm.
Includes 2 papers from another conference. — Bibl. — Index.
ISBN 0-333-21618-0 : £20.00
(B77-31742)

332.4'1 — Finance. Inflation. *Great Britain. Statistics. For consumers*

National Federation of Consumer Groups. Inflation tables for the consumer / National Federation of Consumer Groups. — Sutton (6 Devonshire Rd, Sutton, Surrey SM2 5HQ) : N.F.C.G., [1977]. — [1],13 leaves ; 30cm.
ISBN 0-85202-135-6 Sd : £0.40
(B77-11640)

332.4'1 — Finance. Inflation, 1958-1975

Parkin, Michael. Inflation in the world economy, 1958-1975 / [by] Michael Parkin. — Guildford (Guildford, Surrey GU2 5XH) : University of Surrey, 1976. — [1],19p : ill ; 22cm. — (Surrey papers in economics ; no.11 ISSN 0081-9670)
Bibl.: p.19.
ISBN 0-902599-10-0 Sd : £0.50
(B77-06517)

332.4'1 — Finance. Inflation. Control. *Great Britain. Proposals*

Hardwick, Philip. Inflation and the sinking pound / [by] Philip Hardwick. — London (Room 340, Hamilton House, Mabledon Place, WC1H 9BH) : Economics Association, 1976. — [2],14p : ill ; 21cm. — (Economics Association. Occasional papers ; 2 ISSN 0309-5223)
ISBN 0-901529-12-5 Sd : £0.50(£0.35 to members)
(B77-15131)

332.4'1 — Finance. Inflation. Control. *Proposals*

Ashburnham, George. The thinker / by George R. Ashburnham. — Sutton (22 Effingham Close, Sutton, Surrey SM2 6AG) : [The author].
Part 4. — 1977. — 12p : 1 ill ; 21cm.
Sd : Unpriced
(B77-08263)

332.4'1 — Finance. Inflation. Control. Policies of government. *Great Britain. Social Contract. Communist Party of Great Britain viewpoints*

Ramelson, Bert. Bury the social contract : the case for an alternative policy / [by] Bert Ramelson. — London : Communist Party of Great Britain, [1977]. — [1],36p ; 21cm. — (Communist Party of Great Britain. Pamphlets)

ISBN 0-900302-75-5 Sd : £0.30
(B77-21732)

332.4'1 — Finance. Inflation. Control. Policies of governments. *Conference proceedings*

Institutional arrangements and the inflation problem / editors Karl Brunner, Allan H. Meltzer. — Amsterdam [etc.] ; Oxford : North-Holland Publishing Co., 1976. — [8], 248p : ill ; 24cm. — (Carnegie-Rochester conference series on public policy ; vol.3)
'This ... volume ... offered as a supplement to the Journal of Monetary Economics, contains papers presented at the November 1974 conference' - Introduction. — Bibl.
ISBN 0-7204-0525-4 Pbk : £10.97
(B77-06518)

332.4'1 — Finance. Inflation. Related to unemployment

Friedman, Milton. Inflation and unemployment : the new dimension of politics / [by] Milton Friedman. — London : Institute of Economic Affairs, 1977. — 35p : ill ; 22cm. — (Institute of Economic Affairs. Occasional papers ; 51 ISSN 0073-909x) (Alfred Nobel memorial lectures ; 1976)
Bibl.: p.33-35.
ISBN 0-255-36096-7 Sd : £1.00
(B77-28446)

332.4'1 — Finance. Inflation, to 1976. *Readings*

Inflation / [by] Michael Jefferson ... [et al.] ; with a foreword by John Pardoe. — London : J. Calder : [Distributed by Calder and Boyars], 1977. — 192p : ill ; 23cm. — (Platform books)
Index.
ISBN 0-7145-3539-7 : £5.95
ISBN 0-7245-3547-8 Pbk : £2.25
(B77-16763)

332.4'14 — Money supply. Control

Bain, Andrew David. The control of the money supply / [by] A.D. Bain. — 2nd ed. — Harmondsworth [etc.] : Penguin, 1976. — 176p : ill ; 19cm. — (Penguin modern economics texts : macroeconomics)
Previous ed.: 1970. — Bibl.: p.170-172. — Index.
Pbk : £1.25
ISBN 0-14-080232-0
(B77-03421)

332.4'14 — Money supply. Regulation. Quasi-non-governmental organisations. *Great Britain. Proposals*

Holloway, Edward. Honest money : the case for a Currency Commission / [by] Edward Holloway. — London : Aims for Freedom and Enterprise, 1976. — [2],12p ; 21cm.
Bibl.: p.12.
ISBN 0-7281-0063-0 Sd : £0.25
(B77-02095)

332.4'5 — Exchange control. *Great Britain*

Parker, Anthony, *b.1929.* Exchange control / [by] Anthony Parker. — 2nd ed. — London : Jordan, 1976. — 1v. ; 26cm.
In binder. — xvii,391p. on publication. — Previous ed.: 1975. — Index.
ISBN 0-85308-045-3 Ls : £20.00
(B77-03422)

332.4′5 — Finance. Cooperation. *Eastern European countries, 1945-1975*
Van Brabant, Jozef M. East European cooperation : the role of money and finance / [by] Jozef M. van Brabant. — New York [etc.] ; London : Praeger, 1977. — xxvii,395p : ill ; 24cm. — (Praeger special studies in international business, finance and trade)
Bibl.: p.361-387. — Index.
ISBN 0-275-56650-1 : £16.95
(B77-23195)

332.4′5 — Foreign exchange
Nicholson, John Field. Contemporary problems of foreign exchange and trade / by J.F. Nicholson. — Revised ed. — Aylesbury : Ginn, 1977. — 57p : 2 ill ; 22cm. — (Manchester Economics Project. Satellite books ; 9)
With answers. — Previous ed.: London : Ginn, 1971.
ISBN 0-602-22337-7 Sd : £1.10
Also classified at 382
(B77-20081)

Whiting, Desmond Percival. Finance of foreign trade / [by] D.P. Whiting. — 4th ed. — Plymouth : Macdonald and Evans, 1977. — x, 181p : forms ; 19cm. — (The M. & E. handbook series)
With answers. — Previous ed.: London : Macdonald and Evans, 1973. — Index.
ISBN 0-7121-0629-4 Pbk : £1.95
Also classified at 382
(B77-26165)

Whiting, Desmond Percival. Finance of foreign trade and foreign exchange / by D.P. Whiting. — 3rd ed. — Plymouth : Macdonald and Evans, 1976. — xii,241p : forms ; 22cm.
Previous ed.: London : Macdonald and Evans, 1973. — Index.
ISBN 0-7121-0627-8 Pbk : £3.50
Also classified at 382
(B77-07133)

332.4′5 — International monetary system
Aliber, Robert Zelwin. The international money game / [by] Robert Z. Aliber. — 2nd ed. — London [etc.] : Macmillan, 1977. — xi,312p : ill ; 23cm.
Previous ed. 1973. — Index.
ISBN 0-333-21816-7 : £7.95
ISBN 0-333-21817-5 Pbk : £3.95
(B77-15132)

Crockett, Andrew. International money : issues and analyses / [by] Andrew Crockett. — Sunbury-on-Thames [etc.] : Nelson, 1977. — [7] ,250p : ill ; 22cm.
Bibl. — Index.
ISBN 0-17-712207-2 Pbk : £3.95
(B77-31033)

Grubel, Herbert Gunter. The international monetary system : efficiency and practical alternatives / [by] Herbert G. Grubel. — 3rd ed. — Harmondsworth [etc.] : Penguin, 1977. — 237p : ill ; 19cm. — (Penguin modern economics texts : international economics)
Previous ed.: 1972. — Bibl.: p.219-225. — Index.
Pbk : £1.00
ISBN 0-14-080111-1
(B77-17967)

332.4′5 — International monetary system. *Conference proceedings*
Flexible Exchange Rates and Stabilization Policy *(Conference), Stockholm, 1975.* Flexible exchange rates and stabilization policy / edited by Jan Herin, Assar Lindbeck and Johan Myhrman. — London [etc.] : Macmillan, 1977. — [7],280p : ill ; 23cm.
'... [proceedings of] a conference on "Flexible Exchange Rates and Stabilization Policy", held at Saltsjöbaden, Stockholm, August 26-27, 1975. The conference was organized by the Institute for International Economic Studies at the University of Stockholm ...' - Preface. — 'These proceedings were originally published in "The Scandinavian Journal of Economics", Vol.78, No.2, 1976' - title page verso. — Bibl.
ISBN 0-333-21839-6 : £8.95
(B77-20972)

Paris-Dauphiné Conference on Money and International Monetary Problems, *3rd, Université de Paris, 1974.* Recent issues in international monetary economics : Third Paris-Dauphiné Conference on Money and International Monetary Problems, March 28-30, 1974 / edited by E. Claassen and P. Salin. — Amsterdam [etc.] ; Oxford : North-Holland Publishing Co., 1976. — xiii,428p : ill ; 25cm. — (Studies in monetary economics ; vol.2)
Bibl. — Index.
ISBN 0-7204-0382-0 : £40.76
(B77-03423)

332.4′5 — International monetary system. *Study regions: Western Europe*
Herring, Richard J. National monetary policies and international financial markets / [by] Richard J. Herring and Richard C. Marston. — Amsterdam [etc.] ; Oxford : North-Holland Publishing Co., 1977. — xv,302p : ill ; 23cm. — (Contributions to economic analysis ; 104)
Bibl. — Index.
ISBN 0-7204-0519-x : £18.74
(B77-16764)

332.4′5 — International monetary system, 1945-1976
Solomon, Robert. The international monetary system, 1945-1976 : an insider's view / [by] Robert Solomon. — New York [etc.] ; London : Harper and Row, 1977. — xv,381p ; 25cm.
Index.
ISBN 0-06-013898-x : £9.95
(B77-15133)

332.4′5 — International monetary system, 1945-1977
Tew, Brian. The evolution of the international monetary system, 1945-77 / [by] Brian Tew. — London : Hutchinson, 1977. — 254p : ill ; 23cm. — ([Hutchinson university library])
Bibl.: p.244-245. — Index.
ISBN 0-09-129210-7 : £6.50
ISBN 0-09-129211-5 Pbk : £3.25
(B77-29233)

332.4′5 — International monetary system. Gold exchange standard. Replacement by International Reserve Units. *Proposals*
Economides, Chris. Earned international reserve units : the catalyst of two complementary world problems - the monetary and development / [by] Chris Economides. — Oxford [etc.] : Pergamon, 1976. — xv,24p : 2 ports ; 30cm.
Originally published: in 'World development', vol.1, nos 3 & 4, Mar./Apr. 1973. — Index.
ISBN 0-08-021178-x Sd : £2.50
(B77-09558)

332.4′5 — International monetary system. Influence of monetary policies of United States, 1939-1976
Block, Fred L. The origins of international economic disorder : a study of United States international monetary policy from World War II to the present / [by] Fred L. Block. — Berkeley [etc.] ; London : University of California Press, 1977. — xii,282p ; 25cm.
Bibl.: p.259-274. — Index.
ISBN 0-520-03009-5 : £11.20
(B77-23196)

332.4′5 — International monetary system. Reform. Role of International Monetary Fund. Committee of Twenty, 1971-1974
Williamson, John, *b.1937.* The failure of world monetary reform, 1971-74 / [by] John Williamson. — Sunbury-on-Thames [etc.] : Nelson, 1977. — xiii,221p : 1 ill ; 23cm.
Bibl.: p.204-209. — Index.
ISBN 0-17-711208-5 : £7.50
ISBN 0-17-712208-0 Pbk : £3.25
(B77-28447)

332.4′5 — International monetary system. Role of Euro-dollar market
Einzig, Paul. The Euro-dollar system : practice and theory of international interest rates. — 6th ed. / [by] Paul Einzig and Brian Scott Quinn. — London [etc.] : Macmillan, 1977. — viii, 124p : 1 ill ; 23cm.
Previous ed.: / by Paul Einzig. 1973. — Index.
ISBN 0-333-21401-3 : £8.95 : CIP rev.
(B77-21733)

332.4′5 — International monetary system, to 1976
Wiseley, William. A tool of power : the political history of money / [by] William Wiseley. — New York ; London [etc.] : Wiley, 1977. — xiii,401p ; 24cm.
'A Wiley-Interscience publication'. — Bibl.: p.369-379. — Index.
ISBN 0-471-02235-7 : £12.70
(B77-22415)

332.4′5 — Monetary systems. Integration. Political aspects. *European Community countries*
Tsoukalis, Loukas. The politics and economics of European monetary integration / [by] Loukas Tsoukalis. — London : Allen and Unwin, 1977. — 3-192p : 1 ill ; 23cm.
Index.
ISBN 0-04-382017-4 : £8.50
(B77-20973)

332.4′52 — International monetary system. Gold standard
Gold is money / edited with an introduction by Hans F. Sennholz. — Westport, Conn. ; London : Greenwood Press, 1975. — x,204p ; 22cm. — (Contributions in economics and economic history ; no.12)
Index.
ISBN 0-8371-7804-5 : £9.75
(B77-19254)

332.4′566′094 — Monetary systems. Integration. *European Community countries*
Corden, Warner Max. Monetary union : main issues facing the European community / by W.M. Corden. — London : Trade Policy Research Centre, 1976. — vi,20p ; 21cm. — (International issues ; no.2)
ISBN 0-900842-27-x Sd : £1.00
(B77-10218)

332.4′6 — Monetary policies
Chick, Victoria. The theory of monetary policy / [by] Victoria Chick. — Revised ed. — Oxford : Parkgate Books : Blackwell, 1977. — v,163p : ill ; 24cm.
Previous ed.: London : Gray-Mills Publishing Ltd, 1973. — Bibl.: p.157-163.
ISBN 0-631-18210-1 Pbk : £3.95
(B77-26868)

332.4′6 — Monetary policies. Implications of inflation. *Conference proceedings*
The '**New** Inflation' and monetary policy : proceedings of a conference organised by the Banca Commerciale Italiana and the Department of Economics of Università Bocconi in Milan, 1974 / edited by Mario Monti. — London [etc.] : Macmillan, 1976. — xvii,307p : ill ; 23cm.
Bibl.- Index.
ISBN 0-333-18845-4 : £10.00
(B77-01222)

332.4′6 — Monetary policies. Political aspects. *Conference proceedings*
The **political** economy of monetary reform / edited by Robert Z. Aliber. — London [etc.] : Macmillan, 1977. — xiii,270p : ill ; 23cm.
Proceedings of a conference held at Racine, Wisconsin, 1974. — Bibl. — Index.
ISBN 0-333-19729-1 : £10.00
(B77-17340)

332.4′6′06141 — Mints. *Great Britain. Royal Mint, to 1977*
Royal Mint. The Royal Mint : an outline history. — 6th ed. — London : H.M.S.O., 1977. — ii-vii,42p : ill, plan, port ; 22cm.
Previous ed.: 1970.
ISBN 0-11-887000-9 Sd : £1.00
(B77-23197)

332.4′9 — Money, to 1974
Galbraith, John Kenneth. Money : whence it came, where it went / [by] John Kenneth Galbraith. — Harmondsworth [etc.] : Penguin, 1976. — 335p ; 18cm. — (Pelican books)
Originally published: Boston, Mass. : Houghton Mifflin ; London : Deutsch, 1975. — Index.
ISBN 0-14-022000-3 Pbk : £0.95
(B77-04614)

332.4′917′671 — Islamic countries. Monetary policies. Influence of Islam. Proposed research projects
King Abdul Aziz University. Monetary and fiscal economics of Islam : an outline of some major subjects for research / King Abdul Aziz University. — Leicester (223 London Rd, Leicester LE2 1ZE) : Islamic Foundation for the King Abdul Aziz University, 1977. — 32p ; 21cm.
ISBN 0-86037-018-6 Sd : Unpriced
(B77-28448)

332.4′94 — European Economic Community. Monetary policies, to 1976
Coffey, Peter. Europe and money / [by] Peter Coffey. — London [etc.] : Macmillan, 1977. — 95p : 1 ill ; 23cm.
Index.
ISBN 0-333-21404-8 : £4.95
(B77-26166)

332.4′9427′9 — Monetary system. *Isle of Man. Proposals*
Sound money for the Isle of Man : summary of a report to Tynwald. — [Ramsey] ([Dhoon Plat, Maughold, Ramsey, Isle of Man]) : M.N. Fargher [et al.], 1977. — 8p ; 22cm.
Sd : £0.15
(B77-29234)

332.4'968 — Monetary system. *South Africa*
Goedhuys, D W. Money and banking / [by] D.W. Goedhuys. — Johannesburg ; London [etc.] : McGraw-Hill, 1976. — [11],231p : ill ; 23cm.
Originally published: 1975. — Bibl. — Index.
ISBN 0-07-091222-x : Unpriced
(B77-05249)

332.4'973 — Monetary system. *United States*
Luckett, Dudley G. Money and banking / [by] Dudley G. Luckett. — New York ; London [etc.] : McGraw-Hill, 1976. — xvii,585p : ill ; 25cm.
Index.
ISBN 0-07-038954-3 : £11.60
Also classified at 332.1'0973
(B77-03998)

Ranlett, John Grant. Money and banking : an introduction to analysis and policy / [by] John G. Ranlett. — 3rd ed. — Santa Barbara ; London [etc.] : Wiley, 1977. — x,614p : ill ; 24cm.
'A Wiley/Hamilton Publication'. — Previous ed.: 1969. — Bibl. — Index.
ISBN 0-471-70815-1 : £10.50
Also classified at 332.1'0973
(B77-22416)

332.6 — INVESTMENT
332.6 — Companies. Finance. *Great Britain. Statistics. For investment*
Extel Statistical Services. Extel handbook of market leaders / compiled and published by Extel Statistical Services. — London (37 Paul St., EC2A 4PB) : Extel Statistical Services Ltd.
Supersedes 'Moodies Services Limited Investment Handbook', which ceased publication in January 1976.
[No.1]- ; Sept. 1976-. — [1976]-. — ill ; 24cm.
Two issues a year. — vii,[722]p. in 1st issue.
ISBN 0-903286-23-8 Pbk : £50.00(£37.50 to libraries)
ISSN 0308-9673
(B77-00644)

332.6'0941 — Industries. Investment. Financing. *Great Britain. Proposals*
Bracewell-Milnes, Barry. Industry for the people : investment financing through partially guaranteed securities / [by] Barry Bracewell-Milnes. — London (170 Sloane St., S.W.1) : Selsdon Group, 1976. — [1],vi,31p ; 21cm. — (Selsdon Group. Policy series ; no.4)
ISBN 0-86048-000-3 Sd : £1.00
(B77-12345)

332.6'09411 — Investment. *Scotland. Conference proceedings*
International Forum, *5th, Aviemore, 1974.* Investing in Scotland : an account of the Fifth International Forum, November 1974 / compiled by Jack McGill. — Glasgow [etc.] : Collins for the Scottish Council (Development and Industry), 1975. — 224p : ill, map ; 23cm.
'The Fifth International Forum, sponsored [i.e. organised] by the Scottish Council (Development and Industry), was held at Aviemore, Inverness-shire, on November 6th and 7th 1974' - Introduction. — Bibl.: p.221. — Index.
ISBN 0-00-460119-x : £8.00
(B77-05918)

332.6'2'02541 — Investment dealers. *Great Britain. Directories*
Particulars of dealers in securities and of unit trusts / Department of Trade. — London : H.M.S.O.
1977. — 1977. — 67p ; 25cm.
ISBN 0-11-511127-1 Sd : £1.25
ISSN 0308-2539
(B77-15734)

332.6'3 — Gemstones. Investment. *Manuals*
Zucker, Benjamin. How to invest in gems : a layman's guide to the connoisseur's world of rubies, sapphires, emeralds, diamonds and other precious gemstones / [by] Benjamin Zucker. — Poole : Blandford Press, 1977. — 128p,[16]p of plates : ill(some col), ports ; 24cm.
Originally published: New York : Quadrangle/New York Times Book Co., 1976. — Bibl.: p.119-123. — Index.
ISBN 0-7137-0838-7 : £3.95
(B77-27717)

332.6'32 — Investments: Fixed-interest securities. Investment. *United States. Manuals*
Darst, David M. The complete bond book : a guide to all types of fixed-income securities / [by] David M. Darst. — New York ; London [etc.] : McGraw-Hill, 1975. — xvi,336p : ill, forms ; 24cm.
Index.
ISBN 0-07-017390-7 : £12.50
(B77-13549)

332.6'32'0973 — Investments: Securities. Investment. *United States*
Francis, Jack Clark. Investments : analysis and management / [by] Jack Clark Francis. — 2nd ed. — New York ; London [etc.] : McGraw-Hill, 1976. — xvii,710p : ill, facsims ; 25cm. — (McGraw-Hill series in finance)
Previous ed.: New York : McGraw-Hill, 1972. — Bibl. — Index.
ISBN 0-07-021787-4 : £12.40
(B77-04615)

332.6'322 — Convertible stocks. *Great Britain. Serials. For investment*
Reference manual of convertible stocks and warrants. — [London] ([21 New St., EC2M 4NT]) : [Bishopsgate Press Ltd].
1976. — [1976]. — 130p ; 24cm.
Previously published: as 'Reference manual of convertible stocks'.
ISBN 0-900873-11-6 Pbk : £8.50
(B77-00079)

Reference manual of convertible stocks and warrants. — London (21 New St., EC2M 4NT) : Bishopsgate Press Ltd.
1977. — [1977]. — 120p ; 24cm.
ISBN 0-900873-15-9 Pbk : £8.80
ISSN 0309-9377
(B77-27718)

332.6'322 — Stock exchanges. *London (City). Stock Exchange, London. Stocks & shares. Variation. Mathematical models*
Beckman, R C. The Elliott Wave Principle as applied to the London stock market / [by] R.C. Beckman. — Winchester (Park Rd, Winchester, Hants.) : Tara Books, 1976. — xv,238p : ill ; 23cm.
Bibl.: p.237-238.
ISBN 0-905299-00-0 : £12.50
(B77-14594)

332.6'322 — Stocks & shares. Investment
Firth, Michael Arthur. The valuation of shares and the efficient-markets theory / [by] Michael Firth. — London [etc.] : Macmillan, 1977. — viii,184p : ill ; 23cm. — (Studies in finance and accounting)
Index.
ISBN 0-333-21409-9 : £10.00
ISBN 0-333-21410-2 Pbk : £4.95
(B77-24769)

332.6'322 — Stocks & shares. Investment. *United States*
Crowell, Richard A. Stock market strategy / [by] Richard A. Crowell. — New York ; London [etc.] : McGraw-Hill, 1977. — xi,219p : ill ; 24cm.
Index.
ISBN 0-07-014720-5 : £10.90
(B77-29235)

332.6'322 — Stocks & shares. New issues. *Great Britain. Serials*
Extel Statistical Services. The Extel book of prospectuses and new issues / compiled ... by Extel Statistical Services Limited. — London (37 Paul St., EC2A 4PB) : Extel Statistical Services Ltd.
1976, July to December. — [1977]. — [6], 759p ; 25cm.
Index.
Unpriced
ISSN 0308-7387
(B77-17968)

332.6'322'0941 — Companies. Shareholding. *Great Britain. Manuals*
Harris, L G. Shareholders' rights / [by] L.G. Harris. — London : W.H. Allen, 1977. — 144p ; 23cm.
Index.
ISBN 0-491-01606-9 : £3.95
(B77-28449)

332.6'323 — Government bonds. *Great Britain. Statistics*
Pember and Boyle *(Firm).* British government securities in the twentieth century / [Pember and Boyle]. — [London] ([St Albans House, Goldsmith St., E.C.2]) : Pember and Boyle.
Supplement : [1950-1976]. — [1977]. — xxxviii, 3-430p : ill(incl 1 col) ; 21x33cm.
ISBN 0-9502559-1-2 Sd : Private circulation
(B77-09559)

332.6'323 — Investments: Managed bonds & property bonds. *Great Britain. Serials*
Managed and property bonds / [Fundex Limited]. — London (30 Finsbury Sq., EC2A 1PJ) : [Fundex Limited]. — (A 'Money management and unitholder' publication)
1977 : The guide to single premium investment. — 1977. — 120p : ill ; 24cm.
Index.
ISBN 0-901369-30-6 Pbk : £4.75
(B77-12346)

332.6'324 — Land. Capital investment
Benke, William. All about land investment / [by] William Benke. — New York ; London [etc.] : McGraw-Hill, [1977]. — x,192p : ill, facsims, map, plan ; 24cm.
Published in the United States: 1976. — Index.
ISBN 0-07-004662-x : £12.40
(B77-11108)

332.6'324'0973 — Real property. Investment. *United States*
Maisel, Sherman Joseph. Real estate investment and finance / [by] Sherman J. Maisel, Stephen E. Roulac. — New York ; London [etc.] : McGraw-Hill, [1977]. — ix,516p,fold leaf : ill ; 25cm.
Published in the United States: 1976. — Bibl. — Index.
ISBN 0-07-039730-9 : Unpriced
(B77-12347)

332.6'324'0973 — Real property. Investment. *United States. Manuals*
Henry, Rene A. How to profitably buy and sell land / [by] Rene A. Henry, Jr. — New York ; London [etc.] : Wiley, 1977. — xix,203p ; 24cm. — (Real estate for professional practitioners)
'A Wiley-Interscience publication'. — Index.
ISBN 0-471-37291-9 : £10.60
(B77-12348)

Irwin, Robert, *b.1941.* How to buy and sell real estate for financial security / [by] Robert Irwin. — New York ; London [etc.] : McGraw-Hill, [1976]. — xiv,238p : ill, forms ; 21cm.
Published in the United States: 1975. — Index.
ISBN 0-07-032063-2 : £9.10
(B77-05250)

Unger, Maurice A. How to invest in real estate / [by] Maurice A. Unger. — New York ; London [etc.] : McGraw-Hill, [1976]. — [5],153p ; 21cm.
Published in the United States: 1975. — Index.
ISBN 0-07-065915-x Pbk : £3.30
(B77-05251)

332.6'327 — Investment trusts. *Great Britain*
Arnaud, Anthony Alec. Investment trusts explained / [by] A.A. Arnaud. — Cambridge : Woodhead-Faulkner [for] the Association of Investment Trust Companies, 1977. — vi,154p : ill ; 22cm.
Index.
ISBN 0-85941-051-x : £5.25
ISBN 0-85941-061-7 Pbk : £2.95
(B77-06519)

332.6'327 — Unit trusts. *European Community countries & Switzerland*
Corner, Desmond Carteret. Open-ended investment funds in the EEC and Switzerland / [by] D.C. Corner and D.C. Stafford. — London [etc.] : Macmillan, 1977. — x,254p : ill ; 23cm.
Bibl.: p.244-250. — Index.
ISBN 0-333-15426-6 : £15.00
(B77-11641)

332.6'327 — Unit trusts. Performance. *Great Britain. Statistics*
Unit trusts : graphic survey of historical performance. — Elgin, Ill. : Synergistics International Ltd ; Reading (119 London St., Reading, Berks.) : Distributed by Synergistics International (UK) Ltd.
[1976]. — 1976. — [2],xvi,312p : ill ; 31cm.
In binder. — 2 overlays in pocket. — Index.
Ls : £25.00
(B77-03424)

332.6'34 — Capital investment. Analysis
Beenhakker, Henri L. Handbook for the analysis of capital investments / [by] Henri L. Beenhakker. — Westport, Conn. ; London : Greenwood Press, 1976. — xvi,452,[1]p : ill ; 25cm.
Bibl. — Index.
ISBN 0-8371-8901-2 : £19.95
(B77-17969)

332.6'42'094212 — Stock exchanges. *London (City). Stock Exchange, London. Yearbooks*
Stock Exchange, *London.* The Stock Exchange official year-book. — Croydon : T. Skinner.
1976-77 / edited by Jeffrey Russell Knight, deputy editor David Martin Michael Davies. — 1976. — liii,[i.e. lv],2393,[56]p : ill ; 26cm.
Tab indexed. — Index.
ISBN 0-611-00621-9 : £27.00
ISSN 0305-8050
(B77-07823)

332.6'42'094212 — Stock markets. *London (City), 1972-1975*
Ellinger, Alexander Geoffrey. The post war history of the stock market (cont.), 1972-1975 / written by A.G. Ellinger. — Cambridge (28 Panton St., Cambridge [CB2 1DH]) : Investment Research, 1976. — [1],5 leaves,fold plate : 1 ill ; 30cm.
ISBN 0-901605-09-3 Sd : Unpriced
(B77-05252)

332.6'44 — Commodity markets
Investment Research. Commodities - the best speculation? / [Investment Research]. — [New ed.]. — Cambridge (28 Panton St., Cambridge CB2 1DH) : Investment Research, [1976]. — [1],23[i.e. 25]p : ill ; 21x34cm.
ISBN 0-901605-11-5 Pbk : £2.50
(B77-06520)

332.6'44 — Commodity markets. *Conference proceedings*
The **professional** use of the commodity markets : [conference held at the] International Press Centre, London, May 27-28, 1976 ... — Colchester (Fairfax House, Colchester CO1 1RJ) : City Press, [1976]. — 123,[1]p : ill ; 30cm.
Appendix B, 'Commodities' (48p. : ill ; Sd) in pocket.
ISBN 0-901129-10-0 Pbk : £30.00
(B77-03425)

332.6'44 — Commodity markets. *London (City). Baltic Mercantile and Shipping Exchange, to 1976*
Barty-King, Hugh. The Baltic Exchange : the history of a unique market / [by] Hugh Barty-King. — London : Hutchinson, 1977. — xx,431p,leaf of plate,[30]p of plates(2 fold) : ill(some col), col coat of arms, facsims, map, plan, ports ; 24cm.
Maps on lining papers. — Bibl.: p.391-398. — Index.
ISBN 0-09-128050-8 : £7.50
(B77-24770)

332.6'44 — Commodity markets. Options
Commodity Analysis Limited. Commodity options in practice and theory / [written for Commodity Analysis Limited by D.G. Bean]. — London (194 Bishopsgate, EC2M 4PE) : Commodity Analysis Limited, 1977. — 56p : ill(chiefly col), 2 facsims ; 21cm.
Cover title.
Pbk : £3.00
(B77-26167)

332.6'44 — Futures commodity markets. Trading. *London (City). Manuals*
Brackenbury (M.C.) and Company. Dealing on the London Metal Exchange and Commodity Markets / [prepared by M.C. Brackenbury & Co. and Brackenbury, Barlow & Co.]. — [London] ([19 St Mary at Hill, EC3R 8EE]) : [The authors], [1976]. — [1],116,[1]p : ill ; 22cm.
Cover title.
ISBN 0-9504936-0-0 : £5.00
(B77-03999)

332.6'44 — Metal markets. *London (City). London Metal Exchange*
Wolff's guide to the London Metal Exchange / [compiled] by Rudolf Wolff & Co Limited. — London : Metal Bulletin, 1976. — 280p : ill, facsims, port ; 22cm.
£20.00
(B77-30010)

332.6'44 — Metal markets. *London (City). London Metal Exchange, to 1975*
Gibson-Jarvie, Robert. The London Metal Exchange : a commodity market / [by] Robert Gibson-Jarvie. — Cambridge : Woodhead-Faulkner [for] Metallgesellschaft AG, 1976. — vii,191p : ill, facsims, form ; 23cm.
Index.
ISBN 0-85941-042-0 : £6.50
(B77-04000)

332.6'44 — Metal markets. Trading. *London (City)*
Commodity Analysis Limited. Trading in the London metal markets / [written for Commodity Analysis Limited by D.G. Bean]. — London (194 Bishopsgate, EC2M 4PE) : Commodity Analysis Limited, 1977. — 67p : ill(chiefly col), 2 col maps, plan ; 21cm.
Cover title.
Pbk : £4.00
(B77-26869)

332.6'45 — Stock markets. Options
Gastineau, Gary L. The stock options manual / [by] Gary L. Gastineau. — New York ; London [etc.] : McGraw-Hill, [1976]. — ix, 262p : ill ; 21cm.
Published in the United States: 1975. — Bibl.: p.242-254. — Index.
ISBN 0-07-022969-4 : £10.75
(B77-07134)

332.6'6'094212 — Merchant banks. *London (City). Slater Walker Securities, to 1977*
Raw, Charles. Slater Walker : an investigation of a financial phenomenon / [by] Charles Raw. — London : Deutsch, 1977. — 368p ; 23cm.
Index.
ISBN 0-233-96798-2 : £6.95
(B77-29236)

332.6'7 — Investment. Portfolio analysis
Damant, D C. Technical analysis and the portfolio manager / by D.C. Damant. — Cambridge ([28 Panton St., Cambridge CB2 1DH]) : Investment Research, [1973?]. — [16] p : chiefly ill ; 30cm.
'An address given ... to a meeting of the Society of Investment Analysts at the Institute of Bankers on 3rd February 1972'.
ISBN 0-901605-10-7 Sd : Unpriced
(B77-05253)

332.6'73 — Copper mining industries. Foreign capital investment. *Study regions: Papua New Guinea. Bougainville*
Mikesell, Raymond Frech. Foreign investment in copper mining : case studies of mines in Peru and Papua New Guinea / [by] Raymond F. Mikesell. — Baltimore ; London : Johns Hopkins University Press for Resources for the Future, [1976]. — xxii,143,[1]p : 1 ill ; 24cm.
Published in the United States: 1975. — Index.
ISBN 0-8018-1750-1 : £7.15
Also classified at 332.6'73
(B77-08264)

332.6'73 — Copper mining industries. Foreign capital investment. *Study regions: Peru. Toquepala*
Mikesell, Raymond Frech. Foreign investment in copper mining : case studies of mines in Peru and Papua New Guinea / [by] Raymond F. Mikesell. — Baltimore ; London : Johns Hopkins University Press for Resources for the Future, [1976]. — xxii,143,[1]p : 1 ill ; 24cm.
Published in the United States: 1975. — Index.
ISBN 0-8018-1750-1 : £7.15
Primary classification 332.6'73
(B77-08264)

332.6'73'0947 — Foreign capital investment by Western investors. *Eastern Europe & Soviet Union, 1918-1976*
Spigler, Iancu. Direct Western investment in East Europe / [by] Iancu Spigler. — Oxford : St Antony's College, 1975. — xii,346p ; 22cm. — (St Antony's College. Centre for Soviet and East European Studies. Papers in East European economics ; 48 ISSN 0307-5575)
Index.
ISBN 0-9502802-1-6 Pbk : £6.00
(B77-27719)

332.6'73'0968 — Capital investment by foreign investors. *South Africa. Anti-apartheid viewpoints*
Legassick, Martin. Foreign investment and the reproduction of racial capitalism in South Africa / [by] Martin Legassick & David Hemson. — London : Anti-Apartheid Movement, 1976. — [2],16p ; 28cm. — (Foreign investment in South Africa ; no.2 ISSN 0309-0752)
ISBN 0-900065-01-x Sd : £0.50
(B77-04616)

332.6'7314 — Developing countries. Economic development. Effects of foreign capital investment by multinational companies
Lall, Sanjaya. Foreign investment, transnationals and developing countries / [by] Sanjaya Lall and Paul Streeten. — London [etc.] : Macmillan, 1977. — xii,280p : 2 ill ; 23cm.
Bibl.: p.251-272. — Index.
ISBN 0-333-16898-4 : £10.00
(B77-31743)

332.6'7314 — Foreign investment by multinational companies, 1945-1976. Political factors
Thunell, Lars H. Political risks in international business : investment behavior of multinational corporations / [by] Lars H. Thunell. — New York ; London : Praeger, 1977. — xi,135p : ill ; 25cm. — (Praeger special studies in international business, finance and trade)
Bibl.: p.128-133.
ISBN 0-275-24500-4 : £10.05
(B77-26168)

332.6'7322'4 — Investment by foreign investors. Policies of governments. *Southern Europe. Periodicals. For investors*
Business & government in Southern Europe : a quarterly service for investors. — London : Economist Intelligence Unit.
[No.1]- ; May 1977-. — 1977-. — 30cm.
[1],64p. in 1st issue.
Sd : £100.00 yearly
ISSN 0309-9369
(B77-33660)

332.6'7341'0729 — Foreign investment by British investors. Related to foreign trade by Great Britain. *Study regions: Caribbean region. Commonwealth countries. Inquiry reports*
Great Britain. *Parliament. House of Commons. Select Committee on Overseas Development.* The relationship between UK investment and trading patterns and development with reference to the specific problems of small developing economies : second report from the Select Committee on Overseas Development, session 1975-76, together with the proceedings of the Committee, part of the minutes of evidence and appendices. — London : H.M.S.O., [1976]. — l,193p ; 25cm. — ([1975-76 H.C.]705)
ISBN 0-10-009486-4 Pbk : £4.60
Also classified at 382'.0941'0729
(B77-07135)

332.6'7373 — Foreign capital investment by American companies
Hymer, Stephen. The international operations of national firms : a study of direct foreign investment / [by] Stephen Herbert Hymer. — Cambridge, Mass. ; London : M.I.T. Press, 1976. — xxiii,253p ; 24cm. — (Massachusetts Institute of Technology. MIT monographs in economics ; 14)
Bibl. — Index.
ISBN 0-262-08085-0 : £9.35
(B77-00645)

332.6'7373'043 — Foreign investment by American investors. *Germany, 1922-1944*
Sutton, Antony Cyril. Wall Street and the rise of Hitler / [by] Antony C. Sutton. — Sudbury (The Old Priory, Priory La., Sudbury, Suffolk) : Bloomfield Books [etc.], 1976. — 220p : ill, facsims ; 23cm.
Bibl.: p.207-211. — Index.
Pbk : £2.85
(B77-31034)

332.6'7373'068 — Foreign investment by American investors. *Southern Africa*
Rogers, Barbara. White wealth and black poverty : American investments in Southern Africa / [by] Barbara Rogers. — Westport, Conn. ; London : Greenwood Press, 1976. — xv,333p ; 22cm. — (University of Denver. Center on International Race Relations. Studies in human rights ; no.2)
Index.
ISBN 0-8371-8277-8 : £12.25
(B77-26870)

332.6'78 — Investment. *Manuals*
Maclachlan, D I L. Guide to share investment / [by] D.I.L. Maclachlan. — London [etc.] : Longman, 1977. — x,115p : ill ; 24cm.
Bibl.: p.104. — Index.
ISBN 0-582-45053-5 : £3.75
(B77-23198)

332.6'78'0973 — Investment. *United States. Manuals*
Handbook of wealth management / [edited by] Leo Barnes, Stephen Feldman. — New York ; London [etc.] : McGraw-Hill, 1977. — 1053p in various pagings : ill ; 24cm.
Bibl. — Index.
ISBN 0-07-003765-5 : Unpriced
(B77-31035)

332.7 — CREDIT
332.7'2 — Local authorities. Mortgage schemes. *England. Study regions: West Midlands (Metropolitan County). Birmingham. Reports, surveys*
Karn, Valerie Ann. Priorities for local authority mortgage lending : a case study of Birmingham / by Valerie A. Karn. — Birmingham (J.G. Smith Building, P.O. Box 363, Birmingham B15 2TT) : Centre for Urban and Regional Studies, University of Birmingham, 1976. — [1],iii leaves,45[i.e.46]p ; 30cm. — (University of Birmingham. Centre for Urban and Regional Studies. Research memoranda ; no.52 ISSN 0306-4034)
ISBN 0-7044-0205-x Pbk : £0.75
(B77-15735)

332.7'2 — Privately owned housing. Building society mortgages. Supply & demand. Great Britain. Related to supply & demand of privately owned housing, 1955-1974. Econometric models
Hadjimatheou, George. Housing and mortgage markets : the UK experience / [by] George Hadjimatheou. — Farnborough, Hants. : Saxon House, 1976. — x,179p : ill ; 24cm.
Bibl.: p.165-174. — Index.
ISBN 0-566-00152-7 : £7.95
Also classified at 339.4'8'301540941
(B77-02820)

332.7'2 — Single mothers receiving supplementary benefits. Mortgage payments. Financial assistance. *Great Britain. Child Poverty Action Group viewpoints*
Tunnard, Jo. No father, no home? : a study of 30 fatherless families in mortgaged homes / [by] Jo Tunnard. — London : Child Poverty Action Group, 1976. — [4],43p ; 21cm. — (Poverty pamphlet ; no.28 ISSN 0308-647x)
ISBN 0-903963-35-3 Sd : £0.50
(B77-00646)

332.7'43 — Consumer credit. Rates. *Great Britain. Ready reckoners*
Great Britain. *Office of Fair Trading.* Consumer credit tables to calculate the annual percentage rate of charge / Office of Fair Trading. — London : H.M.S.O.
In 15 vols.
Part 1 : Charge per pound lent, equal weekly instalments up to one year. — 1977. — iii,77p ; 30cm.
ISBN 0-11-280001-7 Pbk : £1.85
(B77-10219)

Part 2 : Charge per pound lent, equal weekly instalments one to two years. — 1977. — [3], 91p ; 30cm.
ISBN 0-11-280002-5 Sd : £2.30
(B77-10220)

Part 3 : Charge per pound lent, equal weekly instalments two years and over. — 1977. — [3], 85p ; 30cm.
ISBN 0-11-280003-3 Sd : £2.05
(B77-10221)

Part 4 : Charge per pound lent, equal monthly instalments up to three years. — 1977. — iii, 62p ; 30cm.
ISBN 0-11-280004-1 Sd : £1.65
(B77-10222)

Part 5 : Charge per pound lent, equal monthly instalments three years and over. — 1977. — [3],117p ; 30cm.
ISBN 0-11-280005-x Sd : £2.95
(B77-10223)

Part 6 : Charge per pound lent, equal quarterly instalments. — 1977. — [3],74p ; 30cm.
ISBN 0-11-280006-8 Sd : £2.05
(B77-10224)

Part 7 : Charge per pound lent, equal half-yearly and yearly instalments. — 1977. — iii,55p ; 30cm.
ISBN 0-11-280007-6 Sd : £1.65
(B77-10225)

Part 8 : Charge per pound lent, single repayment up to 33 weeks-10 months. — 1977. — iii,63p ; 30cm.
ISBN 0-11-280008-4 Sd : £1.85
(B77-10226)

Part 9 : Charge per pound lent, single repayment six months and over. — 1977. — iii, 95p ; 30cm.
ISBN 0-11-280009-2 Sd : £2.30
(B77-10227)

Part 10 : Charge per pound lent, annual percentage rates of 100 per cent and over. — 1977. — iii,69p ; 30cm.
ISBN 0-11-280010-6 Sd : £1.85
(B77-10228)

Part 11 : Flat rate, equal weekly instalments. — 1977. — iii,43p ; 30cm.
ISBN 0-11-280011-4 Sd : £1.20
(B77-10229)

Part 12 : Flat rate, equal monthly instalments. — 1977. — [3],37p ; 30cm.
ISBN 0-11-280012-2 Sd : £1.10
(B77-10230)

Part 13 : Flat rate, equal quarterly, half-yearly and yearly instalments. — 1977. — [3],40p ; 30cm.
ISBN 0-11-280013-0 Sd : £1.20
(B77-10231)

Part 14 : Flat rate, single repayment. — 1977. — [3],43p ; 30cm.
ISBN 0-11-280014-9 Sd : £1.20
(B77-10232)

Part 15 : Period rate on balance outstanding, weekly, monthly, four-weekly, quarterly and half-yearly periods. — 1977. — iii,24p ; 30cm.
ISBN 0-11-280015-7 Sd : £0.90
(B77-10233)

332.7'5'06141 — Great Britain. Department of Trade. Bankruptcy Estates Account & Companies Liquidation Account. *Accounts*
Insolvency Services (Accounting and Investment) Act 1970, accounts ... — London : H.M.S.O.
1975-76. — [1977]. — 11p ; 25cm. — ([1976-77 H.C.] 211)
ISBN 0-10-221177-9 Sd : £0.33
Primary classification 332.7'5'06141
(B77-17341)

332.7'5'06141 — Great Britain. National Debt Commission. Insolvency Services Investment Account. *Accounts*
Insolvency Services (Accounting and Investment) Act 1970, accounts ... — London : H.M.S.O.
1975-76. — [1977]. — 11p ; 25cm. — ([1976-77 H.C.] 211)
ISBN 0-10-221177-9 Sd : £0.33
Also classified at 332.7'5'06141
(B77-17341)

332.7'5'0941 — Bankruptcy. *Great Britain. Statistics*
Bankruptcy : general annual report / Department of Trade. — London : H.M.S.O.
1976. — 1977. — [3],22p ; 21cm.
ISBN 0-11-511364-9 Sd : £0.80
(B77-22417)

332.7'6 — Embossed credit cards. *Standards*
British Standards Institution. Specification for embossed credit cards = Spécification des cartes de crédit en relief = Spezifikation für geprägte Kreditkarten / British Standards Institution. — London : B.S.I.
Part 2 = Partie 2 = Teil 2 : Magnetic stripe encoding for tracks 1 and 2 = Codage de la zone magnétique pour les pistes 1 et 2 = Schlüsseln des magnetischen Streifens für die Spuren 1 und 2. — 1976. — [2],8,[1]p : ill ; 30cm. — (BS5132 : Part 2 : 1976) (ISO 3554-1976)
Pierced for binder.
ISBN 0-580-09660-2 Sd : £2.70
(B77-11109)

332.7'7 — Great Britain. Foreign trade. Bills of exchange
Gillett Brothers Discount Company. The bill on London, or, The finance of trade by bills of exchange / [Gillett Brothers Discount Company]. — 4th revised ed. — London : Methuen, 1976. — 101p : facsims(chiefly col) ; 24cm.
Nine cards (18 sides : col. facsims) in pocket. — Previous ed.: London : Chapman and Hall, 1964. — Index.
ISBN 0-416-85670-5 : £8.00
(B77-16237)

332.8 — INTEREST AND DISCOUNT
332.8'4'094212 — Discount houses. *London (City), to 1975*
Fletcher, Gordon Alan. The discount houses in London : principles, operations and change / [by] G.A. Fletcher. — London [etc.] : Macmillan, 1976. — xiii,298p : ill ; 23cm.
Index.
ISBN 0-333-15046-5 : £10.00
(B77-07136)

333 — LAND ECONOMICS
333 — Natural resources. *Secondary school texts*
World resources. — Exeter : Wheaton.
1 : Energy / [by] D.S. Scott. — 1976. — [7], 71p : ill(some col), maps(some col) ; 29cm. — (Pergamon topic geographies)
ISBN 0-08-019818-x Pbk : £1.60
(B77-04617)

333'.006'11 — Great Britain. Directorate of Overseas Surveys. Land Resources Division. *Reports, surveys. Serials*
Great Britain. *Ministry of Overseas Development. Land Resources Division.* Progress report of the Land Resources Division. — Surbiton : The Division.
April 1974-March 1976. — 1977. — vii,109p, [7]leaves,8p of plates : ill ; 21cm.
Bibl.
Pbk : Unpriced
ISSN 0309-1082
(B77-20082)

333'.00941 — Land. Ownership. *Great Britain*
Green, Daniel. To colonize Eden : land and Jeffersonian democracy / [by] Daniel Green. — London [etc.] : Gordon and Cremonesi, 1977. — [7],200p ; 23cm.
Bibl.: p.192-193. — Index.
ISBN 0-86033-038-9 : £6.90 : CIP rev.
(B77-14105)

333'.0094176 — Natural resources. *Leitrim (County). Reports, surveys*
County Leitrim resource survey. — Dublin (19 Sandymount Ave., Ballsbridge, Dublin 4) : Foras Taluntais.
Part 2 : Some aspects of production : drainage, machinery use, grass production and utilisation, farming systems, animal health, fisheries. — 1975. — iii-x,98p : ill, maps ; 24cm.
ISBN 0-901317-89-6 Pbk : £2.00
(B77-00080)

333'.009595'3 — Land resources. *Sabah. Reports, surveys*
Great Britain. *Ministry of Overseas Development. Land Resources Division.* The land capability classification of Sabah / Land Resources Division [Ministry of Overseas Development]. — Surbiton : The Division. — (Land resource study ; 25 ISSN 0305-6554)
Maps. — [1976]. — Portfolio ([10]fold sheets) : of col maps ; 30cm.
£2.50
(B77-22418)

Vol.1 : The Tawau Residency : (with an introduction and summary for Volumes 1-4) / [written by] P. Thomas, F.K.C. Lo and A.J. Hepburn. — 1976. — xvii,109p,[3]leaves : ill, maps(1 col) ; 30cm.
Bibl.: p.105-109.
Pbk : £2.50
(B77-22419)

Vol.2 : The Sandakan Residency / [written by] P. Thomas, F.K.C. Lo and A.J. Hepburn. — 1976. — xvii,126p(8 fold),leaf : ill, maps(1 col) ; 30cm.
Bibl.: p.123-126.
Pbk : £2.50
(B77-22420)

Vol.3 : The West Coast and Kudat Residences / [written by] P. Thomas, F.K.C. Lo and A.J. Hepburn. — 1976. — xvii,124p, leaf : ill, maps(1 col) ; 30cm.
Bibl.: p.119-124.
Pbk : £2.50
(B77-22421)

Vol.4 : The Interior Residency and Labuan / [written by] P. Thomas, F.K.C. Lo and A.J. Hepburn. — 1976. — xvi,112p,leaf : ill, maps(1 col) ; 30cm.
Bibl.: p.109-112.
Pbk : £2.50
(B77-22422)

333'.009689'4 — Land resources. *Zambia. Luapula Province & Northern Province. Reports, surveys*
Great Britain. *Ministry of Overseas Development. Land Resources Division.* Land resources of the Northern and Luapula Provinces, Zambia : a reconnaissance assessment / Land Resources Division [Ministry of Overseas Development]. — Surbiton : The Division. — (Land resource study ; 19 ISSN 0305-6554)
Vol.6 : The land systems / [by] R.B. King. — 1976. — xiii,236p,fold leaf : ill, maps(1 col) ; 30cm.
Three fold. sheets (3 sides) (maps) in pocket. — Bibl.: p.211-212.
ISBN 0-902409-51-4 Sp : £2.50
(B77-08265)

333'.009729'6 — Land resources. *Bahamas. Reports, surveys*
Great Britain. *Ministry of Overseas Development. Land Resources Division.* Land resources of the Bahamas : a summary / Land Resources Division [Ministry of Overseas Development] ; [written by] Little, B.G. ... [et al.]. — Surbiton : The Division, 1977. — xvii, 130p(4 fold),[6]leaves : ill, col map ; 30cm. — (Land resource study ; 27 ISSN 0305-6554)
Two fold. sheets (2 leaves : col. maps) in pocket. — Bibl.: p.117-120.
Pbk : £2.50
(B77-18604)

333'.00993'5 — Land resources. *Solomon Islands. Reports, surveys*
Great Britain. *Ministry of Overseas Development. Land Resources Division.* Land resources of the Solomon Islands / Land Resources Division [Ministry of Overseas Development]. — Surbiton : The Division. — (Land resource study ; 18 ISSN 0305-6554)
In 8 vols.
Vol.1 : Introduction and recommendations / [written by] J.R.F. Hansell and J.R.D. Wall. — 1976. — xi,148[i.e.146]p(8 fold) : ill, maps ; 30cm.
Seven fold. sheets (4,[3]sides : of maps(chiefly col.)) in pocket. — Bibl.: p.139-148.
Sp : Unpriced
(B77-25440)

Vol.7 : San Cristobal and adjacent islands / [written by] J.R.F. Hansell and J.R.D. Wall. — 1975. — x,123[i.e. 119],[2]p,[5]leaves of plates(3 fold),[4]p of plates(4 fold) : ill(some col), maps(1 col) ; 30cm.
Vol.7 has title: The British Solomon Islands Protectorate. — Eight fold. sheets (col. maps) in portfolio. — Bibl.: p.87-88.
ISBN 0-902409-62-x Sp : Unpriced
(B77-14106)

Vol.8 : Outer islands / [written by] J.R.D. Wall and J.R.F. Hansell. — 1976. — x,154p(10 fold),[2] leaves : ill, maps(some col) ; 30cm.
Ten fold. sheets(col. maps) in portfolio. — Bibl. : p.111-116.
Sp : £2.50
(B77-17970)

333.1 — PUBLIC LAND
333.1 — Great Britain. Crown lands. Administration. *Reports, surveys. Serials*
The **Crown** Estate : report of the Commissioners for the year ended 31st March ... — London : H.M.S.O.
[1975]-1976. — 1976. — iii,26p,plate : ports ; 25cm.
ISBN 0-11-700324-7 Sd : £0.60
(B77-04001)

333.1'06'1429 — Great Britain. Land Authority for Wales. *Accounts*
Great Britain. *Land Authority for Wales.* Account ... / Land Authority for Wales. — London [etc.] : H.M.S.O.
1975-1976 : for the period 12 November 1975-31 March 1976. — [1977]. — Folder (4p) ; 25cm. — ([1976-1977 H.C.]250)
ISBN 0-10-225077-4 : £0.15
(B77-14595)

333.1'0941 — Community land scheme. *Great Britain. Labour Party viewpoints*
Labour Party. Community land / [Labour Party] ; [researched by Philip Wyatt for Transport House]. — London : Labour Party, 1976. — Folder([4]p) : ill ; 30cm. — (Labour Party. Political education discussion papers ; no.3)
Unpriced
(B77-16765)

333.1'0941 — Great Britain. Crown Estate Commissioners. *Accounts*
Crown Estate abstract accounts : abstract accounts of the Crown Estate Commissioners for the year ended 31st March ... — London : H.M.S.O.
1975-76. — [1977]. — 8p ; 25cm. — ([1976-77 H.C.] 233)
ISBN 0-10-223377-2 Sd : £0.25
(B77-12902)

333.1'09411 — Community land scheme. Administration. *Scotland*
Planning Exchange. The community land scheme in Scotland / [Planning Exchange]. — Glasgow (186 Bath St., Glasgow G2 4HG) : Planning Exchange, 1976. — [4],33p ; 30cm. — (Newsheet ; 5 ISSN 0307-1278)
ISBN 0-905011-11-2 Sd : £1.00(£0.50 to contributing local authorities and organisations)
(B77-02821)

333.1'3 — Land. Purchase. Organisations. *Ireland. Irish Land Purchase Fund. Accounts*
Irish Land Purchase Fund account ... for the year ended 31st March ... — London : H.M.S.O.
1975-76. — [1977]. — 6p ; 25cm. — ([1976-77 H.C.] 234)
ISBN 0-10-223477-9 Sd : £0.25
(B77-12903)

333.1'6 — Tax sales. *Iowa, 1840-1900*
Swierenga, Robert P. Acres for cents : delinquent tax auctions in frontier Iowa / [by] Robert P. Swierenga. — Westport, Conn. ; London : Greenwood Press, 1976. — xix,262,[1]p : ill, facsims, 2 maps ; 22cm. — (Contributions in American history ; no.46)
Index.
ISBN 0-8371-8167-4 : £9.95
(B77-24060)

333.3 — PRIVATE LAND
333.3'2 — Great Britain. Land Registry. *Reports, surveys. Serials*
Great Britain. *Land Registry.* Report to the Lord Chancellor on HM Land Registry for the year [ended 31st March] / by the Chief Land Registrar. — London : H.M.S.O.
1976-1977. — 1977. — 16p : 1 ill ; 25cm.
ISBN 0-11-390212-3 Sd : £0.45
(B77-25441)

333.3'2'0723 — Cadastral surveys. *Commonwealth countries*
Dale, P F. Cadastral surveys within the Commonwealth : report / by P.F. Dale. — London : H.M.S.O., 1976. — xxv,281p,3 fold leaves of plates : ill, maps, plans ; 26cm. — (Overseas research publication ; no.23)
ISBN 0-11-880235-6 : £4.35
(B77-08833)

333.3'22'0922 — Kniveton family. *Derbyshire. Cartularies*
Kniveton family. The Kniveton leiger / [prepared by the Derbyshire Archaeological Society] ; edited with an introduction by Avrom Saltman. — London : H.M.S.O., 1977. — xxxiv,316p : geneal tables, map ; 26cm. — (Historical Manuscripts Commission. Joint publications ; no.24) (Derbyshire Archaeological Society. Record series ; no.7)
Latin text, English introduction and notes. — '. .. the early 14th century Leiger or register of title deeds and other evidences of the Kniveton family, now preserved in the muniments of the Dean and Chapter of Lincoln ...' - Bibliographical note. — Index.
ISBN 0-11-440065-2 : £25.00
(B77-28450)

333.3'22'0942 — Land tenure. *England, 1086. Early works. Latin-English parallel texts*
Domesday book / text and translation edited by John Morris. — Chichester : Phillimore. — (History from the sources)
2 : Sussex / edited from a draft translation prepared by Janet Mothersill. — 1976. — [224] p : 4 maps ; 22cm.
Parallel Latin text and English translation. — Index.
ISBN 0-85033-145-5 : £6.00
ISBN 0-85033-146-3 Pbk : Unpriced
(B77-31036)

12 : Hertfordshire / edited from a draft translation prepared by Margaret Newman and Sara Wood. — 1976. — [194]p : map ; 22cm.
Parallel Latin text and English translation. — Index.
ISBN 0-85033-137-4 : £5.00
ISBN 0-85033-138-2 Pbk : £2.50
(B77-00647)

20 : Bedfordshire / edited from a draft translation prepared by Veronica Sankaran and David Sherlock. — 1977. — [176]p : map ; 22cm.
Parallel Latin text and English translation. — Index.
ISBN 0-85033-149-8 : £4.50
ISBN 0-85033-150-1 Pbk : Unpriced
(B77-31037)

23 : Warwickshire / edited from a draft translation prepared by Judy Plaister. — 1976. — [160]p : map ; 22cm.
Parallel Latin text and English translation. — Index.
ISBN 0-85033-141-2 : Unpriced
ISBN 0-85033-142-0 Pbk : Unpriced
(B77-31744)

24 : Staffordshire / edited from a draft translation prepared by Alison Hawkins and Alex Rumble. — 1976. — [120]p : 2 maps ; 22cm.
Parallel Latin text and English translation. — Index.
ISBN 0-85033-143-9 : £2.50
ISBN 0-85033-144-7 Pbk : £1.25
(B77-00648)

28 : Nottinghamshire / edited from a draft translation prepared by Celia Parker and Sara Wood. — 1977. — [166]p : 2 maps ; 22cm.
Parallel Latin text and English translation. — Index.
ISBN 0-85033-147-1 : £4.50
ISBN 0-85033-148-x Pbk : Unpriced
(B77-31038)

333.3'22'0942132 — Collegiate churches. *London. Westminster (London Borough). Westminster Abbey. Ecclesiastical estates, ca 1000-ca 1600*
Harvey, Barbara. Westminster Abbey and its estates in the Middle Ages / by Barbara Harvey. — Oxford : Clarendon Press, 1977. — xii,499p : maps ; 23cm.
Bibl.: p.452-470. — Index.
ISBN 0-19-822449-4 : £15.00 : CIP rev.
(B77-08834)

333.3'22'09422735 — Land tenure. *Hampshire. Winchester, ca 1110 & 1148. Reports, surveys. Early works. Latin-English parallel texts*
[**Winton** Domesday]. Winchester in the early Middle Ages : an edition and discussion of the Winton Domesday / [by] Frank Barlow ... [et al.] ; edited by Martin Biddle. — Oxford : Clarendon Press, 1976 [i.e. 1977]. — xxxiii, 612p,[14]leaves of plates(9 fold),xi p of plates : ill, facsims, maps(some col) ; 29cm. — (Winchester studies ; 1)
Index. — Includes parallel Latin text from Society of Antiquaries of London MS. 154 and English translation edited and translated by Frank Barlow.
ISBN 0-19-813169-0 : £32.00
(B77-10234)

333.3'22'0942414 — Abbeys. *Gloucestershire. Gloucester. Monastery of St Peter's, Gloucester. Ecclesiastical estates, to ca 1400. Documents*
An **ecclesiastical** miscellany. — Bristol (c/o 9A Pembroke Rd, Clifton, Bristol) : Bristol and Gloucestershire Archaeological Society, 1976. — ix,159p : map ; 23cm. — (Bristol and Gloucestershire Archaeological Society. Records Section. Publications ; vol.11)
Index. — Contents: A register of the churches of the monastery of St Peter's, Gloucester / by David Walker - A survey of the Diocese of Gloucester, 1603 / transcribed by Alicia C. Percival ; edited by W.J. Sheils - Wesleyan membership in Bristol, 1783 / by John Kent.
ISBN 0-900197-11-0 : £4.50(£2.50 to members of the Society)
Also classified at 283'.424'14; 287'.1423'93
(B77-12349)

333.3'22'0942417 — Abbeys. *Gloucestershire. Cirencester. Cirencester Abbey. Cartularies. Latin texts*
Cirencester Abbey. The cartulary of Cirencester Abbey, Gloucestershire. — Oxford [etc.] : Oxford University Press.
In 3 vols.
Vol.3 / edited by Mary Devine. — 1977. — xv p,p735-1182,[2]fold leaves of plates : 2 facsims ; 26cm.
Latin text, English introduction and preliminaries. — Index.
ISBN 0-19-711637-x : £15.00
(B77-19255)

333.3'22'0942516 — Chantry chapels. *Derbyshire. Crich. Wakebridge Chantries. Ecclesiastical estates. Cartularies. Latin texts*
The **cartulary** of the Wakebridge Chantries at Crich / edited by Avrom Saltman. — [Derby] ([35 St Mary's Gate, Derby DE1 3JU]) : [Derbyshire Archaeological Society], 1976. — [7],203p : geneal table ; 25cm. — (Derbyshire Archaeological Society. Record series ; vol.6 (1971))
Latin text, English introduction and notes. — Index.
ISBN 0-9501786-6-7 Pbk : £5.30
(B77-12904)

333.3'22'0942579 — Manors. *Oxfordshire. Cuxham. Cuxham (Manor). Archives, ca 1200-1359. Collections. Latin texts*
Cuxham *(Manor).* Manorial records of Cuxham, Oxfordshire, circa 1200-1359 / edited by P.D.A. Harvey. — London : H.M.S.O., 1976. — xviii,839p,ii p of plates : facsims ; 25cm. — (Historical Manuscripts Commission. Joint publications ; 23) (Oxfordshire Record Society. Publications ; no.50)
Index.
ISBN 0-11-440050-4 : £25.00
(B77-01223)

333.3'22'0942841 — Ecclesiastical estates: Estates of Fountains Abbey, Ripon. *North Yorkshire. Craven (District), 1150-1780*
Raistrick, Arthur. Monks & shepherds in the Yorkshire Dales / [by] Arthur Raistrick. — [Leyburn] ([Yorebridge House, Bainbridge, Leyburn, N. Yorkshire]) : Yorkshire Dales National Park Committee, 1976. — [3],22,[1]p : ill, map ; 21cm.
ISBN 0-905455-04-5 Sd : £0.45
(B77-05919)

333.3'23'0942276 — Land. Terriers. *Hampshire. Southampton, 1454. Latin-English parallel texts*
Southampton *(Borough).* The Southampton terrier of 1454 / edited by L.A. Burgess ; with an introduction by L.A. Burgess, P.D.A. Harvey and A.D. Saunders. — London : H.M.S.O., 1976. — x,172p,[8]p of plates : facsims, plans ; 25cm. — (Historical Manuscripts Commission. Joint publications ; 21) (Southampton records series ; no.15)
Map (fold. leaf) in pocket. — Parallel English translation and Latin text, English introduction and notes. — Bibl.: p.ix. — Index.
ISBN 0-11-440031-8 : £13.00
(B77-00081)

333.3'23'0942659 — Open fields: West Field. Land. Terriers. *Cambridgeshire. Cambridge, ca 1360. Latin texts*
Cambridge *(Borough).* [Terrarium Cantabrigiae]. The West Fields of Cambridge / edited by Catherine P. Hall and J.R. Ravensdale. — Cambridge ([c/o The Hon. Sec., Central Library, 7 Lion Yard, Cambridge CB2 3QD]) : Cambridge Antiquarian Records Society, 1976. — xii,168p,fold plate : map ; 25cm. — (Cambridge Antiquarian Records Society. Publications ; vol.3)
'... the manuscript known in the Cambridge University Library as Add.2601, or "Terrarium Cantabrigiae"' - book jacket. — Index.
ISBN 0-904323-02-1 : £9.00
(B77-10235)

333.3'23'096891 — Land tenure. Policies of government. *Rhodesia, 1890-1936*
Palmer, Robin. Land and racial domination in Rhodesia / [by] Robin Palmer. — London [etc.] : Heinemann Educational, 1977. — viii, 307p,[4]p of plates : ill, maps ; 23cm.
Ill. on lining papers. — Bibl.: p.283-298. — Index.
ISBN 0-435-94237-9 : £9.00
(B77-30011)

333.3'23'0985 — Haciendas. *Peru. Coastal regions, to ca 1650*
Keith, Robert G. Conquest and agrarian change : the emergence of the hacienda system on the Peruvian coast / [by] Robert G. Keith. — Cambridge, Mass. ; London : Harvard University Press, 1976. — xi,176p : maps ; 24cm. — (Harvard historical studies ; vol.93)
Bibl.: p.157-169. — Index.
ISBN 0-674-16293-5 : £13.15
(B77-05254)

333.3'23'09931 — Maoris. Land tenure. *New Zealand, 1800-1976*
Kawharu, I H. Maori land tenure : studies of a changing institution / by I.H. Kawharu. — Oxford : Clarendon Press, 1977. — xvi,363p : ill, maps ; 22cm.
Bibl.: p.355-358. — Index.
ISBN 0-19-823177-6 : £13.50 : CIP rev.
(B77-08835)

333.33 — REAL PROPERTY

333.3'3'02541 — Estate agents. *Great Britain. Directories*
The **estate** agents' yearbook and directory. — London : Kemps.
1977. — [1977]. — 330p : ill ; 23cm.
ISBN 0-905255-20-8 : £8.00
(B77-14107)

333.3'3'02541 — Real property development industries. *Great Britain. Directories*
United Kingdom property development companies / [Data Research Group]. — Amersham (Hill House, [Hill Ave.], Amersham, Bucks.) : The Group.
[1976]. — 1976. — 96 leaves in various pagings ; 30cm.
ISBN 0-905570-54-5 Sp : £14.00
(B77-04002)

333.3'3'0621 — Real property. Organisations: International Real Estate Federation. British Chapter. *Directories*
International Real Estate Federation. *British Chapter.* List of members / the British Chapter of the International Real Estate Federation. — [London] ([c/o F.P.R. Short, 29 Lincoln's Inn Fields, WC2A 3ED]) : [The Chapter].
1975-76. — [1975]. — 63p : ill ; 21cm.
Index.
ISBN 0-9505450-1-5 Sd : £1.00
ISSN 0309-1023
(B77-09560)

1976-77. — [1976]. — 46p ; 21cm.
Sd : Unpriced
ISSN 0309-1023
(B77-03426)

333.3'3'0973 — Real property. *United States. For estate agency*
Estes, Jack C. Real estate license preparation course for the uniform examinations : for salespersons and brokers / [by] Jack C. Estes, John Kokus, Jr. — New York ; London [etc.] : McGraw-Hill, 1976. — ix,246,[16]p : ill, forms, maps ; 29cm.
With answers. — Index.
ISBN 0-07-019670-2 : £10.75
(B77-15134)

333.3'32'0941 — Real property. Valuation. *Great Britain*
Turner, D M. An approach to land values / by D.M. Turner. — Berkhamsted : Geographical Publications, 1977. — xiii,223p ; 24cm. — (Studies in land economy)
Bibl.: p.210-213. — Index.
ISBN 0-900394-17-x : £6.25 : CIP rev.
(B77-07824)

333.3'32'0942 — Real property. Valuation. *England. Forms. Collections*
Marshall, Philip Julian Lanagan. Marshall's valuation proformas for real property appraisals : including a 'typical' valuation report / [by] P.J.L. Marshall, J.J. Rose. — [Beckenham] ([39 The Avenue, Beckenham, Kent]) : [P.J.L. Marshall], [1976]. — [40] leaves : forms ; 30cm.
Cover title.
ISBN 0-9504740-1-0 Pbk : £5.00
(B77-02096)

333.3'35 — Agricultural holdings. Improvement. Valuation on termination of tenancies. *England. Proposals*
Committee on Agricultural Valuation. Fourth report of the Committee on Agricultural Valuation. — London : H.M.S.O., 1977. — [3], 54,[1]p : map ; 25cm.
ISBN 0-11-241106-1 Sd : £1.00
(B77-31039)

333.3'35'091724 — Agricultural land. Land tenure. Reform. *Developing countries, ca 1950-1976*
King, Russell. Land reform : a world survey / [by] Russell King. — London : Bell, 1977. — xvi,446p : maps ; 23cm. — (Bell's advanced economic geographies)
Index.
ISBN 0-7135-1995-9 : £10.50
(B77-33105)

333.3'35'0941 — Agricultural land. Ownership. *Great Britain. Reports, surveys*
Royal Institution of Chartered Surveyors. *Land Agency and Agriculture Division.* The agricultural resources of the United Kingdom : the future pattern of land ownership and occupation : a discussion paper of the Land Agency & Agriculture Division, the Royal Institution of Chartered Surveyors. — [London] : [R.I.C.S.], 1977. — [6],69p ; 30cm.
Bibl.
ISBN 0-85406-079-0 Pbk : Unpriced
(B77-12350)

333.3'35'097291 — Agricultural land. Land tenure. Reform. *Cuba, 1930-1976*
Martinez-Alier, Juan. Haciendas, plantations and collective farms : agrarian class societies - Cuba and Peru / [by] Juan Martinez-Alier. — London [etc.] : Cass, 1977. — viii,185p ; 23cm. — (Library of peasant studies ; no.2)
Bibl.: p.171-179. — Index.
ISBN 0-7146-3048-9 : £8.50
Also classified at 333.3'35'0985
(B77-12905)

333.3'35'0985 — Haciendas. Land tenure. Reform. *Peru. Highlands, 1930-1976*
Martinez-Alier, Juan. Haciendas, plantations and collective farms : agrarian class societies - Cuba and Peru / [by] Juan Martinez-Alier. — London [etc.] : Cass, 1977. — viii,185p ; 23cm. — (Library of peasant studies ; no.2)
Bibl.: p.171-179. — Index.
ISBN 0-7146-3048-9 : £8.50
Primary classification 333.3'35'097291
(B77-12905)

333.3'37 — Housing. Rents. Analysis. Applications of theories of ground rent of Marx, Karl. *Urban regions*
Broadbent, Thomas Andrew. An attempt to apply Marx's theory of ground rent to the modern urban economy / [by] T.A. Broadbent. — London : Centre for Environmental Studies, 1975. — 46p : ill ; 30cm. — (Centre for Environmental Studies. Research papers ; 17)
Bibl.: p.46.
Sd : £0.50
(B77-33661)

333.3'37 — Local authority housing. Rents. *Scotland. Statistics*
Rents of public authority houses and rent rebates and allowances in Scotland / Scottish Development Department. — Edinburgh : H.M.S.O.
1976. — [1977]. — 14p ; 25cm. — (Cmnd.6759)
ISBN 0-10-167590-9 Sd : £0.45
(B77-17971)

333.3'37 — Local authority housing. Tenancies. Agreements. Conditions. *England. Reports, surveys*
Housing Services Advisory Group. Tenancy agreements / Housing Services Advisory Group. — [London] : Department of the Environment, 1977. — [1],i,22p ; 30cm.
Pbk : Unpriced
(B77-26871)

333.3'37 — Residences. Purchase. *England. Manuals*
Vickers, Lisa Erica. Buying a house or flat / [by] L.E. Vickers. — [2nd] revised ed. — Harmondsworth [etc.] : Penguin, 1977. — 143p : facsim, forms, map ; 18cm. — (Penguin handbooks)
Previous ed.: i.e. revised ed. published as 'Buying a house'. 1974. — Index.
ISBN 0-14-046279-1 Pbk : £0.70
(B77-33662)

333.3'37 — Residences. Purchase & renting. *Great Britain. Secondary school texts*
Mason, Sheila. Starting a home / [by] Sheila Mason. — Cambridge [etc.] : Cambridge University Press, 1976. — 48p : ill ; 30cm.
ISBN 0-521-20739-8 Sd : £1.00
(B77-03427)

333.3'37 — Residences. Purchase by occupiers. Increase. *London. Proposals*
Oakeshott, J. A consideration of methods of extending owner occupation / by J. Oakeshott ; [for the Greater London Council] Director-General's Department, Policy Studies and Intelligence Branch. — London : G.L.C., 1976. — [1],ii,23p : 2 ill ; 30cm. — (Greater London Council. Intelligence Unit. Research memoranda ; RM495 ISSN 0306-7203)
ISBN 0-7168-0866-8 Sd : £2.30
(B77-15736)

333.3'37 — Residences. Rents. Allowances & rebates. *England. Reports, surveys. Serials*
Great Britain. *Advisory Committee on Rent Rebates and Rent Allowances.* Report / Advisory Committee on Rent Rebates and Rent Allowances. — London : H.M.S.O.
No.2 : July 1974 to December 1976. — 1977. — viii,42p ; 21cm.
Index.
ISBN 0-11-751154-4 Sd : £0.85
(B77-24061)

333.3'37 — Residences. Rents. Allowances & rebates. Administration. *England. Reports, surveys*
Legg, Charles. The administration of the rent rebate and rent allowance schemes / by Charles Legg and Marion Brion. — [London] : Department of the Environment : Welsh Office, 1976. — [5],198p : ill, forms ; 30cm.
Cover title. — Bibl.: p.198.
Pbk : Unpriced
(B77-30012)

333.3'37'0941 — Real property. Management. *Great Britain. Urban regions*
The **management** of urban property / editor T.A. Johnson. — [1st ed. reprinted with minor amendments]. — Reading : College of Estate Management, [1976]. — [7],189p : ill ; 21cm. — (Property studies in the United Kingdom and overseas ; study no.8)
'This book derives from a series of papers delivered to a residential course run at Reading University by the Centre of Advanced Land Use Studies in September 1970' - Introduction. — First ed. originally published: 1972.
ISBN 0-902132-29-6 Pbk : £2.95
(B77-00082)

333.3'8 — Residential property. Speculative development. *Berkshire. Reading region*
Bather, Nicholas John. The speculative residential developer and urban growth : the location decision in a planned environment / [by] Nicholas J. Bather. — Reading (Whiteknights, Reading RG6 1AB) : Department of Geography, University of Reading, 1976. — [2],ii,44p : ill, 2 maps ; 21cm. — (Geographical papers ; no.47 ISSN 0305-5914)
Bibl.: p.35.
ISBN 0-7049-0456-x Sd : £0.70
(B77-03428)

333.5 — RENT
333.5'3'0941 — Privately rented residences. Tenancies. *Great Britain. Labour Party viewpoints*
Labour Party. Home secure home : a charter for private tenants / the Labour Party. — London : Labour Party, [1977?]. — [8]p ; 30cm.
'... based on the Labour Party's evidence to the Government's review of the Rents Acts'.
Sd : £0.20
(B77-32468)

333.7 — LAND UTILISATION
Davis, Kenneth Pickett. Land use / [by] Kenneth P. Davis. — New York ; London [etc.] : McGraw-Hill, 1976. — xi,324p : ill, maps ; 24cm. — (McGraw-Hill series in forest resources)
Bibl.: p.303-318. — Index.
ISBN 0-07-015534-8 : £12.40
(B77-01224)

333.7 — Energy resources
Denby, Erica. Sources of energy / [by] Erica Denby and Chris Swadkin. — [Brighton] : Tyndall, 1975. — 48p : ill ; 24cm. — (World scene)
Bibl.: p.48.
ISBN 0-85949-083-1 : £2.25
(B77-16766)

Energy. — Reading, Mass. ; London [etc.] : Addison-Wesley.
In 3 vols.
Vol.3 : Nuclear energy and energy policies / edited by S.S. Penner. — 1976 [i.e. 1977]. — xxxv,713p : ill ; 24cm.
Ill. on lining papers. — Published in the United States: 1976. — Index.
ISBN 0-201-05564-3 : £24.25
ISBN 0-201-05565-1 Pbk : £13.20
(B77-10751)

Hoyle, *Sir* Fred. Energy or extinction? : the case for nuclear energy / [by] Fred Hoyle. — London : Heinemann Educational, 1977. — ix, 81p : ill, map ; 22cm.
Index.
ISBN 0-435-54430-6 Pbk : £1.50
(B77-25442)

333.7 — Energy resources. *Encyclopaedias*
McGraw-Hill encyclopedia of energy / Daniel N. Lapedes, editor in chief. — New York ; London [etc.] : McGraw-Hill, 1976. — [9], 785p : ill, maps ; 29cm.
'Much of the material in this volume has been published previously in the ... "McGraw-Hill encyclopedia of science and technology", 3rd Edition ... [and] the McGraw-Hill yearbook of science and technology"'. — title page verso. — Index.
ISBN 0-07-045261-x : Unpriced
(B77-30013)

333.7 — Energy resources. *Great Britain. Conference proceedings*
Energy in the 80s *(Conference), Teesside Polytechnic, 1977.* Proceedings of symposium on 'Energy in the 80's' : a symposium organised by the Northern Branch of the Institution of Chemical Engineers at Teesside Polytechnic, Middlesbrough, 5th to 7th April, 1977 ... : 186th event of the European Federation of Chemical Engineering. — Rugby : Institution of Chemical Engineers, 1977. — 435p in various pagings : ill, form ; 30cm. — (Institution of Chemical Engineers. Symposium series ; no.48 ISSN 0307-0492)
Cover title: Energy in the 80s.
ISBN 0-85295-101-9 Pbk : Unpriced
(B77-17972)

333.7 — Energy resources. *Organisation for Economic Co-operation and Development countries. Statistics*
Organisation for Economic Co-operation and Development. Energy balances of OECD countries = Bilans énergétiques des pays de l'OCDE / [Organisation for Economic Co-operation and Development]. — Paris : O.E.C.D. ; [London] : [H.M.S.O.]. 1973-75. — 1977. — 129p ; 27cm.
' ... based on data recently published in "Energy statistics 1973-1975" - Introduction. — Parallel English and French text.
Pbk : £4.90
ISBN 92-64-01608-2
(B77-14596)

333.7 — Energy resources. *Secondary school texts*
Thomas, John Anthony Griffiths. Energy today / [by] John A. G. Thomas. — London : Kaye and Ward [etc.], 1977. — 96p : ill, maps ; 23cm. — ([Today series])
Bibl.: p.91.
ISBN 0-7182-0455-7 : £2.50
(B77-26169)

333.7 — Energy resources. Distribution
Odell, Peter Randon. Energy : needs and resources / [by] Peter Odell. — 2nd ed. — Basingstoke [etc.] : Macmillan, 1977. — v,34p : ill, map ; 22cm. — (Aspects of geography)
Previous ed.: 1974.
ISBN 0-333-23112-0 Sd : £0.85
(B77-20974)

333.7 — Energy resources. Economic aspects & environmental aspects
Commoner, Barry. The poverty of power : energy and the economic crisis / [by] Barry Commoner. — London : Cape, 1976. — [5], 314p ; 23cm.
'A substantial portion of the material in this book appeared in the "New Yorker"' - title page verso. — Also published: New York : Knopf, 1976. — Index.
ISBN 0-224-01336-x : £5.50
(B77-07137)

333.7 — Energy resources. Environmental aspects. Risk-benefit analysis. *Conference proceedings*
Energy and the environment : a risk benefit approach / editors Holt Ashley, Richard L. Rudman, Christopher Whipple. — New York ; Oxford [etc.] : Pergamon, 1976. — ix,305p : ill, maps ; 24cm. — (Pergamon international library)
'... based on nine seminars delivered during Autumn Quarter, 1974, and centered on the theme "Energy and the Environment, a Risk-Benefit Approach"' - Preface. — Bibl.
ISBN 0-08-020873-8 : £6.25
(B77-04003)

333.7 — Energy resources: Geothermal energy & solar energy. *Conference proceedings*
Alternative energy sources / edited by James P. Hartnett. — New York [etc.] ; London : Academic Press ; Washington [D.C.] ; London : Hemisphere Publishing Corporation, 1976. — vii,328p : ill, maps, plans ; 25cm.
' ... proceedings of a conference sponsored [i.e. organized] by the International Centre of Heat and Mass Transfer in the fall of 1975' - Preface. — Bibl. — Index.
ISBN 0-12-328550-x : £20.25
Also classified at 333.8'2
(B77-08836)

333.7 — Energy resources. Policies. *United States*
Hagel, John. Alternative energy strategies : constraints and opportunities / [by] John Hagel, III. — New York [etc.] ; London : Praeger, 1976. — xiii,187p : ill ; 25cm. — (Praeger special studies in international economics and development)
Bibl.: p.160-179. — Index.
ISBN 0-275-56090-2 : £12.95
(B77-07138)

333.7 — Energy resources. Policies of government. *United States*
Energy supply and government policy / edited by Robert J. Kalter and William A. Vogely. — Ithaca ; London : Cornell University Press, 1976. — 356,[1]p : ill ; 22cm.
Index.
ISBN 0-8014-0966-7 : £14.80
ISBN 0-8014-9159-2 Pbk : £4.75
(B77-12906)

Perspectives on U.S. energy policy : a critique of regulation / edited by Edward J. Mitchell. — New York [etc.] ; London : Praeger [for] the American Enterprise Institute for Public Policy Research, 1976. — xiv,257p : ill ; 25cm. — (American Enterprise Institute for Public Policy Research. Perspectives ; 3) (Praeger special studies in US economic, social and political issues)
ISBN 0-275-23640-4 : £12.25
(B77-04619)

333.7 — Energy resources. Policies of government. *United States. Proposals*
Sporn, Philip. Energy in an age of limited availability and delimited applicability / [by] Philip Sporn. — Oxford [etc.] : Pergamon, 1976. — viii,38p ; 28cm. — (Energy Educational Foundation. Visiting professorship lectures) (Pergamon international library)
'Delivered at Manhattan College, April 24, 1975'.
ISBN 0-08-020857-6 Sd : £2.75
(B77-02097)

Task Force on United States Energy Policy. Providing for energy : report of the Twentieth Century Fund Task Force on United States Energy Policy / Background paper by Richard B. Mancke. — New York ; London [etc.] : McGraw-Hill, 1977. — xiii,134p ; 22cm.
ISBN 0-07-065617-7 : £5.95
ISBN 0-07-065618-5 Pbk : £2.95
(B77-26170)

333.7 — Energy resources. Policies of government. Proposals. *Great Britain*
Great Britain. *Department of Energy.* Energy policy review / Department of Energy. — London : H.M.S.O., 1977. — iv,49p : ill ; 25cm. — (Energy papers ; no.22)
ISBN 0-11-410606-1 Sd : £1.75
(B77-20084)

333.7 — Energy resources. Policies of government. Social aspects. *United States. Forecasts*
O'Toole, James. Energy and social change / [by] James O'Toole and the University of Southern California Center for Futures Research. — Cambridge, Mass. ; London : M.I.T. Press, [1977]. — xxi,185p : ill ; 24cm.
Published in the United States: 1976. — Bibl.: p.170-179. — Index.
ISBN 0-262-15018-2 : £7.50
(B77-12907)

333.7 — Energy resources. Policies of governments
Energy policies of the world. — New York ; Oxford [etc.] : Elsevier.
Vol.1 : Canada, China, Arab states of the Persian Gulf, Venezuela, Iran / edited by Gerard J. Mangone. — 1976. — xix,387p : ill, maps ; 22cm.
Bibl. — Index.
ISBN 0-444-00196-4 : £15.62
(B77-06521)

Vol.2 : Indonesia, the North Sea countries, the Soviet Union / edited by Gerard J. Mangone. — 1977. — xv,320p : ill, maps ; 22cm.
Bibl. — Index.
ISBN 0-444-00206-5 : £11.80
(B77-24062)

Lovins, Amory Bloch. Soft energy paths : toward a durable peace / [by] Amory B. Lovins. — Harmondsworth [etc.] : Penguin, 1977. — xx, 231p : ill ; 20cm. — (A pelican original)
ISBN 0-14-022029-1 Pbk : £0.95
(B77-26171)

333.7 — Energy resources. Social aspects. *Conference proceedings*
Energy and humanity / edited by M.W. Thring and R.J. Crookes. — Stevenage : Peregrinus, 1974. — viii,195p : ill, maps ; 24cm. — (PPL series on mankind and the engineer ; vol.2)
'... based ... on papers delivered at a meeting of the same name held at Queen Mary College, London [September 1972] in association with the Society for Social Responsibility in Science' - cover. — Index.
ISBN 0-901223-60-3 Pbk : Unpriced
(B77-19256)

333.7 — Energy resources. Use. *Conference proceedings*
Aspects of Energy Conversion *(Summer School), Oxford, 1975.* Aspects of energy conversion : proceedings of a summer school held at Lincoln College, Oxford, 14-25 July 1975 : organised jointly by Science Research Council, Energy Technology Support Unit and Harwell Education Centre / edited by I.M. Blair, B.D. Jones, A.J. Van Horn. — Oxford [etc.] : Pergamon, 1976. — xvii,847p,plate : ill, charts, maps, plans ; 26cm.
'... contains texts of lectures presented at the Summer School "Aspects of Energy Conversion" together with edited transcripts of the discussions ...' - Preface. — Bibl. — Index.
ISBN 0-08-019975-5 : £17.50
(B77-08266)

333.7 — Environment. Pollution. Economic aspects
Kneese, Allen Victor. Economics and the environment / [by] Allen V. Kneese. — Harmondsworth [etc.] : Penguin, 1977. — 286p : ill, form, maps ; 18cm. — (Penguin education)
Index.
ISBN 0-14-080902-3 Pbk : £1.20
(B77-16767)

333.7 — Great Britain. Environment. Pollution. Control measures. Regulation
Central Unit on Environmental Pollution. Pollution control in Great Britain : how it works : review of legislative and administrative procedures / Department of the Environment, Central Unit on Environmental Pollution. — London : H.M.S.O., 1976. — vi,104p ; 25cm. — (Pollution paper ; no.9)
Bibl.: p.96-104.
ISBN 0-11-751123-4 Pbk : £1.40
(B77-07139)

Environmental standards : a description of United Kingdom practice : the report of an inter-departmental working party / [for the] Department of the Environment. — London : H.M.S.O., 1977. — v,30p ; 25cm. — (Pollution paper ; no.11)
ISBN 0-11-751152-8 Sd : £0.75
(B77-16238)

333.7 — Great Britain. Environment. Pollution. Economic aspects. Monitoring
Marquand, Judith. Economic information for environmental (anti-pollution) policy / [by] Judith Marquand. — London : H.M.S.O., 1977. — iii,47p : ill, form ; 30cm. — (Government Economic Service occasional papers ; 13)
Bibl.: p.46-47.
ISBN 0-11-630289-5 Sd : £2.10
(B77-17342)

333.7 — Land use. Planning. Economic aspects
Harrison, Anthony John. Economics and land use planning / [by] A.J. Harrison. — London : Croom Helm, 1977. — 3-256p : ill ; 23cm.
Bibl.: p.249-253. — Index.
ISBN 0-85664-365-3 : £8.50
ISBN 0-85664-470-6 Pbk : £4.95
(B77-19257)

333.7 — Land use. Policies of governments. *Organisation for Economic Co-operation and Development countries. Reports, surveys*
Organisation for Economic Co-operation and Development. Land use policies and agriculture / [Organisation for Economic Co-operation and Development]. — Paris : O.E.C.D. ; [London] : [H.M.S.O.], 1976. — 84p : ill, col map ; 24cm.
Pbk : £2.00
ISBN 92-64-11558-7
(B77-00649)

333.7 — Nuclear power. Use. *United States*
American Assembly, *50th, New York, 1976.* The nuclear power controversy / [edited by Arthur W. Murphy]. — Englewood Cliffs ; London [etc.] : Prentice-Hall, [1977]. — iv,188p ; 21cm.
'Background papers for the 50th American Assembly, held at Arden House, Hartiman, New York, in April 1976' - Library of Congress Cataloging in Publication Data. — At head of title: The American Assembly, Columbia University. — Published in the United States: 1976. — Index.
ISBN 0-13-625582-5 : £7.95
ISBN 0-13-625574-4 Pbk : £3.20
(B77-11642)

333.7 — Renewable energy resources. *Great Britain. Conference proceedings*
A **symposium** on renewable sources of energy and how far they might be made to meet Britain's energy needs, held at the Society's [i.e. the Royal Society of Arts] house in John Adam Street, London on Wednesday 16 June 1976. — London (John Adam St., WC2N 6EZ) : The Society, [1977]. — [1],137[i.e.165]p : ill, 2 charts ; 31cm.
In binder. — Bibl.
Ls : £5.00
(B77-18605)

333.7'07'2042659 — Land use. Research projects by University of Cambridge. Department of Land Economy. *Serials*
University of Cambridge. *Department of Land Economy.* Research and publications / University of Cambridge, Department of Land Economy. — Cambridge (19 Silver St., Cambridge CB3 9EP) : [The Department].
1975, August-1976, August / compiled by M.-C. Szaz. — [1977]. — [4],28p ; 24cm.
Index.
ISBN 0-901978-71-x Sd : Unpriced
(B77-12908)

333.7'0915'4 — Natural resources. Exploitation. *Semi-arid regions. Conference proceedings*
Resource development in semi-arid lands : a Royal Society discussion [held 17, 18 March 1976] organized by Sir Joseph Hutchinson ... [et al.]. — London : Royal Society, 1977. — iii-x, 176p,[2]leaves of plates : ill, maps ; 31cm.
Pages also numbered 437-614. — Bibl.
ISBN 0-85403-088-3 : £12.00
(B77-29237)

333.7'0941 — Land use. *Great Britain. Proposals*
Land for the people / compiled by Herbert Girardet. — London (8a Leighton Cres., N.W.5) : Crescent Books, [1976]. — 144p : ill, facsim, plan ; 21cm.
Bibl.: p.142-144.
ISBN 0-9505420-0-8 Pbk : £1.20
(B77-04004)

333.7'0941 — Land use. Policies of government. *Great Britain. British Property Federation viewpoints*
British Property Federation. Policy for land / British Property Federation. — London (35 Catherine Place, SW1E 6DY) : The Federation, 1976. — [1],16p ; 21cm.
ISBN 0-900101-06-7 Sd : £1.00
(B77-05255)

333.7'0941 — Natural resources. Exploitation. *Great Britain. Secondary school texts*
Bainbridge, Jack. Resources / [by] Jack Bainbridge ; design by James C. Cairns. — Oxford : Blackwell, 1976. — 64p : ill(some col), facsims, form, col maps, col plan ; 30cm. — (Land marks)
Index.
ISBN 0-631-93950-4 Sd : £1.60
(B77-02098)

333.7'09422'3 — Land use. *Kent. Weald, 450-1380*
Witney, K P. The Jutish forest : a study of the Weald of Kent from 450 to 1380 AD / by K.P. Witney. — London : Athlone Press, 1976. — xvi,339p : maps ; 23cm.
Bibl.: p.xiii-xvi. — Index.
ISBN 0-485-11165-9 : £10.00
(B77-04620)

333.7'09426'752 — Natural resources. *Essex. Chelmsford (District). Rural regions. Reports, surveys*
Chelmsford *(District). Council.* Rural areas study, rural resources / Chelmsford District Council. — Chelmsford ([Civic Centre, Chelmsford CM1 1JE]) : The Council, [1976]. — [3],11[i.e.13]p,4 leaves of plates : 4 maps ; 30cm.
ISBN 0-905110-04-8 Sd : £0.20
(B77-04005)

333.7'09427'31 — Land use. Management. *Greater Manchester (Metropolitan County). Bollin Valley, 1972-1975*
Countryside Commission. The Bollin Valley : a study of land management in the urban fringe / [Countryside Commission] ; compiled by ... Alan Hall ... — [Cheltenham] ([John Dower House, Crescent Place, Cheltenham, Glos. GL50 3RA]) : [The Commission], 1976. — v, 47p(2 fold),[3]fold leaves of plates : ill, col maps ; 30cm. — (CCP ; 97)
ISBN 0-902590-41-3 Sd : £3.00
(B77-04006)

333.7'09744 — Land use. Planning. *Massachusetts. Case studies*
The **land** use controversy in Massachusetts : case studies and policy options / prepared for the Special Commission on the Effects of Growth Patterns on the Quality of Life in the Commonwealth of Massachusetts ; edited by Lawrence Susskind. — Cambridge, Mass. ; London : M.I.T. Press, [1977]. — 148p : ill, maps(chiefly col), ports ; 32cm.
Published in the United States: 1975.
Pbk : Unpriced
(B77-14108)

333.7'09752'32 — Land. Development. *Maryland. Wye Island*
Gibbons, Boyd. Wye Island / [by] Boyd Gibbons. — Baltimore ; London : Johns Hopkins University Press for Resources for the Future, 1977. — xvii,227p : maps ; 24cm.
Map on lining papers.
ISBN 0-8018-1936-9 : Unpriced
(B77-23199)

333.7'2 — Natural resources. Conservation. *Conference proceedings*
Conservation of Resources *(Conference), University of Glasgow, 1976.* Conservation of resources : a symposium held at the University of Glasgow, 5th-9th April 1976 : organised by the Royal Institute of Chemistry and the Industrial Division of the Chemical Society, as part of the Annual Chemical Congress, 1976. — London : Chemical Society, 1976. — ix, 245p : ill, charts, maps ; 21cm. — (Chemical Society. Special publications ; no.27 ISSN 0577-618x)
'... Joint Industrial Division/R.I.C. Symposium on "Conservation of Resources"' - p.1. — Bibl.
ISBN 0-85186-208-x Pbk : £6.00
(B77-06522)

333.7'2 — Natural resources. Conservation. *Teaching kits*
Mackewn, Jenny. Conservation / by Jenny Mackewn and Angela King ; illustrated by David Astin ... [et al.]. — London : Jackdaw [for] Thames Television, 1977. — Portfolio : ill(some col) ; 23x26cm. — (Magpies)
Ten sheets (8 fold)([20] sides), 3 copies each of 2 sheets ([4] sides). — Bibl.: (1p.).
ISBN 0-305-62137-8 : £0.99
(B77-25443)

333.7'3 — Arid regions. Irrigation. Socioeconomic aspects. *Developing countries. Conference proceedings*
Arid land irrigation in developing countries : environmental problems and effects : based on the international symposium, 16-21 February 1976, Alexandria, Egypt / editor E. Barton Worthington. — Oxford [etc.] : Pergamon, 1977. — xi,463p,[4]p of plates : ill, maps ; 26cm.
'COWAR organized the symposium, and a working group of SCOPE ... produce[d] a report which is published as Section 1 [of this book] ...' - Preface. — Includes some contributions in French. — Bibl. — Index.
ISBN 0-08-021588-2 : £35.00
(B77-20085)

333.7'3 — Derelict land. *Wales. Reports, surveys*
Welsh Council. Derelict land in Wales / [prepared by the Welsh Council]. — [Cardiff] ([Crown Building, Cathays Park, Cardiff DF1 3NQ]) : Welsh Council, [1976]. — [2],53p,fold plate : col map ; 30cm.
ISBN 0-904251-14-4 Sp : Unpriced
(B77-01225)

333.7'3 — Derelict land. Reclamation. *Great Britain. Conference proceedings*
Land Reclamation Conference, *Grays, 1976.* Papers of the Land Reclamation Conference held at the Civic Hall, Grays, Essex, 5th, 6th & 7th October, 1976. — Grays (Council Offices, Whitehall La., Grays, Essex) : Thurrock Borough Council, 1976. — [3],2-589p : ill, maps ; 21cm.
Spine title: Land reclamation. — Bibl.
Unpriced
(B77-29238)

333.7'4'0967 — Rangeland. *East Africa*
Rangeland management and ecology in East Africa / edited by D.J. Pratt and M.D. Gwynne ; from contributions by J.R. Blackie ... [et al.]. — London [etc.] : Hodder and Stoughton, 1977. — x,310p,[8]leaves of plates,[16]p of plates : ill, maps(some col) ; 26cm.
Bibl.: p.289-303. — Index.
ISBN 0-340-19766-8 : £7.50
(B77-23200)

333.7'5'0184 — Natural resources: Forests. Exploitation. Optimisation. Mathematical models
Clark, Colin W. Mathematical bioeconomics : the optimal management of renewable resources / [by] Colin W. Clark. — New York ; London [etc.] : Wiley, 1976. — xiii,352p : ill ; 24cm. — (Pure and applied mathematics)
'A Wiley-Interscience publication'. — Bibl.: p.336-346. — Index.
ISBN 0-471-15856-9 : £16.90
Primary classification 333.9'5
(B77-08841)

333.7'5'06142275 — Hampshire. New Forest. Administration. Organisations: Court of Verderers of the New Forest, 1877-1977
Pasmore, Anthony. Verderers of the New Forest : a history of the New Forest, 1877-1977 / [by] Anthony Pasmore ; with decorations by Jean Main. — [Beaulieu] ([John Montague Building, Beaulieu, Hants. SO4 7ZN]) : Pioneer Publications Ltd, [1976]. — viii,298p : ill, facsim, map(on lining papers), plan, ports ; 23cm.
Index.
ISBN 0-9502786-2-9 : £4.95
(B77-20975)

333.7'5'0941 — Natural resources: Forests. Management. *Great Britain. Conference proceedings*
A conference on forestry management held at the Society's house [i.e. the Royal Society of Arts] in John Adam Street, London, on Tuesday 25 November 1975. — London (John Adam St., WC2N 6EZ) : The Society, [1976?]. — [1], 108p ; 31cm.
In binder. — Bibl.
Ls : £3.00
(B77-30014)

333.7'5'0973 — Forests. Exploitation. *United States*
Clawson, Marion. Man, land, and the forest environment / [by] Marion Clawson. — Seattle ; London : University of Washington Press, 1977. — xi,72,[2]p : ill ; 22cm. — (Geo. S. Long Fund. Publication series)
Bibl.: p.71-72.
ISBN 0-295-95540-6 : £5.10
(B77-24063)

333.7'5'0973 — Forests. Exploitation. Policies of government. *United States. Proposals*
Spurr, Stephen H. American forest policy in development / [by] Stephen H. Spurr. — Seattle ; London : University of Washington Press, 1976. — vii,86p ; 21cm. — (Geo. S. Long Fund. Publication series)
Bibl.: p.83-86.
ISBN 0-295-95532-5 : £5.20
(B77-11643)

333.7'6 — Enclosures. *England, 1450-1850*
Yelling, J A. Common field and enclosure in England, 1450-1850 / [by] J.A. Yelling. — London [etc.] : Macmillan, 1977. — viii,255p : ill, maps ; 25cm.
Bibl.: p.234-241. — Index.
ISBN 0-333-15703-6 : £8.95
ISBN 0-333-15704-4 Pbk : £3.95
(B77-28453)

333.7'6 — Enclosures. *Gloucestershire, 1735-1886. Readings from contemporary sources. Facsimiles. Secondary school texts*
Inclosure in Gloucestershire / [compiled by J.H.S. Johnson, B.S. Smith]. — Gloucester (Shire Hall, Gloucester, [Glos.]) : Gloucestershire Record Office, 1976. — [1],x, 30p : 2 ill, facsims, maps ; 30cm. — (A SIGNAL teaching aid)
Pbk : £1.25
(B77-00083)

333.7'6'0941 — Agricultural land. *Great Britain. Glossaries. For historical geography*
Adams, Ian Hugh. Agrarian landscape terms : a glossary for historical geography / by I.H. Adams. — London (1 Kensington Gore, SW7 2AR) : Institute of British Geographers, 1976. — xii,314p : 1 ill ; 25cm. — (Institute of British Geographers. Special publications ; no.9 ISSN 0073-9006)
Bibl.: p.207-276. — Index.
ISBN 0-901989-20-7 Pbk : £4.60
(B77-07140)

333.7'6'0942 — Agricultural land. *England*
Agricultural Development and Advisory Service. Agricultural land classification of England and Wales / Ministry of Agriculture, Fisheries and Food, Agricultural Development and Advisory Service. — Pinner : The Ministry.
Report to accompany Sheet 85, Durham, 1971. — [1977]. — [3]leaves,15p,fold plate : 3 maps ; 21cm. — (ALC 85)
Bibl.: p.15.
ISBN 0-85521-202-0 Sd : £0.70
(B77-11644)

Report to accompany Sheet 120, Burton-upon-Trent, 1972. — [1976]. — [3] leaves,23,[1]p,fold plate : 3 maps ; 21cm. — (ALC 120)
Fold. plate tipped in. — Bibl.: p.22-23.
Sd : £0.70
(B77-17343)

Report to accompany Sheet 122, Melton Mowbray, 1972. — [1976]. — [4],17,[1]p,fold plate : 3 maps ; 21cm. — (ALC 122)
Fold. plate tipped in. — Bibl.: p.17.
Sd : £0.70
(B77-17344)

Report to accompany Sheet 168, Winchester, 1975. — [1977]. — [5],14,[4],fold plate : maps ; 21cm. — (ALC 168)
Bibl.: (1p.).
Sd : £0.70
(B77-18606)

Report to accompany Sheet 183, Eastbourne, 1972. — [1977]. — [4],12,[4]p,fold plate : maps ; 21cm. — (ALC 183)
Bibl.: (1p.).
Sd : £0.70
(B77-18607)

333.7'6'09426712 — Agricultural land use, landscape conservation & nature conservation. Interrelationships. *Essex. Widdington region. Conference proceedings*
Essex Exercise, *Widdington, 1975.* Essex Exercise : farming, wildlife & landscape : held at Widdington in June 1975, [organised by the Farming and Wildlife Advisory Group]. — [Chelmsford] ([Planning Department, County Hall, Chelmsford CM1 1LF]) : Essex County Council, 1976. — [7],58p : ill, maps, plans ; 30cm.
Cover title: Farming, wildlife & landscape.
ISBN 0-901355-70-4 Pbk : £1.00
(B77-09561)

333.7'6'0942786 — Agricultural land use, landscape conservation & recreational land use. Interrelationships. *Cumbria. Hartsop region. Reports, surveys*
Feist, Michael James. A study of the Hartsop Valley : a report to the Countryside Commission and the Lake District Special Planning Board / prepared during 1975 by Rural Planning Services Ltd ; [text by] M.J. Feist, P.M.K. Leat, G.P. Wibberley. — [Cheltenham] ([John Dower House, Crescent Place, Cheltenham, Glos. GL50 3RA]) : [Countryside Commission], 1976. — [1],xii, 146p : ill, maps ; 30cm. — (CCP : 92)
Bibl.: p.145-146.
ISBN 0-902590-49-9 Pbk : £3.00
(B77-00650)

333.7'7 — Industrial estates. *Great Britain. Directories*
United Kingdom industrial estates / [Data Research Group]. — Amersham (Hill House, [Hill Ave.], Amersham, Bucks.) : The Group. [1976]. — 1976. — 42 leaves in various pagings ; 30cm.
ISBN 0-905570-78-2 Sp : £13.00
(B77-07141)

333.7'7 — Land use. Economic aspects. *Urban regions*
Balchin, Paul N. Urban land economics / [by] Paul N. Balchin and Jeffrey L. Kieve. — London [etc.] : Macmillan, 1977. — xviii,278p : ill ; 23cm. — (Macmillan building and surveying series)
Bibl.: p.262-263. — Index.
ISBN 0-333-18083-6 : £6.95
(B77-16768)

Newell, Martin. An introduction to the economics of urban land use / [by] Martin Newell. — London : Estates Gazette, 1977. — ix,348p : ill ; 22cm.
Bibl. — Index.
Pbk : £4.75
(B77-24064)

333.7'7 — Sites available for industries. *East Sussex. Directories. Periodicals*
East Sussex *(County).* Industrial property availability bulletin / County of East Sussex. — Lewes (Southover House, Southover Rd, Lewes, E. Sussex BN7 1YA) : [East Sussex] County Planning Department.
[No.1]- ; [1976]-. — [1976]-. — maps ; 21x30cm.
Quarterly. — [49]p. in 1st issue. — Versos of some leaves blank.
Sd : £0.75
ISSN 0140-0347
(B77-20086)

333.7'7 — Urban regions. Growth. Influence of government policies on land use
Darin-Drabkin, Haim. Land policy and urban growth / by Haim Darin-Drabkin. — Oxford [etc.] : Pergamon, 1977. — viii,442p,4p of plates : ill, maps ; 22cm. — (Urban and regional planning series ; [vol.16] ISSN 0305-5582) (Pergamon international library)
Bibl.: p.423-427. — Index.
ISBN 0-08-020401-5 : £9.00
(B77-32469)

333.7'8 — Canals. *London. Grand Union Canal. Recreation facilities*
London Canals Consultative Committee. London's canal / [London Canals Consultative Committee]. — [New ed.]. — [London] : Greater London Council, [1977]. — [2],21p : ill, col map ; 30cm.
Previous ed.: 1969. — Bibl.: p.21.
ISBN 0-7168-0845-5 Sd : £1.00
(B77-11645)

333.7'8 — Water recreation facilities. Organisations. *England. Water Space Amenity Commission. Reports, surveys. Serials*
Water Space Amenity Commission. Annual report / Water Space Amenity Commission. — London (1 Queen Anne's Gate, SW1H 9BT) : [The Commission].
1975-1976. — [1976]. — 19p ; 30cm.
ISBN 0-905845-00-5 Sd : Unpriced
ISSN 0309-1015
(B77-31053)

333.7'8'0941 — Outdoor recreation facilities. Use. *Great Britain. Rural regions. Statistics*
Countryside Commission. Digest of countryside recreation statistics / [compiled by the Countryside Commission]. — [New ed.]. — [Cheltenham] ([John Dower House, Crescent Place, Cheltenham, Glos. GL50 3RA]) : Countryside Commission [for] the Countryside Recreation Research Advisory Group, 1976. — 1v. : ill, maps(chiefly col) ; 30cm. — (CCP ; 86)
One hundred and fifty six p.(2 fold.) on publication. — Previous ed.: 1975. — Bibl.: p.[153]-[154].
ISBN 0-902590-45-6 Ls : £2.30
(B77-05256)

333.7'8'0941 — Recreation facilities. *Great Britain. Forests*
Goodall, Brian. National forests and recreational opportunities / [by] Brian Goodall. — Reading : Whiteknights, Reading [RG6 2AB] : Department of Geography, University of Reading, 1975. — [2],ii,57p : 2 ill, maps ; 21cm. — (Geographical papers ; no.39 ISSN 0305-5914)
Bibl.: p.55-57.
ISBN 0-7049-0346-6 Sd : £0.70
(B77-06523)

333.7'8'0941 — Recreation facilities. *Great Britain. Forests. Feasibility studies*
Goodall, Brian. Recreation requirements and forest opportunities / [by] Brian Goodall, John B. Whittow. — Reading (Whiteknights, Reading, [Berks.]) : Department of Geography, University of Reading, 1975. — [2],ii,39,[2]p(2 fold) : ill ; 21cm. — (Geographical papers ; no.37 ISSN 0305-5914)
Bibl.: p.37.
Sd : £0.70
(B77-02822)

333.7'8'0941 — Recreation facilities. *Great Britain. Periodicals*
Play times : the journal of the National Playing Fields Association. — London : The Association.
Supersedes: 'Playing fields'.
Issue 1- ; March 1977-. — 1977-. — ill, ports ; 30cm.
Six issues a year. — 12p. in 1st issue.
Sd : Unpriced
ISSN 0309-6041
(B77-18608)

333.7'8'0941 — Recreation facilities. Joint provision & multiple use. *Great Britain. Reports, surveys*
Towards a wider use : Working Party report on joint provision and dual or multiple use of facilities for recreational use by the community. — London (66 Eaton Sq., SW1W 9BH) : Association of County Councils ; London : Association of District Councils : Association of Metropolitan Authorities, [1976]. — 112p ; 21cm.
ISBN 0-901783-10-2 Pbk : £1.25
(B77-02823)

333.7'8'0941 — Recreation facilities. Management. Economic aspects. *Great Britain. Rural regions. Conference proceedings*
Countryside Recreation Research Advisory Group. *Annual Conference, 7th, Durham University, 1976.* The Countryside Recreation Research Advisory Group Conference 1976, Durham University, 22-23 September : proceedings : economic aspects of countryside recreation management. — Cheltenham (John Dower House, Crescent Place, Cheltenham, Glos. GL50 3RA) : Countryside Commission ; Redgorton : Countryside Commission for Scotland, 1976. — [4],194p ; 30cm. — (CCP ; 101)
ISBN 0-902590-46-4 Pbk : £3.00
(B77-08837)

333.7'8'0941 — Recreation facilities. Use. *Great Britain. Rural regions. Periodicals*
Countryside recreation review / Countryside Commission. — Cheltenham (John Dower House, Crescent Place, Cheltenham, Glos. GL50 3RA) : The Commission.
Vol.1-. — 1976-. — ill, maps ; 30cm.
Two issues a year. — [2],46p. in Vol.1. — Supersedes: Recreation news supplement.
Sd : Unpriced
ISSN 0309-2364
(B77-07142)

333.7'8'0941 — Recreation facilities. Visitors. Monitoring. *Great Britain. Forests*
Collings, P S. Monitoring day visitor use of recreational areas / by P.S. Collings and A.J. Grayson. — [London] : H.M.S.O., 1977. — 23p : ill ; 21cm. — (Forest record ; 112)
ISBN 0-11-710183-4 Sd : £0.65
(B77-25444)

333.7'8'0941 — Recreation land. Management. *Great Britain*
Miles, Charles William Noel. Recreational land management / [by] C.W.N. Miles, W. Seabrooke. — London : Spon, 1977. — ix, 147p : ill, map ; 25cm.
Index.
ISBN 0-419-11060-7 : £5.00
(B77-33106)

333.7'8'0941185 — Recreation facilities. Use. *Scotland. Highland Region. Glen Nevis, 1972. Reports, surveys*
Brown, Rosalind, *b.1942.* Glen Nevis : a study of the use of the Glen by summer visitors in 1972 / [by] Rosalind Brown ; for the Countryside Commission for Scotland. — [Edinburgh] : [Countryside Commission for Scotland], [1973]. — 50[i.e.107]leaves(3 fold) : ill, maps ; 30cm.
Three maps in portfolio. — Bibl.: p.[107].
Sp : Unpriced
(B77-01226)

333.7'8'0941425 — Recreation facilities. Use. *Scotland. Loch Lomond region. Reports, surveys*
Brown, Rosalind, *b.1942.* Loch Lomond recreation report / by Rosalind Brown and Vida Chapman ; for the Countryside Commission for Scotland ; presented to the Loch Lomond Technical Group. — Perth (Battleby, Redgorton, Perth) : C.C.S., 1974. — [3],x,203,[32]p,[81]leaves of plates,[8]p of plates : ill, maps ; 30cm. — (Countryside Commission for Scotland. Occasional papers ; no.5)
Bibl.: p.[31]-[32].
ISBN 0-902226-27-4 Sp : £7.00
(B77-02099)

333.7'8'09422 — Farms. Recreation facilities. *South-east England. Reports, surveys*
Bull, Christopher. Farm based recreation in South East England : the experiences of a random sample of farmers in Kent, Surrey and Sussex / by Christopher Bull and Gerald Wibberley. — [Ashford, Kent] : Countryside Planning Unit, School of Rural Economics and Related Studies, Wye College, 1976. — [3],vi, 151p : ill, facsims, form, maps ; 29cm. — (Wye College. School of Rural Economics and Related Studies. Studies in rural land use ; report no.12)
Bibl.: p.135-137.
ISBN 0-901859-64-8 Pbk : £1.75
(B77-25445)

333.7'8'09423592 — Recreation facilities. *Devon. Bickleigh Vale. Reports, surveys*
Devon *(County). Planning Department. Rural and Recreation Section.* Bickleigh Vale recreation study / ... produced by the Rural and Recreation Section of the County Planning Department for consideration by the Amenities and Countryside Committee and the Dartmoor National Park Committee ... — [Exeter] ([County Hall, Exeter, Devon]) : The Department, 1977. — [1],v,54p : ill, maps, col plan ; 30cm.
Sd : £0.60
(B77-20087)

333.7'8'0942648 — Recreation facilities. *Suffolk. Gipping Valley. Reports, surveys. For structure plan making*
Babergh *(District). Council.* Gipping Valley countryside & recreation plan : survey & appraisal / Babergh District Council, Suffolk County Council, Mid Suffolk District Council. — [Ipswich] ([County Hall, Ipswich IP4 2JS]) : [Suffolk County Council] ; [Ipswich] : [Babergh District Council] ; [Eye] : [Mid Suffolk District Council], 1976. — [2],37,[2],xiv p,[6] leaves of plates(5 fold),[8]p of plates : ill, maps(chiefly col) ; 30cm.
Cover title.
ISBN 0-86055-002-8 Pbk : £1.00
(B77-07143)

333.7'8'09426752 — Recreation facilities. *Essex. Chelmsford (District). Rural regions. Reports, surveys*
Chelmsford *(District). Council.* Rural areas study, recreation / Chelmsford District Council. — Chelmsford (Planning Department, Burgess Well Rd, Chelmsford [CM1 1TR]) : [The Council], 1977. — [3],7[i.e.11]p ; 30cm. — (Subject report ; 3)
Sd : £0.20
(B77-17345)

333.7'8'0942881 — Recreation facilities. *Northern England. Countryside adjacent to Hadrian's Wall. Proposals*
Dartington Amenity Research Trust. Hadrian's Wall : a strategy for conservation and visitor services / prepared for the Countryside Commission by Dartington Amenity Research Trust. — [Cheltenham] : [The Commission], 1976. — [2],151p : ill, maps ; 21x30cm. — (DART publication ; no.25) (CCP 98)
ISBN 0-902590-38-3 Pbk : £2.20
Primary classification 623'.19'362881
(B77-04884)

333.7'8'0942931 — Recreation facilities. *Clwyd. Mynydd Hiraethog. Proposals*
Clwyd *(County). Planning Department.* Mynydd Hiraethog : the recreational potential of an upland area : a consultative document / [Clwyd County Planning Department]. — Mold (Shire Hall, Mold, Clwyd) : Clwyd County Council, 1976. — [1],59p : ill, maps(chiefly col) ; 21x31cm. — (County of Clwyd, tourism and recreation research report)
ISBN 0-904444-11-2 Pbk : £1.50
(B77-06524)

333.7'8'0942937 — Recreation facilities. *Clwyd. Dee Valley. Reports, surveys*
Clwyd *(County). Planning Department. Research Section.* Dee Valley recreation survey : with special reference to the Llangollen Canal / [prepared in the Research Section of the County Planning Department, Shire Hall, Mold, Clwyd]. — Mold (Shire Hall, Mold, Clwyd) : Clwyd County Council, [Planning Department], [1976]. — 61p : ill, maps(2 col), plan ; 21x30cm. — (Tourism and recreation research report)
Bibl.: p.61.
ISBN 0-904444-09-0 Pbk : £1.50
(B77-03429)

333.7'8'0942997 — Forests. Scenic drives. Use. *Gwent. Cwmcarn, 1972-1974. Reports, surveys*
Countryside Commission. Cwmcarn scenic forest drive study : a report / by the Countryside Commission. — [Cheltenham] ([John Dower House, Crescent Place, Cheltenham, Glos. GL50 3RA]) : The Commission, 1976. — [1],ii, 41p : ill, 2 maps ; 30cm. — (Countryside Commission. Publications ; 96)
ISBN 0-902590-42-1 Sd : £1.65
(B77-09562)

333.8 — MINERAL RESOURCES

333.8 — Mineral deposits. Economic aspects
Kesler, Stephen E. Our finite mineral resources / [by] Stephen E. Kesler. — New York ; London [etc.] : McGraw-Hill, 1976. — viii,120p : ill, maps ; 23cm. — (McGraw-Hill earth science paperback series)
Index.
ISBN 0-07-034245-8 Pbk : £3.30
(B77-07144)

333.8 — Mineral resources. Conservation. *Juvenile literature*
Constant, Anne Marie. Minerals / written and illustrated by Anne-Marie Constant. — London [etc.] : Burke, 1977. — 31,[1]p : col ill ; 18x19cm. — (Waste not want not)
ISBN 0-222-00520-3 : £0.95
ISBN 0-222-00524-6 Pbk : £0.80
ISBN 0-222-00516-5 Library ed. : £1.50
(B77-20088)

333.8'09'048 — Mineral resources. Exploitation. *Forecasts for 1980-1990*
British-North American Committee. Mineral development in the eighties : prospects and problems : a report / prepared by a group of [British-North American] Committee members, on the basis of a document provided by Ian MacGregor ; with a statistical annex by Sperry Lea. — London (1 Gough Sq., EC4A 3DE) : The Committee, [1976]. — ix,54p : ill ; 23cm. — (British-North American Committee. Publications ; BN-19)
ISBN 0-902594-29-x Sd : £1.50
(B77-08838)

333.8'2 — Fuel resources. Allocation. Mathematical models. *Ireland (Republic)*
Henry, Edmund William. A national model of fuel allocation, a prototype / [by] E.W. Henry and S. Scott. — Dublin : Economic and Social Research Institute, 1977. — 67p(4 fold) : ill ; 25cm. — (Economic and Social Research Institute. Papers ; no.90)
Bibl.: p.60.
ISBN 0-7070-0010-6 Pbk : £2.50
(B77-33107)

333.8'2 — Fuel resources: Coal. *Conference proceedings*
Alternative energy sources / edited by James P. Hartnett. — New York [etc.] ; London : Academic Press ; Washington [D.C.] ; London : Hemisphere Publishing Corporation, 1976. — vii,328p : ill, maps, plans ; 25cm.
' ... proceedings of a conference sponsored [i.e. organized] by the International Centre of Heat and Mass Transfer in the fall of 1975' - Preface. — Bibl. — Index.
ISBN 0-12-328550-x : £20.25
Primary classification 333.7
(B77-08836)

333.8'2 — Natural gas deposits & petroleum deposits. Exploitation. Information sources. *North Sea. Conference proceedings*
Profit opportunities arising from North Sea oil : finding and using the facts : papers presented at [a] conference held at the Piccadilly Hotel, London, on April 22-23, 1975 : ... organised by Ian Maclean, IMAC Research ... — Litchfield (11 Bird St., Litchfield, Staffs.) : Industrial Marketing Research Association, [1977]. — 141 leaves in various pagings : ill ; 30cm.
ISBN 0-9505692-0-8 Sp : £9.50
(B77-15135)

333.8'2 — Natural gas deposits & petroleum deposits. Prospecting & exploitation. *Great Britain. Continental shelf. Reports, surveys. Serials*
Development of the oil and gas resources of the United Kingdom / Department of Energy. — London : H.M.S.O.
1977. — 1977. — iv,48p,[3]fold leaves of plate : ill, 3 maps(2 col) ; 25cm.
ISBN 0-11-410298-8 Sd : £2.25
(B77-15737)

333.8'2 — Natural gas deposits. Prospecting & exploitation. *Great Britain. Continental shelf. Reports, surveys*
Great Britain. *Department of Energy.* Gas from the UK continental shelf / Department of Energy. — [London] ([The Library, Thames House South, Millbank, SW1P 4QJ]) : [Information Directorate, Department of Energy], 1976. — [3],7p ; 30cm. — (Fact sheet ; 3)
ISBN 0-904552-14-4 Sd : Unpriced
(B77-00084)

333.8'2 — Petroleum deposits. Exploitation. Economic aspects. *North Sea*
McRae, Thomas Watson. North Sea oil : Mecca or mirage? / by T.W. McRae. — [Bradford] ([Bradford, W. Yorkshire BD7 1DP]) : University of Bradford, [1976]. — [1],37p : ill ; 21cm. — (University of Bradford. Inaugural lectures)
'... delivered at the University of Bradford on 27 January 1976'. — Bibl.: p.36-37.
Sd : Unpriced
(B77-17346)

333.8'2 — Petroleum deposits. Exploitation. Policies of governments. *North Sea. Comparative studies*
Dam, Kenneth W. Oil resources : who gets what how? / [by] Kenneth W. Dam. — Chicago ; London : University of Chicago Press, 1976. — xi,193p : ill ; 23cm.
Col. ill. on lining papers. — Index.
ISBN 0-226-13497-0 : £7.95
(B77-08839)

333.8'2 — Petroleum deposits. Exploitation. Political aspects. *North Sea. Reports, surveys*
Odell, Peter Randon. Optimal development of the North Sea's oil fields : a study in divergent government and company interests and their reconciliation : a research monograph / by Peter R. O'Dell and Kenneth E. Rosing, (assisted by Hester Vogelaar). — [London] : Kogan Page, [1976]. — 3-189p : ill, maps ; 30cm.
ISBN 0-85038-481-8 Sp : £30.00
(B77-07145)

333.8'2 — Petroleum resources
Grossling, Bernardo. Window on oil : a survey of world petroleum sources / by Bernardo Grossling. — London : 'Financial Times', 1976. — [2],v,140p : ill ; 30cm.
Bibl.: p.134-140.
ISBN 0-900671-78-5 Sp : £50.00
(B77-26872)

333.8'5 — Sand deposits & gravel deposits. Exploitation. *Essex. Stanway region. For environment planning*
Essex *(County). Planning Department.* The Stanway area study : a consultation report on the impact of mineral workings / [prepared by the Essex County Planning Department with the assistance of Colchester Borough Council]. — [Chelmsford] ([County Hall, Chelmsford CM1 1LF]) : The Department, 1977. — [3], 128p : ill, maps, plans ; 21x30cm.
Sp : £1.00
(B77-33663)

333.9 — WATER, AIR, SPACE RESOURCES
333.9'1 — Natural resources: Water. *Juvenile literature*
Best, Gerald Arthur. Water and man / [by] Gerald A. Best, Robert W. Rowatt. — Glasgow [etc.] : Blackie, 1974. — 47p : ill, map ; 21cm. — (Man and his world : series B ; book 6)
Index.
ISBN 0-216-89852-8 Pbk : Unpriced
ISBN 0-216-89850-1 Educational ed. : Unpriced
(B77-20089)

Sowry, Jo. Water / [by] Jo Sowry. — Hove : Priory Press, 1977. — 89p : ill, chart(on lining paper) ; 20x22cm. — (World resources)
Ill. on lining papers. — Bibl.: p.87. — Index.
ISBN 0-85078-235-x : £2.75
(B77-17347)

333.9'1'00184 — Water resource systems. Planning. Mathematical models
Haimes, Yacov Yosseph. Hierarchical analyses of water resources systems : modeling and optimization of large-scale systems / [by] Yacov Y. Haimes. — New York ; London [etc.] : McGraw-Hill, 1977. — xviii,478p : ill ; 25cm. — (McGraw-Hill series in water resources and environmental engineering)
Bibl. — Index.
ISBN 0-07-025507-5 : £23.25
(B77-25446)

333.9'1'002851 — Natural resources: Water. Management. Applications of systems analysis
Systems approach to water management / edited by Asit K. Biswas. — New York ; London [etc.] : McGraw-Hill, 1976. — xvii,429p : ill, maps ; 25cm.
Index.
ISBN 0-07-005480-0 : £17.25
(B77-26873)

333.9'1'005 — Natural resources: Water. *Periodicals*
Advances in water resources. — Southampton (18 Spring Cres., Southampton SO2 1GA) : C.M.L. Publications.
Vol.1, no.1- ; Sept. 1977-. — 1977-. — ill ; 30cm.
Quarterly. — [4],56p. in 1st issue. — Bibl.
Pbk : £35.00 yearly
ISSN 0309-1708
(B77-30015)

333.9'1'005 — Natural resources: Water. Management. *Periodicals*
Aqua : the international journal for the rapid publication of research results and their practical applications in the field of water supply and water management. — Oxford [etc.] : Pergamon.
Vol.1, no.1- ; [Mar.] 1977-. — 1977-. — ill ; 25cm.
Six issues a year. — Cover title. — 252p. in 1st issue.
Pbk : Unpriced
ISSN 0147-3298
(B77-21736)

333.9'1'006142 — Natural resources: Water. Organisations. *England. National Water Council. Reports, surveys. Serials*
National Water Council. Annual report and accounts / National Water Council. — [London] ([1 Queen Anne's Gate, SW1H 9BT]) : The Council.
1975-76. — 1976. — 66p : ill, map ; 30cm.
ISBN 0-904561-15-1 Pbk : £1.50
(B77-01227)

333.9'1'006142 — Natural resources: Water. Planning. Organisations. *England. Central Water Planning Unit. Reports, surveys. Serials*
Central Water Planning Unit. Annual report for the year ending 31st March / Central Water Planning Unit. — Reading (Reading Bridge House, Reading, Berks. RG1 8PS) : The Unit.
[1975]-1976. — 1976. — 66p : ill(some col), maps(some col) ; 30cm.
Bibl.: p.39-43.
ISBN 0-904839-16-8 Sd : Unpriced
(B77-02100)

[1976]-1977. — 1977. — 79p : ill(some col), maps(some col), ports ; 30cm.
Bibl.: p.48-51.
ISBN 0-904839-22-2 Sd : Unpriced
(B77-26172)

333.9'1'0061422 — Regional water authorities. *England. Thames River Basin. Thames Water Authority. Statistics*
Thames Water Authority. Thames Water statistics. — Reading (Nugent House, Vastern Rd, Reading, Berks.) : Thames Water Authority.
1976. [Vol.1]. — [1977]. — 196p in various pagings ; 30cm.
Sp : Unpriced
ISSN 0309-8877
(B77-33664)

1976. Vol.2 : Water quality statistics 1974, 75, 76 / collated and prepared by Central Information Unit, Planning Directorate [Thames Water Authority]. — [1977]. — 258p in various pagings,[1],39 leaves of plates(1 fold) : col maps ; 30cm.
Vol.2 has address: New River Head, Rosebery Ave. EC1R 4TP.
Sp : Unpriced
ISSN 0309-8877
(B77-33665)

333.9'1'0061424 — Regional water authorities. *England. Severn River Basin & Trent River Basin. Severn-Trent Water Authority. Reports, surveys. Serials*
Severn-Trent Water Authority. Report & accounts / Severn Trent Water. — Birmingham (2297 Coventry Rd, Sheldon, Birmingham B26 3PU) : The Authority.
1975-76. — [1976]. — [2],44,xxv p : ill(some col), col maps, port ; 30cm.
ISBN 0-904891-02-x Sd : £2.00
ISSN 0309-0930
(B77-01228)

333.9'1'0061427 — Regional water authorities. *North-west England. North West Water Authority. Reports, surveys. Serials*
North West Water Authority. Annual report / North West Water Authority. — Warrington (Dawson House, Liverpool Rd, Great Sankey, Warrington WA5 3LW) : The Authority.
2nd : 1975-1976. — [1976]. — 121p : ill(some col), maps, ports ; 30cm.
ISBN 0-905843-00-2 Pbk : £1.00
ISSN 0308-1141
(B77-01229)

333.9'1'00614281 — Regional water authorities. *Yorkshire. Yorkshire Water Authority. Reports, surveys. Serials*
Yorkshire Water Authority. Annual report and accounts for the year ended 31 March / Yorkshire Water Authority. — [Leeds] ([67 Albion St., Leeds LS1 5AA]) : [Y.W.A.].
1976. — [1976]. — 44,23p : maps, port ; 30cm.
Cover title.
ISBN 0-905057-06-6 Pbk : £1.00
(B77-02101)

1977. — [1977]. — 50,25p : maps ; 30cm.
Cover title.
ISBN 0-905057-07-4 Pbk : £1.00
(B77-33108)

333.9'1'0061429 — Water authorities. *Wales. Welsh National Water Development Authority*
Welsh National Water Development Authority. Facts & figures / Welsh National Water Development Authority = Awdurdod Cenedlaethol Datblygu Dŵr Cymru. — Brecon (Cambrian Way, Brecon, Powys) : The Authority, [1977]. — Folder([10]p) : ill, 3 maps ; 21x10cm.
ISBN 0-86097-008-6 : Unpriced
(B77-12351)

333.9'1'0061429 — Water authorities. *Wales. Welsh National Water Development Authority. Accounts*
Welsh National Water Development Authority. Annual accounts for the period ending 31st March / Welsh National Water Development Authority = Awdurdod Cenedlaethol Datblygu Dwr Cymru. — Brecon (Cambrian Way, Brecon, Powys) : [The Authority].
[1975]-1976. — 1976. — 44p in various pagings ; 30cm.
ISBN 0-86097-005-1 Pbk : Unpriced
ISSN 0309-4588
(B77-11110)

333.9'1'0061429 — Water authorities. *Wales. Welsh National Water Development Authority. Reports, surveys. Serials*
Welsh National Water Development Authority. Annual report (including the annual accounts) and annual report of the Water Quality Panel for the period ending 31st March / Welsh National Water Development Authority = Awdurdod Cenedlaethol Datblygu Dwr Cymru. — Brecon (Cambrian Way, Brecon, Powys) : [The Authority].
2nd : 1976. — 1976. — [192]p : maps ; 30cm.
Pbk : £1.50
ISSN 0309-2488
(B77-07825)

1st : 1975. — 1975. — [428]p : maps ; 30cm.
Sp : Unpriced
ISSN 0309-2488
(B77-07826)

Welsh National Water Development Authority. Annual report of the Welsh National Water Development Authority. — [Brecon] ([Cambrian Way, Brecon, Powys]) : The Authority.
2nd. Supplement : Fisheries. — 1976. — [3], 87p,[7] leaves ; 30cm.
Cover title.
ISBN 0-86097-004-3 Pbk : £1.00
ISSN 0309-4022
(B77-10236)

2nd. Supplement : Water quality. — 1976. — [10]leaves,[2],75p : 1 ill ; 30cm.
Cover title.
ISBN 0-86097-003-5 Pbk : £0.75
ISSN 0309-4014
(B77-10237)

333.9'1'0061429 — Water authorities. *Wales. Welsh National Water Development Authority. Serials*
Welsh National Water Development Authority. Yearbook / Welsh National Water Development Authority = Awdurdod Cenedlaethol Datblygu Dŵr Cymru. — Brecon (Cambrian Way, Brecon, Powys) : The Authority.
1976. — [1977]. — [1],33,[1]p : 3 maps ; 18cm.
Sd : Unpriced
ISSN 0309-4057
(B77-11111)

333.9'1'0072042 — Natural resources: Water. Research organisations. *England. Water Research Centre. Reports, surveys. Serials*
Water Research Centre. Annual report : for the year ended March 31 / Water Research Centre. — Henley-on-Thames (45 Station Rd, Henley-on-Thames, Oxon. RG9 1BW) : The Centre.
1977. — [1977]. — 116p : ill, 2 ports ; 30cm.
Bibl.: p.80-97.
Sd : Unpriced
(B77-30016)

333.9'1'0094 — Natural resources: Water. Quality. Control. *Europe. Reports, surveys*
Johnson, Ralph W. Cleaning up Europe's waters : economics, management and policies / [by] Ralph W. Johnson, Gardner M. Brown, Jr. — New York [etc.] ; London : Praeger, 1976. — xvii,313,[1]p : ill, maps ; 25cm. — (Praeger special studies in international politics and government)
Index.
ISBN 0-275-56930-6 : £18.50
(B77-06525)

333.9'1'00941 — Natural resources: Water. *Great Britain. Statistics*
Water data / Department of the Environment, Water Data Unit ; prepared in co-operation with ... [others]. — London : H.M.S.O.
1975. — 1977. — iv,72p : ill(some col), maps(1 col) ; 30cm.
Bibl.: p.67-72.
ISBN 0-11-751022-x Sd : £4.75
(B77-10238)

333.9'1'00941 — Natural resources: Water. Exploitation. Optimisation. *Great Britain*
Optimum development of combined sources. — Reading (Reading Bridge House, Reading RG1 8PS) : Central Water Planning Unit.
'This report is the second in a series which presents the results of project studies approved by the Central Water Planning Unit's Steering Committee. It summarises the first stage of the project on Optimum Development of Combined Sources' - Preface.
1 : Unconfined aquifer and surface storage / by D.A. Nutbrown. — 1976. — vi,24p : ill, maps ; 30cm.
Bibl.: p.13.
ISBN 0-904839-17-6 Sd : Free
(B77-08840)

333.9'1'00942 — Natural resources: Water. Quality. Control. *England*
Fish, Hugh. Principles of water quality management / [by] H. Fish. — Harrow (102 College Rd, HA1 1BQ) : Thunderbird Enterprises Ltd, 1973. — [8],257p : ill, map ; 22cm.
Index.
£6.95
(B77-09563)

333.9'1'009429 — Natural resources: Water. Exploitation. *Wales*
Welsh National Water Development Authority. We live in thirsty times / Welsh National Water Development Authority = Awdurdod Cenedlaethol Datblygu Dŵr Cymru. — Brecon (Cambrian Way, Brecon, Powys) : The Authority, [1977]. — Folder([5]p) : ill(chiefly col), chart, maps(chiefly col) ; 21cm.
ISBN 0-86097-009-4 : Unpriced
(B77-12352)

333.9'1'009429 — Natural resources: Water. Exploitation. *Wales. Welsh texts*
Welsh National Water Development Authority. Trigwn mewn cyfnod sychedig / Awdurdod Cenedlaethol Datblygu Dŵr Cymru = Welsh National Water Development Authority. — Aberhonddu [i.e. Brecon] (Cambrian Way, Brecon, Powys) : The Authority, [1977]. — Folder ([5]p) : ill(chiefly col), chart, maps(chiefly col) ; 21cm.
ISBN 0-86097-012-4 : Unpriced
(B77-12353)

333.9'12 — Natural resources: Water. Reservoirs. *England. Wash, The. Feasibility studies*
Central Water Planning Unit. The Wash water storage scheme : report on the feasibility study / Central Water Planning Unit. — London : H.M.S.O., 1976. — [2],vi,51p : ill, col maps, plans(some col) ; 30cm.
ISBN 0-11-751119-6 Sd : £4.20
(B77-07146)

333.9'14 — Tidal power. Exploitation. *England. Severn Estuary. Proposals. Inquiry reports*
Great Britain. *Parliament. House of Commons. Select Committee on Science and Technology.* The exploitation of tidal power in the Severn estuary : fourth report from the Select Committee on Science and Technology, session 1976-77. — London : H.M.S.O., [1977]. — xxvi p,fold plate : map ; 25cm. — ([1976-77 H.C.] 564)
ISBN 0-10-256477-9 Sd : £0.70
(B77-29240)

333.9'162'0941 — Inland waterways. Management. *Great Britain*
British Trust for Conservation Volunteers. Waterways and wetlands / [British Trust for Conservation Volunteers] ; illustrations by Roy Allitt. — London (Zoological Gardens, Regents Park, NW1 4RY) : The Trust, 1976. — 228p : ill(some col), plans ; 30cm.
Bibl.: p.223-227.
ISBN 0-9501643-4-8 Sp : £3.00
Also classified at 333.9'18
(B77-16240)

333.9'164 — Natural resources. Exploitation. *Oceans. Conference proceedings*
International Conference on Technology Assessment, *Monaco, 1975.* Technology assessment and the oceans : proceedings of the International Conference on Technology Assessment, Monaco, 26-30 October 1975, [organised by] Association européenne océanique (Eurocéan) [and the] International Society for Technology Assessment / edited by Philip D. Wilmot, Aart Slingerland. — Guildford : IPC Science and Technology Press [etc.], 1977. — xi,259p : ill, maps, plans, port ; 31cm. — (International Society for Technology Assessment. Documentation series ; no.1)
Includes 2 papers in French, with English summaries.
ISBN 0-902852-61-2 : £12.00
(B77-31040)

333.9'164 — Natural resources. Exploitation. *Oceans. Juvenile literature*
Law, Felicia. Farming the sea / written by Felicia Law ; illustrated by John Shipperbottom. — Glasgow [etc.] : Collins, 1977. — 32p : col ill ; 22cm. — (Dandelions)
Originally published: 1976.
ISBN 0-00-106011-2 : £1.50
(B77-30017)

333.9'164 — Oceans. Bed. Exploitation. International control
Luard, Evan. The control of the sea-bed : who owns the resources of the oceans? / [by] Evan Luard. — Revised ed. — London : Heinemann, 1977. — x,315p : 1 ill ; 23cm.
Ill. on lining papers. — Previous ed.: 1974. — Index.
ISBN 0-434-42952-x : £6.50
(B77-21737)

333.9'164 — Oceans. Exploitation. Environmental aspects
The **marine** environment / general editors John Lenihan and William W. Fletcher. — Glasgow [etc.] : Blackie, 1977. — xiv,170p : ill, maps ; 23cm. — (Environment and man ; vol.5)
Bibl. — Index.
ISBN 0-216-90131-6 : £8.90
ISBN 0-216-90130-8 Pbk : £4.50
(B77-22423)

333.9'164'05 — Oceans. Economic aspects. *Periodicals*
Marine policy. — Guildford : IPC Science and Technology Press ; Haywards Heath (Oakfield House, Perrymount Rd, Haywards Heath, Sussex RH16 3DH) : [Distributed by] IPC Business Press (Sales and Distribution) Ltd.
Vol.1, no.1- ; Jan. 1977-. — 1977-. — ill ; 28cm.
Quarterly. — 88p. in 1st issue.
Pbk : £30.00 yearly
ISSN 0308-597x
(B77-10239)

333.9'164'0916337 — Marine resources. Exploitation. *Western Great Britain. Coastal waters. Conference proceedings*
Oceanic management : conflicting uses of the Celtic Sea and other Western UK waters : report of a conference held at University College of Swansea, 19-22 September 1975 / edited by M.M. Sibthorp, assisted by M. Unwin. — London : Europa for the David Davies Memorial Institute of International Studies, 1977. — xv,220p : ill, maps ; 25cm.
ISBN 0-905118-05-7 : £10.00
(B77-20090)

333.9'17'0973 — Shorelands. Utilisation. *United States. Case studies*
Devanney, J W. Parable Beach : a primer in coastal zone economics / [by] J.W. Devanney III, G. Ashe and B. Parkhurst. — Cambridge, Mass. ; London : M.I.T. Press, [1977]. — xi, 99p : ill, map ; 24cm. — (Ocean engineering series ; 9)
Published in the United States: 1976.
ISBN 0-262-04052-2 : £9.35
(B77-13550)

333.9'17'09746 — Shorelands. Utilisation. *Connecticut. Proposals*
The **urban** sea : Long Island Sound / [by] Lee E. Koppelman ... [et al.]. — New York [etc.] ; London : Praeger, [i.e. 1977]. — viii,223,[1]p : ill, maps ; 23x29cm. — (Praeger special studies : design - environmental planning series)
Published in the United States: 1976. — Bibl. — Index.
ISBN 0-275-28863-3 : £12.60
Primary classification 333.9'17'0974721
(B77-13551)

333.9'17'0974721 — Shorelands. Utilisation. *New York (State). Long Island. Proposals*
The **urban** sea : Long Island Sound / [by] Lee E. Koppelman ... [et al.]. — New York [etc.] ; London : Praeger, [i.e. 1977]. — viii,223,[1]p : ill, maps ; 23x29cm. — (Praeger special studies : design - environmental planning series)
Published in the United States: 1976. — Bibl. — Index.
ISBN 0-275-28863-3 : £12.60
Also classified at 333.9'17'09746
(B77-13551)

333.9'17'097946 — Shorelands: Wetlands. Conservation. Economic aspects. *California. San Francisco Bay area*
Luken, Ralph Andrew. Preservation versus development : an economic analysis of San Francisco Bay wetlands / [by] Ralph Andrew Luken. — New York [etc.] ; London : Praeger ; [London] : [Distributed by Martin Robertson], 1976. — xvii,155p,[1]p : ill, maps ; 24cm. — (Praeger special studies : design-environmental planning series)
Bibl.: p.149-155.
ISBN 0-275-56590-4 : £10.95
(B77-07147)

333.9'18 — Wetlands. Management. *Great Britain*
British Trust for Conservation Volunteers. Waterways and wetlands / [British Trust for Conservation Volunteers] ; illustrations by Roy Allitt. — London (Zoological Gardens, Regents Park, NW1 4RY) : The Trust, 1976. — 228p : ill(some col), plans ; 30cm.
Bibl.: p.223-227.
ISBN 0-9501643-4-8 Sp : £3.00
Primary classification 333.9'162'0941
(B77-16240)

333.9'18 — Wetlands. Utilisation. *Study regions: Cheshire. Conference proceedings*
Report of the wetlands conference : integrating management of intensive lowland farming, pools, ponds, meres, ditches, streams and wildlife conservation, 8, 9, 10 April 1976, Cheshire College of Agriculture, Reaseheath : [organised by] the Farming and Wildlife Advisory Group. — [London] ([Great Westminster House, Horseferry Rd, SW1P 2AE]) : Agricultural Development and Advisory Service, 1976. — iv,59p : ill, col maps ; 30cm.
Cover title: Cheshire wetlands conference report.
ISBN 0-85521-203-9 Sd : Unpriced
(B77-12354)

333.9'5 — Fisheries. Resources. Management. *Irish Sea. Proposals*
Brander, K M. The management of Irish Sea fisheries : a review / [by] K.M. Brander. — Pinner : Ministry of Agriculture, Fisheries and Food, 1977. — [3],40,[6]p : ill, maps ; 30cm. — (Great Britain. Ministry of Agriculture, Fisheries and Food. Directorate of Fisheries Research. Laboratory leaflets ; no.36 ISSN 0072-6699)
Bibl.: p.38-40.
Sd : Unpriced
(B77-26173)

333.9'5 — Oceans. Fisheries. Resources. Exploitation. Optimisation. Mathematical models
Clark, Colin W. Mathematical bioeconomics : the optimal management of renewable resources / [by] Colin W. Clark. — New York ; London [etc.] : Wiley, 1976. — xiii,352p : ill ; 24cm. — (Pure and applied mathematics)
'A Wiley-Interscience publication'. — Bibl.: p.336-346. — Index.
ISBN 0-471-15856-9 : £16.90
Also classified at 333.7'5'0184
(B77-08841)

333.9'5 — Water birds. Habitats: Wetlands. Conservation. *Conference proceedings*
International Conference on the Conservation of Wetlands and Waterfowl, *Heiligenhafen, 1974.* Proceedings [of the] International Conference on the Conservation of Wetlands and Waterfowl, Heiligenhafen, Federal Republic of Germany, 2-6 December 1974 / edited by M. Smart. — Slimbridge ([Slimbridge, Glos., GL1 7BX]) : International Waterfowl Research Bureau, 1976. — [5],v,492p : ill, maps ; 25cm.
Spine title: Conservation of wetlands and waterfowl. — Bibl.
ISBN 0-9505731-0-8 Pbk : £8.50
Also classified at 639'.97'82924
(B77-15738)

334 — COOPERATIVES
334'.03 — Cooperatives. *Dictionaries*
Lamming, Anne. A co-operator's dictionary : a basic list of co-operative and commercial terms for use at primary level in developing countries / compiled by Anne Lamming. — London (11 Upper Grosvenor St., W1X 9PA) : Co-operative Education Materials Advisory Service, International Co-operative Alliance, 1977. — [5],59p ; 20cm.
ISBN 0-904380-26-2 Pbk : £1.00
(B77-15739)

334'.06'241 — Cooperative movements. *Great Britain. Co-operative Union. Conference proceedings*
Co-operative Congress, *106th, Edinburgh, 1975.* Co-operative Congress, 1975, Edinburgh : report of proceedings. — Manchester (Holyoake House, Hanover St., Manchester M60 0AS) : Co-operative Union, [1976]. — [2]p;p129-254 ; 22cm.
'The 106th Annual Co-operative Congress assembled in the Usher Hall, Edinburgh on Monday, May 26th' - p.129.
ISBN 0-85195-111-2 Pbk : £1.00
(B77-03430)

334'.0954'84 — Cooperatives. *India (Republic). Andhra Pradesh. Rural regions, to 1975. Reports, surveys*
Rao, L R. Rural co-operatives : (a study with reference to Andhra Pradesh) / [by] L.R. Rao. — Delhi : Sultan Chand and Sons ; London (32 Coptic St., W.C.1) : [Distributed by] Books from India, [1976]. — iii-xv,220p : map ; 23cm.

Bibl.: p.214-220.
Unpriced
(B77-05257)

334'.0973 — Cooperatives. *United States*
Abrahamsen, Martin Abraham. Cooperative business enterprise / [by] Martin A. Abrahamsen. — New York ; London [etc.] : McGraw-Hill, 1976. — xix,491p : ill ; 25cm.
Bibl. — Index.
ISBN 0-07-000151-0 : £11.55
(B77-04007)

334.1 — BUILDING AND HOUSING COOPERATIVES
334'.1 — Housing associations. *Great Britain, to 1976*
Baker, Charles Vivian. Housing associations / [by] Charles Vivian Baker. — London : Estates Gazette, 1976. — xv,604p : 2 ill, forms ; 23cm.
Bibl.: p.569-576. — Index.
ISBN 0-7282-0031-7 : £7.50
(B77-05258)

334'.1 — Housing associations. *London. Camden (London Borough). St Pancras. St Pancras Housing Association in Camden, to 1975*
Barclay, Irene. People need roots : the story of the St Pancras Housing Association / [by] Irene Barclay. — London : Bedford Square Press, 1976. — 144p : ill, port ; 23cm.
ISBN 0-7199-0918-x : £2.50
ISBN 0-7199-0921-x Pbk. : £1.50
(B77-08267)

334.5 — CONSUMERS' COOPERATIVES
334'.5 — Agricultural products. Cooperative marketing. Organisations. *Great Britain. Central Council for Agricultural and Horticultural Co-operation. Reports, surveys. Serials*
Central Council for Agricultural and Horticultural Co-operation. Annual report / Central Council for Agricultural and Horticultural Co-operation. — London (Market Towers, New Covent Garden Market, SW8 5NQ) : The Council.
1976-77. — 1977. — [1],29p : ill(some col), ports ; 26cm.
Sd : Unpriced
(B77-21738)

334'.5'06541 — Cooperative societies. *Great Britain. Co-operative Wholesale Society, 1938-1976*
Richardson, Sir William, *b.1909.* The CWS in war and peace, 1939-1976 : the Co-operative Wholesale Society Limited in the Second World War and post-war years / by Sir William Richardson. — Manchester [etc.] ([P.O. Box 53, New Century House, Manchester M60 4ES]) : Co-operative Wholesale Society Ltd, 1977. — xiii,399p ; 23cm.
£7.50
(B77-26874)

334.6 — PRODUCTION COOPERATIVES
334'.683'09415 — Agricultural cooperative movements. *Ireland, to 1975*
Bolger, Patrick. The Irish co-operative movement : its history and development / [by] Patrick Bolger. — Dublin : Institute of Public Administration, 1977. — iii-xiv,434p : ill, facsim, ports ; 25cm.
Index.
ISBN 0-902173-75-8 : £9.00
ISBN 0-902173-76-6 Pbk : £4.50
(B77-25447)

334'.683'095694 — Kibbutzim. *Israel*
Barkai, Haim. Growth patterns of the kibbutz economy / [by] Haim Barkai. — Amsterdam [etc.] ; Oxford : North-Holland Publishing Co., 1977. — xix,298p : ill ; 23cm. — (Contributions to economic analysis ; 108)
Bibl.: p.293-295. — Index.
ISBN 0-7204-0556-4 : Unpriced
(B77-31041)

334'.683'92 — Fishing cooperatives. *Conference proceedings*
Modernisation of Fisheries and the Rational Utilisation of Resources : the Role of Co-operatives *(Conference), Tokyo, 1975.* Report of the First Open World Conference on Co-operative Fisheries, Tokyo, 29 September-4 October 1975 : theme "Modernisation of Fisheries and the Rational Utilisation of Resources : the Role of Co-operatives" : the Conference, organised by the International Co-operative Alliance, was held ... at the Keidanren Building, Tokyo, Japan. — [London] ([11 Upper Grosvenor St., W1X 9PA]) : [International Co-operative Alliance], [1976]. — vi,98p : 2 ill, ports ; 23cm.
'... held in Tokyo in September/October 1975 ...' - Acknowledgements.
ISBN 0-904380-24-6 Pbk : £3.00
(B77-15136)

334.7 — BENEFIT SOCIETIES
334'.7'0941 — Friendly societies. *Great Britain. Reports, surveys. Serials*
Great Britain. *Registry of Friendly Societies.* Report of the Chief Registrar of Friendly Societies ... — London : H.M.S.O.
1975. Part 1 : Friendly societies, industrial assurance companies and general : incorporating the report of the Industrial Assurance Commissioner. — 1976. — [2],58p ; 25cm.
ISBN 0-11-600238-7 Sd : £1.15
(B77-07148)

1976. Part 3 : Industrial and provident societies. — 1977. — [2],33p ; 25cm.
ISBN 0-11-600235-2 Sd : £0.85
(B77-29241)

335 — SOCIALISM AND RELATED SYSTEMS
335 — Economics. Theories of New Left Movement
Lindbeck, Assar. The political economy of the New Left : an outsider's view / [by] Assar Lindbeck ; foreword by Paul A. Samuelson. — 2nd ed. — New York [etc.] ; London : Harper and Row, 1977. — xxv,239p : ill ; 21cm.
Previous ed.: 1971. — Bibl.: p.236. — Index. — Includes contributions by others.
ISBN 0-06-044009-0 Pbk : £2.95
(B77-17348)

335 — Socialism
Marx, Carla. Das Socialism / by Carla Marx. — London (22 Bargery Rd, Catford, SE6 2LN) : I.D. Perry Publications, 1977. — [5],150p ; 21cm.
Pbk : Unpriced
(B77-26875)

Russell, Bertrand, *Earl Russell.* Roads to freedom / [by] Bertrand Russell. — 3rd ed. — London : Allen and Unwin, 1977. — 3-158 ; 20cm.
This ed. originally published: 1920. — Index.
ISBN 0-04-335033-x Pbk : £1.50
(B77-20091)

335 — Socialism. *Aims for Freedom and Enterprise viewpoints*
Szamuely, Tibor. Socialism and liberty / [by] Tibor Szamuely. — London : Aims for Freedom and Enterprise, [1977]. — [8],20,[1]p ; 26cm. — (Commemorative Free Enterprise Award ; 1977)
Originally published: as a postscript to 'Half Marx' / by Sir Tufton Beamish. London : Stacey, 1970.
ISBN 0-7281-0072-x Sd : Unpriced
(B77-33666)

335 — Socialism. *Conference proceedings*
Just Society *(Conference), Bradford, 1976.* The just society / edited by Ken Coates and Fred Singleton. — Nottingham : Spokesman Books for the University of Bradford and the Bertrand Russell Peace Foundation, 1977. — [6],183p ; 22cm. — ([European socialist thought series ; no.10])
'... a selection [of papers] from those submitted to the Bradford Seminar, The Just Society ...' - Introductory note.
ISBN 0-85124-181-6 : £6.00
ISBN 0-85124-182-4 Pbk : Unpriced
(B77-30018)

The **socialist** idea : a reappraisal / edited by Leszek Kolakowski and Stuart Hampshire. — London [etc.] : Quartet Books, 1977. — [5], 272p ; 20cm.
'... papers ... presented at the April 1973 international meeting in Reading sponsored by ... Weidenfeld and Nicolson and the Graduate School of Contemporary European Studies Reading University' - Introduction. — Originally published: London : Weidenfeld and Nicolson, 1974. — Bibl.: p.262-263. — Index.
ISBN 0-7043-3109-8 Pbk : £2.95
(B77-20092)

335 — Socialist movements. *Trotskyist viewpoints*
Posadas, J. The meeting of the Socialist International, the Congress of the Spanish PSOE and the world process of the revolution / [by] J. Posadas. — London (24 Cranbourn St., W.C.2) : Revolutionary Workers Party (Trotskyist), 1977. — [3],17,[1]p ; 22cm. — (A 'European Marxist review' publication)
Sd : £0.10
(B77-30019)

335'.005 — Socialism. *Yearbooks*
The **socialist** register. — London : Merlin Press.
1976 / edited by Ralph Miliband and John Saville. — 1976. — [9],226p ; 23cm.
Bibl.
ISBN 0-85036-217-2 : £5.00
(B77-09564)

335'.008 — Socialism. *Essays*
James, Cyril Lionel Robert. The future in the present : selected writings / [by] C.L.R. James. — London : Allison and Busby, 1977. — 271p ; 23cm. — (Motive)
Index.
ISBN 0-85031-148-9 : £6.50
ISBN 0-85031-149-7 Pbk : £2.95
(B77-31042)

335′.008 — Socialism. *Readings*
Essential works of socialism / edited by Irving Howe. — New Haven ; London : Yale University Press, 1976. — [14],850p ; 21cm.
Originally published: as 'Essential works of socialism', New York : Holt, Rinehart and Winston, 1970 ; and as 'A handbook of socialist thought', London : Gollancz, 1972.
ISBN 0-300-01976-9 : £13.20
ISBN 0-300-01977-7 Pbk : £6.60
(B77-03431)

335′.009 — Socialism. Theories, to 1917
Wilson, Edmund. To the Finland Station : a study in the writing and acting of history / [by] Edmund Wilson. — Revised ed. ; with a new introduction. — [London] : Fontana, 1977. — [6],506p ; 18cm. — (Fontana modern classics)
This ed. originally published: London : Macmillan, 1972. — Index.
ISBN 0-00-632420-7 Pbk : £1.50
(B77-17973)

335′.009 — Socialism, to 1976. *Secondary school texts*
Evans, Richard, *b.1950.* Socialism / [by] Richard Evans. — London : Hamilton, 1977. — 96p : ill, facsims, ports ; 25cm. — (People and politics)
Bibl.: p.91-93. — Index.
ISBN 0-241-89441-7 : £3.25
(B77-21739)

335′.009′04 — Socialism, ca 1900-1940
Schumpeter, Joseph Alois. Capitalism, socialism and democracy / [by] Joseph A. Schumpeter. — 5th ed. ; with a new introduction by Tom Bottomore. — London : Allen and Unwin, 1976. — xiv,437p ; 23cm.
Previous ed.: London : Allen and Unwin, 1954. — Index.
ISBN 0-04-335031-3 : £8.00
ISBN 0-04-5032-1 Pbk : £3.95
Also classified at 330.12′2′0904
(B77-08842)

335′.0092′4 — Socialism. Martín-Santos, Luis. *Spain. Biographies*
Hierro, A. Luis Martin Santos : the power of alienation of an organic society, or the beginnings of a meaningful opposition to Franco / [by] A. Hierro. — [London] ([12 Lambs Conduit Passage, Holborn, W.C.1]) : [The author], [1977]. — 37p ; 21cm.
Sd : Unpriced
(B77-23201)

335′.00941 — Socialism. *Great Britain, 1931-1940*
Pimlott, Ben. Labour and the Left in the 1930s / [by] Ben Pimlott. — Cambridge [etc.] : Cambridge University Press, 1977. — xi,259p ; 24cm.
Bibl.: p.245-250. — Index.
ISBN 0-521-21448-3 : £6.50
Primary classification 329.9′41
(B77-24748)

335′.00947 — Socialism. *Eastern Europe & Soviet Union*
Wilczynski, Jozef. The economics of socialism : principles governing the operation of the centrally planned economies in the USSR and Eastern Europe under the new system / by J. Wilczynski. — 3rd ed. — London : Allen and Unwin, 1977. — 3-235p : ill ; 22cm. — (Studies in economics ; 2)
Previous ed.: i.e. Revised ed., 1972. — Bibl. — Index.
ISBN 0-04-335034-8 Pbk : £3.95
(B77-26876)

335′.009495 — Socialist movements. *Greece, 1914-1918*
Leon, George B. The Greek socialist movement and the First World War : the road to unity / [by] George B. Leon. — Boulder : 'East European quarterly' ; New York ; Guildford : Distributed by Columbia University Press, 1976. — x,204p ; 23cm. — (East European monographs ; no.18)
Bibl.: p.187-197. — Index.
ISBN 0-914710-11-7 : Unpriced
(B77-01230)

335′.00951 — Socialism. *China, ca 1890-1907*
Bernal, Martin. Chinese socialism to 1907 / by Martin Bernal. — Ithaca ; London : Cornell University Press, 1976. — ix,259p ; 23cm.
Bibl.: p.237-250. — Index.
ISBN 0-8014-0915-2 : £12.00
(B77-05920)

335′.00984 — Labour movements. *Bolivia, 1848-1971*
Lora, Guillermo. A history of the Bolivian labour movement, 1848-1971 / [by] Guillermo Lora ; edited and abridged by Laurence Whitehead ; translated [from the Spanish] by Christine Whitehead. — Cambridge [etc.] : Cambridge University Press, 1977. — x,408p ; 22cm. — (Cambridge Latin American studies ; 27)
Translation and abridgement of: 'Historia del movimiento obrero boliviano'. Originally published in 5 vols. La Paz : Editorial Los Amigos del Libro, 1967-. — Bibl.: p.395-396. — Index.
ISBN 0-521-21400-9 : £12.50
(B77-30020)

335′.1 — Labour movements. Subversive activities by United States. Central Intelligence Agency
Hirsch, Fred. The CIA and the Labour movement / [by] Fred Hirsch and Richard Fletcher. — Nottingham : Spokesman Books, 1977. — 71p ; 19cm.
ISBN 0-85124-171-9 : £3.95
ISBN 0-85124-170-0 Pbk : Unpriced
(B77-25448)

335′.1′072 — International Association of Labour History Institutions. *Directories*
International Association of Labour History Institutions. Directory / International Association of Labour History Institutions. — [London] ([c/o Labour Party Library, Transport House, Smith Sq., SW1P 3JA]) : [The Association], [1977]. — [48]leaves ; 22cm.
Cover title.
ISBN 0-9505639-0-0 Pbk : £1.50
(B77-12909)

335′.1′0922 — Labour movements. *Great Britain, 1790-1972. Biographical dictionaries*
Dictionary of Labour biography. — London [etc.] : Macmillan.
Vol.3 / [edited by] Joyce M. Bellamy and John Saville. — 1976. — xix,236p ; 25cm.
Bibl. — Index. — Consolidated list of names for vols 1-3.
ISBN 0-333-14415-5 : £20.00
(B77-06526)

Vol.4 / [edited by] Joyce M. Bellamy and John Saville. — 1977. — xix,236p ; 24cm.
Bibl. — Index. — Consolidated list of names for vols 1-4.
ISBN 0-333-19704-6 : £20.00
(B77-30021)

335′.1′0924 — Labour movements. Marx, Eleanor. *Great Britain. Biographies*
Kapp, Yvonne. Eleanor Marx / by Yvonne Kapp. — London : Lawrence and Wishart.
In 2 vols.
Vol.2 : The crowded years (1884-1898). — 1976. — [1],775p,[2]leaves of plates,[16]p of plates : ill, facsims, map, ports ; 23cm.
Index.
ISBN 0-85315-370-1 : £12.00
(B77-05259)

335′.1′0941 — Labour movements. Role of women. *Great Britain, to 1976*
Women in the Labour Movement : the British experience / edited by Lucy Middleton ; foreword by James Callaghan. — London : Croom Helm [etc.], 1977. — 221p ; 23cm.
Bibl.: p.191-194. — Index.
ISBN 0-85664-472-2 : £7.50
(B77-23202)

335.4 — MARXISM
Papers on class, hegemony and party : the Communist University of London / edited by Jon Bloomfield. — London : Lawrence and Wishart, 1977. — 125p ; 22cm.
'These papers were originally delivered at the Communist University, held in London in 1976' - title page verso.
ISBN 0-85315-390-6 Pbk : £1.50
(B77-29242)

Perlman, Selig. Selig Perlman's lectures on capitalism and socialism / [revised and edited by] A.L. Riesch Owen. — Madison ; London : University of Wisconsin Press, 1976. — xviii, 183,[1]p : ill ; 24cm.
Spine title: Perlman on capitalism and socialism. — Bibl.: p.171-175. — Index.
ISBN 0-299-06780-7 : £10.15
(B77-05260)

335.4 — Marxism. *Anarchist viewpoints*
Graham, Marcus. Marxism & a free society : an anarchist reply to Isaac Deutscher's address on 'Socialist man' with particular reference to the minutes of the First International and the sabotaging of the Hague Congress by the Marx clique / [by] Marcus Graham. — Sanday (Sanday, Orkney KW17 2BL) : Simian Publications, 1976. — [1],16p : port ; 22cm.
ISBN 0-904564-13-4 Sd : £0.20
(B77-05261)

335.4 — Marxism. Related to role of Christian church in society
Hebblethwaite, Peter. The Christian-Marxist dialogue : beginnings, present status, and beyond / by Peter Hebblethwaite. — London : Darton, Longman and Todd, 1977. — [3], 122p ; 22cm.
Index.
ISBN 0-232-51390-2 Pbk : £2.50
Primary classification 261.1
(B77-29927)

Vree, Dale. On synthesizing Marxism and Christianity / [by] Dale Vree. — New York ; London [etc.] : Wiley, 1976. — xxiii,206p ; 22cm.
'A Wiley-Interscience publication'. — Bibl.: p.183-201. — Index.
ISBN 0-471-01603-9 : £11.20
Primary classification 261.1
(B77-14041)

335.4′08 — Marxism. *Essays*
Colletti, Lucio. From Rousseau to Lenin : studies in ideology and society / [by] Lucio Colletti ; [translated from the Italian by John Merrington and Judith White]. — London : NLB, 1976. — [6],240p ; 21cm.
This translation originally published: 1972. — Translation of: 'Ideologia e società'. Bari : Laterza, 1969. — Index.
ISBN 0-902308-97-1 Pbk : £2.75
(B77-05921)

Hook, Sidney. Revolution, reform and social justice : studies in the theory and practice of Marxism / [by Sidney Hook]. — Oxford : Blackwell, 1976. — xv,307p ; 21cm.
Originally published: New York : New York University Press, 1975. — Index.
ISBN 0-631-17640-3 : £8.50
(B77-00651)

335.4′09′04 — Marxism. Theories, 1900-1971
Howard, Dick. The Marxian legacy / [by] Dick Howard. — London [etc.] : Macmillan, 1977. — xv,340p ; 23cm.
Index.
ISBN 0-333-19622-8 : £12.00 : CIP rev.
(B77-10752)

335.4′092′4 — Economics. Engels, Friedrich. *Critical studies*
McLellan, David. Engels / [by] David McLellan. — [London] : Fontana, 1977. — 79p ; 18cm. — (Fontana modern masters)
Bibl.: p.76-77.
ISBN 0-00-634231-0 Pbk : £0.75
(B77-27720)

McLellan, David. Engels / [by] David McLellan. — Hassocks : Harvester Press, 1977. — 79p ; 23cm.
Also published: London : Fontana, 1977. — Bibl.: p.76-77.
ISBN 0-85527-710-6 : £4.95 : CIP rev.
(B77-23203)

335.4′092′4 — Economics. Marx, Karl. *Biographies*
McLellan, David. Karl Marx : his life and thought / [by] David McLellan. — St Albans : Paladin, 1976. — xiv,498p,[16]p of plates : ill, facsims, geneal table, map, ports ; 20cm.
Originally published: London : Macmillan, 1973. — Bibl.: p.469-489. — Index.
ISBN 0-586-08201-8 Pbk : £2.50
(B77-07827)

335.4′092′4 — Marxism. Connolly, James. *Ireland. Biographies*
Levenson, Samuel. James Connolly : a biography / [by] Samuel Levenson. — London [etc.] : Quartet Books, 1977. — 349p : port ; 20cm.
Cover title: A biography of James Connolly. — Originally published: London : Martin Brian and O'Keeffe, 1973. — Bibl.: p.337-339. — Index.
ISBN 0-7043-3108-x Pbk : £2.50
(B77-20976)

335.4'092'4 — Marxism. Gramsci, Antonio. *Italy. Critical studies*
Joll, James. Gramsci / [by] James Joll. — [London] : Fontana, 1977. — 128p ; 18cm. — (Fontana modern masters)
Bibl.: p.126-128.
ISBN 0-00-633811-9 Pbk : £0.85
(B77-28454)

335.4'092'4 — Marxism. Hajime, Kawakami. *Japan. Biographies*
Bernstein, Gail Lee. Japanese Marxist : a portrait of Kawakami Hajime, 1879-1946 / [by] Gail Lee Bernstein. — Cambridge, Mass. ; London : Harvard University Press, 1976. — xiv,221p : ports ; 24cm. — (Harvard East Asian series ; 86)
Bibl.: p.199-211. — Index.
ISBN 0-674-47193-8 : £9.75
(B77-20093)

335.4'12 — Economics. Theories. Concepts: Need. Theories of Marx, Karl
Heller, Agnes. The theory of need in Marx / [by] Agnes Heller ; [translated from the German]. — London : Allison and Busby, 1976. — 135p ; 23cm. — (Motive)
Translation of: 'Bedeutung und Funktion des Begriffs Bedürfnis im Denken von Karl Marx'. Milan : Feltrinelli, 1974. — Index.
ISBN 0-85031-168-3 : £5.25
ISBN 0-85031-174-8 Pbk : £2.95
(B77-01231)

335.4'12 — Economics. Theories of Marx, Karl. *Texts*
Marx, Karl. Selected writings [of] Karl Marx / edited by David McLellan. — Oxford [etc.] : Oxford University Press, 1977. — x,625p ; 25cm.
Some of the writings have been translated from the German. — Bibl.: p.599-604. — Index.
ISBN 0-19-876037-x : £7.95 : CIP rev.
ISBN 0-19-876038-8 Pbk : £3.95
(B77-07149)

335.4'12 — Economics. Theories of Marx, Karl & Engels, Friedrich. *Texts*
Marx, Karl. Collected works [of] Karl Marx [and] Frederick Engels. — London : Lawrence and Wishart.
[Vol.7] : [Marx and Engels, 1848] / [translated by Gregor Benton et al.]. — 1977. — xxxiii, 717p,[2] leaves of plates(1 fold),[4]p of plates : facsims, maps ; 23cm.
Includes translations from the German, French, Russian and Italian. — Bibl.: p.681-700. — Index.
ISBN 0-85315-352-3 : £3.00
(B77-15740)

335.4'12'0924 — Economics. Theories of Marx, Karl. *Critical studies*
Rius. Marx for beginners / [by Rius] ; [translated from the Spanish by Richard Appignanesi]. — London (14 Talacre Rd, NW5 3PE) : Writers and Readers Publishing Cooperative (Society Ltd), 1976. — 3-143,[9]p : ill, ports ; 21cm.
Translation of: 'Marx para principiantes'. Mexico : Ediciones de Cultura Popular, 1972.
ISBN 0-904613-27-5 Pbk : £1.00
(B77-07828)

335.43'09'044 — Communism, 1943-1956
Claudin, Fernando. The Communist movement : from Comintern to Cominform / [by] Fernando Claudin ; part one translated by Brian Pearce [part two translated by Francis MacDonagh, translated from the Spanish]. — New York ; London : Monthly Review Press, 1975. — 2v. (ix,644,91,95p) ; 21cm.
This translation also published: Harmondsworth : Penguin, 1975. — Translation of: 'La crisis del movimiento comunista ...'. Paris : Ruedo ibérico, 1970. — Index.
ISBN 0-85345-366-7 : £15.00
(B77-13552)

335.43'09'22 — Communism. Sympathisers, to 1972
Caute, David. The fellow-travellers : a postscript to the Enlightenment / [by] David Caute. — London : Quartet Books, 1977. — [11],433p ; 20cm.
Originally published: London : Weidenfeld and Nicolson, 1973. — Bibl.: p.401-406. — Index.
ISBN 0-7043-3104-7 Pbk : £3.50
(B77-08843)

335.43'092'4 — Communism. Weisbord, Vera Buch. *United States. Autobiographies*
Weisbord, Vera Buch. A radical life / [by] Vera Buch Weisbord. — Bloomington ; London : Indiana University Press, 1977. — xviii,330,[2] p,[2]p of plates : plan, ports ; 24cm.
Index.
ISBN 0-253-34773-4 : £11.25
(B77-28455)

335.43'0947 — Stalinism. *Soviet Union, to ca 1960*
Elleinstein, Jean. The Stalin phenomenon / by Jean Elleinstein ; [translated from the French by Peter Latham]. — London : Lawrence and Wishart, 1976. — 221p ; 23cm.
Translation of: 'Histoire du phénomène Stalinien'. Paris : Grasset, 1975. — Index.
ISBN 0-85315-375-2 : £4.95
ISBN 0-85315-376-0 Pbk : £2.00
(B77-05262)

335.6 — NATIONAL SOCIALISM
335.6'05 — Fascism. *Marxist viewpoints. Periodicals*
Unity against fascism. — London (45 Gooding House, Valley Grove, SE7 8AT) : Daphne Liddle.
No.1 - ; 1976-. — 1976-. — 36cm.
[10]p. in 1st issue.
Sd : £0.20
ISSN 0309-1368
(B77-04008)

335.6'09'04 — Fascism, ca 1915-1975
Fascism : a reader's guide : analyses, interpretations, bibliography / edited by Walter Laqueur. — London : Wildwood House, 1976. — x,478p ; 24cm.
Index.
ISBN 0-7045-0190-2 : £16.95
(B77-10240)

335.6'09'04 — Fascism, to 1976
Purcell, Hugh. Fascism / [by] Hugh Purcell. — London : Hamilton, 1977. — 95p : ill, facsims, ports ; 25cm. — (People and politics)
Bibl.: p.90-92. — Index.
ISBN 0-241-89442-5 : £3.25
(B77-24065)

335.8 — SYNDICALISM, ANARCHISM, ETC
335'.82'0941 — Syndicalism. *Great Britain, 1900-1914*
Holton, Bob. British syndicalism, 1900-1914 : myths and realities / [by] Bob Holton. — London : Pluto Press, 1976. — 232p ; 21cm.
Index.
ISBN 0-904383-17-2 : £6.60
ISBN 0-904383-22-9 Pbk : £2.95
(B77-04621)

335'.83 — Anarchism
Malatesta, Errico. [L'anarchia. English]. Anarchy / by Errico Malatesta ; a new translation from the Italian original [by Vernon Richards]. — London : Freedom Press, 1974. — 54p,plate : port ; 21cm. — (Anarchist classics)
'L'anarchia' originally published: London : Biblioteca dell'Associazione, 1891.
ISBN 0-900384-07-7 Pbk : £0.25
(B77-18609)

335'.83'05 — Anarchism. *Periodicals*
Cienfuegos Press anarchist review. — Sanday : Cienfuegos Press ; London (27 Clerkenwell Close, EC1R 0AT) : Distributed by Publications Distribution Co-operative.
No.1- ; 1976-. — [1976]-. — ill, facsims, maps, ports ; 30cm.
Published at irregular intervals. — [1],66p. in 2nd issue.
Sd : £1.00
ISSN 0309-7285
(B77-26877)

335'.83'076 — Anarchism. *Questions & answers*
Meltzer, Albert. The 'Black flag' anarcho-quiz book / compiled by Albert Meltzer ; (and illustrated mostly by Phil Ruff with ... contributions by others). — Sanday : Simian Publications, 1976. — [2],74p : ill ; 20cm.
Cover title: The anarcho quiz book. — With answers.
ISBN 0-904564-14-2 Sd : £1.00
(B77-18610)

335'.83'08 — Anarchism. *Readings*
The **anarchist** reader / edited by George Woodcock. — [London] : Fontana, 1977. — 383p ; 18cm.
Also published: Hassocks : Harvester Press, 1977. — Bibl.: p.382-383.
ISBN 0-00-634011-3 Pbk : £1.50
(B77-16769)

The **anarchist** reader / edited by George Woodcock. — Hassocks : Harvester Press [etc.], 1977. — 383p ; 23cm.
Also published: London : Fontana, 1977. — Bibl.: p.382-383.
ISBN 0-85527-889-7 : £8.50 : CIP rev.
(B77-08844)

335'.83'0924 — Anarchism. Bakunin, Mikhail Aleksandrovich. *Russia, 1840-1849. Autobiographies*
Bakunin, Mikhail Aleksandrovich. The 'Confession' of Mikhail Bakunin / with the marginal comments of Tsar Nicholas I ; translated [from the Russian] by Robert C. Howes ; introduction and notes by Lawrence D. Orton. — Ithaca ; London : Cornell University Press, 1977. — 200p : port ; 23cm.
'This translation of Bakunin's "Confession" is based upon the text of the document as it appears in "M.A. Bakunin : Sobranie sochinenii i pisem, 1828-1876" ... (1935 ; reprint Düsseldorf and Vaduz, 1970)' - Translator's note. — Index.
ISBN 0-8014-1073-8 : £9.35
(B77-28456)

335'.83'0924 — Anarchism. Mirbeau, Octave. *France*
Carr, Reg. Anarchism in France : the case of Octave Mirbeau / [by] Reg Carr. — Manchester : Manchester University Press, 1977. — xvii,190p ; 23cm.
Bibl.: p.178-186. — Index.
ISBN 0-7190-0668-6 : £7.95
(B77-25449)

335'.83'09468 — Anarchism. *Spain. Andalusia, 1868-1903*
Kaplan, Temma. Anarchists of Andalusia 1868-1903 / [by] Temma Kaplan. — Princeton ; Guildford : Princeton University Press, 1977. — xvii,266,[1]p : ill, map ; 23cm.
Bibl.: p.213-246. — Index.
ISBN 0-691-05236-0 : £10.90
(B77-15741)

336 — PUBLIC FINANCE
336 — Public finance. *Conference proceedings*
The **economics** of public services : proceedings of a conference held by the International Economic Association at Turin, Italy / edited by Martin S. Feldstein, Robert P. Inman. — London [etc.] : Macmillan, 1977. — xiv,529p : ill ; 23cm.
Bibl. — Index.
ISBN 0-333-19543-4 : £20.00
(B77-26174)

336'.02 — Revenue. *Organisation for Economic Co-operation and Development countries. Statistics*
Organisation for Economic Co-operation and Development. Statistiques de recettes publiques des pays membres de l'OCDE = Revenue statistics of OECD member countries : une classification normalisée = a standardized classification. — Paris : O.E.C.D. ; [London] : [H.M.S.O.].
1965-1974. — 1976. — 295p : 2 ill ; 27cm.
English and French text.
Pbk : £4.90
ISBN 92-64-01563-9
(B77-05922)

336.1 — PUBLIC FINANCE. NON-TAX REVENUES
336.1'85 — Rates. Supplementation. Grants from government. *England. Proposals*
Great Britain. *Department of the Environment.* Local government finance (England and Wales), the Rate Support Grant (Increase) (No.2) Order 1976 : report by the Secretary of State for the Environment and the Secretary of State for Transport under section 3(3) as applied by section 4(2) of the Local Government Act 1974 ... — London : H.M.S.O., [1976]. — 10p ; 25cm. — ([1976-77 H.C.]28)
ISBN 0-10-202877-x Sd : £0.25
(B77-07150)

Great Britain. *Department of the Environment.* Local government finance (England and Wales), the Rate Support Grant (Increase) Order 1976 : report by the Secretary of State for the Environment and the Secretary of State for Transport under section 3(3) as applied by section 4(2) of the Local Government Act 1974 ... — London : H.M.S.O., [1976]. — 9p ; 25cm. — ([1976-77 H.C.]27)
ISBN 0-10-202777-3 Sd : £0.25
(B77-07151)

Great Britain. *Department of the Environment.* Local government finance (England and Wales), the Rate Support Grant Order 1976 : report by the Secretary of State for the Environment and the Secretary of State for Transport under Section 3(3) of the Local Government Act 1974. — London : H.M.S.O., [1976]. — 20p ; 25cm. — ([1976-77 H.C.]26)
ISBN 0-10-202677-7 Sd : £0.35
(B77-07152)

Rate Support Grant, eighth period : a report on the Rate Support Grant Order 1976, the Rate Support Grant (Increase) Order 1976, the Rate Support Grant (Increase) (No.1) Order 1976 and the Rate Support Grant Regulations 1976 / Association of County Councils ... [et al.]. — [London] ([66a Eaton Sq., SW1W 9BH]) : The Association [etc.], 1977. — [4],102p ; 30cm.
Sd : £2.00
(B77-17351)

336.1'85 — Rates. Supplementation. Grants from government. *Scotland. Proposals*
Great Britain. *Scottish Office.* The Rate Support Grant (Scotland) Order 1976, report ... / Scottish Office. — Edinburgh : H.M.S.O., [1976]. — 15p ; 25cm. — ([1976-77 H.C.]13)
ISBN 0-10-201377-2 Sd : £0.35
(B77-07153)

336.1'85 — United States. States. Grants from federal government
Harbert, Anita S. Federal grants-in-aid : maximizing benefits to the states / [by] Anita S. Harbert. — New York [etc.] ; London : Praeger, 1976. — xiii,175p : ill ; 25cm. — (Praeger special studies in US economic, social and political issues)
Bibl.: p.157-169. — Index.
ISBN 0-275-23370-7 : £12.20
(B77-10241)

336.1'85'0973 — Revenue sharing. Social aspects. *United States*
Terrell, Paul. The social impact of revenue sharing : planning, participation and the purchase of service / [by] Paul Terrell with the assistance of Stan Weisner. — New York [etc.] ; London : Praeger, 1976. — ix,115p ; 25cm. — (Praeger special studies in US economic, social and political issues)
Bibl.: p.113-114.
ISBN 0-275-23470-3 : £9.25
(B77-10753)

336.2 — PUBLIC FINANCE. TAXATION
336.2 — Taxation. *Organisation for Economic Co-operation and Development countries. Comparative studies*
Bracewell-Milnes, Barry. The camel's back : an international comparison of tax burdens / [by] Barry Bracewell-Milnes. — London (8 Wilfred St., SW1E 6PL) : Centre for Policy Studies, 1976. — 72p ; 21cm.
Bibl.: p.71-72.
ISBN 0-9504392-1-5 Pbk : £1.50
(B77-09565)

336.2'00941 — Taxation. *Great Britain*
Bracewell-Milnes, Barry. Is capital taxation fair? : the tradition and the truth / by Barry Bracewell-Milnes. — London : Institute of Directors, 1974. — 144p ; 19cm.
Pbk : £2.00
(B77-27722)

Field, Frank, *b.1942.* To him who hath : a study of poverty and taxation / [by] Frank Field, Molly Meacher and Chris Pond. — Harmondsworth [etc.] : Penguin, 1977. — 254p : ill ; 19cm. — (A pelican original)
Index.
ISBN 0-14-021976-5 Pbk : £1.00
(B77-18611)

336.2'00941 — Taxation. *Great Britain. Glossaries*
Hart, Gerry Victor. A dictionary of tax definitions / by G.V. Hart. — Horsham (24 London Rd, Horsham, W. Sussex RH12 1LQ) : Grosvenor Tax Publishing Co., 1976. — [2],iv, 135p : port ; 23cm.
In binder.
ISBN 0-905753-00-3 Ls : £4.75
(B77-00652)

336.2'00941 — Taxation. *Great Britain. Proposals*
Confederation of British Industry. The budget 1977 - CBI representations to the Chancellor of the Exchequer. — London : C.B.I., 1977. — 36p : ill ; 30cm.
ISBN 0-85201-131-8 Sd : £1.50
(B77-15137)

336.2'00942 — Taxation. *England. For executors & trustees*
Mellows, Anthony Roger. Taxation for executors and trustees / by Anthony R. Mellows. — 4th ed. — London : Butterworth, 1976. — xxii, 306p ; 23cm. — (A Butterworth taxbook)
Previous ed.: 1972. — Index.
ISBN 0-406-62393-7 : £7.60
(B77-04009)

336.2'00944 — Taxation. *France*
Halpern, Lionel. Taxes in France / by Lionel Halpern. — 2nd ed. — London : Butterworth, 1976. — xvi,250p ; 23cm.
Previous ed.: 1974. — Index.
ISBN 0-406-52083-6 : £9.60
(B77-00653)

336.2'00973 — Taxation. Policies of government. *United States, 1781-1833*
Forsythe, Dall W. Taxation and political change in the young nation, 1781-1833 / [by] Dall W. Forsythe. — New York ; Guildford : Columbia University Press, 1977. — xi,167p : ill ; 24cm.
Bibl.: p.157-162. — Index.
ISBN 0-231-04192-6 : Unpriced
(B77-24772)

336.2'2 — Development land tax. *Great Britain*
Goy, David. Development land tax / by David Goy; with accountancy examples by Nick Kelsey. — London : Sweet and Maxwell, 1976. — xxi,199p ; 25cm.
Index.
ISBN 0-421-22460-6 Pbk : £5.00
(B77-06527)

Hardman, J Philip. Development land tax / by J. Philip Hardman ; with examples by Iain P.A. Stitt and Donald C. Borer. — London : Institute of Chartered Accountants in England and Wales, 1976. — xxiv,252p ; 22cm. — (Chartac taxation guides)
Index.
ISBN 0-85291-160-2 Pbk : Unpriced
(B77-06528)

Maas, Robert William. Development land tax / by Robert W. Maas. — Croydon : Tolley, 1976. — xii,234p ; 24cm.
Index.
ISBN 0-510-49348-3 Pbk : £4.25
(B77-04622)

336.2'2 — Tithe apportionments. *East Sussex. Eastbourne, 1842. Texts*
Great Britain. *Tithe Commissioners.* The Eastbourne tithe schedule. — Eastbourne (c/o J.E. Gryspeerdt, 73 Meads St., Eastbourne, [E. Sussex]) : Eastbourne Local History Society, 1975. — [1],iv,49leaves,[4]leaves of plates : maps ; 21x33cm.
'The instrument itself and the map .... were retained by the Tithe Commissioners and are now in the Public Record Office among the records of the Board of Inland Revenue' - leaf i. — Index.
ISBN 0-9504560-2-0 Sd : £2.50
(B77-02824)

336.2'2'0942 — Rates. *England. Statistics*
Rates and rateable values in England and Wales / Department of the Environment [and] Welsh Office. — London : H.M.S.O.
1975-1976. — 1976. — iv,54p : ill ; 28cm.
ISBN 0-11-750466-1 Sd : £1.50
(B77-02825)

336.2'4 — Income tax. *Countries with double taxation agreements with Great Britain. Reports, surveys*
Income taxes outside the United Kingdom / compiled by direction of the Board of Inland Revenue. — London : H.M.S.O.
[Vol.1. Group 2] : Spain. 1973 to 1975. — 1977. — v,26p ; 25cm.
Pierced for binder. — Index.
ISBN 0-11-640874-x Pbk : £1.25
Also classified at 336.2'4'09171241
(B77-11647)

[Vol.2. Group 6] : Jamaica. 1973 to 1975. — 1976. — vi,42p ; 25cm.
Pierced for binder. — Index.
ISBN 0-11-640917-7 Sd : £1.20
Also classified at 336.2'4'09171241
(B77-02102)

[Vol.4. Group 11] : Pakistan. 1973-1974 to 1975-76. — 1976. — vii,56p ; 25cm.
Pierced for binder. — Index.
ISBN 0-11-640893-6 Sd : £1.45
Also classified at 336.2'4'09171241
(B77-02103)

[Vol.5. Group 12] : Singapore. 1974 to 1976. — 1976. — vi,30p ; 25cm.
Pierced for binder. — Index.
ISBN 0-11-640956-8 Sd : £1.10
Also classified at 336.2'4'09171241
(B77-02104)

[Vol.5. Group 12] : Taiwan. 1975. — 1977. — vi,20p ; 25cm.
Pierced for binder. — Index.
ISBN 0-11-640957-6 Sd : £1.25
Also classified at 336.2'4'09171241
(B77-11112)

[Vol.5. Group 13] : New Zealand. 1973-74 to 1975-76. — 1977. — vi,84p ; 25cm.
Pierced for binder. — Index.
ISBN 0-11-640963-0 Pbk : £2.25
Also classified at 336.2'4'09171241
(B77-11648)

336.2'4 — Taxation. Liability of British emigrants. *Great Britain*
'Tax Haven Review' Technical Services Group. Leaving Britain? : a tax and legal guide for intending emigrants / edited by 'Tax Haven Review' Technical Services Group. — 1st ed., 2nd revision. — London (2 Rothsay St., SE1 4UD) : THR Books Centre, 1977. — 63p ; 21cm.
Previous ed.: i.e. Revised ed., 1976.
ISBN 0-85941-070-6 Pbk : £6.00
(B77-14597)

336.2'4'09171241 — Income tax. *Commonwealth countries. Reports, surveys*
Income taxes outside the United Kingdom / compiled by direction of the Board of Inland Revenue. — London : H.M.S.O.
[Vol.1. Group 2] : Spain. 1973 to 1975. — 1977. — v,26p ; 25cm.
Pierced for binder. — Index.
ISBN 0-11-640874-x Pbk : £1.25
Primary classification 336.2'4
(B77-11647)

[Vol.2. Group 6] : Jamaica. 1973 to 1975. — 1976. — vi,42p ; 25cm.
Pierced for binder. — Index.
ISBN 0-11-640917-7 Sd : £1.20
Primary classification 336.2'4
(B77-02102)

[Vol.4. Group 11] : Pakistan. 1973-1974 to 1975-76. — 1976. — vii,56p ; 25cm.
Pierced for binder. — Index.
ISBN 0-11-640893-6 Sd : £1.45
Primary classification 336.2'4
(B77-02103)

[Vol.5. Group 12] : Singapore. 1974 to 1976. — 1976. — vi,30p ; 25cm.
Pierced for binder. — Index.
ISBN 0-11-640956-8 Sd : £1.10
Primary classification 336.2'4
(B77-02104)

[Vol.5. Group 12] : Taiwan. 1975. — 1977. — vi,20p ; 25cm.
Pierced for binder. — Index.
ISBN 0-11-640957-6 Sd : £1.25
Primary classification 336.2'4
(B77-11112)

[Vol.5. Group 13] : New Zealand. 1973-74 to 1975-76. — 1977. — vi,84p ; 25cm.
Pierced for binder. — Index.
ISBN 0-11-640963-0 Pbk : £2.25
Primary classification 336.2'4
(B77-11648)

336.2'4'0941 — Income tax. *Great Britain*
Budibent, Bryan. The 'Daily telegraph' guide to income tax / [by] Brian Budibent. — New revised ed. — London [etc.] : Collins, 1977. — 126p ; 21cm.
Previous ed.: 1975.
ISBN 0-00-412060-4 : £2.75
ISBN 0-00-412062-0 Pbk : £0.95
(B77-23204)

Chapman, A L. Taxation manual. — 13th ed. / by A.L. Chapman and Percy F. Hughes. — London : Taxation Publishing Co., 1977. — xxxix,728p : 1 ill ; 22cm.
Previous ed.: / by Percy F. Hughes and J.M. Cooper. 1972. — Index.
ISBN 0-900734-43-4 Pbk : £9.00
(B77-15138)

Nelson-Jones, John Austen. Practical tax saving / by J.A. Nelson-Jones and Bertram Smith. — 3rd ed. — London : Butterworth, 1976. — xxiii,317p ; 23cm. — (A Butterworth taxbook)
Previous ed.: 1973. — Index.
ISBN 0-406-53632-5 : £7.60
(B77-05263)

Toch, Henry. Income tax, including corporation tax and capital gains tax / [by] Henry Toch. — 9th ed. — Plymouth : Macdonald and Evans, 1976. — xi,196p ; 19cm. — (The M. & E. handbook series)
With answers. — Previous ed.: 1975. — Bibl.: p.157. — Index.
ISBN 0-7121-0944-7 Pbk : £1.50
(B77-05923)

336.2'4'0941 — Income tax. *Great Britain. Serials*
Check your tax : tax made simple for you. — London [etc.] : Foulsham.
1977-78 / by J.D. Finnigan and G.M. Kitchen. — 1977. — 64p : forms ; 22cm.
Index.
ISBN 0-572-00966-6 Pbk : £0.70
(B77-30022)

'Daily mail' income tax guide. — London : Associated Newspaper Group.
1977-1978 : for the year April 6th, 1977 to April 5th, 1978, in accordance with the changes made by Parliament in July 1977 / edited by Percy F. Hughes. — [1977]. — 127p : ill ; 22cm.
Sd : £0.50
(B77-32471)

Hambros Bank. The Hambro tax guide. — London : Macdonald and Jane's.
1977-78 / by A.S. Silke and W.I. Sinclair ; consulting editor and author of VAT chapter G.S.A. Wheatcroft. — 1977. — [14],258p ; 23cm.
Index.
ISBN 0-354-04115-0 : £4.95
ISSN 0305-6341
(B77-26878)

Key to income tax. — London : Taxation Publishing. — ('Taxation' master key series)
[1977-78 : 83rd ed.] : budget 1977 ed. / [edited by] J.M. Cooper and Percy F. Hughes. — [1977]. — 263p : forms ; 22cm.
Cover title. — Spine title: 'Taxation' key to income tax. — Thumb indexed. — Previously published: as '"Taxation" key to income tax'. — Index.
Pbk : £4.25
(B77-26175)

Smith, Sydney Charles Hudson. Smith's taxation. — Huddersfield : Advertiser Press.
1976-77 / edited and revised by H. Baxter. — [1977]. — 808p ; 20cm.
Index.
ISBN 0-900028-41-6 : £4.50
(B77-08268)

336.2'4'09417 — Income tax. *Ireland (Republic)*
Kelly, Francis Noel. Irish income tax and corporation tax / by F.N. Kelly and K.S. Carmichael. — 9th ed. — London : H.F.L., 1976. — 1v. ; 23cm.
In binder. — xxi,414p. on publication. — Previous ed.: 1975. — Index.
ISBN 0-372-30002-2 Ls : £14.00
(B77-17974)

336.2'42 — Income tax. Liability of craftsmen. *Great Britain*
Federation of British Craft Societies. Income tax and the craftsman / [Federation of British Craft Societies]. — London (80A Southampton Row, WC1B 4BA) : The Federation, 1976. — [1],14p ; 26cm.
Sd : £0.15
(B77-18612)

336.2'42 — Income tax. Tax-credit system. *Great Britain. Proposals*
Clark, Colin, *b.1905.* Poverty before politics : a proposal for a reverse income tax / [by] Colin Clark. — London : Institute of Economic Affairs, 1977. — 69p : ill ; 22cm. — (Hobart papers ; 73 ISSN 0073-2818)
Bibl.: p.69.
ISBN 0-255-36094-0 Pbk : £1.50
(B77-31043)

336.2'42 — Income tax. Tax-credit system. *United States*
Golladay, Frederick L. The economic impacts of tax-transfer policy : regional and distributional effects / [by] Frederick L. Golladay, Robert H. Haveman, with the assistance of Kevin Hollenbeck. — New York [etc.] ; London : Academic Press, 1977. — xvii,198p : 3 ill, map ; 24cm. — (University of Wisconsin. Institute for Research on Poverty. Monograph series)
Index.
ISBN 0-12-288850-2 : £9.95
(B77-20979)

336.2'42 — Personal wealth. Taxation. *Great Britain. Confederation of British Industry viewpoints*
Confederation of British Industry. Wealth tax, the industry view / [Confederation of British Industry]. — London : C.B.I., 1977. — 20p : ill ; 21cm.
Sd : £1.00
(B77-29243)

336.2'42'0941 — Personal income tax. Self-assessment. *Great Britain. Proposals*
Barr, N A. Self-assessment for income tax / [by] N.A. Barr, S.R. James, A.R. Prest. — London : Heinemann Educational for the Institute of Chartered Accountants in England and Wales and the Institute for Fiscal Studies, 1977. — xii,218p : ill, 2 forms ; 25cm.
Index.
ISBN 0-435-84060-6 : £7.50
(B77-17975)

336.2'42'0994 — Personal income tax. Reform, 1975-1976. *Australia*
Collins, D J. The Australian personal income tax reforms, 1975-76 / by D.J. Collins. — [London] : Institute for Fiscal Studies, 1977. — 30p : ill ; 21cm. — (Institute for Fiscal Studies. Lecture series ; no.8 ISSN 0306-5243)
Bibl.: p.30.
Sd : £0.75
(B77-17352)

336.2'422 — Dependent persons. Maintenance allowances. Taxation. *Great Britain*
Williams, Donald Brian. A guide to tax on maintenance payments / [by] Donald B. Williams. — London : Oyez Publishing, 1976. — 45p : form tipped in ; 21cm.
ISBN 0-85120-302-7 Sd : £2.50
(B77-07154)

336.2'43 — Capital gains tax. *Great Britain*
Carmichael, Keith Stanley. Capital gains tax / by K.S. Carmichael. — 2nd ed. — London : H.F.L.
Previous ed.: 1968.
Supplement : (incorporating the provisions of the Finance (No.2) Act 1975 and the Finance Act 1976 so far as these concern capital gains tax). — 1976. — [2]p,22 leaves ; 21cm.
ISBN 0-372-30000-6 Sd : £0.80
(B77-07829)

336.2'43 — Multinational companies. Taxation
Adams, J D R. The international taxation of multinational enterprises in developed countries / [by] J.D.R. Adams, J. Whalley. — London : Associated Business Programmes [for] the Institute of Fiscal Studies, 1977. — viii, 178p : ill ; 23cm.
Index.
ISBN 0-85227-073-9 : £9.95
(B77-25450)

336.2'43'094 — Companies. Taxation. *European countries*
Saunders, M Roy. Tax planning for businesses in Europe / by M. Roy Saunders. — London : Butterworth, 1977. — xii,334p ; 23cm. — (A Butterworth taxbook)
Index.
ISBN 0-406-53550-7 : £12.00
(B77-24773)

336.2'43'0941 — Business firms. Taxation. *Great Britain*
Cope, J M. Business taxation / [by] J.M. Cope. — Sunbury-on-Thames [etc.] : Nelson, 1977. — x,328p : ill ; 23cm.
Originally published: 1972. — Bibl.: p.319-321. — Index.
ISBN 0-17-771052-7 Pbk : £6.50
(B77-23205)

336.2'43'0941 — Corporation tax. *Great Britain*
Topple, Barry Stanley. Corporation tax / [by] B.S. Topple. — 3rd ed. — Plymouth : Macdonald and Evans, 1977. — viii,184p ; 19cm. — (The M & E handbook series)
Previous ed.: 1974. — Index.
ISBN 0-7121-0368-6 Pbk : £1.85
(B77-30023)

336.2'6'0941 — Customs duties. *Great Britain. Reports, surveys. Serials*
Great Britain. *Customs and Excise.* Report of the Commissioners of Her Majesty's Customs and Excise for the year ended 31 March ... — London : H.M.S.O.
[1975]-1976 : 67th. — [1976]. — 146p : ill ; 25cm. — (Cmnd.6694)
ISBN 0-10-166940-2 Pbk : £3.15
Also classified at 336.2'71'0941
(B77-07155)

336.2'63 — Foreign trade. Business firms. Taxation. *Great Britain*
Sharp, Peter. UK fiscal implications of international trade / by Peter Sharp. — London : Institute of Chartered Accountants in England and Wales, 1976. — [9],130p : 1 ill ; 22cm. — (Chartac taxation guides)
Index.
ISBN 0-85291-154-8 Pbk : £4.95
(B77-10242)

336.2'64 — Great Britain. Imports: Dumped goods. Customs duties. *Reports, surveys. Serials*
Customs Duties (Dumping and Subsidies) Act 1969, annual report for the financial year ended 31st March .. / by the Secretary of State for Trade. — London : H.M.S.O.
[1975]-1976. — [1977]. — 6p ; 25cm. — ([1976-77 H.C.] 90)
ISBN 0-10-209077-7 Sd : £0.25
(B77-07156)

336.2'64'0941 — Great Britain. Imports. Customs duties. *Reports, surveys. Serials*
Great Britain. *Department of Trade.* Import Duties Act 1958, annual report by the Department of Trade for the year ended 31st March ... — London : H.M.S.O.
1976. — [1977]. — 26p ; 25cm. — ([1976-77 H.C.] 217)
ISBN 0-10-221777-7 Sd : £0.65
(B77-11649)

336.2'7 — Latin America. Social development. Finance. Betterment levies. *Reports, surveys*
Macón, Jorge. Financing urban and rural development through betterment levies : the Latin American experience / [by] Jorge Macón, José Merino Mañon. — New York ; London : Praeger, 1977. — xv,149p : ill, map ; 25cm. — (Praeger special studies in international politics and government)
'Published in cooperation with the Inter-American Development Bank'. — Bibl.: p.139-142. — Index.
ISBN 0-275-23970-5 : £12.40
(B77-26176)

336.2'71 — Value-added tax. *Great Britain*
Price, A St J. VAT made easy : Value Added Tax explained in simple terms / [by] A. St J. Price. — [2nd ed.]. — York (28 Blossom St., York YO2 2AJ) : Lynxplan (Sheffield) Ltd, [1977]. — 79p in various pagings : 2 forms ; 30cm.
Previous ed.: 1976.
ISBN 0-905859-00-6 Sp : £5.00
(B77-12355)

336.2'71'0941 — Excise. *Great Britain. Reports, surveys. Serials*
Great Britain. *Customs and Excise.* Report of the Commissioners of Her Majesty's Customs and Excise for the year ended 31 March ... — London : H.M.S.O.
[1975]-1976 : 67th. — [1976]. — 146p : ill ; 25cm. — (Cmnd.6694)
ISBN 0-10-166940-2 Pbk : £3.15
Primary classification 336.2'6'0941
(B77-07155)

336.2'76 — Capital transfer tax. *Great Britain*
Capital taxes encyclopaedia : capital transfer tax / [editorial board Sir John Foster, B.J. Sims, E.E. Ray ; editor for Scottish law W.F. Bowes]. — London : Butterworth, 1976. — 1v. ; 26cm.
Tab indexed. — In binder. — Booklet (22p.) in end pocket. — Index.
ISBN 0-406-50509-8 : £32.00
(B77-01232)

Coombes, John. Capital transfer tax / by John Coombes. — Abingdon (Milton Trading Estate, Abingdon, Oxon) : Professional Books Ltd, 1977. — xxi,259p : forms ; 22cm.
Index.
ISBN 0-903486-25-3 Pbk : £6.50
ISBN 0-903486-24-5 Pbk : £3.75
(B77-12910)

Living with capital transfer tax. — London (135 Fleet St., EC4P 4BL) : 'Sunday Telegraph', 1977. — 39p : port ; 21cm.
Sd : £0.45
(B77-16770)

336.2'76 — Capital transfer tax. *Great Britain. Tables*
Capital transfer tax tables. — 2nd ed. ; including grossing of tax free legacies and transitional relief for discretionary settlements. — London : Butterworth, 1977. — 28p ; 25cm.
Previous ed.: 1976.
ISBN 0-406-50530-6 Sd : £2.00
(B77-14598)

336.2'78'30131 — Organisation for Economic Co-operation and Development countries. Environment. Pollution. Control measures: Taxation. *Reports, surveys*

Organisation for Economic Co-operation and Development. *Secretariat.* Pollution charges : an assessment : report / by the Secretariat [of the Organisation for Economic Co-operation and Development]. — Paris : O.E.C.D. ; [London] : [H.M.S.O.], 1976. — 77p : ill ; 24cm.
Pbk : £1.70
ISBN 92-64-11513-7
(B77-00654)

336.3 — PUBLIC FINANCE. FISCAL POLICY

336.3'1'0941 — Financial assistance by government. National Loans Fund. *Great Britain. Accounts*

Accounts relating to issues from the National Loans Fund ... — London : H.M.S.O.
1975-76. — [1977]. — 134p ; 25cm. — ([1976-77 H.C.]194)
ISBN 0-10-219477-7 Pbk : £2.10
(B77-10243)

336.3'1'0941 — Great Britain. Government. Finance. Consolidated Fund. *Accounts*

Consolidated Fund and National Loans Fund accounts ... — London : H.M.S.O.
1975-76. — [1976]. — 18p ; 25cm. — ([1976-77 H.C.] 38)
ISBN 0-10-203877-5 Sd : £0.45
(B77-07830)

1975-76. Supplementary statements. — [1976]. — 65p ; 25cm. — ([1976-77 H.C.] 39)
Index.
ISBN 0-10-203977-1 Sd : £1.75
(B77-07831)

336.3'1'0941 — Great Britain. Government. Finance. Contingencies Fund. *Accounts*

Contingencies Fund accounts ... / [Treasury]. — London : H.M.S.O.
1975-76. — [1977]. — 12p ; 25cm. — ([1976-77 H.C.]232)
ISBN 0-10-223277-6 Sd : £0.33
(B77-12356)

336.3'431 — Local authorities. Capital expenditure. Financial assistance. Loans from government. Organisations. *Great Britain. Public Works Loan Board. Reports, surveys. Serials*

Public Works Loan Board. Annual report of the Public Works Loan Board ... — London : H.M.S.O.
1975-76 : 101st. — [1976]. — 39p,[2]fold leaves ; 25cm.
ISBN 0-11-630683-1 Sd : £1.00
(B77-10244)

336.3'433'0941 — Great Britain. National Debt. Reduction by trust funds. *Reports, surveys. Serials*

National debt : papers relative to the position as at 31st March of certain funds left in trust for the reduction of the national debt / presented to Parliament by the Financial Secretary to the Treasury. — London : H.M.S.O.
1976. — [1976]. — Folder(4p) ; 25cm. — (Cmnd.6671)
ISBN 0-10-166710-8 : £0.15
(B77-05264)

336.3'9'0941 — Great Britain. Government. Expenditure. *Accounts*

Great Britain. *Exchequer and Audit Department.* Appropriation accounts ... / [Exchequer and Audit Department]. — London : H.M.S.O.
1975-76. Vol.2 : Classes 4 and 6-9. — [1977]. — xxxvi,291p ; 25cm. — ([1976-77 H.C.] 92)
Index.
ISBN 0-10-209277-x Pbk : £5.75
(B77-07157)

1975-76. Vol.3 : Classes 10-15 and 17. — [1977] . — xli,2-340p ; 25cm. — ([1976-77 H.C.] 93)
Index.
ISBN 0-10-209377-6 Pbk : £6.80
(B77-11650)

336.3'9'0941 — Great Britain. Government. Expenditure. *Estimates*

Great Britain. *Treasury.* The Government's expenditure plans / presented to Parliament by the Chancellor of the Exchequer ... — London : H.M.S.O., [1977]. — iv,22p ; 25cm. — (Cmnd. 6721-I)
ISBN 0-10-167210-1 Sd : £0.60
(B77-10754)

Great Britain. *Treasury.* The Government's expenditure plans / presented to Parliament by the Chancellor of the Exchequer ... — London : H.M.S.O.
Vol.2. — [1977]. — iv,153p : ill ; 25cm. — (Cmnd.6721-II)
ISBN 0-10-167212-8 Pbk : £2.35
(B77-08845)

Great Britain. *Treasury.* Supply estimates for the year ending 31st March ... / [Treasury]. — London : H.M.S.O.
1976-77. Class 1 : Defence. Supplementary estimates. — [1976]. — vi,46p ; 25cm. — ([1976-77 H.C.]9)
ISBN 0-10-200977-5 Sd : £1.00
(B77-07158)

1976-77. Class 1 : Defence. Supplementary estimates. — [1977]. — vi,41p ; 25cm. — ([1976-77 H.C.] 139)
ISBN 0-10-213977-6 Sd : £1.00
(B77-11651)

1976-77. Class 1-17. Supplementary estimates. — [1977]. — vi,35p ; 25cm. — ([1976-77 H.C.] 173)
ISBN 0-10-217377-x Sd : £1.00
(B77-08846)

1976-77. Class 2-17 : Civil. Supplementary estimates. — [1976]. — xii,306p ; 25cm. — ([1976-77 H.C.]10)
Cover title.
ISBN 0-10-201077-3 Pbk : £4.25
(B77-07159)

1976-77. Class 2-17 : Civil. Supplementary estimates. — [1977]. — xii,453p ; 25cm. — ([1976-77 H.C.]140)
Cover title.
ISBN 0-10-214077-4 Pbk : £8.50
(B77-11652)

1976-77. Class 2-17 : Civil. Supplementary estimates : (machinery of Government changes). — [1976]. — ix,28p ; 25cm. — ([1976-77 H.C.] 8)
ISBN 0-10-200877-9 Sd : £0.67
(B77-07160)

1977-78. Class 1 : Defence. — [1977]. — [1], viii,56p ; 25cm. — ([1976-77 H.C.]174)
Index.
ISBN 0-10-217477-6 Sd : £1.50
(B77-08269)

1977-78. Class 1-17. Supplementary estimates. — [1977]. — [1],viii,94p ; 25cm. — ([1976-77 H.C.] 442)
ISBN 0-10-244277-0 Sd : £2.50
(B77-20977)

1977-78. Class 2 : Overseas services. — [1977]. — [1],xiv,63p ; 25cm. — ([1976-77 H.C.] 231-II)
ISBN 0-10-278377-2 Sd : £1.80
(B77-11653)

1977-78. Class 2-17 : Civil. Revised estimates. — [1977]. — [2],iii,53p ; 25cm. — ([1976-77 H.C.] 442)
ISBN 0-10-244177-4 Sd : £1.25
(B77-20978)

1977-78. Class 3 : Agriculture, fisheries and forestry. — [1977]. — [1],xii,58p ; 25cm. — ([1976-77 H.C.]231-III)
ISBN 0-10-278477-9 Sd : £1.80
(B77-11654)

1977-78. Class 4 : Trade, industry and employment. — [1977]. — [1],xxi,100p ; 25cm. — ([1976-77 H.C.]231-IV)
ISBN 0-10-278577-5 Sd : £2.50
(B77-11655)

1977-78. Class 6 : Roads and transport ; Class 7 : Housing ; Class 8 : Other environmental services. — [1977]. — 162p in various pagings ; 25cm. — ([1976-77 H.C.]231-VI) ([1976-77 H.C.]231-VII) ([1976-77 H.C.]231-VIII)
ISBN 0-10-278677-1 Sd : £3.10
(B77-12357)

1977-78. Class 9 : Law, order and protective services. — [1977]. — [1],xiii,64p ; 25cm. — ([1976-77 H.C.]231-IX)
ISBN 0-10-278777-8 Sd : £1.80
(B77-11656)

1977-78. Class 10 : Education and libraries, science and arts. — [1977]. — [1],xiv,94p ; 25cm. — ([1976-77 H.C.]231-X)
ISBN 0-10-278877-4 Sd : £2.10
(B77-12358)

1977-78. Class 11 : Health and personal social services ; Class 12 : Social security. — [1977]. — [1],xii,39,vii,12p ; 25cm. — ([1976-77 H.C.]231-XI) ([1976-77 H.C.]231-XII)
ISBN 0-10-278977-0 Sd : £2.00
(B77-11657)

1977-78. Class 13 : Other public services ; Class 14 : Common services. — [1977]. — xvi,57,xii, 32p ; 25cm. — ([1976-77 H.C.]231-XIII) ([1976-77 H.C.]231-XIV)
Cover title.
ISBN 0-10-279077-9 Pbk : £2.50
(B77-12359)

1977-78. Class 15 : Northern Ireland. — [1977]. — [1],ix,22p ; 25cm. — ([1976-77 H.C.]231-XV)
ISBN 0-10-279177-5 Sd : £0.90
(B77-12360)

1977-78. Class 17 : Rate support grant, financial transactions, &c. — [1977]. — [1],iv, 21p ; 25cm. — ([1976-77 H.C.]231-XVII)
ISBN 0-10-279277-1 Sd : £0.80
(B77-11658)

1977-78. Memorandum by the Chief Secretary to the Treasury. — [1977]. — vi,48p ; 25cm. — (Cmnd.6769)
ISBN 0-10-167690-5 Sd : £1.10
(B77-12361)

336.3'9'0941 — Great Britain. Government. Expenditure. *Inquiry reports*

Great Britain. *Parliament. House of Commons. Expenditure Committee.* Selected public expenditure programmes : ninth report from the Expenditure Committee, session 1976-77. — London : H.M.S.O., [1977]. — lxiv p ; 25cm. — ([1976-77 H.C.] 466)
ISBN 0-10-246677-7 Sd : £1.10
(B77-23206)

Great Britain. *Parliament. House of Commons. Expenditure Committee.* Selected public expenditure programmes : ninth report from the Expenditure Committee, session 1976-77. — London : H.M.S.O.
Chapter II : Export credit finance : together with the minutes of the evidence taken before the Trade and Industry Sub-committee on 23rd and 30th March 1977 and appendices. — [1977]. — xxvii,64p ; 25cm. — ([1976-77 H.C.] 466-II) ([1976-77 H.C.] 281-i and ii)
ISBN 0-10-299977-5 Sd : £1.85
(B77-32550)

Chapter VI : Stationery and printing (home) : together with the minutes of the evidence taken before the General Sub-committee on 18th May 1977 and appendices. — [1977]. — xiii,34p : ill ; 25cm. — ([1976-77 H.C.] 466-vi) ([1976-77 H.C.] 385-i)
ISBN 0-10-269977-1 Sd : £0.85
(B77-33110)

336.3'9'0941 — Great Britain. Government. Expenditure. *Inquiry reports. Serials*

Great Britain. *Parliament. House of Commons. Committee of Public Accounts.* Report from the Committee of Public Accounts, session 1976-77. — London : H.M.S.O.
4th : together with the proceedings of the Committee, part of the minutes of evidence, appendices and index. — [1977]. — xxiii,104p : ill ; 25cm. — ([1976-77 H.C.]304)
Index.
ISBN 0-10-230477-7 Pbk : £2.25
(B77-20980)

5th : together with the proceedings of the Committee, part of the minutes of evidence, appendices and index. — [1977]. — xxv p,p118-184 ; 25cm. — ([1976-77 H.C.]449)
Index.
ISBN 0-10-244977-5 Pbk : £1.85
(B77-27723)

6th : together with the proceedings of the Committee, part of the minutes of evidence, appendices and index. — [1977]. — xxv,84p ; 25cm. — ([1976-77 H.C.]450)
Index.
ISBN 0-10-245077-3 Pbk : £2.10
(B77-27724)

7th : together with the proceedings of the Committee, part of the minutes of evidence, appendices and index (Northern Ireland). — [1977]. — xvii p,p398-421 ; 25cm. — ([1976-77 H.C.]530)
Index.
ISBN 0-10-253077-7 Sd : £0.85
(B77-28457)

8th : together with the proceedings of the Committee, part of the minutes of evidence, appendices and index. — [1977]. — xliv p,p263-406 ; 25cm. — ([1976-77 H.C.]531)
Index.
ISBN 0-10-253177-3 Pbk : £3.60
(B77-28458)

9th : together with the proceedings of the Committee, part of the minutes of evidence, appendices and index. — [1977]. — xxxviii p,p361-481,fold leaf ; 25cm. — ([1976-77 H.C.]532)
Index.
ISBN 0-10-253277-x Pbk : £3.60
(B77-28459)

10th : together with the proceedings of the Committee, part of the minutes of evidence, appendices and index. — [1977]. — xxviii p,p477-571 ; 25cm. — ([1976-77 H.C.]536)
Index.
ISBN 0-10-253677-5 Sd : £2.10
(B77-30024)

336.3'9'0941 — Great Britain. Government. Expenditure. Control by Great Britain. Parliament. *Conservative and Unionist Party viewpoints*
Du Cann, Edward. Parliament and the purse strings : how to bring public expenditure under parliamentary control / [by] Edward du Cann. — London : Conservative Political Centre, 1977. — 24p ; 21cm. — (Conservative Political Centre. Publications ; no.604)
ISBN 0-85070-598-3 Sd : £0.40
(B77-20094)

336.3'9'0941 — Great Britain. Government. Expenditure. Control. Cash limits. *Inquiry reports*
Great Britain. *Parliament. House of Commons. Select Committee on Public Accounts.* Cash limits : third report from the Select Committee on Public Accounts, session 1976-77, together with the minutes of evidence taken on 16th February 1977 and appendices. — London : H.M.S.O., [1977]. — x p,p73-105 ; 25cm. — ([1976-77 H.C.] 274)
ISBN 0-10-227477-0 Sd : £0.85
(B77-14599)

336.3'9'0941 — Great Britain. Government. Expenditure. Control. Cash limits. *Proposals. Serials*
Cash limits / presented to Parliament by the Chief Secretary to the Treasury ... — London : H.M.S.O.
1977-78. — [1977]. — [1],12p ; 25cm. — (Cmnd.6767)
ISBN 0-10-167670-0 Sd : £0.35
(B77-12911)

336.3'9'0941 — Great Britain. Government. Expenditure. Control. Proposals. Publication. *Inquiry reports*
Great Britain. *Parliament. House of Commons. Expenditure Committee.* Planning and control of public expenditure : thirteenth report from the Expenditure Committee, session 1975-76, together with the minutes of evidence taken before the General Sub-committee in session 1975-76. — London : H.M.S.O., [1976]. — viii, 56p ; 25cm. — ([1975-76 H.C.]718)
ISBN 0-10-009686-7 Sd : £1.60
(B77-08847)

336.3'9'0941 — Great Britain. Government. Expenditure. Great Britain. Treasury. 'Government's expenditure plans'. *Critical studies*
Great Britain. *Parliament. House of Commons. Expenditure Committee.* White paper on the Government's expenditure plans (Cmnd.6721), fourth report from the Expenditure Committee, session 1976-77, together with minutes of evidence taken before the General Sub-committee on 7 March 1977 and appendices. — London : H.M.S.O., 1977. — x, 34p ; 25cm. — ([1976-77 H.C.]258)
ISBN 0-10-225877-5 Sd : £0.85
(B77-15139)

336.3'9'0941 — Great Britain. Government. Expenditure. Related to unemployment
Burgess, Ronald. Full employment and public spending / [by] Ronald Burgess. — London : Aims for Freedom and Enterprise, [1977]. — [3],19p : ill.
ISBN 0-7281-0073-8 Sd : £0.50
Primary classification 331.1'37941
(B77-28436)

336.3'9'0941 — Great Britain. Parliament. House of Commons. Committee of Public Accounts. Reports. *Critical studies*
Great Britain. *Treasury.* Treasury minute on the reports from the Committee of Public Accounts, session 1975-76 and abstract of appropriation accounts. — London : H.M.S.O., [1976]. — 23p ; 25cm. — (Cmnd.6654)
ISBN 0-10-166540-7 Sd : £0.35
(B77-04623)

336.3'9'09416 — Northern Ireland. Government. Excess expenditure. *Reports, surveys*
Northern Ireland. *Department of Finance.* Statement of excesses : a statement of the sums required to be granted in order to make good excesses on certain grants for the year ended 31 March / Department of Finance [Northern Ireland]. — Belfast : H.M.S.O.
1974-75 : eight hundred and fifty-nine thousand, seven hundred and eighty-four pounds. — 1976. — 4p ; 25cm.
ISBN 0-337-23198-2 Sd : £0.20
(B77-04624)

336.3'9'09416 — Northern Ireland. Government. Expenditure. *Accounts*
Northern Ireland appropriation accounts : together with the Consolidated Fund Services Account, and the report of the Comptroller and Auditor-General for Northern Ireland thereon and upon the Revenue Accounts ... / [Northern Ireland Exchequer and Audit Department]. — Belfast : H.M.S.O.
1975-76. — [1977]. — xxxiv,2-217p,[4]leaves ; 25cm. — ([1976-77 H.C.]15)
Index.
ISBN 0-10-201577-5 Pbk : £3.25
(B77-08270)

336.3'9'09416 — Northern Ireland. Government. Expenditure. *Estimates*
Northern Ireland. *Department of Finance.* Main estimates / Department of Finance [Northern Ireland]. — Belfast : H.M.S.O.
1976-77. Further spring supplementary estimate for services under the Government of Northern Ireland. Estimate of a further sum required to be appropriated for the service of the year ending 31 March ... — 1977. — v,11p ; 25cm.
ISBN 0-337-23227-x Sd : £0.50
(B77-26879)

336.3'9'09416 — Northern Ireland. Government. Expenditure. Great Britain. House of Commons. Committee of Public Accounts. Reports. *Critical studies*
Northern Ireland. *Department of Finance.* Memorandum on the reports from the Committee of Public Accounts, session 1975-76 / Northern Ireland Department of Finance. — London : H.M.S.O., [1976]. — 6p ; 25cm. — (Cmnd.6653)
ISBN 0-10-166530-x Sd : £0.20
(B77-07161)

336.4/9 — PUBLIC FINANCE IN SPECIAL LOCALITIES

336.41 — Great Britain. Government. Finance. *Proposals*
Chalmers, Impey and Co. The 1976 spring budget / [Chalmers, Impey and Co.]. — London [etc.] (6 Long La., EC1A 9DP) : Chalmers, Impey and Co., 1976. — [1],24,[1]p ; 21cm.
Sd : Unpriced
(B77-21740)

336.41 — Great Britain. Government. Finance. *Reports, surveys. Serials*
Great Britain. *Treasury.* Financial statement and budget report : ... as laid before the House by the Chancellor of the Exchequer when opening the budget. — London : H.M.S.O.
1977-78. — [1977]. — 35p : ill ; 25cm. — ([1976-77 H.C.]271)
ISBN 0-10-227177-1 Sd : £1.40
(B77-12912)

336.41 — Great Britain. Local government. Finance
Hepworth, Noel Peers. The finance of local government / by N.P. Hepworth. — 3rd ed. — London : Allen and Unwin, 1976. — 3-304p ; 23cm. — (The new local government series ; no.6)
Previous ed.: 1971. — Bibl.: p.286-288. — Index.
ISBN 0-04-352062-6 : £7.95
ISBN 0-04-352063-4 Pbk : £4.95
(B77-00085)

336.41 — Great Britain. Local government. Finance. *Conference proceedings*
Local Government Finance *(Conference), London?, 1973.* Proceedings of a conference on Local Government Finance. — London (1 Bell Yard, WC2A 2JX) : Institute for Fiscal Studies, 1973. — vi,141p : ill ; 21cm. — (Institute for Fiscal Studies. Publications ; no.10 ISSN 0307-2266)
'A conference on Local Government Finance arranged by the Institute for Fiscal Studies was held ... on 22 June 1973' - Introduction.
ISBN 0-902992-09-0 Pbk : £2.00
(B77-06529)

336.41 — Great Britain. Local government. Finance. *Inquiry reports*
Committee of Inquiry into Local Government Finance. Local government finance : report of the Committee of Inquiry / [Committee of Inquiry into Local Government Finance] ; presented to Parliament by the Secretary of State for the Environment, the Secretary of State for Scotland and the Secretary of State for Wales. — London : H.M.S.O.
Chairman : Frank Layfield.
Appendix 2 : Evidence by local authority associations. — 1976. — viii,486p : ill ; 25cm.
ISBN 0-11-751111-0 Pbk : £5.45
(B77-04625)

Appendix 7 : Government grants to local authorities : evidence and commissioned work. — [1976]. — [1],x,147p ; 25cm.
ISBN 0-11-751114-5 Pbk : £1.85
(B77-04626)

Appendix 8 : Local income tax : evidence and commissioned work. — 1976. — x,296p ; 25cm.

ISBN 0-11-751107-2 Pbk : £3.35
(B77-04627)

336.41 — Great Britain. Local government. Finance. Committee of Inquiry into Local Government Finance. 'Local government finance'. *Critical studies*
Cripps, Francis. Local government finance and its reform : a critique of the Layfield Committee's report / by Francis Cripps and Wynne Godley. — Cambridge (Sidgwick Ave., Cambridge CB3 9DE) : University of Cambridge, Department of Applied Economics, 1976. — [4],58,[1]p ; 25cm.

Pbk : £2.40
(B77-27725)

336.411 — Scotland. Local government. Finance. *Proposals*
Great Britain. *Scottish Office.* Local government finance in Scotland ... / Scottish Office. — Edinburgh : H.M.S.O., [1977]. — 23p ; 25cm. — (Cmnd.6811)
ISBN 0-10-168110-0 Sd : £0.55
(B77-21741)

336.411 — Scotland. Local government. Finance. *Statistics*
Local financial returns, Scotland ... / Scottish Office. — Edinburgh : H.M.S.O.
1974-75. — 1977. — 15,[1]p ; 30cm.
ISBN 0-11-491473-7 Sd : £1.00
(B77-26880)

336.416 — Northern Ireland. Government. *Accounts*
Northern Ireland. *Department of Finance.* Financial statement : statement of revenue and expenditure / Department of Finance [Northern Ireland]. — Belfast : H.M.S.O.
1976-77. — 1976. — 9p ; 25cm.
ISBN 0-337-23199-0 Sd : £0.47
(B77-02826)

336.42 — England. Local government. Finance. *Proposals*
Great Britain. *Department of the Environment.* Local government finance / presented to Parliament by the Secretary of State for the Environment and the Secretary of State for Wales ... — London : H.M.S.O., [1977]. — [2], 32p ; 25cm. — (Cmnd.6813)
ISBN 0-10-168130-5 Sd : £0.70
(B77-21742)

336.425'73 — Oxfordshire. Bodicote. Local government, 1700-1822. *Accounts*
Bodicote *(Chapelry).* Parish accounts for the 'Town' of Bodicote, Oxfordshire, 1700-1822 / edited and annotated by J.H. Fearon ; based on a transcription by C.W. Hurst. — Banbury (c/o Banbury Museum, Banbury, Oxon.) : Banbury Historical Society, 1975. — xxvi,34p : 2 ill, map ; 22cm. — (Banbury Historical Society. Publications ; vol.12)
Spine title: Bodicote parish accounts, 1700-1822. — Index.
ISBN 0-900129-12-3 Pbk : £2.00
(B77-00655)

336.429 — Wales. Local government. Finance. *Statistics*
Welsh local government financial statistics = Ystadegau ariannol llywodraeth leol yng Nghymru / [Welsh Office]. — Cardiff : H.M.S.O.
No.1 : 1977. — 1977. — viii,58p : ill, map ; 30cm.
English text, English and Welsh preliminaries.
ISBN 0-11-790088-5 Sd : £2.25
ISSN 0140-4482
(B77-29244)

336.54 — Public finance. *India (Republic)*
Nanjundappa, D M. Studies in public finance / [by] D.M. Nanjundappa. — London : Asia Publishing House, 1976. — ix,315p ; 21cm.
Index.
ISBN 0-210-22265-4 Pbk : £6.50
(B77-10245)

336.9′83′064 — Chile. Economic policies, 1945-1975
Behrman, Jere Richard. Macroeconomic policy in a developing country : the Chilean experience / [by] Jere R. Behrman. — Amsterdam [etc.] ; Oxford : North-Holland Publishing Co., 1977. — xviii,340p : ill ; 23cm. — (Contributions to economic analysis ; 109)
Bibl.: p.305-317.
ISBN 0-7204-0548-3 : Unpriced
(B77-24774)

338 — ECONOMIC ORGANISATION
338 — Industries. *Secondary school texts*
Bell, Evelyn. Industry and resources / [by] Evelyn Bell, Stewart Dunlop. — London [etc.] : Heinemann Educational, 1977. — [4],76p : ill(chiefly col), col maps ; 25cm. — (Place and people ; 5)
ISBN 0-435-34696-2 Sd : £1.25
(B77-16241)

338 — Industries. Economic aspects
An **introduction** to industrial economics / [by] P.J. Devine ... [et al.]. — Revised ed. — London : Allen and Unwin, 1976. — 3-613p : ill ; 22cm. — (Minerva series of students' handbooks ; no.26)
Previous ed.: 1974. — Index.
ISBN 0-04-338081-6 Pbk : £6.50
(B77-25452)

338 — Manufacturing industries. *Organisation for Economic Co-operation and Development countries. Statistics. Periodicals*
Indicateurs économiques à court terme pour les industries manufacturières = Short term economic indicators for manufacturing industries / [prepared by the Industrial Structures Division of the Directorate for Science, Technology and Industry of the Organisation for Economic Co-operation and Development. — Paris : O.E.C.D. ; [London] : [H.M.S.O.].
1- ; 1973?-. — 1973?-. — 27cm.
Quarterly. — 120p. in 7th issue. — English and French text.
Pbk : £2.20
(B77-26177)

338 — Materials. Utilisation. Economic aspects
Page, Talbot. Conservation and economic efficiency : an approach to materials policy / [by] Talbot Page. — Baltimore ; London : Johns Hopkins University Press for Resources for the Future, 1977. — xix,266p : ill ; 24cm.
Index.
ISBN 0-8018-1904-0 : £11.25
ISBN 0-8018-1951-2 Pbk : Unpriced
(B77-28460)

338′.001 — Production. Theories of Marxists
Hindess, Barry. Mode of production and social formation : an auto-critique of 'Pre-capitalist modes of production' / [by] Barry Hindess and Paul Hirst. — London [etc.] : Macmillan, 1977. — vii,82p ; 23cm.
Bibl.: p.78-79. — Index.
ISBN 0-333-22344-6 : £5.95
ISBN 0-333-22345-4 Pbk : £2.20
(B77-20982)

Hindess, Barry. Pre-capitalist modes of production / [by] Barry Hindess, Paul Q. Hirst. — London [etc.] : Routledge and Kegan Paul, 1977. — vi,354p ; 22cm.
Originally published: 1975. — Bibl.: p.342-347. — Index.
ISBN 0-7100-8169-3 Pbk : £3.75
(B77-12913)

338′.0025′41 — Industries producing kitemarked products. *Great Britain. Directories*
British Standards Institution. BSI buyers guide : a complete list of kitemarked products and licensees. — [Hemel Hempstead] ([Maylands Ave., Hemel Hempstead, Herts.]) : Quality Assurance Department, B.S.I.
1976. — [1976]. — [1],88p : ill ; 30cm.
Previously published: as 'Buyer's guide' / British Standards Institution, Quality Assurance Department.
Sd : Unpriced
(B77-20983)

338′.0025′41 — Manufacturing industries allowing visits. *Great Britain. Directories*
Lansbury, Angela. See Britain at work / [by Angela Lansbury]. — Watford (63 Kingsfield Rd, Watford WD1 4PP) : Exley Publications [etc.], 1977. — 208p in various pagings : ill(some col), coats of arms, col facsims, col maps ; 22cm.
Includes: See the South-West at work - See the South at work - See the Midlands at work - See Wales at work - See the North at work - See Scotland at work.
ISBN 0-905521-03-x : £4.95
(B77-28461)

338′.0025′411 — Manufacturing industries. *Scotland. Directories*
Scottish Council (Development and Industry). Guide to sub-contractors in Scotland, 1977 / [Scottish Council (Development and Industry)]. — Edinburgh (1 Castle St., Edinburgh EH2 3AJ) : The Council, [1977]. — 10,[92]p ; 30cm.
Index.
ISBN 0-902527-22-3 Sp : Unpriced
(B77-15742)

338′.0025′411 — Manufacturing industries allowing visits. *Scotland. Directories*
Lansbury, Angela. See Scotland at work : a guide to 68 factories and craft workshops open to visitors ... — Watford (63 Kingsfield Rd, Watford, Herts. WD1 4PP) : Exley Publications Ltd, [1977]. — [1],32,[1]p : ill(some col), col map, ports(1 col) ; 21cm.
Author: Angela Lansbury.
ISBN 0-905521-05-6 Sd : £0.60
(B77-29245)

See Scotland at work / Scottish Tourist Board. — Edinburgh : The Board. — (Scottish Tourist Board. Information booklets)
1977. — [1976]. — 84p : 1 ill ; 21x10cm.
Sd : Unpriced
(B77-29246)

338′.0025′4131 — Manufacturing industries. *Scotland. Central Region. Directories*
Central Region. *Industrial Development Department.* Industrial index : a guide to industries & products in Scotland's Central Region / [Central Regional Council, Industrial Development Department]. — [Stirling] ([Viewforth, Stirling]) : The Department, [1977]. — [48]p : map ; 24cm.
Index.
Sd : Unpriced
(B77-23207)

338′.0025′422 — Manufacturing industries allowing visits. *London & Home Counties. Directories*
Lansbury, Angela. See the South at work : a guide to 62 factories and craft workshops open to visitors ... — Watford (63 Kingsfield Rd, Watford WD1 4PP) : Exley Publications, [1977]. — [1],32,[1]p : ill(some col), col map ; 21cm.
Author: Angela Lansbury.
ISBN 0-905521-07-2 Sd : £0.60
(B77-28462)

338′.0025′423 — Manufacturing industries allowing visits. *South-west England. Directories*
Lansbury, Angela. See the South-West at work : a guide to 46 factories and craft workshops open to visitors .... — Watford (63 Kingsfield Rd, Watford WD1 4PP) : Exley Publications, [1977]. — [1],32,[1]p : ill(some col), col facsim, col map ; 21cm.
Author: Angela Lansbury.
ISBN 0-905521-08-0 Sd : £0.60
(B77-28463)

338′.0025′424 — Manufacturing industries allowing visits. *England. Midlands. Directories*
Lansbury, Angela. See the Midlands at work : a guide to 51 factories and craft workshops open to visitors ... — Watford (63 Kingsfield Rd, Watford WD1 4PP) : Exley Publications, [1977]. — [1],32,[1]p : ill(some col), col map ; 21cm.
Author: Angela Lansbury.
ISBN 0-905521-09-9 Sd : £0.60
(B77-28464)

338′.0025′427 — Manufacturing industries allowing visits. *Northern England. Directories*
Lansbury, Angela. See the North at work : a guide to 52 factories and craft workshops open to visitors ... — Watford (63 Kingsfield Rd, Watford WD1 4PP) : Exley Publications, [1977]. — [1],32,[1]p : ill(some col), coat of arms, col facsim, col map ; 21cm.
Author: Angela Lansbury.
ISBN 0-905521-10-2 Sd : £0.60
(B77-28465)

338′.0025′429 — Manufacturing industries allowing visits. *Wales. Directories*
Lansbury, Angela. See Wales at work : a guide to 55 factories and craft workshops open to visitors ... — Watford (63 Kingsfield Rd, Watford WD1 4PP) : Exley Publications, [1977]. — [1],32,[1]p : ill(some col), col map ; 21cm.
Author: Angela Lansbury.
ISBN 0-905521-06-4 Sd : £0.60
(B77-28466)

338′.006′241 — Industries & trades. Organisations. *Great Britain. Confederation of British Industry. Reports, surveys. Serials*
Confederation of British Industry. CBI annual report. — London : C.B.I.
1976. — 1977. — 28p : port ; 30cm.
Sd : Unpriced
(B77-26178)

338′.0092′2 — Entrepreneurship. Andrews family. *England, 1850-1975*
Andrews, John Francis. Keep moving : the story of Solomon Andrews and his family / by John F. Andrews. — Barry : S. Williams, 1976. — 144p : ill(some col), facsims(some col), plans, ports(some col) ; 21x27cm.
Limited ed. of 1000 copies. — Facsims on lining papers.
ISBN 0-900807-23-7 : £10.00
(B77-04628)

338′.0092′4 — Entrepreneurship. Hughes, Howard. *United States, 1961-1976. Biographies*
Phelan, James. Howard Hughes : the hidden years / [by] James Phelan. — London : Collins, 1977. — xvi,201p ; 22cm.
Originally published: New York : Random House, 1976.
ISBN 0-00-211365-1 : £3.75
(B77-26179)

338′.0092′4 — Entrepreneurship. Hughes, Howard. *United States, 1966-1976. Biographies*
Davenport, Elaine. The Hughes papers / by Elaine Davenport and Paul Eddy with Mark Hurwitz. — London : Deutsch, 1977. — 256p ; 23cm.
At head of title: Howard Hughes' final years - based on an examination of ... — Index.
ISBN 0-233-96924-1 : £4.95
(B77-23208)

Davenport, Elaine. The Hughes papers / by Elaine Davenport and Paul Eddy with Mark Hurwitz. — London : Sphere, 1977. — 256p ; 18cm.
At head of title: Howard Hughes' final years - based on an examination of ... — Also published: New York : Ballantine ; London : Deutsch, 1977. — Index.
ISBN 0-7221-2836-3 Pbk : £0.75
(B77-29247)

338′.0092′4 — Entrepreneurship. Morrison, James, b.1789. *Great Britain. Biographies*
Gatty, Richard. Portrait of a merchant prince : James Morrison, 1789-1857 / by Richard Gatty. — Northallerton (Pepper Arden, Northallerton, [N. Yorkshire]) : [Pamela Gatty], [1977]. — [5],326p,[3]leaves of plates(1 fold),[26]p of plates : ill, facsims(on lining papers), geneal table, ports ; 24cm.
Limited ed. of 250 copies. — Bibl.: p.309-311. — Index.
Unpriced
(B77-22424)

338'.0092'4 — Entrepreneurship. Slater, Jim. *Great Britain. Autobiographies*
Slater, Jim. Return to go : my autobiography / [by] Jim Slater. — London : Weidenfeld and Nicolson, 1977. — [9],278p,[8]p of plates : ill, ports ; 24cm.
Text on lining papers. — Index.
ISBN 0-297-77418-2 : £5.95
(B77-31044)

338'.04 — Entrepreneurship
Bruce, Richard. The entrepreneurs : strategies, motivations, successes and failures / [by] Richard Bruce. — Bedford (Cranfield Book Service, Wharley End, Bedford) : Libertarian Books, 1976. — vii,199p : ill ; 24cm.
Bibl.: p.179-185. — Index.
ISBN 0-905004-02-7 : £5.95
(B77-02105)

338'.06 — Industrialisation. Role of science & technology. *Western world*
Pavitt, Keith. Science, technology and the modern industrial state / [by] Keith Pavitt and Michael Worboys ; [for] Science in a Social Context. — London [etc.] : Butterworth, 1977. — 80p ; 22cm.
Bibl.
ISBN 0-408-71299-6 Pbk : £1.00
Also classified at 355.02
(B77-16242)

338'.06 — Industries. Adaptation. Policies of governments. *Organisation for Economic Co-operation and Development countries. Reports, surveys*
Organisation for Economic Co-operation and Development. Policies for promoting industrial adaptation / [Organisation for Economic Co-operation and Development]. — Paris : O.E.C.D. ; [London] : [H.M.S.O.], 1976. — 48p ; 24cm.
Pbk : £1.10
ISBN 92-64-11550-1
(B77-00661)

338'.06 — Industries. Efficiency. Influence of government. *Great Britain. Conference proceedings*
Industrial Efficiency and the Role of Government *(Conference), London, 1976.* Industrial efficiency and the role of government / edited by Colette Bowe ; [for the] Department of Industry. — London : H.M.S.O., 1977. — iii-viii,282p : ill ; 22cm.
'In 1976 the Department of Industry organised a one-day conference on "Industrial efficiency and the role of government"' - back cover. — Index.
ISBN 0-11-512014-9 Pbk : £4.25
(B77-33109)

338'.06 — Industries. Technological innovation. *Great Britain. Conference proceedings*
An **exposition** of the industrial technologies : presented by the Department of Industry and the Royal Institution of Great Britain at the Royal Institution, 21 Albemarle Street, London W.1, 10-14 March 1975 : proceedings. — [London] : The Department for the Committee for Industrial Technologies, 1975. — 4v. : ill, chart, ports ; 30cm.
Sd : Unpriced
(B77-30025)

338'.06 — Technological development, to 1976. Economic aspects
Heertje, Arnold. Economics and technical change / [by] Arnold Heertje ; [translated from the Dutch by Z. St-Gallay]. — London : Weidenfeld and Nicolson, 1977. — xii,334p : ill ; 23cm.
Translation of: 'Economie en technische ontwikkeling'. Leiden : Stenfert Kroese, 1973. — Index.
ISBN 0-297-77271-6 : £8.50
ISBN 0-297-77268-6 Pbk : £4.50
(B77-21743)

338'.09 — Manufacturing industries. Geographical aspects. *Secondary school texts*
Jarrett, Harold Reginald. A geography of manufacturing / [by] H.R. Jarrett. — 2nd ed. — Plymouth : Macdonald and Evans, 1977. — xvii,366p : ill, maps, plan ; 22cm. — (Aspect geographies)
Previous ed.: 1969. — Bibl. — Index.
ISBN 0-7121-0727-4 Pbk : £3.50
(B77-21744)

338'.09172'4 — Developing countries. Urban regions. Industrial development. Related to supply & demand of manpower
Bienefeld, Manfred A. Capital accumulation and employment in the periphery : a programme of research / by Manfred Bienefeld and Hubert Schmitz. — Brighton : Institute of Development Studies, 1976. — [5],29p ; 30cm. — (Institute of Development Studies. Discussion papers ; no.98 ISSN 0308-5864)
Bibl.: p.27-29.
Sd : £1.00
Primary classification 331.1'26'091724
(B77-18598)

338'.0941 — Business enterprise by government. *Great Britain. Accounts*
Great Britain. *Exchequer and Audit Department.* Trading accounts and balance sheets : accounts and balance sheets of certain trading or commercial services conducted by Government departments, together with the report of the Comptroller and Auditor General thereon ... / [Exchequer and Audit Department]. — London : H.M.S.O.
1975-76. — [1976]. — vi,53p ; 25cm. — ([1976-77 H.C.] 45)
ISBN 0-10-204577-1 Sd : £1.50
(B77-07162)

338'.0941 — Great Britain. Industrial development, 1951-1976. *Secondary school texts*
Stuart, Roderick. Industrial change : cause and consequence / [by] Roderick Stuart. — Glasgow [etc.] : Blackie, 1977. — vi,74p : ill, maps ; 21cm. — (Crossroads, approaches in modern studies)
Bibl.: p.74.
ISBN 0-216-90366-1 Pbk : £1.20
(B77-31745)

338'.0941 — Great Britain. Local industrial development. *Conference proceedings*
Indigenous Industrial Development Seminar, *Peterlee, 1975.* Proceedings of a seminar to consider ways of encouraging indigenous industrial development / edited by R. Clubley. — [Peterlee] ([Shotton Hall, Peterlee, Co. Durham SR8 2NB]) : Aycliffe and Peterlee Development Corporations, 1976. — ii-vii,107 leaves : ill, maps, plans ; 30cm.
'... Indigenous Industrial Development Seminar' - Appendix. — '... took place on the 21st October, 1975 in Peterlee ...' - Introduction.
ISBN 0-905790-00-6 Sp : £1.00
(B77-02827)

338'.0941 — Industrialisation. *Great Britain, ca 1700-ca 1850. Secondary school texts*
Beggs-Humphreys, Mary Eleanor. The Industrial Revolution. — 3rd ed. / [by] Mary Beggs Humphreys, Hugh Gregor and Darlow Humphreys. — London : Allen and Unwin, 1976. — 49p : ill, ports ; 25cm.
Previous ed.: / by Mary Eleanor Beggs Humphreys. 1961. — Bibl.: p.48-49.
ISBN 0-04-942151-4 Sd : £1.00
(B77-02106)

338'.0941 — Industries. *Great Britain*
Great Britain. *Central Office of Information. Reference Division.* Organisation and production / [prepared by Reference Division, Central Office of Information]. — 2nd ed. — London : H.M.S.O., 1977. — [3],30p : 2 maps ; 24cm. — (British industry today) (Central Office of Information reference pamphlet ; 127)
Previous ed.: 1975. — Bibl.: p.30.
ISBN 0-11-700922-9 Sd : £0.75
(B77-15140)

Jarratt, Alex. The case for competition : the text of a speech by Alex Jarratt ... at the fifteenth Council dinner of the Institute of Practitioners in Advertising, Painter-Stainers' Hall, London, on 28 September, 1976. — London : I.P.A., 1976. — 12p : port ; 21cm.
ISBN 0-85294-093-9 Sd : £0.50
(B77-03432)

338'.0941 — Industries. *Great Britain, 1870-1977*
Essays in British business history / edited for the Economic History Society by Barry Supple. — Oxford : Clarendon Press, 1977. — viii,267p ; 24cm.
ISBN 0-19-877087-1 : £7.50 : CIP rev.
ISBN 0-19-877088-x Pbk : £4.50
(B77-31045)

338'.0941 — Industries. *Great Britain. Statistics*
Report on the census of production / ... Business Statistics Office. — London : H.M.S.O. — (Business monitor)
1972. PA1002 : Summary tables ... — 1977. — 2-219,xii p ; 30cm.
ISBN 0-11-511830-6 Pbk : £5.25
(B77-07163)

1973. PA4691.1 : Abrasives. — 1977. — [1],8,v p ; 30cm.
ISBN 0-11-511845-4 Sd : £0.60
(B77-12914)

Wood, Edward Geoffrey. British industries : a comparison of performance : output, employment, wages and salaries, capital expenditure, manpower productivity / researched and compiled by E.G. Wood. — London [etc.] : McGraw-Hill, 1976. — xi,78, 384p ; 30cm.
Index.
ISBN 0-07-084484-4 Pbk : £39.50
(B77-05924)

338'.0941 — Manufacturing industries. *Great Britain*
Great Britain. *Central Office of Information. Reference Division.* Manufacturing industries / [prepared by Reference Division, Central Office of Information]. — 2nd ed. — London : H.M.S.O, 1977. — [3],23p ; 24cm. — (British industry today) (Central Office of Information reference pamphlet ; 126)
Previous ed.: 1975. — Bibl.: p.23.
ISBN 0-11-700920-2 Sd : £0.75
(B77-17976)

338'.0941 — Manufacturing industries established since 1950. *Great Britain. Reports, surveys*
Arthur D. Little Limited. New technology-based firms in the United Kingdom and the Federal Republic of Germany : a report / prepared for the Anglo-German Foundation for the Study of Industrial Society by Arthur D. Little Ltd. — London [etc.] : The Society ; [London] : Distributed by Wilton House Publications, 1977. — ix,323p : ill ; 28cm. — (Anglo-German Foundation for the Study of Industrial Society. Series A ; 0177)
Text in English, introduction and summary in English and German.
ISBN 0-905492-04-8 Pbk : £15.00
Also classified at 338'.0943
(B77-27726)

338'.0941 — Nationalised industries. *Great Britain. Inquiry reports*
National Economic Development Office. A study of UK nationalised industries : their role in the economy and control in the future : a report to the Government from the National Economic Development Office. — London : H.M.S.O., 1976. — 55p : ill ; 30cm.
ISBN 0-11-700844-3 Sd : £1.50
(B77-04010)

National Economic Development Office. A study of UK nationalised industries : their role in the economy and control in the future : a report to the Government from the National Economic Development Office. — London : H.M.S.O. Appendix volume. — 1976. — iv,142p : ill ; 30cm.
ISBN 0-11-700845-1 Pbk : £3.50
(B77-04011)

338'.0941 — Nationalised industries. National Economic Development Office. Study of UK nationalised industries. *Great Britain. Critical studies. Collections*
Comments by nationalised industries on the National Economic Development Office report : second special report from the Select Committee on Nationalised Industries, session 1976-77. — London : H.M.S.O., [1977]. — lxiii p ; 25cm. — ([1976-77 H.C.]345)
ISBN 0-10-234577-5 Sd : £1.10
(B77-29248)

338'.09411 — Industries. *Scotland, ca 1850-ca 1970. Illustrations*
Scotland / [compiled by] I. Donnachie, J. Hume & M. Moss. — Buxton (The Market Place, Hartington, Buxton, Derbyshire SK17 0AL) : Moorland Publishing Company, 1977. — 112p : chiefly ill ; 25cm. — (Historic industrial scenes)
Bibl.: p.111. — Index.
ISBN 0-903485-40-0 : £4.20
(B77-30026)

338'.09411 — Industries. Effects of exploitation of North Sea natural gas & petroleum deposits. *Scotland. Reports, surveys*
Joint Standing Committee of the Scottish Economic Council and the Oil Development Council for Scotland. Scottish industry and offshore markets / [Joint Standing Committee of the Scottish Economic Council and the Oil Development Council for Scotland]. — Edinburgh : H.M.S.O., 1977. — [2],18p ; 21cm.

'Published for the Scottish Office at the request of the Scottish Economic Council and the Oil Development Council for Scotland'.
ISBN 0-11-491480-x Sd : £0.50
(B77-15141)

338'.094113'5 — Scotland. Shetland. Industrial development. Implications of exploitation of petroleum deposits in North Sea
Marshall, Elizabeth, *b.1947.* Shetland's oil era / [compiled by Elizabeth Marshall]. — Lerwick (93 Olaf St., Lerwick, Shetland ZE1 0ES) : Research and Development Department, Shetland Islands Council, [1977]. — 73p : ill, maps, plan ; 30cm.
Bibl.: p.73.
Sd : £3.00
(B77-26881)

338'.09417 — Industries. *Ireland (Republic), 1976-1986. Proposals*
Sinn Fein. *Department of Economic Affairs. Research Section.* The Irish industrial revolution / Research Section, Department of Economic Affairs, Sinn Fein-The Workers' Party. — Dublin (30 Gardiner Place, Dublin 1) : Repsol Publications, 1977. — [4],iii,3-151p : ill ; 26cm. — (Studies in political economy)
ISBN 0-86064-009-4 Pbk : £1.30
Also classified at 330.9'415'08
(B77-12915)

338'.0942 — Industries. *England. Rural regions, 1919-1923. Reports, surveys*
FitzRandolph, Helen E. The rural industries of England & Wales : a survey made on behalf of the Agricultural Economics Research Institute, Oxford / [by Helen E. FitzRandolph, M. Doriel Hay, A.M. Jones]. — Wakefield : EP Publishing.
Index.
1 : Timber and underwood industries and some village workshops / by Helen E. FitzRandolph and M. Doriel Hay. — 1977. — xv,239p,[11] leaves of plates : ill ; 23cm.
Facsimile reprint of: 1st ed. Oxford : Clarendon Press, 1926.
ISBN 0-7158-1229-7 : £5.95 : CIP rev.
(B77-14109)

FitzRandolph, Helen E. The rural industries of England & Wales : a survey made on behalf of the Agricultural Economics Research Institute, Oxford. — Wakefield : EP Publishing.
2 : Osier-growing and basketry and some rural factories / by Helen E. FitzRandolph and M. Doriel Hay. — 1977. — xii,159p,[9] leaves of plates : ill ; 23cm.
Facsimile reprint of: 1st ed. Oxford : Clarendon Press, 1926. — Index.
ISBN 0-7158-1232-7 : £4.95 : CIP rev.
(B77-18613)

338'.09421 — Manufacturing industries. Decline. *London. Reports, surveys*
Weatheritt, L. Manufacturing industry in Greater London / by L. Weatheritt and A.F. Lovett ; [for the Greater London Council] Director-General's Department Policy Studies and Intelligence Branch. — London : G.L.C., 1975. — [1],ii,26[i.e.35]p : ill ; 30cm. — (Greater London Council. Intelligence Unit. Research memoranda ; RM498 ISSN 0306-7203)
ISBN 0-7168-0853-6 Sd : £2.30
(B77-16243)

338'.09422'323 — Industries. *Kent. Lower Medway Valley, 1800-1950*
Preston, J M. Industrial Medway : an historical survey : the industrial development of the lower Medway valley with special reference to the nineteenth and early twentieth centuries / [by] J.M. Preston. — Rochester (Borstal Rd, Rochester, Kent) : The author, 1977. — ix, 218p : ill, maps ; 25cm.
Bibl.: p.209-216. — Index.
ISBN 0-9505733-0-2 : £4.95
(B77-22425)

338'.09422'732 — Industries. *Hampshire. Romsey, to 1975*
Lower Test Valley Archaeological Study Group. Old Romsey at work : a history of industry and transport in Romsey, Hampshire / compiled and published by the Lower Test Valley Archaeological Study Group ; cover illustration by Sybil Panton. — [Romsey] ([c/o Mrs P. Genge, 3 Linden Rd, Romsey, Hants.]) : LVTAS Group, 1976. — [4],43p : ill, maps, ports ; 21cm.
ISBN 0-9503980-2-0 Sd : £0.90
Also classified at 380.5'09422'732
(B77-05925)

338'.09423'41 — Industries & trades. *Jersey, to 1973*
Ahier, Philip. A short parochial and commercial history of Jersey / by Philip Ahier and W.S. Ashworth. — [St Helier] ([5 Burlington House, St Saviour's Rd, St Helier, Jersey, C.I.]) : Ashton and Denton Publishing Co., [1977]. — 145p,[2]p of plates(2 fold) : ill, 2 geneal tables, map ; 22cm.
Sd : £1.75
Primary classification 942.3'41
(B77-23024)

338'.09426'752 — Essex. South Woodham Ferrers. Industrial development. *Proposals*
Essex *(County). Council.* South Woodham Ferrers, phase one, eastern industrial area : development brief / Essex County Council. — [Chelmsford] ([County Hall, Chelmsford, Essex]) : [The Council], 1977. — 44p(6 fold) : ill, 2 maps, plans ; 30cm.
Sp : £2.00
(B77-18614)

338'.09427'34 — Industries. *Greater Manchester (Metropolitan County). Marple & Mellor, to 1976*
Workers' Educational Association. *Marple Branch.* Historic industries of Marple and Mellor / by members of the Marple Branch of the Workers' Educational Association ... ; edited by Owen Ashmore. — [Stockport] ([Bibliographical Services Unit, Torkington Lodge, Hazel Grove, Stockport, Cheshire SK7 4RQ]) : Metropolitan Borough of Stockport Recreation and Culture Division, 1977. — [4], 120,[2]p,[23]leaves of plates,[2]p of plates : ill, maps, port ; 21cm.
ISBN 0-905164-07-5 Sd : £1.00
(B77-29249)

338'.09428'15 — Industries. *West Yorkshire (Metropolitan County). Knottingley, to 1977*
Knottingley District Civic Society. Knottingley : its origins and industries / Knottingley District Civic Society. — [Knottingley] ([The Grove, Marine Villa Rd, Knottingley, W. Yorkshire]) : The Society.
Part 1 / [editor Diana Blanchard]. — 1977. — 52p : ill, facsim ; 21cm.
Bibl.
ISBN 0-9505720-0-4 Sd : £1.00
(B77-15142)

338'.09428'2 — South Yorkshire (Metropolitan County). Industrial development. Related to transport, to 1975
Abell, Paul Henry. Transport and industry in South Yorkshire / by P.H. Abell ; maps by S.A. Harper. — Barnsley (14 The Croft, Elsecar, Barnsley, S. Yorkshire S74 8EB) : The author, 1977. — [1],84p : ill, maps ; 21cm.
Bibl.: p.79-80. — Index.
ISBN 0-901182-02-8 Sd : £1.50
Primary classification 380.5'09428'2
(B77-26987)

338'.0943 — Manufacturing industries established since 1950. *West Germany. Reports, surveys*
Arthur D. Little Limited. New technology-based firms in the United Kingdom and the Federal Republic of Germany : a report / prepared for the Anglo-German Foundation for the Study of Industrial Society by Arthur D. Little Ltd. — London [etc.] : The Society ; [London] : Distributed by Wilton House Publications, 1977. — ix,323p : ill ; 28cm. — (Anglo-German Foundation for the Study of Industrial Society. Series A ; 0177)
Text in English, introduction and summary in English and German.
ISBN 0-905492-04-8 Pbk : £15.00
Primary classification 338'.0941
(B77-27726)

338'.0943 — West Germany. Industrial development. Compared with industrial development in France, 1950-1970
Dyas, Gareth P. The emerging European enterprise : strategy and structure in French and German industry / [by] Gareth P. Dyas, Heinz T. Thanheiser. — London [etc.] : Macmillan, 1976. — viii,337p : ill ; 23cm.
Bibl.: p.330-332. — Index.
ISBN 0-333-17953-6 : £12.00
Also classified at 338'.0944
(B77-05265)

338'.0944 — France. Industrial development. Compared with industrial development in West Germany, 1950-1970
Dyas, Gareth P. The emerging European enterprise : strategy and structure in French and German industry / [by] Gareth P. Dyas, Heinz T. Thanheiser. — London [etc.] : Macmillan, 1976. — viii,337p : ill ; 23cm.
Bibl.: p.330-332. — Index.
ISBN 0-333-17953-6 : £12.00
Primary classification 338'.0943
(B77-05265)

338'.0951 — Business enterprise. *China, ca 1850-1912*
Chan, Wellington K K. Merchants, mandarins and modern enterprise in late Ch'ing China / by Wellington K.K. Chan. — [Cambridge, Mass.] : East Asian Research Center, Harvard University ; Cambridge, Mass. ; London : Distributed by Harvard University Press, 1977. — xiv,323p ; 24cm. — (Harvard East Asian monographs ; 79)
Bibl.: p.279-303. — Index.
ISBN 0-674-56915-6 : £10.50
(B77-27727)

338'.0951 — China. Industrial development, 1949-1975
Andors, Stephen. China's industrial revolution : politics, planning and management, 1949 to the present / by Stephen Andors. — London : Martin Robertson, 1977. — xviii,345p : ill, forms ; 24cm.
Also published: New York : Random House, 1977. — Bibl.: p.323-332. — Index.
ISBN 0-85520-221-1 : £10.00
(B77-26882)

338'.0951 — Industrialisation. *China. Rural regions, 1958-1976*
Sigurdson, Jon. Rural industrialization in China / by Jon Sigurdson. — [Cambridge, Mass.] : East Asian Research Center, Harvard University ; Cambridge, Mass. ; London : Distributed by Harvard University Press, 1977. — xvi,281p : ill, map ; 24cm. — (Harvard East Asian monographs ; 73)
Bibl.: p.259-262. — Index.
ISBN 0-674-78072-8 : £10.25
(B77-30027)

338'.0954 — Industries. *India (Republic). Reports, surveys. For British businessmen*
India 1977 : a report of a British Industrial Co-operation Mission to India, November 1976, organised jointly by the CBI and the India, Pakistan and Bangladesh Association, and supported by the British Overseas Trade Board. — London : Confederation of British Industry, 1977. — 32p ; 30cm.
ISBN 0-85201-129-6 Sd : £8.00
(B77-11113)

338'.0973 — Industries. *United States*
The **structure** of American industry / edited by Walter Adams. — 5th ed. — New York : Macmillan ; London : Collier Macmillan, 1977. — xiii,523p : ill ; 24cm.
Previous ed.: 1971. — Bibl. — Index.
ISBN 0-02-300790-7 Pbk : £7.50
(B77-22426)

338'.0981 — Industrialisation. *Brazil, to 1930*
Martins, José de Souza. Agriculture and industry in Brazil : two studies / by José de Souza Martins. — Cambridge (History Faculty Building, West Rd, Cambridge CB3 9EF) : Centre of Latin American Studies, University of Cambridge, 1977. — [5],30,ii p ; 33cm. — (University of Cambridge. Centre of Latin American Studies. Working papers ; no.27 ISSN 0306-6290)
Sd : Unpriced
(B77-29250)

338.1 — AGRICULTURAL INDUSTRIES
Ritson, Christopher. Agricultural economics : principles and policy / [by] Christopher Ritson. — London : Crosby Lockwood Staples, 1977. — xiii,409p : ill ; 24cm.
Index.
ISBN 0-258-96938-5 : £7.95
(B77-33667)

338.1 — Agricultural industries. Ecological aspects
Radical agriculture / edited by Richard Merrill. — New York [etc.] ; London : Harper and Row, 1976. — xix,459p : ill, map, 2 plans ; 21cm. — (Harper colophon books)
Also published: New York : New York University Press, 1976. — Bibl. — Index.
ISBN 0-06-090337-6 Pbk : £5.20
(B77-02107)

338.1 — Agricultural industries. Geographical aspects. *Secondary school texts*
Walker, Michael J. Agricultural location : concepts and techniques / [by] Michael J. Walker. — Oxford : Blackwell, 1977. — 80p : ill(chiefly col), form, col maps ; 25cm.
Bibl.: p.78.
ISBN 0-631-93660-2 Sd : £1.95
(B77-24066)

338.1 — Part-time agricultural industries. *Organisation for Economic Co-operation and Development countries. Reports, surveys*
Organisation for Economic Co-operation and Development. Part-time farming : Germany, Japan, Norway, United States / [Organisation for Economic Co-operation and Development]. — Paris : O.E.C.D. ; [London] : [H.M.S.O.], 1977. — [157]p : 1 ill, maps ; 30cm. — (Organisation for Economic Co-operation and Development. Agricultural policy reports)
Pbk : £3.20
ISBN 92-64-11630-3
(B77-14110)

338.1 — Part-time agricultural industries. *Western Europe. Reports, surveys*
Part-time farming : its nature and implications : a workshop report. — Ashford, Kent : Centre for European Agricultural Studies, Wye College, 1977. — [6],42,[6]p : 2 ill ; 30cm. — (Wye College. Centre for European Agricultural Studies. Seminar papers ; no.2 ISSN 0307-1111)
'... the Centre invited a small group of academics to take part in a workshop during July 1976' - Foreword. — English text, French and German summaries and contents lists.
ISBN 0-905378-02-4 Sd : £2.00
(B77-23209)

338.1 — Services for agricultural industries. *England. Serials*
At the farmer's service : a handy reference to various services available to farmers in England and Wales / [Ministry of Agriculture, Fisheries and Food]. — Pinner : The Ministry.
[1977-78]. — 1977. — 71,[1]p ; 19cm.
Index.
Sd : Unpriced
(B77-31746)

338.1'05 — Agricultural industries. *Periodicals*
World crops and livestock : the journal of international agriculture. — London (40 Wellington St., WC2E 7BD) : World Crops Publications Ltd.
Vol.29, no.1- ; Jan.-Feb. 1977-. — [1977]-. — ill, maps, ports ; 29cm.
Six issues a year. — Continues: World crops. — p.49-96 in Mar.-Apr. 1977 issue. — English text, French and Spanish summaries.
Pbk : £1.25(£6.00 yearly)
ISSN 0309-7161
(B77-15143)

338.1'06'241 — Agricultural industries. Organisations. *Great Britain. National Farmers' Union. Yearbooks*
National Farmers' Union. Handbook / National Farmers' Union. — London (Agriculture House, Knightsbridge, SW1X 7NJ) : The Union.
1977-78. — [1977]. — 61p : 1 ill, coat of arms ; 22cm.
Sd : £1.00
(B77-20095)

338.1'06'24226 — Agricultural industries. Organisations. *West Sussex. West Sussex Growers' Association. Periodicals*
West Sussex Growers' Association. Newsletter / West Sussex Growers' Association. — Arundel (Westbury House, Queen's La., Arundel, West Sussex BN18 9JW) : The Association.
[No.1]- ; Jan. 1977-. — [1977]-. — 30cm.
Monthly. — 6p. in 1st issue.
Sd : Unpriced
ISSN 0140-6930
(B77-15743)

338.1'06'24229 — Agricultural industries. Organisations. *Berkshire. National Farmers' Union. Oxford and Berkshire County Branch. Yearbooks*
Oxford and Berkshire farmers' year book. — Oxford (269 Banbury Rd, Oxford [OX2 7JE]) : Oxford and Berkshire Executive, National Farmers' Union.
1977. — [1977]. — [1],71p : ill ; 22cm.
Sd : Unpriced
Also classified at 338.1'06'24257
(B77-17353)

338.1'06'24257 — Agricultural industries. Organisations. *Oxfordshire. National Farmers' Union. Oxford and Berkshire County Branch. Yearbooks*
Oxford and Berkshire farmers' year book. — Oxford (269 Banbury Rd, Oxford [OX2 7JE]) : Oxford and Berkshire Executive, National Farmers' Union.
1977. — [1977]. — [1],71p : ill ; 22cm.
Sd : Unpriced
Primary classification 338.1'06'24229
(B77-17353)

338.1'07'23 — Agricultural industries. Farms. Surveys. *Great Britain. Directories*
Register of farm surveys in the United Kingdom and Eire / compiled by a working party formed following a conference on farm surveys in July 1975. — [Exeter] ([c/o W.J.K. Thomas, Agricultural Economics Unit, University of Exeter, Exeter]) : [The Working Party], 1976. — [7],93p : form ; 30cm.
Index.
ISBN 0-901165-61-1 Pbk : £1.00
(B77-11114)

338.1'09172'4 — Agricultural industries. *Developing countries. Conference proceedings*
Rural poverty and agribusiness : conference proceedings / editor Michael Lipton. — Brighton : Institute of Development Studies, 1977. — [6],xiii,86p ; 30cm. — (Institute of Development Studies. Discussion papers ; 104 ISSN 0308-5864)
Sd : £3.00
(B77-18615)

338.1'09172'4 — Agricultural industries. Economic development. *Developing countries*
Growing out of poverty / edited by Elizabeth Stamp. — Oxford [etc.] : Oxford University Press, 1977. — x,165p : 1 ill, maps ; 23cm.
ISBN 0-19-857529-7 : £4.25 : CIP rev.
ISBN 0-19-857528-9 Pbk : £1.95
(B77-22427)

338.1'0941 — Agricultural industries. *Great Britain*
Eltringham, Denham. Agriculture / by D. Eltringham. — Revised ed. — Aylesbury : Ginn, 1977. — 49p : ill ; 22cm. — (Manchester Economics Project. Satellite books ; 5)
With answers. — Previous ed.: London : Ginn, 1970.
ISBN 0-602-22333-4 Sd : £1.10
(B77-19258)

Great Britain. *Central Office of Information. Reference Division.* Agriculture in Britain / [prepared by Reference Division, Central Office of Information]. — 7th ed. — London : H.M.S.O., 1977. — [3],71p ; 24cm. — (Central Office of Information reference pamphlet ; 43)
Bibl.: p.70-71.
ISBN 0-11-700918-0 Sd : £1.40
(B77-17977)

338.1'0941 — Agricultural industries. *Great Britain, 1650-1880. Readings from contemporary sources*
The **agricultural** revolution : changes in agriculture, 1650-1880 / edited and with an introduction by G.E. Mingay. — London : A. and C. Black, 1977. — ix,322p : ill, forms, maps, plans ; 23cm. — (Documents in economic history)
Index.
ISBN 0-7136-1703-9 : £6.95
(B77-15144)

338.1'0941 — Agricultural industries. *Great Britain, 1968-1975. Reports, surveys*
Great Britain. *Ministry of Agriculture, Fisheries and Food.* The changing structure of agriculture, 1968-1975 / Ministry of Agriculture, Fisheries and Food [and] Department of Agriculture and Fisheries for Scotland [and] Department of Agriculture for Northern Ireland. — London : H.M.S.O., 1977. — 78p : 1 ill ; 25cm.
ISBN 0-11-241103-7 Sd : £1.50
(B77-31046)

338.1'0941 — Agricultural industries. *Great Britain. Periodicals*
Big farm weekly. — London (93 Goswell Rd, EC1V 7QA) : Northwood Publications Ltd.
No.1- ; Jan. 21, 1977-. — 1977-. — ill, ports ; 41cm.
Weekly. — 32p. in 1st issue.
Sd : £0.20
ISSN 0309-4766
(B77-08848)

338.1'0941 — Agricultural industries. *Great Britain. Reports, surveys. Serials*
Annual review of agriculture / presented to Parliament by the Secretary of State for Northern Ireland ... [et al.]. — London : H.M.S.O.
1977. — [1977]. — iv,45p ; 25cm. — (Cmnd.6703)
ISBN 0-10-167030-3 Sd : £1.00
(B77-09566)

338.1'0941 — Agricultural industries. *Great Britain. Statistics*
Agricultural statistics, United Kingdom : agricultural censuses and production, with separate figures for England and Wales, Scotland, Great Britain and Northern Ireland, price indices for main agricultural products and materials / Ministry of Agriculture, Fisheries and Food [and] Department of Agriculture and Fisheries for Scotland [and] Department of Agriculture for Northern Ireland. — London : H.M.S.O.
1974. — 1977. — xiii,75p ; 25cm.
ISBN 0-11-241021-9 Pbk : £2.25
ISSN 0065-4590
(B77-13553)

338.1'0941 — Agricultural industries. *Great Britain, to 1964*
Whitlock, Ralph. A short history of farming in Britain / by Ralph Whitlock. — Wakefield : EP Publishing, 1977. — [1],246p,leaf of plate,[22]p of plates : ill ; 21cm.
Originally published: London : J. Baker, 1965. — Bibl.: p.225-227. — Index.
ISBN 0-7158-1208-4 : £6.25
(B77-28467)

338.1'0941 — Agricultural industries. Forecasts. *Great Britain. Food from our own resources. Secondary school texts*
Walton, Brian. Food from our own resources : a student's guide to the April 1975 White Paper on agricultural policy / by Brian Walton, David Richardson, Peter Maunder. — London (Room 340, Hamilton House, Mabledon Place, WC1H 9BH) : Economics Association, 1976. — [2],24,[1]p : ill ; 21cm.
Bibl.: p.24.
Sd : £0.40
(B77-17354)

338.1'0941 — Agricultural products. *Great Britain. Statistics*
Output and utilisation of farm produce in the United Kingdom / Ministry of Agriculture, Fisheries and Food. — [Pinner] : [The Ministry].
1969-70 to 1975-76. — 1977. — [1],46p ; 29cm.
Sd : £3.00
(B77-29251)

338.1'09411 — Agricultural industries. *Scotland, 1700-1900. Secondary school texts*
Simpson, Eric. Farming and the countryside, 1700-1900 / [by] Eric Simpson and Nicholas Tate. — Edinburgh : Holmes McDougall, 1976. — 48p : ill, maps, ports ; 25cm. — (Scottish search series)
Bibl.: p.47-48.
ISBN 0-7157-1476-7 Sd : £1.05
(B77-30028)

338.1'09411 — Agricultural industries. *Scotland. Reports, surveys. Serials*
Agriculture in Scotland report ... / Department of Agriculture and Fisheries for Scotland. — Edinburgh : H.M.S.O.
1976. — [1977]. — viii,89p ; 25cm. — (Cmnd.6756)
Bibl.: p.87-89.
ISBN 0-10-167560-7 Sd : £1.50
(B77-17978)

338.1'094111 — Agricultural industries. *Scotland. Highlands & Islands, 1965-1975*
Bryden, John Marshall. Agrarian change in the Scottish Highlands : the role of the Highlands and Islands Development Board in the agricultural economy of the crofting counties / [by] John Bryden, George Houston. — London : Martin Robertson [for] the Board, 1976. — xiv,152p : ill, maps ; 24cm. — (Glasgow social & economic research studies ; 14)
Bibl.: p.143-145. — Index.
ISBN 0-85520-151-7 : £7.50
(B77-08271)

338.1'09413 — Agricultural industries. *South-east Scotland. Statistics*
Profitability of farming in South East Scotland / the East of Scotland College of Agriculture, Economics and Farm Business Management Department. — Edinburgh (The Librarian, West Mains Rd, Edinburgh EH9 3JG) : E.S.C.A.
1974-75. — 1976. — viii,52p : map ; 21cm. — (East of Scotland College of Agriculture. Bulletins ; no.16 ISSN 0306-8668)
ISBN 0-902164-22-8 Sd : £0.80
(B77-00656)

338.1'09416 — Agricultural industries. *Northern Ireland. Reports, surveys. Serials*
Northern Ireland agriculture : annual general report of the Department of Agriculture [Northern Ireland], year ended 31 March. — Belfast : H.M.S.O.
[1975]-1976 : 35th. — 1976. — 163p : ill ; 25cm.
ISBN 0-337-05175-5 Pbk : £2.00
(B77-07164)

338.1'09417 — Agricultural industries. *Ireland (Republic). Conference proceedings*
Agricultural Development Prospects and Possibilities *(Conference), Dublin, 1976.* Proceedings of conference, Agricultural Development Prospects and Possibilities, [organized by] An Foras Talúntais [Economics & Rural Welfare Research Centre]. — Dublin (19 Sandymount Ave., Dublin 4) : The Centre, [1976]. — [9],145[i.e.151]p : ill ; 21cm.
'... [held] November 25 [1976], Jury's Hotel, Dublin 4' - p.[9].
Sd : £1.50
(B77-11659)

338.1'09417 — Agricultural industries. *Ireland (Republic). Irish Farmers' Association viewpoints*
Llewellyn, Tom. 'Farmers have it easy' / [compiled by Tom Llewellyn] ; design and illustration by Brian Mulvany. — Dublin (Irish Farm Centre, Bluebell, Dublin 12) : Irish Farmers' Association, [1977]. — [2],24p : chiefly col ill, col port ; 30cm.
Sd : £1.00
(B77-20984)

338.1'09417 — Agricultural industries. *Ireland (Republic). Serials*
The **progressive** farmers' annual. — Dublin (3 Lr Abbey St., Dublin 1) : Farming Publications.
[1977]. — [1977]. — [1],92p : ill, map, ports ; 30cm.
Cover title: Progressive farmers' year-book.
ISBN 0-906062-00-4 Sd : £0.75
(B77-15145)

338.1'0942 — Agricultural industries. *England. Statistics*
Agricultural statistics, England and Wales / Ministry of Agriculture, Fisheries and Food. — London : H.M.S.O.
1974 : Acreage and production of crops, numbers of livestock, agricultural workers, agricultural holdings and certain items of agricultural machinery and implements for 1974, prices of agricultural products, store stock, feedingstuffs and fertilisers for the year 1973 and the harvest year 1973-1974. — 1976. — xiv,189p ; 25cm.
ISBN 0-11-241065-0 Pbk : £3.75
(B77-12916)

Farm classification in England and Wales / Ministry of Agriculture, Fisheries and Food. — London : H.M.S.O.
1975. — 1977. — iv,113p ; 25cm.
ISBN 0-11-241055-3 Pbk : £2.50
(B77-12362)

338.1'0942 — Agricultural industries. Farms. *England, to ca 1950*
Seebohm, Mabel Elizabeth. The evolution of the English farm / [by] M.E. Seebohm. — Revised 2nd ed. — Wakefield : EP Publishing, 1976. — 356p,[3] leaves of plates : ill, plans ; 23cm.
This ed. originally published: London : Allen and Unwin, 1952. — Bibl.: p.344-350. — Index.

ISBN 0-7158-1173-8 : £6.25
(B77-05266)

338.1'09422 — Agricultural industries. Farms. *South-east England. Statistics*
Wye College. *Farm Business Unit.* Farm business statistics for south east England / Wye College School of Rural Economics and Related Studies, Farm Business Unit. — [Ashford, Kent] : [The Unit].
1976 supplement. — [1976]. — [1],52p ; 22cm.
ISBN 0-901859-56-7 Sd : £1.20
(B77-11115)

1977 supplement. — [1977]. — [1],44p ; 21cm.
ISBN 0-901859-65-6 Sd : £1.20
(B77-26883)

338.1'09423 — Agricultural industries & trades. *South-west England, to 1900. Essays*
Population and marketing : two studies in the history of the South-west / edited by Walter Minchinton. — [Exeter] : University of Exeter, 1976. — 139p : ill, maps ; 30cm. — (Exeter papers in economic history ; no.11)
Papers from two seminars held at Dartington.
ISBN 0-85989-035-x Pbk : £1.75
Primary classification 301.32'9'423
(B77-20914)

338.1'09423 — Agricultural industries. Farms. *South-west England. Statistics*
Financial results of farming in the Exeter province / University of Exeter, Agricultural Economics Unit. — Exeter (Lafrowda House, St German's Rd, Exeter EX4 6TL) : University of Exeter, Agricultural Economics Unit.
1974-75 and 1975-76 : (based on an identical sample of 257 farms). — 1976. — [2],21p ; 30cm.
ISBN 0-901165-60-3 Sd : £0.50
(B77-04629)

338.1'09423'39 — Agricultural industries. *Dorset. Winkton region, 1855-1875*
Lavender, Ruth. The farmers of Winkton Tithing, 1855-1875 / by Ruth Lavender. — [Dorchester] ([County Hall, Dorchester, Dorset]) : Dorset County Council Education Committee, [1977]. — [3],13[i.e.15]p : map ; 21cm.
ISBN 0-85216-144-1 Sd : £0.25
(B77-17979)

338.1'09424'49 — Agricultural industries. *Hereford and Worcester. Vale of Evesham, 1875-1900*
Robinson, G M. Late Victorian agriculture in the Vale of Evesham / [by] G.M. Robinson. — Oxford (Mansfield Rd, Oxford OX1 3TB) : [University of Oxford] School of Geography, 1976. — 32p : maps ; 22cm. — (University of Oxford. School of Geography. Research papers ; 16 ISSN 0305-8190)
Bibl.: p.29-32.
Sd : Unpriced
(B77-11660)

338.1'09425 — Agricultural industries. *England. East Midlands. Reports, surveys. Serials*
Farming in the East Midlands, financial results / [University of Nottingham, Department of Agriculture and Horticulture]. — Sutton Bonington : The Department.
1975-76 : 25th annual report. — 1977. — 62p : map ; 24cm.
ISBN 0-900573-43-0 Sd : £1.30
(B77-14111)

338.1'09425'8 — Agricultural industries. *South-west Hertfordshire, 1600-1800*
Longman, Grant. A corner of England's garden : an agrarian history of South-west Hertfordshire, 1600-1850 / by Grant Longman. — [Bushey] ([48 Duncan Way, Bushey, Herts.]) : [E.G. Longman], [1977]. — 2v.(iv,96p,[4]p of plates;74p) : ill, maps ; 23cm.
Index.
Sd : £4.50
(B77-17355)

338.1'09427'8 — Agricultural industries. *Cumbria. Yearbooks*
Cumbria farming year book. — Carlisle (12 Lonsdale St., Carlisle) : 'Cumbria Weekly Digest' : 'Lakescene'.
1977-78. — 1977. — 120p : ill ; 22cm.
Sd : Unpriced
ISSN 0309-5940
(B77-17356)

338.1'09428'1 — Agricultural industries. *Yorkshire. Reports, surveys. Serials*
Farming in Yorkshire / [Askham Bryan College of Agriculture and Horticulture, Department of Management, Farm Management Survey Unit]. — [York] ([Askham Bryan, York]) : The Department.
1975-76. — 1976. — 76p in various pagings ; 22x30cm.
Cover title. — Previously published: as 'Types of farming in Yorkshire'.
Pbk : £2.00
ISSN 0309-6114
(B77-16771)

338.1'0947 — Agricultural industries. *Russia, ca 1000-ca 1700*
Smith, Robert Ernest Frederick. Peasant farming in Muscovy / [by] R.E.F. Smith. — Cambridge [etc.] : Cambridge University Press, 1977. — xii,289p,[12]p of plates : ill, geneal tables, maps ; 24cm.
Bibl.: p.266-279. — Index.
ISBN 0-521-20912-9 : £10.50
(B77-15146)

338.1'0947 — Agricultural industries. *Soviet Union, to 1976*
Soviet agriculture : an assessment of its contributions to economic development / edited by Harry G. Shaffer. — New York ; London : Praeger, 1977. — xvii,167p ; 25cm. — (Praeger special studies in international economics and development)
ISBN 0-03-021976-0 : £11.70
(B77-31047)

338.1'09489 — Agricultural industries. *Denmark*
Murray, James William. Growth and change in Danish agriculture / [by] J.W. Murray. — London : Hutchinson, 1977. — 64p : ill(chiefly col), col map ; 23cm.
Index.
ISBN 0-09-127860-0 : £3.50
ISBN 0-09-127861-9 Pbk : £0.95
(B77-26884)

338.1'0951 — Agricultural industries. *China, 1949-1975*
Kuo, Leslie Tse-chiu. Agriculture in the People's Republic of China : structural changes and technical transformation / [by] Leslie T.C. Kuo. — New York [etc.] ; London : Praeger, [1977]. — xx,289p : 2 maps ; 25cm. — (Praeger special studies in international economics and development)
Published in the United States: 1976. — Index.
ISBN 0-275-05870-0 : £16.00
(B77-12363)

338.1'0954 — Agricultural industries. Effects of increases in crop yields. *Eastern India (Republic). Reports, surveys*
Mandal, G C. Economics of the Green Revolution : a study in east India / [by] G.C. Mandal, M.G. Ghosh. — London : Asia Publishing House, 1976. — xvi,115p ; 22cm.
Index.
ISBN 0-210-40571-6 : £5.00
(B77-10755)

338.1'0955 — Agricultural industries. *Iran, 1900-1975*
Aresvik, Oddvar. The agricultural development of Iran / [by] Oddvar Aresvik. — New York [etc.] ; London : Praeger, 1976. — xxv,271,[1] p : ill, maps ; 25cm. — (Praeger special studies in international economics and development)
Bibl.: p.262-271.
ISBN 0-275-00170-9 : £16.75
(B77-05267)

338.1'0966'4 — Agricultural industries. *Sierra Leone*
Levi, John. African agriculture : economic action and reaction in Sierra Leone / by John Levi with contributions by Michael Havinden, Omotunde E.G. Johnson and Gerald L. Karr. — Slough : Commonwealth Agricultural Bureaux, 1976. — [5],xviii,428p : ill, maps ; 22cm. — (Commonwealth Bureau of Agricultural Economics. Miscellaneous publications ; no.2)
Bibl.: p.409-428.
ISBN 0-85198-374-x Pbk : £5.45
(B77-07165)

338.1′0966′51 — Agricultural industries. Development. *Gambia. Feasibility studies*
Great Britain. *Ministry of Overseas Development. Land Resources Division.* The agricultural development of the Gambia : an agricultural, environmental and socioeconomic analysis / Land Resources Division [Ministry of Overseas Development] ; [written by] J.R. Dunsmore ... [et al.]. — Surbiton : The Division, 1976. — xxi,[1],445p(25 fold) : ill(some col), maps(1 col) ; 30cm. — (Land resource study ; 22 ISSN 0305-6554)
Four fold. sheets (col. maps) in pocket. — Bibl. : p.403-431.
Pbk : £2.50
(B77-19259)

338.1′09669′2 — Agricultural industries. Development. Social factors. *Study regions: Nigeria. Western states*
Osuntogun, Adeniyi. Institutional determinants and constraints on agricultural development : case studies from the Western State of Nigeria / by Adeniyi Osuntogun. — [London] ([10 Percy St., W1P 0JB]) : Joint Programme on Agricultural Development Overseas, [1976?]. — [1],iv,57p ; 30cm.
ISBN 0-85003-061-7 Pbk : £1.00
(B77-00657)

338.1′09676′2 — Agricultural industries. *Kenya*
Agricultural development in Kenya : an economic assessment / editors Judith Heyer, J.K. Maitha, W.M. Senga. — Nairobi ; London [etc.] : Oxford University Press, 1976 [i.e. 1977]. — xv,372p,[8]p of plates : ill(some col), maps ; 24cm.
'First published to coincide with the XVI International Association of Agricultural Economists' Conference, Nairobi, Kenya, July 1976'. — Published in Kenya: 1976. — Index.
ISBN 0-19-572377-5 : £12.50
(B77-08849)

338.1′0973 — Agricultural industries. *United States, to 1975. Encyclopaedias*
Schapsmeier, Edward L. Encyclopedia of American agricultural history / [compiled by] Edward L. Schapsmeier, Frederick H. Schapsmeier. — Westport, Conn. ; London : Greenwood Press, 1975. — xii,467p ; 25cm.
Bibl. — Index.
ISBN 0-8371-7958-0 : £18.15
(B77-17357)

338.1′098 — Agricultural industries. *Latin America*
Lehmann, David. A theory of agrarian structure : typology and paths of transformation in Latin America / by David Lehmann. — Cambridge (History Faculty Building, West Rd, Cambridge CB3 9EF) : [University of Cambridge, Centre of Latin American Studies], [1976]. — [2],iv leaves,104[i.e.105]p : 1 ill ; 30cm. — (University of Cambridge. Centre of Latin American Studies. Working papers ; no.25 ISSN 0306-6290)
ISBN 0-904927-16-4 Sd : £0.50
(B77-00086)

338.1′3 — Agricultural industries. *England. Costs & returns*
Farm incomes in England and Wales : a report based on the Farm Management Survey / Ministry of Agriculture, Fisheries and Food. — London : H.M.S.O.
1975-76 : (including a comparison with 1974-75 and some reference to earlier years). — 1977. — [4],131p : map ; 30cm. — (Farm incomes series ; no.29)
ISBN 0-11-241057-x Pbk : £7.00
(B77-08850)

338.1′3 — Agricultural products. Prices. Developing countries. Related to supply. Econometric models
Askari, Hossein. Agricultural supply response : a survey of the econometric evidence / [by] Hossein Askari, John Thomas Cummings. — New York [etc.] ; London : Praeger ; [London] : [Distributed by Martin Robertson], 1976. — xvii,444p : ill ; 25cm. — (Praeger special studies in international economics and development)
Bibl.: p.414-435. — Index.
ISBN 0-275-23260-3 : £24.05
Also classified at 339.4′8′63091724
(B77-05926)

338.1′3 — Sugar beet industries. Research. Finance. Home Grown Sugar Beet (Research and Education) Fund. *Great Britain. Accounts*
Home Grown Sugar Beet (Research and Education) Fund account ... year ended 31st March ... / [Ministry of Agriculture, Fisheries and Food]. — London : H.M.S.O.
1975-76. — [1977]. — 6p ; 25cm. — ([1976-77 H.C.] 261)
ISBN 0-10-226177-6 Sd : £0.25
(B77-12917)

338.1′6 — Agricultural industries. Research & development. *Ireland (Republic)*
Downey, William Kevin. Technological support for the food industry : [a paper] presented at the Institute of Food Science & Technology of Ireland Seminar, The Irish Food Industry, Accelerating Growth for Profit, Jurys Hotel, May 4th 1976 / by W.K. Downey & M.J. Brennan ; [for the National Science Council]. — Dublin (Government Publications Sale Office, G.P.O. Arcade, Dublin 1) : Stationery Office, [1976]. — [3],60p : ill ; 25cm.
Bibl.: p.59-60.
ISBN 0-7076-0017-0 Pbk : £1.00
(B77-00658)

338.1′6 — Agricultural industries. Small farms. Stored maize. Losses. Evaluation. *Africa. Study regions: Zambia. Research reports*
Adams, John Mervyn. The evaluation of losses in maize stored on a selection of small farms in Zambia with particular reference to the development of methodology / [by] J.M. Adams and G.W. Harman. — London : Tropical Products Institute, 1977. — xi,149p : ill, forms, maps ; 30cm. — (G109)
English text, French and Spanish summaries. — Bibl.: p.126-128.
ISBN 0-85954-058-8 Pbk : £2.80
(B77-17980)

338.1′6 — Agricultural industries. Technological development. Ecological aspects
Dickson, Gordon Ross. The problems of technical advance in agriculture : an inaugural lecture delivered before the University of Newcastle upon Tyne on Tuesday, 11th March, 1975 / [by] Gordon R. Dickson. — Newcastle upon Tyne : University of Newcastle upon Tyne, 1975. — 11p ; 21cm. — (University of Newcastle upon Tyne. Inaugural lectures)
ISBN 0-7017-0002-5 Sd : £0.50
(B77-26885)

338.1′6 — Energy. Consumption by agricultural industries. *Great Britain. Conference proceedings*
Reading University Agricultural Club. *Annual Conference, 10th, University of Reading, 1976.* Energy use and British agriculture : proceedings of the Tenth Annual Conference of the Reading University Agricultural Club, 1976 / edited by D.M. Bather and H. Day. — [Reading] (Department of Agriculture and Horticulture, University of Reading, [Earley Gate, Reading] RG6 2AT) : The Club, 1976. — [6],57p : ill ; 30cm.
Bibl.
ISBN 0-7049-0304-0 Pbk : Unpriced
(B77-20083)

338.1′6 — Feedingstuffs. Responses of livestock. Economic aspects. Analysis
Dillon, John Louis. The analysis of response in crop and livestock production / by John L. Dillon. — 2nd ed. — Oxford [etc.] : Pergamon, 1977. — xiii,213p : ill ; 22cm. — (Pergamon international library)
Previous ed.: 1968. — Bibl.: p.177-195. — Index.
ISBN 0-08-021118-6 : £8.00
ISBN 0-08-021115-1 Pbk : £4.50
Also classified at 338.1′6
(B77-17358)

338.1′6 — Fertilisers. Responses of crops. Economic aspects. Analysis
Dillon, John Louis. The analysis of response in crop and livestock production / by John L. Dillon. — 2nd ed. — Oxford [etc.] : Pergamon, 1977. — xiii,213p : ill ; 22cm. — (Pergamon international library)
Previous ed.: 1968. — Bibl.: p.177-195. — Index.
ISBN 0-08-021118-6 : £8.00
ISBN 0-08-021115-1 Pbk : £4.50
Primary classification 338.1′6
(B77-17358)

338.1′6 — Irrigation. *Ethiopia. Lake Zwai region. Feasibility studies*
Great Britain. *Ministry of Overseas Development. Land Resources Division.* Prospects for irrigation development around Lake Zwai, Ethiopia / Land Resources Division [Ministry of Overseas Development] ; [written by] M.J. Makin ... [et al.]. — Surbiton : The Division, 1976. — xvii,316[i.e.318]p(40 fold) : ill(incl 1 col), maps(some col) ; 30cm. — (Land resource study ; 26 ISSN 0305-6554)
Seven fold. sheets (col. maps) in portfolio. — Bibl.: p.213-217.
ISBN 0-902409-45-x Pbk : £2.50
(B77-08851)

338.1′6 — Irrigation. Afl̄aj. Sociopolitical aspects. *Oman, to 1974*
Wilkinson, John Craven. Water and tribal settlement in South-east Arabia : a study of the afl̄aj of Oman / [by] J.C. Wilkinson. — Oxford : Clarendon Press, 1977. — xvi,276p : ill, maps, plan ; 25cm. — (Oxford research studies in geography)
Bibl.: p.249-257. — Index.
ISBN 0-19-823217-9 : £12.50 : CIP rev.
(B77-09567)

338.1′6 — Pesticides. Economic aspects
Pesticides and human welfare / edited by D.L. Gunn and J.G.R. Stevens. — Oxford [etc.] : Oxford University Press, 1976. — xii,278p : ill ; 23cm.
Bibl. — Index.
ISBN 0-19-854522-3 : £5.00
ISBN 0-19-854526-6 Pbk : £1.75
(B77-20985)

338.1′6 — Rice production industries. Effects of technological change. *South Asia. Study regions: India (Republic). Tamil Nadu (State). North Arcot district. Reports, surveys*
Green revolution? : technology and change in rice-growing areas of Tamil Nadu and Sri Lanka / edited by B.H. Farmer ; foreword by Sir Joseph Hutchinson. — London [etc.] : Macmillan, 1977. — xvii,429p : ill, maps ; 23cm. — (Cambridge Commonwealth series)
Bibl. — Index.
ISBN 0-333-19679-1 : £12.00
Also classified at 338.1′6
(B77-27728)

338.1′6 — Rice production industries. Effects of technological change. *South Asia. Study regions: South-eastern Sri Lanka. Reports, surveys*
Green revolution? : technology and change in rice-growing areas of Tamil Nadu and Sri Lanka / edited by B.H. Farmer ; foreword by Sir Joseph Hutchinson. — London [etc.] : Macmillan, 1977. — xvii,429p : ill, maps ; 23cm. — (Cambridge Commonwealth series)
Bibl. — Index.
ISBN 0-333-19679-1 : £12.00
Primary classification 338.1′6
(B77-27728)

338.1′7′3109417 — Cereals industries & trades. *Ireland (Republic). Reports, surveys*
Dunne, W. The grain market in Ireland : an analysis of the components of grain production, processing and utilisation / [by] W. Dunne. — [Dublin] ([19 Sandymount Ave., Dublin 4]) : [An Foras Talúntais], 1976. — [3],61p : ill ; 21cm. — (Agricultural Institute (Republic of Ireland). Economic research series ; no.21)
ISBN 0-905442-09-1 Sd : £1.00
(B77-02828)

338.1′7′310951 — Cereals. Production. *China. Provinces, 1952-1957. Statistics*
Walker, Kenneth Richard. Provincial grain output in China, 1952-57 : a statistical compilation / [by] Kenneth R. Walker. — London : Contemporary China Institute, University of London School of Oriental and African Studies, 1977. — [4],22p ; 24cm. — (Contemporary China Institute. Research notes and studies ; no.3 ISSN 0308-6119)
ISBN 0-7286-0038-2 Sd : £1.25
(B77-20096)

338.1'7'31105 — Wheat industries & trades. *Reports, surveys. Serials*
Review of the world wheat situation = Examen de la situation mondiale du blé = Examen de la situacion triguera mundial = Obzor polozheniia na mirovom rynke pshenitsy / International Wheat Council = Conseil internationale du blé = Consejo Internacional del Trigo = Mezhdunarodnyĭ Sovet po Pshenitse. — London : The Council.
1975-76. — [1977]. — 3-112p : ill(some col), col map ; 28cm.
English text, foreword and summary in English, French, Spanish and Russian.
ISBN 0-901403-15-6 Pbk : Unpriced
(B77-12918)

338.1'7'349106141 — Potato industries. Organisations. *Potato Marketing Board. Reports, surveys. Serials*
Potato Marketing Board. Annual report and accounts / Potato Marketing Board. — London (50 Hans Cres., Knightsbridge SW1X 0NB) : The Board.
1976. — [1976]. — [2],36p : ill, ports ; 23cm.
ISBN 0-903623-16-1 Sd : Unpriced
(B77-02108)

338.1'7'3491094 — Potato industries & trades. *European Community countries. Reports, surveys*
Thompson, N. A diary of a study tour on the EEC potato crop : a report of the study tour undertaken from the 1st to 14th May 1976 / by N. Thompson ... — London (50 Hans Cres., Knightsbridge, SW1X 0NB) : Potato Marketing Board, 1976. — 23[i.e.24]p ; 21cm. — (James E. Rennie award reports ; no.3 ISSN 0309-2240)
Sd : Unpriced
(B77-04630)

338.1'7'349109411 — Potatoes. Certified crops. *Scotland. Lists. Serials*
Register of potato crops certified : comprising stocks graded 'VTSC', 'VTSC NI', 'FS', 'FS NI', 'AA1 & AA' and 'AA1 & AA NI' / Department of Agriculture and Fisheries for Scotland. — Edinburgh : H.M.S.O.
1976. — 1976. — viii,64p ; 25cm.
Index.
ISBN 0-11-491440-0 Sd : £1.80
(B77-02109)

338.1'7'34910942 — Early potato industries. *England, 1975. Reports, surveys*
Lloyd, A. Early potato production in England and Wales, 1975 / by A. Lloyd. — Aberystwyth (School of Agricultural Sciences, Penglais, Aberystwyth, Dyfed SY23 3DD) : Department of Agricultural Economics, University College of Wales, 1977. — [5],35, [16]p ; 30cm. — (Agricultural enterprise studies in England and Wales [economic reports] ; no.44 ISSN 0306-8900)
ISBN 0-902124-17-x Sp : £1.00
(B77-16244)

338.1'7'34910943 — Potato industries. *West Germany. Reports, surveys*
Nicol, A J. Aspects of potato production in France, Germany and Holland : a report of the study tours undertaken during March-April and July 1976 / by A.J. Nicol ... — London (50 Hans Cres., Knightsbridge, SW1X 0NB) : Potato Marketing Board, 1976. — 24p ; 21cm. — (James E. Rennie award reports ; no.2 ISSN 0309-2240)
Sd : Unpriced
Primary classification 338.1'7'34910944
(B77-04631)

338.1'7'34910944 — Potato industries. *France. Reports, surveys*
Nicol, A J. Aspects of potato production in France, Germany and Holland : a report of the study tours undertaken during March-April and July 1976 / by A.J. Nicol ... — London (50 Hans Cres., Knightsbridge, SW1X 0NB) : Potato Marketing Board, 1976. — 24p ; 21cm. — (James E. Rennie award reports ; no.2 ISSN 0309-2240)
Sd : Unpriced
Also classified at 338.1'7'34910943; 338.1'7'349109492
(B77-04631)

338.1'7'349109492 — Potato industries. *Netherlands. Reports, surveys*
Nicol, A J. Aspects of potato production in France, Germany and Holland : a report of the study tours undertaken during March-April and July 1976 / by A.J. Nicol ... — London (50 Hans Cres., Knightsbridge, SW1X 0NB) : Potato Marketing Board, 1976. — 24p ; 21cm. — (James E. Rennie award reports ; no.2 ISSN 0309-2240)
Sd : Unpriced
Primary classification 338.1'7'34910944
(B77-04631)

338.1'7'36091724 — Sugar industries. Effects of demand for sugar. *Developing countries. Reports, surveys*
Grissa, Abdessatar. Structure of the international sugar market and its impact on developing countries / by Abdessatar Grissa. — Paris : Development Centre of the Organisation for Economic Co-operation and Development ; [London] : [H.M.S.O.], 1976. — [2],v,120p : ill ; 27cm. — (Organisation for Economic Co-operation and Development. Development Centre. Studies)
Pbk : £2.20
ISBN 92-64-11473-4
(B77-00659)

338.1'7'361097291 — Cuba. Economic development. Role of cane sugar industries, 1952-1973
Roca, Sergio. Cuban economic policy and ideology : the ten million ton sugar harvest / [by] Sergio Roca. — Beverly Hills ; London : Sage Publications, 1976. — 70,[1]p ; 22cm. — (Sage professional papers in international studies ; vol.4, no.02-044)
Bibl.: p.68-70.
ISBN 0-8039-0623-4 Pbk : £1.75
(B77-15744)

338.1'7'3610985 — Cane sugar industries. *Peru, 1880-1920*
Albert, Bill. An essay on the Peruvian sugar industry, 1880-1922 / [by] Bill Albert. And, The letters of Ronald Gordon, Administrator of the British Sugar Company in the Canete Valley, 1914-1919. — Norwich (University Plain, Norwich [NR4 7TJ]) : School of Social Studies, University of East Anglia, 1976. — 560p in various pagings : ill, facsims, maps, ; 30cm.
Spine title: The Peruvian sugar industry, 1880-1920.
ISBN 0-9505217-0-1 Pbk : £5.00
(B77-04012)

338.1'7'373 — Coffee industries & trades
Campaign Co-op. The world in your coffee cup : how the rich get richer and the poor get poorer on the coffee you drink / [Campaign Co-op and the World Development Movement]. — [Oxford] ([35 Cowley Rd, Oxford]) : Campaign Co-op ; [London] : World Development Movement, [1976]. — 36p : ill, map, port ; 21cm.
Bibl.: p.28.
Sd : £0.40
(B77-25453)

338.1'7'3740966 — Cocoa industries. *Study regions: West Africa. Reviews of research*
Cocoa production : economic and botanical perspectives / edited by John Simmons. — New York [etc.] ; London : Praeger, 1976. — xviii, 413p : ill, map ; 25cm. — (Praeger special studies in international economics and development)
Index.
ISBN 0-275-56030-9 : £18.40
(B77-20986)

338.1'7'4 — Fruit industries & trade. *Directories*
Fruit trades world directory : year book and directory of the world's fruit trade. — London : Haymarket Publishing.
1976 / H.F. Tysser editor. — 1976. — 3-102, D204,[18]p : ill ; 26cm.
Pbk : Unpriced
(B77-24067)

338.1'7'4 — Fruit production industries. *European Community countries. Comparative studies*
Hinton, Wilfred Lynn. The European fruit and vegetable sector : the place of fruit and vegetables in EEC farming / by Lynn Hinton. — [Cambridge] ([16 Silver St., Cambridge CB3 9EP]) : Agricultural Economics Unit, Department of Land Economy, Cambridge University, 1976. — [1],25p : ill ; 30cm. — (University of Cambridge. Department of Land Economy. Agricultural Economics Unit. Occasional papers ; no.20 ISSN 0306-5359)
Sd : £1.00
Primary classification 338.1'7'5094
(B77-02829)

338.1'7'490941 — Forestry industries. Assistance from Forestry Commission. *Great Britain*
Forestry Commission. Advice for woodland owners / Forestry Commission. — [Edinburgh] : [Forestry Commission], 1977. — [3],18p : map ; 21cm.
Bibl.: p.17.
Sd : Unpriced
(B77-31747)

338.1'7'5094 — Vegetable production industries. *European Community countries. Comparative studies*
Hinton, Wilfred Lynn. The European fruit and vegetable sector : the place of fruit and vegetables in EEC farming / by Lynn Hinton. — [Cambridge] ([16 Silver St., Cambridge CB3 9EP]) : Agricultural Economics Unit, Department of Land Economy, Cambridge University, 1976. — [1],25p : ill ; 30cm. — (University of Cambridge. Department of Land Economy. Agricultural Economics Unit. Occasional papers ; no.20 ISSN 0306-5359)
Sd : £1.00
Also classified at 338.1'7'4
(B77-02829)

338.1'7'50941 — Horticultural industries. *Great Britain. Statistics*
Economic results from horticulture. — [Cambridge] ([16 Silver St., Cambridge CB3 9EP]) : Agricultural Economics Unit, Department of Land Economy, University of Cambridge.
1975 harvest year / by W.L. Hinton and W.C. Housden. — 1977. — [4],35p : ill ; 30cm.
Sd : £1.00
(B77-17981)

338.1'7'5094235 — Horticultural industries. *Devon, 1973-1976. Statistics*
University of Exeter. *Agricultural Economics Unit.* Financial results for twelve horticultural holdings in Devon and Cornwall, 1973-74 to 1975-76 / University of Exeter, Agricultural Economics Unit. — Exeter : [The Unit], 1977. — [1],20p ; 30cm.
Sd : £0.50
Also classified at 338.1'7'5094237
(B77-24068)

338.1'7'5094237 — Horticultural industries. *Cornwall, 1973-1976. Statistics*
University of Exeter. *Agricultural Economics Unit.* Financial results for twelve horticultural holdings in Devon and Cornwall, 1973-74 to 1975-76 / University of Exeter, Agricultural Economics Unit. — Exeter : [The Unit], 1977. — [1],20p ; 30cm.
Sd : £0.50
Primary classification 338.1'7'5094235
(B77-24068)

338.1'7'50942836 — Horticultural industries. Role of Dutch immigrants. *Humberside. Cottingham, 1920-1975*
Boersma, D. Dutch settlers in Cottingham and the East Riding / by D. Boersma. — Cottingham (37 Priory Rd, Cottingham, Humberside) : Cottingham Local History Society, 1976. — 15p : ill, ports ; 22cm. — (Cottingham local history series ; no.6 ISSN 0305-0386)
Sd : Unpriced
(B77-29252)

338.1'7'60094284 — National parks. *North Yorkshire. Yorkshire Dales National Park. Livestock industries*
Yorkshire Dales National Park Committee. Farming in the Yorkshire dales / [Yorkshire Dales National Park Committee]. — [Leyburn] ([Yorebridge House, Bainbridge, Leyburn, N. Yorkshire]) : The Committee, 1977. — [1],20p : ill ; 21cm.
ISBN 0-905455-03-7 Sd : Unpriced
(B77-16245)

338.1'7'60883 — Meat. Economic aspects. *Organisation for Economic Co-operation and Development countries. Statistics*
Organisation for Economic Co-operation and Development. Meat balances in OECD member countries = Bilans de la viande dans les pays membres de l'OCDE / [Organisation for Economic Co-operation and Development]. — Paris : O.E.C.D. ; [London] : [H.M.S.O.].
1962-1975. — 1977. — lxvii,129,[1]p ; 32cm.
English and French text.
Pbk : £4.60
ISBN 92-64-01650-3
(B77-17359)

338.1'7'62140942 — Dairy farming industries. *England, 1972-1976. Reports, surveys*
Wragg, Stuart Russell. Milk production in England and Wales 1972-73 to 1975-76 : a review of changes in costs, returns, margins and structure / [by] S.R. Wragg. — [Bristol] : Agricultural Economics Research Unit, University of Bristol, 1976. — 48p ; 30cm.
ISBN 0-900196-10-6 Sd : Unpriced
(B77-12919)

338.1'7'62140942 — Dairy farming industries. *England. Reports, surveys*
Costs and efficiency in milk production / Ministry of Agriculture, Fisheries and Food. — London : H.M.S.O.
1972-1973. — 1976. — x,82p : map ; 21cm.
ISBN 0-11-240513-4 Sp : £1.15
(B77-06530)

338.1'7'6214096894 — Dairy farming industries. *Zambia. Reports, surveys*
Bessell, James Edward. Dairying in Zambia, the traditional sector / by J.E. Bessell and M.G. Daplyn. — Sutton Bonington : University of Nottingham, Department of Agriculture and Horticulture, 1977. — ix,128p : ill, form, 3 maps ; 21cm. — (University of Nottingham's Farm Management Investigations for Zambia. Bulletins ; no.3)
Pbk : £2.50
(B77-30030)

338.1'7'640809426 — Pig production industries. *Eastern England. Statistics. Serials*
University of Cambridge. *Department of Land Economy. Agricultural Economics Unit.* Pig management scheme results / University of Cambridge, Department of Land Economy, Agricultural Economics Unit. — Cambridge (16 Silver St., Cambridge CB3 9EL) : The Unit.
1976 / [by] R.F. Ridgeon. — [1977]. — [1], 32p : ill ; 30cm. — (Agricultural enterprise studies in England and Wales, economic report ; no.51 ISSN 0306-8900)
ISBN 0-901978-70-1 Sd : £0.70
(B77-08272)

338.1'7'6974447 — Mink production industries & mink fur trades. *Conference proceedings*
Fur Breeders' Association of the United Kingdom and Ireland. *Training Course and Conference, 12th, York, 1977.* Twelfth Training Course and Conference ([of the] Fur Breeders' Association of the United Kingdom & Ireland) [held at the] Royal Station Hotel, York, 16-17th April 1977. — London (14 The Quay, Lower Thames St., EC3R 6BU) : Janssen Services, [1977]. — [3], 96p : ill, form, ports ; 34cm.
Sp : £3.50
(B77-20987)

338.1'7'7 — Dairy industries. *Organisation for Economic Co-operation and Development countries. Statistics*
Organisation for Economic Co-operation and Development. Milk, milk products and egg balances in OECD member countries = Bilans du lait, des produits laitiers et des oeufs dans les pays membres de l'OCDE / [Organisation for Economic Co-operation and Development]. — Paris : O.E.C.D. ; [London] : [H.M.S.O.]. 1962-75. — 1977. — liv,196,[1]p ; 32cm.
English and French text.
Pbk : £6.00
ISBN 92-64-01609-0
(B77-17360)

338.1'7'7025 — Dairy industries & trades. *Directories*
Dairy industries international directory. — London : United Trade Press.
1977 / editor Robert Redman. — 1977. — 80p : ill ; 30cm.
Pbk : £5.00
ISSN 0309-7226
(B77-20097)

338.1'7'7094 — Dairy industries & trades. *European Community countries. Statistics*
EEC dairy facts and figures / [Economics Division, Milk Marketing Board]. — Thames Ditton (Thames Ditton, Surrey KT7 0EL) : Milk Marketing Board.
1976 : [5th ed.]. — [1976]. — [2],xiii,151p : 1 ill ; 21cm.
ISBN 0-900543-39-6 Sp : £1.25
(B77-05268)

338.1'7'70941 — Dairy industries & trades. *Great Britain. Statistics*
United Kingdom dairy facts and figures / [Federation of United Kingdom Milk Marketing Boards]. — [Thames Ditton] ([Thames Ditton, Surrey KT7 0EL]) : The Federation.
1976. — [1977]. — xiii,207p : maps ; 20cm.
Index.
ISBN 0-900543-40-x Sp : £1.75
ISSN 0503-3535
(B77-08273)

338.1'7'7106142 — Milk industries. Organisations. *England. Milk Marketing Board. Reports, surveys. Serials*
Milk Marketing Board. Annual report and accounts for the year ended 31st March / Milk Marketing Board. — [Thames Ditton] : [The Board].
44th : [1976]-1977. — [1977]. — 25p : ill, port ; 24cm.
Sd : Unpriced
(B77-28468)

338.1'7'710942 — Channel Islands milk. Production. Economic aspects. Policies of Milk Marketing Board. *England. Inquiry reports*
Report of the Committee of Investigation for England and Wales [on the] complaint by Messrs N.C. Ansdell ... [et al.] as to the operation of the Milk Marketing Scheme 1933 (as amended). — [Pinner] : Ministry of Agriculture, Fisheries and Food ; [Cardiff] : Welsh Office, 1977. — [3],66p : ill, map ; 30cm.
At head of title: The Agricultural Marketing Act 1958.
Sd : £2.10
(B77-10246)

338.1'81 — Agricultural industries. Policies of European Economic Community: Common Agricultural Policy. Regulations. Implementation by British government. Organisations: Intervention Board for Agricultural Produce. *European Community countries. Reports, surveys. Serials*
Intervention Board for Agricultural Produce. Report for the calendar year ... / Intervention Board for Agricultural Produce. — London : H.M.S.O. — (Cmnd.6846)
1976. — [1977]. — 50p ; 24cm.
Bibl.: p.49-50.
ISBN 0-10-168460-6 Sd : £1.00
(B77-20988)

338.1'841 — Agricultural industries. Policies of government. International economic aspects. *Great Britain*
Agriculture and the state : British policy in a world context / edited by Brian Davey, T.E. Josling and Alister McFarquhar. — London : Macmillan for the Trade Policy Research Centre, 1976. — xxiii,280p : ill ; 23cm.
Bibl.: p.270-273. — Index.
ISBN 0-333-21194-4 : £15.00
(B77-04632)

338.1'842 — Agricultural industries. Protection. Policies of government. Influence of farmers. Political aspects. *England, 1815-1852*
Crosby, Travis L. English farmers and the politics of protection, 1815-1852 / [by] Travis L. Crosby. — Hassocks : Harvester Press, 1977. — [8],224p ; 23cm.
Bibl.: p.191-198. — Index.
ISBN 0-85527-116-7 : £5.25 : CIP rev.
(B77-05269)

338.1'843 — Agricultural industries. Influence of Nationalsozialistische Deutsche Arbeiter-Partei. *Germany, 1928-1945*
Farquharson, John Edgar. The plough and the swastika : the NSDAP and agriculture in Germany, 1928-45 / [by] J.E. Farquharson. — London [etc.] : Sage Publications, 1976. — viii, 312p ; 23cm. — (Sage studies in 20th century history ; vol.5)
Bibl.: p.272-279. — Index.
ISBN 0-8039-9949-6 : £8.00
ISBN 0-8039-9997-6 Pbk : £3.50
(B77-07166)

338.1'847 — Agricultural industries. Policies of government. *Soviet Union, 1953-1964*
McCauley, Martin. Khrushchev and the development of Soviet agriculture : the virgin land programme, 1953-1964 / [by] Martin McCauley. — London [etc.] : Macmillan [for] the School of Slavonic and East European Studies, University of London, 1976. — xiii, 232p : maps ; 23cm. — (Studies in Russian and East European history)
Bibl.: p.223-228. — Index.
ISBN 0-333-19834-4 : £10.00
(B77-08274)

338.1'847 — Agricultural industries. Policies of Partiia sotsialistov-revoliutsionerov. *Russia, to 1907*
Perrie, Maureen. The agrarian policy of the Russian Socialist-Revolutionary Party, from its origins through the revolution of 1905-1907 / [by] Maureen Perrie. — Cambridge [etc.] : Cambridge University Press, 1976. — xii,216p : map ; 22cm. — (Soviet and East European studies)
Bibl.: p.206-209. — Index.
ISBN 0-521-21213-8 : £6.75
(B77-08275)

338.1'873 — Agricultural industries. Policies of government. *United States. Reports, surveys*
Organisation for Economic Co-operation and Development. *Working Party on Agricultural Policies.* Recent developments in United States agricultural policies : ... this report has been discussed and adopted by the OECD Working Party on Agricultural Policies and by the Committee for Agriculture ... — Paris : O.E.C.D. ; [London] : [H.M.S.O.], 1976. — [2], ii,65p : ill ; 29cm. — (Organisation for Economic Co-operation and Development. Agricultural Policy Reports)
Pbk : £1.30
ISBN 92-64-11571-4
(B77-00660)

338.1'9 — Food resources
World food prospects and agricultural potential / [by] Marylin Chou ... [et al.]. — New York ; London : Praeger, 1977. — xvi,319p : ill, maps ; 25cm. — (Praeger special studies in international economics and development)
Index.
ISBN 0-275-23770-2 : £13.40
(B77-31748)

338.1'9 — Food supply. *Conference proceedings*
People and Food Tomorrow *(Conference), Cambridge, 1976.* People and food tomorrow / edited by Dorothy Hollingsworth and Elisabeth Morse. — London : Applied Science Publishers, 1976. — xii,173p : ill, map ; 23cm.
'Proceedings of the British Nutrition Foundation conference on "People and food tomorrow", held at Churchill College, Cambridge, 1-4 April, 1976' - half-title verso. — Bibl. — Index.
ISBN 0-85334-701-8 : £10.00
(B77-04013)

338.1'9 — Food supply. *Juvenile literature*
Constant, Anne Marie. Food / written and illustrated by Anne-Marie Constant. — London [etc.] : Burke, 1977. — 31,[1]p : col ill ; 18x19cm. — (Waste not want not)
ISBN 0-222-00519-x : £0.95
ISBN 0-222-00523-8 Pbk : £0.80
ISBN 0-222-00515-7 Library ed. : £1.50
(B77-20098)

338.1'9 — Food supply. Effects of increases in population
Lowry, John Henry. World population and food supply / [by] J.H. Lowry. — 2nd ed. — London : Edward Arnold, 1976. — [6],122p : ill, maps ; 25cm.
Previous ed.: 1970. — Index.
ISBN 0-7131-0092-3 Pbk : £2.50
(B77-10247)

338.1'9 — Food supply. Policies of governments
Tudge, Colin. The famine business / [by] Colin Tudge. — London : Faber, 1977. — iii-ix,141p ; 23cm.
Index.
ISBN 0-571-10887-3 : £3.95 : CIP rev.
(B77-12920)

338.1'9'0901 — Prehistoric agriculture. Origins. Role of increases in population
Cohen, Mark Nathan. The food crisis in prehistory : overpopulation and the origins of agriculture / [by] Mark Nathan Cohen. — New Haven ; London : Yale University Press, 1977. — x,341p ; 22cm.
Bibl.: p.287-330. — Index.
ISBN 0-300-02016-3 : £10.80
(B77-25454)

338.1'9'1724 — Food resources. Effects of policies on food supply of developed countries. *Developing countries*
Jones, David, *b.1942.* Food and interdependence : the effect of food and agricultural policies of developed countries on the food problems of developing countries / [by] David Jones. — London : Overseas Development Institute, 1976. — iv,51p ; 21cm.
ISBN 0-85003-060-9 Sd : £1.00
(B77-00087)

338.1'9'1724 — Food supply. *Developing countries*
Manning, Diana Helen. Society and food : the Third World / [by] Diana H. Manning ; [for] Science in a Social Context. — London [etc.] : Butterworth, 1977. — iv,60p : ill ; 22cm.
Bibl.: p.57-60.
ISBN 0-408-71304-6 Pbk : £1.00
(B77-17361)

338.1'9'1812 — Food supply. Effects of climate. Socioeconomic aspects. *Western world, 1816-1819*
Post, John D. The last great subsistence crisis in the Western world / [by] John D. Post. — Baltimore ; London : Johns Hopkins University Press, 1977. — xv,240p ; 24cm.
Bibl.: p.215-235. — Index.
ISBN 0-8018-1850-8 : £9.70
(B77-33668)

338.1'9'596 — Food supply. Shortages. Effects of policies of United States government. *Cambodia, 1970-1976*
Hildebrand, George. Cambodia, starvation and revolution / [by] George Hildebrand, Gareth Porter. — New York ; London : Monthly Review Press, 1976. — 124p : ill, 2 maps, ports ; 21cm.
ISBN 0-85345-382-9 : £4.40
(B77-04633)

338.1'9'8 — Food supply. *Latin America. Tropical regions. Conference proceedings*
Symposium on Nutrition and Agricultural and Economic Development in the Tropics, *Guatemala City, 1974.* Nutrition and agricultural development : significance and potential for the tropics / edited by Nevin S. Scrimshaw and Moisés Béhar. — New York ; London : Plenum Press, 1976. — xxiv,500p : ill ; 24cm. — (Basic life science ; vol.7)
'... the Symposium on Nutrition and Agricultural and Economic Development in the Tropics, held in Guatemala City December 2-6, 1974 ...' - Preface. — Bibl. — Index.
ISBN 0-306-36507-3 : £24.89
(B77-22428)

338.2 — ECONOMICS OF MINERAL PRODUCTS

338.2'025 — Mining industries. *Directories*
Walter Skinner's mining international yearbook. — London : 'Financial times'.
1977 : [90th year] / editor Wm G. Nightingale. — 1977. — 2-674p : ill, map ; 22cm.
Spine title: 'Mining international year book'. — Previously published: as 'Walter R. Skinner's mining international year book'. — Index. — Previous control number ISBN 0-900671-38-6.
£11.00
(B77-08852)

338.2'05 — Mining industries. *Reports, surveys. Serials*
Mining annual review. — London (15 Wilson St., EC2M 2TR) : Mining Journal Limited.
[1977]. — 1977. — 588p : ill, maps ; 27cm.
Index.
ISBN 0-900117-12-5 Pbk : £10.00
(B77-20099)

338.2'09172'4 — Mining industries. *Developing countries*
Bosson, Rex. The mining industry and the developing countries / [by] Rex Bosson and Bension Varon. — New York ; Oxford [etc.] : Oxford University Press for the World Bank, 1977. — xii,292p : ill ; 24cm.
Bibl.: p.273-283. — Index.
ISBN 0-19-920096-3 : £8.25 : CIP rev.
ISBN 0-19-920099-8 Pbk : £3.50
(B77-22429)

338.2'0941 — Mining industries. *Great Britain. Periodicals*
Quarry & mining news. — [London] ([25 Gateley Rd, SW9 9TA]) : ['Quarry & mining news'].
No.1- ; Apr. 2nd, 1976-. — [1976]-. — ill ; 30cm.
Twenty-six issues a year. — [8]p. in 1st issue.
Sd : £0.25
ISSN 0309-5606
(B77-24775)

338.2'09415 — Metals mining industries. *Ireland. Secondary school texts*
Teeling, John. Tara Mines / text John Teeling ; illustrations Peter Jay. — [Tallaght] : Folens, [1977]. — [1],p.65-96 : col ill, 2 col maps ; 25cm. — (Irish environmental library series ; no.28)
Sd : £0.60
(B77-18616)

338.2'3 — Land disturbed by opencast iron mining. Reclamation. Financial assistance. Ironstone Restoration Fund. *England. Midlands. Accounts*
Mineral Workings Acts 1951 and 1971, account of the Ironstone Restoration Fund ... — London : H.M.S.O.
1975-76. — [1977]. — 7p ; 25cm. — ([1976-77 H.C.]155)
ISBN 0-10-215577-1 Sd : £0.25
(B77-08276)

338.2'3 — Mineral deposits. Prospecting. Financial assistance by government. *Great Britain. Reports, surveys*
Mineral Exploration and Investment Grants Act 1972, annual report ... / by the Department of Industry. — London : H.M.S.O.
1975-1976 : 4th : for the period 1 April to 31 March. — [1976]. — 5p ; 25cm. — ([1976-77 H.C.]4)
ISBN 0-10-200477-3 Sd : £0.25
(B77-06560)

1976-1977 : 5th : for the period 1 April to 31 March. — 1977. — 6p ; 25cm. — ([1976-77 H.C.] 455)
ISBN 0-10-245577-5 Sd : £0.25
(B77-26886)

338.2'3 — Petroleum. Prices. Increases by petroleum exporting countries. International economic aspects
Park, Yoon S. Oil money and the world economy / [by] Yoon S. Park ; with the collaboration of Joseph Aschheim. — London : Wilton House Publications, 1976. — xi,205p : ill ; 24cm.
Also published: Boulder : Westview Press, 1976. — Bibl.: p.199-205.
ISBN 0-904655-22-9 : £10.00
(B77-14600)

338.2'7'202541 — Coal industries. *Great Britain. Directories*
Guide to the coalfields. — Redhill (2 Queensway, Redhill, Surrey RH1 1QS) : 'Colliery Guardian'.
1977 / edited by E.G. Corbin ; assistant editors E. Hammond, G.E. Kusay. — [1977]. — 54, 445p,[38]p : ill, maps ; 19cm.
Index.
Pbk : £6.50
(B77-23210)

338.2'7'20941 — Coal industries. *Great Britain, 1946-1976*
Berkovitch, Israel. Coal on the switchback : the coal industry since nationalisation / [by] Israel Berkovitch ; with a foreword by Sir Derek Ezra. — London : Allen and Unwin, 1977. — 3-237p : ill, 2 maps ; 23cm.
Index.
ISBN 0-04-622002-x : £7.00
ISBN 0-04-622003-8 Pbk : £3.50
(B77-28469)

338.2'7'20941 — Coal industries. *Great Britain, 1946-1976. Reports, surveys*
Great Britain. *Department of Energy.* Coal in the UK / Department of Energy. — [London] ([Thames House South, Millbank, SW1P 4QJ]) : [Information Directorate, Department of Energy], 1977. — [4],18p : map ; 30cm. — (Fact sheet ; 4)
ISBN 0-904552-17-9 Sd : Unpriced
(B77-14112)

338.2'7'20941 — Coal industries. *Great Britain. Reports, surveys*
Coal for the future : progress with 'Plan for coal' and prospects to the year 2000. — London (The Library, Room 1020, Thames House South, Millbank, SW1P 4QJ) : Department of Energy, [1977]. — [1],23p ; 25cm.
'... the third report to come out of meetings of the coal industry's tripartite group ... [of] unions, the National Coal Board and the Government ...' - Foreword.
Sd : Unpriced
(B77-07167)

338.2'7'20941 — Coal industries. *Great Britain, to 1976*
Griffin, Alan Ramsay. The British coalmining industry : retrospect and prospect / [by] A.R. Griffin. — Buxton (The Market Place, Hartington, Buxton, Derbyshire SK17 0AL) : Moorland Publishing Co., 1977. — 224p : ill, facsims, map, plans ; 22cm.
Bibl.: p.210-216. — Index.
ISBN 0-903485-41-9 : £6.00
(B77-15147)

338.2'7'20973 — Coal industries. Environmental aspects. *United States*
Schlottmann, Alan M. Environmental regulation and the allocation of coal : a regional analysis / [by] Alan M. Schlottmann. — New York ; London : Praeger, 1977. — xiv,144p : ill, map ; 25cm. — (Praeger special studies in US economic, social and political issues)
Bibl.: p.137-143.
ISBN 0-275-24090-8 : £11.70
(B77-26181)

338.2'7'28 — Natural gas deposits & petroleum deposits. Exploitation. Offshore drilling rigs. *Registers*
The **offshore** drilling register : a directory of self-contained mobile sea-going rigs / compiled ... by H. Clarkson & Company Limited. — London (52 Bishopsgate, EC2P 2AD) : H. Clarkson and Co. Ltd.
1977. — 1977. — 103p : ill ; 22x32cm.
£12.00
ISSN 0305-4284
(B77-16772)

338.2'7'28 — Services for offshore natural gas & petroleum industries. *Belgium. Directories*
Vendor profiles of suppliers to the offshore industry, Belgium. — London (IPC Industrial Press Ltd, Dorset House, Stamford St., SE1 9LU) : International Offshore Intelligence, 1976. — 3-58p : ill, port ; 28cm.
'Compiled in co-operation with Fabrimetal of Belgium' - cover. — Index.
Sd : Unpriced
(B77-12921)

338.2'7'28 — Services for offshore natural gas & petroleum industries. *Great Britain. Directories*
Great Britain. *Department of Energy. Offshore Supplies Office.* Offshore Supplies Office. — [Glasgow] [etc.] ([Department of Energy, 249 West George St., Glasgow G2 4TL]) : O.S.O., 1975. — [1],144p(2 fold) : col map ; 30cm.
Bibl.: p.33-43.
ISBN 0-904552-15-2 Sp : Unpriced
(B77-02110)

Vendor profiles of suppliers to the offshore industry, United Kingdom. — London (IPC Industrial Press Ltd, Dorset House, Stamford St., SE1 9LU) : International Offshore Intelligence, 1977. — 48p : ill ; 28cm.
'Compiled in co-operation with the Offshore Supplies Office' - cover.
Sd : Unpriced
(B77-19260)

338.2'7'28 — Services for offshore natural gas & petroleum industries. *Ireland (Republic). Directories*
Institute for Industrial Research and Standards. *Library and Information Systems Department.* Suppliers to the offshore industry, Ireland / [compiled by the Library and Information Systems Department, Institute for Industrial Research and Standards]. — Dublin : I.I.R.S., Technical Information Division, 1975. — ii-xii, 140p : ill ; 21cm.
English text, Irish, French and German note. — Index.
ISBN 0-900450-59-2 Pbk : Unpriced
(B77-20100)

Irish Offshore Services Association. Irish offshore services directory / [Irish Offshore Services Association]. — Dublin (Confederation House, Kildare St., Dublin 2) : The Association, [1977]. — [31]p ; 21cm.
Sd : Unpriced
(B77-24069)

338.2'7'28 — Services for offshore natural gas & petroleum industries. *Netherlands. Directories*
Offshore suppliers guide, Netherlands. — London : IPC Industrial Press [for] International Offshore Intelligence [etc.].
1st ed. - ; 1976-. — 1976-. — ill ; 29cm.
vii,42[4],p. in 1st ed.
Sd : £6.50
(B77-08853)

Vendor profiles of suppliers to the offshore industry, Netherlands. — London (IPC Industrial Press Ltd, Dorset House, Stamford St., SE1 9LU) : International Offshore Intelligence, 1977. — 72p : ill, port ; 28cm.
'Compiled in co-operation with IRO [Industriele Raad voor de Oceanologie], [and] NOEM [Netherlands Oil Equipment Manufacturers]' - cover.
Sd : Unpriced
(B77-19261)

338.2'7'28 — Services for offshore natural gas & petroleum industries. *Norway. Directories*
Vendor profiles of suppliers to the offshore industry, Norway. — London (IPC Industrial Press Ltd, Dorset House, Stamford St., SE1 9LU) : International Offshore Intelligence, 1976. — 3-42p : ill ; 28cm.
Sd : Unpriced
(B77-15148)

338.2'7'28 — Services for offshore natural gas & petroleum industries. *West Germany. Directories*
Vendor profiles of suppliers to the offshore industry, Federal Republic of Germany. — London (IPC Industrial Press Ltd, Dorset House, Stamford St., SE1 9LU) : 'Ocean Energy', 1976. — 3-54p : ill, port ; 28cm.
'International Offshore Intelligence'.
Sd : Unpriced
(B77-15149)

338.2'7'28094 — Offshore natural gas & petroleum industries. *Europe. Serials*
The **European** offshore oil & gas yearbook. — London : Kogan Page.
1976-77 / [edited by Ethel de Keyser, assisted by Martha Davis]. — 1976. — 475p : ill, forms, maps, plan ; 29cm.
Index.
ISBN 0-85038-431-1 : £20.00
(B77-05270)

Walter R. Skinner's North Sea and Europe offshore year book and buyers' guide. — London : 'Financial Times'.
[1976] / editor Bart Collins. — [1975]. — 2-331p : ill, maps ; 31cm.
Spine title: North Sea and Europe offshore yearbook and buyers' guide, 1976. — Index.
ISBN 0-900671-49-1 : Unpriced
(B77-13554)

Walter Skinner's North Sea and Europe offshore yearbook & buyers' guide. — London : 'Financial Times'.
1977 / editor Doris M. Birnie. — 1976. — 2-407p : ill, maps ; 31cm.
Spine title: North Sea and Europe offshore yearbook and buyers' guide. — Previously published: as 'Walter R. Skinner's North Sea and Europe offshore yearbook and buyers' guide'.
ISBN 0-900671-37-8 : £19.50
ISSN 0309-4758
(B77-08854)

338.2'7'280941 — Offshore natural gas & petroleum industries. Policies of government. Implementation. Responsibility of government departments. *Great Britain*
Great Britain. *Interdepartmental Committee on Marine Safety.* Marine activities : guide to the responsibilities of Government departments and agencies / prepared by the Interdepartmental Committee on Marine Safety under the chairmanship of the Department of Trade. — London : H.M.S.O., 1977. — iii,49p ; 21cm.
Bibl.: p.30-33.
ISBN 0-11-512032-7 Sd : £1.00
Primary classification 387.5'0941
(B77-29345)

338.2'7'280947 — Natural gas & petroleum industries. *Soviet Union, to 1975*
Campbell, Robert Wellington. Trends in the Soviet oil and gas industry / [by] Robert W. Campbell. — Baltimore ; London : Johns Hopkins University Press for Resources for the Future, 1976. — xvi,125p,leaf : maps ; 23cm.
Bibl.: p.116-119. — Index.
ISBN 0-8018-1870-2 : £7.00
(B77-21745)

338.2'7'282 — Petroleum industries. *Organisation for Economic Co-operation and Development countries. Statistics*
Oil statistics = Statistiques pétrolières : supply and disposal = approvisionnement et consommation / [Organisation for Economic Co-operation and Development]. — Paris : O.E.C.D. ; [London] : [H.M.S.O.].
1975. — 1976. — 295p : col ill ; 27cm.
Parallel English and French preliminaries. — Fold. sheet ([3]p.) as insert.
Pbk : £6.70
ISBN 92-64-01565-5
(B77-06531)

Statistiques pétrolières trimestrielles = Quarterly oil statistics. — Paris : Organisation for Economic Co-operation and Development ; [London] : [H.M.S.O].
Continues: Provisional oil statistics by quarters.
[No.1]- ; 1976, 3e trimestre = 3rd quarter-. — 1977-. — 27cm.
[2],xi,2-17p. in 3rd issue. — Parallel English and French text.
Sd : £2.80 yearly
ISSN 0474-6015
(B77-11116)

338.2'7'282 — Petroleum industries & trades. International political aspects
Blair, John M. The control of oil / [by] John M. Blair. — London [etc.] : Macmillan, 1977. — xxii,442p : ill, 2 maps ; 25cm.
Originally published: New York : Pantheon Books, 1976. — Index.
ISBN 0-333-21751-9 : £12.00
(B77-13555)

338.2'7'2820212 — Petroleum industries. *Statistics*
British Petroleum Company. BP statistical review of the world oil industry : reserves, production, consumption, trade, refining, tankers, energy. — London (Britannic House, Moor La., EC2Y 9BU) : B.P.
1975. — [1976]. — 32p : col ill, col maps ; 30cm.
Sd : Unpriced
(B77-21746)

British Petroleum Company. BP statistical review of the world oil industry. — London (c/o K.A.D. Inglis, Public Affairs and Information Dept., The British Petroleum Company Ltd, Britannic House, Moor La., EC2Y 9BU) : B.P.
1976. — [1977]. — 32p : col ill, col maps ; 30cm.
Sd : Unpriced
(B77-21747)

Institute of Petroleum. *Information Services Department.* Know more about oil : world statistics / the Institute of Petroleum Information Service. — London : The Institute, 1977. — [2],8,[1]p : 1 ill ; 24cm.
Sd : £0.20
(B77-28470)

338.2'7'282025 — Petroleum industries. *Directories*
Walter Skinner's oil and gas international year book. — London : 'Financial Times'.
1977-78. — 1977. — 2-743p : ill(some col), map ; 22cm.
Text on lining papers. — Previously published: as 'Walter R. Skinner's oil and gas international year book'. — Index.
ISBN 0-900671-82-3 : £12.50
ISSN 0078-4273
Primary classification 338.4'7'6657025
(B77-30035)

338.2'7'2820943 — Petroleum industries & trades. *West Germany, 1945-1975*
Mendershausen, Horst. Coping with the oil crisis : French and German experiences / [by] Horst Mendershausen. — Baltimore ; London : Johns Hopkins University Press for Resources for the Future, 1976. — xv,110p : 1 ill ; 24cm.
Index.
ISBN 0-8018-1812-5 : £4.90
ISBN 0-8018-1813-3 Pbk : £1.90
Also classified at 338.2'7'2820944
(B77-07832)

338.2'7'2820944 — Petroleum industries & trades. *France, 1945-1975*
Mendershausen, Horst. Coping with the oil crisis : French and German experiences / [by] Horst Mendershausen. — Baltimore ; London : Johns Hopkins University Press for Resources for the Future, 1976. — xv,110p : 1 ill ; 24cm.
Index.
ISBN 0-8018-1812-5 : £4.90
ISBN 0-8018-1813-3 Pbk : £1.90
Primary classification 338.2'7'2820943
(B77-07832)

338.2'7'2820947 — Petroleum industries. Policies of government. International political aspects. *Soviet Union*
Klinghoffer, Arthur Jay. The Soviet Union & international oil politics / by Arthur Jay Klinghoffer. — New York ; Guildford : Columbia University Press, 1977. — xii,389p : maps ; 24cm.
Index.
ISBN 0-231-04104-7 : £11.00
(B77-23211)

338.2'7'2820951 — Petroleum industries. *China*
Bartke, Wolfgang. Oil in the People's Republic of China, industry structure, production, exports = Chung-hua jen-min kung-he-kuo te shih-yu Kung-ye / by Wolfgang Bartke ; [translated from the German] by Waldtraut Jarke. — London : C. Hurst, 1977. — 125p : 1 ill, 3 maps ; 23cm.
'A publication of the Institute of Asian Affairs, Hamburg'. — Translation of: 'Die Ölwirtschaft der Volksrepublik China'. Hamburg : Institut für Asienkunde, 1975. — Bibl.: p.8.
ISBN 0-903983-64-8 : £6.50 : CIP rev.
(B77-14601)

338.2'7'28209535 — United Arab Emirates. Economic conditions. Effects of petroleum industries
al-Otaiba, Mana Saeed. Petroleum and the economy of the United Arab Emirates / [by] Mana Saeed Al-Otaiba. — London : Croom Helm, 1977. — [7],281,[6]p : map ; 27cm.
Bibl.: p.277-281. — Index.
ISBN 0-85664-563-x : £25.00 : CIP rev.
(B77-23212)

338.2'7'2820956 — Middle East. Economic conditions. Effects of petroleum industries & trades, to 1976
OPEC and the Middle East : the impact of oil on societal development / edited by Russell A. Stone. — New York ; London : Praeger, 1977. — xviii,267p : 2 ill ; 25cm. — (Praeger special studies in international politics and government)
Bibl.: p.246-247. — Index.
ISBN 0-275-24490-3 : Unpriced
(B77-26887)

338.2'7'2820973 — Petroleum industries & trades. Policies of government. *United States*
Engler, Robert. The brotherhood of oil : energy policy and public interest / [by] Robert Engler. — Chicago ; London : University of Chicago Press, 1977. — xi,337p ; 22cm.
Index.
ISBN 0-226-20948-2 : £10.25
(B77-31048)

338.2'7'282098 — Petroleum industries. *Latin America*
O'Shaughnessy, Hugh. Oil in Latin America / by Hugh O'Shaughnessy. — London : 'Financial Times', 1976. — 190p : ill, maps ; 30cm.
ISBN 0-900671-63-7 Sp : £50.00
(B77-26888)

338.2'7'2820987 — Petroleum industries. *Venezuela, to 1975*
Vallenilla, Luis. Oil, the making of a new economic order : Venezuelan oil and OPEC / [by] Luis Vallenilla. — New York ; London [etc.] : McGraw-Hill, [1976]. — xviii,302p : maps(on lining papers) ; 24cm.
Published in the United States: 1975. — Index.
ISBN 0-07-066830-2 : £14.95
(B77-05271)

338.2'7'4094295 — Nonferrous metals mining industries. *Mid Wales. History*
Bick, David Ewart. The old metal mines of mid-Wales / [by] David E. Bick. — Newent ([Market Square, Newent, Glos. GL18 1PS]) : The Pound House.
[Part 4] : West Montgomeryshire. — 1977. — 64p : ill, facsims, maps, port ; 21cm.
ISBN 0-9502040-6-4 Pbk : £1.35
(B77-22430)

338.2'7'4109 — Gold mining industries, to 1976. *Juvenile literature*
Parkins, Trevor. The gold diggers / illustrated by Trevor Parkins ; written by Belinda Hollyer and Vivienne Driscoll. — London : Macdonald Educational, 1977. — [1],44p : col ill, col maps, col ports ; 25cm. — (Toppers history)
Index.
ISBN 0-356-05444-6 : £1.50
(B77-12922)

338.2'7'41099315 — Gold mining industries. *New Zealand. Northern South Island, to ca 1930*
Nolan, Tony. Historic gold trails of Nelson and Marlborough : in the form of a traveller's guide to the goldfields of historic Nelson & Marlborough and a portrayal of the spirited characters and hardy pioneers who opened up the provinces and blazed the trails of their prosperity ... / by Tony Nolan. — Wellington [N.Z.] [etc.] ; London : A.H. and A.W. Reed, 1976. — 95p : ill, 2 facsims, 3 maps, ports ; 27cm. — (Gold star books)
Bibl.: p.90-91. — Index.
Pbk : £3.40
ISBN 0-589-00749-1
(B77-20101)

338.2'7'4210985 — Silver mining industries. *Peru, 1776-1824*
Fisher, John Robert. Silver mines and silver miners in colonial Peru, 1776-1824 / by J.R. Fisher. — [Liverpool] ([P.O. Box 147, Liverpool L69 3BX]) : [University of Liverpool, Centre for Latin American Studies], [1977]. — [4]leaves,149p : 2 ill, map ; 30cm. — (University of Liverpool. Centre for Latin American Studies. Monograph series ; no.7)
Bibl.: p.131-140. — Index.
ISBN 0-902806-06-8 Sp : Unpriced
(B77-30031)

338.2'7'492 — Bauxite & aluminium industries & trades. *Reports, surveys. Serials*
World aluminium survey. — Worcester Park : Metal Bulletin.
[1977] / edited by Norman J. Connell. — 1977. — 3-202p : ill ; 25cm.
Pbk : Unpriced
(B77-29253)

338.3 — ECONOMICS OF PRIMARY INDUSTRIES (OTHER THAN AGRICULTURE AND MINERALS)

338.3'71'3094 — Marine animal production industries. *Western Europe. Conference proceedings*
Fish Farming in Europe : prospects for growth and the problems : conference report [of the conference held] Tuesday and Wednesday 3rd and 4th December, 1974, Cunard International Hotel, London, sponsored by Fish Farming International, organised by Oyez International Business Communications Ltd. — London (1 Hills Place, W.1) : Oyez International Business Communications Ltd, [1977]. — [1],117p : ill, map ; 30cm.
Bibl.: p.9.
Sp : £20.00
(B77-18617)

338.3'71'4110942234 — Oyster fishing industries. *Kent. Whitstable, to 1972*
Stevens, J E. Whitstable natives : a short study of Whitstable and oysters / by J.E. Stevens. — [London] ([15 Chinbrook Cres., S.E.12]) : [K.C. Hall], [1977]. — 48p : ill, chart ; 21cm.
Sd : £0.75
(B77-26182)

338.3'72'53842 — Blue crab fishing industries. *Maryland. Chesapeake Bay*
Warner, William W. Beautiful swimmers : watermen, crabs and the Chesapeake Bay / [by] William W. Warner ; drawings by Consuelo Hanks. — Harmondsworth [etc.] : Penguin, 1977. — xv,304p : ill, chart, map ; 20cm.
Originally published: Boston, Mass. : Little, Brown, 1976.
ISBN 0-14-004405-1 Pbk : £1.50
(B77-24776)

338.3'72'7 — Small scale fishing industries. *Reports, surveys*
Economic state and problems of small-scale fisheries. — Paris : Organisation for Economic Co-operation and Development ; [London] : [H.M.S.O.], 1976. — [2],203p : ill, map ; 30cm.

'... papers prepared at the request of the Committee for Fisheries of O.E.C.D.' - p.1. — Bibl.
Pbk : £3.80
ISBN 92-64-11538-2
(B77-01233)

338.3'72'7 — White fish. British catches. *Statistics. Periodicals*
Fishery Economics Research Unit. Supplies bulletin / White Fish Authority, Fishery Economics Research Unit. — [Edinburgh] ([10 Young St., Edinburgh EH2 4JQ]) : [The Unit]. 1974, no.1-. — 1974-. — ill ; 30cm.
Monthly. — [4],30p. in 1977, no.2.
Sp : Unpriced
ISSN 0309-5517
(B77-17982)

338.3'72'7 — White fish fishing industries. Organisations. *Great Britain. White Fish Authority. Accounts*
Sea Fish Industry Acts 1970 and 1973 Herring Marketing Fund, Herring Industry Board, White Fish Authority, accounts ... — London : H.M.S.O.
1975-76. — [1977]. — 12p ; 25cm. — ([1976-77 H.C.]168)
ISBN 0-10-216877-6 Sd : £0.25
Also classified at 338.3'72'755
(B77-08277)

338.3'72'7 — White fish fishing industries. Organisations. *Great Britain. White Fish Authority. Reports, surveys. Serials*
White Fish Authority. Annual report and accounts for the year ended 31st March / White Fish Authority. — Edinburgh (10 Young St., Edinburgh EH2 4JQ) : W.F.A.
[1973]-1974 : 23rd. — [1974]. — 32p : ill, ports ; 30cm.
ISBN 0-903941-01-5 Sd : £0.75
(B77-02830)

[1975]-1976 : 25th. — 1976. — 32p : ill, map, plan, ports ; 30cm.
ISBN 0-903941-04-x Sd : £0.75
(B77-02831)

[1976-]1977 : 26th. — [1977]. — 36p : ill, ports ; 30cm.
ISBN 0-903941-05-8 Sd : £0.75
(B77-20102)

338.3'72'70941 — Fishing industries. *Great Britain. Reports, surveys*
Fishery Economics Research Unit. A retrospective view of developments in the fishing industry in 1976 and their consequences in 1977 / White Fish Authority [Fishery Economics Research Unit] ; [written by] N. Buchanan. — Edinburgh (White Fish Authority, 10 Young St., Edinburgh EH2 4JQ) : The Unit, 1977. — [1],8[i.e.9]p ; 30cm. — (Fishery Economics Research Unit. Occasional papers series ; no.1 ISSN 0309-605x)

Sp : Unpriced
(B77-21748)

338.3'72'70941 — Fishing industries. *Great Britain, to 1976*
Dyson, John. Business in great waters : the story of British fishermen / [by] John Dyson. — London [etc.] : Angus and Robertson, 1977. — 335,[1]p : ill, facsim, maps ; 24cm.
Ill. on lining papers. — Bibl.: p.324-329. — Index.
ISBN 0-207-95706-1 : £12.00
(B77-21749)

338.3'72'70941 — Fishing industries. Policies of government. *Great Britain. Inquiry reports*
Great Britain. *Parliament. House of Commons. Expenditure Committee.* Inquiry into the fishing industry - progress report : third report from the Expenditure Committee, session 1976-77. — London : H.M.S.O., [1977]. — xv p ; 25cm. — ([1976-77 H.C.]255)
Sd : £0.35
(B77-11661)

338.3'72'70941 — Sea fishing industries. *Great Britain. Statistics*
Sea fisheries statistical tables / Ministry of Agriculture, Fisheries and Food. — London : H.M.S.O.
1975. — 1976. — vi,42p ; 25cm.
ISBN 0-11-241075-8 Sd : £1.25
(B77-06532)

338.3'72'709411 — Fishing industries. *Scotland. Serials*
Scottish Fishermen's Federation. Official year book and diary / Scottish Fishermen's Federation. — Aberdeen (11 Albyn Terrace, Aberdeen AB9 1SE) : Northern Publishers (Aberdeen) Ltd.
1977. — [1977]. — 232p : ill, maps(some col) ; 22cm.
Unpaged diary following p.232.
ISBN 0-9502370-4-3 : £7.02
(B77-10248)

338.3'72'709416 — Fishing industries. *Northern Ireland. Reports, surveys. Serials*
Report on the sea inland fisheries of Northern Ireland / Department of Agriculture [Northern Ireland]. — Belfast : H.M.S.O.
1975. — [1976]. — 29p ; 25cm.
ISBN 0-337-05174-7 Sd : £0.45
(B77-07168)

338.3'72'7094283 — Ports. Economic conditions. Effects of fishing industries. *Humberside. Reports, surveys*
Yorkshire and Humberside Economic Planning Board. *Research Group.* The fishing industry, its economic significance in the Yorkshire and Humberside ports : a report / prepared by the Research Group of the Yorkshire and Humberside Economic Planning Board. — Revised [ed.]. — [Leeds] ([DOE/DTP, Room 1213, City House, Leeds LS1 4JD]) : [The Planning Board], 1977. — [3]leaves,41[i.e.42], A19[i.e.21]p,[4]leaves of plates : ill ; 35cm.
In binder. — Previous ed.: 1976.
Ls : Unpriced
Also classified at 338.3'72'7094284
(B77-31749)

338.3'72'7094284 — Ports. Economic conditions. Effects of fishing industries. *North Yorkshire. Reports, surveys*
Yorkshire and Humberside Economic Planning Board. *Research Group.* The fishing industry, its economic significance in the Yorkshire and Humberside ports : a report / prepared by the Research Group of the Yorkshire and Humberside Economic Planning Board. — Revised [ed.]. — [Leeds] ([DOE/DTP, Room 1213, City House, Leeds LS1 4JD]) : [The Planning Board], 1977. — [3]leaves,41[i.e.42], A19[i.e.21]p,[4]leaves of plates : ill ; 35cm.
In binder. — Previous ed.: 1976.
Ls : Unpriced
Primary classification 338.3'72'7094283
(B77-31749)

338.3'72'755 — Herring fishing industries. Organisations. *Great Britain. Herring Industry Board. Accounts*
Sea Fish Industry Acts 1970 and 1973 Herring Marketing Fund, Herring Industry Board, White Fish Authority, accounts ... — London : H.M.S.O.
1975-76. — [1977]. — 12p ; 25cm. — ([1976-77 H.C.]168)
ISBN 0-10-216877-6 Sd : £0.25
Primary classification 338.3'72'7
(B77-08277)

338.3'72'755 — Herring fishing industries. Organisations. *Great Britain. Herring Industry Board. Reports, surveys. Serials*
Herring Industry Board. Annual report ... / [Herring Industry Board]. — Edinburgh ([Sea Fisheries House, Young St., Edinburgh EH2 4JQ]) : The Board.
42nd : 1976. — 1977. — [1],36p : 1 ill ; 25cm.
ISBN 0-903959-05-4 Sd : £0.50
(B77-25455)

338.3'72'755 — Salmon fisheries. *Scotland*
Association of Scottish District Salmon Fishery Boards. Salmon fisheries of Scotland / Association of Scottish District Salmon Fishery Boards. — Farnham : Fishing News, 1977. — 76p,[2]fold p of plates : ill, map ; 20cm.
Bibl.
ISBN 0-85238-091-7 Pbk : £2.90
(B77-30032)

338.4 — ECONOMICS OF SECONDARY INDUSTRIES

338.4 — Government contracts. Invitations to tender. *Africa. For British businessmen. Polyglot texts. Periodicals*
Africa gazette : government tenders from the whole continent. — London (Wheatsheaf House, Carmelite St., EC4Y 0AX) : African Buyer and Trader Publications Ltd.
Consists of facsimile reprints from government gazettes.
Vol.1, no.1- ; 10 May 1977-. — 1977-. — 42cm.

Fortnightly. — English and French text. — [12]p. in 1st issue.
Sd : £70.00 yearly
(B77-32473)

338.4'0994 — Service industries. *Australia*
The **economics** of the Australian service sector / edited by K.A. Tucker. — London : Croom Helm, 1977. — 443p : ill ; 23cm.
Bibl.: p.433-436. — Index.
ISBN 0-85664-354-8 : £19.95 : CIP rev.
ISBN 0-85664-558-3 Pbk : Unpriced
(B77-17362)

338.4'3 — Beer industries & trades. Profit margins. *Great Britain, 1974-1976. Reports, surveys*
Great Britain. *Price Commission.* Beer prices and margins / Price Commission. — London (Neville House, Page St., SW1P 4LS) : The Commission, 1977. — [6],73p : ill ; 30cm. — (Report ; no.31)
Sd : £2.00
Primary classification 338.4'3663'420941
(B77-26889)

338.4'3 — Book industries & periodical publishing industries. Finance. *Great Britain. Statistics*
Jordan Dataquest Limited. Book and magazine publishing / researched ... by Jordan Dataquest Limited ; market overview by Michael Goldman. — London : Jordan Dataquest, 1976. — [6],157p ; 30cm. — (Dataquest survey)
ISBN 0-85938-069-6 Pbk : £48.00
(B77-04014)

338.4'3 — Catering industries. Companies. Finance. *Great Britain. Statistics*
British catering companies / [Jordan Dataquest Limited]. — London : Jordan Dataquest. — (Dataquest survey)
[1977]. — 1977. — [4],8,[13]leaves ; 30cm.
Notebook format. — Index.
Sp : £28.00
ISSN 0140-3575
(B77-32474)

338.4'3 — Construction industries. Companies. Finance. *Great Britain. Statistics*
British construction companies / [Jordan Dataquest Limited]. — London : Jordan Dataquest. — (Dataquest survey)
[1977]. Part 1 : Companies with over £1M. annual sales. — 1977. — [4],23,[29]leaves ; 30cm.
Notebook format. — Index.
Sp : £28.00(£46.00 for set of 2 vols)
ISSN 0140-3583
(B77-32475)

[1977]. Part 2 : Companies with less than £1M. annual sales. — 1977. — [4],23,[28]leaves ; 30cm.
Notebook format. — Index.
Sp : £28.00(£46.00 for set of 2 vols)
ISSN 0140-3591
(B77-32476)

338.4'3 — Consumer goods in aerosol containers. Costs to consumers. Compared with costs of consumer goods in other containers. *Great Britain. Reports, surveys*
British Aerosol Manufacturers' Association. Cost-effectiveness of aerosol products / [British Aerosol Manufacturers' Association]. — London (93 Albert Embankment, SE1 7TU) : The Association, [1977]. — [2],22p ; 30cm.
Pbk : Unpriced
(B77-24070)

338.4'3 — Electricity supply industries. Growth. Finance. *United States*
Scott, David Logan. Financing the growth of electric utilities / [by] David L. Scott. — New York [etc.] ; London : Praeger, 1976. — xvii, 120,[1]p : ill ; 25cm. — (Praeger special studies in US economic, social and political issues) (Praeger special studies in international business, finance and trade)
Bibl.: p.110-117. — Index.
ISBN 0-275-56460-6 : £11.10
(B77-07169)

338.4'3 — Electricity supply. Marginal costs. Estimation. *United States*
Scherer, Charles R. Estimating electric power system marginal costs / [by] Charles R. Scherer. — Amsterdam [etc.] ; Oxford : North-Holland Publishing Co., 1977. — 338p : ill ; 23cm. — (Contributions to economic analysis ; 107)
Bibl.: p.319.332. — Index.
ISBN 0-7204-0524-6 : Unpriced
(B77-27729)

338.4'3 — Environment. Pollution by industries. Control measures. Costs. *Great Britain*
Atkins, M H. Pollution control costs in industry : an economic study / by M.H. Atkins and J.F. Lowe. — Oxford : Pergamon, 1977. — ix,166p : ill, form ; 26cm.
ISBN 0-08-021851-2 : £7.75
ISBN 0-08-021841-5 Pbk : £4.50
(B77-32477)

338.4'3 — Furniture industries. Finance. *Great Britain. Statistics*
Jordan Dataquest Limited. The British furniture industry / [Jordan Dataquest Ltd]. — London : Jordan Dataquest, 1976. — [3],98,[11]p ; 30cm. — (Dataquest survey)
ISBN 0-85938-066-1 Pbk : £48.00
(B77-06533)

338.4'3 — Health services. *Northern Ireland. Accounts*
Summary of health and personal social services accounts, together with the report of the Comptroller and Auditor-General / [prepared by the] Department of Health and Social Services, Northern Ireland. — Belfast : H.M.S.O.
1974-1975. — [1976]. — 31p ; 25cm.
Contents: Part 1 : Health and social services boards - Part 2 : Northern Ireland Central Services Agency for the Health and Social Services - Part 3 : Northern Ireland Staffs Council for the Health and Social Services.
ISBN 0-337-07131-4 Sd : £0.60
(B77-04634)

338.4'3 — Hotels. Development. Financial incentives of British government. *England, 1968-1973. Reports, surveys*
English Tourist Board. The Hotel Development Incentives Scheme in England / English Tourist Board. — London : The Board, 1976. — 40p : ill, 2 col maps, ports ; 23cm.
ISBN 0-903265-69-9 Pbk : £1.50
(B77-09568)

338.4'3 — Housing. Expenditure by government. Distribution. *Great Britain. Inquiry reports*
Clark, Steve. Who benefits? : a study of the distribution of public expenditure on housing / by Steve Clark. — [London] ([157 Waterloo Rd, S.E.1]) : [Shelter, Housing Research Group], 1977. — [3],v,34p : 1 ill ; 30cm.
'Evidence to the House of Commons Expenditure Sub-committee submitted on behalf of Shelter, the national campaign for the homeless, by the Housing Research Group ...'. — Bibl.: p.33-34.
ISBN 0-9505691-0-0 Sd : £1.00
(B77-15150)

338.4'3 — Inventions. Development. Organisations. *Great Britain. National Research Development Corporation. Accounts*
National Research Development Corporation. Accounts ... / National Research Development Corporation. — London : H.M.S.O.
1975-76. — [1977]. — 19p ; 25cm. — ([1976-77 H.C.]158)
ISBN 0-10-215877-0 Sd : £0.35
(B77-08278)

338.4'3 — Mints. *Great Britain. Royal Mint. Trading operations. Accounts*
Royal Mint Trading Fund accounts : accounts ... as at 31st March, together with the Report of the Comptroller and Auditor General thereon ... — London : H.M.S.O.
1975-76. — 1977. — vi,12,[1]p ; 25cm. — ([1976-77 H.C.] 187)
ISBN 0-10-218777-0 Sd : £0.35
(B77-14113)

338.4'3 — National health services. *England. Accounts*
National Health Service Acts 1946 to 1973, accounts. — London : H.M.S.O.
1975-76. — [1977]. — iv,35p ; 25cm. — ([1976-77 H.C.] 336)
Previously published: as 'National Health Service Acts 1946 to 1968, accounts'.
ISBN 0-10-233677-6 Sd : £0.60
(B77-20103)

338.4'3 — National health services. *Scotland. Accounts*
National Health Service (Scotland) Acts 1947 to 1973, accounts ... for the year ended 31st March. — London : H.M.S.O.
1975-76. — [1977]. — iv,20p ; 25cm. — ([1976-77 H.C.]337)
ISBN 0-10-233777-2 Sd : £0.45
(B77-17983)

338.4'3 — Printing industries. Companies. Finance. *Great Britain. Statistics*
British printing companies / [Jordan Dataquest Limited]. — London : Jordan Dataquest. — (Dataquest survey)
[1977]. Part 1 : Companies with over £650,000 turnover. — 1977. — [4],17,[22]leaves ; 30cm.
Notebook format. — Index.
Sp : £28.00(£46.00 for set of 2 vols)
ISSN 0140-3605
(B77-32478)

[1977]. Part 2 : Companies with less than £650,000 turnover. — 1977. — [4],15,20 leaves ; 30cm.
Notebook format. — Index.
Sp : £28.00(£46.00 for set of 2 vols)
ISSN 0140-3613
(B77-32479)

338.4'3 — Public housing. Organisations. *Northern Ireland. Northern Ireland Housing Executive. Accounts*
Northern Ireland Housing Executive. Accounts of the Northern Ireland Housing Executive for the year ended 31 March ... — Belfast : H.M.S.O.
1975. — [1977]. — 20p ; 25cm.
ISBN 0-337-23225-3 Sd : £0.50
ISSN 0306-9907
(B77-21750)

338.4'3 — Public libraries. Stock: Books. Direct delivery. Cost-benefit analysis. *Pennsylvania*
Hu, Teh-wei. A benefit-cost analysis of alternative library delivery systems / [by] Teh-wei Hu, Bernard H. Booms, and Lynne Warfield Kaltreider. — Westport, Conn. ; London : Greenwood Press, 1975. — xv,287p ; 22cm. — (Contributions in librarianship and information science ; no.13)
Bibl.: p.275-280. — Index.
ISBN 0-8371-7528-3 : £10.95
(B77-15151)

338.4'3 — Research & development. Expenditure. *Great Britain. Statistics*
Great Britain. *Central Statistical Office.* Research and development, expenditure and employment / Central Statistical Office. — [New ed.]. — London : H.M.S.O., 1976. — iii, 54p ; 30cm. — (Studies in official statistics ; no.27)
Previous ed.: published as 'Research and development expenditure'. 1973.
ISBN 0-11-630139-2 Sd : £2.00
Also classified at 331.7'61'607241
(B77-07170)

338.4'3 — Roads. Maintenance. Expenditure. *Great Britain. British Road Federation viewpoints*
British Road Federation. Road maintenance : a British Road Federation report. — London : The Federation, [1977]. — 15,[1]p : ill ; 25cm.
ISBN 0-902060-31-7 Sd : Unpriced
(B77-13556)

338.4'3 — Welfare services. Finance. Sources: Taxation. Political aspects
Wilensky, Harold L. The 'new corporatism', centralization and the welfare state / [by] Harold L. Wilensky. — London [etc.] : Sage Publications, 1976. — 73,[1]p : ill ; 22cm. — (Sage professional papers in contemporary political sociology ; vol.2, no.06-020 ISSN 0305-3842)
Bibl.: p.72-73.
ISBN 0-8039-9863-5 Pbk : £1.75
(B77-09569)

338.4'3'001552 — Non-fiction: Academic books: Books with British imprints. Prices. *Reports, surveys. Serials*
Average prices of British academic books. — Loughborough (Loughborough, Leics. LE11 3TU) : Library Management Research Unit, Loughborough University of Technology. — (Loughborough University of Technology. Library Management Research Unit. Reports ; no.4 ISSN 0309-4804)
1976, Jan.-June / [by] Alan Cooper, J.L. Schofield. — 1976. — 10,[1]p ; 30cm.
ISBN 0-904924-08-4 Sd : £1.00
(B77-12923)

338.4'3'352042 — Local authorities. Services. Charges. *England. Proposals*
Harris, Ralph, *b.1924.* Pricing or taxing? : evidence on charging for local government services invited by the Layfield Committee and a critique of its report / [by] Ralph Harris and Arthur Seldon. — London : Institute of Economic Affairs, 1976. — 103p ; 22cm. — (Hobart paper ; 71)
Bibl.: p.103. — Includes a selection of the oral evidence given to the Committee of Inquiry into Local Government Finance, published in 'Local government finance'.
ISBN 0-255-36084-3 Pbk : £1.50
(B77-05272)

338.4'3'35580941 — Militaria. Prices. *Great Britain. Serials*
The **Lyle** official arms and armour review. — Galashiels (Glenmayne, Galashiels, Selkirkshire) : Lyle Publications.
1977 / [editor Tony Curtis ; compiled by Margaret Anderson et al.]. — 1976. — 5-348p : chiefly ill ; 23cm.
Index.
ISBN 0-902921-57-6 : £6.00
ISSN 0307-7748
(B77-02832)

1978 / [editor Tony Curtis ; compiled by Margaret Anderson et al.]. — 1977. — 3-350p : chiefly ill ; 23cm.
Index.
ISBN 0-902921-60-6 : £6.00
ISSN 0307-7748
(B77-31751)

338.4'3'61460941 — Funeral directors. Fees. *Great Britain. Reports, surveys*
Great Britain. *Price Commission.* Funeral charges / Price Commission. — London : H.M.S.O., 1977. — vi,41p : 1 ill ; 25cm. — (Report ; no.22)
ISBN 0-11-700864-8 Sd : £0.90
(B77-11662)

338.4'3'61510941 — New pharmaceutical products. Pricing. *Great Britain, 1962-1970. Reports, surveys*
Reekie, William Duncan. Pricing new pharmaceutical products / [by] W. Duncan Reekie. — London : Croom Helm, 1977. — 3-34p : ill ; 23cm.
ISBN 0-85664-467-6 Sd : £6.00
(B77-07833)

338.4'3'61789 — Privately prescribed hearing aids. Prices. *Great Britain. Inquiry reports*
Great Britain. *Price Commission.* The prices of privately prescribed hearing aids / Price Commission. — London : H.M.S.O., 1977. — vi,28p ; 25cm. — (Report ; no.28)
ISBN 0-11-700872-9 Sd : £0.80
(B77-23213)

338.4'3'62131 — Electricity supply. Pricing
Turvey, Ralph. Electricity economics : essays and case studies / [by] Ralph Turvey and Dennis Anderson. — Baltimore ; London : John Hopkins University Press for the World Bank, 1977. — xvii,364p : ill, maps ; 24cm. — (International Bank for Reconstruction and Development. World Bank research publications)
Bibl.: p.290-296. — Index.
ISBN 0-8018-1866-4 : £13.45
ISBN 0-8018-1867-2 Pbk : £5.20
(B77-25456)

338.4'3'621310941 — Electricity supply. Charges. Great Britain. Parliament. House of Commons. Select Committee on Nationalised Industries. 'Gas and electricity prices'. *Great Britain. Critical studies*
Great Britain. *Department of Energy.* Gas and electricity prices, the Government's reply to the Fourth Report from the Select Committee on Nationalised Industries, Session 1975-76 H.C.353 / Department of Energy. — London : H.M.S.O., [1977]. — 13p ; 25cm. — (Cmnd. 6806)
ISBN 0-10-168060-0 Sd : £0.35
Also classified at 338.4'3'665740941
(B77-16246)

338.4'3'621388 — Television equipment rentals services. Charges. *Great Britain. Reports, surveys*
Great Britain. *Price Commission.* Television rental charges / Price Commission. — London : H.M.S.O., 1976. — vi,26p : 3 ill ; 25cm. — (Report ; no.19)
ISBN 0-11-700322-0 Sd : £0.60
(B77-00088)

338.4'3'6213892 — Buildings. Burglar alarms. Prices. *Great Britain. Reports, surveys*
Great Britain. *Price Commission.* Intruder alarms / Price Commission. — London : H.M.S.O., 1977. — vi,31p : ill ; 25cm. — (Report ; no.24)
ISBN 0-11-700868-0 Sd : £0.75
(B77-17984)

338.4'3663'420941 — Beers. Prices. *Great Britain, 1974-1976. Reports, surveys*
Great Britain. *Price Commission.* Beer prices and margins / Price Commission. — London (Neville House, Page St., SW1P 4LS) : The Commission, 1977. — [6],73p : ill ; 30cm. — (Report ; no.31)
Sd : £2.00
Also classified at 338.4'3
(B77-26889)

338.4'3'66360941 — Licensed premises. Soft drinks. Prices. *Great Britain, 1973-1976. Inquiry reports*
Great Britain. *Price Commission.* Prices and margins of soft drinks and mixers in licensed premises / Price Commission. — London : H.M.S.O., 1977. — vi,17p ; 25cm. — (Report ; no.23)
ISBN 0-11-700865-6 Sd : £0.60
Also classified at 381'.45'66360941
(B77-14114)

338.4'3'663930941 — Coffee. Prices. *Great Britain, 1974-1977. Reports, surveys*
Great Britain. *Price Commission.* Coffee prices, costs and margins / Price Commission. — London : H.M.S.O., 1977. — vi,34p : ill ; 25cm. — (Report ; no.29)
ISBN 0-11-700873-7 Sd : £0.80
Also classified at 381'.45'66393
(B77-23214)

338.4'3'665740941 — Gas supply. Charges. Great Britain. Parliament. House of Commons. Select Committee on Nationalised Industries. 'Gas and electricity prices'. *Great Britain. Critical studies*
Great Britain. *Department of Energy.* Gas and electricity prices, the Government's reply to the Fourth Report from the Select Committee on Nationalised Industries, Session 1975-76 H.C.353 / Department of Energy. — London : H.M.S.O., [1977]. — 13p ; 25cm. — (Cmnd. 6806)
ISBN 0-10-168060-0 Sd : £0.35
Primary classification 338.4'3'621310941
(B77-16246)

338.4'3'66960212 — Tin. Prices. *Statistics*
Tin prices / International Tin Council = Conseil international de l'étain = Consejo Internacional del Estaño = Mezhdunarodnyĭ sovet po olovu. — London (1 Oxenden St., SW1Y 4EQ) : The Council.
1976. — [1977]. — [13] leaves(8 fold) : ill ; 30cm.
Text on verso of 5 leaves.
ISBN 0-901560-25-1 Sd : £4.00
(B77-15745)

338.4'3'681761 — Sanitary towels & sanitary tampons. Prices. *Great Britain. Reports, surveys*
Great Britain. *Price Commission.* Prices of sanitary towels and tampons / Price Commission. — London : H.M.S.O.
A supplementary report. — 1977. — iv,4p ; 25cm. — (Report ; no.26)
ISBN 0-11-700870-2 Sd : £0.40
(B77-23215)

338.4'3'6838 — Household equipment. Maintenance & repair on site. Charges. *Great Britain. Reports, surveys*
Great Britain. *Price Commission.* Call-out charges / Price Commission. — London : H.M.S.O., 1977. — vi,30p : ill ; 25cm. — (Report ; no.27)
ISBN 0-11-700871-0 Sd : £0.80
(B77-23216)

338.4'3687'15 — Schools. Students. Uniforms. Prices. *Great Britain. Reports, surveys*
Great Britain. *Price Commission.* Prescribed school clothing / Price Commission. — London (Neville House, Page St., SW1P 4LS) : The Commission, [1977?]. — [6],28p ; 30cm. — (Report ; no.30)
Sd : Unpriced
(B77-26890)

338.4'3'7 — Art objects. Auction prices. *Lists. Serials*
Art at auction : the year at Sotheby Parke Bernet. — London (Russell Chambers, Covent Garden, WC2E 8AA) : Sotheby Parke Bernet.
1975-76 : two hundred and forty-second season / [edited by Anne Jackson, assisted by Joan Sarll (UK) and Barbara Evans (USA)]. — 1976. — 488p : chiefly ill(some col), facsims(some col), ports (some col) ; 28cm.
Ill. on lining papers. — Index.
ISBN 0-85667-030-8 : £10.00
(B77-04015)

338.4'3'74510941 — Antiques. Prices. *Great Britain. Serials*
The **Lyle** official antiques review. — Galashiels (Glenmayne, Galashiels, Selkirkshire) : Lyle Publications.
1977 / compiled by Margo Rutherford ; edited by Tony Curtis ; drawings by Peter Knox ... [et al.]. — 1976. — 5-606p : chiefly ill ; 23cm.
Index.
ISBN 0-902921-55-x : £6.00
(B77-02111)

1978 / compiled by Margo Rutherford ; edited by Tony Curtis ; drawings by Peter Knox ... [et al.]. — 1977. — 5-638p : chiefly ill ; 23cm.
Index.
ISBN 0-902921-58-4 : £6.00
(B77-32480)

338.4'3'7488 — British antique glass bottles. Prices
Litherland, Gordon. Antique glass bottles : illustrated price guide / by Gordon Litherland. — Burton-on-Trent (458c Stanton Rd, Burton-on-Trent, [Staffs.]) : Midlands Antique Bottle Publishing, [1976]. — 103p : ill, facsims, port ; 21cm.
ISBN 0-905447-00-x Pbk : £1.85
(B77-03433)

338.4'3'75 — Oil paintings. Auction prices. *Lists. Serials*
The **annual** art sales index. Oil paintings. — Weybridge (Pond House, Weybridge, Surrey) : Art Sales Index Ltd.
1975-76 / edited by Richard Hislop. — [1976]. — 886p : ill, geneal tables ; 23cm.
Text, ill. on lining papers.
ISBN 0-903872-06-4 : £27.00
ISSN 0308-5910
(B77-02112)

338.4'3'75 — Paintings. Auction prices. *Lists. Serials*
The **annual** art sales index. Watercolours and drawings. — Weybridge (Pond House, Weybridge, Surrey) : Art Sales Index Ltd.
1975-76 / edited by Richard Hislop. — [1976]. — 3-336p : geneal tables ; 23cm.
ISBN 0-903872-05-6 : £20.00
ISSN 0308-5902
(B77-02833)

The **Lyle** official arts review. — Galashiels (Glenmayne, Galashiels, Selkirkshire) : Lyle Publications.
1977 / compiled by Marjorie Clark ; edited by Tony Curtis. — 1976. — 4-477p : ill ; 23cm.
ISBN 0-902921-56-8 : £6.00
(B77-02113)

1978 / compiled by Marjorie Clark ; edited by Tony Curtis. — 1977. — 3-478p : ill, ports ; 23cm.
ISBN 0-902921-59-2 : £6.00
(B77-32481)

338.4'5 — Aerospace industries & motor vehicle industries. Machine tools. Requirements. *Great Britain. Forecasts for 1974-1990*
Machine Tool Industry Research Association. The future machine tool requirements of the UK automobile and aerospace industries / the Machine Tool Industry Research Association. — [Macclesfield] ([Hulley Rd, Hurdsfield, Macclesfield, Cheshire]) : [The Association], 1974. — 45,[17]p,[2] leaves of plates : ill, forms ; 31cm.
Sp : Unpriced
(B77-30029)

338.4'5 — Industries. Technology transfer by American business firms. Economic aspects. *Eastern Europe, ca 1965-1975*
Hayden, Eric W. Technology transfer to East Europe : US corporate experience / [by] Eric W. Hayden. — New York [etc.] ; London : Praeger, 1976. — xiii,134,[1]p ; 25cm. — (Praeger special studies in international business, finance and trade)
Bibl.: p.121-130. — Index.
ISBN 0-275-23240-9 : £12.25
(B77-07171)

338.4'562'1312 — Electricity generation industries. Use of coal & nuclear power. Economic aspects. *United States*
Miller, Saunders. The economics of nuclear and coal power / [by] Saunders Miller assisted by Craig Severance. — New York [etc.] ; London : Praeger, [1977]. — xvii,151p : ill ; 25cm. — (Praeger special studies in US economic, social and political issues)
Published in the United States: 1976. — Bibl.: p.147-150.
ISBN 0-275-23710-9 : £11.20
(B77-15152)

338.4'566'91410941 — Iron industries. Technological change. *Great Britain, 1700-1870*
Hyde, Charles K. Technological change and the British iron industry, 1700-1870 / [by] Charles K. Hyde. — Princeton ; Guildford : Princeton University Press, 1977. — xvi,283,[1]p : ill, map ; 23cm.
Bibl.: p.257-272. — Index.
ISBN 0-691-05246-8 : £14.20
(B77-33111)

338.4'566'9722 — Aluminium industries. Adaptation. *Organisation for Economic Co-operation and Development countries. Reports, surveys*

Organisation for Economic Co-operation and Development. *Industry Committee.* Industrial adaptation in the primary aluminium industry / [prepared by the ad hoc Working Party on the aluminium industry of the Industry Committee of the Organisation for Economic Co-operation and Development]. — Paris : O.E.C.D. ; [London] : [H.M.S.O.], 1976. — 87p : ill ; 24cm.
Pbk : £2.20
ISBN 92-64-11520-x
(B77-01234)

338.4'7'0016409417 — Computer industries & trades. *Ireland (Republic). Periodicals*

Irish computer. — Killiney (107 Avondale Rd, Killiney, Co. Dublin) : Computer Publications of Ireland.
Incorporates 'Irish computer weekly', 'Computing Ireland', 'Irish data systems', 'Irish computer'.
Vol.1, no.1- ; Mar. 1977-. — 1977-. — ill, ports ; 30cm.
Monthly. — 16p. in vol.1, no.2.
Sd : £0.30
(B77-17363)

338.4'7'0705025171241 — Publishing industries. *Commonwealth countries. Directories*

Cassell's directory of publishing in Great Britain, the Commonwealth, Ireland, South Africa and Pakistan. — London : Cassell.
1976-1977 : 8th ed. — 1976. — [2],xxiv,581,[2] p : ill, col maps ; 22cm.
Index.
ISBN 0-304-29566-3 Pbk : £7.50
ISSN 0308-7018
(B77-07834)

338.4'7'07050941 — Publishing industries. *Great Britain. Statistics*

Book and periodical publishers / [Business Ratios]. — London (81 City Rd, EC1Y 1BD) : Business Ratios. — (ICC Business Ratio report)
[1976]. — [1976]. — [73]p : ill ; 21x30cm.
Sd : Unpriced
(B77-08855)

338.4'7'070593025 — Publishing industries. Little presses. *Directories*

International directory of little magazines & small presses. — [Paradise, Calif.] : [Dustbooks] ; [New Malden] ([56 Blakes La., New Malden, Surrey KT3 6NX]) : [Distributed by Gerald England].
1973-74 : 9th ed. / [editors Len Fulton, James Boyer May]. — [1973]. — [2],iv,160p : ill ; 21cm.
ISBN 0-913218-08-1 Sd : £1.50
ISSN 0084-9979
Primary classification 052
(B77-09470)

338.4'7'070594 — Academic publishing industries. *Great Britain. Conference proceedings*

Workshop on Trends in Scholarly Publishing, *Leicester, 1976.* Trends in scholarly publishing / British Library Research and Development Department. — London : The Library, 1976. — [2],iv,86p ; 30cm. — (British Library. Research and Development Department. Reports ; no.5299 HC)
'The report of a Workshop on Trends in Scholarly Publishing [at the University of Leicester] on 16th-17th July 1976' - title page verso. — Bibl.: p.80.
ISBN 0-85350-141-6 Sp : £3.50
(B77-02114)

338.4'7'07223 — Newspaper publishing industries. Organisations. *Kent. Kent and Downs Newspaper Publishers' Association, to 1976*

Boorman, Henry Roy Pratt. 'No mean association' : Kent Newspaper Proprietors' Association, now the Kent & Downs Newspaper Publishers' Association, diamond jubilee, 1916-1976 / [by H.R.P. Boorman]. — Bilsington (The Priory, Bilsington, Kent) : The author, 1976. — viii,52,[1]p,plate : ports ; 22cm.
ISBN 0-9505418-0-x : Unpriced
(B77-04635)

338.4'7'30154 — Housing. Economic aspects

Charles, Susan. Housing economics / [by] Susan Charles. — London [etc.] : Macmillan, 1977. — 77p : ill ; 21cm. — (Macmillan studies in economics)
Bibl.: p.71-77.
ISBN 0-333-19827-1 Pbk : £1.75 : CIP rev.
(B77-16773)

338.4'7'3400942 — Legal services. Investigations by Great Britain. Royal Commission on Legal Services. *England. Reports, surveys*

Great Britain. *Royal Commission on Legal Services.* Report on progress, April 1977 / the Royal Commission on Legal Services. — London : H.M.S.O., [1977]. — iii,16p ; 25cm. — (Cmnd.6770)
Chairman: Sir Henry Benson.
ISBN 0-10-167700-6 Sd : £0.50
(B77-14602)

338.4'7'3620420941 — Social problems. Economic aspects. *Great Britain*

Le Grand, Julian. The economics of social problems / [by] Julian Le Grand and Ray Robinson. — London [etc.] : Macmillan, 1976. — xix,245p : ill ; 22cm.
Bibl.: p.233-237. — Index.
ISBN 0-333-18072-0 : £8.95
ISBN 0-333-19531-0 Pbk : £3.95
(B77-05273)

338.4'7'36210941 — National health services. Economic aspects. *Great Britain*

Culyer, Anthony John. Need and the National Health Service : economics and social choice / [by] A.J. Culyer. — London : Martin Robertson, 1976. — xii,163p : ill ; 23cm. — (York studies in economics)
Bibl. — Index.
ISBN 0-85520-092-8 : £6.50
ISBN 0-85520-091-x Pbk : £2.95
(B77-04636)

338.4'7'36211028 — Hospital equipment industries & trades. *Great Britain. Directories*

Sell's Health Service buyers guide : a comprehensive buyers guide to a wide range of suppliers to the National Health Service. — Epsom : Sell's Publications.
1977. — [1977]. — x,198,[2]p : ill ; 30cm.
Index.
ISBN 0-85499-684-2 Pbk : £8.00
ISSN 0308-7107
(B77-16774)

338.4'7'37 — Education. Economic aspects

Blaug, Mark. An introduction to the economics of education / [by] Mark Blaug. — Harmondsworth [etc.] : Penguin, 1976. — xx, 363p : ill ; 20cm. — (Open University. Set books) (Penguin modern economics texts : political economy) (Penguin education)
Originally published: London : Allen Lane, 1970. — Bibl.: p.331-352. — Index. — Previous control number ISBN 0-14-080159-6.
Pbk : £1.50
ISBN 0-14-080159-6
(B77-04637)

338.4'7'370941 — Education. Economic aspects. *Great Britain*

West, Edwin George. Economics, education and the politician / [by] E.G. West. — London : Institute of Economic Affairs, 1976. — 76p : 2 ill ; 22cm. — (Hobart paper ; 42 ISBN 0073-2818)
Originally published: 1968. — Bibl.: p.75-76.
ISBN 0-255-36086-x Sd : £1.00
(B77-12364)

338.4'7'374013 — Vocational education. Economic aspects. Evaluation

Zymelman, Manuel. The economic evaluation of vocational training programs / [by] Manuel Zymelman with the assistance of ... [others]. — Baltimore ; London : Johns Hopkins University Press for the World Bank, 1976. — xi,122p : ill ; 23cm. — (International Bank for Reconstruction and Development. World Bank staff occasional papers ; 21)
ISBN 0-8018-1855-9 Pbk : £3.60
(B77-15153)

338.4'7'37842 — Higher education. Economic aspects. *England*

Morris, Vera. The planning of higher education, the social demand / by Vera Morris, Maureen Woodhall, Adam Westoby ; [for the Open University, Economics and Education Policy Course Team]. — Milton Keynes : Open University Press, 1977. — 94p : ill ; 30cm. — (Educational studies and social sciences, a third level course : economics and education policy ; block 2) (ED322 ; block 2)
With answers. — Bibl.: p.3-4.
ISBN 0-335-06731-x Pbk : Unpriced
(B77-26184)

Westoby, Adam. The planning of higher education, the private demand / [by Adam Westoby, Alan Gordon, Gareth Williams ; for the Open University, Economics and Education Policy Course Team]. — Milton Keynes : Open University Press, 1977. — 79p : ill ; 30cm. — (Educational studies and social sciences, a third level course : economics and education policy ; 1) (ED322 ; block 1)
With answers. — Bibl.: p.3-4.
ISBN 0-335-06730-1 Pbk : Unpriced
(B77-14115)

338.4'7'607241 — Research & development by industries. Economic aspects. *Great Britain*

Green, Kenneth. Research and technology as economic activities / [by] Kenneth Green, Clive Morphet ; [for] Science in a Social Context. — London [etc.] : Butterworth, 1977. — [4],74p : ill ; 22cm.
Bibl.: p.71-72.
ISBN 0-408-71300-3 Pbk : £1.00
(B77-16775)

338.4'7'610941 — Medicine. Economic aspects. *Great Britain*

Clinical practice and economics / edited by C.I. Phillips and J.N. Wolfe. — Tunbridge Wells : Pitman Medical, 1977. — vii,216p : ill, map ; 22cm.
Bibl.: p.202. — Index.
ISBN 0-272-79409-0 Pbk : £2.95 : CIP rev.
(B77-20104)

338.4'7'6151 — Pharmaceutical industries

Coleman, Vernon. The medicine men / [by] Vernon Coleman. — London : Arrow Books, 1977. — [1],190p ; 18cm.
Originally published: London : Temple Smith, 1975. — Index.
ISBN 0-09-915160-x Pbk : £0.70
(B77-29254)

338.4'7'615102541 — Pharmaceutical industries. *Great Britain. Directories*

United Kingdom pharmaceutical & toiletry manufacturers / [Data Research Group]. — Amersham (Hill House, [Hill Ave.], Amersham, Bucks.) : The Group.
[1976]. — 1976. — 69 leaves in various pagings ; 30cm.
ISBN 0-905570-77-4 Sp : £14.00
Also classified at 338.4'7'668502541
(B77-07172)

[1977]. — 1977. — 70 leaves in various pagings ; 30cm.
ISBN 0-86099-061-3 Sp : £14.00
Also classified at 338.4'7'668502541
(B77-31049)

338.4'7'6177005 — Ophthalmic industries. *Yearbooks*

The **international** optical year book and diary. — London : IPC Business Press.
1977 : 73rd ed. / edited by Philip Mullins. — [1976]. — 204,[12]p : ill ; 29cm.
Unpaged diary follows p.204. — Tab indexed. — Index.
£8.00
(B77-04016)

338.4'7'62 — Engineering industries. *Organisation for Economic Co-operation and Development countries. Statistics. French-English parallel texts*

Organisation for Economic Co-operation and Development. The engineering industries in OECD member countries = Les industries mécaniques et électriques dans les pays membres de l'OCDE : basic statistics = statistiques de base. — Paris : O.E.C.D. ; [London] : [H.M.S.O.].
1972-1975 : Deliveries of '100' selected products = Livraisons de '100' produits individuels. — 1977. — 93p ; 20x27cm.
Parallel English and French text.
Pbk : £2.50
ISBN 92-64-01700-3
(B77-25458)

338.4'7'620002541 — Consulting engineers. *Great Britain. Directories*
United Kingdom consulting engineers / [Data Research Group]. — Amersham (Hill House, [Hill Ave.], Amersham, Bucks.) : The Group. [1977]. — 1977. — 95 leaves in various pagings ; 30cm.
Sp : £15.00
(B77-28471)

338.4'7'620002541 — Engineering industries. *Great Britain. Directories*
United Kingdom engineering companies : electrical & electronic, hydraulic, mechanical handling, precicion [i.e. precision] engineers / [Data Research Group]. — Amersham (Hill House, [Hill Ave.], Amersham, Bucks.) : The Group.
[1975]. — 1975. — 412 leaves in various pagings ; 30cm.
ISBN 0-905570-39-1 Pbk : £20.00
(B77-00089)

United Kingdom engineering companies : ... electrical & electronic, mechanical handling, precision engineering & hydraulic ... / [Data Research Group]. — Amersham (Hill House, Amersham, Bucks.) : The Group.
[1977]. — 1977. — 456 leaves in various pagings ; 30cm.
Pbk : 0769045
(B77-20105)

338.4'7'620002541 — Engineering industries & trades. *Great Britain. Directories*
The **engineer** buyers guide. — [London] : [Morgan-Grampian].
1977 ed. — [1977]. — iv,549,[3]p : ill ; 30cm.
Pbk : Unpriced
(B77-16776)

Ryland's : the directory of the engineering industry. — Redhill (2 Queensway, Redhill, Surrey RH1 1QS) : Fuel and Metallurgical Journals Ltd.
1976-77 : forty-second ed. — 1976. — 616, 645-970,[8]p : ill ; 30cm.
Index.
ISBN 0-901994-90-1 Pbk : £17.00
ISSN 0080-505x
(B77-07835)

1977-78 : forty-third ed. — 1977. — 444, 481-972,[8]p : ill ; 30cm.
Index.
ISBN 0-86108-001-7 Pbk : £17.00
ISSN 0080-505x
(B77-31753)

338.4'7'62000941 — Engineering industries. *Great Britain. Periodicals*
Engineering today. — London (54 Regent St., W.1) : 'Engineering today'.
Vol.1, no.1- ; 9th May 1977-. — 1977-. — ill(some col), ports ; 29cm.
Weekly. — 56p. in 1st issue.
Sd : £0.30
ISSN 0140-0088
(B77-20106)

338.4'7'62000941 — Engineering industries. *Great Britain. Proposals*
Engineering Employers' Federation. British engineering : prospects and problems / Engineering Employers' Federation. — London (Broadway House, Tothill St., S.W.1) : E.E.F., 1976. — [2],12p : ill ; 30cm.
ISBN 0-901700-21-5 Sd : £2.00
(B77-00090)

338.4'7'620009413 — Engineering industries. *Scotland. Central Lowlands, 1780-1945*
Moss, Michael Stanley. Workshop of the British Empire : engineering and shipbuilding in the West of Scotland / [by] Michael S. Moss, John R. Hume. — London [etc.] : Heinemann, 1977. — xvi,192p : ill, col maps(on lining papers), plans, port ; 29cm.
Bibl.: p.183-185. — Index.
ISBN 0-435-32590-6 : £9.50(£12.50 after 25th April 1977)
Also classified at 338.4'7'62382009413
(B77-07173)

338.4'7'620416206241 — Ocean engineering industries. Organisations. *Great Britain. Ship and Marine Technology Requirements Board. Reports, surveys. Serials*
Ship and Marine Technology Requirements Board. Report / Ship and Marine Technology Requirements Board. — [London] ([c/o Department of Industry, Research Requirements Division, Room 401, Abell House, John Islip St., S.W.1]) : [S.M.T.R.B.].
1975. — 1976. — [6]p ; 30cm.
Sd : Unpriced
ISSN 0140-5020
(B77-31754)

1976-77. — 1977. — [11]p : ill(some col) ; 30cm.
Sd : Unpriced
ISSN 0140-5020
(B77-31755)

338.4'7'62102541 — Mechanical engineering industries. *Great Britain. Directories*
'Machinery's' annual buyers' guide. — Brighton : Machinery Publishing Co.
1977 : 48th ed. / editor Frederick A.J. Browne. — [1977]. — xvi,1448,A142p : ill ; 21cm.
Previously published: as '"Machinery's" buyers' guide'.
Pbk : £3.75
(B77-20989)

338.4'7'6213 — Electrical contracting industries. *Great Britain. Directories*
Roll of approved electrical installation contractors / National Inspection Council for Electrical Installation Contracting. — London (93 Albert Embankment, SE1 7TB) : The Council.
1976-7 : 18th ed. : as at 30th April, 1976. — [1976]. — 79p : ill, col map ; 25cm.
ISBN 0-85188-065-7 Sd : Unpriced
(B77-06534)

United Kingdom electrical contractors / [Data Research Group]. — Amersham (Hill House, [Hill Ave.], Amersham, Bucks.) : The Group. [1977]. — 1977. — 205 leaves in various pagings ; 30cm.
ISBN 0-86099-074-5 Pbk : £19.00
(B77-33669)

338.4'7'6213 — Electrical contracting industries. Organisations. *Great Britain. Electrical Contractors' Association. Yearbooks*
Electrical Contractors' Association. ECA year book-desk diary / compiled by the Electrical Contractors' Association. — London (34 Palace Court, W2 4HY) : E.C.A.
1977. — [1977]. — 3-76,M73p : ill, 2 maps ; 22cm.
Unpaged diary follows p.76. — Index.
ISBN 0-901452-08-4 : £2.50
(B77-06535)

Electrical Contractors' Association. ECA yearbook-desk diary. — London (55 Catherine Place, SW1E 6ET) : E.C.A.
1975. — [1975]. — 64,101p : ill, map ; 30cm.
Unpaged diary ([54]p.) follows p.64. — Index.
ISBN 0-901452-07-6 Sp : Unpriced
(B77-07836)

1976. — [1976]. — 56,[1],xxvi,70p : ill ; 30cm.
Unpaged diary ([56]p.) follows p.32. — Index.
Sp : £2.50
(B77-07837)

338.4'7'621305 — Electrical engineering industries. *Periodicals. For Middle Eastern businessmen*
Middle East electricity. — London (Dorset House, Stamford St., SE1 9LU) : IPC Electrical-Electronic Press Ltd.
Vol.1, no.1- ; Oct. 1976-. — 1976-. — ill, ports ; 29cm.
Six issues a year. — 56p. in 2nd issue.
Sd : £20.00(yearly)
ISSN 0309-4707
(B77-15746)

338.4'7'6213102541 — Electricity supply industries. *Great Britain. Directories*
Electricity supply handbook. — London ([Dorset House, Stamford St., S.E.1]) : 'Electrical times'.
1977. — [1977]. — 306p : ill, col maps ; 22cm.
Fold. sheet (1 side: col. map) in pocket. — Index.
ISBN 0-617-00188-x : £5.00
(B77-15155)

338.4'7'6213104202541 — Electric equipment industries & trades. *Great Britain. Directories*
Electrical and electronics trades directory. — Stevenage : Peregrinus.
1977 : ninety-fifth ed. — 1977. — xx,652,[16] p : ill(some col) ; 31cm.
Tab indexed. — Index.
ISBN 0-901223-93-x : Unpriced
(B77-13557)

Radio, Electrical and Television Retailers' Association. Year book and directory / Radio, Electrical and Television Retailers' Association (RETRA) Limited. — London (Pembroke House, Campsbourne Rd, N8 7DR) : Batiste Publications Ltd.
1976. — 1976. — 196p : ill ; 21cm.
Pbk : £4.00
ISSN 0140-329x
(B77-26891)

1977. — 1977. — 191p : ill ; 21cm.
Pbk : £4.50
ISSN 0140-329x
(B77-26892)

338.4'7'62131061423 — Electricity supply industries. Consumer protection services. *South-west England. South Western Electricity Consultative Council. Reports, surveys. Serials*
South Western Electricity Consultative Council. South Western Electricity Consultative Council report for the year ended 31st March. — Exeter (Northernhay House, Northernhay Place, Exeter EX4 3RL) : [The Council].
1975. — [1975]. — 26p : map ; 21cm.
Cover title: To help you-.
Sd : Unpriced
(B77-17985)

338.4'7'62131061426 — Electricity supply industries. Consumer protection services. *East Anglia. Electricity Consultative Council (Eastern Area). Reports, surveys. Serials*
Electricity Consultative Council (Eastern Area). Report for the year ended 31st March / Electricity Consultative Council (Eastern Area). — [Ipswich] ([16 Princes St., Ipswich, Suffolk IP1 1QT]) : [The Council].
[1976]-1977. — [1977]. — [34]p : 1 ill, map ; 22cm.
Sd : Unpriced
(B77-20990)

338.4'7'62131061427 — Electricity supply industries. Consumer protection services. *North-west England. North Western Electricity Consultative Council. Reports, surveys. Serials*
Electricity Consultative Council (North West). Report / Electricity Consultative Council (North West). — Manchester (Longridge House, Longridge Place, Corporation St., Manchester M4 3AJ) : The Council.
1977. — 1977. — [6],30p ; 21cm.
Sd : Unpriced
(B77-26185)

North Western Electricity Consultative Council. Report for the year ended 31st March / the North Western Electricity Consultative Council. — Manchester (Longridge House, Corporation St., Manchester M4 3AJ) : [The Council].
1974. — [1974]. — 22p ; 21cm.
Sd : Unpriced
(B77-17986)

338.4'7'621310614281 — Electricity supply industries. Consumer protection services. *Yorkshire. Yorkshire Electricity Consultative Council. Reports, surveys. Serials*
Yorkshire Electricity Consultative Council. Annual report for the year ended 31st March / Yorkshire Electricity Consultative Council. — Leeds (Wetherby Rd, Scarcroft, Leeds LS14 3HS) : The Council.
[1976]-1977. — 1977. — [1],37,[1]p : map ; 30cm.
Sd : £0.50
ISSN 0307-1162
(B77-21751)

338.4'7'621310941 — Electricity supply industries. *Great Britain, to 1977. Chronologies*
Electricity Council. Electricity supply in Great Britain : a chronology from the beginnings of the industry to 31 December 1976 / [Electricity Council]. — 2nd ed. — London : The Council, 1977. — [3],99p ; 30cm. — (RP3)
Previous ed.: published in 'Electricity supply in Great Britain : a chronology ; [and] organisation and development'. 1973. — Bibl.: p.84-85. — Index.
ISBN 0-85188-053-3 Sd : Unpriced
(B77-26186)

338.4'7'621310942 — Electricity supply industries. *England. Reports, surveys. Serials*
Electricity : report of the Secretary of State for Energy for the year ended 31st March. — London : H.M.S.O.
[1975]-1976. — 1976. — [5],14p ; 21cm.
ISBN 0-11-410281-3 Sd : £0.40
(B77-03434)

338.4'7'621310942 — Electricity supply industries. *England. Statistics*
Electricity Council. Statement of accounts and statistics / the Electricity Council. — London : The Council.
1975-76. — [1976]. — 73p ; 21x30cm.
ISBN 0-85188-046-0 Sd : £1.80
ISSN 0307-1839
(B77-07174)

338.4'7'621312132 — Power stations. Heat. Utilisation in district heating. Economic aspects. *Proposals*
District Heating Working Party. District heating combined with electricity generation in the United Kingdom : a discussion document / prepared by the District Heating Working Party of the Combined Heat and Power Group. — London : H.M.S.O., 1977. — 120p : ill ; 30cm. — (Energy paper ; no.20)
ISBN 0-11-410603-7 Pbk : £3.75
(B77-12924)

338.4'7'6213130941 — Power plant industries. *Great Britain. Forecasts for 1977-1990*
Great Britain. *Central Policy Review Staff.* The future of the United Kingdom power plant machinery industry : report / by the Central Policy Review Staff. — London : H.M.S.O., 1976. — xviii,102p : ill, map ; 30cm.
ISBN 0-11-700570-3 Sd : £2.50
(B77-08856)

338.4'7'62138102541 — Electronic equipment industries & trades. *Great Britain. Directories*
Instruments, electronics, automation purchasing directory. — London : Morgan-Grampian with 'Control instrumention' and 'Electronic engineering'.
1977 : 11th [i.e. twelfth] ed. — [1977]. — 320, [10]p : ill ; 30cm.
Cover title: The directory of instruments, electronics and automation.
Pbk : £10.00
ISSN 0074-0578
(B77-16777)

338.4'7'6213810941 — Electronic engineering industries. *Great Britain. Reports, surveys. Serials*
Electronic Engineering Association. Annual report / Electronic Engineering Association. — London (Leicester House, Leicester St., WC2H 7BN) : E.E.A.
1976. — [1977]. — [2],16,[2]p(2 fold) : ill, port ; 29cm.
'General economic background and performance of the industry in 1976' ([7]p. : ill.) as insert.
Sd : Unpriced
ISSN 0070-9859
(B77-20991)

338.4'7'6214 — Energy industries. *Great Britain*
Great Britain. *Central Office of Information. Reference Division.* Energy / [prepared by Reference Division, Central Office of Information]. — 3rd ed. — London : H.M.S.O., 1977. — [3],31p,[4]p of plates : ill, maps(some col) ; 24cm. — (British industry today) (Central Office of Information reference pamphlet ; 124)
Previous ed.: 1975. — Bibl.: p.30-31.
ISBN 0-11-700916-4 Sd : £0.90
(B77-14603)

338.4'7'621480973 — Nuclear power industries. *United States, to 1975*
Dawson, Frank G. Nuclear power : development and management of a technology / by Frank G. Dawson. — Seattle ; London : University of Washington Press, 1976. — xii,320p : ill ; 24cm.
Bibl.: p.305-312. — Index.
ISBN 0-295-95445-0 : £16.00
(B77-05274)

338.4'7'6215602541 — Refrigeration equipment industries. *Great Britain. Directories*
United Kingdom heating, refrigeration & ventilating equipment manufacturers / [Data Research Group]. — Amersham (Hill House, [Hill Ave.], Amersham, Bucks.) : The Group.
[1976]. — [1976]. — 86 leaves in various pagings ; 30cm.
ISBN 0-905570-55-3 Sp : £12.00
Primary classification 338.4'7'697
(B77-06542)

[1977]. — 1977. — 87 leaves in various pagings ; 30cm.
Sp : Unpriced
Primary classification 338.4'7'697
(B77-17994)

338.4'7'6215602541 — Refrigeration equipment industries & trades. *Great Britain. Directories*
Refrigeration and air conditioning year book. — Croydon : Maclaren.
1975. — 1975. — 344,[10]p : ill ; 30cm.
Pbk : £5.00
ISSN 0305-0777
(B77-17987)

Refrigeration and air conditioning year book. — Croydon (Maclaren Group of Companies, Croydon CR9 1QH) : Refrigeration Press Ltd.
1977. — 1977. — 312,[8]p : ill ; 30cm.
Pbk : £8.00
ISSN 0305-0777
(B77-16778)

338.4'7'62175702541 — Packaging industries. *Great Britain. Directories*
'Packaging review' directory & buyers' guide : a reference source for all packaging users and manufacturers. — London : IPC Business Press.
1977 : 2nd ed. — [1977]. — 268p(4 fold) : ill ; 30cm.
ISBN 0-617-00186-3 Pbk : £12.00
(B77-13558)

United Kingdom packers / [Data Research Group]. — Amersham (Hill House, [Hill Ave.], Amersham, Bucks.) : The Group.
[1976]. — 1976. — 56 leaves in various pagings ; 30cm.
Sp : £12.00
(B77-05275)

338.4'7'62190202541 — Machine tools industries. *Great Britain. Directories*
United Kingdom machine tool manufacturers / [Data Research Group]. — Amersham (Hill House, [Hill Ave.], Amersham, Bucks.) : The Group.
[1976]. — 1976. — 62 leaves in various pagings ; 30cm.
ISBN 0-905570-64-2 Sp : £13.00
(B77-08279)

338.4'7'6219020941 — Machine tool industries. Effects of materials. *Great Britain*
Machine Tool Industry Research Association. The influence on the machine tool industry of the development of materials / the Machine Tool Industry Research Association. — [Macclesfield] ([Hulley Rd, Hurdsfield, Macclesfield, Cheshire]) : [The Association], 1974. — [1],69p,[6]leaves of plates : ill, forms ; 31cm.
Sp : Unpriced
(B77-30033)

338.4'7'62193 — Machine tools. Electronic gear cutters. Development by Cranfield Unit for Precision Engineering. Economic aspects. *Inquiry reports*
Great Britain. *Parliament. House of Commons. Select Committee on Science and Technology.* A case study of a machine tool development at the Cranfield Institute of Technology : second report from the Select Committee on Science and Technology, session 1976-77 : report, together with the minutes of evidence taken before the Sub-committee on Technological Innovation and appendices. — London : H.M.S.O., [1977]. — xxxiv,132p,[2]p of plates ; 24cm. — ([1976-77 H.C.] 522)
ISBN 0-10-252277-4 Pbk : £3.60
(B77-30034)

338.4'7'62340973 — Armaments industries. Relations with military forces. *United States, 1800-1976*
War, business and American society : historical perspectives on the military-industrial complex / edited by Benjamin Franklin Cooling. — Port Washington ; London : Kennikat Press, 1977. — [6],205p ; 23cm. — (Kennikat Press national university publications : series in American studies)
Bibl.: p.191-199. — Index.
ISBN 0-8046-9156-8 : £10.60
Also classified at 355'.00973
(B77-25459)

338.4'7'62344250975499 — Arsenals. *West Virginia. Harpers Ferry. Harpers Ferry armory, to 1861*
Smith, Merritt Roe. Harpers Ferry armory and the new technology : the challenge of change / [by] Merritt Roe Smith. — Ithaca ; London : Cornell University Press, 1977. — 363,[37]p : ill, map, ports ; 24cm.
Bibl.: p.349-356. — Index.
ISBN 0-8014-0984-5 : £13.15
(B77-24072)

338.4'7'62381 — Ships. Design. Economic aspects
Buxton, Ian Lyon. Engineering economics and ship design / [by] I.L. Buxton. — 2nd ed. — Wallsend (Wallsend Research Station, Wallsend, Tyne & Wear NE28 6UY) : British Ship Research Association, 1976. — 107p : ill ; 30cm.
Previous ed.: 1971. — Bibl.: p.93-98.
ISBN 0-9502768-2-0 Pbk : £10.00(£5.00 to students)
(B77-02115)

338.4'7'62382002541 — Boatbuilding industries. *Great Britain. Directories*
Boatbuilders' and chandlers' directory of suppliers. — Tonbridge (47 High St., Tonbridge, Kent) : Weald of Kent Publications (Tonbridge) Ltd for Castle Books.
1977. — 1977. — 152p ; 21cm.
Index.
ISBN 0-904238-06-7 Pbk : £2.25
ISSN 0306-3593
Also classified at 381'.45'6238602541
(B77-13559)

338.4'7'62382002541 — Shipbuilding industries. *Great Britain. Directories*
United Kingdom shipping / [Data Research Group]. — Amersham (Hill House, [Hill Ave.], Amersham, Bucks.) : The Group.
[1976]. — 1976. — 200 leaves in various pagings ; 30cm.
ISBN 0-905570-68-5 Pbk : £17.00
Also classified at 381'.45'6238602541; 387'.025'41
(B77-06536)

338.4'7'6238200941 — Shipbuilding industries. *Great Britain*
Chilton, Michael. What goes on in shipbuilding? / [by] Michael Chilton. — Cambridge : Woodhead-Faulkner for Court Shipbuilders Ltd, Austin and Pickersgill Ltd, Scott Lithgow Ltd, A. and P. Appledore (London) Ltd, 1976. — viii,72p : ill, maps ; 22cm.
ISBN 0-85941-041-2 : £1.95
ISBN 0-85941-027-7 Pbk : £1.25
(B77-05276)

338.4'7'62382009413 — Shipbuilding industries. *Scotland. Central Lowlands, 1780-1972*
Moss, Michael Stanley. Workshop of the British Empire : engineering and shipbuilding in the West of Scotland / [by] Michael S. Moss, John R. Hume. — London [etc.] : Heinemann, 1977. — xvi,192p : ill, col maps(on lining papers), plans, port ; 29cm.
Bibl.: p.183-185. — Index.
ISBN 0-435-32590-6 : £9.50(£12.50 after 25th April 1977)
Primary classification 338.4'7'620009413
(B77-07173)

338.4'7'62402541 — Civil engineering industries. *Great Britain. Directories*
United Kingdom civil engineering companies / [Data Research Group]. — Amersham (Hill House, [Hill Ave.], Amersham, Bucks.) : The Group.
[1977]. — 1977. — 119 leaves in various pagings ; 30cm.
ISBN 0-86099-069-9 Sp : £18.00
(B77-31756)

338.4'7'62402541 — Construction industries. *Great Britain. Directories*
B & CJ directory. — Sutton (1 Throwley Way, Sutton, Surrey SM1 4QQ) : IPC Building and Contract Journals Ltd.
1977. — 1977. — clx,878p : ill, maps ; 22cm.
Tab indexed.
£12.00
ISSN 0068-3507
(B77-17365)

Directory of contractors and public works annual. — Sevenoaks [etc.] (Wrotham Place, Wrotham, Sevenoaks, Kent TN15 7AE) : Biggar and Co. (Publishers) Ltd.
1976 ed. — [1976]. — 164,[64]p(6 fold) : ill, maps ; 30cm.
ISBN 0-900167-14-9 Pbk : £7.75
(B77-05277)

1977 ed. — [1977]. — 158,[16]p(3 fold) : ill, maps ; 30cm.
Pbk : £8.80
(B77-31757)

338.4'7'62402541 — Consulting civil engineers. *Great Britain. Directories*
British Data Service. The BDS selective list of consulting engineers (civil and structural). — Frinton-on-Sea (Ashlyns House, Frinton-on-Sea, Essex) : B.D.S.
1974. — [1974]. — [2],66 leaves,15p ; 33cm.
Index.
ISBN 0-905923-00-6 Sp : £15.00
(B77-06537)

338.4'7'624028 — Construction equipment hire services. *Great Britain. Directories*
United Kingdom plant hire companies / [Data Research Group]. — Amersham (Hill House, [Hill Ave.], Amersham, Bucks.) : The Group.
[1976]. — 1976. — 182 leaves in various pagings ; 30cm.
ISBN 0-905570-15-4 Pbk : £16.00
(B77-00091)

338.4'7'6240941 — Construction industries. *Great Britain. Buyers' guides*
Construction industries buyers' guide : materials, plant, services. — Northwood [etc.] (8 High St., Northwood, Middx) : Biggar and Co. (Publishers) Ltd.
1976 ed. — [1976]. — 36,[24]p(2 fold) : ill ; 30cm.
'Published in conjunction with the 'Directory of contractors and public works annual''.
ISBN 0-900167-15-7 Pbk : £2.00
(B77-05278)

1977 ed. — [1977]. — 33,[12]p(2 fold) : ill ; 30cm.
'Published in conjunction with the "Directory of contractors and public works annual"'.
Pbk : Unpriced
(B77-31758)

338.4'7'6240941 — Construction industries. *Great Britain. Forecasts*
Construction forecasts : a report / prepared by the Joint Forecasting Committee of the Building and Civil Engineering EDCs. — London : H.M.S.O. [for the] National Economic Development Office.
1977-1978. — 1977. — v,25p : ill ; 30cm.
ISBN 0-11-700848-6 Sd : £4.00 yearly
ISSN 0308-079x
(B77-07175)

338.4'7'6240941 — Construction industries. *Great Britain. Statistics*
Private contractors' construction census / Department of the Environment. — London : H.M.S.O.
1975. — 1976. — [2],v,34p ; 30cm.
ISBN 0-11-751129-3 Sd : £1.50
ISSN 0308-1834
(B77-10249)

338.4'7'62409411 — Construction industries. *Scotland. Yearbooks*
Scottish building and civil engineering year book. — Edinburgh (Smith's Place House, Edinburgh EH6 8NU) : Edinburgh Pictorial Ltd.
1976. — [1977]. — 125p : ill, maps, 2 ports ; 26cm.
£3.00
ISSN 0085-6002
(B77-20107)

338.4'7'6241 — Quantity surveyors. *Great Britain. Directories*
British Data Service. The BDS selective list of quantity surveyors. — Frinton-on-Sea (Ashlyns House, Frinton-on-Sea, Essex) : British Data Service.
1976. — [1976]. — 127 leaves in various pagings ; 33cm.
Fourteen leaves printed on both sides. — Index.

ISBN 0-905923-02-2 Sp : Unpriced
ISSN 0309-3182
(B77-08857)

United Kingdom quantity surveyors / [Data Research Group]. — Amersham (Hill House, [Hill Ave.], Amersham, Bucks.) : The Group.
1976. — 1976. — 106 leaves in various pagings ; 30cm.
ISBN 0-905570-24-3 Sp : £14.00
(B77-00092)

338.4'7'628 — Water industries. *England. Proposals*
Great Britain. *Department of the Environment.* Review of the water industry in England and Wales : a consultative document / [Department of the Environment, Welsh Office, Ministry of Agriculture, Fisheries and Food]. — [London] ([2 Marsham St., SW1P 3EB]) : The Department : The Welsh Office : The Ministry, [1976]. — [3],33,[4]p : map ; 30cm.
ISBN 0-7184-0077-1 Sd : Unpriced
(B77-08858)

Great Britain. *Department of the Environment.* The water industry in England and Wales : the next steps / presented to Parliament by the Secretary of State the Environment, the Secretary of State for Wales and the Minister of Agriculture, Fisheries and Food ... — London : H.M.S.O., [1977]. — [1],ii,24p ; 25cm. — (Cmnd.6876)
ISBN 0-10-168760-5 Sd : £0.60
(B77-22431)

338.4'7'628 — Water industries. Great Britain. Department of the Environment. Review of the water industry in England and Wales. *England. Critical studies*
Inland Waterways Amenity Advisory Council. Observations on the 'Review of the water industry in England and Wales', the government consultative documents / [Inland Waterways Amenity Advisory Council]. — [London] ([122 Cleveland St., W1P 5DN]) : The Council, 1976. — [5],19[i.e.20],[22]p : ill, 2 maps ; 30cm.
Sp : £0.45
(B77-26893)

338.4'7'628102541 — Water supply industries. *Great Britain. Directories*
Who's who in the water industry : an official publication for the National Water Council. — Watford : Wheatland Journals.
1977. — [1977]. — 342p : ill, map ; 13cm.
ISBN 0-904561-23-2 Pbk : Unpriced
(B77-11664)

338.4'7'62810942 — Water supply systems. Planning by water authorities. *England, 1977. Reports, surveys*
National Water Council. Water supply prospects for 1977 / [National Water Council]. — London (1 Queen Anne's Gate, SW1H 9BT) : The Council, 1976. — 29p ; 30cm.
ISBN 0-904561-16-x Sd : £1.00
(B77-04017)

338.4'7'62872091724 — Water supply. Economic aspects. *Developing countries. Rural regions*
Saunders, Robert J. Village water supply : economics and policy in the developing world / [by] Robert J. Saunders, Jeremy J. Warford. — Baltimore ; London : Johns Hopkins University Press for the World Bank, 1976. — xiii,279p : 2 ill ; 24cm. — (International Bank for Reconstruction and Development. World Bank research publications)
Bibl.: p.241-264. — Index.
ISBN 0-8018-1876-1 : £12.00
ISBN 0-8018-1877-x Pbk : £4.80
(B77-13560)

338.4'7'628922025 — Fire protection industries. *Directories*
Fire protection directory : incorporating 'Fire brigades of the world'. — Tonbridge : 'Fire protection review' : [Distributed by] Benn Bros.

1977 : 37th ed. / [edited by J.L. Eades]. — [1977]. — 535,[8]p : ill ; 19cm.
Tab indexed. — Index.
ISBN 0-510-49508-7 : £10.00
Primary classification 363.3'7'025
(B77-17392)

338.4'7'6292 — Motor vehicle components industries & wholesale motor vehicle components trades. *Great Britain. Directories*
United Kingdom motor factors / [Data Research Group]. — Amersham (Hill House, [Hill Ave.], Amersham, Bucks.) : The Group.
[1976]. — 1976. — 107 leaves in various pagings ; 30cm.
ISBN 0-905570-47-2 Sp : £13.00
(B77-02116)

[1977]. — 1977. — 118 leaves in various pagings ; 30cm.
Sp : £14.00
(B77-16247)

338.4'7'629202541 — Motor vehicle industries & trades. *Great Britain. Directories*
Buyers' guide to the motor industry of Great Britain ... / Society of Motor Manufacturers and Traders. — London : Society of Motor Manufacturers and Traders.
1976-77. — [1976]. — 153p,[3]leaves : ill, map, port ; 30cm.
Text in English, French, German and Spanish, annotations in English. — Index.
Pbk : £3.00
(B77-31759)

1977-78. — [1977]. — 156p,[3]leaves : ill, map, port ; 30cm.
Text in English, French, German and Spanish, annotations in English. — Index.
Pbk : £3.50
(B77-31760)

338.4'7'62920941 — Motor vehicle industries. *Great Britain. Statistics*
The **motor** industry of Great Britain / [Society of Motor Manufacturers and Traders, Statistical Department]. — London : The Society.
1977. — [1977]. — 283p ; 25cm.
Pbk : £15.00(£8.00 to members)
(B77-31761)

338.4'7'6292098 — Motor vehicle industries. *Latin America. Study examples: Argentina, Chile & Mexico*
Jenkins, Rhys Owen. Dependent industrialization in Latin America : the automotive industry in Argentina, Chile and Mexico / [by] Rhys Owen Jenkins. — New York [etc.] ; London : Praeger, 1977. — xix,299p : ill ; 25cm. — (Praeger special studies in international economics and development)
Index.
ISBN 0-275-23220-4 : £14.80
(B77-16248)

338.4'7'62922220941 — Car industries. *Great Britain, 1895-1930*
Making of the motor car, 1895-1930 / [compiled by] Michael E. Ware. — Buxton (The Market Place, Hartington, Buxton, Derbyshire SK17 0AL) : Moorland Publishing Co., 1976. — 112p : chiefly ill, facsims ; 25cm. — (Historic industrial scenes)
Index.
ISBN 0-903485-39-7 : £4.20
(B77-04638)

338.4'7'62922220941 — Car industries. *Great Britain, to 1939*
Richardson, Kenneth, *b.1912.* The British motor industry, 1896-1939 / by Kenneth Richardson, assisted by C.N. O'Gallagher. — London [etc.] : Macmillan, 1977. — xiii,258p : ill, facsims, ports ; 22cm.
Bibl.: p.231-233. — Index.
ISBN 0-333-21925-2 : £8.95 : CIP rev.
(B77-19262)

338.4'7'62922220941 — Car industries. Great Britain. Central Policy Review Staff. Future of the British car industry. *Great Britain. Secondary school texts*
Maunder, Peter, *b.1943.* The UK car industry : a student's guide to the CPR's report, 'The future of the British car industry' / by Peter Maunder, David Richardson and Brian Walton. — London (Hamilton House, Mabledon Place, WC1H 9BH) : Economics Association, 1976. — [2],26p : ill ; 30cm. — ('A' Level economics study guide ; 2 ISSN 0309-5231)
Pierced for binder.
ISBN 0-901529-14-1 Sd : £0.50
(B77-16249)

338.4'7'62922220944 — Car industries. *France, to 1914*

Laux, James Michael. In first gear : the French automobile industry to 1914 / [by] James M. Laux. — Liverpool : Liverpool University Press, 1976. — xiii,239p,[22]p of plates : ill, facsims, maps, ports ; 24cm.
Index.
ISBN 0-85323-213-x : £10.00
(B77-12365)

338.4'7'62922602541 — Caravan industries. *Great Britain. Directories*

'**Caravan** industry' supplies and services directory. — Epsom (172 Kingston Rd, Ewell, Epsom, Surrey) : A.E. Morgan Publications Ltd.
1977 / editor G.D. Ritchie. — 1976. — 108p : ill ; 22cm.
Index.
ISBN 0-905481-03-8 Pbk : £2.00
(B77-09570)

338.4'7'62982 — Automatic vending industries and trades. Organisations. *Great Britain. Automatic Vending Association of Britain. Directories*

Automatic Vending Association of Britain. Handbook and list of members of the Automatic Vending Association of Britain. — London (31 Great Queen St., WC2B 5AA) : The Association.
1976 ed. — [1976]. — 98,[10]p(10 fold) : ill, port ; 21cm.
ISBN 0-904875-05-9 Pbk : £1.00
ISSN 0306-4204
(B77-05927)

1977 ed. — [1977]. — 106,[10]p(10 fold) : ill, port ; 21cm.
Pbk : Unpriced
ISSN 0306-4204
(B77-14604)

338.4'7'63074 — Agricultural exhibitions industries & trades. *Great Britain. Directories*

The **showman's** directory. — Godalming (Brook House, Mint St., Godalming, Surrey GU7 1HE) : S. and J. Lance.
1977 / compiled ... by Stephen & Jean Lance. — 1976. — 152p : ill ; 19cm.
Sd : £0.75
(B77-02834)

338.4'7'633491 — Potato production equipment industries. *Great Britain. Directories*

Potato Marketing Board. Machinery directory : a classified directory of manufacturers and concessionaires supplying machinery, fixed equipment, buildings and supplies associated with the production, storage and marketing of the potato crop / [Potato Marketing Board]. — [London] ([50 Hans Cres., SW1X 0NB]) : The Board.
2nd ed. — [1977]. — [1],47,[1]p ; 21cm.
ISBN 0-903623-20-x Sd : £0.25
ISSN 0309-295x
(B77-14116)

338.4'7'6413005 — Food industries & trades. *Serials*

Food trades directory and food buyer's year book. — London : Newman.
1977-78 : 20th year : 15th ed. — [1977]. — iii-iv,1000p : ill, map, plans ; 22cm.
ISBN 0-7079-6907-7 : £21.00
ISSN 0309-0264
(B77-18618)

338.4'7'6467202541 — Beauty care services. *Great Britain. Directories*

United Kingdom health food shops and beauty salons : including health clubs and sauna baths / [Data Research Group]. — Amersham (Hill House, [Hill Ave.,] Amersham, Bucks.) : The Group.
[1976]. — 1976. — 140p leaves in various pagings ; 30cm.
ISBN 0-905570-57-x Sp : £12.00
Primary classification 381'.45'6646
(B77-07257)

United Kingdom health food shops and beauty salons / [Data Research Group]. — Amersham (Hill House, [Hill Ave.], Amersham, Bucks.) : The Group.
[1977]. — 1977. — 156 leaves in various pagings ; 30cm.
ISBN 0-86099-035-4 Pbk : £14.00
Primary classification 381'.45'6646
(B77-29331)

338.4'7'64794 — Hotel equipment industries & trades. *Great Britain. Directories*

Sell's hotel, restaurant & canteen supplies. — Epsom : Sell's Publications.
1977. — [1976]. — viii,105p : ill ; 30cm.
ISBN 0-85499-664-8 Pbk : £4.00
ISSN 0308-8545
Also classified at 338.4'7'64795
(B77-05279)

338.4'7'6479441 — Hotel industries. *Great Britain. Directories*

United Kingdom hotels with 10 or more bedrooms / [Data Research Group]. — Amersham (Hill House, [Hill Ave.], Amersham, Bucks.) : The Group.
[1975]. — 1975. — 311 leaves in various pagings ; 30cm.
ISBN 0-905570-52-9 Pbk : £20.00
(B77-03435)

338.4'7'647944278 — Hotel industries. *Cumbria. Lake District. Serials*

Lakeland catering and hotel year book. — Carlisle (12 Lonsdale St., Carlisle) : 'Cumbria weekly digest' : 'Lakescene'.
[1st] : [1977]. — 1977. — [2],52p : ill ; 22cm.
Sd : £0.45
ISSN 0309-3999
Also classified at 338.4'7'647954278
(B77-18619)

338.4'7'64795 — Canteen & restaurant equipment industries & trades. *Great Britain. Directories*

Sell's hotel, restaurant & canteen supplies. — Epsom : Sell's Publications.
1977. — [1976]. — viii,105p : ill ; 30cm.
ISBN 0-85499-664-8 Pbk : £4.00
ISSN 0308-8545
Primary classification 338.4'7'64794
(B77-05279)

338.4'7'6479541 — Catering industries. *Great Britain. Directories*

United Kingdom caterers / [Data Research Group]. — Amersham (Hill House, [Hill Ave.], Amersham, Bucks.) : The Group.
[1976]. — 1976. — 95 leaves in various pagings ; 30cm.
ISBN 0-905570-51-0 Sp : £14.00
(B77-03436)

338.4'7'647954278 — Catering industries. *Cumbria. Lake District. Serials*

Lakeland catering and hotel year book. — Carlisle (12 Lonsdale St., Carlisle) : 'Cumbria weekly digest' : 'Lakescene'.
[1st] : [1977]. — 1977. — [2],52p : ill ; 22cm.
Sd : £0.45
ISSN 0309-3999
Primary classification 338.4'7'647944278
(B77-18619)

338.4'7'6485 — Cleaning maintenance services. *Great Britain. Directories*

United Kingdom cleaning contractors / [Data Research Group]. — Amersham (Hill House, [Hill Ave.], Amersham, Bucks.) : The Group.
[1977]. — 1977. — 83 leaves in various pagings ; 30cm.
ISBN 0-86099-050-8 Sp : £13.00
(B77-31762)

338.4'7'64850941 — Buildings. Cleaning maintenance services. *Great Britain. Serials*

Manual of building maintenance. — London : Turret Press.
1977 : 9th ed. — 1977. — 104p : ill ; 30cm.
Bibl.: p.98-101.
Pbk : £9.00
Primary classification 338.4'7'690240941
(B77-32484)

338.4'7'65910941 — Advertising industries. *Great Britain*

Kleinman, Philip. Advertising inside out / [by] Philip Kleinman. — London : W.H. Allen, 1977. — viii,248p ; 23cm.
Bibl.: p.239-240. — Index.
ISBN 0-491-01678-6 : £4.50
(B77-11117)

338.4'7'65910941 — Advertising industries. *Great Britain. Statistics*

Institute of Practitioners in Advertising. IPA vital statistics. — London : I.P.A.
1974-75. — 1976. — [2],11p : ill ; 30cm.
Cover title: How much, how many?.
Sd : £1.00
ISSN 0307-7063
(B77-24777)

1975-76. — 1977. — [2],11p : ill ; 30cm.
Cover title: How much, how many?.
Sd : £1.00
ISSN 0307-7063
(B77-24778)

338.4'7'659202541 — Public relations industries. *Great Britain. Directories*

Hollis press & public relations annual. — Sunbury-on-Thames (Contact House, Sunbury-on-Thames, Middx TW16 5HG) : Hollis Directories.
1977 : 10th ed. — 1977. — 440p : ill, map, port ; 21cm.
Index.
ISBN 0-900967-43-9 Pbk : £7.00
ISSN 0073-3059
(B77-33670)

338.4'7'66 — Chemical industries. *Organisation for Economic Co-operation and Development countries. Statistics*

L'**industrie** chimique = The chemical industry / [Organisation for Economic Co-operation and Development]. — Paris : O.E.C.D. ; [London] : [H.M.S.O.].
1974-1975. — 1976. — 3-138p : 3 ill ; 27cm.
Parallel French and English text.
Pbk : £4.40
ISBN 92-64-01564-7
(B77-05928)

338.4'7'6600254 — Chemical industries. *Western Europe. Directories*

Chemical Data Services. Chemical company profiles Western Europe / [compiled by Chemical Data Services]. — London (Dorset House, Stamford St., SE1 9LU) : Chemical Data Services, IPC Industrial Press, 1976. — iii,323p ; 30cm.
Index.
ISBN 0-905909-00-3 Pbk : £35.00
(B77-07176)

338.4'7'66002541 — Chemical industries. *Great Britain. Directories*

Chemical Data Services. Chemfacts, United Kingdom / [Chemical Data Services]. — London (IPC Industrial Press Ltd, Dorset House, Stamford St., SE1 9LU) : Chemical Data Services, 1977. — viii,141,[4]p : col ill, maps ; 30cm.
Index.
ISBN 0-905909-01-1 Pbk : £35.00
(B77-12925)

Chemical industry directory and who's who. — Tonbridge : E. Benn.
1977. — 1977. — 426p in various pagings : ill ; 29cm.
English text, English, French, German and Spanish list of contents. — Tab indexed. — Index.
ISBN 0-510-48710-6 Pbk : £15.00
(B77-12926)

338.4'7'66006241 — Chemical industries. Organisations. *Great Britain. Chemical Industries Association*

Chemical Industries Association. Serving and representing the chemical industry in Britain / [Chemical Industries Association]. — London (93 Albert Embankment, SE1 7TU) : C.I.A., [1976]. — 20p : map ; 21cm.
ISBN 0-900623-14-4 Sd : Unpriced
(B77-05280)

338.4'7'660094 — Chemical industries. Effects of world chemical industries. *Europe. Conference proceedings*

European Chemical Marketing Research Association. *International Conference, 11th, Madrid, 1976.* The changing world chemical scene - and its impact on Europe : proceedings of the [11th] International Conference of the European Chemical Marketing Research Association, Eurobuilding Hotel, Madrid, 13-15 October 1976 / editor of proceedings N.A. Perkins. — [London] ([c/o N.A. Perkins, 72 Lavington Rd, W13 9LR]) : [E.C.M.R.A.], [1977]. — [6],239p : ill, maps ; 21cm.
Spine title: 1976 ECMRA proceedings. — English text, English and Spanish introduction to the conference.
Pbk : £10.00
(B77-15156)

338.4'7'6600941 — Chemical industries. *Great Britain. Reports, surveys. Serials*

Chemical Industries Association. Activities report / [Chemical Industries Association]. — London (93 Albert Embankment, SE1 7TU) : The Association.
1974-1975. — [1975]. — [3],16,[1]p : ill(some col), ports ; 30cm.
ISBN 0-900623-34-9 Sd : Unpriced
ISSN 0309-2453
(B77-06538)

338.4'7'6600941 — Chemical industries. *Great Britain. Statistics*
UK chemical industry statistics handbook / [Chemical Industries Association]. — London (93 Albert Embankment, SE1 7TU) : The Association.
[1976] : 8th revised ed. — 1976. — 166p ; 21cm.
Index.
Pbk : £10.00
ISSN 0309-2356
(B77-04639)

338.4'7'6600947 — Chemical industries. *Eastern Europe, 1975-1980*
Chemical Data Services. The chemical industry of Eastern Europe, 1975-1980 / prepared by Chemical Data Services. — 4th ed. — [London] : IPC Business Press, 1976. — vii,220p : ill, maps ; 30cm.
Previous ed.: / prepared by ECN Chemical Data Services. Kingston upon Thames : IPC Business Press Information Services, 1974.
Pbk : £35.00
(B77-02835)

338.4'7'661002541 — Industrial chemicals industries. *Great Britain. Directories*
United Kingdom chemical manufacturers / [Data Research Group]. — Amersham (Hill House, [Hill Ave.], Amersham, Bucks.) : The Group.
[1975]. — 1975. — 60 leaves in various pagings ; 30cm.
ISBN 0-905570-45-6 Sp : £13.00
(B77-02117)

338.4'7'663200254 — Wines industries & wines agents allowing visits. *Europe. Directories*
Hogg, Anthony. Guide to visiting vineyards / [by] Anthony Hogg. — London : Joseph, 1976. — 240p : ill, maps ; 22cm.
Bibl. — Index. — Includes sections on spirits and on areas outside Europe.
ISBN 0-7181-1560-0 : £4.50
(B77-04640)

338.4'7'664002541 — Food processing industries. *Great Britain. Directories*
Food processing & packaging directory. — London : IPC Consumer Industries Press.
1977 : sixteenth ed. — [1977]. — [2],664p,[18]p : ill ; 22cm.
Tab indexed. — Index.
ISBN 0-617-00183-9 : £12.00
(B77-12927)

338.4'7'6641094267 — Sugar refining industries. *Essex, to 1975*
Lewis, Frank, *b.1891.* Essex and sugar : historic and other connections / by Frank Lewis ; with a foreword by Lord Lyle of Westbourne. — London [etc.] : Phillimore, 1976. — xi,132p,[4]p of plates : ill, port ; 23cm.
Index.
ISBN 0-85033-107-2 : £3.50
(B77-00662)

338.4'7'664122097291 — Cane sugar processing industries. *Cuba, 1760-1860*
Moreno Fraginals, Manuel. The sugarmill : the socioeconomic complex of sugar in Cuba, 1760-1860 / [by] Manuel Moreno Fraginals ; translated [from the Spanish] by Cedric Belfrage. — New York ; London : Monthly Review Press, 1976. — 182p : ill, facsims, port ; 29cm.
Translation of: 'El ingenio'. La Habana : Comísion Nacional Cubana de la UNESCO, 1964. — Index.
ISBN 0-85345-319-5 : £13.00
(B77-04641)

338.4'7'66415302541 — Confectionery industries. *Great Britain. Directories*
Confectionery, tobacco & newsagency buyers guide : confectionery, tobacco, newspapers & magazines, ice cream, soft drinks, smokers' requisites & allied products. — London (53 Christchurch Ave., North Finchley, N12 0DH) : CTN Enterprises Ltd.
1977. — [1977]. — 143p : ill ; 30cm.
English text, English, French and German preliminaries. — Previously published: as 'Confectionery & tobacco buyers guide'.
Pbk : £2.50
ISSN 0308-289x
Also classified at 338.4'7'679702541
(B77-32482)

338.4'7'66475202541 — Baking industries & trades. *Great Britain. Directories*
'British baker' directory & buyers' guide. — Croydon : Maclaren.
1978. — [1977]. — 176,xii p : ill ; 22cm.
Cover title.
Pbk : Unpriced
(B77-31763)

338.4'7'664752028 — Baking supplies industries. *Great Britain. Directories*
Master bakers' handbook and buyers guide. — London : Turret Press.
1977. — 1977. — 80p : ill ; 30cm.
Index.
ISBN 0-901808-18-0 Pbk : £6.50
(B77-10250)

338.4'7'66475209411 — Baking industries. *Scotland. Yearbooks*
Scottish Association of Master Bakers. Year book / Scottish Association of Master Bakers. — Edinburgh (19 Atholl Cres., Edinburgh EH3 8HJ) : The Association.
1977 / editor J.D. Copeman. — [1977]. — 176p : ill, ports ; 18cm.
ISBN 0-901117-08-0 Pbk : Unpriced
(B77-11118)

338.4'7'6648 — Tropical fruit processing industries. *Developing countries. Reports, surveys*
Vandendriessche, Henri. Tropical fruit processing industry : case studies of the industry in developing countries / by Henri Vandendriessche. — Paris : Development Centre of the Organisation for Economic Co-operation and Development ; [London] : [H.M.S.O.], 1976. — 268p ; 27cm. — (Organisation for Economic Co-operation and Development. Development Centre. Studies)
Bibl.: p.264-268.
Pbk : £5.60
ISBN 92-64-11489-0
(B77-00663)

338.4'7'66540941 — Waste mineral oils. Economic aspects. *Great Britain. Case studies*
Waste Management Advisory Council. An economic case study of waste oil, and its wider significance / Waste Management Advisory Council. — London : H.M.S.O., 1976. — iii, 28p ; 21cm. — (Paper ; no.3)
ISBN 0-11-751009-2 Sd : £0.60
(B77-08859)

338.4'7'6657025 — Gas industries. *Directories*
Walter Skinner's oil and gas international year book. — London : 'Financial Times'.
1977-78. — 1977. — 2-743p : ill(some col), map ; 22cm.
Text on lining papers. — Previously published: as 'Walter R. Skinner's oil and gas international year book'. — Index.
ISBN 0-900671-82-3 : £12.50
ISSN 0078-4273
Also classified at 338.2'7'282025
(B77-30035)

338.4'7'6657406141 — Gas supply industries. Consumer protection services. *Great Britain. National Gas Consumers' Council. Reports, surveys. Serials*
National Gas Consumers' Council. Report of the National Gas Consumers' Council for the year ended March 31. — London (130 Jermyn St., SW1Y 4UL) : The Council.
[1976-]1977. — [1977]. — [5],16,[1]p : ill, map ; 21cm.
ISBN 0-904409-03-1 Sd : Unpriced
ISSN 0305-098x
(B77-20108)

338.4'7'66574061427 — Gas supply industries. Consumer protection services. *Northern England. Northern Gas Consumers' Council. Reports, surveys. Serials*
Northern Gas Consumers' Council. The Northern Gas Consumers' Council report year ended 31st March. — Sunderland (Freeport, Sunderland, Tyne and Wear SR1 1BR) : The Council.
4th : [1976-]1977. — [1977]. — 62,[1]p : ill(some col), col map ; 22cm.
ISBN 0-904447-03-0 Sd : Unpriced
(B77-20109)

338.4'7'66577025 — Gas production industries. *Directories*
Gas directory and who's who. — London : Benn Bros.
1977. — 1977. — 264,[14]p : ill, maps(1 col), ports ; 30cm.
Tab indexed. — Previously published: as 'Gas directory and undertakings of the world'. — 'Incorporating "Gas industry directory", "Gas journal directory" and "Who's who in the gas industry"'.
ISBN 0-510-49609-1 Pbk : £10.00
ISSN 0307-3084
(B77-16779)

338.4'7'665773 — Liquefied petroleum gas industries. *Periodicals*
LP gas review. — London : Benn Bros.
Vol.1, no.1- ; Jan. 1977-. — 1977-. — ill(some col), ports ; 30cm.
Quarterly. — 56p. in 1st issue.
Sd : £0.90(£4.00 yearly)
ISSN 0309-3077
(B77-08280)

338.4'7'665810973 — Fuels: Hydrogen. Economic aspects. *United States. Reports, surveys*
Dickson, Edward M. The hydrogen energy economy : a realistic appraisal of prospects and impacts / [by] Edward M. Dickson, John W. Ryan, Marilyn H. Smulyan. — New York ; London : Praeger, 1977. — xxi,307p : ill, maps ; 25cm. — (Praeger special studies in US economic, social and political issues)
Bibl.: p.30-32. — Index.
ISBN 0-275-24290-0 : £13.40
(B77-30036)

338.4'7'666121 — Glass. Raw materials. Economic aspects
Raw materials for the glass industry / edited by P.W. Harben. — London : Metals Bulletin, 1977. — 3-130p : ill, 2 maps ; 30cm.
'An "Industrial minerals" consumer survey'.
Pbk : £10.00
(B77-30037)

338.4'7'66660941 — Pottery industries. *Great Britain, 250-1700*
Pottery and early commerce : characterization and trade in Roman and later ceramics / edited by D.P.S. Peacock. — London [etc.] : Academic Press, 1977. — xvi,340p,leaf of plate,[4]p of plates : ill, maps ; 24cm.
Bibl. — Index.
ISBN 0-12-547850-x : £12.80
(B77-30038)

338.4'7'6667025 — Refractories industries. *Directories*
International refractories handbook & directory. — London (5 Pond St., NW3 2PN) : London and Sheffield Publishing Co. Ltd.
[1976] / compiled by B.G.R. Lohan. — 1976. — 224p ; 21cm.
ISBN 0-900091-01-0 Pbk : £15.00
(B77-01235)

338.4'7'66689 — Concrete industries & trades. *Great Britain. Directories*
The **concrete** year book / [Cement and Concrete Association]. — Slough : The Association.
1977 : fifty-third ed. — 1977. — 640p : ill ; 30cm. — (Viewpoint publications)
Index.
ISBN 0-7210-1048-2 Pbk : £6.00
(B77-06539)

338.4'7'6671302541 — Laundry services. *Great Britain. Directories*
Laundries / [Data Research Group]. — Amersham (Hill House, [Hill Ave.], Amersham, Bucks.) : The Group.
Includes a section on dry cleaning.
[1976]. — [1976]. — 135 leaves in various pagings ; 30cm.
ISBN 0-905570-66-9 Sp : £14.00
(B77-05929)

United Kingdom laundries & dry cleaners / [Data Research Group]. — Amersham (Hill House, [Hill Ave.], Amersham, Bucks.) : The Group.
[1977]. — 1977. — 125 leaves in various pagings ; 30cm.
Sp : £15.00
(B77-26894)

338.4'7'667602541 — Paints industries. *Great Britain. Directories*
Polymers paint and colour year book. — Redhill (2 Queensway, Redhill, Surrey, RH1 1QS) : Fuel and Metallurgical Journals Ltd.
1977. — [1976]. — 308,[22]p : ill ; 21cm.
Index.
ISBN 0-901994-94-4 Pbk : £7.50
ISSN 0078-7817
(B77-03437)

1978. — [1977]. — 320,[20]p : ill ; 21cm.
Index.
ISBN 0-86108-004-1 Pbk : £8.50
ISSN 0078-7817
(B77-32483)

338.4'7'668302541 — Adhesives industries. *Great Britain. Directories*
Adhesives directory : a directory for the industrial user of adhesives. — Richmond, Surrey (26 Sheen Park, Richmond, Surrey) : A.S. O'Connor and Co. Ltd.
1977. — [1977]. — 194p(2 fold) : ill ; 18cm.
English text, English, French, German and Italian contents list. — Index.
Pbk : £2.75
ISSN 0305-3199
(B77-21752)

338.4'7'668402541 — Plastics industries. *Great Britain. Directories*
United Kingdom plastics industry / [Data Research Group]. — Amersham (Hill House, [Hill Ave.], Amersham, Bucks.) : The Group.
[1976]. — 1976. — 94 leaves in various pagings ; 30cm.
ISBN 0-905570-71-5 Sp : £13.00
(B77-05930)

[1977]. — 1977. — 92 leaves in various pagings ; 30cm.
ISBN 0-86099-071-0 Sp : £15.00
(B77-33671)

338.4'7'6684094 — Plastics industries. *Western Europe. Buyers' guides*
European plastics buyer's guide : guide to the plastics industry of Europe. — London : IPC Industrial Press.
[1977]. — 1977. — viii,644,[48]p : ill ; 30cm.
English, French, German, Italian and Spanish text. — Index.
Pbk : £15.00
ISSN 0306-5502
(B77-21753)

338.4'7'668502541 — Cosmetics, perfumes & toiletries industries. *Great Britain. Directories*
United Kingdom pharmaceutical & toiletry manufacturers / [Data Research Group]. — Amersham (Hill House, [Hill Ave.], Amersham, Bucks.) : The Group.
[1976]. — 1976. — 69 leaves in various pagings ; 30cm.
ISBN 0-905570-77-4 Sp : £14.00
Primary classification 338.4'7'615102541
(B77-07172)

[1977]. — 1977. — 70 leaves in various pagings ; 30cm.
ISBN 0-86099-061-3 Sp : £14.00
Primary classification 338.4'7'615102541
(B77-31049)

338.4'7'66862025 — Fertiliser industries. *Directories*
British Sulphur Corporation. World directory of fertilizer products / British Sulphur Corporation Limited. — 4th ed. — London (25 Wilton Rd, SW1V 1NH) : The Corporation, 1977. — 118p : ill ; 30cm.
Previous ed.: 1975. — Index.
Sp : Unpriced
(B77-28472)

338.4'7'66862028 — Fertiliser manufacturing equipment industries. *Directories*
British Sulphur Corporation. World guide to fertilizer plant equipment / the British Sulphur Corporation Ltd. — 2nd ed. — London (25 Wilton Rd, SW1V 1NH) : The Corporation, 1977. — 198p : ill ; 30cm.
Previous ed.: published as 'World guide to fertilizer plant and equipment'. 1973. — Index.
Sp : £25.00
(B77-24073)

338.4'7'6686206241 — Fertiliser industries. Organisations. *Great Britain. Fertiliser Manufacturers Association, to 1975*
Keatley, W S. The Fertiliser Manufacturers Association : the second fifty years 1925-1975 / by W.S. Keatley. Preceded by a condensed version of the book 'Fifty years of Association history' / written by A.N. Gray in 1926. — [London] ([93 Albert Embankment, SE1 7TU) : [The Association], [1977?]. — 3-72p ; 22cm.
Cover title: 100 years of the Fertiliser Manufacturers Association.
£2.00
(B77-29255)

338.4'7'6690212 — Metals industries. *Statistics*
'Metal bulletin' handbook : (incorporating 'Quin's metal handbook'). — London : Metal Bulletin.
1976 : ninth ed. / edited by Ruby Packard. — [1976]. — 847p : ill ; 23cm.
£12.00
ISSN 0076-664x
(B77-17988)

338.4'7'6691 — Iron & steel industries. *Organisation for Economic Co-operation and Development countries. Statistics*
L'industrie sidérurgique = The iron and steel industry / [Organisation for Economic Co-operation and Development]. — Paris : O.E.C.D. ; [London] : [H.M.S.O.].
1975. — 1977. — 61p(10 fold) : ill ; 27cm.
Parallel French and English text.
Pbk : £2.50
ISBN 92-64-01607-4
(B77-14605)

338.4'7'66910941 — Iron & steel industries. *Great Britain. Statistics*
Iron and steel industry annual statistics for the United Kingdom. — Croydon (P.O. Box 230, 12 Addiscombe Rd, Croydon CR9 6BS) : Iron and Steel Statistics Bureau.
1976. — [1977]. — 100p ; 26cm.
Pbk : £12.00
(B77-27730)

338.4'7'66910942784 — Iron & steel industries. *West Cumbria, to 1976*
Lancaster, J Y. The iron and steel industry of West Cumberland : an historical survey / [by] J.Y. Lancaster and D.R. Wattleworth. — [Workington] ([Workington, Cumbria]) : British Steel Corporation, Workington and Barrow Works, Teesside Division, 1977. — xii,198p,[2] fold leaves of plates : ill(incl 1 col), maps, plans, ports ; 23cm.
Ill., text on lining papers. — Bibl.: p.176-179. — Index.
ISBN 0-9505929-0-0 : £4.75
(B77-31050)

338.4'7'669142 — Stainless steel industries. *Directories*
Stainless steel : a world guide / edited by Raymond Cordero. — London : Metal Bulletin, 1975. — 3-118p : ill ; 25cm.
Pbk : £10.00
(B77-30039)

338.4'7'6697220941 — Aluminium smelting industries. Expenditure by government. *Great Britain*
Jones, Colin, *b.1929.* The £200,000 job! : a study of Government intervention in aluminium smelting - the way the money goes - / [by] Colin Jones. — London (Wilfred St., S.W.1) : Centre for Policy Studies, 1977. — xiv,34p ; 21cm.
ISBN 0-9504392-9-0 Pbk : £1.55
(B77-27731)

338.4'7'671028 — Metal products manufacturing equipment industries. *Great Britain. Directories*
Fab guide : a buyers' directory for welding and fabrication engineers. — Guildford : IPC Science and Technology Press [for] 'Welding and metal fabrication'.
77 / managing editor D. Johnson. — 1977. — 156p : ill ; 30cm.
ISBN 0-902852-74-4 Pbk : £5.00
ISSN 0306-0217
(B77-13561)

338.4'7'671202541 — Foundry industries. *Great Britain. Directories*
The **foundry** directory and register of forges. — Tonbridge : Standard Catalogue Co.
9th ed. : 1977-1978. — [1977]. — xxxii,197, 106p,[4] leaves : ill, maps ; 30cm.
English text, French and German note. — Index.
Pbk : £7.00
ISSN 0071-8730
(B77-20110)

338.4'7'6715202541 — Welding industries. *Great Britain. Directories*
United Kingdom welders / [Data Research Group]. — Amersham (Hill House, [Hill Ave.], Amersham, Bucks.) : The Group.
[1976]. — 1976. — 137 leaves in various pagings ; 30cm.
ISBN 0-905570-60-x Sp : £14.00
(B77-05931)

1977. — [1977]. — 147 leaves in various pagings ; 30cm.
ISBN 0-86099-034-6 Sp : £16.00
(B77-22432)

338.4'7'671702541 — Metals finishing industries. *Great Britain. Directories*
Metal finishers / [Data Research Group]. — Amersham (Hill House, [Hill Ave.], Amersham, Bucks.) : The Group.
[1976]. — 1976. — 69 leaves in various pagings ; 30cm.
ISBN 0-905570-75-8 Sp : £14.00
(B77-07178)

United Kingdom metal finishers / [Data Research Group]. — Amersham (Hill House, [Hill Ave.], Amersham, Bucks.) : The Group.
[1977]. — 1977. — 67 leaves in various pagings ; 30cm.
ISBN 0-86099-059-1 Sp : £16.00
(B77-31764)

338.4'7'671823 — Sheet metal industries. *Great Britain. Directories*
United Kingdom sheet metal workers / [Data Research Group]. — Amersham (Hill House, [Hill Ave.], Amersham, Bucks.) : The Group.
[1976]. — 1976. — 115 leaves in various pagings ; 30cm.
ISBN 0-905570-07-3 Sp : £14.00
(B77-00093)

338.4'7'67284 — Ferrous wire manufacturing industries. *Great Britain, to 1962*
Stones, Frank. The British ferrous wire industry, 1882-1962 / by Frank Stones. — Sheffield : Northend, 1977. — xv,418p,[22]p of plates : facsims, ports ; 26cm.
Jacket title: The history of the British ferrous wire industry, 1882-1962. — Index.
Unpriced
(B77-30040)

338.4'7'6733093622 — Bronze industries. *Southern England, ca B.C.1800-ca B.C.1100*
Rowlands, Michael John. The production and distribution of metalwork in the Middle Bronze Age in southern Britain / [by] M.J. Rowlands. — Oxford : British Archaeological Reports, 1976. — 2v,([7],447,[89]p of plates) : ill, maps ; 30cm. — (British archaeological reports ; 31 ISSN 0306-1205)
Cover title: The organisation of Middle Bronze Age metalworking. — Spine title: Middle Bronze Age metalworking. — Bibl.: p.432-446.
ISBN 0-904531-44-9 Pbk : £7.50
(B77-01236)

338.4'7'674002541 — Timber products industries. *Great Britain. Directories*
Timber trades directory : containing detailed information on firms engaged in the timber and allied trades in England, Wales, Scotland and N. Ireland and throughout the world. — Tonbridge : Benn Bros [for] 'Timber trades journal'.
[1977] : 23rd ed. — 1977. — 376,[22]p : ill(some col) ; 30cm.
Tab indexed.
ISBN 0-510-49815-9 Pbk : £15.00
Also classified at 380.1'45'67402541
(B77-17366)

338.4'7'67409931 — Timber industries. *New Zealand, to 1972*
Simpson, Thomas E. Kauri to radiata : origin and expansion of the timber industry of New Zealand / by Thomas E. Simpson. — Auckland [etc.] ; London : Hodder and Stoughton, 1973. — xviii,442p,[40]p of plates : ill, ports ; 26cm.
Bibl.: p.429-431. — Index.
ISBN 0-340-17738-1 : Unpriced
(B77-18620)

338.4'7'6752025 — Leather working industries. *Directories*
Leather guide : international directory of the industry. — Tonbridge : E. Benn [for] 'Leather'.
1977-8. — 1977. — 264p : ill ; 30cm.
Includes 'A five-language glossary of everyday leather terms' in English, French, German, Spanish and Italian. — Previously published: as 'European leather guide'.
ISBN 0-510-49819-1 Pbk : £12.00
ISSN 0140-413x
(B77-26895)

338.4'7'67614 — Waste paper. Recycling. Economic aspects. *England*
Wray, Margaret. The economics of waste paper reclamation in England / [by] Margaret Wray, Michele Nation. — [Hatfield] ([Hatfield, Herts. AL10 9AD]) : Hatfield Polytechnic, 1977. — xiv,321[i.e.328]p : ill, facsims, 2 forms, map ; 30cm.
Bibl.: p.302-321.
ISBN 0-900458-06-2 Pbk : £5.00
(B77-17989)

338.4'7'6762 — Paper converting industries. *Great Britain. Directories*
The **'Converter'** directory : suppliers and services to the UK converting industry. — [London] ([3 Caledonian Rd, N1 9DX]) : [Embankment Press].
1976. — [1976]. — 160p : ill ; 23cm.
Index.
£6.00
ISSN 0309-2143
(B77-03438)

The '**Converter**' directory : suppliers and services to the UK converting industry. — Wembley (Building 59, G.E.C. Estate, East La., Wembley, Middx) : Embankment Press.
1977. — 1977. — 3-184p : ill ; 22cm.
Index.
£9.00
ISSN 0309-2143
(B77-26187)

338.4'7'6762025 — Paper & paper products industries & trades. *Directories*
Phillips paper trade directory : Europe ; [and], Mills of the world. — London : Benn Bros.
1977. — [1977]. — [8],964p : ill ; 25cm.
ISBN 0-510-49010-7 : £20.00
ISSN 0079-158x
(B77-22433)

338.4'7'676209417 — Paper industries. *Ireland (Republic). Reports, surveys*
Roche, Francis White. Report on the printing and paper industry / presented to the Printing and Paper Industry Training Committee of An Comhairle Oiliuna by F.W. Roche and J.A. Murray of Colin McIver Associates (Ireland) Ltd. — [Dublin] ([49 Upper Mount St., Dublin 2]) : [Colin McIver Associates (Ireland) Ltd], 1977. — vii,109p : forms ; 30cm.
Pbk : Unpriced
Primary classification 338.4'7'686209417
(B77-31765)

338.4'7'6762094235 — Paper manufacturing industries. *Devon, to 1975*
Chitty, Jean. Paper in Devon / by Jean Chitty ; foreword by Christine Tyler. — Exeter ([Exeter Medical Library, Postgraduate Medical Centre, Barrack Rd, Exeter, Devon]) : The author, 1976. — 72p,[20]p of plates,leaf of plate : ill, facsims, form, map ; 26cm.
Bibl.: p.71-72.
Sd : £1.00
(B77-23217)

338.4'7'677 — Textile industries. *Organisation for Economic Co-operation and Development countries. Statistics*
Organisation for Economic Co-operation and Development. L'industrie textile dans les pays de l'OCDE = Textile industry in OECD countries / [Organisation for Economic Co-operation and Development]. — Paris : O.E.C.D. ; [London] : [H.M.S.O.].
1975. — 1977. — 91p ; 20x27cm.
Parallel French and English text.
Pbk : £2.00
ISBN 92-64-01651-1
(B77-20111)

338.4'7'67702822 — Spinning industries. *Great Britain. Directories*
United Kingdom spinners & weavers / [Data Research Group]. — Amersham (Hill House, [Hill Ave.], Amersham, Bucks.) : The Group.
[1976]. — 1976. — 82 leaves in various pagings ; 30cm.
ISBN 0-905570-61-8 Sp : £13.00
Also classified at 338.4'7'67702824
(B77-07180)

[1977]. — 1977. — 66 leaves in various pagings ; 30cm.
ISBN 0-86099-062-1 Sp : £15.00
Also classified at 338.4'7'67702824
(B77-31051)

338.4'7'67702824 — Hand loom weaving industries. *Scotland. Strathclyde Region. Hamilton (District), to 1939*
Walker, Gavin. Hand-loom weaving in Hamilton & district / edited by C. Smith ; written and illustrated by G. Walker. — [Hamilton] ([District Museum, 129 Muir St., Hamilton, Lanarkshire ML3 6BJ]) : Hamilton District Libraries and Museum Dept, [1976]. — 28p : ill, map, plan ; 21cm.
Bibl.: p.28.
ISBN 0-9501983-3-1 Sd : £0.20
(B77-11666)

338.4'7'67702824 — Weaving industries. *Great Britain. Directories*
United Kingdom spinners & weavers / [Data Research Group]. — Amersham (Hill House, [Hill Ave.], Amersham, Bucks.) : The Group.
[1976]. — 1976. — 82 leaves in various pagings ; 30cm.
ISBN 0-905570-61-8 Sp : £13.00
Primary classification 338.4'7'67702822
(B77-07180)

[1977]. — 1977. — 66 leaves in various pagings ; 30cm.
ISBN 0-86099-062-1 Sp : £15.00
Primary classification 338.4'7'67702822
(B77-31051)

338.4'7'678202541 — Rubber industries. *Great Britain. Directories*
United Kingdom rubber industry / [Data Research Group]. — Amersham (Hill House, [Hill Ave.], Amersham, Bucks.) : The Group.
[1976]. — 1976. — 66 leaves in various pagings ; 30cm.
ISBN 0-905570-74-x Sp : £12.00
(B77-05932)

338.4'7'6796 — Brush industries & trades. *Directories*
Directory of the brush and allied trades. — Watford : Wheatland Journals.
1976-7 ed. : 29th ed. — [1976]. — 204p : ill ; 24cm.
Cover title : Brush and allied trades directory. — Index.
ISBN 0-900971-46-0 Pbk : £4.35
ISSN 0305-4861
(B77-03439)

338.4'7'6797025 — Tobacco industries & trades. *Directories*
World tobacco directory. — London (21 John Adam St., WC2N 6JH) : International Trade Publications Ltd [etc.].
25th Jubilee ed. : 1976-1977. — [1977]. — 312p(4 fold) : ill, col maps ; 30cm.
English, German, French and Spanish text. — Index.
£17.50
ISBN 0-901994-66-9
(B77-33672)

338.4'7'679702541 — Tobacco products industries. *Great Britain. Directories*
Confectionery, tobacco & newsagency buyers guide : confectionery, tobacco, newspapers & magazines, ice cream, soft drinks, smokers' requisites & allied products. — London (53 Christchurch Ave., North Finchley, N12 0DH) : CTN Enterprises Ltd.
1977. — [1977]. — 143p : ill ; 30cm.
English text, English, French and German preliminaries. — Previously published: as 'Confectionery & tobacco buyers guide'.
Pbk : £2.50
ISSN 0308-289x
Primary classification 338.4'7'66415302541
(B77-32482)

338.4'7'68 — Rural craft industries & trades. *England. Directories*
Craft workshops in the countryside, England and Wales / [Council for Small Industries in Rural Areas]. — London : CoSIRA.
16th ed. : 1977. — 1977. — [1],192p : ill, map ; 21cm.
Index.
ISBN 0-85407-024-9 Pbk : £0.75
(B77-09571)

338.4'7'68 — Sign manufacturing industries. *Great Britain. Directories*
Sign makers and suppliers year book and directory. — Ewell (172 Kingston Rd, Ewell, Surrey) : A.E. Morgan Publications Ltd.
1977. — [1977]. — 3-42p : ill ; 28cm.
Sd : £1.50
(B77-24074)

338.4'7'68111 — Clockmakers & watchmakers, to 1880. *Lists*
Watchmakers and clockmakers of the world. — London : N.A.G. Press.
In 2 vols.
Vol.2 / [by] Brian Loomes. — 1976. — xiii, 263p ; 23cm.
Bibl.: p.v-vi.
ISBN 0-7198-0080-3 : £4.95
(B77-12366)

338.4'7'68111025 — Clockmakers & watchmakers, 1632-1825. *Directories*
Watchmakers and clockmakers of the world. — London : N.A.G. Press.
In 2 vols.
Vol.1 / by G.H. Baillie. — 3rd ed. — 1976. — xxxv,388p : maps ; 23cm.
This ed. originally published: 1951.
ISBN 0-7198-0040-4 : £3.95
(B77-25460)

338.4'7'68141802541 — Photographic equipment industries & trades. *Great Britain. Directories*
'**ICP**' directory of photographic equipment and services. — Croydon : Maclaren.
[1977]. — [1977]. — 78p : ill ; 30cm.
Spine title: 'The industrial and commercial photographer' directory and buyers guide.
Pbk : Unpriced
ISSN 0305-0866
(B77-07838)

338.4'7'6816 — Printing machinery industries. Organisations. *Great Britain. British Printing Machinery Association. Directories*
British Printing Machinery Association. Index of members and products / British Printing Machinery Association. — London (12 Cliffords Inn, Fetter La., EC4A 1DX) : The Association.
1977. — [1977]. — [1],39,[1]p ; 21cm.
'This booklet is available in English, French, German, Italian and Spanish' - p.1. — Index.
ISBN 0-905303-01-6 Sd : Unpriced
(B77-14117)

338.4'7'6817502541 — Scientific instruments industries. *Great Britain. Directories*
Instrument manufacturers, United Kingdom / Eurolec. — Chelmsford : Rayner.
1977-1978 : 2nd ed. — 1977. — viii,312p : map ; 30cm. — (Eurolec ; 52)
Previously published: in 2 vols.
ISBN 0-900614-52-8 Pbk : £12.00
(B77-20992)

338.4'7'68176105 — Medical equipment industries. *Periodicals. For Middle Eastern businessmen*
MEH : Middle East health supply & service. — Sutton (1 Throwley Way, Sutton, Surrey) : Middle East Publishing Co.
Vol.1, no.1- ; Jan. 1977-. — 1977-. — ill, ports ; 30cm.
Ten issues a year. — 60p. in 1st issue. — English text, Arabic notes.
Sd : £1.50(£15.00 yearly)
ISSN 0309-2003
(B77-15747)

338.4'7'68176302541 — Agricultural equipment industries & trades. *Great Britain. Directories*
Where to buy agricultural and horticultural equipment, supplies, services. — Redhill : 'Where to Buy'.
1977 ed. / editor H.F. Loader. — [1977]. — 116p : ill ; 30cm.
Pbk : £3.00
(B77-04018)

338.4'7'68302541 — Hardware industries & trades. *Great Britain. Directories*
Benn's hardware directory. — Tonbridge : Benn Bros.
1977 / editor D. Muggleton. — [1977]. — 592p in various pagings : ill ; 30cm.
Tab indexed. — Index.
ISBN 0-510-48508-1 : £11.00
(B77-07839)

338.4'7'684002541 — Furnishings industries & trades. *Great Britain. Directories*
Directory to the furnishing trade : comprehensive guide to manufacturers, manufacturers' suppliers and retailers. — London (125 High St., [SW19 2JN]) : Benn Bros [for] 'Cabinet maker and retail furnisher'.
1977 : 19th ed. — 1977. — 442p in various pagings : ill ; 30cm.
Thumb indexed. — Index.
ISBN 0-510-49209-6 : £18.50
(B77-06540)

338.4'7'68502541 — Leather products industries. *Great Britain. Directories*
United Kingdom leather goods manufacturers / [Data Research Group]. — Amersham (Hill House, [Hill Ave.], Amersham, Bucks.) : The Group.
[1976]. — 1976. — 44 leaves in various pagings ; 30cm.
ISBN 0-905570-70-7 Sp : £12.00
(B77-07179)

[1977]. — 1977. — 32 leaves in various pagings ; 30cm.
ISBN 0-86099-044-3 Sp : Unpriced
(B77-26896)

338.4'7'68530254 — Footwear industries & trades. *Europe. Directories*
Shoe retailers manual. — London (84 Great Eastern St., EC2A 3ED) : 'Shoe and Leather News'.
[1977-8]. — 1977. — 144p : ill ; 30cm.
English, French and German text. — Supersedes: Shoe trades directory. Part 2 : A guide to market resources available in Europe to shoe retailers.
Pbk : £8.00
ISSN 0140-5578
(B77-33673)

338.4'7'685302541 — Footwear industries. *Great Britain. Directories*
United Kingdom footwear manufacturers / [Data Research Group]. — Amersham (Hill House, [Hill Ave.], Amersham, Bucks.) : The Group. [1976]. — 1976. — 41 leaves in various pagings ; 30cm.
ISBN 0-905570-79-0 Sp : £12.00
(B77-07840)

1977. — [1977]. — [40] leaves in various pagings ; 30cm.
ISBN 0-86099-047-8 Sp : £14.00
(B77-28473)

338.4'7'68530941 — Footwear industries & trades. *Great Britain. Reports, surveys*
Economists Advisory Group. British footwear, the future : a report prepared for the Department of Industry / by Economists Advisory Group Limited ... — London (54b Tottenham Court Rd, W1P 9RE) : E.A.G., [1976]. — 7v. : ill, forms ; 30cm.
Sp : £50.00
(B77-29256)

Footwear Industry Study Steering Group. Report of the Footwear Industry Study Steering Group. — London : Department of Industry, 1977. — 330p in various pagings ; 30cm.
Chairman: G.W. Marriott.
Pbk : £4.60
(B77-23218)

Shoe and Allied Trades Research Association. Footwear industry study / [Shoe and Allied Trades Research Association]. — Kettering (Rockingham Rd, Kettering, Northants. NN16 9JH) : The Association.
Production efficiency and technology : Group 3 report. Phase 1. Vol.1 : Summary. — 1976. — [2],19p ; 30cm.
Sp : £2.50
(B77-29257)

Production efficiency and technology : Group 3 report. Phase 1. Vol.2 : Papers on processes. — 1976. — [2],44p : 1 ill ; 30cm.
Bibl.: p.7.
Sp : £2.50
(B77-29258)

Production efficiency and technology : Group 3 report. Phase 1. Vol.3 : Papers on materials. — 1976. — [2],39p : 1 ill ; 30cm.
Sp : £2.50
(B77-29259)

Production efficiency and technology : Group 3 report. Phase 1. Vol.4 : Papers on management aspects. — 1976. — [2],136p : 1 ill, map ; 30cm.
Bibl.
Sp : £2.50
(B77-29260)

Production efficiency and technology : Group 3 report. Phase 2. Project S1 : An interfirm comparison of productivity and costs, financial aspects. — 1977. — [3],47p ; 30cm.
Sp : £2.50
(B77-29262)

Production efficiency and technology : Group 3 report. Phase 2. Project S1 : An interfirm comparison of productivity and costs, manufacturing and technical aspects. — 1977. — [4],70p : ill ; 30cm.
Bibl.: p.62.
Sp : £2.50
(B77-29261)

Production efficiency and technology : Group 3 report. Phase 2. Project S2 : Design function audit. — 1976. — [2],55p : form ; 30cm.
Sp : £2.50
(B77-29263)

Production efficiency and technology : Group 3 report. Phase 2. Project S3 : Cost effectiveness of investment machinery. — 1976. — [4],65p ; 30cm.
Sp : £2.50
(B77-29264)

Production efficiency and technology : Group 3 report. Phase 2. Project S4 : The supply of materials and components. — 1976. — [2],69p : ill, form ; 30cm.
Sp : £2.50
(B77-29265)

338.4'7'68541094244 — Leather glove industries. *Hereford and Worcester. Worcester, 1800-1900*
Lyes, D C. The leather glove industry of Worcester in the nineteenth century / by D.C. Lyes. — [Worcester] ([Foregate St., Worcester WR1 1DT]) : Worcester City Museum and Art Gallery, 1976. — 88p : ill, map ; 22cm.
Bibl.: p.86-88.
ISBN 0-903184-01-x Sd : Unpriced
(B77-08281)

338.4'7'686025421 — Book industries & trades. *London, 1775-1800. Directories*
Maxted, Ian. The London book trades, 1775-1800 : a preliminary checklist of members / [by] Ian Maxted. — Folkestone : Dawson, 1977. — xxxv,257p : geneal tables ; 28cm.
Bibl.: p.xiv-xvii.
ISBN 0-7129-0696-7 : Unpriced
(B77-21754)

338.4'7'6860256 — Book industries & trades. *Africa. Directories*
The **African** book world & press, a directory = Répertoire du livre et de la presse en Afrique / compiled by the 'African book publishing record' ; Hans M. Zell, editor. — Oxford (P.O. Box 56, Oxford OX1 3EL) : Hans Zell (Publishers) Ltd, 1977. — xxvi,[1],296,[1]p ; 31cm.
English and French text.
ISBN 0-905450-00-0 : £25.00
Primary classification 021'.0025'6
(B77-23058)

338.4'7'68609424 — Book industries & trades. *England. West Midlands, to 1850. Lists*
Birmingham Bibliographical Society. Working papers for an historical directory of the West Midlands book trade to 1850 / compiled by members of the Birmingham Bibliographical Society and edited by P.B. Freshwater. — Birmingham (Main Library, University of Birmingham, Birmingham B15 2TT) : The Society.
No.3 : 1790-1799 : with addenda to working papers 1 and 2. — 1977. — [3],iv,25p ; 30cm.
Bibl.: p.iii-iv.
ISBN 0-904474-03-8 Sd : £1.00(£0.75 to members)
(B77-17990)

338.4'7'686202541 — Printing industries. *Great Britain. Directories*
National Graphical Association. List of offices recognised by the NGA (fair list). List of offices recognised by SLADE (fair list). — [Bedford] ([63 Bromham Rd, Bedford]) : [N.G.A.].
[1977, as at March]. — [1977]. — 329p ; 19cm.
Cover title. — Index.
Pbk : Unpriced
(B77-27732)

Printing trades directory. — London : Benn Bros [for] 'Printing trades journal'.
1977. — [1977]. — 356p,[12]p : ill(some col) ; 30cm.
Thumb indexed.
ISBN 0-510-49163-4 Pbk : £15.00
(B77-08860)

338.4'7'686206241 — Printing industries. Organisations. *Great Britain. British Printing Industries Federation. Yearbooks*
Printing industries annual / [British Printing Industries Federation]. — London (11 Bedford Row, WC1R 4DX) : The Federation.
1977 : [fifty-eighth year]. — [1977]. — 814,[20] p,plate : ill(some col), map, port ; 23cm.
Thumb indexed. — Index.
ISBN 0-85168-102-6 : £15.00
ISSN 0308-1443
(B77-11667)

338.4'7'68620941 — Printing industries. *Great Britain. Periodicals*
Printing industries. — London (11 Bedford Row, WC1R 4DX) : British Printing Industries Federation.
Previously issued by the Federation, under its earlier name, the British Federation of Master Printers.
Vol.73- ; 1974-. — [1974]-. — ill, ports ; 30cm.
Monthly. — 52p. in Jan. 1977 issue.
Pbk : Controlled circulation
ISSN 0307-7195
(B77-13562)

338.4'7'686209417 — Printing industries. *Ireland (Republic). Reports, surveys*
Roche, Francis White. Report on the printing and paper industry / presented to the Printing and Paper Industry Training Committee of An Comhairle Oiliuna by F.W. Roche and J.A. Murray of Colin McIver Associates (Ireland) Ltd. — [Dublin] ([49 Upper Mount St., Dublin 2]) : [Colin McIver Associates (Ireland) Ltd], 1977. — vii,109p : forms ; 30cm.
Pbk : Unpriced
Also classified at 338.4'7'676209417
(B77-31765)

338.4'7'6862094254 — Private presses. *Leicestershire, 1945-1975*
Morris, Ann. The private press in Leicestershire / [by] Ann Morris. — Loughborough (28 Pantain Rd, Loughborough, Leics.) : Plough Press, 1976. — [4],55p : ill(some col), facsims(some col) ; 26cm.
Bibl.: p.55.
ISBN 0-902813-06-4 Sd : £3.00(special bound edition £6.00)
(B77-02118)

338.4'7'6862094255 — Printing industries. *Northamptonshire, to ca 1890*
Kennedy, Joseph C. An introduction to the history of printing & associated trades in Northamptonshire / by Joseph C. Kennedy. — [Northampton] ([c/o J.C. Kennedy, 242 Obelisk Rise, New Boughton Green, Northampton NN2 8JW]) : Northamptonshire Caxton Quincentenary Committee, 1976. — [15]p ; 21cm.
Bibl.: p.[15].
ISBN 0-9505483-0-8 Sd : £0.15
(B77-05281)

338.4'7'68702541 — Clothing industries. *Great Britain. Directories*
United Kingdom clothing manufacturers / [Data Research Group]. — Amersham (Hill House, [Hill Ave.], Amersham, Bucks.) : The Group.
1976. — [1976]. — 82 leaves in various pagings ; 30cm.
ISBN 0-905570-25-1 Sp : £15.00
(B77-00094)

1977. — [1977]. — [114] leaves in various pagings ; 30cm.
ISBN 0-86099-048-6 Sp : £17.00
(B77-28474)

338.4'7'68702541 — Clothing industries & trades. *Great Britain. Directories*
Clothing Export Council of Great Britain. The Clothing Export Council of Great Britain's directory for the clothing industry / [1977 : fourth ed.] ; edited by P.W. Gamble & D. Price. — London : Kemps, [1977]. — 271,[32] p : ill, facsim, port ; 30cm.
Introduction, section headings and index in English, French, German and Italian. — Index.
ISBN 0-905255-10-0 Pbk : £8.00
(B77-13563)

338.4'7'6870941 — Clothing industries. *Great Britain. Serials*
Hard's clothing industry yearbook / collated, prepared, revised and produced by the editorial staff of 'Manufacturing clothier'. — London : United Trade Press.
1976-7. — 1976. — 110p : ill ; 30cm.
ISBN 0-85471-029-9 Pbk : £5.00
ISSN 0308-9363
(B77-09572)

338.4'7'6870941 — Clothing industries & trades. *Great Britain. Periodicals*
Apparel news. — [London] ([40 Wellington St., W.C.2]) : [Apparel News Ltd].
Supersedes: Apparel.
[No.1]- ; 15th Sept. 1975-. — [1975]-. — ill, ports ; 41cm.
Fortnightly (22 issues a year). — 12p. in 29th Oct. 1976 issue.
Sd : £3.00 yearly
ISSN 0309-4812
(B77-09573)

338.4'7'6871102541 — Men's clothing industries. *Great Britain. Directories*
Buyers guide to British menswear, and brand name index. — London (33 Bedford Place, WC1B 5JX) : Benjamin Dent Publications Ltd.
1977 ed. — [1977]. — 71p : ill, map ; 23x11cm.
English, French and German preliminaries. — English, French, German, Italian and Spanish section headings. — Index.
Pbk : £1.00
ISSN 0309-6556
(B77-18621)

338.4'7'6887202541 — Toy industries & trades. *Great Britain. Directories*
'Games & toys' year book. — London (30 Knightrider St., EC4V 5BL) : 'Games and Toys'.
1977-8 / edited and compiled by Edward L. Simmons. — [1977]. — 224p : ill ; 23cm.
Pbk : Unpriced
(B77-20993)

338.4'7'6887602541 — Sports equipment industries & trades. *Great Britain. Directories*
Camping, caravanning and sports equipment trades directory. — London (4 Spring St., W2 3RB) : Camping and Sports Equipment Ltd.
[1977] : sixth ed. / edited by P. Moloney. — [1977]. — 440p : ill ; 23cm.
Index.
ISBN 0-9501415-3-4 : £6.50
(B77-13564)

338.4'7'69002541 — Building industries. *Great Britain. Directories*
United Kingdom builders / [Data Research Group]. — Amersham (Hill House, [Hill Ave.], Amersham, Bucks.) : The Group.
[1977]. — 1977. — 305 leaves in various pagings ; 30cm.
ISBN 0-86099-064-8 Pbk : £21.00
(B77-30041)

338.4'7'690028 — Building equipment industries & trades. *Great Britain. Directories*
Sell's building index : a buyers' guide for builders, contractors, architects, engineers, surveyors, merchants, government departments, etc.. — Epsom : Sell's Publications.
1977 ed. : 54th year. — [1977]. — xviii,542,[8] p : ill, col map ; 30cm.
Index.
ISBN 0-85499-584-6 Pbk : £10.00
ISSN 0080-8717
(B77-17991)

338.4'7'690062423 — Building industries. Organisations. *South-west England. National Federation of Building Trades Employers. South-Western Region. Directories*
National Federation of Building Trades Employers. *South Western Region.* Year book / National Federation of Building Trades Employers, South Western Region. — Bristol (22 Richmond Hill, Clifton, Bristol BS8 1BD) : The Region.
1975-6. — [1977]. — 168p : ill, coat of arms. 2 forms ; 22cm.
Bibl.: p.65-73.
£2.00(£1.00 to members of the Federation)
(B77-26897)

338.4'7'6900941 — Building industries. Policies of government. *Great Britain. Aims for Freedom and Enterprise viewpoints*
Willan, Bob. A policy for building / [by] Bob Willan. — London : Aims for Freedom and Enterprise, [1976]. — [2],11p ; 21cm.
ISBN 0-7281-0066-5 Sd : £0.25
(B77-04642)

338.4'7'6900941 — Direct labour organisations. Organisation. *Great Britain. Fabian viewpoints*
Tilley, John. Changing prospects for direct labour / [by] John Tilley. — London : Fabian Society, 1976. — [2],15p ; 22cm. — (Initiatives in local government ; 3) (Fabian tract ; 445 ISSN 0307-7535)
ISBN 0-7163-0445-7 Sd : £0.40
(B77-01237)

338.4'7'6900941443 — Direct labour organisations. Organisation. *Great Britain. Study examples: Glasgow (District). Direct Labour Organisation. Aims for Freedom and Enterprise viewpoints*
Hoppé, Malcolm. Glasgow belongs to - whom? / [by] Malcolm Hoppé. — [London] : Aims for Freedom and Enterprise, [1976]. — [2],15p ; 21cm.
ISBN 0-7281-0067-3 Sd : £0.30
(B77-02836)

338.4'7'6900942166 — Wandsworth (London Borough). Building Works Department. Organisation. *Aims for Freedom and Enterprise viewpoints*
Sherman, Alfred. Waste in Wandsworth : how direct labour squanders ratepayers' money and the nation's resources / [by] Alfred Sherman (in collaboration with Dennis Mallam[)]. — London : Aims for Freedom and Enterprise, [1976]. — [2],14p ; 21cm.
ISBN 0-7281-0049-5 Sd : £0.25
(B77-20112)

338.4'7'69018 — Fencing contracting industries. *Great Britain. Directories*
United Kingdom fencing contractors / [Data Research Group]. — Amersham (Hill House, [Hill Ave.], Amersham, Bucks.) : The Group.
[1975]. — 1975. — 75 leaves in various pagings ; 30cm.
ISBN 0-905570-63-4 Sp : £12.00
(B77-07841)

[1977]. — 1977. — 63 leaves in various pagings ; 30cm.
Sp : £13.00
(B77-17992)

338.4'7'690240941 — Buildings. Maintenance services. *Great Britain. Serials*
Manual of building maintenance. — London : Turret Press.
1977 : 9th ed. — 1977. — 104p : ill ; 30cm.
Bibl.: p.98-101.
Pbk : £9.00
Also classified at 338.4'7'64850941
(B77-32484)

338.4'7'690521 — Shopfitting industries. *Great Britain. Directories*
United Kingdom shopfitters & exhibition stand contractors / [Data Research Group]. — Amersham (Hill House, [Hill Ave.], Amersham, Bucks.) : The Group.
1976. — [1976]. — 111 leaves in various pagings ; 30cm.
ISBN 0-905570-32-4 Sp : £14.00
(B77-00095)

338.4'7'691 — Building materials supply industries. *Great Britain. Directories*
United Kingdom builders merchants / [Data Research Group]. — Amersham (Hill House, [Hill Ave.], Amersham, Bucks.) : The Group.
[1976]. — 1976. — 188 leaves in various pagings ; 30cm.
ISBN 0-905570-16-2 Pbk : £16.00
(B77-00096)

[1977]. — 1977. — 210 leaves in various pagings ; 30cm.
Pbk : £17.00
(B77-16780)

338.4'7'691 — Building materials supply industries. Organisations: National Federation of Builders' and Plumbers' Merchants. *Great Britain. Directories*
National Federation of Builders' and Plumbers' Merchants. List of members / National Federation of Builders' and Plumbers' Merchants. — London (15 Soho Sq., W1V 5FB) : The Federation.
1977-1978. — [1977]. — [1],228p : ill ; 30cm.
Cover title. — Index.
Pbk : Unpriced
Also classified at 338.4'7'6961
(B77-33674)

338.4'7'69602541 — Buildings. Engineering services. Consulting engineers. *Great Britain. Directories*
British Data Service. The BDS selective list of consulting engineers (services). — Frinton-on-Sea (Ashlyns House, Frinton-on-Sea, Essex) : B.D.S.
1974. — [1974]. — [2],30,7 leaves ; 33cm.
Index.
ISBN 0-905923-01-4 Sp : £5.00
(B77-06541)

338.4'7'6961 — Plumbing materials supply industries. Organisations: National Federation of Builders' and Plumbers' Merchants. *Great Britain. Directories*
National Federation of Builders' and Plumbers' Merchants. List of members / National Federation of Builders' and Plumbers' Merchants. — London (15 Soho Sq., W1V 5FB) : The Federation.
1977-1978. — [1977]. — [1],228p : ill ; 30cm.
Cover title. — Index.
Pbk : Unpriced
Primary classification 338.4'7'691
(B77-33674)

338.4'7'697 — Air conditioning, heating & ventilation equipment industries. *Great Britain. Directories*
Heating, ventilating, refrigeration & air conditioning year book / sponsored and compiled by Heating and Ventilating Contractors Association ... [et al.]. — London (32 Palace Court, W2 4J9) : The Association.
1977. — [1977]. — 308p,[24]p,[5]leaves : ill, forms, ports ; 30cm.
Previously published: as 'Heating, ventilating and air conditioning yearbook'.
Sp : £8.75
(B77-17993)

United Kingdom heating, refrigeration & ventilating equipment manufacturers / [Data Research Group]. — Amersham (Hill House, [Hill Ave.], Amersham, Bucks.) : The Group.
[1976]. — [1976]. — 86 leaves in various pagings ; 30cm.
ISBN 0-905570-55-3 Sp : £12.00
Also classified at 338.4'7'6215602541
(B77-06542)

[1977]. — 1977. — 87 leaves in various pagings ; 30cm.
Sp : Unpriced
Also classified at 338.4'7'6215602541
(B77-17994)

338.4'7'697 — Heating engineering contracting industries. *Great Britain. Directories*
United Kingdom heating engineering contractors / [Data Research Group]. — Amersham (Hill House [Hill Ave.], Amersham, Bucks.) : The Group.
[1976]. — 1976. — 153 leaves in various pagings ; 30cm.
ISBN 0-905570-82-0 Pbk : £17.00
(B77-10756)

338.4'7'69700941 — Household heating equipment industries. *Great Britain. Periodicals*
Domestic Heating Society. The Domestic Heating Society Newsletter. — London (c/o R.W. Jones, Heating Training Centre, 25 Bagleys La., SW6 2QA) : The Society.
No.1- ; June 1976-. — 1976-. — 30cm.
Two issues a year. — 6p. in 2nd issue.
Sd : Unpriced
ISSN 0308-9614
(B77-02837)

338.4'7'698902541 — Floor coverings contracting industries. *Great Britain. Directories*
United Kingdom flooring contractors / [Data Research Group]. — Amersham (Hill House, [Hill Ave.], Amersham, Bucks.) : The Group.
[1976]. — 1976. — 89 leaves in various pagings ; 30cm.
ISBN 0-905570-67-7 Sp : £13.00
(B77-05933)

338.4'7'70091812 — Arts. Economic aspects. *Western world. Readings*
The **economics** of the arts / edited by Mark Blaug. — London : Martin Robertson, 1976. — [7],272p : ill ; 23cm.
Bibl.: p.259.
ISBN 0-85520-122-3 : £8.45
(B77-07181)

338.4'7'700941 — Arts. Patronage by government. *Great Britain, to 1976*
Minihan, Janet. The nationalization of culture : the development of state subsidies to the arts in Great Britain / [by] Janet Minihan. — London : Hamilton, 1977. — xii,276p ; 23cm.
Bibl.: p.251-265. — Index.
ISBN 0-241-89537-5 : £8.50
(B77-10251)

338.4'7'700941 — Arts. Patronage by Trades Union Congress. *Great Britain. Inquiry reports*
Trades Union Congress. The TUC working party report on the arts. — London : T.U.C., [1976]. — [2],44p ; 24cm. — (A TUC consultative document)
ISBN 0-900878-47-9 Sd : £0.50
(B77-06543)

338.4'7'70094276 — Visual arts. Patronage. *Lancashire, 1760-1860*
Darcy, C P. The encouragement of the fine arts in Lancashire, 1760-1860 / by C.P. Darcy. — Manchester : Manchester University Press for the Chetham Society, 1976. — vi,180p ; 23cm. — (Remains historical and literary connected with the Palatine counties of Lancaster and Chester : third series ; vol.24)
Bibl.: p.165-174. — Index.
ISBN 0-7190-1330-5 : £8.00
(B77-25461)

338.4'7'7202541 — Architectural design. Partnerships. *Great Britain. Directories*

Architectural partnerships / [Data Research Group]. — Amersham (Hill House, [Hill Ave.], Amersham, Bucks.) : The Group.
[1977]. — 1977. — 142 leaves in various pagings ; 30cm.
Sp : £17.00
(B77-17367)

United Kingdom architectural partnerships / [Data Research Group]. — Amersham (Hill House, [Hill Ave.], Amersham, Bucks.) : The Group.
1976. — [1976]. — 138 leaves in various pagings ; 30cm.
ISBN 0-905570-22-7 Sp : £16.00
(B77-00097)

338.4'7'7392702541 — Jewellery industries & trades. *Great Britain. Directories*

United Kingdom jewellers / [Data Research Group]. — Amersham (Hill House, [Hill Ave.], Amersham, Bucks.) : The Group.
[1976]. — 1976. — 60 leaves in various pagings ; 30cm.
ISBN 0-905570-65-0 Sp : £13.00
(B77-06005)

[1977]. — 1977. — 70 leaves in various pagings ; 30cm.
Sp : £14.00
(B77-29266)

338.4'7'770973 — Photographic industries. *United States, to 1925*

Jenkins, Reese V. Images and enterprises : technology and the American photographic industry, 1839 to 1925 / [by] Reese V. Jenkins. — Baltimore ; London : Johns Hopkins University Press, [1976]. — xviii,371,[1]p : ill, facsims, ports ; 26cm. — (Johns Hopkins studies in the history of technology)
Ill. on lining papers. — Published in the United States: 1975. — Bibl.: p.353-357. — Index.
ISBN 0-8018-1588-6 : £16.00
(B77-07842)

338.4'7'78 — Musicians. Agents. *Lists*

British Association of Concert Agents. Composite list of artists showing sole representation by members of the British Association of Concert Agents, as at January 1 / compiled for members of the British Association of Concert Agents. — London (c/o The Secretary, 44 Castelnau Gardens, Arundel Terrace, SW13 9DU) : [The Association].
1977. — [1977]. — [1],79p ; 30cm.
Index.
ISBN 0-904892-02-6 Ls : £3.00
(B77-11119)

338.4'7'7802541 — Music industries & trades. *Great Britain. Directories*

Music trades international directory. — Watford (157 Hagden La., Watford, Herts.) : Trade Papers (London) Ltd.
1977. — [1977]. — 76p : ill ; 30cm.
Cover title: Music trades directory.
ISBN 0-903462-03-6 Pbk : £6.45
ISSN 0307-8523
(B77-08861)

338.4'7'78991025 — Music recording & reproduction industries. *Directories*

Kemp's music and recording industry year book (international) : a comprehensive reference source and marketing guide to the music and recording industry in Great Britain. — London : Kemps.
1977 / executive editor D.I. Price. — [1977]. — [4],268p : ill, form ; 21cm.
ISBN 0-905255-16-x Pbk : £4.50
ISSN 0305-7100
(B77-15157)

338.4'7'792029541 — Theatre industries. *Great Britain. Directories*

British theatre directory. — Eastbourne (18 Terminus Rd, Eastbourne, E. Sussex) : John Offord (Publications) Ltd.
1976. — 1976. — 448p : ill, map, ports ; 23cm.

ISBN 0-903931-09-5 : £4.00
ISSN 0306-4107
(B77-02119)

1977 / [editor John Offord]. — 1977. — 454p : ill, map ; 23cm.
ISBN 0-903931-13-3 : Unpriced
ISSN 0306-4107
(B77-30042)

338.4'7'91 — Tourist industries. *Organisation for Economic Co-operation and Development countries. Reports, surveys. Serials*

Organisation for Economic Co-operation and Development. Tourism policy and international tourism in OECD member countries. — Paris : O.E.C.D. ; [London] : [H.M.S.O.].
[1976] : evolution of tourism in OECD member countries in 1975 and the early months of 1976 : report / adopted in July 1976 by the OECD Tourism Committee. — 1976. — 3-168p(4 fold) : ill ; 27cm.
Pbk : £4.40
ISBN 92-64-11559-5
(B77-00664)

338.4'7'91 — Tourist industries. Planning. *Periodicals*

Tourism international policy : a quarterly journal devoted to the shaping of tourism policy. — London (154 Cromwell Rd, S.W.7) : Tourism International Press.
1st quarter 1976-. — [1976]-. — 30cm.
Twenty p. in 1st issue.
Sd : £16.00 yearly
ISSN 0309-8567
(B77-29267)

Tourism international research : the quarterly research journal of the European Travel Commission. — London ([154 Cromwell Rd, S.W.7]) : Tourism International Press.
Continued by: Tourism international research Europe.
1st quarter 1975-4th quarter 1975. — [1975]-. — ill ; 30cm.
Twenty-four leaves in 1st issue. — Includes articles in French.
Sd : Unpriced
ISSN 0140-0576
(B77-29268)

338.4'7'91 — Travel agencies & tour operators. *Great Britain. Reports, surveys*

Financial Analysis Group. British travel agents and tour operators / researched and compiled jointly by Financial Analysis Group Ltd and Information Research Ltd. — Winnersh : The Group, 1975. — [4],30,xxix[i.e.xxiii]p ; 31cm.
Index.
ISBN 0-85938-057-2 Pbk : Unpriced
(B77-04019)

338.4'7'9102541 — Travel agencies. *Great Britain. Directories*

Travel trade directory. — London : Morgan-Grampian for Travel trade gazette.
'77 : 19th ed. / editor Don Macrae. — [1977]. — 416,[18]p : ill(some col), forms, maps ; 29cm.
Index.
ISBN 0-900865-99-7 Pbk : £6.50
(B77-04643)

338.4'7'9140072 — Tourist industries. Research. *Europe. Periodicals*

Tourism international research Europe : the quarterly research journal of the European Travel Commission. — London (154 Cromwell Rd, S.W.7) : Tourism International Press.
Continues: Tourism international research.
1st quarter 1976-. — [1976]-. — ill ; 30cm.
Twenty p. in 2nd quarter 1976. — Includes articles in French.
Sd : £16.00 yearly
ISSN 0309-8605
(B77-29269)

338.4'7'9141 — Great Britain. Economic development. Role of tourism. *Conference proceedings*

Tourism : a tool for regional development : Leisure Studies Association conference, Edinburgh, 1977 / edited by Brian S. Duffield. — Edinburgh (Department of Geography, High School Yards, Edinburgh EH1 1NR) : Tourism and Recreation Research Unit, University of Edinburgh for the Association, 1977. — 180p in various pagings : ill, 2 maps ; 30cm. — (Leisure Studies Association. Publications ; 7)
Spine title: LSA conference, Edinburgh, 1977.
ISBN 0-904828-28-x Pbk : Unpriced
(B77-30043)

338.4'7'9141 — Tourism. *Great Britain. Secondary school texts. Cards*

Ellis, Veronica. Tourism / [by] Veronica Ellis. — Cambridge [etc.] : Cambridge University Press, 1976. — Portfolio : ill(chiefly col), maps(chiefly col) ; 27cm. — (Geography work cards)
Twenty-one cards ([42] sides) in portfolio.
ISBN 0-521-21118-2 : £2.10(non-net)
(B77-00665)

338.4'7'9141 — Tourist industries. *Great Britain. Periodicals*

Tourism intelligence quarterly. — London (The Secretary, Marketing Intelligence Group, 239 Old Marylebone Rd, NW1 5QT) : British Tourist Authority.
Vol.1, no.1- ; Apr. 1977-. — [1977]-. — 30cm.
viii p. in 1st issue.
Sd : £5.00 yearly
ISSN 0309-8958
(B77-16250)

338.4'7'91411 — Tourism. *Scotland. Reports, surveys*

Travis, Anthony Selwyn. A strategic appraisal of Scottish tourism, 1974 : a report to the Scottish Tourist Board / by A.S. Travis. — Edinburgh : Scottish Tourist Board, 1974. — [3],89p : ill, maps, plans ; 30cm.
Bibl.: p.82.
ISBN 0-85419-114-3 Sp : £2.00
(B77-05934)

338.4'7'91411 — Tourist industries. *Scotland. Directories. For travel agencies*

Travel trade guide, Scotland. — Edinburgh : Scottish Tourist Board.
'Inclusive holidays in Scotland. 1977' (67p: Sd) in pocket.
1977. — 1977. — 96p : ill, col maps, ports ; 30cm.
Pbk : Unpriced
(B77-32485)

338.4'7'91411 — Tourist industries. Information bureaux. *Scotland. Directories*

Tourist information centres / Scottish Tourist Board. — Edinburgh : The Board. — (Scottish Tourist Board. Information booklets)
1977. — [1976]. — 28p : 1 ill ; 21x10cm.
Sd : Unpriced
(B77-23219)

338.4'7'914110072 — Tourism. Research. *Scotland*

Scottish Tourist Board. *Research and Planning Division.* Research and planning information handbook / ... prepared by the Research and Planning Division, the Scottish Tourist Board. — Edinburgh : [The Division], [1976]. — [95]p on publication ; 32cm.
In binder. — Tab indexed.
Ls : Unpriced
(B77-15158)

338.4'7'914170061 — Tourism. Promotion. Organisations. *Ireland (Republic). Irish Tourist Board. Resources. Allocation*

Heneghan, Philip. Resource allocation in tourism marketing / [by] Philip Heneghan in co-operation with Board Failte = Irish Tourist Board and the University of Dublin. — London (154 Cromwell Rd, S.W.7) : Tourism International Press, 1976. — [4],vi,64p : ill ; 30cm.
This book is based on the author's doctoral dissertation presented to the University of Dublin. He is Marketing Planning Manager with the Irish Tourist Board.
ISBN 0-904873-05-6 Pbk : Unpriced
(B77-11668)

338.4'7'9142 — Tourist industries. Financial assistance by English Tourist Board. *England. Development areas, 1971-1976*

English Tourist Board. Investing in tourism : aid to tourist projects in England's development areas, 1971-76 / [English Tourist Board] ; [text] by John Carter. — London : The Board, 1977. — 40p : ill(some col), 3 col maps, 2 ports ; 23cm.
Pbk : £1.50
(B77-23220)

338.4'7'91593 — Tourist industries. *Thailand. Periodicals*

Thailand travel talk. — London (9 Stafford St., W1X 3FE) : Tourist Organization of Thailand.
Vol.1, no.1- ; Aug. 1977-. — [1977]-. — ill ; 30cm.
Monthly. — Folder ([4]p.) as 1st issue.
Sd : Unpriced
ISSN 0140-3796
(B77-31766)

338.4'7'917290072 — Tourist industries. Research. *Caribbean region. Periodicals*

Tourism international research Caribbean : the quarterly research journal of the Caribbean tourism industry. — London (154 Cromwell Rd, S.W.7) : Tourism International Press.
1st quarter 1977-. — [1977]-. — 30cm.
Twenty p. in 1st quarter 1977.
Sd : £16.00 yearly
ISSN 0309-8524
(B77-28475)

338.5 — PRODUCTION ECONOMICS

338.5 — Business firms. Finance. *Japan. Forecasts for 1977-1980*

International Business Information Incorporated. Japanese corporate finance 1977-1980 / by International Business Information Inc. ; ... prepared by C. Tait Ratcliffe ... — London : 'Financial times', 1977. — [12],iv,217[i.e.225]p : ill ; 30cm.
ISBN 0-900671-86-6 Sp : £50.00
(B77-25462)

338.5 — Companies. Finance. *Great Britain. Statistics*

Digest of balance sheets. — London (21 New St., EC2M 4NT) : Bishopsgate Press Ltd.
1976. — [1976]. — 104p ; 19x25cm.
ISBN 0-900873-10-8 Pbk : £3.75
ISSN 0309-0876
(B77-00098)

338.5 — Industries & trades. Finance. *Great Britain. Minutes of evidence*

Committee to Review the Functioning of Financial Institutions. Evidence on the financing of industry and trade / Committee to Review the Functioning of Financial Institutions ; chairman : Sir Harold Wilson. — London : H.M.S.O.
Vol.1 : Treasury, Department of Industry. — 1977. — [3],138p : 1 ill ; 25cm.
ISBN 0-11-630695-5 Pbk : £2.25
(B77-30044)

338.5 — Microeconomics

Armey, Richard K. Price theory : a policy-welfare approach / [by] Richard K. Armey. — Englewood Cliffs ; London [etc.] : Prentice-Hall, 1977. — xv,367p : ill ; 24cm.
Bibl. — Index.
ISBN 0-13-699694-9 : £11.15
(B77-17368)

Bach, George Leland. Microeconomics : analysis and applications / [by] George Leland Bach. — Englewood Cliffs ; London [etc.] : Prentice-Hall, 1977. — ii-xv,439p : ill(chiefly col) ; 24cm.
'This material also appears in "Economics" ... Ninth Edition, by George Leland Bach' - title page verso. — Index.
ISBN 0-13-581306-9 Pbk : £6.35
(B77-23221)

Gwartney, James David. Microeconomics : private and public choice / [by] James D. Gwartney. — New York [etc.] ; London : Academic Press, 1977. — xvii,389p : ill(chiefly col), ports ; 24cm.
Bibl.: p.373-377. — Index.
ISBN 0-12-311065-3 Pbk : £5.70
(B77-23222)

Hewitt, Gordon, *b.1945.* Economics of the market / [by] Gordon Hewitt. — [London] : Fontana, 1976. — vi,343p : ill ; 20cm. — (Fontana introduction to modern economics)
Bibl.: p.332-333. — Index.
ISBN 0-00-633183-1 Pbk : £1.95
(B77-16251)

Heyne, Paul T. Toward understanding microeconomics / [by] Paul Heyne, Thomas Johnson. — Chicago ; Henley-on-Thames [etc.] : Science Research Associates, [1977]. — xiii,459p : ill ; 24cm.
'Material contained herein also appears in books entitled "Toward economic understanding" and "The economic way of thinking"' - title page verso. — Published in the United States: 1976. — Index.
ISBN 0-574-19270-0 Pbk : £5.65
(B77-07182)

Quirk, James Patrick. Intermediate microeconomics / [by] James P. Quirk. — Chicago ; Henley-on-Thames [etc.] : Science Research Associates.
Mathematical notes. — [1977]. — [7],166p ; 24cm.
Published in the United States: 1976.
ISBN 0-574-19267-0 Pbk : £2.05
(B77-09574)

Solutions manual. — [1977]. — [3],49p : ill ; 24cm.
Published in the United States: 1976.
ISBN 0-574-19266-2 Sd : £1.40
(B77-09575)

Solmon, Lewis Calvin. Microeconomics / [by] Lewis C. Solmon. — Reading, Mass. ; London [etc.] : Addison-Wesley, 1977. — xiii,497p : ill(chiefly col) ; 25cm.
'"Microeconomics" and its companion volume, "Macroeconomics", were originally published as one text entitled "Economics", [2nd ed. Reading, Mass. : Addison-Wesley, 1976]' - title page verso. — Bibl.: p.448-455. — Index.
ISBN 0-201-07248-3 Pbk : £7.20
(B77-10252)

Thompson, Arthur A. Economics of the firm : theory and practice / [by] Arthur A. Thompson, Jr. — 2nd ed. — Englewood Cliffs ; London [etc.] : Prentice-Hall, 1977. — xvii, 638p : ill ; 24cm.
Previous ed.: Englewood Cliffs : Prentice-Hall, 1973. — Bibl. — Index.
ISBN 0-13-231407-x : £13.55
(B77-20994)

338.5'1 — Industries. Effects of cost increases in energy resources. *Great Britain*

National Economic Development Office. The increased cost of energy - supplementary calculations of its effects / National Economic Development Office. — London : N.E.D.O., 1975. — 11p ; 30cm. — (NEDO energy series)
ISBN 0-7292-0007-8 Sd : Unpriced
(B77-33112)

338.5'201 — Prices. Theories

Ryan, William James Louden. Price theory / [by] W.J.L Ryan. — Revised ed. / revised by D.W. Pearce. — London [etc.] : Macmillan, 1977. — xvi,399p : ill ; 23cm.
Previous ed.: 1958. — Index.
ISBN 0-333-17912-9 : £12.00
ISBN 0-333-17913-7 Pbk : Unpriced
(B77-21755)

338.5'2'0941 — Recommended retail prices. *Great Britain. Reports, surveys*

Great Britain. *Price Commission.* Recommended retail prices / Price Commission. — London : H.M.S.O., 1977. — vi,86p : ill ; 25cm. — (Report ; no.25)
ISBN 0-11-700869-9 Sd : £2.25
(B77-23223)

338.5'2'0941 — Vat-exclusive prices. *Great Britain. Reports, surveys*

Great Britain. *Consumer Protection Advisory Committee.* VAT-exclusive prices : a report on practices relating to advertising, displaying or otherwise quoting VAT-exclusive prices or charges ... / Consumer Protection Advisory Committee. — London : H.M.S.O., [1977]. — iii,25p ; 25cm. — ([1976-77 H.C.]416)
ISBN 0-10-241677-x Sd : £0.60
(B77-25463)

338.5'23 — Oligopolies. Game theory

Friedman, James W. Oligopoly and the theory of games / [by] James W. Friedman. — Amsterdam [etc.] ; Oxford : North-Holland Publishing Co., 1977. — xiii,311p ; 23cm. — (Advanced textbooks in economics ; vol.8)
Bibl.: p.301-306. — Index.
ISBN 0-7204-0505-x : £15.22
(B77-15748)

338.5'26'0941 — Prices. Control. Policies of government. *Great Britain. Price Code, 1977-1978. For employers*

Confederation of British Industry. The new prices policy (from 1 August 1977) : notes for guidance / [Confederation of British Industry]. — London : C.B.I., 1977. — 31p ; 21cm.
Sd : £1.00
(B77-32486)

338.5'26'0941 — Prices. Control. Policies of government. *Great Britain. Price Code, 1977-1978. Proposals*

Great Britain. *Department of Prices and Consumer Protection.* Prices policy : the Price Code and the safeguard regulations : a consultative document / presented to Parliament by the Secretary of State for Prices and Consumer Protection ... — London : H.M.S.O., [1977]. — iii,48p ; 25cm. — (Cmnd. 6861)
ISBN 0-10-168610-2 Sd : £0.75
(B77-21756)

338.5'4 — Trade cycles. Related to growth of trade unions

Bain, George Sayers. Union growth and the business cycle : an econometric analysis / [by] George Sayers Bain, Farouk Elsheikh. — Oxford : Blackwell, 1976. — xv,155p : ill ; 23cm. — (Warwick studies in industrial relations)
Index.
ISBN 0-631-16650-5 : £10.00
Primary classification 331.88
(B77-02816)

338.5'44 — Great Britain. Economic conditions. Forecasting

McLean, Alan, *b.1941.* Macroeconomic forecasting in the UK / [by] Alan McLean. — London (Hamilton House, Mabledon Place, WC1H 9BH) : Economics Association, 1976. — [2],15p : 1 ill ; 21cm. — (Economics Association. Occasional papers ; 3)
Bibl.: p.15.
ISBN 0-901529-13-3 Sd : Unpriced
(B77-26899)

338.5'442 — Economic forecasting. Applications of time series analysis

Granger, Clive William John. Forecasting economic time series / [by] C.W.J. Granger, Paul Newbold. — New York [etc.] ; London : Academic Press, 1977. — xii,333p : ill ; 24cm. — (Economic theory and mathematical economics)
Bibl.: p.318-325. — Index.
ISBN 0-12-295150-6 : £15.60
(B77-31768)

338.5'442 — United States. Metropolitan regions. Economic conditions. Forecasting. Econometric models. *Study examples: Pennsylvania. Philadelphia*

Glickman, Norman J. Econometric analysis of regional systems : explorations in model building and policy analysis / [by] Norman J. Glickman. — New York [etc.] ; London : Academic Press, 1977. — xi,210p : ill ; 24cm. — (Studies in urban economics)
Bibl.: p.197-206. — Index.
ISBN 0-12-286550-2 : £13.15
(B77-23224)

338.6 — SYSTEMS OF INDUSTRIAL ENTERPRISE

338.6 — Public enterprise. Organisations. *Great Britain. National Enterprise Board. Operation. Regulations*

Great Britain. *Department of Industry.* The National Enterprise Board : guidelines / Department of Industry. — London : [The Department], 1977. — [1],iii,12p ; 21cm.
Sd : Unpriced
(B77-14606)

338.6'042 — Industries. Location. Related to foreign trade. *Conference proceedings*

International Allocation of Economic Activity *(Conference), Stockholm, 1976.* The international allocation of economic activity : proceedings of a Nobel Symposium [the 35th] held at Stockholm / edited by Bertil Ohlin, Per-Ove Hesselborn, Per Magnus Wijkman. — London [etc.] : Macmillan, 1977. — xiv,572p : ill, maps ; 23cm.
'... proceedings of a [conference] ... on The International Allocation of Economic Activity held in Stockholm, 8-11 June, 1976' - Foreword. — Bibl. — Index.
ISBN 0-333-21423-4 : £20.00 : CIP rev.
Also classified at 382
(B77-24779)

338.6'042 — Offices. Location. *Cambridgeshire. Cambridge. Reports, surveys*

Cambridge *(District). Department of Architecture and Planning.* Offices in Cambridge : a report / by the [Cambridge] City Architect and Planning Officer ; ... prepared by D.W. Urwin and D.C. Turner. — [Cambridge] ([The Guildhall, Cambridge]) : [The Department], 1976. — 29 leaves in various pagings : 4 maps ; 30cm.
ISBN 0-902696-04-1 Sd : £0.50
(B77-10757)

338.6'042 — Offices. Relocation. *Great Britain. Statistics*

Office relocation facts and figures : LOB statistical handbook. — London (27 Chancery La., WC2A 1NS) : Location of Offices Bureau. 1975. — [1975]. — [1],60p(2 fold) : col ill, col maps ; 15x21cm.
ISBN 0-901749-14-1 Sd : £1.50
(B77-08862)

338.6'042'01 — Business firms. Location. Central place theory. *Urban regions*

Beavon, Keith S O. Central place theory : a reinterpretation / [by] Keith S.O. Beavon. — London [etc.] : Longman, 1977. — xii,157p : ill, maps ; 24cm.
Bibl.: p.144-150. — Index.
ISBN 0-582-48678-5 : £5.50
ISBN 0-582-48683-1 Pbk : £3.25
(B77-18622)

338.6'042'0941 — Manufacturing industries. Location. *Great Britain*
Keeble, David. Industrial location and planning in the United Kingdom / [by] David Keeble. — London : Methuen, 1976. — [8],317p : ill, maps ; 24cm.
Bibl.: p.290-305. — Index.
ISBN 0-416-80060-2 : £8.50
ISBN 0-416-80070-x Pbk : £4.95
(B77-11120)

338.6'042'094225 — Industries. Location. *East Sussex. Reports, surveys*
East Sussex *(County). Planning Department.* County of East Sussex major industrial sites / [East Sussex County Council, Planning Department]. — Lewes (Southover House, Southover Rd, Lewes, E. Sussex BN7 1YA) : The Department, 1977. — [26]p,fold plate : maps ; 30cm. — (Publication ; no.P/126/1)
Sd : £5.00
(B77-20113)

338.6'048 — Industries. Competition. *Organisation for Economic Co-operation and Development countries. Reports, surveys. Serials*
Organisation for Economic Co-operation and Development. Annual reports on competition policy in OECD member countries. — Paris : O.E.C.D. ; [London] : [H.M.S.O.].
1976. No.2. — 1976. — 175p : 1 ill ; 29cm.
Pbk : £2.80
ISBN 92-64-11575-7
(B77-05935)

338.6'048 — Oligopolistic competition
Metwally, Mokhtar Mohammed. Price and non-price competition : dynamics of marketing / [by] M.M. Metwally. — London : Asia Publishing House, 1976. — x,144p : ill ; 25cm.
Bibl.: p.129-141. — Index.
ISBN 0-210-40568-6 : £7.50
(B77-11669)

338.6'048 — Pharmaceutical industries. Competition. *Great Britain*
Slatter, Stuart St. P. Competition and marketing strategies in the pharmaceutical industry / [by] Stuart St. P. Slatter. — London : Croom Helm, 1977. — 150p : ill ; 23cm.
Bibl.: p.146-148. — Index.
ISBN 0-85664-396-3 : £14.95
Also classified at 381'.45'61510941
(B77-23225)

338.6'048'0941 — Industries. Competition. *Great Britain. Case studies*
Case studies in the competitive process / by Peter J. Barker ... [et al.]. — London [etc.] : Heinemann Educational [for] the Economics Association, 1976. — viii,86p : ill, map ; 20cm. — (Case studies in economic analysis ; 4)
ISBN 0-435-84047-9 Pbk : £1.20
(B77-02838)

Case studies in the competitive process / by Peter J. Barker ... [et al.]. — London [etc.] : Heinemann Educational [for] the Economics Association. — (Case studies in economic analysis ; 4)
[Teacher's guide]. — 1976. — viii,152p : ill, map ; 20cm.
Bibl.
ISBN 0-435-84048-7 Pbk : £1.90
(B77-02839)

338.6'32 — Brewing industries & trades. Guilds. *London (City). Worshipful Company of Brewers, to 1976*
Ball, Mia. The Worshipful Company of Brewers : a short history / [by] Mia Ball. — London : Hutchinson, 1977. — 143p,[4]p of plates : ill(some col), facsims(1 col), ports ; 24cm.
Ill. on lining papers. — Bibl.: p.133-134. — Index.
ISBN 0-09-127850-3 : £5.00
(B77-11121)

338.6'32 — Butchery. Guilds. *London (City). Worshipful Company of Butchers of the City of London, to 1975*
Jones, Philip Edmund. The butchers of London : a history of the Worshipful Company of Butchers of the City of London / [by] Philip E. Jones. — London : Secker and Warburg, 1976. — x,246p,[12]p of plates : ill, facsims, maps, plans, ports ; 24cm.
Bibl.: p.232-235. — Index.
ISBN 0-436-22421-6 : £9.75
(B77-00099)

338.6'32 — Candle making industries & trades. Guilds. *London (City). Worshipful Company of Tallow Chandlers. History*
Monier-Williams, Randall. The tallow chandlers of London / by Randall Monier-Williams. — London : Kaye and Ward.
In 4 vols.
Vol.4 : Ebb and flow. — 1977. — 364p,vi leaves of plates : ill, coat of arms, facsims, map, plan, ports ; 26cm.
Index.
ISBN 0-7182-1132-4 : £5.75
(B77-27733)

338.6'32 — Foundry industries. Guilds. *London (City). Worshipful Company of Founders, to 1975*
Hadley, Guy. Citizens and founders : a history of the Worshipful Company of Founders, London, 1365-1975 / by Guy Hadley. — London [etc.] : Phillimore, 1976. — xi,199p,[8]p of plates : ill(some col), col facsim, map ; 26cm.
Bibl.: p.191. — Index.
ISBN 0-85033-233-8 : £12.00
(B77-30045)

338.6'34 — Agricultural industries. Crofting. Organisations. *Scotland. Highlands & Islands. Crofters Commission. Reports, surveys. Serials*
Crofters Commission. Annual report ... / the Crofters Commission. — Edinburgh : H.M.S.O.
1976. — 1977. — vi,37p : ill, coat of arms ; 25cm.
ISBN 0-11-491487-7 Sd : £0.85
(B77-27734)

338.6'42 — Agricultural industries. Smallholdings. *Trinidad and Tobago. Trinidad. Reports, surveys*
Floyd, B N. Small-scale agriculture in Trinidad : a Caribbean case study in the problems of transforming rural societies in the tropics / [by] B.N. Floyd. — [Durham] : Department of Geography, University of Durham, 1977. — vi, 69p : ill, maps ; 25cm. — (University of Durham. Department of Geography. Occasional publications : new series ; no.10 ISSN 0307-0913)
Bibl.: p.62-69.
Pbk : Unpriced
(B77-22434)

338.6'42'0941 — Small firms. Great Britain. Compared with small firms in West Germany
Bannock, Graham. The smaller business in Britain and Germany / [by] Graham Bannock ; for the Anglo-German Foundation [for the Study of Industrial Society]. — London : Wilton House Publications, 1976. — viii,152p : 2 ill ; 29cm. — (A Wilton House special study)
Bibl.: p.151-152.
ISBN 0-904655-18-0 : £15.00
Also classified at 338.6'42'0943
(B77-24075)

338.6'42'0941 — Small firms. Policies of government. *Great Britain. Conservative and Unionist Party viewpoints*
Small businesses : strategy for survival / [by] Rosemary Brown ... [et al.]. — London : Wilton House Publications, 1976. — 68p ; 23cm.
Also published: London : Conservative Political Centre, 1976. — Bibl.: p.68.
ISBN 0-904655-19-9 : Unpriced
(B77-21757)

338.6'42'0943 — Small firms. West Germany. Compared with small firms in Great Britain
Bannock, Graham. The smaller business in Britain and Germany / [by] Graham Bannock ; for the Anglo-German Foundation [for the Study of Industrial Society]. — London : Wilton House Publications, 1976. — viii,152p : 2 ill ; 29cm. — (A Wilton House special study)
Bibl.: p.151-152.
ISBN 0-904655-18-0 : £15.00
Primary classification 338.6'42'0941
(B77-24075)

338.6'42'09667 — Small firms. *Developing countries. Study regions: Ghana*
Steel, William F. Small-scale employment and production in developing countries : evidence from Ghana / [by] William F. Steel. — New York ; London : Praeger, 1977. — xviii,235,[1] p : ill ; 25cm. — (Praeger special studies in international economics and development)
Bibl.: p.218-232. — Index.
ISBN 0-275-56330-8 : £13.40
(B77-25464)

338.6'44'0903 — Big business, 1750-1976
Parkinson, Cyril Northcote. The rise of big business / [by] C. Northcote Parkinson. — London : Weidenfeld and Nicolson, 1977. — xi, 276p : 1 ill ; 23cm.
Index.
ISBN 0-297-77327-5 : £5.95
(B77-22435)

338.7 — INDUSTRIAL ENTERPRISE. ORGANISATIONS AND THEIR STRUCTURE

338.7 — Business firms. Tenders & contracts. *Great Britain. Periodicals*
Tenders and contracts journal. — Cambridge (10 Jesus La., Cambridge CB5 8BE) : Hotchkiss Lane Associates Ltd.
[No.1]- ; Feb. 1977-. — [1977]-. — ill, ports ; 30cm.
Monthly. — 60p. in 1st issue.
Sd : £15.00 yearly
ISSN 0309-5703
(B77-16252)

338.7'09 — Business firms, to 1970. *Readings*
Business history : selected readings / edited by K.A. Tucker. — London : Cass, 1977. — xvi, 442p : ill, map ; 23cm.
Bibl. — Index.
ISBN 0-7146-3030-6 : £12.00
(B77-11670)

338.7'0941 — Business firms. Financial aspects. *Great Britain*
Davies, Jeffrey Rowe. Managerial economics / [by] J.R. Davies and S. Hughes. — Plymouth : Macdonald and Evans, 1977. — xiv,302p : ill ; 19cm. — (The M. & E. handbook series)
Index.
ISBN 0-7121-1390-8 Pbk : £3.00
(B77-23226)

338.7'0941 — Business firms. Management. Economic aspects. *Great Britain. Conference proceedings*
Management strategy and business development : an historical and comparative study / edited by Leslie Hannah. — London [etc.] : Macmillan, 1976. — xi,267p : ill ; 23cm.
'The present volume has its origins in a conference ... held in London on 10 June 1975' - Preface. — Index.
ISBN 0-333-19816-6 : £10.00
(B77-02120)

338.7'0955 — Business enterprise. *Iran. Reports, surveys. For British businessmen*
Great Britain. *Embassy (Tehran). Commercial Section.* Business practice in Iran / [prepared for the] British Overseas Trade Board [by the Commercial Section of the British Embassy, Tehran]. — [London] : [The Board], [1977]. — iii,23p ; 25cm.
Bibl.: p.23.
Sd : Unpriced
(B77-21758)

338.7'0973 — Business firms. *United States*
Price, Karl Fredrick. Issues in business / [by] Karl F. Price, James W. Walker. — [3rd ed.]. — Santa Barbara ; London [etc.] : Wiley, 1977. — [8],632p : ill(some col), facsims, form, map, ports ; 28cm.
'A Wiley/Hamilton publication'. — Previous ed.: 1974. — Index. — Includes facsimile reprints.
ISBN 0-471-69734-6 Pbk : £9.50
(B77-31052)

338.7'1 — Public companies. Conversion from private companies. *Great Britain*
Vaughan, George Douglas. From private to public : an analysis of the choices, problems and performance of newly floated public companies, 1966-74 / [by] G. Douglas Vaughan, Peter H. Grinyer and Susan J. Birley. — Cambridge : Woodhead-Faulkner, 1977. — 144p : ill ; 22cm.
Index.
ISBN 0-85941-052-8 : £8.50
(B77-15159)

338.7'3 — Estate agency. Partnerships. *England*
The future of partnerships. — Reading : College of Estate Management, 1974. — [5],63,[1]p ; 21cm. — (Occasional papers in estate management ; no.7)
'These papers were originally given at a CALUS conference held in September 1973 ...' - Editorial note.
ISBN 0-902132-18-0 Sd : Unpriced
(B77-19263)

338.7'4 — Defunct companies. *Lists. Serials*
Stock Exchange, *London.* Register of defunct and other companies removed from the Stock Exchange official year-book. — Croydon : T. Skinner.
1976-77 / edited by Jeffrey Russell Knight ; deputy-editor David Martin Michael Davies. — 1976. — vi,563p : coat of arms ; 26cm.
ISBN 0-611-00618-9 : £5.00
(B77-02840)

338.7'4 — Large manufacturing companies. Growth, 1909-1970. *Great Britain*
Prais, Sigbert Jon. The evolution of giant firms in Britain : a study of the growth of concentration in manufacturing industry in Britain, 1909-70 / by S.J. Prais. — Cambridge [etc.] : Cambridge University Press, 1976. — xviii,321p : ill ; 24cm. — (Economic and social studies ; 30)
Bibl.: p.302-315. — Index.
ISBN 0-521-21356-8 : £8.50
(B77-06544)

338.7'4 — Private companies. *Great Britain. Statistics*
Britain's top 1000 private companies / [Jordan Dataquest Limited]. — London : Jordan Dataquest. — (Dataquest survey)
1976. — 1977. — [6],viii,51,[28]p ; 30cm.
Index.
ISBN 0-85938-081-5 Pbk : £12.00
(B77-26900)

338.7'4'0212 — Companies. *Statistics*
'**The Times**' 1000 leading companies in Britain and overseas. — London : Times Newspapers.
1976-1977 / edited by Margaret Allen. — 1976. — 133p : ill ; 29cm.
Index.
ISBN 0-7230-0149-9 : £6.00
(B77-02841)

338.7'4'023 — Companies. *Great Britain. Career guides. For graduates. Serials*
Go. — London ([76 St James's La., N10 3RD]) : New Opportunity Press Ltd.
[19]77 / [editor Denis Curtis]. — 1976. — [1], 844,144p : ill, forms, maps, ports ; 26cm.
Index.
Pbk : £7.50
(B77-33675)

GO. — London ([76 St James's La., N10 3DF]) : New Opportunity Press Ltd.
1976 / [editor Denis Curtis]. — [1976]. — [2], 856p : ill(some col), coat of arms, form, maps, ports ; 25cm.
Index.
ISBN 0-903578-10-7 Pbk : £7.50
(B77-02121)

Go. — London (76 St James' La., N10 3RD) : New Opportunity Press Ltd.
1978 / [editor Denis Curtis]. — 1977. — 982p : ill, forms, maps, ports ; 26cm.
Index.
ISBN 0-903578-26-3 Pbk : £9.15
(B77-28476)

338.7'4'0254 — Companies. *Europe. Directories*
Jane's major companies of Europe. — London : Jane's Yearbooks.
1977 ed. / edited by Jonathan Love. — 1977. — 1133p in various pagings ; 29cm.
Index.
ISBN 0-354-00548-0 : £30.00
(B77-24780)

338.7'4'02541 — Industries. Companies with 100+ personnel. *Great Britain. Directories*
United Kingdom industrial companies with 100 or more employees / [Data Research Group]. — Amersham (Hill House, [Hill Ave.], Amersham, Bucks.) : The Group.
[1976]. — 1976. — 462 leaves in various pagings ; 30cm.
ISBN 0-905570-40-5 Pbk : £24.00
(B77-00100)

[1977]. — 1977. — 471 leaves in various pagings ; 30cm.
Pbk : Unpriced
(B77-14118)

338.7'4'02541 — Industries. Companies with 500+ personnel. *Great Britain. Directories*
United Kingdom industrial companies with 500 or more employees / [Data Research Group]. — Amersham (Hill House, [Hill Ave.], Amersham, Bucks.) : The Group.
1976. — [1976]. — 168 leaves in various pagings ; 30cm.
ISBN 0-905570-35-9 Pbk : £19.00
(B77-00101)

[1977]. — 1977. — 166 leaves in various pagings ; 30cm.
ISBN 0-905570-96-0 Sp : £20.00
(B77-14119)

338.7'4'094 — Large companies. *Western Europe. Statistics. Polyglot texts*
Europe's 5000 largest companies = Die 5000 grössten Unternehmen Europas = Les 5000 plus grandes sociétés de l'Europe. — Oslo : A.S. Okonomisk Literatur ; London [etc.] (26 Clifton St., EC2P 2LY) : Dun and Bradstreet International.
1976. — 1976. — 3-384p : ill ; 31cm.
English, German and French text. — Index.
£24.00
ISBN 82-7018-035-1
(B77-04020)

338.7'4'0941 — Industries. Companies. *Great Britain. Statistics*
Survey of British industry / Clifton Data Research Services. — St Albans (21 Culver Rd, St Albans, Herts.) : Clifton Data Research Services.
1976. — 1976. — [414]p ; 21x31cm.
Index.
£37.50
ISSN 0140-5780
(B77-32487)

338.7'4'09416 — Companies. *Northern Ireland. Statistics*
Companies general annual report ... / Department of Commerce [Northern Ireland]. — Belfast : H.M.S.O.
1975. — [1976]. — 10p ; 25cm.
ISBN 0-337-06072-x Sd : £0.22
ISSN 0308-4078
(B77-08282)

338.7'4'095 — Public companies. *Asia. Conference proceedings*
Colloquium on Public Corporations and the Legal Systems of India, Indonesia, Malaysia and Sri Lanka, *Colombo, 1974.* Law and public enterprise in Asia / [compiled by the] International Legal Center. — New York [etc.] ; London : Praeger ; [London] : [Distributed by Martin Robertson], 1976. — xiii,424p ; 24cm. — (Praeger special studies in international economics and development)
'A Colloquium on Public Corporations and the Legal Systems of India, Indonesia, Malaysia, and Sri Lanka was held in Colombo, Sri Lanka, May 26-31, 1974' - Preface. — Index.
ISBN 0-275-23000-7 : £17.90
(B77-02122)

338.7'4'0973 — Companies. Political aspects. *United States. Conference proceedings*
Conference on Corporate Accountability, *Washington, D.C., 1971.* Corporate power in America : Ralph Nader's Conference on Corporate Accountability / edited by Ralph Nader and Mark J. Green. — Harmondsworth [etc.] : Penguin, 1977. — ix,309p ; 19cm.
'"Corporate Power in America" is the product of our "Conference on Corporate Accountability" held in fall of 1971 in Washington, D.C.' - Preface. — Originally published: New York : Grossman Publishers, 1973. — Bibl.: p.287-295. — Index.
ISBN 0-14-004566-x Pbk : £2.00
(B77-32488)

338.7'61'00164094134 — Computing centres. *Edinburgh. Edinburgh Regional Computing Centre. Services*
Edinburgh Regional Computing Centre. An introduction for Edinburgh users / Edinburgh Regional Computing Centre. — Edinburgh (James Clerk Maxwell Building, The King's Buildings, Mayfield Rd, Edinburgh EH9 3JZ) : E.R.C.C.
1974-75. — [1974]. — 22p : ill, col map, plans ; 22cm.
Sd : Unpriced
(B77-24781)

1975-76. — [1975]. — 24p : ill, col map, plans ; 22cm.
Sd : Unpriced
(B77-24782)

1976-77. — [1976]. — 23p : ill, map, plans ; 22cm.
Sd : Unpriced
(B77-24783)

338.7'61'070509427665 — Publishing industries. *Great Britain. Akros Publications, to 1977*
Glen, Duncan. Forward from Hugh MacDiarmid, or, Mostly out of Scotland : being fifteen years of Duncan Glen, Akros Publications 1962-1977 / by Duncan Glen ; with a check-list of publications, August 1962-August 1977. — Preston : Akros Publications, 1977. — 36p ; 22cm.
Limited ed. of 300 numbered copies, of which nos 1-50 are signed by the author. — Bibl.: p.29-36.
ISBN 0-900036-90-7 Sd : £1.50
ISBN 0-900036-91-5 Signed ed. : £2.50
(B77-14607)

338.7'61'0705793094134 — Map printing & publishing industries. *Edinburgh. John Bartholomew and Son Limited, to 1976*
Gardiner, Leslie. Bartholomew, 150 years / by Leslie Gardiner. — Edinburgh : J. Bartholomew, 1976. — 112p : ill(some col), facsims(some col), maps(chiefly col), plans, ports(some col) ; 28cm.
Col. maps on lining papers.
ISBN 0-85152-791-4 : £4.95
(B77-04644)

338.7'61'07941 — Provincial press. Ownership. *Great Britain. Reports, surveys*
Hartley, Nicholas. Concentration of ownership in the provincial press / [by] Nicholas Hartley, Peter Gudgeon, Rosemary Crafts. — London : H.M.S.O., 1977. — [1],ix,121p ; 25cm. — (Great Britain. Royal Commission on the Press. Research series ; 5) (Cmnd.6810-5)
ISBN 0-10-168105-4 Pbk : £2.10
(B77-28477)

338.7'61'367924 — Clubs. Management. *London, 1945-1976. Personal observations*
O'Connor, Anthony. Clubland : the wrong side of the night people / [by] Anthony O'Connor ; with illustrations by John Farman. — London : Martin Brian and O'Keeffe, 1976. — 142p : ill ; 23cm.
ISBN 0-85616-460-7 : £5.00
(B77-22436)

338.7'61'641300941 — Food industries. Companies. *Great Britain. Statistics*
Companies in the food industry / [compiled by] T.W. Cynog-Jones. — [Watford] ([Grange La., Letchmore Heath, Watford WD2 8DQ]) : Institute of Grocery Distribution, Research Department, 1977. — 66 leaves in various pagings ; 30cm.
Index.
Sp : Unpriced
(B77-31769)

338.7'61'647940924 — Hotels. Management. Laughton, Tom. *North Yorkshire. Scarborough. Autobiographies*
Laughton, Tom. Pavilions by the sea : the memoirs of an hotel-keeper / by Tom Laughton. — London : Chatto and Windus, 1977. — xi,216p,leaf of plate,4p of plates : ill, ports ; 23cm.
Index.
ISBN 0-7011-2205-6 : £4.95
(B77-05936)

338.7'61'700941 — Arts. Patronage. Organisations. *Great Britain. Arts Council of Great Britain. Reports, surveys. Serials*
Arts Council of Great Britain. Annual report and accounts, year ended 31 March / the Arts Council of Great Britain. — London : The Council.
31st : 1976 : The arts in hard times. — 1976. — 35,69p : ill(chiefly col), port ; 30cm.
ISBN 0-7287-0112-x Pbk : £1.00
(B77-02123)

338.7'61'7009429 — Arts. Patronage. Organisations. *Wales. Welsh Arts Council. Reports, surveys. Serials. Welsh-English parallel texts*
Welsh Arts Council. Adroddiad blynyddol = Annual report : am y flwyddyn hyd at 31 Mawrth = for the year ending 31 March / Cyngor Celfyddydau Cymru = Welsh Arts Council. — [Cardiff] : [Welsh Arts Council].
1976. — [1976]. — [38]p : ill, ports ; 30cm.
ISBN 0-905171-14-4 Sd : Unpriced
(B77-03440)

338.7'61'7840924 — Pop music. Beatles. Managing. Williams, Allan, 1959-1962. *Autobiographies*
Williams, Allan. The man who gave the Beatles away / [by] Allan Williams and William Marshall. — Sevenoaks : Coronet, 1976. — 237p,[8]p of plates : ill, ports ; 18cm.
Originally published: London : Elm Tree Books, 1975.
ISBN 0-340-21016-8 Pbk : £0.90
(B77-03441)

338.7'61'7950944949 — Casinos. *Monaco. Monte Carlo. Monte Carlo Casino, to 1976*
Fielding, Xan. The money spinner : Monte Carlo casino / [by] Xan Fielding. — London : Weidenfeld and Nicolson, 1977. — xi,205p,[8]p of plates : ill, plans, ports ; 22cm.
Index.
ISBN 0-297-77201-5 : £5.25
(B77-17369)

338.7'61'796334620942751 — Association football. Clubs. *England. New Brighton Association Football and Athletic Club Company Limited. Inquiry reports*
Rankin, Andrew. New Brighton Association Football and Athletic Club Company Limited : investigation under section 165(b) of the Companies Act 1948 : report / by Andrew Rankin and Thomas White ; [for the] Department of Trade. — London : H.M.S.O., 1977. — [2],iv,112p ; 30cm.
ISBN 0-11-512028-9 Pbk : £2.25
(B77-17995)

338.7'62'000942753 — Engineering industries. *Merseyside (Metropolitan County). Liverpool. Heap and Partners Limited, to 1975*
Millar, John. William Heap and his company, 1866 / by John Millar. — [Hoylake] ([Britannia House, Newton Rd, Hoylake, Merseyside L47 3DG]) : [Heap and Partners Ltd], 1976. — [2], 246p : ill(incl 1 col), facsims, geneal table, plans, ports ; 25cm.
Bibl.: p.235. — Index.
ISBN 0-9505421-0-5 : Private circulation
(B77-03442)

338.7'62'13109413 — Electricity supply industries. *Southern Scotland. South of Scotland Electricity Board. Reports, surveys. Serials*
South of Scotland Electricity Board. Annual report and accounts for the year ended 31 March / South of Scotland Electricity Board. — Glasgow (Cathcart House, Glasgow G44 4BE) : [The Electricity Board].
[1976]-1977. — [1977]. — xvi,55p : ill, 2 maps, ports ; 30cm.
Sd : Unpriced
(B77-22437)

338.7'62'1310942 — Electricity generation industries. *England. Central Electricity Generating Board. Reports, surveys*
Hawkins, *Sir* Arthur. Electricity's balancing act / by Sir Arthur Hawkins. — London : Central Electricity Generating Board, 1976. — 16p ; 21cm.
'... addressing the annual conference of the electricity supply industry's North Western District Joint Advisory Council at Lancaster on 28 September 1976'.
Sd : Unpriced
(B77-02124)

338.7'62'1310942 — Electricity generation industries. *England. Central Electricity Generating Board. Reports, surveys. Serials*
Central Electricity Generating Board. Report and accounts for the year ended 31st March / Central Electricity Generating Board. — London : C.E.G.B.
1977. — 1977. — 60p : ill(chiefly col), 2 maps(1 col), 2 col ports ; 30cm.
Index.
ISBN 0-902543-51-2 Sd : £2.00
(B77-23227)

338.7'62'1310942 — Electricity generation industries. *England. Central Electricty Generating Board. Statistics*
Central Electricity Generating Board. CEGB statistical yearbook. — London : C.E.G.B.
1976-77. — 1977. — 20,[1]p : ill(some col), 2 col maps ; 30cm.
'This Statistical Yearbook supplements information in the CEGB's Annual Report and Accounts for 1976-77. It contains information formerly presented as Appendices to Annual Reports up to and including that for 1962-63' - note.
ISBN 0-902543-52-0 Sd : Unpriced
(B77-23228)

338.7'62'13109428 — Electricity supply industries. *North-east England. North Eastern Electricity Board. Reports, surveys. Serials*
North Eastern Electricity Board. Annual report and statement of accounts for the year ended 31 March / the North Eastern Electricity Board. — [Newcastle-upon-Tyne] ([Carliol House, Newcastle-upon-Tyne NE99 1SE]) : [N.E.E.B]. [1975]-1976. — [1976]. — [5],37[i.e. 38]p : ill(chiefly col), col map ; 30cm.
ISBN 0-904103-03-x Sd : £0.75
ISSN 0308-7905
(B77-02842)

338.7'62'1312134094111 — Hydroelectric power industries. *Northern Scotland. North of Scotland Hydro-Electric Board. Reports, surveys. Serials*
North of Scotland Hydro-Electric Board. Report and accounts 1 April to 31 March / North of Scotland Hydro-Electric Board. — [Edinburgh] ([16 Rothesay Terrace, Edinburgh EH3 7SE]) : [The Board].
1976-1977. — [1977]. — [1],59,[1]p : ill(some col), col chart, 2 col maps, port ; 30cm.
Sd : Unpriced
(B77-28478)

338.7'62'2330942823 — Coal industries. *South Yorkshire (Metropolitan County). Treeton. Treeton Colliery, to 1975*
Rossington, Tom. The story of Treeton Colliery : one hundred years of coal mining, 1875-1975 / [by Tom Rossington]. — Rotherham (Central Library, Walker Place, Rotherham S65 1JH) : Metropolitan Borough of Rotherham Libraries, Museums and Arts Department, 1976. — 60p : ill, ports ; 22cm.
ISBN 0-903666-05-7 Sd : £0.60
(B77-24784)

338.7'62'233820924 — Petroleum industries. Getty, Jean Paul. *United States. Autobiographies*
Getty, Jean Paul. How to be rich / [by] J. Paul Getty. — London : Star Books, 1976. — [7], 214p ; 20cm.
Originally published: Chicago : Playboy Press, 1965 ; London : W.H. Allen, 1966.
Pbk : £0.60
(B77-27735)

338.7'62'233820924 — Petroleum industries. Getty, Jean Paul. *United States. Biographies*
Lund, Robina. Getty : the stately gnome / [by] Robina Lund ; with drawings by the author ; photographs by Catherine Lund. — Walton-on-Thames : M. and J. Hobbs ; London : Joseph, 1977. — 185p,[8]p of plates : ill, ports ; 23cm.
ISBN 0-7181-1616-x : £5.50
(B77-30046)

338.7'62'233820941 — Petroleum industries. *Great Britain. British National Oil Corporation. Finance. National Oil Account. Accounts*
National oil account ... / [Department of Energy]. — London : H.M.S.O.
1976 : for the period 1 January to 31 March 1976. — [1977]. — 8p ; 25cm. — ([1976-77 H.C.] 252)
ISBN 0-10-225277-7 Sd : £0.25
(B77-20995)

338.7'62'23540942929 — Slate mining industries. *Gwynedd. Blaenau Ffestiniog. Llechwedd Slate Mines, to 1976*
Jones, Ivor Wynne. Llechwedd Slate Caverns / by Ivor Wynne Jones. — Blaenau Ffestiniog (Llechwedd Slate Caverns, Blaenau Ffestiniog, Gwynedd LL41 3NB) : Quarry Tours Ltd, 1976. — [1],25p : ill(chiefly col), facsims, col ports ; 19cm.
ISBN 0-9502895-4-x Sd : £0.30
(B77-15749)

338.7'62'34094184 — Munitions industries. *Wicklow (County). Arklow. Kynoch-Arklow Limited, to 1918*
Murphy, Hilary. The Kynoch era in Arklow / by Hilary Murphy. — [Wexford] ([c/o The People Newspapers Ltd, Wexford, Republic of Ireland]) : [The author], [1976]. — 72p : ill, ports ; 19cm.
Sd : £0.75
(B77-21759)

338.7'62'3746 — Military aircraft engines industries. *Great Britain. Rolls-Royce, 1925-1971*
Harker, Ronald W. Rolls-Royce from the wings : military aviation, 1925-71 / [by] Ronald W. Harker. — Oxford : Oxford Illustrated Press, 1976. — viii,168p : ill, ports ; 26cm.
Ill., ports on lining papers.
ISBN 0-902280-38-4 : £4.50
(B77-04021)

338.7'62'38200941441 — Shipbuilding industries. *Scotland. Strathclyde Region. Renfrew (District). Upper Clyde Shipbuilders. Expenditure by British government*
Broadway, Frank. Upper Clyde Shipbuilders : a study of government intervention in industry - the way the money goes / [by] Frank Broadway. — London (Wilfred St., SW1 [E6PL]) : Centre for Policy Studies, 1976. — 58p ; 21cm.
ISBN 0-9504392-3-1 Pbk : £1.55
(B77-06546)

338.7'62'40942 — Construction industries. *England. Edward Wood and Company & Skibben Winton Construction. Inquiry reports*
Clarkson, Derek Joshua. Edward Wood & Company Limited, Skibben Winton Construction Limited : investigations under Section 165 of the Companies Act 1948 : report / by Derek Joshua Clarkson and Kenneth Alexander McKinlay ; [for the] Department of Trade. — London : H.M.S.O., 1977. — [2],89,[85]p : port ; 30cm.
Spine title: Inspectors' report on Edward Wood & Company Limited and Skibben Winton Construction Limited.
ISBN 0-11-512013-0 Pbk : £3.50
(B77-16253)

338.7'62'8109425892 — Water supply industries. *Hertfordshire. Watford. Colne Valley Water Company, to 1973*
Colne Valley Water Company. The Colne Valley Water Company, 1873-1973. — Watford (Blackwell House, Aldenham Rd, Watford WD2 2EY) : The Company, [1973?]. — 77p : ill, maps ; 23cm.
ISBN 0-9505492-0-7 : Unpriced
(B77-04022)

338.7'62'92 — Car equipment industries. *Great Britain. Lucas Industries Limited, 1875-1975*
Nockolds, Harold. Lucas, the first hundred years / [by] Harold Nockolds. — Newton Abbot [etc.] : David and Charles.
In 2 vols.
Vol.1 : The king of the road. — 1976. — 349p, [16]p of plates : ill, facsims, ports ; 25cm.
Bibl.: p.341. — Index.
ISBN 0-7153-7306-4 : £9.50
(B77-04645)

338.7'62'920941 — Motor vehicle industries. *Great Britain. Chrysler United Kingdom Limited. Expenditure of British government. Great Britain. Parliament. House of Commons. Expenditure Committee. Public expenditure on Chrysler UK Ltd. Critical studies*
Great Britain. *Department of Industry.* Public expenditure on Chrysler UK Ltd, the Government's reply to the eighth report from the Expenditure Committee, session 1975-76, HC 596-1 ... / Department of Industry. — London : H.M.S.O., [1977]. — iii,16p ; 25cm. — (Cmnd. 6745)
ISBN 0-10-167450-3 Sd : £0.35
(B77-10758)

338.7'62'920941 — Motor vehicle industries. *Great Britain. Chrysler United Kingdom Limited, to 1976*
Young, Stephen, *b.1944*. Chrysler UK : a corporation in transition / by Stephen Young, Neil Hood. — New York ; London : Praeger, 1977. — xix,343p : ill, maps ; 25cm. — (Praeger special studies in international business, finance and trade)
Index.
ISBN 0-275-23820-2 : £18.40
(B77-22438)

338.7'62'922220941 — Car industries. *Great Britain. TVR Engineering Limited, to 1976*
Filby, Peter. TVR, success against the odds / [by] Peter Filby. — London : Wilton House Gentry, 1976. — 224p : ill, ports ; 25cm.
Index.
ISBN 0-905064-08-9 : £6.50
(B77-14608)

338.7'62'922220945 — Car industries. *Italy. Alfa Romeo (Firm), to 1976*
Owen, David, *b.1939.* Viva! Alfa Romeo / [by] David Owen. — Yeovil : Haynes, 1976. — 3-271p : ill(some col), ports ; 25cm.
'A Foulis motoring book' - title page verso. — Index.
ISBN 0-85429-207-1 : £7.95
(B77-04646)

338.7'64'1300941 — Food industries. Companies. *Great Britain. Statistics*
Institute of Grocery Distribution. *Research Services.* Companies in the food industry : structure and activities / Institute of Grocery Distribution Research Services. — [Watford] ([Letchmore Heath, Watford WD2 8DQ]) : [The Institute], [1977]. — [128]leaves : ill ; 30cm.
Sp : £12.00
(B77-26901)

338.7'66'0025 — Chemical industries. Companies. *Directories*
Worldwide chemical directory / prepared by ECN Chemical Data Services. — London : [IPC Business Press].
1977. — 1977. — iii leaves,424p,[3]leaves ; 30cm.
Previously published by IPC Industrial Press. — Index.
Pbk : £40.00
(B77-26902)

338.7'66'00254 — Chemical industries. Companies. *Western Europe. Directories*
Chemical company profiles, Western Europe. — London : Chemical Data Services, IPC Industrial Press, 1976. — iii,323p ; 30cm.
Index.
Pbk : £35.00
(B77-09576)

338.7'66'143 — Phosphate industries. Organisations. *Nauru & Ocean Island. British Phosphate Commission. Reports, surveys. Serials*
British Phosphate Commission. Report and accounts for the year ended 30 June ... / the British Phosphate Commissioners. — London : H.M.S.O.
[1974]-1975. — [1976]. — 8p ; 25cm. — (Miscellaneous ; no.32(1976)) (Cmnd.6670)
ISBN 0-10-166700-0 Sd : £0.25
(B77-07843)

338.7'66'3224094432 — Champagnes industries. *France. Rheims. Krug et Cie, to 1975*
Arlott, John. Krug, house of Champagne / by John Arlott ; illustrations by Timothy Jaques. — London : Davis-Poynter, 1976. — 224p : ill, facsims, geneal table, ports ; 25cm.
Ill. on lining papers. — Bibl.: p.217-218. — Index.
ISBN 0-7067-0199-2 : £10.00
(B77-02843)

338.7'66'330942523 — Brewing industries. *Nottinghamshire. Mansfield. Mansfield Brewery Company, to 1975*
Bristow, Philip. The Mansfield brew / [by] Philip Bristow. — Ringwood : Navigator Publishing, 1976. — [7],188p : ill, ports ; 23cm.
ISBN 0-902830-03-1 : £4.00
(B77-25465)

338.7'66'63942463 — Pottery & porcelain industries. *Staffordshire. Stoke-on-Trent. Spode Limited, to 1974*
Spode Limited. Spode : notes on the history and manufacture of Spode / [Spode Limited]. — Stoke-on-Trent (Spode Works, Stoke-on-Trent ST4 1BX) : Spode Ltd, 1975. — [36]p : ill, facsims, maps, plan, ports ; 21cm.
Bibl.: p.[35].
ISBN 0-9505540-0-6 Sd : £0.25
(B77-08863)

338.7'66'63942823 — Pottery & porcelain industries. *South Yorkshire (Metropolitan County). Swinton. Rockingham Works, to 1842*
Bennett, Chlöe. The story of the Rockingham Pottery / [by] Chlöe Bennett. — Rotherham (Brian O'Malley Central Library and Arts Centre, Rotherham, [S. Yorkshire] S65 1JH) : Metropolitan Borough of Rotherham, Libraries, Museum and Arts, 1976. — [1],12p : ill, port ; 22cm.
Bibl.: p.12.
ISBN 0-903666-06-5 Sd : £0.25
(B77-32489)

338.7'66'810924 — Surface-active agents industries. *Merseyside (Metropolitan County). Port Sunlight. Knox, Andrew Marshall. Autobiographies*
Knox, Andrew Marshall. Coming clean : a postscript after retirement from Unilever / [by] Andrew M. Knox. — London : Heinemann, 1976. — xii,252p,[16]p of plates : ill, map, ports ; 23cm.
Index.
ISBN 0-434-91066-x : £5.50
(B77-01238)

338.7'66'862094195 — Fertiliser industries. *Cork (County). Gouldings (W.H.M.) and Company. Sinn-Fein-The Workers' Party viewpoints*
Tony O'Reilly's last game : a case history of Irish capitalism. — Dublin (30 Gardiner Place, Dublin 1) : Repsol Publications, 1976. — 34p : 1 ill ; 18cm.
Bibl.: p.34.
ISBN 0-86064-000-0 Sd : £0.25
(B77-23229)

338.7'66'910941 — Iron & steel industries. *Great Britain. British Steel Corporation. Reports, surveys. Serials*
British Steel Corporation. Annual report and accounts / British Steel Corporation. — London : The Corporation.
1976-77. — [1977]. — 52,[1]p : col ill, col maps, port ; 21x30cm.
ISBN 0-901894-53-2 Sd : Unpriced
ISSN 0068-2586
(B77-24076)

338.7'66'910941 — Iron & steel industries. *Great Britain. British Steel Corporation. Statistics*
British Steel Corporation. Annual statistics for the Corporation / British Steel Corporation. — Croydon (12 Addiscombe Rd, Croydon CR9 3JH) : British Steel Corporation Statistical Services.
1976. — [1977]. — 34p ; 30cm.
Sd : Unpriced
(B77-33676)

338.7'66'91410942975 — Iron production industries. *Mid Glamorgan. Dowlais. Dowlais Ironwork Company, to 1970*
Owen, John Alastair. The history of the Dowlais iron works, 1759-1970 / [by] John A. Owen. — Newport, Gwent : Starling Press, 1977. — 161p,[112]p of plates : ill, facsims, plans, ports ; 21cm.
ISBN 0-903434-27-x Pbk : £3.50
(B77-27736)

338.7'66'91420924 — Steel industries. Huntsman, Benjamin. *South Yorkshire (Metropolitan County). Sheffield. Biographies*
Barraclough, Kenneth Charles. Benjamin Huntsman, 1704-1776 / by Kenneth C. Barraclough. — [Sheffield] ([Central Library, Surrey St., Sheffield S1 1XZ]) : Sheffield City Libraries, 1976. — 16p : ill, facsim, maps, 2 plans, port ; 30cm. — (Sheffield City Libraries. Local studies leaflets)
'This paper is essentially the text of the commemorative lecture given ... at the Cutler's Hall, Sheffield on ... Monday 21 June 1976' - p.16.
ISBN 0-900660-30-9 Sd : £0.50
(B77-04023)

338.7'67'7310942817 — Worsted wool industries. *West Yorkshire (Metropolitan County). Saltaire. Salts (Saltaire) Limited, to 1976*
Titus of Salts / [edited by Roger W. Suddards ; photographs by Martin White ; illustrations and drawings by Barrie Birch and Trevor Skempton]. — Bradford ([High St.], Idle, Bradford, [W. Yorkshire BD10 8NL]) : Watmoughs Ltd, 1976. — 64p : ill, plan, port ; 22cm.
Bibl.: p.64.
ISBN 0-903775-05-0 Sd : £0.90
Also classified at 942.8'17
(B77-05282)

338.7'68'17677 — Sewing machine industries. Singer, Isaac Merritt. *United States. Biographies*
Brandon, Ruth. Singer and the sewing machine : a capitalist romance / [by] Ruth Brandon. — London : Barrie and Jenkins, 1977. — xiii,244p, [16]p of plates : ill, plans, ports ; 23cm.
Bibl.: p.233-236. — Index.
ISBN 0-214-20156-2 : £5.95
(B77-21760)

338.7'68'18166242865 — Pipe organ building industries. *Durham (County). Durham. Harrison and Harrison Limited, to 1973*
Elvin, Laurence. The Harrison story : Harrison and Harrison, organ builders, Durham / by Laurence Elvin ; foreword by Sir Ernest Bullock. — 2nd ed. — Lincoln (10 Almond Ave., Swanpool, Lincoln) : The author, 1977. — [3],296p,[62]p of plates : ill, facsims, ports ; 23cm.
Limited ed. of 750 copies. — Previous ed.: 1973. — Bibl.: p.277-282. — Index. — Includes postscript, 1974-77.
ISBN 0-9500049-4-4 : £7.25
(B77-17996)

338.7'68'620942447 — Museums. *London. Kensington and Chelsea (London Borough). Victoria & Albert Museum. Exhibits: Items associated with Stanbrook Abbey Press. Catalogues*
McPherson, G D A. Stanbrook Abbey Press and Sir Sydney Cockerell : a centenary exhibition [held at the Victoria and Albert Museum] 10 November 1976 to 13 February 1977 / exhibition arranged and catalogue compiled by G.D.A. McPherson and J.I. Whalley. — [London] : Victoria and Albert Museum Library, [1976]. — [1],iii,23p ; 30cm.
Sd : £0.50
(B77-08864)

338.7'68'84 — Tobacco pipes industries. *France. GBD, to 1975*
Cole, J W. The GBD St Claude story / [by] J.W. Cole. — London (38 Finsbury Sq., EC2A 1SJ) : Cadogan Investments Ltd, 1976. — 199p,[16]p of plates : ill, ports ; 23cm.
ISBN 0-9505648-0-x : £4.50
(B77-14120)

338.7'69'00942583 — Building industries. *Hertfordshire. Bishop's Stortford. Glasscock (J.L.) Successors (Bishop's Stortford) Ltd, to 1977*
Heath, Cyril. One hundred and fifty years in the - noblest of all arts / by Cyril Heath. — Bishop's Stortford [etc.] (The Causeway, Bishop's Stortford, Herts. CM23 2EQ) : J.L. Glasscock's Successors (Bishop's Stortford) Ltd, 1977. — [20]p : ill, facsim, ports ; 21cm.
Cover title: Noblest of all arts.
Sd : Unpriced
(B77-23230)

338.8 — INDUSTRIAL ENTERPRISE. MONOPOLIES AND MERGERS

338.8'0973 — Combines. *United States*
Reid, Samuel Richardson. The new industrial order : concentration, regulation and public policy / [by] Samuel Richardson Reid. — New York ; London [etc.] : McGraw-Hill, 1976. — xix,299p : ill ; 24cm.
Index.
ISBN 0-07-051779-7 : £7.45
ISBN 0-07-051780-0 Pbk : £5.75
(B77-05937)

338.8'0973 — Combines. *United States, 1896-1905. Statistics*
Bunting, David. Statistical view of trusts : a manual of large American industrial and mining corporations active around 1900 / [by] David Bunting. — Westport, Conn. ; London : Greenwood Press, 1974. — xviii,311,[1]p ; 24cm. — (Contributions in economics and economic history ; no.9)
Bibl.: p.xv-xviii. — Index.
ISBN 0-8371-6624-1 : £11.80
(B77-17997)

338.8'2'0941 — Monopolies. *Great Britain*
Stanlake, George Frederick. Monopolies and restrictive practices / by G. Stanlake. — Revised ed. — Aylesbury : Ginn, 1976. — 49p : 2 ill ; 22cm. — (Manchester Economics Project. Satellite books ; 11)
Previous ed.: London : Ginn, 1970. — Bibl.: p.49.
ISBN 0-602-22339-3 Sd : £1.10
(B77-28479)

338.8'266'4028530941 — Frozen food industries. Monopolies. *Great Britain. Inquiry reports*
Great Britain. *Monopolies and Mergers Commission.* Frozen foodstuffs : a report on the supply in the United Kingdom of frozen foodstuffs for human consumption / the Monopolies and Mergers Commission. — London : H.M.S.O., [1976]. — v,119p : ill ; 25cm. — ([1975-76] H.C.674)
Index.
ISBN 0-10-008886-4 Pbk : £1.50
(B77-07177)

338.8'266'466 — Dogfood & catfood industries & trades. Monopolies. *Great Britain. Inquiry reports*
Great Britain. *Monopolies and Mergers Commission.* Cat and dog foods : a report on the supply in the United Kingdom of cat and dog foods ... / the Monopolies and Mergers Commission. — London : H.M.S.O., [1977]. — iii,86p ; 25cm. — ([1976-77 H.C.]447)
Index.
ISBN 0-10-244777-2 Sd : £1.60
(B77-21761)

338.8'266'4722720941 — Wheat flour milling industries. Monopolies. *Great Britain. Inquiry reports*
Great Britain. *Monopolies and Mergers Commission.* Flour and bread : a report on the supply in the United Kingdom of wheat flour and of bread made from wheat flour ... / the Monopolies and Mergers Commission. — London : H.M.S.O., 1977. — iii,137p : col map ; 25cm. — ([1976-77 H.C.]412)
ISBN 0-10-241277-4 Pbk : £2.25
Also classified at 338.8'26'64752
(B77-22439)

338.8'26'64752 — Bread baking industries. Monopolies. *Great Britain. Inquiry reports*
Great Britain. *Monopolies and Mergers Commission.* Flour and bread : a report on the supply in the United Kingdom of wheat flour and of bread made from wheat flour ... / the Monopolies and Mergers Commission. — London : H.M.S.O., 1977. — iii,137p : col map ; 25cm. — ([1976-77 H.C.]412)
ISBN 0-10-241277-4 Pbk : £2.25
Primary classification 338.8'266'4722720941
(B77-22439)

338.8'268'165 — Indirect electrostatic reprographic equipment industries. Monopolies. *Great Britain. Inquiry reports*
Great Britain. *Monopolies and Mergers Commission.* Indirect electrostatic reprographic equipment : a report on the supply of indirect electrostatic reprographic equipment / the Monopolies and Mergers Commission. — London : H.M.S.O., [1976]. — iii,132p ; 25cm. — ([1975-76 H.C.] 47)
Index.
ISBN 0-10-204777-4 Pbk : £2.10
(B77-07183)

338.8'3 — Engineering industries. *Great Britain. Babcock and Wilcox Limited. Mergers with Herbert Morris Limited. Inquiry reports*
Great Britain. *Monopolies and Mergers Commission.* Babcock & Wilcox Limited and Herbert Morris Limited : a report on the existing and proposed mergers ... / the Monopolies and Mergers Commission. — London : H.M.S.O., [1977]. — v,40p : ill ; 25cm. — ([1976-77 H.C.]175)
ISBN 0-10-217577-2 Sd : £0.85
(B77-33113)

338.8'3 — Freight container industries. *Great Britain. Crane Fruehauf Limited. Mergers with Fruehauf Corporation. Great Britain. Inquiry reports*
Great Britain. *Monopolies and Mergers Commission.* The Fruehauf Corporation and Crane Fruehauf Limited : a report on the proposed mergers ... / the Monopolies and Mergers Commission. — London : H.M.S.O., [1977]. — iv,120p ; 25cm. — (Cmnd.6906)
ISBN 0-10-169060-6 Pbk : £1.60
(B77-32490)

338.8'3 — Ophthalmic glass industries. *Great Britain. UKO International Limited. Mergers with Pilkington Brothers Limited. Inquiry reports*
Great Britain. *Monopolies and Mergers Commission.* Pilkington Brothers Limited and UKO International Limited (formerly UK Optical and Industrial Holdings Limited) : a report on the proposed merger ... / the Monopolies and Mergers Commission. — London : H.M.S.O., [1977]. — v,64p : 1 ill ; 25cm. — ([1976-77 H.C.]267)
ISBN 0-10-226777-4 Sd : £1.35
(B77-12367)

338.8'3 — Petroleum industries. *Great Britain. British Petroleum Company. Mergers with Century Oils Group Limited. Inquiry reports*
Great Britain. *Monopolies and Mergers Commission.* British Petroleum Limited and Century Oils Group Limited : a report on the proposed merger / [Monopolies and Mergers Commission] ; presented to Parliament by the Secretary of State for Prices and Consumer Protection ... — London : H.M.S.O., [1977]. — iv,53p ; 25cm. — (Cmnd.6827)
Sd : £1.10
(B77-17998)

338.8'8 — American multinational companies. *Great Britain. Statistics*
American business in Britain / Clifton Data Research Services. — St Albans (21 Culver Rd, St Albans, Herts.) : Clifton Data Research Services.
1977. — 1977. — [194]p ; 21x30cm.
'Supplement' ([14]p.) as insert. — Index.
Unpriced
ISSN 0140-5799
(B77-32491)

338.8'8 — American multinational companies: Wickes Corporation, to 1975
Bush, George. The wide world of Wickes : an unusual story of an unusual growth company / [by] George Bush. — New York ; London[etc.] : McGraw-Hill, 1976. — xix, 486p : ill., maps, ports ; 24cm.
Maps on lining papers. — Index.
ISBN 0-07-009279-6 : £8.25
(B77-14609)

338.8'8 — British business firms. *Latin America, to 1930*
Business imperialism, 1840-1930 : an inquiry based on British experience in Latin America / edited by D.C.M. Platt. — Oxford : Clarendon Press, 1977. — xvi,449p : maps ; 23cm.
Index.
ISBN 0-19-828271-0 : £12.50 : CIP rev.
(B77-10253)

338.8'8 — British multinational companies: Lonrho Limited. *Inquiry reports*
Heyman, Allan. Lonrho Limited : investigation under Section 165(6) of the Companies Act 1948 : report / by Allan Heyman and Sir William Slimmings ; [for the] Department of Trade. — London : H.M.S.O., 1976. — [3],660, [221]p ; 30cm.
ISBN 0-11-511775-x Pbk : £13.20
(B77-02844)

338.8'8 — British multinational companies: Lonrho Limited, 1961-1974
Cronjé, Suzanne. Lonrho : portrait of a multinational / [by] Suzanne Cronjé, Margaret Ling and Gillian Cronjé. — Harmondsworth [etc.] : Penguin, 1976. — 316p : map ; 19cm. — (Pelican books) (African affairs)
Index. — Previous control number ISBN 0-904014-13-4.
ISBN 0-14-021997-8 Pbk : £1.50
(B77-02845)

Cronjé, Suzanne. Lonrho : portrait of a multinational / [by] Suzanne Cronjé, Margaret Ling and Gillian Cronjé. — London : Friedmann, 1976. — 316p : maps ; 23cm.
Index.
ISBN 0-905290-00-3 : £6.95
(B77-02846)

338.8'8 — Companies. Subsidiaries. *Australia, New Zealand & Far East. Directories*
Who owns whom, Australasia and the Far East : a directory of parent, associate and subsidiary companies ... — London (24 Tufton St., SW1P 3RA) : Who Owns Whom.
1976-77 : 6th ed. — 1976. — xii,807p ; 26cm.
'Addendum' (4p.) as insert. — Index.
£25.00
ISSN 0302-4091
(B77-23231)

338.8'8 — Companies. Subsidiaries. *Western Europe. Directories*
Who owns whom, Continental Europe : a directory of parent, associate and subsidiary companies. — London (24 Tufton St., SW1P 3RA) : Who Owns Whom Ltd.
In 2 vols.
1977 : 16th ed. Vol.1 : Austria, Belgium and Luxembourg, Denmark, Finland, France, Federal Republic of Germany, Holland, Italy, Norway, Portugal, Spain, Sweden, Switzerland. — 1977. — 852p in various pagings ; 26cm.
English, French and German introduction. — Previously published: as 'Who owns whom (Continental edition)'.
£45.00(the 2 vols)
(B77-16254)

338.8'8 — Developing countries. Dependency. Role of multinational companies. Political aspects. *Study examples: Copper mining industries, 1945-1973. Study regions: Chile*
Moran, Theodore Harvey. Multinational corporations and the politics of dependence : copper in Chile / [by] Theodore H. Moran. — Princeton ; Guildford : Princeton University Press, 1977. — xiv,286p : ill ; 22cm.
Originally published: 1974. — Bibl.: p.271-280. — Index.
ISBN 0-691-00359-9 Pbk : £3.80
(B77-26903)

338.8'8 — Developing countries. Economic conditions. Effects of multinational pharmaceutical companies
Heller, Tom. Poor health, rich profits : multinational drug companies and the Third World / by Tom Heller. — Nottingham : Spokesman Books, 1977. — 76p ; 20cm.
ISBN 0-85124-168-9 : £3.95
ISBN 0-85124-169-7 Pbk : Unpriced
(B77-24785)

338.8'8 — Manufacturing industries. American multinational companies. Affiliates. *Great Britain. Reports, surveys*
Dunning, John Harry. US industry in Britain : an EAG business research study / by John H. Dunning ; (with the assistance of R.D. Pearce). — London (40 Buckingham Palace Rd, SW1W 0RE) : Wilton House Publications, 1976. — v, 122p : ill, map ; 30cm. — (Economists Advisory Group. Business research studies)
ISBN 0-904655-14-8 Sp : £30.00
(B77-04647)

338.8'8 — Multinational companies. *Conference proceedings*
Multinational Enterprise in a Hostile World *(Conference), Geneva, 1975.* The Multinational Enterprise in a Hostile World : proceedings of a conference held in Geneva under the auspices of the Graduate Institute of International Studies, l'Institut universitaire d'études européennes and the Center for Education in International Management / edited by Gerard Curzon and Victoria Curzon, with the collaboration of Laurence G. Franko and Henri Schwamm. — London [etc.] : Macmillan, 1977. — x,147p ; 23cm.
'... a conference on "Multinational Enterprise in a Hostile World"' - jacket. — Index.
ISBN 0-333-21467-6 : £7.95
(B77-16781)

338.8'8 — Multinational companies. *Trade union viewpoints*
Edwards, Bob. Multinational companies and the trade unions / [by] Bob Edwards. — Nottingham : Bertrand Russell Peace Foundation [for] Spokesman Books, 1977. — 70p ; 19cm.
ISBN 0-85124-180-8 Pbk : £0.95
(B77-29270)

338.8'8 — Multinational companies. Control. *Fabian viewpoints*
Wilms-Wright, Carl. Transnational corporations : a strategy for control / [by] Carl Wilms-Wright. — London : Fabian Society, 1977. — [2],36p ; 22cm. — (Fabian research series ; 334 ISSN 0305-3555)
ISBN 0-7163-1334-0 Sd : £0.75
(B77-29271)

338.8'8 — Multinational companies. Regulation. *Readings*
Controlling multinational enterprises : problems, strategies, counterstrategies / edited by Karl P. Sauvant and Farid G. Lavipour. — London : Wilton House Publications, 1976. — xiv,335p : ill ; 24cm.
Also published: Boulder : Westview Press, 1976. — Bibl.: p.287-323. — Index.
ISBN 0-904655-21-0 : £12.50
(B77-15160)

338.8'8 — Multinational companies. Relations with states
Vernon, Raymond. Storm over the multinationals : the real issues / [by] Raymond Vernon. — London [etc.] : Macmillan, 1977. — xi,260p : ill ; 24cm.
Originally published: Cambridge, Mass. : Harvard University Press, 1977. — Index.
ISBN 0-333-23060-4 : £10.00
(B77-27737)

338.8'8 — Pharmaceutical industries. Austrian multinational companies: Nicholas International Limited, to 1975
Smith, R Grenville. Aspro - how a family business grew up / by R. Grenville Smith and Alexander Barrie. — Melbourne : Nicholas International Limited ; London ([1 Cresswell Park, SE3 9RG]) : House Information Services Ltd, 1976. — x,182p,[32]p of plates : ill(some col), facsims, ports(some col) ; 23cm.
Col. ill. on lining paper. — Index.
ISBN 0-903716-06-2 : Unpriced
(B77-27738)

338.8'8 — Pharmaceutical industries. Multinational companies. *Forecasts to 1990*
James, Barrie G. The future of the multinational pharmaceutical industry to 1990 / [by] Barrie G. James. — London : Associated Business Programmes, 1977. — xx,283p : ill ; 23cm.
Bibl.: p.265-271. — Index.
ISBN 0-85227-061-5 : £14.95
(B77-26904)

338.8'8'0722 — Multinational companies. *Case studies*
Multinationals from small countries / edited by Tamir Agmon and Charles P. Kindleberger. — Cambridge, Mass. ; London : M.I.T. Press, 1977. — xv,224p : ill ; 24cm.
Papers presented at a conference held at M.I.T. on January 8 and 9, 1976. — Bibl. — Index.
ISBN 0-262-01050-x : £13.30
(B77-23232)

338.8'8'091724 — Multinational companies. *Developing countries. Conference proceedings*
The **multinational** corporation and social change / edited by David E. Apter, Louis Wolf Goodman. — New York [etc.] ; London : Praeger, 1976. — xv,236p : ill ; 24cm. — (Praeger special studies in international economics and development)
'These essays have been selected from a number of papers presented in 1974 at a conference on the multinational corporation at Yale University' - Introduction. — Bibl. p.147. — Index.
ISBN 0-275-23020-1 Pbk : £3.85
(B77-05938)

338.8'8'0941 — Multinational companies. Policies of Labour Party. *Great Britain*
Labour Party. International big business : Labour's policy on the multinationals / the Labour Party. — London : The Party, 1977. — 135,[1]p ; 21cm. — (A policy background paper)
Bibl.: p.83-86.
ISBN 0-86117-003-2 Sd : £0.90
(B77-33677)

338.8'8'0952 — Japanese multinational companies, to 1975
Yoshino, Michael Y. Japan's multinational enterprises / [by] M.Y. Yoshino. — Cambridge, Mass. ; London : Harvard University Press, 1976 [i.e 1977]. — xv,191p ; 24cm.
Published in the United States: 1976. — Index.
ISBN 0-674-47259-4 : £9.35
(B77-13565)

338.8'8'0973 — Multinational companies. *United States. Conference proceedings*
National Conference on Multinational Corporations for Corporate Leaders, *Washington, D.C., 1975.* The case for the multinational corporation / [by] J. Fred Weston ... [et al.] ; edited by Carl H. Madden. — New York [etc.] ; London : Praeger [for] the National Chamber Foundation, 1977. — xvii, 214p : 1 ill ; 25cm. — (Praeger special studies in international business, finance and trade)
'... the National Chamber Foundation's National Conference on Multinational Corporations for Corporate Leaders, held November 25-26, 1975, in Washington, D.C.' - Foreword. — Bibl.
ISBN 0-275-23980-2 : £13.70
(B77-15161)

338.8'8'0994 — Multinational companies. *Australia. Forecasts. Transcripts of discussions*
Australia and the multinational : the proceedings of a seminar on the future of the multinational corporation held at Sydney University on 9 December, 1976 / edited by Michael T. Skully. — Sydney : Dryden Press ; Catterham [i.e. Caterham] (26 Manor Ave., Caterham, Surrey) : Australiana Publications, 1976. — [2], 52p ; 30cm.
Bibl.: p.52.
ISBN 0-909162-01-8 Sd : £3.00
(B77-29272)

338.9 — ECONOMIC PLANNING
Johansen, Leif. Lectures on macroeconomic planning / [by] Leif Johansen. — Amsterdam [etc.] ; Oxford : North-Holland Publishing Co.
Part 1 : General aspects. — 1977. — x,355p : ill ; 23cm.
Bibl. — Index.
ISBN 0-7204-0565-3 : Unpriced
(B77-24786)

338.9 — Economic planning. Optimisation. *Essays*
Kantorovich, Leonid Vital'evich. Essays in optimal planning / [by] L.V. Kantorovich [et al.] ; selected with an introduction by Leon Smolinski ; [translated from the Russian by Arlo Schultz and others]. — Oxford : Blackwell, 1977. — xxxii,251,[1]p ; 24cm.
ISBN 0-631-17760-4 : £7.50
(B77-06547)

338.9'009172'4 — Developing countries. Economic planning
Haq, Mahbub ul. The poverty curtain : choices for the Third World / [by] Mahbub ul Haq. — New York ; Guildford : Columbia University Press, 1976. — xvii,247p ; 24cm.
Bibl.: p.239-240. — Index.
ISBN 0-231-04062-8 : Unpriced
ISBN 0-231-04063-6 Pbk : Unpriced
(B77-02125)

338.91 — Organisation for Economic Co-operation and Development. *Reports, surveys. Serials*
Organisation for Economic Co-operation and Development. Activities of OECD : report / by the Secretary-General. — Paris : O.E.C.D. ; [London] : [H.M.S.O.].
1975. — 1976. — 118p ; 24cm.
Bibl.: p.109-118.
Pbk : £2.20
ISBN 92-64-11522-6
(B77-01239)

1976. — 1977. — 127p ; 24cm.
Bibl.: p.117-127.
Pbk : £4.40
ISBN 92-64-11663-x
(B77-17999)

338.91'09 — Economic integration. Theories, 1459-1976
Machlup, Fritz. A history of thought on economic integration / [by] Fritz Machlup. — London [etc.] : Macmillan, 1977. — xi,323p ; 23cm.
Bibl. — Index.
ISBN 0-333-21344-0 : £10.00
(B77-23233)

338.91'171'241 — Commonwealth developing countries. Economic development. Financial assistance. Organisations: Commonwealth Development Corporation. *Reports, surveys. Serials*
Commonwealth Development Corporation. Commonwealth Development Corporation : partners in development, finance plus management. — London (33 Hill St., W1A 3AR) : C.D.C.
1976. — [1976]. — [2],19p : col ill, col map ; 26cm.
ISBN 0-903799-08-1 Sd : Unpriced
(B77-08865)

338.91'172'4 — Developing countries. Economic development. Foreign assistance. *Conference proceedings*
United Nations Conference on Trade and Development, *4th, Nairobi, 1976.* United Nations Conference on Trade and Development, report of the Conference on its fourth session, Nairobi, 5 to 31 May 1976, with related documents / presented to Parliament by the Secretary of State for Trade ... — London : H.M.S.O., [1977]. — 148p ; 25cm. — (Cmnd. 6708)
ISBN 0-10-167080-x Pbk : £2.35
(B77-08866)

338.91'172'4 — Developing countries. Economic development. Foreign assistance. *Fabian viewpoints*
Westlake, Melvyn. World poverty, the growing conflict / [by] Melvyn Westlake. — London : Fabian Society, 1976. — [2],32,[1]p ; 22cm. — (Young Fabian pamphlets ; 44 ISSN ISSN 0513-5982)
ISBN 0-7163-2044-4 Pbk : £0.70
(B77-00103)

338.91'172'4 — Developing countries. Economic development. Foreign assistance by Organisation for Economic Co-operation and Development countries. *Reports, surveys. Serials*
Development co-operation : efforts and policies of the members of the Development Assistance Committee. — Paris : O.E.C.D ; [London] : [H.M.S.O].
1976 review / report [of the Organisation for Economic Co-operation and Development] by Maurice J. Williams. — 1976. — 273(9 fold) : 2 ill ; 24cm.
Pbk : Unpriced
ISBN 92-64-11589-7
(B77-03443)

338.91'172'4041 — Developing countries. Economic development. Financial assistance by Great Britain. *Reports, surveys. Serials*
Great Britain. *Department of Trade.* Memorandum by the Secretary of State for Trade on the second report of the Committee, session 1976-77 : second special report from the Select Committee on Overseas Development, session 1976-77. — London : H.M.S.O., [1977]. — viii p ; 24cm. — ([1976-77 H.C.] 367)
ISBN 0-10-236777-9 Sd : £0.25
(B77-20996)

338.91'172'4041 — Developing countries. Economic development. Financial assistance by Great Britain. *Statistics*
British aid statistics : statistics of UK economic aid to developing countries / Ministry of Overseas Development. — London : H.M.S.O.
1971-1975. — 1977. — xii,130p : 1 ill ; 30cm.
ISBN 0-11-580204-5 Pbk : £5.50
ISSN 0068-1210
(B77-10254)

338.91'172'4041 — Developing countries. Economic development. Financial assistance by Great Britain. Cooperation between Great Britain. Ministry of Overseas Development & charities. *Inquiry reports*
Great Britain. *Parliament. House of Commons. Select Committee on Overseas Development.* The joint funding scheme : first report from the Select Committee on Overseas Development, session 1976-77, together with the proceedings of the Committee, minutes of evidence and appendices. — London : H.M.S.O., [1977]. — xiii,50p ; 25cm. — ([1976-77 H.C.]72)
ISBN 0-10-207277-9 Sd : £1.10
(B77-11671)

338.91'172'4051 — Developing countries. Technological development. Financial assistance by China, 1957-1974. Economic models
Horvath, Janos. Chinese technology transfer to the Third World : a grants economy analysis / [by] Janos Horvath. — New York [etc.] ; London : Praeger ; [London] : [Distributed by Martin Robertson], 1976. — x,101p ; 24cm. — (Praeger special studies in international economics and development)
Bibl.: p.94-97. — Index.
ISBN 0-275-08670-4 : £9.15
(B77-07184)

338.91'172'4073 — Developing countries. Economic development. Financial assistance by United States. Political aspects
Packenham, Robert A. Liberal America and the Third World : political development ideas in foreign aid and social science / [by] Robert A. Packenham. — Princeton ; Guildford : Princeton University Press, 1976 [i.e. 1977]. — xxii,395p ; 22cm.
Originally published: 1973. — Bibl.: p.369-378. — Index.
ISBN 0-691-07549-2 Pbk : £12.70
ISBN 0-691-02176-7 Pbk : £3.95
(B77-11122)

338.91'4 — European Community countries. Integration. Compared with integration of Central American countries
McCall, Louis A. Regional integration : a comparison of European and Central American dynamics / [by] Louis A. McCall. — Beverly Hills ; London : Sage Publications, 1976. — 77,[1]p : ill ; 22cm. — (Sage professional papers in international studies ; vol.4, no.02-041)
Bibl.: p.70-77.
ISBN 0-8039-0529-7 Pbk : £1.75
Also classified at 338.91'72
(B77-18624)

338.91'4 — European Community countries. Integration. Policies of Sozialdemokratische Partei Deutschlands, 1945-1975
Lodge, Juliet. The European policy of the SPD / [by] Juliet Lodge. — Beverly Hills ; London : Sage Publications, [1977]. — 95,[1]p ; 22cm. — (Sage research papers in the social sciences : contemporary European studies ; vol.5, no.90-035)
Published in the United States: 1976. — Bibl.: p.92-95.
ISBN 0-8039-9954-2 Pbk : £1.75
(B77-11672)

338.91'4 — European Community. Enlargement. *Fabian viewpoints*
Harris, Geoff. A wider Europe / [by] Geoff Harris. — London : Fabian Society, 1976. — [2],20,[1]p ; 22cm. — (Young Fabian pamphlets ; 45 ISSN 0513-5982)
ISBN 0-7163-2045-2 Sd : £0.50
(B77-09577)

338.91'4 — European Economic Community. Enlargement
Edwards, Geoffrey. A wider European community? : issues and problems of further enlargement / [by] Geoffrey Edwards, William Wallace. — London (12A Maddox St., W1R 9PL) : Federal Trust for Education and Research, 1976. — [5],83p ; 30cm. — (Federal Trust for Education and Research. Papers)
ISBN 0-901573-20-5 Pbk : £2.00
(B77-07185)

338.91'4'041 — European Economic Community. Membership of Great Britain. Related to devolution of powers of British government to elected assemblies in Scotland & Wales. *Conservative and Unionist Party viewpoints*
Thomas, Rosamund M. Devolution in the United Kingdom and its relevance to the EEC : a European Policy Group paper / by Rosamund M. Thomas. — London (51 Victoria St., S.W.1) : The Monday Club, 1976. — 6p ; 30cm.
ISBN 0-903900-04-1 Sd : Private circulation
Also classified at 354'.41'082
(B77-09578)

338.91'4'041 — European Economic Community. Membership of Great Britain. Related to devolution of powers of British government to elected assemblies in Scotland & Wales. *Young European Left viewpoints*
Young European Left. 'Devolution, the Left and Europe' / Young European Left. — [London] ([1a Whitehall Place, SW1A 2HA]) : FYEL], [1977]. — [2],31p ; 22cm.
'... based on a seminar held at Gorebridge in Scotland in 1976 and on discussions within YEL since then' - Introduction.
Sd : £0.25
Also classified at 354'.41'082
(B77-18625)

338.91'4'041 — European Economic Community. Role of British elected assemblies
The **British** people : their voice in Europe : report of an independent working party sponsored by the Hansard Society on the effects of membership of the European Community on British representative institutions. — Farnborough, Hants. : Saxon House [for] the Society, 1977. — xii,207p ; 24cm.
ISBN 0-566-00174-8 : Unpriced
(B77-27739)

338.91'4'0429 — Wales. Economic development. Grants from European Economic Community
Commission of the European Communities. Wales in Europe / [Commission of the European Communities]. — [London] ([20 Kensington Palace Gardens, W8 4QQ]) : The Commission, 1976. — [10]p : ill ; 21cm.
ISBN 0-902335-09-x Sd : Unpriced
(B77-16256)

338.91'41 — Great Britain. Economic development. Financial assistance. Loans from International Monetary fund. Conditions. *Proposals*
Sandeman, Edward Kenneth. SOS Britain : appeal to the International Monetary Fund / [by] E.K. Sandeman. — Hindhead (Manor Hotel, Hindhead, Surrey GU26 6RA) : [The author], 1976. — 10 leaves in various pagings ; 26cm.
ISBN 0-9505371-0-1 Sd : £0.85
(B77-02126)

338.91'41 — Great Britain. Foreign Compensation Commission. *Accounts*
Great Britain. *Foreign Compensation Commission.* Accounts ... for the financial year ended 31st March ... / [Foreign Compensation Commission]. — London : H.M.S.O.
1975-76. — [1977]. — 7p ; 25cm.
ISBN 0-10-245777-8 Sd : £0.25
(B77-20997)

338.91'41 — Great Britain. Foreign Compensation Commission. *Reports, surveys. Serials*
Great Britain. *Foreign Compensation Commission.* Annual report of the Foreign Compensation Commission for the financial year ended 31 March ... — London : H.M.S.O.
[1976]-1977 : 27th. — [1977]. — 7p ; 25cm. — (Miscellaneous ; no.13(1977)) (Cmnd.6913)
ISBN 0-10-169130-0 Sd : £0.25
(B77-26905)

338.91'72 — Central American countries. Integration. Compared with integration of European Community countries
McCall, Louis A. Regional integration : a comparison of European and Central American dynamics / [by] Louis A. McCall. — Beverly Hills ; London : Sage Publications, 1976. — 77,[1]p : ill ; 22cm. — (Sage professional papers in international studies ; vol.4, no.02-041)
Bibl.: p.70-77.
ISBN 0-8039-0529-7 Pbk : £1.75
Primary classification 338.91'4
(B77-18624)

338.941 — Great Britain. Economic Advisory Council, to 1939
Howson, Susan. The Economic Advisory Council, 1930-1939 : a study in economic advice during depression and recovery / [by] Susan Howson, Donald Winch. — Cambridge [etc.] : Cambridge University Press, 1977. — viii,424p ; 24cm.
Bibl.: p.405-413. — Index.
ISBN 0-521-21138-7 : £17.50
(B77-09579)

338.941 — Great Britain. Economic planning. *Proposals*
Robens, Alfred, *Baron Robens.* Managing Great Britain Limited / by Lord Robens of Woldingham ... — [Berkhamsted] ([Berkhamsted, Herts. HP4 1NS]) : [Ashridge Management College], [1977]. — 20p ; 21cm. — (The Ashridge lecture ; 1976)
'... delivered ... at the Royal Society of Arts, London on 13th October, 1976'.
ISBN 0-903542-14-5 Sd : £0.75
(B77-09580)

338.941 — Great Britain. Economic planning. *Secondary school texts*
Sandford, Cedric Thomas. National economic planning / [by] C.T. Sandford. — 2nd ed. — London : Heinemann Educational, 1976. — [8],101p : 1 ill ; 20cm. — (Studies in the British economy ; 9)
Previous ed.: 1972. — Bibl.: p.97-98. — Index.
ISBN 0-435-84569-1 Pbk : £1.10
(B77-04648)

338.941 — Great Britain. Economic planning, to 1975. *Case studies*
Sandford, Cedric Thomas. Economic policy / [by] C.T. Sandford, M.S. Bradbury and associates. — 2nd ed. — London [etc.] : Macmillan, 1977. — xii,284p : 2 ill, maps ; 25cm. — (Case studies in economics)
With answers to numerical exercises. — Previous ed.: 1970. — Bibl.
ISBN 0-333-21478-1 : £10.00
ISBN 0-333-21480-3 Pbk : £4.95
(B77-12368)

338.941 — Great Britain. Regional economic development. Financial incentives of government. *For businessmen*
Great Britain. *Central Office of Information.* Incentives for industry in the areas for expansion : special development areas, development areas, intermediate areas, Northern Ireland / [prepared for the Department of Industry by the Central Office of Information]. — [London] : Department of Industry, 1975. — 45,[1]p : col map ; 21cm.
Originally published: 1974.
Sd : Unpriced
(B77-11673)

338.941 — Great Britain. Regional economic development. Financial incentives of government. *Reports, surveys. Serials*
Industry Act 1972, annual report by the Secretaries of State for Industry, Scotland and Wales for the year ended 31 March ... — London : H.M.S.O.
1976. — [1976]. — 100p : col map ; 25cm. — ([1975-76 H.C.] 619)
ISBN 0-10-261976-x Sd : £1.35
(B77-07186)

1977. — [1977]. — 109p : 1 ill, col map ; 25cm. — ([1976-77 H.C.]545)
ISBN 0-10-254577-4 Sd : £1.85
(B77-30048)

338.941 — Great Britain. Rural regions. Economic development. Financial assistance by government. Development Fund. *Accounts*
Development Fund accounts ... / [Treasury]. — London : H.M.S.O.
1975-76. — [1977]. — 11p ; 25cm. — ([1976-77 H.C.] 137)
ISBN 0-10-213777-3 Sd : £0.33
(B77-11674)

338.941 — Industries. Denationalisation. *Great Britain. Aims for Freedom and Enterprise viewpoints*
Gow, Ian. A practical approach to denationalization / [by] Ian Gow. — London : Aims for Freedom and Enterprise, [1977]. — [4],10,[1]p ; 21cm.
ISBN 0-7281-0071-1 Sd : £0.30
(B77-31770)

338.941 — Industries. Financial assistance by government. *Great Britain*
Ganz, Gabriele. Government and industry : the provision of financial assistance to industry and its control / by Gabriele Ganz. — Abingdon : Professional Books, 1977. — xii,112p ; 23cm.
Index.
ISBN 0-903486-34-2 : £5.80
(B77-22440)

338.941 — Industries. Nationalisation. *Great Britain. Labour Party viewpoints*
Labour Party. Public ownership / [Labour Party] ; [researched by Transport House and Michael Meacher]. — London : Labour Party, 1976. — Folder([4]p) : ill ; 30cm. — (Labour Party. Political education discussion papers ; no.2)
Unpriced
(B77-16255)

338.941 — Industries. Planning. *Great Britain*
McIntosh, *Sir* **Ronald.** Future British industrial strategy / by Sir Ronald McIntosh. — Reading (Senior Assistant Registrar, Whiteknights, Reading RG6 2AH) : [University of Reading], [1977]. — 20,[1]p ; 22cm. — (Mercantile Credit lectures ; 1976)
'A lecture delivered at Reading University on 7th December, 1976'.
ISBN 0-7049-0256-7 Sd : Unpriced
(B77-33114)

338.941 — Industries. Policies of government. *Great Britain, 1870-1971*
Skuse, Allen. Government intervention and industrial policy / by Allen Skuse. — 2nd ed. — London : Heinemann Educational, 1976. — [8],95p ; 20cm. — (Studies in the British economy ; 4)
This ed. originally published: 1972. — Bibl.: p.88-89. — Index.
ISBN 0-435-84556-x Pbk : £0.60
(B77-06548)

338.9416 — Business enterprise. Financial assistance by government. *Northern Ireland. Reports, surveys. Serials*
Industrial Advice Grants and Industrial Enterprise Fund : report by the Department of Commerce of proceedings under the Industrial Advice and Enterprise Acts (Northern Ireland) 1964 to 1970 during the period 1 April to 31 March. — Belfast : H.M.S.O.
1975-1976. — [1976]. — 9p ; 25cm.
ISBN 0-337-06071-1 Sd : £0.22
(B77-08867)

338.9417 — Industries. Policies of government. *Ireland (Republic). Proposals*
McKinsey and Company. A new industrial policy : the key to survival : discussion draft / [prepared by McKinsey and Company for the Bank of Ireland]. — [Dublin] ([Lower Baggot St., Dublin 2]) : Bank of Ireland, [1976]. — v, [28]p : ill ; 30cm.
'A business and finance special supplement'.
Sd : Unpriced
(B77-20114)

338.9549'2 — Bangladesh. Economic planning, to 1976
Islam, Nurul. Development planning in Bangladesh : a study in political economy / [by] Nurul Islam. — London : C. Hurst, 1977. — xiii,267p ; 23cm.
Index.
ISBN 0-903983-81-8 : £8.50 : CIP rev.
(B77-14610)

338.961'1 — Tunisia. Economic planning. Mathematical models
Hawrylyshyn, Oli. Planning for economic development : the construction and use of a multisectoral model for Tunisia / [by] Oli Hawrylyshyn with ... [others]. — New York [etc.] ; London : Praeger, [1977]. — xvi,204p : ill ; 25cm. — (Praeger special studies in international economics and development)
'A project of the International Institute of Quantitative Economics'. — Published in the United States: 1976. — Bibl.: p.197-201.
ISBN 0-275-02300-1 : £12.60
(B77-13566)

338.963'2 — Ethiopia. Regional economic planning. *Study regions: Sidamo*
Sadler, Peter. Regional development in Ethiopia : a cost-benefit appraisal / [by] Peter Sadler. — Cardiff : University of Wales Press, 1976. — xiii,88p : maps ; 26cm. — (Bangor occasional papers in economics ; no.8 ISSN 0306-9338)
ISBN 0-7083-0612-8 Pbk : £2.50
(B77-14121)

338.973 — Private enterprise. Regulation by government. *United States*
Economic regulatory policies / edited by James E. Anderson. — Carbondale [etc.] ; Southern Illinois University Press ; London [etc.] : Feffer and Simons, 1977. — xiv,217p : 1 ill ; 21cm.
Originally published: Lexington, Mass. ; London : Lexington Books, 1976. — Index.
ISBN 0-8093-0818-5 Pbk : £3.70
(B77-16257)

338.973 — Social sciences. Policies of governments. Economic aspects. *Study regions: United States. Readings*
The **economic** approach to public policy : selected readings / edited by Ryan C. Amacher, Robert D. Tollison, Thomas D. Willett. — Ithaca ; London : Cornell University Press, 1976. — 528p : ill ; 22cm.
Bibl. — Index.
ISBN 0-8014-0914-4 : £12.95
ISBN 0-8014-9860-0 Pbk : £4.85
(B77-01240)

338.9758 — Georgia (State). Economic development. Assistance by federal government. Administration, 1933-1945
Holmes, Michael S. The New Deal in Georgia : an administrative history / [by] Michael S. Holmes. — Westport, Conn. ; London : Greenwood Press, 1975. — xi,364,[1]p : map ; 22cm. — (Contributions in American history ; no.36)
Bibl.: p.347-353. — Index.
ISBN 0-8371-7375-2 : £12.95
(B77-16258)

339 — MACROECONOMICS
Bach, George Leland. Macroeconomics : analysis and applications / [by] George Leland Bach. — Englewood Cliffs ; London [etc.] : Prentice-Hall, 1977. — ii-xv,426p : ill(chiefly col) ; 24cm.
'This material also appears in "Economics : an introduction to analysis and policy", Ninth Edition, by George Leland Bach [1977]' - title page verso. — Index.
ISBN 0-13-542720-7 Pbk : £6.35
(B77-23234)

Branson, William H. Macroeconomics / [by] William H. Branson, James M. Litvack. — New York [etc.] ; London : Harper and Row, 1976. — xii,433p : ill ; 24cm.
Bibl. — Index.
ISBN 0-06-040934-7 Pbk : £5.50
(B77-24077)

Brooman, Frederick Spencer. Macroeconomics / [by] F.S. Brooman. — 6th ed. — London : Allen and Unwin, 1977. — 384p : ill ; 22cm. — (Minerva series of students' handbooks ; no.9)
Previous ed.: 1973. — Index.
ISBN 0-04-330282-3 Pbk : £3.95
(B77-26188)

Darby, Michael R. Macroeconomics : the theory of income, employment and the price level / [by] Michael R. Darby. — New York ; London [etc.] : McGraw-Hill, 1976. — xii,395p : ill ; 25cm.
With answers to selected exercises. — Bibl. — Index.
ISBN 0-07-015346-9 : £11.20
(B77-03444)

Gwartney, James David. Macroeconomics : private and public choice / [by] James D. Gwartney. — New York [etc.] ; London : Academic Press, 1977. — xvii,426p : ill(chiefly col), ports ; 24cm.
Bibl.: p.409-413. — Index.
ISBN 0-12-311060-2 Pbk : £5.70
(B77-23235)

Heyne, Paul T. Toward understanding macroeconomics / [by] Paul Heyne, Thomas Johnson. — Chicago ; Henley-on-Thames [etc.] : Science Research Associates, [1977]. — x,486p : ill, map ; 24cm.
'Material contained herein also appears in books entitled "Toward economic understanding" and "The economic way of thinking"' - title page verso. — Published in the United States: 1976. — Index.
ISBN 0-574-19275-1 Pbk : £5.65
(B77-07187)

McNown, Robert F. Economics in our time : macro issues / [by] Robert F. McNown, Dwight R. Lee. — Chicago ; Henley-on-Thames [etc.] : Science Research Associates.
Instructor's manual. — [1977]. — [3],107p : ill ; 24cm.
Not the same as B76-11205. — Published in the United States: 1976. — Bibl.
Pbk : Unpriced
ISBN 0-574-21071-7
(B77-09581)

Solmon, Lewis Calvin. Macroeconomics / [by] Lewis C. Solmon. — Reading, Mass. ; London [etc.] : Addison-Wesley, 1977. — xvii,537p : ill(chiefly col), col map ; 25cm.
'"Macroeconomics" and its companion volume, "Microeconomics", were originally published as one text entitled "Economics", [2nd ed. Reading, Mass. : Addison-Wesley, 1976]' - title page verso. — Bibl.: p.484-491. — Index.
ISBN 0-201-07247-5 Pbk : £7.20
(B77-10255)

Venieris, Yiannis P. Macroeconomics [i.e. Macroeconomic] models & policy / [by] Yiannis P. Venieris and Frederick D. Sebold. — Santa Barbara ; London [etc.] : Wiley, 1977. — xiv,655p : ill ; 24cm.
'A Wiley-Hamilton publication'. — Bibl. — Index.
ISBN 0-471-90560-7 : £9.40
(B77-18626)

Westaway, Anthony John. Macroeconomics : theory, evidence and policy / [by] A.J. Westaway and T.G. Weyman-Jones. — London [etc.] : Longman, 1977. — xiv,333p : ill ; 23cm. — (Modern economics)
Bibl.: p.319-326. — Index.
ISBN 0-582-44666-x : Unpriced
ISBN 0-582-44665-1 Pbk : £4.95
(B77-30049)

339'.01'84 — Macroeconomics. Mathematical models
Turnovsky, Stephen J. Macroeconomic analysis and stabilization policies / [by] Stephen J. Turnovsky. — Cambridge [etc.] : Cambridge University Press, 1977. — xiii,390p : ill ; 24cm.
Bibl.: p.376-385. — Index.
ISBN 0-521-21520-x : £12.00
ISBN 0-521-29187-9 Pbk : £4.95
(B77-22441)

339'.08 — Macroeconomics. *Readings*
Macroeconomic themes : edited writings in macroeconomics / with commentaries by M.J.C. Surrey. — London : Oxford University Press, 1976. — ix,524p : ill ; 25cm.
Bibl. — Index.
ISBN 0-19-877059-6 : £8.95
ISBN 0-19-877060-x Pbk : £3.95
(B77-00666)

339.2 — Life. Value. Economic aspects
Mooney, Gavin H. The valuation of human life / [by] Gavin H. Mooney. — London [etc.] : Macmillan, 1977. — xiv,165p : 1 ill ; 23cm.
Index.
ISBN 0-333-21422-6 : £5.95
(B77-31772)

339.2 — Remuneration. Distribution. Inequalities
Phelps-Brown, *Sir* Henry. The inequality of pay / by Henry Phelps Brown. — Oxford [etc.] : Oxford University Press, 1977. — xv, 360p : ill ; 24cm.
Bibl.: p.333-347. — Index.
ISBN 0-19-885097-2 : £7.95 : CIP rev.
ISBN 0-19-888097-9 Pbk : Unpriced
(B77-13567)

339.2'05 — Income. Distribution. *Reports, surveys. Periodicals*
Incomes Data Services. IDS international report. — London (140 Great Portland St., W.1) : I.D.S.
1- ; May 1975-. — 1975-. — 28cm.
Twenty four issues a year. — 8p. in 28th issue. — Pierced for binder.
Sd : Unpriced
ISSN 0308-9320
(B77-03445)

339.2'09172'2 — Income. Distribution. *Developed countries*
Grants and exchange / editor Martin Pfaff. — Amsterdam [etc.] ; Oxford : North-Holland Publishing Co., 1976. — xv,485p ; 23cm.
'The papers included in this volume received their first formulation in a sequence of international conferences held in 1972' - Preface. — Bibl.
ISBN 0-7204-0383-9 : £29.27
(B77-17370)

339.2'0941 — Personal income. Distribution. *Great Britain. Conference proceedings*
The **personal** distribution of incomes / edited by A.B. Atkinson ; for the Royal Economic Society. — London : Allen and Unwin, 1976. — 3-352p : ill ; 22cm.
Bibl. — Index.
ISBN 0-04-332065-1 Pbk : £6.95
(B77-30050)

339.2'0941 — Personal income. Distribution. *Great Britain. Inquiry reports*
Trades Union Congress. The distribution of income and wealth : a TUC digest of the first four reports of the Royal Commission on the Distribution of Income and Wealth. — London : T.U.C., 1976. — 3-31p : col ill ; 21cm.
ISBN 0-900878-48-7 Sd : £0.35
Also classified at 339.4'1'0941
(B77-14122)

339.2'0941 — Personal income. Distribution. *Great Britain. Reports, surveys*
Great Britain. *Royal Commission on the Distribution of Income and Wealth.* Second report on the standing reference / Royal Commission on the Distribution of Income and Wealth ; chairman, Lord Diamond. — London : H.M.S.O., [1976]. — xv,136p(8 fold) : ill ; 25cm. — (Report ; no.4) (Cmnd.6626)
ISBN 0-10-166260-2 Pbk : £1.85
(B77-07188)

339.2'0973 — Income. Distribution. *United States. Proposals*
Jubilee for our times : a practical program for income equality / edited by Alvin L. Schorr. — New York ; Guildford : Columbia University Press, 1977. — xv,320p : 2 ill ; 22cm.
Index.
ISBN 0-231-04056-3 : Unpriced
(B77-18000)

339.2'0973 — Income. Distribution. Inequalities. Effects of taxation & welfare benefits. *United States*
Reynolds, Morgan. Public expenditures, taxes and the distribution of income : the United States, 1950, 1961, 1970 / [by] Morgan Reynolds, Eugene Smolensky. — New York [etc.] ; London : Academic Press, 1977. — xix, 145p : ill ; 24cm. — (University of Wisconsin. Institute for Research on Poverty. Monograph series)
Bibl.: p.133-139. — Index.
ISBN 0-12-586550-3 : £9.95
(B77-24078)

339.2'0985 — Income. Distribution. Policies of government. *Peru, 1963-1973*
Webb, Richard Charles. Government policy and the distribution of income in Peru, 1963-1973 / [by] Richard Charles Webb. — Cambridge, Mass. ; London : Harvard University Press, 1977. — xiii,239p ; 24cm. — (Harvard economic studies ; 147)
Index.
ISBN 0-674-35830-9 : £11.25
(B77-24787)

339.3 — National accounts. *Organisation for Economic Co-operation and Development countires. Statistics. French-English parallel texts*
Organisation for Economic Co-operation and Development. National accounts statistics = Statistique des comptes nationaux / [Organisation for Economic Co-operation and Development]. — Paris : O.E.C.D. ; [London] : [H.M.S.O.].
1974. Vol.2 : Detailed tables = Tableaux détaillés. — 1976. — 371p ; 27cm.
Parallel English and French text.
Pbk : £5.00
ISBN 92-64-01465-9
(B77-01241)

1975. Vol.2 : Detailed tables = Tableaux détaillés. — [1977]. — 370,[1]p ; 27cm.
Parallel English and French text.
Pbk : £5.50
ISBN 92-64-01658-9
(B77-25466)

339.341 — National income. *Great Britain*
Stone, Richard. National income and expenditure / [by] Richard and Giovanna Stone. — 10th ed. — London : Bowes and Bowes, 1977. — 175p : ill ; 21cm.
Previous ed.: 1972. — Bibl.: p.165-175.
ISBN 0-370-10165-0 : £3.75
ISBN 0-370-10166-9 Pbk : £2.50
Also classified at 339.373
(B77-14123)

339.341 — National income. *Great Britain, 1855-1965. Statistics*
Feinstein, Charles Hilliard. Statistical tables of national income, expenditure and output of the UK, 1855-1965 / [by] C.H. Feinstein. — Cambridge [etc.] : Cambridge University Press, 1976. — viii,141p ; 31cm.
Originally published: in 'National income, expenditure and output of the United Kingdom, 1855-1965'. 1972.
ISBN 0-521-21396-7 Pbk : £4.75
Also classified at 339.4'0941
(B77-09582)

339.341 — National income. *Great Britain. Statistics*
Great Britain. *Board of Inland Revenue.* Inland Revenue statistics / Board of Inland Revenue. — London : H.M.S.O.
1976. — 1977. — vi,164p ; 28cm.
ISBN 0-11-640850-2 Pbk : £6.50
(B77-10256)

National income and expenditure / Central Statistical Office. — London : H.M.S.O.
1966-76. — 1977. — viii,2-139p ; 28cm.
ISBN 0-11-630168-6 Pbk : £3.95
Also classified at 339.4'0941
(B77-28480)

339.373 — National income. *United States*
Stone, Richard. National income and expenditure / [by] Richard and Giovanna Stone. — 10th ed. — London : Bowes and Bowes, 1977. — 175p : ill ; 21cm.
Previous ed.: 1972. — Bibl.: p.165-175.
ISBN 0-370-10165-0 : £3.75
ISBN 0-370-10166-9 Pbk : £2.50
Primary classification 339.341
(B77-14123)

339.4'0941 — National expenditure. *Great Britain, 1855-1965. Statistics*
Feinstein, Charles Hilliard. Statistical tables of national income, expenditure and output of the UK, 1855-1965 / [by] C.H. Feinstein. — Cambridge [etc.] : Cambridge University Press, 1976. — viii,141p ; 31cm.
Originally published: in 'National income, expenditure and output of the United Kingdom, 1855-1965'. 1972.
ISBN 0-521-21396-7 Pbk : £4.75
Primary classification 339.341
(B77-09582)

339.4'0941 — National expenditure. *Great Britain. Statistics*
National income and expenditure / Central Statistical Office. — London : H.M.S.O.
1966-76. — 1977. — viii,2-139p ; 28cm.
ISBN 0-11-630168-6 Pbk : £3.95
Primary classification 339.341
(B77-28480)

339.4'1 — Consumers. Purchasing power. *Western Europe. Comparative studies*
Devas, Esmond. The European consumer markets : national and regional purchasing power comparisons / [author Esmond G. Devas]. — London (Suite 433, 52 High Holborn, WC1V 6RL) : Industrial Planning and Economics Ltd, 1976. — [26] leaves : maps ; 30cm.
Sd : £10.00
(B77-19264)

339.4'1 — Cost-benefit analysis. *Kenya. Case studies*
Scott, Maurice FitzGerald. Project appraisal in practice : the Little-Mirrlees method applied in Kenya / by M. FG. Scott, J.D. MacArthur, D.M.G. Newbery. — London : Heinemann Educational, 1976. — xxvii,548p : ill, maps ; 23cm.
Bibl.: p.535-540. — Index.
ISBN 0-435-84786-4 : £9.50
(B77-04649)

339.4'1 — Households. Income. Distribution. *Great Britain, 1957-1972*
Roberti, Paolo. The distribution of household income in the United Kingdom, 1957-72 / [by] Paolo Roberti. — London : H.M.S.O., 1976. — viii,39p : ill ; 28cm. — (Studies in official statistics ; no.30)
At head of title: Central Statistical Office.
ISBN 0-11-630160-0 Sd : £1.15
(B77-04650)

339.4'1 — Wealth. Distribution
Meade, James Edward. The just economy / by J.E. Meade. — London : Allen and Unwin, 1976. — 3-247p : ill ; 22cm. — (Meade, James Edward. Principles of political economy ; vol.4)
Index.
ISBN 0-04-330279-3 Pbk : £4.50
(B77-25467)

339.4'1'091724 — Wealth. Distribution. Developing countries. Rural regions. Compared with distribution of wealth in urban regions
Lipton, Michael. Why poor people stay poor : a study of urban bias in world development / [by] Michael Lipton. — London : Temple Smith, 1977. — 467p : ill ; 24cm.
Bibl.: p.355-357. — Index.
ISBN 0-85117-076-5 : £9.50
(B77-08868)

339.4'1'0941 — Personal wealth. Distribution. *Great Britain. Inquiry reports*
Trades Union Congress. The distribution of income and wealth : a TUC digest of the first four reports of the Royal Commission on the Distribution of Income and Wealth. — London : T.U.C., 1976. — 3-31p : col ill ; 21cm.
ISBN 0-900878-48-7 Sd : £0.35
Primary classification 339.2'0941
(B77-14122)

339.4'6'0941 — Poverty. Economic aspects. *Great Britain, 1953-1973*
Fiegehen, Guy. Poverty and progress in Britain, 1953-73 : a statistical study of low income households, their numbers, types and expenditure patterns / [by] G.C. Fiegehen, P.S. Lansley and A.D. Smith, with a contribution by N.C. Garganas. — Cambridge [etc.] : Cambridge University Press, 1977. — xiv,173p : ill ; 24cm. — (National Institute of Economic and Social Research. Occasional papers ; 29)
Index.
ISBN 0-521-21683-4 : £6.00
(B77-24789)

339.4'6'0941 — Poverty. Economic aspects. *Great Britain. Reports, surveys*
Why the poor pay more / edited by Frances Williams. — London [etc.] : Macmillan for the National Consumer Council, 1977. — viii, 240p : maps ; 21cm.
ISBN 0-333-23643-2 : £8.95
ISBN 0-333-23644-0 Pbk : £2.95
(B77-31054)

339.4'7 — Adolescent girls. Expenditure. *Great Britain. Reports, surveys*
Teenage girls : a market expenditure study. — London : IPC Magazines.
1977. — 1977. — 54,[20]p,[10]leaves : form ; 22x31cm.
Sp : £75.00
(B77-33678)

339.4'7 — Consumer behaviour. Economic aspects
Gordon, Leland James. Economics for consumers / [by] Leland J. Gordon, Stewart M. Lee. — 7th ed. — New York ; London [etc.] : D. Van Nostrand, 1977. — ix,693p : ill, forms ; 24cm.
Previous ed.: New York ; London : Van Nostrand Reinhold, 1972. — Index.
ISBN 0-442-22242-4 : £11.30
(B77-23236)

Green, H A John. Consumer theory / [by] H.A. John Green. — Revised ed. — London [etc.] : Macmillan, 1976. — 344p : ill ; 23cm.
With answers to the exercises. — Previous ed.: Harmondsworth : Penguin, 1971. — Bibl. — Index.
ISBN 0-333-19941-3 : £7.95
ISBN 0-333-19942-1 Pbk : £2.95
(B77-02847)

Scitovsky, Tibor. The joyless economy : an inquiry into human satisfaction and consumer dissatisfaction / [by] Tibor Scitovsky. — Oxford [etc.] : Oxford University Press, 1977. — xxi,310p : ill ; 21cm. — (A Galaxy book)
Originally published: 1976. — Index.
ISBN 0-19-502183-5 Pbk : £1.95
(B77-24079)

339.4'7 — Consumer durables. Purchase. *Great Britain. Reports, surveys*
Pickering, John Frederick. The acquisition of consumer durables : a cross-sectional investigation / [by] J.F. Pickering, with the research assistance of B.C. Isherwood and R.C. Davies. — London : Associated Business Programmes, 1977. — xi,255p : ill ; 25cm.
Bibl.: p.249-252. — Index.
ISBN 0-85227-067-4 : £12.95
(B77-24080)

339.4'7 — Consumer goods. Consumption. *Western Europe. Forecasts for 1975-1980*
Staniland Hall Associates Limited. Discretionary spending in Western Europe : the next five years / [Staniland Hall Associates Ltd] ; contributors include Richard J. Hall, Adam Fforde and Leslie Staniland. — London (1A Camden Walk, N1 8DY) : Staniland Hall Associates Ltd, 1976. — [1],52 leaves : ill ; 21x30cm.
ISBN 0-9504055-3-1 Sp : £45.00
(B77-05283)

339.4'7 — Consumer goods. Consumption. *Western Europe. Statistics*
Consumer Europe. — London : Euromonitor Publications.
1977 : A statistical review of European consumer markets in 1975. — 1977. — [12], 334p ; 31cm.
Index.
£35.00
ISSN 0308-4353
(B77-27740)

339.4'7 — Consumer goods. Consumption. Mathematical models
Private and enlarged consumption : essays in methodology and empirical analysis / edited by L. Solari, J.-N. du Pasquier. — Amsterdam [etc.] ; Oxford : North-Holland Publishing Co., 1976. — ix,301p : ill ; 23cm. — (Association scientifique européenne pour la prévision economique à moyen et à long terme. Publications ; vol.5)
'... partly the result of a European Seminar held in December 1974 in Geneva by the European Scientific Association of Applied Economics' - jacket. — English and French introduction, 3 contributions in French. — Bibl.
ISBN 0-7204-0461-4 : £31.71
(B77-07189)

339.4'7 — Consumer goods. Demand. Econometric models
Theil, Henri. Theory and measurement of consumer demand / [by] Henri Theil. — Amsterdam [etc.] ; Oxford : North-Holland Publishing Co.
In 2 vols.
Vol.2. — 1976. — xvii,490p : ill ; 24cm. — (Studies in mathematical and managerial economics ; vol.21)
Bibl.: p.483-484. — Index.
ISBN 0-7204-3322-3 : £11.18
ISBN 0-7204-3808-x Pbk : Unpriced
(B77-07190)

339.4'7 — Consumer goods. Underconsumption. Theories, ca 1800-ca 1970. *Marxist viewpoints*
Bleaney, M F. Under-consumption theories : a history and critical analysis / by M.F. Bleaney. — London : Lawrence and Wishart, 1976. — 262p ; 22cm.
Bibl.: p.253-258. — Index.
ISBN 0-85315-366-3 Pbk : £3.00
(B77-05284)

339.4'7 — Families. Expenditure. *Great Britain. Statistics*
Family expenditure survey : report / Department of Employment. — London : H.M.S.O.
1975. — 1976. — vii,155p : ill ; 28cm.
Index.
ISBN 0-11-361085-8 Pbk : £4.00
ISSN 0072-5927
(B77-02127)

339.4'7 — Families. Expenditure. *Northern Ireland. Statistics*
Northern Ireland family expenditure survey : report / [Northern Ireland Department of Finance, Statistics and Economics Unit]. — Belfast : H.M.S.O.
1975. — 1977. — v,53p : ill ; 28cm.
ISBN 0-337-23218-0 Sd : £1.85
ISSN 0308-2008
(B77-16259)

339.4'7 — Retired persons. Economic aspects. *South-west England. Reports, surveys*
Gordon, I R. The retirement industry in the South West : a survey of its size, distribution and economic aspects / carried out by I.R. Gordon. — [London] ([2 Marsham St., SW1P 3EB]) : Department of the Environment for the South West Economic Planning Council, 1975. — [8],65,[12]p ; 30cm.
ISBN 0-7184-0075-5 Sd : £1.00
(B77-09583)

339.4'7'015116 — Demand. Combinatorial analysis
Afriat, S N. Combinatorial theory of demand / by S.N. Afriat. — London (3 Wyndham Place, W1H 1AP) : Input-Output Publishing Co., 1976. — [4],26p ; 23cm. — (Input-Output Research Association. Occasional papers ; no.1)
Bibl.: p.25-26.
ISBN 0-904870-05-7 Pbk : £1.00
(B77-13568)

339.4'7'0941 — Consumers. *Great Britain. Statistics. For marketing*
Planning consumer markets : a forecasting service covering population, consumers' incomes and spending for the UK and the regions / the Henley Centre for Forecasting. — [London] ([27 St John's Sq., EC1M 4DP]) : [The Centre].
[No.1]- ; Feb. 1977-. — [1977]-. — ill, col maps ; 30cm.
Quarterly. — [2],84p.,plate in 1st issue.
Sp : £240.00 yearly
ISSN 0308-7751
(B77-17371)

339.4'8'301540941 — Privately owned housing. Supply & demand. Great Britain. Related to supply & demand of building society mortgages, 1955-1974. Econometric models
Hadjimatheou, George. Housing and mortgage markets : the UK experience / [by] George Hadjimatheou. — Farnborough, Hants. : Saxon House, 1976. — x,179p : ill ; 24cm.
Bibl.: p.165-174. — Index.
ISBN 0-566-00152-7 : £7.95
Primary classification 332.7'2
(B77-02820)

339.4'8'3015709427 — Leisure facilities. Demand. Forecasting. Applications of mathematical models. *North-west England. For planning*
Settle, J G. Leisure in the North West : a tool for forecasting / by J.G. Settle. — London : Sports Council ; [Manchester] : North West Council for Sport and Recreation, 1977. — 59p : 1 ill ; 30cm. — (Sports Council. Studies ; no.11 ISSN 0306-8110)
Bibl.: p.59.
ISBN 0-900979-48-8 Sd : £2.00
(B77-20115)

339.4'8'5535 — Naturally occurring aggregates. Demand. *North Wales. Forecasts for 1975-1981*
North Wales Working Party on Aggregates. Interim report of the North Wales Working Party on Aggregates. — [Mold] ([c/o M. Ellis, County Planning Department, Shire Hall, Mold, Clwyd CH7 6NG]) : [The Working Party], 1976. — [5],35p : ill, maps ; 30cm.
ISBN 0-904695-03-4 Sd : £1.25
(B77-06549)

339.4'8'6214 — Energy. Supply & demand. Elasticity. *Great Britain. Reports, surveys*
Working Group on Energy Elasticities. Report of the Working Group on Energy Elasticities. — London : H.M.S.O., 1977. — iv,55p : ill ; 25cm. — (Energy paper ; no.17)
Chairman: T.A. Kennedy.
ISBN 0-11-410296-1 Sd : £2.00
(B77-12369)

339.4'8'622338 — Mobile offshore drilling rigs. Supply & demand. *Forecasts for 1975-1985*
Le Leuch, H. The world market for offshore mobile drilling rigs : the present position and prospects, 1978-1985 / author H. Le Leuch assisted by G. Pointout. — [Revised and updated ed.] / [translated from the French by Sinclair Road]. — London (45 Cornhill, EC3V 9DR) : Energy Reports Ltd.
'Technico-economic data from L'Institut français du pétrole, Département Economie'. — In 2 vols. — Previous ed.: published in French. Rueil-Malmaison : Institut Français du Pétrole, 1976.
Vol.1. — 1976. — 280p in various pagings : ill, plans ; 30cm.
ISBN 0-905793-00-5 Pbk : £140.00(for 2 vols)
(B77-02848)

Vol.2. — 1976. — 282p in various pagings : ill, maps, plans ; 30cm.
ISBN 0-905793-01-3 Pbk : £140.00(for 2 vols.)
(B77-02849)

339.4'8'62810942 — Natural resources: Water. Demand. Trends. *England, 1961-1974. Reports, surveys*
Central Water Planning Unit. Analysis of trends in public water supply / [Central Water Planning Unit]. — Reading (Reading Bridge House, Reading RG1 8PS) : The Unit, 1976. — vi,24p : ill(some col) ; 30cm.
ISBN 0-904839-15-x Sd : Unpriced
(B77-01242)

339.4'8'63 — Agricultural products. Supply & demand. *Reports, surveys*
Organisation for Economic Co-operation and Development. Study of trends in world supply and demand of major agricultural commodities : report / by the Secretary-General [of the Organisation for Economic Co-operation and Development]. — Paris : O.E.C.D. ; [London] : [H.M.S.O.], 1976. — 349p : 1 ill ; 24cm.
Pbk : £6.00
ISBN 92-64-11549-8
(B77-00667)

339.4'8'63091724 — Agricultural products. Supply. Developing countries. Related to prices. Econometric models
Askari, Hossein. Agricultural supply response : a survey of the econometric evidence / [by] Hossein Askari, John Thomas Cummings. — New York [etc.] ; London : Praeger ; [London] : [Distributed by Martin Robertson], 1976. — xvii,444p : ill ; 25cm. — (Praeger special studies in international economics and development)
Bibl.: p.414-435. — Index.
ISBN 0-275-23260-3 : £24.05
Primary classification 338.1'3
(B77-05926)

339.4'8'63904 — Land passenger vehicles. Fuel. Consumption. *Great Britain. Urban regions. Reports, surveys*
Maltby, D. Urban transport planning and energy, a quantitative analysis of energy use / prepared for the Science Research Council by D. Maltby, I.G. Monteith and K.A. Lawler. — [Salford] ([Salford M5 4WT]) : [University of Salford, Centre for Transport Studies], 1976. — [4],vi leaves,178p,[7] leaves of plates : ill ; 31cm. — (University of Salford. Centre for Transport Studies. Working papers ; 3 ISSN 0309-5738)
Bibl.: p.127-130.
Sp : Unpriced
(B77-19265)

339.4'8'66850941 — Cosmetics, perfumes & toiletries. Consumption. *Great Britain. Reports, surveys. Serials*
The **cosmetics** and toiletries survey. — [London] : IPC Magazines.
1957?-. — [1957?]-. — forms ; 23x31cm.
Published at irregular intervals. — [9],129 [i.e. 135], vi,[5]p. in 1973. Second half issue. — Tab indexed.
Sp : £85.00
(B77-30051)

339.4'8'796909411 — Winter sports facilities. Demand. *Scotland. Reports, surveys*
Baker, Michael John. The market for winter sports facilities in Scotland / by Michael J. Baker and Alexander W. Gordon. — Edinburgh : Research and Planning Division, Scottish Tourist Board, 1976. — [3],37 leaves ; 30cm.
'A summary ... of a study carried out for the Scottish Sports Council, The Scottish Tourist Board [and] the Highlands and Islands Development Board' - cover.
ISBN 0-85419-113-5 Pbk : £2.00
(B77-05285)

339.5 — Economic growth
Cornwall, John. Growth and stability in a mature economy / [by] John Cornwall. — London : Martin Robertson, [1977]. — 287p : ill ; 24cm.
Originally published: 1972. — Index.
ISBN 0-85520-100-2 Pbk : £3.45
(B77-11675)

339.5 — Economic growth. Equilibrium theory
Dixit, A K. The theory of equilibrium growth / [by] A.K. Dixit. — London [etc.] : Oxford University Press, 1976. — x,204p : ill ; 21cm.
Bibl.: p.194-202. — Index.
ISBN 0-19-877080-4 : £4.95
ISBN 0-19-877081-2 Pbk : £2.95
(B77-01243)

339.5 — Economic growth. Social aspects. Theories
Mishan, Edward Joshua. The economic growth debate : an assessment / [by] E.J. Mishan. — London : Allen and Unwin, 1977. — 3-277p ; 23cm.
Bibl.: p.268-271. — Index.
ISBN 0-04-330280-7 : £7.50
ISBN 0-04-330281-5 Pbk : £3.50
(B77-22442)

339.5 — Finance. Inflation. Control. Use of tax indexation. *Great Britain. Proposals*
Morgan, David Raymond. Over-taxation by inflation : a study of the effects of inflation on taxation and government expenditure, and of its correction by indexing / [by] David R. Morgan. — [London] : Institute of Economic Affairs, 1977. — 82p : 1 ill ; 22cm. — (Hobart paper ; 72 ISSN 0073-2818)
Bibl.: p.81-82.
ISBN 0-255-36091-6 Pbk : £1.50
(B77-17372)

339.5 — Incomes policy. *Conference proceedings*
The **economics** of price and wage controls / editors Karl Brunner, Allan H. Meltzer. — Amsterdam [etc.] ; Oxford : North-Holland Publishing Co., 1976. — [8],304[i.e. 315]p : ill ; 24cm. — (Carnegie-Rochester conference series on public policy ; vol.2)
' ... papers presented at the November 1973 Conference ... ' - Introduction to the series. — Bibl.
ISBN 0-7204-0458-4 Pbk : Unpriced
(B77-12370)

339.5 — Incomes policy. *Great Britain. Humorous texts*
Johnston, Thomas Lothian. Incomes policy : the long view and the short / [by] T.L. Johnston. — Glasgow (100 Montrose St., Glasgow G4 OL2) : Fraser of Allander Institute, 1977. — 20p ; 22cm. — (Fraser of Allander Institute. Speculative papers ; no.6)
Bibl.: p.20.
ISBN 0-904865-13-4 Sd : £0.80
(B77-28481)

339.5 — Organisation for Economic Co-operation and Development countries. Economic growth. *Reports, surveys*
Towards full employment and price stability, summary of a report to the OECD / by a group of independent experts, Paul McCracken ... [et al.]. — Paris : O.E.C.D. ; [London] : [H.M.S.O.], 1977. — 52p : ill ; 24cm.
Pbk : £2.20
(B77-17373)

339.5 — Personal income. Policies of government. *Great Britain*
Brittan, Samuel. The delusion of incomes policy / [by] Samuel Brittan & Peter Lilley. — London : Temple Smith, 1977. — 254p : ill ; 23cm.
Bibl.: p.238-245. — Index.
ISBN 0-85117-112-5 : £6.50
ISBN 0-85117-121-4 Pbk : £3.00
(B77-09584)

339.5'09172'2 — Developed countries. Economic growth. Social aspects
Hirsch, Fred. Social limits to growth / [by] Fred Hirsch. — London [etc.] : Routledge and Kegan Paul, 1977. — xiii,208p : ill ; 24cm. — (Twentieth Century Fund. Studies)
Originally published: Cambridge, Mass. : Harvard University Press, 1976. — Bibl.: p.193-202. — Index.
ISBN 0-7100-8610-5 : £5.50
(B77-12371)

339.5'0941 — Great Britain. Economic growth. Effects of legislation. *Conservative and Unionist Party viewpoints*
Howe, *Sir* Geoffrey. Too much law? : the effects of legislation on economic growth / [by Sir Geoffrey Howe]. — London : Conservative Political Centre, 1977. — 16p ; 21cm. — (Conservative Political Centre. Publications ; no.610)
'... based on the Address given ... at the Annual General Meeting of the Society of Conservative Lawyers at Gray's Inn Hall, London WC1 on 27th June 1977' - title page verso.
ISBN 0-85070-604-1 Sd : £0.40
(B77-33679)

339.5'0973 — United States. Economic growth. Social aspects
Miles, Rufus E. Awakening from the American dream : the social and political limits to growth / [by] Rufus E. Miles, Jr. — London : Boyars : Distributed by Calder and Boyars, 1977. — x,246p : ill ; 23cm. — ([Open forum])
Originally published: New York : Universe Books, 1976. — Index.
ISBN 0-7145-2601-0 : £5.95
(B77-12929)

339.5'0973 — United States. Economic growth. Theories, 1945-1976
Klein, Burton Harold. Dynamic economics / [by] Burton H. Klein. — Cambridge, Mass. ; London : Harvard University Press, 1977. — xiii,289p : ill ; 24cm.
Index.
ISBN 0-674-24576-8 : £8.20
(B77-33680)

340 — LAW
340 — Law. *Reviews of research*
Current legal problems / [edited] on behalf of the Faculty of Laws, University College, London. — London : Stevens.
1976 : Vol.29 / edited by Lord Lloyd of Hampstead and Roger W. Rideout with Stephen Guest as assistant editor. — 1976. — vii,232p ; 23cm.
Index.
ISBN 0-420-45060-2 : £9.80
(B77-08283)

340 — Law. Decision making. Applications of information systems using digital computer systems
Bing, Jon. Legal decisions and information systems / [by] Jon Bing, Trygve Harvold. — Oslo : Universitetsforlaget ; Henley on Thames (37 Queen St., Henley on Thames, Oxon, RG9 1AJ) : [Distributed by] Global Book Resources Ltd, 1977. — 272p : ill ; 23cm. — (Universitetet i Oslo. Institutt for privatrett. Avdeling for EDB-sporsmal. Publications ; no.5)
Bibl.: p.260-268. — Index.
£12.80
(B77-26906)

340'.023 — Barristers. *France. Toulouse, 1740-1793*
Berlanstein, Lenard R. The barristers of Toulouse in the eighteenth century (1740-1793) / [by] Lenard R. Berlanstein. — Baltimore ; London : Johns Hopkins University Press, 1975. — xii,210p : ill, map ; 24cm. — (Johns Hopkins University. Studies in historical and political science ; 93rd series (1975) ; 1)
Bibl.: p.191-204. — Index.
ISBN 0-8018-1582-7 : £9.35
(B77-20998)

340'.023 — Legal profession
Lawyers in their social setting / edited by D.N. MacCormick. — Edinburgh : Green, 1976. — xii,227p,[2]p of plates : 1 ill, ports ; 25cm. — (Wilson memorial lectures)
'... delivered ... between 1972 and 1975, ... first published in "The Judicial Review" ...' - Editor's foreword. — Index.
ISBN 0-414-00603-8 Pbk : £6.00
(B77-02850)

340'.023 — Legal profession. *Directories*
The **international** law list. — London : Corper-Mordaunt.
1977 : 111th year. — [1976]. — xxxii,1073p ; 23cm.
Index.
£14.50
ISSN 0309-0825
(B77-00668)

1978 : 112th year. — [1977]. — xxxii,1139p ; 23cm.
Index.
£16.82
ISSN 0309-0825
(B77-32492)

Kime's international law directory ... — London (170 Sloane St., SW1X 9QG) : Kime's International Law Directory Ltd.
1977 / edited and compiled by James M. Matthews ... — 1977. — [2],xv,497,245C,[1]p : facsim, forms ; 22cm.
Index.
Unpriced
(B77-21764)

340'.023 — Legal profession. *England. Directories*
The **solicitors'** diary, almanac and legal directory : incorporating the Law Society lists of practising solicitors. — London : Waterlow.
1977 : 133rd year of publication / general editor Sir Desmond Heap. — 1977. — 1234p : ill ; 22cm.
Unpaged diary between p.400-401. — Index.
ISBN 0-900791-31-4 : £8.50
ISBN 0-900791-32-2 De-luxe ed. : Unpriced
ISBN 0-900791-33-0/34-9 De-luxe 2 vol. ed. : Unpriced
ISSN 0305-8263
(B77-08284)

340'.023 — Legal profession. *Scotland. Directories*
The **Scottish** law directory : published so far as relates to certificated solicitors practising in Scotland by the authority of the Law Society of Scotland. — Glasgow : Hodge.
1977 : eighty-sixth year. — 1977. — 616p in various pagings : ill ; 22cm.
Contains unpaged diary. — Index.
ISBN 0-85279-080-5 : £7.25
(B77-14124)

340'.023 — Legal profession. Research projects. *Ghana*
Luckham, Robin. The Ghana legal profession : the natural history of a research project / by Robin Luckham. — Brighton : Institute of Development Studies, 1977. — [3],38p : 1 ill ; 30cm. — (Institute of Development Studies. Discussion papers ; 103 ISSN 0308-5864)
Bibl.: p.28.
Sd : £1.65
(B77-18627)

340'.023 — Solicitors. Complaints by clients. Adjudication. Role of Law Society. *England. Reports, surveys. Serials*
Solicitors Act 1974, annual report of the lay observer / laid before Parliament by the Lord High Chancellor ... — London : H.M.S.O.
2nd : 1976-1977. — [1977]. — [2],8p ; 25cm. — ([1976-77 H.C.] 375)
ISBN 0-10-237577-1 Sd : £0.35
(B77-20999)

340'.023 — Solicitorship. *England*
Gilbert, Michael. The law / [by] Michael Gilbert. — Newton Abbot [etc.] : David and Charles, 1977. — 128p ; 23cm. — (The professions)
Bibl.: p.126. — Index.
ISBN 0-7153-7314-5 : £3.95
(B77-11123)

340'.025'42 — Barristers. *England. Directories*
List of barristers by chambers with index. — London (9 Lincoln's Inn Fields, WC2A 3DW) : Holborn Law Society.
7th ed. : to January 1977. — [1976]. — [1],85,[28]p ; 33cm.
ISBN 0-9504122-1-x Pbk : £3.50
(B77-14611)

340'.05 — Law. *Periodicals*
The **Trent** law journal : journal of the Department of Legal Studies [Trent Polytechnic]. — Nottingham (Burton St., Nottingham) : [The Department].
Vol.1- ; 1977-. — 1977-. — ill ; 23cm.
Annual. — [8],98p. in 1st issue.
Sd : £1.00
ISSN 0309-8990
(B77-32493)

340'.06'24212 — Civilian lawyers. Organisations. *London (City). Doctors' Commons, to 1857*
Squibb, George Drewry. Doctors' Commons : a history of the College of Advocates and Doctors of Law / [by] G.D. Squibb. — Oxford : Clarendon Press, 1977. — xv,244p,v leaves of plates : ill, facsim, geneal table, map ; 23cm.
Bibl.: p.215-218. — Index.
ISBN 0-19-825339-7 : £10.00 : CIP rev.
(B77-22443)

340'.08 — Law. *Essays*
Graveson, Ronald Harry. One law : on jurisprudence and the unification of law / by R.H. Graveson. — Amsterdam [etc.] ; Oxford : North-Holland Publishing Co., 1977. — xvi, 287p,plate : port ; 23cm. — (European studies in law ; vol.2) (Selected readings ; vol.2)
Includes 2 papers in French. — Index.
ISBN 0-7204-0487-8 : Unpriced
(B77-18628)

340'.09171'241 — Commonwealth countries. Law. *Reports, surveys. Serials*
Annual survey of Commonwealth law. — London : Butterworth.
1975 / editor H.W.R. Wade ; associate editor Harold L. Cryer. — 1976. — lxxxiv,733p ; 26cm.
'Prepared under the auspices of the Faculty of Law in the University of Oxford and the British Institute of International and Comparative Law' - p.v. — Bibl. — Index.
ISBN 0-406-10790-4 : £26.50
(B77-07191)

340'.092'4 — England. Law. Robey, Edward. *Autobiographies*
Robey, Edward. The jester and the court : reminiscences / by Edward Robey. — London : Kimber, 1976. — 191p,[12]p of plates : ill, ports ; 25cm.
Index.
ISBN 0-7183-0494-2 : £4.50
(B77-00669)

340'.092'4 — Law. Carlson, Joel. *South Africa. Autobiographies*
Carlson, Joel. No neutral ground / [by] Joel Carlson ; foreword by Peter Hain. — London [etc.] : Quartet Books, 1977. — xxi,241p ; 20cm.
Originally published: London : Davis-Poynter, 1973. — Index.
ISBN 0-7043-3158-6 Pbk : £2.50
(B77-33682)

340'.092'4 — United States. Law. Cox, Hugh Baker. *Biographies*
The **perfect** advocate. — [Oxford] ([c/o The Librarian, Christ Church, Oxford OX1 1DP]) : [Christ Church], [1976]. — [6],84p : port ; 22cm.
Cover title. — 'A memoir of the late Hugh B. Cox, Esquire' - p.[1].
Pbk : Unpriced
(B77-22444)

340'.092'4 — United States. Law. Pound, Roscoe. *Biographies*
Wigdor, David. Roscoe Pound : philosopher of law / [by] David Wigdor. — Westport, Conn. ; London : Greenwood Press, 1974. — xi,356p : port ; 22cm. — (Contributions in American history ; no.[33])
Index.
ISBN 0-8371-6419-2 : £11.95
(B77-15162)

340'.09411 — Scotland. Law. Implications of devolution of powers of British government
Independence and devolution : the legal implications for Scotland / editor John P. Grant. — Edinburgh : Green, 1976. — xvii, 233p ; 22cm.
Index.
ISBN 0-414-00604-6 Pbk : £4.50
(B77-04652)

340'.0942 — England. Civil law. *Secondary school texts*
May, John, *b.1931.* Law in action / [by] John May ; editor R. Giles ; illustrations R. Fereday ; legal consultant J. Harries. — Birmingham : Clearway Publishing Co., 1977. — [1],29p : ill, forms ; 30cm. — (Clearway workshop series)
Pierced for binder. — 'Produced in co-operation with the Law Society'.
ISBN 0-902336-55-x Sd : Unpriced
(B77-21000)

340'.0942 — England. Law
Farrar, John Hynes. Introduction to legal method / [by] John H. Farrar. — London : Sweet and Maxwell, 1977. — xvi,258p : ill ; 22cm.
Bibl. — Index.
ISBN 0-421-21170-9 : £6.90
ISBN 0-421-21190-3 Pbk : £3.25
(B77-18002)

Halsbury, Hardinge Stanley Giffard, *Earl of.* Halbury's laws of England. — 4th ed. / [editor-in-chief] Lord Hailsham of St Marylebone. — London : Butterworth.
In 56 vols. — Previous ed.: in 43 vols, 1952-1964.
Vol.18. — 1977. — 179,1086p ; 26cm.
Index.
ISBN 0-406-03418-4 : £23.80(subscribers only)
ISBN 0-406-03538-5 De luxe ed. : £33.50
(B77-11124)

Halsbury, Hardinge Stanley Giffard, *Earl of.* Halsbury's laws of England. — 3rd ed. — London : Butterworth.
Cumulative supplement 1977 / editor F.M. Walter, assistant editor K.H. Mugford. — 1977. — 2v.(ca 6400 pages in various pagings) ; 26cm.
Booklet (101p.) as insert. — Index.
ISBN 0-406-03165-7 : £68.00
(B77-33683)

Halsbury, Hardinge Stanley Giffard, *Earl of.* Halsbury's laws of England. — 4th ed. / [editor-in-chief] Lord Hailsham of St Marylebone. — London : Butterworth.
In 56 vols. — Previous ed.: in 43 vols, 1952-1964.
Vol.17. — 1976. — 266,877p ; 26cm.
Index.
ISBN 0-406-03417-6 : £23.05(subscribers only)
ISBN 0-406-03537-7 Deluxe ed. : £34.40(£32.45 to subscribers)
(B77-01244)

Vol.19. — 1977. — 77,530p ; 26cm.
Index.
ISBN 0-406-03419-2 : Unpriced
ISBN 0-406-03539-3 De luxe ed. : Unpriced
(B77-31055)

Halsbury, Hardinge Stanley Giffard, *Earl of.* Halsbury's laws of England. — London : Butterworth.
Cumulative supplement 1977 for use by replacement subscribers with fourth edition vols 1-19 and third edition vols 15, 17-19 / editor F.M. Walter, assistant editor K.H. Mugford. — 1977. — ca 1800p in various pagings ; 26cm.
Index.
ISBN 0-406-03661-6 : £68.00(set of 2 vols)
(B77-25468)

Cumulative supplement 1977 for use by replacement subscribers with vols 20 to 43, third edition / editor F.M. Walter, assistant editor K.H. Mugford. — 1977. — ca 3000p in various pagings ; 26cm.
Index.
ISBN 0-406-03662-4 : £68.00(set of 2 vols)
(B77-25469)

James, Philip Seaforth. Introduction to English law / [by] Philip S. James. — 9th ed. / [with a] chapter on revenue law by G.N. Glover. — London : Butterworth, 1976. — xxxvii,498p ; 23cm.
Previous ed.: 1972. — Index.
ISBN 0-406-60496-7 : Unpriced
ISBN 0-406-60497-5 Pbk : Unpriced
(B77-28482)

Newton, Clive Richard. General principles of law / by Clive R. Newton. — 2nd ed. — London : Sweet and Maxwell, 1977. — xxi, 386p ; 22cm. — (Concise college texts)
Previous ed.: 1972. — Bibl.: p.377-378. — Index.
ISBN 0-421-22160-7 Pbk : £3.50
(B77-16782)

Padfield, Colin Frank. Law made simple / [by] C.F. Padfield. — 4th (revised) ed. reprinted with revisions. — London : W.H. Allen, 1977. — xvi,432p : ill, facsims, forms ; 22cm. — (Made simple books ISSN 0464-2902)
This ed. originally published: 1975. — Index.
ISBN 0-491-01021-4 Pbk : £1.75
(B77-24790)

Rolph, C.H. Mr Prone : a week in the life of an ignorant man / [by] C.H. Rolph ; illustrated by David English. — Oxford [etc.] : Oxford University Press, 1977. — [7],166p : ill ; 21cm.
Index.
ISBN 0-19-212966-x : £2.95 : CIP rev.
(B77-20116)

340'.0942 — England. Law. *Dictionaries*
Mozley, Herbert Newman. Mozley & Whiteley's law dictionary. — 9th ed. / by John B. Saunders. — London : Butterworth, 1977. — [9],361p ; 19cm.
Previous ed.: 1970.
ISBN 0-406-62523-9 : Unpriced
ISBN 0-406-62524-7 Pbk : £3.00
(B77-24791)

340'.0942 — Legal services. *England. Labour Party viewpoints*
Labour Party. The citizen & the law : evidence to the Royal Commission on Legal Services / the Labour Party. — London : Labour Party, 1977. — 47p ; 21cm.
Sd : £0.50
(B77-25470)

340'.0967 — Africa south of the Sahara. Law. *Reports, surveys. Serials*
Annual survey of African law. — London : Collings.
Vol.7 : 1973 / edited by N.N. Rubin and E. Cotran. — 1977. — xxi,384p ; 24cm.
Includes chapters in French. — Bibl.: p.358-375. — Index.
ISBN 0-86036-034-2 : £20.00
(B77-25471)

340'.0973 — United States. Law, to 1973
Gilmore, Grant. The ages of American law / [by] Grant Gilmore. — New Haven ; London : Yale University Press, 1977. — x,154p ; 22cm. — (Storrs lectures on jurisprudence)
Index.
ISBN 0-300-01951-3 : £7.20
(B77-24792)

340'.0994 — Australia. Law
Chisholm, Richard, *b.1944.* Understanding law : an introduction to Australia's legal system / by Richard Chisholm and Garth Nettheim. — Melbourne ; London [etc.] : Butterworth, 1975. — vii,112p ; 21cm.
Originally published: 1974. — Bibl.: p.107-108. — Index.
ISBN 0-409-43511-2 Pbk : Unpriced
(B77-23237)

340.1 — LAW. PHILOSOPHY AND THEORY
340.1 — Jurisprudence
Dworkin, Ronald. Taking rights seriously / [by] Ronald Dworkin. — London : Duckworth, 1977. — xv,293p ; 25cm.
Index.
ISBN 0-7156-0715-4 : £9.80
(B77-11125)

Hart, Herbert Lionel Adolphus. The concept of law / by H.L.A. Hart. — [1st ed. reprinted] ; [with a select bibliography of critical writings]. — New York ; London : Oxford University Press, 1961[i.e.1976]. — [8],263p ; 20cm. — (Clarendon law series)
First ed. originally published: 1961. — Bibl.: p.257-258. — Index.
ISBN 0-19-876072-8 Pbk : £2.95
(B77-07844)

Perspectives in jurisprudence / edited by Elspeth Attwooll. — Glasgow : University of Glasgow Press, 1977. — xiii,236,[1]p ; 22cm.
ISBN 0-85261-134-x : £7.50
(B77-19266)

340.1 — Jurisprudence. *Festschriften*
Law, morality and society : essays in honour of H.L.A. Hart / edited by P.M.S. Hacker and J. Raz. — Oxford : Clarendon Press, 1977. — vii, 312p,plate : port ; 23cm.
Bibl.: p.309-312.
ISBN 0-19-824557-2 : £7.50 : CIP rev.
(B77-07845)

340.1'08 — Jurisprudence. *Readings*
The **philosophy** of law / edited by R.M. Dworkin. — Oxford [etc.] : Oxford University Press, 1977. — [9],177p ; 21cm. — (Oxford readings in philosophy)
Bibl.: p.173-176. — Index.
ISBN 0-19-875022-6 Pbk : £1.50
(B77-21001)

340.1'1 — Justice. Philosophical perspectives. Rawls, John. Theory of justice. *Critical studies*
Wolff, Robert Paul. Understanding Rawls : a reconstruction and critique of 'A theory of justice' / by Robert Paul Wolff. — Princeton ; Guildford : Princeton University Press, 1977. — x,224p : ill ; 22cm.
Bibl.: p.211-212. — Index.
ISBN 0-691-01992-4 : £10.20
(B77-22445)

340.1'12'0942 — England. Law. Ethical aspects
Scarman, *Sir* **Leslie.** Common law and ethical principle / [by] Leslie Scarman. — London (Conway Hall, Red Lion Sq., WC1R 4RL) : South Place Ethical Society, [1977]. — 19p ; 22cm. — (Conway memorial lecture ; 57th)
'... [delivered] 16th November 1976' - cover.
Sd : £0.20
(B77-22446)

340.1'15 — Law. *Anthropological perspectives. Conference proceedings*
Social anthropology and law / edited by Ian Hamnett. — London [etc.] : Academic Press, 1977. — x,234p : ill ; 24cm. — (Association of Social Anthropologists of the Commonwealth. Monographs ; 14)
'... conference on social anthropology and law ... held at the University of Keele in March 1974' - title page verso. — Bibl. — Index.
ISBN 0-12-322350-4 : £5.50
(B77-21765)

340.1'15 — Law. *Sociological perspectives*
Ball, Robert Edward. The law and the cloud of unknowing / by R.E. Ball ; with a foreword by Lord Cross of Chelsea. — Ilfracombe : Stockwell, 1976. — 153p ; 22cm.
ISBN 0-7223-0916-3 : £3.30
(B77-11126)

Black, Donald, *b.1941.* The behavior of law / [by] Donald Black. — New York [etc.] ; London : Academic Press, 1976. — xi,175p ; 24cm.
Bibl.: p.139-164. — Index.
ISBN 0-12-102650-7 : £7.60
(B77-05939)

Friedman, Lawrence M. Law and society : an introduction / [by] Lawrence M. Friedman. — Englewood Cliffs ; London [etc.] : Prentice-Hall, 1977. — xiii,177p ; 24cm. — (Prentice-Hall foundations of modern sociology series)
Bibl.: p.169-171. — Index.
ISBN 0-13-526616-5 : £6.35
ISBN 0-13-526608-4 Pbk : £3.15
(B77-24081)

340.1'15 — Law. Social aspects
Hartzler, H Richard. Justice, legal systems and social structure / [by] H. Richard Hartzler. — Port Washington, N.Y. ; London : Kennikat Press, 1976. — x,134p : ill ; 23cm.
'A Dunellen Publishing Company Book'. — Bibl.: p.129-131. — Index.
ISBN 0-8046-7079-x : £9.50
(B77-00670)

Unger, Roberto Mangabeira. Law in modern society : toward a criticism of social theory / [by] Roberto Mangabeira Unger. — New York : Free Press ; London : Collier Macmillan, 1977. — ix,309p ; 21cm.
Originally published: 1976. — Index.
ISBN 0-02-932880-2 Pbk : £3.00
(B77-28483)

340.1'15 — Legal system. Political aspects. *United States*
Eisenstein, James. Politics and the legal process / [by] James Eisenstein. — New York [etc.] ; London : Harper and Row, 1973. — ix, 356p : ill ; 21cm. — (Harper's American political behavior series)
Index.
ISBN 0-06-041883-4 Pbk : £5.20
(B77-22447)

340.1'15'08 — Law. Social aspects. *Readings*
Law and control in society / edited by Ronald L. Akers, Richard Hawkins. — Englewood Cliffs ; London [etc.] : Prentice-Hall, 1975. — xiii, 383p ; 24cm. — (Prentice-Hall sociology series)
Bibl.
ISBN 0-13-526095-7 : £10.35
(B77-31057)

340.1'15'0942 — England. Law. Social aspects. *Secondary school texts*
Bunker, Peter. Law & society / by Peter and John Bunker ; edited by Harry Undy. — London : Christian Education Movement, 1977. — 2-31p : ill, facsims ; 26cm. — (Probe ISSN 0305-3776)
Bibl.: p.31.
ISBN 0-905022-19-x Sd : Unpriced
(B77-23238)

340.3 — LAW REFORM

340'.3'061411 — Scotland. Law. Reform. Organisations: Scottish Law Commission. *Reports, surveys. Serials*
Scottish Law Commission. Annual report [for the year ended 15th June] ... / Scottish Law Commission. — Edinburgh : H.M.S.O.
1975-1976 : 11th. — [1977]. — vii,29p ; 25cm. — (Scot.Law Com. ; no.43) ([1976-77 H.C.]111)
Bibl.: p.24-27.
ISBN 0-10-211177-4 Sd : £0.70
(B77-08285)

340'.3'06142 — England. Law. Reform. Organisations. Law Commission. *Reports, surveys. Serials*
Law Commission. Annual report / the Law Commission. — London : H.M.S.O.
1975-1976 : 11th. — [1977]. — iv,27p ; 25cm. — (Law Com. ; no.78) ([1976-77 H.C.] 94)
ISBN 0-10-209477-2 Sd : £0.70
(B77-07192)

340'.3'0941 — Great Britain. Law. Statutes. Reform. *Proposals*
Law Commission. Statute law revision / the Law Commission and the Scottish Law Commission. — London : H.M.S.O.
8th report : Draft Statute Law (Repeals) Bill ... — [1977]. — ii,76p ; 25cm. — (Law Com. ; no.80) (Scot. Law Com. ; no.44) (Cmnd.6719)
ISBN 0-10-167190-3 Sd : £1.75
(B77-07193)

340'.3'0942 — England. Law. Reform
Edmund-Davies, Herbert Edmund, *Baron Edmund-Davies.* Ferment in the law : being the Presidential Address of Lord Edmund-Davies, President of the Holdsworth Club ... — [Birmingham] (Faculty of Law, University of Birmingham, Edgbaston, Birmingham B15 2TT) : Holdsworth Club of the University of Birmingham, 1977. — [2],19p ; 25cm. — (Holdsworth Club. Presidential addresses ; 1976-77 ISSN 0307-0859)
ISBN 0-7044-0264-5 Sd : £2.00
(B77-33115)

340.9 — CONFLICT OF LAWS

340.9 — England. Conflict of laws with foreign countries. English law
Dicey, Albert Venn. Dicey and Morris on the conflict of laws. — 9th ed. / general editor J.H.C. Morris. — London : Stevens.
Previous ed.: 1967.
4th cumulative supplement : up to date to October 1, 1976 / by J.H.C. Morris ... [et al.]. — 1976. — [76]p ; 24cm.
Index.
ISBN 0-420-45260-5 Sd : £2.50
(B77-07846)

Liddle, Christopher Kingsworth. Cases with a foreign element : some problems for the practitioner / [by] C.K. Liddle. — [Guildford] ([Braboeuf Manor, Portsmouth Rd, St Catherine's, Guildford, Surrey]) : The College of Law, 1973. — [1],15p ; 22cm. — (College of Law. Crash course lectures : 1973)
ISBN 0-905835-36-0 Sd : £0.50
(B77-07847)

340.9 — International Institute for the Unification of Private Law. Constitution. *Treaties*
International Institute for the Unification of Private Law. Statute of the International Institute for the Unification of Private Law, with the amendments adopted at the nineteenth session of the General Assembly on 18 February 1969, Rome, 15 March 1940 ... — London : H.M.S.O., [1977]. — 20p ; 25cm. — (Treaty series ; no.78(1977)) (Cmnd.6946)
French and English text.
ISBN 0-10-169460-1 Sd : £0.35
(B77-31773)

340.9 — Marriage. Conflict of laws. *Treaties*
Hague Conference on Private International Law, *13th, 1976.* Final act of the Thirteenth Session of the Hague Conference on Private International Law including draft conventions and decisions, the Hague, 23 October 1976 ... — London : H.M.S.O., [1977]. — 19p ; 25cm. — (Miscellaneous ; no.11(1977)) (Cmnd.6830)
ISBN 0-10-168300-6 Sd : £0.35
(B77-24082)

340.9'08 — Conflict of laws. *Essays*
Graveson, Ronald Harry. Comparative conflict of laws / by R.H. Graveson. — Amsterdam [etc.] ; Oxford : North-Holland Publishing Co., 1977. — xviii,379p,plate : port ; 23cm. — (European studies in law ; vol.1) (Selected essays ; vol.1)
Index.
ISBN 0-7204-0486-x : Unpriced
(B77-16260)

341 — INTERNATIONAL LAW
Akehurst, Michael Barton. A modern introduction to international law / by Michael Akehurst. — 3rd ed. — London : Allen and Unwin, 1977. — 3-283p ; 23cm. — (Minerva series of students' handbooks ; no.25)
Previous ed.: 1971. — Index.
ISBN 0-04-341013-8 : £10.50
ISBN 0-04-341014-6 Pbk : £4.95
(B77-26190)

Schwarzenberger, Georg. A manual of international law. — 6th ed. / by Georg Schwarzenberger and E.D. Brown. — Milton (Milton Trading Estate, Milton, Oxon) : Professional Books Ltd, 1976. — lix,612p,fold plate : ill ; 23cm.
Previous ed.: / by Georg Schwarzenberger. London : Stevens, 1967. — Bibl.: p.537-546. — Index.
ISBN 0-903486-27-x : £12.50
ISBN 0-903486-26-1 Pbk : £7.50
(B77-01245)

Shaw, Malcolm Nathan. International law / [by] Malcolm N. Shaw ; editorial adviser Ronald Chappell. — Sevenoaks : Teach Yourself Books, 1977. — xiii,546p ; 18cm. — (Teach yourself series)
Bibl.: p.523-528. — Index.
ISBN 0-340-22231-x Pbk : £2.75
(B77-27741)

Starke, Joseph Gabriel. An introduction to international law / by J.G. Starke. — 8th ed. — London : Butterworth, 1977. — xxxii,711, 46p ; 23cm.
Previous ed.: 1972. — Bibl.: p.709-711. — Index.
ISBN 0-406-65954-0 : £15.00
ISBN 0-406-65955-9 Pbk : £13.00
(B77-24793)

341 — International law. *Festschriften*
Toward world order and human dignity : essays in honor of Myres S. McDougal / edited by W. Michael Reisman, Burns H. Weston ; introduction by Harold D. Lasswell ; afterword by Eugene V. Rostow. — New York : Free Press ; London : Collier Macmillan, 1976. — xviii,603p,plate : port ; 24cm.
Bibl.: p.579-593. — Index.
ISBN 0-02-926290-9 : £17.50
(B77-12930)

341 — International law. Political aspects
Levi, Werner. Law and politics in the international society / [by] Werner Levi. — Beverly Hills ; London : Sage Publications, 1976. — 191p ; 22cm. — (Sage library of social research ; vol.32)
Bibl.: p.174-184. — Index.
ISBN 0-8039-0617-x : £7.50
ISBN 0-8039-0618-8 Pbk : £4.00
(B77-14612)

341'.05 — International law. *Serials*
The **British** year book of international law. — Oxford : Clarendon Press.
1974-1975 : forty-seventh year of issue / [editors R.Y. Jennings, Ian Brownlie]. — 1977. — xix,525p,plate : port ; 25cm.
Index.
ISBN 0-19-818168-x : £30.00 : CIP rev.
(B77-06550)

341'.08 — International law. *Essays*
Lauterpacht, *Sir* **Hersch.** International law : being the collected papers of Hersch Lauterpacht / systematically arranged and edited by E. Lauterpacht. — Cambridge [etc.] : Cambridge University Press.
Vol.3 : The law of peace. Parts 2-6. — 1977. — xxv,614p ; 26cm.
Bibl.: p.xix-xxv. — Index.
ISBN 0-521-21207-3 : £30.00
(B77-14125)

341.2 — INTERNATIONAL LEGAL ORGANISATIONS

341.2'05 — Intergovernmental organisations. *Yearbooks*
Political handbook of the world : governments and intergovernmental organizations as of January 1. — New York ; London [etc.] : McGraw-Hill for the Center for Comparative Political Research of the State University of New York at Binghamton and for the Council on Foreign Relations.
1975 / edited by Arthur S. Banks ... [et al.]. — [1976]. — xv,491p : map(on lining papers) ; 29cm.
Published in the United States: 1975.
ISBN 0-07-003713-2 : £14.75
Primary classification 320.9'04'7
(B77-02074)

1976 / edited by Arthur S. Banks ... [et al.]. — 1976. — xi,545p : map(on lining papers) ; 29cm.
ISBN 0-07-003640-3 : £14.75
Primary classification 320.9'04'7
(B77-02075)

Political handbook of the world : governments, regional issues, and intergovernmental organizations as of January 1. — New York [etc.] ; London : McGraw-Hill for the Center for Social Analysis of the State University of New York at Binghamton and for the Council on Foreign Relations.
1977 / edited by Arthur S. Banks ... [et al.]. — 1977. — xii,604p : map(on lining papers) ; 29cm.
Index.
ISBN 0-07-003641-1 : Unpriced
Primary classification 320.9'04'7
(B77-29975)

341.2'09'04 — International organisations, 1919-1976
Bennett, A LeRoy. International organizations : principles and issues / [by] A. LeRoy Bennett. — Englewood Cliffs ; London [etc.] : Prentice-Hall, 1977. — vii,440p : 3 ill ; 24cm.
Bibl.: p.391-399. — Index.
ISBN 0-13-473389-4 : £10.35
(B77-16261)

341.2'09'04 — International organisations, 1945-1976
Luard, Evan. International agencies : the emerging framework of interdependence / [by] Evan Luard. — London [etc.] : Macmillan for the Royal Institute of International Affairs, 1977. — xii,338[i.e.340]p ; 23cm.
Bibl. — Index.
ISBN 0-333-21128-6 : £14.00
(B77-08869)

341.22'43 — League of Nations. Relations with Germany, to 1933
Kimmich, Christoph Martin. Germany and the League of Nations / [by] Christoph M. Kimmich. — Chicago ; London : University of Chicago Press, 1976. — x,266p,plate : 1 ill ; 23cm.
Bibl.: p.251-259. — Index.
ISBN 0-226-43534-2 : £13.15
(B77-07848)

341.23'092'4 — United Nations. Organisation. Role of Webster, Sir Charles, b.1886, 1939-1946
The **historian** as diplomat : Charles Kingsley Webster and the United Nations, 1939-1946 / [edited by] P.A. Reynolds and E.J. Hughes. — London : Martin Robertson, 1976. — [7],198p ; 24cm.
Index. — Includes the text of the Charter of the United Nations.
ISBN 0-85520-131-2 : £7.85
(B77-05940)

341.23'2 — United Nations. General Assembly. Proceedings. *Reports, surveys*
United Nations. *General Assembly.* Report on the proceedings of the thirty-first session of the General Assembly of the United Nations held at New York from 21 September to 22 December, 1976, and on the proceedings of the Security Council in 1976 ... — London : H.M.S.O., [1977]. — viii,129p ; 25cm. — (United Nations ; no.1 (1977)) (Cmnd.6752)
ISBN 0-10-167520-8 Pbk : £2.10
(B77-11676)

341.24'2 — Council of Europe. Consultative Assembly. Representation of Portugal. *Statutes*

Council of Europe. [Statute. Article 26]. Amendment to Article 26 of the Statute of the Council of Europe, Strasbourg, 2 October 1976 ... — London : H.M.S.O., [1977]. — Folder (3p) ; 25cm. — (Treaty series ; no.5(1977)) (Cmnd.6701)
ISBN 0-10-167010-9 : £0.15
(B77-11677)

341.24'2 — European Community. Law

Encyclopedia of European Community law / general editor K.R. Simmonds. — [London] : Sweet and Maxwell ; [Edinburgh] : Green [etc.].

Vol.C. 4 : Community secondary legislation. — [1976]. — 1v : ill, forms ; 26cm.
Vol.C in 5 vols. — 1229p. in various pagings on publication of Vol.C4. — Tab indexed. — In binder.
ISBN 0-421-21960-2 : £30.00
ISBN 0-421-20760-4 Set of 5 vols : £150.00
(B77-01246)

Vol.C. 5 : Community secondary legislation. — [1976]. — lv. : ill, forms ; 26cm.
Vol. C in 5 vols. — 579p. in various pagings on publication of Vol. C.5. — Tab indexed. — In binder.
ISBN 0-421-21970-x Ls : £30.00
ISBN 0-421-20760-4 Set of 5 vols : £150.00
(B77-01247)

Mackenzie Stuart, Alexander John, *Lord Mackenzie Stuart.* The European Communities and the rule of law / by Lord Mackenzie Stuart. — London : Stevens, 1977. — xii,125p ; 19cm. — (The Hamlyn lectures ; 29th series)
'... delivered in April 1977 ... at the Institute of Advanced Legal Studies in London' - p.x.
ISBN 0-420-45190-0 : £4.90
ISBN 0-420-45200-1 Pbk : £1.95
(B77-19267)

341.24'2 — European Community. Law. Secondary legislation. *Reports, surveys. Serials*

Great Britain. *Parliament. House of Commons. Select Committee on European Legislation, etc.* Report from the Select Committee on European Legislation, &c., session 1976-77. — London : H.M.S.O.
31st : Railway undertakings : together with the proceeding[s] of the Committee. — [1977]. — 15p ; 25cm. — ([1976-77 H.C.]41-XXXI)
ISBN 0-10-297777-1 Sd : £0.35
(B77-27742)

3rd : Poultry, Aircraft noise, and, Quality of water : together with the proceedings of the Committee. — [1976]. — 13p ; 25cm. — ([1976-77 H.C.] 41-III)
ISBN 0-10-270977-7 Sd : £0.35
(B77-07194)

29th : Preliminary draft budget 1978 : together with the minutes of evidence taken before the Committee on 6th July 1977. — [1977]. — x p,p57-69 ; 25cm. — ([1976-77 H.C.] 41-xxix) ([1976-77 H.C.] 43-v)
ISBN 0-10-299777-2 Sd : £0.75
(B77-31774)

30th : Greece, Financial protocol, Foodstuff prices (display), Energy : together with the proceedings of the Committee. — [1977]. — 13p ; 25cm. — ([1976-77 H.C.]41-XXX)
ISBN 0-10-295977-3 Sd : £0.35
(B77-27744)

5th : Safety at work, Jute imports, Milk sector : together with the proceedings of the Committee. — [1977]. — 13,[1]p ; 25cm. — ([1976-77 H.C.] 41-v)
ISBN 0-10-272477-6 Sd : £0.35
(B77-07195)

23rd : Contract negotiations away from business premises : together with the minutes of evidence taken before Sub-committee II on 17 May, 1977. — [1977]. — x,65p ; 25cm. — ([1976-77 H.C.]41-xxiii) ([1976-77 H.C.]76-iv)
ISBN 0-10-297977-4 Sd : £1.35
(B77-28484)

11th : Agricultural price review, 1977-78, Aeronautical sector : together with the proceedings of the Committee. — [1977]. — 15p ; 25cm. — ([1976-77 H.C.]41-xi)
ISBN 0-10-280577-6 Sd : £0.35
(B77-16783)

32nd : Jurisdiction in civil and commercial cases : together with the proceedings of the Committee. — [1977]. — 10p ; 25cm. — ([1976-77 H.C.]41-xxxii)
ISBN 0-10-297877-8 Sd : £0.25
(B77-30052)

6th : Life assurance, Dental surgeons, Animal health : together with the proceedings of the Committee. — [1977]. — 17,[1]p ; 25cm. — ([1976-77 H.C.] 41-vi)
ISBN 0-10-273277-9 Sd : £0.35
(B77-07198)

Great Britain. *Parliament. House of Commons. Select Committee on European Legislation, etc.* Report from the Select Committee on European Legislation, &c., session 1976-77. — London : H.M.S.O.
25th : Bird conservation : together with the minutes of evidence taken by Sub-committee I on 11 and 24 May 1977, and appendices. — [1977]. — viii,25p ; 25cm. — ([1976-77 H.C.]41-XXV) ([1976-77 H.C.]297-ii-iii)
ISBN 0-10-293277-8 Sd : £0.60
(B77-27743)

Great Britain. *Parliament. House of Commons. Select Committee on European Legislation, etc.* Report from the Select Committee on European Legislation, &c., session 1976-77. — London : H.M.S.O.
4th : Economic report, Fisheries, Food labelling and advertising, Jute imports, Coke : together with the proceedings of the Committee. — [1977]. — 19,[1]p ; 25cm. — ([1976-77] 41-iv)
ISBN 0-10-271577-7 Sd : £0.35
(B77-07196)

12th : Energy situation, Economic policies and guidelines 1976 and 1977 : together with the proceedings of the Committee. — [1977]. — 15p ; 25cm. — ([1976-77 H.C.]41-XII)
ISBN 0-10-281777-4 Sd : £0.35
(B77-11678)

2nd : Commercial vehicle taxation, Securities-Stock Exchange quotation, Milk sector : together with the proceedings of the Committee. — [1976]. — 15p ; 25cm. — ([1976-77 H.C.]41-II)
ISBN 0-10-270677-8 Sd : £0.35
(B77-07197)

17th : Architects : together with the proceedings of the Committee. — [1977]. — 12p ; 25cm. — ([1976-77 H.C.] 41-xvii)
Sd : £0.25
(B77-29273)

Great Britain. *Parliament. House of Commons. Select Committee on European Secondary Legislation, etc.* Report from the Select Committee on European Secondary Legislation, &c., session 1976-77. — London : H.M.S.O.
1st : Trade co-operation, EAGGF-fifth report 1975, Textile imports Macao : together with the proceedings of the Committee. — [1976]. — 16p ; 25cm. — ([1976-77 H.C.] 41-I)
ISBN 0-10-270277-2 Sd : £0.35
(B77-07199)

Great Britain. *Parliament. House of Commons. Select Committee on European Secondary Legislation, etc.* Report from the Select Committee on European Secondary Legislation, &c., session 1975-76. — London : H.M.S.O.
38th : Agricultural exchange rates, Lead content of petrol, Textile imports - Turkey : together with the proceedings of the Committee. — [1976]. — 18p ; 25cm. — ([1975-76 H.C.] 8-XXXVIII)
ISBN 0-10-009576-3 Sd : £0.35
(B77-07201)

37th : Debates on lawyers and roadworthiness tests, Beef and veal - EAGGF, Agriculture - marketing and processing, Aeronautical sector : together with the proceedings of the Committee. — [1976]. — 19p ; 25cm. — ([1975-76 H.C.] 8-XXVII)
ISBN 0-10-009356-6 Sd : £0.35
(B77-04024)

39th : Round-up of outstanding debates. — [1976]. — 11p ; 25cm. — ([1975-76 H.C.] 8-XXXIX)
ISBN 0-10-009586-0 Sd : £0.25
(B77-07200)

341.24'2 — European Parliament. Members. Direct election. *Treaties*

Decision of the Council of the European Communities, with annexed Act concerning the election of the representatives of the Assembly by direct universal suffrage, Brussels, 20 September 1976 ... — London : H.M.S.O., [1976]. — [1],7p ; 25cm. — (European Communities ; no.23(1976)) (Cmnd.6623)
ISBN 0-10-166230-0 Sd : £0.22
(B77-01248)

341.24'2 — Great Britain. Application of European Community law

Dickens, B M. The EEC and the general practitioner / [by] B.M. Dickens. — [Guildford] ([Braboeuf Manor, Portsmouth Rd, St Catherine's, Guildford, Surrey]) : The College of Law, 1972. — [1],40p ; 22cm. — (College of Law. Crash course lectures : 1972)
ISBN 0-905835-22-0 Sd : £0.45
(B77-08286)

341.24'2 — Nordic Council, to 1976

Solem, Erik. The Nordic Council and Scandinavian integration / [by] Erik Solem. — New York ; London : Praeger, 1977. — xiii, 197,[1]p : ill, map ; 25cm. — (Praeger special studies in international politics and government)

Bibl.: p.181-194. — Index.
ISBN 0-275-24100-9 : £12.40
(B77-21002)

341.3 — RELATIONS BETWEEN STATES. DIPLOMACY AND TREATIES

341.3'3 — British diplomatic service

Moorhouse, Geoffrey. The diplomats : the Foreign Office today / [by] Geoffrey Moorhouse. — London : Cape, 1977. — xii, 405p : 2 ill ; 23cm.
Bibl.: p.393-394. — Index.
ISBN 0-224-01323-8 : £7.50 : CIP rev
(B77-07202)

341.3'3 — British diplomatic service. *Directories*

The **Diplomatic** Service list. — London : H.M.S.O.
1977 : 12th ed. — 1977. — vii,452p ; 22cm.
ISBN 0-11-591645-8 Pbk : £5.25
(B77-16262)

341.3'3 — Consular service. *Treaties beteen Great Britain & East Germany*

Great Britain. *Treaties, etc. Germany (Democratic Republic), May 4, 1976.* Consular convention between the United Kingdom of Great Britain and Northern Ireland and the German Democratic Republic, Berlin, 4 May 1976 ... — London : H.M.S.O., [1976]. — 44p ; 25cm. — (Treaty series ; no.102(1976)) (Cmnd. 6648)
English and German text. — '... previously published as German Democratic Republic No.1 (1976) Cmnd.6501'.
ISBN 0-10-166480-x Sd : £0.55
(B77-05941)

341.3'3 — Consular service. *Treaties between Great Britain & Czechoslovakia*

Great Britain. *Treaties, etc. Czechoslovakia, April 3, 1975.* Consular convention between the United Kingdom of Great Britain and Northern Ireland and the Czechoslovak Socialist Republic, Prague, 3 April 1975 ... — London : H.M.S.O., [1976]. — 39p ; 25cm. — (Treaty series ; no.107 (1976)) (Cmnd.6683)
English and Czech text. — '... previously published as Czechoslovakia No.1 (1975) Cmnd.6069'.
ISBN 0-10-166830-9 Sd : £0.50
(B77-08287)

341.3'3 — Consular service. *Treaties between Great Britain & Mongolia (People's Republic)*

Great Britain. *Treaties, etc. Mongolia (People's Republic), November 21, 1975.* Consular Convention between the United Kingdom of Great Britain and Northern Ireland and the Mongolian People's Republic, London, 21 November 1975 ... — London : H.M.S.O., [1976]. — 40p ; 25cm. — (Treaty series ; no.96(1976)) (Cmnd.6639)
Parallel English and Mongol text. — '... previously published as Mongolia No.1(1976), Cmnd.6299'.
ISBN 0-10-166390-0 Sd : £0.50
(B77-00671)

341.3'3 — Consular service. *Treaties between Great Britain & Poland*

Great Britain. *Treaties, etc. Poland, February 23, 1967. Protocols, amendments, etc., December 16, 1976.* Protocol amending the consular convention between the United Kingdom of Great Britain and Northern Ireland and the Polish People's Republic signed at London on 23 February 1967 (with exchange of notes), London, 16 December 1976 ... — London : H.M.S.O., [1977]. — 12p ; 25cm. — (Poland ; no.1(1977)) (Cmnd.6740)
English text, English and Polish exchange of notes.
ISBN 0-10-167400-7 Sd : £0.25
(B77-11679)

341.3'3 — Diplomatic service
Feltham, Ralph George. Diplomatic handbook / [by] R.G. Feltham. — 2nd ed. — London [etc.] : Longman, 1977. — vi,138p : ill ; 22cm.
Previous ed.: 1970. — Index.
ISBN 0-582-48697-1 Pbk : £2.95
(B77-26191)

341.3'3 — Vatican. Foreign relations. Diplomacy. International legal aspects
Cardinale, Igino. The Holy See and the international order / [by] Hyginus Eugene Cardinale. — Gerrards Cross : Smythe, 1976. — 557p,[4]p of plates : 2 ill, coat of arms, 2 facsims, forms, 2 maps ; 25cm.
Bibl.: p.517-520. — Index.
ISBN 0-900675-60-8 : £17.50
(B77-07849)

341.3'3'0941 — British diplomatic service. *Inquiry reports*
Great Britain. *Central Policy Review Staff.* Review of overseas representation : report / by the Central Policy Review Staff. — London : H.M.S.O., 1977. — xvi,442p : 1 ill ; 30cm.
ISBN 0-11-630803-6 Pbk : £8.50
(B77-28485)

341.3'7 — Bilateral treaties, 1946-1965. *Statistics*
Rohn, Peter H. Treaty profiles / [by] Peter H. Rohn. — Santa Barbara ; Oxford (Woodside House, Hinksey House Hill, Oxford OX1 5BE) : Clio Books, 1976. — [5],257p ; 31cm.
Chiefly note-book format.
ISBN 0-87436-131-1 : Unpriced
(B77-20117)

341.3'7 — Seychelles Islands. Application of British treaties. *Treaties between Great Britain & Seychelles Islands*
Great Britain. *Treaties, etc. Seychelles, June 29, 1976.* Exchange of notes between the Government of the United Kingdom of Great Britain and Northern Ireland and the Government of Seychelles concerning treaty succession, Victoria, 29 June 1976 ... — London : H.M.S.O., [1976]. — Folder ([3]p) ; 25cm. — (Treaty series ; no.109(1976)) (Cmnd. 6687)
ISBN 0-10-166870-8 : £0.15
(B77-10258)

341.4 — JURISDICTION AND JURISDICTIONAL RELATIONS OF STATES
341.4 — Seychelles Islands. Aldabra, Descroches & Farquhar. Transfer from British Indian Ocean Territory, 1976. *Treaties between Great Britain & Seychelles Islands*
Great Britain. *Treaties, etc. Seychelles, June 29,1976.* Exchange of notes between the Government of the United Kingdom of Great Britain and Northern Ireland and the Government of Seychelles concerning the return to Seychelles of the islands of Aldabra, Desroches and Farquhar, Victoria, 29 June 1976 ... — London : H.M.S.O., [1977]. — Folder (4p) ; 25cm. — (Treaty series ; no.8 (1977)) (Cmnd.6713)
ISBN 0-10-167130-x : £0.15
(B77-08870)

341.42 — Antarctic. *Treaties*
[The **Antarctic** Treaty. *Protocols, amendments, etc., June 20, 1975].* The Antarctic Treaty, recommendations of the Eighth Consultative Meeting held at Oslo 9-20 June 1975. — London : H.M.S.O., [1977]. — 38p : maps ; 25cm. — (Miscellaneous ; no.6(1977)) (Cmnd. 6786)
ISBN 0-10-167860-6 Sd : £0.60
(B77-16263)

341.42 — Frontiers between Argentina & Chile. Disputes. Arbitration. *Beagle Channel region. Cases*
Great Britain. Award of Her Britannic Majesty's Government pursuant to the agreement for arbitration (compromiso) of a controversy between the Argentine Republic and the Republic of Chile concerning the region of the Beagle Channel. — London : H.M.S.O., 1977. — [6],a-f,xvii,152p ; 25cm.
Includes the text of relevant legislation in English and Spanish. — Accompanied by portfolio (4 fold. sheets([4]p.) of maps (chiefly col.)). — The report and decision of the Court of Arbitration.
ISBN 0-11-591649-0 Pbk : £15.00
(B77-31058)

341.44'8 — Court of Arbitration on Delimitation of the Continental Shelf between the United Kingdom and France. Privileges. Accordance by Switzerland. *Treaties between Great Britain & France, & Switzerland*
Great Britain. *Treaties, etc. Switzerland, January 14, 1977.* Agreement between the Government of the United Kingdom of Great Britain and Northern Ireland and the Government of the French Republic of the one part, and the Government of the Swiss Confederation, of the other part regarding the status, privileges and immunities of the Court of Arbitration on Delimitation of the Continental Shelf between the United Kingdom and France and persons participating in the work of the Court, Berne, 14 January 1977 ... — London : H.M.S.O., [1977]. — 20p ; 25cm. — (Treaty series ; no.86(1977)) (Cmnd. 6956)
English and French texts.
ISBN 0-10-169560-8 Sd : £0.35
(B77-33116)

341.45 — Oceans. Bed. International law, to 1976
Buzan, Barry. Seabed politics / [by] Barry Buzan. — New York [etc.] ; London : Praeger, 1976. — xix,312p : ill ; 24cm. — (Praeger special studies in international politics and government)
Index.
ISBN 0-275-22850-9 : £14.60
(B77-07203)

341.48'1 — Human rights. International law. Treaties. *Western Europe. European Convention on Human Rights. Critical studies*
Robertson, Arthur Henry. Human rights in Europe : being an account of the European Convention for the Protection of Human Rights and Fundamental Freedoms signed in Rome on 4 November 1950, of the Protocols thereto and of the machinery created thereby : the European Commission of Human Rights and the European Court of Human Rights / by A.H. Robertson. — 2nd ed. — Manchester : Manchester University Press, 1977. — xvii, 329p ; 23cm.
Previous ed.: 1963. — Bibl.: p.320-321. — Index. — Includes the texts of the Convention, the First Protocol, the Second Protocol and the Fourth Protocol.
ISBN 0-7190-0658-9 : £9.95
(B77-08871)

341.48'1'0265 — Human rights. *Treaties*
International Covenant on Economic, Social and Cultural Rights ; and, International Covenant on Civil and Political Rights, adopted by the General Assembly of the United Nations and opened for signature at New York on 19 December 1966 ... — London : H.M.S.O., [1977]. — 47p ; 25cm. — (Treaty series ; no.6 (1977)) (Cmnd.6702)
'... previously published as Miscellaneous No.4 (1967), Cmnd.3220'.
ISBN 0-10-167020-6 Sd : £0.75
(B77-07204)

341.48'8 — Extradition. *Treaties between Great Britain & Finland*
Great Britain. *Treaties, etc. Finland, October 29, 1975.* Extradition treaty between the Government of the United Kingdom of Great Britain and Northern Ireland and the Government of the Republic of Finland (with exchange of notes signed at Helsinki on 12 May 1976 extending the treaty to certain territories), London, 29 October 1975 ... — London : H.M.S.O., [1977]. — 22p ; 25cm. — (Treaty series ; no.23 (1977)) (Cmnd.6741)
English and Finnish text. — 'The Treaty was previously published as Finland No.1 (1976), Cmnd.6365'.
ISBN 0-10-167410-4 Sd : £0.45
(B77-12931)

341.48'8 — Extradition. *Treaties between Great Britain & United States*
Great Britain. *Treaties, etc. United States, June 8, 1972.* Extradition treaty between the Government of the United Kingdom of Great Britain and Northern Ireland and the Government of the United States of America (with protocol of signature), London, 8 June 1972 (together with exchange of notes extending the treaty to certain territories), London, 21 October 1976 ... — London : H.M.S.O., [1977]. — 11p ; 25cm. — (Treaty series ; no.16(1977)) (Cmnd.6723)
'The Treaty was previously published as United States No.2 (1972), Cmnd.5040'.
ISBN 0-10-167230-6 Sd : £0.25
(B77-11680)

341.48'8 — Solomon Islands. Extension of treaties on extradition between Great Britain & Finland. *Treaties between Great Britain & Finland*
Great Britain. *Treaties, etc. Finland, October 29, 1975. Protocols, amendments, etc., January 28, 1977.* Exchange of notes between the Government of the United Kingdom of Great Britain and Northern Ireland and the Government of the Republic of Finland further extending the extradition treaty, signed at London on 29 October 1975, to the Solomon Islands, Helsinki, 28 January 1977 ... — London : H.M.S.O., [1977]. — Folder(4p) ; 25cm. — (Treaty series ; no.53(1977)) (Cmnd. 6843)
ISBN 0-10-168430-4 : £0.15
(B77-21003)

341.6 — LAW OF WAR
341.6 — Bulgarian enemy property. Assets. *Great Britain. Accounts*
Great Britain. *Department of Industry. Finance and Economic Appraisal Division.* Accounts of the administrator of Bulgarian property in the United Kingdom, Channel Islands and the Isle of Man, for the two years ended 31st March ... / [Department of Industry, Finance and Economic Appraisal Division]. — London : H.M.S.O.
[1974]-1976. — [1977]. — 5p ; 25cm. — (Comd.[i.e. Cmnd.]6840)
ISBN 0-10-168400-2 Sd : £0.25
(B77-24083)

Great Britain. *Department of Industry. Finance and Economic Appraisal Division.* Accounts of the administrator of Bulgarian property in the United Kingdom, Channel Islands and the Isle of Man, for the two years ended 31st March / [Department of Industry, Finance and Economic Appraisal Division]. — London : H.M.S.O.
[1972]-1974. — [1976]. — 5p ; 25cm. — (Cmnd. 6588)
Previously issued by the Department of Trade and Industry, Finance and Economic Appraisal Division.
ISBN 0-10-165880-x Sd : £0.20
(B77-06551)

341.6 — German enemy property. Assets. *Great Britain. Accounts*
Distribution of German Enemy Property Acts 1949 and 1952, account ... for the two years ended 31st March ... — London : H.M.S.O.
1974-76. — [1977]. — Folder (4p) ; 25cm. — ([1976-77 H.C.]330)
ISBN 0-10-233077-8 : £0.15
(B77-15163)

341.6 — Hungarian enemy property. Assets. *Great Britain. Accounts*
Great Britain. *Department of Industry. Finance and Economic Appraisal Division.* Accounts of the administrator of Hungarian property in the United Kingdom, Channel Islands and the Isle of Man, for the two years ended 31st March / [Department of Industry, Finance and Economic Appraisal Division]. — London : H.M.S.O.
[1972]-1974. — [1976]. — 5p ; 25cm. — (Cmnd. 6589)
Previously issued by the Department of Trade and Industry, Finance and Economic Appraisal Division.
ISBN 0-10-165890-7 Sd : £0.20
(B77-05942)

Great Britain. *Department of Industry. Finance and Economic Appraisal Division.* Accounts of the administrator of Hungarian property in the United Kingdom, Channel Islands and the Isle of Man, for the two years ended 31st March ... / [Department of Industry, Finance and Economic Appraisal Division]. — London : H.M.S.O.
[1974]-1976. — [1977]. — 5p ; 25cm. — (Cmnd.6841)
ISBN 0-10-168410-x Sd : £0.25
(B77-24084)

341.6 — Romanian enemy property. Assets. *Great Britain. Accounts*
Great Britain. *Department of Industry. Finance and Economic Appraisal Division.* Accounts of the Administrator of Roumanian property in the United Kingdom, Channel Islands and the Isle of Man, for the two years ended 31st March / [Department of Industry, Finance and Economic Appraisal Division]. — London : H.M.S.O.
[1974]-1976. — [1977]. — 5p ; 25cm. — (Cmnd.6839)
ISBN 0-10-168390-1 Sd : £0.25
(B77-18003)

Great Britain. *Department of Industry. Finance and Economic Appraisal Division.* Accounts of the administrator of Roumanian property in the United Kingdom, Channel Islands and the Isle of Man, for the two years ended 31st March / [Department of Industry, Finance and Economic Appraisal Division]. — London : H.M.S.O.
[1972]-1974. — [1976]. — 5p ; 25cm. — (Cmnd. 6587)
Previously issued by the Department of Trade and Industry, Finance and Economic Appraisal Division.
ISBN 0-10-165870-2 Sd : £0.20
(B77-05943)

341.6'3'0265 — Military operations. Military forces. Conduct. *Treaties*
Diplomatic Conference on the Reaffirmation and Development of International Humanitarian Law Applicable in Armed Conflicts, *Geneva, 1974-77.* Final act of the Diplomatic Conference on the Reaffirmation and Development of International Humanitarian Law Applicable in Armed Conflicts, with protocol I, protocol II and resolutions adopted at the fourth session, Geneva, 20 February-29 March 1974, 3 February-18 April 1975, 21 April-11 June 1976, 17 March-10 June 1977 ... — London : H.M.S.O., 1977. — 110p : ill, facsim, forms ; 25cm. — (Miscellaneous ; no.19(1977)) (Cmnd.6927)
ISBN 0-10-169270-6 Pbk : £1.60
(B77-30053)

341.6'9 — German war criminals: Eichmann, Adolf. Trial. *Israel. Jerusalem, 1961-1962*
Arendt, Hannah. Eichmann in Jerusalem : a report on the banality of evil / by Hannah Arendt. — Revised and enlarged ed. — Harmondsworth [etc.] : Penguin, 1976. — vii, 312p ; 20cm.
Revised and enlarged ed. originally published: New York : Viking Press, 1964. — Bibl.: p.299-303. — Index.
ISBN 0-14-004450-7 Pbk : Unpriced
(B77-12372)

341.6'9 — German war criminals. Trials. *West Germany. Nuremberg, 1945-1946*
Smith, Bradley F. Reaching judgement at Nuremberg / [by] Bradley F. Smith. — London : Deutsch, 1977. — xviii,349p,[10]p of plates : ports ; 25cm.
Also published: New York : Basic Books, 1977. — Bibl.: p.335-338. — Index.
ISBN 0-233-96858-x : £6.50
(B77-22448)

341.7 — INTERNATIONAL COOPERATION. LEGAL ASPECTS

341.72'2 — British military forces. Financing. *West Germany, 1977-1980. Treaties between Great Britain & West Germany*
Great Britain. *Treaties, etc. Germany (Federal Republic), October 18, 1977.* Exchange of notes between the Government of the United Kingdom of Great Britain and Northern Ireland and the Government of the Federal Republic of Germany for offsetting the foreign exchange expenditure on British forces in the Federal Republic of Germany, Bonn, 18 October 1977 ... — London : H.M.S.O., [1977]. — 8p ; 25cm. — (Treaty series ; no.101(1977)) (Cmnd.6970)
English and German text.
ISBN 0-10-169700-7 Sd : £0.25
(B77-32495)

341.72'5 — British air bases. Establishment. Treaties between Great Britain & Maldives: Agreement between Her Majesty's Government in the United Kingdom of Great Britain and Northern Ireland and the Government of the Maldive Islands. Termination. *Maldives. Gan. Treaties between Great Britain & Maldives*
Great Britain. *Treaties, etc. Maldives, July 26, 1965. Protocols, amendments, etc., October 6, 1976.* Exchange of notes terminating the agreement signed on 26 July 1965 between Her Majesty's Government in the United Kingdom of Great Britain and Northern Ireland and the Government of the Maldive Islands, Colombo, 6-7 October 1976 ... — London : H.M.S.O., [1977]. — Folder (4)p ; 25cm. — (Treaty series ; no.19 (1977)) (Cmnd. 6728)
ISBN 0-10-167280-2 : £0.15
(B77-11127)

341.73 — Negotiations on disarmament, 1975. *Documents*
United Nations. Further documents on disarmament - the disarmament negotiations, 1975 / presented to Parliament by the Secretary of State for Foreign and Commonwealth Affairs ... — London : H.M.S.O., [1977]. — 296p : ill ; 25cm. — (Miscellaneous ; no.4(1977)) (Cmnd. 6785)
'Proceedings on Disarmament in the CCD, at the Review Conference of the Parties to the Treaty on the Non-Proliferation of Nuclear Weapons and in the United Nations General Assembly, 1975' - p.3.
ISBN 0-10-167850-9 Pbk : £4.10
(B77-14613)

341.73 — Nuclear weapons. Safeguards. *Treaties between Great Britain, Euratom & International Atomic Energy Agency*
Great Britain. *Treaties, etc., September 6, 1976.* Agreement between the United Kingdom of Great Britain and Northern Ireland, the European Atomic Energy Community and the International Atomic Energy Agency for the application of safeguards in the United Kingdom of Great Britain and Northern Ireland in connection with the Treaty on the Non-Proliferation of Nuclear Weapons (with Protocol) (Vienna, 6 September, 1976) ... — London : H.M.S.O., [1977]. — 36p ; 25cm. — (Miscellaneous ; no.2 (1977)) (Cmnd. 6730)
ISBN 0-10-167300-0 Sd : £0.60
(B77-11128)

341.7'5 — Algeria. Economic relations with European Community. *Treaties between European Community countries & Algeria*
Algeria. *Treaties, etc. European Economic Community, April 26, 1976.* Co-operation agreement between the European Economic Community and the People's Democratic Republic of Algeria ; and, Agreement between the member states of the European Coal and Steel Community and the People's Democratic Republic of Algeria (with final act), Algiers, 26 April 1976 ... — London : H.M.S.O., [1977]. — 138p : forms ; 25cm. — (European Communities ; no.23(1977)) (Cmnd.6938)
ISBN 0-10-169380-x Pbk : £2.10
(B77-32496)

341.7'5 — Austria. Economic relations with European Economic Community. *Treaties between Austria & European Economic Community*
Austria. *Treaties, etc. European Economic Community, July 22, 1972. Protocols, amendments, etc., November 29, 1976-December 8, 1976.* Agreements in the form of exchanges of letters amending tables I and II annexed to protocol no.2 and amending annex A to protocol no.1 to the agreement between the European Economic Community and the Republic of Austria, Brussels, 29 November 1976 and 8 December 1976 ... — London : H.M.S.O., [1977]. — 8p ; 25cm. — (European Communities ; no.11(1977)) (Cmnd. 6784)
ISBN 0-10-167840-1 Sd : £0.25
(B77-16784)

341.7'5 — Bangladesh. Economic relations with European Economic Community. *Treaties between Bangladesh & European Economic Community*
Bangladesh. *Treaties etc. European Economic Community, October 19, 1976.* Commercial co-operation agreement between the European Economic Community and the People's Republic of Bangladesh, Luxembourg, 19 October 1976 ... — London : H.M.S.O., [1977]. — 12p ; 25cm. — (European Communities ; no.8(1977)) (Cmnd.6782)
ISBN 0-10-167820-7 Sd : £0.25
(B77-16264)

341.7'5 — Canada. Economic relations with European Economic Community. *Treaties between Canada & European Economic Community*
Canada. *Treaties, etc., July 6, 1976.* Framework agreement for commercial and economic co-operation between the European Communities and Canada, Ottawa, 6 July 1976 ... — London : H.M.S.O., [1976]. — 7p ; 25cm. — (European Communities ; no.26 (1976)) (Cmnd.6646)
'[An agreement] ... between the European Economic Community and the European Atomic Energy Community, of the one part, and Canada, of the other part ...' - p.3.
ISBN 0-10-166460-5 Sd : £0.20
(B77-09585)

341.7'5 — Double taxation. *Treaties between Great Britain & Fiji*
Great Britain. *Treaties, etc. Fiji, November 21, 1975.* Convention between the Government of the United Kingdom of Great Britain and Northern Ireland and the Government of Fiji for the avoidance of double taxation and the prevention of fiscal evasion with respect to taxes on income, Suva, 21 November 1975 ... — London : H.M.S.O., [1977]. — 20p ; 25cm. — (Treaty series ; no.46(1977)) (Cmnd.6809)
'... previously published as Fiji No.1(1976), Cmnd.6451'.
ISBN 0-10-168090-2 Sd : £0.35
(B77-18004)

341.7'5 — Double taxation. *Treaties between Great Britain & Ireland (Republic)*
Great Britain. *Treaties, etc. Ireland (Republic), June 2, 1976. Protocols, amendments, etc., October 28th, 1976.* Convention between the Government of the United Kingdom of Great Britain and Northern Ireland and the Government of the Republic of Ireland for the avoidance of double taxation and the prevention of fiscal evasion with respect to taxes on income and capital gains, with amending protocol, Dublin, 2 June and 28 October 1976 ... — London : H.M.S.O., [1977]. — 24p ; 25cm. — (Treaty series no.43(1977)) (Cmnd. 6815)
'The Convention was previously published as Republic of Ireland No.1(1976), Cmnd.6591'.
ISBN 0-10-168150-x Sd : £0.45
(B77-18005)

341.7'5 — Double taxation. *Treaties between Great Britain & Kenya*
Great Britain. *Treaties, etc. Kenya, July 31, 1973. Protocols, amendments, etc., February 8, 1977.* Exchange of notes amending the protocol of 20 January 1976 to the agreement between the Government of the United Kingdom of Great Britain and Northern Ireland and the Government of the Republic of Kenya for the avoidance of double taxation and the prevention of fiscal evasion with respect to taxes on income and capital gains, signed at Nairobi on 31st July 1973, Nairobi, 8 February 1977 ... — London : H.M.S.O., [1977]. — Folder(4p) ; 25cm. — (Kenya ; no.1(1977)) (Cmnd.6814)
ISBN 0-10-168140-2 : £0.15
(B77-20118)

341.7'5 — Double taxation. *Treaties between Great Britain & Norway*
Great Britain. *Treaties, etc. Norway, January 22, 1969. Protocols, amendments, etc., June 23, 1977.* Protocol between the Government of the United Kingdom of Great Britain and Northern Ireland and the Government of the Kingdom of Norway amending the convention for the avoidance of double taxation and the prevention of fiscal evasion with respect to taxes on income and capital, signed in London on 22 January 1969, London, 23 June 1977 ... — London : H.M.S.O., [1977]. — 8p ; 25cm. — (Norway ; no.1(1977)) (Cmnd.6945)
ISBN 0-10-169450-4 Sd : £0.25
(B77-31059)

341.7'5 — Double taxation. *Treaties between Great Britain & Poland*
Great Britain. *Treaties, etc. Poland, December 16, 1976.* Convention between the Government of the United Kingdom of Great Britain and Northern Ireland and the Government of the Polish People's Republic for the avoidance of double taxation with respect to taxes on income and capital gains, London, 16 December 1976 ... — London : H.M.S.O., [1977]. — 20p ; 25cm. — (Poland ; no.2(1977)) (Cmnd.6761)
ISBN 0-10-167610-7 Sd : £0.35
(B77-14614)

341.7'5 — Double taxation. *Treaties between Great Britain & Romania*
Great Britain. *Treaties, etc. Romania, September 18, 1975.* Convention between the Government of the United Kingdom of Great Britain and Northern Ireland and the Government of the Socialist Republic of Romania for the avoidance of double taxation with respect to taxes on income and capital gains, Bucharest, 18 September, 1975 ... — London : H.M.S.O., [1977]. — 8p ; 25cm. — (Treaty series ; no.14 (1977)) (Cmnd.6724)
English and Romanian text. — ' ... previously published in Romania No.1 (1975), Cmnd.6269'.
ISBN 0-10-167240-3 Sd : £0.60
(B77-08872)

341.7'5 — Double taxation. *Treaties between Great Britain & Spain*
Great Britain. *Treaties, etc. Spain, October 21, 1975.* Convention between the United Kingdom of Great Britain and Northern Ireland and Spain for the avoidance of double taxation and the prevention of fiscal evasion with respect to taxes on income and capital, London, 21 October 1975 ... — London : H.M.S.O., [1977]. — 42p ; 25cm. — (Treaty series ; no.17(1977)) (Cmnd.6726)
English and Spanish text. — '... previously published as Spain No.2 (1975) Cmnd.6362'.
ISBN 0-10-167260-8 Sd : £0.75
(B77-10259)

341.7'5 — Double taxation. *Treaties between Great Britain & United States*
Great Britain. *Treaties, etc. United States, December 31, 1975. Protocols, amendments, etc., August 26, 1976.* Protocol amending the Convention between the Government of the United Kingdom of Great Britain and Northern Ireland and the Government of the United States of America for the avoidance of double taxation and the prevention of fiscal evasion with respect to taxes on income and capital gains, signed at London on 31 December 1975, as amended by notes exchanged at London on 13 April 1976, London, 26 August 1976 ... — London : H.M.S.O., [1976]. — Folder (4p) ; 25cm. — (United States ; no.3 (1976)) (Cmnd. 6642)
ISBN 0-10-166420-6 : £0.12
(B77-03446)

341.7'5 — Double taxation. *Treaties between Great Britain & United States. Texts with commentaries*
Great Britain. *Treaties, etc. United States, December 31, 1975.* [Convention between the Government of the United Kingdom of Great Britain and Northern Ireland and the Government of the United States of America for the avoidance of double taxation and the prevention of fiscal evasion with respect to taxes on income and capital gains, London, 31 December, 1975]. US-UK double tax treaty / with commentary by Perry A. Lerner ; edited by Robert T. Cole. — Revised ed. including protocol. — London (21 Bentinck St., W1M 5RL) : Institute for International Research, 1977. — [4],98p ; 23cm.
Previous ed.: 1976.
ISBN 0-905431-01-4 : £8.95
(B77-12373)

341.7'5 — Economic relations. International legal aspects
Fawcett, James Edmund Sandford. International economic conflicts : prevention and resolution / [by] James Fawcett. — London : Europa for the David Davies Memorial Institute of International Studies, 1977. — v,127p : 1 ill ; 25cm.
Includes the text of relevant legislation.
ISBN 0-905118-06-5 : £5.00
(B77-25472)

341.7'5 — Egypt. Economic relations with European Community. *Treaties between European Community countries & Egypt*
Egypt. *Treaties, etc. European Economic Community, January 18, 1977.* Co-operation agreement between the European Economic Community and the Arab Republic of Egypt ; and, Agreement between the member states of the European Coal and Steel Community and the Arab Republic of Egypt (with final act), Brussels, 18 January 1977 ... — London : H.M.S.O., [1977]. — 116p : forms ; 25cm. — (European Communities ; no.27(1977)) (Cmnd. 6940)
ISBN 0-10-169400-8 Pbk : £1.85
(B77-33117)

341.7'5 — Finland. Economic relations with European Economic Community. *Treaties between Finland & European Economic Community*
European Economic Community. *Treaties, etc. Finland, October 5, 1973. Protocols, amendments, etc., November 29, 1976-December 8, 1976.* Agreements in the form of exchanges of letters amending tables I and II annexed to protocol no.2 and amending annex A to protocol no.1 to the agreement between the European Economic Community and the Republic of Finland, Brussels, 29 November 1976 and 8 December 1976 ... — London : H.M.S.O., [1977]. — 7p ; 25cm. — (European Communities ; no.3 (1977)) (Cmnd. 6777)
ISBN 0-10-167770-7 Sd : £0.25
(B77-14615)

341.7'5 — Greece. Economic relations with European Economic Community. *Treaties between European Economic Community & Greece*
European Economic Community. *Treaties, etc. Greece, February 28, 1977.* Financial protocol between the European Economic Community and Greece, Brussels, 28 February 1977 ... — London : H.M.S.O., [1977]. — 8p ; 25cm. — (European Communities ; no.21 (1977)) (Cmnd. 6917)
ISBN 0-10-169170-x Sd : £0.25
(B77-28486)

341.7'5 — Iceland. Economic relations with European Economic Community. *Treaties between European Economic Community & Iceland*
European Economic Community. *Treaties, etc. Iceland, July 22, 1972. Protocols, amendments, etc., June 29, 1976.* Agreement in the form of an exchange of letters amending protocol no.6 to the agreement between the European Economic Community and the Republic of Iceland, Brussels, 29 June 1976 ... — London : H.M.S.O., [1977]. — Folder(4p) ; 25cm. — (European Communities ; no.1(1977)) (Cmnd. 6737)
ISBN 0-10-167370-1 : £0.15
(B77-16785)

European Economic Community. *Treaties, etc. Iceland, July 22, 1972. Protocols, amendments, etc., November 29, 1976-December 8, 1976.* Agreements in the form of exchanges of letters amending table 1 annexed to protocol no.2 and amending annex A to protocol no.1 to the agreement between the European Economic Community and the Republic of Iceland, Brussels, 29 November 1976 and 8 December 1976 ... — London : H.M.S.O., [1977]. — 7p ; 25cm. — (European Communities ; no.13(1977)) (Cmnd.6794)
ISBN 0-10-167940-8 Sd : £0.25
(B77-15164)

341.7'5 — Malta. Economic relations with European Economic Community. *Treaties between European Economic Community & Malta*
European Economic Community. *Treaties, etc. Malta, December 5, 1970. Protocols, amendments, etc., February 27, 1976.* Agreement extending the provisions governing the first stage of the agreement establishing an association between the European Economic Community and Malta, Brussels, 27 February 1976 ... — London : H.M.S.O., [1976]. — Folder(4p) ; 25cm. — (European Communities ; no.22(1976)) (Cmnd.6641)
ISBN 0-10-166410-9 : £0.12
(B77-09586)

European Economic Community. *Treaties, etc. Malta, December 5, 1970. Protocols, amendments, etc., March 4, 1976.* Protocol laying down certain provisions relating to the agreement establishing an association between the European Economic Community and Malta with financial protocol and final act, Brussels, 4 March 1976, (with association agreement of 5 December 1970 and final act) ... — London : H.M.S.O., [1976]. — [3],164p : forms ; 25cm. — (European Communities ; no.21(1976)) (Cmnd.6640)
ISBN 0-10-166400-1 Pbk : £2.00
(B77-09587)

341.7'5 — Natural resources. Allocation. International legal aspects
Schachter, Oscar. Sharing the world's resources / [by] Oscar Schachter. — New York ; Guildford : Columbia University Press, 1977. — xiii,172p ; 24cm.
Index.
ISBN 0-231-04110-1 : £4.70
(B77-15168)

341.7'5 — Norway. Economic relations with European Economic Community. *Treaties between European Economic Community & Norway*
European Economic Community. *Treaties, etc. Norway, May 14, 1973. Protocols, amendments, etc., November 29, 1976-December 8, 1976.* Agreements in the form of exchanges of letters amending tables I and II annexed to protocol no.2 and amending annex A to protocol no.1 to the agreement between the European Economic Community and the Kingdom of Norway, Brussels, 29 November 1976 and 8 December 1976 ... — London : H.M.S.O., [1977]. — 7p ; 25cm. — (European Communities ; no.12(1977)) (Cmnd.6793)
ISBN 0-10-167930-0 Sd : £0.25
(B77-15165)

341.7'5 — Portugal. Economic relations with European Economic Community. *Treaties between European Economic Community & Portugal*
European Economic Community. *Treaties, etc. Portugal, July 22, 1972. Protocols, amendments, etc., November 29, 1976.* Agreement in the form of an exchange of letters amending tables I and II annexed to protocol no.2 to the agreement between the European Economic Community and the Portuguese Republic, Brussels, 29 November 1976 ... — London : H.M.S.O., [1977]. — Folder (4p) ; 25cm. — (European Communities ; no.9(1977)) (Cmnd. 6789)
ISBN 0-10-167890-8 : £0.15
(B77-16265)

European Economic Community. *Treaties, etc. Portugal, July 22, 1972. Protocols, amendments, etc., September 20, 1976.* Additional protocol to the agreement between the European Economic Community and the Portuguese Republic of 22 July 1972 with financial protocol and final act, Brussels, 20 September 1976 ... — London : H.M.S.O., [1977]. — 38p ; 25cm. — (European Communities ; no.6(1977)) (Cmnd.6781)
ISBN 0-10-167810-x Sd : £0.60
(B77-15750)

European Economic Community. *Treaties, etc. Portugal, September 20, 1976.* Interim agreement between the European Economic Community and the Portuguese Republic (with final act and exchange of letters), Brussels, 20 September 1976 ... — London : H.M.S.O., [1977]. — 26p ; 25cm. — (European Communities ; no.7(1977)) (Cmnd.6780)
ISBN 0-10-167800-2 Sd : £0.50
(B77-15751)

341.7'5 — Sweden. Economic relations with European Economic Community. *Treaties between European Economic Community & Sweden*
European Economic Community. *Treaties, etc. Sweden, July 22, 1972. Protocols, amendments, etc., November 29, 1976-December 8, 1976.* Agreements in the form of exchanges of letters amending tables I and II annexed to protocol no.2 and amending annex A to protocol no.1 to the agreement between the European Economic Community and the Kingdom of Sweden, Brussels, 29 November and 8 December 1976 ... — London : H.M.S.O., [1977]. — 8p ; 25cm. — (European Communities ; no.5(1977)) (Cmnd.6775)
ISBN 0-10-167750-2 Sd : £0.25
(B77-14616)

341.7'5 — Switzerland. Economic relations with European Economic Community. *Treaties between European Economic Community & Switzerland*
European Economic Community. *Treaties, etc. Switzerland, July 22, 1972. Protocols, amendments, etc., December 14, 1976.* Agreement in the form of an exchange of letters amending the English version of table II of protocol 2 to the government between the European Economic Community and the Swiss Confederation, Brussels, 14 December 1976 ... — London : H.M.S.O., [1977]. — Folder(4p) ; 25cm. — (European Communities ; no.2(1977)) (Cmnd.6757)
ISBN 0-10-167570-4 : £0.15
(B77-15166)

European Economic Community. *Treaties, etc. Switzerland, July 22, 1972. Protocols, amendments, etc., November 29, 1976-December 8, 1976.* Agreements in the form of exchanges of letters amending tables I and II annexed to protocol no.2 and amending annex A to protocol no.1 to the agreement between the European Economic Community and the Swiss Confederation, Brussels, 29 November and 8 December 1976 ... — London : H.M.S.O., [1977]. — 8p ; 25cm. — (European Communities ; no.4(1977)) (Cmnd. 6778)
ISBN 0-10-167780-4 Sd : £0.25
(B77-15167)

341.7′5 — Syria. Economic relations with European Community. *Treaties between European Community & Syria*
European Economic Community. *Treaties, etc. Syria, January 18, 1977.* Co-operation agreement between the European Economic Community and the Syrian Arab Republic ; and, Agreement between the member states of the European Coal and Steel Community and the Syrian Arab Republic (with final act), Brussels, 18 January 1977 ... — London : H.M.S.O., [1977]. — 109p : forms ; 25cm. — (European Communities ; no.33(1977)) (Cmnd. 6959)
ISBN 0-10-169590-x Pbk : £1.60
(B77-33119)

341.7′5 — Tunisia. Economic relations with European Community. *Treaties between European Community countries & Tunisia*
European Economic Community. *Treaties, etc. Tunisia, April 25, 1976.* Co-operation agreement between the European Economic Community and the Republic of Tunisia ; and, Agreement between the member states of the European Coal and Steel Community and the Republic of Tunisia (with final act), Tunis, 25 April 1976 ... — London : H.M.S.O., [1977]. — 130p : forms ; 25cm. — (European Communities ; no.18(1977)) (Cmnd.6894)
ISBN 0-10-168940-3 Pbk : £2.10
(B77-29274)

341.7′51 — International Monetary Fund. Constitution. *Treaties*
International Monetary Fund. [Articles of agreement]. The second amendment to the Articles of agreement of the International Monetary Fund / presented to Parliament by the Chancellor of the Exchequer ... — London : H.M.S.O., [1977]. — 66p ; 25cm. — (Cmnd. 6705)
ISBN 0-10-167050-8 Sd : £1.35
(B77-10759)

341.7′52′0266410498 — Foreign investment. *Treaties between Great Britain & Romania*
Great Britain. *Treaties, etc. Romania, March 19, 1976.* Agreement between the Government of the United Kingdom of Great Britain and Northern Ireland and the Government of the Socialist Republic of Romania on the mutual promotion and protection of investments of capital, London, 19 March 1976 ... — London : H.M.S.O., [1977]. — 14p ; 25cm. — (Treaty series ; no.15 (1977)) (Cmnd.6722)
English and Romanian text. — '... previously published as Romania No.2 (1976), Cmnd.6500'.
ISBN 0-10-167220-9 Sd : £0.35
(B77-08873)

341.7′54 — British goods. Purchase by Mozambique. Financial assistance. Loans from Great Britain. *Treaties between Great Britain & Mozambique*
Great Britain. *Treaties, etc. Mozambique, August 17, 1976.* Exchange of notes concerning an interest-free loan by the Government of the United Kingdom of Great Britain and Northern Ireland to the Government of the People's Republic of Mozambique (United Kingdom-Mozambique Programme Loan 1976), Maputo, 17 August 1976 ... — London : H.M.S.O., [1977]. — 28p : forms ; 25cm. — (Treaty series ; no.47(1977)) (Cmnd.6824)
English and Portuguese text.
ISBN 0-10-168240-9 Sd : £0.50
(B77-18006)

341.7′54 — Britons. Commercial transactions with Guineans. Debts. Repayment. *Treaties between Great Britain & Guinea*
Great Britain. *Treaties, etc. Guinea, November 23, 1976.* Agreement between the Government of the United Kingdom of Great Britain and Northern Ireland and the Government of the Republic of Guinea on certain commercial debts, Paris, 23 November 1976 ... — London : H.M.S.O., [1977]. — 15p ; 25cm. — (Treaty series ; no.34(1977)) (Cmnd.6776)
Parallel English and French text.
ISBN 0-10-167760-x Sd : £0.35
(B77-15169)

341.7′54 — European Community countries. Imports from Tunisia. *Treaties between European Economic Community & Tunisia*
European Economic Community. *Treaties, etc. Tunisia, April 25, 1976.* Interim agreement between the European Economic Community and the Republic of Tunisia (with final act), and exchanges of letters concerning the importation into the Community of commodities originating in Tunisia, Tunis, 25 April 1976 ... — London : H.M.S.O., [1977]. — 112p : forms ; 25cm. — (European Communities ; no.29(1977)) (Cmnd.6953)
ISBN 0-10-169530-6 Sd : £1.60
(B77-32497)

341.7′54 — Temporary imports: Packaging. Customs procedures. *Treaties*
Customs Convention on the Temporary Importation of Packings, Brussels, 6 October 1960 ... — London : H.M.S.O., [1976]. — 11p ; 25cm. — (Miscellaneous ; no.31(1976)) (Cmnd. 6685)
ISBN 0-10-166850-3 Sd : £0.25
(B77-07205)

341.7′547′13110265 — Foreign trade in wheat. *Treaties*
[**International** Wheat Agreement, 1971. *Protocols, amendments, etc., March 17, 1976*]. Protocols for the third extension of the Wheat Trade Convention and Food Aid Convention constituting the International Wheat Agreement, 1971, Washington, 17 March-7 April 1976 ... — London : H.M.S.O., [1977]. — 20p ; 25cm. — (Treaty series ; no.24(1977)) (Cmnd.6742)
'... previously published as Miscellaneous No.14(1976), Cmnd.6446'.
ISBN 0-10-167420-1 Sd : £0.35
(B77-15170)

341.7′547′136 — Foreign trade in sugar. *Treaties*
[**International** Sugar Agreement, 1973. *Protocols, amendments, etc., June 18, 1976*]. Resolution to further extend the International Sugar Agreement 1973, approved by the International Sugar Council on 18 June 1976 ... — London : H.M.S.O., [1977]. — 7p ; 25cm. — (Miscellaneous ; no.10(1977)) (Cmnd.6823)
ISBN 0-10-168230-1 Sd : £0.25
(B77-21004)

341.7′547′13610265 — European Community countries. Imports from Barbados: Cane sugar. Prices. *Treaties between Barbados & European Economic Community*
Barbados. *Treaties, etc. European Economic Community, July 14, 1976.* Agreement on cane sugar in the form of an exchange of letters between the European Economic Community and Barbados, Brussels, 14 July 1976 ... — London : H.M.S.O., [1976]. — Folder (4p) ; 25cm. — (European Communities ; no.28(1976)) (Cmnd.6676)
ISBN 0-10-166760-4 : £0.15
(B77-08874)

341.7′547′13610265 — European Community countries. Imports from India (Republic): Cane sugar. *Treaties between European Economic Community & India (Republic)*
European Economic Community. *Treaties, etc. India, July 14, 1976.* Agreement on cane sugar in the form of an exchange of letters between the European Economic Community and the Republic of India, Brussels, 14 July 1976 ... — London : H.M.S.O., [1976]. — Folder (4p) ; 25cm. — (European Communities ; no.25(1976)) (Cmnd.6649)
Bibl.: p.220-221.
£0.12
(B77-08875)

341.7′547′15642 — European Community countries. Imports from Portugal: Preserved tomatoes. *Treaties between European Economic Community & Portugal*
European Economic Community. *Treaties, etc. Portugal, July 22, 1972. Protocols, amendments, etc., April 6, 1977.* Agreement in the form of an exchange of letters relating to article 3 of protocol no.8 to the agreement between the European Economic Community and the Portuguese Republic, Brussels, 6 April 1977 ... — London : H.M.S.O., [1977]. — Folder(4p) ; 25cm. — (European Communities ; no.26(1977)) (Cmnd.6937)
ISBN 0-10-169370-2 : £0.15
(B77-30055)

341.7′547′160883 — United States. Imports from Belize: Meat. *Treaties between Great Britain & United States*
Great Britain. *Treaties, etc. United States, February 8, 1977.* Exchange of notes between the Government of the United Kingdom of Great Britain and Northern Ireland and the Government of the United States of America relating to the importation into the United States of meat from Belize, Washington, 8-9 February 1977 ... — London : H.M.S.O., 1977. — Folder(4p) ; 25cm. — (Treaty series ; no.48(1977)) (Cmnd.6826)
ISBN 0-10-168260-3 : £0.15
(B77-22449)

341.7′547′220265 — Coal industries & trades. *Treaties between Canada & European Coal and Steel Community*
Canada. *Treaties, etc. European Coal and Steel Community, July 26, 1976.* Protocol concerning commercial and economic co-operation between the European Coal and Steel Community and the member states of the European Coal and Steel Community, of the one part, and Canada, of the other part (with final act), Brussels, 26 July 1976 ... — London : H.M.S.O., [1976]. — Folder (4p) ; 25cm. — (European Communities ; no.24(1976)) (Cmnd.6632)
ISBN 0-10-166320-x : £0.12
Also classified at 341.7′547′56691420265
(B77-30056)

341.7′547′220265 — European Community countries. Imports from ACP countries: Coal. Import duties. *Treaties*
Decision of the representatives of the Governments of the member states of the European Coal and Steel Community, meeting within the Council, extending the decision of 24 June 1975 opening tariff preferences for products within the province of that Community originating in the African, Caribbean and Pacific States and in the Overseas countries and territories associated with the Community, Brussels, 23 February 1976 ... — London : H.M.S.O., [1976]. — folder (4p) ; 25cm. — (European Communities ; no.19 (1976)) (Cmnd. 6595)
ISBN 0-10-165950-4 : £0.12
(B77-01249)

341.7′547′220265 — European Community countries. Imports from Austria: Coal. *Treaties*
Decision of the representatives of the Governments of the member states of the European Coal and Steel Community, meeting in Council, establishing supervision for imports of certain products originating in Austria (1976), Brussels, 20 January 1976 ... — London : H.M.S.O., [1977]. — Folder (4p) ; 25cm. — (Treaty series ; no.26(1977)) (Cmnd. 6744)
ISBN 0-10-167440-6 : £0.15
Also classified at 341.7′547′567280265
(B77-13569)

341.7′547′220265 — European Community countries. Imports from Sweden: Coal. *Treaties*
Decision of the representatives of the Governments of the member states of the European Coal and Steel Community, meeting in Council, establishing supervision for imports of certain products originating in Sweden (1976), Brussels, 20 January 1976 ... — London : H.M.S.O., [1977]. — Folder (4p) ; 25cm. — (Treaty series ; no.25(1977)) (Cmnd. 6743)
ISBN 0-10-167430-9 : £0.15
Also classified at 341.7′547′567280265
(B77-13570)

341.7′547′56648 — European Community countries. Imports from Israel: Preserved fruit salads. *Treaties between European Economic Community & Israel*
European Economic Community. *Treaties, etc. Israel, January 28, 1977.* Agreement in the form of an exchange of letters relating to article 9 of protocol no.1 to the agreement between the European Economic Community and the State of Israel and concerning the import into the Community of fruit salads originating in Israel, Brussels, 28 January 1977 ... — London : H.M.S.O., [1977]. — Folder(4p) ; 25cm. — (European Communities ; no.15(1977)) (Cmnd. 6878)
ISBN 0-10-168780-x : £0.15
(B77-28487)

341.7′547′56691420265 — Steel industries & trades. *Treaties between Canada & European Coal and Steel Community*
Canada. *Treaties, etc. European Coal and Steel Community, July 26, 1976.* Protocol concerning commercial and economic co-operation between the European Coal and Steel Community and the member states of the European Coal and Steel Community, of the one part, and Canada, of the other part (with final act), Brussels, 26 July 1976 ... — London : H.M.S.O., [1976]. — Folder (4p) ; 25cm. — (European Communities ; no.24(1976)) (Cmnd.6632)
ISBN 0-10-166320-x : £0.12
Primary classification 341.7′547′220265
(B77-30056)

341.7′547′567280265 — European Community countries. Imports from Austria: Steel products. *Treaties*
Decision of the representatives of the Governments of the member states of the European Coal and Steel Community, meeting in Council, establishing supervision for imports of certain products originating in Austria (1976), Brussels, 20 January 1976 ... — London : H.M.S.O., [1977]. — Folder (4p) ; 25cm. — (Treaty series ; no.26(1977)) (Cmnd. 6744)
ISBN 0-10-167440-6 : £0.15
Primary classification 341.7′547′220265
(B77-13569)

341.7′547′567280265 — European Community countries. Imports from developing countries: Steel products. Import duties. *Treaties*
Decisions of the representatives of the Governments of the member states of the European Coal and Steel Community, meeting in Council, opening, allocating and providing for the administration of tariff quotas and opening tariff preferences for certain steel products originating in developing countries, Brussels, 17 November 1975 ... — London : H.M.S.O., [1977]. — 12p ; 25cm. — (Treaty series ; no.41(1977)) (Cmnd.6807)
ISBN 0-10-168070-8 Sd : £0.25
(B77-16266)

341.7′547′567280265 — European Community countries. Imports from Sweden: Steel products. *Treaties*
Decision of the representatives of the Governments of the member states of the European Coal and Steel Community, meeting in Council, establishing supervision for imports of certain products originating in Sweden (1976), Brussels, 20 January 1976 ... — London : H.M.S.O., [1977]. — Folder (4p) ; 25cm. — (Treaty series ; no.25(1977)) (Cmnd. 6743)
ISBN 0-10-167430-9 : £0.15
Primary classification 341.7′547′220265
(B77-13570)

341.7′547′567628 — European Community countries. Imports from Portugal: Paper products. *Treaties between European Economic Community & Portugal*
European Economic Community. *Treaties, etc. Portugal, September 20, 1976. Protocols, amendments, etc., March 31, 1977.* Agreement in the form of an exchange of letters relating to article 4(3) of the interim agreement between the European Economic Community and the Portuguese Republic and to article 4(3) of the additional protocol, Brussels, 31 March 1977 ... — London : H.M.S.O., [1977]. — Folder (4p) ; 25cm. — (European Communities ; no.24(1977)) (Cmnd.6935)
ISBN 0-10-169350-8 : £0.15
(B77-31775)

341.7′547′567702860265 — European Community countries. Imports from Portugal: Textile products. *Treaties between European Economic Community & Portugal*
European Economic Community. *Treaties, etc. Portugal, September 20, 1976. Protocols, amendments, etc., March 31, 1977.* Agreement in the form of an exchange of letters relating to article 3 of the interim agreement between the European Economic Community and the Portuguese Republic and to article 3 of the additional protocol, Brussels, 31 March 1977 ... — London : H.M.S.O., [1977]. — Folder (4p) ; 25cm. — (European Communities ; no.25(1977)) (Cmnd.6936)
ISBN 0-10-169360-5 : £0.15
(B77-30057)

341.7′547′567702860265 — European Community countries. Imports from South Korea: Textile products. *Treaties between European Economic Community & South Korea*
European Economic Community. *Treaties, etc. Korea (Republic), December 22, 1976.* Agreement between the European Economic Community and the Republic of Korea on trade in textiles, Brussels, 22 December 1976 ... — London : H.M.S.O., 1977. — 16p ; 25cm. — (European communities ; no.20(1977)) (Cmnd. 6912)
ISBN 0-10-169120-3 Sd : £0.35
(B77-26907)

341.7′55 — British electricity supply equipment. Purchase by Ecuador. Financial assistance. Loans from Great Britain. *Treaties between Great Britain & Ecuador*
Great Britain. *Treaties, etc. Ecuador, August 7, 1975.* Exchange of notes concerning a development loan by the Government of the United Kingdom of Great Britain and Northern Ireland to the Government of the Republic of Ecuador (United Kingdom-Ecuador Loan 1975) Quito, 7 August 1975 ... — London : H.M.S.O., [1976]. — 22p : forms ; 25cm. — (Treaty series ; no.41(1976)) (Cmnd.6673)
English and Spanish text.
ISBN 0-10-166730-2 Sd : £0.45
(B77-08876)

341.7′55 — British hydroelectric equipment. Purchase by Ecuador. Financial assistance. Loans from Great Britain. *Treaties between Great Britain & Ecuador*
Great Britain. *Treaties, etc. Ecuador, October 2, 1973. Protocols, amendments, etc., February 2, 1976.* Exchange of notes between the Government of the United Kingdom of Great Britain and Northern Ireland and the Government of the Republic of Ecuador amending the United Kingdom-Ecuador Loan No.(2) 1973 (United Kingdom-Ecuador Loan No.(2) 1973 Amendment 1976) Quito, 2 February-16 June 1976 ... — London : H.M.S.O., [1977]. — Folder(4p) ; 25cm. — (Treaty series ; no.13(1977)) (Cmnd.6725)
English and Spanish text.
ISBN 0-10-167250-0 : £0.15
(B77-08877)

341.7′55 — Hydroelectric power stations. Construction. Financial assistance. *Laos. Nam Ngum. Nam Ngum Development Fund. Treaties*
[**Second** Nam Ngum Development Fund Agreement. *Protocols, amendments, etc., April 12, 1976].* Supplementary agreement, 1976 to the Second Nam Ngum Development Fund Agreement, 1974, Manila, 12 April 1976-31 August 1976 ... — London : H.M.S.O., [1977]. — 7p ; 25cm. — (Treaty series ; no.2(1977)) (Cmnd.6692)
ISBN 0-10-166920-8 Sd : £0.25
(B77-10760)

341.7′55 — Petroleum supply. International cooperation. International Energy Program. *Treaties*
Agreement on an International Energy Program, Paris, 18 November 1974 ... — London : H.M.S.O., [1976]. — 31p ; 25cm. — (Treaty series ; no.111(1976)) (Cmnd.6697)
'... previously published as Miscellaneous No.4(1975) Cmnd.5826'.
ISBN 0-10-166970-4 Sd : £0.60
(B77-08288)

341.7′566 — Shipping. Double taxation. *Treaties between Great Britain & Zaire*
Great Britain. *Treaties, etc. Zaire, October 11, 1976.* Agreement between the United Kingdom of Great Britain and Northern Ireland and the Republic of Zaire for the avoidance of double taxation on revenues arising from the business of shipping and air transport in international traffic, London, 11 October 1976 ... — London : H.M.S.O., [1977]. — Folder(4 p) ; 25cm. — (Zaire ; no.1 (1977)) (Cmnd.6717)
ISBN 0-10-167170-9 : £0.15
Also classified at 341.7′567
(B77-10260)

341.7′566 — Shipping. International law. Conferences: United Nations Conference on the Law of the Sea, 3rd, New York, 1973-1976
Gandhi, D S. Shipowners, mariners and the new law of the sea : the effects of technical, legal and political constraints upon the traditional users of the world's oceans / by D.S. Gandhi. — London (1 Pudding La., EC3R 8AA) : Fairplay Publications Ltd, 1977. — [11],83p : map ; 30cm.
ISBN 0-905045-05-x Sp : £15.00
(B77-26908)

341.7566′8 — Bills of lading. *Treaties*
[**International** Convention for the Unification of Certain Rules of Law Relating to Bills of Lading. *Protocols, amendments, etc., February 23, 1968].* Protocol to amend the International Convention for the Unification of Certain Rules of Law Relating to Bills of Lading signed at Brussels on 25 August 1924, Brussels, 23 February 1968 ... — London : H.M.S.O., [1977]. — 8p ; 25cm. — (Treaty series ; no.83(1977)) (Cmnd.6944)
'... previously published as Miscellaneous No.14(1968) Cmnd.3743'.
ISBN 0-10-169440-7 Sd : £0.25
(B77-31776)

341.7′566′8 — Cereals. Freight transport. Shipping. *Treaties*
[**International** Convention for the Safety of Life at Sea, 1974. Chapter 6]. The IMCO Grain Rules. — London : H.M.S.O., 1976. — iv,31p : ill ; 21cm.
'These Rules are taken directly from the 1974 Safety of Life at Sea Convention, Chapter VI'. — At head of title: Department of Trade.
ISBN 0-11-512012-2 Sd : £0.70
(B77-11681)

341.7′566′8 — International passenger transport. Shipping. *Treaties*
[**Athens** Convention relating to the Carriage of Passengers and their Luggage by Sea. *Protocols, amendments, etc., November 19, 1976].* Protocol to the Athens Convention relating to the Carriage of Passengers and their Luggage by Sea, 1974, London, 19 November 1976 ... — London : H.M.S.O., [1977]. — 6p ; 25cm. — (Miscellaneous ; no.5 (1977)) (Cmnd.6765)
ISBN 0-10-167650-6 Sd : £0.25
(B77-14617)

341.7′567 — Air services. Double taxation. *Treaties between Great Britain & Zaire*
Great Britain. *Treaties, etc. Zaire, October 11, 1976.* Agreement between the United Kingdom of Great Britain and Northern Ireland and the Republic of Zaire for the avoidance of double taxation on revenues arising from the business of shipping and air transport in international traffic, London, 11 October 1976 ... — London : H.M.S.O., [1977]. — Folder(4 p) ; 25cm. — (Zaire ; no.1 (1977)) (Cmnd.6717)
ISBN 0-10-167170-9 : £0.15
Primary classification 341.7′566
(B77-10260)

341.7′567′8 — Air services. Double taxation. *Treaties between Great Britain & Ethiopia*
Great Britain. *Treaties, etc. Ethiopia, February 1, 1977.* Exchange of notes between the Government of the United Kingdom of Great Britain and Northern Ireland and the Provisional Military Government of Socialist Ethiopia for the avoidance of double taxation on profits derived from air transport, Addis Ababa, 1 February 1977 ... — London : H.M.S.O, [1977]. — Folder(4p) ; 25cm. — (Ethiopia ; no.1(1977)) (Cmnd.6857)
ISBN 0-10-168570-x : £0.15
(B77-21005)

341.7′567′8026641045 — Air services. *Treaties between Great Britain & Italy*
Great Britain. *Treaties, etc. Italy, November 22, 1976.* Agreement between the Government of the United Kingdom of Great Britain and Northern Ireland and the Government of the Italian Republic for air services between and beyond their respective territories (with exchange of notes), Rome, 22 November 1976 ... — London : H.M.S.O., [1977]. — 12p ; 25cm. — (Italy ; no.1(1977)) (Cmnd.6873)
English and Italian text.
ISBN 0-10-168730-3 Sd : £0.25
(B77-29275)

341.7'567'802664105952 — Air services. *Treaties between Great Britain & Singapore*
Great Britain. *Treaties, etc. Singapore, January 12, 1971. Protocols, amendments, etc., May 27, 1976.* Exchange of notes between the Government of the United Kingdom of Great Britain and Northern Ireland and the Government of the Republic of Singapore amending the Air Services Agreement of 12 January 1971, Singapore 27 May-14 June 1976 ... — London : H.M.S.O., [1976]. — Folder (4p) ; 25cm. — (Treaty series ; no.93 (1976)) (Cmnd. 6622)
ISBN 0-10-166220-3 : £0.12
(B77-01250)

341.7'567'8026641064 — Air services. *Treaties between Great Britain & Morocco*
Great Britain. *Treaties, etc. Morocco, October 22, 1965. Protocols, amendments, etc., October 25, 1976.* Exchange of notes between the Government of the United Kingdom of Great Britain and Northern Ireland and the Government of the Kingdom of Morocco further amending the agreement for air services between and beyond their respective territories signed on 22 October 1965, Rabat 25 October-20 December 1976 ... — London : H.M.S.O., [1977]. — 6p ; 25cm. — (Treaty series ; no.39(1977)) (Cmnd.6798)
French and English text.
ISBN 0-10-167980-7 Sd : £0.25
(B77-18007)

341.7'567'802664106668 — Air services. *Treaties between Great Britain & Ivory Coast*
Great Britain. *Treaties, etc. Ivory Coast, December 1, 1976.* Agreement between the Government of the United Kingdom of Great Britain and Northern Ireland and the Government of the Republic of the Ivory Coast for air services between and beyond their respective territories, London, 1 December 1976 ... — London : H.M.S.O., [1977]. — 12p ; 25cm. — (Ivory Coast ; no.1 (1977)) (Cmnd. 6736)
ISBN 0-10-167360-4 Sd : £0.25
(B77-11682)

341.7'567'8026641081 — Air services. *Treaties between Great Britain & Brazil*
Great Britain. *Treaties, etc. Brazil, October 31, 1946. Protocols, amendments, etc., January 5, 1977.* Exchange of notes between the Government of the United Kingdom of Great Britain and Northern Ireland and the Government of the Federative Republic of Brazil further amending the air transport agreement of 31 October 1946, Brasilia, 5 January 1977 ... — London : H.M.S.O., [1977]. — 14p ; 25cm. — (Treaty series ; no.52(1977)) (Cmnd.6834)
English and Portuguese text.
ISBN 0-10-168340-5 Sd : £0.35
(B77-21006)

341.7'567'9 — Outer space. Research projects by European Space Research Organisation: Spacelab Programme. Cooperation between United States & European Space Research Organisation countries. *Treaties*
Agreement between the Government of the United States of America and certain Governments, members of the European Space Research Organisation, for a co-operative programme concerning the development, procurement and use of a space laboratory in conjunction with the space shuttle system, Neuilly-sur-Seine, 14 August-24 September 1973 ... — London : H.M.S.O., [1977]. — 12p ; 25cm. — (Treaty series ; no.11(1977)) (Cmnd. 6714)
ISBN 0-10-167140-7 Sd : £0.25
(B77-11683)

341.7'568'2 — British road construction equipment. Purchase by Peru. Financial assistance. Loans from Great Britain. *Treaties between Great Britain & Peru*
Great Britain. *Treaties, etc. Peru, September 28, 1973. Protocols, amendments, etc., July 12, 1976.* Exchange of notes between the Government of the United Kingdom of Great Britain and Northern Ireland and the Government of the Republic of Peru amending the United Kingdom-Peru No.1 Loan Agreement 1973 (United Kingdom-Peru No.1 Loan Agreement 1973 Amendment No.1), Lima, 12 July-1 September 1976 ... — London : H.M.S.O., [1977]. — Folder(4p) ; 25cm. — (Treaty series ; no.43(1977)) (Cmnd.6817)
English and Spanish text.
ISBN 0-10-168170-4 : £0.15
(B77-18008)

341.7'568'8 — Dangerous goods. International road freight transport. Safety measures. *Europe. Treaties*
[European Agreement Concerning the International Carriage of Dangerous Goods by Road (ADR). *Protocols, amendments, etc., 1976].* European Agreement Concerning the International Carriage of Dangerous Goods by Road (ADR), amendment no.1 to the 1976 edition, [issued by the] Department of Transport. — London : H.M.S.O., 1976. — 9p ; 25cm.
'... includes the decisions taken in January 1976 by the Group of Experts on the Transport of Dangerous Goods of the Economic Commission for Europe's Inland Transport Committee'. — Contents: Amendments to 'Annexe A : Provisions concerning dangerous substances and articles' and 'Annexe B : Provisions concerning transport equipment and transport operations'.
ISBN 0-11-550415-x Sd : £0.32
(B77-02851)

341.7'568'80266410438 — International road transport services. *Treaties between Great Britain & Poland*
Great Britain. *Treaties, etc. Poland, September 26, 1975.* Agreement between the Government of the United Kingdom of Great Britain and Northern Ireland and the Government of the Polish People's Republic on international road transport, London, 26 September 1975 ... — London : H.M.S.O., [1977]. — 12p ; 25cm. — (Treaty series ; no.4(1977)) (Cmnd.6700)
English and Polish text. — '... previously published as Poland No.1 (1975), Cmnd.6342'.
ISBN 0-10-167000-1 Sd : £0.25
(B77-10761)

341.7'568'80266410495 — International road freight transport services. *Treaties between Great Britain & Greece*
Great Britain. *Treaties, etc. Greece, February 26, 1974.* Agreement between the Government of the United Kingdom of Great Britain and Northern Ireland and the Government of the Hellenic Republic on the international carriage of goods by road, London, 26 February 1974 ... — London : H.M.S.O., [1977]. — 6p ; 25cm. — (Treaty series; no.10 (1977)) (Cmnd. 6710)
' ... previously published as Greece No.1 (1974), Cmnd. 5590'.
ISBN 0-10-167100-8 Sd : £0.25
(B77-07206)

341.7'577 — British radio equipment. Purchase by Peru. Financial assistance. Loans from Great Britain. *Treaties between Great Britain & Peru*
Great Britain. *Treaties, etc. Peru, September 4, 1975.* Exchange of notes concerning a loan by the Government of the United Kingdom of Great Britain and Northern Ireland to the Government of the Republic of Peru (United Kingdom-Peru Loan Agreement No.2 - 1975), Lima, 4 September 1975 ... — London : H.M.S.O., [1977]. — 21p : forms ; 25cm. — (Treaty series ; no.28(1977)) (Cmnd.6754)
English and Spanish text.
ISBN 0-10-167540-2 Sd : £0.45
(B77-14618)

341.7'577 — Broadcasting. Radio frequency wavebands. Allocation. *Europe. Treaties*
[European Broadcasting Convention. *Protocols, amendments, etc., November 22, 1975].* Additional protocol I relating to the abrogation of the European Broadcasting Convention (Copenhagen, 1948) and the annexed Copenhagen plan, Geneva, 22 November 1975 ... — London : H.M.S.O., [1977]. — Folder (4p) ; 25cm. — (Miscellaneous ; no.18(1977)) (Cmnd.6934)
ISBN 0-10-169340-0 : £0.15
(B77-30058)

341.7'577 — Direct broadcast satellites. International law. Role of United Nations, ca 1960-1975
Signitzer, Benno. Regulation of direct broadcasting from satellites : the UN involvement / [by] Benno Signitzer. — New York [etc.] ; London : Praeger ; [London] : [Distributed by Martin Robertson], 1976. — xiv,112,[1]p ; 24cm. — (Praeger special studies in international politics and government)
Bibl.: p.96-108. — Index.
ISBN 0-275-56800-8 : £9.15
(B77-05286)

341.7'577 — Maritime communications satellites. *Treaties*
Convention on the International Maritime Satellite Organization (INMARSAT) (with the operating agreement), London, 3 September 1976 ... — London : H.M.S.O., [1977]. — 40p ; 25cm. — (Miscellaneous ; no.9(1977)) (Cmnd. 6822)
ISBN 0-10-168220-4 Sd : £0.60
(B77-18629)

International Conference on the Establishment of an International Maritime Satellite System, *London, 1975-1976.* International Conference on the Establishment of an International Maritime Satellite System, 1975-1976 : final act of the conference including the Convention and operating agreement on the International Maritime Satellite Organisation (INMARSAT). — London : Inter-Governmental Maritime Consultative Organization, 1976. — iv,102p : facsims ; 24cm.
' ... the International Conference ... was convened in London on 23 April 1975 and concluded its first session on 9 May 1975 ... a second session from 9 to 27 February 1976 ... a third session from 1 to 3 September 1976 ... ' - p.1.
Pbk : £2.20
ISBN 92-801-1052-7
(B77-08878)

341.7'59 — Agricultural industries. Economic development. Financial assistance by United Nations. International Fund for Agricultural Development. Establishment. *Developing countries. Treaties*
Agreement establishing the International Fund for Agricultural Development adopted by the United Nations conference at Rome on 13 June 1976 and opened for signature at New York on 20 December 1976 ... — London : H.M.S.O., [1977]. — 27p ; 25cm. — (Miscellaneous ; no.7(1977)) (Cmnd.6787)
ISBN 0-10-167870-3 Sd : £0.50
(B77-15171)

341.7'59 — Ammonia industries. Factories. *Turkey. Gemlik. Gemlik Ammonia Plant. Construction. Financial assistance. Loans from Great Britain. Treaties between Great Britain & Turkey*
Great Britain. *Treaties, etc. Turkey, September 7, 1976.* Exchange of notes concerning a development loan by the Government of the United Kingdom of Great Britain and Northern Ireland to the Government of the Republic of Turkey in connection with the Gemlik ammonia plant project (United Kingdom-Turkey (Gemlik Ammonia Plant) Loan Agreement 1976), Ankara, 7 and 30 September 1976 ... — London : H.M.S.O., [1977]. — 12p : forms ; 25cm. — (Treaty series ; no.21(1977)) (Cmnd.6738)
ISBN 0-10-167380-9 Sd : £0.25
(B77-12932)

341.7'59 — Chile. Economic development. Financial assistance. Credit arrangements by Great Britain. Debts. Repayment. *Treaties between Great Britain & Chile*
Great Britain. *Treaties, etc. Chile, November 8, 1974.* Exchange of notes on revised arrangements for the payment of certain debts due from the Government of the Republic of Chile to the Government of the United Kingdom of Great Britain and Northern Ireland, London, 8 November 1974 ... — London : H.M.S.O., [1976]. — Folder(4p) ; 25cm. — (Treaty series ; no.98(1976)) (Cmnd. 6637)
ISBN 0-10-166370-6 : £0.12
(B77-04025)

341.7'59 — Ecuador. Economic development. Financial assistance. Loans from Great Britain. *Treaties between Great Britain & Ecuador*
Great Britain. *Treaties, etc. Ecuador, March 22, 1973. Protocols, amendments, etc., July 14, 1976.* Exchange of notes between the Government of the United Kingdom of Great Britain and Northern Ireland and the Government of the Republic of Ecuador further amending the United Kingdom-Ecuador Loan No.1 1973 (The United Kingdom-Ecuador Loan No.1 1973 Amendment 1976) Quito, 14 July-11 November 1976 ... — London : H.M.S.O., [1977]. — 7p ; 25cm. — (Treaty series ; no.36(1977)) (Cmnd.6792)
English and Spanish text.
ISBN 0-10-167920-3 Sd : £0.25
(B77-15752)

341.7'59 — European Development Fund. Finance. *Treaties*
Agreement amending the internal agreement on the financing and administration of Community aid signed on 11 July 1975, Brussels, 28 March 1977 ... — London : H.M.S.O., [1977]. — 6p ; 25cm. — (European Communities ; no.9(1977)) (Cmnd.6907)
'The Representatives of the Governments of the member states, meeting within the council ...' - p.3.
ISBN 0-10-169070-3 Sd : £0.25
(B77-31060)

341.7'59 — Goods & services. Classification for use in registration of trade marks. *Treaties*
[**Nice** Agreement Concerning the International Classification of Goods and Services for the Purposes of Registration of Marks. *Revision, 1977].* Nice Agreement Concerning the International Classification of Goods and Services for the Purposes of the Registration of Marks of 15 June 1957, as revised at Stockholm on 14 July 1967 and at Geneva on 13 May 1977 ... — London : H.M.S.O., [1977]. — 12p ; 25cm. — (Miscellaneous ; no.16(1977)) (Cmnd. 6898)
ISBN 0-10-168980-2 Sd : £0.25
(B77-28489)

341.7'59 — International Institute for the Management of Technology. Organisation. *Treaties*
Convention on the Establishment of the International Institute for the Management of Technology (with Charter of the Institute), Paris, 6 October 1971 ... — London : H.M.S.O., [1977]. — 19p ; 25cm. — (Treaty series ; no.84(1977)) (Cmnd.6942)
'... previously published as Miscellaneous No.2(1972), Cmnd.4854'.
ISBN 0-10-169420-2 Sd : £0.35
(B77-33120)

341.7'59 — Jordan. Economic development. Financial assistance. Loans from Great Britain. *Treaties between Great Britain & Jordan*
Great Britain. *Treaties, etc. Jordan, March 21, 1977.* Exchange of notes concerning a development loan by the Government of the United Kingdom of Great Britain and Northern Ireland to the Government of the Hashemite Kingdom of Jordan (the United Kingdom-Jordan Loan (1977)), Amman, 21 March 1977 ... — London : H.M.S.O., [1977]. — 18p : forms ; 25cm. — (Treaty series ; no.74(1977)) (Cmnd.6947)
ISBN 0-10-169470-9 Sd : £0.35
(B77-30059)

341.7'59 — Natural resources: Groundwater. Exploitation. Financial assistance. Loans from Great Britain. *Thailand. Sukhothai (Province). Treaties between Great Britain & Thailand*
Great Britain. *Treaties, etc. Thailand, September 29, 1976.* Exchange of notes concerning a loan by the Government of the United Kingdom of Great Britain and Northern Ireland to the Government of the Kingdom of Thailand (United Kingdom-Thailand Loan Agreement 1976), Bangkok, 29 September 1976 ... — London : H.M.S.O., [1977]. — 14p : forms ; 25cm. — (Treaty series ; no.18(1977)) (Cmnd. 6716)
ISBN 0-10-167160-1 Sd : £0.35
(B77-10261)

341.7'59 — Pakistan. Economic development. Financial assistance. Credit arrangements by Great Britain. Debts. Repayment. *Treaties between Great Britain & Pakistan*
Great Britain. *Treaties, etc. Pakistan, November 27, 1976.* Exchange of notes between the Government of the United Kingdom of Great Britain and Northern Ireland and the Government of Pakistan concerning debt relief (United Kingdom/Pakistan Debt Relief Agreement 1976), Islamabad, 27 November 1976. — London : H.M.S.O., [1977]. — 44p ; 25cm. — (Treaty series ; no.35(1977)) (Cmnd. 6779)
ISBN 0-10-167790-1 Sd : £1.00
(B77-15172)

341.7'59 — United Nations. Relief and Works Agency for Palestine Refugees in the Near East. Grants from European Economic Community: Grants for food supply. *Treaties*
United Nations. *Relief and Works Agency for Palestine Refugees in the Near East. Treaties, etc. European Economic Community, December 18, 1972. Protocols, amendments, etc., July 20, 1976.* Convention between the European Economic Community and the United Nations Relief and Works Agency for Palestine Refugees (UNRWA) concerning aid to refugees in the countries of the Near East, Brussels, 20 July 1976 ... — London : H.M.S.O., [1977]. — Folder (4p) ; 25cm. — (European Communities ; no.10(1977)) (Cmnd.6790)
ISBN 0-10-167900-9 : £0.15
(B77-16786)

United Nations. *Relief and Works Agency for Palestine Refugees in the Near East. Treaties, etc. European Economic Community, December 18, 1972. Protocols, amendments, etc., July 20, 1976.* Agreement in the form of an exchange of letters amending the Convention between the European Economic Community and the United Nations Relief and Works Agency for Palestine Refugees (UNRWA) signed on 18 December, 1972, Brussels, 20 July 1976 ... — London : H.M.S.O., [1976]. — Folder (4p) ; 25cm. — (European Communities ; no.27(1976)) (Cmnd.6693)
ISBN 0-10-166930-5 : £0.15
(B77-08289)

341.7'59 — Zaire. Economic development. Cooperation between Great Britain & Zaire. *Treaties between Great Britain & Zaire*
Great Britain. *Treaties, etc. Zaire, October 11, 1976.* General agreement on co-operation in development matters between the Government of the United Kingdom of Great Britain and Northern Ireland and the Executive Council of the Republic of Zaire, London, 11 October 1976 ... — London : H.M.S.O., [1977]. — 7p ; 25cm. — (Treaty series ; no.9 (1977)) (Cmnd. 6707)
English and French text.
ISBN 0-10-167070-2 Sd : £0.25
(B77-07207)

341.7'59 — Zaire. Economic development. Grants from Great Britain. *Treaties between Great Britain & Zaire*
Great Britain. *Treaties, etc. Zaire, October 11, 1976.* Exchange of notes concerning a grant by the Government of the United Kingdom of Great Britain and Northern Ireland to the Executive Council of the Republic of Zaire (United Kingdom-Zaire Grant 1976) London, 11 October 1976 ... — London : H.M.S.O., [1977]. — 25p : forms ; 25cm. — (Treaty series ; no.12(1977)) (Cmnd.6709)
English and French text.
ISBN 0-10-167090-7 Sd : £0.50
(B77-08879)

341.7'59'0265 — Morocco. Social cooperation with European Community countries. *Treaties between European Community countries & Morocco*
European Economic Community. *Treaties, etc. Morocco, April 27, 1976.* Co-operation agreement between the European Economic Community and the Kingdom of Morocco ; and, Agreement between the member states of the European Coal and Steel Community and the Kingdom of Morocco (with final act), Rabat, 27 April 1976 ... — London : H.M.S.O., [1977]. — 138p : forms ; 25cm. — (European Communities ; no.22(1977)) (Cmnd.6920)
ISBN 0-10-169200-5 Pbk : £2.10
(B77-30060)

341.7'6 — Social security benefits. *Treaties between Great Britain & Austria*
Great Britain. *Treaties, etc. Austria, September 16, 1975.* Supplementary convention on social security between the United Kingdom of Great Britain and Northern Ireland and the Republic of Austria, Vienna, 16 September 1975 ... — London : H.M.S.O., [1977]. — 18p ; 25cm. — (Treaty series ; no.29(1977)) (Cmnd.6760)
English and German text. — '... previously published as Austria No.1 (1975), Cmnd.6351'.
ISBN 0-10-167600-x Sd : £0.35
(B77-15173)

341.7'6 — Social security benefits. *Treaties between Great Britain & Spain*
Great Britain. *Treaties, etc. Spain, September 13, 1974. Protocols, amendments, etc., November 4, 1976.* Exchange of notes between the Government of the United Kingdom of Great Britain and Northern Ireland and the Government of Spain amending the Convention on social security signed at London on 13 September 1974, London, 4 November 1976 ... — London : H.M.S.O., [1977]. — 6p ; 25cm. — (Treaty series ; no.1(1977)) (Cmnd.6691)
English and Spanish text.
ISBN 0-10-166910-0 Sd : £0.25
(B77-07850)

341.7'62 — Fisheries. *North-west Atlantic Ocean. Treaties*
[**International** Convention for the Northwest Atlantic Fisheries. *Protocols, amendments, etc., December 20, 1976].* Protocol to the International Convention for the Northwest Atlantic Fisheries relating to the continued functioning of the Commission, Washington, 20 December 1976 ... — London : H.M.S.O., [1977]. — Folder (4p) ; 25cm. — (Miscellaneous ; no.12(1977)) (Cmnd.6844)
ISBN 0-10-168440-1 : £0.15
(B77-29276)

341.7'62 — Fishing. Regulation. *North Atlantic Ocean. Treaties*
Convention on Conduct of Fishing Operations in the North Atlantic, London, 1 June to 30 November 1967 ... — London : H.M.S.O., [1977]. — 20p ; 25cm. — (Treaty series ; no.40(1977)) (Cmnd.6799)
'... previously published in Miscellaneous No.11 (1968), Cmnd.3645'.
ISBN 0-10-167990-4 Sd : £0.35
(B77-18009)

341.7'62 — Foreign trade in organisms in danger of extinction. *Treaties*
Convention on International Trade in Endangered Species of Wild Fauna and Flora, Washington, 3 March 1973 ... — London : H.M.S.O., [1976]. — 45p : form ; 25cm. — (Treaty series ; no.101(1976)) (Cmnd.6647)
'... previously published as Miscellaneous No.25(1975) Cmnd.5459'.
ISBN 0-10-166470-2 Sd : £0.55
(B77-07208)

341.7'62 — Oceans. Pollution by petroleum. Control measures. International legal aspects
Abecassis, D W. Marine oil pollution : the international legal regime relating to the prevention of marine-based oil pollution / [by] D.W. Abecassis. — Cambridge (19 Silver St., Cambridge CB3 9EP) : University of Cambridge, Department of Land Economy, 1976. — [9],123p : ill, map ; 22cm. — (University of Cambridge. Department of Land Economy. Occasional papers ; no.6 ISSN 0306-2384)
Bibl.: p.121-123.
£1.80
(B77-24794)

341.7'62 — Oceans. Pollution by waste materials. Control measures. *Treaties*
Inter-Governmental Conference on the Convention on the Dumping of Wastes at Sea, *London, 1972.* Inter-governmental Conference on the Convention on the Dumping of Wastes at Sea, London, 30 October-13 November 1972 : final act of the conference with technical memorandum and resolution adopted by the Conference and Convention on the Prevention of Marine Pollution by Dumping of Wastes and Other Matter. — London : Inter-Governmental Maritime Consultative Organization, 1976. — 36p : facsims ; 25cm.
Sd : £1.37
ISBN 92-801-1054-3
(B77-08880)

341.7'62 — Pollution by petroleum. Civil liability. *Treaties*
Intergovernmental Conference on the Convention on Civil Liability for Oil Pollution Damage from Offshore Operations, *London, 1975 and 1976.* Final act of the Intergovernmental Conference on the Convention on Civil Liability for Oil Pollution Damage from Offshore Operations, London, 20th to 31 October 1975 and 13 to 17 December 1976 ... — London : H.M.S.O., [1977]. — 28p ; 25cm. — (Miscellaneous ; no.8 (1977)) (Cmnd. 6791)
Parallel English and French text. — Includes the text of the Convention on Civil Liability for Oil Pollution Damage Resulting from Exploration for and Exploitation of Seabed Mineral Resources.
ISBN 0-10-167910-6 Sd : £0.50
(B77-14619)

341.7'62 — Whaling. *Treaties*
[International Whaling Convention. *Protocols, amendments, etc., 1975-76].* Schedule to the International Whaling Convention, 1946, revised to include the amendments adopted at the twenty-seventh and twenty-eighth meetings of the International Whaling Commission ... — London : H.M.S.O., [1977]. — 14p ; 25cm. — (Treaty series ; no.38(1977)) (Cmnd.6797)
'... meetings held in London in 1975 and Cambridge in 1976 ...' - p.2.
ISBN 0-10-167970-x Sd : £0.35
(B77-18010)

341.7'63 — British personnel. Conditions of service. *Botswana. Treaties between Great Britain & Botswana*
Great Britain. *Treaties, etc. Botswana, June 4, 1976.* Exchange of notes between the government of the United Kingdom of Great Britain and Northern Ireland and the Government of Botswana concerning officers designated by the Government of the United Kingdom in the service of specified organisations or institutions in Botswana (The British Expatriates Supplementation (Botswana) Agreement 1976) Gaborone, 4 June 1976 ... — London : H.M.S.O., [1976]. — 6p ; 25cm. — (Treaty series ; no.91(1976)) (Cmnd.6613)
ISBN 0-10-166130-4 Sd : £0.20
(B77-09588)

341.7'63 — British personnel. Conditions of service. *Mauritius. Treaties between Great Britain & Mauritius*
Great Britain. *Treaties, etc. Mauritius, December 8, 1976.* Exchange of notes between the Government of the United Kingdom of Great Britain and Northern Ireland and the Government of Mauritius concerning officers designated by the Government of the United Kingdom in the service of the Government of Mauritius under the provisions of the Overseas Service (Mauritius) Agreement 1971 (The Overseas Service (Mauritius) (Residuary) Agreement 1971-76), Port Louis, 8 December 1976 ... — London : H.M.S.O., [1977]. — Folder(4p) ; 25cm. — (Treaty series ; no.32(1977)) (Cmnd.6773)
ISBN 0-10-167730-8 : £0.15
(B77-15174)

Great Britain. *Treaties, etc. Mauritius, June 30, 1971. Protocols, amendments, etc., December 8, 1976.* Exchange of notes between the Government of the United Kingdom of Great Britain and Northern Ireland and the Government of Mauritius amending and extending the British Expatriates Supplementation (Mauritius) Agreement 1971 (The British Expatriates Supplementation (Mauritius) (Continuance) Agreement 1971-1976), Port Louis, 8 December 1976 ... — London : H.M.S.O., [1977]. — Folder(4p) ; 25cm. — (Treaty series ; no.33(1977)) (Cmnd. 6774)
ISBN 0-10-167740-5 : £0.15
(B77-15175)

341.7'63 — British personnel. Conditions of service. *Tanzania. Treaties between Great Britain & Tanzania*
Great Britain. *Treaties, etc. Tanzania, August 5, 1976.* Exchange of notes between the Government of the United Kingdom of Great Britain and Northern Ireland and the Government of the United Republic of Tanzania concerning officers designated by the Government of the United Kingdom in the service of specified organisations and institutions in Tanzania (The British Expatriates Supplementation (Tanzania) Agreement 1976), Dar-es-Salaam, 5 August 1976 ... — London : H.M.S.O., [1977]. — 7p ; 25cm. — (Treaty series ; no.31(1977)) (Cmnd.6772)
ISBN 0-10-167720-0 Sd : £0.25
(B77-15176)

341.7'63 — British personnel. Conditions of service. *Zambia. Treaties between Great Britain & Zambia*
Great Britain. *Treaties, etc. Zambia, March 31, 1976. Protocols, amendments, etc., August 4, 1976.* Exchange of notes between the Government of the United Kingdom of Great Britain and Northern Ireland and the Government of the Republic of Zambia amending the British Expatriates Supplementation (Zambia) (Continuance) Agreement 1971-1976 (British Expatriates Supplementation (Zambia) (Continuance) Agreement 1971-1976 (Amendment) 1976), Lusaka, 4-10 August 1976 ... — London : H.M.S.O., [1976]. — Folder(4p) ; 25cm. — (Treaty series ; no.108(1976)) (Cmnd.6686)
ISBN 0-10-166860-0 : £0.15
(B77-08881)

341.7'63 — British personnel. Remuneration. *Malawi. Treaties between Great Britain & Malawi*
Great Britain. *Treaties, etc. Malawi, March 27, 1971. Protocols, amendments, etc., June 14, 1976.* Exchange of notes between the Government of the United Kingdom of Great Britain and Northern Ireland and the Government of Malawi amending and extending the British Expatriates Supplementation (Malawi) Agreement 1971 (The British Expatriates Supplementation (Malawi) (Continuance) Agreement 1971-76), Lilongwe, 14 June 1976 ... — London : H.M.S.O., [1977]. — Folder(4p) ; 25cm. — (Treaty series ; no.54(1977)) (Cmnd.6847)
ISBN 0-10-168470-3 : £0.15
(B77-21007)

341.7'63 — Civil service. British designated personnel. Remuneration. *Barbados. Treaties between Great Britain & Barbados*
Great Britain. *Treaties, etc. Barbados, March 26, 1971.* Exchange of notes between the Government of the United Kingdom of Great Britain and Northern Ireland and the Government of Barbados concerning officers designated by the Government of the United Kingdom in the service of the Government of Barbados (The Overseas Service (Barbados) Agreement 1970), Bridgetown, 26-30 March 1971, and exchange of notes amending and extending the 1970 agreement, Bridgetown, 17 February-9 March 1976 ... — London : H.M.S.O., [1976]. — 8p ; 25cm. — (Treaty series ; no.106(1976)) (Cmnd.6682)
ISBN 0-10-166820-1 Sd : £0.20
(B77-10262)

341.7'63 — Civil service. British personnel. Conditions of service. *Barbados. Treaties between Great Britain & Barbados*
Great Britain. *Treaties, etc. Barbados, March 31, 1977.* Exchange of notes between the Government of the United Kingdom of Great Britain and Northern Ireland and the Government of Barbados concerning officers designated by the Government of the United Kingdom in the service of the Government of Barbados (the Overseas Service (Barbados) Agreement 1971-81), Bridgetown, 31 March 1977 ... — London : H.M.S.O., [1977]. — 6p ; 25cm. — (Treaty series ; no.73(1977)) (Cmnd. 6915)
ISBN 0-10-169150-5 Sd : £0.25
(B77-26909)

341.7'63 — Civil service. British personnel. Conditions of service. *Botswana. Treaties between Great Britain & Botswana*
Great Britain. *Treaties, etc. Botswana, December 30, 1970. Protocols, amendments, etc., June 4, 1976.* Exchange of notes between the Government of the United Kingdom of Great Britain and Northern Ireland and the Government of Botswana amending and extending the Overseas Service (Botswana) Agreement 1970 (The Overseas Service (Botswana) (Continuance) Agreement 1970-76) Gaborone, 4 June 1976 ... — London : H.M.S.O., [1976]. — Folder(4p) ; 25cm. — (Treaty series ; no.87(1976)) (Cmnd.6612)
ISBN 0-10-166120-7 : £0.12
(B77-09589)

341.7'63 — Civil service. British personnel. Conditions of service. *Guyana. Treaties between Great Britain & Guyana*
Great Britain. *Treaties, etc. Guyana, March 31, 1977.* Exchange of notes between the Government of the United Kingdom of Great Britain and Northern Ireland and the Government of the Republic of Guyana concerning officers designated by the Government of the United Kingdom in the service of the Government of Guyana (the Overseas Service (Guyana) (Continuance) Agreement 1977-81), Georgetown, 31 March 1977 ... — London : H.M.S.O., [1977]. — 7p ; 25cm. — (Treaty series ; no.71(1977)) (Cmnd. 6911)
ISBN 0-10-169110-6 Sd : £0.25
(B77-26910)

341.7'63 — Civil service. British personnel. Conditions of service. *Malawi. Treaties between Great Britain & Malawi*
Great Britain. *Treaties, etc. Malawi, January 11, 1972. Protocols, amendments, etc., June 14, 1976.* Exchange of notes between the Government of the United Kingdom of Great Britain and Northern Ireland and the Government of Malawi amending and extending the Overseas Service (Malawi) Agreement 1971 (The Overseas Service (Malawi) (Continuance) Agreement 1971-76), Lilongwe, 14 June 1976 ... — London : H.M.S.O., [1977]. — Folder(4p) ; 25cm. — (Treaty series ; no.55(1977)) (Cmnd.6855)
ISBN 0-10-168550-5 : £0.15
(B77-21008)

341.7'63 — Civil service. British personnel. Conditions of service. *Swaziland. Treaties between Great Britain & Swaziland*
Great Britain. *Treaties, etc. Swaziland, February 24, 1971. Protocols, amendments, etc., June 8, 1976.* Exchange of notes between the Government of the United Kingdom of Great Britain and Northern Ireland and the Government of the Kingdom of Swaziland amending and extending The Overseas Service (Swaziland) Agreement 1971 (The Overseas Service (Swaziland) Agreement 1976), Mbabane, 8 June-28 October 1976. — London : H.M.S.O., [1977]. — 6p ; 25cm. — (Treaty series ; no.22(1977)) (Cmnd.6739)
ISBN 0-10-167390-6 Sd : £0.25
(B77-14620)

341.7'63 — Civil service. British personnel. Conditions of service. *Uganda. Treaties between Great Britain & Uganda*
Great Britain. *Treaties, etc. Uganda, March 30, 1971. Protocols, amendments, etc., March 26, 1976.* Exchange of notes between the Government of the United Kingdom of Great Britain and Northern Ireland and the Government of the Republic of Uganda amending and extending the Overseas Service (Uganda) Agreement 1971 (The Overseas Service (Uganda) (Continuance) Agreement 1971-76) Kampala-Entebbe, 26-30 March 1976 ... — London : H.M.S.O., [1976]. — Folder (4p) ; 25cm. — (Treaty series ; no.90(1976)) (Cmnd.6609)
ISBN 0-10-166090-1 : £0.12
(B77-10263)

341.7'63 — Civil service. British personnel. Superannuation. *Botswana. Treaties between Great Britain & Botswana*
Great Britain. *Treaties, etc. Botswana, February 24, 1976.* Agreement between the Government of the United Kingdom of Great Britain and Northern Ireland and the Government of the Republic of Botswana concerning public officers' pensions, Gaborone, 24 February 1976 ... — London : H.M.S.O., [1977]. — 8p ; 25cm. — (Treaty series ; no.3(1977)) (Cmnd.6699)
ISBN 0-10-166990-9 Sd : £0.25
(B77-10264)

341.7'63 — Civil service. British personnel. Superannuation. *St Christopher-Nevis-Anguilla. Treaties between Great Britain & St Christopher-Nevis-Anguilla*
Great Britain. *Treaties, etc. St Christopher-Nevis-Anguilla, November 6, 1975.* Agreement between the Government of the United Kingdom of Great Britain and Northern Ireland and the Government of the Associated State of St Christopher, Nevis and Anguilla concerning public officers' pensions, Basseterre, 6 November 1975 ... — London : H.M.S.O., [1977]. — 8p ; 25cm. — (Miscellaneous ; no.3(1977)) (Cmnd.6731)
ISBN 0-10-167310-8 Sd : £0.25
(B77-10762)

341.7'63 — Civil service. British personnel. Superannuation. *Seychelles Islands. Treaties between Great Britain & Seychelles Islands*
Great Britain. *Treaties, etc. Seychelles, June 29, 1976.* Agreement between the Government of the United Kingdom of Great Britain and Northern Ireland and the Government of Seychelles concerning public officers' pensions, Victoria, 29 June 1976 ... — London : H.M.S.O., [1976]. — 8p ; 25cm. — (Cmnd. 6635)
ISBN 0-10-166350-1 Sd : £0.20
(B77-04026)

341.7'63 — Civil service. British personnel. Superannuation. *Sierra Leone. Treaties between Great Britain & Sierra Leone*
Great Britain. *Treaties, etc. Sierra Leone, July 1, 1976.* Agreement between the Government of the United Kingdom of Great Britain and Northern Ireland and the Government of the Republic of Sierra Leone concerning public officers' pensions, Freetown, 1 July 1976 ... — London : H.M.S.O., [1976]. — 8p ; 25cm. — (Treaty series ; no.105(1976)) (Cmnd.6652)
ISBN 0-10-166520-2 Sd : £0.20
(B77-08290)

341.7'63 — Civil service. British personnel. Superannuation. *Tanzania. Treaties between Great Britain & Tanzania*
Great Britain. *Treaties, etc. Tanzania, March 24, 1976.* Agreement between the Government of the United Kingdom of Great Britain and Northern Ireland and the Government of the United Republic of Tanzania concerning public officers' pensions (the Public Officers' Pensions (Tanzania) Agreement 1976), Dar es Salaam, 24 March 1976 ... — London : H.M.S.O., [1977]. — 10p ; 25cm. — (Treaty series ; no.82(1977)) (Cmnd.6949)
ISBN 0-10-169490-3 Sd : £0.25
(B77-33121)

341.7'63 — Civil services. British personnel. Superannuation. *Jamaica. Treaties between Great Britain & Jamaica*
Great Britain. *Treaties, etc. Jamaica, April 1, 1976.* Agreement between the Government of the United Kingdom of Great Britain and Northern Ireland and the Government of Jamaica concerning public officer's pensions (The Public Officers' Pensions (Jamaica) Agreement 1976), Kingston, 1 April 1976 ... — London : H.M.S.O., [1977]. — 8p ; 25cm. — (Treaty series ; no.27 (1977)) (Cmnd. 6746)
ISBN 0-10-167460-0 Sd : £0.25
(B77-14126)

341.7'63 — Foreign personnel. Employment. Discrimination. Treaties: Treaty of Rome, 1957. *European Community countries. Critical studies*
Sundberg-Weitman, Brita. Discrimination on grounds of nationality : free movement of workers and freedom of establishment under the EEC treaty / [by] Brita Sundberg-Weitman. — Amsterdam [etc.] ; Oxford : North-Holland Publishing Co., 1977. — vii,248p ; 23cm.
Bibl.: p.237-243.
ISBN 0-7204-0477-0 : £17.56
(B77-16787)

341.7'63 — Industrial democracy. European Economic Community law. Proposals: Commission of the European Communities. Employee participation and company structure. *European Community countries. Institute of Personnel Management viewpoints*
Institute of Personnel Management. Participation and the Common Market : IPM comments on the European Commission's green paper 'Employee participation and company structure'. — London : I.P.M., 1976. — [1], 20p ; 30cm.
Sd : £0.50
(B77-05287)

341.7'63 — Personnel. Adult education. Provision of paid leave. *Treaties*
International Labour Convention no.140 : concerning paid educational leave / adopted by the General Conference of the International Labour Organisation at its fifty-ninth session, Geneva, 24 June 1974 ... — London : H.M.S.O., [1977]. — 8p ; 25cm. — (Treaty series ; no.37(1977)) (Cmnd.6796)
'... previously published in Cmnd.6236'.
ISBN 0-10-167960-2 Sd : £0.25
(B77-17374)

341.7'63 — Universities. *Lesotho. Roma. National University of Lesotho. British personnel. Conditions of service. Treaties between Great Britain & Lesotho*
Great Britain. *Treaties, etc. Lesotho, August 2, 1976.* Exchange of notes between the Government of the United Kingdom of Great Britain and Northern Ireland and the Kingdom of Lesotho concerning officers designated by the Government of the United Kingdom in the service of specified organisations or institutions in Lesotho (The British Expatriates Supplementation (Lesotho) Agreement 1976), Maseru, 2 August 1976 ... — London : H.M.S.O., [1977]. — 6p ; 25cm. — (Treaty series ; no.30(1977)) (Cmnd.6766)
ISBN 0-10-167660-3 Sd : £0.25
(B77-14621)

341.7'63 — Universities. *Uganda. Kampala. Makerere University. British personnel. Remuneration. Treaties between Great Britain & Uganda*
Great Britain. *Treaties, etc. Uganda, March 30, 1971. Protocols, amendments, etc., March 26, 1976.* Exchange of notes between the Government of the United Kingdom of Great Britain and Northern Ireland and the Government of the Republic of Uganda amending and extending the British Expatriates Supplementation Scheme (Uganda) Agreement 1971 (The British Expatriates Supplementation Scheme (Uganda) (Continuance) Agreement 1971-76) Kampala-Entebbe, 16-31 March 1976 ... — London : H.M.S.O., [1976]. — Folder (4)p ; 25cm. — (Treaty series ; no.89 (1976)) (Cmnd. 6608)
ISBN 0-10-166080-4 : £0.12
(B77-08882)

341.7'65 — British health service vehicles. Purchase by Peru. Financial assistance. Loans from Great Britain. *Treaties between Great Britain & Peru*
Great Britain. *Treaties, etc. Peru, June 3, 1976.* Exchange of notes concerning a development loan by the Government of the United Kingdom of Great Britain and Northern Ireland to the Government of the Republic of Peru for the purchase of ambulances and ancillary health service vehicles (United Kingdom-Peru Loan Agreement No.1 (1976)) Lima, 3 June 1976 ... — London : H.M.S.O., [1976]. — 19p : forms ; 25cm. — (Treaty series ; no.110 (1976)) (Cmnd.6689)
English and Spanish text.
ISBN 0-10-166890-2 Sd : £0.35
(B77-09590)

341.7'65 — British hospital equipment. Purchase by Nicaragua. Financial assistance. Loans from Great Britain. *Treaties between Great Britain & Nicaragua*
Great Britain. *Treaties, etc. Nicaragua, March 21, 1974. Protocols, amendments, etc., May 17, 1976.* Exchange of notes between the Government of the United Kingdom of Great Britain and Northern Ireland and the Government of Nicaragua further amending the United Kingdom-Nicaragua Loan No.(1) 1974 (United Kingdom-Nicaragua Loan No.(1) 1974 Amendment No.2), San José, 17 May 1976-Managua, 15 June 1976 ... — London : H.M.S.O., [1976]. — Folder (4p) ; 25cm. — (Treaty series ; no.100(1976)) (Cmnd.6636)
English and Spanish text.
ISBN 0-10-166360-9 : £0.12
(B77-02852)

341.7'65 — Medicine. Cooperation between Great Britain & East Germany. *Treaties*
Great Britain. *Treaties, etc. Germany (Democratic Republic), April 14, 1977.* Agreement on co-operation in the field of medicine and public health between the Government of the United Kingdom of Great Britain and Northern Ireland and the Government of the German Democratic Republic, Berlin, 14 April 1977... — London : H.M.S.O., [1977]. — 8p ; 25cm. — (Treaty series ; no.72(1977)) (Cmnd.6914)
English and German text.
ISBN 0-10-169140-8 Sd : £0.25
(B77-28490)

341.7'65 — World Health Organization. Constitution. *Treaties*
World Health Assembly, *26th, Geneva, 1973.* Resolution of the Twenty-sixth World Health Assembly amending articles 34 and 55 of the constitution of the World Health Organization adopted on 22 May, 1973, Geneva, 24 May 1973 ... — London : H.M.S.O., [1977]. — 7p ; 25cm. — (Treaty series ; no.50(1977)) (Cmnd. 6832)
'... previously published as Miscellaneous No.6 (1974), Cmnd.5592.
ISBN 0-10-168320-0 Sd : £0.25
(B77-24085)

World Health Assembly, *29th, Geneva, 1976.* Resolution of the Twenty-ninth World Health Assembly amending Articles 24 and 25 of the Constitution of the World Health Organization, adopted on 17 May 1976 ... — London : H.M.S.O., [1977]. — Folder(4p) ; 25cm. — (Miscellaneous ; no.1 (1977)) (Cmnd. 6711)
ISBN 0-10-167110-5 : £0.15
(B77-07209)

341.7'67 — European Centre for Medium-Range Weather Forecasts. Privileges. Accordance by Great Britain. *Treaties between Great Britain & European Centre for Medium-Range Weather Forecasts*
Great Britain. *Treaties, etc. European Centre for Medium-Range Weather Forecasts, March 1, 1977.* Headquarters agreement between the Government of the United Kingdom of Great Britain and Northern Ireland and the European Centre for Medium-Range Weather Forecasts, London, 1 March 1977 ... — London : H.M.S.O., [1977]. — 66p,fold plate : col map ; 25cm. — (Treaty series ; no.49(1977)) (Cmnd. 6842)
English, Dutch, French, German and Italian text. — 'The English text ... was previously published in draft as Miscellaneous No.1 (1976), Cmnd.6368'.
ISBN 0-10-168420-7 Sd : £1.35
(B77-22450)

341.7'67 — Unesco. Constitution. *Treaties*
Unesco. [Constitution]. Amendments to Articles IV, V and VIII of the Constitution of the United Nations Educational, Scientific and Cultural Organisation adopted by the General Conference of the Organisation at its seventeenth session on 24 and 30 October 1972 ... — London : H.M.S.O., [1976]. — Folder(4p) ; 25cm. — (Treaty series ; no.104(1976)) (Cmnd.6651)
English and French text.
ISBN 0-10-166510-5 : £0.12
(B77-08291)

341.7'67 — Very high flux neutron reactors. Construction & operation. Organisations. *France. Grenoble. Institut Max von Laue-Paul Langevin. Participation of Science Research Council (Great Britain). Treaties between Great Britain, France & West Germany*
Great Britain. *Treaties, etc., July 19, 1974. Protocols, amendments, etc., July 27, 1976.* Protocol to the Convention of 19 January 1967, as amended by the protocol of 6 July 1971, between the Government of the French Republic and the Government of the Federal Republic of Germany on the construction and operation of a very high flux reactor, as further amended by the Agreement of 19 July 1974 between the above mentioned two Governments and the Government of the United Kingdom of Great Britain and Northern Ireland concerning that Government's accession to the Convention, Paris, 27 July 1976 ... — London : H.M.S.O., [1976]. — Folder (4p) ; 25cm. — (Treaty series ; no.42(1976)) (Cmnd.6672)
ISBN 0-10-166720-5 : £0.15
(B77-07851)

341.7'67 — Weather stations. Organisation. *North Atlantic Ocean. Treaties*
Agreement for Joint Financing of North Atlantic Ocean Stations, Geneva, 15 November 1974 ... — London : H.M.S.O., [1977]. — 23p ; 25cm. — (Treaty series ; no.51(1977)) (Cmnd.6833)
'... previously published as Miscellaneous No.10(1975) Cmnd.5937'.
ISBN 0-10-168330-8 Sd : £0.45
(B77-22451)

341.7'67'0266410471 — Great Britain. Cultural relations with Finland. *Treaties between Great Britain & Finland*
Great Britain. *Treaties, etc. Finland, May 26, 1976.* Cultural convention between the Government of the United Kingdom of Great Britain and Northern Ireland and the Government of the Republic of Finland, Helsinki, 26 May 1976 ... — London : H.M.S.O., [1976]. — 8p ; 25cm. — (Treaty series ; no.95(1976)) (Cmnd.6627)
English and Finnish text.
ISBN 0-10-166270-x Sd : £0.20
(B77-01251)

341.7'67'026641072 — Great Britain. Cultural relations with Mexico. *Treaties between Great Britain & Mexico*
Great Britain. *Treaties, etc. Mexico, February 25, 1975.* Agreement on cultural cooperation between the Government of the United Kingdom of Great Britain and Northern Ireland and the Government of the United Mexican States, Tlatelolco, 25 February 1975 ... — London : H.M.S.O., [1977]. — 6p ; 25cm. — (Treaty series ; no.44(1977)) (Cmnd.6818)
English and Spanish text. — '... previously published as Mexico No.1 (1975), Cmnd.6080'.
ISBN 0-10-168180-1 Sd : £0.25
(B77-18011)

341.7'67'026641081 — Brazil. Cultural relations with Great Britain. *Treaties between Great Britain & Brazil*
Great Britain. *Treaties, etc. Brazil, October 14, 1976.* Cultural convention between the Government of the United Kingdom of Great Britain and Northern Ireland and the Government of the Federative Republic of Brazil, London, 14 October, 1976 ... — London : H.M.S.O., [1977]. — Folder (4p) ; 25cm. — (Brazil ; no.1 (1977)) (Cmnd. 6729)
ISBN 0-10-167290-x : £0.15
(B77-11129)

341.7'8 — Civil courts. Evidence. Provision by foreign countries. *Treaties*
Convention on the Taking of Evidence Abroad in Civil or Commercial Matters, The Hague, 18 March 1970 ... — London : H.M.S.O., [1977]. — 19p ; 25cm. — (Treaty series ; no.(20) 1977 [i.e. no.20(1977)]) (Cmnd.6727)
'... previously published as part of Miscellaneous No.11 (1969), Cmnd.3991'.
ISBN 0-10-167270-5 Sd : £0.35
(B77-11130)

341.7'8 — Civil courts. Judgments. Mutual recognition. *Channel Islands, Isle of Man & Italy. Treaties between Great Britain & Italy*
Great Britain. *Treaties, etc. Italy, February 7, 1964. Protocols, amendments, etc., April 12, 1976.* Exchange of notes between the Government of the United Kingdom of Great Britain and Northern Ireland and the Government of the Italian Republic concerning the extension to Jersey, the Bailiwick of Guernsey and the Isle of Man of the Convention providing for the reciprocal recognition and enforcements of judgements in civil and commercial matters signed at Rome on 7 February 1964 as amended by the protocol signed at Rome on 14 July 1970 (with notification of extension), Rome, 12 April 1976 ... — London : H.M.S.O., [1976]. — 6p ; 25cm. — (Treaty series ; no.92 (1976)) (Cmnd. 6617)
English and Italian text.
ISBN 0-10-166170-3 Sd : £0.20
(B77-01252)

341.7'8 — Civil courts. Judgments. Recognition under civil law in Hong Kong. *Italy. Treaties between Great Britain & Italy*
Great Britain. *Treaties, etc. Italy, February 23, 1977.* Exchange of notes between the United Kingdom of Great Britain and Northern Ireland and the Republic of Italy concerning the extension to Hong Kong of the Convention on the Reciprocal Recognition and Enforcement of Judgments in Civil and Commercial Matters signed at Rome on 7 February 1964, as amended by the protocol signed at Rome on 14 July 1970 (with United Kingdom notification of extension), Rome, 23-28 February 1977 ... — London : H.M.S.O., [1977]. — 6p ; 25cm. — (Treaty series ; no.75(1977)) (Cmnd.6925)
English and Italian text.
ISBN 0-10-169250-1 Sd : £0.25
Primary classification 341.7'8
(B77-29277)

341.7'8 — Civil courts. Judgments. Recognition under civil law in Italy. *Hong Kong. Treaties between Great Britain & Italy*
Great Britain. *Treaties, etc. Italy, February 23, 1977.* Exchange of notes between the United Kingdom of Great Britain and Northern Ireland and the Republic of Italy concerning the extension to Hong Kong of the Convention on the Reciprocal Recognition and Enforcement of Judgments in Civil and Commercial Matters signed at Rome on 7 February 1964, as amended by the protocol signed at Rome on 14 July 1970 (with United Kingdom notification of extension), Rome, 23-28 February 1977 ... — London : H.M.S.O., [1977]. — 6p ; 25cm. — (Treaty series ; no.75(1977)) (Cmnd.6925)
English and Italian text.
ISBN 0-10-169250-1 Sd : £0.25
Also classified at 341.7'8
(B77-29277)

341.7'8 — Legal aid. Applications. International transfer. *Western European countries. Treaties*
European Agreement on the Transmission of Applications for Legal Aid (with explanatory report), Strasbourg, 27 January 1977 ... — London : H.M.S.O., [1977]. — 11p ; 25cm. — (Miscellaneous ; no.15(1977)) (Cmnd.6895)
ISBN 0-10-168950-0 Sd : £0.25
(B77-28491)

342 — CONSTITUTIONAL AND ADMINISTRATIVE LAW

342'.00264 — Constitutional law. Cases. *Comparative studies*
Murphy, Walter Francis. Comparative constitutional law : cases and commentaries / [by] Walter F. Murphy, Joseph Tanenhaus. — London [etc.] : Macmillan, 1977. — xxvi,754p ; 24cm.
Also published: New York : St Martin's Press, 1977. — Bibl. — Index. — Includes the texts of constitutional documents.
ISBN 0-333-23108-2 : £20.00
(B77-24795)

342'.4'085 — Individuals. Effects of European Community law. *European Community countries*
European law and the individual / edited by F.G. Jacobs. — Amsterdam [etc.] ; Oxford : North-Holland Publishing Co., 1976. — xi, 211p ; 23cm.
'Papers presented at an annual workshop arranged by the University of London Institute of Advanced Legal Studies, with the support of the Ford Foundation, 1975' - Library of Congress Cataloging in Publication data.
ISBN 0-7204-0473-8 : £12.50
(B77-04653)

342'.41 — Great Britain. Constitutional law
De Smith, Stanley Alexander. Constitutional and administrative law / [by] S.A. de Smith. — 3rd ed. / revised by Harry Street, Barbara de Smith, Rodney Brazier. — Harmondsworth [etc.] : Penguin, 1977. — 729p ; 20cm. — (Foundations of law) (Penguin education)
Previous ed.: Harmondsworth : Penguin Education, 1974. — Index.
Pbk : £3.95
ISBN 0-14-080223-1
Also classified at 342'.41'06
(B77-24086)

342'.41'029 — Great Britain. Constitution, 1485-1968
Keir, *Sir* David Lindsay. The constitutional history of modern Britain since 1485 / by Sir David Lindsay Keir. — 9th ed. — London : A. and C. Black, 1975. — iii-viii,600p ; 23cm.
This ed. originally published: 1969. — Index.
£3.50
ISBN 0-7136-0939-7
(B77-00672)

342'.41'03 — Great Britain. Constitution. Reform. *Proposals*
Hailsham, Quintin Hogg, *Baron.* Elective dictatorship / [by] Lord Hailsham. — London : British Broadcasting Corporation, 1976. — 17p ; 21cm. — (The Richard Dimbleby lecture ; 1976)
'... broadcast on BBC 1 on Thursday, 14 October 1976' - title page verso.
ISBN 0-563-17254-1 Sd : £0.45
(B77-05288)

342'.41'06 — Great Britain. Administrative law
De Smith, Stanley Alexander. Constitutional and administrative law / [by] S.A. de Smith. — 3rd ed. / revised by Harry Street, Barbara de Smith, Rodney Brazier. — Harmondsworth [etc.] : Penguin, 1977. — 729p ; 20cm. — (Foundations of law) (Penguin education)
Previous ed.: Harmondsworth : Penguin Education, 1974. — Index.
Pbk : £3.95
ISBN 0-14-080223-1
Primary classification 342'.41
(B77-24086)

342'.41'066 — Tribunals. Organisations. *Great Britain. Council on Tribunals. Reports, surveys. Serials*
Council on Tribunals. The annual report of the Council on Tribunals ... — London : H.M.S.O.
1975-76 : for the period 1st August to 31st July. — [1977]. — vi,40p ; 25cm. — ([1976-77 H.C.] 236)
ISBN 0-10-223677-1 Sd : £0.85
(B77-11684)

342'.41'07 — Great Britain. Parliament. House of Commons. Members. Elections. Law. *For election agents*
Labour Party. Conduct of Parliamentary elections / [the Labour Party]. — [8th ed.] / [prepared by Donald Storer]. — London : The Party, 1977. — [11],128p : ill, forms ; 24cm.
Previous ed.: 1970?. — Index.
£1.75
(B77-26911)

342'.41'07 — Local authorities. Members. Elections. Expenditure by candidates. Limits. Law. *Great Britain. Statutes*
Great Britain. *Laws, statutes, etc. (Individual titles).* Representation of the People Act 1977 : Elizabeth II. 1977. Chapter 9. — London : H.M.S.O., [1977]. — Folder(4p) ; 25cm.
ISBN 0-10-540977-4 : £0.15
(B77-14622)

342'.41'082 — Immigration to Great Britain. Entry controls. Law. *Regulations*
Great Britain. *Home Office.* Statement of changes in immigration rules for control on entry / [Home Office]. — London : H.M.S.O.
Commonwealth citizens. — [1977]. — Sheet ([2]p) ; 25x16cm. — ([1976-77 H.C.] 238)
ISBN 0-10-223877-4 : £0.10
(B77-21011)

EEC and other non-Commonwealth nationals. — [1977]. — Sheet ([2]p) ; 25x16cm. — ([1976-77 H.C.] 240)
ISBN 0-10-224077-9 : £0.10
(B77-21012)

342'.41'082 — Immigration to Great Britain. Law
Evans, John Maxwell. Immigration law / by J.M. Evans. — London : Sweet and Maxwell, 1976. — xv,152p ; 19cm. — (Modern legal studies)
Index.
ISBN 0-421-20230-0 : £3.75
ISBN 0-421-20240-8 Pbk : £1.75
(B77-04027)

342'.41'082 — Immigration to Great Britain. Law. *Regulations*
Great Britain. *Home Office.* Statement of changes in immigration rules for control after entry / [Home Office]. — London : H.M.S.O.
Commonwealth citizens ... — [1977]. — Folder (3p) ; 25cm. — ([1976-77 H.C.] 239)
ISBN 0-10-223977-0 : £0.15
(B77-21009)

EEC and other non-Commonwealth nationals. — [1977]. — Folder (3p) ; 25cm. — ([1976-77 H.C.] 241)
ISBN 0-10-224177-5 : £0.15
(B77-21010)

342'.41'083 — British citizenship & British nationality. Law
Dummett, Ann. Citizenship and nationality / by Ann Dummett ; with a foreword by J.E.S. Fawcett. — London : Runnymede Trust, 1976. — 88,[1]p : ill ; 21cm.
Bibl.: p.85-88.
Sd : £1.50
(B77-26912)

342'.41'083 — British nationality. Law: British Nationality Act 1948. *Critical studies*
Great Britain. *Home Office.* British nationality law : discussion of possible changes ... / Home Office. — London : H.M.S.O., [1977]. — 26p ; 25cm. — (Cmnd.6795)
ISBN 0-10-167950-5 Sd : £0.60
(B77-15177)

342'.41'085 — Citizens. Rights. Law. *Great Britain. Bill of Rights. Proposals*
Wallington, Peter. Civil liberties and a bill of rights / [by] Peter Wallington and Jeremy McBride. — London (186 Kings Cross Rd, WC1X 9DE) : Cobden Trust, 1976. — 148p ; 21cm.
Bibl.: p.142-146.
ISBN 0-900137-10-x Pbk : £1.50
(B77-13571)

342'.41'085 — Human rights. Law. *Great Britain. Proposals. Inquiry reports*
Legislation on human rights : with particular reference to the European Convention : a discussion document. — [London] ([Whitehall, SW1A 2AP]) : [Home Office], [1976]. — [4], 38p ; 30cm.
Report of a working group representing various government departments.
Sd : Unpriced
(B77-13572)

342'.41'085 — Women. Civil rights. Law. Implementation. *Great Britain. Reports, surveys*
National Council for Civil Liberties. *Rights for Women Unit.* The equality report : one year of - the Equal Pay Act, the Sex Discrimination Act, the Equal Opportunities Commission / ... NCCL Rights for Women Unit ; [written by] Jean Coussins. — London : National Council for Civil Liberties, 1976. — 123p : ill ; 21cm.
ISBN 0-901108-61-8 Pbk : £1.00
(B77-13573)

342'.41'087 — Children. Law. *Great Britain*
Hall, *Sir* William Clarke. Law relating to children and young persons / [by] Clarke Hall and Morrison. — 9th ed. / consulting editor Joseph Jackson ; editors Margaret Booth, Brian Harris ; foreword by Sir George Baker. — London : Butterworth, 1977. — lvi,1295p : forms ; 26cm.
Spine title: Clarke Hall and Morrison on children. — Thumb indexed. — Previous ed.: published as 'Clarke Hall and Morrison's law relating to children and young persons' / by L. Goodman. 1972. — Index. — Includes the text of the relevant legislation.
ISBN 0-406-15807-x : Unpriced
(B77-32498)

342'.41'087 — Race relations. Law. *Great Britain. Race Relations Act 1976. Commentaries*
Great Britain. *Home Office.* Racial discrimination : a guide to the Race Relations Act 1976 / [prepared by the Home Office and the Central Office of Information]. — [London] ([Whitehall, SW1A 2AP]) : Home Office, 1977. — [5],53,[1]p ; 21cm.
Sd : Unpriced
(B77-28492)

342'.41'087 — Race relations. Law. *Great Britain. Race Relations Act 1976. Critical studies*
Macdonald, Ian Alexander, *b.1939.* Race relations : the new law / by Ian A. Macdonald. — London : Butterworth, 1977. — xvii,246p ; 26cm.
Index. — Contains the text of the Race Relations Act, 1976.
ISBN 0-406-28318-4 : £14.50
(B77-18630)

342'.41'087 — Race relations. Law. *Great Britain. Statutes*
Great Britain. *Laws, statutes, etc. (Individual titles).* Race Relations Act 1976 : Elizabeth II. 1976. Chapter 74. — London : H.M.S.O., [1976]. — [1],iv,67p ; 25cm.
ISBN 0-10-547476-2 Sd : £1.35
(B77-08883)

342'.41'087 — Sex discrimination. Law. *Great Britain*
Woodroffe, Geoffrey Frederick. Sex and race discrimination : new rights and new remedies / [by] G.F. Woodroffe. — [Guildford] ([Braboeuf Manor, Portsmouth Rd, St Catherine's, Guildford, Surrey]) : The College of Law, 1976. — [1],24p ; 22cm. — (College of Law. Crash course lectures : 1976)
ISBN 0-905835-31-x Sd : £0.75
(B77-05944)

342'.416'05 — Northern Ireland. Assembly. Membership. Disqualification. Criteria. Law. *Statutes*
Great Britain. *Laws, statutes, etc. (Individual titles).* Northern Ireland Assembly Disqualification Act 1975 : Elizabeth II. 1975. Chapter 25. — London : H.M.S.O., [1977]. — [1],15,[1]p ; 25cm.
'... printed, as amended ... The amendments are those in force on the 1st January 1977'.
ISBN 0-10-850402-6 Sd : £0.35
(B77-10265)

342'.42'07 — Local authorities. Members. Elections. Law. *England. For election agents*
Labour Party. Conduct of local elections (England and Wales) : Greater London, London Borough, County, District / [Labour Party]. — 9th ed. / [revised by Walter Brown]. — London : The Party, 1973. — [3],65p : form ; 22cm.
Previous ed: 1971?. — Index.
ISBN 0-900507-93-4 Sd : £0.20
(B77-14623)

342'.42'085 — Citizens. Rights & duties. *England*
What right have you got? : your rights and responsibilities as a citizen. — London : British Broadcasting Corporation.
Part 2 / [by] Francesca Greenoak ..., with contributions from ... [others] ; edited by John Thomas. — 1977. — 137,[5]p : ill, facsims ; 24cm.
'Published to accompany programmes 11-26 of a BBC radio series, first broadcast on Radio 3 ... on Thursday at 7.00 from 13 January 1977' title page verso. — Bibl.: p.[1]-[3].
ISBN 0-563-16117-5 Pbk : £1.35
(B77-10266)

342'.42'085 — Civil rights. Law. *England*
Street, Harry. Freedom, the individual and the law / [by] H. Street. — 4th ed. — Harmondsworth [etc.] : Penguin, 1977. — 346p ; 19cm. — (A Pelican original)
Previous ed.: 1972. — Index. — Previous control number ISBN 0-14-020646-9.
Pbk : £1.20
ISBN 0-14-020646-9
(B77-23239)

342'.42'087 — Children. Law. *England*
Children and the courts. — [Guildford] ([Braboeuf Manor, Portsmouth Rd, St Catherine's, Guildford, Surrey]) : The College of Law, 1976. — [3],79p ; 22cm. — (College of Law. Lectures : 1976)
' ... contains lectures given at a College of Law course held in September and October 1975 in Birmingham, London and Liverpool' - Introduction.
ISBN 0-905835-27-1 Pbk : £1.50
(B77-05945)

342'.42'0902633 — England. Local government. Law. *Statutes*
Great Britain. *Laws, statutes, etc. (Individual titles).* Local Government (Miscellaneous Provisions) Act 1976 : Elizabeth II. 1976. Chapter 57. — London : H.M.S.O, [1976]. — [1],iv,81p ; 25cm.
ISBN 0-10-545776-0 Sd : £1.35
(B77-07852)

342'.42'0902633 — England. Local government. Law. *Statutes. Texts with commentaries*
Great Britain. *Laws, statutes, etc. (Individual titles).* [Local Government Act 1974]. The text of the Local Government Act 1974 / edited by H. Howard Karslake. — London (115 Ebury St., SW1W 9QT) : Rating and Valuation Association, 1974. — xix,127p ; 22cm.
Cover title. — Spine title: Local Government Act 1974.
Pbk : £2.00
(B77-31777)

342'.669'03 — Nigeria. Constitution. Drafts. Amendment. *Proposals*
Dent, M J. Improving Nigeria's draft constitution : a constructive and detailed study with suggestions for amendment and improvement in the Constituent Assembly / by M.J. Dent. — Keele (42 The Covert, Keele [Staffs.]) : Dark Horse Publications, 1977. — [2],vi,75p ; 21cm.
ISBN 0-906128-00-5 Sd : £1.20
(B77-26913)

342'.6891'03 — Rhodesia. Constitution. *Proposals*
Great Britain. *Foreign and Commonwealth Office.* Rhodesia : proposals for a settlement / presented to Parliament by the Secretary of State for Foreign and Commonwealth Affairs ... — London : H.M.S.O., [1977]. — 24p ; 25cm. — (Cmnd.6919)
ISBN 0-10-169190-4 Sd : £0.45
(B77-28493)

342'.729'023 — West Indies. Constitutions, 1922-1968. *Texts. Collections*
Constitutional development of the West Indies, 1922-1968 : a selection from the major documents / [edited by] Ann Spackman. — St Lawrence, Barbados : Caribbean Universities Press ; Epping : Bowker, 1975. — xxxxiv,619p ; 23cm. — (The Caribbean history bibliographical and documentary series)
Bibl.: p.544-608. — Index.
ISBN 0-85474-030-9 : Unpriced
(B77-20119)

342'.7292 — Jamaica. Constitutional law
Barnett, Lloyd G. The constitutional law of Jamaica / [by] Lloyd G. Barnett. — Oxford [etc.] : Oxford University Press for the London School of Economics and Political Science, 1977. — xxxiv,468p ; 24cm.
Index.
ISBN 0-19-920077-7 : £18.00
(B77-30061)

342'.72983'03 — Trinidad and Tobago. Constitution. Amendment. Adaptation of British law. *Statutes*
Great Britain. *Laws, statutes, etc. (Individual titles).* Trinidad and Tobago Republic Act 1976 : Elizabeth II. 1976. Chapter 54. — London : H.M.S.O., [1976]. — Sheet (2p) ; 25x16cm.
ISBN 0-10-545476-1 : £0.08
(B77-08292)

342'.729841'02 — Dominica. Constitution. *Conference proceedings*
Dominica. *Constitutional Conference, 1977.* Report of the Dominica Constitutional Conference, London, May 1977 ... — London : H.M.S.O., [1977]. — 23p ; 25cm. — (Miscellaneous ; no.14(1977)) (Cmnd.6091)
ISBN 0-10-169010-x Sd : £0.45
(B77-30062)

342'.73 — United States. Constitutional law
Corwin, Edward Samuel. Edward S. Corwin's the Constitution and what it means today. — 13th ed. / revised by Harold W. Chase and Craig R. Ducat. — Princeton ; Guildford : Princeton University Press.
Supplement [1976] : Supreme Court decisions of 1973, 1974, 1975 and 1976 / by Harold W. Chase and Craig R. Ducat. — 1976. — vii, 284p ; 22cm.
Index.
ISBN 0-691-02756-0 Pbk : £2.95
(B77-18012)

Pritchett, Charles Herman. The American constitutional system / [by] C. Herman Pritchett. — 4th ed. — New York ; London [etc.] : McGraw-Hill, [1977]. — x,133p ; 21cm. — (Foundations of American government and political science)
This ed. published in the United States: 1976. — Previous ed.: New York : McGraw-Hill, 1971. — Bibl.: p.107-108. — Index.
ISBN 0-07-050889-5 Pbk : £3.75
(B77-12933)

342'.73'002643 — United States. Constitutional law. Decisions of United States. Supreme Court, to 1975. *Cases*
Cushman, Robert F. Leading constitutional decisions. — 15th ed. / [by] Robert F. Cushman. — Englewood Cliffs ; London [etc.] : Prentice-Hall, 1977. — xvi,464p ; 23cm.
Previous ed.: New York : Appleton-Century-Crofts, 1971. — Includes the text of the Constitution of the United States.
ISBN 0-13-527358-7 Pbk : £6.35
(B77-16788)

342'.73'029 — United States. Constitution. Interpretation, to 1975
Tugwell, Rexford Guy. The compromising of the Constitution (early departures) / [by] Rexford G. Tugwell. — Notre Dame ; London : University of Notre Dame Press, [1976]. — xi, 188p ; 21cm.
Index.
ISBN 0-268-00714-4 : £6.75
(B77-04028)

342'.73'085 — Negroes. Civil rights. Legal aspects. Policies of Republican Party (United States). *United States, 1861-1866*
Belz, Herman. A new birth of freedom : the Republican Party and freedmen's rights, 1861 to 1866 / [by] Herman Belz. — Westport, Conn. ; London : Greenwood Press, 1976. — xv,199,[1]p ; 22cm. — (Contributions in American history ; no.52)
Bibl.: p.183-192. — Index.
ISBN 0-8371-8902-0 : £13.75
(B77-19268)

342'.73'087 — Race relations. Law. Decisions of United States. Supreme Court. *United States, 1880-1970*
Wasby, Stephen Lewis. Desegregation from Brown to Alexander : an exploration of Supreme Court strategies / by Stephen L. Wasby, Anthony A. D'Amato and Rosemary Metrailer ; with a foreword by Victor G. Rosenblum. — Carbondale [etc.] : Southern Illinois University Press ; London [etc.] : Feffer and Simons, 1977. — xx,489p ; 25cm.
Index.
ISBN 0-8093-0805-3 : Unpriced
(B77-25473)

342'.94'02 — Australia. Constitution
Lane, P H. An introduction to the Australian constitution / by P.H. Lane. — Sydney [etc.] : Law Book Co. ; London : Sweet and Maxwell [etc.], 1975. — ix,282p ; 19cm.
Originally published: Sydney : Law Book Co., 1974. — Bibl.: p.229-233. — Index. — Includes the text of the Commonwealth of Australia Constitution Act 1900 with subsequent amendments.
ISBN 0-455-19244-8 Pbk : Unpriced
(B77-26914)

343 — PUBLIC LAW

343.04 — Tax avoidance. *Periodicals*

Tax planning international : the journal of tax incentives and fiscal opportunities. — London (2 Rothsay St., SE1 4UD) : Finax Publications Ltd.
Continues: Tax haven review.
Vol.3 - ; 1976-. — [1976]-. — 30cm.
Monthly. — p.61-80 in Apr. 1977 issue. — Pierced for binder. — 'New development index' (folder ([3]p.)) as insert.
Sd : £60.00 yearly
ISSN 0309-7900
(B77-25474)

343.09'44 — Motor vehicles. Engineering aspects. Standards. Law. *Reports, surveys*

Society of Motor Manufacturers and Traders. *Technical Department.* A summary of international vehicle legislation / prepared by SMM & T, Technical Department. — [London] : [Society of Motor Manufacturers and Traders].
Vol.5. — [1976]. — 274p in various pagings : ill ; 31cm.
In binder.
Ls : Unpriced
ISBN 0-900685-34-4 Set of 8 vols. : £130.00
(B77-01253)

343.09'44 — Motor vehicles. Standards. Legal aspects. *Reports, surveys*

British Standards Institution. *Technical Help to Exporters Section.* Motor vehicles and equipment : an international guide to regulatory, approval and testing organizations / [Technical Help to Exporters, British Standards Institution]. — Hemel Hempstead (Maylands Ave., Hemel Hempstead, Herts. HP2 4SQ) : Technical Help to Exporters, British Standards Institution, 1976. — vi,178p ; 22cm.
ISBN 0-903886-26-x Pbk : £5.00
(B77-15178)

343'.4'055 — Value-added tax. Administration. Harmonisation. Law. Secondary legislation. *European Community countries. Reports, surveys*

Great Britain. *Parliament. House of Commons. Select Committee on European Secondary Legislation, etc.* VAT : twenty-eighth report from the Select Committee on European Secondary Legislation, &c., session 1975-76, together with minutes of evidence and appendices. — London : H.M.S.O, [1976]. — x, 70p ; 25cm. — ([1975-76 H.C. 8-xxviii]) ([1975-76 H.C.] 272 i-iv)
ISBN 0-10-008516-4 Sd : £1.20
(B77-02128)

343'.41'01 — Military forces. Disaffection. Incitement. Law. *Great Britain, to 1975*

Young, Thom. Incitement to disaffection / by Thom Young, assisted by Martin Kettle. — [London] : [Cobden Trust], [1976]. — 117p ; 21cm. — (Cobden Trust. Studies)
ISBN 0-900137-08-8 Pbk : £0.75
(B77-06552)

343'.41'013 — Pensions appeal tribunals. Appeals against decisions of Great Britain. Department of Health and Social Security on assessment of disablement pensions of British military forces personnel. *Great Britain. Practical information*

Pensions appeal tribunals assessment appeals, notes for the guidance of appellants. — 7th ed. — London : H.M.S.O., 1976. — 11p ; 25cm.
Previous ed.: 197-?.
ISBN 0-11-390579-3 Sd : £0.25
(B77-10267)

343'.41'01402633 — British military forces. Discipline. Law. *Statutes*

Great Britain. *Laws, statutes, etc. (Individual titles).* Armed Forces Act 1976 : Elizabeth II. 1976. Chapter 52. — London : H.M.S.O., [1976]. — ii,53p ; 25cm.
ISBN 0-10-545276-9 Sd : £0.75
(B77-04029)

343'.41'015 — Great Britain. Army. Physically handicapped ex-servicemen. Superannuation. Law. *Prerogative instruments*

Great Britain. *Department of Health and Social Security.* Royal Warrant to amend the Royal Warrant of 19th September 1964, concerning pensions and other grants in respect of disablement or death due to service in the military forces during the 1914 World War and after 2nd September 1939 ... / Department of Health and Social Security. — London : H.M.S.O., [1977]. — 6p ; 25cm. — (Cmnd. 6763)
ISBN 0-10-167630-1 Sd : £0.25
(B77-16789)

343'.41'018411151 — Great Britain. Royal Air Force. Physically handicapped ex-servicemen. Superannuation. Law. *Prerogative instruments*

Great Britain. *Department of Health and Social Security.* Order by Her Majesty to amend the order of 24th September 1964, concerning pensions and other grants in respect of disablement or death due to service in the air forces during the 1914 World War and after 2nd September 1939 ... / Department of Health and Social Security. — London : H.M.S.O., [1977]. — 7p ; 25cm. — (Cmnd.6762)
ISBN 0-10-167620-4 Sd : £0.25
(B77-16790)

343'.41'034 — Great Britain. Government. Finance. Consolidated Fund. Law. *Statutes*

Great Britain. *Laws, statutes, etc. (Individual titles).* Consolidated Fund (No.2) Act 1976 : Elizabeth II. 1976. Chapter 84. — London : H.M.S.O., [1976]. — Sheet (2p) ; 25x16cm.
ISBN 0-10-548476-8 : £0.10
(B77-09591)

343'.41'037 — Great Britain. Government. Finance. Appropriations. Law. *Statutes*

Great Britain. *Laws, statutes, etc. (Individual titles).* Appropriation Act 1977 : Elizabeth II. 1976. Chapter 35. — London : H.M.S.O., [1977]. — [1],62p ; 25cm.
ISBN 0-10-543577-5 Sd : £1.10
(B77-27745)

343'.41'04 — Tax avoidance. Role of life assurance. *Great Britain*

Brown, Harry A. Life assurance : its tax implications and practical uses / by Harry A. Brown, Leonard H. Trimm. — London : Witherby, 1977. — [11],344,ix p : 1 ill, forms ; 23cm. — (Monument series)
Index.
ISBN 0-900886-20-x : £7.50
(B77-31061)

343'.41'04 — Taxation. Law. *Great Britain*

Brindley, Louis Peter Kirwan. The Budgets, 1974-1975, and other tax topics / [by] L.P.K. Brindley. — [Guildford] ([Braboeuf Manor, Portsmouth Rd, St Catherine's, Guildford, Surrey]) : The College of Law, 1975. — [1], 32p ; 22cm. — (College of Law. Crash course lectures : 1975)
ISBN 0-905835-12-3 Sd : £0.60
(B77-04654)

Brindley, Louis Peter Kirwan. Tax planning now / [by] L.P.K. Brindley. — [Guildford] ([Braboeuf Manor, Portsmouth Rd, St Catherine's, Guildford, Surrey]) : The College of Law, 1973. — [1],32p ; 22cm. — (College of Law. Crash course lectures : 1973)
ISBN 0-905835-35-2 Sd : £0.50
(B77-04655)

Godfrey, M. The Budget, 1972, and other tax topics / [by] M. Godfrey. — [Guildford] ([Braboeuf Manor, Portsmouth Rd, St Catherine's, Guildford, Surrey]) : The College of Law, 1972. — [1],23p ; 22cm. — (College of Law. Crash course lectures : 1972)
ISBN 0-905835-23-9 Sd : £0.45
(B77-04656)

Lewis, Mervyn, *b.1931 (Nov.).* British tax law : income tax, corporation tax, capital gains tax / [by] Mervyn Lewis. — Plymouth : Macdonald and Evans, 1977. — lxii,528p ; 22cm. — (Legal topics series)
Index.
ISBN 0-7121-0262-0 : Unpriced
ISBN 0-7121-0252-3 Pbk : £7.50
(B77-33684)

Pinson, Barry. Pinson on revenue law : comprising income tax, capital gains tax, development land tax, corporation tax, capital transfer tax, value added tax, stamp duties, tax planning. — 10th ed. / by Barry Pinson ; with sections on value added tax and development land tax by John Gardiner. — London : Sweet and Maxwell, 1976. — lxiii,666p ; 26cm.
Previous ed.: 1975. — Index.
ISBN 0-421-23000-2 : £14.00
ISBN 0-421-23010-x Pbk : £9.75
(B77-01254)

Snow, Raymond Francis. The Budget, 1973, and other tax topics / [by] R.F. Snow. — [Guildford] ([Braboeuf Manor, Portsmouth Rd, St Catherine's, Guildford, Surrey]) : The College of Law, 1973. — [1],22p ; 22cm. — (College of Law. Crash course lectures : 1973)
ISBN 0-905835-38-7 Sd : £0.50
(B77-04657)

Snow, Raymond Francis. The Budget, 1976, and other tax topics / [by] R.F. Snow. — [Guildford] ([Braboeuf Manor, Portsmouth Rd, St Catherine's, Guildford, Surrey]) : The College of Law, 1976. — [1],25p ; 22cm. — (College of Law. Crash course lectures : 1976)
ISBN 0-905835-48-4 Sd : £0.75
(B77-04658)

Tiley, John. Revenue law / by John Tiley. — London : Butterworth, 1976. — lii,853,[9],26p : forms ; 23cm.
Bibl.: p.li-lii. — Index.
ISBN 0-406-66586-9 : £16.00
ISBN 0-406-66587-7 Pbk : £10.00
(B77-00104)

343'.41'04 — Taxation. Law. *Great Britain. Finance Act 1976. Critical studies*

Confederation of British Industry. The Finance Act 1976, an explanatory guide / [Confederation of British Industry]. — London : C.B.I., 1976. — 34p ; 21cm.
ISBN 0-85201-127-x Sd : £2.00
(B77-08884)

Roberts, Derek. Finance Act 1976 taxation changes / prepared by [Derek Roberts for] the Society of Company and Commercial Accountants ... — Birmingham (11 Portland Rd, Edgbaston, Birmingham B16 9HW) : The Society, [1976]. — [3],9p ; 23cm.
ISBN 0-9503913-4-4 Sd : £0.50(free to members)
(B77-05946)

343'.41'0402632 — Direct taxation. Law. *Great Britain. Statutes. Collections. Serials*

Butterworths yellow tax handbook : setting out the amended text of the Income Tax Acts, Corporation Tax Acts and enactments relating to Capital Gains Tax as operative for. — London : Butterworth.
1976-77 : fifteenth ed. / editor David Roberts, assistant editor Moiz Sadikali. — 1976. — viii, 1035,76p ; 25cm. — (A Butterworth taxbook annual)
Previously published: as 'Butterworths tax handbook'. — Index.
ISBN 0-406-50992-1 Pbk : £8.60
(B77-04659)

Great Britain. *Laws, statutes, etc. (Collections).* The Taxes Acts : [as] in force from 6 April ... / Inland Revenue. — London : H.M.S.O.
1971. [1976 ed.] : up to and including the Finance Act 1976. — 1977. — 4v. ; 25cm.
Index.
ISBN 0-11-640848-0 Pbk : £17.50
(B77-10268)

343'.41'0402633 — Taxation. Law. *Great Britain. Statutes*

Great Britain. *Laws, statutes, etc. (Individual titles).* Finance Act 1977 : Elizabeth II, 1977. Chapter 36. — London : H.M.S.O., [1977]. — [1],iii,88p ; 25cm.
ISBN 0-10-543677-1 Sd : £1.60
(B77-26915)

343'.41'040264 — Taxation. Law. *Great Britain. Cases. Serials*

Simon, John Allsebrook, *Viscount Simon.* Simon's tax cases. — London : Butterworth.
1976 / consulting editors R.N.G. Harrison and J. Jeffrey-Cook ; editor Rengan Krishnan. — 1977. — iii,538p ; 24cm.
ISBN 0-406-06977-8 : £10.00
ISSN 0308-8030
(B77-10763)

343'.41'052 — Capital gains tax. Law. *Great Britain*

Di Palma, Vera. Capital gains tax / [by] Vera di Palma. — 3rd ed. — Plymouth : Macdonald and Evans, 1977. — ix,210p ; 19cm. — (The M. & E. handbook series)
Previous ed.: 1973. — Index.
ISBN 0-7121-0363-5 Pbk : £2.00
(B77-25475)

343'.41'052 — Capital gains tax. Law. *Great Britain. Serials*

'Taxation' key to capital gains tax. — London : Taxation Publishing Co.
[1976] : 10th ed. : Finance Act 1976 ed. / [by] K.R. Tingley and Percy F. Hughes. — [1976]. — [1],398p ; 22cm.
Cover title. — Thumb indexed. — Index.
ISBN 0-900734-41-8 Pbk : £4.25
(B77-05289)

343'.41'052 — Income tax. Law. *Great Britain*
Andrews, John M. Taxation of directors and employees : the law under Schedule E / by John M. Andrews. — London : Institute of Chartered Accountants in England and Wales, 1977. — xxiii,244p ; 22cm. — (Chartac taxation guides)
Index.
ISBN 0-85291-184-x Pbk : £5.95
(B77-33685)

343'.41'053 — Capital transfer tax. Law. *Great Britain*
Capital transfer tax. — [Guildford] ([Braboeuf Manor, Portsmouth Rd, St Catherine's, Guildford, Surrey]) : The College of Law, 1975. — v,124p ; 22cm. — (College of Law. Lectures : 1975)
'... the College organised a one-day course in London (twice) and at seven other centres' - Introduction.
ISBN 0-905835-28-x Pbk : £2.00
(B77-05290)

Capital transfer tax and development land tax : prescribed reading for law students issued by the College of Law. — [2nd ed.]. — London : Law Notes Lending Library, 1976. — vii,109p ; 22cm.
Previous ed.: published as 'Capital transfer tax'. Guildford : The College of Law, 1975.
ISBN 0-900516-07-0 Pbk : £1.00
(B77-12934)

Chapman, Anthony Leonard. Capital transfer tax / by A.L. Chapman. — 2nd ed. — Croydon : Tolley, 1977. — xxviii,352p ; 24cm.
Previous ed.: 1975. — Index.
ISBN 0-510-49340-8 Pbk : £5.75
(B77-26916)

343'.41'053 — Capital transfer tax. Law. *Great Britain. Serials*
Key to capital transfer tax. — London : Taxation Publishing Co.
[2nd ed.] : Finance Act 1976 ed. / [by] K.R. Tingley. — [1977]. — 334p ; 22cm. — ('Taxation' master key series)
Cover title. — Thumb indexed. — Previously published: as '"Taxation" key to capital transfer tax'. — Index.
Pbk : £4.25
(B77-16267)

343'.41'053 — Capital transfer tax. Law. *Great Britain. Statutes. Collections*
Great Britain. *Laws, statutes, etc. (Collections).* Capital transfer tax statutes, 1976-77 / edited by A.L. Chapman. — Croydon : Tolley, 1977. — viii,347p ; 24cm.
Cover title: Tolley's capital transfer tax statutes, 1976-77. — 'A Benn Group publication'. — Index.
ISBN 0-510-49346-7 Pbk : £5.25
(B77-17375)

343'.41'053 — Capital transfer tax. Law. *Great Britain. Statutes. Collections. Serials*
Great Britain. *Laws, statutes, etc. (Collections).* The Taxes Acts, the capital transfer tax : enactments in force from 27 March ... / Inland Revenue. — London : H.M.S.O.
1974. [1976 ed.] : up to and including the Finance Act 1976. — 1977. — 208,[40]p ; 25cm.
Index.
ISBN 0-11-640849-9 Pbk : £4.25
(B77-10269)

343'.41'053 — Capital transfer tax. Liability of vendors of private residences. Exemption. Law. *Great Britain*
Godfrey, M. Capital gains tax, the private residence exemption / [by] M. Godfrey. — [Guildford] : [Braboeuf Manor, Portsmouth Rd, St Catherine's, Guildford, Surrey] : The College of Law, 1974. — [1],18p ; 22cm. — (College of Law. Crash course lectures : 1974)
ISBN 0-905835-07-7 Sd : £0.50
(B77-09592)

343'.41'053 — Capital transfer tax. Tax avoidance. *Great Britain*
Ray, Ralph Paul. Practical capital transfer tax planning / [by] Ralph P. Ray, assisted by Margaret W. Ray, Nigel A. Eastaway. — London : Butterworth, 1977. — xxi,274p : forms ; 23cm. — (A Butterworth taxbook)
Index.
ISBN 0-406-53614-7 : £8.50
(B77-12935)

Wright, Edmund Kenneth. Capital transfer tax planning / by E. Kenneth Wright and Malcolm O. Penney. — 2nd ed. — London : Institute of Chartered Accountants in England and Wales, 1976. — 202p ; 21cm.
Previous ed.: 1975.
ISBN 0-85291-165-3 Pbk : £4.50
(B77-00673)

343'.41'054 — Development land tax. Law. *Great Britain*
Development land tax and the Community Land Act 1975. — [Guildford] ([Braboeuf Manor, Portsmouth Rd, St Catherine's, Guildford, Surrey]) : The College of Law, 1976. — v,86p ; 22cm. — (College of Law. Lectures : 1976)
'In March and early April of this year [1976] the College organised a one-day course at eight centres ... This booklet contains the lectures given at the course, revised to take account of changes made up to and including August 1, 1976' - Introduction.
ISBN 0-905835-17-4 Pbk : £2.00
Also classified at 346'.41'0432
(B77-09593)

Matthews, Janek. Development land tax / by Janek Matthews and T.A. Johnson. — London : Estates Gazette, 1977. — xxix,805p : forms ; 23cm.
Index. — Includes the text of the Development Land Tax Act 1976 and relevant statutory instruments.
£13.50
(B77-27746)

Tingley, Kenneth Raymond. Key to development land tax / [by] K.R. Tingley. — Development Land Tax Act, 1976 ed. — London : Taxation Publishing Co., [1976]. — 289p ; 22cm. — ('Taxation' master key series)
Cover title. — Spine title : 'Taxation' key to development land tax. — Thumb indexed.
Pbk : £4.25
(B77-02129)

343'.41'055 — Value-added-tax. Law. *Great Britain*
Value added tax. — [Guildford] ([Braboeuf Manor, Portsmouth Rd, St Catherine's, Guildford, Surrey]) : The College of Law, 1973. — iv,130p ; 22cm. — (College of Law. Lectures : 1972/73)
' ... The College of Law decided to put on a course designed specifically for the needs of solicitors and their staffs' - Introduction.
ISBN 0-905835-19-0 Pbk : £1.50
(B77-05947)

Willoughby, Peter Geoffrey. VAT and the solicitor / [by] P.G. Willoughby. — [Guildford] ([Braboeuf Manor, Portsmouth Rd, St Catherine's, Guildford, Surrey]) : The College of Law, 1972. — [1],29p : forms ; 22cm. — (College of Law. Crash course lectures : 1972)
ISBN 0-905835-05-0 Sd : £0.45
(B77-05948)

Willoughby, Peter Geoffrey. VAT up to date / [by] P.G. Willoughby. — [Guildford] ([Braboeuf Manor, Portsmouth Rd, St Catherine's, Guildford, Surrey]) : The College of Law, 1973. — [1],45p ; 22cm. — (College of Law. Crash course lectures : 1973)
ISBN 0-905835-34-4 Sd : £0.50
(B77-05949)

343'.41'057 — Stamp duties. Law. *Great Britain*
Monroe, John George. The law of stamp duties. — 5th ed. / by J.G. Monroe and R.S. Nock. — London : Sweet and Maxwell, 1976. — xxxii, 281p ; 26cm.
Previous ed.: / by J.G. Monroe. 1964. — Index.
ISBN 0-421-21580-1 : £15.00
(B77-05950)

343'.41'066 — Offshore natural gas & petroleum industries. Taxation. Law. *Great Britain*
Hayllar, R F. UK taxation of offshore oil and gas / [by] R.F. Hayllar, R.T. Pleasance. — London : Butterworth, 1977. — xii,212p : 1 ill ; 26cm.
Index.
ISBN 0-406-22066-2 : £16.50
(B77-24088)

343'.41'066 — Partnerships. Taxation. Law. *Great Britain*
Brindley, Louis Peter Kirwan. Tax and the professional partnership / [by] L.P.K. Brindley. — [Guildford] ([Braboeuf Manor, Portsmouth Rd, St Catherine's, Guildford, Surrey]) : The College of Law, 1976. — [1],30p ; 22cm. — (College of Law. Crash course lectures : 1976)
ISBN 0-905835-45-x Sd : £0.75
(B77-05291)

343'.41'067 — Companies. Taxation. Law. *Great Britain*
Bramwell, Richard. Taxation of companies / by Richard Bramwell ; based on 'Corporation tax' by John E. Talbot and G.S.A. Wheatcroft. — London : Sweet and Maxwell ; Edinburgh : Green. — (British tax encyclopedia)
4th cumulative supplement / by John Dick. — 1977. — [40]p ; 23cm.
ISBN 0-421-22110-0 Sd : Unpriced
(B77-21013)

343'.41'067 — Corporation tax. Law. *Great Britain. Serials*
'Taxation' key to corporation tax. — London : Taxation Publishing Co.
[1976] : Finance Act 1976 ed. / [edited by] T.L.A. Graham and Percy F. Hughes. — [1977]. — 355p ; 22cm.
Cover title. — Thumb indexed. — Index.
ISBN 0-900734-42-6 Pbk : £4.25
(B77-09594)

343'.41'07 — Consumer protection. Law. *Great Britain*
Fair trading and consumer protection. — [Guildford] ([Braboeuf Manor, Portsmouth Rd, St Catherine's, Guildford, Surrey]) : The College of Law, 1974. — [3],96p ; 22cm. — (College of Law. Lectures : 1973)
'... contains the lectures delivered at the one-day course on Fair Trading and Consumer Protection which was held in Liverpool and London in November 1973' - Introduction.
ISBN 0-905835-15-8 Pbk : £1.50
(B77-04660)

Woodroffe, Geoffrey Frederick. Consumer protection up-to-date : (including the enforcement of small claims) / [by] G.F. Woodroffe. — [Guildford] ([Braboeuf Manor, Portsmouth Rd, St Catherine's, Guildford, Surrey]) : The College of Law, 1974. — [1], 21p ; 22cm. — (College of Law. Crash course lectures : 1974)
ISBN 0-905835-10-7 Sd : £0.50
(B77-05951)

343'.41'07202633 — Restrictive practices. Law. *Great Britain. Statutes*
Great Britain. *Laws, statutes, etc. (Individual titles).* Restrictive Trade Practices Act 1977 : Elizabeth II. 1977. Chapter 19. — London : H.M.S.O., [1977]. — 5,[1]p ; 25cm.
ISBN 0-10-541977-x Sd : £0.25
(B77-26192)

343'.41'074 — Industries. Common ownership. Development. Financial assistance by government. Law. *Great Britain. Statutes*
Great Britain. *Laws, statutes, etc. (Individual titles).* Industrial Common Ownership Act 1976 : Elizabeth II. 1976. Chapter 78. — London : H.M.S.O., [1976]. — Folder (4p) ; 25cm.
ISBN 0-10-547876-8 : £0.15
(B77-11685)

343'.41'074 — Industries. Financial assistance by government. Limits. Law. *Great Britain. Statutes*
Great Britain. *Laws, statutes, etc. (Individual titles).* Industry (Amendment) Act 1976 : Elizabeth II. 1976. Chapter 73. — London : H.M.S.O., [1976]. — Sheet(2p) ; 25x16cm.
ISBN 0-10-547376-6 : £0.10
(B77-31778)

343'.41'075 — Weights & measures. Law. *Great Britain. Statutes*
Great Britain. *Laws, statutes, etc. (Individual titles).* Weights and Measures &c. Act 1976 : Elizabeth II. 1976. Chapter 77. — London : H.M.S.O., [1976]. — [2],26p ; 25cm.
ISBN 0-10-547776-1 Sd : £0.50
(B77-08885)

343'.41'076 — Farriers. Registration. Law. *Great Britain. Statutes*
Great Britain. *Laws, statutes, etc. (Individual titles).* Farriers (Registration) (Amendment) Act 1977 : Elizabeth II. 1977. Chapter 31. — London : H.M.S.O., [1977]. — Folder(4p) ; 25cm.
ISBN 0-10-543177-x : £0.15
(B77-25476)

343'.41'076 — Sea fisheries. Boundaries. Law. *Great Britain. Statutes*
Great Britain. *Laws, statutes, etc. (Individual titles).* Fishery Limits Act 1976 : Elizabeth II. 1976. Chapter 86. — London : H.M.S.O., [1976]. — [1],18p ; 25cm.
ISBN 0-10-548676-0 Sd : £0.35
(B77-11132)

343'.41'07602633 — Agricultural industries. Law. *Great Britain. Statutes*
Great Britain. *Laws, statutes, etc. (Individual titles).* Agriculture (Miscellaneous Provisions) Act 1976 : Elizabeth II. 1976. Chapter 55. — London : H.M.S.O., [1976]. — ii,39,[1]p ; 25cm.
ISBN 0-10-545576-8 Sd : £0.75
(B77-08886)

343'.41'077 — Coal industries. *Great Britain. National Coal Board. Law. Statutes*
Great Britain. *Laws, statutes, etc. (Individual titles).* Coal Industry Act 1977 : Elizabeth II. 1977. Chapter 39. — London : H.M.S.O., [1977]. — [1],18p ; 25cm.
ISBN 0-10-543977-0 Sd : £0.35
(B77-29286)

343'.41'077 — Natural gas & petroleum industries. Law. *Great Britain*
A **manual** of United Kingdom oil and gas law / edited by Terence Daintith and G.D.M. Willoughby. — London : Oyez Publishing [for] Thomson Scottish Petroleum Ltd, 1977. — lxxiii,525p : map ; 24cm.
Spine title: United Kingdom oil and gas law. — Index. — Includes the text of relevant legislation.
ISBN 0-85120-318-3 : £40.00
(B77-28494)

343'.41'078 — Nuclear engineering industries. Finance. Law. *Great Britain. Statutes*
Great Britain. *Laws, statutes, etc. (Individual titles).* Nuclear Industry (Finance) Act 1977 : Elizabeth II. 1977. Chapter 7. — London : H.M.S.O., [1977]. — [1],3,[1]p ; 25cm.
ISBN 0-10-540777-1 Sd : £0.25
(B77-14624)

343'.41'078 — Telephone answering machines. Hire. Contracts. Conditions. *Great Britain, 1973-1975. Comparative studies*
Bradbury Controls Limited. The use of telephone answering machines : a survey of the terms of contract stipulated by machine suppliers, 1973-1975 : report / by Bradbury Controls Ltd ... ; for Business Bureaux ... — London (P.O. Box 752, W6 0EF) : Business Bureaux, 1975. — [2],3,[2]p ; 24cm.
Sd : £1.25(£0.25 to members)
(B77-02853)

343'.41'082 — Advertising. Law. *Great Britain*
Woolley, Diana. Advertising law handbook / [by] Diana Woolley. — 2nd ed. — London : Business Books for the Institute of Practitioners in Advertising, 1976. — xiv,106p ; 24cm.
Previous ed.: 1973. — Bibl. — Index.
ISBN 0-220-66306-8 : £6.00
(B77-31062)

343'.41'082 — Consumer goods. Advertising. Law. *Great Britain. Trade Descriptions Act 1968. Reform. Proposals*
Great Britain. *Office of Fair Trading.* Review of the Trade Descriptions Act 1968 : a report / by the Director General of Fair Trading ; presented to Parliament by the Secretary of State for Prices and Consumer Protection ... — London : H.M.S.O., [1976]. — [1],iv,99p ; 25cm. — (Cmnd.6628)
ISBN 0-10-166280-7 Pbk : £1.35
(B77-05952)

343'.41'083 — Goods. Resale prices. Restrictive practices. Law. *Great Britain. Statutes*
Great Britain. *Laws, statutes, etc. (Individual titles).* Resale Prices Act 1976 : Elizabeth II. 1976. Chapter 53. — London : H.M.S.O., [1976]. — ii,18p ; 25cm.
ISBN 0-10-545376-5 Sd : £0.30
(B77-08293)

343'.41'08302633 — Prices. Control. Organisations. *Great Britain. Price Commission. Law. Statutes*
Great Britain. *Laws, statutes, etc. (Individual titles).* Price Commission Act 1977 : Elizabeth II. 1977. Chapter 33. — London : H.M.S.O., [1977]. — [1],ii,35p ; 25cm.
ISBN 0-10-543377-2 Sd : £0.60
(B77-26917)

343'.41'093 — Perishable food. International freight transport. Law. *Great Britain. Statutes*
Great Britain. *Laws, statutes, etc. (Individual titles).* International Carriage of Perishable Foodstuffs Act 1976 : Elizabeth II. 1976. Chapter 58. — London : H.M.S.O., [1976]. — ii,14p ; 25cm.
ISBN 0-10-545876-7 Sd : £0.35
(B77-08887)

343'.41'093 — Transport services. Finance. Law. *Great Britain. Statutes*
Great Britain. *Laws, statutes, etc. (Individual titles).* Transport (Financial Provisions) Act 1977 : Elizabeth II. 1977. Chapter 20. — London : H.M.S.O., [1977]. — Sheet (2p) ; 25x16cm.
ISBN 0-10-542077-8 : £0.10
(B77-26193)

343'.41'094 — Road traffic. Law. *Great Britain*
Treleaven, J. Seat belts, the breathalyzer, and other motoring topics / [by] J. Treleaven. — [Guildford] ([Braboeuf Manor, Portsmouth Rd, St Catherine's, Guildford, Surrey]) : The College of Law, 1976. — [1],19p ; 22cm. — (College of Law. Crash course lectures : 1976)
ISBN 0-905835-46-8 Sd : £0.75
(B77-04661)

Wilkinson, George Stephen. Wilkinson's road traffic offences. — 8th ed. / by P.J. Halnan. — London : Oyez Publishing.
Previous ed.: 1973.
Supplement to 1st August 1976. — 1976. — [4],82,[1]p ; 21cm.
ISBN 0-85120-308-6 Sd : £2.50
(B77-03447)

343'.41'09405 — Road traffic. Law. *Great Britain. Serials*
Kitchin, Leslie Deans. Kitchin's road transport law : a summary of the legislation affecting the construction, equipment and use of motor vehicles. — London : Butterworth.
1977 : [18th ed.] / edited by James Duckworth. — 1977. — ix,244p : ill, forms ; 22cm.
Index.
ISBN 0-406-26467-8 Pbk : £6.80
ISSN 0308-8987
(B77-33686)

343'.41'0948 — Minibuses. Use. Law. *Great Britain. Statutes*
Great Britain. *Laws, statutes, etc. (Individual titles).* Minibus Act 1977 : Elizabeth II. 1977. Chapter 25. — London : H.M.S.O., [1977]. — 5,[1]p ; 25cm.
ISBN 0-10-542577-x Sd : £0.25
(B77-26194)

343'.41'0948 — Public service vehicles. Experimental use. Law. *Great Britain. Statutes*
Great Britain. *Laws, statutes, etc. (Individual titles).* Passenger Vehicles (Experimental Areas) Act 1977 : Elizabeth II. 1977. Chapter 21. — London : H.M.S.O., [1977]. — 8p ; 25cm.
ISBN 0-10-542177-4 Sd : £0.25
(B77-26195)

343'.41'0948 — Road freight transport. Law. *Great Britain. Serials*
Lowe, David. The transport manager's handbook / [by] David Lowe. — London : Kogan Page.
1977 : [7th ed.]. — 1976. — 506p : ill, facsim, forms, map ; 23cm.
Bibl.: p.493-494. — Index.
ISBN 0-85038-441-9 : £6.75
ISSN 0306-9435
(B77-09595)

343'.41'096 — Merchant shipping. British law. *For British shipmasters*
Hopkins, Frederick Neville. Business and law for the shipmaster / by F.N. Hopkins. — 4th ed. / revised by G.G. Watkins. — Glasgow : Brown and Ferguson, 1977. — xiv,922p : ill, facsim, forms ; 22cm.
Previous ed.: 1974. — Index. — Includes the text of relevant legislation.
ISBN 0-85174-273-4 : £11.20
(B77-29278)

343'.41'097 — Aeroplanes. Flying. Statutory regulations. *Great Britain. For private pilots*
Civil Aviation Authority. Aviation law for applicants for the private pilot's licence / [Civil Aviation Authority]. — 4th ed. — London : C.A.A., 1977. — v,50p : ill ; 21cm. — (CAP ; 85)
Previous ed.: 1975.
ISBN 0-86039-031-4 Sd : £0.45
(B77-15753)

343'.41'097602632 — Civil aircraft. Navigation. Law. *Great Britain. Statutory instruments. Collections*
Civil Aviation Authority. Air navigation : the order and the regulations / [Civil Aviation Authority]. — London : C.A.A., 1976. — 1v. : ill, plans ; 32cm. — (CAP 393)
V,111p. in various pagings on publication. — In binder. — Tab indexed. — 'Published for the use of those concerned with air navigation, but not to be treated as authoritative'.
ISBN 0-86039-021-7 Ls : £8.00
(B77-07853)

343'.41'0977 — Airports. *Essex. Foulness. London Airport. Third site. Development. Organisations: Maplin Development Authority. Abolition. Law. Statutes*
Great Britain. *Laws, statutes, etc. (Individual titles).* Maplin Development Authority (Dissolution) Act 1976 : Elizabeth II. 1976. Chapter 51. — London : H.M.S.O., [1976]. — Folder(4 p) ; 25cm.
ISBN 0-10-545176-2 : £0.12
(B77-05292)

343'.41'0992 — Postal services. *Great Britain. Post Office. Members. Numbers. Law. Statutes*
Great Britain. *Laws, statutes, etc. (Individual titles).* Post Office Act 1977 : Elizabeth II. 1977. Chapter 44. — London : H.M.S.O., [1977]. — Sheet(2p) ; 25x16cm.
ISBN 0-10-544477-4 : £0.10
(B77-26196)

343'.411'054 — Real property. Valuation for rates. Exemption. Law. *Scotland. Coastal waters. Statutes*
Great Britain. *Laws, statutes, etc. (Individual titles).* Valuation and Rating (Exempted Classes) (Scotland) Act 1976 : Elizabeth II. 1976. Chapter 64. — London : H.M.S.O., [1976]. — Folder(4p) ; 25cm.
ISBN 0-10-546476-7 : £0.15
(B77-06553)

343'.411'076 — Agricultural industries. Crofting. Law. *Scotland. Highlands & Islands*
Crofters Commission. Guide to the Crofting Acts / the Crofters Commission. — Edinburgh : H.M.S.O., 1976. — 46p ; 21cm.
ISBN 0-11-491437-0 Sd : £0.65
(B77-05953)

343'.411'078 — Licensed premises. Licensing. Law. *Scotland. Statutes*
Great Britain. *Laws, statutes, etc. (Individual titles).* Licensing (Scotland) Act 1976 : Elizabeth II. 1976. Chapter 66. — London : H.M.S.O., [1976]. — [1],v,112p ; 25cm.
ISBN 0-10-546676-x Pbk : £1.85
(B77-08888)

343'.411'092 — Electricity supply industries. Finance. Law. *Scotland. Statutes*
Great Britain. *Laws, statutes, etc. (Individual titles).* Electricity (Financial Provisions) (Scotland) Act 1976 : Elizabeth II. 1976. Chapter 61. — London : H.M.S.O., [1976]. — Folder (4p) ; 25cm.
ISBN 0-10-546176-8 : £0.15
(B77-07210)

343'.411'0942 — Rights of way. Law. *Scotland*
Scottish Rights of Way Society. Right of way : a walker's guide to the law of right of way in Scotland / [Scottish Rights of Way Society]. — Revised ed. — Edinburgh (28 Rutland Sq., Edinburgh EH1 2BW) : The Society, 1977. — 31p ; 18cm.
Previous ed.: 1972.
ISBN 0-9502811-1-5 Sd : £0.25
(B77-16791)

343'.42'025 — Real property affected by public works. Compensation. Law. *England*
Boynton, John Keyworth. Compulsory purchase and compensation / [by] John K. Boynton. — 4th ed. — London : Oyez Publishing, 1977. — xlviii,302p ; 22cm. — (Oyez practice notes ; 53)

Previous ed.: 1974. — Index.
ISBN 0-85120-313-2 Pbk : £9.75
Primary classification 343'.42'025
(B77-21014)

343'.42'025 — Real property. Compulsory purchase. Compensation. Law. *England*
Holbrook, Richard George. Planning and compensation : some recent changes / by R.G. Holbrook. — [Guildford] ([Braboeuf Manor, Portsmouth Rd, St Catherine's, Guildford, Surrey]) : The College of Law, 1973. — [1],16p ; 22cm. — (College of Law. Crash course lectures : 1973)
ISBN 0-905835-39-5 Sd : £0.50
Primary classification 346'.42'045
(B77-05970)

343'.42'025 — Real property. Compulsory purchase. Law. *England*
Boynton, John Keyworth. Compulsory purchase and compensation / [by] John K. Boynton. — 4th ed. — London : Oyez Publishing, 1977. — xlviii,302p ; 22cm. — (Oyez practice notes ; 53)

Previous ed.: 1974. — Index.
ISBN 0-85120-313-2 Pbk : £9.75
Also classified at 343'.42'025
(B77-21014)

343'.42'04 — Taxation. Law. *England. State-of-the-art reviews*
Snow, Raymond Francis. Revenue law, 1976 / [by] R.F. Snow. — [London] : [Law Society], [1976]. — [1],28p ; 21cm. — (Law Society. Refresher lectures ; 1976)
'... delivered on 7th October, 1976' - p.1.
Sd : £0.75
(B77-26918)

343'.42'054 — Valuation for rates. Law. *England. Cases. Serials*
Ryde, Walter Cranley. Ryde's rating cases. — London : Butterworth.
Vol.1-17. Consolidated tables and index. — 1976. — 132p ; 25cm.
Index.
ISBN 0-406-89063-3 Pbk : £7.50
(B77-02854)

Vol.18 : 1971-76 / edited by David Widdicombe, George Bartlett, Matthew Horton. — 1976. — xii,413p ; 26cm.
Index.
ISBN 0-406-89018-8 : £23.00
(B77-07854)

343'.42'07 — Premises. Licensing. Law. *England. Statutes. Collections*
Great Britain. *Laws, statutes, etc. (Collections).* Paterson's licensing acts. — London : Butterworth : Shaw and Sons.
1977 : eighty-fifth ed. / by J.N. Martin. — [1976]. — lxxvii,2161,114p ; 20cm.
Index.
ISBN 0-406-33511-7 : £18.00
(B77-04662)

343'.42'085536800941 — Insurance brokers. Registration. Law. *Great Britain. Statutes*
Great Britain. *Laws, statutes, etc. (Individual titles).* Insurance Brokers (Registration) Act 1977 : Elizabeth II. 1977. Chapter 46. — London : H.M.S.O., [1977]. — ii,24,[1]p ; 25cm.
ISBN 0-10-544677-7 Sd : £0.50
(B77-28495)

343'.42'092 — Water rates. Equalisation. Law. *England. Statutes*
Great Britain. *Laws, statutes, etc. (Individual titles).* Water Charges Equalisation Act 1977 : Elizabeth II. 1977. Chapter 41. — London : H.M.S.O., [1977]. — [1],6p ; 25cm.
ISBN 0-10-544177-5 Sd : £0.25
(B77-28496)

343'.42'0998 — England. Law. *For journalism*
James, Anthony. Media and the law / by Anthony James. — Sale (39 Legh Rd, Sale, Cheshire) : Brennan Publications, 1977. — 32p ; 18cm. — (Media guide ; no.1 ISSN 0140-2056)
Bibl.: p.32.
Sd : £1.20
(B77-31063)

Richards, Anthony, *b.1936.* Law for journalists / [by] Anthony Richards. — Plymouth : Macdonald and Evans, 1977. — xviii,166p ; 19cm. — (The M. & E. handbook series)
Bibl.: p.158. — Index.
ISBN 0-7121-1240-5 Pbk : £2.25
(B77-31064)

343'.4234'052 — Income tax. Law. *Channel Islands. Serials*
Tolley's taxation in the Channel Islands and Isle of Man. — Croydon : Tolley.
1976 : [revised to include the laws at September 1976] / by Leslie J.P. Livens. — 1976. — [5], 90p ; 24cm.
Spine title: Taxation in the Channel Islands and Isle of Man.
ISBN 0-510-49342-4 Pbk : £2.25
Also classified at 343'.4279'052
(B77-03448)

343'.4279'052 — Income tax. Law. *Isle of Man. Serials*
Tolley's taxation in the Channel Islands and Isle of Man. — Croydon : Tolley.
1976 : [revised to include the laws at September 1976] / by Leslie J.P. Livens. — 1976. — [5], 90p ; 24cm.
Spine title: Taxation in the Channel Islands and Isle of Man.
ISBN 0-510-49342-4 Pbk : £2.25
Primary classification 343'.4234'052
(B77-03448)

343'.669'052 — Income tax. Law. *Nigeria*
Ola, C S. Income-tax law & practice in Nigeria / [by] C.S. Ola. — Ibadan ; Edinburgh [etc.] : Heinemann Educational, 1974 [i.e. 1977]. — x, 309p : forms ; 22cm. — (Heinemann studies in Nigerian law)
Published in Nigeria: 1974. — Index.
ISBN 0-435-89671-7 Pbk : £12.00
(B77-13574)

343'.73'025 — Real property affected by government activities. Compensation. Law. Theories. *United States*
Ackerman, Bruce A. Private property and the Constitution / [by] Bruce A. Ackerman. — New Haven ; London : Yale University Press, 1977. — ix,303p ; 22cm.
Index.
ISBN 0-300-02065-1 : £9.40
(B77-25477)

343'.73'072 — Business firms. Restrictive practices. Law. Economic aspects. *United States*
Posner, Richard Allen. Antitrust law : an economic perspective / [by] Richard A. Posner. — Chicago ; London : University of Chicago Press, 1976. — x,262p : ill ; 23cm.
Index.
ISBN 0-226-67557-2 : £10.20
(B77-01255)

343'.73'072 — Industries. Competition. Law. Economic aspects. *United States*
Elzinga, Kenneth Gerald. The antitrust penalties : a study in law and economics / [by] Kenneth G. Elzinga and William Breit. — New Haven ; London : Yale University Press, 1976. — xii, 160p : ill ; 22cm.
Index.
ISBN 0-300-01999-8 : £7.20
(B77-08889)

343'.73'078 — Construction industries. Law. *United States*
Stokes, McNeill. Construction law in contractors' language / [by] McNeill Stokes. — New York [etc.] ; London : McGraw-Hill, 1977. — xv, 285p ; 24cm.
'An "Engineering news-record" book' - cover. — Index.
ISBN 0-07-061635-3 : £14.65
(B77-31065)

343'.73'090264 — Public utilities. Regulation by government. Law. *United States. Cases*
Weiss, Leonard Winchell. Regulation, a case approach / [by] Leonard W. Weiss, Allyn D. Strickland. — New York ; London [etc.] : McGraw-Hill, 1976. — ix,242p : ill ; 23cm.
Index.
ISBN 0-07-069097-9 Pbk : £5.40
(B77-07855)

343'.773'099 — Mass media. Law. *Illinois*
Stonecipher, Harry W. The mass media and the law in Illinois / [by] Harry W. Stonecipher and Robert Trager ; foreword by Howard Rusk Long. — Carbondale [etc.] : Southern Illinois University Press ; London [etc.] : Feffer and Simons, 1976. — xv,207p ; 24cm. — (New horizons in journalism)
Index.
ISBN 0-8093-0788-x : £9.38
(B77-05954)

343'.934'034 — New Hebrides. Government. Budgeting. *Treaties between Great Britain & France*
Great Britain. *Treaties, etc. France, February 10, 1977.* Exchange of notes between the Government of the United Kingdom of Great Britain and Northern Ireland and the Government of the French Republic about the application of the exchange of notes of 29 August 1975 concerning the establishment of a Representative Assembly for the New Hebrides, London, 10 February 1977 ... — London : H.M.S.O., [1977]. — Folder(4p) ; 25cm. — (Treaty series ; no.45(1977)) (Cmnd.6819)
English and French text.
ISBN 0-10-168190-9 : £0.15
(B77-18013)

343'.94'08 — Trade practices. Law. *Australia. Trade Practices Act 1974. For business enterprise*
Taperell, G Q. Trade practices and consumer protection : a guide to the Trade Practices Act 1974 for businessmen and their advisers / by G.Q. Taperell, R.B. Vermeesch, D.J. Harland. — Sydney ; London [etc.] : Butterworth, 1975. — xi,274p ; 24cm.
Originally published: Sydney : Butterworth, 1974. — Bibl. — Index.
ISBN 0-409-38103-9 Pbk : £8.50
(B77-29280)

343'.94'0808 — Trade practices. Law. *Australia. Readings*
Australian trade practices : readings / edited by J.P. Nieuwenhuysen. — 2nd ed. — London : Croom Helm, 1976. — 317p : 1 ill ; 23cm.
Previous ed.: Melbourne : Cheshire, 1970. — Bibl.: p.303-312. — Index.
ISBN 0-85664-169-3 : £8.50
(B77-03449)

344 — SOCIAL LAW

344.04'6 — Damage associated with nuclear power. Third party liability. Law. *Organisation for Economic Co-operation and Development countries*
Nuclear Energy Agency. Nuclear legislation, analytical study, nuclear third party liability / [Nuclear Energy Agency]. — Paris : The Agency ; [London] : [H.M.S.O.], 1976. — 190p ; 24cm.
Spine title: Nuclear third party liability.
Pbk : £6.00
ISBN 92-64-11619-2
(B77-14127)

344.04'65 — Industrial equipment. Safety. Law. *Reports, surveys*
Equipment safety : an international survey / [translated from the German by the Technical Help to Exporters service of the British Standards Institution]. — Hemel Hempstead (Maylands Ave., Hemel Hempstead, Herts. HP2 4SQ) : Technical Help to Exporters, British Standards Institution, 1977. — 1v. ; 24cm.
Four hundred and fifty one p. in various pagings on publication. — In binder. — Tab indexed. — Translation of: 'Maschinenschutz international 1976'. Frankfurt : Maschinenbau-Verlag, 1976. — 'includes the first and second supplements issued in April and October 1976 ... ' - Preface to English edition.
ISBN 0-903886-25-1 Ls : £24.00
(B77-15179)

344'.4'0463 — European Community countries. Environment. Pollution. Law. *Comparative studies*
McLoughlin, James, *b.1921.* The law and practice relating to pollution control in the member states of the European communities : a comparative survey / by J. McLoughlin ; for Environmental Resources Limited. — London : Graham and Trotman for the Commission of the European Communities, 1976. — x,545p ; 23cm.
Index.
ISBN 0-86010-040-5 : £7.50
(B77-02855)

344'.41'01 — Industrial relations. Law. *Great Britain. Industrial Relations Act 1971. Critical studies*
Industrial Relations Act 1971. — [Guildford] ([Braboeuf Manor, Portsmouth Rd, St Catherine's, Guildford, Surrey]) : The College of Law, 1972. — v,64p ; 22cm. — (College of Law. Lectures : 1972)
'... the College of Law organised a one-day course on the Act for solicitors and their staffs in Manchester, Sheffield and London' - Introduction.
ISBN 0-905835-20-4 Pbk : £1.00
(B77-05955)

344'.41'011 — Employment. Law. *Great Britain*
Employment, dismissal and compensation. — [Guildford] ([Braboeuf Manor, Portsmouth Rd, St Catherine's, Guildford, Surrey]) : The College of Law, 1976. — vii,86p ; 22cm. — (College of Law. Lectures : 1976)
'More than 1,000 solicitors attended a course run by the College of Law at five centres in January and February 1976 and this booklet is based on the lectures given at that course' - Preface.
ISBN 0-905835-00-x Pbk : £2.00
(B77-05293)

Hepple, Bob Alexander. Employment law / by B.A. Hepple and Paul O'Higgins. — 2nd ed. — London : Sweet and Maxwell, 1976. — xxxix, 337p ; 25cm.
Previous ed.: published as 'Individual employment law'. 1971. — Bibl.: p.307-313. — Index.
ISBN 0-421-20800-7 Pbk : £7.00
(B77-00105)

Industrial Society. Legal problems of employment / [Industrial Society]. — 6th ed. — London : The Society, 1976. — [7],95p ; 25cm.
Previous ed.: 1973. — Index.
ISBN 0-85290-134-8 Pbk : £4.00
(B77-05294)

Larman Associates Limited. Concise guide to employment law / prepared ... by Larman Associates Ltd. — London (Tavistock House North, Tavistock Sq., WC1H 9HX) : [Larman Associates Limited], 1977. — 281p ; 18cm.
Index.
ISBN 0-9505093-1-0 Pbk : £3.50
(B77-31066)

Marsh, Graham Barrie. Employer and employee : a complete and practical guide to the modern law of employment / by G. Barrie Marsh. — London : Shaw and Sons, 1977. — xxxvi,397p ; 22cm.
Index.
ISBN 0-7219-0740-7 Pbk : £8.00
(B77-23240)

344'.41'011 — Employment. Law. *Great Britain. For management*
Urwick Group. Employment and the law : a management guide to recent legislation / written by the Urwick Group ... — London : Financial Times.
Chapter 1 : Recruitment, selection, training and promotion / [by] Richard Pearson and Frank Kenaghan. — [1976?]. — [2],37p ; 30cm.
ISBN 0-900671-69-6 Sp : Unpriced
(B77-33687)

344'.41'01102632 — Employment. Law. *Great Britain. Statutes. Collections*
Labour law statutes / edited by Peter Wallington. — London : Butterworth, 1977. — xii,493p : forms ; 24cm.
Index.
ISBN 0-406-67789-1 Pbk : £7.00
(B77-26919)

344'.41'01133 — Employment. Race relations. Law. *Great Britain. Race Relations Act 1976. Critical studies*
Incomes Data Services. The new race law and employment / [Incomes Data Services]. — London (140 Great Portland St., W.1) : I.D.S., 1976. — [5],93p ; 21cm. — (Incomes Data Services. Handbook series ; no.4 ISSN 0308-7085)
ISBN 0-905525-03-5 Pbk : £2.50
(B77-11686)

344'.41'012 — Industries. Personnel. Conditions of service. Law. *Great Britain*
Porter, Robert. Guide to employment conditions / [by] Robert Porter. — 2nd ed. — London : Godwin, 1977. — [6],153p ; 21cm.
Previous ed.: 1976. — Index.
ISBN 0-7114-3704-1 : £3.50
(B77-15180)

344'.41'0121 — Low-income personnel. Remuneration. Law. Enforcement. *Great Britain. Reports, surveys*
Winyard, Steve. The weak arm of the law? : an assessment of the new strategy of minimum wage enforcement / by Steve Winyard. — London : Low Pay Unit, 1976. — [2],16 leaves ; 30cm. — (Low pay papers ; no.13)
ISBN 0-905211-15-4 Sd : £0.50
(B77-11133)

344'.41'01255 — Redundancy payments. Rebates. Law. *Great Britain. Statutes*
Great Britain. *Laws, statutes, etc. (Individual titles).* Redundancy Rebates Act 1977 : Elizabeth II. 1977. Chapter 22. — London : H.M.S.O., [1977]. — Folder(4p) ; 25cm.
ISBN 0-10-542277-0 : £0.15
(B77-25478)

344'.41'01255 — Unemployment. Compensation. Law. *Great Britain*
Mesher, John. Compensation for unemployment / by John Mesher. — London : Sweet and Maxwell, 1976. — xvii,138p ; 19cm. — (Modern legal studies)
Bibl.: p.131-133. — Index.
ISBN 0-421-20340-4 : £3.00
ISBN 0-421-20350-1 Pbk : £1.75
(B77-04663)

344'.41'012596 — Personnel. Dismissal. Law. *Great Britain. Algorithms. For employers*
Kelway, John. An employer's guide to fair dismissal and the maternity provisions / [by] John Kelway. — London : Kogan Page, 1977. — 28p ; 30cm.
ISBN 0-85038-092-8 Sd : £1.50
(B77-17376)

344'.41'012596 — Personnel. Lay-offs & short time working. Law. *Great Britain*
Incomes Data Services. Lay-offs and short-time / [Incomes Data Services]. — London (140 Great Portland St., W.1) : I.D.S., 1976. — [5],77p ; 21cm. — (Incomes Data Services. Handbook series ; no.3 ISSN 0308-7085)
Index.
ISBN 0-905525-02-7 Pbk : £2.50(£1.50 to subscribers)
(B77-03450)

344'.41'012596 — Redundancy. Law. *Great Britain. Statutes. Collections. For management*
Redundancy source book / [edited by Incomes Data Services]. — London (140 Great Portland St., W.1) : I.D.S., 1977. — [2],123p ; 21cm. — (Incomes Data Services. Handbook series ; no.6 ISSN 0308-7085)
Pbk : £2.50
(B77-27747)

344'.41'014 — Women personnel. Maternity rights. Legal aspects. *Great Britain*
Coussins, Jean. Maternity rights for working women / by Jean Coussins. — London : National Council for Civil Liberties, [1976]. — [2],24p : 1 ill ; 22cm.
ISBN 0-901108-58-8 Sd : £0.30
(B77-07211)

344'.41'01487 — Factories. Women personnel. Working hours. Law. *Great Britain. Proposals*
National Council for Civil Liberties. Evidence to the Equal Opportunities Commission / [National Council for Civil Liberties] ; [report written] by Tess Gill. — London : N.C.C.L., 1977. — [3],18p ; 30cm. — (National Council for Civil Liberties. Reports ; no.17 ISSN 0306-8994)
ISBN 0-901108-63-4 Sd : £0.30
(B77-15181)

344'.41'0159 — Physically handicapped persons. Workplaces. Access. Law. *Great Britain. Statutes*
Great Britain. *Laws, statutes, etc. (Individual titles).* Chronically Sick and Disabled Persons (Amendment) Act 1976 : Elizabeth II. 1976. Chapter 49. — London : H.M.S.O., [1976]. — Sheet(2p) ; 25x16cm.
ISBN 0-10-544976-8 : £0.08
(B77-05956)

344'.41'0176138715 — Docks. Personnel. Employment. Law. *Great Britain. Statutes*
Great Britain. *Laws, statutes, etc. (Individual titles).* Dock Work Regulation Act 1976 : Elizabeth II. 1976. Chapter 79. — London : H.M.S.O., [1976]. — ii,32,[1]p ; 25cm.
ISBN 0-10-547976-4 Sd : £0.60
(B77-11134)

344'.41'017622338 — Natural gas & petroleum industries. Personnel. Employment. British law. *North Sea*
Kitchen, Jonathan. Labour law and off-shore oil / [by] Jonathan Kitchen. — London : Croom Helm, 1977. — 261,[4]p : ill, map ; 23cm.
Index.
ISBN 0-85664-395-5 : £14.95
(B77-08890)

344'.41'018927 — Industrial relations. Picketing. Law. *Great Britain. Fabian viewpoints*
Ralph, Chris. The picket and the law / [by] Chris Ralph. — London : Fabian Society, 1977. — [2],22p ; 22cm. — (Fabian research series ; 331 ISSN 0305-3555)
Bibl.: p.22.
ISBN 0-7163-1331-6 Sd : £0.60
(B77-18014)

344'.41'02 — Job release schemes. Law. *Great Britain. Statutes*
Great Britain. *Laws, statutes, etc. (Individual titles).* Job Release Act 1977 : Elizabeth II. 1977. Chapter 8. — London : H.M.S.O., [1977]. — Sheet(2p) ; 25x16cm.
ISBN 0-10-540877-8 : £0.10
(B77-14625)

344'.41'02 — Married women & widows. Social security benefits. Great Britain. Department of Health and Social Security. Social Security (Benefit) (Married Women and Widows Special Provisions) Amendment Regulations 1977. Drafts. *Great Britain. Reports, surveys*
National Insurance Advisory Committee. Social Security (Benefit) (Married Women and Widows Special Provisions) Amendment Regulations 1977 (S.I.1977 no.1484), report of the National Insurance Advisory Committee ... preceded by a statement made by the Secretary of State for Social Services ... — London : H.M.S.O., [1977]. — 5p ; 25cm. — (Cmnd. 6929)
ISBN 0-10-169290-0 Sd : £0.25
(B77-31779)

344'.41'02 — National insurance contributions. Surcharges. Law. *Great Britain. Statutes*
Great Britain. *Laws, statutes, etc. (Individual titles).* National Insurance Surcharge Act 1976 : Elizabeth II. 1976. Chapter 85. — London : H.M.S.O., [1976]. — Folder(4p) ; 25cm.
ISBN 0-10-548576-4 : £0.15
(B77-11687)

344'.41'02 — Persons with invalid dependants. Social security benefits. Great Britain. Department of Health and Social Security. Social Security (Invalid Care Allowance) Regulations 1976. Drafts. *Great Britain. Reports, surveys*
National Insurance Advisory Committee. Social Security (Invalid Care Allowance) Regulations 1976 (S.I. 1976 no.409), report of the National Insurance Advisory Committee ... preceded by a statement made by the Secretary of State for Social Services ... — London : H.M.S.O., [1976]. — 8p ; 25cm. — ([1975-76 H.C.] 271)
ISBN 0-10-227176-3 Sd : £0.20
(B77-02887)

344'.41'02 — Social security benefits. Great Britain. Department of Health and Social Security. Social Security (Claims and Payments) Amendment Regulations 1977. Drafts. *Great Britain. Reports, surveys*
National Insurance Advisory Committee. The Social Security (Claims and Payments) (Unemployment Benefit Transitory Provisions) Regulations 1977 (S.I.1977 no.1289) [and] the Social Security (Claims and Payments) Amendment Regulations 1977 (S.I.1977 no.2288), report of the National Insurance Advisory Committee ... preceded by a statement made by the Secretary of State for Social Services ... — London : H.M.S.O., [1977]. — 9p ; 25cm. — (Cmnd.6897)
ISBN 0-10-168970-5 Sd : £0.25
Also classified at 344'.41'024
(B77-33122)

344'.41'02 — Social security benefits. Law. *Great Britain*
Lowe, Robert, *b.1932.* Welfare law, some paths through the jungle / [by] R. Lowe. — [Guildford] ([Braboeuf Manor, Portsmouth Rd, St Catherine's, Guildford, Surrey]) : The College of Law, 1974. — [1],23p ; 22cm. — (College of Law. Crash course lectures : 1974)
ISBN 0-905835-41-7 Sd : £0.50
(B77-05957)

Welfare law and practice. — [Guildford] ([Braboeuf Manor, Portsmouth Rd, St Catherine's, Guildford, Surrey]) : The College of Law, 1975. — iii,80p ; 22cm. — (College of Law. Lectures : 1975)
'To meet the demand for some basic instruction in welfare law matters the College of Law, in association with the Legal Action Group ran an introductory one day course in 1974 ... held in London, Birmingham, Manchester and Leeds ... ' - Introduction.
ISBN 0-905835-18-2 Pbk : £1.50
(B77-05958)

344'.41'02 — Social security. Great Britain. Department of Health and Social Security. Social Security (Miscellaneous Amendments) Regulation 1976. Drafts. *Great Britain. Reports, surveys*
National Insurance Advisory Committee. Social Security (Miscellaneous Amendments) Regulations 1976 (S.I. 1976 no.1736), report of the National Insurance Advisory Committee ... preceded by a statement made by the Secretary of State for Social Services ... — London : H.M.S.O., [1976]. — Folder (3p) ; 25cm. — ([1975-76 H.C.] 667)
ISBN 0-10-008846-5 : £0.12
(B77-02888)

344'.41'02 — Supplementary benefits. Law. *Great Britain*
Legal Action Group. A lawyer's guide to supplementary benefit / Legal Action Group. — London (28a Highgate Rd, NW5 1NS) : L.A.G., 1976. — [2],70p ; 21cm. — (Social law & practice guides ; no.3 ISSN 0307-3483)
Index.
ISBN 0-905099-02-8 Sd : £1.50
(B77-08891)

344'.41'0202633 — Supplementary benefits. Law. *Great Britain. Statutes*
Great Britain. *Laws, statutes, etc. (Individual titles).* Supplementary Benefit (Amendment) Act 1976 : Elizabeth II. 1976. Chapter 56. — London : H.M.S.O., [1976]. — Folder (4p) ; 25cm.
ISBN 0-10-545676-4 : £0.15
(B77-07212)

Great Britain. *Laws, statutes, etc. (Individual titles).* Supplementary Benefits Act 1976 : Elizabeth II. 1976. Chapter 71. — London : H.M.S.O., [1976]. — [1],iii,59p ; 25cm.
ISBN 0-10-547176-3 Sd : £1.10
(B77-08892)

344'.41'0226 — Non-contributory invalidity pensions. Great Britain. Department of Health and Social Security. Social Security (Non-Contributory Invalidity Pension) Amendment Regulations, 1977. Drafts. *Great Britain. Reports, surveys*
National Insurance Advisory Committee. Social Security (Non-Contributory Invalidity Pension) Amendment Regulations 1977 (S.I.1977 no.1312), report of the National Insurance Advisory Committee ... preceded by a statement made by the Secretary of State for Social Services ... — London : H.M.S.O., [1977]. — 11p ; 25cm. — (Cmnd.6900)
ISBN 0-10-169000-2 Sd : £0.25
(B77-33123)

344'.41'023 — State superannuation schemes. Contracting-out. Great Britain. Department of Health and Social Security. Contracted-out Employment (Transitional Arrangements) Regulations 1977. Drafts. *Great Britain. Reports, surveys*
Great Britain. *Occupational Pensions Board.* The Contracted-out Employment (Transitional Arrangements) Regulations 1977 (S.I. no.1615), report of the Occupational Pensions Board preceded by a statement by the Secretary of State for Social Services ... — London : H.M.S.O., [1977]. — 7p ; 25cm. — (Cmnd. 6961)
ISBN 0-10-169610-8 Sd : £0.25
(B77-33124)

344'.41'023 — Superannuation schemes. Great Britain. Department of Health and Social Security. Occupational Pension Schemes (Preservation of Benefit) Amendment Regulations 1977. Drafts. *Great Britain. Reports, surveys*
Great Britain. *Occupational Pensions Board.* The Occupational Pension Schemes (Preservation of Benefit) Amendment Regulations 1977 (S.I.1977 no.1187), report of the Occupational Pensions Board ... preceded by a statement by the Secretary of State for Social Services ... — London : H.M.S.O., [1977]. — 7p ; 25cm. — ([1976-77 H.C.] 454)
ISBN 0-10-245477-9 Sd : £0.25
(B77-33125)

344'.41'023 — Superannuation schemes. Law. *Great Britain. Social Security Pensions Act 1975*
National Association of Pension Funds. Social Security Pensions Act 1975 / [National Association of Pension Funds]. — [Croydon] ([Prudential House, Wellesley Rd, Croydon CR0 2AD]) : [The Association], [1976]. — [1], 14p ; 21cm. — (Notes on pensions ; no.3 ISSN 0309-006x)
ISBN 0-905796-02-0 Sd : £0.50(£0.25 to members)
(B77-01256)

344'.41'024 — Unemployment benefits. Payment. Frequency. Great Britain. Department of Health and Social Security. Social Security (Claims and Payments) (Unemployment Benefit Transitory Provisions) Regulations 1977. Drafts. *Great Britain. Reports, surveys*
National Insurance Advisory Committee. The Social Security (Claims and Payments) (Unemployment Benefit Transitory Provisions) Regulations 1977 (S.I.1977 no.1289) [and] the Social Security (Claims and Payments) Amendment Regulations 1977 (S.I.1977 no.2288), report of the National Insurance Advisory Committee ... preceded by a statement made by the Secretary of State for Social Services ... — London : H.M.S.O., [1977]. — 9p ; 25cm. — (Cmnd.6897)
ISBN 0-10-168970-5 Sd : £0.25
Primary classification 344'.41'02
(B77-33122)

344'.41'0321 — Private medical services. Law. *Great Britain. Statutes*
Great Britain. *Laws, statutes, etc. (Individual titles).* Health Services Act 1976 : Elizabeth II. 1976. Chapter 83. — London : H.M.S.O., [1976]. — ii,37,[1]p ; 25cm.
ISBN 0-10-548376-1 Sd : £0.60
(B77-11688)

344'.41'0327 — Children. Care. Law. *Great Britain. Children Act 1975. Critical studies*
Mumford, Gilbert Henry Francis. A guide to the Children Act 1975 / by Gilbert H.F. Mumford and T.J. Selwood. — [1st ed.] revised reprint. — London : Shaw and Sons, 1976. — xvi,44p ; 19cm.
First ed. originally published: 1976.
ISBN 0-7219-0661-3 Sd : £0.70
(B77-11689)

344'.41'0327 — Children. Care. Law. Great Britain. Parliament. House of Commons. Children Bill. Session 1974-1975. *Great Britain. Critical studies*
British Association of Social Workers. Analysis of Children Bill / British Association of Social Workers. — Birmingham (16 Kent St., Birmingham B5 6RD) : The Association, [1976]. — 1v. ; 30cm.
'The Bill analysed is as amended in the House of Lords prior to consideration in the House of Commons'. — [1],v,39 leaves in folder.
ISBN 0-900102-08-x : £0.75
(B77-05959)

344'.41'041 — National health services. General practitioners. Practical experience. Law. *Great Britain. Statutes*
Great Britain. *Laws, statutes, etc. (Individual titles).* National Health Service (Vocational Training) Act 1976 : Elizabeth II. 1976. Chapter 59. — London : H.M.S.O., [1976]. — Folder (4p) ; 25cm.
ISBN 0-10-545976-3 : £0.15
(B77-09596)

344'.41'042 — Controlled drugs. Law. *Great Britain*
Lydiate, P W H. The law relating to the misuse of drugs / [by] P.W.H. Lydiate. — London : Butterworth, 1977. — xviii,152p ; 22cm.
Index.
ISBN 0-406-27802-4 Pbk : £4.50
(B77-08294)

344'.41'042 — Food. Standards. Law. *Great Britain*
Pearson, David, *b.1919.* Concise guide to food legislation / [by] D. Pearson. — Weybridge ([St George's Ave., Weybridge, Surrey KT13 0DE]) : University of Reading, National College of Food Technology, 1976. — [3],38 leaves ; 30cm.
Index.
ISBN 0-7049-0477-2 Sd : £1.30
(B77-14128)

344'.41'042 — Food. Standards. Law. *Great Britain, 1875-1975. Conference proceedings*
Food quality and safety : a century of progress : proceedings of the symposium celebrating the centenary of the Sale of Food and Drugs Act 1875, London, October 1975, chairman Lord Zuckerman. — London : H.M.S.O., 1976. — vi, 243p ; 21cm.
At head of title: Ministry of Agriculture, Fisheries and Food.
ISBN 0-11-240626-2 Pbk : £5.00
(B77-08893)

344'.41'042 — Household electric equipment. Safety. Standards. Law. *Great Britain. Electrical Equipment (Safety) Regulations 1975 & Electrical Equipment (Safety) (Amendment) Regulations 1976. For manufacturing*
Great Britain. *Department of Prices and Consumer Protection.* Administrative guidance on the Electrical Equipment (Safety) Regulations 1975 and the Electrical Equipment (Safety) (Amendment) Regulations 1976 / Department of Prices and Consumer Protection. — London : H.M.S.O., 1977. — [3],64p : ill ; 30cm.
ISBN 0-11-511831-4 Sd : £1.50
(B77-15754)

344'.41'0463 — Great Britain. Environment. Pollution. Law
McLoughlin, James, *b.1921.* The law and practice relating to pollution control in the United Kingdom / by J. McLoughlin ; for Environmental Resources Limited. — London : Graham and Trotman for the Commission of the European Communities, 1976. — xxxiii, 386p : ill ; 23cm.
Index.
ISBN 0-86010-037-5 : £7.50
(B77-02856)

344'.41'046302632 — Great Britain. Environment. Pollution. Law. *Statutes. Collections. Texts with commentaries*
Control of pollution encyclopaedia / editor J.F. Garner ; assistant editor D.J. Harris. — London : Butterworth, 1977. — 1v. ; 26cm.
Five hundred and seventy three p. in various pagings on publication. — Tab indexed. — Index.
ISBN 0-406-20508-6 Ls : £33.00
(B77-14129)

344'.41'0465 — Factories. Industrial health & industrial safety. Law. *Great Britain. Factories Act 1961*
Great Britain. *Health and Safety Executive.* The Factories Act 1961, a short guide / Health & Safety Executive. — 2nd ed. — [London] : H.M.S.O., 1976. — 22,[1]p ; 24x9cm.
Previous ed.: issued by the Ministry of Labour. 1962.
ISBN 0-11-881111-8 Sd : £0.15
(B77-10270)

344'.41'0465 — Industrial health & industrial safety. Law. *Great Britain. Health and Safety at Work etc. Act 1974. For higher education institutions*
Phillips, David, *b.1923.* Health and Safety at Work Act, implications for colleges / by D. Phillips. — London : Association of Colleges for Further and Higher Education, [1976]. — 12,[1]p ; 21cm.
Delivered at the Summer Meeting of the Association of Colleges for Further and Higher Education, Brighton, June 9th, 10th and 11th, 1976.
Sd : £0.25
(B77-16792)

344'.41'0465 — Mining & quarrying. Safety measures. Law. *Great Britain*
Great Britain. *Department of Trade and Industry.* The law relating to safety and health in mines and quarries / Department of Trade and Industry. — 3rd ed. — London : H.M.S.O.

Previous ed.: published as 'Mines and Quarries Act 1954, the law relating to safety and health' / issued by the Ministry of Power. 1964-65.
Part 1, 2 and 3. Supplement / Health and Safety Executive. — 1977. — v,89p ; 25cm.
Index.
ISBN 0-11-880508-8 Pbk : £1.20
(B77-08894)

Part 4 : Quarries. Supplement no.1 / Health and Safety Executive. — 1976. — 22,[1]p ; 25cm.
ISBN 0-11-880489-8 Sd : £0.25
(B77-21015)

Great Britain. *Health and Safety Executive.* The law relating to safety and health in mines and quarries / Health and Safety Executive. — Consolidated ed. — London : H.M.S.O.
Part 4 and Supplement no.1 : Quarries. — 1976. — iv,216p : forms ; 24cm.
Previous ed.: i.e. 3rd ed. / issued by the Department of Trade and Industry. 1972. — Index. — 'Extracts from the Mines and Quarries Act 1954, the Mines and Quarries (Tips) Act 1969, Regulations and Orders made under these Acts and Approved Specifications and Procedures'.
ISBN 0-11-880488-x Pbk : £3.00
(B77-09597)

344'.41'0465 — Safety representatives & safety committees. Law. *Great Britain. Statutory instruments. Texts with commentaries*
Great Britain. *Health and Safety Commission.* Safety representatives and safety committees / Health and Safety Commission. — [London] : H.M.S.O., 1977. — [1],48,[1]p ; 21x10cm. — (Health and safety at work)
ISBN 0-11-880335-2 Sd : £0.35
(B77-25479)

344'.41'047 — Merchant shipping. Safety measures. Law. *Great Britain. Statutes*
Great Britain. *Laws, statutes, etc. (Individual titles).* Merchant Shipping (Safety Convention) Act 1977 : Elizabeth II. 1977. Chapter 24. — London : H.M.S.O., [1977]. — Folder(4p) ; 25cm.
ISBN 0-10-542477-3 : £0.15
(B77-26197)

344'.41'047 — Motorcyclists. Crash helmets. Compulsory wearing. Exemption of Sikhs. Law. *Great Britain. Statutes*
Great Britain. *Laws, statutes, etc. (Individual titles).* Motor-Cycle Crash Helmets (Religious Exemption) Act 1976 : Elizabeth II. 1976. Chapter 62. — London : H.M.S.O., [1976]. — Sheet(2p) ; 25x15cm.
ISBN 0-10-546276-4 : £0.10
(B77-11690)

344'.41'049 — Livestock. Diseases. Law. *Great Britain. Statutory instruments. Collections*
Great Britain. *Statutory instruments.* Handbook of orders relating to diseases of animals : orders made by the Ministry of Agriculture, Fisheries and Food under the Diseases of Animals Acts. — 3rd ed. — London : H.M.S.O.
Previous ed.: 1968.
Supplement. No.1. — 1976. — 351p in various pagings : forms ; 25cm.
'(also 5th supplement to the Handbook published in 1951) (and 3rd supplement to the Handbook published in 1968)'.
ISBN 0-11-241059-6 Ls : £3.75
(B77-05960)

344'.41'0537 — Buildings. Fire protection. Law. *Great Britain*
Great Britain. *Home Office.* Guides to the Fire Precautions Act 1971 / Home Office [and] Scottish Home and Health Department. — London : H.M.S.O.
3 : Offices, shops and railway premises. — 1977. — iv,49p ; 21cm.
ISBN 0-11-340445-x Sd : £0.85
(B77-25480)

344'.41'0542 — Gambling. Law. Organisations. *Great Britain. Gaming Board for Great Britain. Reports, surveys. Serials*
Gaming Board for Great Britain. Report of the Gaming Board for Great Britain ... — London : H.M.S.O.
1976. — [1977]. — 50p : 1 ill ; 25cm. — ([1976-77 H.C.]253)
ISBN 0-10-225377-3 Sd : £0.90
(B77-12374)

344'.41'097 — Performing arts. Legal aspects. *Great Britain*
Cotterell, Leslie E. Performance / [by] Leslie E. Cotterell. — Eastbourne (P.O. Box 64, Eastbourne, E. Sussex) : John Offord (Publications) Ltd, 1977. — 368p ; 22cm.
Index.
ISBN 0-903931-14-1 : £6.75
ISBN 0-903931-12-5 Pbk : £5.25
(B77-28497)

344'.411'03288 — Victims of crimes. Compensation by offenders. Law. *Scotland. Inquiry reports*
Reparation by the offender to the victim in Scotland : report by the Committee appointed by the Secretary of State for Scotland and the Lord Advocate ... / (chairman Lord Dunpark). — Edinburgh : H.M.S.O., [1977]. — iii,140p ; 25cm. — (Cmnd.6802)
At head of title: Scottish Home and Health Department.
ISBN 0-10-168020-1 Pbk : £2.00
(B77-21767)

344'.411'042 — Food. Processing. Unhygienic factories. Closure. Law. *Scotland. Statutes*
Great Britain. *Laws, statutes, etc. (Individual titles).* Control of Food Premises (Scotland) Act 1977 : Elizabeth II. 1977. Chapter 28. — London : H.M.S.O., [1977]. — 5,[1]p ; 25cm.
ISBN 0-10-542877-9 Sd : £0.25
Primary classification 344'.411'042
(B77-28498)

344'.411'042 — Unhygienic food shops. Closure. Law. *Scotland. Statutes*
Great Britain. *Laws, statutes, etc. (Individual titles).* Control of Food Premises (Scotland) Act 1977 : Elizabeth II. 1977. Chapter 28. — London : H.M.S.O., [1977]. — 5,[1]p ; 25cm.
ISBN 0-10-542877-9 Sd : £0.25
Also classified at 344'.411'042
(B77-28498)

344'.411'078 — Teachers. Retiring age. Law. *Scotland. Statutes*
Great Britain. *Laws, statutes, etc. (Individual titles).* Retirement of Teachers (Scotland) Act 1976 : Elizabeth II. 1976. Chapter 65. — London : H.M.S.O., [1976]. — Sheet(2p) ; 25x15cm.
ISBN 0-10-546576-3 : £0.10
(B77-09598)

344'.416'01283 — Agricultural industries. Personnel. Remuneration. Regulation. Law. *Northern Ireland. Agricultural Wages (Regulation) Act (Northern Ireland) 1939. Administration. Reports, surveys. Serials*
Report of proceedings under the Agricultural Wages (Regulation) Act (Northern Ireland) 1939 for the two years ended 31st December / Department of Agriculture [Northern Ireland]. — Belfast : H.M.S.O.
1975. — [1976]. — 10p ; 25cm.
ISBN 0-337-05169-0 Sd : £0.22
(B77-05295)

344'.417'0463 — Ireland (Republic). Environment. Pollution. Law
Scannell, Yvonne. The law and practice relating to pollution control in Ireland / by Yvonne Scannell ; for Environmental Resources Limited. — London : Graham and Trotman for the Commission of the European Communities, 1976. — xix,223p : map ; 23cm.
Index.
ISBN 0-86010-031-6 : £7.50
(B77-03451)

344'.42'010264 — Industrial relations. Law. *England. Cases. Serials*
Industrial cases, reports : (incorporating reports of restrictive practices cases). — London (3 Stone Buildings, Lincoln's Inn, WC2A 3XN) : Incorporated Council of Law Reporting for England and Wales.
1976 / [editors C.J. Ellis and H. Jellie]. — 1976. — xvi,586p ; 25cm.
Index.
ISBN 0-85289-009-5 : Unpriced
ISSN 0306-2163
(B77-12936)

344'.42'010269 — Industrial tribunals. Procedure. *England*
Goodman, Michael Jack. Industrial tribunals' procedure / by Michael J. Goodman. — London : Oyez Publishing, 1976. — xviii,99p ; 22cm.
Index. — Includes the text of the relevant Statutory Instruments.
ISBN 0-85120-310-8 Pbk : £3.75
(B77-04030)

344'.42'02 — Social security benefits. Law. *England. State-of-the-art reviews*
Ibbett, J P. Welfare law / [by] J.P. Ibbett. — [London] : [Law Society], [1976]. — [1],30p ; 21cm. — (Law Society. Refresher lectures ; 1976)
Sd : £0.75
(B77-26920)

344'.42'031 — Welfare work. Law. *England*
Raisbeck, B L. Law and the social worker / [by] B.L. Raisbeck. — London [etc.] : Macmillan, 1977. — x,153p ; 23cm.
Bibl.: p.149-150. — Index.
ISBN 0-333-19110-2 : £7.95
ISBN 0-333-19111-0 Pbk : Unpriced
(B77-22452)

344'.42'032102633 — National health services. Law. *England. Statutes*
Great Britain. *Laws, statutes, etc. (Individual titles).* National Health Service Act 1977 : Elizabeth II. 1977. Chapter 49. — London : H.M.S.O., [1977]. — [1],vi,130p ; 25cm.
ISBN 0-10-544977-6 Sd : £2.35
(B77-28499)

344'.42'03288 — Victims of crimes. Compensation. Law. *England*
Chiswell, P G. Compensation for victims of crime / [by] P.G. Chiswell. — [Guildford] ([Braboeuf Manor, Portsmouth Rd, St Catherine's, Guildford, Surrey]) : The College of Law, 1973. — [1],24p ; 22cm. — (College of Law. Crash course lectures : 1973)
ISBN 0-905835-40-9 Sd : £0.50
(B77-05961)

344'.42'044 — Mentally ill persons. Treatment. Law. *England. Mental Health Act 1959. For welfare work*
Hoggett, Brenda M. Mental health / by Brenda M. Hoggett. — London : Sweet and Maxwell, 1976. — xxxvii,246p ; 22cm. — (Social work and law)
Bibl.: p.xxviii-xxxvii. — Index.
ISBN 0-421-21450-3 Pbk : £3.00
(B77-02130)

344'.42'044 — Mentally ill persons. Treatment. Law. *England. Mental Health Act 1959. Operation, 1959-1975*
Gostin, Larry Ogalthorpe. A human condition / [by] Larry O. Gostin. — London : MIND. — (MIND. Special reports)
Index.
Vol.2 : The law relating to mentally abnormal offenders : observations, analysis and proposals for reform / edited by Anne Ross. — 1977. — [11],226p : ill ; 21cm.
Pbk : £2.50
ISBN 0-900557-32-x
(B77-18015)

344'.42'044 — Mentally ill persons. Treatment. Law. *England. Mental Health Act 1959. Reform. Proposals. Great Britain. Department of Health and Social Security. Review of the Mental Health Act 1959. MIND viewpoints*
MIND. Observations of MIND (the National Association for Mental Health) on the DHSS consultative document 'A review of the Mental Health Act 1959'. — London : MIND, 1976. — [1],iv,27p ; 30cm.
Sd : £0.35
(B77-18016)

344'.42'0463 — Atmosphere. Pollution. Law. *England*
Garner, John Francis. Clean air - law and practice. — 4th ed. / by J.F. Garner and R.K. Crow. — London : Shaw and Sons, 1976. — xi, 282p : forms ; 22cm.
Previous ed.: 1969. — Bibl.: p.253-262. — Index. — Includes the texts from relevant statutes.
ISBN 0-7219-0680-x Pbk : £6.00
(B77-04664)

344'.42'052 — England. Law. *For police*
Baker, Edward Ronald. General police duties. — 5th ed. / by E.R. Baker and F.B. Dodge. — London : Butterworth, 1977. — xiii,437p : ill ; 19cm. — (Baker, Edward Ronald. Police promotion handbooks ; no.3)
Previous ed. : 1975. — Index.
ISBN 0-406-84140-3 Pbk : £3.30
(B77-18017)

Sloan, Kenneth. Police law primer / by Kenneth Sloan. — London : Butterworth, 1977. — [13], 298p ; 22cm.
Index.
ISBN 0-406-84650-2 Pbk : £3.50
(B77-33688)

344'.42'05233 — Licensed premises. Entry. Powers of police. Law. *England. Statutes*
Great Britain. *Laws, statutes, etc. (Individual titles).* Licensing (Amendment) Act 1977 : Elizabeth II. 1977. Chapter 26. — London : H.M.S.O., [1977]. — Sheet(2p) ; 25x16cm.
ISBN 0-10-542677-6 : £0.10
(B77-25481)

344'.42'06 — Construction. Powers of district councils. Law. *England. Statutes*
Great Britain. *Laws, statutes, etc. (Individual titles).* Local Authorities (Restoration of Works Powers) Act 1977 : Elizabeth II. 1977. Chapter 47. — London : H.M.S.O., [1977]. — Folder(4p) ; 25cm.
ISBN 0-10-544777-3 : £0.15
(B77-28500)

344'.42'063635 — Gypsies. Mobile homes. Sites. Provision. Law. *England. Caravan Sites Act 1968. Operation, to 1976. Reports, surveys*
Cripps, John. Accommodation for gypsies : a report on the working of the Caravan Sites Act 1968 / by John Cripps ; [for the] Department of the Environment [and the] Welsh Office. — London : H.M.S.O., 1977. — viii,50p ; 25cm.
ISBN 0-11-751144-7 Sd : £1.00
(B77-15755)

344'.42'063635 — Homeless persons. Housing. Provision. Powers of local authorities. Law. *Great Britain. Statutes*
Great Britain. *Laws, statutes, etc. (Individual titles).* Housing (Homeless Persons) Act 1977 : Elizabeth II. 1977. Chapter 48. — London : H.M.S.O., [1977]. — ii,19,[1]p ; 25cm.
ISBN 0-10-544877-x Sd : £0.45
(B77-28501)

344'.42'063635 — Housing. Improvement. Law. *England*
Public Health Advisory Service. Area action to deal with housing conditions : Housing Acts 1957-74, etc. / Philag's Public Health Advisory Service. — London (Care House, Bigland St., E1 2ND) : [The Service], 1976. — [1],34p : forms ; 30cm. — (Practice notes ; no.11 ISSN 0307-0301)
ISBN 0-904739-10-4 Sd : £0.50
(B77-00106)

344'.42'0702633 — Education. Law. *England. Statutes*
Great Britain. *Laws, statutes, etc. (Individual titles).* Education Act 1976 : Elizabeth II. 1976. Chapter 81. — London : H.M.S.O., [1976]. — [1],6p ; 25cm.
ISBN 0-10-548176-9 Sd : £0.25
(B77-10764)

344'.42'092 — Public libraries. Legislation. *England, 1850-1976*
Morris, Roger John Bowring. Parliament and the public libraries : a survey of legislative activity promoting the municipal library service in England and Wales, 1850-1976 / [by] R.J.B. Morris. — London : Mansell Information Publishing, 1977. — xiv,477p ; 23cm.
Bibl.: p.422-435. — Index.
ISBN 0-7201-0554-4 : £12.50 : CIP rev.
(B77-06554)

344'.42'094 — Listed buildings. Law. *England. Conference proceedings*
A **future** for old buildings? : listed buildings : the law and the practice : papers from a conference held at Oxford, September 1976, organised by the Bar Council, the Law Society, and the Royal Institution of Chartered Surveyors / foreword by Roger W. Suddards. — London : Sweet and Maxwell, 1977. — [4],108p ; 25cm. — ('Journal of planning and environment law' occasional papers)
ISBN 0-421-23180-7 Sd : £5.00
(B77-28502)

344'.429 — Wales. Rural regions. Social development. Law. *Statutes*
Great Britain. *Laws, statutes, etc. (Individual titles).* Development of Rural Wales Act 1976 : Elizabeth II. 1976. Chapter 75. — London : H.M.S.O., [1976]. — [1],ii,76p ; 25cm.
ISBN 0-10-547576-9 Sd : £1.35
(B77-11135)

344'.43'0463 — West Germany. Environment. Pollution. Law
Steiger, Heinhard. The law and practice relating to pollution control in the Federal Republic of Germany / by Heinhard Steiger and Otto Kimminich ; for Environmental Resources Ltd. — London : Graham and Trotman for the Commission of the European Communities, 1976. — xxxii,420p ; 23cm.
Bibl.: p.411-416. — Index.
ISBN 0-86010-032-4 : £7.50
(B77-02857)

344'.43'0463 — West Germany. Environment. Pollution. Law. *German texts*
Steiger, Heinhard. Umweltschutzrecht -und Verwaltung in der Bundesrepublik Deutschland / von H. Steiger und O. Kimminich ; für Environmental Resources Limited. — London : Graham and Trotman für der Kommission der Europäischen Gemeinschaften, 1976. — xliii,458p : 1 ill ; 23cm.
Bibl.: p.449-454. — Index.
ISBN 0-86010-034-0 : £7.50
(B77-02858)

344'.44'0463 — France. Environment. Pollution. Law
Colliard, Claude Albert. The law and practice relating to pollution control in France / by Claude-Albert Colliard ; for Environmental Resources Limited. — London : Graham and Trotman for the Commission of the European Communities, 1976. — xxiv,190p ; 23cm.
Bibl.: p.187-190. — Index.
ISBN 0-86010-033-2 : £7.50
(B77-02859)

344'.44'0463 — France. Environment. Pollution. Law. *French texts*
Colliard, Claude Albert. Loi et usage concernant le contrôle de la pollution en France / de Claude-Albert Colliard ; pour Environmental Resources Ltd. — London : Graham and Trotman pour la Commission des communautés européennes, 1976. — xx,204p ; 23cm.
Bibl.: p.201-204. — Index.
ISBN 0-86010-035-9 : £7.50
(B77-02860)

344'.45'0463 — Italy. Environment. Pollution. Law
Dell'Anno, P. The law and practice relating to pollution control in Italy / by P. Dell'Anno ; for Environmental Resources Limited. — London : Graham and Trotman for the Commission of the European Communities, 1976. — xxvii,342p : ill, map ; 23cm.
Bibl.: p.327-334. — Index.
ISBN 0-86010-039-1 : £7.50
(B77-02861)

344'.45'0463 — Italy. Environment. Pollution. Law. *Italian texts*
Dell'Anno, P. Legge in materia di controllo dell'inquinamento e sua applicazione in Italia / di P. Dell'Anno ; per la Environmental Resources Limited. — London : Graham and Trotman per la Commissione della Comunità Europee, 1976. — xxxviii,380p : ill, map ; 23cm.
Bibl.: p.361-373. — Index.
ISBN 0-86010-042-1 : £7.50
(B77-02862)

344'.47'063635 — Housing. Law. *Soviet Union, to 1976*
Sawicki, Stanislaw J. Soviet land and housing law : a historical and comparative study / [by] Stanislaw J. Sawicki ; foreword by John Hazard. — New York ; London : Praeger, 1977. — xxv,199,[1]p ; 25cm. — (Praeger special studies in international politics and government)
Index.
ISBN 0-275-24480-6 : £13.05
Primary classification 346'.47'043
(B77-25487)

344'.489'0463 — Denmark. Environment. Pollution. Law
Jensen, C Haagen. The law and practice relating to pollution control in Denmark / by C. Haagen Jensen ; for Environmental Resources Limited. — London : Graham and Trotman for the Commission of the European Communities, 1976. — xxviii,208p ; 23cm.
Bibl.: p.201-203. — Index.
ISBN 0-86010-029-4 : £7.50
(B77-02863)

344'.492'0463 — Netherlands. Environment. Pollution. Law
Graeff, J J de. The law and practice relating to pollution control in the Netherlands / by J.J. de Graeff and J.M. Polack [i.e. Polak] ; for Environmental Resources Limited. — London : Graham and Trotman for the Commission of the European Communities, 1976. — xxi,184p ; 23cm.
Index.
ISBN 0-86010-030-8 : £7.50
(B77-02864)

344'.493'0463 — Belgium. Environment. Pollution. Law
Didier (J.M.) and Associates. The law and practice relating to pollution control in Belgium and Luxembourg / by J.M. Didier and Associates ; for Environmental Resources Limited. — London : Graham and Trotman for the Commission of the European Communities, 1976. — xxvii,496p : ill, maps ; 23cm.
Bibl.: p.483-485. — Index.
ISBN 0-86010-038-3 : £7.50
Also classified at 344'.4935'0463
(B77-02865)

344'.493'0463 — Belgium. Environment. Pollution. Law. *French texts*
Didier (J.M.) and Associates. Loi et usage concernant le contrôle de la pollution en Belgique et Luxembourg / de J.M. Didier & Associates. — London : Graham and Trotman pour la Commission des Communautés européennes, 1976. — xxxiv,478p : ill, maps ; 23cm.
'... pour l'Environmental Resources Limited' - jacket. — Bibl.: p.465-467. — Index.
ISBN 0-86010-041-3 : £7.50
Also classified at 344'.4935'0463
(B77-02866)

344'.4935'0463 — Luxembourg. Environment. Pollution. Law
Didier (J.M.) and Associates. The law and practice relating to pollution control in Belgium and Luxembourg / by J.M. Didier and Associates ; for Environmental Resources Limited. — London : Graham and Trotman for the Commission of the European Communities, 1976. — xxvii,496p : ill, maps ; 23cm.
Bibl.: p.483-485. — Index.
ISBN 0-86010-038-3 : £7.50
Primary classification 344'.493'0463
(B77-02865)

344'.4935'0463 — Luxembourg. Environment. Pollution. Law. *French texts*
Didier (J.M.) and Associates. Loi et usage concernant le contrôle de la pollution en Belgique et Luxembourg / de J.M. Didier & Associates. — London : Graham and Trotman pour la Commission des Communautés européennes, 1976. — xxxiv,478p : ill, maps ; 23cm.
'... pour l'Environmental Resources Limited' - jacket. — Bibl.: p.465-467. — Index.
ISBN 0-86010-041-3 : £7.50
Primary classification 344'.493'0463
(B77-02866)

344'.54'054202633 — Gambling. Law. *India (Republic). Gujarat & Maharashtra. Statutes. Texts with commentaries*
Mujumdar, M B. Commentary on the Bombay Prevention of Gambling Act, 1887 : (Bombay Act no.IV of 1887), as in force in Maharashtra and Gujarat / [by] M.B. Mujumdar ; with a foreword by G.N. Vaidya. — Bombay : Tripathi ; London : Sweet and Maxwell [etc.], 1975. — xix,136p ; 23cm.
Spine title: Bombay Prevention of Gambling Act, 1887. — Index. — Includes the text of the Act.
Unpriced
(B77-05962)

344'.73'0188 — Trade unions. Law. *United States*
Taft, Philip. Rights of union members and the Government / [by] Philip Taft. — Westport, Conn. ; London : Greenwood Press, 1975. — xv,348p ; 22cm. — (Contributions in American history ; no.39)
Index.
ISBN 0-8371-7527-5 : £11.95
(B77-15182)

344'.73'04 — Public health. Law. *United States*
Wing, Kenneth R. The law and the public's health / [by] Kenneth R. Wing. — Saint Louis : Mosby ; London : Distributed by Kimpton, 1976. — ix,167p ; 25cm. — (Issues and problems in health care)
Bibl.
ISBN 0-8016-5601-x Pbk : £5.50
(B77-04031)

344'.73'041 — Man. Genetic control. Legal aspects. *United States. Conference proceedings*
National Symposium on Genetics and the Law, *Boston, Mass., 1975.* Genetics and the law / edited by Aubrey Milunsky and George J. Annas. — New York ; London : Plenum Press, 1976. — xii,532p ; 26cm.
'Proceedings of a National Symposium on Genetics and the Law held in Boston, Mass., May 18-20, 1975 ...' - title page verso. — Bibl.: p.495-515. — Index.
ISBN 0-306-30906-8 : £14.18
(B77-05963)

344'.73'041 — Paediatrics. Legal aspects. *United States*
Holder, Angela Roddey. Legal issues in pediatrics and adolescent medicine / [by] Angela Roddey Holder ; foreword by Howard A. Pearson. — New York ; London [etc.] : Wiley, 1977. — xv, 350p ; 24cm.
'A Wiley medical publication'. — Bibl.: p.319-332. — Index.
ISBN 0-471-40612-0 : £13.90
(B77-21016)

344'.73'044 — Medicine. Psychotherapy. Legal aspects. *United States*
Van Hoose, William H. Ethical and legal issues in counseling and psychotherapy / [by] William H. Van Hoose, Jeffrey A. Kottler. — San Francisco [etc.] ; London : Jossey-Bass, 1977. — xv,224p : 1 ill ; 24cm. — (Jossey-Bass behavioral science series)
Bibl.: p.195-217. — Index.
ISBN 0-87589-317-1 : £10.00
Primary classification 174'.2
(B77-23976)

344'.73'044 — Mental hospitals. Compulsory admission of patients. Legal aspects. *United States. Case studies*
Szasz, Thomas Stephen. Psychiatric slavery / [by] Thomas Szasz. — New York : Free Press ; London : Collier Macmillan, 1977. — xv,159p ; 22cm.
Index.
ISBN 0-02-931600-6 : £6.75
(B77-23241)

344'.73'044 — Mentally ill persons. Treatment. Law. *United States. Conference proceedings*
Amherst Conference on the Right to Treatment, *1973.* The right to treatment for mental patients / edited by Stuart Golann and William J. Fremouw. — New York : Irvington ; New York ; London [etc.] : Distributed by Wiley, 1976. — vii,246p ; 25cm.
'The Amherst Conference on the Right to Treatment was held on May 21-23, 1973' - title page verso. — Index.
ISBN 0-470-15172-2 : £12.70
(B77-15183)

344'.73'046 — United States. Environment. Conservation. Law: National Environmental Policy Act 1969. Operation, to 1975
Liroff, Richard A. A national policy for the environment : NEPA and its aftermath / [by] Richard A. Liroff. — Bloomington ; London : Indiana University Press, 1976. — xi,273p : 1 ill ; 22cm.
Bibl.: p.224-227. — Index.
ISBN 0-253-33973-1 : £8.00
(B77-04032)

344'.73'046 — United States. Environment. Law
Environmental legislation : a sourcebook / edited by Mary Robinson Sive. — New York [etc.] ; London : Praeger, 1976. — xxxv,563p ; 25cm. — (Praeger special studies in US economic, social and political issues)
Bibl.: p.540-561. — Index.
ISBN 0-275-05470-5 : £13.70
(B77-08895)

Heer, John Edward. Environmental assessments and statements / [by] John E. Herr, Jr, D. Joseph Hagerty. — New York [etc.] ; London : Van Nostrand Reinhold, 1977. — xv,367p : ill, forms ; 24cm. — (Van Nostrand Reinhold environmental engineering series)
Bibl.: p.199-201. — Index.
ISBN 0-442-23030-3 : £14.55
(B77-25482)

344'.73'0798 — Schools. Desegregation. Law. *United States, to 1976*
Kluger, Richard. Simple justice : the history of Brown v. Board of Education and black America's struggle for equality / [by] Richard Kluger. — London : Deutsch, 1977. — x,823, xxiii,[1]p ; 25cm.
Originally published: New York : Knopf, 1976. — Bibl.: p.791-795. — Index.
ISBN 0-233-96898-9 : £9.95
(B77-23242)

344'.73'0798 — Schools. Desegregation. Law. Decisions of United States. Supreme Court. *United States, 1954-1976*
Graglia, Lino Anthony. Disaster by decree : the Supreme Court decisions on race and the schools / [by] Lino A. Graglia. — Ithaca ; London : Cornell University Press, 1976. — 351p ; 23cm.
Index.
ISBN 0-8014-0980-2 : £8.05
(B77-00107)

344'.934'0533 — Firearms. Control. *New Hebrides. Treaties between Great Britain & France*
Great Britain. *Treaties, etc. France, August 6, 1914. Protocols, amendments, etc., July 28, 1976.* Exchange of notes between the Government of the United Kingdom of Great Britain and Northern Ireland and the Government of the French Republic concerning amendments to the protocol respecting the New Hebrides signed at London on 6 August 1914, London, 28 July 1976 ... — London : H.M.S.O., [1976]. — Folder(4p) ; 25cm. — (Treaty series ; no.103(1976)) (Cmnd.6650)
English and French text.
ISBN 0-10-166500-8 : £0.12
(B77-07213)

345 — CRIMINAL LAW

345'.00264 — Common law countries. Criminal law. *Cases*
Brett, Peter. Criminal law : cases and text / by Peter Brett and Peter L. Waller. — 3rd ed. — Melbourne ; London [etc.] : Butterworth, 1975. — 943p ; 24cm.
This ed. originally published: 1971. — Index.
ISBN 0-409-43354-3 Pbk : £21.00
(B77-29281)

345.06'4 — Criminal law. Defences: Alibis
Gooderson, R N. Alibi / by R.N. Gooderson. — London : Heinemann Educational, 1977. — xxix,269p ; 23cm. — (Cambridge studies in criminology ; 37) (The Heinemann library of criminology and penal reform)
Bibl.: p.255-258. — Index.
ISBN 0-435-82357-4 : £9.50
(B77-33126)

345.07'09'04 — Crimes. Trials, 1873-1951
Hyde, Harford Montgomery. Crime has its heroes / [by] H. Montgomery Hyde. — London : Constable, 1976. — [11],244p,leaf of plate,[24]p of plates : ill, facsims, ports ; 23cm.
Index.
ISBN 0-09-461550-0 : £5.95
(B77-00674)

345'.4'064 — Criminal courts. Evidence. Provision. Use of torture of defendants. Western Europe. Related to law of proof, to ca 1800
Langbein, John H. Torture and the law of proof : Europe and England in the ancien régime / [by] John H. Langbein. — Chicago ; London : University of Chicago Press, 1977. — x,229p : ill ; 23cm.
Index.
ISBN 0-226-46806-2 : £11.60
(B77-33689)

345'.41'0231 — Terrorism. Prevention. Law. *Great Britain. Prevention of Terrorism (Temporary Provisions) Act 1974. Operation, 1974-1975. Socialist Workers' Party viewpoints*
Berry, Steve. The Prevention of Terrorism Act, legalised terror / by Steve Berry. — London (6 Cottons Gardens, E2 8DN) : Socialist Worker Printers and Publishers, [1977]. — [15]p : ill, ports ; 30cm. — (Socialist Workers' Party. Pamphlets)
ISBN 0-905998-07-3 Sd : £0.10
(B77-16268)

345'.41'0231 — Terrorism. Prevention. Law. *Great Britain. Prevention of Terrorism (Temporary Provisions) Act 1974. Operation, 1974-1976. National Council for Civil Liberties viewpoints*
National Council for Civil Liberties. The Prevention of Terrorisms Acts 1974 and 1976 : a report on the operation of the law / NCCL ; [written by] Catherine Scorer. — London : The Council, 1976. — [2],39p ; 21cm.
ISBN 0-901108-60-x Sd : £0.75
(B77-15184)

345'.41'0247 — Motor vehicles. Parking. Law. *Great Britain. Humorous texts*
Brandreth, Charles. Parking law / [by] Charles Brandreth ; with a foreword by Sir Robert Mark. — Newton Abbot [etc.] : David and Charles, 1977. — 126p : ill ; 23cm.
ISBN 0-7153-7376-5 : £3.50
(B77-21017)

345'.41'02523 — Murder. Trials. *Great Britain, 1911-1947*
McClure, James. Killers / [by] James McClure. — [London] : Fontana, 1976. — 189p ; 18cm.
'A Companion to the Thames Television series by Clive Exton'. — Bibl.: p.189.
ISBN 0-00-634420-8 Pbk : £0.65
(B77-12937)

345'.41'026 — Offences relating to property. Law. Enforcement. *Great Britain. Conference proceedings*
Conference on Major Property Crime in the United Kingdom, *University of Edinburgh, School of Criminology and Forensic Studies, 1975.* Papers presented at a Conference held in September 1975 on major property crime in the United Kingdom - some aspects of law enforcement / edited by P. Young. — Edinburgh : University of Edinburgh, School of Criminology and Forensic Studies, 1976. — 3-180p : ill ; 21cm.
'The School of Criminology and Forensic Studies, in association with the Faculty of Law, organized a Conference on Major Property Crime in the United Kingdom in September 1975' - Foreword.
ISBN 0-905893-00-x Pbk : £2.80
(B77-07214)

345'.41'075 — Criminal courts. Negro defendants. Trials. *Great Britain*
Narayan, Rudy. Black community on trial / by Rudy Narayan. — London (23 Bedford Row, WC1R 5BH) : Blackbird Books Ltd. [Part 1]. — 1976. — [5],41p ; 21cm.
ISBN 0-901813-02-8 Sd : £0.85
(B77-09599)

345'.411'025230924 — Murder of Ross, Rachel. Trial of Meehan, Patrick. *Scotland. Strathclyde Region. Ayr*
Kennedy, Ludovic. A presumption of innocence : the full story of the Ayr murder / [by] Ludovic Kennedy. — St Albans : Panther, 1977. — 3-306p,[8]p of plates : ill, facsim, map, ports ; 18cm.
Originally published: London : Gollancz, 1976.
ISBN 0-586-04633-x Pbk : £1.25
(B77-27748)

345'.411'025302633 — Sex offences. Law. *Scotland. Statutes*
Great Britain. *Laws, statutes, etc. (Individual titles).* Sexual Offences (Scotland) Act 1976 : Elizabeth II. 1976. Chapter 67. — London : H.M.S.O., [1976]. — [1],11,[1]p ; 25cm.
ISBN 0-10-546776-6 Sd : £0.35
(B77-09600)

345'.411'0502633 — Scotland. Criminal law. Justice. Administration. Procedure. Law. *Statutes. Texts with commentaries*
Great Britain. *Crown Office.* Criminal Procedure (Scotland) Act 1975 / Crown Office. — Edinburgh : H.M.S.O., 1976. — 2v. ; 30cm.
'... produced primarily for use by members of the Procurator Fiscal Service. Volume 1 deals with Solemn Procedure and Volume 2 with Summary Procedure. Following each section there are notes, of the derivation, text book references and case law' - p.[3]. — [3],433p.;[3],433p. on publication. — Includes the text of the Act.
ISBN 0-11-491403-6 Ls : £16.00
(B77-07856)

345'.411'07 — Crimes. Trials. *Scotland, 1793-1857*
History is my witness / foreword by James Cameron ; edited by Gordon Menzies. — London : British Broadcasting Corporation, 1976. — 144p : ill, map, port ; 21cm.
'... published in conjunction with a series on BBC1 (Scotland) "History is my witness". First broadcast on Thursdays from 6 January to 3 February 1977' - title page verso. — Bibl.: p.139-140. — Index.
ISBN 0-563-16077-2 Pbk : £2.00
(B77-04665)

345'.411'072 — Scotland. Criminal law. Bail & custody. Imposition by sheriff courts. *Reports, surveys*
Melvin, Michael. Pre-trial bail and custody in the Scottish Sheriff Courts / [by] M. Melvin, P.J. Didcott [for the] Scottish Office, Central Research Unit. — Edinburgh : H.M.S.O., 1976. — vii,82p : ill, forms ; 25cm. — (Great Britain. Scottish Office. Social research studies)
ISBN 0-11-491434-6 Sd : £1.20
(B77-01257)

345'.411'08 — Children's hearings. *Scotland*
Children's hearings / edited by F.M. Martin and Kathleen Murray ; with a foreword by Lord Kilbrandon. — Edinburgh (33 Montgomery St., Edinburgh EH7 5JX) : Scottish Academic Press, 1976. — xv,242p : ill ; 26cm.
Bibl.: p.241-242.
ISBN 0-7073-0123-8 : £5.00
(B77-06555)

345'.416'0231 — Terrorists. Sentences: Imprisonment. Length. Increases. Law. *Northern Ireland. Statutes*
Great Britain. *Laws, statutes, etc. (Individual titles).* Northern Ireland (Emergency Provisions) (Amendment) Act 1977 : Elizabeth II. 1977. Chapter 34. — London : H.M.S.O., [1977]. — Sheet(2)p ; 25x16cm.
ISBN 0-10-543477-9 : £0.10
(B77-26198)

345'.42 — England. Criminal law
Curzon, Leslie Basil. Criminal law / [by] L.B. Curzon. — 2nd ed. — Plymouth : Macdonald and Evans, 1977. — xxxiii,318p ; 19cm. — (M. & E. handbook series)
Previous ed.: 1973. — Bibl.: p.289. — Index.
ISBN 0-7121-0366-x Pbk : £2.75
(B77-16269)

Godfrey, M. Recent developments in criminal law / [by] M. Godfrey. — [Guildford] ([Braboeuf Manor, Portsmouth Rd, St Catherine's, Guildford, Surrey]) : The College of Law, 1975. — [1],18p ; 22cm. — (College of Law. Crash course lectures : 1975)
ISBN 0-905835-14-x Sd : £0.60
(B77-04666)

345'.42 — England. Criminal law. Reform. *Reports, surveys*
Criminal Law Revision Committee. Report / Criminal Law Revision Committee. — London : H.M.S.O.
13th : Section 16 of the Theft Act 1968 ... — [1977]. — 35p ; 25cm. — (Cmnd.6733)
ISBN 0-10-167330-2 Sd : £0.60
(B77-08896)

345'.42'002633 — England. Criminal law. *Statutes*
Great Britain. *Laws, statutes, etc. (Individual titles).* Criminal Law Act 1977 : Elizabeth II. 1977. Chapter 45. — London : H.M.S.O., [1977]. — [1],iv,128p ; 25cm.
ISBN 0-10-544577-0 Sd : £2.10
(B77-29282)

345'.42'00264 — England. Criminal law. *Cases*
Cross, *Sir* Rupert. Cross and Jones' cases and statutes on criminal law. — 6th ed. / [by] Richard Card. — London : Butterworth, 1977. — xxxvi,460p ; 23cm.
Previous ed.: published as 'Cases on criminal law' / by Rupert Cross and P. Asterley Jones. 1973. — Index.
ISBN 0-406-57025-6 : £11.00
ISBN 0-406-47026-4 Pbk : £6.00
(B77-33127)

345'.42'00264 — England. Criminal law. *Cases. For police*
Sloan, Kenneth. Cases for the police / by Kenneth Sloan. — London : Police Review Publishing Co., [1977]. — 81p ; 15cm. — (A Police Review publication)
Index.
ISBN 0-85164-160-1 Sd : £1.25
(B77-15757)

345'.42'01 — England. Criminal law. Cases. Distribution between Crown Court & magistrates' courts. Great Britain. Interdepartmental Committee on the Distribution of Criminal Business Between the Crown Court and Magistrates' Courts. 'Distribution of criminal business between the Crown Court and magistrates' courts. *National Council for Civil Liberties viewpoints*
National Council for Civil Liberties. Trial or error : a reply to the James Committee / [National Council for Civil Liberties] ; [report written] by Peter Thornton. — London : N.C.C.L., [1977]. — [6],23p ; 30cm. — (National Council for Civil Liberties. Reports ; no.16 ISSN 0306-8994)
ISBN 0-901108-66-9 Sd : £0.30
(B77-15756)

345'.42'01 — England. Criminal law. Jurisdiction of magistrates' courts
Harris, Brian, *b.1932*. The criminal jurisdiction of magistrates / by Brian Harris. — 6th ed. — London : Rose : 'Justice of the Peace' Ltd, 1977. — lii,479p ; 26cm.
Previous ed.: 1976. — Index.
ISBN 0-85992-102-6 : £15.00 : CIP rev.
ISBN 0-85992-103-4 Pbk : £12.00
(B77-15185)

345'.42'01 — Legal aid. Law. *England*
Carvell, Ian George. The £25 scheme, and other legal aid topics / [by] I.G. Carvell. — [Guildford] ([Braboeuf Manor, Portsmouth Rd, St Catherine's, Guildford, Surrey]) : The College of Law, 1973. — [1],16p ; 22cm. — (College of Law. Crash course lectures : 1973)
ISBN 0-905835-37-9 Sd : £0.50
(B77-04667)

345'.42'01 — Legal aid. Law. *England. Statutes & statutory instruments. Serials*
Legal aid handbook. — London : H.M.S.O.
1976 : 4th ed. / prepared by the Lord Chancellor's Office and the Law Society. — 1976. — v,281p : forms ; 25cm.
Previously prepared by the Law Society. — Includes the text of the Legal Aid Act 1974 and relevant Statutory Instruments.
ISBN 0-11-390575-0 Pbk : £3.90
(B77-00108)

345'.42'01 — Solicitors undertaking legal aid work. *England. Directories*
Legal aid solicitors referral list / [Law Society]. — London : Law Society.
1976. A : London North. — [1976]. — [2], 67p ; 30cm.
Sd : Unpriced
(B77-32499)

1976. B : London South. — [1976]. — [2],24p ; 30cm.
Sd : Unpriced
(B77-32500)

1976. C : Northumberland, Tyne and Wear, Durham, Cleveland. — [1976]. — [2],26p ; 30cm.
Sd : Unpriced
(B77-32501)

1976. D : North Yorkshire, Humberside. — [1976]. — [2],19p ; 30cm.
Sd : Unpriced
(B77-32502)

1976. E : West Yorkshire. — [1976]. — [2], 20p ; 30cm.
Sd : Unpriced
(B77-32503)

1976. F : Cumbria. — [1976]. — [2],11p ; 30cm.
Sd : Unpriced
(B77-32504)

1976. G : Lancashire. — [1976]. — [2],20p ; 30cm.
Sd : Unpriced
(B77-32505)

1976. H : Merseyside. — [1976]. — [2],18p ; 30cm.
Sd : Unpriced
(B77-32506)

1976. I : Greater Manchester. — [1976]. — [2], 32p ; 30cm.
Sd : Unpriced
(B77-32507)

1976. J : South Yorkshire, Derbyshire. — [1976]. — [2],19p ; 30cm.
Sd : Unpriced
(B77-32508)

1976. K : Nottinghamshire, Lincolnshire. — [1976]. — [2],17p ; 30cm.
Sd : Unpriced
(B77-32509)

1976. L : Cheshire, Staffordshire. — [1976]. — [2],20p ; 30cm.
Sd : Unpriced
(B77-32510)

1976. M : West Midlands. — [1976]. — [2], 25p ; 30cm.
Sd : Unpriced
(B77-32511)

1976. N : Shropshire, Hereford and Worcester, Gloucestershire. — [1976]. — [2],21p ; 30cm.
Sd : Unpriced
(B77-32512)

1976. O : Warwickshire, Northamptonshire, Leicestershire. — [1976]. — [2],19p ; 30cm.
Sd : Unpriced
(B77-32513)

1976. P : Oxfordshire, Berkshire, Buckinghamshire. — [1976]. — [2],22p ; 30cm.
Sd : Unpriced
(B77-32514)

1976. Q : Hertfordshire, Bedfordshire. — [1976] . — [2],19p ; 30cm.
Sd : Unpriced
(B77-32515)

1976. R : Cambridgeshire, Norfolk, Suffolk. — [1976]. — [2],20p ; 30cm.
Sd : Unpriced
(B77-32516)

1976. S : Essex. — [1976]. — [2],20p ; 30cm.
Sd : Unpriced
(B77-32517)

1976. T : Cornwall, Devon. — [1976]. — [2], 22p ; 30cm.
Sd : Unpriced
(B77-32518)

1976. U : Avon. — [1976]. — [2],16p ; 30cm.
Sd : Unpriced
(B77-32519)

1976. V : Somerset, Dorset, Wiltshire. — [1976] . — [2],25p ; 30cm.
Sd : Unpriced
(B77-32520)

1976. W : Hampshire, Isle of Wight. — [1976]. — [2],24p ; 30cm.
Sd : Unpriced
(B77-32521)

1976. WA : Gwynedd, Clwyd, Dyfed, Powys. — [1976]. — [2],19p ; 30cm.
Sd : Unpriced
(B77-32522)

1976. WB : Glamorgan, Gwent. — [1976]. — [2],21p ; 30cm.
Sd : Unpriced
(B77-32523)

1976. X : Surrey. — [1976]. — [2],22p ; 30cm.
Sd : Unpriced
(B77-32524)

1976. Y : West Sussex, East Sussex. — [1976]. — [2],23p ; 30cm.
Sd : Unpriced
(B77-32525)

1976. Z : Kent. — [1976]. — [2],21p ; 30cm.
Sd : Unpriced
(B77-32526)

345'.42'0231 — Treason & sedition. Law. Reform. *England. Proposals*
Law Commission. Second programme, item XVIII, codification of the criminal law, treason, sedition and allied offences / the Law Commission. — London : H.M.S.O., 1977. — v,64p ; 21cm. — (Working paper ; no.72)
ISBN 0-11-730151-5 Sd : £1.50
(B77-26921)

345'.42'0243 — Building industries. Industrial relations. Picketing. Intimidation. Conspiracy. Trial of Shrewsbury six. *Salop. Shrewsbury, 1972. Socialist Workers' Party viewpoints*
Flynn, Laurie. Workers against the law : the truth about the Shrewsbury trials / by Laurie Flynn. — [London] ([Corbridge Works, Corbridge Cres., E2 9DS]) : ['Socialist worker'], [1977]. — 16p : ill, ports ; 30cm. — ('Socialist worker' pamphlet)
ISBN 0-905998-08-1 Sd : £0.10
(B77-16270)

345'.42'025230922 — Murder of Confait, Maxwell. Trial of Lattimore, Colin; Leighton, Ronald & Salih, Ahmet. *London. Lewisham (London Borough). Catford*
Price, Christopher. The Confait confessions / [by] Christopher Price & Jonathan Caplan. — London : Boyars : Distributed by Calder and Boyars, 1977. — 144p,[8]p of plates : 1 ill, facsims, map, ports ; 23cm.
ISBN 0-7145-2564-2 : £4.95
ISBN 0-7145-2565-0 Pbk : £1.95
(B77-21018)

345'.42'025230924 — Murder of Blakely, David. Trial of Ellis, Ruth. *England*
Marks, Laurence. Ruth Ellis : a case of diminished responsibility? / [by] Laurence Marks and Tony Van den Bergh. — London : Macdonald and Jane's, 1977. — [8],v,178p,[8]p of plates : ill, facsims, ports ; 23cm.
Bibl.: p.178.
ISBN 0-354-08509-3 : £4.95
(B77-25483)

345'.42'025230924 — Murder of Bravo, Charles. Inquests. *London. Wandsworth (London Borough)*
Williams, John, *b.1908*. Suddenly at the Priory / [by] John Williams ; foreword by John Dickson Carr. — London : Cardinal, 1976. — 219p,4p of plates : ports ; 20cm.
Originally published: London : Heinemann, 1957. — Index.
ISBN 0-351-18699-9 Pbk : £0.90
(B77-10271)

345'.42'025230924 — Murder of Maybrick, James. Trial of Maybrick, Florence. *Merseyside (Metropolitan County). Liverpool*

Ryan, Bernard. The poisoned life of Mrs Maybrick / [by] Bernard Ryan with Sir Michael Havers ; foreword by Lord Russell of Killowen. — London : Kimber, 1977. — [4], 292p,[16]p of plates : ill, facsims, ports ; 24cm.
Bibl.: p.283-285. — Index.
ISBN 0-7183-0125-0 : £7.50
(B77-30063)

345'.42'025230924 — Murder of Setty, Stanley. Trial of Hume, Donald. *London*

Trials of Brian Donald Hume / with an introduction and edited by Ivan Butler. — Newton Abbot [etc.] : David and Charles, 1976. — 128p,[4]p of plates : ill, map, plan, ports ; 23cm. — (Celebrated trials series)
Contains transcript of trial at Central Criminal Court.
ISBN 0-7153-7118-5 : £4.95
(B77-09601)

345'.42'025230924 — Murder of Stephen, Michael. Trial of Barney, Elvira. *London*

Barney, Elvira. Trial of Elvira Barney / with an introduction and edited by Peter Cotes. — Newton Abbot [etc.] : David and Charles, 1976. — 127p : ill, facsims, ports ; 23cm. — (Celebrated trials series)
ISBN 0-7153-7294-7 : £4.95
(B77-09602)

345'.42'025230924 — Murder of Wallace, Julia. Trial of Wallace, William Herbert. *Merseyside (Metropolitan Borough). Liverpool*

Goodman, Jonathan. The killing of Julia Wallace / [by] Jonathan Goodman ; with a foreword by Edgar Lustgarten. — Revised ed. — London : Severn House : [Distributed by Hutchinson], 1976. — 323p,[16]p of plates : ill, facsims, maps, plans, ports ; 23cm.
Previous ed.: London : Harrap, 1969. — Bibl.: p.309-311. — Index.
ISBN 0-7278-0208-9 : £5.25
(B77-01258)

345'.42'0253 — Crimes: Rape. Law. *England. Statutes*

Great Britain. *Laws, statutes, etc. (Individual titles).* Sexual Offences (Amendment) Act 1976 : Elizabeth II. 1976. Chapter 82. — London : H.M.S.O., [1976]. — [1],9,[1]p ; 25cm.
ISBN 0-10-548276-5 Sd : £0.25
(B77-08897)

345'.42'0253 — Prostitution. Legal aspects. *England*

Sion, Abraham A. Prostitution and the law / [by] Abraham A. Sion. — London : Faber, 1977. — 3-160p ; 23cm.
Bibl.: p.154-157. — Index.
ISBN 0-571-10934-9 : £7.95 : CIP rev.
(B77-23243)

345'.42'0253 — Sex offences against children. Law. Reform. *England. Paedophile Information Exchange viewpoints*

Paedophile Information Exchange. Evidence on the law relating to and penalties for certain sexual offences involving children for the Home Office Criminal Law Revision Committee / [Paedophile Information Exchange]. — London (c/o Release, 1 Elgin Ave., W.9) : P.I.E., 1975. — [1],17 leaves ; 33cm.
Authors: K.R. Hose and M.J. Burbidge.
ISBN 0-905787-00-5 Sd : £0.70
(B77-00109)

345'.42'0253 — Sex offences. Law. Reform. *England. Proposals*

National Council for Civil Liberties. Sexual offences : evidence to the Criminal Law Revision Committee / [National Council for Civil Liberties]. — Revised ed. — London : N.C.C.L., 1976. — [1],23p ; 30cm. — (National Council for Civil Liberties. Reports ; no.13 ISSN 0306-8994)
Previous ed.: 1976. — Bibl.: p.23.
ISBN 0-901108-62-6 Sd : £0.20
(B77-05964)

345'.42'0262 — Theft. Law. *England*

Smith, John Cyril. The law of theft / [by] J.C. Smith. — 3rd ed. — London : Butterworth, 1977. — xxix,255p ; 26cm.
Previous ed.: 1972. — Bibl.: p.xxix. — Index. — Includes the text of the Theft Act 1968.
ISBN 0-406-37904-1 : £9.00
ISBN 0-406-37905-x Pbk : £5.75
(B77-10272)

345'.42'05 — England. Criminal law. Justice. Administration. Plea bargaining. *Sources of data: Great Britain. Crown Court. Study regions: West Midlands (Metropolitan County). Birmingham. Research reports*

Baldwin, John, *b.1945.* Negotiated justice : pressures to plead guilty / [by] John Baldwin & Michael McConville. — London : Martin Robertson, 1977. — xvi,128p ; 23cm. — (Law in society series)
Bibl.: p.121-126. — Index.
ISBN 0-85520-171-1 : £5.85
(B77-31780)

345'.42'052 — Offenders. Formal warnings by police. *England. Reports, surveys*

Ditchfield, John Alan. Police cautioning in England and Wales / by J.A. Ditchfield. — London : H.M.S.O., 1976. — v,27p ; 25cm. — (Great Britain. Home Office. Research studies ; no.37) (Great Britain. Home Office. Research Unit. Reports)
Bibl.: p.27.
ISBN 0-11-340677-0 Sd : £0.65
(B77-01259)

345'.42'052 — Police. Powers. Law. *England*

The **client** in trouble with the police. — [Guildford] ([Braboeuf Manor, Portsmouth Rd, St Catherine's, Guildford, Surrey]) : The College of Law, 1975. — v,106p ; 22cm. — (College of Law. Lectures : 1975)
'... the College of Law arranged in the autumn of 1974 a one-day course entitled "The Client in Trouble with the Law" ... in Liverpool, Bristol and London' - Introduction.
ISBN 0-905835-16-6 Pbk : £1.50
(B77-07857)

345'.42'06 — Criminal courts. Evidence. Law. *England*

Brown, William, *b.1915.* Criminal evidence / by William Brown. — London : Police Review Publishing Co., [1976]. — [2],96p ; 21cm.
Index.
ISBN 0-85164-140-7 Pbk : £1.50
(B77-02131)

345'.42'060243632 — Criminal courts. Evidence. Law. *England. For police*

Baker, Edward Ronald. Criminal evidence and procedure. — 5th ed. / by E.R. Baker and F.B. Dodge. — London : Butterworth, 1976. — x, 262p : 2 ill ; 19cm. — (Baker, Edward Ronald. Police promotion handbooks ; no. 2)
Previous ed.: 1973. — Index.
ISBN 0-406-84129-2 Pbk : £2.80
(B77-03452)

345'.42'072 — England. Criminal law. Bail. Imposition by Great Britain. Magistrates' Court (Camberwell Green). Decision making. Use of information on personal background of defendants. Projects: ILPAS/Vera Bail Project, to 1976. *Reports, surveys*

ILPAS/Vera Bail Project. Report of the first year and proposal for the second year / ILPAS/Vera Bail Project ; [prepared by] William Pearce, Michael Smith. — London (73 Great Peter St., SW1P 2BN) : Inner London Probation and After Care Service, [1976]. — [3] ,61p ; 30cm.
ISBN 0-904909-04-2 Sd : £0.75
(B77-07215)

345'.42'072 — England. Criminal law. Bail. Imposition by magistrates' courts

Bradley, Edgar L. Bail in magistrates' courts / by Edgar L. Bradley and J.J. Senior. — Chichester [etc.] : Rose, 1977. — [3],43p ; 21cm.
ISBN 0-85992-101-8 Sd : £1.65
(B77-29283)

345'.42'072 — England. Criminal law. Bail. Law. *Statutes*

Great Britain. *Laws, statutes, etc. (Individual titles).* Bail Act 1976 : Elizabeth II. 1976. Chapter 63. — London : H.M.S.O., [1976]. — [1],29,[1]p ; 25cm.
ISBN 0-10-546376-0 Sd : £0.60
(B77-11136)

345'.42'072 — England. Criminal law. Summonses & charges. *Forms & precedents. For police*

English, John. Summonses and charges / by J. English and R. Houghton. — London : Police Review Publishing Co., [1977]. — 314p ; 14cm.

Index.
ISBN 0-85164-150-4 Pbk : £1.75
(B77-15758)

345'.42'075 — Criminal courts. Docks. Use. Reform. *England. Proposals*

Howard League Working Party on Custody During Trial. No brief for the dock : report of the Howard League Working Party on Custody During Trial / chairman Lady James of Rusholme ; foreword by Lord Gardiner ; with appendix giving full text of memorandum by the Council of the Law Society on 'The use of the dock in criminal courts'. — Chichester : Rose for the Howard League for Penal Reform, 1976. — 35p ; 21cm.
ISBN 0-85992-089-5 Sd : £1.25
(B77-26922)

345'.42'077 — Great Britain. Crown Court. Sentencing

Morrish, Peter. The Crown Court : an index of common penalties and formalities in cases tried on indictment or committed for sentence and appeals in criminal proceedings. — 8th ed. / by Peter Morrish and Ian McLean. — Chichester : Rose, 1976. — 198p ; 23cm.
Thumb indexed. — Previous ed.: 1975. — Index.
ISBN 0-85992-074-7 : £5.45
(B77-05297)

345'.42'077 — Magistrates' courts. Sentencing. *England*

McLean, Ian, *b.1928.* The magistrates' court : an index of common penalties and formalities in cases before justices / by Ian McLean and Peter Morrish. — 3rd ed. — Chichester : Rose, 1977. — 239p ; 22cm.
Thumb indexed. — Text on lining paper. — Previous ed.: 1975. — Index.
ISBN 0-85992-075-5 : £5.45
(B77-10765)

345'.42'077 — Offenders. Sentences: Imprisonment. Length. *England. Proposals*

Advisory Council on the Penal System. The length of prison sentences, interim report of the Advisory Council on the Penal System. — London : H.M.S.O., 1977. — vi,6p ; 25cm.
ISBN 0-11-340057-8 Sd : £0.35
(B77-21019)

345'.42'08 — Juvenile courts. Proceedings. *England. Tables*

Shaw & Sons' table of proceedings in juvenile courts (with available methods of treatment). — London : Shaw and Sons.
1976 revised to 26th November : incorporating age table and intelligence quotient table. — 1977. — Folder ([4]p) ; 36x13cm.
ISBN 0-7219-0188-3 : Unpriced
(B77-31781)

345'.422'002648 — England. Criminal law. Cases in assize courts in Home Counties, 1558-1625. *Digests*

Cockburn, James Swanston. Calendar of Assize records / edited [i.e. prepared] by J.S. Cockburn. — London : H.M.S.O.
Records preserved in the Public Record Office. — In 11 vols.
Hertfordshire indictments, Elizabeth I. — 1975. — vii,268p ; 26cm.
Index.
ISBN 0-11-440069-5 : £11.00
(B77-01260)

345'.429'08 — Juvenile courts. Defendants. Cooperation between welfare services. *Wales. Inquiry reports*

Working Party on Co-operation and Communication between Agencies concerned with Children and Young Persons appearing before Juvenile Courts in Wales. Children appearing before juvenile courts : a framework of consultation / Working Party on Co-operation and Communication between Agencies concerned with Children and Young Persons appearing before Juvenile Courts in Wales ; chairman Ronald Davie. — Abridged [ed.]. — [Mold] ([Shire Hall, Mold, Clwyd CH7 6NB]) : Childrens Regional Planning Committee for Wales, 1977. — [1],23p ; 21cm.
Full ed.: published as 'Report of the Working Party on Co-operation and Communication between Agencies concerned with Children and Young Persons appearing before Juvenile Courts in Wales'. 1977.
Sd : Unpriced
(B77-26923)

Working Party on Co-operation and Communication between Agencies concerned with Children and Young Persons appearing before Juvenile Courts in Wales. Report of the Working Party on Co-operation and Communication between Agencies concerned with Children and Young Persons appearing before Juvenile Courts in Wales, 1977 = Adroddiad y Pwyllgor Gwaith ar Gydweithrediad a Chyfath rebiad cyd-rhwng y Gwasanaethau sydd yn ymwneud a Phlant a Phersonau Ifanc a ymddengys o flaen Llysoedd Ienctid yng Nghymru, 1977 / chairman = cadeirydd Ronald Davie. — [Mold] ([Shire Hall, Mold, Clwyd CH7 6NB]) : Children's Regional Planning Committee for Wales, 1977. — [3],131p : forms ; 30cm.
Sd : Unpriced
(B77-26924)

345'.47'02310924 — Political prisoners. Trials. *Soviet Union, 1945-1947. Personal observations*
Kopelev, Lev Zalmanovich. No jail for thought / [by] Lev Kopelev ; translated [from the Russian] and edited by Anthony Austin ; foreword by Heinrich Böll ; afterword by Robert G. Kaiser. — Edited and abbreviated [ed.]. — London : Secker and Warburg, 1977. — xx,268p,[8]p of plates : ports ; 25cm.
This ed. also published: Philadelphia : Lippincott, 1977. — Previous ed.: published as 'Khranit' vechno'. Ann Arbor : Ardis, 1975.
ISBN 0-436-23640-0 : £6.00
(B77-27749)

345'.495'0234 — Political prisoners. Torture, 1967-1974. Trial of members of Greece. Ell̄enik̄e Stratiotik̄e Astynomia. *Greece, 1975*
Amnesty International. Torture in Greece : the first torturers' trial, 1975 / [Amnesty International]. — London (53 Theobald's Rd, WC1X 8SP) : Amnesty International Publications, 1977. — 96p,[4]p of plates : ill, ports ; 21cm.
ISBN 0-900058-42-0 Pbk : £0.85
(B77-24796)

345'.498'002632 — Romania. Criminal law. *Penal codes*
Romania. *Laws, statutes, etc. (Individual titles).* The penal code of the Romanian Socialist Republic / translated [from the Romanian] and with an introduction by Simone-Marie Vrăbiescu Kleckner ; research associates Bernard Stamler, Barbara Lacher. — South Hackensack : Fred B. Rothman and Co. ; London : Sweet and Maxwell, 1976. — [15], 143p ; 23cm. — (The American series of foreign penal codes ; 20)
ISBN 0-8377-0040-x : £10.00
(B77-13575)

345'.52'023 — Freedom of speech. Control. Law. *Japan. Peace Preservation Law 1925. Operation, 1925-1941*
Mitchell, Richard Hanks. Thought control in prewar Japan / [by] Richard H. Mitchell. — Ithaca ; London : Cornell University Press, 1976. — 226,[2]p : ill ; 23cm.
Bibl.: p.205-218. — Index.
ISBN 0-8014-1002-9 : £8.75
(B77-01261)

345'.71'05 — Canada. Criminal law. Justice. Administration. Plea bargaining
Klein, John F. Let's make a deal : negotiating justice / [by] John F. Klein. — Lexington, Mass. [etc.] : D.C. Heath ; Farnborough, Hants. (1 Westmead, Farnborough, Hants. GU14 7RU) : Distributed by Teakfield Ltd, 1976. — ix,161p ; 24cm.
'Lexington Books'. — Bibl.: p.151-160.
ISBN 0-669-00796-x : £8.45
(B77-16271)

345'.73'05 — United States. Criminal law. Justice. Administration
Edelstein, Charles D. An introduction to criminal justice / [by] Charles D. Edelstein, Robert J. Wicks. — New York ; London [etc.] : Gregg Division, McGraw-Hill, 1977. — ix,2-296p : ill ; 24cm.
Bibl.: p.245-249. — Index. — Includes the text of the Constitution of the United States.
ISBN 0-07-018980-3 Pbk : £7.45
(B77-24797)

Weinreb, Lloyd L. Denial of justice : criminal process in the United States / [by] Lloyd L. Weinreb. — New York : Free Press ; London : Collier Macmillan, 1977. — xiii,177p ; 25cm.
Index.
ISBN 0-02-934900-1 : £9.75
(B77-21768)

345'.73'05 — United States. Criminal law. Justice. Administration. Role of victims of crimes
Criminal justice and the victim / William F. McDonald, editor. — Beverly Hills ; London : Sage Publications, [1977]. — 288p : 1 ill ; 24cm. — (Sage criminal justice system annuals ; vol.6)
Published in the United States: 1976. — Bibl. — Index.
ISBN 0-8039-0508-4 : £11.00
ISBN 0-8039-0509-2 Pbk : £4.95
(B77-10766)

345'.73'072 — United States. Criminal law. Bail. Imposition. Procedure. Reform, 1961-1975
Thomas, Wayne H. Bail reform in America / [by] Wayne H. Thomas, Jr ; foreword by Floyd Feeney. — Berkeley [etc.] ; London : University of California Press, 1976. — xvi,272p : 1 ill, form ; 23cm.
Index.
ISBN 0-520-03131-8 : £7.00
(B77-22453)

345'.73'077 — Offenders. Sentencing. Reform. *United States. Proposals*
O'Donnell, Pierce. Toward a just and effective sentencing system : agenda for legislative reform / [by] Pierce O'Donnell, Michael J. Churgin, Dennis E. Curtis ; foreword by Edward M. Kennedy. — New York ; London : Praeger, 1977. — xvii,139p ; 25cm. — (Praeger special studies in US economic, social and political issues)
Index.
ISBN 0-275-23990-x : £11.05
(B77-26925)

345'.744'05 — United States. Criminal law. Justice. Administration. Plea bargaining. *Study regions: Massachusetts*
Buckle, Suzann R Thomas. Bargaining for justice : case disposition and reform in the criminal courts / [by] Suzann R. Thomas Buckle, Leonard G. Buckle. — New York ; London : Praeger, 1977. — v,183p ; 25cm. — (Praeger special studies in US economic, social and political issues)
Bibl.: p.170-177. — Index.
ISBN 0-275-56070-8 : £11.70
(B77-27750)

345'.749'025230924 — Murder of Lindbergh, Charles. Trial of Hauptmann, Bruno Richard. *New Jersey. Sourland Mountain*
Scaduto, Anthony. Scapegoat : the truth about the Lindbergh kidnapping / [by] Anthony Scaduto. — London : Secker and Warburg, 1977. — 512p ; 23cm.
Originally published: as 'Scapegoat : the lonesome death of Bruno Richard Hauptmann'. New York : Putnam, 1976. — Index.
ISBN 0-436-44345-7 : £6.50
(B77-14626)

345'.773'025230924 — Murder of Smith, Joseph, b.1805. Trial. *Illinois. Carthage*
Oaks, Dallin Harris. Carthage conspiracy : the trial of the accused assassins of Joseph Smith / [by] Dallin H. Oaks and Marvin S. Hill. — Urbana [etc.] ; London : University of Illinois Press, [1977]. — xiv,248,[1]p,[8]p of plates : ill, map(on lining papers), ports ; 24cm.
Published in the United States: 1975. — Index.
ISBN 0-252-00554-6 : £6.40
(B77-12375)

345'.794'002632 — California. Criminal law. Penal codes, 1955-1971
Berk, Richard Alan. A measure of justice : an empirical study of changes in the California penal code, 1955-1971 / [by] Richard A. Berk, Harold Brackman, Selma Lesser. — New York [etc.] ; London : Academic Press, 1977. — xix, 312p : ill ; 24cm. — (Quantitative studies in social relations)
Index.
ISBN 0-12-091550-2 : £12.40
(B77-28503)

346 — PRIVATE LAW
346.03'8 — Products. Defects. Liability of manufacturers & retailers. *Periodicals*
Journal of products liability. — New York ; Oxford [etc.] : Pergamon.
Vol.1, no.1- ; 1977-. — 1977. — ill ; 26cm.
Quarterly. — [2],62p. in 1st issue.
Sd : Unpriced
ISSN 0363-0404
(B77-15186)

346.04 — Matrimonial property. Apportionment on divorce. Law
Gray, Kevin J. Reallocation of property on divorce / by Kevin J. Gray. — Abingdon : Professional Books, 1977. — xliv,353p ; 23cm.
Index.
ISBN 0-903486-36-9 : £12.50
(B77-24089)

346.05'9 — Trusts. Law. *Commonwealth countries. Comparative studies*
Keeton, George Williams. The comparative law of trusts in the Commonwealth and the Irish Republic / by George W. Keeton & L.A. Sheridan. — Chichester [etc.] : Rose, 1976. — lvi,370p ; 26cm.
Index.
ISBN 0-85992-038-0 : £20.00
(B77-07217)

346'.4'0486 — Patents. Law. *European Community countries*
Confederation of British Industry. Patents and trade marks in the European Community / Confederation of British Industry. — London : C.B.I., 1976. — 39p ; 21cm.
Bibl.: p.39.
Sd : £2.00
Also classified at 346'.4'0488
(B77-00110)

346'.4'0488 — Trade marks. Law. *European Community countries*
Confederation of British Industry. Patents and trade marks in the European Community / Confederation of British Industry. — London : C.B.I., 1976. — 39p ; 21cm.
Bibl.: p.39.
Sd : £2.00
Primary classification 346'.4'0486
(B77-00110)

346'.4'052 — Rural communities. Property. Inheritance. Law. Social aspects. *Western Europe, 1200-1800*
Family and inheritance : rural society in Western Europe, 1200-1800 / edited by Jack Goody, Joan Thirsk, E.P. Thompson. — Cambridge [etc.] : Cambridge University Press, 1976. — vi, 421p : ill, maps ; 23cm. — (Past and present publications)
Index.
ISBN 0-521-21246-4 : £8.80
(B77-02132)

346'.4'0662 — Companies. Law. *European Community countries. For organisation of branches & subsidiaries*
Association européenne d'études juridiques et fiscales. Branches and subsidiaries in the European Common Market : legal and tax aspects. — 2nd ed. (reset, revised, enlarged and updated) / prepared by members of the European Association for Legal and Fiscal Studies, Carel A.V. Aalders ... [et al.]. — London : Kluwer-Harrap [etc.], 1976. — 3-322p ; 24cm.
Previous ed.: / contributions by members of the Association européenne d'études juridiques et fiscales, P.M. Storm et al. 1973. — Bibl.
ISBN 0-903393-21-2 : £11.50
(B77-02133)

346'.41'02 — Contracts. Law. *Great Britain*
Chitty, Joseph. Chitty on contracts. — 24th ed. / [general editor A.G. Guest, editors others]. — London : Sweet and Maxwell, 1977. — 2v.(ccii, 943,64p;clxxxvii,1051,64p) ; 26cm. — (The common law library ; nos 1 [and] 2)
Previous ed.: 1968. — Index.
ISBN 0-421-20170-3 : £40.00
(B77-24798)

346'.41'024 — Employment. Contracts. Law. *Great Britain*
Dix, Dorothy Knight. Dix on contracts of employment. — 5th ed. / [by] D.W. Crump. — London : Butterworth, 1976. — xliv,528p ; 23cm.
Previous ed.: 1972. — Index.
ISBN 0-406-17803-8 : £14.00
(B77-05965)

Incomes Data Services. Employment contracts / [Incomes Data Services]. — London (140 Great Portland St., W.1) : I.D.S., 1976. — [5],119p ; 21cm. — (Incomes Data Services. Handbook series ; no.2 ISSN 0308-7085)
Pbk : £2.50
(B77-10767)

346'.41'03 — Torts. Law. *Great Britain*
Salmond, *Sir* **John William.** Salmond on the law of torts. — 17th ed. / by R.F.V. Heuston. — London : Sweet and Maxwell, 1977. — xc, 629p ; 25cm.
Previous ed.: 1973. — Index.
ISBN 0-421-23050-9 : Unpriced
ISBN 0-421-23060-6 Pbk : £8.50
(B77-24799)

346'.41'038 — Products. Defects. Liability of manufacturers & retailers. Law. Reform. *Great Britain. Proposals*
Law Commission. Liability for defective products / the Law Commission and the Scottish Law Commission. — London : H.M.S.O., [1977]. — iv,96p ; 25cm. — (Law Com ; no.82) (Scot. Law Com. ; no.45) (Cmnd. 6831)
ISBN 0-10-168310-3 Sd : £1.60
(B77-21020)

346'.41'043 — Real property. Development. Law. *Great Britain*
Holbrook, Richard George. Problems for the developer / [by] R.G. Holbrook. — [Guildford] ([Braboeuf Manor, Portsmouth Rd, St Catherine's, Guildford, Surrey]) : The College of Law, 1976. — [1],19p ; 22cm. — (College of Law. Crash course lectures : 1976)
ISBN 0-905835-44-1 Sd : £0.75
(B77-08898)

346'.41'0432 — Land. Common ownership. Law. *Great Britain*
Encyclopedia of planning law and practice, land development series / consultant editor Sir Desmond Heap, general editor J.T. Farrand, assistant general editor Victor Moore. — London : Sweet and Maxwell. — (The local government library)
[Vol.A1]. — 1976. — 1v. ; 26cm.
Three hundred and twenty eight p. in various pagings on publication. — Tab indexed. — In binder. — Index.
ISBN 0-421-22490-8 Ls : £20.00
(B77-02134)

346'.41'0432 — Land. Common ownership. Law. *Great Britain. Community Land Act 1975. Critical studies*
Development land tax and the Community Land Act 1975. — [Guildford] ([Braboeuf Manor, Portsmouth Rd, St Catherine's, Guildford, Surrey]) : The College of Law, 1976. — v,86p ; 22cm. — (College of Law. Lectures : 1976)
'In March and early April of this year [1976] the College organised a one-day course at eight centres ... This booklet contains the lectures given at the course, revised to take account of changes made up to and including August 1, 1976' - Introduction.
ISBN 0-905835-17-4 Pbk : £2.00
Primary classification 343'.41'054
(B77-09593)

Nutley, William George. The Community Land Act 1975 / by W.G. Nutley and C.H. Beaumont. — London : Estates Gazette, 1976. — xix,570p ; 23cm.
Index. — Includes the text of the Act and related statutory instruments.
ISBN 0-7282-0030-9 : £8.50
(B77-01262)

346'.41'04344 — Rented residences. Controlled tenancies. Law. *Great Britain. For landlords & tenants*
Great Britain. *Department of the Environment.* Controlled tenancies and how they can be converted to rent regulation : a guide for private landlords and tenants / [prepared by the Department of the Environment, the Welsh Office and the Central Office of Information]. — [London] : [The Department] : [Welsh Office] : [Central Office of Information], 1977. — [23]p ; 21cm.
Sd : Unpriced
(B77-20120)

346'.41'044 — Residences. Conversion, extension or improvement. Planning permission. Law. *England. For householders*
Great Britain. *Department of the Environment.* Planning permission : a guide for householders / [prepared by the Department of the Environment and the Welsh Office and the Central Office of Information]. — [London] : [Department of the Environment] : [Welsh Office] : [Central Office of Information], 1976. — 20p ; 18cm.
Sd : Unpriced
(B77-28504)

346'.41'045 — New towns. Development corporations. Finance. Law. *Great Britain. Statutes*
Great Britain. *Laws, statutes, etc. (Individual titles).* New Towns Act 1977 : Elizabeth II. 1977. Chapter 23. — London : H.M.S.O., [1977]. — Sheet(2p) ; 25x16cm.
ISBN 0-10-542377-7 : £0.10
(B77-26199)

346'.41'046 — Energy resources. Law. *Great Britain. Statutes*
Great Britain. *Laws, statutes, etc. (Individual titles).* Energy Act 1976 : Elizabeth II. 1976. Chapter 76. — London : H.M.S.O., [1976]. — ii,28,[1]p ; 25cm.
ISBN 0-10-547676-5 Sd : £0.60
(B77-08899)

346'.41'04695 — Birds. Protection. Law. *Great Britain. Statutes*
Great Britain. *Laws, statutes, etc. (Individual titles).* Protection of Birds (Amendment) Act 1976 : Elizabeth II. 1976. Chapter 42. — London : H.M.S.O., [1976]. — Sheet([2]p) ; 25x16cm.
ISBN 0-10-544276-3 : £0.08
(B77-00675)

346'.41'04695 — Great Britain. Foreign trade in organisms in danger of extinction. Law. *Statutes*
Great Britain. *Laws, statutes, etc. (Individual titles).* Endangered Species (Import and Export) Act 1976 : Elizabeth II. 1976. Chapter 72. — London : H.M.S.O., 1976. — [1],29,[1]p ; 25cm.
ISBN 0-10-547276-x Sd : £0.60
(B77-09603)

346'.41'0482 — Copyright. Law. *Great Britain. For teaching. Algorithms*
Crabb, Geoffrey. Copyright clearance : a practical guide / [by] Geoffrey Crabb. — London : Council for Educational Technology for the United Kingdom : Distributed by Councils and Education Press, 1976. — 59p ; 21x30cm. — (Council for Educational Technology for the United Kingdom. Guidelines ; 2 ISSN 0308-0323)
ISBN 0-902204-66-1 Sp : £2.25
(B77-11137)

346'.41'0482 — Copyright. Law. *Great Britain. Inquiry reports*
Committee to Consider the Law on Copyright and Designs. Copyright and designs law : report of the Committee to Consider the Law on Copyright and Designs ... / chairman the Honourable Mr Justice Whitford. — London : H.M.S.O., [1977]. — xiv,272p : 1 ill ; 25cm. — (Cmnd.6732)
Bibl.: p.255-256. — Index.
ISBN 0-10-167320-5 Pbk : £4.10
(B77-09604)

346'.41'0482 — Music. Performing rights. Organisations. *Great Britain. Performing Right Society. Periodicals*
Performing right news / the Performing Right Society Ltd. — London : The Society.
Supersedes: Performing right.
No.1- ; [Sept. 1976]-. — 1976-. — 30cm.
Published at irregular intervals. — 5 leaves in 1st issue.
Sd : Unpriced
ISSN 0309-0019
(B77-04668)

346'.41'0482 — Music. Performing rights. Organisations. *Great Britain. Performing Right Society. Reports, surveys. Serials*
The **performing** right yearbook. — London (29 Berners St., W1P 4AA) : Performing Right Society Ltd.
1977. — 1977. — 80,xvi p : ill, ports ; 30cm.
Cover title. — Folder ([5]p.) as insert.
Pbk : Unpriced
ISSN 0309-0884
(B77-30065)

346'.41'048602633 — Patents. Law. *Great Britain. Statutes*
Great Britain. *Laws, statutes, etc. (Individual titles).* Patents Act 1977 : Elizabeth II. 1977. Chapter 37. — London : H.M.S.O., [1977]. — [1],vi,124p ; 25cm.
ISBN 0-10-543777-8 Sd : £2.10
(B77-26926)

346'.41'0560269 — Inherited property: Estates. Administration. Law. Procedure. *Great Britain. Manuals*
Nelson, Bertram. Nelson's tables of procedure. — 6th ed. / by C.N. Gorman, assisted by R.C. Bailey and A. Robertson. — London : Oyez Publishing, 1975. — vi,65p ; 25cm.
Previous ed.: published as 'Tables of procedure' / by J.W. Mayo and David Foster, 1963.
ISBN 0-85120-259-4 Sd : £2.50
Primary classification 346'.41'0660269
(B77-00111)

346'.41'06305 — Accounting. Law. *Great Britain. Serials*
Current accounting law and practice. — London : Sweet and Maxwell.
1977 / by Robert Willott. — 1977. — xxi, 565p : forms ; 25cm.
Index.
ISBN 0-421-23020-7 Pbk : £9.50
(B77-18631)

346'.41'065 — Business firms. Implications of European Community law. *Great Britain*
The **business** client and the EEC. — [Guildford] : [Braboeuf Manor, Portsmouth Rd, St Catherine's, Guildford, Surrey] : The College of Law, 1973. — [3],100p ; 22cm. — (College of Law. Lectures : 1973)
Lectures given at a course held in London, Leeds and Manchester.
ISBN 0-905835-24-7 Pbk : £1.00
(B77-09605)

346'.41'0652 — Small firms. Law. *Great Britain*
Chesterman, Michael Rainsford. Small businesses / by Michael Chesterman. — London : Sweet and Maxwell, 1977. — xvii, 267p ; 19cm. — (Modern legal studies)
Index.
£4.25
ISBN 0-421-21100-8
ISBN 0-421-21110-5 Pbk : £2.75
(B77-12376)

346'.41'066 — Companies. Law. *Great Britain*
Farrar, Harry. Company law / by Harry Farrar. — 11th ed. / by D.A. Thair. — St Albans : Donnington Press ; London : Cassell, 1976. — xxi,324p ; 23cm.
Previous ed.: / by M.A. Brownlie, 1970. — Index.
ISBN 0-304-29927-8 : £4.75
(B77-27751)

346'.41'066 — Companies. Law. *Great Britain. Companies Act 1976. Commentaries*
Eley, Stanley James Sidney. Company law amendment 1976 : a practical guide and handbook / by S.J.S. Eley. — London (16 Park Cres., W1N 4AH) : Institute of Chartered Secretaries and Administrators, [1976]. — [1],ii leaves,[40],[1]p ; 21cm.
Index.
Sd : £2.00
(B77-27752)

Harkness, W. The Companies Act 1976 : a commentary / by W. Harkness, I.C.M. Robertson. — London : Gee and Co. for the Institute of Chartered Accountants of Scotland, 1976. — 40p ; 22cm.
ISBN 0-85258-155-6 Sd : £1.50
(B77-08900)

346'.41'066 — Companies. Law. *Great Britain. For company secretaryship*
Pitfield, Ronald Reuben. Key to company law and practice. — 4th ed. / [by Ronald R. Pitfield and Percy F. Hughes]. — London (98 Part St., W.1) : Secretaries Journal Ltd, [1976?]. — 253p : forms ; 22cm.
'Companies Act 1976 edition' - cover. — Thumb indexed.
Pbk : £5.00
(B77-31067)

346'.41'066 — Companies. Law. Statutes. *Great Britain, 1976. Critical studies*
Lowe, James Randolph Martin. The 1976 companies legislation / [by] J.R.M. Lowe. — Newcastle upon Tyne (75 Jesmond Park West, Newcastle upon Tyne) : North of England Law Book Publishing Company, 1977. — [1],xi, 160p ; 22cm.
Index. — Includes the texts of the Companies Act, 1976, the Stock Exchange (Completion of Bargains) Act 1976, and those sections of the Insolvency Act 1976 relating to company law.
ISBN 0-905922-00-x Pbk : £2.75
(B77-26927)

346'.41'06602633 — Companies. Law. *Great Britain. Statutes*
Great Britain. *Laws, statutes, etc. (Individual titles).* Companies Act 1976 : Elizabeth II. 1976. Chapter 69. — London : H.M.S.O., [1976]. — iii,53,[1]p ; 25cm.
ISBN 0-10-546976-9 Sd : £1.00
(B77-08901)

346'.41'0660264 — Companies. Law. *Great Britain. Cases*
Oliver, Mary Chichester. Cases in company law / [by] M.C. Oliver. — 2nd ed. — Plymouth : Macdonald and Evans, 1976. — xii, 432p ; 19cm. — (The M & E casebook series)
Previous ed.: 1972. — Index.
ISBN 0-7121-0365-1 Pbk : £2.50
(B77-06556)

346'.41'0660269 — Companies. Law. Procedure. *Great Britain. Manuals*
Nelson, Bertram. Nelson's tables of procedure. — 6th ed. / by C.N. Gorman, assisted by R.C. Bailey and A. Robertson. — London : Oyez Publishing, 1975. — vi,65p ; 25cm.
Previous ed.: published as 'Tables of procedure' / by J.W. Mayo and David Foster, 1963.
ISBN 0-85120-259-4 Sd : £2.50
Also classified at 346'.42'0780269; 346'.41'0560269
(B77-00111)

346'.41'0662 — Companies. Liquidation. Law. *Great Britain*
Chiswell, P G. Company liquidations : some problems for practitioners / [by] P.G. Chiswell. — [Guildford] ([Braboeuf Manor, Portsmouth Rd, St Catherine's, Guildford, Surrey]) : The College of Law, 1974. — [1],25p ; 22cm. — (College of Law. Crash course lectures : 1974)
ISBN 0-905835-11-5 Sd : £0.50
(B77-05966)

Sales, Charles Allison. Sales' the law relating to bankruptcy, liquidations and receiverships. — 6th ed. / by J.H. Thompson. — Plymouth : Macdonald and Evans, 1977. — xliii,332p ; 22cm.
Previous ed.: 1956. — Index.
ISBN 0-7121-1952-3 : £7.50
ISBN 0-7121-1949-3 Pbk : £4.50
Primary classification 346'.42'078
(B77-22455)

346'.41'0662 — Small firms. Take-overs. Law. *Great Britain*
Bullock, R A. Take-over agreements and the small business / [by] R.A. Bullock. — [Guildford] ([Braboeuf Manor, Portsmouth Rd, St Catherine's, Guildford, Surrey]) : The College of Law, 1975. — [1],23p ; 22cm. — (College of Law. Crash course lectures : 1975)
ISBN 0-905835-42-5 Sd : £0.60
(B77-09606)

346'.41'0664 — Companies. Accounts. Law. *Great Britain*
Jones, Frank Horace. Accounting requirements of companies / by Frank H. Jones. — 11th ed. — Bournemouth : Barkeley Book Co., 1977. — 47p ; 22cm.
Previous ed.: 1975. — Index.
ISBN 0-900132-07-8 Sd : £1.00
(B77-11691)

346'.41'0664 — Companies. Auditing. Law. Great Britain. Compared with law of company auditing in Belgium
Anglo-Belgian Liaison Committee of the Institute of Chartered Accountants in England and Wales, Collège National des Experts Comptables de Belgique, Institut des Reviseurs d'Entreprises. Statutory audit requirements in Belgium : a comparison with the requirements in the United Kingdom / [undertaken by the Anglo-Belgian Liaison Committee of the Institute of Chartered Accountants in England and Wales, Collège National des Experts Comptables de Belgique, Institut des Reviseurs d'Entreprises]. — London : The Institute, 1976. — 79p ; 21cm.
ISBN 0-85291-158-0 Pbk : £2.95
Also classified at 346'.493'0664
(B77-08295)

346'.41'0664 — Companies. Published accounts. Law. *Great Britain*
Institute of Chartered Accountants in England and Wales. Guide to the accounting requirements of the Companies Acts : a summary of the statutory requirements contained in the 1948, 1967 and 1976 Acts relating to the production of annual accounts of companies / Institute of Chartered Accountants in England and Wales. — 5th ed. — London : Gee and Co., 1977. — 39p ; 25cm.
Previous ed.: published as 'Guide to the accounting requirements of the Companies Acts 1948-1967'. 1975. — Index.
ISBN 0-85258-156-4 Sd : £1.25
(B77-13576)

346'.41'0664 — Company secretaryship. *Great Britain. Manuals*
Birds, John. Reminders for company secretaries. — 23rd ed. / [by] John Birds. — London : Jordan, 1977. — 122p ; 21cm.
Previous ed.: / by T.M. Stockdale. Bristol : Jordan, 1972.
ISBN 0-85308-048-8 Pbk : £3.00
(B77-26200)

Boulton, Albert Harding. Handbook on company administration. — 3rd ed. / [by] A. Harding Boulton in collaboration with J.E. Neill. — London : Jordan [for] the Institute of Chartered Secretaries and Administrators, 1976 [i.e. 1977]. — xviii,324p : forms ; 21cm.
Previous ed.: / by A. Harding Boulton. 1974. — Index.
ISBN 0-85308-046-1 Pbk : £4.00
(B77-12938)

346'.41'0664 — Periodicals for company secretaries: Periodicals with British imprints. *Texts*
Company secretary's review. — Croydon : Tolley.
No.1- ; 23 Mar. 1977-. — 1977-. — 30cm.
Fortnightly. — 8p. in 1st issue. — Pierced for binder.
Sd : £28.00 yearly
ISSN 0309-703x
(B77-20121)

346'.41'068 — Law. *Great Britain. For self-employed persons*
Croner's reference book for the self employed / edited by Daphne Macara. — New Malden (46 Coombe Rd, New Malden, Surrey KT3 4QL) : Croner Publications Ltd, 1976-. — 1v. : forms ; 22cm.
Ca 400p. on publication. — In binder. — Includes a monthly amendment service. — Index.
Ls : Unpriced
(B77-33691)

346'.41'073 — Consumer credit. Law. *Great Britain. Consumer Credit Act 1974. Critical studies*
Johnson, Howard. The Consumer Credit Act 1974 / by Howard Johnson. — Bradford : MCB, 1976. — [2],48p ; 30cm.
'... first appeared in "Managerial Law" Volume 18, 1976' - title page verso.
ISBN 0-905440-02-1 Sd : £4.50
(B77-18632)

346'.41'073 — Consumer credit. Law. *Great Britain. Consumer Credit Act 1974. Exemption*
Great Britain. *Department of Prices and Consumer Protection.* Consumer Credit Act 1974, exemption of certain consumer credit agreements under Section 16(1) / [Department of Prices and Consumer Protection]. — London (1 Victoria St., SW1H 0ET) : The Department, 1977. — [2],12p ; 21cm.
ISBN 0-86058-004-0 Sd : Unpriced
(B77-11692)

346'.41'073 — Consumer credit. Law. *Great Britain. Consumer Credit (Total Charge for Credit) Regulations 1977. Critical studies*
Great Britain. *Department of Prices and Consumer Protection.* Counting the cost of credit : the Consumer Credit (Total Charge for Credit) Regulations 1977 / [Department of Prices and Consumer Protection]. — [London] ([1 Victoria St., SW1H 0ET]) : [The Department], 1977. — [2],17p ; 21cm.
ISBN 0-86058-005-9 Sd : Unpriced
(B77-12377)

346'.41'073 — Consumer credit. Law. Secondary legislation. *Great Britain*
Goode, Royston Miles. Consumer credit legislation / [by] R.M. Goode. — London : Butterworth, 1977. — 1v. : forms ; 25cm.
In binder. — 384p. in various pagings on publication. — Tab indexed. — Supplements: 'Introduction to the Consumer Credit Act 1974'. 1974. — Includes the text of relevant legislation.
ISBN 0-406-21163-9 Ls : £21.50
(B77-26928)

346'.41'074 — Loans. Securities. Law. *Great Britain*
Sheridan, Lionel Astor. Rights in security / [by] L.A. Sheridan. — London [etc.] : Collins, 1974. — lxxxi,331p ; 23cm. — (Legal topics for business studies)
Index.
ISBN 0-00-460109-2 : £4.50
(B77-07858)

346'.41'078 — Insolvency. Law. Procedure. *Great Britain. Periodicals*
Insolvency administration newsletter. — Chelmsford (16 Taunton Rd, Chelmsford CM1 5JH) : Broken Bench Services.
No.1- ; Easter 1977-. — 1977-. — 30cm.
5 leaves in 1st issue.
Sd : Unpriced
(B77-18633)

346'.41'07802633 — Insolvency. Law. *Great Britain. Statutes*
Great Britain. *Laws, statutes, etc. (Individual titles).* Insolvency Act 1976 : Elizabeth II. 1976. Chapter 60. — London : H.M.S.O., [1976]. — [1],17p ; 25cm.
ISBN 0-10-546076-1 Sd : £0.35
(B77-06557)

346'.41'082 — Banking. Law. *Great Britain. For trustee savings banks*
Doyle, Edward Pemberton. Banking law for TSBS / [by] E.P. Doyle. — [London] ([52 Mortimer St., W1N 7DG]) : [The Savings Banks Institute], [1977]. — [103]leaves : forms ; 31cm.
In binder.
ISBN 0-902772-04-x Ls : Unpriced
(B77-10768)

346'.41'082 — Trustee savings banks. Law. *Great Britain*
Hennessy, J M. TSB legislation and management / [by] J.M. Hennessy. — [London] ([52 Mortimer St., W1N 7DG]) : [Savings Banks Institute], [1977]. — 98 leaves in various pagings ; 31cm.
In binder.
ISBN 0-902772-03-1 Ls : £2.00
(B77-10273)

346'.41'0860264 — Insurance. Law. *Great Britain. Cases*
Ivamy, Edward Richard Hardy. Casebook on insurance law / by E.R. Hardy Ivamy. — 3rd ed. — London : Butterworth, 1977. — xxxii, 267p ; 22cm.
Previous ed.: 1972. — Index.
ISBN 0-406-60262-x Pbk : £7.00
(B77-22454)

346'.411'012 — Presumption of death. Law. *Scotland. Statutes*
Great Britain. *Laws, statutes, etc. (Individual titles).* Presumption of Death (Scotland) Act 1977 : Elizabeth II. 1977. Chapter 27. — London : H.M.S.O., [1977]. — [1],12,[1]p ; 25cm.
ISBN 0-10-542777-2 Sd : £0.35
(B77-26201)

346'.411'015 — Families. Law. *Scotland*
Nichols, David Ian. Marriage, divorce and the family in Scotland / [by] David Ian Nichols. — Edinburgh (12 Queen St., Edinburgh) : Scottish Association of Citizens Advice Bureaux, 1976. — [4],40p ; 21cm.
ISBN 0-905831-00-4 Sd : £0.50
(B77-09607)

346'.411'016602633 — Divorce. Law. *Scotland. Statutes. Texts with commentaries*
Clive, Eric McCredie. The Divorce (Scotland) Act 1976 / by Eric M. Clive. — Edinburgh : Green, 1976. — vii,34p ; 25cm.
Includes the text of the Act.
ISBN 0-414-00602-x Pbk : £3.00
(B77-00112)

346'.411'0430269 — Great Britain. Scottish Land Court. Proceedings. *Reports, surveys. Serials*
Great Britain. *Scottish Land Court.* Report as to proceedings under the Agriculture and the Agricultural Holdings (Scotland) Acts, the Small Landholders (Scotland) Acts 1886 to 1931, the Crofters (Scotland) Acts 1955 and 1961 and the Crofting Reform (Scotland) Act 1976 ... / the Scottish Land Court. — Edinburgh : H.M.S.O.
1976. — [1977]. — 22p ; 25cm. — (Cmnd.6870)
ISBN 0-10-168700-1 Sd : £0.50
(B77-26929)

346'.411'0438 — Real property. Conveyancing. Law. *Scotland. Conveyancing and Feudal Reform (Scotland) Act 1970. Commentaries*
Halliday, John Menzies. The Conveyancing and Feudal Reform (Scotland) Act 1970 / by John M. Halliday. — 2nd ed. — Edinburgh : Green, 1977. — xix,296p : forms ; 25cm.
Previous ed.: 1970. — Index. — Includes the text of the Act and other relevant legislation.
ISBN 0-414-00600-3 : £7.50
ISBN 0-414-00601-1 Pbk : £6.00
(B77-14627)

346'.411'04502633 — Scotland. Environment planning. Law. *Statutes*
Great Britain. *Laws, statutes, etc. (Individual titles).* Town and Country Planning (Scotland) Act 1977 : Elizabeth II. 1977. Chapter 10. — London : H.M.S.O., [1977]. — 7p ; 25cm.
ISBN 0-10-541077-2 Sd : £0.25
(B77-14628)

346'.411'04509 — Scotland. Environment planning. Law, 1973-1976
Planning Exchange. Developments in planning law in Scotland, 1973-76 / [Planning Exchange] ; [written by Eric Young]. — Glasgow (186 Bath St., Glasgow G2 4HG) : The Exchange, 1977. — [5],62p ; 21cm.
Index.
ISBN 0-905011-15-5 Pbk : £5.00(free to members)
(B77-24090)

346'.416'064 — Charities. Law. *Northern Ireland. Charities Act (Northern Ireland) 1964. Administration. Reports, surveys. Serials*
Charities : report by the Department of Finance [Northern Ireland] of proceedings under the Charities Act (Northern Ireland). — Belfast : H.M.S.O.
1964 .. / 1975. — [1976]. — 19p ; 25cm.
ISBN 0-337-23210-5 Sd : £0.30
(B77-07218)

346'.417'015 — Families. Law. *Ireland (Republic)*
Shatter, Alan Joseph. Family law in the Republic of Ireland / [by] Alan Joseph Shatter. — Portmarnock : Wolfhound Press, 1977. — xxxix,360p ; 26cm.
Index. — Includes the text of the Nullity of Marriages Bill, 1976.
ISBN 0-905473-02-7 : £11.00
ISBN 0-905473-03-5 Pbk : £7.25
(B77-19269)

346'.42'015 — Domestic violence. Injunctions. Law. *England. Statutes*
Great Britain. *Laws, statutes, etc. (Individual titles).* Domestic Violence and Matrimonial Proceedings Act 1976 : Elizabeth II. 1976. Chapter 50. — London : H.M.S.O., [1976]. — Folder(4p) ; 25cm.
ISBN 0-10-545076-6 : £0.12
(B77-05298)

346'.42'015 — Families. Law. *England*
Stone, Olive Marjorie. Family law : an account of the law of domestic relations in England and Wales in the last quarter of the twentieth century, with some comparisons / [by] Olive M. Stone. — London [etc.] : Macmillan, 1977. — xxxv,277p ; 25cm.
Bibl.: p.263-271. — Index.
ISBN 0-333-19629-5 : £12.50
ISBN 0-333-19630-9 Pbk : £5.95
(B77-20123)

346'.42'016 — Hide, Bridget. Clandestine marriage to Emerton, John. Legal aspects. *Hertfordshire. Aldbury, 1674-1683*
Davis, Jean, *b.1925.* The case of the pretended marriage : Hide v. Emerton, 1674-1683 / by Jean Davis. — Aldbury (Aldbury [Herts.]) : Church Farm House Publications, 1976. — 38p,[2]p of plates : 1 ill, facsims, 2 geneal tables, maps ; 21cm.
Cover title: The pretended marriage.
Sd : £0.60
(B77-18018)

346'.42'016 — Marriage. Law. *England*
Hopkins, F. Formation and annulment of marriage / [by] F. Hopkins. — London : Oyez Publishing, 1976. — xix,101p ; 22cm. — (Oyez practice notes ; 64)
ISBN 0-85120-309-4 Pbk : £4.75
(B77-04669)

Passingham, Bernard. Marriage breakdown, nullity, separation and divorce / [by] B. Passingham. — [Guildford] ([Braboeuf Manor, Portsmouth Rd, St Catherine's, Guildford, Surrey]) : The College of Law, 1972. — [1], 19p ; 22cm. — (College of Law. Crash course lectures : 1972)
ISBN 0-905835-04-2 Sd : £0.45
(B77-04670)

346'.42'0166 — Divorce. Law. *England*
Rayden, William. Rayden's law and practice in divorce and family matters in all courts. — 12th ed. / editor-in-chief Joseph Jackson. — London : Butterworth.
Previous ed.: 1971.
2nd (cumulative) supplement. — 1976. — xxi, B397p : forms ; 25cm.
Supplement has title: Rayden's law and practice in divorce and family matters in the high court, county courts and magistrates' courts. — Cover title: Rayden on divorce. — Index.
ISBN 0-406-35162-7 : £10.00
(B77-07219)

346'.42'0166 — Divorce. Law. *England. State-of-the-art reviews*
Carvell, Ian George. Divorce law and practice / [by] I.G. Carvell. — [London] : [Law Society], [1976]. — [1],28p ; 21cm. — (Law Society. Refresher lectures ; 1976)
Sd : £0.75
(B77-26930)

346'.42'0166 — Divorce. Maintenance orders. Law. *England*
Lowe, Robert, *b.1932.* Maintenance and matrimonial property orders and their enforcement / [by] R. Lowe. — [Guildford] : [Braboeuf Manor, Portsmouth Rd, St Catherine's, Guildford, Surrey] : The College of Law, 1976. — [1],20p ; 22cm. — (College of Law. Crash course lectures : 1976)
ISBN 0-905835-30-1 Sd : £0.75
Also classified at 346'.42'04
(B77-09608)

346'.42'0166 — Matrimonial causes. Law. *England*
Marriage breakdown, money and tax. — [Guildford] ([Braboeuf Manor, Portsmouth Rd, St Catherine's, Guildford, Surrey]) : The College of Law, 1976. — v,88p ; 22cm. — (College of Law. Lectures : 1976)
'... contains lectures given at a College of Law course held in London and six other centres during 1975' - Preface.
ISBN 0-905835-25-5 Pbk : £2.00
(B77-05299)

346'.42'01660269 — Matrimonial causes. Procedure of magistrates' courts. Reform. *England. Proposals*
Law Commission. Family law, report on matrimonial proceedings in magistrates' courts / the Law Commission ... — London : H.M.S.O., [1976]. — [12],357p ; 25cm. — (Law Com. ; no.77) ([1975-76 H.C.] 637)
ISBN 0-10-263776-8 Pbk : £4.20
(B77-01263)

346'.42'017 — Children. Adoption. Law. *England*
Josling, John Francis. Adoption of children / [by] J.F. Josling. — 8th ed. — London : Oyez, 1977. — xviii,225p : forms ; 22cm. — (Oyez practice notes ; 3)
Previous ed.: 1972. — Index.
ISBN 0-85120-321-3 Pbk : £7.50
(B77-25484)

346'.42'017 — Children. Effects of divorce. Law. *England*
Lowe, Robert, *b.1932.* Marriage breakdown and children / [by] R. Lowe. — [Guildford] : [Braboeuf Manor, Portsmouth Rd, St Catherine's, Guildford, Surrey] : The College of Law, 1975. — [1],17p ; 22cm. — (College of Law. Crash course lectures : 1975)
ISBN 0-905835-43-3 Sd : £0.60
(B77-09609)

346'.42'02 — Contracts. Law. *England*
Davies, Francis Ronald. Contract / by F.R. Davies. — 3rd ed. — London : Sweet and Maxwell, 1977. — xx,233p ; 22cm. — (Concise college texts)
Previous ed.: 1973. — Index.
ISBN 0-421-21860-6 : £4.50
ISBN 0-421-21870-3 Pbk : £2.50
(B77-32527)

346'.42'02 — Contracts. Law. *England. State-of-the-art reviews*
Lowe, Robert, *b.1932.* Contract and mercantile law / [by] R. Lowe. — [London] : [Law Society], [1976]. — [1],22p ; 21cm. — (Law Society. Refresher lectures ; 1976)
Sd : £0.75
Also classified at 346'.42'07
(B77-26931)

346'.42'02 — Joint contracting parties. Liability. Contribution. Law. Reform. *England. Proposals*
Law Commission. Law of contract, report on contribution ... / the Law Commission. — London : H.M.S.O., [1977]. — iii,46p ; 25cm. — (Law Com. ; no.79) ([1976-77 H.C.]181)
ISBN 0-10-218177-2 Sd : £0.85
Also classified at 346'.42'03
(B77-10274)

346'.42'020264 — Contracts. Law. *England. Cases*
Major, William Thomas. Cases in contract law / [by] W.T. Major. — 2nd ed. — Plymouth : Macdonald and Evans, 1977. — xiv,208p ; 18cm. — (The M. & E. casebook series)
Previous ed.: 1972. — Index.
ISBN 0-7121-0367-8 Pbk : £1.50
(B77-32528)

346'.42'022 — Breach of contract. Law. Remedies. *England*
Henderson, Norman. Remedies for breach of contract / [by] N. Henderson. — [Guildford] ([Braboeuf Manor, Portsmouth Rd, St Catherine's, Guildford, Surrey]) : The College of Law, 1976. — [1],16p ; 22cm. — (College of Law. Crash course lectures : 1976)
ISBN 0-905835-33-6 Sd : £0.75
(B77-05967)

346'.42'022 — Contracts. Disputes. Arbitration. Law. *England. Cases*
Parris, John. Casebook of arbitration law / [by] John Parris. — London : Godwin, 1976. — viii, 262p ; 24cm.
Index.
ISBN 0-7114-3311-9 : £7.50
(B77-02135)

346'.42'022 — Contracts. Parol evidence. Law. Reform. *England. Proposals*
Law Commission. Law of contract, the parol evidence rule / the Law Commission. — London : H.M.S.O., 1976. — iv,26p ; 21cm. — (Working paper ; no.70)
ISBN 0-11-730101-9 Sd : £0.55
(B77-01264)

346'.42'029 — Enduring powers of attorney. Law. *England. Proposals*
Law Commission. The incapacitated principal / the Law Commission. — London : H.M.S.O., 1976. — vi,96p ; 21cm. — (Working paper ; no.69)
ISBN 0-11-730100-0 Pbk : £1.35
(B77-02136)

346'.42'029 — Powers of attorney. Law. *England*
Caplin, Charles. Powers of attorney / by Charles Caplin assisted by Arnold Wexler. — 4th ed. revised / by J.F. Josling. — London : Oyez Publishing, 1976. — 103p : forms ; 22cm. — (Oyez practice notes ; no.7)
Fourth ed. originally published: 1971. — Bibl.: p.103. — Includes the text of the relevant Acts and Statutory Instruments.
ISBN 0-85120-304-3 Pbk : £3.00
(B77-01265)

346'.42'03 — Joint tortfeasors. Liability. Contribution. Law. Reform. *England. Proposals*
Law Commission. Law of contract, report on contribution ... / the Law Commission. — London : H.M.S.O., [1977]. — iii,46p ; 25cm. — (Law Com. ; no.79) ([1976-77 H.C.]181)
ISBN 0-10-218177-2 Sd : £0.85
Primary classification 346'.42'02
(B77-10274)

346'.42'03 — Torts. Law. *England*
Baker, Charles David. Tort / by C.D. Baker. — 2nd ed. — London : Sweet and Maxwell, 1976. — xxvii,332p ; 22cm. — (Concise college texts)
Previous ed.: 1972. — Index.
ISBN 0-421-21470-8 : £4.75
ISBN 0-421-21480-5 Pbk : £3.00
(B77-02137)

Tyas, John Gibson Manuel. Law of torts / [by] J.G.M. Tyas. — 3rd ed. — Plymouth : Macdonald and Evans, 1977. — xxvi,246p ; 19cm. — (The M. & E. handbook series)
Previous ed.: 1973. — Bibl.: p.221. — Index.
ISBN 0-7121-1241-3 Pbk : £2.25
(B77-31782)

346'.42'03 — Torts. Law. *England. State-of-the-art reviews*
Henry, Stephen John. Tort / [by] S.J. Henry. — [London] : [Law Society], [1976]. — [1],23p ; 21cm. — (Law Society. Refresher lectures ; 1976)
Sd : £0.75
(B77-26932)

346'.42'030264 — Torts. Law. *England. Cases*
Armour, L A J. Cases in tort / [by] L.A.J. Armour and G.H. Samuel. — Plymouth : Macdonald and Evans, 1977. — xix,332p ; 19cm. — (The M & E casebook series)
Index.
ISBN 0-7121-0356-2 Pbk : £3.25
(B77-30066)

346'.42'032 — Accidents. Personal injuries. Damages. Claims. Law. Procedure. *England*
Pritchard, John M. Personal injury litigation / [by] John M. Pritchard. — London : Oyez Publishing, 1976. — xvi,264p : ill, forms ; 22cm. — (Oyez practice notes ; 63)
Index.
ISBN 0-85120-285-3 Pbk : £6.75
(B77-04033)

346'.42'032 — Negligence. Law. *England, ca 1370-1964*
Prichard, M J. Scott v Shepherd (1773) and the emergence of the tort of negligence / by M.J. Prichard. — London ([c/o The Secretary, Faculty of Laws, Queen Mary College, Mile End Rd, E1 4NS]) : Selden Society, 1976. — [1],43p ; 25cm. — (Selden Society. Annual lectures ; 1973)
'... delivered in the Old Hall of Lincoln's Inn July 4th, 1973'.
Sd : £1.50
(B77-31783)

346'.42'032 — Personal injuries. Damages. Law. *England*
Snow, Raymond Francis. Personal injury claims / [by] R.F. Snow. — [Guildford] ([Braboeuf Manor, Portsmouth Rd, St Catherine's, Guildford, Surrey]) : The College of Law, 1974. — [1],29p ; 22cm. — (College of Law. Crash course lectures : 1974)
ISBN 0-905835-02-6 Sd : £0.50
(B77-05300)

346'.42'032 — Personal injuries. Liability of occupiers of real property. Law. *England. For hospital administration*
Williams, Barry, *b.1940.* Occupiers' Liability Act 1957 and the liability of hospitals / by B. Williams. — Beckenham (P.O. Box 24, 205 Croydon Rd, Beckenham, Kent) : Ravenswood Publications Ltd, 1977. — xi,69p ; 22cm. — (Case studies on health service management law and practice ; vol.6)
Includes the text of the Act.
ISBN 0-901812-20-x : £8.00
ISBN 0-901812-19-6 Sd : £6.00
(B77-05301)

346'.42'032 — Thalidomide. Use. Legal aspects. *England*
Teff, Harvey. Thalidomide : the legal aftermath / [by] Harvey Teff, Colin R. Munro. — Farnborough, Hants. : Saxon House, 1976. — xiii,154,[1]p ; 24cm.
Index.
ISBN 0-566-00120-9 : £4.95
(B77-01266)

346'.42'036 — Real property. Trespassers. Law. *England*
Cooklin, A. Squatters, trespassers and the law : some problems for practitioners / [by] A. Cooklin. — [Guildford] ([Braboeuf Manor, Portsmouth Rd, St Catherine's, Guildford, Surrey]) : The College of Law, 1976. — [1], 19p ; 22cm. — (College of Law. Crash course lectures ; 1976)
ISBN 0-905835-32-8 Sd : £0.75
(B77-05968)

346'.42'036 — Torts: Interference with goods. Law. *England. Statutes*
Great Britain. *Laws, statutes, etc. (Individual titles).* Torts (Interference with Goods) Act 1977 : Elizabeth II. 1977. Chapter 32. — London : H.M.S.O., [1977]. — [2],13,[1]p ; 25cm.
ISBN 0-10-543277-6 Sd : £0.35
(B77-26202)

346'.42'038 — Products. Defects. Liability of manufacturers & retailers. Law. *England*
Miller, C J. Product liability / [by] C.J. Miller, the late P.A. Lovell. — London : Butterworth, 1977. — xxxix,386p ; 23cm.
Index.
ISBN 0-406-29627-8 : £21.00
(B77-15187)

346'.42'04 — Families. Property. Inheritance. Financial provision. Law. *England*
Griffiths, Lionel Robert Humphry. Family provision : the new deal / [by] L.R.H. Griffiths. — [Guildford] ([Braboeuf Manor, Portsmouth Rd, St Catherine's, Guildford, Surrey]) : The College of Law, 1976. — [1], 20p ; 22cm. — (College of Law. Crash course lectures : 1976)
ISBN 0-905835-29-8 Sd : £0.75
(B77-09610)

346'.42'04 — Matrimonial property. Apportionment on divorce. Law. *England*
Griffiths, Lionel Robert Humphry. Matrimonial property and its distribution on divorce / [by] L.R.H. Griffiths. — [Guildford] ([Braboeuf Manor, Portsmouth Rd, St Catherine's, Guildford, Surrey]) : The College of Law, 1974. — [1],17p ; 22cm. — (College of Law. Crash course lectures : 1974)
ISBN 0-905835-01-8 Sd : £0.50
(B77-09611)

Lowe, Robert, *b.1932.* Maintenance and matrimonial property orders and their enforcement / [by] R. Lowe. — [Guildford] : [Braboeuf Manor, Portsmouth Rd, St Catherine's, Guildford, Surrey] : The College of Law, 1976. — [1],20p ; 22cm. — (College of Law. Crash course lectures : 1976)
ISBN 0-905835-30-1 Sd : £0.75
Primary classification 346'.42'0166
(B77-09608)

346'.42'0402632 — Property. Law. *England. Statutes. Collections*
Great Britain. *Laws, statutes, etc. (Collections).* Sweet & Maxwell's property statutes / edited by Sweet & Maxwell's legal editorial staff ; advisory editor J.H.C. Morris. — 3rd ed. — London : Sweet and Maxwell, 1977. — viii, 534p ; 25cm.
Previous ed.: 1972. — Index.
ISBN 0-421-22450-9 : £8.50
ISBN 0-421-22440-1 Pbk : £6.40
(B77-28505)

346'.42'043 — Allotments. Law. *England*
Garner, John Francis. The law of allotments / by J.F. Garner. — 3rd ed. — London : Shaw and Sons, 1977. — xxi,121p ; 22cm.
Previous ed.: 1963. — Index.
ISBN 0-7219-0141-7 Pbk : £3.50
(B77-15759)

346'.42'043 — Real property. Law. *England*
Harwood, Michael. Cases and materials on English land law / by Michael Harwood. — Abingdon (Milton Trading Estate, Abingdon, Oxon) : Professional Books Ltd, 1977. — xxxix, 488p ; 22cm.
Index.
ISBN 0-903486-23-7 : £9.60
ISBN 0-903486-22-9 Pbk : £5.80
(B77-08902)

346'.42'0430264 — Great Britain. Lands Tribunal. *Cases*
Great Britain. *Lands Tribunal.* Lands Tribunal cases. — Chichester : Rose.
Vol.2 : [1974] / edited by Frank Othick. — 1976. — [224]p ; 22cm.
'A regular feature of the weekly journal "Local government review" for the past four years has been "Lands Tribunal Cases" ... This ... volume ... brings together all the published reports in the year ended December 31, 1974 ...' - Introduction. — Index.
ISBN 0-85992-081-x : £5.30
(B77-05302)

Vol.3 : [1975] / edited by Frank Othick. — 1976. — [217]p ; 22cm.
Index.
ISBN 0-85992-086-0 : £5.30
(B77-05303)

346'.42'0432 — Rented residences. Tenants. Eviction. Law. *England. Statutes*
Great Britain. *Laws, statutes, etc. (Individual titles).* Protection from Eviction Act 1977 : Elizabeth II. 1977. Chapter 43. — London : H.M.S.O., [1977]. — [1],10p ; 25cm.
ISBN 0-10-544377-8 Sd : £0.25
(B77-26203)

346'.42'0434 — Tenancies. Law. *England*
Aldridge, Trevor Martin. Rent control and leasehold enfranchisement / by Trevor M. Aldridge. — 7th ed. — London : Oyez Publishing, 1977. — xxxviii,210p ; 22cm.
Previous ed.: 1975. — Index.
ISBN 0-85120-311-6 Pbk : £6.25
(B77-17377)

Hill, Harold Arthur. Hill and Redman's law of landlord and tenant. — 16th ed. / by Michael Barnes assisted by ... [others] ; consulting editor George Dobry. — London : Butterworth.
Previous ed.: 1970.
Supplement : containing developments up to May 15, 1977 / by Michael Barnes and David Hands and Christopher Lockhart-Mummery. — 1977. — xvii,A255p : forms ; 25cm.
Includes the text of relevant new legislation.
ISBN 0-406-22709-8 Pbk : £8.50
(B77-30067)

346'.42'0434 — Tenancies. Law. *England. State-of-the-art reviews*
Donell, Richard Antony. Landlord and tenant / [by] R.A. Donell. — [London] : [Law Society], [1976]. — [1],29p ; 21cm. — (Law Society. Refresher lectures ; 1976)
Sd : £0.75
(B77-26933)

346'.42'04344 — Agricultural industries. Personnel. Rented residences. Tenancies. Law. *England. Statutes*
Great Britain. *Laws, statutes, etc. (Individual titles).* Rent (Agriculture) Act 1976 : Elizabeth II. 1976. Chapter 80. — London : H.M.S.O., [1976]. — [1],iii,64p ; 25cm.
ISBN 0-10-548076-2 Sd : £1.35
(B77-11693)

346'.42'04344 — Rentcharges. Abolition. Law. *England. Statutes*
Great Britain. *Laws, statutes, etc. (Individual titles).* Rentcharges Act 1977 : Elizabeth II. 1977. Chapter 30. — London : H.M.S.O., [1977]. — [1],61,[1]p ; 25cm.
ISBN 0-10-543077-3 Sd : £0.35
(B77-29284)

346'.42'04344 — Rented premises. Tenancies. Law. *England*
Donell, Richard Anthony. Residential and business tenancies up to date / [by] R.A. Donell. — [Guildford] ([Braboeuf Manor, Portsmouth Rd, St Catherine's, Guildford, Surrey]) : The College of Law, 1975. — [1], 18p ; 22cm. — (College of Law. Crash course lectures : 1975)
ISBN 0-905835-13-1 Sd : £0.60
(B77-09612)

346'.42'04344 — Rented residences. Tenancies. Law. *England*
Donell, Richard Antony. Conveyancing, landlord & tenant and bankruptcy up to date / [by] R.A. Donell. — [Guildford] ([Braboeuf Manor, Portsmouth Rd, St Catherine's, Guildford, Surrey]) : The College of Law, 1976. — [1], 33p ; 22cm. — (College of Law. Crash course lectures : 1976)
ISBN 0-905835-47-6 Sd : £0.75
Also classified at 346'.42'0438; 346'.42'078
(B77-10276)

Donell, Richard Antony. Landlord and tenant / [by] R.A. Donell. — [Guildford] ([Braboeuf Manor, Portsmouth Rd, St Catherine's, Guildford, Surrey]) : The College of Law, 1972. — [1],18p ; 22cm. — (College of Law. Crash course lectures : 1972)
ISBN 0-905835-03-4 Sd : £0.45
(B77-10277)

Donell, Richard Antony. Rent control and security of tenure up to date / [by] R.A. Donell. — [Guildford] ([Braboeuf Manor, Portsmouth Rd, St Catherine's, Guildford, Surrey]) : The College of Law, 1974. — [1], 17p ; 22cm. — (College of Law. Crash course lectures : 1974)
ISBN 0-905835-06-9 Sd : £0.50
(B77-10278)

346'.42'04344 — Rented residences. Tenancies. Law. Reform. *England. British Property Federation viewpoints*
British Property Federation. Review of the Rent Acts : submission of evidence in response to Department of Environment Consultation Paper of January 1977 / British Property Federation. — London (35 Catherine Place, SW1E 6DY) : The Federation, 1977. — [2],34,[1]p ; 21cm.
ISBN 0-900101-07-5 Sd : £1.00
(B77-31068)

346'.42'04344 — Rented residences. Tenancies. Law. Reform. *England. Proposals*
Great Britain. *Department of the Environment.* The review of the Rent Acts : a consultation paper / [Department of the Environment]. — [London] ([2 Marsham St., SW1P 3EB]) : The Department, [1977]. — [1],7,13p,[2]leaves ; 30cm.
Sd : Unpriced
(B77-30068)

346'.42'04344 — Residences. Rents. Law. *England*
Prophet, John. Fair rents : a practical guide to the statutory regulation of rents of residential tenancies, including the work of rent officers, rent assessment committees and rent tribunals / by John Prophet. — London : Shaw and Sons, 1976. — iii-xxxiii,299p ; 22cm.
Index.
ISBN 0-7219-0700-8 Pbk : £5.25
(B77-05969)

346'.42'0434402633 — Rented residences. Tenancies. Law. *England. Statutes*
Great Britain. *Laws, statutes, etc. (Individual titles).* Rent Act 1977 : Elizabeth II. 1977. Chapter 42. — London : H.M.S.O., [1977]. — [1],ix,193p ; 25cm.
ISBN 0-10-544277-1 Sd : £2.85
(B77-28506)

346'.42'04346 — Rented residences. Leases. Conditions: Obligations to repair. *England*
Liddle, Christopher Kingsworth. Repairing obligations and their enforcement / [by] C.K. Liddle. — [Guildford] ([Braboeuf Manor, Portsmouth Rd, St Catherine's, Guildford, Surrey]) : The College of Law, 1974. — [1], 19p ; 22cm. — (College of Law. Crash course lectures : 1974)
ISBN 0-905835-08-5 Sd : £0.50
(B77-09613)

346'.42'0436 — Houses. Purchase. Legal aspects. *England*
Consumers' Association. The legal side of buying a house / Consumers' Association. — Amended [ed.] / edited by Edith Rudinger. — London : The Association, 1976. — [4],148p : ill, forms ; 21cm.
Previous ed.: 1975. — Index.
Pbk : £2.15
ISBN 0-85202-112-7
(B77-11138)

346'.42'0438 — Real property. Conveyancing. Law. *England*
Donell, Richard Antony. Conveyancing, landlord & tenant and bankruptcy up to date / [by] R.A. Donell. — [Guildford] ([Braboeuf Manor, Portsmouth Rd, St Catherine's, Guildford, Surrey]) : The College of Law, 1976. — [1], 33p ; 22cm. — (College of Law. Crash course lectures : 1976)
ISBN 0-905835-47-6 Sd : £0.75
Primary classification 346'.42'04344
(B77-10276)

Emmet, Lewis Emanuel. Emmet's notes on perusing titles and on practical conveyancing. — 16th ed. / by J.T. Farrand. — London : Oyez Publishing.
Previous ed.: / by J. Gilchrist Smith and J.T. Farrand. London : Solicitors' Law Stationery Society, 1967.
1st supplement : [to 1st October 1975]. — 1976. — xxv,116p ; 24cm.
ISBN 0-85120-276-4 Pbk : £5.50
(B77-31069)

2 (cumulative) supplement / consultant editor J. Gilchrist Smith. — 1977. — xxxi,170p ; 24cm.
Cover title: Emmet on title.
ISBN 0-85120-319-1 Pbk : £7.50
(B77-26204)

Griffiths, Lionel Robert Humphrey. Conveyancing changes / [by] L.R.H. Griffiths. — [Guildford] ([Braboeuf Manor, St Catherine's, Guildford GU3 1HA]) : College of Law, [1972]. — [1],20p ; 22cm. — (College of Law. Crash course lectures : 1972 ISSN 0309-2771)
Sd : £0.45
(B77-05304)

Holbrook, Richard George. Recent developments in conveyancing / [by] R.G. Holbrook. — [Guildford] ([Braboeuf Manor, Portsmouth Rd, St Catherine's, Guildford, Surrey]) : The College of Law, 1974. — [1],18p ; 22cm. — (College of Law. Crash course lectures : 1974)
ISBN 0-905835-09-3 Sd : £0.50
(B77-04671)

Joseph, Michael, *b.1935.* The conveyancing fraud / [by] Michael Joseph. — London (27 Occupation La., S.E.18) : The author, 1976. — [5],239,[24]p : forms ; 22cm.
Originally published: 1976. — Index.
ISBN 0-9505023-0-8 Pbk : £1.80
(B77-15760)

346'.42'0438 — Real property. Conveyancing. Law. *England. State-of-the-art reviews*
Holbrook, Richard George. Conveyancing / [by] R.G. Holbrook. — [London] : [Law Society], [1976]. — [1],26p ; 21cm. — (Law Society. Refresher lectures ; 1976)
Sd : £0.75
(B77-26934)

346'.42'0438 — Registered land. Conveyancing. Law. *England*
Hayton, David John. Registered land / by David J. Hayton. — 2nd ed. — London : Sweet and Maxwell, 1977. — xx,214p ; 20cm. — (Modern legal studies)
Previous ed.: 1973. — Index.
ISBN 0-421-23290-0 : £5.00
ISBN 0-421-22920-9 Pbk : £2.75
(B77-24800)

346'.42'044 — Offices. Construction. Control. Law. *England. Statutes*
Great Britain. *Laws, statutes, etc. (Individual titles).* Control of Office Development Act 1977 : Elizabeth II. 1977. Chapter 40. — London : H.M.S.O., [1977]. — Sheet(2p) ; 25x16cm.
ISBN 0-10-544077-9 : £0.10
(B77-26205)

346'.42'045 — District councils. Transfer of real property in new towns from new town corporations. Law. *England. Statutes*
Great Britain. *Laws, statutes, etc. (Individual titles).* New Towns (Amendment) Act 1976 : Elizabeth II. 1976. Chapter 68. — London : H.M.S.O., [1976]. — [1],16p ; 25cm.
ISBN 0-10-546876-2 Sd : £0.35
(B77-09614)

346'.42'045 — England. Environment planning. Law
Hamilton, Richard Neville Dalton. A guide to development and planning / by R.N.D. Hamilton. — 6th ed. — London : Oyez Publishing.
Previous ed.: 1970.
Supplement. — 1976. — xx,124p ; 21cm.
Index.
ISBN 0-85120-306-x Pbk : £3.50
(B77-00676)

Holbrook, Richard George. Planning and compensation : some recent changes / by R.G. Holbrook. — [Guildford] ([Braboeuf Manor, Portsmouth Rd, St Catherine's, Guildford, Surrey]) : The College of Law, 1973. — [1], 16p ; 22cm. — (College of Law. Crash course lectures : 1973)
ISBN 0-905835-39-5 Sd : £0.50
Also classified at 343'.42'025
(B77-05970)

Telling, Arthur Edward. Planning law and procedure / [by] A.E. Telling. — 5th ed. — London : Butterworth, 1977. — xxxii,392p ; 22cm.
Previous ed.: 1973. — Index.
ISBN 0-406-66507-9 : £9.20
ISBN 0-406-66508-7 Pbk : £5.20
(B77-19270)

346'.42'04502633 — England. Environment planning. Law. *Statutes*
Great Britain. *Laws, statutes, etc. (Individual titles).* Town and Country Planning (Amendment) Act 1977 : Elizabeth II. 1977. Chapter 29. — London : H.M.S.O., [1977]. — 5,[1]p ; 25cm.
ISBN 0-10-542977-5 Sd : £0.25
(B77-26206)

346'.42'0450264 — England. Environment planning. Law. *Cases*
Purdue, Michael. Cases and materials on planning law / by Michael Purdue. — London : Sweet and Maxwell, 1977. — xxiv, 550p ; 26cm.
Index.
ISBN 0-421-19590-8 : £15.50
ISBN 0-421-19600-9 Pbk : £10.50
(B77-25485)

346'.42'046 — Land. Drainage. Law. *England. Statutes*
Great Britain. *Laws, statutes, etc. (Individual titles).* Land Drainage Act 1976 : Elizabeth II. 1976. Chapter 70. — [London] : [H.M.S.O.], [1976]. — vi,117p ; 25cm.
ISBN 0-10-547076-7 Sd : £1.85
(B77-10769)

346'.42'052 — Probate. Law. *England*
Holloway, Derrick Robert Le Blond. A probate handbook / by D.R. Le B. Holloway. — 4th ed. — London : Oyez Publishing, 1976. — xxiv,311p ; 22cm.
Previous ed.: 1973. — Index.
ISBN 0-85120-299-3 Pbk : £6.00
(B77-04034)

346'.42'052 — Succession. Law. *England*
Mellows, Anthony Roger. The law of succession / by Anthony R. Mellows. — 3rd ed. — London : Butterworth, 1977. — lxiii, 843p ; 22cm.
Previous ed.: 1973. — Index.
ISBN 0-406-62374-0 : £20.00
ISBN 0-406-62375-9 Pbk : £13.00
(B77-24091)

Miller, John Gareth. The machinery of succession / by J. Gareth Miller. — Abingdon : Professional Books, 1977. — iii-xliv,342p ; 22cm.
Index.
ISBN 0-903486-31-8 : £9.50
ISBN 0-903486-32-6 Pbk : £5.50
(B77-15188)

346'.42'054 — Testamentary succession. Implications of capital transfer tax. Legal aspects. *England*
Wills, probate and capital transfer tax. — [Guildford] ([Braboeuf Manor, Portsmouth Rd, St Catherine's, Guildford, Surrey]) : The College of Law, 1977. — v,105p : ill ; 22cm. — (College of Law. Lectures : 1977 ISSN 0309-3166)
'Between October 1976 and January 1977 the College organised nine one-day courses at various centres throughout the country ... This booklet contains the lectures delivered on the course' - Preface.
ISBN 0-905835-50-6 Pbk : £2.25
(B77-16272)

346'.42'054 — Wills. Law. *England*
Consumers' Association. Wills and probate / [Consumers' Association] ; [edited by Edith Rudinger]. — 6th ed. — London : The Association, 1977. — [5],151p : ill ; 19cm. — (A consumer publication)
Previous ed.: 1975. — Index.
ISBN 0-85202-136-4 Pbk : Unpriced
(B77-27753)

346'.42'056 — Inherited property: Estates. Administration. *England. Manuals*
Taylor, James Nigel Rodney. Executorship law and accounts / by J.N.R. Taylor. — 3rd ed. — Estover : Macdonald and Evans, 1977. — xv, 173p ; 19cm. — (The M. & E. handbook series)

With suggested answers to problems. — Previous ed.: 1973. — Index.
ISBN 0-7121-0560-3 Pbk : £1.95
(B77-25486)

346'.42'059 — Trusts. Administration. *England. Manuals*
Sladen, Michael. Practical trust administration / [by] Michael Sladen. — London : Europa, 1977. — xxvi,286p : 2 forms ; 25cm.
Index.
ISBN 0-900362-99-5 : £7.00
(B77-18634)

346'.42'059 — Trusts. Law. *England*
Riddall, John Gervase. Law of trusts / [by] J.G. Riddall. — London : Butterworth, 1977. — xxxv,375p : ill ; 23cm.
Index.
ISBN 0-406-64836-0 : £11.00
(B77-21021)

346'.42'062 — Meetings. Law. *England*
Shackleton, Frank. Shackleton on the law and practice of meetings. — 6th ed. / by A. Harding Boulton. — London [etc.] : Sweet and Maxwell, 1977. — xxvi,369p : forms ; 23cm.
Previous ed.: published as 'The law and practice of meetings'. 1967. — Index. — Includes the text of the relevant legislation.
ISBN 0-421-20870-8 : £6.50
(B77-12939)

346'.42'064 — Charities. Law. Effects. *England. Inquiry reports*
Charity law and voluntary organisations : report of an independent committee of inquiry set up by the National Council of Social Service, under the chairmanship of Lord Goodman, to examine the effect of charity law and practice on voluntary organisations. — London : Bedford Square Press : Distributed by Research Publications Services, 1976. — [7],ii,150p ; 21cm.
ISBN 0-7199-0910-4 Pbk : £2.00
(B77-09615)

346'.42'066 — Companies. Law. *England*
Hadden, Tom. Company law and capitalism / [by] Tom Hadden. — 2nd ed. — London : Weidenfeld and Nicolson, 1977. — xxii,522p : ill ; 23cm. — (Law in context)
Previous ed.: 1972. — Index.
ISBN 0-297-77334-8 : £12.50
ISBN 0-297-77335-6 Pbk : £7.50
(B77-29285)

346'.42'066 — Companies. Law. *England. For company secretaryship*
Pitfield, Ronald Reuben. Duties of a company secretary / by Ronald R. Pitfield and Percy F. Hughes. — 4th ed. — London : Secretaries Journal, 1976. — xv,359p : forms ; 22cm.
Previous ed.: 1967. — Index.
ISBN 0-9505249-4-8 Pbk : £6.00
(B77-04035)

346'.42'068 — Partnerships. Law. *England*
Drake, Charles Dominic. Law of partnership / by Charles D. Drake. — 2nd ed. — London : Sweet and Maxwell, 1977. — xx,266p ; 22cm.
Previous ed.: 1972. — Index.
ISBN 0-421-22130-5 Pbk : £4.00
(B77-20124)

Redmond, Peter William Dawson. Partnership law. — 11th ed. / [by] P.W.D. Redmond. — Plymouth : Macdonald and Evans, 1977. — xii, 145p ; 19cm. — (The M. & E. handbook series)
Previous ed.: / by E.M. Taylor. London : Macdonald and Evans, 1966. — Index.
ISBN 0-7121-1674-5 Pbk : £1.50
(B77-33692)

346'.42'07 — England. Commercial law
Smith, Kenneth, *b.1910.* Mercantile law / [by] Kenneth Smith, Denis J. Keenan. — 4th ed. / by Denis J. Keenan. — London [etc.] : Pitman, 1977. — x,831p ; 22cm.
With answers to self-examination tests. — Previous ed.: published as 'Essentials of mercantile law'. 1973. — Index.
ISBN 0-273-00876-5 Pbk : £4.95 : CIP rev.
(B77-20122)

346'.42'07 — England. Commercial law. *State-of-the-art reviews*
Lowe, Robert, *b.1932.* Contract and mercantile law / [by] R. Lowe. — [London] : [Law Society], [1976]. — [1],22p ; 21cm. — (Law Society. Refresher lectures ; 1976)
Sd : £0.75
Primary classification 346'.42'02
(B77-26931)

346'.42'0703 — England. Commercial law. *Polyglot dictionaries*
Anderson, Ralph James Bushman.
Anglo-Scandinavian law dictionary of legal terms used in professional and commercial practice / by Ralph J.B. Anderson. — Oslo [etc.] : Universitetsforlaget ; Henley on Thames (37 Queen St., Henley on Thames, Oxon. RG9 1AJ) : Distributed by Global Book Resources Ltd, 1977. — 137p ; 21cm.
'Prepared under the auspices of the Royal Norwegian Ministry of Justice' - 'Scandinavian university books'.
Pbk : £7.00
ISBN 82-00-02365-6
Also classified at 346'.48'0703
(B77-27754)

346'.42'072 — Goods. Supply. Contracts. Implied terms. Law. Reform. *England. Proposals*
Law Commission. Law of contract, implied terms in contracts for the supply of goods / the Law Commission. — London : H.M.S.O., 1977. — iv,60p ; 21cm. — (Working paper ; no.71)
ISBN 0-11-730102-7 Sd : £1.10
(B77-10770)

346'.42'074 — Debts. Securities: Floating charges. Law. *England. For banking*
Ryder, Frank Raymond. The floating charge, past, present and future - here and abroad : including in particular banking problems / by F.R. Ryder. — [London] ([Strand, WC2R 2LS]) : King's College, London, [1977]. — [1], 30p ; 24cm. — (Gilbart lectures on banking ; 1977)
'Delivered under the auspices of the University of London King's College'.
ISBN 0-901324-20-5 Sd : £0.80
(B77-14130)

346'.42'077 — Debts. Payment. Enforcement. Law. *England*
Woodroffe, Geoffrey Frederick. Enforcement of judgements, including attachment of earnings / [by] G.F. Woodroffe. — [Guildford] ([Braboeuf Manor, Portsmouth Rd, St Catherine's, Guildford, Surrey]) : The College of Law, 1972. — [1],21p ; 22cm. — (College of Law. Crash course lectures : 1972)
ISBN 0-905835-21-2 Sd : £0.45
(B77-07220)

346'.42'078 — Bankruptcy. Law. *England*
Donell, Richard Antony. Conveyancing, landlord & tenant and bankruptcy up to date / [by] R.A. Donell. — [Guildford] ([Braboeuf Manor, Portsmouth Rd, St Catherine's, Guildford, Surrey]) : The College of Law, 1976. — [1], 33p ; 22cm. — (College of Law. Crash course lectures : 1976)
ISBN 0-905835-47-6 Sd : £0.75
Primary classification 346'.42'04344
(B77-10276)

Sales, Charles Allison. Sales' the law relating to bankruptcy, liquidations and receiverships. — 6th ed. / by J.H. Thompson. — Plymouth : Macdonald and Evans, 1977. — xliii,332p ; 22cm.
Previous ed.: 1956. — Index.
ISBN 0-7121-1952-3 : £7.50
ISBN 0-7121-1949-3 Pbk : £4.50
Also classified at 346'.41'0662
(B77-22455)

346'.42'078 — Insolvency. Law. *England*
Bankruptcy and liquidation. — [Guildford] ([Braboeuf Manor, Portsmouth Rd, St Catherine's, Guildford, Surrey]) : The College of Law, 1976. — iii,71p ; 22cm. — (College of Law. Lectures : 1976)
'This booklet contains lectures given at a course run by the College of Law at London and Nottingham' - Preface.
ISBN 0-905835-26-3 Pbk : £2.00
(B77-07221)

346'.42'0780269 — Insolvency. Law. Procedure. *England. Manuals*
Nelson, Bertram. Nelson's tables of procedure. — 6th ed. / by C.N. Gorman, assisted by R.C. Bailey and A. Robertson. — London : Oyez Publishing, 1975. — vi,65p ; 25cm.
Previous ed.: published as 'Tables of procedure' / by J.W. Mayo and David Foster, 1963.
ISBN 0-85120-259-4 Sd : £2.50
Primary classification 346'.41'0660269
(B77-00111)

346'.43'06602633 — Companies. Law. *West Germany. Statutes. German-English parallel texts*
Germany *(Federal Republic). Laws, statutes, etc. (Individual titles).* [Gesetz betreffend die Gesellschaften mit beschränkter Haftung vom 20 April 1892]. The private company in Germany : a translation and commentary / [by] M.C. Oliver. — Plymouth : Macdonald and Evans, 1976. — vii,120p ; 21cm.
Parallel German text and English translation, English preface and commentary.
ISBN 0-7121-1665-6 Pbk : £2.50
(B77-08296)

346'.45'066 — Companies. Law. *Italy*
Verrucoli, P. Italian company law / by P. Verrucoli. — London : Oyez Publishing, 1977. — xi,218p ; 22cm. — (European commercial law library ; no.5)
Index.
ISBN 0-85120-220-9 Pbk : £8.75
(B77-21770)

346'.47'043 — Real property. Law. *Soviet Union, to 1976*
Sawicki, Stanislaw J. Soviet land and housing law : a historical and comparative study / [by] Stanislaw J. Sawicki ; foreword by John Hazard. — New York ; London : Praeger, 1977. — xxv,199,[1]p ; 25cm. — (Praeger special studies in international politics and government)
Index.
ISBN 0-275-24480-6 : £13.05
Also classified at 344'.47'063635
(B77-25487)

346'.48'0703 — Scandinavia. Commercial law. *Polyglot dictionaries*
Anderson, Ralph James Bushman.
Anglo-Scandinavian law dictionary of legal terms used in professional and commercial practice / by Ralph J.B. Anderson. — Oslo [etc.] : Universitetsforlaget ; Henley on Thames (37 Queen St., Henley on Thames, Oxon. RG9 1AJ) : Distributed by Global Book Resources Ltd, 1977. — 137p ; 21cm.
'Prepared under the auspices of the Royal Norwegian Ministry of Justice' - 'Scandinavian university books'.
Pbk : £7.00
ISBN 82-00-02365-6
Primary classification 346'.42'0703
(B77-27754)

346'.492'066 — Companies. Law. *Netherlands*
Sanders, Pieter. Dutch company law / by P. Sanders. — London : Oyez Publishing, 1977. — xiii,277p ; 21cm. — (European commercial law library ; no.6)
Index.
ISBN 0-85120-216-0 Pbk : £11.50
(B77-26935)

346'.493'0664 — Companies. Auditing. Law. Belgium. Compared with law of company auditing in Great Britain
Anglo-Belgian Liaison Committee of the Institute of Chartered Accountants in England and Wales, Collège National des Experts Comptables de Belgique, Institut des Reviseurs d'Entreprises. Statutory audit requirements in Belgium : a comparison with the requirements in the United Kingdom / [undertaken by the Anglo-Belgian Liaison Committee of the Institute of Chartered Accountants in England and Wales, Collège National des Experts Comptables de Belgique, Institut des Reviseurs d'Entreprises]. — London : The Institute, 1976. — 79p ; 21cm.
ISBN 0-85291-158-0 Pbk : £2.95
Primary classification 346'.41'0664
(B77-08295)

346'.6'070264 — Africa. Common law countries. Commercial law. *Cases. Serials*
The **African** law reports, commercial law series. — Oxford ([Trinity College, Oxford OX1 3BH]) : African Law Reports.
1971. Vol.2 / general editor Alan Milner ... — 1976. — lix,454p ; 24cm.
ISBN 0-903826-04-6 : £13.50
(B77-01267)

1972. Vol.2 / editor in chief Alan Milner ... — 1977. — xlviii,450p ; 24cm.
Index.
ISBN 0-903826-28-3 : £13.50
(B77-31070)

346'.669'015 — Families. Law. *Nigeria*
Nwogugu, Edwin Ifeanyichuwu. Family law in Nigeria / [by] E.I. Nwogugu. — Ibadan ; London [etc.] : Heinemann Educational, 1974 [i.e. 1977]. — xxix,383p ; 22cm. — (Heinemann studies in Nigerian law)
Published in Nigeria: 1974. — Index.
ISBN 0-435-89601-6 Pbk : £12.00
(B77-12940)

346'.669'070264 — Nigeria. Commercial law. *Cases. Serials*
The **Nigerian** commercial law reports. — Oxford : African Law Reports.
1971. Vol.2 / editor in chief Alan Milner ... — 1977. — iii-lviii,454p ; 24cm.
Index.
ISBN 0-903826-24-0 : £10.00
(B77-28507)

346'.73'009033 — United States. Private law, 1780-1860
Horwitz, Morton J. The transformation of American law, 1780-1860 / [by] Morton J. Horwitz. — Cambridge, Mass. ; London : Harvard University Press, 1977. — xix,356p ; 24cm. — (Studies in legal history)
Index.
ISBN 0-674-90370-6 : £12.40
(B77-16273)

346'.73'045 — Housing. Zoning. Law. *United States*
Mann, Mary Sullivan. The right to housing : constitutional issues and remedies in exclusionary zoning / [by] Mary Sullivan Mann. — New York [etc.] ; London : Praeger, [1977]. — ix,3-193p ; 25cm. — (Praeger special studies in US economic, social and political issues)
Published in the United States: 1976. — Bibl.: p.170-182. — Index.
ISBN 0-275-23590-4 : £12.60
(B77-13577)

346'.94'064 — Voluntary organisations. Law. *Australia*
Horsley, Mervyn G. The law & administration of associations in Australia / by Mervyn G. Horsley. — Sydney ; London [etc.] : Butterworth, 1976. — x,296p : forms ; 22cm.
Spine title: Associations in Australia. — 'Published in conjunction with the Australian Division of the Institute of Chartered Secretaries and Administrators'. — Index.
ISBN 0-409-34370-6 Pbk : Unpriced
(B77-23244)

347 — CIVIL PROCEDURE
347.05 — Law courts. Decision making. Research. Applications of multivariate analysis
Kort, Fred. A special and a general multivariate theory of judicial decisions / [by] Fred Kort. — Beverly Hills ; London : Sage Publications, 1977. — 42,[1]p : 1 ill ; 22cm. — (Sage professional papers in American politics ; vol.3, no.04-033)
Bibl.: p.38-42.
ISBN 0-8039-0632-3 Pbk : £1.95
(B77-26936)

347.06 — Law. Cases. Proof. Implications of theories of probabilities. *Philosophical perspectives*
Cohen, Laurence Jonathan. The probable and the provable / [by] L. Jonathan Cohen. — Oxford : Clarendon Press, 1977. — xvi,363p ; 23cm. — (Clarendon library of logic and philosophy)
Index.
ISBN 0-19-824412-6 : £9.50 : CIP rev.
(B77-18635)

347'.385'05 — Law courts. Procedure. *Athenian Empire, B.C.500-B.C.400*
Harrison, James Alexander. The Athenian law courts in the fourth century BC / [by] J.A. Harrison. — London : Bell, 1977. — 32p : ill, 2 plans ; 21cm. — (The ancient world in action)
Bibl.: p.28.
ISBN 0-7135-1958-4 Sd : £1.00
(B77-20125)

347'.41'002633 — Justice. Administration. Law. *Great Britain. Statutes*
Great Britain. *Laws, statutes, etc. (Individual titles).* Administration of Justice Act 1977 : Elizabeth II. 1977. Chapter 38. — London : H.M.S.O., [1977]. — iii,39,[1]p ; 25cm.
ISBN 0-10-543877-4 Sd : £0.75
(B77-28508)

347'.41'09062 — Arbitration. Organisations. *Great Britain. Institute of Arbitrators. Yearbooks*
Institute of Arbitrators. Membership year book / [Institute of Arbitrators]. — London (16 Park Cres., W1N 4BB) : The Institute.
1973. — [1973]. — 107p : forms, port ; 21cm.
Pbk : £1.50
(B77-29287)

347'.411 — Legal system. *Scotland*
Cooper, Thomas Mackay, *Baron Cooper.* The Scottish legal tradition / [by] Lord Cooper. — 4th ed. / revised by Michael C. Meston. — Edinburgh (483 Lawnmarket, Edinburgh EH1 2NT) : Saltire Society, 1977. — 38p ; 19cm. — (Saltire pamphlets ; no.1)
Previous ed.: 1969.
Sd : £0.50
(B77-33693)

Scottish Law Commission. The legal system of Scotland / [prepared by members of the legal staffs of the Scottish Law Commission and of the Office of the Solicitor to the Secretary of State for Scotland]. — 2nd ed. — Edinburgh : H.M.S.O. for the Scottish Office, 1977. — iv, 49p ; 21cm.
Previous ed.: 1975. — Bibl.: p.47-48.
Sd : £1.15
ISBN 0-11-491332-3
(B77-11694)

347'.411'01 — Civil courts. Proceedings. *Scotland. Statistics*
Civil judicial statistics (including licensing and bankruptcy) : statistics relating to the House of Lords (Scottish appeals), the Court of Session, sheriff courts and other civil courts, licensing courts, Lands Tribunal for Scotland, certain legal and public departments, bankruptcy, court fees and fees taken in the departments ... / compiled by the Scottish Courts Administration. — Edinburgh : H.M.S.O.
1975. — [1976]. — 37p : ill ; 25cm. — (Cmnd. 6577)
ISBN 0-10-165770-6 Sd : £0.67
(B77-07859)

347'.416'01 — Law courts. *Northern Ireland. Proposals*
Great Britain. *Lord Chancellor.* Courts in Northern Ireland : the future pattern / presented to Parliament by the Lord High Chancellor and the Secretary of State for Northern Ireland ... — London : H.M.S.O., [1977]. — 19p ; 25cm. — (Cmnd.6892)
ISBN 0-10-168920-9 Sd : £0.35
(B77-29288)

347'.42 — England. Law. Precedent
Cross, *Sir* **Rupert.** Precedent in English law / by Rupert Cross. — 3rd ed. — Oxford : Clarendon Press, 1977. — ix,242p ; 23cm. — (Clarendon law series)
Previous ed.: 1968. — Bibl.: p.234. — Index.
ISBN 0-19-876076-0 : £5.95 : CIP rev.
(B77-17378)

347'.42 — Legal system. *England*
Cecil, Henry, *b.1902.* Learn about English law / [by] Henry Cecil ; illustrated by Edward Ardizzone. — London : Sphere, 1976. — 95p : ill ; 18cm.
This ed. originally published: London : Luscombe, 1974.
ISBN 0-7221-2236-5 Pbk : £0.75
(B77-02138)

Eddey, Keith James. The English legal system / by K.J. Eddey. — 2nd ed. — London : Sweet and Maxwell, 1977. — xv,179p ; 22cm. — (Concise college texts)
Previous ed.: 1971. — Bibl.: p.172-173. — Index.
ISBN 0-421-22140-2 Pbk : £2.60
(B77-20126)

Jackson, Richard Meredith. The machinery of justice in England / [by] R.M. Jackson. — 7th ed. — Cambridge [etc.] : Cambridge University Press, 1977. — xii,627p : map ; 24cm.
Previous ed.: 1972. — Index.
ISBN 0-521-21688-5 : £16.00
ISBN 0-521-29231-x Pbk : £7.95
(B77-33694)

347'.42'009 — Legal system. *England, to 1976*
Radcliffe, Geoffrey Reynolds Yonge. The English legal system / [by] Radcliffe and Cross. — 6th ed. / edited by G.J. Hand and D.J. Bentley ; foreword by Lord Cross of Chelsea. — London : Butterworth, 1977. — [12],464p ; 23cm.
Previous ed.: 1971. — Index.
ISBN 0-406-64703-8 : £12.00
ISBN 0-406-64704-6 Pbk : £7.50
(B77-21772)

347'.42'01 — Civil courts. Proceedings. *England. Statistics*
Judicial statistics : statistics relating to the Judicial Committee of the Privy Council, the House of Lords, the Supreme Court of Judicature, the Crown Court, county courts and other civil courts / compiled by the Lord Chancellor's Department. — London : H.M.S.O.
1975. — [1976]. — xi,112p : ill ; 25cm. — (Cmnd.6634)
This combined report supersedes 'Statistics on judicial administration' and 'Civil judicial statistics'.
ISBN 0-10-166340-4 Pbk : £2.00
(B77-05305)

Judicial statistics, England and Wales : statistics relating to the Judicial Committee of the Privy Council, the House of Lords, the Supreme Court of Judicature, the Crown Court, county courts and other civil courts ... / Lord Chancellor's Office. — London : H.M.S.O.
1976. — [1977]. — xi,113p : ill ; 25cm. — (Cmnd.6875)
Previously published: as 'Judicial statistics'.
ISBN 0-10-168750-8 Pbk : £2.50
(B77-21773)

347'.42'01 — Law courts. Funds in court. *England. Accounts*
Funds in court in England and Wales, accounts ... — London : H.M.S.O.
1975-76 : year ended 29th February ... — [1977]. — 21p ; 25cm. — ([1976-77 H.C.] 365)
ISBN 0-10-236577-6 Sd : £0.60
(B77-23245)

347'.42'01025 — Law courts. *England. Directories*
Shaw's directory of courts in England and Wales. — London : Shaw and Sons.
1977. — 1977. — 236p in various pagings ; 22cm.
Index.
ISBN 0-7219-0444-0 Pbk : £3.80
ISSN 0307-3343
(B77-30069)

347'.42'014 — Judiciary. Role. Political aspects. *England*
Griffith, John Aneurin Grey. The politics of the judiciary / [by] J.A.G. Griffith. — [London] : Fontana, 1977. — 224p ; 18cm. — (Political issues of modern Britain)
Also published: Manchester : Manchester University Press, 1977. — Index.
ISBN 0-00-634176-4 Pbk : £1.25
(B77-33695)

347'.42'02 — County courts. Cases. Costs. *England. Tables. For solicitors*
Orange, Richard Brian. A guide to county court costs as from 19 April 1977 / original notes by R.B. Orange. — 1977 ed. / revised by Hugh C. Collins. — London : Oyez Publishing, 1977. — [1],14p ; 26x11cm.
Cover title: Reminders on county court costs. — Previous ed.: published as 'Reminders on county court costs'. 1971.
ISBN 0-85120-316-7 Sd : £1.25
(B77-32529)

347'.42'02340924 — Judges: Goddard, Rayner, Baron Goddard. *England. Biographies*
Bresler, Fenton Shea. Lord Goddard : a biography of Rayner Goddard, Lord Chief Justice of England / by Fenton Bresler ; with a foreword by Lord Denning. — London : Harrap, 1977. — xiv,336p,leaf of plate,[12]p of plates : ill, ports ; 24cm.
Index.
ISBN 0-245-50955-0 : £7.95
(B77-15761)

347'.42'025 — Magistrates' courts. Court orders. Procedure. *England. Manuals*
Harris, Brian, *b.1932.* The magistrate's companion : guide for magistrates in announcing sentence and other orders of the court / [by] Brian Harris. — Chichester [etc.] : Rose, 1977. — 88p ; 16cm.
ISBN 0-85992-113-1 Sd : £2.00
(B77-32530)

347'.42'025 — Magistrates' courts. Procedure. *England*
Anthony, Ernest. Anthony and Berryman's magistrates' court guide. — London : Butterworth.
1977 / by C.J. Acred. — 1977. — vii,467p ; 19cm.
Index.
ISBN 0-406-10830-7 Pbk : £4.75
(B77-10771)

347'.42'035 — Great Britain. Court of Appeal & Great Britain. High Court of Justice. *Accounts*
Account of receipts and expenditure of the High Court and Court of Appeal for the financial year ended 31st March / laid before Parliament by the Lord High Chancellor ... — London : H.M.S.O.
1975-76. — [1976]. — 6p ; 25cm. — ([1976-77 H.C.]66)
ISBN 0-10-206677-9 Sd : £0.25
(B77-07222)

347'.42'04 — England. Court of Star Chamber. Influence of Wolsey, Thomas
Guy, John Alexander. The cardinal's court : the impact of Thomas Wolsey in Star Chamber / [by] J.A. Guy. — Hassocks : Harvester Press, 1977. — X.191p ; 23cm.
Bibl.: p.179-180. — Index.
ISBN 0-85527-829-3 : £8.50 : CIP rev.
(B77-07223)

347'.42'05 — Civil courts. Procedure. *England*
Langan, Peter St John Hevey. Civil procedure. — [2nd ed.] / by P. St J. Langan and D.G. Lawrence. — London : Sweet and Maxwell, 1976. — xxvi,389p ; 23cm.
Previous ed.: / by P. St J. Langan, published as 'Civil procedure and evidence'. 1970. — Index.
ISBN 0-421-21730-8 : £9.00
ISBN 0-421-21740-5 Pbk : £6.00
(B77-05971)

347'.42'05 — Great Britain. Supreme Court of Judicature. Procedure. *Serials*
Great Britain. *Supreme Court of Judicature.* The Supreme Court practice. — London : Sweet and Maxwell : Stevens : Butterworth.
Vols 1 and 2. 5th cumulative supplement : up to date to August 1, 1977 / [general editor I.H. Jacob]. — 1977. — ca 400p ; 25cm.
ISBN 0-421-18930-4 Pbk : Unpriced
(B77-31071)

347'.42'052 — Limitation of actions. Law. Reform. *England. Proposals*
Law Reform Committee. Final report on limitation of actions ... / Law Reform Committee. — London : H.M.S.O., [1977]. — iv,84p ; 25cm. — (Twenty-first report) (Cmnd. 6923)
ISBN 0-10-169230-7 Sd : £1.40
(B77-29289)

347'.42'055 — England. Civil law. Procedure. *Forms & precedents. Encyclopaedias*
Atkin, James Richard, *Baron Atkin.* Atkin's encyclopaedia of court forms in civil proceedings. — 2nd ed. / by the late Lord Evershed and other lawyers. — London : Butterworth.
Previous ed.: published as 'The encyclopaedia of court forms and precedents in civil proceedings' in 16 vols, 1937-50.
Vol.31 : 1977 issue : Payment into court, peerages and dignities, personal rights, petitions, plant breeders' rights. — 1977. — xxix,407p : forms ; 26cm.
Spine title: Court forms. — Index.
ISBN 0-406-01176-1 : £10.00
(B77-33696)

The **encyclopaedia** of forms and precedents other than court forms. — 4th ed. / managing editor L.G. Jory, assisted by G.D. Dann. — London : Butterworth.
Cumulative noter-up. 1977. — 1977. — 1765p in various pagings ; 26cm.
Index.
£268.00
ISBN 0-406-02299-2
(B77-30070)

347'.42'06 — Law courts. Evidence. Law. *England*
Phipson, Sidney Lovell. Phipson on evidence. — 12th ed. / by John Huxley Buzzard, Richard May, M.N. Howard. — London : Sweet and Maxwell, 1976. — cxciii,1014p ; 26cm. — (The common law library ; no.10)
Previous ed.: / by John H. Buzzard, Roy D. Amlot and Stephen Mitchell. 1970. — Index.
ISBN 0-421-20590-3 : £25.00
(B77-06558)

347'.42187'0236 — Great Britain. Magistrates' Court (Hendon). Duty solicitor schemes. Operation, 1973-1974. *Reports, surveys*
King, Michael, *b.1942.* The effects of a duty solicitor scheme : an assessment of the impact upon a magistrates court / by Michael King ; with an introduction by Susan Marsden-Smedley. — London (186 Kings Cross Rd, WC1X 9DE) : Cobden Trust, 1976. — 52p : 2 ill ; 21cm.
Bibl.: p.43.
ISBN 0-900137-09-6 Sd : £0.70
(B77-14629)

347'.47 — Legal system. *Russia, 1700-1900*
Wortman, Richard. The development of a Russian legal consciousness / [by] Richard S. Wortman. — Chicago ; London : University of Chicago Press, [1977]. — xi,345p ; 24cm.
Published in the United States: 1976. — Bibl.: p.323-336. — Index.
ISBN 0-226-90776-7 : £8.65
(B77-13578)

347'.669'03509 — Nigeria. Supreme Court, to 1970
The **Supreme** Court of Nigeria, 1956-1970 / edited by A.B. Kasunmu. — Ibadan ; London [etc.] : Heinemann Educational, 1977. — xx, 261p : ill ; 23cm. — (Heinemann studies in Nigerian law)
Index.
ISBN 0-435-89057-3 : £12.00
(B77-30071)

347'.73'1 — Law courts. *United States*
McLauchlan, William P. American legal processes / [by] William P. McLauchlan. — New York ; London [etc.] : Wiley, 1977. — xv, 218p : ill ; 22cm. — (Viewpoints on American politics)
Index.
ISBN 0-471-58560-2 : £8.20
ISBN 0-471-58561-0 Pbk : £4.85
(B77-19271)

347'.73'26 — United States. Government. Role of United States. Supreme Court
Abraham, Henry Julian. The judiciary : the Supreme Court in the governmental process / [by] Henry J. Abraham. — 4th ed. — Boston, Mass. ; London [etc.] : Allyn and Bacon, 1977. — xi,228p : 1 ill ; 22cm. — (The Allyn and Bacon series in American government)
Previous ed.: Boston, Mass. : Allyn and Bacon, 1973. — Bibl.: p.191-193. — Index.
ISBN 0-205-05757-8 Pbk : £5.95
(B77-04672)

347'.73'2609 — United States. Supreme Court, 1954-1976
Funston, Richard Y. Constitutional counterrevolution? : the Warren Court and the Burger Court : judicial policy making in modern America / [by] Richard Y. Funston. — Cambridge, Mass. : Schenkman Publishing Co. ; New York ; London [etc.] : [Distributed by] Wiley, 1977. — xv,399p ; 24cm.
Bibl.: p.377-388. — Index.
ISBN 0-470-99022-8 : £13.25
ISBN 0-470-99023-6 Pbk : Unpriced
(B77-29290)

347'.73'265 — United States. Supreme Court. Decisions. *Critical studies. Serials*
The **Supreme** Court review. — Chicago ; London : University of Chicago Press.
1975 / edited by Philip B. Kurland ; [for] the Law School, the University of Chicago. — 1976 [i.e. 1977]. — vi,442p ; 25cm.
Published in the United States: 1976.
ISBN 0-226-46426-1 : £18.70
(B77-10772)

347'.73'265 — United States. Supreme Court. Decisions. Formulation
Jacobsohn, Gary J. Pragmatism, statesmanship, and the Supreme Court / [by] Gary J. Jacobsohn. — Ithaca ; London : Cornell University Press, 1977. — 214,[1]p ; 23cm.
Bibl.: p.199-210. — Index.
ISBN 0-8014-1071-1 : £9.35
(B77-29291)

347'.73'3634 — Supreme courts. Leadership. Role of presiding judges. *United States. States*
Ducat, Craig R. Leadership in state supreme courts : roles of the chief justice / [by] Craig R. Ducat, Victor E. Flango. — Beverly Hills ; London : Sage Publications, [1977]. — 58,[1]p : ill ; 22cm. — (Sage professional papers in American politics ; vol.3, no.04-030)
Published in the United States: 1976. — Bibl.: p.24-26.
ISBN 0-8039-0542-4 Pbk : £1.75
(B77-11695)

347'.73'5 — Litigation by companies. *United States*
Wessel, Milton Ralph. The rule of reason : a new approach to corporate litigation / [by] Milton R. Wessel. — Reading, Mass. ; London [etc.] : Addison-Wesley, [1977]. — xvii,221p ; 22cm.
Published in the United States: 1976.
ISBN 0-201-08583-6 : £8.80
(B77-14630)

347'.934'012 — Law courts. Composition. *New Hebrides. Treaties between Great Britain & France*
Great Britain. *Treaties, etc. France, August 6, 1914. Protocols, amendments, etc., November 10, 1976.* Exchange of notes between the Government of the United Kingdom of Great Britain and Northern Ireland and the Government of the French Republic amending the provisions of the protocol of 6 August 1914 as regards the composition of certain courts in the New Hebrides, London, 10 November 1976 ... — London : H.M.S.O., [1977]. — Folder(4p) ; 25cm. — (Treaty series ; no.68(1977)) (Cmnd. 6904)
English and French text.
ISBN 0-10-169040-1 : £0.15
(B77-26207)

347'.934'012 — Native courts. Jurisdiction. Transfer from New Hebrides. Joint Court. *New Hebrides. Treaties between Great Britain & France*
Great Britain. *Treaties, etc. France, August 6, 1914. Protocols, amendments, etc., November 10, 1976.* Exchange of notes between the Government of the United Kingdom of Great Britain and Northern Ireland and the Government of the French Republic amending the provisions of the protocol of 6 August 1914 to transfer certain jurisdiction from the Joint Court to the native courts in the New Hebrides, London, 10 November 1976 ... — London : H.M.S.O., [1977]. — Folder(4p) ; 25cm. — (Treaty series ; no.69(1977)) (Cmnd.6905)
English and French text.
ISBN 0-10-169050-9 : £0.15
(B77-26208)

347'.94'055 — Australia. Civil law. Procedure. *Forms & precedents. Encyclopaedias*
The **Australian** encyclopaedia of forms and precedents other than court forms / editor-in-chief E.A. Francis. — 2nd ed. — Sydney ; London [etc.] : Butterworth.
Previous ed.: / editor-in-chief L.A. Harris. 1955-.
Vol.6 : Choses in action, Civil Aviation, Clubs, Commission agents, Confirmations, Copyright, Crops, growing products and standing timber, Declarations (statutory), Easements, Enlargement of long terms. — 1975. — xxxvi, 466p : forms ; 25cm.
Index.
ISBN 0-409-30531-6 : £31.50
(B77-31072)

348 — STATUTES, REGULATIONS, CASES

348'.41'022 — Great Britain. Law. *Statutes. Collections*
Great Britain. *Laws, statutes, etc. (Collections).* The Public General Acts and General Synod Measures. — London : H.M.S.O.
1975 : with lists of the Public General Acts and Local Acts and a table of the effect of legislation and an index. — 1976. — a-o,cdxxiii p ; 25cm.
Index.
ISBN 0-11-840150-5 Pbk : £5.00
(B77-08903)

348'.41'022 — Great Britain. Law. Statutes. Repeal. *Statutes*
Great Britain. *Laws, statutes, etc. (Individual titles).* Statute Law (Repeals) Act 1977 : Elizabeth II. 1977. Chapter 18. — London : H.M.S.O., 1977. — [1],38p ; 25cm.
ISBN 0-10-541877-3 Sd : £0.70
(B77-22456)

348'.41'025 — Great Britain. Law. *Statutory instruments. Collections*
Great Britain. *Statutory instruments.* Statutory instruments. — London : H.M.S.O.
1975. Part 2 : [1st May-31st Aug.]. — 1976. — 3v.(cii p,p2653-4809) : ill, forms, maps ; 24cm.
Index.
ISBN 0-11-840142-4 : £34.00
(B77-02867)

1976. Part 1 : [1st Jan.-30 Apr.]. — 1976. — 2v.(1822,liv p) ; 25cm.
Index.
ISBN 0-11-840149-1 : £26.50
(B77-07224)

348'.41'025 — Great Britain. Law. Statutory instruments. *Reports, surveys. Serials*
Great Britain. *Parliament. Joint Committee on Statutory Instruments.* Report from the Joint Committee on Statutory Instruments, session 1976-77. — London : H.M.S.O.
11th. — [1977]. — 5p ; 25cm. — ([1976-77]H.L.73) ([1976-77]H.C.31-xiv)
ISBN 0-10-277077-8 Sd : £0.25
(B77-11139)

348'.41'028 — Great Britain. Law. Government orders. *Indexes. Serials*
Index to government orders in force on 31st December : subordinate legislation, the powers and their exercise. — London : H.M.S.O.
1975. — 1976. — 2v.([7],ccxxxv,1770p) ; 25cm.

Noter up as insert.
ISBN 0-11-840146-7 : £38.50
(B77-15762)

348'.41'028 — Great Britain. Law. Statutes. *Lists. Serials*
Chronological table of the statutes. — London : H.M.S.O.
Covering the period from 1235 to the end of 1975. — 1976. — xii,1542p ; 25cm.
ISBN 0-11-840147-5 : £21.50
(B77-13579)

348'.411 — Scottish legal documents: Letters & brieves. *Forms & precedents, 1286-1424. Latin texts*
Formulary E : Scottish letters and brieves, 1286-1424 / edited by A.A.M. Duncan. — Glasgow ([Glasgow G12 8QQ]) : University of Glasgow, Scottish History Department, 1976. — [1],52p ; 26cm. — (University of Glasgow. Scottish History Department. Occasional papers ISSN 0308-8235)
Latin texts, English introduction and notes. — Texts transcribed from Edinburgh University Library MS. Borland, no.207.
ISBN 0-905493-00-1 Sd : £0.75
(B77-02868)

348'.416'025 — Northern Ireland. Law. *Statutory instruments. Collections*
Northern Ireland. *Statutory instruments.* The statutory rules of Northern Ireland. — Belfast : H.M.S.O.
1975. — 1976. — 2v.(1929,lx p) : ill, forms ; 25cm.
Index.
ISBN 0-337-85000-3 : £27.00
(B77-10279)

348'.42'005 — England. Law. *Yearbooks*
The **lawyer's** remembrancer. — London : Butterworth.
1977 / revised and edited for the year by G.R.N. Cusworth. — 1976. — 368p ; 17cm.
Unpaged diary follows p.368. — Index.
ISBN 0-406-26909-2 : £3.80
(B77-01268)

348'.42'022 — England. Law. *Statutes. Collections*
Great Britain. *Laws, statutes, etc. (Collections).* Butterworths annotated legislation service. Statutes supplements. — London : Butterworth.

No.238 : Miscellaneous acts / annotated by Butterworths legal editorial staff. — 1976. — v, 138p ; 25cm.
Index. — Contents: Nursing Homes Act 1975 - Mobile Homes Act 1975 - Guard Dogs Act 1975 - Safety of Sports Grounds Act 1975 - Lotteries Act 1975 - Housing Finance (Special Provisions) Act 1975 - Local Land Charges Act 1975.
ISBN 0-406-54755-6 : £6.50
(B77-02869)

No.239 : The Finance Act 1976 / edited by J. Jeffrey-Cook, C.P. Cretton ; contributors ... [others]. — 1976. — iv,324p ; 25cm.
Index. — Includes the text of the Act.
ISBN 0-406-54759-9 : £8.00
(B77-02870)

No.240 : The Community Land Act 1975 / general editor George Dobry, editor Michael Barnes, assistant editors ... [others]. — 1976. — 625p in various pagings : forms ; 25cm.
Index. — Includes the text of the Act.
ISBN 0-406-54756-4 : £18.00
(B77-02871)

No.241 : Industry Act 1975 / by Thomas Sharpe. — 1976. — ix,130p ; 25cm.
Index. — Includes the text of the Act.
ISBN 0-406-54753-x : £7.00
(B77-04673)

No.245 : Miscellaneous acts / annotated by Butterworths legal editorial staff. — 1977. — v, 216p ; 25cm.
Index. — Contents: Water Charges Act 1976 - Rating (Caravan Sites) Act 1976 - Food and Drugs (Control of Food Premises) Act 1976 - Drought Act 1976 - Rating (Charity Shops) Act 1976 - Land Drainage Act 1976.
ISBN 0-406-54765-3 : £11.50
(B77-33697)

Great Britain. *Laws, statutes, etc. (Collections).* Halsbury's statutes of England. — 3rd ed. — London : Butterworth.
Cumulative supplement 1976. — 1976. — 2161p in various pagings ; 26cm.
£29.00(£471.00 for the set)
(B77-00677)

Vol.42A : European legislation, 1952-1972. Supplement, 1973-1975 / edited by Kaye McDowell ; contributors Elizabeth Freeman, Chloris Latham. — 1976. — xix,265p ; 25cm.
'Reprinted from "Halsbury's Statutes of England" (3rd Edn.) Cumulative Supplement 1976'.
ISBN 0-406-04249-7 Pbk : £9.00
(B77-00678)

Vol.46 : Continuation volume, 1976. — 1977. — 90,2229p ; 26cm.
Index.
ISBN 0-406-04250-0 : Unpriced
(B77-25488)

Great Britain. *Laws, statutes, etc. (Collections).* The twentieth century statutes : incorporating 'Chitty's annual statutes'. — London : Butterworth.
Vol.75 : containing the public general acts passed in the year 1976 relating to England and Wales. — 1977. — 90,2229p ; 26cm.
Index.
ISBN 0-406-14371-4 : £40.00
(B77-33129)

348'.42'025 — England. Law. *Statutory instruments. Collections*
Great Britain. *Statutory instruments.* Halsbury's statutory instruments : being a companion work to 'Halsbury's statutes of England' / prepared by Butterworths legal editorial staff. — London : Butterworth.
In 24 vols.
Vol.18 : Prisons, prize, public health, rates and rating, real property. — 3rd re-issue / revised for the third re-issue by F.G. Kearney and K.U. Szantyr. — 1976. — vi,344p ; 26cm.
Index.
ISBN 0-406-04682-4 : £14.00
(B77-04036)

348'.42'0405 — England. Law. Cases. *Serials*
The **all** England law reports. — London : Butterworth.
Consolidated tables and index, 1936-1976. — 1977. — 3v.(vi,798p; vi,1625p) ; 24cm.
ISBN 0-406-86214-1 : £39.00
(B77-31073)

348'.42'046 — England. Law. Cases. *Digests*
The **English** and Empire digest with complete and exhaustive annotations. Replacement volumes. — London : Butterworth.
36(2) : Partnership, patents and inventions. — 1976 reissue / [revised by Jane Allen]. — 1976. — lxx p,p583-1351,73p ; 26cm.
Index.
ISBN 0-406-02682-3 : £271.00 the set
(B77-01269)

The **English** and Empire digest with complete and exhaustive annotations. Replacement volumes. — 1977 reissue / [revised by Jane Allen]. — London : Butterworth.
14(1) : Criminal law and procedure : parts 1-8. — 1977. — xv,460,[1],22p ; 26cm.
ISBN 0-406-02571-1 : Unpriced
(B77-31784)

14(2) : Criminal law and procedure : parts 9-15. — 1977. — xcviii p,p463-867,[1],20p ; 26cm.
Index to vols 14(1) and 14(2).
ISBN 0-406-02572-x : Unpriced
(B77-31785)

348'.42'06 — England. Law. *Encyclopaedias*
Jowitt, William Allen, *Earl Jowitt.* Jowitt's dictionary of English law / by the late Earl Jowitt and Clifford Walsh. — 2nd ed. / [edited] by John Burke. — London : Sweet and Maxwell, 1977. — 2v.([11],1935p) ; 26cm.
Previous ed.: published as 'The dictionary of English law'. 1959. — Bibl.: p.1923-1935.
ISBN 0-421-23090-8 : £45.00
(B77-15190)

348'.423'046 — Assize courts. Court orders. *South-west England, 1629-1648. Digests*
Cockburn, James Swanston. Western Circuit Assize Orders, 1629-1648 : a calendar / edited [i.e. prepared] for the Royal Historical Society by J.S. Cockburn. — London : The Society, 1976. — xiv,352p ; 23cm. — (Camden fourth series ; vol.17)
Index.
ISBN 0-901050-29-6 : £5.50
(B77-15191)

348'.4261'046 — Gaol delivery. Cases. *Norfolk, 1307-1316. Digests*
Crime in East Anglia in the fourteenth century / Norfolk gaol delivery rolls, 1307-1316 ; [edited by] Barbara Hanawalt. — Norwich (c/o the Secretary, 425 Unthank Rd, Norwich NR4 7QB) : Norfolk Record Society, 1976. — [9], 150p : 1 ill ; 26cm. — (Norfolk Record Society. Publications ; vol.44)
Index.
ISBN 0-9501370-4-9 : £4.50
(B77-15189)

348'.4279'028 — Isle of Man. Law. Statutes, 1776-1975. *Indexes*
Young, George Vaughan Chichester. Subject guide and chronological table relating to the Acts of Tynwald, 1776-1975 / prepared by G.V.C. Young ; on the directions of H.M. Attorney General for the Isle of Man. — Douglas ([Douglas, Isle of Man]) : Shearwater Press, 1977. — 210p ; 24cm.
Versos of leaves blank in subject guide (p.11-87).
ISBN 0-904980-15-4 : Unpriced
(B77-26209)

348'.6651'022 — Gambia. Law. *Statutes. Collections*
Gambia. *Laws, statutes, etc. (Collections).* The laws of The Gambia, 1966. — Banjul : Government Printer ; London : Sweet and Maxwell.
[Vol.13] : 1974-1975 continuation volume : containing enactments of the period from the 1st January, 1974, to the 31st December, 1975 and prepared under the authority of the Revised Edition of the Laws (Continuation Volumes) Act, 1968 (No.3 of 1968) / by Sir Cecil G. Ames. — 1976. — xx,357p : forms ; 25cm.
Index.
ISBN 0-421-23110-6 : £10.00
(B77-03453)

348'.67'04105 — East African countries. Law. *Cases. Serials*
The **East** Africa law reports. — London : Butterworth.
1974 / editor P. Le Pelley ; assistant editor C.C.K. Ndozireho ; editorial assistant G.M. Fimbo. — 1975. — xxviii,579p ; 25cm.
ISBN 0-406-87114-0 : £30.72
(B77-02139)

350 — PUBLIC ADMINISTRATION
Riggs, Frederick Warren. The ecology of public administration / [by] F.W. Riggs. — London : Asia Publishing House [for] the Indian Institute of Public Administration, 1975. — viii,144p : 1 ill ; 22cm.
Originally published: 1962. — Index.
ISBN 0-210-33842-3 Pbk : £2.50
Also classified at 353; 354'.593; 354'.599
(B77-11696)

Self, Peter. Administrative theories and politics : an enquiry into the structure and processes of modern government / by Peter Self. — 2nd ed. — London : Allen and Unwin, 1977. — [8], 308p ; 22cm. — (Open University. Set books)
Previous ed.: 1972. — Bibl.: p.301-302. — Index.
ISBN 0-04-351053-1 Pbk : £4.50
(B77-20127)

350 — Governments. Policies. Decision making by political elites. Cognitive mapping
Structure of decision : the cognitive maps of political elites / edited by Robert Axelrod. — Princeton ; Guildford : Princeton University Press, 1976. — xvi,404,[1]p : ill ; 25cm.
Bibl.: p.373-393. — Index.
ISBN 0-691-07578-6 : £17.40
ISBN 0-691-10050-0 Pbk : £6.90
(B77-02140)

350 — Governments. Policies. Decision-making. Applications of cybernetics
Steinbruner, John D. The cybernetic theory of decision : new dimensions of political analysis / [by] John D. Steinbruner. — Princeton ; Guildford : Princeton University Press, 1976. — xiii,366,[1]p : 4 ill ; 24cm.
Originally published: Princeton : Princeton University Press, 1974. — Bibl.: p.343-359. — Index.
ISBN 0-691-02175-9 Pbk : £3.95
(B77-16274)

350 — Public administration. Political aspects
Wamsley, Gary L. The political economy of public organizations : a critique and approach to the study of public administration / [by] Gary L. Wamsley, Mayer N. Zald. — Bloomington ; London : Indiana University Press, 1976 [i.e. 1977]. — xi,110p : ill ; 24cm.
Originally published: Lexington, Mass. : Lexington Books, 1973. — Index.
ISBN 0-253-34525-1 Pbk : £2.65
(B77-11697)

350'.001 — Bureaucracy
Schuman, David. Bureaucracies, organizations and administration : a political primer / [by] David Schuman. — New York : Macmillan ; London : Collier Macmillan, 1976. — xii,235p ; 21cm.
Bibl. — Index.
ISBN 0-02-408141-8 Pbk : £4.30
(B77-12941)

351 — CENTRAL GOVERNMENT ADMINISTRATION
351 — Governments. Decision making
Anderson, Charles William. Statecraft : an introduction to political choice and judgment / [by] Charles W. Anderson. — New York ; London [etc.] : Wiley, 1977. — xv,318p : ill ; 24cm.
Bibl. — Index.
ISBN 0-471-02896-7 : £9.00
(B77-25489)

351'.000966 — West Africa. Government, 1765-1973
Adigwe, Francis. Essentials of government for West Africa / [by] Francis Adigwe. — Ibadan ; London [etc.] : Oxford University Press, 1974 [i.e. 1976]. — viii,389p ; 22cm.
Published in Nigeria: 1974. — Bibl.: p.383-384. — Index.
ISBN 0-19-575242-2 : Unpriced
ISBN 0-19-575243-0 Pbk : Unpriced
(B77-11140)

351'.003'094 — Governments. Decision making. *Western Europe. Small countries*
Obler, Jeffrey. Decision-making in smaller democracies : the consociational 'burden' / [by] Jeffrey Obler, Jürg Steiner, Guido Dierickx. — Beverly Hills ; London : Sage Publications, 1977. — 58,[1]p ; 22cm. — (Sage professional papers in comparative politics ; vol.6, no.1-064 ISSN 0080-5343)
Bibl.: p.53-58.
ISBN 0-8039-0759-1 Pbk : £1.95
(B77-26937)

351.003'12 — Africa. Monarchy. Effects of social change. Political aspects
African kingships in perspective : political change and modernization in monarchical settings / edited by René Lemarchand. — London [etc.] : Cass, 1977. — xiv,325p : ill, geneal table ; 24cm.
Bibl.: p.305-314. — Index.
ISBN 0-7146-3027-6 : £12.50
(B77-11700)

351'.003'73096 — Africa. Commonwealth countries. Government. Role of judiciary
Nwabueze, Benjamin Obi. Judicialism in Commonwealth Africa : the role of the courts in government / [by] B.O. Nwabueze ; with a foreword by Rotimi Williams. — London : C. Hurst [etc.], 1977. — xii,324p ; 23cm.
Index.
ISBN 0-903983-56-7 : £9.50 : CIP rev.
(B77-14631)

352 — LOCAL GOVERNMENT

352 — Great Britain. Statistics. Use by local authorities. *Conference proceedings*
Statistics Users Conference, *Royal Society, 1975.* Statistics Users Conference : proceedings of a conference on the theme of statistics for local government held at the Wellcome Hall of the Royal Society on Wednesday, 12 November 1975 : a conference arranged jointly by the Association of County Councils and the Association of Metropolitan Authorities on behalf of the Standing Committee of Statistics Users / [proceedings edited by Kate Kirkland]. — [London] ([c/o Greater London Council, County Hall, London S.E.1]) : Standing Committee of Statistics Users, 1976. — 158p : ill ; 30cm.
'The conference planning committee was serviced by the Greater London Council, which was also its agent in organising the conference' - Preface. — Bibl.: p.49.
Sp : Unpriced
(B77-04674)

352 — Social minorities. Discrimination by local authorities: Discrimination in allocation of resources of federal grants. *United States*
Hope, John. Minority access to federal grants-in-aid : the gap between policy and performance / [by] John Hope, II. — New York [etc.] ; London : Praeger ; [London] : [Distributed by Martin Robertson], 1976. — xxv,269p ; 25cm. — (Praeger special studies in US economic, social and political issues)
Bibl.: p.239-245. — Index.
ISBN 0-275-55920-3 : £14.80
(B77-10280)

352'.00028'54044 — Great Britain. Local government. Applications of minicomputer systems
Local Authorities Management Services and Computer Committee. *Computer Panel.* The use of minicomputers in local government : report of the Computer Panel of LAMSAC. — London : LAMSAC, 1977. — 25,[1]p ; 30cm.
ISBN 0-85497-099-1 Sd : £2.50
(B77-18019)

352'.00028'54044 — United States. Local government. Applications of digital computer systems
Kraemer, Kenneth L. Computers, power and urban management : what every local executive should know / [by] Kenneth L. Kraemer, John Leslie King. — Beverly Hills ; London : Sage Publications, 1976. — 46,[1]p : ill ; 22cm. — (Sage professional papers in administrative and policy studies ; vol.3, no.03-031)
Bibl.: p.43-46.
ISBN 0-8039-0535-1 Pbk : £1.75
(B77-14632)

352'.002'0942 — England. Local government. Corporate planning. Cooperation between local authorities
Local Authorities Management Services and Computer Committee. *General Management Panel.* Corporate planning within and between authorities : interim report of the General Management Panel of LAMSAC. — London : Local Authorities Management Services and Computer Committee, 1977. — 19,[1]p ; 30cm.
ISBN 0-85497-097-5 Sd : £2.50
(B77-17379)

352'.0073 — District councils. Officers: District secretaries. Organisations. *England. Association of District Secretaries. Periodicals*
Association of District Secretaries. ADS journal. — Selby (c/o The Editor, Selby District Council, 2 Abbey Yard, Selby, N. Yorkshire) : The Association.
Vol.1- ; Mar. 1976-. — [1976]-. — 30cm.
Quarterly. — 30p. in 1st issue.
Pbk : Unpriced
ISSN 0309-7307
(B77-21022)

352'.0073 — France. Local government. Prefects. Role
Machin, Howard. The Prefect in French public administration / [by] Howard Machin. — London : Croom Helm, 1977. — 3-210p : 2 maps ; 23cm.
Index.
ISBN 0-85664-236-3 : £8.95
(B77-12378)

352'.0073'06242 — County councils. Organisations. *England. Association of County Councils. Yearbooks*
Association of County Councils. Year book / Association of County Councils. — London (66a Eaton Sq., SW1W 9BH) : The Association.

1977-78. — 1977. — 156p : map ; 21cm.
Sd : £1.00
ISSN 0305-2044
(B77-27755)

352'.0073'09429 — Local authorities. Boundaries. *Wales. Proposals. Welsh-English parallel texts*
Local Government Boundary Commission for Wales. Arolwg ffin = Boundary review / Comisiwn Ffiniau Llywodraeth Leol i Gymru = Local Government Boundary Commission for Wales. — [Cardiff] ([Queens Court, Plymouth St., Cardiff CF1 4DA]) : [The Commission].
Parallel Welsh and English texts.
Adroddiad a chynigion = Report and proposals. Dosbarth Ceredigion a Dosbarth Preseli = District of Ceredigion and District of Preseli. — [1976]. — [1],20p,fold plate : col map ; 30cm.
Sp : Unpriced
(B77-24092)

352'.008'091724 — Local authorities. Organisation structure. *Developing countries. Urban regions. Case studies*
Davies, C J. Problems in urban management / [by] C.J. Davies. — Birmingham (P.O. Box 363, Birmingham B15 2TT) : Development Administration Group, Institute of Local Government Studies, University of Birmingham, 1976. — [3],115[i.e.132]p : ill, map ; 30cm. — (Case studies in development administration ; vol.3)
Bibl.: p.114-115.
ISBN 0-7044-0201-7 Pbk : £1.00
(B77-22457)

352'.008'0924 — Greater Manchester (Metropolitan County). Manchester. Lord Mayors, 1975-1976. *Personal observations*
Ollerenshaw, *Dame* **Kathleen.** First citizen / [by] Kathleen Ollerenshaw. — London : Hart-Davis MacGibbon, 1977. — [10],181p,[18]p of plates : ill, coat of arms, map, ports(1 col) ; 23cm.
Index.
ISBN 0-246-10976-9 : £6.95
(B77-21023)

352'.008'0941 — Great Britain. Community politics. *For Liberal Party*
Lishman, Gordon. Community politics guide / [by] A.G. Lishman. — Manchester (21 Bank Rd, Manchester 8) : North West Community Newspapers Ltd ; [London] : Association of Liberal Councillors, 1974. — [20]p ; 21cm.
Sd : £0.20
(B77-33130)

352'.008'09411 — Community councils. *Scotland. Periodicals*
Community council news. — Edinburgh (c/o Administrative Secretary, Community Council News, 18 Claremont Cres., Edinburgh EH7 4QD) : Scottish Council of Social Service for Scottish Community Councils Publications Council.
Supersedes: Community council news items. [No.1]- ; Spring [1977]-. — [1977]-. — ill ; 30cm.
Monthly (i.e. 10 issues a year). — [2],13,[1]p. in 1st issue.
Sd : £0.25(£2.00 yearly)
ISSN 0309-720x
(B77-24801)

352'.008'09429 — Community councils. Boundaries. *Wales. Proposals. Welsh-English parallel texts*
Local Government Boundary Commission for Wales. Special community review = Arolwg cymdeithas arbennig / Local Government Boundary Commission for Wales = Comisiwn Ffiniau Llywodraeth Leol i Gymru. — Cardiff (Queens Court, Plymouth St., Cardiff CF1 4DA) : The Commission.
Parallel Welsh and English texts.
Draft proposals = Cynigion drafft. Alyn and Deeside = Alun a Glannau Dyfrdwy. — 1976. — [1],20p,fold plate : col map ; 30cm.
Sp : Unpriced
(B77-20128)

Draft proposals = Cynigion drafft. Colwyn. — 1976. — [1],18p ; 30cm.
Fold. sheet (col. map) in pocket.
Sp : Unpriced
(B77-20129)

Draft proposals = Cynigion drafft. Cynon Valley = Cwm Cynon. — 1976. — [1],12p ; 30cm.
Fold. sheet (col. map) in pocket.
Sp : Unpriced
(B77-20130)

Draft proposals = Cynigion drafft. Dwyfor. — 1976. — [1],14p,fold plate : col map ; 30cm.
Sp : Unpriced
(B77-20131)

Draft proposals = Cynigion drafft. Llanelli. — 1976. — [1],20p,fold plate : col map ; 30cm.
Sp : Unpriced
(B77-20132)

Draft proposals = Cynigion drafft. Merthyr Tydfil = Merthyr Tudful. — 1976. — [1],12p, fold plate : col map ; 30cm.
Sp : Unpriced
(B77-20133)

Draft proposals = Cynigion drafft. Newport = Casnewydd. — 1976. — [1],24p,fold plate : col map ; 30cm.
Sp : Unpriced
(B77-20134)

Draft proposals = Cynigion drafft. Ogwr. — 1976. — [1],20p ; 30cm.
Sp : Unpriced
(B77-20135)

Draft proposals = Cynigion drafft. Rhondda. — 1976. — [1],14p,fold plate : col map ; 30cm.

Sp : Unpriced
(B77-20136)

Draft proposals = Cynigion drafft. Swansea = Abertawe. — 1976. — [1],24p,fold plate : col map ; 30cm.
Sp : Unpriced
(B77-20137)

Draft proposals = Cynigion drafft. Vale of Glamorgan = Bro Morgannwg. — 1976. — [1],24p,fold plate : col map ; 30cm.
Sp : Unpriced
(B77-20138)

Report and proposals for Borough of Afan = Adroddiad a chynigion ar gyfer Bwrdeistref Afan. — [1976]. — [1],43p ; 30cm.
Fold. sheet (col. map) in pocket.
Sp : Unpriced
(B77-24093)

352'.008'0973 — Cities. Local government. Political aspects. *United States*
Caraley, Demetrios. City governments and urban problems : a new introduction to urban politics / [by] Demetrios Caraley. — Englewood Cliffs ; London [etc.] : Prentice-Hall, 1977. — xv,448p : ill ; 24cm.
Index.
ISBN 0-13-134973-2 : £10.35
(B77-22458)

352'.008'0973 — Neighbourhood councils. Organisation. *United States. Manuals*
Hallman, Howard Wesley. The organization and operation of neighborhood councils : a practical guide / [by] Howard W. Hallman ; with chapters by ... [others]. — New York ; London : Praeger [for] the Center for Governmental Studies, 1977. — x,159p ; 25cm. — (Praeger special studies in US economic, social and political issues)
Bibl. — Index.
£11.05
(B77-26210)

352'.008'0973 — United States. Urban regions. Local government
Adrian, Charles Raymond. Governing urban America. — 5th ed. / [by] Charles R. Adrian, Charles Press. — New York ; London [etc.] : McGraw-Hill, 1977. — xi,401p : ill ; 25cm.
Previous ed.: 1972. — Bibl.: p.386-393. — Index.
ISBN 0-07-000446-3 : £9.70
(B77-26938)

352'.008'0973 — United States. Urban regions. Local government. *Readings*
Urban administration : management, politics, and change / edited by Alan Edward Bent, Ralph A. Rossum. — Port Washington, N.Y. ; London : Kennikat Press ; London : Distributed by Martin Robertson, 1976. — [6], 385p ; 23cm. — (Kennikat Press national university publications : interdisciplinary urban series)
'A Denellen Company book'. — Index.
ISBN 0-8046-7106-0 : £14.60
ISBN 0-8046-7109-5 Pbk : Unpriced
(B77-15192)

352'.008'0973 — United States. Urban regions. Local government, 1880-1920
Schiesl, Martin J. The politics of efficiency : municipal administration and reform in America, 1800 [i.e. 1880]-1920 / [by] Martin J. Schiesl. — Berkeley [etc.] ; London : University of California Press, 1977. — ix,259p ; 23cm.
Bibl.: p.233-247. — Index.
ISBN 0-520-03067-2 : £8.80
(B77-26211)

352'.008'0973 — United States. Urban regions. Local government. Role of coloured persons
Urban governance and minorities / edited by Herrington J. Bryce. — New York [etc.] ; London : Praeger [for] the Joint Center for Political Studies, [1977]. — xv,220p ; 25cm. — (Praeger special studies in US economic, social and political issues)
Published in the United States: 1976.
ISBN 0-275-23500-9 : £12.60
(B77-14633)

352.041 — Great Britain. Local government. *Statistics*
Local government trends / [Chartered Institute of Public Finance and Accountancy]. — London : C.I.P.F.A.
1976. — 1977. — [5],266p : ill, maps ; 30cm.
Pbk : £6.50
ISSN 0307-0441
(B77-33698)

352.041 — Great Britain. Local government. Performance review
Local Authorities Management Services and Computer Committee. *General Management Panel.* Practical performance review in local government : report of the General Management Panel of LAMSAC. — London : Local Authorities Management Services and Computer Committee, 1977. — 28,[1]p : 2 ill ; 30cm.
ISBN 0-85497-095-9 Sd : £2.50
(B77-15193)

352.041 — Great Britain. Local government. Political aspects
Gyford, John. Local politics in Britain / [by] John Gyford. — London : Croom Helm, 1976. — 3-193p ; 23cm.
Bibl.: p.161-186. — Index.
ISBN 0-85664-319-x : £6.50
ISBN 0-85664-475-7 Pbk : £2.95
(B77-00113)

352.041 — Local authorities. *Great Britain. Directories*
Public authorities directory. — London (Publications Division, 11 Bury St., EC3A 5AP) : Brown, Knight and Truscott (Holdings) Ltd.
1977 / editor Geoffrey Smith ; research Stella Harrington. — [1977]. — 471p ; 21cm.
Index.
ISBN 0-904677-05-2 Pbk : £9.50
ISSN 0306-0470
(B77-16794)

United Kingdom local authorities : new county and district authorities, regional health authorities, new education authorities, gas boards, electricity boards, and regional water authorities / [Data Research Group]. — Amersham (Hill House, [Hill Ave.] Amersham, Bucks.) : The Group.
[1977]. — [1977]. — 103 leaves in various pagings ; 30cm.
ISBN 0-86099-010-9 Sp : £14.00
(B77-14634)

352.041 — Local authorities. Performance. Measurement. *Great Britain. Reports, surveys*
Epping Forest *(District). Council.* Performance measurement in local government : report of a study of five District Councils / Epping Forest District Council. — Epping (323 High St., Epping, Essex) : The Council, [1977]. — 20p ; 21x30cm.
ISBN 0-903930-05-6 Sd : £1.00
(B77-07225)

352.041 — Local authorities. Relations with public. *Great Britain. Case studies*
Local government and the public / edited by Roy Darke and Ray Walker ; contributors Roy Darke ... [et al.]. — London : L. Hill, 1977. — viii,255p : ill, map, plans ; 24cm.
Index.
ISBN 0-249-44154-3 : £6.60
(B77-30072)

352.0411 — Local authorities. *Scotland. Directories*
Scotland's regions : incorporating 'County and municipal year book for Scotland'. — Coupar Angus : Culross.
1976-77 : 45th ed. — [1977]. — [3],xi,326p : maps ; 23cm.
Index.
ISBN 0-900323-22-1 Pbk : Unpriced
ISSN 0305-6562
(B77-27756)

352.0414'25 — Community councils. *Scotland. Strathclyde Region. Cove & Kilcreggan. Proposals*
Cove and Kilcreggan : the establishment of a community council. — [Glasgow] : [Gibson], 1975. — [16]leaves : coat of arms, form ; 30cm.

ISBN 0-7169-3112-5 Sd : Unpriced
(B77-04037)

352.042 — England. Local government
Griffiths, Alan, *b.1924.* Local government administration / by Alan Griffiths. — London : Shaw and Sons, 1976. — xix,312p ; 23cm.
Index.
ISBN 0-7219-0710-5 : £7.00
(B77-12379)

352.042 — England. Local government. *Proposals*
Young, Scot. Shire power : a new dimension in English politics / [by] Scot Young. — London (9 Poland St., W1V 3DG) : Liberal Publication Department, [1977]. — [2],19,[1]p : map ; 21cm.
ISBN 0-900520-55-8 Sd : £0.30
(B77-14131)

352.042 — England. Local government. Reform, 1966-1974
Wood, Bruce. The process of local government reform, 1966-74 / by Bruce Wood ; foreword by Lord Redcliffe-Maud. — London : Allen and Unwin, 1976. — 3-205p ; 23cm. — (The new local government series ; no.14)
Index.
ISBN 0-04-350052-8 : £6.95
(B77-05972)

352.042 — Local authorities. *England. Directories*
The **Oyez** directory of local authorities in England and Wales. — New ed. — London : Oyez Publishing, 1977. — vii,180p ; 25cm.
Previous ed.: published as 'Directory of local authorities in England and Wales'. 1975.
ISBN 0-85120-317-5 Pbk : £6.50
(B77-16795)

352.042 — Local authorities. Cluster analysis. *England. Sources of data: Census data: Social conditions, 1971*
Imber, Valerie. A classification of the English personal social services authorities / by Valerie Imber. — London : H.M.S.O., 1977. — vi,57p : ill ; 28cm. — (Great Britain. Department of Health and Social Security. Statistical and research report series ; no.16)
ISBN 0-11-320237-7 Pbk : £2.10
(B77-13580)

352.042 — Local authorities. Management. *England*
Knowles, Raymond Stewart Brown. Modern management in local government / by Raymond S.B. Knowles. — 2nd ed. — [Chichester] : [Rose], 1977. — x,281p : ill ; 23cm.
Previous ed.: London : Butterworth, 1971. — Index.
ISBN 0-85992-084-4 : £6.00 : CIP rev.
(B77-10281)

352.042 — Local authorities. Organisation structure. *England. Reports, surveys*
In pursuit of corporate rationality : organisational developments in the post-reorganisation period / by Royston Greenwood ... [et al.]. — [Birmingham] ([P.O. Box 363, Birmingham B15 2TT]) : [Institute of Local Government Studies, University of Birmingham], [1976]. — [3],241[i.e.245],vi p : ill ; 29cm.
Pbk : £3.00
(B77-22459)

352.042 — Local government. *Study regions: England*
Stanyer, Jeffrey. Understanding local government / [by] Jeffrey Stanyer. — London : Martin Robertson [etc.], 1976. — 320p : ill ; 21cm. — (Studies in public administration)
Bibl.: p.308-311. — Index.
ISBN 0-85520-140-1 : £7.95
(B77-05306)

352.0421 — Greater London Council. Administration. Participation of personnel
Industrial democracy in local government : papers considered by a working party of GLC/ILEA members [i.e. the Members' Working Party on Industrial Democracy] together with the Working Party's final report. — [London] : Greater London Council, [1977]. — [1],44p : ill ; 30cm.
ISBN 0-7168-0873-0 Sd : £0.60
(B77-18636)

352.0421 — Greater London Council. Services. *Yearbooks*
Greater London services / Greater London Council, Inner London Education Authority. — London : G.L.C. : I.L.E.A.
1976-77. — 1977. — [4],96p : ill, coat of arms, map, port ; 21cm.
Index.
ISBN 0-7168-0837-4 Sd : Unpriced
(B77-13581)

352.0421'2 — London (City). Local government, 1558-1603
Foster, Frank Freeman. The politics of stability : a portrait of the rules in Elizabethan London / [by] Frank Freeman Foster. — London : Royal Historical Society, 1977. — x,209p ; 23cm. — (Royal Historical Society. Studies in history)
Index.
ISBN 0-901050-31-8 : Unpriced
(B77-25491)

352.0422'5 — East Sussex (County). Council, to 1974
Bell, Christopher Richard Vincent. A history of East Sussex County Council, 1889-1974 / by C.R.V. Bell. — London [etc.] : Phillimore for East Sussex County Council, 1975. — [7],119p, leaf of plate,[8]p of plates : ill(incl 1 col), maps, ports ; 26cm.
Index.
ISBN 0-85033-212-5 : £5.75
(B77-02141)

352.0423'38 — Winton (Parish). Council, to 1898
Young, John Anthony. Winton Parish Council, 1894-1898 / [by] J.A. Young. — [Dorchester] ([County Hall, Dorchester, Dorset]) : Dorset County Council Education Committee, [1977]. — [2],21[i.e.23]p : map ; 21cm.
ISBN 0-85216-160-3 Sd : Unpriced
(B77-10773)

352.0423'38 — Winton (Urban District). Council, to 1901
Young, John Anthony. Winton Urban District Council, 1898-1901 / [by] J.A. Young. — [Dorchester] ([County Hall, Dorchester, Dorset]) : Dorset County Council Education Committee, [1977]. — [2],14p ; 21cm.
ISBN 0-85216-162-x Sd : Unpriced
(B77-10774)

352.0424'1 — Gloucestershire (County). Council, to 1974
Kerr, M J. Gloucestershire County Council, 1889-1974 : a short history / compiled from the minutes by M.J. Kerr. — [Gloucester] ([Shire Hall, Gloucester G11 2TN]) : Gloucestershire County Library for the Council, 1977. — [14], 34p : ill, col map, ports ; 25cm.
ISBN 0-904950-04-2 Sd : £1.30
(B77-26939)

352.0424'91 — Wolverhampton. Town Commissioners, to 1848
Mason, F. Wolverhampton, the Town Commissioners, 1777-1848 : their story in their minutes and the files of the 'Wolverhampton chronicle'. — [Wolverhampton] ([Central Library, Snow Hill, Wolverhampton WV1 3AX]) : Wolverhampton Public Libraries, 1976. — [7],71 leaves : facsims ; 30cm.
Author: F. Mason. — Facsims on verso of 9 leaves, some tipped in. — Index.
Pbk : Unpriced
(B77-21774)

352.0425'9 — Buckinghamshire (County). Council. *Reports, surveys. Serials*
Buckinghamshire *(County). Council.* Report / Buckinghamshire County Council. — [Aylesbury] ([County Hall, Aylesbury, Bucks. HP20 1VA]) : [The Council].
1st : 1973-1977. — [1977]. — [2],39p : ill, ports ; 15x21cm.
ISBN 0-902805-69-x Sd : Unpriced
(B77-16275)

352.0426'48 — Freemen. *Suffolk. Sudbury, to 1975*
Berry, Allan. The freedom of Sudbury, Suffolk : a brief history / [by Allan Berry]. — Sudbury ([c/o 10 Blackheath, Colchester, Essex]) : Sudbury Freemen's Society, 1976. — [13]p ; 26cm.
Sd : £1.00
(B77-29292)

352.0429'62 — Haverfordwest (Rural District). Council, to 1974
Dickman, H J. Haverfordwest Rural District Council : history of the Council, 1894-1974 / [by] H.J. Dickman. — [Haverfordwest] ([19 Haven Rd, Haverfordwest, Pembs. SA61 1DU]) : [The author], [1976]. — 136p : ill, map, ports ; 21cm.
Spine title: History of the Council, 1894-1974. — Bibl.: p.132. — Index.
ISBN 0-9505572-0-x Pbk : £2.10
(B77-10282)

352.044 — Local government. Political aspects. France. Compared with political aspects of local government in Italy
Tarrow, Sidney George. Between center and periphery : grassroots politicians in Italy and France / [by] Sidney Tarrow. — New Haven ; London : Yale University Press, 1977. — xv, 272p ; 22cm.
Index.
ISBN 0-300-02047-3 : £10.80
Also classified at 352.045
(B77-24802)

352.045 — Local government. Political aspects. Italy. Compared with political aspects of local government in France
Tarrow, Sidney George. Between center and periphery : grassroots politicians in Italy and France / [by] Sidney Tarrow. — New Haven ; London : Yale University Press, 1977. — xv, 272p ; 22cm.
Index.
ISBN 0-300-02047-3 : £10.80
Primary classification 352.044
(B77-24802)

352.081 — Brazil. Local government, 1949
Leal, Victor Nunes. Coronelismo : the municipality and representative government in Brazil / [by] Victor Nunes Leal ; translated [from the Spanish] by June Henfrey ; with an introduction by Alberto Venancio Filho. — Cambridge [etc.] : Cambridge University Press, 1977. — iii-xvi,237p ; 23cm. — (Cambridge Latin American studies ; 28)
Translation of: 'Coronelismo, enxada e voto'. Brazil : s.n., 1949. — Bibl.: p.230-237.
ISBN 0-521-21488-2 : £7.90
(B77-29293)

352'.1'061411 — Scotland. Local government. Financial management. Organisations: Commission for Local Authority Accounts in Scotland. *Reports, surveys*
Great Britain. *Commission for Local Authority Accounts in Scotland.* Accounts Commission : first report of the Commission for Local Authority Accounts in Scotland. — Edinburgh : H.M.S.O., 1976. — 21p ; 22cm.
ISBN 0-11-491442-7 Sd : £0.50
(B77-07226)

352'.12'0973 — Local authorities. Programme budgeting. *United States*
Babunakis, Michael. Budgets : an analytical and procedural handbook for government and nonprofit organizations / [by] Michael Babunakis. — Westport, Conn. ; London : Greenwood Press, 1976. — xii,257,[1]p : forms ; 25cm.
Bibl.: p.252-255. — Index.
ISBN 0-8371-8900-4 : £11.75
Also classified at 353.9'3'722
(B77-18020)

352'.16'0942 — Local councils. Administration. *England*
Ousby, W H. A practical guide to local council administration : a handbook for clerks and elected members of parish and community councils in England and Wales / [by] W.H. Ousby and B.G. Wright. — London [etc.] : C. Knight, 1976. — 141p : forms ; 22cm.
Index.
ISBN 0-85314-264-5 Pbk : £3.25
(B77-03454)

352'.16'3 — Local authorities. Energy. Conservation. *Great Britain. Reports, surveys*
Local Authorities Management Services and Computer Committee. *O and M and Productivity Panel.* Economic energy consumption : report of the O & M and Productivity Panel of LAMSAC. — London : L.A.M.S.A.C., 1977. — 39,[1]p : form ; 30cm.
Bibl.: p.22.
ISBN 0-85497-101-7 Sd : £2.50
(B77-26212)

352'.17'09417 — Local authorities. Accounting. *Ireland (Republic). Manuals*
Golden, T P. Local authority accounting in Ireland / [by] T.P. Golden. — Dublin : Institute of Public Administration, [1977]. — xii,276p : ill, forms ; 22cm.
Index.
ISBN 0-902173-77-4 Pbk : £5.00
(B77-25492)

352'.17'0942 — Local councils. Accounting. *England. Manuals*
Davies, Richard Ungoed. Parish council and town council accounts : a manual for the officers reponsible [i.e. responsible] for the administration of financial affairs / [by] R.U. Davies. — London [etc.] : C. Knight, 1977. — 160p : forms ; 23cm.
Index.
ISBN 0-85314-288-2 Pbk : £5.75
(B77-25493)

352'.4 — Noise abatement zones. Objections. *England. Manuals*
Great Britain. *Department of the Environment.* Noise abatement zone inquiries : what you need to know / [prepared by the Department of the Environment, the Welsh Office and the Central Office of Information]. — London : H.M.S.O., [1977]. — [1],16p ; 21x8cm.
Sd : Unpriced
(B77-29294)

352'.4'09411 — Local authorities. Relations with health boards. *Scotland. Reports, surveys*
Working Party on Relationships between Health Boards and Local Authorities. Report / Working Party on Relationships between Health Boards and Local Authorities. — Edinburgh : H.M.S.O., 1977. — 26p ; 25cm.
At head of title: Scottish Home and Health Department.
ISBN 0-11-491497-4 Sd : £0.50
Primary classification 362.1'06'1411
(B77-29308)

352'.75 — Housing. Design. Guidance. Provision by local authorities. *England. Reports, surveys*
Llewelyn-Davies, Weeks, Forestier-Walker and Bor *(Firm).* Design guidance survey : report on a survey of local authority design guidance for private residential development / Llewelyn-Davies, Weeks, Forestier-Walker & Bor ... ; commissioned by the Department of the Environment and the Housing Research Foundation. — [London] : Department of the Environment, 1976. — 60[i.e.62],[36]p(1 fold) : ill, forms, plans ; 30cm.
Sd : £2.00
(B77-31075)

352'.75'0942142 — Housing. Policies of Camden (London Borough). Council. *London. Camden (London Borough), 1965-1975. Inquiry reports*
Camden *(London Borough). Housing Review Panel.* Housing Review Panel report / London Borough of Camden [Housing Review Panel]. — [London] ([The Town Hall, Euston Rd, NW1 2RU]) : [London Borough of Camden], 1976. — [1],vi,203p : ill ; 30cm.
Includes Housing Review Panel minority report (9p.; Sd.) as insert.
ISBN 0-902802-12-7 Sp : £1.00
ISBN 0-902802-12-7 (Report)
ISBN 0-902802-11-9 (Minority report)
(B77-03456)

352'.75'094276 — Residences. Conversion & improvement. Policies of Lancashire (County). Council. *Lancashire. For applicants*
Lancashire *(County). Council.* Rural dwellings policy and design notes / [Lancashire County Council]. — [Preston] ([East Cliff County Offices, Preston PR1 3EX]) : Lancashire County Planning Dept, 1977. — [2],16p : ill ; 15x21cm.
Sd : £0.28
(B77-29295)

352'.96'0942498 — Planning. Policies of local authorities. *Great Britain. Study regions: West Midlands (Metropolitan County). Coventry*
Friend, John Kimball. Local government and strategic choice : an operational research approach to the processes of public planning / [by] J.K. Friend and W.N. Jessop. — 2nd ed. — Oxford [etc.] : Pergamon, 1977. — xxvi, 304p,fold plate : ill, maps(1 col) ; 24cm. — (Urban and regional planning series ; vol.14 ISSN 0305-5582) (Pergamon international library)
Previous ed.: London : Tavistock Publications, 1969. — Bibl.: p.297-298. — Index.
ISBN 0-08-021176-3 : £9.00
ISBN 0-08-021451-7 Pbk : £5.85
(B77-23246)

352'.96'0973 — United States. Local government. Planning
Levin, Melvin Richard. Community and regional planning : issues in public policy / [by] Melvin R. Levin. — 3rd ed. — New York ; London : Praeger, 1977. — xxiii,279p ; 24cm. — (Praeger special studies in US economic, social and political issues)
Previous ed.: New York : Praeger, 1972. — Bibl.: p.260-274. — Index.
ISBN 0-275-23690-0 : £14.40
ISBN 0-275-85740-9 Pbk : £5.30
(B77-25494)

353 — FEDERAL AND STATE ADMINISTRATIVE STRUCTURE. UNITED STATES

353 — Government departments. Management by objectives. *United States*
Jun, Jong S. Management by objectives in government : theory and practice / [by] Jong S. Jun. — Beverly Hills ; London : Sage Publications, 1976. — 80p : ill ; 22cm. — (Sage professional papers in administrative and policy studies ; vol.3, no.03-030)
Bibl.: p.79-80.
ISBN 0-8039-0534-3 Pbk : £1.75
(B77-14635)

353 — United States. Government
Ferguson, John Henry. The American Federal Government / [by] John H. Ferguson, Dean E. McHenry. — 13th ed. — New York ; London [etc.] : McGraw-Hill, 1977. — ix,536p : ill, maps ; 25cm.
Previous ed.: New York : McGraw-Hill, 1973. — Bibl. — Index. — Includes the Constitution of the United States.
ISBN 0-07-020524-8 : £9.70
(B77-20139)

353 — United States. Public administration
Gortner, Harold F. Administration in the public sector / [by] Harold F. Gortner. — New York ; London [etc.] : Wiley, 1977. — xvii, 343p : ill ; 24cm.
Bibl. — Index.
ISBN 0-471-31891-4 : £8.50
(B77-20140)

Nigro, Felix Anthony. Modern public administration. — 4th ed. / [by] Felix A. Nigro and Lloyd G. Nigro. — New York [etc.] ; London : Harper and Row, 1977. — xv,492p : ill ; 24cm.
Previous ed.: 1973. — Bibl. — Index.
ISBN 0-06-044843-1 : £10.45
ISBN 0-06-350548-7 Pbk : £5.95
(B77-15195)

Riggs, Frederick Warren. The ecology of public administration / [by] F.W. Riggs. — London : Asia Publishing House [for] the Indian Institute of Public Administration, 1975. — viii,144p : 1 ill ; 22cm.
Originally published: 1962. — Index.
ISBN 0-210-33842-3 Pbk : £2.50
Primary classification 350
(B77-11696)

353 — United States. Public administration. Decision making. Political aspects
Lerner, Allan W. The politics of decision-making : strategy, cooperation and conflict / [by] Allan W. Lerner ; introduction by Martin Landau ; foreword by Harmon Zeigler. — Beverly Hills ; London : Sage Publications, 1976. — 215p ; 22cm. — (Sage library of social research ; vol.34)
Bibl.: p.207-213.
ISBN 0-8039-0694-3 : £7.50
ISBN 0-8039-0695-1 Pbk : £4.00
(B77-15194)

353'.0001 — United States. Government. Theories
Founding principles of American government : two hundred years of democracy on trial / edited by George J. Graham, Jr and Scarlett G. Graham. — Bloomington ; London : Indiana University Press, 1977. — xviii,395p ; 24cm.
Bibl.: p.354-365. — Index. — Includes the text of the Constitution of the United States.
ISBN 0-253-32415-7 : £13.10
(B77-23247)

353'.0009'033 — United States. Government, ca 1780
Conkin, Paul Keith. Self-evident truths : being a discourse on the origins & development of the first principles of American government - popular sovereignty, natural rights, and balance & separation of powers / [by] Paul K. Conkin. — Bloomington ; London : Indiana University Press, [1976]. — xii,211p ; 21cm. — (A Midland book ; 198)
Published in the United States : 1974. — Index.
ISBN 0-253-35150-2 : £7.50
ISBN 0-253-20198-5 Pbk : £2.40
(B77-08904)

353.001'3 — Civil service. Personnel. Employment. Equality of opportunity. Implementation. *United States. Reports, surveys*
Rosenbloom, David Harry. Federal equal employment opportunity : politics and public personnel administration / [by] David H. Rosenbloom. — New York ; London : Praeger, 1977. — xv,185p ; 25cm. — (Praeger special studies in US economic, social and political issues)
Bibl.: p.171-179. — Index.
ISBN 0-275-24420-2 : £12.40
(B77-30073)

353.007'22 — United States. Government. Budgeting
Lee, Robert Dorwin. Public budgeting systems / [by] Robert D. Lee, Jr, Ronald W. Johnson. — 2nd ed. — Baltimore ; London [etc.] : University Park Press, 1977. — xxi,369p ; 24cm.
Previous ed.: 1973. — Bibl.: p.357-362. — Index.
ISBN 0-8391-0988-1 : £10.50
(B77-21775)

353.008'1 — United States. Information Agency. Policies, ca 1950
Bogart, Leo. Premises for propaganda : the United States Information Agency's operating assumptions in the Cold War / [by] Leo Bogart ; abridged by Agnes Bogart. — New York : Free Press ; London : Collier Macmillan, 1976. — xxii,250p ; 24cm.
Originally a five volume study, commissioned in June 1953 by USIA. Now declassified, it has been abridged to about two-fifths of its full length. — Bibl.: p.242-243. — Index.
ISBN 0-02-904390-5 : £11.30
(B77-14132)

353.008'52 — United States. Government. Relations with libraries
Molz, Kathleen. Federal policy and library support / [by] Redmond Kathleen Molz. — Cambridge, Mass. ; London : M.I.T. Press, [1977]. — xiii,118p : 1 ill ; 21cm.
Published in the United States: 1976. — Bibl. — Index.
ISBN 0-262-13120-x : £9.40
Also classified at 021.8'0973
(B77-12942)

353.008'55'0924 — United States. Presidents. Scientific advice from scientific advisers, 1959-1969. *Diaries*
Kistiakowsky, George B. A scientist at the White House : the private diary of President Eisenhower's special assistant for science and technology / by George B. Kistiakowsky ; with an introduction by Charles S. Maier. — Cambridge, Mass. ; London : Harvard University Press, 1976 [i.e. 1977]. — lxx,448p : facsims, ports ; 25cm.
Published in the United States: 1976. — Index.
ISBN 0-674-79496-6 : £11.25
(B77-13582)

353.008'65 — Housing. Financial assistance by United States. Department of Housing and Urban Development. Effectiveness. United States. Compared with effectiveness of state housing finance agencies
Betnun, Nathan S. Housing finance agencies : a comparison between states and HUD / [by] Nathan S. Betnun. — New York [etc.] ; London : Praeger, 1976 [i.e. 1977]. — xv,283p : 1 ill ; 25cm. — (Praeger special studies in US economic, social and political issues)
Published in the United States: 1976. — Bibl.: p.261-270. — Index.
ISBN 0-275-56660-9 : £15.30
(B77-14636)

353.008'77'8 — United States. National Aeronautics and Space Administration. Project management
Anna, Henry J. Task groups and linkages in complex organizations : a case study of NASA / [by] Henry J. Anna. — Beverly Hills ; London : Sage Publications, 1976. — 64p : 1 ill ; 22cm. — (Sage professional papers in administrative and policy studies ; vol.3, no.03-029)
Bibl.: p.64.
ISBN 0-8039-0533-5 Pbk : £1.75
(B77-15196)

353.009'96 — United States. Politics. Watergate affair. *Personal observations*
Colson, Charles W. Born again / [by] Charles W. Colson. — London [etc.] : Hodder and Stoughton, 1977. — 350p,[16]p of plates : ill, facsims, ports ; 23cm.
Originally published: Old Tappan : Chosen Books ; London : Hodder and Stoughton, 1976. — Index.
ISBN 0-340-21330-2 : £4.95
(B77-18637)

Dean, John W. Blind ambition : the White House years / by John W. Dean III. — New York : Simon and Schuster ; [London] ([Strand House, Portugal St., WC2A 2HS]) : Distributed by W.H. Smith and Son Ltd, 1976. — 415p,[16]p of plates : ports ; 24cm.
Index.
ISBN 0-671-22438-7 : £4.95
(B77-14133)

Dean, Maureen. 'Mo' : a woman's view of Watergate / by Maureen Dean ; with Hays Gorey. — Toronto [etc.] ; London : Bantam, 1976. — [9],270,[1]p ; 18cm.
Originally published: New York : Simon and Schuster, 1975. — Index.
ISBN 0-553-02797-2 Pbk : £0.75
(B77-04675)

353.03 — United States. Government agencies. Policies. Decision making. *Reports, surveys*
Shull, Steven A. Interrelated concepts in policy research / [by] Steven A. Shull. — Beverly Hills ; London : Sage Publications, 1977. — 76, [1]p : ill ; 22cm. — (Sage professional papers in American politics ; vol.3, no.04-036)
Bibl.: p.69-71.
ISBN 0-8039-0635-8 Pbk : £1.75
(B77-33131)

353.03 — United States. Government. Policies. Formulation. Role of policy analysts
Meltsner, Arnold Jerry. Policy analysts in the bureaucracy / [by] Arnold J. Meltsner. — Berkeley [etc.] ; London : University of California Press, 1976. — x,310p ; 23cm.
Index.
ISBN 0-520-02948-8 : £8.00
(B77-14134)

353.03'13 — United States. Government. Executive branches. Management by objectives. *Study examples: United States. Office of Management and Budget, ca 1970-1976. Reports, surveys*
Rose, Richard, *b.1933.* Managing Presidential objectives / [by] Richard Rose. — London [etc.] : Macmillan, 1977. — xi,180p ; 24cm.
Originally published: New York : Free Press, 1976. — Bibl.: p.170-175. — Index.
ISBN 0-333-21748-9 : £8.95
(B77-11141)

353.03'4 — United States. Presidency. Succession. Role of vice-presidents
Sindler, Allan Paul. Unchosen presidents : the vice-president and other frustrations of presidential succession / [by] Allan P. Sindler. — Berkeley [etc.] ; London : University of California Press, 1976. — x,118p ; 21cm. — (Quantum books)
ISBN 0-520-03185-7 : £4.15
(B77-00679)

353.6 — United States. Joint Chiefs of Staff, to 1975
Korb, Lawrence J. The Joint Chiefs of Staff : the first twenty-five years / [by] Lawrence J. Korb. — Bloomington ; London : Indiana University Press, 1976. — xiii,210p : ill ; 22cm.
Index.
ISBN 0-253-33169-2 : £8.25
(B77-04038)

353.9 — United States. State governments. Policies. Decision making. Political factors
Schneider, Anne L. Opinions and policies in the American states : the role of political characteristics / [by] Anne L. Schneider. — Beverly Hills ; London : Sage Publications, [1977]. — 47,[1]p : ill ; 22cm. — (Sage professional papers in American politics ; vol.3, no.04-032)
Published in the United States: 1976. — Bibl.: p.42-46.
ISBN 0-8039-0631-5 Pbk : £1.75
(B77-11698)

353.9'3'722 — United States. State governments. Programme budgeting
Babunakis, Michael. Budgets : an analytical and procedural handbook for government and nonprofit organizations / [by] Michael Babunakis. — Westport, Conn. ; London : Greenwood Press, 1976. — xii,257,[1]p : forms ; 25cm.
Bibl.: p.252-255. — Index.
ISBN 0-8371-8900-4 : £11.75
Primary classification 352'.12'0973
(B77-18020)

353.9'744 — Massachusetts. Government. Management
Weinberg, Martha Wagner. Managing the state / [by] Martha Wagner Weinberg. — Cambridge, Mass ; London : M.I.T. Press, 1977. — xi, 244p ; 21cm.
Bibl.: p.233-236. — Index.
ISBN 0-262-23077-1 : £10.25
(B77-31786)

354 — CENTRAL ADMINISTRATIVE STRUCTURE (OTHER THAN UNITED STATES)
354'.31 — Ancient China. Government
Creel, Herrlee Glessner. What is Taoism? and other stories in Chinese cultural history / [by] Herrlee G. Creel. — Chicago ; London : University of Chicago Press, 1977. — viii,192p ; 23cm.
Originally published: 1970. — Index.
ISBN 0-226-12042-2 Pbk : £2.75
Primary classification 299'.514
(B77-31692)

354'.37 — Ancient Rome. Government, 235-337
MacMullen, Ramsay. Roman government's response to crisis, AD 235-337 / [by] Ramsay MacMullen. — New Haven ; London : Yale University Press, 1976. — ix,308p,ii p of plates : ports ; 22cm.
Index.
ISBN 0-300-02008-2 : £11.55
(B77-09616)

354'.37'03 — Ancient Rome. Administration. Officials. Lists: Notitia dignitatum. *Conference proceedings*
Aspects of the 'Notitia dignitatum' : papers presented to the conference in Oxford, December 13 to 15, 1974 / by J.C. Mann ... [et al.] ; edited by R. Goodburn and P. Bartholomew. — Oxford : British Archaeological Reports, 1976. — xix,224p(2 fold) : ill(incl 3 col), facsims, maps ; 30cm. — (British archaeological reports : supplementary series ; 15)
Spine title: Notitia dignitatum.
ISBN 0-904531-58-9 Pbk : £4.20
(B77-23248)

354'.37'0312 — Ancient Rome. Emperorship, B.C.31-A.D.337
Millar, Fergus. The emperor in the Roman world (31BC-AD337) / [by] Fergus Millar. — London : Duckworth, 1977. — xvi,657p(1 fold) ; 25cm.
Bibl.: p.xv-xvi. — Index.
ISBN 0-7156-0951-3 : £15.00
(B77-11142)

354'.4 — European countries. Governments, 1000-1300. *Festschriften*
Church and government in the Middle Ages : essays presented to C.R. Cheney on his 70th birthday and edited by C.N.L. Brooke ... [et al.]. — Cambridge [etc.] : Cambridge University Press, 1976. — xv,312p,[2] leaves of plates : facsim, port ; 24cm.
Bibl.: p.275-284. — Index.
ISBN 0-521-21172-7 : £15.00
Primary classification 274
(B77-07798)

354'.4'0009 — European countries. Government, 1520-1560. *Readings*
Government in Reformation Europe, 1520-1560 / edited by Henry J. Cohn. — New York [etc.] ; London : Harper and Row, 1972[i.e.1976]. — 320p ; 21cm. — (Stratum series)
Published in the United States: 1972. — Originally published: London : Macmillan, 1971. — Bibl.: p.310-314. — Index.
ISBN 0-06-138418-6 Pbk : £3.35
(B77-00114)

354'.41 — Great Britain. Government. Organisation structure
Great Britain. *Central Office of Information. Reference Division.* The central government of Britain / [prepared by Reference Division, Central Office of Information]. — 9th ed. — London : H.M.S.O., 1977. — [3],37p ; 24cm. — (Central Office of Information reference pamphlet ; 40)
Previous ed.: 1974. — Bibl.: p.36-37.
ISBN 0-11-700805-2 Sd : £0.75
(B77-15763)

354'.41 — Great Britain. Government. Policies. Decision making. *Case studies*
Bruce-Gardyne, Jock. The power game : an examination of decision-making in government / [by] Jock Bruce-Gardyne and Nigel Lawson. — London [etc.] : Macmillan, 1976. — [7],204p ; 23cm.
Bibl.: p.190-192. — Index.
ISBN 0-333-14123-7 : £7.95
(B77-04676)

354'.41 — Great Britain. Government. Reform. *Liberal Party viewpoints*
Wallace, William, *b.1941.* Reform of government / [by] William Wallace. — London : Liberal Publication Department, [1977]. — [4],16p ; 21cm. — (Towards a new political agenda ; 4 ISSN 0140-377x)
'... one of a series of papers commissioned by the Standing Committee of the Liberal Party'.
Sd : £0.50
(B77-32531)

354'.41 — Great Britain. Public administration
Smith, Brian Clive. Administering Britain / [by] Brian C. Smith and Jeffrey Stanyer. — [London] : Fontana, 1976. — 288p : ill ; 20cm. — (Studies in public administration).
Also published: London : Robertson, 1976. — Bibl.: p.271-277. — Index.
ISBN 0-00-634157-8 Pbk : £1.95
(B77-00680)

354'.41'0009 — Great Britain. Government, 1800-1900
Cromwell, Valerie. Revolution or evolution : British government in the nineteenth century / [by] Valerie Cromwell. — London : Longman, 1977. — x,230p ; 22cm. — (Problems and perspectives in history)
Bibl.: p.217-219. — Index.
ISBN 0-582-31353-8 Pbk : £2.50
(B77-32532)

354'.41'0009 — Great Britain. Government, 1945-1976. *Documents*
Documents on contemporary British government / edited by Martin Minogue. — Cambridge [etc.] : Cambridge University Press. In 2 vols.
1 : British government and constitutional change. — 1977. — xii,413p : ill ; 24cm.
Bibl.: p.405-413.
ISBN 0-521-21437-8 : £11.00
ISBN 0-521-29148-8 Pbk :£3.95
(B77-20141)

2 : Local government in Britain. — 1977. — xii,470p : ill, maps ; 24cm.
Bibl.: p.465-470.
ISBN 0-521-21429-7 : £11.00
ISSN 0-521-29147-x Pbk : £3.95
(B77-20142)

354'.41'0009 — Great Britain. Government, 1974-1976. *Personal observations*
Haines, Joe. The politics of power / [by] Joe Haines. — London : Cape, 1977. — xi,228p,[8] p of plates : ill, ports ; 23cm.
Index.
ISBN 0-224-01405-6 : £4.95 : CIP rev.
(B77-04677)

Haines, Joe. The politics of power / [by] Joe Haines. — Coronet ed. (revised). — Sevenoaks : Coronet, 1977. — xi,244p ; 18cm.
Previous ed.: London : Cape, 1977. — Index.
ISBN 0-340-22275-1 Pbk : £0.85
(B77-27757)

354'.41'001 — Civil service. *Great Britain. Inquiry reports*
Great Britain. *Parliament. House of Commons. Expenditure Committee.* The Civil Service : eleventh report from the Expenditure Committee, session 1976-77, together with the minutes of evidence taken before the General Sub-committee in sessions 1975-76 and 1976-77 and appendices. — London : H.M.S.O.
Vol.1 : Report. — [1977]. — xcv p ; 25cm. — ([1976-77 H.C.] 535-I)
ISBN 0-10-297477-2 Sd : £1.60
(B77-29296)

Vol.2 : Minutes of evidence : evidence taken from 3 May to 18 October 1976. — [1977]. — 2v.(xiv,839p) ; 25cm. — ([1976-77 H.C.] 535-II)
ISBN 0-10-296177-8 Pbk : £16.50
(B77-29297)

Vol.3 : Appendices. — [1977]. — vi p,p841-1179 : 1 ill, form ; 25cm. — ([1976-77 H.C.] 535-III)
ISBN 0-10-297177-3 Pbk : £4.60
(B77-29298)

354'.41'001 — Civil service. *Great Britain. Statistics*
Civil service statistics / Civil Service Department. — London : H.M.S.O.
1976. — 1977. — 45p : 2 ill ; 30cm.
ISBN 0-11-630276-3 Sd : £2.75
(B77-07860)

354'.41'0013 — Civil service. Administrative grades. Personnel. Recruitment & selection. *Great Britain. Reports, surveys. Serials*
Appointments in administration : memorandum describing the recruitment of Administration Trainees in the Home Civil Service, HM Inspectors of Taxes, Grades 8 and 7 of the Diplomatic Service, Administration Trainees in the Northern Ireland Civil Service, House of Lords Clerks, House of Commons Clerks / Civil Service Commission. — [Basingstoke] ([Alencon Link, Basingstoke, Hants. RG21 1JB]) : [The Commission].
1977. — 1976. — [1],34p ; 30cm.
ISBN 0-903741-28-8 Sd : Unpriced
(B77-00681)

354'.41'00131 — Civil service. Personnel. Recruitment. *Great Britain. Reports, surveys. Serials*
Great Britain. *Civil Service Commission.* Annual report / Civil Service Commission. — Basingstoke ([Alencon Link, Basingstoke, Hants. RG21 1JB]) : The Commission.
1976 : Hundred and tenth report. — 1977. — 41p ; 30cm.
Sd : Unpriced
(B77-19272)

354'.41'002 — Civil service. *Great Britain. Directories*
Civil Service year book / Civil Service Department. — London : H.M.S.O.
1977. — 1977. — xiii p,928 columns,p929-973,[10]leaves ; 25cm.
Index.
ISBN 0-11-630242-9 Pbk : £4.00
ISSN 0302-329x
(B77-12380)

354'.41'005 — Civil service. Superannuation schemes. *Great Britain. Principal Civil Service Pension Scheme. Allocation*
Great Britain. *Civil Service Department.* Civil Service pension scheme, allocation of pension : explanatory memorandum, rules, and tables prepared by the Government Actuary / Civil Service Department. — London : H.M.S.O., 1975. — [3],35p ; 21cm.
Originally published: 1974.
Sd : £0.30
ISBN 0-11-630404-9
(B77-31787)

354'.41'005 — Civil service. Superannuation schemes. *Great Britain. Principal Civil Service Pension Scheme. For personnel*
Great Britain. *Civil Service Department.* Civil Service pensions explained : a guide to the benefits of the Principal Civil Service Pension Scheme and to the arrangements for increasing pensions under the Pensions (Increase) Act 1971 / Civil Service Department. — London : H.M.S.O., 1976. — [5],53p ; 21cm.
At head of title: Civil Service Pension Scheme.
ISBN 0-11-630412-x Sd : £0.85
(B77-06559)

354'.41'00762 — Association football. Betting. Pools. Levies by government. *Great Britain. Feasibility studies*
Great Britain. *Royal Commission on Gambling.* Interim report ... / Royal Commission on Gambling ; chairman the Lord Rothschild. — London : H.M.S.O., [1976]. — 16p ; 25cm. — (Cmnd.6643)
ISBN 0-10-166430-3 Sd : £0.38
(B77-08297)

354'.41'00824 — Patents. Registration. *Great Britain. Manuals*
Patent Office. Applying for a patent / Patent Office. — Revised [ed.]. — London ([25 Southampton Buildings, WC2A 1AY]) : Patent Office, 1976. — 22p ; 21cm.
Previous ed.: 1971. — Index.
ISBN 0-903673-05-3 Sd : Unpriced
(B77-01270)

354'.41'00824 — Patents. Registration. *Great Britain. Reports, surveys. Serials*
Patents, designs and trade marks : report of the Comptroller-General of Patents, Designs and Trade Marks ... — London : H.M.S.O.
1976 : 94th. — [1977]. — iv,39p : ill ; 25cm. — ([1976-77 H.C.]318)
ISBN 0-10-231877-8 Sd : £1.00
(B77-15197)

354'.41'008242 — Iron & steel products industries & textile industries. Levies by government. *Great Britain. Accounts*
Industrial Organisation and Development Act 1947, accounts prepared pursuant to section 9 (4) of the Industrial Organisation and Development Act 1947, of the sums recovered by the Secretary of State for Industry under orders made under section 9 of the Act, and of their disposal, for the year ended 31st March ... — London : H.M.S.O.
1975-76. — [1977]. — 6p ; 25cm. — ([1976-77 H.C.]210)
ISBN 0-10-221077-2 Sd : £0.25
(B77-18021)

354'.41'008243 — Betting industries. Licences & permits. *Great Britain. Statistics*
Betting licensing statistics : for the period ended 31st May ... / [Home Office]. — London : H.M.S.O.
[1975]-1976. — [1976]. — 51p ; 25cm. — ([1975-76 H.C.] 50)
ISBN 0-10-205077-5 Sd : £1.25
(B77-07227)

354'.41'00826 — Great Britain. Office of Fair Trading. *Reports, surveys. Serials*
Great Britain. *Office of Fair Trading.* Annual report of the Director General of Fair Trading to the Secretary of State for Prices and Consumer Protection ... — London : H.M.S.O.
1976 : for the period January 1976 to December 1976. — [1977]. — 100p ; 25cm. — ([1976-77 H.C.] 195)
Bibl.: p.97-99.
ISBN 0-10-219577-3 Pbk : £1.65
(B77-10283)

354'.41'0083 — Great Britain. Certification Office for Trade Unions and Employers' Associations. *Reports, surveys. Serials*
Great Britain. *Certification Office for Trade Unions and Employers' Associations.* Annual report of the Certification Officer. — London : H.M.S.O.
1st : 1976. — 1977. — vi,52p ; 25cm.
ISBN 0-11-885099-7 Sd : £1.15
ISSN 0309-8842
(B77-18638)

354'.41'0084 — Great Britain. Department of Health and Social Security. *Reports, surveys. Serials*
Great Britain. *Department of Health and Social Security.* Annual report ... / Department of Health and Social Security. — London : H.M.S.O.
1976. — [1977]. — vii,70p : ill ; 25cm. — (Cmnd.6931)
Index.
ISBN 0-10-169310-9 Sd : £1.40
(B77-28509)

354'.41'0085 — Buildings of historical importance. Finance. National Land Fund. *Great Britain. Accounts*
National Land Fund account ... for the year ended 31st March, together with the report of the Comptroller and Auditor General thereon ... — London : H.M.S.O.
1975-76. — [1977]. — 7p ; 25cm. — ([1976-77 H.C.]157)
ISBN 0-10-215777-4 Sd : £0.25
(B77-08905)

National Land Fund account ... for the year ended 31st March, together with the report of the Comptroller and Auditor General thereon. — London : H.M.S.O.
1974-75. — [1976]. — 7p ; 25cm. — ([1975-76 H.C.] 170)
ISBN 0-10-217076-2 Sd : £0.20
(B77-02872)

354'.41'00877742 — Great Britain. Air Travel Reserve Fund Agency. *Reports, surveys. Serials*
Great Britain. *Air Travel Reserve Fund Agency.* Report and accounts / Air Travel Reserve Fund Agency. — London : H.M.S.O.
1975-76. — 1977. — [5],14p ; 25cm.
ISBN 0-11-887500-0 Sd : £0.60
ISSN 0309-5215
(B77-11143)

354'.41'008783 — Motor vehicles. Registration. Index marks. *Great Britain. Lists*
Glass's index of suffix marks. — Weybridge (Elgin House, St George's Ave., Weybridge, Surrey KT13 0BX) : Glass's Guide Service Ltd.
1968-1977. — 1977. — 339p ; 15cm.
Pbk : £1.75
(B77-28510)

354'.41'00878344 — Commercial vehicles. Operators' licences. *Great Britain*
Great Britain. *Department of the Environment.* A guide to operators' licensing / Department of the Environment. — 3rd ed. — [London] ([2 Marsham St., SW1P 2EB]) : [The Department], 1975. — v,31p : ill ; 21cm. — (G74)
Previous ed.: 1973.
ISBN 0-7184-0069-0 Sd : Unpriced
(B77-02142)

354'.41'0088 — Trust funds. Administration. Organisations. *Great Britain. Public Trustee. Reports, surveys. Serials*
Public Trustee. Annual report of the Public Trustee. — London : H.M.S.O.
69th : 1976-1977. — [1977]. — 6p ; 25cm.
ISBN 0-11-700876-1 Sd : £0.25
ISSN 0307-6830
(B77-30075)

354'.41'0091 — Great Britain. Parliamentary Commissioner for Administration. Great Britain. Parliament. House of Commons. Select Committee on the Parliamentary Commissioner for Administration. Reports. *Critical studies*
Great Britain. *Lord Privy Seal.* Second report from the Select Committee on the Parliamentary Commissioner for Administration, session 1975-76, observations by the Government / presented to Parliament by the Lord Privy Seal ... — London : H.M.S.O., [1977]. — 6p ; 25cm. — (Cmnd. 6764)
ISBN 0-10-167640-9 Sd : £0.25
(B77-11699)

354'.41'0091 — Great Britain. Public administration. Complaints by public. *Reports, surveys. Serials*
Great Britain. *Parliamentary Commissioner for Administration.* Annual report of the Parliamentary Commissioner for Administration ... — London : H.M.S.O.
1976 : second report, session 1976-77. — [1977] . — [1],48p ; 25cm. — ([1976-77 H.C.]116)
ISBN 0-10-211677-6 Sd : £0.75
(B77-12381)

354'.41'0091 — Great Britain. Public administration. Complaints by public. Procedure
Williams, David W. Maladministration : remedies for injustice : a guide to the powers and practice of the British Ombudsmen and similar bodies / by David W. Williams. — London : Oyez Publishing, 1976. — viii,232p ; 22cm.
Index.
ISBN 0-85120-288-8 Pbk : £7.20
(B77-10284)

354'.41'0312 — Great Britain. Monarchy
Great Britain. *Central Office of Information. Reference Division.* The monarchy in Britain / [prepared by Reference Division, Central Office of Information]. — 3rd ed. — London : H.M.S.O., 1977. — [3],39p,[4]p of plates : geneal table, ports ; 24cm. — (Central Office of Information reference pamphlet ; 118)
Previous ed.: 1975. — Bibl.: p.39.
ISBN 0-11-700915-6 Sd : £0.90
(B77-10285)

Howard, Philip, *b.1933.* The British monarchy in the twentieth century / [by] Philip Howard. — London : Hamilton, 1977. — 208p,xvi p of plates : ill(some col), facsim, geneal table, ports(some col) ; 26cm.
Bibl.: p.204. — Index.
ISBN 0-241-89564-2 : £7.50
(B77-14135)

354'.41'031309 — Great Britain. Government. Role of Great Britain. Prime Minister, to 1976
Wilson, *Sir* **Harold,** *b.1916.* The governance of Britain / [by] Harold Wilson. — London : Sphere, 1977. — 267p ; 18cm.
Originally published: London : Weidenfeld and Nicolson : Joseph, 1976. — Index.
ISBN 0-7221-9212-6 Pbk : £1.50
(B77-29299)

354'.41'038 — Citizens. Effects of public administration. *Great Britain*
Hill, Michael James, *b.1937.* The state, administration and the individual / [by] Michael Hill. — [London] : Fontana, 1976. — 256p ; 20cm. — (Studies in public administration)
Bibl.: p.235-249. — Index.
ISBN 0-00-633821-6 Pbk : £1.95
(B77-07228)

Hill, Michael James, *b.1937.* The state, administration and the individual / [by] Michael Hill. — London : Martin Robertson, 1976. — 256p ; 21cm. — (Studies in public administration)
Bibl.: p.241-249. — Index.
ISBN 0-85520-141-x : £6.95
(B77-05307)

354'.41'05 — Great Britain. Cabinet. Documents. Security. Rules. *Inquiry reports*
Great Britain. *Privy Council.* Report of the Committee of Privy Counsellors on Cabinet document security / presented to Parliament by the Prime Minister ... — London : H.M.S.O., [1976]. — v,10p ; 25cm. — (Cmnd.6677)
Chairman: Lord Houghton of Sowerby.
ISBN 0-10-166770-1 Sd : £0.35
(B77-08298)

354'.41'0509 — Great Britain. Cabinet, to 1976
Mackintosh, John Pitcairn. The British Cabinet / by John P. Mackintosh. — 3rd ed. — London : Stevens, 1977. — xv,656p ; 23cm.
Previous ed.: 1968. — Index.
ISBN 0-420-44670-2 : £5.75
ISBN 0-420-44680-x Pbk : £3.50
(B77-08906)

354'.41'061 — Foreign secretaries. *Great Britain, 1945-1974*
Shlaim, Avi. British foreign secretaries since 1945 / [by] Avi Shlaim, Peter Jones, Keith Sainsbury. — Newton Abbot [etc.] : David and Charles, 1977. — 267p ; 23cm.
Index.
ISBN 0-7153-7381-1 : £6.50
(B77-24803)

354'.41'061 — Great Britain. Colonial Office. Officials, 1794-1870. *Lists*
Sainty, John Christopher. Colonial Office officials : officials of the Secretary of State for War, 1794-1801, of the Secretary of State for War and Colonies, 1801-54, and of the Secretary of State for Colonies, 1854-70 / compiled by J.C. Sainty. — London (Senate House, Malet St., WC1E 7HU) : University of London, Institute of Historical Research, 1976. — x,52p ; 24cm. — (Office-holders in modern Britain ; 6)
Bibl.: p.viii. — Index.
ISBN 0-901179-35-3 : £4.00
(B77-07861)

354'.41'068 — Great Britain. Department of the Environment. Formation, 1970
Draper, Paul. Creation of the DOE / [by] Paul Draper. — London : H.M.S.O., 1977. — [3], 239p(9 fold) : ill ; 25cm. — (Civil Service studies ; no.4)
ISBN 0-11-630234-8 Pbk : £5.00
(B77-25495)

354'.41'082 — Elected assemblies. Devolution of powers of British government. *Scotland & Wales*
Dalyell, Tam. Devolution : the end of Britain? / [by] Tam Dalyell. — London : Cape, 1977. — xiii,321p ; 23cm.
Index.
ISBN 0-224-01559-1 : £4.95 : CIP rev.
ISBN 0-224-01560-5 Pbk : £2.95
(B77-24094)

354'.41'082 — Elected assemblies. Devolution of powers of British government. Proposals: Great Britain. Royal Commission on the Constitution. Royal Commission on the Constitution, 1969-1973. *Scotland & Wales. Critical studies*
Great Britain. *Lord President of the Council.* Devolution within the United Kingdom : some alternatives for discussion / Office of the Lord President of the Council. — London : H.M.S.O., 1976. — 22p ; 25cm.
Originally published: 1974.
Sd : £0.45
ISBN 0-11-700367-0
(B77-10286)

354'.41'082 — Elected assemblies. Devolution of powers of British government. Scotland & Wales. Related to membership of European Economic Community. *Conservative and Unionist Party viewpoints*
Thomas, Rosamund M. Devolution in the United Kingdom and its relevance to the EEC : a European Policy Group paper / by Rosamund M. Thomas. — London (51 Victoria St., S.W.1) : The Monday Club, 1976. — 6p ; 30cm.
ISBN 0-903900-04-1 Sd : Private circulation
Primary classification 338.91'4'041
(B77-09578)

354'.41'082 — Elected assemblies. Devolution of powers of British government. Scotland & Wales. Related to membership of European Economic Community. *Young European Left viewpoints*
Young European Left. 'Devolution, the Left and Europe' / Young European Left. — [London] ([1a Whitehall Place, SW1A 2HA]) : FYEL], [1977]. — [2],31p ; 22cm.
'... based on a seminar held at Gorebridge in Scotland in 1976 and on discussions within YEL since then' - Introduction.
Sd : £0.25
Primary classification 338.91'4'041
(B77-18625)

354'.416'0084 — Northern Ireland. Department of Health and Social Services. Central Services Agency. *Reports, surveys. Serials*
Northern Ireland. *Department of Health and Social Services. Central Services Agency.* Annual report / Northern Ireland Health and Social Services, Central Services Agency. — Belfast (27 Adelaide St., Belfast BT2 8FH) : The Agency.
1976. — 1977. — [2],i,95p : ill, map ; 30cm.
Index.
Pbk : Unpriced
ISSN 0306-9729
(B77-25496)

354'.417 — Public sector. *Ireland (Republic). Sinn-Fein-The Workers' Party viewpoints*
Sinn Fein. *Department of Economic Affairs. Research Section.* The public sector & the profit makers : the case for state workers : Research Section, Department of Economic Affairs, Sinn Fein - The Workers' Party. — Dublin (30 Gardiner Place, Dublin 1) : Repsol Publications, 1976. — [4],20p ; 19cm. — (Studies in political economy ; no.2)
Originally published: 1975.
ISBN 0-86064-004-3 Sd : £0.25
(B77-21776)

354'.42'00761 — Licensed premises. Licences. *England. Statistics*
Liquor licensing statistics, England and Wales / Home Office. — London : H.M.S.O.
1975. — [1977]. — 43p ; 25cm.
Sd : £3.00
(B77-26940)

354'.42'0081 — Registration offices. *England. Lists. Serials*
Great Britain. *Office of Population Censuses and Surveys.* The official list ... / Office of Population Censuses and Surveys, General Register Office. — [London] : [H.M.S.O.].
1977. Part 1 : List of registration officers, etc., corrected to 1st April 1977. — [1977]. — [1],v, 252p ; 30cm.
Index.
Sd : £4.00
(B77-21777)

354'.42'0312 — Lord Protectors' households. *England, 1653-1658*
Sherwood, Roy Edward. The court of Oliver Cromwell / [by] Roy Sherwood. — London : Croom Helm [etc.], 1977. — 3-194p ; 23cm.
Bibl.: p.174-180. — Index.
ISBN 0-85664-549-4 : £6.95 : CIP rev.
(B77-24804)

354'.42'0312 — Royal households. Expenditure. *England, 1285-1286. Accounts*
Records of the Wardrobe and Household, 1285-1286 / edited by Benjamin F. Byerly and Catherine Ridder Byerly. — London : H.M.S.O., 1977. — xlvi,309p ; 26cm.
Latin text, English introduction. — Records deposited in the Public Record Office. — Index. — 'This volume consists of a transcript of the book of the Controller of the Wardrobe for the year 14 Edward I (1285-6) together with all the surviving Household rolls which relate solely to that year' - Preface.
ISBN 0-11-440078-4 : £35.00
(B77-16276)

354'.42'062 — England. Exchequer, 1218-1219. *Accounts. Latin texts*
England. *Exchequer.* The Great Roll of the Pipe for the third year of the reign of King Henry III, Michaelmas 1219 : (Pipe Roll 63) ; now first printed from the original in the Public Record Office / with an introduction by B.E. Harris. — London ([c/o Hon. Secretary, Department of History, University of Reading, Reading RG6 2AA]) : Pipe Roll Society, 1976. — xxvi,314p : coat of arms ; 26cm. — (Pipe Roll Society. Publications : new series ; vol.42)
Latin text, English introduction and notes. — Index.
Unpriced
(B77-28511)

354'.429'0009 — Wales. Government, 1558-1603
Jones, Gareth. The gentry and the Elizabethan state / [by] Gareth Jones. — Swansea : C. Davies, 1977. — 114p,[8]p of plates : ill, facsim, ports ; 22cm. — (A new history of Wales)
Bibl.: p.108-110. — Index.
ISBN 0-7154-0303-6 : £2.95
(B77-18639)

354'.44'0009 — France. Government, 1661-1683. *Readings from contemporary sources*
Government and society in Louis XIV's France / edited by Roger Mettam. — London [etc.] : Macmillan, 1977. — xviii,270p ; 23cm. — (History in depth)
Bibl.: p.xvii. — Index.
ISBN 0-333-06802-5 : £10.00
ISBN 0-333-21430-7 Pbk : £4.95
(B77-22460)

354'.44'770009 — France. Gascony. Government, 1027-1318. English state papers. *Latin texts*
Gascon Register A (series of 1318-1319) / edited from British Museum Cottonian MS. Julius E.i by G.P. Cuttino with the collaboration of J.-P. Trabut-Cussac. — Oxford [etc.] : Oxford University Press for the British Academy.
In 3 vols.
Vol.3 : Index of persons and places. — 1976. — vi p,p719-882 ; 26cm.
ISBN 0-19-725966-9 : £7.00
(B77-06561)

354'.51'0109 — China. Government. Bureaucracy, 618-907
Twitchett, Denis. The birth of the Chinese meritocracy : bureaucrats and examinations in T'ang China / [by] Denis Twitchett. — London (31B Torrington Sq., W.C.1) : China Society, 1976. — 33,[1]p ; 21cm. — (China Society. Occasional papers ; no.18)
'The substance of a lecture delivered to the China Society in London on 17th December, 1974'.
Sd : Unpriced
(B77-21024)

354'.51'25 — Hong Kong. Government
Miners, Norman John. The government and politics of Hong Kong / [by] Norman Miners. — 2nd ed. — Hong Kong ; London [etc.] : Oxford University Press, 1977. — xvi,333p : maps(on inside covers) ; 25cm. — (East Asian social science monographs)
Previous ed.: 1976. — Bibl.: p.314-320. — Index.
ISBN 0-19-580371-x Pbk : £9.00
(B77-24805)

354'.5694'0081 — Israel. Government. Public relations, 1975-1976
Goldsmith, S J. The public relations chaos / [by] S.J. Goldsmith. — London (London N.W.3) : Culmus Publishing, 1976. — [11]p ; 27cm.
Originally published: in 'The American Zionist', June 1975, Sept. 1975 and Feb. 1976.
Sd : £0.25
(B77-26941)

354'.593 — Thailand. Public administration
Riggs, Frederick Warren. The ecology of public administration / [by] F.W. Riggs. — London : Asia Publishing House [for] the Indian Institute of Public Administration, 1975. — viii,144p : 1 ill ; 22cm.
Originally published: 1962. — Index.
ISBN 0-210-33842-3 Pbk : £2.50
Primary classification 350
(B77-11696)

354'.599 — Philippines. Public administration
Riggs, Frederick Warren. The ecology of public administration / [by] F.W. Riggs. — London : Asia Publishing House [for] the Indian Institute of Public Administration, 1975. — viii,144p : 1 ill ; 22cm.
Originally published: 1962. — Index.
ISBN 0-210-33842-3 Pbk : £2.50
Primary classification 350
(B77-11696)

354'.669'5 — Nigeria. Zaria. Government, 1800-1950
Smith, Michael Garfield. Government in Zazzau, 1800-1950 / [by] M.G. Smith. — London [etc.] : Oxford University Press for the International African Institute, 1970 [i.e. 1976]. — xii,372p,[3]fold leaves of plates : ill, geneal table, maps ; 22cm.
Four sheets([4]fold leaves : of geneal. tables) in pocket. — Originally published: 1960. — Bibl.: p.356-357. — Index.
ISBN 0-19-724201-4 Pbk : £4.50
(B77-15198)

354'.72'0009 — Mexico. Public administration, 1970-1975. *Case studies*
Grindle, Merilee Serrill. Bureaucrats, politicians and peasants in Mexico : a case study in public policy / [by] Merilee Serrill Grindle. — Berkeley [etc.] ; London : University of California Press, 1977. — xix,220p : ill ; 24cm.
Bibl.: p.195-212. — Index.
ISBN 0-520-03238-1 : £11.20
(B77-26942)

354'.931'0091 — New Zealand. Parliamentary Commissioner, to 1975
Hill, Larry B. The model ombudsman : institutionalizing New Zealand's democratic experiment / [by] Larry B. Hill. — Princeton ; Guildford : Princeton University Press, 1976. — xviii,411,[1]p ; 23cm.
Bibl.: p.387-403. — Index.
ISBN 0-691-07579-4 : £15.60
(B77-11701)

355 — MILITARY FORCES

355 — Military forces. *Reports, surveys*
Armed forces of the world : a reference handbook. — 4th ed. / edited by Robert C. Sellers. — New York ; London : Praeger, 1977. — vi,278,[1]p ; 25cm. — (Praeger special studies in international politics and government)
Previous ed.: 1971.
ISBN 0-275-23200-x : £13.40
(B77-26943)

355 — Military forces. Management
Downey, J C T. Management in the armed forces : an anatomy of the military profession / [by] J.C.T. Downey, with contributions by ... [others]. — London [etc.] : McGraw-Hill, 1977. — xiv,221p : ill ; 24cm.
Index.
ISBN 0-07-084485-2 : £5.50
(B77-23249)

355'.005 — Military forces. *Serials*
RUSI and Brassey's defence yearbook. — London : Brassey's Naval and Shipping Annual Ltd : Distributed by Seeley.
1976-77 : 87th year of publication / edited by the Royal United Services Institute for Defence Studies, London. — 1976. — vi,377p : ill ; 25cm.
Bibl.: p.351-358.
ISBN 0-904609-09-x : £12.00
ISSN 0305-6155
(B77-04039)

355'.005 — Military history. *Serials*
War and society : a yearbook of military history. — London : Croom Helm.
[1976] : Vol.2 / edited by Brian Bond and Ian Roy. — 1977. — [1],196p ; 23cm.
ISBN 0-85664-404-8 : £8.50
(B77-10775)

355'.007'1174731 — United States. Military Academy, West Point, to 1973
Ellis, Joseph. School for soldiers : West Point and the profession of arms / [by] Joseph Ellis and Robert Moore. — London [etc.] : Oxford University Press, 1976. — xi,291p ; 21cm. — (A galaxy book)
Originally published: New York : Oxford University Press, 1974. — Index.
ISBN 0-19-502022-7 Pbk : £2.50
(B77-01271)

355'.009 — Soldiers, to 1975. *Juvenile literature*
West, John. Soldiers / written by John West ; illustrated by Frank Humphris. — Loughborough : Ladybird Books, 1976. — 52p : col ill ; 18cm. — (Ladybird leaders ; no.16)
Text on lining paper. — Index.
ISBN 0-7214-0388-3 : £0.24
(B77-01272)

355'.009171'3 — North Atlantic Treaty Organisation military forces. Central Europe. Compared with Warsaw Pact military forces
Fischer, Robert Lucas. Defending the central front : the balance of forces / by Robert Lucas Fischer. — London : International Institute for Strategic Studies, 1976. — [3],45p : ill ; 25cm. — (Adelphi papers ; no.127 ISSN 0567-932x)
ISBN 0-900492-99-6 Sd : £0.50
Also classified at 355'.009171'7
(B77-11702)

355'.009171'7 — Warsaw Pact military forces. Central Europe. Compared with North Atlantic Treaty Organisation military forces
Fischer, Robert Lucas. Defending the central front : the balance of forces / by Robert Lucas Fischer. — London : International Institute for Strategic Studies, 1976. — [3],45p : ill ; 25cm. — (Adelphi papers ; no.127 ISSN 0567-932x)
ISBN 0-900492-99-6 Sd : £0.50
Primary classification 355'.009171'3
(B77-11702)

355'.00937 — Ancient Rome. Army, B.C.510-B.C.50. *Essays*
Gabba, Emilio. Republican Rome, the army and the allies / [by] Emilio Gabba ; translated [from the Italian] by P.J. Cuff. — Oxford : Blackwell, 1976. — xi,272p ; 24cm.
'Gabba's articles have recently been collected in "Esercito e Società nella tarda repubblica romana" (Florence [: Nuova Italia editrice,] 1973) and I [the translator] have selected the most important of them for translation ... The text ... used is that in "Esercito e Società", which has incorporated some useful amendments and additions to the original articles' - Preface. — Index.
ISBN 0-631-17150-9 : £12.00
Also classified at 937'.02
(B77-07862)

355'.00938 — Military forces. *Ancient Greece. Juvenile literature*
Connolly, Peter. The Greek armies / written and illustrated by Peter Connolly. — London : Macdonald Educational, 1977. — 4-77p : col ill, col maps, plans(chiefly col) ; 29cm.
Index.
ISBN 0-356-05580-9 : £2.95
(B77-11703)

355'.0094 — European armies, 1812
Pivka, Otto von. Armies of 1812 / [by] Otto von Pivka. — Cambridge : Stephens.
In 2 vols.
Vol.1 : The French Army including foreign regiments in French service and the Confederation of the Rhine. — 1977. — 160p : ill(some col), coats of arms, maps ; 25cm.
ISBN 0-85059-274-7 : £7.95 : CIP rev.
(B77-18640)

355'.0094 — European armies, 1815
North, René. Regiments at Waterloo / [by] René North. — Revised 2nd ed. — London : Almark Publishing.
Previous ed.: in 1 vol. 1971.
Vol.1 : French army uniforms. — 1977. — 48p : ill(some col), plans ; 20x21cm.
ISBN 0-85524-287-6 Pbk : £1.95
(B77-29300)

355'.00941 — Great Britain. Army, 1700-1800
Rogers, Hugh Cuthbert Basset. The British Army of the eighteenth century / [by] H.C.B. Rogers. — London : Allen and Unwin, 1977. — 3-252p,[4]p of plates : ill, maps, plans, port ; 23cm.
Index.
ISBN 0-04-355011-8 : £6.50
(B77-15199)

355'.00941 — Great Britain. Army, 1808-1814
Glover, Michael, *b.1922.* Wellington's army in the Peninsula, 1808-1814 / [by] Michael Glover. — Newton Abbot [etc.] : David and Charles, 1977. — 192p : ill, maps, plan, ports ; 26cm. — (Historic armies and navies)
Bibl.: p.184-188. — Index.
ISBN 0-7153-7369-2 : £5.50
(B77-18641)

355'.00941 — Great Britain. Army, 1850-1914. *Illustrations*
The **British** Army from old photographs : from the National Army Museum / [compiled by] Boris Mollo ; foreword by Sir Gerald Templer. — London : Dent, 1975 [i.e. 1976]. — [204]p : of ill, ports ; 24cm. — (An Aldine paperback)
Originally published: 1975.
ISBN 0-460-02186-9 Pbk : £1.95
(B77-01273)

355'.00941 — Great Britain. Army. Social aspects, 1859-1899
Skelley, Alan Ramsay. The Victorian army at home : the recruitment and terms and conditions of the British Regular, 1859-1899 / [by] Alan Ramsay Skelley. — London : Croom Helm [etc.], 1977. — 3-366p : 1 ill ; 23cm.
Bibl.: p.335-361. — Index.
ISBN 0-85664-335-1 : £9.95 : CIP rev.
(B77-13583)

355'.00941 — Museums. *London. Kensington and Chelsea (London Borough). National Army Museum. Reports, surveys. Serials*
National Army Museum. Report / National Army Museum. — London (Royal Hospital Rd, SW3 4HT) : [The Museum].
1975-76. — [1976]. — 32p : ill, ports ; 22cm.
ISBN 0-901721-05-0 Sd : Unpriced
(B77-04678)

355'.00943 — Germany. Heer, 1918. *Early works. Facsimiles*
Great Britain. *Army. General Staff.* German Army handbook April 1918 / introduction by David Nash. — London : Arms and Armour Press [etc.], 1977. — [6],2-186p(2 fold),[2]p of plates,fold leaf of plate : ill, facsims, maps ; 23cm.
'... compiled by the General Staff in London ...' - Introduction. — Facsimile reprint of: 'Handbook of the German Army in War, April 1918'. London : General Staff, 1918. — Index.
ISBN 0-85368-171-6 : £5.95
(B77-26944)

355'.00945 — Italy. Esercito, 1861-1918. Political aspects
Whittam, John. The politics of the Italian army, 1861-1918 / [by] John Whittam. — London : Croom Helm [etc.], 1977. — 216p ; 23cm.
Bibl.: p.210-213. — Index.
ISBN 0-85664-317-3 : £7.50
(B77-04040)

355'.00954 — India (Dominion). Army, to 1947
Mason, Philip. A matter of honour : an account of the Indian army, its officers and men / [by] Philip Mason. — Harmondsworth [etc.] : Penguin, 1976. — 582p,[16]p of plates : ill, maps, plans, ports ; 20cm. — (Peregrine books)
Originally published: London : Cape, 1974. — Bibl.: p.543-548. — Index.
ISBN 0-14-055116-6 Pbk : £2.50
(B77-08907)

355'.009669'5 — Sokoto (Caliphate) military forces. *Nigeria. Northern states, to 1903*
Smaldone, Joseph P. Warfare in the Sokoto Caliphate : historical and sociological perspectives / [by] Joseph P. Smaldone. — Cambridge [etc.] : Cambridge University Press, 1977. — xii,228p : ill, maps, plans ; 24cm. — (African studies series ; 19 ISSN 0065-406x)
Bibl.: p.203-215. — Index.
ISBN 0-521-21069-0 : £12.50
(B77-18022)

355'.00973 — American military forces. Relations with American armaments industries, ca 1800-1976
War, business and American society : historical perspectives on the military-industrial complex / edited by Benjamin Franklin Cooling. — Port Washington ; London : Kennikat Press, 1977. — [6],205p ; 23cm. — (Kennikat Press national university publications : series in American studies)
Bibl.: p.191-199. — Index.
ISBN 0-8046-9156-8 : £10.60
Primary classification 338.4'7'62340973
(B77-25459)

355.02 — Small scale warfare, to ca 1905. *Manuals. Facsimiles*
Callwell, *Sir* **Charles Edward.** Small wars : their principles and practice / by C.E. Callwell. — 3rd ed. — Wakefield : EP Publishing, 1976. — [1],559p,[10] leaves of plates(3 fold) : maps, plans ; 23cm.
Facsimile reprint of: 3rd ed. London : H.M.S.O., 1906.
ISBN 0-7158-1200-9 : £8.50
(B77-26945)

355.02 — Warfare. Role of science & technology. *Western world*
Pavitt, Keith. Science, technology and the modern industrial state / [by] Keith Pavitt and Michael Worboys ; [for] Science in a Social Context. — London [etc.] : Butterworth, 1977. — 80p ; 22cm.
Bibl.
ISBN 0-408-71299-6 Pbk : £1.00
Primary classification 338'.06
(B77-16242)

355.02'09 — Warfare, to 1920
Delbrück, Hans. History of the art of war within the framework of political history / by Hans Delbrück ; translated from the German by Walter J. Renfroe, Jr. — Westport, Conn. ; London : Greenwood Press.
Vol.1 : Antiquity. — 1975. — 604p : maps ; 24cm. — (Contributions in military history ; no.9)
Translation of: 'Geschichte der Kriegskunst im Rahmen der politischen Geschichte'. Bd 1. 3.Aufl. Berlin : G. Stilke, 1920. — Index.
ISBN 0-8371-6365-x : £19.95
(B77-16277)

355.02'09 — Warfare, to 1976
Dupuy, Richard Ernest. The encyclopedia of military history : from 3500 BC to the present / [by] R. Ernest Dupuy and Trevor N. Dupuy. — Revised ed. — London : Macdonald and Jane's, 1977. — xvii,1464p : ill, maps, plans ; 25cm.
In slip case. — Previous ed.: London : Macdonald and Co., 1970. — Bibl.: p.1347-1354. — Index.
ISBN 0-356-08413-2 : £14.50
(B77-16796)

Williams, John. World atlas of weapons & war / [by] John Williams ; illustrations by Gerry Embleton. — London : Aldus Books, 1976. — 128p : ill(chiefly col), col maps, col plans, ports ; 31cm.
Index.
ISBN 0-490-00390-7 : £3.95
(B77-02143)

355.02'09'03 — Warfare, 1793-1976. *Encyclopaedias*
Parkinson, Roger. Encyclopedia of modern war / [by] Roger Parkinson. — London [etc.] : Routledge and Kegan Paul, 1977. — [9],226p : maps ; 26cm.
Index.
ISBN 0-7100-8560-5 : £7.50
(B77-17380)

355.02'09'04 — Land warfare, 1900-1976
The **encyclopedia** of land warfare in the 20th century / [authors Shelford Bidwell et al. ; editor Ray Bonds]. — London [etc.] : Spring Books, 1977. — 248p : ill(chiefly col), 4 col facsims, col maps, ports ; 31cm. — (A Salamander book)
Col. ill. on lining papers. — Spine title: Land warfare. — Index.
ISBN 0-600-33145-8 : £4.95
(B77-14637)

355.02'09'04 — Warfare, 1945-1975. *Secondary school texts*
Cox, John. On the warpath / [by] John Cox. — London : Oxford University Press, 1976. — [1], 65p : ill, facsims, maps, music, ports ; 20x21cm. — (Standpoints)
Bibl.: p.65.
ISBN 0-19-913234-8 Sd : £0.75
(B77-07229)

355.02'092'4 — Warfare. Theories of Hart, Sir Basil Henry Liddell
Bond, Brian. Liddell Hart : a study of his military thought / [by] Brian Bond. — London : Cassell, 1977. — x,289p : 3 maps ; 23cm.
Bibl.: p.277-280. — Index.
ISBN 0-304-29844-1 : £7.95
(B77-30077)

355.02'0966 — Warfare. *West Africa, to ca 1900*
Smith, Robert S. Warfare and diplomacy in pre-colonial West Africa / [by] Robert S. Smith. — [London] : Methuen, 1976. — vii, 240p ; 19cm. — (Studies in African history ; 15)
Bibl.: p.225-235. — Index.
ISBN 0-416-55060-6 : £5.50
ISBN 0-416-55070-3 Pbk : £2.90
Also classified at 327'.2'0966
(B77-04041)

355.02'17 — Deterrence
Morgan, Patrick M. Deterrence : a conceptual analysis / [by] Patrick M. Morgan. — Beverly Hills ; London : Sage Publications, 1977. — 216p ; 22cm. — (Sage library of social research ; vol.40)
ISBN 0-8039-0819-9 : £8.50
ISBN 0-8039-0820-2 Pbk : £4.50
(B77-30078)

355.02'184 — Guerrilla warfare, to 1975
Asprey, Robert Brown. War in the shadows : the guerilla in history / by Robert B. Asprey. — London : Macdonald and Jane's, 1976. — xlvii, 1615p : maps ; 25cm.
Originally published: Garden City, N.Y. : Doubleday, 1975. — Bibl.: p.1523-1550. — Index.
ISBN 0-356-08352-7 : £15.00
(B77-02873)

Laqueur, Walter. Guerrilla : a historical and critical study / [by] Walter Laqueur. — London : Weidenfeld and Nicolson, 1977. — xiii,462p ; 24cm.
Bibl.: p.446-450. — Index.
ISBN 0-297-77184-1 : £8.95
(B77-06562)

355.03'32'47 — Soviet Union. Military power. *Conference proceedings*
The **future** of Soviet military power / edited by Lawrence L. Whetten. — London : Macdonald and Jane's, 1976. — [6],vii,190p : ill, maps ; 24cm.
'On 1-2 May 1975 an international conference was convened at Ebenhausen, West Germany, under the aegis of the Stiftung für Wissenschaft und Politik and the University of Southern California' - Preface. — Index.
ISBN 0-354-01020-4 : £9.75
(B77-06563)

355.03'32'47 — Soviet Union. Military power. International political aspects. *Conference proceedings*
The **political** implications of Soviet military power / edited by Lawrence L. Whetten. — London : Macdonald and Jane's, 1977. — [3], iii,183p ; 24cm.
'In May 1975 an international conference was convened at Ebenhausen, West Germany, under the auspices of the Stiftung für Wissenschaft und Politik and the University of Southern California' - Preface. — Index.
ISBN 0-354-01021-2 : £9.75
(B77-13584)

355.03'35 — Military policies. *Forecasts for 1977-1990*
Brown, Neville. The future global challenge : a predictive study of world security, 1977-1990 / [by] Neville Brown. — London : Royal United Services Institute for Defence Studies [etc.], 1977. — x,402p ; 23cm.
Index.
ISBN 0-85516-038-1 : £9.95
(B77-29301)

355.03'35'37 — Ancient Rome. Military policies, B.C.27-A.D.305
Luttwak, Edward. The grand strategy of the Roman Empire from the first century AD to the third / [by] Edward N. Luttwak. — Baltimore ; London : Johns Hopkins University Press, 1976. — xiii,255,[2]p : ill, maps, plans ; 24cm.
Bibl.: p.233-246. — Index.
ISBN 0-8018-1863-x : Unpriced
(B77-23250)

355.03'35'41 — Great Britain. Military policies, 1930-1939
Shay, Robert Paul. British rearmament in the thirties : politics and profits / [by] Robert Paul Shay, Jr. — Princeton ; Guildford : Princeton University Press, 1977. — xiii,315p : ill ; 23cm.
Bibl.: p.299-306. — Index.
ISBN 0-691-05248-4 : £14.20
(B77-30079)

355.03'35'41 — Great Britain. Military policies, 1945-1976
British defence policy in a changing world / edited by John Baylis. — London : Croom Helm, 1977. — 295p ; 23cm.
Bibl.: p.283-285. — Index.
ISBN 0-85664-374-2 : £9.95 : CIP rev.
(B77-24096)

355.03'35'73 — United States. Military policies, 1914-1917
Finnegan, John Patrick. Against the specter of a dragon : the campaign for American military preparedness, 1914-1917 / [by] John Patrick Finnegan. — Westport, Conn. ; London : Greenwood Press, 1974. — ix,253,[1]p ; 22cm. — (Contributions in military history ; no.7)
Bibl.: p.235-245. — Index.
ISBN 0-8371-7376-0 : £11.50
(B77-16278)

355.03'35'73 — United States. Military policies, 1941-1945
Sherry, Michael S. Preparing for the next war : American plans for postwar defense, 1941-45 / [by] Michael S. Sherry. — New Haven ; London : Yale University Press, 1977. — x, 260p ; 24cm. — (Yale historical publications : miscellany ; 114)
Bibl.: p.239-252. — Index.
ISBN 0-300-02031-7 : £9.00
(B77-24806)

355.03'35'73 — United States. Military policies. Role of United States. Congress, ca 1965-1975
Frye, Alton. A responsible Congress : the politics of national security / by Alton Frye. — New York ; London [etc.] : McGraw-Hill for the Council on Foreign Relations, [1976]. — xiii, 238p : 1 ill ; 24cm.
Published in the United States: 1975. — Index.
ISBN 0-07-022600-8 : £8.30
(B77-05974)

355.1 — MILITARY LIFE

355.1'092'4 — Great Britain. Army. Officers. Wives. Social life, 1931-1946. *Personal observations*
Davies, Celia. Far to go / by Celia Davies. — Lavenham : Dalton, 1976. — 171p,[24]p of plates : ill, ports ; 23cm.
ISBN 0-900963-71-9 : £3.80
(B77-02874)

355.1'094 — Soldiers. Army life. *Europe, 1550-1650. Juvenile literature*
Parker, Geoffrey, *b.1943.* European soldiers, 1550-1650 / [by] Geoffrey and Angela Parker. — Cambridge [etc.] : Cambridge University Press, 1977. — 64p : ill, facsims, maps, plans, ports ; 21x22cm. — (Cambridge introduction to the history of mankind : topic book)
ISBN 0-521-21020-8 Pbk : £1.30
(B77-19274)

355.1'0941 — Great Britain. Army. Soldiers. Army life, 1642-1965
Laffin, John. Tommy Atkins : the story of an English soldier / [by] John Laffin. — London [etc.] : White Lion Publishers, 1977. — xx, 235p,[24]p of plates : ill, facsim, ports ; 23cm.
Originally published: London : Cassell, 1966. — Bibl.: p.219-221. — Index.
ISBN 0-7274-0306-0 : £4.25
(B77-26946)

355.1'0941 — Great Britain. Army. Soldiers. Army life,1750-1900. *Readings from contemporary sources*
The **rambling** soldier : life in the lower ranks, 1750-1900, through soldiers' songs and writings / edited by Roy Palmer. — Harmondsworth [etc.] : Penguin, 1977. — ix, 310p : ill, facsims, music, ports ; 20cm. — (Peacock books)
Also published: Harmondsworth : Kestrel Books, 1977. — Bibl.: p.295-299. — List of sound discs: p.300-301. — Index.
ISBN 0-14-047103-0 Pbk : £1.75
(B77-26947)

The **rambling** soldier : life in the lower ranks, 1750-1900, through soldiers' songs and writings / edited by Roy Palmer. — Harmondsworth : Kestrel Books, 1977. — ix, 310p : ill, facsims, music, ports ; 21cm.
Also published: Harmondsworth : Puffin Books, 1977. — Bibl.: p.295-299. — List of sound discs: p.300-301. — Index.
ISBN 0-7226-5294-1 : £3.50
(B77-26213)

355.1'15 — Residential institutions for British Army ex-servicemen. *London. Kensington and Chelsea (London Borough). Royal Hospital, Chelsea. Accounts*
Royal Hospital, Chelsea. Army prize money and legacy funds, &c. account ... in the year ended 31st March ... / Royal Hospital, Chelsea. — London : H.M.S.O.
1975-76. — [1977]. — 11p ; 25cm. — ([1976-77 H.C.]249)
ISBN 0-10-224977-6 Sd : £0.33
(B77-15200)

355.1'15 — Residential institutions for physically handicapped ex-servicemen. *London. Ealing (London Borough). St David's Home, to 1976*
Watson, Lavinia. The story of St David's : the Ealing Home for Disabled Ex-Servicemen / by Lavinia Watson. — [Shipley] ([Pannett's, Shipley, Horsham, W. Sussex RH13 8PP]) : [The author], [1977]. — 36p : ill, ports ; 21cm.
ISBN 0-9505710-0-8 Sd : £1.00
(B77-15201)

355.1'151'0941 — War pensions. *Great Britain. Reports, surveys. Serials*
Report on war pensioners / made by the Secretary of State for Social Services, the Secretary of State for Scotland and the Secretary of State for Wales ... — London : H.M.S.O.
1976. — [1977]. — iv,39p,[2]p of plates, leaf of plate : ill, ports ; 25cm. — ([1976-1977 H.C.]472)
Cover title: War pensioners.
ISBN 0-10-247277-7 Sd : £1.00
(B77-26214)

355.1'292 — Great Britain. Army. Officers' messes. Social life, to 1972
Dickinson, Richard John. Officers' mess : being a history of mess origins and customs from a wealth of military records ; enlivened anecdotes of mess times remembered from a host of one-time mess members ; and the progress of Charles Oswald Littlewart from 2 Lieutenant to Major-General / compiled by R.J. Dickinson. — Revised ed. — Tunbridge Wells : Midas Books, 1977. — viii,120p : ill(some col), plan, ports(some col) ; 31cm.
Previous ed.: 1973. — Index.
ISBN 0-85936-094-6 : £6.50
(B77-24097)

355.1'3325 — Great Britain. Army. Military offenders. Corporal punishment: Flogging. Abolition. Effects of inquest into death of White, Frederick John, 1846
Hopkins, Harry. The strange death of Private White : a Victorian scandal that made history / [by] Harry Hopkins. — London : Weidenfeld and Nicolson, 1977. — 273p,[8]p of plates : ill, facsims, ports ; 23cm.
Bibl.: p.257-266. — Index.
ISBN 0-297-77293-7 : £5.95
(B77-19275)

355.1'334 — Great Britain. Army. Scottish Highland regiments. Mutiny, 1743-1804
Prebble, John. Mutiny : Highland regiments in revolt, 1743-1804 / [by] John Prebble. — Harmondsworth [etc.] : Penguin, 1977. — 542p, [16]p of plates : ill, ports ; 19cm.
Originally published: London : Secker and Warburg, 1975. — Bibl.: p.504-509. — Index.
ISBN 0-14-004328-4 Pbk : £1.25
(B77-17381)

355.1'34 — British military forces. Decorations: Victoria Cross, 1854-1945
Smyth, *Sir* **John,** *bart, b.1893.* Great stories of the Victoria Cross / [by] Sir John Smyth. — London : A. Barker, 1977. — xx,192p,[8]p of plates : 1 ill, ports ; 23cm.
Bibl.: p.186. — Index.
ISBN 0-213-16644-5 : £4.95
(B77-23251)

355.1'34 — Great Britain. Army. Hertfordshire yeomanry regiments & Hertfordshire artillery units. Rolls of honour, 1897-1945. *Texts*
Sainsbury, John David. A record of honours and awards to officers and men of Hertfordshire Yeomanry and Artillery units / compiled by J.D. Sainsbury. — Welwyn (Digswell, Welwyn, Herts.) : Hertfordshire Yeomanry and Artillery Historical Trust, 1976. — xiv,138p : ill, facsims, ports ; 25cm.
Index.
ISBN 0-903823-01-2 Pbk : Unpriced
(B77-16279)

355.1'4 — Armies. Guards units. Ceremonial uniforms, 1745-1973
Cassin-Scott, Jack. Ceremonial uniforms of the world / by Jack Cassin-Scott and John Fabb. — Edinburgh [etc.] : J. Bartholomew, 1977. — xxii p,80 leaves of plates : col ill ; 24cm.
Leaves printed on both sides. — Originally published: London : Stephen Hope Books, 1973. — Bibl.: p.xvii-xix.
ISBN 0-7028-1026-6 Pbk : £1.95
(B77-22461)

355.1'4'03 — Armies. Uniforms, to 1976. *Dictionaries*
Carman, William Young. A dictionary of military uniform / [by] W.Y. Carman. — London : Book Club Associates, 1977. — 140p,[28]p of plates : ill(some col) ; 26cm.
Bibl.: p.140.
ISBN 0-7134-0191-5 : £6.50
(B77-24098)

355.1'4'0937 — Ancient Rome. Army. Uniforms in Northern England, 100-400
Robinson, Henry Russell. What the soldiers wore on Hadrian's Wall / by H. Russell Robinson ; coloured paintings by Ronald Embleton. — Newcastle upon Tyne : Graham, 1976. — 40p : ill(some col) ; 25cm.
ISBN 0-85983-093-4 Sd : £1.00
(B77-11646)

355.1'4'094 — European armies. Uniforms, 1700-1800
Funcken, Liliane. The lace wars / [by] Liliane and Fred Funcken ; [translated from the French]. — London : Ward Lock. — (Arms and uniforms)
Translation of: 'L'uniforme et les armes des soldats de la guerre en dentelle'. Tournai : Casterman, 1976.
Part 2 : 1700-1800 : French, British and Prussian cavalry and artillery, other countries : infantry, cavalry and artillery. — 1977. — 5-158p : col ill ; 25cm.
Col. ill. on lining papers. — Index.
ISBN 0-7063-5566-0 : £5.95 : CIP rev.
Also classified at 623'.4'094
(B77-21026)

355.1'4'094 — European armies. Uniforms, 1756-1763
Mollo, John. Uniforms of the Seven Years War, 1756-1763 in colour / [by] John Mollo ; illustrated by Malcolm McGregor. — Poole : Blandford Press, 1977. — 224p : col ill, plans ; 20cm. — ([Blandford colour series])
Bibl.: p.222-224.
ISBN 0-7137-0822-0 : £3.25
(B77-23252)

355.1'4'094 — European military forces. Uniforms, 1812
Haythornthwaite, Philip John. Uniforms of the retreat from Moscow, in colour, 1812 / [by] Philip J. Haythornthwaite ; illustrated by Michael Chappell. — Poole : Blandford Press, 1976. — 203p : ill(chiefly col), plans ; 20cm. — ([Blandford colour series])
Bibl.: p.198-203.
ISBN 0-7137-0788-7 : £2.95
(B77-04042)

355.1'4'0943 — Germany. Heer. Uniforms, 1939-1940
Davis, Brian Leigh. German ground forces, Poland and France, 1939-1940 / by Brian Davis ; colour illustrations by the County Studio and Brian [i.e. Bryan] Foster. — London : Almark Publishing, 1976. — 72p : ill(some col), ports ; 21x22cm. — (The mechanics of war)
Spine title: German forces, 1939-1940. — Bibl.: p.72.
ISBN 0-85524-261-2 : £2.50
(B77-06564)

355.1'4'0943 — Germany. Nationalsozialistische Deutsche Arbeiter-Partei. Schutzstaffel. Uniforms
Uniforms of the SS. — London (27 Emperor's Gate, S.W.7) : Historical Research Unit.
Vol.7 : Waffen-SS badges and unit distinctions, 1939-1945 / [by] Andrew Mollo ; [illustrated by Pierre Turner]. — [1977]. — [2],96p : ill(some col), facsim, ports ; 22x29cm.
Bibl.: p.96.
ISBN 0-901621-14-5 : £6.50
(B77-11144)

355.1'4'0943 — Germany. Nationalsozialistische Deutsche Arbeiter-Partei. Schutzstaffel. Waffenschutzstaffel. Uniforms, 1938-1944
Holzmann, Walther-Karl. Manual of the Waffen-SS : badges, uniforms, equipment / by Walther-Karl Holzmann ; black and white drawings by D.S.V. Fosten ; colour art by R.J. Marrion. — Watford : Argus Books, 1976. — 96p : ill(some col), ports ; 21cm. — (Bellona publications)
ISBN 0-85242-487-6 Pbk : £2.95
(B77-13585)

355.1'5'094 — Military flags. ***Europe, 1792-1815***
Over, Keith. Flags and standards of the Napoleonic wars / compiled and drawn by Keith Over. — London (21 Earl St., EC2A 2AL) : Bivouac Books Ltd [etc.], 1976. — 112p : ill(some col) ; 25cm.
ISBN 0-85680-012-0 Pbk : £3.80
(B77-11704)

355.1'6 — Commonwealth military forces. Dead personnel, 1914- . Commemoration. Organisations: Commonwealth War Graves Commission. ***Reports, surveys. Serials***
Commonwealth War Graves Commission. Annual report [1 April to 31 March] / Commonwealth War Graves Commission. — [Maidenhead] : [The Commission].
57th : [1975-76]. — [1977]. — [2],39p : ill(some col), port ; 25cm.
Previously published by H.M.S.O.
Sd : £0.50
(B77-11705)

355.1'6 — Commonwealth military forces. Dead personnel, 1914-. ***Registers***
Commonwealth War Graves Commission. The war dead of the Commonwealth / Commonwealth War Graves Commission. — Maidenhead : The Commission.
The register of the names of those who fell in the 1914-1918 War and are buried or commemorated in cemeteries, churchyards and gardens of remembrance in Australia. New South Wales. — 1976. — 52p ; 25cm. — (Australia ; 1-138A)
ISBN 0-903099-11-x Sd : £0.50
(B77-02144)

355.2 — MILITARY RESOURCES
355.2'0941 — Military resources. ***Great Britain. Reports, surveys. Serials***
Great Britain. ***Ministry of Defence.*** Statement on the defence estimates / presented to Parliament by the Secretary of State for Defence ... — London : H.M.S.O.
1977. — [1977]. — v,93p,(2 fold) : ill, maps ; 25cm. — (Cmnd.6735)
Index.
ISBN 0-10-167350-7 Sd : £1.50
(B77-09617)

355.2'2'0941 — British military forces. Personnel. ***Statistics***
Great Britain. ***Ministry of Defence.*** Ministry of Defence Votes A for the year ending 31st March ... — London : H.M.S.O.
1977-78. — [1977]. — 7p ; 25cm. — ([1976-77 H.C.]172)
ISBN 0-10-217277-3 Sd : £0.25
(B77-09618)

355.2'29'023 — British military forces. Women personnel. ***Career guides***
Reynolds, Vivienne. Service women : WRNS, WRAC & WRAF / by Vivienne Reynolds, Elizabeth Saxon and Helen Renton ; with a foreword by Sir Peter Hill-Norton. — Reading : Educational Explorers, 1977. — 133p,[8]p of plates : ill, 3 coats of arms, ports ; 22cm. — (My life and my work series)
ISBN 0-85225-762-7 : £2.95 : CIP rev.
(B77-05308)

355.3 — MILITARY ORGANISATION
355.3 — Mercenaries
Burchett, Wilfred Graham. The whores of war : mercenaries today / [by] Wilfred Burchett and Derek Roebuck. — Harmondsworth [etc.] : Penguin, 1977. — 240p ; 18cm. — (A pelican original) (Pelican special)
ISBN 0-14-022027-5 Pbk : £0.75
(B77-26215)

355.3'1 — Armies. Gurkha units, to 1974
Bishop, Edward, *b.1924.* Better to die : the story of the Gurkhas / [by] Edward Bishop. — London : New English Library, 1977. — 143p : ill, maps ; 19cm.
Originally published: 1976. — Bibl.: p.131-133. — Index.
ISBN 0-450-03356-2 Pbk : £0.75
(B77-25497)

355.3'1'0941 — Great Britain. Army. Eighth Army, 1940-1942
Sandars, John. 8th Army in the desert / [by] John Sandars. — Cambridge : Stephens [for] Airfix Products Ltd, 1976. — 64p : ill, map ; 23cm. — ('Airfix magazine' guide ; 20)
ISBN 0-85059-235-6 : £1.40
(B77-02145)

355.3'1'0941 — Great Britain. Army. Household Division, to 1975
Braddon, Russell. All the Queen's men : the Household Cavalry and the Brigade of Guards / by Russell Braddon. — London : Hamilton, 1977. — 288p,[8]p of plates : ill(some col), ports ; 26cm.
Index.
ISBN 0-241-89431-x : £7.50
(B77-10776)

Paget, ***Sir*** **Julian.** The story of the Guards / [by] Julian Paget. — London : Osprey Publishing, 1976. — 304p : ill(some col), col coats of arms, facsim, maps, plans, ports(1 col) ; 30cm.
Bibl.: p.298-299. — Index.
ISBN 0-85045-078-0 : £12.50
(B77-01274)

355.3'31'0922 — France. Armée. Marshals, 1735-1852. ***Biographies***
Dunn-Pattison, R P. Napoleon's marshals / by R.P. Dunn-Pattison. — Wakefield : EP Publishing, 1977. — xix,373p,[20] leaves of plates : 1 ill, ports ; 23cm.
Facsimile reprint of: 1st ed. London : Methuen, 1909. — Index.
ISBN 0-7158-1216-5 : £9.00 : CIP rev.
(B77-08908)

355.3'31'0922 — Germany. Wehrmacht. Generals, 1934-1945
Brett-Smith, Richard. Hitler's generals / [by] Richard Brett-Smith. — London : Osprey Publishing, 1976. — viii,306p,[16]p of plates : maps, ports ; 24cm.
Bibl.: p.297-299. — Index. — Includes chapters on the Luftwaffe and the Waffen SS.
ISBN 0-85045-073-x : £5.95
(B77-02875)

355.3'31'0922 — Polish military forces. Generals, 1918-1944. ***Biographies. Polish texts***
Kryska-Karski, T. Generalowie polski niepodeglej / T. Kryska-Karski, S. Zurakowski. — London (97 Moore Park Rd, SW6 2DA) : Figaro Press, [1976]. — x,178p : ill, ports ; 24cm.
Index.
ISBN 0-9502808-3-6 Pbk : Unpriced
(B77-04679)

355.3'31'0924 — United States. Army. Custer, George Armstrong. ***Biographies***
Anglo, Michael. Custer : man & myth / [by] Michael Anglo. — London : Jupiter Books, 1976. — 144p,[12]p of plates : ill(some col), facsims, maps, ports(some col) ; 31cm.
ISBN 0-904041-49-2 : £4.95
(B77-16797)

355.3'31'0943 — Germany. Heer. Role of Germany. Heer. Generalstab, 1800-1945
Dupuy, Trevor Nevitt. A genius for war : the German army and general staff, 1807-1945 / [by] T.N. Dupuy. — London : Macdonald and Jane's, 1977. — xiii,362p,[24]p of plates : maps, plans, ports ; 24cm.
'A T.N. Dupuy Associates book'. — Also published: Englewood Cliffs : Prentice-Hall, 1977. — Bibl.: p.347-352. — Index.
ISBN 0-354-01084-0 : £6.95
(B77-33699)

355.3'32 — Russia. Armiía. Finnish officers. Recruitment, 1809-1917
Screen, John Ernest Oliver. The entry of Finnish officers into Russian military service, 1809-1917 / [by] J.E.O. Screen. — London ([c/o School of Slavonic and East European Studies, University of London, Senate House, Malet St., WC1E 7HU]) : [The author], 1976. — [3],338p : ill ; 30cm.
Bibl.: p.308-322.
Pbk : Unpriced
Also classified at 359.3'32
(B77-25498)

355.3'32'0924 — Austria. Armee. Eugène, prince de Savoie. ***Biographies***
McKay, Derek. Prince Eugene of Savoy / [by] Derek McKay. — London : Thames and Hudson, 1977. — 288p,[16]p of plates : ill, facsim, maps, ports ; 23cm. — (Men in office)
Bibl.: p.263-269. — Index.
ISBN 0-500-87007-1 : £8.50
(B77-30080)

355.3'32'0924 — Bengal. Army. Sleeman, Sir William Henry. ***Biographies***
Tuker, ***Sir*** **Francis.** The yellow scarf : the story of the life of Thuggee Sleeman, or Major General Sir William Henry Sleeman, KCB, 1788-1856 of the Bengal Army and the Indian Political Service / [by] Sir Francis Tuker. — London [etc.] : White Lion Publishers, 1977. — xvi,211p,leaf of plate,[8]p of plates : ill, facsim, maps, ports ; 23cm.
Originally published: London : Dent, 1961. — Bibl.: p.204. — Index.
ISBN 0-7274-0184-x : £5.25
(B77-08909)

355.3'32'0924 — Germany. Heer. Rommel, Erwin. ***Biographies***
Irving, David. The trail of the fox : the life of Field-Marshal Erwin Rommel / [by] David Irving. — London : Weidenfeld and Nicolson, 1977. — ix,448p,[32]p of plates : ill, ports ; 25cm.
Bibl.: p.415-427. — Index.
ISBN 0-297-77370-4 : £7.95
(B77-31078)

355.3'32'0924 — Great Britain. Army. Auchinleck, Sir Claude. ***Biographies***
Parkinson, Roger. The Auk : Auchinleck, victor at Alamein / [by] Roger Parkinson. — London [etc.] : Hart-Davis MacGibbon, 1977. — 272p, [16]p of plates : ill, maps, plans, ports ; 25cm.
Bibl.: p.262-263. — Index.
ISBN 0-246-10933-5 : £9.50
(B77-23253)

355.3'32'0924 — Great Britain. Army. Fuller, John Frederick Charles. ***Biographies***
Trythall, Anthony John. 'Boney' Fuller : the intellectual general, 1878-1966 / [by] Anthony John Trythall. — London : Cassell, 1977. — xiii,314p,[12]p of plates : ill, facsim, ports ; 23cm.
Bibl.: p.301-303. — Index.
ISBN 0-304-29843-3 : £6.95
(B77-22462)

355.3'32'0924 — Great Britain. Army. Milne, George Francis, Baron Milne. ***Biographies***
Nicol, Graham. Uncle George : Field-Marshal Lord Milne of Salonika and Rubislaw / [by] Graham Nicol. — London (23 Suffolk Rd, S.W.13) : Reedminster Publications, 1976. — [10],341p,24p of plates : maps, ports ; 23cm.
Bibl.: p.333-336. — Index.
ISBN 0-85945-004-x : £6.75
(B77-21027)

355.3'32'0924 — Great Britain. Army. Slim, William, Viscount Slim. ***Biographies***
Lewin, Ronald. Slim : the standardbearer : a biography of Field-Marshal the Viscount Slim / by Ronald Lewin. — London : Cooper, 1976. — xv,350p,leaf of plate,[16]p of plates : ill, maps, ports ; 24cm.
Bibl.: p.331-333. — Index.
ISBN 0-85052-218-8 : £7.50
(B77-01275)

355.3'32'0924 — Russia. Armiía. Kutuzov, Mikhail Ilarionovich, Prince of Smolensk. *Biographies*
Parkinson, Roger. The fox of the north : the life of Kutuzov, general of 'War and peace' / [by] Roger Parkinson. — London : P. Davies, 1976. — ix,253p,4p of plates : ill, maps, ports ; 23cm.

Map on lining papers. — Bibl.: p.245-247. — Index.
ISBN 0-432-11601-x : £6.50
(B77-00115)

355.3'32'0924 — United States. Army. Bullard, Robert Lee. *Biographies*
Millett, Allan R. The general : Robert L. Bullard and officership in the United States Army, 1881-1925 / [by] Allan R. Millett. — Westport, Conn. ; London : Greenwood Press, 1975. — xi,499,[1]p : ill, maps, ports ; 24cm. — (Contributions in military history ; no.10)
Bibl.: p.475-491. — Index.
ISBN 0-8371-7957-2 : £15.75
(B77-31079)

355.3'32'0924 — United States. Army. Pershing, John Joseph. *Biographies*
Vandiver, Frank Everson. Black Jack : the life and times of John J. Pershing / by Frank E. Vandiver. — College Station ; London ([70 Great Russell St., WC1B 3BY]) : Texas A & M University Press, 1977. — 2v.(xxii,1178p,leaf of plate,[32]p of plates) : ill, facsim, maps, ports ; 24cm.
Bibl.: p.1099-1122. — Index.
ISBN 0-89096-024-0 : £26.25
(B77-29302)

355.3'32'0941 — Great Britain. Army. Officers. *Registers*
The **Army** list. — London : H.M.S.O.
1976. Part 2 : Officers in receipt of retired pay. — 1977. — [3],508p ; 21cm.
ISBN 0-11-772127-1 Pbk : £6.25
(B77-28512)

1977. Part 1. — 1977. — ix,726p ; 21cm.
Index.
ISBN 0-11-772199-9 Pbk : £10.00
(B77-28513)

355.3'4 — Great Britain. Army. Postal services, 1903-1929
Kennedy, Alistair. The postal history of the British Army in World War I - before and after, 1903 to 1929 : an illustrated reference book of British Army postmarks and their location at home and abroad during the campaigns of the war and also on manoeuvres, operations and post war occupations, with relevant historical and postal information / by Alistair Kennedy and George Crabb. — Ewell (Charlwood, Howard Ave., Ewell, Epsom, Surrey) : G. Crabb, 1977. — [3]leaves,300[i.e. 301]p : facsims, map, plans ; 30cm.
Limited ed. of 600 numbered copies. — Bibl.: p.300.
ISBN 0-9505719-0-3 Sp : £10.00
(B77-15203)

355.3'432 — Military cryptology. Friedman, William Frederic. *United States. Biographies*
Clark, Ronald William. The man who broke 'Purple' : the life of the world's greatest cryptologist, Colonel William F. Friedman / [by] Ronald W. Clark. — London : Weidenfeld and Nicolson, 1977. — xi,212p,[8]p of plates : ill, ports ; 23cm.
Index.
ISBN 0-297-77279-1 : £5.25
(B77-16280)

355.3'45 — Military hospitals. *Kent. Chatham. Fort Pitt Garrison Hospital, to 1975*
Cooper, John, *b.1947.* Fort Pitt : some notes on the history of a Napoleonic fort, military hospital and technical school / [by] John Cooper. — Maidstone (Springfield, Maidstone, Kent) : Kent County Library, 1976. — [35]p : ill, maps, plans ; 20cm.
ISBN 0-905155-05-x Sd : £0.25
Also classified at 942.2'323
(B77-09619)

355.3'45'0924 — British military forces. Medical services. Dent, William, 1808-1824. *Correspondence*
Dent, William. A young surgeon in Wellington's army : the letters of William Dent / compiled with an introduction by Leonard W. Woodford. — Old Woking (The Gresham Press, Old Woking, Surrey) : Unwin Brothers Ltd, 1976. — [8],68p : ill, facsim, geneal table ; 21cm. — (Looking back ; vol.2)
ISBN 0-9502121-8-0 Pbk : £2.00
(B77-01276)

355.3'45'0924 — Great Britain. Army. Medical services. Barry, James Miranda. *Biographies*
Rose, June. The perfect gentleman : the remarkable life of Dr James Miranda Barry, the woman who served as an officer in the British Army from 1813 to 1859 / [by] June Rose. — London : Hutchinson, 1977. — 160p,[12]p of plates : ill, facsims, ports ; 23cm.
Bibl.: p.154-156. — Index.
ISBN 0-09-126840-0 : £4.50
(B77-11145)

355.3'45'0924 — Indian military forces. Medical services. Kerry, Stephen. *Autobiographies*
Kerry, Stephen. Doctor Sahib / [by] Stephen Kerry. — Large print ed. — Leicester : Ulverscroft, 1977. — [5],399p ; 23cm. — (Ulverscroft large print series : [non-fiction])
Originally published: London : Cassell, 1967.
ISBN 0-85456-532-9 : £2.65
(B77-15764)

355.3'45'0941 — British military forces. Medical services. *Inquiry reports*
Great Britain. *Parliament. House of Commons. Expenditure Committee.* Defence medical services : eleventh report from the Expenditure Committee, session 1975-76, together with the minutes of the evidence taken before the Defence and External Affairs Sub-committee on 10 February 1976 and 29 June 1976 and appendices. — London : H.M.S.O., [1976]. — xvii,56p ; 25cm. — ([1975-76 H.C.]695)
ISBN 0-10-009286-1 Sd : £1.35
(B77-05975)

355.3'45'0941 — British military forces. Medical services. Great Britain. Parliament. House of Commons. Expenditure Committee. 'Defence medical services'. *Critical studies*
Great Britain. *Ministry of Defence.* Defence expenditure, government observations on the eleventh report from the Expenditure Committee, House of Commons paper 695, session 1975-76 ... / Ministry of Defence. — London : H.M.S.O., 1977. — 6p ; 25cm. — (Cmnd.6755)
ISBN 0-10-167550-x Sd : £0.25
(B77-16281)

355.3'46 — Great Britain. Army. Personnel. Entertaining. Organisations: Ensa
Hughes, John Graven. The greasepaint war : show business, 1939-45 / [by] John Graven Hughes. — London : New English Library, 1976. — 216p,[16]p of plates : ill, ports ; 22cm.

ISBN 0-450-03064-4 : £4.95
(B77-06565)

355.3'47 — Welfare services for army personnel. *Great Britain. Inquiry reports*
Army Welfare Inquiry Committee. Report of the Army Welfare Inquiry Committee / chairman, J.C. Spencer. — London : H.M.S.O., 1976. — vii,220p : 1 ill, forms ; 25cm.
ISBN 0-11-771226-4 Pbk : £2.60
(B77-08910)

355.3'47 — Welfare services for army personnel. *Great Britain. Reports, surveys*
Wilders, Malcolm. Army welfare : a survey carried out for the Army Welfare Inquiry Committee (Ministry of Defence) / [by] Malcolm Wilders ; [for the] Office of Population Censuses and Surveys, Social Survey Division. — London : H.M.S.O., 1977. — vi, 28p : form ; 30cm.
ISBN 0-11-700819-2 Sd : £2.25
(B77-33132)

355.3'47'0973 — United States. Army. Chaplains. Social aspects
Abercrombie, Clarence L. The military chaplain / [by] Clarence L. Abercrombie, III ; foreword by Bruce M. Russett. — Beverly Hills ; London : Sage Publications, 1977. — 191p : facsims, forms ; 22cm. — (Sage library of social research ; vol.37)
Bibl.: p.183-189.
ISBN 0-8039-0669-2 : £8.50
ISBN 0-8039-0670-6 Pbk : £4.40
(B77-18642)

355.3'7'0941 — British military forces. Reserves & reinforcements. *Reports, surveys*
Great Britain. *Parliament. House of Commons. Expenditure Committee.* Reserves and reinforcements : sixth report from the Expenditure Committee, session 1976-77, together with part of the minutes of the evidence taken before the Defence and External Affairs Sub-committee on 26 October, 2,9 & 16 November, 7,14 & 16 December 1976, and 18 January 1977, and appendices. — London : H.M.S.O., [1977]. — xlv,183p ; 25cm. — ([1976-77] H.C.393)
ISBN 0-10-239377-x Pbk : £4.60
(B77-27758)

355.3'7'094235 — Militia. Muster rolls. *Devon, 1569. Texts*
Devon *(County).* The Devon muster roll for 1569 / edited by A.J. Howard and T.L. Stoate. — Bristol (Lower Court, Almondsbury, Bristol) : T.L. Stoate, 1977. — [1],xix,283p : map ; 30cm.
Bibl.: p.xvii-xix. — Index.
ISBN 0-9504047-3-x : £4.00
(B77-14638)

355.3'7'0942841 — Militia. Muster rolls. *North Yorkshire. Craven (District), 1803. Texts*
The **Craven** Muster Roll, 1803. — [Northallerton] ([County Hall, Northallerton, N. Yorkshire DL7 8AD]) : North Yorkshire County Council, 1976. — [2],226p ; 30cm. — (North Yorkshire County Record Office. Publications ; no.9)
ISBN 0-9503430-8-0 Sp : £2.00
(B77-11706)

355.4 — MILITARY OPERATIONS

355.4 — Electronic warfare by American military forces, 1960-1976
Dickson, Paul. The electronic battlefield / [by] Paul Dickson. — London : Boyars : [Distributed by Calder and Boyars], 1976. — [9],244p : ill ; 23cm. — ([Open forum])
Originally published: Bloomington : Indiana University Press, 1976. — Bibl.: p.226-237. — Index.
ISBN 0-7145-2606-1 : £6.50
ISBN 0-7145-2607-x Pbk : Unpriced
(B77-24099)

355.4'09 — Military operations. *History. Periodicals*
Battle. — Hemel Hempstead : Model and Allied Publications.
Vol.1, no.1- ; 1974-. — [1974]-. — ill(some col), maps(some col), ports(some col) ; 30cm.
Monthly. — 44,[4]p. in Vol.2, no.5.
Sd : £0.35(£5.75 yearly)
ISSN 0309-7668
(B77-30081)

355.4'09436 — Army operations by Austria. Armee, 1740-1780
Duffy, Christopher. The army of Maria Theresa : the armed forces of Imperial Austria, 1740-1780 / [by] Christopher Duffy. — Vancouver ; London : David and Charles, 1977. — 256p : ill, facsim, maps, ports ; 26cm. — (Historic armies and navies)
Bibl.: p.247-251. — Index.
ISBN 0-7153-7387-0 : £6.50
(B77-26216)

355.4'09438 — Army operations by Poland. Wojsko, 1917-1921. *Polish texts*
Mitkiewicz, Leon. W wojsku polskim, 1917-1921 / Leon Mitkiewicz ; przedmowa Klemens Rudnicki. — London : Veritas Foundation Publication Centre, 1976. — 271p, [3] leaves of plates : ill, ports ; 20cm. — (Biblioteka polska : seria czerwona ; tom.80)
Index.
ISBN 0-901215-63-5 : £3.00
(B77-00116)

355.4'0947 — Military operations by Soviet military forces, 1917-1945
The **Russian** war machine 1917-1945 / edited by S.L. Mayer. — London : Arms and Armour Press, 1977. — 257p : chiefly ill(some col), facsims, col maps, ports ; 31cm.
Index.
ISBN 0-85368-291-7 : £5.95
(B77-21028)

355.4'0952 — Military operations by Japanese military forces, 1868-1945
The **Japanese** war machine / edited by S.L. Mayer. — Feltham : Bison Books : Distributed by Hamlyn, 1976. — 255p : ill(some col), col maps, col plans, ports(some col) ; 31cm.
Col. map on lining papers. — Index.
ISBN 0-600-35247-1 : £4.95
(B77-21029)

355.4'11 — Logistics. *Conference proceedings*
Logistics Research Conference, *7th, Washington, D.C., 1974.* Modern trends in logistics research : proceedings of a conference held at the George Washington University / [contributors] Edward S. Bress III ... [et al.] ; edited by W.H. Marlow. — Cambridge, Mass. ; London : M.I.T. Press, [1977]. — xvi,461p : ill ; 21cm.
'... the May 1974 Logistics Research Conference ...' - Preface. — Published in the United States: 1976. — Bibl. — Index.
ISBN 0-262-13122-6 : £15.00
(B77-11146)

355.4'22 — Blitzkrieg
Messenger, Charles. The art of blitzkrieg / [by] Charles Messenger. — London : Allan, 1976. — 256p,[32]p of plates : ill, map, plans, ports ; 23cm.
Bibl.: p.247-252. — Index.
ISBN 0-7110-0738-1 : £4.50
(B77-02876)

355.6 — MILITARY ADMINISTRATION
355.6'0944 — France. Armée. Intendants, 1630-1670
Baxter, Douglas Clark. Servants of the sword : French intendants of the army, 1630-70 / [by] Douglas Clark Baxter. — Urbana [etc.] ; London : University of Illinois Press, 1976. — xvii,243p ; 24cm.
Bibl.: p.229-235. — Index.
ISBN 0-252-00291-1 : £9.60
(B77-03457)

355.6'213 — American military equipment. Sale. *Great Britain. Accounts*
Disposal of surplus United States Mutual Defence Programme equipment : account ... for the year ended 31st March ... — London : H.M.S.O.
1975-76. — [1977]. — Folder(3p) ; 25cm. — (Cmnd.6808)
ISBN 0-10-168080-5 : £0.15
(B77-18024)

355.6'213 — Oman. Sultan, 1970- (Qaboos bin Said). Gifts of British military equipment by British government. *Proposals*
Great Britain. *Treasury.* Copy of Treasury minute dated 7 March 1977 relative to the gift of assets to His Majesty the Sultan of Oman ... — London : H.M.S.O., [1977]. — Sheet ([2]p) ; 25x16cm. — (Cmnd.6748)
ISBN 0-10-167480-5 : £0.10
(B77-29303)

355.6'22 — British military forces. Expenditure by government, 1974-1976. *Campaign for Nuclear Disarmament viewpoints. Conference proceedings*
Defence cuts and Labour's industrial strategy ... / foreword by Judith Hart. — [London] ([Eastbourne House, Bullards Place, E2 0PT]) : [C.N.D.], [1976]. — [2],31p : 1 ill ; 21cm. — (Campaign for Nuclear Disarmament. Labour Committee. Pamphlets)
'... based on the proceedings of a delegate conference on "Defence cuts and Labour's industrial strategy", called by the Labour Committee of the Campaign for Nuclear Disarmament and held in Holborn Library, London on February 21, 1976' - title page verso.
ISBN 0-9504031-4-8 Sd : £0.25
(B77-01277)

355.6'22 — British military forces. Expenditure by government. Reduction. Cumulative effects. *Reports, surveys*
Great Britain. *Parliament. House of Commons. Expenditure Committee.* Cumulative effect of cuts in defence expenditure : second report from the Expenditure Committee, session 1976-77, together with part of the minutes of the evidence taken before the Defence and External Affairs Sub-committee on 1 February and 17 February 1977 and appendices. — London : H.M.S.O., [1977]. — xx,47p ; 25cm. — ([1976-77]H.C.254)
ISBN 0-10-225477-x Sd : £1.60
(B77-11707)

355.7 — MILITARY ESTABLISHMENTS
355.7'097 — Military institutions. Visits by Great Britain. Parliament. House of Commons. Expenditure Committee. Defence and External Affairs Sub-committee. *North America. Reports, surveys*
Great Britain. *Parliament. House of Commons. Expenditure Committee.* Visit to Canada and the United States : twelfth report from the Expenditure Committee, session 1975-76, together with memoranda. — London : H.M.S.O., [1976]. — vii,43p ; 25cm. — ([1975-76] H.C.696)
ISBN 0-10-009276-4 Sd : £0.75
(B77-07230)

355.7'097 — Military institutions. Visits by Great Britain. Parliament. House of Commons. Expenditure Committee. Defence and External Affairs Sub-committee. Reports. *North America. Critical studies*
Great Britain. *Ministry of Defence.* Defence expenditure, Government observations on the twelfth report from the Expenditure Committee, House of Commons paper 696, session 1975-76 ... / Ministry of Defence. — London : H.M.S.O., [1977]. — 8p ; 25cm. — (Cmnd. 6758)
ISBN 0-10-167580-1 Sd : £0.25
(B77-12382)

355.8 — MILITARY EQUIPMENT AND SUPPLIES
355.8'2 — Military operations. Role of heavy artillery, 1905-1945
Allen, Kenneth. Big guns of the twentieth century and their part in great battles / [by] Kenneth Allen. — Hove (49 Lansdowne Place, Hove, East Sussex BN3 1HS) : Firefly Books Ltd, 1976. — [2],90p : ill, maps, plans, ports ; 29cm.
Ill. on lining papers. — Bibl.: p.88. — Index.
ISBN 0-904724-10-7 : £2.95
(B77-02146)

355.8'3 — Allied forces. Military locomotives, 1939-1955
Tourret, R. Allied military locomotives of the Second World War / by R. Tourret. — [Abingdon] ([5 Byron Close, Abingdon, Oxon. OX14 5PA]) : Tourret Publishing.
In 2 vols.
Book 1 : War Department locomotives. — 1976. — [9],82p : ill, maps, plan ; 31cm.
Index.
ISBN 0-905878-00-0 : £3.90
(B77-18643)

355.8'3 — Germany. Heer. Afrikakorps. Military vehicles, 1941-1943. Camouflage & markings
Jones, Kenneth Matthew. Germany, North Africa / by Kenneth M. Jones. — London : Almark Publishing, 1977. — 36p : ill(some col) ; 20x21cm. — (Focus on armour, camouflage and markings ; no.1)
ISBN 0-85524-279-5 Pbk : £1.25
(B77-20143)

355.8'3 — Great Britain. Army. First Army & Great Britain. Army. Eighth Army. Military vehicles, 1941-1943. Camouflage & markings
Jones, Kenneth Matthew. British, North Africa / by Kenneth M. Jones. — London : Almark Publishing, 1977. — 36p : ill(some col), ports ; 20x22cm. — (Focus on armour, camouflage and markings ; no.2)
ISBN 0-85524-280-9 Pbk : £1.25
(B77-31080)

356 — FOOT FORCES
356'.11'0924 — Great Britain. Army. Welsh units. Silsoe, Malcolm Trustram Eve, Baron, to 1974. *Autobiographies*
Silsoe, Malcolm Trustram Eve, *Baron.* Sixty years a Welsh Territorial / by Lord Silsoe. — [Llandysul] : Gomer Press, 1976. — 148p,[28]p of plates,leaf of plate : ill, facsim, maps, ports ; 22cm.
Maps on lining papers.
ISBN 0-85088-320-2 : £1.95
(B77-08911)

356'.11'0941 — Great Britain. Army. 7th Duke of Edinburgh's Own Gurkha Rifles, to 1973
Smith, Eric David. East of Katmandu : the story of the 7th Duke of Edinburgh's Own Gurkha Rifles / by E.D. Smith. — London : Cooper.
Vol.2 : 1948-1973 / with a foreword by Sir Walter Walker. — 1976. — xx,212p,[8]p of plates : ill, maps, ports ; 23cm.
Maps on lining papers.
ISBN 0-85052-211-0 : £8.50
(B77-02147)

356'.11'0941 — Great Britain. Army. Black Watch, to 1975
Linklater, Eric. The Black Watch : the history of the Royal Highland Regiment / [by] Eric and Andro Linklater. — London : Barrie and Jenkins, 1977. — 240p,[12]p of plates : ill(some col), col facsims, music, plans(some col), ports ; 26cm.
Bibl.: p.233-234. — Index.
ISBN 0-214-20083-3 : £8.95
(B77-18644)

356'.11'0941 — Great Britain. Army. Lancashire infantry regiments, to 1972
Towneley Hall Art Gallery and Museums. The regiments of Lancashire : military exhibition [held at] Towneley Hall Art Gallery and Museum[s], Burnley, 14th April-30th September, 1973. — [Burnley] ([c/o Towneley Hall, Burnley, Lancs. BB11 3RQ]) : County Borough of Burnley, Art Gallery and Museums Sub-committee, 1973. — 23p : ill, facsim ; 25cm.
Sd : £0.12
(B77-07231)

356'.11'0941 — Great Britain. Army. Staffordshire Regiment, to 1976
Great Britain. *Army. Staffordshire Regiment.* Information handbook / the Staffordshire Regiment (The Prince of Wales's). — London : Page, [1976]. — 48p : ill ; 21cm.
ISBN 0-904819-05-1 Sd : Unpriced
(B77-11147)

356'.186 — Great Britain. Army. Infantry. Uniforms, 1700-1800
Funcken, Liliane. British infantry uniforms : from Marlborough to Wellington / [by] Liliane and Fred Funcken. — London : Ward Lock, 1976. — 47p : col ill ; 25cm. — (Arms and uniforms)
ISBN 0-7063-5214-9 : £2.95
ISBN 0-7063-5181-9 Pbk : £1.75
(B77-12383)

356'.186 — United States. Army. Infantry. Army equipment & uniforms, 1815
Warner, Chris. American Civil War, Union infantry uniforms / [by] Chris Warner. — London : Almark Publishing, 1977. — 48p : ill(some col) ; 20x21cm. — (Uniforms and equipment)
Bibl.: p.3.
ISBN 0-85524-284-1 Pbk : £1.95
(B77-33133)

357 — MOUNTED FORCES
357 — Warfare. Role of horses, to 1976
The **military** horse / [edited by Sue Simmons]. — London [etc.] : Marshall Cavendish, 1976. — [2],105,[1]p : ill(some col), ports(some col) ; 29cm.
Ill. on lining papers.
ISBN 0-85685-140-x : £2.50
(B77-12943)

357'.09438 — Poland. Wojsko. 24 Pulk Ulanów, 1920-1947
24 Pulk Ulanów : zarys historii 1920-1947 / opracowal Stefan Komornicki. — Londyn [i.e. London] (12 Freeland Rd, W5 3HR) : Kolo 24 Pulku Ulanów, 1976. — 444p,[40]p of plates : ill(incl 1 col), coats of arms, maps(1 col), music, plans, ports ; 28cm.
Col. maps on lining papers. — Index.
£15.00
(B77-18645)

357'.1'0924 — Great Britain. Army. Light Brigade. Cardigan, James Thomas Brudenell, Earl of. *Biographies*
Thomas, Donald. Charge! hurrah! hurrah! : a life of Cardigan of Balaclava / [by] Donald Thomas. — London : Omega, 1976. — xi, 369p ; 20cm.
Originally published: London : Routledge and Kegan Paul, 1974. — Bibl.: p.351-356. — Index.
ISBN 0-86007-737-3 Pbk : £1.25
(B77-13586)

357'.1'0944 — France. Armée. Chasseurs à cheval regiments, 1800-1815
Bukhari, Emir. Napoleon's line chasseurs / text by Emir Bukhari ; colour plates by Angus McBride. — London : Osprey Publishing, 1977. — 40p,[8]p of plates : ill(some col) ; 25cm. — (Men-at-arms series)
Text accompanying plates in English, French and German. — Bibl.: p.39.
ISBN 0-85045-269-4 Pbk : £1.95
(B77-26948)

357'.1'0944 — France. Armée. Lancer regiments, 1800-1815
De Lee, Nigel. French lancers / by Nigel de Lee ; illustrated by Emir Bukhari. — London : Almark Publishing, 1976. — 48p : ill(chiefly col) ; 21x22cm. — (Nations in arms, 1800-1815)
Bibl.: p.48.
ISBN 0-85524-256-6 : £2.25
(B77-06566)

357'.18 — Army operations by cavalry, 1800-1943
Lunt, James. Charge to glory : a garland of cavalry exploits / [by] James Lunt. — London [etc.] : White Lion Publishers, 1976. — x,265p, [4]p of plates : ill, maps, plans ; 23cm.
Originally published: New York : Harcourt, Brace, 1960 ; London : Heinemann, 1961.
ISBN 0-7274-0255-2 : £4.75
(B77-04043)

357'.188 — France. Armée. Cuirassier regiments & carabinier regiments. Uniforms, 1802-1815
Bukhari, Emir. Napoleon's Cuirassiers and Carabiniers / text by Emir Bukhari ; colour plates by Angus McBride. — London : Osprey Publishing, 1977. — 40p,[8]p of plates : ill(some col) ; 25cm. — (Men-at-arms series)
Bibl.: p.40.
ISBN 0-85045-096-9 Pbk : £1.95
(B77-14136)

357'.188 — Great Britain. Army. Queen's Own Mercian Yeomanry. Uniforms. *Regulations*
Great Britain. *Army. Queen's Own Mercian Yeomanry.* The Queen's Own Mercian Yeomanry, regimental dress regulations and customs, 1975. — Shrewsbury (Territorial House, Sundorne Road, Shrewsbury) : Shropshire Yeomanry Museum Trust, 1976. — [1],12p,plate : ill(some col), coats of arms ; 22cm. — (Shropshire Yeomanry Museum Trust. Publications ; no.3)
'Reproduced from the "Bulletin of the Military Historical Society", June, 1976' - preliminaries.
ISBN 0-905799-00-3 Sd : Unpriced
(B77-02148)

358.1 — ARTILLERY, LAND MISSILE ARMOURED FORCES

358'.12'0941 — Great Britain. Army. 253 Field Regiment, to 1967
Wingfield, A J. The Bolton Artillery : a history, 1860-1975 / by A.J. Wingfield. — Bolton ([231 Tottington Rd, Harwood, Bolton, Lancs. BL2 4DW]) : B.V.A.A., 1976. — [9],78p,fold plate : maps(some col), plan ; 21cm.
Limited ed. of 500 copies. — Bibl.: p.78.
ISBN 0-9505466-0-7 Pbk : £2.00
(B77-05309)

358'.13'0941 — Great Britain. Army. 457 Heavy Air Defence Regiment. Isle of Wight (Princess Beatrice's) Battery, to 1967
Quigley, D J. Princess Beatrice's Isle of Wight Rifles : a regimental history / by D.J. Quigley. — East Cowes (32 Gort Rd, E. Cowes, Isle of Wight) : The author, [1977]. — [3],51,[1]p,[12]p of plates : ill, ports ; 22cm.
Cover title: The Isle of Wight Rifles.
Sd : £1.05
(B77-17382)

358'.17 — Guided missiles. Expenditure by government. Great Britain. Parliament. House of Commons. Expenditure Committee. 'Guided weapons'. *Great Britain. Critical studies*
Great Britain. *Ministry of Defence.* Defence expenditure, government observations on the seventh report from the Expenditure Committee, House of Commons paper 597, session 1975-76 ... / Ministry of Defence. — London : H.M.S.O., [1976]. — 10p ; 25cm. — (Cmnd.6675)
ISBN 0-10-166750-7 Sd : £0.25
(B77-08299)

358'.17 — Guided missiles. Expenditure of government. *Great Britain. Inquiry reports*
Great Britain. *Parliament. House of Commons. Expenditure Committee.* Guided weapons : seventh report from the Expenditure Committee, session 1975-76, together with part of the minutes of the evidence taken before the Defence and External Affairs Sub-committee on 9th, 16th and 23rd March, on 7th and 13th April, on 18th and 25th May, and on 8th June, 1976. — London : H.M.S.O.
Vol.2 : Minutes of evidence and appendices. — [1976]. — viai,232p : 1 ill ; 25cm. — ([1975-76] H.C.597-II)
ISBN 0-10-008876-7 Pbk : £3.90
(B77-00117)

358'.17'540973 — Intercontinental ballistic missiles. Policies of United States. Air Force, 1945-1962
Beard, Edmund. Developing the ICBM : a study in bureaucratic politics / [by] Edmund Beard. — New York ; Guildford : Columbia University Press, 1976. — xvii,273p ; 24cm.
Bibl.: p.247-265. — Index.
ISBN 0-231-04012-1 : £10.41
(B77-03458)

358'.18 — Army operations by armoured combat vehicles, to 1976: Tanks
Humble, Richard. Tanks / [by] Richard Humble. — London : Weidenfeld and Nicolson, 1977. — 144p : ill(some col), ports ; 29cm.
Bibl.: p.142. — Index.
ISBN 0-297-77312-7 : £4.95
(B77-30082)

358'.18 — Military forces. Tank units. Tactics, 1939-1945
Macksey, Kenneth. Tank tactics / by Kenneth Macksey ; with illustrations by Allard Design Group. — London : Almark Publishing, 1976. — 72p : ill(some col), plans ; 21x22cm. — (The mechanics of war)
Cover title: Tank tactics, 1939-1945.
ISBN 0-85524-250-7 : £2.50
(B77-02877)

358.2 — MILITARY FORCES, ENGINEERS

358'.2 — Bombs. Disposal. *Personal observations*
Macdonald, Peter, *b.1928.* Stopping the clock : bomb disposal in the world of terrorism / [by] P.G. Macdonald. — London : Hale, 1977. — 159p,[12]p of plates : ill ; 23cm.
ISBN 0-7091-6191-3 : £3.95
(B77-22463)

358.3 — MILITARY TECHNICAL FORCES

358'.39 — Nuclear weapons. Proliferation. *Campaign for Nuclear Disarmament viewpoints*
Griffiths, David, *b.1952.* How many more? : the spread of nuclear weapons / by David Griffiths & Dan Smith. — London (29 Great James St., WC1N 3EY) : Campaign for Nuclear Disarmament, 1977. — [2],29,[1]p : ill ; 21cm. — (Campaign for Nuclear Disarmament. Pamphlets)
Sd : £0.30
(B77-32533)

358'.39 — Nuclear weapons. Proliferation. Policies of governments
Luttwak, Edward. Strategic power : military capabilities and political utility / [by] Edward N. Luttwak. — Beverly Hills ; London : Sage Publications [for] the Center for Strategic and International Studies, 1976. — 70p ; 22cm. — (The Washington papers ; 38) (A Sage policy paper)
ISBN 0-8039-0659-5 Pbk : £1.75
(B77-11708)

358'.39'0904 — Nuclear weapons, to 1976
Cox, John. Overkill : the story of modern weapons / [by] John Cox ; with a preface by Joseph Rotblat. — Harmondsworth [etc.] : Penguin, 1977. — 205p : ill, facsims, maps, ports ; 20cm. — (Peacock books)
Bibl.: p.194-197. — Index.
ISBN 0-14-047086-7 Pbk : £0.80
(B77-12944)

Cox, John. Overkill : the story of modern weapons / [by] John Cox ; with a preface by Joseph Rotblat. — Harmondsworth : Kestrel Books, 1977. — 205p : ill, facsims, maps, ports ; 21cm.
Bibl.: p.194-197. — Index.
ISBN 0-7226-5343-3 : £2.75
(B77-12945)

358.4 — AIR FORCES

358.4'00941 — Great Britain. Royal Air Force, 1946-1974
James, A E Trevenen. The Royal Air Force : the past 30 years / [by] A.E. Trevenen James. — London : Macdonald and Jane's, 1976. — 230p, [16]p of plates : ill ; 24cm.
Bibl.: p.216-218. — Index.
ISBN 0-356-08425-6 : £5.95
(B77-02149)

358.4'00941 — Museums. *London. Barnet (London Borough). Royal Air Force Museum. Gifts of land by British government. Proposals*
Great Britain. *Treasury.* Copy of a Treasury minute dated 31st August 1977 concerning the conditional gift of land to the Trustees of the Royal Air Force Museum ... — London : H.M.S.O., [1977]. — Sheet([2]p) ; 25x16cm. — (Cmnd.6921)
ISBN 0-10-169210-2 : £0.10
(B77-28514)

358.4'00941 — Museums. *Somerset. Yeovilton. Fleet Air Arm Museum. Gift of Yeovilton RNAS Station by Great Britain. Ministry of Defence. Proposals*
Great Britain. *Treasury.* Copy of a Treasury minute dated 14th June 1977 concerning the conditional gift of land and buildings to the Trustees of the Fleet Air Arm Museum. — London : H.M.S.O., [1977]. — Sheet ([2]p) ; 25x16cm. — (Cmnd.6829)
ISBN 0-10-168290-5 : £0.10
(B77-26217)

358.4'00943 — Germany. Luftwaffe, 1939-1945
Price, Alfred. Luftwaffe handbook, 1939-1945 / [by] Alfred Price. — London : I. Allan, 1977. — 111p : ill, maps, plans, ports ; 24cm.
ISBN 0-7110-0632-6 : £3.50
(B77-21778)

358.4'00947 — Union of Soviet Socialist Republics. Voenno-vozdushnye sily, to 1976
Boyd, Alexander. The Soviet Air Force since 1918 / [by] Alexander Boyd. — London : Macdonald and Jane's, 1977. — xix,259p,[12]p of plates : ill, map, ports ; 24cm.
Bibl.: p.246-253. — Index.
ISBN 0-356-08288-1 : £6.50
(B77-18025)

358.4'11'4 — Air forces. Personnel. Insignia, 1939-1945
Rosignoli, Guido. Air Force badges and insignia of World War 2 / [by] Guido Rosignoli. — Poole : Blandford Press, 1976. — 200p : ill(chiefly col) ; 20cm. — ([Blandford colour series])
Index.
ISBN 0-7137-0777-1 : £3.25
(B77-04044)

358.4'13'320924 — Germany. Luftwaffe. Milch, Erhard. *Biographies*
Irving, David. The rise and fall of the Luftwaffe : the life of Luftwaffe Marshal Erhard Milch / [by] David Irving. — London : Futura Publications, 1976. — xviii,451p,[8]p of plates : ill, ports ; 18cm.
Originally published: London : Weidenfeld and Nicolson, 1973. — Bibl.: p.338-348. — Index.
ISBN 0-86007-253-3 Pbk : £1.50
(B77-08912)

358.4'13'320924 — Great Britain. Royal Air Force. Embry, Sir Basil. *Autobiographies*
Embry, *Sir* Basil. Mission completed / [by] Sir Basil Embry. — London [etc.] : White Lion Publishers, 1976. — 350p,leaf of plate,[16]p of plates : ill, maps, ports ; 23cm.
Originally published: London : Methuen, 1957. — Index.
ISBN 0-7274-0260-9 : £4.95
(B77-33700)

358.4'13'320924 — Great Britain. Royal Air Force. Joubert de la Ferté, Sir Philip. *Autobiographies*
Joubert de la Ferté, *Sir* Philip. The fated sky / [by] Sir Philip Joubert de la Ferté. — London [etc.] : White Lion Publishers, 1977. — 280p, [14]p of plates,leaf of plate : ill, maps, ports ; 23cm.
Originally published: London : Hutchinson, 1952. — Index.
ISBN 0-7274-0249-8 : £5.25
(B77-21030)

358.4'14'0943 — Air operations by Germany. Luftwaffe, 1930-1945
Wood, Tony. Hitler's Luftwaffe : a pictorial history and technical encyclopedia of Hitler's air power in World War 2 / [by] Tony Wood, Bill Gunston. — London (27 Old Gloucester St., W.C.1) : Salamander Books, 1977. — 248p : ill(chiefly col), map, plans, ports ; 31cm.
Index.
ISBN 0-86101-005-1 : £5.95
(B77-33701)

358.4'14'0994 — Air operations by Australia. Royal Australian Air Force, to 1975
Parnell, N M. Australian air force since 1911 / [by] N.M. Parnell & C.A. Lynch. — Sydney [etc.] ; London : A.H. and A.W. Reed, 1976. — 216p : ill, map(on lining paper), ports ; 29cm.
Bibl.: p.210. — Index.
ISBN 0-589-07153-x : £13.00
(B77-24807)

358.4'17'0942453 — Great Britain. Royal Air Force. Aerodromes: Shawbury RAF Station, to 1976
Ferguson, Aldon Patrick. A history of Royal Air Force, Shawbury / by Aldon P. Ferguson. — Liverpool (Room 14, Hangar No.2, Liverpool Airport, Liverpool L24 2QE) : Merseyside Aviation Society Ltd, 1977. — 59p : ill, maps ; 22cm. — (Military airfield history ; no.1)
ISBN 0-902420-20-8 Sd : £1.00
(B77-33702)

358.4'18'3 — General Dynamics F-111 aeroplanes. Development. Policies of government. Decision making. *United States, 1961-1972*
Coulam, Robert F. Illusions of choice : the F-111 and the problem of weapons acquisition reform / [by] Robert F. Coulam. — Princeton, N.J. ; Guildford : Princeton University Press, 1977. — xiii,432,[1]p : ill ; 23cm.
Bibl.: p.395-413. — Index.
ISBN 0-691-07583-2 : £16.20
(B77-26949)

358.4'18'3 — Great Britain. Royal Air Force. Aeroplanes, 1939-1945. Camouflage & markings
British aviation colours of World War Two : the official camouflage, colours & markings of RAF aircraft, 1939-1945. — London : Arms and Armour Press [etc.], 1976. — [6],56,[1]p,fold plate : ill(some col) ; 23cm. — (Royal Air Force Museum. RAF Museum series ; vol.3)
Facsimile reprints. — 'The material ... originally appeared in four publications: a) Air Publication 2656A External Colour of Aircraft, 1944 b) Air Ministry Orders, 1939-1945, c) Ministry of Aircraft Production Colour Standards, d) Ministry of Supply Standards of Colour Gloss and Smoothness for Aircraft Finishes ... produced for official use and internal purposes by the Air Ministry and Ministry of Supply' - title page verso.
ISBN 0-85368-271-2 : £4.95
(B77-02150)

358.4'18'3 — United States. Air Force. Military aircraft. Serial numbers, 1946-1977. *Lists*
Merseyside Aviation Society. United States Air Force serials, 1946 to 1977 / [Merseyside Aviation Society]. — 5th ed. / edited by Peter A. Danby. — Merseyside (Room 14, Hangar 2, Liverpool Airport, Merseyside L24 8QE) : Merseyside Aviation Society, 1977. — 112p : ill ; 21cm.
Previous ed.: 1974.
ISBN 0-902420-18-6 Sd : Unpriced
(B77-33134)

358.4'2'0941 — Great Britain. Royal Air Force. Bomber squadrons, to 1975
Moyes, Philip John Richard. Bomber squadrons of the RAF and their aircraft / [by] Philip J.R. Moyes. — New ed. — London : Macdonald and Jane's, 1976. — 399p : ill, ports ; 29cm.
Previous ed.: London : Macdonald and Co., 1964. — Bibl.: p.378. — Index.
ISBN 0-354-01027-1 : £12.50
(B77-05976)

358.4'3 — Air operations by Supermarine Spitfire aeroplanes, to 1954
Price, Alfred. Spitfire : a documentary history / [by] Alfred Price. — London : Macdonald and Jane's, 1977. — 159p : ill, facsims, map, ports ; 29cm.
Bibl.: p.158.
ISBN 0-354-01077-8 : £5.95
(B77-24808)

358.4'3'0941 — Great Britain. Royal Air Force. Fighter squadrons, to 1975
Rawlings, John Dunstan Richard. Fighter squadrons of the RAF and their aircraft / [by] John D.R. Rawlings. — New revised ed. — London : Macdonald and Jane's, 1976. — 572p : ill, coats of arms ; 29cm.
Previous ed.: London : Macdonald and Co., 1969. — Bibl.: p.544-545. — Index.
ISBN 0-354-01028-x : £12.50
(B77-05977)

359 — NAVAL FORCES

359 — Foreign relations. Role of navies
Booth, Ken. Navies and foreign policy / [by] K. Booth. — London : Croom Helm [etc.], 1977. — 294p : 1 ill ; 23cm.
Index.
ISBN 0-85664-323-8 : £9.95
(B77-11709)

359'.009 — Naval warfare, to 1945
Mordal, Jacques. Twenty-five centuries of sea warfare / [by] Jacques Mordal ; translated [from the French] by Len Ortzen ; with drawings and maps by Michel Fontaine. — London : Futura Publications, 1976. — xix, 428p,[16]p of plates : ill, maps, plans, ports ; 18cm.
Cover title: 25 centuries of sea warfare. — This translation originally published: London : Souvenir Press, 1965. — Translation of: 'Vingt-cinq siècles de guerre sur mer'. Paris : Laffont, 1959. — Index.
ISBN 0-86007-303-3 Pbk : £0.95
(B77-10287)

359'.00947 — Union of Soviet Socialist Republics. Voenno-morskoĭ flot. *Conference proceedings*
Seminar on Soviet Naval Developments, *3rd, Dalhousie University, 1974.* Soviet naval influence : domestic and foreign dimensions / edited by Michael MccGwire, John McDonnell. — New York ; London : Praeger for the Centre for Foreign Policy Studies Department of Political Science, Dalhousie University, 1977. — xxxvi,660p : ill, maps ; 25cm. — (Praeger special studies in international politics and government)
'This book derives from the third annual seminar on Soviet naval developments held at Dalhousie University, Halifax, Nova Scotia, in September 1974' - Introduction.
ISBN 0-275-56290-5 : £23.00
(B77-26950)

359'.00947 — Union of Soviet Socialist Republics. Voenno-morskoĭ flot, to 1976
Morris, Eric. The Russian navy : myth and reality / [by] Eric Morris. — London : Hamilton, 1977. — xiii,150p : map(on lining papers) ; 22cm.
Bibl.: p.145. — Index.
ISBN 0-241-89333-x : £5.95
(B77-18646)

359'.03'0941 — Great Britain. Naval policies. Effects of technological change, 1860-1939
Technical change and British naval policy, 1860-1939 / edited by Bryan Ranft. — London [etc.] : Hodder and Stoughton, 1977. — xii, 178p ; 25cm.
Bibl.: p.147-148. — Index.
ISBN 0-340-21893-2 : £8.50
(B77-22464)

359.1'0941 — Great Britain. Royal Navy. Sailors. Naval life, 1837-1901
Winton, John. Hurrah for the life of a sailor! : life on the lower-deck of the Victorian Navy / [by] John Winton. — London : Joseph, 1977. — 320p : ill, facsims, music, ports ; 25cm.
Bibl.: p.302-314. — Index.
ISBN 0-7181-1580-5 : £6.50
(B77-26951)

359.1'15 — Great Britain. Royal Navy. Ex-servicemen. Financial assistance. Organisations: Greenwich Hospital. *Accounts*
Greenwich Hospital and Travers Foundation accounts ... for the year ended 31st March ... — London : H.M.S.O.
1975-76. — [1977]. — 10p ; 25cm. — ([1976-77 H.C.]225)
ISBN 0-10-222577-x Sd : £0.25
(B77-16798)

359.1'3325 — United States. Navy. Offenders. Treatment. Effects of racial discrimination against negro personnel
Perry, Ronald W. Racial discrimination and military justice / [by] Ronald W. Perry. — New York [etc.] ; London : Praeger, 1977. — xv,103p : 1 ill ; 25cm. — (Praeger special studies in US economic, social and political issues)
Bibl.: p.85-97. — Index.
ISBN 0-275-24180-7 : £9.25
(B77-16282)

359.1'4'0941 — Great Britain. Royal Navy. Uniforms, 1790-1970
Wilkinson-Latham, Robert John. The Royal Navy, 1790-1970 / text by Robert Wilkinson-Latham ; colour plates by G.A. Embleton. — London : Osprey Publishing, 1977. — 40p,[8]p of plates : ill(some col), ports ; 25cm. — (Men-at-arms series)
Text accompanying plates in English, French and German.
ISBN 0-85045-248-1 Pbk : £1.95
(B77-26218)

359.1'4'0941 — Great Britain. Royal Navy. Uniforms, ca 1805
Fabb, John. The uniforms of Trafalgar / [by] John Fabb and Jack Cassin-Scott. — London : Batsford, 1977. — 96p,[4]p of plates : ill(some col), ports ; 26cm.
Bibl.: p.95. — Index.
ISBN 0-7134-0218-0 : £4.50
ISBN 0-7134-0219-9 Pbk : £2.95
Also classified at 359.1'4'0944; 359.1'4'0946
(B77-25499)

359.1'4'0944 — France. Marine. Uniforms, ca 1805
Fabb, John. The uniforms of Trafalgar / [by] John Fabb and Jack Cassin-Scott. — London : Batsford, 1977. — 96p,[4]p of plates : ill(some col), ports ; 26cm.
Bibl.: p.95. — Index.
ISBN 0-7134-0218-0 : £4.50
ISBN 0-7134-0219-9 Pbk : £2.95
Primary classification 359.1'4'0941
(B77-25499)

359.1'4'0946 — Spain. Marina. Uniforms, ca 1805
Fabb, John. The uniforms of Trafalgar / [by] John Fabb and Jack Cassin-Scott. — London : Batsford, 1977. — 96p,[4]p of plates : ill(some col), ports ; 26cm.
Bibl.: p.95. — Index.
ISBN 0-7134-0218-0 : £4.50
ISBN 0-7134-0219-9 Pbk : £2.95
Primary classification 359.1'4'0941
(B77-25499)

359.3'2 — Naval operations by galleons, to ca 1850. *Juvenile literature*
Rutland, Jonathan Patrick. See inside a galleon / [author Jonathan Rutland] ; [illustrations John Berry, Michael Trim]. — London : Hutchinson, 1977. — 4-29p : ill(chiefly col), col map ; 29cm. — (See inside)
Bibl.: p.28. — Index.
ISBN 0-09-128670-0 : £1.50
(B77-32534)

359.3'2'530941 — Naval operations by Great Britain. Royal Navy. Cruisers: Belfast (Ship), to 1976. *Juvenile literature*
Schofield, Roy. The story of HMS Belfast / [pictures by Roy Schofield and story by Joe Martin]. — Cheam (39 Northey Ave., Cheam, Surrey) : Travel About Books, 1977. — [32]p : ill(some col), maps ; 15cm.
ISBN 0-905810-01-5 Sd : £0.40
(B77-32535)

359.3'2'540941 — Naval operations by Great Britain. Royal Navy, 1875-1973. Destroyers
Brookes, Ewart. Destroyer / [by] Ewart Brookes. — Revised ed. / with additional material by Douglas Reeman. — London : Arrow Books, 1977. — 256p,[16]p of plates : ill ; 18cm.
This ed. originally published: 1973. — Bibl.: p.246. — Index. — Previous control number ISBN 0-09-906800-1.
Pbk : £0.75
ISBN 0-09-906800-1
(B77-24809)

359.3'2'5709 — Naval operations by submarines, to 1976
Garrett, Richard. Submarines / [by] Richard Garrett. — London : Weidenfeld and Nicolson, 1977. — 143p : ill(some col), facsims(chiefly col), ports ; 29cm.
Ill. on lining papers. — Bibl.: p.140. — Index.
ISBN 0-297-77276-7 : £4.95
(B77-24810)

359.3'3'10922 — Naval operations. Admirals, 1536-1969. *Biographies*
Hough, Richard. The great admirals / [by] Richard Hough. — London : Weidenfeld and Nicolson, 1977. — 271p : ill(some col), facsim, maps, ports(some col) ; 26cm.
Ill. on lining papers. — Bibl.: p.267. — Index.
ISBN 0-297-77308-9 : £6.50
(B77-23254)

359.3'3'10924 — Great Britain. Admiralty. Beaufort, Sir Francis. *Biographies*
Friendly, Alfred. Beaufort of the Admiralty : the life of Sir Francis Beaufort, 1774-1857 / [by] Alfred Friendly. — London : Hutchinson, 1977. — 362p,[8]p of plates : ill, chart, facsims, maps, plans, ports ; 24cm.
Chart on lining papers. — Bibl.: p.347-352. — Index.
ISBN 0-09-128500-3 : £7.50
(B77-23255)

359.3'32 — Russia. Flot. Finnish officers. Recruitment, 1809-1917
Screen, John Ernest Oliver. The entry of Finnish officers into Russian military service, 1809-1917 / [by] J.E.O. Screen. — London ([c/o School of Slavonic and East European Studies, University of London, Senate House, Malet St., WC1E 7HU]) : [The author], 1976. — [3],338p : ill ; 30cm.
Bibl.: p.308-322.
Pbk : Unpriced
Primary classification 355.3'32
(B77-25498)

359.3'32'0922 — Great Britain. Royal Navy. Captains, 1795-1839
Kennedy, Ludovic. Nelson and his captains / [by] Ludovic Kennedy. — New revised ed. — [London] : Fontana, 1976. — 353p,[4]p of plates : ill, maps, ports ; 18cm.
This ed. originally published: 1975. — Bibl.: p.348-350. — Index.
ISBN 0-00-633719-8 Pbk : £1.00
Also classified at 359.3'32'0924
(B77-02151)

359.3'3'20924 — Great Britain. Royal Navy. Fisher, John Arbuthnot, Baron Fisher. *Biographies*
Hough, Richard. First Sea Lord : an authorized biography of Admiral Lord Fisher / [by] Richard Hough. — [2nd ed.]. — London : Severn House : [Distributed by Hutchinson], 1977. — 3-392p,24p of plates : ill, facsims, ports ; 23cm.
Previous ed.: London : Allen and Unwin, 1969. — Index.
ISBN 0-7278-0293-3 : £6.00
(B77-29304)

359.3'3'20924 — Great Britain. Royal Navy. Le Fanu, Sir Michael. *Biographies*
Baker, Richard, *b.1925.* Dry Ginger : the biography of Admiral of the Fleet Sir Michael Le Fanu, GCB, DSC / [by] Richard Baker. — London : W.H. Allen, 1977. — 254p,leaf of plate,[24]p of plates : ill, ports ; 23cm.
Bibl.: p.247. — Index.
ISBN 0-491-01788-x : £5.00
(B77-15765)

359.3'32'0924 — Great Britain. Royal Navy. Nelson, Horatio, Viscount Nelson
Kennedy, Ludovic. Nelson and his captains / [by] Ludovic Kennedy. — New revised ed. — [London] : Fontana, 1976. — 353p,[4]p of plates : ill, maps, ports ; 18cm.
This ed. originally published: 1975. — Bibl.: p.348-350. — Index.
ISBN 0-00-633719-8 Pbk : £1.00
Primary classification 359.3'32'0922
(B77-02151)

359.3'32'0924 — Great Britain. Royal Navy. Nelson, Horatio, Viscount Nelson. *Biographies*
Bradford, Ernle. Nelson : the essential hero / [by] Ernle Bradford. — London [etc.] : Macmillan, 1977. — 368p,[8]p of plates : ill, maps, plans, ports ; 25cm.
Index.
ISBN 0-333-18561-7 : £6.50
(B77-20144)

Hattersley, Roy. Nelson / [by] Roy Hattersley. — London : Omega, 1976. — 144p,[32]p of plates : ill, facsims, plans, ports ; 20cm. — (The great commanders) (A contact book)
Originally published: London : Weidenfeld and Nicolson, 1974. — Bibl.: p.140-141. — Index.
ISBN 0-86007-731-4 Pbk : £0.95
(B77-08300)

359.3'32'0924 — Great Britain. Royal Navy. Oram, Harry Percy Kendall. *Autobiographies*
Oram, Harry Percy Kendall. Ready for sea / [by] H.P.K. Oram. — London : Futura Publications, 1976. — [5],250p,[8]p of plates : ill, plans, ports ; 18cm.
Originally published: London : Seeley, 1974. — Index.
ISBN 0-86007-302-5 Pbk : £0.75
(B77-09620)

359.3'3'20924 — Great Britain. Royal Navy. Packer, Sir Herbert. *Biographies*
Packer, Joy, *Lady.* Deep as the sea / [by] Joy Packer. — London : Corgi, 1977. — 331p ; 18cm.
Originally published: Johannesburg : Methuen, 1975 ; London : Eyre Methuen, 1976.
ISBN 0-552-10488-4 Pbk : £0.95
(B77-27759)

359.3'32'0941 — Great Britain. Royal Navy. Officers. *Registers*
The **Navy** list. — London : H.M.S.O.
1976. Appendix : Rates of pay, conditions of retirement, entry regulations, etc., etc. (corrected to June). — 1976. — 184p ; 22cm.
ISBN 0-11-772132-8 Pbk : £3.00
(B77-05978)

1977. — 1977. — x,568,21p ; 21cm.
Index.
ISBN 0-11-771581-6 Pbk : £8.00
(B77-16283)

1977. Appendix : Rates of pay, conditions of retirement, entry regulations, etc. etc. (corrected to June). — 1977. — 200p ; 22cm.
ISBN 0-11-772133-6 Pbk : £3.00
(B77-33135)

359.3'38'0924 — Great Britain. Royal Navy. Steel, Arthur. *Autobiographies*
Steel, Arthur. My lifetime story / [by] Arthur Steel. — Ilfracombe : Stockwell.
Book 1. — 1977. — 41p ; 18cm.
ISBN 0-7223-1000-5 Pbk : £0.95
(B77-12384)

359.3'48'0941 — Great Britain. Royal Navy. Women's Royal Naval Service, to 1977
Mason, Ursula Stuart. The Wrens, 1917-77 : a history of the Women's Royal Naval Service / by Ursula Stuart Mason ; with a foreword by Prince Philip, Duke of Edinburgh. — Reading : Educational Explorers, 1977. — 160p : ill, ports ; 22cm.
Bibl.: p.156. — Index.
ISBN 0-85225-774-0 : £4.95 : CIP rev.
ISBN 0-85225-901-8 Pbk : £2.95
(B77-21779)

359.4'09 — Naval operations, to 1945
Pemsel, Helmut. Atlas of naval warfare : an atlas and chronology of conflict at sea from earliest times to the present day / [by] Helmut Pemsel ; translated [from the German] by D.G. Smith. — London [etc.] : Arms and Armour Press, 1977. — 176p : ill, maps, plans ; 26cm.
Translation of: 'Von Salamis bis Okinawa'. München : Lehmann, 1975. — Bibl.: p.165-166. — Index.
ISBN 0-85368-351-4 : £10.95 : CIP rev.
(B77-22242)

359.4'09'04 — Naval operations, 1900-1976
Naval warfare in the twentieth century, 1900-1945 : essays in honour of Arthur Marder / edited by Gerald Jordan. — London : Croom Helm [etc.], 1977. — 243p ; 23cm.
Bibl.: p.233-234. — Index.
ISBN 0-85664-459-5 : £6.95
(B77-21031)

361 — WELFARE WORK
Butrym, Zofia. The nature of social work / [by] Zofia T. Butrym. — London [etc.] : Macmillan, 1976. — xi,167p ; 23cm.
Index.
ISBN 0-333-19124-2 : £7.95
ISBN 0-333-19703-8 Pbk : £3.95
(B77-00118)

Integrating social work methods / edited by Harry Specht and Anne Vickery, with ... [others]. — London : Allen and Unwin, 1977. — 3-260p : ill ; 23cm. — (National Institute for Social Work. Social services library ; no.31)
Index.
ISBN 0-04-361024-2 : £6.50
ISBN 0-04-361025-0 Pbk : £2.95
(B77-19276)

Loewenberg, F M. Fundamentals of social intervention : core concepts and skills for social work practice / [by] F.M. Loewenberg. — New York ; Guildford : Columbia University Press, 1977. — xv,374p ; 24cm.
Bibl.: p.353-364. — Index.
ISBN 0-231-03611-6 : £9.50
(B77-10288)

Timms, Noel. Perspectives in social work / [by] Noel and Rita Timms ; illustrated by Chris Blow. — London [etc.] : Routledge and Kegan Paul, 1977. — vii,233p ; 23cm.
Bibl.: p.221-233.
ISBN 0-7100-8505-2 : £4.95
ISBN 0-7100-8519-2 Pbk : £2.50
(B77-18647)

361 — Community facilities: Converted buses. *Manuals*
Inter-Action Advisory Service. Converting a bus / [Inter-Action Advisory Service] ; [researched and written by Anthony Kendall]. — London (14 Talacre Rd, N.W.5) : Inter-Action Inprint, 1974. — [1],22,[1]p : plans ; 15x21cm. — (Inter-Action Advisory Service. Handbooks ; 1)
ISBN 0-904571-00-9 Sd : £0.30
(B77-20145)

361 — Community work. Networks
Human services and resource networks / [by] Seymour B. Sarason ... [et al.]. — San Francisco [etc.] ; London : Jossey-Bass, 1977. — xvii,201p ; 24cm. — (The Jossey-Bass behavioral science series)
Bibl.: p.189-195. — Index.
ISBN 0-87589-309-0 : £10.50
(B77-30084)

361 — Social services. *Comparative studies*
Meeting human needs. — Beverly Hills ; London : Sage Publications.
2 : Additional perspectives from thirteen countries / editors Daniel Thursz and Joseph L. Vigilante. — 1976. — 286p : ill ; 24cm. — (Social service delivery systems ; vol.2)
Bibl. — Index.
ISBN 0-8039-0590-4 : £10.00
ISBN 0-8039-0591-2 Pbk : £4.50
(B77-14639)

361 — Social services. Policies. *Conference proceedings*
International Conference on Social Welfare, *18th, San Juan, Puerto Rico, 1976.* The struggle for equal opportunity : strategies for social welfare action : proceedings of the XVIIIth International Conference on Social Welfare, San Juan, Puerto Rico, July 18-24, 1976. — New York ; London : Columbia University Press for the International Council on Social Welfare, 1977. — ix,256p ; 24cm.
ISBN 0-231-04346-5 : £12.50
ISBN 0-231-04347-3 Pbk : Unpriced
(B77-30085)

361 — Welfare work. Implications of philosophical theories of personal identity
Ragg, Nicholas M. People not cases : a philosophical approach to social work / [by] Nicholas M. Ragg. — London [etc.] : Routledge and Kegan Paul, 1977. — viii,159p ; 23cm. — (The international library of welfare and philosophy)
Bibl.: p.153-155. — Index.
ISBN 0-7100-8482-x : £4.25
(B77-15204)

361 — Welfare work. Related to sociology
Brewster, Bob. Sociology and social work : new perspectives for practitioners / [by] Bob Brewster and John Whiteford. — Hatfield (c/o G. Newfield, School of Social Sciences, The Hatfield Polytechnic, P.O. Box 109, Hatfield, Herts. AL10 9AB) : Organisation of Sociologists in Polytechnics and Cognate Institutions, 1976. — [2],16p ; 21cm. — (Organisation of Sociologists in Polytechnics and Cognate Institutions. SIP papers ; no.2)
' ... revised version of a paper given to the Annual Conference of SIP at Lanchester Polytechnic in June 1976' - note.
ISBN 0-905509-01-3 Sd : £0.50(free to members)
Primary classification 301
(B77-10168)

361'.0025'41 — Welfare services. *Great Britain. Directories*
Knight, Sally. Help! I need somebody : a guide to national associations for people in need / compiled by Sally Knight. — 2nd ed. — Hertford (County Hall, Hertford SG13 8EJ) : Hertfordshire Library Service, 1977. — [3],30,[3]p ; 21cm.
Previous ed.: 1975. — Index.
ISBN 0-901354-10-4 Sd : £0.30 : CIP rev.
(B77-24811)

361'.0025'417 — Social services. *Ireland (Republic). Directories. For trade unionism*
Irish Transport and General Workers' Union. *Library.* Some information sources and literature of relevance to trade unions / ITGWU, Library, Information Section. — [Dublin] ([10 Palmerston Park, Rathmines, Dublin 6]) : [The Library], 1976. — [1],ii,10 leaves ; 30cm.
Sd : Unpriced
(B77-24100)

361'.0025'4239 — Social services. *Avon. Directories*
Avon *(County). Council.* A-Z pocket guide to services / County of Avon. — Revised ed. — Bristol ([P.O. Box 11], Avon House, The Haymarket, Bristol [BS99 7DE]) : County Director of Public Relations and Publicity, 1976. — [2],87p ; 11x16cm. — (Pocket guide ; no.1 ISSN 0307-5060)
Cover title. — Previous ed.: 1974.
Pbk : Unpriced
(B77-01278)

361'.0025'429 — Welfare services. Organisations. *Wales. Directories. For community action*
Community action in Wales : directory. — Caerphilly (Crescent Rd, Caerphilly, Mid-Glamorgan CF8 1XL) : Council of Social Service for Wales Inc.
'76-77. — [1976]. — [1],25 leaves ; 30cm.
ISBN 0-9500450-3-9 Sd : £0.50
ISSN 0309-1163
(B77-02878)

361'.005 — Social services. *Periodicals. For Scottish community organisations*
In gear : a newsletter of the Community Organisations Group, Scotland. — Edinburgh (19 Claremont Cres., Edinburgh EH7 4QD) : Scottish Council of Social Service.
Supersedes: Scottish community news.
No.1- ; July 1976-. — 1976-. — 30cm.
Quarterly. — [3],10p. in 1st issue.
Sd : £0.20
ISSN 0309-4855
(B77-24101)

361'.006'142 — Personal welfare services. Organisations. *England. Personal Social Services Council. Reports, surveys. Serials*
Personal Social Services Council. Report / Personal Social Services Council. — London (2 Torrington Place, WC1E 7HN) : The Council.
1976. — [1977]. — [2],17,[1]p ; 30cm.
ISBN 0-905250-04-4 Sd : £0.45
(B77-11710)

361'.007 — Social services. Information sources. *Great Britain. For handicapped persons*
Macmorland, Barbara. An ABC of services and information for disabled people / [by] Barbara Macmorland. — [3rd ed.]. — London (28 Commercial St., E1 6LR) : Disablement Income Group Charitable Trust, 1976. — [5],84,[5]p ; 21cm.
Previous ed.: 1975. — Index.
ISBN 0-905179-02-1 Sd : £1.00
(B77-11148)

361'.007'1141 — Community workers. Training. *Great Britain*
Community work : learning and supervision / edited by Catherine Briscoe and David N. Thomas. — London : Allen and Unwin, 1977. — 3-190p : ill ; 23cm. — (National Institute for Social Work. Social services library ; no.32)
Bibl. — Index.
ISBN 0-04-361026-9 : £7.95
ISBN 0-04-361027-7 Pbk : £3.95
(B77-28515)

361'.007'1141 — Social services. Personnel. Training. *Great Britain*
Working Party on Manpower and Training for the Social Services. Manpower and training for the social services : report of the Working Party [on Manpower and Training for the Social Services ; for the] Department of Health and Social Security. — London : H.M.S.O., 1976. — iv,178p : ill ; 25cm.
ISBN 0-11-320221-0 Pbk : £2.00
Also classified at 331.1'1
(B77-06567)

361'.05 — Residential institutions for socially disadvantaged persons. *Scotland, 1847-1901*
Harvey, Colin. Ha'penny help : a record of social improvement in Victorian Scotland / by Colin Harvey. — Milngavie (163 Mugdock Rd, Milngavie, Dunbartonshire) : Heatherbank Press, 1976. — viii,197p : ill, facsims, plans, ports ; 21cm.
ISBN 0-905192-02-8 Pbk : £2.50
(B77-08913)

361'.06 — Advice centres. *Great Britain. Reports, surveys*
National Consumer Council. The fourth right of citizenship : a review of local advice services / National Consumer Council. — London (18 Queen Anne's Gate, SW1H 9AA) : The Council, 1977. — [2],iv,80p : maps ; 21cm. — (Discussion paper ; 4)
ISBN 0-905653-10-6 Pbk : £0.75
(B77-33703)

361'.06 — Community advice centres. *Leicestershire. Braunstone. Braunstone Advice Centre, to 1974. Reports, surveys*
Browse, Barbara. Braunstone Advice Centre : the work of a community advice centre, 1968-1974 / by Barbara Browse. — Leicester (26 Severn St., Leicester LE2) : Leicester Family Service Unit, 1976. — [3],35p ; 30cm.
ISBN 0-905815-00-9 Sd : £0.50
(B77-04045)

361.3 — WELFARE WORK. CASEWORK
Tilbury, D E F. Casework in context : a basis for practice / by D.E.F. Tilbury. — Oxford [etc.] : Pergamon, 1977. — ix,338p : ill ; 22cm. — (Social work series) (Pergamon international library)
Bibl. — Index.
ISBN 0-08-019744-2 : £8.00
ISBN 0-08-019743-4 Pbk : £5.00
(B77-24102)

361.3 — Welfare work. Casework. Task-centred treatment. *Conference proceedings*
Conference on Applications of Task-Centered Treatment, *University of Chicago, 1975.* Task-centered practice / edited by William J. Reid, Laura Epstein. — New York ; Guildford : Columbia University Press, 1977. — xiii,304p : forms ; 24cm.
'... the Conference on Applications of Task-Centered Treatment, held at the University of Chicago in 1975' - Preface. — Bibl. — Index.
ISBN 0-231-04072-5 : £9.35
(B77-12946)

361.3 — Welfare work. Interpersonal relationships. Communication
Day, Peter Russell. Methods of learning communication skills / by P.R. Day. — Oxford [etc.] : Pergamon, 1977. — vii,329p : ill ; 22cm. — (Pergamon international library : social work series)
Bibl.: p.317-323. — Index.
ISBN 0-08-018954-7 : £10.50
ISBN 0-08-018953-9 Pbk : £7.50
(B77-29305)

361.3'2 — Counselling
Concepts of counselling : papers prepared by a working party of the Standing Conference for the Advancement of Counselling / edited by T.D. Vaughan. — London : Bedford Square Press, 1976. — 95,[1]p ; 23cm.
Bibl.
ISBN 0-7199-0909-0 : £2.50
ISBN 0-7199-0908-2 Pbk : £1.50
(B77-04046)

Hansen, James Charles. Counseling : theory and process / [by] James C. Hansen, Richard R. Stevic, Richard W. Warner, Jr. — 2nd ed. — Boston, Mass. ; London [etc.] : Allyn and Bacon, 1977. — x,538p : ill ; 25cm.
Previous ed.: 1972. — Bibl. — Index.
ISBN 0-205-05626-1 : Unpriced
(B77-05979)

361.3'2 — Welfare workers. Clients. Behaviour. Effects of expectations of welfare workers
Smale, Gerald G. Prophecy, behaviour and change : an examination of self-fulfilling prophecies in helping relationships / [by] Gerald G. Smale. — London [etc.] : Routledge and Kegan Paul, 1977. — xi,103p ; 20cm. — (Library of social work ISSN 0305-4381)
Bibl.: p.97-103.
ISBN 0-7100-8470-6 : £3.50
(B77-09621)

361.4 — SOCIAL GROUP WORK
361.4 — Group counselling
Ohlsen, Merle Marvel. Group counseling / [by] Merle M. Ohlsen. — 2nd ed. — New York ; London [etc.] : Holt, Rinehart and Winston, 1977. — xiii,305p ; 25cm.
Previous ed.: 1970. — Bibl. — Index.
ISBN 0-03-089848-x : £7.50
(B77-21032)

361.4'0941 — Welfare work: Group work. *Great Britain. Manuals*
Groups : a handbook / by FSU groupworkers ; [compiled by Martin Jenkins et al. ; graphics Carolyn Gorney et al.]. — [London] ([207 Old Marylebone Rd, N.W.1]) : Family Service Units, 1976. — [2],28,[1]p : ill ; 20x29cm.
Bibl.: p.[1].
ISBN 0-905175-02-6 Sd : £0.50
(B77-04047)

361.5 — DISASTER RELIEF SERVICES
361.5 — Disaster relief
Skeet, Muriel Hilda. Manual for disaster relief work / [by] Muriel Skeet ; foreword by John H. Knowles. — Edinburgh [etc.] : Churchill Livingstone, 1977. — xii,412p : ill ; 24cm.
Bibl.: p.402-405. — Index.
ISBN 0-443-01493-0 : £12.00
(B77-24103)

361.5 — International disaster relief services. *Research reports*
Green, Stephen. International disaster relief : toward a responsive system / [by] Stephen Green. — New York [etc.] ; London : McGraw-Hill, 1977. — xvii,101,[1]p : 2 ill ; 24cm. — (1980s Project. Studies)
Bibl.: p.93-94. — Index.
ISBN 0-07-024287-9 : £5.95
ISBN 0-07-024288-7 Pbk : £2.95
(B77-27760)

361.5'05 — Disaster relief. *Periodicals*
Disasters : the international journal of disaster studies and practice. — Oxford [etc.] : Pergamon.
Vol.1, no.1- ; 1977-. — 1977-. — ill, maps ; 28cm.
Quarterly. — 75p. in 1st issue. — Bibl.
Pbk : Unpriced
ISSN 0361-3666
(B77-10289)

361.5'8 — Lifeboat services. *Ireland. Serials*
Irish lifeboats. — Dublin (10 Merrion Sq., Dublin 2) : Royal National Lifeboat Institution.
1977 : 26th year of issue / editor Brian Clark. — [1977]. — xxxvi,92p : ill(some col), facsim, ports ; 30cm.
ISBN 0-903232-02-2 Sd : £1.00
(B77-15766)

361.5'8 — Lifeboat services. *Lincolnshire. Skegness, to 1977*
Major, F S W. A century and a half of Skegness lifeboats : an account of Skegness Lifeboat Station / from the stories written and collected by F.S.W. Major. — Skegness (c/o C.H. Major & Co., Ltd, 41 Lumley Rd, Skegness, Lincs.) : B.S. Major, 1977. — viii,74p : ill, map, ports ; 21cm.
ISBN 0-9505755-0-x Pbk : £0.75
(B77-16284)

361.5'8 — Lifeboat services. *Scotland. Orkney, to 1976*
'For those in peril' : Orkney life-boat history. — [Stromness] ([52 Alfred St., Stromness, Orkney]) : Stromness Museum, 1977. — [1], 12p : ill, ports ; 22cm.
Sd : Unpriced
(B77-26952)

361.5'8 — Lifeboat services. *West Glamorgan. Mumbles Head, to 1974*
Smith, Carl. The men of the Mumbles Head : the story of the Mumbles life-boat from 1832 / [by] Carl Smith. — Llandysul : Gomer Press, 1977. — [10],87p : ill, map(on lining paper), ports ; 23cm.
Index.
ISBN 0-85088-384-9 : £3.50
(B77-31081)

361.5'8 — Lifeboat services, to 1976
Middleton, Eric William. Lifeboats of the world : a pocket encyclopaedia of sea rescue / [by] E.W. Middleton. — Poole : Blandford Press, 1977. — 256p : ill(some col), maps(1 col), plans ; 20cm. — ([Blandford colour series])
Ill. on lining papers. — Index.
ISBN 0-7137-0842-5 : £3.75
(B77-31790)

361.6 — PUBLIC WELFARE WORK
361.6 — Social services. Professional personnel. Role. *Great Britain. Reports, surveys*
Brunel University. *Health Services Organization Research Unit.* Professionals in health and social services organisations / Health Services Organisation Research Unit [and] Social Services Organisation Research Unit [of Brunel University]. — [Uxbridge] ([Brunel University, School of Social Sciences, Kingston Lane, Uxbridge, Middx UB8 3PH]) : Brunel Institute of Organisation and Social Studies, 1976. — 32p in various pagings : ill ; 30cm. — (Working papers)
Sd : £1.00
Also classified at 362.1'0425
(B77-08301)

361.6'0941 — Public welfare services. *Great Britain*
Wright, Frank Joseph. British social services / [by] F.J. Wright. — 2nd ed. / revised by F. Randall. — Plymouth : Macdonald and Evans, 1976. — xii,259p ; 19cm. — (The M. & E. handbook series)
Previous ed.: London : Macdonald and Evans, 1968. — Bibl.: p.243-246. — Index.
ISBN 0-7121-0253-1 Pbk : £2.25
(B77-07232)

361.6'09411 — Public welfare services. *Scotland. Reports, surveys. Serials*
Social work in Scotland in [the year] ... / Scottish Education Department. — Edinburgh : H.M.S.O.
1976. — [1977]. — 11p ; 25cm. — (Cmnd.6918)
ISBN 0-10-169180-7 Sd : £0.35
(B77-31791)

361.6'3 — Socially disadvantaged persons. Social conditions. Improvement. Role of local authorities. *Great Britain. Urban regions. Reports, surveys*
Stewart, John, *b.1929 (Mar.).* Local government : approaches to urban deprivation : a report / by John Stewart, Kenneth Spencer, Barbara Webster. — [London] ([Horseferry House, Dean Ryle St., SW1P 2AW]) : Home Office Urban Deprivation Unit, [1977]. — [7],v,62p ; 30cm. — (Great Britain. Home Office. Urban Deprivation Unit. Occasional papers ; no.1)
Bibl.: p.62.
ISBN 0-903727-43-9 Sd : £1.20
(B77-13587)

361.6'3'0941 — Local authorities. Personal welfare services. Reform. *Great Britain, ca 1965-1975*
Hall, Phoebe. Reforming the welfare : the politics of change in the personal social services / [by] Phoebe Hall. — London : Heinemann Educational, 1976. — xiv,162p ; 23cm.
Index.
ISBN 0-435-82400-7 : £5.50
(B77-05310)

361.6'3'0941 — Local authorities. Social services. Cooperation with national health services. *Great Britain. Reports, surveys*
Brunel University. *Health Services Organization Research Unit.* Collaboration between health and social services / Health Services Organisation Research Unit [and] Social Services Organisation Research Unit [of Brunel University]. — [Uxbridge] ([Brunel University, School of Social Sciences, Kingston Lane, Uxbridge, Middx UB8 3PH]) : Brunel Institute of Organisation and Social Studies, 1976. — 35p in various pagings : 1 ill ; 30cm. — (Working papers)
Sd : £1.00
Also classified at 362.1'0941
(B77-08302)

361.6'3'097526 — Local authorities. Welfare services. Political aspects. *United States. Study regions: Maryland. Baltimore*
Krefetz, Sharon Perlman. Welfare policy making and city politics / [by] Sharon Perlman Krefetz. — New York [etc.] ; London : Praeger, 1976. — xv,218,[1]p ; 25cm. — (Praeger special studies in US economic, social and political issues)
Index.
ISBN 0-275-23140-2 : £13.70
Also classified at 361.6'3'0979461
(B77-09622)

361.6'3'0979461 — Local authorities. Welfare services. Political aspects. *United States. Study regions: California. San Francisco*
Krefetz, Sharon Perlman. Welfare policy making and city politics / [by] Sharon Perlman Krefetz. — New York [etc.] ; London : Praeger, 1976. — xv,218,[1]p ; 25cm. — (Praeger special studies in US economic, social and political issues)
Index.
ISBN 0-275-23140-2 : £13.70
Primary classification 361.6'3'097526
(B77-09622)

361.7 — PRIVATE WELFARE WORK
361.7 — Voluntary welfare work by young persons. *Great Britain. Reports, surveys*
Ball, Mog. Young people as volunteers / [by] Mog Ball. — Berkhamsted (29 Lower King's Rd, Berkhamsted, Herts. HP4 2AB) : Volunteer Centre, 1976. — [1],60p : ill ; 30cm.
Bibl.: p.60.
ISBN 0-904647-07-2 Sd : £1.00
(B77-04680)

361.7 — Voluntary welfare work by young persons. Effects of television programmes. *Reports, surveys*
Leat, Diana. The role of television in stimulating voluntary action : a pilot study / [by] Diana Leat. — Berkhamsted (29 Lower King's Rd, Berkhamsted, Herts. HP4 2AB) : Volunteer Centre, [1976]. — [5],30p : ill ; 30cm.
ISBN 0-904647-08-0 Sd : £0.60
(B77-04681)

361.7'06'241 — Voluntary social services. Organisations. *Great Britain. National Council of Social Service. Reports, surveys. Serials*
National Council of Social Service. Annual report / National Council of Social Service. — London : [Bedford Square Press].
1975-1976 : 57th. — [1977]. — [1],42p : ill ; 15x22cm.
ISBN 0-7199-0922-8 Sd : £0.20
(B77-08914)

361.7'06'242356 — Councils for voluntary service. *Devon. Exeter. Exeter Council for Voluntary Service. Reports, surveys. Serials*
Exeter Council for Voluntary Service. Annual report / Exeter Council for Voluntary Service. — Exeter (1 Wynards, Magdalen St., Exeter EX2 4HX) : ExVoS.
29th : July 1975-June 1976. — [1976]. — [2], 20,[2]p ; 22cm.
Sd : Unpriced
(B77-17383)

361.7'06'24259 — Councils for voluntary service. *Buckinghamshire. Buckinghamshire Council for Voluntary Service. Periodicals*
Buckinghamshire Council for Voluntary Service. Newsletter / Buckinghamshire Council for Voluntary Service. — Aylesbury (23a Walton St., Aylesbury, Bucks. HP20 1TZ) : [The Council].
No.1- ; Jan. '76-. — 1976. — 30cm.
Quarterly. — 6,[2]p. in 1st issue.
Sd : Unpriced
ISSN 0309-0922
(B77-04682)

361.7'07 — Social services. Voluntary personnel. Training. *Great Britain. Manuals*
Richards, Kay, *b.1932.* Training volunteer organisers / [by] Kay Richards. — [London] ([5 Tavistock Place, WC1H 9SS]) : [National Institute for Social Work], [1977]. — [7],70p : ill ; 30cm. — (National Institute for Social Work. Papers ; no.3)
Bibl.: p.68-69.
Sp : £1.10
(B77-25500)

361.7'0941 — Voluntary welfare services. *Great Britain. Reports, surveys*
Committee on Voluntary Organisations. The future of voluntary organisations : report of the Wolfenden Committee [on Voluntary Organisations]. — London : Croom Helm, 1978. — 286p ; 23cm.
'The Joseph Rowntree Memorial Trust and the Carnegie United Kingdom Trust appointed ... the Committee on Voluntary Organisations' - Preface. — Chairman: Lord Wolfenden. — Index.
ISBN 0-85664-539-7 : £6.50 : CIP rev.
ISBN 0-85664-660-1 Pbk : £2.95
(B77-24812)

361.7'0941 — Voluntary welfare work. *Great Britain*
Murphy, Graham. Voluntary social work : some questions, some comments / by Graham Murphy ; foreword by Geraldine M. Aves. — London (207 Old Marylebone Rd, NW1 5QP) : Family Service Units, 1976. — [2]p,ii,15 leaves ; 30cm.
Originally published: s.l. : s.n., 1972.
Sd : £0.40
(B77-04048)

361.7'0941 — Voluntary welfare work. *Great Britain. Manuals*
Moore, Sheila. Working for free : a practical guide for volunteers / [by] Sheila Moore. — London [etc.] : Pan Books, 1977. — 256p ; 18cm.
Index.
ISBN 0-330-25009-4 Pbk : £0.75
(B77-13588)

Moore, Sheila. Working for free : a practical guide for volunteers / [by] Sheila Moore. — London : Severn House : [Distributed by Hutchinson], 1977. — 256p ; 21cm.
Also published: London : Pan Books, 1977. — Index.
ISBN 0-7278-0265-8 : £3.95
(B77-26953)

361.7'09425'4 — Welfare work. Role of volunteers. *Leicestershire*
Volunteer Centre. Creative partnerships : a study in Leicestershire of voluntary community involvement / [Volunteer Centre]. — Berkhamsted (29 Lower King's Rd, Berkhamsted, Herts. HP4 2AB) : The Centre, [1977]. — 112p : ill ; 30cm.
ISBN 0-904647-09-9 Sd : £1.50
(B77-14640)

361.7'09427'33 — Voluntary welfare work. Projects: Support Project. *Greater Manchester (Metropolitan County). Manchester, 1971-1974*
Davies, Martin, *b.1936.* Support systems in social work / [by] Martin Davies. — London [etc.] : Routledge and Kegan Paul, 1977. — xi,132p : ill ; 23cm. — (Library of social work ISSN 0305-4381)
Bibl.: p.127-128. — Index.
ISBN 0-7100-8616-4 : £4.95 : CIP rev.
ISBN 0-7100-8617-2 Pbk : £2.00
(B77-14137)

361.7'3'0941 — Charities. Fund raising. *Great Britain. Manuals*
Blume, Hilary. Fund raising : a comprehensive handbook / [by] Hilary Blume. — London [etc.] : Routledge and Kegan Paul, 1977. — 188p : forms ; 22cm.
Index.
ISBN 0-7100-8549-4 Pbk : £2.25
(B77-21780)

361.7'3'0941 — Charities. Fund raising. *Great Britain. Serials*
Fund raising annual. — Hastings (197 Queens Rd, Hastings, [E. Sussex]) : Fairlight Publications Ltd.
1976. — [1976]. — 72p : ill, facsim, form, plan ; 25cm.
Index.
ISBN 0-905581-00-8 Pbk : £1.50
ISSN 0309-2089
(B77-04049)

361.7'5 — Christian welfare services. *Great Britain. Christian Action. Collins, Lewis John*
Man of Christian action : Canon John Collins, the man and his work / edited by Ian Henderson. — Guildford [etc.] : Lutterworth Press, 1976. — lx,133p,[8]p of plates : ill, ports ; 23cm.
'... a seventieth birthday tribute ...' - Editor's Preface.
ISBN 0-7188-2271-4 : £3.50
(B77-03459)

361.7'5 — Welfare work. Role of Roman Catholic Church. *Great Britain. For Roman Catholic religious communities*
Cormack, Una. The Church and social work / by Una Cormack. — [Liverpool] ([Christ's College, Woolton Rd, Liverpool L16 8ND]) : Liverpool Institute of Socio-Religious Studies [for] the Conference of Major Religious Superiors of England and Wales, 1977. — [3],32p ; 21cm. — (Pastoral investigation of social trends ; working paper no.7)
Bibl.: p.30-31.
ISBN 0-905052-07-2 Sd : £0.60
(B77-26954)

361.7'6'02541 — Charities. *Great Britain. Directories*
Charities digest : a classified digest of charities. — London : Family Welfare Association : [Distributed by] Macdonald and Evans.
1977 : eighty-fourth ed. — 1977. — 390p : ill ; 21cm.
Index.
Pbk : £3.50
(B77-24104)

Will to charity : the charities' story book. — [London] : [8 Lennox Gardens, SW1X 0DG] : [Will to Charity Ltd].
1976. — [1976]. — 272p : ill, 2 maps, ports ; 21cm.
Cover title. — Index.
ISBN 0-9502497-6-9 Pbk : £1.75
(B77-01279)

361.7'6'02541 — Grant making charities. *Great Britain. Directories*
Directory of grant-making trusts / Charities Aid Foundation. — Tonbridge (48 Pembury Rd, Tonbridge, Kent TN9 2JD) : The Foundation.
5th compilation / [editor H.A. Whittall]. — 1977. — xii,891p ; 24cm.
Index.
ISBN 0-904757-02-1 : £20.00
(B77-30086)

361.7'6'0924 — Philanthropic foundations. Gates, Frederick Taylor. *United States. Autobiographies*
Gates, Frederick Taylor. Chapters in my life / [by] Frederick Taylor Gates ; with the Frederick Taylor Gates lectures by Robert Swain Morison. — New York : Free Press ; London : Collier Macmillan, 1977. — xiii,305p, [8]p of plates : ill, coats of arms, ports ; 24cm.
Index.
ISBN 0-02-911350-4 : £8.25
(B77-29306)

361.7'6'0942 — Great Britain. Charity Commission. *Reports, surveys. Serials*
Great Britain. *Charity Commission.* Report of the Charity Commissioners for England and Wales ... — London : H.M.S.O.
1976. — [1977]. — 47p ; 25cm. — ([1976-1977 H.C.] 389)
ISBN 0-10-238977-2 Sd : £0.85
(B77-18648)

361.9 — SOCIAL SERVICES. HISTORICAL AND GEOGRAPHICAL TREATMENT

361'.92'4 — Social administration. Theories of Titmuss, Richard Morris
Reisman, David Alexander. Richard Titmuss : welfare and society / [by] David Reisman. — London : Heinemann, 1977. — xvi,192p ; 23cm. — (Studies in social policy and welfare)
Index.
ISBN 0-435-82749-9 : £6.00
ISBN 0-435-82750-2 Pbk : £2.50
(B77-32536)

361'.9'24 — Welfare work. *England, 1960-1976. Personal observations*
Evans, Ruth, *b.1915.* Happy families : recollections of a career in social work / [by] Ruth Evans ; foreword by Olive Stevenson. — London : Owen, 1977. — 165p ; 23cm.
ISBN 0-7206-0508-3 : £5.00
(B77-23256)

361'.92'4 — Welfare work. Dickson, Alec, 1930-1975. *Autobiographies*
Dickson, Alec. A chance to serve / [by] Alec Dickson ; edited by Mora Dickson. — London : Dobson, 1976. — 5-174p,[8]p of plates : ill, port ; 22cm.
Bibl. — Index.
ISBN 0-234-77888-1 : £4.25
ISBN 0-234-72022-0 Pbk : £2.50
(B77-04683)

361'.941 — Personal welfare services. *Great Britain*
Sainsbury, Eric. The personal social services / [by] Eric Sainsbury. — London : Pitman, 1977. — xxii,265p ; 24cm. — (Government and administration series)
Bibl.: p.223-257. — Index.
ISBN 0-273-01097-2 : £4.95 : CIP rev.
(B77-21781)

361'.941 — Personal welfare services. *Great Britain. Reports, surveys*
Personal Social Services Council. Personal social services : basic information / [Personal Social Services Council]. — London (2 Torrington Place, WC1E 7HN) : The Council, 1976. — [1] ,23,[1]p : ill ; 30cm.
ISBN 0-905250-01-x Sd : £0.70
(B77-08915)

361'.941 — Short term welfare work. *Great Britain. Readings*
Hutten, Joan M. Short-term contracts in social work / [by] Joan M. Hutten with ... [others]. — London [etc.] : Routledge and Kegan Paul, 1977. — xii,122p ; 23cm. — (Library of social work ISSN 0305-4381)
Bibl.: p.120-122.
ISBN 0-7100-8584-2 : £4.50 : CIP rev.
ISBN 0-7100-8585-0 Pbk : £2.20
(B77-07863)

361'.941 — Social administration. *Great Britain*
Brown, Muriel. Introduction to social administration in Britain / [by] Muriel Brown. — 4th ed. — London : Hutchinson, 1977. — 253p : 1 ill ; 22cm. — (Hutchinson university library)
Previous ed.: 1976. — Bibl. — Index.
ISBN 0-09-131351-1 Pbk : £3.25
(B77-27761)

Foundations of social administration / edited by Helmuth Heisler. — London [etc.] : Macmillan, 1977. — xviii,251p : ill ; 23cm.
Index.
ISBN 0-333-18647-8 : £8.95
ISBN 0-333-18648-6 Pbk : £3.95
(B77-22465)

361'.941 — Social services. *Great Britain*
Baugh, William Ellis. Introduction to the social services / [by] W.E. Baugh. — 3rd ed. — [London] : Macmillan, 1977. — 204p : 1 ill ; 22cm.
Previous ed.: 1975. — Bibl. — Index.
ISBN 0-333-22777-8 Pbk : £1.95
(B77-33136)

361'.941 — Social services. *Great Britain. Encyclopaedias*
Barefoot, Pat. Community services : the health worker's A-Z / [by] Patience Barefoot, P. Jean Cunningham. — London : Faber, 1977. — 3-284p ; 20cm.
ISBN 0-571-11052-5 Pbk : £2.95
(B77-21033)

361'.941 — Social services. Implications of population change. *Great Britain. Reports, surveys*
Great Britain. *Central Policy Review Staff.* Population and the social services : report / by the Central Policy Review Staff. — London : H.M.S.O., 1977. — 106p : ill ; 30cm.
ISBN 0-11-700571-1 Sd : £2.25
(B77-21782)

361'.941 — Welfare services. *Great Britain*
Warham, Joyce. An open case : the organisational context of social work / [by] Joyce Warham. — London [etc.] : Routledge and Kegan Paul, 1977. — x,161p ; 22cm. — (Library of social work ISSN 0305-4381)
Bibl.: p.153-154.
ISBN 0-7100-8608-3 : £4.50 : CIP rev.
ISBN 0-7100-8609-1 Pbk : £2.25
(B77-12947)

361'.941 — Welfare services. *Great Britain. Serials*
The **year** book of social policy in Britain. — London [etc.] : Routledge and Kegan Paul.
1975 / edited by Kathleen Jones ; assistant editor Sally Baldwin. — 1976. — xii,212p : ill, facsim ; 24cm.
ISBN 0-7100-8432-3 : £9.50
ISSN 0307-0476
(B77-03460)

1976 / edited by Kathleen Jones ; assistant editors Muriel Brown and Sally Baldwin. — 1977. — xiii,209p ; 25cm.
ISBN 0-7100-8765-9 : £12.00 : CIP rev.
ISSN 0307-0476
(B77-26955)

361'.941 — Welfare work. *Great Britain. Readings*
Welfare in action / edited by Mike Fitzgerald ... [et al.] at the Open University. — London [etc.] : Routledge and Kegan Paul [for] The Open University Press, 1977. — vii,232p : ill ; 26cm.
Index.
ISBN 0-7100-8738-1 : £5.75 : CIP rev.
ISBN 0-7100-8739-x Pbk : £2.80
(B77-28516)

361'.9425'41 — Community work. Projects. *Leicestershire. Braunstone. Braunstone Neighbourhood Project, to 1973. Reports, surveys*
Twelvetrees, Alan Clyde. Braunstone Neighbourhood Project : the first six years / written by Alan C. Twelvetrees ; for Leicester Family Service Unit. — [Leicester] ([54 Highfield St., Leicester]) : [Leicester Family Service Unit], [1974]. — [3],38p ; 33cm.
ISBN 0-905815-02-5 Sd : £0.40
(B77-04050)

361'.9425'74 — Local authority housing estates. *Oxfordshire. Oxford. Barton Estate. Community work. Projects: Barton Project. Reports, surveys*
Evens, Philip. The Barton project, a kaleidoscopic report of its first two years (1974-1976) prepared as a report for the Calouste Gulbenkian Foundation / by Philip Evens. — Oxford (P.O. Box 70, Headington, Oxford OX3 7NT) : Alistair Shornach Ltd, 1976. — [8],51[i.e.58]p : facsims ; 30cm. — (Occasional paper ; no.1)
Sd : Unpriced
(B77-24813)

Evens, Philip. The Barton project, a study in manipulative inter-action on behalf of a 'forgotten community' / by Philip Evens ; illustrator Geoff Enoch. — Oxford ([P.O. Box 70, Headington, Oxford OX3 7NT]) : Alistair Shornach, [1976]. — [1],172p : ill, facsims ; 25cm. — (Readings in social change ; vol.2)
Cover title. — Bibl.
Pbk : £2.95
(B77-24814)

361'.9426'752 — Social services. *Essex. Chelmsford (District). Rural regions. Reports, surveys*
Chelmsford *(District). Council.* Rural areas study, education and social service provision / [Chelmsford District Council]. — Chelmsford (Planning Department, Burgess Well Rd, Chelmsford [CM1 1TR]) : [The Council], 1977. — [3],7[i.e.9]p ; 30cm. — (Subject report ; 7)
Sd : £0.20
Primary classification 370'.9426'752
(B77-17397)

361'.9427'32 — Community work. Projects. *Greater Manchester (Metropolitan County). Salford. Regent Community Project, to 1975. Reports, surveys*
Regent Community Project. The first year / Regent Community Project ; [prepared by Gill Ormond, Richard Woolrych, June Leeming]. — Salford (8 Regent Sq., Salford 5) : The Project, [1976]. — 18p : ill, map ; 21x30cm.
At head of title : FSU.
ISBN 0-9505429-0-3 Sd : £0.25
(B77-04051)

361'.9428'17 — Community work. Projects. *West Yorkshire (Metropolitan County). Bradford. Lordsville. Lordsville Project. Reports, surveys*
Wardle, Michael. The Lordsville project / [by] Michael Wardle. — [London] ([207 Old Marylebone Rd, NW1 5QP]) : Family Service Units, [1976]. — [1],6p : form ; 24cm.
'Reprinted from "Case conference". Vol.16, no.11 ; March, 1970' - note.
ISBN 0-905175-06-9 Sd : £0.20
(B77-04052)

361'.973 — Social services. *United States. Urban regions*
The **delivery** of urban services : outcomes of change / edited by Elinor Ostrom. — Beverly Hills ; London : Sage Publications, 1976. — 320p : ill ; 24cm. — (Urban affairs annual reviews ; vol.10)
Bibl.
ISBN 0-8039-0469-x : £12.65
ISBN 0-8039-0679-x Pbk : £5.70
(B77-02879)

361'.973 — Social services. Administration. *United States. Reports, surveys*
Gilbert, Neil. Coordinating social services : an analysis of community, organizational and staff characteristics / [by] Neil Gilbert, Harry Specht. — New York ; London : Praeger, 1977. — xvii,84,[1]p : ill, forms ; 25cm. — (Praeger special studies in US economic, social and political issues)
ISBN 0-275-24330-3 : £8.35
(B77-28517)

361'.973 — Welfare work. *United States*
Shaping the new social work / Alfred J. Kahn, editor. — New York ; London : Columbia University Press, 1973 [i.e. 1977]. — xi,221p ; 23cm. — (Social work and social issues)
Originally published: 1973. — Index.
ISBN 0-231-08356-4 Pbk : £4.40
(B77-24815)

362 — SOCIAL WELFARE. PROBLEMS AND SERVICES

362'.042 — Social problems
Loraine, John Alexander. Syndromes of the seventies : population, sex and social change / [by] John A. Loraine ; foreword by Lord Caradon. — London : Owen, 1977. — 217p ; 23cm. — (Contemporary issues series ; 11)
Bibl.: p.191-208. — Index.
ISBN 0-7206-0404-4 : £6.00
(B77-26956)

Nettler, Gwynn. Social concerns / [by] Gwynn Nettler. — New York ; London [etc.] : McGraw-Hill, 1976. — viii,360p : ill ; 24cm.
Bibl.: p.313-353. — Index.
ISBN 0-07-046295-x Pbk : £6.25
(B77-04684)

362'.042'0973 — Social problems. *United States*
Julian, Joseph. Social problems / [by] Joseph Julian. — 2nd ed. — Englewood Cliffs ; London [etc.] : Prentice-Hall, 1977. — xx, 588p : ill, maps, ports ; 25cm.
Previous ed.: New York : Appleton-Century-Crofts, 1973. — Bibl. — Index.
ISBN 0-13-816736-2 : £11.15
(B77-33704)

362'.0425 — Social problems. Alleviation. *Simulation games. Secondary school texts. Cards*
Lynch, Michael. It's your choice : six role-playing exercises / [by] Michael Lynch. — London : Edward Arnold, 1977. — Case : ill, maps ; 22cm.
Eight copies each of 6 cards ([12] sides).
ISBN 0-7131-0146-6 : £5.00 : CIP rev.
(B77-11711)

362'.0425 — Vacations for socially disadvantaged persons. Provision by London local authorities. *Reports, surveys*
English Tourist Board. *Planning and Research Unit.* London boroughs provision of subsidised holidays : 1976 survey and published sources : report to the Social Tourism Study Group of the English Tourist Board / prepared by [the] Planning and Research Unit, English Tourist Board. — London : The Board, 1976. — [3],iii, 28 leaves : form ; 31cm.
Sp : Unpriced
Also classified at 362.4
(B77-33705)

362.1 — WELFARE SERVICES FOR THE PHYSICALLY ILL
362.1 — Community health services. Expounded by general systems theory
Braden, Carrie Jo. Community health : a systems approach / [by] Carrie Jo Braden, Nancy L. Herban. — New York : Appleton-Century-Crofts ; London [etc.] : Prentice-Hall, 1976. — xiii,178p : ill, form, maps ; 23cm.
Bibl. — Index.
ISBN 0-8385-1189-9 Pbk : £7.20
(B77-12385)

362.1 — Drugs. Prescription by general practitioners. *England. Research reports*
University College of Swansea. *Medical Sociology Research Centre.* Prescribing in general practice / the Medical Sociology Research Centre, University College of Swansea, Wales ; [editors Peter A. Parish et al.]. — [Exeter] ([9 Marlborough Rd, Exeter EX2 4TJ]) : Journal of the Royal College of General Practitioners, 1976. — vi,108p ; 25cm. — (Royal College of General Practitioners. 'Journal' supplements ; vol.26, no.1 ISSN 0308-4604)
Bibl.
Pbk : £3.00
(B77-08303)

362.1 — Dying. *For counselling*
Lynch, Loretto. The experience of death : care of the dying and the bereaved / by Loretto Lynch. — Liverpool (Christ's College, Woolton Rd, Liverpool L16 8ND) : Liverpool Institute of Socio-Religious Studies for the Conference of Major Religious Superiors of England and Wales, 1977. — [3],43,[1]p ; 21cm. — (Pastoral investigation of social trends ; working paper no.6)
Bibl.: p.34-36.
ISBN 0-905052-06-4 Sd : £0.60
(B77-30087)

362.1 — Health services for social minorities. *United States*
Weaver, Jerry L. National health policy and the underserved : ethnic minorities, women, and the elderly / [by] Jerry L. Weaver. — Saint Louis : Mosby ; London : Distributed by Kimpton, 1976. — xiii,161p ; 25cm. — (Issues and problems in health care)
ISBN 0-8016-5360-6 Pbk : £5.85
(B77-04685)

362.1 — Health services. Political aspects. *Capitalist countries*
Navarro, Vicente. Medicine under capitalism / [by] Vicente Navarro. — New York : Prodist ; London : Croom Helm, 1976. — [1],xvi,230p : ill ; 24cm.
ISBN 0-88202-116-8 : £7.95
(B77-22466)

362.1 — Medical services. *Conference proceedings*
International aspects of the provision of medical care / edited by P.W. Kent. — Stocksfield [etc.] : Oriel Press ; [London] : [Distributed by] Routledge and Kegan Paul, 1976. — vii,216p : ill ; 23cm.
'The chapters which constitute this volume arise out of contributions made at an international symposium held at Christ Church, Oxford in September 1974 ...' - Preface. — Bibl. — Index.
ISBN 0-85362-160-8 : £8.00
(B77-00682)

362.1 — Medical services. Role of women, to 1973. *Feminist viewpoints*
Ehrenreich, Barbara. Witches, midwives and nurses : a history of women healers / by Barbara Ehrenreich and Deirdre English. — London (14 Talacre Rd, NW5 3PE) : Writers and Readers Publishing Cooperative, 1976. — 63p : ill ; 20cm.
Originally published: New York : Feminist Press, 1973? ; London : Compendium, 1974. — Bibl.: p.62-63.
ISBN 0-904613-24-0 Pbk : £0.65
(B77-14138)

362.1 — Nuclear medicine services. *Reports, surveys*
Joint IAEA/WHO Expert Committee on the Use of Ionizing Radiation and Radioisotopes for Medical Purposes (Nuclear Medicine). Nuclear medicine : report of a Joint IAEA/WHO Expert Committee on the Use of Ionizing Radiation and Radioisotopes for Medical Purposes (Nuclear Medicine). — Geneva : World Health Organization ; [London] : [H.M.S.O.], 1976. — 72p : ill ; 20cm. — (World Health Organization. Technical report series ; no.591)
Bibl.: p.71-72.
Pbk : £1.75
ISBN 92-4-120591-1
(B77-01280)

362.1 — Public health services. Planning. Role of methodology in epidemiology
Epidemiology and health / edited by Walter W. Holland and Susie Gilderdale. — London : Kimpton, 1977. — ix,221p : ill ; 23cm.
Bibl. — Index.
ISBN 0-85313-796-x : £5.50
(B77-12948)

362.1 — Regional health services. Role of higher education institutions. *Conference proceedings*
Health, higher education and the community : towards a regional health university : report of an international conference at OECD, Paris, 15th-18th December, 1975 [organized by the] Centre for Educational Research and Innovation. — Paris : Organisation for Economic Co-operation and Development ; [London] : [H.M.S.O.], 1977. — 350p : ill, map ; 24cm.
Pbk : £8.00
ISBN 92-64-11597-8
(B77-15767)

362.1'01'5195 — Health services. Statistical mathematics
Kilpatrick, Samuel James. Statistical principles in health care information / [by] S. James Kilpatrick, Jr. — 2nd ed. — Baltimore ; London [etc.] : University Park Press, 1977. — xvii,285p : ill, maps ; 24cm.
With answers. — Previous ed.: 1973. — Bibl. — Index.
ISBN 0-8391-1107-x : £10.50
(B77-23257)

362.1'025'41 — Health services. *Great Britain. Directories*
The **hospitals** & health services year book and directory of hospital suppliers : an annual record of the hospitals and health services of Great Britain and Northern Ireland, incorporating 'Burdett's Hospitals and Charities', founded 1889. — London (75 Portland Place, W1N 4AN) : Institute of Health Service Administrators.
1977 / editor N.W. Chaplin ; advisory editor J.F. Milne. — 1977. — 1156p : ill, maps ; 25cm.
Bibl.: p.761-783. — Index.
ISBN 0-901003-15-8 : Unpriced
ISSN 0300-5968
Primary classification 362.1'1'02541
(B77-28520)

United Kingdom nursing homes, hospitals with 100 or more beds [and] regional health authorities / [Data Research Group]. — Amersham (Hill House, [Hill Ave.], Amersham, Bucks.) : The Group.
[1976]. — 1976. — 175 leaves in various pagings ; 30cm.
ISBN 0-905570-53-7 Pbk : £16.00
(B77-04053)

362.1'028 — National health services equipment. *Great Britain. Buyers' guides*
Association of National Health Service Supplies Officers. Members reference book and buyers guide / Association of National Health Service Supplies Officers. — London (86 Edgware Rd, W2 2YW) : Professional Publications.
1977-78. — [1977]. — 3-687,[1]p : ill, ports ; 23cm.
Tab indexed. — Index.
Unpriced
ISSN 0140-4563
(B77-30088)

362.1'028'54 — Health services. Applications of computer systems. *Conference proceedings*
Medical computing : proceedings of an international symposium, Toulouse, 22-25 March 1977, organized by IRIA, Institut de recherche d'informatique et d'automatique / edited by M. Laudet, J. Anderson, F. Begon. — London : Taylor and Francis, 1977. — xii, 602p : ill, forms ; 26cm.
Contributions in English and French, English and French abstracts. — Index.
ISBN 0-85066-131-5 : £30.00
Also classified at 610'.28'54
(B77-31792)

Medical data processing : proceedings of an international symposium, Toulouse, 2-5 March 1976, organized by IRIA Institut de recherche d'informatique et d'automatique / edited by M. Laudet, J. Anderson, F. Begon. — London : Taylor and Francis, 1976. — xi,775p : ill, facsims, forms ; 26cm.
Contributions in English and French. — Bibl. — Index.
ISBN 0-85066-106-4 : £25.00
Also classified at 610'.28'54
(B77-04054)

362.1'0425 — Communities. Health. Self-help groups. *Great Britain*
Robinson, David, *b.1941.* Self-help and health : mutual aid for modern problems / [by] David Robinson and Stuart Henry. — London : Martin Robertson, 1977. — vii,164p ; 23cm.
Bibl.: p.151-155. — Index.
ISBN 0-85520-167-3 : £5.85 : CIP rev.
(B77-21783)

362.1'0425 — Community health services. Nursing. *United States*
Distributive nursing practice : a systems approach to community health / edited by Joanne E. Hall, Barbara R. Weaver. — Philadelphia [etc.] : Lippincott ; London [etc.] : Distributed by Blackwell Scientific, 1977. — xiv,536p : ill ; 24cm.
Bibl. — Index.
ISBN 0-397-54201-1 : £11.00
(B77-33137)

Leahy, Kathleen Mabel. Community health nursing / [by] Kathleen M. Leahy, M. Marguerite Cobb, Mary C. Jones. — 3rd ed. — New York ; London [etc.] : McGraw-Hill, 1977. — xi,432p : ill ; 24cm.
'A Blakiston publication'. — Previous ed.: 1972. — Bibl. — Index.
ISBN 0-07-036832-5 : £8.95
(B77-22467)

362.1'0425 — Community medicine
Farmer, R D T. Lecture notes on community medicine / [by] R.D.T. Farmer, D.L. Miller. — Oxford [etc.] : Blackwell Scientific, 1977. — x, 182p,plate : ill, facsim ; 22cm.
Bibl.: p.174. — Index.
ISBN 0-632-00108-9 Pbk : £4.50 : CIP rev.
(B77-04686)

362.1'0425 — Community medicine. *Great Britain. Conference proceedings*
Seminars in community medicine. — London [etc.] : Oxford University Press. — (Oxford medical publications)
Vol.2 : Health information, planning and monitoring / editors Roy M. Acheson, David Hall, Lesley Aird. — 1976. — xix,189p,fold plate : ill, forms, maps ; 24cm.
'... a seminar entitled "The future of government health statistics" which was held in the London School of Hygiene and Tropical Medicine at the Centre for Extension Training in Community Medicine, in April 1974 ...' - Introduction. — Bibl.: p.167-174. — Index.
ISBN 0-19-261121-6 Pbk : £4.00
(B77-05980)

362.1'0425 — Community medicine. *United States*
Smolensky, Jack. Principles of community health. — 4th ed. / [by] Jack Smolensky. — Philadelphia ; London [etc.] : Saunders, 1977. — vi,472p : ill, facsims, forms, map ; 27cm.
Previous ed.: / by Jack Smolensky, Franklin B. Haar. 1972. — Bibl. — Index.
ISBN 0-7216-8428-9 : £12.00
(B77-26219)

362.1'0425 — General practice. *Gwynedd. Ynys Môn. Stories, anecdotes*
Hywel, William. Doctors' tales / [by] William Hywel. — [Denbigh] : Gwasg Gee, 1976. — 115p ; 19cm.
ISBN 0-7074-0092-9 Pbk : £0.60
(B77-02152)

362.1'0425 — Health services. Professional personnel. Role. *Great Britain. Reports, surveys*
Brunel University. *Health Services Organization Research Unit.* Professionals in health and social services organisations / Health Services Organisation Research Unit [and] Social Services Organisation Research Unit [of Brunel University]. — [Uxbridge] ([Brunel University, School of Social Sciences, Kingston Lane, Uxbridge, Middx UB8 3PH]) : Brunel Institute of Organisation and Social Studies, 1976. — 32p in various pagings : ill ; 30cm. — (Working papers)
Sd : £1.00
Primary classification 361.6
(B77-08301)

362.1'0425 — Health services. Psychologists. Role. *United States*
Dörken, Herbert. The professional psychologist today / [by] Herbert Dörken and associates. — San Francisco [etc.] ; London : Jossey-Bass, 1976. — xxi,394p : 1 ill ; 24cm. — (The Jossey-Bass behavioral science series)
Bibl.: p.293-385. — Index.
ISBN 0-87589-271-x : £12.35
(B77-21034)

362.1'0425 — Health services. Welfare work. *Scotland. Reports, surveys*
Social work services in the Scottish Health Service : report of the Working Party. — Edinburgh : H.M.S.O., 1976. — 45p ; 25cm.
At head of title: Social Work Services Group of Scottish Education Department, Scottish Home and Health Department.
ISBN 0-11-491432-x Sd : £0.65
(B77-01281)

362.1'0425 — Hospitals. Full-time chaplains. *Great Britain. Directories*
Hospital Chaplaincies Council. Directory of whole-time hospital chaplains, hospital church sisters and chaplains' assistants in Great Britain / [Hospital Chaplaincies Council]. — London (Church House, Dean's Yard, SW1P 3NZ) : The Council, 1976. — [3],17p ; 30cm.
Index.
Sd : Unpriced
(B77-00683)

362.1'0425 — National health services. Role of voluntary personnel. *Great Britain. Reports, surveys*
Volunteer Centre. Volunteer involvement in the National Health Service : a paper submitted as evidence to the Royal Commission on the National Health Service / the Volunteer Centre. — Berkhamsted (29 Lower King's Rd, Berkhamsted, Herts. HP4 2AB) : The Centre, 1976. — [1],20,[1]p ; 30cm.
Sd : Unpriced
(B77-26957)

362.1'0425 — Rehabilitation services. *Great Britain, 1950-1976*
Glanville, H J. What is rehabilitation? / by H.J. Glanville. — [Southampton] : University of Southampton, 1976. — 26p : 2 ill ; 21cm. — (University of Southampton. Inaugural lectures)
'Delivered at the University 6 May, 1976'.
ISBN 0-85432-160-8 Sd : £0.50
(B77-15205)

362.1'06'141 — Great Britain. Health Service Commissioner. Reports. *Reports, surveys*
Great Britain. *Parliament. House of Commons. Select Committee on the Parliamentary Commissioner for Administration.* Reports of Health Service Commissioner : first report from the Select Committee on the Parliamentary Commissioner for Administration, session 1976-77, together with the proceedings of the Committee and minutes of evidence taken on 5th May and 27th October, 1976, and on 19th January and 2nd and 9th February 1977. — London : H.M.S.O., [1977]. — xix p,p87-103,47p ; 25cm. — ([1976-77 H.C.]282) ([1976-77 H.C.]107-i)
ISBN 0-10-228277-3 Sd : £1.85
(B77-29307)

362.1'06'1411 — Health services. Health boards. Relations with local authorities. *Scotland. Reports, surveys*
Working Party on Relationships between Health Boards and Local Authorities. Report / Working Party on Relationships between Health Boards and Local Authorities. — Edinburgh : H.M.S.O., 1977. — 26p ; 25cm.
At head of title: Scottish Home and Health Department.
ISBN 0-11-491497-4 Sd : £0.50
Also classified at 352'.4'09411
(B77-29308)

362.1'06'1411 — National health services. Organisations. *Scotland. Scottish Health Service Planning Council. Reports, surveys. Serials*
Scottish Health Service Planning Council. Report ... / Scottish Health Service Planning Council. — Edinburgh : H.M.S.O.
1975. — 1976. — v,22p ; 25cm.
ISBN 0-11-491419-2 Sd : £0.45
(B77-14139)

Scottish Health Service Planning Council. Report / Scottish Health Service Planning Council. — Edinburgh : H.M.S.O.
1976. — 1977. — v,25p ; 25cm.
ISBN 0-11-491472-9 Sd : £0.60
(B77-15768)

362.1'06'1422 — Health services. Regional health authorities. *South-east England. South East Thames Regional Health Authority. Directories*
South East Thames Regional Health Authority. Directory / South East Thames Regional Health Authority. — [Croydon] ([46 Wellesley Rd, Croydon CR9 3QA]) : [The Authority].
1976. — [1976]. — [2],62p : map ; 21cm.
Index.
ISBN 0-9503162-1-0 Sd : Unpriced
ISSN 0308-9967
(B77-04687)

1977. — [1977]. — [2],83p : map ; 21cm.
Index.
Sd : Unpriced
ISSN 0308-9967
(B77-24816)

362.1'07'2 — Health services. Research. Methodology
Stein, Franklin. Anatomy of research in allied health / [by] Franklin Stein. — Cambridge, Mass. : Schenkman ; New York ; London [etc.] : Wiley, 1976. — xvi,294p : ill, forms ; 24cm.
Bibl.: p.281-288. — Index.
ISBN 0-470-15086-6 : £6.90
(B77-08916)

362.1'07'2041 — Research & development by Great Britain. Department of Health and Social Security. *Great Britain. Reports, surveys. Serials*
Great Britain. *Department of Health and Social Security.* Annual report on Departmental research and development / Department of Health and Social Security. — London : H.M.S.O.
1976. — 1977. — v,52p : 1 ill ; 25cm.
Index.
ISBN 0-11-320272-5 Sd : £1.10
ISSN 0307-613x
(B77-16285)

362.1'07'2041 — Welfare services. Research & development supported by Great Britain. Department of Health and Social Security. *Great Britain. Directories*
Great Britain. *Department of Health and Social Security.* DHSS handbook of research and development. — London : H.M.S.O.
1976 : a list of projects supported by the Department in the financial year 1975-76. — 1977. — vi,84p ; 25cm.
Index.
ISBN 0-11-320274-1 Pbk : £2.00
(B77-15206)

362.1'07'2073 — Medical services. Research. Reliability. *United States*
Schach, Elisabeth. Reliability in sociomedical research : implications for cross-national studies / [by] Elisabeth Schach. — Beverly Hills ; London : Sage Publications, 1976. — 43p ; 22cm. — (Sage research papers in the social sciences : cross-national research and documentation in the social sciences series ; vol.4, no.90-032)
Bibl.: p.34-39.
ISBN 0-8039-0549-1 Pbk : £1.75
(B77-15207)

362.1'09172'4 — Health services for families. *Developing countries*
Sai, Fred T. Defining family health needs, standards of care and priorities : with particular reference to family planning / by Fred T. Sai ; with editorial assistance from Penny Kane. — London : International Planned Parenthood Federation, 1977. — 30p : ill ; 21cm. — (Sai, Fred T. Occasional essays ; no.4)
ISBN 0-900924-96-9 Sd : £0.85
(B77-30089)

362.1'092'4 — Health services. Stirling, Leader. *Tanzania. Autobiographies*
Stirling, Leader. Tanzanian doctor / by Leader Stirling ; with an introduction by Julius K. Nyerere. — London : C. Hurst, 1977. — xvi, 138p : ill, 2 maps, ports ; 23cm.
ISBN 0-903983-88-5 : £5.50 : CIP rev.
(B77-14641)

362.1'092'4 — Medical services. *Kenya, 1926-1951. Personal observations*
Carman, John Ambrose. A medical history of the colony and protectorate of Kenya : a personal memoir / [by] John A. Carman. — London : Collings, 1976. — [5],110p,[4]p of plates : ill ; 23cm.
ISBN 0-901720-88-7 : £3.00
(B77-00119)

362.1'0941 — Health services. *Great Britain. Reports, surveys*
Hicks, Donald. Primary health care : a review / by Donald Hicks. — London : H.M.S.O., 1976. — xxii,629p ; 22cm.
At head of title: Department of Health and Social Security. — Index.
ISBN 0-11-320199-0 Pbk : £9.50
(B77-03461)

362.1'0941 — Medical services. *Great Britain. Statistics*
Health and personal social services statistics for England : (with summary tables for Great Britain) / Department of Health and Social Security. — London : H.M.S.O.
1976. — 1977. — 200p : maps ; 28cm.
Bibl.: p.192-193.
ISBN 0-11-320588-0 Pbk : £5.50
ISSN 0307-0824
(B77-15769)

362.1'0941 — Medical services. *Great Britain, to 1975*
Gammon, Max. Health and security : report on the public provision for medical care in Great Britain / by Max Gammon. — London ([80 Highgate West Hill, N6 6LU]) : St Michael's Organization, 1976. — 51p in various pagings,[3] leaves of plates,[2]p of plates : ill ; 30cm.
ISBN 0-905322-02-9 Sd : £4.00
(B77-10777)

362.1'0941 — National health services. *Great Britain*
Conflicts in the National Health Service / edited by Keith Barnard and Kenneth Lee. — London : Croom Helm [etc.], 1977. — 252p ; 23cm.
Bibl.: p.232-247. — Index.
ISBN 0-85664-420-x : £6.95
(B77-18649)

Owen, David, *b.1938.* In sickness and in health : the politics of medicine / [by] David Owen. — London : Quartet Books, 1976. — [11],178p : ill ; 23cm.
Index.
ISBN 0-7043-2133-5 : £4.95
ISBN 0-7043-3123-3 Pbk : £1.95
(B77-00684)

362.1'0941 — National health services. *Great Britain. British Psychological Society viewpoints*
British Psychological Society. *Professional Affairs Board.* Evidence to the Royal Commission on the National Health Service / the British Psychological Society Professional Affairs Board. — Leicester (St Andrews House, Princess Road East, Leicester LE1 7DR) : The Society, 1977. — [2],32p ; 21cm.
Sd : £0.35
(B77-29309)

362.1'0941 — National health services. *Great Britain. Proposals*
Labour Party. The right to health : the Labour Party's evidence to the Royal Commission on the National Health Service. — London : Labour Party, 1977. — 59,[1]p ; 22cm.
Sd : £0.50
(B77-26220)

362.1'0941 — National health services. Cooperation with local authority social services. *Great Britain. Reports, surveys*
Brunel University. *Health Services Organization Research Unit.* Collaboration between health and social services / Health Services Organisation Research Unit [and] Social Services Organisation Research Unit [of Brunel University]. — [Uxbridge] ([Brunel University, School of Social Sciences, Kingston Lane, Uxbridge, Middx UB8 3PH]) : Brunel Institute of Organisation and Social Studies, 1976. — 35p in various pagings : 1 ill ; 30cm. — (Working papers)
Sd : £1.00
Primary classification 361.6'3'0941
(B77-08302)

362.1'0941 — National health services. Effectiveness. *Great Britain*
Cochrane, Archibald Leman. Effectiveness and efficiency : random reflections on health services / [by] A.L. Cochrane. — [London] ([3 Prince Albert Rd, NW1 7SP]) : Nuffield Provincial Hospitals Trust, 1973. — xi,92p : ill ; 22cm. — (The Rock Carling Fellowship ; 1971 ISSN 0305-0688)
Originally published: 1972.
Pbk : £1.50
(B77-03462)

362.1'0941 — National health services. Investigations by Great Britain. Royal Commission on the National Health Service. *Great Britain. Proposals*
Great Britain. *Royal Commission on the National Health Service.* The task of the Commission : a guide for those who wish to submit evidence / Royal Commission on the National Health Service. — London : H.M.S.O., 1976. — [2],10p ; 21cm.
ISBN 0-11-730103-5 Sd : £0.32
(B77-08304)

362.1'0941 — National health services. Reorganisation. Proposals. *Great Britain. Reports, surveys*
Royal College of Nursing. Evidence to the Royal Commission on the National Health Service / the Royal College of Nursing of the United Kingdom. — [London] ([Henrietta Place, W1M 0AB]) : [The College], 1977. — [4],69p ; 30cm.
Sd : Unpriced
(B77-21035)

Royal College of Nursing. Evidence to the Royal Commission on the National Heatlh Service submitted by the Royal College of Nursing of the United Kingdom. — London (Henrietta Place, Cavendish Sq., W1M 0AB) : The College, 1977. — [4],76p ; 21cm.
Sd : £0.60
(B77-21036)

362.1'0941 — National health services. Role of volunteers. *Great Britain. Reports, surveys*
Skeet, Muriel Hilda. Health needs help : results of a study into the role and preparation of volunteers working within the reorganized National Health Service / [by] Muriel Skeet and Elizabeth Crout. — Oxford [etc.] : Blackwell Scientific, 1977. — viii,79p : ill, forms ; 25cm.
'Published as a supplement to "Journal of advanced nursing"' - cover. — Bibl.: p.67.
ISBN 0-632-00025-2 Pbk : £1.95
(B77-16286)

362.1'09411 — Health services. *Scotland. Reports, surveys. Serials*
Health services in Scotland : report ... / Scottish Home and Health Department. — Edinburgh : H.M.S.O.
1976. — [1977]. — vi,96p : ill ; 25cm. — (Cmnd.6812)
ISBN 0-10-168120-8 Sd : £2.00
ISSN 0302-3397
(B77-27762)

362.1'09411 — Health services. *Scotland. Statistics*
Scottish health statistics / ... Information Services Division of the Common Services Agency, Scottish Health Service. — Edinburgh : H.M.S.O.
1975. — 1977. — xiii,190p : ill, map ; 30cm.
ISBN 0-11-880165-1 Pbk : £5.50
(B77-11712)

362.1'09411 — Health services. Resources. Allocation. *Scotland. Reports, surveys*
Working Party on Revenue Resource Allocation. Scottish Health Authorities Revenue Equalisation (SHARE) : report of the Working Party on Revenue Resource Allocation. — Edinburgh : H.M.S.O., 1977. — [7],96p : ill, map ; 16x25cm.
ISBN 0-11-491504-0 Pbk : £2.50
(B77-28518)

362.1'09411 — National health services. Reorganisation. *Scotland. Reports, surveys*
Planning Exchange. Reorganisation of the National Health Service in Scotland / the Planning Exchange. — Glasgow (186 Bath St., Glasgow G2 4HG) : Planning Exchange, [1975]. — [1],31 leaves,plate : map ; 30cm. — (Newsheet ; 3 ISSN 0307-1278)
Bibl.: leaf 31.
ISBN 0-905011-13-9 Sd : £0.40
(B77-08917)

362.1'09417 — Health services. *Ireland (Republic). Sinn Fein viewpoints*
McManus, John, *b.1945.* Health care : the case for socialist medical care / [by] John McManus. — Dublin (30 Gardiner Place, Dublin 1) : Repsol Publications, 1977. — [2], 14p ; 18cm.
'A Repsol/Sinn Fein-The Workers' Party Publication' - cover.
ISBN 0-86064-011-6 Sd : £0.20
(B77-11713)

362.1'0942 — National health services. *England. Proposals*
Great Britain. *Department of Health and Social Security.* The way forward : priorities in the health and social services : further discussion of the Government's national strategy based on the consultative document 'Priorities for health and personal social services in England' / Department of Health and Social Security. — London : H.M.S.O., 1977. — viii,52p : 2 ill ; 25cm.
Bibl.: p.50-52.
ISBN 0-11-320676-3 Sd : £1.00
(B77-29310)

362.1'0942 — National health services. Great Britain. Department of Health and Social Security. 'Priorities for health and personal social services in England'. *England. Radical Statistics viewpoints*
Radical Statistics. *Health Group.* Whose priorities? / Radical Statistics Health Group. — London (c/o The Group, British Society for Social Responsibility in Science, 9 Poland St., W.1) : Radical Statistics, 1976. — [2],36,[2]p : ill ; 20cm. — (Radical Statistics. Pamphlets ; no.1)
Sd : £0.45
(B77-21037)

362.1'09422'17 — Health services. *Surrey. Reigate and Banstead (District), to 1975*
Dulake, Lawrence. Doctors, practices and hospitals through 300 years : a history of general & hospital practice at Reigate & Redhill, including Earlswood & Merstham / by Lawrence Dulake. — [Reigate] ([The White House, Blanford Rd, Reigate, Surrey RH2 7DR]) : The author, 1976. — [4],iv,153[i.e.155] p(2 fold) : ill, facsim, forms, maps, plan, ports ; 21cm.
Cover title: The doctor's tale, 1662-1975, Reigate & Redhill. — Bibl.: p.134-135. — Index.
Pbk : £3.50
(B77-20146)

362.1'09429 — Medical services. *Wales. Statistics*
Health and personal social services statistics for Wales = Ystadegau iechyd a gwasanaethau cymdeithasol personol, Cymru / [Welsh Office = Y Swyddfa Gymreig]. — Cardiff : H.M.S.O.
No.3 : 1976. — 1976. — vii,136p ; 30cm.
Index.
ISBN 0-11-790075-3 Pbk : £3.35
ISSN 0307-0840
(B77-02880)

362.1'095 — Medical services. *Asia. Comparative studies*
Asian medical systems : a comparative study / edited by Charles Leslie. — Berkeley [etc.] ; London : University of California Press, 1976. — xv,419p : ill, facsims ; 25cm.
Bibl. — Index.
ISBN 0-520-02680-2 : £13.25
(B77-14140)

362.1'09597 — Health services. *Vietnam, 1945-1975. Reports, surveys*
Health in the Third World : studies from Vietnam / edited by Joan K. McMichael. — Nottingham : Bertrand Russell Peace Foundation for Spokesman Books, 1976. — 342p : ill, 2 maps, port ; 23cm.
'... edited from ... reports, which were originally published in Hanoi in the series "Vietnamese studies" between 1966 and 1972' - Acknowledgements.
ISBN 0-85124-152-2 : £7.00
(B77-12949)

Health in the third world : studies from Vietnam / edited by Joan K. McMichael. — Nottingham : Bertrand Russell Peace Foundation for Spokesman Books, 1976. — 342p : ill, 2 maps, ports ; 22cm.
ISBN 0-85124-153-0 Pbk : £3.30
(B77-22468)

362.1'0973 — Health services. *United States*
Klaw, Spencer. The great American medicine show : the unhealthy state of US medical care, and what can be done about it / [by] Spencer Klaw. — Harmondsworth [etc.] : Penguin, 1976. — xix,316p ; 20cm.
Originally published: New York : Viking Press, 1975. — Index.
ISBN 0-14-004339-x Pbk : Unpriced
(B77-03463)

Medicine in a changing society / [edited by] Lawrence Corey, Michael F. Epstein, Steven E. Saltman. — 2nd ed. — Saint Louis : Mosby ; London : Distributed by Kimpton, 1977. — xviii,236p : ill ; 23cm.
Previous ed.: 1972. — Bibl. — Index.
ISBN 0-8016-1044-3 Pbk : £4.25
(B77-31082)

Rosser, James M. An analysis of health care delivery / [by] James M. Rosser, Howard E. Mossberg. — New York ; London [etc.] : Wiley, 1977. — x,176p : ill, maps ; 26cm.
'A Wiley-Interscience publication'. — Index.
ISBN 0-471-73760-7 : £14.00
(B77-33139)

362.1'0973 — Health services. Influence of consumers. *United States*
The **consumer** and the health care system : social and managerial perspectives / edited by Harry Rosen, Jonathan M. Metsch, Samuel Levey. — New York : Spectrum Publications ; New York ; London [etc.] : Distributed by Wiley, 1977. — [11],384p : ill ; 24cm. — (Health systems management ; vol.9)
Bibl. — Index.
ISBN 0-89335-005-2 : £13.50
(B77-26958)

362.1'0973 — Health services. Planning. *United States*
Shonick, William. Elements of planning for area-wide personal health services / [by] William Shonick. — Saint Louis : Mosby ; London : Distributed by Kimpton, 1976. — xiii,227p : ill, map ; 25cm. — (Issues and problems in health care)
Bibl.: p.218-227.
ISBN 0-8016-4592-1 Pbk : £6.45
(B77-04688)

362.1'0973 — Health services. Provision. *United States. Reports, surveys*
Lewis, Charles Edwin. A right to health : the problem of access to primary medical care / [by] Charles E. Lewis, Rashi Fein, David Mechanic. — New York ; London [etc.] : Wiley, 1976. — xiii,367p : ill ; 24cm. — (Health, medicine and society)
'A Wiley-Interscience publication'. — Index.
ISBN 0-471-01494-x : £12.90
(B77-00685)

362.1'0973 — Health services. Sociopolitical aspects. *United States*
Krause, Elliott A. Power & illness : the political sociology of health and medical care / [by] Elliott A. Krause. — New York ; Oxford [etc.] : Elsevier, 1977. — xv,383p ; 24cm.
Index.
ISBN 0-444-99037-2 : £11.91
(B77-28519)

362.1'1 — Hospitals. *Cut-out books*
Hospitals / illustrations by Maureen Galvani. — Cambridge : Dinosaur Publications, 1974. — [24]p : ill ; 15x18cm. — (Althea's cut and colour books ; no.1) (Althea's dinosaur books)
ISBN 0-85122-083-5 Sd : Unpriced
(B77-21038)

362.1'1 — Hospitals. National health services facilities. Use by private patients. Abolition. *Great Britain. Proposals*
Great Britain. *Health Services Board.* Withdrawal of authorisations for the use of NHS hospital accommodation and services by private patients : proposals made by the Health Services Board ... — London : H.M.S.O., [1977]. — 23p ; 25cm. — (Cmnd.6963)
ISBN 0-10-169630-2 Sd : £0.45
(B77-33140)

362.1'1 — Hospitals. National health services patients & private patients. Admission. Common waiting lists. *Great Britain. Inquiry reports*
Great Britain. *Health Services Board.* Common waiting lists for NHS and private patients in NHS hospitals : report / by the Health Services Board ... ; presented to Parliament by the Secretaries of State for Social Services, for Wales and for Scotland ... — London : H.M.S.O., [1977]. — 15p ; 25cm. — (Cmnd. 6828)
ISBN 0-10-168280-8 Sd : £0.35
(B77-19277)

362.1'1 — Hospitals. Patients. Visiting. *Great Britain. For Christians*
Autton, Norman. Visiting ours : a layman's guide to hospital visiting / [by] Norman Autton. — Penarth (Education and Communications Centre, Woodland Place, Penarth, S. Glam.) : Church in Wales Publications, 1975. — 3-127p : ill ; 19cm.
Bibl. — Index.
Pbk : £1.00
(B77-17384)

362.1'1 — Independent hospitals. *Great Britain. Directories*
Association of Independent Hospitals and Kindred Organisations. The Association of Independent Hospitals and Kindred Organisations. — 8th ed. — [London] : [The Association], 1976. — [2],80p ; 22cm.
Previous ed.: 1973. — Index.
ISBN 0-9502329-2-0 Sd : £1.00
(B77-14141)

The **register** of approved private hospitals and nursing homes. — [Exeter] ([Northernhay St., Exeter, Devon]) : [Joseph Banks and Son (Printers) Ltd].
[1977] : [3rd ed.]. — [1977]. — [2],69p : ill ; 21cm.
Sd : £1.00
Also classified at 362.1'6'02541
(B77-29311)

362.1'1 — Residential institutions of spiritual healing. *Dorset. Bournemouth. Green Pastures, to 1976*
Hainsworth, Ruth. Led to green pastures / by Ruth Hainsworth. — Evesham : James, 1977. — 75p ; 19cm.
ISBN 0-85305-192-5 Pbk : £1.75
(B77-16287)

362.1'1023 — Hospitals. Occupations. *Great Britain. Career guides*
Ward, Brian. Hospital / [by] Brian Ward. — London : Macdonald Educational, 1977. — 48p : ill(some col) ; 29cm. — (Macdonald insiders)
Bibl.: p.47. — List of films.: p.47. — Index.
ISBN 0-356-05583-3 : £1.95
(B77-25501)

362.1'1'02541 — Hospitals. *Great Britain. Directories*
The **hospitals** & health services year book and directory of hospital suppliers : an annual record of the hospitals and health services of Great Britain and Northern Ireland, incorporating 'Burdett's Hospitals and Charities', founded 1889. — London (75 Portland Place, W1N 4AN) : Institute of Health Service Administrators.
1977 / editor N.W. Chaplin ; advisory editor J.F. Milne. — 1977. — 1156p : ill, maps ; 25cm.
Bibl.: p.761-783. — Index.
ISBN 0-901003-15-8 : Unpriced
ISSN 0300-5968
Also classified at 362.1'025'41
(B77-28520)

362.1'1'0924 — Hospital life. *England. Personal observations. Humorous texts*
Bentley, Nicolas. Pay bed / [by] Nicolas Bentley. — London : Deutsch, 1976. — 123p : ill ; 20cm.
ISBN 0-233-96845-8 : £1.95
(B77-00686)

362.1'1'0924 — Hospitals. *London. Tower Hamlets (London Borough). London Hospital and Medical College. Personal observations*
Toynbee, Polly. Hospital / [by] Polly Toynbee. — London : Hutchinson, 1977. — 279p ; 23cm.
ISBN 0-09-131390-2 : £4.95
(B77-30090)

362.1'1'0941 — Hospitals. *Great Britain. Middle school texts*
Cox, Sarah. Hospitalworker / text by Sarah Cox ; photographs by Robert Golden. — Harmondsworth : Kestrel Books, 1976. — 32p : chiefly ill ; 27cm. — (People working)
ISBN 0-7226-5226-7 : £1.95
(B77-00687)

362.1'1'09411 — Hospitals. In-patients. *Scotland. Statistics*
Scottish hospital in-patient statistics / Information Services Division of the Common Services Agency, Scottish Health Service. — [Edinburgh] ([115 George St., Edinburgh EH2 4YT]) : [The Division].
1974. — [1977]. — [1],ii,109p ; 24x36cm.
Sd : Unpriced
(B77-07234)

362.1'1'0941443 — Hospitals. *Scotland. Strathclyde Region. Glasgow. Western Infirmary, to 1974*
MacQueen, Loudon. The Western Infirmary, 1874-1974 : a century of service to Glasgow / [by] Loudon MacQueen and Archibald B. Kerr. — [Glasgow] ([20 Riverford Rd, Glasgow 3]) : John Horn Limited, 1974. — viii,219p,[12] leaves of plates : ill, ports ; 23cm.
Index.
ISBN 0-9505552-0-7 : £3.00
(B77-05981)

362.1'1'0941835 — Hospitals. *Dublin. Rotunda Hospital. Reports, surveys. Serials*
Rotunda Hospital. Clinical report of the Rotunda Hospital. — [Dublin] ([Parnell St., Dublin 1]) : [The Hospital].
1975. — [1976]. — 82p ; 25cm.
Index.
Pbk : Unpriced
(B77-18650)

362.1'1'0942 — General hospitals. Attitudes of in-patients. *England. Reports, surveys*
Raphael, Winifred. Patients and their hospitals : a survey of patients' views of life in general hospitals / by Winifred Raphael. — 3rd ed. — London : King Edward's Hospital Fund for London, 1977. — 46p : forms ; 30cm.
'Questionnaire' (Sheet ([2]p.)) as insert. — Fold. cover. — Previous ed.: 1973. — Bibl.: p.44. — Index.
ISBN 0-900889-64-0 Pbk : £3.75
(B77-33706)

362.1'1'0942 — Hospitals. In-patients. *England, 1973. Reports, surveys*
Great Britain. *Department of Health and Social Security.* Report on hospital in-patient enquiry for the year 1973 / Department of Health and Social Security [and] Office of Population Censuses and Surveys [and] Welsh Office. — London : H.M.S.O.
Tables. — 1977. — xiv,2-338p : forms ; 28cm.
Index.
ISBN 0-11-690624-3 Pbk : £6.75
(B77-16799)

362.1'1'0942 — Hospitals. In-patients. *England. Statistics*
Hospital in-patient enquiry. Preliminary tables : based on a one in ten sample of NHS patients in hospitals in England and Wales / Department of Health and Social Security, Office of Population Censuses and Surveys, Welsh Office. — London : H.M.S.O.
1974. — 1977. — xii,20p ; 30cm. — (MB4 no.1)
ISBN 0-11-690640-5 Sd : £0.95
ISSN 0140-2595
(B77-33141)

362.1'1'0942144 — Hospitals. *London. Hackney (London Borough). French Protestant Hospital. Applicants & inmates, 1718-1957. Lists*
French Protestant Hospital. The French Protestant Hospital : extracts from the archives of 'La Providence' relating to inmates and applications for admission, 1718-1957, and to recipients of and applicants for the Coqueau charity, 1745-1901 / compiled by Charles F.A. Marmoy. — London (University College, London, Gower St., WC1E 6BT) : Huguenot Society of London, 1977. — 2v.(ca 1200p) ; 28cm. — (Huguenot Society of London. Quarto series ; 52-53)
English and French records.
Pbk : £24.00(£11.00 to members of the Huguenot Society)
(B77-33142)

362.1'1'0942144 — Hospitals. *London. Hackney (London Borough). Reports, surveys*
Hackney Trades Council. Hackney's hospitals : an investigation / by Hackney Trades Council ; ... report ... written by P. Kennedy with additions by G. McMorrow and M. Knowles. — London (35 Spring Hill, E.5) : The Council, [1977]. — [64],25p,[2]p of plates : facsims ; 30cm.
Sd : £0.15
(B77-26223)

362.1'1'0942164 — Hospitals. *London. Southwark (London Borough). Guy's Hospital, to 1976*
Guy's Hospital. Guy's Hospital, 250 years / edited by Clive E. Handler. — London ([16 St Thomas St., S.E.1]) : Guy's Hospital Gazette, 1976. — vi,232p : ill, col coat of arms, facsims, ports ; 22cm.
Bibl.
Pbk : £2.00
(B77-01282)

362.1'1'0942178 — Hospitals. *London. Bromley (London Borough). Bethlem Royal Hospital. Personnel. Accommodation. Land. Leasing by Great Britain. Department of Health and Social Security: Leasing to Bethlem Royal Hospital and the Maudsley Hospital Board of Governors. Proposals*
Great Britain. *Treasury.* Treasury minute dated 13 July 1977 relative to the leasing at a nominal rent of land at the Bethlem Royal Hospital, Beckenham, to the Board of Governors of the Bethlem Royal and Maudsley Hospitals. — London : H.M.S.O., [1977]. — Sheet([2]p) ; 25x16cm. — (Cmnd.6868)
ISBN 0-10-168680-3 : £0.10
(B77-25502)

362.1'1'0942178 — Museums. *London. Bromley (London Borough). Bethlem Historical Museum. Stock. Catalogues*
Bethlem Historical Museum. The Bethlem Historical Museum catalogue / [compiled by] Patricia Allderidge. — [Beckenham] ([Monks Orchard Rd, Beckenham, Kent, BR3 3BX]) : Bethlem Royal Hospital and the Maudsley Hospital, 1976. — [1],60p : ill, 2 coats of arms(1 col), facsims, map, plan, ports ; 21cm.
Index.
ISBN 0-9505519-0-2 Pbk : £0.50
(B77-06568)

362.1'1'0942356 — Hospitals. *Devon. Exeter, to 1948*
Russell, P M G. A history of the Exeter hospitals, 1170-1948 / by P.M.G. Russell ; with a foreword by Sir Derek Jakeway. — Exeter (c/o The Librarian, Barrack Rd, Exeter [EX2 5DW]) : Exeter Medical Post-Graduate Institute [i.e. Exeter Post-Graduate Medical Institute], 1976. — [5],vii,171p,8p of plates : ill, ports ; 21cm.
Bibl.: p.159-164. — Index.
ISBN 0-9505609-0-1 Pbk : £4.00
(B77-09623)

362.1'1'0942733 — Hospitals. *Greater Manchester (Metropolitan County). Manchester. Crumpsall Hospital, to 1976*
Hall, Susan, *b.1933.* Crumpsall Hospital, 1876-1976 : the story of a hundred years / by Susan Hall and D.L. Perry. — [Crumpsall] ([Crumpsall, Lancs.]) : [Crumpsall Hospital], [1977]. — [2],43,[2]p : ill, facsims, map, ports ; 21cm.
ISBN 0-9505625-0-5 Sd : Unpriced
(B77-11149)

362.1'2 — Public amenities. Location. Mathematical models. *Study examples: Health services. Clinics*
Rosenberg, Mark. Some thoughts on a model for the location of public facilities / [by] Mark Rosenberg. — London : London School of Economics and Political Science, Graduate Geography School, 1977. — [1],10,[8],plate : 1 ill ; 30cm. — (London School of Economics and Political Science. Graduate School of Geography. Discussion papers ; no.60 ISSN 0307-1960)
Bibl.(2p.).
Sd : Unpriced
(B77-32537)

362.1'4'071141 — Health visitors. Professional education. Organisations. *Great Britain. Council for the Education and Training of Health Visitors. Accounts*
Health Visiting and Social Work (Training) Act 1962, Local Authority Social Services Act 1970, accounts ... of the receipts and payments of the Council for the Education and Training of Health Visitors and of the Central Council for Education and Training in Social Work for the year ended 31st March ... — London : H.M.S.O.
1975-76. — [1977]. — 8p ; 25cm. — ([1976-77 H.C.]331)
ISBN 0-10-233177-4 Sd : £0.25
(B77-15208)

362.1'4'076 — Health visitors. Professional education. Examinations. *Great Britain. Reports, surveys*
Fader, Wendy. Qualifying procedures for health visitors / by Wendy Fader. — [Windsor] : NFER, 1976 [i.e. 1977]. — [1],xi,124p : ill ; 30cm.
Bibl.: p.123-124.
ISBN 0-85633-111-2 Pbk : £3.00
(B77-25503)

362.1'6'02541 — Nursing homes. *Great Britain. Directories*
The **register** of approved private hospitals and nursing homes. — [Exeter] ([Northernhay St., Exeter, Devon]) : [Joseph Banks and Son (Printers) Ltd].
[1977] : [3rd ed.]. — [1977]. — [2],69p : ill ; 21cm.
Sd : £1.00
Primary classification 362.1'1
(B77-29311)

362.1'9'6123 — Personal adjustment to coronary heart diseases
Finlayson, Angela. Coronary heart disease and patterns of living / [by] Angela Finlayson and James McEwen. — London : Croom Helm [etc.], 1977. — 222p ; 23cm.
Index.
ISBN 0-85664-457-9 : £7.50
(B77-19278)

362.1'9'613200973 — Man. Blood. Hypertension. Prevention & control. Economic aspects. *United States*
Weinstein, Milton C. Hypertension : a policy perspective / [by] Milton C. Weinstein, William B. Stason, with contributions by David Blumenthal ... [et al.]. — Cambridge, Mass. ; London : Harvard University Press, 1976 [i.e. 1977]. — xxiii,243p : ill ; 24cm.
Published in the United States: 1976. — Bibl.: p.229-240. — Index.
ISBN 0-674-43900-7 : £11.25
(B77-12950)

362.1'9'681 — Periodicals for persons with strokes: Periodicals with British imprints. *Texts*
Look forward / the Chest, Heart and Stroke Association. — Great Missenden (St Martin's, Grimm's Hill, Great Missenden, Bucks. HP16 9BG) : 'Look forward'.
Issue no.1- ; Spring 1977-. — [1977]-. — ill, ports ; 42cm.
Quarterly. — Folder ([4]p.) as 1st issue.
£0.50 yearly
(B77-18651)

362.1'9'6853005 — Epileptics. *Periodicals*
Epilepsy news. — [London] ([3 Alfred Place, WC1E 7ED]) : [British Epilepsy Association].
Vol.1, no.1- ; [Sept. 1976]-. — [1976]-. — ports ; 38cm.
Four issues a year. — 8p. in 1st issue.
Sd : £0.15
ISSN 0308-9703
(B77-02153)

362.1'9'6994 — Patients with cancer. Rehabilitation. *Manuals*
Smith, Elizabeth A. A comprehensive approach to rehabilitation of the cancer patient : a self-instructional text / [by] Elizabeth A. Smith. — New York ; London [etc.] : McGraw-Hill, 1976. — vi,234p ; 24cm.
'A Blakiston Publication'. — With answers. — Bibl.
ISBN 0-07-058492-3 Pbk : £4.10
(B77-04689)

362.1'9'699400924 — Persons with terminal illnesses: Persons with cancer. *Personal observations*
Lewis, Jacquie. Let me tell you how I live with cancer / by Jacquie Lewis. — Stoke-on-Trent (c/o Cancer Research in the Department of Radio-therapy and Oncology, North Staffordshire Royal Infirmary, Hartshill, Stoke-on-Trent, Staffs. ST4 7LN) : Andy Ridler, 1977. — 43p : port ; 21cm.
ISBN 0-905074-02-5 Pbk : £0.50
(B77-23258)

362.1'9'699800948 — Lepers. Social conditions. *Northern Europe, ca 1100-ca 1960*
Richards, Peter. The medieval leper and his northern heirs / [by] Peter Richards. — Cambridge : Brewer [etc.], 1977. — xvi,178p, plate : ill(incl 1 col), facsim, 2 maps, 2 plans, ports ; 24cm.
Map on lining papers. — Bibl.: p.170-171. — Index.
ISBN 0-85991-026-1 : £6.00
(B77-22469)

362.1'9'7600973 — Dental services. *United States. Consumers' guides*
Denholtz, Melvin. How to save your teeth and your money : a consumer's guide to better, less costly dental care / [by] Melvin Denholtz & Elaine Denholtz. — New York ; London [etc.] : Van Nostrand Reinhold, 1977. — xv,263,[7]p : ill, forms ; 24cm.
Index.
ISBN 0-442-22080-4 : £7.25
ISBN 0-442-22081-2 Pbk : Unpriced
(B77-21039)

362.1'9'82 — Midwifery. Role of doctors. *Great Britain, to 1976*
Donnison, Jean. Midwives and medical men : a history of inter-professional rivalries and women's rights / [by] Jean Donnison. — London : Heinemann Educational, 1977. — vi, 250p,leaf of plate,4p of plates : ill, facsims ; 23cm.
Bibl.: p.225-228. — Index.
ISBN 0-435-32250-8 : £6.50
(B77-12386)

362.1'9'8200973 — Maternity health services. *United States. Reports, surveys*
Shaw, Nancy Stoller. Forced labor : maternity care in the United States / by Nancy Stoller Shaw. — New York ; Oxford [etc.] : Pergamon, [1976]. — viii,166p : ill ; 24cm. — (Pergamon studies in critical sociology)
Published in the United States: 1974. — Bibl.: p.155-161.
ISBN 0-08-017835-9 : £5.50
ISBN 0-08-017834-0 Pbk : £2.75
(B77-03464)

362.2 — WELFARE SERVICES FOR THE MENTALLY ILL

362.2 — Lodging schemes for mentally ill persons. *England. Case studies*
MIND. 'Room to let' : a report on nine social service lodgings schemes / MIND. — London [etc.] : MIND, [1977]. — [3],14p ; 30cm. — (Report ; 15 ISSN 0306-8625)
Sd : £0.65
(B77-20147)

362.2 — Medicine. Psychiatry. Political aspects
Lader, Malcolm. Psychiatry on trial / [by] Malcolm Lader. — Harmondsworth [etc.] : Penguin, 1977. — 202p ; 18cm. — (A Pelican original)
Bibl.: p.200-202.
ISBN 0-14-021992-7 Pbk : £0.80
(B77-22470)

362.2 — Medicine. Psychiatry. Social aspects
Social psychiatry. — New York ; London : Grune and Stratton [for] the American Association for Social Psychiatry.
Vol.1 : 1974 / editors Jules H. Masserman, John J. Schwab. — 1974. — xii,200p ; 24cm.
'An annual publication of the American Association for Social Psychiatry'. — Bibl. — Index.
ISBN 0-8089-0001-3 : Unpriced
(B77-18652)

362.2 — Psychopaths. *United States*
Harrington, Alan. Psychopaths / [by] Alan Harrington. — St Albans : Panther, 1974. — 283p ; 18cm.
Originally published: New York : Simon and Schuster, 1972 ; London : IF Books, 1974. — Index.
ISBN 0-586-04004-8 Pbk : £0.75
(B77-19279)

362.2 — Schizophrenics. *Personal observations*
Reed, David. Anna / [by] David Reed. — Harmondsworth [etc.] : Penguin, 1977. — 189p ; 19cm.
Originally published: London : Secker and Warburg, 1976.
ISBN 0-14-004422-1 Pbk : £0.70
(B77-24105)

Vonnegut, Mark. The Eden Express / [by] Mark Vonnegut. — Toronto [etc.] ; London : Bantam, 1976. — [11],274,[1]p ; 18cm.
Originally published: New York : Praeger, 1975 ; London : Cape, 1976.
ISBN 0-552-10419-1 Pbk : £0.85
Also classified at 301.44'94'0924
(B77-17385)

362.2 — Schizophrenics. *Personal observations. Collections*
Schizophrenia from within / edited by John Wing. — Surbiton (29 Victoria Rd, Surbiton, Surrey KT6 4JT) : National Schizophrenia Fellowship, 1975. — [3],65p ; 22cm.
Bibl.: p.65.
ISBN 0-904854-06-x Pbk : £1.50
(B77-07235)

362.2 — Schizophrenics. Organisations. *Great Britain. National Schizophrenia Fellowship*
National Schizophrenia Fellowship. What is the National Schizophrenia Fellowship?. — Surbiton (29 Victoria Rd, Surbiton, Surrey KT6 4JT) : The Fellowship, [1976]. — [1],6p ; 21cm.
ISBN 0-904854-05-1 Sd : Unpriced
(B77-02154)

362.2'0425 — Mentally ill persons. Treatment, 1300-1976. *Sources of data: Bethlem Royal Hospital*
Masters, Anthony. Bedlam / [by] Anthony Masters. — London : Joseph, 1977. — 206p, [12]p of plates : ill, facsim, ports ; 23cm.
Bibl.: p.198-200. — Index.
ISBN 0-7181-1546-5 : £6.50
(B77-29312)

362.2'0425 — National health services. Psychologists. Role. *Great Britain. Reports, surveys*
Standing Mental Health Advisory Committee. *Sub-Committee on the Role of Psychologists in the Health Services.* The role of psychologists in the health services : report of the Sub-Committee [on the Role of Psychologists in the Health Services, Standing Mental Health Advisory Committee]. — London : H.M.S.O., 1977. — iv,33p ; 25cm.
ISBN 0-11-320275-x Sd : £0.70
(B77-26224)

362.2'0425 — Patients with mental disorders. Rehabilitation. *United States*
Goldstein, Arnold Paul. Skill training for community living : applying structured learning therapy / [by] Arnold P. Goldstein, Robert P. Sprafkin, N. Jane Gershaw. — New York ; Oxford [etc.] : Pergamon [for] Structured Learning Associates, [1977]. — vii,273p : ill, forms ; 24cm. — (Pergamon international library)
Published in the United States: 1976. — Bibl.: p.146-152. — Index.
ISBN 0-08-021109-7 : £8.75
ISBN 0-08-021108-9 Pbk : £6.00
(B77-11150)

362.2'07'1141 — Welfare work with mentally ill persons. Welfare workers. In-service training. *Great Britain*
In-service training for social work with the mentally ill : report of a MIND working party. — London : MIND, [1976?]. — [1],32,[1]p ; 30cm.
Bibl.: p.27-30. — List of films: p.31-32.
Sd : £0.75
(B77-17386)

362.2'07'1141 — Welfare workers. Professional education. Curriculum subjects: Welfare work with mentally ill persons. *Great Britain. Reports, surveys*
MIND. The mental illness and health component of basic social work training : report of a MIND working party. — [London] : MIND, 1976. — [4],22p ; 30cm.
Sd : £1.00
(B77-18026)

362.2'092'4 — Persons with mental disorders. *Personal observations*
Gotkin, Janet. Too much anger, too many tears : a personal triumph over psychiatry / [by] Janet and Paul Gotkin. — London : Cape, 1977. — iii-xv,395p ; 24cm.
Originally published: New York : Quadrangle, 1975.
ISBN 0-224-01203-7 : £7.95
(B77-08918)

362.2'0941 — Mental health services. Provision. *Great Britain*
Holloway, Clive. Mental health service provision / prepared for the [Open University] Course Team by Clive Holloway. — Milton Keynes : Open University Press, 1976. — 162p : ill, facsims ; 30cm. — ([Technology], a third level course : systems performance, human factors and systems failures ; unit 13-14) (TD342 ; 13-14)
With answers. — Bibl.: p.142-144.
ISBN 0-335-06256-3 Pbk : Unpriced
(B77-14642)

362.2'0942 — Mental health services. *England. Statistics*
Mental health statistics / MIND. — [London] : [MIND].
[1976]. — 1976. — [1],2,17p ; 30cm.
Sd : £0.60
ISSN 0306-8684
(B77-17387)

362.2'1 — Mental illness hospitals. Patients. Compulsory admission. Procedure. *England. Tables*
Edwards, Arthur Hubert. Shaw's summary of procedural requirements in respect of compulsory admission to hospital and guardianship. — London : Shaw and Sons, 1976. — Folder ([3]p)(1 fold)) ; 28x11cm.
'... extracted from "Mental health services" ... by Arthur Hubert Edwards' - note.
ISBN 0-7219-0195-6 : £0.24
(B77-15209)

362.2'1 — Psychiatric hospitals. In-patients. *England. Statistics*
In-patient statistics from the mental health inquiry for England / Department of Health and Social Security. — London : H.M.S.O.
1974. — 1977. — iii,125p : ill, form ; 28cm. — (Great Britain. Department of Health and Social Security. Statistical and research report series ; no.17)
Bibl.: p.125.
ISBN 0-11-320239-3 Pbk : £3.50
(B77-07236)

362.2'1 — Psychiatric hospitals. Suicidal patients. *United States. Personal observations*
Reynolds, David Kent. Suicide : inside and out / [by] David K. Reynolds and Norman L. Farberow. — Berkeley [etc.] ; London : University of California Press, 1976. — xi, 226p ; 24cm.
Bibl.: p.221-224. — Index.
ISBN 0-520-03103-2 : £7.65
(B77-00120)

362.2'1'0924 — Psychiatric hospitals. *England. Personal observations*
Arden, Noele. Child of a system / [by] Noele Arden ; foreword by Anthony Storr ; coda by Bridget C. Downer. — London : Quartet Books, 1977. — [8],118p ; 23cm.
ISBN 0-7043-2134-3 : £3.95
(B77-13589)

362.2'1'0941 — Mental illness hospitals. Patients. Transfer to hostels for mentally ill persons. Financial resources: Mental illness hospital land. *Great Britain. Proposals*
Campaign for the Mentally Handicapped. Hospital land : a resource for the future? / Campaign for the Mentally Handicapped, MIND, the Spastics Society. — Bristol (11 Henceaze Ave., Bristol BS9 4EZ) : C.M.H. ; Leeds : MIND ; London : Spastics Society, 1975. — [3],9,3p ; 30cm.
Sd : £0.25
(B77-25504)

362.2'1'09417 — Psychiatric hospitals. Patients. *Ireland (Republic). Statistics*
Activities of Irish psychiatric hospitals and units / the Medico-Social Research Board. — Dublin (73 Lower Baggot St., Dublin 2) : The Board.
1971 and 1972 / by Aileen O'Hare and Dermot Walsh. — [1977]. — [1],87p : ill, 2 forms ; 25cm.
Sd : Unpriced
(B77-22471)

362.2'1'0942 — Psychiatric hospitals. *England. Statistics*
The **facilities** and services of mental illness and mental handicap hospitals in England / Department of Health and Social Security. — London : H.M.S.O.
1974. — 1976. — ix,125p : ill ; 28cm. — (Great Britain. Department of Health and Social Security. Statistical and research report series ; no.15)
Continues: The facilities and services of mental illness and mental handicap hospitals in England and Wales.
ISBN 0-11-320224-5 Pbk : £3.00
(B77-08919)

362.2'1'0942 — Psychiatric hospitals. Attitudes of in-patients. *England. Reports, surveys*
Raphael, Winifred. Psychiatric hospitals viewed by their patients. — 2nd ed. / by Winifred Raphael. — London : King Edward's Hospital Fund for London, 1977. — 50p : forms ; 30cm.

'Questionnaire' (Sheet ([2]p.)) as insert. — Fold. cover. — Previous ed.: / by Winifred Raphael, Valerie Peers. 1972. — Bibl.: p.48. — Index.
ISBN 0-900889-65-9 Pbk : £3.75
(B77-33707)

362.2'1'0942 — Psychiatric hospitals. Patients: Londoners. Admission. *England, 1973. Reports, surveys*
Davies, Hywel. Admissions of residents of Greater London to psychiatric hospitals and units, 1973 / by Hywel Davies ; [for the Greater London Council] Director-General's Department Policy Studies and Intelligence Branch. — London : G.L.C., 1976. — [3],iii, 75p : form ; 30cm. — (Greater London Council. Intelligence Unit. Research memoranda ; RM481 ISSN 0306-7203)
ISBN 0-7168-0838-2 Sd : £2.30
(B77-16288)

362.2'2 — Emergency psychiatric services. *United States. Conference proceedings*
Emergency and disaster management : a mental health source book / [edited by] Howard J. Parad, H.L.P. Resnik, Libbie G. Parad. — Bowie, Md : Charles Press Publishers ; London [etc.] : Prentice-Hall, 1976. — xxix,497p : ill, form ; 24cm.
This book is a compilation of the material presented at a continuing education seminar on emergency mental health, sponsored by the National Institute of Mental Health in Washington, D.C., June 1973. — Bibl.: p.475-497.
ISBN 0-913486-77-9 : £20.80
(B77-08305)

362.2'2'09421 — Day care centres for mentally ill persons. *London, 1966-1974. Reports, surveys*
Thompson, Richard. Residential and day care services for the mentally handicapped and mentally ill in the London boroughs, 1966-1974 / by Richard Thompson ; [for the Greater London Council] Director-General's Department, Policy Studies and Intelligence Branch. — London : G.L.C., 1976. — [3],37, [96]p ; 30cm. — (Greater London Council. Intelligence Unit. Research memoranda ; RM489 ISSN 0306-7203)
ISBN 0-7168-0839-0 Sd : £2.30
Primary classification 362.3
(B77-16289)

362.2'3'09421 — Residential institutions for mentally ill persons. *London, 1966-1974. Reports, surveys*
Thompson, Richard. Residential and day care services for the mentally handicapped and mentally ill in the London boroughs, 1966-1974 / by Richard Thompson ; [for the Greater London Council] Director-General's Department, Policy Studies and Intelligence Branch. — London : G.L.C., 1976. — [3],37, [96]p ; 30cm. — (Greater London Council. Intelligence Unit. Research memoranda ; RM489 ISSN 0306-7203)
ISBN 0-7168-0839-0 Sd : £2.30
Primary classification 362.3
(B77-16289)

362.2'9 — Addictive drugs. Social aspects, to 1974
Inglis, Brian. The forbidden game : a social history of drugs / [by] Brian Inglis. — Sevenoaks : Coronet, 1977. — 256p ; 18cm.
Originally published: London : Hodder and Stoughton, 1975. — Bibl.: p.234-243. — Index.
ISBN 0-340-21575-5 Pbk : £0.90
(B77-21040)

362.2'9 — Alcoholism & drug abuse
Worick, W Wayne. Alcohol, tobacco and drugs : their use and abuse / [by] W. Wayne Worick, Warren E. Schaller. — Englewood Cliffs ; London [etc.] : Prentice-Hall, 1977. — vi,170p : ill, facsims, map ; 24cm.
Bibl. — Index.
ISBN 0-13-021444-2 : Unpriced
ISBN 0-13-021436-1 Pbk : Unpriced
(B77-23259)

362.2'92 — Alcoholism
Alcoholism : development, consequences and interventions / [edited by] Nada J. Estes, M. Edith Heinemann. — Saint Louis : Mosby ; London : Distributed by Kimpton, 1977. — xi, 2-332p : ill, forms ; 26cm.
Index.
ISBN 0-8016-1529-1 Pbk : £7.40
(B77-28521)

362.2'92 — Alcoholism. *Conference proceedings*
Alcoholism : new knowledge and new responses / edited by Griffith Edwards and Marcus Grant. — London : Croom Helm, 1977. — 359p : ill ; 23cm.
Based on papers presented at a conference held at the Institute of Psychiatry in September 1976. — Bibl. — Index.
ISBN 0-85664-479-x : £11.95 : CIP rev.
(B77-13590)

362.2'92'0942 — Alcoholism. Control. *England*
Brake, George Thompson. Alcohol : its consumption and control : objective facts about a widespread habit, the personal and social problems involved in its abuse, and efforts to control it by legislation in other European countries / by G. Thompson Brake. — [London] ([12 Caxton St., SW1H 0QS]) : [Christian Economic and Social Research Foundation], [1976]. — [5],42p ; 22cm.
Index.
ISBN 0-905651-01-4 Pbk : £0.30
(B77-02155)

362.2'93'0941 — Drug abuse. *Great Britain. Secondary school texts*
Hardman, Peter. Drugs / [text by Peter Hardman and Eric Jay]. — London : S.C.M. Press [for] the Christian Education Movement, 1976. — 31p : ill ; 23cm. — (Probe ; 2 ISSN 0305-3776)
Originally published: 1969. — Bibl.: p.31.
Sd : £0.15
ISBN 0-334-00341-5
(B77-11151)

362.3 — WELFARE SERVICES FOR THE MENTALLY RETARDED

362.3 — Day care centres for mentally handicapped persons & residential institutions for mentally handicapped persons. *London, 1966-1974. Reports, surveys*
Thompson, Richard. Residential and day care services for the mentally handicapped and mentally ill in the London boroughs, 1966-1974 / by Richard Thompson ; [for the Greater London Council] Director-General's Department, Policy Studies and Intelligence Branch. — London : G.L.C., 1976. — [3],37, [96]p ; 30cm. — (Greater London Council. Intelligence Unit. Research memoranda ; RM489 ISSN 0306-7203)
ISBN 0-7168-0839-0 Sd : £2.30
Also classified at 362.2'2'09421; 362.2'3'09421
(B77-16289)

362.3 — Mental handicap hospitals. Long-stay patients. Care. Participation of public
One-to-one : an experiment with community participation in long-stay hospitals / edited by Pete Limbrick. — London (14 Talacre Rd, NW5 3PE) : Inter-Action Inprint, 1976. — iv, 36p : ill, 2 plans ; 30cm. — (Inter-Action Advisory Service. Handbooks)
ISBN 0-904571-08-4 Sd : £0.75
(B77-12951)

362.3 — Mentally handicapped persons. Rehabilitation
Rosen, Marvin. Habilitation of the handicapped : new dimensions in the programs for the developmentally disabled / by Marvin Rosen, Gerald R. Clark, Marvin S. Kivitz ; with a foreword by H.C. Gunzburg. — Baltimore ; London [etc.] : University Park Press, 1977. — xix,371p : 4 ill ; 24cm.
Bibl. — Index.
ISBN 0-8391-1137-1 : £13.25
(B77-24817)

362.3′0973 — Mentally retarded persons. *United States, ca 1840-ca 1970. Readings from contemporary sources*
The **history** of mental retardation : collected papers / edited by Marvin Rosen, Gerald R. Clark, Marvin S. Kivitz. — Baltimore ; London [etc.] : University Park Press, 1976. — 2v.(xxiv, 400p;ix,453p) ; 24cm.
Bibl. — Index.
ISBN 0-8391-0827-3 : £21.25
(B77-03465)

362.3′0973 — Mentally retarded persons. Social aspects. *United States*
Mental retardation : social and educational perspectives / [edited by] Clifford J. Drew, Michael L. Hardman, Harry P. Bluhm ; with a foreword by Burton Blatt. — Saint Louis : Mosby ; London : Distributed by Kimpton, 1977. — xvi,248p : ill ; 26cm.
Bibl. — Index.
ISBN 0-8016-1462-7 Pbk : £6.10
(B77-19280)

362.4 — WELFARE SERVICES FOR THE PHYSICALLY HANDICAPPED
362.4 — Physically handicapped persons. *Teaching kits*
Physical handicap / [edited by Ann Griffith]. — London (237 Pentonville Rd, N1 9NJ) : Community Service Volunteers, 1976. — Portfolio : ill, ports ; 21x31cm. — (A school and community kit)
Twenty-two items. — Bibl.: (1p.). — List of films (1p.).
Unpriced
(B77-18653)

362.4 — Physically handicapped persons. Rehabilitation
Gingras, Gustave. Feet was I to the lame / by Gustave Gingras ; translated [from the French] by Joan Chapman. — London : Souvenir Press, 1977. — 262,[1]p,[8]p of plates : ill, ports ; 23cm. — (Human horizons series) (A condor book)
Translation of: 'Combats pour la survie'. Paris : Opera Mundi, 1975.
ISBN 0-285-64836-5 : £5.00 : CIP rev.
ISBN 0-285-64837-3 Pbk : £3.25
(B77-12952)

Hirschberg, Gerald Gunter. Rehabilitation : a manual for the care of the disabled and elderly. — 2nd ed. / [by] Gerald G. Hirschberg, Leon Lewis, Patricia Vaughan. — Philadelphia [etc.] : Lippincott ; London [etc.] : Distributed by Blackwell Scientific, 1976. — xvi,474p : ill, forms ; 24cm.
Previous ed.: / by G.G. Hirschberg, Leon Lewis, Dorothy Thomas. Philadelphia : Lippincott ; London : Pitman Medical, 1964. — Bibl. — Index.
ISBN 0-397-54195-3 : £10.20
ISBN 0-397-54190-2 Pbk : £5.75
(B77-08306)

362.4 — Physically handicapped persons. Rehabilitation. *South Wales. Proposals*
Rehabilitation services in industrial South Wales : report of a working party appointed by the Secretary of State for Wales. — [Cardiff] ([Cathays Park, Cardiff CF1 3NQ]) : [Welsh Office], 1975. — [5]leaves,92p ; 30cm.
Sp : Unpriced
(B77-19281)

362.4 — Vacations for handicapped persons. Provision by London local authorities. *Reports, surveys*
English Tourist Board. *Planning and Research Unit.* London boroughs provision of subsidised holidays : 1976 survey and published sources : report to the Social Tourism Study Group of the English Tourist Board / prepared by [the] Planning and Research Unit, English Tourist Board. — London : The Board, 1976. — [3],iii, 28 leaves : form ; 31cm.
Sp : Unpriced
Primary classification 362′.0425
(B77-33705)

362.4′028 — Equipment for physically handicapped persons. *Great Britain. Buyers' guides*
Equipment for the disabled. — 3rd ed. / [edited by E.R. Wilshere, E.M. Hollings, P.J.R. Nichols ; investigator B.H. Rostance]. — Horsham : National Fund for Research into Crippling Diseases ; [Portslade] ([2 Foredown Drive, Portslade, Sussex BN4 2BB]) : [Distributed by Equipment for the Disabled]. In 9 vols. — Previous ed.: i.e. Revised and enlarged ed., published in 4 vols. 1966.
4 : Disabled mother. — 1973. — [6],34p : ill ; 30cm.
Index.
Sd : £1.50
(B77-26959)

5 : Personal care. — 1973. — [8],55p : ill, plans ; 30cm.
Index.
Sd : £1.50
(B77-26960)

6 : Leisure & gardening. — 1973. — [6],54p : ill, plans ; 30cm.
Bibl.: p.31. — Index.
Sd : £1.50
(B77-26961)

7 : Housing & furniture. — 1974. — [6],50p : ill, plans ; 30cm.
Bibl.: p.4-5. — Index.
Sd : £1.50
(B77-26962)

8 : Hoists, walking aids. — 1974. — [6],48p : ill ; 30cm.
Index.
Sd : £1.50
(B77-26963)

9 : Disabled child. — 1974. — [6],53p : ill, form ; 30cm.
Bibl.: p.51. — Index.
Sd : £1.50
(B77-26964)

Equipment for the disabled. — 4th ed. — [Oxford] : Oxford Regional Health Authority ; [Portslade] ([2 Foredown Drive, Portslade, Sussex BN4 2BB]) : [Distributed by Equipment for the Disabled].
Previous ed.: / issued by the National Fund for Research into Crippling Diseases. London : The Fund, 1972-74.
Home management. — 1976. — [4],80p : ill ; 30cm.
Bibl.: p.77. — Index.
Pbk : £1.50
(B77-06765)

362.4′028 — Equipment for physically handicapped persons. *Periodicals*
Design for special needs : the journal of the Centre on Environment for the Handicapped. — [London] ([126 Albert St., NW1 7NF]) : [C.E.H.].
No.10- ; May-Aug. 1976-. — [1976]-. — ill, ports ; 30cm.
Three issues a year. — [2],24p. in issue no.11. — Continues: Newsletter / Centre on Environment for the Handicapped. — Bibl.
Sd : £4.50 yearly
ISSN 0309-3042
Primary classification 721
(B77-10872)

362.4′028 — Equipment for physically handicapped persons. Research & development. *Great Britain. Reports, surveys. Serials*
Research and development work on equipment for the disabled : [report] / [by the Secretary of State for Social Services, the Secretary of State for Scotland and the Secretary of State for Wales] ... — London : H.M.S.O.
1976. — [1977]. — [1],20p ; 25cm. — ([1976-77 H.C.]448)
ISBN 0-10-244877-9 Sd : £0.45
(B77-26225)

362.4′0941 — Physically handicapped persons. Social adjustment. *Great Britain. Reports, surveys*
Blaxter, Mildred. The meaning of disability : a sociological study of impairment / [by] Mildred Blaxter. — London : Heinemann Educational, 1976. — xi,250,[1]p : ill ; 23cm. — (Sociology of social and medical care series)
Index.
ISBN 0-435-82033-8 : £6.00
(B77-02156)

Working Party on Integration of the Disabled. Integrating the disabled : report of the Snowdon working party / [the Working Party on Integration of the Disabled] ; [editor Rosemary Thorpe-Tracey]. — Horsham (1 Springfield Rd, Horsham, W. Sussex RH12 2PN) : National Fund for Research into Crippling Diseases, [1976]. — 71p : ill ; 30cm.
Cover title. — Chairman: Earl of Snowdon.
ISBN 0-900931-17-5 Pbk : £2.50
(B77-07237)

362.4′0941 — Welfare services for physically handicapped persons. *Great Britain. Periodicals*
Royal Association for Disability and Rehabilitation. The bulletin / Royal Association for Disability and Rehabilitation. — London (25 Mortimer St., W1N 8AB) : The Association.
Continues: Central Council for the Disabled. CCD bulletin.
No.54- ; Aug. [1977]-. — [1977]-. — 30cm.
Monthly. — 24p. in 1st issue.
Sd : Unpriced
ISSN 0140-2692
(B77-32539)

362.4′09411 — Social services for physically handicapped persons. *Scotland. Periodicals*
Scottish Information Service for the Disabled. SISD news. — Edinburgh (18 Claremont Cres., Edinburgh EH7 4QD) : The Service.
Mar.-Apr. 1977-. — [1977]-. — 30cm.
Six issues a year. — 8p. in 1st issue.
Sd : £1.00 yearly
ISSN 0309-4863
(B77-22472)

362.4′09413′4 — Welfare services for physically handicapped persons: Craigentinny-Lochend Welfare Services Project. *Edinburgh. Reports, surveys*
Craigentinny-Lochend Welfare Services Project. Report on the first year of the [Craigentinny-Lochend Welfare Services] Project / by Dave Du Feu, Project Co-ordinator. — Edinburgh (Craigentinny House, Loaning Rd, Edinburgh EH7 6JE) : [The Project], [1976]. — 24,[5]leaves : forms ; 24cm.
Cover title.
ISBN 0-9505350-0-1 Pbk : Unpriced
Also classified at 362.6′09413′4
(B77-00688)

362.4′1 — Blind persons. Tactile perception
Weiss, Malcolm E. Seeing through the dark : blind and sighted - a vision shared / by Malcolm E. Weiss ; introduction by Doris E. Hadary. — New York ; London : Harcourt Brace Jovanovich, [1977]. — xi,84p : ill, port ; 22cm.
Published in the United States: 1976. — Bibl.: p.79. — Index.
ISBN 0-15-272815-5 : Unpriced
(B77-11152)

362.4′1′0924 — Personal adjustment to blindness. *Personal observations*
Hickford, Jessie. I never walked alone / [by] Jessie Hickford. — London : Joseph, 1977. — 127p ; 23cm.
ISBN 0-7181-1565-1 : £3.00
(B77-09624)

Hocken, Sheila. Emma and I / by Sheila Hocken. — London : Gollancz, 1977. — 191p, [8]p of plates : ill, ports ; 23cm.
ISBN 0-575-02349-x : £3.95
(B77-26226)

362.4'3 — Wheelchairs provided by national health services. *Great Britain. Reports, surveys*
Fenwick, David. Wheelchairs and their users : a survey among users of National Health Service wheelchairs in England and Wales, to establish their characteristics and attitudes to their wheelchairs and to the operation of the wheelchair service / [by] David Fenwick ; [for the] Office of Population Censuses and Surveys, Social Survey Division [on behalf of the Department of Health and Social Security]. — London : H.M.S.O., 1977. — x,78p : ill, form ; 30cm.
ISBN 0-11-700818-4 Pbk : £3.65
(B77-10778)

362.5 — WELFARE SERVICES FOR THE POOR

362.5 — Almshouses. *London. Southwark (London Borough). Hopton's Almshouses, to 1976*
Charles Hopton and the foundings of the almshouses. — [London] ([25 Hopton's Gardens, Hopton St., London S.E.1]) : [Hopton's Charity], [1977]. — 32p : ill, facsim, plans ; 22cm.
Sd : £0.50
(B77-18027)

362.5 — Income maintenance programmes. Applications of income tax. Tax-credit system. *New Jersey*
The **New** Jersey income-maintenance experiment. — New York [etc.] ; London : Academic Press. — (University of Wisconsin. Institute for Research on Poverty. Monograph series)
In 3 vols.
Vol.1 : Operations, surveys and administration / [by] David Kershaw and Jerilyn Fair [et al.] ; with a foreword by Robert J. Lampman. — 1976. — xxii,232p : ill, forms ; 24cm.
Index.
ISBN 0-12-405001-8 : £9.15
(B77-02157)

362.5 — Man. Malnutrition. Relief. Policies of governments. *Developing countries. Reports, surveys*
Reutlinger, Shlomo. Malnutrition and poverty : magnitude and policy options / [by] Shlomo Reutlinger, Marcelo Selowsky. — Baltimore ; London : Johns Hopkins University Press for the World Bank, [1977]. — xiii,82p : ill ; 23cm. — (International Bank for Reconstruction and Development. World Bank staff occasional papers ; no.23)
Published in the United States: 1976.
ISBN 0-8018-1868-0 Pbk : £3.80
(B77-13591)

362.5 — Society. Role of social movements. *Study examples: Neighbors in Need*
Perry, Ronald W. Social movements and the local community / [by] Ronald W. Perry, David F. Gillespie, Howard A. Parker. — Beverly Hills ; London : Sage Publications, 1976. — 66,[1]p : ill, maps ; 22cm. — (Sage research papers in the social sciences : social ecology of the community series ; vol.5, no.90-037)
Bibl.: p.60-66.
ISBN 0-8039-0750-8 Pbk : £1.95
(B77-20148)

362.5'0941 — Poverty relief. Means-tested schemes. *Great Britain. Reports, surveys*
National Consumer Council. Means tested benefits : a discussion paper / National Consumer Council. — London (18 Queen Anne's Gate, SW1H 9AA) : The Council, 1976. — 111p ; 21cm.
ISBN 0-905653-03-3 Pbk : £0.75
(B77-08920)

362.5'09427'36 — Poverty relief. *Greater Manchester (Metropolitan County). Leigh, 1660-1860*
Wilson, M D. The paupers of Leigh : their persecution and poor relief, 1660-1860 / by M.D. Wilson. — Leigh ([Hon. Secretary, c/o Leigh Library, Leigh, Lancs. WN7 1EB]) : Leigh Local History Society, 1976. — 32p : facsims ; 26cm. — (Leigh Local History Society. Publications ; no.4 ISSN 0307-8892)
Bibl.: p.29-32.
ISBN 0-905235-03-7 Sd : £0.50
(B77-02881)

362.5'095694 — Poverty relief. *Israel*
Greenberg, Harold I. Poverty in Israel : economic realities and the promise of social justice / [by] Harold I. Greenberg, Samuel Nadler. — New York ; London : Praeger, 1977. — xiii,177p ; 25cm. — (Praeger special studies in international economics and development)
Bibl.: p.163-169. — Index.
ISBN 0-275-24300-1 : £12.40
(B77-26227)

362.5'0972 — Poverty relief. Policies of government. *Mexico. Urban regions, 1910-1976*
Eckstein, Susan. The poverty of revolution : the state and the urban poor in Mexico / [by] Susan Eckstein. — Princeton ; Guildford : Princeton University Press, 1977. — xv,300p : ill, form, maps, plan ; 25cm.
Bibl.: p.267-290. — Index.
ISBN 0-691-09367-9 : £13.40
(B77-29313)

362.5'8'09411 — Legal aid. *Scotland. Reports, surveys. Serials*
Law Society of Scotland. Report of the Law Society of Scotland on the legal aid scheme from 1st April to 31st March. — Edinburgh : H.M.S.O.
1975-1976 : twenty-sixth. — 1977. — 44p(8 fold) ; 25cm.
At head of title: Scottish Home and Health Department.
ISBN 0-11-491476-1 Sd : £1.00
(B77-33143)

362.5'8'09411 — Legal aid. Finance. Legal Aid (Scotland) Fund. *Scotland. Accounts*
Legal Aid (Scotland) Fund account ... — London : H.M.S.O.
1975-76. — [1977]. — 9p ; 25cm. — ([1976-77 H.C.]476)
Previously published: as 'Legal Aid (Scotland) Act 1967 account ...'.
ISBN 0-10-247677-2 Sd : £0.25
(B77-21784)

362.5'8'0942 — Legal aid. Finance. Legal Aid Fund. *England. Accounts*
Legal Aid Fund account ... — London : H.M.S.O.
1975-76. — [1977]. — 10p ; 25cm. — ([1976-77 H.C.]475)
Previously published: as 'Legal Aid Act 1974 accounts ...'.
ISBN 0-10-247577-6 Sd : £0.25
(B77-21785)

362.6 — WELFARE SERVICES FOR OLD PEOPLE

362.6 — Welfare services for sick old persons. *Great Britain. Reports, surveys*
Dowdell, T C. The role of the social services in the care of the elderly sick / [by] T.C. Dowdell. — London (11 Dartmouth St., SW1H 9BN) : Socialist Medical Association, [1976]. — [2], 17p ; 23cm. — (Socialist Medical Association. Discussion documents)
ISBN 0-900687-11-8 Sd : £0.20
(B77-07238)

362.6'06'242 — Welfare services for old persons. Organisations. *England. Age Concern. Reports, surveys*
Age Concern. Age Concern at work. — Mitcham : Age Concern, [1976]. — 28p : ill, ports ; 21x30cm.
ISBN 0-904502-69-4 Sd : Unpriced
(B77-02158)

362.6'0941 — Old persons. Care. Great Britain. Compared with care of old persons in United States. *Conference proceedings*
Care of the elderly : meeting the challenge of dependency : proceedings of a conference sponsored [i.e. organized] jointly by the Institute of Medicine, National Academy of Medicine, Washington, DC, the Royal Society of Medicine and the Royal Society of Medicine Foundation Inc., held at the National Academy of Sciences, Washington, DC, USA, 17-19 May 1976 / edited by A.N. Exton-Smith and J. Grimley Evans. — London : Academic Press [etc.], 1977. — xi,312p : ill ; 24cm.
Bibl. — Index.
ISBN 0-12-244950-9 : £11.80
Also classified at 362.6'0973
(B77-24106)

362.6'0941 — Old persons. Social problems. *Great Britain*
Scott-Moncrieff, Joanna. The sixty plus book : a guide to health and activity in later years / [by] Joanna Scott-Moncrieff. — London : Arrow Books, 1977. — 95p : ill ; 20cm. — (Arrow family handbooks)
Index.
ISBN 0-09-913730-5 Pbk : £0.70
(B77-10290)

362.6'09413'4 — Welfare services for old persons: Craigentinny-Lochend Welfare Services Project. *Edinburgh. Reports, surveys*
Craigentinny-Lochend Welfare Services Project. Report on the first year of the [Craigentinny-Lochend Welfare Services] Project / by Dave Du Feu, Project Co-ordinator. — Edinburgh (Craigentinny House, Loaning Rd, Edinburgh EH7 6JE) : [The Project], [1976]. — 24,[5]leaves : forms ; 24cm.
Cover title.
ISBN 0-9505350-0-1 Pbk : Unpriced
Primary classification 362.4'09413'4
(B77-00688)

362.6'09429 — Welfare services for old persons. *Wales. Reports, surveys*
Welsh Council. Services for the elderly in Wales / Cyngor Cymru = Welsh Council. — [Cardiff] ([c/o Welsh Office, Cathays Park, Cardiff CF1 3NQ]) : [The Council], 1976. — [5],68p ; 30cm.
ISBN 0-904251-13-6 Sp : Unpriced
(B77-01283)

362.6'0973 — Old persons. Care. United States. Compared with care of old persons in Great Britain. *Conference proceedings*
Care of the elderly : meeting the challenge of dependency : proceedings of a conference sponsored [i.e. organized] jointly by the Institute of Medicine, National Academy of Medicine, Washington, DC, the Royal Society of Medicine and the Royal Society of Medicine Foundation Inc., held at the National Academy of Sciences, Washington, DC, USA, 17-19 May 1976 / edited by A.N. Exton-Smith and J. Grimley Evans. — London : Academic Press [etc.], 1977. — xi,312p : ill ; 24cm.
Bibl. — Index.
ISBN 0-12-244950-9 : £11.80
Primary classification 362.6'0941
(B77-24106)

362.6'15 — Old persons. Day care. Role of residential institutions for old persons. *England*
National Corporation for the Care of Old People. Day care for the elderly : the role of residential homes / [National Corporation for the Care of Old People]. — London (Nuffield Lodge, Regent's Park, NW1 4RS) : The Corporation, 1976. — [1],8,[1]p ; 15x21cm. — (Homes advice broadsheets ; 2)
Bibl.: p.8.
ISBN 0-904139-04-2 Sd : £0.25
(B77-11714)

362.6'15 — Old persons. Residential care
Brearley, Christopher Paul. Residential work with the elderly / [by] C. Paul Brearley. — London [etc.] : Routledge and Kegan Paul, 1977. — vii,107p ; 23cm. — (Library of social work ISSN 0305-4381)
Bibl.: p.103-107.
ISBN 0-7100-8587-7 : £4.75 : CIP rev.
ISBN 0-7100-8588-5 Pbk : £2.25
(B77-07239)

362.6'15'0942498 — Residential homes for old persons. *Great Britain. Study examples: Craven House. Conference proceedings*
A life style for the elderly : report of a seminar held in conjunction with Coventry Social Services Department at Craven House home for the elderly, 18-20 July 1974, [organised by the] Department of Health and Social Security, Development Group-Social Work Service. — London : H.M.S.O., 1976. — [3],84p : ill, plans ; 30cm. — (Great Britain. Department of Health and Social Security. Social Work Service. Development Group. Report series)
Plan (fold. sheet)(1 side) in pocket. — Bibl.: p.58-59.
ISBN 0-11-320634-8 Pbk : £1.15
(B77-05312)

362.6'15'0973 — Old persons. Effects of residential care. *United States*
Tobin, Sheldon S. Last home for the aged / [by] Sheldon S. Tobin, Morton A. Lieberman. — San Francisco [etc.] ; London : Jossey-Bass, 1976. — xv,304p : 1 ill ; 24cm. — (The Jossey-Bass behavioral science series)
Bibl.: p.281-295. — Index.
ISBN 0-87589-280-9 : £9.00
(B77-07240)

362.6'3 — Catering services for old persons: Meals on wheels. *Scotland. Reports, surveys*
Stanley, Gillian. Meals services for the elderly in Scotland / [by] Gillian Stanley, W. Lutz. — [Edinburgh] ([New St Andrew's House, St James Centre, Edinburgh EH1 3TF]) : Scottish Home and Health Department, 1976. — xv, 266p : ill, forms, map ; 30cm. — (Scottish Health Service studies ; no.35)
Bibl.: p.98-99.
Pbk : £4.80
(B77-12953)

362.7 — WELFARE SERVICES FOR CHILDREN

362.7 — Adventure playgrounds. Social aspects. *Staffordshire. Stoke-on-Trent. Chell Heath. Feasibility studies*
Duggan, Edward Patrick. A report to the Social Science Research Council on a feasibility study of the social and educational effects of adventure playgrounds / by E.P. Duggan. — [Keele] : Centre for Social Science Research, University of Keele, [1975]. — 61[i.e.66]p : ill, forms ; 30cm.
ISBN 0-905851-00-5 Sd : Unpriced
(B77-02882)

362.7 — Children. Effects of housing. *Great Britain*
Shelter. No place to grow up / [Shelter] ; [written] by Zoë Fairbairns and Jim Wintour. — London (157 Waterloo Rd, SE1 8UU) : Shelter, 1977. — 28p : ill, facsims, ports ; 21cm.
Sd : £0.60
(B77-18028)

362.7 — Cities. Homeless single young persons. Accommodation. *Great Britain. Manuals*
Akehurst, Michael. Running to the city / by Michael Akehurst. — Nuneaton : National Association of Youth Clubs, [1977]. — [1],14, [1]p : 1 ill ; 21cm.
Bibl.: p.11-13.
ISBN 0-901528-77-3 Sd : £0.30
(B77-32540)

362.7 — Homeless single young persons. Accommodation. *Great Britain. Reports, surveys*
Waugh, Sarah. Needs and provision for young single homeless people : a review of information and literature / by Sarah Waugh. — London (27 Endell St., W.C.2) : Campaign for the Homeless and Rootless, Campaign for Single Homeless People, 1976. — [2],56p ; 26cm.
Bibl.: p.54-56.
Sd : Unpriced
(B77-26966)

362.7 — Play leaders. Training. *Great Britain. Reports, surveys*
Training for leadership : a discussion paper. — London (237 Pentonville Rd, N.1) : Fair Play For Children, 1976. — [2],61p ; 21cm.
Report of a working party commissioned by the Campaign in December 1973.
ISBN 0-9505533-0-1 Sd : £0.50
(B77-06569)

362.7 — Runaway young persons. Social conditions. *London*
Deakin, Michael. Johnny go home / [by] Michael Deakin & John Willis. — London : Futura Publications : Quartet Books, 1976. — 191p,[8]p of plates : ill, facsims, ports ; 18cm.
'Published in association with Yorkshire Television' - cover.
ISBN 0-86007-339-4 Pbk : £0.65
(B77-11153)

362.7 — Socially disadvantaged children. Care. *Great Britain. Reports, surveys*
Holman, Robert. Inequality in child care / [by] Robert Holman. — London : Child Poverty Action Group, 1975. — [2],38p ; 21cm. — (Poverty pamphlet ; 26 ISSN 0308-647x)
ISBN 0-903963-34-5 Sd : £0.50
(B77-02883)

362.7 — Welfare services for young people in ethnic minorities. *Great Britain. Conference proceedings*
Seen but not served : black youth and the youth service : report of a series of six seminars held in 1975-76 to examine statutory provision for young people from racial minorities. — London : Youth and Community Section, Community Relations Commission, 1977. — 42p : form ; 21cm.
Sd : Unpriced
(B77-21041)

362.7 — Welfare services for young persons with sexual problems. Role of Albany Trust. *Great Britain*
Albany Trust. The Albany Trust, the youth service and the psychosexual health of young people : an introduction. — London : 16 Strutton Ground, SW1P 2HP : The Trust, [1977]. — Folder([4]p) ; 30cm.
Unpriced
(B77-23260)

362.7 — Welfare work with adolescent girls. *England. Case studies*
Marchant, Harold. Adolescent girls at risk / by Harold Marchant and Helen M. Smith. — Oxford [etc.] : Pergamon, 1977. — xv,103p : forms ; 26cm. — (Pergamon international library : social work series)
Bibl.: p.103.
ISBN 0-08-018914-8 : Unpriced
ISBN 0-08-020634-4 Pbk : £2.50
(B77-30091)

362.7 — Welfare work with children. Assessment. *Reports, surveys*
Assessment of children and their families : a report / produced by a MIND working party under the chairmanship of P. Righton. — London : MIND : King's Fund Centre, 1975. — 41p ; 30cm.
Bibl.: p.27-28. — Previous control number ISBN 0-900557-32-x.
ISBN 0-900557-33-8 Sp : £0.50
(B77-00121)

362.7 — Welfare work with young persons. Contact techniques
Farrant, Michael Roger. Making contact : a stage in the detached work process / [by] Michael R. Farrant, Harold J. Marchant. — [Revised ed.]. — [London] ([31a Torridon Rd, S.E.6]) : [Youth AID], [1977]. — [1],36,[1]p ; 22cm.
Previous ed.: i.e. 1st ed., published as 'Making contact with unreached youth'. Manchester : Youth Development Trust (Manchester and District), 1971. — Bibl.: p.36.
ISBN 0-9505695-0-x Sd : £0.80(£2.00 for 3 copies, £7.00 for 10 copies)
(B77-15210)

362.7'06'11 — United Nations International Children's Emergency Fund, to 1973. *Teaching kits*
The **history** of UNICEF / compiled by Vivian Russell. — New York : Grossman ; London : Jackdaw [etc.], 1974. — Portfolio : ill(some col), facsims, map ; 23x35cm. — ([American] jackdaw ; no.A23)
Introductory leaflet ([4]p.) and 28 items. — English text, French, Norwegian and Ceylonese items. — Bibl.
ISBN 0-305-62097-5 : £1.95
(B77-02159)

362.7'06'241 — Welfare services for children. Organisations. *Great Britain. National Children's Home*
Many pieces, one aim : a practitioner approach to the multi-disciplinary concerns of an international voluntary child care organisation / edited by Gordon E. Barritt. — London (85 Highbury Park, N5 1UD) : National Children's Home, 1975. — [6],130p : ill, port ; 23cm.
Pbk : £1.00
(B77-32541)

362.7'092'2 — Services for children. *United States. Biographical dictionaries*
Who's who biographical record, child development professionals / compiled by the editors of 'Who's who in America'. — Chicago : Marquis Who's Who ; London : Distributed by Prior, 1976. — xiv,515p ; 26cm.
ISBN 0-8379-3701-9 : £31.50
(B77-15211)

362.7'092'4 — Voluntary welfare services for homeless children. *Vietnam. Saigon, 1972-1975. Personal observations*
Thomas, Liz. Dust of life : children of the Saigon streets / [by] Liz Thomas. — London : Hamilton, 1977. — viii,199p,[8]p of plates : ill, 2 maps, ports ; 23cm.
ISBN 0-241-89489-1 : £4.50
(B77-08307)

362.7'0941 — Welfare work with young persons. *Great Britain*
Collins, Nigel. No man's landmarks / [by] Nigel Collins and Liz Hoggarth. — Leicester : National Youth Bureau, [1977]. — [2],138p : ill ; 21cm. — (National Youth Bureau. Reports ; 6)
Bibl.: p.133-135.
ISBN 0-902095-57-9 Pbk : £2.50
(B77-32542)

362.7'0951 — Children. Care. *China*
Sidel, Ruth. Women and child care in China : a firsthand report / by Ruth Sidel ; photographs by Victor W. Sidel. — London : Sheldon Press, 1974. — xiv,207p : ill, ports ; 21cm.
Originally published: New York : Hill and Wang, 1972. — Bibl.: p.193-194. — Index.
ISBN 0-85969-034-2 Sd : £1.95
(B77-20149)

362.7'0973 — Children. Care. *United States. Transcripts of interviews*
Speaking out for America's children / [compiled by] Milton J.E. Senn. — New Haven ; London : Yale University Press, 1977. — xxi, 214p ; 21cm.
Bibl.: p.209-212. — Index.
ISBN 0-300-02107-0 : Unpriced
ISBN 0-300-02113-5 Pbk : £3.60
(B77-24818)

362.7'1 — Childminding. *England. Reports, surveys*
Mayall, Berry. Minder, mother and child / [by] Berry Mayall and Pat Petrie ; foreword by Jack Tizard. — London : University of London, Institute of Education ; Windsor : Distributed by NFER, 1977. — 97p : 1 ill, forms ; 22cm. — (Studies in education : new series ; 5)
Bibl.: p.83-84.
ISBN 0-85473-073-7 Pbk : £2.25
(B77-25506)

362.7'1 — Children. Non-accidental injury. *Somerset. Case studies*
Somerset Area Review Committee for Non-accidental Injury to Children. Wayne Brewer : report of the review panel [appointed by the] Somerset Area Review Committee for Non-accidental Injury to Children. — [Taunton] ([County Hall, Taunton, Somerset TA1 4DY]) : [The Committee], [1977]. — [3] leaves,51p ; 30cm.
Sd : Unpriced
(B77-20150)

362.7'1 — Ethnic minorities. Children, to 4 years. Day care. *Great Britain. Reports, surveys*
Community Relations Commission. *Reference and Technical Services Division.* Caring for under-fives in a multi-racial society / [Community Relations Commission, Reference and Technical Services Division]. — London : The Division, 1977. — 60p ; 22cm.
Bibl.: p.53-56. — Lists of films : p.56-57.
ISBN 0-902355-70-8 Sd : £0.60
(B77-12387)

362.7'1 — Pre-school children. Day care. *Great Britain*
Pre-school Playgroups Association. At work together : day nurseries in factories, hospitals and colleges / [Pre-school Playgroups Association]. — London (Alford House, Aveline St., SE11 5DH) : P.P.A., 1976. — 34p : 1 ill ; 30cm.
Bibl.: p.34.
ISBN 0-901755-13-3 Sd : £1.25
(B77-04690)

362.7'1 — Pre-school children. Day care. *London, 1966-1974. Reports, surveys*
Armistead, Nigel. Children's day care facilities in London, 1966-1974 / by Nigel Armistead, David Plank and Jean Sackett ; [for the] Director-General's Department, Intelligence Unit. — London : Greater London Council. Supplement. Data for 1975 / by Nigel Armistead. — 1976. — [1],ii,26p : ill ; 30cm. — (Greater London Council. Intelligence Unit. Research memoranda ; RM493 ISSN 0306-7203)
'The statistical series is the result of teamwork within the Personal Services Studies Section of the Policy Studies and Intelligence Branch' - Preface.
ISBN 0-7168-0842-0 Sd : £2.30
(B77-14142)

362.7'1 — Pre-school children. Day care. Policies of government. *United States, 1960-1975*
Greenblatt, Bernard. Responsibility for child care / [by] Bernard Greenblatt. — San Francisco [etc.] ; London : Jossey-Bass, 1977. — xvii,317p ; 24cm. — (The Jossey-Bass behavioral science series)
Bibl.: p.287-306. — Index.
ISBN 0-87589-315-5 : £11.00
Also classified at 372.21'0973
(B77-24107)

362.7'1 — Working mothers. Children. Day care. *United States. Reports, surveys*
Levitan, Sar A. Child care & ABC's too / [by] Sar A. Levitan, Karen Cleary Alderman. — Baltimore ; London : Johns Hopkins University Press, [1976]. — ix,125,[1]p : ill ; 24cm.
Published in the United States: 1975. — Index.
ISBN 0-8018-1733-1 : £6.80
(B77-03466)

362.7'3 — Homeless young persons. *Great Britain. Urban regions. Reports, surveys*
Working Group on Homeless Young People. Report / Working Group on Homeless Young People. — London ([Alexander Fleming House, Elephant and Castle, SE1 6BY]) : Department of Health and Social Security, 1976. — [5],81[i.e.84]p : facsims, forms ; 30cm.
ISBN 0-902650-11-4 Sd : Unpriced
(B77-06570)

362.7'32 — Children in care. Assessment. *England*
Assessment of children and their families : a report produced by a MIND working party ... — London : MIND : King's Fund Centre, 1975. — [3],41p ; 30cm.
Bibl.: p.27-28.
Sp : £0.50
(B77-20151)

362.7'32 — Coloured children. Residential care. *Great Britain. Reports, surveys*
Community Relations Commission. A home from home? : some policy considerations on black children in residential care / [Community Relations Commission]. — London : The Commission, 1977. — 39p : 2 forms ; 21cm.
Bibl.: p.35-39.
Sd : Unpriced
(B77-26228)

362.7'32 — Houseparents. *London. Personal observations*
Stone, Margaret. A housemother's dilemma / [by] Margaret Stone. — Ilfracombe : Stockwell, 1976. — 35p ; 19cm.
ISBN 0-7223-0939-2 Pbk : £0.75
(B77-25507)

362.7'32'08 — Children. Residential care. *Readings*
Children in care / edited by Robert J.N. Tod ; with a foreword by Sir Alan Moncrieff. — London : Longman, 1976. — xiii,115p ; 22cm. — (Papers on residential work ; vol.1)
This collection originally published: 1968. — Bibl.: p.114. — Index.
Pbk : £1.95
ISBN 0-582-42852-1
(B77-31083)

Children in care / edited by Robert J.N. Tod ; with a foreword by Alan Moncrieff. — London : Longman, 1974. — xiii,115p ; 22cm. — (Papers on residential work ; vol.1)
Originally published: 1968. — Bibl.: p.114. — Index.
ISBN 0-582-42852-1 Pbk : £1.40
(B77-18655)

362.7'32'0941 — Child care services. *Great Britain. For teaching*
Fitzherbert, Katrin. Child care services and the teacher / [by] Katrin Fitzherbert. — London : Temple Smith, 1977. — x,226p ; 23cm.
Bibl.: p.217-222. — Index.
ISBN 0-85117-110-9 : £4.65
(B77-13592)

362.7'32'09413 — Children. Residential care. *South-east Scotland. Reports, surveys*
Newman, Nancy. A roof over their heads? : residential provision for children in SE Scotland / by Nancy Newman, Harriet Mackintosh ; illustrations by Margaret Reynolds. — [2nd ed.]. — [Edinburgh] ([7 Buccleuch Place, Edinburgh EH8 9LW]) : University of Edinburgh, Department of Social Administration, [1977]. — 374p in various pagings : ill, facsims, forms, 2 maps ; 30cm.
Previous ed.: 1975?. — Bibl.(4p.). — Index.
ISBN 0-902174-04-5 Sp : £3.00
(B77-13593)

362.7'32'0942 — Local authorities. Child care services. *England. Statistics*
Children in care in England and Wales : a report / by the Secretaries of State for Social Services and for Wales ... — London : H.M.S.O.
1976, March. — [1977]. — 16p ; 25cm. — ([1976-77 H.C.]506)
ISBN 0-10-250677-9 Sd : £0.45
ISSN 0307-675x
(B77-26229)

362.7'32'0942753 — Residential institutions for young persons. *Merseyside (Metropolitan County). Liverpool. Brooks House, to 1975*
Redfern, Margaret, *b.1949.* Brooks House : an experiment in the provision of accommodation for young people at risk / [by] Margaret Redfern. — Liverpool (14 Castle St., Liverpool L2 0NJ) : Liverpool Council for Voluntary Service, 1977. — 76p ; 19cm.
Pbk : £0.60
(B77-23261)

362.7'33 — Children. Personal adjustment to foster care. Role of welfare workers
O'Connell, Marie. Helping the child to use foster family care : an in-service training and teaching aid / [by] Marie O'Connell. — London (4 Southampton Row, WC1B 4AA) : Association of British Adoption and Fostering Agencies, 1976. — [2],20p ; 21cm.
' ... based on talks given ... at a regional conference of the Child Welfare League of America' - Foreword. — Also published: New York : Child Welfare League of America, 1976.
ISBN 0-903534-21-5 Sd : £0.40
(B77-08921)

362.7'33'06241 — Children. Foster care. Organisations. *Great Britain. Association of British Adoption and Fostering Agencies. Reports, surveys*
Association of British Adoption and Fostering Agencies. Annual report / [the Association of British Adoption & Fostering Agencies]. — London (4 Southampton Row, WC1B 4AA) : The Association.
1975-76. — [1976]. — 23p ; 21cm.
Sd : Unpriced
Also classified at 362.7'34'06241
(B77-32543)

362.7'33'0941 — Children. Foster care. *Great Britain*
Stevenson, Olive. Someone else's child / [by] Olive Stevenson. — Revised ed. — London [etc.] : Routledge and Kegan Paul, 1977. — v, 122p ; 19cm.
Previous ed.: 1965. — Bibl.: p.14.
ISBN 0-7100-8706-3 Pbk : £1.60 : CIP rev.
(B77-19282)

362.7'33'094225 — Children. Foster care. *East Sussex*
East Sussex *(County). Social Services Department.* Foster care : a guide to practice in East Sussex / [Social Services Department, East Sussex County Council]. — [Lewes] ([P.O. Box 5, County Hall, St Anne's Cres., Lewes, E. Sussex]) : [The Department], [1977]. — [1],ii, 28,[4]p ; 21cm.
ISBN 0-900348-51-8 Sp : £9.50
(B77-08922)

362.7'34 — Coloured children. Adoption by white parents. *United States*
Simon, Rita James. Transracial adoption / [by] Rita James Simon, Howard Altstein. — New York ; London [etc.] : Wiley, 1977. — x,197p ; 24cm.
'A Wiley-Interscience publication'. — Index.
ISBN 0-471-79208-x : £11.00
(B77-21042)

362.7'34'06241 — Children. Adoption. Organisations. *Great Britain. Association of British Adoption and Fostering Agencies. Reports, surveys*
Association of British Adoption and Fostering Agencies. Annual report / [the Association of British Adoption & Fostering Agencies]. — London (4 Southampton Row, WC1B 4AA) : The Association.
1975-76. — [1976]. — 23p ; 21cm.
Sd : Unpriced
Primary classification 362.7'33'06241
(B77-32543)

362.7'34'0924 — Natural parents. Discovery by adopted persons. *United States. Personal observations*
Lifton, Betty Jean. Twice born : memoirs of an adopted daughter / [by] Betty Jean Lifton. — Harmondsworth [etc.] : Penguin, 1977. — [5], 281p ; 18cm.
Originally published: New York : McGraw-Hill, 1975.
ISBN 0-14-004404-3 Pbk : Unpriced
(B77-14643)

362.7'34'0924 — Natural parents of Hulse, Jody. Discovery. *United States. Personal observations*
Hulse, Jerry. Jody / by Jerry Hulse. — London : W.H. Allen, 1977. — 3-145p ; 23cm.
Originally published: New York : McGraw-Hill, 1976.
ISBN 0-491-01988-2 : £2.95
(B77-23262)

362.7'34'0941 — Children. Adoption. *Great Britain*
Kornitzer, Margaret. Adoption / [by] Margaret Kornitzer. — 5th ed. — London : Putnam, 1976. — 186p ; 21cm.
Previous ed.: 1973. — Bibl.: p.177-178. — Index.
ISBN 0-370-10058-1 : £4.95
ISBN 0-370-10059-x Pbk : £3.50
(B77-01284)

362.7'34'0941 — Children. Adoption. *Great Britain. Practical information*
Association of British Adoption and Fostering Agencies. Adopting a child : a brief guide for prospective adopters / the Association of British Adoption & Fostering Agencies. — Revised ed. — London (4 Southampton Row, WC1B 4AA) : The Association, 1977. — 24p ; 22cm.
Previous ed.: 1972. — Bibl.: p.10.
ISBN 0-903534-22-3 Sd : £0.30
(B77-15212)

362.7'34'0973 — Children. Adoption. Failures. *United States. Conference proceedings*
Disruption Workshop, *Chelsea, Mich., 1975.* Looking back on disruption : breakdown in family placements : papers given at a Disruption Workshop organised by Spaulding for Children, Michigan, USA. — London (4 Southampton Row, WC1B 4AA) : Association of British Adoption and Fostering Agencies, 1977. — 16,[1]p ; 21cm.
Also published: Chelsea, Mich. : Spaulding for Children, 1977.
Sd : £0.40
(B77-29314)

362.7'4 — Maladjusted children. Foster care. *Great Britain. Personal observations*
Swain, John. Spit once for luck : fostering Julie, a disturbed child / [by] John Swain ; foreword by Jean S. Heywood. — London : Elek : Pemberton, 1977. — 136p ; 23cm.
ISBN 0-236-40091-6 : £3.50
(B77-25508)

362.7'4 — Welfare work with deviant children. Projects. *South Glamorgan. Reports, surveys*
Great Britain. *Department of Health and Social Security. Social Work Service. Development Group.* Working together for children and their families : report of a project undertaken with South Glamorgan County Council / by Social Work Service, Development Group, Department of Health & Social Security ; [for the] Welsh Office. — London : H.M.S.O., 1977. — 207p : map ; 21cm.
'... project ... undertaken by the Social Work Service Development Group of the Department of Health and Social Security at the request of the Welsh Office ...' - Foreword. — Bibl.: p.169-190.
ISBN 0-11-320273-3 Pbk : £3.00
(B77-14644)

362.7'4'0924 — Welfare work with maladjusted young persons. *Great Britain. Personal observations*
Hart, Tom. Safe on a seesaw : a book of children / [by] Tom Hart. — London : Quartet Books, 1977. — [7],151p ; 23cm.
ISBN 0-7043-2089-4 : £4.25
(B77-09625)

362.7'8'10941 — Community health services for children. *Great Britain*
Child health in the community : a handbook of social and community paediatrics / edited by Ross G. Mitchell ; foreword by S.D.M. Court. — Edinburgh [etc.] : Churchill Livingstone, 1977. — xi,313p : ill ; 24cm.
Bibl. — Index.
ISBN 0-443-01507-4 : £8.00
(B77-10291)

362.7'8'10941 — Health services for children. *Great Britain. Inquiry reports*
Committee on Child Health Services. Fit for the future : report of the Committee on Child Health Services. — London : H.M.S.O.
In 2 vols. — Chairman: S.D.M. Court.
Vol.1. — [1976]. — xvii,448p : ill, maps ; 25cm. — (Cmnd.6684)
ISBN 0-10-166840-6 Pbk : £6.50
(B77-08308)

Vol.2. — [1976]. — [2],222p(14 fold) : 2 maps ; 25cm. — (Cmnd.6684-1)
ISBN 0-10-166841-4 Pbk : £4.00
(B77-08309)

362.7'8'10941 — Health services. Requirements of children. *Great Britain. Reports, surveys*
Franklin, Alfred White. Widening horizons of child health : a study of the medical health needs of children in England and Wales / by Alfred White Franklin with the help of working party of the British Paediatric Association and the Royal College of General Practitioners. — Lancaster : M.T.P. Press, 1976. — [10],279p ; 24cm.
Bibl.: p.269-276. — Index.
ISBN 0-85200-165-7 : £5.95
(B77-03467)

362.7'8'1094212 — Health services for children. *London (City)*
City and Hackney Health District. Profile of services for children / City and Hackney Health District. — [London] ([D.M.T. Office, Queen Mary's Nurses Home, St Bartholomew's Hospital, West Smithfield, EC1A 7BE]) : [The District], [1977]. — [4],112[i.e. 114]p : maps ; 33cm.
In binder.
Ls : Unpriced
Also classified at 362.7'8'10942144
(B77-18656)

362.7'8'10942144 — Health services for children. *London. Hackney (London Borough)*
City and Hackney Health District. Profile of services for children / City and Hackney Health District. — [London] ([D.M.T. Office, Queen Mary's Nurses Home, St Bartholomew's Hospital, West Smithfield, EC1A 7BE]) : [The District], [1977]. — [4],112[i.e. 114]p : maps ; 33cm.
In binder.
Ls : Unpriced
Primary classification 362.7'8'1094212
(B77-18656)

362.7'8'11 — Hospitals. Patients: Children. Care. *For parents*
Sail, Teresa. Children in hospital / by Teresa and Lawrence Sail. — Gloucester : Thornhill Press, 1976. — 30p ; 20cm. — (A Thornhill guide ; 2)
ISBN 0-904110-37-0 Sd : £0.40
(B77-12388)

362.7'8'11 — Hospitals. Patients: Children. Play therapy. *Great Britain. Sociological perspectives. Case studies*
Hall, David J. Social relations and innovation : changing the state of play in hospitals / [by] David J. Hall. — London [etc.] : Routledge and Kegan Paul, 1977. — x,222p : ill, plans ; 23cm. — (Medicine, illness and society)
Bibl.: p.201-212. — Index.
ISBN 0-7100-8607-5 : £5.25 : CIP rev.
(B77-21043)

362.7'8'110941835 — Hospitals. *Dublin. Rotunda Hospital. Department of Paediatrics. Reports, surveys. Serials*
Rotunda Hospital. Paediatric report / Rotunda Hospital. — Dublin ([Parnell St., Dublin 1]) : [The Hospital].
1975. — [1976]. — [1],8p ; 25cm.
Sd : Unpriced
(B77-20152)

362.7'8'19615500924 — Children with leukaemia. *Personal observations*
Mitson, Eileen Nora. Beyond the shadows / [by] Eileen Mitson. — London : Lakeland, 1973. — 128p ; 18cm.
Originally published: London : Oliphants, 1968.
ISBN 0-551-00469-x Pbk : £0.40
(B77-19283)

362.7'8'19639 — Children. Malnutrition. Relief. *Developing countries. Manuals*
Koppert, Joan. Nutrition rehabilitation : its practical application / by Joan Koppert ; with contributions by Sue Cole-King and William Cutting ; foreword by David Morley. — London (5 Tudor Cottage, Lovers Walk, Finchley, N3 1JH) : Tri-Med Books Ltd, 1977. — xiv,130p : ill, plans ; 22cm.
Bibl. — Index.
ISBN 0-905402-01-4 Pbk : £1.00
(B77-24820)

362.7'8'196858842 — Children with Down's syndrome. Foster care. *Great Britain. Personal observations*
Smithson, Margaret. Lesley, the child we chose : foster care of a mongol baby / [by] Margaret Smithson. — London (Pembridge Hall, Pembridge Sq., W2 4EP) : National Society for Mentally Handicapped Children, 1977. — [1], 21p ; 21cm.
ISBN 0-85537-041-6 Sd : £0.50
(B77-23263)

362.7'8'2 — Autistic children
Wing, Lorna. Children apart : autistic children and their families / [by] Lorna Wing. — Revised ed. — London : MIND, 1976. — 24p : ill ; 21cm.
Previous ed.: i.e. Revised ed., London : National Association for Mental Health, 1973.
ISBN 0-902502-12-3 Sd : £0.40
(B77-17388)

362.7'8'2 — Autistic children. *Personal observations*
Copeland, James. For the love of Ann / [by] James Copeland ; based on a diary by Jack Hodges. — Revised [ed.]. — London : Severn House : [Distributed by Hutchinson], 1976. — 156p,[16]p of plates : ill, ports ; 19cm.
Previous ed.: London : Arrow Books, 1973.
ISBN 0-7278-0151-1 : £3.95
(B77-04691)

362.7'8'2 — Dyslexic children. Psychosocial aspects
Morris, John C. The Education Act, how it provides for handicapped children : basic legal information which applies to the education of all handicapped pupils and to the dyslexic in particular / by John C. Morris. A dyslexic child in the family : a psychiatrist's sensitive and helpful consideration of the emotional tight-rope to be negotiated by parents / by A.F. Cheyne. — London (78 Whitehall Park, N19 3TN) : London Dyslexia Association, [1977]. — [12]p ; 30cm.
'Transcripts of two lectures given at a Conference of the North London Dyslexia Association, March 1976'.
Sd : £0.70
Primary classification 371.9'14
(B77-17400)

362.7'8'2 — Psychotic children
Guild of Teachers of Backward Children. *Annual Conference, Leicester, 1963.* Communication and the withdrawn child : papers presented at the annual conference of the Guild of Teachers of Backward Children, Leicester, 1963. — [London] : The Guild ; London (The NSMHC Bookshop, Pembridge Hall, Pembridge Sq., W2 4EP) : National Society for Mentally Handicapped Children, 1976. — 28p ; 21cm.
ISBN 0-85537-042-4 Sd : £0.30
(B77-21786)

362.7'8'2042 — Children undergoing psychotherapy. Rights
Children's rights and the mental health professions / edited by Gerald P. Koocher. — New York ; London [etc.] : Wiley, 1976. — xi, 259p ; 24cm. — (Wiley series on personality processes)
'A Wiley-Interscience publication'. — Bibl. — Index.
ISBN 0-471-01736-1 : £11.45
(B77-24108)

362.7'8'20973 — Mental health services for children. *United States*
Hetznecker, William. On behalf of children / [by] William Hetznecker, Marc A. Forman ; with a foreword by Leon Eisenberg. — New York [etc.] ; London : Grune and Stratton, 1974. — xviii,232p ; 23cm.
Index.
ISBN 0-8089-0844-8 Pbk : Unpriced
(B77-18657)

362.7'8'20973 — Mental health services for children. *United States. Reports, surveys*
Joint Commission on Mental Health of Children. *Task Force IV.* The mental health of children : services, research and manpower : reports of Task Forces IV and V and the report of the Committee on Clinical Issues by [i.e. of] the Joint Commission on Mental Health of Children. — New York [etc.] ; London : Harper and Row, 1973. — ix,446p : ill ; 24cm.
Bibl. — Index.
ISBN 0-06-012227-7 : Unpriced
(B77-18658)

362.7'8'20973 — Mental health services for young persons. *United States. Reports, surveys*
Joint Commission on Mental Health of Children. Mental health : from infancy through adolescence : reports of Task Forces I, II and III and the committees on education and religion by [i.e. of] the Joint Commission on Mental Health of Children. — New York [etc.] ; London : Harper and Row, 1973. — ix, 470p : 1 ill ; 24cm.
Bibl. — Index.
ISBN 0-06-012228-5 : £8.25
(B77-18659)

362.7'8'29209417 — Alcoholic drinks. Consumption by adolescents, to 18 years. Welfare aspects. *Ireland (Republic). Reports, surveys*
Teenage Drinking Committee. Teenage drinking : a cause for concern / [Teenage Drinking Committee]. — Dublin (6 Waterloo Rd, Dublin 4) : National Youth Council of Ireland, 1976. — [5],27p ; 21cm.
Bibl.: p.26-27.
Sd : £0.50
(B77-20153)

362.7'8'3 — Mentally handicapped children
Burt, *Sir* **Cyril.** The subnormal mind / by Sir Cyril Burt. — 3rd ed. re-issued ; with a new foreword. — Oxford [etc.] : Oxford University Press, 1977. — xxxv,391p ; 23cm. — (Heath Clark lectures ; 1933) ([Oxford medical publications])
'... delivered at The London School of Hygiene and Tropical Medicine'. — This ed. originally published: 1955. — Bibl.: p.381-383. — Index.
ISBN 0-19-261130-5 : £5.95
(B77-20154)

362.7'8'3 — Mentally handicapped children. Care
Intervention strategies for high risk infants and young children / edited by Theodore D. Tjossem. — Baltimore ; London [etc.] : University Park Press, [1977]. — xxxvii,787p : ill, facsim, forms, plans ; 25cm. — (National Institute of Child Health and Human Development. Mental Retardation Research Centers series)
'Based on the conference, "Early Intervention with High Risk Infants and Young Children", held at the University of North Carolina at Chapel Hill, May 5-8, 1974' - half title page verso. — Published in the United States: 1976. — Bibl. — Index.
ISBN 0-8391-0760-9 : £17.50
(B77-12389)

362.7'8'30942142 — Welfare work with mentally handicapped children. Projects: Kith and Kids. *London. Camden (London Borough), 1975*
Jones, Ann, *b.1946.* Two-to-One : a Kith and Kids community project / by Ann Jones ; preface by Albert Kushlick. — London (14 Talacre Rd, NW5 3PE) : Inter-Action Imprint, 1976. — 48p : ill, facsim ; 15x21cm. — (Inter-Action Advisory Service. Handbooks)
ISBN 0-904571-10-6 Sd : £0.60
(B77-14645)

362.7'8'30942659 — Services for mentally handicapped children. *Cambridgeshire*
Guide to services for the mentally handicapped and their parents / [produced by the collaboration of members of the Cambridge, Ely and Wisbech Societies for Mentally Handicapped Children et al.]. — [Cambridge] ([Castle Court, Shire Hall, Castle Hill, Cambridge CB3 0AP]) : Cambridgeshire County Council, Social Services Department, 1976. — [6],29p ; 30cm.
ISBN 0-905951-00-x Sd : £0.50
(B77-10292)

362.7'8'4 — Handicapped adolescents. Care. *For nursing*
The **nurse** and the developmentally disabled adolescent / edited by Mary Lou de Leon Siantz. — Baltimore ; London [etc.] : University Park Press, 1977. — xv,248p : ill, plans ; 23cm.
Bibl. — Index.
ISBN 0-8391-1131-2 Pbk : £7.25
(B77-31084)

362.7'8'4 — Handicapped children. Activities: Movement. Teaching. *Manuals*
Mortimore, Frederick. Making movement fun / [by] Frederick Mortimore. — London (Pembridge Hall, 17 Pembridge Sq., W2 4EP) : National Society for Mentally Handicapped Children, 1977. — [24]p : ill ; 21cm. — (National Society for Mentally Handicapped Children. Advisory leaflets)
Sd : £0.50
(B77-25505)

362.7'8'402541 — Services for handicapped children. *Great Britain. Directories. For parents*
Stone, Judith. A handbook for parents with a handicapped child / by Judith Stone and Felicity Taylor. — [New ed.]. — London : Arrow Books, 1977. — 424p ; 20cm.
Previous ed.: i.e. 2nd ed., 1972. — Index.
ISBN 0-09-914610-x Pbk : £2.50
(B77-30092)

362.7'8'40254281 — Services for handicapped children. *Yorkshire. Directories*
Winkworth, Fay. Public library facilities for handicapped children in Yorkshire : survey and directory / compiled by Fay Winkworth and Helen Sunderland. — [Leeds] ([c/o Margaret Marshall, School of Librarianship, 28 Park Place, Leeds LS1 2SY]) : Library Association, Yorkshire Branch of the Youth Libraries Group, [1976]. — [1],116p ; 25cm.
Bibl.: p.88-110. — Index.
ISBN 0-85365-650-9 Sd : £3.50
(B77-32544)

362.7'8'40924 — Physically handicapped children. *Personal observations*
Wallace, Marjorie. On giant's shoulders : the story of Terry Wiles / [by] Marjorie Wallace and Michael Robson. — London : Corgi, 1977. — 157p,[4]p of plates : ports ; 18cm.
Originally published: London : Time Books, 1976.
ISBN 0-552-10472-8 Pbk : £0.65
(B77-22473)

362.7'8'40941 — Handicapped children. *Great Britain*
Davie, Ronald. Children and families with special needs / by Ronald Davie. — Cardiff ([P.O. Box 78, Cardiff CF1 1XL]) : University College, [1975]. — 17p : 1 ill ; 21cm. — (University College, Cardiff. Inaugural lectures)
'... given on 22 January 1975 at University College, Cardiff'. — Bibl.: p.17.
Sd : Unpriced
(B77-00122)

362.7'8'42 — Partially hearing children. Communication. Development. *United States*
Berg, Frederick S. Educational audiology : hearing and speech management / [by] Frederick S. Berg. — New York [etc.] ; London : Grune and Stratton, [1977]. — viii, 312p : ill ; 24cm.
Published in the United States: 1976. — Bibl. — Index.
ISBN 0-8089-0973-8 : £11.30
(B77-12954)

362.7'8'43 — Children with spina bifida. *Great Britain*
Anderson, Elizabeth Marian. The child with spina bifida / [by] Elizabeth M. Anderson & Bernie Spain. — London : Methuen, 1977. — ix,352p : ill, map ; 23cm.
Bibl. — Index.
ISBN 0-416-55900-x : £7.50
ISBN 0-416-55910-7 Pbk : £4.95
(B77-21787)

362.8 — WELFARE SERVICES FOR FAMILIES, UNMARRIED MOTHERS, MINORITY GROUPS ETC.

362.8 — Housing. Organisations. *Great Britain. Shelter, to 1975*
Shelter. Shelter 1976 : ten years on : a progress report. — [London] ([157 Waterloo Rd, SE1 8UU]) : Shelter, National Campaign for the Homeless Ltd, 1976. — [2],26p : ill, col map, port ; 15x21cm.
ISBN 0-901242-38-1 Sd : Free
(B77-08310)

362.8 — Missing persons. Tracing. Role of Salvation Army
Williams, Richard. Missing! / by Richard Williams. — Abridged ed. — London [etc.] : Hodder and Stoughton, 1976. — 192p ; 18cm. — (Hodder Christian paperbacks)
Previous ed.: 1969.
ISBN 0-340-20438-9 Pbk : £0.80
(B77-08311)

362.8 — Welfare services for deviants. *England. Directories*
Directory of projects (England & Wales) for adult offenders, alcoholics, drug takers, homeless single people and people with histories of mental illness / co-produced by CCA, Camberwell Council on Alcoholism ... [et al.]. — [Chichester] : Rose.
1976-77. — [1976]. — [2],xiv,277p : map ; 21cm.
'Previously published: as 'Directory of projects for adult offenders, alcoholics, drug takers and homeless single people'. — Index.
Pbk : £2.00
ISSN 0309-0221
(B77-00689)

362.8 — Welfare services for persons with sexual problems. Organisations. *Great Britain. Albany Trust. Periodicals*
At work. — London (16 Strutton Ground, SW1P 2HP) : Albany Trust.
No.1- ; Autumn 1976-. — [1976]-. — ill, ports ; 42cm.
Quarterly. — 8p. in 1st issue.
Sd : Unpriced
ISSN 0309-7188
(B77-23264)

362.8 — Welfare services for widows. *New York (City). Widows Consultation Center*
Hiltz, Starr Roxanne. Creating community services for widows : a pilot project / [by] Starr Roxanne Hiltz. — Port Washington ; London : Kennikat Press, 1977. — x,166p : ill, facsims, forms ; 23cm. — (National university publications)
Bibl.: p.162-164. — Index.
ISBN 0-8046-9157-6 : £8.45
(B77-22474)

362.8 — Women. Attitudes of welfare services. *Great Britain, 1837-1976*
Wilson, Elizabeth, *b.1936.* Women & the welfare state / [by] Elizabeth Wilson. — London : Tavistock Publications, 1977. — 208p ; 20cm. — (Tavistock women's studies)
Bibl.: p.188-202. — Index.
ISBN 0-422-76050-1 : £5.50
ISBN 0-422-76060-9 Pbk : £2.50
(B77-23265)

362.8'2 — Battered wives. *Great Britain. Reports, surveys*
Great Britain. *Parliament. House of Commons. Select Committee on Violence in the Family.* Battered wives : second report from the Select Committee on Violence in the Family, session 1976-77, together with the proceedings of the Committee and appendices. — London : H.M.S.O., [1977]. — xvi p ; 25cm. — ([1976-77 H.C.]431)
ISBN 0-10-030595-4 Sd : £0.35
(B77-28522)

362.8'2 — Families with children conceived by artificial insemination of donor sperm. *Personal observations*
Blizzard, Joseph. Blizzard and the Holy Ghost : artificial insemination : a personal account. — London : Owen, 1977. — 191p ; 22cm.
ISBN 0-7206-0374-9 : £5.25
(B77-08923)

362.8'2 — Families with mentally handicapped children. Self-help. Organisations. *Great Britain. Kith and Kids (Group). Personal observations*
Collins, Maurice. Kith and kids : self-help for families of the handicapped / by Maurice and Doreen Collins. — London : Souvenir Press, 1976. — [6],192p,[8]p of plates : ill, ports ; 22cm. — (Human horizons series) (A condor book)
ISBN 0-285-64818-7 : £4.00
ISBN 0-285-64819-5 Pbk : £2.50
(B77-02160)

362.8'2 — Family allowances. *Great Britain. Power of Women Collective viewpoints*
Fleming, Suzie. The family allowance under attack / [by] Suzie Fleming. — 2nd ed. — Bristol (79 Richmond Road, Montpelier, Bristol BS6 5EP) : Falling Wall Press Ltd ; [London] : Power of Women Collective, 1973. — [2],14p ; 21cm.
Previous ed.: 1973.
Sd : £0.08
(B77-15213)

362.8'2 — Family planning services. *Botswana. Reports, surveys*
Cook, Sheila. Evaluation of family planning programmes : an example from Botswana / by Sheila Cook. — London : Evaluation and Social Sciences Department, International Planned Parenthood Federation, 1976. — [1],13p ; 21cm. — (Research for action ; no.2 ISSN 0309-2615)
ISBN 0-900924-77-2 Sd : £0.35
(B77-09626)

362.8'2 — Family planning services. *Reports, surveys. Spanish texts*
International Planned Parenthood Federation. La planificación familiar en cinco continentes / [Federation International de Planificacion de la Familia]. — Londres [i.e. London] : The Federation, 1974. — [2],41p ; 21x30cm.
ISBN 0-900924-60-8 Sd : £0.25
Also classified at 312
(B77-21044)

362.8'2 — Family planning services. Clinics. Location. *London. Reports, surveys*
Price, D G. Family planning clinics in London : a geographical view / by D.G. Price and Alison J. Cummings. — [London] ([32 Wells St., W1P 3FG]) : [Polytechnic of Central London, School of the Social Sciences and Business Studies], [1977]. — 46 leaves in various pagings : maps ; 30cm. — (Polytechnic of Central London. School of the Social Sciences and Business Studies. Research working papers ; no.2)
Pbk : Unpriced
(B77-22475)

362.8'2 — Family planning services. Evaluation. *Reports, surveys*
Organisation for Economic Co-operation and Development. *Development Centre.* Measuring the impact of family planning : a short guide / [Organisation for Economic Co-operation and Development, Development Centre]. — Paris : The Centre ; [London] : [H.M.S.O.], 1977. — 73p : ill ; 24cm. — (Organisation for Economic Co-operation and Development. Development Centre. Studies)
Bibl.: p.62.
Pbk : £2.00
ISBN 92-64-11613-3
(B77-15214)

362.8'2 — Local authorities. Welfare services for homeless families: Temporary accommodation: Local authority hostels. *Great Britain. Reports, surveys*
Shelter. Hostel for a home / [Shelter] ; [written] by Bob Widdowson. — London (157 Waterloo Rd, SE1 8UU) : Shelter, [1977]. — [1],21p : ill ; 27cm.
ISBN 0-901242-39-x Sd : £0.60
(B77-11715)

362.8'2 — Low-income families. Standard of living. Effects of cost of school students' bus fares. *England. Child Poverty Action Group viewpoints*
Tunnard, Jo. Taken for a ride / by Jo Tunnard. — London : Child Poverty Action Group, 1976. — [3],21[i.e.22]p ; 30cm. — (Welfare in action)
Sd : £0.40
(B77-17389)

362.8'2 — Low-income families. Standard of living. Effects of fuel prices. Alleviation. *Great Britain*
National Consumer Council. Paying for fuel : report by the National Consumer Council to the Secretary of State for Prices and Consumer Protection. — London : H.M.S.O., 1976. — viii,238p : ill ; 21cm. — (Report ; no.2)
Bibl.: p.145.
ISBN 0-11-880237-2 Pbk : £3.50
(B77-05982)

362.8'2 — Marriage bureaux. *Ireland (Republic). Personal observations*
O'Beirne, Michael. People people marry, people people don't / [by] Michael O'Beirne. — Dublin : Veritas Publications, 1976. — 142p ; 19cm.
ISBN 0-905092-15-5 Pbk : £0.90
(B77-05313)

362.8'2 — Marriage counselling
Ables, Billie S. Therapy for couples / [by] Billie S. Ables in collaboration with Jeffrey M. Brandsma. — San Francisco [etc.] ; London : Jossey-Bass, 1977. — xvii,364p : form ; 24cm. — (The Jossey-Bass behavioral science series)
Index.
ISBN 0-87589-312-0 : £11.00
(B77-21045)

362.8'2 — Married persons. Sexual problems. Research projects by National Marriage Guidance Council. *Great Britain. National Marriage Guidance Council Marital Sexual Dysfunction Project. Reports, surveys*
National Marriage Guidance Council. An account of the NMGC marital sexual dysfunction project / by David Barkla, Development Officer, NMGC. — [Rugby] : The Council, [1977]. — [1],13p ; 22cm.
ISBN 0-85351-048-2 Sd : £0.75
(B77-14646)

362.8'2 — Problem families. Interpersonal relationships with welfare workers. *Great Britain. Case studies*
Jennens, Roger. Casework with a family at risk / by Roger Jennens. — London (207 Old Marylebone Rd, NW1 [5QP]) : Family Service Units, 1976. — [1],29p ; 30cm.
ISBN 0-905175-04-2 Sd : £0.50
(B77-02884)

362.8'2 — Welfare services for low-income families. *Great Britain, 1960-1970*
Abel-Smith, Brian. Child poverty / [by] Brian Abel-Smith. — London (207 Old Marylebone Rd, NW1 [5QP]) : Family Service Units, [1976]. — 22p ; 30cm.
'... address ... given to the A.G.M. of Family Service Units in December, 1971' - p.22. — 'Reprinted from F.S.U. Quarterly No.1'.
ISBN 0-905175-03-4 Sd : £0.20
(B77-04055)

362.8′2 — Welfare work with families where parents neglect their children. *Great Britain*
Martel, Sheila. Non-accidental injury : two papers on diagnosis, prevention, treatment and administrative procedures, with case material as appendices / by Sheila Martel. — London (207 Old Marylebone Rd, NW1 5QP) : Family Service Units, 1977. — [1],54p ; 30cm.
Sd : £1.20
(B77-17390)

362.8′2 — Welfare work with inarticulate mothers. Group work. *West Yorkshire (Metropolitan County). Personal observations*
Walker, Lorna, *b.1920.* Groupwork with the inarticulate : an account of a Bradford FSU Mothers Group / [by] Lorna Walker ; with a complimentary paper by Elizabeth E. Irvine. — [London] ([207 Old Marylebone Rd, NW1 5QP]) : [Family Service Units], [1976]. — [3], 33p ; 30cm.
Originally published: s.l. : s.n., 1970. — Bibl.: p.8.
ISBN 0-905175-05-0 Sd : £0.40
(B77-04056)

362.8′2 — Women with unwanted pregnancies. Counselling
Cheetham, Juliet. Unwanted pregnancy and counselling / [by] Juliet Cheetham. — London [etc.] : Routledge and Kegan Paul, 1977. — xii, 234p ; 23cm.
Bibl.: p.225-232. — Index.
ISBN 0-7100-8499-4 : £4.95
(B77-10293)

362.8′2′0941 — Families. Members. Care. Responsibility of government & families. *Great Britain*
Moroney, Robert. The family and the state : considerations for social policy / [by] Robert M. Moroney. — London [etc.] : Longman, 1976. — xii,142p ; 22cm.
Index.
ISBN 0-582-48493-6 Pbk : £2.50
(B77-31085)

362.8′2′0942 — Welfare work with problem families by family service units. *England. Case studies*
Halliwell, Rex. Time limited work with a family at point of being prosecuted for child neglect / [by] Rex Halliwell. — [London] ([207 Old Marylebone Rd, NW1 5QP]) : Family Service Units, [1976]. — [1],6p ; 24cm.
'Reprinted from "Case Conference" vol.15. No.9 January, 1969' - p.6.
ISBN 0-905175-01-8 Sd : £0.20
(B77-02161)

362.8′2′094215 — Welfare work with problem families. Family service units. *London. Tower Hamlets (London Borough). East London Family Service Unit*
East London Family Service Unit. Families and groups : a unit at work : a description and analysis of work with families, groups and the neighbourhood undertaken at the East London Family Service Unit / Donald Smith, editor. — London (169 Malden Rd, NW5 4HT) : Bookstall Publications, 1974. — 68p ; 21cm. — (Family Service Units. Monographs ; no.2)
ISBN 0-903075-11-3 Pbk : £0.90
(B77-04057)

362.8′3′09411 — Unmarried pregnant women. *Great Britain. Sociological perspectives. Study regions: Scotland*
Macintyre, Sally. Single and pregnant / [by] Sally Macintyre. — London : Croom Helm [etc.], 1977. — 201p ; 23cm.
Bibl.: p.190-198. — Index.
ISBN 0-85664-402-1 : £6.95
(B77-17391)

362.8′4 — New Commonwealth immigrants. Dependants. Registers. *Great Britain. Feasibility studies*
Great Britain. *Parliament.* A register of dependants : report of the Parliamentary Group on the feasibility and usefulness of a register of dependants ; presented to Parliament by the Secretary of State for the Home Department ... — London : H.M.S.O., [1977]. — [2],ii,30p ; 25cm. — (Cmnd.6698)
ISBN 0-10-166980-1 Sd : £0.60
(B77-09627)

362.8′4 — Welfare work with negro communities. *United States*
Solomon, Barbara Bryant. Black empowerment : social work in oppressed communities / [by] Barbara Bryant Solomon. — New York ; Guildford : Columbia University Press, 1976 [i.e. 1977]. — ix,438p ; 24cm.
Published in the United States: 1976. — Index.
ISBN 0-231-04086-5 : £13.88
(B77-10294)

362.8′5 — Social services for returning migrant personnel. *Organisation for Economic Co-operation and Development countries. Reports, surveys*
Gendt, Rien van. Return migration and reintegration services / [by] Rien van Gendt in consultation with G. Garcia Passigli. — Paris : Organisation for Economic Co-operation and Development ; [London] : [H.M.S.O.], 1977. — 64p ; 24cm.
Pbk : £2.00
ISBN 92-64-11612-5
(B77-11154)

362.8′8 — Criminal injuries. Compensation. Organisations. *Great Britain. Criminal Injuries Compensation Board. Reports, surveys. Serials*
Criminal Injuries Compensation Board. Report [and] accounts for the year ended 31st March / Criminal Injuries Compensation Board .... — London : H.M.S.O.
12th : [1975]-1976. — [1976]. — 34p ; 25cm. — (Cmnd. 6656)
ISBN 0-10-166560-1 Sd : £0.50
(B77-04058)

362.9 — SPECIALISED WELFARE SERVICES. HISTORICAL AND GEOGRAPHICAL TREATMENT

362′.92′4 — United States. Social reform. Du Bois, William Edward Burghardt. *Biographies*
Rampersad, Arnold. The art and imagination of W.E.B. Du Bois / [by] Arnold Rampersad. — Cambridge, Mass. ; London : Harvard University Press, 1976. — ix,325p : ports ; 24cm.
Index.
ISBN 0-674-04711-7 : £10.50
(B77-08312)

363 — SECURITY AND OTHER PUBLIC SERVICES

363 — Environment. Pollution. Control measures. Planning. Role of public inquiries
Open University. *Environmental Control and Public Health Course Team.* Planning and pollution : areas of concern / prepared by the Course Team [i.e. The Environmental Control and Public Health Course Team]. — Milton Keynes : Open University Press, 1975. — 86p : ill, col maps ; 30cm. — (PT272 ; 16) (Technology, a post experience and second level course : environmental control and public health ; unit 16)
With answers to self-assessment questions. — Bibl.
ISBN 0-335-06007-2 Pbk : £1.95
(B77-27763)

363 — Great Britain. Politics. Dissent. Control. Techniques
Royal Town Planning Institute. List of members / Royal Town Planning Institute. — London : The Institute.
1975, as at August. — [1977]. — [2],162p ; 21cm.
Pbk : £6.00(£0.90 to members)
(B77-09838)

The **technology** of political control / by Carol Ackroyd ... [et al.]. — Harmondsworth [etc.] : Penguin, 1977. — 320p ; 18cm. — (Pelican books)
Index.
ISBN 0-14-021943-9 Pbk : £1.25
(B77-18660)

363 — Public services. Innovation. Policies of governments. *Organisation for Economic Co-operation and Development countries*
Organisation for Economic Co-operation and Development. Policies for innovation in the service sector, identification and structure of relevant factors / [Organisation for Economic Co-operation and Development]. — Paris : O.E.C.D. ; [London] : [H.M.S.O.], 1977. — 235p ; 24cm.
Pbk : £5.50
ISBN 92-64-11627-3
(B77-14143)

363 — Security services. *Directories*
International security directory. — St Albans (117 Hatfield Rd, St Albans, Herts. AL1 4JS) : Security Gazette Ltd.
1976-7 : 14th ed. — 1976. — x,355p : ill, maps ; 22cm.
Index.
ISBN 0-901718-16-5 Pbk : £7.00
ISSN 0074-7890
(B77-04059)

1977-8 : 15th ed. — 1977. — vi,376p,[3]p of plates : ill, maps ; 22cm.
Index.
Pbk : £7.00
ISSN 0074-7890
(B77-31793)

363′.025′42184 — Public services. *London. Ealing (London Borough). Directories*
The **London** Borough of Ealing information handbook. — 3rd ed. — London : Burrow, [1977]. — [1],52p : ill ; 21cm.
Sd : Unpriced
(B77-18029)

363′.025′42394 — Public services. *Avon. Kingswood (District). Directories*
Kingswood District Council services information handbook. — Carshalton : Forward Publicity, [1977]. — 40,[1]p : ill ; 21cm.
ISBN 0-7174-0738-1 Sd : Unpriced
(B77-12390)

363′.09172′4 — Public services. Provision by local authorities. *Developing countries. Urban regions. Case studies*
Pasteur, David. The Metroville water supply exercise : a case study in project appraisal and implementation in a large scale infrastructure project / [by] D. Pasteur. — Birmingham (P.O. Box 363, Birmingham B15 2TT) : Development Administration Group, Institute of Local Government Studies, University of Birmingham, 1976. — [3],33[i.e.41]p(4 fold),[4]leaves of plates(3 fold) : ill, map ; 30cm. — (Case studies in development administration ; vol.1)
Page size varies.
ISBN 0-7044-0198-3 Pbk : £0.50
(B77-22476)

363′.09173′2 — Public services. *Urban regions*
Comparing urban service delivery systems : structure and performance / edited by Vincent Ostrom and Frances Pennell Bish. — Beverly Hills ; London : Sage Publications, 1977. — 304p : ill ; 24cm. — (Urban affairs annual reviews ; vol.12)
Bibl.
ISBN 0-8039-0470-3 : £12.00
ISBN 0-8039-0680-3 Pbk : £4.95
(B77-27764)

363′.0973 — Public services. Distribution. *United States. Urban regions*
Lineberry, Robert Leon. Equality and urban policy : the distribution of municipal public services / [by] Robert L. Lineberry. — Beverly Hills ; London : Sage Publications, 1977. — 207p : 1 ill ; 22cm. — (Sage library of social research ; vol.39)
Bibl.: p.199-202. — Index.
ISBN 0-8039-0742-7 : £8.00
ISBN 0-8039-0743-5 Pbk : £4.50
(B77-25509)

363′.0973 — Public services. Mathematical models. *United States*
Beltrami, Edward John. Models for public systems analysis / [by] Edward J. Beltrami. — New York [etc.] ; London : Academic Press, 1977. — xv,218p : ill ; 24cm. — (Operations research and industrial engineering)
Bibl. — Index.
ISBN 0-12-085565-8 : £10.30
(B77-25510)

363.2 — POLICE

363.2′092′2 — Police. Greenberg, David & Hantz, Robert. *New York (City). Personal observations*
Whittemore, L H. The super cops : the story of the cops known as Batman and Robin / [by] L.H. Whittemore. — London : Futura Publications, 1976. — 383p ; 18cm.
Originally published: New York : Stein and Day, 1973 ; London : Macdonald and Jane's, 1974.
ISBN 0-86007-001-8 Pbk : £0.80
(B77-27765)

363.2′092′4 — Police. Corruption. Exposure. Serpico, Frank. *New York (City)*
Maas, Peter. Serpico / [by] Peter Maas. — [London] : Fontana, 1977. — 252p ; 18cm.
Originally published: New York : Viking Press ; London : Collins, 1973.
ISBN 0-00-634905-6 Pbk : £0.80
(B77-14144)

363.2'092'4 — Police. Williams, Ken. *Wales. Autobiographies*
Williams, Ken, *b.1929.* Wildlife in custody / [by] Ken Williams and Ian Skidmore. — London : Cassell, 1977. — x,195p,[8]p of plates, ill, maps, ports ; 23cm.
ISBN 0-304-29826-3 : £4.50
(B77-21046)

363.2'092'4 — Texas. Texas Rangers, 1875-1881. *Personal observations*
Gillett, James B. Six years with the Texas Rangers, 1875 to 1881 / by James B. Gillett ; edited, with an introduction, by M.M. Quaife. — [New ed. reprinted] ; with a foreword by Oliver Knight. — Lincoln [Neb.] ; London : University of Nebraska Press, 1976. — iii-xxxvi, 259p,[10]leaves of plates : ill, ports ; 22cm.
'A Bison book'. — Facsimile reprint of: New ed.: New Haven : Yale University Press, 1925. — Index.
ISBN 0-8032-0889-8 : £9.60
ISBN 0-8032-5844-5 Pbk : £3.20
(B77-04692)

363.2'0941 — Police. *Great Britain. Lectures, speeches*
Mark, *Sir* **Robert.** Policing a perplexed society / by Sir Robert Mark. — London : Allen and Unwin, 1977. — 3-132p ; 23cm.
Index.
ISBN 0-04-363005-7 : £5.00
ISBN 0-04-363006-5 Pbk : £2.50
(B77-10295)

363.2'0941 — Police. Role. *Great Britain. Forecasts*
Lewis, Roy, *b.1913.* A force for the future : the role of the police in the next ten years / [by] Roy Lewis. — London : Temple Smith, 1976. — 316p ; 23cm.
Index.
ISBN 0-85117-111-7 : £7.50
(B77-00690)

363.2'0941 — Police. Role. Political aspects. *Great Britain, to 1975*
Bunyan, Tony. The history and practice of the political police in Britain / [by] Tony Bunyan. — Revised [ed.]. — London : Quartet Books, 1977. — xi,324p : ill, facsims ; 20cm.
Previous ed.: London : Friedmann, 1976. — Bibl.: p.310-313. — Index.
ISBN 0-7043-3128-4 Pbk : £2.50
(B77-11716)

363.2'09411 — Police. *Scotland. Reports, surveys. Serials*
Great Britain. *Scottish Home and Health Department. Police and Fire Services Division.* Her Majesty's Chief Inspector of Constabulary for Scotland : report ... — Edinburgh : H.M.S.O.
1976. — [1977]. — 63p ; 25cm. — (Cmnd.6891)
ISBN 0-10-168910-1 Sd : £1.00
(B77-31794)

363.2'0942 — Police. *England. Reports, surveys. Serials*
Great Britain. *Police Department.* Report of Her Majesty's Chief Inspector of Constabulary for the year ... — London : H.M.S.O.
1976. — [1977]. — viii,103p : ill ; 25cm. — ([1976-77 H.C.]414)
ISBN 0-10-241477-7 Pbk : £1.65
(B77-22477)

363.2'09421 — Police. *London. Metropolitan Police. Reports, surveys. Serials*
Metropolitan Police. *Commissioner.* Report of the Commissioner of Police of the Metropolis / presented to Parliament by the Secretary of State for the Home Department ... — London : H.M.S.O.
1976. — [1977]. — 132p : ill ; 25cm. — (Cmnd.6821)
ISBN 0-10-168210-7 Pbk : £2.10
(B77-18030)

363.2'09421 — Police. *London. Metropolitan Police, to 1911. Secondary school texts*
Wilkes, John, *b.1937.* The London police in the nineteenth century / [by] John Wilkes. — Cambridge [etc.] : Cambridge University Press, 1977. — 48p : ill, maps, ports ; 21x22cm. — (Cambridge introduction to the history of mankind : topic book)
ISBN 0-521-21406-8 Sd : Unpriced
(B77-27766)

363.2'0952 — Police. Behaviour. Japan. Compared with police behaviour in United States
Bayley, David Hume. Forces of order : police behavior in Japan and the United States / [by] David H. Bayley. — Berkeley [etc.] ; London : University of California Press, 1976. — xvi, 201p ; 25cm.
Index.
ISBN 0-520-03069-9 : £7.65
Also classified at 363.2'0973
(B77-00123)

363.2'0973 — Police. *United States*
Sullivan, John Lawrence, *b.1908.* Introduction to police science / [by] John L. Sullivan. — 3rd ed. — New York ; London [etc.] : McGraw-Hill, 1977. — xii,356p : ill, forms ; 24cm.
Previous ed.: New York : McGraw-Hill, 1971. — Bibl.: p.341-345. — List of films: p.333-338. — Index.
ISBN 0-07-062430-5 : £8.95
(B77-24111)

363.2'0973 — Police. *United States. Sociological perspectives*
Drummond, Douglas S. Police culture / [by] Douglas S. Drummond. — Beverly Hills ; London : Sage Publications, 1976. — 45,[1]p ; 22cm. — (Sage professional papers in administrative and policy studies ; vol.3, no.03-032)
Bibl.: p.41-44.
ISBN 0-8039-0536-x Pbk : £1.75
(B77-14145)

363.2'0973 — Police. *United States, to 1975. Readings*
Focus on police : police in American society / [edited by] Christian P. Potholm, Richard E. Morgan. — Cambridge, Mass. : Schenkman Publishing Co. ; New York ; London [etc.] : Distributed by Wiley, 1976. — [6],412p : 1 ill ; 24cm.
ISBN 0-470-15075-0 : £12.55
ISBN 0-470-15077-7 Pbk : £4.75
(B77-11155)

363.2'0973 — Police. Behaviour. United States. Compared with police behaviour in Japan
Bayley, David Hume. Forces of order : police behavior in Japan and the United States / [by] David H. Bayley. — Berkeley [etc.] ; London : University of California Press, 1976. — xvi, 201p ; 25cm.
Index.
ISBN 0-520-03069-9 : £7.65
Primary classification 363.2'0952
(B77-00123)

363.2'0994 — Police. *Australia. Australia. Corps of Native Police, 1849-1859*
Skinner, L E. Police of the pastoral frontier : native police, 1849-59 / [by] L.E. Skinner. — St Lucia : University of Queensland Press ; Hemel Hempstead : Distributed by Prentice-Hall, [1976]. — x,455p,[8]p of plates : ill, facsim, maps, ports ; 23cm.
Published in Australia: 1975. — Index.
ISBN 0-7022-0977-5 : £9.35
(B77-02162)

363.2'42 — Police. *Northern Ireland. Royal Ulster Constabulary. Complaints by public. Administration. Procedure. Proposals*
The **handling** of complaints against the police, report of the Working Party for Northern Ireland / presented to Parliament by the Secretary of State for Northern Ireland. — Belfast : H.M.S.O., [1976]. — [1],iii,56p ; 25cm. — (Cmnd.6475)
Chairman: Sir Harold Black.
ISBN 0-10-164750-6 Sd : £0.75
(B77-03468)

363.3 — PUBLIC ORDER SERVICES

363.3 — Riot control
Deane-Drummond, Anthony. Riot control / by Anthony Deane-Drummond. — London (25 Haymarket, S.W.1) : Thornton Cox Ltd [etc.], 1975. — 158p ; 24cm.
Also published: London : Royal United Services Institute for Defence Studies, 1975.
ISBN 0-902726-21-8 : £3.25
(B77-19284)

363.3 — Western world. Politics. Violence. Control. Policies of governments
Gregory, Frank. Protest and violence : the police response: a comparative analysis of democratic methods / by Frank Gregory. — London : Institute for the Study of Conflict, 1976. — [2], 15p ; 30cm. — (Conflict studies ; no.75 ISSN 0069-8792)
ISBN 0-903366-51-7 Sd : £2.00
(B77-02163)

363.3'7'025 — Fire brigades. *Directories*
Fire protection directory : incorporating 'Fire brigades of the world'. — Tonbridge : 'Fire protection review' : [Distributed by] Benn Bros.
1977 : 37th ed. / [edited by J.L. Eades]. — [1977]. — 535,[8]p : ill ; 19cm.
Tab indexed. — Index.
ISBN 0-510-49508-7 : £10.00
Also classified at 338.4'7'628922025
(B77-17392)

363.3'7'09411 — Fire brigades. *Scotland. Reports, surveys. Serials*
Great Britain. *Scottish Home and Health Department. Police and Fire Services Division.* Report ... / Her Majesty's Inspector of Fire Services for Scotland. — Edinburgh : H.M.S.O.
1976. — [1977]. — 27p ; 25cm. — (Cmnd.6816)
ISBN 0-10-168160-7 Sd : £0.55
(B77-21047)

363.3'7'0942 — Fire brigades. *England. Reports, surveys. Serials*
Great Britain. *Home Office. Fire Department.* Report of Her Majesty's Chief Inspector of Fire Services (Metropolitan counties and non-metropolitan counties, England and Wales and Greater London Council) ... — London : H.M.S.O.
1976. — [1977]. — v,61p ; 25cm. — (Cmnd.6859)
ISBN 0-10-168590-4 Sd : £1.40
(B77-21788)

363.3'7'0942212 — Fire brigades. *Surrey. Sunbury-on-Thames, to 1973*
Heselton, Kenneth Yeaman. Sunbury mills and fire services / [by] Kenneth Y. Heselton. — Sunbury-on-Thames (12 Heathcroft Ave., Sunbury-on-Thames, [Middx]) : Sunbury and Shepperton Local History Society, 1977. — [2], 12p ; 26cm. — (Sunbury and Shepperton Local History Society. Occasional publications ; no.4 ISSN 0309-2070)
Sd : £0.20
Also classified at 664'.7207
(B77-15770)

363.3'7'094273 — Fire brigades. *Greater Manchester (Metropolitan County), to 1975*
Turnbull, George. The Fire Service / by G. Turnbull. — Manchester (c/o Mrs M. Beeston, 53 Sunningdale Drive, Irlam, Manchester) : Irlam and Cadishead Historical Society, 1976. — [1],15 leaves ; 30cm.
Bibl.: leaf 15.
Sd : £0.15
(B77-31795)

363.5 — PUBLIC WORKS SERVICES

363.5 — Ethnic minorities. Public housing. *England. Reports, surveys*
Smith, David, *b.1941.* Racial minorities & public housing / [by] David Smith and Anne Whalley. — London : P.E.P., [1975]. — vi,119p ; 21cm. — (Political and Economic Planning. Broadsheets ; no.556)
ISBN 0-85374-142-5 Pbk : £3.00
(B77-00044)

363.5 — Greater London Council housing. Tenancies. Allocation. Alleged racial discrimination. London. Investigated by comparison of social conditions of coloured & white tenants. *Inquiry reports*
Parker, John, *b.1936.* Colour and the allocation of GLC housing : the report of the GLC lettings survey, 1974-75 / by John Parker and Keith Dugmore. — London : Greater London Council, 1976. — 105p in various pagings : ill, forms, maps ; 30cm. — (Greater London Council. Research reports ; 21)
Bibl.: p.73-74.
ISBN 0-7168-0862-5 Sd : £5.00
(B77-13594)

363.5 — Housing services for old persons. *United States*
Huttmann, Elizabeth D. Housing and social services for the elderly : social policy trends / [by] Elizabeth D. Huttmann, with a chapter by Ilse J. Volinn. — New York ; London : Praeger, 1977. — xv,295p ; 25cm. — (Praeger special studies in US economic, social and political issues)
Index.
ISBN 0-275-23830-x : £14.40
(B77-26230)

363.5 — Local authority housing. Coloured tenants. Records. *London. Proposals*
London Housing Research Group. *Working Party on Race and Housing.* Race and local authority housing : information on ethnic groups : a report / by a Working Party [on Race and Housing] of the London Housing Research Group. — London : Community Relations Commission, 1977. — 16p ; 21cm.
'In October 1976 the London Housing Research Group (LHRG) set up a Working Party on Race and Housing ...' - Foreword.
Sd : Unpriced
(B77-18661)

363.5 — Public amenities. Provision. *London. Enfield (London Borough). Edmonton, 1890-1903*
Charlton, Connie. Civilisation comes to Edmonton / by Connie Charlton. — [Enfield] : Edmonton Hundred Historical Society, [1977]. — [1],18p,[2]p of plates : ill ; 30cm. — (Edmonton Hundred Historical Society. Occasional papers : new series ; no.34)
Sd : £0.40
(B77-23266)

363.5 — Public housing. Organisations. *Northern Ireland. Northern Ireland Housing Executive. Reports, surveys. Serials*
Northern Ireland Housing Executive. Annual report / Housing Executive. — Belfast (1 College Square East, Belfast BT1 6BQ) : Northern Ireland Housing Executive.
5th : 1st April 1975 to 31st March 1976. — [1976]. — 52p : col ill ; 30cm.
ISBN 0-9503906-2-3 Sd : Unpriced
(B77-06571)

363.5 — Sub-standard rented residences. Acquisition & improvement. Policies of local authorities. *England. Reports, surveys*
Study Group on Programmes of Social Ownership and Renovation of Council Dwellings. Study Group on Programmes of Social Ownership and Renovation of Council Dwellings, first report. — [London] ([2 Marsham St., SW1P 3EB]) : Department of the Environment : Association of District Councils : Association of Metropolitan Authorities : Greater London Council : London Boroughs Association, [1976]. — [50]p in various pagings ; 30cm.
ISBN 0-7184-0076-3 Sd : Unpriced
(B77-08924)

363.5'06'1416 — Public works. Organisations. *Northern Ireland. Enterprise Ulster. Reports, surveys. Serials*
Enterprise Ulster. Report and statement of accounts ... / Enterprise Ulster. — Belfast : H.M.S.O.
[1974-1975] : 2nd : 1 April 1974 to 31 March 1975. — [1976]. — 44p : ill, maps ; 25cm.
ISBN 0-337-07132-2 Sd : £0.55
(B77-04060)

363.6 — PUBLIC UTILITY SERVICES
363.6 — Sanitary services. *Ireland (Republic)*
Flannery, Michael. Sanitation, conservation and recreation services in Ireland / [by] Michael Flannery. — Dublin : Institute of Public Administration, 1976. — [8],178p ; 23cm.
Index.
ISBN 0-902173-73-1 Pbk : £5.75
(B77-04693)

363.6'09426'752 — Public utilities. *Essex. Chelmsford (District). Rural regions. Reports, surveys*
Chelmsford *(District).* *Council.* Rural areas study, public utilities / Chelmsford District Council. — Chelmsford ([Civic Centre, Chelmsford CM1 1JE]) : The Council, [1976]. — [3],13[i.e. 14]p,plate : map ; 30cm. — (Subject report ; 4)
ISBN 0-905110-03-x Sd : £0.20
(B77-04061)

363.6'1'091724 — Water supply. Provision by local authorities. *Developing countries. Case studies*
Davies, C J. Urban services / [by] C.J. Davies. — Birmingham (P.O. Box 363, Birmingham B15 2TT) : Development Administration Group, Institute of Local Government Studies, University of Birmingham, 1976. — [3],129[i.e. 143],[2]p : ill, maps, plans ; 30cm. — (Case studies in development administration ; vol.2)
Bibl.(2p.).
ISBN 0-7044-0200-9 Pbk : £1.25
(B77-22478)

363.6'1'091724 — Water supply systems. Development. Social aspects. *Developing countries*
Intermediate Technology Development Group. *Water Panel.* Water for the thousand millions / written by the Water Panel of the Intermediate Technology Development Group ... ; compiled and edited by Arnold Pacey ... — Oxford [etc.] : Pergamon, 1977. — vi,58p : ill, plans ; 25cm.
Bibl.: p.58.
ISBN 0-08-021805-9 Sd : £1.25
(B77-20155)

364 — CRIMINOLOGY
364 — Crime & punishment
Quinney, Richard. The problem of crime : a critical introduction to criminology. — 2nd ed. / [by] Richard Quinney, John Wildeman. — New York [etc.] ; London : Harper and Row, 1977. — x,198p : ill, ports ; 24cm.
Previous ed.: / by Richard Quinney. New York : Dodd, Mead, 1970. — Bibl.: p.175-186. — Index.
ISBN 0-06-045311-7 Pbk : £6.40
(B77-14146)

Radzinowicz, *Sir* **Leon.** The growth of crime : the international experience / [by] Sir Leon Radzinowicz and Joan King. — London : Hamilton, 1977. — x,342p ; 22cm.
Index.
ISBN 0-241-89609-6 : £6.95
(B77-21048)

364 — Victims of crimes. Surveys. *Organisation for Economic Co-operation and Development countries. Reports, surveys*
Organisation for Economic Co-operation and Development. Data sources for social indicators of victimisation suffered by individuals : with special reference to the potential of victim surveys / [Organisation for Economic Co-operation and Development]. — Paris : O.E.C.D. ; [London] : [H.M.S.O.], 1976. — 57p ; 24cm. — (Organisation for Economic Co-operation and Development. Social Indicator Development Programme special studies ; no.3)
Pbk : £1.30
ISBN 92-64-11556-0
(B77-05983)

364.1 — CRIMES
364.1 — White-collar crimes. *United States*
Conklin, John Evan. 'Illegal but not criminal' : business crime in America / [by] John E. Conklin. — Englewood Cliffs ; London [etc.] : Prentice-Hall, 1977. — xiii,153p ; 21cm.
'A spectrum book'. — Index.
ISBN 0-13-450890-4 : Unpriced
ISBN 0-13-450882-3 Pbk : £3.15
(B77-33708)

White-collar crime : offenses in business, politics and the professions. — Revised ed. / edited, with introduction and notes by Gilbert Geis and Robert F. Meier. — New York : Free Press ; London : Collier Macmillan, 1977. — xii,356p : 2 ill ; 24cm.
Previous ed.: published as 'White-collar criminal' / edited by Gilbert Geis. New York : Atherton, 1968. — Bibl.: p.337-345. — Index.
ISBN 0-02-911590-6 : £9.75
ISBN 0-02-911600-7 Pbk : £5.25
(B77-21789)

364.1'06 — Chinese secret societies: Triads
Robertson, Frank. Triangle of death : the inside story of the Triads - the Chinese Mafia / [by] Frank Robertson. — London [etc.] : Routledge and Kegan Paul, 1977. — vii,184p,[12]p of plates : ill, ports ; 23cm.
Bibl.: p.183-184.
ISBN 0-7100-8732-2 : £3.95 : CIP rev.
(B77-18662)

364.1'092'2 — Criminals. *United States, 1750-1972. Biographies*
Gish, Anthony. American outlaws / by Anthony Gish and Anton S. Booker. — St Ives, Cornwall : Pike, 1973. — 123p ; 21cm. — ([Compelling literature series])
ISBN 0-900850-88-4 : £1.50
(B77-19285)

364.1'092'4 — Crimes. Boyle, Jimmy. *Scotland. Strathclyde Region. Glasgow. Autobiographies*
Boyle, Jimmy. A sense of freedom / [by] Jimmy Boyle. — London [etc.] : Pan Books, 1977. — [6],264p ; 18cm.
Also published: Edinburgh : Canongate Publishing, 1977.
ISBN 0-330-25303-4 Pbk : £0.80
(B77-26231)

Boyle, Jimmy. A sense of freedom / [by] Jimmy Boyle. — Edinburgh : Canongate Publishing, 1977. — vi,264p ; 23cm.
Also published: London : Pan Books, 1977.
ISBN 0-903937-19-0 : £3.95
(B77-30093)

364.1'092'4 — Crimes. Probyn, Walter. *England. Autobiographies*
Probyn, Walter. Angel face : the making of a criminal / by Walter Probyn ; with an introduction and commentary by Stan Cohen. — London [etc.] : Allen and Unwin, 1977. — 3-254p ; 23cm.
ISBN 0-04-923070-0 : £4.95
(B77-29315)

364.1'092'4 — Mafia. *New York (City). Personal observations*
Diapoulos, Peter. The sixth family / by Peter Diapoulos and Steven Linakis ; foreword by Nicholas Gage. — Toronto [etc.] ; London : Bantam, 1977. — [1],xiii,239,[1]p : col ill(on inside front cover) ; 18cm.
Originally published: New York : Dutton, 1976.
ISBN 0-552-10439-6 Pbk : £0.75
(B77-26967)

364.1'092'4 — Mafia. Costello, Frank. *New York (City). Biographies*
Katz, Leonard. Uncle Frank : the biography of Frank Costello / [by] Leonard Katz ; foreword by Anthony Quinn. — London : Star Books, 1975. — 268p,[8]p of plates : ill, facsim, ports ; 18cm.
Originally published: New York : Drake Publishers, 1973 ; London : W.H. Allen, 1974.
ISBN 0-352-30063-9 Pbk : £0.75
(B77-20156)

Wolf, George. Frank Costello : Prime Minister of the underworld / [by] George Wolf with Joseph DiMona. — London : Futura Publications, 1976. — xv,270,[1]p ; 18cm.
Originally published: New York : Morrow, 1974 ; London : Hodder and Stoughton, 1975.
ISBN 0-86007-349-1 Pbk : £0.75
(B77-08925)

364.1'092'4 — Mafia. Luciano, Charles. *United States. Biographies*
Scaduto, Anthony. Lucky Luciano : the man who modernized the Mafia / [by] Tony Scaduto. — London : Sphere, 1976. — 208p ; 18cm.
Originally published: United States : s.n., 1975.
ISBN 0-7221-7657-0 Pbk : £0.60
(B77-12955)

364.1'092'4 — Mafia. Siegel, Benjamin. *United States*
Carpozi, George. Bugsy : the godfather of Las Vegas / [by] George Carpozi, Jr. — London : Everest, 1976. — 190p,[16]p of plates : ill, ports ; 18cm.
Originally published: New York : Pinnacle Books, 1973. — Index.
ISBN 0-905018-09-5 Pbk : £0.65
(B77-14147)

364.1'09411 — Crimes. *Scotland. Statistics*
Criminal statistics, Scotland : statistics relating to police apprehensions and criminal proceedings ... / Scottish Home and Health Department. — Edinburgh : H.M.S.O.
1975. — [1976]. — 83p : ill ; 25cm. — (Cmnd.6631)
ISBN 0-10-166310-2 Sd : £1.35
ISSN 0307-6717
(B77-07241)

Criminal statistics, Scotland : statistics relating to crime and criminal proceedings ... / Scottish Home and Health Department. — Edinburgh : H.M.S.O.
1976. — [1977]. — 79p : ill ; 25cm. — (Cmnd.6885 ISSN 0307-6717)
ISBN 0-10-168850-4 Sd : £1.75
(B77-28523)

364.1'0942 — Crimes. *England. Statistics*
Criminal statistics, England and Wales : statistics relating to crime and criminal proceedings ... / Home Office. — London : H.M.S.O.
1976. — [1977]. — 390p : ill, map ; 25cm. — (Cmnd.6909)
ISBN 0-10-169090-8 Pbk : £7.15
(B77-26968)

364.12'09'04 — Criminal investigation, 1945-1975. *Case studies*
Henderson, Bruce. The super sleuths / [by] Bruce Henderson and Sam Summerlin. — London : Cassell, 1977. — xii,291p : 1 ill, ports ; 22cm.
Originally published: New York : Macmillan, 1976.
ISBN 0-304-29886-7 : £4.95
(B77-29316)

364.12'8 — Forensic science
Ellen, David. Science and crime / [by] David Ellen. — Exeter : Wheaton, 1977. — [11],51p : ill, facsims, port ; 25cm. — (Science in action)
Bibl.: p.51.
ISBN 0-08-020597-6 Pbk : £1.20
ISBN 0-08-020226-8 (non-net) : £0.90
(B77-15771)

Saferstein, Richard. Criminalistics : an introduction to forensic science / [by] Richard Saferstein. — Englewood Cliffs ; London [etc.] : Prentice-Hall, 1977. — viii,439p : ill, facsims, map, ports ; 24cm.
With answers. — Bibl. — Index.
ISBN 0-13-193359-0 : £11.95
(B77-15772)

364.12'8 — Suspects. Interrogation by police. Tape recording. Projects. *England. Feasibility studies*
The **feasibility** of an experiment in the tape-recording of police interrogations : report of a Committee appointed by the Home Secretary ... — London : H.M.S.O., [1976]. — [1],ii,35p ; 25cm. — (Cmnd. 6630)
ISBN 0-10-166300-5 Sd : £0.50
(B77-06572)

364.1'31 — Police. *London. Metropolitan Police. Bomb Squad. Huntley, Bob. Autobiographies*
Huntley, Bob. Bomb squad : my war against the terrorists : the autobiography of Ex-Commander Bob Huntley. — London : W.H. Allen, 1977. — x,198p,[16]p of plates : ill, ports ; 23cm.
Index.
ISBN 0-491-01978-5 : £4.95
(B77-20157)

364.1'31'0924 — Political crimes. Hiss, Alger. *United States. Biographies*
Smith, John Chabot. Alger Hiss : the true story / [by] John Chabot Smith. — Harmondsworth [etc.] : Penguin, 1977. — xiii,495p,[24]p of plates : ill, facsims, ports ; 20cm.
Originally published: New York : Holt, Rinehart and Winston, 1976. — Bibl.: p.455-458. — Index.
ISBN 0-14-004427-2 Pbk : Unpriced
(B77-27767)

364.1'33 — Smuggling
Green, Timothy. The smuggling business / [by] Timothy Green. — London : Aldus Books, 1977. — 144p : ill(some col), facsims, ports(1 col) ; 27cm. — (Undercover)
Index.
ISBN 0-490-00370-2 : £3.95
(B77-09628)

364.1'33 — Smuggling. *England, to ca 1850. Juvenile literature*
Sutton, Harry Thomas. Honest rogues : the inside story of smuggling / [by] Harry T. Sutton. — London (21 Little Russell St., W.C.1) : Heritage Books, 1977. — 48p : ill(some col), map ; 21cm.
'A National Trust series for children'.
ISBN 0-906045-01-0 Pbk : £0.85
(B77-30094)

364.1'35 — International Criminal Police Organisation. *Juvenile literature*
Noble, Iris. Interpol : international crime fighter / by Iris Noble ; illustrated with photographs. — New York ; London : Harcourt Brace Jovanovich, 1975. — ix,116p, [8]p of plates : ill, facsim, map, ports ; 22cm.
Index.
ISBN 0-15-238733-1 : Unpriced
(B77-19286)

364.1'38'0924 — German war criminals: Bormann, Martin. Alleged residence. *South America, 1948-1974*
Farago, Ladislas. Aftermath : Martin Bormann and the Fourth Reich / [by] Ladislas Farago. — London [etc.] : Pan Books, 1976. — [10], 550,[1]p : ports ; 18cm.
Originally published: New York : Simon and Schuster, 1974 ; London : Hodder and Stoughton, 1975. — Bibl.: p.518-533. — Index.
ISBN 0-330-24557-0 Pbk : £1.25
(B77-00124)

364.1'38'0943 — German war crimes, 1939-1945
Russell, Edward, *Baron Russell of Liverpool.* The scourge of the swastika / [by] Lord Russell of Liverpool. — London : Corgi, 1976. — 221p,[8] p of plates : ill, facsim, ports ; 18cm.
Originally published: London : Cassell, 1954.
ISBN 0-552-10300-4 Pbk : £0.65
(B77-04694)

364.1'38'0952 — Japanese war crimes, 1939-1945
Russell, Edward, *Baron Russell of Liverpool.* The knights of Bushido / [by] Lord Russell of Liverpool. — London : Corgi, 1976. — 253p,[8] p of plates : ill, ports ; 18cm.
Originally published: London : Cassell, 1958.
ISBN 0-552-10301-2 Pbk : £0.65
(B77-04695)

364.1'5'0924 — Crimes. Spring Heeled Jack. *London*
Haining, Peter. The legend and bizarre crimes of Spring Heeled Jack / [by] Peter Haining. — London : Muller, 1977. — x,179p : ill, facsims, map, ports ; 23cm.
Index.
ISBN 0-584-10276-3 : £4.75 : CIP rev.
(B77-24114)

364.1'5'0973 — Crimes of violence. *United States. Rural regions, ca 1850-ca 1900*
Hollon, W Eugene. Frontier violence : another look / [by] W. Eugene Hollon. — London [etc.] : Oxford University Press, 1976. — xiii, 279p : ill, facsim, ports ; 21cm.
Originally published: New York : Oxford University Press, 1974. — Bibl.: p.237-265. — Index.
ISBN 0-19-502098-7 Pbk : £2.25
(B77-05315)

364.1'522 — Suicide. Cultural factors. *Comparative studies*
Suicide in different cultures / edited by Norman L. Farberow. — Baltimore ; London [etc.] : University Park Press, 1975. — xviii,286p ; 24cm.
Bibl. — Index.
ISBN 0-8391-0843-5 : £13.95
(B77-04062)

364.1'523'0904 — Murder, 1875-1970. *Case studies*
Crimes of horror / [edited by Angus Hall]. — London [etc.] : Spring Books, 1976. — 192p : ill, facsims, ports ; 29cm.
Ill. on lining papers. — 'This material first appeared in "Crimes and punishment"' - title page verso.
ISBN 0-600-31936-9 : £2.95
(B77-00691)

364.1'523'0904 — Murder, 1892-1976. *Case studies*
Gribble, Leonard. Compelled to kill / [by] Leonard Gribble. — London : Long, 1977. — 184p ; 21cm.
ISBN 0-09-129010-4 : £3.95
(B77-26969)

364.1'523'0904 — Murder. Criminal investigation, 1900-1974. *Case studies*
Grex, Leo. Detection stronger than fiction / [by] Leo Grex. — London : Hale, 1977. — 176p ; 23cm.
ISBN 0-7091-6472-6 : £3.95
(B77-31796)

364.1'523'0922 — Murder by Manson family. *California. Los Angeles. Hollywood*
Bugliosi, Vincent. Helter skelter : an investigation into motive / [by] Vincent Bugliosi ; with Curt Gentry. — Abridged ed. — Harmondsworth [etc.] : Penguin, 1977. — 623p,[16]p of plates : ill, maps, plan, ports ; 19cm.
Previous ed.: i.e. full ed. published as 'Helter skelter', New York : Norton, 1974, and as 'The Manson murders', London : Bodley Head, 1975. — Index.
ISBN 0-14-004296-2 Pbk : £0.95
(B77-16290)

364.1'523'0922 — Murder of Hill, Joan Olive & Hill, John Robert. *Texas. Houston*
Thompson, Thomas, *b.1933.* Blood and money / [by] Thomas Thompson. — London : New English Library, 1977. — [4],450p ; 24cm.
Originally published: Garden City, N.Y. : Doubleday, 1976.
ISBN 0-450-03213-2 : £4.95
(B77-15215)

364.1'523'0924 — Murder. Evertsz, Carlos. *Dominican Republic*
Robbins, Christopher. Assassin / [by] Christopher Robbins ; illustrated by Bob Gale. — London : Star Books, 1977. — 143p : ill ; 18cm.
ISBN 0-352-39626-1 Pbk : £0.70
(B77-28524)

364.1'523'0924 — Murder of Foster, Evelyn. *Northumberland. Otterburn*
Goodman, Jonathan. The burning of Evelyn Foster / [by] Jonathan Goodman. — Newton Abbot : David and Charles, 1977. — 152p : 1 ill, 2 maps ; 23cm.
Index.
ISBN 0-7153-7374-9 : £5.50
(B77-30095)

364.1'523'0924 — Murderers: Crippen, Hawley Harvey. *London. Biographies*
Cullen, Tom. Crippen : the mild murderer / [by] Tom Cullen. — London [etc.] : Bodley Head, 1977. — 224p,[8]p of plates : facsims, ports ; 23cm.
ISBN 0-370-10465-x : £4.95
(B77-26232)

364.1'523'0924 — Murderers: Jack the Ripper. *London*
Jones, Elwyn, *b.1923.* The Ripper file : the documentary investigation by Detective Chief Superintendents Charles Barlow and John Watt / [by] Elwyn Jones and John Lloyd. — London : Futura Publications, 1975. — 204p ; 18cm.
Based on six BBC Television programmes. — Also published: London : Barker, 1975. — Bibl. : p.203-204.
ISBN 0-86007-118-9 Pbk : £0.50
(B77-08313)

364.1'523'094 — Murder. *Europe, 1968-1974. Case studies*
Dunning, John. Truly murderous : horrific modern European murders reconstructed / by John Dunning ; introduction by Colin Wilson. — Blandford [etc.] : Harwood-Smart, 1977. — viii,226p ; 23cm.
ISBN 0-904507-18-1 : £3.95
(B77-22479)

364.1'524'0924 — Assassination of Kennedy, John Fitzgerald. *United States*
Roffman, Howard. Presumed guilty / [by] Howard Roffman. — South Brunswick ; New York : Barnes ; London : Yoseloff, 1976. — 299p,[10]p of plates : ill, plans, ports ; 22cm.
Originally published: Rutherford : Fairleigh Dickinson University Press, 1975. — Bibl.: p.290-294. — Index.
ISBN 0-498-01933-0 : £4.50
(B77-24821)

364.1'53 — Crimes: Rape. *England*
Toner, Barbara. The facts of rape / [by] Barbara Toner. — London : Hutchinson, 1977. — 208p ; 23cm.
ISBN 0-09-128210-1 : £3.75
(B77-10296)

Toner, Barbara. The facts of rape / [by] Barbara Toner. — London : Arrow Books, 1977. — 208p ; 18cm.
ISBN 0-09-914570-7 Pbk : £0.90
(B77-10297)

364.1'53 — Crimes: Rape. *United States*
Forcible rape : the crime, the victim, and the offender / Duncan Chappell, Robley Geis, and Gilbert Geis, editors. — New York ; Guildford : Columbia University Press, 1977. — xi,393p ; 24cm.
Bibl.: p.356-382. — Index.
ISBN 0-231-03839-9 : £10.70
(B77-31086)

364.1'53 — Crimes: Rape. Social aspects, to 1974. *Feminist viewpoints*
Brownmiller, Susan. Against our will : men, women and rape / [by] Susan Brownmiller. — Harmondsworth [etc.] : Penguin, 1977. — 472p ; 18cm.
Originally published: New York : Simon and Schuster ; London : Secker and Warburg, 1975. — Index.
ISBN 0-14-004244-x Pbk : £0.95
(B77-12956)

364.1'54'0924 — Diment, Eunice. Kidnapping by Moro National Liberation Front. *Philippines. Mindanao. Zamboanga. Diaries*
Diment, Eunice. Kidnapped! : Eunice Diment's story. — Exeter : Paternoster Press, 1976. — 79p : ill, maps, ports ; 18cm.
ISBN 0-85364-199-4 Pbk : £0.75
(B77-08926)

364.1'54'0924 — Herrema, Tiede. Kidnapping by Irish Republican Army. Provisional IRA. *Kildare (County). Monasterevin*
Connolly, Colm. Herrema : siege at Monasterevin / by Colm Connolly. — Dublin (21 Great Denmark St., Dublin 1) : Olympic Press Ltd, 1977. — [4],116p,[24]p of plates : ill, ports ; 21cm.
Pbk : £1.25
(B77-30096)

364.1'55 — Old age pensioners. Mugging. Effects of extension of opening hours of licensed premises. Monitoring. Methodology. *England. Proposals*
Christian Economic and Social Research Foundation. Monitoring the social effects of changes in the licensing laws / [Christian Economic and Social Research Foundation]. — London (12 Caxton St., SW1H 0QS) : The Foundation, [1977]. — [12]p : ill, maps ; 30cm.

Sd : Unpriced
(B77-21049)

364.1'55'09 — Highway robbers, to 1976
Evans, Hilary. Hero on a stolen horse : the highwayman and his brothers-in-arms, the bandit and the bushranger / [by] Hilary and Mary Evans ; with illustrations from the Mary Evans Picture Library. — London : Muller, 1977. — xi,177p : ill, facsims, ports ; 26cm.
Ill. on lining papers. — Bibl.: p.xi. — Index.
ISBN 0-584-10340-9 : £6.95 : CIP rev.
(B77-21791)

364.1'55'0922 — Highwaymen & outlaws. *Biographies. Juvenile literature*
Stein, Nora. Highwaymen and brigands / [written and planned by Nora Stein ; illustrators Peter Dennis, Tony Payne, Gary Rees]. — London : Macdonald Educational, 1977. — 2-47p : ill(chiefly col), music, col ports ; 29cm. — (Topic books)
Index.
ISBN 0-356-05449-7 : £1.60
(B77-26970)

364.1'55'0922 — Highwaymen & outlaws, to 1968. *Biographies. Juvenile literature*
Gilbert, John, *b.1926.* Highwaymen and outlaws / [by] John Gilbert ; text illustrations by Edward Mortlemans. — London : Severn House : [Distributed by Hutchinson], 1977. — 123p : ill ; 21cm.
Originally published: London : Pan Books, 1971.
ISBN 0-7278-0261-5 : £2.75
(B77-14647)

364.1'55'0924 — Robbery. Brodie, William. *Edinburgh. Biographies*
Gibson, John Sibbald. Deacon Brodie : father to Jekyll and Hyde / [by] John S. Gibson. — Edinburgh : P. Harris, 1977. — 158p,[8]p of plates : ill, map, ports ; 23cm.
Bibl.: p.152-154. — Index.
ISBN 0-904505-24-3 : £4.50
(B77-17393)

364.1'55'0924 — Trains. Robbery. Biggs, Ronald. *Great Britain, 1958-1974. Biographies*
Mackenzie, Colin, *b.1942.* The most wanted man : the story of Ronald Biggs / [by] Colin Mackenzie. — St Albans : Panther, 1976. — 303p,[8]p of plates : ill, facsims, ports ; 18cm.
Originally published: London : Hart-Davis MacGibbon, 1975.
ISBN 0-586-04349-7 Pbk : £0.75
(B77-00692)

364.1'55'0924 — Trains. Robbery. Biggs, Ronald. Arrest & release in Brazil, 1974. Role of journalists. *Great Britain*
Delano, Anthony. Slip up : how Fleet Street caught Ronnie Biggs and Scotland Yard lost him : the story behind the scoop / [by] Anthony Delano. — London : Deutsch, 1977. — 174p ; 23cm.
Originally published: New York : Quadrangle / New York Times Book Co., 1975.
ISBN 0-233-96885-7 : £4.50
(B77-27768)

364.1'55'0978 — Outlaws. *United States. Western states, 1760-1895. Juvenile literature*
Ulyatt, Kenneth. Outlaws / [by] Kenneth Ulyatt ; illustrated with contemporary material. — Harmondsworth : Kestrel Books, 1976. — [4],90p : ill, map, music, ports ; 25cm.
Index.
ISBN 0-7226-5165-1 : £2.95
(B77-09629)

364.1'62 — Burglary. *Stories, anecdotes*
Stone, Jago. The burglar's bedside companion / [by] Jago Stone. — London : Everest, 1975. — 127p ; 18cm.
ISBN 0-903925-18-4 Pbk : £0.40
(B77-19287)

364.1'62 — Crimes: Fiddling. *England. Sociological perspectives. Study examples: Baking industries & trades. Case studies*
Ditton, Jason. Part-time crime : an ethnography of fiddling and pilferage / [by] Jason Ditton. — London [etc.] : Macmillan, 1977. — viii,195p : ill ; 23cm.
Bibl.: p.185-192. — Index.
ISBN 0-333-21466-8 : £10.00
(B77-23268)

364.1'62 — Stolen goods. Receiving. *United States*
Walsh, Marilyn E. The fence : a new look at the world of property theft / [by] Marilyn E. Walsh. — Westport, Conn. ; London : Greenwood Press, 1977. — xvi,215,[1]p : ill ; 22cm. — (Contributions in sociology ; no.21)
Bibl.: p.203-206. — Index.
ISBN 0-8371-8910-1 : £9.50
(B77-21792)

364.1'62'0924 — Theft. Hoff, Armand. *Netherlands. Autobiographies*
Hoff, Armand. The Panther / [by] Armand Hoff. — St Albans : Mayflower, 1977. — 327p ; 18cm.
Originally published: London : Muller, 1975.
ISBN 0-583-12612-x Pbk : £0.95
(B77-23269)

364.1'63 — Forgery. Baudin, Robert. *Autobiographies*
Baudin, Robert. Fake : the passing fortunes of a counterfeiter / [by] Robert Baudin. — Sydney [etc.] : Methuen of Australia ; London : Eyre Methuen, 1977. — [7],376p : map(on lining papers) ; 23cm.
ISBN 0-454-00034-0 : £4.95
(B77-32545)

364.1'73'0942 — Crimes: Drunkenness. *England. Statistics*
Offences of drunkenness, England and Wales ... / Home Office. — London : H.M.S.O.
1976. — [1977]. — 17p : ill ; 25cm. — (Cmnd.6952)
ISBN 0-10-169520-9 Sd : £0.50
(B77-30097)

364.2 — CAUSES OF CRIME AND DELINQUENCY
364.2'4 — Man. Criminal behaviour. Related to personality
Eysenck, Hans Jürgen. Crime and personality / [by] H.J. Eysenck. — [3rd ed.]. — London [etc.] : Routledge and Kegan Paul, 1977. — 222p : ill ; 23cm.
Previous ed.: St Albans : Paladin, 1970. — Index.
ISBN 0-7100-8487-0 : £4.50
(B77-23270)

Eysenck, Hans Jürgen. Crime and personality / [by] H.J. Eysenck. — [3rd revised ed.]. — St Albans : Paladin, 1977. — 222p : ill ; 20cm.
Previous ed.: London : Paladin, 1970. — Index.

Pbk : £1.25
ISBN 0-586-08007-4
(B77-22480)

364.2'5 — Juvenile delinquency. Social factors. *England. Urban regions. Study examples: Boys, 8-18 years. Study regions: London*
West, Donald James. The delinquent way of life : third report of the Cambridge study in delinquent development / by D.J. West and D.P. Farrington ; with the assistance of ... [others]. — London : Heinemann Educational, 1977. — xi,209p : 2 ill ; 23cm. — (Cambridge studies in criminology ; 35) (The Heinemann library of criminology and penal reform)
Bibl.: p.196-203. — Index.
ISBN 0-435-82935-1 : £6.00
(B77-09630)

364.2'5 — Probationers: Boys. Reconviction. Social factors. *Dublin. Reports, surveys*
Hart, Ian. Factors relating to reconviction among young Dublin probationers / [by] Ian Hart. — Dublin : Economic and Social Research Institute, 1974. — 124p : ill ; 24cm. — (Economic and Social Research Institute. Papers ; no.76)
Bibl.: p.121-124.
ISBN 0-901809-89-6 Pbk : £1.50(£0.75 to students)
(B77-19288)

364.2'5'072041 — Crimes. Social aspects. Research sponsored by Great Britain. Home Office. Research Unit. *Great Britain. Directories*
Great Britain. *Home Office. Research Unit.* Programme of research / Home Office Research Unit. — [London] ([Romney House, Marsham St., SW1P 3DY]) : [The Unit].
1977-1978. — [1977]. — [1],v[i.e.vii],20[i.e.24] p ; 30cm.
Bibl.: p.15-20.
Sd : Unpriced
(B77-21050)

364.2'55 — Man. Criminal behaviour. Role of drug abuse
Street ethnography : selected studies of crime and drug use in natural settings / Robert S. Weppner, editor. — Beverly Hills ; London : Sage Publications, 1977. — 288p ; 24cm. — (Sage annual reviews of drug and alcohol abuse ; vol.1)
Bibl. — Index.
ISBN 0-8039-0808-3 : £12.00
ISBN 0-8039-0809-1 Pbk : £5.25
(B77-33145)

364.3 — CRIMINALS
364.3 — Crimes. Psychological aspects
Feldman, Maurice Philip. Criminal behaviour : a psychological analysis / [by] M. Philip Feldman. — London [etc.] : Wiley, 1977. — xvi,330p : 1 ill ; 24cm.
Bibl.: p.286-313. — Index.
ISBN 0-471-99401-4 : £9.50
(B77-14148)

364.3'0973 — Criminals. Psychology. *United States*
Menninger, Karl. The crime of punishment / by Karl Menninger. — Harmondsworth [etc.] : Penguin, 1977. — xiii,396p ; 20cm.
Originally published: New York : Viking Press, 1968. — Bibl.: p.293-296. — Index.
ISBN 0-14-004488-4 Pbk : £1.20
(B77-27769)

364.36 — Juvenile delinquency. Social aspects. *Reports, surveys*
Malewska, Hanna. Juvenile delinquency and development : a cross-national study / [by] Hanna Malewska, Vincent Peyre. — Beverly Hills ; London : Sage Publications, 1976. — 40p ; 22cm. — (Sage research papers in the social sciences : cross-national research and documentation in the social sciences series ; vol.4, no.90-031)
'This paper was presented at the Budapest Round Table Conference on Theory and Practice in Cross-National Survey Research organised in July 1972 ...' - Foreword. — Bibl.: p.35-37.
ISBN 0-8039-0548-3 Pbk : £1.25
(B77-13595)

364.36 — Murder by adolescents. Psychosocial aspects. *United States. Case studies*
Gardiner, Muriel. The deadly innocents : portraits of children who kill / [by] Muriel Gardiner ; with a preface by Stephen Spender. — London : Hogarth Press, 1977. — xxv,190p ; 23cm.
Originally published: New York : Basic Books, 1976.
ISBN 0-7012-0426-5 : £5.50 : CIP rev.
(B77-05316)

364.36'09421'91 — Juvenile delinquency. Social aspects. *Great Britain. Urban regions. Study regions: London. Croydon (London Borough). Reports, surveys*
Child guidance and delinquency in a London borough / [by] Dennis Gath ... [et al.]. — Oxford [etc.] : Oxford University Press, 1977. — xiii,190p : ill, forms, maps ; 26cm. — (Maudsley monographs ; no.24)
Bibl.: p.177-183. — Index.
ISBN 0-19-712146-2 : £7.00
Primary classification 364.6
(B77-03469)

364.36'0973 — Juvenile delinquency. *United States. Readings*
Delinquency, crime and society / edited by James F. Short, Jr. — Chicago ; London : University of Chicago Press, 1976. — ix,325p : 1 ill ; 23cm.
'The papers for chapters 3, 5, 6, 7, 8, 9 and 10 ... were prepared initially for a symposium honoring Henry D. McKay, held at the University of Chicago in the late fall of 1972' - Preface. — Bibl. — Index.
ISBN 0-226-75468-5 : £10.20
(B77-01285)

364.36'0973 — Juvenile delinquency. Theories. *United States, to 1975*
Finestone, Harold. Victims of change : juvenile delinquents in American society / [by] Harold Finestone. — Westport, Conn. ; London : Greenwood Press, 1976. — xvii,235,[1]p ; 22cm. — (Contributions in sociology ; no.20)
Bibl.: p.220-228. — Index.
ISBN 0-8371-8897-0 : £11.95
(B77-16800)

364.3'74 — Women murderers. *England & France, ca 1840-ca 1890. Case studies*
Hartman, Mary S. Victorian murderesses : a true history of thirteen respectable French and English women accused of unspeakable crimes / [by] Mary S. Hartman. — London : Robson Books, 1977. — x,318p : ports ; 24cm.
Also published: New York : Schocken Books, 1977. — Bibl.: p.307-312. — Index.
ISBN 0-86051-008-5 : £5.25 : CIP rev.
(B77-16291)

364.3'74 — Women offenders. Social aspects. *Feminist viewpoints*
Smart, Carol. Women, crime and criminology : a feminist critique / [by] Carol Smart. — London [etc.] : Routledge and Kegan Paul, 1977. — xv, 208p ; 23cm.
Bibl.: p.197-204. — Index.
ISBN 0-7100-8449-8 : £4.95
(B77-00125)

364.4 — CRIME PREVENTION
364.4'0973 — Crimes. Prevention. *United States. Proposals*
Morris, Norval. Letter to the President on crime control / [by] Norval Morris and Gordon Hawkins. — Chicago ; London : University of Chicago Press, 1977. — vii,96p : 1 ill ; 21cm.
Bibl.: p.87-96.
ISBN 0-226-53998-9 Pbk : £1.35
(B77-33146)

364.4'4 — Juvenile delinquency. Prevention. Role of schools. *United States*
Delinquency prevention and the schools : emerging perspectives / edited by Ernst A. Wenk. — Beverly Hills ; London : Sage Publications, 1976 [i.e. 1977]. — 128p : 1 ill, form ; 22cm. — (Sage contemporary social science issues ; 29)
Published in the United States: 1976. — '... originally appeared as a special issue of "Criminal justice and behavior" (Volume 2, Number 4, December 1975)' - title page verso. — Bibl.
ISBN 0-8039-0730-3 Pbk : £2.50
(B77-10298)

364.6 — PUNISHMENT OF CRIME
364.6 — Community treatment. *Great Britain & United States*
Scull, Andrew T. Decarceration : community treatment and the deviant : a radical view / [by] Andrew T. Scull. — Englewood Cliffs ; London : Prentice-Hall, 1977. — vii,184p ; 22cm.
Bibl.: p.161-181. — Index.
ISBN 0-13-197657-5 : £7.20
ISBN 0-13-197640-0 Pbk : £3.15
(B77-16801)

364.6 — Juvenile delinquency. Intermediate treatment. *England. Conference proceedings*
Conference on Intermediate Treatment, *Birmingham, 1974.* Intermediate treatment : report of a residential conference held at Birmingham, 2-5 December 1974. — London : H.M.S.O., 1976. — [3],91p : ill ; 30cm. — (Great Britain. Department of Health and Social Security. Social Work Service. Development Group. Report series)
'After the Conference of Regional Planning Committees ... there was a need for a Conference on Intermediate Treatment' - p.7.
ISBN 0-11-320631-3 Pbk : £1.55
(B77-05317)

364.6 — Juvenile delinquency. Intermediate treatment. *Wales. Reports, surveys*
The **development** of intermediate treatment : report of the residential workshops held at Carmarthen and Llandudno in March 1976 [organised by the] Welsh Office, Social Work Service. — [Cardiff] ([Pearl Assurance House, Greyfriars Rd, Cardiff CF1 3JL]) : [The Service], [1977]. — [1],131p : 1 ill ; 30cm.
Sp : Unpriced
(B77-19289)

364.6 — Juvenile delinquency. Intermediate treatment. Role of family advice centres. *England. Research reports*
National Children's Bureau. Intermediate treatment : a community-based action-research study / [National Children's Bureau] ; [written by] Aryeh Leissner, Terry Powley, Dave Evans. — London (8 Wakley St., EC1V 7QE) : The Bureau, 1977. — viii,86p : ill ; 24cm.
Bibl.
ISBN 0-902817-11-6 Sd : Unpriced
(B77-23271)

364.6 — Juvenile delinquency. Treatment. Role of child guidance clinics. *Great Britain. Urban regions. Study regions: London. Croydon (London Borough). Reports, surveys*
Child guidance and delinquency in a London borough / [by] Dennis Gath ... [et al.]. — Oxford [etc.] : Oxford University Press, 1977. — xiii,190p : ill, forms, maps ; 26cm. — (Maudsley monographs ; no.24)
Bibl.: p.177-183. — Index.
ISBN 0-19-712146-2 : £7.00
Also classified at 364.36'09421'91
(B77-03469)

364.6 — Offenders. Community service orders. Effectiveness. *England, 1972-1976*
Pease, Kenneth. Community service assessed in 1976 / by K. Pease, S. Billingham and I. Earnshaw. — London : H.M.S.O., 1977. — vi, 26p ; 25cm. — (Great Britain. Home Office. Research studies ; no.39) (Great Britain. Home Office. Research Unit. Reports)
Bibl.: p.26.
ISBN 0-11-340679-7 Sd : £0.75
(B77-18663)

364.6 — Offenders. Community service orders. Operation. *Nottinghamshire. Nottingham, 1973-1974. Reports, surveys*
Community service by offenders (the Nottinghamshire experiment) / introduced and edited by John Harding. — London (125 Kennington Park Rd, S.E.11) : National Association for the Care and Resettlement of Offenders ; [London] : Howard League for Penal Reform, [1974]. — [3],63p,[4]p of plates : ill, ports ; 21cm. — (National Association for the Care and Resettlement of Offenders. Papers and reprints ; 9)
Bibl.: p.59.
ISBN 0-85069-014-5 Sd : £0.60
(B77-01286)

364.6 — Offenders. Treatment. *Conference proceedings*
Treating the offender : problems and issues / edited by Marc Riedel, Pedro A. Vales. — New York [etc.] ; London : Praeger, 1977. — ix, 180p ; 25cm. — (Praeger special studies in US economic, social and political issues)
'In November 1973, the American Society of Criminology held its annual meeting in New York ... [this] volume is a selection of papers that were delivered at the ... meeting' - Preface. — Bibl.
ISBN 0-275-56350-2 : £11.10
(B77-15216)

364.6 — Young offenders. Treatment. *England. Study regions: Avon. Bristol. Reports, surveys*
Priestley, Philip. Justice for juveniles : the 1969 Children and Young Persons Act : a case for reform? / [by] Philip Priestley, Denise Fears, Roger Fuller. — London [etc.] : Routledge and Kegan Paul, 1977. — viii,120p : ill ; 23cm. — (Library of social work ISSN 0305-4381)
ISBN 0-7100-8703-9 : £3.95 : CIP rev.
Also classified at 364.6
(B77-21793)

364.6 — Young offenders. Treatment. *England. Study regions: Wiltshire. Reports, surveys*
Priestley, Philip. Justice for juveniles : the 1969 Children and Young Persons Act : a case for reform? / [by] Philip Priestley, Denise Fears, Roger Fuller. — London [etc.] : Routledge and Kegan Paul, 1977. — viii,120p : ill ; 23cm. — (Library of social work ISSN 0305-4381)
ISBN 0-7100-8703-9 : £3.95 : CIP rev.
Primary classification 364.6
(B77-21793)

364.6 — Young offenders. Treatment. *United States*
Pursuing justice for the child / edited by Margaret K. Rosenheim ; with a foreword by Robert Maynard Hutchins. — Chicago ; London : University of Chicago Press, [1977]. — xix,361p ; 23cm. — (Studies in crime and justice)
Published in the United States: 1976. — Bibl. — Index.
ISBN 0-226-72789-0 : £9.75
(B77-11717)

364.6'09 — Penal systems. Influence of slavery, to 1900
Sellin, Thorsten. Slavery and the penal system / [by] J. Thorsten Sellin. — New York ; Oxford [etc.] : Elsevier, 1976. — ix,202p ; 24cm.
Index.
ISBN 0-444-99027-5 : £9.15
(B77-07242)

364.6'2'061411 — Prisoners. Parole. Organisations. *Scotland. Parole Board for Scotland. Reports, surveys. Serials*
Parole Board for Scotland. Report ... / Parole Board for Scotland. — Edinburgh : H.M.S.O.
1976. — [1977]. — 19p ; 25cm. — ([1976-77 H.C.]461)
ISBN 0-10-246177-5 Sd : £0.50
(B77-21051)

364.6'2'06142 — Prisoners. Parole. Organisations. *England. Parole Board. Reports, surveys. Serials*
Parole Board. Report of the Parole Board ... — London : H.M.S.O.
1976. — [1977]. — v,36p : form ; 25cm. — ([1976-77 H.C.]388)
ISBN 0-10-238877-6 Sd : £0.90
(B77-21052)

364.6'2'0942 — Prisoners. Parole. *England*
Cavadino, Paul. Parole : the case for change / [by] Paul Cavadino, Nicholas Hinton, Stephanie Mackey. — Chichester [etc.] : Rose [for the National Association for the Care and Resettlement of Offenders], [1977]. — 40,[1]p ; 21cm.
Bibl.: p.30-31.
ISBN 0-85992-100-x Sd : £1.00
(B77-28525)

364.6'2'0942 — Prisoners. Parole. *England. Research reports*
Nuttall, Christopher Peter. Parole in England and Wales / [by] C.P. Nuttall, with ... [others]. — London : H.M.S.O., 1977. — vi,87p : ill ; 25cm. — (Great Britain. Home Office. Research studies ; no.38) (Great Britain. Home Office. Research Unit. Reports)
Bibl.: p.85-87.
ISBN 0-11-340678-9 Sd : £1.75
(B77-08927)

364.6'2'0942 — Prisoners. Parole. Criteria. *England*
Hawkins, Keith. The parole decision : a guide / compiled from official sources by Keith Hawkins. — Chichester : Rose [for] the Howard League for Penal Reform, 1977. — 25p ; 21cm.
Index.
ISBN 0-85992-105-0 Sd : £0.75
(B77-25511)

364.6'3'06241 — Probation officers. Organisations. *Great Britain. National Association of Probation Officers. Regulations*
National Association of Probation Officers. Constitution / NAPO. — Thornton Heath (1st Floor, Ambassador House, Brigstock Rd, Thornton Heath, Surrey CR4 7JG) : National Association of Probation Officers, 1976. — 11p ; 21cm.
ISBN 0-901617-10-5 Sd : Unpriced
(B77-04063)

364.6'3'0942 — Probation services. *England*
Great Britain. *Central Office of Information.* The probation and after-care service in a changing society / [prepared for the Home Office by the Central Office of Information]. — [London] ([Whitehall, SW1A 2AP]) : [Home Office], 1976. — [2],30p(2 fold) : ill ; 21x22cm.
Page width varies. — Bibl.: p.30.
ISBN 0-903723-15-8 Sd : Unpriced
Also classified at 364.8'0942
(B77-13596)

364.6'3'0942 — Probation services. *England. Manuals*
Jarvis, Frederick Victor. Probation officers' manual / by F.V. Jarvis. — 2nd ed. — London : Butterworth.
Previous ed.: 1969.
Supplement. — 1976. — iv,64p ; 22cm.
ISBN 0-406-25603-9 Sd : £1.80
(B77-02164)

364.6'3'0942 — Probation services. *England. Statistics*
Probation service statistics, based on estimates / the Conference of Chief Probation Officers, the Society of County Treasurers. — Leicester : [The Conference] ; Reading : [The Society].
1977-78 / [compiler J. Unsworth]. — 1977. — [1],9p ; 30cm.
Sd : Unpriced
(B77-31087)

364.6'3'0942 — Probation services. *England, to 1975. Reports, surveys*
Bochel, Dorothy. Probation and after-care : its development in England and Wales / [by] Dorothy Bochel. — Edinburgh : Scottish Academic Press ; London : Distributed by Chatto and Windus, 1976. — viii,289p ; 23cm.
Bibl.: p.241-248. — Index.
ISBN 0-7011-2179-3 : £7.50
Also classified at 364.8'0942
(B77-03470)

364.6'3'0942 — Probation services. Influence of social change. *England*
Marshall, George, *b.1933.* Probation and social change / by George Marshall. — Thornton Heath (Ambassador House, Brigstock Rd, Thornton Heath, Surrey CR4 7JG) : National Association of Probation Officers, 'Role and Structure' Committee, 1976. — 8p ; 21cm. — (No.2)
ISBN 0-901617-09-1 Sd : £0.25(free to members)
(B77-04696)

364.6'3'0942 — Probation services. Role of voluntary personnel. *England. Reports, surveys*
Volunteer Centre. A survey of the involvement of volunteers with probation and after-care services in England and Wales / the Volunteer Centre. — Berkhamsted (29 Lower King's Rd, Berkhamsted, Herts. HP4 2AB) : The Centre, [1977?]. — [2],19,[1]p ; 30cm.
Sd : £0.35
Also classified at 364.8'0942
(B77-28526)

364.6'3'09421 — Probation services. *Inner London. Inner London Probation and After Care Service. Reports, surveys*
ILPAS '76 : a report on aspects of the work of the Inner London Probation and After-Care Service - to commemorate the centenary of probation in London. — London (73 Great Peter St., S.W.1) : I.L.P.A.S., [1977]. — 128p ; 21cm.
ISBN 0-904909-03-4 Pbk : £1.25
(B77-09631)

364.6'3'0973 — Probation & parole. *United States*
Carney, Louis P. Probation and parole : legal and social dimensions / [by] Louis P. Carney. — New York ; London [etc.] : McGraw-Hill, Gregg Division, 1977. — vi,346p : ill, forms, 2 ports ; 24cm.
Index.
ISBN 0-07-010126-4 : £9.70
(B77-21794)

364.6'6'0922 — Executioners. *England, to ca 1900*
Bleackley, Horace. The hangmen of England : how they hanged and whom they hanged : the life story of 'Jack Ketch' through two centuries / by Horace Bleackley. — Wakefield : EP Publishing, 1976. — xix,272p,[20]leaves of plates : ill, facsims, map, ports ; 23cm.
Facsimile reprint of: 1st ed. London : Chapman and Hall, 1929. — Index.
ISBN 0-7158-1184-3 : £5.95
(B77-24822)

364.6'6'0924 — Executioners: Pierrepoint, Albert. *Great Britain. Autobiographies*
Pierrepoint, Albert. Executioner, Pierrepoint / [by] Albert Pierrepoint. — London : Coronet, 1977. — 208p,[8]p of plates : ill, ports ; 18cm.
Originally published: London : Harrap, 1974.
ISBN 0-340-21307-8 Pbk : £0.70
(B77-28527)

364.6'8 — Victims of crimes. Compensation by offenders. *England. Proposals*
Howard League for Penal Reform. Making amends : criminals, victims and society, compensation - reparation - reconciliation : a discussion paper / by the Howard League [for Penal Reform]. — Chichester : Rose, 1977. — 18p ; 21cm.
ISBN 0-85992-104-2 Sd : £1.00
(B77-26971)

364.8 — DISCHARGED PRISONERS

364.8'0942 — Discharged prisoners. Aftercare services. *England*
Great Britain. *Central Office of Information.* The probation and after-care service in a changing society / [prepared for the Home Office by the Central Office of Information]. — [London] ([Whitehall, SW1A 2AP]) : [Home Office], 1976. — [2],30p(2 fold) : ill ; 21x22cm.
Page width varies. — Bibl.: p.30.
ISBN 0-903723-15-8 Sd : Unpriced
Primary classification 364.6'3'0942
(B77-13596)

364.8'0942 — Discharged prisoners. Aftercare services. *England, to 1975. Reports, surveys*
Bochel, Dorothy. Probation and after-care : its development in England and Wales / [by] Dorothy Bochel. — Edinburgh : Scottish Academic Press ; London : Distributed by Chatto and Windus, 1976. — viii,289p ; 23cm.
Bibl.: p.241-248. — Index.
ISBN 0-7011-2179-3 : £7.50
Primary classification 364.6'3'0942
(B77-03470)

364.8'0942 — Discharged prisoners. Aftercare services. Role of voluntary personnel. *England. Reports, surveys*
Volunteer Centre. A survey of the involvement of volunteers with probation and after-care services in England and Wales / the Volunteer Centre. — Berkhamsted (29 Lower King's Rd, Berkhamsted, Herts. HP4 2AB) : The Centre, [1977?]. — [2],19,[1]p ; 30cm.
Sd : £0.35
Primary classification 364.6'3'0942
(B77-28526)

364.9 — CRIMINOLOGY. HISTORICAL AND GEOGRAPHICAL TREATMENT

364'.903 — Crime. Political aspects, 1750-1976
Gurr, Ted Robert. The politics of crime and conflict : a comparative history of four cities / [by] Ted Robert Gurr, Peter N. Grabosky, Richard C. Hula ; with contributions by ... [others]. — Beverly Hills ; London : Sage Publications, 1977. — xii,792,[1]p : ill ; 24cm.
Index.
ISBN 0-8039-0677-3 : £20.00
Also classified at 301.6'3'09
(B77-19290)

364'.904 — Crime and punishment, 1920-1976
Chambers, Aidan. Aidan Chambers' book of cops and robbers / illustrated by Allan Manham and with photographs. — Harmondsworth : Kestrel Books, 1977. — 127p : ill, facsims, ports ; 23cm.
Bibl.: p.125. — Index.
ISBN 0-7226-5217-8 : £3.75
(B77-13597)

364'.941 — Crime. *Great Britain. Periodicals*
Crime & community forum. — London (125 Kennington Park Rd, SE11 4JP) : Howard League for Penal Reform.
No.1- ; Winter 1976-. — 1976-. — 30cm.
Quarterly? - Folder(4p.) as 1st issue.
Unpriced
(B77-21053)

364'.941 — Crime. *Great Britain. Sociological perspectives*
The **sociology** of crime and delinquency in Britain. — London : Martin Robertson.
Vol.2 : The new criminologies / edited by Paul Wiles. — 1976. — viii,237p ; 23cm.
ISBN 0-85520-111-8 : £6.45
ISBN 0-85520-110-x Pbk : £2.95
(B77-04697)

364'.942 — Crime & punishment. *England, 1700-1800*
Albion's fatal tree : crime and society in eighteenth-century England / [by] Douglas Hay ... [et al.]. — Harmondsworth [etc.] : Penguin, 1977. — 352p,[12]p of plates : ill, facsims, 2 maps, port ; 21cm. — (Peregrine books)
Originally published: London : Allen Lane, 1976. — Index.
ISBN 0-14-055130-1 Pbk : £3.25
(B77-26972)

364'.9421 — Crime. *London, 1558-1603*
Salgādo, Gāmini. The Elizabethan underworld / [by] Gāmini Salgādo. — London : Dent [etc.], 1977. — 221p : ill, facsims, map(on lining papers), ports ; 24cm.
Bibl.: p.209-211. — Index.
ISBN 0-460-12010-7 : £5.50 : CIP rev.
(B77-15217)

364'.9424'9 — Crime. *West Midlands (Metropolitan County). Black Country, 1835-1860*
Philips, David. Crime and authority in Victorian England : the Black Country, 1835-1860 / [by] David Philips. — London : Croom Helm [etc.], 1977. — 3-321p : ill, map ; 23cm.
Bibl.: p.302-314. — Index.
ISBN 0-85664-568-0 : £8.50 : CIP rev.
(B77-18031)

364'.943 — Crime. *Germany, 1800-1900. Sociological perspectives*
Zehr, Howard. Crime and the development of modern society : patterns of criminality in nineteenth century Germany and France / [by] Howard Zehr. — London : Croom Helm [etc.], 1976. — 188p : ill ; 23cm.
Bibl.: p.177-185. — Index.
ISBN 0-85664-235-5 : £7.50
Also classified at 364'.944
(B77-02165)

364'.944 — Crime. *France, 1800-1900. Sociological perspectives*
Zehr, Howard. Crime and the development of modern society : patterns of criminality in nineteenth century Germany and France / [by] Howard Zehr. — London : Croom Helm [etc.], 1976. — 188p : ill ; 23cm.
Bibl.: p.177-185. — Index.
ISBN 0-85664-235-5 : £7.50
Primary classification 364'.943
(B77-02165)

364'.968 — Crime & punishment. *South Africa*
Crime and punishment in South Africa / edited by James Midgley, Jan H. Steyn, Roland Graser. — Johannesburg ; London [etc.] : McGraw-Hill, 1975. — [8],261,[2]p : maps ; 24cm.
Bibl.
ISBN 0-07-091250-5 : Unpriced
(B77-01287)

364'.973 — Crime. *United States. Sociological perspectives*
Gibbons, Don Cary. Society, crime and criminal careers : an introduction to criminology / [by] Don C. Gibbons. — 3rd ed. — Englewood Cliffs ; London [etc.] : Prentice-Hall, 1977. — x,582p : ill ; 25cm.
Previous ed.: 1973. — Index.
ISBN 0-13-820100-5 : £11.15
(B77-31088)

364'.9747 — Crime & punishment. *New York (Colony), 1691-1776*
Greenberg, Douglas. Crime and law enforcement in the colony of New York, 1691-1776 / [by] Douglas Greenberg. — Ithaca ; London : Cornell University Press, 1976. — 259,[1]p : map ; 23cm.
Bibl.: p.237-252. — Index.
ISBN 0-8014-1020-7 : £12.00
(B77-14648)

365 — DETENTION INSTITUTIONS

365.3 — British criminals. Transportation. *Tasmania, ca 1840. Case studies. Secondary school texts*
O'Neill, Judith. Transported to Van Diemen's Land : the story of two convicts / [by] Judith O'Neill. — Cambridge [etc.] : Cambridge University Press, 1977. — 48p : ill, facsims, geneal table, map, plans, ports ; 21x22cm. — (Cambridge introduction to the history of mankind : topic books)
ISBN 0-521-21231-6 Pbk : £1.10(non-net)
(B77-09632)

365.3 — British criminals. Transportation. Voyages by sailing ships. *Australia, 1787-1868*
Bateson, Charles. The convict ships, 1787-1868 / by Charles Bateson. — 2nd ed. — Sydney [etc.] ; London : A.H. and A.W. Reed, 1974. — x,421p,[8]p of plates : ill, facsim, map, port ; 21cm.
This ed. originally published: Glasgow : Brown, Son and Ferguson, 1969. — Index.
ISBN 0-589-07146-7 Pbk : £6.50
(B77-02166)

365'.3 — Floating prisons. *London. Greenwich (London Borough). Woolwich, 1770-1857*
Rigden, Reg. The floating prisons of Woolwich and Deptford / [by] Reg Rigden. — [London] ([232 Plumstead High St., SE18 1JL]) : London Borough of Greenwich, 1976. — [1],25p ; 21cm.
Bibl.: p.25.
Sd : £0.15
Also classified at 365'.3
(B77-08314)

365'.3 — Floating prisons. *London. Lewisham (London Borough). Deptford, 1770-1857*
Rigden, Reg. The floating prisons of Woolwich and Deptford / [by] Reg Rigden. — [London] ([232 Plumstead High St., SE18 1JL]) : London Borough of Greenwich, 1976. — [1],25p ; 21cm.
Bibl.: p.25.
Sd : £0.15
Primary classification 365'.3
(B77-08314)

365'.3 — Open prisons. *Great Britain*
Jones, Howard, *b.1918.* Open prisons / [by] Howard Jones and Paul Cornes ; assisted by Richard Stockford. — London [etc.] : Routledge and Kegan Paul, 1977. — x,275p : ill, forms ; 23cm. — (International library of social policy)
ISBN 0-7100-8602-4 : £7.95 : CIP rev.
(B77-18664)

365'.42 — Community homes. Security. *England. Howard League for Penal Reform viewpoints*
'Unruly' children in a human context : types, costs and effects of security : report of a Howard League working party. — Chichester [etc.] : Rose [for the] Howard League for Penal Reform, 1977. — [1],iv,34p ; 21cm.
ISBN 0-85992-087-9 Sd : £1.20
(B77-17394)

365'.42'0973 — Child prisoners. *United States*
Wooden, Kenneth. Weeping in the playtime of others : America's incarcerated children / by Kenneth Wooden. — New York ; London [etc.] : McGraw-Hill, 1976. — xii,264p ; 22cm.
Bibl.: p.249-251. — Index.
ISBN 0-07-071642-0 : £6.70
ISBN 0-07-071643-9 Pbk : £2.90
(B77-18665)

365'.45 — Psychiatric hospitals. Patients: Political dissidents. Detention. *Soviet Union*
Bloch, Sidney. Russia's political hospitals : the abuse of psychiatry in the Soviet Union / [by] Sidney Bloch and Peter Reddaway. — London : Gollancz, 1977. — 510p,[16]p of plates : ill, facsim, plan, ports ; 23cm.
Index.
ISBN 0-575-02318-x : £6.95
(B77-30098)

365'.45'0621 — Amnesty International. *Reports, surveys. Serials*
Amnesty International. The Amnesty International report. — London (53 Theobald's Rd, WC1X 8SP) : Amnesty International Publications.
1 June 1975-31 May 1976. — 1976. — 220p : ill ; 21cm.
Supersedes: Amnesty International. Annual report.
ISBN 0-900058-31-5 Pbk : £1.50
ISSN 0309-068x
(B77-00693)

365'.45'0947 — Political prisoners. *Soviet Union, 1918-1956*
Solzhenitsyn, Aleksandr Isaevich. The Gulag Archipelago, 1918-56 : an experiment in literary investigation / [by] Alexander Solzhenitsyn. — [London] : Fontana.
[Vol.1] : [Part] 1 [and] 2 / translated from the Russian by Thomas P. Whitney. — 1976. — xii,660p,[2] leaves of plates : ports ; 18cm.
'This present English-language edition of Parts I and II of "The Gulag Archipelago" differs very slightly, as a result of author's corrections and other corrections, from the Russian-language first edition of these parts ...' - Translator's notes. — Parts of this work previously appeared in "The Observer" and the "New York Times"' - title page verso. — This translation originally published: New York : Harper and Row ; London : Collins : Harvill Press, 1974. — Translation of 'Arkhipelag Gulag', Vol.1. Paris : YMCA Press, 1973. — Index.
Pbk : £1.25
(B77-02167)

365'.45'09598 — Political prisoners. *Indonesia, 1965-1976. Reports, surveys*
Amnesty International. Indonesia : an Amnesty International report. — London (10 Southampton St., WC2E 7HF) : Amnesty International Publications, 1977. — 146p : ill, 2 maps, ports ; 21cm.
ISBN 0-900058-63-3 Pbk : £2.00
(B77-32546)

365'.45'096891 — Political prisoners. *Rhodesia. Reports, surveys*
International Defence and Aid Fund. Ian Smith's hostages : political prisoners in Rhodesia / [International Defence and Aid Fund]. — London (104 Newgate St., [EC1A 7AP]) : The Fund, 1976. — [2],38p : 1 ill, map ; 30cm.
ISBN 0-904759-16-4 Sd : £1.00
(B77-08928)

365'.45'097285 — Political prisoners. *Nicaragua, 1975-1977. Reports, surveys*
Amnesty International. The Republic of Nicaragua : an Amnesty International report including the findings of a mission to Nicaragua, 10-15 May 1976. — London ([53 Theobald's Rd, WC1X 8SP]) : Amnesty International Publications, 1977. — 75p : facsim, map ; 30cm.
Bibl.: p.75.
ISBN 0-900058-62-5 Sd : £0.75
(B77-31797)

365'.6 — Prisoners. Protest movements. *Western world, to 1976*
Fitzgerald, Mike. Prisoners in revolt / [by] Mike Fitzgerald. — Harmondsworth [etc.] : Penguin, 1977. — 278p ; 18cm. — (Pelican books)
Bibl.: p.267-268. — Index.
ISBN 0-14-021922-6 Pbk : £1.00
(B77-14149)

365'.6'08 — Prison life. *Collections*
The **experience** of prison : an anthology of prose, drama, verse, and picture / edited by David Ball. — London : Longman, 1977. — viii, 168p : ill ; 19cm. — (Longman imprint books)
Bibl.: p.163-164.
ISBN 0-582-23343-7 Pbk : £1.00
(B77-32547)

365'.6'0922 — Castles. *London. Tower Hamlets (London Borough). Tower of London. Prisoners, 1478-1774. Biographies. Juvenile literature*
Picard, Barbara Leonie. The Tower and the traitors / [by] Barbara Leonie Picard. — London [etc.] : Beaver Books, 1976. — 206p : ill, plan ; 20cm.
Originally published: as 'The Tower of London & the traitors'. London : Batsford, 1961. — Index.
ISBN 0-600-38747-x Pbk : £0.65
(B77-14649)

365'.6'0924 — German prisoners of war. Prison life. *East Germany & Soviet Union, 1945-1954. Personal observations*
Linke, Maria Zeitner. East wind : the story of Maria Zeitner Linke / written by Ruth Hunt. — Berkhamsted : Lion Publishing, 1977. — 228p,8p of plates : facsims, form, ports ; 20cm. — (An Aslan book)
ISBN 0-85648-080-0 Pbk : £0.95
(B77-31798)

365'.6'0924 — Labour camps. *Russia (RSFSR). Siberia, 1940-1953. Personal observations*
Ciszek, Walter Joseph. He leadeth me / by Walter J. Ciszek, with Daniel L. Flaherty. — London [etc.] : Mowbrays, 1973 [i.e. 1977]. — 216p ; 22cm.
Originally published: Garden City, N.Y. : Doubleday, 1973 ; London : Hodder and Stoughton, 1974.
ISBN 0-264-66455-8 Pbk : £3.25
(B77-32548)

365'.6'0924 — Penal colonies. *French Guiana, 1932-1945. Personal observations*
Charrière, Henri. Papillon / [by] Henri Charrière ; translated from the French by June P. Wilson and Walker B. Michaels ; a condensation by the editors of Reader's Digest Condensed Books. — Large print ed. — Leicester : Ulverscroft, 1976. — [5],250p ; 23cm. — (Ulverscroft large print series : [fiction])
Full ed. of this translation originally published: New York : Morrow, 1970 ; St Albans : Panther, 1971. — Translation of: 'Papillon'. Paris : Laffont, 1959.
ISBN 0-85456-549-3 : £2.65
(B77-00694)

365'.6'0924 — Political prisoners. *United States, 1919-1920. Personal observations*
O'Hare, Kate Richards. In prison / by Kate Richards O'Hare. — [1st ed. reprinted] ; introduction by Jack M. Holl. — Seattle ; London : University of Washington Press, 1976. — xli p,p21-211 ; 23cm. — (Americana library)

Facsimile reprint of: 1st ed. New York : Knopf, 1923. — Index.
ISBN 0-295-95451-5 : £11.25
(B77-29317)

365'.6'0924 — Political prisoners. Kearney, Peadar. Internment. *Ireland. Correspondence with Kearney, Eva*
Kearney, Peadar. My dear Eva : letters written from Ballykinlar Internment Camp (1921) / by Peadar Kearney ; introduced by Seamus de Burca. — Dublin (64 Dame St., Dublin) : P.J. Bourke, 1976. — [5],43[5]p : 1 ill, facsims, ports ; 23cm.
ISBN 0-85163-032-4 Sd : £1.00
(B77-00695)

365'.6'0924 — Political prisoners. Ten Boom, Corrie. *Netherlands, 1944. Correspondence*
Ten Boom, Corrie. Corrie ten Boom's prison letters. — London [etc.] : Hodder and Stoughton ; London : Christian Literature Crusade, 1976. — 94p,[4]p of plates : 1 ill, ports ; 18cm. — (Hodder Christian paperbacks)

Originally published: Old Tappan, N.J. : F.H. Revell, 1975.
ISBN 0-340-20580-6 Pbk : £0.60
(B77-16292)

365'.6'0924 — Prison life. *India (Republic). Personal observations*
Tyler, Mary. My years in an Indian prison / by Mary Tyler ; with illustrations by Dilip Ray. — London : Gollancz, 1977. — 191p : ill, plan ; 23cm.
ISBN 0-575-02210-8 : £5.20
(B77-05984)

365'.6'0924 — Prisons. *United States. Personal observations*
Harsh, George. Lonesome road / [by] George Harsh. — London : Sphere, 1976. — 188p ; 18cm.
Originally published: New York : Norton, 1971 ; Harlow : Longman, 1972.
ISBN 0-7221-4405-9 Pbk : £0.65
(B77-07864)

365'.64 — Mentally ill offenders. Treatment. *Canada. Personal observations*
Pollock, Donald. Call me a good thief / by Donald Pollock. — London : H. Baker, 1976. — [2],236p,[4]p of plates : facsims, ports ; 23cm.
ISBN 0-7030-0088-8 : £3.50
ISBN 0-7030-0095-0 Pbk : £1.25
(B77-02168)

365'.64 — Political prisoners. Torture. *Argentina. Reports, surveys*
Amnesty International. Report of an Amnesty International mission to Argentina, 6-15 November 1976. — London (53 Theobald's Rd, WC1X 8SP) : Amnesty International Publications, 1977. — 92p ; 30cm.
ISBN 0-900058-47-1 Sd : £1.00
(B77-16802)

365'.64 — Political prisoners. Torture. *Philippines. Reports, surveys*
Amnesty International. Report of an Amnesty International Mission to the Republic of the Philippines, 22 November-5 December 1975. — 2nd ed. — London (53 Theobald's Rd, WC1X 8SP) : Amnesty International Publications, 1977. — 95p ; 21cm.
Previous ed.: 1976. — Includes the reply of the Philippines Government.
ISBN 0-900058-43-9 Pbk : £1.00
(B77-18032)

365'.641 — Prisons. *Isle of Wight. Medina (District). Albany Prison. Administration. Protest by Irish Republican Army. Provisional IRA prisoners, 1976*
Amnesty International. A dossier concerning treatment of prisoners during and after a disturbance at Albany Prison in September 1976 / Amnesty International, Howard League for Penal Reform, National Council for Civil Liberties. — [London] ([53 Theobald's Rd, WC1X 8SP]) : [Amnesty International] ; [London] : [Howard League for Penal Reform] : [N.C.C.L.], [1977]. — [2],23p ; 30cm.

ISBN 0-900058-55-2 Sd : Unpriced
(B77-16293)

365'.641 — Prisons. Leicestershire. Leicester. Leicester Prison. Escape of Hughes, William Thomas, 1977. Related to security of Leicester Prison. *Inquiry reports*
Great Britain. *Prison Department. Inspectorate.* Report of an inquiry by the Chief Inspector of the Prison Service into security at HM Prison Leicester and the arrangements for conducting prisoners to courts (escape of William Thomas Hughes on 12 January 1977). — London : H.M.S.O., [1977]. — ii,57p : facsims, forms ; 25cm. — ([1976-77 H.C.]202)
ISBN 0-10-220277-x Sd : £1.10
(B77-11718)

365'.66 — Prisoners. Higher education. *United States. Case studies*
Seashore, Marjorie J. Prisoner education : Project NewGate and other college programs / [by] Marjorie J. Seashore, Steven Haberfeld with ... [others]. — New York [etc.] ; London : Praeger, 1976. — xv,[2]p : ill, form ; 25cm. — (Praeger special studies in US economic, social and political issues)
Bibl.: p.326-329.
ISBN 0-275-56040-6 : £15.90
(B77-08929)

365'.66 — Prisons. Drug addicts. Treatment. *United States*
Newman, Charles L. Jails and drug treatment / [by] Charles L. Newman, Barbara R. Price. — Beverly Hills ; London : Sage Publications, 1977. — 223p : ill ; 22cm. — (Sage library of social research ; vol.36)
Bibl.: p.209-214. — Index.
ISBN 0-8039-0696-x : £8.00
ISBN 0-8039-0697-8 Pbk : £4.50
(B77-18033)

365'.7'0924 — Prisons. Reform. Howard, John, b.1726. *England. Biographies*
Godber, Joyce. John Howard the philanthropist / by Joyce Godber. — [Bedford] ([County Hall, Bedford MK42 9AP]) : Arts and Recreation Department, Bedfordshire County Council, 1977. — [2],17,[2]p,[4]p of plates : ill, maps, port ; 22cm.
Sd : £0.30
(B77-32549)

365'.7'0924 — Prisons. Reform. Paul, Sir George Onesiphorus, bart. *Gloucestershire*
Whiting, John Roger Scott. Prison reform in Gloucestershire, 1776-1820 : a study of the work of Sir George Onesiphorus Paul, Bart / by J.R.S. Whiting. — London [etc.] : Phillimore, 1975. — xxii,287p,[6]p of plates : facsim, map, plans, ports ; 23cm.
Bibl.: p.270-273. — Index.
ISBN 0-85033-208-7 : £8.75
(B77-02169)

365'.7'0973 — Correctional institutions. Reform. *United States. Conference proceedings*
Reform in corrections : problems and issues / edited by Harry E. Allen, Nancy J. Beran. — New York ; London : Praeger [for] the American Society of Criminology, 1977. — xi, 131p : 2 ill ; 25cm. — (Praeger special studies in US economic, social and political issues)
'Papers originally presented at the annual meeting of the American Society of Criminology, Chicago, 1974' - Library of Congress Cataloging in Publication Data. — Bibl.
ISBN 0-275-24270-6 : £10.05
(B77-27770)

365'.92'4 — Concentration camps. Administration. Stangl, Franz. *Poland*
Sereny, Gitta. Into that darkness : an examination of conscience / [by] Gitta Sereny. — London : Pan Books, 1977. — [2],380p,[8]p of plates : ill, map, plans, ports ; 20cm. — (Picador)
Originally published: London : Deutsch, 1974. — Bibl.: p.369-372. — Index.
ISBN 0-330-25016-7 Pbk : £1.50
(B77-10299)

365'.942 — Prisons. *England, ca 1775. Early works. Facsimiles*
Howard, John. The state of the prisons / by John Howard. — Bicentennial ed. ; with a preface by Martin Wright. — Abingdon : Professional Books, 1977. — xv,512p,[3]fold leaves of plates : ill, plans ; 28cm.
Facsimile reprint of: 1st ed.: Warrington : s.n., 1777.
ISBN 0-903486-41-5 : £13.50
(B77-26973)

365'.942 — Prisons. *England. Conservative and Unionist Party viewpoints*
The **proper** use of prisons : a Conservative study group report. — London : Conservative Political Centre, 1977. — 28p ; 21cm. — (Conservative Political Centre. Publications ; no.609)
ISBN 0-85070-603-3 Sd : £0.50
(B77-30099)

365'.942 — Prisons. *England. Reports, surveys. Serials*
Great Britain. *Prison Department.* Report on the work of the Prison Department ... — London : H.M.S.O.
1976. — [1977]. — iv,90p,[4]p of plates : ill ; 25cm. — (Cmnd.6877)
ISBN 0-10-168770-2 Sd : £1.65
(B77-21795)

1976. Statistical tables. — [1977]. — iii,87p : ill ; 25cm. — (Cmnd.6884)
ISBN 0-10-168840-7 Sd : £2.15
(B77-21796)

365'.942 — Prisons. *England, to 1975*
Morris, Rosamund. Prisons / [by] Rosamund Morris. — London : Batsford, 1976. — 95p : ill, facsims, plans, ports ; 26cm. — (Past-into-present series)
Bibl.: p.92-93. — Index.
ISBN 0-7134-3242-x : £2.95
(B77-00696)

365'.942 — Prisons. Social aspects. *England. Secondary school texts*
Foster, John Louis. Prisons / [by] John L. Foster. — London : Edward Arnold, 1976. — 16p : ill, port ; 30cm. — (Checkpoint ; 5)
ISBN 0-7131-0049-4 Sd : £2.50(set of 5 copies)
(B77-09633)

365'.9423'89 — Prisons. Social conditions. *Somerset. Ilchester, ca 1820. Early works. Facsimiles*
Visits to a prison, a peep at the prisoners and a description of the interior of Ilchester gaol, 1821 ; also, Saint Henry of Ilchester / edited by J. Stevens Cox. — St Peter Port : Toucan Press, 1977. — [2],17[i.e.19],[1]p : 1 ill ; 26cm. — (Ilchester and district occasional papers ; no.8)
'Visits to a prison ...' originally published: Ilminster : John Moore, 1821. — Facsimile reprint.
Sd : Unpriced
(B77-22481)

365'.9427'59 — Boys community home schools. *Merseyside (Metropolitan County). Formby. St Vincent's Community Home. Administration. Reports, surveys*
Approved school to community home : report of an exercise held in conjunction with Liverpool Catholic Children's and Social Services at St Vincent's, Formby, Lancashire / [edited by Barbara Kahan]. — London : H.M.S.O., 1976. — [3],73p : ill, plans ; 30cm. — (Great Britain. Department of Health and Social Security. Social Work Service. Development Group. Report series)
ISBN 0-11-320639-9 Pbk : £1.25
(B77-08315)

365'.9428'37 — Prisons. *Humberside. Hull. Hull Prison. Prisoners. Riots, 1976. Inquiry reports*
Great Britain. *Prison Department. Inspectorate.* Report of an inquiry by the Chief Inspector of the Prison Service into the cause and circumstances of the events at HM Prison Hull during the period 31st August to 3rd September, 1976. — London : H.M.S.O., [1977]. — ii,121p,[2]fold leaves of plates,[4]p of plates : ill, plans ; 25cm. — ([1976-77 H.C.]453)
ISBN 0-10-245377-2 Pbk : £2.10
(B77-22482)

365'.9429'37 — Prisons. *Clwyd. Ruthin. Ruthin Gaol, to 1916*
Clwyd Record Office. Ruthin gaol / [Clwyd Record Office]. — Hawarden (The Old Rectory, Hawarden, Deeside CH5 3NR) : Clwyd Record Office, 1977. — [1],9p,fold plate : 1 ill, 2 facsims, plan ; 22cm.
Sd : £0.15
(B77-24825)

365'.973 — Prisons. *United States*
Mitford, Jessica. The American prison business / [by] Jessica Mitford. — Harmondsworth [etc.] : Penguin, 1977. — 329p : 1 ill ; 19cm.
Originally published: as 'Kind and usual punishment', New York : Knopf, 1973 ; and as 'The American prison business', London : Allen and Unwin, 1975. — Index.
ISBN 0-14-004152-4 Pbk : £1.00
(B77-12957)

366 — ASSOCIATIONS

366'.09421 — Secret societies. *London. Ancient and Benevolent Order of the Friendly Brothers of St Patrick. London Knots, to 1973*
Portlock, Ronald. History of the London Knots, 1775 to 1973 / by Ronald Portlock ; [for] the Ancient and Benevolent Order of the Friendly Brothers of St Patrick. — London ([1 Smith Court, Chelsea, S.W.3]) : The author, [1973?]. — [3],110p : coat of arms ; 22cm.
Index.
ISBN 0-9505427-0-9 : Unpriced
(B77-03471)

366'.0951 — Secret societies. *China, 1840-1911*
Davis, Fei-Ling. Primitive revolutionaries of China : a study of secret societies in the late nineteenth century / [by] Fei-Ling Davis ; [translated from the Italian]. — London [etc.] : Routledge and Kegan Paul, 1977. — vii,254p : facsims, map, plan ; 23cm.
Translation of: 'Le società segrete in Cina, 1840-1911'. Torino : Einaudi, 1971. — Bibl.: p.240-248. — Index.
ISBN 0-7100-8186-3 : £4.95
(B77-24826)

366'.1'02542 — Freemasons. *England. Freemasons. United Grand Lodge of England. Directories*
Masonic year book. — London (Freemasons' Hall, Great Queen St., WC2B 5AZ) : United Grand Lodge of England.
1976-7. — 1976. — 3-769p ; 16cm.
ISBN 0-901075-07-8 Pbk : £2.50 to members only
(B77-00126)

366'.1'0254221 — Freemasons. *Surrey. Freemasons. Grand Lodge (Surrey). Directories*
Freemasons. *Grand Lodge (Surrey).* Surrey Provincial calendar and list of craft lodges ... / [Provincial Grand Lodge of Surrey]. — [Croydon] ([c/o 71 Oakfield Rd, Croydon, CR0 2UX]) : The Grand Lodge.
1976, September. — [1976]. — 315 columns,xxxix p ; 17cm.
Cover title.
ISBN 0-9504553-1-8 Pbk : £0.40
(B77-01288)

366'.1'0254267 — Freemasons. *Essex. Freemasons. Grand Lodge (Essex). Directories*
Freemasons. *Grand Lodge (Essex).* The Freemasons' handbook of the Province of Essex. — Ilford (19 The Crescent, Gants Hill, Ilford IG2 6JJ) : [The Provincial Grand Lodge].
1976-1977 : 92nd year of publication / compiled by the Provincial Grand Secretary ... L.K. Corbett. — 1976. — xxv,440p ; 15cm.
ISBN 0-9505234-1-0 Pbk : £0.50
(B77-09634)

366'.1'09 — Freemasonry, to 1976
Pick, Fred Lomax. The pocket history of Freemasonry / by Fred L. Pick and G. Norman Knight. — 6th ed. / revised by G. Norman Knight and Frederick Smyth. — London : Muller, 1977. — 348p ; 18cm.
Previous ed.: 1969. — Bibl.: p.319-320. — Index.
ISBN 0-584-10256-9 : £3.30
(B77-25512)

366'.1'0942 — Freemasons. *England. Grand Lodge of Mark Master Masons. Yearbooks*
Grand Lodge of Mark Master Masons. Year book / Grand Lodge of Mark Master Masons of England and Wales and the Dominions and Dependencies of the British Crown. — London (Mark Mason's Hall, 40 Upper Brook St., W1Y 2DX) : [The Grand Lodge].
1976 : ninety-first year of issue. — [1976]. — 391p ; 16cm.
Cover title: Mark year book 1976.
ISBN 0-904990-04-4 Pbk : £1.75
(B77-11156)

1976-1977 : ninety-second year of issue. — [1977]. — 397p ; 16cm.
Cover title: Mark year book, 1977. — Index.
ISBN 0-904990-03-6 Pbk : £1.75
(B77-10300)

367 — SOCIAL CLUBS

367'.025'41 — Ex-servicemen's clubs. *Great Britain. Directories*
United Kingdom ex-servicemen's clubs / [Data Research Group]. — Amersham (Hill House, [Hill Ave.], Amersham, Bucks.) : The Group. [1976]. — 1976. — 125 leaves in various pagings ; 30cm.
ISBN 0-905570-81-2 Sp : £15.00
(B77-11157)

367'.025'41 — Political social clubs. *Great Britain. Directories*
United Kingdom political clubs / [Data Research Group]. — Amersham (Hill House [Hill Ave.], Amersham, Bucks.) : The Group. [1977]. — 1977. — 123 leaves in various pagings ; 30cm.
ISBN 0-905570-83-9 Sp : £15.00
(B77-13598)

367'.025'41 — Workingmen's clubs. *Great Britain. Directories*
United Kingdom workingmens' clubs / [Data Research Group]. — Amersham (Hill House, [Hill Ave.], Amersham, Bucks.) : The Group. 1977. — 1977. — 119 leaves in various pagings ; 30cm.
ISBN 0-905570-85-5 Sd : Unpriced
(B77-13599)

367'.941 — Social clubs. *Great Britain. Directories*
United Kingdom social clubs / [Data Research Group]. — Amersham (Hill House, [Hill Ave.], Amersham, Bucks.) : The Group. 1975. — [1975]. — 253 leaves in various pagings ; 30cm.
ISBN 0-905570-36-7 Pbk : £16.00
(B77-00127)

367'.9421 — Clubs for handicapped persons. *London. Directories*
Greater London Association for the Disabled. Directory of clubs in Greater London / Greater London Association for the Disabled. — London (183 Queensway, W2 5HL) : G.L.A.D.
4th ed. — [1976]. — 80p ; 30cm.
Cover title.
ISBN 0-901828-02-5 Pbk : £0.40
ISSN 0309-0337
(B77-02885)

367'.9421 — Dining clubs. *London. Royal Society Club, to 1974*
Allibone, Thomas Edward. The Royal Society and its dining clubs / by T.E. Allibone. — Oxford [etc.] : Pergamon, 1976. — xv,457p : 1 ill, facsims, 2 maps(on lining papers) ; 26cm.
Index.
ISBN 0-08-020493-7 : £16.50
Also classified at 506'.241
(B77-04698)

368 — INSURANCE
Cockerell, Hugh Anthony Lewis. Insurance / [by] H.A.L. Cockerell. — 3rd ed. — London : Teach Yourself Books, 1976. — ix,237p ; 18cm. — (Teach yourself books)
Previous ed.: London : English Universities Press, 1964. — Bibl.: p.228-230. — Index.
ISBN 0-340-20770-1 Pbk : £1.25
(B77-25513)

368 — Captive insurance companies. *Great Britain. Reports, surveys*
Captive insurance companies : the Association of Insurance and Risk Managers in Industry and Commerce Study Group report. — London ([97 The Avenue, W13 8LA]) : The Association, 1976. — [5],33p ; 30cm.
ISBN 0-9504063-1-7 Sp : £2.00(free to members of the Association)
(B77-12958)

368 — Voluntary organisations. Insurance. *Great Britain*
British Insurance Association. Insurance protection for voluntary organisations and voluntary workers / [prepared by the British Insurance Association]. — London : National Council of Social Service, 1977. — [2],14p ; 21cm.
ISBN 0-7199-0923-6 Sd : £0.30
(B77-22483)

368'.001'51 — Insurance. Mathematics. *Essays*
Borch, Karl. The mathematical theory of insurance : an annotated selection of papers on insurance published 1960-1972 / [by] Karl Borch. — Lexington, Mass. [etc.] ; London : D.C. Heath, 1974. — xvi,373p : 1 ill ; 24cm.
'Lexington Books'. — Bibl. — Index.
ISBN 0-669-86942-2 : £10.60
(B77-15773)

368'.001'84 — Insurance. Risks. Mathematical models
Beard, Robert Eric. Risk theory : the stochastic basis of insurance / [by] R.E. Beard, T. Pentikäinen, E. Pesonen. — 2nd ed. — London : Chapman and Hall, 1977. — iii-xvi, 195p : ill ; 23cm. — (Monographs on applied probability and statistics)
'A Halstead Press book'. — With answers. — Previous ed.: London : Methuen, 1969. — Bibl.: 185-189. — Index.
ISBN 0-412-15100-6 : £5.00
(B77-26233)

368'.0025 — Insurance companies. *Directories*
The **'Financial** times' world insurance yearbook. — London : 'Financial Times'.
1976-77 / compiled and edited by the Business Year Books Department, the Financial Times Limited. — 1976. — 296p : ill ; 30cm.
Index.
ISBN 0-900671-68-8 : £15.00
(B77-04064)

368'.006'5416 — Insurance companies. *Northern Ireland. Reports, surveys. Serials*
Insurance companies general annual report / Department of Commerce [Northern Ireland]. — Belfast : H.M.S.O.
1975. — [1976]. — 15p ; 24cm.
ISBN 0-337-06070-3 Sd : £0.28
(B77-03472)

368'.0092'2 — Insurance. *Great Britain. Biographical dictionaries*
Who's who in insurance / edited by R.T.D. Wilmot. — London : Graham and Trotman, 1975. — [5],xv,303p : ports ; 24cm.
ISBN 0-86010-023-5 : £12.00
(B77-04065)

368'.01'06241 — Actuaries. Organisations. *Great Britain. Institute of Actuaries. Yearbooks*
Institute of Actuaries. The Institute of Actuaries year book. — Oxford : Alden Press.
1976-1977 : [49th ed.]. — 1976. — xiv,282p, plate : port ; 21cm.
Booklet (11p.) as insert. — Index.
ISBN 0-900040-19-x Pbk : £1.00
(B77-04699)

368'.01'062411 — Actuaries. Organisations. *Scotland. Faculty of Actuaries. Yearbooks*
Faculty of Actuaries. Year book / Faculty of Actuaries. — Edinburgh ([23 St Andrew Sq., Edinburgh, EH2 1AQ]) : [The Faculty].
1976-77. — 1976. — 196p ; 22cm.
'Additions to the library' (4p.) as insert.
Pbk : £1.00
ISSN 0305-7216
(B77-03473)

368'.011 — Insurance. Pricing. Related to loss prevention incentives
Doherty, Neil Alexander. Insurance and loss prevention / [by] Neil Doherty. — Farnborough, Hants. : Saxon House [etc.], 1976. — ix,134,[1]p : ill ; 24cm.
Index.
ISBN 0-347-01097-0 : £5.50
Primary classification 368'.015
(B77-11719)

368'.015 — Insurance. Losses. Prevention. Incentives. Related to insurance pricing
Doherty, Neil Alexander. Insurance and loss prevention / [by] Neil Doherty. — Farnborough, Hants. : Saxon House [etc.], 1976. — ix,134,[1]p : ill ; 24cm.
Index.
ISBN 0-347-01097-0 : £5.50
Also classified at 368'.011
(B77-11719)

368.2 — TRANSPORT INSURANCE
368.2'2'00924 — Shipping. Insurance. Ledwith, Frank. *Autobiographies*
Ledwith, Frank. Ships afloat in the city / [by] Frank Ledwith. — London : Hale, 1977. — 203p ; 23cm.
Index.
ISBN 0-7091-6161-1 : £4.50
(B77-21797)

368.3 — INSURANCE AGAINST DEATH, OLD AGE, ILLNESS, INJURY
368.3'2'00941 — Life assurance. *Great Britain. Reports, surveys. Serials*
Life assurance in the United Kingdom / [the Life Offices' Association, Associated Scottish Life Offices, Industrial Life Offices Association in collaboration with the Linked Life Assurance Group]. — London [etc.] (Aldermary House, Queen St., EC4N 1TP) : The authors.
1971-75. — [1976]. — 24p : col ill, ports ; 21cm.
ISBN 0-905856-00-7 Sd : Unpriced
(B77-02886)

368.3'2'00968 — Life assurance. *South Africa. Tables*
Stone & Cox South African Ordinary Branch life assurance tables / compiled from official sources. — London : Stone and Cox.
1976-77. — 1976. — 124p ; 17cm.
ISBN 0-85443-071-7 Pbk : £2.40
(B77-00697)

368.3'2'00973 — Life assurance. *United States. Programmed texts*
Prudential Insurance Company of America. Life insurance fundamentals / prepared by the Prudential Insurance Company of America ; [editors Judy Wilson and Irene Brownstone]. — New York ; London [etc.] : Wiley, 1976. — ix, 303p : ill ; 26cm. — (Self-teaching guides)
Booklet ([3],62p.; Sd) as insert. — 'To prepare for the life insurance agents' license examination' - cover. — Index.
ISBN 0-471-01938-0 Pbk : £6.55
(B77-07865)

368.3'2'00994 — Life assurance. *Australia. Tables*
Stone & Cox Australasian Ordinary Branch life assurance tables / compiled from official sources. — London : Stone and Cox.
1976-77. — [1976]. — 144p ; 17cm.
ISBN 0-85443-072-5 Pbk : £2.40
(B77-00128)

368.3'2'011 — Life assurance. Risks. Medical selection & rating
Brackenridge, Robert David Campbell. Medical selection of life risks / [by] R.D.C. Brackenridge. — London : Undershaft Press : Distributed by Witherby, 1977. — xii,765p : ill ; 23cm.
Index.
£15.00
(B77-21798)

368.3'2'0110184 — Life assurance. Risks. Rating. Mathematical models
Neill, Alistair. Life contingencies / by Alistair Neill. — London : Heinemann for the Institute of Actuaries and the Faculty of Actuaries, 1977. — xi,452p : ill ; 23cm.
Bibl.: p.448. — Index.
ISBN 0-434-91440-1 : £10.50
(B77-30100)

368.3'82'00973 — Health insurance. *United States. Programmed texts*
Prudential Insurance Company of America. Health insurance fundamentals / prepared by the Prudential Insurance Company of America ; [editors Judy Wilson and Irene Brownstone]. — New York ; London [etc.] : Wiley, 1976. — viii,161p ; 26cm. — (Self-teaching guides)
With answers. — Booklet ([2],32p.;Sd) as insert. — 'To prepare for the health insurance license examination' - cover. — Index.
ISBN 0-471-01937-2 Pbk : £3.95
(B77-07866)

368.3'82'00973 — Private health insurance. *United States*
Morrow, Carol Klaperman. Health care guidance : commercial health insurance and national health policy / [by] Carol Klaperman Morrow. — New York [etc.] ; London : Praeger, 1976. — ix,141p ; 25cm. — (Praeger special studies in US economic, social and political issues)
Bibl.: p.133-138. — Index.
ISBN 0-275-56950-0 : £11.10
(B77-11720)

368.4 — NATIONAL INSURANCE
368.4 — Handicapped persons. Social security benefits. Policies of government. *United States*
Berkowitz, Monroe. Public policy toward disability / [by] Monroe Berkowitz, William G. Johnson, Edward H. Murphy. — New York [etc.] ; London : Praeger, 1976. — xv,151p : ill ; 25cm. — (Praeger special studies in US economic, social and political issues)
Bibl. — Index.
ISBN 0-275-23290-5 : £12.25
(B77-05985)

368.4 — Women. Social security benefits. *Great Britain. Claimants Union Movement viewpoints*
Claimants Union Movement. Women and social security : a handbook from the Claimants Union Movement. — London (c/o 172 Lavender Hill, S.E. 11) : The Movement, [1977]. — [2],33p : ill, facsims, form ; 31cm.
Sd : Unpriced
(B77-10301)

368.4'007'2041 — Social security. Research. *Great Britain. Conference proceedings*
Social security research : papers presented at a DHSS seminar on 7-9 April 1976. — London : H.M.S.O., 1977. — [6],217p : 2 ill ; 25cm.
'... organised by the Department of Health and Social Security (DHSS) at its residential centre at Sunningdale on 7-9 April 1976' - Introduction. — Bibl.
ISBN 0-11-760016-4 Pbk : £3.00
(B77-28528)

368.4'00941 — Industries. Strikers. Social security benefits. *Great Britain*
National Federation of Claimants Unions. Claimants handbook for strikers / [National Federation of Claimants Unions]. — [Birmingham] ([19 Carlyle Rd, Birmingham B16 9BM]) : [The Federation], [1977]. — [2], 48,[2]p : ill, facsims ; 22cm.
Originally published: 1974.
ISBN 0-9502670-4-x Sd : £0.25
(B77-10779)

368.4'00941 — National insurance benefits. *Great Britain*
Drabble, Richard. Contributory benefits : unemployment, sickness & death, maternity, pensions, child benefits / [by] Richard Drabble. — London : Child Poverty Action Group, 1977. — 62p ; 21cm. — (Rights guide ; 3 ISSN 0307-6342)
Sd : £0.60
(B77-21054)

368.4'00941 — Social security. *Great Britain. Statistics*
Social security statistics / Department of Health and Social Security. — London : H.M.S.O.
1975. — 1977. — 258p, plate : map ; 28cm.
ISBN 0-11-760317-1 Pbk : £7.00
(B77-07244)

368.4'00941 — Social security benefits. *Great Britain*
Great Britain. *Central Office of Information. Reference Division.* Social security in Britain / [prepared by Reference Division, Central Office of Information]. — 4th ed. — London : H.M.S.O., 1977. — [4],44p ; 24cm. — (Central Office of Information reference pamphlet ; 90)
Previous ed.: 1975. — Bibl.: p.43-44.
ISBN 0-11-700807-9 Sd : £0.90
(B77-11158)

368.4'00941 — Social security benefits. *Great Britain. For retired persons*
Age Concern. Your rights : for pensioners. — 4th ed. / prepared by Age Concern Information Department from the original concept by Patricia Hewitt. — Mitcham : Age Concern, 1976. — [2],60p ; 15cm.
Previous ed.: / by Patricia Hewitt and Paul Lewis. 1975.
ISBN 0-904502-66-x Sd : £0.25
(B77-03474)

368.4'00941 — Supplementary benefits. *Great Britain*
Great Britain. *Supplementary Benefits Commission.* Supplementary benefits handbook : a guide to claimants' rights / Supplementary Benefits Commission, Department of Health and Social Security. — 5th ed. — London : H.M.S.O., 1977. — 115p ; 22cm. — (Supplementary benefits administration papers ; 2)
Previous ed.: 1975. — Index.
ISBN 0-11-760435-6 Pbk : £0.65
(B77-16294)

368.4'00941 — Supplementary benefits. *Great Britain. Claimants Union Movement viewpoints*
National Federation of Claimants Unions. A guaranteed minimum income : Claimants Union report to the TUC / [National Federation of Claimants Unions]. — [Birmingham] ([Havelock Rd, Birmingham B20 31R]) : [The Federation], [1977]. — [1],12p : ill ; 31cm.
'... produced ... in response to a recent TUC questionnaire "Review of the Supplementary Benefit Scheme"' - Introduction.
Sd : Unpriced
(B77-33709)

368.4'00941 — Supplementary benefits. *Great Britain. Reports, surveys. Serials*
Great Britain. *Supplementary Benefits Commission.* Report of the Supplementary Benefits Commission ... — London : H.M.S.O.
1976-. — [1977]. — xvi,260,[8]p of plates : ill, form ; 25cm. — (Cmnd.6910)
Cover title: Supplementary Benefits Commission annual report 1976. — Bibl.: p.233.
ISBN 0-10-169100-9 Pbk : £4.15
(B77-27771)

Great Britain. *Supplementary Benefits Commission.* Report of the Supplementary Benefits Commission. — London : H.M.S.O.
1975. — [1976]. — vii,140p,[4]p of plates : ill, facsim, form ; 25cm. — (Cmnd.6615)
Cover title: Supplementary Benefits Commission annual report 1975.
ISBN 0-10-166150-9 Pbk : £1.85
(B77-01289)

368.4'00941 — Unemployed persons. Social security benefits. *Great Britain*
National Federation of Claimants Unions. The fight to live : the Claimants Union handbook for the unemployed / [National Federation of Claimants Unions]. — Birmingham ([19 Carlyle Rd, Ladywood, Birmingham 16]) : The Federation, [1977]. — [2],57p : ill ; 22cm.
ISBN 0-9502670-5-8 Sd : £0.30
(B77-11721)

368.4'009416 — Supplementary benefits. *Northern Ireland. Reports, surveys. Serials*
Northern Ireland. *Supplementary Benefits Commission.* Report of the Supplementary Benefits Commission [for Northern Ireland]. — Belfast : H.M.S.O.
1975. — 1976. — 80p ; 24cm.
ISBN 0-337-07135-7 Sd : £1.25
(B77-20158)

368.4'00947 — Social security. *Eastern Europe & Soviet Union, 1917-1976*
Porket, J L. Main features of social security in Eastern Europe / by J.L. Porket. — Oxford : St Antony's College, Centre for Soviet and East European Studies, [1977]. — 98p in various pagings ; 33cm. — (St Antony's College. Centre for Soviet and East European Studies. Papers in East European economics ; 51 ISSN 0307-5575)

'The research, under the direction of Michael Kaser, is supported by the Social Science Research Council. This is a first draft of one of the chapters in the study on the Economic History of Eastern Europe 1950-1975'.
Sd : Unpriced
(B77-24827)

368.4'014'0941 — Social security benefits. Claims. *Great Britain. Periodicals*
The **claimant,** and 'Claimants newspaper'. — [London] ([c/o Camberwell CU, Union Place, 122 Vassall Rd, S.W.9]) : [National Federation of Claimants Unions].
Issue no.6 ; [1976]. — [1976]. — 16p : ill ; 31cm.
Continues: Claimants newspaper. — Continued by: Claimants unite.
Sd : £0.15
(B77-18666)

Claimants newspaper. — [London] ([c/o Camberwell CU, Union Place, 122 Vassall Rd, S.W.9]) : [National Federation of Claimants Unions].
No.1-5 ; Summer 1974-Autumn 1975. — [1974] -[1975]. — ill ; 30cm.
Monthly. — 20p. in Autumn 1975 issue. — Continued by: The claimant.
Sd : £0.15
(B77-11722)

Claimants unite : incorporating 'Claimants newspaper'. — [London] ([c/o Camberwell CU, Union Place, 122 Vassall Rd, S.W.9]) : [National Federation of Claimants Unions].
No.7- ; Apr. 1976-. — [1976]-. — ill ; 31cm.
Monthly. — [10]p. in issue no.7, Apr. 1976. — Continues: The claimant.
Sd : £0.15
ISSN 0309-5576
(B77-11723)

368.4'015'0941 — National insurance. *Great Britain. Accounts*
National Insurance Fund account : account ... for the year ended 31st March ... — London : H.M.S.O.
1975-76. — [1977]. — 15p ; 25cm. — ([1976-77 H.C.]278)
ISBN 0-10-227877-6 Sd : £0.45
(B77-14650)

368.4'015'0941 — Social security benefits. Increase. Great Britain. Department of Health and Social Security. Social Security Benefits Up-rating Order 1977. Drafts. Financial aspects. *Great Britain. Reports, surveys*
Great Britain. *Government Actuary.* Report by the Government Actuary on the draft of the Social Security Benefits Up-rating Order 1977 ... — London : H.M.S.O., [1977]. — 9p ; 25cm. — (Cmnd.6848)
ISBN 0-10-168480-0 Sd : £0.25
(B77-25514)

368.4'015'0941 — Social security contributions. Great Britain. Department of Health and Social Security. Social Security (Contributions, Re-rating) Order 1976. Drafts. Financial aspects. *Great Britain. Reports, surveys*
Great Britain. *Government Actuary.* Report by the Government Actuary on the draft of the Social Security (Contributions, Re-rating) Order 1976. — London : H.M.S.O., [1976]. — 8p ; 25cm. — (Cmnd.6688)
ISBN 0-10-166880-5 Sd : £0.25
(B77-08930)

368.4'1 — Man. Diseases caused by vinyl chloride monomer. Health insurance benefits. Provision. *Great Britain. Inquiry reports*
Industrial Injuries Advisory Council. Vinyl chloride monomer : report by the Industrial Injuries Advisory Council in accordance with section 141 of the Social Security Act 1975 on the question whether there is any condition resulting from exposure to vinyl chloride monomer which should be prescribed as an industrial disease under the Act and if so for what occupations ... — London : H.M.S.O., [1976]. — 15p ; 25cm. — (Cmnd.6620)
ISBN 0-10-166200-9 Sd : £0.28
(B77-07867)

368.4'24 — Unsupported mothers. Social security benefits. *Great Britain*
Unsupported mothers handbook. — [Birmingham] ([19 Carlyle Rd, Birmingham B16 9BM]) : [National Federation of Claimants Unions], [1977]. — [2],32p : ill ; 22cm.
'We [the authors] are a group of unsupported mothers who are members of Claimants Unions ...' - text. — Originally published: 1974.
Sd : £0.10(£0.05 to claimants)
(B77-12959)

368.4'3'00941 — State superannuation schemes. Age of eligibility. Sex discrimination. Abolition. *Great Britain. Proposals*
Equal Opportunities Commission. Sex equality and the pension age : a choice of routes / Equal Opportunities Commission. — Manchester (Manchester M3 3HN) : The Commission, [1977]. — 23p : 1 ill ; 21cm.
ISBN 0-905829-00-x Sd : £0.60
(B77-14651)

368.4'3'00941 — State superannuation schemes. Great Britain. Related to occupational superannuation schemes
National Association of Pension Funds. State and occupational pension schemes / [National Association of Pension Funds]. — [Croydon] ([Prudential House, Wellesley Rd, Croydon CR0 2A5) : [The Association], [1976]. — [1], 15p ; 21cm. — (Notes on pensions ; no.1 ISSN 0309-006x)
ISBN 0-905796-03-9 Sd : Unpriced
Primary classification 331.2'52'0941
(B77-01214)

368.4'4'00941 — Unemployment insurance. Administration. *Great Britain, 1920-1931*
Deacon, Alan, *b.1946.* In search of the scrounger : the administration of Unemployment Insurance in Britain, 1920-1931 / [by] Alan Deacon. — London : Bell [for the Social Administration Research Trust], 1976. — 110p ; 21cm. — (Occasional papers on social administration ; no.60)
ISBN 0-7135-1992-4 Pbk : £2.95
(B77-07245)

368.4'4'00973 — Unemployment insurance. *United States. Reports, surveys*
Hamermesh, Daniel Selim. Jobless pay and the economy / [by] Daniel S. Hamermesh. — Baltimore ; London : Johns Hopkins University Press, 1977. — ix,114,[1]p ; 21cm. — (Policy studies in employment and welfare ; no.29)
Bibl.: p.112-114.
ISBN 0-8018-1927-x : £6.40
ISBN 0-8018-1928-8 Pbk : Unpriced
(B77-33147)

368.8 — INSURANCE. MISCELLANEOUS TYPES
368.8'15'00941 — Business firms. Consequential losses. Insurance. *Great Britain, to 1975*
Pembroke, R J. Consequential loss insurance / by R.J. Pembroke. — London [etc.] : Financial Times, [1976]. — [5],76p : ill ; 30cm.
ISBN 0-900671-45-9 Sp : £20.50
(B77-04066)

368.9 — INSURANCE. HISTORICAL AND GEOGRAPHICAL TREATMENT
368'.9'41 — Insurance. *Great Britain. Directories*
Insurance facts and figures / [British Insurance Association]. — London (P.O. Box 538, Aldermary House, Queen St., EC4P 4JD) : The Association.
1975. — 1976. — [2],22p : col ill ; 21cm.
Sd : Unpriced
ISSN 0308-8308
(B77-31799)

369.4 — YOUTH ORGANISATIONS
369.4'0941 — Welfare work with young persons. Youth clubs. *Great Britain. For part-time youth workers. Periodicals*
Youth clubs. — Nuneaton : National Association of Youth Clubs.
[No.1]- ; Spring 1977-. — [1977]-. — ill, ports ; 30cm.
Three issues a year. — 20p. in 1st issue.
Sd : Unpriced
ISSN 0309-7315
(B77-20159)

369.4'0941 — Young persons' organisations. *Great Britain. Juvenile literature*
Gundrey, Elizabeth. Joining things / [by] Elizabeth Gundrey ; cover and text illustrations by Peter Gregory. — London : Pan Books, 1977. — 96p : ill ; 20cm. — (Piccolo original)
ISBN 0-330-24763-8 Pbk : £0.45
(B77-08316)

369.4'0941 — Youth movements. *Great Britain, 1883-1940*
Springhall, John. Youth, empire and society : British youth movements, 1883-1940 / [by] John Springhall. — London : Croom Helm [etc.], 1977. — 163p,[8]p of plates : ill, ports ; 23cm.
Bibl.: p.140-150. — Index.
ISBN 0-85664-102-2 : £6.95
(B77-11724)

369.4'0941 — Youth work. *Great Britain. Reports, surveys*
Eggleston, John. Adolescence and community : the youth service in Britain / [by] John Eggleston with the assistance of Patricia Allatt. — London : Edward Arnold, 1976. — ix,253p : ill, forms ; 23cm.
Bibl.: p.242-248. — Index.
ISBN 0-7131-5886-7 : £7.00
ISBN 0-7131-5887-5 Pbk : £3.50
(B77-10302)

369.42'0941 — Boys' clubs. *Great Britain*
Haselhurst, Alan. A time for heroes / [by] Alan Haselhurst. — London (17 Bedford Sq., WC1B 3JJ) : National Association of Boys' Clubs, [1976]. — 12p : port ; 21cm. — (Basil Henriques memorial lecture ; 1976)
'The thirteenth ... lecture delivered at Warwick University during the National Association of Boys' Clubs Conference'.
ISBN 0-901192-21-x Sd : £0.15
(B77-02889)

369'.43 — Scouting. Leaders. Selection. *Great Britain. Regulations*
Scout Association. The appointment of adult leaders / [Scout Association]. — 2nd ed. — London : The Association, 1976. — [2],16p ; 18cm.
Previous ed.: 1972. — Bibl.: p.16.
ISBN 0-85165-127-5 Sd : £0.10
(B77-04067)

369.43'092'4 — Scouting. Rowallan, Thomas Godfrey Polson Corbett, Baron. *Autobiographies*
Rowallan, Thomas Godfrey Polson Corbett, *Baron.* Rowallan : the autobiography of Lord Rowallan. — Edinburgh : P. Harris, 1976. — xi,223p,leaf of plate,[12]p of plates : ill, ports ; 23cm.
Index.
ISBN 0-904505-11-1 : £6.00
(B77-00129)

369.43'0941 — Boys' organisations. *Great Britain. Scout Association. Regulations*
Scout Association. The policy, organisation and rules of the Scout Association. — [1977 ed., 1st ed.]. — London : The Association.
In 2 vols. — Previous ed.: published as 4 parts in 2v. 1974.
Part 1 : Organisation. — 1977. — 160p ; 18cm.
Index.
ISBN 0-85165-128-3 Pbk : £0.40
(B77-24828)

Part 2 : Training. — 1977. — 272p : ill ; 18cm.
Index.
ISBN 0-85165-129-1 Pbk : £0.55
(B77-24829)

369.463 — Brownie guides. Activities. *Great Britain. Colouring books*
Brown, Rosalie. Brownie journey colouring book / devised and drawn by Rosalie Brown. — Wendover (70 Carrington Cres., Wendover, Bucks.) : John Goodchild, Publishers [for] the Girl Guides Association.
In 4 vols.
No.1. — 1976. — [24]p : of ill ; 30cm.
ISBN 0-903445-23-9 Sd : £0.45
(B77-14150)

No.2. — 1976. — [24]p : of ill ; 30cm.
ISBN 0-903445-24-7 Sd : £0.45
(B77-14151)

No.3. — 1976. — [24]p : of ill ; 30cm.
ISBN 0-903445-25-5 Sd : £0.45
(B77-14152)

No.4. — 1976. — [24]p : of ill ; 30cm.
ISBN 0-903445-26-3 Sd : £0.45
(B77-14153)

369.463 — Brownie Guides. Activities. *Manuals*
The **book** of Brownie skills. — Maidenhead : Purnell, 1976. — 192p : col ill, col chart, 3 col maps ; 19cm.
ISBN 0-361-03577-2 Pbk : £1.35
(B77-08931)

369.463'092'4 — Girls' organisations. *Great Britain. Girl Guides Association. Baden-Powell, Olave, Baroness Baden-Powell. Autobiographies*
Baden-Powell, Olave, *Baroness Baden-Powell.* Window on my heart : the autobiography of Olave, Lady Baden Powell, GBE / as told to Mary Drewery. — London [etc.] : Hodder and Stoughton, 1977. — 287p,[16]p of plates : ill, map, ports ; 18cm.
Originally published: 1973. — Index.
ISBN 0-340-21667-0 Pbk : £1.25
(B77-23272)

369.463'0941 — Girls' organisations. *Great Britain. Girl Guides Association, to 1975*
Kerr, Rose. Story of the Girl Guides / [by Rose Kerr and Alix Liddell]. — London : Girl Guides Association.
In 2 vols.
[Vol.1] : 1908-1938 / by Rose Kerr. — New ed. / edited by Alix Liddell. — 1976. — 223p, leaf of plate,[12]p of plates : ill, ports ; 21cm.
Previous ed.: i.e. New ed. revised, 1954. — Index.
ISBN 0-85260-007-0 Pbk : £1.60
(B77-11725)

Kerr, Rose. Story of the Girl Guides / [by Rose Kerr and Alix Liddell]. — London : Girl Guides Association.
In 2 vols.
[Vol.2] : 1938-1975 / by Alix Liddell. — 1976. — 120p,leaf of plate,[12]p of plates : ill, ports ; 21cm.
Bibl.: p.109. — Index.
ISBN 0-85260-008-9 Pbk : £1.10
(B77-11726)

369.5 — SERVICE CLUBS
369.5 — Rotary clubs. *Ireland, 1911-1976*
Duncan, Terence Stuart. The hub of the wheel : the story of the Rotary movement in Ireland, District 116 (earlier 5, 6 and 16) 1911-1976 / compiled by Terence S. Duncan. — [Belfast] ([c/o Ulster Bank House, Shaftesbury Sq., Belfast BT2 7BY]) : [The author], 1976. — 134p(3 fold) : ill, facsims, ports ; 23cm.
Pbk : Unpriced
(B77-01290)

369.5 — Round Tables. *Great Britain. National Association of Round Tables of Great Britain and Ireland, to 1977*
Barty-King, Hugh. Round Table : the search for fellowship, 1927-1977 / [by] Hugh Barty-King. — London : Heinemann, 1977. — xviii,298p, [16]p of plates : ill, ports ; 23cm.
Bibl.: p.290-291. — Index.
ISBN 0-434-04901-8 : £4.50
(B77-12391)

370 — EDUCATION
Holt, John, *b.1923.* Instead of education : ways to help people do things better / [by] John Holt. — Harmondsworth [etc.] : Penguin, 1977. — 252p ; 18cm. — (A pelican original)
Originally published: New York : Dutton, 1976. — Bibl.: p.250-252.
ISBN 0-14-021999-4 Pbk : £0.80
(B77-18034)

370 — Education. Implications of technological development
Hidden factors in technological change / editors Edward Semper ... [et al.]. — Oxford [etc.] : Pergamon [for the] Standing Conference on Schools' Science and Technology, 1976. — xiii, 252p : map ; 21cm.
Bibl.
ISBN 0-08-021007-4 Pbk : £5.00
Primary classification 301.24'3
(B77-10175)

370 — Education. Policies of governments. *Organisation for Economic Co-operation and Development countries. Reports, surveys*
Organisation for Economic Co-operation and Development. Reviews of national policies for education / Organisation for Economic Co-operation and Development. — Paris : O.E.C.D. ; [London] : [H.M.S.O.].
Austria : higher education and research. — 1976. — 121p : 1 ill ; 24cm.
Pbk : £2.60
ISBN 92-64-11555-2
(B77-05986)

Netherlands : contours of a future education system. — 1976. — 91p : 1 ill ; 24cm.
Pbk : £1.80
ISBN 92-64-11552-8
(B77-01291)

370.1 — Deschooling
Illich, Ivan. After deschooling, what? / [by] Ivan Illich. — [1st ed. reprinted] / with an introduction [i.e. an essay] by Ian Lister. — London (14 Talacre Rd, NW5 3PE) : Writers and Readers Publishing Cooperative, 1976. — 55p ; 20cm.
'After deschooling, what?' originally published: 1974.
ISBN 0-904613-36-4 Pbk : £0.35
(B77-12960)

370.1 — Education. *Philosophical perspectives*
Elvin, Lionel. The place of commonsense in educational thought / [by] Lionel Elvin. — London : Allen and Unwin, 1977. — 3-165p ; 23cm. — (Unwin education books ; 35)
Index.
ISBN 0-04-370078-0 : £6.50
ISBN 0-04-370079-9 Pbk : £2.95
(B77-22484)

Warnock, Mary. Schools of thought / [by] Mary Warnock. — London : Faber, 1977. — 3-176p ; 23cm.
Index.
ISBN 0-571-10963-2 : £5.50
ISBN 0-571-11161-0 Pbk : £2.95
(B77-20160)

370.1 — Education. *Philosophical perspectives. Essays*
Peters, Richard Stanley. Education and the education of teachers / [by] R.S. Peters. — London [etc.] : Routledge and Kegan Paul, 1977. — xii,195p ; 23cm. — (International library of the philosophy of education)
Index.
ISBN 0-7100-8469-2 : £4.95
(B77-10303)

370.1 — Education. *Philosophical perspectives. For teaching*
Wilson, John. Philosophy and practical education / [by] John Wilson. — London [etc.] : Routledge and Kegan Paul, 1977. — x, 130p ; 23cm. — (Students library of education)
Bibl.: p.129-130.
ISBN 0-7100-8675-x : £3.95 : CIP rev.
(B77-17395)

370.1 — Education. Theories
Novak, Joseph D. A theory of education / by Joseph D. Novak ; with a foreword by Ralph W. Tyler. — Ithaca ; London : Cornell University Press, 1977. — 295,[1]p : ill ; 23cm.
Bibl.: p.277-288. — Index.
ISBN 0-8014-1104-1 : Unpriced
(B77-33710)

Piaget, Jean. To understand is to invent : the future of education / [by] Jean Piaget ; [translated from the French by George-Anne Roberts]. — Harmondsworth [etc.] : Penguin, 1976. — ix,148p ; 18cm.
These translations originally published: New York : Grossman, 1973. — Index.
ISBN 0-14-004378-0 Pbk : £0.90
(B77-08932)

370.11'2 — Liberal education
Valett, Robert Edward. Humanistic education : developing the total person / [by] Robert E. Valett. — Saint Louis : Mosby ; London : Distributed by Kimpton, 1977. — xiv,232p : ill, forms ; 25cm.
Bibl.: p.220-227. — Index.
ISBN 0-8016-5212-x Pbk : £6.45
(B77-31800)

370.11'3'0941 — Vocational education. *Great Britain. Proposals*
Great Britain. *Department of Employment.* Training for vital skills : a consultative document / Department of Employment [and the] Manpower Services Commission. — London (8 St James's Sq., SW1Y 4JB) : Department of Employment, Public Enquiry Office, 1976. — [3],33p : ill ; 30cm.
ISBN 0-903314-25-8 Sd : Unpriced
(B77-16295)

370.11'4 — Moral education
Hirst, Paul Heywood. Moral education in a secular society / [by] Paul A. Hirst. — London : University of London Press [for the] National Children's Home, 1974 [i.e. 1977]. — viii,123p ; 23cm. — (National Children's Home. Convocation lectures ; 1974)
Originally published: 1974. — Index.
£3.30
ISBN 0-340-19434-0
ISBN 0-340-19433-2 Pbk (Unibooks) : £1.65
(B77-27772)

370.11'4 — Primary schools. Moral education. *England. Reports, surveys*
Working Party on Moral and Religious Education in County Primary Schools. Moral and religious education in county primary schools : report of a working party to the Social Morality Council / [Working Party on Moral and Religious Education in County Primary Schools] ; H.J. Blackham, editor. — Windsor : NFER, 1976. — 60p ; 22cm.
ISBN 0-85633-115-5 Sd : £2.10
Primary classification 372.8
(B77-09641)

370.11'5 — Social education
Rendall, Mary Philip. Development education / by Mary Philip Rendall. — [Liverpool] ([Christ's College, Woolton Rd, Liverpool L16 8ND]) : Liverpool Institute of Socio-Religious Studies [for] the Conferences of Major Religious Superiors of England and Wales, 1976. — [3], 42,[1]p : 1 ill ; 21cm. — (Pastoral investigation of social trends ; working paper no.5)
Bibl.: p.38.
ISBN 0-905052-05-6 Sd : £0.50
(B77-09635)

370.15 — Education. *Behaviourist perspectives*
Herman, Therese M. Creating learning environments : the behavioral approach to education / [by] Therese M. Herman. — Boston, [Mass.] ; London [etc.] : Allyn and Bacon, 1977. — x,278p : ill, 2 forms ; 24cm.
With answers. — Bibl.: p.257-263. — Index.
ISBN 0-205-05591-5 : Unpriced
ISBN 0-205-05567-2 Pbk : Unpriced
(B77-03475)

370.15 — Education. Behaviour modification. *Conference proceedings*
Symposium on Behavior Modification, *2nd, Mexico City, 1972.* Behavior modification, applications to education / edited by Fred S. Keller, Emilio Ribes-Inesta. — New York ; London : Academic Press, 1974. — xvi,211p : ill ; 24cm.
'Most of the studies ... were reported at the Second Symposium on Behavior Modification held at the National Autonomous University of Mexico, in Mexico City, January 24-25, 1972' - Preface. — Bibl. — Index.
ISBN 0-12-403950-2 : Unpriced
(B77-18668)

370.15 — Education. Psychological aspects
The **live** classroom : innovation through confluent education and Gestalt / edited by George Isaac Brown with Thomas Yeomans and Liles Grizzard. — Harmondsworth [etc.] : Penguin, 1976. — xv,304p : ill, form ; 20cm. — (Esalen books)
Originally published: New York : Viking Press, 1975. — Bibl.: p.301-304.
ISBN 0-14-004421-3 Pbk : £1.10
(B77-08933)

Wilson, John Abraham Ross. Psychological foundations of learning and teaching / [by] John A.R. Wilson, Mildred C. Robeck, William B. Michael. — 2nd ed. — New York ; London [etc.] : McGraw-Hill, 1974. — xvi,589p : ill ; 24cm.
Previous ed.: New York : McGraw-Hill, 1969. — Bibl.: p.553-574. — Index.
ISBN 0-07-070855-x : Unpriced
ISBN 0-07-070856-8 Pbk : Unpriced
(B77-18669)

370.15 — Education. Psychological aspects. *Essays*
Piaget, Jean. Science of education and the psychology of the child / [by] Jean Piaget ; translated from the French by Derek Coltman. — Harmondsworth [etc.] : Penguin, 1977. — [6],186p ; 18cm.
This translated selection originally published: New York : Orion Press, 1970 ; Harlow : Longman, 1971. — Translation of: 'Psychologie et pédagogie'. Paris : Denoël, 1969. — Index.
ISBN 0-14-004377-2 Pbk : £1.25
(B77-10304)

370.15 — Education. Psychological aspects. *For teaching*
Child, Dennis. Psychology and the teacher / [by] Dennis Child. — 2nd ed. — London [etc.] : Holt, Rinehart and Winston, 1977. — xiv, 396p : ill ; 23cm.
Previous ed.: 1973. — Bibl. — Index.
ISBN 0-03-910161-4 Pbk : £2.75
(B77-19291)

Galloway, Charles. Psychology for learning and teaching / [by] Charles Galloway. — New York ; London [etc.] : McGraw-Hill, 1976. — xv,520p : ill, facsims, forms ; 24cm.
With answers. — Bibl. — Index.
ISBN 0-07-022737-3 Pbk : £9.90
(B77-06573)

Sprinthall, Richard Clark. Educational psychology : a developmental approach / [by] Richard C. Sprinthall, Norman A. Sprinthall. — 2nd ed. — Reading, Mass. ; London [etc.] : Addison-Wesley, 1977. — xxv,647,[36]p : ill(some col), facsim, ports ; 24cm. — (Addison-Wesley series in education)
Previous ed.: New York ; London : Van Nostrand Reinhold, 1969. — Bibl. — Index.
ISBN 0-201-06821-4 Pbk : £9.60
(B77-29318)

Yelon, Stephen L. A teacher's world : psychology in the classroom / [by] Stephen L. Yelon, Grace W. Weinstein ; consultant Paul D. Weener. — New York ; London [etc.] : McGraw-Hill, 1977. — xiv,593p : ill, forms ; 24cm.
With answers. — Bibl.: p.559-580. — Index.
ISBN 0-07-072267-6 Pbk : £8.95
(B77-20161)

370.15 — Education. Psychological aspects. *Readings*
Human dynamics in psychology and education : selected readings / [compiled by] Don E. Hamachek. — 3rd ed. — Boston [Mass.] ; London [etc.] : Allyn and Bacon, 1977. — xi, 344p : ill ; 24cm.
Previous ed.: Boston, Mass. : Allyn and Bacon, 1972. — Bibl. — Index.
ISBN 0-205-05583-4 Pbk : Unpriced
(B77-08317)

370.15 — Education. Psychological aspects. *Readings. For teaching*
Readings in psychology for the teacher / [edited by] Dennis Child. — London [etc.] : Holt, Rinehart and Winston, 1977. — xi,441p : ill ; 23cm.
Bibl.
ISBN 0-03-910162-2 Pbk : Unpriced
(B77-23273)

Transpersonal education : a curriculum for feeling and being / edited by Gay Hendricks, James Fadiman. — Englewood Cliffs ; London [etc.] : Prentice-Hall, 1976. — viii,184p : ill ; 22cm. — (Transpersonal books)
'A Spectrum book'. — Bibl.: p.178-184.
ISBN 0-13-930479-7 : £8.99
ISBN 0-13-930461-4 Pbk : £3.10
(B77-08318)

370.15 — Education. Psychological aspects. *United States. Readings*
Contemporary issues in educational psychology / edited by Harvey F. Clarizio, Robert C. Craig, William A. Mehrens. — 3rd ed. — Boston [Mass.] ; London [etc.] : Allyn and Bacon, 1977. — xv,338p : ill ; 24cm.
Previous ed.: Boston, Mass. : Allyn and Bacon, 1974. — Bibl. — Index.
ISBN 0-205-05627-x Pbk : Unpriced
(B77-08934)

370.15 — Education. Psychological aspects. Theories
Snelbecker, Glenn E. Learning theory, instructional theory, and psychoeducational design / [by] Glenn E. Snelbecker. — New York ; London [etc.] : McGraw-Hill, 1974. — xvi,527p : ill ; 24cm.
Bibl.: p.501-515. — Index.
ISBN 0-07-059450-3 : Unpriced
(B77-18670)

370.15 — Educational psychology
Williams, Phillip. Children and psychologists / [by] Phillip Williams. — London [etc.] : Hodder and Stoughton, 1977. — viii,88p : ill, form, map ; 22cm.
Previous ed.: London : National Children's Home, 1976. — Bibl.: p.81-86. — Index.
ISBN 0-340-21942-4 Pbk : £1.75
(B77-23274)

370.15 — Educational psychology. Teaching
Handbook on teaching educational psychology / edited by Donald J. Treffinger, J. Kent Davis, Richard E. Ripple. — New York [etc.] ; London : Academic Press, 1977. — xv,352p : 1 ill, forms ; 24cm. — (Educational psychology)
Bibl. — Index.
ISBN 0-12-697750-x : £12.80
(B77-23275)

370.15'2 — Education. Applications of learning theories
Gagné, Robert Mills. The conditions of learning / [by] Robert M. Gagné. — 3rd ed. — New York ; London [etc.] : Holt, Rinehart and Winston, 1977. — xii,339p : ill ; 25cm.
Previous ed.: 1970. — Bibl.: p.314-330. — Index.
ISBN 0-03-089965-6 : £6.50
(B77-23276)

Travers, Robert Morris William. Essentials of learning / [by] Robert M.W. Travers. — 4th ed. — New York : Macmillan ; London : Collier Macmillan, 1977. — xi,626p : ill ; 24cm.
Previous ed.: 1972. — Bibl.: p.565-599. — Index.
ISBN 0-02-421350-0 : £10.50
(B77-24830)

370.15'2 — Learning by primary school students. *Great Britain. For teaching*
Rae, Gordon. Learning in the primary school : a systematic approach / [by] Gordon Rae, W.N. McPhillimy. — London [etc.] : Hodder and Stoughton, 1976. — 126p : ill ; 23cm.
Bibl.: p.117-121. — Index.
ISBN 0-340-21037-0 : £3.25
ISBN 0-340-21038-9 Pbk : £1.50
(B77-02170)

370.15'2 — Learning by school students
Levin, Joel Richard. Learner differences : diagnosis and prescription / [by] Joel R. Levin. — New York ; London [etc.] : Holt, Rinehart and Winston, 1977. — xiii,146p : ill ; 21cm. — (Principles of educational psychology series)
Bibl.: p.135-142. — Index.
ISBN 0-03-015296-8 Pbk : £2.50
(B77-20162)

Riding, R J. School learning : mechanisms and processes / [by] R.J. Riding. — London : Open Books, 1977. — viii,167p : ill ; 21cm. — (Psychology and education)
Bibl.: p.158-165. — Index.
ISBN 0-7291-0066-9 : £4.50
ISBN 0-7291-0061-8 Pbk : £1.95
(B77-15218)

370.15'2 — Learning by school students. Influence of personality
Bloom, Benjamin Samuel. Human characteristics and school learning / [by] Benjamin S. Bloom. — New York ; London [etc.] : McGraw-Hill, 1976. — xiii,284p : ill ; 24cm.
Bibl. — Index.
ISBN 0-07-006117-3 : £8.20
(B77-22485)

370.15'2 — Learning by secondary school students. *Great Britain. Reviews of research*
Dennis, Hamlyn. School learning : a literature survey / [by] Hamlyn Dennis. — [Watford] : [Engineering Industry Training Board Library], 1976. — [7],30p ; 30cm. — (Engineering Industry Training Board. Library. Literature survey series ; no.3/1976)
Bibl.: p.27-30.
Sp : £0.75
(B77-16296)

370.15'2 — Learning by secondary school students. Role of oral communication in small groups. *Research reports*
Barnes, Douglas. Communication and learning in small groups / [by] Douglas Barnes and Frankie Todd. — London [etc.] : Routledge and Kegan Paul, 1977. — x,139p : 1 ill ; 24cm.
'Routledge direct editions'. — Index.
ISBN 0-7100-8512-5 Pbk : £2.50
(B77-16803)

370.15'2 — Schools. Students. Cognitive development
Cognitive learning in children : theories and strategies / edited by Joel R. Levin, Vernon L. Allen. — New York [etc.] ; London : Academic Press, 1976. — xvi,297p : ill ; 24cm. — (Educational psychology)
Bibl. — Index.
ISBN 0-12-444850-x : £10.15
(B77-00698)

Klausmeier, Herbert John. Conceptual learning and development : a cognitive view / [by] Herbert J. Klausmeier, Elizabeth Schwenn Ghatala, Dorothy A. Frayer. — New York ; London : Academic Press, 1974. — xi,283p : ill ; 24cm.
Bibl. — Index.
ISBN 0-12-411360-5 : Unpriced
(B77-18671)

370.15'3 — Primary schools. Students, 5-8 years. Development. Role of play. *For teaching*
Structuring of Play in the Infant/First School *(Project).* Structuring play in the early years at school / Schools Council Project, the Structuring of Play in the Infant-First School ; [written by] Kathleen Manning and Ann Sharp. — London : Ward Lock ; Cardiff : Drake Educational Associates, 1977. — 223p,[4]p of plates : ill, forms ; 23cm.
Bibl. — Index.
ISBN 0-7062-3609-2 : £3.25
ISBN 0-7062-3602-5 Pbk : £1.75
(B77-21055)

370.15'3 — Schools. Students. Personality. Development. Theories
Fontana, David. Personality and education / [by] David Fontana. — London : Open Books, 1977. — viii,178p : ill ; 21cm. — (Psychology and education)
Bibl.: p.166-175. — Index.
ISBN 0-7291-0087-1 : £4.50
ISBN 0-7291-0082-0 Pbk : £1.95
(B77-15219)

370.15'4 — Schools. Students. Motivation
Motivation in education / edited by Samuel Ball. — New York [etc.] ; London : Academic Press, 1977. — xv,204p : ill ; 24cm. — (Educational psychology)
Bibl. — Index.
ISBN 0-12-077450-x : £8.85
(B77-26234)

370.15'6 — Schools. Students. Reading skills. Psychological aspects
Dechant, Emerald Victor. Psychology in teaching reading / [by] Emerald V. Dechant, Henry P. Smith. — 2nd ed. — Englewood Cliffs ; London [etc.] : Prentice-Hall, 1977. — x,436p : ill, 2 forms ; 24cm.
Previous ed.: / by Henry P. Smith and Emerald V. Dechant. 1961. — Bibl. — Index.
ISBN 0-13-736686-8 : £10.35
(B77-23277)

370.19 — Education. Psychosocial aspects
Bany, Mary A. Educational social psychology / [by] Mary A. Bany, Lois V. Johnson. — New York : Macmillan ; London : Collier Macmillan, [1976]. — xi,451p : ill ; 24cm.
Published in the United States: 1975. — Bibl. — Index.
ISBN 0-02-305780-7 Pbk : £8.65
(B77-00045)

370.19 — Schools. Inequalities. Sociopolitical aspects. *United States*
Morgan, Edward P, *b.1945.* Inequality in classroom learning : schooling and democratic citizenship / [by] Edward P. Morgan. — New York ; London : Praeger, 1977. — xii,225p : 2 ill ; 25cm. — (Praeger special studies in US economic, social and political issues)
Bibl.: p.208-216. — Index.
ISBN 0-275-24510-1 : £13.40
(B77-25515)

370.19'3 — Great Britain. Society. Role of universities
Edwards, E G. The relevant university : a public lecture / by E.G. Edwards. — [Bradford] ([Bradford, W. Yorkshire BD7 1DP]) : University of Bradford, 1977. — [1],27p ; 21cm.
'[Delivered] 18th February, 1977'.
Sd : Unpriced
(B77-28529)

370.19'3 — Society. Role of education
Russell, Bertrand, *Earl Russell.* Education and the social order / [by] Bertrand Russell. — London : Allen and Unwin, 1977. — 3-158p ; 20cm.
Originally published: 1932. — Index.
ISBN 0-04-370080-2 Pbk : £1.50
(B77-21056)

370.19'3 — Society. Role of schools
Society, state and schooling : readings on the possibilities for radical education / edited and introduced by Michael Young and Geoff Whitty. — Ringmer (Broome House, Delves Close, Ringmer BN8 5JW) : Falmer Press, 1977. — [4],283p ; 23cm. — ([Politics and education series])
Bibl. — Index.
ISBN 0-905273-02-8 : £7.50
ISBN 0-905273-01-x Pbk : £2.95
(B77-16297)

370.19'3'0973 — Education. Social aspects. *United States*
The **social** context of learning and development / edited by John C. Glidewell. — New York : Gardner Press ; New York ; London [etc.] : Distributed by Wiley, 1977. — xi,239p : ill ; 24cm.
Bibl. — Index.
ISBN 0-470-15078-5 : £14.20
(B77-20163)

370.19'3'0973 — United States. Society. Role of education
Persell, Caroline Hodges. Education and inequality : a theoretical and empirical synthesis / [by] Caroline Hodges Persell. — New York : Free Press ; London : Collier Macmillan, 1977. — xi,244p : ill ; 25cm.
Bibl.: p.179-233. — Index.
ISBN 0-02-925140-0 : £9.75
(B77-28530)

370.19'3'09931 — New Zealand. Society. Role of schools. *Readings*
Schools in New Zealand society : a book of readings / edited by G.H. Robinson, B.T. O'Rourke. — Sydney ; London [etc.] : Wiley, 1973. — viii,311p : ill ; 25cm.
ISBN 0-471-72817-9 : Unpriced
ISBN 0-471-72818-7 Pbk : Unpriced
(B77-19292)

370.19'31 — Parents & students. Relations with schools & local education authorities. *Great Britain. Codes of conduct*
National Consumer Council. Advise and consent : proposals for a code of practice to guide relations between the providers of the school education service and its consumers / prepared by the National Consumer Council in association with ... [others]. — London (18 Queen Anne's Gate, SW1H 9AA) : The Council, 1977. — [8]p ; 30cm.
Sd : £0.10
(B77-26974)

370.19'344'09794 — Schools. Racial discrimination. *California, 1855-1975*
Wollenberg, Charles. All deliberate speed : segregation and exclusion in California schools, 1855-1975 / [by] Charles Wollenberg. — Berkeley [etc.] ; London : University of California Press, 1976. — vi,201p ; 23cm.
Bibl.: p.187. — Index.
ISBN 0-520-03191-1 : £8.00
(B77-14652)

370.19'4 — Community education. *Conference proceedings*
Research into Aspects of Community Education *(Conference), Sutton Centre, 1977.* Community education '77 / edited by Colin Fletcher. — Sutton-in-Ashfield (High Pavement, Sutton-in-Ashfield, Notts.) : Research Office, Sutton Centre ; Nottingham : Sutton Centre Research Project, Department of Adult Education, University of Nottingham, [1977]. — [7],112p : ill ; 30cm.
'Between the 7th and 8th January, 1977, some 120 teachers and professors, students and community workers met together at the Sutton Centre for a Conference on "Research into Aspects of Community Education"' - Introduction.
Sp : Unpriced
(B77-17396)

370.19'4'0711411 — Community education. Personnel. Professional education. *Scotland. Inquiry reports*
Working Party on Professional Training for Community Education. Professional education and training for community education / [Working Party on Professional Training for Community Education]. — Edinburgh : H.M.S.O., 1977. — viii,59p ; 25cm.
At head of title: Scottish Education Department. — '[The] Working Party on Professional Training for Community Education. We were appointed in the summer of 1975 by the Standing Consultative Council [on Youth and Community Service] and the Scottish Institute of Adult Education ...' - p.iii.
ISBN 0-11-491486-9 Sd : £1.50
(B77-18672)

370.19'5'018 — Comparative education. Methodology
Trethewey, A R. Introducing comparative education / [by] A.R. Trethewey. — Rushcutters Bay ; Oxford [etc.] : Pergamon, 1976. — ix,141p : 1 ill ; 22cm.
Index.
ISBN 0-08-020563-1 : £6.65
ISBN 0-08-020562-3 Pbk : £3.50
(B77-21800)

370.19'6 — Higher education. International educational exchanges with United States. *Soviet Union, 1958-1975*
Byrnes, Robert Francis. Soviet-American academic exchanges, 1958-1975 / [by] Robert F. Byrnes. — Bloomington ; London : Indiana University Press, [1977]. — xii,275p ; 24cm.
Published in the United States: 1976. — Bibl.: p.255-268. — Index.
ISBN 0-253-35402-1 Pbk : £7.50
(B77-11159)

370'.23 — Education. *Great Britain. Career guides. Serials*
'The **Times** educational supplement' guide to careers in education. — Sunbury-on-Thames [etc.] : Nelson.
1977-78 / general editor Tony Howarth. — 1977. — viii,440p : ill, maps ; 22cm.
Spine title: TES guide to careers in education. — Bibl. — Index.
ISBN 0-17-771191-4 Pbk : £2.95
(B77-11160)

370'.25'41 — Vacation courses. *Great Britain. Directories*
Britain, holiday courses / [British Tourist Authority]. — London : B.T.A.
[1977]. — 1977. — [2],31,[2]p : map ; 21cm. — (British Tourist Authority. Information sheets ; no. 311/77/14)
English text, French, German, Dutch, Italian and Spanish introduction and key. — Index.
ISBN 0-85630-386-0 Sd : £0.15
(B77-11161)

370'.25'4259 — Educational institutions. *Buckinghamshire. Directories*
Buckinghamshire *(County). Education Department.* Directory / Buckinghamshire County Council, Education Department. — [Aylesbury] ([County Hall, Aylesbury, Bucks. HP20 1UZ]) : [The Council].
1976. — [1976]. — [2],49p ; 21cm.
ISBN 0-902805-58-4 Sd : Unpriced
ISSN 0309-0841
(B77-03476)

370'.3 — Education. *Dictionaries*
Page, Graham Terry. International dictionary of education / [compiled by] G. Terry Page & J.B. Thomas, with A.R. Marshall. — London : Kogan Page [etc.], 1977. — 381p : ill ; 24cm.
ISBN 0-85038-301-3 : £10.00
(B77-32552)

370'.3 — Education. *Glossaries*
Fergus, Andrew. What they are doing to your child at school : A-Z of the new education : a handbook for parents who can no longer understand their children's homework / by Andrew Fergus. — Kingswood : Elliot Right Way Books, 1976. — 126p : ill, plan ; 18cm. — (Paperfronts)
Ixex.
ISBN 0-7160-0628-6 Pbk : £0.40
(B77-00699)

370'.6'041 — Education. Organisations. *Great Britain. Directories*
The **education** authorities directory and annual. — Redhill : School Government Publishing Co.

1977 : 74th year of publication. — 1977. — iii-lxxxii,1216p : ill ; 22cm.
Index.
ISBN 0-900640-09-x : £9.60
(B77-12961)

370'.71'0942 — Teachers. Professional education. *England, 1800-1975*
Dent, Harold Collett. The training of teachers in England and Wales, 1800-1975 / [by] H.C. Dent. — London [etc.] : Hodder and Stoughton, 1977. — [7],163p ; 23cm.
Bibl.: p.157. — Index.
ISBN 0-340-19751-x : £4.95
ISBN 0-340-19750-1 Pbk : Unpriced
(B77-26975)

370'.71'0942 — Teachers. Professional education. *England. Proposals*
Hencke, David. The re-organization of teacher training : where do we go from here? : a paper presented to the CTFE-CISE Annual Study Conference, 1976 / by David Hencke. — London : Library Association, Colleges of Technology and Further Education Section ; Cambridge (c/o The Librarian, Cambridgeshire College of Arts and Technology, Collier Rd, Cambridge CB1 2AJ) : Distributed by F.J. Chambers, 1976. — [2],8p ; 21cm. — (Library Association. Colleges of Technology and Further Education Section. Occasional publications ; 2)
ISBN 0-85365-209-0 Sd : £0.40
(B77-11162)

370'.73 — Church of England colleges of education. *England. Reports, surveys*
Niblett, William Roy. The church's colleges of higher education : a report, with recommendations, from Professor W.R. Niblett. — London : Church Information Office, 1976. — 31p ; 21cm.
Sd : £0.65
(B77-14154)

370'.73 — Teachers. Professional education. Courses. Entrance requirements. *Scotland. Reports, surveys. Serials*
Memorandum on entry requirements to courses of teacher training in Scotland / Scottish Education Department. — Edinburgh : H.M.S.O.
1977. — 1977. — 42p ; 25cm.
ISBN 0-11-491491-5 Sd : £1.00
(B77-22486)

370'.73'0942142 — Universities. *London. Camden (London Borough). University of London. Institute of Education. Calendars*
University of London. *Institute of Education.* Calendar / University of London Institute of Education. — London : [The Institute].
1976-77. — 1976. — 283p ; 21cm.
'Amendments to regulations and syllabuses for the Certificate in Education' ([2],10p.) as insert.

ISBN 0-85473-069-9 Pbk : £1.00
ISSN 0307-563x
(B77-01292)

370'.73262 — Primary schools. Teachers. Professional education. Projects: Applied Education Project. *North-west England. Reports, surveys*
Ross, Alec, *b.1922.* An experiment in teacher education / [by] Alec Ross, David McNamara and Jean Whittaker. — Guildford : Society for Research into Higher Education, 1977. — v, 133p ; 21cm. — (Research into higher education monographs ; 29 ISSN 0085-1523)
Bibl.: p.91-93.
ISBN 0-900868-55-4 Pbk : £4.15(£3.10 to members)
Also classified at 370'.73263
(B77-30101)

370'.73263 — Middle schools. Teachers. Professional education. Projects: Applied Education Project. *North-west England. Reports, surveys*
Ross, Alec, *b.1922.* An experiment in teacher education / [by] Alec Ross, David McNamara and Jean Whittaker. — Guildford : Society for Research into Higher Education, 1977. — v, 133p ; 21cm. — (Research into higher education monographs ; 29 ISSN 0085-1523)
Bibl.: p.91-93.
ISBN 0-900868-55-4 Pbk : £4.15(£3.10 to members)
Primary classification 370'.73262
(B77-30101)

370'.733 — Microteaching
Investigations of microteaching / edited by Donald McIntyre, Gordon MacLeod and Roy Griffiths. — London : Croom Helm, 1977. — 3-269p : ill ; 23cm.
Bibl. — Index.
ISBN 0-85664-537-0 : £8.95 : CIP rev.
(B77-18035)

370'.733 — Teachers. Professional education. Teaching practice. *Manuals*
Cohen, Louis. A guide to teaching practice / [by] Louis Cohen & Lawrence Manion. — London : Methuen, 1977. — xvii,266p : ill, forms, map, plans ; 25cm.
Bibl.: p.250-257. — Index.
ISBN 0-416-55530-6 : £6.75
ISBN 0-416-55540-3 Pbk : £3.95
(B77-23278)

370'.78 — Education. Research. Methodology
Cohen, Louis. Educational research in classrooms and schools : a manual of materials and methods / [by] Louis Cohen. — London [etc.] : Harper and Row, 1976. — xvi,426p : ill, forms, plans ; 26cm.
Bibl. — Index.
ISBN 0-06-318047-2 : £8.50
(B77-01293)

370'.78 — Education. Research. Statistical methods
Novick, Melvin Robert. Statistical methods for educational and psychological research / [by] Melvin R. Novick, Paul H. Jackson. — New York ; London [etc.] : McGraw-Hill, 1974. — xviii,456p : ill ; 24cm. — (McGraw-Hill series in psychology)
Text on lining paper. — Lining paper perforated at inside edge. — Bibl.: p.xvii-xviii. — Index.
ISBN 0-07-047550-4 : Unpriced
Also classified at 150'.7'2
(B77-18673)

370'.78'041 — Education. Research by British educational institutions. *Directories*
Register of educational research in the United Kingdom / [compiled at the National Foundation for Educational Research in England and Wales]. — Slough : NFER.
1973-76. — 1977. — 27,[336]p ; 30cm.
Index.
ISBN 0-85633-117-1 Pbk : £12.00
(B77-08935)

370'.78'073 — Education. Research. Methodology. *United States. Manuals*
Best, John Wesley. Research in education / [by] John W. Best. — 3rd ed. — Englewood Cliffs ; London [etc.] : Prentice-Hall, 1977. — xii, 403p : ill, facsims, forms, map ; 24cm.
With answers to statistics exercises. — Previous ed.: 1970. — Bibl. — Index.
ISBN 0-13-774018-2 : £9.55
(B77-18674)

370'.8 — Education. *Readings*
Six questions : controversy and conflict in education / edited by J.A. Johnston. — Sydney ; London [etc.] : John Wiley and Sons, Australasia, [1977]. — viii,292p : 1 ill ; 25cm.
Published in Australia: 1975. — Bibl.: p.291-292.
ISBN 0-471-44636-x Pbk : £8.55
(B77-09636)

370.9 — EDUCATION. HISTORICAL AND GEOGRAPHICAL TREATMENT

370'.9172'4 — Nonformal education. *Developing countries. State-of-the-art reviews*
Simkins, Tim. Non-formal education and development : some critical issues / by Tim Simkins. — [Manchester] ([Manchester M13 3LP]) : [University of Manchester, Department of Adult and Higher Education], [1977]. — iv, 77p : 1 ill ; 21cm. — (Manchester monographs ; 8 ISSN 0305-4152)
Bibl.: p.72-77.
Pbk : £2.00
(B77-33148)

370'.918'2 — Education. *Western world, ca 1530-1940*
Schooling and society : studies in the history of education / edited by Lawrence Stone. — Baltimore ; London : Johns Hopkins University Press, [1977]. — xvii,263,[1]p ; 24cm.
Published in the United States: 1976.
ISBN 0-8018-1749-8 : £11.20
(B77-14155)

370'.92'4 — Education. Owen, Sir Hugh, b.1804. *Wales. Biographies. Welsh-English parallel texts*
Davies, Brynmor Lewis. Hugh Owen, 1804-1881 / [by] B.L. Davies. — [Cardiff] : University of Wales Press, 1977. — 98p,leaf of plate,[4]p of plates : ill, port ; 21cm.
Parallel Welsh text and English translation. — Bibl.: p.98.
ISBN 0-7083-0641-1 Pbk : £1.00
(B77-15220)

370'.92'4 — Education. Tomlinson, Joan. *England. Autobiographies*
Tomlinson, Joan. On a May morning / by Joan Tomlinson. — [Richmond] ([8 The Green, Richmond, Surrey]) : Hickey Press Ltd, 1977. — [7],165p ; 22cm.
ISBN 0-900644-02-8 Pbk : £1.80
(B77-26235)

370'.94 — Education. *Europe. Forecasts for 2000*
Education without frontiers : a study of the future of education from the European Cultural Foundation's 'Plan Europe 2000' / edited by Gabriel Fragnière ; with a foreword by John Vaizey. — London : Duckworth, 1976. — xiv, 207p ; 23cm.
Index.
ISBN 0-7156-0988-2 : £8.95
(B77-08936)

370'.941 — Circulars & administrative memoranda published by Great Britain. Department of Education and Science. *Serials*
Great Britain. *Department of Education and Science.* Circulars and administrative memoranda issued / Department of Education and Science. — London : H.M.S.O.
1976. — 1977. — iv,171p : 1 ill ; 21cm.
ISBN 0-11-270419-0 Pbk : £2.60
(B77-15774)

370'.941 — Education. *Great Britain*
Bell, Robert, *b.1930.* Patterns of education in the British Isles / [by] Robert Bell, Nigel Grant. — London [etc.] : Allen and Unwin, 1977. — 3-223p : ill, maps ; 23cm. — (Unwin education books ; 37)
Bibl.: p.219-220. — Index.
ISBN 0-04-370082-9 : £6.95
ISBN 0-04-370083-7 Pbk : £3.50
(B77-33711)

Great Britain. *Central Office of Information. Reference Division.* Education in Britain / [prepared by Reference Division, Central Office of Information]. — 7th ed. — London : H.M.S.O., 1977. — [3],30p : 1 ill ; 24cm. — (Central Office of Information reference pamphlet ; 7)
Previous ed.: 1975. — Bibl.: p.28-30.
ISBN 0-11-700808-7 Sd : £0.75
(B77-15775)

370'.941 — Education. *Great Britain. Essays*
Black paper 1977 / edited by C.B. Cox and Rhodes Boyson. — London : Temple Smith, 1977. — 128p ; 25cm.
Bibl.: p.125-126.
ISBN 0-85117-117-6 Pbk : £1.65
(B77-13600)

370'.941 — Education. *Great Britain. National Front viewpoints*
National Front. Education for national survival / National Front. — Teddington (91 Connaught Rd, Teddington, Middx) : National Front Policy Department, [1976]. — [3],13p : ill ; 28cm.
ISBN 0-905109-02-3 Sd : £0.20
(B77-00700)

370'.941 — Education. Attitudes of underground press. *Great Britain, 1968-1976*
Smith, Mike, *b.1933.* The underground and education : a guide to the alternative press / [by] Mike Smith. — London : Methuen, 1977. — [6],153p : ill, facsims ; 19cm.
Bibl.: p.136-152.
ISBN 0-416-85540-7 Pbk : £1.60
(B77-26976)

370'.9411 — Education. *Scotland. Reports, surveys. Serials*
Education in Scotland : a report of the Secretary of State for Scotland / Scottish Education Department. — Edinburgh : H.M.S.O.
1976. — [1977]. — 16p ; 25cm. — (Cmnd.6804)
Bibl.: p.10-16.
ISBN 0-10-168040-6 Sd : £0.50
(B77-20164)

370'.9411 — Education. *Scotland. Statistics*
Scottish educational statistics / [Scottish Education Department]. — [Edinburgh] : H.M.S.O.
1974. — [1976]. — v,238p ; 30cm.
Cover title. — 'Basic educational statistics (Scotland)' (card ([2] sides)) as insert.
ISBN 0-11-491399-4 Pbk : £5.15
ISSN 0582-2963
(B77-07246)

370'.9416 — Education. *Northern Ireland. Statistics*
Education statistics / Northern Ireland Department of Education. — Belfast : H.M.S.O.
21. — 1976. — vii,113p ; 31cm.
Cover title: Northern Ireland education statistics.
ISBN 0-337-04066-4 Pbk : £1.50
(B77-04068)

Northern Ireland education statistics / Northern Ireland Department of Education. — Belfast : H.M.S.O.
22 : Finance and further education, examinations and school leavers. — 1977. — v, 115p ; 31cm.
Cover title.
Pbk : £1.50
(B77-14653)

370'.942 — Education. *England, 1851-1881*
Jones, Donald K. The making of the education system, 1851-81 / [by] Donald K. Jones. — London [etc.] : Routledge and Kegan Paul, 1977. — x,88p ; 23cm. — (Students library of education)
Bibl.: p.84-88.
ISBN 0-7100-8707-1 : £3.95 : CIP rev.
(B77-23279)

370'.942 — Education. *England, 1939-1945*
Gosden, Peter Henry John Heather. Education in the Second World War : a study in policy and administration / [by] P.H.J.H. Gosden. — London : Methuen, 1976. — x,527p ; 24cm.
Index.
ISBN 0-416-75900-9 : £15.00
(B77-03477)

370'.942 — Education. *England. Forecasts*
Education estimates statistics / [the Chartered Institute of Public Finance and Accountancy and the Society of County Treasurers]. — London : C.I.P.F.A.
1976-77. — 1976. — [2],49p ; 31cm.
Previously published: as 'Education statistics. Estimates'.
ISBN 0-85299-181-9 Sd : £3.00
(B77-00130)

370'.942 — Education. *England. Reports, surveys. Serials*
Education and science : a report of the Department of Education and Science ... — London : H.M.S.O.
1976. — 1977. — viii,62p : 1 ill ; 25cm.
Bibl.: p.60-62.
ISBN 0-11-270455-7 Sd : £1.50
Also classified at 509'.41
(B77-26236)

370'.942 — Education. *England. Statistics*
Statistics of education / Department of Education and Science. — London : H.M.S.O.
1974. Vol.3 : Further education. — 1976. — xx,97p ; 28cm.
ISBN 0-11-270434-4 : £3.75
(B77-02171)

1974. Vol.6 : Universities / [compiled by the] University Grants Committee. — 1976. — xxx, 135p ; 28cm.
ISBN 0-11-270375-5 Pbk : £7.00
(B77-05987)

1975. Vol.1 : Schools. — 1976. — xviii,61p ; 28cm.
ISBN 0-11-270431-x Pbk : £4.75
(B77-06574)

1975. Vol.2 : School leavers CSE and GCE. — 1977. — xxix,66p ; 28cm.
ISBN 0-11-270429-8 Pbk : £4.25
(B77-14654)

1975. Vol.5 : Finance and awards. — 1977. — xxv,45p : 2 ill ; 28cm.
ISBN 0-11-270424-7 Pbk : £2.70
(B77-18036)

1976. Vol.1 : Schools. — 1977. — xx,55p ; 28cm.
ISBN 0-11-270432-8 Pbk : £4.75
(B77-28531)

370'.9422'34 — Education. *Kent. Canterbury, ca 1560-1975*
Canterbury chapters : a Kentish heritage for tomorrow / joint editors M.H.A. Berry, J.H. Higginson. — Liverpool (83 The Albany, Old Hall St., Liverpool) : Dejall and Meyorre International Publishers Ltd [for] Christ Church College, Canterbury, 1976. — [4],139p : ill, facsims, maps, plan, ports ; 30cm.
Bibl.: p.17.
ISBN 0-905603-00-1 Pbk : £3.95
(B77-27773)

370'.9425'32 — Education. *Lincolnshire. Horncastle, 1329-1970*
Clarke, Joseph Norman. Education in a market town : Horncastle, 1329-1970 / by J.N. Clarke. — London [etc.] : Phillimore, 1976. — xv, 183p : ill, facsims, map, plans ; 23cm.
Map on lining paper. — Bibl.: p.177-178. — Index.
ISBN 0-900592-74-5 : £3.75
(B77-02890)

370'.9426'752 — Education. *Essex. Chelmsford (District). Rural regions. Reports, surveys*
Chelmsford *(District). Council.* Rural areas study, education and social service provision / [Chelmsford District Council]. — Chelmsford (Planning Department, Burgess Well Rd, Chelmsford [CM1 1TR]) : [The Council], 1977. — [3],7[i.e.9]p ; 30cm. — (Subject report ; 7)
Sd : £0.20
Also classified at 361'.9426'752
(B77-17397)

370'.9429 — Education. *Wales. Statistics*
Statistics of education in Wales = Ystadegau addysg yng Nghymru / [prepared by the Welsh Office]. — Cardiff : H.M.S.O.
No.1 : 1976. — 1976. — viii,87p : 2 col maps ; 30cm.
ISBN 0-11-790083-4 Pbk : £3.00
(B77-11163)

370'.946 — Education. *Spain. Secondary school texts*
Newcombe, Norman William. Education in Spain / [by] N.W. Newcombe. — London : Harrap, 1977. — 32p : ill, forms ; 14x22cm. — (Discovering Spain)
ISBN 0-245-53049-5 Sd : £0.60
(B77-14156)

370'.947 — Education. Influence of Marxism. *Soviet Union*
Price, Ronald Francis. Marx and education in Russia and China / [by] Ronald F. Price. — London : Croom Helm [etc.], 1977. — 376p : ill ; 23cm.
Bibl.: p.349-369. — Index.
ISBN 0-85664-507-9 : £9.95 : CIP rev.
Also classified at 370'.951
(B77-23280)

370'.951 — Education. Influence of Marxism. *China*
Price, Ronald Francis. Marx and education in Russia and China / [by] Ronald F. Price. — London : Croom Helm [etc.], 1977. — 376p : ill ; 23cm.
Bibl.: p.349-369. — Index.
ISBN 0-85664-507-9 : £9.95 : CIP rev.
Primary classification 370'.947
(B77-23280)

370'.954 — Education. *India (Republic)*
Biswas, A. The new educational pattern in India / [by] A. Biswas, Sunitee Dutt, R.P. Singhal. — Delhi [etc.] : Vikas ; Hemel Hempstead (66 Wood Lane End, Hemel Hempstead, Herts.) : Distributed by International Book Distributors Ltd, 1976. — vii,164p ; 22cm.
Bibl. — Index.
ISBN 0-7069-0384-6 : Unpriced
(B77-16298)

370'.97292 — Education. *Jamaica, to 1976*
Whyte, Millicent. A short history of education in Jamaica / [by] Millicent Whyte. — London [etc.] : Hodder and Stoughton, 1977. — 128p : ill ; 22cm.
ISBN 0-340-22477-0 Pbk : £1.90 : CIP rev.
(B77-26977)

370'.973 — Education. *United States*
Foundations of education : planning for competence / [edited by] Joseph F. Callahan, Leonard H. Clark. — New York : Macmillan ; London : Collier Macmillan, 1977. — xi,283p : ill ; 26cm.
With answers. — Pages perforated at inside edge. — Bibl.
ISBN 0-02-318200-8 Pbk : £5.25
(B77-30102)

370'.973 — Education. *United States, 1636-1973. Readings*
The **dimensions** of American education / edited by Theodore Rawson Crane. — Reading, Mass. ; London [etc.] : Addison-Wesley, 1974. — x,265p ; 21cm. — (Themes and social forces in American history series)
Bibl.: p.249-265.
ISBN 0-201-01212-x Pbk : £4.80
(B77-20165)

370'.973 — Education. *United States. Readings*
Kaleidoscope : readings in education / [compiled by] Kevin Ryan, James M. Cooper. — 2nd ed. — Boston [Mass.] [etc.] ; London : Houghton Mifflin, 1975. — x,273p : ill ; 24cm.
Previous ed.: Boston, Mass. : Houghton Mifflin, 1972. — Bibl.
ISBN 0-395-18623-4 Pbk : £5.50
(B77-31089)

370'.973 — Education. *United States. Yearbooks*
Standard education almanac. — Chicago : Marquis Academic Media ; London : Distributed by Prior.
1976-77 : 9th ed. — 1976. — vii,687p : ill ; 29cm.
Index.
ISBN 0-8379-2103-1 : £22.50
(B77-09637)

370'.973 — Education. Innovation. Planning. *United States*
Zaltman, Gerald. Dynamic educational change : models, strategies, tactics and management / [by] Gerald Zaltman, David H. Florio, Linda A. Sikorski. — New York : Free Press ; London : Collier Macmillan, 1977. — xvi, 364p : ill ; 25cm.
Bibl.: p.336-350. — Index.
ISBN 0-02-935750-0 : £12.00
(B77-23281)

370'.973 — Education. United States. Related to economic conditions
Bowles, Samuel. Schooling in capitalist America : educational reform and the contradictions of economic life / [by] Samuel Bowles and Herbert Gintis. — London [etc.] : Routledge and Kegan Paul, 1977. — ix,340p : ill ; 22cm.
Originally published: New York : Basic Books ; London : Routledge and Kegan Paul, 1976. — Bibl.: p.297. — Index.
ISBN 0-7100-8486-2 Pbk : £2.95
Also classified at 330.9'73'0925
(B77-02891)

370'.983 — Educational systems. *Chile, 1973-1975*
Bulé, P. Notes on the current cultural and educational system in Chile / by P. Bulé. — London (260 High Rd, N15 4AJ) : World University Service (U.K.) [for Academics for Chile], 1976. — [2],17,[1]leaves ; 31cm.
Sd : £0.20
(B77-16804)

370'.995'3 — Education. *Papua New Guinea. Readings*
Papua New Guinea education / edited by E. Barrington Thomas. — Melbourne ; London [etc.] : Oxford University Press, 1976 [i.e. 1977]. — viii,272p ; 23cm.
Published in Australia: 1976. — Index.
ISBN 0-19-550460-7 : £13.00
(B77-11727)

371 — SCHOOLS
371 — Community schools. *Devon, to 1976*
Devon *(County). Education Department.* Sharing and growing : a short account of the growth and activity of community colleges in Devon / Devon County Council Education Department. — [Exeter] ([County Hall, Exeter EX2 4QG]) : The Department, 1977. — 66p ; 21cm.
Bibl.: p.62.
ISBN 0-903896-02-8 Sd : £0.40
(B77-23282)

371 — Community schools. *England. Reports, surveys*
Smith, George, *b.1941.* Community schools in England and Wales : a review / by George and Teresa Smith. — [Edinburgh] ([New St Andrew's House, Scotland EH1 3SY]) : [Scottish Education Department], [1974]. — [1], 44p ; 25cm. — (Great Britain. Scottish Education Department. Inspectorate. Bulletin : occasional papers ; 3)
Bibl.: p.43-44.
ISBN 0-903907-15-1 Sd : Unpriced
(B77-02892)

371 — Rudolf Steiner schools. *Great Britain. Directories*
Practical activities : a guide to institutions founded on the work of Rudolf Steiner. — Revised ed. — Chislehurst (c/o The Secretary, Claverley Cottage, Lubbock Rd, Chislehurst, Kent BR7 5LA) : Rudolf Steiner Special Schools and Homes Information Centre, 1974. — [2],42p ; 23cm.
Previous ed.: i.e. 9th revised ed., 1969.
Sd : £0.35
(B77-00701)

371'.006'242 — Schools. Organisations. *England. Schools Council. Reports, surveys. Serials*
Schools Council. Schools Council report / Schools Council, Pwyllgor Cymru'r Cyngor Ysgolion. — London : Evans Bros : Methuen.
1976-77. — 1977. — 76p ; 21cm.
ISBN 0-423-50530-0 Pbk : £1.50
ISSN 0306-0306
(B77-33149)

371'.0094 — Schools. *Western Europe. Comparative studies*
Newcombe, Norman William. Europe at school : a study of primary and secondary schools in France, West Germany, Italy, Portugal & Spain / [by] Norman Newcombe. — London : Methuen, 1977. — viii,264p ; 23cm.
Index.
ISBN 0-416-82880-9 : £6.50
ISBN 0-416-82890-6 Pbk : £3.95
(B77-10305)

371'.009419'3 — Boys' schools. *Clare (County). Kilrush Christian Brothers' School, to 1974. Irish & English texts*
Kilrush CBS centenary souvenir, 1874-1974 / editor Noel MulQueen, assistant editor Donal M. Ryan ... — Kilrush ([c/o Brothers of the Christian Schools, Kilrush, Eire]) : Executive of the Past Pupils' Union, Kilrush, [1977]. — 144p : ill, facsim, ports ; 30cm.
Cover title: Christian Brothers, Kilrush, 1874-1974. — Includes three articles in Irish and one parallel English-Irish article.
Sd : Unpriced
(B77-21801)

371'.00942 — Schools. *England*
Wright, Nigel. Progress in education : a review of schooling in England and Wales / [by] Nigel Wright. — London : Croom Helm, 1977. — 3-225p : ill ; 23cm.
Bibl.: p.206-219. — Index.
ISBN 0-85664-500-1 : £6.50 : CIP rev.
ISBN 0-85664-615-6 Pbk : £2.95
(B77-24116)

371'.00942 — Schools. *England. Conference proceedings*
The **scope** of education : opportunities for the teacher : March education conference, 1976 : [a one day conference arranged by the School of Education, Goldsmiths' College in conjunction with the Goldsmiths' College Association, Saturday March 6th 1976] / [editor A.V. Kelly]. — London ([6 Dixon Rd, S.E.14]) : The College, [1977]. — [3],32p ; 21cm.
ISBN 0-901542-36-9 Sd : £0.65
(B77-13601)

371'.00942 — Schools. *England. Reports, surveys*
Great Britain. *Department of Education and Science.* Education in schools : a consultative document / presented to Parliament by the Secretary of State for Education and Science and the Secretary of State for Wales ... — London : H.M.S.O., [1977]. — [3],54p : ill ; 25cm. — (Cmnd.6869)
ISBN 0-10-168690-0 Sd : £1.10
(B77-21802)

371'.009423'15 — Schools. *Wiltshire. Holt, 1834-1935*
Bucknall, G V S. Two into one : Holt schools, 1834-1935 / by G.V.S. Bucknall. — Holt, Wilts. (c/o Editorial Secretary, 'Cranfield', Ham Green, Holt, Trowbridge, Wilts. BA14 6PX) : 'Holt magazine', 1976. — [4],71p,[4]p of plates : ill, ports ; 21cm.
ISBN 0-9503284-2-1 Sd : £0.50
(B77-06575)

371'.009425'98 — Schools. *Buckinghamshire. Stoke Poges, 1876-1976*
Tarrant, John, *b.1898.* The village school : education in Stoke Poges / by John Tarrant. — [Slough] ([c/o Clerk to the Council, 14 Neville Close, Stoke Poges, Slough, Berks.]) : Stoke Poges Parish Council, 1976. — [1],64,[1]p : ill, 2 facsims, map, plans, ports ; 24cm.
ISBN 0-9505541-0-3 Sd : £1.00
(B77-08937)

371'.009428'65 — Schools. *Durham (County). Framwellgate Moor. Framwellgate Moor School, to 1935. Personal observations. Collections*
Framwellgate Moor schools, 1877-1977 : extracts from the school log books / selected by R. Hopkinson ... [et al.]. — [Durham] ([Newton Drive, Framwellgate Moor, Durham DH1 5BQ]) : [Framwellgate Moor Comprehensive School], [1977]. — [3],60[i.e.64]p ; 15x22cm.
Sp : Unpriced
(B77-26982)

371'.009429'21 — Schools. *Gwynedd. Ynys Môn, 1700-1902*
Pretty, David A. Two centuries of Anglesey schools, 1700-1902 / [by] David A. Pretty. — Llangefni ([c/o Huw Roberts, Area Education Office, Shire Hall, Llangefni, Anglesey, Gwynedd]) : Anglesey Antiquarian Society, 1977. — 383p,[6]p of plates : ill, facsims, maps, ports ; 22cm. — (Studies in Anglesey history ; vol.5)
Bibl.: p.354-372. — Index.
£4.50
(B77-31090)

371'.00973 — Schools. *United States*
Tye, Kenneth Austin. Schools in transition : the practitioner as change agent / [by] Kenneth A. Tye and Jerrold M. Novotney ; foreword by Samuel G. Sava ; introduction by John I. Goodlad. — New York ; London [etc.] : McGraw-Hill, [1976]. — xvii,178p : ill ; 24cm. — (Institute for Development of Educational Activities. Reports on schooling : series on educational change)
'A Charles F. Kettering Foundation Program'. — Published in the United States: 1975. — Bibl.: p.163-172. — Index.
ISBN 0-07-065690-8 : £7.45
(B77-05318)

371'.00973 — Schools. Political aspects. *United States, to 1975*
Greer, Colin. The great school legend : a revisionist interpretation of American public education / [by] Colin Greer. — Harmondsworth [etc.] : Penguin, 1976. — xvii, 206p ; 20cm.
Originally published: New York : Basic Books, 1972. — Bibl.: p.186-202. — Index.
ISBN 0-14-004447-7 Pbk : Unpriced
(B77-14157)

371'.02'02541 — Independent schools. *Great Britain. Directories*
Schools : a geographical directory of independent schools, universities, polytechnics arranged in order of counties and towns in Great Britain and Northern Ireland, including information regarding recognised public schools for boys (and co-educational) indicating those with sixth form courses for girls, tutorial colleges, career training courses, schools on the continent of Europe. — London : Truman and Knightley.
1977 : (fifty-fourth ed.). — [1977]. — 848p : ill ; 21cm.
Index.
Pbk : £2.50
(B77-16299)

United Kingdom schools, private / [Data Research Group]. — Amersham (Hill House, [Hill Ave.], Amersham, Bucks.) : The Group. [1976]. — 1976. — 164 leaves in various pagings ; 30cm.
Includes sections on universities, colleges of education and new education authorities.
ISBN 0-905570-48-0 Pbk : £16.00
(B77-03478)

371'.02'025411 — Independent schools. *Scotland. Directories*
Independent Schools Information Service. *Scotland.* Independent Schools Information Service (Scotland). — Edinburgh (18 Hanover St., Edinburgh EH2 2EP) : [ISIS Scotland].
[1976-1977]. — [1976]. — [1],19,[3]p : map ; 21cm.
Sd : Unpriced
ISSN 0309-619x
(B77-18037)

371'.02'025422 — Independent schools. *South-east England. Directories*
Independent Schools Information Service. *London and South East.* ISIS : [the] Independent Schools Information Service, London and South East. — London (47 Victoria St., SW1H 0EQ) : ISIS [London and South East].
1976. — [1976]. — 80,[1]p ; 15x21cm.
Fold. sheet (1 side ; map) as insert.
Sd : Unpriced
ISSN 0309-4162
(B77-09638)

1977. — [1977]. — 86p ; 15x21cm.
Fold sheet ([2]p.: 2 maps) as insert.
ISBN 0-902533-17-7 Sd : Free
ISSN 0309-4162
(B77-08938)

371'.02'025423 — Independent schools. *South-west England. Directories*
Independent Schools Information Service. *South and West.* The Independent Schools Information Service. South and West. — Somerset (Oldway Lodge, Hinton St George, Somerset) : [ISIS South and West].
1977. — [1977]. — [2],42,[4]p : forms ; 15x21cm.
Fold. sheet ([1] side: col. map) as insert.
Sd : Unpriced
ISSN 0309-6203
(B77-18038)

371'.02'025424 — Independent schools. *England. Midlands. Directories*
Independent Schools Information Service. *Central England.* The Independent Schools Information Service. Central England. — Bewdley (Kinlet Hall, Bewdley, Worcs.) : [ISIS Central England].
1976-77. — [1976]. — [2],55,[2]p : form ; 15x21cm.
Fold. sheet ([1] side: col. map) as insert.
Sd : Unpriced
ISSN 0309-6165
(B77-18039)

371'.02'025426 — Independent schools. *East Anglia. Directories*
Schools in eastern England : Norfolk, Suffolk, Cambridgeshire, Essex, Hertfordshire / Independent Schools Information Service - East. — Cambridge (9 Woodlark Rd, Cambridge CB3 0HT) : ISIS (East).
1976-7 : [seventh ed.]. — [1976]. — 44,[3],4p ; 21cm.
Fold. sheet ([1] side: map) as insert.
Sd : Unpriced
ISSN 0309-6173
(B77-18040)

371'.02'025427 — Independent schools. *Northern England. Directories*
Independent Schools Information Service. *North.* Independent Schools Information Service. North. — Gwynedd (c/o Mrs W.E. Lane, Mynydd Nefyn, Gwynedd LL53 6TN) : [ISIS North].
1976-77. — [1976]. — [3],32,[4]p : forms ; 16x21cm.
Fold. sheet ([1] side : col. map) as insert. — Previous issue published by ISIS North England and North Wales.
Sd : Unpriced
ISSN 0309-6181
(B77-17398)

371'.02'0254294 — Independent schools. *South Wales. Directories*
Independent Schools Information Service. *South Wales.* Independent schools in South Wales / ISIS [South Wales]. — Brecon (3 Orchard Gardens, Brecon, Powys LD3 8AP) : ISIS South Wales, [1977]. — [2],9p : map ; 15x21cm.
Sd : Unpriced
(B77-29319)

371'.02'0941 — Independent schools. *Great Britain. For parents*
Independent Schools Information Service. Private schools, would they be right for my child? / [Independent Schools Information Service]. — London (47 Victoria St., SW1H 0EQ) : I.S.I.S., [1977]. — [8]p : ill ; 21cm.
Sd : Unpriced
(B77-27774)

Truman and Knightley Educational Trust. Independent schools / the Truman & Knightley Educational Trust. — London : The Trust, [1977]. — [2],20p ; 16cm.
Sd : Unpriced
(B77-33712)

371'.02'0942733 — Schools run by Cross Street Chapel, Manchester. *Greater Manchester (Metropolitan County). Manchester, to 1942*
Burney, Lester. Cross Street Chapel Schools, Manchester, 1734-1942 / by Lester Burney. — [Manchester] ([114 Atwood Rd, Didsbury, Manchester M20 0DJ]) : [The author], 1977. — [2],94p : ill, ports ; 21cm.
Bibl.: p.94.
Sd : £1.30
(B77-24831)

371'.02'095414 — Anglo-Indian schools. *India (Republic). Bengal, to 1960*
D'Souza, Austin A. Anglo-Indian education : a study of its origins and growth in Bengal up to 1960 / [by] Austin A. D'Souza. — Delhi ; London [etc.] : Oxford University Press, 1976. — x,344p ; 22cm.
Bibl.: p.333-338. — Index.
ISBN 0-19-560354-0 : £6.95
(B77-16300)

371.1 — TEACHING AND TEACHING PERSONNEL

371.1'0092'2 — British governesses. *Soviet Union, ca 1900-1941*
Pitcher, Harvey John. When Miss Emmie was in Russia : English governesses before, during and after the October Revolution / [by] Harvey Pitcher. — London : J. Murray, 1977. — xiii, 246p,[14]p of plates : 1 ill, maps, ports ; 23cm.
Bibl.: p.239-241. — Index.
ISBN 0-7195-3332-5 : £5.95
(B77-15776)

371.1'00941 — Teaching. *Great Britain. Socialist viewpoints. Periodicals*
'Rank & file' occasional journal. — London (5 Lavender Grove, E.8) : Rank and File.
No.1- ; Spring 1977-. — 1977-. — ill, ports ; 30cm.
Published at irregular intervals. — [2],29p. in 1st issue.
Sd : £0.25
ISSN 0309-4790
(B77-14655)

371.1'02 — Children. Classroom behaviour. Behaviour modification
Sulzer-Azaroff, Beth. Applying behavior-analysis procedures with children and youth / [by] Beth Sulzer-Azaroff and G. Roy Mayer. — New York ; London [etc.] : Holt, Rinehart and Winston, 1977. — xiii,541p : ill, forms ; 25cm.
Bibl. — Index.
ISBN 0-03-018236-0 : £9.75
(B77-22487)

371.1'02 — Children. Classroom behaviour. Behaviour modification. *Readings*
Classroom management : the successful use of behavior modification / [edited by] K. Daniel O'Leary and Susan G. O'Leary. — 2nd ed. — New York ; Oxford [etc.] : Pergamon, 1977. — xvii,444p : ill ; 24cm. — (Pergamon general psychology series) (Pergamon international library)
Previous ed.: 1972. — Bibl.: p.427-440. — Index.
ISBN 0-08-021396-0 : £8.55
ISBN 0-08-021395-2 Pbk : £4.00
(B77-24117)

371.1'02 — Schools. Students, 8-13 years. Teaching
Teaching the eight to thirteens / editors Michael Raggett and Malcolm Clarkson. — London : Ward Lock. — (The middle years curriculum series)
Vol.2. — 1976. — 267p : ill, music ; 23cm.
Bibl. — Index.
ISBN 0-7062-3542-8 : £4.00
ISBN 0-7062-3543-6 Pbk : £2.50
(B77-21057)

371.1'02 — Schools. Students. Personality assessment by teachers
Downey, Meriel Elaine. Interpersonal judgements in education / [by] Meriel Downey. — London [etc.] : Harper and Row, 1977. — [4],123p ; 22cm.
Index.
ISBN 0-06-318051-0 : £3.95 : CIP rev.
ISBN 0-06-318052-9 Pbk : £1.95
(B77-07868)

371.1'02 — Schools. Teachers. Interpersonal relationships with students
Wragg, Edward Conrad. Classroom interaction / prepared for the [Open University, Personality and Learning] Course Team by Edward Wragg, John Oates and Paul Gump. — Milton Keynes : Open University Press, 1976. — 97p : ill, form ; 30cm. — (Educational studies, a second level course : personality and learning ; block 11) (E201 ; block 11)
Bibl.
ISBN 0-335-06511-2 Pbk : Unpriced
(B77-04069)

371.1'02 — Schools. Teaching. *Manuals*
Gray, William A. Learning by doing : developing teaching skills / [by] William A. Gray III, Brian A. Gerrard. — Reading, Mass. ; London [etc.] : Addison-Wesley, 1977. — vi,409p : ill, plan ; 24x22cm.
Fill-in book. — Bibl.: p.406-409.
ISBN 0-201-02547-7 Pbk : £4.80
(B77-21803)

Kohl, Herbert Ralph. On teaching / [by] Herbert R. Kohl. — London : Methuen, 1977. — [1], 185p : ill ; 20cm.
Originally published: New York : Schocken, 1976. — Bibl.: p.179-181. — Index.
ISBN 0-416-85800-7 : £3.95
ISBN 0-416-85820-1 Pbk : £1.80
(B77-21058)

371.1'02 — Small groups. Teaching. *Readings*
Small group teaching : selected papers / [compiled by Helen Simons and Geoffrey Squires in collaboration with Jean Rudduck] ; [for the] Group for Research & Innovation in Higher Education. — London : Nuffield Foundation, 1976. — [4],133p : ill ; 21cm.
Bibl.: p.15.
ISBN 0-904956-14-8 Pbk : Unpriced
(B77-02172)

371.1'02 — Teaching
Evans, Ellis D. Transition to teaching / [by] Ellis D. Evans. — New York ; London [etc.] : Holt, Rinehart and Winston, 1976. — xv,156p : forms ; 21cm. — ([Holt, Rinehart and Winston principles of education psychology series])
Bibl.: p.141-150. — Index.
ISBN 0-03-089811-0 Pbk : £2.50
(B77-08939)

Pullias, Earl V. A teacher is many things / [by] Earl V. Pullias and James D. Young. — 2nd ed. — Bloomington ; London : Indiana University Press, 1977. — xxiii,295p ; 22cm.
Previous ed.: Bloomington : Indiana University Press, 1968. — Index.
ISBN 0-253-18691-9 : £7.25
ISBN 0-253-35680-6 Pbk : £3.75
(B77-21059)

371.1'02 — Teaching. *Manuals*
Implementing teacher competencies : positive approaches to personalizing education / James E. Weigand, editor. — Englewood Cliffs ; London [etc.] : Prentice-Hall, 1977. — viii, 280p : ill, forms ; 24cm.
Bibl.: p.279-280.
ISBN 0-13-451948-5 : £9.55
ISBN 0-13-451930-2 Pbk : £5.20
(B77-23283)

371.1'02'019 — Schools. Teaching. Psychological aspects
Vargas, Julie S. Behavioral psychology for teachers / [by] Julie S. Vargas. — New York [etc.] ; London : Harper and Row, 1977. — xvii,319p : ill, forms ; 25cm.
With answers. — Index.
ISBN 0-06-046813-0 : £6.70
(B77-33151)

371.1'02'019 — Teaching. Psychological aspects. *Programmed texts*
Becker, Wesley C. Teaching / [by] Wesley C. Becker, Siegfried Engelmann, Don R. Thomas. — Revised ed. — Chicago ; Henley-on-Thames [etc.] : Science Research Associates.
In 3 vols. — Previous ed.: published in 1 vol. as 'Teaching : a course in applied psychology'. Chicago : Science Research Associates, 1971.
3 : Evaluation of instruction / [by] Wesley C. Becker, Siegfried Engelmann. — [1977]. — viii, 343p : ill, facsim, forms ; 26cm.
Vol,3 of this ed. published in the United States: 1976. — Index. — Previous control number ISBN 0-574-18025-7.
ISBN 0-574-23035-1 Pbk : £5.55
(B77-08940)

371.1'02'0941 — Schools. Teaching. *Great Britain*
Explorations in the politics of school knowledge / edited and introduced by Geoff Whitty and Michael Young. — Driffield (Nafferton, Driffield, [Humberside] YO25 0JL) : Studies in Education Ltd, 1976. — [5], 265p ; 22cm. — (Issues in sociology, politics and education)
'Nafferton Books'. — Index.
ISBN 0-905484-00-2 : £5.95
ISBN 0-905484-05-3 Pbk : £2.95
(B77-14158)

371.1'02'0973 — Schools. Teaching. *United States*
Good, Thomas L. Teachers make a difference / [by] Thomas L. Good, Bruce J. Biddle, Jere E. Brophy. — New York [etc.] ; London : Holt, Rinehart and Winston, [1976]. — xv,271p : ill, facsims, music ; 23cm.
Published in the United States: 1975. — Bibl.: p.243-256. — Index.
ISBN 0-03-012591-x Pbk : £4.75
(B77-02893)

371.1'03 — Education. Participation of parents
Midwinter, Eric. Education for sale / [by] Eric Midwinter. — London : Allen and Unwin, 1977. — 95p ; 23cm. — (Classroom close-ups ; 5)
Bibl.: p.95.
ISBN 0-04-371049-2 : £4.50
ISBN 0-04-371050-6 Pbk : £2.50
(B77-21804)

371.1'03 — School life. Involvement of parents. *Proposals*
Wood, Anthony, *b.1938.* Involving parents in the curriculum / by Anthony Wood and Lena Simpkins ; appendix 'Involvement at the secondary stage' by Peter Preston. — Gravesend [etc.] : Home and School Council Publications, 1976. — [1],24p : ill, music ; 21cm.
ISBN 0-901181-23-4 Sd : £0.40
(B77-14159)

371.1'04 — Schools. Teachers. Stress. *Great Britain*
Stress in schools. — Hemel Hempstead (Swan Court, Waterhouse St., Hemel Hempstead, Herts.) : National Association of Schoolmasters and Union of Women Teachers, 1976. — 62p : 1 ill ; 24cm.
Bibl.
ISBN 0-901930-33-4 Pbk : £2.00
(B77-16301)

371.1'04 — Schools. Teaching. Social aspects
Cortis, Gerald. The social context of teaching / [by] Gerald Cortis. — London : Open Books, 1977. — x,169p : ill ; 21cm. — (Psychology and education)
Bibl.: p.158-167. — Index.
ISBN 0-7291-0018-9 : £4.50
ISBN 0-7291-0013-8 Pbk : £1.95
(B77-15221)

371.1'06'09417 — Schools. Decision making. Participation of teachers. Effects of organisation structure. *Ireland (Republic). Reports, surveys*
Conway, James A. Organizational structure and teacher participation in decision making in selected schools in Ireland / author James A. Conway ; editorial adviser S.V.O. Súilleabháin. — Galway (Galway, Republic of Ireland) : Social Sciences Research Centre, University College, Galway, 1976. — 28p : forms ; 22cm. — (University College, Galway. Social Sciences Research Centre. Research papers ; no.8)
Bibl.: p.26-28.
Sd : £0.50
(B77-22019)

371.1'412 — Schools. Teachers. Duties: Covering. *Great Britain. National Union of Teachers viewpoints*
No cover. — London (c/o M. Hurford, 18 Williamson St., N.7) : ['Rank and file'], [1977]. — [2],11p : ill ; 22cm. — (Action against the cuts ; no.1) (A 'Rank & file' pamphlet)
Sd : £0.05
(B77-26237)

371.1'44'0973 — Teachers. Evaluation. *United States. Readings*
The appraisal of teaching : concepts and processes / [edited by] Gary D. Borich ; with the assistance of Kathleen S. Fenton. — Reading, Mass. ; London [etc.] : Addison-Wesley, 1977. — iii-xvi,396p : ill, form ; 25cm.
Bibl. — Index.
ISBN 0-201-00841-6 : £9.60
(B77-18041)

371.1'46'09423 — Teachers. In-service training. *South-west England. Conference proceedings*
Staff development in the teaching service in the South West : report of the conference held at Weymouth in September 1973. — [Bristol] : University of Bristol, School of Education, 1974. — 94p in various pagings : ill ; 30cm.
ISBN 0-903024-28-4 Pbk : £0.50
(B77-02894)

371.2 — SCHOOL ADMINISTRATION
371.2 — Educational institutions. Efficiency
Wagner, Leslie. The internal efficiency of education institutions / [prepared by Leslie Wagner and Donald Verry ; for the Open University Economics and Education Policy Course Team]. — Milton Keynes : Open University Press, 1977. — 119p : ill ; 30cm. — (Educational studies and social sciences, a third level course : economics and education policy ; 3) (ED322 ; block 3)
With answers. — Bibl.: p.3.
ISBN 0-335-06732-8 Pbk : Unpriced
(B77-28532)

371.2'0092'2 — Schools. Administration. *United States. Biographical dictionaries*
Who's who biographical record, school district officials / compiled by the editors of 'Who's who in America'. — Chicago : Marquis Who's Who ; London : Distributed by Prior, 1976. — xiv,666p ; 26cm.
ISBN 0-8379-3801-5 : Unpriced
(B77-09639)

371.2'009669 — Schools. Administration. *Nigeria. Manuals*
Ozigi, A O. A handbook on school administration and management / [by] A.O. Ozigi. — London [etc.] : Macmillan, 1977. — viii,144p ; 22cm.
Bibl.: p.139-140. — Index.
ISBN 0-333-21325-4 Pbk : £1.47
(B77-30103)

371.2'00973 — Schools. Administration. *United States*
Campbell, Roald Fay. Introduction to educational administration. — 5th ed. / [by] Roald F. Campbell, Edwin M. Bridges, Raphael O. Nystrand. — Boston, Mass. ; London [etc.] : Allyn and Bacon, 1977. — xii,396p : ill ; 24cm.

Previous ed.: / by Roald F. Campbell et al. Boston, Mass. : Allyn and Bacon, 1971. — Bibl. — Index.
ISBN 0-205-05678-4 : Unpriced
(B77-15222)

371.2'012'0924 — Boarding schools. *Suffolk. Leiston. Summerhill School. Neill, Alexander Sutherland. Autobiographies*
Neill, Alexander Sutherland. Neill! Neill! Orange peel! : a personal view of ninety years / [by] A.S. Neill. — [Revised ed.]. — London [etc.] : Quartet Books, 1977. — [7],264p ; 20cm.
This ed. originally published: London : Weidenfeld and Nicolson, 1973. — Index.
ISBN 0-7043-3112-8 Pbk : £2.50
(B77-26238)

371.2'51'0941 — Schools. Classes. Size. Regulation. Role of National Union of Teachers. *Great Britain, 1962-1976*
Rosenberg, Chanie. Class size and the relationship between official and unofficial action in the NUT / by Chanie Rosenberg. — London (c/o C. Rosenberg, 58 Allerton Rd, N16 5UF) : ['Rank and file'], [1977]. — [2], 15p : ill ; 22cm. — (Action against the cuts ; no.2) (A 'Rank & file' pamphlet)
Sd : £0.06
(B77-16805)

371.2'6 — Schools. Students. Assessment
Leverett, S M. Assessment and related topics in teaching : (a study-source paper) / by S.M. Leverett. — [Revised ed.]. — Chelmsford (Chelmer Institute of Higher Education, Victoria Rd South, Chelmsford CM1 1LL) : Advisory Unit for Computer Education in Essex, 1977. — [4],22p : ill ; 30cm.
'... a revised version of a paper originally printed for a mathematics teachers' conference, entitled "Testing", and published in September, 1976' - Note. — Bibl.: p.20-22.
Sd : £0.50
(B77-26978)

371.2'6 — Schools. Students. Tests
Brown, Frederick G. Principles of educational and psychological testing / [by] Frederick G. Brown. — 2nd ed. — New York ; London [etc.] : Holt, Rinehart and Winston, [1977]. — viii,504p : ill, forms ; 25cm.
This ed. published in the United States: 1976. — Previous ed.: Hinsdale : Dryden Press, 1970. — Bibl.: p.479-494. — Index.
ISBN 0-03-089051-9 : £9.50
(B77-11164)

371.2'64 — Schools. Students. Academic achievement. Assessment. Methods. *Scotland. Scottish Council for Research in Education Profile Assessment System. Manuals*
Scottish Council for Research in Education. SCRE profile assessment system : manual. — [Edinburgh] ([16 Moray Place, Edinburgh EH3 6DR]) : The Council, 1977. — [2],34p : forms ; 22cm.
ISBN 0-901116-10-6 Sd : £0.50
(B77-23284)

371.2'64 — Schools. Students. Academic achievement. Effects of self-image
Covington, Martin. Self-worth and school learning / [by] Martin V. Covington, Richard G. Beery. — New York ; London [etc.] : Holt, Rinehart and Winston, [1977]. — ix,166p : ill ; 21cm. — (The principles of educational psychology series)
Published in the United States: 1976. — Bibl.: p.149-162. — Index.
ISBN 0-03-015286-0 Pbk : £2.25
(B77-11728)

371.2'64 — Schools. Students. Academic achievement. Effects of social class of students. *Great Britain*
Swift, Arnold. Education & inequalities / prepared by Arnold Swift and Richard Skellington ; for the [Open University] Course Team. — Milton Keynes : Open University Press, 1976. — 34p : ill ; 30cm. — (Social science, a third level course : patterns of inequality ; section 2 : inequality within nations ; unit 12) (D302 ; 12)
Bibl.: p.33-34.
ISBN 0-335-07164-3 Sd : Unpriced
(B77-04070)

371.2'64 — Schools. Students. Assessment. *Great Britain. For teaching*
Macintosh, Henry Gordon. Assessing attainment in the classroom / [by] Henry G. Macintosh. — London [etc.] : Hodder and Stoughton, 1976. — 2-47p : 1 ill ; 28cm. — (Canterbury study books)
Bibl.: p.45-47.
ISBN 0-340-19181-3 Sd : £0.80
(B77-06576)

371.2'64 — Students. Academic achievement. Assessment
Gronlund, Norman Edward. Measurement and evaluation in teaching / [by] Norman E. Gronlund. — 3rd ed. — New York : Macmillan ; London : Collier Macmillan, 1976. — x,590p : ill, facsims, forms, map ; 24cm.
Previous ed.: 1971. — Bibl. — Index.
ISBN 0-02-979400-5 Pbk : £6.25
(B77-24118)

Readings in measurement and evaluation in education and psychology / [edited by] William A. Mehrens. — New York ; London [etc.] : Holt, Rinehart and Winston, 1976. — x,374p : ill, forms ; 23cm.
Bibl. — Index.
ISBN 0-03-089680-0 Pbk : £6.00
(B77-02173)

371.2'64 — Students. Academic achievement. Assessment. Analysis
Rowntree, Derek. Assessing students : how shall we know them? / [by] Derek Rowntree. — London [etc.] : Harper and Row, 1977. — ix, 269p : ill, form ; 22cm.
Bibl.: p.244-258. — Index.
ISBN 0-06-318062-6 : Unpriced : CIP rev.
(B77-10306)

371.2'64 — Students. Academic achievement. Assessment. Techniques
Martuza, Victor R. Applying norm-referenced and criterion-referenced measurement in education / [by] Victor R. Martuza. — Boston, Mass. ; London [etc.] : Allyn and Bacon, 1977. — viii,352p : ill, forms ; 24cm.
With answers. — Bibl. — Index.
ISBN 0-205-05545-1 : Unpriced
(B77-18042)

371.2'64 — Students. Academic achievement. Assessment. Techniques. *Conference proceedings*
International Symposium on Educational Testing, *2nd, Montreux, 1975.* Advances in psychological and educational measurement / edited by Dato N.M. De Gruijter and Leo J. Th. van der Kamp. — London [etc.] : Wiley, 1976. — x,320p : ill ; 24cm.
'... proceedings of the Second International Symposium on Educational Testing, held in Montreux, Switzerland, June 30-July 13 1975 ...' - Foreword. — Bibl. — Index.
ISBN 0-471-01817-1 : £14.00
(B77-04071)

371.2'722'014 — Schools. Students. School reports. Terminology. *Great Britain. Lists*
Triggers. — [Maidstone] ([c/o K.F.C. Pearce, 54 Allinston Way, Maidstone, Kent]) : ['Triggers'], [1977]. — [1],27p ; 21cm.
Sd : £1.25
(B77-18043)

371.3 — TEACHING METHODS
371.3 — Distance study
Harris, William Jack Augustus. A handbook on distance education : (a handbook to brief and help administrators, educationalists, politicians and all others engaged in distance education in countries seeking to introduce, extend or improve correspondence education for adults) / by W.J.A. Harris and J.D.S. Williams ; preface and appendix by C.J.J. Wiedhaup. — [Manchester] ([Manchester M13 9PL]) : Department of Adult and Higher Education, University of Manchester, 1977. — [1],vi,77p : ill, plan ; 21cm. — (Manchester monographs ; 7 ISSN 0305-4152)
Bibl.: p.76-77.
Pbk : £1.80
(B77-15223)

Holmberg, Börje. Distance education : a survey and bibliography / [by] Börje Holmberg. — London : Kogan Page [etc.], 1977. — 167p ; 23cm.
Index.
ISBN 0-85038-062-6 : £8.00
(B77-22488)

371.3 — Distance study. Organisations. *Great Britain. International Extension College, to 1976*
International Extension College. Food from learning : the International Extension College, 1971-1976 / edited by Hilary Perraton. — Cambridge (131 Hills Rd, Cambridge CB2 1PD) : The College, 1976. — 37p ; 21cm.
ISBN 0-903632-11-x Sd : £1.00
(B77-05319)

371.3 — Rudolf Steiner schools. Teaching methods
Carlgren, Frans. Education towards freedom : Rudolf Steiner education : a survey of the work of Waldorf schools throughout the world / text Frans Carlgren ; [translated from the German] ; prefaces Rudolf Grosse and Alan Howard. — English ed. / [edited by] Joan and Siegfried Rudel. — East Grinstead (Peredur, East Grinstead, [Sussex]) : Lanthorn Press, 1976. — 208p : ill(some col), col facsims, col maps, ports(chiefly col) ; 25x35cm.
Translation of: 'Erziehung zur Freiheit'. Stuttgart : Freies Geistesleben, 1972.
£7.00
(B77-26979)

371.3 — Schools. Teaching methods
Steiner, Rudolf. Practical advice to teachers : fourteen lectures given at the foundation of the Waldorf School, Stuttgart, from 21 August to 5 September 1919 / [by] Rudolf Steiner. — 2nd ed. / translated [from the German] by Johanna Collis. — London : Rudolf Steiner Press, 1976. — 205p : ill ; 23cm.
Previous ed.: / translated by Harry Collison. 1937.
ISBN 0-85440-302-7 : £3.75
ISBN 0-85440-303-5 Pbk : £2.00
(B77-02895)

371.3'0282 — Confluent education. *United States*
Brown, George Isaac. Human teaching for human learning : an introduction to confluent education / [by] George Isaac Brown. — Harmondsworth [etc.] : Penguin, 1977. — xvii, 298p ; 18cm. — (Esalen books)
Originally published: New York : Viking Press, 1971. — Bibl.: p.295-298.
ISBN 0-14-004496-5 Pbk : Unpriced
(B77-24119)

371.3'078 — Educational technology. *Conference proceedings*
Aspects of educational technology. — London : Kogan Page.
Vol.10 : Educational technology for individualised learning / edited for the Association for Programmed Learning and Educational Technology by John Clarke and John Leedham. — 1976. — 315p : ill, forms, plans ; 24cm.
Proceedings of the tenth annual conference of the Association for Programmed Learning and Educational Technology, held at Dundee College of Education in April 1976. — Bibl.
ISBN 0-85038-461-3 : £10.50
(B77-07869)

Schramm, Wilbur. Big media, little media : tools and technologies for instruction / [by] Wilbur Schramm. — Beverly Hills ; London : Sage Publications, 1977. — 315p : ill ; 23cm. — (People and communication ; 2)
Bibl.: p.281-296. — Index.
ISBN 0-8039-0740-0 : £12.00
ISBN 0-8039-0745-1 Pbk : £4.95
(B77-30104)

371.3'078 — Educational technology. *Great Britain*
Black, Joseph, *b.1921.* The challenge of the new media : systems approach to educational technology / by J. Black. — [London] : [Association of Colleges for Further and Higher Education], [1976]. — [1],5p ; 21cm.
'[A paper presented at the] Summer Meeting [of] The Association of Colleges for Further and Higher Education [held at] Brighton 9th, 10th, 11th June, 1976'.
ISBN 0-900096-70-5 Sd : £0.25
(B77-02174)

371.3'078 — Educational technology. Organisations. *Great Britain. Council for Educational Technology for the United Kingdom. Reports, surveys. Serials*
Council for Educational Technology for the United Kingdom. Annual report for the year October-September / Council for Educational Technology for the United Kingdom. — London : C.E.T.
1975-1976. — 1976. — 112p ; 21cm.
ISBN 0-902204-69-6 Pbk : Unpriced
ISSN 0307-921x
(B77-12962)

371.3'078 — Higher education institutions. Curriculum subjects: Educational technology. *Great Britain*
Coffey, John. Educational technology courses for teachers in training / [by] John Coffey. — [London] : [Council for Educational Technology for the United Kingdom], [1977]. — 24p ; 21cm. — (Council for Educational Technology for the United Kingdom. Discussion documents)
Bibl.: p.15-17.
Sd : Unpriced
(B77-14160)

371.3'078 — Higher education institutions. Curriculum subjects: Educational technology. Courses. *Great Britain. Directories*
Courses leading to qualifications in educational technology / Council for Educational Technology. — [London] : [C.E.T.].
1977-1978. — [1977]. — [5],44p ; 21cm.
Sd : Unpriced
ISSN 0309-4839
(B77-13602)

371.3'078 — Schools. Resource centres. Organisation. *Manuals*
Scottish Educational Film Association. The setting up of a resources centre / [Scottish Educational Film Association, Publications Working Party]. — Glasgow : The Association.

2 : Planning & staffing / by Richard N. Tucker. — 1976. — iv,56p : ill, plans ; 30cm.
Bibl.: p.55. — Index.
ISBN 0-86011-003-6 Pbk : £1.50
(B77-14161)

3 : Retrieval systems / editor Adam H. Malcolm. — 1976. — xii,46p : ill, facsims, forms ; 30cm.
Bibl.: p.vii-viii. — Index.
ISBN 0-86011-005-2 Pbk : £1.00
(B77-14162)

371.3'078 — Schools. Teaching aids: Play-games. *Collections*
Owen, Dilys. Play-games / [by] Dilys Owen. — London : Muller, 1977. — [7],72p ; 23cm.
ISBN 0-584-62053-5 : £1.95 : CIP rev.
(B77-11729)

371.3'078 — Schools. Teaching. Use of educational resources. *England*
Beswick, Norman Wilfred. Resource-based learning / [by] Norman Beswick. — London : Heinemann Educational, 1977. — xiv,264p ; 23cm. — (Heinemann organization in schools series)
Bibl.: p.243-256. — Index.
ISBN 0-435-80077-9 : £6.50
(B77-16806)

371.3'078 — Teachers' centres. Attitudes of school teachers. *Great Britain. Study examples: Kirkby-in-Ashfield Teachers' Centre. Reports, surveys*
Flood, Pamela. How teachers regard their centre, its functions, aims and use and how they feel it should be equipped and organised / by Pamela Flood. — [Nottingham] ([University Park, Nottingham NG7 2RD]) : University of Nottingham, School of Education, Further Professional Training Division, [1977]. — [1], 13p ; 30cm.
Sd : Unpriced
(B77-27775)

371.3'078 — Teaching aids. Selection. *For training*
Anderson, Ronald H. Selecting and developing media for instruction / [by] Ronald H. Anderson ; with illustrations by Pat Lynch. — Madison : American Society for Training and Development ; New York ; London [etc.] : Van Nostrand Reinhold, 1976. — x,138p : ill(some col), form ; 26cm.
Bibl.: p.133-136. — Index.
ISBN 0-442-20350-0 : £11.75
(B77-20166)

371.33'07'2041 — Education. Audio-visual aids. Research in British institutions, 1945-. *Reports, surveys*
Survey of British research in audio-visual aids. — London (33 Queen Anne St., W1M 0AL) : National Committee for Audio-Visual Aids in Education : Educational Foundation for Visual Aids.
Supplement no.3 : 1975 : (including cumulative index, 1945-1975) / compiled by Susie Rodwell. — [1976]. — 43p ; 22cm.
Index.
Pbk : £0.80
(B77-26239)

371.33'0973 — Education. Audio-visual aids. *United States. Serials*
Educational media yearbook. — New York ; London : Bowker.
1977 / edited by James W. Brown. — 1977. — xi,433p ; 24cm.
Index.
ISBN 0-8352-0948-2 : £15.75
ISSN 0000-037x
(B77-16302)

371.33'2 — Education. Teaching methods: Drama
Siks, Geraldine Brain. Drama with children / [by] Geraldine Brain Siks. — New York [etc.] ; London : Harper and Row, 1977. — xvi,252p : ill ; 24cm.
Bibl.: p.209-214. — List of audiovisual and instructional materials: p.242-244. — Index.
ISBN 0-06-046151-9 : £7.45
(B77-16303)

371.33'31'091724 — Schools. Students. Education. Use of radio programmes. *Developing countries*
Wells, Stuart. Instructional technology in developing countries : decision-making processes in education / [by] Stuart Wells. — New York [etc.] ; London : Praeger, 1976[i.e.1977]. — xii, 179p : ill ; 25cm. — (Praeger special studies in international economics and development)
Published in the United States: 1976. — Bibl.: p.165-174. — Index.
ISBN 0-275-23750-8 : £11.20
Also classified at 371.33'58'091724
(B77-12963)

371.33'58 — Educational institutions. Television services. Planning. *Manuals*
Hancock, Alan. Planning for educational mass media / [by] Alan Hancock. — London [etc.] : Longman, 1977. — viii,383p : ill, form, plans ; 23cm.
Bibl.: p.363-373. — Index.
ISBN 0-582-41055-x : £10.00
(B77-23285)

371.33'58'091724 — Schools. Students. Education. Use of television programmes. *Developing countries*
Wells, Stuart. Instructional technology in developing countries : decision-making processes in education / [by] Stuart Wells. — New York [etc.] ; London : Praeger, 1976[i.e.1977]. — xii, 179p : ill ; 25cm. — (Praeger special studies in international economics and development)
Published in the United States: 1976. — Bibl.: p.165-174. — Index.
ISBN 0-275-23750-8 : £11.20
Primary classification 371.33'31'091724
(B77-12963)

371.3'8 — Farms. Visits by school students. *Manuals. For teaching*
Young, Isabel Vivien. Farm visits / [by] I.V. Young. — 2nd ed. — London (16 Strutton Ground, SW1P 2HP) : Association of Agriculture, 1977. — [1],23p ; 21cm.
Previous ed.: 1972.
Sd : Unpriced
(B77-23286)

371.3'8 — Visits by British school students. Organisation. *For teaching*
Arkinstall, Michael James. Organizing school journeys / [by] Michael James Arkinstall. — London : Ward Lock, 1977. — 157p : ill, forms, maps ; 22cm.
Bibl.: p.153-154. — Index.
ISBN 0-7062-3608-4 Pbk : £2.50
(B77-18044)

371.39'4 — Schools. Students. Individualised instruction
Nussel, Edward J. The teacher and individually guided education / [by] Edward J. Nussel, Joan D. Inglis, William Wiersma. — Reading, Mass. ; London [etc.] : Addison-Wesley, [1977]. — xiii,322p : ill, facsim, forms ; 24cm. — (Leadership series in individually guided education)
Published in the United States: 1976. — Bibl. — Index.
ISBN 0-201-19011-7 : £8.50
(B77-12964)

371.3'94 — Schools. Tutoring by students
Children as teachers : theory and research on tutoring / edited by Vernon L. Allen. — New York [etc.] ; London : Academic Press, 1976. — xv,276p : ill ; 24cm. — (Educational psychology)
Bibl. — Index.
ISBN 0-12-052640-9 : £8.55
(B77-07870)

371.39'445 — Schools. Teaching methods. Applications of computer systems
Ellis, Allan B. The use & misuse of computers in education / [by] Allan B. Ellis. — New York ; London [etc.] : McGraw-Hill, 1974. — xiii, 226p : ill ; 24cm.
Bibl.: p.217-222. — Index.
ISBN 0-07-019236-7 : £10.15
(B77-19293)

371.39'6 — Lecturing. *Manuals*
Borrell, Peter. Lecturing / [by] Peter Borrell ; cartoons by Monica Law. — Keele ([Keele University, Keele, Staffs. ST5 5BG]) : Keele University Library, 1977. — iv,39p : ill, form ; 21cm. — (University of Keele. Library. Occasional publications ; no.14)
Bibl.: p.39.
Sd : Unpriced
(B77-31801)

371.4 — EDUCATION. GUIDANCE AND COUNSELLING

371.4'0941 — Educational institutions. Students. Counselling. *Great Britain, 1964-1974. Reports, surveys*
Daws, Peter Philip. Early days : a personal review of the beginnings of counselling in English education during the decade 1964-74 / [by] Peter P. Daws. — Cambridge : Hobsons Press [for] the Careers Research and Advisory Centre, 1976. — [2],1,64p ; 21cm. — (Careers Research and Advisory Centre. Aspects of guidance series)
Bibl.: p.57-61. — Index.
ISBN 0-86021-059-6 Pbk : £4.00
(B77-13603)

371.4'0942 — Schools. Students. Counselling. *England. Christian viewpoints*
Are our schools Christian? : a call to pastoral care / [edited] by John Callaghan and Michael Cockett. — Great Wakering : Mayhew-McCrimmon, 1975. — 144p : ill ; 21cm.
ISBN 0-85597-093-6 Pbk : £2.00
(B77-05320)

371.4'0973 — Educational institutions. Students. Counselling. *United States*
Counseling methods / edited by John D. Krumboltz, Carl E. Thoresen. — New York ; London [etc.] : Holt, Rinehart and Winston, 1976. — xvi,576p : ill, forms ; 25cm.
Bibl. — Index.
ISBN 0-03-089471-9 : £9.50
(B77-02175)

371.4'25 — Cooperative education. *United States*
Bennett, Robert L. Careers through cooperative work experience / [by] Robert L. Bennett. — New York ; London [etc.] : Wiley, 1977. — xi, 172p : ill, forms ; 23cm.
Bibl.: p.165-166. — Index.
ISBN 0-471-06634-6 Pbk : £4.50
(B77-12392)

371.4'25'08 — Careers guidance. *Readings*
Vocational guidance and career development : selected readings / [edited by] Herman J. Peters, James C. Hansen. — 3rd ed. — New York : Macmillan ; London : Collier Macmillan, 1977. — xi,481p : ill ; 24cm.
Previous ed.: New York : Macmillan, 1971. — Bibl.
ISBN 0-02-394670-9 : £7.50
(B77-32554)

371.4'25'0942 — Local education authorities. Careers guidance services. *England. Proposals*
Great Britain. *Department of Employment.* The Careers Service : guidance to local education authorities in England and Wales / [Department of Employment]. — London ([c/o Careers Service Branch, 97 Tottenham Court Rd, W1P 0ER]) : Department of Employment, 1975. — 34p ; 25cm.
ISBN 0-903314-24-x Sd : Unpriced
(B77-06577)

371.4'25'0973 — Careers guidance. *United States*
Hoppock, Robert. Occupational information : where to get it and how to use it in career education, career counseling, and career development / [by] Robert Hoppock. — 4th ed. — New York ; London [etc.] : McGraw-Hill, 1976. — xiii,383p ; 25cm.
Previous ed.: New York : McGraw-Hill, 1967. — Bibl.: p.351-369. — Index.
ISBN 0-07-030330-4 : £11.60
(B77-06578)

371.4'6 — Schools. Curriculum subjects: Solution of personal problems. Teaching. *United States*
Morrison, Donald W. Personal problem solving in the classroom : the reality technique / [by] Donald W. Morrison. — New York ; London [etc.] : Wiley, 1977. — xiii,186p ; 22cm.
Bibl.: p.170-174. — Index.
ISBN 0-471-61610-9 Pbk : £4.50
(B77-14656)

371.4'6 — Schools. Students. Interpersonal relationships. Teaching. *Manuals*
Human relations development : a manual for educators / [by] George M. Gazda ... [et al.]. — 2nd ed. — Boston [Mass.] ; London [etc.] : Allyn and Bacon, 1977. — viii,232p : ill ; 24cm.
Previous ed.: Boston, Mass. : Allyn and Bacon, 1973. — Bibl. — Index.
ISBN 0-205-05566-4 : Unpriced
ISBN 0-205-05558-3 Pbk : Unpriced
(B77-10307)

371.4'6 — Schools. Welfare officers. *Great Britain*
Clark, Janet, *b.1921.* Education welfare officers : a study of the work of education welfare officers and consideration of the future development of the service / [by] Janet Clark. — [Potters Bar] ([33 Heathfield Close, Potters Bar, Herts. EN1 1SP]) : [The author], [1977]. — viii,87p ; 21cm.
'Dissertation submitted in part fulfillment of the requirements for the degree of M.A. in Education of the University of London, Institute of Education 1976'. — Bibl.: p.84-87.
Pbk : Unpriced
(B77-16807)

371.4'6'0942 — Local authority education welfare services. *England*
MacMillan, Keith, *b.1945.* Education welfare : strategy and structure / [by] Keith MacMillan. — London [etc.] : Longman, 1977. — vii,165p : form ; 23cm.
Bibl.: p.157-160. — Index.
ISBN 0-582-48688-2 : £4.50
ISBN 0-582-48689-0 Pbk : £2.50
(B77-29320)

371.5 — SCHOOL DISCIPLINE
371.5 — Truancy. *Scotland. Inquiry reports*
Truancy and indiscipline in schools in Scotland : the Pack report : report of a Committee of Inquiry appointed by the Secretary of State for Scotland / (chairman D.C. Pack). — [Edinburgh] : H.M.S.O., 1977. — xi,139p : 1 ill, form ; 25cm.
'Scottish Education Department'. — Bibl.: p.137-139.
ISBN 0-11-491496-6 Pbk : £2.50
Also classified at 371.5'09411
(B77-30105)

371.5'09411 — Schools. Discipline. *Scotland. Inquiry reports*
Truancy and indiscipline in schools in Scotland : the Pack report : report of a Committee of Inquiry appointed by the Secretary of State for Scotland / (chairman D.C. Pack). — [Edinburgh] : H.M.S.O., 1977. — xi,139p : 1 ill, form ; 25cm.
'Scottish Education Department'. — Bibl.: p.137-139.
ISBN 0-11-491496-6 Pbk : £2.50
Primary classification 371.5
(B77-30105)

371.6 — SCHOOL BUILDINGS AND EQUIPMENT
371.6'2'0942 — Schools. Buildings. *England, 1370-1970*
Seaborne, Malcolm. The English school : its architecture and organization / [by] Malcolm Seaborne. — London [etc.] : Routledge and Kegan Paul.
In 2 vols.
Vol.2 : 1870-1970 / [by] Malcolm Seaborne and Roy Lowe. — 1977. — xix,240p,[32]p of plates : ill, map, plans ; 26cm.
Bibl.: p.215-225. — Index.
ISBN 0-7100-8408-0 : £15.00
(B77-18675)

371.6'2'0973 — Schools. Buildings. Space & facilities. Allocation. *United States*
Planning flexible learning places / [by] Stanton Leggett ... [et al.]. — New York ; London [etc.] : McGraw-Hill, 1977. — viii,183p : ill, forms, plans ; 25cm.
Index.
ISBN 0-07-037060-5 : Unpriced
(B77-23287)

371.6'24'0973 — Schools. Physical education facilities. Planning. *United States*
Penman, Kenneth Albert. Planning physical education & athletic facilities in schools / [by] Kenneth A. Penman. — New York ; London [etc.] : Wiley, 1977. — ix,443p : ill, plans ; 24cm.
Bibl. — Index.
ISBN 0-471-67915-1 : £9.85
(B77-31091)

371.7 — SCHOOL HYGIENE
371.7'12 — Schools. Nursing services. *England, 1973. Reports, surveys*
Thurmott, Priscilla. Health and the school : an exploratory survey of the school nursing service in an English county / [by] Priscilla Thurmott. — London : Henrietta Place, Cavendish Sq., W1M 0AB : The Royal College of Nursing of the United Kingdom, 1976. — 71p : forms ; 22cm. — (Royal College of Nursing. Research series)
Bibl.: p.70-71.
ISBN 0-902606-51-4 Pbk : £2.00
(B77-10308)

371.7'7 — Schools. Safety measures. *Manuals*
Great Britain. *Department of Education and Science.* Safety at school : general advice / Department of Education and Science. — London : H.M.S.O., 1977. — iv,47p ; 21cm. — (DES safety series ; no.6)
Index.
ISBN 0-11-270441-7 Sd : £0.90
(B77-20167)

371.7'75 — Schools. Laboratories. Safety measures. *Great Britain. Manuals*
Armitage, Phillip. Laboratory safety : a science teachers' source book / [by] Phillip Armitage, Johnson Fasemore. — London : Heinemann Educational, 1977. — vi,82p : ill, forms ; 22cm.
Bibl.: p.57-58. — Index.
ISBN 0-435-57050-1 Sd : £1.20
(B77-27776)

371.8 — EDUCATION. STUDENTS
371.8'1 — Schools. Damage by students. *Great Britain*
Stone, Judith. Vandalism in schools / [written by Judith Stone and Felicity Taylor]. — [London] ([157 Clapham Rd, SW9 0PT]) : [Save the Children Fund], [1977]. — [1],52p : ill ; 15x21cm.
Bibl.: p.49.
Sd : £1.00
(B77-26240)

371.8'1 — Schools. Students. Behaviour problems. *Staffordshire. Reports, surveys*
Disruptive pupils in schools : report of a working party established by the Staffordshire Education Committee. — [Stafford] ([County Education Offices, Earl St., Stafford]) : [Staffordshire Education Committee], 1977. — [1],120p ; 21cm.
Pbk : Unpriced
(B77-16809)

371.8'1 — Schools. Students. Behaviour problems. Treatment. *Great Britain. Urban regions. For teaching. Case studies*
Successful teaching in the urban school / introduced and edited by Paul Widlake. — London : Ward Lock, 1976. — 157p : ill ; 22cm.
Bibl.: p.149-154. — Index.
ISBN 0-7062-3484-7 Pbk : £2.50
(B77-00131)

371.8'1 — Schools. Students. Development. Role of drama. *Great Britain. For teaching*
Slade, Peter. Child drama and its value in education / [by] Peter Slade. — [Bromley] ([1 Hawthorndene Rd, Hayes, Bromley, Kent BR2 7DZ]) : Educational Drama Association, 1974. — 18p ; 21cm.
'Given at the 1st Drama Conference of the Department of Education and Science for Wales, Bangor University, April 1965'. — Originally published: 1966.
ISBN 0-9501295-6-9 Sd : Unpriced
(B77-06579)

371.9 — EDUCATION. EXCEPTIONAL PUPILS
371.9 — Children. Learning disorders. Neuropsychological aspects. *Conference proceedings*
International Conference on Neuropsychology of Learning Disorders, *Korsor, 1975.* The neuropsychology of learning disorders : theoretical approaches / edited by Robert M. Knights and Dirk J. Bakker. — Baltimore ; London [etc.] : University Park Press, [1977]. — xvii,532p : ill ; 24cm.
'Proceedings of the International Conference on Neuropsychology of Learning Disorders, held at Korsor, Denmark, June 15-18, 1975' - half title page verso. — Published in the United States: 1976. — Bibl.: p.469-521. — Index.
ISBN 0-8391-0951-2 : £13.95
(B77-12965)

371.9 — Children. Learning disorders. Psychological aspects
Ross, Alan Otto. Psychological aspects of learning disabilities & reading disorders / [by] Alan O. Ross. — New York ; London [etc.] : McGraw-Hill, 1976. — xiii,191p : ill ; 25cm. — (McGraw-Hill series in special education)
Bibl.: p.170-178. — Index.
ISBN 0-07-053845-x : £9.10
(B77-04700)

371.9 — Children with learning disorders & deviant children. Education. *For teaching*
Leach, D J. Learning and behaviour difficulties in school / [by] D.J. Leach and E.C. Raybould. — London : Open Books, 1977. — viii,168p : 2 ill ; 21cm. — (Psychology and education)
Bibl.: p.158-167. — Index.
ISBN 0-7291-0076-6 : £4.50
ISBN 0-7291-0071-5 Pbk : £1.95
(B77-15224)

371.9 — Children with learning disorders. Remedial education
Johnson, Stanley W. Learning disabilities / [by] Stanley W. Johnson, Robert L. Morasky. — Boston, Mass. ; London [etc.] : Allyn and Bacon, 1977. — xi,415p : ill, form ; 25cm.
Bibl. — Index.
ISBN 0-205-05546-x : Unpriced
(B77-12966)

371.9 — Children with learning disorders. Remedial education. Linguistic aspects
Gurney, Roger. Language, learning and remedial teaching / [by] Roger Gurney. — London : Edward Arnold, 1976. — 108p ; 22cm. — (Explorations in language study)
Bibl.: p.108.
ISBN 0-7131-0081-8 Pbk : £2.40
(B77-03479)

371.9 — Crammers. *Great Britain*
Palmer, Carey. Crammers / [by] Carey Palmer. — London : Duckworth, 1977. — [6],62p : ill ; 23cm.
ISBN 0-7156-1105-4 : £3.95
ISBN 0-7156-1106-2 Pbk : £0.95
(B77-30106)

371.9 — Educationally disadvantaged persons. Adult education. *Great Britain. Conference proceedings*
Jones, Henry Arthur, *b.1917.* Education and disadvantage / by H.A. Jones. — [Leicester] ([The University, Leicester LE1 7RH]) : University of Leicester, Department of Adult Education, 1977. — [3],18p ; 21cm. — (Vaughan paper ; no.22 ISSN 0308-9258)
'Keynote address at the conference of the European Bureau of Adult Education at Farnham Castle, England on 6-10 September 1976'.
ISBN 0-901507-10-5 Sd : £0.35
(B77-26241)

371.9 — Handicapped children. Education
Bender, Michael. Teaching the moderately and severely handicapped : curriculum objectives, strategies and activities / [by] Michael Bender, Peter J. Valletutti. — Baltimore ; London [etc.] : University Park Press.
In 3 vols.
Vol.2 : Communication, socialization, safety and leisure time skills / [by] Michael Bender, Peter J. Valletutti with Rosemary Bender. — [1977]. — xi,420p : ill, forms ; 23cm.
Published in the United States: 1976. — Bibl.
ISBN 0-8391-0868-0 Sp : £11.95
(B77-11730)

Vol.3 : Functional academics for the mildly and moderately handicapped / [by] Michael Bender, Peter J. Valletutti and Rosemary Bender. — [1977]. — viii,263p : ill ; 23cm.
Published in the United States: 1976. — Bibl.: p.258-263.
ISBN 0-8391-0963-6 Sp : £9.95
(B77-11731)

Teaching special children / edited by Norris G. Haring and Richard L. Schiefelbusch ; technical editor Robert K. Hoyt, Jr. — New York ; London [etc.] : McGraw-Hill, 1976. — xiii, 417p : ill, forms ; 25cm. — (McGraw-Hill series in special education)
Bibl.: p.387-405. — Index.
ISBN 0-07-026430-9 : £10.75
(B77-03480)

371.9 — Handicapped children. Education. Behavioural aspects
Gardner, William I. Learning and behavior characteristics of exceptional children and youth : a humanistic behavioral approach / [by] William I. Gardner. — Boston, Mass. ; London [etc.] : Allyn and Bacon, 1977. — xiii,593p : ill, forms ; 24cm.
Bibl. — Index.
ISBN 0-205-05586-9 : Unpriced
(B77-17399)

371.9 — Handicapped children. Teaching
Donlon, Edward T. The severely and profoundly handicapped : a practical approach to teaching / [by] Edward T. Donlon, Louise F. Burton. — New York [etc.] ; London : Grune and Stratton, 1976. — x,262p : 1 ill, forms ; 24cm.
Bibl. — Index.
ISBN 0-8089-0952-5 : £10.05
(B77-01294)

371.9 — Hospital schools. *England. Reports, surveys*
National Association of Head Teachers. Hospital schools in England and Wales : a report / prepared by the National Association of Head Teachers. — [Haywards Heath] ([41 Bottro Rd, Haywards Heath, W. Sussex RH16 1BJ]) : [The Association], [1976]. — [1],24p ; 21cm.
ISBN 0-904840-01-8 Sd : £0.20
(B77-14163)

371.9 — Secondary schools. Children with learning disorders. *United States*
Goodman, Libby. Learning disabilities in the secondary school : issues and practice / [by] Libby Goodman, Lester Mann. — New York [etc.] ; London : Grune and Stratton, [1977]. — xi,256p ; 24cm.
Published in the United States: 1976. — Bibl.: p.171-247. — Index.
ISBN 0-8089-0949-5 : £10.05
(B77-13604)

371.9'043 — Handicapped children. Education in camps. *Manuals*
Shea, Thomas Michael. Camping for special children / [by] Thomas M. Shea. — Saint Louis : Mosby ; London : Distributed by Kimpton, 1977. — xi,244p : ill, forms ; 26cm.
Bibl. — Index.
ISBN 0-8016-4566-2 : £8.55
(B77-19294)

371.9'043'0973 — Children with learning disorders. Education. Teaching methods. *United States*
Gearheart, Bill Ray. Learning disabilities : educational strategies / [by] Bill R. Gearheart. — 2nd ed. — Saint Louis : Mosby ; London : Distributed by Kimpton, 1977. — xv,258p : ill ; 27cm.
Previous ed.: 1973. — Bibl. — Index.
ISBN 0-8016-1767-7 : £9.55
(B77-18676)

371.9'044 — Handicapped persons. Physical education
Arnheim, Daniel David. Principles and methods of adapted physical education and recreation / [by] Daniel D. Arnheim, David Auxter, Walter C. Crowe. — 3rd ed. — Saint Louis : Mosby ; London : Distributed by Kimpton, 1977. — ix, 528p : ill, forms, plans ; 27cm.
Previous ed.: published as 'Principles and methods of adapted physical education'. 1973. — Bibl. — Index.
ISBN 0-8016-0320-x : £11.25
(B77-22489)

371.9'0942 — Remedial education. *England. Readings*
Remedial education : programmes and progress : a reader / edited and introduced by Paul Widlake ; for the National Association for Remedial Education from the journal 'Remedial education'. — London : Longman for the National Association for Remedial Education, 1977. — xvi,368p : ill ; 22cm.
Bibl.
ISBN 0-582-36317-9 : £6.95
ISBN 0-582-36314-4 Pbk : £3.25
(B77-16304)

371.9'0973 — Handicapped children. Education. *United States. Reviews of research*
The **third** review of special education / Lester Mann, editor, David A. Sabatino, editor. — New York [etc.] ; London : Grune and Stratton, [1977]. — viii,277p : 3 ill ; 24cm.
Published in the United States: 1976. — Bibl. — Index.
ISBN 0-8089-0979-7 : £16.25
(B77-13605)

371.9'1 — Further education institutions. Physically handicapped students. *Great Britain. Reports, surveys*
Child, Derek. The disabled student / [by Derek Child and Graham Markall]. — [London] ([49 Victoria St., S.W.1]) : Action Research for the Crippled Child ; [London] : NUS Publications, 1976. — vi,41p : forms ; 21cm.
Sd : £0.40
(B77-26242)

371.9'1 — Physically handicapped children. Education
Haskell, Simon Hai. The education of motor and neurologically handicapped children / [by] Simon H. Haskell, Elizabeth K. Barrett, [and] Helen Taylor. — London : Croom Helm [etc.], 1977. — 3-195p : ill.
'A Halsted Press book'. — Bibl.: p.187-193. — Index.
ISBN 0-85664-149-9 : £6.95 : CIP rev.
(B77-23288)

371.9'1 — Physically handicapped children. Education. Curriculum subjects: Home economics
Handscomb, Sue. The disabled schoolchild and kitchen sense / [by] Sydney Foott, editor ; Sue Handscomb, Marian Lane ; [illustrated by] Brenda Naylor. — London : Heinemann Health for the Disabled Living Foundation, 1976. — xii,96p : ill ; 21cm.
Bibl.: p.88-89. — Index.
ISBN 0-433-10666-2 Pbk : £1.75
(B77-08319)

371.9'1 — Physically handicapped children. Physical education. *United States. Manuals. For teaching*
Crowe, Walter Campbell. Laboratory manual in adapted physical education and recreation : experiments, activities, and assignments / [by] Walter C. Crowe, Daniel D. Arnheim, David Auxter. — Saint Louis : Mosby ; London : Distributed by Kimpton, 1977. — xi,244p : ill, forms ; 27cm.
Pages perforated at inside edge. — Pierced for binder. — Bibl.
ISBN 0-8016-1099-0 Pbk : £7.15
(B77-31802)

371.9'1'0942189 — Physically handicapped children. Education. *London. Enfield (London Borough). Reports, surveys*
Enfield Association for Education. Education for the physically handicapped and for the delicate : report of study group 1973-76 / Enfield Association for Education ; [report compiled by Valerie Brooker et al.]. — London (25 Forestdale, N14 7DY) : The Association, [1977]. — [1],60p ; 22cm. — (Special children ; 4)
Chairman of study group: Valerie Brooker, and, Molly Woodley. — Bibl.: p.60.
ISBN 0-9500529-4-9 Sd : £0.80
(B77-14657)

371.9'11'0942 — Schools. Blind students & partially sighted students. Integration into schools. *England*
Jamieson, Monika. Towards integration : a study of blind and partially sighted children in ordinary schools / [by] Monika Jamieson, Malcolm Parlett and Keith Pocklington. — Windsor : NFER, 1977. — 251p ; 22cm. — (National Foundation for Educational Research in England and Wales. Reports)
Bibl.: p.237-238.
ISBN 0-85633-119-8 Pbk : £6.25
(B77-15777)

371.9'12 — Deaf school leavers. *Great Britain. Reports, surveys*
National Deaf Children's Society. The deaf school-leaver / [National Deaf Children's Society]. — London (31 Gloucester Place, W1H 3EA) : The Society, [1977]. — 13,[4]leaves ; 30cm.
Sd : £0.30
(B77-26980)

371.9'12'05 — Deaf children. Education. *Periodicals*
The **teacher** of the deaf : the journal of the British Association of Teachers of the Deaf. — Bolton (20 Devonshire Rd, Bolton, Lancs.) : The Association.
Vol.1, no.1- ; Jan. 1977-. — [1977]-. — ill, ports ; 25cm.
Six issues a year. — [2], 56p. in 1st issue. — Previously issued by the National College of Teachers of the Deaf. — Bibl.
Sd : £0.75
ISSN 0040-0459
(B77-08941)

371.9'14 — Children with speech disorders. Remedial education
Eisenson, Jon. Speech correction in the schools / [by] Jon Eisenson, Mardel Ogilvie. — 4th ed. — New York : Macmillan ; London : Collier Macmillan, 1977. — vii,452p : ill ; 25cm.
Previous ed.: 1971. — Bibl. — Index.
ISBN 0-02-332070-2 : £9.75
(B77-24832)

371.9'14 — Dyslexic children. Education. Effects of Education Act 1944. *England*
Morris, John C. The Education Act, how it provides for handicapped children : basic legal information which applies to the education of all handicapped pupils and to the dyslexic in particular / by John C. Morris. A dyslexic child in the family : a psychiatrist's sensitive and helpful consideration of the emotional tight-rope to be negotiated by parents / by A.F. Cheyne. — London (78 Whitehall Park, N19 3TN) : London Dyslexia Association, [1977]. — [12]p ; 30cm.
'Transcripts of two lectures given at a Conference of the North London Dyslexia Association, March 1976'.
Sd : £0.70
Also classified at 362.7'8'2
(B77-17400)

371.9'14 — Dyslexic children. Speech disorders. *For remedial teaching*
Hamilton-Fairley, Daphne. Dyslexia, speech therapy and the dyslexic / by Daphne Hamilton-Fairley. — London (14 Crondace Rd, SW6 4BB) : Helen Arkell Dyslexia Centre, 1976. — [2],26p : ill ; 21cm.
ISBN 0-9503626-8-9 Sd : £0.65
(B77-02176)

371.9'14 — Persons with dyslexia. Writing skills. Teaching. *Manuals*
Hornsby, Bevé. Alpha to omega : the A-Z of teaching reading, writing and spelling / by Bevé Hornsby and Frula Shear. — 2nd ed. (revised and reset). — London : Heinemann Educational, 1976. — x,286p : ill ; 22cm.
'First published (privately) 1974 ; first published by Heinemann Educational Books 1975' - title page verso. — Bibl.: p.266-268. — Index.
Sp : £2.75
ISBN 0-435-10380-6
(B77-02177)

Hornsby, Bevé. Alpha to omega : the A-Z of teaching reading, writing and spelling / by Bevé Hornsby and Frula Shear. — 2nd ed.(revised and reset). — London : Heinemann Educational.
'First published (privately) 1974 ; first published by Heinemann Educational Books 1975' - title page verso.
Flash cards. — 1976. — Case : ill ; 9x14x10cm.

Two hundred and thirty nine cards ([322] sides).
ISBN 0-435-10381-4 : £5.67
(B77-02896)

371.9'2 — Autistic children. Education. *For teaching*
Autistic children : teaching, community and research approaches / compiled and edited by Barbara Furneaux and Brian Roberts with contributions from Sybil Elgar ... [et al.]. — London [etc.] : Routledge and Kegan Paul, 1977. — xiv,193p ; 23cm. — (Special needs in education)
ISBN 0-7100-8704-7 : £5.50 : CIP rev.
(B77-21805)

371.9'2 — Autistic children. Speech. Teaching. Use of behaviour modification
Lovaas, Ole Ivar. The autistic child : language development through behavior modification / by O. Ivar Lovaas. — New York : Irvington ; New York ; London [etc.] : Distributed by Wiley, 1977. — ix,246[i.e.262]p : ill ; 25cm.
Bibl. — Index.
ISBN 0-470-15065-3 : £11.00
(B77-23289)

371.9'2 — Educationally subnormal children. Assessment. *United States. Manuals*
Lambert, Nadine M. The educationally retarded child : comprehensive assessment and planning for slow learners and the educable mentally retarded / [by] Nadine M. Lambert, Margaret R. Wilcox, W. Preston Gleason. — New York ; London : Grune and Stratton, 1974. — xiii, 197p : ill ; 23cm.
Index.
ISBN 0-8089-0836-7 Pbk : Unpriced
(B77-19295)

371.9'2'0924 — Schools for educationally subnormal children. *London. Hackney (London Borough). Downsview School. Personal observations*
Wakefield, Tom. Special school / [by] Tom Wakefield. — London [etc.] : Routledge and Kegan Paul, 1977. — xi,8-159p ; 22cm.
Originally published: as 'He's much better, he can smile now'. Newton Abbot : David and Charles, 1974.
ISBN 0-7100-8750-0 Pbk : £2.25 : CIP rev.
(B77-24833)

371.9'26 — Schools. Slow learning students. Teaching
Haigh, Gerald. Teaching slow learners / [by] Gerald Haigh. — London : Temple Smith, 1977. — 155p ; 23cm.
Bibl.: p.153-155.
ISBN 0-85117-128-1 : £5.50
ISBN 0-85117-131-1 Pbk : £3.00
(B77-24120)

371.9'26 — Secondary schools. Slow learning students. Curriculum subjects: English language. Teaching. *Scotland. Inquiry reports*
Scottish Central Committee on English. English for slower learning children in the Scottish secondary school : the report of a sub-committee / Scottish Education Department, Scottish Central Committee on English. — Edinburgh : H.M.S.O., 1977. — vii, 79p : ill, forms ; 25cm.
Bibl.
ISBN 0-11-491467-2 Sd : £2.50
(B77-14658)

371.9'26 — Slow learning children. *Reports, surveys*
Jackson, Charles Herbert. 'They say my child's backward' : a guide to the understanding and development of backward children for parents, educationalists, psychologists and others / by Charles Herbert Jackson. — [New ed.]. — London (Pembridge Hall, Pembridge Sq., W2 4EP) : National Society for Mentally Handicapped Children, 1976. — [6],24p ; 22cm.

Previous ed.: 1970.
ISBN 0-85537-036-x Sd : £0.50
(B77-02178)

371.9'26 — Slow learning children. Education. Curriculum subjects: Music. Teaching
Ward, David, *b.1932 (Sept.).* Hearts and hands and voices : music in the education of slow learners / [by] David Ward. — London [etc.] : Oxford University Press, 1976. — vii,87p,8p of plates : ill, music ; 19cm.
Bibl.: p.86. — List of music : p.80-84. — List of sound discs : p.84-85.
ISBN 0-19-314921-4 Pbk : £1.95
(B77-04701)

371.9'26 — Slow learning children. Teaching
Haring, Norris Grover. Teaching the learning disabled child / [by] Norris G. Haring, Barbara Bateman with ... [others]. — Englewood Cliffs ; London [etc.] : Prentice-Hall, 1977. — viii, 343p : ill ; 24cm. — (The Prentice-Hall series in special education)
Bibl. — Index.
ISBN 0-13-893503-3 : £9.55
(B77-23290)

371.9'28 — Mentally handicapped adolescents, 16-21 years. Education. *England*
The **education** of mentally handicapped young adults / editors R.J. Kedney and E. Whelan. — Bolton (Chadwick St., Bolton BL2 1JW) : Bolton College of Education (Technical), 1976. — [2],vi,137p : ill, form ; 21cm.
'This is a report of the proceedings of a study-conference of three one-day meetings ...' - Foreword. — Bibl.
ISBN 0-9504588-2-1 Pbk : £2.00
(B77-11732)

371.9'28 — Mentally handicapped children. Sex education. *For parents*
Shennan, Victoria. Help your child to understand sex / [by] Victoria Shennan. — London (Pembridge Hall, Pembridge Sq., W2 4EP) : National Society for Mentally Handicapped Children, 1976. — 8p ; 21cm.
ISBN 0-85537-039-4 Sd : £0.30
(B77-08942)

371.9'28 — Mentally handicapped children. Sex education. *For teaching*
Lee, George William. Sex education and the mentally retarded / [by] George W. Lee. — London (Pembridge Hall, Pembridge Sq., W2 4EP) : National Society for Mentally Handicapped Children, 1976. — 13p ; 21cm.
'Based on an address given by George W. Lee at an International Symposium on Sexuality and the Mentally Handicapped. Marburg, Germany, September 1975' - note. — Bibl.: p.13.
ISBN 0-85537-040-8 Sd : £0.50
(B77-10309)

371.9'28 — Mentally handicapped children. Sex education. Role of television programmes. *Great Britain*
Lowes, Lindsay. Sex and social training : a programme for young adults / [by] Lindsay Lowes. — London (Pembridge Hall, Pembridge Sq., W2 4EP) : National Society for Mentally Handicapped Children, 1977. — 7p ; 21cm.
Bibl.: p.7.
Sd : £0.30
(B77-32555)

371.9'28 — Mentally retarded children. Education
Kolstoe, Oliver Paul. Teaching educable mentally retarded children / [by] Oliver P. Kolstoe. — 2nd ed. — New York [etc.] ; London : Holt, Rinehart and Winston, 1976. — x,308p : ill ; 24cm.
Previous ed.: 1970. — Index.
ISBN 0-03-089724-6 : £6.75
(B77-01295)

371.9'28 — Mentally retarded children. Teaching
Smith, Robert McNeil. Clinical teaching : methods of instruction for the retarded / [by] Robert M. Smith. — 2nd ed. — New York ; London [etc.] : McGraw-Hill, 1974. — ix, 366p : ill, form ; 24cm. — (McGraw-Hill series in special education)
Previous ed.: 1968. — Bibl. — Index.
ISBN 0-07-058906-2 : Unpriced
(B77-18677)

371.9'28'09794 — Mentally handicapped children. Education. *California*
Milofsky, Carl. Special education : a sociological study of California programs / [by] Carl Milofsky. — New York [etc.] ; London : Praeger, 1976. — xxv,177,[1]p : ill ; 25cm. — (Praeger special studies in US economic, social and political issues)
Bibl.: p.166-174. — Index.
ISBN 0-275-56940-3 : £12.95
(B77-15225)

371.9'283 — Trainable mentally retarded children. Education
Baumgartner, Bernice B. Helping every trainable mentally retarded child / [by] Bernice B. Baumgartner. — [Revised ed.]. — New York ; London : Teachers College Press, 1975. — xi, 97p : 2 ill ; 21cm. — (Teachers College series in special education)
Previous ed.: published as 'Helping the trainable mentally retarded child'. New York : Bureau of Publications, Teachers College, Columbia University, 1960. — Bibl.: p.92-97.
ISBN 0-8077-2472-6 Pbk : Unpriced
(B77-19296)

371.9'284 — Severely mentally handicapped persons. Education
Teaching the severely handicapped / edited by Norris G. Haring, Louis J. Brown. — New York [etc.] ; London : Grune and Stratton.
In 2 vols.
Vol.1. — [1977]. — x,335p : ill, forms ; 24cm.
'The papers ... are outgrowths of presentations made at a seminar in Kansas City in November 1974' - Preface. — Published in the United States: 1976. — Bibl. — Index.
ISBN 0-8089-0945-2 : £13.85
(B77-12967)

Vol.2. — 1977. — vi,346p : ill, forms ; 24cm.
Papers presented at the Second Annual Conference of the American Association for the Education of the Severely/Profoundly Handicapped, Kansas City, Missouri, November 12-14, 1975. — Bibl. — Index.
ISBN 0-8089-0980-0 : £13.85
(B77-17401)

371.9'284 — Severely subnormal children. Education. Curriculum subjects: Music. *Research reports*
Hunt, Ann. Listen, let's make music / by Ann Hunt. — London : Bedford Square Press for the Standing Conference for Amateur Music, 1976. — 43p : ill, music ; 21cm.
Bibl.: p.37.
ISBN 0-7199-0920-1 Sd : £0.70
(B77-09640)

371.9'284'0973 — Severely subnormal children. Education. *United States*
Educating the severely and profoundly retarded / compiled and edited by Robert M. Anderson, and John G. Greer ; with a foreword by Robert M. Smith. — Baltimore ; London [etc.] : University Park Press, 1976. — xvii,422p : ill, ports ; 22cm.
Bibl. — Index.
ISBN 0-8391-0945-8 Pbk : £10.75
(B77-06580)

371.9'4 — Maladjusted children. Remedial education. *Colorado. Case studies*
Simon, Sidney B. Developing values with exceptional children / [by] Sidney B. Simon, Robert D. O'Rourke. — Englewood Cliffs ; London [etc.] : Prentice-Hall, 1977. — xiii, 140p : ill ; 23cm.
ISBN 0-13-205310-1 Pbk : £4.80
(B77-28533)

371.9'4'0941 — Maladjusted children. Education. *Great Britain*
Laslett, Robert. Educating maladjusted children / [by] Robert Laslett. — London : Crosby Lockwood Staples, 1977. — x,269p ; 23cm.
Bibl.: p.256-265. — Index.
ISBN 0-258-96957-1 : £7.50
(B77-12968)

371.9'5 — Gifted children. Education
Vernon, Philip Ewart. The psychology and education of gifted children / [by] Philip E. Vernon, Georgina Adamson and Dorothy F. Vernon. — London : Methuen, 1977. — viii, 216p : ill ; 23cm.
Bibl.: p.197-208. — Index.
ISBN 0-416-84390-5 : £5.95
ISBN 0-416-84400-6 Pbk : £2.95
Also classified at 155.4'5'5
(B77-18046)

371.9'5'0941 — Comprehensive schools & middle schools. Gifted students. *Great Britain. Reports, surveys*
Great Britain. *Department of Education and Science. HM Inspectorate (England).* Gifted children in middle and comprehensive secondary schools : a discussion paper / by a working party of Her Majesty's Inspectorate. — London : H.M.S.O., 1977. — [2],ii,103p ; 25cm. — (Matters for discussion ; 4 ISSN 0309-5746)
ISBN 0-11-270444-1 Pbk : £1.75
(B77-25516)

371.9'67 — Dublin. Socially disadvantaged pre-school children. Compensatory education. Projects
Kellaghan, Thomas. The evaluation of an intervention programme for disadvantaged children / [by] Thomas Kellaghan. — Windsor : NFER, 1977. — 3-145p : ill ; 22cm.
Bibl.: p.128-145.
ISBN 0-85633-124-4 Pbk : £4.75
(B77-24121)

371.9'67 — Infant schools. Socially disadvantaged students. *England. Research reports*
Schools Council Research and Development Project in Compensatory Education. Studies of infant school children / Schools Council Research and Development Project in Compensatory Education. — Oxford : Blackwell.
1 : Deprivation and school progress / [by] Maurice Chazan ... [et al.]. — 1976. — xvi, 499p : ill, forms ; 26cm.
Bibl.: p.341-345. — Index.
ISBN 0-631-17050-2 : £30.00
(B77-11733)

371.9'67 — Political refugees. Education. *Great Britain. Reports, surveys*
World University Service (UK). Education for refugees / [World University Service (UK)]. — London (260 High Rd, N15 4AJ) : W.U.S. (U.K.), 1977. — [4],86p ; 30cm.
Pbk : £1.00
(B77-23291)

371.9'67 — Socially disadvantaged children, 2-8 years. Compensatory education. *Conference proceedings*
Hyman Blumberg Symposium on Research in Early Childhood Education, *2nd, Johns Hopkins University, 1972.* Compensatory education for children ages two to eight : recent studies of educational intervention : proceedings of the Second Annual Hyman Blumberg Symposium on Research in Early Childhood Education / edited by Julian C. Stanley. — Baltimore ; London : Johns Hopkins University Press, 1973. — ix,212,[1]p : ill ; 24cm.
Bibl. — Index.
ISBN 0-8018-1457-x : Unpriced
ISBN 0-8018-1461-8 Pbk : Unpriced
(B77-18678)

371.9'67 — Socially disadvantaged persons. Vocational education. United States. Related to employment. *Forecasts for 1976-1985*
Lecht, Leonard Abe. Occupational choices and training needs : prospects for the 1980s / [by] Leonard A. Lecht. — New York ; London : Praeger [for] the Conference Board, 1977. — xv,205p ; 25cm. — (Praeger special studies in US economic, social and political issues)
Index.
ISBN 0-275-23960-8 : £12.40
Primary classification 331.5
(B77-24765)

371.9'67 — Socially disadvantaged pre-school children. Compensatory education. Projects. *Berkshire. Slough. Research reports*
National Foundation for Educational Research in England and Wales. *Pre-School Project.* An experiment in nursery education : report of the NFER Pre-School Project / [by] H.L. Williams ... [et al.] ; edited by Martin Woodhead. — Windsor : NFER, 1976. — 123p : ill ; 22cm.
Bibl.: p.119-123.
ISBN 0-85633-122-8 Pbk : £3.95
(B77-15226)

371.9'67 — Socially disadvantaged pre-school children. Compensatory education. Projects: West Riding EPA Project. *West Yorkshire (Metropolitan County). Reports, surveys*
West Riding EPA Project. Red House early education programmes / West Riding EPA Project. — [Oxford] ([40 Wellington St., Oxford]) : Department of Social and Administrative Studies, Oxford University.
Part A : The impact of preschool : a review of American experience and an account of the local setting. — [1975]. — [5],29p ; 30cm. — (Follow up studies)
Bibl.: p.20-21.
ISBN 0-905627-02-4 Sd : Unpriced
(B77-02897)

Part B : Preschool follow-up study : a longitudinal investigation of the Preschool Groups which participated in the Red House Education Centre Preschool Experiment, 1969-71. — [1975]. — 3,92[i.e.98]p : ill ; 30cm. — (Follow up studies)
ISBN 0-905627-01-6 Sd : Unpriced
(B77-02898)

Part C : Preschool and home-visiting programmes, 1972-3 : a concurrent evaluation of the preschool and home-visited groups operated by the Red House Social Education Centre, September 1972-July 1973. — [1975]. — [5],129[i.e.132]p ; 30cm. — (Follow up studies)
ISBN 0-905627-03-2 Sd : Unpriced
(B77-02899)

371.9'67 — Special education. Influence of education of feral children: Victor of Aveyron
Lane, Harlan. The wild boy of Aveyron / [by] Harlan Lane. — London : Allen and Unwin, 1977. — [14],351p : facsim, ports ; 24cm.
Originally published: Cambridge, Mass. : Harvard University Press, 1976. — Bibl.: p.293-317. — Index.
ISBN 0-04-155007-2 : £6.95
(B77-15227)

371.9'672'0941 — Socially disadvantaged children. Education. *Great Britain. Urban regions. Conference proceedings*
Education and the urban crisis / edited by Frank Field. — London [etc.] : Routledge and Kegan Paul, 1977. — vii,149p ; 23cm.
'... papers which were prepared for the two Calouste Gulbenkian conferences on education and the urban crisis' - Preface. — Not the same as B73-03544.
ISBN 0-7100-8535-4 : £3.50
(B77-08320)

371.9'672'0973 — Socially disadvantaged children. Compensatory education. *United States. Urban regions*
Boyd, John, *b.1935.* Community education and urban schools / [by] John Boyd. — London [etc.] : Longman, 1977. — vii,82p ; 22cm.
Bibl.: p.77-79. — Index.
ISBN 0-582-48945-8 Pbk : £1.95
(B77-33152)

371.9'7 — Bilingual education
The **bilingual** child : research and analysis of existing educational themes / edited by António Simões, Jr. — New York [etc.] ; London : Academic Press, 1976. — xv,272p : ill, forms ; 24cm. — (Educational psychology)
Bibl. — Index.
ISBN 0-12-644050-6 : £10.05
(B77-06581)

371.9'7 — Immigrants. Adult education. *Western world*
Education for adult immigrants / edited by A.K. Stock and D. Howell. — [Leicester] : National Institute of Adult Education, [1976]. — 142p ; 22cm.
Proceedings of a seminar held at Burton Manor College. — Bibl.: p.114-115.
ISBN 0-900559-38-1 Pbk : £1.20
(B77-06582)

371.9'7'6872073 — Ethnic minorities. Education. Cultural factors. *United States. Study examples: Mexican people*
Ramírez, Manuel. Cultural democracy, bicognitive development, and education / [by] Manuel Ramírez III, Alfredo Castañeda. — New York [etc.] ; London : Academic Press, 1974. — xiv,189p : ill, forms ; 24cm.
Bibl. — Index.
ISBN 0-12-577250-5 : £5.75
(B77-00132)

371.9'7'914 — South Asian non-English speaking women students. Education. Curriculum subjects: English language. Teaching. *England*
Mobbs, Michael C. Meeting their needs : an account of the language tuition schemes for ethnic minority women / by Michael C. Mobbs ; on behalf of the Community Relations Commission's Education Department and Reference Division. — London : Community Relations Commission, Reference and Technical Services Division, 1977. — 64p : forms ; 22cm.
Bibl.: p.64.
Sd : £0.80
(B77-18679)

371.9'7'969729041 — Schools. West Indian students. Academic achievement. Effects of English-Creole languages. *Great Britain*
Edwards, Viv. West Indian language : attitudes and the school / [by] Viv Edwards. — [Slough] ([c/o Otto Poling, Northbrook Centre, William Penn School, Penn Rd, Slough, Bucks.]) : National Association for Multiracial Education, 1976. — [13]p ; 30cm. — (National Association for Multi-racial Education. NAME handbooks)
ISBN 0-9504539-1-9 Sd : Unpriced
(B77-06583)

372 — PRIMARY EDUCATION

372 — Primary education. *For teaching*
Frostig, Marianne. Education for dignity / [by] Marianne Frostig. — New York [etc.] ; London : Grune and Stratton ; London : Distributed by Academic Press, 1976. — xiii, 208p : ill, forms ; 20cm.
Index.
ISBN 0-8089-0951-7 : £7.95
(B77-07247)

372.1 — PRIMARY SCHOOLS

372.1'1'00924 — Primary schools. *Scotland. Strathclyde Region. Clydeside. St Swithin's Primary School. Teaching, 1967-1970. Personal observations*
Bowie, Janetta. Penny change : Clydeside schools in the 'seventies / [by] Janetta Bowie ; illustrations by Susan Shields. — London : Constable, 1977. — 216p : ill ; 23cm.
ISBN 0-09-461800-3 : £4.75
Also classified at 373.1'1'00924
(B77-32557)

372.1'1'02 — Junior schools. Teaching. *Great Britain. Periodicals*
Junior education : incorporating 'Teachers world'. — London : Evans Bros.
Vol.1, no.1- ; Feb. 1977-. — 1977. — ill(some col), music, ports ; 30cm.
Monthly. — [4],viii,40,[4]p. in 1st issue.
Sd : £0.45
ISSN 0309-3484
(B77-17402)

372.1'1'020973 — Primary schools. Teaching. *United States. For teachers' aides*
Welty, Don A. The teacher aide in the instructional team / [by] Don A. Welty, Dorothy R. Welty. — New York ; London [etc.] : McGraw-Hill, 1976. — xvii,205p : ill, forms ; 23cm.
Bibl. — Index.
ISBN 0-07-069263-7 Pbk : £4.95
(B77-05988)

372.1'1'020973 — Primary schools. Teaching. *United States. Manuals*
Callahan, Joseph F. Teaching in the elementary school : planning for competence / [by] Joseph F. Callahan, Leonard H. Clark. — New York : Macmillan ; London : Collier Macmillan, 1977. — xi,320p : ill, forms ; 26cm.
With answers. — Bibl.
ISBN 0-02-318070-6 Pbk : Unpriced
(B77-24122)

372.1'1'480941 — Primary schools. Team teaching. *Great Britain*
O'Neil, Margaret. Team teaching in a primary school / [by] Margaret O'Neil, Michael Worrall. — Newcastle upon Tyne (Newcastle upon Tyne NE1 7RU) : Newcastle University Institute of Education, [1977]. — [34]p : plan ; 21cm.
Bibl.: p.34.
Sd : £0.40
(B77-27777)

372.1'2'64 — Primary schools. Students. Academic achievement. Assessment. Techniques
Cartwright, Carol A. Developing observation skills / [by] Carol A. Cartwright, G. Phillip Cartwright. — New York ; London [etc.] : McGraw-Hill, 1974. — x,168p : ill, forms ; 24cm. — (McGraw-Hill series in special education)
Pages perforated at inside edge.
ISBN 0-07-010184-1 Pbk : Unpriced
(B77-20168)

372.1'3 — Pre-school children. Education. Teaching methods: Discovery method. *United States*
Sava, Samuel G. Learning through discovery for young children / [by] Samuel G. Sava. — New York ; London [etc.] : McGraw-Hill, [1976]. — xiii,156p : ill ; 24cm.
Published in the United States: 1975. — Bibl.: p.137-156.
ISBN 0-07-054963-x : £6.60
(B77-06584)

372.1'3 — Primary schools. Open plan education. *Scotland. Case studies*
Hamilton, David, *b.1943.* In search of structure : essays from a new Scottish open-plan primary school / [by] David Hamilton. — London [etc.] : Hodder and Stoughton for the Scottish Council for Research in Education, 1977. — vi, 110p ; 23cm. — (Scottish Council for Research in Education. Publications ; 68)
Bibl.: p.108. — Index.
ISBN 0-340-22060-0 : £6.00
ISBN 0-340-22053-8 Pbk : £3.50
(B77-30107)

372.1'33'58 — Pre-school children. Education. Role of educational television programmes
Lesser, Harvey. Television and the preschool child : a psychological theory of instruction and curriculum development / [by] Harvey Lesser. — New York [etc.] ; London : Academic Press, 1977. — x,261p : ill ; 24cm. — (Educational psychology)
Bibl.: p.243-255. — Index.
ISBN 0-12-444250-1 : £11.35
(B77-28534)

372.1'39'40973 — Primary schools. Students. Individualised instruction. *United States*
Individually guided elementary education : concepts and practices / edited by Herbert J. Klausmeier, Richard A. Rossmiller, Mary Saily. — New York [etc.] ; London : Academic Press, 1977. — xviii,376p : ill, forms ; 24cm.
Bibl. — Index.
ISBN 0-12-411340-0 : £10.65
(B77-21806)

372.1'8'0924 — Primary schools. School life. *Great Britain, ca 1930-1955. Personal observations*
Trevor, William. Old school ties / [by] William Trevor ; illustrations by Magnus Lohkamp. — London : Lemon Tree Press, 1976. — 146p : ill ; 19cm.
'... combines stories and episodes from the Trevor novels, with hitherto unpublished material on the author's own school days ...' - jacket.
ISBN 0-904291-12-x : £3.60
ISBN 0-904291-13-8 Pbk : £1.60
(B77-24123)

372.1'8'1 — Education. Organisations. *Inner London. Inner London Education Authority. Primary schools. Students. Behaviour problems. Treatment. Nurture groups*
Boxall, Marjorie. The nurture group in the primary school / by Marjorie Boxall. — [London] : Inner London Education Authority, [1976]. — [15]p ; 21cm.
Sd : Unpriced
(B77-16808)

372.1'8'1 — Primary schools. Attitudes of students, 7 years. *Sources of data: Parents' personal observations. Study regions: Nottinghamshire. Nottingham. Reports, surveys*
Newson, John. Perspectives on school at seven years old / [by] John and Elizabeth Newson and Peter Barnes. — London : Allen and Unwin, 1977. — 3-216p : form ; 23cm.
Bibl.: p.211-213. — Index.
ISBN 0-04-136017-6 : £6.95
(B77-33713)

372.1'8'1 — Primary schools. Students. Socialisation. *England, 1812-1904*
Popular education and socialization in the nineteenth century / edited by Phillip McCann. — London : Methuen, 1977. — xii,276p : ill, facsims, maps, ports ; 23cm.
Index.
ISBN 0-416-81110-8 : £6.90
(B77-23292)

372.1'9 — Children, 3-6 years. Education. Curriculum
Eliason, Claudia Fuhriman. A practical guide to early childhood curriculum / [by] Claudia Fuhriman Eliason, Loa Thomson Jenkins. — Saint Louis : Mosby ; London : Distributed by Kimpton, 1977. — ix,297p : ill ; 26cm.
Bibl. — Lists of sound discs. — Lists of films and filmstrips. — Index.
ISBN 0-8016-1508-9 Pbk : Unpriced
(B77-24834)

372.1'9 — Children, 3-7 years. Education. Curriculum. *United States*
Fromberg, Doris Pronin. Early childhood education : a perceptual models curriculum / [by] Doris Pronin Fromberg. — New York ; London [etc.] : Wiley, 1977. — xviii,342p : ill ; 24cm.
Bibl.: p.311-326. — Index.
ISBN 0-471-28286-3 : £8.25
(B77-19297)

372.1'9 — Primary schools. Activities connected with sickness. *For teaching*
Michael, Bill. Something to say about feeling poorly / [by] Bill Michael. — London : Evans Bros, 1977. — 48p : ill ; 25cm. — (Practical language development)
ISBN 0-237-29174-6 Sd : £0.95
(B77-23293)

372.1'9 — Primary schools. Activities connected with travel. *For teaching*
Michael, Bill. Something to say about going places / [by] Bill Michael. — London : Evans Bros, 1977. — 47p : ill ; 25cm. — (Practical language development)
ISBN 0-237-29175-4 Sd : £0.95
(B77-23294)

372.1'9 — Primary schools. Activities connected with water. *For teaching*
Michael, Bill. Something to say about water / [by] Bill Michael. — London : Evans Bros, 1977. — 48p : ill ; 25cm. — (Practical language development)
ISBN 0-237-29176-2 Sd : £0.95
(B77-23295)

372.1'9 — Primary schools. Activities connected with winds. *For teaching*
Michael, Bill. Something to say about the wind / [by] Bill Michael, Bill Moffat. — London : Evans Bros, 1977. — 48p : ill ; 25cm. — (Practical language development)
ISBN 0-237-29173-8 Sd : £0.95
(B77-23296)

372.2 — LEVELS OF PRIMARY EDUCATION
372.21 — Children, to 8 years. Education
Margolin, Edythe. Young children : their curriculum and learning processes / [by] Edythe Margolin. — New York : Macmillan ; London : Collier Macmillan, 1976. — xvii, 361p : ill, ports ; 24cm.
Bibl. — Index.
ISBN 0-02-376010-9 : £8.25
(B77-12969)

372.21 — Pre-school children. Education
Van Der Eyken, Willem. The pre-school years / [by] Willem van der Eyken. — 4th ed. — Harmondsworth [etc.] : Penguin, 1977. — 262p ; 19cm. — (Penguin education)
Previous ed.: 1974. — Bibl.: p.232-253. — Index.
Pbk : £0.80
ISBN 0-14-080001-8
(B77-24124)

372.21 — Pre-school children. Education. *Organisation for Economic Co-operation and Development countries. Reports, surveys*
Austin, Gilbert R. Early childhood education : an international perspective / [by] Gilbert R. Austin. — New York [etc.] ; London : Academic Press, 1976. — xiii,369p : ill ; 24cm. — (Educational psychology)
Bibl. — Index. — Includes a section on the United States.
ISBN 0-12-068550-7 : £10.65
(B77-08321)

372.21'01'9 — Pre-school children. Education. Psychological aspects
Psychological processes in early education / edited by Harry L. Hom, Jr, Paul A. Robinson. — New York [etc.] ; London : Academic Press, 1977. — xix,334p : ill ; 24cm. — (Educational psychology)
Bibl. — Index.
ISBN 0-12-354450-5 : £12.40
(B77-23297)

372.21'0941 — Pre-school children. Education. *Great Britain. For parents. Readings*
The **best** of 'Where' on pre-schooling. — Cambridge : Advisory Centre for Education, 1976. — 3-85p : ill ; 20x21cm.
'... compilation of some of the best articles on pre-schooling to have appeared in "Where" during the last ten years' - p.6. — Bibl.
ISBN 0-900029-46-3 Pbk : £1.50
(B77-00133)

372.21'0973 — Pre-school children. Education. *United States*
Frost, Joe L. The young child and the educative process / [by] Joe L. Frost, Joan B. Kissinger. — New York [etc.] ; London : Holt, Rinehart and Winston, 1976. — x,390p : ill, forms, plan, ports ; 25cm.
Bibl. — Index.
ISBN 0-03-085290-0 : £9.00
(B77-02900)

Robison, Helen F. Exploring teaching in early childhood education / [by] Helen F. Robison. — Boston, Mass. ; London [etc.] : Allyn and Bacon, 1977. — xi,2-550p : ill, forms ; 25cm.
Bibl. — List of films. — Index.
ISBN 0-205-05550-8 : Unpriced
(B77-14659)

Todd, Vivian Edmiston. The years before school : guiding preschool children / [by] Vivian Edmiston Todd, Helen Heffernan. — 3rd ed. — New York : Macmillan ; London : Collier Macmillan, 1977. — xi,724p : ill, forms ; 24cm.

Previous ed.: 1970. — Bibl. — Index.
ISBN 0-02-420880-9 : £10.50
(B77-30108)

372.21'0973 — Pre-school children. Education. Policies of government. *United States, 1960-1975*
Greenblatt, Bernard. Responsibility for child care / [by] Bernard Greenblatt. — San Francisco [etc.] ; London : Jossey-Bass, 1977. — xvii,317p ; 24cm. — (The Jossey-Bass behavioral science series)
Bibl.: p.287-306. — Index.
ISBN 0-87589-315-5 : £11.00
Primary classification 362.7'1
(B77-24107)

372.21'09794'67 — Pre-school children. Education. *California. Berkeley*
Joffe, Carole E. Friendly intruders : childcare professionals and family life / by Carole E. Joffe. — Berkeley [etc.] ; London : University of California Press, 1977. — xiii,172p ; 23cm.
Bibl.: p.154-166. — Index.
ISBN 0-520-02925-9 : £8.25
(B77-28535)

372.21'6 — Children, to 3 years. Education
Ibuka, Masaru. Kindergarten is too late / by Masaru Ibuka. — London : Souvenir Press, 1977. — 160p ; 23cm.
ISBN 0-285-64814-4 : £3.50 : CIP rev.
(B77-12970)

372.21'6 — Further education institutions. Students: Parents. Curriculum subjects: Playgroups. Teaching. *Great Britain*
Pre-school Playgroups Association. Guidelines for a playgroup foundation course / [Pre-school Playgroups Association]. — [London] ([Alford House, Aveline St., SE11 5DH]) : P.P.A., [1976]. — [5],24p : ill, form ; 30cm.
Originally published: 1975. — Bibl. — Lists of films.
ISBN 0-901755-11-7 Sd : £1.10
(B77-02179)

372.21'6 — Groups for mothers & children, to 3 years. *Great Britain. Proposals*
Mother and toddlers clubs : a basis for discussion / [edited by Joyce Donoghue]. — London (Alford House, Aveline St., SE11 5DH) : Pre-school Playgroups Association, 1976. — 23p ; 15x21cm.
ISBN 0-901755-12-5 Sd : £0.30
(B77-02180)

372.21'6 — Nursery education
Baker, Katherine Read. The nursery school : human relationships and learning / [by] Katherine H. Read. — 6th ed. — Philadelphia ; London [etc.] : Saunders, 1976. — viii,394p : ill ; 26cm.
Previous ed.: 1971. — Bibl. — Index.
ISBN 0-7216-7488-7 : £7.75
(B77-05989)

372.21'6 — Nursery schools. *For teaching*
Dowling, Marion. The modern nursery / [by] Marion Dowling. — London [etc.] : Longman, 1976. — xv,152p ; 23cm. — (Longman early childhood education)
Bibl.: p.150-152.
ISBN 0-582-25004-8 : Unpriced
ISBN 0-582-25005-6 Pbk : £2.00
(B77-15228)

372.21'6 — Playgroups. *Great Britain*
Crowe, Brenda. The playgroup movement / by Brenda Crowe. — 3rd ed. — London : Allen and Unwin [for] the Pre-school Playgroups Association, 1977. — 3-212p ; 22cm.
Previous ed.: 1975. — Bibl.: p.208-210. — List of films: p.210-212.
ISBN 0-04-372024-2 : £5.50
ISBN 0-04-372025-0 Pbk : £2.95
(B77-33714)

372.21'6 — Playgroups. *Inner London. Reports, surveys*
Inner London Pre-school Playgroups Association. Playgroups : a shared adventure / [Inner London Pre-school Playgroups Association] ; [compiled and co-ordinated by Margaret Hanton]. — London (57 Beak St., W.1) : The Association, [1976]. — 32p : ill, 2 maps ; 30cm.
ISBN 0-901755-18-4 Sd : £0.50
(B77-06585)

372.21'6 — Playgroups. Administration. *Manuals*
Attfield, Janet. The business side of playgroups / [by] Janet Attfield and Sally Black. — London (Alford House, Aveline St., SE11 5DH) : Pre-school Playgroups Association, 1976. — 50p : ill ; 21cm.
ISBN 0-901755-15-x Sd : £0.40
(B77-01296)

372.21'6 — Playgroups. Administration. Role of feminism. *West Midlands (Metropolitan County). Birmingham. Calthorpe Park*
Birmingham Women's Liberation. *Playgroup Pamphlet Group.* Out of the pumpkin shell : running a Women's Liberation playgroup / [Birmingham Women's Liberation, Playgroup Pamphlet Group]. — Birmingham (65 Prospect Rd, Moseley, Birmingham 13) : The Group, 1975. — [2],52,[1]p : ill ; 21x30cm.
Bibl.: p.50-51.
Sd : £0.35
(B77-17403)

372.21'6 — Playgroups. Organisation. *Great Britain. Manuals*
Smith, Helen. Starting a playgroup / [by] Helen Smith. — Revised ed. — London (Alford House, Aveline St., SE11 5DH) : Pre-school Playgroups Association, 1975. — [2],17p : ill ; 24cm. — (Pre-school Playgroups Association. Publications)
Sd : £0.40
(B77-02901)

372.21'6 — Playgroups. Role of playgroup leaders. *Manuals*
Smith, Helen. Notes for playgroup leaders & committees / [by] Helen Smith ; [illustrations by Ruth Bartlett]. — [New ed.]. — London (Alford House, Aveline St., SE11 5DH) : Pre-school Playgroups Association, 1976. — 46p : ill ; 21cm.
Previous ed.: published as 'The supervisor's handbook' / by Pre-school Playgroups Association. 1970.
ISBN 0-901755-14-1 Sd : £0.40
(B77-01297)

372.21'6'0924 — Nursery education. McMillan, Margaret. *England. Biographies*
Bradburn, Elizabeth. Margaret McMillan : framework and expansion of nursery education / [by] Elizabeth Bradburn. — Redhill : Denholm House Press, 1976. — 192p, leaf of plate,[16]p of plates : ill, facsim, maps, ports ; 23cm.
Index.
ISBN 0-85213-151-8 : £8.00
ISBN 0-85213-152-6 Pbk : £3.00
(B77-24835)

372.24'1'0941 — Infant education. *Great Britain*
Lancaster, Janet. Developments in early childhood education / [by] Janet Lancaster and Joan Gaunt. — London : Open Books, 1976. — ix,145p : 1 ill ; 21cm. — (The changing classroom)
Bibl.: p.140-141. — Index.
ISBN 0-7291-0027-8 : £3.90
ISBN 0-7291-0022-7 Pbk : £1.75
(B77-02181)

372.24'1'0941 — Infant schools. *Great Britain*
Yardley, Alice. The organisation of the infant school / [by] Alice Yardley. — London : Evans Bros, 1976. — 95p : ill, plans ; 25cm.
Bibl.
ISBN 0-237-29139-8 Pbk : £2.10
(B77-03481)

372.3/8 — PRIMARY SCHOOL CURRICULUM
372.3'5'044 — Primary schools. Curriculum subjects: Science. Teaching
Gega, Peter Christopher. Science in elementary education / [by] Peter C. Gega. — 3rd ed. — New York ; London [etc.] : Wiley, 1977. — ix, 284p : ill(some col) ; 25cm.
Previous ed.: 1970. — Bibl.: p.277-278. — Index.
ISBN 0-471-29508-6 : £9.00
(B77-18047)

372.3'5'04409425 — Primary schools. Curriculum subjects: Science. Teaching. *England. East Midlands. Reports, surveys*
Bradley, Howard. A survey of science teaching in primary schools : pointers for I.N.S.E.T. / [by] Howard Bradley. — [Nottingham] ([University Park, Nottingham NG7 2RD]) : University of Nottingham, School of Education, 1976. — [5], 16[i.e.17]p : ill ; 30cm.
ISBN 0-85359-043-5 Sd : £0.30
(B77-05321)

372.3'7 — Primary schools. Curriculum subjects: Man. Health. Teaching. *Great Britain*
Schools Council Health Education 5-13 Project. All about me : teacher's guide for the early years of schooling (5-8) / Schools Council Health Education 5-13 Project, project team Trefor Williams ... [et al.]. — Sunbury-on-Thames : Nelson for the Schools Council, 1977. — [6],134p : ill ; 25cm.
Bibl.: p.120-134.
ISBN 0-17-423067-2 Pbk : £2.95
(B77-17404)

372.4 — Children, to 10 years. Reading skills. Acquisition. Theories. *For primary school teaching*
Smith, Donald Eugene Phillip. A technology of reading and writing / [by Donald E.P. Smith, Judith M. Smith and James R. Brink]. — New York [etc.] ; London : Academic Press.
In 4 vols.
Vol.2 : Criterion-referenced tests for reading and writing / [by] Judith M. Smith, Donald E.P. Smith, James R. Brink. — 1977. — xii, 279p : forms ; 25cm. — (Educational psychology)
Bibl. — Index. — Includes 'Standard achievement recording system' / by Donald E.P. Smith and Judith M. Smith. Revised ed. Chelsea, Mich. : Ed-Ventures, 1976.
ISBN 0-12-651702-9 : £8.85
Also classified at 372.6'23
(B77-22490)

Smith, Donald Eugene Phillip. A technology of reading and writing / [by Donald E.P. Smith, Judith M. Smith and James R. Brink]. — New York [etc.] ; London : Academic Press. — (Educational psychology)
In 4 vols.
Vol.3 : The adaptive classroom / [by] Donald E.P. Smith. — 1976. — x,320p : ill, forms ; 25cm.
With answers. — Bibl.: p.313-316. — Index.
ISBN 0-12-651703-7 : £10.30
Also classified at 372.6'23
(B77-26245)

372.4 — Children, to 5 years. Reading skills. Teaching. *Great Britain*
Berg, Leila. Reading and loving / [by] Leila Berg. — London [etc.] : Routledge and Kegan Paul, 1977. — [5],136p ; 21cm.
ISBN 0-7100-8475-7 : £2.75
ISBN 0-7100-8476-5 Pbk : £1.20
(B77-06586)

372.4 — Children, to 7 years. Reading skills. Development
Clay, Marie M. Reading : the patterning of complex behaviour / [by] Marie M. Clay. — London [etc.] : Heinemann Educational, 1977. — [6],168p : ill ; 23cm. — (Open University. Set books)
Originally published: 1973. — Bibl. — Index.
ISBN 0-86863-251-1 Pbk : £1.95
(B77-28536)

372.4 — Pre-school children. Reading skills. Teaching. *For parents*
Smethurst, Wood. Teaching young children to read at home / [by] Wood Smethurst. — New York ; London [etc.] : McGraw-Hill, [1976]. — xii,237p : ill ; 24cm.
Published in the United States: 1975. — Bibl.: p.216-224. — Index.
ISBN 0-07-058443-5 : £6.60
(B77-04702)

372.4 — Primary schools. Curriculum subjects: Reading. Teaching
Duffy, Gerald G. How to teach reading systematically. — 2nd ed. / [by] Gerald G. Duffy, George B. Sherman and Laura R. Roehler. — New York [etc.] ; London : Harper and Row, 1977. — x,363p : ill, plan ; 24cm.
With answers. — Previous ed.: / by Gerald G. Duffy and George B. Sherman, with others. New York : Harper and Row, 1973. — Bibl.
ISBN 0-06-041784-6 Pbk : £5.95
(B77-17405)

Fry, Edward B. Elementary reading instruction / [by] Edward B. Fry. — New York ; London [etc.] : McGraw-Hill, 1977. — xi,339p : ill, facsims, forms ; 25cm.
Bibl. — Index.
ISBN 0-07-022585-0 : £8.95
(B77-20169)

Harris, Larry Allen. Reading instruction : diagnostic teaching in the classroom / [by] Larry A. Harris, Carl B. Smith. — 2nd ed. — New York ; London [etc.] : Holt, Rinehart and Winston, 1976. — xiii,498p : ill, facsims, forms, plan ; 25cm.
Previous ed.: published as 'Reading instruction through diagnostic teaching'. 1972. — Bibl.: p.477-489. — Index.
ISBN 0-03-089682-7 : £9.50
(B77-02182)

372.4'03 — Primary schools. Curriculum subjects: Reading. *Dictionaries*
Hughes, John Malcolm. The reading handbook : a dictionary guide to the teaching of reading / [by] John M. Hughes. — London : Evans Bros, 1977. — 84p ; 21cm.
Bibl. — Index.
ISBN 0-237-29190-8 Sd : £1.20
(B77-28537)

372.4'1'0973 — Primary schools. Students. Reading skills. Teaching. *United States*
An **experience-based** approach to language and reading / edited by Carl Braun and Victor Froese. — Baltimore ; London [etc.] : University Park Press, 1977. — xi,284p : ill, forms ; 24cm.
Bibl.: p.251-266. — Index.
ISBN 0-8391-1146-0 : £11.25
Primary classification 372.6'044'0973
(B77-33154)

372.4'14 — Infant & junior schools. *Gwent. Newport. Tredegar Wharf School. Reading schemes: Colour Story Reading*
Price, M J W. The teaching of reading : a lecture on colour story reading / by M.J.W. Price. — Crosskeys, Gwent ([c/o] William G. Smith, College of Further Education, Crosskeys, Gwent) : College of Preceptors, South Wales Executive, [1975]. — 31p ; 21cm.
'... given ... at a College of Preceptors' Course held at Caerleon College on Saturday, 16th November, 1974 - p.7.
ISBN 0-9505453-0-9 Sd : £0.35
(B77-03482)

372.4'14 — Primary schools. Reading schemes: Pirate reading scheme. *Great Britain. For teaching*
McCullagh, Sheila Kathleen. The pirate reading scheme handbook / [by] Sheila K. McCullagh. — Revised ed. — Leeds : E.J. Arnold, 1977. — v,122p : ill, music ; 23cm.
Previous ed.: 1973.
ISBN 0-560-05010-0 Pbk : £2.50
(B77-30109)

372.5'044 — Primary schools. Curriculum subjects: Appreciation of visual arts. Teaching. *United States*

Hurwitz, Al. The joyous vision : a source book for elementary art appreciation / [by] Al Hurwitz, Stanley S. Madeja. — Englewood Cliffs ; London [etc.] : Prentice-Hall, 1977. — xi,302p : ill, form ; 24cm.
Bibl.: p.292-294. — Index.
ISBN 0-13-511600-7 : £10.35
(B77-23298)

372.5'044'0973 — Primary schools. Curriculum subjects: Visual arts. Teaching. *United States*

MacGregor, Ronald N. Art plus / [by] Ronald N. MacGregor. — Toronto ; London [etc.] : McGraw-Hill Ryerson, 1977. — x,109p : ill ; 23cm.
ISBN 0-07-082450-9 Pbk : £3.70
(B77-33715)

372.5'5 — Primary schools. Curriculum subjects: Handicrafts. Teaching

Linderman, Earl W. Crafts for the classroom / by Earl W. Linderman, Marlene M. Linderman. — New York : Macmillan ; London : Collier Macmillan, 1977. — xxiii,497p,[8]p of plates : ill(some col), facsim, ports(2 col) ; 26cm.
Bibl. — Index.
ISBN 0-02-370780-1 : £9.75
(B77-31092)

372.6 — Children, to 10 years. Language skills. Acquisition. Teaching

Meers, Hilda J. Helping our children talk : a guide for teachers of young or handicapped children / [by] Hilda J. Meers. — London [etc.] : Longman, 1976. — v,162p : ill ; 23cm. — (Longman early childhood education)
Bibl.: p.152-157. — Index.
ISBN 0-582-25014-5 : £4.00
ISBN 0-582-25010-2 Pbk : £2.00
(B77-12393)

372.6 — Primary schools. Students. Language skills. *West Sussex. Reports, surveys*

West Sussex Language Development Working Party. Children and language / [West Sussex Language Development Working Party]. — Basingstoke (Houndmills, Basingstoke, Hants. RG21 2XS) : Globe Education [for] West Sussex County Council, 1976. — xiii,117p,[16]p of plates : ill ; 30cm.
Bibl.: p.116-117.
ISBN 0-333-19919-7 Pbk : Unpriced
(B77-16810)

372.6'044 — Primary schools. Students. Language skills. Teaching. *Manuals*

Boyd, Gertrude A. Teaching communication skills in the elementary school. — 2nd ed. / [by] Gertrude A. Boyd, Daisy M. Jones. — New York ; London [etc.] : D. Van Nostrand, 1977. — viii,342p : ill ; 25cm.
Previous ed.: / by Gertrude A. Boyd. New York : London : Van Nostrand-Reinhold, 1971. — Bibl. — Index.
ISBN 0-442-20737-9 : £9.70
(B77-20170)

Cullingford, Cedric. Teaching children English : a language policy for primary and middle schools / [by] Cedric Cullingford. — London : Ward Lock, 1977. — 120p ; 22cm.
ISBN 0-7062-3549-5 Pbk : £2.25
(B77-17406)

372.6'044'0973 — Primary schools. Students. Language skills. Teaching. *United States*

An **experience-based** approach to language and reading / edited by Carl Braun and Victor Froese. — Baltimore ; London [etc.] : University Park Press, 1977. — xi,284p : ill, forms ; 24cm.
Bibl.: p.251-266. — Index.
ISBN 0-8391-1146-0 : £11.25
Also classified at 372.4'1'0973
(B77-33154)

372.6'1 — Primary schools. Curriculum subjects: English language. Words. Meaning. Recognition. Teaching. *United States*

Durkin, Dolores. Strategies for identifying words : a workbook for teachers and those preparing to teach / [by] Dolores Durkin. — Boston [Mass.] ; London [etc.] : Allyn and Bacon, 1976. — x,139p : 1 ill ; 24cm.
With answers. — Bibl.: p.125. — Index.
ISBN 0-205-05565-6 Sp : Unpriced
ISBN 0-205-05564-8 Pbk : £4.95
(B77-02902)

372.6'22 — Primary schools. Students. Speech skills. Teaching aids. *United States*

Carlson, Ruth Kearney. Speaking aids through the grades / [by] Ruth Kearney Carlson. — New York ; London : Teachers College Press, 1975. — vii,87p ; 21cm.
Bibl. — Index.
ISBN 0-8077-2421-1 Sp : Unpriced
(B77-18680)

372.6'23 — Children, to 10 years. Writing skills. Acquisition. Theories. *For primary school teaching*

Smith, Donald Eugene Phillip. A technology of reading and writing / [by Donald E.P. Smith, Judith M. Smith and James R. Brink]. — New York [etc.] ; London : Academic Press.
In 4 vols.
Vol.2 : Criterion-referenced tests for reading and writing / [by] Judith M. Smith, Donald E.P. Smith, James R. Brink. — 1977. — xii, 279p : forms ; 25cm. — (Educational psychology)
Bibl. — Index. — Includes 'Standard achievement recording system' / by Donald E.P. Smith and Judith M. Smith. Revised ed. Chelsea, Mich. : Ed-Ventures, 1976.
ISBN 0-12-651702-9 : £8.85
Primary classification 372.4
(B77-22490)

Smith, Donald Eugene Phillip. A technology of reading and writing / [by Donald E.P. Smith, Judith M. Smith and James R. Brink]. — New York [etc.] ; London : Academic Press. — (Educational psychology)
In 4 vols.
Vol.3 : The adaptive classroom / [by] Donald E.P. Smith. — 1976. — x,320p : ill, forms ; 25cm.
With answers. — Bibl.: p.313-316. — Index.
ISBN 0-12-651703-7 : £10.30
Primary classification 372.4
(B77-26245)

372.6'34'0941 — Primary schools. Curriculum subjects: Handwriting. Teaching. *Great Britain*

Smith, Peter, *b.1924.* Developing handwriting / [by] Peter Smith. — London [etc.] : Macmillan, 1977. — xiv,95p : ill ; 22cm. — (The language project) (Language guides)
Bibl.: p.81-83. — Index.
ISBN 0-333-15700-1 Pbk : £2.25
(B77-31803)

372.6'4 — Children's stories in English. Story-telling

Sawyer, Ruth. The way of the storyteller / [by] Ruth Sawyer. — Revised ed. — Harmondsworth [etc.] : Penguin, 1976. — 5-356p : music ; 18cm.
This ed. originally published: New York : Viking Press, 1962. — Bibl.: p.334-348. — Index.
ISBN 0-14-004436-1 Pbk : Unpriced
Also classified at 823'.9'1J
(B77-16305)

372.6'4 — Primary schools. Curriculum subjects: Children's literature in English. *United States. For teaching*

Huck, Charlotte S. Children's literature in the elementary school. — 3rd ed. / [by] Charlotte S. Huck. — New York ; London [etc.] : Holt, Rinehart and Winston, 1976. — xiv,815p,[16]p of plates : ill(some col), facsims, map ; 25cm.
Previous ed.: / by Charlotte S. Huck and Doris Young Kuhn. 1968. — Bibl. — Index.
ISBN 0-03-010051-8 : £10.25
(B77-02183)

372.6'4 — Primary schools. Curriculum subjects: Concrete poetry in English. *For teaching*

Cook, Stanley. Seeing your meaning : concrete poetry in language and education / [by] Stanley Cook. — [Huddersfield] ([Queensgate, Huddersfield HD1 3DH]) : Department of English Studies, The Polytechnic, Huddersfield, 1975. — [2],50p : ill ; 21cm.
Bibl.: p.2.
ISBN 0-905767-00-4 Sd : £0.15
(B77-01298)

372.6'5'078 — Primary schools. Curriculum subjects: Languages. Audio-visual aids. *Great Britain. Reports, surveys. Serials*

Birmingham Educational Development Centre. A-V aids for language teaching in primary schools : EDC project three : report / [Birmingham Educational Development Centre]. — Birmingham (Garrison La., Birmingham B9 4BS) : The Centre.
3rd : Teachers' use of certain technological aids for language teaching in primary schools. — 1972. — [1],26p : 1 ill ; 21cm.
Bibl.: p.24-25.
Sd : Unpriced
(B77-11734)

372.6'6 — Infant schools. Curriculum subjects: Drama. Teaching

Whittam, Penny. Teaching speech and drama in the infant school / [by] Penny Whittam. — London : Ward Lock, 1977. — 127p : ill, music, plans ; 23cm.
Bibl.: p.122-125. — Index.
ISBN 0-7062-3590-8 : £4.00
ISBN 0-7062-3591-6 Pbk : £2.25
(B77-16306)

372.6'6 — Primary schools. Curriculum subjects: Drama. Teaching. *England*

Lutley, Phyllis. Teaching with a purpose : using child drama with younger children / [by] Phyllis Lutley. — [3rd ed.]. — [Bromley] ([1 Hawthorndene Rd, Hayes, Bromley BR2 7DZ]) : Educational Drama Association, [1973]. — 19p ; 21cm. — (Educational Drama Association. Publications)
Previous ed.: 197-?.
ISBN 0-9501295-4-2 Sd : £0.35
(B77-03483)

372.7'3'044 — Primary schools. Curriculum subjects: Mathematics. Teaching

Evans, Dorothy, *b.1927.* Mathematics, friend or foe? : a review of some ideas about learning and teaching mathematics in the primary school / [by] Dorothy Evans. — London [etc.] : Allen and Unwin, 1977. — 3-140p : ill, forms ; 23cm. — (Classroom close-ups ; 4)
Bibl.: p.136-137. — Index.
ISBN 0-04-372022-6 : £5.50
ISBN 0-04-372023-4 Pbk : £2.50
(B77-31093)

Inner London Education Authority. *Inspectorate.* Primary school mathematics / [Inner London Education Authority Inspectorate]. — [Revised ed.]. — London (County Hall, London S.E.1) : The Inspectorate. — (Inner London Education Authority. ILEA curriculum guidelines)
Previous ed.: published in 1 vol. as 'Guide lines for primary school mathematics'. 1973.
1 : Mathematical content. — 1976. — [16]p : ill(some col) ; 21x30cm.
ISBN 0-7085-0016-1 Sd : £0.30
(B77-16307)

National Association of Teachers in Further and Higher Education. *Mathematical Education Section.* Teaching primary mathematics : strategy and evaluation : a report of the Mathematical Education Section of the National Association of Teachers in Further and Higher Education / edited on behalf of the section by J.A. Glenn. — London [etc.] : Harper and Row, 1977. — ix,110p : ill ; 22cm.
Bibl.: p.103-105. — Index.
ISBN 0-06-318071-5 : £3.95 : CIP rev.
Pbk : £1.95
(B77-08943)

372.7'3'044 — Primary schools. Curriculum subjects: Mathematics. Teaching aids: Games

Dumas, Enoch. Math activities for child involvement / [by] Enoch Dumas, C.W. Schminke. — 2nd ed. — Boston [Mass.] ; London [etc.] : Allyn and Bacon, 1977. — xiv, 341p : ill, facsims, maps ; 24cm.
Previous ed.: Boston, Mass. : Allyn and Bacon, 1971. — Index.
ISBN 0-205-05592-3 : Unpriced
ISBN 0-205-05577-x Pbk : Unpriced
(B77-07871)

372.7'3'0440941 — Infant schools. Curriculum subjects: Mathematics. Teaching. *Great Britain*

Thyer, Dennis. Teaching mathematics to young children / [by] Dennis Thyer, John Maggs ; diagrams drawn by B.S. Pugh. — London [etc.] : Holt, Rinehart and Winston, 1976. — xii,266p : ill ; 23cm.
Originally published: 1971. — Index.
Pbk : £2.75
ISBN 0-03-910120-7
(B77-01299)

372.7'3'0442 — Primary schools. Curriculum subjects: Mathematics. *For parents*

Stewart, Shirley. Modern maths explained / by Shirley Stewart. — Billericay ; Gravesend : Home and School Council Publications, 1977. — 24,[1]p : ill ; 21cm.
ISBN 0-901181-24-2 Sd : Unpriced
(B77-16811)

372.8 — Primary schools. Curriculum subjects: Road safety for pedestrians. *Great Britain. For teaching*
Road Safety Education Project. Children & traffic / author Ken Jolly ; [for the] Road Safety Education Project. — London [etc.] : Macmillan.
In 3 vols.
[2] : The young traveller. — 1977. — 63p : ill(some col), facsim, maps, col plans ; 20x21cm.
Bibl.: p.62-63.
ISBN 0-333-21793-4 Pbk : £0.64
(B77-25518)

372.8 — Primary schools. Curriculum subjects: Road safety for riding of bicycles. *Great Britain. For teaching*
Road Safety Education Project. Children & traffic / author Ken Jolly ; [for the] Road Safety Education Project. — London [etc.] : Macmillan.
In 3 vols.
[3] : Preparing for the road. — 1977. — 64p : ill(some col), facsims(some col) ; 20x21cm.
Bibl.: p.64.
ISBN 0-333-21794-2 Pbk : £0.64
(B77-25519)

372.8 — Primary schools. Religious education. *England. Reports, surveys*
Working Party on Moral and Religious Education in County Primary Schools. Moral and religious education in county primary schools : report of a working party to the Social Morality Council / [Working Party on Moral and Religious Education in County Primary Schools] ; H.J. Blackham, editor. — Windsor : NFER, 1976. — 60p ; 22cm.
ISBN 0-85633-115-5 Sd : £2.10
Also classified at 370.11'4
(B77-09641)

372.8'3'0967 — Primary schools. Curriculum subjects: Social studies. *Africa south of the Sahara. English speaking countries. For teaching*
Thompson, Fred, *b.1923.* Social studies : a guide for primary school teachers in Africa / by Fred Thompson, Patrick Bailey, Hugh Hawes. — London : Longman, 1977. — vi,198p : ill, coat of arms, facsim, maps, plans ; 22cm.
Bibl.: p.163-166.
ISBN 0-582-60761-2 Pbk : £1.00
(B77-16812)

372.8'6 — Students, to 11 years. Motor skills. Development. Use of physical education
Gallahue, David L. A conceptual approach to moving and learning / by David L. Gallahue, Peter H. Werner, George C. Luedke. — New York ; London [etc.] : Wiley, 1975. — xxii, 423p : ill, maps, music ; 24cm.
Bibl. — Index.
ISBN 0-471-29043-2 : Unpriced
(B77-20171)

372.8'6'044 — Primary schools. Curriculum subjects: Physical education. Teaching
Cameron, William McDonald. The games lesson in primary schools / [by] W.McD. Cameron, Shirley Munday. — Cambridge [etc.] : Cambridge University Press, 1977. — vi,74p : ill ; 21x22cm.
Bibl.: p.74.
ISBN 0-521-21426-2 Pbk : £2.30
(B77-16813)

Platts, B J. Games and primary children / by B.J. Platts. — [Nottingham] ([University Park, Nottingham NG7 2RD]) : University of Nottingham, School of Education, Further Professional Training Division, [1977?]. — [1], 27p : ill ; 30cm.
Bibl.: p.27.
Sd : Unpriced
(B77-26981)

372.8'6'0440973 — Primary schools. Curriculum subjects: Physical education. Teaching. *United States*
Physical education for children : a focus on the teaching process / [by] Bette J. Logsdon ... [et al.]. — Philadelphia ; Lea and Febiger ; London : Kimpton, 1977. — xi,328p : ill, forms ; 27cm.
Bibl. — Index.
ISBN 0-8121-0588-5 : £11.00
(B77-28538)

372.8'6'0973 — Primary schools. Curriculum subjects: Physical education. *United States*
Fait, Hollis Francis. Experiences in movement : physical education for the elementary school child. — 3rd ed. / [by] Hollis F. Fait, with the collaboration of Gladene Hansen Fait ; illustrated by Gregory Fait and Gerry Fait. — Philadelphia ; London [etc.] : Saunders, 1976. — ii-xvii,525p : ill, forms, plan ; 26cm.
Previous ed.: published as 'Physical education for the elementary school child' / by Hollis F. Fait. 1971. — Bibl. — Index.
ISBN 0-7216-3532-6 : £9.75
(B77-16814)

372.8'7'044 — Primary schools. Curriculum subjects: Music. Teaching
Nye, Robert Evans. Music in the elementary school / [by] Robert Evans Nye, Vernice Trousdale Nye. — 4th ed. — Englewood Cliffs ; London [etc.] : Prentice-Hall, 1977. — xvii,471p : ill, music ; 25cm.
Previous ed.: 1970. — Bibl. — Index.
ISBN 0-13-608117-7 : £8.80
(B77-21807)

372.8'72 — Primary schools. Curriculum subjects: Music. Appreciation. Teaching
Craddock, Eveline. Musical appreciation in an infant school / [by] Eveline Craddock. — London : Oxford University Press, 1977. — [4], 45p : ill, music ; 26cm.
List of records: p.41-44.
ISBN 0-19-321055-x Sd : £1.75
(B77-18681)

372.9 — PRIMARY EDUCATION. HISTORICAL AND GEOGRAPHICAL TREATMENT

372.9'4 — Primary education. Western Europe. Compared with primary education in Great Britain
Wilkinson, Max. Lessons from Europe : a comparison of British and West European schooling / [by] Max Wilkinson. — London (Wilfred St., [SW1E 6PL]) : Centre for Policy Studies, 1977. — viii,128p : ill ; 21cm.
ISBN 0-905880-02-1 Pbk : £2.95
Primary classification 372.9'41
(B77-25520)

372.9'41 — Primary education. Great Britain. Compared with primary education in Western Europe
Wilkinson, Max. Lessons from Europe : a comparison of British and West European schooling / [by] Max Wilkinson. — London (Wilfred St., [SW1E 6PL]) : Centre for Policy Studies, 1977. — viii,128p : ill ; 21cm.
ISBN 0-905880-02-1 Pbk : £2.95
Also classified at 372.9'4; 373.41; 373.4
(B77-25520)

372.9'41 — Primary schools. *Great Britain*
Yardley, Alice. Primary schools today / by Alice Yardley. — [Gravesend] : Home and School Council Publications, 1976. — 24p : ill ; 21cm.
ISBN 0-901181-22-6 Sd : £0.40
(B77-06587)

372.9'41 — Primary schools. *Great Britain. For parents*
O'Connor, Maureen. Your child's primary school : the teaching methods, the systems and the options explained / [by] Maureen O'Connor. — London [etc.] : Pan Books, 1977. — 160p ; 18cm. — (Pan original)
Index.
ISBN 0-330-25153-8 Pbk : £0.75
(B77-24125)

O'Connor, Maureen. Your child's primary school : the teaching methods, the systems and the options explained / [by] Maureen O'Connor. — London : Severn House : [Distributed by Hutchinson], 1977. — 160p ; 21cm.
Bibl. — Index.
ISBN 0-7278-0346-8 : £3.95
(B77-28539)

372.9'417 — Primary education. *Ireland (Republic), 1922-1960*
Akenson, Donald Harman. A mirror to Kathleen's face : education in independent Ireland, 1922-1960 / [by] Donald Harman Akenson. — Montreal ; London : McGill-Queen's University Press, 1975. — x, 224p : ill ; 23cm.
Bibl.: p.207-220. — Index.
ISBN 0-7735-0203-3 : Unpriced
Also classified at 373.417
(B77-15778)

372.9'42 — Primary education. *England. Proposals*
Educating our children : four subjects for debate : a background paper for the regional conferences, February and March 1977. — London : Department of Education and Science, [1977]. — [1],14p ; 30cm.
Also issued by the Welsh Education Office as 'Educating our children = Addysgu ein Plant', containing an extra paper 'Welsh in the schools of Wales'.
ISBN 0-85522-085-6 Sd : Unpriced
Also classified at 373.42
(B77-11735)

372.9'421'43 — Infant & junior schools. *London. Islington (London Borough). William Tyndale Infants School & William Tyndale Junior School, 1973-1975. Personal observations. Collections*
William Tyndale : the teachers' story / [by] Terry Ellis ... [et al.]. — London : Writers and Readers Publishing Cooperative, 1977. — [5], 171p ; 20cm.
ISBN 0-904613-31-3 Pbk : £1.00
(B77-23299)

372.9'421'43 — Infant & junior schools. *London. Islington (London Borough). William Tyndale Infants School & William Tyndale Junior School. Conservative and Unionist Party viewpoints*
Williams, Paul. The lessons of Tyndale : an examination of the William Tyndale School affair / [by] Paul Williams. — London : Conservative Political Centre, 1977. — 16p ; 21cm. — (Conservative Political Centre. Publications ; no.599)
ISBN 0-85070-593-2 Sd : £0.40
(B77-15779)

372.9'421'88 — Primary schools. *London. Haringey (London Borough). Highgate Primary School, to 1977*
Jobson, Ruby. The story of a school, 1877-1977 / written by and contributions edited by Ruby Jobson. — [London] ([Highgate Primary School, North Hill, Highgate N6 4ED]) : Highgate Primary School Association, [1977]. — [5],79p : ill, facsim, ports ; 22cm.
Sd : £0.80
(B77-26246)

372.9'423'38 — Primary schools. *Dorset. Bournemouth. St Walburga's School, to 1977*
Young, John Anthony. Saint Walburga's School, 1877-1977 / [by] J.A. Young. — Bournemouth ([40 Morley Rd, Bournemouth BH5 2JL]) : St Walburga's School, 1977. — [2],28,[1]p : ill ; 21cm.
Bibl.: p.[2].
ISBN 0-9505898-0-2 Sd : Unpriced
(B77-32558)

372.9'426'19 — Primary schools. *Norfolk. Tacolneston. Tacolneston School, 1877-1977. Personal observations. Collections*
Tacolneston School centenary anniversary, 1877-1977. — [Tacolneston] ([c/o Mrs R.J. Buckingham, 32 Norwich Rd, Tacolneston, Norwich NR16 1DD]) : [Tacolneston School Centenary Committee], [1977]. — [28]p : ill ; 15x21cm.
Sd : £0.45
(B77-28540)

372.9'427'37 — Primary schools. *Greater Manchester (Metropolitan County). Prestolee. Prestolee School, 1918-1952*
Holmes, Gerald. The idiot teacher : a book about Prestolee School and its headmaster E.F. O'Neill / by Gerald Holmes. — Nottingham : Bertrand Russell Peace Foundation for Spokesman Books, 1977. — xvi,194p,plate : port ; 22cm.
Originally published: London : Faber, 1952.
ISBN 0-85124-179-4 Pbk : £1.95
(B77-25517)

372.9'429 — Primary education. *Wales. Proposals*
Educating our children = Addysgu ein plant : a background paper for the conference in Wales, 22 March 1977 = papur cefndir ar gyfer y gynhadledd yng Nghymru, 22 Mawrth 1977. — [Cardiff] ([31 Cathedral Rd, Cardiff CF1 9UJ]) : Welsh Office (Welsh Education Office), [1977]. — [1],18p ; 30cm.
Includes one paper in English and Welsh. — Also issued by the Department of Education and Science as 'Educating our children : four subjects for debate', without the paper 'Welsh in the schools of Wales'.
ISBN 0-903702-04-5 Sd : Unpriced
Also classified at 373.429
(B77-11736)

372.9'429'54 — Primary schools. *Powys. Whitton. Whitton School, to 1973*
Smith, Denys J. Whitton School and the Dame Anna Child's Charity, Radnorshire, 1703-1973 / [by] D.J. Smith. — [Knighton] ([c/o Dame Anna Child's Endowed School, Whitton, Knighton, Radnor]) : [The author], [1973]. — [1],48p,[4]p of plates : ill, ports ; 22cm.
Sd : Unpriced
(B77-23300)

372.9'624 — Primary education. *Sudan, 1930-1970*
Griffiths, Vincent Llewellyn. Teacher-centred : quality in Sudan primary education, 1930 to 1970 / [by] V.L. Griffiths ; with a foreword by L.C. Taylor ... — London : Longman, 1975. — xiii,146p : ill ; 23cm.
Index.
ISBN 0-582-78063-2 : £5.75
(B77-11165)

373.1 — SECONDARY SCHOOLS

373.1'1'00924 — Secondary schools. *Scotland. Strathclyde Region. Clydeside. Wallace Secondary School. Teaching, 1970-1973. Personal observations*
Bowie, Janetta. Penny change : Clydeside schools in the 'seventies / [by] Janetta Bowie ; illustrations by Susan Shields. — London : Constable, 1977. — 216p : ill ; 23cm.
ISBN 0-09-461800-3 : £4.75
Primary classification 372.1'1'00924
(B77-32557)

373.1'1'02 — Secondary schools. Reluctant learners, 15-16 years. Interpersonal relations with trainee teachers. *Study examples: Hillview project*
Hannam, Charles. Young teachers and reluctant learners : an account of the Hillview project, an experiment in teacher education, and a discussion of its educational implications / [by] Charles Hannam, Pat Smyth and Norman Stephenson. — 2nd ed. — Harmondsworth [etc.] : Penguin, 1977. — 173p ; 18cm. — (Penguin education) (Penguin papers in education)
Previous ed.: 1971. — Bibl.: p.172-173.
Pbk : £0.70
ISBN 0-14-080246-0
(B77-10310)

373.1'1'020924 — Secondary schools. Teaching. *New Zealand. Personal observations*
Bream, Freda. I'm sorry, Amanda / [by] Freda Bream. — Auckland ; London : Collins, 1974 [i.e. 1976]. — 211p ; 22cm.
Published in New Zealand: 1974.
ISBN 0-00-222540-9 : Unpriced
(B77-04703)

373.1'2'02 — Secondary schools. Administrative personnel & technical personnel. *Scotland. Reports, surveys*
Ancillary staff in secondary schools : administrative and clerical staff, technicians, auxiliaries : report of a working party appointed by the Secretary of State for Scotland. — Edinburgh : H.M.S.O., 1976. — [6],41p : 1 ill ; 25cm.
Chairman: B.T. Ruthven. — At head of title: Scottish Education Department.
ISBN 0-11-491452-4 Sd : £1.75
(B77-08944)

373.1'2'02 — Secondary schools. Non-teaching professional personnel. *Scotland. Reports, surveys*
Non-teaching staff in secondary schools : youth and community workers, librarians, instructors : report of a working party appointed by the Secretary of State for Scotland. — Edinburgh : H.M.S.O., 1976. — [5],53p ; 25cm.
Chairman: D.E. Stimpson. — At head of title: Scottish Education Department. — Bibl.: p.49.
ISBN 0-11-491453-2 Sd : £2.00
(B77-08945)

373.1'2'62 — Secondary schools. C.S.E. examinations & G.C.E. (O level) examinations. Grading standards. Comparability. *England. Reports, surveys*
Willmott, Alan Stewart. CSE and GCE grading standards : the 1973 comparability study / [by] Alan S. Willmott. — Basingstoke [etc.] : Macmillan, 1977. — xxiv,208p : ill ; 24cm. — (Schools Council. Research studies ISSN 0306-0292)
'A report to the Schools Council from the Examinations and Tests Research Unit of the National Foundation for Educational Research in England and Wales' - half title page verso. — Bibl.: p.201-202. — Index.
ISBN 0-333-22025-0 : £4.95 : CIP rev.
ISBN 0-333-22370-5 Pbk : £2.95
(B77-05990)

373.1'2'62 — Secondary schools. G.C.E. examinations. Setting & marking. *England*
Associated Examining Board for the General Certificate of Education. How examination papers are set and marked / the Associated Examining Board for the General Certificate of Education. — Aldershot (Wellington House, Aldershot, Hants. GU11 1BQ) : The Board, [1977]. — [2],16p ; 21cm.
Sd : Unpriced
(B77-33716)

373.1'2'62 — Secondary schools. Malawi Certificate of Education examinations. Organisation. Role of Associated Examining Board for the General Certificate of Education. *Malawi*
James, R. The Malawi Certificate of Education / by R. James. — Aldershot (Wellington House, Aldershot, Hants. GU11 1BQ) : Associated Examining Board for the General Certificate of Education, [1977]. — [5],38,[1]p : ill(incl 2 col), map ; 22cm.
Sd : £0.45
(B77-17407)

373.1'2'6209416 — Secondary schools. Examinations. Administration. *Northern Ireland. Reports, surveys. Serials*
Northern Ireland Schools Examinations Council. Report of the Northern Ireland Schools Examinations Council. — Belfast : H.M.S.O.
4th, for the year 1974-75. — 1976. — 35p ; 25cm.
ISBN 0-337-04068-0 Sd : £0.60
ISSN 0306-5324
(B77-20172)

373.1'2'64 — School leavers. Academic achievement. *England. Inquiry reports*
Great Britain. *Parliament. House of Commons. Expenditure Committee.* The attainments of the school leaver : tenth report from the Expenditure Committee, session 1976-77, together with the minutes of evidence taken before the Education, Arts and Home Office Sub-committee in session 1976-77, appendices and index. — London : H.M.S.O.
[Vol.1]. — [1977]. — lx p : 1 ill ; 25cm. — ([1976-77 H.C.] 526-I)
ISBN 0-10-252677-x Sd : £1.10
(B77-29321)

Vol.2 : Minutes of evidence, 29th November 1976-28th February 1977. — [1977]. — xii, 480p ; 25cm. — ([1976-77 H.C.] 525[i.e.526]-II)
ISBN 0-10-296677-x Pbk : £6.60
(B77-29322)

Vol.3 : Minutes of evidence, 7 March-24 May, and appendices. — [1977]. — xii p,p481-873 ; 25cm. — ([1976-77 H.C.] 526-III)
ISBN 0-10-296777-6 Pbk : £7.60
(B77-29323)

373.1'2'64 — Secondary schools. Students. Academic achievement. Assessment. *Great Britain. For teaching*
Macintosh, Henry Gordon. Assessment and the secondary school teacher / [by] H.G. Macintosh in collaboration with D.E. Hale. — London [etc.] : Routledge and Kegan Paul, 1976. — xiii,131p : ill, forms ; 20cm. — (Students library of education)
Bibl.: p.129-131.
ISBN 0-7100-8472-2 : £3.50
ISBN 0-7100-8473-0 Pbk : £1.75
(B77-04072)

373.1'2'64 — Secondary schools. Third forms & fourth forms. Students. Assessment. *Scotland. Inquiry reports*
Great Britain. *Committee to Review Assessment in the Third and Fourth Years of Secondary Education in Scotland.* Assessment for all : report of the Committee to Review Assessment in the Third and Fourth Years of Secondary Education in Scotland. — Edinburgh : H.M.S.O., 1977. — 139p : ill, forms ; 25cm.
Bibl.
ISBN 0-11-491505-9 Pbk : £2.00
(B77-31094)

373.1'2'709411 — Secondary schools. Students. Academic achievement. Assessment by teachers. *Scotland. Reports, surveys*
Scottish Council for Research in Education. Pupils in profile : making the most of teachers' knowledge of pupils / [Scottish Council for Research in Education]. — London [etc.] : Hodder and Stoughton, 1977. — xii,172p : ill, forms ; 23cm. — (Scottish Council for Research in Education. Publications)
A study carried out by the Council in conjunction with a Working Party set up by the Headteachers' Association of Scotland. — Bibl.: p.169-170. — Index.
ISBN 0-340-22059-7 : £5.00
ISBN 0-340-22052-x Pbk : £2.50
(B77-18048)

373.1'2'9140942496 — Secondary schools. Transfer of primary school students. *West Midlands (Metropolitan County). Birmingham. Reports, surveys*
Birmingham Educational Development Centre. Continuity in education : EDC project five / City of Birmingham Education Department, Educational Development Centre. — Birmingham (Garrison La., Birmingham B9 4BS) : The Centre.
Final report. — 1975. — [1],103p : ill, forms, map ; 30cm.
Cover title: Continuity in education (junior to secondary). — Bibl.: p.100-101.
Sd : Unpriced
(B77-11166)

373.1'3'0973 — Secondary schools. Teaching methods. *United States*
Hoover, Kenneth H. The professional teacher's handbook : a guide for improving instruction in today's middle and secondary schools / [by] Kenneth H. Hoover. — Abridged 2nd ed. — Boston, Mass. ; London [etc.] : Allyn and Bacon, [1977]. — xv,445p : ill, forms ; 25cm.
'Portions of this material were taken from "Learning and teaching in the secondary school", third edition, by Kenneth H. Hoover ...' - title page verso. — Abridged 2nd ed. published in the United States: 1976. — Previous ed.: i.e. 1st ed., Boston, Mass. : Allyn and Bacon, 1973. — Bibl. — Lists of films. — Index.
ISBN 0-205-05582-6 : Unpriced
(B77-09642)

373.1'3'9445 — Secondary schools. Teaching methods. Applications of digital computer systems. *Organisation for Economic Co-operation and Development countries. Reports, surveys*
Centre for Educational Research and Innovation. The use of the computer in teaching secondary school subjects / Centre for Educational Research and Innovation. — Paris : Organisation for Economic Co-operation and Development ; [London] : [H.M.S.O.], 1976. — 73p ; 24cm.
Pbk : £1.80
ISBN 92-64-11517-x
(B77-00702)

373.1'4'0941 — Secondary schools. Students. Counselling. *Great Britain*
Jones, Anne. Counselling adolescents in school / [by] Anne Jones. — [Revised and updated ed.]. — London : Kogan Page, 1977. — 200p ; 23cm.
Previous ed.: published as 'School counselling in practice'. London : Ward Lock, 1970. — Bibl.: p.193-196. — Index.
ISBN 0-85038-132-0 : £4.95
(B77-19299)

373.1'4'09411 — Secondary schools. Students. Counselling. *Scotland. Reports, surveys*
Great Britain. *Scottish Education Department. Inspectorate.* Guidance in Scottish secondary schools : a progress report / by HM Inspectors of Schools ; [for the] Scottish Education Department. — Edinburgh : H.M.S.O., 1976. — 23p ; 25cm.
ISBN 0-11-491435-4 Sd : £0.70
(B77-01300)

373.1'4'0973 — Secondary schools. Students. Counselling. *United States*
Byrne, Richard Hill. Guidance : a behavioral approach / [by] Richard Hill Byrne. — Englewood Cliffs ; London [etc.] : Prentice-Hall, 1977. — xiii,386p : ill, plan ; 24cm.
Bibl. — Index.
ISBN 0-13-368001-0 : £9.55
(B77-15780)

373.1'4'25 — School leavers. Vocational preparation. *Great Britain*
Getting ready for work, 16-19 : conference [held] 23-24 March, 1976. — [London] : Department of Education and Science, [1976]. — [3],21p ; 30cm.
ISBN 0-85522-086-4 Sp : Unpriced
(B77-16308)

373.1'4'25 — Sixth forms. Careers guidance. Courses: Challenge of industry conferences. Organisation. *Great Britain. Manuals. For teaching*
Industrial Society. Challenge of industry conferences : an operational manual for school organisers / [The Industrial Society]. — [London] : [The Society], [1976]. — [7],70p ; 26cm.
Cover title: Challenge of industry manual.
ISBN 0-85290-141-0 Ls : £25.00
(B77-13606)

373.1'4'250941 — Secondary schools. Careers guidance. *Great Britain. Serials*
National Union of Teachers. NUT guide to careers work. — [London] ([76 St James's La., N10 3RD]) : [New Opportunity Press Ltd].
1977 : 21st ed. / [editor Henry Clother] ; [assistant editor Susan Johnstone]. — [1977]. — [1],100p : ill, port ; 27cm.
Bibl.: p.30-35.
Sd : £0.40
ISSN 0309-9261
(B77-30110)

373.1'4'250942 — Secondary schools. Careers guidance. *England. Reports, surveys*
Law, Bill. Schools, careers and community : a study of some approaches to careers education in schools / [by] Bill Law and A.G. Watts. — London : CIO Publishing for the General Synod Board of Education, 1977. — v,149p : ill ; 21cm.
Bibl.: p.148-149.
ISBN 0-7151-9029-6 Pbk : £1.60
(B77-25521)

373.1'4'25094254 — Secondary schools. Careers guidance. *Leicestershire. Reports, surveys*
Keil, E T. The induction of school-leavers into work in Leicestershire / by E.T. Keil. — [Leicester] : [Leicestershire Committee for Education and Industry], 1976. — 283p in various pagings : forms ; 30cm.
Cover title: Becoming a worker.
Sp : Unpriced
Primary classification 658.31'242'094254
(B77-27957)

373.1'7'75 — Secondary schools. Laboratories. Safety measures. *Manuals*
Everett, Kenneth. A safety handbook for science teachers / [by] K. Everett, E.W. Jenkins. — 2nd ed. — London : J. Murray, 1977. — [8], 100p : ill(some col) ; 24cm.
Previous ed.: 1973. — Bibl.: p.67-70. — Index.
ISBN 0-7195-3336-8 : £2.60
(B77-18045)

373.1'9 — Middle schools. Activities. *Middle school texts. Cards*
Baker, Peter, *b.1943.* Interplay / [by] Peter Baker. — London [etc.] : Macmillan.
In 3 vols.
2 : Fantasia / [cards designed and illustrated by Janet Sterling]. — 1976. — 1v. : ill(some col) ; 20x21cm.
Teachers' notes (folder : ([4]p.)), 20 cards (14 fold.) ([70]p.).
ISBN 0-333-18024-0 : £4.95
(B77-11167)

373.1'9 — Sixth forms. Examinations. Syllabuses. Development. *England. Reports, surveys*
Schools Council Project on Syllabus Construction and Examining Techniques for Advanced Sixth Form Work. Sixth form syllabuses and examinations : a new look : final report from the Schools Council Project on Syllabus Construction and Examining Techniques for Advanced Sixth Form Work / prepared by the Joint Steering Committee. — London [etc.] : Macmillan, 1976. — vii,54,[1]p ; 24cm. — (Schools Council. Research studies)
Bibl.: p.52.
ISBN 0-333-21461-7 Pbk : £2.45
(B77-05322)

373.1'9'09411 — Secondary schools. Third forms & fourth forms. Curriculum. *Scotland. Reports, surveys*
Consultative Committee on the Curriculum. The structure of the curriculum in the third and fourth years of the Scottish secondary school / Scottish Education Department, Consultative Committee on the Curriculum. — Edinburgh : H.M.S.O., 1977. — 76p ; 25cm.
ISBN 0-11-491501-6 Sd : £1.50
(B77-31095)

373.1'9'0942 — Secondary schools. Curriculum. *England*
Devlin, Tim. What must we teach? / [by] Tim Devlin and Mary Warnock. — London : Temple Smith, 1977. — 160p ; 23cm.
ISBN 0-85117-136-2 : £5.00
ISBN 0-85117-137-0 Pbk : £2.55
(B77-33717)

373.1'9'0973 — Secondary schools. Curriculum. *United States. Readings*
Curriculum handbook : the disciplines, current movements, instructional methodology, administration and theory / [edited by] Louis Rubin. — Abridged ed. — Boston [Mass.] ; London [etc.] : Allyn and Bacon, 1977. — x, 590p : ill ; 24cm.
Full ed.: in 2 vols. Boston, Mass. : Allyn and Bacon, 1977. — Bibl. — Index.
ISBN 0-205-05910-4 Pbk : £7.35
(B77-28541)

373.2 — SECONDARY SCHOOLS. SPECIAL TYPES

373.2'22'02541 — Boys' public schools. *Great Britain. Directories*
The **public** and preparatory schools year book : the official book of reference of the Headmasters' Conference and of the Incorporated Association of Preparatory Schools. — London : A. and C. Black.
1977 : eighty-seventh year of publication / edited by J.F. Burnet. — [1977]. — xxxvi, 1207p : ill ; 19cm.
Index.
ISBN 0-7136-1711-x : £4.50
(B77-16309)

373.2'22'02541 — Boys' public schools. *Great Britain. Directories. For parents*
The **bedside** book of boys public schools / compiled and edited by Nigel Hadow ; illustrations by John Grant. — Lewes (Sandhill, Halland, Lewes, Sussex BN8 6PP) : Nigel Hadow Publications, 1976. — 146p : ill ; 22cm.

ISBN 0-905698-00-2 Pbk : £1.50
Primary classification 082
(B77-01991)

373.2'22'0941 — Boys' public schools. *Great Britain, to 1976*
The **world** of the public school / introduced by George Macdonald Fraser. — London : Weidenfeld and Nicolson, 1977. — [7],210p,[16] p of plates : ill, ports ; 25cm.
ISBN 0-297-77228-7 : £5.95
(B77-23301)

373.2'38'0942496 — Secondary schools & sixth form colleges. Students, 16-19 years. Education. *Great Britain. Study regions: West Midlands (Metropolitan County). Birmingham. Reports, surveys. Serials*
Birmingham Educational Development Centre. Education 16 to 19 : EDC project two : report / Birmingham Educational Development Centre. — Birmingham (Garrison La., Birmingham B9 4BS) : The Centre.
2nd. — 1971. — [1],59p ; 21cm.
Sd : £0.35
Also classified at 374.9'424'96
(B77-11737)

373.2'38'0942659 — Secondary schools & sixth form colleges. Students, 16-19 years. Education. *Cambridgeshire. Cambridge region. Proposals*
Cambridgeshire *(County). Education Committee.* Post-16 education in the Cambridge area : a consultative document / Cambridgeshire Education Committee. — Cambridge (Shire Hall, [Castle Hill], Cambridge [CB3 0AP]) : Cambridgeshire Education Committee], 1976. — [3],18p ; 30cm.
ISBN 0-9500179-8-1 Sd : Unpriced
Also classified at 374.9'426'59
(B77-14660)

373.2'4'0941 — Grammar schools. *Great Britain, ca 1560-1870*
Thomas, Keith. Rule and misrule in the schools of early modern England / by Keith Thomas. — [Reading] (Publications Officer, Department of History, Faculty of Letters, University of Reading, [Reading] RG6 2AA) : University of Reading, 1976. — 35p ; 24cm. — (The Stenton lectures ; 9 ISSN 0309-0469)
ISBN 0-7049-0206-0 Sd : £0.65
(B77-03484)

373.2'5'0941 — Comprehensive schools. *Great Britain. For parents*
O'Connor, Maureen. Your child's comprehensive school : the teaching methods, the systems and the options explained / [by] Maureen O'Connor. — London [etc.] : Pan Books, 1977. — 156p ; 18cm. — (Pan original)
Bibl. — Index.
ISBN 0-330-25152-x Pbk : £0.75
(B77-24126)

O'Connor, Maureen. Your child's comprehensive school : the teaching methods, the systems and the options explained / [by] Maureen O'Connor. — London : Severn House : [Distributed by Hutchinson], 1977. — 156p ; 21cm.
Bibl. — Index.
ISBN 0-7278-0345-x : £4.25
(B77-29324)

373.3/9 — SECONDARY EDUCATION. HISTORICAL AND GEOGRAPHICAL TREATMENT

373.4 — Secondary education. Western Europe. Compared with secondary education in Great Britain
Wilkinson, Max. Lessons from Europe : a comparison of British and West European schooling / [by] Max Wilkinson. — London (Wilfred St., [SW1E 6PL]) : Centre for Policy Studies, 1977. — viii,128p : ill ; 21cm.
ISBN 0-905880-02-1 Pbk : £2.95
Primary classification 372.9'41
(B77-25520)

373.41 — Secondary education. Great Britain. Compared with secondary education in Western Europe
Wilkinson, Max. Lessons from Europe : a comparison of British and West European schooling / [by] Max Wilkinson. — London (Wilfred St., [SW1E 6PL]) : Centre for Policy Studies, 1977. — viii,128p : ill ; 21cm.
ISBN 0-905880-02-1 Pbk : £2.95
Primary classification 372.9'41
(B77-25520)

373.411 — Secondary education. *Scotland. Conference proceedings*
Signpost for Education *(Conference), 1976.* Signpost for Education : conference report, 1976. — [Edinburgh] ([c/o Scottish Education Department, New St Andrew's House, Edinburgh EH1 3SY]) : [Convention of Scottish Local Authorities], [1976]. — [1],100p ; 21cm.
At head of title: 'Scotsman', COSLA, EIS. — Bibl.
ISBN 0-9505267-0-3 Sd : £1.00
(B77-06588)

373.417 — Secondary education. *Ireland (Republic), 1922-1960*
Akenson, Donald Harman. A mirror to Kathleen's face : education in independent Ireland, 1922-1960 / [by] Donald Harman Akenson. — Montreal ; London : McGill-Queen's University Press, 1975. — x, 224p : ill ; 23cm.
Bibl.: p.207-220. — Index.
ISBN 0-7735-0203-3 : Unpriced
Primary classification 372.9'417
(B77-15778)

373.42 — Secondary education. *England*
A question of schooling / edited by John E.C. MacBeath. — London [etc.] : Hodder and Stoughton, 1976. — vi,201p : ill ; 23cm.
Index.
ISBN 0-340-20893-7 : £4.75
ISBN 0-340-20894-5 Pbk : £2.40
(B77-06589)

373.42 — Secondary education. *England. Proposals*
Educating our children : four subjects for debate : a background paper for the regional conferences, February and March 1977. — London : Department of Education and Science, [1977]. — [1],14p ; 30cm.
Also issued by the Welsh Education Office as 'Educating our children = Addysgu ein Plant', containing an extra paper 'Welsh in the schools of Wales'.
ISBN 0-85522-085-6 Sd : Unpriced
Primary classification 372.9'42
(B77-11735)

Judge, Harry. The future of secondary education / by Harry Judge. — [Swansea] ([Singleton Park, Swansea SA2 3PP]) : University College of Swansea, [1976]. — 16p ; 21cm. — (The Charles Gittins memorial lecture)
'... delivered at the University College of Swansea on March 11, 1976'.
ISBN 0-901626-99-6 Sd : Unpriced
(B77-04073)

373.42 — Secondary schools. *England. Inquiry reports*
Great Britain. *Department of Education and Science. HM Inspectorate (England).* Ten good schools : a secondary school enquiry : a discussion paper / by some members of HM Inspectorate of Schools. — London : H.M.S.O., 1977. — 36p ; 25cm. — (Matters for discussion ; 1 ISSN 0309-5746)
ISBN 0-11-270452-2 Sd : £0.75
(B77-14164)

373.422'19 — Girls' public schools. *Surrey. Haslemere. Royal Naval School, to 1975*
Unwin, Philip. The Royal Naval School, 1840-1975 / by Philip Unwin ; with an introduction by Earl Mountbatten of Burma. — Haslemere (Farnham La., Haslemere, Surrey [GU27 1HQ]) : The School, 1976. — 122p,leaf of plate,[8]p of plates : ill, ports ; 23cm.
Index.
ISBN 0-9505370-0-4 : £2.80
(B77-00134)

373.422'91 — Boys' public schools. *Berkshire. Bradfield. Bradfield College, to 1975*
Blackie, John. Bradfield, 1850-1975 / [by] John Blackie. — Bradfield ([Bradfield, Berks. RG7 6AU]) : Warden and Council of St Andrew's College, 1976. — xii,255p,[8]p of plates : ill, coat of arms, col map(on lining papers), ports ; 24cm.
Bibl.: p.243-246. — Index.
£6.50
(B77-01301)

373.425'41 — Comprehensive schools. *Leicestershire. Countesthorpe. Countesthorpe College, to 1975. Personal observations. Collections*
The **Countesthorpe** experience : the first five years / editor John Watts. — London : Allen and Unwin, 1977. — 3-217p : facsim, plan ; 23cm. — (Unwin education books ; 34)
Bibl.: p.212-213. — Index.
ISBN 0-04-373003-5 : £5.95
ISBN 0-04-373004-3 Pbk : £2.50
(B77-08946)

373.425'41 — Comprehensive schools. *Leicestershire. Countesthorpe. Countesthorpe College, to 1975. Teaching kits*
Portrait of Countesthorpe College / [edited by William Prescott ; for the Open University Curriculum Design and Development Course Team]. — Milton Keynes : Open University Press, 1976. — Portfolio : ill, plan, ports ; 23x33cm. — (Educational studies, a second level course : curriculum design and development ; case study 5) (E203 ; case study 5)
Three booklets, sheet ([2] sides).
ISBN 0-335-06566-x : Unpriced
(B77-04704)

373.425'79 — Grammar schools. *Oxfordshire. Dorchester-on-Thames. Dorchester-on-Thames Grammar School, to 1713. Early works*
Dorchester-on-Thames Grammar School. Dorchester-on-Thames Grammar School. — [Dorchester-on-Thames] ([Dorchester Abbey, Dorchester-on-Thames, Oxon.]) : Dorchester-on-Thames Archaeology and Local History Group, [1976]. — [1],ii-ix,35p ; 21cm.
Contains 'Statutes and ordinances for the ordering of the schoole master and schoole of Dorchester made the twenty ninth day of September 1652 ...' and 'A register of the names of the schollers with the time of their admission' (rearranged alphabetically).
ISBN 0-9505683-0-9 Sd : Unpriced
(B77-14165)

373.426'12 — Boys' grammar schools. *Norfolk. North Walsham. Paston School, to 1974*
Forder, Charles Robert. A history of the Paston School, North Walsham, Norfolk / by Charles Forder. — 2nd ed., revised and enlarged. — North Walsham ([Paston Grammar School, School House, North Walsham, Norfolk]) : The Governors [of Paston School], 1975. — xv, 200p,[6]leaves of plates : ill, col coat of arms, facsims, port ; 21cm.
Previous ed.: 1934. — Index.
ISBN 0-9505598-0-6 Pbk : £2.50
(B77-10311)

373.426'49 — Boys' public schools. *Suffolk. Ipswich. Ipswich School. Students, to 1857. Lists*
Ipswich School : an alphabetical list of Ipswichians known to have been educated at the school from its earliest days to the end of the headmastership of the Reverend S.J. Rigaud in 1857 / compiled by W.M. Morfey. — [Ipswich] ([Ipswich, Suffolk]) : [Ipswich School], 1976. — [1],38p ; 22cm.
ISBN 0-9505354-0-0 Sd : £0.50
(B77-00703)

373.426'59 — Boys' public schools. *Cambridgeshire. Cambridge. Perse School, to 1976*
Mitchell, S J D. Perse : a history of the Perse School, 1615-1976 / [by] S.J.D. Mitchell. — Cambridge : Oleander Press, 1976. — viii, 263p : ill, coat of arms, map, plans, ports ; 22cm. — ([Cambridge town, gown and county ; 7])
Index.
ISBN 0-902675-71-0 : £4.95
(B77-02184)

373.428'17 — Boys' secondary schools. *West Yorkshire (Metropolitan County). Bradford. Belle Vue Boys' School, to 1919*
Jackson, John C. Belle Vue Boys' School / by John C. Jackson. — [Bradford] ([Thorn Lane, Haworth Rd, Bradford BD9 6ND]) : [The School], [1977]. — [1],29[i.e.30]p ; 30cm.
Sd : Unpriced
(B77-24836)

373.428'17 — Comprehensive schools. *West Yorkshire (Metropolitan County). Bradford. Belle Vue Boys' School, to 1977. Personal observations. Collections*
Belle Vue Boys' School. Belle Vue Boys' School, Bradford, 1877-1977. — [Bradford] ([Thorn La., Bradford BD9 6ND]) : [The School], [1977]. — 84p : ill, ports ; 30cm.
Cover title.
Pbk : £0.90
(B77-25522)

373.429 — Secondary education. *Wales. Proposals*
Educating our children = Addysgu ein plant : a background paper for the conference in Wales, 22 March 1977 = papur cefndir ar gyfer y gynhadledd yng Nghymru, 22 Mawrth 1977. — [Cardiff] ([31 Cathedral Rd, Cardiff CF1 9UJ]) : Welsh Office (Welsh Education Office), [1977]. — [1],18p ; 30cm.
Includes one paper in English and Welsh. — Also issued by the Department of Education and Science as 'Educating our children : four subjects for debate', without the paper 'Welsh in the schools of Wales'.
ISBN 0-903702-04-5 Sd : Unpriced
Primary classification 372.9'429
(B77-11736)

373.44 — Secondary education. *France, to 1903*
Durkheim, Emile. The evolution of educational thought : lectures on the formation and development of secondary education in France / [by] Emile Durkheim ; translated [from the French] by Peter Collins. — London [etc.] : Routledge and Kegan Paul, 1977. — xxx,354p ; 23cm.
Translation of: 'L'évolution pédagogique en France'. 2.éd. Paris : Presses universitaires de France, 1969. — Index.
ISBN 0-7100-8446-3 : £7.50 : CIP rev.
(B77-08947)

373.73 — Secondary education. *United States. Reports, surveys*
Task Force '74. The adolescent, other citizens and their high schools : a report to the public and the profession / Task Force '74 ... — New York ; London [etc.] : McGraw-Hill, [1976]. — xix,119p ; 22cm.
Published in the United States: 1975.
ISBN 0-07-062918-8 : £7.45
ISBN 0-07-062920-x Pbk : £3.30
(B77-05991)

373.73 — Secondary schools. *United States*
Smith, Frederick R. Secondary schools in a changing society / [by] Frederick R. Smith, C. Benjamin Cox. — New York ; London [etc.] : Holt, Rinehart and Winston, 1976. — xvii, 201p : ill, map ; 24cm.
Index.
ISBN 0-03-089179-5 : £6.75
(B77-02185)

374 — ADULT AND FURTHER EDUCATION

374 — Adult education. *Festschriften*
Wiltshire, Harold. The spirit and the form : essays in adult education by and in honour of Professor Harold Wiltshire / edited by Alan Rogers. — [Nottingham] ([14 Shakespeare St., Nottingham NG1 4FJ]) : Department of Adult Education, University of Nottingham, 1976. — [7],159p,plate : port ; 23cm. — (Nottingham studies in the theory and practice of the education of adults)
Index.
ISBN 0-902031-38-4 : £4.75
(B77-02903)

374 — Adult education. *Organisation for Economic Co-operation and Development countries. Reports, surveys*
Organisation for Economic Co-operation and Development. Learning opportunities for adults / [Organisation for Economic Co-operation and Development]. — Paris : O.E.C.D. ; [London] : [H.M.S.O.].
Vol.1 : General report. — 1977. — 81p ; 24cm.

Pbk : £2.20
ISBN 92-64-11621-4
(B77-14166)

374 — Colleges of further education. *London. Camden (London Borough). Kingsway-Princeton College. Students. Counselling*
Lee, Rosemary. Students at risk : an account of the full-time tutorial (FTT) course at Kingsway-Princeton College / [by] Rosemary Lee. — Cambridge : Hobsons Press, 1976. — [3],99p ; 21cm. — (Careers Research and Advisory Centre. Aspects of guidance series)
Bibl.: p.99.
ISBN 0-86021-060-x Pbk : Unpriced
(B77-27778)

374 — Colleges of further education. Machinery. Safety measures. *Great Britain. Manuals*
Southern Regional Council for Further Education. *Safety Working Party.* Safety and machinery / Southern Regional Council for Further Education, Safety Working Party ; [written by R.J. Hailes]. — [Reading] ([26 Bath Rd, Reading RG1 6NT]) : [The Council], [1976]. — [12]p ; 30cm. — (Safety booklet ; no.1)
ISBN 0-901271-27-6 Sd : £0.30
(B77-08322)

374 — Further education. Examinations. *Great Britain. Association of Teachers in Technical Institutions viewpoints*
National Association of Teachers in Further and Higher Education. Assessment / National Association of Teachers in Further and Higher Education. — [London] : [The Association], [1977]. — [2],46p : ill ; 21cm.
Bibl.: p.45-46.
Sd : £0.50(£4.00 for 10 copies, £10.50 for 30 copies, £15.00 for 50 copies)
(B77-16815)

374 — Further education institutions. Teachers. Training. *Great Britain. Reports, surveys*
Haycocks, Norman. The training of full-time teachers in further education : an ACSTT report / by N. Haycocks. — London : Association of Colleges for Further and Higher Education, [1977]. — [1],4,[1]p ; 21cm.
Address delivered at the Annual General Meeting of the Association of Colleges for Further and Higher Education held on Thursday and Friday, 24th and 25th February 1977 at the Institution of Electrical Engineers, Savoy Place, London W.C.2.
Sd : £0.50
(B77-27779)

374 — Lifelong education
Foundations of lifelong education / edited by R.H. Dave. — Oxford [etc.] : Pergamon for UNESCO Institute for Education, 1976. — vi, 382p : ill ; 22cm. — (Studies in lifelong education)
Bibl.
ISBN 0-08-021192-5 : £8.75
ISBN 0-08-021191-7 Pbk : £5.00
(B77-00135)

374 — Lifelong education. *Great Britain. Inquiry reports*
Open University. *Committee on Continuing Education.* Report of the Committee on Continuing Education. — Milton Keynes : Open University Press, 1976. — 126,[1]p : 1 ill ; 21cm.
Pbk : Unpriced
(B77-07872)

374 — Lifelong education. *Organisation for Economic Co-operation and Development countries. Reports, surveys*
Centre for Educational Research and Innovation. Recurrent education : policy and development in OECD member countries / Centre for Educational Research and Innovation. — Paris : Organisation for Economic Co-operation and Development ; [London] : [H.M.S.O.].
France / by Jean-Michel Belorgey. — 1976. — 30p : ill ; 24cm.
Sd : £1.10
ISBN 92-64-11515-3
(B77-01303)

Centre for Educational Research and Innovation. Recurrent education : policy and development in OECD member countries / Centre for Educational Research and Innovation. — Paris : O.E.C.D. ; [London] : [H.M.S.O.].
Japan / by Kazufusa Moro-Oka. — 1976. — 59p : ill ; 24cm.
Pbk : £1.50
ISBN 92-64-11579-x
(B77-05992)

Centre for Educational Research and Innovation. Recurrent education, policy and development in OECD member countries / Centre for Educational Research and Innovation. — Paris : Organisation for Economic Co-operation and Development ; [London] : [H.M.S.O.].
Denmark / by Berrit Hansen. — 1976. — 33p : ill ; 24cm.
Sd : £1.10
ISBN 92-64-11536-6
(B77-01302)

Switzerland / by N. Bottani ... [et al.]. — 1976. — 114p ; 24cm.
Bibl.: p.110-111.
Pbk : £1.80
ISBN 92-64-11546-3
(B77-00704)

374 — Lifelong education. Psychological aspects
Cropley, Arthur John. Lifelong education : a psychological analysis / [by] A.J. Cropley. — Oxford [etc.] : Pergamon, 1977. — [4],196p : ill ; 22cm. — (Advance studies in lifelong education ; vol.3)
Bibl.: p.166-184. — Index.
ISBN 0-08-021814-8 : £7.75
ISBN 0-08-021815-6 Pbk : Unpriced
(B77-30111)

374 — Lifelong education. Theories
Illich, Ivan. Imprisoned in the global classroom / [by] Ivan Illich and Etienne Verne. — London (14 Talacre Rd, NW5 3PE) : Writers and Readers Publishing Cooperative, 1976. — 63p ; 20cm.
Includes 'Political inversion' / by Ivan Illich.
ISBN 0-904613-30-5 Pbk : £0.45
(B77-04705)

374 — Old persons. Education. *Great Britain. Conference proceedings*
Education for the Elderly *(Conference), University of Keele, 1975.* Education and the over-60s : a report of the seminar 'Education for the Elderly' arranged by the Department of Adult Education, University of Keele, and the Beth Johnson Foundation at Keele from 26 to 28 September 1975 / [report written by] Frank Glendenning ; with an essay by Sidney Jones. — Stoke-on-Trent (Parkfield House, Princes Rd, Hartshill, Stoke-on-Trent) : Beth Johnson Foundation, 1976. — 50p ; 22cm.
ISBN 0-9505771-0-3 Sd : £1.25
(B77-14167)

374'.0025'41 — Adult education. *Great Britain. Directories*
Year book of adult education : the year book of the National Institute of Adult Education (England and Wales). — [Leicester] : [The Institute].
1977-78. — [1977]. — 127p ; 25cm.
Cover title. — Index.
Pbk : £2.00
ISSN 0084-3601
(B77-28542)

374'.0025'41 — Further education. Courses. *Great Britain. Directories*
Directory of further education / CRAC. — Cambridge : Hobson Press [for] CRAC.
1976-77 / [editors J.C. Tomlinson and Mary Lawson]. — 1976. — [1],750p : ill ; 22cm.
Bibl.: p.721-722. — Index.
ISBN 0-86021-090-1 : £22.50
ISBN 0-86021-089-8 Pbk : £20.00
(B77-03485)

374'.006'242 — Further education. Organisations. *England. Standing Conference of Regional Advisory Councils for Further Education. Reports, surveys. Serials*
Standing Conference of Regional Advisory Councils for Further Education. Report to the regional advisory councils in England and Wales / Standing Conference of Regional Advisory Councils in England and Wales. — London (Tavistock House South, Tavistock Sq., WC1H 9LR) : The Standing Conference.
1975-76. — [1976]. — 12p ; 21cm.
ISBN 0-85394-047-9 Sd : £0.25
(B77-05993)

374'.012 — Adult literacy education. *Conference proceedings*
International Symposium for Literacy, *Persepolis, 1975.* A turning point for literacy : adult education for development : the spirit and declaration of Persepolis : proceedings of the International Symposium for Literacy, Persepolis, Iran 3 to 8 September 1975 / edited by Leon Bataille. — Oxford [etc.] : Pergamon, 1976. — viii,277p : ill ; 26cm. — (Pergamon international library)
ISBN 0-08-021385-5 : £9.00
ISBN 0-08-021386-3 Pbk : £6.00
(B77-18682)

374'.012 — Adult literacy education. Teaching methods
Singh, Sohan. Learning to read and reading to learn : an approach to a system of literacy instruction / [by] Sohan Singh. — Amersham : Hulton [for] the International Institute for Adult Literacy Methods, 1976. — 116p : ill, forms ; 23cm. — (Literacy in development)
ISBN 0-7175-0765-3 Pbk : £1.75
(B77-08948)

374'.012 — Adult literacy education. Use of programmed texts. *For teaching*
Thiagarajan, Sivasailam. Programmed instruction for literacy workers : a guide for developing self-instructional materials and strategies for adult learners, literacy teachers and discussion leaders / [by] Sivasailam Thiagarajan. — Amersham : Hulton [for] the International Institute for Adult Literacy Methods, 1976. — 136p : ill, forms ; 23cm. — (Literacy in development)
ISBN 0-7175-0764-5 Pbk : £1.95
(B77-04706)

374'.012'02542144 — Adult literacy education institutions. *London. Hackney (London Borough). Directories*
Directory of adult literacy teaching in Hackney. — London (c/o G. Harding, Shoreditch District Library, Pitfield St., N.1) : Hackney Library Services.
1977. — [1977]. — [24]p ; 31cm.
Sd : Unpriced
(B77-25523)

374'.012'06341 — Adult literacy education. Organisations. *Great Britain. Adult Literacy Resource Agency, 1975-1976. Reports, surveys*
Adult Literacy Resource Agency. *Management Committee.* Adult literacy : progress in 1975-76 / report to the Secretaries of State for Education and Science and for Scotland by the Adult Literacy Resource Agency's Management Committee on the first year's operations. — London : H.M.S.O., 1976. — x,58p ; 25cm.
ISBN 0-11-270379-8 Sd : £0.95
(B77-01304)

374'.012'0941 — Teachers of illiterate adults. Teaching. *Great Britain. Teaching kits*
Lesson kit for trainers of adult literacy tutors / [written and produced by a group convened by the British Association of Settlements and Social Action Centres]. — [London] : Adult Literacy Resource Agency ; Oxford [etc.] : Distributed by Pergamon, 1975. — Portfolio : ill ; 32cm.
Seven folders, sound tape. — Bibl.
ISBN 0-08-020981-5 : £12.50
(B77-04707)

374'.013 — Vocational courses: Short courses. Planning. *Great Britain. Manuals*
Ruddick, Jennifer. Staff development in the social services : planning short courses : a handbook for organisers / [by Jennifer Ruddick, Priscilla Whiffen]. — London (Clifton House, Euston Rd, NW1 2RS) : Central Council for Education and Training in Social Work, [1976]. — [2],32,[1]p : 1 ill ; 21cm. — (Central Council for Education and Training in Social Work. Papers ; 14 ISSN 0306-4433)
ISBN 0-903720-34-5 Sd : £0.50
(B77-04074)

374'.013'02541 — Further education institutions. Vocational courses. *Great Britain. Directories*
Directory of technical and further education. — London : Godwin.
1977 : 17th ed. / general editor Paul J. Edmonds, compiling editor Annabel Swinnerton. — 1977. — viii,787p : maps ; 23cm.
Previously published as: Year book of technical education and training for industry. — Bibl.: p.764-765. — Index.
ISBN 0-7114-3411-5 : £12.00
ISSN 0309-5290
Also classified at 378'.01'302541
(B77-15229)

374'.02 — Adult education. Teaching methods. *Great Britain*
Rogers, Jennifer. Adults learning / [by] Jennifer Rogers. — 2nd ed. — Milton Keynes [etc.] : Open University Press, 1977. — 256p ; 18cm.
Previous ed.: Harmondsworth : Penguin, 1971. — Bibl.: p.250-252. — Index.
ISBN 0-335-00044-4 Pbk : £1.75
(B77-30112)

374'.4 — Correspondence courses. Lessons. Editing
Jenkins, Janet. Editing distance teaching texts : a handbook for those involved in preparing printed course materials / [by] Janet Jenkins. — Cambridge (131 Hills Rd, Cambridge CB2 1PD) : International Extension College, 1976. — [5],iii,61p : ill, facsims ; 21cm. — (International Extension College. Broadsheets on distance learning ; no.9 ISSN 0307-7322)
Bibl.: p.61.
ISBN 0-903632-12-8 Sd : Unpriced
(B77-11168)

374.8 — Vocational education institutions. Advisory committees. Organisation. *United States. Manuals*
Riendeau, Albert J. Advisory committees for occupational education : a guide to organization and operation / [by] Albert J. Riendeau. — New York ; London [etc.] : Gregg Division, McGraw-Hill, 1977. — vi,90p : forms ; 21cm.
Bibl.: p.88. — Index.
ISBN 0-07-052680-x Sd : £2.20
(B77-33155)

374.8'425'37 — Adult education institutions. *Lincolnshire. Boston. Pilgrim College, 1945-1975*
Champion, Alan. Pilgrim's progress, Boston, 1945-1975 / by Alan Champion. — Boston, Lincs. (80 Sleaford Rd, Boston, Lincs. PE21 8EU) : Richard Kay for the Governors of Pilgrim College [and] the Department of Adult Education, University of Nottingham, 1976. — 60p : ill, facsims, plan ; 21cm.
ISBN 0-902662-40-6 : £2.35
ISBN 0-902662-41-4 Pbk : £1.25
(B77-08949)

374.9 — ADULT AND FURTHER EDUCATION. HISTORICAL AND GEOGRAPHICAL TREATMENT

374.9'172'4 — Adult education. *Developing countries*
Townsend Coles, Edwin. Adult education in developing countries / by Edwin K. Townsend Coles. — 2nd ed. — Oxford [etc.] : Pergamon, 1977. — xviii,199p : ill ; 22cm. — (Pergamon international library)
Previous ed.: 1969. — Bibl.: p.195-196. — Index.
ISBN 0-08-021293-x : £5.00
(B77-24127)

374.9'41 — Adult education. *Great Britain*
Richards, Elfyn John. Adult education : a challenge to all / by E.J. Richards. — Cardiff ([P.O. Box 78, Cardiff CF1 1XL]) : University College, [1975]. — 18p ; 21cm.
'A Public Lecture given at University College, Cardiff, on 6 May 1975'.
ISBN 0-901426-14-8 Sd : £0.35
(B77-00136)

Rogers, Jennifer. Right to learn : the case for adult equality / [by] Jennifer Rogers and Brian Groombridge ; photographs by Fay Godwin. — London [etc.] : Arrow Books, 1976. — 202p, [16]p of plates : ill ; 18cm.
Index.
ISBN 0-09-914030-6 Pbk : £1.25
(B77-01305)

374.9'41 — Further education. *Great Britain. Conference proceedings*
Association of Colleges for Further and Higher Education. *Annual General Meeting, Institution of Electrical Engineers, 1976.* The future of further and higher education : [two papers with discussion report presented at the] Annual General Meeting [of] the Association of Colleges for Further and Higher Education [held] Thursday and Friday, 26th and 27 February 1976 [at] the Institution of Electrical Engineers, Savoy Place, London W.C.2. — London : The Association, 1976. — [1],22p ; 21cm.
Contents: Paper 1 / by E.H. Simpson - Paper II / by Roy P. Harding - Report of the discussion / by K.R. Bishop.
ISBN 0-900096-68-3 Sd : £0.25
Also classified at 378.41
(B77-02186)

374.9'41 — Further education. *Great Britain. For school leavers*
Jackson, Florence Emma. Student hindsight : on from school : choosing the next step : advice from those who have chosen / [by] Florence E. Jackson. — Cambridge : Hobsons Press [for] the Careers Research and Advisory Centre, 1976. — [3],64p ; 22cm.
ISBN 0-86021-095-2 : £4.00
ISBN 0-86021-061-8 Pbk : £1.25
(B77-02187)

374.9'41 — Further education. *Great Britain. Periodicals*
Journal of further and higher education. — London : National Association of Teachers in Further and Higher Education.
Supersedes: Education for teaching.
Vol.1, no.1- ; Spring 1977-. — 1977-. — ill ; 24cm.
Three issues a year. — Cover title. — [2],140p. in 1st issue. — Bibl.
Pbk : £4.00 yearly
ISSN 0309-877x
(B77-24128)

374.9'41 — Further education institutions. Administration. *Great Britain*
Wheeler, G E. Management of a further education college / by G.E. Wheeler. — London : Association of Colleges for Further and Higher Education, [1977]. — [1],15,[1]p ; 21cm.
Address delivered at the Annual General Meeting of the Association of Colleges for Further and Higher Education held on Thursday and Friday, 24th and 25th, February 1977 at the Institution of Electrical Engineers, Savoy Place, London W.C.2.
Sd : £0.50
(B77-27780)

374.9'41 — Local communities. Role of further education institutions. *Great Britain. Reports, surveys*
Aitken, Robert, *b.1928.* The colleges in the community / by Robert Aitken. — [London] : [Association of Colleges for Further and Higher Education], [1976]. — [1],10p : 3 ill ; 21cm.
'[A paper presented at the] Summer Meeting [of] The Association of Colleges for Further and Higher Education [held at] Brighton 9th, 10th, 11th June, 1976'.
ISBN 0-900096-69-1 Sd : £0.25
(B77-02188)

374.9'42 — Adult education. Role of universities. *England*
Ellwood, Caroline. Adult learning today : a new role for the universities? / [by] Caroline Ellwood. — London [etc.] : Sage Publications, [1977]. — [6],265,[1]p : ill, maps ; 23cm. — (Sage studies in social and educational change ; vol.4)
Published in the United States: 1976. — Bibl.: p.261-265.
ISBN 0-8039-9979-8 : £6.00
ISBN 0-8039-0853-8 Pbk : £3.00
(B77-11738)

374.9'42 — Colleges of further education. *England*
Bristow, Adrian. Inside the colleges of further education / [by] Adrian Bristow. — 2nd ed. — London : H.M.S.O. [for the Department of Education and Science], 1976. — vi,158p,[20]p of plates : ill ; 18cm.
Previous ed.: 1970.
ISBN 0-11-270331-3 Pbk : £1.20
(B77-13607)

374.9'424'96 — Further education institutions. Students, 16-19 years. Education. *Great Britain. Study regions: West Midlands (Metropolitan County). Birmingham. Reports, surveys. Serials*
Birmingham Educational Development Centre. Education 16 to 19 : EDC project two : report / Birmingham Educational Development Centre. — Birmingham (Garrison La., Birmingham B9 4BS) : The Centre.
2nd. — 1971. — [1],59p ; 21cm.
Sd : £0.35
Primary classification 373.2'38'0942496
(B77-11737)

374.9'426'59 — Colleges of further education. Students, 16-19 years. Education. *Cambridgeshire. Cambridge region. Proposals*
Cambridgeshire *(County). Education Committee.* Post-16 education in the Cambridge area : a consultative document / Cambridgeshire Education Committee. — Cambridge (Shire Hall, [Castle Hill], Cambridge [CB3 0AP]) : Cambridgeshire Education Committee], 1976. — [3],18p ; 30cm.
ISBN 0-9500179-8-1 Sd : Unpriced
Primary classification 373.2'38'0942659
(B77-14660)

374.9'429'29 — Adult education institutions. *Gwynedd. Harlech. Coleg Harlech, to 1977*
Stead, Peter. Coleg Harlech : the first fifty years / by Peter Stead. — Cardiff : University of Wales Press, 1977. — xv,135p,[16]p of plates : ill, ports ; 25cm.
Index.
ISBN 0-7083-0657-8 Pbk : £4.00
(B77-33156)

375 — CURRICULUM
Kelly, Albert Victor. The curriculum : theory and practice / [by] A.V. Kelly. — London [etc.] : Harper and Row, 1977. — [10],202p ; 22cm.
Bibl.: p.187-194. — Index.
ISBN 0-06-318053-7 : £4.95 : CIP rev.
ISBN 0-06-318054-5 Pbk : £2.75
(B77-07248)

375 — Schools. Curriculum subjects: Integrated studies
Integrated Studies Working Party. Integrated studies : aims and objectives / Integrated Studies Working Party. — [Nottingham] : University of Nottingham, School of Education, 1976. — [5],30,[1]p ; 30cm. — (Integrated studies working paper ; no.1)
Cover title.
ISBN 0-85359-045-1 Pbk : £0.50
(B77-10312)

375 — Waldorf schools. Curriculum
Carlgren, Frans. Education towards freedom : Rudolph Steiner education : a survey of the work of Waldorf schools throughout the world / text Frans Carlgren ; prefaces Rudolf Grosse and Alan Howard ; layout Arne Klingborg ; English edition Joan and Siegfried Rudel ; [translated from the German]. — East Grinstead (Peredur, East Grinstead, W. Sussex) : Lanthorn Press, 1976. — 208p : ill(chiefly col), col facsims, col maps, col ports ; 25x35cm.
Translation and revision of: 'Erziehung zur Freiheit'. Stuttgart : Verlag Freies Geistesleben, 1972. — Bibl.: p.204.
£7.00
(B77-29325)

375'.001 — Schools. Curriculum. Innovation
Innovation, the school and the teacher. — Milton Keynes : Open University Press.
2 / prepared by Eric Hoyle and Robert McCormick ; [for the Open University Curriculum Design and Development Course Team]. — 1976. — 90p : ill, plan, ports ; 30cm. — (Educational studies, a second level course : curriculum design and development ; units 29 and 30) (E203 ; units 29 and 30)
Bibl.
ISBN 0-335-06561-9 : Unpriced
(B77-02189)

375'.001'0941 — Schools. Curriculum. Development. *Great Britain. Conference proceedings*
Standing Conference on Curriculum Studies, *4th, Worcester College of Higher Education, 1976.* New contexts for teaching, learning and curriculum studies : proceedings of the Fourth Standing Conference on Curriculum Studies / edited by Colin Richards. — [Leicester] ([c/o The editor, University of Leicester, School of Education, The University Centre, Leicester Parade, Barrack Rd, Northampton NN2 6AF]) : Association for the Study of the Curriculum, [1977]. — [157p] ; 30cm.
'Held at Worcester College of Higher Education in April 1976' - Foreword. — Bibl.
Sd : £3.00
(B77-18683)

375'.001'0941 — Schools. Curriculum. Planning. Great Britain. Related to accountability. *Lectures, speeches*
Whitfield, Richard Charles. Curriculum planning, teaching and educational accountability / [by] Richard C. Whitfield. — Birmingham (Gosta Green, Birmingham B4 7ET) : Department of Educational Enquiry, University of Aston in Birmingham, [1976]. — [4],28p : ill ; 21cm. — (University of Aston in Birmingham. Inaugural lectures) (Aston educational enquiry monograph ; no.6)
'... [delivered on] 21st October 1976'.
Sd : £0.35
(B77-26247)

375'.001'0973 — Schools. Curriculum. Development. *United States*
Oliver, Albert I. Curriculum improvement : a guide to problems, principles, and process / [by] Albert I. Oliver. — 2nd ed. — New York [etc.] ; London : Harper and Row, 1977. — viii,392p : ill ; 24cm.
Previous ed.: New York : Dodd, Mead, 1965. — Bibl. — Index.
ISBN 0-06-044912-8 : £8.95
(B77-20173)

375'.006 — Schools. Curriculum. Innovation. Evaluation. *Great Britain. Reports, surveys*
Munro, R G. Innovation : success or failure? / [by] R.G. Munro. — London [etc.] : Hodder and Stoughton, 1977. — x,70p ; 25cm. — (Curriculum research papers ; 1)
Bibl.: p.68-70.
ISBN 0-340-20900-3 Pbk : £1.75
(B77-13608)

375'.006'08 — Schools. Curriculum. Evaluation. *Readings*
Beyond the numbers game : a reader in educational evaluation / edited by David Hamilton ... [et al.]. — Basingstoke [etc.] : Macmillan, 1977. — viii,360p : 2 ill ; 24cm.
Bibl.: p.356-360.
ISBN 0-333-19872-7 : £6.25
ISBN 0-333-21274-6 Pbk : £4.95
(B77-26983)

375'.0094 — Schools. Curriculum. Control. *Western Europe. Conference proceedings*
British Educational Administration Society. *Annual Conference, 5th, London, 1976.* Control of the curriculum : issues and trends in Britain and Europe : proceedings of the Fifth Annual Conference of the British Educational Administration Society, London, September 1976 / edited for the Society by Ron Glatter. — [London] : University of London Institute of Education ; Windsor : Distributed by NFER, 1977. — 147p : ill ; 22cm. — (Studies in education : new series ; 4 ISSN 0458-2101)
Bibl.: p.94-95.
ISBN 0-85473-072-9 Pbk : £2.75
(B77-14661)

375'.00941 — Schools. Curriculum. Reform. *Great Britain. Proposals*
White, J P. Towards a compulsory curriculum / [by] J.P. White. — London [etc.] : Routledge and Kegan Paul, 1977. — ix,112p ; 22cm. — (Students library of education)
Originally published: 1973. — Bibl.: p.106-107. — Index.
ISBN 0-7100-8720-9 : £1.75
(B77-29326)

376 — EDUCATION OF WOMEN

376 — Women. Vocational education. *Great Britain, 1965-1975*

London and Home Counties Regional Advisory Council for Technological Education. *Committee on Vocational Courses for Women.* The vocational education of women : the report of the Council's [i.e. the London and Home Counties Regional Advisory Council for Technological Education] Vocational Courses for Women Committee, 1965-1975. — [London] : [The Council], 1976. — [1],29p ; 21cm.
Bibl.: p.20.
Sd : £0.60
(B77-16816)

376'.63 — Girls' public schools. *Great Britain. Directories*

The **girls'** school year book. — London : A. and C. Black.
1977 : seventy-first year of publication. — [1977]. — xxxiv,750p : ill ; 19cm.
Index.
ISBN 0-7136-1712-8 : £3.25
ISSN 0072-4564
(B77-16310)

376'.65'0973 — Women. Higher education. Equality of opportunity. *United States*

Fitzpatrick, Blanche. Women's inferior education : an economic analysis / [by] Blanche Fitzpatrick. — New York [etc.] ; London : Praeger, 1976. — xv,190p : ill ; 25cm. — (Praeger special studies in US economic, social and political issues)
Bibl.: p.182-189.
ISBN 0-275-56670-6 : £12.20
(B77-05323)

377 — SCHOOLS AND RELIGION

377'.1 — Middle schools. Morning assembly. Stories. *Anthologies*

Stories of great lives / edited by D.M. Prescott. — Poole : Blandford Press, 1977. — viii,178p ; 19cm. — (School assembly books)
ISBN 0-7137-0850-6 Pbk : £2.50
(B77-31804)

377'.1 — Schools. Morning assembly. Activities. *For teaching*

Taylor, Dorothy Jean. Explorations in assembly with children : suggestions for assembly in the junior school / by Dorothy J. Taylor. — Guildford [etc.] : Lutterworth Press, 1973. — 94p ; 20cm.
Bibl.: p.85-91.
ISBN 0-7188-2042-8 Sp : £1.10
(B77-05994)

377'.1 — Secondary schools. Morning assembly. Activities. Special themes: Harvest

Christian Aid. The harvesters : Harvest Assembly suggestions for secondary schools / prepared jointly by Christian Aid and Christian Education Movement ; [compiled and written by Harry Undy and Andrew Hutchinson]. — London (P.O. Box no.1 SW1W 9BW) : Christian Aid ; London (2 Chester House, Pages La., N10 1PR) : Christian Education Movement, 1976. — 14p : port ; 21cm.
Bibl.: p.5-5.
Sd : Unpriced
(B77-03486)

377'.1 — Secondary schools. Morning assembly. Stories. *Anthologies*

Cheston, Molly. Pause for thought / twenty-five stories for assembly with follow-up work ; [by] Molly Cheston. — Glasgow [etc.] : Blackie, 1976. — viii,87p ; 22cm.
ISBN 0-216-90262-2 Pbk : £1.55
(B77-11739)

377'.1 — Secondary schools. Morning assembly. Themes. *Great Britain. Secondary school texts*

Mullen, Peter. Assembling / [by] Peter Mullen. — London : Edward Arnold, 1977. — xi,107p ; 22cm.
Index.
ISBN 0-7131-0173-3 Pbk : £1.75 : CIP rev.
(B77-28543)

377'.8'2 — Roman Catholic schools. *Roman Catholic viewpoints*

Roman Catholic Church. *Congregatio pro Institutione Catholica.* The Catholic school / the Sacred Congregation for Catholic Education. — Rome : Vatican Polyglot Press ; London : Distributed by the Catholic Truth Society, 1977. — 3-36,[1]p ; 21cm.
Sd : £0.40
(B77-28544)

377'.8'2417 — Roman Catholic schools. *Ireland (Republic)*

Is integrated schooling the answer? / by a group of Catholic parents ; edited by Vera Verba. — Dublin (55 Lower Gardiner St., Dublin 1) : Vera Verba Publications, [1977]. — [1],68,[2]p ; 18cm. — (Education and the Irish child ; vol.1, no.2)
Bibl.: p.68.
Sd : £0.50
(B77-24129)

378 — HIGHER EDUCATION

378 — Universities. *Transcripts of interviews*

Urban, George Robert. Hazards of learning : an international symposium on the crisis of the university / edited by G.R. Urban. — London : Temple Smith, 1977. — xix,294p ; 21cm.
'This symposium consists of edited versions of conversations originally broadcast in 1973 and 1974, by Radio Free Europe' - title page verso.
ISBN 0-85117-120-6 : £6.75
(B77-19300)

378'.001 — Colleges. Theories

Abbs, Peter. Proposal for a new college / by Peter Abbs and Graham Carey. — London : Heinemann Educational, 1977. — [4],92p ; 19cm.
Bibl.: p.88-91.
ISBN 0-435-80013-2 Pbk : £1.50
(B77-28545)

378'.001 — Higher education. *Philosophical perspectives*

Brubacher, John Seiler. On the philosophy of higher education / [by] John S. Brubacher. — San Francisco [etc.] ; London : Jossey-Bass, 1977. — xiii,143p ; 24cm. — (The Jossey-Bass series in higher education)
Bibl.: p.125-136. — Index.
ISBN 0-87589-306-6 : £7.50
(B77-23302)

378'.001'84 — Higher education institutions. Applications of operations research. *Periodicals*

New directions for institutional research. — San Francisco [etc.] ; London : Jossey-Bass.
1- ; Spring 1974-. — 1974-. — ill ; 24cm.
Quarterly. — xii,117p. in no.13. — Nos 1-9 lack London imprint.
Pbk : £4.00
(B77-25524)

378'.0025'171241 — Universities. *Commonwealth countries. Directories*

Commonwealth universities yearbook : a directory to the universities of the Commonwealth and the handbook of their Association / [Association of Commonwealth Universities]. — London : The Association.
1976 : [fifty-third ed.] / [joint editors Sir Hugh W. Springer, T. Craig, assistant editor Eileen A. Archer]. — 1976. — 4v.(xxv,2467p) : maps ; 28cm.
In slip case. — Bibl.: p.2141-2158. — Index.
ISBN 0-85143-042-2 Pbk : Unpriced
ISSN 0069-7745
(B77-02904)

378'.0028'54 — Higher education institutions. Digital computer systems. Policies of government. *Great Britain. Proposals*

Computer Board for Universities and Research Councils. Computers in higher education and research : the next decade : a statement of future policy by the Computer Board for Universities and Research Councils for discussion with universities, research councils, and other interested bodies / [for the] Department of Education and Science. — London : H.M.S.O., 1976. — [2],24p ; 25cm.
ISBN 0-11-270440-9 Sd : £0.60
(B77-10313)

378'.0028'54 — Universities. *Great Britain. Open University. Digital computer systems. Implementation. Reports, surveys*

British Computer Society. *Bedfordshire Branch. Seminar, Open University, 1976.* Database implementation experience : [proceedings of the] British Computer Society (Bedfordshire Branch) seminar, the Open University, 13th October 1976. — [London] : The Society, [1977]. — [5], 65p : ill ; 30cm.
ISBN 0-901865-20-6 Pbk : £6.00
(B77-16311)

378'.0028'54 — Universities. Applications of computer system networks

Jarratt, P. Only connect / [by] P. Jarratt. — [Birmingham] : University of Birmingham, 1977. — [2],15p ; 21cm. — (University of Birmingham. Inaugural lectures)
'... delivered in the University of Birmingham on 11 May 1976' - title page verso.
ISBN 0-7044-0240-8 Sd : Unpriced
(B77-15230)

378'.007'2 — Higher education. Research

Beard, Ruth Mary. On the growth of research into higher education / by Ruth Beard. — [Bradford] ([Bradford, W. Yorkshire BD7 1DP]) : [University of Bradford], 1976. — [2], 26p ; 21cm. — (University of Bradford. Inaugural lectures)
'... delivered at the University of Bradford on 14 October 1975'. — Bibl.: p.25-26.
ISBN 0-901945-24-2 Sd : Unpriced
(B77-00705)

378'.009172'4 — Higher education. Projects. *Developing countries*

Thompson, Kenneth Winfred. Higher education and social change : promising experiments in developing countries / [by] Kenneth W. Thompson, Barbara R. Fogel. — New York [etc.] ; London : Praeger. — (Praeger special studies in international economics and development)
Vol.1 : Reports. — 1976. — xiv,224,[1]p ; 25cm.
Index.
ISBN 0-275-23150-x : £12.20
(B77-05324)

Thompson, Kenneth Winfred. Higher education and social change : promising experiments in developing countries / by Kenneth W. Thompson, Barbara R. Fogel. — New York [etc.] ; London : Praeger. — (Praeger special studies in international economics and development)
Vol.2 : Case studies / edited by Kenneth W. Thompson, Barbara R. Fogel, Helen E. Danner. — 1977. — xxiii,565p : ill ; 25cm.
Published for the International Council for Educational Development. — Index.
ISBN 0-275-23390-1 : £22.20
(B77-14168)

378'.01'302541 — British qualifications. *Directories*

Priestley, Barbara. British qualifications : a comprehensive guide to educational, technical, professional and academic qualifications in Britain / compiled by Barbara Priestley. — 6th ed. — London : Kogan Page, 1975. — 1008p : ill ; 23cm.
Previous ed.: 1974. — Index.
ISBN 0-85038-281-5 : £8.50
(B77-00706)

Priestley, Barbara. British qualifications : a comprehensive guide to educational, technical, professional and academic qualifications in Britain / compiled by Barbara Priestley. — 7th ed. — London : Kogan Page, 1976. — 829p : ill ; 23cm.
Previous ed.: 1975. — Index.
ISBN 0-85038-401-x : £9.00
(B77-07249)

378'.01'302541 — Higher education institutions. Vocational courses. *Great Britain. Directories*

Directory of technical and further education. — London : Godwin.
1977 : 17th ed. / general editor Paul J. Edmonds, compiling editor Annabel Swinnerton. — 1977. — viii,787p : maps ; 23cm.
Previously published as: Year book of technical education and training for industry. — Bibl.: p.764-765. — Index.
ISBN 0-7114-3411-5 : £12.00
ISSN 0309-5290
Primary classification 374'.013'02541
(B77-15229)

378'.01'30941 — Professional education. *Great Britain. Yearbooks*

Education and training : your guide to over 4,000 training and employment opportunities in industry, commerce, hospitals and public service / Confederation of British Industry. — Cambridge : Hobsons Press for CRAC.
1976-77. — [1976]. — [2],30,375p : ill, maps ; 31cm.
Cover title. — Index.
ISBN 0-86021-054-5 : £7.00
ISSN 0309-0027
(B77-01306)

The **job** book : the yearbook of education and training : training and career choices for school and college leavers. — [Cambridge] : Hobsons Press for the Careers Research and Advisory Centre [and] the Confederation of British Industry.
1977. — [1976]. — 308,[1]p : ill, maps ; 30cm.
Cover title. — Previously published: as 'Education and training'. — Bibl. — Index.
ISBN 0-86021-103-7 Pbk : Unpriced
ISBN 0-86021-012-9 Pbk : Unpriced
ISSN 0309-9059
(B77-30113)

378'.01'30973 — Professional education. *United States. Conference proceedings*
Crossfire in Professional Education : Students, the Professions, and Society *(Conference), Evanston, 1975.* Crossfire in professional education : students, the professions and society : proceedings of a conference sponsored by Northwestern University Schools of Dentistry, Education, Engineering, Journalism, Law, Management, Medicine, October 16-17, 1975, Evanston, Illinois / edited by Bruno A. Boley. — New York ; Oxford [etc.] : Pergamon, 1977. — x,108p : ill, ports ; 24cm.
'Northwestern University Conference "Crossfire in Professional Education : Students, the Professions, and Society" ...' - p.ix.
ISBN 0-08-021429-0 : £5.00
(B77-26984)

378.1 — HIGHER EDUCATION. ORGANISATION AND ADMINISTRATION

378.1 — Higher education institutions. Authority & power. *Great Britain. Conference proceedings*
Society for Research into Higher Education. *Annual Conference, 11th, 1975.* Power and authority in higher education : papers presented at the eleventh annual conference of the Society [for Research into Higher Education] in December 1975 / edited by Colin Flood Page and Mary Yates. — Guildford : The Society, 1976. — [5],94p ; 21cm. — (Society for Research into Higher Education. Occasional papers)
ISBN 0-900868-53-8 Pbk : £3.60(£2.70 to members)
(B77-06590)

378.1 — Large communities. Communication networks. Research. Small World Method. *United States. Study examples: Large universities*
Shotland, Robert Lance. University communication networks : the small world method / [by] R. Lance Shotland. — New York ; London [etc.] : Wiley, 1976. — xi,179p : ill, forms ; 23cm.
Bibl.: p.136-145. — Index.
ISBN 0-471-78855-4 Pbk : £5.50
(B77-07875)

378.1'009 — Universities. *Canada, England & United States, to 1975. Comparative studies*
Ross, Murray George. The university : the anatomy of academe / [by] Murray G. Ross ; [editors Nancy Frank, Cheryl Love and Michael Hennelly]. — New York ; London [etc.] : McGraw-Hill, 1976. — xiii,310p ; 24cm.
Bibl.: p.283-295. — Index.
ISBN 0-07-053876-x : £8.85
(B77-02190)

378.1'03 — Community development. Role of higher education institutions. *United States*
College leadership for community renewal : beyond community-based education / [by] James F. Gollattscheck ... [et al.]. — San Francisco [etc.] ; London : Jossey-Bass, 1976. — xv,160p ; 24cm. — (The Jossey-Bass series in higher education)
Bibl.: p.145-157. — Index.
ISBN 0-87589-299-x : £8.65
(B77-11169)

378.1'03 — Universities. Services for industries. *Great Britain. Directories*
Directory of university-industry liaison services / edited by Brunel Industrial Services Bureau. — 4th ed. — Uxbridge (Kingston La., Uxbridge, Middx UB8 3PH) : Brunel University, 1976. — 57p : map ; 22cm.
Two sheets ([2] sides) in pocket. — Previous ed.: 1975.
Sd : Unpriced
(B77-07876)

378.1'05'60941 — Polytechnics. Council for National Academic Awards courses. Admission. Applications. *Great Britain. Manuals*
Cross, Penelope. Choosing a polytechnic : a guide to degree course opportunities outside university / by Penelope Cross. — Cambridge : Advisory Centre for Education, 1976. — [3], 38p ; 22cm. — (Advisory Centre for Education. Advisory booklets ; no.6)
Bibl.: p.32-38.
ISBN 0-900029-45-5 Sd : £1.20
(B77-00137)

378.1'05'60941 — Universities. Admission. Applications. *Great Britain. Manuals*
Hatton, Stella. Choosing a university : a guide for applicants / by Stella Hatton. — 2nd revised ed. — Cambridge : Advisory Centre for Education, 1974. — [4],43,[1]p ; 21cm. — (Advisory Centre for Education. Advisory booklets ; no.5)
Previous ed.: 1972. — Bibl.: p.36-43.
ISBN 0-900029-37-4 Sd : £0.70
(B77-18684)

Hatton, Stella. Choosing a university : a guide for applicants / by Stella Hatton. — 3rd revised ed. — [Cambridge] : Advisory Centre for Education, 1976. — [4],43p ; 21cm. — (Advisory Centre for Education. Advisory booklets ; no.5)
Previous ed.: 1974. — Bibl.: p.37-43.
ISBN 0-900029-44-7 Sd : £1.20
(B77-00138)

378.1'05'7 — Universities. Entrance requirements: Public examinations in computer science. Recognition. *Great Britain. Reports, surveys*
Leverett, S M. The recognition of computer studies examinations as entrance qualifications to universities / by S.M. Leverett. — Chelmsford (c/o Chelmer Institute of High Education, Victoria Rd South, Chelmsford, Essex CM1 1LL) : Advisory Unit for Computer Education in Essex, 1976. — [3],5,ii[i.e. iii]p ; 30cm.
Sd : £0.50
(B77-10314)

378.1'05'941 — Universities. Students. Population. *Great Britain. Forecasts for 1977-1988*
Association of University Teachers. University student numbers / Association of University Teachers. — London (1 Pembridge Rd, W11 3HJ) : [The Association], [1977]. — 11p : ill ; 30cm.
Sd : Unpriced
(B77-17408)

378.1'1'0924 — Colleges. *Leicestershire. Loughborough. Loughborough College. Schofield, Herbert*
Harvey, Joan Margaret. Herbert Schofield and Loughborough College / by Joan M. Harvey. — Diseworth (42 Hall Gate, Diseworth, Derby DE7 2QJ) : The author, [1976]. — [3],92p : ill, coat of arms, map, ports ; 22cm.
Bibl.: p.92.
ISBN 0-9505928-0-3 Sd : £1.50
(B77-09643)

378.1'1'0924 — Universities. Colleges. *Oxfordshire. Oxford. New College, Oxford. Spooner, William Archibald. Biographies*
Hayter, *Sir* William. Spooner : a biography / [by] William Hayter. — London : W.H. Allen, 1977. — 191p,leaf of plate,[8]p of plates : ill, ports ; 23cm.
Bibl.: p.182. — Index.
ISBN 0-491-01658-1 : £4.95
(B77-11170)

378.1'11'0924 — Negroes. Professional education. Washington, Booker Taliaferro. *United States. Documents*
Washington, Booker Taliaferro. The Booker T. Washington papers. — Urbana [etc.] ; London : University of Illinois Press.
Vol.5 : 1899-1900 / Louis R. Harlan and Raymond W. Smock, editors, Barbara S. Kraft, assistant editor. — 1976. — xxviii,747p : 1 ill ; 25cm.
Bibl.: p.711-715. — Index.
ISBN 0-252-00627-5 : £13.10
(B77-32560)

378.1'2 — Higher education institutions. Teaching. Evaluation. *Great Britain. Conference proceedings*
Evaluating teaching in higher education : a collection of conference papers. — London (55 Gordon Sq., WC1H 0NT) : University Teaching Methods Unit, 1975. — xii,111p : 1 ill, form ; 21cm.
'The papers ... were all read at a conference organised by the University of London Teaching Methods Unit and held in April 1975' - Preface. — Bibl.
ISBN 0-85473-053-2 Pbk : £2.30
(B77-02191)

378.1'2'071141 — Universities. Teachers. Training. *Great Britain. Conference proceedings*
Issues in staff development : a collection of conference papers. — London (55 Gordon Sq., WC1H 0NT) : University Teaching Methods Unit, 1975. — [7],128p : ill ; 21cm. — (Staff development in universities programme)
'... it was decided that the University Teaching Methods Unit and the Department of Educational Administration should co-operate in a joint Staff Development in Universities programme ... In 1974 the organisers ... felt it would be useful to bring together workers in the field ...' - Preface.
ISBN 0-85473-052-4 Pbk : £2.20
(B77-02192)

378.1'21 — Universities. Academic freedom. *Germany, 1900-1910*
Weber, Max. Max Weber on universities : the power of the state and the dignity of the academic calling in imperial Germany / translated [from the German], edited and with an introductory note by Edward Shils. — Chicago ; London : University of Chicago Press, 1974. — [5],62p ; 23cm. — (A phoenix book)
'Reprinted from "Minerva", vol.11, no.4 (October 1973)' - title page verso.
ISBN 0-226-87726-4 Pbk : Unpriced
(B77-19301)

378.1'22 — Higher education institutions. Departments. Organisation. *United States*
McHenry, Dean E. Academic departments / [by] Dean E. McHenry and associates. — San Francisco [etc.] ; London : Jossey-Bass, 1977. — iii-xxi,240p ; 24cm. — (The Jossey-Bass series in higher education)
Bibl.: p.225-233. — Index.
ISBN 0-87589-307-4 : £10.60
(B77-21060)

378.1'54 — Polytechnics. Courses. *England. Directories*
Polytechnic courses in England and Wales : full-time and sandwich advanced courses. — London : Lund Humphries for the Committee of Directors of Polytechnics.
1977-8 : 6th ed. — 1976. — 359p : ill, map ; 21cm.
Previously published: as 'Handbook of polytechnic courses in England and Wales'. — Index.
ISBN 0-905564-01-4 Pbk : £3.35
(B77-18049)

378.1'55 — Universities. Expansion. Forecasting. *Great Britain. Reports, surveys*
Conference of University Administrators. *Group on Forecasting and University Expansion.* Interim report, 1977 / Conference of University Administrators, Group on Forecasting and University Expansion. — Glasgow (M.G.E. Paulson-Ellis, Conference of University Administrators, University of Strathclyde, Royal College Building, George St., Glasgow G1 1XW) : The Conference, 1977. — [8],62p : ill ; 30cm.
Sp : £1.00
(B77-32561)

378.1'55'06241 — Universities. Administration. Organisations. *Great Britain. Committee of Vice-Chancellors and Principals of the Universities of the United Kingdom. Reports, surveys*
Committee of Vice-Chancellors and Principals of the Universities of the United Kingdom. Report on the period 1972-76 / the Committee of Vice-Chancellors and Principals of the Universities of the United Kingdom. — [London] ([29 Tavistock Sq., WC1H 9EZ]) : [The Committee], [1976]. — 74p ; 21cm.
ISBN 0-85143-051-1 Sd : Unpriced
(B77-14169)

378.1'55'0941 — Universities. Administration. *Great Britain. Reports, surveys. Serials*
University Grants Committee. University Grants Committee annual survey [for the] academic year ... — London : H.M.S.O.
1975-76. — [1977]. — 58p ; 25cm. — (Cmnd.6750)
ISBN 0-10-167500-3 Sd : £1.00
(B77-16817)

378.1'55'09411 — Universities. Administrative powers. Devolution. *Scotland. Proposals*
Grant, Nigel. Scottish universities, the case for devolution / [by Nigel Grant, Alex Main]. — [Edinburgh] ([c/o University of Edinburgh, Department of Educational Studies, 11 Buccleuch Place, Edinburgh EH8 9JT]) : [The authors], [1976]. — [1],24p : 1 ill ; 21cm.
ISBN 0-902148-04-4 Sd : £0.20
(B77-14170)

378.1'552 — Higher education institutions. Modular degree courses. *Great Britain. Reports, surveys*
Mansell, Tony. The container revolution : a study of unit and modular schemes / ... by Tony Mansell with ... [others] ; [for the] Group for Research and Innovation in Higher Education. — London : Nuffield Foundation, 1976. — 38p ; 22cm.
ISBN 0-904956-13-x Sd : Unpriced
(B77-02193)

378.1'552'02541 — Council for National Academic Awards courses: First degree courses. *Great Britain. Directories*
Directory of first degree courses / [Council for National Academic Awards]. — London (344 Gray's Inn Rd, WC1X 8BP) : C.N.A.A.
[1976]. — 1976. — 159p ; 21cm.
Index.
ISBN 0-902071-05-x Sd : Unpriced
ISSN 0308-8057
(B77-04708)

378.1'552'02541 — Higher education institutions. First degree courses. *Great Britain. Directories*
Degree course guides : guides to first-degree courses in UK universities and colleges / CRAC. — Cambridge : Hobsons Press.
1976-77. — 1976. — 815p in various pagings ; 22cm.
'... comprises the collected edition of the 21 Degree Course Guides published in 1976' - jacket. — Bibl. — Index.
ISBN 0-86021-091-x : Unpriced
ISSN 0309-0485
(B77-02194)

378.1'553'02541 — Council for National Academic Awards courses: Postgraduate courses. *Great Britain. Directories*
Directory of postgraduate courses / [Council for National Academic Awards]. — London (344 Gray's Inn Rd, WC1X 8BP) : C.N.A.A.
[1976]. — 1976. — 75p ; 21cm.
Index.
ISBN 0-902071-02-5 Sd : Unpriced
ISSN 0308-8065
(B77-00139)

378.1'553'02541 — Postgraduate courses. *Great Britain. Directories*
Graduate studies / Careers Research and Advisory Centre. — Cambridge : Hobsons Press.
1976-77 / [editor Jenny Knight]. — 1976. — i, 31,773p ; 22cm.
Index.
ISBN 0-86021-052-9 : £35.00
ISSN 0309-0949
(B77-00707)

378.1'553'0924 — Universities. *Switzerland. Fribourg. Université de Fribourg. American students. Postgraduate education. Personal observations*
Hitner, John. Two for the road : Ph D European plan / [by] John and Elizabeth Hitner. — Ilfracombe : Stockwell, 1977. — 195p,[2]leaves of plates,[8]p of plates : ill(incl 1 col), facsims ; 22cm.
Index.
ISBN 0-7223-0997-x : £4.25
Primary classification 914'.04'55
(B77-29799)

378.1'554'09421 — Extra-mural education. Role of University of London. *London, to 1976*
Burrows, John, *b.1919.* University adult education in London : a century of achievement / [by] John Burrows. — [London] : University of London ; Leicester : Distributed by National Institute of Adult Education, 1976. — x,122p ; 21cm.
Fold. cover. — Index.
ISBN 0-7187-0428-2 Pbk : £1.25
(B77-06591)

378.1'66'4 — Higher education institutions. Students. Academic achievement. *Great Britain. Case studies*
Entwistle, Noel James. Degrees of excellence : the academic achievement game / [by] Noel J. Entwistle and John D. Wilson assisted by ... [others]. — London [etc.] : Hodder and Stoughton, 1977. — ix,226p : ill, forms ; 24cm.
Bibl.: p.169-177. — Index.
ISBN 0-340-20901-1 : £7.95
(B77-23303)

378.1'66'4 — Higher education institutions. Students. Academic achievement. Assessment
Heywood, John, *b. 1930.* Assessment in higher education / [by] John Heywood. — London [etc.] : Wiley, 1977. — xiii,289p : ill, forms ; 24cm.
Bibl.: p.258-284. — Index.
ISBN 0-471-99404-9 : £10.00
(B77-14662)

378.1'66'4 — Higher education institutions. Students. Academic achievement. Assessment. *Great Britain*
Klug, Brian. The grading game / [by] Brian Klug. — [2nd ed.]. — London : NUS Publications, 1977. — 94p : ill ; 21cm.
Previous ed.: published as 'Pro-profiles'. 1974. — Bibl.: p.83-86. — Index.
ISBN 0-900544-63-5 Pbk : £2.20
(B77-14171)

378.1'66'4 — Higher education institutions. Students. Academic achievement. Assessment. *Ireland (Republic). Conference proceedings*
Student Assessment in Third Level Education *(Conference), Dublin, 1975.* Student assessment in third level education : papers presented at a seminar organised jointly by the Association of Vocational Education Colleges, (AVEC) [and] the National Council for Educational Awards, (NCEA), held at College of Technology, Bolton Street, Dublin, 19th/20th September, 1975. — [Dublin] ([26 Mountjoy Sq., Dublin 1]) : N.C.E.A., [1977]. — 83p : ill ; 21cm. — (National Council for Educational Awards. Publications ; 4)
'... a two-day seminar on "Student Assessment in Third Level Education"' - Introduction. — Bibl.
Pbk : Unpriced
(B77-21061)

378.1'7'02812 — Universities. *Great Britain. Open University. Study techniques. Manuals*
Open University. How to study : a guide to studying at the Open University. — [Milton Keynes] ([Walton Hall, Milton Keynes MK7 6AA]) : [Open University], [1976]. — 28,[1]p : 1 ill, forms ; 30cm.
Sd : Unpriced
(B77-24838)

378.1'7'078 — Higher education institutions. Resource centres. *Great Britain. Conference proceedings*
New approaches to learning resources in higher education : selected papers delivered at a DES/ATCDE/LA [i.e. Department of Education and Science/Association of Teachers in Colleges and Departments of Education/Library Association] joint conference held at the Windermere Hydro Hotel, Bowness-on-Windermere, Cumbria, 21-24 October 1975 / edited by Jean Stearns. — Wakefield (c/o A. Macdonald, The Library, Bretton Hall College, West Bretton, Wakefield) : National Association of Teachers in Further and Higher Education, Library Section, 1976. — 87p : ill ; 22cm.
ISBN 0-901390-19-4 Sd : £2.00
(B77-16818)

378.1'7'078 — Polytechnics. Resource centres. *Great Britain. Directories*
Register of educational development services in polytechnics : a brief statement of terms of reference, staff, resources and services provided in educational development services, including educational technology and AV/TV units, pertaining to the position in January, in 21 polytechnics. — Newcastle upon Tyne (c/o R. Fothergill, Petras, Pandon Building, Newcastle upon Tyne Polytechnic, Newcastle upon Tyne NE1 8ST) : The Conference.
1976 / compiled by Stuart Trickey ; on behalf of SCEDSIP Committee, Standing Conference on Educational Development Services in Polytechnics. — 1976. — [3],56,[1]p ; 21cm.
Sp : £2.50
(B77-27781)

378.1'7'0941 — Higher education institutions. Teaching. *Great Britain. Reports, surveys*
Group for Research and Innovation in Higher Education. Making the best of it : reconciling ends, means and resources in higher education : the final report of the Group for Research and Innovation in Higher Education. — London : Nuffield Foundation, 1976. — [6],37,[1]p ; 21cm.
ISBN 0-904956-16-4 Sd : £0.50
(B77-14172)

378.1'7'0973 — Higher education institutions. Teaching. *United States*
Eble, Kenneth Eugene. The craft of teaching / [by] Kenneth E. Eble. — San Francisco [etc.] ; London : Jossey-Bass, 1976. — xv,179p ; 24cm. — (The Jossey-Bass series in higher education)
Bibl.: p.173-176. — Index.
ISBN 0-87589-284-1 : £8.65
(B77-05325)

378.1'7'3 — Universities. *Great Britain. Open University. Teaching aids. Telecommunication systems*
Open University. *Telecommunication Systems Course Team.* Teaching by telephone / prepared by the [Open University Telecommunication Systems] Course Team. — Milton Keynes : Open University Press, 1976. — 56p : ill(some col), map ; 30cm. — (Technology, a third level course : telecommunication systems ; unit 16) (T321 ; 15)
With answers to self-assessment questions.
ISBN 0-335-06106-0 Pbk : £2.95
(B77-04709)

378.1'7'94 — Higher education. Tutoring. *Great Britain*
Bramley, Wyn. Personal tutoring in higher education / [by] Wyn Bramley. — Guildford : Society for Research into Higher Education, 1977. — iii,136p : ill ; 21cm. — (Research into higher education monographs ; 30 ISSN 0085-1523)
Bibl.: p.131-132.
ISBN 0-900868-56-2 Pbk : £4.10(£3.05 to members)
(B77-30114)

378.1'79'4450973 — Higher education institutions. Teaching methods. Applications of computer systems. *United States*
Rockart, John Fralick. Computers and the learning process in higher education : a report / prepared for the Carnegie Commission on Higher Education by John Fralick Rockart and Michael S. Scott Morton. — New York ; London [etc.] : McGraw-Hill, [1976]. — xxi, 356p : ill ; 24cm.
Published in the United States: 1975. — Bibl.: p.337-346. — Index.
ISBN 0-07-010122-1 : £14.55
(B77-07250)

378.1'94'0924 — Higher education institutions. Students. Counselling. Swainson, Mary. *Great Britain. Autobiographies*
Swainson, Mary. The spirit of counsel : the story of a pioneer in student counselling / [by] Mary Swainson. — London : Spearman, 1977. — 256p,[4]p of plates : 1 ill, ports ; 23cm.
Bibl. — Index.
ISBN 0-85435-103-5 : £4.50
(B77-29327)

378.1'94'0973 — Higher education institutions. Students. Counselling. *United States*
Miller, Theodore K. The future of student affairs / [by] Theodore K. Miller, Judith S. Prince. — San Francisco [etc.] ; London : Jossey-Bass, 1976. — xix,220p : ill ; 24cm. — ([Jossey-Bass series in higher education])
Bibl.: p.201-215. — Index.
ISBN 0-87589-298-1 : £8.95
(B77-15231)

378.1'96'7 — Universities. Computer systems. *Great Britain. Reports, surveys. Serials*
Computer Board for Universities and Research Councils. Report of the Computer Board ... / Computer Board for Universities and Research Councils. — London : H.M.S.O.
1975-1976 : for the period 1st April 1975-31st March 1976. — [1976]. — ii,19p ; 25cm. — (Cmnd.6696)
ISBN 0-10-166960-7 Sd : £0.45
(B77-07251)

378.1'98 — Higher education institutions. Students. Success. *Manuals*
Cassie, William Fisher. Student's guide to success / [by] W. Fisher Cassie, T. Constantine. — London [etc.] : Macmillan, 1977. — vi, 170p : ill ; 24cm.
Index.
ISBN 0-333-23277-1 Pbk : £2.95 : CIP rev.
(B77-22491)

378.1'98'0941 — Universities. *Great Britain. Open University. Students, 1971. Reports, surveys*
Open University. *Survey Research Department.* A degree of difference : a study of the first year's intake of students into the Open University of the United Kingdom / [Open University Survey Research Department] ; [written] by Naomi E. McIntosh with Judith A. Calder and Betty Swift. — Guildford : Society for Research into Higher Education, 1976. — [2],xviii,320p : ill, forms ; 21cm. — (Research into higher education monographs ; 26 ISSN 0085-1523)
Bibl. — Index.
ISBN 0-900868-48-1 Pbk : £4.80
(B77-00140)

378.1'98'1 — Higher education institutions. Protest by students. *United States, 1798-1815*
Novak, Steven J. The rights of youth : American colleges and student revolt, 1798-1815 / [by] Steven J. Novak. — Cambridge, Mass. ; London : Harvard University Press, 1977. — xi, 218p : ill ; 23cm.
Bibl.: p.209-213. — Index.
ISBN 0-674-77016-1 : £6.80
(B77-31805)

378.1'98'1 — Higher education institutions. Protest by students. Psychosocial aspects. *United States*
Gold, Alice Ross. Fists and flowers : a social psychological interpretation of student dissent / [by] Alice Ross Gold, Richard Christie, Lucy Norman Friedman. — New York [etc.] ; London : Academic Press, 1976. — xi,204p : ill, forms ; 24cm. — (Social psychology)
Bibl.: p.197-199. — Index.
ISBN 0-12-287650-4 : £7.00
(B77-06592)

378.1'98'1 — Higher education institutions. Students from social minorities. *United States, 1960-1975. Reports, surveys*
Brown, Frank. Minorities in US institutions of higher education / [by] Frank Brown, Madelon D. Stent. — New York ; London : Praeger, 1977. — xvii,179p ; 25cm. — (Praeger special studies in US economic, social and political issues)
Bibl.: p.161-173. — Index.
ISBN 0-275-55540-2 : £11.70
(B77-26244)

378.1'98'433510941 — Higher education institutions. Students. Labour movements. Organisations. *Great Britain. National Organisation of Labour Students. Periodicals*
Labour student : newsletter of the National Organisation of Labour Students. — [London] : Labour Party.
[1976]-. — [1976]-. — ill ; 30cm.
Published at irregular intervals. — 10p. in Autumn 1976 issue. — Supersedes: Socialist student.
Sd : £0.05
ISSN 0309-3689
(B77-10780)

378.1'98'9 — Universities. *Cambridgeshire. Cambridge. University of Cambridge. Students. Escapades, to 1977*
Reeve, Frank Albert. Varsity rags and hoaxes / [by] F.A. Reeve. — Cambridge : Oleander Press, 1977. — 48p : ill ; 22cm. — (Cambridge town, gown and county ; vol.17)
Bibl.: p.39.
ISBN 0-900891-16-5 Sd : £1.30 : CIP rev.
(B77-18050)

378.1'99'09753 — Universities. Curriculum. Development. *United States. Study examples: Columbia University*
Belknap, Robert L. Tradition and innovation : general education and the reintegration of the university : a Columbia report / [by] Robert L. Belknap & Richard Kuhns. — New York ; Guildford : Columbia University Press, 1977. — ix,130p ; 22cm.
Bibl.
ISBN 0-231-04322-8 : £8.60
ISBN 0-231-04323-6 Pbk : £2.90
(B77-27782)

378.3 — HIGHER EDUCATION. STUDENT FINANCES

378.3 — Higher education institutions. Students. Grants. Organisations. *United States. Directories*
Annual register of grant support. — Chicago : Marquis Academic Media ; London : Distributed by Prior.
1976-77 : 10th ed. — 1976. — xxiii,708p ; 29cm.
Index.
ISBN 0-8379-1903-7 : £23.75
(B77-08950)

378.3 — Postgraduate courses. Awards. *Directories*
The **grants** register. — London : St James Press [etc.].
1977-1979 / editor Roland Turner ; assistant editor David Cumming. — 1977. — xxv,764p ; 26cm.
Index.
ISBN 0-900997-84-2 : £9.00
(B77-14663)

378.3'4 — Great Britain. Marshall Aid Commemoration Commission. *Accounts*
Great Britain. *Marshall Aid Commemoration Commission.* Marshall Aid Commemoration Commission account ... for the financial year ended 31st March ... — London : H.M.S.O.
1975-76. — [1977]. — Folder (3p) ; 25cm. — ([1976-77 H.C.] 86)
ISBN 0-10-208677-x : £0.25
(B77-07877)

378.3'4 — Great Britain. Marshall Aid Commemoration Commission. *Reports, surveys. Serials*
Great Britain. *Marshall Aid Commemoration Commission.* Annual report of the Marshall Aid Commemoration Commission for the year ending 30 September ... — London : H.M.S.O.
23rd [1975]-1976. — [1977]. — 16p ; 25cm. — (United States ; no.1 (1977)) (Cmnd.6720)
ISBN 0-10-167200-4 Sd : £0.35
(B77-10315)

378.3'4 — Higher education. Scholarships. Provision. Commonwealth Scholarship and Fellowship Plan. *Commonwealth countries. Reports, surveys. Serials*
Commonwealth Scholarship Commission. Annual report of the Commonwealth Scholarship Commission in the United Kingdom for the year ending 30th September. — London : H.M.S.O.
16th : [1974]-1975. — [1976]. — 78p ; 25cm. — ([1975-76 H.C.] 636)
At head of title : Ministry of Overseas Development.
ISBN 0-10-263676-1 Sd : £0.95
(B77-04075)

378.3'4 — Higher education. Scholarships. Provision. Organisations. *Commonwealth countries. Commonwealth Scholarship Commission. Reports, surveys. Serials*
Commonwealth Scholarship Commission. Annual report of the Commonwealth Scholarship Commission in the United Kingdom for the year ending 30th September ... — London : H.M.S.O.
17th : [1975]-1976. — [1977]. — 79p ; 25cm. — ([1976-77 H.C.] 159)
At head of title: Ministry of Overseas Development.
ISBN 0-10-215977-7 Sd : £1.25
(B77-08951)

378.4/9 — HIGHER EDUCATION. HISTORICAL AND GEOGRAPHICAL TREATMENT

378.4 — Higher education. Equality of opportunity. *Western Europe, 1945-1975. Research reports*
Neave, Guy Richard. Patterns of equality : the influence of new structures in European higher education upon the equality of educational opportunity / [by] Guy Neave. — Windsor : NFER, 1976. — 150p ; 22cm.
'... originally a report to the European Commission prepared by the Institute of Education of the European Cultural Foundation' - p.8. — Index.
ISBN 0-85633-114-7 Pbk : £4.60
(B77-08952)

378.4 — Universities. *Europe. Conference proceedings. French texts*
Standing Conference of Rectors and Vice-Chancellors of the European Universities. *General Assembly, 5th, Bologna, 1974.* Les universités européennes, 1975-1985. — Oxford [etc.] : Pergamon, 1975. — viii,240p : 1 ill ; 21cm.
'Assemblée générale de la Conférence permanente des recteurs et vice-chanceliers des Universités européennes réunie à Bologne du 1er au 7 septembre 1974' - preliminaries.
ISBN 0-08-019711-6 Pbk : Unpriced
(B77-19302)

378.41 — Higher education. *Great Britain*
Graduation addresses / by Lord Robbins. — [Stirling] ([Stirling FK9 4LA]) : [University of Stirling], [1976]. — [1],16p ; 23cm.
Delivered on Graduation days, 21 February and 25 June 1976 by the Chancellor, Lord Robbins, and on 25 June? 1976 by Dr. W.A. Cramond. — Contents: Graduation addresses / by Lord Robbins - Laureation address / by W.A. Cramond.
ISBN 0-901636-14-2 Sd : Unpriced
(B77-01307)

378.41 — Higher education. *Great Britain. Conference proceedings*
Association of Colleges for Further and Higher Education. *Annual General Meeting, Institution of Electrical Engineers, 1976.* The future of further and higher education : [two papers with discussion report presented at the] Annual General Meeting [of] the Association of Colleges for Further and Higher Education [held] Thursday and Friday, 26th and 27 February 1976 [at] the Institution of Electrical Engineers, Savoy Place, London W.C.2. — London : The Association, 1976. — [1],22p ; 21cm.
Contents: Paper 1 / by E.H. Simpson - Paper II / by Roy P. Harding - Report of the discussion / by K.R. Bishop.
ISBN 0-900096-68-3 Sd : £0.25
Primary classification 374.9'41
(B77-02186)

378.41 — Higher education. *Great Britain. Periodicals*
New universities quarterly : culture, education & society. — Oxford : Blackwell.
Continues: 'Universities quarterly'.
Vol.30, no.1- ; Dec. 1975-. — 1975-. — 22cm.
128p. in Vol.31, no.1.
Pbk : £2.25(£7.50 yearly to institutions, £6.00 yearly to individuals)
ISSN 0307-8612
(B77-11171)

378.41 — Higher education. *Great Britain. Proposals*
Burgess, Tyrrell. Education after school / [by] Tyrrell Burgess. — Harmondsworth [etc.] : Penguin, 1977. — 256p ; 18cm. — (Pelican books)
Bibl.: p.242-244. — Index.
ISBN 0-14-021956-0 Pbk : £0.80
(B77-10781)

Burgess, Tyrrell. Education after school / [by] Tyrrell Burgess. — London : Gollancz, 1977. — 256p ; 23cm.
Bibl.: p.242-244. — Index.
ISBN 0-575-02237-x : £6.95
(B77-10782)

378.41 — Higher education institutions. Influence of left-wing radical movements. *Great Britain. Reports, surveys*
Institute for the Study of Conflict. The attack on higher education : Marxist and radical penetration : report of a study group of the Institute for the Study of Conflict / [written] by Julius Gould. — London : The Institute, 1977. — [2],55p ; 30cm. — (Institute for the Study of Conflict. Special reports)
Summary (sheet [2]p.) as insert. — Bibl.: p.55.
Sd : £5.00
(B77-30115)

378.41 — Polytechnics & universities. *Great Britain. Directories*
Payne, Vicky. The alternative prospectus of universities and polytechnics / [by] Vicky Payne and Vivien Lipschitz. — Revised ed. — London : Wildwood House, 1977. — [6],279p ; 25cm.
Previous ed.: 1975.
ISBN 0-7045-0288-7 : £6.50
(B77-24839)

378.41 — Universities. *Great Britain. Open University, to 1975*
Perry, *Sir* Walter. Open University : a personal account / by Walter Perry. — Milton Keynes : Open University Press, 1976. — xv,298p,[2],8p of plates(2 fold) : ill, coat of arms, ports ; 24cm.
Index.
ISBN 0-335-00042-8 : £7.50
(B77-03487)

378.41 — Universities. Marketing. *Great Britain*
Doyle, Peter. Marketing and the responsive university / by P. Doyle. — [Bradford] ([Bradford, W. Yorkshire BD7 1DP]) : [University of Bradford], [1976]. — [1],26p : 3 ill ; 21cm. — (University of Bradford. Inaugural lectures)
'... delivered at the University of Bradford on 13 January 1976'.
ISBN 0-901945-23-4 Sd : Unpriced
(B77-02195)

378.411 — Universities. Implications of devolution of powers of British government to elected assemblies. *Scotland*
Drever, James. The Scottish universities and devolution / [by] James Drever, Nigel Grant, Arnold Morrison. — Stirling (Stirling FK9 4LA) : Department of Education, University of Stirling, 1977. — [2],vi,40p ; 30cm. — (Stirling educational monographs ; no.3 ISSN 0308-8758)
ISBN 0-901636-15-0 Pbk : £1.00
(B77-16819)

378.412'35 — Universities. *Scotland. Grampian Region. Aberdeen. University of Aberdeen. Calendars*
University of Aberdeen. Aberdeen University calendar. — Aberdeen ([Aberdeen AB9 1FX]) : The University.
1977-1978. — [1977]. — 604p : coat of arms ; 21cm.
Index.
Pbk : £2.00
ISBN 0-902604-23-6
ISSN 0305-6295
(B77-33718)

378.412'7 — Universities. *Scotland. Tayside Region. Dundee. University of Dundee. Calendars*
University of Dundee. Calendar / University of Dundee. — Dundee (c/o The Secretary, University of Dundee, Dundee DD1 4HN) : The University.
1977-78. — [1977]. — 347p : coat of arms ; 21cm.
Index.
Pbk : £3.00
ISSN 0305-456x
(B77-31096)

378.412'92 — Universities. *Scotland. Fife Region. St Andrews. University of St Andrews. Calendars*
University of St Andrews. St Andrews University calendar. — [Edinburgh] : [Blackwood for] the Senatus Academicus.
1977-78. — 1977. — 537p ; 22cm.
Index.
Pbk : £3.00
ISSN 0308-972x
(B77-30116)

378.413'4 — Universities. *Edinburgh. University of Edinburgh. Calendars*
University of Edinburgh. Edinburgh University calendar. — Edinburgh : Thin.
1977-78. — 1977. — 738p : coat of arms ; 21cm.
Index.
Pbk : £3.00
0305-6058
(B77-32562)

378.414'43 — Universities. *Scotland. Strathclyde Region. Glasgow. University of Glasgow. Calendars*
University of Glasgow. Calendar / University of Glasgow. — Glasgow (The Registrar, The University, Glasgow G12 8QQ) : The University.
1976-77. — 1976. — xcvii,3-870p ; 22cm.
Bibl. — Index.
ISBN 0-85261-135-8 Pbk : £2.50
ISSN 0305-5434
(B77-06593)

University of Glasgow. University of Glasgow calendar. — Glasgow : The University.
1977-78. — 1977. — 741p : coat of arms ; 22cm.
Index.
Pbk : £2.50
ISBN 0-85261-135-8
ISSN 0305-5434
(B77-31097)

378.414'43 — Universities. *Scotland. Strathclyde Region. Glasgow. University of Glasgow, to 1577*
Durkan, John. The University of Glasgow, 1451-1577 / by John Durkan and James Kirk. — [Glasgow] : University of Glasgow Press, 1977. — xiv,498p,leaf of plate,[4]p of plates : ill(incl 1 col), facsims, ports ; 22cm.
Bibl.: p.449-470. — Index.
ISBN 0-85261-137-4 : £15.00
(B77-26985)

378.414'43 — Universities. *Scotland. Strathclyde Region. Glasgow. University of Strathclyde. Calendars*
University of Strathclyde. Calendar / University of Strathclyde. — Glasgow : The University.
1977-78. — [1977]. — 606,xxx p : coat of arms ; 22cm.
ISBN 0-902013-20-3 : £4.00
ISBN 0-902013-21-1 Pbk : Unpriced
ISSN 0305-3180
(B77-30117)

378.416'7 — Universities. *Belfast. Queen's University of Belfast. Calendars*
Queen's University of Belfast. Calendar / the Queen's University of Belfast. — Belfast : The University.
1976-7. — 1976. — [2],473p : coat of arms, map ; 21cm.
Index.
ISBN 0-85389-108-7 Pbk : £4.00
(B77-00709)

378.417 — Universities. *Ireland (Republic). National University of Ireland. Calendars*
National University of Ireland. Calendar for the year / Ollscoil na hEireann = the National University of Ireland. — Dublin : The University.
1976. — 1977. — 395p : coat of arms ; 19cm.
Pbk : £1.00
(B77-33719)

378.418'35 — Universities. *Dublin. Trinity College, Dublin. Calendars*
Trinity College, *Dublin.* Dublin University calendar. — Dublin : Hodges, Figgis.
1977-8. — 1977. — 842p : ill(on lining paper), coat of arms, plan(on lining paper) ; 22cm.
Bibl.: p.750-790. — Index.
Unpriced
(B77-33720)

378.418'35 — Universities. Colleges. *Dublin. University College, Dublin. Calendars*
University College, *Dublin.* Calendar / University College, Dublin. — [Dublin] ([The Registrar, University College, Belfield, Dublin 4]) : [The College].
1977-78. — [1977]. — 749p in various pagings : coat of arms ; 22cm.
ISBN 0-901120-50-2 Pbk : £2.00
(B77-33721)

378.418'35 — Universities. Colleges. *Dublin. University College, Dublin, to 1976*
University College, *Dublin.* The past, the present, the plans / University College, Dublin. — Dublin (Publications Office, Administration Building, Belfield, Dublin 4) : The College, 1976. — [1],81p : ill, coat of arms, facsims, plan, ports ; 15x21cm.
Cover title. — Bibl.: p.77.
ISBN 0-901120-48-0 Pbk : £0.70
(B77-23304)

378.419'56 — Universities. Colleges. *Cork (County). Cork. University College, Cork. Calendars*
University College, *Cork.* Féilire = Calendar / University College, Cork. — Cork (University College, Cork) : The College.
1976-77. — [1976]. — 389p : 2 maps ; 22cm.
Index.
ISBN 0-9502440-2-3 : Unpriced
ISBN 0-9502440-1-5 Pbk : Unpriced
(B77-00141)

378.42 — Polytechnics. Students & teachers. *England. Reports, surveys*
Whitburn, Julia. People in polytechnics : a survey of polytechnic staff and students, 1972-3 / [by] Julia Whitburn, Maurice Mealing, Caroline Cox. — Guildford : Society for Research into Higher Education, 1976. — vi, 212p : ill ; 21cm. — (Research into higher education monographs ISSN 0085-1523)
Bibl.: p.205-208. — Index.
ISBN 0-900868-52-x Pbk : £4.00(£3.00 to members)
(B77-02196)

378.421 — Universities. *London. University of London. Calendars*
University of London. Calendar / University of London. — London : The University.
1976-77. — 1976. — xi,468p : coat of arms ; 21cm.
Index.
ISBN 0-7187-0422-3 Pbk : £6.00
ISSN 0309-4103
(B77-01308)

1977-78. — 1977. — xi,478p ; 21cm.
Index.
ISBN 0-7187-0465-7 Pbk : £6.00
ISSN 0309-4103
(B77-31098)

378.421 — Universities. *London. University of London. Regulations*
University of London. Regulations for internal students / University of London. — [London] : The University.
1977-78. — 1977. — 1109p in various pagings : coat of arms ; 21cm.
ISBN 0-7187-0463-0 Pbk : Unpriced
(B77-33157)

378.421'32 — Universities. Colleges. *London. Westminster (London Borough). King's College, London. Calendars*
King's College, *London.* Calendar / King's College, London. — [London] ([Strand, WC2R 2LS]) : [King's College, London].
1977-1978 : University of London King's College and King's College Theological Department. — [1977]. — 222p : coat of arms ; 22cm.
Index.
Pbk : £1.00
ISSN 0305-4489
(B77-31099)

378.421'42 — Universities. Colleges. *London. Camden (London Borough). University College, London. Calendars*
University College, London. University College calendar / [University College, London]. — London ([Gower St., WC1E 6BT]) : The College.
1977-78. — [1977]. — 186p ; 23cm.
Index.
£6.00
ISSN 0305-4764
(B77-32563)

378.421'83 — Universities. *London. Hillingdon (London Borough). Brunel University, to 1975*
Faherty, Janette. From technical college to university : a case study of Brunel College / [by] Janette Faherty. — Uxbridge (Uxbridge, Middx [UB8 3PH]) : Department of Building Technology, Brunel University, 1976. — [1],iii, 214p : ill, map, plans, port ; 30cm.
Bibl.: p.208-213.
Pbk : £5.00
(B77-01309)

378.422'11 — Universities. Colleges. *Surrey. Egham. Royal Holloway College. Calendars*
Royal Holloway College. The calendar of the Royal Holloway College, University of London. — Egham (Egham Hill, Egham, Surrey TW20 0EX) : The College.
1977-78. — [1977]. — xxii,35p ; 19cm.
Sd : Unpriced
ISSN 0305-4462
(B77-32564)

378.422'56 — Universities. *East Sussex. Brighton. University of Sussex. Guidebooks*
University of Sussex. The University of Sussex guide. — [Brighton] ([Essex House, Falmer, Brighton, E. Sussex]) : [University of Sussex].
1976-77. — [1976]. — [1],89,[1]p : coat of arms, 2 maps ; 21cm.
ISBN 0-85446-006-3 Sd : Unpriced
ISSN 0309-1090
(B77-00142)

378.422'76 — Universities. *Hampshire. Southampton. University of Southampton. Calendars*
University of Southampton. Calendar / University of Southampton. — [Southampton] : Southampton University Press.
1977-78. — [1977]. — [2],491p : coat of arms ; 22cm.
Index.
ISBN 0-85432-177-2 Pbk : Unpriced
ISSN 0561-0796
(B77-31100)

378.422'93 — Universities. *Berkshire. Reading. University of Reading. Calendars*
University of Reading. Calendar / University of Reading. — [Reading] : [The University].
1977-78. — 1977. — 674p ; 21cm.
Index.
ISBN 0-7049-0009-2 Pbk : £4.00
ISSN 0305-473x
(B77-30118)

378.422'93 — Universities. *Berkshire. Reading. University of Reading. Reports, surveys. Serials*
University of Reading. Proceedings of the University / University of Reading. — [Reading] ([Reading, Berkshire RG6 2AH]) : [The University].
1975-76. — [1977]. — 374p ; 22cm.
Bibl.
ISBN 0-7049-0063-7 Pbk : Unpriced
(B77-17409)

378.423'13 — Higher education institutions. *Wiltshire. Swindon. Swindon Technocentre. Proposals*
A **university** of the community : a study / prepared by the Working Party on Education for the 'Technology and you' project ... — [Swindon] ([Civic Offices, Swindon]) : [Swindon Technocentre Advisory Committee], [1976]. — [8],42p ; 21cm.
'... an expanded version of the working paper that was presented to a conference in Swindon on 17th October, 1974, as part of the "Technology and you" project ...' - Foreword.
ISBN 0-86080-005-9 Sd : Unpriced
(B77-14664)

378.423'56 — Universities. *Devon. Exeter. University of Exeter. Calendars*
University of Exeter. Calendar / University of Exeter. — Exeter : The University.
1977-78. — 1977. — v,702p : coat of arms ; 22cm.
Index.
ISBN 0-85989-077-5 : Unpriced
ISSN 0305-5388
(B77-33722)

378.423'93 — Universities. Colleges. *Avon. Bristol. University College, Bristol, to 1909*
Sherborne, James Wilson. University College, Bristol, 1876-1909 / [by] J.W. Sherborne. — Bristol (c/o P. Harris, 74 Bell Barn Rd, Stoke Bishop, Bristol [BS9 2DG]) : Bristol Branch of the Historical Association, 1977. — [2],26p,[4]p of plates : 1 ill, facsim, ports ; 22cm. — (Historical Association. Bristol Branch. Local history pamphlets ; 40)
ISBN 0-901388-17-3 Sd : £0.50
(B77-15232)

378.424'62 — Universities. *Staffordshire. Keele. University of Keele. Calendars*
University of Keele. Calendar / University of Keele. — Keele : The University.
1977-78. — [1977]. — [1],199,[141]p,2 fold leaves of plates,[2]fold p of plates : plans ; 21cm.
Pbk : £0.50
ISSN 0305-3792
(B77-31101)

378.424'96 — Universities. *West Midlands (Metropolitan County). Birmingham. University of Birmingham. Calendars*
University of Birmingham. Calendar / University of Birmingham. — Birmingham : The University.
1977-78. — 1977. — 188p : coat of arms ; 21cm.
Index.
ISBN 0-7044-0273-4 Pbk : Unpriced
ISSN 0306-0098
(B77-32565)

378.424'98 — Universities. *West Midlands (Metropolitan County). Coventry. University of Warwick. Calendars*
University of Warwick. Calendar / University of Warwick. — Coventry (Academic Registrar, Coventry CV4 7AL) : The University.
1976-77. — [1977]. — [4],271p : coat of arms ; 21cm.
Pbk : £2.00
ISSN 0140-0614
(B77-22492)

1977-78. — [1977]. — [5],264p : coat of arms ; 21cm.
Pbk : £2.00
ISSN 0140-0614
(B77-31102)

378.425'27 — Universities. *Nottinghamshire. Nottingham. University of Nottingham. Calendars*
University of Nottingham. The calendar of the University of Nottingham. — [Nottingham] : The University.
Session 1977-78. — 1977. — 449p : coat of arms ; 21cm.
Index.
Pbk : Unpriced
(B77-29328)

378.425'47 — Higher education institutions. *Leicestershire. Loughborough, to 1976*
Cantor, Leonard Martin. Loughborough from college to university : a history of higher education at Loughborough, 1909-1966 / [by] Leonard M. Cantor and Geoffrey F. Matthews. — [Loughborough] ([Loughborough, Leics.]) : Loughborough University of Technology, 1977. — iii-199p : ill, map, plan, ports ; 22cm.
Index.
ISBN 0-902761-19-6 : £8.50
ISBN 0-902761-18-8 Pbk : £4.95
(B77-18051)

378.425'47 — Universities. *Leicestershire. Loughborough. Loughborough University of Technology. Calendars*
Loughborough University of Technology. Calendar / Loughborough University of Technology. — [Loughborough] ([Loughborough, Leics.]) : [The University].
1976-77. — [1976]. — 158p : map ; 21cm.
ISBN 0-902761-17-x Pbk : £1.00
(B77-01310)

378.425'74 — Universities. *Oxfordshire. Oxford. University of Oxford. Courses. Regulations. Serials*
University of Oxford. Examination decrees and regulations / University of Oxford. — Oxford : Clarendon Press.
1977 : for the academic year 1977-8. — 1977. — xi,834p : coat of arms ; 22cm.
'... incorporates all changes made until the end of the Trinity Term 1978' - Preface. — Index.
ISBN 0-19-951076-8 Pbk : £3.50
ISSN 0302-3567
(B77-31103)

378.425'74 — Universities. *Oxfordshire. Oxford. University of Oxford. Social life, 1919-1971. Personal observations. Collections*
My Oxford / [by] Martin Amis ... [et al.] ; edited and introduced by Ann Thwaite. — London : Robson, 1977. — 213p,[4]p of plates : ill, ports ; 23cm.
Ill. on lining papers.
ISBN 0-903895-83-8 : £4.75
(B77-18685)

378.425'74 — Universities. Colleges. *Oxfordshire. Oxford. Brasenose College, to 1976*
Evans, Robert John Weston. Brasenose College : a short guide / by R.J.W. Evans and B.A. Richards ; photographs by J.W. Thomas. — Oxford ([Brasenose College, Oxford]) : [The College], 1977. — 16p,[4]p of plates : ill, coat of arms, plan ; 19cm.
Bibl.: p.16.
Sd : Unpriced
(B77-23305)

378.426'15 — Universities. *Norfolk. Norwich. University of East Anglia. Calendars*
University of East Anglia. Calendar / University of East Anglia. — Norwich (Norwich NR4 7TJ) : The University.
1977-78. — [1977]. — 385p : coat of arms ; 21cm.
Index.
Pbk : £2.75
ISSN 0305-3326
(B77-30119)

378.426'59 — Universities. *Cambridgeshire. Cambridge. University of Cambridge. Calendars*
Cambridge University, a prospectus by students. — Cambridge (3 Round Church St., Cambridge CB5 8AD) : Varsity Publications Ltd for Cambridge Students' Union.
1976 : 4th ed., fully revised. — [1976]. — [1], 72,[1]p : ill, map ; 22cm.
Sd : Unpriced
(B77-01311)

University of Cambridge. The Cambridge University handbook. — Cambridge : Cambridge University Press.
1976-77. — 1976. — x,553p : 1 ill ; 19cm.
Bibl. — Index.
ISBN 0-521-21278-2 Pbk : Unpriced
ISSN 0305-3148
(B77-30120)

378.426'59 — Universities. *Cambridgeshire. Cambridge. University of Cambridge. Regulations*
University of Cambridge. Statutes [and ordinances] of the University of Cambridge and passages from acts of Parliament relating to the University. — Cambridge : Cambridge University Press.
[1976]. — 1976. — xiii,[2],140,xi,988p : 1 ill, coat of arms ; 26cm.
Index.
ISBN 0-521-21470-x : £12.00
(B77-01312)

378.426'59 — Universities. *Cambridgeshire. Cambridge. University of Cambridge. Social life, 1924-1971. Personal observations. Collections*
My Cambridge / [by] Muriel Bradbrook ... [et al.] ; edited and introduced by Ronald Hayman. — London : Robson, 1977. — 224p,[4]p of plates : ill, ports ; 23cm.
Ill. on lining papers.
ISBN 0-903895-84-6 : £4.75
(B77-18686)

378.426'59 — Universities. Colleges. *Cambridgeshire. Cambridge. Trinity Hall, to 1975*
Crawley, Charles. Trinity Hall : the history of a Cambridge college, 1350-1975 / by Charles Crawley. — Cambridge (Trinity Hall, Cambridge) : The College, 1976. — xvi,289p, [16]p of plates : ill, plan, ports ; 24cm.
Ill. on lining papers. — Bibl.: p.xiv-xv. — Index.
ISBN 0-9505122-0-6 : £6.00
(B77-04710)

378.427'32 — Universities. *Greater Manchester (Metropolitan County). Salford. University of Salford. Calendars*
University of Salford. Calendar / University of Salford. — [Salford] ([Salford M5 4WT]) : [The University].
1977-78. — 1977. — [2],467p : coat of arms ; 21cm.
Index.
Pbk : £2.00
(B77-31104)

378.427'33 — Universities. *Greater Manchester (Metropolitan County). Manchester. University of Manchester. Graduates. Lists. Serials*
University of Manchester. Register of graduates and holders of diplomas and certificates. Supplementary register (second series) / University of Manchester. — Manchester (Manchester M13 9PL) : The University.
7 : 1975. — [1976]. — [4],137p ; 22cm.
ISBN 0-7190-1290-2 Pbd : Unpriced
(B77-02905)

378.427'53 — Universities. *Merseyside (Metropolitan County). Liverpool. University of Liverpool. Calendars*
University of Liverpool. Calendar / the University of Liverpool. — Liverpool (P.O. Box 147, Liverpool L69 3BX) : [The University].
Session 1976-77. — 1976. — xi,669p : coat of arms ; 21cm.
Index.
ISBN 0-9501618-8-8 Pbk : £5.00
ISSN 0305-9227
(B77-04711)

378.428'17 — Universities. *West Yorkshire (Metropolitan County). Bradford. University of Bradford. Calendars*
University of Bradford. Calendar / University of Bradford. — Bradford (Bradford, W. Yorkshire BD7 1DP) : The University.
1976-77. — [1976]. — [4],603p : coat of arms ; 21cm.
Index.
ISBN 0-901945-26-9 Pbk : £2.00
ISSN 0306-7459
(B77-00710)

1977-78. — [1977]. — [4],617p : coat of arms ; 21cm.
Index.
Pbk : £2.00
ISSN 0306-7459
(B77-32566)

378.428'19 — Universities. *West Yorkshire (Metropolitan County). Leeds. University of Leeds. Calendars*
University of Leeds. The calendar of the University of Leeds. — Leeds (Leeds LS2 9JT) : The University.
1976-77. — 1976. — 1287p in various pagings ; 22cm.
Index.
ISBN 0-85316-113-5 : £2.90
(B77-07878)

378.428'37 — Universities. *Humberside. Hull. University of Hull. Calendars*
University of Hull. Calendar / University of Hull. — [Hull] : [The University].
1977-78. — [1977]. — 636p in various pagings : coat of arms ; 21cm.
Index.
Pbk : £2.50
ISSN 0307-6210
(B77-31105)

378.428'65 — Universities. *Durham (County). Durham. University of Durham. Calendars*
University of Durham. Calendar / University of Durham. — Durham : The University.
1977-78. — [1977]. — iv,869[i.e.789]p : coat of arms, map ; 22cm.
Index.
Pbk : £4.00
ISSN 0305-3903
(B77-31106)

378.428'76 — Universities. *Tyne and Wear (Metropolitan County). Newcastle upon Tyne. University of Newcastle upon Tyne. Calendars*
University of Newcastle upon Tyne. Calendar / University of Newcastle upon Tyne. — Newcastle upon Tyne (The Registrar, The University, Newcastle upon Tyne NE1 7RU) : The University.
1977-78. — 1977. — vii,1066p : coat of arms ; 21cm.
Index.
ISBN 0-7017-0005-x Pbk : £5.00
ISSN 0545-8005
(B77-31107)

378.429 — Universities. *Wales. University of Wales. Calendars*
University of Wales. Calendar for the academic year / University of Wales. — Cardiff (c/o The Registrar, University Registry, Cathays Park, Cardiff CF1 3NS) : The University.
1977-78. — [1977]. — xx,584p : ill, coat of arms ; 21cm.
Index.
Pbk : £1.00
(B77-33158)

378.429'87 — Universities. Colleges. *Cardiff. University College, Cardiff. Calendars*
University College, *Cardiff.* Calendar / University College, Cardiff. — [Cardiff] ([Cathays Park, Cardiff]) : [The College].
1976-77. — [1976]. — 349p in various pagings ; 21cm.
Index.
Pbk : £0.75
(B77-05326)

378.43 — Universities. *West Germany, 1967-1975*
Tilford, Roger Bertram. The West German university : the problem of social responsibility / by R. Tilford. — [Bradford] : [University of Bradford], [1977]. — [2],19p ; 21cm. — (University of Bradford. Inaugural lectures)
'... delivered at the University of Bradford on 16 March 1976'. — Bibl.: p.19.
ISBN 0-901945-20-x Sd : Unpriced
(B77-17410)

378.73 — Colleges. *United States. Directories*
Cass, James. Comparative guide to American colleges : for students, parents and counselors / by James Cass and Max Birnbaum. — 7th ed. — New York [etc.] ; London : Harper and Row, [1976]. — xxxv,749p ; 25cm.
This ed. published in the United States: 1975. — Previous ed: New York : Harper and Row, 1973. — Index.
ISBN 0-06-010657-3 : £5.20
ISBN 0-06-010649-2 Pbk : £4.40
(B77-05995)

378.73 — Higher education. *United States. Conference proceedings*
Boyer Workshop on State University Systems, *Aspen, 1975.* The Monday morning imagination : report from the Boyer Workshop on State University Systems / edited by Martin Kaplan. — New York ; London : Praeger [for] the Aspen Institute for Humanistic Studies, 1977. — xix,158,[1]p ; 24cm. — (Praeger special studies in US economic, social and political issues)
'... the workshop [was held at Aspen] during the summer of 1975' - Preface. — Index.
ISBN 0-03-021481-5 : £11.05
(B77-24131)

378.73 — Higher education. *United States. Serials*
Current issues in higher education. — San Francisco [etc.] ; London : Jossey-Bass. — (The Jossey-Bass series in higher education)
1976 : Individualizing the system / Dyckman W. Vermilye, editor ; associate editor William Ferris. — 1976. — xxi,217p ; 24cm.
'A publication of the American Association for Higher Education' - 'My thanks to Dick Martin, who not only served as chairman of the planning group for the 31st National Conference on Higher Education but who also helped select the conference papers to be included in this book ...' - Preface. — Index.
ISBN 0-87589-288-4 : £8.65
(B77-04712)

378.73 — Higher education institutions. *United States. Yearbooks*
Yearbook of higher education. — Chicago : Marquis Academic Media ; London : Distributed by Prior.
1976-77 : 8th ed. — 1976. — x,727p : ill ; 29cm.
Index.
ISBN 0-8379-2003-5 : £24.50
(B77-08953)

378.73 — Higher education institutions. Administration. *United States*
Corson, John Jay. The governance of colleges and universities : modernizing structure and process / [by] John J. Corson. — Revised ed. — New York ; London [etc.] : McGraw-Hill, [1976]. — xiii,297p ; 24cm. — (The Carnegie series in American education)
This ed. published in the United States: 1975. — Previous ed.: 1960. — Index.
ISBN 0-07-013205-4 : £8.30
(B77-05327)

378.73 — Higher education institutions. Administration. Decision making. Effects of surveys of students. *United States. Reports, surveys*
Astin, Alexander William. Academic gamesmanship : student-oriented change in higher education / [by] Alexander W. Astin. — New York [etc.] ; London : Praeger [for] the Higher Education Research Institute ; [London] : [Distributed by Martin Robertson], 1976. — xi,209,[1]p : forms ; 25cm. — (Praeger special studies in US economic, social and political issues)
Index.
ISBN 0-275-56720-6 : £11.40
(B77-02906)

378.73 — Higher education. Psychosocial aspects. *United States*
Cottle, Thomas J. College : reward and betrayal / [by] Thomas J. Cottle. — Chicago ; London : University of Chicago Press, 1977. — viii,190p ; 23cm.
ISBN 0-226-11599-2 : £7.00
(B77-33723)

378.73 — Political authority. Attitudes of public. *United States. Study examples: Attitudes of students to university administration*
Wise, Charles R. Clients evaluate authority : the view from the other side / [by] Charles R. Wise. — Beverly Hills ; London : Sage Publications, 1976. — 91,[1]p : ill ; 22cm. — (Sage professional papers in administrative and policy studies ; vol.3, no.03-034)
Bibl.: p.89-91.
ISBN 0-8039-0628-5 Pbk : £1.75
(B77-14665)

378.73 — Universities. Role of women. *United States, 1970-1975. Feminist viewpoints*
Women and the power to change / edited by Florence Howe. — New York [etc.] ; London : McGraw-Hill, [1976]. — ix,182p ; 24cm.
'A volume of essays sponsored by the Carnegie Commission on Higher Education'. — Published in the United States: 1975. — Bibl. — Index.
ISBN 0-07-010124-8 : £5.90
(B77-02197)

378.749'67 — Universities. *New Jersey. Princeton. College of New Jersey. Graduates, 1748-1768. Biographies*
McLachlan, James. Princetonians, 1748-1768 : a biographical dictionary / by James McLachlan. — Princeton ; Guildford : Princeton University Press, 1976. — xxviii,706p : ports ; 25cm.
Index.
ISBN 0-691-04639-5 : £22.50
(B77-23306)

378.773 — Higher education. Political aspects. *United States. Study regions: Illinois*
Nowlan, James Dunlap. The politics of higher education : lawmakers and the Academy in Illinois / [by] James Dunlap Nowlan. — Urbana [etc.] ; London : University of Illinois Press, 1976. — xiii,109p : ill ; 23cm. — (An Illini book)
Bibl.: p.101-105. — Index.
ISBN 0-252-00558-9 Pbk : £2.25
(B77-23307)

378.94 — Colleges of advanced education. *Australia*
Treyvaud, E R. Equal but cheaper : the development of Australian colleges of advanced education / [by] E.R. Treyvaud, John McLaren. — Carlton, Vic. : Melbourne University Press ; Hemel Hempstead : [Distributed by] Prentice-Hall, 1976. — viii, 103p ; 22cm. — (The second century in Australian education)
Index.
ISBN 0-522-84105-8 Pbk : £3.15
(B77-30121)

379.1/2 — PUBLIC EDUCATION

379'.1214'0941 — Universities. Capital investment. Grants. Procedure of University Grants Committee. *Great Britain*
University Grants Committee. Notes on procedure, capital grants / University Grants Committee. — 6th ed. — London : H.M.S.O., 1977. — [2],54p : forms ; 30cm.
Previous ed.: 1974.
ISBN 0-11-700862-1 Sd : £1.60
(B77-26248)

379'.1214'0941 — Universities. Resources. Allocation. *Great Britain. Reports, surveys*
University of Bradford. *School of Social Sciences.* Incentives to the efficient use of resources in universities : report of research financed by the Social Science Research Council in the School of Social Sciences at the University of Bradford / project leader J.E. Dunworth, Senior Research Fellow W.R. Cook. — Bradford ([Bradford, W. Yorkshire BD7 1DP]) : The School, 1975. — [1],iv,198 leaves : ill ; 30cm.
Bibl.: p.196-198.
ISBN 0-905913-00-0 Pbk : £2.40
(B77-06594)

379'.15 — Education. Evaluation. *Organisation for Economic Co-operation and Development countries. Reports, surveys*
Stake, Robert Earl. Evaluating educational programmes : the need and the response : a collection of resource materials / prepared by Robert E. Stake ; [for the] Centre for Educational Research and Innovation. — Paris : Organisation for Economic Co-operation and Development ; [London] : [H.M.S.O.], 1976. — 89p ; 24cm.
Bibl.: p.85-89.
Pbk : £2.00
ISBN 92-64-11535-8
(B77-00711)

379'.15 — Education. Evaluation. *Periodicals*
Evaluation in education : international progress : an international review series. — Oxford [etc.] : Pergamon.
Vol.1, no.1- ; 1977-. — 1977-. — ill, maps ; 25cm.
Quarterly. — Cover title. — 72p. in 1st issue. — Bibl.
Pbk : Unpriced
ISSN 0145-9228
(B77-18052)

379'.15 — Schools. Inspection. *England, 1936-1970. Personal observations*
Clark, Leonard, *b.1905.* The inspector remembers : diary of one of Her Majesty's Inspectors of Schools, 1936-1970 / [by] Leonard Clark. — London : Dobson, 1976. — 192p ; 23cm.
ISBN 0-234-77948-9 : £4.75
(B77-04076)

379'.151 — Primary education. Law. Administration by Great Britain. Education Department. *England, 1870-1885*
Roper, Henry. Administering the Elementary Education Acts, 1870-1885 / by Henry Roper. — [Leeds] ([Leeds LS2 9JT]) : Museum of [the] History of Education, University of Leeds, 1976. — [2],50p ; 21cm. — (Educational administration and history monographs ; no.5)
ISBN 0-904427-03-x Sd : £1.75
(B77-11740)

379'.153 — Education. Innovation. Role of local authority advisory services. *England. Reports, surveys*
Bolam, Raymond. Local education authority advisers and educational innovation : a report on a research project funded by the Department of Education and Science and carried out from 1972-1975 at the School of Education Research Unit [of the University of Bristol] / by R. Bolam, G. Smith and H. Canter. — [Bristol] ([Lyndale House, Berkeley Sq., Bristol BS8 1HF]) : University of Bristol, School of Education, 1976. — 419p in various pagings : ill, facsim ; 30cm.
Cover title. — Bibl.: (9p.).
Pbk : £4.00
(B77-32567)

379'.153'0941 — Education. Role of local authorities. *Great Britain*
Regan, David Edward. Local government and education / by D.E. Regan. — London : Allen and Unwin, 1977. — 265p ; 23cm. — (The new local government series ; no.15)
Bibl.: p.244-251. — Index.
ISBN 0-04-352064-2 : £6.50
ISBN 0-04-352065-0 Pbk : Unpriced
(B77-05996)

379'.153'0942 — Local education authorities. Policies. Decision making. Political aspects. *England*
Jennings, Robert E. Education and politics : policy-making in local education authorities / [by] Robert E. Jennings. — London : Batsford, 1977. — ix,214p ; 23cm.
Bibl.: p.206-211. — Index.
ISBN 0-7134-0474-4 : Unpriced
ISBN 0-7134-0475-2 Pbk : £3.35
(B77-22493)

379'.1531'0942 — Schools. Governing boards & managing boards. Role. *England. Inquiry reports*
Great Britain. *Committee of Enquiry into the Management and Government of Schools.* A new partnership for our schools : report of a Committee of Enquiry [i.e. the Committee of Enquiry into the Management and Government of Schools] appointed jointly by the Secretary of State for Education and Science and the Secretary of State for Wales / under the chairmanship of Tom Taylor. — London : H.M.S.O., 1977. — xv,228p ; 25cm.
Index.
ISBN 0-11-270457-3 Pbk : £3.25
(B77-29329)

379'.1531'0942 — Schools. Governing boards & managing boards. Role. Committee of Enquiry into the Management and Government of Schools. New partnership for our schools. *England. Critical studies*
Sallis, Joan. School managers and governors : Taylor and after / [by] Joan Sallis. — London : Ward Lock, 1977. — 128p ; 22cm.
Bibl.: p.120-121. — Index.
ISBN 0-7062-3626-2 Pbk : £2.25
(B77-33159)

379'.24'091724 — Adults. Literacy programmes. Role of British organisations. *Developing countries. Reports, surveys*
British Committee on Literacy. Illiteracy in the developing world / the British Committee on Literacy ; [edited by John Spencer]. — Reading (c/o The Secretary, Agricultural Extension and Rural Development Centre, The University, 16 London Rd, Reading RG1 5AQ) : British Committee on Literacy, 1976. — viii,64p : ill ; 21cm.
'The report of a survey, undertaken for the British Committee on Literacy, of resources available in British institutions and organisations ... together with the report of a Conference held at Brighton in October 1975 on the British contribution to adult literacy work overseas' - title page verso.
ISBN 0-9505439-0-x Sd : Unpriced
(B77-04077)

379'.24'0973 — Illiteracy. *United States. Reports, surveys*
Toward a literate society : the report of the Committee on Reading of the National Academy of Education, with a series of papers commissioned by the committee / John B. Carroll and Jeanne S. Chall, editors. — New York ; London [etc.] : McGraw-Hill, [1976]. — xiii,370p : ill ; 24cm.
Published in the United States: 1975. — Bibl. — Index.
ISBN 0-07-010130-2 : £12.45
(B77-06595)

379.3 — PRIVATE EDUCATION AND THE STATE

379'.324'0973 — Higher education institutions. Endowments. *United States. Reports, surveys*
Task Force on College and University Endowment Policy. Funds for the future : report of the Twentieth Century Fund Task Force on College and University Endowment Policy / [with] background paper by J. Peter Williamson. — New York ; London [etc.] : McGraw-Hill, [1976]. — ix,206p : ill ; 24cm.
'... the trustees of the Twentieth Century Fund decided to assemble an independent Task Force to consider and report on the controversial and significant issue of endowment policy' - Foreword. — Published in the United States: 1975.
ISBN 0-07-065619-3 : £6.60
ISBN 0-07-065620-7 Pbk : £3.75
(B77-07252)

379.4/9 — PUBLIC EDUCATION IN SPECIAL COUNTRIES

379.41 — Education. Policies of government. Protest by students & teachers. *Great Britain. Communist Party of Great Britain viewpoints*
Bloomfield, Jon. Into action : the campaign on teacher unemployment / by Jon Bloomfield. — London : Communist Party of Great Britain, [1976]. — [1],15p ; 23cm. — (Communist Party of Great Britain. Pamphlets)
Sd : £0.10
(B77-06596)

379.41 — Vocational education. Policies of government. *Great Britain. Proposals*
Great Britain. *Department of Education and Science.* Unified vocational preparation : a pilot approach : a government statement / [Department of Education and Science]. — [London] : [The Department], [1976]. — [1], 16p ; 21cm.
ISBN 0-85522-084-8 Sd : Unpriced
(B77-02198)

379.42 — Education. Policies of Great Britain. Department of Education and Science. Decision making. Great Britain. Parliament. House of Commons. Expenditure Committee. Policy making in the Department of Education and Science. *England. Critical studies*
Great Britain. *Department of Education and Science.* The Government's reply to the tenth report from the Expenditure Committee, session 1975-76, H.C.621 'Policy making in the Department of Education and Science' / presented to Parliament by the Secretary of State for Education and Science ... — London : H.M.S.O., [1976]. — 8p ; 25cm. — (Cmnd. 6678)
ISBN 0-10-166780-9 Sd : £0.25
(B77-07253)

379.51'249 — Education. Policies of Japanese government. *Taiwan, 1895-1945*
Tsurumi, E Patricia. Japanese colonial education in Taiwan, 1895-1945 / [by] E. Patricia Tsurumi. — Cambridge, Mass. ; London : Harvard University Press, 1977. — xiii,334p ; 24cm. — (Harvard East Asian series ; 88)
Bibl.: p.311-324. — Index.
ISBN 0-674-47187-3 : £14.00
(B77-28547)

379.81 — Higher education. Political aspects. *Brazil, to 1975*
Haar, Jerry. The politics of higher education in Brazil / [by] Jerry Haar. — New York [etc.] ; London : Praeger [for] the Institute of Higher Education, Teachers College, Columbia University, 1977. — xv,223p : 2 ill ; 25cm. — (Praeger special studies in international politics and government)
Bibl.: p.203-222.
ISBN 0-275-55630-1 : £13.70
(B77-15233)

380 — COMMERCE
Gartside, Leonard. Commerce : a guide to the business world for sixth forms, professional examination students and the general reader / [by] L. Gartside. — Plymouth : Macdonald and Evans, 1977. — xxvi,545p : ill, forms, map ; 22cm.
Includes facsimile reprints. — Index.
ISBN 0-7121-0349-x Pbk : £3.50
(B77-20174)

Jones, Henry Leonard. Groundwork of commerce / [by] H.L Jones, R.P. Jones. — 6th ed. — London : Edward Arnold.
In 2 vols.
Book 1. — 1977. — vii,255p : ill, forms, map ; 22cm.
Previous ed.: 1971. — Index.
ISBN 0-7131-0083-4 Pbk : £1.95
(B77-19303)

380 — Commerce. *For West African students. Secondary school texts*
Anderson, David John. Commerce for West Africa / [by] David J. Anderson. — London [etc.] : Macmillan, 1977. — [4],252p : ill, forms, map ; 22cm.
Index.
ISBN 0-333-21418-8 Pbk : £1.47
(B77-23308)

380 — Commerce. *Secondary school texts*
Gow, Marion. First steps in commerce / [by] M. Gow and M. Moyle. — London [etc.] : Pitman, 1977. — iii,124p : ill, forms ; 22cm.
ISBN 0-273-00728-9 Pbk : £1.30
(B77-10316)

Outhwaite, Walter. Commerce for schools / [by] Walter Outhwaite. — 2nd ed. — London [etc.] : McGraw-Hill, 1977. — [4],103p : ill, forms, 2 maps, plan ; 25cm.
Previous ed.: i.e. Decimal money ed., 1971. — Index.
ISBN 0-07-084219-1 Pbk : £1.30
(B77-22494)

Plume, Robert. Commerce comes alive / [by] Robert Plume. — Glasgow [etc.] : Blackie, 1977. — 88p : ill, facsims, forms, map ; 25cm.
Bibl. — Index.
ISBN 0-216-90399-8 Pbk : £1.55
(B77-33160)

380'.03 — Commerce. *Dictionaries*
Thomas, David John. A dictionary of commerce / [by] D.J. Thomas. — London : Bell, 1977. — [7],101p : ill, facsims, forms ; 21cm.
ISBN 0-7135-1977-0 Pbk : £1.95
(B77-20175)

380.1 — TRADE

380.1 — Forwarding agents & shipping agents. *Great Britain. Directories*
United Kingdom shipping & forwarding agents / [Data Research Group]. — Amersham (Hill House, [Hill Ave.], Amersham, Bucks.) : The Group.
1977. — [1977]. — 102 leaves in various pagings ; 30cm.
ISBN 0-86099-037-0 Sp : £14.00
(B77-23309)

380.1'025 — Industries & trades. *Directories*
Kelly's manufacturers and merchants directory, including industrial services : the British purchasing directory. — Kingston upon Thames : Kelly's Directories.
1977-78 : 91st ed. — 1977. — xx,2160p : ill ; 29cm.
List of products in French, German and Spanish. — Tab indexed. — Previously published: in 2 vols.
ISBN 0-610-00507-3 : £15.00
(B77-30123)

World trade index. — Croydon (62 High St., Croydon, Surrey) : Eagle Publishing Co.
1976-77 ed. — [1976]. — [446]p ; 25cm.
ISBN 0-905782-00-3 Pbk : £7.00
(B77-01313)

380.1'025'174927 — Industries & trades. *Arab countries. Directories*
The **Arab** business yearbook. — London : Graham and Trotman.
[1976] / compiled by Giselle Bricault, Michael Donovan ; with contributions from ... [others]. — 1977. — v-xvii,579p : ill ; 24cm.
Originally published: 1976.
ISBN 0-86010-048-0 : £12.00
ISSN 0140-1874
(B77-25525)

380.1'025'41 — Industries & trades. *Great Britain. Directories*
Kemp's directory, merchants, manufacturers, shippers, import & export, engineers, professional & general trade. — London : Kemp's.
1976-77 ed. — [1976]. — 3v.(lxiv,1096p;740p in various pagings;497p in various pagings) : ill ; 30cm.
ISBN 0-905255-05-4 Pbk : £15.00
(B77-03488)

Kemp's directory, merchants, manufacturers, shippers, import & export, engineers, professional & general trades. — London : Kemps.
1977-78 ed. — [1977]. — 3v.(860,76p;426,286p; 461p in various pagings) : ill ; 30cm.
ISBN 0-905255-26-7 Pbk : £17.50
(B77-30124)

Kompass [United Kingdom] : register of British industry and commerce. — Haywards Heath : Kompass [for the Confederation of British Industries].
15th ed. : [1977]. — 1977. — 2v.(2498,[172]p; 1897,[156]p) : ill, 2 maps, port ; 31cm.
English, French, German, Italian and Spanish text. — Vol.1 thumb indexed. — Map on lining paper. — Index.
ISBN 0-900505-70-2 : Unpriced
(B77-21062)

Sell's directory of products & services. — Epsom : Sell's Publications.
1977 ed. : ninety second year. [Vol.1] : Alphabetical. — [1977]. — [4],532p : ill ; 30cm.
ISBN 0-85499-504-8 Pbk : £7.00(£12.00 set with classified ed.)
ISSN 0300-5046
(B77-15234)

1977 ed. : ninety second year. [Vol.2] : Classified. — [1977]. — x,574p : ill ; 30cm.
ISBN 0-85499-524-2 Pbk : £7.00(£12.00 set with alphabetical ed.)
ISSN 0305-3512
(B77-15235)

Sell's government & municipal contractors register. — Epsom : Sell's Publications.
1977. — [1976]. — 420p : ill ; 24cm.
ISBN 0-85499-564-1 Pbk : £8.00
ISSN 0308-8553
(B77-05328)

Stubbs buyers' guide : incorporating Stubbs directory. — London (6 Bonhill St., EC2A 4BU) : Stubbs Ltd.
1977 ed. — 1977. — 1851p in various pagings : ill ; 31cm.
English text, English, French, German and Italian index. — Index.
ISBN 0-900714-12-3 : Unpriced
(B77-12971)

Town & county trades guide. — London (62 Oxford Circus House, W.1) : B.M.R. United Publications Ltd.
1976-7. — [1976]. — 590p in various pagings ; 24cm.
Pbk : £3.00
(B77-27783)

380.1'025'41 — Industries & trades. *Great Britain. Directories. For European Community countries*
Kelly's British industry & services in the Common Market. — Kingston upon Thames : Kelly's Directories.
76 : 4th ed. — 1975. — viii,973,[325]p : ill, port ; 28cm.
English text, list of products and services in English, French, German and Italian. — Previously published: as 'British industry & services in the Common Market'. — Index.
ISBN 0-610-00471-9 Pbk : Unpriced
(B77-20176)

77 : 5th ed. — 1976. — 1337p in various pagings : ill, port ; 28cm.
English text, list of products and services in English, French, German and Italian. — Index.
ISBN 0-610-00490-5 Pbk : £12.00
(B77-04078)

380.1'025'41 — Industries & trades. *Great Britain. Directories. For North Sea natural gas & petroleum industries*
Great Britain. *Department of Industry.* The offshore supply market : with special reference to Yorkshire and Humberside industry. — [New ed.] / prepared by the Department of Industry and the Central Office of Information. — Leeds (Priestley House, Park Row, Leeds LS1 5LF) : Department of Industry, Research Section, 1976. — 291p ; 30cm.
Previous ed.: / by Department of Industry, Research Section. 1975. — Index.
Pbk : Unpriced
(B77-22495)

380.1'025'411 — Industries & trades. *Scotland. Directories*
Chambers trades register of Scotland & North East England. — London : Kemps.
1977 ed. — [1977]. — 264p ; 30cm.
Previously published: as 'Chambers trades register of Scotland'.
ISBN 0-905255-23-2 Pbk : £4.50
ISSN 0309-5630
Also classified at 380.1'025'428
(B77-15781)

The **Scottish** national register of classified trades. — Epsom : Sell's Publications.
1976-7. — 1976. — vi,399p : ill ; 30cm.
Index.
ISBN 0-85499-603-6 Pbk : £6.50
ISSN 0080-8148
(B77-02199)

380.1'025'4111 — Industries & trades. *Scotland. Highlands & Islands. Directories*
Highlands and Islands Development Board. Business in the Highlands and Islands : directory of industry, commerce and public administration .. / Highlands and Islands Development Board. — 2nd ed. — Inverness : The Board, 1977. — 447p : ill, maps ; 21cm.
Previous ed.: published as 'Directory of industry, commerce and public administration'. 1973. — Index.
ISBN 0-902347-45-4 Pbk : £8.00
(B77-15236)

380.1'025'421 — Industries & trades. *London. Directories*
The **London** directory : covering London and the Home counties. — London : Kemps.
1977 ed. — [1977]. — 1040p ; 30cm.
ISBN 0-905255-11-9 Pbk : £6.50
(B77-14173)

380.1'025'42189 — Industries & trades. *London. Enfield (London Borough). Directories*
Enfield, Edmonton and Southgate Chamber of Trade. Year book / Enfield, Edmonton & Southgate Chamber of Trade. — South Croydon (21 Brighton Rd, South Croydon, Surrey) : Geoffrey Mowbray Ltd.
1976-77. — [1976]. — 104p : ill, port ; 21cm.
Index.
ISBN 0-901485-13-6 Pbk : Unpriced
(B77-05329)

380.1'025'4223 — Industries & trades. *Kent. Directories*
Kent area trades directory. — Harrow (386 Kenton Rd, Harrow HA3 9HA) : Area Trades Directory Ltd.
[1977-1978]. — [1976]. — [12],276p : ill, map ; 30cm.
Cover title.
ISBN 0-901770-33-7 Pbk : £5.50
ISSN 0308-986x
(B77-01314)

380.1'025'423 — Industries & trades. *South-west England. Directories*
Chambers trades register of South Wales and South-West England : general trades, including retail and distributing, professions, engineers, manufacturing and merchants. — London : Chambers Trades Register and Directories.
1977 ed. — [1977]. — 328p : 1 ill ; 30cm.
ISBN 0-905255-14-3 Pbk : £4.50
Also classified at 380.1'025'4294
(B77-14666)

380.1'025'4246 — Industries & trades. *Staffordshire. Directories*
Staffordshire guide, industry & commerce. — Stockport (Borough Chambers, St Petersgate, Stockport SK1 1EB) : G.W. Foster Associates Ltd.
1st ed. : 1977-78 / compiled ... [for] Staffordshire Development Association. — [1977]. — 168,[2]p(2 fold) : ill, col map ; 22cm.
Pbk : Unpriced
ISSN 0140-038x
(B77-28548)

380.1'025'4251 — Industries & trades. *Derbyshire, 1835. Directories. Facsimiles*
James Pigot and Company. [James Pigot and Co's national commercial directory, 1835. Derbyshire section]. Pigot & Co's commercial directory for Derbyshire, 1835. — Matlock ([c/o County Offices, Matlock, Derbyshire DE4 3AG]) : Derbyshire County Library, 1976. — [4]p,p9-84 ; 24cm.
Facsimile reprint. — Originally published: London : James Pigot and Co., 1835.
ISBN 0-903463-01-6 Pbk : Unpriced
(B77-01315)

380.1'025'4251 — Industries & trades. *Derbyshire. Directories*
Derby's artrad. — [Harrow] ([386 Kenton Rd, Harrow HA3 9HA]) : Artrad.
1976-1977. — [1976]. — [11],126p : ill, map ; 30cm.
Cover title: Derby's area trades directory.
ISBN 0-901770-32-9 Pbk : £3.75
ISSN 0308-9851
(B77-01316)

380.1'025'4254 — Industries & trades. *Leicestershire. Directories*
Leicestershire & Northants. — Harrow (386 Kenton Rd, Harrow, Middx HA3 9HA) : Area Trades Directory Ltd.
1977-1978. — [1977]. — 212,[10]p : 1 ill ; 28cm.
Cover title: Leics & Northants area trades directory. — Index.
Pbk : £5.50
Also classified at 380.1'025'4255
(B77-30125)

380.1'025'4255 — Industries & trades. *Northamptonshire. Directories*
Leicestershire & Northants. — Harrow (386 Kenton Rd, Harrow, Middx HA3 9HA) : Area Trades Directory Ltd.
1977-1978. — [1977]. — 212,[10]p : 1 ill ; 28cm.
Cover title: Leics & Northants area trades directory. — Index.
Pbk : £5.50
Primary classification 380.1'025'4254
(B77-30125)

380.1'025'426723 — Industries & trades. *Essex. Colchester. Directories*
Colchester and District Chamber of Trade and Commerce. Official year book and classified trade directory of members / Colchester and District Chamber of Trade and Commerce Limited. — South Croydon (21 Brighton Rd, South Croydon, Surrey) : Geoffrey Mowbray Ltd.
1976-77. — [1977]. — 95p : ill, form ; 21cm.
ISBN 0-901485-14-4 Pbk : £0.65
ISSN 0305-9278
(B77-12972)

380.1'025'427393 — Industries & trades. *Great Manchester (Metropolitan County). Oldham. Directories*
Oldham companies. — Oldham ([Central Library, Union St., Oldham OL1 1DN]) : [Oldham] Libraries, Art Galleries and Museums : [Oldham] Estates Department.
[Part 1]. — [1976]. — [62]p : 2 ill, 2 maps ; 21cm.
ISBN 0-902809-11-3 Sd : £1.00
(B77-05330)

380.1'025'4278 — Industries & trades. *Cumbria. Directories*
Cumbria guide, industry & commerce. — Stockport (Borough Chambers, St Petersgate, Stockport SK1 1EB) : G.W. Foster Associates Ltd.
3rd ed. : 1975. — [1975]. — 188p,fold plate : ill, 2 maps(1 col) ; 22cm.
Pbk : £3.00
ISSN 0309-8338
(B77-25526)

4th ed. : 1976-77. — [1976]. — 218p,fold plate : ill, 2 maps(1 col) ; 21cm.
Pbk : £3.50
ISSN 0309-8338
(B77-25527)

380.1'025'428 — Industries & trades. *North-east England. Directories*
Buyers' guide to North East industry / North of England Development Council. — Newcastle upon Tyne (Bank House, Carliol Sq., Newcastle upon Tyne NE1 6XE) : The Council.
1976-77. — [1977]. — 264p : ill, map ; 21cm.
Pbk : £2.50
ISSN 0305-6406
(B77-22496)

Chambers trades register of Scotland & North East England. — London : Kemps.
1977 ed. — [1977]. — 264p ; 30cm.
Previously published: as 'Chambers trades register of Scotland'.
ISBN 0-905255-23-2 Pbk : £4.50
ISSN 0309-5630
Primary classification 380.1'025'411
(B77-15781)

380.1'025'4294 — Industries & trades. *South Wales. Directories*
Chambers trades register of South Wales and South-West England : general trades, including retail and distributing, professions, engineers, manufacturing and merchants. — London : Chambers Trades Register and Directories.
1977 ed. — [1977]. — 328p : 1 ill ; 30cm.
ISBN 0-905255-14-3 Pbk : £4.50
Primary classification 380.1'025'423
(B77-14666)

380.1'025'72983 — Industries & trades. *Trinidad and Tobago. Directories*
Trinidad & Tobago trade directory : classified trade index. — London : Thrower for the Diplomatic Press.
1976 : 2nd ed. — [1976]. — [18]p ; 21cm.
ISBN 0-900334-01-0 Sd : £1.25
(B77-00143)

380.1'06'242296 — Industries & trades. Organisations. *Berkshire. Maidenhead region. Maidenhead and District Chamber of Commerce, to 1976*
Maidenhead and District Chamber of Commerce. Golden jubilee handbook, [1926-1976] / Maidenhead and District Chamber of Commerce. — London : Burrow, [1976]. — 24p : ill, map, ports ; 22cm.
ISBN 0-85026-635-1 Sd : Unpriced
(B77-02200)

380.1'09'01 — Prehistoric trade. *Conference proceedings*
Exchange systems in prehistory / edited by Timothy K. Earle, Jonathon E. Ericson. — New York [etc.] ; London : Academic Press, 1977. — xiii,274p : ill, maps ; 24cm. — (Studies in archeology)
'Preliminary versions of most of the papers ... were presented at two symposia ... "Prehistoric Raw Material Trade and Archaeo-economic Processes" ... held at the 38th Annual Meeting of the Society for American Archaeology in San Francisco on May 3, 1973 ... [and] "Archaeoeconomics - Part I : Goals, Theories and Models" ... held at the 40th Annual Meeting of the Society ... in Dallas, Texas on May 9, 1975' - Acknowledgments. — Bibl. — Index.
ISBN 0-12-227650-7 : £14.20
(B77-24841)

380.1'0954'14 — British merchants. *India. Bengal, 1700-1800*
Marshall, Peter James. East Indian fortunes : the British in Bengal in the eighteenth century / by P.J. Marshall. — Oxford : Clarendon Press, 1976. — ix,284p : 2 maps ; 23cm.
Bibl.: p.272-274. — Index.
ISBN 0-19-821566-5 : £7.75
(B77-06597)

380.1'41'0941 — Agricultural products. Marketing. *Great Britain. Reports, surveys. Serials*
Report on agricultural marketing schemes ... / Ministry of Agriculture, Fisheries and Food ... [et al.]. — London : H.M.S.O.
1974-75. — [1976]. — vi,97p ; 25cm. — ([1976-77 H.C.]40)
ISBN 0-10-204077-x Pbk : £2.25
(B77-08323)

380.1'41'37 — Cocoa, coffee & tea. Marketing. Economic aspects
Coffee, tea and cocoa : market prospects and development lending / [by] Shamsher Singh ... [et al.]. — Baltimore ; London : Johns Hopkins University Press for the World Bank, 1977. — xii,129p ; 23cm. — (International Bank for Reconstruction and Development. World Bank staff occasional papers ; no.22)
ISBN 0-8018-1869-9 : £4.15
(B77-26986)

380.1'41'50941 — Horticultural products. Marketing. *Great Britain. Statistics*
Folley, Roger Roland Westwell. The horticultural marketing year / compiled by R.R.W. Folley. — [Ashford, Kent] : Wye College, Agricultural Economics Unit, 1977. — [3],40p ; 30cm.
Versos of leaves 7-31 blank.
ISBN 0-901859-66-4 Sp : £0.60
(B77-30126)

380.1'45'070573 — Books. Auctions by Sotheby Parke Bernet (Firm), 1963-1976
Sotheby Parke Bernet *(Firm).* Sotheby's book department : some notable sales, 1963-1976 / [Sotheby Parke Bernet & Co.]. — London [etc.] (34 New Bond St., W1A 2AA) : Sotheby's, 1977. — 47,[1]p,fold plate : ill(some col), facsims, port ; 25cm.
Pbk : Unpriced
(B77-33161)

380.1'45'620002541 — Engineering trades. *Great Britain. Directories*
United Kingdom engineers merchants / [Data Research Group]. — Amersham (Hill House, [Hill Ave.], Amersham, Bucks.) : The Group.
[1976]. — 1976. — 81 leaves in various pagings ; 30cm.
ISBN 0-905570-42-1 Sp : £12.00
(B77-03489)

[1977]. — 1977. — 82 leaves in various pagings ; 30cm.
ISBN 0-86099-049-4 Sp : Unpriced
(B77-24842)

380.1'45'621312133 — Diesel generating sets. Marketing. *Spain. Reports, surveys*
Economist Intelligence Unit. A study on the generating sets market in Spain / [Economist Intelligence Unit]. — London : E.I.U., 1977. — [3],63 leaves ; 30cm. — (An EIU multi-client project)
Sp : £200.00
(B77-33725)

380.1'45'62138102541 — Electronic equipment trades. *Great Britain. Directories*
EI distributor survey. — London (375 Upper Richmond Road West, SW14 7NX) : Lesterstar Ltd.
[1976]. — 1976. — 156p : ill ; 30cm.
'A Supplement to "Electronics Industry"' - cover. — Index.
Pbk : £2.50
(B77-27784)

[1977-78] / editor Roy Atterbury. — 1977. — 140p : ill ; 30cm.
'A Supplement to "Electronics Industry"' - cover. — Index.
Pbk : £3.50
(B77-27785)

380.1'45'629225 — Construction motor vehicles. Marketing. *Japan. Reports, surveys*
Economist Intelligence Unit. A study on the Japanese market for construction equipment / [Economist Intelligence Unit]. — London : E.I.U., 1977. — [9],170p : 1 ill ; 30cm. — (An EIU multi-client project)
Sp : £1075.00
(B77-33726)

380.1'45'629225 — Construction motor vehicles. Marketing. *Spain. Reports, surveys*
Economist Intelligence Unit. A study on the construction equipment market in Spain / [Economist Intelligence Unit]. — London : E.I.U., 1977. — [4],173p ; 30cm. — (An EIU multi-client project)
Sp : £425.00
(B77-33727)

380.1'45'629225 — Diesel agricultural vehicles. Marketing. *Spain. Reports, surveys*
Economist Intelligence Unit. A study on the agricultural vehicles market in Spain / [Economist Intelligence Unit]. — London : E.I.U., 1977. — [4],94 leaves : map ; 30cm. — (An EIU multi-client project)
Sp : £300.00
(B77-33728)

380.1'45'66410212 — Sugar trades. *Statistics*
Sugar year book / [International Sugar Organization]. — London (28 Haymarket, SW1Y 4SP) : International Sugar Organization.
1975. — [1976]. — [2],vii,375p ; 14cm.
£5.00
(B77-01317)

380.1'45'6641206141 — Sugar trades. Organisations. *Great Britain. Sugar Board. Accounts*
Sugar Board. Accounts ... / Sugar Board. — London : H.M.S.O.
1976 : for the period 1st January to 30th November. — [1977]. — 12p ; 25cm. — ([1976-77 H.C.] 162)
ISBN 0-10-216277-8 Sd : £0.33
(B77-12973)

Sugar Board. Accounts / Sugar Board. — London : H.M.S.O.
1975. — [1976]. — 11p ; 25cm. — ([1976-77 H.C.]18)
Sd : £0.36
(B77-05997)

380.1'45'669142025 — Steel trades. *Directories*
Steel traders of the world. — Worcester Park : Metal Bulletin.
1976 : 1st ed. / edited by Raymond Cordero ; compiled by Sylvia Danon. — 1976. — 551p : ill ; 23cm.
Index.
£20.00
ISSN 0308-8006
(B77-20177)

380.1'45'6730941 — Nonferrous metal products trades. *Great Britain. Directories*
Where to buy non-ferrous metals in the UK : wrought products, castings, scrap. — Betchworth (39 Hillside Gardens, Brockham, Betchworth, Surrey) : Modern Metals Publications Ltd, 1976. — 63p : ill ; 21cm.
ISBN 0-905816-00-5 Sd : £1.95
(B77-03490)

380.1'45'67402541 — Timber trades. *Great Britain. Directories*
Timber trades directory : containing detailed information on firms engaged in the timber and allied trades in England, Wales, Scotland and N. Ireland and throughout the world. — Tonbridge : Benn Bros [for] 'Timber trades journal'.
[1977] : 23rd ed. — 1977. — 376,[22]p : ill(some col) ; 30cm.
Tab indexed.
ISBN 0-510-49815-9 Pbk : £15.00
Primary classification 338.4'7'674002541
(B77-17366)

380.1'45'67405 — Timber trades. *Yearbooks*
The **timber** year book and diary. — Rickmansworth (120 Heronsgate Rd, Chorleywood, Rickmansworth, Herts. WD3 5BP) : Lomax Wilmoth and Co. Ltd.
1977. — [1976]. — 3-214p : ill, maps ; 25cm.
Unpaged diary follows p.214.
Unpriced
(B77-01318)

380.1'45'677310942 — Wool trades. *England, 1066-1485*
Lloyd, Terence Henry. The English wool trade in the Middle Ages / [by] T.H. Lloyd. — Cambridge [etc.] : Cambridge University Press, 1977. — xi,351p : 2 maps ; 24cm.
Bibl.: p.338-344. — Index.
ISBN 0-521-21239-1 : £12.50
(B77-11741)

380.1'45'745102541 — Antiques trades. *Great Britain. Directories*
Guide to the antique shops of Britain. — [Woodbridge] : Antique Collectors' Club.
1978 / compiled by Rosemary Ferguson. — [1977]. — 1009p : ill, maps ; 23cm.
Index.
ISBN 0-902028-65-0 : £4.95
(B77-22497)

International art & antiques yearbook. — London (Chestergate House, Vauxhall Bridge Rd, SW1V 1HF) : Art and Antiques Yearbooks.
1977 / [editor Marcelle d'Argy Smith]. — 1977. — 1248p : ill(some col), maps ; 19cm.
Thumb indexed. — Previously published: as 'The international antiques yearbook'. — Index.
ISBN 0-900305-15-0 : £10.00
ISSN 0309-7455
(B77-11172)

380.1'45'745109412 — Antiques trades. *Scotland. Grampian Region & Tayside Region*
Holbrook, Bernard. A guide to antique dealers in the North-east : a peep into Scotland's yesteryear / compiled by Bernard Holbrook. — Aberdeen ([123 Crown St., AB1 2HN]) : Aberdeen Advertiser, [1976]. — 34p : ill, facsims, map ; 30cm.
Bibl.
ISBN 0-9505379-0-x Sd : £0.50
(B77-01319)

380.1'45'76956025 — Philatelic trades. *Directories*
International stamp dealers' directory. — London : Harris Publications.
1974 : ninth ed. / edited by O.W. Newport. — [1974]. — 238p : ill, map ; 22cm.
ISBN 0-906033-00-4 Pbk : Unpriced
(B77-15237)

380.3 — COMMUNICATION SERVICES
380.3'09172'4 — Mass communication services. Policies of governments. *Developing countries*
Communications policy for national development : a comparative perspective / edited by Majid Teheranian, Farhad Hakimzadeh, Marcello L. Vidale. — London [etc.] : Routledge and Kegan Paul [for] the Iran Communications and Development Institute and the International Institute of Communications, 1977. — xii,286p : ill ; 23cm.
'... based on the contributions of Iranian and international communications specialists to a symposium held in Mashad, Iran [from 25 June to 1 July 1975]' - jacket.
ISBN 0-7100-8597-4 : £7.50 : CIP rev.
(B77-07879)

380.5 — TRANSPORT
380.5 — Transport. Geographical aspects. *Secondary school texts*
Dinkele, Geoffrey William. Transport / [by] Geoff Dinkele, Stephen Cotterell, Ian Thorn. — London : Harrap, 1976. — 87p : ill, maps ; 28cm. — (Harrap's course in reformed geography)
ISBN 0-245-52382-0 Sd : £1.75
(B77-01320)

380.5 — Transport services. *Proposals*
Bendixson, Terence. Instead of cars / [by] Terence Bendixson. — Revised ed. — Harmondsworth [etc.] : Penguin, 1977. — 254p : ill, maps ; 18cm. — (Pelican books)
Previous ed.: London : Temple Smith, 1974. — Index.
ISBN 0-14-021952-8 Pbk : £1.00
(B77-12394)

380.5 — Transport services. Environmental aspects
Hutchins, John G B. Transportation and the environment / [by] John G.B. Hutchins. — London : Elek, 1977. — vi,106p ; 22cm. — (Environmental studies)
Index.
ISBN 0-236-40023-1 Pbk : £3.25
(B77-11173)

380.5'094 — Transport services. *Western Europe. Serials*
European Conference of Ministers of Transport. Annual report and resolutions of the Council of Ministers / European Conference of Ministers of Transport. — Paris : E.C.M.T. ; [London] : [H.M.S.O.].
22nd : 1975 : Copenhagen, 18th-19th June 1975, Paris, 2nd December 1975. — 1976. — 399p(2 fold) : ill ; 27cm.
Pbk : £8.00
ISBN 92-821-1039-7
(B77-06598)

380.5'0941 — Great Britain. Society. Role of transport. *Liberal Party viewpoints*
Macpherson, Gavin. Transport - its role in society / by Gavin Macpherson. — London : Liberal Publication Department, 1977. — 5,[1] p ; 30cm. — (Liberal Party. Study papers ; no.5 ISSN 0308-9657)
Sd : £0.20
(B77-33162)

380.5'0941 — Transport. *Great Britain*
Great Britain. *Central Office of Information. Reference Division.* Inland transport in Britain / [prepared by Reference Division, Central Office of Information]. — 2nd ed. — London : H.M.S.O., 1977. — [3],20p : 2 maps ; 24cm. — (Central Office of Information reference pamphlets ; 138)
Previous ed.: 1976. — Bibl.: p.19-20.
ISBN 0-11-700919-9 Sd : £0.60
(B77-15782)

380.5'0941 — Transport. *Great Britain, 1965-1975. Statistics*
Transport statistics, Great Britain, 1965-1975 / Department of Transport, Scottish Development Department, Welsh Office. — London : H.M.S.O., 1977. — xiv,213p : ill, maps ; 30cm.
Index.
ISBN 0-11-550432-x Pbk : £5.50
(B77-11742)

380.5'0941 — Transport. *Great Britain. Conservative and Unionist Party viewpoints*
Fowler, Norman. The right track : a paper on Conservative transport policy / by Norman Fowler. — London : Conservative Political Centre, 1977. — 39p ; 21cm. — (Conservative Political Centre. Publications ; no.612)
ISBN 0-85070-606-8 Sd : £0.60
(B77-32568)

380.5'0941 — Transport. *Great Britain. Secondary school texts*
Scudamore, C N J. Transport problems / [by] C.N.J. Scudamore. — Exeter : Wheaton, 1976. — [7],56p : ill, maps ; 30cm. — (Pergamon topic geographies)
ISBN 0-08-019716-7 Pbk : £1.45
(B77-06599)

380.5'0941 — Transport networks. *Great Britain*
Robinson, Roger. Ways to move : the geography of networks and accessibility / [by] Roger Robinson. — Cambridge [etc.] : Cambridge University Press, 1977. — vi,90p : ill, facsims, maps, plans ; 26cm. — (Cambridge topics in geography series)
Index.
ISBN 0-521-21271-5 : £4.40
ISBN 0-521-29081-3 Pbk : £2.25
(B77-22498)

380.5'0941 — Transport. Planning. Social aspects. *Great Britain, to 1974*
Planning Exchange. Transport planning : the new framework / the Planning Exchange. — Glasgow (186 Bath St., Glasgow G2 4HG) : Planning Exchange, [1975]. — [3],15p ; 30cm. — (Newsheet ; 4 ISSN 0307-1278)
Bibl.: p.15.
ISBN 0-905011-14-7 Sd : £0.30
(B77-08324)

380.5'0941 — Transport. Policies of government. *Great Britain*
Starkie, David Nicholas Martin. Transportation planning, policy and analysis / by D.N.M. Starkie. — Oxford [etc.] : Pergamon, 1976. — xii,145p : ill ; 22cm. — (Urban and regional planning series ; vol.13 ISSN 0305-5582) (Pergamon international library)
Bibl.: p.119-122. — Index.
ISBN 0-08-020909-2 Pbk : £6.75
ISBN 0-08-020908-4 Pbk : £3.50
Also classified at 711'.7'0941
(B77-07254)

380.5'0941 — Transport. Policies of government. *Great Britain. Conference proceedings*
A policy for transport? : papers presented to a conference at Nuffield Lodge / with an introduction by C.D. Foster. — London : Nuffield Foundation, 1977. — [4],84p : ill ; 22cm.
Conference held 8-9 April 1976.
ISBN 0-904956-15-6 Pbk : £1.00
(B77-12395)

380.5'0941 — Transport. Policies of government. Great Britain. Department of the Environment. Transport policy. *Great Britain. Critical studies*
Railway Conversion League. Transport policy : comments by the Railway Conversion League Ltd on the government's consultation document published in April, 1976. — Chertsey (Shouson Hill, Ruxbury Rd, Chertsey KT16 9NH) : The League, 1976. — 20p ; 25cm.
ISBN 0-904698-02-5 Sd : £0.50
(B77-01321)

380.5'0941 — Transport services. *Great Britain. Christian Socialist Movement viewpoints*
Bagwell, Philip Sidney. Transport, private privilege or public service? / by Philip S. Bagwell. — London (Kingsway Hall, Kingsway, W.C.2) : Christian Socialist Movement Central London Branch, [1977]. — [1],14,[1]p ; 21cm.
ISBN 0-900286-00-8 Sd : £0.25
(B77-12396)

380.5'0941 — Transport services. *Great Britain. Periodicals*
Warwickshire Area Transport Society. Newsletter / Warwickshire Area Transport Society. — [Nuneaton] ([c/o The editor, Mendip Drive, Stockington, Nuneaton, Warwickshire CV10 8PT]) : [The Society].
No.1- ; Sept. 1976-. — 1976-. — 30cm.
Monthly. — 2 leaves in 1st issue.
Sd : £1.50 yearly
ISSN 0309-0272
(B77-04079)

380.5'09422'732 — Transport services. *Hampshire. Romsey, to 1975*
Lower Test Valley Archaeological Study Group. Old Romsey at work : a history of industry and transport in Romsey, Hampshire / compiled and published by the Lower Test Valley Archaeological Study Group ; cover illustration by Sybil Panton. — [Romsey] ([c/o Mrs P. Genge, 3 Linden Rd, Romsey, Hants.]) : LVTAS Group, 1976. — [4],43p : ill, maps, ports ; 21cm.
ISBN 0-9503980-2-0 Sd : £0.90
Primary classification 338'.09422'732
(B77-05925)

380.5'09425'3 — Transport. *Lincolnshire. Reports, surveys. For structure plan making*
Lincolnshire *(County). Planning Department.* Transportation : a background paper to the Lincolnshire structure plan / [Lincolnshire County Planning Department]. — [Lincoln] ([County Offices, Lincoln LN1 1YJ]) : The Department, 1977. — 36p : ill, maps(some col) ; 30cm. — (Report of survey ; part 9)
Cover title: Lincolnshire structure plan, background paper, transportation. — Summary (sheet ([2]p.) as insert.
Sp : £0.75
(B77-24132)

380.5'09428'2 — Transport. South Yorkshire (Metropolitan County). Related to industrial development, to 1975
Abell, Paul Henry. Transport and industry in South Yorkshire / by P.H. Abell ; maps by S.A. Harper. — Barnsley (14 The Croft, Elsecar, Barnsley, S. Yorkshire S74 8EB) : The author, 1977. — [1],84p : ill, maps ; 21cm.
Bibl.: p.79-80. — Index.
ISBN 0-901182-02-8 Sd : £1.50
Also classified at 338'.09428'2
(B77-26987)

380.5'096 — Transport networks. Political aspects. *Africa*
Arnold, Guy. Strategic highways of Africa / [by] Guy Arnold and Ruth Weiss. — London : Friedmann, 1977. — [1],178p : maps ; 23cm.
Bibl.: p.166-167. — Index.
ISBN 0-904014-12-6 : £5.95
ISBN 0-904014-13-4 Pbk : Unpriced
(B77-22499)

380.5'1 — Railway services. Replacement by bus services. *Great Britain*
Railway Invigoration Society. Can bus replace train?, or, Will they never learn? / [compiled by a study group of the Railway Invigoration Society, R.V. Banks et al.]. — London (BM/RIS, WC1V 6XX) : The Society, 1977. — [1],24p : maps ; 22cm.
Sd : £0.30
(B77-31806)

380.5'2 — Cargo handling. Organisations: International Cargo Handling Coordination Association. *Directories*
International Cargo Handling Co-ordination Association. Directory of members / [International Cargo Handling Co-ordination Association]. — [London] ([15 Wilton Rd, SW1V 1LX]) : The Association.
1977. — [1977]. — 163p : ill ; 18cm.
Cover title.
Pbk : Unpriced
(B77-30127)

380.5'2 — Food. Refrigerated transport. *Periodicals*
Temperature controlled storage & distribution. — Redhill (2 Queensway, Redhill RH1 1QS) : Retail Journals Ltd.
No.1- ; Sept. 1977-. — [1977]-. — ill(some col), ports ; 30cm.
48p. in preview issue.
Sd : Unpriced
Primary classification 664'.02852'05
(B77-21278)

380.5'2 — Freight transport. Containerisation. *Serials*
'Containerisation international' year book. — London : National Magazine Co.
1977 / editor R.F. Gibney ; compiled by Leo Denton and the staff of 'Containerisation international'. — [1977]. — 392p : ill, form ; 29cm.
Bibl.: p.373-376. — Index.
ISBN 0-85223-115-6 : £12.50
ISSN 0305-7402
(B77-14667)

380.5'2 — Freight transport. Energy. Conservation. *Great Britain. Proposals*
Advisory Council on Energy Conservation. Freight transport : short and medium term considerations / Advisory Council on Energy Conservation. — London : H.M.S.O., 1976. — iv,22p ; 25cm. — (Advisory Council on Energy Conservation. Papers ; 6) (Energy paper ; no.24)
ISBN 0-11-410610-x Sd : £1.50
(B77-27786)

380.5'2 — International freight transport. *Ireland. Periodicals*
International transport. — [Dublin] ([64 Northumberland Rd, Dublin 4]) : [International Transport Journals Ltd].
Jan. 1977-. — [1977]-. — ill, ports ; 30cm.
Monthly. — [1],64p. in Apr. 1977 issue includes 1 contribution in Danish.
Sd : £0.50(£8.00 yearly)
(B77-15783)

380.5'2 — Long-distance passenger transport services. Planning. *Western Europe. Reports, surveys*
Organisation for Economic Co-operation and Development. The future of European passenger transport : final report on the OECD study on European intercity passenger transport requirements (study undertaken in liaison with the ECMT and the EEC). — [Paris] : O.E.C.D. ; [London] : [H.M.S.O.], [1977]. — 3v.([2],xiv,602;[2],307p;portfolio) : ill, maps(some col) ; 30cm.
Thirty sheets ([31] sides) ([27] fold) in portfolio. — English text, French and English parallel text in portfolio.
£14.60
ISBN 92-64-11678-8
(B77-25529)

Organisation for Economic Co-operation and Development. The future of European passenger transport : final report on the OECD study on European intercity passenger transport requirements (study undertaken in liaison with the ECMT and the EEC), report by the Steering Committee. — [Paris] : O.E.C.D. ; [London] : [H.M.S.O.], [1977]. — [2],28p ; 30cm.
Sd : Unpriced
(B77-25528)

380.5'2 — Passenger transport. *Juvenile literature*
The way we travel. — London : Dean, 1977. — [30]p : chiefly col ill ; 32cm.
ISBN 0-603-08503-2 : £0.85
(B77-31807)

380.5'2 — Passenger transport services. Choice by governments. Organisation for Economic Co-operation and Development countries. Related to town planning. *Reports, surveys*
Round Table on Transport Economics, *33rd, Paris, 1976.* Report of the Thirty-third Round Table on Transport Economics held in Paris on 26th and 27th February, 1976 on the following topic, 'Impact of the structure and extent of urban development on the choice of modes of transport : the case of large conurbations' / [by P. Merlin]. — Paris : European Conference of Ministers of Transport, Economic Research Centre ; [London] : [H.M.S.O.], 1976. — 48p : ill, maps, plan ; 24cm. — (ECMT round table ; 33 ISSN 0531-9528)
Bibl.: p.36.
Pbk : £1.80
ISBN 92-821-1038-9
Also classified at 711'.4
(B77-05998)

381 — DOMESTIC TRADE
381 — Auctioneering firms. *England. East Midlands. William H. Brown and Son, to 1976. Chronologies*
William H. Brown and Son. The history of William H. Brown & Son, 1896-1976. — [Sleaford] ([Northgate House, Sleaford, Lincs.]) : [William H. Brown & Son], [1977]. — [10]p ; 23cm.
Sd : Unpriced
(B77-31108)

381 — Cash and carry depots. *Great Britain. Directories*
United Kingdom cash & carry warehouses / [Data Research Group]. — Amersham (Hill House, [Hill Ave.], Amersham, Bucks.) : The Group.
[1977]. — 1977. — 108 leaves in various pagings ; 30cm.
Previously published: as 'United Kingdom cash and carry companies'. — Index.
Sp : £16.00
(B77-27787)

381 — Department stores. *Great Britain. Directories*
United Kingdom department stores / [Data Research Group]. — Amersham (Hill House, [Hill Ave.], Amersham, Bucks.) : The Group.
[1976]. — 1976. — 77 leaves in various pagings ; 30cm.
ISBN 0-905570-44-8 Sp : Unpriced
(B77-02201)

[1977]. — 1977. — 70 leaves in various pagings ; 30cm.
ISBN 0-905570-94-4 Sp : £14.00
(B77-15238)

381 — Gift shops. *Great Britain. Directories*
United Kingdom gift shops / [Data Research Group]. — Amersham (Hill House, [Hill Ave.], Amersham, Bucks.) : The Group.
1976. — [1976]. — 146 leaves in various pagings ; 30cm.
ISBN 0-905570-31-6 Sp : £16.00
(B77-00144)

381 — Hypermarkets & supermarkets. *Great Britain. Reports, surveys*
House of Commons Seminar on Hypermarkets and Superstores, *1976.* Hypermarkets and superstores : report of a House of Commons seminar. — Reading (229 King's Rd, Reading RG1 4LS) : The Unit for Retail Planning Information Ltd, 1976. — [5],30p,plate : ill, map ; 26cm. — (Unit for Retail Planning Information. Reports ; U1 ISSN 0309-2925)
'... papers given at a House of Commons Seminar on Hypermarkets and Superstores on 4th February 1976 ... presented by the Unit for Retail Planning Information in conjunction with the All-Party Parliamentary Retail Trade Group' - Preface. — Bibl.: p.30.
Sd : £4.50(£2.50 to members)
(B77-08325)

381 — Hypermarkets & superstores. *Great Britain. Lists*
Unit for Retail Planning Information. List of UK hypermarkets & superstores / [the Unit for Retail Planning Information Limited]. — 3rd ed. — Reading (229 King's Rd, Reading RG1 4LS) : U.R.P.I., 1976. — [2],8 leaves ; 30cm.
ISBN 0-905912-01-2 Sd : Unpriced
(B77-07255)

381 — Mail-order firms. *Great Britain. Directories*
United Kingdom mail order companies / [Data Research Group]. — Amersham (Hill House, [Hill Ave.], Amersham, Bucks.) : The Group.
[1977]. — 1977. — 21 leaves in various pagings ; 30cm.
ISBN 0-86099-043-5 Sp : Unpriced
(B77-26249)

381 — Multiple shops. *Great Britain. Directories*
United Kingdom multiple shops with three or more outlets / [Data Research Group]. — Amersham (Hill House, [Hill Ave.], Amersham, Bucks.) : The Group.
1976. — [1976]. — 433 leaves in various pagings ; 30cm.
ISBN 0-905570-37-5 Pbk : £25.00
(B77-00145)

381 — Supermarkets. *Great Britain. Directories*
United Kingdom supermarkets / [Data Research Group]. — Amersham (Hill House, [Hill Ave.], Amersham, Bucks.) : The Group.
1975. — [1975]. — 176 leaves in various pagings ; 30cm.
Index.
ISBN 0-905570-20-0 Pbk : £15.00
(B77-00146)

381 — Wholesale fancy goods trades. *Great Britain. Directories*
United Kingdom fancy goods & toy wholesalers / [Data Research Group]. — Amersham (Hill House, [Hill Ave.], Amersham, Bucks.) : The Group.
[1976]. — 1976. — 43 leaves in various pagings ; 30cm.
ISBN 0-905570-62-6 Sp : £13.00
Primary classification 381'.45'6887202541
(B77-07259)

381'.01'84 — Shopping behaviour. Spatial models. *Cumbria. Reports, surveys*
Moseley, Janet. Cumbria shopping model, preliminary calibration / [by] Janet Moseley. — Reading (229 King's Rd, Reading RG1 4LS) : Unit for Retail Planning Information, 1976. — [3],46p : ill, maps ; 26cm. — (Unit for Retail Planning Information. Reports ; U3 ISSN 0309-2925)
Sd : £7.50(£4.50 to sponsors)
(B77-08954)

381'.025'41 — Retail trades. *Great Britain. Directories*
Stores, shops, supermarkets retail directory : UK department stores, multiple shops, variety chains, supermarkets, hypermarkets, discount stores, co-operative societies, cash and carry. — London : Newman Books.
1978 : [32nd ed.]. — [1977]. — 1275p : ill, maps ; 22cm.
ISBN 0-7079-6908-5 : £23.00
ISSN 0305-4012
(B77-32569)

381'.025'421 — Shops. *London. Directories*
Sherwood, James. James Sherwood's discriminating guide [to] London : fine dining and shopping, with a special section on museums and art galleries. — London : Heinemann.
[1977] / edited by Susan Blackburn ; illustrations by Rodney Shackell. — 1977. — viii,419,[15]p : ill, col maps ; 20cm.
Index.
ISBN 0-448-14057-8 : £4.50
Primary classification 647'.95421
(B77-21977)

381'.07'23 — Shopping behaviour. Surveys. Methodology. *Berkshire*
Royal Institute of Public Administration. *Local Government Operational Research Unit.* Shopping in Berkshire : survey methods : a report of the Local Government Operational Research Unit / [written by] Janet Moseley. — Reading (229 King's Rd, Reading RG1 4LS) : Unit for Retail Planning Information, 1975. — [9],32p : facsim, forms, map ; 30cm. — (Unit for Retail Planning Information. Reports ; G1 ISSN 0309-2917)
Sd : £2.00(£1.50 to members)
(B77-08326)

381'.0941 — Local shopping facilities. *Great Britain. Reports, surveys*
Local shops : problems and prospects / Peter Jones and Rosemary Oliphant, editors. — Reading (229 King's Rd, Reading RG1 4LS) : Unit for Retail Planning Information, 1976. — [4],103p ; 26cm. — (Unit for Retail Planning Information. Reports ; U2 ISSN 0309-2925)
Bibl.: p.103.
Pbk : £7.00(£4.00 to members)
(B77-08955)

381'.0941 — Shopping. *Great Britain. Secondary school texts*
Leafe, Margaret. Shopping around : a textbook in consumer protection / [by] Margaret Leafe. — London : Cassell, 1977. — 64p : ill, form ; 22cm.
ISBN 0-304-29832-8 Sd : £1.00
(B77-25530)

381'.0941 — Shopping centres. *Great Britain. Urban regions. Statistics*
Shopping centre data. — London (70 Jermyn St., SW1Y 6PE) : Donaldsons, 1977. — [18]leaves ; 30cm. — (Donaldson and Sons. Research notes ; 1)
Pbk : £2.00
(B77-30128)

381'.0941 — Shops. *Great Britain, to ca 1950. Juvenile literature*
Mountfield, Anne. Shops and shopping / [by] Anne Mountfield. — Hove : Wayland, 1976. — 96p : ill, facsims, ports ; 24cm. — (Eyewitness books)
Bibl.: p.94. — Index.
ISBN 0-85340-438-0 : £2.95
(B77-00147)

381'.0942 — Domestic trade. *England, 1500-1700*
Chartres, J A. Internal trade in England, 1500-1700 / prepared for the Economic History Society by J.A. Chartres. — London [etc.] : Macmillan, 1977. — 79p ; 21cm. — (Studies in economic and social history)
Bibl.: p.68-76. — Index.
ISBN 0-333-18358-4 Pbk : £1.60
(B77-21808)

381'.0942 — Free-standing shopping facilities. Planning. Proposals. Inquiry reports. *England. Reports, surveys*
Lee, Michael. Planning inquiry study / [by] Michael Lee, Elizabeth Kent. — London (70 Jermyn St., SW1Y 6PE) : Donaldsons, 1976. — viii,161p : 1 ill, map ; 30cm. — (Donaldson and Sons. Research reports ; 3)
Pbk : £10.00
(B77-30129)

381'.09421 — Shops. *London. Guidebooks*
Donald, Elsie Burch. London shopping guide / [by] Elsie Burch Donald. — 2nd ed. — Harmondsworth [etc.] : Penguin, 1977. — 307p ; 18cm. — (Penguin handbooks)
Previous ed.: 1975. — Index.
Pbk : £0.90
ISBN 0-14-046222-8
(B77-27788)

381'.09422'5 — Shopping. *East Sussex. Reports, surveys. For structure plan making*
East Sussex *(County). Planning Department.* County structure plan, 1976 review : County Council approved / East Sussex [County Planning Department]. — Lewes (Southover House, Southover Rd, Lewes, E. Sussex BN7 1YA) : The Department, 1976. — [3],10p ; 30cm.
ISBN 0-900348-47-x Sd : £0.60
(B77-02202)

381'.09422'7 — Shopping. *Hampshire. Reports, surveys*
Southampton Chamber of Commerce. Southampton Chamber of Commerce sub-committee report on 'Shopping in Hampshire'. — [Southampton] ([53 Bugle St., Southampton SO9 4WP]) : [The Chamber of Commerce], [1977]. — [30]p ; 33cm.
Includes copies of correspondence with the Department of the Environment and Eastleigh Borough Council, and the Southampton Chamber of Commerce retail shopping report.
Sd : Unpriced
(B77-29330)

381'.09422'93 — Retail trades. Location. *Berkshire. Reading. Reports, surveys*
Guy, Clifford. The location of shops in the Reading area / [by] Clifford Guy. — Reading (Whiteknights, Reading RG6 2AB) : Department of Geography, University of Reading, 1976. — [2],ii,52p : ill, maps ; 21cm. — (Geographical papers ; no.46 ISSN 0305-5914)
Bibl.: p.38.
ISBN 0-7049-0455-1 Sd : £0.65
(B77-02907)

381'.09426'752 — Shopping facilities. *Essex. Chelmsford (District). Rural regions. Reports, surveys*
Chelmsford *(District). Council.* Rural areas study, subject report, shopping and services / Chelmsford District Council. — Chelmsford (Planning Department, Burgess Well Rd, Coval La., Chelmsford, [Essex]) : [The Council], 1976. — [2] leaves,7[i.e.9]p ; 30cm.
ISBN 0-905110-02-1 Sd : £0.20
(B77-02203)

381'.41'4 — Retail fruit trades. *Dublin. Reports, surveys*
Bowbrick, P. Fruit and vegetable retailing in Dublin / [by] P. Bowbrick and D. Twohig. — [Dublin] : Foras Taluntais, 1976. — [6],30p ; 21cm.
ISBN 0-905442-12-1 Sd : £0.50
Also classified at 381'.41'50941835
(B77-30130)

381'.41'506242165 — Horticultural products. Wholesaling. Markets. Organisations. *London. Lambeth (London Borough). Covent Garden Market Authority. Reports, surveys. Serials*
Covent Garden Market Authority. Report and accounts for the accounting period ended 30th September / Covent Garden Market Authority. — London (1 Nine Elms La., SW8 5NX) : The Authority.
1976 : [Fifteenth report]. — [1977]. — [4],21p ; 30cm.
ISBN 0-905976-00-2 Sd : £0.50
(B77-15784)

381'.41'50941835 — Retail vegetable trades. *Dublin. Reports, surveys*
Bowbrick, P. Fruit and vegetable retailing in Dublin / [by] P. Bowbrick and D. Twohig. — [Dublin] : Foras Taluntais, 1976. — [6],30p ; 21cm.
ISBN 0-905442-12-1 Sd : £0.50
Primary classification 381'.41'4
(B77-30130)

381'.42'206141 — Coal trades. Consumer protection services. *Great Britain. Domestic Coal Consumers' Council. Reports, surveys. Serials*
Domestic Coal Consumers' Council. Annual report ... / Domestic Coal Consumers' Council. — London : H.M.S.O.
1976. — [1977]. — [2],25p ; 25cm. — ([1976-77 H.C.] 18)
ISBN 0-10-213877-x Sd : £0.65
(B77-08956)

381'.45'070573 — Antiquarian booksellers & out-of-print booksellers. *Great Britain. Directories*
Annual directory of booksellers in the British Isles specialising in antiquarian and out-of-print books. — Birmingham (75 Worlds End Rd, Handsworth Wood, Birmingham B20 2NS) : The Clique Ltd.
1977 : 8th ed. — 1977. — 2-132p : ill ; 22cm.
ISBN 0-901909-07-6 Pbk : £3.00
(B77-31109)

381'.45'070573 — Antiquarian booksellers & second-hand booksellers. *London. Illustrations*
Brown, Richard, *b.1932.* The London bookshop : a pictorial record of the antiquarian book trade : portraits & premises / [by] Richard Brown & Stanley Brett. — Pinner ('Ravelston', South View Rd, Pinner, Middx) : Private Libraries Association.
Part 2. — 1977. — 75,[1]p : chiefly ill, ports ; 19x25cm.
ISBN 0-900002-23-9 : £5.00(£2.50 to members of the Association)
(B77-23310)

381'.45'070573 — Antiquarian booksellers & second-hand booksellers. *North America. Directories*
Bookdealers in North America : a directory of dealers in secondhand and antiquarian books in Canada and the United States of America. — London : Sheppard Press.
1976-78 : seventh ed. — 1976. — xxiv,259p : ill ; 19cm.
Previously published: as 'Book dealers in North America'.
ISBN 0-900661-13-5 : £6.00
(B77-02908)

381'.45'070573 — Antiquarian booksellers & second-hand booksellers. *South Asia. Directories*
Bookdealers in India, Pakistan, Sri Lanka &c. : a directory of dealers in secondhand and antiquarian books in the Sub-Continent of South Western Asia / [edited by Kunnuparampil P. Punnoose]. — London : Sheppard Press, 1977. — xxiv,108p : ill, map ; 20cm.
Index.
ISBN 0-900661-14-3 : £3.50
(B77-25531)

381'.45'070573 — Books for higher education institutions. Booksellers. *Great Britain. Directories*
List of college and university booksellers / the Booksellers Association of Great Britain and Ireland. — London : The Association.
1976. — 1976. — [2],11p ; 21cm.
ISBN 0-901690-37-6 Sd : £1.00
(B77-05999)

381'.45'070573 — Books for schools. Booksellers. *Great Britain. Directories*
List of school suppliers / the Booksellers Association of Great Britain and Ireland. — London : The Association.
1976. — 1976. — [2],16p ; 21cm.
ISBN 0-901690-32-5 Sd : £1.00
(B77-06000)

381'.45'070573 — Books on religion. Booksellers. *Great Britain. Directories*
List of religious booksellers / the Booksellers Association of Great Britain and Ireland. — London : The Association.
1976. — [1976]. — [2],16p ; 21cm.
ISBN 0-901690-35-x Sd : £1.00
(B77-06001)

381'.45'070573 — Books with foreign imprints. Booksellers. *Great Britain. Directories*
List of export and foreign booksellers / the Booksellers Association of Great Britain and Ireland. — London : The Association.
1976. — 1976. — [2],14p ; 21cm.
ISBN 0-901690-33-3 Sd : £1.00
Also classified at 382'.45'07057302541
(B77-06002)

381'.45'070573 — Children's books. Booksellers. *Great Britain. Directories*
List of childrens booksellers / the Booksellers Association of Great Britain and Ireland. — London : The Association.
1976. — 1976. — [2],11p ; 21cm.
ISBN 0-901690-34-1 Sd : £1.00
(B77-06003)

381'.45'07057302541 — Libraries. Stock: Books. Booksellers. *Great Britain. Directories*
List of library suppliers / the Booksellers Association of Great Britain and Ireland. — London : The Association.
1976. — 1976. — [2],16p ; 21cm.
ISBN 0-901690-36-8 Sd : £1.00
(B77-06004)

381'.45'07057302541 — Wholesale book trades. *Great Britain. Directories*
A directory of book wholesalers in Great Britain and Ireland and their terms / [Booksellers Association]. — London : The Association. [1976-77]. — 1976. — viii,71p ; 21cm.
Index.
ISBN 0-901690-40-6 Pbk : £2.00
(B77-06600)

381'.45'07057306241 — Bookselling. Organisations. *Great Britain. Booksellers Association. Charter Group. Directories*
Booksellers Association. List of charter members / The Booksellers Association of Great Britain and Ireland. — London : The Association.
1976. — 1976. — [2],iii,21p ; 21cm.
ISBN 0-901690-31-7 Sd : Unpriced
(B77-16820)

381'.45'36800941 — Insurance agents & insurance brokers. Regulation. *Great Britain. Proposals*
Great Britain. *Department of Trade.* Insurance intermediaries .. / Department of Trade. — London : H.M.S.O., [1977]. — iii,19p ; 25cm. — (Cmnd.6715)
ISBN 0-10-167150-4 Sd : £0.45
(B77-07256)

381'.45'615102541 — Wholesale pharmaceutical trades. *Great Britain. Directories*
United Kingdom chemists wholesalers / [Data Research Group]. — Amersham (Hill House, [Hill Ave.], Amersham, Bucks.) : The Group.
[1975]. — 1975. — 30 leaves in various pagings ; 30cm.
ISBN 0-905570-46-4 Sp : £10.00
(B77-02204)

[1977]. — 1977. — 44 leaves in various pagings ; 30cm.
ISBN 0-905570-93-6 Sp : Unpriced
(B77-14174)

381'.45'61510924 — Pharmaceutical products. Retailing. Greenwood, J E. *Great Britain. Autobiographies*
Greenwood, J E. A cap for boots : an autobiography / [by] J.E. Greenwood. — London : Hutchinson, 1977. — xvii,254p,fold leaf of plate,[36]p of plates : ill, facsims, geneal table, ports ; 23cm.
Index.
ISBN 0-09-128890-8 : £4.95
(B77-23311)

381'.45'61510941 — Pharmaceutical industries. Marketing. Economic aspects. *Great Britain*
Slatter, Stuart St. P. Competition and marketing strategies in the pharmaceutical industry / [by] Stuart St. P. Slatter. — London : Croom Helm, 1977. — 150p : ill ; 23cm.
Bibl.: p.146-148. — Index.
ISBN 0-85664-396-3 : £14.95
Primary classification 338.6'048
(B77-23225)

381'.45'6200028 — Wholesale engineering equipment trades. *Great Britain. Periodicals*
Engineering distributors journal. — Tonbridge : E. Benn.
Vol.1, no.1- ; Mar. 1977-. — 1977-. — ill, ports ; 29cm.
Six issues a year. — 76p. in 1st issue.
Pbk : £6.00 yearly
ISSN 0309-6092
(B77-18053)

381'.45'6213104202541 — Wholesale electric equipment trades. *Great Britain. Directories*
United Kingdom electrical wholesalers / [Data Research Group]. — Amersham (Hill House, [Hill Ave.], Amersham, Bucks.) : The Group.
[1976]. — 1976. — 84 leaves in various pagings ; 30cm.
ISBN 0-905570-41-3 Sp : Unpriced
(B77-02205)

381'.45'6238602541 — Ships' chandlers. *Great Britain. Directories*
Boatbuilders' and chandlers' directory of suppliers. — Tonbridge (47 High St., Tonbridge, Kent) : Weald of Kent Publications (Tonbridge) Ltd for Castle Books.
1977. — 1977. — 152p ; 21cm.
Index.
ISBN 0-904238-06-7 Pbk : £2.25
ISSN 0306-3593
Primary classification 338.4'7'62382002541
(B77-13559)

United Kingdom shipping / [Data Research Group]. — Amersham (Hill House, [Hill Ave.], Amersham, Bucks.) : The Group.
[1976]. — 1976. — 200 leaves in various pagings ; 30cm.
ISBN 0-905570-68-5 Pbk : £17.00
Primary classification 338.4'7'62382002541
(B77-06536)

381'.45'6238605 — Ships' chandlers. *Periodicals*
Marine stores international. — Redhill (2 Queensway, Redhill, Surrey RH1 1QS) : International Trade Publications Ltd.
[No.1]- ; Feb.-Mar. 1977-. — 1977-. — ill, forms, maps, ports ; 30cm.
Six issues a year. — 54p. in 1st issue.
Sd : Unpriced
ISSN 0140-2498
(B77-33165)

381'.45'6292 — Car accessories shops. *Great Britain. Directories*
United Kingdom car accessory shops / [Data Research Group]. — Amersham (Hill House, [Hill Ave.], Amersham, Bucks.) : The Group.
[1977]. — 1977. — 134 leaves in various pagings ; 30cm.
Sp : £16.00
(B77-26988)

381'.45'629222209422 — Newspapers consisting of advertisements for car trades in London & Home Counties. *Texts*
Car buyer. — London (191 King's Cross Rd, W.C.1) : Shaw's Car Buyer Ltd.
[No.1]- ; 20-26 May 1976-. — [1976]-. — ill ; 30cm.
Weekly. — 48p. in 1st issue.
Sd : £0.10
ISSN 0308-9460
(B77-02206)

381'.45'631 — Agricultural equipment & materials trades. *Great Britain. Directories*
United Kingdom agricultural merchants / [Data Research Group]. — Amersham (Hill House, [Hill Ave.], Amersham, Bucks.) : The Group.
[1976]. — 1976. — 186 leaves in various pagings ; 30cm.
ISBN 0-905570-30-8 Pbk : £15.00
(B77-00148)

381'.45'6413 — Retail food trades. Supermarkets. *United States*
Cross, Jennifer. The supermarket trap : the consumer and the food industry / [by] Jennifer Cross. — Revised and enlarged ed. — Bloomington ; London : Indiana University Press, 1976. — xiii,306p : ill ; 22cm.
Previous ed.: i.e. 1st ed. 1970. — Bibl.: p.261-269. — Index.
ISBN 0-253-35582-6 : £10.00
ISBN 0-253-20199-3 Pbk : £2.80
(B77-05331)

381'.45'6413002541 — Wholesale grocery trades. *Great Britain. Directories*
Grocery wholesalers / [Data Research Group]. — Amersham (Hill House, [Hill Ave.], Amersham, Bucks.) : The Group.
[1976]. — 1976. — 62 leaves in various pagings ; 30cm.
ISBN 0-905570-76-6 Sp : £12.00
(B77-08957)

United Kingdom grocery wholesalers / [Data Research Group]. — Amersham (Hill House, [Hill Ave.], Amersham, Bucks.) : The Group.
[1977]. — 1977. — 78 leaves in various pagings ; 30cm.
ISBN 0-86099-046-x Sp : £14.00
(B77-28549)

381'.45'641300941 — Grocery trades. *Great Britain. Periodicals*
Grocery trade bulletin / Institute of Grocery Distribution, Research Services. — [Watford] ([Grange La., Letchmore Heath, Watford WD2 8DQ]) : [The Institute].
Supersedes: News / Institute of Grocery Distribution.
[No.1]- ; [1977]-. — [1977]-. — 30cm.
Monthly. — [53]p. in June 1977 issue.
Sd : £20.00(free to members of the Institute)
ISSN 0140-0371
(B77-21809)

381'.45'641300941 — Retail grocery trades. *Great Britain, 1961-1976. Reports, surveys*
Lambert, Geoffrey, *b.1950.* Developments in the retail grocery trade / by G. Lambert. — [Watford] ([Letchmore Heath, Watford WD2 8DQ]) : Institute of Grocery Distribution, Research Services, 1977. — [3],32 leaves : ill ; 30cm.
Sp : £15.00(£5.00 to members)
(B77-31808)

381'.45'66360941 — Licensed premises. Soft drinks trades. Profit margins. *Great Britain, 1973-1976. Inquiry reports*
Great Britain. *Price Commission.* Prices and margins of soft drinks and mixers in licensed premises / Price Commission. — London : H.M.S.O., 1977. — vi,17p ; 25cm. — (Report ; no.23)
ISBN 0-11-700865-6 Sd : £0.60
Primary classification 338.4'3'66360941
(B77-14114)

381'.45'66393 — Coffee trades. Profit margins. *Great Britain, 1974-1977. Reports, surveys*
Great Britain. *Price Commission.* Coffee prices, costs and margins / Price Commission. — London : H.M.S.O., 1977. — vi,34p : ill ; 25cm. — (Report ; no.29)
ISBN 0-11-700873-7 Sd : £0.80
Primary classification 338.4'3'663930941
(B77-23214)

381'.45'6640285302541 — Freezer centres. *Great Britain. Directories*
United Kingdom freezer centres / [Data Research Group]. — Amersham (Hill House, [Hill Ave.], Amersham, Bucks.) : The Group.
[1976]. — 1976. — 102 leaves in various pagings ; 30cm.
ISBN 0-905570-59-6 Sp : £15.00
(B77-07880)

[1977]. — 1977. — 110 leaves in various pagings ; 30cm.
Sp : £16.00
(B77-17411)

381'.45'6646 — Food for special diets. Marketing. *Great Britain. Reports, surveys*
Economist Intelligence Unit. A study of the United Kingdom market for slimming, dietetic and health foods / [Economist Intelligence Unit]. — London : E.I.U., 1977. — [8],365p ; 30cm. — (An EIU multi-client project)
Sp : £450.00
(B77-24843)

381'.45'6646 — Health food trades. *Great Britain. Directories*
United Kingdom health food shops and beauty salons : including health clubs and sauna baths / [Data Research Group]. — Amersham (Hill House, [Hill Ave.,] Amersham, Bucks.) : The Group.
[1976]. — 1976. — 140p leaves in various pagings ; 30cm.
ISBN 0-905570-57-x Sp : £12.00
Also classified at 338.4'7'6467202541
(B77-07257)

United Kingdom health food shops and beauty salons / [Data Research Group]. — Amersham (Hill House, [Hill Ave.], Amersham, Bucks.) : The Group.
[1977]. — 1977. — 156 leaves in various pagings ; 30cm.
ISBN 0-86099-035-4 Pbk : £14.00
Also classified at 338.4'7'6467202541
(B77-29331)

381'.45'66492 — Multiple butcher's shops. *Great Britain. Directories*
United Kingdom multiple butchers / [Data Research Group]. — Amersham (Hill House, [Hill Ave.], Amersham, Bucks.) : The Group.
[1975]. — 1975. — 40 leaves in various pagings ; 30cm.
ISBN 0-905570-03-0 Sp : £13.00
(B77-00712)

381'.45'66553827025411 — Petrol filling stations. *Scotland. Directories*
Petrol stations in Scotland / Scottish Tourist Board. — Edinburgh : The Board. — (Scottish Tourist Board. Information booklets)
Notebook format.
1977. — [1976]. — 36p : 1 ill, map ; 21x10cm.
Sd : Unpriced
(B77-22500)

381'.45'665773 — Garages selling liquefied petroleum gas. *Great Britain. Directories*
Dods, John Rollier. The auto-gas directory. — Richmond [N. Yorkshire] (23 Maple Rd, Richmond [N. Yorkshire DL10 4BW]) : The author, [1976]. — [1],69[i.e.70],[1]p : maps ; 15cm.
Author: J.R. Dods.
ISBN 0-9505329-0-8 Sd : £0.25
(B77-00149)

381'.45'667602541 — Paints trades. *Great Britain. Directories*
United Kingdom paint merchants / [Data Research Group]. — Amersham (Hill House, [Hill Ave.], Amersham, Bucks.) : The Group.
1975. — [1976]. — 71 leaves in various pagings ; 30cm.
ISBN 0-905570-72-3 Sp : £12.00
(B77-07258)

381'.45'67402541 — Wholesale timber trades. *Great Britain. Directories*
United Kingdom timber merchants / [Data Research Group]. — Amersham (Hill House, [Hill Ave.], Amersham, Bucks.) : The Group.
[1976]. — 1976. — 172 leaves in various pagings ; 30cm.
ISBN 0-905570-27-8 Pbk : £16.00
(B77-00150)

[1977]. — 1977. — 163 leaves in various pagings ; 30cm.
ISBN 0-86099-038-9 Pbk : £18.00
(B77-33730)

381'.45'676282302541 — Stationery trades. *Great Britain. Directories*
Stationery trade reference book and buyers' guide. — Maidstone (Earl House, Maidstone, Kent ME14 1PE) : Whitehall Press Ltd.
1977 : [22nd ed.] / compiled by the information staff of 'Stationery trade review'. — [1976]. — 276p : ill ; 24cm.
ISBN 0-903175-07-x Pbk : £6.00
(B77-05332)

381'.45'676282302541 — Wholesale stationery trades. *Great Britain. Directories*
United Kingdom stationers, wholesale / [Data Research Group]. — Amersham (Hill House, [Hill Ave.], Amersham, Bucks.) : The Group.
[1976]. — 1976. — 55 leaves in various pagings ; 30cm.
ISBN 0-905570-50-2 Sp : £13.00
(B77-04080)

[1977]. — [1977]. — 47 leaves in various pagings ; 30cm.
ISBN 0-86099-058-3 Sp : £15.00
(B77-31809)

381'.45'677643 — Wholesale carpet trades. Companies. Finance. *Great Britain. Statistics*
British carpet wholesalers / [Jordan Dataquest Limited]. — London : Jordan Dataquest. — (Dataquest survey)
[1977]. — 1977. — [4],9,[13]leaves ; 30cm.
Notebook format. — Index.
Sp : £28.00
ISSN 0140-3567
(B77-32570)

381'.45'68302541 — Retail hardware trades. *Great Britain. Directories*
United Kingdom hardware & ironmongery retailers / [Data Research Group]. — Amersham (Hill House, [Hill Ave.], Amersham, Bucks.) : The Group.
1975. — [1975]. — 321 leaves in various pagings ; 30cm.
ISBN 0-905570-38-3 Pbk : £19.00
(B77-00151)

[1977]. — 1977. — 327 leaves in various pagings ; 30cm.
ISBN 0-86099-065-6 Pbk : £21.00
(B77-31810)

381'.45'68302541 — Wholesale hardware trades. *Great Britain. Directories*
United Kingdom hardware & ironmongery wholesalers / [Data Research Group]. — Amersham (Hill House, [Hill Ave.], Amersham, Bucks.) : The Group.
1976. — [1976]. — 46 leaves in various pagings ; 30cm.
ISBN 0-905570-14-6 Sp : £13.00
(B77-00152)

[1977]. — 1977. — 44 leaves in various pagings ; 30cm.
Sp : £14.00
(B77-17412)

381'.45'6840802541 — Do-it-yourself trades. *Great Britain. Directories*
United Kingdom do-it-yourself shops / [Data Research Group]. — Amersham (Hill House, [Hill Ave.], Amersham, Bucks.) : The Group.
[1976]. — 1976. — 141 leaves in various pagings ; 30cm.
ISBN 0-905570-43-x Sp : £16.00
(B77-02207)

381'.45'6855302541 — Retail camping equipment trades. *Great Britain. Directories*
United Kingdom sport shops and camping equipment / [Data Research Group]. — Amersham (Hill House, [Hill Ave.], Amersham, Bucks.) : The Group.
[1976]. — 1976. — 114 leaves in various pagings ; 30cm.
ISBN 0-905570-49-9 Sp : £14.00
Primary classification 381'.45'6887602541
(B77-04081)

United Kingdom sports shops and camping equipment / [Data Research Group]. — Amersham (Hill House, [Hill Ave.], Amersham, Bucks.) : The Group.
[1977]. — 1977. — 140 leaves in various pagings ; 30cm.
ISBN 0-86099-020-6 Sp : £15.00
Primary classification 381'.45'6887602541
(B77-15785)

381'.45'687025421 — Clothing shops. *London. Directories*
The **fashion** guide / [editor Kaori O'Connor]. — London (3 Culmstock Rd, S.W.11) : Farrol Kahn for The Fashion Guide.
1976. — [1976]. — 3-269p : ill ; 19cm.
Previously published: as 'The London fashion guide'. — Index.
ISBN 0-9504175-1-3 Pbk : £1.10
(B77-00713)

The **fashion** guide / [written and edited by] Kaori O'Connor. — Sevenoaks : Coronet.
1977. — 1977. — 379p : ill ; 18cm.
Index.
ISBN 0-340-21798-7 Pbk : £1.25
(B77-15239)

381'.45'68780654212 — Haberdashery trades. *London (City). Williams (W.) and Son (Bread Street) Limited, to 1975*
Hayman, Leslie Crease Ridd. An account of W. Williams & Son (Bread Street) Limited, (formerly the partnership business of W. Williams & Sons), 1819-1975 / by Leslie C.R. Hayman. — [London] ([17c Abbey Rd, N.W.8]) : [Mrs L. Hayman], [1975]. — 28p : ill, ports ; 25cm.
ISBN 0-9505353-0-3 : For private circulation only
(B77-00714)

381'.45'6887202541 — Wholesale toy trades. *Great Britain. Directories*
United Kingdom fancy goods & toy wholesalers / [Data Research Group]. — Amersham (Hill House, [Hill Ave.], Amersham, Bucks.) : The Group.
[1976]. — 1976. — 43 leaves in various pagings ; 30cm.
ISBN 0-905570-62-6 Sp : £13.00
Also classified at 381
(B77-07259)

381'.45'6887602541 — Retail sports equipment trades. *Great Britain. Directories*
United Kingdom sport shops and camping equipment / [Data Research Group]. — Amersham (Hill House, [Hill Ave.], Amersham, Bucks.) : The Group.
[1976]. — 1976. — 114 leaves in various pagings ; 30cm.
ISBN 0-905570-49-9 Sp : £14.00
Also classified at 381'.45'6855302541
(B77-04081)

United Kingdom sports shops and camping equipment / [Data Research Group]. — Amersham (Hill House, [Hill Ave.], Amersham, Bucks.) : The Group.
[1977]. — 1977. — 140 leaves in various pagings ; 30cm.
ISBN 0-86099-020-6 Sp : £15.00
Also classified at 381'.45'6855302541
(B77-15785)

381'.45'69802541 — Decorators' merchants. *Great Britain. Directories*
United Kingdom decorators' merchants / [Data Research Group]. — Amersham (Hill House, [Hill Ave.], Amersham, Bucks.) : The Group.
[1977]. — 1977. — 66 leaves in various pagings ; 30cm.
ISBN 0-86099-006-0 Sp : £13.00
(B77-16312)

382 — FOREIGN TRADE
Nicholson, John Field. Contemporary problems of foreign exchange and trade / by J.F. Nicholson. — Revised ed. — Aylesbury : Ginn, 1977. — 57p : 2 ill ; 22cm. — (Manchester Economics Project. Satellite books ; 9)
With answers. — Previous ed.: London : Ginn, 1971.
ISBN 0-602-22337-7 Sd : £1.10
Primary classification 332.4'5
(B77-20081)

382 — Foreign trade. Finance
Whiting, Desmond Percival. Finance of foreign trade / [by] D.P. Whiting. — 4th ed. — Plymouth : Macdonald and Evans, 1977. — x, 181p : forms ; 19cm. — (The M. & E. handbook series)
With answers. — Previous ed.: London : Macdonald and Evans, 1973. — Index.
ISBN 0-7121-0629-4 Pbk : £1.95
Primary classification 332.4'5
(B77-26165)

Whiting, Desmond Percival. Finance of foreign trade and foreign exchange / by D.P. Whiting. — 3rd ed. — Plymouth : Macdonald and Evans, 1976. — xii,241p : forms ; 22cm.
Previous ed.: London : Macdonald and Evans, 1973. — Index.
ISBN 0-7121-0627-8 Pbk : £3.50
Primary classification 332.4'5
(B77-07133)

382 — Foreign trade. Instability
Coppock, Joseph David. International trade instability / [by] Joseph D. Coppock. — Farnborough, Hants. : Saxon House, 1977. — xii,218,[1]p,[2] fold leaves of plates : ill ; 24cm.
Index.
ISBN 0-566-00154-3 : Unpriced
(B77-25532)

382 — Foreign trade. Related to location of industries. *Conference proceedings*
International Allocation of Economic Activity *(Conference), Stockholm, 1976.* The international allocation of economic activity : proceedings of a Nobel Symposium [the 35th] held at Stockholm / edited by Bertil Ohlin, Per-Ove Hesselborn, Per Magnus Wijkman. — London [etc.] : Macmillan, 1977. — xiv,572p : ill, maps ; 23cm.
'... proceedings of a [conference] ... on The International Allocation of Economic Activity held in Stockholm, 8-11 June, 1976' - Foreword. — Bibl. — Index.
ISBN 0-333-21423-4 : £20.00 : CIP rev.
Primary classification 338.6'042
(B77-24779)

382'.01'2 — Great Britain. Foreign trade. Commodities. *Classification schedules. Serials*
Guide to the classification for overseas trade statistics / published under the authority of the Commissioners of Her Majesty's Customs and Excise. — London : H.M.S.O.
1977. Vol.1 (January to June). — 1977. — 560p ; 22cm. — (OUT 603-7-2)
Index.
ISBN 0-11-260349-1 Pbk : £6.10
(B77-08958)

382'.09172'4 — Developing countries. Economic conditions. Effects of foreign trade
Emmanuel, Arghiri. Unequal exchange : a study of the imperialism of trade / [by] Arghiri Emmanuel ; with additional comments by Charles Bettelheim ; translated from the French by Brian Pearce. — London : NLB, 1972 [i.e. 1977]. — xlii,453p : ill ; 21cm.
This translation originally published: 1972. — Translation of: 'L'échange inégal'. Paris : F. Maspero, 1969. — Bibl.: p.432-441. — Index.
ISBN 0-902308-32-7 Pbk : £4.00
(B77-14175)

382'.09172'4 — Developing countries. Foreign trade
Morton, Kathryn. Trade and developing countries / [by] Kathryn Morton and Peter Tulloch. — London : Croom Helm [for] the Overseas Development Institute, 1977. — 3-376p ; 23cm.
Bibl.: p.351-356. — Index.
ISBN 0-85664-303-3 : £9.95
(B77-21810)

382'.0937'0398 — Ancient Rome. Foreign trade with Dacia, B.C.200-A.D.105
Glodariu, Ioan. Dacian trade with the Hellenistic and Roman world / [by] Ioan Glodariu ; revised by the author ; translated from the Romanian by Nubar Hampartumian. — Oxford : British Archaeological Reports, 1976. — [8],275p(4 fold),[4],[52]p of plates,[3] leaves of plates(1 fold) : ill, maps ; 30cm. — (British archaeological reports : supplementary series ; 8)
Translation and revision of: 'Relaţii comerciale ale Daciei cu lumea elenistică şi roman˜a'. Cluj : 'Dacia', 1974. — Bibl.: p.269-274.
ISBN 0-904531-40-6 Sd : £6.80
Primary classification 382'.0939'8038
(B77-00153)

382'.0938'0398 — Ancient Greece. Foreign trade with Dacia, B.C.200-A.D.105
Glodariu, Ioan. Dacian trade with the Hellenistic and Roman world / [by] Ioan Glodariu ; revised by the author ; translated from the Romanian by Nubar Hampartumian. — Oxford : British Archaeological Reports, 1976. — [8],275p(4 fold),[4],[52]p of plates,[3] leaves of plates(1 fold) : ill, maps ; 30cm. — (British archaeological reports : supplementary series ; 8)
Translation and revision of: 'Relaţii comerciale ale Daciei cu lumea elenistică şi roman˜a'. Cluj : 'Dacia', 1974. — Bibl.: p.269-274.
ISBN 0-904531-40-6 Sd : £6.80
Primary classification 382'.0939'8038
(B77-00153)

382'.0939'8037 — Dacia. Foreign trade with Ancient Rome, B.C.200-A.D.105
Glodariu, Ioan. Dacian trade with the Hellenistic and Roman world / [by] Ioan Glodariu ; revised by the author ; translated from the Romanian by Nubar Hampartumian. — Oxford : British Archaeological Reports, 1976. — [8],275p(4 fold),[4],[52]p of plates,[3] leaves of plates(1 fold) : ill, maps ; 30cm. — (British archaeological reports : supplementary series ; 8)
Translation and revision of: 'Relaţii comerciale ale Daciei cu lumea elenistică şi roman˜a'. Cluj : 'Dacia', 1974. — Bibl.: p.269-274.
ISBN 0-904531-40-6 Sd : £6.80
Primary classification 382'.0939'8038
(B77-00153)

382'.0939'8038 — Dacia. Foreign trade with Ancient Greece, B.C.200-A.D.105
Glodariu, Ioan. Dacian trade with the Hellenistic and Roman world / [by] Ioan Glodariu ; revised by the author ; translated from the Romanian by Nubar Hampartumian. — Oxford : British Archaeological Reports, 1976. — [8],275p(4 fold),[4],[52]p of plates,[3] leaves of plates(1 fold) : ill, maps ; 30cm. — (British archaeological reports : supplementary series ; 8)
Translation and revision of: 'Relaţii comerciale ale Daciei cu lumea elenistică şi roman˜a'. Cluj : 'Dacia', 1974. — Bibl.: p.269-274.
ISBN 0-904531-40-6 Sd : £6.80
Also classified at 382'.0938'0398; 382'.0939'8037; 382'.0937'0398
(B77-00153)

382'.094 — Europe. Foreign trade, 1500-1630
Ball, J N. Merchants and merchandise : the expansion of trade in Europe, 1500-1630 / [by] J.N. Ball. — London : Croom Helm, 1977. — 3-226p : map ; 23cm.
Bibl.: p.207-220. — Index.
ISBN 0-85664-494-3 : £7.95 : CIP rev.
(B77-08327)

382'.094'05 — Europe. Foreign trade with Far East, 1600-1800
Furber, Holden. Rival empires of trade in the orient, 1600-1800 / by Holden Furber. — Minneapolis : University of Minnesota Press ; London : Oxford University Press, 1976. — xix, 408p : ill, maps, ports ; 24cm. — (Europe and the world in the age of expansion ; 2)
Index.
ISBN 0-8166-0787-7 : £12.25
Also classified at 382'.095'04
(B77-04713)

382'.0941 — Great Britain. Foreign trade. *Statistics*
Annual statement of the overseas trade of the United Kingdom / published under the authority of the Commissioners of HM Customs and Excise. — London : H.M.S.O.
1974. Vol.1 : Summary tables of imports and exports. — 1976. — xxi,[298],37p ; 29cm.
Index.
ISBN 0-11-260294-0 : £17.50
(B77-10783)

1974. Vol.2 : Imports of commodities analysed by country. — 1976. — xviii,672,37p ; 29cm.
Index.
ISBN 0-11-260295-9 : £33.50
(B77-14176)

1974. Vol.3 : Exports of commodities analysed by country. — 1976. — xix,645,37p ; 29cm.
Index.
ISBN 0-11-260296-7 : £32.00
(B77-14177)

1974. Vol.4 : Country figures of imports and exports. — 1976. — xxiii,261p ; 29cm.
ISBN 0-11-260297-5 : £14.50
(B77-10784)

1974. Vol.5 : Trade at ports. — 1976. — xii, 165p ; 29cm.
Index.
£13.00
(B77-10785)

Statistics of trade through United Kingdom ports. [Annual ed.] / HM Customs and Excise. — London : H.M.S.O.
[1976]. — 1977. — 325p in various pagings ; 30cm.
ISBN 0-11-725099-6 Pbk : £6.00
ISSN 0309-3107
(B77-29332)

382'.0941 — Great Britain. Foreign trade. *Statistics. Periodicals*
Statistics of trade through United Kingdom ports. — London : H.M.S.O.
[No.1]- ; 1976-. — 1976-. — 30cm.
Quarterly. — [324]p. various pagings in 1st issue. — At head of title: HM Customs and Excise.
ISBN 0-11-260344-0 Pbk : £6.00
ISSN 0309-3107
(B77-04714)

382'.0941 — Great Britain. Foreign trade, 1850-1975. *Secondary school texts*
Anthony, Vivian Stanley. Britain's overseas trade : the recent history of British trade / by Vivian S. Anthony. — 3rd ed. — London : Heinemann Educational, 1976. — [6],113p : ill, maps ; 20cm. — (Studies in the British economy ; 3)
Previous ed.: 1971. — Index.
ISBN 0-435-84566-7 Pbk : £1.10
(B77-30131)

382'.0941 — Great Britain. Seaborne foreign trade. Defence, 1689-1815
Crowhurst, Patrick. The defence of British trade, 1689-1815 / [by] Patrick Crowhurst. — Folkestone : Dawson, 1977. — 281p : maps ; 23cm.
Bibl.: p.265-273. — Index.
ISBN 0-7129-0699-1 : £8.00 : CIP rev.
(B77-14178)

382'.0941'0492 — Great Britain. Foreign trade with Netherlands. *For British businessmen. Serials*
Netherlands-British trade directory / Netherlands-British Chamber of Commerce. — London (307 High Holborn, WC1V 7LS) : Netherlands-British Chamber of Commerce.
1976-7. — [1976]. — 300p : ill ; 19cm.
Index.
Pbk : Free to members
ISSN 0308-1273
Also classified at 382'.09492'041
(B77-00154)

382'.0941'051 — Great Britain. Foreign trade with China, 1800-1900
Steeds, David. China, Japan and 19th century Britain / [by] David Steeds, Ian Nish. — Dublin : Irish University Press, 1977. — 136p : map ; 23cm. — (Commentaries on British parliamentary papers)
Bibl.: p.125-133. — Index.
ISBN 0-7165-2225-x : £6.00
Also classified at 382'.0951'041; 382'.0941'052; 382'.0952'041
(B77-30132)

382'.0941'052 — Great Britain. Foreign trade with Japan
Japan. *Embassy (Great Britain). Information Centre.* British trade with Japan / [Japan Information Centre]. — London ([9 Grosvenor Sq., W.1]) : Japan Information Centre, Embassy of Japan, 1977. — 33p ; 26cm.
Bibl.: p.28.
ISBN 0-9505706-0-5 Sd : Unpriced
Also classified at 382'.0952'041
(B77-14669)

382'.0941'052 — Great Britain. Foreign trade with Japan, 1800-1900
Steeds, David. China, Japan and 19th century Britain / [by] David Steeds, Ian Nish. — Dublin : Irish University Press, 1977. — 136p : map ; 23cm. — (Commentaries on British parliamentary papers)
Bibl.: p.125-133. — Index.
ISBN 0-7165-2225-x : £6.00
Primary classification 382'.0941'051
(B77-30132)

382'.0941'071 — Great Britain. Foreign trade with Canada. *Yearbooks*
Canada-UK year book. — London (3 Lower Regent St., SW1Y 4NZ) : Canada-United Kingdom Chamber of Commerce.
1973-4. — [1976]. — xx,72p : port ; 21cm.
ISBN 0-905840-01-1 Pbk : £0.50(free to members)
ISSN 0309-0329
Also classified at 382'.0971'041
(B77-04715)

1975. — [1976]. — xxiv,68p : ill, port ; 21cm.
ISBN 0-905840-00-3 Pbk : £0.50(free to members)
ISSN 0309-0329
Also classified at 382'.0971'041
(B77-04716)

382'.0941'0729 — Great Britain. Foreign trade. Related to foreign investment by British investors. *Study regions: Caribbean region. Commonwealth countries. Inquiry reports*
Great Britain. *Parliament. House of Commons. Select Committee on Overseas Development.* The relationship between UK investment and trading patterns and development with reference to the specific problems of small developing economies : second report from the Select Committee on Overseas Development, session 1975-76, together with the proceedings of the Committee, part of the minutes of evidence and appendices. — London : H.M.S.O., [1976]. — l,193p ; 25cm. — ([1975-76 H.C.]705)
ISBN 0-10-009486-4 Pbk : £4.60
Primary classification 332.6'7341'0729
(B77-07135)

382'.0941'073 — Great Britain. Foreign trade with United States. *Directories*
Anglo American trade directory / [American Chamber of Commerce (United Kingdom)]. — London (75 Brook St., W1Y 2EB) : American Chamber of Commerce (United Kingdom).
1977-8. — 1977. — 491p : ill, ports ; 31cm.
£25.00
Also classified at 382'.0973'041
(B77-29333)

382'.0945'10458 — Northern Italy. Foreign trade with Sicily, 1100-1200
Abulafia, David. The two Italies : economic relations between the Norman Kingdom of Sicily and the northern communes / [by] David Abulafia. — Cambridge [etc.] : Cambridge University Press, 1977. — xx,310p : ill, maps ; 23cm. — (Cambridge studies in medieval life and thought : 3rd series ; vol.9)
Bibl. — Index.
ISBN 0-521-21211-1 : £14.50
Also classified at 382'.09458'0451
(B77-14179)

382'.09458'0451 — Sicily. Foreign trade with Northern Italy, 1100-1200
Abulafia, David. The two Italies : economic relations between the Norman Kingdom of Sicily and the northern communes / [by] David Abulafia. — Cambridge [etc.] : Cambridge University Press, 1977. — xx,310p : ill, maps ; 23cm. — (Cambridge studies in medieval life and thought : 3rd series ; vol.9)
Bibl. — Index.
ISBN 0-521-21211-1 : £14.50
Primary classification 382'.0945'10458
(B77-14179)

382'.0947 — Eastern Europe. Foreign trade. Finance
Garland, John S. Financing foreign trade in Eastern Europe : problems of bilateralism and currency inconvertibility / [by] John S. Garland. — New York [etc.] ; London : Praeger, 1977. — xv,169p ; 25cm. — (Praeger special studies in international business, finance and trade)
Bibl.: p.151-166. — Index.
ISBN 0-275-23800-8 : £12.20
(B77-14670)

382'.09492'041 — Netherlands. Foreign trade with Great Britain. *For British businessmen. Serials*
Netherlands-British trade directory / Netherlands-British Chamber of Commerce. — London (307 High Holborn, WC1V 7LS) : Netherlands-British Chamber of Commerce.
1976-7. — [1976]. — 300p : ill ; 19cm.
Index.
Pbk : Free to members
ISSN 0308-1273
Primary classification 382'.0941'0492
(B77-00154)

382'.095'04 — Far East. Foreign trade with Europe, 1600-1800
Furber, Holden. Rival empires of trade in the orient, 1600-1800 / by Holden Furber. — Minneapolis : University of Minnesota Press ; London : Oxford University Press, 1976. — xix, 408p : ill, maps, ports ; 24cm. — (Europe and the world in the age of expansion ; 2)
Index.
ISBN 0-8166-0787-7 : £12.25
Primary classification 382'.094'05
(B77-04713)

382'.0951'041 — China. Foreign trade with Great Britain, 1800-1900
Steeds, David. China, Japan and 19th century Britain / [by] David Steeds, Ian Nish. — Dublin : Irish University Press, 1977. — 136p : map ; 23cm. — (Commentaries on British parliamentary papers)
Bibl.: p.125-133. — Index.
ISBN 0-7165-2225-x : £6.00
Primary classification 382'.0941'051
(B77-30132)

382'.0952'041 — Japan. Foreign trade with Great Britain
Japan. *Embassy (Great Britain). Information Centre.* British trade with Japan / [Japan Information Centre]. — London ([9 Grosvenor Sq., W.1]) : Japan Information Centre, Embassy of Japan, 1977. — 33p ; 26cm.
Bibl.: p.28.
ISBN 0-9505706-0-5 Sd : Unpriced
Primary classification 382'.0941'052
(B77-14669)

382'.0952'041 — Japan. Foreign trade with Great Britain, 1800-1900
Steeds, David. China, Japan and 19th century Britain / [by] David Steeds, Ian Nish. — Dublin : Irish University Press, 1977. — 136p : map ; 23cm. — (Commentaries on British parliamentary papers)
Bibl.: p.125-133. — Index.
ISBN 0-7165-2225-x : £6.00
Primary classification 382'.0941'051
(B77-30132)

382'.0971'041 — Canada. Foreign trade with Great Britain. *Yearbooks*
Canada-UK year book. — London (3 Lower Regent St., SW1Y 4NZ) : Canada-United Kingdom Chamber of Commerce.
1973-4. — [1976]. — xx,72p : port ; 21cm.
ISBN 0-905840-01-1 Pbk : £0.50(free to members)
ISSN 0309-0329
Primary classification 382'.0941'071
(B77-04715)

1975. — [1976]. — xxiv,68p : ill, port ; 21cm.
ISBN 0-905840-00-3 Pbk : £0.50(free to members)
ISSN 0309-0329
Primary classification 382'.0941'071
(B77-04716)

382'.0973 — United States. Foreign trade. Organisation, 1913-1921
Kaufman, Burton I. Efficiency and expansion : foreign trade organization in the Wilson Administration, 1913-1921 / [by] Burton I. Kaufman. — Westport, Conn. ; London : Greenwood Press, 1974. — xviii,300p ; 22cm. — (Contributions in American history ; no.34)
Bibl.: p.267-291. — Index.
ISBN 0-8371-7338-8 : £11.95
(B77-15240)

382'.0973 — United States. Foreign trade. Related to labour market
Mitchell, Daniel Jesse Brody. Labor issues of American international trade and investments / [by] Daniel J.B. Mitchell. — Baltimore ; London : Johns Hopkins University Press, 1976. — xiii,112p ; 22cm. — (Policy studies in employment and welfare ; no.24)
ISBN 0-8018-1848-6 : £5.95
ISBN 0-8018-1849-4 Pbk : £2.05
Also classified at 331.1'2'0973
(B77-01322)

382'.0973'041 — United States. Foreign trade with Great Britain. *Directories*
Anglo American trade directory / [American Chamber of Commerce (United Kingdom)]. — London (75 Brook St., W1Y 2EB) : American Chamber of Commerce (United Kingdom). 1977-8. — 1977. — 491p : ill, ports ; 31cm. £25.00
Primary classification 382'.0941'073
(B77-29333)

382'.0981 — Brazil. Foreign trade. Policies of government, 1930-1939
Hilton, Stanley Eon. Brazil and the great powers, 1930-1939 : the politics of trade rivalry / by Stanley E. Hilton ; foreword by José Honório Rodrigues. — Austin ; London : University of Texas Press, [1976]. — xxii,304p ; 24cm. — (Latin American monographs ; no.38)
Published in the United States: 1975. — Bibl.: p.282-294. — Index.
ISBN 0-292-70713-4 : Unpriced
(B77-03491)

382.1 — ECONOMIC RELATIONS
Corden, Warner Max. Inflation, exchange rates and the world economy : lectures on international monetary economics / by W.M. Corden. — Oxford : Clarendon Press, 1977. — viii,160p : ill ; 23cm.
Index.
ISBN 0-19-877096-0 : £4.50 : CIP rev.
(B77-06601)

Friedrich, Klaus. International economics : concepts and issues / [by] Klaus Friedrich. — New York ; London [etc.] : McGraw-Hill, 1974. — xiv,322p : ill ; 24cm.
Bibl. — Index.
ISBN 0-07-022435-8 : Unpriced
(B77-19304)

Menon, B P. Global dialogue : the new international economic order / [by] B.P. Menon. — Oxford [etc.] : Pergamon, 1977. — vii,110p : ill, facsims ; 22cm. — (Pergamon international library)
Index.
ISBN 0-08-021498-3 : Unpriced
ISBN 0-08-021499-1 Pbk : £3.00
(B77-24133)

Salvatore, Dominick. Schaum's outline of theory and problems of international economics / by Dominick Salvatore. — New York ; London [etc.] : McGraw-Hill, [1976]. — [7],191p : ill ; 28cm. — (Schaum's outline series)
Cover title: Theory and problems of international economics. — With answers. — Published in the United States: 1975. — Index.
ISBN 0-07-054496-4 Pbk : £3.30
(B77-04082)

382.1'04 — Economic imperialism. Theories, 1800-1976
Hodgart, Alan. The economics of European imperialism / [by] Alan Hodgart. — London : Edward Arnold, 1977. — xi,88p ; 22cm. — (Foundations of modern history)
Bibl.: p.82-86. — Index.
ISBN 0-7131-5911-1 : £5.95
ISBN 0-7131-5912-x Pbk : £2.25
(B77-24844)

382.1'06 — International economic organisations. *Conference proceedings*
Colloquium on the Future of International Economic Organizations, *Washington, D.C., 1975.* The future of international economic organizations / edited by Don Wallace, Jr, Helga Escobar. — New York ; London : Praeger [for] the Institute for International and Foreign Trade Law, Georgetown University Law Center, 1977. — xii,188p ; 25cm. — (Praeger special studies in international business, finance and trade)
'... proceedings of a Colloquium on the Future of International Economic Organizations, ... [held] in Washington, D.C., on October 31, 1975' - Preface. — Index.
ISBN 0-275-22990-4 : £12.40
(B77-27789)

382.1'09'046 — Economic relations, 1960-1976. International political aspects
Shonfield, Andrew. International economic relations : the western system in the 1960s and 1970s / [by] Andrew Shonfield. — Beverly Hills ; London : Sage Publications [for] the Center for Strategic and International Studies, Georgetown University, 1976. — 88p ; 22cm. — (The Washington papers ; vol.4, no.42) (A Sage policy paper)
Spine title: International economics. — Bibl.: p.87-88.
ISBN 0-8039-0790-7 Pbk : £1.75
(B77-23312)

382.1'09171'7 — Communist countries. Economic relations with United States. Role of American multinational companies
Brookstone, Jeffrey M. The multinational businessman and foreign policy : entrepreneurial politics in east-west trade and investment / [by] Jeffrey M. Brookstone. — New York [etc.] ; London : Praeger, 1976. — xv,183,[1]p : ill ; 25cm. — (Praeger special studies in international business, finance and trade)
Bibl.: p.158-172. — Index.
ISBN 0-275-23360-x : £12.20
Primary classification 382.1'0973
(B77-08959)

382.1'09172'2 — Developed countries. Economic relations with developing countries
Singer, Hans Wolfgang. Rich and poor countries / by Hans W. Singer and Javed A. Ansari. — London : Allen and Unwin, 1977. — 3-228p : ill ; 23cm. — (Studies in economics ; 12)
Index.
ISBN 0-04-330274-2 : £6.50
ISBN 0-04-330275-0 Pbk : £2.95
Also classified at 382.1'09172'4
(B77-07881)

Singh, Jyoti Shankar. A new international economic order : toward a fair redistribution of the world's resources / [by] Jyoti Shankar Singh. — New York ; London : Praeger, 1977. — xiv,137p : ill ; 25cm. — (Praeger special studies in international economics and development)
Bibl.: p.127-129. — Index.
ISBN 0-275-24170-x : £10.05
Also classified at 382.1'09172'4
(B77-20178)

382.1'09172'4 — Developing countries. Economic relations
Rothstein, Robert Lewis. The weak in the world of the strong : the developing countries in the international system / [by] Robert L. Rothstein. — New York ; Guildford : Columbia University Press [for the Institute of War and Peace Studies, Columbia University], 1977. — xiii,384p ; 24cm.
Index.
ISBN 0-231-04338-4 : £11.20
Also classified at 327'.09172'4
(B77-31811)

382.1'09172'4 — Developing countries. Economic relations with developed countries
Singer, Hans Wolfgang. Rich and poor countries / by Hans W. Singer and Javed A. Ansari. — London : Allen and Unwin, 1977. — 3-228p : ill ; 23cm. — (Studies in economics ; 12)
Index.
ISBN 0-04-330274-2 : £6.50
ISBN 0-04-330275-0 Pbk : £2.95
Primary classification 382.1'09172'2
(B77-07881)

Singh, Jyoti Shankar. A new international economic order : toward a fair redistribution of the world's resources / [by] Jyoti Shankar Singh. — New York ; London : Praeger, 1977. — xiv,137p : ill ; 25cm. — (Praeger special studies in international economics and development)
Bibl.: p.127-129. — Index.
ISBN 0-275-24170-x : £10.05
Primary classification 382.1'09172'2
(B77-20178)

382.1'09172'4 — Developing countries. Economic relations with European Community countries
McQueen, Matthew. Britain, the EEC and the developing world / [by] Matthew McQueen. — London [etc.] : Heinemann Educational, 1977. — viii,119p : ill ; 20cm. — (Studies in the British economy ; 17)
Bibl.: p.116. — Index.
ISBN 0-435-84562-4 Pbk : £1.25
Also classified at 382.1'094
(B77-30133)

382.1'094 — European Community countries. Economic relations with developing countries
McQueen, Matthew. Britain, the EEC and the developing world / [by] Matthew McQueen. — London [etc.] : Heinemann Educational, 1977. — viii,119p : ill ; 20cm. — (Studies in the British economy ; 17)
Bibl.: p.116. — Index.
ISBN 0-435-84562-4 Pbk : £1.25
Primary classification 382.1'09172'4
(B77-30133)

382.1'094 — European Community countries. Economic relations with Scandinavia, 1945-1975. Political aspects
Miljan, Toivo. The reluctant Europeans : the attitudes of the Nordic countries towards European integration / [by] Toivo Miljan. — London : C. Hurst, 1977. — viii,325p ; 23cm.
Bibl.: p.301-318. — Index.
ISBN 0-903983-74-5 : £7.50
Primary classification 382.1'0948
(B77-29334)

382.1'0941 — Great Britain. Economic relations. *Case studies*
Case studies in international economics / edited by Peter Maunder ; [contributors] Peter Barker ... [et al.]. — London [etc.] : Heinemann Educational [for] the Economics Association, 1977. — [5],87p : ill ; 20cm. — (Case studies in economic analysis ; 6)
ISBN 0-435-84471-7 Pbk : £1.30
(B77-22501)

Case studies in international economics / edited by Peter Maunder ; [contributors] Peter Barker ... [et al.]. — London [etc.] : Heinemann Educational [for] the Economics Association. — (Case studies in economic analysis ; 6)
[Teacher's guide]. — 1977. — [5],135p ; 20cm.
ISBN 0-435-84472-5 Pbk : £2.30
(B77-22502)

382.1'0948 — Scandinavia. Economic relations with European Community countries, 1945-1975. Political aspects
Miljan, Toivo. The reluctant Europeans : the attitudes of the Nordic countries towards European integration / [by] Toivo Miljan. — London : C. Hurst, 1977. — viii,325p ; 23cm.
Bibl.: p.301-318. — Index.
ISBN 0-903983-74-5 : £7.50
Also classified at 382.1'094
(B77-29334)

382.1'0973 — United States. Economic relations
Cohen, Stephen David. The making of United States international economic policy : principals, problems, and proposals for reform / [by] Stephen D. Cohen ; foreword by C. Fred Bergsten. — New York ; London : Praeger, 1977. — xxiv,209p ; 24cm. — (Praeger special studies in international business, finance and trade)
Index.
ISBN 0-03-021926-4 : Unpriced
ISBN 0-03-021921-3 Pbk : £4.60
(B77-33731)

382.1'0973 — United States. Economic relations, 1970-1976. International political aspects
Hudson, Michael. Global fracture : the new international economic order / [by] Michael Hudson. — New York [etc.] ; London : Harper and Row, 1977. — viii,296p : ill ; 21cm.
Index.
ISBN 0-06-012004-5 : £7.50
(B77-33732)

382.1'0973 — United States. Economic relations with communist countries. Role of American multinational companies
Brookstone, Jeffrey M. The multinational businessman and foreign policy : entrepreneurial politics in east-west trade and investment / [by] Jeffrey M. Brookstone. — New York [etc.] ; London : Praeger, 1976. — xv,183,[1]p : ill ; 25cm. — (Praeger special studies in international business, finance and trade)
Bibl.: p.158-172. — Index.
ISBN 0-275-23360-x : £12.20
Also classified at 382.1'09171'7
(B77-08959)

382.1'7 — Balance of payments. Improvement. Use of import controls. *Great Britain*
Clark, Colin, *b.1905.* The balance of payments, or, Are import restrictions necessary? / by Colin Clark ; with a foreword by Sir Alec Cairncross. — London (55 Park La., W1Y 3DH) : Overseas Trade Research Fund, Economic Research Council, [1977]. — [7], 28p : ill ; 21cm.
Sd : £0.50
(B77-33164)

382.1'7 — Balance of payments. Related to monetary systems
The **monetary** approach to the balance of payments / edited by Jacob A. Frenkel, Harry G. Johnson. — London : Allen and Unwin, 1977. — 5-388p : ill ; 22cm.
Originally published: 1976. — Bibl. — Index.
ISBN 0-04-330276-9 Pbk : £6.95
Also classified at 332.4
(B77-13609)

382.1'7 — Foreign trade in primary commodities. Negotiations between developed countries & developing countries. Policies of British government. *Inquiry reports*
Great Britain. *Parliament. House of Commons. Select Committee on Overseas Development.* The forthcoming UNCTAD negotiations : second report from the Select Committee on Overseas Development, session 1976-77, together with the proceedings of the Committee. — London : H.M.S.O., [1977]. — xvi p ; 25cm. — ([1976-77 H.C.]222)
ISBN 0-10-222277-0 Sd : £0.35
(B77-11174)

382.1'7'0184 — Balance of payments. Mathematical models
Kyle, John F. The balance of payments in a monetary economy / [by] John F. Kyle. — Princeton ; Guildford : Princeton University Press, 1976. — xiii,192p : ill ; 23cm. — (Irving Fisher Award monographs ; 4)
Bibl.: p.181-185. — Index.
ISBN 0-691-04208-x : £8.70
(B77-02208)

382'.17'0941 — Balance of payments. *Great Britain. Proposals*
On how to cope with Britain's trade position / by Hugh Corbet ... [et al.]. — London : Trade Policy Research Centre, 1977. — viii,72p : ill ; 22cm. — (Thames essays ; no.8 ISSN 0306-6991)
ISBN 0-900842-29-6 Sd : £2.00
(B77-12397)

382.1'7'0941 — Balance of payments. Effects of exploitation of petroleum deposits in North Sea. *Great Britain*
Robinson, Colin, *b.1932.* Effects of North Sea oil on the United Kingdom's balance of payments / by Colin Robinson and Jon Morgan. — London (1 Gough Sq., EC4A 3DE) : Trade Policy Research Centre, [1976]. — iii,39 leaves : ill ; 30cm. — (Trade Policy Research Centre. Guest papers ; no.5 ISSN 0306-5987)
ISBN 0-900842-28-8 Pbk : £1.00
(B77-04717)

382.4 — FOREIGN TRADE. SPECIAL COMMODITIES AND SERVICES

382'.4 — Coastal foreign trade & short-sea foreign trade in bulk cargoes. *Europe. Reports, surveys*
Drewry (H.P.) (Shipping Consultants) Limited. *Research Division.* Bulk cargo in European coastal and short-sea trades / prepared by the Research Division, H.P. Drewry (Shipping Consultants) Limited. — London (1 Argyll St., W1V 1AD) : H.P. Drewry (Shipping Consultants) Ltd, 1976. — [3],77p : ill, col map ; 30cm. — (An economic study ; no.48 ISSN 0307-4919)
ISBN 0-904726-28-2 Sd : £30.00(£100.00 for nos 41-50)
(B77-02209)

382'.4'09595 — Developing countries. Exports: Primary commodities. Related to economic development. *Study regions: Malaysia*
Thoburn, John T. Primary commodity exports and economic development : theory, evidence and a study of Malaysia / [by] John T. Thoburn. — London [etc.] : Wiley, 1977. — xvi,310p : map ; 24cm.
Bibl.: p.287-302. — Index.
ISBN 0-471-99441-3 : £9.00
Primary classification 330.9'595'05
(B77-24055)

382'.4'098 — Latin America. Foreign trade in primary commodities. *Periodicals*
Latin America commodities report. — London (90 Cowcross St., EC1M 6BL) : Latin American Newsletters Ltd.
Vol.O, no.1- ; Friday 3 Dec. 1976-. — 1976-. — 28cm.
Weekly (fifty issues a year). — Folder (4p.) as 1st issue.
£55.00 yearly
ISSN 0309-300x
(B77-08960)

382'.41 — Foreign trade in agricultural products. Negotiations between European Economic Community & United States, 1973-1976
Harris, Simon. EEC trade relations with the USA in agricultural products : multilateral tariff negotiations / by Simon Harris. — Ashford, Kent : Centre for European Agricultural Studies, Wye College, 1977. — 57, [17]p ; 30cm. — (Wye College. Centre for European Agricultural Studies. Occasional papers ; no.3 ISSN 0306-2902)
English text, French and German summaries and contents lists.
ISBN 0-905378-00-8 Sd : £2.00
(B77-22503)

382'.41'09624 — Sudan. Economic development. Role of exports of agricultural products, 1900-1967
Beshai, Adel Amin. Export performance & economic development in Sudan, 1900-1967 / [by] Adel Amin Beshai. — London : Ithaca Press for the Middle East Centre, St Anthony's College, 1976. — [11],358p : ill ; 23cm. — (St Antony's College. Middle East Centre. Monographs ; no.3)
Bibl.: p.343-350. — Index.
ISBN 0-903729-15-6 : £6.50
(B77-02909)

382'.41'34 — Great Britain. Imports: Fruit. Competition
Hinton, Wilfred Lynn. Competition in fruit and vegetable imports to the United Kingdom / by Lynn Hinton. — [Cambridge] ([16 Silver St., Cambridge CB3 9EP]) : Agricultural Economics Unit, Department of Land Economy, University of Cambridge, [1976]. — [1],20 leaves ; 30cm.
'Paper given at IXe Congrès International Norcofel (Congrès International de la Normalisation et de la Commercialisation des Fruits et Légumes), Dijon, 3-5 November, 1976'.
ISBN 0-901978-69-8 Sd : £0.50
Primary classification 382'.41'35
(B77-01323)

382'.41'35 — Great Britain. Imports: Vegetables. Competition
Hinton, Wilfred Lynn. Competition in fruit and vegetable imports to the United Kingdom / by Lynn Hinton. — [Cambridge] ([16 Silver St., Cambridge CB3 9EP]) : Agricultural Economics Unit, Department of Land Economy, University of Cambridge, [1976]. — [1],20 leaves ; 30cm.
'Paper given at IXe Congrès International Norcofel (Congrès International de la Normalisation et de la Commercialisation des Fruits et Légumes), Dijon, 3-5 November, 1976'.
ISBN 0-901978-69-8 Sd : £0.50
Also classified at 382'.41'34
(B77-01323)

382'.42'2820611 — Organisation of Petroleum Exporting Countries, to 1975
Rustow, Dankwart Alexander. OPEC, success and prospects / by Dankwart A. Rustow and John F. Mugno. — London : Martin Robertson, 1977. — xi,179p ; 22cm.
'A Council on Foreign Relations Book'. — Originally published: New York : New York University Press, 1976. — Index.
ISBN 0-85520-154-1 : £7.85
(B77-21811)

382'.42'453 — Foreign trade in tin, 1960-1974. *Reports, surveys*
International Tin Council. Trade in tin, 1960-1974 / prepared on behalf of the Committee on Development of the Fourth International Tin Agreement [by the] International Tin Council = Conseil International de l'Etain = Consejo Internacional del Estaño = Mezhdunarodnyi Sovet po Olovu. — London (1 Oxendon St., SW1 4EQ) : The Council, [1976]. — [2],89p : ill, maps ; 30cm.
Bibl.: p.89.
ISBN 0-901560-24-3 Sd : £10.00
(B77-02210)

382'.42'453 — International Tin Council. *Reports, surveys. Serials*
International Tin Council. Annual report / the International Tin Council. — London (1 Oxendon St., SW1Y 4EQ) : The Council.
1975-1976. — [1977]. — 56p ; 24cm.
Sd : £2.00
(B77-23313)

382'.44'09 — Slave trade, to ca 1860. *Juvenile literature*
Hook, Richard. The slave trade / illustrated by Richard Hook ; planned and written by Belinda Hollyer ; edited by Vivienne Driscoll. — London : Macdonald Educational, 1977. — [1], 44p : col ill, col maps, col ports ; 25cm. — (Toppers history)
Index.
ISBN 0-356-05445-4 : £1.50
(B77-12974)

382'.44'0924 — Slave trade. *Africa, 1820-1850. Personal observations*
Conneau, Theophilus. A slaver's log book, or, 20 years' residence in Africa : the original manuscript / by Theophilus Conneau. — London : Hale, 1977. — xiv,370p : facsim ; 24cm.
This transcription originally published: Englewood Cliffs : Prentice-Hall, 1976. — Index.
ISBN 0-7091-6401-7 : £5.95
(B77-29335)

382'.44'0941 — Great Britain. Slave trade, to 1807. *Reviews of research*
Liverpool, the African slave trade and abolition : essays to illustrate current knowledge and research / edited by Roger Anstey and P.E.H. Hair. — [Widnes] ([c/o Mrs E.M. Schofield, 272 Liverpool Rd, Widnes, Cheshire WA8 7HT]) : Historic Society of Lancashire and Cheshire, 1976. — ix,244p : 1 ill ; 23cm. — (Historic Society of Lancashire and Cheshire. Occasional series ; vol.2 ISSN 0305-9375)
Index.
ISBN 0-9503591-2-2 : £8.00
(B77-09644)

382'.44'0961 — Africa. Barbary states. Slave trade, ca 1500-1800
Clissold, Stephen. The Barbary slaves / [by] Stephen Clissold. — London : Elek, 1977. — viii,181p,[8]p of plates : ill, map, ports ; 23cm.
Bibl.: p.167-168. — Index.
ISBN 0-236-40084-3 : £5.75
(B77-13610)

382'.45 — Great Britain. Exports to France: Consumer goods. Marketing. *Reports, surveys. For British businessmen*
British Overseas Trade Board. Marketing consumer goods in France / British Overseas Trade Board. — London : The Board, [1977]. — vi,54,[1]p : map ; 25cm.
ISBN 0-85605-271-x Sd : Unpriced
(B77-11743)

382'.45'07057302541 — Exports: Books. Booksellers. *Great Britain. Directories*
List of export and foreign booksellers / the Booksellers Association of Great Britain and Ireland. — London : The Association.
1976. — 1976. — [2],14p ; 21cm.
ISBN 0-901690-33-3 Sd : £1.00
Primary classification 381'.45'070573
(B77-06002)

382'.45'591042 — Great Britain. Imports: Animals in danger of extinction. *Reports, surveys. Serials*
Animals Act 1964 (Restriction on Importation), report of the Advisory Committee [for the] year ending 31 December. — [London] ([2 Marsham St., SW1P 3EB]) : Department of the Environment.
1974. — [1974]. — iii leaves,29p ; 30cm.
ISBN 0-7184-0074-7 Sp : Unpriced
(B77-11744)

382'.45'6200044 — Great Britain. Exports to Japan: Measuring instruments. Marketing. *Reports, surveys. For British businessmen*
Peat, Marwick, Mitchell and Company. The Japanese market for metrology and tooling equipment / prepared by Peat, Marwick, Mitchell & Co. [for the] British Overseas Trade Board. — [London] : The Board ; [London] ([1 Victoria St., SW1H 0ET]) : [Distributed by Department of Industry Central Library], 1976. — 88 leaves in various pagings : 1 ill ; 30cm.
Two leaves printed on both sides.
ISBN 0-85605-232-9 Sp : £20.00(to British manufacturers only)
Also classified at 382'.45'621902
(B77-00715)

382'.45'620112 — Great Britain. Exports to Japan: Materials testing equipment. Marketing. *Reports, surveys. For British businessmen*
Dodwell Marketing Consultants. The Japanese market for materials testing equipment / prepared by Dodwell Marketing Consultants. — [London] : British Overseas Trade Board : Distributed by Department of Industry Central Library, 1976. — [4],119,35 leaves ; 30cm.
ISBN 0-85605-287-6 Sp : £20.00(to British manufacturers only)
(B77-10317)

382'.45'62138195832 — Great Britain. Exports to Japan: Digital computers. Peripheral equipment. Marketing. *Reports, surveys. For British businessmen*
Overseas Affiliates Pty Ltd. The Japanese market for business and reproduction equipment and computer peripherals / prepared by Overseas Affiliates Pty Ltd and PA International Management Consultants. — [London] : British Overseas Trade Board : Distributed by Department of Industry Central Library, 1977. — [2],147 leaves : ill ; 31cm.
Sp : £20.00(to British manufacturers only)
Primary classification 382'.45'6816
(B77-29336)

382'.45'621757 — Great Britain. Exports to Iran: Packaging equipment. Marketing. *Reports, surveys. For British businessmen*
MSR Associates. The Iran market for packaging equipment / prepared by MSR Associates. — [London] : British Overseas Trade Board : Distributed by Department of Industry Central Library, [1977]. — [4],53 leaves ; 30cm.
ISBN 0-85605-285-x Sp : £10.00(to British manufacturers only)
(B77-10318)

382'.45'62186 — Great Britain. Exports to Japan: Mechanical handling equipment. Marketing. *Reports, surveys. For British businessmen*
International Business Information. The Japanese market for mechanical handling equipment / prepared by International Business Information. — [London] : British Overseas Trade Board : [Distributed by Department of Industry Central Library], 1976. — [2],44 leaves : ill ; 30cm.
ISBN 0-85605-245-0 Sd : £5.00(to British manufacturers only)
(B77-01324)

382'.45'621902 — Great Britain. Exports to Japan: Machine tools. Marketing. *Reports, surveys. For British businessmen*
International Business Information. The Japanese market for machine tools / prepared by International Business Information. — [London] : British Overseas Trade Board : Distributed by Department of Industry Central Library, 1977. — [3],36 leaves : ill ; 30cm.
ISBN 0-85605-288-4 Sp : £5.00(to British manufacturers only)
(B77-10319)

Peat, Marwick, Mitchell and Company. The Japanese market for metrology and tooling equipment / prepared by Peat, Marwick, Mitchell & Co. [for the] British Overseas Trade Board. — [London] : The Board ; [London] ([1 Victoria St., SW1H 0ET]) : [Distributed by Department of Industry Central Library], 1976. — 88 leaves in various pagings : 1 ill ; 30cm.
Two leaves printed on both sides.
ISBN 0-85605-232-9 Sp : £20.00(to British manufacturers only)
Primary classification 382'.45'6200044
(B77-00715)

382'.45'62340904 — Weapons trades, 1862-1976
Sampson, Anthony. The arms bazaar : the companies, the dealers, the bribes : from Vickers to Lockheed / [by] Anthony Sampson. — London [etc.] : Hodder and Stoughton, 1977. — 352p ; 24cm.
Index.
ISBN 0-340-21331-0 : £5.95
(B77-23314)

382'.45'6285 — Great Britain. Exports to Japan: Pollution control equipment & pollution measuring equipment. Marketing. *Reports, surveys. For British businessmen*
International Business Information. The Japanese market for pollution control and measuring equipment / prepared by International Business Information. — [London] : British Overseas Trade Board : [Distributed by Department of Industry Central Library], 1976. — [2],37[i.e. 38]leaves : ill ; 30cm.
ISBN 0-85605-244-2 Sp : £5.00(to British manufacturers only)
(B77-01325)

382'.45'641300941 — Great Britain. Foreign trade in food. *Statistics*
Statistical review of the UK food industry / the Campden Food Preservation Research Association. — Chipping Campden (Chipping Campden, Glos.) : The Association.
1976. Part 1 : UK exports of fresh, processed and semi-preserved fruits and vegetables for the period 1st January-31st December 1975 / by C. Newman. — 1976. — [1],68p ; 30cm.
Cover title.
ISBN 0-905942-02-7 Pbk : Unpriced
(B77-06602)

1976. Part 3 : UK trade imports in fresh, processed and semi-preserved fruits and vegetables for the period 1st January-31st December 1975 / by C. Newman. — 1976. — [2],126p ; 30cm.
Cover title.
ISBN 0-9504399-8-3 Pbk : Unpriced
(B77-06603)

1976. Part 4 : UK trade imports in fresh, preserved and semi-preserved meat, poultry, fish, milk, cream, butter and cheese for the period 1st January-31st December 1975. — 1976. — [2],83p ; 30cm.
Cover title.
ISBN 0-9504399-9-1 Pbk : Unpriced
(B77-06604)

1976. Part 5 : UK food industry, 1975, processed foods and agricultural statistics. — 1976. — [2],iii,130p ; 30cm.
Cover title.
ISBN 0-905942-00-0 Pbk : Unpriced
(B77-06605)

382'.45'664152 — Great Britain. Exports to Japan: Food: Jams & spreads. Marketing. *Reports, surveys. For British businessmen*
International Business Information. The Japanese market for jams and spreads / prepared by International Business Information. — [London] : British Overseas Trade Board : [Distributed by Department of Industry Central Library], 1975. — [2],15 leaves : ill ; 30cm.
ISBN 0-85605-243-4 Sp : £5.00(to British manufacturers only)
(B77-01326)

382'.45'666 — Ceramic tableware importers. *London. Camden (London Borough). Holborn Tableware Co. Ltd*
Holborn Tableware Co. Ltd. Holborn Tableware, 1951-1976. — [London] ([36 Hatton Garden, E.C.1]) : Holborn Tableware, 1976. — [24]p : ill(some col), ports ; 30cm.
Sd : Unpriced
(B77-21812)

382'.45'67091724 — Developing countries. Exports: Manufactured goods
Morrison, Thomas K. Manufactured exports from developing countries / [by] Thomas K. Morrison. — New York [etc.] ; London : Praeger, 1976. — xiii,109p ; 25cm. — (Praeger special studies in international economics and development)
Bibl.: p.97-103. — Index.
ISBN 0-275-56880-6 : £10.00
(B77-09645)

382'.45'6728 — Foreign trade in stainless steel. *Statistics*
Inco Europe Limited. *Market Research.* Stainless steel statistics : post-war historical series / produced by Market Research, Inco Europe Limited. — London : Inco Europe Ltd ; Worcester Park : Distributed by Metal Bulletin, 1977. — [3],iv,161p ; 31cm.
'... a supplement to the 1977 Edition of "World Stainless Steel Statistics"' - p.1. — Index.
£25.00
(B77-33733)

International Nickel. *Market Research Department.* World stainless steel statistics : a comprehensive review of stainless steel production and international trade in the non-communist countries of the world / produced by the Market Research Department, International Nickel Limited ... from numerous official and original sources. — [London] : [The Department] : Distributed by Metal Bulletin, 1976. — [1],iv,70,A77 leaves : ill ; 30cm.
Pbk : £28.00
(B77-30134)

382'.45'6816 — Great Britain. Exports to Japan: Office equipment. Marketing. *Reports, surveys. For British businessmen*
Overseas Affiliates Pty Ltd. The Japanese market for business and reproduction equipment and computer peripherals / prepared by Overseas Affiliates Pty Ltd and PA International Management Consultants. — [London] : British Overseas Trade Board : Distributed by Department of Industry Central Library, 1977. — [2],147 leaves : ill ; 31cm.
Sp : £20.00(to British manufacturers only)
Also classified at 382'.45'62138195832
(B77-29336)

382'.45'6838 — Great Britain. Exports to Japan: Kitchen equipment. Marketing. *Reports, surveys. For British businessmen*
International Business Information. The Japanese market for kitchenware / prepared by International Business Information. — [London] : British Overseas Trade Board : Distributed by Department of Industry Central Library, 1977. — [3],17 leaves : plans ; 30cm.
Sp : £5.00(to British manufacturers only)
(B77-21813)

382'.45'684100941 — Great Britain. Exports: Furniture. *Serials. English-French-German parallel texts*
British furniture for the world. — London : E. Benn [for 'Cabinet maker and retail furnisher' and British Furniture Manufacturers Exports Ltd].
1977-78. — [1977]. — iv,116p : ill(some col), 2 ports ; 30cm.
English, German and French text. — Index.
Pbk : £1.00
ISSN 0140-6337
(B77-31812)

382'.45'687 — Clothing importers. *Great Britain. Directories*
The **directory** of British clothing and textiles importers / sponsored by the British Importers Confederation ; compiled ... by Trade Research Publications. — Berkhamsted (7 Oxfield Close, Berkhamsted, Herts. HP4 3NE) : [Trade Research Publications], 1977. — 311p in various pagings : ill, port ; 30cm.
ISBN 0-904783-01-4 Sp : £20.00
(B77-12398)

382'.45'69397 — Great Britain. Exports to Japan: Prefabricated houses. Marketing. *Reports, surveys. For British businessmen*
International Business Information. The Japanese market for prefabricated housing / prepared by International Business Information. — [London] : British Overseas Trade Board : [Distributed by Department of Industry Central Library], 1976. — [1],20 leaves ; 30cm.
ISBN 0-85605-246-9 Sd : £5.00(to British manufacturers only)
(B77-02211)

382'.45'7 — Illegal trade in art objects, 1900-1975
Meyer, Karl Ernest. The plundered past : the traffic in art treasures / [by] Karl E. Meyer. — Revised ed. — Harmondsworth [etc.] : Penguin, 1977. — 303p,[8]p of plates : ill, ports ; 19cm. — (Pelican books)
Previous ed.: New York : Atheneum, 1973 ; London : Hamilton, 1974. — Bibl.: p.267-290. — Index.
ISBN 0-14-021990-0 Pbk : £1.50
(B77-22504)

382.5 — IMPORTS
382'.5 — Imports: Dumped goods. Protection of states. Role of General Agreement on Tariffs and Trade
Lloyd, Peter John. Anti-dumping actions and the GATT system / by Peter Lloyd. — London : Trade Policy Research Centre, 1977. — v,53p ; 22cm. — (Thames essays ; no.9 ISSN 0306-6991)
Sd : £2.00
(B77-29337)

382'.5'0941 — Import controls. *Great Britain. Fabian viewpoints*
Cable, Vincent. Import controls : the case against / [by] Vincent Cable. — London : Fabian Society, 1977. — [1],32p ; 22cm. — (Fabian research series ; 335 ISSN 0305-3555)
ISBN 0-7163-1335-9 Sd : £0.70
(B77-32571)

382.6 — EXPORTS
382'.6 — Exporting. Financial incentives. *Organisation for Economic Co-operation and Development countries. Reports, surveys*
Organisation for Economic Co-operation and Development. The export credit financing systems in OECD member countries / [Organisation for Economic Co-operation and Development]. — Paris : O.E.C.D. ; [London] : [H.M.S.O.], 1976. — 140p ; 24cm.
Pbk : £2.40
ISBN 92-64-11574-9
(B77-00716)

382'.6 — Exporting. Subsidies by governments
Walker, William N. International limits to government intervention in the market-place : focus on subsidies to the private sector / by William N. Walker. — London : Trade Policy Research Centre, 1976. — viii,15p ; 22cm. — (Lectures in commercial diplomacy ; no.1 ISSN 0309-1961)
ISBN 0-900842-26-1 Sd : £1.00
(B77-06606)

382'.6'02541 — Exporters. *Great Britain. Directories*
British exports. — Haywards Heath : Kompass.
77 : Ninth ed. — 1977. — 1672p in various pagings : ill, col maps, port ; 30cm.
English text, French, German and Spanish indexes.
ISBN 0-900505-69-9 Pbk : £18.00
ISSN 0068-1970
(B77-06607)

Sell's British exporters. — Epsom : Sell's Publications.
1977. — [1977]. — xxxviii,202p : ill, ports ; 30cm.
English text, French, German, Italian, Portuguese and Spanish preface.
ISBN 0-85499-544-7 Pbk : £7.00
ISSN 0080-8709
(B77-24846)

382'.6'0941 — Great Britain. Exports. Finance using foreign currencies. *Conference proceedings*
Export finance in foreign currencies : a look at the problems associated with obtaining medium and long term finance for larger projects and associated matters : conference addresses. — London : Confederation of British Industry, 1977. — [1],36p ; 30cm.
Sd : £5.00
(B77-30135)

382'.6'0954 — India (Republic). Exports, 1960-1969
Nayyar, Deepak. India's exports and export policies in the 1960s / [by] Deepak Nayyar. — Cambridge [etc.] : Cambridge University Press, 1976 [i.e. 1977]. — xviii,392p : 1 ill ; 23cm. — (Cambridge South Asian studies ; no.19)
Bibl.: p.378-381. — Index.
ISBN 0-521-21135-2 : £12.50
(B77-15241)

382'.6'095694 — Israeli goods. Boycotts by Arab countries, 1945-1975
Chill, Dan S. The Arab boycott of Israel : economic aggression and world reaction / [by] Dan S. Chill. — New York [etc.] ; London : Praeger ; [London] : [Distributed by Martin Robertson], 1976. — xi,123p : form ; 25cm. — (Praeger special studies in international economics and development)
Bibl.: p.113-118. — Index.
ISBN 0-275-56810-5 : £10.35
(B77-05333)

382.7 — TARIFF POLICIES
382.7'0973 — Tariffs. *United States, ca 1830*
Friends of Domestic Industry. Journal of the proceedings of the Friends of Domestic Industry ; and, British opinions on the protecting system / by Alexander Everett. [2nd ed.]. — Garland ed. ; with an introduction by Michael Hudson. — New York ; London : Garland, 1974 [i.e. 1976]. — 274p in various pagings ; 23cm. — (The neglected American economists)
This facsimile reprint published in the United States: 1974. — 'Journal of the proceedings of the Friends of Domestic Industry' originally published: Baltimore : By order of the Convention, 1831. — This ed. of 'British opinions on the protecting system' originally published: Boston, Mass. : Nathan Hale, 1830.
ISBN 0-8240-1003-5 : £21.00
(B77-04718)

382.7'0973 — Tariffs. Policies of government. *United States, ca 1820. Proposals. Early works*
Carey, Mathew. Addresses of the Philadelphia Society for the Promotion of National Industry / [by] Mathew Carey. [5th ed.] ; [and], Essay on the expediency and practicability of improving or creating home markets / [by] George Tibbits. — Garland ed. ; with introductions by Michael Hudson. — New York ; London : Garland, 1974 [i.e. 1976]. — 389p in various pagings ; 23cm. — (The neglected American economists)
This facsimile reprint published in the United States: 1974. — This ed. of 'Addresses of the Philadelphia Society for the Promotion of National Industry' originally published: Philadelphia : J. Maxwell, 1820. — 'Essay on the expediency and practicability of improving or creating home markets' originally published: Philadelphia : J.R.A. Skerrett, 1827.
ISBN 0-8240-1000-0 : £21.00
(B77-04719)

382.7'3'091724 — Developed countries. Foreign trade with developing countries. Policies of developed countries: Generalised Systems of Preferences, to 1976
Murray, Tracy. Trade preferences for developing countries / [by] Tracy Murray. — London [etc.] : Macmillan, 1977. — xiv,172p : ill ; 24cm. — (Problems of economic integration)
Bibl.: p.169-170. — Index.
ISBN 0-333-18969-8 : £8.95
ISBN 0-333-18970-1 Pbk : £3.95
(B77-24134)

382.9 — TRADE AGREEMENTS
382'.9142 — European Community. *Conservative and Unionist Party viewpoints*
Heath, Edward. Our community / [by] Edward Heath. — London : Conservative Political Centre, 1977. — 23p ; 21cm. — (Conservative Political Centre. Publications ; no.613)
'... based on the address delivered by [the author] to the Conservative Political Centre meeting held at Blackpool on 12th October, 1977' - title page verso.
ISBN 0-85070-607-6 Sd : £0.40
(B77-33166)

382'.9142 — European Community. *For British businessmen*
Great Britain. *EEC Information Unit.* EEC, your questions answered : a businessman's guide / EEC Information [Unit]. — [New ed.]. — London (Department of Industry, 1 Victoria St., SW1H 0ET) : The Unit, [1977]. — 3-128, [1]p : ill(some col), 2 col maps ; 30cm.
Fold. sheet ([1]p.) (ill.) as insert. — 'The Unit's main concert is with EEC aspects of those subjects for which the Departments of Industry, Trade and Prices and Consumer Protection are responsible' - Introduction. — Previous ed.: 1974. — Bibl.: p.110-116. — Index.
Pbk : Unpriced
(B77-09646)

382'.9142 — European Community countries. Foreign trade. Policies of European Economic Community: Association System, to 1976
Matthews, Jacqueline D. Association system of the European Community / [by] Jacqueline D. Matthews. — New York [etc.] ; London : Praeger, 1977. — xix,169p : map ; 25cm. — (Praeger special studies in international business, finance and trade)
Bibl.: p.156-163. — Index.
ISBN 0-275-23270-0 : £12.20
(B77-16313)

382'.9142 — European Community. Policies. Decision making
Decision making in the European Community / [by] Christoph Sasse ... [et al.]. — New York ; London : Praeger [for] the European Community Institute for University Studies, 1977. — xvii,354p ; 25cm. — (Praeger special studies in international politics and government)
ISBN 0-275-23900-4 : £18.40
(B77-22505)

Policy-making in the European Communities / edited by Helen Wallace, William Wallace and Carole Webb. — London [etc.] : Wiley, 1977. — xiv,341p : ill ; 24cm.
Index.
ISBN 0-471-99423-5 : £10.50
(B77-15786)

382'.9142 — European Economic Community. Organisation structure
Sutton, Mary. The institutions of the EEC : how development cooperation policy is formulated / by Mary Sutton. — Dublin (169 Booterstown Ave., [Blackrock], Co. Dublin) : Trócaire : Irish Commission for Justice and Peace, 1976. — [2], vi,82[i.e.83]p : ill ; 23cm. — (Joint Development Education Programme)
Bibl.: p.81-82.
ISBN 0-905911-00-8 Sd : £0.60
(B77-08961)

382'.9142'08 — European Community, to 1973. *Readings from contemporary sources*
Europe, the quest for unity / compiled by Leith McGrandle ; with an etching by Pietro Annigoni. — London ([770 Fulham Rd, SW6 5SJ]) : Ranelagh Editions, 1975. — iii-xxiii,87, [1]p,plate : 1 ill ; 48cm.
Limited ed. of 475 copies. — Full leather. — In slip case.
ISBN 0-904862-00-3 : £170.00
(B77-26251)

382'.9142'09 — European Economic Community, to 1976
Kerr, Anthony John Crawford. The Common Market and how it works / by Anthony J.C. Kerr. — Oxford [etc.] : Pergamon, 1977. — xv, 210p,[3]leaves of plates(1 fold),[6]p of plates : ill, maps, port ; 24cm. — (Pergamon international library) (Pergamon Oxford geography series)
Bibl.: p.200-206. — Index.
ISBN 0-08-021142-9 : £6.50
ISBN 0-08-021141-0 Pbk : £3.50
(B77-24135)

382'.9142'09047 — European Community, 1977. *Reports, surveys*
Great Britain. *Foreign and Commonwealth Office.* Developments in the European communities, the United Kingdom presidency / presented to Parliament by the Secretary of State for Foreign and Commonwealth Affairs ... — London : H.M.S.O., 1977. — iii,40p ; 25cm. — (European communities ; no.17(1977)) (Cmnd.6887)
ISBN 0-10-168870-9 Sd : £0.75
(B77-26252)

383 — POSTAL SERVICES
383'.06'1411 — Postal services. Consumer protection services. *Scotland. Post Office Users' Council for Scotland. Reports, surveys. Serials*
Post Office Users' Council for Scotland. Report on the exercise and performance of its functions for the accounting year ended 31st March / Post Office Users' Council for Scotland. — London : H.M.S.O.
[1975]-1976. — [1976]. — 10p ; 25cm. — ([1975-76 H.C.]684)
ISBN 0-10-009016-8 Sd : £0.22
(B77-04083)

Post Office Users' Council for Scotland. Report on the exercise and performance of its functions for the accounting year ended 31st March ... / Post Office Users' Council for Scotland. — London : H.M.S.O.
1977. — [1977]. — 10p ; 25cm. — ([1976-77 H.C.]552)
ISBN 0-10-255277-0 Sd : £0.25
(B77-28550)

383'.06'1416 — Postal services. Consumer protection services. *Northern Ireland. Post Office Users' Council for Northern Ireland. Reports, surveys. Serials*

Post Office Users' Council for Northern Ireland. Report on the exercise and performance of its functions for the accounting year ended 31st March / Post Office Users' Council for Northern Ireland. — London : H.M.S.O.
[1975]-1976. — [1976]. — 7p ; 25cm. — ([1975-76 H.C.]683)
ISBN 0-10-009026-5 Sd : £0.20
(B77-04084)

383'.06'142 — Postal services. Consumer protection services. *England. Post Office Users' National Council. Reports, surveys. Serials*

Post Office Users' National Council. Report on the exercise and performance of its functions for the accounting year ended 31st March ... / Post Office Users' National Council. — London : H.M.S.O.
[1976]-1977. — [1977]. — 29p : 1 ill ; 25cm. — ([1976-77 H.C.] 561)
ISBN 0-10-256177-x Sd : £0.70
(B77-31813)

383'.06'1429 — Postal services. Consumer protection services. *Wales. Post Office Users' Council for Wales. Reports, surveys. Serials*

Post Office Users' Council for Wales. Report on the exercise and performance of its functions for the accounting year ended 31st March / Post Office Users' Council for Wales. — London : H.M.S.O.
[1975]-1976. — [1976]. — 16p : map ; 25cm. — ([1975-76 H.C.]685)
ISBN 0-10-009036-2 Sd : £0.30
(B77-04085)

383'.0941 — Postal services. *Great Britain. Serials*

Post Office. Post Office guide. — [London] : H.M.S.O.
1976, November. — 1976. — 679p : ill ; 21cm.
Index.
ISBN 0-11-880476-6 Pbk : £0.50
(B77-08328)

383'.09423'38 — Postal services. *Dorset. Bournemouth, 1839-1899*

Young, John Anthony. An outline of postal services in Bournemouth, 1839-1899 / by J.A. Young. — [Dorchester] ([County Hall, Dorchester, Dorset DT1 1XJ]) : Dorset County Council, Education Committee, [1977]. — [2], 17p : 1 ill ; 21cm.
Bibl.: p.12. — Includes facsimile reprints.
ISBN 0-85216-157-3 Sd : £0.20
(B77-18054)

383'.09426'1 — Postal services: Penny posts. *Norfolk, 1792-1840*

Pegg, R E F. Norfolk penny posts / [by] R.E.F. Pegg. — [Bishops Stortford] ([c/o 6 Church Manor, Bishops Stortford, Herts. CM23 5AE]) : [East Anglia Postal History Study Circle], [1977?]. — [3],80p : facsims, maps ; 30cm.
Sp : £1.70
(B77-31814)

383'.09428'47 — Postal services. *North Yorkshire. Whitby, to 1975*

Bullamore, Colin P. History of Whitby's post / by Colin P. Bullamore. — [Whitby] ([Carr Hill Farm, Sleights, Whitby, N. Yorkshire YO21 1RS]) : The author, 1975. — 2-87p : ill, facsims, map ; 22cm. — (Yorkshire Postal History Society. Series ; 10)
Bibl.: p.85-87.
ISBN 0-9504109-0-x : £2.00
(B77-11745)

383'.09595'3 — Postal services. *Sabah. History*

Sarawak Specialists' Society. The stamps and postal history of North Borneo / Sarawak Specialists' Society. — [Mablethorpe] ([c/o L.H. Shipman, 8 Hillside Ave., Sutton-on-Sea, Mablethorpe, Lincs. LN12 2JH]) : The Society.
Part 1 : 1883-1893 / [compiled] by L.H. Shipman. — [1976]. — 347p : ill, facsims, map ; 25cm.
Index.
ISBN 0-905844-00-9 Pbk : £7.50
(B77-04720)

383'.122'0941 — Letter post: Post Office. Great Britain. Parliament. House of Commons. Select Committee on Nationalised Industries. Post Office: second report. *Great Britain. Critical studies*

The **Post** Office's letter post services, observations by the Secretary of State for Industry, the Chancellor of the Exchequer, the Secretary of State for Prices and Consumer Protection and the Post Office on the second report from the Select Committee on Nationalised Industries, House of Commons paper 73, session 1975-76 ... — London : H.M.S.O., [1976]. — 12p ; 25cm. — (Cmnd. 6629)
ISBN 0-10-166290-4 Sd : £0.22
(B77-06006)

383'.143 — Travelling post offices. *Great Britain, to 1971*

Wilson, Harold Salter. TPO : a history of the Travelling Post Offices of Great Britain / by H.S. Wilson. — Leicester (20 Rockley Rd, Leicester LE4 0GJ) : Railway Philatelic Group.
Index.
Part 1 : England, 'the specials' & associated T.P.O.s. — Revised ed. / edited by Peter Johnson. — 1977. — 76p : ill, facsims, map ; 24cm.
Previous ed.: Altrincham : Railway Philatelic Group, 1971.
ISBN 0-901667-09-9 Sd : £3.25
(B77-15787)

383'.143 — Travelling post offices. *Great Britain, to 1976*

Goodbody, A M. An introduction and guide to the travelling post offices of Great Britain / [by] A.M. Goodbody ; edited by Peter Johnson. — Leicester (20 Rockley Rd, Leicester LE4 0GJ) : Railway Philatelic Group, 1977. — 16p : ill, facsims, map ; 22cm.
Bibl.: p.14.
ISBN 0-901667-10-2 Sd : £0.75
(B77-17413)

383'.49'41 — Postal services. *Great Britain. Post Office. Efficiency. Reports, surveys*

Bradbury Controls Limited. The Post Office, submission to the Post Office Review Committee (the Carter Committee) / by Bradbury Controls Ltd. — Ross-on-Wye (P.O. Box 4, Ross-on-Wye, [Herefordshire] HR9 6EB) : Bradbury Controls Ltd, 1976. — [1],6p ; 25cm.
Sd : Unpriced
(B77-02212)

383'.49'41 — Postal services. *Great Britain. Post Office. Inquiry reports*

Post Office Review Committee. Report of the Post Office Review Committee. — London : H.M.S.O., [1977]. — vi,141p ; 25cm. — (Cmnd.6850)
Chairman: C.F. Carter.
ISBN 0-10-168500-9 Pbk : £3.25
(B77-25533)

383'.49'41 — Postal services. *Great Britain. Post Office. Reports, surveys. Serials*

Post Office. Report and accounts for the year ended 31 March / Post Office. — London : H.M.S.O.
[1976]-1977. — 1977. — 105p : col ill, facsim ; 30cm.
ISBN 0-11-886001-1 Pbk : £2.00
(B77-25534)

384 — TELECOMMUNICATION SERVICES

384'.05 — Telecommunication services. *Periodicals*

Telecommunications policy. — Guildford : IPC Science and Technology Press.
Vol.1, no.1- ; Dec. 1976-. — 1976-. — ill ; 28cm.
Quarterly. — 96p. in 1st issue.
Pbk : £30.00 yearly
ISSN 0308-5961
(B77-08962)

384'.06'541 — Telecommunication services: Post Office. *Great Britain. Statistics*

Telecommunications statistics / [Post Office, Telecommunications Management Services Department]. — London (2 Gresham St., EC2V 7AG) : The Department.
1976. — 1976. — 99p ; 30cm.
Pbk : £1.60
(B77-18055)

384'.07'2041 — Telecommunication services: Post Office. Research & development. *Great Britain*

Post Office. R & D / [Post Office]. — London (Telecommunications System Strategies Department (TSS 10.7), 2 Gresham St., EC2V 7AG) : Post Office Telecommunications, 1975. — [5],84p(2 fold) : ill(chiefly col), col map ; 20x22cm.
ISBN 0-903419-02-5 Sp : Private circulation
(B77-01327)

384.54 — Broadcasting services. Audiences. Research by British Broadcasting Corporation. Audience Research Department. *Great Britain. Reports, surveys. Serials*

British Broadcasting Corporation. Annual review of BBC audience research findings. — London : B.B.C.
Research conducted by the Audience Research Department of the BBC.
No.1 : 1973-74. — 1974. — 54p : 3 ill ; 21cm.
Bibl.: p.53-54.
ISBN 0-563-12836-4 Pbk : £1.00
ISSN 0309-6289
(B77-17414)

No.3 : 1975-76. — 1977. — [2],84p : 1 ill ; 21cm.
ISBN 0-563-17275-4 Pbk : £1.00
ISSN 0309-6289
(B77-17415)

384.54 — Broadcasting services. Sociopolitical aspects

Cruise O'Brien, Rita. Professionalism in broadcasting, issues of international dependence / by Rita Cruise O'Brien. — Brighton : Institute of Development Studies, 1976. — [7],56p : ill ; 30cm. — (Institute of Development Studies. Discussion papers ; 100 ISSN 0308-5864)
Sd : £1.80
(B77-22506)

384.54'025'41 — Broadcasting services. *Great Britain. Directories*

The **blue** book of British broadcasting / [Tellex Monitors]. — London (50 Grosvenor St., W.1) : Tellex Monitors.
1977. — 1977. — [5],ii,216p ; 30cm.
Index.
Pbk : £15.00
ISBN 0-85227-042-9
(B77-22507)

384.54'06'541 — Broadcasting services. *Great Britain. British Broadcasting Corporation. Autonomy*

Swann, *Sir* Michael. The autonomy of the broadcasters : constitution and convention : a speech given by Sir Michael Swann, chairman of the BBC, to the Royal Television Society, Midland Centre, 22 October 1974. — London : British Broadcasting Corporation, [1974?]. — 12,[1]p ; 23cm.
ISBN 0-563-12842-9 Sd : Unpriced
(B77-31111)

384.54'06'541 — Broadcasting services. *Great Britain. British Broadcasting Corporation. Yearbooks*

British Broadcasting Corporation. BBC handbook. — London : B.B.C.
1977 : incorporating the annual report and accounts 1975-76. — 1976. — 352p : ill(some col), maps(some col), ports(some col) ; 21cm.
Bibl.: p.333-336. — Index.
ISBN 0-563-17196-0 Pbk : £1.50
(B77-06007)

384.54'092'4 — Broadcasting services. Thomas, Howard, b.1909. *Great Britain. Autobiographies*

Thomas, Howard, *b.1909*. With an independent air : encounters during a lifetime of broadcasting / [by] Howard Thomas. — London : Weidenfeld and Nicolson, 1977. — [7],248p,[12]p of plates : ill, ports ; 23cm.
Index.
ISBN 0-297-77278-3 : £5.95
(B77-17416)

384.54'0941 — Broadcasting services. *Great Britain. Inquiry reports*

Committee on the Future of Broadcasting. Report of the Committee on the Future of Broadcasting ... / chairman Lord Annan. — London : H.M.S.O., [1977]. — xv,522p : 1 ill ; 25cm. — (Cmnd.6753)
ISBN 0-10-167530-5 Pbk : £7.25
(B77-12399)

384.54'0941 — Broadcasting services. *Great Britain. Proposals*
Institute of Practitioners in Advertising. IPA submission to the Annan Committee. — London : I.P.A., 1975. — [1],14p ; 21cm.
Sd : £0.25
(B77-24847)

384.54'0941 — Broadcasting services. Committee on the Future of Broadcasting. Report of the Committee on the Future of Broadcasting. *Great Britain. Critical studies*
Independent Television Companies Association. The Annan report, an ITV view : a submission to the Home Secretary in response to the report of the Annan Committee on the Future of Broadcasting / Independent Television Companies Association. — London : Independent Television Books Ltd ; [London] ([52 Mortimer St., W1N 8AN]) : [The Association], 1977. — 58,[1]p ; 30cm.
Sd : £2.00
(B77-30136)

384.54'0941 — Commercial broadcasting services. *Great Britain. Yearbooks*
Television and radio : guide to Independent Television and Independent Local Radio. — [London] ([Independent Broadcasting Authority]) ; [London] ([247 Tottenham Court Rd, W1P 0AU]) : [Distributed by Independent Television Publications Ltd].
1977 / [editor Eric Croston]. — [1977]. — 224p : ill(chiefly col), col maps, ports(some col) ; 23cm.
Previously published: as 'TV & radio'. — Index.
ISBN 0-900485-24-8 Pbk : £1.40
(B77-07260)

384.54'09492 — Broadcasting services. *Netherlands*
Haak, Kees van der. Broadcasting in the Netherlands / [by] Kees van der Haak with Joanna Spicer. — London [etc.] : Routledge and Kegan Paul [for the] International Institute of Communications, 1977. — xi,93p ; 22cm. — (Case studies on broadcasting systems)
Bibl.: p.92-93.
ISBN 0-7100-8780-2 Pbk : £3.50 : CIP rev.
(B77-26989)

384.54'09595'1 — Broadcasting services. *West Malaysia*
Adhikarya, Ronny. Broadcasting in peninsular Malaysia / [by] Ronny Adhikarya with ... [others]. — London [etc.] : Routledge and Kegan Paul [for the] International Institute of Communications, 1977. — xi,102p : ill, maps ; 22cm. — (Case studies on broadcasting systems)
Bibl.: p.101-102.
ISBN 0-7100-8530-3 Pbk : £2.95
(B77-13611)

384.54'0965 — Broadcasting services. Sociopolitical aspects. *Study regions: Algeria*
Cruise O'Brien, Rita. Professionalism in broadcasting, case studies of Algeria and Senegal / by Rita Cruise O'Brien. — Brighton : Institute of Development Studies, 1976. — [5], 50p : ill ; 30cm. — (Institute of Development Studies. Discussion papers ; 101 ISSN 0308-5864)
Sd : £1.40
Also classified at 384.54'0966'3
(B77-22508)

384.54'0966'3 — Broadcasting services. Sociopolitical aspects. *Study regions: Senegal*
Cruise O'Brien, Rita. Professionalism in broadcasting, case studies of Algeria and Senegal / by Rita Cruise O'Brien. — Brighton : Institute of Development Studies, 1976. — [5], 50p : ill ; 30cm. — (Institute of Development Studies. Discussion papers ; 101 ISSN 0308-5864)
Sd : £1.40
Primary classification 384.54'0965
(B77-22508)

384.54'0968 — Radio services. *South Africa, to 1973*
Rosenthal, Eric. You have been listening : the early history of radio in South Africa / [by] Eric Rosenthal. — Cape Town ; London [etc.] : Purnell [for] South African Broadcasting Corporation, 1974. — vii,165p,[24]p of plates : ill, facsims, ports ; 25cm.
Index.
ISBN 0-360-00267-6 : Unpriced
(B77-18688)

384.54'0971 — Broadcasting services. *Canada*
Hallman, E S. Broadcasting in Canada / [by] E.S. Hallman with H. Hindley. — London [etc.] : Routledge and Kegan Paul [for] the International Institute of Communications, 1977. — xi,90p : ill, map ; 22cm. — (Case studies on broadcasting systems)
ISBN 0-7100-8528-1 Pbk : £2.95
(B77-13612)

384.54'43 — Broadcasting services. *Great Britain. British Broadcasting Corporation. Adult educational broadcasting services*
British Broadcasting Corporation. An introduction to further education broadcasts / [British Broadcasting Corporation]. — Revised [ed.] / by Neil H. Barnes. — London : B.B.C., 1977. — 27p ; 24cm.
Previous ed.: 1974.
ISBN 0-563-16182-5 Sd : Unpriced
(B77-18689)

384.54'43 — Broadcasting services. *Great Britain. British Broadcasting Corporation. News & current affairs reporting services. Organisation*
Curran, *Sir* Charles. BBC journalism : the relevance of structures : a speech given by Sir Charles Curran, Director-General of the British Broadcasting Corporation at Goldsmiths' College, University of London, 1 March 1977. — London : British Broadcasting Corporation, [1977]. — 16p ; 21cm.
ISBN 0-563-17375-0 Sd : Unpriced
(B77-28551)

384.54'43 — Broadcasting services: External services to Warsaw Pact countries. Policies of Warsaw Pact countries. *West Germany*
Wettig, Gerhard. Broadcasting and détente : Eastern policies and their implications for East-West relations / by Gerhard Wettig ; [translated from the German by George Campbell]. — London : C. Hurst, 1977. — x, 110p ; 23cm.
Translation of articles originally appearing in 'Deutschland Archiv' and 'Aus Politik und Zeitgeschichte', 1976. — Index.
ISBN 0-903983-91-5 : £5.50 : CIP rev.
(B77-07261)

384.54'43 — Educational radio services. *Tanzania, 1969-1974*
Hall, Budd L. Voices for development : the Tanzanian national radio study campaigns / [by] Budd L. Hall and Tony Dodds. — Cambridge (131 Hills Rd, Cambridge CB2 1PD) : International Extension College, 1974. — 53p ; 21cm. — (International Extension College. Broadsheets on distance learning ; no.6)
Bibl.: p.53.
ISBN 0-903632-07-1 Sd : Unpriced
(B77-19306)

384.54'43 — International radio services. International political aspects
Abshire, David Manker. International broadcasting : a new dimension of Western diplomacy / [by] David M. Abshire. — Beverly Hills ; London : Sage Publications [for] the Center for Strategic and International Studies, 1976. — 89p : 2 ill ; 22cm. — (The Washington papers ; 35) (A Sage policy paper)
Bibl.: p.88-89.
ISBN 0-8039-0657-9 Pbk : £1.75
(B77-14180)

384.54'52 — Broadcasting services. *Great Britain. British Broadcasting Corporation. Local radio services, to 1977*
British Broadcasting Corporation. Serving neighbourhood and nation / BBC. — London : B.B.C., [1977]. — [2],65p : ill(some col), maps(some col), ports(some col) ; 21cm.
Includes an article in Welsh.
ISBN 0-563-17281-9 Sd : £0.30
(B77-16314)

384.54'52 — Commercial local radio services. *Great Britain*
Independent Broadcasting Authority. Independent local radio / [Independent Broadcasting Authority]. — London (70 Brompton Rd, SW3 1EY) : I.B.A., 1974. — 64p : ill(some col), col map, plan, ports ; 23cm. — (Independent Broadcasting Authority. IBA technical reviews ; 5 ISSN 0308-423x)
Pbk : Unpriced
(B77-25535)

384.54'53 — Offshore radio services. *Europe, to 1976*
Harris, Paul, *b.1948.* Broadcasting from the high seas : the history of offshore radio in Europe 1958-1976 / [by] Paul Harris. — Edinburgh : P. Harris, 1977. — 361p : ill, facsims, ports ; 23cm.
' ... incorporates much of the text of ... [the author's] first work, "When pirates ruled the waves" [Aberdeen : Impulse Publications, 1968]' - jacket. — Ill., facsims on lining papers.
ISBN 0-904505-07-3 : £7.50
(B77-12400)

384.54'53 — Public broadcasting services. *United States*
The **future** of public broadcasting / [edited by] Douglass Cater, Michael J. Nyhan. — New York [etc.] ; London : Praeger [for] the Aspen Institute Program on Communications and Society ; London : [Distributed by Martin Robertson], 1976. — x,372,[1]p ; 24cm. — (Praeger special studies in US economic, social and political issues)
Bibl.: p.333-352. — Index.
ISBN 0-275-56990-x Pbk : £12.05
ISBN 0-275-64590-8 Pbk : Unpriced
(B77-00155)

384.54'56 — Communications satellites. Economic aspects
Economic and policy problems in satellite communications / edited by Joseph N. Pelton, Marcellus S. Snow. — New York [etc.] ; London : Praeger, 1977. — x,244p : 2 ill ; 25cm. — (Praeger special studies in international economics and development)
Index.
ISBN 0-275-23730-3 : £12.40
(B77-25536)

384.55'4'025 — Television services. *Directories*
International film and TV year book. — London (142 Wardour St., W1V 4BR) : 'Screen international'.
1977-8 : 32nd year / founded and edited by Peter Noble. — [1977]. — xlviii,688p : ill, ports ; 23cm.
Unpriced
Also classified at 384.8'025
(B77-32572)

Kemp's film and television year book (international). — London : Kemp's.
1976-1977. — [1976]. — [2],322,385,[18]p : ill ; 21cm.
Index.
ISBN 0-905255-01-1 Pbk : £6.50
Also classified at 384.8'025
(B77-03492)

1977-1978. — [1977]. — [2],823,[22]p : ill ; 22cm.
Index.
ISBN 0-905255-25-9 : £7.50
Also classified at 384.8'025
(B77-26990)

384.55'4'06541 — Television services. *Great Britain. ATV Network Limited. Yearbooks*
Associated Television. ATV yearbook. — [London] ([17 Great Cumberland Place, W1A 1AG]) : [ATV Network Ltd].
1976-77. — [1977]. — 28p(2 fold) : col ill, col ports ; 30cm.
Sd : Unpriced
ISSN 0308-8286
(B77-32573)

384.55'4'0941 — Television services. Political aspects. *Great Britain, 1934-1976*
Goldie, Grace Wyndham. Facing the nation : television and politics, 1936-1976 / [by] Grace Wyndham Goldie. — London [etc.] : Bodley Head, 1977. — 368p ; 23cm.
Bibl.: p.353-356. — Index.
ISBN 0-370-01383-2 : £7.50
(B77-13613)

384.55'4'09429 — Television services in Welsh. *Wales. Proposals. Welsh texts*
Welsh Language Society. Darlledu : dogfen drafod / Cymdeithas yr Iaith Gymraeg. — Aberystwyth ([5 Maes Albert, Aberystwyth, Dyfed]) : Y Gymdeithas, 1977. — [2],13p ; 26cm.
Sd : Unpriced
(B77-33167)

384.55'44'3 — Commercial television services. *Great Britain. Thames Television. Educational television services. Serials*
Independent television for schools and colleges, Thames : annual programme, age 4-18. — [London] ([306 Euston Rd, NW1 3BB]) : [Thames Television Ltd].
1977-78. — [1977]. — [2],37p ; 21cm.
ISBN 0-904416-02-x Sd : Unpriced
(B77-15788)

384.55'44'3 — Educational television services. *Developing countries*
Educational television : a policy critique and guide for developing countries / edited by Robert F. Arnove. — New York [etc.] ; London : Praeger ; [London] : [Distributed by Martin Robertson], 1976. — xxi,224p : ill ; 24cm. — (Praeger special studies in international politics and government)
ISBN 0-275-55510-0 : £12.95
(B77-06008)

384.55'47'0973 — Cable television services. Operation. *United States. Manuals*
Woodard, Charles C. Cable television : acquisition and operation of CATV systems / [by] Charles C. Woodard, Jr. — New York ; London [etc.] : McGraw-Hill, 1974. — xi, 274p : ill, forms ; 29cm.
Index.
ISBN 0-07-071635-8 : Unpriced
(B77-20179)

384.6'5 — Telephone exchange equipment. Purchase by telecommunication services: Post Office. *Great Britain. Inquiry reports*
Posner, Michael Vivian. Post Office orders for telecommunication switching equipment : report to the Secretary of State for Industry / [by M.V. Posner]. — [London] : [Department of Industry], 1977. — [57]p : ill, map ; 30cm.
Sd : Unpriced
(B77-20180)

384.8 — CINEMA INDUSTRIES
384.8'025 — Cinema industries. *Directories*
International film and TV year book. — London (142 Wardour St., W1V 4BR) : 'Screen international'.
1977-8 : 32nd year / founded and edited by Peter Noble. — [1977]. — xlviii,688p : ill, ports ; 23cm.
Unpriced
Primary classification 384.55'4'025
(B77-32572)

Kemp's film and television year book (international). — London : Kemp's.
1976-1977. — [1976]. — [2],322,385,[18]p : ill ; 21cm.
Index.
ISBN 0-905255-01-1 Pbk : £6.50
Primary classification 384.55'4'025
(B77-03492)

1977-1978. — [1977]. — [2],823,[22]p : ill ; 22cm.
Index.
ISBN 0-905255-25-9 : £7.50
Primary classification 384.55'4'025
(B77-26990)

384'.8'0922 — Cinema industries. *California. Los Angeles. Hollywood, to 1967. Personal observations. Collections*
The **real** tinsel / [compiled by] Bernard Rosenberg and Harry Silverstein. — New York : Macmillan ; London : Collier Macmillan, [1976]. — xi,436p : ill, ports ; 23cm.
Originally published: 1970. — Index.
ISBN 0-02-012550-x : £2.95
(B77-01328)

384'.8'0973 — Cinema industries. *United States, to 1975. Readings*
The **American** film industry / edited by Tino Balio. — Madison ; London : University of Wisconsin Press, 1976. — ix,501p : ill, ports ; 24cm.
Bibl.: p.474-481. — Index.
ISBN 0-299-07000-x : £11.25
ISBN 0-299-07004-2 Pbk : £5.25
(B77-24848)

384.8'3 — Cinema industries. Financial assistance. Organisations. *Great Britain. British Film Fund Agency. Reports, surveys. Serials*
British Film Fund Agency. Annual report and statement of accounts / British Film Fund Agency. — London : H.M.S.O.
18th : [1974]-1975 : for the fifty-two weeks ended 27 September 1975. — [1976]. — 10p ; 25cm. — ([1975-76 H.C.] 588)
ISBN 0-10-258876-7 Sd : £0.22
(B77-04086)

384'.8'3 — Cinema industries. Financial assistance. Organisations. *Great Britain. National Film Finance Corporation. Reports, surveys. Serials*
National Film Finance Corporation. Annual report and statement of accounts for the year ended 31st March ... / National Film Finance Corporation. — London : H.M.S.O.
[1975]-1976. — [1976]. — [2],15p ; 25cm. — (Cmnd. 6633)
ISBN 0-10-166330-7 Sd : £0.30
(B77-04087)

385 — RAILWAY SERVICES
Nock, Oswald Stevens. Railways of the world / [by] O.S. Nock. — London : A. and C. Black.
4 : Railways of Western Europe. — 1977. — xvi,264p,leaf of plate,32p of plates : ill(incl 1 col), maps ; 24cm.
Bibl.: p.256. — Index.
ISBN 0-7136-1686-5 : £7.50 : CIP rev.
(B77-06608)

385 — Railways. *Juvenile literature*
Kerrod, Robin. Railways / [by Robin Kerrod] ; [illustrator Mike Atkinson]. — Maidenhead : Sampson Low, 1977. — 5-44p : ill(chiefly col), facsims, port ; 28cm. — (New horizon library)
Index.
ISBN 0-562-00062-3 : £1.75
(B77-24136)

The **super** book of trains. — London : Macdonald Educational, 1977. — 32p : ill(some col), facsim, maps ; 28cm.
Adaptation of: 'Trains'. London : Macdonald, 1971.
ISBN 0-356-05595-7 Sd : £0.50
(B77-18056)

385'.025 — Railway services. *Directories*
Railway directory & year book / compiled from official sources under the direction of the editor of 'Railway gazette international'. — London : IPC Transport Press.
1977 : 82nd year of publication. — 1976. — 3-73D,4p,96p,[10]fold leaves of plates : ill, maps ; 22cm.
Tab indexed. — Bibl.: p.656-658. — Index.
ISBN 0-617-00184-7 : £8.00
ISSN 0079-9513
(B77-09647)

385'.05 — Railway services. *Serials*
The **railway** & steam enthusiasts' handbook. — Bristol (9 Poplar Ave., Westbury-on-Trym, Bristol B59 2BE) : Avon-Anglia Publications and Services.
No.7 / edited by Geoffrey Body and Ian G. Body. — 1977. — 120p : ill ; 23cm.
Bibl.
Unpriced
ISSN 0485-9170
(B77-32574)

385'.06'242398 — Railway services. Organisations. *Avon. Bath. Bath Railway Society, to 1976*
Lawrance, F W J. The Bath Railway Society : a brief history / by F.W.J. Lawrance. — [Weston-super-Mare] ([57 Burnham Drive, Bleadon Hill, Weston-super-Mare, Avon BS24 9LF]) : The author, 1976. — 56p : ill, ports ; 22cm.
ISBN 0-9505579-0-0 Sd : £1.00
(B77-11175)

385'.09 — Railway services. *History. Serials*
'**Railway** world' annual. — London : Allan.
1977 / edited by Alan Williams. — 1976. — [2],130p : ill(some col) ; 25cm.
Ill. on lining papers.
ISBN 0-7110-0720-9 : £2.50
(B77-00156)

'**Railway** world' annual. — London : I. Allan.
1978 / edited by Alan Williams. — 1977. — [2],130p : ill(some col) ; 25cm.
Ill., text on lining papers.
ISBN 0-7110-0813-2 : £2.75
(B77-31815)

385'.09 — Railways, to 1975
History of railways / [edited by E.L. Cornwell]. — [London] : Hamlyn : New English Library, 1976. — 512p : ill(chiefly col), col coats of arms, facsims(chiefly col), col maps, ports(some col) ; 35cm.
Index.
ISBN 0-600-37587-0 : £6.95
(B77-07262)

Manning, Rosemary. Rosemary Manning's book of railways and railwaymen. — Harmondsworth : Kestrel Books, 1977. — 143p : ill, facsims, map, ports ; 23cm.
Spine title: Railways and railwaymen. — Bibl.: p.139. — Index.
ISBN 0-7226-5351-4 : £3.75
(B77-31816)

World of trains / edited by Patrick B. Whitehouse ; picture research Patricia E. Hornsey. — London [etc.] : Hamlyn ; London : New English Library, 1976. — 144p : ill(chiefly col), col coats of arms, col facsims, plan ; 31cm.
ISBN 0-600-39345-3 : £1.95
(B77-07263)

385'.092'4 — Railway services. *England. British Rail. Western Region. Steam locomotives. Operation, 1923-1960. Personal observations*
Drayton, John. On the footplate : memories of a GWR engineman / [by] John Drayton. — Truro : Barton, 1976. — 111p : ill, map, ports ; 22cm. — (Bradford Barton pictorial railway series)
ISBN 0-85153-299-3 Pbk : £1.50
(B77-06609)

385'.092'4 — Railway services. *Yorkshire, 1923-1970. Personal observations*
Bedale, Len. Station master : my lifetime's railway service in Yorkshire / by Len Bedale ; as told to C.T. Goode. — Sheffield ([745 Abbeydale Rd, Sheffield S7 2BG]) : Turntable Publications, 1976. — 80p,[24]p of plates : ill, maps, plans, port ; 22cm.
ISBN 0-902844-38-5 : £2.50
ISBN 0-902844-36-9 Pbk : £1.75
(B77-04721)

385'.092'4 — Railway services, 1907-1976. *Personal observations*
Nock, Oswald Stevens. Out the line / [by] O.S. Nock. — London : Elek, 1976. — x,163p,[16]p of plates : ill, maps, ports ; 23cm.
Bibl.: p.158-160. — Index.
ISBN 0-236-40070-3 : £5.95
(B77-02213)

385'.092'4 — Railway services. Stephen, George, 1st Baron Mount Stephen. *North America. Biographies*
Gilbert, Heather. The life of Lord Mount Stephen / [by] Heather Gilbert. — [Aberdeen] : Aberdeen University Press.
In 2 vols.
Vol.2 : 1891-1921 : The end of the road. — 1977. — xiii,442p,[8]leaves of plates : 2 col maps(on lining papers), ports ; 23cm.
Index.
ISBN 0-900015-38-1 : £10.00
(B77-24849)

385'.0941 — Railway services. *Great Britain, 1870-1973. For systems analysis*
Spear, Roger. The British railways system. — 2nd ed. / prepared by Roger Spear ; for the [Open University, Systems Management] Course Team. — Milton Keynes : Open University Press, 1975. — 71p : ill, facsims, maps(1 col) ; 30cm. — (Technology, a second level course : systems management ; unit 2) (T242 ; 2)
Previous ed. / by Chris Hirst. 1974.
ISBN 0-335-02727-x Pbk : £1.60
(B77-26991)

385'.0941 — Railway services. *Great Britain. British Rail. Inquiry reports*
Great Britain. *Parliament. House of Commons. Select Committee on Nationalised Industries.* The role of British Rail in public transport : first report from the Select Committee on Nationalised Industries, session 1976-77, together with the proceedings of the Committee, minutes of evidence taken before Sub-committee A and appendices. — London : H.M.S.O.
Vol.1 : Report and proceedings of the Committee. — [1977]. — cxxxvi p : ill ; 25cm. — ([1976-77 H.C.] 305-I)
ISBN 0-10-285477-7 Pbk : £2.10
(B77-17417)

Vol.2 : Minutes of evidence. — [1977]. — vii, 431p,[2]fold leaves of plates : ill, 2 maps ; 25cm. — ([1976-77 H.C.] 305-II)
ISBN 0-10-285577-3 Pbk : £8.10
(B77-17418)

Vol.3 : Appendices. — [1977]. — v p,p432-675 : ill, form, map ; 25cm. — ([1976-77 H.C.] 305-III)
ISBN 0-10-285677-x Pbk : £3.10
(B77-17419)

385'.0941 — Railway services. *Great Britain. British Rail. London-Glasgow line, 1913-1974*
Nock, Oswald Stevens. Sixty years of West Coast express running / [by] O.S. Nock. — London : Allan, 1976. — 264p,48p of plates : ill ; 22cm.
Jacket title: 60 years of West coast express running. — Index.
ISBN 0-7110-0618-0 : £4.95
(B77-02214)

385'.0941 — Railway services. *Great Britain. British Rail. London-Glasgow line, to 1975*
The **west** coast route to Scotland : the history and romance of the railway between Euston and Glasgow / [compiled] by Geoffrey Kichenside. — Newton Abbot [etc.] : David and Charles, 1976. — 96p : chiefly ill, facsims, maps ; 26cm.
Bibl.: p.96.
ISBN 0-7153-7210-6 : £3.95
(B77-06009)

385'.0941 — Railway services. *Great Britain. British Rail. Middle school texts*
Cox, Sarah. Railwayworker / text by Sarah Cox ; photographs by Robert Golden. — Harmondsworth : Kestrel Books, 1976. — 32p : chiefly ill ; 27cm. — (People working)
ISBN 0-7226-5229-1 : £1.95
(B77-00157)

385'.0941 — Railway services. *Great Britain. London and North Eastern Railway, to 1947*
Allen, Geoffrey Freeman. Salute to the LNER / [by] G. Freeman Allen. — London : I. Allan, 1977. — 100p : ill ; 25cm.
ISBN 0-7110-0789-6 : £2.50
(B77-23315)

385'.0941 — Railway services. *Great Britain. Rural regions, to 1968*
Thomas, David St John. The country railway / by David St John Thomas. — Newton Abbot [etc.] : David and Charles, 1976. — 160p : ill, facsims, maps, ports ; 24cm.
Index.
ISBN 0-7153-7285-8 : £3.95
(B77-05334)

385'.0941 — Railway services. *Great Britain, to 1923*
Bucknall, Rixon. Our railway history / by Rixon Bucknall. — 3rd ed., revised and enlarged. — London : Allen and Unwin, 1970 [i.e. 1977]. — 234p,[8]leaves of plates : ill(some col) ; 22cm.
This ed. originally published: 1970. — Bibl.: p.11-12.
ISBN 0-04-385064-2 Pbk : £2.25
(B77-06610)

385'.0941 — Railway services. *Great Britain, to 1976*
Britain's main-line railways / edited by P.B. Whitehouse. — London : New English Library, 1977. — 224p : ill(chiefly col), col coats of arms, col facsims, col maps ; 35cm.
ISBN 0-450-02836-4 : £6.50
(B77-30137)

385'.0941 — Railways. Branch lines. *Great Britain, to 1976. Illustrations*
Gammell, Christopher John. The branch line age : the minor railways of the British Isles in memoriam and retrospect / [by] C.J. Gammell. — Buxton (The Market Place, Harlington, Buxton, Derbyshire SK17 0AL) : Moorland Publishing Co., 1976. — 96p : of ill ; 25cm.
Bibl.: p.96.
ISBN 0-903485-38-9 : £3.50
(B77-03493)

385'.09411 — Railway services. *Scotland, to 1976*
Thomas, John, *b.1914.* The Scottish railway book / [by] John Thomas. — Newton Abbot [etc.] : David and Charles, 1977. — 96p : ill, facsims, plan, ports ; 26cm.
ISBN 0-7153-7324-2 : £3.50
(B77-16821)

385'.094115 — Railway services. *Scotland. Highlands. British Rail. Scottish Region. West Highland line, to 1964*
Thomas, John, *b.1914.* The West Highland Railway / by John Thomas. — 2nd ed. ; with new introduction [by the author]. — Newton Abbot [etc.] : David and Charles, 1976. — 5-172p,[24]p of plates : ill, facsims, maps, plans ; 23cm.
Previous ed.: London : Macdonald and Co., 1965. — Bibl.: p.168. — Index.
ISBN 0-7153-7281-5 : £2.95
(B77-07264)

385'.09414'36 — Railway services. *Scotland. Strathclyde Region. Strathkelvin (District). Monkland and Kirkintilloch Railway, to 1975*
Martin, Don. The Monkland & Kirkintilloch Railway / [by Don Martin]. — [Glasgow] ([District Library HQ, 170 Kirkintilloch Rd, Bishopbriggs, Glasgow G64]) : Strathkelvin District Libraries and Museums, 1976. — [1], 15,[1]p,[4]p of plates : ill, facsim, map ; 21cm. — (Auld Kirk Museum. Publications ; no.2)
ISBN 0-904966-02-x Sd : £0.50
Also classified at 385'.09414'46
(B77-00158)

385'.09414'46 — Railway services. *Scotland. Strathclyde Region. Monklands (District). Monkland and Kirkintilloch Railway, to 1975*
Martin, Don. The Monkland & Kirkintilloch Railway / [by Don Martin]. — [Glasgow] ([District Library HQ, 170 Kirkintilloch Rd, Bishopbriggs, Glasgow G64]) : Strathkelvin District Libraries and Museums, 1976. — [1], 15,[1]p,[4]p of plates : ill, facsim, map ; 21cm. — (Auld Kirk Museum. Publications ; no.2)
ISBN 0-904966-02-x Sd : £0.50
Primary classification 385'.09414'36
(B77-00158)

385'.09414'7 — Railway services. *Scotland. Dumfries and Galloway Region. Stranraer-Dumfries line. Reopening. Feasibility studies*
Scottish Association for Public Transport. The Stranraer-Dumfries railway : a case for reopening / Scottish Association for Public Transport. — Glasgow (113 West Regent St., Glasgow G2 2RX) : The Association, 1977. — [2],ii,19p : 2 maps ; 30cm. — (Scottish Association for Public Transport. Study papers ; 8 ISSN 0306-8005)
Sd : £1.00
(B77-20181)

385'.0942 — Railway services. *England. British Rail. London Midland Region*
Palmer, John, *b.1948.* The Midland line to London / [by] John Palmer. — Brampton (34 Glenthorne Close, Brampton, Chesterfield S40 3AR) : Grayson Publications, 1976. — [1],53p : ill, map ; 21cm. — (A 'read as you go' guide)
ISBN 0-900709-07-3 Pbk : £1.20
Also classified at 914.25
(B77-06010)

385'.0942 — Railway services. *England. Great Western Railway, ca 1890-ca 1910. Illustrations*
The **Great** Western at the turn of the century / [compiled] by A.R. Kingdom. — Oxford : Oxford Publishing, 1976. — 112p : of ill, coat of arms, facsims ; 23x27cm.
Ill., facsims on lining papers.
ISBN 0-902888-93-5 : £3.60
(B77-09648)

385'.09421 — Railway services. *London. British Rail. Southern Region. North Kent Line, to 1976*
Kidner, Roger Wakely. The North Kent Line / [by] R.W. Kidner. — Blandford : Oakwood Press, 1977. — 62,[1]p : ill, maps, plans ; 22cm. — (Locomotion papers ; no.104 ISSN 0305-5493)
Sd : £1.50
Primary classification 385'.09422'3
(B77-26992)

385'.09421'89 — Railway services. *London. Enfield (London Borough). British Rail. Eastern Region. Hertford Loop, to 1975*
Hodge, Peter, *b.1943.* The Hertford Loop : the first hundred years of a local railway / by Peter Hodge. — London (c/o Vicars Moor La., N.21) : Southgate Civic Trust, 1976. — 32p : ill, map ; 21cm.
Bibl.: p.32.
ISBN 0-905494-00-8 Sd : £0.60
Also classified at 385'.09425'8
(B77-03494)

385'.09422 — Railway services. *South-east England. London, Brighton and South Coast Railway, to 1922*
Turner, John Howard. The London Brighton and South Coast Railway / [by] John Howard Turner. — London : Batsford.
In 2 vols.
1 : Origins and formation. — 1977. — xv,287p, [8]p of plates : ill, maps, plans ; 23cm.
Index.
ISBN 0-7134-0275-x : £5.95
(B77-23316)

385'.09422 — Railway services. *Southern England. British Rail. Southern Region. Branch lines, 1955-1965. Illustrations*
Gammell, Christopher John. Southern branch lines, 1955-1965 / by C.J. Gammell. — Oxford : Oxford Publishing, 1976. — [96]p : of ill, maps ; 28cm.
Bibl.: p.[4].
ISBN 0-902888-76-5 : £3.90
(B77-15242)

385'.09422 — Railway services. Disused routes. *South-east England*
White, Henry Patrick. South East England / [by] H.P. White. — Newton Abbot [etc.] : David and Charles, 1976. — 192p,fold plate : ill, map ; 23cm. — (Forgotten railways)
Index.
ISBN 0-7153-7286-6 : £3.95
(B77-05335)

385'.09422'3 — Railway services. *Kent. British Rail. Southern Region. North Kent Line, to 1976*
Kidner, Roger Wakely. The North Kent Line / [by] R.W. Kidner. — Blandford : Oakwood Press, 1977. — 62,[1]p : ill, maps, plans ; 22cm. — (Locomotion papers ; no.104 ISSN 0305-5493)
Sd : £1.50
Also classified at 385'.09421
(B77-26992)

385'.09422'36 — Railway services. *Kent. Sevenoaks (District), to 1976*
Devereux, Charles M. Railways to Sevenoaks / [by] Charles M. Devereux. — Tarrant Hinton : Oakwood Press, 1977. — 60,[1]p : ill, facsims, map, plans ; 22cm. — (Locomotion papers ; no.102 ISSN 0305-5493)
ISBN 0-85361-211-0 Sd : £1.35
(B77-15243)

385'.09422'91 — Railway services. *Berkshire. Newbury (District). Lambourn Valley Railway, to 1964*
Price, Martin Randall Connop. The Lambourn Valley Railway / [by] M.R.C. Price. — Blandford : Oakwood Press, [1977]. — 25,[1]p, [8]p of plates : ill, map, plans ; 22cm. — (Locomotion papers ; no.32 ISSN 0305-5493)
Originally published: Lingfield : Oakwood Press, 1964.
ISBN 0-85361-091-6 Sd : £1.05
(B77-11176)

385'.09423 — Railway services. *Southern England. London and South Western Railway, 1838-1925. Illustrations*
London & South Western Railway album / [compiled by] D.L. Bradley. — London : Allan, 1976. — 96p,plate : chiefly ill(incl 1 col), ports ; 25cm.
ISBN 0-7110-0744-6 : £3.25
(B77-02215)

385'.09423'12 — Railway services. *Wiltshire. North Wiltshire (District). Malmesbury Railway, to 1962*
Fenton, D M. The Malmesbury Railway : to commemorate the centenary of its opening, 1877-1977 / [by] D.M. Fenton. — [Tarrant Hinton] : Oakwood Press, 1977. — 57p,plate : ill, facsims, map, plans, ports ; 22cm. — (The Oakwood library of railway history ; no.41)
Bibl.: p.57.
Sd : £1.60
(B77-33168)

385'.09423'31 — Railway services. *Dorset. West Dorset (District). British Rail. Western Region. Bridport Branch, to 1975*
Jackson, B L. The Bridport Branch / by B.L. Jackson and M.J. Tattershall. — Oxford : Oxford Publishing, 1976. — 208p : ill, facsims, maps, plans, ports ; 22cm.
ISBN 0-902888-85-4 Pbk : £2.40
(B77-04088)

385'.09423'55 — Railway services. *Devon. Teignbridge (District). Great Western Railway. Ashburton branch, to 1969*
Kingdom, Anthony Richard. The Ashburton Branch (and the Totnes Quay Line) / by Anthony R. Kingdom. — Oxford : Oxford Publishing, 1977. — 152p : ill, coat of arms, facsims, maps, plans, port ; 22cm.
Bibl.: p.6.
ISBN 0-902888-84-6 Pbk : £2.40
Primary classification 385'.09423'592
(B77-15244)

385'.09423'592 — Railway services. *Devon. South Hams (District). Great Western Railway. Ashburton branch, to 1969*
Kingdom, Anthony Richard. The Ashburton Branch (and the Totnes Quay Line) / by Anthony R. Kingdom. — Oxford : Oxford Publishing, 1977. — 152p : ill, coat of arms, facsims, maps, plans, port ; 22cm.
Bibl.: p.6.
ISBN 0-902888-84-6 Pbk : £2.40
Also classified at 385'.09423'55
(B77-15244)

385'.09423'83 — Railway services. *Somerset. Mendip (District). East Somerset Railway, to 1972*
Maggs, Colin Gordon. The East Somerset Railway, 1858-1872 / by Colin G. Maggs. — Bristol (9 Poplar Ave., Westbury-on-Trym, Bristol BS9 2BE) : Avon-Anglia Publications and Services [for] the East Somerset Railway Co. Ltd, 1977. — 28p : ill, map, plans ; 16x24cm.
Bibl.: p.27.
ISBN 0-905466-09-8 Sd : £0.40
(B77-33734)

385'.09424 — Railway services. *England. Midlands. Oxford, Worcester and Wolverhampton Railway, to 1976*
Jenkins, Stanley Charles. The Oxford, Worcester & Wolverhampton Railway : a history of the 'Cotswold Line' and its branches from the 1840s to the present day / [by] S.C. Jenkins, H.I. Quayle. — [Blandford] : Oakwood Press, 1977. — 128p,[12]p of plates : ill, facsims, map, plan ; 22cm. — (The Oakwood library of railway history ; no.40)
Index.
ISBN 0-85361-203-x Pbk : £3.00
(B77-15789)

385'.09424 — Railway services. *England. South Midlands, to 1976*
Chilterns and Cotswolds / [compiled by] R. Davies and M.D. Grant. — Newton Abbot [etc.] : David and Charles, 1977. — 96p : ill, facsim, maps ; 26cm. — (Railway history in pictures) ([David & Charles picture history series])
Not the same as B75-10073. — Index.
ISBN 0-7153-7299-8 : £3.95
(B77-28552)

385'.09425'11 — Railway services. *England. Peak District, to 1976. Illustrations*
Main lines in the Peak District / compiled by Christopher P. Nicholson. — Clapham, N. Yorkshire : Dalesman, 1977. — 80p : chiefly ill, maps ; 18x21cm.
ISBN 0-85206-371-7 Pbk : £1.50
(B77-16315)

385'.09425'4 — Railway services. *Leicestershire. Leicester and Swannington Railway, to 1976*
Clinker, Charles Ralph. The Leicester & Swannington Railway : a detailed history of one of Britain's earlies railways / by C.R. Clinker. — Bristol (9 Poplar Ave, Westbury-on-Trym, Bristol BS9 2BE) : Avon Anglia Publications and Services, 1977. — 72p : ill, map ; 22cm.
'... reprinted from the "Transactions of the Leicestershire Archaeological Society" Volume 30, 1954'. — Bibl.: p.71.
ISBN 0-905466-04-7 Pbk : £2.50
(B77-17420)

385'.09425'74 — Railway services. *Oxfordshire. Oxford region. British Rail. Western Region. Branch lines. Guidebooks*
Oxfordshire rambler : (Morris Cowley-Abingdon-Wallingford-Bicester/ Bletchley branches) : a souvenir booklet of photographs depicting local scenes. — Oxford : Oxford Publishing Co., [1976]. — [15]p : chiefly ill, facsims, map ; 22cm.
Sd : £0.20
(B77-21814)

385'.09425'8 — Railway services. *Hertfordshire. British Rail. Eastern Region. Hertford Loop, to 1975*
Hodge, Peter, *b.1943.* The Hertford Loop : the first hundred years of a local railway / by Peter Hodge. — London (c/o Vicars Moor La., N.21) : Southgate Civic Trust, 1976. — 32p : ill, map ; 21cm.
Bibl.: p.32.
ISBN 0-905494-00-8 Sd : £0.60
Primary classification 385'.09421'89
(B77-03494)

385'.09426 — Railway services. Disused routes. *East Anglia, to 1973*
Joby, R S. East Anglia / [by] R.S. Joby. — Newton Abbot [etc.] : David and Charles, 1977. — 175p, fold plate : ill, maps ; 23cm. — (Forgotten railways)
Bibl.: p.166-169. — Index.
ISBN 0-7153-7312-9 : £3.95
(B77-12401)

385'.09426'51 — Railway services. *Cambridgeshire. Peterborough (District). Nene Valley Railway. Guidebooks*
Brown, Clive. Nene Valley Railway : a visitor's guide / compiled by Peter Waszak and members of Peterborough Railway Society ; written by Clive Brown. — Peterborough (c/o Peterborough Development Corporation, Touthill Close, Peterborough) : Peterborough Railway Society, 1977. — 3-34p : ill(some col), facsims, 2 maps, 2 col plans ; 21cm.
Sd : £0.50
(B77-21063)

385'.09427'3 — Railway services. *Greater Manchester (Metropolitan County). Liverpool and Manchester Railway, 1830. Illustrations*
Bury, T T. Coloured views on the Liverpool and Manchester Railway / [by] T.T. Bury. — [1st ed. reprinted] ; with an historical introduction to the railway by George Ottley. — Oldham (Aveyard Broadbent Co., [Spring La.], Lees, Oldham OL4 5AL) : Hugh Broadbent, 1976. — xi,8p,[16] leaves of plates(3 fold) : chiefly col ill, map ; 35cm.
'[Includes] ... three large extra plates which were issued as optional supplements to the original publication' - jacket. — Also available in a de luxe limited ed. — Facsimile reprint of: 1st ed. London : R. Ackermann, 1831. — Bibl.: p.vi.
ISBN 0-904848-02-7 : £16.50
ISBN 0-904848-03-5 De luxe limited ed. : £50.00
Also classified at 385'.09427'5
(B77-06011)

385'.09427'5 — Railway services. *Merseyside (Metropolitan County). Liverpool and Manchester Railway, 1830. Illustrations*
Bury, T T. Coloured views on the Liverpool and Manchester Railway / [by] T.T. Bury. — [1st ed. reprinted] ; with an historical introduction to the railway by George Ottley. — Oldham (Aveyard Broadbent Co., [Spring La.], Lees, Oldham OL4 5AL) : Hugh Broadbent, 1976. — xi,8p,[16] leaves of plates(3 fold) : chiefly col ill, map ; 35cm.
'[Includes] ... three large extra plates which were issued as optional supplements to the original publication' - jacket. — Also available in a de luxe limited ed. — Facsimile reprint of: 1st ed. London : R. Ackermann, 1831. — Bibl.: p.vi.
ISBN 0-904848-02-7 : £16.50
ISBN 0-904848-03-5 De luxe limited ed. : £50.00
Primary classification 385'.09427'3
(B77-06011)

385'.09427'6 — Railway services. *Lancashire, to 1974. Illustrations*
Railways in Lancashire : a pictorial history / compiled by David Joy. — 2nd ed. — Clapham, N. Yorkshire : Dalesman, 1976. — 96p : chiefly ill, maps ; 18x22cm.
Previous ed.: 1975. — Bibl.: p.5.
ISBN 0-85206-346-6 Pbk : £1.50
(B77-16316)

385'.09427'83 — Railway services. *Cumbria. South Lakeland (District). Lakeside and Haverthwaite Railway, to 1975*
Quayle, H I. Lakeside and Haverthwaite Railway / by H.I. Quayle and S.C. Jenkins. — Clapham, N. Yorkshire : Dalesman, 1977. — 72p : ill, maps, plans ; 21cm. — (A Dalesman paperback)
Bibl.: p.72.
ISBN 0-85206-409-8 Pbk : £0.95
(B77-30138)

385'.09428 — Railway services. *North-east England, 1925-1975*
Hoole, Kenneth. The East Coast main line since 1925 / [by] K. Hoole. — London : I. Allan, 1977. — 128p : ill ; 24cm.
ISBN 0-7110-0780-2 : £3.95
(B77-25538)

385'.09428'1 — Railways. *Yorkshire, to 1976. Illustrations*
Railways in Yorkshire. — Clapham, N. Yorkshire : Dalesman.
In 3 vols.
2 : East Riding / compiled by K. Hoole. — 1976. — 80p : chiefly ill, facsim, map ; 18x21cm.
ISBN 0-85206-356-3 Pbk : £1.50
(B77-15790)

385'.09428'35 — Railway services. *Humberside. Boothferry (District). Goole and Selby Railway, to 1964*
Goode, Charles Tony. The Goole and Selby Railway / [by] C.T. Goode. — Blandford : Oakwood Press, 1976. — 42p : ill, maps, plans ; 22cm. — (Locomotion papers ; no.100 ISSN 0305-5493)
ISBN 0-85361-205-6 Sd : £1.05
Also classified at 385'.09428'45
(B77-08329)

385'.09428'45 — Railway services. *North Yorkshire. Selby (District). Goole and Selby Railway, to 1964*
Goode, Charles Tony. The Goole and Selby Railway / [by] C.T. Goode. — Blandford : Oakwood Press, 1976. — 42p : ill, maps, plans ; 22cm. — (Locomotion papers ; no.100 ISSN 0305-5493)
ISBN 0-85361-205-6 Sd : £1.05
Primary classification 385'.09428'35
(B77-08329)

385'.09428'46 — Railway services. *North Yorkshire. Ryedale (District). North Yorkshire Moors Railway, to 1973*
Mead, Harry. Around the Railway / researched and written by Harry Mead. — [Pickering] ([Pickering Station, Pickering, N. Yorkshire]) : North York Moors Historical Railway Trust, 1974. — [17]p : col ill, col map ; 18cm.
Sd : £0.25
Also classified at 385'.09428'47
(B77-31817)

385'.09428'47 — Railway services. *North Yorkshire. Scarborough (District). North Yorkshire Moors Railway, to 1973*
Mead, Harry. Around the Railway / researched and written by Harry Mead. — [Pickering] ([Pickering Station, Pickering, N. Yorkshire]) : North York Moors Historical Railway Trust, 1974. — [17]p : col ill, col map ; 18cm.
Sd : £0.25
Primary classification 385'.09428'46
(B77-31817)

385'.09428'47 — Railway services. *North Yorkshire. Scarborough (District). Scarborough and Whitby Railway, to 1965*
The **Scarborough** & Whitby Railway : a photographic & historical survey / [compiled] by J. Robin Lidster. — Nelson : Hendon Publishing Co., 1977. — [1],44,[1]p : ill, facsims, maps, plans, ports ; 21x29cm.
ISBN 0-86067-016-3 Sd : £1.60
(B77-21815)

385'.09428'51 — Railway services. *Cleveland. Stockton-on-Tees (District). Stockton and Darlington Railway, to 1925. Illustrations*
150th anniversary, Stockton and Darlington Railway / [text by A. Suddes and K. Taylor]. — [Darlington] : Darlington S and D 150 Committee, [1975?]. — Portfolio : ill, facsims, maps ; 34cm.
Twelve sheets ([12]p.).
Unpriced
Also classified at 385'.09428'63
(B77-31818)

385'.09428'62 — Railways. *Durham (County). Shildon, to 1900*
Corkin, Robert. Shildon, cradle of the railways / story Robert Corkin ; photographs Ken Beetham. — Newcastle upon Tyne : F. Graham, 1977. — 38p : ill, coats of arms, facsim ; 22cm. — (Northern history booklet ; no.76 ISSN 0550-855x)
ISBN 0-85983-014-4 Sd : £0.60
(B77-24137)

385'.09428'63 — Railway services. *Durham (County). Darlington (District). Stockton and Darlington Railway, to 1925. Illustrations*
150th anniversary, Stockton and Darlington Railway / [text by A. Suddes and K. Taylor]. — [Darlington] : Darlington S and D 150 Committee, [1975?]. — Portfolio : ill, facsims, maps ; 34cm.
Twelve sheets ([12]p.).
Unpriced
Primary classification 385'.09428'51
(B77-31818)

385'.09428'8 — Railway services. Routes. *Northumberland, to 1974*
Warn, Christopher Robert. Rails across Northumberland / by C.R. Warn. — Newcastle upon Tyne : Graham.
Part 1 : Waggonways and early railways of Northumberland, 1605-1840. — 1976. — 56p : ill, maps ; 22cm. — (Northern history booklets ; no.78 ISSN 0550-855x)
ISBN 0-85983-034-9 Sd : £1.00
(B77-18057)

385'.09429 — Railway services. *Wales. Cambrian Railways, to 1922*
Cambrian Railways album / [compiled by] C.C. Green. — London : I. Allan, [1977]. — 112p, plate : ill(incl 1 col), facsims, map, ports ; 25cm.
ISBN 0-7110-0784-5 : £3.95
(B77-24138)

385'.09429'6 — Railway services. *Dyfed. Whitland and Cardigan Railway, to 1963*
Price, Martin Randall Connop. The Whitland & Cardigan Railway / [by] M.R.C. Price. — Blandford : Oakwood Press, 1976. — 71p,[8]p of plates : ill, facsim, maps, plans, ports ; 22cm. — (Oakwood library of railway history ; 39)
Bibl.: p.72.
ISBN 0-85361-194-7 Pbk : £1.60
(B77-07265)

385'.0957'5 — Railway services. *Russia (RSFSR). Eastern Siberia. Baykal-Amur Railroad. Economic aspects*
Shabad, Theodore. Gateway to Siberian resources : (the BAM) / [by] Theodore Shabad and Victor L. Mote. — Washington, D.C. : Scripta Publishing ; New York ; London [etc.] : Distributed by Wiley, 1977. — viii,189p : ill, maps ; 24cm. — (Scripta series in geography)
'A Halsted Press book'. — Bibl. — Index.
ISBN 0-470-99040-6 : Unpriced
(B77-24850)

385'.0971 — Railway services. *Canada. Canadian Pacific Railway, to 1976*
Lamb, William Kaye. History of the Canadian Pacific Railway / [by] W. Kaye Lamb. — New York : Macmillan ; London : Collier Macmillan, 1977. — ii-xix,491p : ill, facsim, maps, ports ; 25cm. — (Railroads of America ; vol.5)
Bibl.: p.467-476. — Index.
ISBN 0-02-567660-1 : £13.50
(B77-27791)

385'.0973 — Railway services. *United States. Chicago, Burlington and Quincy Railroad, to 1964*
Overton, Richard C. Burlington route : a history of the Burlington lines / [by] Richard C. Overton. — Lincoln [Neb.] ; London : University of Nebraska Press, 1976. — xxviii, 623,xl p,[32]p of plates : ill, maps, ports ; 23cm.
'A Bison book'. — Originally published: New York : Knopf, 1965. — Bibl.: p.601-623. — Index.
ISBN 0-8032-5853-4 Pbk : £6.75
(B77-18058)

385'.0973 — Railways. *United States, ca 1935-1955. Illustrations*
Logan, Ian. Lost glory : great days of the American railways / [by] Ian Logan. — London (51 Endell St., WC2H 9AJ) : Mathews Miller Dunbar Ltd, 1977. — [84]p : of col ill ; 21cm.
ISBN 0-903811-21-9 Pbk : £2.95
(B77-23317)

385'.0978 — Railway services. *United States. Western states, to ca 1900*
Brown, Dee. Hear that lonesome whistle blow / [by] Dee Brown. — London : Chatto and Windus, 1977. — viii,311p : ill, facsims, maps, ports ; 24cm.
Map on lining papers. — Also published: New York : Holt, Rinehart and Winston, 1977. — Bibl.: p.293-303. — Index.
ISBN 0-7011-2232-3 : £5.95 : CIP rev.
(B77-09649)

385'.0978 — Railways. *United States. Western states, to ca 1910*
Riegel, Robert Edgar. The story of the Western railroads : from 1852 through the reign of the giants / by Robert Edgar Riegel. — Lincoln [Neb.] ; London : University of Nebraska Press, [1977]. — xvii,345p ; 21cm.
'A Bison book'. — Facsimile reprint: of 1st ed., New York : Macmillan, 1926. — Bibl.: p.321-337. — Index.
ISBN 0-8032-0903-7 : £11.20
ISBN 0-8032-5159-9 Pbk : £3.00
(B77-17421)

385'.1'09 — Railway services. Economic aspects, to 1975
O'Brien, Patrick. The new economic history of the railways / [by] Patrick O'Brien. — London : Croom Helm, 1977. — 3-121p : 2 ill ; 23cm.
Bibl.: p.115-118. — Index.
ISBN 0-85664-531-1 : £5.95 : CIP rev.
(B77-23318)

385'.2'09429 — Railway services. *Wales. Cambrian Railways, 1904. Timetables. Facsimiles*
Cambrian Railways timetables & working timetables of 1904. — [Oxford] : Oxford Publishing, 1977. — 134p in various pagings,[2]fold p of plates : ill, maps ; 25cm.
Spine title. — Facsimile reprints.
ISBN 0-86093-008-4 Pbk : £1.80
(B77-26253)

385'.22 — Rail travel. Commuting. Effects of increases in prices of petroleum. *Merseyside (Metropolitan County), 1974-1976. Reports, surveys*
Maltby, D. A monitoring study of rail commuting on Merseyside with particular reference to the effects of increases in the price of petrol / prepared for the Science Research Council by D. Maltby, K.A. Lawler and I.G. Monteath. — [Salford] ([Salford M5 4WT]) : University of Salford, Centre for Transport Studies, 1976. — [7],ix,169p,[4] leaves of plates,[2]p of plates : ill, form, map ; 31cm. — (University of Salford. Centre for Transport Studies. Working papers ; 4 ISSN 0309-5738)
Bibl.: p.87-88.
Sp : Unpriced
(B77-29338)

385'.22'06141 — Railway passenger transport services. Consumer protection services. *Great Britain. Central Transport Consultative Committee for Great Britain. Reports, surveys. Serials*
Central Transport Consultative Committee for Great Britain. Annual report ... / Central Transport Consultative Committee for Great Britain. — London : H.M.S.O.
1976. — [1977]. — 29p ; 25cm. — ([1976-77 H.C.] 122)
ISBN 0-10-212277-6 Sd : £0.60
(B77-11746)

385'.22'061411 — Railway passenger transport services. Consumer protection services: Transport Users Consultative Committee for Scotland. *Scotland. Reports, surveys. Serials*
Transport Users Consultative Committee for Scotland. Annual report to the Secretary of State for Transport and Secretary of State for Prices and Consumer Protection ... / Transport Users Consultative Committee for Scotland. — London : H.M.S.O.
1976. — [1977]. — 10p ; 25cm. — ([1976-77 H.C.] 123)
ISBN 0-10-212377-2 Sd : £0.25
(B77-11747)

385'.22'061429 — Railway passenger transport services. Consumer protection services. *Wales. Transport Users Consultative Committee for Wales. Reports, surveys. Serials*
Transport Users Consultative Committee for Wales. Annual report ... / Transport Users Consultative Committee for Wales. — London : H.M.S.O.
1976. — [1977]. — 12p ; 25cm. — ([1976-77 H.C.] 124)
ISBN 0-10-212477-9 Sd : £0.25
(B77-11748)

385'.3'0942 — Railway services. *England. London and North Western Railway. Structures. For modelling*
Nelson, Jack. LNWR portrayed : a survey of the design and construction methods of the Premier Line / by Jack Nelson. — Seaton : Peco, 1975. — 192p : ill, plans ; 26cm.
Bibl.: p.190. — Index.
ISBN 0-900586-45-1 : £6.50
(B77-02216)

385'.314 — Railways. Stations. *North Yorkshire. York. York Station, to 1977*
Rankin, Stuart. York 100, 1877-1977 : the story of a station / [by] Stuart Rankin & David Thompson ; with a foreword by Kenneth Appleby. — York (c/o Public Relations Officer, British Rail, Eastern Region, York) : C.W.F. Cook, [1977]. — [1],37p : ill, facsim, plans ; 22cm.
Bibl.: p.37.
Sd : Unpriced
(B77-26254)

385'.314 — Railways. Stations: Halts. *Dorset. Bournemouth. Meyrick Park Halt, to 1917*
Barker, John. The Meyrick Park Halt / by John Barker. — [Bournemouth] ([Portman House, Richmond Hill, Bournemouth BH2 6ER]) : [Dorset County Council, Education Committee], 1976. — [2],5[i.e. 6]p : map ; 21cm. — (Dorset (County). Education Committee. Local studies) (Environmental studies)
Sd : £0.10
(B77-04722)

385'.314'0942 — Railway services. *England. Great Western Railway. Branch lines. Terminals, 1873-1967*
Great Western branch line termini. — Oxford : Oxford Publishing Co.
Vol.1 / [compiled] by Paul Karau. — 1977. — 124p,8 fold leaves of plates : chiefly ill, facsims, maps, plans ; 28cm.
Ill. on lining papers. — Bibl.
ISBN 0-902888-89-7 : £4.95
(B77-25539)

385'.36'09 — Locomotives, to 1975
Gordon, Sally Patricia. Trains : an illustrated history of locomotive development / [by] S.P. Gordon. — [London] ([59 Grosvenor St., W.1]) : [Cathay Books] for W.H. Smith and Son Ltd, 1976. — 192p : ill(some col), map ; 29cm.
Ill. on lining papers. — Index.
ISBN 0-904644-19-7 : £1.95
(B77-00159)

385'.36'0941 — Railway services. *Great Britain. British Rail. Locomotives, 1950-1959. Illustrations*
British Rail in the fifties. — London : I. Allan.
No.5 : Scottish Region. — [1977]. — 32p : of ill ; 13x19cm.
ISBN 0-7110-0818-3 Sd : £0.25
(B77-24851)

No.6 : Western Region. — [1977]. — 32p : of ill ; 13x19cm.
ISBN 0-7110-0819-1 Sd : £0.25
(B77-24852)

No.7 : London Midland Region. — [1977]. — 32p : of ill ; 13x19cm.
ISBN 0-7110-0820-5 Sd : £0.25
(B77-24853)

No.8 : Southern Region. — [1977]. — 32p : of ill ; 13x19cm.
ISBN 0-7110-0821-3 Sd : £0.25
(B77-24854)

No.9 : Eastern and North Eastern Regions. — [1977]. — 32p : of ill ; 13x19cm.
ISBN 0-7110-0822-1 Sd : £0.25
(B77-24855)

385'.36'0941 — Railway services. *Great Britain. British Rail. Locomotives. Lists*
Locomotive stock of British Railways : including detail differences. — Rugeley : Railway Correspondence and Travel Society.
1977 / [by] Roger B. Wood and P. Mallaband. — [1977]. — 49p ; 21cm.
Cover title.
ISBN 0-901115-42-8 Pbk : £0.80
(B77-32575)

385'.36'0941 — Railway services. *Great Britain. British Rail. Rolling stock: Locomotives & multiple units. Lists*
British Railways locoshed book. — London : Allan.
1977 ed. — [1977]. — 78p : ill ; 16cm.
ISBN 0-7110-0752-7 Sd : £0.40
(B77-16822)

385'.36'09423 — Railway services. *South-west England. British Rail. Southern Region. Locomotives, 1935-1964. Illustrations*
Southern's south western memories / [compiled by] Robert Antell. — London : I. Allan, 1977. — 112p : chiefly ill, facsim, map ; 25cm.
ISBN 0-7110-0824-8 : £3.95
(B77-23319)

385'.36'1 — 4-6-0 steam locomotives. *Great Britain, 1894-1975*
Clay, John Frederic. The British 4-6-0 / [by] John F. Clay. — London : New English Library, 1977. — 96p : ill(some col) ; 31cm.
ISBN 0-450-03218-3 : £4.95
(B77-31819)

385'.36'106242579 — Preserved steam locomotives. Organisations. *Oxfordshire. Didcot. Great Western Society*
Great Western Society. Didcot / the Great Western Society. — Didcot (Didcot, Oxon OX11 7NJ) : The Society, [1977]. — 32,iv p : ill(some col), plan ; 16x22cm.
Sd : Unpriced
(B77-33169)

385'.36'109034 — Railway services. Steam locomotives, 1825-1969
Cook, Chris. A history of the great trains / [by] Chris Cook. — London : Weidenfeld and Nicolson, 1977. — 144p : ill(some col), facsims, ports ; 29cm.
Ill. on lining papers. — Index.
ISBN 0-297-77348-8 : £4.95
(B77-29339)

385'.36'10904 — Steam locomotives, ca 1910-ca 1965
Ellis, Cuthbert Hamilton. The engines that passed / [by] Hamilton Ellis. — London : Allen and Unwin, 1968 [i.e. 1976]. — 3-133p, [4] leaves of plates : ill(some col) ; 25cm.
Originally published: 1968.
ISBN 0-04-385065-0 Pbk : £2.25
(B77-09650)

385'.36'109046 — Steam locomotives, ca 1960-1975
Hunt, John, *b.1945.* On and off the beaten track / [by] John Hunt and Ian Krause. — London : New English Library, 1976. — [128] p : chiefly ill ; 22x28cm.
ISBN 0-450-02958-1 : £6.95
(B77-04089)

385'.36'10941 — Preserved steam locomotives. *Great Britain, 1968-1976. Illustrations*
Nixon, L A. Steam around Britain in the seventies / [by] L.A. Nixon. — Truro : Barton, 1977. — 96p : of ill ; 23cm.
ISBN 0-85153-313-2 : £3.75
(B77-30139)

385'.36'10941 — Railway services. *Great Britain. British Rail. Steam locomotives, 1952-1973. Illustrations*
Carter, James Roy. Working steam / [by] J.R. Carter. — Douglas (1 Hope St., Douglas, Isle of Man) : Viking Publications, 1976. — [109]p : of ill ; 26cm.
ISBN 0-905389-00-x : £4.50
(B77-06012)

385'.36'10941 — Railway services. *Great Britain. British Rail. Steam locomotives, 1956-1958. Illustrations*
Blenkinsop, Richard James. Echoes of the big four / [by] R.J. Blenkinsop. — Oxford : Oxford Publishing, 1976. — [96]p : of ill ; 30cm.
Notebook format.
ISBN 0-902888-77-3 : £3.30
(B77-04090)

385'.36'10941 — Railway services. *Great Britain. British Rail. Steam locomotives, 1957-1968. Illustrations*
Pope, M. Steam ramble / [by] M. Pope. — London : Allan.
No.1 : South and west. — 1976. — 96p : chiefly ill, port ; 30cm.
ISBN 0-7110-0729-2 : £3.25
(B77-02217)

No.2 : North and west. — 1976. — 96p : chiefly ill, ports ; 30cm.
ISBN 0-7110-0730-6 : £3.25
(B77-02218)

385'.36'10941 — Railway services. *Great Britain. London and North Eastern Railway. Steam locomotives, 1923-1948. Illustrations*
Casserley, Henry Cecil. LNER locomotives, 1923-1948 / [by] H.C. Casserley. — Truro : Barton, 1977. — 96p : of ill ; 22cm.
ISBN 0-85153-298-5 : £3.75
(B77-30140)

Casserley, Henry Cecil. LNER steam, 1923-1948 / [by] H.C. Casserley. — Truro : Barton, 1977. — 96p : of ill ; 23cm.
ISBN 0-85153-296-9 : £3.75
(B77-30141)

385'.36'10941 — Railway services. *Great Britain. London, Midland and Scottish Railway. Steam locomotives, 1945-1965*
Powell, Alec John. Living with London Midland locomotives / [by] A.J. Powell. — London : I. Allan, 1977. — 156p,[24]p of plates : ill, plans ; 23cm.
ISBN 0-7110-0728-4 : £3.95
(B77-21064)

385'.36'10941 — Steam locomotives. *Great Britain, 1925-1975. Illustrations*
Peters, Ivo. Somewhere along the line : fifty years love of trains / by Ivo Peters. — Oxford : Oxford Publishing, 1976. — [208]p : of ill ; 30cm.
ISBN 0-902888-80-3 : £6.30
(B77-10321)

385'.36'10941 — Steam locomotives. *Great Britain, ca 1835-1972*
British steam : a profile / edited by Patrick B. Whitehouse ; picture research Patricia E. Hornsey. — [London] : New English Library, 1976. — 112p : ill(chiefly col), 3 col coats of arms, col map, col port ; 30cm.
ISBN 0-450-03147-0 : £2.75
(B77-04723)

385'.36'10941 — Steam locomotives built by British companies, 1940-1975. *Illustrations*
Westwood, John Norton. British-built steam locos overseas / [photographs by] J.N. Westwood [et al.]. — Truro : Barton, 1977. — 96p : chiefly ill ; 22cm.
ISBN 0-85153-284-5 : £3.75
(B77-30142)

385'.36'109411 — Railways. Branch lines. Steam locomotives. *Scotland, 1946-1966. Illustrations*
Scottish branch line steam / edited by Jack Kernahan ; for the Scottish Railway Preservation Society. — Truro : Barton, 1977. — 96p : of ill ; 22cm.
ISBN 0-85153-310-8 : £3.75
(B77-30143)

385'.36'109411 — Steam locomotives. *Scotland, ca 1920-1930. Illustrations*
Stephen, R D. Scottish steam miscellany / [by] R.D. Stephen. — Truro : Barton, 1977. — 96p : of ill ; 22cm.
ISBN 0-85153-279-9 : £3.75
(B77-17422)

385'.36'10942 — Railway services. *England. British Rail. Western Region. Steam locomotives, to 1966. Illustrations*
Hornby, Frank. Western Region steam / by Frank Hornby & Norman Browne. — London : Almark Publishing, 1977. — [72]p : chiefly ill ; 20x21cm. — (Railways in view)
ISBN 0-85524-282-5 : £2.95
(B77-29340)

385'.36'10942 — Railway services. *England. Great Western Railway. Doubleheaded trains. Steam locomotives, 1948-1973. Illustrations*
More Great Western steam doubleheaded / [compiled by] Colin L. Williams. — Truro : Barton, 1977. — 96p : of ill ; 22cm.
ISBN 0-85153-251-9 : £3.50
(B77-18059)

385'.36'10942 — Railway services. *England. Great Western Railway. Preserved steam locomotives*
Elliott, Richard James. Preserved locomotives of the Great Western Railway / compiled by R.J. Elliott. — [Buckfastleigh] ([Buckfastleigh Station, Devon]) : Dumbleton Hall Preservation Society, 1977. — 36p : ill ; 15cm. — (Preserved locomotives ; 1)
Cover title: Great Western Railway.
ISBN 0-9505827-0-0 Sd : £0.40
(B77-30144)

385'.36'10942 — Railway services. *England. Great Western Railway. Steam locomotives, 1899-1947. Illustrations*
Great Western steam through the years / edited by Tony Fairclough and Alan Wills. — Truro : Barton, 1976. — 96p : chiefly ill ; 22cm.
ISBN 0-85153-286-1 : £3.50
(B77-00160)

385'.36'10942 — Railway services. *England. Great Western Railway. Steam locomotives, 1948-1965. Illustrations*
Great Western steam in action / [compiled by] L.M. Collins. — Truro : Barton.
6. — 1977. — 96p : chiefly ill ; 22cm.
ISBN 0-85153-292-6 : £3.50
(B77-05336)

Great Western steam miscellany / edited by C.L. Williams. — Truro : Barton.
1. — 1977. — 96p : of ill ; 23cm.
ISBN 0-85153-287-x : £3.75
(B77-30145)

385'.36'109422 — Railway services. *Southern England. British Rail. Southern Region. Branch lines. Steam locomotives, 1950-1966. Illustrations*
Southern branch line steam / [compiled by] Tony Fairclough and Alan Wills. — Truro : Barton.
1. — 1976. — 96p : of ill ; 23cm.
ISBN 0-85153-300-0 : £3.50
(B77-06611)

Vol.2. — 1977. — 96p : of ill ; 23cm.
ISBN 0-85153-315-9 : £3.75
(B77-30146)

385'.36'109422 — Railway services. *Southern England. British Rail. Southern Region. Doubleheaded trains. Steam locomotives, 1936-1966. Illustrations*
Southern steam doubleheaded / [compiled by] Tony Fairclough and Alan Wills. — Truro : Barton, 1977. — 96p : of ill ; 23cm.
ISBN 0-85153-291-8 : £3.50
(B77-18060)

385'.36'109422 — Railway services. *Southern England. British Rail. Southern Region. Steam locomotives, 1948-1967. Illustrations*
Southern steam in action / [compiled by] Tony Fairclough and Alan Wills. — Truro : Barton.
3. — 1976. — 96p : of ill ; 22cm.
ISBN 0-85153-290-x : £3.50
(B77-17423)

Southern steam in camera / [compiled by] John Adams and Patrick Whitehouse. — London : I. Allan, 1977. — 64p : chiefly ill ; 24cm.
ISBN 0-7110-0811-6 : £1.95
(B77-22509)

385'.36'109422 — Railway services. *Southern England. Southern Railway. Maunsell Mogul locomotives, to ca 1950*
Rowledge, John Westbury Peter. The Maunsell Moguls / [by] J.W.P. Rowledge. — Blandford : Oakwood Press, 1976. — 64p : ill ; 22cm. — (Locomotion papers ; no.99 ISSN 0305-5493)
ISBN 0-85361-199-8 Sd : £1.50
(B77-07266)

385'.36'109422 — Railway services. *Southern England. Southern Railway. Steam locomotives, 1919-1939. Illustrations*
Casserley, Henry Cyril. Recollections of the Southern between the wars / [by] H.C. Casserley. — Truro : Barton, 1976. — 96p : of ill, port ; 23cm.
Ill. on lining papers.
ISBN 0-85153-278-0 : £3.50
(B77-00717)

385'.36'109422 — Railway services. *Southern England. Southern Railway. Steam locomotives, 1923-1966. Illustrations*
Southern trains. — London : Allan, [1977]. — 80p : of ill ; 25cm.
ISBN 0-7110-0692-x : £1.50
(B77-18061)

385'.36'109422 — Railway services. *Southern England. Southern Railway. Steam locomotives, to 1968. Illustrations*
Southern steam locomotive survey. — Truro : Barton. — (Southern steam series)
The Drummond classes / edited by Tony Fairclough & Alan Wills. — 1977. — 96p : ill, port ; 23cm.
ISBN 0-85153-276-4 : £3.75
(B77-30147)

385'.36'109424 — Steam locomotives. *England. North Midlands, 1867-1957. Illustrations*
Steam in the north Midlands / [compiled by] Brian Hinchliffe ; [photographs by Ken Boulter et al.]. — Sheffield (745 Abbeydale Rd, Sheffield) : Turntable Publications, 1976. — 96p : of ill, map ; 23cm.
ISBN 0-902844-34-2 : £3.50
(B77-04724)

385'.36'109427 — Railway services. *Northern England. British Rail. Steam locomotives, 1958-1968. Illustrations*
Gifford, Colin Telfer. Steam finale north / [by] Colin T. Gifford. — London : Allan, 1976. — 96p : chiefly ill, facsim, 2 maps(on lining papers) ; 29cm.
ISBN 0-7110-0737-3 : £3.50
(B77-02219)

385'.36'109428 — Steam locomotives. *England. Pennines, ca 1950-1960. Illustrations*
Field, Kenneth. Pennine steam / [by] Kenneth Field & Brian Stephenson. — London : I. Allan, 1977. — 128p : of ill ; 24cm.
ISBN 0-7110-0793-4 : £3.25
(B77-23320)

385'.36'10944 — Steam locomotives. *France, 1945-1972. Illustrations*
Last steam locomotives of France / [compiled by] Yves Broncard ; [text by Bernard Collardey, Jacques Renaud ; photographs by Yves Broncard et al.]. — London : I. Allan, 1977. — 192p : chiefly ill, maps ; 30cm.
ISBN 0-7110-0724-1 : £5.95
(B77-24139)

385'.36'109821 — Railway services. *Southern Argentina. Ferrocarril General Roca. British steam locomotives, 1924-1967*
Purdom, D S. British steam on the pampas : the locomotives of the Buenos Aires Great Southern Railway / [by] D.S. Purdom ; for[e]word by Andrew B. Henderson. — London [etc.] : Mechanical Engineering Publications, 1977. — [9],118p,[16]p of plates : ill, maps ; 26cm.
Index.
ISBN 0-85298-353-0 : £4.95
(B77-29341)

385'.36'109931 — Steam locomotives. *New Zealand, 1864-1951*
Stewart, W W. When steam was king / [by] W.W. Stewart. — Wellington [etc.] ; London : A.H. and A.W. Reed, 1974. — 144p : ill(some col), facsims, map, ports ; 29cm.
Ill. on lining papers. — Originally published: 1970. — Bibl.: p.143.
ISBN 0-589-00382-8 : £11.25
(B77-01329)

385'.36'30904 — Electric locomotives, to 1976. *Illustrations*
Electric locomotives of the world / [compiled by] F.J.G. Haut. — Truro : Barton, 1977. — 96p : chiefly ill ; 23cm.
ISBN 0-85153-256-x : £3.95
(B77-30148)

385'.36'309422 — Railway services. *Southern England. British Rail. Southern Region. Rolling stock: Electric multiple units, to 1970. Illustrations*
Southern electric album / [compiled by] Alan Williams. — London : I. Allan, 1977. — 2-91p : chiefly ill ; 25cm.
Ill. on lining papers.
ISBN 0-7110-0806-x : £2.75
(B77-32576)

385'.36'60941 — Railway services. *Great Britain. British Rail. Doubleheaded trains. Diesel locomotives, 1957-1976. Illustrations*
BR diesels doubleheaded / [compiled by] G. Weekes. — Truro : Barton, 1977. — 96p : of ill ; 22cm.
ISBN 0-85153-301-9 : £3.50
(B77-18062)

385'.36'620941 — Railway services. *Great Britaih. British Rail. Deltic class diesel-electric locomotives. Essays*
The Deltics : a symposium / [by] Cecil J. Allen ... [et al.]. — 2nd ed. — London : Allan, 1977. — 79p,[24]p of plates : ill, plans ; 23cm.
Previous ed.: Shepperton : Allan, 1972.
ISBN 0-7110-0799-3 : £1.95
(B77-18690)

385'.36'62094115 — Railway services. *Scotland. Highlands. British Rail. Diesel-electric locomotives, ca 1955-1975*
BR diesels in the Highlands / [compiled by] G. Weekes. — Truro : Barton, 1976. — 96p : of ill ; 22cm.
Spine title: Diesels in the Highlands.
ISBN 0-85153-241-1 : £3.50
(B77-06612)

385'.36'640942 — Railway services. *England. British Rail. Western Region. Western class diesel-hydraulic locomotives, to 1975*
'Western' Locomotive Association. The Western Region Class 52s / ['Western' Locomotive Association and Diesel and Electric Group] ; written by Michael Oakley. — Bolton (99 Aintree Rd, Little Lever, Bolton BL3 1ES) : 'Western' Locomotive Association ; Sutton Coldfield : Diesel and Electric Group, 1976. — 24p : ill, map ; 30cm.
Sd : Unpriced
(B77-32577)

385'.5 — Coal industries. Industrial railway services. *Dyfed. South Pembrokeshire (District). Saundersfoot Railway, to 1939*
Price, Martin Randall Connop. The Saundersfoot Railway / [by] M.R.C. Price. — [1st ed. reprinted] ; [with a postscript]. — Lingfield [i.e. Blandford] : Oakwood Press, 1964 [i.e. 1976]. — 22p,[8]p of plates : ill, maps ; 21cm. — (Locomotion papers ; no.28 ISSN 0305-5493)
First ed. originally published: Lingfield : Oakwood Press, 1964. — Bibl.: p.21.
ISBN 0-85361-189-0 Sd : £0.75
(B77-04725)

385'.5 — Coal industries. Industrial railway services. Steam locomotives. *Great Britain, ca 1970-1976. Illustrations*
Heavyside, G T. Steam in the coalfields / [by] G.T. Heavyside. — Newton Abbot [etc.] : David and Charles, 1977. — 96p : chiefly ill, maps ; 26cm.
ISBN 0-7153-7323-4 : £3.95
(B77-19307)

385'.5 — Industrial railway services. Locomotives. *Durham (County)*
Mountford, Colin Edwin. Industrial locomotives of Durham / compiled by Colin E. Mountford and L.G. Charlton. — Market Harborough : Industrial Railway Society ; London (47 Waverley Gardens, NW10 7EE) : Distributed by IRS Publications, 1977. — [5],vii,403p,leaf of plate,[72]p of plates : ill, maps ; 21cm. — (Industrial Railway Society. Handbook series ; L)
Index.
ISBN 0-901096-30-x Pbk : Unpriced
ISBN 0-901096-31-8 Pbk : Unpriced
(B77-30149)

385'.5 — Industrial railway services. Locomotives. *South-west England*
Industrial locomotives of South Western England / compiled by Roger Hateley. — Greenford : Industrial Railway Society ; Greenford (44 Hicks Ave., Greenford, Middx) : Distributed by IRS Publications, 1977. — xxx, H135[i.e.164]p,[32]p of plates : ill, maps ; 21cm. — (Industrial Railway Society. Handbook series ; H)
Index.
ISBN 0-901096-23-7 Pbk : Unpriced
(B77-24856)

385'.5 — Municipal engineering. Industrial railway services. *Surrey. Sunbury-on-Thames. Metropolitan Water Board Light Railway, to ca 1940*
Heselton, Kenneth Yeaman. Sunbury and the Metropolitan Water Board Light Railway / [by] Kenneth Y. Heselton. — Sunbury-on-Thames (12 Heathcroft Ave., Sunbury-on-Thames, [Middx]) : Sunbury and Shepperton Local History Society, 1976. — [8] p, plate : map ; 30cm. — (Sunbury and Shepperton Local History Society. Occasional publications ; no.1 ISSN 0309-2070)
Bibl.: p.[8].
ISBN 0-905178-02-5 Sd : £0.10
(B77-06013)

385'.5'094196 — Narrow gauge railway services. *Kerry (County). Tralee and Dingle Railway, 1893-1953. Illustrations*
The **Tralee** & Dingle Railway / [compiled] by David G. Rowlands ; with drawings by David Pinniger. — Truro : Barton, 1977. — 96p : ill, facsims, map, plans ; 23cm.
Bibl.: p.96.
ISBN 0-85153-267-5 : £3.95
(B77-31820)

385'.5'09422395 — Narrow gauge railway services. *Kent. Shepway (District). Romney, Hythe and Dymchurch Light Railway, 1927. Guidebooks. Facsimiles*
The **Romney,** Hythe & Dymchurch Railway. — New Romney ([c/o C.S. Wolfe, 6 Quadrant Rd, Thornton Heath, Surrey CR4 7DA]) : The Romney, Hythe and Dymchurch Railway Association, 1977. — [2],26p : ill, map ; 14x22cm.
Facsimile reprint of: 1st ed. London : Locomotive Publishing, 1927.
Sd : £0.50
(B77-29342)

385'.5'0942459 — Light railway services. *Salop. Bridgnorth (District). Cleobury Mortimer and Ditton Priors Light Railway, to 1965*
Price, Martin Randall Connop. The Cleobury Mortimer and Ditton Priors Light Railway / [by] M.R.C. Price. — Blandford : Oakwood Press, [1977]. — 32,[1]p,[8]p of plates : ill, map, plans ; 22cm. — (Locomotion papers ; no.21 ISSN 0305-5493)
Originally published: Lingfield : Oakwood Press, 1963. — Bibl.: p.32.
ISBN 0-85361-069-x Sd : £1.20
(B77-11177)

385'.5'0942817 — Railway services. *West Yorkshire (Metropolitan County). Bradford (District). Keighley and Worth Valley Railway. Preserved rolling stock*
Keighley and Worth Valley Railway stockbook. — 5th ed. / compiled by Robin Lush and Ian Holt. — Keighley (Haworth Station, Keighley, W. Yorkshire BD22 8NJ) : Keighley and Worth Valley Railway Preservation Society, 1976. — 64p : ill(incl 2 col) ; 21cm.
Cover title: Worth Valley Railway stockbook. — Previous ed.: / compiled by Robin Lush, John Holroyd and Gavin Morrison. 1973. — Index.
ISBN 0-902438-17-4 Sd : £0.60
(B77-08330)

385'.5'0942929 — Narrow gauge railway services. *Gwynedd. Ffestiniog Railway, to 1976. Juvenile literature*
Schofield, Roy. The story of Merddin Emrys and the Festiniog Railway / [pictures by Roy Schofield and story by Joe Martin]. — Cheam (39 Northey Ave., Cheam, Surrey) : Travel About Books, 1977. — [32]p : ill(some col), map ; 15cm.
ISBN 0-905810-00-7 Sd : £0.40
(B77-31112)

385'.5'0942951 — Narrow gauge railway services. *Powys. Montgomery (District). Welshpool and Llanfair Railway, 1901-1974. Illustrations*
The **Welshpool** & Llanfair Light Railway in pictures. — [Llanfair Caereinion] ([The Station, Llanfair Caereinion, Welshpool, Powys]) : Welshpool and Llanfair Light Railway Preservation Company Ltd, 1975. — 18,[2]p : chiefly ill, map ; 25cm.
Sd : Unpriced
(B77-31821)

386 — INLAND WATERWAYS TRANSPORT, FERRY TRANSPORT

386'.06'141 — Inland waterways. Organisations. *Great Britain. British Waterways Board. Reports, surveys. Serials*
British Waterways Board. Annual report and accounts ... / British Waterways Board. — London : The Board : Distributed by H.M.S.O.

1976. — 1977. — x,75p,leaf,[8]p of plates : ill(some col), ports ; 25cm.
ISBN 0-903218-16-x Pbk : £1.40
ISSN 0068-2683
(B77-18691)

386'.09424'1 — Inland waterways. *Gloucestershire, to 1976. Documents*
Gloucestershire waterways / [compiled by P.A. Howard and B.S. Smith]. — [Gloucester] ([Shire Hall, Gloucester]) : Gloucestershire Record Office, 1977. — x,30p : ill, facsims, maps ; 30cm. — (A 'SIGNAL' teaching aid)
Cover title.
Pbk : £1.25
(B77-31822)

386'.22'340941 — Passenger transport. Shipping: Ferry boats. Fleets. *Great Britain. Lists*
Clegg, William Paul. European ferry fleets / by W. Paul Clegg. — [2nd ed.]. — Deal (95 Beach St., Deal, Kent [CT14 6NY]) : Marinart Ltd, 1976. — 73p : ill ; 16cm. — (Pocket book series : second series)
Previous ed.: 1974.
ISBN 0-904478-10-6 Sd : £1.20
(B77-16317)

386'.32'062422323 — Kent. Medway River. Maintenance. Organisations: Medway Navigation Company, to 1910
Hilton, John Anthony. A history of the Medway Navigation Company / compiled from various sources by John Hilton. — Hadlow ([19 Lonewood Way, Hadlow, Tonbridge, Kent]) : The author, [1977]. — [1],36p : facsims, maps ; 21cm. — (Tonbridge tales)
ISBN 0-900465-10-7 Sd : £0.60
(B77-15791)

386'.4042'40924 — Canals. Freight transport. *England. Midlands, 1941. Personal observations*
Smith, Emma, *b.1923.* Maidens' trip / [by] Emma Smith. — Large print ed. — Bath : Chivers, 1977. — [7],336p ; 23cm.
Originally published: London : Putnam, 1948.
ISBN 0-85997-254-2 : £5.20(£3.90 to members of the Library Association)
(B77-25540)

386'.46'0941 — Broad canals. *Great Britain*
Gagg, John. Broad canals / [by] John Gagg. — Princes Risborough (Shootacre House, Princes Risborough, Bucks.) : The author, 1977. — 32p : ill, map ; 21cm. — (Looking at inland waterways)
ISBN 0-9504226-5-7 Sd : £0.50
(B77-21065)

386'.46'0941 — Canals. *Great Britain*
Gagg, John. Canals in a nutshell / [by] John Gagg. — Princes Risborough (Shootacre House, Princes Risborough, Aylesbury, Bucks. HP17 9NN) : The author, 1977. — 33p : ill, map ; 21cm. — (Looking at inland waterways)
ISBN 0-9504226-4-9 Sd : £0.50
(B77-18063)

386'.46'0941 — Canals. *Great Britain, to 1976*
Ransom, Philip John Greer. Your book of canals / [by] P.J.G. Ransom. — London : Faber, 1977. — 3-80p : ill, maps ; 16x22cm. — (The your book series)
Bibl.: p.75. — Index.
ISBN 0-571-10971-3 : £2.35 : CIP rev.
(B77-08331)

386'.46'09411 — Canals. *Scotland, 1700-1900. Secondary school texts*
Donnachie, Ian Lowe. Roads and canals, 1700-1900 / [by] Ian Donnachie. — Edinburgh : Holmes-McDougall, 1977. — 48p : ill, facsims, maps, ports ; 25cm. — (Scottish search series)
Bibl.: p.48.
ISBN 0-7157-1475-9 Sd : £1.05
Primary classification 388.1'09411
(B77-12979)

386'.46'0942 — Canals. *England. Juvenile literature*
Rice, Peter. Narrow boats / by Peter Rice ; illustrated by the author. — Cambridge : Dinosaur Publications for the National Trust, 1976. — [31]p : chiefly col ill, col map ; 23cm. — (National Trust. Picture books)
ISBN 0-85122-121-1 Sd : £0.45
(B77-00718)

386'.46'0971 — Canals. *Canada, to 1974*
Legget, Robert Ferguson. Canals of Canada / by Robert F. Legget. — Vancouver : Douglas, David and Charles ; Newton Abbot : David and Charles, 1976. — x,261p : ill, maps ; 23cm. — (Canals of the world)
Bibl.: p.244. — Index.
ISBN 0-7153-7195-9 : £6.50
(B77-06014)

386'.48 — Canals controlled by British Waterways Board: Remainder waterways. Upgrading. *England. Proposals*
Inland Waterways Amenity Advisory Council. Upgrading of remainder waterways : a report to the Secretary of State for the Environment / [Inland Waterways Amenity Advisory Council]. — [London] ([122 Cleveland St., W1P 5DN]) : The Council, 1974. — [5],9 leaves ; 30cm.
Sp : £0.30
(B77-26993)

386'.48 — Canals controlled by British Waterways Board. Water supply. Shortages. *Great Britain, 1973-1974. Reports, surveys*
Inland Waterways Amenity Advisory Council. Water shortages on British Waterways Board system : a report to the Secretary of State for the Environment / [Inland Waterways Amenity Advisory Council]. — [London] ([122 Cleveland St., W1P 5DN]) : The Council, 1974. — [3],6 leaves ; 30cm.
Sp : Unpriced
(B77-26994)

386'.48'0941436 — Canals. *Scotland. Strathclyde Region. Strathkelvin (District). Forth and Clyde Canal, to 1963*
Martin, Don. The Forth & Clyde canal : Kirkintilloch view / [by Don Martin]. — [Glasgow] ([District Library HQ, 170 Kirkintilloch Rd, Bishopbriggs, Glasgow G64]) : Strathkelvin District Libraries and Museums, 1977. — 32,[1]p : ill, facsims, map, port ; 21cm. — (Auld Kirk Museum. Publications ; no.3)
Bibl.: p.32.
ISBN 0-904966-03-8 Sd : Unpriced
(B77-32578)

386'.48'09424 — Canals. *England. Midlands. Oxford Canal, to 1975*
Compton, Hugh J. The Oxford Canal / [by] Hugh J. Compton. — Newton Abbot [etc.] : David and Charles, 1976. — 171p : ill, facsims, form, maps, plans ; 23cm. — (Inland waterways histories)
Bibl.: p.162-163. — Index.
ISBN 0-7153-7238-6 : £3.95
(B77-17424)

386'.48'09427 — Canals. *Northern England. Leeds and Liverpool Canal. Illustrations*
Lyons, David C. The Leeds & Liverpool Canal : a photographic journey / [text and photographs by David C. Lyons]. — Nelson : Hendon Publishing Co., 1977. — [66]p : chiefly ill, 3 maps ; 19x25cm.
Cover title.
ISBN 0-86067-024-4 Pbk : £1.80
(B77-33170)

386'.48'09427 — Canals. *North-west England. Ellesmere Canal, to 1963*
Wilson, E A. The Ellesmere and Llangollen Canal : an historical background / by E.A. Wilson. — Chichester : Phillimore, 1975. — xii, 148p(2 fold),[16]p of plates : ill, maps, plan ; 23cm.
Bibl.: p.140-141. — Index.
ISBN 0-85033-109-9 : £3.50
(B77-02220)

386'.48'0942719 — Canals. *North-west England. Bridgewater Canal*
The **Bridgewater** Canal handbook. — [New ed.]. — London : Burrow, [1977]. — 84p : ill, facsims, col map, port ; 22cm.
Pbk : Unpriced
(B77-22510)

386'.48'09429 — Canals. *Wales*
Wright, Ian L. Canals in Wales / [by] Ian L. Wright. — Truro : Barton, 1977. — 96p : chiefly ill, facsims, 2 maps, ports ; 23cm.
ISBN 0-85153-314-0 : £3.95
(B77-29343)

386'.6'06542413 — Ferry services. *England. Severn Estuary. Old Passage Severn Ferry Company, to 1967*
Jordan, Christopher. Severn enterprise : the story of the old and new passage ferries / [by] Christopher Jordan. — Ilfracombe : Stockwell, 1977. — 112p,[32]p of plates : ill, 4 facsims, map, plans(on lining papers), ports ; 22cm.
Bibl.: p.106-107.
ISBN 0-7223-0967-8 : £3.00
(B77-23321)

386'.6'094131 — Queensferry-North Queensferry ferry services. *Scotland. Firth of Forth, to 1964*
Brodie, Ian. Queensferry Passage / Ian Brodie author. — Edinburgh (c/o Hon. Sec. Patrick Cadell, 11a Tippertinn Rd, Edinburgh EH10 5ET) : West Lothian History and Amenity Society, 1976. — [4],25p : ill, chart ; 21cm.
Bibl.: p.24.
ISBN 0-9504721-1-5 Sd : £0.60
(B77-14671)

386'.6'09481 — Ferry services. *Norway. Reports, surveys*
Highlands and Islands Development Board. *Policy and Research Division.* The Norse way : a study of Norwegian ferry operations / [Highlands and Islands Development Board, Policy and Research Division]. — [Inverness] : [The Board], 1977. — [5],16p,[9]leaves : map ; 30cm. — (Transport research paper ; 1 ISSN 0309-8818)
Pbk : Unpriced
(B77-30150)

386'.6'09944 — Ferry services. *New South Wales. Sydney, to 1974*
Andrews, Graeme. The ferries of Sydney / [by] Graeme Andrews. — Sydney [etc.] ; London : A.H. and A.W. Reed, 1976. — 128p,[4]p of plates : ill(some col), col map(on lining papers) ; 19x27cm.
Originally published: Sydney : A.H. & A.W. Reed, 1975. — Bibl.: p.128. — Index.
ISBN 0-589-07172-6 Pbk : £6.00
(B77-20182)

386'.8'0942998 — Gwent. Port of Chepstow, to 1882
Waters, Ivor. The port of Chepstow / by Ivor Waters. — Chepstow ([c/o Hon. Secretary, Wyebank Close, Tutshill, Chepstow, Gwent NP6 7ET]) : The Chepstow Society, 1977. — 43p,16p of plates : ill, maps ; 22cm. — (Chepstow Society. Pamphlet series ; no.30)
Bibl.: p.41-43.
ISBN 0-900278-37-4 Sd : £1.25
(B77-23322)

387 — SHIPPING
Branch, Alan Edward. The elements of shipping / [by] Alan E. Branch. — 4th ed. — London : Chapman and Hall, 1977. — xv, 238p : ill, plans ; 22cm.
Previous ed.: 1975. — Index.
ISBN 0-412-15080-8 Pbk : £3.95
(B77-16318)

387 — Shipping. Regulation. *Proposals*
Inter-Governmental Maritime Consultative Organization. *Assembly, 5th Extraordinary Session, London, 1974.* Resolutions and other decisions (resolutions 315-370) : Fifth Extraordinary Session, 16-18 October 1974 and Ninth Session, 3-14 November 1975 / [Inter-Governmental Maritime Consultative Organization] Assembly. — London : Inter-Governmental Maritime Consultative Organization, 1976. — 281p : ill, forms ; 30cm.
Pbk : £3.65
(B77-05337)

387'.021'2 — Shipping. *Statistics*
World shipping statistics / prepared by the Research Division, H.P. Drewry (Shipping Consultants) Limited. — London (34 Brook St., W1Y 2LL) : H.P. Drewry (Shipping Consultants) Limited.
1976. — 1977. — [1],74p : ill(chiefly col) ; 32cm.
Sp : £30.00
(B77-23323)

387'.025 — Shipping. *Directories*
Directory of shipowners, shipbuilders & marine engineers. — London : IPC Industrial Press [for] 'Marine Week'.
1977 : seventy-fifth year of publication. — 1977. — 1386,3-58,xl p : ill ; 22cm.
Tab indexed. — Index.
£15.00
(B77-14181)

International shipping and shipbuilding directory. — London : Benn Bros.
1977 : eighty-ninth ed. / editor Richard Daykin ... — 1977. — 8,892,[24]p : ill ; 29cm.
Tab indexed. — Index.
ISBN 0-510-49710-1 : £23.00
(B77-26255)

387'.025'41 — Shipping. *Great Britain. Directories*
United Kingdom shipping / [Data Research Group]. — Amersham (Hill House, [Hill Ave.], Amersham, Bucks.) : The Group.
[1976]. — 1976. — 200 leaves in various pagings ; 30cm.
ISBN 0-905570-68-5 Pbk : £17.00
Primary classification 338.4'7'62382002541
(B77-06536)

387′.05 — Shipping. *Serials*
Nautical review : joint Nautical Institute and Lloyd's of London Press publication. — London : Lloyd's of London.
Vol.1, no.1- ; Mar.-Apr. 1977-. — 1977-. — ill, ports ; 30cm.
Six issues a year. — 94p. in 1st issue.
Sd : £1.00
ISSN 0309-6254
(B77-17425)

387′.05 — Shipping. *Yearbooks*
The **'Financial** times' world shipping year book. — London : 'Financial Times'.
1977 / editor David J. Sanders. — 1976. — 3-634p : ill(incl 1 col) ; 22cm.
'In association with "Fairplay International Shipping Weekly"'. — Text on lining papers. — Index.
ISBN 0-900671-76-9 : £14.00
(B77-07882)

Lloyd's calendar. — London (Lime St., EC3M 7HA) : Lloyd's of London Press Ltd.
1977. — 1977. — xx,610p : ill, forms, map ; 21cm.
Index.
ISBN 0-904093-22-0 : £4.50
ISSN 0076-0196
(B77-04091)

387′.06′11 — Inter-Governmental Maritime Consultative Organization. *Periodicals*
Inter-Governmental Maritime Consultative Organization. IMCO news. — London : I.M.C.O.
Also published: in French.
No.1- ; [May/June] 1977-. — [1977]-. — ill(some col), col maps, ports ; 30cm.
Six issues a year. — 12p. in 2nd issue.
Sd : Unpriced
ISSN 0140-6434
(B77-33735)

387′.09 — Shipping, to ca 1850
A **history** of seafaring based on underwater archaeology / edited by George F. Bass. — London : Omega, 1974. — 320p : ill(some col), facsim, maps, plans ; 27cm.
Originally published: London : Thames and Hudson, 1972. — Bibl.: p.307-311. — Index.
ISBN 0-86007-705-5 Pbk : £2.95
(B77-09651)

387′.0941 — Shipping. *Great Britain. Statistics*
British shipping statistics / General Council of British Shipping. — [London] ([30 St Mary Axe, E.C.3]) : [The Council].
1975. — [1976]. — 116p : ill ; 30cm.
Cover title. — Previously issued by the Chamber of Shipping of the United Kingdom.
ISBN 0-905883-00-4 Pbk : Unpriced
(B77-05338)

387′.094112′7 — Shipping. *Scotland. Tayside Region. Dundee. Coastal waters, 1797-1966*
Perkins, John, *b.1944.* Sagas of the sea : tales of Dundee's maritime past / compiled by John Perkins. — [Dundee] ([Albert Sq., Dundee DD1 1DA]) : City of Dundee District Council, Civic Amenities Division, Museums and Art Galleries Department, 1976. — [2],53p : ill, facsims, maps, ports ; 30cm.
Sd : £0.80
(B77-11178)

387′.09423 — Shipping. *Western England. Coastal waters, 1850-1950*
Stammers, M K. West coast shipping / [by] M.K. Stammers. — Aylesbury : Shire Publications, 1976. — 88p : ill, ports ; 21cm. — (History in camera)
Bibl.: p.86. — Index.
ISBN 0-85263-361-0 Pbk : £1.50
(B77-11749)

387′.09429′2 — Shipping. *Gwynedd, ca 1800-1913*
Ships & seamen of Gwynedd / [Gwynedd Archives Service] ; [compilation and text by] Aled Eames. — [Caernarfon] ([County Offices, Caernarfon, Gwynedd]) : The Service, 1976. — [44]p : of ill, facsims, ports ; 21cm.
A selection of photographs from Gwynedd Archives Service's travelling exhibition 'Ships and seamen of Gwynedd'.
ISBN 0-901337-12-9 Sd : £1.00
(B77-26995)

387′.099312′2 — Shipping. *New Zealand. Auckland Harbour, 1927-1974*
Jackson, Gainor Wilmott. Reflections on Auckland Harbour / [by] Gainor W. Jackson. — Auckland ; London : Collins, 1975. — 96p(2 fold) : ill(some col), map(on lining papers) ; 29cm.
Unpriced
(B77-24140)

387.1 — Ports. *Juvenile literature*
Connell, Stephanie. Ports and ships / written by Stephanie Connell and Vivienne Driscoll. — London : Macdonald Educational, 1977. — [1], 32p : col ill ; 18cm. — (Readabout)
Adaptation of: 'Ports and harbours'. London : Macdonald and Co., 1972. — Index.
ISBN 0-356-05544-2 Sd : £0.35
(B77-12975)

387.1′025 — Ports. *Directories*
Ports of the world. — London : Benn Bros.
1977 : 30th ed. / editor Richard Daykin ; deputy editor John Riethmuller. — [1976]. — 14,[14],923p : ill ; 30cm.
Tab indexed. — Index.
ISBN 0-510-49152-9 : £25.00
(B77-02910)

387.1′06′141 — Ports. Organisations. *Great Britain. National Ports Council. Reports, surveys. Serials*
National Ports Council. Annual report and statement of accounts / National Ports Council. — London : The Council.
1976. — [1977]. — vii,53p,[4]p of plates : ill ; 25cm.
ISBN 0-86073-004-2 Sd : £0.75
ISSN 0072-6974
(B77-18692)

387.1′0941 — Ports. *Great Britain. Statistics*
Annual digest of port statistics / [National Ports Council]. — London : The Council.
1975. Vol.2. — [1976]. — p145-268 ; 29cm.
Index.
ISBN 0-901058-96-3 Pbk : £10.00
ISSN 0305-3156
(B77-08963)

Quarterly bulletin of port statistics. — London : Economics and Statistics Division, National Ports Council.
Quarter 1- ; [Sept?] 1976-. — 1976-. — 30cm.
Twenty-six leaves in 1st issue.
Sp : £6.00
ISSN 0308-7409
(B77-00161)

387.1′09414′23 — Scotland. Strathclyde Region. Bute. Rothesay Harbour, 1752-1975
Maclagan, Ian. Rothesay Harbour : an historical survey from 1752 to 1975 / by Ian Maclagan. — [Rothesay] ([c/o The Museum, Stuart St., Rothesay, Buteshire]) : [Buteshire Natural History Society], [1976]. — 106p,[8]p of plates : ill, maps ; 21cm. — (Buteshire Natural History Society. Transactions ; vol.19)
Bibl.: p.106.
ISBN 0-905812-00-x Sd : £1.25
(B77-02911)

387.1′09423′37 — Dorset. Port of Poole. *Guidebooks*
The **port** of Poole : Dorset's principal port. — [New ed.]. — London : Burrow, [1977]. — 56, [2]p(2 fold) : ill, chart ; 19cm.
Sd : Unpriced
(B77-20183)

387.1′09423′93 — Avon. Port of Bristol. *Reports, surveys. Serials*
Port of Bristol Authority. Annual report and accounts, for the year ended 31st March / Port of Bristol Authority. — [Bristol] ([St Andrew's Rd, Avonmouth, Bristol BS11 9DQ]) : [The Authority].
[1975]-1976. — [1976]. — [1],19p : coat of arms ; 30cm.
ISBN 0-902919-04-0 Sd : Unpriced
(B77-04092)

387.1′09423′93 — Avon. Port of Bristol, 1500-1600
Vanes, Jean. The port of Bristol in the sixteenth century / by Jean Vanes. — Bristol (c/o P. Harris, 74 Bell Barn Rd, Stoke Bishop, Bristol [BS9 2DG]) : Bristol Branch of the Historical Association, 1977. — [2],26p,[4]p of plates : 2 facsims, 2 maps ; 22cm. — (Historical Association. Bristol Branch. Local history pamphlets ; 39)
Sd : £0.50
(B77-17426)

387.1′09423′93 — Avon. Port of Bristol, 1914-1918
Neale, Wilfred Groves. The tides of war and the Port of Bristol, 1914-1918 / [by] W.G. Neale. — Bristol ([St Andrews Rd, Avonmouth, Bristol BS11 9DQ]) : Port of Bristol Authority, 1976. — xiii,315,[33]p,plate : ill, facsim, maps, ports ; 28cm.
Index.
ISBN 0-902919-02-4 : £9.50
(B77-10322)

387.1′09426 — Ports. *East Anglia, to 1975*
Wren, Wilfrid John. Ports of the Eastern Counties : the development of harbours on the coast of the Eastern Counties from Boston in Lincolnshire to Rochford in Essex / [by] Wilfrid J. Wren. — Lavenham : Dalton, 1976. — 207p : ill, facsim, maps, plans, ports ; 24cm.
Bibl.: p.196-200. — Index.
ISBN 0-900963-70-0 : £5.40
(B77-03495)

387.1′09426′49 — Suffolk. Port of Ipswich. *Serials*
Ipswich Port Authority. Handbook / Port of Ipswich. — Ipswich (Old Custom House, Key St., Ipswich IP4 1BY) : Ipswich Port Authority.
1977. — [1977]. — [1],xvi,20p : ill, maps ; 23cm.
'Tide table 1977' (fold. sheet) in pocket.
ISBN 0-901029-08-4 Sd : Unpriced
(B77-10323)

387.1′09427′665 — Lancashire. Port of Preston. *Guidebooks*
Official handbook, the port of Preston. — London : Burrow.
1976-7. — [1976]. — 32,[2]p(2 fold) : ill, maps ; 21cm.
ISBN 0-85026-640-8 Sd : Unpriced
(B77-00162)

387.1′09427′87 — Cumbria. Port of Maryport, to 1976
Robinson, Annie. The maritime history of Maryport / compiled by Annie Robinson. — [Carlisle] ([12 Lonsdale St., Carlisle CA1 1DD]) : [Border Press Agency Ltd].
Part 1. — [1977]. — [8],45p : ill, ports ; 21cm.
Sd : £0.50
(B77-30151)

387.1′09428′5 — Ports. *Cleveland. Tees Estuary, 1776-1976*
The **River** Tees, two centuries of change : an album of plans with descriptive notes illustrating the development of the River Tees Estuary into a major port during the past 200 years. — [Middlesbrough] (Victoria Sq., Middlesbrough, Cleveland TS1 2AY]) : Cleveland County Libraries : Cleveland and Teesside Local History Society, [1977]. — 1v. : ill, facsims, chiefly maps(1 col), plans ; 34cm.
Booklet ([12]p.) and 20 sheets(18 fold.) in plastic bag.
ISBN 0-904784-04-5 : £1.65
(B77-12976)

387.1′0973 — Deepwater ports. Environmental aspects. *United States*
Winters, Tobey L. Deepwater ports in the United States : an economic and environmental impact study / [by] Tobey L. Winters. — New York ; London : Praeger, 1977. — xv,201p : ill, map ; 25cm. — (Praeger special studies in US economic, social and political issues)
Bibl.: p.179-195. — Index.
ISBN 0-275-23250-6 : £13.40
(B77-22511)

387.1′0973 — Ports. Policies of government. *United States*
Federal port policy in the United States / [by] Henry S. Marcus ... [et al.]. — Cambridge, Mass. ; London : M.I.T. Press, 1976. — [11], 371p : ill ; 26cm.
Bibl.: p.347-359. — Index.
ISBN 0-262-13125-0 : £15.00
(B77-07267)

387.1′53 — Ports capable of handling large bulk carrying ships. *Reports, surveys*
Drewry (H.P.) (Shipping Consultants) Limited. *Research Division.* Ports and terminals for large bulk carriers / prepared by the Research Division, H.P. Drewry (Shipping Consultants) Limited. — London (1 Argyll St., W1V 1AD) : H.P. Drewry (Shipping Consultants) Ltd, 1976. — [3],114p : maps ; 30cm. — (An economic study ; no.46 ISSN 0307-4919)
ISBN 0-904726-29-0 Sd : £30.00(£100.00 for nos.41-50)
(B77-02912)

387.1′64 — Freight transport. Shipping. Cargoes. Trimming. *Tables*
Griffith, Emrys. Griffith's trimming tables. — 3rd ed. — Glasgow : Brown and Ferguson, 1976. — 49p : ill ; 19cm.
Previous ed.: 1950.
ISBN 0-85174-238-6 Sd : £1.20
(B77-10324)

387.1'64 — Ports. Cargo handling. Accidents. Costs. *Great Britain. Reports, surveys*
Bearham, John. The cost of accidents within the port transport industry : an analysis and comparison of the direct and indirect costs of personal accidents and accidents involving plant and cargo at sample conventional general cargo, roll-on and container berths over one year / by J. Bearham. — London : National Ports Council, 1976. — vi,34p : ill ; 30cm.
ISBN 0-901058-89-0 Sd : £8.00
(B77-00164)

387.1'64 — Ports. Cargo handling. Effects of technological innovation. *California*
Lowndes, Richard. Technological innovation : capital and labour : two case histories of the port industry of California / by Richard Lowndes. — Chadwell Heath : Nelpress, 1977. — [2],ii,39,[2]p ; 22cm. — (Management series ISSN 0309-3794)
Originally published: Romford : Anglian Regional Management Centre, 1976.
Sd : £1.50
(B77-26996)

387.1'66 — Shipping. Pilotage, to 1976. *Juvenile literature*
Martin, Nancy, *b.1899.* Sea and river pilots / by Nancy Martin. — Lavenham : T. Dalton, 1977. — 156p : ill, coat of arms, 2 facsims, form, map(on lining papers), ports ; 24cm.
Bibl.: p.151. — Index.
ISBN 0-900963-72-7 : £4.80
(B77-20184)

387.2 — Boat hire services. *Scotland. Directories*
Boat and yacht charter / Scottish Tourist Board. — Edinburgh : The Board. — (Scottish Tourist Board. Information booklets)
1977. — [1976]. — 20p : 1 ill ; 21x10cm.
Sd : Unpriced
(B77-23324)

387.2 — Harbour craft. Fleets. *Great Britain. Lists*
Richardson, S C E. British harbour craft / by S.C.E. Richardson. — Deal (95 Beach St., Deal, Kent [CT14 6NY]) : Marinart Ltd, 1976. — 64p : ill ; 16cm.
ISBN 0-904478-20-3 Sd : £0.90
(B77-16319)

387.2 — Ships. Scrapping due to obsolescence, 1972-1976
Drewry (H.P.) (Shipping Consultants) Limited. *Research Division.* Ship obsolescence and scrapping / prepared by the Research Division, H.P. Drewry (Shipping Consultants) Limited. — London (34 Brook St., W1Y 2LL) : H.P. Drewry (Shipping Consultants) Limited, 1977. — [3],61p : ill ; 30cm. — (An economic study ; no.51 ISSN 0307-4919)
Sd : £30.00(£115.00 for nos 51-60 inclusive)
(B77-23325)

387.2'021'2 — Merchant ships. *Statistics*
Lloyd's Register of Shipping. Statistical tables / [Lloyd's Register of Shipping]. — London : Lloyd's Register of Shipping.
1976. — 1976. — 73p ; 29cm.
ISBN 0-900528-82-6 Sd : £3.00
(B77-04093)

387.2'021'6 — Merchant ships. *Registers*
Lloyd's Register of Shipping. Register book / Lloyd's Register of Shipping. — London : [Lloyd's Register of Shipping].
1976-77. List of shipowners, index to former names of ships, compound names of ships. — [1976]. — 471,[214]p ; 30cm.
ISBN 0-900528-81-8 : £12.00
ISSN 0305-8425
(B77-01330)

The **mercantile** navy list. — London : H.M.S.O.
1975. Part 1 : Steam and sailing vessels : corrected to 31st December 1975 from official and other sources by the Registrar-General of Shipping and Seamen. — 1976. — 1v. ; 22x28cm.
Pierced for binder. — xxxi,393p. on publication.
ISBN 0-11-511706-7 Ls : £32.00
(B77-00719)

387.2'021'6 — Merchant ships built in 1976. *Lists*
Merchant ships - newbuildings / edited by D.T. Hornsby. — Sandwich : Marinart ; London : Kogan Page, 1977. — 250p : ill, plans ; 22cm.
ISBN 0-904478-30-0 : £6.95
ISBN 0-904478-31-9 Pbk : £3.95
ISBN 0-85038-059-6 (Kogan Page) : £6.95
ISBN 0-85038-069-3 (Kogan Page) Pbk : £3.95
(B77-32579)

387.2'09 — Shipping. Ships, to 1970
Heine, William Colburne. Historic ships of the world / [by] William C. Heine. — Newton Abbot [etc.] : David and Charles, 1977. — 156p : ill(some col), chart, map, ports ; 25cm.
Bibl.: p.152. — Index.
ISBN 0-7153-7410-9 : £5.95
(B77-30152)

387.2'09'04 — Shipping. Ships, 1900-1976
Ships of the twentieth century / [editor Pat Hornsey]. — London : New English Library, 1977. — 160p : ill(chiefly col), 3 maps(2 col), plans, port ; 35cm.
'Much of the material ... appeared originally in the partwork, "History of Ships" ...' - title page verso. — Index.
ISBN 0-450-03462-3 : £4.95
(B77-32580)

387.2'09163'36 — Merchant ships. Fleets. *England. Solent. Lists*
Hornsby, D T. Southampton & Solent shipping / by D.T. Hornsby & N.V. Robinson. — Deal ([95 Beach St., Deal, Kent CT14 6NY]) : Marinart Ltd, 1975. — [1],49p : ill, 2 maps ; 16cm. — (Pocket book series ; 12)
ISBN 0-904478-18-1 Sd : £0.50
(B77-16823)

387.2'09931 — Shipping. Preserved ships. *New Zealand*
Andrews, Graeme. Veteran ships of Australia and New Zealand / [by] Graeme Andrews. — Sydney [etc.] ; London : A.H. and A.W. Reed, 1976. — 136p,[4]p of plates : ill(some col), port ; 20x28cm.
Bibl.: p.134. — Index.
ISBN 0-589-07190-4 : £9.50
Primary classification 387.2'0994
(B77-23326)

387.2'0994 — Shipping. Preserved ships. *Australia*
Andrews, Graeme. Veteran ships of Australia and New Zealand / [by] Graeme Andrews. — Sydney [etc.] ; London : A.H. and A.W. Reed, 1976. — 136p,[4]p of plates : ill(some col), port ; 20x28cm.
Bibl.: p.134. — Index.
ISBN 0-589-07190-4 : £9.50
Also classified at 387.2'09931
(B77-23326)

387.2'2 — Shipping. Merchant sailing ships, ca 1850-ca 1920
The **medley** of mast and sail ... / with an introduction by Frank G.G. Carr. — Brighton (P.O. Box 430, Brighton, Sussex BN1 6GT) : Teredo Books, 1976. — xxii,330p : ill ; 25cm. — (A camera record ; [1])
'... accompanied by comment and description by Frank G.G. Carr ... and others'. — Ill. on lining papers.
ISBN 0-903662-03-5 : £13.80
(B77-03496)

387.2'2 — Shipping. Sail training ships, to 1975
Drummond, Maldwin. Tall ships : the world of sail training / text by Maldwin Drummond ; illustrated by Mike Willoughby ; foreword by the Duke of Edinburgh. — London [etc.] : Angus and Robertson [for] the Sail Training Association, 1976. — 160p : ill(some col) ; 27x36cm.
Ill. on lining papers. — Bibl.: p.158. — Index.
ISBN 0-207-95629-4 : £15.00
(B77-01331)

387.2'2 — Yachts. *Registers*
Lloyd's Register of Shipping. Lloyd's register of yachts. — London : Lloyd's Register of Shipping.
1977 : [90th ed.]. — 1977. — xxviii,1300,[1]p ; 19x23cm.
Previously published: as 'Register of yachts'.
£8.50
ISSN 0306-6207
(B77-17427)

387.2'2'0941 — Shipping. Sailing ships. *Great Britain, 1860-1976*
Simper, Robert. British sail / [by] Robert Simper. — Newton Abbot [etc.] : David and Charles, 1977. — 160p : chiefly ill, map, ports ; 26cm.
Index.
ISBN 0-7153-7263-7 : £7.95
(B77-23327)

387.2'2'09429 — Shipping. Sailing ships. *Wales, to ca 1925*
Campbell-Jones, Susan. Welsh sail : a pictorial history / by Susan Campbell-Jones ; with a foreword by Alun Richards. — Llandysul : Gomer Press, 1976. — 103p : ill, ports ; 23cm.
Bibl.: p.101. — Index.
ISBN 0-85088-353-9 : £2.50
(B77-08964)

387.2'43 — Passenger transport. Shipping: Liners. *North Atlantic Ocean, 1840-1974*
Coleman, Terry. The liners : a history of the North Atlantic crossing / [by] Terry Coleman. — Harmondsworth [etc.] : Penguin, 1977. — 232p : ill(some col), facsims, maps, plans, ports(1 col) ; 25cm.
Originally published: London : Allen Lane, 1976. — Bibl.: p.221-223. — Index.
ISBN 0-14-004398-5 Pbk : £1.95
(B77-27792)

387.2'43'09034 — Passenger transport. Shipping: Ships, 1858-1975. *Illustrations*
Kludas, Arnold. Great passenger ships of the world / [by] Arnold Kludas ; translated [from the German] by Charles Hodges. — Cambridge : Stephens.
In 5 vols. — Translation of 'Die grossen Passagierschiffe der Welt'. Oldenburg : G. Stalling, 1972-.
Vol.3 : 1924-1935. — 1976. — 240p : ill ; 25cm.
Bibl.: p.238. — Index.
ISBN 0-85059-245-3 : £8.95
(B77-08965)

Vol.4 : 1936-1950. — 1977. — 232p : ill ; 25cm.
Bibl.: p.228-229. — Index.
ISBN 0-85059-253-4 : £8.95
(B77-16824)

Vol.5 : 1951-1976. — 1977. — 226p : ill ; 25cm.
Bibl.: p.212. — Index.
ISBN 0-85059-265-8 : £9.95 : CIP rev.
(B77-21816)

387.2'45 — Freight transport. BP Tanker Company ships: Oil tankers. *Study examples: British Respect (Ship) & British Avon (Ship)*
MacLeod, R F. Two ships : the work of the BP Tanker Company seen through two voyages by two vessels plying the international oil trade / by R.F. MacLeod. — London (Britannic House, Moor La., EC2Y 9BR) : The Company, [1977]. — 47p : ill(some col), form, port ; 21cm.
Pbk : Unpriced
(B77-29344)

387.2'45 — Freight transport. Bulk carrying ships. *Registers*
The **bulk** carrier register / compiled ... by H. Clarkson & Company Limited. — London (52 Bishopsgate, EC2P 2AD) : H. Clarkson and Co. Ltd.
1977. — 1977. — xxx,475,[8]p : ill ; 22x32cm.
£30.00
ISSN 0305-0122
(B77-16825)

387.2'45 — Freight transport. Bulk carrying ships. Fleets. *Lists*
Jordan, Roger William. Ocean bulk carrier fleets / by R.W. Jordan. — Deal ([95 Beach St., Deal, Kent CT14 6NY]) : Marinart Ltd, 1976. — [1],73p : ill ; 16cm. — (Pocket book series ; 11)
Originally published: 1975.
ISBN 0-904478-17-3 Sd : £0.90
(B77-16320)

387.2'45 — Freight transport. Bulk carrying ships for transporting liquefied gases. *Registers*
Liquid gas carrier register / compiled ... by H. Clarkson & Company Limited. — London (52 Bishopsgate, EC2P 2AD) : H. Clarkson and Co. Ltd.
1977. — 1977. — 135,[1]p : ill(some col) ; 22x32cm.
£12.00
ISSN 0305-1803
(B77-16826)

387.2'45 — Freight transport. Cargo ships: Coasters. Fleets. *Germany & Netherlands. Lists*
Ridley-Chesterton, D. Dutch & German coaster fleets / by D. Ridley-Chesterton & R.S. Fenton. — Deal (95 Beach St., Deal, Kent CT14 6NY) : Marinart Ltd, 1975. — [1],73p : ill ; 16cm.
ISBN 0-904478-06-8 Sd : £0.90
(B77-16827)

387.2'45 — Freight transport. Cargo ships: Steam coasters. *Scotland. Strathclyde Region. Clyde River, to 1969*
McDonald, Dan. The Clyde puffer / [by] Dan McDonald. — Newton Abbot [etc.] : David and Charles, 1977. — 48p : ill, map, plan ; 26cm.
ISBN 0-7153-7443-5 : £2.95
(B77-24858)

387.2'45 — Freight transport. Ships: Tankers. *Registers*
The **tanker** register / compiled ... by H. Clarkson & Company Limited. — London (52 Bishopsgate, EC2P 2AD) : H. Clarkson and Co. Ltd.
1977. — 1977. — xxx,475,[16]p : ill ; 22x32cm.

£30.00
ISSN 0305-179x
(B77-16828)

387.2'45 — Offshore supply ships. *Registers*
The **offshore** service vessel register / compiled ... by H. Clarkson & Company Limited. — London (52 Bishopsgate, EC2P 2AD) : The Company.
1977. — 1977. — 251p : ill ; 22x32cm.
£30.00
ISSN 0309-040x
(B77-27793)

387.2'45 — Ships: 100000-175000 ton oil tankers. *Statistics. For marketing. Periodicals*
Oil tanker & combined carrier tonnage 100,000-175,000 DWT / E.A. Gibson Shipbrokers Limited. — London (PO Box 278, 61 Holborn Viaduct, EC1P 1HP) : E.A. Gibson Shipbrokers Ltd.
July 1976-. — [1976]-. — col ill ; 30cm.
Four issues a year. — [1],59,[1]p. in 1st issue. — Index.
Sp : £20.00
ISSN 0140-3710
(B77-30153)

387.2'45 — Ships: 70000-175000 ton oil tankers. *Statistics. For marketing*
Drewry (H.P.) (Shipping Consultants) Limited. *Research Division.* The market for medium-sized tankers (70-175,000 DWT) / prepared by the Research Division, H.P. Drewry (Shipping Consultants) Limited. — London (1 Argyll St., W1V 1AD) : H.P. Drewry (Shipping Consultants) Ltd, 1976. — [1],58p : 1 ill ; 30cm. — (An economic study ; no.47 ISSN 0307-4919)
ISBN 0-904726-30-4 Sd : £30.00(£100.00 for nos 41-50 inclusive)
(B77-04726)

387.2'45 — Ships: Large crude carriers. *Statistics. For marketing. Periodicals*
Large crude carriers in excess of 175,000 DWT / E.A. Gibson Shipbrokers. — London (P.O. Box 278, 61 Holborn Viaduct, EC1P 1HP) : E.A. Gibson Shipbrokers Ltd.
1 Jan. 1975-. — [1975]-. — col ill ; 30cm.
Four issues a year. — [1],40,[1]p. in 1st issue. — Index.
Sd : £20.00
ISSN 0140-3702
(B77-30154)

387.5'092'4 — Merchant shipping. *Great Britain, ca 1920. Personal observations*
Lloyd, Jack Ivester. Don't fall off your boat : a salty tale of the sea / [by] Jack Ivester Lloyd. — Kineton : Roundwood Press, 1976. — xii, 159p ; 23cm.
ISBN 0-900093-61-7 : £3.75
(B77-10325)

387.5'0941 — Merchant shipping. Policies of government. Implementation. Responsibility of government departments. *Great Britain*
Great Britain. *Interdepartmental Committee on Marine Safety.* Marine activities : guide to the responsibilities of Government departments and agencies / prepared by the Interdepartmental Committee on Marine Safety under the chairmanship of the Department of Trade. — London : H.M.S.O., 1977. — iii,49p ; 21cm.
Bibl.: p.30-33.
ISBN 0-11-512032-7 Sd : £1.00
Also classified at 338.2'7'280941
(B77-29345)

387.5'0994 — Merchant shipping. *Australia, 1788-1975*
Bach, John. A maritime history of Australia / [by] John Bach. — London : Hamilton, [1977]. — xiv,481p,plate : ill, facsim, map, ports ; 24cm.
Ill. on lining papers. — Originally published: West Melbourne, Vic. : Thomas Nelson (Australia), 1976. — Bibl.: p.443-458. — Index.

ISBN 0-241-89793-9 : £9.50
(B77-29346)

387.5'1 — Freight transport. Shipping. Economic aspects
Advances in maritime economics / edited by R.O. Goss. — Cambridge [etc.] : Cambridge University Press, 1977. — viii,294p : ill ; 24cm.

Index.
ISBN 0-521-21232-4 : £10.50
(B77-21066)

387.5'1 — Freight transport. Shipping. Time charters. *Conference proceedings*
Time Charters, Why the Confusion? *(Conference), London Press Centre, 1977.* 'Time Charters, Why the Confusion?' : a two-day seminar sponsored by F.O.N.A.S.B.A., organised by Lloyd's of London Press Ltd [at] the London Press Centre, March 24-25, 1977. — [London] ([16 Bride La., EC4Y 8EB]) : [Lloyd's of London Press Ltd], [1977]. — 139 leaves in various pagings : forms ; 31cm.
Time charters in plastic pocket.
ISBN 0-904093-32-8 : £1.00
(B77-33736)

387.5'1 — Shipping: Eurocanadian Shipholdings Limited. Mergers with Furness, Withy and Company & Manchester Liners Limited. *Inquiry reports*
Great Britain. *Monopolies and Mergers Commission.* Eurocanadian Shipholdings Limited and Furness, Withy & Company, Limited and Manchester Liners Limited : a report on the existing and proposed mergers ... / the Monopolies and Mergers Commission. — London : H.M.S.O., [1976]. — iv,141p ; 25cm. — (Cmnd.[i.e. 1975-76 H.C.]639)
ISBN 0-10-263976-0 Pbk : £1.80
(B77-11750)

387.5'42'061411 — Passenger transport services. Shipping. Consumer protection services: Transport Users Consultative Committee for Scotland. *Scotland. Reports, surveys. Serials*
Transport Users Consultative Committee for Scotland. Annual report to the Secretary of State for Scotland and Secretary of State for Prices and Consumer Protection ... / Transport Users Consultative Committee for Scotland. — Edinburgh : H.M.S.O.
1976. — [1977]. — 10p ; 25cm. — ([1976-77 H.C.] 120)
ISBN 0-10-212077-3 Sd : £0.25
(B77-11751)

387.5'44 — Freight transport. Shipping. Political aspects. *Conference proceedings*
Trade Ships and Politics *(Conference), New York, 1976.* Trade Ships and Politics : New York Hilton, November 8-9, 1976. — Colchester : Seatrade Publications, [1977]. — 125p ; 30cm. — ('Seatrade' conferences)
Booklet ([7],5p.) 'Exhibits relating to remarks of Nicholas J. Coolidge at "Trade Ships and Politics", Seatrade conference' in pocket.
Pbk : Unpriced
(B77-19308)

387.5'44 — Freight transport. Shipping. Roll on/roll off services. *Conference proceedings*
RoRo 76 *(Conference), London, 1976.* RoRo 76, London Hilton, Park Lane, 6-7 July 1976. — Rickmansworth (2 Station Rd, Rickmansworth, Herts. WD3 1QP) : BML Business Meetings Ltd, 1976. — x,245p : ill, maps, plans, ports ; 30cm.
'International Conference on Marine Transport Using Roll-on/Roll-off Methods, London Hilton, 6-7 July 1976' - cover. — Originally published: in 2 vols. 1976.
ISBN 0-904930-03-3 Pbk : £40.00
(B77-14182)

387.5'44 — Freight transport. Shipping. Roll on/roll off services. Routes. *Directories*
RoRo worldwide : Wilstow's guide to worldwide routes & services. — London (64 Queen St., EC4R 1AD) : Wilstow Ltd.
1976 / editor A.A. Howell. — 1976. — 3-320p : ill, maps, port ; 30cm.
Index.
ISBN 0-905801-00-8 Pbk : £6.50
ISSN 0308-9711
(B77-02221)

387.5'44 — Freight transport. Small bulk carrying ships. Demand. *Forecasts for 1974-1980*
Lambert Brothers Shipping Limited. *Research and Development Department.* Small bulk carriers : supply-demand analysis and forecast : bulk carriers of 18,000-35,000 dwt, 1974-1980 / Lambert Brothers Shipping Ltd [Research and Development Department]. — London (P.O. Box 431, 53 Eastcheap, EC3P 3HL) : The Department, 1976. — [2],ii,59 leaves : 1 ill ; 31cm.
ISBN 0-9504170-3-3 Sp : £75.00
(B77-04094)

387.5'44 — Fuels. International transport by ships: Tankers. *Forecasts for 1975-1985*
Hawdon, David. World transport of energy, 1975 to 1985 / [by] David Hawdon. — London (42 Colebrooke Row, N1 8AF) : Staniland Hall Associates Ltd, 1977. — [3],67[i.e.68]p : ill ; 22x31cm. — (Economic, industrial and market forecasts)
Sp : £70.00
(B77-29347)

387.5'44 — Motor vehicles. Freight transport. Shipping. *Reports, surveys*
Drewry (H.P.) (Shipping Consultants) Limited. *Research Division.* The growth of the car-carrying fleet / prepared by the Research Division, H.P. Drewry (Shipping Consultants) Limited. — London : [HPD Shipping Publications], 1977. — [1],74p ; 30cm. — (An economic study ; no.52 ISSN 0307-4919)
Bibl.: p.6.
Sd : £30.00(£115.00 for nos 51-60 inclusive)
(B77-20185)

387.5'44 — Petroleum. Transport by ships. Role of independently owned oil tankers. *Reports, surveys*
Drewry (H.P.) (Shipping Consultants) Limited. *Research Division.* The role of independent tanker owners / prepared by the Research Division, H.P. Drewry (Shipping Consultants) Limited. — London (1 Argyll St., W1V 1AD) : H.P. Drewry (Shipping Consultants) Limited, 1976. — [6],80p ; 30cm. — (An economic study ; no.49 ISSN 0307-4919)
ISBN 0-904726-31-2 Sd : £30.00(£100.00 for nos 41-50 inclusive)
(B77-11179)

387.5'44'03 — Freight transport. Shipping. *Dictionaries*
Branch, Alan Edward. Dictionary of shipping/international trade terms and abbreviations / by Alan E. Branch. — London : Witherby, 1976. — ix,117p ; 22cm. — (Monument series)
ISBN 0-900886-16-1 Pbk : £3.00
(B77-04727)

387.5'44'0981 — Freight transport. Shipping. *Brazil*
Hayman, Christopher. Brazil / ... by Christopher Hayman. — Colchester [etc.] : Seatrade Publications, 1977. — 84p : ill, col map, ports ; 30cm. — (A 'Seatrade' study)
Sd : Unpriced
(B77-18064)

387.7 — AIR SERVICES
387.7 — Aviation. Social aspects. *Conference proceedings*
Anglo-American Aeronautical Conference, *15th, London, 1977.* The place of aviation in society : 15th Anglo-American Aeronautical Conference, London, 31 May-2 June 1977. — London (4 Hamilton Place, W1V 0BQ) : Royal Aeronautical Society, [1977]. — 421p in various pagings : ill, maps ; 30cm.
Bibl.
Pbk : £15.00
(B77-31823)

387.7'06'141 — Air services. Organisations. *Great Britain. Civil Aviation Authority. Accounts*
Civil Aviation Authority. Accounts : accounts of the Civil Aviation Authority ... for the year ending 31st March, together with the report of the Comptroller and Auditor General thereon ... — London : H.M.S.O.
1976-77. — [1977]. — 33p ; 25cm. — ([1976-77 H.C.] 547)
ISBN 0-10-254777-7 Sd : £0.60
(B77-29348)

387.7'06'141 — Air services. Organisations. *Great Britain. Civil Aviation Authority. Reports, surveys. Serials*
Civil Aviation Authority. Annual report and accounts / Civil Aviation Authority. — London : C.A.A.
1975-76. — 1976. — 88p : ill(some col), maps(chiefly col) ; 30cm.
Bibl.: p.62. — List of films: p.61.
ISBN 0-86039-014-4 Pbk : £3.00
ISSN 0306-3569
(B77-02222)

1976-77. — 1977. — 48p : col ill, col map ; 30cm.
ISBN 0-86039-046-2 Sd : £2.50
ISSN 0306-3569
(B77-31113)

387.7'06'141 — Airlines. *Great Britain. British Airways. Organisation structure. Reports, surveys. Serials*
British Airways. *Board.* Report on organisation / British Airways Board. — London : H.M.S.O.
4th. — [1976]. — 11p ; 25cm. — ([1975-76 H.C.]722)
ISBN 0-10-009316-7 Sd : £0.25
(B77-04095)

387.7'06'541 — Airlines. *Great Britain. British Airways. Reports, surveys. Serials*
British Airways. British Airways annual report and accounts for the year ended 31 March / [British Airways Board]. — [London] (Air Terminal, Victoria, S.W.1) : British Airways Board.
1974. — [1974]. — [1],37,[1]p,[8]p of plates : col ill, col coat of arms, facsims(chiefly col) ; 30cm.
Cover title: Annual report 1973-4.
ISBN 0-900031-04-2 Sd : £1.00
(B77-02913)

1975. — [1975]. — [1],51,[1]p,[4]p of plates : col ill, col coat of arms, facsims(chiefly col) ; 30cm.
ISBN 0-900031-08-5 Sd : £1.00
(B77-02914)

1976. — [1976]. — 52p : col ill, coat of arms ; 30cm.
ISBN 0-900031-09-3 Sd : £1.00
(B77-02915)

387.7'0941 — Civil aviation. *Great Britain. Statistics*
Civil Aviation Authority. CAA annual statistics. — Cheltenham : The Authority.
1974 and 1975. — 1976. — vii,137,[3]p(88 fold) : forms ; 30cm. — (CAP 386)
ISBN 0-86039-012-8 Pbk : £10.00
(B77-08332)

1976. — 1977. — vi,111p ; 30cm. — (CAP 406)
ISBN 0-86039-047-0 Pbk : £10.00
(B77-31114)

387.7'0941 — Independent airlines. *Great Britain, 1946-1975*
Jones, A C Merton. British independent airlines since 1946 / by A.C. Merton Jones. — Uxbridge (21 Barchester Close, Uxbridge UB8 2JY) : LAAS International ; Liverpool : Merseyside Aviation Society Ltd.
In 4 vols.
Vol.3 : Irish Air Charter to Sagittair. — 1976. — p241-372 : ill ; 30cm.
ISBN 0-902420-09-7 Sd : £2.50
(B77-16321)

387.7'1 — Airlines. *Great Britain. Accounts*
Financial results, United Kingdom airlines / [Civil Aviation Authority]. — London : C.A.A.
1968-1974. — 1975. — v,45p(12 fold) : forms ; 30cm. — (CAP 376)
ISBN 0-903083-77-9 Sd : £4.25
(B77-01332)

387.7'33'0904 — Air services. Aircraft. *History. Serials*
Aircraft annual. — London : Allan.
1977 / edited by Philip J.R. Moyes. — 1976. — [1],129p : ill(some col), ports(some col) ; 25cm.
Ill. on lining papers.
ISBN 0-7110-0721-7 : £2.75
(B77-02916)

Aircraft annual. — London : I. Allan.
1978 / edited by E.L. Cornwell. — 1977. — [2] ,130p : ill(some col), ports ; 25cm.
Ill. on lining papers.
ISBN 0-7110-0815-9 : £2.75
(B77-31824)

387.7'33'40423 — Civil aircraft. *Austria, Benelux countries & Switzerland. Registers*
The **Benelux,** Swiss and Austrian civil registers. — Saffron Walden : Air-Britain.
1975 / co-ordinating editor D. Partington. — 1975. — 72p,[8]p of plates : ill ; 24cm.
ISBN 0-85130-042-1 Sd : Unpriced
(B77-19309)

387.7'33'40423 — Civil aircraft. *France. Registers*
Civil aircraft registers of France. — Saffron Walden : Air-Britain.
1975 / edited by D. Partington, in collaboration with ... [others]. — 1975. — 110p,[4]p of plates, leaf of plate : ill, map ; 24cm.
ISBN 0-85130-041-3 Sd : Unpriced
(B77-18693)

387.7'33'40423 — Civil aircraft. Markings. *Lists. Serials*
Civil aircraft markings. — London : Allan.
1977 : twenty-seventh ed. / [edited by] John W.R. Taylor. — 1977. — 168p : ill ; 19cm.
ISBN 0-7110-0750-0 Pbk : £0.65
(B77-12402)

387.7'33'4097281 — Civil aeroplanes. *Guatemala. Registers*
Registers of Guatemala and Belize / edited by I.P. Burnett. — Hornchurch (9 Rook Close, Elm Park, Hornchurch, Essex RM12 5QH) : Air-Britain, 1976. — 20p ; 21cm.
ISBN 0-85130-050-2 Sd : £0.60
Also classified at 387.7'33'4097282
(B77-09652)

387.7'33'4097282 — Civil aeroplanes. *Belize. Registers*
Registers of Guatemala and Belize / edited by I.P. Burnett. — Hornchurch (9 Rook Close, Elm Park, Hornchurch, Essex RM12 5QH) : Air-Britain, 1976. — 20p ; 21cm.
ISBN 0-85130-050-2 Sd : £0.60
Primary classification 387.7'33'4097281
(B77-09652)

387.7'33'5 — Helicopter services. Organisations. *Great Britain. British Helicopter Advisory Board. Directories*
British Helicopter Advisory Board. Information handbook / British Helicopter Advisory Board. — London (111 Cheyne Walk, SW10 0DJ) : Hereford Press Ltd.
1977. — [1977]. — [2],60p : ill, map ; 21cm.
ISBN 0-905356-01-2 Sd : Unpriced
(B77-12977)

387.7'36 — Airports. *Conference proceedings*
World Airports Conference, *5th, London, 1976.* Airports, the challenging future : proceedings of the 5th World Airports Conference on technological and economic change, 5-7 May, 1976 / [editor Mary Monro]. — London : Institution of Civil Engineers, 1976. — [3], 251p : ill, maps, plans ; 31cm.
ISBN 0-7277-0017-0 : £20.00
(B77-12978)

387.7'36 — Airports. *Juvenile literature*
Gascoyne, David, *b.1939.* Airports / by David Gascoyne ; illustrations by Robert Hodgson. — Oxford : Blackwell, 1977. — 59p,[4]leaves of plates : ill(some col) ; 21cm. — (Blackwell's learning library ; no.96)
Ill. on lining paper. — Index.
ISBN 0-631-13450-6 : £0.95
(B77-18694)

Rutland, Jonathan Patrick. See inside an airport / [author Jonathan Rutland ; illustrations John Berry, John Green, Michael Kelly]. — London : Hutchinson, 1977. — 4-29p : ill(chiefly col) ; 29cm. — (See inside)
Bibl.: p.28. — Index.
ISBN 0-09-131480-1 : £1.50
(B77-30155)

387.7'36 — Airports. *Teaching kits*
Petty, Mike. The airport / by Mike Petty ; illustrated by Steve Forster ... [et al.]. — London : Jackdaw [for] Thames Television, 1977. — Portfolio : ill(some col) ; 23x27cm. — (Magpies)
Eleven sheets (8 fold.)([21] sides). — Bibl.: (1p.).
ISBN 0-305-62135-1 : £0.99(non-net)
Also classified at 629.133'34
(B77-25542)

387.7'36'02541 — Airports. *Great Britain. Directories. For air services*
Air touring flight guide, United Kingdom. — [Boreham Wood] (Elstree Aerodrome, [Boreham Wood], Herts.) : Airtour Associates International Limited.
1977, Jan. : [14th ed.] / compiled and edited by Robert Pooley. — [1977]. — 283p : ill, maps ; 20cm.
Cover title: United Kingdom & Ireland air touring flight guide.
£4.50
(B77-27794)

387.7'36'0942183 — Airports. *London. Hillingdon (London Borough). London Airport (Heathrow). Development. Proposals. Reports, surveys*
British Airports Authority. Heathrow Airport, London master development plan report / British Airports Authority. — [New ed.]. — [London] ([2 Buckingham Gate, SW1E 6JL]) : [B.A.A.], 1976. — [1],18p,[12]leaves(1 fold) : map, plans ; 30cm.
Previous ed.: 1972. — Bibl.: p.18.
ISBN 0-903460-08-4 Sp : £1.50
(B77-01333)

387.7'36'094261 — Aerodromes. *Norfolk, to 1976*
Norfolk and Suffolk Aviation Museum. Airfields of Norfolk and Suffolk / [Norfolk and Suffolk Aviation Museum]. — [Norwich] ([c/o H.J. Fairhead, 48 Monks Cottages, Langley, Norwich, Norfolk NR14 6DG]) : [The Museum].
[Part 1]. — 1977. — [2],22p : map ; 30cm.
Sd : Unpriced
Also classified at 387.7'36'094264
(B77-32581)

387.7'36'094264 — Aerodromes. *Suffolk, to 1976*
Norfolk and Suffolk Aviation Museum. Airfields of Norfolk and Suffolk / [Norfolk and Suffolk Aviation Museum]. — [Norwich] ([c/o H.J. Fairhead, 48 Monks Cottages, Langley, Norwich, Norfolk NR14 6DG]) : [The Museum].
[Part 1]. — 1977. — [2],22p : map ; 30cm.
Sd : Unpriced
Primary classification 387.7'36'094261
(B77-32581)

387.7'36'09426795 — Airports. *Essex. Southend-on-Sea. Southend Airport. Practical information*
Southend Airport official handbook. — 6th ed. — London : Burrow, [1976]. — 32p : ill, map, port ; 19x25cm.
ISBN 0-85026-629-7 Sd : Unpriced
(B77-00165)

387.7'36'0942765 — Airports. *Lancashire. Blackpool. Blackpool Airport. Practical information*
Blackpool Airport : information handbook. — London : Burrow, [1977]. — 44p : ill ; 21cm.
Sd : Unpriced
(B77-30156)

387.7'362 — Airports. *West Sussex. London Airport (Gatwick). Civil aeroplanes. Arrival & departure. Delays. Effects of capacity of runways. Reports, surveys*
Goldstein, M G. Aircraft delays and the runway capacity at Gatwick Airport / [by] M.G. Goldstein, G.A. Paulson. — London : Civil Aviation Authority, 1977. — [2],vi,31,[9]p : ill ; 30cm. — (Civil Aviation Authority. Papers ; 77023) (Civil Aviation Authority. Directorate of Operational Research and Analysis. Reports ; 7705)
ISBN 0-86039-051-9 Sd : £3.00
(B77-31115)

387.7'4042 — Air services. Delays. Avoidance. Use of simulations. *Great Britain*
Paulson, G A. A technique to achieve pre-planned balancing of schedules and some results of its application / [by] G.A. Paulson, V.W. Attwooll. — London : Civil Aviation Authority, 1977. — vi,30p : ill ; 30cm. — (Civil Aviation Authority. Directorate of operational Research and Analysis. Research papers ; no.7701) (Civil Aviation Authority. Papers ; 77005)
ISBN 0-86039-039-x Sd : £3.50
(B77-15792)

387.7'4'094 — International air traffic. *Western Europe. Forecasts for 1975-1980*
British Airports Authority. Air traffic forecasts for Western Europe / [British Airports Authority in association with Coopers & Lybrand Associates Ltd and Frankfurt Airport]. — [London] ([2 Buckingham Gate, SW1E 6JL]) : [B.A.A.], 1976. — [1],108p : ill ; 30cm.
Study initiated by the Western European Airports Association. — Bibl.: p.99-104.
Sp : £50.00
(B77-17428)

British Airports Authority. Air traffic forecasts for Western Europe / [British Airports Authority in association with Coopers & Lybrand Associates Ltd and Frankfurt Airport]. — [London] ([2 Buckingham Gate, SW1E 6JL]) : [B.A.A.].
Study initiated by the Western European Airports Association.
Summary report. — 1976. — [1],20p ; 30cm.
Sp : £5.00
(B77-17429)

387.7'42 — Airports. Passengers. Baggage. Handling. *Great Britain. Reports, surveys*
Air Transport and Travel Industry Training Board. A survey of baggage handling / Air Transport and Travel Industry Training Board. — Staines (158 High St., Staines, Middx) : The Board, [1977]. — [7],30[i.e.40],[5]p : ill, form, plans ; 30cm.
Sp : Unpriced
(B77-26256)

387.7'42 — International air passenger transport services. Fares. *Europe. Reports, surveys*
Airline Users Committee. European air fares : a report / by the Airline Users Committee ; to the Civil Aviation Authority. — London : Civil Aviation Authority, 1976. — 52p : ill, form ; 30cm.
ISBN 0-86039-023-3 Sd : £1.75
(B77-08966)

British Airways. Civil air transport in Europe / [prepared for the British Civil Aviation Authority by] British Airways. — [London] ([Victoria Terminal, S.W.1]) : [British Airways], 1977. — [3],84,[55]p : ill(some col), facsims(1 col), maps ; 32cm.
ISBN 0-901515-03-5 Sp : £10.00
(B77-11752)

387.7'42'09411 — Airports. Passengers. Origins & destinations. *Scotland. Reports, surveys*
Civil Aviation Authority. Passengers at major airports in Scotland and central England : origin and destination survey, July-November 1975 / [Civil Aviation Authority]. — London : C.A.A., 1976. — [2],72p : ill, forms, maps ; 30cm. — (CAP ; 394)
ISBN 0-86039-024-1 Sd : £8.00
Also classified at 387.7'42'09424
(B77-11753)

387.7'42'0942183 — Airports. *London. Hillingdon (London Borough). London Airport (Heathrow). Transfer passengers, 1975. Reports, surveys*
British Airports Authority. 1975 survey on transfer passengers, Heathrow : summary of results / British Airports Authority. — [London] ([2 Buckingham Gate, SW1E 6JL]) : [B.A.A.], 1976. — [45]leaves(2 fold) : ill, form, maps, plan ; 30cm.
ISBN 0-903460-09-2 Sp : £3.00
(B77-01334)

387.7'42'09424 — Airports. Passengers. Origins & destinations. *England. Midlands. Reports, surveys*
Civil Aviation Authority. Passengers at major airports in Scotland and central England : origin and destination survey, July-November 1975 / [Civil Aviation Authority]. — London : C.A.A., 1976. — [2],72p : ill, forms, maps ; 30cm. — (CAP ; 394)
ISBN 0-86039-024-1 Sd : £8.00
Primary classification 387.7'42'09411
(B77-11753)

387.7'44'0941 — Air freight transport. *Great Britain. Proposals*
Civil Aviation Authority. Air freight policy : a consultation document / [Civil Aviation Authority]. — London : The Authority, 1977. — [2],16p ; 30cm. — (CAP 405)
ISBN 0-86039-045-4 Sd : £1.50
(B77-29349)

387.7'44'0941 — Air freight transport. Demand. *Great Britain. Reports, surveys*
Civil Aviation Authority. Air freight demand : a survey of UK shippers / [Civil Aviation Authority]. — London : The Authority, 1977. — [2],16,[21]p : ill, facsims, form ; 30cm. — (CAP 401)
ISBN 0-86039-041-1 Sd : £3.00
(B77-18065)

387.7'44'0956 — Air freight transport. *Middle East. Periodicals*
Hereford's air cargo Middle East. — London (111 Cheyne Walk, SW10 ODJ) : Hereford Press Ltd.
Vol.1, no.1- ; Jan. 1976-. — 1976-. — ill(some col), maps, ports ; 30cm.
Two issues a year. — 104p. in July-Dec. 1976 issue.
Pbk : Unpriced
ISSN 0308-9932
(B77-01335)

388 — LAND TRANSPORT

388'.0941 — Land transport. Environmental aspects. *Great Britain*
Sharp, Clifford. Transport and the environment / [by] Clifford Sharp and Tony Jennings. — [Leicester] : Leicester University Press, 1976. — x,229p : ill ; 22cm.
Bibl.: p.215-216. — Index.
ISBN 0-7185-1133-6 Pbk : £3.50
(B77-06015)

388'.09426'4 — Land transport. *Suffolk. Proposals*
Suffolk *(County). Department of the County Surveyor.* Transport policies and programmes / Suffolk County Council [Department of the County Surveyor]. — Ipswich (St Peter's House, Cutler St., Ipswich IP1 2UU) : [The Department].
1978-79. — 1977. — 112p in various pagings,[8] leaves of plates : ill, facsims, col maps ; 30cm.
ISBN 0-86055-030-3 Sp : Unpriced
(B77-33171)

Suffolk *(County). Department of the County Surveyor.* Transport policies and programmes [i.e. programme] / Suffolk County Council [Department of the County Surveyor]. — [Ipswich] ([St Peter's House, Cutler St., Ipswich IP1 1UU]) : [The Department].
1977-1978. — [1976]. — 99p in various pagings,[15] leaves of plates : ill, facsim, maps(chiefly col) ; 30cm.
ISBN 0-86055-000-1 Sp : £1.00
(B77-07883)

388.1 — ROAD TRANSPORT

388.1'0941 — Roads. *Great Britain. Statistics*
Basic road statistics / British Road Federation. — London : British Road Federation.
1977. — [1977]. — [2],36p : ill, map ; 30cm.
Bibl.: p.36.
Sd : £2.00
ISSN 0309-3638
(B77-32582)

388.1'09411 — Roads. *Scotland, 1700-1900. Secondary school texts*
Donnachie, Ian Lowe. Roads and canals, 1700-1900 / [by] Ian Donnachie. — Edinburgh : Holmes-McDougall, 1977. — 48p : ill, facsims, maps, ports ; 25cm. — (Scottish search series)
Bibl.: p.48.
ISBN 0-7157-1475-9 Sd : £1.05
Also classified at 386'.46'09411
(B77-12979)

388.1'09411 — Roads. *Scotland. Reports, surveys. Serials*
Roads in Scotland report ... / Scottish Development Department. — Edinburgh : H.M.S.O.
1975. — [1976]. — 22p : map ; 25cm. — (Cmnd.6681)
ISBN 0-10-166810-4 Sd : £0.45
ISSN 0307-7659
(B77-07268)

388.1'0985 — Roads. *Peru. Royal Highway of the Incas, to 1967*
Von Hagen, Victor Wolfgang. The royal road of the Inca / [by] Victor Wolfgang von Hagen. — London : Gordon and Cremonesi, 1976. — [4], 200p,[40]p of plates : ill(some col), maps, plan, ports(1 col) ; 27cm.
In slip case. — Index.
ISBN 0-86033-009-5 : £15.00
(B77-04096)

388.1'1 — Industrial antiquities: Tollhouses. *Devon*
Kanefsky, John. Devon tollhouses / [by] John Kanefsky. — Exeter (Department of Economic History, University of Exeter, [Amory Building, Rennes Drive, Exeter EX4 4RJ]) : Exeter Industrial Archaeology Group, 1976. — [1], 36p : ill, 2 maps ; 22cm. — (Exeter papers in industrial archaeology ; 6)
Bibl.: p.35-36.
Sd : £0.30
(B77-04097)

388.1'1 — Transport. Related to economic development. Study examples: Turnpike roads. Related to economic development. *Great Britain, 1700-1800. Study regions: England*
Pawson, Eric. Transport and economy : the turnpike roads of eighteenth century Britain / [by] Eric Pawson. — London [etc.] : Academic Press, 1977. — xx,407p : ill, maps ; 24cm.
Bibl.: p.370-393. — Index.
ISBN 0-12-546950-0 : £9.60
(B77-16829)

388.1'1 — Turnpike trusts. *Hampshire. Andover region, 1775-1887. Readings from contemporary sources*
Turnpikes near Andover, 1775-1887 / [compiled by J.E.H. Spaul]. — Andover (c/o Public Library, Andover SP10 1LT) : Andover Local Archives Committee, 1977. — 37p : facsim, map ; 30cm.
ISBN 0-903755-08-4 Sd : £0.40
(B77-26257)

388.1'2 — Bus lanes. *Reports, surveys*
Organisation for Economic Co-operation and Development. *Road Research Group on Bus Lanes and Busway Systems.* Bus lanes and busway systems : a report / prepared by an OECD Road Research Group [i.e. the Road Research Group on Bus Lanes and Busway Systems]. — Paris : O.E.C.D. ; [London] : [H.M.S.O.], 1977. — 125p : ill, maps ; 27cm. — (Road research)
Pbk : £3.40
ISBN 92-64-11628-1
(B77-26997)

388.1'2 — Footpaths. *Greater Manchester (Metropolitan County). Flixton. Bottoms Path. Rights of way. Preservation, 1826-1827*
Lee, Donald W. The Flixton footpath battle / compiled by Donald W. Lee. — [Manchester] ([c/o Hon. Secretary, 10 Albert Rd, Eccles, Manchester M30 9QJ]) : Peak and Northern Footpaths Society, 1976. — [1],23,[2]p : ill, 2 maps ; 22cm.
Bibl.: p.22.
ISBN 0-9505470-0-x Sd : £0.50
(B77-06613)

388.1'2 — Public paths. *Essex. Proposals*
Essex *(County). Council.* Rights of way in the Essex countryside : a discussion paper / [Essex County Council] ; [written by J.M. Hunter et al.]. — [Chelmsford] ([County Hall, Chelmsford CM1 1LX]) : The Council, 1976. — 18p ; 30cm.
ISBN 0-901355-71-2 Sp : £0.25
(B77-14672)

388.1'2 — Trunk roads. *Great Britain. Great North Road, to 1973*
Webster, Norman William. The Great North Road / [by] Norman W. Webster. — Bath : Adams and Dart, 1974. — vi,144p,[32]p of plates : ill, facsims ; 21cm.
Index.
ISBN 0-239-00142-7 : £3.65
(B77-04728)

388.1'3 — Bridges: Baldwin's Bridge. Maintenance. Organisations. *Berkshire. Eton. Baldwin's Bridge Trust, to 1976*
Wilson, F I. A history of the Baldwin's Bridge Trust of Eton / [by] F.I. Wilson. — [Windsor] ([52 Tilstone Close, Eton Wick, Windsor, Berks.]) : [The author], [1977]. — [9],42p,[9] leaves of plates : ill, map ; 24cm.
ISBN 0-9505670-0-0 Sd : £1.75
(B77-14673)

388.3'09426'752 — Road transport services. *Essex. Chelmsford (District). Rural regions. Reports, surveys*
Chelmsford *(District). Council.* Rural areas study, transportation / Chelmsford District Council. — Chelmsford (Planning Department, Burgess Well Rd, Chelmsford [CM1 1TR]) : The Council, [1977]. — [3],7[i.e. 11]p ; 30cm. — (Subject report ; 9)
Sd : £0.20
(B77-17430)

388.3'09429'3 — Public road transport. *Clwyd. Reports, surveys*
Clwyd *(County). Transport Section.* New ways forward = Ffyrdd newydd ymlaen : alternatives in public transport in Clwyd = dewis mewn cludiad cyhoeddus yng Nghlwyd / [prepared by the Transport Section of Clwyd County Council]. — [Mold] ([Shire Hall, Mold, Clwyd CH7 6NR]) : Clwyd County Council, [1977]. — [1],95p : 1 ill, facsims, forms, maps ; 30cm.
Pbk : Unpriced
(B77-20186)

388.3'1 — Road traffic & road traffic services
Salter, Richard John. Highway traffic analysis and design / [by] R.J. Salter. — Revised ed. — London [etc.] : Macmillan, 1976. — vii,378p : ill, forms, maps ; 24cm.
Previous ed.: 1974. — Index.
£6.95
(B77-01336)

388.3'12 — Motorway M6. Anti-dazzle fences. Attitudes of motor vehicle drivers and passengers. *Warwickshire, 1974. Reports, surveys*
Dunnell, Karen. Attitudes to an anti-dazzle fence : a survey on drivers' and passengers' attitudes to an anti-dazzle fence on the M6 motorway / carried out for the Transport & Road Research Laboratory, Department of the Environment [by] Karen Dunnell. — London : H.M.S.O., 1976. — [6],59p : 2 ill, form ; 30cm. — (SS1058)
At head of title: Office of Population Censuses and Surveys, Social Survey Division.
ISBN 0-11-700817-6 Sd : £2.30
(B77-02917)

388.3'14 — Road traffic. Accidents. *Buckinghamshire. Statistics*
Buckinghamshire *(County). Engineer's Department.* Road safety statistics & traffic flows / Buckinghamshire County Council, County Engineer's Department. — [Aylesbury] ([c/o County Library Headquarters, Walton St., Aylesbury, Bucks. HP20 1UU]) : [The Council].
1976. — 1977. — [1],52p : ill, maps ; 30cm.
Previously published: as 'Accident statistics & road traffic flows'.
ISBN 0-902805-77-0 Sd : £1.00
Primary classification 388.3'14'094259
(B77-19310)

388.3'14 — Road traffic. Routes. Choice. *England. East Midlands. Reports, surveys*
Outram, V E. Route choice : report / [by] V.E. Outram ; [for the] Mathematical Advisory Unit, [Department of the Environment]. — [London] : The Department, 1976. — [3],13p,[6] leaves,[5] leaves of plates : ill, form, map ; 30cm. — (Great Britain. Department of the Environment. Mathematical Advisory Unit. Notes ; 256)
Sp : Unpriced
Primary classification 388.3'14
(B77-17431)

388.3'14 — Road traffic. Routes. Choice. *Humberside. Hull. Reports, surveys*
Outram, V E. Route choice : report / [by] V.E. Outram ; [for the] Mathematical Advisory Unit, [Department of the Environment]. — [London] : The Department, 1976. — [3],13p,[6] leaves,[5] leaves of plates : ill, form, map ; 30cm. — (Great Britain. Department of the Environment. Mathematical Advisory Unit. Notes ; 256)
Sp : Unpriced
Also classified at 388.3'14
(B77-17431)

388.3'14'0285424 — Road traffic. Zone planning. Data. Calculations. Applications of digital computer systems. Programs: ZONREG program. *Great Britain. Manuals*
Dale, H M. ZONREG : a system for weighted zonal regression : technical paper / [by] H.M. Dale & S. Johnsen ; [for the] Mathematical Advisory Unit, [Department of the Environment]. — [London] : The Department, 1976. — [44]leaves ; 30cm. — (Great Britain. Department of the Environment. Mathematical Advisory Unit. Notes ; 257)
Three leaves printed on both sides.
Sd : Unpriced
(B77-16830)

388.3'14'094259 — Road traffic. *Buckinghamshire. Statistics*
Buckinghamshire *(County). Engineer's Department.* Road safety statistics & traffic flows / Buckinghamshire County Council, County Engineer's Department. — [Aylesbury] ([c/o County Library Headquarters, Walton St., Aylesbury, Bucks. HP20 1UU]) : [The Council].
1976. — 1977. — [1],52p : ill, maps ; 30cm.
Previously published: as 'Accident statistics & road traffic flows'.
ISBN 0-902805-77-0 Sd : £1.00
Also classified at 388.3'14
(B77-19310)

388.3'14'094293 — Road traffic generated by visitors. *Clwyd. Rural regions. Reports, surveys. For environment planning*
Clwyd *(County). Planning Department. Research Section.* Recreational traffic in rural Clwyd / [prepared in the Research Section of the County Planning Department] ; [report by Ian Martin]. — Mold ([Shire Hall, Mold, Clwyd CH7 6NG]) : [The Department], 1976. — [4], 21p : ill, maps ; 30cm.
ISBN 0-904444-10-4 Ls : £1.00
(B77-08333)

388.3'22'0254 — Bus services & coach services. *Western Europe. Directories*
Road passenger transport directory for the British Isles and Western Europe : the little red book. — Shepperton : Allan.
1976. — [1976]. — 288p : ill, maps ; 23cm.
Spine title: Passenger transport industry. — Index.
ISBN 0-7110-0674-1 : £5.00
(B77-04729)

Road passenger transport directory for the British Isles and Western Europe : the little red book. — Shepperton : I. Allan.
1977. — [1977]. — 288p : ill, maps ; 22cm.
Spine title: Passenger transport industry. — Index.
ISBN 0-7110-0756-x : £5.95
(B77-26998)

388.3'22042'0942517 — Bus services. Effects of traffic re-routing. *Derbyshire. Derby. Reports, surveys*
Working Group on Bus Demonstration Projects. *Technical Sub-committee.* Derby : traffic management with bus priorities in the central area / [Working Group on Bus Demonstration Projects, Technical Sub-committee]. — [London] : Department of the Environment, 1976. — [4],15p : col ill, col maps ; 30cm. — (Bus Demonstration Project summary report ; no.9)
'This report is an abridged version of a more detailed report on this work' - Introduction.
Sd : Unpriced
(B77-16831)

388.3'22'062424 — Bus services & coach services. *England. South Midlands. United Counties Omnibus Company Limited. History*
Warwick, Roger M. An illustrated history of the United Counties Omnibus Company Limited / by Roger M. Warwick. — Northampton (101 Broadway East, Northampton NN3 2PP) : The author.
Part 1 : The Wellingborough Motor Omnibus Company Limited 1913-1921. — 1977. — 31p : ill, facsim, map ; 22cm.
Index.
Sd : £1.25
(B77-19311)

388.3'22'06542 — Bus services. *England. National Bus Company. Reports, surveys. Serials*
National Bus Company. Annual report / National Bus Company. — [London] ([25 New Street Sq., EC4A 3AP]) : [The Company].
1976 : [8th]. — [1977]. — [1],48p : col ill, col map ; 30cm.
ISBN 0-902950-08-8 Sd : £1.00
(B77-18066)

388.3'22'065428 — Bus services. *North-east England. Underwood Bus Company, 1929-1934*
Dunabin, John Edward. Underwood of Sunderland / by J.E. Dunabin. — London (103A Streatham Hill, SW2 4UD) : Omnibus Society, 1977. — 12p : ill, map ; 25cm.
ISBN 0-901307-24-6 Sd : £0.65
(B77-30157)

388.3'22'0941 — Bus services. *Great Britain. History. Serials*
Buses annual. — London : I. Allan.
1978 / edited by Gavin Booth. — 1977. — [1], 129p : ill(some col) ; 25cm.
Ill. on lining papers.
ISBN 0-7110-0814-0 : £2.75
(B77-31825)

388.3'22'0941 — Road transport. Coaching. *Great Britain, ca 1730-1975*
Richards, John, *b.1943.* Stagecoach : the real story of coaching across the land, based on the BBC TV 'Nationwide' film series / written by John Richards. — [Bradford] ([High St., Idle, Bradford, W. Yorkshire BD10 8NL]) : Watmoughs Ltd ; [s.l.] : Horse Drawn Carriages Ltd, 1976. — 96p : ill(some col), facsims(some col), col map, music, plan, ports(some col) ; 30cm.
ISBN 0-903775-04-2 Pbk : £1.50
(B77-04098)

388.3'22'0941 — Stagecoaching. *Great Britain, to ca 1840. Juvenile literature*
Grant, Neil, *b.1938.* Stagecoaches / [by] Neil Grant ; illustrated by Anthony Colbert. — Harmondsworth : Kestrel Books, 1977. — [32] p : ill(some col), facsim, 2 col maps, 2 ports ; 25cm. — (History in pictures)
ISBN 0-7226-5305-0 : £3.25
(B77-26999)

388.3'22'0942 — Stagecoaching. *England, 1800-1850. Juvenile literature*
Sutton, Harry Thomas. Ride a cock horse : the inside story of the stagecoach / [by] Harry T. Sutton. — London (21 Little Russell St., W.C.1) : Heritage Books, 1977. — 46p : ill(some col), map ; 21cm.
'A National Trust series for children'.
ISBN 0-906045-03-7 Pbk : £0.85
(B77-29350)

388.3'22'09426 — Independent bus services. *East Anglia, 1976. Lists*
Clark, Peter, *b.1943.* List of independent bus and coach services in East Anglia (Eastern Traffic Area) / [by] P.F. Clark. — Revised [ed.]. — London (103A Streatham Hill, SW2 4UD) : Omnibus Society, 1976. — [23]p ; 30cm.
Previous ed.: 1971.
Sd : £0.30
(B77-11754)

388.3'24'02541 — Road freight transport services. *Great Britain. Directories*
United Kingdom road hauliers / [Data Research Group]. — Amersham (Hill House, [Hill Ave.], Amersham, Bucks.) : The Group.
[1976]. — 1976. — 263 leaves in various pagings ; 30cm.
ISBN 0-905570-21-9 Pbk : £17.00
(B77-00166)

1977. — [1977]. — 272 leaves in various pagings ; 30cm.
Pbk : £18.00
(B77-22512)

388.3'24'0941 — Road freight transport. *Great Britain. Manuals. Serials*
Road Haulage Association. RHA haulage manual. — London (22 Upper Woburn Place, WC1H 0ES) : The Association.
1977. — [1976]. — 176p : ill, forms ; 25cm.
Cover title: Haulage manual. — Index.
Pbk : £4.50
(B77-05339)

388.34 — Bus services. Battery electric buses. *Great Britain, to 1975*
Kaye, David, *b.1929.* British battery electric buses / [by] David Kaye. — Blandford : Oakwood Press, 1976. — 18,[1]p,[8]p of plates : ill ; 22cm. — (Locomotion papers ; no.98)
ISBN 0-85361-192-0 Sd : £1.05
(B77-01337)

388.34 — Car, motor van & truck hire services. *Great Britain. Directories*
United Kingdom car & van hire companies / [Data Research Group]. — Amersham (Hill House, [Hill Ave.], Amersham, Bucks.) : The Group.
[1977]. — 1977. — 147 leaves in various pagings ; 30cm.
ISBN 0-86099-051-6 Pbk : £16.00
(B77-33737)

388.34 — Traction engines. Driving. *England, 1908-1966. Personal observations*
Smith-Powell, Harry. On the roads and in the fields : fifty years a Fowler driver, 1912-1965 / [by] Harry Smith-Powell. — Ilfracombe : Stockwell, 1976. — 46p : 1 ill ; 19cm.
ISBN 0-7223-0944-9 Pbk : £1.00
(B77-02223)

388.34 — Trolley bus services. Trolleybuses. *Europe. Illustrations*
Round Europe by trolleybus : a pictorial review of the European trolleybus scene / edited by M.J. Russell. — Strood (57 Yantlet Drive, Strood, Kent ME2 2TH) : 'Trolleybooks' Joint Publications Panel, 1977. — 49p : chiefly ill ; 16x22cm.
ISBN 0-904235-05-x Sd : £0.90
(B77-24141)

388.34'1 — Road transport. Horse-drawn vehicles, 1760-1966
Ingram, Arthur. Horse-drawn vehicles since 1760, in colour / by Arthur Ingram ; colour plates by David Dowland and Joyce Smith. — Poole : Blandford Press, 1977. — 207p : col ill ; 20cm. — ([Blandford colour series])
ISBN 0-7137-0820-4 : £3.50
(B77-23328)

388.34'22 — Car hire services. *Scotland. Directories*
Car hire in Scotland / Scottish Tourist Board. — Edinburgh : The Board. — (Scottish Tourist Board. Information booklets)
1977. — [1976]. — 20p : 1 ill ; 21x10cm.
Sd : Unpriced
(B77-22513)

388.34'2'2 — Cars. Number plates. *Great Britain. Lists*
Woodall, Noel. Car numbers, 1977 / compiled by Noel Woodall. — Brentford : Transport Bookman Publications, 1976. — [5],386p : ill, ports ; 25cm.
ISBN 0-85184-017-5 : Unpriced
(B77-31116)

388.34'2'330941 — Bus services. Buses. *Great Britain, 1970-1976. Illustrations*
Britain's buses in the seventies / edited by E.L. Cornwell and John Parke. — Shepperton : Allan, 1976. — [80]p : chiefly ill ; 25cm.
ISBN 0-7110-0741-1 : £2.25
(B77-01338)

388.34'2'3309421 — Bus services. Single-deck buses. *London, 1950-1960*
Wagstaff, John Stephen. The London single-deck bus of the fifties / [by] J.S. Wagstaff. — Blandford : Oakwood Press, 1976. — 40p : ill ; 22cm. — (Locomotion papers ; no.101 ISSN 0305-5493)
ISBN 0-85361-198-x Sd : £1.05
(B77-07269)

388.34'2'3309422 — Bus services. *England. Home Counties. London Country Bus Services. Buses. Registers. Serials*
London Country buses and Green Line coaches. — Stanmore (White Leas, Clamp Hill, Stanmore, Middx) : Capital Transport Publishing.
1977-78 ed. / [by] Mark Chapman ; incorporating fleet at 1st August 1977 compiled by David Stewart. — 1977. — 60p : ill ; 21cm.
ISBN 0-904711-06-4 Sd : £1.20
(B77-31117)

388.34'2'3309423 — Bus services. Buses. *South-west England, 1936-1975. Illustrations*
Buses in camera, South West / [compiled by] Norman Aish. — London : Allan, 1977. — 128p : chiefly ill(some col) ; 24cm. — (Buses in camera)
ISBN 0-7110-0732-2 : £3.50
(B77-10786)

388.34'2'3309424 — Buses. *England. West Midlands. Registers*
Buses of the West Midlands / edited by R. Heathcote and A. Witton. — Manchester (42 Warwick Rd, Manchester M21 1AX) : [A.M. Witton], 1975. — 65p : ill ; 15cm. — (Fleetbook ; no.6)
ISBN 0-86047-006-7 Sd : £0.50
(B77-07270)

388.34'2'33094244 — Independent bus & coach services. Buses & motor coaches. *Hereford and Worcester. Lists*
PSV Circle. The independent stage carriage operators of Hereford and Worcester / [PSV Circle and the Omnibus Society]. — London (42 Old Park Ridings, N21 2ES) : PSV Circle : Omnibus Society, [1976]. — [2],60p,[4]p of plates : ill ; 30cm. — (Fleet history ; 2PB8)
ISBN 0-905517-02-4 Sd : Unpriced
(B77-02918)

388.34'2'33094248 — Independent bus & coach services. Buses & motor coaches. *Warwickshire. Lists*
PSV Circle. The independent stage carriage operators of Warwickshire and West Midlands / [PSV Circle and the Omnibus Society]. — London (52 Old Park Ridings, N21 2ES) : PSV Circle : Omnibus Society, [1976]. — [2],41p,[2]p of plates : ill ; 30cm. — (Fleet history ; 2PD14)
ISBN 0-905517-03-2 Sd : Unpriced
Also classified at 388.34'2'33094249
(B77-02919)

388.34'2'33094249 — Independent bus & coach services. Buses & motor coaches. *West Midlands (Metropolitan County). Lists*
PSV Circle. The independent stage carriage operators of Warwickshire and West Midlands / [PSV Circle and the Omnibus Society]. — London (52 Old Park Ridings, N21 2ES) : PSV Circle : Omnibus Society, [1976]. — [2],41p,[2]p of plates : ill ; 30cm. — (Fleet history ; 2PD14)
ISBN 0-905517-03-2 Sd : Unpriced
Primary classification 388.34'2'33094248
(B77-02919)

388.34'2'3309425 — Buses. *England. East Midlands. Registers*
Buses of the East Midlands / edited ... by A.M. Witton. — Manchester (42 Warwick Rd, Manchester M21 1AX) : [A.M. Witton], 1976. — 65p : ill ; 15cm. — (Fleetbook ; no.7)
ISBN 0-86047-007-5 Sd : £0.50
(B77-07271)

388.34'2'33094273 — Buses. *Greater Manchester (Metropolitan County). Registers*
Buses of Greater Manchester / edited ... by A.M. Witton. — 2nd ed. — Manchester (42 Warwick Rd, Manchester M21 1AX) : [A.M. Witton], 1975. — 56p : ill ; 16cm. — (Fleetbook ; no.1)
ISBN 0-86047-001-6 Sd : £0.40
(B77-07272)

388.34'2'33094275 — Buses. *Merseyside (Metropolitan County). Registers*
Buses of Merseyside & North Wales / edited ... by A.M. Witton. — Manchester (42 Warwick Rd, Manchester M21 1AX) : [A.M. Witton], 1975. — 56,[1]p : ill ; 15cm. — (Fleetbook ; no.5)
ISBN 0-86047-005-9 Sd : £0.40
Also classified at 388.34'2'33094291
(B77-07273)

388.34'2'33094276 — Buses. *Lancashire. Registers*
Buses of Lancashire & Cumbria / edited ... by A.M. Witton ; with the assistance of the Ribble Enthusiasts' Club and the Coronation Tramcar Preservation Society. — Manchester (42 Warwick Rd, Manchester M21 1AX) : [A.M. Witton], 1975. — 65p : ill ; 15cm. — (Fleetbook ; no.4)
ISBN 0-86047-004-0 Sd : £0.40
Also classified at 388.34'2'33094278
(B77-07274)

388.34'2'33094278 — Bus services. *Cumbria. Cumberland Motor Services Limited. Buses, 1947-1976. Registers*
PSV Circle. Cumberland Motor Services Limited / [PSV Circle]. — London (52 Old Park Ridings, Grange Park, N21 2ES) : The Circle, 1976. — 13p ; 33cm. — (P51R2)
ISBN 0-905517-04-0 Sd : Unpriced
(B77-05340)

388.34'2'33094278 — Buses. *Cumbria. Registers*
Buses of Lancashire & Cumbria / edited ... by A.M. Witton ; with the assistance of the Ribble Enthusiasts' Club and the Coronation Tramcar Preservation Society. — Manchester (42 Warwick Rd, Manchester M21 1AX) : [A.M. Witton], 1975. — 65p : ill ; 15cm. — (Fleetbook ; no.4)
ISBN 0-86047-004-0 Sd : £0.40
Primary classification 388.34'2'33094276
(B77-07274)

388.34'2'3309428 — Buses. *North-east England. Registers*
Buses of North-east England / edited ... by A.M. Witton. — Manchester (42 Warwick Rd, Manchester M21 1AX) : [A.M. Witton], 1976. — 57p : ill ; 15cm. — (Fleetbook ; no.8)
ISBN 0-86047-008-3 Sd : £0.50
(B77-07275)

388.34'2'33094281 — Bus services. Buses. *West Yorkshire (Metropolitan County). Registers*
Buses of West Yorkshire / edited by A.M. Witton. — 2nd ed. revised. — Manchester (Room 20, City Buildings, 69 Corporation St., Manchester M4 2DE) : The editor, 1976. — [1],57p : ill ; 15cm. — (Fleetbook ; no.3)
Previous ed.: 1974.
ISBN 0-86047-032-6 Sd : £0.50
(B77-33738)

388.34'2'33094287 — Bus services: Northern General Transport Company Limited. Subsidiaries. Buses. *Tyne and Wear (Metropolitan County), to 1975. Lists*
PSV Circle. The subsidiary companies of Northern General Transport / [PSV Circle and the Omnibus Society]. — London (c/o 52 Old Park Ridings, N21 2ES) : PSV Circle : Omnibus Society.
Part 1 : The Gateshead and District Omnibus Company Limited ; the Jarrow and District Electric Traction Company Limited ; the Sunderland District Omnibus Company Limited. — 1976. — [4],48p,[2]p of plates : ill ; 30cm. — (Publication ; PA4)
ISBN 0-905517-01-6 Sd : Unpriced
Also classified at 388.4'6'094287
(B77-01339)

388.34'2'33094291 — Buses. *North Wales. Registers*
Buses of Merseyside & North Wales / edited ... by A.M. Witton. — Manchester (42 Warwick Rd, Manchester M21 1AX) : [A.M. Witton], 1975. — 56,[1]p : ill ; 15cm. — (Fleetbook ; no.5)
ISBN 0-86047-005-9 Sd : £0.40
Primary classification 388.34'2'33094275
(B77-07273)

388.34'2'33094294 — Buses. *South Wales. Registers*
Buses of South Wales / edited ... by A.M. Witton. — Manchester (42 Warwick Rd, Manchester M21 1AX) : [A.M. Witton], 1976. — 64p : ill ; 15cm. — (Fleetbook ; no.9)
ISBN 0-86047-091-1 Sd : £0.50
(B77-07276)

388.34'2'4094264 — Road freight transport services. Motor vehicles: Heavy trucks. *Suffolk. Reports, surveys*
Suffolk *(County). Highways Department.* Heavy lorries in Suffolk : a paper for public consultation / [Suffolk County Highways Department]. — [Ipswich] ([St Peters House, Cutler St., Ipswich IP1 UU]) : The Department, [1977]. — [3],10p,fold plate : plan ; 30cm.
ISBN 0-86055-010-9 Sd : Unpriced
(B77-12403)

388.34'72 — Bicycle hire services. *Scotland. Directories*
Bicycle hire in Scotland / Scottish Tourist Board. — Edinburgh : The Board. — (Scottish Tourist Board. Information booklets)
1977. — [1976]. — 8p : 1 ill ; 21x10cm.
Sd : Unpriced
(B77-22514)

388.4 — URBAN TRANSPORT
388.4 — Passenger transport services. Environmental aspects. *Urban regions. Conference proceedings*
Passenger transport and the environment : the integration of public passenger transport with the urban environment / edited by Roy Cresswell. — London : L. Hill, 1977. — xvi, 299p : ill, form, maps, plans ; 24cm.
'Proceedings of the Conference held at the University of York in March 1976 and organized by the Construction Industry Conference Centre Limited in association with ... [others]' - p.viii.
ISBN 0-249-44153-5 : £11.00
(B77-15793)

388.4 — Transport. Planning. Economic aspects. *North America. Urban regions*
Abouchar, Alan. Transportation economics and public policy : with urban extensions / [by] Alan Abouchar. — New York ; London [etc.] : Wiley, 1977. — xvii,326p : ill, map ; 24cm.
'A Wiley-Interscience publication'. — Bibl. — Index.
ISBN 0-471-02101-6 : £12.50
(B77-25543)

388.4 — Transport. Planning. Methodology. Economic aspects. *Urban regions*
Jones, Ian Shore. Urban transport appraisal / [by] Ian S. Jones. — London [etc.] : Macmillan, 1977. — x,144p : ill ; 23cm. — (Studies in planning)
Index.
ISBN 0-333-17783-5 : £7.95
ISBN 0-333-21379-3 Pbk : £2.95
(B77-14183)

388.4'042 — Passenger transport services. Demand. Mathematical models. *Organisation for Economic Co-operation and Development countries. Urban regions*
Round Table on Transport Economics, *32nd, Paris, 1975.* Report of the thirty-second Round Table on Transport Economics, held in Paris on 4th and 5th December 1975 on the following topic, 'Passenger transport demands in urban areas : methodology for analysing and forecasting' / [by A. Bonnafous ; annex by B. Gerardin]. — Paris : Economic Research Centre, European Conference of Ministers of Transport ; [London] : [H.M.S.O.], 1976. — 81p : ill ; 24cm. — (ECMT round table ; 32 ISSN 0531-9528)
Pbk : £1.30
ISBN 92-821-1037-0
(B77-00720)

388.4'042 — Passenger transport services. Fares. Collection
Wyse, William John. Presidential address to a meeting of the [Transport Ticket] Society in London on Saturday 22 November 1975 / by W.J. Wyse. — Luton (18 Villa Rd, Luton LU2 7NT) : Transport Ticket Society, [1976]. — [1], 17p ; 30cm.
'... I chose the title of "A Computer Man looks at ticket and fare systems" as the subject of my address ...' - p.1.
ISBN 0-903209-06-3 Sd : £0.25
(B77-05341)

388.4'042 — Public transport services. Expenditure by government. Proposed reduction. *London. Save Public Transport Campaign Committee viewpoints*
Save Public Transport Campaign Committee. Save our public transport services background briefing material / information prepared by the Save Public Transport Campaign Committee. — London (4th Floor, Greater London House, Hampstead Rd, NW1 7QP) : [The Committee], 1976. — [3],13p ; 30cm.
ISBN 0-9505599-0-3 Sd : £1.50 for 10 copies
(B77-10326)

388.4'042'0941 — Transport. Economic aspects. *Great Britain. Urban regions*
Button, Kenneth John. The economics of urban transport / [by] K.J. Button. — Farnborough, Hants. : Saxon House, 1977. — x,181,[1]p : ill ; 24cm.
Bibl.: p.164-177. — Index.
ISBN 0-566-00148-9 : £9.50
(B77-11755)

388.4'09421 — Passenger transport. *London. Practical information*
Britain, travelling around London / [British Tourist Authority]. — London : B.T.A. [1977]. — 1977. — [1],13p : 1 ill, maps ; 21cm. — (British Tourist Authority. Information sheets ; no.359/77/14)
ISBN 0-85630-379-8 Sd : Unpriced
(B77-14184)

388.4'09421 — Passenger transport services. *London, to 1970*
Barker, Theodore Cardwell. A history of London transport : passenger travel and the development of the metropolis / by T.C. Barker and Michael Robbins. — London : Allen and Unwin for the London Transport Executive.
Vol.2 : The twentieth century to 1970. — [1st ed. reprinted] with minor revisions. — 1976. — xx,550p,leaf of plate,[88]p of plates : ill, facsims, maps, ports(1 col) ; 25cm.
First ed. originally published: 1974. — Bibl.: p.500-503. — Index.
£7.50
ISBN 0-04-385063-4
ISBN 0-04-385067-7 Pbk : £4.50
(B77-01340)

Barker, Theodore Cardwell. A history of London transport : passenger travel and the development of the metropolis / by T.C. Barker and Michael Robbins. — London : Allen and Unwin for the London Transport Executive.
Vol.1 : The nineteenth century. — [1st ed.] revised. — 1975. — xxxii,414p,leaf of plate,[58]p of plates : ill, facsims, maps, ports ; 24cm.
First ed. originally published: 1963.
ISBN 0-04-385002-2 : £5.50
ISBN 0-04-389066-9 Pbk : £3.75
(B77-01341)

388.4'09421 — Transport. Greater London Council. Greater London Transportation Survey. Screenlines. Validation. *London. Reports, surveys*
Kinlock, A G. Greater London Transportation Survey, screenline validation / by A.G. Kinlock and M.P. Ness ; [for the Greater London Council] Department of Planning and Transportation, Transportation Branch. — London : G.L.C., 1976. — [4],35[i.e.37]p,[2]p of plates : ill, map ; 30cm. — (Greater London Council. Intelligence Unit. Research memoranda ; RM308 ISSN 0306-7203)
ISBN 0-7168-0830-7 Sp : £2.30
(B77-16322)

388.4'09421 — Transport. Policies of Greater London Council. *London, 1978-1983. Proposals*
Greater London Council. Transport policies and programme, 1978-83 / [Greater London Council]. — [London] : G.L.C., [1977]. — [1], 108p(2 fold) : 1 ill, maps ; 30cm.
Versos of some leaves blank.
ISBN 0-7168-0929-x Sd : £1.60
(B77-33739)

388.4'09423'56 — Public transport services. *Devon. Exeter, 1882-1975. Illustrations*
Sambourne, Roy Charles. Exeter, a century of public transport / by R.C. Sambourne. — Falmouth ([Falmouth, Cornwall]) : Glasney Press, 1976. — 104p : chiefly ill, maps, ports ; 27cm.
ISBN 0-9502825-3-7 : £4.25
(B77-06016)

388.4'131'4 — Motor vehicles. Travel time between traffic lights. Mathematical models
Gipps, P G. The estimation of a measure of vehicle delay from detector output / [by] P.G. Gipps. — Newcastle upon Tyne (The University, Newcastle upon Tyne NE1 7RU) : Transport Operations Research Group, University of Newcastle upon Tyne, 1977. — 18p : ill ; 30cm. — (University of Newcastle upon Tyne. Transport Operations Research Group. Working papers ; no.25 ISSN 0306-3402)
Sd : Unpriced
(B77-17432)

388.4'1321 — Taxi services. Organisations. *Ireland (Republic). Irish Taxi Federation. Periodicals*
Taxi news : official journal of the Irish Taxi Federation. — [Dublin] ([7 Marlboro St., Dublin 1]) : [The Federation].
Vol.1, no.1- ; Nov. 1976-. — 1976-. — ill ; 21cm.
Monthly. — [2],25p. in 1st issue.
Sd : Unpriced
(B77-29351)

388.4'1322 — Bus services. Routes. Operation. Travel time. *Urban regions. Study regions: Tyne and Wear (Metropolitan County). Newcastle upon Tyne. Research reports*
Chapman, R A. Factors affecting the operation of urban bus routes / [by] R.A. Chapman, H.E. Gault and I.A. Jenkins. — Newcastle upon Tyne (The University, Newcastle upon Tyne NE1 7RU) : Transport Operations Research Group, 1976. — 103p : ill ; 30cm. — (University of Newcastle upon Tyne. Transport Operations Research Group. Working papers ; no.23 ISSN 0306-3402)
Bibl.: p.85-88.
ISBN 0-903259-27-3 Sd : £5.23
(B77-12980)

388.4'1322'0941 — Trolleybus services. *Great Britain, to 1972*
Cormack, Ian Leslie. Trams and trolleybuses : an illustrated history / [by] Ian L. Cormack & David Kaye. — Bourne End : Spurbooks, [1977?]. — 160p : ill, facsims ; 23cm.
Ill. on lining papers. — Bibl.: p.157-159. — Index.
ISBN 0-904978-11-7 : £5.00
Primary classification 388.4'6'0941
(B77-08967)

388.4'1322'09421 — Bus services. *London. Serials*
The London bus review. — [Stanmore] ([White Leas, Clamp Hill, Stanmore, Middx]) : London Omnibus Traction Society.
1974 / compiled by Leon Daniels ... [et al.] ; edited by James Whiting. — 1975. — [1],57p : ill(some col), facsims, map ; 30cm.
ISBN 0-9503219-3-1 Sd : £1.50
(B77-33172)

388.4'1322'0942565 — Bus services. Use. *Bedfordshire. Dunstable, 1975-1976. Reports, surveys*
Bedfordshire *(County). Planning Department.* Luton, Dunstable and Houghton Regis bus users survey, summary report / [Bedfordshire] County Planning Department. — [Bedford] ([County Hall, Bedford]) : The Department, 1977. — [1],118[i.e.133],[1]p(14 fold) : ill, forms, maps ; 30cm.
Cover title: Bus users survey 1975-76.
Sd : £3.00
Primary classification 388.4'1322'0942567
(B77-30158)

388.4'1322'0942567 — Bus services. Use. *Bedfordshire. Luton, 1975-1976. Reports, surveys*
Bedfordshire *(County). Planning Department.* Luton, Dunstable and Houghton Regis bus users survey, summary report / [Bedfordshire] County Planning Department. — [Bedford] ([County Hall, Bedford]) : The Department, 1977. — [1],118[i.e.133],[1]p(14 fold) : ill, forms, maps ; 30cm.
Cover title: Bus users survey 1975-76.
Sd : £3.00
Also classified at 388.4'1322'0942565
(B77-30158)

388.4'1322'0942821 — Bus services. *South Yorkshire (Metropolitan County). Sheffield, to 1974*
Hall, Charles C. Sheffield transport / by Chas. C. Hall. — Glossop (Glossop, Derbyshire) : Transport Publishing Co., 1977. — 330p : ill(some col), facsims(some col), maps, plans, ports ; 30cm.
Fold. sheet (map) tipped in. — Map on lining paper.
ISBN 0-903839-04-0 : £12.00
Also classified at 388.4'6'0942821
(B77-31826)

388.4'1322'0942875 — Trolleybus services. *Tyne and Wear (Metropolitan County). South Shields, to 1964*
Burrows, G. The trolleybuses of South Shields, 1936-1964 / by G. Burrows. — [Strood] ([57 Yantlet Drive, Strood, Kent ME2 2TH]) : Trolleybooks Joint Publications Panel, 1976. — 100p,fold plate : ill, map, ports ; 21cm.
Map tipped in. — Bibl.: p.100.
ISBN 0-904235-04-1 Pbk : £1.50
(B77-04099)

388.4'1324 — Shops. Goods. Deliveries. *Tyne and Wear (Metropolitan County). Newcastle upon Tyne. Northumberland Street. Reports, surveys*
Smith, K J G. Analysis of goods deliveries to a semi-pedestrianised shopping street / [by] K.J.G. Smith. — Newcastle upon Tyne (The University, Newcastle upon Tyne NE1 7RU) : Transport Operations Research Group, University of Newcastle upon Tyne, 1976. — 128p : ill, facsims, forms, maps, plan ; 30cm. — (University of Newcastle upon Tyne. Transport Operations Research Group. Working papers ; no.22 ISSN 0306-3402)
Bibl.: p.81-82.
ISBN 0-906044-00-6 Sd : £7.80
(B77-14185)

388.4'2 — Underground railway services. *Scotland. Strathclyde Region. Glasgow, to 1977*
Kelly, Paul J. Glasgow Subway, 1896-1977 / by Paul J. Kelly and M.J.D. Willsher. — London : Light Railway Transport League, [1977]. — 28p : ill, facsims, maps ; 22cm.
'... reprinted from "Modern Tramway" ...' - p.14.
ISBN 0-900433-68-x Sd : £0.30
(B77-30159)

388.4'2 — Underground railways. Stations. Opening dates & origins of names. *London*
Harris, Cyril Michael. What's in a name? : the origins of station names on the London Underground / by Cyril M. Harris. — Tunbridge Wells : Midas Books [for] London Transport, 1977. — 96p : ill, map ; 17cm.
Bibl.: p.94-96.
ISBN 0-85936-060-1 Pbk : £0.95
(B77-12981)

388.4'6'0941 — Tram services. *Great Britain, to 1970*
Cormack, Ian Leslie. Trams and trolleybuses : an illustrated history / [by] Ian L. Cormack & David Kaye. — Bourne End : Spurbooks, [1977?]. — 160p : ill, facsims ; 23cm.
Ill. on lining papers. — Bibl.: p.157-159. — Index.
ISBN 0-904978-11-7 : £5.00
Also classified at 388.4'1322'0941
(B77-08967)

388.4'6'0941 — Tram services. Trams. *Great Britain, to 1976*
Turner, Keith. Discovering trams and tramways / [by] Keith Turner. — Aylesbury : Shire Publications, 1977. — 62p,[16]p of plates : ill ; 18cm. — (Discovering series ; no.231)
Bibl.: p.60. — Index.
ISBN 0-85263-384-x Pbk : £0.60
(B77-33740)

388.4'6'0941443 — Tram services. *Scotland. Strathclyde Region. Glasgow, ca 1875-1962. Illustrations*
Glasgow by tram / [compiled by] Ian G.McM. Stewart. — [Glasgow] ([46 Wellshop Drive, Cambuslang, Glasgow G72 8BN]) : Scottish Tramway Museum Society, 1977. — 48p : chiefly ill, facsim ; 22cm.
ISBN 0-900648-16-3 Sd : £0.85
(B77-31827)

388.4'6'0941443 — Tram services. *Scotland. Strathclyde Region. Glasgow, to 1960. Illustrations*
Wiseman, Richard Joseph Stewart. Glasgow / [by] R.J.S. Wiseman. — 3rd (enlarged) ed. — Huddersfield : Advertiser Press, 1977. — 48p : ill ; 22cm. — (British tramways in pictures ; 2)
Previous ed.: 1971.
Sd : Unpriced
(B77-27000)

388.4'6'0941443 — Tram services. Trams: Green Goddesses. *Scotland. Strathclyde Region. Glasgow, 1953-1960*
Cormack, Ian Leslie. Green goddesses go east : a brief history of the ex-Liverpool trams in Glasgow, 1953-60 / by Ian L. Cormack. — [New ed.]. — [Glasgow] ([46 Wellshot Drive, Cambuslang, Glasgow G72 8BN]) : Scottish Tramway Museum Society, [1977]. — [1],21p : ill, plan ; 22cm.
Previous ed.: 1961.
Sd : £0.35
(B77-22515)

388.4'6'09423 — Tram services. *South-west England, to ca 1950. Illustrations*
West Country electric trams / [compiled] by John B. Appleby. — Glossop (22 Longmoor Rd, Simmondley, Glossop, Derbyshire) : Transport Publishing Co., 1975. — [2],38p : chiefly ill, ports ; 21x30cm.
ISBN 0-903839-09-1 Sd : £1.50
(B77-05342)

388.4'6'0942496 — Tram services. Trams. *West Midlands (Metropolitan County). Birmingham, to 1953. Illustrations*
Wiseman, Richard Joseph Stewart.
Birmingham / [by] R.J.S. Wiseman. — 2nd ed. — Huddersfield : Advertiser Press, 1977. — 40p : ill ; 22cm. — (British tramways in pictures ; 3)
Previous ed.: 1972.
ISBN 0-900028-42-4 Sd : £0.80
(B77-16323)

388.4'6'0942734 — Tram services. *Greater Manchester (Metropolitan County). Stockport, to 1951*
Marshall, Maurice. Stockport Corporation Tramways / by Maurice Marshall. — Rochdale (1020 Manchester Rd, Castleton, Rochdale, Lancs.) : Manchester Transport Museum Society, 1975. — 160p, fold plate : ill, facsims, maps, ports ; 25cm.
ISBN 0-900857-10-2 : £4.00
ISBN 0-900857-11-0 Pbk : £3.00
(B77-14186)

388.4'6'0942765 — Tram services. Trams. *Lancashire. Blackpool, to 1976*
Turner, Brian Richard. Blackpool to Fleetwood / [by] Brian Turner. — London : Light Railway Transport League, [1977]. — 100p : ill, facsims, maps, plans ; 21cm.
'... reprinted, with additions, from the 1975 and 1976 issues of "Modern tramway" ...' - p.5.
ISBN 0-900433-67-1 Sd : £1.20
(B77-29352)

388.4'6'0942821 — Tram services. *South Yorkshire (Metropolitan County). Sheffield, to 1960*
Hall, Charles C. Sheffield transport / by Chas. C. Hall. — Glossop (Glossop, Derbyshire) : Transport Publishing Co., 1977. — 330p : ill(some col), facsims(some col), maps, plans, ports ; 30cm.
Fold. sheet (map) tipped in. — Map on lining paper.
ISBN 0-903839-04-0 : £12.00
Primary classification 388.4'1322'0942821
(B77-31826)

388.4'6'094287 — Tram services: Northern General Transport Company Limited. Subsidiaries. Trams. *Tyne and Wear (Metropolitan County), to 1951. Lists*
PSV Circle. The subsidiary companies of Northern General Transport / [PSV Circle and the Omnibus Society]. — London (c/o 52 Old Park Ridings, N21 2ES) : PSV Circle : Omnibus Society.
Part 1 : The Gateshead and District Omnibus Company Limited ; the Jarrow and District Electric Traction Company Limited ; the Sunderland District Omnibus Company Limited. — 1976. — [4],48p,[2]p of plates : ill ; 30cm. — (Publication ; PA4)
ISBN 0-905517-01-6 Sd : Unpriced
Primary classification 388.34'2'33094287
(B77-01339)

388.4'6'09437 — Tram services. *Czechoslovakia*
Taplin, Michael Redvers. Tramways of Czechoslovakia and Poland / [by] M.R. Taplin. — London : Light Railway Transport League, [1977]. — 44,[2]p : maps ; 21cm.
Bibl.: p.44. — Index.
ISBN 0-900433-61-2 Sd : £1.00
Also classified at 388.4'6'09438
(B77-15245)

388.4'6'09438 — Tram services. *Poland*
Taplin, Michael Redvers. Tramways of Czechoslovakia and Poland / [by] M.R. Taplin. — London : Light Railway Transport League, [1977]. — 44,[2]p : maps ; 21cm.
Bibl.: p.44. — Index.
ISBN 0-900433-61-2 Sd : £1.00
Primary classification 388.4'6'09437
(B77-15245)

388.4'6'096822 — Tram services. *South Africa. Johannesburg, to 1961*
Spit, Tony. Johannesburg tramways : a history of the tramways of the City of Johannesburg / by Tony Spit ; revised and with additional material by Brian Patton. — London : Light Railway Transport League, 1976. — 137p : ill, maps ; 23cm.
ISBN 0-900433-55-8 : £4.25
(B77-07277)

388.4'74 — Motor vehicles. Parking in private non-residential spaces. Control. *London. Reports, surveys*
Powers to control private non-residential parking / by a joint working party of the GLC-DOE-LBA ; [for the Greater London Council] Department of Planning and Transportation, Transportation Branch. — London : G.L.C., 1975. — [1],ii,12p ; 30cm. — (Greater London Council. Intelligence Unit. Research memoranda ; RM483 ISSN 0306-7203)
ISBN 0-7168-0836-6 Sd : £2.30
(B77-15794)

388.5 — PIPELINE TRANSPORT
388.5 — Gas gathering pipelines. *North Sea. Proposals*
Great Britain. *Department of Energy.* Gas gathering pipeline systems in the North Sea : note / by the Department of Energy. — [London] (Thames House South, Millbank, SW1P 4QJ) : The Department, 1976. — [2],8p : 1 ill ; 21cm.
ISBN 0-904552-19-5 Sd : Unpriced
(B77-15246)

389.1 — WEIGHTS AND MEASURES
389'.1'0212 — Measures. *Tables*
'The **economist**' measurement guide and reckoner. — 3rd ed., revised and enlarged. — London (25 St James's St., SW1A 1HG) : Economist Newspaper Ltd, 1975. — 232p : ill(chiefly col), col map ; 27cm.
Previous ed.: published as '"The economist" guide to weights and measures'. 1962. — Index.
ISBN 0-85058-040-4 : £8.50
(B77-04100)

389'.152'014 — S.I. units. Notation & terminology. *Manuals*
Metrication Board. How to write metric : a style guide for teaching and using SI units / [Metrication Board]. — London : H.M.S.O., 1977. — [1],33,[1]p,fold leaf : ill ; 21cm.
Index.
ISBN 0-11-700867-2 Sd : £0.50
(B77-31828)

389'.152'0212 — Measurement. Système International d'Unités. *Standards*
British Standards Institution. The international system of units (SI) = Système International des unités (SI) = Das internationale Einheitssystem (SI) / British Standards Institution. — 2nd revision. — London : B.S.I., 1976. — [2],8,[2]p ; 30cm. — (BS 3763 : 1976)
Pierced for binder.
ISBN 0-580-09148-1 Sd : £2.40
(B77-00721)

389'.152'0212 — Measurement. Système International d'Unités. *Tables*
Qasim, S H. SI units in engineering and technology / by S.H. Qasim. — Oxford [etc.] : Pergamon, 1977. — vii,54p ; 25cm. — (Pergamon international library)
Index.
ISBN 0-08-021278-6 Pbk : £2.50
(B77-19312)

389'.152'071273 — Secondary schools. Curriculum subjects: Metric system. Teaching. *United States. Manuals*
Cunningham, James Barrett. Teaching metrics simplified / [by] James B. Cunningham. — Englewood Cliffs ; London [etc.] : Prentice-Hall, 1976. — viii,184p : ill ; 24cm.
Index.
ISBN 0-13-893883-0 : £8.55
ISBN 0-130-893875-x Pbk : £4.80
(B77-02224)

389'.152'0941 — Metrication. *Great Britain. Reports, surveys*
Great Britain. *Department of Prices and Consumer Protection.* Metrication : report to Parliament / by the Department of Prices and Consumer Protection. — London : H.M.S.O., 1977. — v,25p ; 21cm.
ISBN 0-11-512068-8 Sd : £0.70
(B77-21067)

389'.152'0941 — Metrication. *Great Britain. Reports, surveys. Serials*
Metrication Board. Report of the Metrication Board. — London : H.M.S.O.
1976 : Going metric : 1976, the final stage begins. — 1977. — 32p ; 30cm.
ISBN 0-11-700325-5 Sd : £1.20
(B77-15795)

390 — CUSTOMS AND FOLKLORE
390'.09423'4 — Channel Islands customs, to 1975
Lemprière, Raoul. Customs, ceremonies and traditions of the Channel Islands / [by] Raoul Lemprière. — London : Hale, 1976. — 224p, [24]p of plates : ill, ports ; 23cm.
Bibl.: p.213-216. — Index.
ISBN 0-7091-5842-4 : £5.00
(B77-02225)

390'.09425'1 — Derbyshire customs, to 1975
Porteous, Crichton. The ancient customs of Derbyshire / by Crichton Porteous. — [New ed.]. — Derby (Lodge La., Derby) : Derbyshire Countryside Ltd, 1976. — [2],18p : ill(some col) ; 24cm.
Previous ed.: 1971.
Sd : £0.30
(B77-18067)

390'.0996'13 — Samoan customs. *Samoan-English parallel texts*
Stuebel, C. Myths and legends of Samoa = Tala o le vavau / Samoan text by C. Stuebel ; English translation by Brother Herman ; illustrated by Iosua Toafa. — Wellington [N.Z.] [etc.] ; London : A.H. and A.W. Reed [etc.], 1976. — [4],157p : ill ; 25cm.
ISBN 0-589-00968-0 Pbk : £3.05
Primary classification 398.2'0996'13
(B77-04102)

391 — COSTUME AND PERSONAL APPEARANCE
391 — Working clothing. *England, 1776-1976*
Lansdell, Avril. Occupational costume and working clothes, 1776-1976 / [by] Avril Lansdell. — Aylesbury : Shire Publications, 1977. — 33p : ill ; 21cm. — (Shire album ; 27)
Bibl.: p.33.
ISBN 0-85263-383-1 Sd : £0.50
(B77-32583)

391'.009 — Costume, to 1976
Lowndes, Rosemary. Make your own history of costume / written and designed by Rosemary Lowndes and Claude Kaïler. — London : Macdonald and Jane's, 1977. — [95]p : chiefly col ill ; 30cm.
ISBN 0-356-08418-3 Pbk : £3.50
Primary classification 745.59'22
(B77-25784)

391'.009 — Western costume, to 1976. *Middle school texts*
Healey, Tim. History of costume / [by] Tim Healey ; [illustrators Shirley Bellwood et al.]. — London : Macdonald Educational, 1977. — 2-46p : ill(chiefly col), 2 col maps ; 25cm. — (Macdonald new reference library ; 3)
Text on lining paper. — Bibl.: p.44. — Index.
ISBN 0-356-05802-6 : £1.50
(B77-24142)

391'.00937'5 — Etruscan costume, ca B.C.750-ca B.C.100
Bonfante, Larissa. Etruscan dress / [by] Larissa Bonfante. — Baltimore ; London : Johns Hopkins University Press, [1976]. — xi,243p : ill ; 27cm.
Published in the United States: 1975. — Bibl.: p.213-230. — Index.
ISBN 0-8018-1640-8 : £8.00
(B77-08334)

391'.00941 — British costume, B.C.43-
Sichel, Marion. Costume reference / [by] Marion Sichel. — London : Batsford.
In 6 vols.
1 : Roman Britain and the Middle Ages. — 1977. — 72p,[4]p of plates : ill(some col) ; 26cm.
Bibl.: p.71. — Index.
ISBN 0-7134-0334-9 : £2.95
(B77-24143)

3 : Jacobean, Stuart and Restoration. — 1977. — 70p,[4]p of plates : ill(some col) ; 26cm.
Bibl.: p.68. — Index.
ISBN 0-7134-0338-1 : £2.95
(B77-21068)

391'.00942 — Museums. *Surrey. Chertsey. Chertsey Museum. Exhibits: English costume, 1700-1800. Catalogues*
Chertsey Museum. Costume in Chertsey Museum, 1700-1800 / [catalogue compiled by] Christina Rowley. — [Chertsey] ([The Cedars, Windsor St., Chertsey, Surrey KT16 8AT]) : [The Museum], 1976. — [3],16p : ill ; 21cm.
Bibl.: p.16.
Sd : Unpriced
(B77-22516)

391'.009429 — Welsh costume, 1700-1900
Etheridge, Ken. Welsh costume : in the 18th & 19th century / [by] Ken Etheridge. — Swansea : C. Davies, 1977. — 112p : ill(some col) ; 18cm.
Not the same as B58-15726. — Index.
ISBN 0-7154-0411-3 Pbk : £1.50
(B77-33173)

391'.00947 — Eastern European traditional costume. *Juvenile literature*
Fox, Lilla Margaret. Folk costumes from Eastern Europe / [by] Lilla M. Fox ; illustrated by the author. — London : Chatto and Windus, 1977. — 64p : ill(some col), col map ; 22cm. — (The signpost library)
Index.
ISBN 0-7011-5092-0 : £2.50 : CIP rev.
(B77-10327)

391'.00947 — Russian costume, 1682-1894
In the Russian style / edited by Jacqueline Onassis ; with the co-operation of the Metropolitan Museum of Art ; introduction by Audrey Kennett ; designed by Bryan Holme. — London : Thames and Hudson, 1977. — 184p : ill(some col), facsim, ports ; 29cm.
Originally published: New York : Viking Penguin, 1976. — Bibl.: p.183.
ISBN 0-500-23266-0 : £10.00
Also classified at 745'.0947
(B77-21069)

391'.02'2 — Great Britain. Elizabeth II, Queen of Great Britain. Costume, to 1976
Robb. The Queen's clothes / illustrations by Robb ; text by Anne Edwards ; introduction by Sir Norman Hartnell. — London : Rainbird Publishing Group : Distributed by Elm Tree Books, 1977. — 128p,[24]p of plates : ill(some col), ports(some col) ; 25cm.
'An "Express" book'.
ISBN 0-241-89709-2 : £5.95
(B77-24859)

391'.413'09 — Shoes, to 1973
Wilson, Eunice. A history of shoe fashions : a study of shoe design in relation to costume and shoe designers, pattern cutters, manufacturers, fashion students and dress designers etc. / by Eunice Wilson ; with shoe drawings by the author, costume drawings by Gay Lloyd. — London : Pitman [etc.], 1974. — xvi,334p,[12]p of plates : ill, ports ; 25cm.
Originally published: 1969. — Bibl.: p.318-320. — Index.
ISBN 0-273-00471-9 Pbk : £2.50
(B77-16832)

391'.43 — Printers' paper hats, 1800-1900
The **hat** story : in honour of the Caxton Quincentenary / [edited by W.A. Shepherd]. — [Plymouth ([Palace St., Plymouth]) : Department of Printing, Plymouth College of Art and Design, 1976. — 20p : ill, facsim, ports ; 19cm.
ISBN 0-905797-00-0 Sd : £1.00
(B77-03497)

391'.45 — England. Squire, Gwen. Private collections: British livery buttons, 1800-1900. Collections: Pitt Collection. *Catalogues*
Squire, Gwen. Livery buttons : the Pitt Collection / [by] Gwen Squire. — Pulborough ([Bury], Pulborough, Sussex) : Leghorn Co., 1976. — lvix p,100 leaves of plates : chiefly ill, port ; 28cm.
Leaves printed on both sides. — Bibl.: p.lxix. — Index.
ISBN 0-9504748-0-0 : £10.00
(B77-10328)

391'.45'06241 — Buttons. Collecting. Organisations. *Great Britain. British Button Society. Periodicals*
British Button Society. Intermediate lines / the British Button Society. — Rayleigh (c/o Mrs L.M. Graham, 32 Crown Hill, Rayleigh, Essex) : [The Society].
No.1- ; Mar. 1976-. — 1976-. — 32cm.
3 leaves in 1st issue.
Sd : Unpriced
(B77-04730)

Button lines / the British Button Society. — Rayleigh (c/o Hon. Secretary, 32 Crown Hill, Rayleigh, Essex) : The Society.
No.1- ; Jan. 1976-. — [1976]-. — 30cm.
Quarterly. — 13p. in 2nd issue.
Sd : Unpriced
ISSN 0309-121x
(B77-04731)

391'.45'094 — European buttons, to ca 1910. *Collectors' guides*
Houart, Victor. Buttons : a collector's guide / by Victor Houart. — London : Souvenir Press, 1977. — 128p : ill ; 23cm.
ISBN 0-285-62277-3 : £4.95
(B77-27795)

392 — CUSTOMS OF LIFE CYCLE AND DOMESTIC LIFE
392 — Rites of passage. *Anthropological perspectives*
Gennep, Arnold van. The rites of passage / by Arnold van Gennep ; translated [from the French] by Monika B. Vizedom and Gabrielle L. Caffee ... — London [etc.] : Routledge and Kegan Paul, 1977. — vii,198p ; 22cm.
This translation originally published: / with introduction by Solon T. Kimball, 1960. — Translation of: 'Les rites de passage'. Paris : Nourry, 1908. — Index.
ISBN 0-7100-8744-6 Pbk : £2.25
(B77-31118)

392'.4'09429 — Welsh courtship customs, to ca 1900. *Welsh texts*
Stevens, Catrin. Arferion caru / gan Catrin Stevens. — Llandysul : Gwasg Gomer, 1977. — 118p,[8]p of plates : ill ; 19cm.
Index.
ISBN 0-85088-482-9 Pbk : £0.90
(B77-31119)

392'.5'09 — Marriage customs, to 1976
Baker, Margaret, *b.1928.* Wedding customs and folklore / [by] Margaret Baker. — Newton Abbot [etc.] : David and Charles [etc.], 1977. — 144p : ill, facsim, ports ; 23cm.
Bibl.: p.139-140. — Index.
ISBN 0-7153-7325-0 : £3.95
(B77-16324)

392'.6 — Courtly love. Theories, 1500-1975
Boase, Roger. The origin and meaning of courtly love : a critical study of European scholarship / [by] Roger Boase. — Manchester : Manchester University Press [etc.], 1977. — xii,171p,viii p of plates : ill ; 23cm.
Bibl.: p.140-166. — Index.
ISBN 0-7190-0656-2 : £7.50
(B77-21817)

393 — DEATH CUSTOMS
393 — Body snatching, to 1974. *Juvenile literature*
Cohen, Daniel. The body snatchers / [by] Daniel Cohen. — London [etc.] : Dent, 1977. — 159p : ill ; 22cm. — (The weird and horrible library)
Originally published: Philadelphia : Lippincott, 1975. — Index.
ISBN 0-460-06812-1 : £2.50 : CIP rev.
(B77-19313)

393.2'68282'0942444 — Christmas. *Hereford and Worcester. Kingsland, ca 1928*
Belloc, Hilaire. A remaining Christmas / by Hilaire Belloc. — Worcester ([Callow End, Worcester WR2 4TD]) : Stanbrook Abbey Press, 1976. — [1],xi,12p : ill ; 19cm.
Limited ed. of 400 copies of which the first 100 are numbered ; nos 1-35 bound in full leather, nos 36-100 quarter bound in leather. — Originally published : s.l. : s.n., 1928.
£12.75
(B77-31829)

393'.3'0932 — Ancient Egyptian mummies. *Juvenile literature*
Pace, Mildred Mastin. Wrapped for eternity : the story of the Egyptian mummy / [by] Mildred Mastin Pace ; egyptologist and content consultant Kenneth Jay Linsner ; line drawings by Tom Huffman. — Guildford [etc.] : Lutterworth Press, 1977. — 191p : ill, map, plans ; 24cm.
Originally published: New York : McGraw-Hill, 1974. — Bibl.: p.186-189. — Index.
ISBN 0-7188-2311-7 : £3.75
(B77-29353)

394 — PUBLIC AND SOCIAL CUSTOMS
394 — Traditional seasonal activities. *Middle school texts*
Feasts & seasons. — Glasgow [etc.] : Blackie.
Autumn / [compiled by] Anthony Adams, Robert Leach, Roy Palmer. — 1977. — [6], 58p : ill, music, plan ; 25cm.
ISBN 0-216-90263-0 Pbk : £1.50
(B77-27796)

Winter / [compiled by] Anthony Adams, Robert Leach, Roy Palmer. — 1977. — [6], 58p : ill, facsims, music ; 25cm.
Bibl.: p.57.
ISBN 0-216-90354-8 Pbk : £1.50
(B77-27797)

394'.09425'1 — Derbyshire social customs
Daniel, Clarence. Derbyshire customs / by Clarence Daniel. — Clapham, N. Yorkshire : Dalesman, 1976. — 80p : ill ; 21cm.
ISBN 0-85206-358-x Pbk : £0.90
(B77-15247)

394.1'2 — Breakfasts, to 1976
Pomeroy, Ralph. First things first : a connoisseur's companion to breakfast / [by] Ralph Pomeroy. — New York ; London : Paddington Press, 1977. — 156p : ill, facsims, ports ; 18x26cm.
Index.
ISBN 0-448-22835-1 Pbk : £2.95
(B77-14674)

394.1'3 — Beer festivals. *Cambridgeshire. Cambridge. Cambridge Beer Festival, 3rd, 1976*
3rd Beer Festival : 21-24 July 1976 at the Corn Exchange, Cambridge / [editors Peter B. Pearce and Stephen G. Cornford]. — [Fenstanton] ([8 Rookery Way, Fenstanton, Cambs.]) : Campaign for Real Ale, [Cambridge and District Branch], [1976]. — [2],24,[2]p : ill ; 22cm.
Bibl.: p.24.
ISBN 0-9505687-0-8 Sd : £0.15
(B77-16325)

394.2'0938'5 — Festivals. *Ancient Greece. Athens*
Parke, Herbert William. Festivals of the Athenians / [by] H.W. Parke. — London : Thames and Hudson, 1977. — 208p,[32]p of plates : ill, plan ; 23cm. — (Aspects of Greek and Roman life)
Bibl.: p.202. — Index.
ISBN 0-500-40033-4 : £9.50
(B77-11756)

394.2'6'0941 — British calendar customs
Sykes, Homer W. Once a year : some traditional British customs / [by] Homer Sykes ; introduction by Paul and Georgina Smith. — London : Gordon Fraser Gallery, 1977. — 168p : ill, map ; 25cm.
Bibl.: p.168.
ISBN 0-900406-68-2 Pbk : £5.95 : CIP rev.
(B77-18068)

394.2'6'0942 — English calendar customs
Long, George, *b.1882.* The folklore calendar / by George Long. — Wakefield : EP Publishing, 1977. — [9],240p,[24]leaves of plates : ports ; 22cm.
Facsimile reprint of: 1st ed. London : Philip Allan, 1930. — Index.
ISBN 0-7158-1227-0 : £5.50 : CIP rev
(B77-13614)

394.2'6'09427 — Northern English calendar customs
Poulson, Joan. North country traditions / by Joan Poulson. — Nelson : Hendon Publishing Co.
Part 1 : January-June. — 1977. — 48p : ill ; 14x22cm.
ISBN 0-86067-019-8 Sd : £1.00
(B77-32584)

394.2'68282 — Christmas. *Juvenile literature*
The **sugar-plum** Christmas book : a book for Christmas and all the days of the year / [compiled by] Jean Chapman ; illustrated by Deborah Niland ; song settings by Margaret Moore. — Sydney ; London [etc.] : Hodder and Stoughton, 1977. — [2],190p : ill(chiefly col), music ; 27cm.
Text on lining papers. — Index.
ISBN 0-340-22049-x : £4.95
(B77-25544)

394.2'68282'0941 — Christmas. *Great Britain, ca 1850-1900. Readings from contemporary sources. Facsimiles*
Christmas past / compiled by Dulcie M. Ashdown ; foreword by Jilly Cooper. — London : Arrow Books, 1977. — [1],152p : ill ; 24cm.
Facsimile reprints. — This selection originally published: London : Elm Tree Books, 1976.
ISBN 0-09-915260-6 Pbk : £1.95
(B77-33741)

Christmas past : a selection from Victorian magazines / compiled by Dulcie M. Ashdown ; foreword by Jilly Cooper. — London : Elm Tree Books, 1976. — 152p : ill ; 24cm.
Facsimile reprints.
ISBN 0-241-89461-1 : £4.50
(B77-00167)

394.2'68282'0941 — Christmas customs. *Great Britain, to 1974*
Muir, Frank. Christmas customs and traditions / [by] Frank Muir. — London : Sphere, 1975. — 111p,[32]p of plates : ill(some col), facsims, ports ; 20cm.
Index.
ISBN 0-7221-6262-6 Pbk : £0.90
(B77-18695)

394.2'69'411 — Public holidays. *Scotland. Calendars*
Public holidays in Scotland / Scottish Tourist Board. — Edinburgh : The Board. — (Scottish Tourist Board. Information booklets)
1977. — [1976]. — 24p : 1 ill ; 21x10cm.
Also published: Edinburgh : Scottish Tourist Board ; Glasgow : Glasgow Chamber of Commerce, 1977.
Sd : Unpriced
(B77-21070)

Public holidays in Scotland / Scottish Tourist Board, Glasgow Chamber of Commerce. — Edinburgh : Scottish Tourist Board ; Glasgow (30 George Sq., Glasgow G2 1EQ) : Glasgow Chamber of Commerce.
1977. — [1977]. — 22p ; 21x10cm.
ISBN 0-85419-115-1 Sd : Unpriced
(B77-12404)

394.3 — Circuses. Factions. *Ancient Rome*
Cameron, Alan, *b.1938.* Circus factions : Blues and Greens at Rome and Byzantium / by Alan Cameron. — Oxford : Clarendon Press, 1976. — x,364p,plate : 1 ill ; 23cm.
Bibl.: p.347-352. — Index.
ISBN 0-19-814804-6 : £16.50
(B77-01342)

394'.3'0942 — Gentry. Outdoor sports. Social aspects. *England. Rural regions, to 1918*
Longrigg, Roger. The English squire and his sport / [by] Roger Longrigg. — London : Joseph, 1977. — 302p : ill, plan, ports ; 24cm.
Ill. on lining papers. — Index.
ISBN 0-7181-1554-6 : £7.50
(B77-09653)

394'.4 — Royal charities: Royal Maundy. *Great Britain, to 1976*
Robinson, Brian. The Royal Maundy / [by] Brian Robinson. — London : Kaye and Ward, 1977. — 84p,[24]p of plates : ill, ports ; 23cm.
ISBN 0-7182-1151-0 : £3.25
(B77-17433)

394.5 — Processions. Special themes: Dragons. *Norfolk. Norwich, to 1975*
Lane, Richard. Snap, the Norwich dragon / by Richard Lane ; original photography by Alan Howard. — Norwich (White Lodge Trading Estate, Hall Rd, Norwich) : Trend Litho, 1976. — 34p : ill, ports ; 21cm.
Bibl.: p.33.
ISBN 0-9505361-0-5 Sd : £0.45
(B77-00168)

394'.5'062 — Medieval pageantry societies. *Periodicals*
The **Norseman** : the monthly journal of the Norse Film & Pageant Society incorporating the kindred interests of the mediaeval societies. — [London] ([95 Dartford Ave., N.9]) : Norse Film and Pageant Society.
Vol.1, no.1- ; [May?, 1974]-. — 1974-. — ill, ports ; 30cm.
[16]p. in 1st issue.
Sd : £0.25
ISSN 0309-5762
(B77-18696)

394'.5'0942 — Pageantry. Special subjects: England. Elizabeth I, Queen of England. *England, 1558-1603*
Strong, Roy. The cult of Elizabeth : Elizabethan portraiture and pageantry / [by] Roy Strong. — [London] : Thames and Hudson, 1977. — 227p : ill(incl 1 col), facsim, geneal table, ports(3 col) ; 26cm.
Index.
ISBN 0-500-23263-6 : £11.50
Primary classification 757'.0942
(B77-27265)

394.6 — Fairs. *Oxfordshire. Oxford. St Giles' Fair, 1927-1946. Traction engines. Personal observations*
Kirk, Viv. Memories of St Giles' Fair / by Viv Kirk ; edited and introduced by Ran Hawthorne. — Loughton (c/o G.F. Beck, 127 Greensted Rd, Loughton, Essex) : [National Traction Engine Club], [1976]. — 56p : ill, port ; 22cm. — (A 'Steaming' publication : series A ; no.5)
ISBN 0-905818-00-8 Sd : Unpriced
(B77-04732)

394'.6'0941 — Customs: Fairs. *Great Britain. Secondary school texts*
Fairs & circuses / [compiled by] John Foster & Rod Hunt. — Basingstoke [etc.] : Macmillan, 1977. — [1],32p : ill, facsim ; 20x21cm. — (Investigations)
Bibl.
ISBN 0-333-16839-9 Sd : £0.55
Also classified at 791.3'0941
(B77-27798)

394'.6'0941 — Customs: Fairs. *Great Britain, to 1975*
Jewell, Brian. Fairs and revels / [by] Brian Jewell. — Tunbridge Wells : Midas Books, 1976. — 127p : ill, plan, port ; 26cm.
Ill. on lining papers. — Bibl.: p.123. — Index.
ISBN 0-85936-068-7 : £5.50
(B77-04101)

394'.6'0942786 — Horse fairs. *Cumbria. Appleby. Appleby New Fair. Illustrations*
Hall, Wilfred. A time to come alive : a pictorial souvenir of Appleby Horse Fair / [written, photographed, designed and produced by Wilfred Hall]. — Harrogate (44 St Mark's Ave., Harrogate, N. Yorkshire HG2 8AE) : Wilfred Hall Associates, 1976. — [28]p : chiefly ill, ports ; 21x30cm.
ISBN 0-9504992-0-x Sd : £1.00
(B77-08968)

394'.7'03 — Chivalry. *Encyclopaedias*
Uden, Grant. A dictionary of chivalry / [by] Grant Uden ; illustrated by Pauline Baynes. — Harmondsworth : Kestrel Books, 1977. — [7], 352p : ill(some col), coats of arms(some col), geneal table, map, ports(some col) ; 25cm.
Ill. on lining papers. — Originally published: London : Longmans Young Books, 1968. — Index.
ISBN 0-7226-5372-7 : £5.95
(B77-31830)

395 — ETIQUETTE
Walker, Gladys. Points of order / by Gladys Walker. — 3rd ed. — London : Shaw and Sons, 1976. — 171p ; 19cm.
Previous ed.: 1971. — Bibl.: p.161-162. — Index.
ISBN 0-7219-0401-7 Pbk : £1.50
(B77-02920)

395'.4 — Forms of address & titles
Montague-Smith, Patrick Wykeham. Debrett's correct form : an inclusive guide to everything from drafting wedding invitations to addressing an archbishop / compiled and edited by Patrick Montague-Smith. — Revised ed. — Kingston-upon-Thames : Debrett's Peerage Ltd [etc.] ; London [etc.] : Distributed by Hamlyn, 1976. — x,423p,plate : forms, col port ; 23cm.
Previous ed.: Kingston upon Thames: Kelly's Directories, 1970. — Index.
ISBN 0-905649-00-1 : £4.95
(B77-05343)

398 — FOLKLORE
398'.092'4 — Welsh folklore. Peate, Iorwerth Cyfeiliog. *Autobiographies. Welsh texts*
Peate, Iorwerth Cyfeiliog. Rhwng dau fyd : darn o hunangofiant / [gan] Iorwerth C. Peate. — [Denbigh] : Gwasg Gee, 1976. — 200p,8p of plates : ill, ports ; 22cm.
ISBN 0-7074-0093-7 : £3.00
(B77-02921)

398'.0941 — British folklore. *Encyclopaedias*
Folklore, myths and legends of Britain / [edited and designed by the Reader's Digest Association]. — 2nd ed. — London : Reader's Digest Association, 1977. — 552p : ill(some col), facsims(some col), maps, ports(some col) ; 29cm.
Previous ed.: 1973. — Index.
£7.95
(B77-31831)

398'.094111 — Scottish folklore: Highlands & Islands folklore
Robertson, Ronald Macdonald. Selected Highland folk tales / gathered orally by R. Macdonald Robertson ; edited and with a new introduction by Jeremy Bruce-Watt. — Newton Abbot [etc.] : David and Charles, 1977. — xii,212p ; 23cm.
This collection originally published: Edinburgh : Oliver and Boyd, 1961. — Index.
ISBN 0-7153-7436-2 : £3.95
(B77-21071)

398'.09416 — Northern Irish folklore
Andrews, Elizabeth. Ulster folklore / by Elizabeth Andrews. — Wakefield : EP Publishing, 1977. — xiii,121p,12 leaves of plates : ill, plans ; 22cm.
Facsimile reprint of: 1st ed. London : Elliot Stock, 1913. — Index.
ISBN 0-7158-1231-9 : £3.95 : CIP rev.
(B77-16326)

398'.09416'58 — Rostrevor folklore
Crowe, William Haughton. Village in seven hills : the story and stories of Rostrevor, Co. Down / by W. Haughton Crowe. — Dundalk : Dundalgan Press, 1973. — ix,106p,[2] leaves of plates,[22]p of plates : ill, map, ports ; 19cm.
Originally published: 1972. — Bibl.: p.102. — Index.
Pbk : Unpriced
Primary classification 941.6'58
(B77-05781)

398'.094172 — Sligo (County) folklore: Coney Island folklore
Finnegan, T A. Sligo : Sinbad's yellow shore / by T.A. Finnegan. — Sligo (Castle St., Sligo, [Eire]) : J.M. Keohane ; Dublin : Dolmen Press, 1977. — 91p ; 22cm.
ISBN 0-85105-332-7 Pbk : £2.00
(B77-23330)

398'.0942 — English folklore. *Collections*
A **country** compendium / [compiled by] Godfrey Baseley ; text illustrations by Alex Jardine. — London : Sidgwick and Jackson, 1977. — 254p : ill ; 21cm.
Index.
ISBN 0-283-98222-5 : £5.50
(B77-16327)

398′.09422′9 — Berkshire folklore
Millson, Cecilia. Tales of old Berkshire / [by] Cecilia Millson. — Thatcham (4 Turners Drive, Thatcham, Berks. [RG13 4QB]) : Countryside Books, 1977. — [10],86p : map ; 22cm.
ISBN 0-905392-01-9 Pbk : £1.95
(B77-23331)

398′.09423′5 — Devon folklore
Hewett, Sarah. Nummits and crummits : Devonshire customs, characteristics, and folk-lore / by Sarah Hewett ; with frontispiece by George Martin. — Wakefield : EP Publishing, 1976. — [4],vii,219p : 1 ill ; 20cm.
Facsimile reprint of: 1st ed. London : Thomas Burleigh, 1900.
ISBN 0-7158-1170-3 : £3.45
(B77-16833)

398′.09424′17 — Cotswolds folklore
Bloom, James Harvey. Folk lore, old customs and superstitions in Shakespeare land / by J. Harvey Bloom. — Wakefield : EP Publishing, 1976. — [1],viii,167p ; 23cm.
Facsimile reprint of: 1st ed. London : Mitchell Hughes and Clarke, 1930. — Bibl.: p.viii. — Index.
ISBN 0-7158-1185-1 : £4.75
(B77-24144)

398′.09425′8 — Hertfordshire folklore
Jones-Baker, Doris. The folklore of Hertfordshire / [by] Doris Jones-Baker. — London : Batsford, 1977. — 240p : ill, map, music, plan ; 23cm. — (The folklore of the British Isles)
Bibl.: p.229-231. — Index.
ISBN 0-7134-3266-7 : £3.95
(B77-24145)

398′.09427′8 — Lake District folklore
Findler, Gerald. Lake District folk lore / by Gerald Findler. — Abridged ed. — Clapham, N. Yorkshire : Dalesman, 1977. — 48p : ill ; 19cm. — (A Dalesman mini-book)
Full ed. published: as 'Folk lore of the Lake Counties'. 1968.
ISBN 0-85206-382-2 Pbk : £0.50
(B77-33742)

398′.09427′83 — Cumbrian folklore: Kendal folklore
Preston, Kathleen. Tales of Old Kendal / by Kathleen Preston ; photographs, H. Bell ... [et al.]. — [Kendal] ([Rowan Bank, High Park, Oxenholme, Kendal, Cumbria]) : [The author], 1977. — 72p : ill ; 21cm. — (The years look down)
Bibl.: p.72.
Pbk : Unpriced
(B77-23332)

398′.09429 — Welsh folklore
Owen, Elias. Welsh folk-lore : a collection of the folk-tales and legends of North Wales : being the prize essay of the National Eisteddfod 1887 / by Elias Owen ; revised and enlarged by the author. — Wakefield : EP Publishing, 1976. — [1],xii,359p ; 23cm.
Facsimile reprint of: 1896 ed. Oswestry : Woodall and Minshall, 1896. — Index.
ISBN 0-7158-1179-7 : £5.95
(B77-25545)

398′.09498 — Romanian folklore
Mackenzie, Andrew. Dracula country : travels and folk beliefs in Romania / [by] Andrew Mackenzie. — London : A. Barker, 1977. — xv,176p : map ; 23cm.
Bibl.: p.169-170. — Index.
ISBN 0-213-16658-5 : £4.95
(B77-25546)

398′.152′02462 — Measurement. Système International d'Unités. *For engineering*
Walshaw, Arthur Clifford. SI calculations in engineering science / [by] A.C. Walshaw. — London [etc.] : Newnes-Butterworths, 1977. — [7],88p : ill ; 22cm.
Index.
ISBN 0-408-00284-0 Pbk : £1.95
(B77-25547)

398.2 — TALES AND LEGENDS
398.2 — Tales & legends. *Anthologies*
Černý, Václav. Tales of the uncanny / [by] Václav Černý, Zlata Černá, Miroslav Novák ; [translated from the Czech by Helen Notzl]. — London [etc.] : Hamlyn, 1976. — 211p : ill(some col) ; 29cm.
Ill. on lining papers.
ISBN 0-600-38716-x : £2.50
(B77-14675)

398.2′0917′43 — Germanic tales & legends. *Anthologies*
The **Faber** book of northern legends / edited by Kevin Crossley-Holland ; illustrated by Alan Howard. — London : Faber, 1977. — 3-236p : ill ; 24cm.
Bibl.: p.229-231. — Index.
ISBN 0-571-10912-8 : £4.50 : CIP rev.
(B77-18069)

398.2′0941 — British tales & legends. *Anthologies*
British folk tales and legends : a sampler / [compiled by] Katharine M. Briggs. — St Albans [etc.] : Paladin, 1977. — xv,315p ; 20cm.
'[The author has] taken [her] "Dictionary of British Folk-Tales" (Part A, 2 volumes published in 1970 and Part B, 2 volumes published in 1971 ...) and selected a sampler ...' - Introduction. — This selection originally published: London : Routledge and Kegan Paul, 1977.
ISBN 0-586-08237-9 Pbk : £1.50
(B77-23333)

A **sampler** of British folk-tales / [compiled by] Katharine M. Briggs. — London [etc.] : Routledge and Kegan Paul, 1977. — xv,315p ; 24cm.
Selections from: 'A dictionary of British folk tales in the English language'. 1970-71. — Bibl.: p.11-12.
ISBN 0-7100-8553-2 : £4.95
(B77-14676)

398.2′0941 — British tales & legends. *Anthologies. Juvenile literature*
Stuart, Forbes. The dancer of Burton Fair : folk tales from Britain / [retold by] Forbes Stuart ; illustrated by Charles Keeping. — London : Abelard-Schuman, 1976. — 82p : ill ; 22cm.
Ill. on lining papers.
ISBN 0-200-72460-6 : £2.95
(B77-08969)

398.2′09411 — Scottish tales & legends. *Anthologies*
Scottish fairy and folk tales / selected and edited, with an introduction by Sir George Douglas, bart ; twelve illustrations by James Torrance. — Wakefield : EP Publishing, 1977. — xxxii[i.e. xxxiv],301p,[12]leaves of plates : ill ; 19cm.
Facsimile reprint of: 1st ed. London : W. Scott, 1893.
ISBN 0-7158-1230-0 : £4.95 : CIP rev.
(B77-14187)

398.2′09423′5 — Devon folklore
Whitlock, Ralph. The folklore of Devon / [by] Ralph Whitlock ; illustrated by Gay John Galsworthy. — London : Batsford, 1977. — [2],214p : ill, map ; 23cm. — (The folklore of the British Isles)
Bibl.: p.201-202. — Index.
ISBN 0-7134-3265-9 : £3.95
(B77-27799)

398.2′09429 — Welsh tales & legends. *Anthologies. Juvenile literature*
Strange, Morfudd. Chwedlau ddoe o Fro Hiraethog / [gan] Morfudd Strange. — Abertawe [i.e. Swansea] : C. Davies, 1977. — 52p ; 22cm.
ISBN 0-7154-0420-2 Pbk : £0.40
(B77-24146)

398.2′09429′4 — South Wales tales & legends. *Anthologies*
Styles, Showell. Welsh walks & legends, South Wales / [by] Showell Styles. — Cardiff (41 Lochaber St., Cardiff CF2 3LS) : John Jones Cardiff Ltd, 1977. — 63p : ill, map ; 22cm.
ISBN 0-902375-06-7 : Unpriced
ISBN 0-902375-07-5 Pbk : £1.25
Primary classification 914.29′4′04857
(B77-23841)

398.2′0951 — Chinese tales & legends. *Anthologies*
Manton, Jo. The flying horses : tales from China / [by] Jo Manton ; with verses in Chinese style by Robert Gittings ; illustrated by Derek Collard. — London : Methuen, 1977. — 172p : ill ; 24cm.
ISBN 0-416-83440-x : £3.95
(B77-30160)

398.2′09676′29 — Nyanza tales & legends. *Anthologies*
Harman, Humphrey. Tales told near a crocodile : a book of African stories / [by] Humphrey Harman. — London [etc.] : Beaver Books, 1976. — 2-157p : ill, map ; 20cm.
This collection originally published: London : Hutchinson, 1962.
ISBN 0-600-38748-8 Pbk : £0.55
(B77-14677)

398.2′09764 — Texan negro tales & legends. *Anthologies*
Brewer, J Mason. Dog ghosts, and other Texas negro folk tales ; [and], The word on the Brazos : negro preacher tales from the Brazos Bottoms of Texas / [by] J. Mason Brewer. — Austin ; London : University of Texas Press, 1976. — 124,109,[33]p,[2]leaves of plates : ill ; 23cm.
'Dog ghosts and other Texas negro folk tales' originally published: Austin : University of Texas Press, 1958. — 'Word on the Brazos' originally published: Austin : University of Texas Press, 1953.
ISBN 0-292-71512-9 Pbk : £3.75
(B77-17434)

398.2′09764′932 — Texan tales & legends: Big Bend region tales & legends. *Anthologies*
Miles, Elton. Tales of the Big Bend / by Elton Miles. — College Station ; London ([c/o 70 Great Russell St., WC1B 3BY]) : Texas A & M University Press, 1976. — 189p,[8]p of plates : ill, map, ports ; 23cm.
Index.
ISBN 0-89096-021-6 : £7.50
(B77-22517)

398.2′09767′1 — Missouri tales: Ozark erotic tales. *Anthologies*
Pissing in the snow, and other Ozark folktales / [compiled by] Vance Randolph ; introduction by Rayna Green ; annotations by Frank A. Hoffmann. — Urbana [etc.] ; London : University of Illinois Press, 1976. — [1],xxxiii, 153p : music ; 21cm.
Bibl.: p.151-153.
ISBN 0-252-00618-6 : £6.00
(B77-15796)

398.2′0994 — Australian aboriginal tales & legends. *Anthologies*
Reed, Alexander Wyclif. Myths and legends of Australia / by A.W. Reed ; illustrated by Roger Hart. — Sydney [etc.] ; London : A.H. and A.W. Reed, 1976. — 256p : ill ; 21cm.
Originally published: 1965. — Bibl.: p.255-256.
ISBN 0-589-07041-x : £6.90
(B77-24860)

398.2′0996′13 — Samoan tales & legends. *Anthologies. Samoan-English parallel texts*
Stuebel, C. Myths and legends of Samoa = Tala o le vavau / Samoan text by C. Stuebel ; English translation by Brother Herman ; illustrated by Iosua Toafa. — Wellington [N.Z.] [etc.] ; London : A.H. and A.W. Reed [etc.], 1976. — [4],157p : ill ; 25cm.
ISBN 0-589-00968-0 Pbk : £3.05
Also classified at 390′.0996′13
(B77-04102)

398.2′1 — Fairy tales. *Critical studies*
Lüthi, Max. Once upon a time : on the nature of fairy tales / [by] Max Lüthi ; translated [from the German] by Lee Chadeayne and Paul Gottwald ; with additions by the author ; introduction and reference notes by Francis Lee Utley. — Bloomington ; London : Indiana University Press, 1976. — [7],179p ; 21cm. — (A Midland book)
This translation originally published: New York : F. Ungar, 1970. — Translation of: 'Es war einmal'. 3., durchgesehene Aufl. Gottingen : Vandenhoeck und Ruprecht, 1968. — Index.
ISBN 0-253-20203-5 Pbk : £1.60
(B77-09654)

398.2′1 — Tales. *Anthologies*
The **Penguin** book of world folk tales / edited by Milton Rugoff ; illustrations by Joseph Low. — Harmondsworth [etc.] : Penguin, 1977. — xviii, 734p : ill ; 20cm.
Originally published: as 'A harvest of world folk tales'. New York : Viking Press, 1949. — Index.
ISBN 0-14-004525-2 Pbk : £2.75
(B77-33174)

398.2′1 — Tales. *Anthologies. Juvenile literature*
Favourite fairy tales / [edited by Howard Jennings]. — London : Octopus Books, 1977. — 128p : col ill ; 31cm.
Title page has author statement: Edited by Diana Bremer.
ISBN 0-7064-0632-x : £1.99
(B77-31120)

Green, Roger Lancelyn. Once upon a time : fairy tales of the world / retold by Roger Lancelyn Green ; illustrations by V. Kubašta. — [New ed.]. — London [etc.] : Hamlyn, [1977]. — 4-301p : col ill ; 30cm.
Previous ed.: New York : Golden Press, 1962 ; Feltham : Hamlyn, 1969.
ISBN 0-600-36745-2 : £2.95
(B77-30161)

398.2'1'09174927 — Arabic tales. *Anthologies*
Petrus Alfonsi. The 'Disciplina clericalis' of Petrus Alfonsi / translated [from the Latin] and edited by Eberhard Hermes ; translated into English [from the German and the Latin] by P.R. Quarrie. — London [etc.] : Routledge and Kegan Paul, 1977. — x,203p ; 22cm. — (The Islamic world series)
'The translation of the 'Disciplina Clericalis' itself, and that of any passages quoted from other works of Petrus Alfonsi in the body of the introduction, has been made anew from the original Latin, with reference to the German version of Herr Hermes. The text used for the "Disciplina Clericalis" was the Heidelberg, 1911 edition of Hilka and Söderhjelm' - Translator's note. — Bibl.: p.192-196. — Index.
ISBN 0-7100-7477-8 : £5.95
(B77-07278)

398.2'1'094 — European tales. *Anthologies*
Tales from times past / edited by Bryan Holme. — London : Heinemann, 1977. — 176p : ill(some col) ; 24cm.
ISBN 0-434-34541-5 : £4.75
(B77-24861)

398.2'1'0941 — British tales. *Anthologies*
Folk tales of the British Isles / edited by Michael Foss ; illustrated by Ken Kiff. — London [etc.] : Macmillan, 1977. — 176p : ill(some col) ; 25cm.
ISBN 0-333-23436-7 : £4.95
(B77-33175)

398.2'1'094115 — Highland Scottish tales. *Anthologies*
Temperley, Alan. Tales of the North Coast : the beautiful and remote north coast of Scotland from Melvich to Tongue / gathered and written by Alan Temperley and the pupils of Farr Secondary School ; illustrations by the pupils under the direction of Elliot Rudie ; and with a foreword by James Scotland. — London : Research Publishing Co., 1977. — 252p : ill, map ; 22cm.
Bibl.: p.247-248.
ISBN 0-7050-0045-1 : £3.20
ISBN 0-7050-0046-x Pbk : £1.90
(B77-25548)

398.2'1'0943 — German tales. *Anthologies*
Grimm, Jacob. [Fairy tales]. Grimm's fairy tales / edited by Edric Vredenburg ; pictured by Mabel Lucie Attwell. — London : Pan Books, 1977. — 139p,[8]p of plates : ill(some col) ; 23cm. — (Piccolo gift book series)
Facsimile reprint of: 1st ed. of this selection. London : R. Tuck, 1902.
ISBN 0-330-24532-5 Pbk : £1.25
(B77-12982)

Grimm, Jacob. [Fairy tales]. Grimm's fairy tales : a selection. — Maidenhead : Purnell, 1976. — 128p : ill ; 21cm. — (A Purnell classic)
ISBN 0-361-03546-2 : £0.50
(B77-06017)

Grimm, Jacob. [Fairy tales]. Grimm's fairy tales / illustrated by Charles Folkard. — London : Dent. — (Dent dolphins)
Book 1. — 1977. — [5],166p : ill ; 19cm.
ISBN 0-460-02730-1 Pbk : £0.50
(B77-06615)

Book 2. — 1977. — [3],172p : ill ; 19cm.
ISBN 0-460-02731-x Pbk : £0.50
(B77-06616)

Grimm, Jacob. [Fairy tales]. The juniper tree, and other tales from Grimm / selected by Lore Segal and Maurice Sendak ; translated [from the German] by Lore Segal, with four tales translated by Randall Jarrell ; pictures by Maurice Sendak. — London : Bodley Head, 1977. — [12],332,[1]p : ill ; 18cm.
These translations originally published: New York : Farrar, Straus and Giroux, 1973 ; London : Bodley Head, 1974.
ISBN 0-370-30059-9 Pbk : £2.50
(B77-33743)

398.2'1'0943 — German tales. *Juvenile literature. Irish texts*
Grimm, Jacob. [Die Bremer Stadtmusikanten. Irish]. Amhránaithe Bhremen / na Deartháireacha Grimm ; Svend Otto S. a rinne na pictiúir ; Eoghan Ó Colla a chuir an leagan Gaeilge in oiriúint do leanaí 6-8 mbliana d'aois. — Baile Atha Cliath [i.e. Dublin] : Oifig an tSolathair, 1977. — [24]p : chiefly col ill ; 26cm.
Translation of: 'Stadsmusikanterne fra Bremen'. Kobenhavn : Gyldendal, 1974.
Unpriced
(B77-31121)

Grimm, Jacob. An gabhar agus na meannáin / na Deartháireacha Grimm ; Máire Aine Ní Dhonnchadha a d' aistrigh do leanaí 7-9 mbliana d'aois ; learáidí Xavier Saint-Justh. — Baile Atha Cliath [i.e. Dublin] ([Bothar an Phoirt Thoir, Baile Atha Cliath 3, Eire]) : Oifig an tSoláthair, 1976. — [29]p : col ill ; 31cm.
Translation of: 'La Chèvre et les biquets'. Paris : Editions Bias, 1973.
ISBN 0-905621-10-7 : £0.90
(B77-06614)

398.2'1'09439 — Hungarian tales. *Texts. Juvenile literature*
Illyés, Gyula. Matt the gooseherd : a story from Hungary / retold for this edition by Gyula Illyés ; illustrated by Károly Reich ; [translated from the Hungarian MS. by Paul Tabori]. — Harmondsworth [etc.] : Puffin Books, 1976. — [32]p : col ill ; 19cm. — (Puffin folktales of the world ; 3)
'An Andreas Landshoff book' - title page verso.
ISBN 0-14-030803-2 Pbk : £0.50
(B77-04103)

398.2'1'09492 — Dutch tales. *Texts. Juvenile literature*
Bouhuys, Mies. The lady of Stavoren : a story from Holland / retold for this edition by Mies Bouhuys ; illustrated by Francien van Westering ; [translated from the Dutch MS. by Elizabeth Willems-Treeman]. — Harmondsworth [etc.] : Puffin Books, 1976. — [32]p : col ill ; 19cm. — (Puffin folktales of the world ; 2)
'An Andreas Landshoff book' - title page verso.
ISBN 0-14-030802-4 Pbk : £0.50
(B77-04104)

398.2'1'09495 — Greek tales. *Anthologies*
Folktales of Greece / edited by Georgios A. Megas ; translated [from the Greek] by Helen Colaclides ; foreword by Richard M. Dorson. — Chicago ; London : University of Chicago Press, 1977. — lvii,287p ; 21cm. — (Folktales of the world)
This translation originally published: 1970. — Translation of: 'Hell̄enika paramythia'. Ath̄enai (Athens) : Kollarou, 1963. — Bibl.: p.257-263. — Index.
ISBN 0-226-51786-1 Pbk : £3.40
(B77-33744)

398.2'1'09515 — Tibetan tales. *Texts. Juvenile literature*
Tsultim, Yeshe. The mouse king : a story from Tibet / retold for this edition by Yeshe Tsultim ; illustrated by Kusho Ralla ; [translated from the Tibetan MS. by Frederick Hyde-Chambers]. — Harmondsworth [etc.] : Puffin Books, 1976. — [32]p : col ill ; 19cm. — (Puffin folktales of the world ; 4)
'An Andreas Landshoff book' - title page verso.
ISBN 0-14-030804-0 Pbk : £0.50
(B77-04105)

398.2'1'0952 — Japanese tales. *Anthologies*
Freeman-Mitford, Algernon Bertram, *Baron Redesdale.* Tales of Old Japan / by A.B. Mitford (Lord Redesdale) ; with illustrations drawn and cut on wood by Japanese artists. — Rutland [Vt] [etc.] : Tuttle ; London : Distributed by Kegan Paul, Trench, Trubner, 1975. — 429p : ill ; 19cm.
Facsimile reprint of: 1st ed., originally published in 2 vols. London : Macmillan, 1871.
ISBN 0-8048-1160-1 Pbk : £3.30
(B77-29354)

398.2'1'0956 — Sufi tales. *Anthologies*
Idries Shah. The pleasantries of the incredible Mulla Nasrudin / [by] Idries Shah ; drawings by Richard Williams and Errol le Cain. — London : Pan Books, 1977. — 220p : ill ; 20cm. — (Picador)
Originally published: London : Cape, 1968.
Pbk : £0.90
ISBN 0-330-25485-6
(B77-33745)

398.2'1'09794 — Tales of Indians of California. *Texts*
Angulo, Jaime de. Indian tales / [by] Jaime de Angulo ; illustrations by Jaime de Angulo ; introduction by Richard Cupidi. — London : Abacus, 1976. — 202p : ill ; 20cm. — (American Indian visions)
Originally published: New York : A.A. Wyn, 1953.
ISBN 0-349-10020-9 Pbk : £1.50
(B77-02922)

398.2'1'09931 — Maori tales. *Anthologies*
Reed, Alexander Wyclif. Favourite Maori legends / by A.W. Reed ; illustrated by Roger Hart. — Wellington [N.Z.] [etc.] ; London : A.H. and A.W. Reed, 1977. — 142p : ill ; 19cm.
Originally published: Wellington, N.Z. : A.H. and A.W. Reed, 1965.
ISBN 0-589-00461-1 Pbk : £1.65
(B77-22518)

Reed, Alexander Wyclif. Legends of Rotorua and the hot lakes / by A.W. Reed ; with illustrations by Dennis Turner. — Wellington [N.Z.] [etc.] ; London : A.H. and A.W. Reed, 1973. — 144p : ill ; 19cm.
Originally published: Wellington, N.Z. : Reed, 1958 ; London : Bailey and Swinfen, 1959.
ISBN 0-589-00184-1 Pbk : £1.65
(B77-25549)

398.2'2 — Legends. Arthur, King. *Texts*
Steinbeck, John. The acts of King Arthur and his noble knights - : from the Winchester MSS. of Thomas Malory and other sources / [by] John Steinbeck ; edited by Chase Horton. — London : Heinemann, 1976. — xiv,364p ; 24cm.
ISBN 0-434-74022-5 : £6.50
(B77-03498)

398.2'2'03 — Legends. *Encyclopaedias*
Pears encyclopaedia of myths and legends. — London : Pelham.
In 4 vols.
[Book 2] : Northern Europe, Southern and Central Africa / by Sheila Savill ; advisory editor Geoffrey Parrinder, general editors Mary Barker and Christopher Cook. — 1977. — 191p,[8]p of plates : ill (some col), facsims(1 col) ; 26cm.
Bibl. — Index.
ISBN 0-7207-0931-8 : £5.50
Primary classification 291.1'3'03
(B77-12851)

[Book 3] : The Orient / by Sheila Savill ; advisory editor Geoffrey Parrinder ; general editors Mary Barker and Christopher Cook. — 1977. — 247p,[8]p of plates : ill(some col), facsims, ports ; 26cm.
Bibl. — Index.
ISBN 0-7207-1001-4 : £7.50
Primary classification 291.1'3'03
(B77-30975)

398.2'2'0933 — Ancient Israeli legends. *Texts. Juvenile literature*
Elkin, Benjamin. The wisest man in the world : a legend of Ancient Israel / retold by Benjamin Elkin ; pictures by Anita Lobel. — Tadworth : World's Work, 1976. — [38]p : col ill ; 26cm.
Col. ill. on lining papers. — Originally published: New York : Parents' Magazine Press, 1968 ; Tadworth : World's Work, 1971.
£2.60
ISBN 0-437-37450-5
(B77-12405)

398.2'2'0938 — Ancient Greek legends. *Anthologies. Juvenile literature*
Reeves, James. Heroes and monsters : legends of Ancient Greece / retold by James Reeves ; illustrated by Sarah Nechamkin. — Glasgow [etc.] : Blackie, 1977. — xvi,112p : ill, map ; 22cm.
Originally published: London : Blackie, 1969.
ISBN 0-216-90445-5 : £2.50
ISBN 0-216-90443-9 Pbk : Unpriced
(B77-33746)

398'.2'20938 — Ancient Greek legends. *Texts*
Pater, Walter. Cupid and Psyche / [by] Walter Pater ; illustrated by Errol le Cain. — London : Faber, 1977. — [48]p : ill ; 30cm.
'The text is a shortened and slightly adapted version of the story of 'Cupid and Psyche' from 'Marius the Epicurean' - title page verso.
ISBN 0-571-11115-7 : £3.95 : CIP rev.
(B77-23334)

398.2'2'0941 — British legends. *Anthologies. Juvenile literature*
Picard, Barbara Leonie. Hero tales from the British Isles / retold by Barbara Leonie Picard ; illustrations by Gay Galsworthy. — Harmondsworth [etc.] : Puffin Books, 1976. — 187p : ill ; 18cm. — (Puffin books)
This collection originally published: London : Ward, 1963.
ISBN 0-14-030279-4 Pbk : £0.50
(B77-04733)

398.2'2'09415 — Irish legends. *Anthologies*
O'Sullivan, Sean. Legends from Ireland / [by] Sean O'Sullivan ; drawings by John Sketton. — London : Batsford, 1977. — 176p : ill, map ; 22cm.
Bibl.: p.169-170. — Index.
ISBN 0-7134-0733-6 : £4.25
ISBN 0-7134-0734-4 Pbk : £2.75
(B77-33747)

398.2'2'09415 — Irish legends. *Anthologies. For Irish students. Secondary school texts*
Curriculum Development Unit. The Celtic way of life / [Curriculum Development Unit] ; [editor Agnes McMahon]. — Dublin (11 Clare St., Dublin 2) : O'Brien Press, 1976. — 136p : ill, maps ; 22cm.
Includes portions from 'The Ulster cycle' with one story in Irish.
ISBN 0-905140-19-2 : £3.95
Primary classification 940'.04'916
(B77-09412)

398.2'2'09415 — Irish legends. *Irish texts*
Cussen, Cliodna. Buile Shuibhne : leagan Nua-Ghaeilge agus léaráidi / le Cliodna Cussen. — Baile Átha Cliath [i.e. Dublin] (Conradh na Gaeilge, 6 Sráid Fhearchair, Baile Átha Cliath 2) : Clódhanna Tta, 1976. — 32p : ill, maps ; 20cm.
ISBN 0-905027-08-6 Sd : £0.45
(B77-00722)

398.2'2'09426 — Fenland legends. *Anthologies*
Marlowe, Christopher, *fl.1926.* Legends of the Fenland people / by Christopher Marlowe. — Wakefield : EP Publishing, 1976. — xiii,240p ; 20cm.
Facsimile reprint of: 1st ed. London : Cecil Palmer, 1926. — Bibl.: p.xiii.
ISBN 0-7158-1172-x : £4.00
(B77-17435)

398.2'2'0956 — Sufi legends. *Anthologies*
Afl¯ak¯i, Shams al-Din Ahmad. Legends of the Sufis : selected anecdotes from the work entitled 'The acts of the adepts' ('Men¯aqibu 'l ''Arif in) / by Shemsu-'d-D¯in Ahmed, el Efl¯ak¯i ; translated [from the Arabic] by James W. Redhouse. — 3rd and revised ed. ; preface by Idries Shah. — London [etc.] : Theosophical Publishing House, 1976. — xii,125p,plate : port ; 23cm.
Previous ed. of this translation: i.e. 1st ed. published in 'The Mesnevi ... illustrated by a selection of anecdotes, as collected by ... Meol¯an¯a Shemsu 'd D¯in Ahmed'. London : Trübner and Co., 1881.
ISBN 0-7229-5050-0 : £3.25
ISBN 0-7229-5051-9 Pbk : £2.25
(B77-01343)

398.2'42 — Tales. Special subjects: Plants. *Anthologies. Juvenile literature*
The **enchanted** garden : legends and tales about trees and flowers / illustrated by Dagmar Berková ; [translated from the Czech] by Paul Wilson. — London [etc.] : Hamlyn, [1977]. — 195p : ill(some col) ; 29cm. — ([World fairy tales series])
Col. ill on lining papers.
ISBN 0-600-33131-8 : £2.50
(B77-14188)

398.2'45'09729 — Caribbean tales. Special subjects: Animals. *Anthologies*
Sherlock, *Sir* **Philip.** The iguana's tail : crick crack stories from the Caribbean / [by] Sir Philip Sherlock ; illustrated by Gioia Flammenghi. — London : Deutsch, 1976. — [5],97p : ill ; 23cm.
This collection originally published: New York : Crowell, 1969.
ISBN 0-233-96687-0 : £2.25
(B77-11757)

398.2'452'82 — Tales. Special subjects: Birds. *Anthologies. Juvenile literature*
Haddon, Tessa. A magic book of birds / [by] Tessa Haddon ; illustrated by James Hutcheson. — Edinburgh : Canongate Publishing, 1976. — [7],101p : ill ; 23cm.
ISBN 0-903937-20-4 : £2.95
(B77-15797)

398.2'5'09427 — Northern English tales. Special subjects: Ghosts. *Anthologies*
Dane, Rebecca. Further tales of - phantoms, fear and fantasy around the north of England ... / by Rebecca Dane and Craig MacNeale ; [illustrations by Peter Murray and Rod Wesson]. — [Darlington] ([P.O. Box 38, Darlington, Co. Durham, DL3 7TR]) : Nordales (Five-Counties) Publications, 1976. — [1],48p : ill ; 22cm.
ISBN 0-9504314-1-9 Sd : £0.35
(B77-10329)

398.2'7 — Edo tales. Special themes: Justice. *Anthologies*
Umobuarie, David. Black justice / [by] David Umobuarie. — Ibadan ; Oxford [etc.] : Oxford University Press, 1976. — vii,195p ; 21cm. — (A three crowns book)
ISBN 0-19-575232-5 Pbk : £4.00
(B77-28553)

398.3/4 — FOLKLORE OF SPECIAL SUBJECTS

398'.352 — British legends. Special subjects: Outlaws, to ca 1400. *Critical studies*
Keen, Maurice Hugh. The outlaws of medieval legend / by Maurice Keen. — Revised ed. — London [etc.] : Routledge and Kegan Paul [etc.], 1977. — xxi,235p : ill, facsim ; 23cm. — (Studies in social history)
Previous ed.: 1961. — Bibl.: p.223-227. — Index.
ISBN 0-7100-8682-2 : £5.95
(B77-24862)

398'.352 — European legends. Characters: Santa Claus. Historicity. *Juvenile literature*
Ebon, Martin. Saint Nicholas : life and legend / [by] Martin Ebon. — New York [etc.] ; London : Harper and Row, [1976]. — [8], 120p : ill, facsims, ports ; 24cm.
Published in the United States: 1975. — Bibl.: p.119.
ISBN 0-06-062113-3 : £6.70
Primary classification 270.2'092'4
(B77-00020)

398'.362'0938 — Ancient Greek legends. Special subjects: Solar system. Planets. *Anthologies. Juvenile literature*
Moore, Patrick. Legends of the planets / [by] Patrick Moore. — London : Luscombe, 1976. — [5],115p : ill(some col) ; 27cm.
ISBN 0-86002-122-x : £4.50
(B77-10330)

398'.368 — Folklore. Special subjects: Gardening
Boland, Bridget. Gardener's magic & other old wives' lore / [by] Bridget Boland. — London [etc.] : Bodley Head, 1977. — 64p : ill ; 21cm.
Index.
ISBN 0-370-30053-x : £1.95
(B77-29355)

398'.368 — Plants. Symbolism
Gordon, Lesley. Green magic : flowers, plants & herbs in lore & legend / [by] Lesley Gordon. — [London] : Ebury Press, 1977. — 200p : ill(some col), facsims(1 col), ports ; 25cm.
Bibl.: p.193-195. — Index.
ISBN 0-85223-117-2 : £6.95
Also classified at 581.6'1
(B77-30162)

398'.368'213 — Flowers. Symbolism. *Dictionaries*
Greenaway, Kate. Language of flowers / illustrated by Kate Greenaway. — Revised ed. — London [etc.] : F. Warne, 1977. — [64]p : col ill ; 17cm.
Previous ed.: London : Routledge, 1884.
ISBN 0-7232-2006-9 : £1.95
(B77-26258)

398'.41 — American superstitions. *Juvenile literature*
Schwartz, Alvin. Cross your fingers, spit in your hat : superstitions and other beliefs / collected by Alvin Schwartz ; illustrated by Glen Rounds. — London : Deutsch, 1976. — 3-146p : ill ; 22cm.
Originally published: Philadelphia : Lippincott, 1974. — Bibl.: p.138-144.
ISBN 0-233-96832-6 : £3.25
ISBN 0-233-96841-5 Pbk : £1.50
(B77-01344)

398'.42 — Atlantean civilization. Historical sources: Antiquities. *Great Britain. Readings*
Roberts, Anthony. Atlantean traditions in ancient Britain / by Anthony Roberts. — London : Rider, 1977. — xv,120p : ill, maps, plans ; 26cm.
Originally published: Llanfynydd : Unicorn Bookshop, 1975. — Bibl.: p.114-115. — Index.
ISBN 0-09-128751-0 Pbk : £2.95
(B77-18697)

398'.42 — Atlantis
Berlitz, Charles. The mystery of Atlantis / [by] Charles Berlitz. — [British ed.]. — St Albans : Panther, 1977. — 188p,[8]p of plates : ill, maps ; 18cm.
This ed. originally published: London : Souvenir Press, 1976. — Bibl.: p.185-187.
ISBN 0-586-04403-5 Pbk : £0.75
(B77-14678)

Donnelly, Ignatius. Atlantis : the antediluvian world / by Ignatius Donnelly. — [1st ed. reprinted] ; with a new introduction by E.F. Bleiler. — New York : Dover Publications [etc.] ; London : Constable, 1976. — iii-xxii, 490p : ill, chart, maps, port ; 21cm.
Facsimile reprint of: 1st ed. New York : Harper, 1882. — Bibl.: p.xx. — Index.
ISBN 0-486-23371-5 Pbk : £3.60
(B77-21072)

Scrutton, Robert J. The other Atlantis / by Robert J. Scrutton ; edited by Ken Johnson. — St Helier : Neville Spearman (Jersey) Ltd ; Sudbury : Distributed by Spearman, 1977. — 260p,leaf of plate,[2]p of plates : ill, maps ; 23cm.
ISBN 0-85978-021-x : £4.25
(B77-22519)

398'.42 — Atlantis. Theories, to 1975
Stemman, Roy. Atlantis and the lost lands / by Roy Stemman. — London : Aldus Books, 1976. — 144p : ill(some col), facsim, maps(some col), ports(some col) ; 27cm.
ISBN 0-490-00343-5 : £3.25
(B77-08970)

398'.42 — Atlantis. Theories, to 1976
Steiger, Brad. Atlantis rising / [by] Brad Steiger. — London : Sphere, 1977. — 157p ; 18cm.
Originally published: New York : Dell, 1973. — Bibl.: p.155-157.
ISBN 0-7221-8132-9 Pbk : £0.65
(B77-14189)

398'.42 — Shambhala
Tomas, Andrew. Shambhala : oasis of light / [by] Andrew Tomas. — London : Sphere, 1977. — 175p,[8]p of plates : ill, map, port ; 18cm.
Bibl.: p.173-175.
ISBN 0-7221-8554-5 Pbk : £0.85
(B77-33749)

398'.42 — Subterranean worlds. Theories
Smith, Warren. This hollow earth / [by] Warren Smith. — London : Sphere, 1977. — 188p ; 18cm.
ISBN 0-7221-7937-5 Pbk : £0.65
(B77-08335)

398'.45 — Fabulous beings. *Secondary school texts*
Legendary & fantastic / [compiled by] John Foster & Rod Hunt. — Basingstoke [etc.] : Macmillan, 1977. — [1],32p : ill ; 20x21cm. — (Investigations)
Bibl.
ISBN 0-333-19833-6 Sd : £0.55
(B77-27801)

398'.45 — Fairies
Arrowsmith, Nancy. Field guide to the Little People / [by] Nancy Arrowsmith with George Moorse ; illustrated by Heinz Edelmann ; calligraphy by Kevin Reilly. — London [etc.] : Macmillan, 1977. — 296p : ill ; 24cm.
Bibl.: p.282-287. — Index.
ISBN 0-333-21307-6 : £5.95
(B77-28554)

398'.45 — Fairies. *Great Britain*
Briggs, Katharine Mary. The fairies in tradition and literature / [by] K.M. Briggs. — London [etc.] : Routledge and Kegan Paul, 1977. — x, 261p,13p of plates : ill ; 22cm.
Originally published: 1967. — Bibl.: p.241-250. — Index.
ISBN 0-7100-8687-3 Pbk : £2.95 : CIP rev.
(B77-11758)

398'.45 — Fairies. Sexual aspects. *Great Britain*
Duffy, Maureen. The erotic world of faery / [by] Maureen Duffy. — St Albans : Panther, 1974. — 336p,[8]p of plates : ill, facsims ; 18cm.
Originally published: London : Hodder and Stoughton, 1972. — Bibl.: p.311-317. — Index.
ISBN 0-586-03940-6 Pbk : £0.90
(B77-19314)

398'.45'03 — Fabulous beings. *Encyclopaedias*
Briggs, Katharine Mary. A dictionary of fairies : hobgoblins, brownies, bogies and other supernatural creatures / [by] Katharine Briggs. — Harmondsworth [etc.] : Penguin, 1977. — xxi,481p,[16]p of plates : ill ; 20cm.
Originally published: London : Allen Lane, 1976. — Bibl.: p.455-462. — Index.
ISBN 0-14-004753-0 Pbk : £1.50
(B77-33750)

398′.469 — Dragons
Gould, Charles. The dragon / [by] Charles Gould and others ; edited by Malcolm Smith. — London : Wildwood House, 1977. — 104p : ill ; 30cm.
ISBN 0-7045-0277-1 Pbk : £2.50
(B77-11759)

398′.469 — Fabulous beasts. *Juvenile literature*
Blythe, Richard. Fabulous beasts / by Richard Blythe ; illustrated by Fiona French and Joanna Troughton. — London : Macdonald Educational, 1977. — 4-61p : ill(chiefly col) ; 31cm.
ISBN 0-356-05546-9 : £2.95
(B77-26259)

398.6 — FOLKLORE. RIDDLES
398.6′0942 — Riddles in English. *Anthologies. Juvenile literature*
Leach, Maria. Riddle me, riddle me, ree / [by] Maria Leach ; illustrated by William Wiesner. — Harmondsworth [etc.] : Puffin Books, 1977. — 143p : ill ; 20cm. — (Puffin books)
Originally published: New York : Viking Press, 1970. — Bibl.: p.139-142.
Pbk : Unpriced
(B77-31832)

Low, Joseph. 5 men under 1 umbrella, & other riddles / [by] Joseph Low. — Tadworth : World's Work, 1977. — 64p : chiefly col ill ; 22cm.
Originally published: New York : Macmillan, 1975.
ISBN 0-437-56000-7 : £2.20
(B77-26260)

398.8 — FOLKLORE. RHYMES, FOLK SONGS, GAMES
398.8 — British children's customs, ca 1950-1960
Opie, Iona. The lore and language of schoolchildren / [by] Iona and Peter Opie. — St Albans : Paladin, 1977. — 446p : ill, maps ; 20cm.
Originally published: Oxford : Clarendon Press, 1959. — Index.
ISBN 0-586-08311-1 Pbk : £2.50
(B77-17436)

398.8 — Children's counting rhymes in English. *Texts*
Stobbs, William. A gaping wide-mouthed waddling frog : a counting book / with pictures by William Stobbs. — London : Pelham, 1977. — [24]p : chiefly col ill ; 26cm.
ISBN 0-7207-0849-4 : £2.95
(B77-16328)

398.8 — Nursery rhymes in English. *Anthologies*
Little Bo-Peep, and other nursery rhymes / [selected and] illustrated by Dorothy Stevens. — Tadworth : World's Work, 1977. — [32]p : col ill ; 19x26cm.
ISBN 0-437-77575-5 : £2.60
(B77-33177)

The **magic** of rhymes / compiled by Lucy Kincaid ; illustrated by Eric Kincaid. — Cambridge : Brimax Books, 1976. — [74]p : col ill ; 28cm.
Col. ill on lining papers.
ISBN 0-904494-27-6 : £1.65
(B77-12983)

My favourite nursery rhymes / illustrated by Fel. — Maidenhead : Purnell, 1977. — [20]p : col ill ; 25cm. — (A Purnell fireside tale)
Col. ill., text on lining papers.
ISBN 0-361-03862-3 : £0.45
(B77-14679)

Nicola Bayley's book of nursery rhymes / [illustrated by Nicola Bayley]. — Revised ed. — London : Cape, 1977. — [32]p : col ill ; 26cm.
This ed. originally published: 1976.
ISBN 0-224-01337-8 : £2.50
(B77-30163)

The **Oxford** dictionary of nursery rhymes / edited by Iona and Peter Opie. — London [etc.] : Oxford University Press, 1975. — xxvii, 467p,[20] leaves of plates,[4]p of plates : ill, facsims ; 23cm.
Originally published: Oxford : Clarendon Press, 1951. — Index.
ISBN 0-19-869111-4 : £6.50
(B77-16329)

Pat-a-cake nursery rhymes / illustrated by Rene Cloke. — [Maidenhead] : Popular Press, 1977. — [20]p : col ill ; 27cm.
Col. ill., text on lining papers.
ISBN 0-361-03996-4 : £0.30
(B77-18070)

Red herrings : traditional rhymes / chosen by Peggy Blakeley ; with pictures by Frank Francis. — London : A. and C. Black, 1977. — 5-30p : col ill ; 20x27cm. — (Fact and fancy books ; 23)
Index.
ISBN 0-7136-1801-9 : £1.75
(B77-30164)

Three little ghostesses : traditional rhymes / chosen by Peggy Blakeley ; with pictures by Frank Francis. — London : A. and C. Black, 1977. — 5-30p : col ill ; 20x27cm. — (Fact and fancy books ; 24)
Index.
ISBN 0-7136-1802-7 : £1.75
(B77-30165)

398.8 — Nursery rhymes in English. *Texts*
Tinker, tailor - : a nursery rhyme board book. — Cambridge : Brimax Books, [1976]. — [10]p : col ill ; 27cm.
Cover title.
ISBN 0-904494-19-5 Pbd : £0.80
(B77-07279)

Tozer, Mary. The tale of Old Mother Hubbard and her dog / illustrated by Mary Tozer. — Tadworth : World's Work, 1977. — [40]p : chiefly col ill ; 21cm.
ISBN 0-437-79418-0 : £2.60
(B77-27001)

398.8 — Nursery rhymes in English. *Texts. Facsimiles*
The **death** and burial of Cock Robin : as taken from the original manuscript in the possession of Master Meanwell. — [St Peter Port] : Toucan Press, 1977. — 16p : ill ; 11cm.
Facsimile reprint of: 1st ed. Lichfield : M. Morgan, 1800?.
Sd : Unpriced
(B77-24147)

398.8 — Rhymes in English, 1837-1901. *Anthologies*
Victorian jingles / collected by Dorothy Baker ; drawings by James Dolby. — Gloucester : Thornhill Press, 1976. — [4],59p : ill ; 14cm.
ISBN 0-904110-27-3 Pbk : £0.65
(B77-12406)

398.8 — Rhymes in English. Origins
Harrowven, Jean. The origins of rhymes, songs and sayings / [by] Jean Harrowven. — London : Kaye and Ward, 1977. — xii,356p : ill, ports ; 23cm.
Bibl.: p.333-334. — Index.
ISBN 0-7182-1123-5 : £5.25
Also classified at 784′.0942
(B77-28555)

398.8 — Tongue-twisters in English. *Anthologies. Juvenile literature*
Williams, Ferelith Eccles. One old Oxford ox / [by] Ferelith Eccles Williams. — Tadworth : World's Work, 1976. — [32]p : of col ill ; 19x25cm.
ISBN 0-437-86006-x : £1.95
(B77-02226)

398.9 — FOLKLORE. PROVERBS
398.9′21 — Proverbs in English. *Anthologies. Juvenile literature*
Make hay while the sun shines : a book of proverbs / chosen by Alison M. Abel ; illustrated by Shirley Hughes. — London : Faber, 1977. — [48]p : ill ; 22cm.
ISBN 0-571-11006-1 : £1.80
(B77-15248)

398.9′9162 — Proverbs in Irish. *Anthologies*
Proverbs & sayings of Ireland / edited by Sean Gaffney & Seamus Cashman. — Dublin (19c Garville Rd, Rathgar, Dublin) : Wolfhound Press, 1976. — 124p : ill ; 22cm.
Originally published: 1974. — Index.
ISBN 0-9503454-4-x Pbk : £1.00
(B77-10331)

400 — LANGUAGE
400 — Languages
Katzner, Kenneth. The languages of the world / [by] Kenneth Katzner. — London [etc.] : Routledge and Kegan Paul, 1977. — x,374p : ill ; 23cm.
Originally published: New York : Funk and Wagnalls, 1975. — Bibl.: p.361-367. — Index.
ISBN 0-7100-8717-9 : £5.95 : CIP rev.
(B77-23335)

400 — Modern languages. *Reviews of research*
The **year's** work in modern language studies. — London (c/o The Hon. Treasurer, King's College, Strand, WC2R 2LS) : Modern Humanities Research Association.
1975 : Vol.37 / edited by Glanville Price and David A. Wells. — 1976. — xi,1006p ; 23cm.
Index.
ISBN 0-900547-44-8 : £16.00
Also classified at 809′.894
(B77-14680)

401 — Language. *Phenomenological viewpoints*
Edie, James M. Speaking and meaning : the phenomenology of language / [by] James M. Edie. — Bloomington ; London : Indiana University Press, 1976. — xiii,271p ; 24cm. — (Studies in phenomenology and existential philosophy)
Bibl.: p.245-271.
ISBN 0-253-35425-0 : £10.00
(B77-14681)

401 — Language. *Philosophical perspectives*
Fraser, Russell. The language of Adam : on the limits and systems of discourse / [by] Russell Fraser. — New York ; Guildford : Columbia University Press, 1977. — xvi,288p ; 24cm.
Bibl.: p.257-274. — Index.
ISBN 0-231-04256-6 : Unpriced
(B77-30166)

401′.2 — Languages. Classification
Voegelin, C F. Classification and index of the world's languages / [by] C.F. and F.M. Voegelin. — New York ; Oxford [etc.] : Elsevier, 1977. — viii,658p ; 26cm. — (Foundations of linguistics series)
′ ... based in part upon [the authors′] earlier survey of the literature, "Languages of the World," published [in] the journal "Anthropological Linguistics" (1964-66)′ - Acknowledgments. — Bibl.: p.359-383.
ISBN 0-444-00155-7 : £22.95
(B77-14682)

401′.9 — Children, 5-7 years. Language skills. Related to social class
Adlam, Diana S. Code in context / [by] Diana S. Adlam ; with the assistance of Geoffrey Turner and Lesley Lineker. — London [etc.] : Routledge and Kegan Paul, 1977. — xvii,253p : ill ; 23cm. — (Primary socialization, language and education)
Bibl.: p.245-247. — Index.
ISBN 0-7100-8481-1 : £6.25
Also classified at 301.44
(B77-16331)

401′.9 — Children. Language skills. Acquisition
Tough, Joan. The development of meaning : a study of children's use of language / [by] Joan Tough. — London : Allen and Unwin, 1977. — [9],198p ; 23cm. — (Unwin education books ; 33)
Bibl.: p.193-195. — Index.
ISBN 0-04-372020-x : £6.00
ISBN 0-04-372021-8 Pbk : £2.95
(B77-08971)

401′.9 — Children. Language skills. Acquisition. *For teaching*
Derrick, June. The child's acquisition of language / [by] June Derrick. — Windsor : NFER, 1977. — [5],53p ; 22cm.
Bibl.: p.50-53.
ISBN 0-85633-110-4 Sd : £1.75
(B77-18071)

401′.9 — Children. Language skills. Acquisition. Related to social class. *Essays*
Bernstein, Basil. Class, codes and control / [by] Basil Bernstein [et al.]. — 2nd ed. — London [etc.] : Routledge and Kegan Paul. — (Primary socialization, language and education ; 4)
Vol.1 : Theoretical studies towards a sociology of language / [by] Basil Bernstein. — 1977. — xiv,266p : ill ; 22cm.
This ed. originally published: 1974. — Bibl. — Index.
ISBN 0-7100-8654-7 Pbk : £2.40
(B77-18698)

401′.9 — Children. Language skills. Acquisition. Research. Applications of linguistics
Crystal, David. Child language, learning and linguistics : an overview for the teaching and therapeutic professions / [by] David Crystal. — London : Edward Arnold, 1976. — 106p : ill, form ; 22cm.
Index.
ISBN 0-7131-5890-5 : £4.25
ISBN 0-7131-5891-3 Pbk : £1.95
(B77-11180)

401'.9 — Children. Language skills. Acquisition. Role of listening
Slade, Peter. Listening and language development : sounds and music / [by] Peter Slade. — [Bromley] : Educational Drama Association, [1977]. — [1],16p ; 22cm.
Sd : £0.40
(B77-29356)

401'.9 — Children. Language skills. Development
Dale, Philip S. Language development : structure and function / [by] Philip S. Dale. — 2nd ed. — New York ; London [etc.] : Holt, Rinehart and Winston, 1976. — x,358p : ill ; 23cm.
Previous ed.: Hinsdale : Dryden Press, 1972. — Bibl.: p.332-352. — Index.
ISBN 0-03-089705-x Pbk : £5.00
(B77-13615)

Moerk, Ernst L. Pragmatic and semantic aspects of early language development / by Ernst L. Moerk. — Baltimore ; London [etc.] : University Park Press, 1977. — xi,330p : ill ; 24cm.
Bibl.: p.279-315. — Index.
ISBN 0-8391-1118-5 : £13.25
(B77-22520)

401'.9 — Children. Language skills. Tests: Bankson Language Screening Test. *Manuals*
Bankson, Nicholas W. Bankson language screening test / by Nicholas W. Bankson. — Baltimore ; London [etc.] : University Park Press, 1977. — vi,73p : ill(chiefly col), forms ; 22x29cm.
Notebook format. — Bibl.: p.5.
ISBN 0-8391-1126-6 Sp : £10.75
(B77-29357)

401'.9 — Children. Speech skills. Development
Gallagher, Miriam. Let's help our children talk / [by] Miriam Gallagher. — Dublin (11 Clare St., Dublin 2) : O'Brien Press, 1977. — 160p : ill ; 20cm.
Bibl. — Index.
ISBN 0-905140-20-6 : £4.00
ISBN 0-905140-21-4 Pbk : £1.50
(B77-25551)

401'.9 — Children, to 10 years. Language skills. Development
Language and learning in early childhood / edited by Alan Davies. — London : Heinemann Educational [for the] SSRC and SCRE, 1977. — [7],222p ; 23cm.
'... [papers] from seminars organized by the SSRC and the Scottish Council for Research in Education [held] in Leeds and Bristol ... [and] a report for the Scottish Education Department' - jacket. — Bibl.: p.187-215. — Index.
ISBN 0-435-10191-9 : £4.75
(B77-12407)

401'.9 — Children, to 6 years. Language skills: Pragmatics. Acquisition. *Study examples: Italian language*
Bates, Elizabeth. Language and context : the acquisition of pragmatics / [by] Elizabeth Bates. — New York [etc.] ; London : Academic Press, 1976. — xv,375p : ill ; 24cm. — (Language, thought and culture)
Bibl.: p.355-365. — Index.
ISBN 0-12-081550-8 : £12.20
(B77-02923)

401'.9 — Language. Psychological aspects
New approaches to language mechanisms : a collection of psycholinguistic studies / editors, R.J. Wales, Edward Walker. — Amsterdam [etc.] ; Oxford : North-Holland Publishing Co., 1976. — vii,296p : ill ; 23cm. — (North-Holland linguistic series ; 30)
Bibl.: p.285-287p. — Index.
ISBN 0-7204-0523-8 Pbk : £11.95
(B77-05344)

401'.9 — Language. Psychological aspects. *State-of-the-art reviews*
Psycholinguistics series / edited by John Morton and John C. Marshall. — London : Elek.
1 : Developmental and pathological / [by] Eve V. Clark ... [et al.]. — 1977. — vii,160p : ill ; 23cm.
Bibl.
ISBN 0-236-31049-6 : £4.95
(B77-11760)

401'.9 — Man. Language skills. Development
Fry, Dennis Butler. Homo loquens : man as a talking animal / [by] Dennis Fry. — Cambridge [etc.] : Cambridge University Press, 1977. — vii,177p : ill ; 21cm.
Bibl.: p.170. — Index.
ISBN 0-521-21705-9 : £5.95
ISBN 0-521-29239-5 Pbk : £1.95
(B77-32585)

401'.9 — Man. Speech skills. Psycholinguistic aspects. Experiments
Bradshaw, John, *b.1924.* Experimental studies of adult patterns of speech : (experiments in psycholinguistics) / by John Bradshaw. — Birmingham (Gosta Green, Birmingham B4 7ET) : Department of Educational Enquiry, University of Aston in Birmingham, 1976. — [3],121p : ill ; 21cm. — (Aston educational enquiry monograph ; no.5)
Bibl.: p.116-121.
ISBN 0-903807-32-7 Sd : £1.50
(B77-26261)

401'.9 — Psycholinguistics
Cairns, Helen S. Psycholinquistics : a cognitive view of language / [by] Helen S. Cairns, Charles E. Cairns. — New York ; London [etc.] : Holt, Rinehart and Winston, 1976. — xi,252p : ill ; 24cm.
Bibl.: p.229-241. — Index.
ISBN 0-03-007851-2 Pbk : £6.00
(B77-04734)

Taylor, Insup. Introduction to psycholinguistics / [by] Insup Taylor. — New York [etc.] ; London : Holt, Rinehart and Winston, 1976. — xiii,434p : ill, facsim ; 24cm.
Bibl.: p.396-423. — Index.
ISBN 0-03-012981-8 : £9.25
(B77-01345)

401'.9 — Schools. Students. Mental development. Role of language skills
Smith, E Brooks. Language and thinking in school / [by] E. Brooks Smith, Kenneth S. Goodman, Robert Meredith. — 2nd ed. — New York ; London [etc.] : Holt, Rinehart and Winston, 1976. — x,438p : ill ; 24cm.
Previous ed.: published as 'Language and thinking in the elementary school'. 1970. — Index.
ISBN 0-03-089248-1 : £8.00
(B77-02924)

408 — Language. *Essays*
Halliday, Michael Alexander Kirkwood. Halliday, system and function in language / selected papers edited by G.R. Kress. — London : Oxford University Press, 1976. — xxi, 250p : ill ; 23cm.
Bibl.: p.235-237. — List of works : p.238-241. — Index.
ISBN 0-19-437127-1 : £7.50
ISBN 0-19-437062-3 Pbk : £5.00
(B77-14683)

409'.2'4 — Language. Theories of Jakobson, Roman
Holenstein, Elmar. Roman Jakobson's approach to language : phenomenological structuralism / [by] Elmar Holenstein ; translated [from the German] by Catherine Schelbert and Tarcisius Schelbert. — Bloomington ; London : Indiana University Press, 1976. — viii,215p : ill ; 24cm.

Translation of: 'Roman Jakobsons phänomenologischer Strukturalismus'. Frankfurt am Main : Suhrkamp, 1975. — Bibl.: p.194-209. — Index.
ISBN 0-253-35018-2 : £7.50
(B77-33178)

409'.67'73 — Languages. Political aspects. *Somalia*
Laitin, David D. Politics, language and thought : the Somali experience / [by] David D. Laitin. — Chicago ; London : University of Chicago Press, 1977. — xii,268p : ill, map ; 24cm.
Bibl.: p.247-255. — Index.
ISBN 0-226-46791-0 : £13.30
(B77-23336)

410 — LINGUISTICS
Chomsky, Noam. Reflections on language / [by] Noam Chomsky. — [London] : Fontana, 1976. — vi,269p ; 20cm.
Originally published: New York : Pantheon Books, 1975 ; London : Temple Smith, 1976. — Bibl.: p.255-265. — Index.
ISBN 0-00-634299-x Pbk : £1.50
(B77-15249)

Robins, Robert Henry. General linguistics : an introductory survey / [by] R.H. Robins. — 2nd ed. — London : Longman, [1977]. — xx,398p : ill ; 22cm. — (Longman linguistics library)
This ed. originally published: Harlow : Longman, 1971. — Bibl. — Index.
ISBN 0-582-55049-1 Pbk : £2.75
(B77-09655)

Wardhaugh, Ronald. Introduction to linguistics / [by] Ronald Wardhaugh. — 2nd ed. — New York ; London [etc.] : McGraw-Hill, 1977. — ix,268p : ill ; 24cm.
Previous ed.: New York : McGraw-Hill, 1972. — Bibl.: p.255-261. — Index.
ISBN 0-07-068152-x Pbk : £6.70
(B77-20187)

410 — Generative linguistics. *Readings*
Bever, Thomas G. An integrated theory of linguistic ability / [by] Thomas G. Bever, Jerrold J. Katz and D. Terence Langendoen. — Hassocks : Harvester Press, 1977. — ix,432p ; 25cm. — (The language and thought series)
Originally published: New York : Crowell, 1976. — Bibl.: p.425. — Index.
ISBN 0-85527-899-4 : £14.95 : CIP rev.
(B77-04735)

410 — Historical linguistics. *Conference proceedings*
Directions for historical linguistics : a symposium / edited by W.P. Lehmann and Yakov Malkiel. — Austin ; London : University of Texas Press, [1976]. — xiii,199p : ill, map ; 23cm.
Originally published: 1968. — Bibl.: p.189-195. — Index.
ISBN 0-292-71511-0 Pbk : £2.60
(B77-02925)

International Conference on Historical Linguistics, *2nd, Tucson, 1976.* Current progress in historical linguistics : proceedings of the Second International Conference on Historical Linguistics, Tucson, Arizona, 12-16 January 1976 / editor William M. Christie, Jr. — Amsterdam [etc.] : North-Holland Publishing Co., 1976. — x,409p : ill, maps ; 23cm. — (North-Holland linguistic series ; 31)
Bibl.
ISBN 0-7204-0533-5 : £24.39
(B77-06018)

410 — Language. Change
Harris, Roy, *b.1931.* On the possibility of linguistic change / by Roy Harris. — Oxford : Clarendon Press, 1977. — 23p ; 22cm. — (University of Oxford. Inaugural lectures)
'Delivered ... on 18 November 1976'.
ISBN 0-19-951511-5 Sd : £0.90 : CIP rev.
(B77-06019)

410 — Mathematical linguistics
Prague studies in mathematical linguistics. — Amsterdam [etc.] ; Oxford : North-Holland Publishing Co.
Vol.5 / scientific editors, Ján Horecký, Petr Sgall, Marie Těšitelová. — 1977. — 320p : ill ; 25cm.
Includes one article in Russian with English summary. — Bibl.
ISBN 0-7204-8034-5 : £16.81
(B77-16834)

410 — Systemic linguistics
Berry, Margaret. An introduction to systemic linguistics / [by] Margaret Berry. — London : Batsford.
In 2 vols.
2 : Levels and links. — 1977. — viii,142p : ill ; 23cm.
Bibl.: p.134-138. — Index.
ISBN 0-7134-3256-x : £5.95
ISBN 0-7134-3257-8 Pbk : £2.95
(B77-26262)

410 — Transformational-generative linguistics
Jacobsen, Bent. Transformational-generative grammar : an introductory survey of its genesis and development / [by] Bent Jacobsen. — Amsterdam [etc.] ; Oxford : North-Holland Publishing Co., 1977. — xv,525p : ill ; 23cm. — (North-Holland linguistic series ; 17)
Bibl.: p.491-508. — Index.
ISBN 0-7204-0761-3 : Unpriced
(B77-28556)

410'.028'54044 — Linguistics. Applications of digital computer systems. *Conference proceedings*
International Symposium on the Use of the Computer in Linguistic and Literary Research, *3rd, Cardiff, 1974.* The computer in literary and linguistic studies : (proceedings of the Third International Symposium) / edited by Alan Jones and R.F. Churchhouse. — Cardiff : University of Wales Press, 1976. — viii,362p : ill, facsims ; 23cm.
'The Third International Symposium on the Use of the Computer in Linguistic and Literary Research ... held at Cardiff in April 1974' - Introduction. — Bibl. — Index.
ISBN 0-7083-0590-3 : £10.00
Also classified at 801'.95'02854044
(B77-02227)

410'.1 — Linguistics. Hypotheses. Testing. *Conference proceedings*
Testing Linguistic Hypotheses *(Conference), University of Wisconsin-Milwaukee, 1974.* Testing Linguistic Hypotheses / edited by David Cohen and Jessica R. Wirth. — Washington, D.C. ; London : Hemisphere Publishing Corporation ; New York ; London [etc.] : Wiley, [1977]. — xii,227p : ill ; 24cm.
'A Halsted Press book'. — 'On May 10 and 11, 1974 a symposium was held at the University of Wisconsin-Milwaukee on the topic, Testing Linguistic Hypotheses ...' - Preface. — Published in the United States: 1975. — Bibl. — Index.
ISBN 0-470-16419-0 : £9.55
(B77-11181)

410'.1'8 — Linguistics. Methodology. *Conference proceedings*
Assessing linguistic arguments / edited by Jessica R. Wirth. — Washington [D.C.] ; London : Hemisphere Publishing Corporation ; New York ; London [etc.] : Distributed by Wiley, 1976. — viii,280p : ill ; 24cm.
'... the fourth annual linguistic foundations symposium at the University of Wisconsin-Milwaukee May 9-10, 1975. This volume includes the revised versions of the papers presented ... there, with the addition of three other papers' - Preface. — 'A Halsted Press Book'. — Bibl. — Index.
ISBN 0-470-98916-5 : £11.90
(B77-08972)

410'.5 — Linguistics. *Periodicals*
University of East Anglia. UEA papers in linguistics. — Norwich (University Plain, Norwich NR4 7TJ) : The University.
1- ; Apr. 1976-. — 1976-. — 30cm.
Published at irregular intervals. — [3],64,[1]p. in 1st issue. — Bibl.
ISBN 0-902171-12-7 Sp : £0.55
(B77-06617)

410'.7'1141 — Universities. Linguistics teachers. *Great Britain. Directories*
Mruck, Martin L. Handbook of university teachers of English language and literature, linguistics and Celtic studies in Great Britain and Ireland / [compiled and] edited by Martin L. Mruck. — London (11 Arlington St., S.W.1) : Deutscher Akademischer Austauschdienst, 1975. — vii,235p ; 24cm.
Index.
Pbk : Unpriced
Primary classification 420'.7'1141
(B77-22523)

410'.92'4 — Linguistics. Jones, Richard Robert. *Biographies*
Howe, Marjorie. Georgian drop-out : a biography of Richard Robert Jones - 'Dic Aberdaron', the self-taught Welsh linguist of the nineteenth century / by Marjorie Howe. — [Rhyl] ([38 Trellewelyn Rd, Rhyl, Clwyd LL18 4ET]) : [The author], 1977. — [4],61,[8]p : ill, ports ; 21cm.
Bibl.: (1p.).
Sd : £1.00
(B77-27002)

410'.92'4 — Linguistics. Theories of Chomsky, Noam
Lyons, John. Chomsky / [by] John Lyons. — 2nd ed. — Hassocks : Harvester Press, 1977. — 184p : ill ; 23cm.
This ed. also published: London : Fontana, 1977. — Previous ed. London : Fontana, 1970. — Bibl.: p.176-181.
ISBN 0-85527-690-8 : £5.95 : CIP rev.
(B77-22521)

410'.92'4 — Linguistics. Theories of Saussure, Ferdinand de
Culler, Jonathan. Ferdinand de Saussure / [by] Jonathan Culler. — Harmondsworth [etc.] : Penguin, 1977. — xix,140p ; 18cm. — (Penguin modern masters)
Originally published: as 'Saussure'. Hassocks : Harvester Press ; London : Fontana, 1976. — Bibl.: p.133-135. — Index.
ISBN 0-14-004369-1 Pbk : Unpriced
(B77-32586)

Culler, Jonathan. Saussure / [by] Jonathan Culler. — Hassocks : Harvester Press, 1976. — 127p ; 23cm.
Also published: London : Fontana, 1976. — Bibl.: p.125-127.
ISBN 0-85527-379-8 : £4.50
(B77-01346)

411 — Non-alphabetic writing systems. Linguistic aspects
Writing without letters / [by] Ernst Pulgram ... [et al.] ; edited by W. Haas. — Manchester : Manchester University Press [etc.], 1976. — viii,216p : ill ; 23cm. — (Mont Follick series ; vol.4)
'The papers ... are based on lectures given ... in the University of Manchester' - half title page verso. — Bibl. — Index.
ISBN 0-7190-0618-x : £4.50
(B77-03499)

412 — Etymological dictionaries
Malkiel, Yakov. Etymological dictionaries : a tentative typology / [by] Yakov Malkiel. — Chicago ; London : University of Chicago Press, 1976. — ix,144p ; 23cm.
Bibl.: p.101-129. — Index.
ISBN 0-226-50292-9 : £11.25
(B77-01347)

412 — Etymology. Expounding ancient civilizations
Cohane, John Philip. The key / [by] John Philip Cohane ; preface by Cyrus H. Gordon. — [London] : Fontana, 1975. — 224p,8p of plates : ill ; 18cm.
Originally published: New York : Crown Publishers, 1969 ; London : Turnstone Books, 1973. — Bibl.: p.201-207. — Index.
ISBN 0-00-633724-4 Pbk : £0.80
Also classified at 930
(B77-06618)

412 — Generative semantics. Theories
Fodor, Janet Dean. Semantics : theories of meaning in generative grammar / [by] Janet Dean Fodor. — Hassocks : Harvester Press, 1977. — xiii,225p : ill ; 24cm. — (The language and thought series)
Also published: New York : Crowell, 1977. — Bibl.: p.215-222. — Index.
ISBN 0-85527-500-6 : £12.95
(B77-14190)

412 — Language. Origins
Englefield, F R H. Language : its origin and its relation to thought / by F.R.H. Englefield ; edited by G.A. Wells and D.R. Oppenheimer. — London : Elek : Pemberton, 1977. — xvi, 192p : ill ; 23cm.
Bibl.: p.186-189. — Index.
ISBN 0-301-76101-9 : £6.00
ISBN 0-301-76102-7 Pbk : £3.00
(B77-08336)

412 — Semantics
Kempson, Ruth M. Semantic theory / [by] Ruth M. Kempson. — Cambridge [etc.] : Cambridge University Press, 1977. — xi,216p : ill ; 24cm. — (Cambridge textbooks in linguistics)
Bibl.: p.197-208. — Index.
ISBN 0-521-21613-3 : £8.50
ISBN 0-521-29209-3 Pbk : £2.95
(B77-27003)

Lyons, John. Semantics / [by] John Lyons. — Cambridge [etc.] : Cambridge University Press. In 2 vols.
Vol.1. — 1977. — xiii,371p : ill ; 24cm.
Bibl.: p.336-356. — Index.
ISBN 0-521-21473-4 : £12.00
ISBN 0-521-29165-8 Pbk : £3.95
(B77-23337)

Vol.2. — 1977. — xiv p,p373-897 ; 24cm.
Bibl.: p.850-879. — Index.
ISBN 0-521-21560-9 : £15.00
ISBN 0-521-29186-0 Pbk : £4.95
(B77-31122)

Shaumian, S K. Applicational grammar as a semantic theory of natural language / [by] S.K. Shaumyan ; [translated from the Russian by J.E. Miller]. — Edinburgh : Edinburgh University Press, 1977. — viii,184p : ill ; 22cm.

Translation of: 'Applikativnaia grammatika kak semanticheskaia teoriia estestvennykh iazykov'. Moskva : Nauka, 1974. — Index.
ISBN 0-85224-076-7 : £8.00
(B77-32587)

Syntax and semantics. — New York [etc.] ; London : Academic Press.
Vol.7 : Notes from the linguistic underground / edited by James D. McCawley. — 1976. — xxi, 453p : ill ; 24cm.
Bibl.: p.433-450. — Index.
ISBN 0-12-613507-x : £12.05
Primary classification 415
(B77-12408)

Vol.8 : Grammatical relations / edited by Peter Cole, Jerrold M. Sadock. — 1977. — xxiv, 347p ; 24cm.
Bibl. — Index.
ISBN 0-12-613508-8 : £13.85
Primary classification 415
(B77-14685)

412'.01 — Language. Origins. Theories, ca 1700-ca 1900
Stam, James H. Inquiries into the origin of language : the fate of a question / [by] James H. Stam. — New York [etc.] ; London : Harper and Row, 1976. — xii,307p : facsims ; 24cm. — (Studies in language)
Index.
ISBN 0-06-046403-8 : £11.20
(B77-08973)

413 — Abbreviations. *Dictionaries*
Pugh, Eric. Third dictionary of acronyms & abbreviations : more abbreviations in management, technology and information science / [compiled by] Eric Pugh. — London : Bingley [etc.], 1977. — 208p ; 23cm.
'[Contains] ... more than 5,000 entries additional to, and in some cases updating, those in the first and second dictionaries ...' - jacket. — Index.
ISBN 0-85157-224-3 : £4.50
(B77-05345)

414 — Generative phonology
Hooper, Joan B. An introduction to natural generative phonology / [by] Joan B. Hooper. — New York [etc.] ; London : Academic Press, [1977]. — xvii,254p ; 24cm.
Published in the United States: 1976. — Bibl.: p.243-249. — Index.
ISBN 0-12-354750-4 : £13.15
(B77-13616)

414 — Phonemes
Jones, Daniel. The phoneme : its nature and use / [by] Daniel Jones. — 3rd ed. / with an appendix on the history and meaning of the term 'phoneme'. — Cambridge [etc.] : Cambridge University Press, 1976. — [1], ii-xviii,284p : ill ; 23cm.
This ed. originally published: Cambridge : Heffer, 1967. — Bibl.: p.270-275. — Index.
ISBN 0-521-21351-7 : £6.50
(B77-04736)

414 — Phonetics
Carrell, James Aubrey. Phonetics : theory and application. — 2nd ed. / by William R. Tiffany, James Carrell. — New York ; London [etc.] : McGraw-Hill, 1977. — xv,426p : ill ; 24cm. — (McGraw-Hill series in speech)
With keys to the exercises. — Previous ed.: published as 'Phonetics : theory and application to speech improvement' / by James Carrell, William R. Tiffany. 1960. — Bibl.: p.357-362. — Index.
ISBN 0-07-064575-2 : £11.20
(B77-24148)

Catford, John Cunnison. Fundamental problems in phonetics / [by] J.C. Catford. — Edinburgh : Edinburgh University Press, 1977. — [8],278p : ill ; 22cm.
Bibl.: p.256-262. — Index.
ISBN 0-85224-279-4 : £8.00
(B77-16332)

414 — Phonology
Sommerstein, Alan Herbert. Modern phonology / [by] Alan H. Sommerstein. — London : Edward Arnold, 1977. — x,282p : ill ; 24cm. — (Theoretical linguistics ; 2)
Bibl.: p.263-272. — Index.
ISBN 0-7131-5961-8 : £12.00 : CIP rev.
ISBN 0-7131-5962-6 Pbk : £5.95
(B77-25552)

414 — Phonology. Theories
Kenstowicz, Michael. Topics in phonological theory / [by] Michael Kenstowicz, Charles Kisseberth. — New York [etc.] ; London : Academic Press, 1977. — xi,242p ; 24cm.
Bibl.: p.231-235. — Index.
ISBN 0-12-405150-2 : £12.40
(B77-27004)

415 — Generative linguistics
Parisi, Domenico. Essentials of grammar / [by] Domenico Parisi, Francesco Antinucci ; translated [from the Italian] by Elizabeth Bates. — New York [etc.] ; London : Academic Press, 1976. — x,181p : ill ; 24cm. — (Language, thought and culture)
Translation of: 'Elementi di grammatica'. Turin : Boringhieri, 1973. — Bibl.: p.117-178. — Index.
ISBN 0-12-544650-0 : £6.10
(B77-00169)

415 — Grammar. Daughter-dependency theory
Hudson, Richard Anthony. Arguments for a non-transformational grammar / [by] Richard A. Hudson. — Chicago ; London : University of Chicago Press, [1977]. — x,214p : ill ; 21cm.

Published in the United States: 1976. — Bibl.: p.207-211. — Index.
ISBN 0-226-35799-6 : £6.80
(B77-14684)

415 — Language. Discourse
Dijk, Teun Adrianus van. Text and context : explorations in the semantics and pragmatics of discourse / [by] Teun A. van Dijk. — London [etc.] : Longman, 1977. — xix,261p ; 23cm. — (Longman linguistics library ; no.21)
Bibl.: p.249-255. — Index.
ISBN 0-582-55085-8 : £6.50
(B77-32588)

415 — Languages. Sentences. Production
Sentence production : developments in research and theory / edited by Sheldon Rosenberg. — Hillsdale : Erlbaum ; New York ; London [etc.] : Distributed by Wiley, 1977. — xii,323p : ill ; 24cm.
Bibl. — Index.
ISBN 0-470-99114-3 : £13.45
(B77-22522)

415 — Syntax
Stockwell, Robert Paul. Foundations of syntactic theory / [by] Robert P. Stockwell. — Englewood Cliffs ; London [etc.] : Prentice-Hall, 1977. — xix,217p : ill ; 24cm. — (Prentice-Hall foundations of modern linguistics series)
Bibl.: p.206-211. — Index.
ISBN 0-13-329987-2 : £9.55
ISBN 0-13-329979-1 Pbk : £5.55
(B77-10332)

Syntax and semantics. — New York [etc.] ; London : Academic Press.
Vol.7 : Notes from the linguistic underground / edited by James D. McCawley. — 1976. — xxi, 453p : ill ; 24cm.
Bibl.: p.433-450. — Index.
ISBN 0-12-613507-x : £12.05
Also classified at 412
(B77-12408)

Vol.8 : Grammatical relations / edited by Peter Cole, Jerrold M. Sadock. — 1977. — xxiv, 347p ; 24cm.
Bibl. — Index.
ISBN 0-12-613508-8 : £13.85
Also classified at 412
(B77-14685)

415 — Utterances. Production & comprehension
Schlesinger, I M. Production and comprehension of utterances / [by] I.M. Schlesinger. — Hillsdale : Erlbaum ; New York ; London [etc.] : Distributed by Wiley, 1977. — xiii, 235p : ill ; 24cm.
Bibl.: p.217-226. — Index.
ISBN 0-470-99136-4 : £11.20
(B77-27802)

417'.2 — Creole languages. *West Indies*
Taylor, Douglas. Languages of the West Indies / [by] Douglas Taylor. — Baltimore ; London : Johns Hopkins University Press, 1977. — xix, 278,[1]p ; 24cm. — (Johns Hopkins studies in Atlantic history and culture)
Bibl.: p.270-278.
ISBN 0-8018-1729-3 : £12.00
Primary classification 497
(B77-33191)

417'.7 — Runic writing
Pennick, Nigel. Runic / by Nigel Pennick. — Cambridge (113 Shelford Rd, Trumpington, Cambridge CB2 2NB) : Megalithic Visions, Etcetera, 1974. — [1],12p : ill ; 30cm.
ISBN 0-9505400-0-5 Sd : Unpriced
(B77-03500)

417'.7 — Written records. Palaeographic aspects. *Scotland, 1150-1650*
Simpson, Grant Gray. Scottish handwriting, 1150-1650 : an introduction to the reading of documents / [by] Grant G. Simpson. — Aberdeen : Aberdeen University Press, 1977. — viii,140p : facsims ; 26cm.
Originally published: Edinburgh : Bratton Publishing, 1973. — Bibl.: p.135-138.
ISBN 0-900015-41-1 : £4.50
(B77-33180)

417'.7'093 — Ancient inscriptions. Decipherment, to 1976
Cottrell, Leonard. Reading the past : the story of deciphering ancient languages / [by] Leonard Cottrell. — London : Dent, [1977]. — ix,182p : ill ; 22cm.
Originally published: New York : Crowell-Collier, 1971 ; London : Dent, 1972. — Bibl.: p.171-173. — Index.
ISBN 0-460-02184-2 Pbk : £0.75
(B77-08337)

King, Charles, *b.1911.* Hieroglyphs to alphabets / [by] Charles King. — London : Muller, 1977. — 133p : ill ; 23cm.
Index.
ISBN 0-584-10134-1 : £3.95
(B77-14191)

418 — Language. Variety. *Readings*
A **reader** on language variety / edited by C.S. Butler and R.R.K. Hartmann. — [Exeter] : University of Exeter, 1976. — [2],iv,131p ; 21cm. — (Exeter linguistic studies ; vol.1 ISSN 0309-4375)
Bibl.: p.121-131.
ISBN 0-85989-051-1 Pbk : £1.00
(B77-13617)

418'.007 — Schools. Modern languages teachers. In-service training. *Conference proceedings*
Continuing Training of Modern Language Teachers *(Conference), London, 1976.* The continuing training of modern language teachers : the first year and after : papers arising from a conference convened in April, 1976. — London (20 Carlton House Terrace, SW1Y 5AP) : Centre for Information on Language Teaching and Research, 1976. — 54p ; 21cm. — (Centre for Information on Language Teaching and Research. Reports and papers ; 15 ISSN 0590-6075)
'The Centre for Information on Language Teaching and Research, with the collaboration of the National Association of Language Advisers, convened a specialist conference on "The continuing training of modern language teachers", which was held in London, 9-11 April 1976' - Foreword.
ISBN 0-903466-12-0 Pbk : £1.50
(B77-09656)

418'.007 — Teachers. Professional education. Curriculum subjects: Modern languages. *Great Britain. Reports, surveys*
Spicer, Arthur. Initial training of teachers of modern languages / [by] A. Spicer, D.C. Riddy. — [Abridged ed.]. — Leeds : E.J. Arnold, 1977. — [1],v,74p ; 30cm.
Full ed.: originally published in 2 parts as 'The initial training of teachers in modern foreign languages in colleges and departments of education'. Part 1. York : University of York, 1973 ; Part 2. Colchester : University of Essex, 1974.
ISBN 0-560-00539-3 Sd : Unpriced
(B77-20188)

418'.007'1041 — Educational institutions. Curriculum subjects: Modern languages. *Great Britain. Conference proceedings*
Modern languages for the 1980s : report of a colloquium held at the University of Sussex, 16-18 September 1976, organised by the School of European Studies in cooperation with the Centre for Information on Language Teaching and Research (CILT) / edited by C.G. Bearne and C.V. James. — London (20 Carlton House Terrace, 5W1Y 5AP) : C.I.L.T. for the University of Sussex, 1976. — [2];25p ; 21cm.
ISBN 0-903466-13-9 Sd : £0.50
(B77-04106)

418'.007'1042 — Schools. Curriculum subjects: Modern languages. *England. Reports, surveys*
Great Britain. *Department of Education and Science. HM Inspectorate (England).* Mathematics, science and modern languages in maintained schools in England : an appraisal of problems in some key subjects / by HM Inspectorate. — [London] ([Elizabeth House, York Rd, SE1 7PH]) : [HM Inspectorate], 1977. — 40p in various pagings ; 30cm.
ISBN 0-85522-087-2 Sp : Unpriced
Primary classification 507'.1042
(B77-14204)

418'.007'1073 — Schools. Curriculum subjects: Foreign languages. Teaching. *United States*
Grittner, Frank M. Teaching foreign languages / [by] Frank M. Grittner. — 2nd ed. — New York [etc.] ; London : Harper and Row, 1977. — xix,379p : ill, form ; 24cm.
Previous ed.: New York : Harper and Row, 1968. — Bibl. — Index.
ISBN 0-06-042524-5 : £9.70
(B77-16333)

418'.007'1141 — Higher education institutions. Curriculum subjects: Modern languages. Students. Effects of overseas residence. *Great Britain. Reports, surveys*
University of Bradford. *Modern Languages Centre.* Residence abroad and the student of modern languages : a preliminary survey / [University of Bradford Modern Languages Centre and Postgraduate School of Studies in Research in Education] ; [written] by Frank Willis ... [et al.]. — Bradford (Bradford BD7 1DP) : University of Bradford, Modern Languages Centre and Postgraduate School of Studies in Research in Education, 1977. — [7], 119p : forms ; 30cm.
Bibl.: p.93-95.
Pbk : £2.50
(B77-29358)

418'.007'1241 — Secondary schools. Curriculum subjects: Foreign languages. Teaching. Role of foreign language assistants. *Great Britain*
National Association of Language Advisers. Using the foreign language assistant : a guide to good practice / National Association of Language Advisers in cooperation with the Central Bureau for Educational Visits and Exchanges and the Centre for Information on Language Teaching and Research. — London (20 Carlton House Terrace, SW1Y 5AP) : Centre for Information on Language Teaching and Research, 1977. — [2],29p ; 22cm.
Bibl.: p.24-28.
ISBN 0-903466-14-7 Sd : £0.60
(B77-32589)

418'.007'1242 — Comprehensive schools. Curriculum subjects: Modern languages. *England, 1975-1976. Inquiry reports*
Great Britain. *Department of Education and Science. HM Inspectorate (England).* Modern languages in comprehensive schools : a discussion paper / by some members of HM Inspectorate of Schools, based on a survey of 83 schools in 1975-76. — London : H.M.S.O., 1977. — [3],51p ; 25cm. — (Matters for discussion ; 3 ISSN 0309-5746)
ISBN 0-11-270443-3 Sd : £0.90
(B77-14192)

418'.008 — Applied linguistics. *Readings*
The **Edinburgh** course in applied linguistics. — London : Oxford University Press. — (Language and language learning)
In 4 vols.
Vol.4 : Testing and experimental methods / edited by J.P.B. Allen and Alan Davies. — 1977. — x,233p : ill ; 24cm.
With answers to practical work. — Bibl.: p.224-226. — Index.
ISBN 0-19-437125-5 : £8.00
ISBN 0-19-437060-7 Pbk : Unpriced
(B77-12984)

419 — Deaf persons. Sign languages: American Sign Language
On the other hand : new perspectives on American Sign Language / edited by Lynn A. Friedman. — New York [etc.] ; London : Academic Press, 1977. — xii,245p : ill ; 24cm. — (Language, thought and culture)
'... an outgrowth of a course on the structure of the American Sign Language (ASL) given at U.C. Berkeley during the winter and spring quarters, 1975' - Preface. — Bibl.: p.237-241. — Index.
ISBN 0-12-267850-8 : £10.65
(B77-24150)

420 — ENGLISH LANGUAGE
420'.6'241 — English language. Organisations. *Great Britain. Directories*
English Association. The English Association handbook of societies and collections / edited by Alicia C. Percival. — London : Library Association for the English Association, 1977. — [1],xii,139p ; 21cm.
Index.
ISBN 0-85365-449-2 Pbk : £2.50(£2.00 to members of the associations) : CIP rev.
Also classified at 820'.6'241
(B77-23338)

420'.7 — Education. Curriculum subjects: English language. *Periodicals*
English language teaching. — London (State House, High Holborn, WC1R 4SZ) : British Council, English Teaching Information Centre. An index to twenty-five years of 'English language teaching', 1946-1971. — 1972. — [1], 88p ; 22cm.
Index.
ISBN 0-900229-08-x Sd : £0.60
(B77-11761)

420'.7'1041 — Schools. Curriculum subjects: English language. *Great Britain. Proposals*
Wesker, Arnold. Words as definitions of experience / [by] Arnold Wesker. — London : Writers and Readers Publishing Cooperative, 1976. — 43p ; 20cm.
Includes Finding one's own voice / by Richard Appignanesi.
ISBN 0-904613-26-7 Pbk : £0.75
(B77-04737)

420'.7'1141 — Universities. English language teachers. *Great Britain. Directories*
Mruck, Martin L. Handbook of university teachers of English language and literature, linguistics and Celtic studies in Great Britain and Ireland / [compiled and] edited by Martin L. Mruck. — London (11 Arlington St., S.W.1) : Deutscher Akademischer Austauschdienst, 1975. — vii,235p ; 24cm.
Index.
Pbk : Unpriced
Also classified at 820'.7'1141; 410'.7'1141; 940'.04'916
(B77-22523)

420'.7'12411 — Secondary schools. Mixed ability groups. Curriculum subjects: English language. Teaching. *Scotland. Proposals*
Grampian *(Region). Banff English Committee.* English for mixed ability classes in the common course : some suggestions for designing of programmes and for the structuring of a session's work / the Education Committee of Grampian Regional Council, Banff English Committee [formerly the Banff County Council Education Committee, County English Committee]. — 2nd ed. [i.e. 1st ed. reprinted]. — [Aberdeen] ([St Peter's School, Nelson St., Aberdeen AB2 3EQ]) : [Grampian Regional Council Education Committee, Schools Library Service], [1976]. — 113p ; 30cm.
Cover title: The Banffshire report. — Originally published: 1974.
Sd : Unpriced
(B77-33751)

420'.7'1242 — Secondary schools. Curriculum subjects: English language. Teaching. *England*
Marland, Michael. Language across the curriculum : the implementation of the Bullock Report in the secondary school / [by] Michael Marland ; with specialist contributions by Douglas Barnes ... [et al.]. — London : Heinemann Educational, 1977. — x,309p : ill ; 23cm. — (Heinemann organization in schools series)
Bibl.: p.302-304. — Index. — Previous control number ISBN 0-435-80631-9.
ISBN 0-435-80578-9 : £6.80
ISBN 0-435-80631-9 Pbk : £2.95
(B77-24151)

420'.7'1273 — Secondary schools. Curriculum subjects: English language. Teaching. *United States*
Language programs in the public schools / edited by Jewell A. Friend. — Carbondale [etc.] : Southern Illinois University Press ; London [etc.] : Feffer and Simons, 1977. — vii,133p : ill, maps ; 24cm.
Index.
ISBN 0-8093-0794-4 : £6.00
ISBN 0-8093-0811-8 Pbk : £2.96
(B77-31123)

Mersand, Joseph. The English teacher : basic traditions and successful innovations / [by] Joseph Mersand. — Port Washington ; London : Kennikat Press, 1977. — x,290p ; 24cm. — (Kennikat Press national university publications)
Bibl. — Index.
ISBN 0-8046-9170-3 : £11.00
ISBN 0-8046-9175-4 Pbk : Unpriced
(B77-23339)

420'.9 — English language, to 1949
Wrenn, Charles Leslie. The English language / by C.L. Wrenn. — London : Methuen, 1977. — iii-viii,236p ; 17cm. — (University paperbacks)
Originally published: 1949. — Bibl.: p.218-224. — Index.
ISBN 0-416-85810-4 Pbk : £1.55
(B77-18072)

421 — ENGLISH LANGUAGE. WRITTEN AND SPOKEN CODES
421 — English language. Punctuation. *Exercises, worked examples*
Williams, Eric, *b.1942.* Assignments in punctuation and spelling : for reinforcement and revision / [by] Eric Williams. — London : Edward Arnold, 1977. — [6],170p ; 23cm.
ISBN 0-7131-0101-6 Pbk : £1.95
Primary classification 428'.1
(B77-24153)

421 — English language. Punctuation. *Secondary school texts*
Ledgard, T G. Punctuation / [by] T.G. Ledgard. — London : Cassell.
In 4 vols.
Book 1. — 1977. — 39p ; 22cm.
ISBN 0-304-29771-2 Sd : £0.55
(B77-25553)

Book 2. — 1977. — 40p ; 22cm.
ISBN 0-304-29772-0 Sd : £0.55
(B77-25554)

Book 3. — 1977. — 40p ; 22cm.
ISBN 0-304-29773-9 Sd : £0.55
(B77-25555)

Book 4. — 1977. — 55p ; 22cm.
ISBN 0-304-29774-7 Sd : £0.55
(B77-25556)

421.1 — ENGLISH LANGUAGE. NOTATION
421'.1 — English language. Alphabets. *Juvenile literature*
Easy to learn ABC / illustrated by Jo Eaves. — [Maidenhead] : Popular Press, 1977. — [20]p : col ill ; 27cm.
Col. ill., text on lining papers.
ISBN 0-361-03997-2 : £0.30
(B77-18073)

Fredman, Alan. Dean's picture fun with the alphabet / illustrated by Alan Fredman. — London : Dean, 1974. — 3-30p : chiefly col ill ; 28cm.
With answers.
ISBN 0-603-05772-1 : Unpriced
(B77-20189)

Hargreaves, Roger. Albert the alphabetical elephant / story and pictures by Roger Hargreaves. — Leicester : Hodder and Stoughton, 1977. — [29]p : chiefly col ill ; 25cm.
Col. ill. on lining papers.
ISBN 0-340-21395-7 : £2.40
(B77-06619)

Kincaid, Lucy. The Skittles ABC / [written and illustrated by Lucy and Eric Kincaid]. — [Cambridge] : Brimax Books, 1976. — [20]p : chiefly col ill ; 26cm.
Cover title. — Col. ill., text on lining papers.
ISBN 0-904494-13-6 : £0.65
(B77-06620)

Williams, Ferelith Eccles. The Oxford ox's alphabet / [by] Ferelith Eccles Williams. — Tadworth : World's Work, 1977. — [32]p : chiefly col ill ; 19x25cm.
ISBN 0-437-86007-8 : £2.60
(B77-27803)

421'.1 — English language. Alphabets. *Juvenile literature. Facsimiles*
The **Noah's** ark ABC and 8 other Victorian alphabet books in color / edited by Ruari McLean. — New York : Dover Publications [etc.] ; London : Constable, 1976. — 64p : of col ill ; 29cm.
Col. ill. on inside front cover. — Facsimile reprints.
ISBN 0-486-23355-3 Pbk : £2.85
(B77-24864)

422 — ENGLISH LANGUAGE. ETYMOLOGY
422 — English language. Semantics
Bolinger, Dwight. Meaning and form / [by] Dwight Bolinger. — London [etc.] : Longman, 1977. — xi,212p ; 23cm. — (English language series ; 11)
Bibl.: p.201-204. — Index.
ISBN 0-582-55103-x : £6.50
Also classified at 425
(B77-32590)

423 — ENGLISH LANGUAGE. DICTIONARIES
Chambers everyday paperback dictionary / edited by A.M. Macdonald and E.M. Kirkpatrick. — Edinburgh : W. and R. Chambers, 1977. — xii, 851p ; 20cm.
Originally published: as 'Chambers everyday dictionary'. 1975.
ISBN 0-550-18014-1 Pbk : £1.75
(B77-22524)

Chambers twentieth century dictionary. — New ed. / edited by A.M. Macdonald ; with supplement. — Edinburgh : W. and R. Chambers, 1977. — xii,1652p ; 22cm.
This ed. originally published: 1972.
ISBN 0-550-10226-4 : £5.95
ISBN 0-550-10227-2 Presentation ed. : £7.50
ISBN 0-550-10228-0 Quarter leather ed. : £9.75
ISBN 0-550-10229-9 Full leather ed. : £12.50
ISBN 0-550-10230-2 Half leather hand bound ed. : £21.00
ISBN 0-550-10231-0 Full leather hand bound ed. : £26.00
(B77-33752)

Ehrlich, Eugene. Basic vocabulary builder / [by] Eugene Ehrlich, Daniel Murphy. — New York [etc.] ; London : McGraw-Hill, [1976]. — iii-xiii,187p ; 21cm.
Published in the United States: 1975.
ISBN 0-07-019105-0 Pbk : £2.45
(B77-04107)

The **Merriam-Webster** dictionary for large print users. — London : Prior [etc.], 1977. — xi, 1119p ; 28cm.
ISBN 0-86043-067-7 : £14.95
(B77-28557)

The **Nelson** contemporary English dictionary / [general editor W.T. Cunningham]. — Sunbury-on-Thames : Nelson, 1977. — xiv, 610p : ill ; 19cm.
ISBN 0-17-443302-6 Pbk : £1.25
(B77-30167)

Nuttall's concise standard dictionary of the English language / based on the labours of the most eminent lexicographers. — [New ed.] / edited and revised by Lawrence H. Dawson. — London [etc.] : F. Warne, 1976. — xvi,1104p ; 21cm.
This ed. originally published: 1973.
ISBN 0-7232-1700-9 : £2.50
(B77-09657)

Ostler, George. The little Oxford dictionary of current English / compiled by George Ostler. — 4th ed. / edited by Jessie Coulson. — Leicester : Ulverscroft, 1977. — ix,687p ; 28cm. — ([Ulverscroft large print series])
This ed. originally published: Oxford : Clarendon Press, 1969.
ISBN 0-7089-0118-2 : £8.75
(B77-31834)

West, Michael. The new method English dictionary / [by] Michael West and James Gareth Endicott. — 5th ed. / revised ... by Ian Elliott and Lloyd Humberstone. — London : Longman, 1976. — ix,310p : ill ; 22cm.
Previous ed.: 1953.
ISBN 0-582-55522-1 Pbk : £0.98
(B77-10333)

423 — English language. *Dictionaries. For non-English speaking students*
Carver, David J. Collins English learner's dictionary / [compiled] by David J. Carver, Michael J. Wallace, John Cameron. — London [etc.] : Collins, 1977. — xviii,622p : ill ; 22cm.
Originally published: 1974.
ISBN 0-00-433112-5 : £2.95
(B77-31124)

Pollmann, Friedrich. Macmillan Lensing new basic dictionary / [by] Friedrich Pollmann with the assistance of Christopher Scott. — London [etc.] : Macmillan, 1976. — viii,247p : ill, form, maps ; 19cm.
ISBN 0-333-21213-4 Pbk : £1.00
(B77-07280)

West, Michael. An international reader's dictionary. — New ed. / [by] Michael West and James Gareth Endicott ; revised for this edition by Ian Elliott and Lloyd Humberstone. — London : Longman, 1977. — ix,310p : ill ; 20cm.
Previous ed.: 1965.
ISBN 0-582-55535-3 : £1.20
(B77-18074)

423 — English language. *Dictionaries. Juvenile literature*

Bevington, Jeffrey Dixey. My first dictionary all in colour / [by] J.D. Bevington ; illustrated by Jennifer Parsons. — London [etc.] : Hamlyn, 1977. — 4-61p : col ill ; 28cm.
ISBN 0-600-32924-0 : £1.50
(B77-23340)

Child's first dictionary. — London (43 Dover St., W1X 3RE) : Nile and Mackenzie Ltd, 1976. — [2],78p : chiefly col ill ; 18cm.
ISBN 0-86031-018-3 Pbk : £0.95
(B77-31835)

The **illustrated** dictionary / [edited by] Patrick Hanks, Alan Isaacs, and John Daintith ; educational consultant Mary Waddington. — London (59 Grosvenor Street, W.1) : Sundial, 1977. — [1],v,242p : col ill, col charts, col maps ; 29cm.
Spine title: The St Michael illustrated dictionary. — Col. ill. on lining papers.
ISBN 0-904230-40-6 : £2.99
(B77-29359)

Macmillan dictionary for children / William D. Halsey, editorial director, Christopher G. Morris, editor. — New York : Macmillan Publishing Co. ; London : Collier Macmillan, 1976. — xii,724p : col ill, col coat of arms ; 27cm.
Published in the United States: 1975. — 'This dictionary is also published in a text edition, with a different introduction, under the title "Macmillan beginning dictionary"' - title page verso.
ISBN 0-02-547580-0 : £8.25
(B77-10334)

Owen, Bernard. Bernard's children's dictionary / by Bernard Owen. — London [etc.] : Regency Press, 1977. — 204p ; 23cm.
Half title page has title: Bernard's children's dictionary and young typists' guide.
ISBN 0-7212-0486-4 : £4.00
(B77-16334)

Priestley, Harold Edford. Hamlyn shorter all-colour children's dictionary / [by] Harold E. Priestley. — London [etc.] : Hamlyn, 1977. — 254p : col ill ; 19cm.
'The illustrations in this book appeared originally in "The Hamlyn all-colour dictionary"' - title page verso.
ISBN 0-600-32931-3 : £1.75
(B77-19315)

423 — English language. Usage. *Dictionaries*

Butt, Margot. English usage / [by] Margot Butt. — [London] : Collins, 1976. — xvi,492p ; 12cm. — (Gem dictionary)
Cover title: Dictionary of English usage. — Originally published: as 'Collins gem dictionary of English usage'. 1970. — Bibl.: p.xiii.
ISBN 0-00-458750-2 : £0.75
(B77-14686)

Hudson, Kenneth. The dictionary of diseased English / [by] Kenneth Hudson. — London [etc.] : Macmillan, 1977. — xxviii,267p ; 23cm.
Bibl.: p.261-267.
ISBN 0-333-21394-7 : £7.95 : CIP rev.
(B77-19316)

423'.02'07 — English language. *Dictionaries. Humorous texts. Juvenile literature*

Rosenbloom, Joseph. Daffy dictionary : funabridged definitions from aardvark to Zuider Zee / by Joseph Rosenbloom ; illustrations by Joyce Behr. — New York : Sterling [etc.] ; London : Distributed by Ward Lock, 1977. — 256p : ill ; 22cm.
Index.
ISBN 0-7061-2544-4 : £2.95
(B77-25557)

423'.1 — English language. Antonyms & synonyms. *Dictionaries*

Allen, F Sturges. Allen's synonyms and antonyms / by F. Sturges Allen. — Revised and enlarged ed. / edited by T.H. Vail Motter. — New York [etc.] ; London : Barnes and Noble, [1976]. — xi,427p ; 21cm. — (Everyday handbooks)
This ed. originally published: 1972.
ISBN 0-06-463328-4 Pbk : £1.90
(B77-02926)

423'.1 — English language. Catch phrases. *Dictionaries*

Partridge, Eric. A dictionary of catch phrases : British and American, from the sixteenth century to the present day / [by] Eric Partridge. — London [etc.] : Routledge and Kegan Paul, 1977. — xv,278p ; 25cm.
ISBN 0-7100-8537-0 : £7.95 : CIP rev.
(B77-11182)

425 — ENGLISH LANGUAGE. GRAMMAR

425 — English language. Grammar. Theories

Herndon, Jeanne Hefner. A survey of modern grammars / [by] Jeanne H. Herndon. — 2nd ed. — New York ; London [etc.] : Holt, Rinehart and Winston, 1976. — x,374p : ill, map ; 24cm.
Previous ed.: 1970. — Bibl.: p.362-367. — Index.
ISBN 0-03-089675-4 Pbk : £6.00
(B77-01348)

Stageberg, Norman Clifford. An introductory English grammar / [by] Norman C. Stageberg ; with a chapter on transformational grammar by Ralph M. Goodman. — 3rd ed. — New York [etc.] ; London : Holt, Rinehart and Winston, 1977. — xiv,459p : ill ; 24cm.
With answers. — Previous ed.: 1971. — Index.
ISBN 0-03-089919-2 Pbk : Unpriced
(B77-33753)

425 — English language. Grammar. Theories. *For non-English speaking students*

Tomori, Sunday Hezekiah Olu. The morphology and syntax of present-day English : an introduction / [by] S.H. Olu Tomori ; with appendices by John Milne, Ayo Banjo and A. Afolayan. — London [etc.] : Heinemann Educational, 1977. — vii,137p ; 22cm.
Index.
ISBN 0-435-92894-5 Pbk : £2.50
(B77-33754)

425 — English language. Sentences. Stress

Schmerling, Susan F. Aspects of English sentence stress / by Susan F. Schmerling. — Austin ; London : University of Texas Press, 1976. — xi,127p ; 24cm.
Bibl.: p.119-123. — Index.
ISBN 0-292-70312-0 : £7.20
(B77-05346)

425 — English language. Syntax

Bolinger, Dwight. Meaning and form / [by] Dwight Bolinger. — London [etc.] : Longman, 1977. — xi,212p ; 23cm. — (English language series ; 11)
Bibl.: p.201-204. — Index.
ISBN 0-582-55103-x : £6.50
Primary classification 422
(B77-32590)

Fries, Charles Carpenter. The structure of English : an introduction to the construction of English sentences / [by] Charles Carpenter Fries. — London : Longman, 1977. — xi,304p ; 20cm.
Originally published: New York : Harcourt, Brace, 1952. — Index.
ISBN 0-582-52141-6 Lp : £1.75
(B77-20190)

425 — English language. Syntax. Transformational-generative theories

Lester, Mark. Introductory transformational grammar of English / [by] Mark Lester. — 2nd ed. — New York ; London [etc.] : Holt, Rinehart and Winston, 1976. — vi,353p : ill, facsim ; 24cm.
With answers. — Previous ed.: 1971. — Index.
ISBN 0-03-088345-8 Pbk : £6.75
(B77-02228)

425 — Syntax. Lexical aspects. *Study examples: English language*

Gruber, Jeffrey S. Lexical structures in syntax and semantics / [by] Jeffrey S. Gruber. — Amsterdam [etc.] ; Oxford : North-Holland Publishing Co., 1976. — xi,375p : ill ; 23cm. — (North-Holland linguistic series ; 25)
Bibl.: p.369-370. — Index.
ISBN 0-7204-0410-x Pbk : £15.85
(B77-08974)

427 — ENGLISH LANGUAGE. EARLY FORMS, SLANG, DIALECTS

427 — English language. Dialects

Wakelin, Martyn Francis. English dialects : an introduction / [by] Martyn F. Wakelin. — Revised ed. — London : Athlone Press, 1977. — xvi,208p : maps ; 22cm.
Previous ed.: 1972. — Bibl.: p.170-179. — Index.
ISBN 0-485-12031-3 Pbk : £3.50
(B77-31125)

427'.5'18 — English language. Erewash dialect. *Collections*

Scollins, Richard. Ey up, mi duck! : an affectionate look at the speech, history and folklore of Ilkeston and the Erewash Valley / by Richard Scollins and John Titford ; illustrations by Richard Scollins. — Ilkeston (49 St Mary St., Ilkeston [Derbyshire]) : Scollins and Titford.
Part 1. — 1976. — 64p : ill, facsims, maps, port ; 22cm.
ISBN 0-9505292-0-6 Pbk : £0.95
(B77-08338)

Part 2. — 1976. — 64p : ill, facsims, map ; 22cm.
Bibl.: p.60-64.
ISBN 0-9505292-1-4 Pbk : £0.95
(B77-12985)

427'.5'3 — English language. Lincolnshire dialect

Campion, George Edward. Lincolnshire dialects / by G. Edward Campion ; with a foreword by J.D.A. Widdowson. — Boston (80 Sleaford Rd, Boston, Lincs. PE21 8EU) : Richard Kay, 1976. — 61p ; 21cm.
Bibl.: p.61.
ISBN 0-902662-30-9 : £2.25
ISBN 0-902662-31-7 Pbk : £1.20
(B77-07281)

427'.5'45 — English language. Rutland dialect, to 1891. *Dictionaries*

Dialect in Rutland : a dictionary of Rutland words / [compiled by A.R. Traylen]. — Oakham (Rutland County Museum, Oakham, Rutland) : Rutland Local History Society, 1977. — 19p ; 25cm.
Sd : Unpriced
(B77-23341)

427'.7'6 — English language. Lancashire dialect

Wright, Peter, *b.1923.* Lancashire dialect / by Peter Wright ; [maps by E. Gower]. — Clapham, N. Yorkshire : Dalesman, 1976. — 80p : 1 ill, 2 maps ; 21cm.
Bibl.: p.79. — Index.
ISBN 0-85206-354-7 Pbk : £0.90
(B77-00170)

427'.9'73 — English language. American usage. *Dictionaries*

Flesch, Rudolf. Look it up : a deskbook of American spelling and style / [by] Rudolf Flesch. — London [etc.] : Routledge and Kegan Paul, 1977. — xi,431p ; 20cm.
Also published: New York : Harper and Row, 1977.
ISBN 0-7100-8795-0 : £5.75 : CIP rev.
(B77-24152)

427'.9'73 — English language. American usage, to 1975

Flexner, Stuart Berg. I hear America talking : an illustrated treasury of American words and phrases / by Stuart Berg Flexner. — New York ; London [etc.] : Van Nostrand Reinhold, 1976. — xii,505p : ill, facsims, maps, ports ; 29cm.
'A Hudson group book'. — Index.
ISBN 0-442-22413-3 : £14.20
(B77-14687)

427'.9'73 — English language. Usage by negroes in urban regions of United States

Labov, William. Language in the inner city : studies in the black English vernacular / [by] William Labov. — Oxford : Blackwell, 1977. — xxv,412p : ill ; 24cm.
Originally published: Philadelphia : University of Pennsylvania Press, 1972. — Bibl.: p.397-405. — Index.
ISBN 0-631-17670-5 : £10.00
(B77-15798)

427'.9'764 — English language. Texan usage. Vocabulary

Atwood, Elmet Bagby. The regional vocabulary of Texas / by E. Bagby Atwood. — Austin ; London : University of Texas Press, 1975[i.e.1976]. — xiv,273p : maps ; 23cm.
Published in the United States: 1975. — Originally published: Austin : University of Texas Press, 1962. — Index.
ISBN 0-292-77008-1 Pbk : £3.00
(B77-06020)

427'.9'931 — English language. Usage of children in New Zealand. Effects of social class. Statistical analysis

Hawkins, P R. Social class, the nominal group and verbal strategies / [by] P.R. Hawkins. — London [etc.] : Routledge and Kegan Paul, 1977. — xii,242p ; 23cm. — (Primary socialization, language and education ; 8)
Bibl.: p.233-235. — Index.
ISBN 0-7100-8375-0 : £7.50
(B77-14688)

427'.9'94 — English language. Australian usage. *Dictionaries*
The **Australian** pocket Oxford dictionary / edited by Grahame Johnston. — Melbourne ; London [etc.] : Oxford University Press, 1976. — xxiv, 975p ; 18cm.
'Based on "The pocket Oxford dictionary of current English"'.
ISBN 0-19-550537-9 : £6.50
(B77-14689)

428 — ENGLISH LANGUAGE USAGE
McIntyre, J R L. English for professional examinations / [by] J.R.L. McIntyre. — 2nd ed. — Plymouth : Macdonald and Evans, 1977. — viii,167p ; 19cm. — (The M. & E. handbook series)
With suggested answers to progress tests. — Previous ed.: published as 'Intermediate English'. 1968. — Bibl.: p.164. — Index.
ISBN 0-7121-0559-x Pbk : £2.25
(B77-18075)

428 — English language. *Exercises, worked examples*
Burton, Samuel Holroyd. Using English : a language course for advanced students / [by] S.H. Burton. — London : Longman, 1976. — x,181p in various pagings ; 22cm.
'The seven Sections of this Course are also available as separate booklets ... ' - title page verso.
ISBN 0-582-42198-5 Pbk : £2.20
(B77-02927)

428 — English language. *Exercises, worked examples. For illiterate adults. Cards*
Roach, Margaret. Disco pack / [by] Margaret Roach and Joan Tate. — London [etc.] : Cassell and Collier Macmillan, 1976. — Portfolio : ill, form, map ; 27cm.
Thirty-two cards ([64] sides) in portfolio. — '... based on Disco books 1 & 2 ...'.
ISBN 0-304-29756-9 : £4.50
(B77-02928)

428 — English language. *Exercises, worked examples. For slow learning children. Primary school texts. Fill-in books*
Gunn, Ivy. Know how to write a story / devised and illustrated by Ivy Gunn. — Glasgow : Gibson, [1977]. — [1],24,[1]p : ill ; 30cm. — ('Know-how' books ; 3)
'With teacher's notes'.
ISBN 0-7169-0052-1 Sd : £0.35
(B77-15799)

Gunn, Ivy. Know-how to read and write / devised and illustrated by Ivy Gunn. — Glasgow : Gibson, [1977]. — [1],24,[1]p : ill ; 30cm. — ('Know how' books ; 1)
'With teacher's notes'.
ISBN 0-7169-0050-5 Sd : £0.35
(B77-15800)

Gunn, Ivy. Know-how to write / devised and illustrated by Ivy Gunn. — Glasgow : Gibson, [1977]. — [1],24,[1]p : ill ; 30cm. — ('Know-how' books ; 2)
'With teacher's notes'.
ISBN 0-7169-0051-3 Sd : £0.35
(B77-15801)

428 — English language. *Exercises, worked examples. For West Indian students. Middle school texts*
Messenger, Yvonne. Let's revise English / [by] Yvonne Messenger. — St Albans : Hart-Davis Educational, 1977. — [9],230p ; 20cm.
Index.
ISBN 0-247-12608-x Pbk : £0.95
(B77-15250)

428 — English language. *Exercises, worked examples. Middle school texts*
Eagle, Ralph Fletcher. Stride ahead in English / [by] R.F. Eagle. — Exeter [etc.] : Wheaton.
Book 5. — 1976. — 96p : ill ; 24cm.
With answers to crosswords.
ISBN 0-08-020552-6 Pbk : Unpriced
(B77-02229)

Sanders, Eileen. English for the middle years / [by] Eileen Sanders. — Glasgow [etc.] : Blackie.

1. — 1977. — [4],108p : ill ; 21cm.
Bibl.: p.108.
ISBN 0-216-90434-x Pbk : £1.45
(B77-33755)

428 — English language. *Exercises, worked examples. Primary school texts*
Anderson, Kenneth, *b.1919.* On the way! / [by] Kenneth Anderson ; illustrations by Dorothy Ralphs. — Amersham : Hulton.
Book 3. — 1976. — 176p : ill(some col) ; 22cm.
ISBN 0-7175-0756-4 Pbk : £1.50
(B77-02929)

Gagg, John Colton. Exploration English / [by] J.C. Gagg. — Revised ed. — London : Evans Bros.
In 4 vols.
Book 1. — 1977. — 64p : ill(some col) ; 25cm.
Previous ed.: 1969.
ISBN 0-237-29195-9 Sd : £1.10
(B77-33756)

Book 2. — 1977. — 80p : ill, 2 plans ; 25cm.
Previous ed.: 1969.
ISBN 0-237-29196-7 Sd : £1.10
(B77-33757)

Book 3. — 1977. — 64p : ill ; 25cm.
Previous ed.: 1969.
ISBN 0-237-29197-5 Sd : £1.10
(B77-33758)

Book 4. — 1977. — 64p : ill, maps ; 25cm.
Previous ed.: 1969.
ISBN 0-237-29198-3 Sd : £1.10
(B77-33759)

Mellgren, Lars. Yes! : English for children / [by] Lars Mellgren, Michael Walker. — Reading, Mass. ; London [etc.] : Addison-Wesley.
Book A : Listening, speaking / [illustrations by Akihito Shirakawa]. — 1977. — 64p : of ill(some col) ; 25cm.
ISBN 0-201-04940-6 Sd : £1.30
(B77-31126)

Book B : Listening, speaking, reading / [illustrations by Akihito Shirakawa]. — 1977. — 64p : chiefly ill(some col) ; 25cm.
ISBN 0-201-04942-2 Sd : £1.30
(B77-31127)

428 — English language. *Exercises, worked examples. School texts*
Thorpe, Eustace George. Complete English / [by] E.G. Thorpe. — London : Heinemann Educational.
Book 5. Key. — 1976. — iv,91p ; 19cm.
ISBN 0-435-01899-x Sd : £1.50
(B77-06621)

428 — English language. *Exercises, worked examples. Secondary school texts*
Finn, Frederick Edward Simpson. Practice in English for 16+ examinations / [by] F.E.S. Finn. — London : J. Murray, 1977. — vii,88p : ill, map ; 22cm.
ISBN 0-7195-3421-6 Sd : £0.80
(B77-33181)

Finn, Frederick Edward Simpson. Practice in English for 16+ examinations / [by] F.E.S. Finn. — London : J. Murray.
[Teachers' ed.]. — 1977. — vii,88,T11p : ill, map ; 22cm.
With answers.
ISBN 0-7195-3423-2 Sd : £1.00
(B77-33182)

Ockenden, Michael. Talking points / [by] Michael Ockenden. — London : Longman, 1977. — ix,34p : ill, map, plan ; 21cm.
ISBN 0-582-55323-7 Sd : £0.60
(B77-26263)

Rowe, Albert. Language matters / [by] Albert Rowe. — Exeter : Wheaton, 1977. — vi,103p : ill, facsim, map ; 21cm.
ISBN 0-08-021770-2 Pbk : £1.50
(B77-33760)

428 — English language. *Exercises, worked examples. Secondary school texts. Cards*
Abbs, Brian. Picture sets and practice packs : visuals and work cards for language development / [by] Brian Abbs, Evelyn Davies, Peter Town. — London : Longman.
1 : The Olympics. — 1976. — Case : ill(chiefly col), ports(some col) ; 31cm.
Teacher's booklet ([2],30p.), 4 fold. sheets ([4]p.), 10 copies each of 4 folders ([12]p.).
ISBN 0-582-55317-2 : £16.00
(B77-18076)

428 — English language. *For Australian students. Secondary school texts*
Finney, Judith. The language of living : a new English text for the middle years of the secondary school / [by] Judith Finney, Peter Smart. — Sydney [etc.] ; London : Reed Education, 1975. — 150p : ill, facsims ; 19x27cm.
Bibl.: p.149-150.
ISBN 0-589-09162-x Pbk : £3.90
(B77-22525)

428 — English language. *Middle school texts*
Murphy, Aubrey. A treasury of English / by Aubrey Murphy & Declan Murphy. — Dublin : Folens.
1 : Grammar through nature study ; suitable for middle standards. — [1977]. — 80p : ill, forms, music ; 25cm.
Pbk : Unpriced
(B77-30169)

428 — English language. *Middle school texts. Teaching kits*
Menzies, David, *b.1934.* Flannan Isle file / [by] David Menzies. — [Glasgow etc.] : Blackie, [1977]. — Portfolio : ill, map ; 19x25cm. — (Options for English)
Teacher's guide (16p.) 30 copies of each of one folder ([4]p.), two sheets ([4]p.), 6 copies of each of three sheets ([6]p.). — Bibl.: Teacher's guide p.15.
ISBN 0-216-90350-5 : £5.00
(B77-27005)

428 — English language. *Primary school texts*
Gregory, Olive Barnes. Workbooks in primary English / by O.B. Gregory. — 2nd ed. — Exeter : Wheaton.
1. — 1976. — [1],45p : ill ; 21cm.
Fill-in book. — Previous ed.: 1968.
ISBN 0-08-021069-4 Sd : £0.35
(B77-02930)

Rudd, Elizabeth. One two three go! / [by] Elizabeth Rudd. — London : Hodder and Stoughton.
Picture book 1 / [illustrations by Andrew Sier]. — 1976. — 32p : of col ill ; 25cm.
ISBN 0-340-19402-2 Sd : £0.75
Primary classification 428'.2'43931
(B77-01349)

Reading workbook 1 / [illustrations by Andrew Sier]. — 1976. — 31p : ill ; 25cm.
ISBN 0-340-19404-9 Sd : £0.40
Primary classification 428'.2'43931
(B77-01350)

Story figurines 1. — 1976. — 1v. : col ill ; 41cm.
Four cards (4 sides) in envelope. — Story figurines 1 has subtitle: A primary course in English.
ISBN 0-340-19401-4 : £2.95
Primary classification 428'.2'43931
(B77-01351)

Teacher's book 1 / [translator, Pim Gerner]. — 1976. — 1v. ; 22cm.
Pierced for binder.
ISBN 0-340-19405-7 Ls : £6.00
Primary classification 428'.2'43931
(B77-03505)

Stagg, Sidney Alfred. Mind your language / [by] S.A. Stagg and J.A. Wynne. — London : Longman, 1977. — [1],48p : ill ; 21cm.
ISBN 0-582-18719-2 Sd : £0.50
(B77-16835)

428 — English language. *Secondary school texts*
Contemporary English / [compiled by] John Foster. — Basingstoke [etc.] : Macmillan.
1. — 1977. — 125p : ill, facsims, ports ; 30cm.
Bibl.
ISBN 0-333-19670-8 Pbk : £1.95
(B77-21073)

2. — 1977. — 118p : ill, facsims, port ; 30cm.
Bibl.
ISBN 0-333-19671-6 Pbk : £1.95
(B77-21074)

Madgwick, Mary. Crossroads : a course in the language arts / by Mary Madgwick and Norman McCulla ; edited by Alan Proud. — London : Edward Arnold, 1976. — 159p : ill ; 19x25cm.
Originally published: Terrey Hills, N.S.W. : Reed Education, 1974. — Index.
ISBN 0-7131-0100-8 Pbk : £2.25
(B77-19318)

Rowe, Albert Ward. English through experience / [by] Albert Rowe & Peter Emmens. — 2nd ed. — St Albans : Hart-Davis Educational.
In 5 vols.
1. — 1974. — x,211p : ill ; 22cm.
Previous ed.: London : Blond Educational, 1963.
ISBN 0-219-51853-x Pbk : Unpriced
(B77-18699)

2. — 1974. — xii,261p : ill, facsims, 2 maps, music ; 22cm.
Previous ed.: London : Blond Educational, 1963.
ISBN 0-219-51854-8 Pbk : Unpriced
(B77-18700)

3. — 1975. — x,268p : ill, 2 facsims ; 22cm.
Previous ed.: London : Blond Educational, 1964.
ISBN 0-219-51855-6 Pbk : Unpriced
(B77-18701)

428 — English language. *Secondary school texts. Teaching kits*
Andrews, Janet. The pied piper file / [by] Janet Andrews. — [Glasgow] : Blackie, [1977]. — 1v. : ill ; 19x26cm. — (Options for English)
Teacher's guide, 30 copies each of booklet ([8]p.), 6 copies each of 2 sheets ([4]p.), 30 copies each of sheet ([2]p.), 30 copies each of folder ([4]p.) in folder. — Bibl.: Teacher's guide p.15.
ISBN 0-216-90351-3 : £7.50
(B77-23342)

428 — English language. *Study examples: Signs in English. Questions & answers. For non-English speaking students*
Pearce, M R. English sign language : reading comprehension activities / [by] M.R. Pearce. — London : Harrap, 1977. — 68p : ill, facsims ; 22cm.
ISBN 0-245-53127-0 Sd : £1.50
(B77-28560)

428 — English language. Errors. *Primary school texts*
Groves, Paul. Smudge and Chewpen : a book of exercises for correction of the common errors made in writing / [by] Paul Groves and Nigel Grimshaw. — London : Edward Arnold, 1976. — [4],73p ; 22cm.
ISBN 0-7131-0090-7 Sd : Unpriced
(B77-10513)

428 — English language. Sentences. *Exercises, worked examples. Primary school texts. Fill-in books*
Hughes, John Malcolm. Sounds in sentences / [by] John M. Hughes ; [illustrated by Colin Hawkins]. — Sunbury-on-Thames [etc.] : Nelson.
In 4 vols.
Book 1. — 1977. — 30p : ill ; 28cm.
Fill-in book.
ISBN 0-17-424221-2 Sd : £0.32
(B77-24865)

Book 2. — 1977. — 30p : ill ; 28cm.
Fill-in book.
ISBN 0-17-424222-0 Sd : £0.32
(B77-24866)

Book 3. — 1977. — 30p : ill ; 28cm.
Fill-in book.
ISBN 0-17-424223-9 Sd : £0.32
(B77-24867)

Book 4. — 1977. — 30p : ill ; 28cm.
Fill-in book.
ISBN 0-17-424224-7 Sd : £0.32
(B77-24868)

428 — English language. Special subjects: Change & communication. *For New Zealand students. Secondary school texts*
Catherwood, V J. Communication and change / [by] V.J. Catherwood. — Christchurch, [N.Z.] [etc.] ; London : Whitcoulls, 1976. — 80p : ill(some col) ; 24cm. — (Beacon series ; 3)
Bibl.: p.80.
ISBN 0-7233-0460-2 Sd : £2.68
(B77-07282)

428 — English language. Usage. *Middle school texts*
Deadman, Ronald. Ways of knowing, awareness / [by] Ronald Deadman and Arthur Razzell. — London [etc.] : Macmillan.
In 2 vols. — EP records also available.
1. — 1977. — 80p : ill ; 25cm.
ISBN 0-333-19379-2 Pbk : £0.95
(B77-31128)

428 — English language. Usage. *Secondary school texts*
Acland, Robin. Target English / by Robin Acland. — [Oxford] : Blackwell.
[Approval pack]. — 1977. — 1v. : ill, facsims, maps ; 30cm.
Teacher's book (15p.), 6 booklets ([196]p.) in plastic envelope.
ISBN 0-631-93470-7 : £3.00
(B77-18077)

428.1 — ENGLISH LANGUAGE USAGE. SPELLING AND PRONUNCIATION

428'.1 — English language. Comparative adjectives. *Juvenile literature*
Freudberg, Judy. Some more most / written by Judy Freudberg ; illustrated by Richard Hefter. — Glasgow [etc.] : Collins, 1977. — [30]p : col ill ; 24cm. — (A strawberry book)
Originally published: United States : One Strawberry, 1976.
ISBN 0-00-138216-0 : £1.50
(B77-18078)

428'.1 — English language. Pronunciation. *Exercises, worked examples. For non-English speaking students*
Baker, Ann. Ship or sheep? : introducing English pronunciation / [by] Ann Baker ; with cartoons by Leslie Marshall. — Cambridge [etc.] : Cambridge University Press, 1977. — [6],229p : ill ; 21cm. — (Cambridge English language learning)
ISBN 0-521-21312-6 Pbk : £2.00(non-net)
(B77-31129)

Lewis, J Windsor. People speaking : phonetic readings in current English / [by] J. Windsor Lewis. — Berlin : Cornelson ; Berlin ; Oxford : Oxford University Press, 1977. — iv,92p ; 22cm.
Text on inside front and back covers. — 'A 60-minute companion cassette tape ... is also available' - back cover.
Pbk : £2.00
ISBN 3-8109-0403-1
(B77-31838)

428'.1 — English language. Spelling. *Exercises, worked examples*
Williams, Eric, *b.1942.* Assignments in punctuation and spelling : for reinforcement and revision / [by] Eric Williams. — London : Edward Arnold, 1977. — [6],170p ; 23cm.
ISBN 0-7131-0101-6 Pbk : £1.95
Also classified at 421
(B77-24153)

428'.1 — English language. Spelling. *Exercises, worked examples. Juvenile literature*
Smith, John, *b.1921.* Spelling / by John Smith. — London : Cassell.
Book 6. — 1977. — [8],40p : ill ; 19cm.
ISBN 0-304-29815-8 Sd : £0.42
(B77-14690)

Book 7. — 1977. — [8],40p : ill ; 19cm.
ISBN 0-304-29816-6 Sd : £0.42
(B77-14691)

Book 8. — 1977. — [8],40p : ill ; 19cm.
ISBN 0-304-29817-4 Sd : £0.42
(B77-14692)

428'.1 — English language. Spelling. *Exercises, worked examples. Primary school texts*
Ballance, Denis. Nelson spelling / [by] Denis and Helen Ballance. — Sunbury-on-Thames [etc.] : Nelson.
In 4 vols.
1. — 1977. — 48p : ill(some col) ; 25cm.
ISBN 0-17-424231-x Pbk : £0.60
(B77-28561)

2. — 1977. — 48p : ill(some col) ; 25cm.
ISBN 0-17-424232-8 Pbk : £0.60
(B77-28562)

3. — 1977. — 48p : ill(some col) ; 25cm.
ISBN 0-17-424233-6 Pbk : £0.60
(B77-28563)

4. — 1977. — 48p : ill(some col) ; 25cm.
ISBN 0-17-424234-4 Pbk : £0.60
(B77-28564)

428'.1 — English language. Spelling. *Manuals. Juvenile literature*
Arvidson, Gordon Lincoln. Alphabetical spelling list.
[Book 1] : Targets 1, 2, 3. — [Exeter] : Wheaton, 1977. — [66]p : ill ; 24x9cm.
Author: Gordon Lincoln Arvidson. — Originally published: 1963.
ISBN 0-08-021399-5 Sd : £0.50
(B77-18079)

[Book 2] : Targets 1-7. — [Exeter] : Wheaton, 1977. — [1],63,[1]p : ill ; 24x9cm.
Author: Gordon Lincoln Arvidson. — Originally published: 1963.
ISBN 0-08-021400-2 Sd : £0.40
(B77-18080)

Arvidson, Gordon Lincoln. Alphabetical spelling list / [by] G.L. Arvidson. — Exeter : Wheaton.

Learning to spell : a manual for use with the 'Alphabetical spelling list'. — 1977. — 47p : 1 ill ; 22cm.
Originally published: 1963.
ISBN 0-08-021772-9 Sd : £0.90
(B77-24869)

Arvidson, Gordon Lincoln. Alphabetical spelling list. — [Exeter] : Wheaton.
Target 1 : Introductory book. — 1977. — [18] p ; 24x9cm.
Author: Gordon Lincoln Arvidson. — Originally published: 1963.
ISBN 0-08-021038-4 Sd : £0.20
(B77-08339)

428'.1 — English language. Spelling. *School texts*
Allan, B V. Logical spelling / [by] B.V. Allan ; illustrated by A. & W. Rodger. — Glasgow [etc.] : Collins, 1977. — 128p : ill(some col) ; 23cm.
With answers. — Index.
ISBN 0-00-314316-3 Pbk : £1.25
(B77-29360)

428'.1 — English language. Words
De Bono, Edward. Wordpower : an illustrated dictionary of vital words / [compiled by] Edward De Bono ; illustrated by George Craig. — London ([17 Oakley Rd, N1 3LL]) : Pierrot Publishing Ltd, 1977. — [2],269p : ill ; 21cm.
ISBN 0-905310-06-3 : £4.95
ISBN 0-905310-02-0 Pbk : £1.95
(B77-30170)

Triesman, Susan. Verballistics / prepared for the [Open University, Art and Environment] Course Team by Susan Triesman (text), John Barr (layout). — [Milton Keynes] : [Open University Press], 1976. — [16]p : ill ; 42cm. — ([Technology/arts/social sciences], a second level interdisciplinary course : art and environment ; unit 9) (TAD292 ; 9)
Bibl.: p.[16].
ISBN 0-335-06208-3 Sd : Unpriced
(B77-14693)

428'.1 — English language. Words. *For pre-school children*
Scarry, Richard. Short and tall / with illustrations by Richard Scarry. — London [etc.] : Hamlyn, 1977. — [24]p : col ill ; 21cm. — (A golden look-look book)
Originally published: New York : Golden Press, 1976.
ISBN 0-600-38252-4 Sd : £0.40
(B77-31839)

428'.1 — English language. Words. *Illustrations. For non-English speaking students*
Parnwell, Eric Charles. Oxford English picture dictionary / [by] E.C. Parnwell ; illustrated by Corinne Clarke and Ray Burrows. — Oxford [etc.] : Oxford University Press, 1977. — 92p : col ill, col maps ; 23cm.
Index.
ISBN 0-19-431214-3 : £1.75
ISBN 0-19-431160-0 Pbk : £0.80
(B77-27006)

428'.1 — English language. Words. *Juvenile literature*
Sims, Charles Alfred. Another word / [by] C.A. Sims ; illustrated by G. Quinn, J.B. Ridyard and D. Etchell. — Huddersfield : Schofield and Sims, 1976. — [3],51p : chiefly col ill ; 30cm.
Index.
ISBN 0-7217-0293-7 Pbk : £1.00
ISBN 0-7217-0292-9 Non-net : £0.75
(B77-09658)

428'.1 — English language. Words. *Juvenile literature. Illustrations*
Ricketts, Michael. Indoors / illustrated by Michael and Ann Ricketts. — [London] : Angus and Robertson, 1977. — [12]p : chiefly col ill ; 32cm. — (A word hunter picture book)

Cover title. — Col. ill., text on lining papers.
ISBN 0-207-95755-x : £1.50
(B77-20191)

Ricketts, Michael. Outdoors / illustrated by Michael and Ann Ricketts. — [London] : Angus and Robertson, 1977. — [12]p : chiefly col ill ; 32cm. — (A word hunter picture book)

Cover title. — Col. ill., text on lining papers.
ISBN 0-207-95753-3 : £1.50
(B77-20192)

Scarry, Richard. Early words / [by] Richard Scarry. — Glasgow [etc.] : Collins, [1977]. — [14]p : chiefly col ill ; 20cm.
ISBN 0-00-138244-6 Pbd : £0.85
(B77-18081)

Words for topics. — [London] : Macmillan.
[Set 2]. A baron and his castle / illustrated by Malcolm Stokes. — 1976. — [15]p : chiefly col ill ; 25cm.
ISBN 0-333-18993-0 Sd : £0.42
(B77-06622)

[Set 2]. Around our town / illustrated by Kathleen Wapham. — 1976. — [15]p : chiefly col ill ; 25cm.
ISBN 0-333-18988-4 Sd : £0.42
(B77-06623)

[Set 2]. At the airport / illustrated by Peter Kesteven. — 1976. — [15]p : chiefly col ill ; 25cm.
ISBN 0-333-18989-2 Sd : £0.42
(B77-06624)

[Set 2]. At the docks / illustrated by Peter Kesteven. — 1976. — [15]p : chiefly col ill ; 25cm.
ISBN 0-333-18990-6 Sd : £0.42
(B77-06625)

[Set 2]. Early animals and people / illustrated by Graham Allen. — 1976. — [15]p : chiefly col ill ; 25cm.
ISBN 0-333-18991-4 Sd : £0.42
(B77-06626)

[Set 2]. Romans / illustrated by Malcolm Stokes. — 1976. — [15]p : chiefly col ill ; 25cm.
ISBN 0-333-18992-2 Sd : £0.42
(B77-06627)

428'.1 — English language. Words. *Juvenile literature. Questions & answers*
What am I? project ... — St Ives, Cornwall : Pike, 1974. — 32p : ill, form ; 26cm. — (Look learn projects)
Fill-in book. — With answers. — '... with a merit award certificate'.
ISBN 0-85932-048-0 Sd : £0.30
(B77-18702)

428'.1 — English language. Words. *Primary school texts*
Fergus, Andrew. Activity words / [by] Andrew Fergus. — Amersham : Hulton.
Book 6. — 1977. — [3],123p : ill(chiefly col) ; 21cm.
ISBN 0-7175-0689-4 Pbk : £1.60
(B77-30171)

428'.1 — English language. Words difficult to spell. *Exercises, worked examples. For typing*
Smith, Marion. Type to spell / by Marion Smith and Dorothy L. Butterfield. — London [etc.] : McGraw-Hill, 1976. — 64p : facsims ; 25cm.
Index.
ISBN 0-07-084214-0 Sp : £1.35
(B77-07283)

428'.1 — English language. Words. Usage
Howard, Philip, *b.1933.* New words for old / [by] Philip Howard. — London : Hamilton, 1977. — xv,127p ; 23cm.
Index.
ISBN 0-241-89722-x : £3.95
(B77-24870)

428'.1 — English language. Words. Usage. *Readings*
More words / [by] Dannie Abse ... [et al.]. — London : British Broadcasting Corporation, 1977. — 127p ; 24cm.
Selections from the Radio 3 programme 'Words'.
ISBN 0-563-17298-3 : £4.25
(B77-33761)

428'.1'05 — English language. Words. *Periodicals*
Logophile : the Cambridge journal of words. — Cambridge (The Editor, 'Logophile', Trinity College, Cambridge CB2 1TQ) : Logophile Press.
No.1- ; Lent term 1977-. — 1977-. — ill ; 31cm.
12p. in 1st issue.
Sd : £0.15
ISSN 0309-6270
(B77-20193)

428'.1'076 — English language. Vocabulary. *Exercises, worked examples. For non-English speaking students*
Hill, Leslie, Alexander. Contextualized vocabulary tests / [by] L.A. Hill. — London : Oxford University Press.
2 / illustrated by Edward McLachlan. — 1973. — [63]p : ill ; 24cm.
Originally published: 1970. — Previous control number ISBN 0-19-432565-2.
Sd : £0.65
ISBN 0-19-432565-2
(B77-07285)

Hill, Leslie Alexander. Contextualized vocabulary tests / [by] L.A. Hill. — London : Oxford University Press.
1 / illustrated by Colin King. — 1976. — [71] p : ill(some col) ; 24cm.
Originally published: 1970. — Previous control number ISBN 0-19-432564-4.
Sd : £0.70
ISBN 0-19-432564-4
(B77-07284)

428'.1'076 — English language. Words. *Questions & answers*
Word power from 'Reader's digest'. — London [etc.] : Reader's Digest Association, 1976. — 128p ; 19cm.
With answers. — Originally published: 1967.
ISBN 0-276-00154-0 Pbk : £6.95
(B77-07286)

428.2 — ENGLISH LANGUAGE USAGE. GRAMMAR

428'.2 — English language. Comprehension. *Exercises, worked examples. Middle school texts*
Reading for concepts / William Liddle, general editor. — [2nd ed.]. — New York ; London [etc.] : McGraw-Hill.
In 8 vols. — Previous ed.: St Louis : McGraw-Hill, 1970-.
Book A. — 1977. — 176p : ill ; 24cm.
ISBN 0-07-037661-1 Pbk : £2.70
(B77-30172)

Book B. — 1977. — 176p : ill ; 24cm.
ISBN 0-07-037662-x Pbk : £2.70
(B77-30173)

Book C. — 1977. — 176p : ill, map ; 24cm.
ISBN 0-07-037663-8 Pbk : £2.70
(B77-30174)

Book D. — 1977. — 176p : ill, ports ; 24cm.
ISBN 0-07-037664-6 Pbk : £2.70
(B77-30175)

Book E. — 1977. — 176p : ill ; 24cm.
ISBN 0-07-037665-4 : £2.70
(B77-30176)

Book F. — 1977. — 192p : ill, map, ports ; 24cm.
ISBN 0-07-037666-2 Pbk : £2.70
(B77-30177)

Book G. — 1977. — 192p : ill, chart, maps, ports ; 24cm.
ISBN 0-07-037667-0 Pbk : £2.70
(B77-30178)

Book H. — 1977. — 192p : ill, maps, ports ; 24cm.
ISBN 0-07-037668-9 Pbk : £2.70
(B77-30179)

Scope for reading / [edited by] C. Allan, G. Livingstone, J. Love. — Edinburgh : Holmes-McDougall.
Book 1 : On the lines / [illustrations by Penny Abrahams et al.]. — [1975]. — [1],96p : ill(some col), facsims, form, port ; 30cm.
ISBN 0-7157-1349-3 Pbk : £1.40
ISBN 0-7157-1350-7 Teacher's ed. : £2.00
(B77-04108)

428'.2 — English language. Comprehension. *Exercises, worked examples. Secondary school texts*
English comprehension tests. — Slough : Foulsham. — (Copymasters)
Book 1 / by Gordon Chapman. — 1976. — [24]leaves ; 28cm.
Contains ready cut stencils. — 2 leaves printed on both sides. — Answers to the multiple choice test.
ISBN 0-572-00945-3 Pbk : £4.95
(B77-02230)

Fisher, Clifford Henry. An introduction to CSE multiple choice English / [by] Clifford H. Fisher. — London : Edward Arnold, 1976. — 155p : ill ; 22cm.
ISBN 0-7131-0068-0 Pbk : Unpriced
(B77-02231)

Lamb, Geoffrey Frederick. Exercises in composition and comprehension (CSE standard) / by G.F. Lamb. — London : Harrap, 1976. — 159p : ill, map ; 20cm.
Originally published: 1968.
ISBN 0-245-53038-x Pbk : £1.70
Also classified at 808'.042'076
(B77-10788)

428'.2 — English language. Extracts from printed directions. Comprehension. *Exercises, worked examples. Secondary school texts*
Ridgway, Bill. What's this all about? / [by] Bill Ridgway. — London : Edward Arnold, 1977. — 48p : ill, facsims, forms, map ; 25cm.
ISBN 0-7131-0073-7 Sd : £1.10
(B77-15802)

428'.2 — English language. Grammar
Barnard, John Burra Clothier. Examination English. — 7th ed. / [by] J.B.C. Barnard. — Plymouth : Macdonald and Evans, 1976. — viii,244p ; 22cm.
Previous ed.: 1964. — Index.
ISBN 0-7121-0557-3 Pbk : £2.50
(B77-08340)

Ehrlich, Eugene. Schaum's outline of English grammar / by Eugene Ehrlich and Daniel Murphy. — New York ; London [etc.] : McGraw-Hill, 1976. — [13],139p ; 28cm. — (Schaum's outline series)
Spine title: English grammar. — With answers.
ISBN 0-07-019098-4 Pbk : £2.90
(B77-07287)

428'.2 — English language. Grammar. *Exercises, worked examples*
Brendel, Leroy A. English usage drills and exercises : programmed for the typewriter / [by] Leroy A. Brendel, Elsie L. Leffingwell. — 2nd ed. — New York ; London [etc.] : McGraw-Hill, 1977. — vi,122p ; 28cm.
With answers to tests. — Previous ed.: New York : McGraw-Hill, 1968.
ISBN 0-07-007485-2 Pbk : £3.05
(B77-33184)

Harkess, Shiona. Cue for a drill / [by] Shiona Harkess & John Eastwood. — London [etc.] : Oxford University Press, 1976. — 127p : ill, forms, maps ; 22cm.
Index.
ISBN 0-19-432780-9 Pbk : £1.75
(B77-06628)

428'.2 — English language. Grammar. *Primary school texts*
Agar, Kenneth. On target / [by] K. Agar and P.W.R. Foot. — Basingstoke [etc.] : Macmillan.

Book 1 / illustrated by Val Biro. — 1977. — 40p : ill ; 20x26cm.
ISBN 0-333-19099-8 Sd : £0.50
(B77-24155)

Book 2 / illustrated by Sumiko Davis. — 1977. — 48p : ill ; 21x26cm.
ISBN 0-333-19100-5 Sd : £0.55
(B77-24156)

Book 3 / illustrated by Rowan Barnes Murphy. — 1977. — 56p : ill ; 21x26cm.
ISBN 0-333-19101-3 Sd : £0.60
(B77-31840)

Book 4 / illustrated by Frank Boyle. — 1977. — 64p : ill, map ; 21x26cm.
ISBN 0-333-19102-1 Sd : £0.65
(B77-31841)

428'.2 — English language. Précis. Writing. *Secondary school texts*
Proud, Alan. English in brief : a course in summary writing / [by] Alan Proud. — London : Edward Arnold, 1977. — 96p ; 22cm.

Index.
ISBN 0-7131-0157-1 Sd : £1.10 : CIP rev.
(B77-16335)

428'.2'03 — English language. Grammar. *Encyclopaedias*
Thompson, Denys. The Nelson guide to good English / [by] Denys Thompson. — Sunbury-on-Thames [etc.] : Nelson, 1976. — [10],178p ; 19cm.
ISBN 0-17-443303-4 Pbk : £2.50
(B77-02931)

428.24 — ENGLISH LANGUAGE. FOR FOREIGN STUDENTS

428'.2'4 — English language. *Exercises, worked examples. For Caribbean students. Secondary school texts*
Gray, Cecil, *b.1923.* Language for living : a Caribbean English course. — Revised ed. / [by] Cecil Gray. — [Port of Spain] : Longman Caribbean ; London : Longman.
Stage 1. — 1977. — [9],204p ; 21cm.
Previous ed.: / by Cecil Gray, John Barker. 1968.
ISBN 0-582-76551-x Pbk : £1.15
(B77-25558)

Messenger, Yvonne. Let's revise English / [by] Yvonne Messenger. — St Albans : Hart-Davis Educational.
Answers. — 1977. — [2],62p ; 20cm.
ISBN 0-247-12797-3 Sd : £0.95
(B77-18703)

428'.2'4 — English language. *Exercises, worked examples. For non-English speaking students*

Access to English. — Oxford [etc.] : Oxford University Press.
[Part 1] : Starting out. Workbook B / [by] Michael Coles and Basil Lord ; illustrated by Ivan Ripley. — 1977. — 48,[1]p : ill ; 22cm.
ISBN 0-19-453716-1 Sd : £0.65
(B77-12986)

[Part 3] : Turning point / [by] Michael Coles and Basil Lord ; designed and illustrated by Peter Edwards. — 1976. — 176p : ill, facsims, music ; 22cm.
ISBN 0-19-453740-4 Pbk : £1.80
(B77-08341)

Test pack 2 / [by] Michael Coles and Basil Lord. — 1976. — 1v. : ill ; 22cm.
Eighteen copies of 1 folder (8p.). — Fill-in sheets. — With answers.
ISBN 0-19-453791-9 : £2.00
(B77-02932)

Alexander, L.G. Mainline skills / [by] L.G. Alexander, R.H. Kingsbury, M.C. Vincent. — London : Longman. — (New concept English)

B. Students' book / [by] L.G. Alexander, R.H. Kingsbury. — 1976. — iii,125p : ill, facsims, maps, ports ; 24cm.
With answers.
ISBN 0-582-51953-5 Pbk : £1.50
(B77-06629)

B. Teacher's book / [by] L.G. Alexander, R.H. Kingsbury. — 1977. — [3],180p : ill ; 22cm.
With answers.
ISBN 0-582-51966-7 Pbk : £1.75
(B77-30180)

Archer, Margaret. Cambridge Certificate English : a course for First Certificate / [by] Margaret Archer and Enid Nolan-Woods. — Sunbury-on-Thames [etc.] : Nelson.
Key. — 1977. — 32p ; 22cm.
ISBN 0-17-555194-4 Sd : £0.95
(B77-31130)

Fowler, William Scott. Proficiency English / [by] W.S. Fowler. — Sunbury-on-Thames [etc.] : Nelson.
Book 2 : Reading comprehension. — 1977. — 192p : ill ; 22cm.
ISBN 0-17-555118-9 Pbk : £1.75
(B77-25559)

Johnson, Capper. First Certificate skills / [by] Capper Johnson. — London : Evans Bros, 1977. — iv,116p : ill, forms, ports ; 22cm.
ISBN 0-237-28968-7 Pbk : £1.40
(B77-27804)

MacIver, Angus. Concise first aid in English / [by] Angus MacIver ; edited and arranged by D.A. McLennan. — Glasgow : Gibson.
Answer book / [by] D.A. McLennan. — 1974. — 40p ; 21cm.
ISBN 0-7169-4071-x Sd : Unpriced
(B77-19319)

Millington-Ward, John. Practice in structure and usage for intermediate students / [by] John Millington Ward. — London : Longman.
[Practice 11-15]. — 1976. — [4],44p ; 20cm.
This supplement has the title 'Practice in structure and usage : fifty exercises'. — With answers.
ISBN 0-582-55251-6 Sd : £0.35
(B77-06630)

Millington-Ward, John. Proficiency in the use of English : 10 lessons of guidance and practice / [by] John Millington Ward. — London : Longman, 1975. — [1],iii,108p : ill ; 20cm.
ISBN 0-582-55341-5 Sd : £1.00
(B77-11762)

Swan, Hazel Ann. New English proficiency course / [by] H.A. Swan. — Amersham : Hulton.
Answer book. — 1977. — 61p ; 21cm.
ISBN 0-7175-0774-2 Sd : £1.00
(B77-28565)

Thomas, B J. Practical information : comprehension and composition practice / [by] B.J. Thomas. — London : Edward Arnold, 1977. — 64p : ill, forms, maps ; 25cm.
ISBN 0-7131-0151-2 Sd : £1.35 : CIP rev.
(B77-10335)

White, Colin. Broader context English / [by] Colin White, Paul Davies. — London [etc.] : Macmillan. — (ACE series)
Key to exercises. — 1976. — 36p ; 22cm.
ISBN 0-333-21629-6 Sd : £1.25
(B77-04109)

428'.2'4 — English language. *Exercises, worked examples. For non-English speaking students. Secondary school texts*

Archer, Margaret. Cambridge Certificate English : a course for First Certificate / [by] Margaret Archer and Enid Nolan-Woods. — Sunbury-on-Thames [etc.] : Nelson, 1977. — [6],199p : ill, form ; 25cm.
Index.
ISBN 0-17-555195-2 Pbk : £2.25
(B77-26264)

Low, Ona. First Certificate in English practice / [by] Ona Low. — London : Edward Arnold, 1977. — iv,113p : ill ; 23cm.
ISBN 0-7131-0127-x Pbk : £1.50
(B77-25560)

Low, Ona. First Certificate in English practice / [by] Ona Low. — London : Edward Arnold.
Key. — 1977. — 28p ; 22cm.
ISBN 0-7131-0131-8 Sd : £0.80
(B77-25561)

428'.2'4 — English language. *For non-English speaking students*

Byrne, Donn, *b.1931.* Insight : a language practice and composition book at intermediate level / [by] Donn Byrne and Susan Holden. — London : Longman, 1976. — xiii,99p : ill, forms, maps ; 25cm.
ISBN 0-582-55249-4 Pbk : £1.60
(B77-02933)

Guide to language and study skills for college students of English as a second language / [by] Anne V. Martin ... [et al.]. — Englewood Cliffs ; London [etc.] : Prentice-Hall, 1977. — xii,276p : ill, forms ; 24cm.
Index.
ISBN 0-13-370452-1 Pbk : £5.55
(B77-25562)

Merat, Ferokh. Creative reading and writing / [by] F. Merat and M. Fabre. — London : Collier Macmillan, 1976. — 127p ; 22cm.
With answers.
ISBN 0-02-970440-5 Pbk : £1.75
(B77-04110)

Mosback, Gerald Peter. Practical faster reading : an intermediate/advanced course in reading and vocabulary / [by] Gerald Peter Mosback, Vivienne Mosback. — Cambridge [etc.] : Cambridge University Press, 1976. — xi,120p ; 25cm. — (Cambridge English language learning)
With answers.
ISBN 0-521-21346-0 Pbk : £1.50
(B77-04111)

O'Neill, Robert. Interaction : practice modules at the First Certificate level / [by] Robert O'Neill. — London : Longman, 1976. — ix,87p : ill ; 25cm. — (First Certificate in English)
Booklet (7p.) in pocket.
ISBN 0-582-55243-5 Pbk : £1.50
(B77-00171)

428'.2'4 — English language. *For non-English speaking students. Primary school texts*

Broughton, Geoffrey. Go / [by] Geoffrey Broughton. — London : Longman.
3. Picture reader / illustrated by Jenny Williams. — 1977. — [3],12p : chiefly ill(chiefly col) ; 22x28cm.
ISBN 0-582-55094-7 Sd : £0.75
(B77-12987)

3. Teacher's book. — 1977. — iv,28p : music ; 22cm.
ISBN 0-582-55091-2 Sd : £0.80
(B77-10336)

Broughton, Geoffrey. Go / by Geoffrey Broughton. — London : Longman.
3. Workbook / illustrated by Jenny Williams. — 1976. — 32p : ill ; 21x28cm.
ISBN 0-582-55092-0 Sd : £0.60
(B77-03501)

Schools Council Project in English for Immigrant Children. Scope stage 2 / [Schools Council Project in English for Immigrant Children]. — London : Longman for the Schools Council.
Travel. Work cards / by Josie Levine ; illustrations by Andrew Sier. — 1976. — Portfolio : ill, maps ; 22x23cm.
Sheet ([2]p.), 18 cards ([36] sides).
ISBN 0-582-09168-3 : £1.25
(B77-05347)

Water. Work cards / by Josie Levine ; illustrations by Andrew Sier. — 1976. — Portfolio : ill, map, port ; 22x23cm.
Sheet ([2]p.), 18 cards ([36] sides).
ISBN 0-582-09166-7 : £1.25
(B77-05348)

Webster, Diana. Play and say with Paddy and Pip. — 2nd ed. / [by] Diana Webster, Hiroyoshi Hatori ; illustrated by Keith Rawling. — London [etc.] : Macmillan.
Picture book 1. — 1977. — 36,[1]p : chiefly col ill ; 25cm.
Previous ed.: / by Diana Webster. 1973.
ISBN 0-333-22652-6 Sd : Unpriced
(B77-21075)

Picture book 2. — 1977. — 36,[1]p : chiefly col ill ; 25cm.
Previous ed.: / by Diana Webster. 1973.
ISBN 0-333-22653-4 Sd : Unpriced
(B77-21076)

Play book 1. — 1977. — 40p : chiefly col ill ; 25cm.
Previous ed.: / by Diana Webster. 1973.
ISBN 0-333-22656-9 Sd : Unpriced
(B77-21077)

Play book 2. — 1977. — 36,[1]p : chiefly col ill ; 25cm.
Previous ed.: / by Diana Webster. 1973.
ISBN 0-333-22657-7 Sd : Unpriced
(B77-21078)

Webster, Diana. Play and say with Paddy and Pip / [by] Diana Webster ; illustrated by Keith Rawling. — [London etc.] : Macmillan.
Picture book 4. — [1974]. — 36p : of col ill ; 26cm.
Five laminated cards as inserts.
ISBN 0-333-16730-9 : Unpriced
(B77-20194)

Wright, Andrew, *b.1937.* Kaleidoscope : English for juniors / [by Andrew Wright, David Betteridge and Nicolas Hawkes]. — London [etc.] : Macmillan [for the] University of York.
Stage 1 : units 1-6. Step-by-step teacher's guide. — 1976. — iv,234p : ill ; 21cm.
ISBN 0-333-21260-6 Pbk : £2.80
(B77-02934)

428'.2'4 — English language. *For non-English speaking students. Secondary school texts*

Alexander, L.G. Target : an audio-visual English course for secondary schools / by L.G. Alexander, J. Tadman, R.H. Kingsbury. — London : Longman.
1. Workbook / by L.G. Alexander, J. Tadman, D.K. Swan ; illustrated by John Geipel. — 1977. — 63p : ill ; 24cm.
Fill-in book.
ISBN 0-582-51879-2 Sd : £0.50
(B77-31131)

Cox, Alwyn. English examined / [by] Alwyn Cox, Neville Grant, Helen O'Neill ; based on the BBC radio series designed and produced by Terry O'Neill ; cassette recordings produced by Terry O'Neill ; illustrations by Peter Joyce and Dick Vine. — Sunbury-on-Thames [etc.] : Nelson for the British Broadcasting Corporation and the British Council, on behalf of the British Ministry of Overseas Development, 1976. — viii,245p : ill ; 22cm.
With answers.
ISBN 0-17-555131-6 Pbk : £1.30
(B77-07884)

428'.2'4 — English language. *For West Indian students. Secondary school texts*

Gray, Cecil, *b.1923.* Language for living : a Caribbean English course. — Revised ed. / [by] Cecil Gray. — [Port of Spain] : Longman Caribbean ; London : Longman.
Stage 3. — 1976. — viii,184p : ill ; 21cm.
Previous ed.: / by Cecil Gray, Joan Barker, Alan Gilchrist. 1971. — Bibl.: p.181-183.
ISBN 0-582-76552-8 Pbk : £1.10
(B77-00723)

428'.2'4 — English language. Comprehension. *Exercises, worked examples. For non-English speaking students*

Banjo, Ladipo Ayo. Effective use of English : a developmental language course for colleges and universities / [by] L. Ayo Banjo and S.O. Unoh. — Sunbury-on-Thames [etc.] : Nelson, 1976. — viii,184p : form ; 22cm.
With answers.
ISBN 0-17-511391-2 Pbk : £1.75
(B77-24871)

Byrne, Donn, *b.1929.* Functional comprehension / [by] Donn Byrne. — London : Longman, 1977. — viii,84p : ill, facsims, forms ; 24cm.
ISBN 0-582-55242-7 Sd : £0.90
(B77-12988)

Chaplen, Frank. Communication practice in written English / [by] Frank Chaplen. — Oxford [etc.] : Oxford University Press.
Teacher's book. — 1977. — 48p ; 22cm.
ISBN 0-19-432796-5 Sd : £1.75
(B77-30181)

Keane, Leila Louise. The Egyptian cat / [by] L.L. Keane. — London : Longman, 1977. — [1],30,[1]p : ill ; 23cm. — (Longman integrated comprehension and composition series)
ISBN 0-582-55327-x Sd : £0.40
(B77-31842)

National Council of Teachers of English. English for today / the National Council of Teachers of English ; project director William R. Slager ; chief reviser William R. Slager ; senior consultant Albert H. Marckwardt. — 2nd ed. — New York ; London [etc.] : McGraw-Hill.
Book 6 : Literature in English. — [1976]. — [12],259p : ill, ports ; 23cm.
This ed. published in the United States: 1975. — Previous ed.: 1964.
ISBN 0-07-045819-7 Pbk : Unpriced
(B77-03502)

Readings in English / [compiled by] Walter Pauk, Josephine M. Wilson. — London [etc.] : McGraw-Hill.
Book 2. — 1976. — 271p : col ill ; 23cm.
Some portions of the selections have been rewritten.
ISBN 0-07-094442-3 Pbk : £2.50
(B77-04112)

Book 3. — 1976. — 277p : col ill ; 23cm.
ISBN 0-07-094443-1 Pbk : £2.50
(B77-03503)

Book 4. — 1976. — 301p : col ill ; 23cm.
ISBN 0-07-094444-x Pbk : £2.50
(B77-03504)

Richards, Brian. Nobody sings like Ted / [by] Brian Richards. — London : Longman, 1977. — [1],30,[1]p : ill ; 23cm. — (Longman integrated comprehension and composition series)
ISBN 0-582-55329-6 Sd : £0.40
(B77-20195)

428'.2'4 — English language. Comprehension. *For mature non-English speaking students*

Lewis, Richard, *b.1930.* Reading for adults / [by] Richard Lewis, M.C. Vincent, Susan Weir. — London : Longman.
3. — 1977. — 96p : ill(some col), ports ; 24cm.

ISBN 0-582-52792-9 Pbk : £1.25
(B77-30182)

428'.2'4 — English language. Determiners. *For non-English speaking students*

Close, Reginald Arthur. Determiners / [by] R.A. Close. — London : Longman for the British Council. — (English language units ; unit 33)
Part 3 : (Some, any, no, either, neither).
Teacher's book. — 1976. — [6],57p ; 22cm.
Bibl.: p.56.
ISBN 0-582-53931-5 Sd : £0.21
(B77-07288)

Part 3. Students' book. — 1976. — 8p ; 22cm.
ISBN 0-582-53930-7 Sd : £0.21
(B77-07289)

428'.2'4 — English language. Grammar. *Exercises, worked examples. For non-English speaking students*

Rainsbury, Robert. Written English : an introduction for beginning students of English as a second language / [by] Robert Rainsbury. — Englewood Cliffs ; London [etc.] : Prentice-Hall, 1977. — xiii,111p ; 28cm.
Pages perforated at inside edge and pierced for binder.
ISBN 0-13-970673-9 Pbk : £3.95
(B77-31132)

428'.2'4 — English language. Grammar. *For non-English speaking students*

Close, Reginald Arthur. English as a foreign language : its constant grammatical problems / [by] R.A. Close. — 2nd ed. — London : Allen and Unwin, 1977. — 3-192p : ill ; 23cm.
Previous ed.: 1962. — Bibl.: p.180-181. — Index.
ISBN 0-04-425023-1 : £5.95
ISBN 0-04-425024-x Pbk : £2.95
(B77-21079)

Naidoo, Pauline. Office practice / [by] Pauline Naidoo, Maryvonne Bolch, Margaret Walker. — London : Cassell and Collier Macmillan. — (Special English)
Book 2 : Secretarial duties / [by] Pauline Naidoo and Maryvonne Bolch. — 1973. — vii, 117p : ill, facsims, forms ; 21cm.
With answers.
ISBN 0-02-974840-2 Pbk : Unpriced
(B77-19320)

Spankie, Greig Marshall. English in use / [by] G.M. Spankie. — London [etc.] : Nelson.
Key. — 1977. — [2],28p ; 22cm.
ISBN 0-17-555182-0 Sd : £0.80
(B77-27805)

Success with English : the Penguin course / [general editor Geoffrey Broughton]. — Harmondsworth [etc.] : Penguin. — (Penguin education)
[Stage] 1. Coursebook / [by] Geoffrey Broughton ; illustrations by Quentin Blake. — Revised ed. — 1977. — 303p : ill ; 21cm.
Previous ed.: 1968. — Index.
ISBN 0-14-080007-7 Pbk : £0.95
(B77-15803)

[Stage] 1. Teachers' handbook / [by] J.A. Barnett, Geoffrey Broughton and Thomas Greenwood. — Revised ed. — 1977. — 137p ; 21cm.
Previous ed.: 1968. — Index.
ISBN 0-14-080010-7 Pbk : £1.50
(B77-15804)

[Stage] 2. Coursebook / [by] Geoffrey Broughton ; illustrations by Quentin Blake. — Revised ed. — 1977. — 317p : ill ; 21cm.
Previous ed.: 1969. — Index.
Pbk : £0.95
ISBN 0-14-080077-8
(B77-15805)

[Stage] 2. Teachers' handbook / [by] Geoffrey Broughton and Thomas Greenwood. — Revised ed. — 1977. — 134p ; 22cm.
Previous ed.: / by J.A. Barnett, Geoffrey Broughton and Thomas Greenwood. 1969. — Index.
Pbk : £1.50
ISBN 0-14-080272-x
(B77-15806)

[Stage] 3. Coursebook / [by] Geoffrey Broughton ; illustrations by Quentin Blake. — Revised ed. — 1977. — 253p : ill ; 21cm.
Previous ed.: 1970. — Index.
Pbk : £1.10
ISBN 0-14-080180-4
(B77-15807)

[Stage] 3. Teachers' handbook / [by] Geoffrey Broughton and Thomas Greenwood. — Revised ed. — 1977. — 134p ; 21cm.
Previous ed.: 1968. — Index.
Pbk : £1.50
ISBN 0-14-080181-2
(B77-15808)

Success with English : the Penguin course / [general editor Geoffrey Broughton]. — Harmondsworth [etc.] : Penguin. — (Penguin education)
[Stage 1]. A first reader / [by] Alexander Baird ... [et al.] ; illustrations by Maureen Roffey. — 1977. — 89p : ill ; 21cm.
Originally published: 1968.
ISBN 0-14-080008-5 Pbk : £0.50
(B77-15809)

[Stage] 1. Objective test book / [by] Geoffrey Broughton ; illustrations by Quentin Blake. — 1977. — 2-30,[1]p : ill ; 21cm.
Originally published: 1971.
ISBN 0-14-080293-2 Sd : £0.25
(B77-15810)

[Stage 1]. Workbook / [by] Geoffrey Barnard ; illustrations by John Vernon Lord. — 1977. — 3-45p : ill ; 21cm.
With answers. — Originally published: 1968.
ISBN 0-14-080009-3 Sd : £0.30
(B77-15811)

[Stage 2]. Crossword book / [by] Geoffrey Broughton. — 1977. — [64]p ; 22cm.
With answers. — Originally published: 1968.
ISBN 0-14-080078-6 Sd : £0.40
(B77-15812)

[Stage] 2. Objective test book / [by] Geoffrey Broughton ; illustrations by Quentin Blake. — 1977. — 2-31p : ill ; 21cm.
Originally published: 1971.
ISBN 0-14-080294-0 Sd : £0.25
(B77-15813)

[Stage] 3. Objective test book / [by] Geoffrey Broughton ; illustrations by Quentin Blake. — 1971. — 2-19p ; 21cm.
ISBN 0-14-080295-9 Sd : £0.25
(B77-15814)

428'.2'4 — English language. Indirect statements. *For non-English speaking students*

Higgins, Muriel Fyfe. Indirect statements / [by] M.F. Higgins. — London : Longman for the British Council. — (English language units ; unit 31)
Part 2. Students' book. — 1976. — 15p ; 22cm.

ISBN 0-582-53926-9 Sd : £0.21
(B77-06021)

Part 2. Teacher's book. — 1976. — [6],72p ; 22cm.
Bibl.: p.68.
ISBN 0-582-53927-7 Sd : £0.21
(B77-06022)

428'.2'4 — English language. Negative questions. Answers. *For non-English speaking students*

Coe, Norman. Answers to negative questions / [by] Norman Coe. — London : Longman for the British Council. — (English language units ; unit 30)
Teacher's book. — 1975. — [6],59p : map ; 22cm.
Bibl.: p.56.
ISBN 0-582-53925-0 Sd : Unpriced
(B77-18704)

428'.2'4 — English language. Sentences. *For non-English speaking students*

English alive. — London : Edward Arnold.
In 3 vols.
1 / [by] Sandra Nicholls, Patrick O'Shea, Tony Yeadon. — 1977. — [2],78p : ill, map ; 25cm.
Fill-in book.
ISBN 0-7131-0115-6 Pbk : £1.30
(B77-31843)

428'.2'4 — English language. Verbs. Tenses. *Exercises, worked examples. For non-English speaking students*

Barnes, Ronald. Get your tenses right / [by] Ronald Barnes ; drawings by David Bryant. — Cambridge [etc.] : Cambridge University Press, 1977. — [9],158p : ill ; 21cm. — (Cambridge English language learning)
Cassette also available.
ISBN 0-521-21296-0 Pbk : £1.50(non-net)
(B77-16836)

428'.2'402461 — English language. *For medicine. For non-English speaking students*

Brasnett, Clive. English for medical students / [by] Clive Brasnett. — London [etc.] : Methuen, 1976. — 170p ; 22cm.
ISBN 0-423-49760-x Pbk : £1.75
(B77-01352)

428'.2'4024658 — English language. *For marketing. For non-English speaking students*

Kruse, Benedict. English for business, marketing / [by] Benedict Kruse and Bettijune Kruse. — New York ; London [etc.] : McGraw-Hill, 1976. — vii,120p ; 23cm.
Two tape cassettes also available. — Index.
ISBN 0-07-035557-6 Pbk : £1.90
(B77-04113)

428'.2'407 — Non-English speaking students. Education. Curriculum subjects: English language. Courses: 'Kaleidoscope'. *For teaching*

Wright, Andrew, *b.1937.* Introducing kaleidoscope : English for juniors / [by Andrew Wright, David Betteridge and Nicolas Hawkes]. — London [etc.] : Macmillan [for the] University of York, 1976. — [2],31p : ill(some col) ; 29cm.
Index.
ISBN 0-333-21296-7 Sd : £2.60
(B77-04738)

428'.2'407 — Non-English speaking students. Education. Curriculum subjects: English language for science. *Readings*

English-Teaching Information Centre. English for academic study : with special reference to science and technology : problems and perspectives / the British Council, English Teaching Information Centre. — London (10 Spring Gardens, SW1A 2BN) : The Centre, 1975. — [3],69p : ill ; 30cm. — (Occasional paper)
Bibl.
Sd : £1.00
(B77-10789)

428'.2'4071 — Schools. Non-English speaking students. Curriculum subjects: English language. Teaching

Derrick, June. Language needs of minority group children : learners of English as a second language / [by] June Derrick. — Windsor : NFER, 1977. — [5],59p ; 22cm.
Bibl.: p.56-59.
ISBN 0-85633-118-x Sd : £2.10
(B77-19321)

428'.2'4076 — Non-English speaking students. Education. Curriculum subjects: English language. Examinations & tests

English-Teaching Information Centre. Examinations and tests in English for speakers of other languages / the British Council, English Teaching Information Centre. — [London] ([10 Spring Gardens, SW1A 2BN]) : [The Centre], 1976. — [3],63p ; 29cm. — (Information guide ; 6)
Bibl.: p.48-57.
ISBN 0-901618-11-x Sd : £1.00
(B77-12989)

428'.2'4076 — Secondary schools. Non-English speaking students. Curriculum subjects: English language. Examinations set by Joint Matriculation Board. Test in English (Overseas). *England, 1966-1976. Reports, surveys*

McEldowney, Patricia L. Test in English (Overseas) : the position after ten years / [by] Patricia L. McEldowney. — Manchester : Joint Matriculation Board, 1976. — 51,[1]p : ill, map, plans ; 21cm. — (Joint Matriculation Board. Occasional publications ; 36)
ISBN 0-901628-09-3 Sd : £0.30
(B77-14193)

428'.2'43931 — English language. *For Dutch speaking students. Secondary school texts*

Rudd, Elizabeth. One two three go! / [by] Elizabeth Rudd. — London : Hodder and Stoughton.
Picture book 1 / [illustrations by Andrew Sier]. — 1976. — 32p : of col ill ; 25cm.
ISBN 0-340-19402-2 Sd : £0.75
Also classified at 428
(B77-01349)

Reading workbook 1 / [illustrations by Andrew Sier]. — 1976. — 31p : ill ; 25cm.
ISBN 0-340-19404-9 Sd : £0.40
Also classified at 428
(B77-01350)

Story figurines 1. — 1976. — 1v. : col ill ; 41cm.
Four cards (4 sides) in envelope. — Story figurines 1 has subtitle: A primary course in English.
ISBN 0-340-19401-4 : £2.95
Also classified at 428
(B77-01351)

Teacher's book 1 / [translator, Pim Gerner]. — 1976. — 1v. ; 22cm.
Pierced for binder.
ISBN 0-340-19405-7 Ls : £6.00
Also classified at 428
(B77-03505)

428'.2'4927 — English language. *For Arabic speaking students. Primary school texts*

Allen, William Stannard. Living English for the Arab world / [by] W. Stannard Allen & Ralph Cooke. — London : Longman.
Pupils' book 2. — 1977. — 144p : col ill ; 19cm.
Cover title. — Originally published: 1963.
ISBN 0-582-74007-x Pbk : Unpriced
(B77-27007)

428'.2'4927 — English language. *For Arabic speaking students. School texts*

Allen, William Stannard. Living English for the Arab world / [by] W. Stannard Allen & Ralph Cooke. — London : Longman.
1. Pupils' book / drawings by Cliff Rowe ; calligraphy by Denys Baker. — [Revised ed.]. — 1977. — [2],90p : col ill ; 19cm.
This ed. originally published: 1966.
ISBN 0-582-74003-7 Sd : £0.26
(B77-29361)

428'.2'4927 — English language. *For Arabic speaking students. Secondary school texts*

Allen, William Stannard. Progressive living English for the Arab world / [by] W. Stannard Allen [J.M. Morgan, Alan C. McLean]. — London : Longman.
Pupils' book 4 / [by] W. Stannard Allen, Alan C. McLean. — 1977. — 80p : ill(chiefly col), maps ; 24cm.
ISBN 0-582-76199-9 Pbk : £1.20
(B77-24873)

Tapescript 3 / [by] W. Stannard Allen, Alan C. McLean. — 1976. — 47p ; 22cm.
ISBN 0-582-76178-6 Sd : Unpriced
(B77-01353)

Teacher's book 4 / [by] W. Stannard Allen, Alan C. McLean. — 1977. — xii,159p ; 22cm.
ISBN 0-582-76127-1 Pbk : £1.75
(B77-32592)

428'.2'4927 — English language. *For Jordanian students. Secondary school texts*

Mackin, Ronald. Oxford secondary English course, Jordan / [by] Ronald Mackin, David Carver, Shahir El-Hassan. — London : Oxford University Press.
In 3 vols.
Anthology 3A. — 1976. — [4],114p ; 24cm.
ISBN 0-19-433443-0 Pbk : £0.80
(B77-00724)

Anthology 3B. — 1976. — [4],125p ; 24cm.
ISBN 0-19-433444-9 Pbk : £0.95
(B77-00725)

Book 3. — 1976. — [10],141p : ill, ports ; 24cm.
Index.
ISBN 0-19-433441-4 Pbk : £0.95
(B77-00726)

428'.2'4927 — English language. Grammar. *For Libyan students. Secondary school texts*

Gusbi, Mustafa. Further English for Libya / [by] M. Gusbi and R. John. — Revised ed. — London : Longman.
Book 2. Teacher's guide. — 1977. — 76p ; 22cm.
Previous ed.: 1971.
ISBN 0-582-76158-1 Sd : £0.56
(B77-28566)

Gusbi, Mustafa. Further English for Libya / [by] Mustafa Gusbi and Roland John ; drawings by Dennis Barker. — London : Longman.
Pupils' book 2. — Revised ed. — 1977. — [3], 218p : ill ; 21cm.
Previous ed.: Harlow : Longman, 1971.
ISBN 0-582-76157-3 Pbk : £1.70
(B77-24874)

428'.2'495911 — English language. *Exercises, worked examples. For Thai students. Secondary school texts*

Methold, Ken. Read it, write it / [by] Ken Methold. — Bangkok : Thai Watana Panich ; London : Longman.
2. — 1975. — 2,61p : ill ; 22x28cm.
ISBN 0-582-70802-8 Sd : Unpriced
(B77-19322)

428'.2'496 — English language. *Exercises, worked examples. For West African students. Secondary school texts*

Grant, Neville J H. Secondary English project : an English course for secondary schools in West Africa / [by] Neville J.H. Grant, D. Olu Olagoke, K.R. Southern. — [London] : Longman.
Book 2. — 1977. — [6],184p : ill, maps ; 25cm.

ISBN 0-582-60154-1 Pbk : £1.30
(B77-28567)

428'.2'496 — English language. *Exercises, worked examples. For West African students. Secondary school texts. Fill-in books*

Rulka, Constance. Objective questions and answers in English / [by] C. Rulka. — London [etc.] : Macmillan.
Book 3. — 1977. — [4],105,[3]p ; 28cm.
Fill-in book. — With answers.
ISBN 0-333-21327-0 Pbk : £0.95
(B77-14194)

428'.2'496 — English language. *For Gambian students. Primary school texts*

Primary English for The Gambia. — London : Longman.
Teacher's programme 2 / [edited by] Elizabeth Hyde and J.M. Stitt. — 1977. — [2],vi,173p : music ; 30cm.
'The material in this book is taken from the new edition of "Sierra Leone Primary English, Teacher's Programme 2"' - title page verso.
ISBN 0-582-59199-6 Sp : £1.50
(B77-30183)

428'.2'496 — English language. *For Sierra Leonean students. Primary school texts*

Sierra Leone primary English. — New ed. — [Harlow] : Longman.
Pupils' book 1. — 1975. — [2],48,[1]p : col ill ; 25cm.
Two sheets in pocket. — Previous ed.: 1966.
ISBN 0-582-59197-x Sd : Unpriced
(B77-16336)

Teacher's programme 2 / [by] Elizabeth Hyde and J.M. Stitt. — New ed. — 1977. — [2],vi, 173p : music ; 30cm.
Previous ed.: 1969.
ISBN 0-582-59801-x Sp : £1.50
(B77-27806)

428'.2'496 — English language. *For West African students. Secondary school texts*

Berry, Ann. Evans primary English course / [by] A. Berry. — Ibadan : Evans Brothers (Nigeria Publishers) ; London : Evans Bros.
Pupils' transition book. — New ed. ; with new exercises. — 1976. — 128p : ill ; 21cm.
Previous ed.: 1961.
ISBN 0-237-50087-6 Pbk : £0.75
(B77-00172)

Stoddart, John. English language for the Certificate year / [by] John Stoddart, Frances Stoddart. — Revised ed. — London [etc.] : Allen and Unwin, 1977. — 140p ; 22cm.
With answers. — Previous ed.: 1969.
ISBN 0-04-370081-0 Pbk : £1.50
(B77-24875)

428.3 — ENGLISH LANGUAGE. SPOKEN EXPRESSION

428'.3 — Children, 5-11 years. Spoken English language. Narratives. Structure. *Study regions: Londonderry (County). Research reports*

McClements, Roberta Jane. Aspects of the structure of narrative speech in children aged 5,7,9 & 11 years / [by] Roberta Jane McClements. — Coleraine (Coleraine, [Co. Derry]) : Board of Studies in Linguistics, New University of Ulster, 1976. — [1],iii,76,[2]p : ill ; 21cm. — (Occasional papers in linguistics and language learning ; no.2 ISSN 0308-2075)
Bibl.: p.71.
ISBN 0-901229-16-4 Sd : Unpriced
(B77-11763)

428'.3 — Spoken English language

Brown, Gillian. Listening to spoken English / [by] Gillian Brown. — London : Longman, 1977. — xv,175p : ill ; 22cm. — (Applied linguistics and language study)
Bibl.: p.173. — Index.
ISBN 0-582-55077-7 Pbk : £2.25
(B77-33762)

428'.3 — Spoken English language. *For teaching non-English speaking students*

Innes, Peggy. Let's talk English : and feel at home with your acquired language / [by] Peggy Innes. — Southport (32 Roe La., Southport, Merseyside PR9 9EA) : English Speaking Board (International), 1976. — [4],99p ; 22cm.
Bibl.: p.67-69.
ISBN 0-9502789-7-1 Pbk : £1.50
(B77-13618)

428'.3'024658 — Spoken English language. *Exercises, worked examples. For management*

O'Reilly, Máire. Talking business / [by] M. O'Reilly, P.E. Moran, N. Ferguson. — London [etc.] : Macmillan.
Drills. — 1976. — [4],34p ; 14x22cm.
'... based on extracts from the dialogues ... on the dialogue tape' - Instructions.
ISBN 0-333-21649-0 Sd : £1.00
(B77-04114)

428'.3'4 — Spoken English language. *Conversation primers. For non-English speaking students*

Alexander, L.G. I think you think : 30 discussion topics for adults / [by] L.G. Alexander, R.H. Kingsbury. — London : Longman, 1976. — ix, 63p : ill, maps, ports ; 21cm.
ISBN 0-582-55510-8 Sd : £0.80
(B77-06631)

428'.3'4 — Spoken English language. *Exercises, worked examples. For non-English speaking students*

Abbs, Brian. Starting strategies : an integrated language course for beginners of English / [by] Brian Abbs, Ingrid Freebairn. — [London] : Longman.
Strategies 1. [Students' book]. — [1977]. — 134p : ill, forms, maps ; 26cm.
ISBN 0-582-51905-5 Pbk : £1.55
(B77-27807)

Strategies 1. Teacher's book / [by] Ingrid Freebairn. — 1977. — ix,130p : ill, forms, maps ; 26cm.
ISBN 0-582-51915-2 Pbk : £2.05
(B77-27808)

Maddock, Vivienne. Speak English English / [by] Vivienne Maddock. — London : University Tutorial Press, 1977. — 143p : ill ; 21cm.
With answers.
ISBN 0-7231-0737-8 Pbk : £1.10
(B77-27809)

Nash, Doreen Mary. Hear, talk and write / [by] Doreen Nash. — London : Duckworth.
'... a work-book of oral tests for the First Cambridge Certificate' - cover. — In 2 vols. — With answers.
Vol.1. — 1977. — 96p ; 22cm.
ISBN 0-7156-0776-6 Pbk : £0.95
(B77-14195)

Vol.2. — 1977. — 95p ; 22cm.
ISBN 0-7156-1059-7 Pbk : £0.95
(B77-14196)

Templer, J C. Intermediate oral skills / [by] J.C. Templer and Keith Nettle. — London : Heinemann Educational.
Students' book. — 1977. — 64p : ill, 2 facsims ; 22cm.
ISBN 0-435-28743-5 Sd : £0.55
(B77-31844)

Teachers' book. — 1977. — 96p : ill, 2 facsims ; 22cm.
ISBN 0-435-28744-3 Pbk : £1.75
(B77-31845)

428'.3'4 — Spoken English language. *For non-English speaking students*

Andrews, John, *b.1934.* Say what you mean in English / [by] John Andrews. — Sunbury-on-Thames [etc.] : Nelson.
Workbook. 1. — 1976. — [61]p ; 25cm.
ISBN 0-17-555188-x Pbk : £0.70
(B77-10337)

428'.3'4 — Spoken English language. Comprehension. *Exercises, worked examples. For non-English speaking students*

Alexander, L.G. Question and answer : graded oral comprehension exercises / [by] L.G. Alexander. — New ed. / revised by Peter Ferguson. — London : Longman, 1977. — xi, 146p ; 22cm.
Previous ed.: 1968.
ISBN 0-582-55206-0 Pbk : £1.00
(B77-27008)

428'.3'4 — Spoken English language. Dialogues. *For non-English speaking students*

Long, Michael Hugh. Face to face / [by] Michael H. Long. — London : Evans Bros, 1977. — [4], 52p : ill ; 19cm.
Index.
ISBN 0-237-50046-9 Sd : Unpriced
(B77-29362)

428'.3'4 — Spoken English language. Grammar. *For non-English speaking students*

Palmer, Harold Edward. A grammar of spoken English / by Harold E. Palmer and F.G. Blandford. — 3rd ed. / revised and rewritten by Roger Kingdon. — Cambridge [etc.] : Cambridge University Press, 1976. — xx,341p ; 23cm.
This ed. originally published: 1969. — Index.
ISBN 0-521-21097-6 : £6.50
ISBN 0-521-29040-6 Pbk : £2.95
(B77-02232)

428'.3'4 — Spoken English language. Verbs. Tenses. *For non-English speaking students*

Tense time : extension material in spoken English / developed from materials written and used by the staff of the British Council's English Language Teaching Institute ; edited by Patricia Ahrens. — London : Longman.
In 3 vols, each accompanied by a set of 3 tapes.

Book 2. — 1977. — [4],76p : ill, forms ; 24cm.
ISBN 0-582-55360-1 Sd : £1.00
(B77-32593)

428'.3'495922 — Spoken English language. *Phrase books. For Vietnamese speaking persons*

Nguyen-dinh-Hoa. English phrase book for Vietnamese speakers : useful and practical phrases and expressions needed by Vietnamese / by Nguyen-dinh-Hoa. — Rutland, Vt [etc.] : Tuttle ; London : Prentice-Hall, 1976. — [8],39p : ill ; 13x19cm.
Cover title: Hoa's English phrase book for Vietnamese speakers.
ISBN 0-8048-1193-8 Pbk : £1.55
(B77-01354)

428.4 — ENGLISH LANGUAGE. READING

428'.4 — Children. Reading skills. Development. *For teaching*

Open University. *Reading Development Course Team.* Developing independence in reading / prepared by John Merritt ... [et al.] ; for the [Open University, Reading Development] Course Team. — Milton Keynes : Open University Press, 1977. — 154p : ill, facsims ; 30cm. — ([Educational studies], a post-experience and second level undergraduate course : reading development ; block 2, units 5, 6, 7 and 8) (PE231 ; block 2, units 5, 6, 7 and 8)
Bibl.: p.149-150. — Index.
ISBN 0-335-06692-5 Pbk : Unpriced
(B77-28568)

428'.4 — Reading skills. Assessment. *For teaching*

Pumfrey, Peter David. Measuring reading abilities : concepts, sources and applications / [by] Peter D. Pumfrey. — London [etc.] : Hodder and Stoughton, 1977. — viii,216p : ill, forms ; 23cm.
Bibl. — Index.
ISBN 0-340-18797-2 : £6.35 : CIP rev.
ISBN 0-340-18796-4 Pbk : £2.85
(B77-24876)

428'.4'019 — Reading. Learning by man. Psychological aspects. *Conference proceedings*

Toward a psychology of reading : the proceedings of the CUNY conferences / edited by Arthur S. Reber, Don L. Scarborough. — Hillsdale : Erlbaum ; New York ; London [etc.] : Distributed by Wiley, 1977. — xiii,337p : ill ; 24cm.
'The contributions ... are based upon presentations at two conferences held at the City University of New York in the Spring of 1974' - Preface. — Index.
ISBN 0-470-99010-4 : £13.50
(B77-22526)

428'.4'07 — Reading skills. Teaching

Spooncer, Frank A. The development of reading / [by] Frank A. Spooncer. — London [etc.] : Hodder and Stoughton, 1976. — 2-31p ; 28cm. — (Canterbury study books)
With answers. — Bibl.: p.29-31.
ISBN 0-340-19074-4 Sd : £0.60
(B77-06023)

Spooncer, Frank A. The evaluation of reading / [by] Frank A. Spooncer. — London [etc.] : Hodder and Stoughton, 1976. — 2-31p ; 28cm. — (Canterbury study books)
With answers. — Bibl.: p.29-31.
ISBN 0-340-05097-7 Sd : £0.60
(B77-06024)

428'.4'07 — Reading skills. Teaching. *Periodicals*

Reading education. — Sunderland (c/o S.V. Heatlie, 63 Laurel Grove, Sunderland, Tyne and Wear SR2 9EE) : United Kingdom Reading Association.
No.2 : 1977 / editors Bruce Gillham, Douglas Dennis, Valerie Nickson. — [1977]. — 52p : ill ; 21cm.
Cover title: Reading education, UK. — Bibl.
Sd : Unpriced
ISSN 0309-8176
(B77-26265)

428'.4'07 — Reading. Teaching methods, to 1965

Mathews, Mitford McLeod. Teaching to read, historically considered / [by] Mitford M. Mathews. — Chicago ; London : University of Chicago Press, 1976. — xi,218p : facsim, music ; 22cm.
Originally published: 1966. — Bibl.: p.209-214. — Index.
ISBN 0-226-51013-1 Pbk : £3.05
(B77-01355)

428'.4'071 — Schools. Curriculum subjects: Reading. Teaching

Duffy, Gerald G. Systematic reading instruction / [by] Gerald G. Duffy, George B. Sherman. — 2nd ed. — New York [etc.] ; London : Harper and Row, 1977. — viii,519p ; 24cm.
Previous ed.: 1972. — Bibl.: p.484-489.
ISBN 0-06-041794-3 Pbk : £6.70
(B77-17437)

428'.4'071041 — Schools. Curriculum subjects: Reading. Projects. *Great Britain. Case studies. For teaching*

Hoffman, Mary. Reading, writing and relevance / [by] Mary Hoffman. — London : Hodder and Stoughton [for] the United Kingdom Reading Association, 1976. — 109p ; 22cm. — (Open University. Set books) (Teaching of reading monographs)
Index.
ISBN 0-340-21025-7 Pbk : £1.35
Also classified at 808'.042'071041
(B77-06632)

428'.4'0710411 — Schools. Students, 8-15 years. Curriculum subjects: Reading. *Scotland. Reports, surveys*

Maxwell, James, *b.1911.* Reading progress from 8 to 15 : a survey of attainment and teaching practices in Scotland / [by] James Maxwell. — Windsor : NFER, 1977. — 148p ; 22cm.
Index.
ISBN 0-85633-120-1 Lp : £5.40
(B77-18705)

428'.4'071042 — Schools. Curriculum subjects: Reading. Teaching. *England, 1800-1850*

Chalmers, G S. Reading easy, 1800-50 : a study of the teaching of reading with a list of the books which were used and a selection of facsimile pages / [by] G.S. Chalmers. — London (c/o John Foreman, 15 Mortimore Terrace, N.W.5) : The Broadsheet King, 1976. — [9],185p : ill, ports ; 21cm.
Bibl. — Index. — Includes facsimile reprints.
ISBN 0-902617-16-8 Pbk : £2.50
(B77-02233)

428'.4'0712 — Secondary schools. Curriculum subjects: Reading. *For teaching*

Piercey, Dorothy. Reading activities in content areas : an ideabook for middle and secondary schools / [by] Dorothy Piercey. — Abridged ed. — Boston [Mass.] ; London [etc.] : Allyn and Bacon, [1977]. — xii,2-369p : ill, facsims ; 24cm.
This ed. published in the United States: 1976. — Full ed.: Boston, Mass. : Allyn and Bacon, 1976. — Bibl.: p.11. — Index.
ISBN 0-205-05510-9 Pbk : Unpriced
(B77-10338)

428'.4'072041 — Reading. Research. *Great Britain. Directories*

British register of reading research. — [Reading] ([29 Eastern Ave., Reading RG1 5RU]) : Centre for the Teaching of Reading, University of Reading School of Education.
No.1 / compiled by Elizabeth J. Goodacre. — [1976]. — [1],16 leaves ; 21x30cm.
ISBN 0-7049-0396-2 Sd : Unpriced
(B77-18706)

428'.4'076 — English language. Reading. *Exercises, worked examples. Primary school texts. Fill-in books*

Jackson, Stephen. Oxford junior workbook / by Stephen Jackson. — Oxford [etc.] : Oxford University Press.
1A / illustrated by Phyllida Legg. — 1977. — 31p : chiefly ill ; 31cm.
ISBN 0-19-838009-7 Sd : £0.25
(B77-08975)

2A / illustrated by Jane Lewington. — 1977. — 32p : chiefly ill ; 31cm.
ISBN 0-19-838010-0 Sd : £0.25
(B77-08976)

3A / illustrated by Phyllida Legg. — 1977. — 32p : chiefly ill ; 31cm.
ISBN 0-19-838011-9 Sd : £0.25
(B77-08977)

4A / illustrated by Jane Lewington, Phyllida Legg and Philip Martin. — 1977. — 32p : ill ; 31cm.
ISBN 0-19-838012-7 Sd : £0.25
(B77-08978)

428'.4'0942753 — School leavers. Reading skills. *Great Britain. Study regions: Merseyside (Metropolitan County). Liverpool. Reports, surveys*

Irvine, D G. The reading ability of school-leavers : a study of the extent of reading difficulties among school-leavers in Liverpool / by D.G. Irvine. — [Liverpool] ([1 Abercromby Sq., P.O. Box 147, Liverpool L69 3BX]) : University of Liverpool, Institute of Extension Studies, 1976. — [4],31p : 1 ill, map ; 21cm. — (University of Liverpool. Institute of Extension Studies. Adult Education Division. Monographs in educational research ; no.1)
ISBN 0-903762-01-3 Sd : £0.75
(B77-02234)

428'.4'09429 — School leavers. Reading skills. *Wales. Reports, surveys*
Confederation of British Industry. Standards of numeracy and literacy in Wales : a CBI [Wales] working party report. — Cardiff (Pearl Assurance House, Greyfriars Rd, Cardiff CF1 3JR) : Confederation of British Industry Wales, 1977. — 35p : ill, form ; 30cm.
Sd : £1.50
Also classified at 513
(B77-27009)

428'.4'2076 — English language. Reading. *Exercises, worked examples. For slow readers*
Piggin, Elsie. Chartway to reading / by Elsie Piggin. — Wokingham (336 Nine Mile Ride, Wokingham, Berks. RG11 3NJ) : Chartway Publications.
Student book 1. — 1977. — 28p,fold plate : ill ; 21cm.
Sd : £0.40
(B77-31846)

Student book 2. — 1977. — [1],27p,fold plate : ill ; 21cm.
Sd : £0.40
(B77-31847)

Student book 3. — 1977. — [1],31p,fold plate : ill ; 21cm.
Sd : £0.40
(B77-31848)

Teacher's manual. — 1977. — [6],42p ; 21cm.
With answers.
Sd : £0.40
(B77-31849)

428'.4'3 — Reading skills. Development
Chapman, L John. Developing fluent reading / prepared by L. John Chapman and Mary Hoffman ; for the [Open University, Reading Development] Course Team ; in collaboration with J.E. Merritt. — Milton Keynes : Open University Press, 1977. — 173p : ill, facsims, forms ; 30cm. — ([Educational studies], post-experience and second level undergraduate course : reading development ; block 1, units 1, 2, 3 and 4) (PE231 ; block 1, units 1, 2, 3 and 4)
Bibl. — Index.
ISBN 0-335-06690-9 Pbk : Unpriced
(B77-13619)

Shute, Helen A K. Underlying factors in reading success and failure / by Helen A.K. Shute. — Birmingham (Gosta Green, Birmingham B4 7ET) : Department of Educational Enquiry, University of Aston in Birmingham, 1976. — [4],91p : ill ; 21cm. — (Aston educational enquiry monographs ; no.3)
Bibl.: p.81-91.
Sd : £1.35
(B77-26266)

428.4'3 — Speed reading. *Manuals*
Buzan, Tony. Speed reading / [by] Tony Buzan. — [New ed., revised and updated]. — Newton Abbot [etc.] : David and Charles, 1977. — 159p : ill ; 23cm.
With answers. — Previous ed.: London : Sphere, 1971.
ISBN 0-7153-7366-8 : £1.95
(B77-12409)

Dudley, Geoffrey A. Rapid reading : the high speed way to increase your learning power / by Geoffrey A. Dudley. — Wellingborough : Thorsons, 1977. — 160p ; 22cm.
Not the same as B65-5273.
ISBN 0-7225-0393-8 : £3.25
(B77-30184)

428'.4'307 — Children. Reading skills. Development. Information sources
Dale, Sheila. Using the literature / prepared by Sheila M. Dale ; for the [Open University, Reading Development] Course Team. — Milton Keynes : Open University Press, 1977. — 43p ; 30cm. — ([Educational studies], a post-experience and second level undergraduate course : reading development) (PE 231 ; UL)
Bibl.
ISBN 0-335-06691-7 Pbk : Unpriced
(B77-14694)

428.6 — ENGLISH LANGUAGE. READING BOOKS

428'.6 — English language. Reading books
Barnes, Hanne. Goodbye Ann and Susie / [by] Viola Wahlstedt ; translated and adapted by Hanne Barnes ; illustrated by Ilon Wikland. — London [etc.] : Burke, 1977. — 64p : ill(some col) ; 21cm. — (A words your children use book, I love to read)
Translation and adaptation of: 'Hej da, Anna och Susanna'. Stockholm : Rabén och Sjögren, 1970.
ISBN 0-222-00633-1 : £1.00
ISBN 0-222-00634-x Pbk : £0.90
ISBN 0-222-00632-3 Library ed. : £1.50
(B77-23343)

Barnes, Hanne. John sails his boat / [by] Harry Iseborg ; translated and adapted by Hanne Barnes ; illustrated by Stig Södersten. — London [etc.] : Burke, 1977. — 64p : ill(some col) ; 21cm. — (A words your children use book, I love to read)
Translation and adaptation of: 'Jan seglar "Bidewind"'. Stockholm : Rabén och Sjögren, 1963?.
ISBN 0-222-00630-7 : £1.00
ISBN 0-222-00631-5 Pbk : £0.90
ISBN 0-222-00629-3 Library ed. : £1.50
(B77-23344)

428'.6 — English language. Reading books. *For parents of pre-school children*
Keen, Margaret. Talkabout bedtime / compiled by Margaret Keen ; illustrated by Harry Wingfield. — Loughborough : Ladybird Books, 1977. — [52]p : chiefly ill(chiefly col) ; 18cm. — (Ladybird talkabout books)
Text on lining papers.
ISBN 0-7214-0398-0 : £0.24
(B77-31850)

West, Margaret. Talkabout holidays / compiled by Margaret West ; illustrated by Robert Ayton and Martin Aitchison. — Loughborough : Ladybird Books, 1977. — [52]p : chiefly ill(chiefly col) ; 18cm. — (Ladybird talkabout books)
Text on lining papers.
ISBN 0-7214-0441-3 : £0.24
(B77-06633)

West, Margaret. Talkabout starting school / compiled by Margaret West and Ethel Wingfield ; illustrated by Harry Wingfield. — Loughborough : Ladybird Books, 1977. — [52] p : chiefly ill(chiefly col) ; 18cm. — (Ladybird talkabout books)
Text on lining papers.
ISBN 0-7214-0412-x : £0.24
(B77-06634)

428'.6 — English language. Reading books. *For pre-school children*
Dewar, Ferguson. Dusty the donkey / illustrated by Ferguson Dewar. — London : Macdonald Educational, 1977. — [25]p : of col ill ; 16cm. — (Macdonald picture tales)
ISBN 0-356-05121-8 Sd : £0.40
(B77-16337)

Goffe, Toni. Kipper the kitten / illustrated by Toni Goffe. — London : Macdonald Educational, 1977. — [25]p : of col ill ; 16cm. — (Macdonald picture tales)
ISBN 0-356-05118-8 Sd : £0.40
(B77-16338)

Hunia, Fran. Billy goats Gruff / by Fran Hunia ; illustrated by John Dyke. — Loughborough : Ladybird Books, 1977. — [48]p : col ill ; 18cm. — (Read it yourself : fiction : reading level 2 ; 2) ([Ladybird books] : series 777)
ISBN 0-7214-0469-3 : £0.25
(B77-27010)

Hunia, Fran. Gingerbread man / [by] Fran Hunia ; illustrated by Brian Price Thomas. — Loughborough : Ladybird Books, 1977. — [50] p : col ill ; 18cm. — (Read it yourself : fiction : reading level 4 ; 1) ([Ladybird books] : series 777)
ISBN 0-7214-0472-3 : £0.24
(B77-27011)

Hunia, Fran. Goldilocks and the three bears / by Fran Hunia ; illustrated by John Dyke. — Loughborough : Ladybird Books, 1977. — [50] p : col ill ; 18cm. — (Read it yourself : fiction : reading level 2 ; 1) ([Ladybird books] : series 777)
ISBN 0-7214-0468-5 : £0.24
(B77-27012)

Hunia, Fran. Jack and the beanstalk / by Fran Hunia ; illustrated by Brian Price Thomas. — Loughborough : Ladybird Books, 1977. — [50] p : col ill ; 18cm. — (Read it yourself : fiction : reading level 4 ; 2) ([Ladybird books] : series 777)
ISBN 0-7214-0473-1 : £0.24
(B77-27013)

Hunia, Fran. Red Riding Hood / by Fran Hunia ; illustrated by Kathie Layfield. — Loughborough : Ladybird Books, 1977. — [48] p : col ill ; 18cm. — (Read it yourself : fiction : reading level 3 ; 2) ([Ladybird books] : series 777)
ISBN 0-7214-0471-5 : £0.24
(B77-27014)

Hunia, Fran. Three little pigs / by Fran Hunia ; illustrated by Kathie Layfield. — Loughborough : Ladybird Books, 1977. — [48] p : col ill ; 18cm. — (Read it yourself : fiction : reading level 3 ; 1) ([Ladybird books] : series 777)
ISBN 0-7214-0470-7 : £0.24
(B77-27015)

Lewis, Wendy Diane. Bouncer the bear / illustrated by Wendy Lewis. — London : Macdonald Educational, 1977. — [25]p : of col ill ; 16cm. — (Macdonald picture tales)
ISBN 0-356-05120-x Sd : £0.40
(B77-16339)

Linsell, Tony. Scamper the squirrel / illustrated by Tony Linsell. — London : Macdonald Educational, 1977. — [25]p : of col ill ; 16cm. — (Macdonald picture tales)
ISBN 0-356-05119-6 Sd : £0.40
(B77-16340)

Scadding, Ann. Periwinkle Pig / written and drawn by Ann Scadding. — London : Longman, 1977. — [1],32p : ill(some col) ; 21cm. — (Creative story time ; 1) (Longman tadpole books)
ISBN 0-582-25001-3 Sd : £0.65
(B77-28569)

Scadding, Ann. The picnic / written and drawn by Ann Scadding. — London : Longman, 1977. — [1],32p : ill(some col) ; 21cm. — (Creative story time ; 2) (Longman tadpole books)
ISBN 0-582-25002-1 Sd : £0.65
(B77-28570)

Scarry, Richard. All day long / with illustrations by Richard Scarry. — London [etc.] : Hamlyn, 1977. — [24]p : col ill ; 21cm. — (A golden look-look book)
Originally published: as 'Richard Scarry's all day long'. New York : Golden Press, 1976.
ISBN 0-600-32959-3 Sd : £0.40
(B77-28571)

Scarry, Richard. All year long / with illustrations by Richard Scarry. — London [etc.] : Hamlyn, 1977. — [24]p : col ill ; 21cm. — (A golden look-look book)
Originally published: New York : Golden Press, 1976.
ISBN 0-600-39533-2 Sd : £0.40
(B77-28572)

Scarry, Richard. In my town / with illustrations by Richard Scarry. — London [etc.] : Hamlyn, 1977. — [24]p : col ill ; 21cm. — (A golden look-look book)
Originally published: New York : Golden Press, 1976.
ISBN 0-600-38766-6 Sd : £0.40
(B77-28573)

Steps forward, images and ideas arranged for children of 4 to 5 years. — St Ives, Cornwall : Pike, 1974. — 2-30p : ill(incl 2 col), 2 maps ; 26cm.
Cover title: Steps forward, educational activity for 4-5 year olds. — Originally published: 1972.
ISBN 0-85932-037-5 Sd : £0.35
(B77-18707)

428'.6 — English language. Reading books. *Middle school texts*
Discoveries / edited by Brian Thompson ; from material prepared by Bank Street College of Education ... — London : Longman.
Originally published: Boston, Mass. : Houghton Mifflin, 1972.
Born wild. — 1976. — 64p : ill(chiefly col) ; 24cm.
ISBN 0-582-18471-1 Sd : £0.90
(B77-08979)

Don't read this. — 1976. — 64p : ill(chiefly col), facsims, ports ; 24cm.
ISBN 0-582-18472-x Sd : £0.90
(B77-08980)

Discoveries / edited by Brian Thompson ; from material prepared by Bank Street College of Education. — London : Longman.
Originally published: Boston, Mass. : Houghton Mifflin, 1972.
Giant steps. — 1976. — 64p : ill(chiefly col), facsims, ports(1 col) ; 24cm.
ISBN 0-582-18473-8 Sd : £0.90
(B77-08981)

Discoveries / edited by Brian Thompson ; from material prepared by Bank Street College of Education ... — London : Longman.
Originally published: Boston, Mass. : Houghton Mifflin, 1972.
Paint the sky green. — 1976. — [1],64p : ill(chiefly col) ; 24cm.
ISBN 0-582-18474-6 Sd : £0.90
(B77-08982)

428′.6 — English language. Reading books. ***Primary school texts***

Berg, Leila. Grandad's clock / [by] Leila Berg ; pictures by Joan Beales. — London [etc.] : Macmillan, 1976. — [1],16p : col ill ; 22cm. — (Nippers : [red books])
ISBN 0-333-18097-6 Sd : Unpriced
(B77-06635)

Bird, Bettina. Sammy Long-name / [by] Bettina Bird and Ian Falk ; illustrated by Hilary Jackman. — Potts Point ; Oxford [etc.] : Pergamon, 1975. — [2],18p : col ill ; 22cm. — (Kidsbooks)
ISBN 0-08-019905-4 Sd : Unpriced
(B77-22527)

Blance, Ellen. Monster and the magic umbrella / [by] Ellen Blance and Ann Cook ; illustrated by Quentin Blake. — London : Longman, 1976. — [2],16p : chiefly col ill ; 21cm. — (Longman tadpole books)
Originally published: as part of 'Monster series'. 1973.
ISBN 0-582-18593-9 Sd : £0.35
(B77-05349)

Blance, Ellen. Monster at school / [by] Ellen Blance and Ann Cook ; illustrated by Quentin Blake. — London : Longman, 1976. — [2], 24p : chiefly col ill ; 21cm. — (Longman tadpole books)
Originally published: as part of 'Monster series'. 1973.
ISBN 0-582-18597-1 Sd : £0.35
(B77-05350)

Blance, Ellen. Monster cleans his house / [by] Ellen Blance and Ann Cook ; illustrated by Quentin Blake. — London : Longman, 1976. — [2],16p : chiefly col ill ; 21cm. — (Longman tadpole books)
Originally published: as part of 'Monster series'. 1973.
ISBN 0-582-18590-4 Sd : £0.35
(B77-05351)

Blance, Ellen. Monster goes to school / [by] Ellen Blance and Ann Cook ; illustrated by Quentin Blake. — London : Longman, 1976. — [2],24p : chiefly col ill ; 21cm. — (Longman tadpole books)
Originally published: as part of 'Monster series'. 1973.
ISBN 0-582-18596-3 Sd : £0.35
(B77-05352)

Blance, Ellen. Monster goes to the museum / [by] Ellen Blance and Ann Cook ; illustrated by Quentin Blake. — London : Longman, 1976. — [2],24p : chiefly col ill ; 21cm. — (Longman tadpole books)
Originally published: as part of 'Monster series'. 1973.
ISBN 0-582-18594-7 Sd : £0.35
(B77-05353)

Blance, Ellen. Monster goes to the zoo / [by] Ellen Blance and Ann Cook ; illustrated by Quentin Blake. — London : Longman, 1976. — [2],24p : chiefly col ill ; 21cm. — (Longman tadpole books)
Originally published: as part of 'Monster series'. 1973.
ISBN 0-582-18599-8 Sd : £0.35
(B77-05354)

Blance, Ellen. Monster has a party / [by] Ellen Blance and Ann Cook ; illustrated by Quentin Blake. — London : Longman, 1976. — [2], 24p : chiefly col ill ; 21cm. — (Longman tadpole books)
Originally published: as part of 'Monster series'. 1973.
ISBN 0-582-18598-x Sd : £0.35
(B77-05355)

Blance, Ellen. Monster looks for a friend / [by] Ellen Blance and Ann Cook ; illustrated by Quentin Blake. — London : Longman, 1976. — [2],16p : chiefly col ill ; 21cm. — (Longman tadpole books)
Originally published: as part of 'Monster series'. 1973.
ISBN 0-582-18591-2 Sd : £0.35
(B77-05356)

Blance, Ellen. Monster looks for a house / [by] Ellen Blance and Ann Cook ; illustrated by Quentin Blake. — London : Longman, 1976. — [2],16p : chiefly col ill ; 21cm. — (Longman tadpole books)
Originally published: as part of 'Monster series'. 1973.
ISBN 0-582-18589-0 Sd : £0.35
(B77-05357)

Blance, Ellen. Monster meets lady monster / [by] Ellen Blance and Ann Cook ; illustrated by Quentin Blake. — London : Longman, 1976. — [2],16p : chiefly col ill ; 21cm. — (Longman tadpole books)
Originally published: as part of 'Monster series'. 1973.
ISBN 0-582-18592-0 Sd : £0.35
(B77-05358)

Blance, Ellen. Monster on the bus / [by] Ellen Blance and Ann Cook ; illustrated by Quentin Blake. — London : Longman, 1976. — [2], 24p : chiefly col ill ; 21cm. — (Longman tadpole books)
Originally published: as part of 'Monster series'. 1973.
ISBN 0-582-18595-5 Sd : £0.35
(B77-05359)

Boyce, Ella Ruth. Cat and dog / [by] E.R. Boyce ; [illustrated by Toni Goffe]. — London [etc.] : Macmillan, 1977. — [14]p : col ill ; 16x21cm. — (The gay way introductory series)
ISBN 0-333-21113-8 Sd : £0.25
(B77-20196)

Boyce, Ella Ruth. The fat pig / [by] E.R. Boyce ; [illustrated by Toni Goffe]. — London [etc.] : Macmillan, 1977. — [14]p : col ill ; 16x21cm. — (The gay way introductory series)
ISBN 0-333-21117-0 Sd : £0.25
(B77-20197)

Boyce, Ella Ruth. The gay way series / by E.R. Boyce. — London [etc.] : Macmillan.
The green book. — [1st ed. reprinted] / illustrated by Gerald Rose. — 1977. — 48p : col ill ; 21cm.
Originally published: 1950.
ISBN 0-333-21586-9 Sd : £0.42
(B77-27810)

Boyce, Ella Ruth. The gay way series / by E.R. Boyce. — London [etc.] : Macmillan.
The red book. — [1st ed. reprinted] / illustrated by Toni Goffe. — 1977. — 32p : col ill ; 21cm.
Originally published: 1949.
ISBN 0-333-21585-0 Sd : £0.42
(B77-27811)

The blue book. — [Revised ed.] / illustrated by Maureen Williams. — 1977. — 64p : col ill ; 21cm.
Previous ed.: 1950.
ISBN 0-333-21587-7 Sd : £0.48
(B77-27812)

Boyce, Ella Ruth. The gay way series / by E.R. Boyce. — London [etc.] : Macmillan.
[Violet book, 2nd book] : Boo the kangaroo / illustrated by Keith Rawling. — 1977. — 32p : ill(some col) ; 21cm.
ISBN 0-333-21121-9 Sd : £0.42
(B77-29363)

[Violet book, 3rd book] : Beany and Brownie / illustrated by Terry Burton. — 1977. — 32p : ill(some col) ; 21cm.
ISBN 0-333-21122-7 Sd : £0.42
(B77-29364)

[Yellow book, 2nd book] : Miss Min and Mr Badman / illustrated by Derek Walstow. — 1977. — 32p : ill(some col) ; 21cm.
ISBN 0-333-21123-5 Sd : £0.42
(B77-28574)

[Yellow book, 3rd book] : Pancake Day / illustrated by Kate Lloyd-Jones. — 1977. — 32p : ill(some col) ; 21cm.
ISBN 0-333-21124-3 Sd : £0.42
(B77-28575)

Boyce, Ella Ruth. A house to live in / [by] E.R. Boyce ; [illustrated by Toni Goffe]. — London [etc.] : Macmillan, 1977. — [14]p : col ill ; 16x21cm. — (The gay way introductory series)
ISBN 0-333-21120-0 Sd : £0.25
(B77-20198)

Boyce, Ella Ruth. Pig, pots and pans / [by] E.R. Boyce ; [illustrated by Toni Goffe]. — London [etc.] : Macmillan, 1977. — [14]p : col ill ; 16x21cm. — (The gay way introductory series)
ISBN 0-333-21115-4 Sd : £0.25
(B77-20199)

Boyce, Ella Ruth. The red fox / [by] E.R. Boyce ; [illustrated by Toni Goffe]. — London [etc.] : Macmillan, 1977. — [14]p : col ill ; 16x21cm. — (The gay way introductory series)
ISBN 0-333-21119-7 Sd : £0.25
(B77-20200)

Boyce, Ella Ruth. The red lorry / [by] E.R. Boyce ; [illustrated by Toni Goffe]. — London [etc.] : Macmillan, 1977. — [14]p : col ill ; 16x21cm. — (The gay way introductory series)
ISBN 0-333-21118-9 Sd : £0.25
(B77-20201)

Boyce, Ella Ruth. The red pig / [by] E.R. Boyce ; [illustrated by Toni Goffe]. — London [etc.] : Macmillan, 1977. — [14]p : col ill ; 16x21cm. — (The gay way introductory series)
ISBN 0-333-21114-6 Sd : £0.25
(B77-20202)

Boyce, Ella Ruth. Who is it? / [by] E.R. Boyce ; [illustrated by Toni Goffe]. — London [etc.] : Macmillan, 1977. — [14]p : col ill ; 16x21cm. — (The gay way introductory series)
ISBN 0-333-21116-2 Sd : £0.25
(B77-20203)

Bradburne, Elizabeth Sutton. Through the rainbow / by E.S. Bradburne. — Huddersfield : Schofield and Sims.
Finding out about phonics. Book 1. — 1977. — 2-15p : ill ; 30cm.
Fill-in book.
ISBN 0-7217-0303-8 Sd : £0.15
(B77-31133)

Finding out about phonics. Book 2. — 1977. — 2-15p ; 30cm.
Fill-in book.
ISBN 0-7217-0304-6 Sd : £0.15
(B77-31134)

Finding out about phonics. Book 3. — 1977. — 2-15p ; 30cm.
Fill-in book.
ISBN 0-7217-0305-4 Sd : £0.15
(B77-31135)

Finding out about phonics. Book 4. — 1977. — 2-15p ; 30cm.
Fill-in book.
ISBN 0-7217-0306-2 Sd : £0.15
(B77-31136)

Finding out about phonics. Book 5. — 1977. — 2-15p : ill ; 30cm.
Fill-in book.
ISBN 0-7217-0307-0 Sd : £0.15
(B77-31137)

Finding out about phonics. Book 6. — 1977. — 2-15p ; 30cm.
Fill-in book.
ISBN 0-7217-0308-9 Sd : £0.15
(B77-31138)

Finding out about phonics. Book 7. — 1977. — 2-15p ; 30cm.
Fill-in book.
ISBN 0-7217-0309-7 Sd : £0.15
(B77-31139)

Finding out about phonics. Book 8. — 1977. — 2-15p : ill ; 30cm.
Fill-in book.
ISBN 0-7217-0310-0 Sd : £0.15
(B77-31140)

Finding out about phonics. Book 9. — 1977. — 2-15p ; 30cm.
Fill-in book.
ISBN 0-7217-0311-9 Sd : £0.15
(B77-31141)

Breinburg, Petronella. Tiger, Paleface and me / [by] Petronella Breinburg ; pictures by Richard Rose. — London [etc.] : Macmillan, 1976. — 32p : col ill ; 22cm. — (Nippers : [red books])
ISBN 0-333-17308-2 Sd : £0.30
(B77-06636)

Butterworth, Ben. Grandpa and the mammoth / by Ben Butterworth ; pictures by Lorraine Calaora. — Leeds : E.J. Arnold, 1976. — [2], 32p : chiefly col ill ; 21cm. — (Butterworth, Ben. That boy Trog)
Originally published: London : Methuen, 1973.
ISBN 0-560-03519-5 Sd : £0.60
(B77-16837)

Butterworth, Ben. Grandpa goes hunting / by Ben Butterworth ; pictures by Lorraine Calaora. — Leeds : E.J. Arnold, 1976. — [2],32p : chiefly col ill ; 21cm. — (Butterworth, Ben. That boy Trog)
Originally published: London : Methuen, 1973.
ISBN 0-560-03521-7 Sd : £0.60
(B77-16838)

Butterworth, Ben. Grandpa the birdman / by Ben Butterworth ; pictures by Lorraine Calaora. — Leeds : E.J. Arnold, 1976. — [2],32p : chiefly col ill ; 21cm. — (Butterworth, Ben. That boy Trog)
Originally published: London : Methuen, 1973.
ISBN 0-560-03520-9 Sd : £0.60
(B77-16839)

Butterworth, Ben. Grandpa's horse race / by Ben Butterworth ; pictures by Lorraine Calaora. — Leeds : E.J. Arnold, 1976. — [2],32p : chiefly col ill ; 21cm. — (Butterworth, Ben. That boy Trog)
Originally published: London : Methuen, 1973.
ISBN 0-560-03518-7 Sd : £0.60
(B77-16840)

Carr, James Lloyd. The green children of the woods / [by] J.L. Carr ; [illustrated by Bill Sanderson]. — London : Longman, 1976. — [1] ,32p : ill(some col) ; 21cm. — (Whizz bang series : whizz bang books)
ISBN 0-582-19326-5 Sd : £0.50
(B77-06025)

Causley, Charles. When Dad felt bad / [by] Charles Causley ; illustrated by Richard Rose. — [Basingstoke] : Macmillan, 1975[i.e.1977]. — [1],12p : chiefly col ill ; 15cm. — (Little nippers)
Originally published: 1975.
ISBN 0-333-18746-6 Sd : £0.20
(B77-22528)

Flowerdew, Phyllis. More interest / [by] Phyllis Flowerdew. — Edinburgh : Oliver and Boyd, 1977. — 128p : ill(chiefly col) ; 20cm. — (Wide range reading)
ISBN 0-05-002968-1 Pbk : £0.85
(B77-26267)

Flowerdew, Phyllis. More interest / [by] Phyllis Flowerdew. — Edinburgh : Oliver and Boyd. — (Wide range reading)
2. — 1977. — 128p : ill(chiefly col) ; 20cm.
ISBN 0-05-002970-3 Pbk : £0.85
(B77-26268)

Quiz book 1. — 1977. — 31p : ill ; 21cm.
ISBN 0-05-003063-9 Sd : £0.40
(B77-32594)

Quiz book 2. — 1977. — 31p : ill ; 21cm.
ISBN 0-05-003064-7 Sd : £0.40
(B77-32595)

Gilroy, Beryl. Arthur Small / [by] Beryl Gilroy ; pictures by Dorothy Clarke. — London [etc.] : Macmillan, 1976. — [1],16p : col ill ; 22cm. — (Nippers : [red books])
ISBN 0-333-18098-4 Sd : £0.30
(B77-06637)

Gilroy, Beryl. New shoes / [by] Beryl Gilroy ; pictures by Ferelith Eccles-Williams. — London [etc.] : Macmillan, 1976. — [1],16p : col ill ; 22cm. — (Nippers : [red books])
ISBN 0-333-18099-2 Sd : £0.30
(B77-06638)

Glynn, Dorothy Maud. Dominoes / [by] Dorothy M. Glynn. — Edinburgh : Oliver and Boyd.
Teacher's guide. — 3rd ed. — 1976. — Portfolio ; 21cm.
Six booklets. — Previous ed.: 1974.
ISBN 0-05-003041-8 : £3.25
(B77-05360)

Hardcastle, Michael. First contact / [by] Michael Hardcastle ; illustrated by Maureen and Gordon Gray. — Glasgow [etc.] : Collins.
In 4 vols.
1 : Go and find him. — 1977. — 32p : ill ; 21cm.
ISBN 0-00-325345-7 Sd : £1.50
ISBN 0-00-325349-x Set of 4 vols : Unpriced
(B77-31851)

2 : River of danger. — 1977. — 32p : ill ; 21cm.
ISBN 0-00-325346-5 Sd : £1.50
ISBN 0-00-325349-x Set of 4 vols : Unpriced
(B77-31852)

3 : The great bed race. — 1977. — 32p : ill ; 21cm.
ISBN 0-00-325347-3 Sd : £1.50
ISBN 0-00-325349-x Set of 4 vols : Unpriced
(B77-31853)

4 : Night raid. — 1977. — 32p : ill ; 21cm.
ISBN 0-00-325348-1 Sd : £1.50
ISBN 0-00-325349-x Set of 4 vols : Unpriced
(B77-31854)

Workbook / [by] Gordon Gibson ; illustrated by Dorothy Hamilton. — 1977. — [1],29p : ill, map ; 25cm.
Fill-in book. — With answers.
ISBN 0-00-325354-6 Sd : £1.80 for 6 copies
(B77-31855)

Harper, Anita. How we live / by Anita Harper ; with pictures by Christine Roche. — Harmondsworth : Kestrel Books, 1977. — [28] p : chiefly col ill ; 19x20cm.
Col. ill. on lining papers.
ISBN 0-7226-5348-4 : £1.50
(B77-33185)

Harper, Anita. How we work / by Anita Harper ; with pictures by Christine Roche. — Harmondsworth : Kestrel Books, 1977. — [28] p : chiefly col ill ; 19x20cm.
Col. ill. on lining papers.
ISBN 0-7226-5349-2 : £1.50
(B77-33186)

Huddy, Delia. Catch the plane! / by Delia Huddy ; illustrated by Val Biro. — London [etc.] : E. Benn, 1977. — 28p : col ill ; 21cm. — (Beginning to read books)
ISBN 0-510-08509-1 : £1.25
ISBN 0-510-08512-1 Pbk : £0.95
(B77-21080)

Kent, Jill. Fred, Mags and Creep / by Jill Kent and Ron van der Meer. — London [etc.] : Macmillan.
Fred, Mags and Creep decorate. — 1976. — [20]p : chiefly col ill ; 21x26cm.
ISBN 0-333-19541-8 Sd : £0.45
(B77-00727)

Fred, Mags and Creep go to the farm. — 1976. — [20]p : chiefly col ill ; 21x26cm.
ISBN 0-333-19534-5 Sd : £0.45
(B77-00728)

Fred, Mags and Creep go to the playground. — 1976. — [20]p : chiefly col ill ; 21x26cm.
ISBN 0-333-19533-7 Sd : £0.45
(B77-00729)

Fred, Mags and Creep go to the supermarket. — 1976. — [20]p : chiefly col ill ; 21x26cm.
ISBN 0-333-19538-8 Sd : £0.45
(B77-00730)

Fred, Mags and Creep have a bath. — 1976. — [20]p : chiefly col ill ; 21x26cm.
ISBN 0-333-19539-6 Sd : £0.45
(B77-00731)

Fred, Mags and Creep in the garden. — 1976. — [20]p : chiefly col ill ; 21x26cm.
ISBN 0-333-19536-1 Sd : £0.45
(B77-00732)

Fred, Mags and Creep meet a conjurer. — 1976. — [20]p : chiefly col ill ; 21x26cm.
ISBN 0-333-19542-6 Sd : £0.45
(B77-00733)

Fred, Mags and Creep see the doctor. — 1976. — [20]p : chiefly col ill ; 21x26cm.
ISBN 0-333-19535-3 Sd : £0.45
(B77-00734)

Language in action, level 2, core. — London [etc.] : Macmillan. — (The language project)
Fly high magpie! / [author Mary Cockett ; artist Jeroo Roy]. — 1976. — [1],24,[1]p : chiefly col ill ; 22cm.
ISBN 0-333-19944-8 Sd : £0.35
(B77-04739)

Seals from the sea / [author Richard Parker ; artist Jolyne Knox]. — 1976. — [1],24,[1]p : chiefly col ill ; 22cm.
ISBN 0-333-19945-6 Sd : £0.35
(B77-04740)

Language in action, level 2, special features. — London [etc.] : Macmillan. — (The language project)
Sam wishes / [author and artist Terry Reid]. — 1976. — [1],16,[1]p : chiefly col ill ; 22cm.
ISBN 0-333-19946-4 Sd : £0.30
(B77-04741)

Language in action, level 3, core. — London [etc.] : Macmillan. — (The language project)
An ear-ring for Anna Beer / [author Jim Carr ; artist Trevor Ridley]. — 1976. — [1],24,[1]p : chiefly col ill ; 22cm.
ISBN 0-333-19954-5 Sd : £0.35
(B77-04742)

Billy Brewer goes on tour / [author Janet McNeill ; artist Keith Rawling]. — 1976. — [1] ,24,[1]p : chiefly col ill ; 22cm.
ISBN 0-333-19955-3 Sd : £0.35
(B77-04743)

Clare at the fair / [authors Pip and Jane Baker ; artist John Glover]. — 1976. — [1],24, [1]p : chiefly col ill ; 22cm.
ISBN 0-333-19953-7 Sd : £0.35
(B77-04744)

Down-in-the-mouth clown / [author Geraldine Kaye ; artist Charles Front]. — 1976. — [1],24, [1]p : chiefly col ill ; 22cm.
ISBN 0-333-19951-0 Sd : £0.35
(B77-04745)

More than acorns / [author Helen Solomon ; artist Gareth Floyd]. — 1976. — [1],24,[1]p : chiefly col ill ; 22cm.
ISBN 0-333-19949-9 Sd : £0.35
(B77-04746)

Paul Shaw calling! / [author Helen Solomon ; artist Gareth Floyd]. — 1976. — [1],24,[1]p : chiefly col ill ; 22cm.
ISBN 0-333-19948-0 Sd : £0.35
(B77-04747)

Roy and the Pointon Express / [author Roy Brown ; artist Val Biro]. — 1976. — [1],24,[1] p : chiefly col ill ; 22cm.
ISBN 0-333-19952-9 Sd : £0.35
(B77-04748)

The hermit's purple shirts / [author Janet McNeill ; artist Keith Rawling]. — 1976. — [1] ,24,[1]p : chiefly col ill ; 22cm.
ISBN 0-333-19950-2 Sd : £0.35
(B77-04749)

The rook that took a cookery-book / [author and artist Terry Reid]. — 1976. — [1],24,[1]p : chiefly col ill ; 22cm.
ISBN 0-333-19947-2 Sd : £0.35
(B77-04750)

Language in action. — London [etc.] : Macmillan. — (The language project)
Resource book, a practical manual for teachers. (Supplement 2) / [by] Joyce M. Morris. — 1976. — 82p ; 21cm.
ISBN 0-333-19956-1 Pbk : £0.95
(B77-06639)

Le Jeune, Marvyn. Super Butch books / [by Marvyn and Peter Le Jeune]. — London : Cassell.
[Set 1 : Look books. Look at Butch, ball]. — 1977. — [10]p : of col ill ; 14x22cm.
ISBN 0-304-29795-x Sd : £0.15
(B77-07290)

[Set 1 : Look books. Look at Butch, hedgehog]. — 1977. — [10]p : of col ill ; 14x22cm.
ISBN 0-304-29796-8 Sd : £0.15
(B77-07291)

[Set 1 : Look books. Look at Butch, milk]. — 1977. — [10]p : of col ill ; 14x22cm.
ISBN 0-304-29798-4 Sd : £0.15
(B77-07292)

[Set 1 : Look books. Look at Butch, rabbit]. — 1977. — [10]p : of col ill ; 14x22cm.
ISBN 0-304-29797-6 Sd : £0.15
(B77-07293)

[Set 2 : At home. Butch and his ball]. — 1977. — [18]p : col ill ; 14x22cm.
ISBN 0-304-29800-x Sd : £0.35
(B77-07294)

[Set 2 : At home. Butch and his balloon]. — 1977. — [18]p : col ill ; 14x22cm.
ISBN 0-304-29802-6 Sd : £0.35
(B77-07295)

[Set 2 : At home. Butch and his bone]. — 1977. — [18]p : col ill ; 14x22cm.
ISBN 0-304-29801-8 Sd : £0.35
(B77-07296)

[Set 2 : At home. Butch on the farm]. — 1977. — [18]p : col ill ; 14x22cm.
ISBN 0-304-29799-2 Sd : £0.35
(B77-07297)

[Set 3 : At large. Butch by the river]. — 1977. — [18]p : col ill ; 14x22cm.
ISBN 0-304-29803-4 Sd : £0.35
(B77-07298)

[Set 3 : At large. Butch goes walking]. — 1977. — [18]p : col ill ; 14x22cm.
ISBN 0-304-29806-9 Sd : £0.35
(B77-07299)

[Set 3 : At large. Butch in his boat]. — 1977. — [18]p : col ill ; 14x22cm.
ISBN 0-304-29804-2 Sd : £0.35
(B77-07300)

[Set 3 : At large. Butch in the park]. — 1977. — [18]p : col ill ; 14x22cm.
ISBN 0-304-29805-0 Sd : £0.35
(B77-07301)

[Set 4 : Through the year. Butch by the sea]. — 1977. — [18]p : col ill ; 22cm.
ISBN 0-304-29808-5 Sd : £0.35
(B77-07302)

[Set 4 : Through the year. Butch in the garden]. — 1977. — [18]p : col ill ; 22cm.
ISBN 0-304-29807-7 Sd : £0.35
(B77-07303)

[Set 4 : Through the year. Butch in the snow]. — 1977. — [18]p : col ill ; 22cm.
ISBN 0-304-29810-7 Sd : £0.35
(B77-07304)

[Set 4 : Through the year. Butch in the wood]. — 1977. — [18]p : col ill ; 22cm.
ISBN 0-304-29809-3 Sd : £0.35
(B77-07305)

[Set 5 : Having fun. Butch and the paddling-pool]. — 1977. — [18]p : col ill ; 22cm.
ISBN 0-304-29813-1 Sd : £0.35
(B77-07306)

[Set 5 : Having fun. Butch and the see-saw]. — 1977. — [18]p : col ill ; 22cm.
ISBN 0-304-29814-x Sd : £0.35
(B77-07307)

[Set 5 : Having fun. Butch and the slide]. — 1977. — [18]p : col ill ; 22cm.
ISBN 0-304-29811-5 Sd : £0.35
(B77-07308)

[Set 5 : Having fun. Butch and the snake]. — 1977. — [18]p : col ill ; 22cm.
ISBN 0-304-29812-3 Sd : £0.35
(B77-07309)

McCullagh, Sheila Kathleen. The cross old man / [by] Sheila McCullagh ; [illustrated by Carmen Miranda]. — London : Longman, 1976. — [1],32p : ill(some col) ; 21cm. — (Whizz bang series : whizz bang books)
ISBN 0-582-19321-4 Sd : £0.50
(B77-06026)

McCullagh, Sheila Kathleen. Escape by night / [by] Sheila K. McCullagh ; illustrated by Pat Cook. — Leeds : E.J. Arnold, 1977. — [1], 32p : col ill ; 21cm. — (McCullagh, Sheila Kathleen. Tim and the hidden people) (Flightpath to reading : C series ; 6)
ISBN 0-560-01383-3 Sd : £0.45
(B77-32596)

McCullagh, Sheila Kathleen. How Kilora became a queen / [by] Sheila McCullagh ; [illustrated by Oscar Zarate]. — London : Longman, 1976. — [1],32p : ill(some col) ; 21cm. — (Whizz bang series : whizz bang books)
ISBN 0-582-19323-0 Sd : £0.50
(B77-06027)

McCullagh, Sheila Kathleen. Mandrake's castle / [by] Sheila K. McCullagh ; illustrated by Pat Cook. — Leeds : E.J. Arnold, 1977. — [1], 32p : col ill ; 21cm. — (McCullagh, Sheila Kathleen. Tim and the hidden people) (Flightpath to reading : C series ; 5)
ISBN 0-560-01382-5 Sd : £0.45
(B77-32597)

McCullagh, Sheila Kathleen. On the road to the North / [by] Sheila K. McCullagh ; illustrated by Pat Cook. — Leeds : E.J. Arnold, 1977. — [1],32p : col ill ; 21cm. — (McCullagh, Sheila Kathleen. Tim and the hidden people) (Flightpath to reading : C series ; 3)
ISBN 0-560-01380-9 Sd : £0.45
(B77-31856)

McCullagh, Sheila Kathleen. The pool by the whispering trees / [by] Sheila K. McCullagh ; illustrated by Pat Cook. — Leeds : E.J. Arnold, 1977. — [1],32p : col ill ; 21cm. — (McCullagh, Sheila Kathleen. Tim and the hidden people) (Flightpath to reading : C series ; 1)
ISBN 0-560-01378-7 Sd : £0.45
(B77-31857)

McCullagh, Sheila Kathleen. Princess Ugly-face / [by] Sheila McCullagh ; [illustrated by Mary Dinsdale]. — London : Longman, 1976. — [1], 32p : ill(some col) ; 21cm. — (Whizz bang series : whizz bang books)
ISBN 0-582-19322-2 Sd : £0.50
(B77-06028)

McCullagh, Sheila Kathleen. Riding into danger / [by] Sheila K. McCullagh ; illustrated by Pat Cook. — Leeds : E.J. Arnold, 1977. — [1],32p : col ill ; 21cm. — (McCullagh, Sheila Kathleen. Tim and the hidden people) (Flightpath to reading : C series ; 4)
ISBN 0-560-01381-7 Sd : £0.45
(B77-31858)

McCullagh, Sheila Kathleen. Three fires on the Dark Tower / [by] Sheila K. McCullagh ; illustrated by Pat Cook. — Leeds : E.J. Arnold, 1977. — [1],32p : col ill ; 21cm. — (McCullagh, Sheila Kathleen. Tim and the hidden people) (Flightpath to reading : C series ; 7)
ISBN 0-560-01384-1 Sd : £0.45
(B77-32598)

McCullagh, Sheila Kathleen. Tim in trouble / [by] Sheila K. McCullagh ; illustrated by Pat Cook. — Leeds : E.J. Arnold, 1977. — [1], 32p : col ill ; 21cm. — (McCullagh, Sheila Kathleen. Tim and the hidden people) (Flightpath to reading : C series ; 2)
ISBN 0-560-01379-5 Sd : £0.45
(B77-31859)

McCullagh, Sheila Kathleen. Tim rides on the ghost bus / [by] Sheila K. McCullagh ; illustrated by Pat Cook. — Leeds : E.J. Arnold, 1977. — [1],32p : col ill ; 21cm. — (McCullagh, Sheila Kathleen. Tim and the hidden people) (Flightpath to reading : C series ; 8)
ISBN 0-560-01385-x Sd : £0.45
(B77-31860)

McKay, Gwendda. Walking to school / [by] Gwendda McKay ; illustrated by Hilary Jackman. — Potts Point ; Oxford [etc.] : Pergamon, 1975. — [2],18p : col ill ; 22cm. — (Kidsbooks)
ISBN 0-08-019909-7 Sd : Unpriced
(B77-22529)

McNeill, Janet. The day Mum came home / [by] Janet McNeill ; pictures by Prudence Seward. — London [etc.] : Macmillan, 1976. — [1], 16p : col ill ; 22cm. — (Nippers : [red books])
ISBN 0-333-18220-0 Sd : £0.30
(B77-06640)

McNeill, Janet. Look who's here / [by] Janet McNeill ; pictures by Gerald Rose. — London [etc.] : Macmillan, 1976. — [1],16p : col ill ; 22cm. — (Nippers : [red books])
ISBN 0-333-18221-9 Sd : Unpriced
(B77-06641)

Muller, Gerda. Tiny and Tufty, the little koalas / illustrations by Gerda Muller ; text by Lucy Kincaid. — Cambridge : Brimax Books, 1976. — 4-45p : col ill ; 20cm. — ('Real life' readers)

These illustrations originally published: with French text. Paris : Gautier-Languereau, 1975.
ISBN 0-904494-31-4 : £0.75
(B77-10790)

Nixon, Joan Lowery. The mysterious prowler / by Joan Lowery Nixon ; illustrated by Berthe Amoss. — New York ; London : Harcourt Brace Jovanovich, 1976. — [61]p : ill(some col) ; 22cm. — (Let me read books)
ISBN 0-15-256355-5 : £3.05
IBN 0-15-256356-3 Pbk : £1.20
(B77-12990)

Oakley, Barry. A letter from hospital / [by] Barry Oakley ; illustrated by Hilary Jackman. — Potts Point ; Oxford [etc.] : Pergamon, 1975. — [2],18p : col ill ; 22cm. — (Kidsbooks)
ISBN 0-08-019906-2 Sd : Unpriced
(B77-22530)

O'Donnell, Mabel. Horizons / by Mabel O'Donnell and Philippa Murray. — Welwyn : Nisbet, 1976. — 128p : col ill ; 21cm.
ISBN 0-7202-1012-7 Pbk : £1.20
(B77-08983)

O'Donnell, Mabel. Horizons / by Mabel O'Donnell and Philippa Murray. — Welwyn : Nisbet.
Work cards. — 1977. — Portfolio : ill ; 24cm.
Sixteen cards ([16] sides).
ISBN 0-7202-1156-5 : £0.55
(B77-15815)

Reid, Jessie. Link-up / [by Jessie Reid, Joan Low]. — Edinburgh : Holmes McDougall.
Teacher's manual : The written word. — Revised and enlarged ed. — 1977. — 84p : ill ; 21cm.
Previous ed.: 1973. — Bibl. — Index.
ISBN 0-7157-1650-6 Pbk : Unpriced
(B77-32599)

Reid, Jessie. Link-up / [by Jessie Reid, Joan Low]. — Edinburgh : Holmes McDougall.
Build-up book 1c : My day / [illustrator Anne Rodger]. — 1973. — [2],16p : col ill ; 21cm.
ISBN 0-7157-1624-7 Sd : £0.45
(B77-32600)

Build-up book 2c : Karen at the zoo / [illustrator Anne Rodger]. — 1973. — [2],16p : col ill ; 21cm.
ISBN 0-7157-1625-5 Sd : £0.45
(B77-32601)

Build-up book 3c : Safe across the road / [illustrator Anne Rodger]. — 1973. — [2],16p : col ill ; 21cm.
ISBN 0-7157-1626-3 Sd : £0.45
(B77-32602)

Build-up book 4c : Nicky and the yellow car / [illustrator Anne Rodger]. — 1973. — [2],16p : col ill ; 21cm.
ISBN 0-7157-1627-1 Sd : £0.45
(B77-32603)

Schonell, *Sir* Fred Joyce. Wide range readers / by Fred J. Schonell. — Edinburgh : Oliver and Boyd.
Green book 6. Wide range quiz. — 2nd ed. — 1976. — [2],43,[2]p : ill ; 21cm.
Previous ed.: 1970.
ISBN 0-05-002418-3 Sd : £0.40
(B77-11183)

Schonell, *Sir* Fred Joyce. Wide range readers / [by] Fred J. Schonell, Phyllis Flowerdew. — Edinburgh : Oliver and Boyd.
Blue book 1. — 3rd ed. — 1976. — 128p : ill(chiefly col) ; 20cm.
Previous ed.: 1965.
ISBN 0-05-002911-8 Pbk : £0.75
(B77-01356)

Blue book 2. — 3rd ed. — 1976. — 128p : ill(chiefly col) ; 20cm.
Previous ed.: 1965.
ISBN 0-05-002912-6 Pbk : £0.75
(B77-01357)

Blue book 3. — 3rd ed. — 1976. — 128p : ill(chiefly col) ; 20cm.
Previous ed.: 1965.
ISBN 0-05-002913-4 Pbk : £0.75
(B77-01358)

Blue book 4. — 3rd ed. — 1976. — 144p : ill(chiefly col) ; 20cm.
Previous ed.: 1965.
ISBN 0-05-002914-2 Pbk : £0.85
(B77-01359)

Blue book 5. — 3rd ed. — 1976. — 143p : ill(chiefly col) ; 20cm.
Previous ed.: 1965.
ISBN 0-05-002915-0 Pbk : £0.85
(B77-01360)

Blue book 6. — 3rd ed. — 1976. — 176p : ill(chiefly col) ; 20cm.
Previous ed.: 1965.
ISBN 0-05-002916-9 Pbk : £0.95
(B77-01361)

Green book 1. — 3rd ed. — 1976. — 128p : ill(chiefly col) ; 20cm.
Previous ed.: 1965.
ISBN 0-05-002917-7 Pbk : £0.85
(B77-05361)

Green book 3. — 3rd ed. — 1976. — 128p : ill(chiefly col) ; 20cm.
Previous ed.: 1965.
ISBN 0-05-002919-3 Pbk : £0.75
(B77-06642)

Green book 4. — 3rd ed. — 1976. — 144p : ill(chiefly col) ; 20cm.
Previous ed.: 1965.
ISBN 0-05-002920-7 Pbk : £0.95
(B77-05362)

Green book 5 / [illustrated by Barry Wilkinson]. — 3rd ed. — 1976. — 144p : ill(some col), col map ; 20cm.
Previous ed.: 1965.
ISBN 0-05-002921-5 Pbk : £0.85
(B77-06643)

Green book 6. — 3rd ed. — 1976. — 176p : ill(chiefly col) ; 20cm.
Previous ed.: 1965.
ISBN 0-05-002922-3 Pbk : £0.95
(B77-05363)

Scott, Rachel. The school trip / [by] Rachel Scott ; pictures by Nicole Goodwin. — London [etc.] : Macmillan, 1976. — [1],16p : col ill ; 22cm. — (Nippers : [red books])
ISBN 0-333-18102-6 Sd : £0.30
(B77-06644)

Simon, Romain. Kimba the lion / illustrations by Romain Simon ; text by Rosalind Sutton. — Cambridge : Brimax Books, 1976. — 5-45p : ill(chiefly col) ; 20cm. — ('Real life' readers)
These illustrations originally published: with French text. Paris : Gautier-Languereau, 1971.
ISBN 0-904494-30-6 : £0.75
(B77-10791)

Simon, Romain. Rusty and Mitzi / illustrations by Romain Simon ; text by Rosalind Sutton. — Cambridge : Brimax Books, 1976. — 5-45p : ill(chiefly col) ; 20cm. — ('Real life' readers)
These illustrations originally published: with French text. Paris : Gautier-Languereau, 1971.
ISBN 0-904494-28-4 : £0.75
(B77-10792)

Solomon, Helen. Dad's pie / [by] Helen Solomon ; pictures by Trevor Stubley. — London [etc.] : Macmillan, 1976. — [1],16p : col ill ; 22cm. — (Nippers : [red books])
ISBN 0-333-18101-8 Sd : £0.30
(B77-06645)

Solomon, Helen. Gran's glasses / [by] Helen Solomon ; pictures by Richard Rose. — London [etc.] : Macmillan, 1976. — [1],16p : col ill ; 22cm. — (Nippers : [red books])
ISBN 0-333-18529-3 Sd : £0.30
(B77-06646)

Sparks, stage five (pink) / [text by R.M. Fisher et al.]. — [Glasgow] : [Blackie].
5 : The Easter egg / [pictures by Douglas Phillips]. — [1976]. — 16p : col ill ; 23cm.
ISBN 0-216-90258-4 Sd : £0.48
(B77-01362)

6 : The birthday present / [pictures by Anna Dzierzek]. — [1976]. — 16p : col ill ; 23cm.
ISBN 0-216-90259-2 Sd : £0.48
(B77-01363)

7 : The holiday bus / [pictures by Lynette Hemmant]. — [1976]. — 16p : col ill ; 23cm.
ISBN 0-216-90260-6 Sd : £0.48
(B77-01364)

8 : The Punch and Judy show / [pictures by Gareth Floyd]. — [1976]. — 16p : col ill ; 23cm.
ISBN 0-216-90261-4 Sd : £0.48
(B77-01365)

Tansley, Albert Edward. Racing to read / by A.E. Tansley & R.H. Nicholls ; illustrated by William H. Robertshaw. — Leeds : E.J. Arnold.
Book 6 : Fire! fire!. — 2nd revised ed. — 1977. — 24p : col ill ; 18x20cm.
Previous ed.: 1970.
ISBN 0-560-13622-6 Sd : Unpriced
(B77-29365)

Taylor, James Peter. Read and discover / by James P. Taylor. — Oxford [etc.] : Pergamon.
Book 2. — 1975. — x,119p : ill, maps ; 22cm. — (Pergamon Oxford English series)
Originally published: 1968.
Pbk : £0.85
ISBN 0-08-013426-2
(B77-02935)

Waugh, Daphne. First time stories / [by] Daphne Waugh, Glennis Allison. — Sunbury-on-Thames [etc.] : Nelson, 1976. — 6v. : chiefly col ill ; 22cm.
ISBN 0-17-412301-9 Sd : £1.30
(B77-09659)

West, Michael. Five famous fairy tales / simplified by Michael West. — 3rd ed. / revised by D.K. Swan ; illustrated by Ron McTrusty. — London : Longman, 1977. — [4], 59p : ill ; 19cm. — ([New method supplementary readers] : stage 1)
'500 word vocabulary'. — Previous ed. of these adaptations: published as 'Seven famous fairy tales'. London : Longmans, Green, 1957.
ISBN 0-582-53521-2 Sd : £0.35
(B77-16841)

West, Michael. Rip Van Winkle ; and, The legend of Sleepy Hollow / [by] Washington Irving ; simplified by Michael West ; illustrated by Richard Rose. — 2nd ed. — London : Longman, 1977. — [4],44p : ill ; 19cm. — ([New method supplementary readers] : stage 2)
'850 word vocabulary'. — Previous ed.: 1967.
ISBN 0-582-53530-1 Sd : £0.35
(B77-08984)

West, Michael. Tales from the Arabian Nights / retold within the vocabulary of New Method Reader 2 by Michael West ; illustrated by Victor Ambrus. — London : Longman, 1973. — viii,88p : ill ; 19cm. — (New method supplementary readers : stage 2)
These adaptations originally published: London : Longmans, 1963.
ISBN 0-582-53437-2 Sd : £0.35
(B77-31142)

428'.6 — English language. Reading books. *Secondary school texts*

Douglas, N. Sixteen fathoms down, and other stories / by N. Douglas ; illustrations for the stories John Jamieson, illustrations for 'Themes for enquiry' Clive Jackson. — Glasgow : Gibson, 1977. — 208p : ill, maps, ports ; 21cm. — (World wide adventures ; book 5)
ISBN 0-7169-5513-x Pbk : £1.00
(B77-14695)

Groves, Paul. 13 weird tales : a collection of original strange stories with suggestions for varied work in English / [by] Paul Groves and Nigel Grimshaw. — London : Edward Arnold, 1977. — [4],108p ; 22cm.
ISBN 0-7131-0174-1 Pbk : £1.10 : CIP rev.
(B77-25564)

Heaton, John Brian. Stories from Shakespeare / simplified by Brian Heaton and Michael West ; illustrated by Whitear. — New ed. — London : Longman, 1977. — [4],76p : ill ; 19cm. — ([New method supplementary readers] : stage 3)
Previous ed.: 1966.
ISBN 0-582-53529-8 Sd : £0.35
(B77-17438)

Johnston, Frances. Lord Jim / [by] Joseph Conrad ; simplified and brought within the vocabulary of New Method Supplementary Readers, Stage 5, by Frances Johnston ; illustrated by Ivan Lapper. — London : Longman, 1976. — [4],76p : ill ; 19cm. — (New method supplementary readers : stage 5)
ISBN 0-582-53420-8 Sd : £0.35
(B77-01366)

Johnston, Frances. Three adventures of Sherlock Holmes / [by] Sir Arthur Conan Doyle ; simplified and brought within the 1500 word vocabulary of New Method Supplementary Readers Stage 4 by Frances Johnston. — London : Longman, 1976. — [4],59p : ill ; 19cm. — (New method supplementary readers : stage 4)
Contents: The speckled band - The five orange pips - The crown of diamonds.
ISBN 0-582-53470-4 Sd : £0.35
(B77-02235)

Maison, Margaret Mary. The last of the Mohicans / [by] J. Fenimore Cooper ; simplified and brought within the 1500 word vocabulary of New Method Supplementary Reader[s] Stage 4 by Margaret Maison and Michael West ; illustrated by Drake Brookshaw. — London : Longman, 1977. — [6] ,82p : ill, map ; 19cm. — (New method supplementary readers : stage 4)
This adaptation originally published: London : Longmans, 1963.
ISBN 0-582-53492-5 Sd : £0.40
(B77-27016)

Maison, Margaret Mary. Oliver Twist / [by] Charles Dickens ; simplified and brought within the vocabulary of New Method Supplementary Readers Stage 4 by Margaret Maison and Michael West ; illustrated by Whitear. — [1st ed. reprinted] with corrections. — London : Longman, 1977. — [4],107p : ill ; 19cm. — (New method supplementary readers : stage 4)
First ed. of this adaptation originally published: London : Longmans, 1966.
ISBN 0-582-53496-8 Sd : £0.40
(B77-27017)

Swan, Douglas Kelso. The magic slippers, and other stories / [by] B. Lumsden Milne ; illustrated by Rosemary Brown. — 2nd ed. / simplified and brought within the 850 word vocabulary of New Method Supplementary Readers Stage 2 by D.K. Swan. — London : Longman, 1976. — [3],59p : ill ; 19cm. — ([New method supplementary readers] : stage 2)
Previous ed.: 1951.
ISBN 0-582-53531-x Sd : £0.35
(B77-06029)

West, Michael. Gulliver's travels, and other stories / simplified and brought within the 850 word vocabulary of the New Method Supplementary Readers Stage 2 by Michael West ; illustrated by Victor Ambrus. — Revised [ed.]. — London : Longman, 1976. — [3],91p : ill ; 19cm. — ([New method supplementary readers] : stage 2)
This ed. of these adaptations originally published: London : Longmans, 1963. — Contents: Gulliver's travels: a journey to Lilliput / by Jonathan Swift - The King of the Golden River / by John Ruskin - Chaunticlere and Pertelote / by Geoffrey Chaucer.
ISBN 0-582-53425-9 Sd : £0.40
(B77-30185)

West, Michael. King Arthur and the Knights of the Round Table / simplified and brought within the 500 word vocabulary of New Method Supplementary Readers Stage 1, by Michael West. — 2nd ed. / ... revised by D.K. Swan. — London : Longman, 1976. — [4],60p : ill ; 19cm. — (New method supplementary readers : stage 1)
Previous ed. of this adaptation : London : Longmans, Green, 1955.
ISBN 0-582-53415-1 Sd : £0.35
(B77-02236)

West, Michael. Little women / [by] Louisa M. Alcott ; simplified and brought within the 1500 world vocabulary of New Method Supplementary Reader[s] Stage 4 by Michael West and E.P. Hart ; illustrated by Cyril Deakins. — 2nd ed. — London : Longman, 1976. — [4],131p : ill ; 19cm. — (New method supplementary readers : stage 4)
'... based on ... "Little women" and "Good wives"' - p.[4]. — This ed. of this adaptation originally published: London : Longmans, 1965.
ISBN 0-582-53489-5 Pbk : £0.40
(B77-27018)

West, Michael. The mystery of the island / by Jules Verne ; simplified and brought within the vocabulary of New Method Supplementary Readers, Stage 2, by Michael West ; illustrated by Christopher Evans. — New ed. — London : Longman, 1977. — 40p : ill ; 19cm. — (New method supplementary readers : stage 2)
This ed. originally published: 1967.
ISBN 0-582-53429-1 Sd : £0.40
(B77-33188)

West, Michael. The prince and the pauper / [by] Mark Twain ; simplified and brought within the 850 word vocabulary of the New Method Supplementary Readers Stage 2, by Michael West. — 2nd ed. / ... revised by D.K. Swan. — London : Longman, 1976. — [4],44p : ill ; 19cm. — (New method supplementary readers : stage 2)
Previous ed. of this adaptation: London : Longmans, Green, 1957.
ISBN 0-582-53422-4 Sd : £0.35
(B77-02237)

West, Michael. Robin Hood / simplified and brought within the 500 word vocabulary of New Method Supplementary Readers Stage 1 by Michael West ; illustrated by Mark Peppé. — [1st ed.] reprinted with amendments. — London : Longman, 1976. — [4],76p : ill ; 19cm. — (New method supplementary readers : stage 1)
First ed. of this adaptation originally published: 1972.
Sd : £0.35
ISBN 0-582-53412-7
(B77-02238)

West, Michael. Treasure Island / [by] Robert Louis Stevenson ; simplified and brought within the 1,800 word vocabulary of the New Method Supplementary Readers Stage 5 by Michael West ; illustrated by Adrian Bailey. — 2nd ed. — London : Longman, 1977. — 160p : ill, map ; 19cm. — (New method supplementary readers : stage 5)
This ed. of this adaptation originally published: London : Longmans, Green, 1952.
ISBN 0-582-53504-2 Pbk : £0.40
(B77-27019)

West, Michael. The waterbabies / [by] Charles Kingsley ; simplified by Michael West. — 2nd ed. / revised by D.K. Swan ; illustrated by Rosemary Honeybourne. — London : Longman, 1977. — [4],36p : ill ; 19cm. — (New method supplementary readers : stage 1)
Previous ed.: London : Longmans, Green, 1957.
ISBN 0-582-53532-8 Pbk : £0.35
(B77-31143)

428'.6 — English language. Reading books. Special subjects: Animals. *Primary school texts*

Harper, Clive. PM animal books / by Clive Harper and Beverley Randell ; illustrated by Ernest Papps. — Sunbury-on-Thames : Nelson, 1977. — 8v. : col ill ; 21cm.
Originally published: Wellington, N.Z. : Price Milburn, 1973.
ISBN 0-17-412321-3 Sd : £2.25
(B77-17439)

428'.6 — English language. Reading books. Special subjects: Colour

Althea. Colours and cars / by Althea ; illustrated by the author. — London : Souvenir Press, 1977. — [24]p : ill(chiefly col) ; 19cm. — (Althea's brightstart books)
ISBN 0-285-62262-5 : £1.00
(B77-14197)

428'.6 — English language. Reading books. Special subjects: Costume, to 1973

Oram, Sandie. Clothes and costume / [written and planned by Sandie Oram ; illustrated by Sarah [i.e. Sara] Silcock]. — London : Macdonald Educational, 1974. — 28p : chiefly col ill ; 21cm. — (Starters long ago books)
Text on lining papers. — Index.
ISBN 0-356-04637-0 : £0.45
(B77-18708)

428'.6 — English language. Reading books. Special subjects: Hospitals. *Primary school texts*

Althea. I go to hospital / by Althea ; illustrated by Ljiljana Rylands. — London : Souvenir Press, 1977. — [24]p : col ill ; 19cm. — (Althea's brightstart books)
ISBN 0-285-62261-7 : £1.00
(B77-13620)

428'.6 — English language. Reading books. Special subjects: Malaysian legends

West, Michael. Tales from the East / simplified by Michael West, K.J. Fielding and B.M. Parker ; illustrated by Joanna Troughton. — 2nd ed. — London : Longman, 1977. — [4], 44p : ill ; 19cm. — (New method supplementary readers : stage 1)
Previous ed.: 1958.
ISBN 0-582-53533-6 Sd : Unpriced
(B77-29366)

428'.6 — English language. Reading books. Special subjects: Monsters

Groves, Paul. Monsters of myth and legend / [by] Paul Groves, Nigel Grimshaw. — London : Edward Arnold, 1977. — 96p : ill ; 22cm.
ISBN 0-7131-0096-6 Sd : £1.20
(B77-18709)

428'.6 — English language. Reading books. Special subjects: Tales. *Primary school texts*

Abbott, Gerry. What next? / [by] Gerry Abbott. — London : Longman.
Teacher's handbook. — 1976. — [3],78p : 2 ill ; 22cm.
ISBN 0-582-55316-4 Sd : £0.90
(B77-01367)

428'.6 — English language. Reading books: Strip cartoons. *Primary school texts*

Alexander, L.G. Operation Janus / [by] L.G. Alexander ; illustrated by Gil Potter. — London : Longman, 1976. — 16p : col ill ; 20cm. — (Longman structural readers : fiction : stage 1)
ISBN 0-582-53713-4 Sd : £0.25
(B77-00735)

428'.6'2 — English language. Reading books. *For illiterate adults*

Spence, Peter. Next move / by Peter Spence and Jim McManus ; drawings by Dave Cockcroft. — London : British Broadcasting Corporation, 1977. — 78p : ill, ports ; 21cm.
'... accompanies the "Next Move" programmes, ... broadcast on BBC Radio' - half title page verso.
ISBN 0-563-16138-8 Sd : £0.90
(B77-12991)

428'.6'2 — English language. Reading books. *For slow learning adolescents*

Baker, Geoffrey. Running hot and cold / [by] Geoffrey Baker. — Sunbury-on-Thames [etc.] : Nelson, 1976. — 93p ; 18cm. — (Getaway)
ISBN 0-17-432079-5 Pbk : £0.40
(B77-02564)

Berman, Kathleen. A night out / written and illustrated by Kathleen Berman. — Pinner : Grail Publications, 1976. — 44p : ill, port ; 18cm. — (Waxwell books ; no.4)
ISBN 0-901829-35-8 Sd : £0.55
(B77-08342)

Berman, Kathleen. The week-end / written and illustrated by Kathleen Berman. — Pinner : Grail Publications, 1976. — 44p : ill, port ; 18cm. — (Waxwell books ; no.5)
ISBN 0-901829-36-6 Sd : £0.55
(B77-08343)

Carew, Jan. Save the last dance for me, and other stories / [by] Jan Carew. — London : Longman, 1976. — 64p : ill ; 20cm. — (Knockouts)
Cassette also available.
ISBN 0-582-21173-5 Pbk : £0.40
(B77-04751)

Carew, Jan. Stranger than tomorrow : three stories of the future / [by] Jan Carew. — London : Longman, 1976. — 80p : ill ; 20cm. — (Knockouts)
ISBN 0-582-22223-0 Pbk : £0.45
(B77-05364)

Foster, John Louis. Recordbreakers / [by] John L. Foster. — London : Edward Arnold, 1977. — 48p : ill, map, ports ; 19cm. — (Headlines ; 4)
ISBN 0-7131-0072-9 Sd : £0.75
(B77-18710)

Hardcastle, Michael. Crash car / [by] Michael Hardcastle ; illustrated by Gareth Floyd. — London [etc.] : E. Benn, 1977. — 46p : ill ; 19cm. — (Inner ring hipsters : green circle hipsters)
ISBN 0-510-07721-8 Pbk : £0.75
(B77-30187)

Hardcastle, Michael. Fire on the sea / [by] Michael Hardcastle ; illustrated by Gareth Floyd. — London [etc.] : E. Benn, 1977. — 45p : ill ; 19cm. — (Inner ring hipsters : green circle hipsters)
ISBN 0-510-07723-4 Pbk : £0.75
(B77-30188)

Hardcastle, Michael. Holiday house / [by] Michael Hardcastle ; illustrated by Gareth Floyd. — London [etc.] : E. Benn, 1977. — 46p : ill ; 19cm. — (Inner ring hipsters : green circle hipsters)
ISBN 0-510-07724-2 Pbk : £0.75
(B77-30189)

Hardcastle, Michael. Strong arm / [by] Michael Hardcastle ; illustrated by Gareth Floyd. — London [etc.] : E. Benn, 1977. — 46p : ill ; 19cm. — (Inner ring hipsters : green circle hipsters)
ISBN 0-510-07722-6 Pbk : £0.75
(B77-30190)

Hunt, Roderick. Remarkable animals / [by] Rod Hunt. — London : Edward Arnold, 1977. — 48p : ill ; 19cm. — (Headlines ; 3)
ISBN 0-7131-0071-0 Sd : £0.75
(B77-18711)

Hunt, Roderick. Survivors from the sea / [by] Rod Hunt. — London : Edward Arnold, 1977. — 48p : ill, ports ; 19cm. — (Headlines ; 2)
ISBN 0-7131-0070-2 Sd : £0.75
(B77-18712)

King, Clive. Accident / [by] Clive King ; illustrated by Jacqueline Atkinson. — London [etc.] : E. Benn, 1976. — 46p : ill ; 19cm. — (Inner ring hipsters : green circle hipsters)
ISBN 0-510-07746-3 Pbk : £0.65
(B77-00472)

King, Clive. The secret / [by] Clive King ; illustrated by Jacqueline Atkinson. — London [etc.] : E. Benn, 1976. — 45p : ill ; 19cm. — (Inner ring hipsters : green circle hipsters)
ISBN 0-510-07747-1 Pbk : £0.65
(B77-00473)

Layton, George. A northern childhood : the balaclava story, and other stories / [by] George Layton ; [photographs by Lance Browne]. — London : Longman, 1976. — 94p : ill ; 20cm. — (Knockouts)
Sound tape also available. — This collection originally published: 1975. — 'The balaclava story' originally published: London : British Broadcasting Corporation, 1971.
ISBN 0-582-23345-3 Pbk : £0.45
(B77-10339)

Loxton, Margaret. The job / [by] Margaret Loxton. — London : Longman, 1977. — 80p ; 20cm. — (Knockouts)
ISBN 0-582-22159-5 Pbk : £0.50
(B77-31144)

McLeish, Kenneth. Odysseus returns / Homer's 'Odyssey' retold by Kenneth McLeish. — London : Longman, 1977. — 160p : ill ; 20cm. — (Knockouts)
ISBN 0-582-22219-2 Pbk : £0.70
(B77-31145)

McLeish, Kenneth. The robe of blood, and other stories / [by] Kenneth McLeish. — London : Longman, 1976. — 77p : ill ; 19cm. — (Knockouts)
ISBN 0-582-22220-6 Pbk : £0.45
(B77-04752)

Pepper, Dennis. Company K / [by] William March ; abridged [and simplified] by Dennis Pepper. — Sunbury-on-Thames [etc.] : Nelson, 1976. — [2],110p ; 19cm. — (Getaway)
Adaptation of: 'Company K'. New York : H. Smith and R. Haas ; London : Gollancz, 1933.
ISBN 0-17-432083-3 Pbk : £0.40
(B77-02608)

Robinson, Rony. Six summers / [by] Rony Robinson. — Sunbury-on-Thames [etc.] : Nelson, 1976. — 95p ; 18cm. — (Getaway)
ISBN 0-17-432082-5 Pbk : £0.40
(B77-03506)

Sains, Charles. Trapped / [by] Charles Sains. — London [etc.] : Macmillan, 1977. — [1],32,[1] p : ill(some col) ; 14x22cm. — (Sains, Charles. Trackers)
ISBN 0-333-21517-6 Sd : £0.45
(B77-23345)

Samuda, Mike. Daredevils / [by] Mike Samuda. — London : Edward Arnold, 1977. — 48p : ill, ports ; 19cm. — (Headlines ; 1)
ISBN 0-7131-0069-9 Sd : £0.75
(B77-18713)

Tate, Joan. Luke's garden / [by] Joan Tate. — London : Longman, 1976. — 101p : ill ; 19cm. — (Knockouts)
'... published in a short version by Heinemann Educational [1968]' - title page verso.
ISBN 0-582-22217-6 Pbk : £0.50
(B77-04753)

Tate, Joan. The runners / [by] Joan Tate ; [photographs by David Thompson]. — London : Longman, 1977. — 95p : ill ; 20cm. — (Knockouts)
Originally published: with illustrations by Douglas Phillips. Newton Abbot : David and Charles, 1974.
ISBN 0-582-23132-9 Pbk : £0.50
(B77-31146)

Tate, Joan. See you, and other stories / [by] Joan Tate. — London : Longman, 1977. — 80p : ill ; 20cm. — (Knockouts)
ISBN 0-582-22218-4 Pbk : £0.50
(B77-31147)

Thorpe, John, *b.1928.* A scramble for Steve / [by] John Thorpe ; illustrations by Brian J. Wilkins. — Amersham : Hulton, 1977. — [4], 100p : ill ; 19cm. — (Speedswinger ; 1)
ISBN 0-7175-0781-5 Pbk : £0.95
(B77-32605)

Thorpe, John, *b.1928.* Steve takes a chance / [by] John Thorpe ; illustrations by Brian J. Wilkins. — Amersham : Hulton, 1977. — [4],107p : ill ; 19cm. — (Speedswinger ; 2)
ISBN 0-7175-0784-x Pbk : £0.95
(B77-32606)

Through time and space / edited by Dennis Pepper. — Sunbury-on-Thames [etc.] : Nelson, 1976. — 112p ; 19cm. — (Getaway)
ISBN 0-17-432081-7 Pbk : £0.40
(B77-02630)

428'.6'2 — English language. Reading books. *For slow learning children. Middle school texts*

Breinburg, Petronella. One day, another day / [by] Petronella Breinburg ; [illustrator Mary Dinsdale]. — Basingstoke [etc.] : Macmillan, 1977. — 64p : ill ; 18cm. — (Rockets)
ISBN 0-333-21544-3 Pbk : Unpriced : CIP rev.
(B77-04754)

Chambers, Aidan. Snake river / [by] Aidan Chambers ; [illustrator Peter Morgan]. — Basingstoke [etc.] : Macmillan, 1977. — 77p : ill ; 18cm. — (Rockets)
Originally published: Stockholm : Almqvist and Wiksell, 1975.
ISBN 0-333-21524-9 Pbk : Unpriced : CIP rev.
(B77-05365)

Chilton, Irma. A spray of leaves / [by] Irma Chilton ; [illustrator Mark Peppé]. — Basingstoke [etc.] : Macmillan, 1977. — 64p : ill ; 18cm. — (Rockets)
ISBN 0-333-21545-1 Pbk : Unpriced : CIP rev.
(B77-04755)

Jenkins, Ray. The world of Col Kelly / [by] Ray Jenkins ; [illustrator Rowan Barnes-Murphy]. — Basingstoke [etc.] : Macmillan, 1977. — 72p : ill ; 18cm. — (Rockets)
ISBN 0-333-21549-4 Pbk : Unpriced : CIP rev.
(B77-04756)

Kirkham, John. Beasts of plenty / [by] John Kirkham. — Basingstoke [etc.] : Macmillan, 1977. — 80p : ill ; 18cm. — (Rockets)
ISBN 0-333-21547-8 Pbk : Unpriced : CIP rev.
(B77-05366)

Morpurgo, Michael. Friend or foe / [by] Michael Morpurgo ; [illustrator Trevor Stubley]. — Basingstoke [etc.] : Macmillan, 1977. — 88p : ill ; 18cm. — (Rockets)
ISBN 0-333-21543-5 Pbk : Unpriced : CIP rev.
(B77-05367)

Rankin, Jodie. Eleventh hour / [by] Jodie Rankin ; illustrations by Hilary Jackman. — Melbourne [etc.] : Cheshire Publishing ; Aylesbury : Distributed by Ginn, 1975. — [4], 89p : ill ; 19cm. — (Trend books)
ISBN 0-7015-1685-2 Pbk : Unpriced
(B77-31148)

Rowe, Albert. Pollen girl / [by] Albert Rowe. — Basingstoke [etc.] : Macmillan, 1977. — 64p : ill ; 18cm. — (Rockets)
ISBN 0-333-21548-6 Pbk : Unpriced : CIP rev.
(B77-05368)

Smith, Leonard. Pop's shed / [by] Leonard Smith ; [illustrator Trevor Stubley]. — Basingstoke [etc.] : Macmillan, 1977. — 64p : ill ; 18cm. — (Rockets)
ISBN 0-333-21525-7 Pbk : Unpriced : CIP rev.
(B77-05369)

428'.6'2 — English language. Reading books. *For slow reading adults*

Carey, Steve. Murder at night / [by] John Creasey ; re-told by Steve Carey. — Bath : Chivers, 1976. — [7],81p ; 20cm. — (Aerial books : intermediate level)
ISBN 0-85997-214-3 : £2.40
ISBN 0-85997-215-1 Pbk : £0.80
(B77-07310)

Cox, Anne-Marie. Fair exchange / [by] Anne-Marie Cox. — Bath : Chivers, 1976. — [6],90p ; 19cm. — (Aerial books : preliminary level)
ISBN 0-85997-210-0 : £2.40
ISBN 0-85997-211-9 Pbk : £0.80
(B77-06647)

Leete, Ann. Second chance for love / [by] Ann Leete. — Bath : Chivers, 1976. — [4],122p ; 20cm. — (Aerial books : preliminary level)
ISBN 0-85997-212-7 : £2.40
ISBN 0-85997-213-5 Pbk : £0.80
(B77-06648)

Leete-Hodge, Lornie. Dangerous guest / [by] Lornie Leete-Hodge. — Bath : Chivers, 1976. — [6],119p ; 19cm. — (Aerial books : preliminary level)
ISBN 0-85997-216-x : £2.40
ISBN 0-85997-217-8 Pbk : £0.80
(B77-06649)

428'.6'2 — English language. Reading books. *For slow-learning students*

Alderson, Jim. The witch princess / [by] Jim Alderson. — London : Hutchinson, 1977. — 39p ; 21cm. — (Spirals series)
ISBN 0-09-129951-9 Sd : £0.45
(B77-30186)

Jackson, Anita. Pentag / [by] Anita Jackson. — London : Hutchinson, 1977. — 54p ; 21cm. — (Spirals series)
ISBN 0-09-131011-3 Sd : £0.45
(B77-30191)

428'.6'2 — English language. Reading books. Special subjects: Athletics. Track & field events. *For illiterate adults*

Honig, Donald. Running harder / by Donald Honig ; photographs by Bill Powers ; consultants Harold N. Friedman, Corinne Bloomer. — New York ; London : F. Watts, 1976. — 47p : col ill ; 19x25cm. — (A target book)
ISBN 0-85166-605-1 : £1.95
(B77-01368)

428'.6'2 — English language. Reading books. Special subjects: Authority. *For slow readers. Secondary school texts. Teaching kits*

Authority. — London : Evans Bros.
Teacher's box / editors Margaret Dobson, John Vockings ; contributors Barbara Boyers ... [et al.]. — 1977. — 1v. : ill(some col), facsims(some col), map, ports ; 27x34cm. — (Checkers)
Two booklets, 2 folders, 10 cards, 17 sheets (3 fold.) in box. — Bibl.
ISBN 0-237-29062-6 : Unpriced
(B77-18714)

428'.6'2 — English language. Reading books. Special subjects: Ski racing. Slalom. *For illiterate adults*

Luray, Martin. Ski racer / written and photographed by Martin Luray ; consultants Harold N. Friedman, Corinne Bloomer. — New York ; London : F. Watts, 1976. — 47p : col ill ; 19x25cm. — (A target book)
ISBN 0-85166-603-5 : £1.95
(B77-01369)

428'.6'2 — English language. Reading books. Special subjects: Swimming. Competitions. *For illiterate adults*

Honig, Donald. Going the distance / by Donald Honig ; photographs by Bill Powers ; consultants Harold N. Friedman, Corinne Bloomer. — New York ; London : F. Watts, 1976. — 47p : col ill ; 19x25cm. — (A target book)
ISBN 0-85166-604-3 : £1.95
(B77-01370)

428'.6'2 — English language. Reading books. Special subjects: Wrestling. *For illiterate adults*

Powers, Bill. Break him down! / written and photographed by Bill Powers. — New York ; London : F. Watts, 1977. — 48p : col ill ; 19x25cm. — (A target book)
ISBN 0-85166-646-9 : £2.50
(B77-30192)

428'.6'4 — English language. Reading books. *For Caribbean students. Middle school texts*

Archer, Fred, *b.1920.* The happiest Christmas / [by] Fred Archer. — London [etc.] : Macmillan, 1977. — [2],22p : col ill ; 22cm. — (Yellow bird stories)
ISBN 0-333-21456-0 Sd : £0.50
(B77-30193)

Bailey, Nadina. The golden mongoose / [by] Nadina Bailey. — London [etc.] : Macmillan, 1977. — [3],44p : col ill ; 22cm. — (Yellow bird stories)
ISBN 0-333-21454-4 Sd : £0.60
(B77-24157)

Mills, Therese. The canefield fire ; and, The Picoplat boy / [by] Therese Mills. — London [etc.] : Macmillan, 1977. — [2],33p : ill ; 22cm. — (Yellow bird readers)
ISBN 0-333-22366-7 Sd : Unpriced
(B77-30194)

428'.6'4 — English language. Reading books. *For non-English speaking students*

Alexander, L.G. Clint Magee / [by] L.G. Alexander ; illustrated by John Holder. — London : Longman, 1976. — [4],59p : ill, map ; 20cm. — (Longman structural readers : fiction : stage 3)
Originally published: as 'Look, listen and learn'. Link reader 4. 1972.
ISBN 0-582-53682-0 Sd : £0.35
(B77-07885)

Amis, Kingsley. Interesting things / [by] Kingsley Amis ; [edited by Michael Swan]. — Cambridge [etc.] : Cambridge University Press, 1977. — [1],16,[2]p ; 21cm. — (Cambridge English language learning : [level] 5)
ISBN 0-521-21503-x Sd : £0.35
(B77-18082)

Berman, Aaron. Forestville tales / [by] Aaron Berman. — New York ; London : Collier Macmillan, 1977. — 2-71p : ill ; 22cm. — (Collier Macmillan English readers) (Collier Macmillan English program)
ISBN 0-02-971280-7 Pbk : £1.60
(B77-27813)

Chisholm, Richard. Scottish adventure / [by] Richard Chisholm ; illustrated by Peter Edwards. — London [etc.] : Heinemann Educational, 1977. — [7],67p : ill, maps ; 18cm. — (Heinemann guided readers : intermediate level ; 16)
ISBN 0-435-27044-3 Pbk : £0.28
(B77-16341)

Christian, Carol. The legend of Sleepy Hollow / [by] Washington Irving ; adapted by Carol Christian. — London [etc.] : Macmillan, 1976. — [4],62p : ill ; 21cm. — (Ranger fiction : range 6)
ISBN 0-333-21285-1 Sd : £0.45
(B77-07311)

Dahl, Roald. The sound machine / [by] Roald Dahl ; [edited by Alan Duff]. — Cambridge [etc.] : Cambridge University Press, 1977. — [2],20,[1]p ; 21cm. — (Cambridge English language learning : level 5)
Originally published: in 'Some one like you'. New York : Knopf, 1953 ; London : Secker and Warburg, 1954.
ISBN 0-521-21722-9 Sd : £0.50
(B77-27815)

Dent, John. Mark and Jennifer / [by] John Dent. — London : Longman, 1977. — [3],71p : ill, map ; 20cm. — (Longman structural readers : fiction : stage 3)
ISBN 0-582-53845-9 Sd : £0.40
(B77-15251)

Gibbs, Frances. Old Yeller / [by] Fred Gipson ; retold by Frances Gibbs ; illustrated by Douglas Bisset. — Sunbury-on-Thames [etc.] : Nelson, 1977. — vi,90p : ill ; 19cm. — (Streamline books)
This adaptation originally published: 1966.
ISBN 0-17-555208-8 Pbk : £0.45
(B77-16842)

Gilbert, Michael. The amateur / [by] Michael Gilbert ; [edited by Ronald Barnes]. — Cambridge [etc.] : Cambridge University Press, 1977. — [1],14,[2]p ; 21cm. — (Cambridge English language learning : [level] 5)
ISBN 0-521-21762-8 Sd : £0.50
(B77-30195)

Gregory, T S. The invisible man / [by] H.G. Wells ; simplified and abridged by T.S. Gregory. — 3rd ed. — London : Longman, 1977. — 78p ; 18cm. — (Longman simplified English series)
Previous ed. of this adaptation: London : Longmans, Green, 1952.
ISBN 0-582-53697-9 Pbk : £0.40
(B77-11764)

Harmer, Jeremy. I spy / [by] Jeremy Harmer. — London [etc.] : Macmillan, 1976. — [4],80p : ill ; 21cm. — (Ranger fiction : range 6)
ISBN 0-333-21268-1 Sd : Unpriced
(B77-09660)

Harris, William. Dangerous game / [by] William Harris ; edited by L.G. Alexander. — London : Longman, 1977. — [4],60p : ill ; 20cm. — (Longman structural readers : fiction : stage 3)
ISBN 0-582-53681-2 Sd : £0.35
(B77-10340)

Hill, David, *b.1940.* A town like Alice / [by] Nevil Shute ; retold by D.R. Hill ; illustrated by Kay Mary Wilson. — London : Heinemann Educational, 1977. — [6],89p : ill, map ; 18cm. — (Heinemann guided readers : intermediate level ; 18)
ISBN 0-435-27048-6 Pbk : £0.45
(B77-21818)

Jacobson, Dan. Stop thief ; and, A way of life / [by] Dan Jacobson ; [edited by Alan Duff]. — Cambridge [etc.] : Cambridge University Press, 1977. — [2],24,[2]p ; 21cm. — (Cambridge English language learning : [level] 5)
ISBN 0-521-21162-x Sd : £0.50
(B77-27816)

Johnston, Olivia. The L-shaped room / [by] Lynne Reid Banks ; abridged and simplified by Olivia Johnston ; photographs by Lance Brown. — London : Longman, 1977. — [4],108p : ill ; 20cm. — (Longman structural readers : fiction : stage 6)
ISBN 0-582-53835-1 Sd : £0.45
(B77-29367)

Keane, Peter. The controllers / [by] Peter Keane. — London [etc.] : Macmillan, 1977. — [4], 80p : ill ; 21cm. — (Ranger fiction : range 5)
ISBN 0-333-22009-9 Sd : £0.50
(B77-29368)

Laude, Anthony. Sherlock Holmes short stories / [by] Sir Arthur Conan Doyle ; chosen and simplified by Anthony Laude. — London : Longman, 1977. — [4],120p ; 18cm. — (Longman simplified English series)
ISBN 0-582-52911-5 Pbk : £0.40
(B77-07886)

Lessing, Doris. A mild attack of locusts / [by] Doris Lessing ; [edited by Alan Duff]. — Cambridge [etc.] : Cambridge University Press, 1977. — [1],14,[1]p ; 21cm. — (Cambridge English language learning : [level] 5)
ISBN 0-521-21164-6 Sd : £0.35
(B77-18083)

McCallum, George Patrick. The man in black, and other stories / by George P. McCallum ; illustrated by Peter Joyce. — Sunbury-on-Thames [etc.] : Nelson, 1976. — [3] ,44p : ill ; 19cm. — (Nelson elementary English readers)
ISBN 0-17-555125-1 Sd : £0.30
(B77-01371)

McFarlan, Donald Maitland. Dr Jekyll and Mr Hyde ; and, The Suicide Club / [by] Robert Louis Stevenson ; retold by Donald M. McFarlan ; illustrated by Dick Hart. — Sunbury-on-Thames [etc.] : Nelson, 1977. — [6] ,90p : ill ; 19cm. — (Streamline books)
These adaptations originally published: 1966.
ISBN 0-17-555207-x Pbk : £0.45
(B77-16843)

McFarlan, Donald Maitland. A journey to the centre of the earth / [by] Jules Verne ; retold by Donald M. McFarlan ; illustrated by Ivan Lapper. — Sunbury-on-Thames [etc.] : Nelson, 1977. — [7],86p : ill ; 19cm. — (Streamline books)
This adaptation originally published: 1969.
ISBN 0-17-555205-3 Pbk : £0.45
(B77-16844)

McFarlan, Donald Maitland. Twenty thousand leagues under the sea / [by] Jules Verne ; retold by Donald M. McFarlan ; illustrated by Douglas Bisset. — Sunbury-on-Thames [etc.] : Nelson, 1977. — viii,88p : ill ; 19cm. — (Streamline books)
This adaptation originally published: 1966.
ISBN 0-17-555206-1 Pbk : £0.45
(B77-16845)

McLean, Alan Campbell. Garry's first season / [by] Alan C. McLean ; [illustrated by Jerry Malone]. — London : Longman, 1977. — [1], 16,[1]p : col ill ; 20cm. — (Longman structural readers : fiction : stage 1)
ISBN 0-582-53688-x Sd : £0.25
(B77-16846)

Mansfield, Katherine. The little governess / [by] Katherine Mansfield ; [edited by Ann Brumfit]. — Cambridge [etc.] : Cambridge University Press, 1976. — [1],22,[2]p ; 21cm. — (Cambridge English language learning : [level] 5)
ISBN 0-521-21165-4 Sd : £0.35(non-net)
(B77-03507)

Naipaul, Vidiadhar Surajprasad. The perfect tenants ; and, The mourners / [by] V.S. Naipaul ; [edited by Francis Curtis]. — Cambridge [etc.] : Cambridge University Press, 1977. — [1],30,[1]p ; 21cm. — (Cambridge English language learning : [level] 5)
ISBN 0-521-21363-0 Sd : £0.45
(B77-18084)

Nasr, Raja Tewfik. Patchwork : stories around the world for students of English / [by] Raja T. Nasr. — London : Longman, 1977. — iv,140p : ill ; 19cm.
ISBN 0-582-76129-8 Pbk : £0.65
(B77-30196)

O'Connor, Frank. Public opinion / [by] Frank O'Connor ; [edited by Alan Duff]. — Cambridge [etc.] : Cambridge University Press, 1976. — [1],14,[2]p ; 21cm. — (Cambridge English language learning : [level] 5)
ISBN 0-521-20991-9 Sd : £0.30(non-net)
(B77-03508)

Password. — Harmondsworth : Penguin.
1 / [editor Valerie Mendes]. — 1977. — [2],32, [1]p : ill(some col), col port ; 23cm.
ISBN 0-14-081297-0 Sd : £0.60
(B77-16342)

2 / [editor Valerie Mendes]. — 1977. — [2],32, [1]p : ill(some col), col port ; 23cm.
ISBN 0-14-081298-9 Sd : £0.60
(B77-16343)

3 / [editor Valerie Mendes]. — 1977. — [2],32, [1]p : ill(some col), col port ; 23cm.
ISBN 0-14-081299-7 Sd : £0.60
(B77-16344)

Ronaldson, Alan. The hound of the Baskervilles / by Sir Arthur Conan Doyle ; simplified by Alan Ronaldson. — London : Longman, 1976. — [5],72p ; 18cm. — (Longman simplified English series)
ISBN 0-582-52910-7 Pbk : £0.40
(B77-01372)

Samphire, and other modern stories / edited by Michael Swan. — Cambridge [etc.] : Cambridge University Press, 1977. — viii,127p ; 18cm. — (Cambridge English language learning)
ISBN 0-521-21537-4 Pbk : Unpriced
(B77-24158)

Scott-Buccleuch, Robert Lascelles. The promise / [by] R.L. Scott-Buccleuch ; illustrated by Gareth Floyd. — London : Heinemann Educational, 1977. — [5],55p : ill, map ; 18cm. — (Heinemann guided readers : elementary level ; E10)
ISBN 0-435-27043-5 Pbk : £0.38
(B77-33189)

Stevens, Sydney Frank. The missing scientist / by S.F. Stevens. — Hong Kong ; Oxford [etc.] : Oxford University Press, 1976 [i.e. 1977]. — [6] ,69p : col ill ; 22cm. — (Oxford progressive English readers : grade 2) (Oxford in Asia)
Published in Hong Kong: 1976.
ISBN 0-19-581015-5 Pbk : £0.75
(B77-10793)

Stevenson, Robert M. North American short stories / [adapted by] Robert M. Stevenson, Jane L. Stevenson. — Sunbury-on-Thames [etc.] : Nelson.
Book 1. — 1976. — x,85p ; 22cm.
ISBN 0-17-555090-5 Pbk : £0.95
(B77-04115)

Book 2. — 1976. — viii,88p ; 22cm.
ISBN 0-17-555096-4 Pbk : £0.95
(B77-04116)

Tarner, Margaret. Rebecca / [by] Daphne Du Maurier ; retold by Margaret Tarner ; illustrated by Kay Mary Wilson. — London : Heinemann Educational, 1977. — [6],136p : ill ; 18cm. — (Heinemann guided readers : upper level ; 9)
ISBN 0-435-27041-9 Pbk : £0.50
(B77-11184)

Taylor, Elizabeth, *b.1912.* The wrong order / [by] Elizabeth Taylor ; [edited by Ronald Barnes]. — Cambridge [etc.] : Cambridge University Press, 1977. — [1],22,[2]p ; 21cm. — (Cambridge English language learning : [level] 5)
ISBN 0-521-21761-x Sd : £0.50
(B77-30197)

Thomas, Maurice Walton. Tales of mystery and imagination / [by] E.A. Poe ; retold by M.W. Thomas ; illustrated by Robert Broomfield. — Sunbury-on-Thames [etc.] : Nelson, 1977. — 96p : ill ; 19cm. — (Streamline books)
These adaptations originally published: 1966.
ISBN 0-17-555203-7 Pbk : £0.45
(B77-16847)

Thomas, Maurice Walton. Tom Sawyer / [by] Mark Twain ; retold by M.W. Thomas ; illustrated by Denis K. Turner. — Sunbury-on-Thames [etc.] : Nelson, 1977. — vi, 90p : ill ; 19cm. — (Streamline books)
This adaptation originally published: 1966.
ISBN 0-17-555204-5 Pbk : £0.45
(B77-16848)

Wain, John. A visit at tea-time ; and, Manhood / [by] John Wain ; [edited by Michael Donley]. — Cambridge [etc.] : Cambridge University Press, 1977. — [1],32,[1]p ; 21cm. — (Cambridge English language learning : [level] 5)
These stories originally published: in 'Death of the hind legs, and other stories'. London : Macmillan, 1966.
ISBN 0-521-21359-2 Sd : £0.45
(B77-18085)

Wells, Herbert George. The Country of the Blind / [by] H.G. Wells ; [edited by Simon Freeman]. — Cambridge [etc.] : Cambridge University Press, 1977. — [4],24,[2]p : map ; 21cm. — (Cambridge English language learning : [level] 5)
ISBN 0-521-21721-0 Sd : £0.50
(B77-27817)

Whitney, Norman Frederick. The sky's the limit / [by] Norman F. Whitney ; illustrated by Leslie Branton. — London : Heinemann Educational, 1977. — [1],30p : ill ; 18cm. — (Heinemann guided readers : beginner level ; 8)
ISBN 0-435-27042-7 Sd : £0.27
(B77-15252)

Whitney, Norman Frederick. The stranger / [by] Norman Whitney ; illustrated by Peter Edwards. — London : Heinemann Educational, 1977. — [5],55p : ill ; 18cm. — (Heinemann guided readers : elementary level ; 9)
ISBN 0-435-27046-x Pbk : £0.35
(B77-24877)

Words! / [edited by] Alan Maley, Alan Duff. — Cambridge [etc.] : Cambridge University Press, 1976. — [5],186p : ill ; 18cm. — (Cambridge English language learning : [level] 5)
ISBN 0-521-21357-6 Pbk : £0.95
(B77-03509)

428'.6'4 — English language. Reading books. *For non-English speaking students. Primary school texts*

Christian, Carol. The girl who laughed / [by] Carol Christian ; illustrated [by] David Harris. — London [etc.] : Evans Bros, 1976. — [4], 21p : ill(some col) ; 19cm. — (Evans English readers : stage 3)
ISBN 0-237-49964-9 Sd : £0.22
(B77-02936)

Curtis, Arnold. The white duck / [by] Arnold Curtis ; illustrated [by] Sally Michel. — London [etc.] : Evans Bros, 1977. — [3],14,[1] p : col ill ; 19cm. — (Evans English readers : stage 1)
ISBN 0-237-49993-2 Sd : £0.28
(B77-27814)

Jolly, Dorothy Edna. The kind firefly / [by] Dorothy Jolly ; illustrated [by] Linda Broad. — London [etc.] : Evans Bros, 1977. — [2],15p : col ill ; 19cm. — (Evans English readers : stage 2)
ISBN 0-237-50051-5 Sd : £0.28
(B77-25565)

Stuart, Melvine. The village shoe maker [i.e. shoemaker] and other stories / [by] Melvine Stuart ; illustrated [by] Mary Shillabeer. — London [etc.] : Evans Bros, 1976. — [4],22p : ill(some col) ; 19cm. — (Evans English readers : stage 4)
ISBN 0-237-49996-7 Sd : £0.22
(B77-02937)

428'.6'4 — English language. Reading books. *For non-English speaking students. Secondary school texts*

Chia, Benjamin. Madam White Snake / retold by Benjamin Chia. — Hong Kong ; Oxford [etc.] : Oxford University Press, 1976. — [7],58p : col ill ; 22cm. — (Oxford progressive English readers : grade 1) (Oxford in Asia)
ISBN 0-19-581016-3 Pbk : £0.75
(B77-02239)

Davies, Suzan. Islands in the sky / by Arthur C. Clarke ; [retold by Suzan Davies]. — Hong Kong [etc.] ; Oxford : Oxford University Press, 1976. — [6],66p : col ill ; 22cm. — (Oxford progressive English readers : grade 1) (Oxford in Asia)
ISBN 0-19-581033-3 Pbk : Unpriced
(B77-19323)

Hill, David, *b.1940.* Twenty thousand leagues under the sea / by Jules Verne ; [retold by David Hill]. — Hong Kong [etc.] ; Oxford : Oxford University Press, 1976. — [8],119p : col ill ; 22cm. — (Oxford progressive English readers : grade 3) (Oxford in Asia)
ISBN 0-19-581001-5 Pbk : £0.75
(B77-02938)

Hill, Leslie Alexander. Niagara Falls, and other stories / by Roderick Hunt ; rewritten by L.A. Hill for elementary students ; illustrated by Roger Walker. — Sunbury-on-Thames [etc.] : Nelson, 1976. — [5],40p : ill ; 19cm. — (Nelson elementary English readers)
ISBN 0-17-555126-x Sd : £0.30
(B77-00173)

Hill, Leslie Alexander. UFOs, and other stories / by Roderick Hunt ; rewritten by L.A. Hill for elementary students ; illustrated by Peter North. — Sunbury-on-Thames [etc.] : Nelson, 1976. — [5],36p : ill ; 19cm. — (Nelson elementary English readers)
ISBN 0-17-555174-x Sd : £0.30
(B77-00174)

Letley, Emma. The house of sixty fathers / by Meindert Dejong ; [retold by Emma Letley]. — Hong Kong [etc.] ; Oxford : Oxford University Press, 1976. — [6],64p : ill(chiefly col) ; 22cm. — (Oxford progressive English readers : grade 1) (Oxford in Asia)
ISBN 0-19-581034-1 Pbk : Unpriced
(B77-19324)

Letley, Emma. Kidnapped / by R.L. Stevenson ; [retold by Emma Letley]. — Hong Kong [etc.] ; Oxford : Oxford University Press, 1976. — [11],107p : col ill, col map ; 22cm. — (Oxford progressive English readers : grade 3) (Oxford in Asia)
ISBN 0-19-581000-7 Pbk : £0.75
(B77-02939)

McCallum, George Patrick. The sightseers, and other stories / by George P. McCallum ; illustrated by Peter North. — Sunbury-on-Thames [etc.] : Nelson, 1976. — [3],44p : ill ; 19cm. — (Nelson intermediate English readers)
'For intermediate students'.
ISBN 0-17-555173-1 Sd : £0.30
(B77-00175)

Mattock, Kate. Journey to the centre of the earth / by Jules Verne ; [retold by K. Mattock ; simplified according to the language grading scheme especially compiled by D.H. Howe]. — Hong Kong ; Oxford [etc.] : Oxford University Press, 1976. — [6],124p : col ill ; 22cm. — (Oxford progressive English readers : grade 3) (Oxford in Asia)
ISBN 0-19-581014-7 Pbk : £0.75
(B77-02240)

Oxley, J. King Solomon's mines / by H. Rider Haggard ; [retold by J. Oxley]. — Hong Kong [etc.] ; Oxford : Oxford University Press, 1976. — [6],131p : col ill, map ; 22cm. — (Oxford progressive English readers : grade 3) (Oxford in Asia)
ISBN 0-19-581013-9 Pbk : £0.75
(B77-02940)

428'.6'4 — English language. Reading books: Humour in English. *For non-English speaking students*

Wilson, Ken. Laugh! : an introduction to English humour / [by] Ken Wilson. — London [etc.] : Evans Bros, 1977. — [4],44p : ill, ports ; 19cm. — (Evans graded reading : grade 3)
ISBN 0-237-50028-0 Sd : £0.60
(B77-15816)

428'.6'4 — English language. Reading books: Poetry. *For non-English speaking students*

Asimov, Isaac. Liar! / [by] Isaac Asimov ; [edited by Rosemary Border]. — Cambridge [etc.] : Cambridge University Press, 1977. — [2],22,[2]p ; 21cm. — (Cambridge English language learning : level 5)
Originally published: in 'I robot'. New York : Gnome Press, 1950 ; London : Grayson and Grayson, 1952.
ISBN 0-521-21718-0 Sd : £0.50
(B77-27818)

Asimov, Isaac. Little lost robot / [by] Isaac Asimov ; [edited by Rosemary Border]. — Cambridge [etc.] : Cambridge University Press, 1977. — [2],30,[2]p ; 21cm. — (Cambridge English language learning : level 5)
Originally published: in 'I robot'. New York : Gnome Press, 1950 ; London : Grayson and Grayson, 1952.
ISBN 0-521-21717-2 Sd : £0.60
(B77-27819)

Dahl, Roald. Mrs Bixby and the Colonel's coat / [by] Roald Dahl ; [edited by Rosemary Border]. — Cambridge [etc.] : Cambridge University Press, 1977. — [2],16,[2]p ; 21cm. — (Cambridge English language learning : level 5)

Originally published: in 'Kiss kiss'. New York : Knopf ; London : Joseph, 1960.
ISBN 0-521-21720-2 Sd : £0.45
(B77-27820)

Dahl, Roald. Parson's pleasure / [by] Roald Dahl ; [edited by Rosemary Border]. — Cambridge [etc.] : Cambridge University Press, 1977. — [2],24,[2]p ; 21cm. — (Cambridge English language learning : level 5)
Originally published: in 'Kiss kiss'. New York : Knopf ; London : Joseph, 1960.
ISBN 0-521-21719-9 Sd : £0.50
(B77-27821)

Evans graded verse / [compiled by] Michael Knight, Ronald Ridout. — London : Evans Bros.
1-3. Teacher's guide. — 1977. — [3],23p : music ; 21cm.
ISBN 0-237-50142-2 Sd : Unpriced
(B77-28576)

428'.6'4 — English language. Reading books. Special subjects: Australia. *For non-English speaking students*

Stories from down under / chosen, simplified and abridged by A.G. Eyre ; illustrated by Gordon King. — London : Longman, 1976. — [4],75p : ill ; 20cm. — (Longman structural readers : fiction : stage 5)
ISBN 0-582-53798-3 Sd : £0.40
(B77-01373)

428'.6'4 — English language. Reading books. Special subjects: Biology. *For non-English speaking students*

Adamson, Donald, *b.1943.* Biology / [by] Donald Adamson, Martin Bates. — London : Longman, 1977. — [2],110p : ill ; 24cm. — (Nucleus)
Bibl.: p.110.
ISBN 0-582-51302-2 Pbk : £1.35
(B77-11765)

Adamson, Donald, *b.1943.* Biology / [by] Donald Adamson, Martin Bates. — London : Longman. — (Nucleus)
Teacher's notes. — 1977. — vi,72p ; 24cm.
With answers.
ISBN 0-582-55354-7 Sd : £1.00
(B77-32608)

428'.6'4 — English language. Reading books. Special subjects: Cinema industries, to 1974. *For non-English speaking students*

Ellis-Jones, Barrie. The cinema / [by] Barrie Ellis-Jones. — London : Heinemann Educational, 1977. — 93p : ill, ports ; 18cm. — (Heinemann guided readers : upper level ; U8)
ISBN 0-435-27031-1 Pbk : £0.50
(B77-26269)

428'.6'4 — English language. Reading books. Special subjects: Clothing, to 1975. *For non-English speaking students*

Holden, Susan. Clothes and fashion / [by] Susan Holden. — London : Evans Bros, 1976. — [4],44p : ill, form ; 19cm. — (Evans graded reading : grade 4)
ISBN 0-237-50050-7 Sd : £0.60
(B77-20204)

428'.6'4 — English language. Reading books. Special subjects: Great Britain. Family life. *For non-English speaking students*

Gill, Vivienne. Family life / [by] Vivienne Gill. — London [etc.] : Evans Bros, 1976. — [4],44p : ill ; 19cm. — (Evans graded reading : grade 4)
ISBN 0-237-49966-5 Sd : £0.50
(B77-12992)

428'.6'4 — English language. Reading books. Special subjects: Great Britain. Food. *For non-English speaking students*

Holden, Susan. What's cooking? / [by] Susan Holden. — London [etc.] : Evans Bros, 1976. — [4],44p : ill ; 19cm. — (Evans graded reading : grade 5)
ISBN 0-237-49991-6 Sd : £0.50
(B77-12410)

428'.6'4 — English language. Reading books. Special subjects: Great Britain. Occupations. *For non-English speaking students*

Giese, Diana. Making a living / [by] Diana Giese. — London [etc.] : Evans Bros, 1977. — [4],44p : ill, ports ; 19cm. — (Evans graded reading : grade 3)
ISBN 0-237-50065-5 Sd : £0.50
(B77-12993)

428'.6'4 — English language. Reading books. Special subjects: Great Britain. Theatre. *For non-English speaking students*

Holden, Susan. Theatre in Britain / [by] Susan Holden. — London : Evans Bros, 1976. — [4],44p : ill, 2 facsims, plans ; 19cm. — (Evans graded reading : grade 3)
ISBN 0-237-50049-3 Sd : £0.60
(B77-07312)

428'.6'4 — English language. Reading books. Special subjects: London, to 1976. *For non-English speaking students*

Prowse, Philip. This is London / [by] Philip Prowse. — London : Heinemann Educational, 1977. — [2],29,[1]p : ill, map ; 18cm. — (Heinemann guided readers : beginner level ; 7)

ISBN 0-435-27045-1 Sd : £0.27
(B77-15253)

428'.6'4 — English language. Reading books. Special subjects: United States. Western states, 1800-1900. *For non-English speaking students*

Clarke, Waldo. The wild west / [by] Waldo Clarke. — London [etc.] : Evans Bros, 1977. — [4],44p : ill, maps, ports ; 19cm. — (Evans graded reading : grade 4)
ISBN 0-237-50047-7 Sd : £0.50
(B77-12411)

428'.6'4 — Non-English speaking students. Reading schemes: Heinemann graded readers. *For teaching*

Milne, John, *b.1927.* Heinemann guided readers handbook / [by] John Milne. — London : Heinemann Educational, 1977. — [4],28p ; 22cm.
ISBN 0-435-27039-7 Sd : £0.50
(B77-09661)

428'.6'4071 — Schools. Non-English speaking students. Curriculum subjects: English language. Reading. Teaching

Swan, Douglas Kelso. Longman guide to graded reading / [by D.K. Swan]. — London : Longman, 1977. — [3],27p : forms ; 20cm.
ISBN 0-582-53670-7 Sd : £0.35
(B77-16345)

428'.6'495 — English language. Reading books. *For South-east Asian students. Middle school texts*

Comber, Leon. Favourite stories from Taiwan / retold by Leon Comber & Charles Shuttleworth ; illustrated by Lo Koon-chiu. — Hong Kong [etc.] ; London : Heinemann Educational, 1976. — [5],51p : ill(col) ; 19cm.
Originally published: 1975.
Sd : Unpriced
(B77-25566)

Pordes, Ilse. Favourite stories from Japan / retold by Ilse Pordes ; illustrated by Lo Koon-chiu. — Hong Kong [etc.] ; London : Heinemann Educational, 1976. — [4],50p : ill ; 19cm.
Originally published: 1975.
Sd : Unpriced
(B77-25567)

428'.6'495 — English language. Reading books. *For South-east Asian students. Secondary school texts*

Lee, Frances. The things from the South China Sea / by Frances Lee ; illustrated by Patrick Printer. — Hong Kong [etc.] ; London : Heinemann Educational, 1975. — [5],126p : ill ; 19cm. — (Heinemann Asian secondary readers)

Originally published: 1970.
Pbk : Unpriced
(B77-16849)

428.6'4951 — English language. Reading books. *For Chinese speaking students. Primary school texts*

Ho Man Yee. More favourite Chinese stories / [by] Ho Man Yee. — Hongkong [etc.] : Heinemann Educational Books (Asia) ; London : Heinemann Educational, 1975. — vi,34p : ill ; 19cm. — (Favourite stories series ; 2)

Originally published: as 'More favourite stories for Chinese schools'. 1969.
Sd : Unpriced
(B77-27020)

428'.6'4956 — English language. Reading books. Special subjects: Europe. *For Japanese tourists*

Booth, Alan, *b.1946.* Let's see Europe : a book for travellers and the people who help them / by Alan Booth and Takashi Hashimoto. — London [etc.] : Macmillan, 1977. — [4],108p : ill(chiefly col), facsims, col maps ; 22cm.
ISBN 0-333-19976-6 Pbk : £1.05
(B77-22531)

429 — OLD ENGLISH LANGUAGE
429'.5 — Old English language. Grammar
Hill, Joyce. Beginning Old English : materials for a one-year course / [by] Joyce Hill, A.R. Taylor, R.L. Thomson. — [Leeds] ([Leeds LS2 9JT]) : University of Leeds, School of English, 1977. — vii,130p ; 21cm. — (Leeds studies in English)
Pbk : £2.50
(B77-29369)

An **outline** of Old English grammar. — [Leeds] ([The University, Leeds LS2 9JT]) : University of Leeds, School of English, 1976. — [1],33p ; 21cm. — (Leeds studies in English)
ISBN 0-902296-17-5 Sd : £0.50
(B77-00736)

430 — GERMANIC LANGUAGES
430'.07'1142142 — Universities. *London. Camden (London Borough). University of London. Institute of Germanic Studies. Reports, surveys. Serials*
University of London. *Institute of Germanic Studies.* Annual report / University of London, Institute of Germanic Studies. — London (29 Russell Sq., WC1B 5DP) : [The Institute].
26th : 1st August 1975-31st July 1976. — [1976]. — 16p ; 22cm.
ISBN 0-85457-073-x Sd : Unpriced
(B77-13621)

430'.7'1073 — Educational institutions. Curriculum subjects: German language. Teaching. *United States*
German studies in the United States : assessment and outlook / edited by Walter F.W. Lohnes, Valters Nollendorfs. — Madison ; London : University of Wisconsin Press for 'Monatshefte', 1976. — viii,263,[1]p : ill ; 24cm. — ('Monatshefte' occasional volume ; no.1)
ISBN 0-299-97009-4 : £11.25
ISBN 0-299-97010-8 Pbk : £5.65
(B77-21819)

430'.9 — German language, to 1975
Waterman, John Thomas. A history of the German language : with special reference to the cultural and social forces that shaped the standard literary language / by John T. Waterman. — Revised ed. — Seattle ; London : University of Washington Press, 1976. — xiv, 284p : ill, facsims, maps ; 24cm.
Previous ed.: 1966. — Bibl.: p.233-273. — Index.
ISBN 0-295-73807-3 : £8.40
(B77-03510)

433 — GERMAN LANGUAGE. DICTIONARIES
433'.2'1 — German language. *German-English, English-German dictionaries*
Langenscheidt's encyclopaedic dictionary of the English and German languages / based on the original work by E. Muret and D. Sanders. — Completely revised [ed.] / edited by Otto Springer. — London : Hodder and Stoughton.
In 4 vols.
Part 2 : German-English. Vol.2 : L-Z. — 1975. — [7]p,p974-2024 ; 30cm.
Second title page in German. — This ed. originally published: Berlin : Langenscheidt ; London : Hodder and Stoughton, 1974?.
ISBN 0-340-15389-x : Unpriced
(B77-09662)

Laurence Urdang Associates. Hamlyn German dictionary : German-English, English-German / [compiled by Laurence Urdang Associates]. — London [etc.] : Hamlyn, 1976. — [10],306p ; 15cm.
ISBN 0-600-36564-6 Pbk : £0.75
(B77-19325)

433'.2'1 — German language. Synonyms. *English-German dictionaries*
Farrell, Ralph Barstow. Dictionary of German synonyms / [by] R.B. Farrell. — 3rd ed. — London [etc.] : Cambridge University Press, 1977. — x,412p ; 23cm.
Previous ed.: 1971.
ISBN 0-521-21189-1 : £10.50
ISBN 0-521-29068-6 Pbk : £3.95
(B77-16346)

438 — GERMAN LANGUAGE USAGE
438 — German language. *Exercises, worked examples*
Baer, Edith Ruth. Der arme Millionär : a BBC Radio course in everyday German based on Erich Kästner's novel 'Drei Männer im Schnee' / radio adaptation Edith R. Baer ; notes, grammar and linguistic advice L. Löb. — London : British Broadcasting Corporation, 1976. — 111p ; 23cm.
First broadcast March-August 1967, re-broadcast 4 May-28 September 1977. — German text, English and German exercises. — Originally published: 1967.
ISBN 0-563-07118-4 Pbk : £1.50
(B77-16347)

438 — German language. *Exercises, worked examples. Secondary school texts*
Anderson, Walter Ewart. Aufenthalt in Deutschland / [by] Walter E. Anderson. — London : Harrap.
In 2 vols.
[Vol.2] : with vocabularies to both volumes / with ... photographs ... and line illustrations in the text by Arthur Whitney. — 1976. — 166p, [8]p of plates : ill, map ; 19cm.
Originally published: 1949.
ISBN 0-245-53035-5 Pbk : £1.50
(B77-10341)

Hawkin, Terry. A German fun book / [by] Terry Hawkin. — London : Longman, 1977. — [2], 33p : ill ; 16x22cm. — (Longman German workbooks)
Fill-in book.
ISBN 0-582-21521-8 Sd : £0.35
(B77-31861)

438 — German language. *Secondary school texts*
Foster, Joseph Reginald. Die mündliche Prüfung : an 'O' Level course in reproduction, dictation, reading and conversation / by J.R. Foster. — London : Harrap.
Pupil's book. — 1974. — 104p : ill, map ; 19cm.
Originally published: 1960.
ISBN 0-245-56894-8 Sd : £1.60
(B77-10342)

Paxton, Norman. Wir lernen Deutsch / by N. Paxton and R.J. Brake ; drawings by Frances Winder. — 2nd ed. — London [etc.] : Hodder and Stoughton.
Previous ed.: London : English Universities Press, 1971.
1. Teil. — 1976. — [4],92p : ill(chiefly col), map ; 19x25cm.
ISBN 0-340-21427-9 Pbk : £1.35
(B77-02941)

Paxton, Norman. Wir lernen Deutsch / [by] N. Paxton and R.J. Brake. — 2nd ed. — London : Hodder and Stoughton.
Previous ed.: London : English Universities Press, 1970.
1. Teil : Teacher's handbook / produced in collaboration with H. Keith ; edited by P.J. Downes. — 1977. — 63p ; 19x25cm.
ISBN 0-340-21428-7 Sd : £1.50
(B77-17440)

Rowlinson, William. Lies mal Deutsch! / [von] W. Rowlinson, G. Lehnigk. — Oxford [etc.] : Oxford University Press.
2C / [von] W. Rowlinson ; photographs by the author and others. — 1976. — 1v. : ill, maps ; 20cm.
Ten booklets ([160]p.) in folder. — In plastic envelope. — German text and comprehension questions in English.
ISBN 0-19-832480-4 : £3.25
(B77-02942)

Stevenson, Jack. Ich kann's! : an illustrated German course / [by] Jack Stevenson. — London : Bell.
Book 3. — 1976. — viii,192p : ill, maps, plan ; 21cm.
ISBN 0-7135-1975-4 Pbk : £6.50
(B77-04757)

Wightwick, Charles Christopher Brooke. Longman audio-lingual German / [by] C.C.B. Wightwick, H.W. Strubelt. — [London] : Longman.
Stage 2 : Die Welt ist rund. [Pupil's book]. — [1977]. — [2],126p : ill(some col), col maps, plans(some col) ; 24cm.
Text on inside back cover. — Tapes (recorded at 3 3/4 i.p.s.) also available. — Index.
ISBN 0-582-36115-x Pbk : £1.95
(B77-25568)

438 — German language. *Study examples: Signs in German. Questions & answers*
Sawers, Robin. German sign language : reading comprehension activities / [by] Robin Sawers. — London : Harrap, 1977. — [60]p : ill ; 21cm.
ISBN 0-245-53091-6 Sd : £1.50
(B77-27822)

438'.1 — German language. Vocabulary. *Primary school texts*
Colyer, Penrose. I can read German : my first English-German word book / compiled by Penrose Colyer, German by Ruth Jahnke ; illustrations by Colin Mier and Wendy Lewis. — [London] ([2 Queen's Drive, W3 0HA]) : Peter Lowe, 1976. — 4-116p : ill(chiefly col) ; 28cm.
ISBN 0-85654-026-9 : £2.75
(B77-05370)

438'.3'421 — Spoken German language idioms
Adrienne. Der Gimmick gesprochenes Deutsch / von Adrienne ; adapted [i.e. translated] by Michèle Tavernier, with assistance from Wanda Bortel and Ursel Bähr. — London : Hutchinson, 1977. — vi,162p ; 21cm.
English and German text. — Translation of: 'Der Gimmick gesprochenes Deutsch'. Paris : Flammarion, 1975.
ISBN 0-09-127161-4 Pbk : £2.50
(B77-27021)

438'.6'421 — German language. Reading books. *Secondary school texts*
Das **Feuerschiff** / [von] Siegfried Lenz ; [gekürzt und vereinfacht]. — Kopenhagen : Grafisk Forlag ; London : J. Murray [etc.], [1977]. — 85p : ill ; 20cm. — (Easy readers = Leicht zu lesen : B)
This adaptation originally published: Kopenhagen : Grafisk Forlag, 1975. — Bibl.: p.5.
ISBN 0-7195-3331-7 Pbk : £0.80
(B77-15817)

Kein Schnaps für Tamara / [von] Hansjörg Martin ; [gekürzt und vereinfacht]. — Kopenhagen : Grafisk Forlag ; London : J. Murray [etc.], [1977]. — 85p : ill ; 19cm. — (Easy readers = Leicht zu lesen : B)
This adaptation originally published: Kopenhagen : Grafisk Forlag, 1975.
ISBN 0-7195-3351-1 Pbk : £0.80
(B77-15818)

438'.6'421 — German language. Reading books. Special subjects: Europe. Rhine River region. *Secondary school texts*
Sargent, Malcolm B. Mit zum Rhein! / [von] Malcolm B. Sargent. — Sevenoaks : Hodder and Stoughton, 1977. — 31p : ill, coats of arms, facsims, maps, music, port ; 25cm.
ISBN 0-340-18391-8 Sd : £0.75
(B77-18715)

439.7 — SWEDISH LANGUAGE
439.7'8'02 — Swedish language. Translation from English language. *Exercises, worked examples*
Swedish proses / [editor Laurie Thompson]. — Aberystwyth (Aberystwyth, Dyfed SY23 3DY) : Department of German, Swedish and Russian, University College of Wales, 1976. — 2v.(47; 87p) ; 21cm.
Contents: Part 1. Texts (in English) - Part 2. Keys (Swedish text, English foreword and notes) Pbk.
ISBN 0-905884-00-0 Sd : £0.40
(B77-10343)

443 — FRENCH LANGUAGE. DICTIONARIES
443'.2'1 — French language. *French-English, English-French dictionaries*
Laurence Urdang Associates. Hamlyn French dictionary : French-English, English-French / [compiled by Laurence Urdang Associates]. — London [etc.] : Hamlyn, 1976. — [12],305p ; 15cm.
ISBN 0-600-36563-8 Pbk : £0.75
(B77-20205)

448 — FRENCH LANGUAGE USAGE
448 — French language. *Exercises, worked examples*
Allez France! : third stage French : a BBC Radio course to follow 'Ensemble' and 'Sur le vif' / course writer John Ross ... — London : British Broadcasting Corporation, 1977. — 228p : ill(some col), forms, maps(chiefly col) ; 23cm.
'Published to accompany a series of programmes prepared in consultation with the BBC Further Education Advisory Council' - title page verso. — English and French text. — With answers.
ISBN 0-563-16146-9 Pbk : £2.75
(B77-27823)

Sur le vif : second stage French : a BBC radio course to follow 'Ensemble'. — London : British Broadcasting Corporation.
'An LP record and tape cassette containing identical material accompany this book ...' title page verso.
Book 2 : Programmes 11-20 / course designer Madeleine Le Cunff. — 1976. — 136p : ill(some col), form, maps(chiefly col), ports ; 23cm.
With answers to exercises.
ISBN 0-563-16101-9 Pbk : £1.25
(B77-07313)

448 — French language. *Exercises, worked examples. Secondary school texts*

Brockman, Pat. Go to a town in France / [written by Pat Brockman and Dave Crossland]. — London : Longman, 1976. — [2] ,30p : ill, 2 maps ; 21cm.
ISBN 0-582-21556-0 Sd : £3.50
(B77-05371)

Mountjoy, Margaret Eva. Aspects de la vie / [by] D. and K. Matthes ; adapted by M.E. Mountjoy. — London : Edward Arnold, 1977. — 112p : ill, map, ports ; 21cm. — (Etudes françaises)
ISBN 0-7131-0093-1 Pbk : £1.25
(B77-14198)

Pryce, Denis Kirk. Certificate French / by D.K. Pryce ; illustrated by A.C. Eccott and J.S. Goodall. — London : Harrap, 1976. — 392p : ill, maps ; 20cm.
Originally published: 1967.
ISBN 0-245-53034-7 Pbk : £2.50
(B77-10794)

Whitmarsh, William Frederick Herbert. Examination French / [by] W.F.H. Whitmarsh. — [Harlow] : Longman, 1977. — vi,218p : ill ; 20cm.
ISBN 0-582-33109-9 Pbk : £1.30
(B77-24159)

Whitmore, Paul Crowe. French for CSE : a complete fifth year course / [by] P.C. Whitmore. — 2nd ed. — London : Bell, 1977. — xii,250p : ill ; 22cm.
Previous ed.: 1967.
ISBN 0-7135-1989-4 Pbk : £1.65
(B77-12412)

Wildbore, Alison M. Qu'as-tu fait? / [by] Alison M. Wildbore. — London : Edward Arnold, 1977. — 64p : ill, map ; 22cm.
French and English text.
ISBN 0-7131-0097-4 Sd : £0.90
(B77-31149)

448 — French language. *Middle school texts*

Symonds, Pamela. French from France / [by] Pamela Symonds. — London : Longman.
1 : En France. — 1976. — [2],17p : ill, maps ; 21cm.
French text, English introduction.
ISBN 0-582-20718-5 Sd : £0.25
(B77-02241)

[2] : En Normandie. — 1976. — [1],32p : ill, maps ; 21cm.
French text, English introduction.
ISBN 0-582-20719-3 Sd : £0.35
(B77-02242)

3 : À Coutances. — 1976. — [1],48p : ill, facsims, maps ; 21cm.
French text, English introduction.
ISBN 0-582-20720-7 Sd : £0.50
(B77-08344)

448 — French language. *Secondary school texts*

Hawkins, Eric. Le français pour tout le monde / [by] Eric Hawkins and Bryan Howson. — Edinburgh : Oliver and Boyd.
Book 4. — 1977. — 176p : ill, maps, music ; 20x26cm.
ISBN 0-05-002541-4 Pbk : £2.50
(B77-24160)

Joiner, Elizabeth G. First-year French / [by] Elizabeth G. Joiner, Georges A. Perla, Stanley L. Shinall. — New York [etc.] ; London : Holt, Rinehart and Winston, 1977. — xvi,483,xlii p,[24]p of plates : ill(some col), facsims, form, col maps, plans ; 25cm.
Index.
ISBN 0-03-015006-x : £7.50
(B77-20206)

Kellett, Arnold. Basic French / [by] Arnold Kellett. — Plymouth : Macdonald and Evans, 1977. — xii,240p : ill, map ; 19cm. — (The M & E handbook series)
Index.
ISBN 0-7121-0250-7 Pbk : £1.75
(B77-30198)

Mountjoy, Margaret Eva. Passeport pour la France d'aujourd'hui / [par] M.E. Mountjoy. — London : Edward Arnold.
In 3 vols.
Book 1. — 1977. — 64p : ill, facsims, maps, music ; 25cm.
English and French text.
ISBN 0-7131-0045-1 Sd : £1.50
(B77-18716)

Nott, David Owen. Actualités françaises : a complete course for advanced students / [by] D.O. Nott, J.E. Trickey. — 2nd ed. — London [etc.] : Hodder and Stoughton.
Previous ed.: London : English Universities Press, 1971.
Part 1. — 1976. — x,211p : ill, map, ports ; 25cm.
French text, English preface and notes. — Index.
ISBN 0-340-20921-6 Pbk : £2.45
(B77-02945)

Part 1. Tape booklet. — 1976. — 48p ; 19cm.
French text, English introduction. — Index.
ISBN 0-340-20029-4 Sd : £0.75
(B77-02946)

Symonds, Pamela. Let's speak French / by Pamela Symonds. — 2nd ed. — Oxford [etc.] : Oxford University Press.
1. — 1977. — vi,175p : ill(some col), music ; 23cm.
Previous ed.: 1962.
ISBN 0-19-832289-5 Pbk : £1.75
(B77-12413)

2. — 1977. — vi,229p : ill, maps ; 23cm.
French text, English preface and notes. — Previous ed.: 1963.
ISBN 0-19-832290-9 Pbk : £1.75
(B77-24878)

448'.002'465 — French language. *For business enterprise*

Bower, Malcolm. French for business / [by] Malcolm Bower and Lucette Barbarin. — London [etc.] : Hodder and Stoughton, 1977. — x,142p : ill, facsims, 2 maps ; 20cm.
ISBN 0-340-16266-x Pbk : £1.25
(B77-24879)

448'.1'076 — French language. Vocabulary. *Exercises, worked examples. Secondary school texts*

Sewell, Penelope Mary. Le mot juste / [by] F.F. de Haan, A.E. van de Ven ; adapted by P.M. Sewell. — English school ed. — Harlow : Longman, 1976. — 128p : ill ; 21cm.
Adaptation of: 'Pesez vos mots'. Groningen : Wolters Noordhoff, 1974.
ISBN 0-582-33112-9 Pbk : £0.80
(B77-02243)

448'.2'421 — French language. Comprehension. *Exercises, worked examples. Secondary school texts*

Leech, Christopher Thomas Gill. Une question de choix : a programme of reading comprehension with multiple choice answers / [by] C.T. Gill Leech. — London : Heinemann Educational, 1977. — viii,88p : ill, ports ; 25cm.
French text, English introduction and notes. — With answers.
ISBN 0-435-37610-1 Pbk : £1.50
(B77-29370)

Mackereth, John Derrick. France-choix : advanced multiple-choice comprehension / [by] Derrick Mackereth, Lilian M. Derham. — London : Harrap.
Livre de l'étudiant. — 1976. — 144p ; 22cm.
French and English text, English introduction.
ISBN 0-245-52907-1 Pbk : £1.95
(B77-05372)

Livre du professeur. — 1976. — 3-66p ; 22cm.
French text, English introduction. — With answers.
ISBN 0-245-52908-x Sd : £2.40
(B77-05373)

Vercambre, Michel. Nous allons nous entendre : listening and reading comprehension tests with multiple choice questions for 'A' Level French / [by] Michel Vercambre, Moira Atkinson. — London : Heinemann Educational.

Pupil's book. — 1976. — [4],44p ; 22cm.
ISBN 0-435-37900-3 Sd : £0.65
(B77-04758)

Teacher's book. — 1976. — viii,32p ; 22cm.
French text, English acknowledgements and foreword.
ISBN 0-435-37901-1 Sd : £1.00
(B77-04759)

448'.2'421 — French language. Grammar

Butturff, Diane L. French : language and life styles / [by] Diane L. Butturff, Mary E. Coffman. — New York ; London [etc.] : McGraw-Hill, [1977]. — xvii,493p : ill ; 25cm.
Published in the United States: 1976. — Index.
ISBN 0-07-009455-1 : £10.75
(B77-12414)

Fraser, William Henry. Heath's practical French grammar / [by] W.H. Fraser and J. Squair ; with an introduction by William Robertson. — London : Harrap, 1976. — viii,394,[92]p ; 19cm.
Originally published: Boston, Mass. : D.C. Heath, 19-? ; London : Harrap, 1922. — Index.

ISBN 0-245-53042-8 Pbk : £2.95
(B77-11185)

Jackson, Eugene. French made simple / [by] Eugene Jackson and Antonio Rubio ; advisory editor Jacqueline Janvier. — Revised [ed.]. — London : W.H. Allen, 1976. — xv,317p ; 22cm. — (Made simple books ISSN 0464-2902)
With answers. — This ed. originally published: 1967.
ISBN 0-491-01332-9 Pbk : £1.50
(B77-20207)

Mansion, Jean Edmond. A grammar of present-day French / by J.E. Mansion. — [2nd ed., without exercises]. — London : Harrap, 1976. — 247p ; 18cm.
This ed. originally published: 1952. — Index.
ISBN 0-245-53032-0 Pbk : £1.45
(B77-10795)

448'.2'49162 — French language. *Exercises, worked examples. For Irish students. Secondary school texts*

Byrne, Brendan. Intermediate Certificate French / [by] Brendan Byrne. — Dublin : Helicon, 1976. — [4],112p : ill ; 21cm. — (Study assessment series)
French and English text.
ISBN 0-904916-60-x Sd : £1.32
(B77-02943)

Byrne, Brendan. Intermediate Certificate French / [by] Brendan Byrne. — Dublin : Helicon. — (Study assessment series)
Teacher's book. — 1976. — [4],19p ; 21cm.
Teacher's book has title: Intermediate French. — French and English text.
ISBN 0-904916-61-8 Sd : £0.66
(B77-02944)

448'.3'421 — Spoken French language. *Conversation primers*

Gilbert, Mark. Let's talk French / [by] Mark Gilbert. — London [etc.] : Hodder and Stoughton, 1977. — xii,212p : ill ; 20cm.
ISBN 0-340-20644-6 Pbk : £1.50
(B77-23346)

448'.3'421 — Spoken French language. *Exercises, worked examples. For slow learning students. Secondary school texts*

Chouette!. — Leeds : E.J. Arnold.
Slides and tape also available.
A. [Pupil's book]. — 1976. — 23p : ill ; 30cm.
French text, English instructions. — 'Published ... in association with the Inner London Education Authority, Media Resources Centre' - p.3.
ISBN 0-560-03021-5 Sd : £0.30
(B77-07314)

A. Teacher's guide. — 1976. — 23p ; 21x30cm.

English text, French dialogues. — 'Published ... in association with the Inner London Education Authority, Media Resources Centre' - title page verso.
ISBN 0-560-03020-7 Sd : £0.60
(B77-07315)

B. [Pupil's book]. — 1976. — 23p : ill, form ; 30cm.
French text, English instructions. — 'Published ... in association with the Inner London Education Authority, Learning Materials Service' - p.3.
ISBN 0-560-03023-1 Sd : £0.30
(B77-07316)

B. Teacher's guide. — 1976. — 23p ; 21x30cm.

English text, French dialogues. — 'Published ... in association with the Inner London Education Authority, Media Resources Centre' - title page verso.
ISBN 0-560-03022-3 Sd : £0.60
(B77-07317)

448'.3'421 — Spoken French language. *For slow learning students. Secondary school texts*

Ellis, David Leslie. Destination France : survival language course / by D.L. Ellis and M.R. Pearce. — London : Harrap.
Part 1. Student's book. — 1976. — 96p : ill(some col), facsims ; 21cm.
ISBN 0-245-52910-1 Pbk : £1.50
(B77-07318)

Part 1. Teacher's book. — 1976. — 80p : ill ; 21cm.
ISBN 0-245-52911-x Pbk : £2.25
(B77-07319)

448'.3'421 — Spoken French language. Grammar. *Secondary school texts*

Moore, Sidney. Longman audio-visual French / [by] S. Moore, A.L. Antrobus, G.F. Pugh. — London : Longman.
Introductory stage. Bienvenue. Teacher's book. — 1977. — 80p : ill ; 24cm.
ISBN 0-582-20256-6 Sd : £2.00
(B77-31863)

448'.3'421 — Spoken French language. Special subjects: Transport. *Secondary school texts. Teaching kits*

Transport / [by Colin Asher et al.]. — [Cambridge, etc.] : Cambridge University Press, 1976. — Case : ill(chiefly col), col maps ; 22x31x8cm. — (Something to talk about)
'Teacher's handbook' ([2],46p.), wallchart, 35 of each of 3 work cards, 6 sets of materials (board and 20 cards) for each of 2 games, sound tape (1 reel 5 in.). 3 3/4 in. per sec.).
ISBN 0-521-20722-3 : £32.00(non-net + VAT in UK)
(B77-00737)

448'.3'42107 — Educational institutions. Curriculum subjects: Spoken French language. Teaching. *Great Britain. For French language assistants. French texts*

Fontier, Geneviève. Guide de l'assistant de français ou Comment stimuler le français oral / [par] Geneviève Fontier, Madeleine le Cunff ; collaboration de Michel Blanc et Penny Sewell. — London : Longman, 1975. — xii,208p : ill, form, maps ; 20cm. — (Education today : language teaching)
Index.
ISBN 0-582-36304-7 Pbk : £2.50
(B77-11766)

448'.6'421 — French language. Reading books

Les **enfants** terribles / [par] Jean Cocteau ; [abregé et simplifié]. — Copenhague [i.e. Copenhagen] : Grafisk Forlag ; Londres [i.e. London] : J. Murray [etc.], 1977. — 94p : ill ; 19cm. — (Easy readers = Facile à lire : B)
This adaptation originally published: Copenhagen : Grafisk Forlag, 1975.
ISBN 0-7195-3364-3 Pbk : Unpriced
(B77-25569)

Les **petits** enfants du siècle / [par] Christiane Rochefort ; [abrégé et simplifié]. — Copenhague [i.e. Copenhagen] : Grafisk Forlag ; Londres [i.e. London] : J. Murray [etc.], 1976. — 80p : ill ; 19cm. — (Easy readers = Facile à lire : B)
This adaptation originally published: Copenhagen : Grafisk Forlag, 1974.
ISBN 0-7195-3304-x Pbk : £0.80
(B77-17441)

La **tête** sur les épaules / [par] Henri Troyat ; [abregé et simplifié]. — Copenhague [i.e. Copenhagen] : Grafisk Forlag ; Londres [i.e. London] : J. Murray [etc.], 1977. — 95p : ill ; 19cm. — (Easy readers = Facile à lire : C)
This adaptation originally published: Copenhagen : Grafisk Forlag, 1975.
ISBN 0-7195-3367-8 Pbk : Unpriced
(B77-25570)

448'.6'421 — French language. Reading books. *Secondary school texts*

Buckby, Michael. La course à la mort / [par] N.M. Buckby. — London : Harrap, 1977. — [2],16,[2]p : ill, facsim, map, port ; 13x20cm. — (Collection vécue ; 8)
ISBN 0-245-52920-9 Sd : £0.30
(B77-11186)

Buckby, Michael. La Croix-Rouge / [par] N.M. Buckby. — London : Harrap, 1977. — [1],16, [2]p : ill, port ; 13x19cm. — (Collection vécue ; 10)
ISBN 0-245-52922-5 Sd : £0.35
(B77-11187)

Buckby, Michael. Entre ciel et terre / [par] N.M. Buckby. — London : Harrap, 1977. — [1],16, [2]p : ill, ports ; 13x20cm. — (Collection vécue ; 9)
ISBN 0-245-52921-7 Sd : £0.30
(B77-11188)

Colyer, Penrose. Voyage en Normandie / [by] Penrose Colyer ... — London : Longman, 1977. — [4],76p : ill(some col), coat of arms, facsims(chiefly col), 2 forms(1 col), maps(2 col), ports ; 21cm.
Map on inside front cover, text on inside back cover.
ISBN 0-582-31340-6 Pbk : £0.95
(B77-30199)

Davoust, Eugène Pierre. Deux mois sous terre / [by] E.-P. Davoust. — London : Harrap, 1977. — [1],16,[2]p : ill, maps, ports ; 13x20cm. — (Collection vécue ; 7)
ISBN 0-245-52919-5 Sd : £0.30
(B77-12994)

Davoust, Eugène Pierre. En pleine mer / [par] E.-P. Davoust. — London : Harrap, 1977. — [1],16,[2]p : ill, maps, port ; 13x20cm. — (Collection vécue ; 6)
ISBN 0-245-52918-7 Sd : £0.30
(B77-11189)

Davoust, Eugène Pierre. La traversée de la Manche / [by] E.-P. Davoust. — London : Harrap, 1977. — [1],16,[2]p : ill, ports ; 13x20cm. — (Collection vécue ; 5)
ISBN 0-245-52917-9 Sd : £0.30
(B77-12995)

Kiil, Hans. Servez-vous / [par] Hans Kiil. — London : Edward Arnold, 1977. — 48p : ill, map ; 22cm.
Originally published: Stockholm : Almquist och Wiksell, 1972.
ISBN 0-7131-0137-7 Sd : £0.75
(B77-29371)

448'.6'421 — French language. Reading books. Special subjects: Europe. Alps. Mont Blanc range. Mountain rescue. *Secondary school texts*

Desmaison, René. Sauvetage à 3000 mètres / [par] René Desmaison. — Leeds : E.J. Arnold, 1974. — [2],14p : ill, map, ports ; 25cm. — (West Riding modern language reading project : level 2 ; 2)
Based on: 'La montagne à mains nues'. Paris : Flammarion, 1971.
ISBN 0-560-09314-4 Sd : Unpriced
(B77-20208)

448'.6'421 — French language. Reading books. Special subjects: France. Champagnes industries, to 1973. *Secondary school texts*

Harcourt, L M d'. L'histoire du champagne / [par] L.M. d'Harcourt. — Leeds : E.J. Arnold, 1974. — [2],14p : ill, map, port ; 25cm. — (West Riding modern language reading project : level 2 ; 3)
French text, English introduction and notes.
ISBN 0-560-09317-9 Sd : Unpriced
(B77-20209)

448'.6'421 — French language. Reading books. Special subjects: France. Women's clothing. Fashion, 1920-1975. *Secondary school texts*

Griffith, Simone Wyn. Les Révolutions de la mode / [par] Simone Wyn Griffith. — London : Hodder and Stoughton, 1976. — 48p : ill, facsims, ports ; 25cm. — (Découvrons la France)
ISBN 0-340-18460-4 Sd : Unpriced
(B77-10344)

448'.6'421 — French language. Reading books. Special subjects: French costume, 1625-ca 1920. *Secondary school texts*

Griffith, Simone Wyn. L'évolution du costume / [par] Simone Wyn Griffith. — London : Hodder and Stoughton, 1976. — [2],45p : ill, ports ; 25cm. — (Découvrons la France)
ISBN 0-340-17957-0 Sd : Unpriced
(B77-08345)

448'.6'421 — French language. Reading books. Special subjects: Petroleum industries, to 1973. *Secondary school texts*

Weiss, Henri. L'histoire du pétrole / [par] Henri Weiss. — Leeds : E.J. Arnold, 1974. — [2], 14p : ill, map, port ; 25cm. — (West Riding modern language reading project : level 2 ; 1)
French text, English introduction and notes.
ISBN 0-560-09311-x Sd : Unpriced
(B77-20210)

453 — ITALIAN LANGUAGE. DICTIONARIES

453'.2'1 — Italian language. *Italian-English, English-Italian dictionaries*

Laurence Urdang Associates. Hamlyn Italian dictionary : Italian-English, English-Italian / [compiled by Laurence Urdang Associates]. — London [etc.] : Hamlyn, 1976. — [14],301p ; 15cm.
ISBN 0-600-36566-2 Pbk : £0.75
(B77-19326)

455 — ITALIAN LANGUAGE. GRAMMAR

455 — Italian language. Syntax. Transformational-generative linguistics

Radford, Andrew. Italian syntax : transformational and relational grammar / [by] Andrew Radford. — Cambridge [etc.] : Cambridge University Press, 1977. — ix,271p : ill ; 24cm. — (Cambridge studies in linguistics ; 21)
Bibl.: p.260-267. — Index.
ISBN 0-521-21643-5 : £11.50
(B77-28577)

458 — ITALIAN LANGUAGE USAGE

458'.2'421 — Italian language. Grammar

Hugo's Language Books. Italian in three months / [Hugo's Language Books]. — [New ed.] / revised and rewritten by M.G. Dawson-Bellone. — London : Hugo's Language Books, 1976. — 144p ; 18cm. — (Hugo's simplified system)
With key to grammar exercises. — English and Italian text. — Previous ed.: / Hugo's Language Institute. London : Hugo's Language Institute, 1969.
ISBN 0-85285-053-0 Pbk : £0.75
(B77-16850)

Speroni, Charles. Basic Italian / [by] Charles Speroni, Carlo L. Golino. — 4th ed. — New York [etc.] ; London : Holt, Rinehart and Winston, 1977. — xxxvi,471p : ill(some col), facsim, col maps(on lining papers), ports ; 25cm.
Previous ed.: New York : Holt, Rinehart and Winston, 1972. — Index.
ISBN 0-03-089955-9 : £7.50
(B77-26270)

458'.3'421 — Spoken Italian language. *Conversation primers*

Negro, Ottavio. Beginners' Italian : an introduction to conversational Italian / [by] Ottavio Negro. — 3rd ed. — London [etc.] : Hodder and Stoughton, 1977. — xiii,111p ; 20cm.
Previous ed.: / by Ottavio Negro and Joseph Harvard. London : University of London Press, 1969.
ISBN 0-340-21508-9 Pbk : £1.25
(B77-24880)

458'.3'421 — Spoken Italian language. *Study examples: Interviews*

Conversazioni : second stage Italian / editor Maddalena Fagandini ; language commentaries Joseph A. Cremona. — London : British Broadcasting Corporation, 1977. — 96p : ill, maps, ports ; 30cm.
Italian text, English notes and preliminaries. — '[A collection of interviews] prepared to complement "Conversazioni", a series of ten BBC television programmes on contemporary Italy, first broadcast on BBC-1 between April and June 1977' - cover.
ISBN 0-563-16108-6 Sd : £1.80
(B77-27824)

458'.6'421 — Italian language. Reading books

La **ragazza** di Bube / [di] Carlo Cassola ; [abbreviata e semplificata]. — Copenaghen [i.e. Copenhagen] : Grafisk Forlag ; Londra [i.e. London] : J. Murray [etc.], 1977. — 95p : ill, map ; 19cm. — (Easy readers = Facili letture : C)
This adaptation originally published: Copenhagen : Grafisk Forlag, 1976.
ISBN 0-7195-3365-1 Pbk : Unpriced
(B77-25571)

Ti ho sposato per allegria : commedia in tre atti / [per] Natalia Ginzburg ; [semplificata ad uso]. — Copenaghen [i.e. Copenhagen] : Grafisk Forlag ; Londra [i.e. London] : J. Murray [etc.], 1976. — 48p : ill ; 19cm. — (Easy readers = Facili letture : A)
This adaptation originally published: Kopenhagen : Grafisk Forlag, 1974.
ISBN 0-7195-3305-8 Pbk : £0.70
(B77-15819)

Vino e pane / [di] Ignazio Silone ; [abbreviata e semplificata]. — Copenaghen [i.e. Copenhagen] : Grafisk Forlag ; Londra [i.e. London] : J. Murray [etc.], 1976. — 96p : ill, map ; 19cm. — (Easy readers = Facili letture : B)
This adaptation originally published: Copenhagen : Grafisk Forlag, 1974.
ISBN 0-7195-3418-6 Pbk : £0.80
(B77-17442)

463 — SPANISH LANGUAGE. DICTIONARIES
463'.2'1 — Spanish language. *Spanish-English, English-Spanish dictionaries*
Castillo, Carlos. The University of Chicago Spanish dictionary : a new concise Spanish-English and English-Spanish dictionary of words and phrases basic to the written and spoken language of today, plus a list of 1,000 Spanish idioms and sayings with variants and English equivalents / compiled by Carlos Castillo & Otto F. Bond, with the assistance of Barbara M. Garcia. — 3rd ed., revised and enlarged / revised by D. Lincoln Canfield. — Chicago ; London : University of Chicago Press, 1977. — vi,488p ; 23cm.
Second title page in Spanish. — Previous ed.: 1972.
ISBN 0-226-09673-4 : £6.75
ISBN 0-226-09674-2 Pbk : £2.00
(B77-30200)

Laurence Urdang Associates. Hamlyn Spanish dictionary : Spanish-English, English-Spanish / [compiled by Laurence Urdang Associates]. — London [etc.] : Hamlyn, 1976. — [11],305p ; 14cm.
ISBN 0-600-36565-4 Pbk : £0.75
(B77-12996)

465 — SPANISH LANGUAGE. GRAMMAR
465 — Spanish language. Words. Order
Teskey, Patrick David. Theme and rheme in Spanish and English / [by] Patrick David Teskey. — Coleraine (Coleraine, [Co. Derry]) : Board of Studies in Linguistics, New University of Ulster, 1976. — [4],56 leaves ; 21cm. — (Occasional papers in linguistics and language learning ; no.1 ISSN 0308-2075)
Bibl.: leaves 53-56.
ISBN 0-901229-11-3 Sd : £0.50
(B77-00176)

468 — SPANISH LANGUAGE USAGE
468 — Spanish language. *Exercises, worked examples*
Roberts, Margaret Christine Maud. Eso es / [by Joaquin] Masoliver, [Ulla] Hakonson, [Hans L.] Beeck ; adapted [and translated from the Swedish] by M.C.M. Roberts [and Sonia Rouve]. — London : Longman.
Translation and adaptation of: 'Eso es'. Stockholm : Almqvist och Wiksell, 1973-.
2. Workbook / illustrated by George Bessis. — 1977. — [1],65p : ill, maps ; 26cm.
ISBN 0-582-22252-4 Sd : Unpriced
(B77-31864)

468 — Spanish language. *Exercises, worked examples. For Caribbean students. Secondary school texts*
Colibri readers / [edited by] Dorothy Figueroa. — [Aylesbury] : Ginn [etc.].
Book 1 : La familia Gómez / drawings by Val Biro. — 1977. — [1],97p : ill, map ; 23cm.
Spanish text, English foreword.
ISBN 0-602-22317-2 Sd : Unpriced
(B77-31151)

468 — Spanish language. *Secondary school texts*
Schmitt, Conrad J. Español, a descubrirlo / [por] Conrad J. Schmitt, Protase E. Woodford, Randall G. Marshall. — 4th ed. — New York ; London [etc.] : McGraw-Hill, 1977. — xiv, 338p,[32]p of plates : ill(chiefly col), facsims, col maps ; 25cm.
Spanish text, English introductory material. — Previous ed.: New York : McGraw-Hill, 1972. — Index.
ISBN 0-07-055395-5 : £8.10
(B77-24161)

Woodford, Protase E. Español, a sentirlo / [por] Protase E. Woodford, Randall G. Marshall, Conrad J. Schmitt. — 4th ed. — New York ; London [etc.] : McGraw-Hill, 1977. — vi,378p, [16]p of plates : ill(some col), maps(chiefly col), ports ; 25cm.
Spanish text, English introductory material. — Previous ed.: New York : McGraw-Hill, 1972. — Index.
ISBN 0-07-071656-0 : £8.10
(B77-24162)

468 — Spanish language. *Study examples: Signs in Spanish. Questions & answers*
Bawcutt, G J. Spanish sign language : reading comprehension activities / [by] G.J. Bawcutt. — London : Harrap, 1977. — 60p : chiefly ill, facsims, forms ; 21cm.
ISBN 0-245-52993-4 Sd : £1.25
(B77-24881)

468 — Spanish language. Usage. *Exercises, worked examples. Spanish texts*
Hickey, Leo. Usos y estilos del español moderno / [por] Leo Hickey. — London : Harrap, 1977. — 142p : ill, facsims, forms ; 22cm.
ISBN 0-245-52328-6 Pbk : £4.50
(B77-27022)

468'.1 — Spanish language. Vocabulary. *Primary school texts*
Colyer, Penrose. I can read Spanish : my first English-Spanish word book / compiled by Penrose Colyer, Spanish by María Dolores García Moliner ; illustrated by Colin Mier and Wendy Lewis. — [London] ([2 Queen's Drive, W3 0HA]) : Peter Lowe, 1976. — 4-116p : ill(chiefly col) ; 28cm.
ISBN 0-85654-025-0 : £2.75
(B77-05374)

468'.2'421 — Spanish language. Grammar
Noble, Judith. Spanish : a basic course. — 2nd ed. / [by] Judith Noble, Jaime Lacasa. — New York [etc.] ; London : Holt, Rinehart and Winston, 1977. — xvi,462,16p : ill(some col), maps(chiefly col), plan ; 25cm.
Previous ed.: / by Judith Noble, Elizabeth Fouad, Jaime Lacasa. New York : Holt, Rinehart and Winston, 1971. — Index.
ISBN 0-03-089744-0 : £7.50
(B77-26271)

468'.3'421 — Spoken Spanish language. Idioms
Adrienne. El Gimmick Español hablado / por Adrienne ; adapted [i.e. translated] by Catherine Audousset. — London : Hutchinson, 1977. — vi,162p ; 21cm.
English and Spanish text. — Translation of: 'El Gimmick Español hablado'. Paris : Flammarion, 1974.
ISBN 0-09-127151-7 Pbk : £2.50
(B77-26272)

468'.3'42102461 — Spoken Spanish language. *For medicine*
Kelz, Rochelle K. Conversational Spanish for medical personnel : essential expressions, questions and directions for medical personnel to facilitate conversation with Spanish-speaking patients and coworkers / [by] Rochelle K. Kelz. — New York ; London [etc.] : Wiley, 1977. — xiii,313p : ill ; 26cm.
'A Wiley medical publication'. — Index.
ISBN 0-471-02154-7 Pbk : £7.50
(B77-24163)

468'.6'4 — Spanish language. Reading books. *For West Indian students. Secondary school texts*
Moss, Hazel. Escenas antillanas : a Caribbean Spanish reader / [by] Hazel Moss ; illustrated by Lennox Honychurch. — Trinidad : Columbus ; London : University Tutorial Press, 1977. — 112p : ill ; 22cm.
Spanish text, English preface.
ISBN 0-7231-0742-4 Pbk : £0.75
(B77-14199)

468'.6'421 — Spanish language. Reading books
Marcelino pan y vino / [de] José María Sánchez-Silva ; [resumida y simplificada]. — Copenhague [i.e. Copenhagen] : Grafisk Forlag ; Londres [i.e. London] : J. Murray [etc.], 1976. — 48p : ill ; 19cm. — (Easy readers = Lecturas fáciles : A)
This adaptation originally published: Copenhagen : Grafisk Forlag, 1975.
ISBN 0-7195-3355-4 Pbk : £0.70
(B77-17443)

469 — PORTUGUESE LANGUAGE
469'.08 — Portuguese language. *Readings*
Readings in Portuguese linguistics / edited by Jürgen Schmidt-Radefeldt. — Amsterdam [etc.] ; Oxford : North-Holland Publishing Co., 1976. — xiii,479p : ill ; 23cm. — (North-Holland linguistic series ; 22)
Bibl. — Index.
ISBN 0-7204-6203-7 Pbk : £19.32
(B77-04760)

473 — LATIN LANGUAGE. DICTIONARIES
473'.2'1 — Latin language. *Latin-English dictionaries*
Oxford Latin dictionary. — Oxford : Clarendon Press.
Fasc.6 : Pactus-Qualitercumque / edited by P.G.W. Glare. — 1977. — [4]p,p1281-1536 ; 31cm.
ISBN 0-19-864219-9 Pbk : £12.50 : CIP rev.
(B77-24882)

Smith, *Sir* **William,** *b.1813.* Chambers Murray Latin-English dictionary / by Sir William Smith and Sir John Lockwood. — Edinburgh : W. and R. Chambers ; London : J. Murray, 1976. — [8],817,[6]p ; 21cm.
Originally published: as 'A smaller Latin-English dictionary'. Revised ed. / by J.F. Lockwood. London : J. Murray, 1933.
ISBN 0-550-19004-x : £4.70
ISBN 0-7195-3343-0 (J. Murray) : £4.70
ISBN 0-550-19003-1 Pbk : £2.90
ISBN 0-7195-3323-6 (J. Murray) Pbk : Unpriced
(B77-02244)

477 — LATIN LANGUAGE. OLD, POSTCLASSICAL, VULGAR LATIN
477 — Vulgar Latin language. Usage. Sources of evidence: Terentianus, Claudius. Correspondence
Adams, J N. The vulgar Latin of the letters of Claudius Terentianus (P.Mich.VIII, 467-72) / [by] J.N. Adams. — Manchester : Manchester University Press, 1977. — viii,100p ; 23cm. — (University of Manchester. Faculty of Arts. Publications ; no.23)
Bibl.: p.90-95. — Index.
ISBN 0-7190-1289-9 : £7.50 : CIP rev.
(B77-11767)

478 — LATIN LANGUAGE USAGE
478'.6'421 — Latin language. Reading books
Cambridge Latin course. — Cambridge [etc.] : Cambridge University Press.
Unit 5. Teacher's handbook. — 1977. — viii, 112p : geneal table, map ; 22cm.
Bibl.
ISBN 0-521-08544-6 Pbk : £2.00
(B77-24164)

485 — GREEK LANGUAGE. GRAMMAR
485 — Greek language. Grammar
Abbott, Evelyn. A primer of Greek grammar. Accidence / by Evelyn Abbott and E.D. Mansfield. Syntax / by E.D. Mansfield / with a preface by John Percival. — London : Duckworth, 1977. — 220p ; 21cm.
Facsimile reprint of: 1st ed. London : Rivington, Percival, 1893.
ISBN 0-7156-1257-3 : £5.95
ISBN 0-7156-1258-1 Pbk : £2.25
(B77-23347)

489.3 — MODERN GREEK LANGUAGE
489'.3'8 — Modern Greek language. *Secondary school texts*
Tofallis, Kypros. A textbook of modern Greek : for beginners up to GCE 'O' level / [by] Kypros Tofallis. — London (34 Bush Hill Rd, N21 2DS) : The Greek Institute, 1977. — 148p : ill, ports ; 20cm.
ISBN 0-905313-02-x : £3.00
(B77-30201)

489'.3'802 — Modern Greek language. Translation from English language. *Exercises, worked examples*
Tofallis, Kypros. English-Greek translation / [by] Kypros Tofallis. — 2nd ed. — London (34 Bush Hill Rd, N21 2DS) : Greek Institute, 1976. — 56p ; 20cm.
Cover title. — Previous ed.: published as 'Exercises in English-Greek translation'. London : The author, 1968.
ISBN 0-9500138-9-7 Pbk : £1.20
(B77-07320)

491.1 — INDO-IRANIAN LANGUAGES
491.1'07 — Ethnic minorities. Native languages. Teaching. *Great Britain. Study examples: South Asian languages. Conference proceedings*
The **teaching** of the mother tongue and the Asian community : background papers on seminars, organized by Yuvak Sangh (London) and National Association of Indian Youth. — Southall (46 High St., Southall, Middx) : Scope Communication ; London : Yuvak Sangh (London), 1976. — 16p in various pagings ; 30cm.
Sd : £0.15
(B77-17444)

491.2/4 — INDIC LANGUAGES
491'.2'82421 — Sanskrit language. Grammar
Coulson, Michael. Sanskrit : an introduction to the classical language / by Michael Coulson. — Sevenoaks : Teach Yourself Books, 1976. — xxx,493p ; 18cm. — (Teach yourself books)
With key to exercises in Roman and N¯agar¯i script.
ISBN 0-340-05982-6 Pbk : £2.95
(B77-15820)

491'.419 — Siraiki language. Grammar
Shackle, Christopher. The Siraiki language of Central Pakistan : a reference grammar / [by] C. Shackle. — London : University of London School of Oriental and African Studies, 1976. — [8],198p : maps ; 23cm.
Bibl.: p.187-189.
ISBN 0-7286-0026-9 Pbk : Unpriced
(B77-02245)

491'.42'82421 — Punjabi language. Grammar. *For teaching of English language to Punjabi speaking students*
Gill, David. English and Punjabi grammar & syntax : a comparison / [by David Gill, K.S. Bath]. — [Slough] ([c/o Otto Poling, Northbrook Centre, William Penn School, Penn Rd, Slough, Bucks.]) : National Association for Multiracial Education, 1976. — [8]p ; 30cm.
ISBN 0-9504539-2-7 Sd : Unpriced
(B77-06650)

491'.49 — Nepali language. Grammar
Clark, Thomas Welbourne. Introduction to Nepali : a first-year language course / by T.W. Clark. — Revised ed. / by John Burton-Page. — London : University of London School of Oriental and African Studies, 1977. — xviii, 421p ; 23cm.
Previous ed.: Cambridge : Heffer, 1963.
ISBN 0-7286-0024-2 Pbk : £6.00
(B77-18717)

491.5 — IRANIAN LANGUAGES
491'.5 — Inscriptions in Ancient Iranian languages. *Collections*
Corpus Inscriptionum Iranicarum. — London : Lund Humphries.
Part 2 : Inscriptions of the Seleucid and Parthian periods and of Eastern Iran and Central Asia. Vol.2 : Parthian. Parthian economic documents from Nisa. Plates 2 / by I.M. Diakonoff and V.A. Livshits ; edited by D.N. Mackenzie. — 1977. — [8],3p,p124-330 of plates : chiefly ill ; 32cm.
Spine title: Parthian economic documents from Nisa. — Accompanied by 'Parthian economic documents from Nisa. Texts I pp.1-80' (80p.) for use with 'Plates 1' and 'Plates 2'.
ISBN 0-85331-399-7 : £72.00
(B77-16349)

491.6 — CELTIC LANGUAGES
491.6'2'09417 — Irish language. Policies of government. *Ireland (Republic). Irish texts*
Ó Snodaigh, Pádraig. An bealach Romhainn : léacht a tugadh in Áras an Chonartha faoi bhráid Choiste na Cathrach, Baile Átha Cliath, mí Márta, 1974 / le Pádraig Ó Snodaigh. — Baile Átha Cliath [i.e. Dublin] ([Conradh na Gaeilge, 6 Sráid Fhearchair, Baile Átha Cliath 2]) : Clódhanna Teo., 1974. — [2],14p ; 22cm.
Sd : £0.10
(B77-06651)

491.6'2'5 — Irish language. Grammar
Ó Huallacháin, Colmán. Irish grammar / [by] Colmán Ó Huallacháin, Micheál Ó Murchú. — Coleraine ([Coleraine, Northern Ireland]) : The University of Ulster, 1976. — [2],xxvii,171p, plate : 1 ill ; 30cm. — (New University of Ulster. Irish studies)
Text in Irish and English, English introduction and notes.
Pbk : Unpriced
(B77-24883)

491.6'2'5 — Irish language. Grammar. Theories
Ó Huallacháin, Colmán. Irish grammar / [le] Colmán Ó Huallacháin, Mícheál Ó Murchú. — Coleraine ([Coleraine, Co. Londonderry]) : New University of Ulster, Irish Studies, 1976. — [1], xxvii,171,[1]p : 1 ill ; 30cm.
Sd : £3.00(sold only with 'Irish grammar (morphology)')
(B77-21820)

491.6'2'5 — Irish language. Morphology
Ó Huallacháin, Colmán. Irish grammar (morphology) / [le] Colmán Ó Huallacháin, Mícheál Ó Murchú. — Coleraine ([Coleraine, Co. Londonderry]) : New University of Ulster, Irish Studies, 1977. — [1]p,p171-194 ; 30cm.
Sd : £3.00(sold only with 'Irish grammar')
(B77-21821)

491.6'2'8 — Irish language. *Exercises, worked examples. For Irish speaking students. Primary school texts*
Seal ag obair. — Baile Átha Cliath [i.e. Dublin] : Comhlacht Oideachais na hÉireann.
Leabhar D / [le] Seán Ó Domhnaill. — 1976. — [2],33p : ill ; 19x21cm.
Fill-in book.
Sd : £0.35
(B77-14699)

Leabhar E / [le] Seasamh Ó Tuathail. — 1977. — [2],33p : ill ; 20x21cm.
Sd : £0.38
(B77-31152)

491.6'2'86 — Irish language. Reading books. *For Irish speaking students. Primary school texts*
Ní Mhaoláin, Páraicín. Seal ag súgradh / [le] Páraicín Ní Mhaoláin, Treasa Ní Ailpín ; [Jon Donohoe a mhaisigh an leabhar seo]. — Baile Átha Cliath [i.e. Dublin] : Comhlacht Oideachais na hÉireann : Longman Brún agus Ó Nualláin.
Leabhar 1. — 1977. — [2],17p : col ill ; 21cm.
Sd : £0.38
(B77-14700)

Leabhar 2. — 1977. — [2],17p : col ill ; 21cm.
Sd : £0.38
(B77-14701)

O Conchubhair, Uinsionn. Seal ag L¯eamh / [by] Uinsionn Ó Conchubhair. — Baile Átha Cliath [i.e. Dublin] : Comhlacht Oideachais na hÉireann.
Leabhar F. — 1977. — [2],40,[1]p : col ill ; 22cm.
Sd : £0.66
(B77-27825)

491.6'2'86 — Irish language. Reading books. *For Irish speaking students. Secondary school texts*
Linus, *Bráthair.* Peig : achomaireachtaí agus léirmheas / [le] Br Linus. — Bhaile Átha Cliath [i.e. Dublin] : Folens, [1977]. — 27p ; 22cm.
Sd : £0.56
(B77-23348)

Linus, *Bráthair.* Rotha mór an tsaoil : achomaireachtaí agus léirmheas / [le] Br Linus. — Bhaile Átha Cliath [i.e. Dublin] : Folens, [1977]. — 56p ; 22cm.
Pbk : £0.72
(B77-23349)

491.6'3'09411 — Gaelic language. *Scotland. Gaelic & English texts*
Gaelic in Scotland = Gaidhlig ann an Albainn : a blueprint for official and private initiatives / edited by Derick Thomson = deasaichte le Ruaraidh MacThómais. — Glaschu [i.e. Glasgow] (29 Sràid Bhatairliù, Glaschu G2) : Gairm, 1976. — iv,92p : 1 ill ; 18cm.
English and Gaelic text with Gaelic and English synopses.
ISBN 0-901771-54-6 Pbk : £1.20
(B77-12415)

491.6'3'83421 — Spoken Gaelic language. Comprehension. *Exercises, worked examples*
Listening comprehension passages : Ordinary and Higher Grade Gaelic (learners) / [edited by] Lachlaim Dick & Donnchadh Mac Guaire. — [Inverness] ([Abertarff House, Inverness]) : An Comunn Gàidhealach, 1976. — [6],70p ; 21cm.
Cover title: Earainn eisdeachd. — Gaelic text, English instructions and questions.
ISBN 0-9502727-1-x Pbk : £1.80
(B77-12416)

491.6'6'0715 — Adult education. Curriculum subjects: Welsh language. Teaching. *Wales. Inquiry reports. Welsh-English parallel texts*
Council for the Welsh Language. Dysgu Cymraeg i oedolion = Welsh for adults : adroddiad i'r Gwir Anrhydeddus John Morris Q.C., A.S., Ysgrifennydd Gwladol Cymru = a report to the Right Hon. John Morris Q.C., M.P., Secretary of State for Wales / Cyngor yr Iaith Gymraeg = Council for the Welsh Language. — Cardiff : H.M.S.O., 1976. — viii,63p ; 30cm.

Parallel Welsh and English texts.
ISBN 0-11-790086-9 Pbk : £1.25
(B77-11190)

491.6'6'5 — Welsh language. Verbs. Passive voice. Transformational-generative theories
Awbery, G M. The syntax of Welsh : a transformational study of the passive / [by] G.M. Awbery. — Cambridge [etc.] : Cambridge University Press, 1976. — viii,243p ; 24cm. — (Cambridge studies in linguistics ; [18])
Bibl.: p.238-239. — Index.
ISBN 0-521-21341-x : £8.50
(B77-08346)

491.6'6'7 — Welsh language. Usage of school students. Gwynedd. Lleyn Peninsula. Related to social class. *Reports, surveys. Welsh texts*
Griffith, William Ll. Iaith plant llŷn : astudiaeth mewn ieithyddiaeth gymdeithasol / gan William Ll. Griffith. — Caerdydd [i.e. Cardiff] : Gwasg Prifysgol Cymru, 1976. — 230p : ill, map ; 22cm. — (Ysgrifau ar addysg ; vol.6)
ISBN 0-7083-0633-0 Pbk : £3.00
(B77-04761)

491.6'6'83421 — Spoken Welsh language. Grammar
Jones, Gwen Pritchard. 'Speak Welsh' : an introduction to the Welsh language combining a simple grammar, phrase book and dictionary / by Gwen Pritchard Jones. — Cardiff (41 Lochaber St., Cardiff CF2 3LS) : John Jones Cardiff Ltd, 1977. — 51p : ill ; 22cm.
ISBN 0-902375-04-0 Sd : £0.40
(B77-23350)

Jones, T J Rhys. Living Welsh / [by] T.J. Rhys Jones. — Sevenoaks : Teach Yourself Books, 1977. — 445p ; 18cm. — (Teach yourself books)
With key to the exercises. — Index.
ISBN 0-340-21846-0 Pbk : £1.95
(B77-26273)

491.6'6'86 — Welsh language. Reading books. *For Welsh speaking students. Primary school texts*
Jenkins, Edna. Nel a'r teganau / [gan] Edna Jenkins. — Abertawe [i.e. Swansea] : C. Davies, 1976. — [15]p : chiefly ill(chiefly col) ; 19cm.
ISBN 0-7154-0373-7 Sd : £0.45
(B77-01374)

Jenkins, Edna. Nel yn sâl / [gan] Edna Jenkins. — Abertawe [i.e. Swansea] : C. Davies, 1976. — [19]p : chiefly ill(chiefly col) ; 19cm.
ISBN 0-7154-0376-1 Sd : £0.45
(B77-01375)

Jenkins, Edna. Nel yn siopa / [gan] Edna Jenkins. — Abertawe [i.e. Swansea] : C. Davies, 1976. — [19]p : chiefly ill(chiefly col) ; 19cm.
ISBN 0-7154-0377-x Sd : £0.45
(B77-01376)

Jenkins, Edna. Nel yn syrthio / [gan] Edna Jenkins. — Abertawe [i.e. Swansea] : C. Davies, 1976. — [19]p : chiefly ill(chiefly col) ; 19cm.
ISBN 0-7154-0370-2 Sd : £0.45
(B77-01377)

Jenkins, Edna. Nel yn y dref / [gan] Edna Jenkins. — Abertawe [i.e. Swansea] : C. Davies, 1976. — [19]p : chiefly ill(chiefly col) ; 19cm.
ISBN 0-7154-0375-3 Sd : £0.45
(B77-01378)

Jenkins, Edna. Nel yn y glaw / [gan] Edna Jenkins. — Abertawe [i.e. Swansea] : C. Davies, 1976. — [19]p : chiefly ill(chiefly col) ; 19cm.
ISBN 0-7154-0372-9 Sd : £0.45
(B77-01379)

Jenkins, Edna. Nel yn yr ardd / [gan] Edna Jenkins. — Abertawe [i.e. Swansea] : C. Davies, 1976. — [15]p : chiefly ill(chiefly col) ; 19cm.
ISBN 0-7154-0374-5 Sd : £0.45
(B77-01380)

Jenkins, Edna. Nel yn yr ysgol / [gan] Edna Jenkins. — Abertawe [i.e. Swansea] : C. Davies, 1976. — [19]p : chiefly ill(chiefly col) ; 19cm.
ISBN 0-7154-0378-8 Sd : £0.45
(B77-01381)

Williams, Buddug Medi. Y gwcw / gan Buddug Medi Williams ; arluniwyd gan Bryan Gibbons. — Y Bala : Llyfrau'r Faner, [1977]. — [16]p : ill ; 22cm. — (Cyfres Huw a Mair)
ISBN 0-901695-28-9 Sd : £0.65
(B77-14200)

Williams, Buddug Medi. Y gwdihŵ / gan Buddug Medi Williams ; arluniwyd gan Bryan Gibbons. — Y Bala : Llyfrau'r Faner, [1977]. — [20]p : ill ; 22cm. — (Cyfres Huw a Mair)
ISBN 0-901695-30-0 Sd : £0.65
(B77-14201)

Williams, Buddug Medi. Y Robin goch / gan Buddug Medi Williams ; arluniwyd gan Bryan Gibbons. — Y Bala : Llyfrau'r Faner, [1977]. — [20]p : ill ; 22cm. — (Cyfres Huw a Mair)
ISBN 0-901695-29-7 Sd : £0.65
(B77-14202)

Williams, Buddug Medi. Y wennol / gan Buddug Medi Williams ; arluniwyd gan Bryan Gibbons. — Y Bala : Llyfrau'r Faner, [1977]. — [20]p : ill ; 22cm. — (Cyfres Huw a Mair)
ISBN 0-901695-31-9 Sd : £0.65
(B77-14203)

491.6'6'864 — Welsh language. Reading books. *For non-Welsh speaking students. Primary school texts*

Evans, Leonard. Mic a'r dewin / [gan] Len Evans. — Abertawe [i.e. Swansea] : C. Davies, 1977. — [51]p : ill ; 22cm.
ISBN 0-7154-0423-7 Sd : Unpriced
(B77-24884)

491.6'6'86421 — Welsh language. Reading books. *Primary school texts*

Scarry, Richard. Bore tan nos / ymgynghorwr iaith John Albert Evans ; lluniau gan Richard Scarry. — Caerdydd [i.e. Cardiff] : Gwasg y Dref Wen, 1976. — [22]p : chiefly col ill ; 21cm. — (Scarry, Richard. Geiriau Cymraeg)
ISBN 0-904910-19-9 Pbk : £0.45
(B77-02247)

491.6'6'86421 — Welsh language. Reading books. Special subjects: Agricultural industries. Farms. *Primary school texts*

Scarry, Richard. Ar y fferm / ymgynghorwr iaith John Albert Evans ; lluniau gan Richard Scarry. — Caerdydd [i.e. Cardiff] : Gwasg y Dref Wen, 1976. — [22]p : chiefly col ill ; 21cm. — (Scarry, Richard. Geiriau Cymraeg)
ISBN 0-904910-18-0 Pbk : £0.45
(B77-02246)

491.6'6'86421 — Welsh language. Reading books. Special subjects: Animals. *Primary school texts*

Scarry, Richard. Gyda'r anifeiliaid / ymgynghorwr iaith John Albert Evans ; lluniau gan Richard Scarry. — Caerdydd [i.e. Cardiff] : Gwasg y Dref Wen, 1976. — [22]p : chiefly col ill ; 21cm. — (Scarry, Richard. Geiriau Cymraeg)
ISBN 0-904910-21-0 Pbk : £0.45
(B77-02248)

491.6'6'86421 — Welsh language. Reading books. Special subjects: Homes. *Primary school texts*

Scarry, Richard. Yn y tŷ / ymgynghorwr iaith John Albert Evans ; lluniau gan Richard Scarry. — Caerdydd [i.e. Cardiff] : Gwasg y Dref Wen, 1976. — [22]p : chiefly col ill ; 21cm. — (Scarry, Richard. Geiriau Cymraeg)
ISBN 0-904910-24-5 Pbk : £0.45
(B77-02249)

491.6'6'86421 — Welsh language. Reading books. Special subjects: Vacations. *Primary school texts*

Scarry, Richard. Gwyliau / ymgynghorwr iaith John Albert Evans ; lluniau gan Richard Scarry. — Caerdydd [i.e. Cardiff] : Gwasg y Dref Wen, 1976. — [22]p : chiefly col ill ; 21cm. — (Scarry, Richard. Geiriau Cymraeg)
ISBN 0-904910-20-2 Pbk : £0.45
(B77-02250)

491.6'6'86421 — Welsh language. Reading books. Special subjects: Work. *Primary school texts*

Scarry, Richard. Yn y gwaith / ymgynghorwr iaith John Albert Evans ; lluniau gan Richard Scarry. — Caerdydd [i.e. Cardiff] : Gwasg y Dref Wen, 1976. — [22]p : chiefly col ill ; 21cm. — (Scarry, Richard. Geiriau Cymraeg)
ISBN 0-904910-23-7 Pbk : £0.45
(B77-02251)

491.6'8'82421 — Breton language. Grammar

Delaporte, Raymond. Brezhoneg-buan hag aes : a beginner's course in Breton / adapted from the French by Per Denez by Raymond Delaporte ; preface by Pádraig Í Riain ; illustrations by Nono. — [Cork] : Cork University Press, 1977. — 255p : ill ; 22cm.
Translation and revision of: 'Brezhoneg buan hag aes' / by Per Denez. Paris : S.I.R.S. Omnivox, 1972.
ISBN 0-902561-11-1 Pbk : Unpriced
(B77-33763)

491.7 — RUSSIAN LANGUAGE

491.7'8'2421 — Russian language. Grammar

Frewin, Michael, *b.1931.* Russian / [by] Michael Frewin. — Sevenoaks : Teach Yourself Books, 1977. — xv,425p ; 18cm. — (Teach yourself books)
Index.
ISBN 0-340-21281-0 Pbk : £1.95
(B77-23351)

491.7'8'6421 — Russian language. Reading books

Chuk i Gek / Arkadiĭ Gaĭdar ; [abridged and simplified]. — Copenhagen : Grafisk Forlag ; London : J. Murray [etc.], 1977. — 55p : ill ; 19cm. — (Easy readers = Lëgkoe chtenie : A)
Russian title transliterated. — This adaptation originally published: Copenhagen : Grafisk Forlag, 1972.
ISBN 0-7195-3296-5 Pbk : £0.80
(B77-18718)

Taman' / M. IU. Lermontov ; [abridged and simplified]. — Copenhagen : Grafisk Forlag ; London : J. Murray [etc.], 1976. — 46p : ill ; 19cm. — (Easy readers = Lëgkoe chtenie)
Russian title transliterated.
ISBN 0-7195-3419-4 Pbk : £0.80
(B77-19327)

491.9 — BALTIC AND OTHER INDO-EUROPEAN LANGUAGES

491'.91 — Old Prussian language. *State-of-the-art reviews*

Schmalstieg, William Riegel. Studies in Old Prussian : a critical review of the relevant literature in the field since 1945 / [by] William R. Schmalstieg. — University Park ; London : Pennsylvania State University Press, 1976. — ix,420p ; 24cm.
Index.
ISBN 0-271-01231-5 : £11.00
(B77-30202)

492 — SEMITIC LANGUAGES

492 — Semitic languages. Writing systems, to ca B.C.400

Driver, Godfrey Rolles. Semitic writing : from pictograph to alphabet / by G.R. Driver. — Newly revised ed. / edited by S.A. Hopkins. — London : Oxford University Press for the British Academy, 1976. — xviii,276,[1]p,66p of plates : ill ; 24cm. — (Schweich lectures)
Previous ed.: 1954. — Index.
ISBN 0-19-725917-0 : £12.00
(B77-09664)

492.4 — HEBREW LANGUAGE

492.4'2 — Hebrew language. Semantics

Studies in modern Hebrew syntax and semantics : the transformational-generative approach / editor Peter Cole. — Amsterdam [etc.] ; Oxford : North-Holland Publishing Co., 1976. — xi,285p : ill ; 23cm. — (North-Holland linguistic series ; 32)
Bibl.
ISBN 0-7204-0543-2 Pbk : £15.04
Also classified at 492.4'5
(B77-06652)

492.4'5 — Hebrew language. Syntax

Studies in modern Hebrew syntax and semantics : the transformational-generative approach / editor Peter Cole. — Amsterdam [etc.] ; Oxford : North-Holland Publishing Co., 1976. — xi,285p : ill ; 23cm. — (North-Holland linguistic series ; 32)
Bibl.
ISBN 0-7204-0543-2 Pbk : £15.04
Primary classification 492.4'2
(B77-06652)

492.4'7 — Biblical Hebrew language. Grammar. *For Welsh speaking students*

Jones, Gwilym Henry. Gramadeg Hebraeg y Beibl / [gan] Gwilym H. Jones a Dafydd R. Ap-Thomas. — Caerdydd [i.e. Cardiff] : Gwasg Prifysgol Cymru, 1976. — [2],ix,164p ; 26cm. — (Cyfres Beibl a chrefydd ; 1)
Bibl.: p.vii.
ISBN 0-7083-0632-2 Pbk : £2.00
(B77-03511)

492.7 — ARABIC LANGUAGE

492'.7'17 — Papyri in Arabic. *Textual criticisms*

Abbott, Nabia. Studies in Arabic literary papyri / by Nabia Abbott. — Chicago ; London : University of Chicago Press.
In 3 vols.
3 : Language and literature. — 1972. — xvi, 216p,[10]p of plates(2 fold),leaf of plate : facsims ; 31cm. — (University of Chicago. Oriental Institute. Publications ; vol.77)
Includes Arabic texts. — Bibl.: p.xi-xvi. — Index.
ISBN 0-226-62178-2 : Unpriced
(B77-20211)

492'.7'321 — Arabic language. *Arabic-English dictionaries*

Wehr, Hans. A dictionary of modern written Arabic / [by] Hans Wehr ; edited by J. Milton Cowan. — 3rd ed. — London : Harrap [etc.], 1976. — xvii,1110p ; 17cm.
This ed. originally published: Ithaca, N.Y. : Spoken Language Services, 1971.
ISBN 0-87950-001-8 Pbk : £6.50
(B77-12417)

492'.7'86421 — Arabic language. Reading books

Beeston, Alfred Felix Landon. Samples of Arabic prose in its historical development : (a manual for English-speaking students) / [by] A.F.L. Beeston. — Oxford [etc.] : Oxford University Press for the Board of Management of the James Mew Fund, 1977. — [4],47p ; 26cm.
English text, Arabic examples.
ISBN 0-19-920086-6 Sd : £1.80
(B77-23352)

492.9 — SOUTH ARABIAN LANGUAGES

492'.9 — Harsūsi language. *Harsūsi-English dictionaries*

Johnstone, Thomas Muir. Harsūsi lexicon and English-Harsūsi word-list / by T.M. Johnstone. — London [etc.] : Oxford University Press, 1977. — xxix,181p ; 23cm.
Harsūsi and English text, English introduction. — Bibl.: p.xxvii-xxviii. — Index.
ISBN 0-19-713580-3 : £13.00
(B77-18719)

493 — HAMITIC AND CHAD LANGUAGES

493'.1 — Ancient Egyptian animal necropolises. *Egypt. North Saqqâra. Serapeum of Memphis. Inscriptions. Texts*

Hor of Sebennytos. The archive of Hor / [translated from the Greek and Egyptian] by J.D. Ray. — London : Egypt Exploration Society, 1976. — xv,192p,xxxix leaves of plates : ill, 2 maps ; 32cm. — (Excavations at North Saqqâra : documentary series ; 1) (Texts from excavations ; 2nd memoir ISSN 0307-5125)
Includes photographs of the ostraca from which the translations have been made. — Some leaves printed on both sides. — Index.
ISBN 0-85698-061-7 : £27.00
(B77-11768)

493'.1 — Inscriptions in Old Egyptian, ca B.C.1350-B.C.1090. *Collections*

Ramesside inscriptions : historical and biographical / compiled by K.A. Kitchen. — Oxford : Blackwell.
Egyptian hieroglyphic text, English notes.
2. Fasc.7. — 1976. — [1],353-416p ; 29cm.
Pbk : £1.50
(B77-30203)

493'.7 — Kanakuru language. Grammar

Newman, Paul, *b.1937.* The Kanakuru language / by Paul Newman. — Leeds (Leeds LS2 9JT) : Institute of Modern English Language Studies, University of Leeds ; [Leeds] : West African Linguistic Society, 1974. — x,139p ; 26cm. — (West African language monograph series ; 9 ISSN 0083-8179)
Bibl.: p.139.
ISBN 0-904550-00-1 Pbk : Unpriced
(B77-02947)

493'.72'321 — Hausa language. *Hausa-English dictionaries*

Modern Hausa-English dictionary / compiled by Paul Newman and Roxana ma Newman ; assisted by Ibrahim Yaro Yahaya and Linda Dresel and Centre for the Study of Nigerian Languages, Bayero University College, Kano. — Ibadan ; [Oxford] : Oxford University Press, 1977. — xiii,153p ; 19cm.
Second title page in Hausa.
ISBN 0-19-575303-8 Pbk : £3.50
(B77-33190)

494.1/3 — ALTAIC LANGUAGES

494'.35'82421 — Turkish language. Grammar

Underhill, Robert. Turkish grammar / [by] Robert Underhill. — Cambridge, Mass. ; London : M.I.T. Press, 1976. — xix,474p ; 24cm.
Index.
ISBN 0-262-21006-1 : £15.00
(B77-04762)

494.4/5 — URALIC LANGUAGES

494'.511'83421 — Spoken Hungarian language. Grammar

Whitney, Arthur Harold. Colloquial Hungarian / by Arthur H. Whitney ; illustrated by the author. — 2nd ed. — London [etc.] : Routledge and Kegan Paul, 1977. — xiii,264p : ill ; 19cm. — (Trubner's colloquial manuals)
This ed. originally published: 1950.
ISBN 0-7100-8550-8 Pbk : £2.50
(B77-05375)

495.6 — JAPANESE LANGUAGE
495.6'8'02 — Japanese language. Translations from English language. *Algorithms*
Jelínek, Jiří. Classical Japanese-English grammar dictionary / [by] Jiří Jelínek. — [Sheffield] ([Sheffield S10 2TN]) : University of Sheffield, Centre of Japanese Studies, 1976. — [1],v,59 leaves ; 30cm. — (University of Sheffield. Centre of Japanese studies. Scientific and technical Japanese series ; 003)
Fold. sheet as insert. — Tab indexed.
ISBN 0-904787-03-6 Sp : £3.50
(B77-06030)

495.9 — THAI, AND OTHER SOUTHEAST ASIAN LANGUAGES
495.9'2'283421 — Spoken Vietnamese language. *Phrase books*
Nguyen-dinh-Hoa. Vietnamese phrase book / by Nguyen-dinh-Hoa. — Rutland, Vt [etc.] : Tuttle ; London : Prentice-Hall, 1976. — [9], 109p : ill ; 13x19cm.
Cover title: Hoa's Vietnamese phrase book.
ISBN 0-8048-1196-2 Pbk : £1.75
(B77-01382)

496 — AFRICAN LANGUAGES
Gregersen, Edgar A. Language in Africa : an introductory survey / [by] Edgar A. Gregersen. — New York [etc.] ; London : Gordon and Breach, 1977. — xvii,237p : ill, maps, ports ; 24cm. — (Library of anthropology)
Bibl.: p.215-226. — Index.
ISBN 0-677-04380-5 : £13.00
(B77-16350)

496 — Sub-Saharan languages. Syntax
Welmers, Wm E. African language structures / [by] Wm E. Welmers. — Berkeley [etc.] ; London : University of California Press, 1973. — xi,488p ; 26cm.
Bibl.: p.478-484. — Index.
ISBN 0-520-02210-6 : £15.00
(B77-16351)

497 — NORTH AMERICAN INDIAN LANGUAGES
497 — Languages of Indians of West Indies
Taylor, Douglas. Languages of the West Indies / [by] Douglas Taylor. — Baltimore ; London : Johns Hopkins University Press, 1977. — xix, 278,[1]p ; 24cm. — (Johns Hopkins studies in Atlantic history and culture)
Bibl.: p.270-278.
ISBN 0-8018-1729-3 : £12.00
Also classified at 417'.2
(B77-33191)

497'.3 — Puget Salish language. *Puget Salish-English dictionaries*
Hess, Thom. Dictionary of Puget Salish / [by] Thom Hess. — Seattle ; London : University of Washington Press, 1976. — xvii,771p : map ; 29cm.
Bibl.: p.771. — Index.
ISBN 0-295-95436-1 : £12.00
(B77-07321)

497'.4 — Maya hieroglyphs. Decipherment
Kelley, David Humiston. Deciphering the Maya script / [by] David Humiston Kelley. — Austin ; London : University of Texas Press, 1976. — xvii,334p(2 fold),[9]fold leaves of plates,[10]fold p of plates : ill, facsims ; 31cm.
Bibl.: p.299-316. — Index.
ISBN 0-292-71504-8 : £20.60
(B77-12997)

497'.4 — Uto-Aztecan languages. Grammar
Langacker, Ronald Wayne. Non-distinct arguments in Uto-Aztecan / by Ronald W. Langacker. — Berkeley [etc.] ; London : University of California Press, 1976. — xiii, 241p : ill ; 26cm. — (University of California. University of California publications in linguistics ; vol.82)
Bibl.: p.205-241.
ISBN 0-520-09539-1 Pbk : Unpriced
(B77-02948)

499.1 — NONAUSTRONESIAN LANGUAGES OF OCEANIA
499'.15 — Yidin language. Grammar
Dixon, Robert Malcolm Ward. A grammar of Yidin / [by] R.M.W. Dixon. — Cambridge [etc.] : Cambridge University Press, 1977. — xxiii,563p,4p of plates : ill, map, ports ; 24cm. — (Cambridge studies in linguistics ; [19])
Bibl.: p.540-545. — Index.
ISBN 0-521-21462-9 : £24.00
(B77-28578)

499.2 — MALAYAN LANGUAGES
499'.221 — Bahasa Malaysia language. *Bahasa Malaysia-English, English-Bahasa Malaysia dictionaries*
Abdul Rahman Bin Yusop. Collins gem dictionary, Bahasa Malaysia-English, English-Bahasa Malaysia / [by] Abdul Rahman bin Yusop. — Revised ed. — London [etc.] : Collins, 1976. — xxiv,614p ; 12cm.
Cover title: Collins gem Malay-English, English-Malay dictionary. — This ed. originally published: as 'Collins Malay gem dictionary'. 1975.
ISBN 0-00-458660-3 : £0.75
(B77-01383)

499.4 — POLYNESIAN LANGUAGES
499'.4 — Maori language. *Exercises, worked examples. For New Zealand students. School texts*
Paora, Roka. Learn Maori with Parchau and Sharon / [by] Roka Paora. — Christchurch [N.Z.] [etc.] ; London : Whitcoulls.
Book 3 / illustrated by Cathie Penetito. — 1976. — 32p : ill, forms ; 24cm.
ISBN 0-7233-0475-0 Sd : £1.46
(B77-04763)

499'.4 — Maori language. Grammar
Harawira, K T. Teach yourself Maori / by K.T. Harawira. — 2nd ed. — Wellington, N.Z. [etc.] ; London : A.H. and A.W. Reed, 1974. — 121p ; 19cm. — (Reed Maori library)
This ed. originally published: Wellington, N.Z. : A.H. and A.W. Reed, 1954.
ISBN 0-589-00907-9 Pbk : £1.75
(B77-00738)

499.9 — MINOR LANGUAGES (INCLUDING ARTIFICIAL LANGUAGES)
499'.95 — Inscriptions in Sumerian. *Collections*
British Museum. Cuneiform texts from Babylonian tablets in the British Museum. — London : British Museum Publications Ltd.
Part 52 : Old Babylonian letters / [edited] by C.B.E. Walker. — 1976. — [14]p,61p of plates : of facsims ; 35cm.
ISBN 0-7141-1091-4 : £7.00
(B77-01384)

499'.95 — Museums. *Oxfordshire. Oxford. Ashmolean Museum. Stock: Inscriptions in Sumerian*
Sumerian literary texts in the Ashmolean Museum / [compiled] by Oliver R. Gurney and Samuel Noah Kramer. — Oxford : Clarendon Press, 1976. — vii,113p,ii p of plates : ill ; 31cm. — (Oxford editions of cuneiform texts ; vol.5 ISSN 0309-0701)
ISBN 0-19-815450-x Pbk : £10.00
(B77-03512)

499'.992 — Esperanto language. *Esperanto texts*
Goodheir, Albert. Lingvo kaj logiko / Albert Goodheir. — Glasgow (16 Woodlands Drive, Coatbridge, [Lanarkshire] ML5 1LE) : Eldonejo Kardo, 1977. — 20,[1]p ; 19cm.
ISBN 0-905149-03-3 Sd : £0.30
(B77-08347)

499'.992'83421 — Spoken Esperanto language. *Exercises, worked examples*
Wells, John Christopher. Jen nia mondo : an introductory series of lessons in Esperanto, the living language which aims to solve the world's language problem by becoming a second language, neutral and simple, for all mankind / [by] J.C. Wells and others. — [London] ([140 Holland Park Ave., W11 4UF]) : Group Five, 1974. — [6],56p : ill ; 21cm.
Bibl.: p.56.
ISBN 0-902756-10-9 Sp : £0.75
(B77-08348)

500 — SCIENCE
Great world encyclopedia of science / [editor in chief Michael W. Dempsey]. — Maidenhead : Sampson Low, 1977. — 280p : ill(some col), maps(some col), ports(1 col) ; 31cm.
Jacket title: the Sampson Low great world encyclopedia of science. — Index.
ISBN 0-562-00042-9 : £6.50
(B77-12998)

Hoyle, *Sir* Fred. Ten faces of the universe / [by] Fred Hoyle. — London : Heinemann, 1977. — xi,207p : ill, charts, maps, ports ; 24cm.
Bibl. — Index.
ISBN 0-435-54427-6 : £4.80
(B77-27023)

McGlashan, Alan. Gravity and levity / by Alan McGlashan. — London : Chatto and Windus, 1976. — 140p ; 21cm.
ISBN 0-7011-2186-6 : £3.50
(B77-15254)

500 — Science. *For Caribbean students. Secondary school texts*
Integrated science for Caribbean schools / [by] Florence Commissiong ... [et al.] ; foreword by D.H. Irvine. — Kingston [Jamaica] ; London : Heinemann Educational.
In 3 vols.
Book 2. — 1976. — [10],147p : ill(chiefly col), col map, col port ; 24cm.
Index.
ISBN 0-435-57580-5 Pbk : £2.00
(B77-02252)

500 — Science. *For Irish students. Secondary school texts*
Collins, Kevin. Intermediate Certificate science / [by] Kevin Collins. — Dublin : Helicon, 1977. — iv,92p ; 21cm. — (Study assessment series)
Sd : £1.10
(B77-16851)

Henly, Randal L. Investigating science in school / by Randal L. Henly, Anthony J. Fox, Danielle Mooney. — Dublin : Folens.
In 2 vols.
Book 1. — [1977]. — 208p : ill, map, ports ; 25cm. — (Intermediate Certificate)
Index.
Pbk : £1.80
(B77-19328)

500 — Science. *For Nigerian students. Primary school texts*
Nicholson, J. Science step by step / [by] J. Nicholson, M. Okoye ; project adviser E.A. Yoloye. — London [etc.] : Macmillan. — (The Macmillan primary science project)
1 : Teachers' book. — 1976. — vi,91p : ill ; 22cm.
ISBN 0-333-19724-0 Sd : £0.94
(B77-18720)

500 — Science. *Juvenile literature*
Houwink, Roelof. Sizing up science / [by] R. Houwink. — London : Beaver Books, 1977. — 3-139p : ill, maps ; 20cm.
Originally published: London : J. Murray, 1975. — Bibl.: p.136-137. — Index.
ISBN 0-600-38211-7 Pbk : £0.55
(B77-30204)

Laithwaite, Eric Roberts. Why does a glow-worm glow? / [by] Eric Laithwaite ; illustrated by Mike Jackson. — London [etc.] : Beaver Books, 1977. — 93p : ill ; 20cm.
ISBN 0-600-33128-8 Pbk : £0.45
(B77-33192)

Ward Lock's children's encyclopedia of science / edited by John Paton ; designed and illustrated by John Marshall. — London : Ward Lock, 1977. — 3-62p : ill(chiefly col), col ports ; 33cm.
Index.
ISBN 0-7063-5337-4 : £2.50
(B77-33764)

500 — Science. *Middle school texts*
Kincaid, Doug. Science in a topic / [by] Doug Kincaid and Peter S. Coles. — London : Hulton.
Food / illustrated by Chris Hoggett. — 1977. — 64p : ill(some col), port ; 25cm.
ISBN 0-7175-0769-6 Pbk : £1.50
Also classified at 600
(B77-22532)

Summerfield, John. Nelson science 11-13 / [by] John Summerfield. — Sunbury-on-Thames [etc.] : Nelson.
Stage 1. — 1976. — 80p : ill(chiefly col) ; 25cm.
ISBN 0-17-438311-8 Pbk : £1.10
(B77-04764)

Stage 1. Worksheets. — 1976. — [74]p : ill ; 28cm.
ISBN 0-17-438312-6 Sd : £7.00
(B77-04765)

500 — Science. *Primary school texts*
Hampson, Brian Lloyd. Science from the beginning / [by] B.L. Hampson and K.C. Evans. — New ed. — Edinburgh : Oliver and Boyd.
Pupils' book 1. — 1976. — 79p : ill(some col) ; 25cm.
Previous ed.: 1960.
ISBN 0-05-002907-x Sd : £0.90
(B77-06031)

Pupils' book 2. — 1977. — 79p : ill(chiefly col) ; 25cm.
Previous ed.: 1961.
ISBN 0-05-002908-8 Sd : £0.90
(B77-06032)

Pupils' book 3. — 1977. — 79p : ill(chiefly col) ; 25cm.
Previous ed.: 1962.
ISBN 0-05-002909-6 Sd : £0.90
(B77-19329)

Pupils' book 4. — 1977. — 79p : ill(chiefly col) ; 25cm.
Previous ed.: 1966.
ISBN 0-05-002910-x Sd : £0.90
(B77-29372)

James, Albert. Active science / [by] Albert James. — Huddersfield : Schofield and Sims.
1 / illustrated by David Leek. — 1977. — 79p : ill(chiefly col) ; 26cm.
Index.
ISBN 0-7217-3543-6 Pbk : £0.85
(B77-24885)

1. Teacher's notes. — 1977. — [2],16,[1]p : ill ; 22cm.
ISBN 0-7217-3547-9 Sd : £0.35
(B77-24886)

Parker, Sheila. Sciencewise / [by] Sheila Parker and Alan Ward. — [Sunbury-on-Thames] : Nelson.
2 / [illustrated by Rowan Barnes-Murphy]. — 1977. — [1],32p : ill(chiefly col) ; 28cm.
ISBN 0-17-423013-3 Sd : £0.70
(B77-19330)

3 / [illustrated by Colin Mier]. — 1977. — [1], 32p : ill(chiefly col) ; 28cm.
ISBN 0-17-423015-x Sd : £0.70
(B77-19331)

Parker, Sheila. Sciencewise / [by] Sheila Parker and Alan Ward. — [Sunbury-on-Thames] : [Nelson].
3. Teachers' book / [illustrated by Colin Mier]. — [1977]. — [4],32,[2]p : ill(chiefly col) ; 28cm.
Bibl.: (1p.).
ISBN 0-17-423016-8 Sd : £1.00
(B77-19332)

500 — Science. *Primary school texts. Cards*
Nuffield Combined Science Continuation Project.
Nuffield combined science themes for the middle years / [Nuffield Combined Science Continuation Project] ; general editor C.D. Bingham. — [Harlow] : Longman for the Nuffield Foundation.
Colour / authors of this theme, Peter Coles and Doug Kincaid. — 1977. — 1v. : ill(some col) ; 30cm.
'Teachers' notes' (booklet; 10p.), 4 copies each of 4 study cards ([8] sides), 2 copies each of 16 activity cards ([32] sides). — Bibl.: p.9 (Teacher's notes).
ISBN 0-582-04572-x : £8.95
(B77-16852)

Out of doors / contributors to this theme, Betty Fitzgerald ... [et al.]. — 1977. — 1v. : ill(some col) ; 30cm.
'Teachers' notes' (booklet; 12p.), 4 copies each of 4 study cards ([8] sides), 2 copies each of 16 activity cards ([32] sides). — Bibl.: p.11-12 (Teachers' notes).
ISBN 0-582-04573-8 : £8.95
(B77-16853)

500 — Science. *Primary school texts. Irish texts*
Hampson, Brian Lloyd. An eolaíocht ón tús / [le] B.L. Hampson, K.C. Evans. — Baile Átha Cliath [i.e. Dublin] ([Oriel House, Beggar's Bush, Dublin 4]) : Oifig an tSoláthair.
Leabhar an dalta 1 / Livín Ó Murchú a d'aistrigh ; C.S. MacDonald a léirigh. — 1976. — 79p : ill(chiefly col) ; 24cm.
Translation of: 'Science from the beginning. Pupil's book 1'. Edinburgh : Oliver and Boyd, 1960.
ISBN 0-905621-09-3 Sd : £0.77
(B77-04117)

500 — Science. *Secondary school texts*
Combined science worksheets / [by] S.M. Arkless ... [et al.]. — Exeter : Wheaton.
Teacher's guide. — 1976. — [3],91p : ill ; 21cm.
ISBN 0-08-019888-0 Pbk : £1.00
(B77-08985)

Hanson, Edward Latham. Introducing science / [by] E.L. Hanson. — [Amersham] : Hulton.
Book 1. — [1976]. — 160p : ill(some col), chart, maps, ports ; 26cm.
Cover title. — Index.
ISBN 0-7175-0668-1 Pbk : £2.00
(B77-02949)

Windridge, Charles. General science / by Charles Windridge ; edited by Patrick J. Kenway ; illustrated by Barry Davies. — 3rd (revised) ed. — Huddersfield : Schofield and Sims.
In 5 vols.
Book 1. — 1976. — 88p : ill, ports ; 25cm.
With answers to selected exercises. — Previous ed.: 1969. — Index.
ISBN 0-7217-3556-8 Pbk : £1.25
ISBN 0-7217-3551-7 : £0.95(non-net)
(B77-09665)

Book 2. — 1976. — 88p : ill, port ; 25cm.
With answers to selected exercises. — Previous ed.: 1969. — Index.
ISBN 0-7217-3557-6 Pbk : £1.25
ISBN 0-7217-3552-5 : £0.95(non-net)
(B77-09666)

Book 3. — 1977. — 88p : ill, maps, ports ; 25cm.
With answers to numerical exercises. — Previous ed.: 1969. — Index.
ISBN 0-7217-3558-4 Pbk : £1.25
ISBN 0-7217-3553-3 : £0.95(non-net)
(B77-15821)

Book 4. — 1977. — 88p,plate : ill(incl 1 col), maps, ports ; 25cm.
With answers to numerical exercises. — Previous ed.: 1969. — Index.
ISBN 0-7217-3559-2 Pbk : £0.95
ISBN 0-7217-3554-1 Unpriced : (non-net)
(B77-30205)

Wreake Valley School. *Science Department.*
Integrated science / Wreake Valley School Science Department ; general editors Dirk Tinbergen and Phil Thorburn ; authors Dave Barlex ... [et al.]. — London : Edward Arnold.
Book 1A. — 1976. — vi,106p : ill, map ; 25cm.
ISBN 0-7131-0103-2 Pbk : £1.50
(B77-01385)

Book 2. — 1976. — vii,104p : ill, maps ; 25cm.
ISBN 0-7131-0011-7 Pbk : £1.75
(B77-01386)

Book 3. — 1976. — vii,136p : ill ; 25cm.
ISBN 0-7131-0043-5 Pbk : £2.25
(B77-08349)

500.2 — Physical sciences
Barnhill, Maurice Victor. Physical science with modern applications / [by] Maurice V. Barnhill III. — Philadelphia ; London [etc.] : Saunders.
Student's guide. — 1976. — vi,212p : ill ; 26cm. — (Saunders golden sunburst series)
With answers.
ISBN 0-7216-1567-8 Pbk : £4.50
(B77-01387)

Marion, Jerry Baskerville. Physical science in the modern world / [by] Jerry B. Marion. — New York ; London : Academic Press, 1974. — xv,717p : ill,charts, maps, ports ; 24cm.
With answers to odd-numbered numerical exercises. — Text on lining papers. — Bibl. — Index.
ISBN 0-12-472260-1 : Unpriced
(B77-19333)

Merken, Melvin. Physical science with modern applications / [by] Melvin Merken. — Philadelphia ; London [etc.] : Saunders, 1976. — xv,699p,plate : ill(some col), maps(some col), ports ; 27cm. — (Saunders golden sunburst series)
Text on lining papers. — With answers to selected exercises. — Bibl. — Index.
ISBN 0-7216-6273-0 : £11.75
(B77-01388)

Monroe, James. Physical science : an inquiry approach / [by] James Monroe, Bonnie Jackson. — San Francisco [etc.] ; London : Harper and Row, 1977. — xvii,605p : ill, facsim, maps, ports ; 24cm.
With answers. — Index.
ISBN 0-06-384225-4 : £11.20
(B77-30206)

Turk, Jonathan. Physical science : with environmental and other practical applications / [by] Jonathan Turk, Amos Turk. — Philadelphia ; London [etc.] : Saunders, 1977. — xii,595p,xii p of plates : ill(some col), charts, maps ; 28cm. — (Saunders golden sunburst series)
With selected answers. — Text on lining paper. — Bibl. — Index.
ISBN 0-7216-8929-9 : £13.00
(B77-21081)

500.2 — Physical sciences. *For East African students. Secondary school texts*
Johnson, Harvey. Energy and matter : an introduction to physical science / [by] Harvey Johnson ; photographs John Clifford. — London : Edward Arnold, 1977. — 180p : ill ; 25cm.
With answers. — Index.
ISBN 0-7131-0066-4 Pbk : £1.80
(B77-22533)

Usher, N. Physical science : an introductory course / [by] N. Usher, D. Brook and D. Parker. — London : Longman, 1977. — [2], 174p : ill ; 25cm.
Index.
ISBN 0-582-60676-4 Pbk : £1.50
(B77-33765)

500.2 — Physical sciences. *Secondary school texts*
Mee, Arthur James. Certificate physical science / [by] A.J. Mee and A.C.E. Jarvis. — Singapore ; London [etc.] : Heinemann Educational.
Book 1 : Theories and models. — 1976. — x, 242p : ill, facsim, ports ; 19x25cm.
With answers. — Index.
ISBN 0-435-57581-3 Pbk : £1.80
(B77-24887)

Book 2 : Science applies its theories. — 1977. — vi,170p : ill ; 19x25cm.
With answers. — Index.
ISBN 0-435-57582-1 Pbk : £1.50
(B77-24888)

500.2'03 — Physical sciences. *Dictionaries*
A **dictionary** of physical sciences / edited by John Daintith. — London [etc.] : Macmillan, 1976. — [5],333p : ill ; 22cm.
ISBN 0-333-19434-9 : £5.95
(B77-10345)

500.2'05 — Physical sciences. Conferences. *Reports, surveys. Serials*
Conference reports, physical and chemical sciences. — London : Applied Science Publishers.
Vol.1, [no.1]- ; 1977-. — 1977-. — 24cm.
Quarterly. — [1],83p. in 1st issue. — Index.
Pbk : £16.00(yearly)
ISSN 0309-5894
Also classified at 660'.05
(B77-15822)

500.2'09 — Physical sciences. *History. Serials*
Historical studies in the physical sciences. — Princeton ; London : Princeton University Press.
7th annual vol. / Russell McCormmach, editor. — 1976. — xxxv,489p : ill, facsims, port ; 24cm.
ISBN 0-691-08169-7 : £19.80
(B77-02253)

Historical studies in the physical sciences. — Baltimore ; London : Johns Hopkins University Press.
8th annual vol. / Russell McCormmach and Lewis Pyenson, editors. — 1977. — xi,300p : ill, ports ; 24cm.
ISBN 0-8018-1907-5 : £13.15
(B77-30207)

500.5 — Space sciences. *Juvenile literature*
Highland, Harold Joseph. The how and why wonder book of planets and interplanetary travel / written by Harold J. Highland ; illustrated by Denny McMains ; edited under the supervision of Paul E. Blackwood. — Revised ed. / revised by the London Planetarium. — London : Transworld, 1976. — 48p : ill(some col), charts(some col), ports ; 28cm.
Previous ed.: 1965.
ISBN 0-552-86507-9 Pbk : £0.45
(B77-00739)

500.5 — Space sciences. *Secondary school texts*
Stoneman, Colin Frank. Space biology / [by] C.F. Stoneman. — Harmondsworth : Kestrel Books, 1976. — 94p : ill, facsims, map, ports ; 23cm.
Originally published: Harmondsworth : Penguin, 1972. — Bibl.: p.90-92. — Index.
ISBN 0-7226-5292-5 : £2.75
(B77-06033)

500.5'03 — Space sciences. *Encyclopaedias*
The **illustrated** encyclopedia of astronomy and space / editor Ian Ridpath. — London [etc.] : Macmillan, 1976. — 240p,[8]p of plates : ill(some col), ports ; 28cm.
Spine title: Encyclopedia of astronomy and space. — Index.
ISBN 0-333-21365-3 : £7.95
Primary classification 520'.3
(B77-03521)

500.9 — Natural history. *Poems. Juvenile literature*
Berenstain, Stan. The bears' nature guide : almost everything small bears and kids need to know about - the animals, the plants, the earth itself, with actual facts about frogs, possums, birds, fish, trees, rocks, ladybirds, earthquakes - and lots more / by Stan and Jan Berenstain. — London [etc.] : Collins, 1977. — 64p : col ill ; 29cm. — (Bear facts library)
Col. ill. on lining papers. — Originally published: New York : Random House, 1975.
ISBN 0-00-183712-5 : £2.25
(B77-18721)

500.9'025'41 — Nature trails. *Great Britain. Directories*
Britain, nature trails / [British Tourist Authority]. — London : B.T.A.
1977. — 1976. — [3],83p : map ; 21cm. — (British Tourist Authority. Information sheets ; no. 317/77/14)
English text, French, German, Dutch, Italian and Spanish introduction and key.
ISBN 0-85630-104-3 Sd : £0.35
(B77-08986)

500.9'028 — Natural history. Use of magnifying glasses
Headstrom, Richard. Adventures with a hand lens / [by] Richard Headstrom ; illustrated by the author. — Revised [ed.]. — New York : Dover Publications [etc.] ; London : Constable, 1976. — 220p : ill ; 20cm.
Previous ed.: Philadelphia : Lippincott, 1962.
ISBN 0-486-23330-8 Pbk : £1.80
(B77-13622)

500.9'074 — Natural history museums. *Juvenile literature*
Facklam, Margery. Frozen snakes and dinosaur bones : exploring a natural history museum / [by] Margery Facklam. — New York ; London : Harcourt Brace Jovanovich, 1976. — viii,114p : ill ; 24cm.
Bibl.: p.109-110. — Index.
ISBN 0-15-230275-1 : £3.25
(B77-16352)

500.9'162 — Underwater sciences. *Reviews of research*
Progress in underwater science : report of the Underwater Association. — London [etc.] (Estover Rd, Plymouth, Devon) : Pentech Press [etc.].
Vol.2 (new series) : Proceedings of the 10th Symposium of the Underwater Association, at the British Museum (Natural History), March 26-27th, 1976 / edited by K. Hiscock, A.D. Baume. — 1977. — vii,134p : ill, map ; 24cm.
Continues: Underwater Association report. — Bibl.
ISBN 0-7273-1605-2 : £7.50
(B77-10796)

500.9'2'4 — Natural history. Frohawk, Frederick William. *Great Britain. Biographies*
Bolingbroke, Valezina. Frederick William Frohawk : a memoir / by his daughter Valezina Bolingbroke. — Faringdon : Classey, 1977. — [2],16p : ports ; 21cm.
ISBN 0-900848-98-7 Sd : £1.00
(B77-29373)

500.9'2'4 — Natural history. Grey Owl. *Canada. Biographies*
Dickson, Lovat. Wilderness man : the strange story of Grey Owl / [by] Lovat Dickson. — London : Abacus, 1976. — [8],279p,[16]p of plates : ill, 2 maps, ports ; 20cm.
Originally published: Toronto : Macmillan, 1973 ; London : Macmillan, 1974. — Bibl.: p.269-272. — Index.
ISBN 0-349-10764-5 Pbk : £1.50
(B77-07322)

500'.92'4 — Natural history. Waterton, Charles. *Biography*
Phelps, Gilbert. Squire Waterton / by Gilbert Phelps. — Wakefield : EP Publishing, 1976. — viii,167p : ill, coat of arms, facsim, ports ; 21cm.
Bibl.: p.165-167.
ISBN 0-7158-1196-7 : £4.25
(B77-25572)

500.9'41 — Natural history. *Great Britain. Highland regions*
Burton, Robert, *b.1941.* Exploring hills and moors / by Robert Burton. — Wakefield : EP Publishing, 1976. — 116p : ill, charts, maps ; 21cm. — (Countryside leisure)
ISBN 0-7158-0468-5 : £3.25
(B77-25573)

500.941 — Natural history. *Great Britain. Wetlands*
Whitlock, Ralph. Exploring rivers, lakes and canals / by Ralph Whitlock. — Wakefield : EP Publishing, 1976. — 115p : ill, chart, maps ; 21cm. — (Countryside leisure)
ISBN 0-7158-0467-7 : £3.25
(B77-24889)

500.9'4114 — Natural history. *Scotland. Hebrides*
Knowlton, Derrick. The naturalist in the Hebrides / [by] Derrick Knowlton. — Newton Abbot [etc.] : David and Charles, 1977. — 183p : ill, maps ; 23cm. — (The regional naturalist)
Bibl.: p.168-175. — Index.
ISBN 0-7153-7446-x : £5.95
(B77-24890)

500.9'413'1 — Natural history. *Scotland. Forth River region. Periodicals*
The **Forth** naturalist & historian. — Stirling ([c/o D.M. Dickie, Room 239, Viewforth, Stirling]) : Central Regional Council.
Vol.1- ; 1976-. — 1976-. — ill, maps ; 21cm.
Annual. — 173p. in 1976 issue. — Bibl.
Pbk : £1.00
ISSN 0309-7560
Also classified at 941.3'1
(B77-12999)

500.9'415 — Nature trails. *Ireland. Secondary school texts*
Nairn, Richard. Irish nature trails / text Richard Nairn ; illustrations Peter Jay. — [Tallaght] : Folens, [1977]. — [1],32p : col ill, col map ; 25cm. — (Irish environmental library series ; no.26)
Sd : £0.60
(B77-18722)

500.9'418'3 — Natural history. *Dublin (County). North Bull Island. Coastal regions*
North Bull Island, Dublin Bay : a modern coastal natural history / edited by D.W. Jeffrey, general editor ... [et al.]. — [Dublin] ([Thomas Prior House, Ballsbridge, Dublin 4]) : Royal Dublin Society, 1977. — 158p,[8]p of plates : ill(some col), maps ; 30cm.
Bibl.: p.125-129. — Index.
ISBN 0-86027-001-7 : £6.50
ISBN 0-86027-002-5 Pbk : £3.60
(B77-27024)

500.9'422'323 — Natural history. *Kent. Rochester region*
Natural history in the Rochester area / edited by I.K. Champion and E.E. Floodgate. — Rainham (14 London Rd, Rainham, Kent) : Meresborough Books [for the] Rochester and District Natural History Society, 1977. — 114p : ill, maps ; 23cm.
Limited ed. of 1,000 copies. — Bibl.
ISBN 0-905270-00-2 : £2.50
(B77-18723)

500.9'422'392 — Nature reserves. *Kent. Ashford (District). Wye and Crundale Downs National Nature Reserve. Nature trails. Guidebooks*
Nature Conservancy Council. Wye and Crundale Downs National Nature Reserve nature trail / Nature Conservancy Council. — Banbury : The Council, 1977. — [16]p : ill, col map ; 21cm.
With answers.
ISBN 0-901204-40-4 Sd : £0.10
(B77-29374)

500.9'422'51 — Country parks. *East Sussex. Wealden (District). Seven Sisters Country Park. Nature trails: Seven Sisters Park Trail. Walkers' guides*
East Sussex *(County). Planning Department.* Seven Sisters Park Trail / [East Sussex County Planning Department]. — Lewes (Southover House, Southover Rd, Lewes, E. Sussex) : The Department, 1976. — [20]p : ill, col map ; 26x11cm.
ISBN 0-900348-53-4 Sd : £0.15
(B77-13000)

500.9'422'62 — Nature reserves. *West Sussex. Bedham. Mens, The. Natural history*
Natural history of the Mens, Sussex / edited by Andrew and Ruth Tittensor. — Horsham (c/o Mr A. Coxon, 33 Churchill Ave., Horsham, Sussex) : Horsham Natural History Society, 1977. — [1],34,[1]p : ill, maps ; 21cm.
Report of a survey by members of the Horsham Natural History Society and Sussex Trust for Nature Conservation.
ISBN 0-9505739-0-6 Sd : £0.50
(B77-16353)

500.9'422'62 — Nature reserves. *West Sussex. Chichester (District). Kingley Vale National Nature Reserve. Nature trails. Walkers' guides*
Nature Conservancy Council. Kingley Vale National Nature Reserve, nature trail / Nature Conservancy Council. — Banbury : The Council, [1977]. — 16p : col ill, col map ; 21cm.
With answers.
ISBN 0-901204-21-8 Sd : £0.10
(B77-29375)

500.9'422'74 — Natural history. *Hampshire. Selborne. Early works*
White, Gilbert. The natural history of Selborne / [by] Gilbert White. — [1st ed. reprinted] / edited with an introduction and notes by Richard Mabey. — Harmondsworth [etc.] : Penguin, 1977. — xxxi,283p : 2 maps ; 18cm. — (Penguin English library)
Originally published: London : B. White and Son, 1789[i.e.1788]. — Bibl.: p.xxiii-xxv.
ISBN 0-14-043112-8 Pbk : £0.95
(B77-21082)

500.9'423'36 — Nature reserves. *Dorset. Purbeck (District). Studland Heath National Nature Reserve. Guidebooks*
Nature Conservancy Council. Studland Heath National Nature Reserve / Nature Conservancy Council. — Banbury (Calthorpe House, Calthorpe St., Banbury, Oxon. OX16 8EX) : The Council, 1976. — Folder ([16]p) : ill, col maps ; 15x21cm.
ISBN 0-901204-17-x : £0.10
(B77-00740)

500.9'423'36 — Nature reserves. *Dorset. Purbeck (District). Studland Heath National Nature Reserve. Nature trails: Woodland Trail. Walkers' guides*
Nature Conservancy Council. Studland Heath National Nature Reserve, woodland trail / Nature Conservancy Council. — 2nd ed. — Taunton (Roughmoor, Bishop's Hull, Taunton, Somerset TA1 5AA) : Nature Conservancy Council, South West Region, 1976. — 10p ; 22cm.
This ed. originally published: 1975.
ISBN 0-901226-08-4 Sd : Unpriced
(B77-00741)

500.9'425'98 — Buckinghamshire. Beaconsfield (District). Nature trails: Black Park Nature Trail. *Walkers' guides*
Buckinghamshire *(County). Council.* Black Park Nature Trail / Buckinghamshire County Council. — [Aylesbury] ([County Hall, Aylesbury, Bucks.]) : [The Council], [1977]. — [2],18p : ill, map ; 15x22cm.
Bibl.: p.18.
ISBN 0-902805-10-x Sd : £0.05
(B77-09667)

500.9'425'98 — Buckinghamshire. Beaconsfield (District). Nature trails: Langley Park Trail. *Walkers' guides*
Buckinghamshire *(County). Council.* Langley Park Trail / Buckinghamshire County Council. — [Aylesbury] ([County Hall, Aylesbury, Bucks.]) : [The Council], [1977]. — [2],27p : ill, map ; 15x22cm.
ISBN 0-902805-59-2 Sd : £0.05
(B77-09668)

500.9'426'12 — Nature reserves. *Norfolk. North Norfolk (District). Holkham National Nature Reserve. Natural history*
Nature Conservancy Council. Holkham National Nature Reserve / Nature Conservancy Council. — Banbury (Calthorpe House, Calthorpe St., Banbury, Oxon. OX16 8EX) : The Council, [1976]. — [1],20p : ill, map ; 15x21cm.
Bibl.: p.20.
ISBN 0-901204-18-8 Sd : £0.10
(B77-02254)

500.9'426'56 — Nature reserves. *Cambridgeshire. Wicken. Wicken Fen. Walkers' guides. School texts. Fill-in books*
Hoad, Brian. Wander round Wicken Fen / [devised and written by Brian Hoad]. — Ely (Back Hill, Ely, Cambs.) : EARO, Ely Resource and Technology Centre, 1976. — [1], 10p : ill, maps ; 21x30cm.
Two-way paging. — Notebook format.
Sd : £0.15
(B77-11769)

500.9′426′7 — Natural history. *Essex. Rural regions*
Essex Rural and Environmental Studies Association. Essex : a guide to the countryside / [Essex Rural and Environmental Studies Association]. — Letchworth (19 Baldock Rd, Letchworth, Herts. SG6 3JX) : County Guide Publications, 1976. — [7],100p, fold plate : ill, maps ; 15x22cm.
Bibl.
ISBN 0-905858-01-8 Pbk : £1.50
(B77-05376)

500.9′427′393 — Natural history. *Greater Manchester (Metropolitan County). Oldham (District)*
Kidd, Leonard. Oldham's natural history / written by Leonard Kidd ; illustration and design by David McRae. — Oldham ([Central Library, Union St., Oldham OL1 1DN]) : Oldham Libraries, Art Galleries and Museums, 1977. — [1],41p : ill, maps ; 25x19cm.
Index.
Sd : £1.50
(B77-28579)

500.9′427′86 — Nature reserves. *Cumbria. Eden (District). Moor House National Nature Reserves. Guidebooks*
Nature Conservancy Council. Moor House National Nature Reserve / Nature Conservancy Council. — Banbury (Calthorpe House, Calthorpe St., Banbury, Oxon. OX16 8EX) : The Council, [1976]. — [2],12,[1]p : ill, map ; 15x21cm.
ISBN 0-901204-19-6 Sd : £0.15
(B77-01389)

500.9′429′25 — Nature reserves. *Gwynedd. Arfon (District). Coedydd Aber National Nature Reserve. Nature trails. Guidebooks*
Nature Conservancy Council. Coedydd Aber National Nature Reserve nature trail / Nature Conservancy Council. — Revised [ed.]. — Bangor (Penrhos Rd, Bangor, Gwynedd LL57 2LQ) : The Council, 1977. — [12]p : ill, col map ; 21cm.
Previous ed.: 1975.
ISBN 0-901204-36-6 Sd : £0.10
(B77-29376)

500.9′71 — Natural history. *Canada. Mountainous regions. Personal observations*
Blacklock, Les. The high West / photographs by Les Blacklock ; text by Andy Russell. — Harmondsworth [etc.] : Penguin, 1976. — 141p : chiefly col ill ; 28cm.
Originally published: New York : Viking Press, 1974.
ISBN 0-14-004425-6 Pbk : Unpriced
Primary classification 500.9′78
(B77-06034)

500.9′78 — Natural history. *United States. Western states. Mountainous regions. Personal observations*
Blacklock, Les. The high West / photographs by Les Blacklock ; text by Andy Russell. — Harmondsworth [etc.] : Penguin, 1976. — 141p : chiefly col ill ; 28cm.
Originally published: New York : Viking Press, 1974.
ISBN 0-14-004425-6 Pbk : Unpriced
Also classified at 500.9′71
(B77-06034)

501 — Science. *Philosophical perspectives*
Chalmers, A F. What is this thing called science? : an assessment of the nature and status of science and its methods / [by] A.F. Chalmers. — St Lucia, Queensland : University of Queensland Press ; Hemel Hempstead : Distributed by Prentice-Hall, 1976. — xvii, 157p ; 23cm.
Bibl.: p.149-153. — Index.
ISBN 0-7022-1342-x : Unpriced
ISBN 0-7022-1341-1 Pbk : Unpriced
(B77-33193)

Laudan, Larry. Progress and its problems : towards a theory of scientific growth / [by] Larry Laudan. — London [etc.] : Routledge and Kegan Paul, 1977. — x,257p ; 23cm.
Bibl.: p.247-254. — Index.
ISBN 0-7100-8749-7 : £5.95 : CIP rev.
(B77-24891)

Maxwell, Nicholas. What's wrong with science? : towards a people's rational science of delight and compassion / by Nicholas Maxwell. — [Hayes] ([91 Wimborne Ave., Hayes, Middx]) : Bran's Head Books Ltd, 1976. — xi,260p ; 22cm. — (The library of science criticism)
Bibl.: p.259-260.
ISBN 0-905220-05-6 : £5.50
(B77-07323)

502.8 — Electron microscopy
Dietrich, I. Superconducting electron-optic devices / [by] I. Dietrich. — New York ; London : Plenum Press, 1976. — ix,140p : ill ; 24cm. — (International cryogenics monograph series)
Bibl.: p.129-135. — Index.
ISBN 0-306-30882-7 : Unpriced
(B77-30208)

Practical methods in electron microscopy / edited by Audrey M. Glauert. — Amsterdam ; Oxford : North-Holland Publishing Co. [etc.].
[Vol.5. Part 1] : Staining methods for sectional material / [by] P.R. Lewis, D.P. Knight. — 1977. — xv,311p : ill ; 23cm.
Bibl. — Index.
ISBN 0-7204-0606-4 Pbk : £11.20
(B77-23353)

Practical methods in electron microscopy / edited by Audrey M. Glauert. — Amsterdam [etc.] ; Oxford : North-Holland Publishing Co.
Vol.5 : [Part 1. Staining methods for sectioned materials / by P.R. Lewis and D.P. Knight ; and, Part 2. X-ray microanalysis in the electron microscope / by John A. Chandler]. — 1977. — xxi,547p : ill ; 23cm.
Bibl. — Index.
ISBN 0-7204-0605-6 : Unpriced
(B77-24166)

[Vol.5. Part 2] : [X-ray microanalysis in the electron microscope] / [by John A. Chandler]. — 1977. — [4]p,p317-547 : ill ; 23cm.
Bibl. — Index.
ISBN 0-7204-0607-2 Pbk : £8.80
(B77-25574)

502.8 — Microscopy. *Juvenile literature*
Darlington, Arnold. Experiments with your microscope / [by] Arnold Darlington ; illustrated by Rowan Barnes Murphy and Arnold Darlington. — London : Carousel Books, 1977. — 109p : ill ; 20cm. — (Carousel books)
Index.
ISBN 0-552-54115-x Pbk : £0.45
(B77-17446)

502.8 — Secondary schools. Laboratory techniques. *For teaching*
Creedy, John. A laboratory manual for schools and colleges / [by] John Creedy. — London : Heinemann Educational, 1977. — x,255p : ill, form ; 26cm.
Bibl. — Index.
ISBN 0-435-57130-3 : £10.00
(B77-09669)

502.8′5 — Science. Data processing. *Conference proceedings*
International CODATA Conference, *5th, University of Colorado, 1976.* The proceedings of the Fifth Biennial International CODATA Conference, June 28-July 1, 1976, held at the University of Colorado, Boulder, Colorado, USA at the invitation of the National Academy of Sciences / edited by Bertrand Dreyfus. — Oxford [etc.] : Pergamon, 1977. — xxvi,642p : ill, forms, maps ; 31cm.
Bibl. — Index.
ISBN 0-08-021291-3 : £27.75
ISBN 0-08-021290-5 Pbk : Unpriced
Also classified at 602′.8′5
(B77-29377)

502.8′54044 — Laboratory techniques. Applications of digital computer systems
Digital electronics and laboratory computer experiments / [by] Charles L. Wilkins ... [et al.]. — New York ; London : Plenum Press, [1976]. — viii,283p : ill ; 24cm.
Published in the United States: 1975. — Bibl.: p.273-276. — Index.
ISBN 0-306-30822-3 : £9.00
(B77-02950)

502.8′54044 — Science. Applications of digital computer systems. *Conference proceedings*
ICASE Conference on Scientific Computing, *3rd, Williamsburg, 1976.* Computer science and scientific computing : proceedings of the Third ICASE Conference on Scientific Computing, Williamsburg, Virginia, April 1 and 2, 1976 / edited by James M. Ortega. — New York [etc.] ; London : Academic Press, 1976 [i.e. 1977]. — x,306p : ill, maps ; 24cm.
Published in the United States: 1976. — Bibl.
ISBN 0-12-528540-x : £9.45
(B77-10346)

503 — Science. *Dictionaries*
Lucas, David J. A first science dictionary / [compiled by] David J. Lucas, Harold I. James, John Simpson. — London : Edward Arnold, 1976. — 206,2p : ill ; 22cm.
ISBN 0-7131-0027-3 Pbk : £1.95
(B77-01390)

503 — Science. *Encyclopaedias*
McGraw-Hill encyclopedia of science and technology : an international reference work ... — New York ; London [etc.] : McGraw-Hill.
Reader's guide / compiled by the editorial staff of the 'Encyclopedia of science and technology'. — [2nd ed.]. — 1977. — [5],33p : ill ; 28cm.
Previous ed.: New York : McGraw-Hill, 1971.
ISBN 0-07-045336-5 Sd : Unpriced
Also classified at 603
(B77-24167)

Study guide / compiled by the editorial staff of the 'Encyclopedia of science and technology'. — [2nd ed.]. — 1977. — [4],50p : ill ; 28cm.
Previous ed.: New York : McGraw-Hill, 1971.
ISBN 0-07-045337-3 Sd : Unpriced
Also classified at 603
(B77-24168)

McGraw-Hill encyclopedia of science and technology : an international reference work ... — [4th ed.]. — New York ; London [etc.] : McGraw-Hill, 1977. — 15v. : ill(chiefly col), charts(chiefly col), maps(chiefly col), plans(chiefly col) ; 29cm.
Previous ed.: New York : McGraw-Hill, 1971. — Bibl. — Index.
ISBN 0-07-079590-8 : £295.00 the set
Also classified at 603
(B77-24169)

Van Nostrand's scientific encyclopedia. — 5th ed. / edited by Douglas M. Considine. — New York ; London [etc.] : Van Nostrand Reinhold, 1976. — xi,2370p : ill, maps ; 31cm.
Previous ed.: Princeton ; London : Van Nostrand, 1968. — Bibl.
ISBN 0-442-21629-7 : £55.00
Also classified at 603
(B77-05377)

503 — Science. *French-English dictionaries*
De Vries, Louis. French-English science and technology dictionary / [by] Louis DeVries. — 4th ed. / revised and enlarged by Stanley Hochman. — New York ; London [etc.] : McGraw-Hill, 1976. — xiii,683p ; 21cm.
Previous ed.: published as 'French-English science dictionary'. 1962.
ISBN 0-07-016629-3 : £11.20
Also classified at 603
(B77-01391)

505 — Science. *Serials*
Royal Institution of Great Britain. Proceedings of the Royal Institution of Great Britain. — London : Applied Science Publishers.
Vol.49 : 1976. — 1977. — vi,337p : ill, facsims, port ; 23cm.
ISBN 0-85334-718-2 : £12.00
ISSN 0035-8959
(B77-11770)

Yearbook of science and the future. — Chicago ; London[etc.] : Encyclopaedia Britannica.
1976 / [editor Dave Calhoun]. — 1975. — 447,[1]p : ill(some col), col charts, map, ports(some col) ; 29cm.
Bibl. — Index.
ISBN 0-85229-307-0 : £10.50
Also classified at 605
(B77-13001)

1977 / [editor David Calhoun]. — 1976. — 447,[1]p : ill(some col), maps(some col), ports ; 29cm.
Bibl. — Index.
ISBN 0-85229-319-4 : £13.00
Also classified at 605
(B77-13002)

505 — Science. *Yearbooks*
McGraw-Hill yearbook of science and technology / compiled by the staff of the 'McGraw-Hill encyclopedia of science and technology'. — New York ; London [etc.] : McGraw-Hill.
1976 : comprehensive coverage of the important events of the year. — 1977. — [10],454[i.e.450] p : ill, maps, ports ; 29cm.
Bibl. — Index.
ISBN 0-07-045344-6 : £22.15
Also classified at 605
(B77-32609)

506'.025 — Science. Organisations. *Directories*
Commonwealth Science Council. International activities in science and technology : register of organisations of interest to Commonwealth countries / Commonwealth Science Council. — London : Commonwealth Secretariat, 1976. — [4],58p ; 29cm.
Index.
ISBN 0-85092-119-8 Pbk : £2.00
Also classified at 606'.025
(B77-02255)

506'.241 — Science. Organisations. *Great Britain. Royal Society, to 1974*
Allibone, Thomas Edward. The Royal Society and its dining clubs / by T.E. Allibone. — Oxford [etc.] : Pergamon, 1976. — xv,457p : 1 ill, facsims, 2 maps(on lining papers) ; 26cm.
Index.
ISBN 0-08-020493-7 : £16.50
Primary classification 367'.9421
(B77-04698)

506'.241 — Science. Organisations. *Great Britain. Royal Society. Yearbooks*
Royal Society. The year book of the Royal Society of London. — London : Royal Society.
1977. — [1977]. — 421p ; 23cm.
Index.
ISBN 0-85403-084-0 : £3.50
(B77-11771)

506'.2411 — Science. Organisations. *Scotland. Royal Society of Edinburgh. Yearbooks*
Royal Society of Edinburgh. Year book of the Royal Society of Edinburgh. — Edinburgh (22 George St., Edinburgh EH2 2PQ) : The Society.
1976 : (Session 1974-75). — 1976. — 180p ; 25cm.
Bibl. — Index.
Pbk : £2.50
ISSN 0080-4576
(B77-20212)

1977 : (Session 1975-76). — 1977. — 164p ; 25cm.
Index.
Pbk : Unpriced
ISSN 0080-4576
(B77-31865)

507'.1 — Schools. Curriculum subjects: Science. Learning by students. Influence of cognitive development. *For teaching*
Good, Ronald G. How children learn science : conceptual development & implications for teaching / [by] Ronald G. Good. — New York : Macmillan ; London : Collier Macmillan, 1977. — xiii,337p : ill ; 25cm.
Bibl. — Index.
ISBN 0-02-344640-4 : £8.25
(B77-32610)

507'.1042 — Schools. Curriculum subjects: Science. *England. Reports, surveys*
Great Britain. *Department of Education and Science. HM Inspectorate (England).* Mathematics, science and modern languages in maintained schools in England : an appraisal of problems in some key subjects / by HM Inspectorate. — [London] ([Elizabeth House, York Rd, SE1 7PH]) : [HM Inspectorate], 1977. — 40p in various pagings ; 30cm.
ISBN 0-85522-087-2 Sp : Unpriced
Also classified at 418'.007'1042
(B77-14204)

507'.1073 — Schools. Curriculum subjects: Science. Teaching. Individualised instruction. *United States*
Haney, Richard E. Individually guided science / [by] Richard E. Haney, Juanita S. Sorenson. — Reading, Mass. ; London [etc.] : Addison-Wesley, 1977. — xviii,219p : ill, forms ; 24cm. — (Leadership series in individually guided education)
Sound film and 2 sound filmstrips also available. — Bibl. — Index.
ISBN 0-201-19511-9 Pbk : £4.30
(B77-13003)

507'.11'42134 — Universities. Colleges. *London. Kensington and Chelsea (London Borough). Chelsea College of Science and Technology, to 1976*
Chelsea College, a history / [edited by Harold Silver and S. John Teague]. — London ([Information Officer, Chelsea College Annexe, Chelsea Manor St., SW3 3TW]) : Chelsea College, 1977. — 96p : ill, facsims, ports ; 25cm.
Bibl.: p.85.
Pbk : £3.50
(B77-31153)

507'.11'422 — Higher education institutions. Curriculum subjects: Science. Courses. *London & Home Counties. Serials*
London and Home Counties Regional Advisory Council for Technological Education. Science education in the region : a guide to courses in universities, polytechnics and technical colleges in the region / [London and Home Counties Regional Advisory Council for Technological Education]. — London : The Council.
1977-78. — [1977]. — [2],2-48p ; 21cm.
Index.
ISBN 0-85394-053-3 Sd : £0.70
(B77-33766)

507'.12 — Secondary schools. Curriculum subjects: Science. Applications of mathematics. *For teaching*
School Mathematics Project. Modern mathematics in the science lesson / The School Mathematics Project. — Cambridge [etc.] : Cambridge University Press, 1977. — 39p : ill ; 21cm.
Index.
ISBN 0-521-21328-2 Sd : £0.60
(B77-16854)

507'.12'41 — Secondary schools. Mixed ability groups. Curriculum subjects: Science. Teaching. *Great Britain. Manuals*
Sturges, L M. Non-streamed science : a teacher's guide / by L.M. Sturges. — Hatfield ([College La., Hatfield, Herts.]) : Association for Science Education, 1976. — [7],106p : ill, forms, map ; 30cm. — (Association for Science Education. Study series ; no.7 ISSN 0305-1404)
Bibl.: p.100.
ISBN 0-902786-21-0 Sd : £1.00
(B77-27025)

507'.12'411 — Secondary schools. Curriculum subjects: Science. Favourable attitudes of students. Encouragement. *Scotland*
Brown, Sally A. Attitude goals in secondary school science / [by] Sally A. Brown. — Stirling ([Stirling FK9 4LA]) : Department of Education, University of Stirling, 1976. — [2], vi,75 leaves ; 30cm. — (Stirling educational monographs ; no.1 ISSN 0308-8758)
Bibl.: p.71-72. — Index.
ISBN 0-901636-08-8 Pbk : £1.00
(B77-04118)

507'.12'411 — Secondary schools. Curriculum subjects: Science. Innovation. Implementation. *Scotland. Research reports*
Innovations : an investigation of teachers' views / [by] Sally Brown ... [et al.]. — Stirling (Stirling FK9 4LA) : Department of Education, University of Stirling, 1976. — [3],iv,89p ; 30cm. — (Stirling educational monographs ; no.2 ISSN 0308-8758)
Variant title: Innovations in integrated science in Scottish secondary schools. — Bibl.: p.89.
ISBN 0-901636-12-6 Pbk : £1.50
(B77-10347)

507'.12'42313 — Secondary schools. Students, 11-14 years. Mixed ability groups. Curriculum subjects: Science. Teaching. Projects. *Wiltshire. Swindon. Swindon Area Mixed Ability Exercise in Science. Reports, surveys*
Whitehead, Jack. Improving learning for 11 to 14 yr olds in mixed ability science groups / [by] Jack Whitehead. — Swindon ([Sanford St., Swindon]) : Wiltshire Curriculum Development Centre, [1976]. — 43,[1]p : ill, form ; 30cm.
Sd : Unpriced
(B77-27026)

507'.12'425 — Secondary schools. Curriculum subjects: Science. Teaching. *England. East Midlands. Reports, surveys*
Bradley, Howard. A survey of science teaching in secondary schools as a guide to I.N.S.E.T. planning / [by] Howard Bradley. — [Nottingham] ([University Park, Nottingham NG7 2RD]) : University of Nottingham, School of Education, 1976. — [5],23p : ill ; 30cm.
ISBN 0-85359-044-3 Sd : £0.40
(B77-06035)

507'.2 — Science. Policies of governments. *Organisation for Economic Co-operation and Development countries. Reports, surveys*
Organisation for Economic Co-operation and Development. Reviews of national science policy / Organisation for Economic Co-operation and Development. — Paris : O.E.C.D. ; [London] : [H.M.S.O.].
Australia. — 1977. — 217p : ill ; 24cm.
Pbk : £4.90
ISBN 92-64-11636-2
(B77-31866)

507'.2 — Science. Research & development. Surveys. *Organisation for Economic Co-operation and Development countries. Standards*
Organisation for Economic Co-operation and Development. The measurement of scientific and technical activities : proposed standard practice for surveys of research and experimental development : 'Frascati manual' / [Organisation for Economic Co-operation and Development]. — [3rd ed.]. — Paris : O.E.C.D. ; [London] : [H.M.S.O.], 1976. — 139p : ill, form ; 24cm.
English text, parallel English and French bibliography. — Previous ed.: 1970. — Bibl.: p.111-119. — Index.
Pbk : £2.70
ISBN 92-64-11548-x
(B77-00742)

507'.2'041 — Science. Research in British institutions. Registers. Compilation. *Reports, surveys*
Chettle, Peter Michael. Studies for a British register of current research in the sciences and technology : final report / by P.M. Chettle. — [Southampton] ([Highfield, Southampton SO9 5NH]) : Southampton University Library, 1976. — 146p in various pagings : forms ; 30cm. — (Register of scientific research project [report] ; [3]) (SoUL/RSR3)
'Final Report to the Research & Development Department of the British Library on project S1/G/052' - preliminaries. — Includes facsims.
ISBN 0-85432-168-3 Sd : £2.35
(B77-18724)

507'.2041 — Science. Research in British universities. Related to research & development by industries in Great Britain. *Inquiry reports*
Great Britain. *Parliament. House of Commons. Select Committee on Science and Technology.* University-industry relations : third report from the Select Committee on Science and Technology, session 1975-76. — London : H.M.S.O., [1976]. — 96p : 1 ill ; 25cm. — ([1975-76 H.C.]680)
ISBN 0-10-009216-0 Sd : £1.15
(B77-06036)

507'.2041 — Science. Research in British universities. Related to research & development by industries in Great Britain. Great Britain. Parliament. House of Commons. Select Committee on Science and Technology. Industry and scientific research. *Critical studies*
Great Britain. *Department of Education and Science.* University-industry relations : the Government's reply to the third report of the Select Committee on Science and Technology, session 1975-76 / presented to Parliament by the Secretary of State for Education and Science and the Secretary of State for Industry ... — London : H.M.S.O., [1977]. — [1],23p ; 25cm.
ISBN 0-10-169280-3 Sd : £0.50
(B77-33194)

507'.2041 — Science. Research in higher education institutions in Great Britain. Related to research & development by industries in Great Britain. *Inquiry reports*
Great Britain. *Parliament. House of Commons. Select Committee on Science and Technology. Science Sub-committee.* Industry and scientific research : [report from] the Select Committee on Science and Technology (Science Sub-committee), session 1975-76. — London : H.M.S.O.
Further memoranda. Part 4. — [1976]. — cviii p : ill ; 25cm. — ([1975-76 H.C.] 136-iv)
ISBN 0-10-008986-0 Pbk : £1.35
(B77-06037)

507'.2'041 — Science. Research organisations. *Great Britain. Science Research Council (Great Britain). Reports, surveys. Serials*
Science Research Council *(Great Britain).* Report of the Council for the year [ended 31st March] ... / Science Research Council. — London : H.M.S.O.
1976-77. — [1977]. — v,117p,[8]p of plates : ill, port ; 25cm. — ([1976-77 H.C.] 568)
ISBN 0-10-256877-4 Pbk : £2.50
(B77-31867)

507'.2'4 — Science. Experiments. *Juvenile literature*
Carrick, Malcolm. Science experiments / [by] Malcolm Carrick. — Ealing : Carousel Books, 1977. — [64]p : ill ; 20cm. — (Carousel books)
ISBN 0-552-54120-6 Pbk : £0.45
(B77-31154)

Goldstein-Jackson, Kevin. Experiments with everyday objects / by Kevin Goldstein-Jackson ; illustrated by Jonathan Harvey. — London : Souvenir Press, 1976. — 187p : ill ; 22cm.
ISBN 0-285-62245-5 : £3.00
(B77-01392)

507'.2'4 — Science. Experiments. *Secondary school texts*
Combined science worksheets / [by] S.M. Arkless ... [et al.]. — Exeter : Wheaton.
Year 1. — 1976. — [4],68p : ill ; 30cm.
ISBN 0-08-019886-4 Pbk : £0.90
(B77-08987)

Year 1. — 1977. — [4]p,68 leaves : ill ; 28cm.
Spirit masters. — Leaves perforated at inner edge.
ISBN 0-08-020555-0 Pbk : £9.00
(B77-15255)

Year 2. — 1976. — [4],60p : ill ; 30cm.
ISBN 0-08-019887-2 Pbk : £0.90
(B77-08988)

Combined science worksheets / [by] S.M. Arkless ... [et al.. — Exeter : Wheaton.
Year 2. — 1977. — [4],60 leaves : ill ; 28cm.
Spirit masters. — Leaves perforated at inner edge.
ISBN 0-08-020556-9 Pbk : £9.00
(B77-15256)

507'.6 — Science. *Exercises, worked examples. Secondary school texts*
School Certificate science papers, 1969-75. — Christchurch, N.Z. [etc.] ; London : Whitcoulls.

Part A : Selected multiple-choice questions / compiled by D. Metzger and D. Robinson. — 1976. — 103p : ill, form ; 25cm.
With answers.
ISBN 0-7233-0492-0 Sd : Unpriced
(B77-11772)

507'.9 — Scientists. Awards. *Ireland (Republic). Directories*
Murphy, Diarmuid. Fellowships and scholarships available to Irish scientists and technologists / compiled by Diarmuid Murphy and Michael Fitzgerald (with the assistance of Rachel Brew) ; [for the] National Science Council = An Chomhairle Eolaíochta. — Dublin (Government Publications Sales Office, GPO, Dublin 1) : Stationery Office, 1976. — 85p ; 24cm.
Index.
ISBN 0-7076-0023-5 Pbk : £0.45
Also classified at 607'.9
(B77-08350)

508'.1 — Science. *Essays*
Asimov, Isaac. The left hand of the electron / [by] Isaac Asimov. — St Albans : Panther, 1976. — 236p : ill ; 18cm. — (Panther science)
This collection originally published: Garden City, N.Y. : Doubleday, 1972 ; London : White Lion Publishers, 1975. — Contains essays reprinted from 'The magazine of fantasy and science fiction'.
ISBN 0-586-04121-4 Pbk : £0.75
(B77-04119)

Asimov, Isaac. Today and tomorrow / [by] Isaac Asimov. — London : Coronet, 1976. — 176p ; 18cm.
This collection originally published: as the first part of 'Today and tomorrow and-'. Garden City, N.Y. : Doubleday, 1973 ; London : Abelard-Schuman, 1974.
ISBN 0-340-19999-7 Pbk : £0.60
(B77-01393)

Asimov, Isaac. Towards tomorrow / [by] Isaac Asimov. — Sevenoaks : Coronet, 1977. — 173p ; 18cm.
'[This collection] first published in Great Britain 1974 by Abelard-Schuman Limited as the second part of "Today and Tomorrow And ..."' - title page verso.
ISBN 0-340-21785-5 Pbk : £0.70
(B77-28580)

509 — SCIENCE. HISTORICAL AND GEOGRAPHICAL TREATMENT
509 — Science, 1700-1930. *Juvenile literature*
Roberts, David, *b.1926.* The age of machines / [written by David Roberts] ; compiled and edited by Kenneth Bailey. — Glasgow [etc.] : Collins, 1977. — 3-63p : col ill, col ports ; 31cm. — (Collins wide world encyclopedias)
Text on lining papers. — Selection from: 'Science and invention'. 1974. — Index.
ISBN 0-00-106303-0 : £1.50
Also classified at 609
(B77-26275)

509'.034 — Science, 1850-1976
Stableford, Brian M. The mysteries of modern science / [by] Brian M. Stapleford. — London [etc.] : Routledge and Kegan Paul, 1977. — [5], 270p : ill ; 23cm.
Index.
ISBN 0-7100-8697-0 : £4.95 : CIP rev.
(B77-17447)

509'.181'2 — Science. *Western world, 1600-1975*
Knight, David Marcus. The nature of science : the history of science in western culture since 1600 / [by] David Knight. — London : Deutsch, 1976. — 215p ; 23cm.
Bibl.: p.205-209. — Index.
ISBN 0-233-96814-8 : £4.95
(B77-14205)

509'.2'2 — Science. Organisations. *Great Britain. Royal Society. Fellows. Biographies*
Royal Society. Biographical memoirs of Fellows of the Royal Society. — London : Royal Society.
Vol.22 : 1976. — 1976. — [5],653p,[22]leaves of plates : ill, geneal tables, ports ; 26cm.
Bibl.
ISBN 0-85403-083-2 : Unpriced
ISSN 0080-4606
(B77-02951)

509'.2'2 — Scientists. *United States. Biographical dictionaries*
American men and women of science / edited by the Jaques Cattell Press. — 13th ed. — New York ; London : Bowker.
In 7 vols. — Previous ed.: New York : Jaques Cattell Press ; New York ; Epping : Bowker, 1971-1973.
Discipline and geographic indexes. — 1976. — ix,733p ; 29cm.
ISBN 0-8352-0872-9 : £28.50
ISSN 0065-9347
(B77-15263)

Vol.1 : A-C. — 1976. — xiii,913p ; 29cm.
ISBN 0-8352-0866-4 : £28.50
ISSN 0065-9347
(B77-15257)

Vol.2 : D-G. — 1976. — xiii p,p915-1689 ; 29cm.
ISBN 0-8352-0867-2 : £28.50
ISSN 0065-9347
(B77-15258)

Vol.3 : H-K. — 1976. — xiii p,p1691-2466 ; 29cm.
ISBN 0-8352-0868-0 : £28.50
ISSN 0065-9347
(B77-15259)

Vol.4 : L-O. — 1976. — xiii p,p2467-3335 ; 29cm.
ISBN 0-8352-0869-9 : £28.50
ISSN 0065-9347
(B77-15260)

Vol.5 : P-Sr. — 1976. — xiii p,p3337-4255 ; 29cm.
ISBN 0-8352-0870-2 : £28.50
ISSN 0065-9347
(B77-15261)

Vol.6 : St-Z. — 1976. — xiii p,p4257-5043 ; 29cm.
ISBN 0-8352-0871-0 : £28.50
ISSN 0065-9347
(B77-15262)

American men and women of science / edited by the Jaques Cattell Press. — New York ; London : Bowker.
1977. Chemistry. — 1977. — xiii,1672p ; 29cm.

'... entries from the recently published 13th edition are grouped by subject' - p.vii. — Index.

ISBN 0-8352-1011-1 : £32.50
ISSN 0146-0056
(B77-29378)

509'.2'4 — Science. Darwin, Erasmus. *Biographies*
King-Hele, Desmond. Doctor of revolution : the life and genius of Erasmus Darwin / by Desmond King-Hale. — London : Faber, 1977. — 3-361p,[12]p of plates : ill, facsims, geneal table, map, ports ; 23cm.
Bibl.: p.339-343. — Index.
ISBN 0-571-10781-8 : £12.50 : CIP rev.
(B77-23354)

509'.2'4 — Science. Hunt, Robert, b.1807. *Biographies*
Pearson, Alan. Robert Hunt (1807-1887) / by A. Pearson. — [St Austell] ([c/o Mrs S. Trenberth, Bronruth, Garker Rd, Trethurgy, St Austell]) : Federation of Old Cornwall Societies, 1976. — 123p : ill, ports ; 21cm.
Bibl.: p.117-123.
ISBN 0-902660-19-5 Pbk : £0.90
(B77-02256)

509'.2'4 — Science. Oldenburg, Henry. *Correspondence*
Oldenburg, Henry. The correspondence of Henry Oldenburg / edited and translated by A. Rupert Hall & Marie Boas Hall. — London : Mansell Information Publishing.
May 1674 - September 1675 : Letters 2490-2754. — 1977. — xxiv,543p : ill ; 25cm.
Includes letters in French and Latin. — Index.
ISBN 0-7201-0630-3 : £25.00 : CIP rev.
(B77-11191)

509'.4 — Science. *Europe, 1600-1700. Readings from contemporary sources*
European science in the seventeenth century / [edited by] John Redwood. — Newton Abbot [etc.] : David and Charles [etc.], 1977. — 208p : ill ; 23cm.
Bibl.: p.200-201. — Index. — Previous control number ISBN 0-7153-7388-9.
ISBN 0-7153-6466-9 : £6.50
(B77-21083)

509'.41 — Science. *Great Britain. Reports, surveys. Serials*
Education and science : a report of the Department of Education and Science ... — London : H.M.S.O.
1976. — 1977. — viii,62p : 1 ill ; 25cm.
Bibl.: p.60-62.
ISBN 0-11-270455-7 Sd : £1.50
Primary classification 370'.942
(B77-26236)

Great Britain. *Parliament. House of Commons. Select Committee on Science and Technology.* Special report from the Select Committee on Science and Technology, session 1976-77. — London : H.M.S.O.
1st. — [1977]. — v p ; 25cm. — ([1976-77 H.C.] 88)
ISBN 0-10-208877-2 Sd : £0.25
Also classified at 609'.41
(B77-08351)

2nd. — [1977]. — Folder(iv p) ; 25cm. — ([1976-77 H.C.] 269)
ISBN 0-10-226977-7 : £0.15
Also classified at 609'.41
(B77-11773)

509'.423'98 — Science. *Avon. Bath, 1700-1800*
Turner, Anthony John. Science and music in eighteenth century Bath : [catalogue of] an exhibition in the Holburne of Menstrie Museum, Bath, 22 September 1977-29 December 1977 / catalogue by A.J. Turner, with the assistance of I.D. Woodfield and contributions by H.S. Torrens. — Bath (Claverton Down, Bath, Avon BA2 7AY) : University of Bath, 1977. — viii,131p : ill, facsims, music, ports ; 21cm.
Bibl.: p.117-123.
ISBN 0-900843-83-7 Sd : Unpriced
Primary classification 520'.92'4
(B77-33778)

509'.73 — Science. *United States, 1650-1815. Readings*
Early American science / Brooke Hindle, editor. — New York : Science History Publications ; Folkestone : [Distributed by] Dawson, 1976. — xiv,213,[1]p : facsims ; 24cm. — (History of science, selections from 'Isis')
Bibl.: p.134.
ISBN 0-88202-151-6 : £5.50
(B77-33767)

510 — MATHEMATICS
Gudder, Stanley. A mathematical journey / [by] Stanley Gudder. — New York ; London [etc.] : McGraw-Hill, 1976. — xiii,434p : ill ; 25cm.
With answers to selected odd-numbered exercises. — Index.
ISBN 0-07-025105-3 : £10.75
(B77-04120)

Joint Schools Project. Joint Schools Project mathematics. — Metric ed. — [Harlow] : Longman.
1. Teacher's guide / [edited by M.C. Mitchelmore, B. Raynor]. — 1977. — [5], 133p : ill ; 22cm.
With answers. — Previous ed.: 1967.
ISBN 0-582-60696-9 Pbk : £1.20
(B77-31155)

2. Teacher's guide / [edited by M.C. Mitchelmore, B. Raynor]. — 1976. — [6], 134p : ill ; 22cm.
Teacher's guide 2 has title: JSP modern mathematics. — With answers. — Previous ed.: Harlow : Longmans, 1968.
ISBN 0-582-60697-7 Pbk : £1.20
(B77-13004)

3. Teacher's guide / [edited by M.C. Mitchelmore, B. Raynor]. — 1976. — [6], 145p : ill ; 22cm.
Teacher's guide 3 has title: JSP modern mathematics. — With answers. — Previous ed.: Harlow : Longmans, 1969.
ISBN 0-582-60698-5 Pbk : £1.30
(B77-13005)

Moore, Hal G. Pre-calculus mathematics / [by] Hal G. Moore. — 2nd ed. — New York ; London [etc.] : Wiley, 1977. — x,517p : ill ; 27cm.
With answers to selected exercises. — Previous ed.: 1973. — Index.
ISBN 0-471-61454-8 : £9.50
(B77-16855)

Person, Russell Vernon. Practical mathematics / [by] Russell V. Person, Vernon J. Person. — New York ; London [etc.] : Wiley, 1977. — xv, 589p : ill ; 25cm.
With answers to most odd-numbered exercise problems. — Index.
ISBN 0-471-68216-0 : £9.00
(B77-16354)

Practical mathematics. — 6th ed. / [by] Claude Irwin Palmer ... [et al.]. — New York ; London [etc.] : McGraw-Hill, 1977. — xviii,557p : ill ; 25cm.
With answers to odd-numbered exercises. — Previous ed.: / by Claude Irwin Palmer, Samuel Fletcher Bibb ; revised by John A. Jarvis, Leonard A. Mrachek. New York : McGraw-Hill, 1970. — Index.
ISBN 0-07-048253-5 : Unpriced
(B77-27827)

Stewart, Ian. The foundations of mathematics / [by] Ian Stewart and David Tall. — Oxford [etc.] : Oxford University Press, 1977. — xi, 263p : ill ; 23cm.
Bibl.: p.259. — Index.
ISBN 0-19-853164-8 : £7.50 : CIP rev.
ISBN 0-19-853165-6 Pbk : £3.95
(B77-07887)

The **VNR** concise encyclopedia of mathematics / editors W. Gellert ... [et al.]. — New York ; London [etc.] : Van Nostrand Reinhold, 1977. — 760p,56p of plates : ill(chiefly col), facsims, ports ; 24cm.
This translation originally published: as 'Mathematics at a glance'. 1.Aufl. Leipzig : Bibliographisches Institut, 1975. — Translation of: 'Mathematik'. 5.Aufl. Leipzig : Verlag Enzyklopädie, 1970. — Index.
ISBN 0-442-22646-2 : £12.10
ISBN 0-442-22647-0 Pbk : Unpriced
(B77-24170)

510 — Applied mathematics. *Conference proceedings*
Los Alamos Symposium on Mathematics in the Natural Sciences, *1st, 1974?.* Surveys in applied mathematics : essays dedicated to S.M. Ulam / edited by N. Metropolis, S. Orszag, G.-C. Rota. — New York [etc.] ; London : Academic Press, 1976 [i.e. 1977]. — xvii,297p : ill, port ; 24cm.
'Proceedings of the First Los Alamos Symposium on Mathematics in the Natural Sciences' - half title page verso. — Published in the United States: 1976. — Bibl. — Index.
ISBN 0-12-492150-7 : £9.95
(B77-09670)

510 — Applied mathematics. *Secondary school texts*
Bostock, Linda. Applied mathematics / [by] L. Bostock, S. Chandler. — Cheltenham (32 Malmesbury Rd, Kingsditch Estate, Cheltenham GL51 9PL) : Stanley Thornes (Publishers) Ltd.
2. — 1976. — xii,379p : ill ; 24cm.
With answers. — Index.
ISBN 0-85950-024-1 Pbk : £3.85
(B77-13623)

510 — Finite mathematics
Bittinger, Marvin Lowell. Finite mathematics : a modeling approach / [by] Marvin L. Bittinger, J. Conrad Crown. — Reading, Mass. ; London [etc.] : Addison-Wesley, 1977. — xiii,375,A62, I6p : ill ; 25cm.
With answers. — Index.
ISBN 0-201-00832-7 : £11.20
(B77-21822)

Goodman, Adolph Winkler. Finite mathematics with applications / [by] A.W. Goodman, J.S. Ratti. — 2nd ed. — New York : Macmillan ; London : Collier Macmillan, 1975. — xiv, 541p : ill(chiefly col) ; 25cm.
With answers. — Previous ed.: 1971. — Index.
ISBN 0-02-344810-5 : £12.40
(B77-17448)

Liu, Chung Laung. Elements of discrete mathematics / [by] C.L. Liu. — New York ; London [etc.] : McGraw-Hill, 1977. — x,294p : ill ; 25cm. — (McGraw-Hill computer science series)
Bibl. — Index.
ISBN 0-07-038131-3 : £12.70
(B77-22534)

Swift, William C. Principles of finite mathematics / [by] William C. Swift, David E. Wilson. — Englewood Cliffs ; London [etc.] : Prentice-Hall, 1977. — xi,455p : ill ; 24cm.
With solutions for odd-numbered exercises. — Index.
ISBN 0-13-701359-0 : £11.15
(B77-20213)

510 — Finite mathematics. *For computer sciences*
Stanat, Donald F. Discrete mathematics in computer science / [by] Donald F. Stanat, David F. McAllister. — Englewood Cliffs ; London [etc.] : Prentice-Hall, 1977. — xiii, 401p : ill ; 25cm.
With answers to selected problems. — Bibl.: p.391-392. — Index.
ISBN 0-13-216150-8 : £12.80
(B77-24171)

510 — Finite mathematics. *For management*
Vazsonyi, Andrew. Finite mathematics : quantitative analysis for management / [by] Andrew Vazsonyi. — Santa Barbara, Calif. ; London [etc.] : Wiley, 1977. — [18],493p : ill ; 24cm. — (Wiley/Hamilton series in management, accounting and information systems)
With answers. — Index.
ISBN 0-471-90480-5 : £10.60
(B77-11774)

510 — Mathematics. *Conference proceedings. Serials*
Symposia Mathematica, *Rome, 1967-.* Symposia mathematica. — Roma : Istituto nazionale di alta matematica ; London [etc.] : Distributed by Academic Press. — (Istituto nazionale di alta matematica. Pubblicazioni)
Vol.20 : [convegni del marzo e dell'ottobre 1975]. — 1976. — 3-576p ; 25cm.
Includes a paper in Italian. — Bibl. — Index.
£17.70
(B77-26276)

510 — Mathematics. *For Caribbean students. Secondary school texts*
Joint Schools Project. JSP Caribbean maths / [Joint Schools Project]. — Metric ed. — [Port of Spain] : Longman Caribbean ; London : Longman.
Previous ed.: published as 'Joint Schools Project mathematics'. Caribbean ed. Port of Spain : Longman Caribbean ; Harlow : Longman, 1967-1972.
Textbook 4 / editors M.C. Mitchelmore, B. Raynor ; Caribbean editor Ian Isaacs. — 1976. — v,376p : ill, map ; 25cm.
With answers. — Index.
ISBN 0-582-76542-0 Pbk : £2.20
(B77-00177)

SMP basic mathematics / editors S.H. Holloway, R. de Four. — Cambridge [etc.] : Cambridge University Press [etc.].
'... developed from material prepared by the School Mathematics Project for the SMP Main School Course ...' - Preface.
Book 1. — 1977. — vi,285p : ill ; 23cm.
With selected answers.
ISBN 0-521-21491-2 Pbk : £2.00
(B77-28581)

510 — Mathematics. *For Irish students. Secondary school texts*
Holland, Frederick Joseph. Mathematics / [by] Frederick J. Holland, Alphonsus D. Madden. — Dublin : Educational Company of Ireland.
6. — 1977. — [4],186p : ill ; 20cm.
With answers.
ISBN 0-904916-62-6 Pbk : £2.86
(B77-13624)

510 — Mathematics. *For primary school teaching*
Begle, Edward Griffith. The mathematics of the elementary school / [by] Edward G. Begle. — New York ; London [etc.] : McGraw-Hill, [1976]. — xi,453p : ill ; 25cm.
With answers. — Published in the United States: 1975. — Index.
ISBN 0-07-004325-6 : £11.20
(B77-04121)

Devine, Donald Francis. Elementary mathematics / [by] Donald F. Devine, Jerome E. Kaufmann. — New York ; London [etc.] : Wiley, 1977. — xiii,525p : ill ; 26cm.
With answers to selected problems. — Text on lining papers. — Bibl.: p.xiii. — Index.
ISBN 0-471-20970-8 : £9.35
(B77-10348)

Larsen, Max Dean. Essentials of elementary school mathematics / [by] Max D. Larsen, James L. Fejfar. — New York ; London : Academic Press, 1974. — xx,410p,[4]p of plates : ill(chiefly col), plan ; 24cm.
With answers to selected exercises. — Bibl.: p.365-372. — Index.
ISBN 0-12-438640-7 : Unpriced
(B77-19334)

Riedesel, C Alan. Elementary school mathematics for teachers / [by] C. Alan Riedesel, Leroy G. Callahan. — New York [etc.] ; London : Harper and Row, 1977. — vii,311p : ill ; 24cm.
With answers. — Index.
ISBN 0-06-045412-1 Pbk : £6.70
(B77-21084)

510 — Mathematics. *For West African students. Secondary school texts*
Certificate mathematics / series editor A.O. Kalejaiye. — Cambridge [etc.] : Cambridge University Press.
Book 2. Teachers guide. — 1976. — vii,191p : ill ; 23cm.
ISBN 0-521-20862-9 Pbk : Unpriced
(B77-01394)

510 — Mathematics. *Middle school texts*
School Mathematics Project. SMP 7-13 / the School Mathematics Project. — Cambridge [etc.] : Cambridge University Press.
Unit 1. Teacher's handbook. — 1977. — [6], 49p : ill ; 21cm.
ISBN 0-521-21413-0 Sd : £0.70
(B77-33768)

Unit 2. Teacher's handbook. — 1977. — [6], 44p : ill ; 21cm.
ISBN 0-521-21414-9 Sd : £0.70
(B77-33769)

510 — Mathematics. *Primary school texts*
Glenn, John Albert. Towards mathematics / [by] J.A. Glenn, D.A. Sturgess. — Huddersfield : Schofield and Sims.
Set 5. — 1976. — Case : ill(chiefly col), facsim, forms ; 22x33x17cm.
Handbook (207p.), 10 copies each of core units 21-25, core units answers (62p.), 60 work cards ([70] sides), work cards handbook (40p.), 40 work card records.
ISBN 0-7217-2218-0 : £18.50
(B77-09671)

Halsall, John. Mathematics for primary schools / [by] John Halsall. — New ed. — Sunbury-on-Thames [etc.] : Nelson.
Book 2. — 1977. — 80p : ill, map ; 25cm.
Text on inside front and back covers. — Previous ed.: 1961.
ISBN 0-17-421147-3 Pbk : £0.85
(B77-31868)

Book 3. — 1977. — 96p : ill, plans ; 25cm.
Text on inside front and back covers. — Previous ed.: 1961.
ISBN 0-17-421148-1 Pbk : £0.95
(B77-31869)

Book 4. — 1977. — 96p : ill ; 25cm.
Text on inside front and back covers. — Previous ed.: 1961.
ISBN 0-17-421149-x Pbk : £0.95
(B77-31870)

Books 1-4. Complete answers. — 1977. — [2], 44p : ill ; 25cm.
Previous ed.: in 4 vols, 1965.
ISBN 0-17-421150-3 Sd : £1.50
(B77-27828)

Hollands, Roy Derrick. Headway maths / [by] Roy Hollands and Howell Moses. — St Albans : Hart-Davis Educational.
1. — 1977. — 96p : ill(some col) ; 28cm.
Fill-in book.
ISBN 0-247-12728-0 Pbk : £1.50
(B77-18725)

2. — 1977. — 96p : ill(some col), col maps ; 28cm.
ISBN 0-247-12729-9 Pbk : £1.50
(B77-23355)

2. Teacher's book. — 1977. — 59p : ill ; 22cm.
ISBN 0-247-12734-5 Sd : £1.50
(B77-31871)

Marshall, George, *b.1923.* A world of mathematics / [by] G. Marshall. — Sunbury-on-Thames [etc.] : Nelson.
Activity book 1. — 1976 [i.e. 1977]. — 2p, leaves 3-32 : ill ; 25cm.
Fill-in book. — Originally published: 1973.
ISBN 0-17-431250-4 Pbk : £6.00
(B77-09672)

Scottish Primary Mathematics Group. Primary mathematics / Scottish Primary Mathematics Group. — London : Heinemann Educational.
Stage 3. Answers book. — 1976. — [2],39p : ill ; 30cm.
Stage 3. Answers book has subtitle: A development through activity.
ISBN 0-435-02914-2 Sd : £2.35
(B77-02257)

Stage 3. Teachers' notes. — 1976. — [2],57p : ill ; 30cm.
Stage 3. Teachers' notes has subtitle: A development through activity.
ISBN 0-435-02913-4 Sd : £2.50
(B77-02258)

Stanfield, Jan. Maths adventure / written by Jan Stanfield ; illustrated by Anna Potworowska. — London : Evans Bros.
5. Activity book. — 1977. — [2],45p : chiefly ill ; 25cm.
ISBN 0-237-29087-1 Sd : £0.86
(B77-11192)

5. Pupil's book / advisory editor Peter Kaner. — 1977. — [4],92p : ill(some col), map ; 19x25cm.
ISBN 0-237-29085-5 Sd : £1.35
(B77-14206)

5. Teacher's book. — 1977. — [2],43p : ill ; 25cm.
With answers.
ISBN 0-237-29086-3 Sd : £0.95
(B77-14207)

510 — Mathematics. *Primary school texts. Cards*

Mathematics Appreciation Project Group. Mathematics for general education / [Mathematics Appreciation Project Group]. — [Basingstoke, etc.] : Macmillan.
Set C. Interest cards. — 1976. — 1v. : ill ; 21cm.
Sheet ([1]p.), 8 cards ([15] sides).
ISBN 0-333-19359-8 : £1.35
(B77-01395)

Set C. Workcards. — 1976. — 1v. : ill ; 21cm.
Sheet ([1]p), 17 cards ([17] sides).
ISBN 0-333-19357-1 : £2.25
(B77-01396)

Slater, Joseph Derrick. Link workcards : a four unit series of workcards for the 7-11 year age range : a programme of mathematical games and activities to extend and enrich any main course scheme / [by] J.D. Slater. — Amersham : Hulton.
Unit 4. — 1977. — Portfolio : ill(some col) ; 30cm.
Thirty-nine cards (42 sides).
ISBN 0-7175-0776-9 Ls : £3.00
(B77-16355)

510 — Mathematics. *Primary school texts. Teaching kits*

Scottish Primary Mathematics Group. Primary mathematics / Scottish Primary Mathematics Group. — London : Heinemann Educational.
Stage 2. Answers book. — 1976. — [2],40p : ill ; 30cm.
Stage 2. Answers book has subtitle: A development through activity.
ISBN 0-435-02916-9 Sd : £1.90
(B77-01397)

Stage 3. Textbook. — 1976. — [5],102p : ill(chiefly col), col map ; 30cm.
Stage 3. Textbook has subtitle: A development through activity.
ISBN 0-435-02910-x Sd : £1.35
(B77-01398)

Stage 3. Workbook. — 1976. — 40p : ill ; 30cm.
Stage 3. Workbook has subtitle: A development through activity.
ISBN 0-435-02911-8 Sd : £0.35
(B77-01399)

Stage 3. Workcards. — 1976. — 1v. : ill(chiefly col) ; 21cm.
Thirty-two cards ([64] sides).
ISBN 0-435-02912-6 : £4.75
(B77-01400)

Stage 4. Textbook. — 1977. — [2],115p : ill(chiefly col), col maps ; 30cm.
Stage 4. Textbook has subtitle: A development through activity.
ISBN 0-435-02925-8 Sd : £1.40
(B77-27027)

Stage 4. Workbook. — 1977. — [2],24,[1]p : ill ; 30cm.
Stage 4. Workbook has subtitle : A development through activity. — Fill-in book.
ISBN 0-435-02926-6 Sd : £0.30
(B77-24893)

510 — Mathematics. *Secondary school texts*

Bass, Doris. O Level mathematics / [by] Doris Bass, Ann Farnham. — London : Cassell and Collier Macmillan.
Part 2. — 1977. — [6],160p : ill ; 22cm.
ISBN 0-304-29684-8 Pbk : £1.65
(B77-17449)

Part 2. [With answers]. — 1977. — [6],174p : ill ; 22cm.
ISBN 0-304-29683-x Pbk : £2.15
(B77-17450)

Blakey, Joseph. Intermediate pure mathematics : SI units / [by] J. Blakey. — 5th ed. — London [etc.] : Macmillan, 1977. — viii,530p : ill ; 22cm.
With answers. — Previous ed.: 1964. — Index.
ISBN 0-333-22377-2 Pbk : £2.95
(B77-27829)

Bolt, Ronald Leonard. Mathematics to sixteen / by R.L. Bolt and C. Reynolds. — London : University Tutorial Press.
In 4 vols. — Also available without answers.
Book 1. [With answers]. — 1977. — [6],215p : ill ; 22cm.
ISBN 0-7231-0743-2 Pbk : £1.65
ISBN 0-7131-0752-1 Without answers: £1.55
(B77-24172)

Book 2. [With answers]. — 1977. — [6],226p : ill ; 22cm.
ISBN 0-7231-0744-0 Pbk : £1.75
ISBN 0-7231-0753-x Without answers: £1.65
(B77-24173)

Channon, John Bredin. New general mathematics revision / [by] J.B. Channon, A. McLeish Smith, H.C. Head. — London : Longman, 1976. — ix,432p : ill ; 20cm.
With answers.
ISBN 0-582-33201-x Pbk : £2.30
(B77-06653)

Cheah Tat Huat. Modern mathematics / [by] Cheah Tat Huat, Tan Beng Theam, Khor Gark Kim. — Kuala Lumpur ; Oxford [etc.] : Oxford University Press, 1976. — iv,155p : ill ; 25cm. — (Modern certificate guides)
With answers.
ISBN 0-19-581023-6 Pbk : £1.95
(B77-18726)

Jarman, Eric Arthur. Modern mathematics / [by] E.A. Jarman. — London : Longman, 1976. — [5],153p : ill ; 20cm. — (Longman certificate notes)
ISBN 0-582-60661-6 Pbk : £0.55
(B77-00743)

Joy, Richard Raymond. Essential topics in modern maths / [by] R.R. Joy. — Basingstoke [etc.] : Macmillan, 1977. — vii,136p : ill, geneal tables, maps ; 24cm.
With answers. — Index.
ISBN 0-333-19107-2 Pbk : £1.45 : CIP rev.
(B77-08352)

Mathematics Appreciation Project Group. Mathematics for general education / Mathematics Appreciation Project Group. — [Basingstoke, etc.] : Macmillan.
Set A. Unit 1 : Delivering the goods. — [1976]. — 16p : ill, maps ; 20x21cm.
ISBN 0-333-19332-6 Sd : £3.75(10 copies)
(B77-02952)

Set A. Unit 2 : The champions. — [1976]. — 12p : ill ; 20x21cm.
ISBN 0-333-19333-4 Sd : £3.25(10 copies)
(B77-02953)

Set A. Unit 3 : Angling. — [1976]. — 16p : ill ; 20x21cm.
ISBN 0-333-19334-2 Sd : £3.25(10 copies)
(B77-02954)

Set A. Unit 5 : Go electric. — [1976]. — 12p : ill ; 20x21cm.
ISBN 0-333-19335-0 Sd : £3.25(10 copies)
(B77-02955)

Set A. Unit 6 : Time and time again. — 1976. — 12p : ill ; 20x21cm.
ISBN 0-333-19329-6 Sd : £3.25(10 copies)
(B77-02956)

Set A. Workcards. — [1976]. — 1v. : ill ; 21cm.
Nine cards ([15] sides).
ISBN 0-333-19336-9 : £1.25
(B77-02957)

Set A. Worksheets. — 1976. — [32]p : ill ; 28cm.
Cover title.
ISBN 0-333-19338-5 Pbk : £3.25
(B77-02958)

Mathematics Appreciation Project Group. Mathematics for general education / [Mathematics Appreciation Project Group]. — [Basingstoke, etc.] : Macmillan.
Set B. Apparatus and interest cards. — 1976. — 1v. : ill, map, port ; 21cm.
Sheet ([1]p.), 18 cards ([27] sides).
ISBN 0-333-19348-2 : £2.85
(B77-00178)

[Set B. Unit 2] : Cardboard engineering. — 1976. — 12p : ill ; 20x21cm.
ISBN 0-333-19340-7 Sd : £3.25(for 10 copies)
(B77-00179)

[Set B. Unit 3] : Working to rule. — 1976. — 12p : ill ; 20x21cm.
ISBN 0-333-19341-5 Sd : £3.25(for 10 copies)
(B77-00180)

[Set B. Unit 5] : Can you afford it?. — 1976. — 12p : ill ; 20x21cm.
ISBN 0-333-19342-3 Sd : £3.25(for 10 copies)
(B77-00181)

[Set B. Unit 7] : Roundabout. — 1976. — 12p : ill ; 20x21cm.
ISBN 0-333-19343-1 Sd : £3.25(for 10 copies)
(B77-00182)

[Set B. Unit 8] : Drunken sailor. [Games board]. — 1976. — Fold sheet : ill ; 30cm.
ISBN 0-333-19345-8 : £1.25
(B77-00183)

[Set B. Unit 10] : Pandora. — 1976. — [1], 16p : ill ; 20x21cm.
ISBN 0-333-19346-6 Sd : £3.75(for 10 copies)
(B77-00184)

Set B. Workcards. — 1976. — 1v. : ill ; 21cm.
Sheet ([1]p.), 25 cards ([30]sides).
ISBN 0-333-19347-4 : £3.50
(B77-00185)

Set B. Worksheets. — 1976. — [29] leaves : of ill, forms ; 28cm.
Cover title. — Consists chiefly of spirit duplicator masters.
ISBN 0-333-19349-0 Pbk : £7.95
(B77-02259)

[Set C. Unit 1] : Time-tables. — 1976. — 12p : ill ; 20x21cm.
ISBN 0-333-19351-2 Sd : £3.25(for 10 copies)
(B77-00186)

[Set C. Unit 2] : Designing a kitchen. — 1976. — 16p : ill, plans ; 20x21cm.
ISBN 0-333-19352-0 Sd : £3.75(for 10 copies)
(B77-00187)

[Set C. Unit 3] : Spy trap. — 1976. — 12p : ill ; 20x21cm.
ISBN 0-333-19353-9 Sd : £3.25(for 10 copies)
(B77-00188)

[Set C. Unit 5] : Taking a 'pot shot'. — 1976. — 16p : ill ; 20x21cm.
ISBN 0-333-19354-7 Sd : £3.75(for 10 copies)
(B77-00189)

Set C. Unit 8 : Catch cran. — 1976. — Fold sheet : of ill ; 30cm.
Games board.
ISBN 0-333-19355-5 : £1.25
(B77-02959)

[Set C. Unit 10] : Find your bearings. — 1976. — 12p : ill ; 20x21cm.
ISBN 0-333-19356-3 Sd : £3.25(for 10 copies)
(B77-00190)

Set C. Worksheets. — 1976. — [35] leaves : ill, map ; 28cm.
Cover title. — Consists chiefly of spirit duplicator masters.
ISBN 0-333-19360-1 Pbk : Unpriced
(B77-02960)

Morgan, John Butler. Unified mathematics / [by] J.B. Morgan and the late K.S. Snell. — Cambridge [etc.] : Cambridge University Press.
In 5 vols. — With answers.
Book 4. — 1977. — x,346p : ill ; 23cm.
Index.
ISBN 0-521-21298-7 Pbk : £1.80(non-net)
(B77-24894)

Oxford comprehensive mathematics. — Oxford [etc.] : Oxford University Press.
Book 5 / [by] C.S. Banwell, K.D. Saunders ; illustrated by Peter Edwards. — 1977. — 160p : ill(some col) ; 24cm.
A 'green cover' book for CSE students.
ISBN 0-19-914208-4 Pbk : £1.75
(B77-27830)

Book 5 / [by] J.E. Hiscocks, M.E. Wardle, C.J. Weeks ; illustrated by Peter Edwards. — 1977. — 160p : ill(some col) ; 24cm.
A 'blue cover' book for GCE students.
ISBN 0-19-914205-x Pbk : £1.75
(B77-27831)

Teacher's book 5. C.S.E. / [by] C.S. Banwell, K.D. Saunders. — 1977. — [3],25,90p : ill ; 24cm.
With answers to questions. — Index to books 3, 4 and 5 CSE and books 3, 4 and 5 GCE.
ISBN 0-19-914224-6 Pbk : £3.50
(B77-27832)

Teacher's book 5. GCE / [by] J.E. Hiscocks, M.E. Wardle, C.J. Weeks. — 1977. — [3],43, 98p : ill ; 24cm.
With answers to questions. — Index to books 3, 4 and 5 GCE and books 3, 4 and 5 CSE.
ISBN 0-19-914221-1 Pbk : £3.50
(B77-27833)

Workbook 4. — 1976. — [32]p : of ill ; 21cm.
ISBN 0-19-914215-7 Sd : £0.20
(B77-06038)

Reynolds, H E. Essentials of modern maths : a revision course for first examinations / [by] H.E. Reynolds. — London : Edward Arnold, 1976. — [6],137p : ill ; 22cm.
With answers. — Index.
ISBN 0-7131-0040-0 Sd : £1.50
(B77-02260)

School Mathematics Project. The School Mathematics Project. — Cambridge [etc.] : Cambridge University Press.
Computing in mathematics. Computer orientated mathematics package / [edited by Rosemary Fraser]. Main pack. — 1976. — 1v. : ill(some col) ; 21cm.
'SMP compack'. — 'Teacher's guide' (29p.), 100 cards ([199] sides).
ISBN 0-521-20814-9 : £10.00
(B77-18086)

Computing in mathematics. Computer orientated mathematics package / [edited by Rosemary Fraser]. Preliminary pack. — 1976. — 1v. : ill ; 21cm.
'SMP compack'. — 'Teacher's guide' (29p.), 20 cards ([39] sides).
ISBN 0-521-20813-0 : £4.50
(B77-18087)

Supplementary booklet 1 / [by Judy Bonsall et al.] ; based on the content of SMP books 1, A and B. — 1977. — v,84p : ill ; 23cm.
With answers.
ISBN 0-521-21220-0 Sp : £0.95(non-net)
(B77-31156)

Supplementary booklet 2 / [by Judy Bonsall et al.] ; based on the content of SMP 2, C and D. — 1977. — v,101p : ill ; 23cm.
With answers.
ISBN 0-521-21221-9 Sp : £0.95(non-net)
(B77-31157)

Supplementary booklet 3 / [by Judy Bonsall et al.] ; based on the content of SMP books 3, E and F. — 1977. — v,83p : ill ; 23cm.
With answers.
ISBN 0-521-21222-7 Sp : £0.95(non-net)
(B77-31158)

Supplementary booklet 4 / [by Judy Bonsall et al.] ; based on the content of SMP books 4, G, H and X. — 1977. — vi,131p : ill ; 23cm.
With answers.
ISBN 0-521-21223-5 Sp : £1.05
(B77-31159)

Supplementary booklet 5 / [by Judy Bonsall et al.] ; based on the content of SMP books 5, Y and Z. — 1977. — v,85p : ill ; 23cm.
With answers.
ISBN 0-521-21224-3 Sd : £1.05
(B77-31160)

Shaw, Harold Alan. Discovering mathematics : a course for secondary schools / [by] H.A. Shaw, F.E. Wright ; illustrated by A.G. Standley. — 3rd (metric) ed. — London : Edward Arnold.
4. — 1976. — 237p : ill, facsim ; 22cm.
With answers. — Previous ed.: i.e. 2nd (decimal) ed. 1970.
ISBN 0-7131-0044-3 Pbk : £1.90
(B77-01401)

Turner, Leonard Keith. Advanced mathematics : a unified course / [by] L.K. Turner, [F.J. Budden, D. Knighton]. — London : Longman.
In 2 vols.
Book 1 : including 'Introduction to vectors and mechanics'. — 1976. — xv,382p : ill, map ; 23cm.
With answers. — Book 1 originally published: 1973 ; 'Introduction to vectors and mechanics' (Book T) originally published: 1975.
ISBN 0-582-35237-1 Pbk : £2.95(non-net)
(B77-06039)

510 — Mathematics. *Secondary school texts. Teaching kits*

Maths resource sheets. — Slough : Foulsham. — (Copymasters)
Book 1 / by M. Wallace. — 1976. — [26] leaves : of ill ; 28cm.
Contains ready cut stencils. — 4 leaves printed on both sides.
ISBN 0-572-00946-1 Pbk : £4.95
(B77-02261)

510 — Mathematics. Applications

Hunkins, Dalton R. Mathematics, tools and models / [by] Dalton R. Hunkins, Thomas L. Pirnot. — Reading, Mass. ; London [etc.] : Addison-Wesley, 1977. — xiv,393p : ill, maps, ports ; 25cm.
With answers to selected exercises. — Bibl. — Index.
ISBN 0-201-03046-2 : £11.20
(B77-30209)

510 — Mathematics. Calculation. *Secondary school texts*

Mathematics Appreciation Project Group. Mathematics for general education / [Mathematics Appreciation Project Group]. — Basingstoke [etc.] : Macmillan.
Advanced number skills. — 1977. — [6],98p : ill ; 21cm.
ISBN 0-333-19328-8 Pbk : £0.95 : CIP rev.
(B77-04766)

Mathematics Appreciation Project Group. Mathematics for general education / Mathematics Appreciation Project Group. — Basingstoke [etc.] : Macmillan.
Advanced number skills. Teacher's ed. — 1977. — [5],214p : ill ; 22cm.
With answers.
ISBN 0-333-19326-1 : £4.75 : CIP rev.
(B77-04767)

510'.21'2 — Mathematics. *Tables. For social sciences*

Kmietowicz, Zbigniew Wawrzyniec. Mathematical, statistical and financial tables for the social sciences / [by] Z.W. Kmietowicz and Y. Yannoulis. — London [etc.] : Longman, 1976. — x,54p ; 24cm.
ISBN 0-582-44062-9 Sd : £0.95
(B77-02262)

510'.22'2 — Mathematics. *Illustrations. School texts*

Ely Resource and Technology Centre. Orange book / [by Mary Cullen ... et al. for the Ely Resource and Technology Centre]. — London [etc.] : Hutchinson for Leapfrogs, 1975. — [1], 28,[1]p : of ill(some col) ; 21x30cm. — (Network : with few words)
ISBN 0-09-125461-2 Sd : £0.35(non-net)
(B77-02263)

510'.2'433 — Mathematics. *For economics*

Gartenberg, Michael. Mathematics for financial analysis / by Michael Gartenberg and Barry Shaw. — Oxford [etc.] : Pergamon, 1976. — x, 210p : ill ; 26cm. — (Pergamon international library)
With answers to selected problems. — Index.
ISBN 0-08-019599-7 : £6.50
(B77-05378)

510'.2'4574 — Mathematics. *For biology*

Causton, David R. A biologist's mathematics / [by] David R. Causton. — London : Edward Arnold, 1977. — xii,326p : ill ; 22cm. — (Contemporary biology)
With answers. — Index.
ISBN 0-7131-2604-3 : £9.95
ISBN 0-7131-2605-1 Pbk : £4.95
(B77-18088)

Pollard, John Hurlstone. A handbook of numerical and statistical techniques : with examples mainly from the life sciences / [by] J.H. Pollard. — Cambridge [etc.] : Cambridge University Press, 1977. — xvi,349p : ill ; 24cm.
Bibl.: p.332-335. — Index.
ISBN 0-521-21440-8 : £13.50
(B77-19335)

510'.2'46 — Mathematics. *For technicians*

Bird, J O. Technician mathematics / [by] J.O. Bird, A.J.C. May. — London [etc.] : Longman. — (Longman technician series : mathematics and sciences)
In 3 vols.
Vol.1. — 1977. — viii,403p : ill ; 22cm.
Index.
ISBN 0-582-41160-2 Pbk : £3.50
(B77-24174)

Schofield, Clarence Ward. Basic mathematics for technicians / [by] C.W. Schofield. — London : Edward Arnold, 1977. — [7],119p : ill ; 22cm.
With answers to revision questions and numerical exercises.
ISBN 0-7131-3379-1 Pbk : £1.50
(B77-18089)

510'.2'462 — Mathematics. *For engineering*

Bajpai, Avinash Chandra. Advanced engineering mathematics / [by] A.C. Bajpai, L.R. Mustoe, D. Walker. — London [etc.] : Wiley, 1977. — x,578p : ill ; 24cm.
With answers. — Bibl.: p.549. — Index.
ISBN 0-471-99521-5 : £11.50
ISBN 0-471-99520-7 Pbk : 4.75
(B77-25575)

Engineering mathematics. — New York ; London [etc.] : Van Nostrand Reinhold.
Vol.1 / [by] A.J.M. Spencer ... [et al.]. — 1977. — xii,536p : ill ; 25cm.
With answers. — Bibl. — Index.
ISBN 0-442-30146-4 : £11.50
ISBN 0-442-30147-2 Pbk : £5.50
(B77-24175)

Engineering mathematics / [by] A.J.M. Spencer ... [et al.]. — New York ; London [etc.] : Van Nostrand Reinhold.
In 2 vols.
Vol.2. — 1977. — xi,400p : ill ; 24cm.
With answers. — Bibl. — Index.
ISBN 0-442-30206-1 : £12.50
ISBN 0-442-30208-8 Pbk : £5.50
(B77-31161)

510'.2'46213 — Mathematics. *For electronic engineering*

Cooke, Nelson Magor. Basic mathematics for electronics. — 4th ed. / [by] Nelson M. Cooke, Herbert F.R. Adams. — New York ; London [etc.] : McGraw-Hill, 1976. — vi,617p : ill(some col) ; 25cm.
With answers to odd-numbered problems. — Text on lining papers. — Previous ed.: 1970. — Index.
ISBN 0-07-012512-0 : £10.75
(B77-02961)

510'.2'46238 — Mathematics. *For deck officers*

Earl, George Edwin. Munro's mathematics for deck officers. — 5th ed. / by G.E. Earl, D.M. Robinson and J. Ward. — Glasgow : Munro, [1976]. — 407p : ill ; 22cm.
With answers. — Previous ed.: i.e. 3rd ed. revised, 1971.
Pbd : £3.60
(B77-04122)

510'.2'4624 — Mathematics. *For construction*

Jones, M K. Construction mathematics / [by] M.K. Jones. — London [etc.] : Longman.
In 2 vols.
Vol.2. — [1976]. — viii,186p : ill ; 22cm. — (Longman technician series : construction and civil engineering)
With answers. — Index.
ISBN 0-582-42021-0 : £5.50
ISBN 0-582-42022-9 Pbk : £3.25
(B77-07324)

510'.2'4658 — Mathematics. *For business studies*
Green, Terry. Managing mathematically / [by] Terry Green and John Webster. — London [etc.] : Macmillan, 1976. — xvi,205p : ill ; 24cm. — (Macmillan business, management and administration series)
Index.
ISBN 0-333-19113-7 Pbk : £4.95
(B77-27834)

Ochs, Robert. Contemporary business mathematics / [by] Robert Ochs, James Gray. — Philadelphia ; London [etc.] : Saunders.
Student's workbook. — [1976]. — vii,195p ; 26cm.
With answers. — Published in the United States: 1975.
ISBN 0-7216-6893-3 Pbk : £3.75
(B77-02264)

510'.28 — Electronic calculators. *Manuals*
Wyld, B A. The calculator revolution : how to make the most of your calculator / [by] B.A. Wyld and D.A. Bell. — London [etc.] : White Lion Publishers, 1977. — [7],207p : ill ; 23cm.
With answers to exercises. — Index.
ISBN 0-7274-0111-4 : £4.95
ISBN 0-7285-0019-1 Pbk : £2.50
(B77-22535)

510'.28 — Pocket electronic calculators. *Exercises, worked examples*
Goult, Raymond John. The pocket calculator pocket book / by R.J. Goult and M.J. Pratt. — Cheltenham (32 Malmesbury Rd, Kingsditch Trading Estate, Cheltenham GL51 9PL) : Stanley Thornes (Publishers) Ltd, 1976. — 63p : ill ; 22cm.
ISBN 0-85950-034-9 Pbk : £1.00
(B77-14208)

510'.28 — Pocket electronic calculators. *Manuals*
Gilbert, Jack. Advanced applications for pocket calculators / [by] Jack Gilbert ; with a specially written chapter for the guidance of the English reader by W. Oliver. — Slough : Foulsham-Tab, 1977. — viii,7-304p : ill ; 21cm.

Originally published: Blue Ridge Summit, Pa. : G/L Tab Books, 1975. — Index.
ISBN 0-7042-0176-3 Pbk : £3.50
(B77-26277)

Jansson, Lars. Make the most of your pocket calculator / [by Lars Jansson]. — London [etc.] : Foulsham, 1977. — 72p ; 17cm.
ISBN 0-572-00962-3 Pbk : £0.75
(B77-33770)

510'.7'1 — Schools. Curriculum subjects: Mathematics. Teaching methods
Heimer, Ralph T. Strategies for teaching children mathematics / [by] Ralph T. Heimer, Cecil R. Trueblood. — Reading, Mass. ; London [etc.] : Addison-Wesley, 1977. — xii,320p : ill ; 25cm.
Bibl. — Index.
ISBN 0-201-02882-4 : £9.60
(B77-21823)

510'.7'1041 — Schools. Curriculum subjects: Mathematics. *Great Britain. For parents*
Tammadge, Alan. A parents' guide to school mathematics / [by] Alan Tammadge, Phyllis Starr ; cartoons by David and Mark Ingram. — Cambridge [etc.] : Cambridge University Press, 1977. — vii,182p : ill, 2 facsims, plan ; 24cm. — (School Mathematics Project. Handbooks)
With answers. — Index.
ISBN 0-521-21108-5 : £6.50
(B77-14702)

510'.7'1041 — Schools. Curriculum subjects: Mathematics. Teaching. Implications of requirement by industries of school leavers with mathematical skills. *Great Britain. Conference proceedings*
Mathematics at the School/Industry Interface *(Conference), Yeovil, 1975.* Mathematics at the school-industry interface : proceedings of a symposium organized by the Education Department, Somerset County Council, held in Yeovil in March 1975. — [Southend-on-Sea] ([Maitland House, Warrior Sq., Southend-on-Sea, Essex SS1 2JY]) : Institute of Mathematics and its Applications, [1975]. — v, 77p : ill ; 20cm. — (Institute of Mathematics and its Applications. Symposium proceedings series ; no.12)
'The conference on Mathematics at the School/Industry Interface ...' - Foreword.
Sp : £2.50
(B77-06654)

510'.7'1073 — Schools. Curriculum subjects: Mathematics. Teaching. Individualised instruction. *United States*
Romberg, Thomas A. Individually guided mathematics / [by] Thomas A. Romberg [et al.]. — Reading, Mass. ; London [etc.] : Addison-Wesley, [1977]. — xi,196p : ill, forms ; 24cm. — (Leadership series in individually guided education)
Sound film and 3 sound filmstrips also available. — Published in the United States: 1976. — Bibl. — Index.
ISBN 0-201-19411-2 Pbk : £4.80
(B77-12418)

510'.7'1141 — Universities. *Great Britain. Open University. Curriculum subjects: Mathematics. Courses: Elementary mathematics for science and technology*
Open University. *Elementary Mathematics for Science and Technology Course Team.* A guide to the course, Elementary mathematics for science and technology / prepared by the Course Team. — 2nd ed. — Milton Keynes : Open University Press, 1973. — 16p ; 30cm. — (Mathematics/science/technology, an inter-faculty second level course) (MST281 ; G)

Previous ed.: 1971.
Sd : Unpriced
(B77-04123)

510'.7'1141 — Universities. Curriculum subjects: Mathematics. *Great Britain. For sixth formers*
Mathematical Association. *Universities and Schools Committee.* Mathematics at the university : an introduction to university mathematics for students / [prepared by the Universities and Schools Committee of the Mathematical Association ; edited by M.L. Cornelius and H. Neill]. — [London] : Bell for the Mathematical Association, [1977]. — [2], 7p ; 22cm.
'These notes ... appeared originally in the issue for December 1975 (Vol.59, No.410) of the "Mathematical gazette"' - title page verso.
Sd : £0.25
(B77-11775)

510'.7'12 — Secondary schools. Curriculum subjects: Mathematics. Teaching
Mathematics teaching / [by] Kenneth J. Travers ... [et al.]. — New York [etc.] ; London : Harper and Row, 1977. — xi,591p : ill, facsims, form, map, ports ; 25cm.
Bibl.: p.549-572. — Index.
ISBN 0-06-045233-1 : £10.45
(B77-32611)

510'.7'1241 — Secondary schools. Curriculum subjects: Mathematics. *Great Britain. For further education teaching*
Yorkshire and Humberside Council for Further Education. What is modern mathematics? : a guide to teachers in further education / Yorkshire & Humberside Council for Further Education. — [Leeds] ([Bowling Green Terrace, Leeds LS11 9SX]) : [The Council], 1976. — [2], 39p : ill ; 30cm.
ISBN 0-9502705-1-2 Sd : £0.70
(B77-00744)

510'.76 — Mathematics. *Exercises, worked examples. For Irish students. Primary school texts*
New primary maths. — Tallaght : Folens.
5 : Senior standards. Part 1 / [by] J.J. O'Neill. — [1977]. — 136p : ill(some col), maps ; 25cm.

Pbk : £1.20
(B77-18090)

510'.76 — Mathematics. *Exercises, worked examples. For slow learning children. Secondary school texts*
Boyde, Florence Colonna. Simple modern maths / [by] F.C. Boyde, R.A. Court, with A.M. Court and J.C. Hawdon. — Sunbury-on-Thames [etc.] : Nelson.
In 2 vols.
2. Pupil's book. — 1977. — 223,[1]p : ill(some col) ; 24cm.
ISBN 0-17-431006-4 Pbk : £1.95
(B77-24895)

Boyde, Florence Colonna. Simple modern maths / by F.C. Boyde, R.A. Court, with A.M. Court and J.C. Hawdon. — Sunbury-on-Thames [etc.] : Nelson.
In 2 vols.
2. Teacher's book. — 1977. — 283p : ill(some col) ; 24cm.
With answers.
ISBN 0-17-431008-0 Pbk : £2.25
(B77-25576)

Hill, Ian P. First aid maths / [by] Ian P. Hill and John Culpin. — Glasgow : Gibson.
1. — 1976. — [2],38p : ill, map ; 28cm.
Fill-in book.
ISBN 0-7169-3113-3 Sd : Unpriced
(B77-24896)

1. [Teachers' book]. — 1976. — [2],38p : ill, map ; 28cm.
With answers.
ISBN 0-7169-3115-x Sd : Unpriced
(B77-24897)

2. — 1976. — [2],38p : ill ; 28cm.
Fill-in book.
ISBN 0-7169-3114-1 Sd : Unpriced
(B77-24898)

2. [Teachers' book]. — 1976. — [2],38p : ill ; 28cm.
With answers.
ISBN 0-7169-3116-8 Sd : Unpriced
(B77-24899)

510'.76 — Mathematics. *Exercises, worked examples. Primary school texts*
Atkinson, Stanley Leonard Richard. Modern mathematics practice / [by] S.L.R. Atkinson and S. Newbold. — 2nd ed., metric. — London [etc.] : Oxford University Press, 1974. — 5v. : ill, map ; 20cm.
This ed. originally published: 1971.
ISBN 0-19-834719-7 Sd : £2.95
(B77-07325)

Griffiths, Alan Lionel. Key maths / [by] A.L. Griffiths. — Edinburgh : Oliver and Boyd.
Level 1. [Book] 7. — 1976. — [2],60p : chiefly ill(some col) ; 26cm.
Fill-in book.
ISBN 0-05-002956-8 Sd : £0.35
(B77-16356)

O & B maths tests. — Edinburgh : Oliver and Boyd.
Originally published: Hawthorn : Australian Council for Educational Research, 19-.
Test 1 : Numeration, counting and number patterns. — 1977. — Folder (4p) : 1 ill ; 28cm.
ISBN 0-05-003100-7 : £0.50 for 10 copies
(B77-29379)

Test 2 : Place value. — 1977. — Folder (4p) : ill ; 28cm.
ISBN 0-05-003101-5 : £0.50 for 10 copies
(B77-29380)

Test 3 : Sets. — 1977. — 5p : ill ; 28cm.
ISBN 0-05-003102-3 Sd : £1.00 for 10 copies
(B77-29381)

Test 4 : Whole numbers, mathematical ideas. — 1977. — Folder (4p) : ill ; 28cm.
ISBN 0-05-003103-1 : £0.50 for 10 copies
(B77-29382)

Test 5 : Whole numbers, mathematical terms, applications. — 1977. — Folder (4p) ; 28cm.
ISBN 0-05-003104-x : £0.50 for 10 copies
(B77-29383)

Test 6 : Whole numbers, computation. — 1977. — 8p ; 28cm.
ISBN 0-05-003105-8 Sd : £1.00 for 10 copies
(B77-29384)

Test 7 : Money. — 1977. — Folder (4p) ; 28cm.
ISBN 0-05-003106-6 : £0.50 for 10 copies
(B77-29385)

Test 8 : Common fractions, mathematical ideas. — 1977. — 5p : ill ; 28cm.
ISBN 0-05-003107-4 Sd : £1.00 for 10 copies
(B77-29386)

Test 9 : Common fractions, mathematical terms, applications. — 1977. — Folder (4p) ; 28cm.
ISBN 0-05-003108-2 : £0.50 for 10 copies
(B77-29387)

Test 10 : Common fractions, computation. — 1977. — Folder (4p) ; 28cm.
ISBN 0-05-003109-0 : £0.50 for 10 copies
(B77-29388)

Test 11 : Decimal fractions, mathematical ideas. — 1977. — Folder (4p) : ill ; 28cm.
ISBN 0-05-003110-4 : £0.50 for 10 copies
(B77-29389)

Test 12 : Decimal fractions, mathematical terms, applications. — 1977. — Folder (4p) ; 28cm.
ISBN 0-05-003111-2 : £0.50 for 10 copies
(B77-29390)

Test 13 : Decimal fractions, computation. — 1977. — Folder (4p) ; 28cm.
ISBN 0-05-003112-0 : £0.50 for 10 copies
(B77-29391)

Test 14 : Spatial relations. — 1977. — 7p : ill ; 28cm.
ISBN 0-05-003113-9 Sd : £1.00 for 10 copies
(B77-29392)

Test 15 : Length. — 1977. — Folder (4p) : ill ; 28cm.
ISBN 0-05-003114-7 : £0.50 for 10 copies
(B77-29393)

Test 16 : Area. — 1977. — Folder (4p) : ill ; 28cm.
ISBN 0-05-003115-5 : £0.50 for 10 copies
(B77-29394)

Test 17 : Weight. — 1977. — 6p : ill ; 28cm.
ISBN 0-05-003116-3 Sd : £1.00 for 10 copies
(B77-29395)

Test 18 : Capacity and volume. — 1977. — 6p : ill ; 28cm.
ISBN 0-05-003117-1 Sd : £1.00 for 10 copies
(B77-29396)

Test 19 : Time. — 1977. — Folder (4p) : ill ; 28cm.
ISBN 0-05-003118-x : £0.50 for 10 copies
(B77-29397)

Test 20 : Graphs. — 1977. — 5p : ill ; 28cm.
ISBN 0-05-003119-8 Sd : £1.00 for 10 copies
(B77-29398)

510'.76 — Mathematics. *Exercises, worked examples. Primary school texts. Cards*

Slater, Joseph Derrick. Link workcards : a programme of mathematical games and activities to extend and enrich any main course scheme / [by] J.D. Slater. — Amersham : Hulton.
Unit 2. — 1977. — Portfolio : ill(chiefly col) ; 30cm.
'A four unit series of workcards for the 7-11 year age range'. — 38 cards (38 sides).
ISBN 0-7175-0771-8 : £3.00
(B77-13006)

Units 1-4. Teachers' answer book. — 1977. — [7],27p ; 20cm.
ISBN 0-7175-0770-x Sd : £0.65
(B77-27835)

510'.76 — Mathematics. *Exercises, worked examples. Secondary school texts*

Dada, S A. Exercises in certificate mathematics. — Revised ed. / [by] S.A. Dada, G.M. Hocking. — London [etc.] : Macmillan, 1976. — 190p : ill ; 22cm.
With answers. — Previous ed.: in 2 vols. / by G.M. Hocking. 1974.
ISBN 0-333-19687-2 Pbk : £1.41
(B77-12419)

Elvin, R. Mathematics, revision and practice / [by] R. Elvin, C. Oliver, S.K. Whitehead. — Ibadan ; Oxford [etc.] : Oxford University Press, 1977. — [4],262p : ill ; 24cm.
With answers.
ISBN 0-19-832527-4 Pbk : £2.20
(B77-27028)

Fletcher, G. Multiple choice tests in mathematics / [by] G. Fletcher. — Basingstoke [etc.] : Macmillan, 1976. — 111p : ill ; 21cm.
With answers.
ISBN 0-333-17829-7 Pbk : £0.95
(B77-15823)

Fox, Ronald William. Basic skills in mathematics / [by] R.W. Fox. — London : Edward Arnold.
Book 4. — 1977. — [8],135p : ill, map ; 18cm.
ISBN 0-7131-0079-6 Sd : £1.25
(B77-17451)

Book 4. Answers. — 1977. — [2],29p ; 23cm.
ISBN 0-7131-0080-x Sd : £0.80
(B77-17452)

House maths / [by] N.S. Armstrong ... [et al.]. — Glasgow [etc.] : Blackie, 1976. — 32p : ill, form, plan ; 25cm. — (Mathematics for living)
ISBN 0-216-90211-8 Sd : £0.60
(B77-02265)

House maths / [by] N.S. Armstrong ... [et al.]. — Glasgow [etc.] : Blackie.
Teacher's guide. — 1976. — 11,[1]p : ill, form ; 25cm. — (Mathematics for living)
With answers.
ISBN 0-216-90212-6 Sd : £0.90
(B77-02266)

Raven, Arthur John. Metric mechanical mathematics / [by] A.J. Raven. — London : Heinemann Educational.
Book 3. — 1976. — [3],126p : ill ; 22cm.
ISBN 0-435-50810-5 Pbk : £0.90
(B77-02962)

Raven, Arthur John. Modern mathematics check-up / by A.J. Raven and K.K. Look. — London : Heinemann Educational, 1977. — ix, 117p : ill ; 25cm.
With answers.
ISBN 0-435-50812-1 Pbk : £1.60
(B77-29399)

510'.76 — Mathematics. *Questions & answers. Secondary school texts*

Benzie, H R H. Modern mathematics multiple choice tests / [by] H.R.H. Benzie. — London : J. Murray, 1977. — 48p : ill ; 25cm.
With answers.
ISBN 0-7195-3219-1 Sd : £0.95
(B77-07888)

510'.76 — Secondary schools. Examinations. Development. *Ireland (Republic). Study examples: Mathematics. Reports, surveys*

Public Examinations Evaluation Project. The Public Examinations Evaluation Project : a progress report / by J. Heywood, S. McGuinness, D. Murphy. — Dublin (School of Education, Trinity College, Dublin 2) : The Project, 1977. — ii,32,10 leaves ; 30cm. — (Public Examinations Evaluation Project. Reports ; vol. 1, no.3)
Sd : Unpriced
Also classified at 907'.6
(B77-31162)

510'.7'8 — Schools. Curriculum subjects: Mathematics. Teaching aids: Games

Kohl, Herbert Ralph. Writing, maths & games in the open classroom / [by] Herbert R. Kohl. — London : Methuen, 1977. — xi,200p : ill ; 21cm.
Originally published: as 'Math, writing & games in the open classroom'. New York : New York Review, 1974.
ISBN 0-416-83930-4 : £4.00
ISBN 0-416-83940-1 Pbk : £2.35
Also classified at 808'.042'071
(B77-12420)

510'.8 — Mathematics. *Essays. Early works*

Newton, *Sir* Isaac. The mathematical papers of Isaac Newton. — Cambridge [etc.] : Cambridge University Press.
Vol.7 : 1691-1695 / edited by D.T. Whiteside ; with the assistance in publication of A. Prag. — 1976. — xlviii,706p,[1],iv leaves of plates : ill, facsims ; 29cm.
Parallel Latin text and English translation. — Index.
ISBN 0-521-08720-1 : £52.00
(B77-04768)

510'.9 — Mathematics, to 1975

Bunt, Lucas Nicolaas Hendrik. The historical roots of elementary mathematics / [by] Lucas N.H. Bunt, Phillip S. Jones, Jack D. Bedient. — Englewood Cliffs ; London [etc.] : Prentice-Hall, 1976. — xiii,299p : ill, facsims ; 24cm.
With hints and answers to selected exercises. — Bibl. — Index.
ISBN 0-13-389015-5 : £9.35
(B77-07326)

Eves, Howard. An introduction to the history of mathematics / [by] Howard Eves. — 4th ed. — New York ; London [etc.] : Holt, Rinehart and Winston, 1976. — xvii,588p : ill, facsims, geneal table, maps, ports ; 25cm.
With answers. — Previous ed.: 1970. — Bibl. — Index.
ISBN 0-03-089539-1 : £12.50
(B77-02963)

510'.9 — Universities. *Great Britain. Open University. Curriculum subjects: Mathematics, to 1975. Courses: History of mathematics*

Introduction to the course / prepared by Graham Flegg for the [Open University] Course Team. — Milton Keynes (Walton Hall, Milton Keynes MK7 6AA) : Open University, 1975. — 34p : ill ; 30cm. — (Arts/mathematics, an interfaculty second level course : history of mathematics) (AM289 ; IC)
Bibl.: p.32-33.
Sd : Unpriced
(B77-14703)

510'.9'032 — Mathematics. Discoveries, 1600-1750

Griffiths, P L. Mathematical discoveries, 1600-1750 / [by] P.L Griffiths. — Ilfracombe : Stockwell, 1977. — 121p ; 19cm.
ISBN 0-7223-1006-4 : £2.75
(B77-33771)

510'.917'671 — Muslim mathematics, 600-1300

al-Daffa', Ali Abdullah. The Muslim contribution to mathematics / [by] Ali Abdullah al-Daffa'. — London : Croom Helm [etc.], 1977. — 121p : ill ; 23cm.
Bibl.: p.103-118. — Index.
ISBN 0-85664-464-1 : £7.95 : CIP rev.
(B77-09673)

510'.92'2 — Women mathematicians, 370-1935. *Biographies*

Osen, Lynn M. Women in mathematics / [by] Lynn M. Osen. — Cambridge, Mass. ; London : M.I.T. Press, 1974. — xii,185p : ports ; 21cm.
Bibl.: p.173-178. — Index.
ISBN 0-262-15014-x : Unpriced
(B77-19336)

510'.92'4 — Mathematics. Green, George. *Biographies*

George Green, miller, Snienton. — [Nottingham] ([The Castle, Nottingham NG1 6EL]) : Nottingham Castle, City of Nottingham Leisure Services, 1976. — 96p : ill, facsims, maps ; 21cm.
Bibl.: p.95-96. — Contents: George Green, his achievements and place in science / by R.M. Bowley, L.J. Challis and F.W. Sheard - George Green, his family and background / by Frieda M. Wilkins-Jones - George Green, his academic career / by David Phillips.
ISBN 0-905634-01-2 Sd : £0.75
(B77-10349)

511 — MATHEMATICS. GENERALITIES

511'.2 — Intuitionistic mathematics

Dummett, Michael. Elements of intuitionism / by Michael Dummett, with the assistance of Roberto Minio. — Oxford : Clarendon Press, 1977. — xii,467p : ill ; 24cm. — (Oxford logic guides)
Bibl.: p.452-461. — Index.
ISBN 0-19-853158-3 : £9.00
(B77-23356)

511'.3 — Formal languages. *Conference proceedings*

International Colloquium on Automata, Languages and Programming, *3rd, University of Edinburgh, 1976.* Automata, languages and programming : Third International Colloquium at the University of Edinburgh, 20, 21, 22, 23 July 1976 / edited by S. Michaelson and R. Milner. — Edinburgh : Edinburgh University Press, 1976. — viii,559p : ill ; 24cm.
'Third International Colloquium on Automata, Languages and Programming' - half title page. — Includes 4 papers in French. — Bibl.
ISBN 0-85224-308-1 : £8.00
(B77-00191)

511'.3 — Mathematical logic

Bell, John Lane. A course in mathematical logic / by J.L. Bell and M. Machover. — Amsterdam [etc.] ; Oxford : North-Holland Publishing Co., 1977. — xix,599p : ill ; 23cm.
Bibl.: p.576-583. — Index.
ISBN 0-7204-2844-0 : £10.00
(B77-21824)

Copi, Irving Marmer. Symbolic logic / [by] Irving M. Copi. — 4th ed. — New York : Macmillan ; London : Collier Macmillan, [1977]. — xiii,350,[2]p ; 24cm.
With solutions to selected exercises. — This ed. originally published: 1973. — Index.
ISBN 0-02-979680-6 Pbk : £5.85
(B77-28582)

Curry, Haskell Brooks. Foundations of mathematical logic / [by] Haskell B. Curry. — New York : Dover Publications [etc.] ; London : Constable, 1977. — viii,408p : ill ; 21cm.
Originally published: New York ; London : McGraw-Hill, 1963. — Bibl.: p.369-390. — Index.
ISBN 0-486-63462-0 Pbk : £4.25
(B77-31872)

511'.3 — Mathematical logic. *Conference proceedings*

Latin-American Symposium on Mathematical Logic, *3rd, Campinas, 1976.* Non-classical logics, model theory, and computability : proceedings of the Third Latin-American Symposium on Mathematical Logic, Campinas, Brazil, July 11-17, 1976 / edited by A.I. Arruda, N.C.A. da Costa, R. Chuaqui. — Amsterdam [etc.] ; Oxford : North-Holland Publishing Co., 1977. — xviii,307p : ill ; 23cm. — (Studies in logic and the foundations of mathematics ; vol.89)
Bibl.
ISBN 0-7204-0752-4 : Unpriced
(B77-24176)

511'.3 — Mathematical logic. Truth-value semantics
Leblanc, Hugues. Truth-value semantics / [by] Hugues Leblanc. — Amsterdam [etc.] ; Oxford : North-Holland Publishing Co., 1976. — xii,319p ; 23cm.
Bibl.: p.303-310. — Index.
ISBN 0-7204-2824-6 : £25.00
(B77-06040)

511'.3 — Mathematics. Sets. *Juvenile literature*
Oram, Sandie. Families / original story by Vivian Cohen and Colette Deblé ; illustrations by Colette Deblé ; [translated from the French and adapted by Sandie Oram]. — London : Macdonald Educational, 1975. — [24]p : chiefly col ill ; 26cm. — (Play school books)
These illustrations originally published: with French text. France : Le Livre de Paris, 1973.
ISBN 0-356-04786-5 Sd : £0.30
(B77-21086)

511'.3 — Model theory
Bridge, Jane. Beginning model theory : the completeness theorem and some consequences / by Jane Bridge. — Oxford : Clarendon Press, 1977. — viii,143p ; 25cm. — (Oxford logic guides)
Bibl.: p.138-140. — Index.
ISBN 0-19-853157-5 : £4.50
(B77-33772)

511'.3 — Propositional calculus
Foster, Alan W. Propositional logic : a student introduction / by Alan W. Foster and Graham J. Shute. — Birmingham (Gosta Green, Birmingham B4 7ET) : Department of Educational Enquiry, University of Aston in Birmingham, 1976. — [2],vii,305p ; 21cm. — (Aston educational enquiry monograph ; no.4)
With answers.
Pbk : Unpriced
(B77-27836)

511'.3 — Set theory
Fundamentals for mathematics : a foundation for decisions / [by] James Robinson ... [et al.]. — Reading, Mass. ; London [etc.] : Addison-Wesley, 1976. — viii,82p : ill ; 24cm.
With answers.
ISBN 0-201-06507-x Pbk : £2.40
Also classified at 512
(B77-13007)

Kuratowski, Kazimierz. Set theory : with an introduction to descriptive set theory / [by] K. Kuratowski and A. Mostowski ; [translated from the Polish by M. Mączyńoki and R. Kowalsky]. — 2nd, completely revised ed. — Amsterdam [etc.] ; Oxford : North-Holland Publishing Co. [etc.], 1976. — xiv,514p ; 23cm. — (Studies in logic and the foundations of mathematics ; vol.86)
Previous ed. of this translation: 1968. — Translation of: 'Teoria mnogości'. Wyd. 2., rozsz. Warszawa : Państwowe Wydawn. Naukowe, 1966. — Bibl.: p.476-495. — Index.
ISBN 0-7204-0470-3 : £21.25
(B77-04124)

511'.3 — Set theory. Concepts: Classes. *Festschriften*
Sets and classes : on the work by Paul Bernays / edited by Gert H. Müller. — Amsterdam [etc.] ; Oxford : North-Holland Publishing Co., 1976. — xxiii,358p : port ; 23cm. — (Studies in logic and the foundations of mathematics ; vol.84)
Bibl. — Index.
ISBN 0-7204-2284-1 : £27.91
(B77-02267)

511'.4 — Mathematics. Approximation. *Conference proceedings*
Symposium on Approximation Theory, *Austin, 1976.* Approximation theory II / edited by G.G. Lorentz, C.K. Chui, L.L. Schumaker. — New York [etc.] ; London : Academic Press, 1976. — xi,588p : ill ; 24cm. — (Academic Press rapid manuscript reproduction)
'... proceedings of a Symposium on Approximation Theory which was held in Austin on January 18-21, 1976' - Preface. — Bibl.
ISBN 0-12-455760-0 : £14.35
(B77-01402)

511'.5 — Graph theory
Berge, Claude. Graphs and hypergraphs / [by] Claude Berge ; translated [from the French] by Edward Minieka. — 2nd revised ed. — Amsterdam ; London : North-Holland Publishing Co. [etc.], 1976. — xiv,528p : ill ; 23cm. — (North-Holland mathematical library ; vol.6)
Previous ed. of this translation: 1973. — Translation and revision of: 'Graphes et hypergraphes'. Paris : Dunod, 1970. — Bibl.: p.498-522. — Index.
Unpriced
ISBN 0-7204-2453-4
(B77-18091)

Bondy, John Adrian. Graph theory with applications / [by] J.A. Bondy and U.S.R. Murty. — 1st ed. [reprinted] ; with corrections and some revision. — London [etc.] : Macmillan, 1977. — x,264p : ill ; 24cm.
Originally published: 1976. — Bibl.: p.254-255. — Index.
ISBN 0-333-22694-1 Pbk : £5.95
(B77-21825)

511'.5'02491 — Graph theory. *For geography*
Tinkler, Keith J. An introduction to graph theoretical methods in geography / by Keith J. Tinkler. — Norwich (University of East Anglia, Norwich NR4 7TJ) : Geo Abstracts Ltd, 1977. — [1],56,[1]p : ill ; 21cm. — (Concepts and techniques in modern geography ; no.14 ISSN 0306-6142)
Bibl.: p.53-56.
ISBN 0-902246-68-2 Sd : Unpriced
(B77-21826)

511'.6 — Combinatorial analysis
Brualdi, Richard A. Introductory combinatorics / [by] Richard A. Brualdi. — New York ; Oxford [etc.] : North-Holland Publishing Co., 1977. — x,374p : ill ; 24cm.
With answers to selected exercises. — Bibl.: p.359. — Index.
ISBN 0-7204-8610-6 : £13.00
(B77-21087)

511'.6 — Combinatorial analysis. *Conference proceedings*
British Combinatorial Conference, *6th, Royal Holloway College, 1977.* Combinatorial surveys : proceedings of the Sixth British Combinatorial Conference / edited by Peter J. Cameron. — London [etc.] : Academic Press, 1977. — vii,226p : ill ; 24cm.
'... held at Royal Holloway College in July 1977 ...' - Preface. — Bibl. — Index.
ISBN 0-12-157150-5 : £7.00
(B77-25577)

511'.6 — Combinatorial analysis. Algorithms
Reingold, Edward Martin. Combinatorial algorithms : theory and practice / [by] Edward M. Reingold, Jurg Nievergelt, Narsingh Deo. — Englewood Cliffs ; London [etc.] : Prentice-Hall, 1977. — xii,433p : ill ; 25cm.
Bibl. — Index.
ISBN 0-13-152447-x : £15.15
(B77-23357)

511'.6 — Combinatorial analysis. Applications of matroids
Welsh, Dominic James Anthony. Matroid theory / [by] D.J.A. Welsh. — London [etc.] : Academic Press, 1976. — xi,433p : ill ; 24cm. — (London Mathematical Society. Monographs ; 8 ISSN 0076-0560)
Bibl.: p.402-403. — Index.
ISBN 0-12-744050-x : £15.00
(B77-02964)

511'.64 — Permutations. *School texts*
Orders / [by Ray Hemmings ... et al.]. — London [etc.] : Hutchinson for Leapfrogs, 1976. — [1],16,[1]p : ill ; 21cm. — (Network : action books)
ISBN 0-09-127041-3 Sd : £0.35(non-net)
(B77-02268)

511'.7 — Numerical analysis
Johnson, Lee W. Numerical analysis / [by] Lee W. Johnson, R. Dean Riess. — Reading, Mass. ; London [etc.] : Addison-Wesley, 1977. — xi,370p : ill ; 24cm. — (World student series)
Bibl.: p.359-360. — Index.
Pbk : £6.00
(B77-24178)

511'.7 — Numerical analysis. *Conference proceedings*
Conference on the State of the Art in Numerical Analysis, *University of York, 1976.* The state of the art in numerical analysis : proceedings of the Conference on the State of the Art in Numerical Analysis held at the University of York, April 12th-15th, 1976, organized by the Institute of Mathematics and its Applications / edited by D. Jacobs. — London [etc.] : Academic Press, 1977. — xix,978p : ill ; 24cm.
Bibl. — Index.
ISBN 0-12-378650-9 : £20.00
(B77-23358)

511'.7 — Numerical methods. *Programmed texts*
Bajpai, Avinash Chandra. Numerical methods for engineers and scientists : a students' course book / [by] A.C. Bajpai, I.M. Calus, J.A. Fairley. — London [etc.] : Wiley, 1977. — xii, 380p : ill ; 25cm.
With answers. — Originally published: London : Taylor and Francis, 1975. — Bibl.: p.377. — Index.
ISBN 0-471-99542-8 Pbk : £4.95
(B77-24900)

511'.8 — Algorithms
Goodman, Seymour Evan. Introduction to the design and analysis of algorithms / [by] S.E. Goodman, S.T. Hedetniemi. — New York ; London [etc.] : McGraw-Hill, 1977. — xi, 371p : ill, map ; 25cm. — (McGraw-Hill computer science series)
Bibl.: p.332-336. — Index.
ISBN 0-07-023753-0 : £13.45
(B77-23359)

511'.8 — Mathematical models
Mathematical modelling / edited by J.G. Andrews and R.R. McLone. — London [etc.] : Butterworth, 1976. — xvii,260p : ill ; 24cm.
Bibl. — Index.
ISBN 0-408-10601-8 Pbk : £5.00
(B77-03513)

Open University. *Modelling by Mathematics Course Team.* Graphs and symbols / prepared by the [Open University, Modelling by Mathematics] Course Team. — Milton Keynes : Open University Press, 1977. — 64,60,55p : ill(some col), maps(1 col) ; 30cm. — (Technology/mathematics, a second level course : modelling by mathematics ; block 1) (TM281 ; 1-3)
With answers.
ISBN 0-335-06290-3 Pbk : Unpriced
(B77-26278)

512 — ALGEBRA
Barnett, Raymond A. College algebra / [by] Raymond A. Barnett. — New York ; London [etc.] : McGraw-Hill, [1976]. — xiii,418p : ill ; 25cm.
'Based on the author's "College algebra with trigonometry", with sections on trigonometry omitted [New York : McGraw-Hill, 1974]' - Library of Congress Cataloguing in Publication data. — With answers. — Published in the United States: 1974. — Index.
ISBN 0-07-003764-7 : £10.75
(B77-04125)

Carman, Robert Archibald. Basic algebra : a guided approach / [by] Robert A. Carman, Marilyn J. Carman. — New York ; London [etc.] : Wiley, 1977. — x,566p : ill(chiefly col) ; 28cm.
Pages perforated at inside edge. — With answers. — Index.
ISBN 0-471-13499-6 Pbk : £8.00
(B77-18092)

Fuller, Gordon. College algebra / [by] Gordon Fuller. — 4th ed. — New York ; London [etc.] : D. Van Nostrand, 1977. — xii,467p : ill ; 24cm.
With answers to selected problems. — Text on lining papers. — Previous ed.: i.e. 3rd ed. revised, New York ; London : Van Nostrand Reinhold, 1974. — Index.
ISBN 0-442-22516-4 : £10.50
(B77-21827)

Fundamentals for mathematics : a foundation for decisions / [by] James Robinson ... [et al.]. — Reading, Mass. ; London [etc.] : Addison-Wesley, 1976. — viii,82p : ill ; 24cm.
With answers.
ISBN 0-201-06507-x Pbk : £2.40
Primary classification 511'.3
(B77-13007)

512 — Algebra. *Festschriften*
Algebra, topology and category theory : a collection of papers in honor of Samuel Eilenberg / edited by Alex Heller, Myles Tierney. — New York [etc.] ; London : Academic Press, 1976. — xi,225p : ill, port ; 24cm.
'Many of these papers ... were read at a conference held May 3 and 4, 1974, on the occasion of Professor Eilenberg's sixtieth birthday, at the Graduate Center of the City University of New York' - Preface. — Bibl.
ISBN 0-12-339050-8 : £16.15
Also classified at 514
(B77-02269)

512'.02 — Abstract algebra
Birkhoff, Garrett. A survey of modern algebra / [by] Garrett Birkhoff, Saunders MacLane. — 4th ed. — New York : Macmillan ; London : Collier Macmillan, 1977. — xi,500p : ill ; 25cm.
Previous ed.: 1965. — Bibl.: p.438-485. — Index.
ISBN 0-02-310070-2 : £10.15
(B77-22536)

Brisley, Warren. A basis for linear algebra / [by] Warren Brisley. — Sydney ; London [etc.] : Wiley, 1973. — viii,189p : ill ; 25cm.
With answers. — Index.
ISBN 0-471-10460-4 : Unpriced
ISBN 0-471-10461-2 Pbk : Unpriced
(B77-18727)

Chow, Yutze. Modern abstract algebra / [by] Yutze Chow. — New York ; London [etc.] : Gordon and Breach, 1976. — 2v.([40],742p) ; 24cm.
Index.
ISBN 0-677-03880-1 : £34.30
(B77-00192)

Cohn, Paul Moritz. Algebra / [by] P.M. Cohn. — London [etc.] : Wiley.
In 2 vols.
Vol.2. — 1977. — xiii,483p : ill ; 24cm.
Bibl.: p.468-471. — Index.
ISBN 0-471-01823-6 : £8.95
(B77-11193)

Gilbert, William J. Modern algebra with applications / [by] William J. Gilbert. — New York ; London [etc.] : Wiley, [1977]. — xiii, 348p : ill ; 24cm.
'A Wiley-Interscience publication'. — With answers to odd-numbered exercises. — Published in the United States: 1976. — Bibl.: p.319-323. — Index.
ISBN 0-471-29891-3 : £16.45
(B77-10797)

512'.2 — Algebra. Groups. Characters & representations
Hill, Victor E. Groups, representations and characters / [by] Victor E. Hill. — New York : Hafner Press ; London : Collier Macmillan, 1975. — x,182p : ill ; 24cm.
Bibl.: p.175-177. — Index.
ISBN 0-02-846790-6 : £9.00
(B77-11776)

512'.2 — Algebra. Groups. Representations
Mackey, George Whitelaw. The theory of unitary group representations / [by] George W. Mackey. — [New ed.]. — Chicago ; London : University of Chicago Press, 1976. — x,372p ; 21cm. — (Chicago lectures in mathematics)
Previous ed.: published as 'The theory of group representations'. Chicago : Department of Mathematics, University of Chicago, 1955. — Bibl.
ISBN 0-226-50051-9 : £9.00
ISBN 0-226-50052-7 Pbk : £3.75
(B77-05379)

512'.2 — Finite groups. Modular representations
Puttaswamaiah, B M. Modular representations of finite groups / [by] B.M. Puttaswamaiah, John D. Dixon. — New York [etc.] ; London : Academic Press, 1977. — xv,242p ; 24cm. — (Pure and applied mathematics)
Bibl.: p.229-237. — Index.
ISBN 0-12-568650-1 : £16.70
(B77-18093)

512'.22 — Combinatorial group theory
Magnus, Wilhelm. Combinatorial group theory : presentations of groups in terms of generators and relations / [by] Wilhelm Magnus, Abraham Karrass, Donald Solitar. — 2nd revised ed. — New York : Dover Publications [etc.] ; London : Constable, 1976. — xii,444p ; 21cm.
Previous ed.: New York ; London : Interscience, 1966. — Bibl.: p.421-435. — Index.
ISBN 0-486-63281-4 Pbk : £4.50
(B77-04769)

512'.22 — Finite groups. Characters
Ledermann, Walter. Introduction to group characters / [by] Walter Ledermann. — Cambridge [etc.] : Cambridge University Press, 1977. — viii,174p : 1 ill ; 24cm.
With answers. — Bibl.: p.172. — Index.
ISBN 0-521-21486-6 : £9.50
ISBN 0-521-29170-4 Pbk : £3.30
(B77-27837)

512'.24 — Enveloping algebras
Dixmier, Jacques. Enveloping algebras / [by] Jacques Dixmier ; [translated from the French]. — Amsterdam [etc.] ; Oxford : North-Holland Publishing Co. [etc.], 1977. — xvi,375p ; 23cm. — (North-Holland mathematical library ; vol.14)
Translation of: 'Algèbres enveloppantes'. Paris : Gauthiers-Villars, 1974. — Bibl.: p.359-370. — Index.
ISBN 0-7204-0430-4 : £21.08
(B77-15264)

512'.4 — Algebra. Rings with involutions
Herstein, Israel Nathan. Rings with involution / [by] I.N. Herstein. — Chicago ; London : University of Chicago Press, [1977]. — x,247p ; 21cm. — (Chicago lectures in mathematics)
Published in the United States: 1976. — Bibl.
ISBN 0-226-32805-8 : £9.00
ISBN 0-226-32806-6 Pbk : £4.15
(B77-11194)

512'.4 — Near-rings
Pilz, Günter. Near-rings : the theory and its applications / [by] Günter Pilz. — Amsterdam [etc.] ; Oxford : North-Holland Publishing Co., 1977. — xiv,393p : ill ; 24cm. — (North-Holland mathematics studies ; 23)
Bibl.: p.350-387. — Index.
ISBN 0-7204-0566-1 Pbk : £14.64
(B77-14704)

512'.4 — Nonassociative rings. Applications of digital computer systems
Computers in nonassociative rings and algebras / edited by Robert E. Beck, Bernard Kolman. — New York [etc.] ; London : Academic Press, 1977. — ix,297p : ill ; 23cm.
'... an outgrowth of the Special Session on Computers in the Study of Nonassociative Rings and Algebras, which was held at the 82nd annual meeting of the American Mathematical Society in San Antonio, January 22-26, 1976' - Preface. — Bibl. — Index.
ISBN 0-12-083850-8 : £9.95
(B77-26279)

512'.4 — Skew fields
Cohn, Paul Moritz. Skew field constructions / [by] P.M. Cohn. — Cambridge [etc.] : Cambridge University Press, 1977. — xii,253p : ill ; 23cm. — (London Mathematical Society. Lecture note series ; 27)
Bibl.: p.234-250. — Index.
ISBN 0-521-21497-1 Pbk : £7.50
(B77-15265)

512'.5 — Linear algebra
Anton, Howard. Elementary linear algebra / [by] Howard Anton. — 2nd ed. — New York ; London [etc.] : Wiley, 1977. — xv,315,[36]p : col ill ; 24cm.
With answers. — Previous ed.: 1973. — Index.
ISBN 0-471-03244-1 : £9.35
(B77-18094)

512'.5 — Linear algebra. Applications
Noble, Benjamin. Applied linear algebra. — 2nd ed. / [by] Ben Noble, James W. Daniel. — Englewood Cliffs ; London [etc.] : Prentice-Hall, 1977. — xvii,477p : ill ; 24cm.
With answers to selected exercises. — Previous ed.: / by Ben Noble. 1969. — Bibl.: p.459-463. — Index.
ISBN 0-13-041343-7 : £12.75
(B77-21088)

Rorres, Chris. Applications of linear algebra / by Chris Rorres, Howard Anton. — New York ; London [etc.] : Wiley, 1977. — ix,233p : ill ; 23cm.
With answers.
ISBN 0-471-02398-1 Pbk : £3.25
(B77-20214)

512'.522 — Algebra. Modules
Solian, Alexandru. Theory of modules : (an introduction to the theory of module categories) / [by] Alexandru Solian ; translated from the Romanian by Mioara Buiculescu. — Bucureşti (Editura Academiei) ; London [etc.] : Wiley, 1977. — xi,420p : ill ; 25cm.
'A Wiley-Interscience Publication'. — Translation and revision of: 'Teoria modulelor'. Bucareşti : Editura Academiei Republicii Socialiste România, 1972. — Bibl.: p.401-405. — Index.
ISBN 0-471-99462-6 : £12.75
(B77-30210)

512'.522 — Linear algebra. Modules
Blyth, Thomas Scott. Module theory : an approach to linear algebra / [by] T.S. Blyth. — Oxford : Clarendon Press, 1977. — xi,400p : ill ; 24cm.
Index.
ISBN 0-19-853162-1 : £9.50 : CIP rev.
(B77-06655)

512'.55 — Discrete groups. Homological & cohomological dimensions
Bieri, Robert. Homological dimension of discrete groups / [by] Robert Bieri. — London ([Mile End Rd, E1 4NS]) : Mathematics Department, Queen Mary College, [1977]. — [1],iii,190p : ill ; 25cm. — (Queen Mary College. Mathematics notes)
'These Notes grew out of a course of advanced lectures given at Queen Mary College, London, in the Spring of 1975' - Introduction. — Bibl.: p.184-190.
Sd : £2.50
(B77-09674)

512'.55 — Lie groups
Price, John F. Lie groups and compact groups / [by] John F. Price. — Cambridge [etc.] : Cambridge University Press, 1977. — ix,177p ; 23cm. — (London Mathematical Society. Lecture note series ; 25)
Bibl.: p.169-173. — Index.
ISBN 0-521-21340-1 Pbk : £4.95
(B77-16856)

512'.55 — Locally compact abelian groups. Pontryagin duality
Morris, Sidney A. Pontryagin duality and the structure of locally compact abelian groups / [by] Sidney A. Morris. — Cambridge [etc.] : Cambridge University Press, 1977. — viii,128p : ill ; 23cm. — (London Mathematical Society. Lecture note series ; 29 ISSN 0076-0552)
Bibl.: p.119-120. — Index.
ISBN 0-521-21543-9 Pbk : £4.95
(B77-21828)

512'.55 — Topological algebras
Beckenstein, Edward. Topological algebras / [by] Edward Beckenstein, Lawrence Narici, Charles Suffel. — Amsterdam [etc.] ; Oxford : North-Holland Publishing Co., 1977. — xii, 370p : ill ; 24cm. — (Notas de matemática ; (60)) (North-Holland mathematics studies ; 24)
Bibl.: p.349-362. — Index.
ISBN 0-7204-0724-9 Pbk : £12.00
(B77-24901)

512'.7 — Algebra. Lattices. *Conference proceedings*
Lattice theory / edited by A.P. Huhn and E.T. Schmidt. — Amsterdam ; Oxford [etc.] : North-Holland Publishing Co. [etc.], 1976. — 462p : ill ; 25cm. — (Bolyai János Matematikai Társulat. Colloquia Mathematica Societatis János Bolyai ; 14)
'The conference was held in Szeged from 27 August to 30 August 1974 ...' - Preface. — Bibl.
ISBN 0-7204-0498-3 : £29.27
(B77-14705)

512'.7 — Complex numbers. *Secondary school texts*
Wilbraham, A N S. Advanced Level complex numbers / by A.N.S. Wilbraham. — London (2 Minford Gardens, W.14) : The author, 1977. — [5],175p : ill ; 23cm.
With answers. — Previous control number B77-26280.
ISBN 0-9505981-0-0 Pbk : £2.60
(B77-26280)

512'.7 — Number theory
Malcolm, W G. Number and structure / [by] W.G. Malcolm. — Wellington [N.Z.] ; London [etc.] : Reed Education, 1975. — ix,176p : ill ; 22cm. — (Studies in mathematics)
With answers. — Bibl.: p.165. — Index.
ISBN 0-589-05088-5 Pbk : £5.15
(B77-18728)

512'.7 — Real numbers
Flegg, Henry Graham. The real numbers / prepared by Graham Flegg ; for the [Open University] Course Team. — Milton Keynes : Open University Press, 1974. — 24p : ill, facsims ; 30cm. — (Arts/mathematics, an interfaculty second level course : history of mathematics ; unit 2) (AM289 ; 2)
With answers. — Bibl.: p.24.
ISBN 0-335-05005-0 Sd : £0.90
(B77-13625)

512'.73 — Integers. Partitions
Andrews, George E. The theory of partitions / [by] George E. Andrews. — Reading, Mass. ; London : Addison-Wesley, 1976. — xiv,255p : ill ; 24cm. — (Encyclopedia of mathematics and its applications ; vol.2)
Text on lining paper. — Bibl. — Index.
ISBN 0-201-13501-9 : £13.20
(B77-31873)

512'.74 — Algebraic number fields
Janusz, Gerald J. Algebraic number fields / [by] Gerald J. Janusz. — New York ; London : Academic Press, 1973. — x,220p ; 24cm. — (Pure and applied mathematics ; vol.55)
Bibl.: p.218. — Index.
ISBN 0-12-380250-4 : Unpriced
(B77-19337)

512'.74 — Algebraic number fields. *Conference proceedings*
Algebraic number fields (L-functions and Galois properties) : proceedings of a Symposium organised by the London Mathematical Society with the support of the Science Research Council and the Royal Society / edited by A. Fröhlich. — London [etc.] : Academic Press, 1977. — xii,704p : ill ; 24cm.
'... held from 2 to 12 September 1975, in the University of Durham' - Preface. — Includes two chapters in French. — Bibl.
ISBN 0-12-268960-7 : £16.00
(B77-20215)

512.9'0076 — Algebra. *Exercises, worked examples. Secondary school texts*
Johnson, Mildred. How to solve word problems in algebra : a solved problem approach / by Mildred Johnson. — New York ; London [etc.] : McGraw-Hill, 1976. — [7],166p : ill ; 20cm.
With answers.
ISBN 0-07-032620-7 Pbk : £3.30
(B77-05380)

512.9'042 — Algebra. *Introductions, primers*
Drooyan, Irving. Elementary algebra : structure and skills / [by] Irving Drooyan, Walter Hadel, Frank Fleming. — 4th ed. — New York ; London [etc.] : Wiley, 1977. — x,390p : ill(some col) ; 24cm.
With answers. — Text, ill. on lining papers. — Previous ed.: 1973. — Index.
ISBN 0-471-22249-6 : £8.65
(B77-10798)

512.9'43 — Linear algebra. Matrices
Campbell, Hugh G. An introduction to matrices, vectors and linear programming / [by] Hugh G. Campbell. — 2nd ed. — Englewood Cliffs ; London [etc.] : Prentice-Hall, 1977. — xv, 316p : ill ; 24cm.
With answers to odd-numbered exercises. — Previous ed.: New York : Appleton-Century-Crofts, 1965. — Index.
ISBN 0-13-487439-0 : £8.80
(B77-31163)

512.9'43 — Linear algebra. Matrices. Applications of Gaussian processes
Jacobson, David Harris. Extensions of linear-quadratic control, optimization and matrix theory / [by] David H. Jacobson. — London [etc.] : Academic Press, 1977. — x, 217p ; 24cm. — (Mathematics in science and engineering ; vol.133)
Index.
ISBN 0-12-378750-5 : £6.50
Primary classification 519.2
(B77-23365)

513 — ARITHMETIC
513 — Arithmetic. *For users of electronic calculators*
Hyatt, Herman Robert. Arithmetic with pushbutton accuracy / [by] Herman R. Hyatt, Irving Drooyan, Charles C. Carico. — New York ; London [etc.] : Wiley, 1977. — ix,304p : ill ; 28cm.
With answers. — Index.
ISBN 0-471-22308-5 Pbk : £7.95
(B77-11777)

513 — Arithmetic. *Primary school texts*
Jex, Stanley Frank. Number skills / [by] S.F. Jex. — London : Cassell and Collier Macmillan.
Answers. Books 1-6. — 1977. — 80p ; 25cm.
ISBN 0-304-29770-4 Pbk : £1.99
(B77-18729)

Sussex House School. *Mathematics Department.* Notes on number and geometry / [Sussex House School, Mathematics Department]. — [London] ([68 Cadogan Sq., SW1X 0EA]) : [The Department], [1976]. — [104]p : ill ; 22cm.
Limited ed. of 180 copies. — Index.
ISBN 0-9505511-0-4 Sd : Unpriced
Also classified at 516
(B77-06042)

513 — School leavers. Computational skills. *Great Britain. Reports, surveys*
Report of Working Party set up to investigate the reported decline in basic calculation skills among recruits to further education, industry and commerce. — Southampton ([Grosvenor Rd, Southampton]) : Southampton Curriculum Development Centre, [1974]. — 39p in various pagings : ill, form ; 31cm.
At head of title: Hampshire Education Committee, Southampton Area Education Office.
ISBN 0-903626-02-0 Sp : £0.75
(B77-02965)

513 — School leavers. Computational skills. *Wales. Reports, surveys*
Confederation of British Industry. Standards of numeracy and literacy in Wales : a CBI [Wales] working party report. — Cardiff (Pearl Assurance House, Greyfriars Rd, Cardiff CF1 3JR) : Confederation of British Industry Wales, 1977. — 35p : ill, form ; 30cm.
Sd : £1.50
Primary classification 428'.4'09429
(B77-27009)

513'.02'433 — Arithmetic. *For economics*
Bamford, George Gordon. Arithmetical and statistical methods / by G.G. Bamford. — Aylesbury : Ginn, 1976. — [2],60p : ill ; 22cm. — (Manchester Economics Project. Satellite books ; 1)
With answers. — Originally published: London : Ginn, 1969.
ISBN 0-602-22329-6 Sd : £1.10
Also classified at 519.5'02'433
(B77-21829)

513'.02'4613 — Arithmetic. *Programmed texts. For nursing*
Lipsey, Sally Irene. Mathematics for nursing science : a programmed text / [by] Sally Irene Lipsey. — 2nd ed. — New York ; London [etc.] : Wiley, 1977. — xv,252p : ill ; 26cm.
'A Wiley medical publication'. — Previous ed.: New York : Wiley, 1965. — Index.
ISBN 0-471-01798-1 Pbk : £5.60
(B77-20216)

513'.07 — Arithmetic. Learning by children
Ginsburg, Herbert. Children's arithmetic : the learning process / [by] Herbert Ginsburg. — New York [etc.] ; London : D. Van Nostrand, 1977. — ix,197p : ill ; 23cm.
Bibl.: p.191-194. — Index.
ISBN 0-442-22695-0 Pbk : £4.00
(B77-25578)

513'.076 — Arithmetic. *Exercises, worked examples. Primary school texts*
Bullock, G V. Way ahead / [by] G.V. Bullock. — [Andover] : Philograph.
Number work book 1. — 1976. — [1],15p ; 16cm.
ISBN 0-85370-322-1 Sd : £0.60(for pack of 10 copies)
(B77-02966)

Number work book 2. — 1976. — [1],15p ; 16cm.
ISBN 0-85370-323-x Sd : £0.60(for pack of 10 copies)
(B77-02967)

Number work book 3. — 1976. — [1],15p ; 16cm.
ISBN 0-85370-324-8 Sd : £0.60(for pack of 10 copies)
(B77-02968)

Number work book 4. — 1976. — [1],15p ; 16cm.
ISBN 0-85370-325-6 Sd : £0.60(for pack of 10 copies)
(B77-02969)

Number work book 5. — 1976. — [1],15p ; 16cm.
ISBN 0-85370-326-4 Sd : £0.60(for pack of 10 copies)
(B77-02970)

Crew, C C. Seek and find arithmetic / by C.C. Crew. — New ed. with decimal currency, use of bases and metric units. — Exeter : Wheaton, 1976. — 80p : ill ; 25cm.
Previous ed.: 1970.
ISBN 0-08-021359-6 Sd : £0.45
ISBN 0-08-021358-8 Teacher's ed. : £0.50
(B77-02270)

Hesse, Kenneth Anderson. Graded workbooks / by K.A. Hesse. — London : Longman.
Workbook 6 : An introduction to decimals. — Teacher's ed. — 1977. — [2],46p : ill ; 25cm.
With answers.
ISBN 0-582-18223-9 Sd : £0.65
(B77-31874)

Hesse, Kenneth Anderson. Graded workbooks / by K.A. Hesse. — London : Longman.
Workbook 6 : An introduction to decimals. — 1977. — [2],46p : ill ; 25cm.
Fill-in book.
ISBN 0-582-18222-0 Sd : £0.49
(B77-31875)

Watson, Thomas Frizzell. Modern comprehensive arithmetic / [by] T.F. Watson, J. Freedland, [T.A. Quinn]. — Edinburgh : Holmes-McDougall.
1. — 1976. — 96p : ill ; 24cm.
ISBN 0-7157-1480-5 Pbk : £1.00
(B77-04770)

Watson, Thomas Frizzell. Modern comprehensive arithmetic / [by] T.F. Watson, J. Freeland, [T.A. Quinn]. — Edinburgh : Holmes-McDougall.
1. Answer book. — 1976. — [1],20p ; 24cm.
ISBN 0-7157-1485-6 Sd : £0.50
(B77-17453)

2. — 1976. — 96p : ill ; 24cm.
ISBN 0-7157-1481-3 Pbk : £1.00
(B77-04771)

2. Answer book. — 1976. — [1],22,[1]p ; 24cm.
ISBN 0-7157-1486-4 Sd : £0.50
(B77-17454)

3. — 1976. — 96p : ill ; 24cm.
ISBN 0-7157-1482-1 Pbk : £1.10
(B77-04772)

3. Answer book. — 1976. — [1],18,[1]p ; 24cm.
ISBN 0-7157-1487-2 Sd : £0.50
(B77-17455)

4. Answer book. — 1977. — [1],17p ; 24cm.
ISBN 0-7157-1488-0 Sd : £0.50
(B77-17456)

5. — 1977. — 96p : ill, maps ; 24cm.
ISBN 0-7157-1484-8 Sd : £1.15
(B77-17457)

513'.076 — Middle schools. Students. Computational skills. Assessment. Tests: Basic Number Screening Test. *Manuals*
Gillham, William Edwin Charles. Basic number screening test / prepared by W.E.C. Gillham and K.A. Hesse. — London : Hodder and Stoughton, 1976. — Portfolio : ill ; 22x27cm.
Manual (14p.), form A (folder ([4]p.)), form B (folder ([4]p.)). — With answers.
ISBN 0-340-21289-6 : £0.90(specimen set)
(B77-04126)

513'.2 — Arithmetic. Fundamental operations. *School texts*
Briten, Paul. Clearway maths / [by] Paul Briten. — Oxford [etc.] : Oxford University Press, 1977. — 4v. : ill(chiefly col), col map ; 25cm.
ISBN 0-19-832528-2 Sd : £2.50
(B77-31164)

513'.2 — Arithmetic. Multiplication. *Tables. Juvenile literature*
The **easy** times table book. — Slough [etc.] : Foulsham, 1977. — [24]p ; 20cm.
ISBN 0-572-00990-9 Sd : £0.40
(B77-33195)

513'.2 — Numbers. *Illustrations. Juvenile literature*
Anno, Mitsumasa. Anno's counting book. — London [etc.] : Bodley Head, 1977. — [29]p : of col ill ; 25x26cm.
These illustrations originally published: with Japanese text. Tokyo : Kodansha, 1975.
ISBN 0-370-30009-2 : £2.95
(B77-18096)

Eichenberg, Fritz. Dancing in the moon : counting rhymes / by Fritz Eichenberg. — New York ; London : Harcourt Brace Jovanovich, 1975. — [27]p : chiefly col ill ; 26cm. — (Voyager picture books)
Originally published: New York : Harcourt Brace, 1955.
ISBN 0-15-623811-x Pbk : £1.25
(B77-06043)

Hay, Dean. I can count / photographs by Dean Hay. — Revised ed. — London [etc.] : Collins, 1977. — [31]p : of col ill ; 21cm.
Previous ed.: published as part of 'Now I can count'. 1968.
ISBN 0-00-195354-0 : £1.25
(B77-33773)

Spencer, Herbert, *b.1924.* The book of numbers / [by] Herbert & Mafalda Spencer. — [New ed.]. — London : Latimer New Dimensions, 1977. — [96]p : chiefly ill ; 20x21cm.
Previous ed.: 1974.
ISBN 0-901539-65-1 Pbk : £2.00
(B77-23360)

513'.2 — Numbers. *Juvenile literature*
Kincaid, Lucy. The Skittles counting book / [written and illustrated by Lucy and Eric Kincaid]. — [Cambridge] : Brimax Books, 1976. — [20]p : chiefly col ill ; 26cm.
Cover title. — Text, col. ill. on lining papers.
ISBN 0-904494-14-4 : £0.65
(B77-07889)

513'.26'014 — Arithmetic. Fractions. Notation, to ca 900
Waerden, Bartel Leendert van der. Written fractions / prepared by B.L. van der Waerden. — Milton Keynes : Open University Press, 1976. — 50p : ill, facsims, port ; 30cm. — (AM289 ; N4) (Arts/mathematics, an interfaculty second level course : history of mathematics : counting, numerals and calculation ; 4)
ISBN 0-335-05019-0 Pbk : £1.80
(B77-27029)

513'.5 — Numeration
Waerden, Bartel Leendert van der. Counting / prepared by B.L. van der Waerden and Graham Flegg ; for the [Open University] Course Team. — Milton Keynes : Open University Press.
1 : Primitive and more developed counting systems. — 1975. — 46p : ill, facsim, maps(1 col), port ; 30cm. — (Arts/mathematics, an interfaculty second level course : history of mathematics : counting, numerals and calculation ; 1) (AM289 ; N1)
With answers. — Bibl.: p.10.
ISBN 0-335-05016-6 Pbk : £1.40
(B77-14209)

2 : Decimal number words ; [and], Tallies and knots. — 1975. — 46p : ill, facsims, 2 maps, port ; 30cm. — (Arts/mathematics, an interfaculty second level course : history of mathematics : counting, numerals and calculation ; 2) (AM289 ; N2)
With answers.
ISBN 0-335-05017-4 Pbk : £1.50
(B77-14210)

513'.5 — Numeration. *Juvenile literature*
Berenstain, Stan. The bears' counting book / [by] Stan and Jan Berenstain. — Glasgow [etc.] : Collins, 1977. — [13]p : of col ill ; 20cm.
Originally published: as 'The Berenstain bears' counting book'. New York : Random House, 1976.
ISBN 0-00-138246-2 Pbd : £0.85
(B77-18097)

Brychta, Alex. Numbers 1 to 10, and back again / [by] Alex Brychta. — London : Dent, 1977. — [25]p : chiefly col ; 18x28cm.
ISBN 0-460-06786-9 : £1.75 : CIP rev.
(B77-06044)

My first book : counting rhymes, numbers, telling the time. — [Maidenhead] : Popular Press, 1977. — [20]p : col ill ; 27cm.
Col. ill., text on lining papers.
ISBN 0-361-03995-6 : Unpriced
(B77-18098)

Scarry, Richard. Learn to count / with illustrations by Richard Scarry. — London [etc.] : Hamlyn, 1977. — [24]p : col ill ; 21cm. — (A golden look-look book)
Originally published: New York : Golden Press, 1976.
ISBN 0-600-31972-5 Sd : £0.40
(B77-28583)

Scarry, Richard. Richard Scarry's best counting book ever. — Glasgow [etc.] : Collins, 1977. — [44]p : chiefly col ill ; 31cm.
Col. ill., text on lining papers. — Originally published: New York : Random House, 1976.
ISBN 0-00-138220-9 : £1.95
(B77-18099)

513'.5'0222 — Numeration. *Colouring books*
Counting. — Maidenhead : Purnell, 1977. — [48] p : ill ; 28cm. — (Colour and learn)
Fill-in book.
Pbk : £0.15
(B77-09675)

513'.5'09 — Numeration, to 1975. *Juvenile literature*
Charlton, Robert Foster. Number past & present / [by] R.F. Charlton, R.G. Russell. — Folkestone : Bailey and Swinfen, 1976. — [6], 121p : ill, maps ; 23cm.
With answers.
ISBN 0-561-00282-7 : £3.25
(B77-02271)

513'.92 — Mental arithmetic. *Exercises, worked examples. School texts*
Adams, John William. Mental arithmetic / compiled by J.W. Adams and R.P. Beaumont ; edited by T.R. Goddard. — Huddersfield : Schofield and Sims.
1. — 1976. — 47p : ill ; 30cm.
Fill-in book.
ISBN 0-7217-2240-7 Sd : Unpriced
(B77-03514)

1. [Teacher's notes and answers]. — 1976. — 47p : ill ; 30cm.
ISBN 0-7217-2245-8 Sd : Unpriced
(B77-03515)

2. — 1976. — 47p : ill ; 30cm.
Fill-in book.
ISBN 0-7217-2241-5 Sd : Unpriced
(B77-03516)

2. [Teacher's notes and answers]. — 1976. — 47p : ill ; 30cm.
ISBN 0-7217-2246-6 Sd : Unpriced
(B77-03517)

3. — 1976. — 47p : ill ; 30cm.
Fill-in book.
ISBN 0-7217-2242-3 Sd : £0.30
(B77-03518)

3. [Teacher's notes and answers]. — 1976. — 47p : ill ; 30cm.
ISBN 0-7217-2247-4 Sd : £0.45
(B77-03519)

4. — 1976. — 47p : ill ; 30cm.
Fill-in book.
ISBN 0-7217-2243-1 Sd : £0.30
(B77-09676)

[4]. Teacher's notes and answers. — 1976. — 47p : ill ; 30cm.
ISBN 0-7217-2248-2 Sd : Unpriced
(B77-09677)

Adams, John William. Mental arithmetic / compiled by J.W. Adams and R.B. Beaumont ; edited by T.R. Goddard. — Huddersfield : Schofield and Sims.
5. — 1977. — 47p : ill ; 30cm.
Fill-in book.
ISBN 0-7217-2244-x Sd : £0.30
(B77-12421)

Adams, John William. Mental arithmetic / compiled by J.W. Adams and R.P. Beaumont ; edited by T.R. Goddard. — Huddersfield : Schofield and Sims.
5. [Teacher's notes and answers]. — 1977. — 47p : ill ; 30cm.
ISBN 0-7217-2249-0 Sd : £0.45
(B77-12422)

Jex, Stanley Frank. Mental arithmetic / [by] S.F. Jex. — London : Cassell.
Book 1. — 1977. — [32]p : ill(some col) ; 22cm.
ISBN 0-304-29836-0 Sd : £0.45
(B77-16857)

Book 2. — 1977. — [32]p : ill(some col) ; 22cm.
ISBN 0-304-29837-9 Sd : £0.45
(B77-16858)

513'.93 — Business arithmetic
Harvey, John Henry. Arithmetic for the business student / by J.H. Harvey. — 7th ed. — London : Cassell, 1977. — 224p : ill, form ; 22cm.
With answers. — Previous ed.: 1972.
ISBN 0-304-29872-7 Pbk : £2.50
(B77-23361)

Harvey, John Henry. The arithmetic of commerce / [by] J.H. Harvey. — London : Cassell.
First course. — [Standard ed., metric units ed., 16th ed.]. — 1977. — 192p : ill ; 20cm.
With answers. — Previous ed.: i.e. Nigerian ed., 1973.
ISBN 0-304-29824-7 Pbk : £1.50
(B77-27030)

Harvey, John Henry. Commercial arithmetic / [by] J.H. Harvey. — 4th ed. — Sevenoaks : Teach Yourself Books, 1977. — 208p : ill, form ; 18cm. — (Teach yourself books)
With answers. — Previous ed.: 1972.
ISBN 0-340-21845-2 Pbk : £0.95
(B77-31165)

513'.93'02462 — Business arithmetic. *For engineering*
Kurtz, Max. Engineering economics for professional engineers' examinations / [by] Max Kurtz. — 2nd ed. — New York ; London [etc.] : McGraw-Hill, [1976]. — xvii,311p : ill ; 21cm.
This ed. published in the United States: 1975. — Previous ed.: New York : McGraw-Hill, 1959. — Bibl.: p.301-303. — Index.
ISBN 0-07-035675-0 : £14.55
(B77-06045)

513'.93'076 — Business arithmetic. *Exercises, worked examples*
Greer, Alec. Arithmetic for commerce / [by] A. Greer. — Cheltenham ([Baunton La., Cirencester, Glos. GL7 2LL]) : Stanley Thornes (Publishers) Ltd, 1976. — ix,243p : ill ; 25cm.
With answers. — Index.
ISBN 0-85950-028-4 Pbk : £2.20
(B77-12423)

514 — TOPOLOGY
Sims, Benjamin T. Fundamentals of topology / [by] Benjamin T. Sims. — New York : Macmillan ; London : Collier Macmillan, 1976. — xi,179p : ill ; 24cm.
Bibl.: p.169-173. — Index.
ISBN 0-02-410640-2 : £8.50
(B77-17458)

514 — Topology. *Festschriften*
Algebra, topology and category theory : a collection of papers in honor of Samuel Eilenberg / edited by Alex Heller, Myles Tierney. — New York [etc.] ; London : Academic Press, 1976. — xi,225p : ill, port ; 24cm.
'Many of these papers ... were read at a conference held May 3 and 4, 1974, on the occasion of Professor Eilenberg's sixtieth birthday, at the Graduate Center of the City University of New York' - Preface. — Bibl.
ISBN 0-12-339050-8 : £16.15
Primary classification 512
(B77-02269)

514'.2 — H-spaces
Zabrodsky, Alexander. Hopf spaces / [by] Alexander Zabrodsky. — Amsterdam [etc.] ; Oxford : North-Holland Publishing Co., 1976. — x,223p : ill ; 24cm. — (North-Holland mathematics studies ; 22) (Notas de matemática ; 59)
Bibl.: p.211-218. — Index.
ISBN 0-7204-0553-x Pbk : £10.54
(B77-14706)

514'.223 — Topological spaces: Stiefel manifolds
James, I M. The topology of Stiefel manifolds / [by] I.M. James. — Cambridge [etc.] : Cambridge University Press, 1976 [i.e. 1977]. — viii,168p ; 23cm. — (London Mathematical Society. Lecture note series ; 24 ISSN 0076-0552)
Bibl.: p.155-165. — Index.
ISBN 0-521-21334-7 Pbk : £3.95
(B77-06046)

514'.23 — Algebraic topology. Homology theory
Giblin, P J. Graphs, surfaces and homology : an introduction to algebraic topology / [by] P.J. Giblin. — London : Chapman and Hall [etc.], 1977. — xv,329p : ill ; 22cm. — (Chapman and Hall mathematics series)
'A Halsted Press book'. — Bibl.: p.309-312. — Index.
ISBN 0-412-21440-7 Pbk : £4.95
(B77-11195)

514'.3 — Topological spaces. Dynamical systems
Brown, James R. Ergodic theory and topological dynamics / [by] James R. Brown. — New York [etc.] ; London : Academic Press, 1976. — x, 190p : ill ; 24cm. — (Pure and applied mathematics)
Bibl.: p.181-185. — Index.
ISBN 0-12-137150-6 : £11.90
Primary classification 515'.42
(B77-06047)

514'.32 — Topological spaces. Fixed points. Theories. *Conference proceedings*
Fixed Point Theory and Its Applications *(Conference), Dalhousie University, 1975.* Fixed Point Theory and Its Applications / edited by Srinivasa Swaminathan. — New York [etc.] ; London : Academic Press, 1976. — xv,216p : ill ; 24cm.
'... proceedings of the seminar on Fixed Point Theory and Its Applications held at Dalhousie University, Halifax, Nova Scotia, June 9-12, 1975' - Preface. — Bibl. — Index.
ISBN 0-12-678650-x : £8.50
(B77-15824)

514'.7 — Differential topology
Chillingworth, D R J. Differential topology with a view to applications / [by] D.R.J. Chillingworth. — London [etc.] : Pitman, 1976. — [10],291p : ill ; 25cm. — (Research notes in mathematics ; 9)
Bibl.: p.273-283. — Index.
ISBN 0-273-00283-x Pbk : £4.50
(B77-03520)

514'.7 — Foliations. Characteristic classes
Pittie, H V. Characteristic classes of foliations / [by] H.V. Pittie. — London [etc.] : Pitman, 1976. — [7],107p ; 25cm. — (Research notes in mathematics ; 10)
Bibl.: p.106-107.
ISBN 0-273-00311-9 Pbk : £4.40
(B77-04127)

515 — CALCULUS
Bers, Lipman. Calculus. — 2nd ed. / [by] Lipman Bers in collaboration with Frank Karal. — New York ; London [etc.] : Holt, Rinehart and Winston, 1976. — xi,783p : ill ; 25cm.
With answers to odd numbered problems. — Previous ed.: / by Lipman Bers. 1969. — Index.
ISBN 0-03-089268-6 : £11.00
(B77-00745)

Binmore, K G. Mathematical analysis : a straightforward approach / [by] K.G. Binmore. — Cambridge [etc.] : Cambridge University Press, 1977. — x,257p : ill ; 24cm.
With answers. — Bibl.: p.251-252. — Index.
ISBN 0-521-21480-7 : £9.75
ISBN 0-521-29167-4 Pbk : £3.75
(B77-20217)

Choquet, Gustave. Lectures on analysis / [by] Gustave Choquet ; edited by J. Marsden, T. Lance and S. Gelbart. — Reading, Mass. ; London [etc.] : Benjamin.
'Advanced Book Program'. — In 3 vols. — Originally published: New York : Benjamin, 1969.
Vol.1 : Integration and topological vector spaces. — 1976. — xx,360,27p ; 23cm. — (Mathematics lecture note series ; 24)
Index.
ISBN 0-8053-6955-4 Pbk : £7.60
(B77-11778)

Vol.2 : Representation theory. — 1976. — xx, 315,21p : ill ; 23cm. — (Mathematics lecture note series ; 25)
Index.
ISBN 0-8053-6957-0 Pbk : £7.60
(B77-11779)

Vol.3 : Infinite dimensional measures and problem solutions. — 1976. — xix,320,21p : ill ; 23cm. — (Mathematics lecture note series ; 26)
Index.
ISBN 0-8053-6959-7 Pbk : £7.60
(B77-11780)

Flanders, Harley. A second course in calculus / [by] Harley Flanders, Robert R. Korfhage, Justin J. Price. — New York ; London : Academic Press, 1974. — xii,687p : ill ; 25cm.
With answers to selected exercises. — Text on lining papers. — Index.
ISBN 0-12-259662-5 : Unpriced
(B77-19339)

Grossman, Stanley Irwin. Calculus / [by] Stanley I. Grossman. — New York [etc.] ; London : Academic Press, 1977. — xviii,1005,A136p : ill(chiefly col) ; 24cm.
With answers to odd-numbered problems and review exercises. — Index.
ISBN 0-12-304350-6 : £13.50
(B77-23362)

Kline, Morris. Calculus : an intuitive and physical approach / [by] Morris Kline. — 2nd ed. — New York ; London [etc.] : Wiley, 1977. — xvi,943p : ill ; 26cm.
Previous ed.: in 2 vols. 1967. — Index.
ISBN 0-471-49116-0 : £14.00
(B77-32612)

Loomis, Lynn Harold. Calculus / [by] Lynn Loomis. — 2nd ed. — Reading, Mass. ; London [etc.] : Addison-Wesley, 1977. — xiii, 801,A78,I9 : ill ; 26cm.
With answers to selected odd-numbered problems. — Previous ed.: Reading, Mass. : Addison-Wesley, 1974. — Index.
ISBN 0-201-04326-2 : £15.20
(B77-21090)

Rudin, Walter. Principles of mathematical analysis / [by] Walter Rudin. — 3rd ed. — New York ; London [etc.] : McGraw-Hill, 1976. — x,342p ; 24cm. — (International series in pure and applied mathematics)
Previous ed.: 1964. — Bibl.: p.335-336. — Index.
ISBN 0-07-054235-x : £12.85
(B77-04774)

Wonnacott, Thomas. Calculus : an applied approach / [by] Thomas Wonnacott. — New York ; London [etc.] : Wiley, 1977. — xiv, 514p : ill ; 24cm.
With answers to odd-numbered problems. — Index.
ISBN 0-471-95959-6 : £9.70
(B77-18100)

515 — Calculus. *Secondary school texts*
Dakin, Albert. Elementary analysis / by A. Dakin and R.I. Porter. — Metricated ed. — London : Bell, 1975. — xii,378p : ill ; 19cm.
With answers. — This ed. originally published: 1971. — Index.
ISBN 0-7135-1540-6 : £1.75
(B77-25579)

515 — Fixed points. Applications. *Conference proceedings*
International Conference on Computing Fixed Points with Applications, *1st, Clemson University, 1974.* Fixed points : algorithms and applications / edited by Stepan Karamardian in collaboration with C.B. Garcia. — New York [etc.] ; London : Academic Press, 1977. — x, 494p : ill ; 24cm.
'The first International Conference on Computing Fixed Points with Applications was held in the Department of Mathematical Sciences at Clemson University, Clemson, South Carolina, June 26-28, 1974' - Preface. — Bibl.
ISBN 0-12-398050-x : £13.85
(B77-31876)

515 — Infinitesimals
Stroyan, K D. Introduction to the theory of infinitesimals / [by] K.D. Stroyan, in collaboration with W.A.J. Luxemburg. — New York [etc.] ; London : Academic Press, 1976 [i.e. 1977]. — xv,326p : ill ; 24cm. — (Pure and applied mathematics)
Published in the United States: 1976. — Bibl.: p.316-321. — Index.
ISBN 0-12-674150-6 : £17.40
(B77-12424)

515 — Mathematics. Optimisation. Theories
Neustadt, Lucien Wolf. Optimization : a theory of necessary conditions / [by] Lucien W. Neustadt. — Princeton ; Guildford : Princeton University Press, 1976 [i.e. 1977]. — xiii,424,[1] p ; 25cm.
Published in the United States: 1976. — Bibl.: p.413-421. — Index.
ISBN 0-691-08141-7 : £15.70
(B77-11781)

515 — Nonlinear optimisation
Adby, P R. Introduction to optimization methods / [by] P.R. Adby and M.A.H. Dempster. — London : Chapman and Hall, 1974. — x,204p : ill ; 22cm. — (Chapman and Hall mathematics series)
Bibl.: p.196-198. — Index.
ISBN 0-412-11040-7 Pbk : £2.50
(B77-20218)

515 — Nonstandard mathematical analysis
Davis, Martin, *b.1928.* Applied nonstandard analysis / [by] Martin Davis. — New York ; London [etc.] : Wiley, 1977. — xiii,181p ; 24cm. — (Pure and applied mathematics)
'A Wiley-Interscience publication'. — Bibl.: p.178. — Index.
ISBN 0-471-19897-8 : Unpriced
(B77-23363)

515 — Optimisation. Applications. *Conference proceedings*
Conference on Optimization in Action, *University of Bristol, 1975.* Optimization in action : proceedings of the Conference on Optimization in Action held at the University of Bristol in January 1975, organised by the Institute of Mathematics and its Applications / edited by L.C.W. Dixon. — London [etc.] : Academic Press, 1976. — xi,622p : ill ; 24cm.
Bibl. — Index.
ISBN 0-12-218550-1 : £13.50
(B77-04775)

515'.02'43 — Calculus. *For social sciences*
Goodman, Adolph Winkler. Calculus for the social sciences / [by] A.W. Goodman. — Philadelphia ; London [etc.] : Saunders, 1977. — ii-xx,442p : ill(some col) ; 27cm.
Text, ill. on lining papers. — With answers. — Index.
ISBN 0-7216-4162-8 : £10.75
(B77-11782)

515'.09'032 — Calculus, 1600-1670
Baron, Margaret Eleanor. Indivisibles and infinitesimals / prepared by Margaret E. Baron ; for the [Open University] Course Team. — Milton Keynes : Open University Press, 1974. — 47p : ill, facsims, ports ; 30cm. — (Arts/mathematics, an interfaculty second level course : history of mathematics : origins and development of the calculus ; 2) (AM289 ; C2)
With answers.
ISBN 0-335-05001-8 Pbk : £1.60
(B77-14211)

515'.09'033 — Calculus, 1700-1800
The **calculus** in the eighteenth century. — Milton Keynes : Open University Press.
2 : Techniques and applications / prepared by H.J.M. Bos ; for the [Open University] Course Team. — 1975. — 43p : ill, facsims, ports ; 30cm. — (Arts/mathematics, an interfaculty second level course : history of mathematics : origins and development of the calculus ; 5) (AM289 ; C5)
With answers.
ISBN 0-335-05015-8 Pbk : £1.70
(B77-13008)

515'.092'2 — Calculus. Theories of Newton, Sir Isaac & Leibniz, Gottfried Wilhelm von
Baron, Margaret Eleanor. Newton and Leibniz / prepared by Margaret E. Baron and H.J.M. Bos ; for the [Open University] Course Team. — Milton Keynes : Open University Press, 1974. — 58p : ill, facsims, ports ; 30cm. — (Arts/mathematics, an interfaculty second level course : history of mathematics : origins and development of the calculus ; 3) (AM289 ; C3)
With answers.
ISBN 0-335-05002-6 Pbk : £1.80
(B77-14707)

515'.15 — Calculus & analytic geometry
Protter, Murray Harold. College calculus with analytic geometry / [by] Murray H. Protter, Charles B. Morrey, Jr. — 3rd ed. — Reading, Mass. ; London [etc.] : Addison-Wesley, 1977. — ix,771,[141]p : ill ; 26cm. — (Addison-Wesley series in mathematics)
Text on lining papers. — With answers to odd-numbered problems. — Previous ed.: 1970.
ISBN 0-201-06030-2 : £15.20
(B77-24904)

Protter, Murray Harold. [College calculus with analytical geometry. *Selections].* Calculus with analytic geometry : a first course / [by] Murray H. Protter, Charles B. Morrey, Jr. — 3rd ed. — Reading, Mass. ; London [etc.] : Addison-Wesley, 1977. — ix,563,[127]p : ill ; 26cm. — (Addison-Wesley series in mathematics)
With answers to odd-numbered problems. — Text on lining papers. — Previous ed.: Reading, Mass. : Addison-Wesley, 1970. — 'This text also appears as part of the larger work "College Calculus with Analytic Geometry", Third Edition...' - title page verso. — Index.
£12.80
(B77-24903)

515'.223 — Calculus. Analytic functions
Open University. Properties of analytic functions / prepared by the [Open University] Course Team. — Milton Keynes : Open University Press, 1975. — 83p : ill ; 30cm. — (M332 ; unit 13) (Mathematics, a third level course : complex analysis ; unit 13)
With solutions. — Index.
ISBN 0-335-05554-0 Pbk : £2.30
(B77-27031)

515'.2432 — Calculus. Singular perturbations. Applications
O'Malley, Robert E. Introduction to singular perturbations / [by] Robert E. O'Malley, Jr. — New York ; London : Academic Press, 1974. — viii,206p : ill ; 24cm. — (Applied mathematics and mechanics ; vol.14)
Bibl.: p.190-201. — Index.
ISBN 0-12-525950-6 : Unpriced
(B77-19340)

515'.2433 — Fourier series
Tolstov, Georgiĭ Pavlovich. Fourier series / [by] Georgi P. Tolstov ; translated from the Russian [and revised] by Richard A. Silverman. — New York : Dover Publications [etc.] ; London : Constable, 1976. — xi,336p : ill ; 21cm.
With answers. — This English ed. originally published: Englewood Cliffs : London : Prentice-Hall, 1962. — Translation and revision of: 'Riady Fur'e'. Izd.2.ispr. Moskva : Gos. izd-vo fiziko-matematicheskoĭ lit-ry, 1960. — Bibl.: p.331. — Index.
ISBN 0-486-63317-9 Pbk : £3.60
(B77-13626)

515'.35 — Boundary value problems. Solution. Integral operators
Colton, David Lem. Solution of boundary value problems by the method of integral operators / [by] D.L. Colton. — London [etc.] : Pitman, 1976. — [7],148p ; 25cm. — (Research notes in mathematics ; 6)
Bibl.: p.144-148.
ISBN 0-273-00307-0 Pbk : £5.60
(B77-00193)

515'.35 — Degenerate differential equations & singular differential equations. Solution. Cauchy's theorem
Carroll, Robert Wayne. Singular and degenerate Cauchy problems / [by] R.W. Carroll, R.E. Showalter. — New York [etc.] ; London : Academic Press, 1976 [i.e. 1977]. — viii,333p ; 24cm. — (Mathematics in science and engineering ; vol.127)
Published in the United States: 1976. — Bibl.: p.276-327. — Index.
ISBN 0-12-161450-6 : £10.30
(B77-12425)

515'.35 — Differential equations
Boyce, William Edward. Elementary differential equations / [by] William E. Boyce and Richard C. DiPrima. — 3rd ed. — New York ; London [etc.] : Wiley, 1977. — xiv,451,A38,I7p : ill ; 24cm.
With answers. — Previous ed.: 1969. — Bibl. — Index.
ISBN 0-471-09339-4 : £12.50
(B77-20219)

515'.35 — Differential equations. Geometrical theory
Lefschetz, Solomon. Differential equations : geometric theory / [by] Solomon Lefschetz. — 2nd ed. — New York : Dover Publications [etc.] ; London : Constable, 1977. — x,390p : ill ; 21cm.
This ed. originally published: New York ; London : Interscience, 1963. — Bibl.: p.376-385. — Index.
ISBN 0-486-63463-9 Pbk : £3.60
(B77-33774)

515'.35 — Differential equations. Initial value problems. Solution. Integration methods
Houwen, P J van der. Construction of integration formulas for initial value problems / [by] P.J. van der Houwen. — Amsterdam [etc.] ; Oxford : North-Holland Publishing Co., 1977. — xi,269p : ill ; 23cm. — (North-Holland series in applied mathematics and mechanics ; vol.19)
Bibl.: p.261-266. — Index.
ISBN 0-7204-2372-4 : £19.91
(B77-18101)

515'.35 — Linear dynamical systems. States. Analysis. State space methods
Wiberg, Donald M. Schaum's outline of theory and problems of state space and linear systems / by Donald M. Wiberg. — New York ; London [etc.] : McGraw-Hill, 1971. — [6],237p : ill ; 28cm. — (Schaum's outline series)
With answers. — Cover title: Theory and problems of state space and linear systems. — Spine title: State space and linear systems. — Index.
ISBN 0-07-070096-6 Pbk : £4.40
(B77-04128)

515'.35 — Nonlinear differential equations. Applications. *Conference proceedings*
International Conference on Nonlinear Systems and Applications, *University of Texas, Arlington, 1976.* Nonlinear systems and applications : an international conference / edited by V. Lakshmikantham. — New York [etc.] ; London : Academic Press, 1977. — xvi, 700p : ill ; 24cm.
'Proceedings of an International Conference on Nonlinear Systems and Applications held at the University of Texas at Arlington, July 19-23, 1976' - half-title page verso.
ISBN 0-12-434150-0 : £17.75
(B77-28584)

515'.35 — Nonlinear differential equations. Applications. *Periodicals*
Nonlinear analysis : theory, methods & applications: an international multidisciplinary journal. — Oxford [etc.] : Pergamon.
Vol.1, no.1- ; Sept. 1976-. — 1976-. — ill ; 25cm.
Six issues a year. — [2],90p. in 1st issue. — Bibl.
Pbk : Unpriced
Also classified at 515'.45
(B77-09678)

515'.352 — Nonlinear ordinary differential equations
Jordan, Dominic William. Nonlinear ordinary differential equations / [by] D.W. Jordan and P. Smith. — Oxford : Clarendon Press, 1977. — viii,360p : ill ; 23cm. — (Oxford applied mathematics and computing science series)
With hints and answers to the exercises. — Bibl.: p.355-356. — Index.
ISBN 0-19-859620-0 : £12.00 : CIP rev.
ISBN 0-19-859621-9 Pbk : £6.50
(B77-13009)

515'.352 — Ordinary differential equations
Etgen, Garret J. An introduction to ordinary differential equations : with difference equations, numerical methods, and applications / [by] Garret J. Etgen, William L. Morris. — New York [etc.] ; London : Harper and Row, 1977. — x,517p : ill ; 25cm.
With answers to selected exercises. — Index.
ISBN 0-06-041913-x : £11.20
(B77-24905)

515'.353 — Mathematics. Finite element methods
Oden, John Tinsley. An introduction to the mathematical theory of finite elements / [by] J.T. Oden, J.N. Reddy. — New York ; London [etc.] : Wiley, 1976. — xiii,429p : ill ; 24cm. — (Pure and applied mathematics)
'A Wiley-Interscience publication'. — Index.
ISBN 0-471-65261-x : £17.90
(B77-11783)

Tong, Pin. Finite-element method : basic technique and implementation / [by] Pin Tong, John N. Rossettos. — Cambridge, Mass. ; London : M.I.T. Press, 1977. — xi,332p : ill ; 24cm.
Bibl.: p.315-322. — Index.
ISBN 0-262-20032-5 : £15.00
(B77-28585)

515'.353 — Mathematics. Finite element methods. *Conference proceedings*
Conference on the Mathematics of Finite Elements and Applications, *2nd, Brunel University, 1975.* The mathematics of finite elements and applications II, MAFELAP 1975 : proceedings of the Brunel University Conference of the Institute of Mathematics and Its Applications held in April 1975 / edited by J.R. Whiteman. — London [etc.] : Academic Press, 1976. — xiii,573p : ill ; 24cm.
'... the 2nd Conference on the Mathematics of Finite Elements and Applications ... was held at Brunel University during ... 7-10 April, 1975' - Preface. — Bibl. — Index.
ISBN 0-12-747252-5 : £21.00
(B77-15825)

515'.353 — Mathematics. Finite element methods. *For civil engineering*
Bathe, Klaus-Jürgen. Numerical methods in finite element analysis / [by] Klaus-Jürgen Bathe, Edward L. Wilson. — Englewood Cliffs ; London [etc.] : Prentice-Hall, 1976. — xv, 528p : ill ; 24cm. — ([Prentice-Hall civil engineering and engineering mechanics series])
Bibl. — Index.
ISBN 0-13-627190-1 : £21.15
(B77-01403)

515'.353 — Mathematics. Finite element methods. Applications of computer systems
Hinton, E. Finite element programming / [by] E. Hinton and D.R.J. Owen. — London [etc.] : Academic Press, 1977. — xiii,305p : ill, map ; 24cm. — (Computational mathematics and applications ; vol.1)
Index.
ISBN 0-12-349350-1 : £11.80
(B77-24906)

515'.353 — Partial differential equations. Solution. Applications of differentiable dynamical systems
Benton, Stanley H. The Hamilton-Jacobi equation : a global approach / [by] Stanley H. Benton, Jr. — New York [etc.] ; London : Academic Press, 1977. — xi,147p : 2 ill ; 24cm. — (Mathematics in science and engineering ; vol.131)
Bibl.: p.133-143. — Index.
ISBN 0-12-089350-9 : £9.60
(B77-23364)

515'.353 — Partial differential equations. Solution. Finite element methods
Mitchell, Andrew Ronald. The finite element method in partial differential equations / [by] A.R. Mitchell and R. Wait. — London [etc.] : Wiley, 1977. — x,198p : ill ; 24cm.
'A Wiley-Interscience publication'. — Bibl.: p.191-195. — Index.
ISBN 0-471-99405-7 : £6.95
(B77-11784)

515'.42 — Ergodic theory
Brown, James R. Ergodic theory and topological dynamics / [by] James R. Brown. — New York [etc.] ; London : Academic Press, 1976. — x, 190p : ill ; 24cm. — (Pure and applied mathematics)
Bibl.: p.181-185. — Index.
ISBN 0-12-137150-6 : £11.90
Also classified at 514'.3
(B77-06047)

Sinaĭ, IA G. Introduction to ergodic theory / [by] YA. G. Sinai ; translated [from the Russian] by V. Scheffer. — Princeton ; Guildford : Princeton University Press, 1976. — [3],144,[1]p : ill ; 24cm. — (Mathematical notes ; 18)
Originally published: in Russian. USSR : Erevan State University, 1973.
ISBN 0-691-08182-4 Pbk : £4.90
(B77-18730)

515'.45 — Integral equations
Moiseiwitsch, Benjamin Lawrence. Integral equations / [by] B.L. Moiseiwitsch. — London [etc.] : Longman, 1977. — ix,161p : ill ; 22cm. — (Longman mathematical texts)
Bibl.: p.157. — Index.
ISBN 0-582-44288-5 Pbk : £3.95
(B77-11196)

515'.45 — Nonlinear integral equations. Applications. *Periodicals*
Nonlinear analysis : theory, methods & applications: an international multidisciplinary journal. — Oxford [etc.] : Pergamon.
Vol.1, no.1- ; Sept. 1976-. — 1976-. — ill ; 25cm.
Six issues a year. — [2],90p. in 1st issue. — Bibl.
Pbk : Unpriced
Primary classification 515'.35
(B77-09678)

515'.5 — Mathematics. Special functions. Sets
Higgins, J R. Completeness and basic properties of sets of special functions / [by] J.R. Higgins. — Cambridge [etc.] : Cambridge University Press, 1977. — x,134p ; 23cm. — (Cambridge tracts in mathematics ; 72)
Bibl.: p.126-129. — Index.
ISBN 0-521-21376-2 : £9.80
(B77-18103)

515'.53 — Mathematics. Subharmonic functions
Hayman, Walter Kurt. Subharmonic functions / [by] W.K. Hayman and the late P.B. Kennedy. — London [etc.] : Academic Press. — (London Mathematical Society. Monographs ; 9 ISSN 0076-0560)
Vol.1. — 1976. — xvii,284p : ill ; 24cm.
Bibl.: p.277-281. — Index.
ISBN 0-12-334801-3 : £11.60
(B77-04776)

515'.55 — Mathematics. Multiple hypergeometric functions
Exton, Harold. Multiple hypergeometric functions and applications / [by] Harold Exton. — Chichester : Ellis Horwood [etc.] ; New York ; London [etc.] : Distributed by Wiley, 1976. — 312p ; 24cm. — (Mathematics and its applications)
Bibl.: p.296-304. — Index.
ISBN 0-85312-047-1 : £11.00
(B77-08355)

515'.62 — Boundary value problems. Solution. Applications of inequalities
Sigillito, V G. Explicit a priori inequalities with applications to boundary value problems / [by] V.G. Sigillito. — London [etc.] : Pitman, 1977. — [7],103p : 1 ill ; 25cm. — (Research notes in mathematics ; no.13)
Bibl.: p.99-103.
ISBN 0-273-01022-0 Pbk : £5.50 : CIP rev.
(B77-11785)

515'.63 — Irreducible tensor analysis. *For chemistry*
Silver, Brian L. Irreducible tensor methods : an introduction for chemists / [by] Brian L. Silver. — New York [etc.] ; London : Academic Press, 1976 [i.e. 1977]. — xvii,226p : ill ; 24cm. — (Physical chemistry ; vol.36)
Published in the United States: 1976. — Bibl.: p.219-221. — Index.
ISBN 0-12-643650-9 : £18.80
(B77-12426)

515'.63 — Tensor analysis & vector analysis
Bourne, Donald Edward. Vector analysis and Cartesian tensors / [by] D.E. Bourne and P.C. Kendall. — 2nd ed. — Sunbury-on-Thames : Nelson, 1977. — ix,256p : ill ; 23cm.
With answers. — Previous ed.: London : Oldbourne, 1967. — Index.
ISBN 0-17-761051-4 : £7.50
ISBN 0-17-771016-0 Pbk : £2.95
(B77-27838)

Bowen, Ray M. Introduction to vectors and tensors / [by] Ray M. Bowen and C.-C. Wang. — New York ; London : Plenum Press. — (Mathematical concepts and methods in science and engineering)
In 2 vols.
Vol.1 : Linear and multilinear algebra. — 1976. — xxii,241p ; 24cm.
Index.
ISBN 0-306-37508-7 : £12.29
(B77-17459)

Vol.2 : Vector and tensor analysis. — 1976. — xxii p,p243-434 ; 24cm.
Index.
ISBN 0-306-37509-5 : £12.29
(B77-17460)

515'.63'02453 — Vector analysis. *For physics*
Kemmer, N. Vector analysis : a physicist's guide to the mathematics of fields in three dimensions / [by] N. Kemmer. — Cambridge [etc.] : Cambridge University Press, 1977. — xiv,254p : ill ; 24cm.
With answers. — Index.
ISBN 0-521-21158-1 : £12.00
ISBN 0-521-29064-3 Pbk : £3.95
(B77-07327)

515'.7 — Mathematics. Vector-valued functions. Approximation
Prolla, João B. Approximation of vector valued functions / [by] João B. Prolla. — Amsterdam [etc.] ; Oxford : North-Holland Publishing Co., 1977. — xiii,219p ; 24cm. — (Notas de matemática ; 61) (North-Holland mathematics studies ; v.25)
Bibl.: p.206-212. — Index.
ISBN 0-444-85030-9 Pbk : £12.94
(B77-33196)

515'.723 — Calculus. Laplace transforms
Open University. Laplace transforms / prepared by the [Open University] Course Team. — Milton Keynes : Open University Press, 1975. — 75p : ill ; 30cm. — (M332 ; unit 14) (Mathematics, a third level course : complex analysis ; unit 14)
With solutions. — Index.
ISBN 0-335-05555-9 Pbk : £2.00
(B77-25580)

515'.723 — Calculus. Laplace transforms & Z-transforms
Muth, Eginhard J. Transform methods with applications to engineering and operations research / [by] Eginhard J. Muth. — Englewood Cliffs ; London [etc.] : Prentice-Hall, 1977. — xi,372p : ill ; 24cm.
Bibl.: p.343-344. — Index.
ISBN 0-13-928861-9 : £17.55
(B77-24181)

515'.73 — Banach spaces. Dunford-Pettis properties
Ryan, R A. Dunford-Pettis properties / [by] R.A. Ryan. — Dublin (School of Mathematics, Trinity College, Dublin 2) : Trinity College, Dublin, 1977. — [3],12 leaves ; 30cm.
Bibl.: leaf [12].
Sd : Unpriced
(B77-33775)

515'.73 — Banach spaces. Nonlinear functional analysis
Martin, Robert Harold. Nonlinear operators and differential equations in Banach spaces / [by] Robert H. Martin, Jr. — New York ; London [etc.] : Wiley, 1976. — xiii,440p ; 24cm. — (Pure and applied mathematics)
'A Wiley-Interscience publication'. — Bibl.: p.429-433. — Index.
ISBN 0-471-57363-9 : £21.20
(B77-00746)

515'.73 — Ordered vector spaces. Linear operators
Cristescu, Romulus. Ordered vector spaces and linear operators / [by] Romulus Cristescu ; [translated from the Romanian by Silviu Teleman ; translation editor J.C. Hammel]. — Bucureşti [i.e. Bucharest] : Editura Academiei ; Tunbridge Wells : Abacus Press, 1976. — 339p ; 25cm.
Translation and revision of: 'Spatii liniare ordonate si operatori liniari'. Bucureşti : Editura Academiei, 1970. — Bibl.: p.315-335. — Index.
ISBN 0-85626-090-8 : £14.85
(B77-07890)

515'.785 — Harmonic oscillations. Analysis
Katznelson, Yitzhak. An introduction to harmonic analysis / [by] Yitzhak Katznelson. — 2nd corrected ed. — New York : Dover Publications [etc.] ; London : Constable, 1976. — iii-xv,264p ; 21cm.
Previous ed.: New York : Wiley, 1968. — Bibl.: p.261-262. — Index.
ISBN 0-486-63331-4 Pbk : £2.85
(B77-15266)

515'.8 — Calculus. Functions of real variables
Artémiadis, Nicolas K. Real analysis / by Nicolas K. Artémiadis. — Carbondale [etc.] : Southern Illinois University Press ; London [etc.] : Feffer and Simons, 1976. — xiii,581p ; 24cm.
Bibl.: p.567-569. — Index.
ISBN 0-8093-0727-8 : Unpriced
(B77-00747)

515'.9 — Calculus. Functions of complex variables
Churchill, Ruel Vance. Complex variables and applications. — 3rd ed. / [by] Ruel V. Churchill, James W. Brown, Roger F. Verhey. — New York ; London [etc.] : McGraw-Hill, 1974. — xi,332p : ill ; 24cm.
Previous ed.: / by Ruel V. Churchill. 1960. — Bibl.: p.311-313. — Index.
ISBN 0-07-010855-2 : Unpriced
(B77-18731)

Henrici, Peter. Applied and computational complex analysis / [by] Peter Henrici. — New York ; London [etc.] : Wiley. — (Pure and applied mathematics)
In 3 vols.
Vol.2 : Special functions, integral transforms, asymptotics, continued fractions. — 1977. — ix, 662p : ill ; 24cm.
'A Wiley Interscience publication'. — Bibl.: p.642-649. — Index.
ISBN 0-471-01525-3 : £24.40
(B77-25581)

Lang, Serge. Complex analysis / [by] Serge Lang. — Reading, Mass. ; London [etc.] : Addison-Wesley, 1977. — xi,321p : ill ; 25cm. — (Addison-Wesley series in mathematics)
Index.
ISBN 0-201-04137-5 : £12.00
(B77-24182)

Saff, E B. Fundamentals of complex analysis for mathematics, science and engineering / [by] E.B. Saff, A.D. Snider. — Englewood Cliffs ; London [etc.] : Prentice-Hall, 1976. — xv, 444p : ill ; 24cm.
With answers to selected problems. — Bibl. — Index.
ISBN 0-13-332148-7 : £15.05
(B77-04129)

515'.9 — Complex spaces. Global theory. Applications of algebraic methods
Branică, Constantin. Algebraic methods in the global theory of complex spaces / [by] Constantin Bănică and Octavian Stănăşilă ; [translated from the Romanian]. — Bucureşti [i.e. Bucharest] : Editura Academiei ; London [etc.] : Wiley, 1976. — 296p ; 25cm.
Translation and revision of: 'Metode algebrice în teoria globală a spaţiilor complexe'. Bucharest : Editura Academiei, 1974. — Bibl.: p.293-296.
ISBN 0-471-01809-0 : £9.75
(B77-13627)

515'.9 — Complex variables
Pennisi, Louis Legendre. Elements of complex variables / [by] Louis L. Pennisi with the collaboration of Louis I. Gordon, Sim Lasher. — 2nd ed. — New York ; London [etc.] : Holt, Rinehart and Winston, 1976. — viii,517p : ill ; 24cm.
With answers to selected exercises. — Previous ed.: 1963. — Bibl.: p.493-494. — Index.
ISBN 0-03-014426-4 : £13.25
(B77-01404)

515'.93 — Calculus. Functions of one complex variable
Tall, David Orme. Functions of a complex variable ... / by D.O. Tall. — London : Routledge and Kegan Paul [etc.], [1977]. — 72, 80p ; 19cm. — (Library of mathematics)
With answers. — Originally published: in 2 vols. 1970. — Index.
ISBN 0-7100-8655-5 Pbk : £1.75
(B77-14212)

515'.983 — Mathematics. Elliptic modular functions
Rankin, Robert A. Modular forms and functions / [by] Robert A. Rankin. — Cambridge [etc.] : Cambridge University Press, 1977. — xiii,384p : ill ; 24cm.
Bibl.: p.361-367. — Index.
ISBN 0-521-21212-x : £16.50
(B77-27839)

516 — GEOMETRY
Open University. *Modelling by Mathematics Course Team.* Position and movement / prepared by the [Open University, Modelling by Mathematics] Course Team. — Milton Keynes : Open University Press, 1977. — 68,59,62p : ill(some col) ; 30cm. — (Technology/ mathematics, a second level course : modelling by mathematics ; block 2) (TM281 ; 4-6)
With answers.
ISBN 0-335-06291-1 Pbk : Unpriced
Also classified at 531
(B77-25582)

516 — Coloured elastic bands. Patterns. Mathematical aspects. *School texts*
Bands / [by Ray Hemmings ... et al.]. — London [etc.] : Hutchinson for Leapfrogs, 1976. — [1], 16,[1]p : of ill ; 21cm. — (Network : action books)
ISBN 0-09-127421-4 Sd : £0.35(non-net)
(B77-02971)

516 — Doodles. Mathematical aspects. *School texts*
Doodles / [by Ray Hemmings ... et al.]. — London [etc.] : Hutchinson for Leapfrogs, 1975. — [1],16,[1]p : ill ; 21cm. — (Network : action books)
ISBN 0-09-124931-7 Sd : £0.30(non-net)
(B77-02272)

516 — Geometry. *Primary school texts*
Sussex House School. *Mathematics Department.* Notes on number and geometry / [Sussex House School, Mathematics Department]. — [London] ([68 Cadogan Sq., SW1X 0EA]) : [The Department], [1976]. — [104]p : ill ; 22cm.
Limited ed. of 180 copies. — Index.
ISBN 0-9505511-0-4 Sd : Unpriced
Primary classification 513
(B77-06042)

516 — Geometry. *Secondary school texts*
Posamentier, Alfred S. Geometry : its elements and structure. — 2nd ed. / [by] Alfred S. Posamentier, J. Houston Banks, Robert L. Bannister. — New York ; London [etc.] : McGraw-Hill, 1977. — xi,612p : ill(some col) ; 25cm. — (Elements and structure series)
Previous ed.: / by J. Houston Banks, Alfred S. Posamentier, Robert L. Bannister. New York : McGraw-Hill, 1972. — Bibl.: p.603. — Index.
ISBN 0-07-050551-9 : £8.45
(B77-22538)

516 — Illustrations. Mathematical aspects. *School texts*
Links : a book of pictures & diagrams which have been selected with certain mathematical ideas in mind, not to illustrate these ideas but to show parts of the real world from which mathematics comes / [by Ray Hemmings ... et al.]. — London [etc.] : Hutchinson for Leapfrogs, 1975. — 64,[1]p : of ill ; 20cm. — (Network : link books)
ISBN 0-09-124941-4 Sd : £0.95
(B77-02273)

516 — Length. *Juvenile literature*
Long and short. — Cambridge : Brimax Books, 1976. — [12]p : chiefly col ill ; 16cm. — ('Show baby opposites' series)
ISBN 0-904494-42-x Pbd : £0.60
(B77-14708)

516 — Patterns. Mathematical aspects. *Illustrations. School texts*
Hemmings, Ray. Leads : a book of pictures & diagrams which have been selected with certain mathematical ideas in mind, not to illustrate these ideas but to show parts of the real world from which mathematics comes ... / [by Ray Hemmings and Dick Tahta]. — London [etc.] : Hutchinson for Leapfrogs, 1976. — 64p : of ill, facsim, maps, ports ; 20x21cm. — (Network : link books)
ISBN 0-09-126381-6 Sd : £0.95
(B77-00194)

516 — Shapes. *Juvenile literature*
Smeltzer, Patricia. The circle / [by] Patricia and Victor Smeltzer. — London [etc.] : Burke, 1976. — [18]p : ill(chiefly col) ; 20cm. — (Surprise shapes)
ISBN 0-222-00474-6 : £1.00
ISBN 0-222-00478-9 Pbk : £0.40
ISBN 0-222-00552-1 Pbd : £0.50
(B77-02972)

Smeltzer, Patricia. The rectangle / [by] Patricia and Victor Smeltzer. — London [etc.] : Burke, 1976. — [18]p : ill(chiefly col) ; 20cm. — (Surprise shapes)
ISBN 0-222-00477-0 : £1.00
ISBN 0-222-00481-9 Pbk : £0.40
ISBN 0-222-00555-6 Pbd : £0.50
(B77-02973)

Smeltzer, Patricia. The square / [by] Patricia and Victor Smeltzer. — London [etc.] : Burke, 1976. — [18]p : ill(chiefly col) ; 20cm. — (Surprise shapes)
ISBN 0-222-00475-4 : £1.00
ISBN 0-222-00479-7 Pbk : £0.40
ISBN 0-222-00553-x Pbd : £0.50
(B77-02974)

Smeltzer, Patricia. The triangle / [by] Patricia and Victor Smeltzer. — London [etc.] : Burke, 1976. — [18]p : ill(chiefly col) ; 20cm. — (Surprise shapes)
ISBN 0-222-00476-2 : £1.00
ISBN 0-222-00480-0 Pbk : £0.40
ISBN 0-222-00554-8 Pbd : £0.50
(B77-02975)

516 — Sizes. *Juvenile literature*
Big and small. — Cambridge : Brimax Books, 1976. — [12]p : chiefly col ill ; 16cm. — ('Show baby opposites' series)
ISBN 0-904494-40-3 Pbd : £0.60
(B77-13628)

516'.15 — Conic sections. Applications of imaginary numbers
Francis, Philip Harwood. Mathematics of the universe : the universe of the mind / by P.H. Francis. — [Chichester] : [The author] ; Cambridge [etc.] : Distributed by Oleander Press, 1977. — vii,120p : ill ; 22cm.
With answers. — Index.
ISBN 0-902675-75-3 Pbk : £4.95
(B77-25583)

516'.15 — Cubes. *School texts*
Cubes / [by Ray Hemmings ... et al.]. — London [etc.] : Hutchinson for Leapfrogs, 1975. — [1], 16,[1]p : ill ; 21cm. — (Network : action books)
ISBN 0-09-124921-x Sd : £0.30(non-net)
(B77-02274)

516'.15 — Polyhedra
Pugh, Anthony. Polyhedra : a visual approach / by Anthony Pugh. — Berkeley [etc.] ; London : University of California Press, 1976. — x,118p : ill ; 23cm.
Bibl.: p.117-118.
ISBN 0-520-02926-7 : £10.00
ISBN 0-520-03056-7 Pbk : £3.50
(B77-14213)

516'.22 — Pythagorean geometry. *Ancient China*
Swetz, Frank. Was Pythagoras Chinese? : an examination of right triangle theory in Ancient China / by Frank J. Swetz and T.I. Kao. — University Park ; London : Pennsylvania State University Press [for the] National Council of Teachers of Mathematics, 1977. — 75p : ill ; 23cm. — (Pennsylvania State University. Studies ; no.40)
Bibl.: p.73-74. — Includes an annotated translation of the 9th chapter of the 'Chiu chang' together with its solution commentaries.
ISBN 0-271-01238-2 Pbk : £2.95
(B77-30211)

516'.23 — Inside & outside. *Juvenile literature*
Inside and outside. — Cambridge : Brimax Books, 1976. — [12]p : chiefly col ill ; 16cm. — ('Show baby opposites' series)
ISBN 0-904494-41-1 Pbd : £0.60
(B77-14709)

516'.24 — Plane trigonometry. *Exercises, worked examples*
Washington, Allyn Jarvis. Plane trigonometry / [by] Allyn J. Washington, Carolyn E. Edmond. — Menlo Park ; London [etc.] : Cummings, 1977. — [10],372p : ill(some col) ; 24cm.
With answers to odd-numbered exercises. — Ill. on lining papers. — Index.
ISBN 0-8465-8622-3 : £14.40
(B77-30212)

516'.24 — Trigonometry
Drooyan, Irving. Essentials of trigonometry / [by] Irving Drooyan, Walter Hadel, Charles C. Carico. — 2nd ed. — New York : Macmillan ; London : Collier Macmillan, 1977. — viii, 328p : ill(chiefly col) ; 24cm.
With answers to odd-numbered problems. — Text on lining papers. — Previous ed.: New York : Macmillan, 1971. — Index.
ISBN 0-02-330220-8 : £9.40
(B77-28586)

516'.35 — Lattice point geometry
Hammer, Joseph. Unsolved problems concerning lattice points / [by] J. Hammer. — London [etc.] : Pitman, 1977. — [8],101p ; 25cm. — (Research notes in mathematics ; no.15)
Bibl.: p.67-101.
ISBN 0-273-01103-0 Pbk : £5.00 : CIP rev.
(B77-17461)

516'.36 — Differential geometry
Guggenheimer, Heinrich W. Differential geometry / by Heinrich W. Guggenheimer. — New York : Dover Publications [etc.] ; London : Constable, 1977. — iii-x,378p : ill ; 21cm.
With answers to selected exercises. — Originally published: New York : McGraw-Hill, 1963. — Bibl. — Index.
ISBN 0-486-63433-7 Pbk : £4.25
(B77-24183)

516'.362 — Integral geometry
Santaló, Luis A. Integral geometry and geometric probability / [by] Luis A. Santaló ; with a foreword by Mark Kac. — Reading, Mass. ; London [etc.] : Addison-Wesley, 1976. — xix, 404p : ill ; 24cm. — (Encyclopedia of mathematics and its applications ; vol.1)
Text on lining paper. — Bibl.: p.363-394. — Index.
ISBN 0-201-13500-0 : £15.60
(B77-16860)

516'.6 — Three-dimensional descriptive geometry
Slaby, Steve M. Fundamentals of three-dimensional descriptive geometry / [by] Steve M. Slaby. — 2nd ed. — New York ; London [etc.] : Wiley, 1976. — xiii,416p : ill(some col) ; 24cm.
Ill., text on lining papers. — Previous ed.: New York : Harcourt, Brace and World, 1966. — Bibl.: p.409. — Index.
ISBN 0-471-79621-2 : Unpriced
(B77-05381)

Slaby, Steve M. Fundamentals of three-dimensional descriptive geometry / [by] Steve M. Slaby. — 2nd ed. — New York ; London [etc.] : Wiley.
Previous ed.: New York : Harcourt, Brace and World, 1966.
Workbook ; [and], Solutions for workbook ; [and], Instructor's manual and solutions. — 1976. — 1v. : chiefly ill ; 31cm.
Workbook ([7]p., 80 leaves : pbk), Solutions for workbook ([2],80p. : sd), Instructor's manual and solutions (booklet (23p.), 162 sheets ([162] sides) in envelope.
ISBN 0-471-79622-0 : £15.40
(B77-11197)

516'.9 — Non-Euclidean tesselations
Magnus, Wilhelm. Noneuclidean tesselations and their groups / [by] Wilhelm Magnus. — New York ; London : Academic Press, 1974. — xv, 207p : ill ; 24cm. — (Pure and applied mathematics)
Bibl.: p.199-204. — Index.
ISBN 0-12-465450-9 : Unpriced
(B77-21091)

519 — PROBABILITIES AND APPLIED MATHEMATICS
519 — Applied finite mathematics
Anton, Howard. Applied finite mathematics / [by] Howard Anton, Bernard Kolman. — New York ; London : Academic Press, 1974. — xv, 475p : ill(chiefly col), col maps ; 24cm.
With answers to selected exercises. — Index.
ISBN 0-12-059550-8 : Unpriced
(B77-20220)

519 — Probabilities & statistical mathematics
Hodge, Susan Elizabeth. Statistics and probability / [by] S.E. Hodge, M.L. Seed. — 2nd ed. — Glasgow [etc.] : Blackie ; Edinburgh [etc.] : W. and R. Chambers, 1977. — [7], 264p : ill ; 22cm.
With answers. — Previous ed.: 1972. — Index.
ISBN 0-216-90450-1 Pbk : Unpriced
ISBN 0-550-75998-0 (W. and R. Chambers) : Unpriced
(B77-30213)

Mathai, A M. Probability and statistics / [by] A.M. Mathai, P.N. Rathie. — Delhi [etc.] : Macmillan Company of India ; London [etc.] : Macmillan, 1977. — xvii,406p,fold plate : ill ; 22cm.
With answers. — Bibl.: p.355-356. — Index.
ISBN 0-333-19056-4 Pbk : £4.95
(B77-19341)

Seber, George Arthur Frederick. Elementary statistics / [by] G.A.F. Seber. — Sydney ; London [etc.] : Wiley, [1977]. — x,216p : ill ; 24cm.
With answers. — Published in Australia: 1974. — Index.
ISBN 0-471-77092-2 Pbk : £8.55
(B77-08989)

Spiegel, Murray Ralph. Schaum's outline of theory and problems of probability and statistics / by Murray R. Spiegel. — New York ; London [etc.] : McGraw-Hill, [1976]. — [9],372p : ill ; 28cm. — (Schaum's outline series)
Spine title: Probability and statistics. — Cover title: Theory and problems of probability and statistics. — With answers to supplementary problems. — Published in the United States: 1975. — Index.
ISBN 0-07-060220-4 Pbk : £4.95
(B77-04130)

Turner, John Christopher. Modern applied mathematics : probability, statistics, operational research / [by] J.C. Turner. — London : English Universities Press, 1972. — ix,502p : ill ; 23cm.
With answers. — Originally published: 1970. — Bibl.: p.453-454. — Index.
£3.95
ISBN 0-340-05056-x
ISBN 0-340-11456-8 Pbk : Unpriced
(B77-30214)

Wolf, Frank Louis. Elements of probability and statistics / [by] Frank L. Wolf. — 2nd ed. — New York ; London [etc.] : McGraw-Hill, 1974. — xiv,450p : ill ; 24cm. — (McGraw-Hill series in probability and statistics)
Previous ed.: 1962. — Index.
ISBN 0-07-071341-3 : Unpriced
(B77-19342)

519'.02'433 — Probabilities & statistical mathematics. *For economics*
Hoel, Paul Gerhard. Basic statistics for business and economics / [by] Paul G. Hoel and Raymond J. Jessen. — 2nd ed. — Santa Barbara ; London [etc.] : Wiley, 1977. — xiii, 536p : ill(chiefly col) ; 24cm. — (The Wiley/Hamilton series in management and administration)
With answers. — Previous ed.: 1971. — Index.
ISBN 0-471-40268-0 : £10.00
(B77-19343)

519'.02'462 — Probabilities & statistical mathematics. *For engineering*
Miller, Irwin. Probability and statistics for engineers / [by] Irwin Miller, John E. Freund. — 2nd ed. — Englewood Cliffs ; London [etc.] : Prentice-Hall, 1977. — xii,529p : ill ; 24cm.
With answers to odd-numbered exercises. — Previous ed.: Englewood Cliffs : Prentice-Hall, 1965. — Bibl.: p.472-475. — Index.
ISBN 0-13-711945-3 : £13.20
(B77-16357)

519.2 — Functions of random variables & functions of random vectors
Open University. Vector random variables ; [and], Distributions of functions of random variables / prepared by the [Open University] course team. — Milton Keynes : Open University Press, 1977. — 95p : ill ; 30cm. — (Mathematics, a third level course : fundamentals of statistical inference ; units 4 and 5) (M341 ; units 4 and 5)
With answers. — Index.
ISBN 0-335-05751-9 Pbk : Unpriced
(B77-27032)

519.2 — Mathematics. Optimisation. Applications of Gaussian processes
Jacobson, David Harris. Extensions of linear-quadratic control, optimization and matrix theory / [by] David H. Jacobson. — London [etc.] : Academic Press, 1977. — x, 217p ; 24cm. — (Mathematics in science and engineering ; vol.133)
Index.
ISBN 0-12-378750-5 : £6.50
Also classified at 512.9'43
(B77-23365)

519.2 — Probabilities
Fortet, Robert. Elements of probability / [by] Robert Fortet ; [translated from the French]. — London [etc.] : Gordon and Breach, 1977. — xix,524p : ill ; 24cm.
Translation of: 'Eléments de la théorie des probabilités'. Vol.1. 2.éd. Paris : Centre national de la recherche scientifique, 1965. — Bibl.: p.509-519. — Index.
ISBN 0-677-02110-0 : £30.00
(B77-06048)

Hogg, Robert Vincent. Probability and statistical inference / by Robert V. Hogg and Elliot A. Tanis. — New York : Macmillan ; London : Collier Macmillan, 1977. — xi,450p : ill ; 24cm.
With answers to selected exercises. — Bibl.: p.415-416. — Index.
ISBN 0-02-355650-1 Pbk : £6.75
Also classified at 519.5'4
(B77-21830)

Mathematical statistics : its setting and scope ; [and], Univariate distributions / prepared by the [Open University] Course Team. — Milton Keynes : Open University Press, 1977. — 94p : ill ; 30cm. — (Mathematics, a third level course : fundamentals of statistical inference ; units 1 and 2) (M341 ; units 1 and 2)
With answers. — Index.
ISBN 0-335-05750-0 Pbk : Unpriced
(B77-13629)

Milton, J Susan. Probability theory with the essential analysis / [by] J. Susan Milton, Chris P. Tsokos. — Reading, Mass. ; London [etc.] : Addison-Wesley, 1976 [i.e. 1977]. — xxi,339p ; 24cm. — (Applied mathematics and computation ; 10)
With answers. — Published in the United States: 1976. — Bibl. — Index.
ISBN 0-201-07604-7 : £18.20
ISBN 0-201-07605-5 Pbk : £10.80
(B77-10350)

Nosal, Miloslav. Basic probability and applications / [by] Miloslav Nosal. — Philadelphia ; London [etc.] : Saunders, 1977. — x,370p : ill, port ; 27cm.
With answers to selected exercises. — Index.
ISBN 0-7216-6865-8 : £9.50
(B77-33197)

Orkin, Michael. Vital statistics / [by] Michael Orkin, Richard Drogin. — New York ; London [etc.] : McGraw-Hill, [1976]. — xi,388p : ill ; 24cm.
With answers to odd-numbered problems. — Published in the United States: 1974. — Index.
ISBN 0-07-047720-5 : £10.40
Primary classification 519.5
(B77-01407)

Weaver, Warren. Lady luck : the theory of probability / [by] Warren Weaver. — Harmondsworth [etc.] : Penguin, 1977. — 298p : ill ; 19cm. — (Pelican books)
With answers. — Originally published: Garden City, N.Y. : Doubleday, 1963 ; London : Heinemann ; 1965. — Index.
ISBN 0-14-021931-5 Pbk : £1.00
(B77-07328)

Woodroofe, Michael. Probability with applications / [by] Michael Woodroofe. — New York ; London [etc.] : McGraw-Hill, [1976]. — x,372p : ill ; 24cm.
With answers to selected problems. — Published in the United States: 1975. — Bibl.: p.356-257. — Index.
ISBN 0-07-071718-4 : £10.00
(B77-00195)

519.2 — Probabilities. *School texts*
Chance / [by Ray Hemmings ... et al.]. — London [etc.] : Hutchinson for Leapfrogs, 1975. — [1],16,[1]p : ill ; 21cm. — (Network : action books)
ISBN 0-09-124911-2 Sd : £0.30(non-net)
(B77-02275)

519.2 — Random variables
Kallenberg, Olav. Random measures / [by] Olav Kallenberg. — Berlin : Akademie-Verlag ; London [etc.] : Academic Press, 1976. — [6], 104p ; 25cm.
Originally published: Berlin : Akademie-Verlag, 1975. — Bibl.: p.97-100. — Index.
ISBN 0-12-394950-5 : £6.00
(B77-27033)

519.2 — Stochastic dynamical systems. *Conference proceedings*
Stochastic systems : modeling, identification and optimization / edited by Roger J.-B. Wets. — Amsterdam [etc.] ; Oxford : North-Holland Publishing Co.
'... the proceedings of a symposium held in Lexington, Kentucky, in June 1975' - Preface. — In 2 vols.
1 / [contributors] V. Beneš ... [et al.]. — 1976. — ix,243p : ill ; 24cm. — (Mathematical programming studies ; 5)
Bibl.
ISBN 0-7204-0569-6 Pbk : £11.24
(B77-17462)

2 / [contributors] L. Choi ... [et al.]. — 1976. — x,263p : ill ; 24cm.
Bibl.
ISBN 0-7204-0570-x Pbk : £11.43
(B77-25584)

519.2 — Stochastic integral equations
Tsokos, Chris P. Random integral equations with applications to life sciences and engineering / [by] Chris P. Tsokos, W.J. Padgett. — New York ; London : Academic Press, 1974. — x, 278p : ill ; 24cm. — (Mathematics in science and engineering ; vol.108)
Bibl.: p.260-273. — Index.
ISBN 0-12-702150-7 : Unpriced
(B77-19344)

519.2 — Stochastic processes
Cox, David Roxbee. The theory of stochastic processes / [by] D.R. Cox, H.D. Miller. — London : Chapman and Hall, 1977. — x,398p : ill ; 24cm.
Originally published: London : Methuen, 1965. — Bibl.: p.378-385. — Index.
ISBN 0-412-15170-7 Pbk : £4.95
(B77-13010)

Theory of stochastic processes. — New York [etc.] : Wiley ; Jerusalem ; London : Israel Program for Scientific Translations ; Chichester : Distributed by Wiley.
No.1 / I.I. Gikhman, editor ; translated from Russian by D. Louvish. — [1977]. — v,157p ; 25cm.
'A Halsted Press book'. — This translation published in the United States: 1974. — Translation of 'Teoriia sluchaĭnykh protsessov. Vyp.1'. Kiev : Naukova Dumka, 1973. — Bibl.
ISBN 0-7065-1433-5 : £14.05
(B77-09679)

519.2 — Stochastic processes: Brownian motion processes
Petersen, K E. Brownian motion, Hardy spaces and bounded mean oscillation / [by] K.E. Petersen. — Cambridge [etc.] : Cambridge University Press, 1977. — [5],105p : ill ; 23cm. — (London Mathematical Society. Lecture note series ; 28)
Bibl.: p.98-101. — Index.
ISBN 0-521-21512-9 Pbk : £3.95
(B77-18732)

519.2 — Stochastic processes. Probability methods
Kushner, Harold Joseph. Probability methods for approximations in stochastic control and for elliptic equations / [by] Harold J. Kushner. — New York [etc.] ; London : Academic Press, 1977. — xvii,243p : ill ; 24cm. — (Mathematics in science and engineering ; vol.129)
Bibl.: p.237-239. — Index.
ISBN 0-12-430140-1 : £16.35
(B77-27034)

519.2'09 — Probabilities. Theories, to 1966
Maistrov, L E. Probability theory : a historical sketch / [by] L.E. Maistrov ; translated [from the Russian] and edited by Samuel Kotz. — New York ; London : Academic Press, 1974. — xiii,281p : ill ; 24cm. — (Probability and mathematical statistics ; 23)
Translation of: 'Teoriiâ veroiâtnosteĭ : istoricheskiĭ ocherk'. Moscow : Izdatel'stvo Nauka, 1967. — Bibl.: p.265-274. — Index.
ISBN 0-12-465750-8 : Unpriced
(B77-19345)

519.2'32 — Time series. Spectral analysis
Koopmans, Lambert Herman. The spectral analysis of time series / [by] L.H. Koopmans. — New York ; London : Academic Press, 1974. — xiv,366p : ill ; 24cm. — (Probability and mathematical statistics)
Bibl.: p.354-358. — Index.
ISBN 0-12-419250-5 : Unpriced
(B77-21092)

519.2'33 — Markov processes. Parameters. Estimation. *For economics*
Lee, Tsoung-Chao. Estimating the parameters of the Markov probability model from aggregate time series data / [by] T.C. Lee, G.G. Judge, A. Zellner. — 2nd, revised ed. — Amsterdam [etc.] ; Oxford : North-Holland Publishing Co., 1977. — 260p ; 23cm. — (Contributions to economic analysis ; 65)
Previous ed.: Amsterdam : London : North-Holland Publishing Co., 1970. — Bibl.: p.249-255. — Index.
Unpriced
ISBN 0-7204-3163-8
(B77-18733)

519.2'33 — Nonlinear diffusion. Mathematical models. *Conference proceedings*
Nonlinear diffusion / W.E. Fitzgibbon (III) & H.F. Walker (editors). — London [etc.] : Pitman, 1977. — [8],232p : ill ; 25cm. — (Research notes in mathematics ; no.14)
'... a five-day regional conference ... was held at the University of Houston in June, 1976' - Preface. — Bibl.
ISBN 0-273-01066-2 Pbk : £7.50 : CIP rev.
(B77-16861)

519.2'4 — Probabilities. Density functions. Superpositions. Decomposition
Medgyessy, Pál. Decomposition of superpositions of density functions and discrete distributions / [by] Pál Medgyessy. — Bristol (Techno House, Redcliffe Way, Bristol BS1 6NX) : Hilger, 1977. — 308p : ill ; 25cm.
Bibl.: p.267-294. — Index.
ISBN 0-85274-294-0 : £12.00
Also classified at 519.5'32
(B77-12427)

519.2'87 — Calculus. Integration. Stochastic processes. Martingales
Kussmaul, A U. Stochastic integration and generalized martingales / [by] A.U. Kussmaul. — London [etc.] : Pitman, 1977. — [10],163p ; 25cm. — (Research notes in mathematics ; 11)
Bibl.: p.155-157. — Index.
ISBN 0-273-01030-1 Pbk : £6.90
(B77-18104)

519.4 — Algebraic coding theory
Blake, Ian Fraser. An introduction to algebraic and combinatorial coding theory / [by] Ian F. Blake, Ronald C. Mullin. — New York [etc.] ; London : Academic Press, 1976. — xiii,229p : ill ; 23cm.
Originally published: as ch. 1-3 of 'The mathematical theory of coding'. New York ; London : Academic Press, 1975. — Bibl.: p.215-222. — Index.
ISBN 0-12-103560-3 Pbk : £6.75
(B77-14214)

519.4 — Computation by digital computer systems
Hennie, Frederick Clair. Introduction to computability / [by] Fred Hennie. — Reading, Mass. ; London [etc.] : Addison-Wesley, 1977. — ix,374p : ill ; 25cm. — (Addison-Wesley series in computer science and information processing)
Bibl.: p.363-364. — Index.
ISBN 0-201-02848-4 : £16.80
(B77-31167)

519.4 — Computation by digital computer systems. Arithmetic error coding
Rao, T R N. Error coding for arithmetic processors / [by] T.R.N. Rao. — New York ; London : Academic Press, 1974. — xiv,216p : ill ; 24cm. — (Electrical science)
Index.
ISBN 0-12-580750-3 : Unpriced
(B77-19346)

519.4 — Computational complexity
Savage, John E. The complexity of computing / [by] John E. Savage. — New York ; London [etc.] : Wiley, 1976. — xv,391p : ill ; 24cm.
'A Wiley-Interscience Publication'. — Bibl.: p.373-386. — Index.
ISBN 0-471-75517-6 : £17.20
(B77-17463)

519.4 — Digital computer systems. Mathematics
Mathematical methods for digital computers. — New York ; London [etc.] : Wiley.
Vol.3 : Statistical methods for digital computers / edited by Kurt Enslein, Anthony Ralston, Herbert S. Wilf. — 1977. — ix,454p : ill ; 26cm.
'A Wiley-Interscience Publication'. — Bibl. — Index.
ISBN 0-471-70690-6 : £18.70
(B77-17464)

519.4 — Digital computer systems. Mathematics. *Conference proceedings*
Symposium on New Directions and Recent Results in Algorithms and Complexity, *Carnegie-Mellon University, 1976.* Algorithms and complexity : new directions and recent results / edited by J.F. Traub. — New York [etc.] ; London : Academic Press, 1976 [i.e. 1977]. — ix,523p ; 24cm.
'Proceedings of a Symposium on New Directions and Recent Results in Algorithms and Complexity held by The Computer Science Department, Carnegie-Mellon University, April 7-9, 1976' - half title page verso. — Published in the United States: 1976. — Bibl.
ISBN 0-12-697540-x : £13.85
(B77-12428)

519.4 — Linear algebra. Matrices. Computation by digital computer systems
Jennings, Alan. Matrix computation for engineers and scientists / [by] Alan Jennings. — London [etc.] : Wiley, 1977. — xv,330p : ill ; 24cm.
'A Wiley-Interscience publication'. — Bibl. — Index.
ISBN 0-471-99421-9 : £10.50
(B77-13011)

519.4 — Mathematics. Applications of digital computer systems. *Festschriften*
Computers and mathematics with applications : in memory of Cornelius Lánczos / edited by Ervin Y. Rodin. — Oxford [etc.] : Pergamon, 1976. — ix p,p257-428 : ill, port ; 28cm.
'Published as a special issue of the journal "Computers and mathematics with applications" Volume 1, Number 3/4 ...' - title page verso.
ISBN 0-08-020521-6 : £10.00
(B77-01405)

519.4 — Numerical analysis. Applications of digital computer systems. Programming languages: Fortran language
Forsythe, George Elmer. Computer methods for mathematical computations / [by] George E. Forsythe, Michael A. Malcolm, Cleve B. Moler. — Englewood Cliffs ; London [etc.] : Prentice-Hall, 1977. — xi,259p : ill ; 24cm. — (Prentice-Hall series in automatic computation)
Bibl. — Index.
ISBN 0-13-165332-6 : £12.80
(B77-24184)

519.5 — Statistical analysis. Significance. Tests. Power. *For behavioural sciences*
Cohen, Jacob. Statistical power analysis for the behavioral sciences / [by] Jacob Cohen. — Revised ed. — New York [etc.] ; London : Academic Press, 1977. — xv,474p ; 24cm.
Previous ed.: 1969. — Bibl.: p.465-467. — Index.
ISBN 0-12-179060-6 : £17.40
(B77-30215)

519.5 — Statistical mathematics
Ary, Donald. Introduction to statistics : purposes and procedures / [by] Donald Ary, Lucy Cheser Jacobs. — New York ; London [etc.] : Holt, Rinehart and Winston, 1976. — xiii, 461p : ill ; 24cm.
With answers. — Index.
ISBN 0-03-088412-8 : £9.00
(B77-01406)

Bhattacharyya, Gouri K. Statistical concepts and methods / [by] Gouri K. Bhattacharyya, Richard A. Johnson. — New York ; London [etc.] : Wiley, 1977. — xv,639p : ill ; 24cm. — (Wiley series in probability and mathematical statistics)
With answers to selected odd-numbered exercises. — Bibl. — Index.
ISBN 0-471-07204-4 : £11.25
(B77-22539)

Chase, Clinton Irvin. Elementary statistical procedures / [by] Clinton I. Chase. — 2nd ed. — New York ; London [etc.] : McGraw-Hill, 1976. — ix,277p : ill ; 24cm.
With answers. — Previous ed.: 1967. — Index.
ISBN 0-07-010681-9 : £9.10
(B77-04777)

Downie, Norville Morgan. Descriptive and inferential statistics / [by] N.M. Downie, A.R. Starry. — New York ; London [etc.] : Harper and Row, 1977. — ix,362p : ill ; 24cm.
With answers to selected exercises. — Bibl.: p.353. — Index.
ISBN 0-06-041721-8 : £8.65
(B77-24186)

Dudewicz, Edward J. Introduction to statistics and probability / [by] Edward J. Dudewicz. — New York ; London [etc.] : Holt, Rinehart and Winston, 1976. — xi,512p : ill ; 24cm. — (International series in decision processes)
With answers to selected problems. — Bibl.: p.469-470. — Index.
ISBN 0-03-086688-x : £12.50
(B77-00748)

Elementary statistics. — 3rd ed. / [by] Janet T. Spence ... [et al.]. — Englewood Cliffs ; London [etc.] : Prentice-Hall, 1976. — vi,282p : ill ; 24cm. — (Century psychology series)
Previous ed.: New York : Appleton-Century-Crofts, 1968. — Index.
ISBN 0-13-260109-5 : £8.75
(B77-21831)

Fried, Robert. Introduction to statistics / [by] Robert Fried. — Revised ed. — New York : Gardner Press ; New York ; London [etc.] : Distributed by Wiley, 1976. — xvi,304p : ill ; 24cm.
'A Halsted Press book'. — Previous ed.: London : Oxford University Press, 1969. — Bibl.: p.299-302. — Index.
ISBN 0-470-15184-6 : £10.05
(B77-00196)

Gilbert, Norma. Statistics / [by] Norma Gilbert. — Philadelphia ; London [etc.] : Saunders, 1976. — ix,364p : ill(some col) ; 27cm.
Text on lining papers. — With answers. — Index.
ISBN 0-7216-4127-x : £10.75
(B77-00749)

Haber, Audrey. General statistics / [by] Audrey Haber, Richard P. Runyon. — 3rd ed. — Reading, Mass. [etc.] ; London : Addison-Wesley, 1977. — 343,[135]p : ill ; 25cm. — (Addison-Wesley series in statistics)
With answers to selected exercises. — Previous ed.: 1973. — Bibl.: p.342-343. — Index.
ISBN 0-201-02729-1 : £10.40
(B77-21093)

Ingram, John A. Elementary statistics / [by] John A. Ingram. — Menlo Park ; London [etc.] : Cummings, 1977. — [12],445p : ill(some col), map ; 25cm.
Text on lining paper. — With selected answers. — Index.
ISBN 0-8465-2660-3 : £11.20
(B77-21094)

Kendall, *Sir* **Maurice George.** The advanced theory of statistics / [by] Sir Maurice Kendall and Alan Stuart. — 4th ed. — London [etc.] : Griffin.
In 3 vols.
Vol.1 : Distribution theory. — 1977. — xii, 472p : ill ; 26cm.
Previous ed.: 1969. — Bibl.: p.441-455. — Index.
ISBN 0-85264-242-3 : £14.50
(B77-31168)

Kuebler, Roy R. Statistics : a beginning / [by] Roy R. Kuebler and Harry Smith, Jr. — New York ; London [etc.] : Wiley, 1976. — xvi, 320p : ill ; 24cm.
With answers. — Index.
ISBN 0-471-50928-0 : £9.50
(B77-04778)

Orkin, Michael. Vital statistics / [by] Michael Orkin, Richard Drogin. — New York ; London [etc.] : McGraw-Hill, [1976]. — xi,388p : ill ; 24cm.
With answers to odd-numbered problems. — Published in the United States: 1974. — Index.
ISBN 0-07-047720-5 : £10.40
Also classified at 519.2
(B77-01407)

Pollard, Alfred Hurlstone. Introductory statistics : a service course / [by] A.H. Pollard. — 2nd ed., revised and enlarged. — Rushcutters Bay ; Oxford [etc.] : Pergamon, 1975. — [8],262p : ill ; 22cm.
With solutions to exercises. — This ed. originally published: 1972. — Index.
Pbk : £3.75
ISBN 0-08-017352-7
(B77-22540)

Romano, Albert. Applied statistics for science and industry / [by] Albert Romano. — Boston, Mass. ; London [etc.] : Allyn and Bacon, 1977. — xiv,513p : ill ; 25cm.
With answers to selected exercises. — Bibl.: p.385-390. — Index. — Previous control number B7715826.
ISBN 0-205-05575-3 : Unpriced
(B77-15826)

Sanders, Donald H. Statistics : a fresh approach / [by] Donald H. Sanders and A. Franklin Murph, Robert J. Eng. — New York ; London [etc.] : McGraw-Hill, 1976. — xv, 367p : ill ; 25cm.
With answers to self-testing review questions. — Index.
ISBN 0-07-054635-5 : £10.75
(B77-04131)

Schutte, Jerald G. Everything you always wanted to know about elementary statistics (but were afraid to ask) / [by] Jerald G. Schutte. — Englewood Cliffs ; London [etc.] : Prentice-Hall, 1977. — x,230p : ill ; 23cm. — (Prentice-Hall methods of social science series)
Bibl. — Index.
ISBN 0-13-293506-6 Pbk : £5.55
(B77-22541)

Steel, Robert George Douglas. Introduction to statistics / [by] Robert G.D. Steel, James H. Torrie. — New York ; London [etc.] : McGraw-Hill, 1976. — xiv,382p : ill ; 25cm. — (McGraw-Hill series in probability and statistics)
With answers to selected problems. — Bibl.: p.355-358. — Index.
ISBN 0-07-060918-7 : £11.60
(B77-04132)

Wonnacott, Thomas Herbert. Introductory statistics for business and economics / [by] Thomas H. Wonnacott and Ronald J. Wonnacott. — 2nd ed. — Santa Barbara ; London [etc.] : Wiley, 1977. — xxii,753p : ill(some col), maps ; 24cm. — (Wiley series in probability and mathematical statistics)
'A Wiley/Hamilton publication'. — With answers to odd numbered problems. — Text on lining papers. — Previous ed.: 1972. — Index.
ISBN 0-471-95980-4 : £11.50
(B77-22542)

Zirkel, Gene. Beginning statistics / [by] Gene Zirkel, Robert Rosenfeld. — New York ; London [etc.] : McGraw-Hill, 1976. — xiii,318, [2]p : ill ; 24cm.
With answers to selected assignments. — Bibl.: p.285. — Index.
ISBN 0-07-072840-2 Pbk : £8.25
(B77-04133)

519.5 — Statistical mathematics. *Conference proceedings*
European Meeting of Statisticians, *Grenoble, 1976.* Recent developments in statistics : proceedings of the European Meeting of Statisticians, Grenoble, 6-11 September, 1976 / edited by J.R. Barra ... [et al.]. — Amsterdam [etc.] ; Oxford : North-Holland Publishing Co., 1977. — x,808p : ill ; 23cm.
Includes a paper in French. — Bibl. — Index.
ISBN 0-7204-0751-6 : £36.00
(B77-23366)

519.5'02'07 — Statistical mathematics. *Humorous texts*
Runyon, Richard Porter. Winning with statistics : a painless first look at numbers, ratios, percentages, means, and inference / [by] Richard P. Runyon. — Reading, Mass. ; London [etc.] : Addison-Wesley, 1977. — iii-xii, 210p : ill ; 24cm.
Index.
ISBN 0-201-06654-8 Pbk : £4.80
(B77-25585)

519.5'02'415 — Statistical mathematics. *For psychometrics*

Ferguson, George Andrew. Statistical analysis in psychology & education / [by] George A. Ferguson. — 4th ed. — New York ; London [etc.] : McGraw-Hill, 1976. — xi,529p : ill ; 25cm. — (McGraw-Hill series in psychology)
With answers. — Previous ed.: New York : McGraw-Hill, 1971. — Bibl.: p.480-483. — Index.
ISBN 0-07-020480-2 : £11.60
Also classified at 519.5'02'437
(B77-06049)

Horowitz, Leonard M. Elements of statistics for psychology and education / [by] Leonard M. Horowitz. — New York ; London [etc.] : McGraw-Hill, 1974. — xv,464p : ill ; 24cm. — (McGraw-Hill series in psychology)
With answers. — Text on lining papers. — Index.
ISBN 0-07-030390-8 : Unpriced
Also classified at 519.5'02'437
(B77-20221)

Insko, Chester A. Introductory statistics for psychology / [by] Chester A. Insko and Douglas W. Schoeninger. — 2nd ed. — Boston, Mass. ; London [etc.] : Allyn and Bacon, 1977. — x,450p : ill ; 24cm.
Text on lining papers. With exercise answers. — Previous ed.: published as 'Introductory statistics for the behavioral sciences' / by Douglas W. Schoeninger and Chester A. Insko. 1971. — Bibl.: p.425-426. — Index. — Previous control number ISBN 0-205-05575 3.
Unpriced
(B77-09680)

519.5'02'43 — Statistical analysis. *For behavioural sciences*

Denenberg, Victor Hugo. Statistics and experimental design for behavioral and biological researchers : an introduction / [by] Victor H. Denenberg. — Washington ; London : Hemisphere Publishing Corporation ; New York ; London [etc.] : Distributed by Wiley, 1976. — viii,344p : ill ; 24cm.
'A Halsted Press book'. — With answers. — Bibl.: p.341. — Index.
ISBN 0-470-15202-8 : £13.25
Also classified at 519.5'02'4574
(B77-01408)

519.5'02'43 — Statistical mathematics. *For behavioural sciences*

Hardyck, Curtis D. Introduction to statistics for the behavioral sciences / [by] Curtis D. Hardyck, Lewis F. Petrinovich. — 2nd ed. — Philadelphia ; London [etc.] : Saunders, 1976. — ii-viii,336p : ill ; 26cm. — (Saunders books in psychology)
With answers. — Previous ed.: 1969. — Index.
ISBN 0-7216-4521-6 : £9.25
(B77-01409)

Johnson, Marcia K. Statistics : tool of the behavioral sciences / [by] Marcia K. Johnson, Robert M. Liebert. — Englewood Cliffs ; London [etc.] : Prentice-Hall, 1977. — xv, 237p : ill ; 24cm.
Index.
ISBN 0-13-844704-7 : £8.75
(B77-19347)

519.5'02'43 — Statistical mathematics. *For social sciences*

Levin, Jack, *b.1941.* Elementary statistics in social research / [by] Jack Levin. — 2nd ed. — New York [etc.] ; London : Harper and Row, 1977. — x,293p : ill ; 25cm.
With answers to selected problems. — Previous ed.: 1973. — Bibl.: p.285-286. — Index.
ISBN 0-06-043985-8 : £9.70
(B77-20222)

Palumbo, Dennis J. Statistics in political and behavioral science / [by] Dennis J. Palumbo. — Revised ed. — New York ; Guildford : Columbia University Press, 1977. — xv,469p : ill ; 24cm.
Previous ed.: New York : Appleton-Century-Crofts, 1969. — Bibl. — Index.
ISBN 0-231-04010-5 : £11.00
(B77-23367)

519.5'02'43 — Statistical mathematics. *Programmed texts. For behavioural sciences*

Young, Robert Kehoe. Introductory statistics for the behavioral sciences / [by] Robert K. Young, Donald J. Veldman. — 3rd ed. — New York ; London [etc.] : Holt, Rinehart and Winston, 1977. — xii,594p : ill ; 25cm.
With answers to the problems. — Previous ed.: 1972. — Index.
ISBN 0-03-089677-0 : £11.50
(B77-21095)

519.5'02'433 — Statistical mathematics. *For economics*

Bamford, George Gordon. Arithmetical and statistical methods / by G.G. Bamford. — Aylesbury : Ginn, 1976. — [2],60p : ill ; 22cm. — (Manchester Economics Project. Satellite books ; 1)
With answers. — Originally published: London : Ginn, 1969.
ISBN 0-602-22329-6 Sd : £1.10
Primary classification 513'.02'433
(B77-21829)

Davies, Brinley. Statistics for economics : an introductory course / [by] Brinley Davies and John M. Foad. — London : Heinemann Educational, 1977. — [6],89p : ill ; 25cm.
With answers. — Bibl.: p.85-86. — Index.
ISBN 0-435-84330-3 Pbk : £1.95
(B77-33776)

Dyckman, Thomas Richard. Fundamental statistics for business and economics / [by] Thomas R. Dyckman, L. Joseph Thomas. — Englewood Cliffs ; London [etc.] : Prentice-Hall, 1977. — xvii,715p : ill ; 24cm.
With answers to starred problems. — Index.
ISBN 0-13-344523-2 : £13.55
(B77-19348)

Mills, Richard L. Statistics for applied economics and business / [by] Richard L. Mills. — New York ; London [etc.] : McGraw-Hill, 1977. — xvii,618p : ill ; 25cm.
With answers to selected exercises. — Bibl.: p.610-612. — Index.
ISBN 0-07-042372-5 : £11.95
(B77-24188)

519.5'02'437 — Statistical mathematics. *For education*

Ferguson, George Andrew. Statistical analysis in psychology & education / [by] George A. Ferguson. — 4th ed. — New York ; London [etc.] : McGraw-Hill, 1976. — xi,529p : ill ; 25cm. — (McGraw-Hill series in psychology)
With answers. — Previous ed.: New York : McGraw-Hill, 1971. — Bibl.: p.480-483. — Index.
ISBN 0-07-020480-2 : £11.60
Primary classification 519.5'02'415
(B77-06049)

Horowitz, Leonard M. Elements of statistics for psychology and education / [by] Leonard M. Horowitz. — New York ; London [etc.] : McGraw-Hill, 1974. — xv,464p : ill ; 24cm. — (McGraw-Hill series in psychology)
With answers. — Text on lining papers. — Index.
ISBN 0-07-030390-8 : Unpriced
Primary classification 519.5'02'415
(B77-20221)

519.5'02'4574 — Statistical mathematics. *For biology*

Denenberg, Victor Hugo. Statistics and experimental design for behavioral and biological researchers : an introduction / [by] Victor H. Denenberg. — Washington ; London : Hemisphere Publishing Corporation ; New York ; London [etc.] : Distributed by Wiley, 1976. — viii,344p : ill ; 24cm.
'A Halsted Press book'. — With answers. — Bibl.: p.341. — Index.
ISBN 0-470-15202-8 : £13.25
Primary classification 519.5'02'43
(B77-01408)

519.5'02'461 — Statistical mathematics. *For medicine*

Duncan, Robert C. Introductory biostatistics for the health sciences / [by] Robert C. Duncan, Rebecca G. Knapp, M. Clinton Miller III. — New York ; London [etc.] : Wiley, 1977. — ix, 163p : ill ; 23cm.
'A Wiley medical publication'. — Index.
ISBN 0-471-01604-7 Pbk : £5.70
(B77-18734)

Hill, *Sir* Austin Bradford. A short textbook of medical statistics / by Sir Austin Bradford Hill. — [10th ed.]. — London [etc.] : Hodder and Stoughton, 1977. — ix,325p : ill ; 23cm. — (University medical texts)
Previous ed.: published as 'Principles of medical statistics'. London : 'The lancet', 1971. — Index.
ISBN 0-340-21957-2 : £6.75
ISBN 0-340-21958-0 Pbk : £3.45
(B77-28587)

519.5'02'461 — Statistical mathematics. *Programmed texts. For medicine*

Castle, Winifred Mary. Statistics in small doses / [by] Winifred M. Castle. — 2nd ed. — Edinburgh [etc.] : Churchill Livingstone, 1977. — viii,220p : ill ; 22cm.
With answers. — Previous ed.: 1972.
ISBN 0-443-01491-4 Pbk : £3.00
(B77-08356)

519.5'02'461 — Statistical mathematics. *Readings. For medicine*

Swinscow, Thomas Douglas Victor. Statistics at square one / [by] T.D.V. Swinscow. — 2nd ed. — London : British Medical Association, 1977. — viii,86p : ill ; 22cm.
'... based on a series of articles, here revised and extended, which were published in the "British Medical Journal" in 1976' - Introduction. — Previous ed.: 1976. — Bibl.: p.84.
ISBN 0-7279-0022-6 Pbk : £2.00
(B77-17465)

Swinscow, Thomas Douglas Victor. Statistics at square one / [by T.D.V. Swinscow]. — London : British Medical Association, 1976. — vi,86p : ill ; 22cm.
'... based on a series of articles, here revised and extended, which were published in the "British Medical Journal" in 1976' - Introduction. — Bibl.: p.84. — Index.
ISBN 0-7279-0018-8 Pbk : £1.50
(B77-02276)

519.5'02'462 — Statistical mathematics. *For engineering*

Johnson, Norman Lloyd. Statistics and experimental design in engineering and the physical sciences / by Norman L. Johnson, Fred C. Leone. — 2nd ed. — New York ; London [etc.] : Wiley. — (Wiley series in probability and mathematical statistics)
In 2 vols.
Vol.1. — 1977. — xv,592,9p : ill ; 24cm.
'A Wiley publication in applied statistics'. — With answers to selected exercises. — Previous ed.: 1964. — Bibl. — Index.
ISBN 0-471-01756-6 : £18.00
(B77-28588)

519.5'02'465 — Statistical mathematics. *For business enterprise*

Clelland, Richard Cook. Basic statistics with business applications. — 2nd ed. / [by] Richard C. Clelland, John S. deCani, Francis E. Brown. — New York ; London [etc.] : Wiley, 1973. — xii,691p : ill ; 24cm. — (Wiley series in probability and mathematical statistics)
With answers to selected exercises. — Previous ed.: / by Richard C. Clelland et al. 1966. — Bibl.: p.685-686. — Index.
ISBN 0-471-16051-2 : Unpriced
(B77-18735)

Kazmier, Leonard J. Schaum's outline of theory and problems of business statistics / by Leonard J. Kazmier. — New York ; London [etc.] : McGraw-Hill, 1976. — [8],375p : ill ; 28cm. — (Schaum's outline series)
Spine title: Business statistics. — Cover title: Theory and problems of business statistics. — With answers. — Index.
ISBN 0-07-033460-9 Pbk : £3.70
(B77-17466)

Letchford, Stanley. Business mathematics and statistics / by S. Letchford. — 2nd ed. — Reading : Donnington Press ; London [etc.] : Distributed by Cassell and Collier Macmillan, 1977. — x,546p : ill ; 22cm.
'A Cassell professional handbook' - cover. — With answers. — Previous ed.: 1974. — Index.
ISBN 0-304-29760-7 Pbk : £8.00
(B77-29400)

Miller, Robert B. Intermediate business statistics : analysis of variance, regression and time series / [by] Robert B. Miller, Dean W. Wichern. — New York ; London [etc.] : Holt, Rinehart and Winston, 1977. — xv,525p : ill ; 25cm. — (Series in quantitative methods for decision making)
Bibl.: p.513-515. — Index.
ISBN 0-03-089101-9 : £11.50
(B77-25586)

Wheldon, Harold James. Wheldon's business statistics and statistical method. — 8th ed. / [by] G.L. Thirkettle. — Plymouth : Macdonald and Evans, 1976. — xi,244p : ill, forms, maps ; 22cm.
Cover title: Wheldon's business statistics. — Previous ed.: 1972. — Index.
ISBN 0-7121-2331-8 Pbk : £2.00
(B77-06050)

519.5'02'4658 — Statistical mathematics. *For management*
Ashford, John Robert. Statistics for management / [by] John Ashford. — London : Institute of Personnel Management, 1977. — [6],394p : ill ; 23cm. — (Management in perspective)
Index.
ISBN 0-85292-152-7 : £6.25
ISBN 0-85292-155-1 Pbk : £4.95
(B77-30216)

519.5'02'4658 — Statistical mathematics. *For management decision making*
Brite, Robert L. Introduction to business statistics / [by] Robert L. Brite. — Reading, Mass. ; London [etc.] : Addison-Wesley, 1977. — xiii,365p : ill ; 24cm.
With answers to marginal exercises and odd-numbered problems. — Index.
ISBN 0-201-00593-x Pbk : £8.80
(B77-24189)

Jedamus, Paul. Statistical analysis for business decisions / [by] Paul Jedamus, Robert Frame, Robert Taylor. — New York ; London [etc.] : McGraw-Hill, 1976. — xiii,622p ; 24cm.
With answers. — Index.
ISBN 0-07-032302-x : £11.60
(B77-06051)

519.5'02'466 — Statistical mathematics. *For chemical engineering*
Statistical methods in research and production : with special reference to the chemical industry. — 4th revised ed. (reprinted with corrections) / edited by Owen L. Davies and Peter L. Goldsmith. — London : Longman for Imperical Chemical Industries Ltd, 1976. — xiii,478p : ill ; 24cm.
Fourth revised ed. originally published: 1972. — Index.
ISBN 0-582-03040-4 : £6.50
(B77-07329)

519.5'02'491 — Statistical mathematics. *For geography*
Ebdon, David. Statistics in geography : a practical approach / [by] David Ebdon. — Oxford : Blackwell, 1977. — viii,195p : ill, maps ; 25cm.
With answers to exercises. — Bibl.: p.142. — Index.
ISBN 0-631-16880-x : £5.50
(B77-13630)

519.5'028'54044 — Statistical analysis. Applications of digital computer systems
McNeil, Donald R. Interactive data analysis : a practical primer / [by] Donald R. McNeil. — New York ; London [etc.] : Wiley, 1977. — xiii,186p : ill ; 23cm.
'A Wiley-Interscience publication'. — Index.
ISBN 0-471-02631-x Pbk : £7.00
(B77-25587)

519.5'09 — Statistical mathematics, to 1975
Hollingdale, Stuart Havelock. Mathematics and man / prepared by S.H. Hollingdale, R.L. Wilder and Graham Flegg ; for the [Open University] Course Team. — Milton Keynes : Open University Press, 1976. — 47p : ill, facsims ; 30cm. — (Arts/mathematics, an interfaculty second level course : history of mathematics ; unit 11) (AM 289 ; 11)
Bibl.
ISBN 0-335-05014-x Sd : £1.25
Primary classification 001.6'4'0904
(B77-03862)

519.5'2 — Statistical mathematics. Sampling. Techniques
Cochran, William Gemmell. Sampling techniques / [by] William G. Cochran. — 3rd ed. — New York ; London[etc.] : Wiley, 1977. — xvi,428p : ill ; 24cm. — (Wiley series in probability and mathematical statistics)
With answers. — Previous ed.: 1963. — Bibl.: p.400-411. — Index.
ISBN 0-471-16240-x : £12.50
(B77-29401)

519.5'3 — Factor analysis. *For social sciences*
Mulaik, Stanley A. The foundations of factor analysis / [by] Stanley A. Mulaik. — New York ; London [etc.] : McGraw-Hill, 1972. — xvii,453p : ill ; 24cm. — (McGraw-Hill series in psychology)
Bibl.: p.429-436. — Index.
ISBN 0-07-043980-x : Unpriced
(B77-21096)

519.5'3 — Multivariate analysis
Giri, Narayan C. Multivariate statistical inference / [by] Narayan C. Giri. — New York [etc.] ; London : Academic Press, 1977. — xvi, 319p ; 24cm. — (Probability and mathematical statistics)
Bibl. — Index.
ISBN 0-12-285650-3 : £17.50
(B77-24190)

Gnanadesikan, R. Methods for statistical data analysis of multivariate observations / [by] R. Gnanadesikan. — New York ; London [etc.] : Wiley, 1977. — xi,311p : ill ; 24cm. — (Wiley series in probability and mathematical statistics)

'A Wiley publication in applied statistics' - half title page verso. — Bibl.: p.287-299. — Index.
ISBN 0-471-30845-5 : £15.00
(B77-13012)

Green, Paul Edgar. Mathematical tools for applied multivariate analysis / [by] Paul E. Green with contributions by J. Douglas Carroll. — New York [etc.] ; London : Academic Press, 1976. — xiii,376p : ill ; 24cm.
With answers. — Bibl.: p.364-367. — Index.
ISBN 0-12-297550-2 : £14.95
(B77-06052)

Morrison, Donald Franklin. Multivariate statistical methods / [by] Donald F. Morrison. — 2nd ed. — New York ; London [etc.] : McGraw-Hill, 1976. — xv,415p : ill ; 24cm. — (McGraw-Hill series in probability and statistics)
Previous ed.: 1967. — Bibl.: p.346-361. — Index.
ISBN 0-07-043186-8 : £13.25
(B77-04134)

519.5'3 — Multivariate analysis. *For behavioural sciences*
Bennett, Spencer. An introduction to multivariate techniques for social and behavioural sciences / [by] Spencer Bennett and David Bowers. — London [etc.] : Macmillan, 1976. — xii,156p : ill ; 25cm.
Spine title: Multivariate techniques for the social and behavioural sciences. — Bibl.: p.151-152. — Index.
ISBN 0-333-18277-4 : £10.00
(B77-02976)

Bock, R Darrell. Multivariate statistical methods in behavioral research / [by] R. Darrell Bock. — New York ; London [etc.] : McGraw-Hill, [1976]. — xv,623p : ill ; 24cm. — (McGraw-Hill series in psychology)
Published in the United States: 1975. — Bibl.: p.589-605. — Index.
ISBN 0-07-006305-2 : £12.40
(B77-02977)

Maxwell, Albert Ernest. Multivariate analysis in behavioural research / [by] A.E. Maxwell. — London : Chapman and Hall [etc.], 1977. — ix, 164p : ill ; 22cm. — (Monographs on applied probability and statistics)
Bibl.: p.153-157. — Index.
ISBN 0-412-14300-3 Pbk : £3.95
(B77-15827)

519.5'3 — Multivariate analysis. Applications of digital computer systems. Programming. *Manuals*
Youngman, Michael Brendon. Programmed methods for multivariate data / [by] M.B. Youngman. — Version 5. — [Nottingham] : University of Nottingham, School of Education, 1976. — 255p in various pagings : ill, forms ; 30cm.
Cover title: PMMD. — Previous ed.: 1975. — Bibl.
ISBN 0-85359-039-7 Sp : £2.50
(B77-05382)

519.5'3 — Statistical hypotheses. Testing. Nonparametric methods
Gibbons, Jean Dickinson. Nonparametric method for quantitative analysis / [by] Jean Dickinson Gibbons. — New York ; London [etc.] : Holt, Rinehart and Winston, [1977]. — xv,463p : ill ; 24cm. — (International series in decision processes)
With answers to even-numbered problems. — Published in the United States: 1976. — Bibl.: p.445-452. — Index.
ISBN 0-03-007811-3 : £9.75
(B77-11198)

Lehmann, E L. Nonparametrics : statistical methods based on ranks / [by] E.L. Lehmann with the special assistance of H.J.M. D'Abrera. — San Francisco : Holden-Day ; New York ; London [etc.] : McGraw-Hill, [1976]. — xvi, 457p : ill ; 24cm. — (Holden-Day series in probability and statistics)
With answers to selected problems. — Published in the United States: 1975. — Bibl. — Index.
ISBN 0-07-037073-7 : £12.95
(B77-02277)

519.5'3 — Statistical mathematics. Canonical correlation & factor comparison
Levine, Mark S. Canonical analysis and factor comparison / [by] Mark S. Levine. — Beverly Hills ; London : Sage Publications, 1977. — 62, [1]p : ill ; 22cm. — (Quantitative applications in the social sciences ; 07-006) (Sage university papers)
Bibl.: p.59-62.
ISBN 0-8039-0655-2 Pbk : £1.95
(B77-27035)

519.5'3 — Statistical mathematics. Contingency tables. Analysis
Everitt, Brian. The analysis of contingency tables / [by] B.S. Everitt. — London : Chapman and Hall [etc.], 1977. — ix,128p ; 23cm. — (Monographs on applied probability and statistics)
Bibl.: p.122-125. — Index.
ISBN 0-412-14970-2 : £3.75
(B77-27036)

519.5'32 — Statistical mathematics. Discrete distributions. Superpositions. Decomposition
Medgyessy, Pál. Decomposition of superpositions of density functions and discrete distributions / [by] Pál Medgyessy. — Bristol (Techno House, Redcliffe Way, Bristol BS1 6NX) : Hilger, 1977. — 308p : ill ; 25cm.
Bibl.: p.267-294. — Index.
ISBN 0-85274-294-0 : £12.00
Primary classification 519.2'4
(B77-12427)

519.5'32 — Statistical mathematics. Distributions. Curve fitting. Least squares method. Applications of programs written in Basic language
Till, Roger. Programs in BASIC for non-linear and multivariate least-squares methods : (with worked examples) / by Roger Till ; (with programs by Duncan Cowan, Margaret Moss and Sue Watts). — Reading (Reading RG6 2AB) : Geology Department, University of Reading, 1977. — [4],87p : ill ; 30cm. — (University of Reading. Department of Geology. Geological reports ; no.12) (Computer-based packages for teaching earth science report ; no.6)
Bibl.
ISBN 0-7049-0282-6 Sp : £1.50
(B77-18736)

519.5'35 — Statistical mathematics. Analysis of variance. Applications of multiple linear regression analysis
Wesolowsky, George O. Multiple regression and analysis of variance : an introduction for computer users in management and economics / [by] George O. Wesolowsky. — New York ; London [etc.] : Wiley, [1977]. — xi,292p : ill ; 24cm.
'A Wiley-Interscience publication'. — Published in the United States: 1976. — Index.
ISBN 0-471-93373-2 : £14.65
(B77-11199)

519.5'36 — Statistical mathematics. Linear regression analysis
Seber, George Arthur Frederick. Linear regression analysis / [by] G.A.F. Seber. — New York ; London [etc.] : Wiley, 1977. — xix, 465p : ill ; 24cm. — (Wiley series in probability and mathematical statistics)
With outline solutions to exercises. — Bibl.: p.433-457. — Index.
ISBN 0-471-01967-4 : £22.00
(B77-18105)

519.5'37 — Quadrat analysis
Thomas, R W. An introduction to quadrat analysis / by R.W. Thomas. — Norwich (University of East Anglia, Norwich NR4 7TJ) : Geo Abstracts Ltd, 1977. — [1],41,[1]p : ill ; 21cm. — (Concepts and techniques in modern geography ; no.12 ISSN 0306-6142)
Bibl.: p.37-40.
ISBN 0-902246-66-6 Sd : Unpriced
(B77-21097)

519.5'4 — Decision theory. *Conference proceedings*
Statistical Decision Theory and Related Topics *(Conference), 2nd, Purdue University, 1976.*
Statistical decision theory and related topics, II : proceedings of a symposium held at Purdue University, May 17-19, 1976 / edited by Shanti S. Gupta and David S. Moore. — New York [etc.] ; London : Academic Press, 1977. — xiii, 478p : ill ; 24cm.
'... papers presented at an international symposium on Statistical Decision Theory and Related Topics' - Preface. — Bibl.
ISBN 0-12-307560-2 : £17.40
(B77-21832)

519.5'4 — Forecasting
Gilchrist, Warren. Statistical forecasting / [by] Warren Gilchrist. — London [etc.] : Wiley, 1976. — xiii,308p : ill ; 24cm.
'A Wiley-Interscience publication'. — Bibl. — Index.
ISBN 0-471-99402-2 : £9.50
ISBN 0-471-99403-0 Pbk : £4.50
(B77-08357)

519.5'4 — Forecasting. Applications of time series analysis. *For production management*
Montgomery, Douglas C. Forecasting and time series analysis / [by] Douglas C. Montgomery, Lynwood A. Johnson. — New York ; London [etc.] : McGraw-Hill, 1976. — xi,304p : ill ; 24cm.
Bibl.: p.297-299. — Index.
ISBN 0-07-042857-3 : £10.75
(B77-04779)

519.5'4 — Parameters. Estimation. *For engineering & science*
Beck, James V. Parameter estimation in engineering and science / [by] James V. Beck and Kenneth J. Arnold. — New York ; London [etc.] : Wiley, 1977. — xix,501p : ill ; 24cm. — (Wiley series in probability and mathematical statistics)
Index.
ISBN 0-471-06118-2 : £18.75
(B77-25588)

519.5'4 — Parameters. Estimation. *For social sciences*
Hanushek, Eric A. Statistics methods for social scientists / [by] Eric A. Hanushek, John E. Jackson. — New York [etc.] ; London : Academic Press, 1977. — xiii,374p : ill ; 24cm. — (Quantitative studies in social relations)
Bibl.: p.367-368. — Index.
ISBN 0-12-324350-5 : £13.50
(B77-16358)

519.5'4 — Statistical analysis. Prediction
Hildebrand, David K. Prediction analysis of cross classifications / [by] David K. Hildebrand, James D. Laing, Howard Rosenthal. — New York ; London [etc.] : Wiley, 1977. — xvii, 311p : ill ; 24cm. — (Wiley series in probability and mathematical statistics)
Bibl. — Index.
ISBN 0-471-39575-7 : £16.80
(B77-14215)

519.5'4 — Statistical inference
Hogg, Robert Vincent. Probability and statistical inference / by Robert V. Hogg and Elliot A. Tanis. — New York : Macmillan ; London : Collier Macmillan, 1977. — xi,450p : ill ; 24cm.
With answers to selected exercises. — Bibl.: p.415-416. — Index.
ISBN 0-02-355650-1 Pbk : £6.75
Primary classification 519.2
(B77-21830)

Huntsberger, David Vernon. Elements of statistical inference / [by] David V. Huntsberger, Patrick Billingsley. — 4th ed. — Boston, Mass. ; London [etc.] : Allyn and Bacon, 1977. — ix,385p : ill(chiefly col) ; 25cm.
With answers to odd-numbered questions. — Previous ed.: 1973. — Bibl. — Index.
ISBN 0-205-05734-9 : Unpriced
(B77-16862)

519.5'4 — Statistical mathematics. Estimation. Maximum likelihood method. Use of small samples
Shenton, L R. Maximum likelihood estimation in small samples / [by] L.R. Shenton, K.O. Bowman. — London [etc.] : Griffin, 1977. — x, 186p : ill ; 22cm. — (Griffin's statistical monographs and courses ; no.38)
Bibl. — Index.
ISBN 0-85264-238-5 Pbk : £6.80
(B77-33777)

519.5'4'02491 — Statistical inference. *For geography*
Norcliffe, G B. Inferential statistics for geographers : an introduction / [by] G.B. Norcliffe. — London : Hutchinson, 1977. — 272p : ill, maps ; 23cm.
Bibl.: p.245-252. — Index.
ISBN 0-09-128620-4 : £6.95
ISBN 0-09-128621-2 Pbk : £3.50
(B77-30217)

519.7 — Mathematical programming
Mitra, G. Theory and application of mathematical programming / [by] G. Mitra. — London [etc.] : Academic Press, 1976. — ix, 214p : ill ; 24cm.
Bibl.: p.163-165.
ISBN 0-12-500450-8 : £8.20
(B77-05383)

519.7'03 — Dynamic programming
Bertsekas, Dimitri P. Dynamic programming and stochastic control / [by] Dimitri P. Bertsekas. — New York [etc.] ; London : Academic Press, 1976. — xv,397p : ill ; 24cm. — (Mathematics in science and engineering ; vol.125)
Bibl.: p.387-394. — Index.
ISBN 0-12-093250-4 : £13.70
(B77-07891)

Dreyfus, Stuart Ernest. The art and theory of dynamic programming / [by] Stuart E. Dreyfus, Averill M. Law. — New York [etc.] ; London : Academic Press, 1977. — xv,284p : ill ; 24cm. — (Mathematics in science and engineering ; vol.130)
With answers. — Bibl. — Index.
ISBN 0-12-221860-4 : £13.15
(B77-21833)

519.7'2 — Linear programming
Bazaraa, Mokhtar S. Linear programming and network flows / [by] Mokhtar S. Bazaraa, John J. Jarvis. — New York ; London [etc.] : Wiley, 1977. — x,565p : ill ; 24cm.
Bibl.: p.530-558. — Index.
ISBN 0-471-06015-1 : £15.75
(B77-18737)

Gass, Saul Irving. Linear programming : methods and applications / [by] Saul I. Gass. — 4th ed. — New York ; London [etc.] : McGraw-Hill, [1976]. — x,406p : ill ; 24cm.
This ed. published in the United States: 1975. — Previous ed.: 1969. — Bibl.: p.371-401. — Index.
ISBN 0-07-022968-6 : £16.20
(B77-04780)

Murty, Katta G. Linear and combinatorial programming / [by] Katta G. Murty. — New York ; London [etc.] : Wiley, 1976. — xxiii, 567p : ill ; 26cm.
Bibl.: p.559-560. — Index.
ISBN 0-471-57370-1 : £12.00
(B77-24191)

Van de Panne, Cornelius. Linear programming and related techniques / [by] C. van de Panne. — 2nd, revised ed. — Amsterdam [etc.] ; Oxford : North-Holland Publishing Co., 1976. — x,438p : ill ; 23cm.
With answers to odd-numbered exercises. — Previous ed.: 1971. — Bibl.: p.429-430. — Index.
ISBN 0-7204-0532-7 Pbk : £13.29
(B77-04135)

519.7'2 — Linear programming. Transportation problem
Hay, Alan. Linear programming : elementary geographical applications of the transportation problem / by Alan Hay. — Norwich (University of East Anglia, Norwich NR4 7TJ) : Geo Abstracts Ltd, 1977. — [1],29,[1]p : ill, maps ; 21cm. — (Concepts and techniques in modern geography ; no.11 ISSN 0306-6142)
Bibl.: p.28-29.
ISBN 0-902246-65-8 Sd : £0.50
(B77-15267)

519.7'6 — Nonlinear programming
Avriel, Mordecai. Nonlinear programming : analysis and methods / [by] Mordecai Avriel. — Englewood Cliffs ; London [etc.] : Prentice-Hall, 1976. — xv,512p : ill ; 24cm. — (Prentice-Hall series in automatic computation)
Bibl. — Index.
ISBN 0-13-623603-0 : £19.95
(B77-27037)

520 — ASTRONOMY
Abell, George. Realm of the universe / [by] George O. Abell. — Brief ed. revised. — New York [etc.] ; London : Holt, Rinehart and Winston, 1976. — iii-x,431p,[34]p of plates : ill(some col), charts, maps(some col) ; 24cm.
'... a complete revision of ... [the author's] previous brief edition of "Exploration of the Universe" [1969, and] ... a short and updated companion to the third (1975) edition of "Exploration of the Universe"' - Preface. — Bibl.: p.369-370. — Index.
ISBN 0-03-014996-7 Pbk : £9.50
(B77-06657)

Bash, Frank N. Astronomy / Frank N. Bash, consulting author. — New York ; London [etc.] : Harper and Row, 1977. — xii,468p,[16]p of plates : ill(some col), charts(some col), facsims, maps, ports ; 24cm. — (A Leogryph book)
Index.
ISBN 0-06-043853-3 Pbk : £8.95
(B77-29402)

The **Cambridge** encyclopaedia of astronomy / editor-in-chief Simon Mitton ; foreword by Sir Martin Ryle. — London : Cape, 1977. — 495p : ill(some col), charts(chiefly col), maps(1 col) ; 27cm.
ISBN 0-224-01418-8 : £15.00 : CIP rev.
(B77-21834)

Fredrick, Laurence William. Astronomy. — 10th ed. / [by] Laurence W. Fredrick, Robert H. Baker. — New York ; London [etc.] : D. Van Nostrand, 1976. — xvi,559p,[8]p of plates : ill(some col), charts(some col), maps(some col) ; 24cm.
Previous ed.: / by Robert H. Baker, Laurence W. Fredrick. New York ; London : Van Nostrand Reinhold, 1971. — Bibl. — Index.
ISBN 0-442-22444-3 : £13.75
(B77-18106)

International Science School for High School Students, *16th, University of Sydney, 1973.*
Focus on the stars / [by] B.J. Bok ... [et al.] ; edited by H. Messel, S.T. Butler. — London : Heinemann Educational, 1977. — 291p : ill, ports ; 22cm.
Text on lining paper. — 'This book is an edited version of a course of lectures contributed in the sixteenth International Science School for High School Students at the University of Sydney, sponsored by the Science Foundation for Physics' p.4. — Originally published: Gladesville, N.S.W. : Shakespeare Head Press, 1976. — Bibl. — Index.
ISBN 0-435-68282-2 : £4.80
(B77-21098)

Jastrow, Robert. Astronomy : fundamentals and frontiers / [by] Robert Jastrow, Malcolm H. Thompson. — 3rd ed. — New York ; London [etc.] : Wiley, 1977. — [16],144,452p,[26]p of plates : ill(some col), charts(some col), maps(some col), ports ; 25cm.
Charts on lining papers. — Previous ed.: New York : Wiley, 1974. — Index.
ISBN 0-471-01845-7 : £10.30
(B77-22543)

Maloney, Terry. Astronomy / [by] Terry Maloney. — [London] : [Macdonald Educational], [1977]. — 96p : ill(some col), charts, col map ; 20cm. — (Macdonald guidelines ; 13)
Bibl.: p.88-89. — Index.
ISBN 0-356-06013-6 Pbk : £1.00
(B77-21099)

Pasachoff, Jay M. Contemporary astronomy / [by] Jay M. Pasachoff. — Philadelphia ; London [etc.] : Saunders, 1977. — xvi,588,[52] p,[24]p of plates : ill(some col), charts, facsims, map, ports ; 28cm. — (Saunders golden sunburst series)
Col. charts on lining papers. — Bibl.: (3p.). — Index.
ISBN 0-7216-7101-2 : £13.25
(B77-20223)

Rosemergy, John C. Celestial horizons : a concise view of the universe / [by] John C. Rosemergy. — Boston, Mass. ; London [etc.] : Allyn and Bacon, 1977. — xii,260p : ill, charts, facsims, ports ; 24cm.
Bibl. — Index.
ISBN 0-205-05571-0 Pbk : £7.95
(B77-07892)

Roy, Archie Edmiston. Astronomy, principles and practice / [by] A.E. Roy, D. Clarke. — Bristol : Hilger, 1977. — xv,342p : ill ; 29cm.
With answers to problems. — Bibl.: p.332-333. — Index.
ISBN 0-85274-292-4 : £10.00
ISBN 0-85274-346-7 Pbk : £7.50
(B77-14216)

Stars & space 77 / editor Ian Ridpath. — London : Independent Newspapers Ltd ; London (181 Queen Victoria St., EC4V 4DD) : Distributed by Independent Magazines (Publishing) Ltd, 1976. — 96p : ill, charts, maps, ports ; 29cm.
Bibl.: p.94.
ISBN 0-905583-00-0 Sd : £1.00
(B77-16863)

Wickramasinghe, Nalin Chandra. The cosmic laboratory / by N.C. Wickramasinghe. — Cardiff ([P.O. Box 78, Cardiff CF1 1XL]) : University College, [1975]. — 30p : ill ; 21cm. — (University College, Cardiff. Inaugural lectures)
'... given on 20 May 1975 at University College, Cardiff'.
ISBN 0-901426-15-6 Sd : £0.35
(B77-00197)

520 — Astronomy. *Juvenile literature*

Children's encyclopedia of earth, stars and planets / compiled and edited by Kenneth Bailey ; [written by Anthony Harvey, Barry Cork, Maurice Allward ; illustrated by Max Ansell ... et al.]. — Glasgow [etc.] : Collins, 1976. — 3-189p : col ill, col charts, col maps, col ports ; 31cm. — ([Collins children's encyclopaedia])
Cover title: Collins children's encyclopedia of earth, stars and planets. — Index.
ISBN 0-00-106165-8 : £2.95
Primary classification 550
(B77-26305)

Wicks, Keith. Stars and planets / [by Keith Wicks]. — Maidenhead : Sampson Low, 1977. — 5-44p : ill(chiefly col), col charts, col facsim, ports ; 28cm. — ([New horizon library])
Index.
ISBN 0-562-00063-1 : £1.75
(B77-14710)

520 — Astronomy. *Reviews of research*

Vistas in astronomy. — Oxford [etc.] : Pergamon.
Vol.18 : Kepler : four hundred years : proceedings of conferences held in honour of Johannes Kepler / edited by Arthur Beer and Peter Beer. — 1975. — xx,1034p : ill(incl 1 col), facsims, maps,(some col) ; 26cm.
'Sixteen World-wide Symposia, in particular the joint Symposium sponsored by The Franklin Institute and the American Association for the Advancement of Science (AAAS), held at Philadelphia ; the joint Symposium of the International Astronomical Union (IAU) and the Académie Internationale d'Histoire des Sciences (IHS), held at Leningrad ; and specially contributed papers' - title page verso. — Ill. on lining papers. — Bibl. — Index.
ISBN 0-08-017879-0 : £75.00
(B77-06053)

Vol.19 : History and philosophy, celestial mechanics, instrumentation, radio telescopes, solar physics, planetary studies, stellar work, galactic structure, cosmic rays, X-ray astronomy, black holes / edited by Arthur Beer and Peter Beer. — 1977. — [6],ii,412p,[6]leaves of plates,[34]p of plates : ill ; 28cm.
Bibl. — Index.
ISBN 0-08-018280-1 : £35.00
(B77-19349)

520'.3 — Astronomy. *Encyclopaedias*

The **illustrated** encyclopedia of astronomy and space / editor Ian Ridpath. — London [etc.] : Macmillan, 1976. — 240p,[8]p of plates : ill(some col), ports ; 28cm.
Spine title: Encyclopedia of astronomy and space. — Index.
ISBN 0-333-21365-3 : £7.95
Also classified at 500.5'03
(B77-03521)

Weigert, Alfred. Concise encyclopedia of astronomy / [by] A. Weigert and H. Zimmermann ; translated [from the German] by J. Home Dickson. — 2nd English ed. / revised by H. Zimmermann. — London : Hilger, 1976. — 532p,16p of plates : ill ; 25cm.
Five fold. leaves (ill., charts) as inserts. — Previous ed. of this translation: published as 'ABC of astronomy'. London : Hilger, 1967. — Translation of: 'Brockhaus-ABC Astronomie'. 3 Aufl. / von H. Zimmermann überarbeitet. Leipzig : Brockhaus, 1971.
ISBN 0-85274-099-9 : £9.00
(B77-00198)

520'.5 — Astronomy. *Serials*

British Astronomical Association. Handbook / British Astronomical Association. — [London] ([Burlington House, Piccadilly, W1V 0NL]) : [The Association].
1978 : fifty-seventh year of publication. — 1977. — [1],xii,100,[1]p : ill, charts, map ; 23cm.
Sd : £1.50(free to members)
ISSN 0068-130x
(B77-25589)

Yearbook of astronomy. — London : Sidgwick and Jackson.
1978 / [edited by] Patrick Moore. — 1977. — 230p : ill, charts ; 21cm.
Bibl.: p.221.
ISBN 0-283-98392-2 : £4.50
ISBN 0-283-98393-0 Pbk : £2.25
ISSN 0084-3660
(B77-30218)

520'.8 — Astronomy. *Essays. Early works. Latin-English parallel texts*

Richard of Wallingford. Richard of Wallingford : an edition of his writings / with introductions, English translation and commentary by J.D. North. — Oxford : Clarendon Press, 1976. — 3v.(xxii,567p;[5],387p;viii,319p,leaf of plate,xxiv p of plates) : ill, facsims, maps, port ; 24cm.
Parallel Latin text and English translation, including some Middle English. — Bibl.: p.292-300. — Index (Vol.3).
ISBN 0-19-858139-4 : £75.00
(B77-00750)

520'.8 — Astronomy. *Readings*

Modern astronomy : selections from the 'Yearbook of astronomy' / by the editor Patrick Moore. — London : Sidgwick and Jackson [etc.], 1977. — 3-184p : ill ; 21cm.
ISBN 0-283-98322-1 : £4.50
ISBN 0-283-98369-8 Pbk : £2.50
(B77-13013)

Space science and astronomy : escape from earth / edited by Thornton Page and Lou Williams Page. — New York : Macmillan ; London : Collier Macmillan, 1976. — xix, 467p : ill, charts, map, ports ; 24cm. — ('Sky and telescope' library of astronomy ; vol.9)
'... articles that first appeared in ... "Sky and Telescope", "The Sky", and "The Telescope"' - half title page verso. — Bibl.: p.450-452. — Index.
ISBN 0-02-594310-3 : £10.50
Also classified at 629.4'09'04
(B77-11786)

520'.92'4 — Astronomy. Herschel, Sir John, 1st bart. *Biographies*

Turner, Anthony John. Science and music in eighteenth century Bath : [catalogue of] an exhibition in the Holburne of Menstrie Museum, Bath, 22 September 1977-29 December 1977 / catalogue by A.J. Turner, with the assistance of I.D. Woodfield and contributions by H.S. Torrens. — Bath (Claverton Down, Bath, Avon BA2 7AY) : University of Bath, 1977. — viii,131p : ill, facsims, music, ports ; 21cm.
Bibl.: p.117-123.
ISBN 0-900843-83-7 Sd : Unpriced
Also classified at 780'.9423'98; 509'.423'98
(B77-33778)

520'.951 — Astronomy. *China. Periodicals*

Chinese astronomy. — [Oxford etc.] : [Pergamon].
'A selected translation of "Acta Astronomica Sinica"' - cover.
Vol.1, no.1- ; [June 1977]-. — [1977]-. — ill ; 25cm.
Two issues a year. — [2],i,196p. in 1st issue.
Pbk : Unpriced
ISSN 0146-6364
(B77-21100)

521 — THEORETICAL ASTRONOMY

521'.1'0924 — Celestial mechanics. Theories of Galilei, Galileo

Morphet, Clive. Galileo and Copernican astronomy : a scientific world view defined / [by] Clive Morphet ; [for] Science in a Social Context. — London [etc.] : Butterworth, 1977. — 80p : ill ; 22cm.
Bibl.: p.75-80.
ISBN 0-408-71303-8 Pbk : £1.00
(B77-17467)

521'.54 — Solar system. Planets. Motion. Theories. *Early works*

Copernicus, Nicolaus. [De revolutionibus orbium coelestium. English]. Copernicus, on the revolutions of the heavenly spheres / a new translation from the Latin, with an introduction and notes by A.M. Duncan. — Newton Abbot [etc.] : David and Charles [etc.], 1976. — 328p : ill ; 26cm.
'De revolutionibus orbium coelestium' originally published: Nuremberg : John Petreius, 1543. — Bibl.: p.327.
ISBN 0-7153-6927-x : £12.50
(B77-07330)

522 — PRACTICAL AND SPHERICAL ASTRONOMY

522 — Astronomical bodies. Observation. *Amateurs' manuals*

Knox, Richard. Discover the sky with telescope and camera / [by] Richard Knox. — Chislehurst (PO Box 11, Chislehurst, Kent) : R. Morgan Publishing, 1976. — 186p : ill, charts ; 23cm.
Bibl.: p.182. — Index.
ISBN 0-902979-01-9 : £4.95
(B77-16864)

522 — Naked eye astronomy. *Amateurs' manuals*

Knox, Richard. Experiments in astronomy for amateurs / [by] Richard Knox. — Shaldon : K. Reid, 1975. — 206p : ill, charts ; 22cm.
Bibl.: p.201. — Index.
ISBN 0-904094-15-4 : £6.50
(B77-18107)

522'.1'0973 — Astronomical observatories. *United States. Guidebooks*

Kirby-Smith, H T. US observatories : a directory and travel guide / by H.T. Kirby-Smith. — New York [etc.] ; London : Van Nostrand Reinhold, 1976. — 173p : ill, map ; 24cm.
Bibl.: p.165-167. — Index.
ISBN 0-442-24451-7 : £8.50
ISBN 0-442-24450-9 Pbk : £4.75
(B77-15828)

522'.19'4134 — Astronomical observatories. *Edinburgh. Royal Observatory, Edinburgh. Reports, surveys. Serials*

Royal Observatory, Edinburgh. Annual report for the year ending 30 September / Royal Observatory, Edinburgh. — Edinburgh (Blackford Hill, Edinburgh EH9 3HJ) : The Observatory.
1976. — [1977]. — 47p : ill ; 30cm.
ISBN 0-902553-16-x Sd : Unpriced
ISSN 0309-0108
(B77-08990)

522'.19'42162 — Astronomical observatories. *London. Greenwich (London Borough). Royal Greenwich Observatory, 1676*

Howse, Derek. Francis Place and the early history of the Greenwich Observatory / [by] Derek Howse. — New York : Science History Publications ; Folkestone : [Distributed by] Dawson, 1975. — 64p : ill, facsims, plans, ports ; 24x31cm.
Bibl.: p.62. — Index.
ISBN 0-88202-031-5 : £9.00
(B77-33779)

522'.19'42251 — Astronomical observatories. *East Sussex. Herstmonceux. Royal Greenwich Observatory. Reports, surveys. Serials*

Royal Greenwich Observatory. The Royal Greenwich Observatory report for January to September. — Hailsham (Herstmonceux Castle, Hailsham, E. Sussex BN27 1RP) : The Observatory.
1975. — 1976. — 55p,viii p of plates : ill, map, ports ; 25cm.
At head of title: Science Research Council. — Bibl.: p.47-49.
Sd : £1.00
ISSN 0308-3322
(B77-21835)

Royal Greenwich Observatory. The Royal Greenwich Observatory report for October to September. — Hailsham (Herstmonceaux Castle, Hailsham, E. Sussex BN27 1RP) : The Observatory.
1975-1976. — 1977. — 64p,iv p of plates : ill, ports ; 25cm.
At head of title: Science Research Council. — Bibl.: p.53-57.
Sd : £1.00
ISSN 0308-3322
(B77-21836)

Royal Greenwich Observatory. The Royal Greenwich Observatory report for the year ending 31 December. — Hailsham (Herstmonceaux Castle, Hailsham, E. Sussex BN27 1RP) : The Observatory.
1974. — 1975. — 43p,iv p of plates : ill ; 25cm.
At head of title: Science Research Council. — Bibl.: p.34-38.
ISBN 0-901660-28-0 Sd : £0.40
ISSN 0308-3322
(B77-06658)

522'.6 — Gamma ray astronomy. *Great Britain. Reports, surveys*
Panel to Review the Future of Gamma-ray Astronomy in the UK. Report of the Panel to Review the Future of Gamma-ray Astronomy in the UK. — [London] ([State House, High Holborn, WC1R 4TA]) : [Science Research Council], 1977. — 73p in various pagings : ill ; 30cm.
Bibl.: p.[37]-[38].
Sd : Unpriced
(B77-17468)

522'.682'0941 — Radioastronomy. *Great Britain, to 1975*
Edge, David Owen. Astronomy transformed : the emergence of radio astronomy in Britain / [by] David O. Edge, Michael J. Mulkay. — New York ; London [etc.] : Wiley, 1976. — xvii, 482p : ill ; 24cm. — (Science, culture and society)
'A Wiley-Interscience publication'. — Index.
ISBN 0-471-23273-4 : £19.25
(B77-00751)

522'.7 — Spherical astronomy
Smart, William Marshall. Textbook on spherical astronomy / by W.M. Smart. — 6th ed. / revised by R.M. Green. — Cambridge [etc.] : Cambridge University Press, 1977. — xiii,431p : ill ; 23cm.
Previous ed.: 1962. — Index.
ISBN 0-521-21516-1 : £11.50
ISBN 0-521-29180-1 Pbk : £5.50
(B77-29403)

523 — DESCRIPTIVE ASTRONOMY
523 — Astronomical bodies
Clotfelter, Beryl E. The universe and its structure / [by] Beryl E. Clotfelter. — New York ; London [etc.] : McGraw-Hill, 1976. — x,437p : ill(some col), charts, ports ; 25cm.
Col. ill. on lining papers. — Bibl.: p.426-432. — Index.
ISBN 0-07-011385-8 : £11.20
(B77-04781)

Moore, Patrick. The stars above / [by] Patrick Moore. — Norwich : Jarrold and Sons, 1976. — [34]p : ill(chiefly col), port ; 20cm.
ISBN 0-85306-665-5 Sd : £0.40
(B77-11200)

523 — Astronomical bodies. *Juvenile literature*
Connell, Stephanie. Stars and planets / written by Stephanie Connell and Vivienne Driscoll. — London : Macdonald Educational, 1977. — [1], 32p : col ill, col charts ; 18cm. — (Readabout)
Adaptation of: 'The universe'. 1971. — Index.
ISBN 0-356-05540-x Sd : £0.35
(B77-13014)

523 — Black holes
Asimov, Isaac. The collapsing universe / [by] Isaac Asimov. — London : Hutchinson, 1977. — [9],204p ; 23cm.
Index.
ISBN 0-09-131770-3 : £4.50
(B77-29404)

523 — Celestial masers
Cook, Alan Hugh. Celestial masers / [by] A.H. Cook. — Cambridge [etc.] : Cambridge University Press, 1977. — viii,135p : ill ; 24cm. — (Cambridge monographs on physics)
Bibl.: p.124-132. — Index.
ISBN 0-521-21344-4 : £7.50
(B77-24907)

523 — Descriptive astronomy. *Study regions: Universe visible from southern hemisphere*
Calder, David. Seeing the southern sky / [by] David Calder. — Christchurch, N.Z. [etc.] ; London : Whitcoulls, 1977. — 159p : ill, charts ; 22cm. — (Practical guides series)
Bibl.: p.146-147. — Index.
ISBN 0-7233-0490-4 : Unpriced
(B77-23368)

Warner, Lionel. Astronomy for the southern hemisphere : a practical guide to the sky at night / [by] Lionel Warner. — Wellington [etc.] ; London : A.H. and A.W. Reed, 1975. — xiv,159p : ill, map, ports ; 30cm.
Ill. on lining papers. — Index.
ISBN 0-589-00864-1 : £10.85
(B77-33780)

523 — Extragalactic astronomy
Vaucouleurs, Gérard de. Topics in extragalactic astronomy : with special reference to the southern hemisphere / by Gérard de Vaucouleurs. — Edinburgh (Blackford Hill, Edinburgh EH9 3HJ) : Royal Observatory, Edinburgh, 1977. — [1],vi[i.e. viii],125p,[62]p of plates,[8]leaves of plates : ill, charts ; 30cm. — (Royal Observatory, Edinburgh. Occasional reports ; no.2 ISSN 0309-099x)
Bibl.
ISBN 0-902553-17-8 Sp : £5.00 : CIP rev.
(B77-05385)

523 — Pulsars
Smith, Francis Graham. Pulsars / [by] F.G. Smith. — Cambridge [etc.] : Cambridge University Press, 1977. — xii,239p : ill ; 24cm. — (Cambridge monographs on physics)
Bibl. — Index.
ISBN 0-521-21241-3 : £9.50
(B77-14711)

523.01 — Astrophysics. *Reviews of research*
Kuchowicz, Bronislaw. Nuclear and relativistic astrophysics and nuclidic cosmochemistry, 1963-1967 / [compiled by] B. Kuchowicz. — New York ; London [etc.] : Gordon and Breach.
Originally published: in 2 vols. Warsaw : Nuclear Energy Information Center, 1968.
Vol.1. — 1976. — xiv,366p : ill ; 23cm.
ISBN 0-677-02760-5 : £21.10
(B77-00752)

523.01 — Relativistic astrophysics
Kaufmann, William John. Relativity and cosmology / [by] William J. Kaufmann, III. — 2nd ed. — New York [etc.] ; London : Harper and Row, 1977. — vi,154p : ill, charts ; 24cm.
Previous ed.: 1973. — Index.
ISBN 0-06-043572-0 Pbk : £2.95
(B77-16359)

523.1 — ASTRONOMY. UNIVERSE
Motz, Lloyd. The universe : its beginning and end. — [1st ed. reprinted] ; foreword by Patrick Moore. — London : Abacus, 1977. — xvi,343p, [16]p of plates : ill, charts ; 20cm.
Originally published: New York : Scribner, 1975 ; London : Millington, 1976. — Bibl.: p.331-332. — Index.
ISBN 0-349-12404-3 Pbk : £1.95
(B77-31170)

Motz, Lloyd. The universe : its beginning and end / [by] Lloyd Motz. — [1st ed. reprinted] ; foreword by Patrick Moore. — London [etc.] : Millington, 1976. — xvi,343,[1]p,[22]p of plates : ill ; 22cm.
Originally published: New York : Scribner, 1975. — Bibl.: p.331-332. — Index.
ISBN 0-86000-071-0 : £5.00
(B77-08991)

Narlikar, Jayant. The structure of the universe / [by] Jayant Narlikar. — London [etc.] : Oxford University Press, 1977. — [8],264p : ill ; 21cm.
Bibl.: p.259. — Index.
ISBN 0-19-217653-6 : £4.25
ISBN 0-19-289082-4 Pbk : £1.95
(B77-13015)

Rowan-Robinson, Michael. Cosmology / [by] Michael Rowan-Robinson. — Oxford : Clarendon Press, 1977. — x,plate,159p : ill, charts ; 23cm. — (Oxford physics series ; no.15)
Bibl.: p.146. — Index.
ISBN 0-19-851838-2 : £6.00 : CIP rev.
ISBN 0-19-851839-0 Pbk : £2.95
(B77-07331)

523.1'01 — Universe. Theories
Moore, Patrick. Can you speak Venusian? : a guide to the independent thinkers / by Patrick Moore. — 2nd ed. — Hornchurch : I. Henry, 1977. — 158p : ill, charts, 2 facsims, maps ; 21cm.
Previous ed.: Newton Abbot : David and Charles, 1972. — Bibl.: p.151-152. — Index.
ISBN 0-86025-802-5 : £3.95
(B77-29405)

523.1'12 — Radio galaxies. Physical properties
Pacholczyk, A G. Radio galaxies : radiation transfer, dynamics, stability and evolution of a synchrotron plasmon / by A.G. Pacholczyk. — Oxford [etc.] : Pergamon, 1977. — xi,293p : ill ; 26cm. — (International series in natural philosophy ; vol.89) (Pergamon international library)
Index.
ISBN 0-08-021031-7 : £13.95
(B77-25590)

523.1'13 — Milky Way
Bok, Bart Jan. The Milky Way / [by] Bart J. Bok and Priscilla F. Bok. — 4th ed. revised and enlarged. — Cambridge, Mass. ; London : Harvard University Press, 1976 [i.e. 1977]. — [7],273p : ill, charts ; 24cm. — (The Harvard books on astronomy)
This ed. originally published: 1974. — Index.
ISBN 0-674-57501-6 : £11.25
ISBN 0-674-57502-4 Pbk : £4.50
(B77-12429)

523.1'2 — Cosmogony
Weinberg, Steven. The first three minutes : a modern view of the origin of the universe / [by] Steven Weinberg. — London : Deutsch, 1977. — x,188p,[10]p of plates : ill, ports ; 23cm.
Also published: New York : Basic Books, 1977. — Bibl.: p.177-180. — Index.
ISBN 0-233-96906-3 : £4.50
(B77-25591)

523.1'2'09 — Cosmogony, to 1975. *Polish texts*
Knappik, Jerzy Jan. Dynamiczna ekspansja kosmosu : poustawanie, rozwój i koniec wszechświata / Jerzy Jan Knappik. — London : Veritas Foundation Publication Centre, 1976. — 134p ; 20cm. — (Biblioteka polska : seria zielona ; tom 14)
Bibl.: p.7-21. — Index.
ISBN 0-901215-66-x : £1.90
(B77-04782)

523.2 — ASTRONOMY. SOLAR SYSTEM
523.2 — Solar system. *Teaching kits*
Fairley, Peter. Space / by Peter Fairley ; illustrated by Kuo Kang Chen ... [et al.]. — London : Jackdaw [for] Thames Television, 1977. — Portfolio : ill(some col), charts, maps ; 22x26cm. — (Magpies)
Eleven sheets (8 fold) ([22] sides). — Bibl.(1p.).
ISBN 0-305-62133-5 : £0.99
(B77-25592)

523.3 — ASTRONOMY. MOON
Kondo, Herbert. The moon / by Herbert Kondo. — Revised ed. — London [etc.] : F. Watts, 1977. — [10],86p : ill, 2 maps ; 23cm.
Previous ed.: i.e. New ed., New York : F. Watts, 1971 ; London : F. Watts, 1972. — Index.
ISBN 0-85166-674-4 : £1.95
(B77-33781)

Moore, Patrick. Guide to the moon / by Patrick Moore. — Revised and new ed. — Guildford [etc.] : Lutterworth Press, 1976. — 320p,xvi p of plates : ill, maps ; 23cm.
Previous ed.: London : Collins, 1957. — Index.
ISBN 0-7188-1720-6 : £4.95
(B77-03522)

523.3 — Moon. *Juvenile literature*
Shapp, Martha. Let's find out about the moon / by Martha and Charles Shapp. — Revised full-colour ed. / pictures by Brigitte Hartmann. — London [etc.] : F. Watts, 1977. — 43p : col ill ; 23cm.
Previous ed.: / pictures by Yukio Tashiro. 1971.
ISBN 0-85166-583-7 : £1.75
(B77-23369)

523.4 — ASTRONOMY. PLANETS
Firsoff, Valdemar Axel. The solar planets / [by] V.A. Firsoff. — Newton Abbot [etc.] : David and Charles [etc.], 1977. — 184p : ill ; 23cm.
Index.
ISBN 0-7153-7352-8 : £5.50
(B77-18108)

523.4 — Solar system. Giant planets. Chemical constituents. *Conference proceedings*
Chemical evolution of the giant planets / edited by Cyril Ponnamperuma. — New York [etc.] ; London : Academic Press, 1976. — xi,240p : ill ; 24cm.
'[Proceedings of] a colloquium sponsored [i.e. organized] by the Laboratory of Chemical Evolution of the University of Maryland, October 1974' - jacket. — Bibl. — Index.
ISBN 0-12-561350-4 : £6.65
(B77-08358)

523.4'0901 — Solar system. Planets. Observations. Effects of ephemeris time, ca B.C.2000-A.D.1019
Newton, Robert Russell. Ancient planetary observations and the validity of ephemeris time / [by] Robert R. Newton. — Baltimore ; London : Johns Hopkins University Press, [1977]. — xviii,749p : ill ; 24cm.
Published in the United States: 1976. — Bibl.: p.727-740. — Index.
ISBN 0-8018-1842-7 : £20.00
(B77-13016)

523.4'3 — Mars. Astronomical data. Related to dimensions of Great Pyramid
Saunders, Michael William. Pyramid-Mars connection : true or false?. — 2nd ed. — Caterham (Caterham, Surrey) : Downs Books, 1977. — 14 columns : ill, plan ; 21x30cm.
Author: M.W. Saunders. — Previous ed.: 1976. — Previous control number ISBN 0-9502260-6-8.
Sd : £0.40
ISBN 0-9502260-6-8
Also classified at 932
(B77-15268)

523.4'3 — Mars. Surface features. Observation, to 1977
Moore, Patrick. Guide to Mars / by Patrick Moore. — Guildford [etc.] : Lutterworth Press, 1977. — 214p,xvi p of plates : ill, charts, maps ; 23cm.
Not the same as B65-13259. — Index.
ISBN 0-7188-2316-8 : £5.95
(B77-27038)

523.5 — ASTRONOMY. METEORS AND ZODIACAL LIGHT
523.5'1 — Iron meteorites
Buchwald, Vagn F. Handbook of iron meteorites : their history, distribution, composition and structure / by Vagn F. Buchwald. — Berkeley [etc.] ; London : University of California Press for the Center for Meteorite Studies, Arizona State University, 1975. — 3v.(xii,1418,[24]p) : ill, maps ; 29cm.
In slip case. — Bibl.: p.175-243. — Index.
ISBN 0-520-02934-8 : £98.00
(B77-20224)

523.5'1'07402134 — Museums. *London. Kensington and Chelsea (London Borough). British Museum (Natural History). Stock: Meteorites. Catalogues*
British Museum (Natural History). Catalogue of meteorites, with special reference to those represented in the collection of the British Museum (Natural History). — 3rd revised and enlarged ed. / by Max H. Hey. — London : The Museum.
Previous ed.: 1953.
Appendix to the catalogue of meteorites / by R. Hutchison, A.W.R. Bevan and J.M. Hall. — 1977. — xxvii,297p ; 23cm. — (Publication ; no.789)
ISBN 0-565-00789-0 : £18.00
(B77-27039)

523.7 — ASTRONOMY. SUN
523.7 — Sun. *Juvenile literature*
Shapp, Martha. Let's find out about the sun / by Martha and Charles Shapp. — Revised full-colour ed. / revised by Henry Pluckrose ; pictures by Stephanie Later. — London [etc.] : F. Watts, 1977. — 39p : col ill, col charts ; 23cm.
Previous ed.: / pictures by Yukio Tashiro. 1971.
ISBN 0-85166-584-5 : £1.75
(B77-22544)

523.8 — ASTRONOMY. STARS
523.8'44 — Variable stars. Observation. *Amateurs' manuals*
Glasby, John Stephen. The variable star observer's handbook / [by] John S. Glasby. — London : Sidgwick and Jackson, [1977]. — 213p : ill, charts ; 21cm.
Originally published: 1971. — Index.
ISBN 0-283-98259-4 Pbk : £1.75
(B77-13631)

523.8'446 — Novae & supernovae. Observation by Far Eastern astronomers, to 1976
Clark, David H. The historical supernovae / by David H. Clark and F. Richard Stephenson. — Oxford [etc.] : Pergamon, 1977. — x,233p : ill, charts, maps ; 26cm. — (Pergamon international library)
Bibl.: p.223-228. — Index.
ISBN 0-08-020914-9 : £8.50
ISBN 0-08-021639-0 Pbk : £3.95
(B77-21837)

523.8'7 — Stars. Spectra. Energy. Distribution. *For spectrophotometric observations*
Tereshchenko, V M. Zonal spectrophotometric standards : a study of energy distribution in the spectra of 109 stars, in absolute units / [by] V.M. Tereshchenko and A.V. Kharitonov ; translated [from the Russian] by P.A.J. Graham. — Boston Spa : British Library Lending Division, 1977. — [4],191p : ill ; 24cm.

Translation of: 'Zonal'nye spektrofotometricheskie standarty'. Alma-Ata : Astrofizicheskiĭ Institut AN Kazakhskoĭ SSR, 1972. — Bibl.: p.99-102.
ISBN 0-85350-163-7 : £6.00
(B77-20225)

523.8'9'024526 — Stars. *Tables. For land surveying*
The **star** almanac for land surveyors / prepared by H.M. Nautical Almanac Office ; published by order of the Science Research Council. — London : H.M.S.O.
1978. — 1977. — xvi,80p : charts ; 25cm.
Index.
ISBN 0-11-881396-x Pbk : £1.10
(B77-27840)

525 — ASTRONOMY. PLANETS. EARTH
525 — Planets: Earth. *Juvenile literature*
Knight, David Carpenter. Let's find out about earth / by David C. Knight. — Revised full colour ed. / pictures by Linda Chen. — London [etc.] : F. Watts, 1977. — [1],41p : col ill, col maps ; 23cm.
Previous ed.: / pictures by Don Miller. New York : F. Watts, 1968 ; London : F. Watts, 1971.
ISBN 0-85166-581-0 : £1.75
(B77-22545)

525'.1 — Earth. Shape & size. Theories, to 1969. *Juvenile literature*
Asimov, Isaac. How did we find out the earth is round? / [by] Isaac Asimov ; illustrated by Matthew Kalmenoff. — London [etc.] : White Lion Publishers, 1976. — 63p : ill, maps ; 21cm.
Originally published: New York : Walker, 1973. — Index.
ISBN 0-85686-221-5 : £2.25
(B77-04136)

525'.69 — Tides. *Tables*
Admiralty tide tables / [Hydrographic Department]. — [Taunton] : Hydrographer of the Navy.
1978. Vol.1 : European waters, including Mediterranean Sea. — 1977. — xxx,411p : ill, map ; 30cm. — (NP200-78)
Index.
Pbk : £4.00
ISSN 0309-1066
(B77-20226)

1978. Vol.2 : Atlantic and Indian Oceans, including tidal stream tables. Parts 1 & 2. — 1977. — xxxiv,432p : ill, map ; 30cm. — (NP201-78)
Index.
Pbk : £4.00
ISSN 0305-5175
(B77-28589)

525'.69'0941 — Great Britain. Coastal waters. Tides. *Tables*
Tide, distance and speed tables : daily tide tables for 24 British ports, world-wide distance tables, data for principal British rivers and a valuable collection of tables and information useful to all branches of the shipping industry. — Glasgow : Brown and Ferguson.
1977. — [1976]. — [7],256p : ill(some col) ; 12cm.
ISBN 0-85174-298-x : £0.90
(B77-14712)

525'.69'09421 — Port of London. Tides. *Tables*
Port of London Authority. Handbook of tide tables, particulars of docks, &c. / Port of London Authority. — London (World Trade Centre, E.1) : Port of London Authority.
1977. — [1976]. — 111p ; 16cm.
Conversion tables, feet to metres and metres to feet ([2]p.) as insert.
ISBN 0-900598-09-3 : £0.55
(B77-02278)

1978. — [1977]. — 109p ; 16cm.
Conversion tables, feet to metres and metres to feet ([2]p.) as insert.
£0.67
(B77-33198)

526 — GEODESY, CARTOGRAPHY
526 — Cartography
Mapping for field scientists : a problem-solving approach / [by] W. Ritchie ... [et al.]. — Newton Abbot [etc.] : David and Charles, 1977. — [1],327p : ill, maps ; 23cm.
Bibl.: p.319-320. — Index.
ISBN 0-7153-7272-6 : £7.50
(B77-24908)

526'.028'54044 — Cartography. Applications of digital computer systems
Margerison, T A. Computer and the renaissance of cartography / [by] T.A. Margerison. — London (Royal College of Art, 6a Cromwell Place, SW7 2JN) : Natural Environment Research Council, Experimental Cartography Unit, [1976]. — [1],20p,[8]p of plates : ill, maps(chiefly col) ; 21cm.
Bibl.: p.18-20.
ISBN 0-9505590-0-8 Sd : £1.00
(B77-09681)

526'.03 — Cartography, to 1900. Glossaries
International Cartographic Association.
Map-making to 1900 = La cartographie jusqu'à 1900 : an historical glossary of cartographic innovations and their diffusion = un lexique historique des innovations cartographiques et leur diffusion / International Cartographic Association = Association cartographique ; edited by Helen Wallis = édité par Helen Wallis. — London : Royal Society, 1976. — xix,52p ; 23cm.
'Preliminary study, presented on the occasion of the Eighth International Conference on Cartography, Moscow, USSR, 3-10 August 1976. — English and French preliminaries. — Bibl.
ISBN 0-85403-082-4 Sd : £1.95
(B77-15829)

526'.06'141 — Cartography. Organisations. *Great Britain. Ordnance Survey. Reports, surveys. Serials*
Ordnance Survey. Annual report / the Ordnance Survey. — Southampton (Romsey Rd, Maybush, Southampton SO9 4DH) : Ordnance Survey.
1975-76. — 1976. — 24p,6 leaves of plates(1 fold) : 1 ill, col maps ; 30cm.
ISBN 0-319-00002-8 Sd : £1.35
(B77-31877)

526'.7'0285424 — Gravitational fields. Surveying. Applications of programs written in Basic language
McCann, Clive. The collection and reduction of gravity and magnetic survey data / by C. McCann. — Reading (c/o Assistant Librarian, Whiteknights, Reading RG6 2AB) : Geology Department, University of Reading, 1976. — [3],49p,plate : ill, form ; 30cm. — (University of Reading. Department of Geology. Geological reports ; no.8) (Computer-based packages for teaching earth science report ; no.2)
Bibl.
ISBN 0-7049-0278-8 Sp : £0.75
Also classified at 538'.78'0285424
(B77-10351)

526.8 — Orienteering maps. Design. *Manuals*
Harvey, Robin. Mapmaking for orienteers / [by] Robin Harvey. — Matlock (Lea Green, Matlock, Derbyshire DE4 5GJ) : British Orienteering Federation, [1977]. — 107p : ill, maps ; 22cm.
Cover title. — Text on inside front cover.
Pbk : £1.95
(B77-29406)

526.8'09 — Cartography, to 1900
Bricker, Charles. Landmarks of mapmaking : an illustrated survey of maps and mapmakers / maps chosen and displayed by R.V. Tooley ; text written by Charles Bricker ; preface by Gerald Roe Crone. — Oxford : Phaidon, 1976 [i.e. 1977]. — 276p : ill(some col), facsims, maps(chiefly col), ports ; 41cm.
Originally published: Amsterdam, etc. : Elsevier, 1968. — Bibl.: p.269. — Index.
ISBN 0-7148-1758-9 : £27.50
(B77-07894)

526.9 — SURVEYING

526.9 — Glaciers. Surveying. *Northern Iceland. Manuals*

North Iceland glacier inventory : manual for the use of field survey parties / prepared by E.A. Escritt ; [for the] Young Explorers' Trust. — [Stockport] ([238 Wellington Rd South, Stockport, Cheshire SK2 6NW]) : Young Explorers' Trust, [1977]. — [6],60[i.e. 68]p : ill, maps ; 22cm.
Map (fold. sheet) as insert. — Bibl.: p.55-58.
ISBN 0-905965-00-0 Pbk : £1.00
(B77-13632)

526.9 — Land. Surveying

Bannister, Arthur. Surveying / [by] A. Bannister and S. Raymond. — 4th ed. — London : Pitman, 1977. — viii,632p : ill, maps ; 23cm. — (A Pitman international text)
Previous ed.: 1972. — Index.
ISBN 0-273-00799-8 Pbk : £5.95 : CIP rev.
(B77-17469)

526.9'01'51 — Surveying. Mathematics. *For civil engineering*

Murchison, D E. Surveying and photogrammetry : computation for civil engineers / [by] D.E. Murchison. — London [etc.] : Newnes-Butterworths, 1977. — vii, 113p : ill ; 22cm.
Bibl.: p.109. — Index.
ISBN 0-408-00293-x Pbk : £4.00
(B77-25593)

526.9'02'462 — Surveying. *For engineering*

Shepherd, Frank Arnold. Engineering surveying : problems and solutions / [by] F.A. Shepherd. — London : Edward Arnold, 1977. — xiv, 370p : ill ; 22cm.
'Based on material first published in Imperial units as "Surveying problems and solutions", 1968' - title page verso. — Bibl.
ISBN 0-7131-3370-8 Pbk : £5.95
(B77-15269)

526.9'06'11 — Great Britain. Directorate of Overseas Surveys. *Reports, surveys. Serials*

Great Britain. *Directorate of Overseas Surveys.* Annual report for the year ended 31st March / Directorate of Overseas Surveys. — London : H.M.S.O.
1975. — 1976. — [4],59p,[4]p of plates : ill ; 25cm.
Nine sheets ([9]fold leaves: of col. maps) in pocket. — Bibl.: p.56.
ISBN 0-11-580205-3 Sd : £2.40
(B77-04137)

526.9'06'241 — Surveying. Organisations. *Great Britain. Royal Institution of Chartered Surveyors. Directories*

Royal Institution of Chartered Surveyors. Yearbook / the Royal Institution of Chartered Surveyors. — Haywards Heath : T. Skinner.
1976-1977. — 1977. — li,772p,p765-1335 : ill, port ; 31cm.
ISBN 0-611-00622-7 : £12.50
ISSN 0308-1451
(B77-26282)

1976-1977. [Geographical section]. — 1977. — li p,p765-1335 : ill, port ; 30cm.
Pbk : £12.50
ISSN 0308-1451
(B77-26283)

526.9'0956 — Surveying. *Middle East. For chartered surveyors*

Franklin, C Philip. Surveying and land administration in the Middle East : prospects for chartered surveyors : report of a tour of Middle East countries / by C. Philip Franklin and Robert Steel ; on behalf of the Royal Institution of Chartered Surveyors. — London : [The Institution], [1976]. — [1],xvi,48p : maps ; 30cm.
Bibl.: p.xiii.
ISBN 0-85406-080-4 Sd : £3.00
(B77-11787)

526.9'82'08 — Photogrammetry. *Essays*

Thompson, Edgar Hynes. Photogrammetry & surveying : a selection of papers / by E.H. Thompson ; [compiled and edited by K.B. Atkinson]. — London (c/o Department of Photogrammetry and Surveying, University College London, Gower St., WC1E 6BT) : Photogrammetric Society, 1977. — [15],359p : ill, port ; 25cm.
Includes one paper in French, with French and English abstracts and French and German abstracts of some of the other papers. — Bibl.
ISBN 0-9504376-1-1 : £10.00
(B77-22546)

526.9'9'023 — Hydrographic surveying. *Career guides*

Hydrographic Society. Hydrographic surveying as a career / [Hydrographic Society]. — [London] ([c/o Dept of Surveying, North East London Polytechnic, E17 4JB]) : [The Society], [1977?]. — 19p : 1 ill ; 21cm. — (Special publication ; no.3 ISSN 0309-8303)
Sd : Unpriced
(B77-27040)

526.9'9'06141 — Great Britain. Hydrographic Department. *Reports, surveys. Serials*

Great Britain. *Hydrographic Department.* Report by the Hydrographer of the Navy ... — Taunton : [Hydrographer of the Navy]. — (NP130)
1976. — 1977. — [5],40p,[2]fold leaves of plates : ill, col maps ; 30cm.
Sd : Unpriced
(B77-26284)

526.9'9'0922 — Hydrographic surveying. Voyages by Great Britain. Hydrographic Department. Adventurer (Ship) & Beagle (Ship). *South America. Coastal waters, 1826-1836. Personal observations. Collections*

FitzRoy, Robert. [Narrative of the surveying voyages of His Majesty's Ships 'Adventure' and 'Beagle' between the years 1826 and 1836. *Selections].* A narrative of the voyage of HMS Beagle : being passages from the 'Narrative' written by Captain Robert FitzRoy, R.N., together with extracts from his logs, reports and letters, additional material from the diary and letters of Charles Darwin, notes from Midshipman Philip King and letters from Second Lieutenant Bartholomew Sulivan / selected and edited by David Stanbury. — London : Folio Society, 1977. — 360p,[12] leaves of plates : col ill, map(on lining papers), col ports ; 25cm.
'Narrative of the surveying voyages ...' originally published: London : McColburn, 1839.
£7.50 (to members only)
(B77-25594)

527 — CELESTIAL NAVIGATION

527'.02'47971 — Seamanship. Celestial navigation. *Amateurs' manuals. For sailing*

Rantzen, Mannas Joel. Little ship astro-navigation / by M.J. Rantzen ; illustrated by M.A. Moffat. — 4th (N.P.401/H.O.229) ed. — London : Barrie and Jenkins, 1977. — 162p : ill, maps ; 21cm.
With answers. — Previous ed.: 1973. — Index.
ISBN 0-214-20373-5 : £4.25
(B77-24192)

528 — NAUTICAL ALMANACS

528'.8'41 — Navigation. *British nautical almanacs*

The **astronomical** ephemeris / issued by Her Majesty's Nautical Almanac Office. — United Kingdom ed. — London : H.M.S.O.
1978. — 1976. — viii,573p : ill ; 25cm.
Index.
ISBN 0-11-880627-0 : £8.50
(B77-10352)

The **astronomical** ephemeris / issued by Her Majesty's Nautical Almanac Office. — London : H.M.S.O.
1977. — 1975. — viii,572p : ill ; 25cm.
Index.
ISBN 0-11-880597-5 : £7.10
(B77-14217)

Brown's nautical almanac daily tide tables. — Glasgow : Brown and Ferguson.
1978 : 101st year / edited by R. Ingram-Brown ; assistant editor Charles H. Cotter. — [1977]. — 2-20,24,959p : ill, charts, maps ; 23cm.
'Dover, 1978, times of high water' sheet (2 sides) as insert. — Index.
ISBN 0-85174-285-8 : £7.20
ISSN 0068-290x
(B77-30219)

Burton, Stephen Merceron. A set of nautical tables for general navigational purposes / compiled by the late Stephen M. Burton. — 8th ed. / revised and edited by the late Gilbert F. Cunningham. - Metric ed. / prepared by D.R. Derrett. — London : Stanford Maritime, 1974. — [2],xviii,344p ; 28cm.
Cover title: Burton's nautical tables. — Text on lining paper. — Previous ed.: i.e. 7th ed., 1967.
ISBN 0-540-07380-6 : £2.25
(B77-19350)

The **nautical** almanac. — London : H.M.S.O.
1978. — 1977. — 4,276,xxxvi p : charts, maps ; 27cm. — (NB314-78)
'Altitude correction tables and index to selected stars' ([2]p.) as insert.
ISBN 0-11-771599-9 Pbk : £5.00
(B77-17470)

529 — TIME

529 — Time. *Juvenile literature*

Kincaid, Lucy. The Skittles clock book / [written and illustrated by Lucy and Eric Kincaid]. — [Cambridge] : Brimax Books, 1976. — [20]p : chiefly col ill ; 27cm.
Cover title. — Text, col. ill. on lining papers.
ISBN 0-904494-16-0 : £0.65
(B77-06659)

529'.7 — Time. Measurement. *Juvenile literature*

Hay, Dean. I can tell the time / photographs by Dean Hay. — New ed. — London [etc.] : Collins, 1977. — [31]p : of col ill ; 21cm.
Previous ed.: published as part of 'Now I can count'. 1968.
ISBN 0-00-195355-9 : £1.25
(B77-33782)

Pullen, George. Time / [by] Werner Kirst ; [translated from the German and adapted by George Pullen]. — St Albans : Hart-Davis Educational, 1977. — 2-47p : ill(some col), col map, ports(some col) ; 23x25cm. — (Reporter books)
Originally published: in German. Stuttgart : Deutsche Verlags-Anstalt, 1974.
ISBN 0-247-12726-4 : £1.95
(B77-11201)

529'.7 — Time. Measurement. *Stories for children*

Woodward, Ken. Telling the time : the king's clocks / written and illustrated by Ken Woodward. — Maidenhead : Purnell, 1976. — [26]p : col ill ; 25cm. — (My first colour library)
ISBN 0-361-03490-3 : £0.60
(B77-08359)

530 — PHYSICS

Bolton, William, *b.1933.* Physical science for technicians : a first level unit / [by] W. Bolton. — London [etc.] : McGraw-Hill, 1976. — [10], 136p : ill ; 23cm.
Bibl. — Index.
ISBN 0-07-084216-7 Pbk : £2.25
(B77-04138)

Bueche, Frederick. Technical physics / [by] F. Bueche. — New York [etc.] ; London : Harper and Row, 1977. — xix,738p,plate : ill(incl 1 col) ; 24cm.
Text on lining papers. — With answers to odd-numbered problems. — Index.
ISBN 0-06-041033-7 : £12.70
(B77-15270)

Faughn, Jerry S. Physics for people who think they don't like physics / [by] Jerry S. Faughn, Karl F. Kuhn. — Philadelphia ; London [etc.] : Saunders, 1976. — ii-xvi,570p,4p of plates : ill(some col) ; 28cm. — (Saunders golden sunburst series)
Index.
ISBN 0-7216-3582-2 : £12.25
(B77-13633)

Hooper, Henry O. Physics and the physical perspective / [by] Henry O. Hooper, Peter Gwynne. — New York [etc.] ; London : Harper and Row, 1977. — xiv,850p : ill(some col), ports ; 24cm.
With answers to odd-numbered problems. — Index.
ISBN 0-06-042901-1 : £12.70
(B77-30220)

Landau, Lev Davidovich. Course of theoretical physics / by L.D. Landau and E.M. Lifshitz. — 3rd ed. — Oxford [etc.] : Pergamon. — (Pergamon international library)
Vol.1 : Mechanics / translated from the Russian by J.B. Sykes and J.S. Bell. — 1976. — xxvii,169p : ill, port ; 26cm.
Translation of: 'Teoreticheskaia fizika. T.1 : Mekhanika'. Izd. 3-e, islr. i dol. Moskva : 'Nauka', 1973. — Previous ed. of 'Mechanics' : 1969. — Index.
ISBN 0-08-021022-8 : £6.25
(B77-02978)

Marion, Jerry Baskerville. Essential physics in the world around us / [by] Jerry B. Marion. — New York ; London [etc.] : Wiley, 1977. — ix, 444p : ill(chiefly col), col map ; 24cm.
Index.
ISBN 0-471-56905-4 : £9.95
(B77-33783)

Martin, Martin C. Elements of classical physics / [by] Martin C. Martin and Charles A. Hewett. — New York ; Oxford [etc.] : Pergamon, [1976]. — x,359p : ill ; 26cm. — ([Pergamon international library])
With answers to odd-numbered problems. — Published in the United States: 1975. — Index.
ISBN 0-08-017098-6 : £8.00
(B77-01410)

Nelkon, Michael. Revision notes in physics for Advanced Level and intermediate students / by M. Nelkon. — 4th ed. — London : Heinemann Educational. — (Heinemann books for Advanced Level physics)
Book 2 : Waves, optics, sound, heat, properties of matter. — 1977. — [5],162p : ill ; 22cm.
Previous ed.: 1971.
ISBN 0-435-68658-5 Pbk : £1.80
(B77-33784)

Resnick, Robert. Physics / [by] Robert Resnick, David Halliday. — 3rd ed. — New York ; London [etc.] : Wiley.
In 2 vols. — Also available in 1 vol. — Previous ed.: 1966.
Part 1. — 1977. — xi,564,A44p : ill ; 26cm.
With answers to odd-numbered problems. — Text on lining papers. — Index.
ISBN 0-471-71716-9 : £10.00
(B77-30221)

Ridley, B K. Time, space and things / [by] B.K. Ridley. — Harmondsworth [etc.] : Penguin, 1976. — 169p : ill ; 20cm. — (Peregrine books)
Index.
ISBN 0-14-055113-1 Pbk : £1.75
(B77-02979)

Schaum, Daniel. Schaum's outline of theory and problems of college physics / by Daniel Schaum. — SI (metric) ed. / edited by Carel W. van der Merwe ; adapted for SI units by William J. Duffin. — New York ; London [etc.] : McGraw-Hill, 1977. — [8],289p : ill ; 28cm. — (Schaum's outline series)
Cover title: Theory and problems of college physics. — Spine title: College physics. — Previous ed.: i.e. 6th ed. / edited by Carel W. van der Merwe. New York : Schaum Pub. Co., 1961. — Index.
ISBN 0-07-084365-1 Pbk : £3.95
(B77-16360)

Sears, Francis Weston. University physics. — 5th ed. / [by] Francis W. Sears, Mark W. Zemansky, Hugh D. Young. — Reading, Mass. [etc.] ; London : Addison-Wesley, 1976. — xiii, 811,[33]p : ill ; 24cm. — (Addison-Wesley world student series)
With answers to odd-numbered problems. — This ed. also published in 2 vols. 1976. — Previous ed.: 1970. — Index.
ISBN 0-201-06924-5 Pbk : £5.75
(B77-01411)

Williams, George A. Elementary physics : atoms, waves, particles / [by] George A. Williams. — 2nd ed. — New York ; London [etc.] : McGraw-Hill, 1976. — xv,458p,[3]p of plates : ill(some col), charts, facsims, ports ; 25cm.
Text on lining papers. — With answers. — Previous ed.: 1969. — Bibl. — Index.
ISBN 0-07-070402-3 : £12.40
(B77-04783)

530 — Physics. *For African students. Secondary school texts*

Vinall, N P. Physics : a revision scheme for students preparing for the East African Certificate of Education and the West African School Certificate ('O' level) and the Cambridge Overseas School Certificate / [by] N.P. Vinall. — London [etc.] : Evans Bros, 1977. — 64p : ill ; 19cm. — (Evans pocket facts)
ISBN 0-237-50073-6 Sd : Unpriced
(B77-18109)

Ward, A H. Essential senior physics in SI units / [by] A.H. Ward, E.H. Ward. — Sunbury-on-Thames : Nelson.
In 4 vols.
[1] : Mechanics. — 1977. — vi,137p : ill ; 25cm.
With answers. — Index.
ISBN 0-17-511497-8 Pbk : £1.45
(B77-27041)

[2] : Energy, heat and the structure of matter. — 1977. — iv,124p : ill ; 25cm.
With answers. — Index.
ISBN 0-17-511498-6 Pbk : £1.45
(B77-27042)

[3] : Light and sound. — 1977. — iv,124p : ill ; 25cm.
With answers. — Index.
ISBN 0-17-511499-4 Pbk : £1.45
(B77-27043)

[4] : Magnetism, electricity and atomic physics. — 1977. — iv,124p : ill ; 25cm.
With answers. — Index.
ISBN 0-17-511500-1 Pbk : £1.45
(B77-27044)

530 — Physics. *Secondary school texts*

Abbott, Arthur Frederick. Ordinary Level physics / [by] A.F. Abbott ; with a foreword by Sir John Cockcroft. — 3rd ed. — London : Heinemann Educational, 1977. — xxvi,598p : ill, ports ; 25cm.
With answers. — Previous ed.: 1969. — Index.
ISBN 0-435-67005-0 Pbk : £3.60
(B77-23370)

Bolton, William, *b.1933.* A foundation course in physics / [by] W. Bolton. — Cambridge [etc.] : Cambridge University Press, 1977. — vii,213p : ill ; 30cm.
Index.
ISBN 0-521-21300-2 Pbk : £3.95
(B77-21838)

Chaplin, Sylvia. Focus on physics / [by] Sylvia Chaplin, John Keighley ; illustrated by Lacey Hawkins. — 2nd ed. — Exeter : Wheaton, 1977. — [12],440p : ill(some col) ; 17x25cm.
With answers. — Text on inside cover. — Previous ed.: Oxford : Pergamon, 1974. — Index.
ISBN 0-08-021016-3 Pbk : £2.60
(B77-27045)

College physics. — 5th ed. / [by] Robert L. Weber ... [et al.]. — New York ; London [etc.] : McGraw-Hill, 1974. — x,917p,[3]p of plates : ill(some col), charts, ports ; 25cm.
Previous ed.: / by Robert L. Weber, Kenneth V. Manning and Marsh W. White. New York : McGraw-Hill, 1965. — Bibl. — Index.
ISBN 0-07-068827-3 : Unpriced
(B77-19351)

Folivi, Louis Ekue. New Certificate physics, in SI units / [by] L.E. Folivi, A. Godman. — New ed. — London : Longman, 1977. — [5],591p : ill(chiefly col) ; 25cm.
With answers to numerical questions. — Previous ed.: 1974. — Index.
ISBN 0-582-65015-1 Pbk : £3.40
(B77-33199)

Last, Allan. Certificate physical science / [by] Allan Last. — London [etc.] : Macmillan, 1977. — vi,176,[1]p : ill ; 25cm.
With answers. — Index.
ISBN 0-333-21147-2 Pbk : £1.95
Also classified at 540
(B77-33785)

Nelkon, Michael. Advanced Level physics / [by] M. Nelkon, P. Parker. — 4th ed. — London : Heinemann Educational, 1977. — x,1014p : ill ; 24cm.
With answers. — Previous ed.: 1970. — Index.
ISBN 0-435-68610-0 : £6.50
(B77-33200)

Nelkon, Michael. Principles of physics / [by] M. Nelkon. — 6th ed., with SI units. — St Albans : Hart-Davis Educational, 1977. — xiv, 689p : ill, chart ; 24cm.
With answers. — This ed. originally published: 1975. — Index.
ISBN 0-7010-0633-1 Pbk : £2.25
(B77-19352)

Noakes, George Robert. Structure of physics / [by] G.R. Noakes. — Basingstoke [etc.] : Macmillan, 1977. — vi,602p : ill ; 26cm.
With answers. — Index.
ISBN 0-333-19424-1 : £6.95
(B77-19353)

Nuffield Foundation Science Teaching Project. Revised Nuffield physics / [Nuffield Foundation Science Teaching Project] ; general editors Eric M. Rogers, E.J. Wenham. — Revised ed. — London : Longman for the Nuffield Foundation.
Previous ed.: i.e. 1st ed., published as 'Physics'. 1966-.
General introduction. — 1977. — x,91p : ill ; 25cm.
Index.
ISBN 0-582-04686-6 Pbk : £2.65
(B77-10800)

Year 3. Pupils' text / contributors H.F. Boulind ... [et al.]. — 1976. — x,276p : ill(chiefly col) ; 25cm.
ISBN 0-582-04673-4 Pbk : £3.90
(B77-10801)

Year 3. Teachers' guide / contributors D.W. Harding, J.L. Lewis. — 1977. — xxv,257p : ill ; 25cm.
Index.
ISBN 0-582-04683-1 Pbk : £7.95
(B77-10802)

Powney, Derek J. Advanced Level physical science / [by] D.J. Powney and B.J. Stokes. — London : Edward Arnold, 1977. — vii,394p : ill ; 25cm.
Index.
Pbk : £5.95
Also classified at 540
(B77-33786)

530 — Spatial relations. *Juvenile literature*

Oram, Sandie. Hide-and-seek with Snuff / original story by Vivian Cohen and Colette Deblé ; illustrations by Colette Deblé ; [translated from the French and adapted by Sandie Oram]. — London : Macdonald Educational, 1975. — [24]p : chiefly col ill ; 26cm. — (Play school books)
These illustrations originally published: with French text. France : Le Livre de Paris, 1973.
ISBN 0-356-04787-3 Sd : £0.30
(B77-21101)

Pluckrose, Henry. Things up and down / by Henry Pluckrose ; photographs by G.W. Hales. — London [etc.] : F. Watts, 1976. — 32p : ill ; 18x22cm.
ISBN 0-85166-600-0 : £1.25
(B77-01412)

530 — Spatial relations. *Teaching kits*

Sowter, Nita. Up and down / illustrated by Nita Sowter. — London : Jackdaw [for] Thames Television Ltd [etc.], 1977. — 1v : chiefly col ill ; 22x26cm. — (Rainbows)
Twelve sheets (16 fold) in plastic envelope. — 'Playpacks from ITV's "Rainbow" programme'.
ISBN 0-305-62123-8 : £0.99(non-net)
(B77-26285)

530'.01'51 — Physics. Calculations. *Manuals*

Tuma, Jan Joseph. Handbook of physical calculations : definitions, formulas, technical applications, physical tables, conversion tables, graphs, dictionary of physical terms / [by] Jan J. Tuma. — New York ; London [etc.] : McGraw-Hill, 1976. — x,370p : ill, map ; 25cm.
Text on lining papers. — Bibl.: p.339-340. — Index.
ISBN 0-07-065438-7 : £12.40
(B77-06054)

530'.02'46 — Physics. *For technicians*

Pollard, A B. Basic physical science for technicians / [by] A.B. Pollard and C.W. Schofield. — London : Edward Arnold, 1977. — vii,168p : ill ; 22cm.
With answers to numerical exercises. — Index.
ISBN 0-7131-3384-8 Pbk : £2.00
(B77-30222)

530'.02'469 — Physics. *For building construction*

Smith, Brian John. Construction science / [by] B.J. Smith. — London [etc.] : Longman. — (Longman construction series)
Vol.1. — 1976. — viii,152p : ill ; 23cm.
With answers. — Index.
ISBN 0-582-42012-1 : £4.95
ISBN 0-582-42013-x Pbk : £2.75
(B77-01413)

530'.03 — Physics. *Encyclopaedias*

The **Penguin** dictionary of physics / editor Valerie H. Pitt. — Harmondsworth [etc.] : Penguin, 1977. — 428p : ill ; 20cm. — (Penguin reference books)
An abridged version of 'A new dictionary of physics'. London : Longman, 1975.
ISBN 0-14-051071-0 Pbk : £2.00
(B77-12430)

530'.06'241 — Physics. Organisations. *Great Britain. Institute of Physics. Directories*

Institute of Physics. Membership list / [Institute of Physics]. — London [etc.] : The Institute.
1974. — 1974. — vii,132p ; 31cm.
£20.00
ISBN 0-85498-028-8 Pbk : £2.00(Members only)
(B77-25595)

1974. — 1974. — vii,132p ; 31cm.
ISBN 0-85498-028-8 : £20.00
Pbk : £2.00(members only)
(B77-31878)

530'.07'1141 — Higher education institutions. Curriculum subjects: Physics. Attitudes of students. *Great Britain. Reports, surveys*
Bliss, Joan. Students' reactions to undergraduate science / [by] Joan Bliss, Jon Ogborn in association with [others] ; [for the] Higher Education Learning Project (Physics). — London : Heinemann Educational for the Nuffield Foundation, 1977. — viii,152p : ill ; 21cm.
Bibl.: p.145-146. — Index.
ISBN 0-435-69583-5 Pbk : £5.00
(B77-33201)

530'.07'1142 — Higher education institutions. Curriculum subjects: Physics. Independent learning. *England. Reports, surveys*
Higher Education Learning Project (Physics). Individual study in undergraduate science / Higher Education Learning Project (Physics) ; contributors Peter S. Allen ... [et al.] ; editors Will Bridge, Lewis Elton. — London : Heinemann Educational for the Nuffield Foundation, 1977. — [1],ix,217p : ill, form ; 21cm.
Bibl.: p.212-214. — Index.
ISBN 0-435-69580-0 Pbk : £5.00
(B77-33202)

530'.07'1142 — Higher education institutions. Curriculum subjects: Physics. Teaching methods: Group methods. *England*
Higher Education Learning Project (Physics). Small group teaching in undergraduate science / Higher Education Learning Project (Physics) ; contributors P.J. Black ... [et al.] ; editor Jon Ogborn. — London : Heinemann Educational for the Nuffield Foundation, 1977. — ix,189p : ill ; 21cm.
Bibl. — Index.
ISBN 0-435-69581-9 Pbk : £5.00
(B77-33203)

530'.07'1142769 — Universities. *Lancashire. Lancaster. University of Lancaster. Humanities students. Curriculum subjects: Physics*
Heywood, John, *b.1930.* Science for arts students : a case study in curriculum development / [by] John Heywood & Hubert Montagu-Pollock. — Guildford : Society for Research into Higher Education, 1977. — [2],v, 123[i.e.124]p : ill, form ; 21cm. — (Research into higher education monographs ; 28 ISSN 0085-1523)
Index.
ISBN 0-900868-47-3 Pbk : Unpriced
(B77-16865)

530'.07'24 — Higher education institutions. Curriculum subjects: Physics. Experiments. Teaching methods. *England. Reports, surveys*
Higher Education Learning Project (Physics). Practical work in undergraduate science / Higher Education Learning Project (Physics) ; contributors E.R. Davies ... [et al.] ; editor Jon Ogborn. — London : Heinemann Educational for the Nuffield Foundation, 1977. — [1],x, 201p ; 21cm.
Bibl. — Index.
ISBN 0-435-69582-7 Pbk : £5.00
(B77-33204)

530'.07'24 — Physics. Experiments
Squires, Gordon Leslie. Practical physics / [by] G.L. Squires. — Revised ed. — London [etc.] : McGraw-Hill, 1976. — x,224p : ill ; 22cm.
With answers. — Previous ed.: 1968. — Bibl.: p.217-219. — Index.
ISBN 0-07-084070-9 Pbk : £4.25
(B77-03523)

Tyler, Frank. A laboratory manual of physics / [by] F. Tyler. — 5th ed., SI version. — London : Edward Arnold, 1977. — viii,264p : ill ; 25cm.
Previous ed.: 1970.
ISBN 0-7131-0170-9 Pbk : £3.50
(B77-30223)

530'.07'24 — Physics. Experiments. *Secondary school texts*
Bolton, William, *b.1933.* Physics investigations / [by] W. Bolton. — Exeter : Wheaton, 1977. — xii,50p : ill ; 25cm.
ISBN 0-08-020481-3 Pbk : £1.15
(B77-15271)

Lewis, John Logan. Physics 11-13 / [by] John L. Lewis. — London : Longman, 1977. — 263p : ill ; 21cm.
ISBN 0-582-20877-7 Pbk : £2.25
(B77-21839)

530'.076 — Physics. *Exercises, worked examples. Secondary school texts*
Folland, Clive Bryan. Graded examples for 'O' Level physics / [by] C.B. Folland. — New ed. — London : J. Murray, 1977. — 101p ; 22cm.
With answers. — Previous ed.: 1970.
ISBN 0-7195-3392-9 Pbk : £0.90
(B77-33205)

Harris, Brian Kempster. Advanced problems in physics / [by] B.K. Harris and G.R. Noakes. — Basingstoke [etc.] : Macmillan, 1977. — vi, 112p : ill ; 21cm.
With answers.
ISBN 0-333-19096-3 Pbk : £1.60 : CIP rev.
(B77-20227)

530'.08 — Physics. *Lectures, speeches*
Cargèse lectures in physics. — New York ; London [etc.] : Gordon and Breach.
Vol.7 / edited by M. Lévy ; authors R. Barbieri ... [et al.]. — 1977. — x,501p : ill ; 24cm.
'... the record of lectures and seminars that were delivered at the Institut d'Etudes Scientifiques of Cargèse during the summer of 1972' - Preface. — English text, English and French preface.
ISBN 0-677-15750-9 : £33.00
(B77-18110)

530'.09 — Physics, to 1935. *Marxist viewpoints. Early works*
Caudwell, Christopher. The concept of freedom / by Christopher Caudwell. — London : Lawrence and Wishart, 1977. — 260p ; 22cm.
This collection originally published: 1965. — Index.
ISBN 0-85315-393-0 Pbk : £2.00
Primary classification 909'.09'812082
(B77-28270)

530'.092'4 — Physics. Morse, Philip McCord. *Autobiographies*
Morse, Philip McCord. In at the beginnings : a physicist's life / [by] Philip M. Morse. — Cambridge, Mass. ; London : M.I.T. Press, 1977. — ix,375p,12p of plates : ports ; 21cm.
Index.
ISBN 0-262-13124-2 : £10.25
(B77-31171)

530'.092'4 — Physics. Newton, Sir Isaac. *Biographies*
English, James Seymour. '- and all was light' : the life and work of Sir Isaac Newton / by J.S. English. — [Lincoln] ([Brayford House, Lucy Tower St., Lincoln LN1 1XN]) : Lincolnshire Library Service, 1977. — 32p : ill, facsim, port ; 21cm. — (Lincolnshire history series)
Bibl.: p.21-32.
Sd : £0.30
(B77-17471)

530.1 — PHYSICS. THEORIES
Ash, Anna Mary. The Tower of Truth / script and illustrations by Anna Mary Ash ; text and appendix figures by David A. Ash. — Dolsdon (Beachcott, Dolsdon, Boyton, Cornwall) : D. and A. Ash, 1977. — [2],18,26p : ill ; 21x30cm.

'Based on the Lecture "The development of a Theory to challenge Scientific Materialism", delivered by David A. Ash ... [at] The Royal Institution of Great Britain ... January 15th 1975'.
Sd : £3.00
(B77-29407)

530.1'1 — Fourth dimension. Theories
Rucker, Rudolf V.B. Geometry, relativity and the fourth dimension / by Rudolf V.B. Rucker. — New York : Dover Publications [etc.] ; London : Constable, 1977. — [9],133p : ill ; 22cm.
Bibl.: p.119-133.
ISBN 0-486-23400-2 Pbk : £1.95
(B77-27841)

530.1'1 — Physics. General theory of relativity, special theory of relativity & unified field theory
Bergmann, Peter Gabriel. Introduction to the theory of relativity / by Peter Gabriel Bergmann ; with a foreword by Albert Einstein. — Enlarged ed. — New York : Dover Publications [etc.] ; London : Constable, 1976. — xii,307p : ill ; 22cm.
Previous ed.: New York : Prentice-Hall, 1942. — Index.
ISBN 0-486-63282-2 Pbk : £2.85
(B77-13017)

530.1'1 — Physics. Relativity
Moller, Christian. The theory of relativity / by C. Moller. — 2nd ed. — Delhi ; London [etc.] : Oxford University Press, 1974. — xiii,557p : ill ; 22cm. — (The international series of monographs on physics)
This ed. originally published: Oxford : Clarendon Press, 1972. — Bibl.: p.544-550. — Index.
ISBN 0-19-560539-x Pbk : £5.95
(B77-32616)

Russell, Bertrand, *Earl Russell.* ABC of relativity / [by] Bertrand Russell. — 3rd revised ed. / edited by Felix Pirani. — London : Allen and Unwin, 1977. — 3-160p : ill ; 20cm.
This ed. originally published: 1969.
ISBN 0-04-521002-0 Pbk : £1.50
(B77-20228)

530.1'1 — Space & time
Davies, Paul Charles William. Space and time in the modern universe / [by] P.C.W. Davies. — Cambridge [etc.] : Cambridge University Press, 1977. — viii,232p : ill ; 23cm.
Index.
ISBN 0-521-21445-9 : £6.50
ISBN 0-521-29151-8 Pbk : £2.95
(B77-18738)

530.1'2 — Physics. Non-relativistic quantum theory
Landau, Lev Davidovich. Quantum mechanics : non-relativistic theory / by L.D. Landau and E.M. Lifshitz ; translated from the Russian by J.B. Sykes and J.S. Bell. — 3rd ed., revised and enlarged. — Oxford [etc.] : Pergamon, 1977. — xiv,673p : ill ; 26cm. — (Course of theoretical physics ; vol.3)
Previous ed. of this translation: 1965. — Translation of: 'Kvantovaia mekhanika'. 3.e. Moscow : Nauka, 1974. — Index.
ISBN 0-08-020940-8 : £13.85
(B77-29408)

530.1'2 — Physics. Quantum theory
Davies, Edward Brian. Quantum theory of open systems / [by] E.B. Davies. — London [etc.] : Academic Press, 1976. — x,171p ; 24cm.
Bibl.: p.161-167. — Index.
ISBN 0-12-206150-0 : £7.50
(B77-01414)

Davydov, Aleksandr Sergeevich. Quantum mechanics / by A.S. Davydov ; translated [from the Russian], edited and with additions by D. ter Haar. — 2nd ed. — Oxford [etc.] : Pergamon, 1976. — xiii,636p : ill ; 25cm. — (International series in natural philosophy ; vol.1) (Pergamon international library)
Previous English ed.: 1965. — Translation of 'Kvantovaia mekhanika'. Izd. 2-e. Moskva : Nauka, 1973. — Index.
ISBN 0-08-020438-4 : £15.00
ISBN 0-08-020437-6 Pbk : £9.00
(B77-01415)

Espagnat, Bernard d'. Conceptual foundations of quantum mechanics / [by] Bernard d'Espagnat. — 2nd ed. completely revised, enlarged, reset. — Reading, Mass. ; London [etc.] : Benjamin, 1976 [i.e. 1977]. — xxxix,301[i.e. 305]p ; 25cm. — (Mathematical physics monograph series ; vol.20)
This ed. published in the United States: 1976. — Previous ed.: Menlo Park, Calif. : Benjamin, 1971. — Bibl. — Index.
ISBN 0-8053-2384-8 : £19.20
ISBN 0-8053-2383-x Pbk : £11.90
(B77-10803)

530.1'2 — Physics. Quantum theory. Applications of symmetry
Wolbarst, Anthony B. Symmetry and quantum systems / [by] Anthony B. Wolbarst. — New York ; London [etc.] : Van Nostrand Reinhold, 1977. — xviii,249p : ill ; 23cm. — (The modern university physics series)
Originally published: as 'Symmetry and quantum mechanics'. New York : Van Nostrand Reinhold, 1976. — Bibl.: p.238-240. — Index.
ISBN 0-442-30163-4 : £9.95
ISBN 0-442-30180-4 Pbk : £3.50
(B77-24193)

530.1'2 — Physics. Quantum theory. Applications of uncertainty principle
The **uncertainty** principle and foundations of quantum mechanics : a fifty years' survey / edited by William C. Price, Seymour S. Chissick. — London [etc.] : Wiley, 1977. — xvii,572p : ill ; 24cm.
'A Wiley-Interscience publication'. — Bibl. — Index.
ISBN 0-471-99414-6 : £19.50
(B77-27046)

530.1'2 — Quantum theory. Applications of qualitative methods
Migdal, Arkadiĭ Beĭnusovich. Quantitative methods in quantum theory / [by] A.B. Migdal ; translated from the Russian edition by Anthony J. Leggett. — Reading, Mass. ; London [etc.] : Benjamin, 1977. — xxiii,437p : ill ; 24cm. — (Frontiers in physics ; vol.48)
Text on lining paper. — Translation of: 'Kachestvennye metody v kvantovoĭ teorii'. Moscow : Nauka, 1975. — Index.
ISBN 0-8053-7064-1 : £17.20
(B77-31172)

530.1'3 — Statistical mechanics
Mayer, Joseph Edward. Statistical mechanics / [by] Joseph Edward Mayer and the late Maria Goeppert Mayer. — 2nd ed. — New York ; London [etc.] : Wiley, 1977. — xvii,491p : ill ; 24cm.
'A Wiley-Interscience publication'. — Previous ed.: New York : Wiley ; London : Chapman and Hall, 1940. — Index.
ISBN 0-471-57985-8 : £17.50
(B77-13018)

530.1'3 — Statistical mechanics. *Conference proceedings*
Statistical physics : proceedings of the International Conference, 25-29 August 1975, Budapest, Hungary / edited by L. Pál and P. Szépfalusy. — Amsterdam ; Oxford [etc.] : North-Holland Publishing Co., 1976. — 251p : ill, port ; 25cm.
'The International Conference on Statistical Physics ... was organized by the International Union of Pure and Applied Physics through its Commission on Thermodynamics and Statistical Mechanics' - Preface. — Index.
ISBN 0-7204-0431-2 : £20.73
(B77-05388)

530.1'3'0246213 — Statistical mechanics. *For electrical engineering*
Beck, Arnold Hugh William. Statistical mechanics, fluctuations and noise / [by] A.H.W. Beck. — London : Edward Arnold, 1976. — xii,231p : ill ; 24cm. — (Contemporary electrical engineering)
Index.
ISBN 0-7131-3362-7 : £12.50
ISBN 0-7131-3363-5 Pbk : £7.50
(B77-04139)

530.1'4 — High energy physics. Field theory & gauge theories. *Conference proceedings*
Conference on Gauge Theories and Modern Field Theory, *Boston, Mass., 1975.* Gauge theories and modern field theory : proceedings of a conference held at Northeastern University, Boston, September 26 and 27, 1975 / edited by Richard Arnowitt and Pran Nath. — Cambridge, Mass. ; London : M.I.T. Press, 1976. — xi,428p : ill ; 26cm.
'The Conference on Gauge Theories and Modern Field Theory was held at Northeastern University on September 26 and 27, 1975' - Preface.
ISBN 0-262-01046-1 : £11.25
(B77-00199)

530.1'41 — Electric fields & magnetic fields
Oatley, *Sir* Charles William. Electric and magnetic fields : an introduction / [by] Sir Charles Oatley. — Cambridge [etc.] : Cambridge University Press, 1976. — x,262p : ill ; 24cm. — (Electronics texts for engineers and scientists)
With answers. — Index.
ISBN 0-521-21228-6 : £9.75
ISBN 0-521-29076-7 Pbk : £3.50
(B77-06055)

530.1'41'0246213 — Electromagnetic fields & waves. *For electrical engineering*
Rao, Nannapaneni Narayana. Elements of engineering electromagnetics / [by] N. Narayana Rao. — Englewood Cliffs ; London [etc.] : Prentice-Hall, 1977. — xv,479p : ill ; 24cm.
With answers to odd-numbered problems. — Bibl.: p.455. — Index.
ISBN 0-13-264150-x : £15.95
(B77-25596)

530.1'42 — Physics. Unified field theory
Baden Fuller, Arthur John. Worked examples in engineering field theory / by A.J. Baden Fuller. — Oxford [etc.] : Pergamon, 1976. — x,321p : ill ; 25cm. — (Pergamon international library : applied electricity and electronics division)
Index.
ISBN 0-08-018143-0 : £10.00
ISBN 0-08-018142-2 Pbk : £5.00
(B77-06660)

530.1'43 — Physics. Quantum field theory. *Conference proceedings*
Université de Grenoble. *École d'été de physique théorique, Session 28, Les Houches, 1975.* Méthodes en théorie des champs = Methods in field theory : Les Houches, Session XXVIII, 28 juillet-6 septembre 1975 / édité par Roger Balian et Jean Zinn-Justin. — Amsterdam [etc.] ; Oxford : North-Holland Publishing Co., 1976. — xx,386p : ill, ports ; 23cm.
English text, English and French prefaces.
ISBN 0-7204-0433-9 : £23.42
(B77-16362)

530.1'44 — Physics. Many-body problem. Solution. Applications of Feynman diagrams
Mattuck, Richard David. A guide to Feynman diagrams in the many-body problem / [by] Richard D. Mattuck. — 2nd ed. — New York ; London [etc.] : McGraw-Hill, 1976. — xv,429p : ill ; 25cm.
With answers. — Previous ed.: 1967. — Bibl.: p.414-421. — Index.
ISBN 0-07-040954-4 : £12.50
(B77-04784)

530.1'5 — Physics. Field theory. *Conference proceedings*
Quark Binding *(Conference), University of Rochester, 1976.* Quark confinement and field theory : proceedings of a conference at the University of Rochester, Rochester, New York, June 14-18, 1976 / edited by D.R. Stump, D.H. Weingarten. — New York ; London [etc.] : Wiley, 1977. — ix,253p : ill ; 24cm.
'A Wiley-Interscience publication'. — 'During the week of June 14, 1976 a workshop on quark binding was held at the University of Rochester ... The title, "Quark Binding" was chosen ... ' - Preface.
ISBN 0-471-02721-9 : £18.70
Primary classification 539.7'216
(B77-28591)

530.1'5 — Physics. Mathematics
Wyld, H W. Mathematical methods for physics / [by] H.W. Wyld. — Reading, Mass. ; London [etc.] : Benjamin, 1976 [i.e. 1977]. — xix,628p : ill ; 24cm. — (Lecture notes and supplements in physics ; no.15)
Published in the United States: 1976. — Index.
ISBN 0-8053-9856-2 : £22.55
ISBN 0-8053-9857-0 Pbk : £13.20
(B77-10353)

530.1'5 — Physics. Mathematics. Dimensionless parameters
Becker, H A. Dimensionless parameters : theory and methodology / [by] H.A. Becker. — London : Applied Science Publishers, 1976. — xiv,128p ; 23cm. — (Fuel and energy science series)
Bibl.: p.107-112. — Index.
ISBN 0-85334-689-5 : £8.00
(B77-03524)

530.1'5'02854 — Physics. Mathematics. Applications of computer systems. *Reviews of research*
Methods in computational physics : advances in research and applications. — New York [etc.] ; London : Academic Press.
Vol.16 : Controlled fusion / volume editor John Killeen. — 1976. — xiii,445p : ill ; 24cm.
Bibl. — Index.
ISBN 0-12-460816-7 : £27.25
(B77-03525)

Vol.17 : General circulation models of the atmosphere / volume editor Julius Chang. — 1977. — ix,337p : ill, charts ; 24cm.
Bibl. — Index.
ISBN 0-12-460817-5 : £25.20
(B77-24194)

530.1'5'563 — Physics. Vector analysis
Shercliff, John Arthur. Vector fields : vector analysis developed through its application to engineering and physics / [by] J.A. Shercliff. — Cambridge [etc.] : Cambridge University Press, 1977. — xi,329p : ill ; 24cm.
With answers. — Index.
ISBN 0-521-21306-1 : £13.50
ISBN 0-521-29092-9 Pbk : £4.25
(B77-16866)

530.4 — PHYSICS. STATES OF MATTER
530.4 — Superfluids. *Conference proceedings*
Symposium on Quantum Statistics and Many-Body Problems, *1st, Sanibel Island, 1975.* Quantum statistics and the many-body problem / edited by Samuel B. Trickey, Wiley P. Kirk and James W. Dufty. — New York ; London : Plenum Press, [1976]. — xii,288p : ill ; 26cm.
'Proceedings of the first Symposium on Quantum Statistics and Many-Body Problems held on Sanibel Island, January 26-29, 1975' - title page verso. — Published in the United States: 1975. — Index.
ISBN 0-306-30887-8 : £17.33
(B77-04785)

530.4'1 — Amorphous materials. Structure. *Conference proceedings*
The **structure** of non-crystalline materials : proceedings of the symposium held in Cambridge, England on 20-23 September 1976 / edited by P.H. Gaskell. — London : Taylor and Francis [for] the Society of Glass Technology, 1977. — [10],262p : ill ; 31cm. — (A 'Physics and chemistry of glasses' conference volume)
Index.
ISBN 0-85066-120-x : £15.00
(B77-27842)

530.4'1 — Crystalline solids. Quantum theory
Animalu, Alexander O E. Intermediate quantum theory of crystalline solids / [by] Alexander O.E. Animalu. — Englewood Cliffs ; London [etc.] : Prentice-Hall, 1977. — xi,516p : ill ; 24cm. — (Prentice-Hall physics series)
Bibl. — Index.
ISBN 0-13-470799-0 : £18.00
(B77-18739)

530.4'1 — Nonmetallic solids. Defects. *Conference proceedings*
Defects and their structure in nonmetallic solids / edited by B. Henderson and A.E. Hughes. — New York ; London : Plenum Press [for the] NATO Scientific Affairs Division, 1976. — xi,505p : ill ; 26cm. — (NATO Advanced Study Institutes : series B, physics ; vol.19)
'Proceedings of a NATO Advanced Study Institute held at the University of Exeter, August 24-September 6, 1975' - title page verso. — Bibl. — Index.
ISBN 0-306-35719-4 : £28.35
(B77-14218)

530.4'1 — Nonmetallic thin films. Structure & physical properties. *Conference proceedings*
NATO Summer School on Metallic and Nonmetallic Thin Films, *2nd, Corsica, 1974.* Physics of nonmetallic thin films / edited by C.H.S. Dupuy and A. Cachard. — New York ; London : Plenum Press [for the] NATO Scientific Affairs Division, 1976. — viii,510p : ill ; 26cm. — (NATO Advanced Study Institutes : series B, physics ; vol.14)
'Lectures presented at the Second NATO Summer School on Metallic and Nonmetallic Thin Films held in Corsica, Serra di Ferro, September 1-5, 1974' - title page verso. — Index.
ISBN 0-306-35714-3 : £31.19
(B77-14219)

530.4'1 — Semimetals. Preparation & properties
Lovett, D R. Semimetals & narrow-bandgap semiconductors / [by] D.R. Lovett. — London : Pion, 1977. — [4],viii,256p : ill ; 24cm. — (Applied physics series ; 10)
Bibl. — Index.
ISBN 0-85086-060-1 : £8.50
Also classified at 537.6'22
(B77-21102)

530.4'1 — Solid state physics
Ashcroft, Neil W. Solid state physics / [by] Neil W. Ashcroft, N. David Mermin. — New York ; London [etc.] : Holt, Rinehart and Winston, [1977]. — xxi,826p : ill ; 25cm.
Ill., text on lining papers. — Published in the United States: 1976. — Index.
ISBN 0-03-083993-9 : £11.00
(B77-11788)

530.4'1 — Solids. Electrons. Transport phenomena. *Conference proceedings*
NATO Advanced Study Institute on Linear and Nonlinear Electronic Transport in Solids, *Rijksuniversitair Centrum te Antwerpen, 1975.* Linear and nonlinear electronic transport in solids / edited by J.T. Devreese and V.E. van Doren. — New York ; London : Plenum Press [for the] NATO Scientific Affairs Division, 1976. — ix,634p : ill ; 26cm. — (NATO Advanced Study Institutes : series B, physics ; vol.17)
'Lectures presented at the NATO Advance[d] Study Institute on Linear and Nonlinear Electronic Transport in Solids held at the State University of Antwerp (Ruca), Antwerp, Belgium, July 21-August 2, 1975' - title page verso. — Index.
ISBN 0-306-35717-8 : £31.19
(B77-18111)

530.4'1 — Solids. Implantation of ions. *Technical data*
Ion implantation range and energy deposition distributions. — New York [etc.] : IFI/Plenum ; London : Plenum Press.
In 2 vols.
Vol.2 : Low incident energies / [by] K. Bruce Winterbon. — [1976]. — vii,341p : ill ; 28cm.
Published in the United States: 1975.
ISBN 0-306-67402-5 : £31.19
(B77-02980)

530.4'1 — Solids. Interactions with radiation
Lehmann, Chr. Interaction of radiation with solids and elementary defect production / [by] Chr. Lehmann. — Amsterdam [etc.] ; Oxford : North-Holland Publishing Co., 1977. — xviii, 341p : ill ; 23cm. — (Defects in crystalline solids ; vol.10)
Text on lining paper. — Bibl.: p.276-306. — Index.
ISBN 0-7204-0416-9 : £28.10
(B77-17472)

530.4'1 — Solids. Microstructure. Research. Applications of electron microscopy
Grundy, P J. Electron microscopy in the study of materials / [by] P.J. Grundy and G.A. Jones. — London : Edward Arnold, 1976. — [12], 174p : ill ; 24cm. — (The structures and properties of solids ; 7)
Bibl.: p.165-169. — Index.
ISBN 0-7131-2521-7 : £8.00
ISBN 0-7131-2522-5 Pbk : £3.75
(B77-02279)

530.4'1 — Solids. Structure & physical properties
Busch, Georg. Lectures on solid state physics / by Georg Busch and Horst Schade ; translated [from the German] by Ferdinand Cap ; translation editor D. ter Haar. — Oxford [etc.] : Pergamon, 1976. — xv,535p : ill ; 25cm. — (International series in natural philosophy ; vol.79)
Translation of: 'Vorlesungen über Festkörperphysik'. Basel : Birkhäuser, 1973. — Bibl. — Index.
ISBN 0-08-016894-9 : £17.50
ISBN 0-08-021653-6 Pbk : £10.00
(B77-02981)

530.4'1 — Solids. Surfaces. Interactions with gases
Goodman, Frank Oxenham. Dynamics of gas-surface scattering / [by] Frank O. Goodman, Harold Y. Wachman. — New York [etc.] ; London : Academic Press, 1976. — xxiii,327p : ill ; 24cm.
Index.
ISBN 0-12-290450-8 : £17.10
Primary classification 533'.2
(B77-00753)

530.4'1 — Solids. Surfaces. Properties. Measurement. Use of ion beams. *Conference proceedings*
International Conference on Ion Beam Surface Layer Analysis, *Karlsruhe, 1975.* Ion beam surface layer analysis / edited by O. Meyer, G. Linker and F. Käppeler. — New York ; London : Plenum Press.
In 2 vols.
Vol.1. — 1976. — 494,xxvi p : ill ; 26cm.
'Proceedings of the first half of the International Conference on Ion Beam Surface Layer Analysis held at Karlsruhe, Germany, September 15-19, 1975' - title page verso. — Index.
ISBN 0-306-35045-9 : £23.63
(B77-18112)

Vol.2. — 1976. — xvii p,p495-985 : ill ; 26cm.
'Proceedings of the second half of the International Conference on Ion Beam Surface Layer Analysis held at Karlsruhe, Germany, September 15-19, 1975' - title page verso. — Bibl. — Index.
ISBN 0-306-35046-7 : £23.63
(B77-18113)

530.4'1 — Thin films. Structure & physical properties. *Reviews of research*
Physics of thin films : advances in research and development. — New York [etc.] ; London : Academic Press.
Index.
Vol.9 : 1977 / edited by Georg Hass, Maurice H. Francombe, Richard W. Hoffman. — 1977. — xv,316p : ill ; 24cm.
ISBN 0-12-533009-x : £22.35
(B77-20230)

530.4'1 — Transparent solids. Optical properties. *Conference proceedings*
International Conference on Optical Properties of Highly Transparent Solids, *Waterville Valley, 1975.* Optical properties of highly transparent solids / edited by Shashanka S. Mitra and Bernard Bendow. — New York ; London : Plenum Press, [1976]. — xix,538p : ill ; 26cm. — (Optical physics and engineering)
'Proceedings of the International Conference on Optical Properties of Highly Transparent Solids held at Waterville Valley, New Hampshire, February 3-5, 1975' - title page verso. — Published in the United States: 1975. — Index.
ISBN 0-306-30861-4 : £24.89
(B77-04140)

530.4'2 — Liquids. Atoms. Dynamics
March, Norman Henry. Atomic dynamics in liquids / [by] N.H. March and M.P. Tosi. — London [etc.] : Macmillan, 1976. — vii,330p : ill ; 24cm.
Bibl.: p.315-324. — Index.
ISBN 0-333-11278-4 : £25.00
(B77-05389)

530.4'2 — Liquids. Physical properties
Watts, R O. Liquid state chemical physics / [by] R.O. Watts, I.J. McGee. — New York ; London [etc.] : Wiley, [1977]. — xv,334p : ill ; 24cm.
'A Wiley-Interscience Publication'. — Published in the United States: 1976. — Index.
ISBN 0-471-91240-9 : £18.70
(B77-14220)

530.4'2 — Liquids. Statistical mechanics
Hansen, Jean Pierre. Theory of simple liquids / [by] Jean Pierre Hansen, Ian R. McDonald. — London [etc.] : Academic Press, 1976. — xv, 395p : ill ; 24cm.
Bibl.: p.370-379. — Index.
ISBN 0-12-323850-1 : £14.00
(B77-06661)

530.4'4 — High-beta plasmas. *Conference proceedings*
Topical Conference on High Beta Plasmas, *3rd, Culham Laboratory, 1975.* Pulsed high beta plasmas : proceedings of the third topical conference held at UKAEA Culham Laboratory, Abingdon, Oxfordshire, U.K., 9-12 September 1975 / edited by D.E. Evans. — Oxford [etc.] : Pergamon, 1976. — xii,625p : ill ; 26cm.
'... the Third Topical Conference on High Beta Plasmas'. — Preface. — 'Published as a Supplement to the Journal "Plasma Physics"'. — Bibl. — Index.
ISBN 0-08-020941-6 : £15.00
(B77-04141)

530.4'4 — Magnetosphere. Hot plasmas. *Conference proceedings*
Physics of the hot plasma in the magnetosphere / edited by Bengt Hultqvist and Lennart Stenflo. — New York ; London : Plenum Press, 1975. — x,369p : ill ; 26cm.
'Proceedings of the thirteenth Nobel Symposium held April 2-4, 1975 at Kiruna Geophysical Institute, Kiruna, Sweden' - title-page verso. — Bibl. — Index.
ISBN 0-306-33700-2 : £15.75
(B77-02982)

530.4'4 — Plasma columns. Physical properties
Franklin, Raoul Norman. Plasma phenomena in gas discharges / by Raoul N. Franklin. — Oxford : Clarendon Press, 1976. — x,249p : ill ; 24cm. — (The Oxford engineering science series)
Bibl.: p.238-245. — Index.
ISBN 0-19-856113-x : £15.00
(B77-10354)

530.4'4 — Plasmas
Laing, Ernest William. Plasma physics / [by] E.W. Laing. — London : Chatto and Windus for Sussex University Press [etc.], 1976. — viii, 163p : ill ; 24cm. — (Graduate student series in physics)
Bibl.: p.159. — Index.
ISBN 0-85621-057-9 Pbk : £5.00
(B77-31879)

530.4'4 — Plasmas. Effects of lasers
Principles of laser plasmas / edited by George Bekefi. — New York ; London [etc.] : Wiley, 1976. — xix,695p : ill ; 24cm.
'A Wiley-Interscience Publication'. — '... this book celebrates Sanborn C. Brown ...' - Foreword. — Bibl. — Index.
ISBN 0-471-06345-2 : £26.00
(B77-13634)

530.4'4 — Plasmas. Effects of lasers. *Reviews of research*
Laser interaction and related plasma phenomena / edited by Helmut J. Schwarz and Heinrich Hora. — New York ; London : Plenum Press.
Vol.3A. — [1976]. — 395,lxiii p : ill ; 26cm.
'First half of the Proceedings of the Third Workshop on Laser Interaction and Related Plasma Phenomena held at Rensselaer Polytechnic Institute, Troy, New York, August 13-17, 1973' - title page verso. — Published in the United States: 1974. — Index.
ISBN 0-306-37143-x : £20.48
(B77-01416)

530.4'4 — Plasmas. Turbulence
Weiland, Jan. Coherent non-linear interaction of waves in plasmas / by J. Weiland and H. Wilhelmsson. — Oxford [etc.] : Pergamon, 1977. — xiv,353p : ill ; 26cm. — (International series in natural philosophy ; vol.88) (Pergamon international library)
Index.
ISBN 0-08-020964-5 : £15.50
(B77-29409)

531 — MECHANICS
Open University. *Modelling by Mathematics Course Team.* Position and movement / prepared by the [Open University, Modelling by Mathematics] Course Team. — Milton Keynes : Open University Press, 1977. — 68,59,62p : ill(some col) ; 30cm. — (Technology/ mathematics, a second level course : modelling by mathematics ; block 2) (TM281 ; 4-6)
With answers.
ISBN 0-335-06291-1 Pbk : Unpriced
Primary classification 516
(B77-25582)

531 — Continuous media. Mechanics
Fung, Yuan Cheng. A first course in continuum mechanics / [by] Y.C. Fung. — 2nd ed. — Englewood Cliffs ; London [etc.] : Prentice-Hall, 1977. — xii,340p : ill ; 24cm.
Previous ed.: 1969. — Bibl. — Index.
ISBN 0-13-318311-4 : £15.95
(B77-21840)

Hunter, S C. Mechanics of continuous media / [by] S.C. Hunter. — Chichester : Ellis Horwood [etc.], 1976. — 567p : ill ; 24cm. — (Mathematics and its applications)
With answers to selected problems. — Bibl.: p.559-560. — Index.
ISBN 0-85312-042-0 : £15.00
ISBN 0-85312-043-9 Student ed.: £6.90
(B77-08992)

Truesdell, Clifford. A first course in rational continuum mechanics / [by] C. Truesdell. — New York [etc.] ; London : Academic Press. — (Pure and applied mathematics)
Vol.1 : General concepts. — 1977. — xxiii, 280p ; 24cm.
'Parts 1 through 4 of this work ... from my text of 1972 ... were published in December, 1973 by Masson et Cie in a single volume with the title "Introduction à la Mécanique Rationnelle des Milieux Continus". Parts 1 through 5 appeared in 1975 in Russian, ... Since that time I have been able to add some material ... Volume 1 contains Part 1 only' - p.xiii-xiv. — With answers. — Index.
ISBN 0-12-701301-6 : £16.35
(B77-30224)

531 — Strength. *Juvenile literature*
Kentzer, Michal. Collins young scientist's book of strength / [by Michal Kentzer]. — Glasgow [etc.] : Collins, [1977]. — 3-46p : col ill, col maps ; 31cm.
Spine title: Strength. — Col. ill. on lining papers. — Index.
ISBN 0-00-106280-8 : £2.50
(B77-30225)

531'.01'515 — Mechanics. Calculus
Fowles, Grant Robert. Analytical mechanics / [by] Grant R. Fowles. — 3rd ed. — New York ; London [etc.] : Holt, Rinehart and Winston, 1977. — [11],334p : ill ; 25cm.
With answers to selected odd-numbered problems. — Previous ed.: 1970. — Bibl.: p.309. — Index.
ISBN 0-03-089725-4 : £9.75
(B77-22547)

531'.01'51563 — Mechanics. Vector analysis. *For engineering*
Beer, Ferdinand P. Vector mechanics for engineers / [by] Ferdinand P. Beer, E. Russell Johnston, Jr. — 3rd ed. — New York ; London [etc.] : McGraw-Hill.
In 2 vols. — With answers to even-numbered problems. — Previous ed.: New York : McGraw-Hill, 1972.
Dynamics. — 1977. — xvi p,p435-976 : ill(chiefly col) ; 25cm.
Text, ill. on lining papers. — Index.
ISBN 0-07-004281-0 : £12.40
(B77-25597)

Statics. — 1977. — xiv,448p : ill(chiefly col) ; 25cm.
Text, ill. on lining papers. — Index.
ISBN 0-07-004278-0 : £12.40
(B77-25598)

531.1 — DYNAMICS, STATICS, PARTICLE MECHANICS
531'.11 — Dynamics
Ginsberg, Jerry H. Dynamics / [by] Jerry H. Ginsberg, Joseph Genin. — New York ; London [etc.] : Wiley, 1977. — xi,558p : ill(chiefly col) ; 25cm.
With answers to odd-numbered problems. — Text on lining papers. — Index.
ISBN 0-471-29606-6 : £11.50
(B77-26286)

Greenwood, Donald Theodore. Classical dynamics / [by] Donald T. Greenwood. — Englewood Cliffs ; London [etc.] : Prentice-Hall, 1977. — xi,337p : ill ; 24cm. — (Prentice-Hall international series in dynamics)
With answers to selected problems. — Index.
ISBN 0-13-136036-1 : £15.20
(B77-28590)

531'.112 — Speed. *Juvenile literature*
Fast and slow. — Cambridge : Brimax Books, 1976. — [12]p : chiefly col ill ; 16cm. — ('Show baby opposites' series)
ISBN 0-904494-39-x Pbd : £0.60
(B77-13635)

McCarthy, M L. Speed / [text by M.L. McCarthy] ; [planned and edited by Dale Gunthorp]. — London : Macdonald Educational, 1977. — 3-46p : ill(chiefly col), col port ; 25cm. — (Action world)
Col. ill., text on lining papers. — Index.
ISBN 0-356-05560-4 : £1.25
(B77-16867)

North, Peter. Fast and slow / [illustrated by Peter North]. — London : Macdonald Educational, 1976. — [29]p : of col ill ; 16x20cm. — (Opposites ; 5)
ISBN 0-356-05115-3 : £0.60
(B77-04786)

531'.1133 — Waves
Open University. *Introduction to Materials Course Team.* Strong materials ; [and], Electrons and waves / prepared by the [Open University, Introduction to Materials] Course Team. — 3rd ed. — Milton Keynes : Open University Press, 1977. — [9],31,61p : ill(chiefly col) ; 30cm. — (A second level course : an introduction to materials ; units 1A and 1B) (TS251 ; 1A and 1B)
With answers. — Previous ed.: 1974.
Pbk : Unpriced
Primary classification 620.1'12
(B77-26349)

Pain, Herbert John. The physics of vibrations and waves / [by] H.J. Pain. — 2nd ed. — London [etc.] : Wiley, 1976. — xvi,357p : ill ; 24cm.
Previous ed.: Chichester : Wiley, 1968. — Index.
ISBN 0-471-99407-3 : £9.75
ISBN 0-471-99408-1 Pbk : £4.25
Also classified at 531'.32
(B77-02280)

531'.1133 — Waves. *Juvenile literature*
Kentzer, Michal. Collins young scientist's book of waves / [by Michal Kentzer]. — Glasgow [etc.] : Collins, [1977]. — 3-46p : ill(chiefly col) ; 31cm.
Spine title: Waves. — Col. ill. on lining papers. — Index.
ISBN 0-00-106285-9 : £2.50
(B77-30226)

531'.163 — Brownian motion & spin relaxation
Lenk, Rudolf. Brownian motion and spin relaxation / [by] R. Lenk. — Amsterdam ; Oxford [etc.] : Elsevier, 1977. — x,250p : ill ; 24cm.
Bibl. — Index.
ISBN 0-444-41592-0 : £22.00
(B77-23371)

531.3 — DYNAMICS
531'.32 — Nonlinear vibration & random vibration. Mathematics
Dincă, Florea. Nonlinear and random vibrations / [by] Florea Dincă, Cristian Teodosiu ; [translated from the Romanian by Cristian Teodosiu]. — Bucureşti [i.e. Bucharest] (Editura Academiei) ; New York ; London : Academic Press, 1973. — 413p : ill ; 25cm.
Translation and revision of: 'Vibraţii neliniare şi aleatoare'. Bucharest : Editura Academiei, 1969. — Bibl.: p.399-404. — Index.
ISBN 0-12-216750-3 : Unpriced
(B77-19354)

531'.32 — Vibration
Meirovitch, Leonard. Elements of vibration analysis / [by] Leonard Meirovitch. — New York ; London [etc.] : McGraw-Hill, [1976]. — xvi,495p : ill ; 25cm.
Published in the United States: 1975. — Bibl.: p.484. — Index.
ISBN 0-07-041340-1 : £11.50
(B77-02281)

Pain, Herbert John. The physics of vibrations and waves / [by] H.J. Pain. — 2nd ed. — London [etc.] : Wiley, 1976. — xvi,357p : ill ; 24cm.
Previous ed.: Chichester : Wiley, 1968. — Index.
ISBN 0-471-99407-3 : £9.75
ISBN 0-471-99408-1 Pbk : £4.25
Primary classification 531'.1133
(B77-02280)

531'.381 — Solids. Elasticity. Constants. Measurement
Schreiber, Edward. Elastic constants and their measurement / [by] Edward Schreiber, Orson L. Anderson, Naohiro Soga. — New York ; London [etc.] : McGraw-Hill, 1973. — xi, 196p : ill ; 24cm.
Index.
ISBN 0-07-055603-2 : Unpriced
(B77-19355)

531'.382 — Hardness. *Juvenile literature*
Pluckrose, Henry. Things hard and soft / by Henry Pluckrose ; photographs by G.W. Hales. — London [etc.] : F. Watts, 1976. — 32p : chiefly ill ; 18x22cm.
ISBN 0-85166-601-9 : £1.25
(B77-01417)

531.5 — MASS, GRAVITY, BALLISTICS
531'.5 — Gravitation. *Conference proceedings*
International School of Physics 'Enrico Fermi', *56th, Varenna, 1972.* Experimental gravitation : proceedings of the International School of Physics 'Enrico Fermi', course LVI, Varenna on Lake Como, Villa Monastero, 17th-29th July 1972 / edited by B. Bertotti. — New York ; London : Academic Press, 1974. — ii-xv,574p, [3]leaves of plates : ill(incl 1 col), map, ports ; 25cm.
At head of title: Italian Physical Society. — Second title page in Italian. — Cover title: Gravitazione sperimentale.
ISBN 0-12-368856-6 : £30.15
(B77-23372)

531.6 — ENERGY
531'.6 — Energy. *Juvenile literature*
Sibley, C Bruce. The how and why wonder book of energy and power / written by C. Bruce Sibley ; illustrated by Raymond Turvey. — London : Transworld, 1976. — 48p : ill(some col), col ports ; 28cm.
Index.
ISBN 0-552-86577-x Pbk : £0.50
(B77-07895)

531'.6'076 — Energy. *Questions & answers. Secondary school texts*
Lyth, Mike. Energy and man / [by] Mike Lyth ; [design and illustrations by Alex Fung]. — St Albans : Hart-Davis Educational, 1977. — [1], 56p : ill ; 25cm. — (Science testers)
ISBN 0-247-12604-7 Sd : £1.35
(B77-16363)

531.7 — TRANSPORT PHENOMENA IN SOLIDS
531'.7 — Solids. Diffusion
Stark, J P. Solid state diffusion / [by] J.P. Stark. — New York ; London [etc.] : Wiley, 1976. — xiii,237p : ill ; 24cm.
'A Wiley-Interscience Publication'. — Bibl.: p.225-226. — Index.
ISBN 0-471-82073-3 : £12.00
(B77-06056)

531.8 — MECHANICS OF SIMPLE MACHINES
531'.8 — Wheels. *Juvenile literature*
Ramsbottom, Edward. Wheels / [by] Edward Ramsbottom and Joan Redmayne ; illustrated by Malcolm Stokes. — London [etc.] : Macmillan, 1977. — 16p : col ill ; 30cm. — (Bright ideas)
ISBN 0-333-19643-0 Sd : £0.48
(B77-21841)

532 — FLUIDS. MECHANICS
Giles, Ranald V. Schaum's outline of theory and problems of fluid mechanics and hydraulics / by Ranald V. Giles. — SI (metric) ed. / adapted for SI units by David J. Pollard and Edward H. Wilson. — New York ; London [etc.] : McGraw-Hill, 1977. — x,275p : ill ; 28cm. — (Schaum's outline series)
Cover title: Theory and problems of fluid mechanics and hydraulics. — Spine title: Fluid mechanics and hydraulics. — Previous ed.: i.e. 2nd ed. New York : Schaum Publishing Co., 1962. — Index.
ISBN 0-07-084368-6 Pbk : £3.65
(B77-25599)

Vennard, John King. Elementary fluid mechanics. — 5th ed. SI version / [by] John K. Vennard, Robert L. Street. — New York ; London [etc.] : Wiley, 1976. — xix,740p : ill ; 24cm.
Text on lining paper. — Fifth ed. originally published: 1975. — Bibl. — Index.
ISBN 0-471-90589-5 : £13.85
(B77-00200)

Welty, James Richard. Fundamentals of momentum, heat and mass transfer / [by] James R. Welty, Charles E. Wicks, Robert E. Wilson. — 2nd ed. — New York ; London [etc.] : Wiley, 1976. — xix,789p : ill ; 24cm.
With answers to selected problems. — Text on lining papers. — Previous ed.: 1969. — Index.
ISBN 0-471-93354-6 : £17.00
(B77-06662)

532'.002'462 — Fluids. Mechanics. *For engineering*
Daugherty, Robert Long. Fluid mechanics with engineering applications. — 7th ed. / [by] Robert L. Daugherty, Joseph B. Franzini. — New York ; London [etc.] : McGraw-Hill, 1977. — xxi,564p : ill ; 24cm.
Text on lining papers. — Previous ed.: 1965. — Bibl.: p.546-548. — Index.
ISBN 0-07-015427-9 : £13.90
(B77-24197)

532'.05 — Fluids. Dynamics
Tritton, D J. Physical fluid dynamics / [by] D.J. Tritton. — New York ; London [etc.] : Van Nostrand Reinhold, 1977. — xv,362p : ill, charts, maps ; 24cm. — (The modern university physics series)
Bibl.: p.346-353. — Index.
ISBN 0-442-30131-6 : £11.50
ISBN 0-442-30132-4 Pbk : £5.50
(B77-18114)

Université de Grenoble. *École d'été de physique théorique, Les Houches, 1973.* Fluid dynamics = Dynamique des fluides : Les Houches, juillet 1973, cours de l'École d'Été de Physique Théorique, organe d'intérêt commun de l'USMG et INPG, subventionné par le Commissariat à l'Energie Atomique / edited by R. Balian and J.-L. Peube. — London [etc.] : Gordon and Breach, 1977. — xiv,677p : ill ; 24cm.
English and French text. — Bibl.
ISBN 0-677-10170-8 : £46.00
(B77-27843)

532'.051 — Fluids. Flow & pressure. Measurement
Benedict, Robert P. Fundamentals of temperature, pressure and flow measurements / [by] Robert P. Benedict. — New York ; London [etc.] : Wiley, 1977. — xvi,517p : ill ; 24cm.
'A Wiley-Interscience Publication'. — With answers. — Previous ed.: New York : Wiley, 1969. — Index.
ISBN 0-471-06561-7 : £22.50
Primary classification 536'.5
(B77-31880)

532'.051 — Fluids. One-dimensional compressible flow
Daneshyar, H. One-dimensional compressible flow / [by] H. Daneshyar. — Oxford [etc.] : Pergamon, 1976. — xi,179p : ill ; 26cm. — (Thermodynamics and fluid mechanics series) (Pergamon international library)
Index.
ISBN 0-08-020414-7 : £7.50
ISBN 0-08-020413-9 Pbk : £3.75
(B77-11789)

532'.052 — Fluids. Unsteady flow. Measurement
Measurement of unsteady fluid dynamic phenomena / edited by Bryan E. Richards. — Washington [D.C.] ; London : Hemisphere ; New York ; London [etc.] : McGraw-Hill, 1977. — xii,340p : ill ; 24cm. — (Series in thermal and fluids engineering)
'A von Karman Institute book'. — 'A lecture series on measurement of unsteady fluid dynamic phenomena was organized in January 1975 at the von Karman Institute for Fluid Dynamics, Belgium' - Preface. — Bibl. — Index.
ISBN 0-07-052280-4 : £20.60
(B77-25600)

532'.0527 — Fluids. Turbulence
Hinze, Julius Oscar. Turbulence / [by] J.O. Hinze. — 2nd ed. — New York ; London [etc.] : McGraw-Hill, [1976]. — x,790p : ill ; 24cm.
This ed. published in the United States: 1975. — Previous ed.: 1959. — Index.
ISBN 0-07-029037-7 : £23.65
(B77-04142)

532.5 — HYDRODYNAMICS
532'.54 — Liquids. Unsteady flow in pipes
Fox, J A. Hydraulic analysis of unsteady flow in pipe networks / [by] J.A. Fox. — London [etc.] : Macmillan, 1977. — xvi,216p : ill ; 24cm.
Bibl.: p.209. — Index.
ISBN 0-333-19142-0 : £12.95
(B77-13019)

533.2 — GASES. DYNAMICS
533'.2 — Gases. Dynamics
Zucrow, Maurice Joseph. Gas dynamics / [by] Maurice J. Zucrow, Joe D. Hoffman. — New York ; London [etc.] : Wiley.
In 2 vols.
Vol.1. — 1976. — ix,772p : ill ; 26cm.
Text on lining papers. — Index.
ISBN 0-471-98440-x : £19.45
(B77-24909)

533'.2 — Gases. Interactions with surfaces of solids
Goodman, Frank Oxenham. Dynamics of gas-surface scattering / [by] Frank O. Goodman, Harold Y. Wachman. — New York [etc.] ; London : Academic Press, 1976. — xxiii,327p : ill ; 24cm.
Index.
ISBN 0-12-290450-8 : £17.10
Also classified at 530.4'1
(B77-00753)

533'.28 — Perfect gases. Compressible flow. *Tables*
Stockport College of Technology. *Department of Mechanical Engineering.* Compressible flow tables : perfect gas ... [gamma equals] 1.4 / Stockport College of Technology, Department of Mechanical Engineering. — [Stockport] ([Wellington Road South, Stockport SK1 3UQ]) : The College, 1976. — [3]p,22 leaves ; 30cm.
Notebook format.
ISBN 0-9505376-0-8 Sp : £1.00
(B77-14221)

533.6 — AEROMECHANICS
533'.62 — Aerodynamics
Kuethe, Arnold Martin. Foundations of aerodynamics : bases of aerodynamic design. — 3rd ed. / [by] Arnold M. Kuethe, Chuen-Yen Chow. — New York ; London [etc.] : Wiley, 1976. — xii,527p,fold plate : ill ; 24cm.
Text on lining papers. — Previous ed.: / by Arnold M. Kuethe and J.D. Schetzer. New York : Wiley ; London : Chapman and Hall, 1959. — Bibl.: p.508-518. — Index.
ISBN 0-471-50953-1 : £17.50
(B77-02983)

533'.62 — Air. Flow. Measurement
Ower, Ernest. The measurement of air flow / by E. Ower and R.C. Pankhurst. — 5th ed. (in SI units). — Oxford [etc.] : Pergamon, 1977. — xi, 362p,[4] leaves of plates,[2]p of plates : ill ; 24cm.
Previous ed.: 1966. — Index.
ISBN 0-08-021282-4 : Unpriced
ISBN 0-08-021281-6 Pbk : £7.25
(B77-30227)

534 — SOUND AND RELATED VIBRATIONS
534 — Acoustics
Acoustics and vibration progress. — London : Chapman and Hall.
Vol.2 / edited by R.W.B. Stephens and H.G. Leventhall. — 1976. — vii,203p : ill ; 24cm.
Bibl. — Index.
ISBN 0-412-14680-0 : £10.00
(B77-02282)

Physical acoustics : principles and methods / edited by Warren P. Mason and R.N. Thurston. — New York [etc.] ; London : Academic Press.
Vol.12. — 1976 [i.e. 1977]. — xiii,389p : ill ; 24cm.
Published in the United States: 1976. — Bibl. — Index.
ISBN 0-12-477912-3 : £28.05
(B77-08993)

534 — Sound. *Juvenile literature*
Knight, David, *b.1922.* Let's find out about sound / by David Knight ; pictures by Ulrick Schramm. — London [etc.] : F. Watts, 1977. — 41p : col ill ; 23cm.
ISBN 0-85166-582-9 : £1.75
(B77-21104)

Sanday, Alan Philip. Sounds / written by Allan [i.e. Alan] Sanday ; illustrated by Bernard H. Robinson. — Loughborough : Ladybird Books, 1975. — 52p : col ill ; 18cm. — (Ladybird leaders ; no.17)
Text, col. ill. on lining papers. — Index.
ISBN 0-7214-0393-x : £0.24
(B77-00201)

534'.05 — Acoustics. *Periodicals*
Acoustics letters. — [London] ([The Old Mill, Dorset Place, E15 1DJ]) : Multi-Science Publishing Co. Ltd.
Published at irregular intervals. — [5],1,30p. in 1st issue. — Pierced for binder.
Vol.1- ; 1977-. — [1977]-. — ill ; 30cm.
Sd : Unpriced
ISSN 0140-1599
(B77-24910)

534'.22 — Solids. Sound waves
Pollard, H F. Sound waves in solids / [by] H.F. Pollard. — London : Pion, 1977. — [4],xiii, 366p : ill ; 24cm. — (Applied physics series)
With answers. — Bibl. — Index.
ISBN 0-85086-053-9 : £10.50
(B77-24200)

534'.24 — Aeroacoustics
Goldstein, Marvin E. Aeroacoustics / [by] Marvin E. Goldstein. — New York ; London [etc.] : McGraw-Hill, 1976. — xvii,293p : ill ; 25cm.
Index.
ISBN 0-07-023685-2 : £16.45
(B77-24201)

535 — LIGHT AND PARAPHOTIC PHENOMENA
535 — Optics
Jenkins, Francis Arthur. Fundamentals of optics / [by] Francis A. Jenkins, Harvey E. White. — 4th ed. — New York ; London [etc.] : McGraw-Hill, 1976. — xxi,746p : ill ; 24cm.
Previous ed.: 1957. — Index.
ISBN 0-07-032330-5 : £14.05
(B77-00202)

535 — Optics. *Reviews of research*
Progress in optics. — Amsterdam [etc.] ; Oxford : North-Holland Publishing Co.
Vol.14 / edited by E. Wolf ; contributors J.C. Dainty ... [et al.]. — 1976. — xvii,422p : ill ; 23cm.
Bibl. — Index.
ISBN 0-7204-1514-4 : £32.79
(B77-15830)

535'.1 — Light. Theories
Waldron, Richard Arthur. The wave and ballistic theories of light : a critical review / [by] R.A. Waldron. — London : Muller, 1977. — xiii, 201p : ill ; 24cm.
Bibl.: p.193-195. — Index.
ISBN 0-584-10148-1 : £14.50
(B77-15272)

535'.15 — Quantum optics
Yariv, Amnon. Introduction to optical electronics / [by] Amnon Yariv. — 2nd ed. — New York ; London [etc.] : Holt, Rinehart and Winston, 1976. — ix,438p : ill ; 25cm.
Previous ed.: 1971. — Index.
ISBN 0-03-089892-7 : £15.00
(B77-23374)

535'.33 — Optical equipment. Surfaces
Jurek, Bohumil. Optical surfaces : aspherical optical systems, X-ray optics, reflecting microscopes, reflectors, measurements / by Bohumil Jurek. — Amsterdam ; Oxford [etc.] : Elsevier Scientific [etc.], 1977. — 217p,2p of plates : ill ; 25cm.
At head of half-title: Czechoslovak Academy of Sciences. — Bibl.: p.210-212. — Index.
ISBN 0-444-99868-3 : £20.49
(B77-16364)

535.5'2 — Ellipsometry
Azzam, Rasheed Mohammed Abdel-Gawad. Ellipsometry and polarized light / [by] R.M.A. Azzam and N.M. Bashara. — Amsterdam [etc.] ; Oxford : North-Holland Publishing Co., 1977. — xvii,529p : ill ; 23cm.
Index.
ISBN 0-7204-0694-3 : Unpriced
(B77-30228)

535.5'8 — Lasers. Theories
Sargent, Murray. Laser physics / [by] Murray Sargent III, Marlan O. Scully, Willis E. Lamb, Jr. — Reading, Mass. ; London [etc.] : Addison-Wesley, 1977. — xxix,432p : ill ; 25cm.
Originally published: 1974. — Bibl. — Index.
ISBN 0-201-06912-1 : £19.60
ISBN 0-201-06913-x Pbk : £11.60
(B77-23375)

535.6 — Colour. *Juvenile literature*
Campbell, Ann. Let's find out about colour / by Ann Campbell. — Full colour ed. / pictures by Boche Kaplan and Roz Abisch. — London [etc.] : F. Watts, 1977. — 39p : col ill ; 23cm.
Previous ed.: / pictures by the author. New York : F. Watts, 1966.
ISBN 0-85166-585-3 : £1.75
(B77-22548)

Duvoisin, Roger. See what I am / [by] Roger Duvoisin. — Tadworth : World's Work, 1977. — [31]p : col ill ; 26cm.
Originally published: New York : Lothrop, Lee and Shepard, 1974.
ISBN 0-437-35953-0 : £2.60
(B77-25601)

Kincaid, Lucy. The Skittles colours book / [written and illustrated by Lucy and Eric Kincaid]. — Cambridge] : Brimax Books, 1976. — [20]p : chiefly col ill ; 26cm.
Cover title. — Text, col. ill. on lining papers.
ISBN 0-904494-15-2 : £0.65
(B77-06663)

Oram, Sandie. Colours / original story by Vivian Cohen and Colette Deblé ; illustrations by Colette Deblé ; [translated from the French and adapted by Sandie Oram]. — London : Macdonald Educational, 1975. — [24]p : chiefly col ill ; 26cm. — (Play school books)
These illustrations originally published: with French text. France : Le Livre de Paris, 1973.
ISBN 0-356-04784-9 Sd : £0.30
(B77-21105)

Scarry, Richard. Colour book / [by] Richard Scarry. — Glasgow [etc.] : Collins, [1977]. — [13]p : chiefly col ill ; 20cm.
ISBN 0-00-138245-4 Pbd : £0.85
(B77-18115)

535'.84 — Atomic spectroscopy & laser spectroscopy. *State-of-the-art reviews*
Corney, Alan. Atomic and laser spectroscopy / [by] Alan Corney. — Oxford : Clarendon Press, 1977. — xvii,763p : ill ; 24cm.
Bibl. — Index.
ISBN 0-19-851138-8 : £16.00
(B77-25602)

535'.84 — Beam-foil spectroscopy. *Conference proceedings*
International Conference on Beam-Foil Spectroscopy, *4th, Gatlinburg, 1975.* Beam-foil spectroscopy / edited by Ivan A. Sellin and David J. Pegg. — New York ; London : Plenum Press.
In 2 vols.
Vol.1 : Atomic structure and lifetimes. — 1976. — xxv,459p : ill ; 26cm.
'Proceedings of the first half of the Fourth International Conference on Beam-Foil Spectroscopy held in Gatlinburg, Tennessee, September 15-19, 1975' - title page verso. — Bibl. — Index.
ISBN 0-306-37126-x : £28.35
(B77-18740)

Vol.2 : Collisional and radiative processes. — 1976. — xx p,p461-987 : ill ; 26cm.
'Proceedings of the second half of the Fourth International Conference on Beam-Foil Spectroscopy held in Gatlinburg, Tennessee, September 15-19, 1975' - title page verso. — Bibl. — Index.
ISBN 0-306-37127-8 : £28.35
(B77-18741)

535'.84 — Fluorescence spectroscopy. *Reviews of research*
Modern fluorescence spectroscopy / edited by E.L. Wehry. — London [etc.] : Heyden, 1976. — 2v.(xvi,238p; xx,459p) : ill ; 24cm. — ([Modern analytical chemistry])
Also published: New York : Plenum Press, 1976. — Index.
ISBN 0-85501-213-7 : £35.00
(B77-01418)

535'.84 — Laser spectroscopy. *Conference proceedings*
Université de Grenoble. *École d'été de physique théorique, Session 27, Les Houches, 1975.* Aux frontières de la spectroscopie laser = Frontiers in laser spectroscopy : Les Houches, session XXVII, 30 juin-26 juillet 1975 / édité par Roger Balian, Serge Haroche, Sylvain Liberman. — Amsterdam [etc.] ; Oxford : North-Holland Publishing Co.
In 2 vols.
Vol.1. — 1977. — xxv,472p : ill, port ; 23cm.
English text, English and French preface.
ISBN 0-7204-0457-6 : Unpriced
(B77-24913)

Vol.2. — 1977. — [6]p,p xxvii-xxxv,p473-907 : ill, port ; 23cm.
ISBN 0-7204-0695-1 : Unpriced
(B77-24914)

535'.84 — Molecular spectroscopy. *Conference proceedings*
Conference on Molecular Spectroscopy, *6th, University of Durham, 1976.* Molecular spectroscopy : proceedings of the Sixth Conference on Molecular Spectroscopy, organized by the Institute of Petroleum, Hydrocarbon Research Group, and held at the University of Durham, 30 March-2 April, 1976 / edited by A.R. West. — London [etc.] : Heyden [for] the Institute of Petroleum, 1977. — xx,578p : ill, ports ; 25cm.
Bibl.: p.123-126. — Index.
ISBN 0-85501-303-6 : £30.00
(B77-15831)

535'.84 — Molecular spectroscopy. *Reviews of research*
Molecular spectroscopy : modern research. — New York [etc.] ; London : Academic Press.
Vol.2 / edited by K. Narahari Rao. — 1976. — xiv,279p : ill ; 24cm.
Bibl. — Index.
ISBN 0-12-580642-6 : £18.00
(B77-04787)

Molecular spectroscopy. — London : Chemical Society. — (Chemical Society. Specialist periodical reports)
Vol.4 : a review of the literature published during 1974 and early 1975 / senior reporters R.F. Barrow, D.A. Long, J. Sheridan ... — 1976. — viii,279p : ill ; 23cm.
Index.
ISBN 0-85186-536-4 : £17.25
ISSN 0305-9782
(B77-03526)

535'.84 — Molecular spectroscopy. Spectra. *Technical data*
Pearse, Reginald William Blake. The identification of molecular spectra / [by] R.W.B. Pearse and A.G. Gaydon. — 4th ed. — London : Chapman and Hall [etc.], 1976. — viii,407p,12p of plates : ill ; 26cm.
'A Halsted Press book'. — Previous ed.: 1963. — Bibl. — Index.
ISBN 0-470-15164-1 : £20.00
(B77-01419)

535'.84 — Spectrophotometers
Tinker, Robert F. The spectrophotometer : a module on the spectral properties of light / [by] Robert F. Tinker, John W. McWane ; [for] TERC. — New York ; London [etc.] : McGraw-Hill, [1976]. — [5],74p : ill, facsims ; 28cm. — (Physics of technology)
'... produced by the Tech Physics Project ... written and tested at the curriculum Development Laboratory of the Technical Education Research Centers ...' - title page verso. — Published in the United States: 1975.
ISBN 0-07-001731-x Sd : £2.10
(B77-07332)

535'.84 — Spectroscopy
Spectrometric techniques. — New York [etc.] ; London : Academic Press.
Vol.1 / edited by George A. Vanasse. — 1977. — xi,355p : ill ; 24cm.
Bibl. — Index.
ISBN 0-12-710401-1 : £20.95
(B77-26287)

Spectroscopy / edited by Dudley Williams. — New York [etc.] ; London : Academic Press. — (Methods of experimental physics ; vol.13)
In 2 parts.
Part A. — 1976. — xvii,366p : ill ; 24cm.
Index.
ISBN 0-12-475913-0 : £26.60
(B77-00203)

Part B. — 1976. — xv,364p : ill ; 24cm.
Index.
ISBN 0-12-475954-8 : £26.60
(B77-00204)

535'.842 — Infrared spectroscopy. *Reviews of research*
Advances in infrared and Raman spectroscopy. — London [etc.] : Heyden.
Vol.2 / edited by R.J.H. Clark, R.E. Hester. — 1976. — xv,343p,leaf of plate,[2]p of plates : ill ; 25cm.
Index.
ISBN 0-85501-182-3 : £17.50
(B77-30229)

535'.842 — Vibration spectroscopy. *Reviews of research*
Vibrational spectra and structure : a series of advances. — Amsterdam ; Oxford [etc.] : Elsevier.
Vol.6 / edited by James R. Durig. — 1977. — xiv,397p : ill ; 24cm.
Index.
ISBN 0-444-41588-2 : Unpriced
(B77-20231)

535'.842'0212 — Infrared spectroscopy. Spectra. *Tables*
Dolphin, David. Tabulation of infrared spectral data / [by] David Dolphin, Alexander Wick. — New York ; London [etc.] : Wiley, 1977. — xvii,549p : ill ; 24cm.
'A Wiley-Interscience publication'. — Text on lining papers. — Index.
ISBN 0-471-21780-8 : £14.65
(B77-23376)

535'.844 — Ultraviolet photoemission spectroscopy
Rabalais, J Wayne. Principles of ultraviolet photoelectron spectroscopy / by J. Wayne Rabalais. — New York ; London [etc.] : Wiley, 1977. — xvii,454p : ill ; 24cm. — (Wiley-Interscience monographs in chemical physics)
'A Wiley-Interscience publication'. — Bibl.: p.420-448. — Index.
ISBN 0-471-70285-4 : £22.50
(B77-23377)

535'.846 — Raman spectroscopy
Long, Derek Albert. Raman spectroscopy / [by] D.A. Long. — New York [etc.] ; London : McGraw-Hill, 1977. — xiii,276,16p,[2]leaves of plates : ill(some col) ; 26cm.
Bibl.: p.244-253. — Index.
ISBN 0-07-038675-7 : £14.40
(B77-25603)

536 — HEAT
536'.2 — Heat transfer
Cornwell, Keith. The flow of heat / [by] Keith Cornwell. — New York ; London [etc.] : Van Nostrand Reinhold, 1977. — xv,245p : ill ; 25cm.
Bibl.: p.238-240. — Index.
ISBN 0-442-30177-4 : £10.00
ISBN 0-442-30168-5 Pbk : £4.95
(B77-20232)

Holman, Jack Philip. Heat transfer / [by] J.P. Holman. — 4th ed. — New York ; London [etc.] : McGraw-Hill, 1976. — xvii,530p : ill ; 25cm.
Text on lining papers. — With answers to selected problems. — Previous ed.: 1972. — Index.
ISBN 0-07-029598-0 : £15.35
(B77-02984)

Özişk, M Necati. Basic heat transfer / [by] M. Necati Özişk. — New York ; London [etc.] : McGraw-Hill, 1977. — xv,572p : ill ; 25cm.
Text on lining papers. — Index.
ISBN 0-07-047980-1 : £13.90
(B77-30230)

Whitaker, Stephen. Fundamental principles of heat transfer / [by] Stephen Whitaker. — New York ; Oxford [etc.] : Pergamon, 1977. — xviii, 556p : ill ; 29cm.
Index.
ISBN 0-08-017866-9 : £27.50
(B77-14222)

536'.2 — Heat transfer. *Reviews of research*
Advances in heat transfer. — New York [etc.] ; London : Academic Press.
Vol.13 / edited by James P. Hartnett, Thomas F. Irvine, Jr. — 1977. — xiii,280p : ill ; 24cm.
Index.
ISBN 0-12-020013-9 : £21.30
(B77-26288)

536'.2'002462 — Heat transfer. *For engineering*
Butterworth, D. Introduction to heat transfer / [by] D. Butterworth. — [Oxford] : Oxford University Press for the Design Council, the British Standards Institution and the Council of Engineering Institutions, 1977. — [2],43p : ill ; 30cm. — (Engineering design guides ; 18)
Bibl.: p.42-43.
ISBN 0-19-859153-5 Sd : £2.25
(B77-10355)

Wong, H Y. Handbook of essential formulae and data on heat transfer for engineers / [by] H.Y. Wong. — London [etc.] : Longman, 1977. — xi,236p : ill ; 22cm.
Spine title: Heat transfer for engineers. — Index.
ISBN 0-582-46050-6 Pbk : £4.95
(B77-27844)

536'.2'002854044 — Heat transfer. Analysis. Applications of digital computer systems
Adams, J Alan. Computer-aided heat transfer analysis / [by] J. Alan Adams, David F. Rogers. — New York ; London [etc.] : McGraw-Hill, 1973. — xiii,426p : ill ; 24cm.
Index.
ISBN 0-07-000285-1 : Unpriced
(B77-20233)

536'.2012 — Solids. Thermal conductivity
Berman, R. Thermal conduction in solids / by R. Berman. — Oxford : Clarendon Press, 1976. — xi,193p : ill ; 24cm. — (Oxford studies in physics)
Bibl.: p.179-186. — Index.
ISBN 0-19-851429-8 : £9.75
(B77-06057)

536'.2'01515625 — Heat transfer. Calculation. Use of finite difference equations
Croft, David R. Heat transfer calculations using finite difference equations / [by] David R. Croft and David G. Lilley. — London : Applied Science Publishers, 1977. — xi,283p : ill ; 23cm.
Bibl. — Index.
ISBN 0-85334-720-4 : £16.00
(B77-24202)

536'.401 — Phase transitions. Critical phenomena
Pfeuty, Pierre. Introduction to the renormalization group and to critical phenomena / [by] Pierre Pfeuty and Gérard Toulouse ; translation [from the French by] G. Barton. — London [etc.] : Wiley, 1977. — xi, 190p : ill ; 24cm.
'A Wiley-Interscience Publication'. — Translation of: 'Introduction au groupe de renormalisation et à ses applications'. Grenoble : Presses universitaires de Grenoble, 1975. — Bibl. — Index.
ISBN 0-471-99440-5 : £9.00
(B77-15273)

536'.401 — Phase transitions. Critical phenomena. *Reviews of research*
Phase transitions and critical phenomena. — London [etc.] : Academic Press.
In 6 vols.
Vol.5b / edited by C. Domb and M.S. Green. — 1976. — xvii,412p : ill ; 24cm.
Bibl. — Index.
ISBN 0-12-220351-8 : £13.50
(B77-00205)

Vol.6 / edited by C. Domb and M.S. Green. — 1976. — xviii,575p : ill ; 24cm.
Bibl. — Index.
ISBN 0-12-220306-2 : £21.50
(B77-04788)

536'.41 — High pressure. *Conference proceedings*
European High Pressure Research Group. *Annual Meeting, 14th, Trinity College, Dublin, 1976.* High pressure techniques for science and technology : EHPRG 14th Annual Meeting, Trinity College ... Ireland, 6-8 Sept. 1976 / [editor W.G.S. Scaife]. — Dublin : E.H.P.R.G. ; Dublin (6 Trimleston Ave., Booterstown, Dublin) : [Distributed by] Typografia Hiberniae, 1976. — [3],32,[2]p ; 21cm.
ISBN 0-903448-01-7 Sd : £2.00
(B77-15274)

536'.443 — Gases. Nucleation
Nucleation phenomena / edited by A.C. Zettlemoyer. — Amsterdam ; Oxford [etc.] : Elsevier, 1977. — viii,418p : ill ; 25cm.
'These papers have been published as a special issue of "Advances in Colloid and Interface Science", vol.7, 1977'. — Bibl.
£24.00
(B77-26289)

536'.5 — Temperature. Measurement
Benedict, Robert P. Fundamentals of temperature, pressure and flow measurements / [by] Robert P. Benedict. — New York ; London [etc.] : Wiley, 1977. — xvi,517p : ill ; 24cm.
'A Wiley-Interscience Publication'. — With answers. — Previous ed.: New York : Wiley, 1969. — Index.
ISBN 0-471-06561-7 : £22.50
Also classified at 532'.051
(B77-31880)

536'.54 — Thermometry below 1°K
Betts, David Sheridan. Refrigeration and thermometry below one kelvin / [by] D.S. Betts. — London : Chatto and Windus for Sussex University Press [etc.], 1976. — x,283p : ill ; 24cm. — (Graduate student series in physics)
Index.
ISBN 0-85621-028-5 Pbk : £8.00
Primary classification 536'.56
(B77-15832)

536'.56 — Cryogenics. *Juvenile literature*
Haines, Gail Kay. Supercold, superhot : cryogenics and controlled thermonuclear fusion / by Gail Kay Haines. — New York ; London : F. Watts, 1976. — [7],81,[1]p : ill ; 25cm. — (An impact book)
Index.
ISBN 0-531-01203-4 : £2.50
(B77-18116)

536'.56 — Refrigeration below 1°K
Betts, David Sheridan. Refrigeration and thermometry below one kelvin / [by] D.S. Betts. — London : Chatto and Windus for Sussex University Press [etc.], 1976. — x,283p : ill ; 24cm. — (Graduate student series in physics)
Index.
ISBN 0-85621-028-5 Pbk : £8.00
Also classified at 536'.54
(B77-15832)

536'.7 — Fluids. Thermodynamic properties. *Tables*
Thermodynamic Tables Project. International thermodynamic tables of the fluid state / International Union of Pure and Applied Chemistry, Division of Physical Chemistry, Commission on Thermodynamics and Thermochemistry, Thermodynamic Tables Project. — Oxford [etc.] : Pergamon.
[Vol.3] : Carbon dioxide / edited and compiled ... by S. Angus, B. Armstrong, K.M, de Reuck ; on the basis of surveys and equations produced by V.V. Altunin ... [et al.]. — 1976. — xxviii,385p : ill ; 26cm.
English text, English, French, German and Russian preface and introduction.
ISBN 0-08-020924-6 : £25.00
(B77-02283)

536'.7 — Thermodynamics
Redlich, Otto. Thermodynamics : fundamentals, applications / [by] Otto Redlich. — Amsterdam ; Oxford [etc.] : Elsevier, 1976. — xiv,277p : ill ; 25cm.
Index.
ISBN 0-444-41487-8 : £23.29
(B77-02985)

Wark, Kenneth. Thermodynamics / [by] Kenneth Wark. — 3rd ed. — New York ; London [etc.] : McGraw-Hill, 1977. — xviii,909p : ill ; 25cm.
With answers to selected problems. — Previous ed.: New York : McGraw-Hill, 1971. — Bibl. — Index.
ISBN 0-07-068280-1 : £16.50
(B77-21842)

536'.7 — Thermodynamics. *Secondary school texts*
Johnstone, Alexander Henry. Energy, chaos and chemical change : concepts and applications of chemical thermodynamics / [by] A.H. Johnstone, G. Webb. — London [etc.] : Heinemann Educational, 1977. — x,110p : ill ; 22cm.
With answers. — Index.
ISBN 0-435-65525-6 Pbk : £1.30
(B77-08994)

536'.7 — Thermodynamics. Continuous media mechanics aspects
Ziegler, Hans. An introduction to thermomechanics / [by] Hans Ziegler. — Amsterdam [etc.] ; Oxford : North-Holland Publishing Co., 1977. — xi,308p : ill ; 23cm. — (North-Holland series in applied mathematics and mechanics ; vol.21)
Index.
ISBN 0-7204-0432-0 : £21.08
(B77-31173)

536'.7'0212 — Thermodynamics. *Tables*
Ražnjević, Kuzman. Handbook of thermodynamic tables and charts / [by] Kuzman Ražnjević ; [translated from the Serbo-Croatian by Marijan Bošković and Rickard Podhorsky]. — Washington [D.C.] ; London : Hemisphere ; New York ; London [etc.] : McGraw-Hill, 1976. — viii,392p : ill ; 29cm.
Two fold. sheets (col. ill.) in pocket. — Translation of: 'Termodinamičke tablice i dijagrami'. s.l. : s.n., 1970?. — Index.
ISBN 0-07-051270-1 : £24.50
(B77-02986)

536'.7'024553 — Thermodynamics. *For geology*
Wood, Bernard James. Elementary thermodynamics for geologists / [by] B.J. Wood and D.G. Fraser. — Oxford [etc.] : Oxford University Press, 1976. — xiii,303p : ill ; 23cm.
With answers to problems. — Bibl.: p.283-298. — Index.
ISBN 0-19-859926-9 : £6.00
ISBN 0-19-859927-7 Pbk : £2.95
(B77-10356)

537 — ELECTRICITY
Basford, Leslie. Electricity made simple / [by] Leslie Basford. — [1st ed.] reprinted ; with revision questions. — London : W.H. Allen, 1976. — x,230p : ill ; 22cm. — (Made simple books ISSN 0464-2902)
With answers. — This ed. originally published: 1968. — Index.
ISBN 0-491-01741-3 Pbk : £1.25
(B77-23378)

Turnbull, Kenneth Denham. The alignment pattern : a new basic theory of electricity and magnetism / [by] K.D. Turnbull. — Ilfracombe : Stockwell, 1977. — 44p : ill ; 19cm.
ISBN 0-7223-1028-5 Pbk : £1.00
Also classified at 538
(B77-24915)

537 — Electricity. *Secondary school texts*
Morris, Noel Malcolm. Study notes in electrical science / [by] Noel M. Morris. — London [etc.] : Macmillan, 1977. — x,118p : ill ; 24cm.
ISBN 0-333-21216-9 Pbk : £2.95
(B77-23379)

537'.07'8 — Electromagnetism. Teaching kits: Griffin Westminster electromagnetic kit. *For teaching*
Teacher's guide to the use of the Westminster electromagnetic kit. — [Wembley] ([285 Ealing Rd, Alperton, Wembley, Middx HA0 1HJ]) : Griffin and George Ltd, [1975]. — [2],28p : ill ; 21cm. — (IS 1317)
Cover title: Experiments with the Griffin Westminster electromagnetic kit.
Sd : Unpriced
(B77-17473)

537.2 — ELECTROSTATICS
537.2 — Electrostatics. *State-of-the-art reviews*
Bright, Alfred W. A serious change / by A.W. Bright. — [Southampton] ([Highfield, Southampton SO9 5NH]) : University of Southampton, 1976. — 26p : ill ; 21cm. — (University of Southampton. Inaugural lectures)
'... delivered at the University 11 March, 1976'.
ISBN 0-85432-159-4 Sd : £0.40
(B77-02284)

537.2'4 — Anisotropic dielectrics. *Conference proceedings*
Dielectrics Society. *Meeting, Cambridge, 1977.* Anisotropic dielectrics : [proceedings of the] 1977 meeting [of] the Dielectrics Society. — [Salford] ([c/o Dr C.W. Smith, Department of Electrical Engineering, University of Salford, Salford M5 4WT]) : [The Society], [1977]. — [34] leaves,[8]p ; 30cm.
Bibl.
Sp : Unpriced
(B77-18117)

537.2'44 — Ferroelectrics
Lines, M E. Principles and applications of ferroelectrics and related materials / by M.E. Lines and A.M. Glass. — Oxford : Clarendon Press, 1977. — xiii,680p : ill ; 25cm. — (The international series of monographs on physics)
Bibl.: p.633-662. — Index.
ISBN 0-19-851286-4 : £25.00 : CIP rev.
(B77-09682)

537.5 — ELECTRONICS
537.5 — Electronics. *Reviews of research*
Advances in electronics and electron physics. — New York ; London [etc.] : Academic Press.
Vol.40B / edited by L. Marton, assistant editor Claire Marton. — 1976. — xviii p,p519-1074 : ill ; 24cm.
Contains '"Photo-Electronic Image Devices" proceedings of the sixth symposium held at Imperial College, London, September 9-13, 1974' / edited by B.L. Morgan, R.W. Airey and D. McMullan. — Index.
ISBN 0-12-014554-5 : £18.50
(B77-01420)

Vol.41 / edited by L. Marton, assistant editor Claire Marton. — 1976. — x,389p : ill ; 24cm.
Bibl. — Index.
ISBN 0-12-014541-3 : £20.15
(B77-05391)

Vol.42 / edited by L. Marton, assistant editor Claire Marton. — 1976 [i.e. 1977]. — xi,304p : ill ; 24cm.
Published in the United States: 1976. — Bibl. — Index.
ISBN 0-12-014642-8 : £20.95
(B77-11790)

Vol.43 / edited by L. Marton, assistant editor Claire Marton. — 1977. — xi,259p : ill ; 24cm.
Bibl. — Index.
ISBN 0-12-014643-6 : £19.20
(B77-16365)

537.5'021'2 — Electronics. Formulae. *Tables*
Turner, Rufus Paul. Electronic conversions, symbols & formulas / [by] Rufus P. Turner ; with a specially written chapter for the guidance of the English reader by W. Oliver. — Slough : Foulsham-Tab, 1977. — vii,5-224p : ill ; 21cm.
Originally published: Blue Ridge Summit, Pa. : Tab Books, 1975. — Index.
ISBN 0-7042-0174-7 Pbk : £2.75
(B77-20234)

537.5'34 — Electrically conductive bodies. High frequency electromagnetic waves. Diffraction & scattering. Analysis. Applications of geometrical theory of diffraction
James, Graeme L. Geometrical theory of diffraction for electromagnetic waves / [by] Graeme L. James. — Stevenage : Peregrinus [for] the Institution of Electrical Engineers, 1976. — viii,253p : ill ; 23cm. — (Institution of Electrical Engineers. IEE electromagnetic waves series ; 1)
Bibl. — Index.
ISBN 0-901223-83-2 : £13.50
(B77-01421)

537.5'352 — In-beam gamma-ray spectroscopy
Morinaga, H. In-beam gamma-ray spectroscopy / [by] H. Morinaga, T. Yamazaki. — Amsterdam [etc.] ; Oxford : North-Holland Publishing Co., 1976. — xiv,527p : ill ; 23cm.
Bibl. — Index.
ISBN 0-7204-0297-2 : £35.13
(B77-16366)

537.5'352 — Spectroscopy. Mössbauer effect. Methodology. *Conference proceedings*
Mössbauer effect methodology. — New York ; London : Plenum Press.
Vol.5 : Proceedings of the Fifth Symposium on Mössbauer Effect Methodology, New York City, February 2, 1969 / edited by Irwin J. Gruverman. — 1970 [i.e. 1976]. — viii,278p : ill ; 24cm.
'A Publication of the New England Nuclear Corporation'. — Published in the United States: 1970. — Index.
ISBN 0-306-38805-7 : £17.33
(B77-03527)

Vol.6 : Proceedings of the Sixth Symposium on Mössbauer Effect Methodology, New York City, January 25, 1970 / edited by Irwin J. Gruverman. — 1971 [i.e. 1976]. — viii,237p : ill ; 24cm.
'A Publication of the New England Nuclear Corporation'. — Published in the United States: 1971. — Index.
ISBN 0-306-38806-5 : £17.33
(B77-03528)

Vol.7 : Proceedings of the Seventh Symposium on Mössbauer Effect Methodology, New York City, January 31, 1971 / edited by Irwin J. Gruverman. — 1971 [i.e. 1976]. — xii,308p : ill ; 24cm.
'A Publication of the New England Nuclear Corporation'. — Published in the United States: 1971.
ISBN 0-306-38807-3 : £17.33
(B77-03529)

Vol.8 : Proceedings of the Eighth Symposium on Mössbauer Effect Methodology, New York City, January 28, 1973 / edited by Irwin J. Gruverman and Carl W. Seidel. — [1976]. — xii,281p : ill ; 24cm.
'A Publication of the New England Nuclear Corporation'. — Published in the United States: 1973. — Index.
ISBN 0-306-38808-1 : £17.33
(B77-03530)

537.5'4 — Photoconductivity
Photoconductivity and related phenomena / edited by J. Mort and D.M. Pai. — Amsterdam ; Oxford [etc.] : Elsevier, 1976. — xiii,502p : ill ; 25cm.
Index.
ISBN 0-444-41463-0 : £36.30
(B77-16367)

537.5'6 — Materials. Effects of ion beams. *Conference proceedings*
International Conference on Applications of Ion Beams to Materials, *University of Warwick, 1975.* Applications of ion beams to materials : invited and contributed papers from the International Conference on Applications of Ion Beams to Materials, held at the University of Warwick, 8-12 September 1975 / edited by G. Carter, J.S. Colligon and W.A. Grant. — London [etc.] : Institute of Physics, 1976. — xi, 364p : ill ; 24cm. — (Institute of Physics. Conference series ; no.28 ISSN 0305-4632)
Bibl. — Index.
ISBN 0-85498-118-7 : £19.00
(B77-01422)

537.6 — ELECTRIC CURRENTS
537.6'22 — Gallium arsenide semiconductors. *Conference proceedings*
International Symposium on Gallium Arsenide and Related Compounds, *6th, Edinburgh and St Louis, 1976.* Gallium arsenide and related compounds (Edinburgh), 1976 : proceedings of the Sixth International Symposium on Gallium Arsenide and Related Compounds, Edinburgh Conference, 20-22 September 1976 / edited by C. Hilsum. — Bristol [etc.] : Institute of Physics, 1977. — x,438p : ill ; 24cm. — (Institute of Physics. Conference series ; no.33a ISSN 0305-2346)
Bibl. — Index.
ISBN 0-85498-123-3 : £20.00 : CIP rev.
(B77-07333)

International Symposium on Gallium Arsenide and Related Compounds, *6th, Edinburgh and St Louis, 1976.* Gallium arsenide and related compounds (St Louis) 1976 : proceedings of the Sixth International Symposium on Gallium Arsenide and Related Compounds, St Louis Conference, 26-29 September 1976 / edited by Lester F. Eastman. — Bristol [etc.] : Institute of Physics, 1977. — x,358p : ill ; 24cm. — (Institute of Physics. Conference series ; no.33b ISSN 0305-2346)
Bibl. — Index.
ISBN 0-85498-124-1 : £18.00 : CIP rev.
(B77-07334)

537.6'22 — Narrow bandgap semiconductors. Preparation & properties
Lovett, D R. Semimetals & narrow-bandgap semiconductors / [by] D.R. Lovett. — London : Pion, 1977. — [4],viii,256p : ill ; 24cm. — (Applied physics series ; 10)
Bibl. — Index.
ISBN 0-85086-060-1 : £8.50
Primary classification 530.4'1
(B77-21102)

537.6'22 — Semiconductors. Domains
Bonch-Bruevich, V L. Domain electrical instabilities in semiconductors / [by] V.L. Bonch-Bruevich, I.P. Zvyagin and A.C. Mironov ; translated from Russian by Albin Tybulewicz. — New York ; London (8 Scrubs La., Harlesden, NW10 6SE) : Consultants Bureau, [1976]. — x,398p : ill ; 24cm. — (Studies in Soviet science : physical sciences)
This translation published in the United States: 1975. — Translation of 'Domennaia ėlektricheskaia neustoĭchivost' v poluprovodnikakh'. Moskva : Nauka, 1972.
ISBN 0-306-10911-5 : £22.63
(B77-07335)

537.6'22 — Semiconductors. Effects of radiation. *Conference proceedings*
International Conference on Radiation Effects in Semiconductors, *Dubrovnik, 1976.* Radiation effects in semiconductors, 1976 : invited and contributed papers from the International Conference on Radiation Effects in Semiconductors held in Dubrovnik, 6-9 September 1976 / edited by N.B. Urli and J.W. Corbett. — Bristol [etc.] : Institute of Physics, 1977. — xii,534p : ill ; 24cm. — (Institute of Physics. Conference series ; no.31 ISSN 0305-2346)
Bibl. — Index.
ISBN 0-85498-121-7 : £22.00 : CIP rev.
(B77-06664)

537.6'22 — Semiconductors. Optical properties
Pankove, Jacques I. Optical processes in semiconductors / [by] Jacques I. Pankove. — New York : Dover Publications [etc.] ; London : Constable, 1975 [i.e. 1976]. — iii-xix, 422p : ill ; 21cm.
Originally published: Englewood Cliffs ; London : Prentice-Hall, 1971. — Index.
ISBN 0-486-60275-3 Pbk : £4.15
(B77-05392)

537.6'22 — Semiconductors. Physical properties. *Conference proceedings*
Physics of semiconductors : proceedings of the 13th International Conference, Rome, August 30-September 3, 1976 / editor F.G. Fumi. — Amsterdam [etc.] ; Oxford : North-Holland Publishing Co., 1976. — xiii,1328p : ill ; 25cm.
Index.
ISBN 0-7204-0571-8 : £58.55
(B77-15833)

537.6'22 — Semiconductors. Structure & physical properties
Fraser, D A. The physics of semi-conductor devices / [by] D.A. Fraser. — Oxford : Clarendon Press, 1977. — ix,149p : ill ; 23cm. — (Oxford physics series ; 16)
With answers to selected problems. — Bibl.: p.145. — Index.
ISBN 0-19-851826-9 : £5.95
ISBN 0-19-851827-7 Pbk : £2.95
(B77-30231)

537.6'22 — Semiconductors. Surfaces. Electronic properties. *Conference proceedings*
International Conference on the Electronic Properties of Quasi-Two-Dimensional Systems, *Brown University, 1976.* Electronic properties of quasi-two-dimensional systems : proceedings of the International Conference on the Electronic Properties of Quasi-Two-Dimensional Systems, Brown University, Providence, RI, USA, 24-28 August, 1976 / guest editors John J. Quinn and Phillip J. Stiles. — Amsterdam [etc.] ; Oxford : North-Holland Publishing Co., 1976. — iii-xi,353p : ill ; 25cm.
'Reprinted from: "Surface Science" 58 (1976)' - title page verso. — Index.
ISBN 0-7204-0503-3 : £31.71
(B77-07336)

537.6'22 — Semiconductors. Tunnelling. Theories
Roy, D K. Tunnelling and negative resistance phenomena in semiconductors / by D.K. Roy ; edited by B.R. Pamplin. — Oxford [etc.] : Pergamon Press, 1977. — xv,213p : ill ; 26cm. — (International series in the science of the solid state ; vol.11)
Bibl.: p.177-209. — Index.
ISBN 0-08-021044-9 : £9.75
Primary classification 621.3815'22
(B77-15326)

537.6'23 — Superionic conductors. *Conference proceedings*
Conference on Supersonic Conductors : Chemistry, Physics, and Applications, *General Electric Research and Development Center, 1976.* Superionic conductors / edited by Gerald D. Mahan and Walter L. Roth. — New York ; London : Plenum Press, 1976. — xvii,438p : ill ; 24cm. — (Physics of solids and liquids)
'Proceedings of a Conference on Superionic Conductors : Chemistry, Physics, and Applications held at the General Electric Research and Development Center, Schenectady, New York, May 10-12, 1976' - title page verso. — Index.
ISBN 0-306-30975-0 : £24.89
(B77-26290)

538 — MAGNETISM
Turnbull, Kenneth Denham. The alignment pattern : a new basic theory of electricity and magnetism / [by] K.D. Turnbull. — Ilfracombe : Stockwell, 1977. — 44p : ill ; 19cm.
ISBN 0-7223-1028-5 Pbk : £1.00
Primary classification 537
(B77-24915)

538 — Magnetism. *Conference proceedings*
International Conference on Magnetism, *Amsterdam, 1976.* Proceedings of the International Conference on Magnetism, ICM '76, Amsterdam, the Netherlands, September 6-10, 1976 / editors P.F. de Châtel and J.J.M. Franse. — Amsterdam [etc.] ; Oxford : North-Holland Publishing Co., 1977. — 3v. ([28],1502p) : ill, map ; 27cm.
'Reprinted from "Physica" Volumes 86-88 B + C ...' - title page verso. — Bibl. — Index.
£95.00
(B77-25604)

Proceedings of the 1976 Arbeitsgemeinschaft Magnetismus Conference, 23-25 March 1976, Bad Nauheim, Germany / editors A.J. Freeman, Karl Schüler. — Amsterdam ; Oxford [etc.] : North-Holland Publishing Co., 1977. — viii,381p : ill ; 27cm.
English and German papers and summaries. — 'Reprinted from "Journal of magnetism and magnetic materials" vol.4, nos 1-4' - title page verso. — Index.
ISBN 0-7204-0576-9 : £46.84
(B77-16368)

538'.05 — Magnetism. *Periodicals*
Magnetism letters : an international journal. — New York ; London [etc.] : Gordon and Breach.
Vol.1, no.1- ; Aug. 1976-. — 1976-. — ill ; 23cm.
Six issues a year. — [2],32p. in 1st issue.
Sd : £39.00 yearly
ISSN 0308-6011
(B77-03531)

538'.3 — Magneto-optics. *Conference proceedings*
International Conference on Magneto-Optics, *Zürich, 1976.* Proceedings of the International Conference on Magneto-Optics, Zürich, September 1-3, 1976 / editor P. Wachter. — Amsterdam [etc.] ; Oxford : North-Holland Publishing, 1977. — ix,301p : ill ; 27cm.
Index.
ISBN 0-7204-0737-0 : Unpriced
(B77-26291)

538'.3 — Nuclear magnetic resonance spectroscopy. Applications of Fourier transforms
Müllen, K. Fourier transform NMR techniques : a practical approach / [by] K. Müllen, P.S. Pregosin. — London [etc.] : Academic Press, 1976. — x,149p : ill ; 24cm.
With answers. — Index.
ISBN 0-12-510450-2 : £6.80
(B77-08995)

Shaw, Derek, *b.1940.* Fourier transform NMR spectroscopy / [by] Derek Shaw. — Amsterdam ; Oxford [etc.] : Elsevier, 1976. — xvii,357p : ill, port ; 24cm.
Index.
ISBN 0-444-41466-5 : £30.05
(B77-04789)

538'.4 — Metals & metal compounds. Magnetism. *Conference proceedings*
Winter School of Theoretical Physics, *11th, Karpacz, 1974.* Magnetism in metals and metallic compounds / edited by Jan T. Lopuszański, Andrzej Pekalski and Jerzy Przystawa. — New York ; London : Plenum Press, 1976. — xiii,626p : ill ; 26cm.
'Proceedings of the 11th Winter School of Theoretical Physics organized by the University of Wroclaw and held at Karpacz, Poland, February 19-March 4, 1974' - title page verso. — Index.
ISBN 0-306-30865-7 : £31.19
(B77-18118)

538'.42 — Molecules. Diamagnetism
Theory and applications of molecular diamagnetism / [edited by] L.N. Mulay, E.A. Boudreaux. — New York ; London [etc.] : Wiley, 1976. — xiii,321p : ill ; 24cm.
'A Wiley-Interscience publication'. — Index.
ISBN 0-471-62358-x : £23.45
(B77-26292)

538.7 — GEOMAGNETISM AND RELATED PHENOMENA

538'.78'0285424 — Geomagnetic fields. Surveying. Applications of programs written in Basic language

McCann, Clive. The collection and reduction of gravity and magnetic survey data / by C. McCann. — Reading (c/o Assistant Librarian, Whiteknights, Reading RG6 2AB) : Geology Department, University of Reading, 1976. — [3],49p,plate : ill, form ; 30cm. — (University of Reading. Department of Geology. Geological reports ; no.8) (Computer-based packages for teaching earth science report ; no.2)
Bibl.
ISBN 0-7049-0278-8 Sp : £0.75
Primary classification 526'.7'0285424
(B77-10351)

539 — MODERN PHYSICS

Calder, Nigel. The key to the universe : a report on the new physics / [by] Nigel Calder. — London : British Broadcasting Corporation, 1977. — 196p : ill(some col), ports ; 27cm.
'The television programme, "The Key to the Universe", was first transmitted on BBC2 on 27 January, 1977' - title page verso. — Bibl.: p.193. — Index.
ISBN 0-563-17091-3 : £5.95
(B77-22549)

Thomas, Edward John. From quarks to quasars : an outline of modern physics / by Edward Thomas. — London : Athlone Press, 1977. — ix,294p : ill ; 22cm.
Index.
ISBN 0-485-12024-0 Pbk : £3.95
(B77-13020)

Young, Hugh David. Fundamentals of waves, optics and modern physics / [by] Hugh D. Young. — 2nd ed. — New York ; London [etc.] : McGraw-Hill, 1976. — xix,549p,[3]p of plates : ill(some col) ; 25cm. — (McGraw-Hill series in fundamentals of physics)
With answers to odd-numbered problems. — Text on lining papers. — Previous ed.: published as 'Fundamentals of optics and modern physics'. 1968. — Index.
ISBN 0-07-072521-7 : £12.85
(B77-04143)

539 — Atoms & molecules. Structure. *Reviews of research*

Advances in atomic and molecular physics. — New York [etc.] ; London : Academic Press.
Vol.12 / edited by D.R. Bates, Benjamin Bederson. — 1976 [i.e. 1977]. — xi,440p : ill ; 24cm.
Published in the United States: 1976. — Bibl. — Index.
ISBN 0-12-003812-9 : £31.25
(B77-08996)

539 — Modern physics. *Festschriften*

Rudolf Peierls and theoretical physics : proceedings of the symposium held in Oxford on July 11th & 12th 1974, to mark the occasion of the retirement of Professor Sir Rudolf E. Peierls, FRS, CBE / edited by I.J.R. Aitchison and J.E. Paton. — Oxford [etc.] : Pergamon, 1977. — vii,119p,plate : 1 ill, ports ; 26cm. — (Progress in nuclear physics ; vol.13)
ISBN 0-08-020606-9 : £15.00
ISBN 0-08-021621-8 Pbk : £5.00
(B77-15275)

539.1 — STRUCTURE OF MATTER

539'.12'0151222 — Molecules. Structure. Determination. Applications of group theory

Ferraro, John Ralph. Introductory group theory and its application to molecular structure / [by] John R. Ferraro and Joseph S. Ziomek. — 2nd ed. — New York ; London : Plenum Press, [1976]. — xv,292p : ill ; 24cm.
This ed. published in the United States: 1975. — Previous ed.: New York : Plenum Press, 1969. — Bibl. — Index.
ISBN 0-306-30768-5 : £12.60
(B77-06058)

539.2 — RADIATION

539.2'05 — Radiation. *Periodicals*

Radiation physics and chemistry. — Oxford [etc.] : Pergamon.
Continues: International journal for radiation physics and chemistry.
Vol.9, no.1- ; 1977-. — 1977. — ill ; 25cm.
Six issues a year. — Cover title. — [1],xx,401p. in Vol.9, nos 1-3. — Bibl.
Pbk : Unpriced
ISSN 0146-5724
(B77-18119)

539.2'092'4 — Radiation. Theories of Planck, Max, 1880-1901

Kangro, Hans. Early history of Planck's radiation law / [by] Hans Kangro ; [translated from the German by R.E.W. Maddison in collaboration with the author]. — London : Taylor and Francis, 1976. — xvii,282p : ill ; 26cm.
Translation of: 'Vorgeschichte des Planckschen Stahlungsgesetzes'. Wiesbaden : F. Steiner, 1970. — Bibl.: p.245-265. — Index.
ISBN 0-85066-063-7 : £25.00
(B77-00206)

539.6 — MOLECULAR PHYSICS

539'.6 — Molecules. Relaxation processes. *Conference proceedings*

Symposium on Newer Aspects of Molecular Relaxation Processes, *London, 1976.* Newer aspects of molecular relaxation processes. — London : Faraday Division, Chemical Society, 1977. — 180p : ill ; 26cm. — (Faraday Society. Symposia ; no.11 ISSN 0301-5696)
'A Symposium on Newer Aspects of Molecular Relaxation Processes was held in the Royal Institution, London on 13th and 14th December 1976' - p.3.
ISBN 0-85186-928-9 Pbk : £11.00
(B77-30232)

539.6 — Small molecules. Electrons. Correlations

Hurley, A C. Electron correlation in small molecules / [by] A.C. Hurley. — London [etc.] : Academic Press, 1976. — viii,276p : ill ; 24cm. — (Theoretical chemistry ; vol.6)
Index.
ISBN 0-12-362450-9 : £10.50
(B77-09683)

539.6 — Small molecules. Electrons. Theories

Hurley, A C. Introduction to the electron theory of small molecules / [by] A.C. Hurley. — London [etc.] : Academic Press, 1976. — x, 329p : ill ; 24cm.
Index.
ISBN 0-12-362460-6 : £12.00
(B77-09684)

539.7 — NUCLEAR PHYSICS

Burge, Edward James. Atomic nuclei and their particles / [by] E.J. Burge. — Oxford : Clarendon Press, 1977. — [10],194p : ill ; 23cm. — (Oxford physics series ; 13)
With answers to numerical problems. — Index.
ISBN 0-19-851834-x : £6.00
ISBN 0-19-851835-8 Pbk : £3.25
(B77-31174)

539.7 — Atoms & ions. Physical properties. *Tables*

Fraga, Serafin. Handbook of atomic data / [by] Serafin Fraga, Jacek Karwowski, K.M.S. Saxena. — Amsterdam ; Oxford [etc.] : Elsevier, 1976. — [8],551p : ill ; 25cm.
Bibl.: p.535-545. — Index.
ISBN 0-444-41461-4 : £31.16
(B77-03532)

539.7 — Nuclear physics. *Conference proceedings*

International School of Physics 'Enrico Fermi', *53rd, Varenna, 1971.* Developments and borderlines of nuclear physics : proceedings of the International School of Physics 'Enrico Fermi', course LIII, Varenna on Lake Como, Villa Monastero, 19th-31st July 1971 / edited by H. Morinaga. — New York ; London : Academic Press, 1972. — ii-xi,214p,[2]leaves of plates : ill, ports ; 25cm.
At head of title: Italian Physical Society. — Second title page in Italian. — Cover title: Sviluppi e limiti della fisica nucleare.
ISBN 0-12-368853-1 : £14.90
(B77-23381)

539.7 — Nuclear physics. *Festschriften*

Atomic processes and applications : in honour of David R. Bates' 60th birthday / edited by P.G. Burke and B.L. Moiseiwitsch. — Amsterdam [etc.] ; Oxford : North-Holland Publishing Co., 1976. — x,533p : ill, port ; 23cm.
Bibl. — Index.
ISBN 0-7204-0444-4 : £38.64
(B77-16868)

539.7'07'2 — Nuclear physics. Research organisations. *Directories*

Nuclear research index : (incorporating 'World nuclear directory') : a guide to world nuclear research. — 5th ed. / advisory editor Ales I. Fort ; editor Ann Pernet. — [St Peter Port] : Hodgson, 1976. — 682p ; 26cm.
Previous ed.: published as 'World nuclear directory'. London : Harrap, 1970. — Index.
ISBN 0-85280-151-3 : Unpriced
(B77-23382)

539.7'07'2042579 — Nuclear physics laboratories. *Oxfordshire. Chilton. Rutherford Laboratory. Reports, surveys. Serials*

Rutherford Laboratory. The work of the Rutherford Laboratory. — Didcot (Rutherford Laboratory, Chilton, Didcot, Oxon. OX11 0QX) : Science Research Council.
1976 / edited by Gordon Fraser ; compiled by the Laboratory Information Panel. — 1977. — xi,127p : ill, plans ; 30cm.
Pbk : Unpriced
(B77-26293)

539.7'07'2042718 — Nuclear physics laboratories. *Cheshire. Daresbury. Daresbury Nuclear Physics Laboratory. Reports, surveys. Serials*

Daresbury Nuclear Physics Laboratory. Daresbury / [Daresbury Nuclear Physics Laboratory]. — Daresbury (Daresbury, Warrington WA4 4AD) : The Laboratory.
1976. — 1977. — [4],60p : ill ; 30cm.
Bibl.: p.55-60.
Pbk : Unpriced
ISSN 0307-7993
(B77-27047)

539.7'2 — Charged particles. Beams

Lawson, J D. The physics of charged-particle beams / by J.D. Lawson. — Oxford : Clarendon Press, 1977. — xxi,462p : ill ; 24cm. — (The international series of monographs on physics)
Bibl.: p.436-455. — Index.
ISBN 0-19-851278-3 : £16.50
(B77-30233)

539.7'2 — High energy physics

Proceedings of the school for young high energy physicists, Rutherford Laboratory, September 6-24 1976 / editor P.G. Murphy. — Didcot (Chilton, Didcot, Oxon. OX11 0QX) : Science Research Council, Rutherford Laboratory, 1977. — [7],459 columns in various pagings : ill ; 21x30cm. — (RL ; 76-120)
Bibl.
Sd : Unpriced
(B77-18742)

539.7'21 — Elementary particles. *Conference proceedings*

Brentwood Summer Institute on Nuclear and Particle Physics at Intermediate Energies, *1975.* Nuclear and particle physics at intermediate energies / edited by J.B. Warren. — New York ; London : Plenum Press [for the] NATO Scientific Affairs Division, 1976. — viii,608p : ill ; 26cm. — (NATO Advanced Study Institutes : series B, physics ; vol.15)
'Lectures presented at the Brentwood Summer Institute on Nuclear and Particle Physics at Intermediate Energies held at Brentwood College, Victoria, Canada, June 23-July 2, 1975' - title page verso. — Index.
ISBN 0-306-35715-1 : £31.19
(B77-17474)

Methods in subnuclear physics. — New York [etc.] ; London : Gordon and Breach.
Vol.5 : Proceedings of the International School of Elementary Particle Physics, Herceg-Novi (Yugoslavia) / edited by M. Nikolić. — 1977. — 2v.(vii,496p;vii,364p) : ill ; 24cm.
'The fifth session of the International School of Elementary Particle Physics took place at Herceg Novi from September 15 to 28, 1969' - Foreword.
ISBN 0-677-15910-2 : £73.30
(B77-30234)

539.7'21 — High energy particles. *Conference proceedings*

Orbis Scientiae *(Conference), 2nd, University of Miami, 1975.* Theories and experiments in high-energy physics / ... editors Arnold Perlmutter, Susan M. Widmayer ... — New York ; London : Plenum Press, [1976]. — ix, 486p : ill ; 26cm. — (Studies in the natural sciences ; vol.9)
'Part of the Proceedings of Orbis Scientiae held by the Center for Theoretical Studies, University of Miami, January 20-24, 1975' - title page verso. — Published in the United States: 1975. — Index.
ISBN 0-306-36909-5 : £24.89
(B77-03533)

539.7'2112 — Electron spectroscopy. *Reviews of research*

Electron spectroscopy : theory, techniques and applications / edited by C.R. Brundle and A.D. Baker. — London [etc.] : Academic Press.
Vol.1. — 1977. — xv,459p : ill ; 24cm.
Index.
ISBN 0-12-137801-2 : £24.00
(B77-22550)

539.7'216 — Hadrons. Interactions. Regge theory
Collins, P D B. An introduction to Regge theory & high energy physics / [by] P.D.B. Collins. — Cambridge [etc.] : Cambridge University Press, 1977. — xiii,445p : ill ; 24cm. — (Cambridge monographs on mathematical physics ; [4])
Bibl.: p.430-439. — Index.
ISBN 0-521-21245-6 : £29.00
(B77-18743)

539.7'216 — Quarks. *Conference proceedings*
Quark Binding *(Conference), University of Rochester, 1976.* Quark confinement and field theory : proceedings of a conference at the University of Rochester, Rochester, New York, June 14-18, 1976 / edited by D.R. Stump, D.H. Weingarten. — New York ; London [etc.] : Wiley, 1977. — ix,253p : ill ; 24cm.
'A Wiley-Interscience publication'. — 'During the week of June 14, 1976 a workshop on quark binding was held at the University of Rochester ... The title, "Quark Binding" was chosen ... ' - Preface.
ISBN 0-471-02721-9 : £18.70
Also classified at 530.1'5
(B77-28591)

539.7'2164 — Baryon resonance spectroscopy. *Conference proceedings*
Topical Conference on Baryon Resonances, *Oxford, 1976.* Proceedings of the Topical Conference on Baryon Resonances, St Catherine's College, Oxford, 5th to 9th July 1976 : ... organised by Rutherford Laboratory ... / editors R.T. Ross, D.H. Saxon. — Didcot (Chilton, Didcot, Oxon. OX11 0QX) : Rutherford Laboratory, [1976]. — [7],526p : ill, port ; 21x30cm.
ISBN 0-902376-41-1 Pbk : £6.00
(B77-06059)

539.7'222 — X-rays. *Questions and answers*
Bushong, Stewart Carlyle. Radiologic science : workbook and laboratory manual / [by] Stewart C. Bushong. — Saint Louis : Mosby ; London : Distributed by Kimpton, 1977. — xi,202p : ill ; 28cm.
Pages perforated at inside edge and pierced for binder.
ISBN 0-8016-0925-9 Pbk : Unpriced
(B77-31175)

539.7'3 — Ion accelerators. Applications
New uses of ion accelerators / edited by James F. Ziegler. — New York ; London : Plenum Press, [1976]. — xiii,482p : ill ; 26cm.
Published in the United States: 1975. — Index.
ISBN 0-306-30853-3 : £17.64
(B77-04144)

539.7'4 — Atoms. Nuclei. Structure
Eisenberg, Judah Moshe. Nuclear theory / [by] Judah M. Eisenberg, Walter Greiner. — [2nd ed.]. — Amsterdam [etc.] ; Oxford : North-Holland Publishing Co.
In 3 vols.
Vol.3 : Microscopic theory of the nucleus. — 1976. — xv,519p : ill ; 23cm.
Previous ed.: 1972. — Bibl.: p.493-508. — Index.
ISBN 0-7204-0484-3 Pbk : £18.29
(B77-05393)

Eisenberg, Judah Moshe. Nuclear theory / [by] Judah M. Eisenberg, Walter Greiner. — Amsterdam [etc.] ; Oxford : North-Holland Publishing Co.
In 3 vols.
Vol.2 : Excitation mechanisms of the nucleus. — 2nd, revised ed. — 1976. — xiii,421p : ill ; 23cm.
Previous ed.: 1970. — Bibl.: p.401-414. — Index.
ISBN 0-7204-0483-5 Pbk : £17.50
(B77-02987)

539.7'4 — Atoms. Nuclei. Structure & properties
Barrett, Roger C. Nuclear sizes and structure / by Roger C. Barrett and Daphne F. Jackson. — Oxford : Clarendon Press, 1977. — x,566p : ill ; 25cm. — (The international series of monographs on physics)
Bibl.: p.515-559. — Index.
ISBN 0-19-851272-4 : £17.50
(B77-31176)

Towner, I S. A shell model description of light nuclei / [by] I.S. Towner. — Oxford : Clarendon Press, 1977. — x,383p : ill ; 25cm. — (Oxford studies in nuclear physics)
Bibl.: p.371-379. — Index.
ISBN 0-19-851508-1 : £11.00
(B77-23383)

Wildermuth, K. A unified theory of the nucleus / [by] K. Wildermuth, Y.C. Tang. — New York [etc.] ; London : Academic Press, 1977. — x, 389p : ill ; 24cm.
Bibl.: p.377-387. — Index.
ISBN 0-12-751950-5 : £27.35
(B77-21106)

539.7'44 — Nuclear spectroscopy
Nuclear spectroscopy and reactions / edited by Joseph Cerny. — New York ; London : Academic Press.
In 4 parts.
Part C. — 1974. — xvi,590p : ill ; 24cm. — (Pure and applied physics ; vol.40-C)
Bibl. — Index.
ISBN 0-12-165203-3 : Unpriced
Also classified at 539.7'5
(B77-18744)

539.7'5 — Nuclear reactions
Nuclear spectroscopy and reactions / edited by Joseph Cerny. — New York ; London : Academic Press.
In 4 parts.
Part C. — 1974. — xvi,590p : ill ; 24cm. — (Pure and applied physics ; vol.40-C)
Bibl. — Index.
ISBN 0-12-165203-3 : Unpriced
Primary classification 539.7'44
(B77-18744)

539.7'54 — Elementary particles. Interactions. *Conference proceedings*
NATO Advanced Study Institute on Photoionization and Other Probes of Many-Electron Interactions, *Carry-le-Rouet, 1975.* Photoionization and other probes of many-electron interactions / edited by F.J. Wuilleumier. — New York ; London : Plenum Press [for] NATO Scientific Affairs Division, 1976. — xv,472p : ill ; 26cm. — (NATO Advanced Study Institutes : series B, physics ; vol.18)
'Proceedings of the NATO Advanced Study Institute on Photoionization and Other Probes of Many-Electron Interactions held at the Centre "Les Cigales" in Carry-le-Rouet, France, August 31-September 13, 1975' - title page verso. — Index.
ISBN 0-306-35718-6 : £28.35
(B77-17475)

539.7'54 — Elementary particles. Weak interactions
Bailin, David. Weak interactions / [by] David Bailin. — London : Chatto and Windus for Sussex University Press, 1977. — ix,406p ; 24cm. — (Graduate student series in physics)
Index.
ISBN 0-85621-023-4 Pbk : £9.00 : CIP rev.
(B77-08997)

539.7'54 — High energy particles. Interactions. *Conference proceedings*
Cargèse Summer Institute on Weak and Electromagnetic Interactions at High Energies, *1975.* Weak and electromagnetic interactions at high energies, Cargèse, 1975 / edited by Maurice Lévy ... [et al.]. — New York ; London : Plenum Press [for] NATO Scientific Affairs Division. — (NATO Advanced Study Institutes : series B, physics ; vol.13)
'The Cargèse Summer Institute 1975 on Weak and Electromagnetic Interactions at High Energies ... held at Cargèse [June 30-July 25]' - Preface. — In 2 vols.
Part A. — 1976. — xi,467p : ill ; 26cm.
Index.
ISBN 0-306-35795-x : £24.89
(B77-17476)

539.7'54 — Solids. Nuclear tracks. Detection. *Periodicals*
Nuclear track detection. — Oxford [etc.] : Pergamon.
Vol.1, no.1- ; 1977-. — 1977-. — ill ; 25cm.
Quarterly. — [2],84p. in 1st issue. — Bibl.
Pbk : Unpriced
ISSN 0145-224x
(B77-15835)

539.7'7 — Ionising radiation. Detectors
Ouseph, P J. Introduction to nuclear radiation detectors / [by] P.J. Ouseph. — New York ; London : Plenum Press, [1976]. — xii,194p : ill ; 24cm. — (Laboratory instrumentation and techniques ; vol.2)
Published in the United States: 1975. — Bibl. — Index.
ISBN 0-306-35302-4 : £11.66
(B77-01423)

539.7'75 — Ionising radiation. Measurement. Use of liquid scintillation counters. *Conference proceedings*
Liquid scintillation counting. — London [etc.] : Heyden.
Vol.4 : Proceedings of a symposium on liquid scintillation counting organised by Radiochemical Methods Group (Analytical Division, The Chemical Society) Bath, England, September 16-19, 1975 / editors M.A. Crook, P. Johnson. — 1977. — ix,269p : ill ; 27cm.
Index.
ISBN 0-85501-209-9 : £16.00
(B77-21107)

539.7'75 — Liquid scintillation counters. *Conference proceedings*
International Conference on Liquid Scintillation : Science and Technology, *Banff Centre, Alta, 1976.* Liquid scintillation : science and technology / edited by A.A. Noujaim, C. Ediss, L.I. Weibe. — New York [etc.] ; London : Academic Press, 1976. — xiv,352p : ill ; 24cm.
'Proceedings of the International Conference on Liquid Scintillation : Science and Technology held at the Banff Centre in Alberta, Canada on June 14-17, 1976' - half title page verso. — 'Academic Press Rapid Manuscript Reproduction'. — Index.
ISBN 0-12-522350-1 : £12.40
(B77-08360)

540 — CHEMISTRY (INCLUDING CRYSTALLOGRAPHY, MINERALOGY)
540 — Chemistry
Amend, John R. Introductory chemistry : models and basic concepts / [by] John R. Amend. — New York ; London [etc.] : Wiley, 1977. — xvii,470p : ill(chiefly col), 2 col maps ; 24cm.
Text on lining papers. — With answers to odd-numbered problems. — Index.
ISBN 0-471-02533-x : £9.70
(B77-18120)

Bloomfield, Molly M. Chemistry and the living organism / [by] Molly M. Bloomfield. — New York ; London [etc.] : Wiley, 1977. — [7], 536p : ill(chiefly col), ports ; 26cm.
Text on lining papers. — Bibl. — Index.
ISBN 0-471-08255-4 : £9.35
(B77-21843)

Brown, Theodore Lawrence. Chemistry, the central science / [by] Theodore L. Brown, H. Eugene LeMay, Jr. — Englewood Cliffs ; London [etc.] : Prentice-Hall, 1977. — xvi, 815p : ill(chiefly col), ports ; 26cm.
With answers to selected exercises. — Text on lining papers. — Index.
ISBN 0-13-128769-9 : £12.75
(B77-23384)

Chadwick, Thomas Fowler. Chemistry : a modern introduction for sixth forms and colleges / [by] T.F. Chadwick. — 2nd ed. — London : Allen and Unwin.
In 3 vols.
Part 1 : General and inorganic chemistry. — 1977. — 214p : ill ; 22cm.
Previous ed.: 1971. — Bibl.: p.207. — Index.
ISBN 0-04-546003-5 Pbk : £2.95
(B77-13021)

Part 2 : Organic chemistry. — 1977. — 175p : ill ; 22cm.
Previous ed.: 1971. — Bibl.: p.170. — Index.
ISBN 0-04-547003-0 Pbk : £2.95
(B77-13022)

Part 3 : Physical chemistry. — 1977. — 266p : ill ; 22cm.
With answers to exercises. — Previous ed.: 1972. — Bibl.: p.251. — Index.
ISBN 0-04-541004-6 Pbk : £3.25
(B77-13023)

Chemistry, man and society / [by] Mark M. Jones ... [et al.]. — 2nd ed. — Philadelphia ; London [etc.] : Saunders, 1976. — 774p in various pagings : ill(some col), facsims, forms, col map, ports(some col) ; 28cm. — (Saunders golden sunburst series)
Text, ill. on lining papers. — With answers to self tests. — Previous ed.: 1972. — Bibl. — Index.
ISBN 0-7216-5220-4 : £11.75
(B77-01424)

Keenan, Charles William. General college chemistry. — 5th ed. / [by] Charles W. Keenan, Jesse H. Wood and Donald C. Kleinfelter. — New York [etc.] ; London : Harper and Row, 1976. — xiv,754p,[8]p of plates : ill(chiefly col) ; 27cm.
With answers. — Previous ed.: / by Charles W. Keenan and Jesse H. Wood. 1971. — Bibl. — Index.
ISBN 0-06-043613-1 Pbk : £6.50
(B77-04790)

King, George Brooks. College chemistry / [by] G. Brooks King, William E. Caldwell, Max B. Williams. — 7th ed. — New York ; London [etc.] : D. Van Nostrand, 1977. — xiii,804p : ill(chiefly col) ; 25cm.
Text on lining papers. — With answers to numerical problems. — Previous ed.: New York : Van Nostrand Reinhold, 1972. — Bibl. — Index.
ISBN 0-442-24417-7 : £12.50
(B77-24916)

Lippincott, William Thomas. Chemistry : a study of matter. — 3rd ed. / [by] W.T. Lippincott, Alfred B. Garrett, Frank Henry Verhoek. — New York [etc.] ; London : Wiley, 1977. — xvii,761p : ill(chiefly col) ; 26cm.
With answers. — Col. ill., text on lining papers. — Previous ed.: / by Alfred B. Garrett, W.T. Lippincott, Frank Henry Verhoek. Lexington : Xerox College Pub., 1972. — Bibl. — Index.
ISBN 0-471-29246-x : Unpriced
(B77-21844)

Long, M J. Fundamental chemistry : a revision book for First Certificate / [by] M.J. Long and J.H. White. — London : Heinemann Educational, 1977. — viii,255p : ill ; 23cm.
Index.
ISBN 0-435-64520-x Pbk : £1.60
(B77-29410)

Masterton, William Lewis. Chemical principles / [by] William L. Masterton, Emil J. Slowinski. — 4th ed. / illustrated by George Kelvin. — Philadelphia ; London [etc.] : Saunders, 1977. — ii-xv,636,52,xx p,12p of plates : ill(some col) ; 28cm. — (Saunders golden sunburst series)
Text on lining papers. — With answers. — Previous ed.: 1973. — Index.
ISBN 0-7216-6173-4 : £9.50
(B77-24204)

Masterton, William Lewis. Chemical principles / [by] William L. Masterton, Emil J. Slowinski. — 4th ed. / illustrated by George Kelvin. — Philadelphia ; London [etc.] : Saunders. — (Saunders golden sunburst series)
Previous ed.: 1973.
Student's guide. — 3rd ed. / [by] Ray Boyington, William L. Masterton. — 1977. — xi,348p : ill ; 25cm.
With answers. — Previous ed.: 1975. — Bibl.
ISBN 0-7216-1902-9 Pbk : £5.00
(B77-24205)

Mortimer, Charles Edgar. Introduction to chemistry / [by] Charles E. Mortimer. — New York ; London [etc.] : D. Van Nostrand, 1977. — xv,720p : ill(some col) ; 24cm.
With answers. — Text on lining papers. — Index.
ISBN 0-442-25569-1 : £12.90
(B77-28592)

Petrucci, Ralph Herbert. General chemistry : principles and modern applications / [by] Ralph H. Petrucci. — 2nd ed. — New York : Macmillan ; London : Collier Macmillan, 1977. — xxi,790p : ill(chiefly col) ; 24cm.
With answers. — Text on lining papers. — Previous ed.: 1972. — Index.
ISBN 0-02-394980-5 : £12.00
ISBN 0-02-979540-0 Pbk : £8.95
(B77-28593)

Routh, Joseph Isaac. Essentials of general, organic and biochemistry / [by] Joseph I. Routh, Darrell P. Eyman, Donald J. Burton. — 3rd ed. — Philadelphia ; London [etc.] : Saunders, 1977. — ii-x,631,xx p : ill(some col), port ; 27cm. — (Saunders golden sunburst series)
With answers. — Text on lining papers. — Previous ed.: 1973. — Index.
ISBN 0-7216-7762-2 : £12.75
(B77-24917)

Routh, Joseph Isaac, *b.1910.* A brief introduction to general, organic and biochemistry / [edited by] Joseph I. Routh, Darrell P. Eyman, Donald J. Burton. — 2nd ed. — Philadelphia ; London [etc.] : Saunders, 1976. — xiv,438p : ill(some col) ; 27cm. — (Saunders golden sunburst series)
With answers. — Text on lining papers. — Previous ed.: 1971. — Bibl. — Index.
ISBN 0-7216-7769-x : £10.00
(B77-01425)

Sienko, Michell Joseph. Chemical principles and properties / [by] Michell J. Sienko, Robert A. Plane. — 2nd ed. — New York ; London [etc.] : McGraw-Hill, 1974. — xi,788p : ill(chiefly col) ; 24cm.
Text on lining papers. — With answers. — Previous ed.: published as 'Chemistry, principles and properties'. 1966. — Bibl.: p.771-772. — Index.
ISBN 0-07-057364-6 : Unpriced
(B77-19356)

Sienko, Michell Joseph. Chemistry / [by] Michell J. Sienko, Robert A. Plane. — 5th ed. — New York ; London [etc.] : McGraw-Hill, 1976. — xi,624p : ill(some col) ; 25cm.
Text on lining papers. — With answers to selected questions. — Previous ed.: 1971. — Bibl.: p.604-605. — Index.
ISBN 0-07-057335-2 : £12.40
(B77-03534)

540 — Chemistry. *Conference proceedings*
International Union of Pure and Applied Chemistry. *Conference, 28th, Madrid, 1975.*
Comptes rendus 28th Conference, Madrid, 2-11 September 1975 [of the] International Union of Pure and Applied Chemistry. — Oxford [etc.] : Pergamon.
In 2 vols.
Part B. — 1976. — ix,433p ; 21cm.
ISBN 0-08-021357-x Pbk : £13.00
(B77-11203)

Part A. — 1976. — [2],vi,141p,fold plate : 1 ill ; 21cm.
Index.
ISBN 0-08-021155-0 Pbk : £7.00
(B77-11202)

540 — Chemistry. *Reviews of research*
Annual reports on the progress of chemistry. Section A : Physical and inorganic chemistry. — London : Chemical Society.
Vol.73 : 1976. — 1977. — xiii,273p : ill ; 23cm.
Index.
ISBN 0-85186-090-7 : £14.00
ISSN 0308-6003
(B77-30235)

Annual reports on the progress of chemistry. Section B : Organic chemistry. — London : Chemical Society.
Vol.73 : 1976. — 1977. — xvi,456p ; 23cm.
Index.
ISBN 0-85186-091-5 : £15.00
ISSN 0069-3030
(B77-32617)

540 — Chemistry. *Secondary school texts*
Henderson, Euan Scott. Chemistry today / [by] Euan S. Henderson. — Basingstoke [etc.] : Macmillan, 1977. — viii,447p : ill, facsim, maps, port ; 23cm.
Originally published: 1976. — Index.
ISBN 0-333-22737-9 Pbk : £1.95
(B77-22551)

Holderness, Albert. A new Certificate chemistry / [by] A. Holderness, John Lambert. — 5th ed. / revised in collaboration with J.J. Thompson. — London : Heinemann Educational, 1977. — viii,519p : ill ; 23cm.
With answers. — This ed. originally published: 1976. — Index.
ISBN 0-435-64424-6 Pbk : £2.20
(B77-10357)

Last, Allan. Certificate physical science / [by] Allan Last. — London [etc.] : Macmillan, 1977. — vi,176,[1]p : ill ; 25cm.
With answers. — Index.
ISBN 0-333-21147-2 Pbk : £1.95
Primary classification 530
(B77-33785)

McDuell, Bob. Foundation chemistry / [by] Bob McDuell. — Sunbury on Thames [etc.] : Nelson, 1976. — 186p : ill(some col), ports ; 26cm.
Index.
ISBN 0-17-438301-0 Pbk : £1.95
(B77-05394)

Powney, Derek J. Advanced Level physical science / [by] D.J. Powney and B.J. Stokes. — London : Edward Arnold, 1977. — vii,394p : ill ; 25cm.
Index.
Pbk : £5.95
Primary classification 530
(B77-33786)

540 — Chemistry. *State-of-the-art reviews*
Sherwood, Martin. New worlds in chemistry / by Martin Sherwood. — London : Faber, 1977. — 3-234p : ill ; 23cm.
'An earlier, longer version of this book [was] published in the United States of America by Basic Books Inc., [1974] as "The New Chemistry"' - Acknowledgements. — Bibl.: p.226-230. — Index.
ISBN 0-571-10753-2 : £6.95
(B77-15276)

540 — Chemistry. Masterton, William Lewis. Chemical principles. *Study outlines*
Clouser, Joseph L. Keller plan for self-paced study using Masterton and Slowinski's 'Chemical principles' / [by] Joseph L. Clouser. — 2nd ed. — Philadelphia ; London [etc.] : Saunders, 1977. — xi,305p : 1 ill ; 25cm. — (Saunders golden sunburst series)
With answers. — Previous ed.: 1974.
ISBN 0-7216-2611-4 Pbk : £5.50
(B77-29411)

540'.1 — Alchemy
The **supernatural.** — [United States] : Danbury Press ; London : Aldus Books.
Alchemy, the ancient science / by Neil Powell. — 1976. — 144p : ill(some col), ports(some col) ; 27cm.
ISBN 0-490-00346-x : £3.25
(B77-13024)

540'.1 — Alchemy. *Manuals*
Albertus, *Frater.* The alchemist's handbook : (manual for practical laboratory alchemy) / by Frater Albertus. — Revised ed. — London [etc.] : Routledge and Kegan Paul, 1976. — [2], 124p : ill ; 24cm.
This ed. originally published: New York : S. Weiser, 1974.
ISBN 0-7100-8477-3 : £5.50
(B77-13636)

540'.1 — Chemistry. *Early works. Latin-English parallel texts*
Marius. [De elementis. English & Latin]. On the elements / Marius ; a critical edition and translation [from the Latin] by Richard C. Dales. — Berkeley [etc.] : University of California Press, 1976. — viii,206p,[4]p of plates : facsims ; 24cm. — (University of California at Los Angeles. Center for Medieval and Renaissance Studies. Publications ; 10)
Parallel transcription and translation of British Library MS. Cotton Galba E.IV, folios 190-200 (saec.XIIex.). — Bibl.: p.185-189. — Index.
ISBN 0-520-02856-2 : £8.50
(B77-27048)

540'.23 — Chemistry as a profession. *Great Britain, 1800-1976*
Russell, Colin Archibald. Chemists by profession : the origins and rise of the Royal Institute of Chemistry / [by] Colin A. Russell with Noel G. Coley, Gerrylynn K. Roberts. — Milton Keynes : Open University Press [for] the Institute, 1977. — x,342p,[12]p of plates : ill, coats of arms, ports ; 24cm.
Index.
ISBN 0-335-00041-x : £9.50
(B77-21108)

540'.2'461 — Chemistry. *For auxiliary personnel in health services in United States*
Ucko, David A. Living chemistry / [by] David A. Ucko. — New York [etc.] ; London : Academic Press, 1977. — xxi,593p : ill ; 25cm.
Text on lining papers. — With answers to numerical problems. — Index.
ISBN 0-12-705950-4 : £9.95
(B77-20235)

Ucko, David A. Living chemistry / [by] David A. Ucko. — New York [etc.] ; London : Academic Press.
Experiments for 'Living chemistry' / [by] David A. Ucko. — 1977. — xvii,189p : ill ; 28cm.
Fill-in book. — Pierced for binder. Pages perforated at inside edge.
ISBN 0-12-705956-3 Pbk : £3.90
(B77-26294)

Student guide for 'Living chemistry' / [by] David A. Ucko, Barbara C. Ucko. — 1977. — ix,257p : ill ; 24cm.
Fill-in book. — With answers.
ISBN 0-12-705955-5 Pbk : £2.85
(B77-26295)

540'.3 — Chemistry. *Dictionaries*
The **condensed** chemical dictionary. — 9th ed. / revised by Gessner G. Hawley. — New York ; London [etc.] : Van Nostrand Reinhold, 1977. — xv,957p : ill ; 24cm.
Previous ed.: 1971.
ISBN 0-442-23240-3 : £26.35
(B77-24206)

540'.5 — Chemistry. *Research reports. Periodicals*
Journal of chemical research, miniprint. — London : Chemical Society.
Issue 1- ; [Jan.] 1977-. — 1977-. — ill ; 30cm.
Monthly. — [44]p. in 1st issue. — Also available in microfiche. — English, French and German text.
Sd : Unpriced
ISSN 0308-2350
(B77-24918)

Journal of chemical research, synopses. — London : Chemical Society.
Issue 1- ; [Jan.] 1977-. — 1977-. — ill ; 30cm.
Monthly. — [4],33p. in 1st issue.
Sd : £10.00 yearly
ISSN 0308-2342
(B77-24919)

540'.6'241 — Chemistry. Organisations. *Great Britain. Chemical Society & Royal Institute of Chemistry. Directories*
Chemical Society. Register of members / the Chemical Society [and] the Royal Institute of Chemistry. — London : Chemical Society. 1976. — 1976. — viii,427p ; 30cm.
ISBN 0-85186-669-7 Pbk : £3.50(controlled circulation)
(B77-13025)

540'.7'104 — Educational institutions. Curriculum subjects: Chemistry. *Europe. Reports, surveys*
Chemical education in Europe / edited by P.J. Farago, M.J. Frazer, S.D. Walker. — London : Chemical Society, 1976. — vii,380p : ill ; 21cm.
Includes one paper in French. — Bibl.: p.375-377. — Index.
ISBN 0-85186-659-x Pbk : £3.50
(B77-19357)

540'.7'1141 — Universities. *Great Britain. Open University. Curriculum subjects: Chemistry. Courses: Nature of Chemistry*
Open University. *S304(S352) Course Team.* Introduction and guide to the course / [Open University S304(S352) Course Team]. — Milton Keynes (Walton Hall, Milton Keynes MK7 6AA) : Open University, 1977. — 22p ; 30cm. — (Science, a third level course : the nature of chemistry) (S304(S352) ; G)
Bibl.: p.18-21.
Sd : Unpriced
(B77-14223)

540'.7'2 — Chemistry. Research. Applications of digital computer systems
Computers in chemical and biochemical research. — New York ; London : Academic Press.
Vol.2 / edited by C.E. Klopfenstein, C.L. Wilkins. — 1974. — xii,276p : ill ; 24cm.
Bibl. — Index.
ISBN 0-12-151302-5 : Unpriced
(B77-19358)

540'.76 — Chemistry. *Exercises, worked examples. Secondary school texts*
Chemistry (Advanced Level). — 4th ed. / [compiled] by L.A. Linton and K. Morgan. — Horsham : Artemis, 1976. — 71p : ill ; 22cm. — (General Certificate of Education model answers)
Previous ed.: / compiled by L.A. Linton. 1971.
ISBN 0-85141-289-0 Pbk : £0.90
(B77-13637)

Mathews, John Charles. Calculations in modern chemistry with worked examples / [by] J.C. Mathews. — 3rd ed. — London : Hutchinson, 1977. — 104p ; 22cm. — (Modern chemistry series)
With answers. — Previous ed.: 1973.
ISBN 0-09-128901-7 Pbk : £1.25
(B77-27845)

540'.76 — Chemistry. *Questions & answers. Secondary school texts*
Hill, James William. A question guide to CSE chemistry / [by] J.W. Hill. — London : Cassell, 1977. — [4],59p : ill ; 22cm.
With answers to short questions.
ISBN 0-304-29869-7 Sd : £0.95
(B77-21109)

Simpson, Oswald John. Multiple choice chemistry : over 1000 factual, reasoning and analytical questions / by O.J. Simpson. — 2nd ed. — London : Edward Arnold, 1977. — vi, 158p : ill ; 22cm.
Previous ed.: 1969.
ISBN 0-7131-0130-x Pbk : £1.70
(B77-18121)

Swain, J R L. Structured questions in A Level chemistry / [by] J.R.L. Swain, J.S. Clarke. — London [etc.] : Hodder and Stoughton, 1977. — vi,122p : ill ; 22cm.
With answers to some numerical questions.
ISBN 0-340-20831-7 Pbk : £1.75
(B77-13638)

540'.76 — Educational institutions. Curriculum subjects: Chemistry. Academic achievement of students. Assessment. Techniques. *Conference proceedings*
Research in assessment : proceedings of a symposium, University of Reading, September 1975 / edited by R. Kempa, D.E. Hoare, R.J.D. Rutherford. — London : Education Division, Chemical Society, [1976]. — [7],94p : ill ; 21cm.
'This Symposium was organised by the Chemical Society Assessment Group, and formed part of the Autumn Meeting of the Chemical Society ...' - Introduction. — Bibl.
ISBN 0-85186-739-1 Pbk : £2.50(£1.50 to members of the Chemical Society, Education Division)
(B77-06060)

540'.7'7 — Chemistry. *Programmed texts*
Hanna, Melvin W. Foundation studies in general chemistry : a self-study guide / [by] Melvin W. Hanna. — Menlo Park, Calif. ; London [etc.] : Benjamin, [1977]. — [4],204p : ill ; 24cm.
Published in the United States: 1976.
ISBN 0-8053-3704-0 Pbk : £3.00
(B77-10358)

Houk, Clifford C. Chemistry : concepts and problems / [by] Clifford C. Houk, Richard Post. — New York ; London [etc.] : Wiley, 1977. — [2],xiii,370p : ill ; 26cm. — (Self-teaching guides)
With answers to self-tests. — Index.
ISBN 0-471-41500-6 Pbk : £4.35
(B77-12431)

540'.9 — Chemistry, to 1975
Jaffe, Bernard, *b.1896.* Crucibles : the story of chemistry from ancient alchemy to nuclear fission / [by] Bernard Jaffe. — 4th ed., new revised and updated. — New York : Dover Publications [etc.] ; London : Constable, 1976. — ix,368p : ill ; 22cm.
Previous ed.: New York : Simon and Schuster, 1948. — Index.
ISBN 0-486-23342-1 Pbk : £3.60
(B77-20236)

540'.92'4 — Chemistry. Curie, Marie. *Biographies. Juvenile literature*
Henrie, Jacqueline. Marie Curie : discoverer of radium / by Jacqueline Henrie ; illustrated by Louis Joos. — Edinburgh : W. and R. Chambers, 1977. — [28]p : ill(chiefly col), col ports ; 19x20cm. — (History makers)
ISBN 0-550-31933-6 : £1.40
(B77-32618)

540'.92'4 — Chemistry. Curie, Marie. *Biographies. Secondary school texts*
Birch, Beverley. Marie Curie : radium scientist / written and planned by Beverley Birch ; illustrated by Jenny Thorne/Linda Rogers Associates. — London : Macdonald Educational, 1977. — 47p : ill(chiefly col), ports ; 29cm. — (Macdonald famous people)
Index.
ISBN 0-356-05165-x : £1.60
(B77-06665)

540'.92'4 — Chemistry. Playfair, Lyon, Baron Playfair. *Great Britain. Autobiographies*
Playfair, Lyon, *Baron Playfair.* Memoirs and correspondence of Lyon Playfair / [edited with biographical material by] Thomas Wemyss Reid. — [1st ed. reprinted] ; [with] a new introduction by Colin Armstrong. — Jemimaville : P.M. Pollak ; [Altrincham] ([4 Arthog Rd, Hale, Altrincham, Cheshire WA15 0NA]) : [Distributed by Peter Bell], 1976. — [12],ii-xii,487p,plate : ports ; 23cm.
Limited ed. of 250 copies. — Facsimile reprint of: 1st ed. London : Cassell, 1899. — Index.
ISBN 0-9505343-0-7 : £10.00
(B77-04145)

541 — PHYSICAL AND THEORETICAL CHEMISTRY

541 — Chemistry. Applications of modern physics
Modern physics in chemistry / edited by E. Fluck and V.I. Goldanskii. — London [etc.] : Academic Press.
Vol.1. — 1976. — xiii,406p : ill ; 24cm.
Index.
ISBN 0-12-261201-9 : £18.50
(B77-32619)

541'.042 — Fluids. Chemical properties
Reid, Robert Clark. The properties of gases and liquids. — 3rd ed. / [by] Robert C. Reid, John M. Prausnitz, Thomas K. Sherwood. — New York ; London [etc.] : McGraw-Hill, 1977. — xv,688p : ill ; 24cm. — (McGraw-Hill chemical engineering series)
Previous ed.: / by Robert C. Reid, Thomas K. Sherwood. 1966. — Bibl. — Index.
ISBN 0-07-051790-8 : £20.65
(B77-23385)

541'.042'1 — Solids. Chemical properties
Treatise on solid state chemistry / edited by N.B. Hannay. — New York ; London : Plenum Press.
In 6 vols.
Vol.4 : Reactivity of solids. — 1976. — xvii, 721p : ill ; 26cm.
Index.
ISBN 0-306-35054-8 : £22.05
ISBN 0-306-35050-5 Set of 6 vols : £97.29
(B77-01426)

541'.042'2 — Liquids. Structure & chemical properties
Marcus, Yizhak. Introduction to liquid state chemistry / [by] Y. Marcus. — London [etc.] : Wiley, 1977. — xviii,357p : ill ; 24cm.
'A Wiley-Interscience Publication'. — Bibl.: p.x. — Index.
ISBN 0-471-99448-0 : £12.50
(B77-22552)

541.2 — THEORETICAL CHEMISTRY

541'.22 — Inorganic compounds. Electrons. Properties. *Reviews of research*
Electronic structure and magnetism of inorganic compounds. — London : Chemical Society. — (Chemical Society. Specialist periodical reports)
Vol.5 : a review of the literature published during 1974 and 1975 / senior reporter P. Day, reporters ... [others]. — 1977. — viii,248p : ill ; 23cm.
Index.
ISBN 0-85186-291-8 : £21.00
ISSN 0305-9766
(B77-31883)

541'.22 — Molecules. Properties. Influence of connectivity
Kier, Lemont Burwell. Molecular connectivity in chemistry and drug research / [by] Lemont B. Kier, Lowell H. Hall. — New York [etc.] ; London : Academic Press, 1976. — xiii,257p : ill ; 24cm. — (Medicinal chemistry ; vol.14)
Published in the United States: 1976. — Index.
ISBN 0-12-406560-0 : £19.20
(B77-13639)

541'.22 — Molecules. Structure. Determination. Applications of diffraction. *Reviews of research*
Molecular structure by diffraction methods. — London : Chemical Society. — (Chemical Society. Specialist periodical reports)
Vol.4 : a review of the literature published between April 1974 and September 1975 / senior reporters G.A. Sim, L.E. Sutton ... — 1976. — xiv,439p : ill ; 22cm.
Index.
ISBN 0-85186-537-2 : £28.50
ISSN 0305-9790
(B77-06061)

541'.22 — Molecules. Symmetry. Applications of group theory. *Programmed texts*
Vincent, Alan, *b.1938.* Molecular symmetry and group theory : a programmed introduction to chemical applications / [by] Alan Vincent. — London [etc.] : Wiley, 1977. — x,156p : ill ; 24cm.
Bibl.: p.138. — Index.
ISBN 0-471-01867-8 : £5.90
ISBN 0-471-01868-6 Pbk : £2.75
(B77-18745)

541'.223'077 — Stereochemistry. *Programmed texts*
Pearce, John, *b.1940.* Stereochemistry : an introductory programme with models / by John Pearce, Erica Glynn. — London [etc.] : Wiley, 1976. — v,171p : ill ; 23cm.
With answers to self-assessment test.
ISBN 0-471-67467-2 Sd : £1.00
(B77-08361)

541'.224 — Valency
Cartmell, Edward. Valency and molecular structure / [by] E. Cartmell and G.W.A. Fowles. — 4th ed. — London [etc.] : Butterworth, 1977. — [10],341p : ill ; 24cm.
Previous ed.: 1966. — Index.
ISBN 0-408-70809-3 Pbk : £4.95 : CIP rev.
(B77-11204)

541'.2242 — Vapours: Coordination compounds. Stereochemistry
Hargittai, Magdolna. The molecular geometries of coordination compounds in the vapour phase / by Magdolna Hargittai and István Hargittai. — Amsterdam ; Oxford [etc.] : Elsevier, 1977. — 276p : ill ; 21cm.
Translation and revision of: 'Koordinációs vegyületek gözfázisú molekulageometriája'. Budapest : Akadémiai Kiadó, 1974. — Bibl.: p.237-258. — Index.
ISBN 0-444-99832-2 : £17.33
(B77-14713)

541'.2253 — Metal coordination compounds. Chelation
Bell, Colin Frank. Principles and applications of metal chelation / [by] Colin F. Bell. — Oxford : Clarendon Press, 1977. — viii,149p : ill ; 23cm. — (Oxford chemistry series)
Jacket title: Metal chelation. — With answers. — Bibl.: p.141-143. — Index.
ISBN 0-19-855485-0 : £4.95
(B77-27049)

541'.226 — Molecules. Dispersion forces
Mahanty, J. Dispersion forces / [by] J. Mahanty, B.W. Ninham. — London [etc.] : Academic Press, 1976. — xi,236p : ill ; 24cm. — (Colloid science)
Bibl. — Index.
ISBN 0-12-465050-3 : £9.20
(B77-11205)

541'.28 — Chemical compounds. Spectroscopy. Spectra. *Technical data*
Spectroscopic data. — New York [etc.] : IFI/Plenum ; London : Plenum Press.
Vol.2 : Homonuclear diatomic molecules / edited by S.N. Suchard and J.E. Melzer. — 1976. — vii,585p : ill ; 28cm.
ISBN 0-306-68312-1 : £36.23
(B77-04791)

541'.28 — Inorganic compounds. Spectroscopy. *Reviews of research*
Spectroscopic properties of inorganic and organometallic compounds. — London : Chemical Society. — (Chemical Society. Specialist periodical reports)
Vol.9 : a review of the literature published during 1975 / senior reporter N.N. Greenwood ... — 1976. — xiii,544p : ill ; 23cm.
Bibl.: p.500-506. — Index.
ISBN 0-85186-083-4 : £28.56
ISSN 0584-8555
Also classified at 547'.05
(B77-06062)

541'.28 — Molecules. Excited states. *Reviews of research*
Excited states. — New York [etc.] ; London : Academic Press.
Vol.2 / edited by Edward C. Lim. — 1975. — ix,403p : ill ; 24cm.
Bibl. — Index.
ISBN 0-12-227202-1 : Unpriced
(B77-19359)

541'.28 — Molecules. Excited states. Spectroscopy. *Conference proceedings*
NATO Advanced Study Institute on the Spectroscopy of the Excited State, *Erice, 1975.* Spectroscopy of the excited state / edited by Baldassare di Bartolo ; assistant editors Dennis Pacheco and Velda Goldberg. — New York ; London : Plenum Press [for the] NATO Scientific Affairs Division, 1976. — xiv,416p : ill ; 26cm. — (NATO Advanced Study Institutes : series B, physics ; vol.12)
'Proceedings of the NATO Advanced Study Institute on the Spectroscopy of the Excited State held at Erice, Italy, June 9-24, 1975' - title page verso. — Index.
ISBN 0-306-35712-7 : £20.48
(B77-03535)

541'.28 — Molecules. Structure. Determination. Applications of neutron scattering
Bacon, George Edward. Neutron scattering in chemistry / [by] G.E. Bacon. — London [etc.] : Butterworth, 1977. — [6],186p : ill ; 24cm.
Bibl. — Index.
ISBN 0-408-70800-x : £12.50
(B77-26296)

541'.28 — Molecules. Structure. Determination. Nuclear magnetic resonance spectroscopy. *Reviews of research*
Nuclear magnetic resonance. — London : Chemical Society. — (Chemical Society. Specialist periodical reports)
Vol.5 : a review of the literature published between June 1974 and May 1975 / senior reporter R.K. Harris ... — 1976. — xxix,342p : ill ; 23cm.
Bibl.: p.xxi-xxix. — Index.
ISBN 0-85186-292-6 : £15.50
ISSN 0305-9804
(B77-06063)

Vol.6 : a review of the literature published between June 1975 and May 1976 / senior reporter R.J. Abraham ... — 1977. — xxix, 269p : ill ; 23cm.
Bibl.: p.xxi-xxix. — Index.
ISBN 0-85186-302-7 : Unpriced
ISSN 0305-9804
(B77-29412)

541'.28 — Pure substances. Spectroscopy
Spectrochemical analysis of pure substances / edited by Kh. I. Zil'bershtein ; translated [from the Russian] by J.H. Dixon. — Bristol : Hilger, 1977. — xv,435p : ill ; 26cm.
Translation and revision of: 'Spektral'nyĭ analiz chistykh veshchestv'. Leningrad : Khimiia, 1971. — Index.
ISBN 0-85274-264-9 : £27.00
(B77-14714)

541.3 — PHYSICAL CHEMISTRY
Chang, Raymond. Physical chemistry with applications to biological systems / [by] Raymond Chang. — New York : Macmillan ; London : Collier Macmillan, 1977. — xv,538p : ill(some col) ; 26cm.
With answers to numerical problems. — Text on lining paper. — Bibl. — Index.
ISBN 0-02-321020-6 : £11.25
ISBN 0-02-979370-x Pbk : £6.75
(B77-21845)

Fried, Vojtech. Physical chemistry / [by] Vojtech Fried, Hendrik F. Hameka, Uldis Blukis. — New York : Macmillan ; London : Collier Macmillan, 1977. — 2 leaves,xix,983p : ill ; 26cm.
With answers. — Index.
ISBN 0-02-339760-8 Pbk : £12.25
(B77-28594)

Moncrief, J William. Elements of physical chemistry / [by] J. William Moncrief, William H. Jones. — Reading, Mass. ; London [etc.] : Addison-Wesley, 1977. — xxvii,450p : ill ; 24cm. — (Addison-Wesley series in chemistry)
With answers to selected problems. — Index.
ISBN 0-201-04897-3 : £12.80
(B77-16869)

Physical methods of chemistry / edited by Arnold Weissberger and Bryant W. Rossiter. — New York ; London [etc.] : Wiley. — (Techniques of chemistry ; vol.1)
In 6 parts. — 'Incorporating fourth completely revised and augumented edition of ... "Physical methods of organic chemistry"'. — Previous ed.: i.e. 3rd ed., 1960.
Part 6 : Supplement and cumulative index ... — 1977. — xi,323p : ill ; 24cm.
Bibl.: p.216.
ISBN 0-471-92899-2 : £17.25
(B77-17477)

541'.3 — Physical chemistry. *Reviews of research*
Advances in chemical physics / edited by I. Prigogine and Stuart A. Rice. — New York ; London [etc.] : Wiley.
Vol.27 : Aspects of the study of surfaces. — [1977]. — xi,656p : ill ; 24cm.
'An Interscience publication'. — Published in the United States: 1974. — Index.
ISBN 0-471-69932-2 : £15.50
(B77-08362)

Vol.36. — 1977. — xi,541p : ill ; 24cm.
Bibl. — Index.
ISBN 0-471-02274-8 : £27.40
(B77-21110)

541'.3'024574 — Physical chemistry. *For biology*
Barrow, Gordon Milne. Physical chemistry for the life sciences / [by] Gordon M. Barrow. — New York ; London [etc.] : McGraw-Hill, 1974. — x,405p : ill ; 24cm.
Ill., text on lining papers. — With answers to selected problems. — Bibl. — Index.
ISBN 0-07-003855-4 : Unpriced
(B77-18746)

Wallwork, Stephen Collier. Physical chemistry : for students of pharmacy and biology. — 3rd ed. / by S.C. Wallwork and D.J.W. Grant. — London [etc.] : Longman, 1977. — xiv,607p : ill ; 22cm.
With answers. — Previous ed.: i.e. 2nd ed. revised, 1960. — Index.
ISBN 0-582-44254-0 Pbk : £7.95
Primary classification 541'.3'024615
(B77-33787)

541'.3'024615 — Physical chemistry. *For pharmacy*
Wallwork, Stephen Collier. Physical chemistry : for students of pharmacy and biology. — 3rd ed. / by S.C. Wallwork and D.J.W. Grant. — London [etc.] : Longman, 1977. — xiv,607p : ill ; 22cm.
With answers. — Previous ed.: i.e. 2nd ed. revised, 1960. — Index.
ISBN 0-582-44254-0 Pbk : £7.95
Also classified at 541'.3'024574
(B77-33787)

541'.3'076 — Physical chemistry. *Exercises, worked examples*
Metz, Clyde R. Schaum's outline of theory and problems of physical chemistry / by Clyde R. Metz. — New York ; London [etc.] : McGraw-Hill, 1976. — [8],424p : ill ; 28cm. — (Schaum's outline series)
Cover title: Theory and problems of physical chemistry. — Spine title: Physical chemistry. — With answers. — Index.
ISBN 0-07-041709-1 Pbk : £5.75
(B77-01427)

541'.34 — Solid-liquid equilibria
Nývlt, Jaroslav. Solid-liquid phase equilibria / [by] Jaroslav Nývlt. — Amsterdam ; Oxford [etc.] : Elsevier, 1977. — 248p : ill ; 25cm.
At head of half title page: Czechoslovak Academy of Sciences. — Bibl.: p.180. — Index.
ISBN 0-444-99850-0 : £46.43
(B77-28595)

541'.3423 — Non-aqueous solvents
The **chemistry** of nonaqueous solvents / edited by J.J. Lagowski. — New York [etc.] ; London : Academic Press.
Vol.4 : Solution phenomena and aprotic solvents. — 1976. — xiv,311p : ill ; 24cm.
Index.
ISBN 0-12-433804-6 : £19.20
(B77-05395)

541'.3423 — Solutions of metals in liquid ammonia
Thompson, J C. Electrons in liquid ammonia / by J.C. Thompson. — Oxford : Clarendon Press, 1976. — xii,297p : ill ; 23cm. — (Monographs on the physics and chemistry of materials)
Bibl. — Index.
ISBN 0-19-851343-7 : £14.50
(B77-03536)

541'.345 — Colloids & surface phenomena. *Conference proceedings*
International Conference on Colloids and Surfaces, *San Juan, 1976.* Colloid and interface science : proceedings of the International Conference on Colloids and Surfaces - 50th Colloid and Surface Science Symposium, held in San Juan, Puerto Rico on June 21-25, 1976. — New York [etc.] ; London : Academic Press.
In 5 vols.
Vol.2 : Aerosols, emulsions, and surfactants / edited by Milton Kerker. — 1976. — xx,481p : ill ; 24cm.
ISBN 0-12-404502-2 : £14.90
(B77-13026)

Vol.3 : Adsorption, catalysis, solid surfaces, wetting, surface tension, and water / edited by Milton Kerker. — 1976. — xx,548p : ill ; 24cm.
ISBN 0-12-404503-0 : £15.95
(B77-13027)

Vol.4 : Hydrosols and rheology / edited by Milton Kerker. — 1976. — xviii,587p : ill ; 24cm.
ISBN 0-12-404504-9 : £15.60
(B77-13028)

Vol.5 : Bicolloids, polymers, monolayers, membranes, and general papers / edited by Milton Kerker. — 1976. — xvii,507p : ill ; 24cm.
ISBN 0-12-404505-7 : £15.60
(B77-13029)

541'.3451 — Colloids. *Reviews of research*
Surface and colloid science. — New York ; London [etc.] : Wiley.
Vol.9 / editor Egon Matijević. — 1976. — xi, 382p : ill ; 24cm.
'A Wiley-Interscience publication'. — Index.
ISBN 0-471-57638-7 : £26.90
Also classified at 541'.3453
(B77-06064)

541'.34513 — Colloids: Clay
Van Olphen, H. An introduction to clay colloid chemistry : for clay technologists, geologists, and soil scientists / [by] H. van Olphen. — 2nd ed. — New York ; London [etc.] : Wiley, 1977. — xviii,318p : ill ; 24cm.
'A Wiley-Interscience publication'. — Previous ed.: 1963. — Bibl.: p.294-301. — Index.
ISBN 0-471-01463-x : £15.00
(B77-22554)

541'.34514 — Liquids. Foams. *Conference proceedings*
Symposium on Foams, *Brunel University, 1975.*
Foams : proceedings of a symposium organized by the Society of Chemical Industry, Colloid and Surface Chemistry Group, and held at Brunel University, September 8-10, 1975 / edited by R.J. Akers. — London [etc.] : Academic Press, 1976. — x,301p : ill ; 24cm.
'Symposium on Foams, 1975' - half title page verso. — Index.
ISBN 0-12-047350-x : £12.00
(B77-14224)

541'.3453 — Adhesion. *Conference proceedings*
Adhesion. — London : Applied Science Publishers.
1 / edited by K.W. Allen. — 1977. — ix,315p : ill ; 23cm.
'... based on papers presented at the 13th and 14th annual conferences on Adhesion and Adhesives held at the City University, London' - half title page verso. — Index.
ISBN 0-85334-735-2 : £16.00
(B77-31884)

541'.3453 — Chemisorption
Wedler, Gerd. Chemisorption : an experimental approach / [by] Gerd Wedler ; translated [from the German] by Derek F. Klemperer. — Revised English language ed. — London [etc.] : Butterworth, 1976. — [8],250p : ill ; 24cm.
Previous ed.: published as 'Adsorption'. Weinheim/Bergstr. Verlag Chemie, 1970. — Bibl.: p.201-225. — Index.
ISBN 0-408-10611-5 : £12.00
(B77-04146)

541'.3453 — Surface phenomena
Adamson, Arthur Wilson. Physical chemistry of surfaces / [by] Arthur W. Adamson. — 3rd ed. — New York ; London [etc.] : Wiley, 1976. — xviii,698p : ill ; 24cm.
'A Wiley-Interscience publication'. — Previous ed.: 1967. — Bibl. — Index.
ISBN 0-471-00794-3 : £17.75
(B77-06065)

541'.3453 — Surface phenomena. *Reviews of research*
Progress in surface and membrane science. — New York [etc.] ; London : Academic Press.
Vol. 11 / edited by D.A. Cadenhead, J.F. Danielli. — 1976. — xi,345p : ill ; 24cm.
Bibl. — Index.
ISBN 0-12-571811-x : £15.25
(B77-06666)

Surface and colloid science. — New York ; London [etc.] : Wiley.
Vol.9 / editor Egon Matijević. — 1976. — xi, 382p : ill ; 24cm.
'A Wiley-Interscience publication'. — Index.
ISBN 0-471-57638-7 : £26.90
Primary classification 541'.3451
(B77-06064)

Surface and defect properties of solids. — London : Chemical Society. — (Chemical Society. Specialist periodical reports)
Vol.4 : a review of the recent literature published up to April 1974 / senior reporters M.W. Roberts, J.M. Thomas. — 1975. — ix, 255p : ill ; 23cm.
Index.
ISBN 0-85186-280-2 : £14.00
ISSN 0305-3873
Also classified at 548'.81
(B77-08998)

541'.35 — Photochemistry. *Reviews of research*
Advances in photochemistry. — New York ; London [etc.] : Wiley.
Vol.10 / editors James N. Pitts, Jr, George S. Hammond, Klaus Gollnick. — 1977. — xi, 475p : ill ; 24cm.
'An Interscience Publication'. — Index.
ISBN 0-471-02145-8 : £22.50
(B77-18747)

Photochemical and photobiological reviews. — New York ; London : Plenum Press.
Vol.1 / edited by Kendric C. Smith. — 1976. — xi,391p : ill ; 24cm.
Bibl. — Index.
ISBN 0-306-33801-7 : £20.48
Primary classification 574.1'9153
(B77-19371)

Photochemistry. — London : Chemical Society. — (Chemical Society. Specialist periodical reports)
Vol.7 : a review of the literature published between July 1974 and June 1975 / senior reporter D. Bryce-Smith ... — 1976. — xx, 617p : ill ; 23cm.
Index.
ISBN 0-85186-065-6 : £32.00
ISSN 0556-3860
(B77-06066)

Vol.8 : a review of the literature published between July 1975 and June 1976 / senior reporter D. Bryce-Smith, reporters ... [others]. — 1977. — xix,644p : ill ; 23cm.
Index.
ISBN 0-85186-075-3 : £37.00
ISSN 0556-3860
(B77-27050)

541'.361 — Combustion. *Juvenile literature*
Connell, Stephanie. Fire / written by Stephanie Connell and Vivienne Driscoll. — London : Macdonald Educational, 1977. — [1],32p : col ill ; 18cm. — (Readabout)
Adaptation of: 'Fire'. London : Macdonald and Co., 1971. — Index.
ISBN 0-356-05542-6 Sd : £0.35
(B77-13030)

541'.361 — Fire. *Juvenile literature*
Ralphs, Dorothy Howarth. Fire / written and illustrated by Dorothy Ralphs. — London [etc.] : F. Watts, 1977. — 48p : ill(chiefly col) ; 22cm. — (A first look book)
Index.
ISBN 0-85166-629-9 : £1.75
(B77-09685)

Webster, James. Fire / by James Webster ; with illustrations by Frank Humphris. — Loughborough : Ladybird Books, 1977. — 2-52p : ill(chiefly col) ; 18cm. — (Ladybird leaders ; 29)
Text, col. ill. on lining papers. — Index.
ISBN 0-7214-0414-6 : £0.24
(B77-08363)

541'.363 — Phase diagrams. Coordination with thermal analysis data. Applications of computer systems. Projects: CALPHAD. *Periodicals*
Calphad : computer coupling of phase diagrams and thermochemistry. — Oxford [etc.] : Pergamon.
Vol.1, no.1- ; [Jan.] 1977-. — 1977-. — ill ; 25cm.
Quarterly. — Cover title. — 95p. in 1st issue.
Pbk : Unpriced
ISSN 0364-5916
Also classified at 543'.086
(B77-07896)

541'.3686 — Cryochemistry
Cryochemistry / edited by Martin Moskovits, Geoffrey A. Ozin. — New York ; London [etc.] : Wiley, 1976. — xi,532p : ill ; 24cm.
'A Wiley-Interscience Publication'. — Bibl.: p.520-523. — Index.
ISBN 0-471-61870-5 : £25.85
(B77-05396)

541'.3687 — High temperature chemical reactions. Kinetics. *Technical data*
Evaluated kinetic data for high temperature reactions. — London [etc.] : Butterworth.
Vol.3 : Homogeneous gas phase reactions of the O2-O3 system, the CO-O2-H2 system, and sulphur-containing species / [by] D.L. Baulch ... [et al.]. — 1976. — xiii,593p : ill ; 31cm.
Index.
ISBN 0-408-70787-9 : £29.50
(B77-02285)

541'.369 — Chemical reactions. Thermodynamics
Smith, Eric Brian. Basic chemical thermodynamics / [by] E. Brian Smith. — 2nd ed. — Oxford : Clarendon Press, 1977. — xii, 132p : ill ; 22cm. — (Oxford chemistry series)
With answers. — Previous ed.: 1973. — Bibl.: p.127. — Index.
ISBN 0-19-855508-3 Pbk : £2.25
(B77-30236)

541'.369 — Gases. Chemical reactions. Thermodynamics. Related to kinetics
Benson, Sidney William. Thermochemical kinetics : methods for the estimation of thermochemical data and rate parameters / [by] Sidney W. Benson. — 2nd ed. — New York ; London [etc.] : Wiley, 1976. — xiii,320p : ill ; 24cm.
'A Wiley-Interscience publication'. — Previous ed.: 1968. — Index.
ISBN 0-471-06781-4 : £16.00
Also classified at 541'.39
(B77-07897)

541'.369'0212 — Chemical reactions. Thermodynamics. *Technical data*
Computer analysis of thermo chemical data : CATCH tables. — [Brighton] ([Falmer, Brighton BN1 9QJ]) : [University of Sussex, School of Molecular Science].
Bibl.: p.2.
Cr, Mo and W compounds / data selection by D.S. Barnes ; data processing by J.B. Pedley ... [et al.]. — 1974. — [2],30p ; 30cm.
ISBN 0-905939-00-x Sd : £2.00
(B77-06667)

541'.37 — Electrochemistry
Selley, Nicholas John. Experimental approach to electrochemistry / [by] N.J. Selley. — London : Edward Arnold, 1977. — viii,211p : ill ; 24cm.
With selected answers. — Bibl.: p.207. — Index.
ISBN 0-7131-2540-3 : £9.00
ISBN 0-7131-2541-1 Pbk : £4.50
(B77-29413)

541'.37 — Electrochemistry. *Reviews of research*
Advances in electrochemistry and electrochemical engineering. — New York ; London [etc.] : Wiley.
'A Wiley-Interscience Publication'.
Vol.10 / edited by Heinz Gerischer and Charles W. Tobias. — 1977. — xiii,491p : ill ; 24cm.
Index.
ISBN 0-471-87527-9 : £22.50
(B77-17478)

541'.38 — Radiochemistry. *Reviews of research*
Advances in inorganic chemistry and radiochemistry. — New York [etc.] ; London : Academic Press.
Vol.19 : 1976 / editors H.J. Emeléus, A.G. Sharpe. — [1977]. — vii,322p : ill ; 24cm.
Published in the United States: 1976. — Bibl. — Index.
ISBN 0-12-023619-2 : £22.35
Primary classification 546
(B77-11791)

Vol.20 : 1977 / editors H.J. Emeléus, A.G. Sharpe. — 1977. — vii,374p : ill ; 24cm.
Bibl. — Index.
ISBN 0-12-023620-6 : £27.70
Primary classification 546
(B77-31885)

Advances in radiation chemistry. — New York ; London [etc.] : Wiley.
Vol.5 / edited by Milton Burton and John L. Magee. — 1976. — xiii,337p : ill ; 24cm.
'A Wiley-Interscience publication'. — Index.
ISBN 0-471-01669-1 : £28.60
(B77-04792)

Radiochemistry. — London : Chemical Society. — (Chemical Society. Specialist periodical reports)
Vol.3 : a review of the literature published during 1974 and 1975 / senior reporter G.W.A. Newton, reporters ... [others]. — 1976. — viii, 141p : ill ; 23cm.
Index.
ISBN 0-85186-274-8 : £11.50
ISSN 0301-0716
(B77-13640)

541'.39 — Chemical reactions. Kinetics
Comprehensive chemical kinetics / edited by C.H. Bamford and C.F.H. Tipper. — Amsterdam ; Oxford [etc.] : Elsevier.
Vol.8 : Proton transfer. — 1977. — xi,261p : ill ; 25cm.
Index.
ISBN 0-444-41512-2 : £19.50
(B77-18123)

Vol.14A : Free-radical polymerisation. — 1976. — xiii,594p : ill ; 25cm.
Index.
ISBN 0-444-41486-x : £58.31
(B77-13641)

Latham, Joseph Lionel. Elementary reaction kinetics. — 3rd ed. / [by] J.L. Latham and A.E. Burgess. — London [etc.] : Butterworth, 1977. — x,182p : ill ; 22cm.
Previous ed.: / by J.L. Latham. 1969. — Bibl.: p.175. — Index.
ISBN 0-408-46102-0 Pbk : £2.95
(B77-20238)

541'.39 — Gases. Chemical reactions. Energy transfer & kinetics. *Reviews of research*

Gas kinetics and energy transfer. — London : Chemical Society. — (Chemical Society. Specialist periodical reports)
Vol.2 : a review of the literature published up to early 1976 / senior reporters P.G. Ashmore, R.J. Donovan, reporters ... [others]. — 1977. — xii,392p : ill ; 23cm.
Continues: Reaction kinetics. — Index.
ISBN 0-85186-766-9 : Unpriced
ISSN 0309-6890
(B77-14225)

541'.39 — Gases. Chemical reactions. Kinetics. Related to thermodynamics

Benson, Sidney William. Thermochemical kinetics : methods for the estimation of thermochemical data and rate parameters / [by] Sidney W. Benson. — 2nd ed. — New York ; London [etc.] : Wiley, 1976. — xiii,320p : ill ; 24cm.
'A Wiley-Interscience publication'. — Previous ed.: 1968. — Index.
ISBN 0-471-06781-4 : £16.00
Primary classification 541'.369
(B77-07897)

541'.39 — Inorganic compounds. Synthesis. *Reviews of research*

Annual reports in inorganic and general syntheses. — New York [etc.] ; London : Academic Press. — (Academic Press rapid manuscript reproduction)
1975 / edited by Hans Zimmer, Kurt Niedenzu. — 1976. — ix,344p : ill ; 26cm.
Index.
ISBN 0-12-040704-3 Pbk : £11.00
(B77-05397)

Inorganic syntheses. — New York ; London [etc.] : McGraw-Hill.
Vol.12 / editor-in-chief Robert W. Parry. — [1976]. — xvii,344p : ill ; 24cm.
Published in the United States: 1970. — Index.
ISBN 0-07-048517-8 : £14.65
(B77-03537)

541'.39 — Solids. Chemical reactions

Schmalzried, Hermann. Solid state reactions / [by] Hermann Schmalzried ; translated [from the German] by A.D. Pelton. — Weinheim/ Bergstr. : Verlag Chemie ; New York ; London : Academic Press, 1974. — x,214p : ill ; 24cm. — (Materials science and technology)
Text on lining paper. — Translation and revision of: 'Festkörperreaktionen'. Weinheim/Bergstr. : Verlag Chemie, 1971. — Index.
ISBN 0-12-625850-3 : Unpriced
(B77-21111)

541'.39 — Solids. Chemical reactions with gases

Szekely, Julian. Gas-solid reactions / [by] Julian Szekely, James W. Evans, Hong Yong Sohn. — New York [etc.] ; London : Academic Press, 1976. — xiii,400p : ill ; 24cm.
Bibl.: p.393-394. — Index.
ISBN 0-12-680850-3 : £24.10
(B77-08364)

541'.39'028 — Ion cyclotron resonance spectrometry

Lehman, Thomas A. Ion cyclotron resonance spectrometry / [by] Thomas A. Lehman, Maurice M. Bursey. — New York ; London [etc.] : Wiley, 1976. — xiii,230p : ill ; 24cm.
'A Wiley-Interscience publication'. — Index.
ISBN 0-471-12530-x : £17.00
(B77-07898)

541'.392 — Aqueous solutions. Chemical reactions. Equilibria

Guenther, William Benton. Chemical equilibrium : a practical introduction for the physical and life sciences / [by] William B. Guenther. — New York ; London : Plenum Press, [1976]. — xiii,248p : ill ; 24cm.
With answers to selected problems. — Published in the United States: 1975. — Bibl.: p.238-239. — Index.
ISBN 0-306-30850-9 : £12.29
(B77-04147)

541'.392 — Metal coordination compounds. Equilibria. *Technical data*

Martell, Arthur Earl. Critical stability constants / by Arthur E. Martell and Robert M. Smith. — New York ; London : Plenum Press.
In 3 vols.
Vol.1 : Amino acids. — [1976]. — xv,469p ; 28cm.
Published in the United States: 1974. — Bibl.: p.411-452. — Index.
ISBN 0-306-35211-7 : £18.59
(B77-02286)

541'.394 — Fast chemical reactions. Rates. Measurement. Relaxation techniques

Bernasconi, Claude F. Relaxation kinetics / [by] Claude F. Bernasconi. — New York [etc.] ; London : Academic Press, 1976. — xi,288p : ill ; 24cm.
Index.
ISBN 0-12-092950-3 : £18.00
(B77-08999)

541'.395 — Catalysis. *Reviews of research*

Advances in catalysis. — New York [etc.] ; London : Academic Press.
Vol.26 / edited by D.D. Eley, Herman Pines, Paul B. Weisz. — 1977. — xix,413p : ill, port ; 24cm.
Index.
ISBN 0-12-007826-0 : £28.05
(B77-18124)

Catalysis. — London : Chemical Society. — (Chemical Society. Specialist periodical reports)
Vol.1 : a review of the literature published up to mid-1976 / senior reporter C. Kemball ... — 1977. — xiv,425p : ill ; 23cm.
Index.
ISBN 0-85186-534-8 : £27.00
ISSN 0140-0568
(B77-21846)

541'.395 — Catalysts. Preparation & examination. *Reviews of research*

Experimental methods in catalytic research. — New York [etc.] ; London : Academic Press.
In 3 vols.
Vol.2 : Preparation and examination of practical catalysts / edited by Robert B. Anderson and Peter T. Dawson. — 1976. — xiv,283p : ill ; 24cm. — (Physical chemistry ; vol.15-II)
Bibl. — Index.
ISBN 0-12-058660-6 : £16.15
(B77-06067)

Vol.3 : Characterization of surface and absorbed species / edited by Robert B. Anderson and Peter T. Dawson. — 1976. — xiv,327p : ill ; 24cm. — (Physical chemistry ; vol.15-III)
Bibl. — Index.
ISBN 0-12-058662-2 : £20.95
(B77-12432)

541'.395 — Catalysts: Zeolites. Structure & physical properties

Jacobs, Peter A. Carboniogenic activity of zeolites / [by] Peter A. Jacobs. — Amsterdam ; Oxford [etc.] : Elsevier, 1977. — xvi,253p : ill ; 24cm.
Index.
ISBN 0-444-41556-4 : £14.40
(B77-20239)

541'.395 — Heterogeneous catalysis. *Conference proceedings*

Battelle Colloquium in the Materials Sciences, *9th, Gstaad, 1974.* The physical basis for heterogeneous catalysis / edited by Edmund Drauglis, Robert I. Jaffee. — New York ; London : Plenum Press, [1977]. — xxvi,596p : ill ; 26cm.
'... proceedings of the ninth Battelle Colloquium in the Materials Sciences, held in Gstaad, Switzerland, September 2-6, 1974' - Preface. — 'Battelle Institute materials science colloquia'. — Published in the United States: 1975. — Index.
ISBN 0-306-30912-2 : £28.35
(B77-10804)

541'.395 — Homogeneous catalysis. Metal coordination compounds

Taqui Khan, M M. Homogenous catalysis by metal complexes / [by] M.M. Taqui Khan, Arthur E. Martell. — New York ; London : Academic Press.
In 2 vols.
Vol.1 : Activation of small inorganic molecules. — 1974. — xiii,422p : ill ; 24cm.
Index.
ISBN 0-12-406101-x : Unpriced
(B77-20240)

541'.395 — Porous catalysts. Transport phenomena

Jackson, Roy. Transport in porous catalysts / [by] R. Jackson. — Amsterdam ; Oxford [etc.] : Elsevier, 1977. — ix,197p : ill ; 25cm. — (Chemical engineering monographs ; vol.4)
Index.
ISBN 0-444-41593-9 : £14.60
(B77-26297)

542 — CHEMISTRY. LABORATORIES, APPARATUS, EQUIPMENT

542 — Chemistry. Experiments

Bauer, Joseph M. Laboratory experiments for chemistry and the living organism / [by] Joseph M. Bauer, Molly M. Bloomfield. — New York ; London [etc.] : Wiley, 1977. — vi,272p : ill, forms ; 28cm.
Fill-in book. — Pierced for binder.
ISBN 0-471-05921-8 Pbk : Unpriced
(B77-26298)

Introductory experimental chemistry. — 2nd ed. / [by] Robert J. Ouellette ... [et al.]. — New York [etc.] ; London : Harper and Row, 1975. — vii,213p : ill ; 28cm.
Fill-in book. — Pages perforated at inside edge and pierced for binder. — Previous ed.: / by Robert J. Ouellette, Carole W. Bohn, John S. Swenton. New York : Harper and Row, 1970.
ISBN 0-06-044957-8 Pbk : Unpriced
(B77-20241)

542 — Chemistry. Research. Use of lasers

Chemical and biochemical applications of lasers / edited by C. Bradley Moore. — New York [etc.] ; London : Academic Press.
Vol.2. — 1977. — ix,288p : ill ; 24cm.
Index.
ISBN 0-12-505402-5 : £10.65
(B77-22555)

543 — CHEMICAL ANALYSIS

Christian, Gary D. Analytical chemistry / [by] Gary D. Christian. — 2nd ed. — New York ; London [etc.] : Wiley, 1977. — xvii,648p : ill ; 26cm.
Text on lining papers. — Previous ed.: Waltham, Mass. : Xerox College Publications, 1971. — Bibl.: p.624-625. — Index.
ISBN 0-471-15617-5 : £11.35
(B77-17479)

Comprehensive analytical chemistry / edited by Cecil L. Wilson and David W. Wilson. — Amsterdam ; Oxford [etc.] : Elsevier.
Vol.8 : Enzyme electrodes in analytical chemistry ; [and], Molecular fluorescence spectroscopy ; [and], Photometric titrations ; [and], Analytical applications of interferometry / edited by G. Svehla ; [contributors G.G. Guilbault, M.A. Leonard, W. Nebe]. — 1977. — xvi,589p : ill ; 24cm.
Index.
ISBN 0-444-41523-8 : £44.50
(B77-14226)

Modern methods of chemical analysis. — 2nd ed. / by Robert L. Pecsok ... [et al.]. — New York ; London [etc.] : Wiley, 1977. — xviii, 573p : ill ; 26cm.
Text on lining papers. — Previous ed.: / by Robert L. Pecsok and L. Donald Shields. 1968. — Index.
ISBN 0-471-67662-4 : £12.65
(B77-23386)

Skoog, Douglas Arvid. Fundamentals of analytical chemistry / [by] Douglas A. Skoog, Donald M. West. — 3rd ed. — New York ; London [etc.] : Holt, Rinehart and Winston, 1976. — xi,804p : ill ; 25cm.
With answers. — Text on lining papers. — Previous ed.: London : Holt, Rinehart and Winston, 1970. — Bibl.: p.777-780. — Index.
ISBN 0-03-089495-6 : £10.00
(B77-07337)

Treatise on analytical chemistry / edited by I.M. Kolthoff and Philip J. Elving. — New York ; London [etc.] : Wiley.
Part 1 : Theory and practice. Vol.12 : index, volumes 1 to 11 / edited by I.M. Kolthoff and Philip J. Elving with the assistance of Ernest B. Sandell. — 1976. — xviii p,p7235-7428 ; 25cm.
'An Interscience publication'.
ISBN 0-471-49968-4 : £17.35
(B77-05398)

Treatise on analytical chemistry / [edited by I.M. Kolthoff, Philip J. Elving]. — New York ; London [etc.] : Wiley.
Part 3 : Analytical chemistry in industry. Vol.3 / edited by I.M. Kolthoff, Philip J. Elving and Fred H. Stross. — 1976. — xxiii, 598p : ill, ports ; 25cm.
'An Interscience publication'. — Bibl. — Index.
ISBN 0-471-50012-7 : £27.70
(B77-12433)

543 — Chemical analysis. *Festschriften*
Essays on analytical chemistry : in memory of Professor Anders Ringbom / editor-in-chief Erkki Wänninen, editorial board ... [others]. — Oxford [etc.] : Pergamon, 1977. — xiv,607p, plate : ill, port ; 26cm.
Cover title: Analytical chemistry. — Bibl.: p.xi-xiv. — Index.
ISBN 0-08-021596-3 : £27.50
(B77-25605)

543 — Chemical analysis. *Reviews of research*
Selected annual reviews of the analytical sciences. — London (Burlington House, W1V 0BN) : Chemical Society.
Vol.4 : [1976] / editor L.S. Bark. — 1976. — v, 73p : ill ; 21cm.
ISBN 0-85990-204-8 Pbk : £9.50
ISSN 0300-9963
(B77-00207)

543'.0028 — Chemical analysis. Laboratory techniques
Methodicum chimicum : a critical survey of proven methods and their application in chemistry, natural science, and medicine / editor-in-chief Friedhelm Korte. — New York ; London [etc.] : Academic Press [etc.].
[Vol.8] : [Preparation of transition metal derivatives] / [edited by Kurt Niedenzu, Hans Zimmer]. — 1976. — x,579p : ill ; 28cm.
Bibl. — Index.
ISBN 0-12-460708-x : £67.00
(B77-24920)

543'.006'141 — Chemical analysis. Organisations. *Great Britain. Laboratory of the Government Chemist. Reports, surveys. Serials*
Laboratory of the Government Chemist. Report of the Government Chemist. — London : H.M.S.O.
1975. — 1976. — iv,158p,fold leaf of plate,[4]p of plates : ill(incl 1 col) ; 21cm.
Bibl.: p.141-145. — Index.
ISBN 0-11-511626-5 Pbk : £2.10
ISSN 0307-6814
(B77-03538)

1976. — 1977. — iv,166p,fold leaf of plate,4p of plates : ill(incl 1 col) ; 21cm.
Bibl.: p.146-150. — Index.
ISBN 0-11-511627-3 Pbk : £3.00
ISSN 0307-6814
(B77-21847)

543'.08 — Chemical analysis. Use of selective ion sensitive electrodes
Bailey, Peter L. Analysis with ion-selective electrodes / [by] Peter L. Bailey. — London [etc.] : Heyden, 1976. — xii,228p : ill ; 25cm. — (Heyden international topics in science)
Index.
ISBN 0-85501-223-4 : £6.80
(B77-09000)

543'.08 — Gas chromatography & pyrolysis mass spectrometry. *Conference proceedings*
International Symposium on Analytical Pyrolysis, *3rd, Amsterdam, 1976.* Analytical pyrolysis : proceedings of the third International Symposium on Analytical Pyrolysis, held in Amsterdam, September 7-9, 1976 / edited by C.E. Roland Jones and Carl A. Cramers. — Amsterdam ; Oxford [etc.] : Elsevier, 1977. — ix,424p : ill ; 25cm.
ISBN 0-444-41558-0 : Unpriced
(B77-22556)

543'.08 — Instrumental chemical analysis
Ewing, Galen Wood. Instrumental methods of chemical analysis / [by] Galen W. Ewing. — 4th ed. — New York ; London [etc.] : McGraw-Hill, [1976]. — ix,560p : ill ; 25cm.
Published in the United States: 1975. — Previous ed.: 1969. — Index.
ISBN 0-07-019853-5 : £11.20
(B77-01428)

543'.085 — Chemical analysis. Atomic absorption spectrometry. Use of electrothermal atomisers
Fuller, C W. Electrothermal atomization for atomic absorption spectrometry / [by] C.W. Fuller. — London : Chemical Society, 1977. — viii,127p : ill ; 23cm. — (Analytical sciences monographs ; [no.4] ISSN 0583-8894)
Index.
ISBN 0-85186-777-4 : £6.75
(B77-12434)

543'.085 — Chemical analysis. Atomic spectroscopy
Schrenk, William George. Analytical atomic spectroscopy / [by] William G. Schrenk. — New York ; London : Plenum Press, [1976]. — xvii,375p : ill ; 24cm. — (Modern analytical chemistry)
Published in the United States: 1975. — Bibl. — Index.
ISBN 0-306-33902-1 : £20.48
(B77-03539)

543'.085 — Chemical analysis. Atomic spectroscopy. *Reviews of research*
Annual reports on analytical atomic spectroscopy. — London (Burlington House, W1V 0BN) : Chemical Society.
Vol.5 : reviewing 1975 / editor C.W. Fuller. — 1976. — viii,267p ; 21cm.
Index.
ISBN 0-85186-757-x Pbk : £15.00
ISSN 0306-1353
(B77-00208)

543'.085 — Chemical analysis. Electron spectroscopy
Carlson, Thomas A. Photoelectron and Auger spectroscopy / [by] Thomas A. Carlson. — New York ; London : Plenum Press, [1976]. — xiii,417p : ill ; 24cm. — (Modern analytical chemistry)
Published in the United States: 1975. — Index.
ISBN 0-306-33901-3 : £20.00
(B77-04148)

543'.085 — Chemical analysis. Fluorescence spectroscopy & phosphorescence spectroscopy
Schulman, Stephen G. Fluorescence and phosphorescence spectroscopy : physicochemical principles and practice / by Stephen G. Schulman. — Oxford [etc.] : Pergamon, 1977. — x,288p : ill ; 26cm. — (International series in analytical chemistry ; vol.59)
Index.
ISBN 0-08-020499-6 : £11.00
(B77-16369)

543'.085 — Chemical analysis. Optical techniques
Olsen, Eugene Donald. Modern optical methods of analysis / [by] Eugene D. Olsen. — New York ; London [etc.] : McGraw-Hill, [1976]. — ix,629p : ill ; 24cm.
Published in the United States: 1975. — Bibl. — Index.
ISBN 0-07-047697-7 : £14.75
(B77-01429)

543'.085 — Gases. Infrared spectrometry. Spectra. *Tables. For calibration of infrared spectrometers*
International Union of Pure and Applied Chemistry. *Commission on Molecular Structure and Spectroscopy.* Tables of wavenumbers for the calibration of infrared spectrometers / International Union of Pure and Applied Chemistry, Commission on Molecular Structure and Spectroscopy. — 2nd ed. / compiled by A.R.H. Cole. — Oxford [etc.] : Pergamon, 1977. — xi,219p : ill ; 26cm.
Previous ed.: London : Butterworth, 1961. — Index.
ISBN 0-08-021247-6 : £12.50
(B77-23387)

543'.086 — Thermal analysis. *Conference proceedings*
European Symposium on Thermal Analysis, *1st, University of Salford, 1976.* Proceedings of the First European Symposium on Thermal Analysis, ESTA 1, University of Salford, UK, 20-24 September 1976, organized by the Thermal Methods Group of the Analytical Division of the Chemical Society / edited by David Dollimore. — London [etc.] : Heyden, 1976. — xxxv,458p : ill ; 25cm.
Includes 2 papers in French.
ISBN 0-85501-172-6 : £11.50
(B77-01430)

543'.086 — Thermal analysis. *Graphs*
Atlas of thermoanalytical curves : (TG-, DTG-, DTA-curves measured simultaneously) / edited by G. Liptay. — London [etc.] : Heyden.
2. — 1973. — 7p,leaves 51-125,p159-161 : ill(chiefly col) ; 25cm.
Leaves printed on both sides. — In binder. — Index.
ISBN 0-85501-152-1 Ls : £17.50
(B77-02988)

5. — 1976. — 15p,p276-350,p167-169 : col ill ; 25cm.
In binder. — Bibl. — Index.
ISBN 0-85501-155-6 Ls : £17.50
(B77-02989)

543'.086 — Thermal analysis data. Coordination with phase diagrams. Applications of computer systems. Projects: CALPHAD. *Periodicals*
Calphad : computer coupling of phase diagrams and thermochemistry. — Oxford [etc.] : Pergamon.
Vol.1, no.1- ; [Jan.] 1977-. — 1977-. — ill ; 25cm.
Quarterly. — Cover title. — 95p. in 1st issue.
Pbk : Unpriced
ISSN 0364-5916
Primary classification 541'.363
(B77-07896)

543'.087 — Chemical analysis. Electrochemical techniques
Galus, Z. Fundamentals of electrochemical analysis / [by] Z. Galus ; [translated from the Polish by Stefan Marcinkiewicz] ; translation editor G.F. Reynolds. — Chichester : Ellis Horwood Ltd ; New York ; London [etc.] : Wiley, 1976. — xviii,520p : ill ; 24cm. — (Ellis Horwood series in analytical chemistry)
Translation of: 'Teoretyczne podstawy elektroanalizy chemicznej'. Warszwaw : Pánstwowe Wydawn. Naukowe, 1971. — Index.
ISBN 0-85312-036-6 : £23.50
(B77-06068)

543'.087 — Chemical analysis. Isotachophoresis
Everaerts, Frans M. Isotachophoresis : theory, instrumentation and applications / [by] Frans M. Everaerts, Jo L. Beckers, Theo P.E.M. Verheggen. — Amsterdam ; Oxford [etc.] : Elsevier, 1976. — xiv,418p : ill(some col) ; 25cm. — ('Journal of chromatography' library ; vol.6)
Bibl.: p.397-408. — Index.
ISBN 0-444-41430-4 : £37.20
(B77-22557)

543'.087 — Chemical analysis. Stripping voltammetry
Vydra, František. Electrochemical stripping analysis / [by] František Vydra, Karel Štulík, Eva Juláková ; [translated from the Czech] ; translation editor Julian Tyson. — Chichester : Ellis Horwood [etc.], 1976. — 283p : ill ; 24cm. — (Ellis Horwood series in analytical chemistry)
Index.
ISBN 0-85312-017-x : £17.50
(B77-09686)

543'.088 — Chemical analysis. Applications of ionising radiation
Nuclear analytical chemistry. — Baltimore ; London [etc.] : University Park Press [etc.].
1 : Introduction to nuclear analytical chemistry / [by] J. Tölgyessy, Š. Varga and V. Kriváň ; English translation [from the Czech MS. by] P. Tkáč. — 1971[i.e.1976]. — 271p : ill ; 25cm.
Published in the United States: 1971. — Index.
ISBN 0-8391-0079-5 : £21.25
(B77-02287)

4 : Analysis based on the interaction of nuclear radiation with matter / [by] J. Tölgyessy and Š. Varga ; English translation [from the Czech MS.] V. Kačena, M. Rakovič. — 1975[i.e.1976]. — 300p : ill ; 25cm.
Published in the United States: 1975. — Index.
ISBN 0-8391-0082-5 : £21.25
(B77-02288)

5 : Tables, nomograms and schemes / [by] J. Tölgyessy ... [et al.] ; [translated from the Czech MS.]. — 1976. — 493p : ill ; 25cm.
Index.
ISBN 0-8391-0083-3 : £21.25
(B77-02289)

543'.088 — Chemical analysis. Radiochemical techniques
Radiochemical methods in analysis / edited by D.I. Coomber. — New York ; London : Plenum Press, [1976]. — ix,498p : ill ; 24cm.
Published in the United States: 1975. — Index.
ISBN 0-306-30738-3 : £17.33
(B77-00209)

544 — QUALITATIVE ANALYSIS
544'.1 — Ultracentrifugation. *Conference proceedings*
Fifty Years of the Ultracentrifuge *(Conference), Bethesda, 1975.* Proceedings of the conference Fifty Years of the Ultracentrifuge, Bethesda, Maryland, February 24-26, 1975 / editors Marc S. Lewis and George H. Weiss. — Amsterdam [etc.] ; Oxford : North-Holland Publishing Co., 1976. — [8],286p : ill, ports ; 27cm.
'Reprinted from "Biophysical Chemistry", Vol.5 (1, 2), 1976' - title page verso. — Index.
ISBN 0-7204-0511-4 : £28.05
(B77-06668)

544'.85 — Qualitative analysis: Semimicroanalysis
Sorum, Clarence Harvey. Introduction to semimicro qualitative analysis. — 5th ed. / [by] C.H. Sorum, J.J. Lagowski. — Englewood Cliffs ; London [etc.] : Prentice-Hall, 1977. — x,310p : ill, forms ; 23cm.
Previous ed.: / by C.H. Sorum. 1967. — Bibl.: p.8-9. — Index.
ISBN 0-13-496059-9 Pbk : £7.15
(B77-26299)

544'.92 — High performance thin layer chromatography
HPTLC : high performance thin-layer chromatography / editors A. Zlatkis, R.E. Kaiser. — Amsterdam ; Oxford [etc.] : Elsevier [for the] Institute of Chromatography, 1977. — 240p : ill(some col) ; 25cm. — ('Journal of chromatography' library ; vol.9)
Index.
ISBN 0-444-41525-4 : £27.50
(B77-07338)

544'.924 — Liquid chromatography
Bristow, P A. Liquid chromatography in practice / [by] P.A. Bristow. — Handforth (10 Langley Drive, Handforth, Wilmslow, Cheshire SK9 3BQ) : Letp, 1976. — [7],265p : ill ; 22cm.
Text on lining papers. — Also available on microfiche. — Index.
ISBN 0-9504833-1-1 : Unpriced
ISBN 0-9504833-0-3 Pbk : Unpriced
(B77-28596)

544'.926 — Gas chromatography
Modern practice of gas chromatography / edited by Robert L. Grob. — New York ; London [etc.] : Wiley, 1977. — xix,654p : ill ; 24cm.
'A Wiley-Interscience publication'. — Index.
ISBN 0-471-01564-4 : Unpriced
(B77-22558)

544'.926 — Pyrolysis-gas chromatography
May, R W. Pyrolysis-gas chromatography / [by] R.W. May, E.F. Pearson & D. Scothern. — London : Chemical Society, 1977. — vii,109p : ill ; 22cm. — (Analytical sciences monographs ISSN 0583-8894)
ISBN 0-85186-767-7 : £7.20
(B77-25606)

545 — QUANTITATIVE ANALYSIS
545 — Trace elements. Quantitative analysis. Contamination. Control measures. *State-of-the-art reviews*
Zief, Morris. Contamination control in trace element analysis / [by] Morris Zief, James W. Mitchell. — New York ; London [etc.] : Wiley, 1976. — xv,262p : ill ; 24cm. — (Chemical analysis ; vol.47)
'A Wiley-Interscience Publication'. — Index.
ISBN 0-471-61169-7 : £17.35
(B77-09002)

545'.2 — Volumetric analysis. *Secondary school texts*
Atkinson, Arthur. Elementary volumetric analysis / by Arthur Atkinson. — New SI ed. — London : Longman, 1976. — viii,40p ; 19cm.
With answers. — Previous ed.: i.e. S.I. ed., 1973.
ISBN 0-582-69807-3 Sd : £0.42
(B77-16870)

545'.33 — Mass spectrometry
Majer, J R. The mass spectrometer / [by] J.R. Majer. — London [etc.] : Wykeham Publications, 1977. — xii,159p : ill ; 22cm. — (The Wykeham science series ; 44)
Bibl.: p.155. — Index.
ISBN 0-85109-590-9 : £6.50
ISBN 0-85109-550-x Pbk : £3.50
(B77-30237)

545'.33 — Mass spectrometry. *Reviews of research*
Mass spectrometry. — London : Chemical Society. — (Chemical Society. Specialist periodical reports)
Vol.4 : a review of the literature published between July 1974 and June 1976 / senior reporter R.A.W. Johnstone, reporters ... [others]. — 1977. — xii,357p : ill ; 23cm.
Index.
ISBN 0-85186-288-8 : Unpriced
ISSN 0305-9987
(B77-15836)

545'.812 — Colorimetric analysis. *Laboratory manuals*
Thomas, Leslie Charles. Colorimetric chemical analytical methods. — 8th ed. / [by] L.C. Thomas, G.J. Chamberlin. — Salisbury [etc.] : Tintometer Ltd ; London [etc.] : Distributed by Wiley, 1974. — [3],xli,626p : ill ; 27cm.
Previous ed.: / by Tintometer Limited. 1967.
ISBN 0-471-99525-8 : £20.00
(B77-27051)

546 — INORGANIC CHEMISTRY
546 — Inorganic compounds
Jolly, William Lee. The principles of inorganic chemistry / [by] William L. Jolly. — New York ; London [etc.] : McGraw-Hill, 1976. — viii,376p : ill ; 25cm.
Text on lining papers. — With answers to selected problems. — Index.
ISBN 0-07-032758-0 : £13.30
(B77-02990)

Lee, John David. A new concise inorganic chemistry / by J.D. Lee. — 3rd ed. — New York ; London [etc.] : Van Nostrand Reinhold, 1977. — xxi,505p : ill ; 24cm.
Previous ed.: published as 'Concise inorganic chemistry'. 1965. — Bibl. — Index.
ISBN 0-442-30169-3 : £12.00
ISBN 0-442-30165-0 Pbk : Unpriced
(B77-29414)

Purcell, Keith F. Inorganic chemistry / [by] Keith F. Purcell, John C. Kotz. — Philadelphia ; London [etc.] : Saunders, 1977. — xix,1116p : ill ; 28cm. — (Saunders golden sunburst series)
Text on lining papers. — Index.
ISBN 0-7216-7407-0 : £9.50
(B77-25607)

Rochow, Eugene George. Modern descriptive chemistry / [by] Eugene G. Rochow. — Philadelphia ; London [etc.] : Saunders, 1977. — viii,253p,2p of plates : ill(some col), ports ; 27cm. — (Saunders golden sunburst series)
Index.
ISBN 0-7216-7628-6 Pbk : £5.75
(B77-21848)

546 — Inorganic compounds. *Reviews of research*
Advances in inorganic chemistry and radiochemistry. — New York [etc.] ; London : Academic Press.
Vol.19 : 1976 / editors H.J. Emeléus, A.G. Sharpe. — [1977]. — vii,322p : ill ; 24cm.
Published in the United States: 1976. — Bibl. — Index.
ISBN 0-12-023619-2 : £22.35
Also classified at 541'.38
(B77-11791)

Vol.20 : 1977 / editors H.J. Emeléus, A.G. Sharpe. — 1977. — vii,374p : ill ; 24cm.
Bibl. — Index.
ISBN 0-12-023620-6 : £27.70
Also classified at 541'.38
(B77-31885)

546 — Inorganic compounds. Compounds of main group elements. *Reviews of research*
Inorganic chemistry of the Main-group elements. — London : Chemical Society. — (Chemical Society. Specialist periodical reports)
Vol.14 : a review of the literature published between October 1974 and September 1975 / senior reporter C.C. Addison, reporters ... [others]. — 1977. — xi,454p : ill ; 23cm.
Index.
ISBN 0-85186-782-0 : £26.00
ISSN 0305-697x
(B77-16370)

546'.028 — Inorganic chemistry. Experiments. *Manuals*
Angelici, Robert Joe. Synthesis and technique in inorganic chemistry / [by] Robert J. Angelici. — 2nd ed. — Philadelphia ; London [etc.] : Saunders, 1977. — xiv,237p : ill ; 24cm. — (Saunders golden sunburst series)
Text on lining paper. — Previous ed.: 1969. — Bibl. — Index.
ISBN 0-7216-1281-4 : £10.00
(B77-24207)

546'.22 — Water. Chemical analysis. Laboratory techniques
Mitchell, John, *b.1913.* Aquametry / [by] John Mitchell, Jr, and Donald Milton Smith. — 2nd ed. — New York ; London [etc.] : Wiley. — (Chemical analysis ; vol.5)
Previous ed.: in 1 vol. New York : Interscience, 1948.
Part 1 : A treatise on methods for the determination of water. — 1977. — xiii,632p : ill ; 24cm.
'A Wiley-Interscience publication'. — Bibl. — Index.
ISBN 0-471-02264-0 : £22.45
(B77-33788)

546'.22 — Water. Properties
Water : a comprehensive treatise / edited by Felix Franks. — New York ; London : Plenum Press.
In 5 vols.
Vol.1 : The physics and physical chemistry of water. — [1976]. — xix,396p : ill ; 24cm.
Published in the United States: 1972. — Bibl.: p.545-577. — Index.
ISBN 0-306-37181-2 : £23.63
(B77-00754)

Vol.2 : Water in crystalline hydrates, aqueous solutions of simple nonelectrolytes. — 1973 [i.e. 1976]. — xix,684p : ill ; 24cm.
Published in the United States: 1973. — Bibl.: p.625-661. — Index.
ISBN 0-306-37182-0 : £23.63
(B77-00755)

Vol.3 : Aqueous solutions of simple electrolytes. — 1973 [i.e. 1976]. — xvii,472p : ill ; 24cm.
Published in the United States: 1973. — Bibl.: p.433-455. — Index.
ISBN 0-306-37183-9 : £23.63
(B77-00756)

Vol.4 : Aqueous solutions of amphiphiles and macromolecules. — 1975. — xxi,839p : ill ; 24cm.
Bibl.: p.759-801. — Index.
ISBN 0-306-37184-7 : £19.90
(B77-01431)

546'.3 — Liquid metals. *Conference proceedings*
International Conference on Liquid Metals, *3rd, University of Bristol, 1976.* Liquid metals, 1976 : invited and contributed papers from the Third International Conference on Liquid Metals held at the University of Bristol, 12-16 July 1976 / edited by R. Evans and D.A. Greenwood. — Bristol [etc.] : Institute of Physics, 1977. — xiii,672p : ill ; 24cm. — (Institute of Physics. Conference series ; no.30 ISSN 0305-2346)
Bibl. — Index.
ISBN 0-85498-120-9 : Unpriced
(B77-13031)

546'.3 — Metals. Impurities: Magnetic ions. Electron spin resonance spectroscopy
Taylor, R H. Magnetic ions in metals : a review of their study by electron spin resonance / [by] R.H. Taylor. — London : Taylor and Francis, 1977. — [7],118p : ill ; 26cm. — (Taylor & Francis monographs on physics)
Originally published: in 'Advances in physics. Vol.24, no.6, November 1975'. — Bibl.: p.109-113. — Index.
ISBN 0-85066-100-5 : £6.00
(B77-14715)

546'.3 — Metals. Interactions with gases
Fast, Johan Diedrich. Gases in metals / [by] J.D. Fast. — Updated and reorganised ed. — London [etc.] : Macmillan, 1976. — ix,260p : ill ; 24cm. — (Philips technical library)
Previous ed.: published as 'Interaction of metals and gases'. 1971. — Index.
ISBN 0-333-21214-2 Pbk : £5.95
(B77-04793)

546'.3 — Metals. Surfaces. Chemical properties. *Conference proceedings*
NATO Advanced Study Institute on Electronic Structure and Reactivity of Metal Surfaces, *Namur, 1975.* Electronic structure of reactivity of metal surfaces / edited by E.G. Derouane and A.A. Lucas. — New York ; London : Plenum Press [for the] NATO Scientific Affairs Division, 1976. — xiii,633p : ill ; 26cm. — (NATO Advanced Study Institutes : series B, physics ; vol.16)
'Lectures presented at the NATO Advanced Study Institute on Electronic Structure and Reactivity of Metal Surfaces held at the Facultés Universitaires Notre-Dame de la Paix, Namur, Belgium, August 31-September 13, 1975' - title page verso. — Index.
ISBN 0-306-35716-x : £31.19
(B77-14227)

546'.6 — Transition metal compounds. Experiments. *Secondary school texts*
King, Joseph Norman. Transition element chemistry / [by] J.N. King and P. McManus. — London : Heinemann Educational. — (Heinemann experimental chemistry series ; 4)
Students' text. — 1976. — x,78p : ill ; 24cm.
ISBN 0-435-65956-1 Sd : £1.25
(B77-00210)

Teachers' guide. — 1976. — xi,91p : ill ; 22cm.

ISBN 0-435-65957-x Sd : £1.90
(B77-00211)

546'.6 — Transition metals
Open University. *S304 (S351) Course Team.* Transition-metal chemistry / prepared by an Open University Course Team [i.e. the S304 (S351) Course Team]. — Milton Keynes : Open University Press.
2. — 1976. — 39,45p : ill(some col) ; 30cm. — (Science, a third level course : the nature of chemistry ; units 15 and 16) (S304 (S351) ; 15 and 16)
With answers.
ISBN 0-335-04235-x Pbk : Unpriced
(B77-02991)

546'.6 — Transition metals. *Reviews of research*
Inorganic chemistry of the transition elements. — London : Chemical Society. — (Chemical Society. Specialist periodical reports)
Vol.5 : a review of the literature published between Oct. 1974 and Sept. 1975 / senior reporter B.F.G. Johnson ... — 1977. — xvi, 524p : ill ; 23cm.
Index.
ISBN 0-85186-540-2 : £29.00
ISSN 0305-9774
(B77-10359)

546'.63 — Platinum metals. Chemical analysis
Analytical chemistry of platinum metals / [by] S.I. Ginzburg ... [et al.] ; [editor I.P. Alimarin] ; translated [from the Russian] by N. Kaner ; [translation] edited by P. Shelnitz. — New York [etc.] : Wiley ; Jerusalem ; London : Israel Program for Scientific Translations ; London : Distributed by Wiley, [1977]. — xii, 673p ; 25cm. — (Analytical chemistry of the elements)
'A Halsted Press book'. — This translation published in the United States: 1975. — Translation of: 'Analiticheskaia khimiia platinovykh metallov'. Moscow : Nauka, 1972. — Bibl.: p.583-654. — Index.
ISBN 0-7065-1405-x : £35.60
(B77-11206)

546'.663'2 — Mercury compounds
The **chemistry** of mercury / edited by C.A. McAuliffe. — London [etc.] : Macmillan, 1977. — viii,288p : ill ; 25cm. — (Aspects of inorganic chemistry)
Bibl.: p.42. — Index.
ISBN 0-333-17863-7 : £25.00
(B77-20242)

546'.683'24 — Silicates. *State-of-the-art reviews*
Eitel, Wilhelm. Silicate science / by Wilhelm Eitel. — New York [etc.] ; London : Academic Press.
Vol.8 : Industrial glass : glazes and enamels. — 1976 [i.e 1977]. — xvi,396p : ill ; 25cm.
Published in the United States: 1976. — Index.
ISBN 0-12-236308-6 : £27.70
(B77-09003)

546'.711'2 — Nitrogen oxides. Chemical reactions. Catalysis. *Conference proceedings*
Symposium on the Catalytic Chemistry of Nitrogen Oxides, *General Motors Research Laboratories, 1974.* The catalytic chemistry of nitrogen oxides / edited by Richard L. Klimisch and John G. Larson. — New York ; London : Plenum Press, 1975 [i.e. 1976]. — ix, 340p : ill ; 26cm.
'Proceedings of the Symposium on the Catalytic Chemistry of Nitrogen Oxides held at the General Motors Research Laboratories, Warren, Michigan, October 7-8, 1974' - title page verso. — Published in the United States: 1975. — Index.
ISBN 0-306-30875-4 : £17.33
(B77-02290)

546'.712'2 — Phosphorus compounds
Topics in phosphorus chemistry. — New York ; London [etc.] : Wiley.
Vol.8 / authors Margot Becke-Goehring ... [et al.] ; editors Edward J. Griffith, Martin Grayson ... — 1976. — ix,664p : ill ; 24cm.
'An Interscience Publication'. — Bibl. — Index.

ISBN 0-471-32789-1 : £30.70
(B77-27052)

546'.712'2 — Phosphorus compounds. *Reviews of research*
Topics in phosphorus chemistry. — New York ; London [etc.] : Wiley.
Vol.9 / authors H.M. Buck ... [et al.] ; editors Edward J. Griffith, Martin Grayson. — 1977. — ix,516p : ill ; 24cm.
'An Interscience publication'. — Bibl. — Index.

ISBN 0-471-32782-4 : £32.65
(B77-26301)

546'.712'205 — Phosphorus compounds. *Periodicals*
Phosphorus and sulfur and the related elements. — New York ; London [etc.] : Gordon and Breach.
Vol.1, no.1- ; Aug. 1976. — 1976-. — ill ; 28cm.
Published at irregular intervals. — Each volume consists of 3 double-sized issues. — Cover title. — [3],128p. in 1st issue. — Supersedes: 'International journal of sulfur chemistry' and 'Phosphorus and the related Group V elements'.

Pbk : £71.50 for each volume
ISSN 0308-664x
Also classified at 546'.723'205
(B77-01432)

546'.723'205 — Sulphur compounds. *Periodicals*
Phosphorus and sulfur and the related elements. — New York ; London [etc.] : Gordon and Breach.
Vol.1, no.1- ; Aug. 1976. — 1976-. — ill ; 28cm.
Published at irregular intervals. — Each volume consists of 3 double-sized issues. — Cover title. — [3],128p. in 1st issue. — Supersedes: 'International journal of sulfur chemistry' and 'Phosphorus and the related Group V elements'.

Pbk : £71.50 for each volume
ISSN 0308-664x
Primary classification 546'.712'205
(B77-01432)

546'.75 — Solidified inert gases
Rare gas solids / edited by M.L. Klein and J.A. Venables. — London [etc.] : Academic Press.
In 2 vols. — Index.
Vol.2. — 1977. — xiii p,p609-1252 : ill ; 24cm.
Bibl.
ISBN 0-12-413502-1 : £26.00
(B77-22559)

547 — ORGANIC CHEMISTRY
Neckers, Douglas Carlyle. Organic chemistry / [by] Douglas C. Neckers, Michael P. Doyle. — New York [etc.] ; London : Wiley, 1977. — xxxvi,1147p : ill ; 26cm.
With answers to selected problems. — Text, ill. on lining papers. — Bibl.: p.1083-1090. — Index.
ISBN 0-471-63091-8 : £16.50
(B77-23388)

Rodd, Ernest Harry. Rodd's chemistry of carbon compounds : a modern comprehensive treatise. — 2nd ed. / edited by S. Coffey. — Amsterdam ; Oxford [etc.] : Elsevier.
Previous ed.: published as 'Chemistry of carbon compounds'. Amsterdam : Elsevier, 1951-.
Vol.4 : Heterocyclic compounds. Part F : Six membered heterocyclic compounds with a single nitrogen atom in the ring, pyridine, polymethylenepyridines, quinoline, isoquinoline and their derivatives. — 1976. — xvii,486p ; 24cm.
Index.
ISBN 0-444-41503-3 : £43.33
(B77-14228)

Ternay, Andrew L. Contemporary organic chemistry / [by] Andrew L. Ternay, Jr. — Philadelphia ; London [etc.] : Saunders, 1976. — 1095p in various pagings : ill ; 27cm. — (Saunders golden sunburst series)
Text, ill. on lining papers. — With answers to selected problems. — Index.
ISBN 0-7216-8794-6 : £17.50
(B77-06069)

547 — Organic chemistry. *Reviews of research*
Advances in organic chemistry : methods and results / E.C. Taylor, editor. — New York ; London [etc.] : Wiley.
[Vol.9] : Iminium salts in organic chemistry. Part 1 / edited by H. Böhme, H.G. Viehe. — [1977]. — xiii,631p : ill ; 24cm.
'An Interscience Publication'. — Published in the United States: 1976. — Index.
ISBN 0-471-90692-1 : £32.00
(B77-13642)

547 — Organic compounds
March, Jerry. Advanced organic chemistry : reactions, mechanisms and structure / [by] Jerry March. — 2nd ed. — New York ; London [etc.] : McGraw-Hill, 1977. — xv, 1328p : ill ; 25cm.
Previous ed.: 1968. — Index.
ISBN 0-07-040247-7 : £20.25
(B77-33789)

Meislich, Herbert. Schaum's outline of theory and problems of organic chemistry / by Herbert Meislich, Howard Nechamkin and Jacob Sharefkin. — New York ; London [etc.] : McGraw-Hill, 1977. — [11],480p : ill ; 28cm. — (Schaum's outline series)
Cover title: Theory and problems of organic chemistry. — Spine title: Organic chemistry. — Index.
ISBN 0-07-041457-2 Pbk : £5.20
(B77-31177)

O'Leary, Marion H. Contemporary organic chemistry : molecules, mechanisms and metabolism / [by] Marion H. O'Leary. — New York ; London [etc.] : McGraw-Hill, [1977]. — xv,396p : ill(some col) ; 25cm.
With answers to selected problems. — Published in the United States: 1976. — Bibl. — Index.
ISBN 0-07-047694-2 : £12.40
(B77-11207)

Rodd, Ernest Harry. Rodd's chemistry of carbon compounds : a modern comprehensive treatise. — 2nd ed. / edited by S. Coffey. — Amsterdam ; Oxford [etc.] : Elsevier.
Previous ed.: published as 'Chemistry of carbon compounds'. Amsterdam : Elsevier, 1951-.
Vol.1 : Aliphatic compounds. Part G : Tetrahydric alcohols, their analogues, derivatives and oxidation products. Cumulative index vol.1, parts A-G. — 1976. — xiv,344p ; 24cm.
Index.
ISBN 0-444-41447-9 : £32.61
(B77-07899)

Vol.4 : Heterocyclic compounds. Part E : Six-membered monoheterocyclic compounds containing oxygen, sulphur, selenium, tellurium, silicon, germanium, tin, lead or iodine as the hetero-atom. — 1977. — xvi,521p ; 24cm.
Index.
ISBN 0-444-41363-4 : £45.67
(B77-33790)

Simpson, J Ernest. An outline of organic chemistry : problems and answers. — 3rd ed. / [by] J. Ernest Simpson, Corwin Hansch, George K. Helmkamp. — New York ; London [etc.] : McGraw-Hill, [1976]. — xiii,447p : ill ; 28cm.
This ed. published in the United States: 1975. — Previous ed.: published as 'Organic chemistry' / by Corwin Hansch, George Helmkamp. 1963. — Index.
ISBN 0-07-057436-7 Pbk : £5.30
(B77-01433)

547 — Organic compounds. *Reviews of research*
International review of science. Organic chemistry. Series two / [consultant editor D.H. Hey]. — London [etc.] : Butterworth.
Vol.10 : Free radical reactions / edited by W.A. Waters. — 1975. — [11],375p : ill ; 24cm.
Index.
ISBN 0-408-70622-8 : £15.00
(B77-11792)

547 — Organic compounds containing double bonds. *Reviews of research*
The **chemistry** of double-bonded functional groups / edited by Saul Patai. — London [etc.] : Wiley, 1977. — 2v.(xv,1343p) : ill ; 24cm. — (The chemistry of functional groups : supplement A)
'An Interscience Publication'. — Index.
ISBN 0-471-66940-7 : £58.50
(B77-18748)

547 — Organic selenium compounds & organic tellurium compounds. *Reviews of research*
Organic compounds of sulphur, selenium, and tellurium. — London : Chemical Society. — (Chemical Society. Specialist periodical reports)
Vol.2 : A review of the literature published between April 1970 and March 1972 / senior reporter D.H. Reid, reporters ... [others]. — 1973. — xxxii,827p : ill ; 23cm.
Index.
ISBN 0-85186-269-1 : Unpriced
ISSN 0305-9812
Primary classification 547'.06
(B77-19361)

Vol.3 : A review of the literature published between April 1972 and March 1974 / senior reporter D.H. Reid, reporters ... [others]. — 1975. — xxv,805p : ill ; 23cm.
Index.
ISBN 0-85186-279-9 : Unpriced
ISSN 0305-9812
Primary classification 547'.06
(B77-19362)

Vol.4 : a review of the literature published between April 1974 and March 1976 / senior reporter D.R. Hogg ; reporters ... [others]. — 1977. — xxiii,527p ; 23cm.
Index.
ISBN 0-85186-289-6 : £35.00
ISSN 0305-9812
Primary classification 547'.06
(B77-31886)

547'.0028 — Organic chemistry. Experiments. *Laboratory manuals*
Brewster, Ray Quincy. Unitized experiments in organic chemistry / [by] Ray Q. Brewster, Calvin A. Vanderwerf, William E. McEwen. — 4th ed. — New York ; London [etc.] : D. Van Nostrand, 1977. — xxiii,577p : ill, form ; 23cm.
Previous ed.: New York ; London : Van Nostrand Reinhold, 1970. — Bibl.: p.520. — Index.
ISBN 0-442-21051-5 Pbk : £8.85
(B77-22560)

Pavia, Donald L. Introduction to organic laboratory techniques : a contemporary approach / [by] Donald L. Pavia, Gary M. Lampman, George S. Kriz, Jr. — Philadelphia ; London [etc.] : Saunders, 1976. — xiv,699,viii p : ill ; 27cm. — (Saunders golden sunburst series)
Text on lining papers. — Index.
ISBN 0-7216-7121-7 : £8.25
(B77-17480)

Routh, Joseph Isaac. Experiments in organic and biochemistry / [by] Joseph I. Routh. — Philadelphia ; London [etc.] : Saunders, 1974 [i.e. 1976]. — viii,172p : ill ; 25cm. — (Saunders golden series)
Pages perforated at inside edge. — Published in the United States: 1974. — Students laboratory manual for the textbook 'Essentials of organic and biochemistry' / by Donald J. Burton and Joseph I. Routh. '... designed to strengthen and illustrate material in the textbook, as well as in any other book that covers the two fields of chemistry' - Preface.
ISBN 0-7216-7730-4 Pbk : £4.00
Also classified at 574.1'92'028
(B77-04794)

547'.0028 — Organic chemistry. Laboratory techniques. Applications of biochemical laboratory techniques
Applications of biochemical systems in organic chemistry / edited by J. Bryan Jones, Charles J. Sih, D. Perlman. — New York ; London [etc.] : Wiley. — (Techniques of chemistry ; vol.10)
Part 1. — 1976. — xiii,505,I16p : ill ; 24cm.
'A Wiley-Interscience publication'. — Index.
ISBN 0-471-93267-1 : £24.25
(B77-08365)

Part 2. — 1976. — xiii,I16p,p507-1065 : ill ; 24cm.
'A Wiley-Interscience publication'. — Index.
ISBN 0-471-93270-1 : £26.65
(B77-08366)

547'.003 — Organic compounds. *Dictionaries*
Dictionary of organic compounds : the constitution and physical, chemical and other properties of the principal carbon compounds and their derivatives, together with relevant literature references. — 4th ed. — London : Eyre and Spottiswoode : Spon.
12th supplement : incorporating new material published in and before 1975 / editor J.B. Thomson. — 1976. — [5],264p : ill ; 27cm.
Index.
ISBN 0-413-60810-7 : £22.50
(B77-00212)

547'.02 — Organic fluorine compounds
Hudlický, Miloš. Chemistry of organic fluorine compounds : a laboratory manual with comprehensive literature coverage / [by] Miloš Hudlický. — 2nd (revised) ed. — Chichester : Ellis Horwood [etc.], 1976. — xiv,903p,4p of plates : ill ; 24cm.
Previous ed.: Oxford : Pergamon, 1961. — Bibl. : p.729-859. — Index.
ISBN 0-85312-008-0 : £35.50
(B77-01434)

547'.02 — Organic fluorine compounds. *Reviews of research*
Fluorocarbon and related chemistry. — London : Chemical Society. — (Chemical Society. Specialist periodical reports)
Vol.3 : a review of the literature published during 1973 and 1974 / senior reporters R.E. Banks, M.G. Barlow ... — 1976. — ix,491p : ill ; 23cm.
Index.
ISBN 0-85186-524-0 : £35.00
ISSN 0301-8938
(B77-09004)

547'.036 — Aldehydes. Chemical analysis. Photometry
Sawicki, Eugene. Aldehydes, photometric analysis / [by] Eugene Sawicki and Carole R. Sawicki. — London [etc.] : Academic Press. — (The analysis of organic materials ; 9)
In 7 vols.
Vol.4 : Aldehyde precursors : formation and analysis of aldehydes (Part II). — 1976. — xiii, 285p : ill ; 24cm.
Index.
ISBN 0-12-620504-3 : £12.00
(B77-08367)

547'.05 — Organometallic compounds. *Reviews of research*
Organometallic chemistry reviews / edited by D. Seyferth ... [et al.]. — Amsterdam ; Oxford [etc.] : Elsevier, 1977. — vii,342p : ill ; 25cm. — ('Journal of organometallic chemistry' library ; 3)
ISBN 0-444-41538-6 : £24.12
(B77-15837)

Organometallic chemistry. — London : Chemical Society. — (Chemical Society. Specialist periodical reports)
Vol.5 : a review of the literature published during 1975 / senior reporters E.W. Abel, F.G.A. Stone ... — 1976. — xviii,520p : ill ; 22cm.
Bibl. — Index.
ISBN 0-85186-541-0 : £29.00
ISSN 0301-0074
(B77-06070)

547'.05 — Organometallic compounds. Chemical reactions. Mechanisms. *Reviews of research*
Matteson, Donald S. Organometallic reaction mechanisms of the nontransition elements / [by] Donald S. Matteson. — New York ; London : Academic Press, 1974. — xii,353p : ill ; 24cm. — (Organometallic chemistry)
Index.
ISBN 0-12-481150-7 : Unpriced
(B77-19360)

547'.05 — Organometallic compounds. Infrared spectroscopy & Raman spectroscopy
Maslowsky, Edward. Vibrational spectra of organometallic compounds / [by] Edward Maslowsky, Jr. — New York ; London [etc.] : Wiley, 1977. — xiii,528p : ill ; 24cm.
'A Wiley-Interscience publication'. — Index.
ISBN 0-471-58026-0 : £18.75
(B77-22561)

547'.05 — Organometallic compounds. Spectroscopy. *Reviews of research*
Spectroscopic properties of inorganic and organometallic compounds. — London : Chemical Society. — (Chemical Society. Specialist periodical reports)
Vol.9 : a review of the literature published during 1975 / senior reporter N.N. Greenwood ... — 1976. — xiii,544p : ill ; 23cm.
Bibl.: p.500-506. — Index.
ISBN 0-85186-083-4 : £28.56
ISSN 0584-8555
Primary classification 541'.28
(B77-06062)

547'.05'51 — Organic hafnium compounds, organic titanium compounds & organic zirconium compounds
Wailes, P C. Organometallic chemistry of titanium, zirconium and hafnium / [by] P.C. Wailes, R.S.P. Coutts, H. Weigold. — New York ; London : Academic Press, 1974. — x, 302p : ill ; 24cm. — (Organometallic chemistry)
Bibl.: p.262-286. — Index.
ISBN 0-12-730350-2 : Unpriced
(B77-21112)

547'.05686 — Organic tin compounds. *Reviews of research*
Organometallic chemistry reviews, annual surveys, silicon-tin-lead / edited by D. Seyferth, R.B. King. — Amsterdam ; Oxford [etc.] : Elsevier, 1977. — [7],547p : ill ; 25cm. — ('Journal of organometallic chemistry' library ; 4)
Index.
Unpriced
ISBN 0-444-41591-2
Primary classification 547'.08
(B77-25608)

547'.06 — Organic sulphur compounds. *Reviews of research*
Organic compounds of sulphur, selenium, and tellurium. — London : Chemical Society. — (Chemical Society. Specialist periodical reports)
Vol.2 : A review of the literature published between April 1970 and March 1972 / senior reporter D.H. Reid, reporters ... [others]. — 1973. — xxxii,827p : ill ; 23cm.
Index.
ISBN 0-85186-269-1 : Unpriced
ISSN 0305-9812
Also classified at 547
(B77-19361)

Vol.3 : A review of the literature published between April 1972 and March 1974 / senior reporter D.H. Reid, reporters ... [others]. — 1975. — xxv,805p : ill ; 23cm.
Index.
ISBN 0-85186-279-9 : Unpriced
ISSN 0305-9812
Also classified at 547
(B77-19362)

Vol.4 : a review of the literature published between April 1974 and March 1976 / senior reporter D.R. Hogg ; reporters ... [others]. — 1977. — xxiii,527p ; 23cm.
Index.
ISBN 0-85186-289-6 : £35.00
ISSN 0305-9812
Also classified at 547
(B77-31886)

547'.06 — Organic sulphur compounds. Chemical analysis
Ashworth, Michael Raymond Frederick. The determination of sulphur-containing groups / [by] M.R.F. Ashworth. — London [etc.] : Academic Press.
Vol.3 : Analytical methods for sulphides and disulphides. — 1977. — xi,220p : ill ; 24cm. — (The analysis of organic materials ; 2)
Bibl. — Index.
ISBN 0-12-065003-7 : £11.00
(B77-24921)

547'.07 — Organic phosphorus compounds. *Reviews of research*
Organophosphorus chemistry. — London : Chemical Society. — (Chemical Society. Specialist periodical reports)
Vol.8 : a review of the literature published between July 1975 and June 1976 / senior reporter S. Trippett ... — 1977. — xii,289p ; 23cm.
Index.
ISBN 0-85186-076-1 : £22.00
ISSN 0306-0713
(B77-20243)

547'.08 — Organic silicon compounds. *Reviews of research*
Organometallic chemistry reviews, annual surveys, silicon-tin-lead / edited by D. Seyferth, R.B. King. — Amsterdam ; Oxford [etc.] : Elsevier, 1977. — [7],547p : ill ; 25cm. — ('Journal of organometallic chemistry' library ; 4)
Index.
Unpriced
ISBN 0-444-41591-2
Also classified at 547'.05686
(B77-25608)

Organometallic chemistry reviews, organosilicon reviews / edited by D. Seyferth ... [et al.]. — Amsterdam ; Oxford [etc.] : Elsevier, 1976. — [7],404p : ill ; 25cm. — ('Journal of organometallic chemistry' library ; 2)
Bibl.: p.384-404.
ISBN 0-444-41488-6 : £25.12
(B77-06669)

547'.1'22 — Organic compounds. Colour. Effects of molecular structure
Griffiths, John, *b.1942 (Dec.).* Colour and constitution of organic molecules / [by] John Griffiths. — London [etc.] : Academic Press, 1976. — x,281p : ill ; 24cm.
Index.
ISBN 0-12-303550-3 : £9.50
(B77-08368)

547'.1'22077 — Organic compounds. Molecules. Structure. *Programmed texts*
Weeks, Daniel P. Electron movement : a guide for students of organic chemistry / [by] Daniel P. Weeks. — Philadelphia ; London [etc.] : Saunders, 1976. — ii-xv,133p : ill ; 26cm. — (Saunders golden sunburst series)
With answers.
ISBN 0-7216-9143-9 Pbk : £4.50
(B77-03540)

547'.1'224 — Organic compounds. Free radicals. Reactivity
Hay, John Munro. Reactive free radicals / [by] J.M. Hay. — London [etc.] : Academic Press, 1974. — viii,158p : ill ; 24cm.
Index.
ISBN 0-12-333550-7 : £4.40
(B77-19363)

547'.1'28 — Organic compounds. Chemical reactions. Mechanisms. Effects of stereochemistry of molecular orbitals
Fleming, Ian, *b.1935.* Frontier orbitals and organic chemical reactions / [by] Ian Fleming. — London [etc.] : Wiley, 1976. — vii,249p : ill ; 24cm.
'A Wiley-Interscience publication'. — Index.
ISBN 0-471-01820-1 : £8.95
ISBN 0-471-01819-8 Pbk : £3.95
(B77-25609)

547'.1'28 — Organic compounds. Molecules. Structure. Determination. Spectroscopy
Organic structural analysis / [by] Joseph B. Lambert ... [et al.]. — New York : Macmillan ; London : Collier Macmillan, 1976. — xii,596p : ill ; 26cm. — (A series of books in organic chemistry)
Index.
ISBN 0-02-367290-0 : £17.25
(B77-10805)

547'.1'3 — Organic compounds. Physical chemistry
Perkins, Michael John. The question of looking-glass milk / [by] M.J. Perkins. — [London] ([Chelsea College Annexe, Chelsea Manor St., SW3 3TW]) : [Chelsea College of Science and Technology, University of London], [1976]. — [1],21p : ill ; 21cm. — (Chelsea College of Science and Technology. Inaugural lectures)
'Inaugural Lecture 30th October 1975' - cover.
ISBN 0-902889-08-7 Sd : Unpriced
(B77-00757)

547'.1'3 — Physical organic chemistry. *Reviews of research*
Advances in physical organic chemistry. — London [etc.] : Academic Press.
Vol.14 / edited by V. Gold, associate editor D. Bethell. — 1977. — viii,374p : ill ; 24cm.
Bibl. — Index to vol.14 and cumulative index.
ISBN 0-12-033514-x : £16.00
(B77-20244)

Progress in physical organic chemistry. — New York ; London [etc.] : Wiley.
Vol.12 / editor Robert W. Taft. — 1976. — xiii,368p : ill ; 24cm.
'An Interscience publication'. — Index.
ISBN 0-471-01738-8 : £25.40
(B77-06670)

547'.1'372 — Carbonium ions
Carbonium ions / edited by George A. Olah, Paul von R. Schleyer. — New York ; London [etc.] : Wiley-Interscience.
Vol.5 : Miscellaneous ions, theory and structure. — [1977]. — xii p,p1961-2491 : ill ; 24cm. — (Reactive intermediates in organic chemistry)
Published in the United States: 1976. — Index.
ISBN 0-471-65342-x : £30.90
(B77-11793)

547'.1'3722 — Organic acids. Ionisation. Thermodynamic properties. *Technical data*
Christensen, James J. Handbook of proton ionization heats and related thermodynamic quantities / [compiled by] James J. Christensen, Lee D. Hansen, Reed M. Izatt. — New York ; London [etc.] : Wiley, 1976. — xv,269p ; 26cm. — (Brigham Young University. Center for Thermochemical Studies. Contributions ; no.85)
'A Wiley-Interscience publication'. — Index.
ISBN 0-471-01991-7 : £17.35
(B77-04149)

547'.1'388 — Organic compounds. Isotopes
Isotopes in organic chemistry / edited by E. Buncel and C.C. Lee. — Amsterdam ; Oxford [etc.] : Elsevier.
Vol.2 : Isotopes in hydrogen transfer processes. — 1976. — xvi,318p : ill ; 25cm.
Index. — Previous control number B7702992.
ISBN 0-444-41353-7 : £37.50
(B77-02992)

547'.1'39 — Organic compounds. Chemical reactions. *Reviews of research*
Organic reactions. — New York ; London [etc.] : Wiley.
Vol.24 / editorial board William G. Dauben, editor-in-chief ... [et al.]. — 1976. — xi,431p : ill ; 24cm.
Index. — Includes index to vols 1-24.
ISBN 0-471-19625-8 : £20.20
ISSN 0078-6179
(B77-17481)

547'.1'39 — Organic compounds. Chemical reactions. Mechanisms. *Reviews of research*
Organic reaction mechanisms : an annual survey. — London [etc.] : Interscience.
1975 : covering the literature dated December 1974 through November 1975 / edited by A.R. Butler, M.J. Perkins. — 1977. — [7],624p ; 24cm.
Index.
ISBN 0-471-01864-3 : £27.50
(B77-09005)

547'.1'39 — Organic compounds. Pericyclic reactions
Pericyclic reactions / edited by Alan P. Marchand, Roland E. Lehr. — New York [etc.] ; London : Academic Press.
In 2 vols.
Vol.1. — 1977. — xi,286p : ill ; 24cm. — (Organic chemistry ; vol.35)
Bibl. — Index.
ISBN 0-12-470501-4 : £19.90
(B77-22562)

547'.1'395 — Organic compounds. Chemical reactions catalysed by enzymes. Kinetics & mechanisms. Effects of isotope-labelled reagents. Conference proceedings
Harry Steenbock Symposium, *6th, Madison, Wis., 1976.* Isotope effects on enzyme-catalyzed reactions / edited by W. Wallace Cleland, Marion H. O'Leary, Dexter B. Northrop. — Baltimore ; London [etc.] : University Park Press, 1977. — xiii,303p : ill ; 24cm.
'Proceedings of the Sixth Annual Harry Steenbock Symposium, held in Madison, Wisconsin, on June 4 and 5, 1976' - half title page verso. — Bibl. — Index.
ISBN 0-8391-0851-6 : £28.25
(B77-30238)

547'.2 — Organic compounds. Synthesis. *Reviews of research*
Annual reports in organic synthesis. — New York [etc.] ; London : Academic Press.
1975 / edited by R. Bryan Miller, L.G. Wade, Jr. — 1976. — xiii,555p ; 23cm.
ISBN 0-12-040806-6 Pbk : £11.00
(B77-04796)

547'.2 — Organic compounds. Synthesis. Photochemical techniques. *Laboratory manuals*
Organic photochemical syntheses / editor R. Srinivasan. — New York ; London [etc.] : Wiley.
Vol.2 / associate editors T.D. Roberts, Jan Cornelisse. — 1976. — xi,109p : ill ; 24cm.
'A Wiley-Interscience Publication'. — Index.
ISBN 0-471-81921-2 : £15.00
(B77-02291)

547'.2 — Organic compounds. Synthesis. Reagents
Synthetic reagents / [editor J. Pizey]. — Chichester : Ellis Horwood ; New York ; London [etc.] : [Distributed by] Wiley.
Lithium aluminium hydride / [by] J.S. Pizey. — 1977. — [4],234p ; 24cm.
'Reprinted from "Synthetic Reagents Volume 1" by J.S. Pizey ([Chichester] Ellis Horwood, Ltd) 1974' - title page verso. — Index.
ISBN 0-85312-081-1 : Unpriced
(B77-32620)

547'.2 — Organic compounds. Synthesis. Use of metal carbonyls
Organic syntheses via metal carbonyls / edited by Irving Wender and Piero Pino. — New York ; London [etc.] : Wiley.
In 2 vols.
Vol.2. — 1977. — xv,743p : ill ; 24cm.
'A Wiley-Interscience publication'. — Index.
ISBN 0-471-93367-8 : £33.75
(B77-24922)

547'.2 — Organic compounds. Synthesis. Use of organic transition metal compounds. *Reviews of research*
Transition metal organometallics in organic synthesis. — New York [etc.] ; London : Academic Press. — (Organic chemistry ; vol.33)
Vol.1 / edited by Howard Alper. — 1976. — ix,258p : ill ; 24cm.
Bibl. — Index.
ISBN 0-12-053101-1 : £18.80
(B77-04797)

547'.2'05 — Organic compounds. Synthesis. *Serials*
Organic syntheses : an annual publication of satisfactory methods for the preparation of organic chemicals. — New York ; London [etc.] : Wiley.
Vol.56 : 1977 / George H. Büchi, editor-in-chief. — 1977. — xviii,144,[13]p : 1 ill ; 24cm.
Index.
ISBN 0-471-02218-7 : Unpriced
(B77-27846)

547'.21 — Organic compounds. Friedel-Crafts reaction
Olah, George Andrew. Friedel-Crafts chemistry / by George A. Olah. — New York ; London [etc.] : Wiley, 1973. — [7],581p,[12]p of plates : ill, facsims ; 24cm. — (Interscience monographs on organic chemistry)
'A Wiley-Interscience publication'. — Bibl. — Index.
ISBN 0-471-65315-2 : Unpriced
(B77-19364)

547'.28 — Polymerisation. *Conference proceedings*
Midland Macromolecular Meeting, *3rd, Midland Macromolecular Institute, 1974?.*
Polymerization of organized systems / edited by Hans Georg Elias. — New York ; London [etc.] : Gordon and Breach, 1977. — viii,230p : ill ; 24cm. — (Midland macromolecular monographs ; vol.3)
'... the third Midland Macromolecular Meeting ... [held at the Midland Macromolecular Institute, Michigan]. — Index.
ISBN 0-677-15930-7 : £19.30
(B77-18125)

547'.308'5 — Organic compounds. Carbon-13 nuclear magnetic resonance spectroscopy
Wehrli, F W. Interpretation of carbon-13 NMR spectra / [by] F.W. Wehrli and T. Wirthlin. — London [etc.] : Heyden, 1976. — xiv,310p,fold plate : ill(incl 1 col) ; 24cm.
With answers. — Index.
ISBN 0-85501-207-2 : £9.30
(B77-06671)

547'.308'5 — Organic compounds. Spectroscopy. *Exercises, worked examples*
Shapiro, Robert H. Exercises in organic spectroscopy. — 2nd ed. / [by] Robert H. Shapiro, Charles H. DePuy. — New York ; London [etc.] : Holt, Rinehart and Winston, 1977. — [3],171p : ill ; 24cm.
Notebook format. — Previous ed.: published as 'Spectral exercises in structural determination of organic compounds' / by Robert H. Shapiro. New York : Holt, Rinehart and Winston, 1969.
ISBN 0-03-089712-2 Sp : £6.50
(B77-26302)

547'.34'65 — Organic compounds. Chemical analysis. Ultraviolet spectroscopy. Spectra. *Technical data. Serials*
Organic electronic spectral data. — New York ; London [etc.] : Wiley.
Vol.11 : 1969 / John P. Phillips ... [et al.] editors. — [1976]. — xiii,1057p ; 24cm.
'An Interscience publication'. — Published in the United States: 1975.
ISBN 0-471-68802-9 : £23.50
(B77-06071)

547'.4 — Aliphatic compounds. *Reviews of research*
Aliphatic chemistry. — London : Chemical Society. — (Chemical Society. Specialist periodical reports)
Vol.4 : a review of the literature published during 1974 / senior reporter A. McKillop ... — 1976. — x,281p ; 23cm.
Index.
ISBN 0-85186-572-0 : £18.00
ISSN 0305-618x
(B77-22563)

Vol.5 : a review of the literature published during 1975 / senior reporter A. McKillop ... — 1977. — xi,337p ; 23cm.
Index.
ISBN 0-85186-602-6 : £23.50
ISSN 0305-618x
(B77-22564)

547'.5 — Alicyclic compounds. *Reviews of research*
Alicyclic chemistry. — London : Chemical Society. — (Chemical Society. Specialist periodical reports)
Vol.4 : a review of the literature published during 1974 / senior reporter W. Parker ... — 1976. — ix,511p : ill ; 22cm.
Index.
ISBN 0-85186-582-8 : £27.50
ISSN 0305-6201
(B77-06072)

Vol.5 : a review of the literature published during 1975 / senior reporter W. Parker, reporters ... [others]. — 1977. — ix,439p ; 23cm.
Index.
ISBN 0-85186-612-3 : Unpriced
ISSN 0305-6201
(B77-15838)

547'.59 — Heterocyclic compounds
Acheson, Richard Morrin. An introduction to the chemistry of heterocyclic compounds / [by] R.M. Acheson. — 3rd ed. — New York ; London [etc.] : Wiley, 1976. — xix,501p ; 24cm.
'A Wiley-Interscience Publication'. — Previous ed.: 1967. — Index.
ISBN 0-471-00268-2 : £17.75
(B77-06672)

547'.59 — Heterocyclic compounds. *Reviews of research*
Advances in heterocyclic chemistry. — New York [etc.] ; London : Academic Press.
Vol.20 / edited by A.R. Katritzky, A.J. Boulton. — 1976 [i.e. 1977]. — ix,324p : ill ; 24cm.
Published in the United States : 1976. — Index.
ISBN 0-12-020620-x : £23.80
(B77-09006)

Vol.21 / edited by A.R. Katritzky, A.J. Boulton. — 1977. — ix,486p : ill ; 24cm.
Index.
ISBN 0-12-020621-8 : £34.00
(B77-22565)

547'.59 — Heterocyclic compounds. Stereochemistry
Armarego, W L F. Stereochemistry of heterocyclic compounds / [by] W.L.F. Armarego. — New York ; London [etc.] : Wiley. — (General heterocyclic chemistry series)
Part 1 : Nitrogen heterocycles. — 1977. — xvii, 433p ; 24cm.
'A Wiley-Interscience Publication'. — Index.
ISBN 0-471-01892-9 : £27.00
(B77-18749)

Part 2 : Oxygen, sulfur, mixed N, O, and S, and phosphorus heterocycles / with a chapter on phosphorus heterocycles by M.J. Gallagher. — 1977. — xvii,494p : ill ; 24cm.
'A Wiley-Interscience publication'. — Index.
ISBN 0-471-03322-7 : £32.65
(B77-24923)

547'.59 — Saturated heterocyclic compounds. *Reviews of research*
Saturated heterocyclic chemistry. — London : Chemical Society. — (Chemical Society. Specialist periodical reports)
Vol.3 : a review of the literature published during 1973 / senior reporter M.F. Ansell ; reporters D.J. Maitland ... [et al.]. — 1975. — ix,301p : ill ; 23cm.
Index.
ISBN 0-85186-562-3 : £13.00
ISSN 0305-6198
(B77-04798)

547'.593 — Heterocyclic nitrogen compounds. Electrochemistry
Dryhurst, Glenn. Electrochemistry of biological molecules / [by] Glenn Dryhurst. — New York [etc.] ; London : Academic Press, 1977. — xii, 601p : ill ; 24cm.
Index.
ISBN 0-12-222650-x : £33.50
(B77-32621)

547'.593 — Pyrroles
Jones, Richard Alan. The chemistry of pyrroles / [by] R. Alan Jones and Gerritt P. Bean. — London [etc.] : Academic Press, 1977. — ix, 525p : ill ; 24cm. — (Organic chemistry ; vol.34)
Index.
ISBN 0-12-389840-4 : £21.00
(B77-22566)

547'.596 — Nucleic acids
Basic principles in nucleic acid chemistry. — New York ; London : Academic Press.
Vol.2 / edited by Paul O.P. Ts'o. — 1974 [i.e. 1976]. — xi,519p : ill ; 24cm.
Published in the United States: 1974. — Index.
ISBN 0-12-701902-2 : £24.50
(B77-00758)

547'.6 — Aromatic compounds. *Reviews of research*
Aromatic and heteroaromatic chemistry. — London : Chemical Society. — (Chemical Society. Specialist periodical reports)
Vol.5 : a review of the literature abstracted between July 1975 and June 1976 / senior reporters C.W. Bird and G.W.H. Cheeseman, reporters ... [others]. — 1977. — xv,566p : ill ; 23cm.
Index.
ISBN 0-85186-793-6 : £35.00
ISSN 0305-9715
(B77-27053)

547'.6 — Aromaticity
Open University. *S304(S352) Course Team.*
Aromaticity / prepared by an Open University course team [i.e. the S304(S352) Course Team]. — Milton Keynes : Open University Press, 1977. — 41,63,51p : ill(some col) ; 30cm. — (Science, a third level course : the nature of chemistry ; 17, 18, 19) (S304(S352) ; 17-19)
With answers.
ISBN 0-335-04238-4 Pbk : Unpriced
(B77-24924)

547'.71 — Essential oils. Constituents. *Technical data*
Masada, Yoshiro. Analysis of essential oils by gas chromatography and mass spectrometry / [by] Yoshiro Masada. — [New ed.]. — New York ; London [etc.] : Wiley, 1976. — iii-xv,334p : ill ; 27cm.
'A Halsted Press book'. — English text, Japanese chapter summaries. — 'Encouraged by the success of the first edition of my book "Analysis of Essential Oils by Gas Chromatography", [1968] I decided to attempt an English edition' - preface. — Index.
ISBN 0-470-15019-x : £28.90
(B77-01435)

547'.71 — Terpenoids. *Reviews of research*
Terpenoids and steroids. — London : Chemical Society. — (Chemical Society. Specialist periodical reports)
Vol.7 : a review of the literature published between September 1975 and August 1976 / senior reporter J.R. Hanson ; reporters ... [others]. — 1977. — x,349p ; 23cm.
Index.
ISBN 0-85186-316-7 : £25.00
ISSN 0300-5992
Also classified at 547'.73
(B77-31887)

547'.72 — Alkaloids. *Reviews of research*
The **alkaloids**. — London : Chemical Society. — (Chemical Society. Specialist periodical reports)
Vol.6 : a review of the literature published between July 1974 and June 1975 / senior reporter M.F. Grundon ... — 1976. — x,310p : ill ; 23cm.
Index.
ISBN 0-85186-307-8 : £19.50
ISSN 0305-9707
(B77-11794)

Vol.7 : a review of the literature published between July 1975 and June 1976 / senior reporter M.F. Grundon ... — 1977. — x,332p : ill ; 23cm.
Index.
ISBN 0-85186-317-5 : £25.00
ISSN 0305-9707
(B77-30239)

547'.72'03 — Alkaloids. *Encyclopaedias*
Glasby, John Stephen. Encyclopedia of the alkaloids / [compiled by] John S. Glasby. — New York ; London : Plenum Press, [1976]. — 2v.([7],1423p) ; 24cm.
Published in the United States: 1975. — Bibl.
ISBN 0-306-30845-2 : £53.55
(B77-01436)

547'.73 — Steroids. *Reviews of research*
Terpenoids and steroids. — London : Chemical Society. — (Chemical Society. Specialist periodical reports)
Vol.7 : a review of the literature published between September 1975 and August 1976 / senior reporter J.R. Hanson ; reporters ... [others]. — 1977. — x,349p ; 23cm.
Index.
ISBN 0-85186-316-7 : £25.00
ISSN 0300-5992
Primary classification 547'.71
(B77-31887)

547'.73 — Steroids. Chromatography
Heftmann, Erich. Chromatography of steroids / [by] Erich Heftmann. — Amsterdam ; Oxford [etc.] : Elsevier, 1976. — xiii,203p : ill ; 25cm. — ('Journal of chromatography' library ; vol.8)
Bibl.: p.127-192. — Index.
ISBN 0-444-41441-x : £15.93
(B77-23389)

547'.73 — Steroids. Colorimetric analysis & fluorimetric analysis
Bartos, J. Colorimetric and fluorimetric analysis of steroids / [by] J. Bartos and M. Pesez. — London [etc.] : Academic Press, 1976. — xii, 274p : ill ; 24cm. — (Tha analysis of organic materials ; 11)
Bibl. — Index.
ISBN 0-12-080150-7 : £9.80
(B77-09687)

547'.73 — Steroids. Molecular crystals. Structure. *Technical data*
Atlas of steroid structure. — New York [etc.] : IFI/Plenum ; London : Plenum Press.
Vol.1 / edited by William L. Duax and Dorita A. Norton. — [1976]. — xiii,572p : ill ; 29cm.
Published in the United States: 1975. — Index.
ISBN 0-306-66101-2 : £31.19
(B77-04150)

547'.734 — Prostaglandins. Synthesis
Bindra, Jasjit Singh. Prostaglandin synthesis / [by] Jasjit S. Bindra, Ranjna Bindra. — New York [etc.] ; London : Academic Press, 1977. — xiii,522p : ill ; 24cm.
Bibl.: p.511-516. — Index.
ISBN 0-12-099460-7 : £17.05
(B77-22567)

547'.75 — Amino acids, peptides & proteins. *Reviews of research*
Amino-acids, peptides and proteins. — London : Chemical Society. — (Chemical Society. Specialist periodical reports)
Vol.8 : a review of the literature published during 1975 / senior reporter R.C. Sheppard. — 1976. — xvii,504p,leaf of plate,[4]p of plates : ill ; 23cm.
Index.
ISBN 0-85186-074-5 : £28.00
ISSN 0306-0004
(B77-10360)

547'.75 — Iron-sulphur proteins
Iron-sulfur proteins / edited by Walter Lovenberg. — New York [etc.] ; London : Academic Press. — (Molecular biology)
Vol.3 : Structure and metabolic mechanisms. — 1977. — xiv,443p : ill ; 24cm.
Bibl. — Index.
ISBN 0-12-456003-2 : £28.05
(B77-16371)

547'.756 — Peptides. Synthesis
Bodanszky, Miklos. Peptide synthesis. — 2nd ed. / [by] Miklos Bodanszky, Yakir S. Klausner, Miguel A. Ondetti. — New York ; London [etc.] : Wiley, 1976. — xv,208p : ill ; 24cm. — (Interscience monographs on organic chemistry)
'A Wiley-Interscience publication'. — Previous ed.: / by Miklos Bodanszky and Miguel A. Ondetti. 1966. — Bibl.: p.2-4. — Index.
ISBN 0-471-08451-4 : £15.50
(B77-05399)

547'.756 — Synthetic peptides
Pettit, George Robert. Synthetic peptides / [by] George R. Pettit. — Amsterdam ; Oxford [etc.] : Elsevier.
Vol.4. — 1976. — xvii,477p : ill ; 23cm.
Bibl.: p.448-477.
ISBN 0-444-41521-1 : £35.13
(B77-15277)

547'.758 — Enzymes. Chemical reactions. Kinetics
Engel, Paul C. Enzyme kinetics : the steady-state approach / [by] Paul C. Engel. — London : Chapman and Hall [etc.], 1977. — 96p : ill ; 22cm. — (Outline studies in biology)
'A Halsted Press Book'. — Index.
ISBN 0-470-99097-x Pbk : £1.75
(B77-24210)

Open University. *S322 Course Team.* Enzyme kinetics ; [and], Microenvironments / prepared by an Open University Course Team [i.e. the S322 Course Team]. — Milton Keynes : Open University Press, 1977. — 66,60,41p : ill(some col) ; 30cm. — (Science, a third level course : biochemistry and molecular biology ; blocks B, C, units 5-7) (S322 ; 5-7)
With answers. — Bibl.
ISBN 0-335-04412-3 Pbk : Unpriced
Also classified at 574.8'76
(B77-28597)

Roberts, D V. Enzyme kinetics / [by] D.V. Roberts. — Cambridge [etc.] : Cambridge University Press, 1977. — x,326p : ill ; 23cm. — (Cambridge chemistry texts)
Bibl.: p.312-318. — Index.
ISBN 0-521-21274-x : £15.00
ISBN 0-521-29080-5 Pbk : £5.50
(B77-15839)

547'.78 — Carbohydrates. *Reviews of research*
Advances in carbohydrate chemistry and biochemistry. — New York [etc.] ; London : Academic Press.
Vol.33 / editors R. Stuart Tipson, Derek Horton. — 1976. — xii,464p : ill, port ; 24cm.
Index.
ISBN 0-12-007233-5 : £31.25
(B77-05400)

Carbohydrate chemistry. — London : Chemical Society. — (Chemical Society. Specialist periodical reports)
Vol.9 : a review of the literature published during 1975 / senior reporter J.S. Brimacombe ... — 1977. — xiii,485p : ill ; 23cm.
Index.
ISBN 0-85186-082-6 : £29.00
ISSN 0576-7172
(B77-10361)

547'.8 — Block copolymers
Noshay, Allen. Block copolymers : overview and critical survey / [by] Allen Noshay, James E. McGrath. — New York [etc.] ; London : Academic Press, 1977. — xvi,516p : ill ; 24cm.
Bibl.: p.457-473. — Index.
ISBN 0-12-521750-1 : £31.95
(B77-22568)

547'.84 — Chitin
Muzzarelli, Riccardo A A. Chitin / by Riccardo A.A. Muzzarelli. — Oxford [etc.] : Pergamon, 1977. — xv,309p : ill ; 26cm.
Bibl.: p.267-305. — Index.
ISBN 0-08-020367-1 : £21.25
(B77-21850)

547'.84 — Crosslinked polymers. Structure & chemical properties. *Conference proceedings*
Chemistry and Properties of Crosslinked Polymers *(Conference), San Francisco, 1976.*
Chemistry and properties of crosslinked polymers / edited by Santokh S. Labana. — New York [etc.] ; London : Academic Press, 1977. — xiii,581p : ill ; 24cm.
'Proceedings of the ACS [i.e. American Chemical Society] Symposium on "Chemistry and Properties of Crosslinked Polymers"' - half title page verso. — Index.
ISBN 0-12-432250-6 : £20.95
(B77-24925)

547'.84 — Ion-containing polymers. Structure & physical properties
Eisenberg, A. Ion-containing polymers : physical properties and structure / [by] A. Eisenberg and M. King. — New York [etc.] ; London : Academic Press, 1977. — xvi,287p : ill ; 24cm. — (Polymer physics ; vol.2)
Index.
ISBN 0-12-235050-2 : £19.55
(B77-25610)

547'.84 — Polymers
Elias, Hans-Georg. Macromolecules / [by] Hans-Georg Elias ; translated from the German by John W. Stafford. — London [etc.] : Wiley.
In 2 vols. — Translation of: 'Makromoleküle'. 3. völlig überarb. Aufl. Basel : Hüthig and Wepf, 1975.
[Vol.] 1 : Structure and properties. — 1977. — xlxxx,532p : ill ; 24cm.
Index.
ISBN 0-471-99487-1 : £24.00
(B77-25611)

[Vol.] 2 : Synthesis and materials. — 1977. — xlxxx p,p533-1131 : ill ; 24cm.
Index.
ISBN 0-471-99488-x : £24.00
(B77-25612)

547'.84 — Polymers. Dielectric spectroscopy
Hedvig, Péter. Dielectric spectroscopy of polymers / [by] Péter Hedvig. — Bristol : Hilger, 1977. — 431p : ill ; 24cm.
Bibl.: p.411-425. — Index.
ISBN 0-85274-247-9 : £17.50
(B77-15840)

547'.84 — Polymers. Gas chromatography
Berezkin, V G. Gas chromatography of polymers / [by] V.G. Berezkin, V.R. Alishoyev and I.B. Nemirovskaya. — Amsterdam ; Oxford [etc.] : Elsevier, 1977. — xii,225p : ill ; 25cm. — ('Journal of chromatography' library ; vol.10)
Translation and revision of: 'Gazovaia khromatografiia v khimii polimerov'. Moscow : Nauka, 1972.
ISBN 0-444-41514-9 : £24.12
(B77-16871)

547'.84 — Polymers. Relaxation processes
Relaxation phenomena in polymers / G.M. Bartenev and Yu. V. Zelenev, editors ; translated from Russian by Th. Pelz ; translation edited by P. Shelnitz. — New York [etc.] : Wiley ; Jerusalem ; London : Israel Program for Scientific Translations ; Chichester : Distributed by Wiley, [1977]. — x, 349p : ill ; 25cm.
'A Halsted Press book'. — '... based on lectures held in October 1969 in Leningrad at the Theoretical Course on Relaxation in Phenomena in Polymers, which were revised and supplemented' - Introduction. — This translation published in the United States: 1974. — Translation of: 'Relaksatsionnye iavleniia v polimerakh'. Leningrad : Khimiia, 1972. — Index.
ISBN 0-470-05429-8 : £21.90
(B77-11208)

547'.84 — Polymers. Structure & chemical properties
Open University. *S322 Course Team.* Macromolecules / prepared by an Open University Course Team [i.e. the S322 Course Team]. — Milton Keynes : Open University Press.
In 2 vols.
[Vol.1]. — 1977. — 56,61p : ill(some col) ; 30cm. — (Science, a third level course : biochemistry and molecular biology ; block A, units 1-2) (S322 ; 1-2)
With answers. — Bibl.
ISBN 0-335-04410-7 Pbk : Unpriced
(B77-26303)

[Vol.2]. — 1977. — 68,31p : ill(some col) ; 30cm. — (Science, a third level course : biochemistry and molecular biology ; block A, units 3-4) (S322 ; 3-4)
With answers. — Bibl.
ISBN 0-335-04411-5 Pbk : Unpriced
(B77-26304)

547'.84 — Polymers. Structure & physical properties
Krevelen, Dirk Willem van. Properties of polymers : their estimation and correlation with chemical structure / by D.W. van Krevelen with the collaboration of P.J. Hoftyzer. — 2nd, completely revised ed. — Amsterdam ; Oxford [etc.] : Elsevier, 1976. — xxxiii,620p : ill ; 25cm.
Previous ed.: 1972. — Bibl. — Index.
ISBN 0-444-41467-3 : £44.26
(B77-03541)

Treloar, Leslie Ronald George. Introduction to polymer science / [by] L.G.R. Treloar. — London [etc.] : Wykeham Publications, 1974. — vii,182p : ill ; 22cm. — (The Wykeham science series ; 9)
Originally published: 1970. — Bibl.: p.179. — Index.
ISBN 0-85109-480-5 : £2.25
(B77-18750)

547'.84 — Polymers. Synthesis. Laboratory techniques. *Serials*
Macromolecular syntheses : a periodic publication of methods for the preparation of macromolecules. — New York ; London [etc.] : Wiley.
Vol.6 : 1977 / James E. Mulvaney, editor. — 1977. — xi,116p : ill ; 24cm.
Index.
ISBN 0-471-02131-8 : £14.65
(B77-23390)

547'.84 — Solutes: Polymers. *Conference proceedings*
Structure-Solubility Relationships in Polymers *(Conference), San Francisco, 1976.*
Structure-solubility relationships in polymers / edited by Frank W. Harris, Raymond B. Seymour. — New York [etc.] ; London : Academic Press, 1977. — xiii,271p : ill ; 24cm.
'Proceedings of the Symposium on Structure-Solubility Relationships in Polymers held by the American Chemical Society in San Francisco, California, on August 30-September 3, 1976' - half title-page verso. — Index.
ISBN 0-12-327450-8 : £9.25
(B77-22569)

547'.84 — Solutes: Polymers. Dynamics
Dynamics of polymeric liquids. — New York ; London [etc.] : Wiley.
In 2 vols.
Vol.1 : Fluid mechanics / [by] R. Byron Bird, Robert C. Armstrong, Ole Hassager. — 1977. — xv,470,[89]p : ill ; 26cm.
Index.
ISBN 0-471-07375-x : £22.00
(B77-23391)

Vol.2 : Kinetic theory / [by] R. Byron Bird ... [et al.]. — 1977. — xiii,p471-727,[31]p : ill ; 27cm.
Index.
ISBN 0-471-01596-2 : £20.00
(B77-21852)

547'.86 — Synthetic dyes
Abrahart, Edward Noah. Dyes and their intermediates / [by] E.N. Abrahart. — 2nd ed. — London : Edward Arnold, 1977. — xiii, 265p : ill ; 24cm.
Previous ed.: Oxford : Pergamon, 1968. — Bibl. : p.245-247. — Index.
ISBN 0-7131-2580-2 : £15.00
(B77-22570)

547'.86 — Synthetic dyes. Chemical analysis
The **analytical** chemistry of synthetic dyes / edited by K. Venkataraman. — New York ; London [etc.] : Wiley, 1977. — xxv,591p : ill ; 24cm.
'A Wiley-Interscience publication'. — Index.
ISBN 0-471-90575-5 : £31.90
(B77-25613)

548 — CRYSTALLOGRAPHY
Glasser, L S Dent. Crystallography and its applications / [by] L.S. Dent Glasser. — New York [etc.] ; London : Van Nostrand Reinhold, 1977. — viii,224p : ill ; 24cm.
With answers. — Bibl.: p.211-214. — Index.
ISBN 0-442-30135-9 : £10.50
ISBN 0-442-30136-7 Pbk : £4.95
(B77-21114)

548'.5 — Crystals. Growth. *Conference proceedings*
Growth of crystals. — New York ; London : Consultants Bureau.
Translation and revision of: 'Rost kristallov'. Moskva : Izd-vo Akademii nauk SSSR, 1957-.
Vol.9 / edited by N.N. Sheftal' and E.I. Givargizov ; translated [from the Russian] by J.E.S. Bradley. — 1975. — x,329p : ill, ports ; 28cm.
'Proceedings of E.S. Fedorov All-Union Symposium on Crystal Growth, Jubilee Meeting, May 21-24, 1969' - title page verso.
ISBN 0-306-18109-6 : £22.05
(B77-04799)

548'.5'05 — Crystals. Growth. *Periodicals*
Progress in crystal growth and characterization : an international review journal. — Oxford [etc.] : Pergamon.
Vol.1, no.1- ; 1977-. — 1977-. — ill, ports ; 25cm.
Quarterly. — Cover title. — 91,iv p. in 1st issue. — Bibl.: p.18.
Pbk : Unpriced
ISSN 0146-3535
(B77-21853)

548'.7 — Crystallography. Applications of three-dimensional nets & three-dimensional polyhedra
Wells, Alexander Frank. Three-dimensional nets and polyhedra / [by] A.F. Wells. — New York ; London [etc.] : Wiley, 1977. — xiii, 268p : ill ; 24cm. — (Wiley monographs in crystallography)
'A Wiley-Interscience publication'. — Index.
ISBN 0-471-02151-2 : £22.00
(B77-27847)

548'.81 — Crystals. Atoms. Thermal vibration. Symmetry
Poulet, Henri. Vibration spectra and symmetry of crystals / by H. Poulet and J.P. Mathieu ; translated [from the French] by A. Simievic. — New York ; London [etc.] : Gordon and Breach, 1976. — xiv,571p : ill ; 24cm.
Translation of: 'Spectres de vibration et symétrie des cristaux'. Paris : Gordon et Breach, 1970. — Bibl.: p.559-563. — Index.
ISBN 0-677-30180-4 : £22.30
(B77-02292)

548'.81 — Crystals. Defects. *Reviews of research*
Surface and defect properties of solids. — London : Chemical Society. — (Chemical Society. Specialist periodical reports)
Vol.4 : a review of the recent literature published up to April 1974 / senior reporters M.W. Roberts, J.M. Thomas. — 1975. — ix, 255p : ill ; 23cm.
Index.
ISBN 0-85186-280-2 : £14.00
ISSN 0305-3873
Primary classification 541'.3453
(B77-08998)

548'.81 — Crystals. Point defects
Watts, R K. Point defects in crystals / [by] R.K. Watts. — New York ; London [etc.] : Wiley, 1977. — xiii,312p : ill ; 24cm.
'A Wiley-Interscience Publication'. — Index.
ISBN 0-471-92280-3 : £16.50
(B77-18751)

548'.83 — Crystallography. Applications of x-ray topography
Tanner, B K. X-ray diffraction topography / by B.K. Tanner. — Oxford [etc.] : Pergamon, 1976. — xiv,174p : ill ; 26cm. — (International series in the science of the solid state ; vol.10) (Pergamon international library)
Bibl. — Index.
ISBN 0-08-019692-6 : £6.25
(B77-05401)

548'.83 — Crystals. Molecules. Structure. Determination. Applications of x-ray diffraction
Speakman, James Clare. Molecular structure : its study by crystal diffraction / [by] J. Clare Speakman. — London : Chemical Society, 1977. — iii,53p,plate : ill ; 22cm. — (Chemical Society. Monographs for teachers ; no.30)
Bibl.: p.53.
ISBN 0-85186-689-1 Sd : £1.20(£0.90 to members)
(B77-27054)

548'.83 — Low temperature x-ray diffraction
Rudman, Reuben. Low-temperature x-ray diffraction : apparatus and techniques / [by] Reuben Rudman. — New York ; London : Plenum Press, [1976]. — xvi,344p : ill ; 24cm. — (Monographs in low-temperature physics)
Bibl.: p.255-338. — Index.
ISBN 0-306-30923-8 : £22.05
(B77-30240)

548'.83 — X-ray crystallography. Applications of statistical mathematics
Srinivasan, Ramachandran. Some statistical applications in X-ray crystallography / by R. Srinivasan and S. Parthasarathy. — Oxford [etc.] : Pergamon, 1976. — xix,246p : ill ; 26cm. — (International series in natural philosophy ; vol.83)
Bibl.: p.229-236. — Index.
ISBN 0-08-018046-9 : £11.25
(B77-07339)

548'.83 — X-ray crystallography. Rotation methods
The **rotation** method in crystallography : data collection from macromolecular crystals / edited by U.W. Arndt and A.J. Wonacott. — Amsterdam [etc.] ; Oxford : North-Holland Publishing Co., 1977. — xvii,275p : ill ; 25cm.
Bibl.: p.269-275. — Index.
ISBN 0-7204-0594-7 : £20.80
(B77-31178)

548'.83 — X-ray diffraction
X-ray diffraction / [by] Leonid V. Azároff ... [et al.]. — New York ; London [etc.] : McGraw-Hill, 1974. — xix,664p : ill ; 24cm. — (International series in pure and applied physics)
Bibl.: p.619-649. — Index.
ISBN 0-07-002672-6 : Unpriced
(B77-19365)

548'.842 — Ionic crystals. Plastic deformation
Sprackling, Michael Thomas. The plastic deformation of simple ionic crystals / [by] M.T. Sprackling. — London [etc.] : Academic Press, 1976. — ix,242p : ill ; 24cm. — (Materials science and technology)
Bibl.: p.207-236. — Index.
ISBN 0-12-657850-8 : £9.20
(B77-08369)

548'.9 — Crystals. Optical properties
Wood, Elizabeth Armstrong. Crystals and light : an introduction to optical crystallography / [by] Elizabeth A. Wood. — 2nd revised ed. — New York : Dover Publications [etc.] ; London : Constable, 1977. — iv,156p,8p of plates : ill(some col) ; 22cm.
Previous ed: Princeton, N.J. ; London : Van Nostrand, 1964. — Bibl.: p.152. — Index.
ISBN 0-486-23431-2 Pbk : £1.95
(B77-24926)

548'.9 — Liquid crystals
Chandrasekhar, Sivaramakrishna. Liquid crystals / [by] S. Chandrasekhar. — Cambridge [etc.] : Cambridge University Press, 1977. — xi, 342p : ill ; 24cm. — (Cambridge monographs on physics)
Index.
ISBN 0-521-21149-2 : £18.00
(B77-20246)

Leadbetter, A J. Solid liquids and liquid crystals / [by] A.J. Leadbetter. — [Exeter] : University of Exeter, 1976. — 35p : ill ; 21cm. — (University of Exeter. Inaugural lectures)
'... delivered in the University of Exeter on 20 November, 1975'.
ISBN 0-85989-081-3 Sd : £0.50
Primary classification 666'.1042
(B77-15373)

548'.9 — Liquid crystals. *Readings*
Introduction to liquid crystals / edited by E.B. Priestley, Peter J. Wojtowicz, Ping Sheng. — New York ; London : Plenum Press, [1976]. — xi,356p : ill ; 24cm.
Published in the United States: 1975. — Index.
ISBN 0-306-30858-4 : £14.18
(B77-04151)

548'.9 — Liquid crystals. *Reviews of research*
Advances in liquid crystals. — New York [etc.] ; London : Academic Press.
Vol.2 / edited by Glenn H. Brown. — 1976. — xi,308p : ill ; 24cm.
Index.
ISBN 0-12-025002-0 : £18.30
(B77-04152)

549 — MINERALOGY
Sanborn, William B. Oddities of the mineral world / [by] William B. Sanborn ; with photographs by the author. — New York ; London [etc.] : Van Nostrand Reinhold, 1976. — 142p,[4]p of plates : ill(some col), port ; 24cm.
Bibl.: p.134-135. — Index.
ISBN 0-442-27346-0 : £7.60
(B77-01437)

549'.06'241 — Mineralogy. Organisations. *Great Britain. Mineralogical Society. Rules*
Mineralogical Society. Bye-laws / the Mineralogical Society. — London (41 Queen's Gate, SW7 5HR) : The Society, 1976. — [1], 10p ; 26cm.
ISBN 0-903056-07-0 Sd : £2.50
(B77-02293)

549'.1 — Minerals. Analysis. Non-destructive techniques
Physicochemical methods of mineral analysis / edited by Alastair W. Nicol. — New York ; London : Plenum Press, 1975. — xv,508p : ill ; 24cm.
'This book has developed from a short residential course organised by the Department of Minerals Engineering and the Department of Extra Mural Studies of the University of Birmingham' - Foreword. — Index.
ISBN 0-306-30739-1 : £21.74
(B77-02294)

549'.125 — Minerals. Optical properties
Kerr, Paul Francis. Optical mineralogy. — 4th ed. / [by] Paul F. Kerr. — New York ; London [etc.] : McGraw-Hill, 1977. — xvii, 492p,[2]leaves of plates : ill(incl 1 col) ; 24cm.
Previous ed.: 1959. — Bibl. — Index.
ISBN 0-07-034218-0 : £16.90
(B77-25614)

549'.133 — Minerals. Chemical analysis. *Laboratory manuals. For prospecting*
Stanton, Ronald Ernest. Analytical methods for use in geochemical exploration / [by] R.E. Stanton. — London : Edward Arnold, 1976. — v,55p : ill ; 22cm.
Bibl.: p.53-54. — Index.
ISBN 0-7131-2581-0 Pbk : £2.20
(B77-04800)

550 — EARTH
Ojakangas, Richard W. The earth, past & present / [by] Richard W. Ojakangas, David G. Darby. — New York ; London [etc.] : McGraw-Hill, 1976. — xi,260p : ill, maps ; 23cm. — (McGraw-Hill earth science paperback series)
Index.
ISBN 0-07-047676-4 Pbk : £4.40
(B77-00213)

550 — Earth. *Juvenile literature*
Children's encyclopedia of earth, stars and planets / compiled and edited by Kenneth Bailey ; [written by Anthony Harvey, Barry Cork, Maurice Allward ; illustrated by Max Ansell ... et al.]. — Glasgow [etc.] : Collins, 1976. — 3-189p : col ill, col charts, col maps, col ports ; 31cm. — ([Collins children's encyclopaedia])
Cover title: Collins children's encyclopedia of earth, stars and planets. — Index.
ISBN 0-00-106165-8 : £2.95
Also classified at 520
(B77-26305)

Lockie, Patricia. Earth : our planet in full colour with a children's atlas / [by] Patricia Lockie ; design and artwork by the Diagram Group. — London : Sidgwick and Jackson, 1977. — 80p : ill(chiefly col), col maps, col plans ; 27cm.
With answers. — Index.
ISBN 0-283-98248-9 : £3.50
(B77-28598)

Lucas, Angela. Focus on earth / [by] Angela & Derek Lucas. — London : Methuen, 1977. — 48p : col ill, col maps ; 22cm.
Index.
ISBN 0-416-82400-5 : £1.85
(B77-14230)

Lye, Keith. Our planet Earth / [author Keith Lye] ; [editor Jane Olliver]. — London : Ward Lock, 1977. — 120p : chiefly ill(chiefly col), charts(some col), maps(some col) ; 33cm.
Col. ill. on lining papers. — Index.
ISBN 0-7063-5348-x : Unpriced
(B77-28599)

Moore, Patrick. Wonder why book of the earth / [by] Patrick Moore ; illustrated by Raymond Turvey. — London : Transworld, 1977. — [2], 32p : col ill, col maps ; 29cm.
Index. — Previous control number ISBN 0-552-57002-8.
ISBN 0-552-98036-6 : £1.35
ISBN 0-552-57002-8 Sd : £0.50
(B77-11209)

Watts, Lisa. The children's book of the Earth / [by] Lisa Watts and Jenny Tyler ; illustrated by Bob Hersey and designed by Bob Scott. — London : Usborne, 1976. — 32p : ill(chiefly col), col maps ; 28cm. — (Children's guides)
Index.
ISBN 0-86020-062-0 Pbk : £0.75
(B77-11795)

550 — Geology
Davis, Stanley N. Geology : our physical environment / [by] Stanley N. Davis, Paul H. Reitan, Raymond Pestrong. — New York ; London [etc.] : McGraw-Hill, 1976. — viii, 470p : ill(some col), maps(some col) ; 25cm.
Bibl. — Index.
ISBN 0-07-015680-8 : £12.40
(B77-02993)

Geology, the science of a changing earth / by Ira S. Allison ... [et al.]. — 6th ed. — New York ; London [etc.] : McGraw-Hill, 1974. — x,498p : ill(some col), maps(some col) ; 24cm.
Previous ed.: published as 'Geology, principles and processes' / by William H. Emmons et al. 1960. — Bibl. — Index.
ISBN 0-07-001118-4 : Unpriced
ISBN 0-07-001119-2 Pbk : Unpriced
(B77-19366)

Holmes, Arthur. Principles of physical geology / [by] Arthur Holmes. — 2nd ed. completely revised. — Sunbury-on-Thames [etc.] : Nelson, 1977. — xv,1288p : ill, charts, maps ; 22cm.
This ed. originally published: London : Nelson, 1965. — Bibl. — Index.
ISBN 0-17-771298-8 Pbk : £8.50
(B77-27848)

Planet Earth : an encyclopedia of geology / consultant editor A. Hallam, [editors Peter Hutchinson, Paul Barnett]. — Oxford : Elsevier-Phaidon, 1977. — 319,[1]p : ill(chiefly col), col maps, ports ; 29cm.
Index.
ISBN 0-7290-0055-9 : £7.95
(B77-29415)

550 — Geology. *Juvenile literature*
Shepherd, Walter. Our landscape : discovering how it was made / [by] Walter Shepherd ; illustrated by Walter Shepherd. — London (247 Tottenham Court Rd, W1P 0AU) : Independent Television Books Ltd ; London : Arrow Books, 1977. — 96p : ill, maps ; 20cm. — (Look-in books)
Bibl.: p.93. — Index.
ISBN 0-09-915470-6 Pbk : £0.65
(B77-23392)

550 — Geology. *Secondary school texts*
Greensmith, John Trevor. Geology for schools / [by] J.T. Greensmith. — 3rd ed. — Glasgow [etc.] : Blackie, 1976. — [4],188p,[6]p of plates : ill, maps ; 22cm.
This ed. originally published: Aylesbury : Intertext, 1973. — Bibl.: p.179. — Index.
ISBN 0-216-90319-x Pbk : £2.25
(B77-02295)

550'.2'46231 — Geology. *For military engineering*
Applied geology for engineers : sponsored jointly by the Ministry of Defence and the Institution of Civil Engineers. — London : H.M.S.O., 1976. — xxxv,378p,[5]fold leaves of plates : ill, maps(some col) ; 21cm. — (Military engineering ; vol.15) (Army ; code no.71044)
Bibl. — Index.
ISBN 0-11-771597-2 Pbk : £9.00
(B77-12435)

550'.25 — Geology. *Directories*
The **geologists'** year book. — Poole : Dolphin Press.
1977. — 1977. — 299p : ill ; 23cm.
ISBN 0-85642-048-4 : £8.00
ISSN 0309-8966
(B77-20247)

550'.6'24281 — Geology. Organisations. *Yorkshire. Yorkshire Geological Society. Directories*
Yorkshire Geological Society. Membership list of the Yorkshire Geological Society. — [Leeds] ([c/o J. Hartley, Department of Earth Sciences, The University, Leeds LS2 9JT]) : The Society.
1976, December. — [1977]. — 51p ; 21cm.
Sd : Unpriced
(B77-33206)

550'.7'1041 — Schools. Curriculum subjects: Geology. *Great Britain. Reports, surveys*
Schools Council Geology Curriculum Review Group. Geology in the school curriculum : the report of the Schools Council Geology Curriculum Review Group (1973-5). — London : Evans Bros : Methuen, 1977. — 96p : ill ; 21cm. — (Schools Council. Working papers ; 58 ISSN 0533-1668)
ISBN 0-423-50390-1 Pbk : £1.85
(B77-30241)

550'.7'1241 — Secondary schools. Curriculum subjects: Geology. Teaching. *Great Britain. Periodicals*
Geology teaching : journal of the Association of Teachers of Geology. — Milton Keynes (Dept of Earth Sciences, The Open University, Milton Keynes MK7 6AA) : The Association.
Supersedes: Geology.
Vol.1, no.1- ; March 1976-. — 1976-. — ill, maps ; 30cm.
Quarterly. — 28p. in 1st issue. — Bibl.
Sd : £3.00 yearly
ISSN 0308-1567
(B77-09688)

550'.7'23 — Geology. Field studies. *Great Britain*
Simpson, Ian Morven. Fieldwork in geology / [by] I.M. Simpson. — London [etc.] : Murby : Allen and Unwin, 1977. — 72p : ill, maps ; 24cm. — (Introducing geology ; 5)
Index.
ISBN 0-04-550025-8 Sd : £1.75
(B77-27055)

550'.7'8 — Museums. *Cardiff. National Museum of Wales. Schools Service. Stock: Teaching aids on geology: Items available for loan. Lists*
National Museum of Wales. *Schools Service.* Catalogue of loan material in geology / National Museum of Wales, Schools Service = Amgueddfa Genedlaethol Cymru, Gwasanaeth i'r Ysgolion. — 6th ed. — Cardiff : The Museum, 1976. — 56p ; 21cm.
Cover title: Geology, catalogue of loan material. — Previous ed.: 1972.
ISBN 0-7200-0095-5 Sd : £0.50
(B77-02994)

550'.8 — Earth sciences. *Essays*
Jeffreys, *Sir* **Harold.** Collected papers of Sir Harold Jeffreys on geophysics and other sciences. — London [etc.] : Gordon and Breach.
In 6 vols.
Vol.6 : Mathematics, probability and miscellaneous other sciences / edited by Sir Harold Jeffreys and Bertha Swirles (Lady Jeffreys). — 1977. — xviii,622p : ill, maps ; 24cm.
Bibl. — Index.
ISBN 0-677-03220-x : £35.30
(B77-12436)

550'.941 — Geology. *Great Britain, 1660-1815*
Porter, Roy. The making of geology : earth science in Britain, 1660-1815 / [by] Roy Porter. — Cambridge [etc.] : Cambridge University Press, 1977. — xi,288p ; 23cm.
Bibl.: p.239-278. — Index.
ISBN 0-521-21521-8 : £8.95
(B77-22571)

551 — GEOPHYSICAL PROCESSES
Calder, Nigel. Restless earth : a report on the new geology / [by] Nigel Calder. — London : Omega, 1975. — [2],125p,32p of plates : ill, maps ; 20cm.
'The television programme "The Restless Earth" was broadcast on BBC2 on 16 February 1972' - Author's note. — Originally published: London : British Broadcasting Corporation, 1972. — Bibl.: p.6. — Index.
ISBN 0-86007-719-5 Pbk : £0.95
(B77-09007)

Cazeau, Charles J. Physical geology : principles, processes, and problems / [by] Charles J. Cazeau, Robert D. Hatcher, Jr, Francis T. Siemankowski. — New York [etc.] ; London : Harper and Row, 1976. — x,518p : ill(some col), maps(chiefly col) ; 25cm.
Text on lining papers. — Bibl. — Index.
ISBN 0-06-041209-7 : £10.45
(B77-01438)

Flint, Richard Foster. Physical geology / [by] Richard Foster Flint, Brian J. Skinner. — 2nd ed. — New York ; London [etc.] : Wiley, 1977. — x,594,[75]p : ill(chiefly col), maps(chiefly col) ; 26cm.
Col. maps on lining papers. — Previous ed.: 1974. — Bibl. — Index.
ISBN 0-471-26442-3 : £11.00
(B77-17483)

Gribbin, John. Our changing planet / [by] John Gribbin. — London : Wildwood House, 1977. — [6],165p : ill, maps, port ; 23cm.
Bibl.: p.153-154. — Index.
ISBN 0-7045-0247-x : £5.95
(B77-32622)

Stacey, Frank Donald. Physics of the earth / [by] Frank D. Stacey. — 2nd ed. — New York ; London [etc.] : Wiley, 1977. — xi,414p : ill, maps ; 24cm.
Previous ed.: 1969. — Bibl.: p.361-396. — Index.
ISBN 0-471-81956-5 : £13.40
(B77-18126)

Strahler, Arthur Newell. Principles of physical geology / [by] Arthur N. Strahler. — New York [etc.] ; London : Harper and Row, 1977. — xii,419p : ill(some col), col maps ; 28cm.
Col. map, text on lining papers. — Bibl.: p.379-391. — Index.
ISBN 0-06-046457-7 : £11.20
(B77-15278)

551 — Earth. Evolution
Dott, Robert H. Evolution of the earth / [by] Robert H. Dott, Jr, Roger L. Batten ; maps and diagrams by Randall D. Sale. — 2nd ed. — New York ; London [etc.] : McGraw-Hill, 1976. — viii,504p : ill(some col), maps(chiefly col) ; 25cm.
Col. ill. on lining papers. — Previous ed.: New York : McGraw-Hill, 1971. — Bibl. — Index.
ISBN 0-07-017619-1 : £13.30
(B77-04801)

551 — Earth. Expansion. Theories
Carey, S Warren. The expanding earth / [by] S. Warren Carey. — Amsterdam ; Oxford [etc.] : Elsevier, 1976. — x,488p : ill, charts, maps ; 25cm. — (Developments in geotectonics ; 10)
Bibl.: p.462-478. — Index.
ISBN 0-444-41485-1 : £20.14
(B77-16872)

551 — Geophysical processes. *Secondary school texts*
Bunnett, R B. Physical geography in diagrams / [by] R.B. Bunnett. — 3rd, metric ed. — London : Longman, 1976. — viii,196p : ill, charts, maps ; 25cm.
Previous ed.: i.e. Metric ed., 1973. — Index.
ISBN 0-582-34122-1 Pbk : £1.25
(B77-23393)

Robinson, Harry, *b.1915.* Physical geography / [by] H. Robinson. — 2nd ed. — Plymouth : Macdonald and Evans, 1977. — x,242p : ill, maps ; 19cm. — (The M. & E. handbook series)
Previous ed.: 1971. — Index.
ISBN 0-7121-1670-2 Pbk : £1.75
(B77-15841)

551 — Geophysics. Applications of high pressure research. *Conference proceedings*
High-pressure research : applications in geophysics / edited by Murli H. Manghnani, Syun-Iti Akimoto. — New York [etc.] ; London : Academic Press, 1977. — xvi,642p : ill ; 24cm.
'... a four-day U.S.-Japan joint seminar was held in Honolulu, Hawaii, 6-9 July 1976' - Preface. — Bibl. — Index.
ISBN 0-12-468750-4 : £20.95
(B77-27056)

551 — Geothermal processes
Goguel, Jean. Geothermics / [by] Jean Goguel ; English language edition edited by Sydney P. Clark, Jr ; translated [from the French] by Alan Rite. — New York ; London [etc.] : McGraw-Hill, 1976. — xi,200p : ill ; 24cm. — (McGraw-Hill international series in the earth and planetary sciences)
Translation of: 'La géothermie'. Paris : Doin, 1975. — Index.
ISBN 0-07-023518-x : £12.35
(B77-06673)

551 — Natural disasters. Geophysical processes
Forces of nature / edited by Sir Vivian Fuchs ; [contributors] Martin Holdgate ... [et al.]. — London : Thames and Hudson, 1977. — 303p : ill(some col), charts, maps(some col) ; 28cm.
Bibl. — Index.
ISBN 0-500-01153-2 : £9.50
(B77-15279)

551'.028'5 — Geophysics. Use of digital filters
Kulhánek, Ota. Introduction to digital filtering in geophysics / by Ota Kulhánek. — Amsterdam ; Oxford [etc.] : Elsevier, 1976. — xi,168p : ill ; 24cm. — (Developments in solid earth geophysics ; 8)
Bibl.: p.154-162. — Index.
ISBN 0-444-41331-6 : £14.05
(B77-16873)

551'.028'5424 — Geophysical analysis. Applications of programs written in Basic language
McCann, Clive. Computer programs in 'BASIC' for the interpretation of gravity, magnetic and resistivity profiles / by C. McCann ; (with programs by S. Watts). — Reading (Reading RG6 2AB) : Geology Department, University of Reading, 1977. — [3],100p : ill ; 30cm. — (University of Reading. Department of Geology. Geological reports ; no.9) (Computer-based packages for teaching earth science report ; no.3)
Bibl.
ISBN 0-7049-0279-6 Sp : £1.50
(B77-18752)

551.1'3 — Continental drift
Sullivan, Walter. Continents in motion : the new earth debate / by Walter Sullivan. — London [etc.] : Macmillan, 1977. — xv,399p,[16]p of plates : ill(some col), maps(1 col) ; 29cm.
Text, ill. on lining papers. — Originally published: New York : McGraw-Hill, 1974. — Bibl.: p.357-384. — Index.
ISBN 0-333-21683-0 : £6.95 : CIP rev.
(B77-05402)

Tarling, Donald Harvey. Continental drift : a study of the earth's moving surface / [by] D.H. Tarling and M.P. Tarling. — 2nd ed. — Harmondsworth [etc.] : Penguin, 1977. — 154p, [4]p of plates : ill, maps ; 19cm. — (Pelican books)
Previous ed.: London : Bell, 1971. — Bibl.: p.145-147. — Index.
Pbk : £0.80
ISBN 0-14-021533-6
(B77-27850)

551.1'3 — Lithosphere. Evolution. Effects of plate tectonics
Condie, Kent C. Plate tectonics and crustal evolution / [by] Kent C. Condie. — New York ; Oxford [etc.] : Pergamon, 1976. — ix, 288p : ill, maps ; 29cm.
Col. map on fold. sheet in pocket. — Bibl.: p.263-279. — Index.
ISBN 0-08-019594-6 : £11.25
(B77-31179)

551.1'3 — Plate tectonics
Windley, Brian Frederick. The evolving continents / [by] Brian F. Windley. — London [etc.] : Wiley, 1977. — xviii,385p : ill, maps ; 26cm.
Bibl.: p.341-371. — Index.
ISBN 0-471-99475-8 : £14.00
ISBN 0-471-99476-6 Pbk : £5.75
(B77-24211)

Young, Patrick. Drifting continents, shifting seas : an introduction to plate tectonics / by Patrick Young ; illustrated by Rod Slater. — New York ; London : F. Watts, 1976. — [6],89, [1]p : ill, maps ; 25cm. — (An impact book)
Bibl.: p.82-84. — Index.
ISBN 0-531-00848-7 : £2.25
(B77-15280)

551.2 — Plutonic phenomena
Oakeshott, Gordon B. Volcanoes & earthquakes : geologic violence / [by] Gordon B. Oakeshott. — New York ; London [etc.] : McGraw-Hill, 1976. — xv,143p : ill, maps ; 23cm. — (McGraw-Hill earth science paperback series)
Bibl.: p.123-128. — Index.
ISBN 0-07-047492-3 Pbk : £3.30
(B77-05403)

551.2'1 — Volcanoes
Bullard, Fred Mason. Volcanoes of the earth / by Fred M. Bullard. — Revised ed. — Austin ; London : University of Texas Press, 1976. — [18],579p,[16]p of plates : ill(some col), maps ; 26cm.
Map. on lining papers. — Previous ed.: published as 'Volcanoes : in history, in theory, in eruption'. Austin : Texas University Press ; Edinburgh : Nelson, 1962. — Bibl.: p.547-563. — Index.
ISBN 0-292-78701-4 : £20.25
(B77-15842)

551.2'1 — Volcanoes. *Juvenile literature*
Law, Felicia. Volcanoes / written by Felicia Law ; illustrated by Tony Morris. — Glasgow [etc.] : Collins, 1977. — 32p : col ill, col map ; 22cm. — (Dandelions)
ISBN 0-00-106006-6 : £1.50
(B77-32623)

551.2'2 — Earthquakes
Gribbin, John. The Jupiter effect / [by] John Gribbin and Stephen Plagemann ; with a foreword by Isaac Asimov. — [London] : Fontana, 1977. — 156p : ill, maps ; 18cm.
Originally published: London : Macmillan, 1974. — Bibl.: p.146-151. — Index.
ISBN 0-00-634419-4 Pbk : £0.70
(B77-13032)

551.2'22 — Earth. Mantle. Viscoelastic materials. Seismic waves. Propagation
Ricker, Norman Hurd. Transient waves in visco-elastic media / [by] Norman Hurd Ricker. — Amsterdam ; Oxford [etc.] : Elsevier, 1977. — x,278p : ill ; 24cm. — (Developments in solid earth geophysics ; 10)
Bibl.: p.273-275. — Index.
ISBN 0-444-41526-2 : £24.00
(B77-23394)

551.3'02 — Great Britain. Coasts. Erosion
Pennick, Nigel. Lost towns of the sunken lands / by Nigel Pennick. — Cambridge (142 Pheasant Rise, Bar Hill, Cambridge CB3 8SD) : Fenris-Wolf, 1975. — [1],11p : maps ; 30cm. — (Megalithic visions antiquarian papers ; no.6)
ISBN 0-9505403-2-3 Sd : £0.20
(B77-14231)

551.3'03 — Ancient sedimentary environments
Selley, Richard Curtis. Ancient sedimentary environments : a brief survey / [by] Richard C. Selley. — London : Chapman and Hall, 1973. — xvi,237p : ill, maps ; 23cm.
Originally published: 1970. — Bibl. — Index.
£7.00
ISBN 0-412-10100-9
(B77-07900)

551.3'04 — Coarse-grained sediments. Compaction
Compaction of coarse-grained sediments / edited by George V. Chilingarian and Karl H. Wolf. — Amsterdam ; Oxford [etc.] ; Elsevier.
In 2 vols.
2. — 1976. — x,808p(18 fold) : ill, chart, facsims, maps ; 25cm. — (Developments in sedimentology ; 18B)
Bibl. — Index.
ISBN 0-444-41361-8 : £39.80
(B77-15843)

551.3'04'028 — Sediments. Analysis. Techniques
Briggs, David. Sediments / [by] David Briggs. — London [etc.] : Butterworth, 1977. — 192p : ill, maps ; 15x21cm. — (Sources and methods in geography)
Bibl.: p.186-190. — Index.
ISBN 0-408-70815-8 Pbk : £1.95
(B77-22572)

551.3'1 — Glaciation
John, Brian Stephen. The ice age : past and present / [by] Brian S. John. — London : Collins, 1977. — 254p,32p of plates : ill, maps ; 23cm.
Bibl.: p.237-240. — Index.
ISBN 0-00-219457-0 : £4.95
(B77-16874)

551.3'12 — Glaciers. Development. Effects of climate
Thompson, Russell Duncan. The influence of climate on glaciers and permafrost / [by] R.D. Thompson. — Reading (Whiteknights, Reading RG6 2AB) : Department of Geography, University of Reading, 1977. — [2],ii,42p : ill ; 21cm. — (University of Reading. Department of Geography. Geographical papers ; no.57 ISSN 0305-5914)
Bibl.: p.41-42.
ISBN 0-7049-0467-5 Sd : £0.70
Also classified at 551.3'84'0971
(B77-27851)

551.3'5'072 — Water-produced landforms. Research. *Proposals*
Working Party on Geomorphology of Water-Produced Landforms. Research on geomorphology of water-produced landforms : report of the NERC [Natural Environment Research Council] Working Party on Geomorphology of Water-Produced Landforms. — London (27 Charing Cross Rd, WC2H 0AX) : N.E.R.C., 1976. — [1],iv,36p : ill, maps ; 30cm. — (Natural Environment Research Council. Publications : series B ; no.16)
ISBN 0-901875-46-5 Sd : Unpriced
(B77-11210)

551.3'6 — Estuarine suspended sediments. Transport. *Reports, surveys*
Buller, Antony Treverton. Fluctuations of suspended sediment in estuaries : a descriptive review / by Buller, A.T., McManus, J. — [Newport-on-Tay] ([Old Ferry Pier, Newport-on-Tay, Fife DD6 8EX]) : Tay Estuary Research Centre, 1976. — [1],iii,39p : ill ; 21cm. — (Tay Estuary Research Group. Reports ; no.3)
Bibl.: p.36-39.
ISBN 0-9502931-2-1 Sd : £0.40
(B77-04153)

551.3'6'094225 — East Sussex. Coasts. Erosion. *For environment planning*
East Sussex *(County). Planning Department.* Report on the problems of coastal erosion / East Sussex County Planning Department. — Lewes (Southover House, Southover Rd, Lewes, E. Sussex BN7 1YA) : The Department, 1977. — [5],13,[8]p,[8]leaves of plates(5 fold),[2]p of plates : ill, maps ; 30cm.
Bibl.: p.[8].
Sd : £1.00
(B77-18128)

551.3'84'0971 — Permafrost. Effects of climate. *Canada*
Thompson, Russell Duncan. The influence of climate on glaciers and permafrost / [by] R.D. Thompson. — Reading (Whiteknights, Reading RG6 2AB) : Department of Geography, University of Reading, 1977. — [2],ii,42p : ill ; 21cm. — (University of Reading. Department of Geography. Geographical papers ; no.57 ISSN 0305-5914)
Bibl.: p.41-42.
ISBN 0-7049-0467-5 Sd : £0.70
Primary classification 551.3'12
(B77-27851)

551.4 — GEOMORPHOLOGY
551.4 — Deserts. Geomorphology
Cooke, Ronald Urwick. An empty quarter / [by] R.U. Cooke. — London (Regent's Park, London NW1 4NS) : Bedford College, 1977. — 20p,[4]p of plates : ill, 2 maps ; 25cm. — (Bedford College. Inaugural lectures)
Presented in the Tuke Hall of Bedford College in London, 17th May 1976.
ISBN 0-900145-36-6 Sd : Unpriced
(B77-27058)

551.4 — Geomorphology. Temporal aspects. Research. Methodology
Thornes, John. Geomorphology and time / [by] J.B. Thornes and D. Brunsden. — London : Methuen, 1977. — xvi,208p : ill, maps ; 24cm. — (The field of geography)
Bibl.: p.186-199. — Index.
ISBN 0-416-80080-7 : £6.00
ISBN 0-416-80090-4 Pbk : £3.45
(B77-17484)

551.4 — Landforms
Butzer, Karl Wilhelm. Geomorphology from the earth / [by] Karl W. Butzer. — New York [etc.] : Harper and Row, 1976. — xiii,463p : ill, maps ; 25cm. — (Harper and Row series in geography)
Bibl. — Index.
ISBN 0-06-041097-3 : £14.20
(B77-06674)

551.4 — Landforms. *Secondary school texts*
Robinson, Harry, *b.1915.* Morphology and landscape / by Harry Robinson. — 3rd ed. — London : University Tutorial Press, 1977. — viii,392p,leaf of plate,xxiv p of plates : ill, maps ; 22cm.
Previous ed.: 1973. — Bibl.: p.380-385. — Index.
ISBN 0-7231-0756-4 Pbk : £3.00
(B77-30243)

551.4'028 — Geomorphology. Applications of remote sensing
Verstappen, H Th. Remote sensing in geomorphology / [by] H. Th. Verstappen. — Amsterdam ; Oxford [etc.] : Elsevier, 1977. — ix,214p : ill(some col), facsim, maps, ports ; 31cm.
Bibl. — Index.
ISBN 0-444-41086-4 : £19.60
(B77-25615)

551.4'09411 — Scotland. Landforms. Effects of geological structure
Whittow, John Byron. Geology and scenery in Scotland / [by] J.B. Whittow. — Harmondsworth [etc.] : Penguin, 1977. — 362p, [40]p of plates : ill, maps ; 20cm. — (Pelican geography and environmental studies)
Col. map on back cover verso. — Bibl.: p.341-342. — Index.
ISBN 0-14-021867-x Pbk : £1.95
(B77-23395)

551.4'094111 — Scotland. Highlands & Islands. Landforms
Price, Robert John. Highland landforms / [by Robert J. Price]. — Inverness : Highlands and Islands Development Board ; Glasgow [etc.] : [Distributed by] Collins, 1976. — 3-110p : ill(some col), maps(1 col), port ; 21x23cm. — (Highland life series)
Bibl.: p.106. — Index.
ISBN 0-00-411163-x Pbk : £2.50
(B77-09008)

551.4'09429'25 — National parks. *Gwynedd. Snowdonia National Park.* **Landforms**
Evans, David Emlyn. Snowdonia National Park scenery : a geological interpretation / ... written by D. Emlyn Evans. — Cardiff : National Museum of Wales, 1977. — [1],416p : col ill, maps(some col) ; 16x23cm.
ISBN 0-7200-0094-7 Sd : £0.70
(B77-16372)

551.4'0961 — Maghreb. Landforms. Evolution
Smith, Bernard J. Four geomorphological studies of Morocco and the Northwest Sahara / [by] Bernard J. Smith, Philip A. Whittel. — Reading (Whiteknights, Reading RG6 2AB) : Department of Geography, University of Reading, 1977. — [2],iii,60p : ill, maps ; 21cm. — (Geographical papers ; no.53 ISSN 0305-5914)
Bibl.: p.49-60.
ISBN 0-7049-0463-2 Sd : £0.70
(B77-17485)

551.4'09945 — Australia. Victoria. Landforms
Hills, Edwin Sherbon. Physiography of Victoria : an introduction to geomorphology / [by] E. Sherbon Hills. — New ed. — London [etc.] : Whitcombe and Tombs, 1975. — x,373p : ill(some col), maps(some col) ; 25cm.
Maps on lining papers. — Previous ed., i.e. 4th ed. : Melbourne : Whitcombe and Tombs, 1960. — Index.
ISBN 0-7233-5288-7 : Unpriced
(B77-22573)

551.4'0997'11 — British Antarctic Territory. Deception Island, South Orkney Islands & South Shetland Islands. Landforms
Clapperton, Chalmers Moyes. Scenery of the South : Falkland Islands, South Georgia, sub-Antarctic islands / [by] Chalmers M. Clapperton, David E. Sugden. — Aberdeen (162 Broomhill Rd, Aberdeen AB1 6HY) : David E. Sugden, 1975. — [2],17p : ill, maps ; 21cm.
ISBN 0-9505496-0-6 Sd : £0.50
Also classified at 551.4'0997'11; 551.4'0998'9
(B77-12437)

551.4'0997'11 — Falkland Islands & Falkland Islands Dependencies. Landforms
Clapperton, Chalmers Moyes. Scenery of the South : Falkland Islands, South Georgia, sub-Antarctic islands / [by] Chalmers M. Clapperton, David E. Sugden. — Aberdeen (162 Broomhill Rd, Aberdeen AB1 6HY) : David E. Sugden, 1975. — [2],17p : ill, maps ; 21cm.
ISBN 0-9505496-0-6 Sd : £0.50
Primary classification 551.4'0997'11
(B77-12437)

551.4'0998'9 — British Antarctic Territory. Antarctic Peninsula. Landforms
Clapperton, Chalmers Moyes. Scenery of the South : Falkland Islands, South Georgia, sub-Antarctic islands / [by] Chalmers M. Clapperton, David E. Sugden. — Aberdeen (162 Broomhill Rd, Aberdeen AB1 6HY) : David E. Sugden, 1975. — [2],17p : ill, maps ; 21cm.
ISBN 0-9505496-0-6 Sd : £0.50
Primary classification 551.4'0997'11
(B77-12437)

551.4'2 — Coral reefs. Formation. *Early works*
Darwin, Charles. [The geology of the voyage of the 'Beagle'. Part 1]. The structure and distribution of coral reefs / [by] Charles Darwin ; foreword by H.W. Menard. — Berkeley [etc.] ; London : University of California Press, 1976. — xii,214,[4]p,[21]p of plates : ill, maps(some col) ; 21cm. — (California library reprint series)
Facsimile reprint of: 'Geological observations on coral reefs, volcanic islands, and on South America'. Part 1. London : Smith, Elder, 1851. — Originally published: as 'The geology of the voyage of the "Beagle"'. Part 1. London : Smith, Elder, 1842. — Index.
ISBN 0-520-03282-9 : £11.60
(B77-13643)

551.4'3 — Mountains. *Juvenile literature*
Armstrong, Patrick Hamilton. Mountains / by P.H. Armstrong ; with illustrations by Gerald Witcomb. — Loughborough : Ladybird Books, 1977. — 52p : chiefly col ill, col maps ; 18cm. — (Ladybird leaders ; 33)
Text, col. map on lining papers. — Index.
ISBN 0-7214-0458-8 : £0.24
(B77-25616)

551.4'3 — Upland regions. Geophysical processes. *Primary school texts*
Davies, Margaret Lloyd. Mountains and hills / [by] Margaret Lloyd Davies ; illustrated by Angela Lewer. — London : Muller, 1977. — 48p : ill, map ; 24cm.
With answers.
ISBN 0-584-63546-x : £2.35
(B77-08370)

551.4'4 — Caves. *Juvenile literature*
Wilkins, Frances. Caves / by Frances Wilkins ; illustrations by Kathleen Gell. — Oxford : Blackwell, 1977. — 59p,[4]leaves of plates : ill(some col), map ; 21cm. — (Blackwell's learning library ; no.98)
Ill. on lining paper. — Index.
ISBN 0-631-13430-1 : £0.95
(B77-20248)

551.4'4 — Karst. Morphogenesis
Jakucs, László. Morphogenetics of karst regions : variants of karst evolution / by László Jakucs ; [translated from the Hungarian by B. Balkay]. — Bristol : Hilger [etc.], 1977. — 294p : ill, maps ; 25cm.
Translation and revision of: 'A karsztok morfogenetikája'. Budapest : Akademiai Kiadó, 197-?. — Bibl.: p.245-268. — Index.
ISBN 0-85274-309-2 : £17.00
(B77-15281)

551.4'5 — Beaches. Geophysical processes
Komar, Paul D. Beach processes and sedimentation / [by] Paul D. Komar. — Englewood Cliffs ; London [etc.] : Prentice-Hall, 1976. — xvii,429p : ill, maps, port ; 25cm.
Bibl. — Index.
ISBN 0-13-072595-1 : £19.65
(B77-04154)

551.4'5 — Coasts. Geophysical processes. *Primary school texts*
Davies, Margaret Lloyd. The coast / [by] Margaret Lloyd Davies ; illustrated by Angela Lewer. — London : Muller, 1977. — 61p : ill ; 24cm.
With answers.
ISBN 0-584-63544-3 : £2.35
(B77-08371)

551.4'5 — Coasts. Geophysical processes. Development
Davies, John Lloyd. Geographical variation in coastal development / [by] J.L. Davies ; edited by K.M. Clayton. — [1st ed.], 2nd impression with revisions and corrections. — London [etc.] : Longman, 1977. — vii,204p : ill, charts, maps ; 25cm. — (Geomorphology texts ; 4)
First ed. originally published: Edinburgh : Oliver and Boyd, 1972. — Bibl.: p.187-197. — Index.
ISBN 0-582-48434-0 Pbk : £5.00
(B77-31180)

551.4'5 — Lowland regions. Geophysical processes. *Primary school texts*
Davies, Margaret Lloyd. Lowlands / [by] Margaret Lloyd Davies ; illustrated by Angela Lewer. — London : Muller, 1977. — 47p : ill ; 23cm.
With answers.
ISBN 0-584-63545-1 : £2.35
(B77-08372)

551.4'5 — National parks. *Dyfed. Preseli (District) & South Pembrokeshire. Pembrokeshire Coast National Park. Coastal regions. Landforms*
Ellis-Gruffydd, Dyfed. Coastal scenery of the Pembrokeshire Coast National Park / [by] Dyfed Ellis-Gruffydd. — Newport, Dyfed (Brian S. John, Trefelin, [Cilgwyn], Newport, Dyfed) : Greencroft Books for the Pembrokeshire Coast National Park Committee, 1977. — [1],32p : ill, map ; 22cm. — (Pembrokeshire Coast National Park Committee. Information booklets ; no.2 ISSN 0140-2323)
Bibl.: p.32.
ISBN 0-905559-05-3 Sd : £0.50
(B77-27059)

551.4'6 — Oceanography
Gross, M Grant. Oceanography : a view of the earth / [by] M. Grant Gross. — 2nd ed. — Englewood Cliffs ; London [etc.] : Prentice-Hall, 1977. — xi,497p : ill, charts, maps ; 28cm.
Maps on lining papers. — Previous ed.: 1972. — Bibl. — Index.
ISBN 0-13-629675-0 : £13.55
(B77-21116)

McCormick, J Michael. Elements of oceanography / [by] J. Michael McCormick, John V. Thiruvathukal. — Philadelphia ; London [etc.] : Saunders, 1976. — vi,346p : ill, maps ; 28cm.
Text on lining papers. — Bibl.: p.333-338. — Index.
ISBN 0-7216-5900-4 : £12.00
(B77-02296)

Monin, Andreĭ Sergeevich. Variability of the oceans / [by] Andrey S. Monin, Vladimir M. Kamenkovich, Vladimir G. Kort ; John L. Lumley, editor of the English translation [from the Russian]. — New York ; London [etc.] : Wiley, 1977. — xiii,241p : ill, charts ; 24cm.
'A Wiley-Interscience publication'. — Translation of: 'Izmenchivost' mirovogo okeana'. Leningrad : Gidrometeoizdat, 1974. — Index.
ISBN 0-471-61328-2 : £14.95
(B77-33207)

Ross, David A. Introduction to oceanography / [by] David A. Ross. — [2nd ed.]. — Englewood Cliffs ; London [etc.] : Prentice-Hall, 1977. — x,438p,[8]p of plates : ill(some col), charts ; 24cm.
Previous ed.: New York : Appleton-Century-Crofts, 1970. — Bibl.: p.413-421. — Index.
ISBN 0-13-491332-9 : £11.95
(B77-15282)

551.4'6 — Oceanography. *Reviews of research*
Oceanography and marine biology : an annual review. — [Aberdeen] : Aberdeen University Press.
Vol.15 / Harold Barnes, editor. — 1977. — 3-571p,leaf of plate,[2]p of plates : ill, maps ; 26cm.
Bibl. — Index.
ISBN 0-900015-39-x : £28.00
ISSN 0078-3218
Also classified at 574.92
(B77-31889)

The sea : ideas and observations on progress in the study of the seas. — New York ; London [etc.] : Wiley.
Vol.6 : Marine modelling / edited by E.D. Goldberg ... [et al.]. — 1977. — xv,1048p : ill, maps, port ; 26cm.
'A Wiley-Interscience publication'. — Bibl. — Index.
ISBN 0-471-31091-3 : £34.75
(B77-18129)

551.4'6 — Oceans
Duxbury, Ken. Seastate and tides / [by] Kenneth Duxbury. — London : Stanford Maritime, 1977. — [8],84p : ill, maps ; 22cm.
Bibl.: p.80. — Index.
ISBN 0-540-07267-2 Pbk : £2.25 : CIP rev.
(B77-24927)

Harvey, John G. Atmosphere and ocean : our fluid environments / by John G. Harvey. — Horsham : Artemis Press, 1976. — 143p : ill, charts, maps ; 26cm.
Bibl.: p.133-135. — Index.
ISBN 0-85141-296-3 : £4.95
ISBN 0-85141-295-5 £3.75
Also classified at 551.5
(B77-15844)

551.4'6 — Oceans. *Juvenile literature*
Pick, Christopher. The young scientist book of the undersea / [written by Christopher Pick] ; [illustrators Malcolm English et al.]. — London : Usborne, 1977. — 32p : ill(chiefly col), col maps ; 28cm. — (Young scientist books)
Spine title: Undersea. — Bibl.: p.32. — Index.
ISBN 0-86020-092-2 Pbk : £0.95
(B77-28600)

Tyler, Jenny. The children's book of the seas / [by] Jenny Tyler, assisted by Lisa Watts ; illustrated by Bob Hersey and designed by Bob Scott. — London : Usborne, 1976. — 32p : ill(chiefly col), col maps ; 28cm. — (Children's guides)
Index.
ISBN 0-86020-064-7 Pbk : £0.75
(B77-11796)

551.4'6 — Oceans. Upper layers. Mathematical models. *Conference proceedings*
Advanced Study Institute on Modelling and Prediction of the Upper Layers of the Ocean, *Urbino, 1975.* Modelling and prediction of the upper layers of the ocean : proceedings of a NATO Advanced Study Institute / edited by E.B. Kraus. — Oxford [etc.] : Pergamon, 1977. — xiii,325p : ill, maps ; 26cm. — (Pergamon marine series ; vol.1) (A NATO Advanced Study Institute)
'... an Advanced Study Institute on "Modelling and Prediction of the Upper Layers of the Ocean" ...' - Preface. — '... Urbino, Italy, 1975' - cover. — Bibl.: p.291-321. — Index.
ISBN 0-08-020611-5 : £10.95
ISBN 0-08-020610-7 Pbk : £6.95
(B77-18753)

551.4'6 — Sea level. Variation. *Statistics*
Permanent Service for Mean Sea Level. Monthly and annual mean heights of sea level / Permanent Service for Mean Sea Level, Federation of Astronomical and Geophysical Services (FAGS). — Birkenhead (Institute of Oceanographic Sciences, Bidston Observatory, Birkenhead, Merseyside L43 7RA) : The Service.
In 3 vols. — Updated and amended pages to be issued annually.
[Vol.1] : [Europe, Africa, India and the Far East]. — [1977]-. — 1v. ; 22x30cm.
Ca 300 leaves on publication. — Notebook format.
Ls : Unpriced
(B77-32624)

551.4'6'0028 — Oceanography. Use of submersibles
Submersibles and their use in oceanography and ocean engineering / edited by Richard A. Geyer. — Amsterdam ; Oxford [etc.] : Elsevier, 1977. — xxi,383p : ill, charts, maps ; 25cm. — (Elsevier oceanography series ; 17)
Bibl. — Index.
ISBN 0-444-41545-9 : £28.24
(B77-31181)

551.4'6'0072 — Oceanography. Research institutions. *Directories*
Ocean research index : a guide to ocean and freshwater research including fisheries research. — 2nd ed. / editor Allen Varley, associate editor Stella E.L. Wheeler. — [St Peter Port] : Hodgson, 1976. — 637p ; 26cm.
Previous ed.: 1970. — Bibl.: p.503-548. — Index.
ISBN 0-85280-141-6 : Unpriced
Also classified at 574.5'2632'072
(B77-23396)

551.4'6'0072041 — Oceanography. Research organisations. *Great Britain. Institute of Oceanographic Sciences. Reports, surveys. Serials*
Institute of Oceanographic Sciences. Annual report / Institute of Oceanographic Sciences. — Wormley ([Wormley, Godalming, Surrey GU8 5UB]) : The Institute.
June 1973-December 1974. — 1976. — iii,72p, plate : map, port ; 30cm.
Bibl.: p.51-56.
ISBN 0-904175-03-0 Pbk : £1.00
ISSN 0309-4472
(B77-10362)

551.4'601 — Oceans. Chemical composition & chemical properties
Chemical oceanography. — 2nd ed. — London [etc.] : Academic Press.
Previous ed.: in 2 vols. 1965.
Vol.6 / edited by J.P. Riley and R. Chester. — 1976. — xiv,414p : ill, maps ; 24cm.
Bibl. — Index.
ISBN 0-12-588606-3 : £14.00
(B77-00214)

551.4'601 — Oceans. Optical properties
Jerlov, Nils Gunnar. Marine optics / by N.G. Jerlov. — 2nd revised and enlarged ed. — Amsterdam ; Oxford [etc.] : Elsevier, 1976. — xiv,231p : ill, maps ; 25cm. — (Elsevier oceanography series ; 14)
Previous ed.: published as 'Optical oceanography'. Amsterdam ; Barking : Elsevier, 1968. — Bibl.: p.205-226. — Index.
ISBN 0-444-41490-8 : £17.94
(B77-04802)

551.4'607 — Oceans. Benthic regions. Boundary layer. *Conference proceedings*
NATO Science Committee Conference on the Benthic Boundary Layer, *Les Arcs, 1974.* The benthic boundary layer / edited by I.N. McCave. — New York ; London : Plenum Press [for] NATO Scientific Affairs Division, 1976. — x,323p : ill, charts, maps ; 24cm.
'Proceedings of the NATO Science Committee Conference on the Benthic Boundary Layer held at Les Arcs, France, November 4-9, 1974' - title page verso. — Bibl. — Index.
ISBN 0-306-30886-x : £17.33
(B77-20249)

551.4'608 — Continental shelf. Geological features. Surveying
McQuillin, Robert. Exploring the geology of shelf seas / [by] R. McQuillin, D.A. Ardus. — London : Graham and Trotman, 1977. — xiii, 234p : ill, charts, maps ; 24cm.
Bibl.: p.219-221. — Index.
ISBN 0-86010-012-x : £9.50
(B77-30244)

551.4'609 — Estuaries. *Conference proceedings*
International Estuarine Research Conference, *3rd, Galveston, 1975.* Estuarine processes / edited by Martin Wiley. — New York [etc.] ; London : Academic Press.
In 2 vols.
Vol.1 : Uses, stresses and adaptation to the estuary. — 1976. — xviii,541p : ill, maps ; 24cm.
'... the Third International Estuarine Research Conference [organized by] the Estuarine Research Federation ... [held] in Galveston, Texas, October 7-9, 1975' - Preface. — Bibl. — Index.
ISBN 0-12-751801-0 : £15.60
(B77-11797)

Vol.2 : Circulation, sediments and transfer of material in the estuary. — 1976. — xviii,428p : ill, maps ; 24cm.
' ... the Third International Estuarine Conference [organized by] the Estuarine Research Federation ... [held] in Galveston, Texas, October 7-9, 1975' - Preface. — Bibl. — Index.
ISBN 0-12-751802-9 : £13.85
(B77-11798)

551.4'609 — Estuaries. Chemical properties. *Reviews of research*
Estuarine chemistry / edited by J.D. Burton and P.S. Liss. — London [etc.] : Academic Press, 1976. — xii,229p : ill, maps ; 24cm.
'... based upon lectures given at a meeting on Estuarine Chemistry held in London on 16th May, 1974, under the auspices of the Estuarine and Brackish-Water Sciences Association and the Marine Chemistry Discussion Group' - Preface. — Bibl. — Index.
ISBN 0-12-147350-3 : £8.00
(B77-04155)

551.4'613'7 — England. Severn Estuary. Proposed barrage region. Bed. Geological features. *Reports, surveys*
Green, Gilbert Wilson. The geology of the Severn barrage area / by G.W. Green and B.N. Fletcher. — Leeds [etc.] (Ring Rd, Halton, Leeds LS15 8TQ) : Institute of Geological Sciences, 1976. — [4],8p : maps ; 30cm.
'... prepared by the Institute of Geological Sciences for the Department of Energy. — Bibl. : p.8.
Sd : Unpriced
(B77-20250)

551.4'613'7 — Ireland. Coastal waters. Physical properties & chemical properties. *Tables. Serials*
University College, *Galway. Department of Oceanography.* Data report / University College, Galway, [Department of] Oceanography. — [Galway] ([College Rd, Galway, Republic of Ireland]) : [The Department].
1972-73. — [1974]. — [1],2,[96]p : of forms ; 30cm.
Sd : Unpriced
(B77-16875)

1974. — [1975]. — [3],77 leaves ; 28cm.
Sd : Unpriced
(B77-16876)

551.4'65'51 — Bering Strait. Physical properties
Coachman, L K. Bering Strait : the regional physical oceanography / [by] L.K. Coachman, K. Aagaard, R.B. Tripp. — Seattle ; London : University of Washington Press, [1976]. — [13], 172p : ill, maps ; 24cm.
Published in the United States: 1975. — Bibl.: p.165-168. — Index.
ISBN 0-295-95442-6 : £16.00
(B77-05404)

551.4'7 — Estuaries. Hydrodynamics. *For hydraulic engineering*
McDowell, Donald Malcolm. Hydraulic behaviour of estuaries / [by] D.M. McDowell and B.A. O'Connor. — London [etc.] : Macmillan, 1977. — viii,292p : ill, maps ; 24cm. — (Civil engineering hydraulics series)
Index.
ISBN 0-333-12231-3 : £12.50
(B77-22574)

551.4'7 — Oceans. Benthic regions. Boundary layer. Turbulence. *Conference proceedings*
International Liège Colloquium on Ocean Hydrodynamics, *8th, 1976?.* Bottom turbulence : proceedings of the 8th International Liège Colloquium on Ocean Hydrodynamics / edited by Jaques [i.e. Jacques] C.J. Nihoul. — Amsterdam ; Oxford [etc.] : Elsevier, 1977. — xiv,306p : ill, charts, maps ; 25cm. — (Elsevier oceanography series ; 19)
Bibl. — Index.
ISBN 0-444-41574-2 : £19.05
(B77-25617)

551.4'71 — North Atlantic Ocean. Currents
Worthington, L V. On the North Atlantic circulation / by L.V. Worthington. — Baltimore ; London : Johns Hopkins University Press, 1976. — 110,[1]p : ill, maps(some col) ; 29cm. — (The Johns Hopkins oceanographic studies ; no.6)
Bibl.: p.107-110.
ISBN 0-8018-1742-0 : £12.40
(B77-29416)

551.4'71'36 — Great Britain. Coastal waters. Currents. *For dinghy racing*
Proctor, Ian. Sailing strategy : wind and current / by Ian Proctor ; illustrated by the author. — 3rd ed. — London : Coles, 1977. — 189p,8p of plates : ill, charts, maps ; 23cm.
Previous ed.: published as 'Sailing : wind and current'. 1964. — Index.
ISBN 0-229-11552-7 : £4.95
Also classified at 551.5'185'0941
(B77-21854)

551.4'8 — Hydrology
Miller, David Hewitt. Water at the surface of the earth : an introduction to ecosystem hydrodynamics / [by] David H. Miller. — New York [etc.] ; London : Academic Press, 1977. — xii,557p : ill, charts, maps ; 24cm. — (International geophysics series ; vol.21)
Bibl. — Index.
ISBN 0-12-496750-7 : £33.70
(B77-21855)

551.4'8 — Hydrology. *Reviews of research*
Working Party on Hydrology. Research in hydrology : the report of a NERC Working Party on hydrological research. — London : Natural Environment Research Council, 1976. — [1],iv,20p : ill ; 30cm. — (Natural Environment Research Council. Publications : series B ; no.19)
'Report of the Working Party on Hydrology' - p.i.
ISBN 0-901875-48-1 Sd : Unpriced
(B77-16373)

551.4'8'0184 — Surface water. Mathematical models. *Conference proceedings*
Workshop on Mathematical Models in Hydrology, *Pisa, 1974.* Mathematical models for surface water hydrology : proceedings of the Workshop held at the IBM Scientific Center, Pisa, Italy / edited by Tito A. Ciriani, Ugo Maione, James R. Wallis. — London [etc.] : Wiley, 1977. — xv,423p : ill, maps ; 24cm.
'A Wiley-Interscience publication'. — '... the IBM Scientific Center, Pisa, and the Hydraulics Institute of the University of Pavia co-sponsored a Workshop on Mathematical Models in Hydrology held in Pisa, December 9-12, 1974' - Introduction. — Bibl.: p.385-391. — Index.
ISBN 0-471-99400-6 : £14.00
(B77-20251)

551.4'8'024627 — Hydrology. *For hydraulic engineering*
Linsley, Ray Keyes. Hydrology for engineers / [by] Ray K. Linsley, Jr, Max A. Kohler, Joseph L.H. Paulhus. — 2nd ed. — Tokyo ; London [etc.] : McGraw-Hill, [1977]. — xxiii, 482p : ill, charts, maps ; 22cm. — (McGraw-Hill series in water resources and environmental engineering)
This ed. originally published: 1975. — Bibl. — Index.
ISBN 0-07-085428-9 Pbk : £7.30
(B77-24928)

551.4'82'09931 — New Zealand. Lakes. *Readings*
New Zealand lakes / edited by V.H. Jolly and J.M.A. Brown. — [Auckland] : Auckland University Press ; [Oxford] : Oxford University Press, 1975 [i.e. 1976]. — 388p : ill, maps ; 25cm.
Published in New Zealand: 1975. — Bibl.: p.338-350. — Index.
ISBN 0-19-647936-3 : £16.75
(B77-00215)

551.4'83 — Great Britain. Rivers. Flow. Calculation. Use of rainfall statistics. Mathematical models. *Study examples: England. Thames River*
Wright, C E. Monthly catchment regression models, Thames Basin / by C.E. Wright. — Reading (Reading Bridge House, Reading RG1 8PS) : Central Water Planning Unit, 1975. — [3],32p : ill, map ; 30cm. — (Central Water Planning Unit. Technical notes ; no.8)
Bibl.: p.32.
ISBN 0-904839-08-7 Sp : Unpriced
(B77-31182)

551.4'83 — Rivers. *Juvenile literature*
Wrigley, Denis. The living world of the river / [by] Denis Wrigley. — Guildford [etc.] : Lutterworth Press, 1977. — 31,[1]p : col ill ; 22cm. — (Wrigley, Denis. Wrigley eye openers)
ISBN 0-7188-2202-1 : £1.50
(B77-32625)

551.4'98 — Stormwater. Mathematical models
Overton, Donald E. Stormwater modeling / [by] Donald E. Overton, Michael E. Meadows. — New York [etc.] ; London : Academic Press, 1976 [i.e. 1977]. — xii,358p : ill, charts, maps ; 24cm.
Published in the United States: 1976. — Index.
ISBN 0-12-531550-3 : £15.95
(B77-13644)

551.5 — METEOROLOGY
Byers, Horace Robert. General meteorology / [by] Horace Robert Byers. — 4th ed. — New York ; London [etc.] : McGraw-Hill, 1974. — xv,461p : ill, charts ; 24cm.
Previous ed.: 1959. — Index.
ISBN 0-07-009500-0 : Unpriced
(B77-19367)

Hardy, David Andrews. Air and weather / written and illustrated by David A. Hardy ; foreword by Peter Fairley. — Tadworth : World's Work, 1977. — 61p : col ill, col charts ; 24cm. — (Hardy, David Andrews. Advance of science)
Index.
ISBN 0-437-45198-4 : £3.50
(B77-31183)

551.5 — Atmosphere
Wallace, John M. Atmospheric science : an introductory survey / [by] John M. Wallace, Peter V. Hobbs. — New York [etc.] ; London : Academic Press, 1977. — xvii,467p : ill, charts, maps ; 25cm.
Col. ill. on lining paper. — With answers. — Index.
ISBN 0-12-732950-1 : £12.80
(B77-31890)

551.5 — Atmosphere. Chemical composition & properties
Heicklen, Julian. Atmosphere chemistry / [by] Julian Heicklen. — New York [etc.] ; London : Academic Press, 1976 [i.e. 1977]. — xiv,406p : ill ; 24cm.
Published in the United States: 1976. — Bibl. — Index.
ISBN 0-12-336740-9 : £27.00
(B77-13033)

551.5 — Atmosphere. Meteorological conditions. Measurement
Schwerdtfeger, Peter. Physical principles of micro-meteorological measurements / by Peter Schwerdtfeger. — Amsterdam ; Oxford [etc.] : Elsevier, 1976. — ix,113p : ill ; 25cm. — (Developments in atmospheric science ; 6)
Bibl.: p.109-110. — Index.
ISBN 0-444-41489-4 : £15.70
(B77-06073)

551.5 — Atmosphere. Physical properties
Houghton, John Theodore. The physics of atmospheres / [by] John T. Houghton. — Cambridge [etc.] : Cambridge University Press, 1977. — xiii,203p : ill, charts ; 24cm.
With answers. — Bibl.: p.187-189. — Index.
ISBN 0-521-21443-2 : £6.50
(B77-24214)

551.5 — Meteorology. *Juvenile literature*
Dalton, Frank. The weather / [by] Frank Dalton. — Hove : Priory Press, 1977. — 88p : ill, charts, ports ; 24cm. — (Science in action)
Ill. on lining papers. — Bibl.: p.84. — Index.
ISBN 0-85078-215-5 : £3.25
(B77-20252)

551.5 — Weather
Frick, Martin. The weather : an introduction to meteorology / [by] Martin Frick ; [translated from the German by Stanley Crawford]. — Yeovil : Haynes, 1976. — 85p : ill(chiefly col), charts ; 17cm. — (Foulis spectrum books)
Translation of: 'Wetterkunde'. Bern : Hallwag, 197- ?.
ISBN 0-85429-501-1 Pbk : £0.85
(B77-04156)

Harvey, John G. Atmosphere and ocean : our fluid environments / by John G. Harvey. — Horsham : Artemis Press, 1976. — 143p : ill, charts, maps ; 26cm.
Bibl.: p.133-135. — Index.
ISBN 0-85141-296-3 : £4.95
ISBN 0-85141-295-5 £3.75
Primary classification 551.4'6
(B77-15844)

551.5'022'2 — Weather. *Illustrations. Juvenile literature*
Blanco, Josette. The weather / by Josette Blanco ; illustrated by Claude d'Ham. — Purton (Restrop Manor, Purton, Wilts.) : Child's Play (International) Ltd, [1977]. — [20] p : chiefly col ill ; 22cm. — (Child's Play moments ; book 3)
Page width varies.
ISBN 0-85953-041-8 : £0.90
ISBN 0-85953-037-x Pbk : £0.45
(B77-13034)

551.5'02'479 — Weather. *For outdoor activities*
Brown, Terence Henry Charles. The Spur book of weather lore / by Terry Brown and Rob Hunter. — Bourne End, Bucks. : Spurbooks, 1976. — 63p : ill, charts, maps ; 19cm. — (A Spurbooks venture guide)
ISBN 0-904978-21-4 Pbk : £0.75
(B77-04157)

551.5'06'141 — Meteorology. Organisations. *Great Britain. Meteorological Office. Reports, surveys. Serials*
Meteorological Office. Annual report on the Meteorological Office. — London : H.M.S.O. 1976. — 1977. — xiv,145p,iv p of plates : ill(incl 1 col), chart, map ; 25cm. — (Met.O. ; 907)
Bibl.: p.124-131.
ISBN 0-11-400303-3 Pbk : £2.75
ISSN 0072-6605
(B77-26306)

551.5'1 — Air. *Juvenile literature*
Lucas, Angela. Focus on air / [by] Angela & Derek Lucas. — London : Methuen, 1977. — 48p : col ill ; 22cm.
Index.
ISBN 0-416-82410-2 : £1.85
(B77-14232)

551.5'113 — Atmosphere. Aerosols
Twomey, S. Atmospheric aerosols / by S. Twomey. — Amsterdam ; Oxford [etc.] : Elsevier, 1977. — xiv,302p : ill ; 25cm. — (Developments in atmospheric science ; 7)
Bibl. — Index.
ISBN 0-444-41527-0 : Unpriced
(B77-21117)

551.5'142 — Stratosphere. Monitoring in France, Great Britain & United States, 1976-1977. *Reports, surveys*
Tripartite agreement on stratospheric monitoring between France, the United Kingdom and the United States of America, joint annual report, 1976-77. — London : H.M.S.O., 1977. — vii, 106p : ill ; 25cm. — (Pollution paper ; no.13)
Bibl.: p.103-106. — Includes the text of the agreement.
ISBN 0-11-751239-7 Pbk : £2.75
(B77-30246)

551.5'153 — Atmosphere. Dynamics
Dutton, John A. The ceaseless wind : an introduction to the theory of atmospheric motion / [by] John A. Dutton. — New York ; London [etc.] : McGraw-Hill, [1977]. — xix, 579p : ill, charts ; 25cm.
Text on lining papers. — Published in the United States: 1976. — Bibl. — Index.
ISBN 0-07-018407-0 : £17.00
(B77-13645)

551.5'185'0941 — Great Britain. Coastal waters. Winds. *For dinghy racing*
Proctor, Ian. Sailing strategy : wind and current / by Ian Proctor ; illustrated by the author. — 3rd ed. — London : Coles, 1977. — 189p,8p of plates : ill, charts, maps ; 23cm.
Previous ed.: published as 'Sailing : wind and current'. 1964. — Index.
ISBN 0-229-11552-7 : £4.95
Primary classification 551.4'71'36
(B77-21854)

551.5'2'028 — Meteorology. Organisations. *Great Britain. Meteorological Office. Wet bulb meteorological thermometers. Psychrometer coefficient. Research reports*
Folland, C K. The psychrometer coefficient of the wet-bulb thermometers used in the Meteorological Office large thermometer screen / by C.K. Folland. — London : H.M.S.O., 1977. — [2],38p : ill ; 25cm. — (Meteorological Office. Scientific papers ; no.38) (Met.O. ; 902)
Bibl.: p.35-36.
ISBN 0-11-400302-5 Sd : £1.25
(B77-14716)

551.5'271 — Sunshine. *Juvenile literature*
Law, Felicia. Sunshine / written by Felicia Law ; illustrated by Jenny Thorne. — Glasgow [etc.] : Collins, 1977. — 32p : chiefly col ill ; 22cm. — (Dandelions)
ISBN 0-00-106008-2 : £0.50
(B77-32626)

551.5'66 — Light. Scattering in atmosphere
McCartney, Earl J. Optics of the atmosphere : scattering by molecules and particles / [by] Earl J. McCartney. — New York ; London [etc.] : Wiley, 1976. — xvii,408p : ill ; 24cm. — (Wiley series in pure and applied optics)
Bibl.: p.360-391. — Index.
ISBN 0-471-01526-1 : £19.20
(B77-00216)

551.5'781'213 — Rainfall. *Tropical regions*
Jackson, Ian Joseph. Climate, water and agriculture in the tropics / [by] I.J. Jackson. — London [etc.] : Longman, 1977. — xii,248p : ill, charts, maps ; 22cm.
Bibl.: p.214-228. — Index.
ISBN 0-582-48528-2 : £6.95
ISBN 0-582-48529-0 Pbk : £3.75
(B77-22575)

551.5'781'3 — Great Britain. Long duration rainfall. Variability. Calculation. Statistical methods
Tabony, R C. The variability of long-duration rainfall over Great Britain / by R.C. Tabony. — London : H.M.S.O., 1977. — [3],40p : ill, charts ; 25cm. — (Meteorological Office. Scientific papers ; no.37) (Met.O.901)
Bibl.: p.38-39.
ISBN 0-11-400301-7 Sd : £0.85
(B77-13035)

551.6 — CLIMATE AND WEATHER
World survey of climatology / editor-in-chief H.E. Landsberg. — Amsterdam ; Oxford [etc.] : Elsevier.
Vol.6 : Climates of central and southern Europe / edited by C.C. Walten. — 1977. — ix,248[i.e.244]p(2 fold) : ill, charts, maps ; 30cm.
Bibl. — Index.
ISBN 0-444-41336-7 : Unpriced
(B77-24929)

Vol.7 : Climates of the Soviet Union / by Paul E. Lydolph. — 1977. — xi,443p : ill, charts ; 30cm.
Bibl. — Index.
ISBN 0-444-41516-5 : £46.84
(B77-14233)

551.6 — Applied climatology. *Reviews of research*
Working Party on Applied Climatology. Research in applied and world climatology : the reports of the NERC Working Parties on Applied Climatology and on World Climatology. — London : Natural Environment Research Council, 1977. — [1],11,46p : ill, maps ; 29cm. — (Natural Environment Research Council. Publications : series B ; no.17)
ISBN 0-901875-49-x Sd : Unpriced
(B77-16374)

551.6 — Climate. Changes
Wright, Peter Brian. Portrait of climatic change : a survey of the field and a review of recent books / by Peter B. Wright. — Norwich [etc.] (Environmental Sciences, University of East Anglia, Norwich NR4 7TJ) : Dr T.D. Davies (PCC), 1977. — [2],46p : 1 ill ; 21cm.
Bibl.: p.41-45.
ISBN 0-9505614-0-1 Sd : £3.50
(B77-33208)

551.6 — Dendroclimatology
Fritts, H C. Tree rings and climate / [by] H.C. Fritts. — London [etc.] : Academic Press, 1976. — xiii,567p : ill, charts, maps, ports ; 24cm.
Bibl.: p.511-529. — Index.
ISBN 0-12-268450-8 : £16.00
(B77-07901)

551.6'3 — Public weather reports & forecasts. *Great Britain. Reports, surveys*
Meteorological Office. Weather advice to the community / Meteorological Office. — [Bracknell] ([Bracknell, Berks. RG12 2SZ]) : [Meteorological Office], 1975. — [1],11p : 2 maps ; 21cm. — (Met.O. leaflet ; no.1)
Sheet ([2]p.) as insert.
Sd : Unpriced
(B77-06074)

551.6'3 — Weather. Observation. *Manuals. For sailors*
Meteorological Office. The marine observer's handbook / Meteorological Office. — 10th ed. — London : H.M.S.O., 1977. — vii,157,[3]p(3 fold),[12],viii,xxiv,12p of plates : ill ; 25cm. — (Met. O. 887)
Previous ed.: 1969. — Index.
ISBN 0-11-400297-5 : £5.50
(B77-20253)

551.6'32 — Weather. Reporting by shipping. Coding. *Manuals*
Meteorological Office. Ships' code and decode book : incorporating the international meteorological codes for weather reports from and to ships and the analysis code for use of shipping / Meteorological Office. — 9th ed. — London : H.M.S.O., 1977. — [2],62p,fold plate : ill, col chart, map ; 25cm. — (Met.O. 509)
Previous ed.: 1975. — Index.
ISBN 0-11-400310-6 Pbk : £1.50
(B77-33209)

551.6'34 — Great Britain. Weather. Forecasting. Meteorological Office Operational 10-level Numerical Weather Prediction Model
Burridge, D M. The Meteorological Office operational 10-level numerical weather prediction model (December 1975) / by D.M. Burridge and A.J. Gadd. — London : H.M.S.O., 1977. — vii,39p : ill ; 25cm. — (Meteorological Office. Scientific papers ; no.34) (Met.O.890)
Bibl.: p.38-39.
ISBN 0-11-400300-9 Sd : £1.25
(B77-24215)

551.6'9'13 — Tropical regions. Climate
Nieuwolt, S. Tropical climatology : an introduction to the climates of the low latitudes / by S. Nieuwolt. — London [etc.] : Wiley, 1977. — ix,207p : ill, charts, maps ; 24cm.
Bibl. — Index.
ISBN 0-471-99406-5 : £6.95
(B77-13646)

551.6'9'154 — Arid regions. Climate
Thompson, Russell Duncan. The climatology of the arid world / [by] R.D. Thompson. — Reading (Whiteknights, Reading, [Berks.]) : Department of Geography, University of Reading, 1975. — [2],iii,39p : 2 ill, charts, maps ; 21cm. — (Geographical papers ; no.35 ISSN 0305-5914)
Bibl.: p.38-39.
Sd : £0.50
(B77-02995)

551.6'9'4 — Europe. Weather. *For tourists. Statistics*
Meteorological Office. Your holiday weather / [United Kingdom Meteorological Office]. — Bracknell (London Rd, Bracknell, Berks. RG12 2SZ) : The Office, 1977. — [2],18p : col charts ; 30cm. — (London Weather Centre. Memoranda ; no.27)
Sd : £0.90
(B77-18754)

551.6'9'41 — Great Britain. Climate
The **climate** of the British Isles / edited by T.J. Chandler and S. Gregory. — London [etc.] : Longman, 1976. — xvii,390p : ill, maps ; 25cm.
Bibl.: p.343-369. — Index.
ISBN 0-582-48558-4 : £7.95
(B77-04803)

551.6'9'41 — Great Britain. Climate. *Statistics. For agriculture*
Smith, Lionel Percy. The agricultural climate of England and Wales : areal averages, 1941-70 / [by] L.P. Smith. — London : H.M.S.O., 1976. — vi,147p : maps ; 25cm. — (Great Britain. Ministry of Agriculture, Fisheries and Food. Technical bulletins ; 35)
ISBN 0-11-240896-6 Pbk : £2.40
(B77-01439)

551.6'9'42282 — Isle of Wight. Ryde. Weather, 1918-1975. *Statistics*
Hosking, Kenneth J. A lifetime of island weather : a statistical analysis prepared from the official meteorological records at Ryde, Isle of Wight, 1918 to 1975 / [by] Kenneth J. Hosking. — Newport (Upper St James St., Newport, Isle of Wight) : Isle of Wight Teachers' Centre, 1975. — [4],40p : ill, facsims ; 30cm.
ISBN 0-9504958-1-6 Sp : £1.75
(B77-03542)

551.6'9'52 — Japan. Climate
The **climate** of Japan / ed[itor] E. Fukui. — Tokyo : Kodansha ; Amsterdam ; Oxford [etc.] : Elsevier, 1977. — x,317p : ill, charts ; 25cm. — (Developments in atmospheric science ; 8)
Bibl. — Index.
ISBN 0-444-99818-7 : £25.00
(B77-18130)

551.6'9'78 — North America. Great Plains. Climate, 1800-1850. Models
Lawson, Merlin Paul. The climate of the Great American Desert : reconstruction of the climate of Western Interior United States, 1800-1850 / [by] Merlin Paul Lawson. — Landmark ed. — Lincoln [Neb.] ; London : University of Nebraska Press, 1976. — viii,135p : ill, charts, facsims, maps ; 24cm.
Originally published: Lincoln, Neb. : University of Nebraska Press, 1974. — Bibl.: p.128-134.
ISBN 0-8032-0226-1 : £8.00
(B77-07340)

551.7 — STRATIGRAPHY
551.7'1'091813 — Northern hemisphere. Pre-Cambrian strata
Salop, L J. Precambrian of the northern hemisphere : and general features of early geological evolution / by L.J. Salop ; English translation [from the Russian] edited by G.M. Young. — Amsterdam ; Oxford [etc.] : Elsevier, 1977. — ix,378p : ill, maps ; 25cm. — (Developments in palaeontology and stratigraphy ; 3)
Two fold. sheets ([3]sides) in pocket. — Translation of: 'Obshchaia stratigraficheskaia shkala dokembriia'. Leningrad : Nedra, 1973. — Bibl.: p.329-360. — Index.
ISBN 0-444-41510-6 : Unpriced
(B77-25618)

551.7'12 — Lower pre-Cambrian strata. Stratigraphy. *Conference proceedings*
College Park Colloquium on Chemical Evolution, *2nd, University of Maryland, 1975.* Chemical evolution of the early Precambrian / edited by Cyril Ponnamperuma. — New York [etc.] ; London : Academic Press, 1977. — xi,221p : ill, map ; 24cm.
'... the invited papers (edited and updated) presented at the Second College Park Colloquium on Chemical Evolution held at the University of Maryland from October 19 to November 1, 1975. These meetings have been organized by the Laboratory of Chemical Evolution ...' - Preface. — Bibl. — Index.
ISBN 0-12-561360-1 : £9.60
Also classified at 560'.171
(B77-29417)

551.7'8'05 — Cainozoic era. *Periodicals*
Tertiary research. — West Wickham (c/o The editor, 121 Hayes Chase, West Wickham, Kent BR4 0HY) : Tertiary Research Group.
Vol.1, no.1- ; Sept. 1976-. — 1976-. — ill ; 30cm.
Two issues a year. — Cover title. — 30p. in 1st issue. — Bibl.
Pbk : £2.00
ISSN 0308-9649
(B77-02297)

551.7'9'0916337 — Irish Sea. Quaternary strata
The **quaternary** history of the Irish Sea / edited by C. Kidson and M.J. Tooley ; [for the] International Union for Quaternary Research, Commission on Shore Lines, Subcommission on Shorelines of Northwestern Europe. — Liverpool (Seel St., Liverpool L1 4AY) : Seel House Press, 1977. — [10],345p,[8]fold leaves of plates : ill(some col), maps(some col) ; 25cm. — ('Geological journal' special issues ; no.7 ISSN 0435-3951)
Bibl. — Index.
ISBN 0-902354-07-8 : £16.00
(B77-25619)

551.7'9'0941 — Great Britain. Quaternary strata. *For field studies*
International Union for Quaternary Research. *Congress, 10th, 1977.* X INQUA Congress excursion guides / [editor D.Q. Bowen]. — Norwich ([c/o] Geo Abstracts Ltd, University of East Anglia, Norwich NR4 7TJ) : [I.N.Q.U.A.].
In 16 vols.
[A1 and C1] : [East Anglia] / [excursion organiser and leader R.G. West]. — [1977]. — [1],65p : ill, maps ; 21cm.
Bibl.: p.61-64.
ISBN 0-902246-70-4 Sd : £1.25
(B77-33210)

[A2] : [The English Midlands] / [excursion organiser and leader F.W. Shotton]. — [1977]. — [1],51p : ill, maps ; 21cm.
Bibl.: p.48-50.
ISBN 0-902246-71-2 Sd : £1.25
(B77-33211)

[A4] : [The Isle of Man, Lancashire Coast and Lake District] / [excursion organiser and leader M.J. Tooley]. — [1977]. — [1],61p : ill, maps ; 21cm.
Bibl.: p.55-60.
ISBN 0-902246-72-0 Sd : £1.25
(B77-33212)

[A5] : [South East England and the Thames Valley] / [excursion organisers and leaders E.R. Shephard-Thorn and J.J. Wyner]. — [1977]. — [1],76p : ill, maps ; 21cm.
Bibl.: p.72-75.
ISBN 0-902246-73-9 Sd : £1.25
(B77-33213)

[A6 and C6] : [South West England] / [excursion organiser and leader D.N. Mottershead]. — [1977]. — [1],61p : ill, maps ; 21cm.
Bibl.: p.56-59.
ISBN 0-902246-75-5 Sd : £1.25
(B77-33214)

[A8 and C8] : [Wales and the Cheshire-Shropshire Lowland] / [excursion organiser and leader D.Q. Bowen, assisted by E.H. Brown]. — [1977]. — [1],65p : ill, maps ; 21cm.
Bibl.: p.61-64.
ISBN 0-902246-76-3 Sd : £1.25
(B77-33215)

[A10 and C10] : [The Northern Highlands of Scotland] / [excursion organiser and leader C.M. Clapperton]. — [1977]. — [1],45p : ill, maps ; 21cm.
Bibl.: p.42-43.
ISBN 0-902246-78-x Sd : £1.25
(B77-33216)

[A11 and C11] : [The Scottish Highlands] / [excursion organiser and leader J.B. Sissons]. — [1977]. — [1],51p : ill, maps ; 21cm.
Bibl.: p.47-49.
ISBN 0-902246-79-8 Sd : £1.25
(B77-33217)

[A12] : [Western Scotland, 1] / [excursion organiser and leader R.J. Price]. — [1977]. — [1],49p : ill, maps ; 21cm.
Bibl.: p.47-49.
ISBN 0-902246-80-1 Sd : £1.25
(B77-33218)

[A14] : [South East Ireland] / [excursion organiser and leader David Huddart]. — [1977] . — [1],56p : ill, maps ; 21cm.
Bibl.: p.54-55.
ISBN 0-902246-82-8 Sd : £1.25
(B77-33219)

[A15] : [South and South West Ireland] / [excursion organiser and leader C.A. Lewis]. — [1977]. — [1],53p : ill, maps ; 21cm.
Bibl.: p.51-52.
ISBN 0-902246-83-6 Sd : £1.25
(B77-33220)

[C7] : [Yorkshire and Lincolnshire] / excursion organiser and leader J.A. Catt, assisted by ... [others]. — [1977]. — [1],57p : ill, maps ; 21cm.
Bibl.: p.53-56.
ISBN 0-902246-74-7 Sd : £1.25
(B77-33221)

[C9] : [Mid and North Wales] / [excursion organisers and leaders D.F. Ball, E. Watson, assisted by Sybil Watson]. — [1977]. — [1], 49p : ill, maps ; 21cm.
Bibl.: p.46-48.
ISBN 0-902246-77-1 Sd : £1.25
(B77-33222)

[C13] : [Western Scotland, 2] / [excursion organiser and leader J.H. Dickson]. — [1977]. — [1],36p : ill, maps ; 21cm.
Bibl.: p.33-35.
ISBN 0-902246-81-x Sd : £1.25
(B77-33223)

[C16] : [Western Ireland] / [excursion organiser and leader T.F. Finch]. — [1977]. — [1],40p : ill, maps ; 21cm.
Bibl.: p.38-39.
ISBN 0-902246-84-4 Sd : £1.25
(B77-33224)

[C17] : [Southern shores of the North Sea (continental excursion)] / [excursion organiser and leader R. Paepe, assisted by W.H. Zagwijn]. — [1977]. — [1],63p : ill, maps ; 21cm.
Bibl.: p.57-59.
ISBN 0-902246-85-2 Sd : £1.25
(B77-33225)

551.7'9'0941 — Great Britain. Quaternary strata. *Reviews of research*
British Quaternary studies : recent advances / edited by F.W. Shotton. — Oxford : Clarendon Press, 1977. — xii,298p : ill, charts, maps ; 24cm.
Bibl.
ISBN 0-19-854414-6 : £10.00 : CIP rev.
(B77-16375)

551.7'92'0941 — Glacial epoch. *North-western Europe. Study regions: Great Britain*
West, Richard Gilbert. Pleistocene geology and biology : with especial reference to the British Isles / [by] R.G. West. — 2nd ed. — London [etc.] : Longman, 1977. — xi,440p,16p of plates : ill, maps ; 22cm.
Previous ed.: 1968. — Bibl. — Index.
ISBN 0-582-44620-1 Pbk : £6.95
(B77-27060)

551.7'92'09411 — Scotland. Pleistocene strata
Studies in the Scottish Lateglacial environment / edited by J.M. Gray and J.J. Lowe. — Oxford [etc.] : Pergamon, 1977. — xiii,197p : ill, maps ; 22x31cm.
Bibl.: p.183-194. — Index.
ISBN 0-08-020498-8 : £7.95
(B77-23397)

551.7'92'097 — Ice ages. *North America*
Matsch, Charles L. North America and the great Ice Age / [by] Charles L. Matsch. — New York [etc.] ; London : McGraw-Hill, 1976. — xii,131p : ill, maps, port ; 23cm. — (McGraw-Hill earth science paperback series)
Bibl.: p.124-125. — Index.
ISBN 0-07-040935-8 Pbk : £3.80
(B77-03543)

551.8 — STRUCTURAL GEOLOGY
551.8 — Geological maps. *Exercises, worked examples*
Blyth, Francis George Henry. Geological maps and their interpretation / [by] F.G.H. Blyth. — 2nd ed. (metric). — London : Edward Arnold, 1976. — 48p : ill, maps ; 22x28cm.
Previous ed.: 1965. — Index.
ISBN 0-7131-2568-3 Sd : £1.75
(B77-02298)

551.8 — Geological maps. Map reading. *Secondary school texts*
Johnson, W E. Simple geological mapwork : an introduction to problem maps without strike lines / [by] W.E. Johnson. — London : Edward Arnold, 1976. — iv,44p : ill, maps ; 25cm.
ISBN 0-7131-0023-0 Sd : £1.15
(B77-02996)

Thomas, John Albert Gay. An introduction to geological maps / [by] J.A.G. Thomas. — 2nd ed. — London : Murby : Allen and Unwin, 1977. — 67p : ill, maps ; 25cm.
Previous ed.: i.e. Metricated ed., London : Murby, 1973.
ISBN 0-04-550024-x Sd : £0.70(non-net)
(B77-09689)

551.8'7 — Strata. Folds
Johnson, Arvid M. Styles of folding : mechanics and mechanisms of folding of natural elastic materials / by Arvid M. Johnson, with shorter contributions by ... [others]. — Amsterdam ; Oxford [etc.] : Elsevier, 1977. — xx,406[i.e.404] p(2 fold) : ill, maps ; 25cm. — (Developments in geotectonics ; 11)
Bibl. — Index.
ISBN 0-444-41496-7 : £24.40
(B77-25620)

552 — PETROLOGY
552 — Rocks
Dineley, David. Rocks / [by] David Dineley. — London : Collins, 1976. — 160p,24p of plates : ill ; 22cm. — (Collins countryside series ; 6)
Bibl.: p.154. — Index.
ISBN 0-00-219354-x : £2.50
(B77-05405)

552'.03 — Crystalline rocks. Formation
The **evolution** of the crystalline rocks / edited by D.K. Bailey and R. Macdonald. — London [etc.] : Academic Press, 1976. — xi,484p : ill ; 24cm.
Bibl. — Index.
ISBN 0-12-073450-8 : £16.00
(B77-06075)

552'.4 — Laterite. *State-of-the-art reviews*
McFarlane, M J. Laterite and landscape / [by] M.J. McFarlane. — London [etc.] : Academic Press, 1976. — xiii,151p,[8]p of plates, fold leaf of plate : ill(some col), map ; 24cm.
Bibl.: p.127-140. — Index.
ISBN 0-12-484450-2 : £5.80
(B77-10363)

552'.5 — Sedimentary basins. Formation. *Conference proceedings*
Sedimentary basins of continental margins and cratons / edited by M.H.P. Bott. — Amsterdam ; Oxford [etc.] : Elsevier, 1976. — [5],314p(2 fold) : ill, maps ; 25cm. — (Inter-Union Commission on Geodynamics. Scientific reports ; no.27) (Developments in geotectonics ; 12)
'... papers presented at the Durham symposium ... held from 5th to 9th April, 1976' - p.1. — 'Reprinted from "Tectonophysics". Vol.36'. — Bibl.
ISBN 0-444-41549-1 : £21.08
(B77-16376)

552'.5 — Sedimentary rocks
Pettijohn, Francis. Sedimentary rocks / [by] F.J. Pettijohn. — 3rd ed. — New York [etc.] ; London : Harper and Row, [1976]. — xii,628p : ill, maps ; 26cm.
Published in the United States: 1975. — Previous ed.: New York : Harper, 1957. — Bibl. — Index.
ISBN 0-06-045191-2 Pbk : £7.80
(B77-04158)

552'.5 — Sedimentary rocks. Deformation
Stearns, D W. Deformation characteristics of layered sedimentary rocks important to hydrocarbon exploration / by D.W. Stearns. — [London] : [Burlington House, Piccadilly, W1V 0JU] : [Geological Society], 1977. — [1],45p : ill ; 30cm. — (Geological Society of London. Miscellaneous papers ; no.6 ISSN 0305-0394)
'A[merican] A[ssociation of] P[etroleum] G[eologists] Lecture Series ... sponsored by Geological Society of London, Petroleum Exploration Society of Great Britain'. — Bibl.
Sd : £1.00
(B77-30247)

552'.5 — Stromatolites
Stromatolites / edited by M.R. Walter. — Amsterdam ; Oxford [etc.] : Elsevier, 1976. — xi,790p : ill, maps ; 25cm. — (Developments in sedimentology ; 20)
Bibl.: p.705-771. — Index.
ISBN 0-444-41376-6 : £60.33
(B77-03544)

553 — ECONOMIC GEOLOGY
553 — Minerals
Almond, D C. Rocks, minerals and crystals / [by] D.C. Almond, D.G.A. Whitten ; illustrated by Max Ansell and John Smith. — London [etc.] : Hamlyn, 1976. — 128p : col ill, col maps ; 18cm. — (Hamlyn all-colour paperbacks)
Bibl.: p.124-125. — Index.
ISBN 0-600-31873-7 Pbk : £0.75
(B77-00759)

The **encyclopedia** of minerals and gemstones / edited by Michael O'Donoghue. — London : Orbis Books, 1976. — 304p : ill(chiefly col), facsim, port ; 30cm.
Ill. on lining papers. — Bibl.: p.296-297. — Index.
ISBN 0-85613-209-8 : £7.95
(B77-07902)

553 — Minerals. *Conference proceedings*
'Industrial minerals' International Congress, *2nd, Munich, 1976.* Industrial minerals : proceedings of the 2nd 'Industrial minerals' International Congress, held at the Sheraton Hotel, Munich, on 17-19 May 1976 / edited by R.F.S. Fleming. — London : Metal Bulletin, 1977. — [3],viii, 252p : ill, maps ; 30cm.
Includes a contribution in German, with English translation. — Bibl.
Pbk : £25.00
(B77-30248)

553 — Minerals. Use by prehistoric man
Shackley, Myra. Rocks and man / [by] Myra Shackley. — London [etc.] : Allen and Unwin, 1977. — 3-159p : ill, maps ; 23cm.
Bibl.: p.149-152. — Index.
ISBN 0-04-913018-8 : £4.95
(B77-29418)

553 — Ore deposits. Formation. Role of volcanicity. *Conference proceedings*
Volcanic processes in ore genesis : proceedings of a joint meeting of the Volcanic Studies Group of the Geological Society of London and the Institution of Mining and Metallurgy, held in London on 21 and 22 January, 1976. — [London] ([44 Portland Place, W1N 8BR]) : The Institution ; [London] : The Geological Society, 1977. — vi,188p : ill, maps ; 30cm.
Bibl. — Index.
ISBN 0-900488-33-6 Pbk : £11.00(£8.50 to members of the Institution of Mining and Metallurgy and the Geological Society of London)
(B77-31184)

553 — Stratabound ore deposits & stratiform ore deposits
Handbook of strata-bound and stratiform ore deposits / edited by K.H. Wolf. — Amsterdam ; Oxford [etc.] : Elsevier.
In 7 vols.
1 : Principles and general studies. Vol.1 : Classifications and historical studies. — 1976. — x,338p(12 fold) : ill, maps ; 25cm.
Bibl.
ISBN 0-444-41401-0 : £29.04
(B77-14717)

1 : Principles and general studies. Vol.2 : Geochemical studies. — 1976. — xi,363p : ill, maps ; 25cm.
Bibl.
ISBN 0-444-41402-9 : £29.04
(B77-14718)

1 : Principles and general studies. Vol.3 : Supergene and surficial ore deposits : textures and fabrics. — 1976. — xi,353p : ill, maps ; 25cm.
Bibl.
ISBN 0-444-41403-7 : £29.04
(B77-14719)

1 : Principles and general studies. Vol.4 : Tectonics and metamorphism. — 1976. — x, 429p(4 fold) : ill, maps ; 25cm.
Bibl. — Indexes vols 1-4.
ISBN 0-444-41404-5 : £29.04
(B77-14720)

2 : Regional studies and specific deposits. Vol.5 : Regional studies. — 1976. — xi,319p : ill, maps ; 25cm.
Bibl.
ISBN 0-444-41405-3 : £29.04
(B77-14721)

2 : Regional studies and specific deposits. Vol.6 : Cu, Zn, Pb and Ag deposits. — 1976. — xvi,585p(12 fold) : ill, maps ; 25cm.
Bibl.
ISBN 0-444-41406-1 : £50.36
(B77-14722)

2 : Regional studies and specific deposits. Vol.7 : Au, U, Fe, Mn, Hg, Sb, W and P deposits. — 1976. — xii,656p(2 fold) : ill, maps ; 25cm.
Bibl. — Indexes vols 5-7.
ISBN 0-444-41407-x : £50.36
(B77-14723)

553'.03 — Minerals. *Encyclopaedias*
Sorrell, Charles A. The rocks and minerals of the world / [by] Charles A. Sorrel[l], George F. Sandstrom ; original project editor Herbert S. Zimm [i.e. Zim]. — London : Collins, 1977. — 288p : ill(chiefly col), 2 maps(1 col) ; 20cm.
Originally published: as 'Minerals of the world'. New York : Golden Press, 1973. — Bibl.: p.270-278. — Index.
ISBN 0-00-219694-8 : £3.95
ISBN 0-00-219682-4 Pbk : £2.50
(B77-23398)

553'.09425'1 — Derbyshire. Minerals
Grayson, Peter James. Derbyshire minerals & rocks (with especial reference to the Peak District) / [by] Peter J. Grayson. — 2nd ed. — Chesterfield (34 Glenthorne Close, Brampton, Chesterfield, S40 3AR) : Grayson Publications, [1976]. — [3],34p : ill, form, map ; 16cm.
Previous ed.: Bakewell : M.N. and P.J. Grayson, 1971. — Bibl.: p.31. — Index.
ISBN 0-900709-05-7 Sd : £0.30
(B77-00217)

553'.0947 — Soviet Union. Ore deposits
Ore deposits of the USSR / edited by V.I. Smirnov ; [translated from the Russian by D.A. Brown]. — London [etc.] : Pitman.
In 3 vols. — Translation of: 'Rudnye mestorozhdeniia SSSR'. Moscow : Nebra, 1974.

Vol.1. — 1977. — [8],352p : ill, maps ; 26cm.
Bibl.
ISBN 0-273-01034-4 : £12.00 : CIP rev.
ISBN 0-273-01073-5 Set of 3 vols : £38.00
(B77-07903)

Vol.2. — 1977. — [10],3-424p : ill, maps ; 26cm.
Bibl.
ISBN 0-273-01037-9 : £14.00 : CIP rev.
ISBN 0-273-01073-5 Set of 3 vols : £38.00
(B77-07904)

Vol.3. — 1977. — [11],3-492p : ill, maps ; 26cm.
Bibl.
ISBN 0-273-01039-5 : £16.50 : CIP rev.
ISBN 0-273-01073-5 Set of 3 vols : £38.00
(B77-07905)

553'.43 — Copper deposits
Bowen, Robert. Copper : its geology and economics / [by] Robert Bowen and Ananda Gunatilaka. — London : Applied Science Publishers, 1977. — xi,366p : ill(some col), maps ; 23cm.
Index.
ISBN 0-85334-726-3 : £25.00
(B77-24930)

553'.493 — Uranium deposits. *Conference proceedings*
Geology, mining and extractive processing of uranium : an international symposium, co-sponsored [i.e. organised] by the Institution of Mining and Metallurgy and the Commission of the European Communities, London, 17-19 January, 1977 / edited by M.J. Jones. — [London] ([44 Portland Place, W1N 8BR]) : The Institution, [1977]. — vii,171p : ill(some col), maps(some col) ; 30cm.
Includes 2 papers in French and 1 in German. — English, French and German synopses. — 'Thanks ... to the Directorate-General for Energy, Commission of the European Communities, for organizational and financial support ...' - Foreword. — Bibl.
ISBN 0-900488-35-2 Pbk : £16.00
(B77-10364)

553'.493 — Uranium deposits. Hydrothermal properties. *Reports, surveys*
Rich, Robert A. Hydrothermal uranium deposits / [by] Robert A. Rich, Heinrich D. Holland, Ulrich Petersen. — Amsterdam ; Oxford [etc.] : Elsevier, 1977. — xx,264p : ill(incl 1 col), maps ; 25cm. — (Developments in economic geology ; 6)
Based on ERDA report GJO-1640 / by R.A. Rich and H.D. Holland, 1975. — Bibl. — Index.
ISBN 0-444-41551-3 : £20.24
(B77-23399)

553'.5 — Northern Ireland. Mineral deposits yielding aggregates. *Reports, surveys*
Cameron, Ian Burnett. Sources of aggregate in Northern Ireland / [by] I.B. Cameron. — 2nd ed. / [by] E.N. Calvert-Harrison. — London : H.M.S.O., 1977. — vi,21p : maps ; 30cm. — (Institute of Geological Sciences. Reports ; no.77-1)
Previous ed.: 1970. — Bibl.: p.21.
ISBN 0-11-881279-3 Sd : £0.70
(B77-10806)

553'.5 — Scotland. Highlands & Islands. Mineral deposits yielding aggregates. *Reports, surveys*
Chatten, J R. Evaluation of the aggregate resources of the northern and western part of the Crofter Counties of Scotland / by J.R. Chatten ; for [the] Highlands and Islands Development Board. — [London] ([7 Catherine Place, S.W.1]) : Robertson Research International Limited, 1973. — [2],33 leaves : map ; 30cm. — (Robertson Research International. Technical reports ; no.3036)
Fold. sheet(1 side) (map) in pocket.
ISBN 0-9505556-0-6 Sp : Unpriced
(B77-06076)

553'.51'0942513 — Derbyshire. Monyash region. Limestone deposits & dolomite deposits
Cox, F C. The limestone and dolomite resources of the country around Monyash, Derbyshire : description of 1: 25 000 resource sheet SK16 / [by] F.C. Cox and D.McC. Bridge ; with a contribution by J.I. Chisholm and N. Aitkenhead ; [for the] Institute of Geological Sciences, Natural Environment Research Council. — London : H.M.S.O., 1977. — vi, 137p,plate : ill, maps ; 30cm. — (Mineral assessment reports ; 26)
Cover title: Limestone resources. — Spine title: SK16 Monyash, Derbyshire. — Fold. sheet (col. ill., col. map) in pocket. — Bibl.: p.137.
ISBN 0-11-881263-7 Pbk : £7.00
(B77-21118)

553'.53 — Great Britain. Sandstone deposits
Harris, P M. Sandstone / compiled by P.M. Harris. — London : H.M.S.O., 1977. — v,37p : ill, map ; 30cm. — (Mineral dossier ; no.17)
ISBN 0-11-510841-6 Sd : £1.50
(B77-15283)

553'.62'0942534 — Lincolnshire. Lincoln region. Sand deposits & gravel deposits
Jackson, Ian, *b.1950.* The sand and gravel resources of the country west and south of Lincoln, Lincolnshire : description of 1:25000 resource sheets SK95, SK96 and SK97 / [by] I. Jackson. — London : H.M.S.O., 1977. — vi, 89p : ill, maps ; 30cm. — (Mineral assessment reports ; no.27)
Two fold. sheets (col. maps; [2]p.) in pocket. — English text, French and German summaries. — Bibl.: p.89.
ISBN 0-11-884003-7 Pbk : £6.00
(B77-17486)

553'.62'0942571 — Oxfordshire. Eynsham region. Sand deposits & gravel deposits
Harries, W J R. The sand and gravel resources of the country around Eynsham, Oxfordshire : description of 1:25000 resource sheet SP 40 and part of SP 41 / [by] W.J.R. Harries with a contribution by M. Vincent. — London : H.M.S.O., 1977. — vi,88p : ill, maps ; 30cm. — (Mineral assessment reports ; no.28)
Col. map (fold. sheet ; 1 side) in pocket. — Bibl.: p.88.
ISBN 0-11-884012-6 Pbk : £3.00
(B77-20254)

553'.62'0942831 — Humberside. Scunthorpe region. Sand deposits & gravel deposits
Lovell, J H. The sand and gravel resources of the country south-west of Scunthorpe, Humberside : description of 1 : 25000 resource sheet SE80 / [by] J.H. Lovell. — London : H.M.S.O., 1977. — vi,101p : ill, map ; 30cm. — (Mineral assessment report ; 29)
Fold. sheet (col. map) in pocket. — Bibl.: p.101.
ISBN 0-11-884013-4 Pbk : £3.50
(B77-30249)

553'.7 — Water. *Juvenile literature*
Hunt, Patricia Joan. Water / by P.J. Hunt ; illustrated by Kenneth Ody. — London [etc.] : F. Watts, 1977. — 48p : ill(chiefly col) ; 22cm. — (A first look book)
Index.
ISBN 0-85166-623-x : £1.75
(B77-09691)

553'.7 — Water. *Secondary school texts*
Sanderson, Mike. Why we need water / [by] Mike Sanderson. — London : Macdonald Educational, 1977. — [1],24,[1]p : ill(chiefly col), col map, ports ; 27cm. — (Biology colour units)
ISBN 0-356-05526-4 Sd : £0.85
(B77-16377)

553'.8 — Gemstones
Frank, Joan. All gemstones are precious : an introduction to the world of jewels / by Joan Frank. — Kings Langley : Model and Allied Publications, 1976. — 48p,[4]p of plates : ill(some col) ; 20cm.
Text on lining paper.
ISBN 0-85242-477-9 : £1.95
(B77-04159)

553'.8'0941 — Gemstones. *Great Britain*
Weller, Sam. Let's collect British gemstones / with text by Sam Weller. — Norwich : Jarrold and Sons, 1976. — [34]p : ill(chiefly col), map, port ; 19cm. — (Jarrold collectors series)
ISBN 0-85306-663-9 Sd : £0.40
(B77-04160)

553'.8'097 — Gemstones. *North America*
Sinkankas, John. Gemstones of North America / [by] John Sinkankas. — New York ; London [etc.] : Van Nostrand Reinhold.
In 2 vols.
Vol.2. — 1976. — xvi,494p,[8]p of plates : ill(some col), maps, ports ; 24cm.
Bibl.: p.374-462. — Index.
ISBN 0-442-27627-3 : £12.65
(B77-01440)

554/559 — GEOLOGY OF SPECIAL LOCALITIES

554 — Europe. Geological features. *Conference proceedings*
Meeting of European Geological Societies, *1st, Reading, 1975.* Europe from crust to core : keynote addresses from the First Meeting of European Geological Societies, Reading (UK), September 1975 / edited by D.V. Ager and M. Brooks. — London [etc.] : Wiley, 1977. — viii, 202p : ill, maps ; 24cm.
'A Wiley-Interscience publication'. — Bibl. — Index.
ISBN 0-471-99420-0 : £9.75
(B77-14724)

554.118'5 — Scotland. Highland Region. Ardnamurchan peninsula. Geological features. *For field studies*
Gribble, C D. Ardnamurchan : a guide to geological excursions / [by] C.D. Gribble, E.M. Durrance and J.N. Walsh. — Edinburgh (c/o Grant Institute of Geology, West Mains Rd, Edinburgh EH9 3JW) : Edinburgh Geological Society, 1976. — ix,122p : 2 ill, maps(1 col) ; 18cm.
Map on fold. leaf in pocket. — Bibl.: p.68-71.
ISBN 0-904440-02-8 Pbk : £2.00
(B77-06077)

554.12'92 — Scotland. Fife Region. Eastern North East Fife (District). Geological features
Forsyth, Ian Hunter. The geology of East Fife : (explanation of the Fife portion of One-inch Geological Sheet 41 and part of Sheet 49) / by I.H. Forsyth and J.I. Chisholm ; with contributions by ... [others]. — Edinburgh : H.M.S.O., 1977. — ix,284p,[4]p of plates,[5]leaves of plates : ill, maps ; 25cm. — (Memoirs of the geological survey of Great Britain, Scotland)
Spine title: East Fife. — Bibl. — Index.
ISBN 0-11-880164-3 : £10.00
(B77-11211)

554.19'6 — Kerry (County). Dingle Peninsula. Geological features. *For field studies*
Horne, Ralph R. Geological guide to the Dingle Peninsula / [by] Ralph R. Horne. — [Dublin] ([14 Hume St., Dublin 2]) : [Department of Industry and Commerce], 1976. — [3],53p,[2] fold leaves of plates : ill, maps ; 25cm. — (Geological Survey of Ireland. Guide series ; no.1)
Bibl.: p.52.
ISBN 0-905910-00-1 Pbk : Unpriced
(B77-06675)

554.22'5 — England. Weald. Geological features. *For field studies*
Kirkaldy, John Francis. The Weald / by J.F. Kirkaldy. — 3rd ed., revised / revised by F.A. Middlemiss, L.J. Allchin and H.G. Owen. — London : Geologists' Association ; Norwich (30 St Benedict's St., Norwich NOR 24J) : [Distributed by] 'The Scientific Anglian', 1976. — [1],27,[1]p : map ; 22cm. — (Geologists' Association. Guides ; no.29)
Previous ed.: i.e. Revised ed. Published as 'Geology of the Weald' / edited by S.W. Hester. Colchester : Benham, 1967. — Bibl.
ISBN 0-900717-13-0 Sd : £0.50
(B77-06676)

554.23 — South-west England. Geological features. *For field studies*
Geological excursions in the Bristol district / edited by R.J.G. Savage. — Bristol (c/o Department of Geology, University of Bristol, Queen's Building, Bristol BS8 1TR) : University of Bristol, 1977. — iii-xv,196p : ill, maps ; 22cm.
Bibl.: p.187-196.
ISBN 0-901239-22-4 Pbk : Unpriced
(B77-31891)

554.23'3 — Dorset. Geological features
Perkins, John William. Geology explained in Dorset / by John W. Perkins ; illustrations by the author. — Newton Abbot [etc.] : David and Charles, 1977. — 224p : ill, maps ; 23cm.
Bibl.: p.207-211. — Index.
ISBN 0-7153-7319-6 : £3.95
(B77-14725)

554.24'63 — Staffordshire. Stoke-on-Trent region. Geological features. *For field studies*
Cope, Fred Wolverson. The area around Stoke-on-Trent / by F. Wolverson Cope. — London : Geologists' Association ; Norwich (30 St Benedict's St., Norwich NOR 24J) : [Distributed by] 'The Scientific Anglian', 1976. — [1],26p : 1 ill, maps ; 22cm. — (Geologists' Association. Guides ; no.8)
Previous ed.: Colchester : Benham, 1960. — Bibl.
ISBN 0-900717-14-9 Sd : £0.50
(B77-06677)

554.25'1 — Derbyshire. Geological features
Rodgers, Peter Rowland. Derbyshire geology / by Peter R. Rodgers. — Clapham, N. Yorkshire : Dalesman, 1977. — 128p : ill, maps ; 21cm.
Bibl.: p.125. — Index.
ISBN 0-85206-377-6 Pbk : £1.50
(B77-15284)

554.25'3 — Lincolnshire. Geological features
Swinnerton, Henry Hurd. The geology of Lincolnshire : from the Humber to the Wash / by H.H. Swinnerton and P.E. Kent. — 2nd ed. / with revisions and additions by Sir Peter Kent. — Lincoln ([Headquarters, City and County Museum, Lincoln]) : Lincolnshire Naturalists' Union, 1976. — xiv,130p,[8]p of plates : ill, maps ; 22cm. — (Lincolnshire natural history brochure ; no.7)
Bibl.: p.120-128. — Index.
ISBN 0-9500353-5-1 Pbk : £3.45
(B77-09009)

554.27'8 — Cumbria. Lake District. Geological features
Prosser, Robert. Geology explained in the Lake District / [by] Robert Prosser ; illustrated by the author. — Newton Abbot [etc.] : David and Charles, 1977. — 189p : ill, maps ; 23cm.
Bibl.: p.179-183. — Index.
ISBN 0-7153-7397-8 : £4.95
(B77-27852)

554.28'61 — Durham (County). Middle Teesdale. Geological features
Mills, D A C. Geology of the country around Barnard Castle : explanation of One-inch Geological Sheet 32, (New Series) / by D.A.C. Mills and J.H. Hull with contributions by ... [others]. — London : H.M.S.O., 1976. — xii, 385p,[16]leaves of plates(10 fold),[8]p of plates : ill(incl 3 col), maps(incl 2 col) ; 25cm. — (Memoirs of the geological survey of Great Britain, England and Wales ; [32])
Spine title: Barnard Castle. — Bibl. — Index.
ISBN 0-11-880742-0 : £18.00
(B77-11212)

554.29'62 — National parks. *Dyfed. Preseli (District) & South Pembrokeshire (District). Pembrokeshire Coast National Park. Geological features*
Ellis-Gruffydd, Dyfed. Rocks and landforms of the Pembrokeshire Coast National Park / [by] Dyfed Ellis-Gruffydd. — Newport, Dyfed (Brian S. John, Trefelin, [Cilgwyn], Newport, Dyfed) : Greencroft Books for the Pembrokeshire Coast National Park Committee, 1977. — [1],36p : ill, maps ; 22cm. — (Pembrokeshire Coast National Park Committee. Information booklets ; no.1 ISSN 0140-2323)
Bibl.: p.36.
ISBN 0-905559-04-5 Sd : £0.50
(B77-26307)

554.84'5 — Norway. Okstindan region. Geological features. *Reports, surveys. Serials*
Okstindan Research Project. Preliminary report / Okstindan Research Project. — Reading (Department of Geography, University of Reading, Reading RG6 2AB) : The Project. 1974 / edited by Robert B. Parry and Peter Worsley. — 1976. — x,81p,plate : ill, maps ; 30cm.
Bibl.
ISBN 0-7049-0343-1 Sd : £1.00
(B77-31892)

555.91 — Burma. Neyaungga region & Ye-ngan region. Geological features
Garson, Magnus Sinclair. The geology of the area around Neyaungga and Ye-ngan, Southern Shan States, Burma / [by] M.S. Garson, B.J. Amos, A.H.G. Mitchell. — London : H.M.S.O., 1976. — 2-70p : ill, maps(1 col) ; 29cm. — (Institute of Geological Sciences. Overseas memoirs ; 2 ISSN 0308-5325)
Fold. sheet ([1]side) (col. map) in pocket. — Bibl.: p.66-67. — Index.
ISBN 0-11-880715-3 : £8.00
(B77-09692)

556.76'27 — Kenya. Turkana region. Geological features. *Conference proceedings*
Stratigraphy, Paleoecology and Evolution in the Lake Rudolf Basin *(Conference), National Museum, Nairobi, 1973.* Earliest man and environments in the Lake Rudolf Basin : stratigraphy, paleoecology and evolution / edited by Yves Coppens ... [et al.]. — Chicago ; London : University of Chicago Press, 1976. — xxii,615p,[20]p of plates : ill, maps ; 25cm. — (Prehistoric archeology and ecology)
'... proceedings of a workshop-symposium ... held in East Africa from 9 to 19 September 1973 ... entitled "Stratigraphy, Paleoecology and Evolution in the Lake Rudolf Basin"' - Preface. — Bibl.
ISBN 0-226-11577-1 : £13.10
Primary classification 560'.9676'27
(B77-27062)

557.282 — Belize. Maya Mountains. Geological features
Bateson, J H. The geology of the Maya Mountains, Belize / [by] J.H. Bateson and I.H.S. Hall. — London : H.M.S.O., 1977. — iv, 43p : ill, maps ; 29cm. — (Institute of Geological Sciences. Overseas memoirs ; 3 ISSN 0308-5325)
Col. map(fold. sheet) in pocket. — Bibl. — Index.
ISBN 0-11-880765-x : Unpriced
(B77-31893)

557.94 — California. Geological features
Norris, Robert M. Geology of California / [by] Robert M. Norris, Robert W. Webb. — New York ; London [etc.] : Wiley, [1977]. — xi,365, 13p : ill, maps ; 26cm.
Text on lining paper. — Published in the United States: 1976. — Bibl. — Index.
ISBN 0-471-61566-8 : £9.35
(B77-13036)

557.94'4 — California. Sierra Nevada. Geological features
Hill, Mary. Geology of the Sierra Nevada / by Mary Hill ; maps by Adrienne E. Morgan ; drawings by Alex Eng and others. — Berkeley [etc.] ; London : University of California Press, 1975. — [5],232p,[8]p of plates : ill(some col), facsims, maps ; 21cm. — (California natural history guides)
Bibl.: p.192-193. — Index.
ISBN 0-520-02801-5 : £6.70
ISBN 0-520-02698-5 Pbk : £3.15
(B77-25621)

557.97'98 — National parks. *Washington (State). Olympic National Park. Geological features. Guidebooks*
Tabor, Rowland W. Guide to the geology of Olympic National Park / [by] Rowland W. Tabor. — Seattle ; London : University of Washington Press, 1975. — xv,144p : ill, maps, 2 ports ; 23cm.
Two maps on fold. leaves in pocket. — Bibl.: p.133-136. — Index.
ISBN 0-295-95395-0 Pbk : £4.50
(B77-21119)

559.9'1 — Moon. Geological features
French, Bevan Meredith. The Moon book / [by] Bevan M. French. — Harmondsworth [etc.] : Penguin, 1977. — 287p,[32]p of plates : ill, maps ; 20cm.
Bibl.: p.275-276. — Index.
ISBN 0-14-004340-3 Pbk : £1.95
(B77-33226)

Geological Museum. Moon, Mars and meteorites / Geological Museum ; [text by Peter Adams]. — [London] : H.M.S.O. for the Institute of Geological Sciences, 1977. — [2], 38p : ill(chiefly col), col maps ; 20x22cm.
Bibl.: p.36.
ISBN 0-11-880672-6 Sd : £0.70
(B77-30250)

Guest, John Edward. Geology on the moon / [by] J.E. Guest, R. Greeley. — London [etc.] : Wykeham Publications, 1977. — x,235p : ill, maps ; 23cm. — (The Wykeham science series)
Bibl.: p.222-227. — Index.
ISBN 0-85109-580-1 : Unpriced
ISBN 0-85109-540-2 Pbk : £4.00
(B77-22577)

Leonardi, Piero. Volcanoes and impact craters on the moon and Mars / [by] Piero Leonardi ; with the collaboration of Alfred Rittmann and Elio Sommavilla ; [translated from the Italian]. — Amsterdam ; Oxford [etc.] : Elsevier, 1976. — 3-463p : ill(some col), charts, maps(some col) ; 31cm.
Col. ill. on lining papers. — Fold. sheet (1 side : col. map) as insert. — Translation of: 'Vulcani e bolidi sulla luna e su marte'. Calliano : Vallagarina, 1971. — Bibl.: p.419-463.
ISBN 0-444-99821-7 : £46.84
(B77-14726)

559.9'1 — Moon. Geological features. *Conference proceedings*
Lunar Science Conference, *6th, Houston, 1975.* Proceedings of the Sixth Lunar Science Conference, Houston, Texas, March 17-21, 1975 / compiled by the Lunar Science Institute. — New York ; Oxford [etc.] : Pergamon, 1975. — 3v.([41],3637,[94]p,[10]p of plates) : ill(some col), maps ; 25cm. — ('Geochimica et cosmochimica acta' supplement ; 6)
Bibl. — Index.
ISBN 0-08-020566-6 : £65.00
(B77-07341)

The **moon** : a new appraisal from space missions and laboratory analyses : a Royal Society discussion held 9-12 June 1975, and arranged by the British National Committee on Space Research under the leadership of Sir Harrie Massey ... [et al.]. — London : Royal Society, 1977. — vi,606p,[13] leaves of plates,[2]p of plates : ill, maps(some col) ; 31cm.
Also published: in 'Philosophical Transactions of the Royal Society', Series A. vol.285. 1977. — Bibl. — Index.
ISBN 0-85403-085-9 : £38.00
(B77-18131)

559.9'23 — Mars. Geological features
The **geology** of Mars / [by] Thomas A. Mutch ... [et al.]. — Princeton ; Guildford : Princeton University Press, [1977]. — ix,400p,[2]p of plates : ill(some col), maps ; 29cm.
Published in the United States: 1976. — Bibl.: p.366-381. — Index.
ISBN 0-691-08173-5 : £24.80
(B77-09010)

560 — PALAEONTOLOGY

560 — Evolution. *Sources of data: Fossils*
Cowen, Richard, *b.1940.* History of life / [by] Richard Cowen. — New York ; London [etc.] : McGraw-Hill, 1976. — xi,145p : ill, maps ; 23cm. — (McGraw-Hill earth science paperback series)
Bibl.: p.135. — Index.
ISBN 0-07-013260-7 Pbk : £3.30
(B77-05406)

Patterns of evolution : as illustrated by the fossil record / edited by A. Hallam. — Amsterdam ; Oxford [etc.] : Elsevier, 1977. — xiii,591p : ill ; 25cm. — (Developments in palaeontology and stratigraphy ; 5)
Bibl. — Index.
ISBN 0-444-41495-9 : Unpriced
(B77-27061)

560 — Fossils
Moody, Richard Thomas Jones. The fossil world / [by] Richard Moody. — London [etc.] : Hamlyn, 1977. — 5-124p : ill(chiefly col) ; 31cm.
Col. ill. on lining papers. — Bibl.: p.121. — Index.
ISBN 0-600-33609-3 : £2.95
(B77-33793)

560 — Fossils. *Juvenile literature*
Cartner, William Carruthers. Fun with fossils / [by] William C. Cartner. — London : Kaye and Ward [etc.], 1977. — 64p : ill, 2 maps ; 26cm. — ([Learning with fun])
Originally published: as 'Fun with palaeontology'. 1970.
ISBN 0-7182-1312-2 : £2.25
(B77-29419)

Halstead, Lambert Beverly. Fossil hunting / [by] Beverly Halstead ; illustrated by Peter North, Richard Orr and Gwen Simpson. — London (90 Great Russell St., WC1B 3PT) : Scimitar, 1977. — [1],32p : ill(chiefly col) ; 14cm. — (Scatterbox)
ISBN 0-241-89713-0 Pbk : £0.40
(B77-30251)

560 — Prehistoric animals. *Juvenile literature*
Cox, Barry, *b.1931.* Prehistoric animals / by Barry Cox and Maurice Wilson ; in association with Thames Television. — Guildford [etc.] : Lutterworth Press, 1976. — [46]p : ill(chiefly col), col maps ; 11x14cm. — ('Magpie' pocket books)
ISBN 0-7188-2275-7 Pbk : £0.35
(B77-02997)

560'.171 — Organisms. Evolution. *Lower pre-Cambrian strata. Conference proceedings*
College Park Colloquium on Chemical Evolution, *2nd, University of Maryland, 1975.* Chemical evolution of the early Precambrian / edited by Cyril Ponnamperuma. — New York [etc.] ; London : Academic Press, 1977. — xi,221p : ill, map ; 24cm.
'... the invited papers (edited and updated) presented at the Second College Park Colloquium on Chemical Evolution held at the University of Maryland from October 19 to November 1, 1975. These meetings have been organized by the Laboratory of Chemical Evolution ...' - Preface. — Bibl. — Index.
ISBN 0-12-561360-1 : £9.60
Primary classification 551.7'12
(B77-29417)

560'.172 — Fossil plants. *Great Britain. Carboniferous strata*
Fossil plants of the carboniferous rocks of Great Britain. — London : H.M.S.O.
2nd section, pt 7 : [Unrelated forms and gymnospermous fructifications] / by Robert Crookall. — 1976. — p xxxv-xli,841-1004,leaves of plates clx-clxxiii,[12]p : ill ; 31cm. — (Memoirs of the geological survey of Great Britain, palaeontology ; vol.4, part 7)
Leaves printed on both sides. — Bibl.: p.957-978. — Index.
ISBN 0-11-880735-8 Pbk : £25.00
(B77-08373)

560'.28 — Fossil animals. Preparation & conservation. *Manuals*
Rixon, A E. Fossil animal remains : their preparation and conservation / by A.E. Rixon. — London : Athlone Press, 1976. — viii,304p : ill, form ; 22cm.
Bibl. — Index.
ISBN 0-485-12028-3 Pbk : £5.25
(B77-05407)

560'.75 — Fossils. Collecting. *England*
Hamilton, William Roger. Finding fossils / [by] Roger Hamilton and Allan N. Insole. — Harmondsworth [etc.] : Penguin, 1977. — 160p : ill, maps ; 20cm. — (Peacock books)
Bibl.: p.157-158. — Index.
ISBN 0-14-047091-3 Pbk : £0.75
(B77-21856)

Hamilton, William Roger. Finding fossils / [by] Roger Hamilton and Allan N. Insole. — Harmondsworth : Kestrel Books, 1977. — 160p : ill, maps ; 21cm.
Bibl.: p.157-158. — Index.
ISBN 0-7226-5287-9 : £2.75
(B77-21857)

560'.75 — Fossils. Collecting. *United States. Manuals*
MacFall, Russell P. Fossils for amateurs : a guide to collecting and preparing invertebrate fossils / [by] Russell P. MacFall & Jay Wollin. — New York ; London [etc.] : Van Nostrand Reinhold, [1976]. — ix,341p : ill, maps, ports ; 23cm.
Originally published: 1972. — Bibl.: p.324-331. — Index.
ISBN 0-442-25061-4 Pbk : £4.25
(B77-05408)

560'.909'1821 — Fossil microorganisms. *Atlantic region. Conference proceedings*
Stratigraphic micropaleontology of Atlantic basin and borderlands / edited by F.M. Swain. — Amsterdam ; Oxford [etc.] : Elsevier, 1977. — vii,603p : ill, maps ; 25cm. — (Developments in palaeontology and stratigraphy ; 6)
'[Proceedings of] a symposium on the stratigraphic micropaleontology of the Atlantic basin and margins ... convened at the University of Delaware, June 14-16, 1976' - Preface. — Bibl. — Index.
ISBN 0-444-41554-8 : £27.38
(B77-28601)

560'.941 — Fossils. *Great Britain*
Mathieson, Andrew. Let's collect fossils / text by Andrew Mathieson and photographs by Heather Angel. — Norwich : Jarrold and Son, 1977. — [34]p : ill(chiefly col), port ; 20cm. — (Jarrold collectors series)
ISBN 0-85306-712-0 Sd : £0.40
(B77-31894)

560'.941 — Palaeo-ecology. Archaeological sources. *Great Britain*
Dimbleby, Geoffrey William. Ecology and archaeology / [by] Geoffrey W. Dimbleby. — London : Edward Arnold, 1977. — iv,55p : ill ; 23cm. — (Institute of Biology. Studies in biology ; no.77)
Bibl.: p.55.
ISBN 0-7131-2631-0 : £3.00
ISBN 0-7131-2632-9 Pbk : £1.50
(B77-24216)

560'.9411 — Fossils. *Scotland. Queenslie Marine Band. Reports, surveys*
Brand, P J. The fauna and distribution of the Queenslie Marine Band (Westphalian) in Scotland / [by] P.J. Brand. — London : H.M.S.O., 1977. — iv,9p : ill, 3 maps ; 30cm. — (Institute of Geological Sciences. Reports ; no.77-18)
English text, French and German summaries. — Bibl.: p.7-8.
ISBN 0-11-884011-8 Sd : £0.60
(B77-24931)

560'.9676'27 — Prehistoric animals. *Kenya. Lake Turkana region. Conference proceedings*
Stratigraphy, Paleoecology and Evolution in the Lake Rudolf Basin *(Conference), National Museum, Nairobi, 1973.* Earliest man and environments in the Lake Rudolf Basin : stratigraphy, paleoecology and evolution / edited by Yves Coppens ... [et al.]. — Chicago ; London : University of Chicago Press, 1976. — xxii,615p,[20]p of plates : ill, maps ; 25cm. — (Prehistoric archeology and ecology)
'... proceedings of a workshop-symposium ... held in East Africa from 9 to 19 September 1973 ... entitled "Stratigraphy, Paleoecology and Evolution in the Lake Rudolf Basin"' - Preface. — Bibl.
ISBN 0-226-11577-1 : £13.10
Also classified at 556.76'27
(B77-27062)

560'.973 — Palaeontology. *United States, to 1970*
Howard, Robert West. The dawnseekers : the first history of American paleontology / [by] Robert West Howard ; foreword by Gilbert F. Stucker. — New York ; London : Harcourt Brace Jovanovich, 1975. — xv,314p,[16]p of plates : ill, map, ports ; 22cm.
Bibl.: p.295-299. — Index.
ISBN 0-15-123973-8 : £3.95
(B77-21120)

561 — FOSSIL PLANTS
561'.93 — Fossil calcareous algae
Wray, John Lee. Calcareous algae / [by] John L. Wray. — Amsterdam ; Oxford [etc.] : Elsevier, 1977. — xiv,185p : ill ; 25cm. — (Developments in palaeontology and stratigraphy ; 4)
Bibl.: p.169-180. — Index.
ISBN 0-444-41536-x : £16.39
(B77-16378)

562 — FOSSIL INVERTEBRATES
563'.71 — Graptoloidea. Rhabdosomes
Kirk, Nancy Hartshorne. More thoughts on the construction and functioning of the rhabdosome in the Graptoloidea in the light of their ultrastructure / [by] Nancy Hartshorne Kirk. — Aberystwyth (Aberystwyth, [Dyfed]) : University College of Wales, Department of Geology, 1975. — [2],24 leaves,[5] leaves of plates : col ill ; 32cm. — (University College of Wales. Department of Geology. Publications ; no.7 ISSN 0305-7038)
Bibl.: leaves 22-24.
ISBN 0-903812-06-1 Sd : £0.70
(B77-00218)

564 — Fossil shells
Wright, Anthony David, *b.1934.* Rotten shells / [by] A.D. Wright. — [Belfast] : Queen's University of Belfast, 1976. — 26p : ill, map ; 21cm. — (Queen's University of Belfast. New lecture series ; no.88)
'An Inaugural Lecture delivered before The Queen's University of Belfast on 19 February, 1975'.
ISBN 0-85389-096-x Sd : £0.40
(B77-09693)

564'.53 — Ammonites
Kennedy, William James. Aspects of ammonite biology, biogeography and biostratigraphy / by W.J. Kennedy and W.A. Cobban. — London : Palaeontological Association ; Oxford (Broad St., Oxford OX1 3BQ) : [Distributed by] B.H. Blackwell, 1976. — [5],94p : ill, maps ; 25cm. — (Special papers in palaeontology ; no.17)
Bibl.: p.82-94.
Pbk : £6.00
(B77-17487)

564'.53'07402134 — Museums. *London. Kensington & Chelsea (London Borough). British Museum (Natural History). Exhibits: Mesozoic ammonites. Type-specimens & figured-specimens. Catalogues*
British Museum (Natural History). Catalogue of the type and figured specimens of mesozoic Ammonoidea in the British Museum (Natural History) / by D. Phillips. — [London] : The Museum, 1977. — iii,220p ; 30cm.
Bibl.: p.190-208. — Index.
ISBN 0-565-00790-4 Pbk : £8.00
(B77-27063)

564'.53'095491 — Ammonites. *Northern Pakistan. Neocomian strata. Illustrations*
Fatmi, Ali Nasir. Neocomian ammonites from northern areas of Pakistan / by Ali Nasir Fatmi. — London : British Museum (Natural History), 1977. — p255-296,[1]p,[22]p of plates,leaf of plate : ill, map ; 25cm. — (British Museum (Natural History). Bulletins of the British Museum (Natural History) : geology ; vol.28, no.4 ISSN 0007-1471)
Bibl.: p.292-293. — Index.
Pbk : £6.25
(B77-18132)

564'.8'0941643 — Fossil Brachiopoda. *Tyrone (County). Pomeroy. Ordovician strata*
Mitchell, W I. The Ordovician brachiopoda from Pomeroy, Co. Tyrone / [by] W.I. Mitchell. — London ([c/o Institute of Geological Sciences, Exhibition Rd, SW7 2DE]) : Palaeontographical Society, 1977. — [2],140p,[55]p of plates : ill, maps ; 28cm. — (Palaeontographical Society. Monographs)
Bibl.: p.127-131. — Index.
ISBN 0-902682-08-3 Pbk : £15.00
(B77-13647)

565'.33 — Fossil Ostracoda. Shells. *Stereographs*
A **stereo-atlas** of ostracod shells / edited by R.H. Bate ... [et al.]. — Welwyn Garden City (Welwyn Garden City, Herts.) : Broadwater Press Ltd.
Vol.3, part 2. — 1976. — [38]leaves : ill ; 31cm.
Leaves [37]-[38] printed on both sides.
Sp : £12.00
(B77-08374)

A **stereo-atlas** of ostracod shells / edited by R.H. Bate ... [et al.]. — Llandudno ('Ty'n-Y-Coed', Llanrhos, Llandudno, Gwynedd, North Wales LL30 1SA) : Robertson Research International Ltd [for] the British Micropalaeontological Society.
Vol.4, part 1. — 1977. — [2]p,[39] leaves : ill ; 31cm.
Sp : £15.00
(B77-21858)

566 — FOSSIL VERTEBRATES
566 — Prehistoric vertebrates. *Juvenile literature*
Hinde, Cecilia. Wonder why book of the first life on earth / [by] Cecilia Hinde ; illustrated by John Barber. — London : Transworld, 1977. — [2],32p : col ill ; 29cm.
Index. — Previous control number ISBN 0-552-57003-6.
ISBN 0-552-98037-4 : £1.35
ISBN 0-552-57003-6 Sd : £0.50
(B77-12438)

567 — Fossil fish. *State-of-the-art reviews*
Casteel, Richard W. Fish remains in archaeology and paleo-environmental studies / [by] Richard W. Casteel. — London [etc.] : Academic Press, 1976. — x,180p : ill ; 24cm. — (Studies in archaeological science)
Bibl.: p.142-165. — Index.
ISBN 0-12-163850-2 : £6.80
(B77-09011)

567'.2 — Fossil Ostracoderma. *Northwest Territories. Mackenzie Mountain region. Siluro-Devonian strata. Reports, surveys*
Dineley, David. Ostracoderm faunas of the Delorme and associated Siluro-Devonian formations, North West Territories Canada / by D.L. Dineley and E.J. Loeffler. — London : Palaeontological Association ; [Oxford] ([Broad St., Oxford OX1 3BQ]) : [Distributed by B.H. Blackwell], 1976. — v,214p : ill, map ; 25cm. — (Special papers in palaeontology ; no.18)
Bibl.: p.208-214.
Pbk : £20.00
(B77-24932)

568'.1'0941223 — Fossil reptiles. *Scotland. Grampian Region. Elgin region*
Benton, Michael. The Elgin reptiles / [by Michael Benton]. — [Elgin] ([1 High St., Elgin, Grampian]) : [Elgin Museum], 1977. — 19p : ill, map ; 22cm.
Bibl.: p.18-19.
Sd : £0.25
(B77-26308)

568'.19 — Dinosaurs
Tweedie, Michael. The world of dinosaurs / [by] Michael Tweedie. — London : Weidenfeld and Nicolson, 1977. — 143p : ill(some col), col coat of arms, map ; 31cm.
Ill. on lining papers. — Bibl.: p.139. — Index.
ISBN 0-297-77352-6 : £4.95
(B77-33227)

568'.19 — Dinosaurs. *Cut-out books*
Make and know dinosaurs. — [London] ([Wheatsheaf House, Carmelite St., E.C.4]) : GeminiScan Ltd, 1974. — [2],24,[1]p : ill(chiefly col), col map, ports ; 33cm.
Six leaves, with versos blank, are perforated for making press-out models.
ISBN 0-85691-006-6 Sd : £0.85
(B77-20255)

568'.19 — Dinosaurs. *Juvenile literature*
Bastable, Tony. A dictionary of dinosaurs / [by] Tony Bastable ; cover and text illustrations by Mary I. French. — London : Pan Books, 1977. — 123p : ill ; 20cm. — (Piccolo original)
ISBN 0-330-25127-9 Pbk : £0.60
(B77-26309)

Halstead, Lambert Beverly. A closer look at prehistoric reptiles / [by] Beverly Halstead ; illustrated by Richard Orr. — London : Hamilton, [1977]. — 3-30p : col ill ; 27cm. — (A closer look book ; 16)
Col. ill., text on lining papers.
ISBN 0-241-89558-8 : £1.75
(B77-18133)

569 — Prehistoric mammals. *Juvenile literature*
Hinde, Cecilia. Wonder why book of prehistoric mammals / [by] Cecilia Hinde ; illustrated by John Barber. — London : Transworld, 1977. — [2],32p : ill(chiefly col) ; 29cm.
Spine title: Prehistoric mammals. — Index.
ISBN 0-552-98044-7 : £1.35
ISBN 0-552-57009-5 Sd : £0.50
(B77-28602)

McCord, Anne. The children's picture prehistory / [by] Anne McCord ; illustrated by Bob Hersey ; designed by Graham Round. — London : Usborne.
Prehistoric mammals. — 1977. — 32p : ill(chiefly col) ; 28cm.
Bibl.: p.32. — Index.
ISBN 0-86020-129-5 : £1.95
ISBN 0-86020-128-7 Pbk : £0.95
(B77-28603)

569'.9 — Man. Evolution. *Sources of data: Fossils*
Poirier, Frank Eugene. Fossil evidence : the human evolutionary journey / [by] Frank E. Poirier. — 2nd ed. — Saint Louis : Mosby ; London : Distributed by Kimpton, 1977. — xiii,342p : ill, maps ; 26cm.
Previous ed.: published as 'Fossil man'. 1973. — Bibl. — Index.
ISBN 0-8016-3951-4 Pbk : £6.45
(B77-27853)

572 — ETHNOLOGY
572 — Race. Biological aspects
Goldsby, Richard Allen. Race and races / [by] Richard A. Goldsby. — 2nd ed. — New York : Macmillan ; London : Collier Macmillan, 1977. — xiii,158p : ill(some col), col maps, ports ; 25cm.
Previous ed.: 1971. — Bibl.: p.149-152. — Index.
ISBN 0-02-344310-3 Pbk : £4.15
(B77-27854)

572'.01 — Race. Theories, 1800-1976
Banton, Michael. The idea of race / [by] Michael Banton. — London : Tavistock Publications, 1977. — vi,190p ; 23cm.
Bibl.: p.173-181. — Index.
ISBN 0-422-76170-2 : £6.50
(B77-24933)

572.8'96073 — Negroes. Racial inferiority. Biosocial aspects. Theories. *United States, 1859-1900*
Haller, John Samuel. Outcasts from evolution : scientific attitudes of racial inferiority, 1859-1900 / [by] John S. Haller, Jr. — New York ; London [etc.] : McGraw-Hill, 1975 [i.e. 1976]. — xii,228p : ill ; 20cm.
Originally published: Urbana ; London : University of Illinois Press, 1971. — Bibl.: p.211-222. — Index.
ISBN 0-07-025625-x Pbk : £3.30
(B77-07342)

573 — PHYSICAL ANTHROPOLOGY
Brace, Charles Loring. Human evolution : an introduction to biological anthropology / [by] C.L. Brace and Ashley Montagu. — 2nd ed. — New York : Macmillan ; London : Collier Macmillan, 1977. — xi,493p : ill, facsims, maps, ports ; 24cm.
Previous ed.: published as 'Man's evolution'. 1965. — Bibl. — Index.
ISBN 0-02-313190-x : £9.75
(B77-21121)

Lasker, Gabriel Ward. Physical anthropology / [by] Gabriel Ward Lasker. — 2nd ed. — New York ; London [etc.] : Holt, Rinehart and Winston, [1977]. — xiii,420p : ill, maps ; 25cm.
Map on lining papers. — This ed. published in the United States: 1976. — Previous ed.: New York : Holt, Rinehart and Winston, 1973. — Bibl.: p.381-405. — Index.
ISBN 0-03-089757-2 : £10.00
(B77-09694)

573 — Man. *Physical anthropological perspectives*
Population structure and human variation / edited by G.A. Harrison. — Cambridge [etc.] : Cambridge University Press, 1977. — xvii, 342p : ill, maps(some col) ; 24cm. — (International Biological Programme. Publications ; 11)
Bibl. — Index.
ISBN 0-521-21399-1 : £17.50
(B77-27855)

573'.01 — Physical anthropology. Theories
Gooch, Stan. The Neanderthal question / [by] Stan Gooch. — London : Wildwood House, 1977. — xv,178p : ill ; 23cm.
Bibl.: p.170-173. — Index.
ISBN 0-7045-0260-7 : £5.95
ISBN 0-7045-0261-5 Pbk : Unpriced
(B77-22578)

573.2 — Man. Evolution
Leakey, Richard E. Origins : what new discoveries reveal about the emergence of our species and its possible future / [by] Richard E. Leakey and Roger Lewin. — London : Macdonald and Jane's, 1977. — 264p : ill(some col), maps(some col), ports(1 col) ; 25cm.
Bibl.: p.257. — Index.
ISBN 0-354-04162-2 : £8.95
(B77-28604)

The **rise** of man / [editor Frances M. Clapham ; assistant editor Abigail Frost ; contributors Peter Andrews et al. ; illustrators John Barber et al.]. — Maidenhead : Sampson Low, 1976. — 160p : ill(chiefly col), facsims, maps ; 29cm. — ([The Sampson Low visual world library])
Index.
ISBN 0-562-00043-7 : £4.50
Primary classification 930
(B77-06974)

Tomkins, S P. The origin and evolution of man : the story of human evolution with special reference to the continent of Africa / [by] S.P. Tomkins. — London [etc.] : Macmillan Education, 1977. — [5],28,[1]p : ill, maps ; 22cm. — (Advanced readers in tropical biology)
ISBN 0-333-19475-6 Sd : £0.41
(B77-11799)

Wood, Bernard. The evolution of early man / text by Bernard Wood ; illustrations by Giovanni Caselli. — [London] ([Eurobook Ltd, 2 Queens Drive, W3 0HA]) : Peter Lowe, 1976. — 5-124p : ill(chiefly col), col maps ; 28cm.
Bibl.: p.120. — Index.
ISBN 0-85654-023-4 : £2.95
(B77-04161)

573.2'07'7 — Man. Evolution. *Programmed texts*
Pawson, Ivan G. Physical anthropology : human evolution / [by] Ivan G. Pawson. — New York ; London [etc.] : Wiley, 1977. — x,246p : ill, 2 maps ; 26cm. — (A self-teaching guide)
Fill-in book. — With answers. — Bibl.: p.viii. — Index.
ISBN 0-471-67280-7 Pbk : £3.75
(B77-32628)

573.2'1 — Man. Genetics
Carter, Cedric Oswald. Human heredity / [by] C.O. Carter. — 2nd ed. — Harmondsworth [etc.] : Penguin, 1977. — 286p,4p of plates : ill, 2 maps ; 18cm. — (A pelican original)
Previous ed.: 1962. — Bibl.: p.277-278. — Index.
ISBN 0-14-020523-3 Pbk : £1.25
(B77-24934)

Human genetics / prepared by a Course Team for the Open University. — Milton Keynes : Open University Press, 1976. — p615-689 : ill, maps ; 30cm. — (Science, a second level course : genetics) (S299 ; 14 and 15)
With answers. — Bibl.: p.688-689.
ISBN 0-335-04289-9 Pbk : £1.40
(B77-02299)

Novitski, Edward. Human genetics / [by] Edward Novitski. — New York : Macmillan ; London : Collier Macmillan, 1977. — xxi, 458p : ill, maps, geneal table, ports ; 26cm.
Bibl. — Index.
ISBN 0-02-388550-5 : £10.50
(B77-27064)

Rothwell, Norman V. Human genetics / [by] Norman V. Rothwell. — Englewood Cliffs ; London [etc.] : Prentice-Hall, 1977. — xv, 429p : ill ; 24cm. — (Prentice-Hall biological sciences series)
With answers to review questions. — Bibl. — Index.
ISBN 0-13-445080-9 : £11.60
(B77-17488)

573.2'1 — Man. Genetics. *Reviews of research*
Advances in human genetics / edited by Harry Harris and Kurt Hirschhorn. — New York ; London : Plenum Press.
6. — 1976. — xv,382p : ill, maps ; 24cm.
Bibl. — Index.
ISBN 0-306-39606-8 : £18.59
(B77-05409)

573.2'21 — Man. Chromosomes. Abnormalities
New chromosomal syndromes / edited by Jorge J. Yunis. — New York [etc.] ; London : Academic Press, 1977. — xi,404p : ill ; 24cm. — (Chromosomes in biology and medicine)
Bibl. — Index.
ISBN 0-12-775165-3 : £20.60
(B77-23400)

573.2'21 — Man. Chromosomes. Abnormalities. *Conference proceedings*
Symposium on Human Population Cytogenetics, *Albany, 1975.* Population cytogenetics : studies in humans : proceedings of a Symposium on Human Population Cytogenetics sponsored by the Birth Defects Institute of the New York State Department of Health, held in Albany, New York, October 14-15, 1975 / edited by Ernest B. Hook and Ian H. Porter. — New York [etc.] ; London : Academic Press, 1977. — xv,374p : ill ; 24cm. — (Birth Defects Institute. Symposia ; 6th)
Index.
ISBN 0-12-355460-8 : £12.40
(B77-27065)

573.2'2'1 — Man. Physiology. Variation. Genetic factors. *Conference proceedings*
Physiological variation and its genetic basis / edited by J.S. Weiner. — London : Taylor and Francis, 1977. — xi,178p : ill, map ; 23cm. — (Society for the Study of Human Biology. Symposia ; vol.17 ISSN 0081-153x)
Bibl. — Index.
ISBN 0-85066-108-0 : £7.00
(B77-32629)

573'.3 — Prehistoric man. Migration. Research. *Soviet Union. State-of-the-art reviews*
McBurney, Charles Brian Montagu. Early man in the Soviet Union : the implications of some recent discoveries / by C.B.M. McBurney. — London [etc.] : Oxford University Press for the British Academy, 1976. — 55p,fold leaf of plate,xvi p of plates : ill, maps ; 25cm. — (Albert Reckitt archaeological lecture ; 1975)
'Read in shortened form 14 May 1975' - note. — Bibl.: p.53-55.
ISBN 0-19-725731-3 Sd : £1.00
(B77-07906)

573'.8 — Giants: Cotter, Patrick. *Ireland*
Frankcom, Graham. The Irish giant / [by] G. Frankcom & J.H. Musgrave. — London : Duckworth, 1976. — 128p : ill, facsims, plan, ports ; 26cm.
Ill. on lining paper. — Bibl.: p.125-127. — Index.
ISBN 0-7156-1021-x : £3.95
(B77-00219)

574 — BIOLOGY
Jones, Kenneth C. Introductory biology / [by] Kenneth C. Jones, Anthony J. Gaudin. — New York ; London [etc.] : Wiley, 1977. — xvi, 619p : ill(some col), col maps, ports ; 29cm.
Index.
ISBN 0-471-44875-3 : £10.50
(B77-18134)

Villee, Claude Alvin. Biological principles and processes / [by] Claude A. Villee, Vincent G. Dethier. — 2nd ed. — Philadelphia ; London [etc.] : Saunders, 1976. — xvii,999p : ill(some col), maps ; 28cm.
Col. ill. on lining papers. — Previous ed.: 1971. — Bibl. — Index.
ISBN 0-7216-9029-7 : £13.00
(B77-00760)

574 — Biology. *Reviews of research*
Advances in the biosciences. — Oxford [etc.] : Pergamon [etc.].
13 : Hormones and embryonic development / editor G. Raspé, associate editor S. Bernhard. — 1974. — vi,252p : ill, ports ; 22cm.
Bibl. — Index.
ISBN 0-08-018239-9 : £15.00
(B77-11800)

Progress in theoretical biology. — New York [etc.] ; London : Academic Press.
Vol.4 / edited by Robert Rosen and Fred M. Snell. — 1976. — xii,297p : ill ; 24cm.
Bibl. — Index.
ISBN 0-12-543104-x : £19.20
(B77-04162)

574 — Biology. *Secondary school texts*
Focus on biology : a course for first examinations / edited by C.D. Gould. — Exeter : Wheaton, 1977. — 152p,plate : ill(incl 1 col), map ; 30cm.
Adaptation of: 'Natural science'. Units C, F, I, L. Oxford : Pergamon, 1968. — Index.
ISBN 0-08-020592-5 Pbk : £1.60
(B77-18135)

Tinbergen, Dirk. Biology step by step / [by] D. Tinbergen, M.R. Pattinson. — London : Edward Arnold, 1977. — vi,170p : ill, forms ; 25cm.
ISBN 0-7131-0042-7 Pbk : £2.95
(B77-19368)

574 — Biology. *State-of-the-art reviews*
Medawar, *Sir* Peter Brian. The life science : current ideas of biology / [by] P.B. Medawar, J.S. Medawar. — London : Wildwood House, 1977. — [2],196p ; 23cm.
Index.
ISBN 0-7045-0243-7 : £4.95
(B77-09695)

574 — Biology. Measurement. Système International d'Unités. Symbols & abbreviations. *Directories*
Units, symbols, and abbreviations : a guide for biological and medical editors and authors / editor D.N. Baron. — 3rd ed. — London (Publications Office, 2 Queen Anne St., W1M 0BR) : Royal Society of Medicine, 1977. — 48p ; 23cm.
Previous ed.: 1972.
ISBN 0-905958-00-4 Sd : £2.00
Also classified at 610
(B77-21859)

574 — Organisms
Allen, Robert Day. The science of life / by Robert Day Allen and contributors. — New York [etc.] ; London : Harper and Row, 1977. — xxvi,438p : ill(chiefly col), col map ; 29cm.
Bibl. — Index.
ISBN 0-06-040207-5 : £11.20
(B77-14727)

Baker, Jeffrey John Wheeler. The study of biology / [by] Jeffrey J.W. Baker, Garland E. Allen. — 3rd ed. — Menlo Park ; London [etc.] : Addison-Wesley, 1977. — xviii,1122,[85] p,iv p of plates : ill(some col), col maps ; 24cm. — (Addison-Wesley series in life science)
Previous ed.: 1971. — Bibl. — Index.
ISBN 0-201-00409-7 : £13.60
(B77-23401)

Chute, Robert M. An introduction to biology / [by] Robert M. Chute. — New York [etc.] ; London : Harper and Row, 1976. — xv,455p : ill, chart, maps ; 24cm.
Bibl. — Index.
ISBN 0-06-041293-3 Pbk : £8.20
(B77-06078)

Davis, P William. The world of biology : life, society, ecosphere / [by] P. William Davis, Eldra Pearl Solomon. — New York ; London [etc.] : McGraw-Hill, 1974. — xvi,674p : ill(some col) ; 24cm.
Bibl. — Index.
ISBN 0-07-015548-8 : Unpriced
ISBN 0-07-015547-x Pbk : Unpriced
(B77-19369)

Goldsby, Richard Allen. Basic biology / [by] Richard A. Goldsby. — New York [etc.] ; London : Harper and Row, [1976]. — [20],x, 500[i.e.578]p,[32]p of plates : ill(some col), 2 col maps, ports ; 25cm.
'A Leogryph book'. — Bibl.: p.469-479. — Index.
ISBN 0-06-162400-4 : £9.70
(B77-06678)

Villee, Claude Alvin. Biology / [by] Claude A. Villee. — 7th ed. — Philadelphia ; London [etc.] : Saunders, 1977. — xviii,980p : ill ; 28cm.
Ill. on lining papers. — Previous ed.: 1972. — Bibl.: p.938-950. — Index.
ISBN 0-7216-9023-8 : £12.50
(B77-21860)

Weisz, Paul B. Elements of biology. — 4th ed. / [by] Paul B. Weisz, Richard N. Keogh. — New York ; London [etc.] : McGraw-Hill, 1977. — x,593p : ill(some col), col maps, port ; 25cm.
Text, col. ill. on lining papers. — Previous ed.: / by Paul B. Weisz. 1969. — Bibl. — Index.
ISBN 0-07-069137-1 : £11.20
(B77-21861)

574 — Organisms. *For East & West African students. Secondary school texts*
Ayerst, Peter William. Biology : a revision scheme for students preparing for the West African School Certificate ('O' Level) and the East African Certificate of Education / [by] P.W. Ayerst. — [New ed.]. — London [etc.] : Evans Bros, 1976. — 64p : ill ; 19cm. — (Evans pocket facts)
Previous ed.: s.l. : Progress Publications, 1970.
ISBN 0-237-49971-1 Sd : Unpriced
(B77-09012)

574 — Organisms. *For West African students. Secondary school texts*
Mackean, Donald Gordon. Introduction to biology / [by] D.G. Mackean. — West African ed. — [Ibadan] : Heinemann Educational Books (Nigeria) ; [London] : J. Murray, 1977. — 224p : ill, map ; 30cm.
Previous ed.: i.e. Tropical ed., London : J. Murray, 1969. — Index.
ISBN 0-7195-3315-5 Pbk : £2.50
ISBN 97-8129-087-0 (Heinemann Educational Books (Nigeria))
(B77-14728)

574 — Organisms. *Gaelic texts*
MacLeod, Ronald. Bith-eolas : a' chealla, gintinneachd is mean-fhàs / le Raghnall MacLeòid ; eadar -theangaichte le Ruariadh MacThómais. — Glaschu [i.e. Glasgow] (29 Sràid Bhatairliù, Glaschu G2) : Gairm, 1976. — 152p : ill, maps ; 23cm.
Gaelic text, English foreword.
ISBN 0-901771-53-8 : £2.00
(B77-11801)

574 — Organisms. *Irish texts*
Ó Ceallacháin, C N. An domhan beo / [le] C.N. Ó Ceallacháin. — Baile Átha Cliath [i.e. Dublin] ([Oriel House, Beggar's Bush, Dublin 4]) : Oifig an tSoláthair, 1976. — [11],263p : ill(some col), ports ; 25cm.
Text, ill. on lining papers. — Index.
ISBN 0-905621-16-6 : £2.40
(B77-09013)

574 — Organisms. *Juvenile literature*
Discovering nature. — Revised ed. — London : Macdonald Educational, 1977. — 4-189p : ill(chiefly col) ; 27cm. — (Macdonald's discovery library)
Previous ed.: published as 'Purnell's discovering nature'. London : Macdonald and Co., 1972. — Index.
ISBN 0-356-05169-2 : £2.95
(B77-24935)

574 — Organisms. *Secondary school texts*
Head, John Juan. Science through biology / [by] J.J. Head ; illustrated by Derek Whiteley. — London : Edward Arnold, 1976. — vi,306p : ill(some col), col maps ; 25cm.
Index.
ISBN 0-7131-1972-1 Pbk : £4.75
(B77-09014)

Strathclyde Biology Group. The science of life / Strathclyde Biology Group. — Glasgow [etc.] : Blackie ; London : J. Murray.
Experimental guide. — 1977. — 64p : ill ; 25cm.
ISBN 0-216-90247-9 Sd : £1.10
ISBN 0-7195-3280-9 (J. Murray) Sd : £1.10
(B77-28605)

Student's unit 1 : Maintaining the species. — 1977. — 64p : ill ; 25cm.
ISBN 0-216-90241-x Sd : £0.75
ISBN 0-7195-3338-4 (J. Murray) Sd : £0.75
(B77-28606)

Student's unit 2 : Energy and life. — 1977. — 48p : ill ; 25cm.
ISBN 0-216-90242-8 Sd : £0.70
ISBN 0-7195-3339-2 (J. Murray) Sd : £0.70
(B77-28607)

Student's unit 3 : Exchanging materials. — 1977. — 48p : ill ; 25cm.
ISBN 0-216-90243-6 Sd : £0.70
ISBN 0-7195-3281-7 (J. Murray) Sd : £0.70
(B77-28608)

Student's unit 4 : Movement and control. — 1977. — 64p : ill ; 25cm.
ISBN 0-216-90244-4 Sd : £0.75
ISBN 0-7195-3340-6 (J. Murray) Sd : £0.75
(B77-28609)

Student's unit 5 : Interactions. — 1977. — 48p : ill ; 25cm.
ISBN 0-216-90245-2 Sd : £0.70
ISBN 0-7195-3341-4 (J. Murray) Sd : £0.70
(B77-28610)

Teacher's resource book. — 1977. — 188p : ill ; 25cm.
Bibl. — Lists of films.
ISBN 0-216-90246-0 Pbk : £4.95
ISBN 0-7195-3282-5 (J. Murray) Pbk : £4.95
(B77-28611)

Technician's manual. — 1977. — 62p : ill ; 25cm.
ISBN 0-216-90248-7 Sd : £1.95
ISBN 0-7195-3337-6 (J. Murray) Sd : £1.95
(B77-28612)

574 — Organisms. *Stories for children*
Sucksdorff, Astrid Bergman. The magnifying glass / [by] Astrid Bergman Sucksdorff ; [translated from the Swedish by Francesca Greenoak]. — London : A. and C. Black, 1977. — [41]p : chiefly col ill ; 29cm.
Translation of: 'Förstoringsglaset'. Stockholm : Rabén och Sjögren, 1975.
ISBN 0-7136-1704-7 : £2.75
(B77-06079)

574'.01'4 — Organisms. Names
Jeffrey, Charles. Biological nomenclature / [by] Charles Jeffrey ; for the Systematics Association ; foreword by V.H. Heywood. — 2nd ed. — London : Edward Arnold, 1977. — viii,72p ; 24cm.
Previous ed.: 1973. — Bibl.: p.53-54. — Index.
ISBN 0-7131-2614-0 : £4.75
ISBN 0-7131-2615-9 Pbk : £1.95
(B77-26310)

574'.028 — Biology. Use of ultrasonic waves
Wells, Peter Neil Temple. Biomedical ultrasonics / [by] P.N.T. Wells. — London [etc.] : Academic Press, 1977. — x,635p : ill ; 24cm. — (Medical physics series)
Bibl.: p.511-594. — Index.
ISBN 0-12-742940-9 : £24.00
Primary classification 610'.28
(B77-23429)

574'.03 — Biology. *Dictionaries*
A dictionary of life sciences / edited by E.A. Martin. — London [etc.] : Macmillan, 1976. — [5],374p,fold plate : ill ; 22cm.
ISBN 0-333-19436-5 : £5.95
(B77-10365)

McGraw-Hill dictionary of the life sciences / Daniel N. Lapedes, editor in chief. — New York ; London [etc.] : McGraw-Hill, 1976. — xiv,907,A1-A38 : ill ; 24cm.
'Much of the material in this Dictionary has been published previously in the "McGraw-Hill dictionary of scientific and technical terms" ... 1974' - title page verso.
ISBN 0-07-045262-8 : Unpriced
(B77-27856)

574'.05 — Biology. Conferences. *Reports, surveys. Serials*
Conference reports, agriculture, food and biology. — London : Applied Science Publishers.
Vol.1, [no.1]- ; 1977-. — 1977-. — 24cm.
Quarterly. — [1],79p. in 1st issue. — Index.
Pbk : £16.00(yearly)
ISSN 0309-5886
Primary classification 630'.5
(B77-15924)

574'.074 — Terrariums. *Amateurs' manuals*
White, William, *b.1934.* A terrarium in your home / [by] William White, Jr & Sara Jane White. — New York : Sterling [etc.] ; London : Distributed by Ward Lock, 1976. — 92p : ill ; 21cm.
Index.
ISBN 0-7061-2522-3 : £2.95
(B77-21122)

574'.092'4 — Biology. Bates, Henry Walter
Moon, H P. Henry Walter Bates FRS, 1825-1892 : explorer, scientist and Darwinian / [by] H.P. Moon. — Leicester (96 New Walk, Leicester LE1 6TD) : Leicestershire Museums, Art Galleries and Records Service, 1976. — [2], 99p : ill(incl 1 col), facsim, port ; 21cm.
Bibl.: p.85-91.
ISBN 0-904671-19-4 Sd : £1.00
(B77-15285)

574'.092'4 — Marine biology. M'Intosh, William Carmichael. *Great Britain. Biographies*
Gunther, Albert Everard. The life of William Carmichael M'Intosh, M.D., F.R.S., of St Andrews, 1838-1931, a pioneer in marine biology / by A.E. Gunther. — Edinburgh : Scottish Academic Press for the University of St Andrews, 1977. — 214p,leaf of plate,[10]p of plates : ill, facsims, geneal tables, maps, ports ; 30cm. — (University of St Andrews. Publications ; no.61)
Index.
ISBN 0-7073-0138-6 Sd : Unpriced
(B77-33794)

574.1 — ORGANISMS. PHYSIOLOGY
574.1 — Organisms. Cybernetics aspects
Calow, Peter. Biological machines : a cybernetic approach to life / [by] Peter Calow. — London : Edward Arnold, 1976. — vii,134p : ill ; 24cm. — (Special topics in biology series)
Bibl.: p.126-128. — Index.
ISBN 0-7131-2582-9 : £7.95
ISBN 0-7131-2583-7 Pbk : £3.95
(B77-01441)

574.1'3 — Organisms. Nutrition. *Secondary school texts*
Gray, Don. What happens to food / [by] Don Gray. — London : Macdonald Educational, 1977. — [1],24,[1]p : ill(chiefly col) ; 27cm. — (Biology colour units)
ISBN 0-356-05521-3 Sd : £0.85
(B77-16379)

574.1'33 — Organisms. Drugs. Metabolism. *Festschriften*
Symposium on Drug Metabolism, *University of Surrey, 1976.* Drug metabolism : from microbe to man : a symposium in honour of Richard Tecwyn Williams / editors D.V. Parke, R.L. Smith. — London : Taylor and Francis, 1977. — xii,460p : ill, port ; 26cm.
'Proceedings of the International Symposium held at the University of Surrey, April 1976' - jacket. — 'Symposium on Drug Metabolism ...' - p.v. — Bibl. — Index.
ISBN 0-85066-105-6 : £25.00
(B77-14729)

574.1'33 — Organisms. Metal ions. Metabolism
Phipps, D A. Metals and metabolism / [by] D.A. Phipps. — Oxford : Clarendon Press, 1976. — ix,134p : ill ; 23cm. — (Oxford chemistry series)
Bibl.: p.130-131. — Index.
ISBN 0-19-855452-4 : £5.00
ISBN 0-19-855413-3 Pbk : £2.50
(B77-15286)

574.1'7 — Organisms. Cells. Differentiation
Maclean, Norman, *b.1932.* The differentiation of cells / [by] Norman Maclean. — London : Edward Arnold, 1977. — viii,216p : ill ; 22cm. — (Genetics - principles and perspectives ; 1)
Bibl.: p.193-207. — Index.
ISBN 0-7131-2566-7 : £12.00
ISBN 0-7131-2567-5 Pbk : £5.95
(B77-19370)

574.1'8 — Organisms. Responses. *Secondary school texts*
Morgan, Carol. Co-ordination / [by] Carol Morgan. — London : Macdonald Educational, 1977. — [1],24,[1]p : ill(chiefly col) ; 27cm. — (Biology colour units)
ISBN 0-356-05522-1 Pbk : £0.85
(B77-08375)

574.1'9 — Biophysics & biochemistry. *Reviews of research*
Horizons in biochemistry and biophysics. — Reading, Mass. ; London [etc.] : Addison-Wesley.
Vol.2 / E. Quagliariello, editor-in-chief ; F. Palmieri, managing editor ; Thomas P. Singer, consulting editor ... — 1976 [i.e. 1977]. — xvii, 340p : ill ; 25cm.
Published in the United States: 1976.
ISBN 0-201-02712-7 : £12.75
ISSN 0096-2708
ISBN 0-201-02722-4 Pbk : £6.20
(B77-12439)

574.1'9'09162 — Marine organisms. Biophysics & biochemistry. *Reviews of research*
Biochemical and biophysical perspectives in marine biology / edited by D.C. Malins and J.R. Sargent. — London [etc.] : Academic Press.
Vol.3. — 1976. — xv,447p : ill ; 24cm.
Bibl. — Index.
ISBN 0-12-466603-5 : £14.00
(B77-11802)

574.1'91 — Biophysics
Sybesma, C. An introduction to biophysics / [by] C. Sybesma. — New York [etc.] ; London : Academic Press, 1977. — x,278p : ill ; 24cm.
Bibl.: p.264-265. — Index.
ISBN 0-12-679750-1 : £13.85
(B77-23402)

574.1'91 — Biophysics. *Reviews of research*
Advances in biological and medical physics. — New York ; London : Academic Press.
Vol.15 / edited by John H. Lawrence and John W. Gofman ; assistant editor Thomas L. Hayes. — 1974. — x,310p : ill ; 24cm.
Bibl. — Index.
ISBN 0-12-005215-6 : £21.30
(B77-22579)

Current topics in bioenergetics. — New York [etc.] ; London : Academic Press.
Vol.6 / edited by D. Rao Sanadi. — 1977. — xii,324p : ill ; 24cm.
Bibl. — Index.
ISBN 0-12-152506-6 : £22.70
(B77-24936)

Progress in biophysics and molecular biology. — Oxford [etc.] : Pergamon.
[Vol.] 30 / editors J.A.V. Butler, D. Noble. — 1976. — vi,263p,2p of plates : ill ; 28cm.
Bibl. — Index.
ISBN 0-08-020207-1 : £25.00
ISSN 0079-6107
(B77-06679)

574.1'91 — Organisms. Biological rhythms
Saunders, David Stanley. An introduction to biological rhythms / [by] David S. Saunders. — Glasgow [etc.] : Blackie, 1977. — viii,170p : ill ; 21cm. — (Tertiary level biology)
Bibl.: p.156-163. — Index.
ISBN 0-216-90226-6 : £5.50
(B77-12440)

574.1'91'028 — Biophysics. Laboratory techniques
New techniques in biophysics and cell biology. — London [etc.] : Wiley.
Vol.3 / edited by R.H. Pain, B.J. Smith. — 1976. — vii,245p,plate : ill(incl 2 col) ; 24cm.
'A Wiley-Interscience Publication'. — Bibl. — Index.
ISBN 0-471-01814-7 : £10.00
Also classified at 574.8'7'028
(B77-01442)

574.1'9121 — Bioenergetics. *Reviews of research*
Topics in bioelectrochemistry and bioenergetics. — London [etc.] : Wiley.
Vol.1 / edited by G. Milazzo. — 1976. — xvi, 378p : ill ; 24cm.
'A Wiley-Interscience publication'.
ISBN 0-471-01356-0 : £19.50
Primary classification 574.1'9283
(B77-22581)

574.1'9121 — Bioenergetics. Mechanisms
Racker, Efraim. A new look at mechanisms in bioenergetics / [by] Efraim Racker. — New York [etc.] ; London : Academic Press, 1976. — xiv,197p : ill ; 22cm.
Bibl.: p.177-188. — Index.
ISBN 0-12-574670-9 : £6.75
ISBN 0-12-574672-5 Pbk : £2.45
(B77-01443)

574.1'915 — Organisms. Effects of nonionising radiation. *Conference proceedings*
International Conference on Environmental Toxicity, *7th, Rochester, 1974.* Fundamental and applied aspects of nonionizing radiation / edited by Sol M. Michaelson ... [et al.]. — New York ; London : Plenum Press, 1975. — xvi, 470p : ill ; 26cm.
'Proceedings of a conference organized by the Department of Radiation Biology and Biophysics, the School of Medicine and Dentistry of the University of Rochester, held at Rochester, New York, June 5-7, 1974' - title page verso. — 'This is the Seventh International Conference on Environmental Toxicity' - p.xv. — Bibl. — Index.
ISBN 0-306-30901-7 : £24.89
(B77-03545)

574.1'915 — Radiobiology
Stewart, John Charles. A manual of radiobiology / by John C. Stewart and David M. Hawcroft. — London : Sidgwick and Jackson, 1977. — xi,202p : ill ; 23cm. — (Biology series)
Bibl.: p.197-199. — Index.
ISBN 0-283-98343-4 : £7.50
ISBN 0-283-98344-2 Pbk : £3.95
(B77-17489)

574.1'9153 — Organisms. Effects of light
Björn, L O. Light and life / [by] L.O. Björn. — London [etc.] : Hodder and Stoughton, 1976. — vi,249p,[16]p of plates : ill, map ; 19cm.
Translation and revision of: 'Ljus oc hliv'. Stockholm : Aldus : Bonnier, 1973. — Bibl.: p.242-246. — Index.
ISBN 0-340-06762-4 : £3.45
ISBN 0-340-04996-0 Pbk : £1.95
(B77-07343)

574.1'9153 — Photobiology. *Reviews of research*
Photochemical and photobiological reviews. — New York ; London : Plenum Press.
Vol.1 / edited by Kendric C. Smith. — 1976. — xi,391p : ill ; 24cm.
Bibl. — Index.
ISBN 0-306-33801-7 : £20.48
Also classified at 541'.35
(B77-19371)

574.1'92 — Biochemistry
Biochemistry : a case-oriented approach / [by] Rex Montgomery ... [et al.]. — 2nd ed. — Saint Louis : Mosby ; London : Distributed by Kimpton, 1977. — xix,769p : ill ; 26cm.
Previous ed.: 1974. — Bibl. — Index.
ISBN 0-8016-3469-5 Pbk : £8.60
(B77-21862)

Comprehensive biochemistry / edited by Marcel Florkin and Elmer H. Stotz. — Amsterdam ; Oxford [etc.] : Elsevier.
Vol.32 : A history of biochemistry. Part 4 : Early studies on biosynthesis / by Marcel Florkin. — 1977. — xx,362p : ill, ports ; 23cm.
Index.
ISBN 0-444-41544-0 : £23.33
(B77-27066)

Suttie, John Weston. Introduction to biochemistry / [by] John W. Suttie. — 2nd ed. — New York ; London [etc.] : Holt, Rinehart and Winston, 1977. — xiv,434p : ill(some col) ; 25cm.
With answers. — Previous ed.: New York : Holt, Rinehart and Winston, 1972. — Bibl. — Index.
ISBN 0-03-089713-0 : £7.50
(B77-20256)

574.1'92 — Biochemistry. *Reviews of research*
Essays in biochemistry. — London [etc.] : Academic Press for the Biochemical Society.
Vol.12 / edited for the Biochemical Society by P.N. Campbell, W.N. Aldridge. — 1976. — ix, 154p : ill ; 23cm.
Index.
ISBN 0-12-158112-8 Pbk : £3.20
(B77-06680)

International review of biochemistry. — Baltimore ; London [etc.] : University Park Press.
Vol.14 : Biochemistry of lipids, 2 / edited by T.W. Goodwin. — 1977. — xi,386p : ill ; 24cm.
Index.
ISBN 0-8391-1078-2 : £21.25
(B77-23403)

574.1'92 — Environmental change. Biochemical adaptation of organisms. *Conference proceedings*
Biochemical adaptation to environmental change : organized by R.M.S. Smellie / and edited by R.M.S. Smellie and J.F. Pennock. — London (7 Warwick Court, WC1R 5DP) : Biochemical Society, 1976. — ix,240p,[3] leaves of plates : ill ; 26cm. — (Biochemical Society. Symposia ; no.41 ISSN 0067-8694)
'... held at the University of Liverpool, July 1975'. — Bibl. — Index.
ISBN 0-904498-01-8 : £10.00
(B77-21863)

574.1'92'028 — Biochemistry. Applications of mass spectrometry. *Reviews of research*
Advances in mass spectrometry in biochemistry and medicine. — New York : Spectrum Publications ; New York ; London [etc.] : Distributed by Wiley.
Vol.2 : Proceedings of the 3rd International Symposium of Mass Spectrometry in Biochemistry and Medicine, Mario Negri Institute for Pharmacological Research, June, 1975, Milan, Italy / edited by Alberto Frigerio. — 1977. — [22],609p : ill ; 24cm.
Bibl. — Index.
ISBN 0-470-99039-2 : £35.00
(B77-15287)

574.1'92'028 — Biochemistry. Experiments. *Laboratory manuals*
Routh, Joseph Isaac. Experiments in organic and biochemistry / [by] Joseph I. Routh. — Philadelphia ; London [etc.] : Saunders, 1974 [i.e. 1976]. — viii,172p : ill ; 25cm. — (Saunders golden series)
Pages perforated at inside edge. — Published in the United States: 1974. — Students laboratory manual for the textbook 'Essentials of organic and biochemistry' / by Donald J. Burton and Joseph I. Routh. '... designed to strengthen and illustrate material in the textbook, as well as in any other book that covers the two fields of chemistry' - Preface.
ISBN 0-7216-7730-4 Pbk : £4.00
Primary classification 547'.0028
(B77-04794)

574.1'92'028 — Biochemistry. Laboratory techniques
Cooper, Terrance G. The tools of biochemistry / [by] Terrance G. Cooper. — New York ; London [etc.] : Wiley, 1977. — xvii,423p : ill ; 24cm.
'A Wiley-Interscience publication'. — Index.
ISBN 0-471-17116-6 : £13.95
(B77-33229)

Laboratory techniques in biochemistry and molecular biology / edited by T.S. Work, E. Work. — Amsterdam [etc.] ; Oxford : North-Holland Publishing Co.
Vol.6. Part 1 : Density gradient centrifugation / [by] Richard Hinton and Miloslav Dobrota. — 1976. — [2],290p : ill ; 20cm.
Bibl.: p.274-286. — Index.
ISBN 0-7204-4217-6 Pbk : £11.00
(B77-15845)

574.1'92'028 — Biochemistry. Laboratory techniques. *Reviews of research*
Techniques of biochemical and biophysical morphology. — New York ; London [etc.] : Wiley.
Vol.3 / edited by David Glick and Robert M. Rosenbaum. — 1977. — ix,214p : ill ; 24cm.
Bibl.: p.194-197. — Index.
ISBN 0-471-02219-5 : £17.25
(B77-17490)

574.1'92'071141 — Universities. *Great Britain. Open University. Curriculum subjects: Biochemistry. Courses: 'Biochemistry and molecular biology'*
Open University. *S322 Course Team.* S322, introduction and guide to the course / [Open University, S322 Course Team]. — Milton Keynes : Open University Press, 1977. — 10p ; 30cm. — (Science, a third level course : biochemistry and molecular biology) (S322 ; IG)
Bibl.: p.8-9.
Sd : Unpriced
(B77-27067)

574.1'921 — Biochemistry. Role of metal compounds
Hanzlik, Robert P. Inorganic aspects of biological and organic chemistry / [by] Robert P. Hanzlik. — New York [etc.] ; London : Academic Press, 1976. — xvii,402p : ill ; 24cm.
Index.
ISBN 0-12-324050-6 : £22.55
(B77-09015)

574.1'921 — Organisms. Inorganic compounds
Ochiai, Ei-ichiro. Bioinorganic chemistry : an introduction / [by] Ei-ichiro Ochiai. — Boston, Mass. ; London [etc.] : Allyn and Bacon, 1977. — xi,515p : ill ; 24cm. — (The Allyn and Bacon chemistry series)
Bibl.: p.29. — Index.
ISBN 0-205-05508-7 : Unpriced
(B77-18755)

574.1'9214 — Organisms. Trace elements
Bowen, Humphrey John Moule. Trace elements in biochemistry / [by] H.J.M. Bowen. — London [etc.] : Academic Press, 1976. — ix, 241p : ill ; 23cm.
Originally published: 1966. — Bibl.: p.211-234. — Index.
ISBN 0-12-120956-3 Pbk : £6.00
(B77-04163)

574.1'924 — Biopolymers. Spectroscopy
Introduction to the spectroscopy of biological polymers / edited by D.W. Jones. — London [etc.] : Academic Press, 1976. — xii,328p : ill ; 24cm.
Bibl. — Index.
ISBN 0-12-389250-3 : £11.60
(B77-09016)

574.1'924 — Biopolymers. Structure & physical properties. *Conference proceedings*
Cleveland Symposium on Macromolecules, *1st, 1976.* Proceedings of the First Cleveland Symposium on Macromolecules : structure and properties of biopolymers / edited by A.G. Walton. — Amsterdam ; Oxford [etc.] : Elsevier, 1977. — vii,309p : ill ; 25cm.
ISBN 0-444-41561-0 : £23.21
(B77-25622)

574.1'924 — Organisms. Aldehydes
Schauenstein, E. Aldehydes in biological systems : their natural occurrence and biological activities / [by] E. Schauenstein, H. Esterbauer, H. Zollner ; translator [from the German MS.] P.H. Gore. — London : Pion, 1977. — [9],205p,2p of plates : ill(some col) ; 24cm. — ([Pion advanced biochemistry series ; 5])
Index.
ISBN 0-85086-059-8 : £9.00
(B77-18136)

574.1'924 — Secondary metabolites
Luckner, Martin. Secondary metabolism in plants and animals / [by] Martin Luckner ; translated [from the German] by T.N. Vasudevan with the assistance of J.L. Wray. — London : Chapman and Hall, 1977. — xix,404p : ill ; 24cm.
This translation originally published: 1972. — Translation of: 'Der Sekundärstoffwechsel in Pflanze und Tier'. Stuttgart : G. Fischer, 1969. — Bibl. — Index.
ISBN 0-412-15050-6 Pbk : £5.00
(B77-16380)

574.1'924 — Solutes: Biopolymers: Polyelectrolytes. Biophysics
Eisenberg, Henryk. Biological macromolecules and polyelectrolytes in solution / by Henryk Eisenberg. — Oxford : Clarendon Press, 1976. — xviii,272p : ill ; 24cm. — (Monographs on physical biochemistry ISSN 0309-0698)
Bibl.: p.247-264. — Index.
ISBN 0-19-854612-2 : £16.00
(B77-02998)

574.1'9243 — Steroids. Biochemistry
Nes, William R. Biochemistry of steroids and other isopentenoids / [by] William R. Nes and Margaret Lee McKean. — Baltimore ; London [etc.] : University Park Press, 1977. — xi,690p : ill ; 24cm.
Index.
ISBN 0-8391-1127-4 : £28.25
(B77-31185)

574.1'9245 — Concanavalin A. Applications
Concanavalin A as a tool / edited by H. Bittiger and H.P. Schnebli. — London [etc.] : Wiley, 1976. — xv,639p : ill ; 24cm.
'A Wiley-Interscience Publication'. — Index.
ISBN 0-471-01350-1 : £19.50
(B77-01444)

574.1'9245 — Organisms. Kinins. *Conference proceedings*
International Symposium on Vasopeptides, *Fiesole, 1975.* Kinins : pharmacodynamics and biological roles / edited by F. Sicuteri, Nathan Back and G.L. Haberland. — New York ; London : Plenum Press, 1976. — xi,398p : ill ; 26cm. — (Advances in experimental medicine and biology ; vol.70)
'Proceedings of the International Symposium on Vasopeptides "Kinin '75" held in Fiesole-Villa Medici (Auditorium Hoechst), Florence, Italy, July 15-17, 1975' - title-page verso. — Bibl. — Index.
ISBN 0-306-39070-1 : £23.63
(B77-18756)

574.1'9245 — Organisms. Peptides. Transport & hydrolysis. *Conference proceedings*
Symposium on Peptide Transport and Hydrolysis, *Ciba Foundation, 1976.* Peptide transport and hydrolysis / [editors Katherine Elliott and Maeve O'Connor]. — Amsterdam ; Oxford [etc.] : Elsevier [etc.], 1977. — ix,385p : ill ; 25cm. — (Ciba Foundation. Symposia : new series ; 50)
'Symposium on Peptide Transport and Hydrolysis, held at the Ciba Foundation, London 9th-11th November, 1976' - p.vii. — Bibl. — Index.
ISBN 0-444-15272-5 : £18.59
(B77-30254)

574.1'9247 — Organisms. Lipids. *Reviews of research*
Progress in the chemistry of fats and other lipids. — Oxford [etc.] : Pergamon.
Vol.14 / editor Ralph T. Holman. — 1975. — [5],296p,[5] leaves of plates,[4]p of plates : ill, facsims ; 26cm.
Originally published: in 4 vols. 1973-1975?. — Bibl. — Index.
ISBN 0-08-017808-1 : Unpriced
(B77-21123)

574.1'925 — Organisms. Enzymes
Ferdinand, W. The enzyme molecule / [by] W. Ferdinand. — London [etc.] : Wiley, 1976. — xvi,289p : ill ; 24cm.
Index.
ISBN 0-471-01822-8 : £9.50
ISBN 0-471-01821-x Pbk : £4.50
(B77-00761)

574.1'925 — Organisms. Enzymes. Immune reactions
Immunochemistry of enzymes and their antibodies / edited by Milton R.J. Salton. — New York ; London [etc.] : Wiley, 1977. — ix, 230p : ill ; 26cm. — (Developments in medical microbiology and infectious diseases)
'A Wiley Medical Publication'. — Index.
ISBN 0-471-74995-8 : £14.25
(B77-13037)

574.1'925'028 — Biology. Enzymology. Laboratory techniques
Methods in enzymology / editors-in-chief Sidney P. Colowick, Nathan O. Kaplan. — New York [etc.] ; London : Academic Press.
Vol.44 : Immobilized enzymes / edited by Klaus Mosbach. — 1976. — xx,999p : ill ; 24cm.
Index.
ISBN 0-12-181944-2 : £34.10
(B77-17491)

Vol.45 : Proteolytic enzymes. Part B / edited by Laszlo Lorand. — 1976. — xix,939p : ill, port ; 24cm.
Index.
ISBN 0-12-181945-0 : £34.10
(B77-09696)

574.1'927 — Hormones. Biochemistry
Butt, Wilfred Roger. Hormone chemistry / [by] W.R. Butt. — 2nd (revised) ed. — Chichester : Ellis Horwood ; New York ; London [etc.] : [Distributed by] Wiley.
In 2 vols. — Previous ed.: in 1 vol. 1967.
Vol.1 : Protein, polypeptide & peptide hormones. — 1975. — xiv,272p : ill ; 24cm.
Bibl. — Index.
ISBN 0-85312-037-4 : £13.50
(B77-11213)

Vol.2 : Steroids, thyroid hormones, biogenic amines and prostaglandins / with chapters by B.T. Rudd and R. Morris. — 1976. — 272p : ill ; 24cm.
Bibl. — Index.
ISBN 0-85312-038-2 : £16.00
(B77-31186)

574.1'927 — Organisms. Hormones. Action. Molecular biology. *Conference proceedings*
Society for Developmental Biology. *Symposium, 34th, Orono, 1975.* The molecular biology of hormone action / edited by John Papaconstantinou. — New York [etc.] ; London : Academic Press, 1976 [i.e. 1977]. — xiii,197p : ill ; 24cm.
'The Thirty-Fourth Symposium of the Society for Developmental Biology, Orono, Maine, June 1-4, 1975' - half title page verso. — Published in the United States: 1976. — Bibl. — Index.
ISBN 0-12-612980-0 : £11.70
(B77-15288)

574.1'9282 — Biochemistry. Quantum theory
Simon, Zeno. Quantum biochemistry and specific interactions / [by] Zeno Simon ; [translated from the Romanian by Zeno Simon and Vasile Vasilescu]. — Tunbridge Wells : Abacus Press, 1976. — 251p : ill ; 24cm.
Translation and revision of: 'Biochimie cuantică şi interacţii specifice'. Bucarest : Editura Stiinţifica, 1973.
ISBN 0-85626-087-8 : £11.95
(B77-05410)

574.1'9283 — Bioelectrochemistry. *Reviews of research*
Topics in bioelectrochemistry and bioenergetics. — London [etc.] : Wiley.
Vol.1 / edited by G. Milazzo. — 1976. — xvi, 378p : ill ; 24cm.
'A Wiley-Interscience publication'.
ISBN 0-471-01356-0 : £19.50
Also classified at 574.1'9121
(B77-22581)

574.1'9283 — Cryobiochemistry
Douzou, Pierre. Cryobiochemistry : an introduction / [by] Pierre Douzou. — London [etc.] : Academic Press, 1977. — x,286p : ill ; 24cm.
Index.
ISBN 0-12-221050-6 : £12.60
(B77-23404)

574.1'9285 — Biochemistry. Chemical analysis. *Reviews of research*
Methods of biochemical analysis. — New York ; London [etc.] : Wiley.
Vol.23 / edited by David Glick. — 1976. — ix, 435p : ill ; 24cm.
'An Interscience Publication'. — Contains index to volumes 1-23 and supplement. — Bibl.: p.338-345. — Index.
ISBN 0-471-01413-3 : £19.20
(B77-06080)

574.1'9285 — Biochemistry. Chemical analysis. Isoelectric focusing
Isoelectric focusing / edited by Nicholas Catsimpoolas. — New York [etc.] ; London : Academic Press, 1976 [i.e. 1977]. — xii,265p : ill ; 25cm.
Published in the United States: 1976. — Bibl. — Index.
ISBN 0-12-163950-9 : £16.70
(B77-13648)

574.1'9296 — Proteins. Biosynthesis
Molecular mechanisms of protein biosynthesis / edited by Herbert Weissbach, Sidney Pestka. — New York [etc.] ; London : Academic Press, 1977. — xiii,720p : ill ; 24cm. — (Molecular biology)
Bibl. — Index.
ISBN 0-12-744250-2 : £39.50
(B77-31187)

574.2 — ORGANISMS. DISEASES
574.2 — Organisms. Decomposition
Mason, C F. Decomposition / [by] C.F. Mason. — London : Edward Arnold, 1977. — [4],58p : ill ; 23cm. — (Institute of Biology. Studies in biology ; no.74)
Bibl.: p.56-58.
ISBN 0-7131-2588-8 : £2.80
ISBN 0-7131-2589-6 Pbk : £1.40
(B77-15846)

574.2'9 — Immunochemistry
Steward, M W. Immunochemistry / [by] M.W. Steward. — London : Chapman and Hall [etc.], 1976. — 64p : ill ; 21cm. — (Outline studies in biology)
'A Halsted Press book'. — Originally published: 1974. — Bibl.: p.60. — Index.
Pbk : £1.50
ISBN 0-412-12450-5
(B77-31188)

Steward, M W. Immunochemistry / [by] M.W. Steward. — London : Chapman and Hall, 1974. — 64p : ill ; 21cm. — (Outline studies in biology)
Bibl.: p.60. — Index.
ISBN 0-412-12450-5 Pbk : £0.95
(B77-21124)

574.2'9 — Immunology
An **introduction** to immunology / edited by E.M. Lance, P.B. Medawar, E. Simpson. — London : Wildwood House, 1977. — xii,158p : ill ; 20cm.
Index.
ISBN 0-7045-0209-7 : £5.95
(B77-20257)

Kabat, Elvin Abraham. Structural concepts in immunology and immunochemistry / [by] Elvin A. Kabat. — 2nd ed. — New York [etc.] ; London : Holt, Rinehart and Winston, 1976. — xi,547p : ill ; 25cm.
Previous ed.: 1968. — Bibl. — Index.
ISBN 0-03-089542-1 : £11.75
(B77-04164)

Methods in immunology and immunochemistry / edited by Curtis A. Williams, Merrill W. Chase. — New York [etc.] ; London : Academic Press.
Vol.5 : Antigen-antibody reactions in vivo. — 1976. — xxvi,559p : ill ; 24cm.
Index.
ISBN 0-12-754405-4 : £24.85
(B77-12441)

Sell, Stewart. Immunology, immunopathology and immunity / [by] Stewart Sell. — 2nd ed. — Hagerstown [etc.] ; London : Harper and Row, Medical Department, 1976]. — xiii,384p : ill ; 24cm.
This ed. published in the United States: 1975. — Previous ed.: 1972. — Index.
ISBN 0-06-142371-8 Pbk : £11.20
(B77-05411)

574.2'9 — Immunology. *Reviews of research*
Advances in immunology. — New York [etc.] ; London : Academic Press.
Vol.23 / edited by Henry G. Kunkel, Frank J. Dixon. — 1976 [i.e. 1977]. — xi,242p : ill ; 24cm.
Published in the United States: 1976. — Bibl. — Index.
ISBN 0-12-022423-2 : £15.95
(B77-08376)

Vol.24 / edited by Frank J. Dixon, Henry G. Kunkel. — 1976 [i.e. 1977]. — xi,338p : ill ; 24cm.
Published in the United States: 1976. — Bibl. — Index.
ISBN 0-12-022424-0 : £19.55
(B77-11214)

Contemporary topics in immunobiology. — New York ; London : Plenum Press.
Vol.5 / edited by William O. Weigle. — 1976. — xvi,341p : ill ; 24cm.
Bibl. — Index.
ISBN 0-306-37805-1 : Unpriced
ISSN 0093-4054
(B77-33795)

574.2'9 — Molecular immunology. *Reviews of research*
Contemporary topics in molecular immunology / [general editor F.P. Inman]. — New York ; London : Plenum Press.
Vol.5 / edited by H.N. Eisen and R.A. Reisfeld. — 1976. — xv,234p : ill ; 24cm.
Bibl. — Index.
ISBN 0-306-36105-1 : Unpriced
(B77-27068)

574.2'9'05 — Immunology. *Periodicals*
Developmental and comparative immunology : an international journal on immunological diversification. — New York ; Oxford : Pergamon.
Vol.1, no.1- ; Jan. 1977-. — 1977-. — ill ; 26cm.
Quarterly. — Cover title. — [1],72p. in 1st issue.
Pbk : Unpriced
ISSN 0145-305x
(B77-14234)

574.2'92 — Antigens
The **antigens.** — New York [etc.] ; London : Academic Press.
Vol.4 / edited by Michael Sela. — 1977. — xiv, 582p : ill ; 24cm.
Bibl. — Index.
ISBN 0-12-635504-5 : £29.10
(B77-23405)

574.3 — ORGANISMS. DEVELOPMENT
Berrill, Norman John. Development / [by] N.J. Berrill, Gerald Karp. — New York ; London [etc.] : McGraw-Hill, [1977]. — ix,566p : ill ; 25cm.
Published in the United States: 1976. — Bibl. — Index.
ISBN 0-07-005021-x : £13.25
(B77-14235)

574.3 — Organisms. Development. Role of control systems. *Conference proceedings*
Control mechanisms in development : activation, differentiation and modulation in biological systems / edited by Russel H. Meints and Eric Davies. — New York ; London : Plenum Press, [1976]. — xiii,226p : ill ; 26cm. — (Advances in experimental medicine and biology ; vol.62)
'Proceedings of a Symposium to inaugurate the School of Life Sciences at the University of Nebraska-Lincoln, held October 14-16, 1974' - title page verso. — Published in the United States: 1975. — Index.
ISBN 0-306-39062-0 : £12.29
(B77-04165)

574.3'1 — Organisms. Growth. Regulation. Role of hormones
Humoral control of growth and differentiation / edited by Joseph LoBue, Albert S. Gordon. — New York ; London : Academic Press.
In 2 vols.
Vol.2 : Nonvertebrate neuroendocrinology and aging. — 1973. — xiv,319p : ill ; 24cm.
Bibl. — Index.
ISBN 0-12-453802-9 : £19.55
(B77-19372)

574.5 — ECOLOGY
Dajoz, R. Introduction to ecology / [by] R. Dajoz ; translated [from the French] by A. South. — London [etc.] : Hodder and Stoughton, 1977. — vii,416p : ill, maps ; 23cm.
Translation of: 'Précis d'écologie'. 2.éd. Paris : Dunod, 1971. — 'The third edition of "Précis d'écologie" appeared after this translation had been prepared for publication. While it has not been possible to make a complete revision of the text, the section on population ecology (chapters 6, 7 and 8) has been partly rewritten' - Translator's foreword. — Bibl.: p.389-411. — Index.
ISBN 0-340-16254-6 : £7.50
ISBN 0-340-19559-2 Pbk : £3.50
(B77-05412)

Smith, Robert Leo. Elements of ecology and field biology / [by] Robert Leo Smith. — New York [etc.] ; London : Harper and Row, 1977. — xii, 497p : ill, maps ; 25cm.
Bibl.: p.459-488. — Index.
ISBN 0-06-046328-7 : £10.45
(B77-25623)

574.5 — Ecosystems
Franke, Robert G. Man and the changing environment / [by] Robert G. Franke and Dorothy N. Franke. — New York ; London [etc.] : Holt, Rinehart and Winston, [1976]. — vi,442p : ill, maps, ports ; 25cm.
Published in the United States: 1975. — Bibl. — Index.
ISBN 0-03-084714-1 : £9.25
(B77-02300)

574.5 — Ecosystems. *For East African students. Secondary school texts*
Moss, Stanley. Beginning ecology / [by] S. Moss and D. Theobald. — London [etc.] : Macmillan. — (Macmillan ecology project)
Student's workbook. — 1976. — [2],29p : ill, forms, map ; 25cm.
ISBN 0-333-19656-2 Sd : £0.25
(B77-17492)

Moss, Stanley. Beginning ecology / [by] S. Moss, D.J. Theobald. — London [etc.] : Macmillan. — (The Macmillan ecology project)
Teachers' guide. — 1976. — v,26p : ill ; 22cm.
ISBN 0-333-21131-6 Sd : £0.65
(B77-17493)

574.5 — Ecosystems. *Juvenile literature*
Billington, Elizabeth Thain. Ecology today / by Elizabeth T. Billington ; illustrations by Robert Galster. — London : Kaye and Ward, 1977. — 96p : ill, maps ; 23cm. — (Today series)
Originally published: as 'Understanding ecology'. New York : F. Warne, 1968 ; London : Kaye and Ward, 1971. — Bibl.: p.94-95.
£2.25
ISBN 0-7182-0451-4
(B77-29421)

574.5 — Ecosystems. Effects of alien animals, to 1975
Roots, Clive. Animal invaders / [by] Clive Roots. — Newton Abbot [etc.] : David and Charles, 1976. — 203p : ill, maps ; 23cm.
Bibl.: p.189-196. — Index.
ISBN 0-7153-6846-x : £5.95
(B77-02301)

574.5 — Ecosystems. Primary productivity. *Reviews of research*
Primary productivity of the biosphere / edited by Helmut Lieth and Robert H. Whittaker ; with 67 figures. — Berlin [etc.] : Springer-Verlag ; London : Distributed by Chapman and Hall, [1976]. — viii,339p : ill, maps ; 25cm. — (Ecological studies ; vol.14)
Bibl. — Index.
ISBN 0-387-07083-4 : £14.50
(B77-02302)

574.5 — Natural environment
Grzimek's encyclopedia of ecology / editor-in-chief Bernhard Grzimek ; [edited by Bernhard Grzimek, Joachim Illies, Wolfgang Klausewitz ; translated from the German by Marguerite A. Biederman-Thorson]. — New York ; London [etc.] : Van Nostrand Reinhold, 1976. — 3-705p : ill(chiefly col), maps(chiefly col), plans ; 25cm.
Col. ill. on lining papers. — Translation of: 'Unsere Unwelt als Lebensraum, ökologie'. Zürich : Kindler, 1973. — Bibl.: p.683-686. — Index.
ISBN 0-442-22948-8 : £30.00
(B77-04804)

574.5'01'84 — Ecology. Mathematical models
Pielou, Evelyn Chris. Mathematical ecology / [by] E.C. Pielou. — [2nd ed.]. — New York ; London [etc.] : Wiley, 1977. — xi,385p : ill ; 24cm.
'A Wiley-Interscience Publication'. — Previous ed.: published as 'An introduction to mathematical ecology'. New York ; London : Wiley-Interscience, 1969. — Bibl.: p.364-375. — Index.
ISBN 0-471-01993-3 : £13.00
(B77-26311)

Systems analysis and simulation in ecology / edited by Bernard C. Patten. — New York [etc.] ; London : Academic Press.
Vol.4. — 1976 [i.e. 1977]. — xx,593p : ill ; 24cm.
Published in the United States: 1976. — Bibl. — Index.
ISBN 0-12-547204-8 : £23.45
(B77-12442)

574'.5'071141 — Ecology. Postgraduate education. *Great Britain. Reports, surveys*
Natural Environment Research Council. Postgraduate training in the sciences of the natural environment / [Natural Environment Research Council]. — [London] : The Council, 1977. — [2],9p ; 30cm.
Sd : Unpriced
(B77-26312)

574.5'07'2041 — Natural environment. Research organisations. *Great Britain. Natural Environment Research Council. Reports, surveys. Serials*
Natural Environment Research Council. Report of the Council for the period 1 April-31 March ... / Natural Environment Research Council. — London : H.M.S.O.
1976-1977. — [1977]. — vi,162p : ill, chart, map ; 25cm. — ([1976-77 H.C.]567)
Index.
ISBN 0-10-256777-8 Pbk : £4.00
(B77-28613)

574.5'0967 — Ecology. *East Africa*
Berglund, Björn. Noah's ark is stranded / by Björn Berglund ; photographs by Ingemar Berling ; translated from the Swedish by Sheila La Farge. — London : Macdonald and Jane's, 1977. — xiv,210p : ill, map ; 26cm.
This translation originally published: New York : Delacorte Press, 1976. — Translation of: 'Noaks ark har strandat i gräset'. Stockholm : Forum, 1973. — Bibl.: p.207-208. — Index.
ISBN 0-354-04051-0 : £6.95
(B77-22582)

574.5'24 — Organisms. Population
Emmel, Thomas C. Population biology / [by] Thomas C. Emmel. — New York [etc.] ; London : Harper and Row, 1976. — xii,371p : ill, maps ; 25cm.
Bibl.: p.341-355. — Index.
ISBN 0-06-041904-0 : £15.95
(B77-08377)

574.5'24 — Organisms. Population. Dynamics
Ecological relationships / [by] N. Gilbert ... [et al.]. — Reading [etc.] : W.H. Freeman, 1976. — [9],157p : ill ; 23cm.
Bibl.: p.149-154. — Index.
ISBN 0-7167-0486-2 : £3.50
(B77-08378)

574.5'24 — Organisms. Population. Dynamics. *Case studies. Teaching kits*
Murphy, Patrick Joseph. Coexist : unit on population dynamics / [by] P.J. Murphy. — London : Edward Arnold [for the] Chelsea Science Simulation Project, 1975. — 2v.(16p; 16p) : ill ; 28cm.
'Students' notes' and 'Teachers' guide'. — Bibl.
ISBN 0-7131-1928-4 Sd : Unpriced
(B77-19373)

574.5'24 — Parasites. *Conference proceedings*
International Symposium on the Biochemistry of Parasites and Host-Parasite Relationships, *2nd, Beerse, 1976.* Biochemistry of parasites and host-parasite relationships : proceedings of the Second International Symposium on the Biochemistry of Parasites and Host-Parasite Relationships, Beerse, Belgium, 28 June-1 July 1976, organized by the Janssen Research Foundation / editor H. van den Bossche. — Amsterdam [etc.] ; Oxford : North-Holland Publishing Co., 1976. — xi,664p : ill ; 25cm.
Bibl. — Index.
ISBN 0-7204-0592-0 : £31.62
(B77-16381)

574.5'24 — Parasitology
Schmidt, Gerald Dee. Foundations of parasitology / [by] Gerald D. Schmidt, Larry S. Roberts. — St Louis : Mosby ; London : Distributed by Kimpton, 1977. — ix,604p : ill, facsims, maps ; 26cm.
Bibl. — Index.
ISBN 0-8016-4345-7 Pbk : Unpriced
(B77-27069)

574.5'24'0941 — Ecological communities. Monitoring. *Great Britain. Reports, surveys*
Marine Biological Surveillance Working Party. Biological surveillance : reports of the NERC [Natural Environment Research Council] Working Parties on biological surveillance in the marine, freshwater and terrestrial environments [i.e. the Marine Biological Surveillance Working Party, the Freshwater Biological Surveillance Working Party, the Terrestrial Biological Surveillance Working Party]. — London (27 Charing Cross Rd, WC2H 0AX) : N.E.R.C., 1976. — [1],iv,30,[1] p : ill, maps ; 30cm. — (Natural Environment Research Council. Publications : series B ; no.18)
ISBN 0-901875-47-3 Sd : Unpriced
(B77-11215)

574.5'26 — Urban ecosystems. *Secondary school texts*
Gilman, David. Urban ecology / [by] David Gilman. — London : Macdonald Educational, 1977. — [1],24,[1]p : ill(chiefly col) ; 27cm. — (Biology colour units)
ISBN 0-356-05523-x Pbk : £0.85
(B77-08379)

574.5'2632 — Lakes & reservoirs. Eutrophication. *Conference proceedings*
Eutrophication of lakes and reservoirs : symposium papers, September 1976. — [London] ([32 Eccleston Sq., S.W.1]) : Institution of Public Health Engineers, [1977?]. — [126]p : ill, maps ; 30cm.
Bibl.: p.B29-B33.
Pbk : Unpriced
(B77-27070)

574.5'2632 — Ponds. Ecology. *Great Britain*
Burton, Robert, *b.1941.* Ponds : their wildlife and upkeep / [by] Robert Burton. — Newton Abbot [etc.] : David and Charles, 1977. — 142p : ill ; 23cm.
Bibl.: p.139. — Index.
ISBN 0-7153-7390-0 : £3.95
(B77-28614)

574.5'2632'072 — Freshwater ecosystems. Research institutions. *Directories*
Ocean research index : a guide to ocean and freshwater research including fisheries research. — 2nd ed. / editor Allen Varley, associate editor Stella E.L. Wheeler. — [St Peter Port] : Hodgson, 1976. — 637p ; 26cm.
Previous ed.: 1970. — Bibl.: p.503-548. — Index.
ISBN 0-85280-141-6 : Unpriced
Primary classification 551.4'6'0072
(B77-23396)

574.5'2636 — Marine ecosystems
Parsons, Timothy Richard. Biological oceanographic process. — 2nd ed. / [by] Timothy R. Parsons and Masayuki Takahashi and Barry Hargrave. — Oxford [etc.] : Pergamon, 1977. — xi,332p : ill, maps ; 26cm. — (Pergamon international library)
Previous ed.: / by Timothy R. Parsons and Masayuki Takahashi. 1973. — Bibl.: p.281-323. — Index.
ISBN 0-08-021502-5 : Unpriced
ISBN 0-08-021501-7 Pbk : £7.95
(B77-27857)

574.5'2636 — Seashore ecosystems. *Juvenile literature*
Lambert, David, *b.1932.* Seashore / [by David Lambert] ; [illustrators Graham Allen, Phil Weare, Brian Pearce]. — Maidenhead : Sampson Low, 1977. — 5-44p : col ill ; 28cm. — (New horizon library)
Index.
ISBN 0-562-00066-6 : £1.75
(B77-33796)

574.5'2636 — Wet coastal ecosystems
Wet coastal ecosystems / edited by V.J. Chapman. — Amsterdam ; Oxford [etc.] : Elsevier, 1977. — xi,428p,fold plate : ill, chart, maps(2 col) ; 27cm. — (Ecosystems of the world ; 1)
Col. map on lining papers. — Bibl. — Index.
ISBN 0-444-41560-2 : £29.05
(B77-18757)

574.5'2636'08 — Marine ecosystems. *Readings*
Marine ecology : selected readings / edited by J. Stanley Cobb and Marilyn M. Harlin. — Baltimore ; London [etc.] : University Park Press, [1977]. — xi,546p : ill, maps ; 28cm.
Published in the United States: 1976. — Bibl.
ISBN 0-8391-0959-8 Pbk : £11.95
(B77-11803)

574.5'264 — Forest ecosystems & garden ecosystems. *North America. Juvenile literature*
White, William, *b.1934.* Forest and garden / [by] William H. White, Jr ; photographs by the author. — New York : Sterling [etc.] ; London : Distributed by Ward Lock, [1977]. — 96p,A-Dp of plates : ill(some col) ; 21cm. — (Living nature series)
Published in the United States: 1976. — Index.
ISBN 0-7061-2516-9 : £2.95
(B77-13038)

574.5'264 — Forests. *Juvenile literature*
Armstrong, Patrick Hamilton. Forests / by P.H. Armstrong ; with illustrations by Gerald Witcomb. — Loughborough : Ladybird Books, 1977. — 52p : col ill, col maps ; 18cm. — (Ladybird leaders)
Text, col. map on lining papers. — Index.
ISBN 0-7214-0477-4 : £0.24
(B77-25624)

Law, Felicia. Forests / written by Felicia Law ; illustrated by Annie Bennett. — London [etc.] : Collins, 1976. — 32p : col ill ; 22cm. — (Dandelions)
ISBN 0-00-651187-2 Sd : £0.50
(B77-02303)

574.5'264 — Garden ecosystems. *Great Britain*
Chinery, Michael. The natural history of the garden / [by] Michael Chinery ; with illustrations by Marjorie Blamey ... [et al.]. — London : Collins, 1977. — 287p,24p of plates : ill(some col) ; 24cm.
Bibl.: p.273-274. — Index.
ISBN 0-00-219606-9 : £4.50
(B77-18758)

574.5'264 — Mountain ecosystems. *Juvenile literature*
Condry, William. The world of a mountain / [by] William Condry ; with line drawings by Wilhelmina Mary Guymer. — London : Faber, 1977. — 3-127p : ill ; 22cm.
Bibl.: p.111-113. — Index.
ISBN 0-571-10779-6 : £3.50 : CIP rev.
(B77-23406)

574.5'264 — Roadside ecosystems. *Great Britain. Rural regions*
Burton, Robert, *b.1941.* Nature by the roadside / by Robert Burton. — Wakefield : EP Publishing, 1977. — 115p : ill ; 21cm. — (Countryside leisure)
ISBN 0-7158-0471-5 : £3.50
(B77-30255)

574.5'264 — Tree ecosystems. *Juvenile literature*
Paterson, Allen. Wonder why book of the world of a tree / [by] Allen Paterson ; illustrated by Elsie Wrigley. — London : Transworld, 1977. — [2],32p : ill(chiefly col) ; 29cm.
Spine title: The world of a tree. — Index.
ISBN 0-552-98043-9 : £1.35
ISBN 0-552-57010-9 Sd : £0.50
(B77-29422)

574.5'264 — Woodland ecosystems. *Great Britain. Juvenile literature*
Leutscher, Alfred. The ecology of woodlands / by Alfred Leutscher ; illustrated by Derick Bown. — London [etc.] : F. Watts, 1977. — 128p : ill(chiefly col) ; 18x22cm.
Index.
ISBN 0-85166-628-0 : £3.75
(B77-21864)

574.5'264 — Woodlands. *Juvenile literature*
Wrigley, Denis. The living world of the woodland / [by] Denis Wrigley. — Guildford [etc.] : Lutterworth Press, 1977. — 31,[1]p : col ill ; 22cm. — (Wrigley, Denis. Wrigley eye openers)
ISBN 0-7188-2203-x : £1.50
(B77-32630)

574.5'265 — Arid region ecosystems
Cloudsley-Thompson, John Leonard. Man and the biology of arid zones / [by] J.L Cloudsley-Thompson. — London : Edward Arnold, 1977. — ix,182p : ill, maps ; 22cm. — (Contemporary biology)
Bibl.: p.172-177. — Index.
ISBN 0-7131-2578-0 : £10.00
ISBN 0-7131-2579-9 Pbk : £4.95
(B77-15847)

574.5'4 — Phenology. *Conference proceedings*
Phenology and seasonality modeling / edited by Helmut Lieth. — London : Chapman and Hall [etc.], 1974. — xv,444p,[5] leaves of plates : ill(some col), 2 forms, maps(1 col) ; 25cm. — (Ecological studies ; vol.8)
Text, col. ill., maps on lining papers. — '... a symposium ... [was] held during the 25th Annual AIBS meeting in Minneapolis, Minnesota, in August 1972. Most of the chapters in this volume were presented as papers at the symposium' - Preface. — 'Contribution No.85, Eastern Deciduous Forest Bionne US-IBP' - title page verso. — Bibl. — Index.
ISBN 0-412-13290-7 : Unpriced
(B77-19374)

574.5'42 — Ecology. *Mediterranean climatic regions*
Mediterranean type ecosystems : origin and structure / edited by Francesco di Castri and Harold A. Mooney. — London : Chapman and Hall [etc.], 1973. — xii,405p : ill, maps ; 25cm. — (Ecological studies ; vol.7)
Bibl. — Index.
ISBN 0-412-68420-9 : Unpriced
(B77-18759)

574.5'42'0621 — Biometeorology. Organisations: International Society of Biometeorology
Links : bulletin of the International Society of Biometeorology. — Cambridge (c/o Dr M. Klinowska, Anatomy Department, Downing St., Cambridge CB2 3DY) : International Society of Biometeorology.
Vol.1, no.1- ; Autumn 1976-. — 1976-. — 21cm.
Four issues a year. — [1],14p. in 1st issue.
Sd : Unpriced
ISSN 0309-2836
(B77-08380)

574.5'43 — Seasons. *Juvenile literature*
Davies, Geoffrey. Round the year / by Geoffrey Davies ; illustrations by Ultra Art Ltd. — Edinburgh : Holmes-McDougall, [1974]. — 48p : col ill ; 21cm. — (Exploring your world : man ; section D : our surroundings ; book 3D)
Index.
ISBN 0-7157-1188-1 Pbk : Unpriced
ISBN 0-7157-1072-9 Pbk : Unpriced(non-net)
Also classified at 301.31
(B77-19375)

574.5'43 — Seasons. Ecological aspects. *Juvenile literature*
White, William, *b.1934.* The cycle of the seasons / by William White, Jr ; photographs by the author. — New York : Sterling [etc.] ; London : Distributed by Ward Lock, 1977. — 80p,[4]p of plates : ill(some col), maps ; 21cm.
Index.
ISBN 0-7061-2543-6 : £2.95
(B77-30256)

574.5'43'0941 — Organisms. Seasonal variation. *Great Britain*
Adams, Richard, *b.1920.* Nature through the seasons / [by] Richard Adams ; illustrated by David A. Goddard ; science texts by Max Hooper ; illustrated by Adrian Williams. — Harmondsworth [etc.] : Penguin, 1977. — 108, [2]p : ill(some col) ; 25cm.
Originally published: Harmondsworth : Kestrel Books, 1975. — Index.
Pbk : £1.75
ISBN 0-14-004205-9
(B77-21125)

574.6 — ECONOMIC BIOLOGY

574.6 — Organisms beneficial to man & organisms deleterious to man. *Secondary school texts*
Sanderson, Mike. Helpful and harmful organisms / [by] Mike Sanderson. — London : Macdonald Educational, 1977. — [1],24,[1]p : ill(chiefly col) ; 27cm. — (Biology colour units)
ISBN 0-356-05524-8 Pbk : £0.85
(B77-09017)

574.8 — ORGANISMS. HISTOLOGY AND CYTOLOGY

574.8 — Organisms. Cells & tissues. Development
Wessells, Norman K. Tissue interactions and development / [by] Norman K. Wessells. — Menlo Park, Calif. ; London [etc.] : Benjamin, 1977. — xi,2-276p : ill ; 24cm.
Bibl. — Index.
ISBN 0-8053-9619-5 : Unpriced
ISBN 0-8053-9620-9 Pbk : £8.00
(B77-27858)

574.8'21 — Organisms. Non-muscle tissues. Contractile processes. *Conference proceedings*
International Symposium on Contractile Systems in Non-muscle Tissues, *Bressanone, 1976.* Contractile systems in non-muscle tissues : proceedings of the International Symposium on Contractile Systems in Non-muscle Tissues, Bressanone, Italy, 19-22 September 1976, sponsored by the Consiglio Nazionale delle Ricerche / editors S.V. Perry, A. Margreth, R.S. Adelstein. — Amsterdam ; Oxford [etc.] : North-Holland Publishing Co., 1976. — xi, 360p : ill ; 25cm.
Bibl. — Index.
ISBN 0-7204-0616-1 : £18.74
(B77-16382)

574.8'7 — Cytology. *Reviews of research*
International review of cytology. — New York [etc.] ; London : Academic Press.
Vol.47 / edited by G.H. Bourne, J.F. Danielli, assistant editor K.W. Jeon. — 1976. — ix, 377p : ill ; 24cm.
Bibl. — Index.
ISBN 0-12-364347-3 : £23.05
(B77-05413)

Vol.48 / edited by G.H. Bourne, J.F. Danielli, assistant editor K.W. Jeon. — 1977. — ix, 405p : ill ; 24cm.
Bibl. — Index.
ISBN 0-12-364348-1 : £27.00
(B77-11804)

Vol.49 / edited by G.H. Bourne, J.F. Danielli, assistant editor K.W. Jeon. — 1977. — ix, 381p : ill ; 24cm.
Bibl. — Index.
ISBN 0-12-364349-x : £24.50
(B77-20258)

Methods in cell biology. — New York [etc.] ; London : Academic Press.
Vol.14 / edited by David M. Prescott. — 1976[i.e.1977]. — xxi,411p : ill ; 24cm.
Published in the United States: 1976. — Bibl. — Index.
ISBN 0-12-564114-1 : £19.20
(B77-11216)

Vol.15 / edited by David M. Prescott. — 1977. — xix,478p : ill ; 24cm.
Bibl. — Index.
ISBN 0-12-564115-x : £24.85
(B77-20259)

Vol.16 : Chromatin and chromosomal protein research. 1 / edited by Gary Stein and Janet Stein, Lewis J. Kleinsmith. — 1977. — xix, 494p : ill ; 24cm.
Index.
ISBN 0-12-564116-8 : £27.00
(B77-27071)

574.8'7 — Organisms. Cells
De Witt, William. Biology of the cell : an evolutionary approach / [by] William de Witt. — Philadelphia ; London [etc.] : Saunders, 1977. — ix,568p : ill ; 27cm.
Bibl. — Index.
ISBN 0-7216-3045-6 : £11.50
(B77-11805)

Novikoff, Alex Benjamin. Cells and organelles / [by] Alex B. Novikoff, Eric Holtzman. — 2nd ed. — New York ; London [etc.] : Holt, Rinehart and Winston, 1976. — xii,400p : ill(some col) ; 24cm. — (Modern biology series)
Previous ed.: 1970. — Bibl. — Index.
ISBN 0-03-089721-1 Pbk : £6.25
(B77-02999)

Swanson, Carl Pontius. The cell. — 4th ed. / [by] Carl P. Swanson, Peter L. Webster. — Englewood Cliffs ; London [etc.] : Prentice-Hall, 1977. — xvi,304p : ill(some col) ; 24cm. — (Prentice-Hall foundations of modern biology series)
Previous ed.: / by Carl P. Swanson. 1969. — Bibl. — Index.
ISBN 0-13-121707-0 : £10.35
ISBN 0-13-121699-6 Pbk : £7.15
(B77-28615)

574.8'7 — Organisms. Chromaffin cells, enterochromaffin cells & amine-storing mast cells. *Conference proceedings*
Chromaffin, enterochromaffin & related cells : a Naito Foundation symposium / edited by R.E. Coupland, T. Fujita. — Amsterdam ; Oxford [etc.] : Elsevier, 1976. — xiii,400p : ill ; 27cm.
'... proceedings ... held in the Naito Memorial Hall' - Preface. — Bibl. — Index.
ISBN 0-444-41448-7 : £31.25
(B77-07346)

574.8'7'028 — Cytology. *Laboratory manuals*
De Witt, William. Biology of the cell, laboratory explorations / by William De Witt and Eleanor R. Brown. — Philadelphia ; London [etc.] : Saunders, 1977. — vi,205p : ill, forms ; 26cm.
Pages perforated at inside edge. — Bibl.
ISBN 0-7216-3047-2 Pbk : £5.75
(B77-14730)

574.8'7'028 — Cytology. Laboratory techniques
New techniques in biophysics and cell biology. — London [etc.] : Wiley.
Vol.3 / edited by R.H. Pain, B.J. Smith. — 1976. — vii,245p,plate : ill(incl 2 col) ; 24cm.
'A Wiley-Interscience Publication'. — Bibl. — Index.
ISBN 0-471-01814-7 : £10.00
Primary classification 574.1'91'028
(B77-01442)

574.8'7'05 — Cytology. *Periodicals*
Cell biology international reports. — London [etc.] : Academic Press for the International Federation for Cell Biology.
Vol.1, no.1- ; Jan. 1977-. — 1977-. — ill ; 25cm.
Six issues a year. — Cover title. — [2],122p. in 1st issue.
Pbk : £10.00 yearly
ISSN 0309-1651
(B77-09697)

574.8'72 — Organisms. Cells. Ultrastructure. *Micrographs*
Student's collection of electron micrographs / selected and introduced by J.J. Head. — London : Edward Arnold, 1976. — [2],46p : of ill ; 28cm.
Originally published: s.l. : The author, 1975.
ISBN 0-7131-0084-2 Sd : £2.50
(B77-02304)

574.8'732 — Chromosomes
Rees, H. Chromosome genetics / [by] H. Rees, R.N. Jones. — London : Edward Arnold, 1977. — viii,151p : ill ; 22cm. — (Genetics, principles and perspectives ; 3)
Bibl.: p.138-146. — Index.
ISBN 0-7131-2626-4 : £10.50
ISBN 0-7131-2627-2 Pbk : £5.25
(B77-31902)

574.8'732 — Chromosomes. *Conference proceedings*
Kew Chromosome Conference, *1976.* Current chromosome research : proceedings of the Kew Chromosome Conference held at the Jodrell Laboratory, The Royal Botanic Gardens, Kew, England, July 1st-3rd, 1976 / editors K. Jones and P.E. Brandham. — Amsterdam [etc.] ; Oxford : North-Holland Publishing Co., 1976. — xv,240p : ill ; 25cm.
Index.
ISBN 0-7204-0595-5 : £14.90
(B77-04166)

574.8'732 — Organisms. Cells. Chromosomes. Effects of caffeine
Kihlman, Bengt Anders. Caffeine and chromosomes / [by] Bengt A. Kihlman. — Amsterdam [etc.] ; Oxford : Elsevier, 1977. — xviii,504p : ill ; 25cm.
Bibl.: p.417-468. — Index.
ISBN 0-444-41491-6 : £36.90
(B77-23407)

574.8'732 — Organisms. Cells. Development. Regulation. Nuclei
D'Amato, F. Nuclear cytology in relation to development / [by] F. D'Amato. — Cambridge [etc.] : Cambridge University Press, 1977. — viii,283p : ill ; 24cm. — (Developmental and cell biology series ; 6)
Bibl.: p.229-276. — Index.
ISBN 0-521-21508-0 : £15.00
(B77-26313)

574.8'732 — Organisms. Cells. Nuclei
The **cell** nucleus / edited by Harris Busch. — New York ; London : Academic Press.
In 3 vols.
Vol.3. — 1974. — xxiii,584p : ill ; 24cm.
Bibl. — Index.
ISBN 0-12-147603-0 : £34.10
(B77-06081)

574.8'732 — Organisms. Chromatin & chromosomes. Structure
Chromatin and chromosome structure / edited by Hsueh Jei Li, Ronald A. Eckhardt. — New York [etc.] ; London : Academic Press, 1977. — xiii,357p : ill ; 24cm.
ISBN 0-12-450550-3 : £11.70
(B77-20260)

574.8'732 — Organisms. Cyclic nucleotides
Cyclic 3', 5'-nucleotides : mechanisms of action / edited by Hinrich Cramer, Joachim Schultz. — London [etc.] : Wiley, 1977. — xiv,554p : ill ; 24cm.
'A Wiley-Interscience Publication'. — Bibl.: p.435-537. — Index.
ISBN 0-471-99456-1 : £17.50
(B77-29423)

574.8'732 — Organisms. DNA. Addition reactions. *Conference proceedings*
Proteins and Other Adducts to DNA : Their Significance to Aging, Carcinogenesis, and Radiation Biology *(Conference), Williamsburg, 1975.* Aging, carcinogenesis, and radiation biology : the role of nucleic acid addition reactions / edited by Kendric C. Smith. — New York ; London : Plenum Press, 1976. — xi,561p : ill ; 26cm.
'Proceedings of an International Conference entitled "Proteins and Other Adducts to DNA : Their Significance to Aging, Carcinogenesis, and Radiation Biology" held in Williamsburg, Virginia on May 2-6, 1975' - title page verso. — Bibl. — Index.
ISBN 0-306-30911-4 : £24.89
(B77-07347)

574.8'732 — Organisms. DNA. Repair. Mechanisms. *Conference proceedings*
Molecular Mechanisms for Repair of DNA *(Conference), Squaw Valley, Calif., 1974.* Molecular mechanisms for repair of DNA / edited by Philip C. Hanawalt and Richard B. Setlow. — New York ; London : Plenum Press.

Part A. — [1976]. — 481,xliii p : ill, port ; 24cm. — (Basic life sciences ; vol.5a)
'First half of the Proceedings of a workshop conference on Molecular Mechanisms for Repair of DNA held in Squaw Valley, California, February 25-March 1, 1974' - title page verso. — Published in the United States: 1975. — Bibl. — Index.
ISBN 0-306-36593-6 : £20.48
(B77-02305)

574.8'732 — Organisms. Nucleic acids. Biochemistry. *Reviews of research*
Progress in nucleic acid research and molecular biology. — New York [etc.] ; London : Academic Press.
Vol.18 / edited by Waldo E. Cohn. — 1976. — xii,339p : ill ; 24cm.
Index.
ISBN 0-12-540018-7 : £17.00
(B77-03546)

Vol.19 : mRNA : the relation of structure to function / edited by Waldo E. Cohn and Elliot Volkin. — 1976[i.e.1977]. — xxxiii,523p : ill, port ; 24cm.
Published in the United States: 1976. — Index.
ISBN 0-12-540019-5 : £24.85
(B77-11806)

574.8'734 — Organisms. Cells. Mitochondria. Biosynthesis & genetics. *Conference proceedings*
Interdisciplinary Conference on the Genetics and Biogenesis of Chloroplasts and Mitochondria, *Munich, 1976.* Genetics and biogenesis of chloroplasts and mitochondria : Interdisciplinary Conference on the Genetics and Biogenesis of Chloroplasts and Mitochondria, Munich, Germany, August 2-7, 1976, held under the auspices of the Bayerische Akademie der Wissenschaften, Mathematisch-Naturwissenschaftliche Klasse / editors Th. Bücher ... [et al.]. — Amsterdam [etc.] ; Oxford : North-Holland Publishing Co., 1976. — xiii,895p : ill ; 25cm.
Index.
ISBN 0-7204-0604-8 : £40.98
Primary classification 581.8'733
(B77-15850)

574.8'734 — Organisms. Cells. Mitochondria. Membranes. Formation
Membrane biogenesis : mitochondria, chloroplasts and bacteria / edited by Alexander Tzagoloff. — New York ; London : Plenum Press, [1976]. — xvii,460p : ill ; 24cm.
Published in the United States: 1975. — Index.
ISBN 0-306-30825-8 : £18.59
Also classified at 589.9'08'75
(B77-04167)

574.8'75 — Organisms. Cells. Membranes. Enzymes
The **enzymes** of biological membranes. — London [etc.] : Wiley.
In 4 vols.
Vol.3 : Membrane transport / edited by Anthony Martonosi. — 1976. — xv,459p : ill ; 26cm.
Originally published: New York : Plenum Press, 1976. — Bibl. — Index.
ISBN 0-471-99429-4 : £21.00
(B77-04168)

Vol.4 : Electron transport systems and receptors / edited by Anthony Martonosi. — 1976. — xv,431p : ill ; 26cm.
Originally published: New York : Plenum Press, 1976. — Bibl. — Index.
ISBN 0-471-99430-8 : £20.00
(B77-04169)

574.8'75 — Organisms. Cells. Membranes. Transport phenomena
Current topics in membranes and transport. — New York [etc.] ; London : Academic Press.
Vol.9 / edited by Felix Bronner and Arnost Kleinzeller. — 1977. — xv,394p : ill ; 24cm.
Bibl. — Index.
ISBN 0-12-153309-3 : £25.55
(B77-27072)

Water Relations in Membranes in Plants and Animals *(Conference), University of Pennsylvania, 1976.* Water relations in membrane transport in plants and animals / edited by Arthur M. Jungreis ... [et al.]. — New York [etc.] ; London : Academic Press, 1977. — xiv,393p : ill ; 24cm.
'The chapters of this book were prepared for presentation in a symposium dealing with Water Relations in Membranes in Plants and Animals, during the 27th Annual Fall Meeting of the American Physiological Society held at the University of Pennsylvania, August 17-19, 1976' - Preface. — Bibl. — Index.
ISBN 0-12-392050-7 : £12.80
(B77-26314)

574.8'75 — Organisms. Cells. Plasma membranes
Gomperts, B D. The plasma membrane : models for structure and function / [by] B.D. Gomperts. — London [etc.] : Academic Press, 1977. — ix,224p ; 24cm.
Index.
ISBN 0-12-289450-2 : £11.40
(B77-13649)

574.8'75 — Organisms. Membranes. Electrical phenomena. *Conference proceedings*
Sociétié de chimie physique. *International Meeting, 29th, Orsay, 1976.* Electrical phenomena at the biological membrane level : proceedings of the 29th International Meeting of the Société de chimie physique, Orsay, 12-15 October 1976 / edited by E. Roux. — Amsterdam ; Oxford [etc.] : Elsevier, 1977. — xv,565p : ill ; 25cm.
Includes four chapters in French.
ISBN 0-444-41572-6 : £11.91
(B77-25625)

574.8'75 — Organisms. Membranes. Enzymes
The **enzymes** of biological membranes / edited by Anthony Martonosi. — London [etc.] : Wiley.
In 4 vols.
Vol.1 : Physical and chemical techniques. — 1976. — xiii,257p : ill ; 26cm.
Originally published: New York : Plenum Press, 1976. — Bibl. — Index.
ISBN 0-471-99427-8 : £10.50
(B77-01445)

Vol.2 : Biosynthesis of cell components. — 1976. — xvii,654p : ill ; 26cm.
Originally published: New York : Plenum Press, 1976. — Bibl. — Index.
ISBN 0-471-99428-6 : £28.00
(B77-01446)

574.8'76 — Organisms. Cells. Biochemistry
Metzler, David E. Biochemistry, the chemical reactions of living cells / [by] David E. Metzler. — New York [etc.] ; London : Academic Press, 1977. — xxxiii,1129p : ill ; 24cm.
Index.
ISBN 0-12-492550-2 : £17.75
(B77-22583)

Open University. *S322 Course Team.* Enzyme kinetics ; [and], Microenvironments / prepared by an Open University Course Team [i.e. the S322 Course Team]. — Milton Keynes : Open University Press, 1977. — 66,60,41p : ill(some col) ; 30cm. — (Science, a third level course : biochemistry and molecular biology ; blocks B, C, units 5-7) (S322 ; 5-7)
With answers. — Bibl.
ISBN 0-335-04412-3 Pbk : Unpriced
Primary classification 547'.758
(B77-28597)

574.8'76 — Organisms. Cells. Hybridisation
Ringertz, Nils R. Cell hybrids / [by] Nils R. Ringertz, Robert E. Savage. — New York [etc.] ; London : Academic Press, 1976[i.e.1977]. — xiv,366p : ill ; 24cm.
Published in the United States: 1976. — Bibl.: p.301-348. — Index.
ISBN 0-12-589150-4 : £20.95
(B77-13039)

574.8'76 — Organisms. Cells. Interactions
Receptors and recognition. — London : Chapman and Hall [etc.].
Series A.2 / edited by P. Cuatrecasas and M.F. Greaves. — 1976. — viii,229p : ill ; 24cm.
Bibl.: p.152-163.
ISBN 0-412-13810-7 : £10.00
ISBN 0-412-14280-5 Pbk : Unpriced
(B77-04170)

Series A.3 / edited by P. Cuatrecasas and M.F. Greaves. — 1977. — viii,166p : ill ; 24cm.
'A Halsted Press book'. — Bibl.: p.93-100.
ISBN 0-412-14310-0 : £10.00
ISBN 0-412-14320-8 Pbk : £6.00
(B77-25626)

Receptors and recognition / general editors P. Cuatrecasas and M.F. Greaves. — London : Chapman and Hall [etc.].
Series A.4 / edited by P. Cuatrecasas and M.F. Greaves. — 1977. — xii,258p,[2]p of plates : ill ; 25cm.
Bibl.
ISBN 0-412-14330-5 : £11.50
ISBN 0-412-14340-2 Pbk : £7.50
(B77-27073)

Receptors and recognition / general editors P. Cuatrecasas and M.F. Greaves. — London : Chapman and Hall [etc.].
Series B. Vol.1 : The specificity and action of animal, bacterial and plant toxins / edited by P. Cuatrecasas. — 1977. — ix,345p : ill ; 24cm.
'A Halsted Press book'. — Bibl. — Index.
ISBN 0-412-09730-3 : £15.00
(B77-09698)

574.8'76 — Organisms. Cells. Physiology
Goodwin, Brian Carey. Analytical physiology of cells and developing organisms / [by] B.C. Goodwin. — London [etc.] : Academic Press, 1976. — x,249p : ill ; 24cm.
Bibl.: p.227-240. — Index.
ISBN 0-12-289360-3 : £8.50
(B77-06082)

Tedeschi, Henry. Cell physiology : molecular dynamics / [by] Henry Tedeschi. — New York ; London : Academic Press, 1974. — xiv, 724p : ill ; 24cm.
Bibl. — Index.
ISBN 0-12-685150-6 : Unpriced
(B77-20261)

574.8'761 — Organisms. Cells. Development. Regulation. Role of polymers. *Conference proceedings*
Society for Developmental Biology. *Symposium, 30th, Seattle, 1971.* Macromolecules regulating growth and development / edited by Elizabeth D. Hay, Thomas J. King, John Papaconstantinou. — New York ; London : Academic Press, 1974. — xi,244p : ill ; 24cm.
'The thirtieth Symposium, the Society for Developmental Biology, Seattle, Washington, June 17-19, 1971' - half title page verso. — Bibl. — Index.
ISBN 0-12-612973-8 : Unpriced
(B77-18760)

574.8'761 — Organisms. Cells. Energy metabolism
Goldsby, Richard Allen. Cells and energy / [by] Richard A. Goldsby. — 2nd ed. — New York : Macmillan ; London : Collier Macmillan, 1977. — ix,162p : ill ; 24cm.
Bibl.: p.156. — Index.
ISBN 0-02-344300-6 Pbk : £3.75
(B77-27074)

574.8'761 — Organisms. Cells in vitro. Growth, metabolism & nutrition
Growth, nutrition and metabolism of cells in culture / edited by George H. Rothblat and Vincent J. Cristofalo. — New York [etc.] ; London : Academic Press.
Vol.3. — 1977. — xiv,548p : ill ; 24cm.
Bibl. — Index.
ISBN 0-12-598303-4 : £18.45
(B77-27859)

574.8'761 — Organisms. Cells. Metabolism. Regulation. *Reviews of research*
Current topics in cellular regulation. — New York [etc.] ; London : Academic Press.
Vol.11 : 1976 / edited by Bernard L. Horecker, Earl R. Stadtman. — [1977]. — xv,251p : ill ; 24cm.
Published in the United States: 1976. — Bibl. — Index.
ISBN 0-12-152811-1 : £14.20
(B77-09018)

Vol.12 : 1977 / edited by Bernard L. Horecker, Earl R. Stadtman. — 1977. — xii,280p : ill ; 24cm.
Bibl. — Index.
ISBN 0-12-152812-x : £20.95
(B77-21865)

574.8'762 — Organisms. Eukaryotic cells. Reproduction
Prescott, David Marshall. Reproduction of eukaryotic cells / [by] David M. Prescott. — New York [etc.] ; London : Academic Press, 1976. — ix,177p : ill ; 24cm.
Bibl.: p.141-168. — Index.
ISBN 0-12-564150-8 : £8.85
(B77-08381)

574.8'764 — Organisms. Cells. Rearrangement. Mathematical models. *Readings*
Mathematical models for cell rearrangement / [G.D. Mostow, editor]. — New Haven ; London : Yale University Press, 1975 [i.e. 1976]. — ix,271p : ill ; 24cm. — ([Yale mathematical monographs])
Published in the United States: 1975. — Bibl.: p.249-271.
ISBN 0-300-01598-4 : £11.50
(B77-03000)

574.8'8 — Molecular biology
Hopfinger, Anton Joseph. Intermolecular interactions and biomolecular organization / [by] A.J. Hopfinger. — New York ; London [etc.] : Wiley, 1977. — xix,395p : ill ; 24cm.
'A Wiley-Interscience publication'. — Bibl. — Index.
ISBN 0-471-40910-3 : £19.50
(B77-20262)

574.8'8 — Molecular biology. Applications of systems analysis
Savageau, Michael A. Biochemical systems analysis : a study of function and design in molecular biology / [by] Michael A. Savageau ; with a foreword by Robert Rosen. — Reading, Mass. ; London [etc.] : Addison-Wesley, 1976. — xix,379p : ill ; 25cm.
Bibl. — Index.
ISBN 0-201-06738-2 : £21.20
ISBN 0-201-06739-0 Pbk : £13.20
(B77-16383)

574.8'8 — Organisms. Molecules. Kinetics
Norwich, Kenneth H. Molecular dynamics in biosystems : the kinetics of tracers in intact organisms / by Kenneth H. Norwich. — Oxford [etc.] : Pergamon, 1977. — xi,405p : ill ; 26cm.
With answers to selected problems. — Bibl. — Index.
ISBN 0-08-020420-1 : £22.00
(B77-23408)

574.8'8'028 — Molecular biology. Applications of electron spin resonance spectroscopy. Spin labelling
Likhtenshteĭn, G I. Spin labeling methods in molecular biology / [by] G.I. Likhtenshtein ; translated [from the Russian] by Philip S. Shelnitz. — New York ; London [etc.] : Wiley, 1976. — xiii,258p : ill ; 24cm.
'A Wiley-Interscience Publication'. — Translation of: 'Metod spinovykh metok v molekuliarnoĭ biologii'. Moskva : Nauka, 1974. — Bibl.: p.236-254. — Index.
ISBN 0-471-53415-3 : £26.00
(B77-07907)

574.9 — BIOLOGY. GEOGRAPHICAL TREATMENT
574.9 — Biogeography
Tivy, Joy. Biogeography : a study of plants in the ecosphere / [by] Joy Tivy. — Edinburgh : Oliver and Boyd, 1977. — ix,394p : ill, charts, maps ; 22cm.
Originally published: 1971. — Bibl. — Index.
ISBN 0-05-003122-8 Pbk : £3.05
(B77-28623)

574.9 — Biogeography. Organisations. *Great Britain. Biogeography Study Group. Serials*
Biogeography Study Group. Directory / Biogeography Study Group. — Newtownabbey (c/o D.W. Clement, Geography Section, Northern Ireland Polytechnic, Newtownabbey, County Antrim BT37 0QB) : [The Group].
1976 / edited by Robert A. Pullan, Jane Roberts, David W. Clement ; art by David Houghton. — [1976]. — 73p in various pagings : ill ; 30cm.
Bibl.(23p.).
Sp : Unpriced
(B77-24938)

574.909'42 — Organisms. *Coral reefs*
Campbell, Andrew Campbell. The coral seas / [by] Andrew C. Campbell. — London : Orbis Books, 1976. — 128p : ill(chiefly col) ; 31cm.
Col.ill on lining papers. — Bibl.: p.128. — Index.
ISBN 0-85613-232-2 : £4.95
(B77-06681)

574.909'46 — Organisms. *Seashore. Juvenile literature*
Kilpatrick, Cathy. Let's look at the seashore / written by Cathy Kilpatrick ; illustrated by Graham Allen ; edited by Jennifer Justice. — London : Ward Lock, 1977. — 4-29p : col ill ; 33cm.
Spine title: The seashore. — Col. ill. on lining papers. — Index.
ISBN 0-7063-5341-2 : £1.50
(B77-29424)

574.909'73'2 — Organisms. *Towns. Middle school texts*
Gilman, David. Nature in towns / [by] David Gilman. — London : Macdonald Educational, 1977. — 2-46p : ill(chiefly col) ; 25cm. — (Macdonald new reference library)
Bibl.: p.44. — Index.
ISBN 0-356-05801-8 : £1.50
(B77-30257)

574.909'9 — Space biology. *Conference proceedings*
Life sciences and space research. — Oxford [etc.] : Pergamon.
Vol.15 : Proceedings of the open meeting of the Working Group on Space Biology of the Nineteenth Plenary Meeting of COSPAR, Philadelphia, Pennsylvania, USA, 8-19 June 1976 / scientific editor R. Holmquist ; executive editor A.C. Stickland. — 1977. — ix, 316p,plate : ill(incl 1 col) ; 26cm.
Index.
ISBN 0-08-021635-8 : Unpriced
(B77-27075)

574.92 — Marine benthic organisms. *Conference proceedings*
European Symposium on Marine Biology, *11th, Galway, 1976.* Biology of benthic organisms : 11th European Symposium on Marine Biology, Galway, October 1976 / edited by B.F. Keegan and P. Ó Céidigh and P.J.S. Boaden. — Oxford [etc.] : Pergamon, 1977. — xxxiii,630p : ill, charts, maps ; 26cm.
Includes 8 papers in French, English abstracts. — Bibl.
ISBN 0-08-021378-2 : £27.50
(B77-30258)

574.92 — Marine biology. *Reviews of research*
Advances in marine biology. — London [etc.] : Academic Press.
Vol.14 / edited by Sir Frederick S. Russell and Sir Maurice Yonge. — 1976. — xii,497p,plate : ill(incl 1 col), maps ; 24cm.
Bibl. — Index.
ISBN 0-12-026114-6 : £19.20
(B77-06682)

Oceanography and marine biology : an annual review. — [Aberdeen] : Aberdeen University Press.
Vol.15 / Harold Barnes, editor. — 1977. — 3-571p,leaf of plate,[2]p of plates : ill, maps ; 26cm.
Bibl. — Index.
ISBN 0-900015-39-x : £28.00
ISSN 0078-3218
Primary classification 551.4'6
(B77-31889)

574.92 — Marine organisms
Marvels and mysteries of the seas. — London [etc.] : Reader's Digest Association, 1977. — [1],33p : ill(chiefly col), col maps ; 21cm.
Sd : £0.40
(B77-30259)

574.92 — Marine organisms. *Juvenile literature*
Barthelemy, Georgette. Secrets of the sea / [by Georgette Barthelemy] ; [translated from the French by Richard Marsden] ; [illustrations Jean Reschofsky]. — London : Marshall Cavendish, 1974. — 5-77p : col ill, col map ; 27cm. — (A question and answer book) (A 'Golden hands' book)
Ill. on lining papers. — Translation of: 'La mer et ses secrets'. Paris : Nathan, 1972.
ISBN 0-85685-079-9 : £1.25
(B77-18761)

574.92'1 — Marine research stations. *Atlantic region. Directories*
Royal Society. *Naples Zoological Station Committee.* Guide to the marine stations of the North Atlantic and European waters / compiled on behalf of the Royal Society's Naples Zoological Station Committee by J.E. Webb. — London : Royal Society.
Part 3 : Iceland, the West Atlantic Coast and the Caribbean Sea : with supplement to parts 1 and 2. — 1977. — 256p : maps ; 22cm.
ISBN 0-85403-090-5 Pbk : £4.85
Primary classification 574.92'13
(B77-29425)

574.92'13 — Marine biology. Organisations. *North-east Atlantic Ocean. Porcupine. Periodicals*
Porcupine. Porcupine newsletter. — South Shields ([c/o F.R. Woodward, South Shields Museum, Ocean Rd, South Shields, Tyne and Wear) : [Porcupine].
Vol.1, no.1- ; Nov. 1976-. — 1976-. — 30cm.
Three issues a year. — 6p. in 1st issue.
Sd : Unpriced
ISSN 0309-3085
(B77-10366)

574.92'13 — Marine research stations. *Western Europe. Coastal regions. Directories*
Royal Society. *Naples Zoological Station Committee.* Guide to the marine stations of the North Atlantic and European waters / compiled on behalf of the Royal Society's Naples Zoological Station Committee by J.E. Webb. — London : Royal Society.
Part 3 : Iceland, the West Atlantic Coast and the Caribbean Sea : with supplement to parts 1 and 2. — 1977. — 256p : maps ; 22cm.
ISBN 0-85403-090-5 Pbk : £4.85
Also classified at 574.92'1
(B77-29425)

574.92'5'76 — Marine organisms. *Queensland. Great Barrier Reef*
Gillett, K. The Australian Great Barrier Reef in colour / [by] K. Gillett. — Sydney [etc.] ; London : A.H. and A.W. Reed, 1976. — 112p : ill(chiefly col), maps ; 18x19cm. — ([Reed colourbook series])
Ill. on lining papers. — Originally published: 1968. — Index.
ISBN 0-589-07009-6 : £4.75
(B77-18762)

574.92'9'41 — Organisms. *Great Britain. Rivers*
Angel, Heather. Life in our rivers / photographs and text Heather Angel. — Norwich : Jarrold and Sons, 1977. — [33]p : col ill ; 20cm. — (Jarrold nature series : fresh and saltwater life)
Index.
ISBN 0-85306-718-x Sd : £0.40
(B77-27076)

574.941 — Organisms. *Great Britain. Estuaries*
Angel, Heather. Life in our estuaries / text and photographs by Heather Angel. — Norwich : Jarrold and Sons, 1977. — [33]p : chiefly col ill ; 20cm. — (Jarrold aquatic life series ; book 2)
Index.
ISBN 0-85306-672-8 Sd : £0.40
(B77-12443)

574.941 — Organisms. *Great Britain. Juvenile literature*
In the country. — St Ives, Cornwall : Pike, 1974. — 31p : ill ; 26cm. — (Look learn projects)
Fill-in book. — With answers. — '... with a merit award certificate'.
ISBN 0-85932-053-7 Sd : £0.30
(B77-18763)

574.941 — Organisms. *Great Britain. Seashore. Illustrations. Juvenile literature*
Mills, Caroline. Henry discovers - the seaside / [by Caroline Mills]. — London (27 Chancery La., WC2A 1NF) : Foxwood Publishing Ltd, 1977. — [7]leaves,[2]p(1 fold) : of col ill ; 25x20cm. — (Turn-over picture books) (Foxcub books)
Leaves in 3 separated horizontal segments. — Notebook format.
ISBN 0-904897-48-6 Sp : £1.25
(B77-28616)

574.9422'357 — Organisms. *Kent. Broadstairs. Seashore. Juvenile literature*
Reynolds, Christopher. Creatures of the bay / written and illustrated by Christopher Reynolds. — London : Target Books, 1975. — 148p : ill ; 20cm.
Originally published: London : Deutsch, 1974. — Index.
ISBN 0-426-10823-x Pbk : £0.40
(B77-19376)

574.9422'51 — Country parks. *East Sussex. Wealden (District). Seven Sisters Country Park. Organisms. Walkers' guides. Periodicals*
Wildlife : what to look for in Seven Sisters Country Park / East Sussex [County Planning Department]. — Lewes (Southover House, Southover Rd, Lewes, [E. Sussex] BN7 1YA) : [The Department].
[No.1]- : [Jan. 1977]-. — [1977]-. — ill ; 30cm.
Six issues a year. — Folder ([4]p.) as Feb./Mar. 1977 issue.
ISBN 0-900348-56-9 : £0.10
(B77-15848)

574.9422'67 — Organisms. *West Sussex. Pagham Harbour*
The natural history of Pagham Harbour. — [Bognor Regis] ([c/o V. Cavill, Seven Apples, Fish La., Bognor Regis, W. Sussex]) : Bognor Regis Natural Science Society.
Part 2 : Plants and animals other than birds and mammals / edited by R.W. Rayner ; [line drawings by E.M. Venables and I. Kraunsoe]. — 1975. — 69p,plate : ill, maps ; 24cm.
Part 1 published: without work title as 'The birds and mammals of Pagham Harbour' / by W.W.A. Phillips. 1965.
ISBN 0-9500652-4-2 Sd : £1.00
(B77-00220)

574.9423'41 — Organisms. *Jersey*
Le Sueur, Frances. A natural history of Jersey / by Frances le Sueur ; with illustrations by Richard le Sueur. — London [etc.] : Phillimore, 1976. — x,221p,plate : ill(incl 1 col), maps ; 23cm.
Bibl.: p.207-210. — Index.
ISBN 0-85033-238-9 : £4.75
(B77-24219)

574.9423'5 — Organisms. *Devon. Wetlands*
Devon wetlands : a guide to some of Devon's estuaries, lakes, canals and other wet places / [compiled by P.J. Hunt and G.L. Wills, with assistance from A.E. Symmons ; for the Conservation Section of the Devon County Planning Department]. — [Exeter] ([County Hall, Exeter EX2 4QH]) : Devon County Council, [1977]. — v,86p : ill, maps ; 25cm.
'Water & wildlife' - cover.
Sd : £1.00
(B77-21126)

574.9424'97 — Organisms. *West Midlands (Metropolitan County). Olton, to 1906. Diaries. Facsimiles*
Holden, Edith, *b.1871.* The country diary of an Edwardian lady : a facsimile reproduction of a naturalist's diary for the year 1906 / Edith Holden recorded in words and paintings the flora and fauna of the British countryside through the changing seasons of the year. — London : Joseph ; Exeter : Webb and Bower, 1977. — [5],177,[9]p : col ill ; 24cm.
ISBN 0-7181-1581-3 : £5.50
(B77-23409)

574.9425'9 — Organisms. *Buckinghamshire. Rural regions*
Uttley, Alison. A year in the country / by Alison Uttley ; illustrated by C.F. Tunnicliffe. — London : H. Baker, 1976. — 222p : ill ; 23cm.
Originally published: London : Faber, 1957.
ISBN 0-7030-0100-0 : £3.75
(B77-11807)

574.9426'7 — Organisms. *South-east Essex*
The wild life of South East Essex / edited by John F. Skinner. — [Southend-on-Sea] ([c/o Central Library, Victoria Ave., Southend-on-Sea, Essex SS2 6ER]) : Museums Service, Borough of Southend-on-Sea, 1976. — 41p : ill ; 21cm. — (Southend-on-Sea Museums Service. Publications ; no.18)
Bibl.: p.41.
ISBN 0-900690-13-5 Sd : £0.40
(B77-02306)

574.9429 — Organisms. *Wales. Reports, surveys. Serials*
Biological Recording Working Group for Wales. Reports and records of field meetings / Biological Recording Working Group for Wales. — Cardiff : National Museum of Wales.

1974-1975 / editors James A. Bateman, June E. Chatfield. — 1976. — [3],145[i.e.153]p : maps ; 30cm.
ISBN 0-7200-0098-x Pbk : Unpriced
(B77-28617)

574.967 — Organisms. Distribution. *Africa. Tropical regions. For West African students*
Bishop, Owen Neville. The distribution of organisms / [by] O.N. Bishop. — London [etc.] : Macmillan Education, 1977. — [1],iv,28,[1]p : ill, maps ; 22cm. — (Advanced readers in tropical biology)
ISBN 0-333-21396-3 Sd : £0.41
(B77-13040)

574.978 — Organisms. *South-western United States. Deserts. Personal observations*
Krutch, Joseph Wood. The desert year / [by] Joseph Wood Krutch ; decorations by Rudolf Freund. — Harmondsworth [etc.] : Penguin, 1977. — [13],270p : ill ; 20cm.
Originally published: New York : Sloane, 1952.
ISBN 0-14-004448-5 Pbk : Unpriced
(B77-11808)

574.979 — Marine organisms. *California. Coastal waters*
North, Wheeler J. Underwater California / by Wheeler J. North ; with sections on underwater photography by Robert Hollis ; illustrated by Laurence G. Jones. — Berkeley [etc.] ; London : University of California Press, 1976. — [3],276p,[8]p of plates : ill(some col), charts ; 21cm. — (California natural history guides ; 39)
Bibl.: p.259-265. — Index.
ISBN 0-520-03025-7 : £8.00
ISBN 0-520-03039-7 Pbk : £4.75
(B77-14731)

574.9794 — Organisms. *California. Deserts. Personal observations*
Cowles, Raymond Bridgman. Desert journal : a naturalist reflects on arid California / by Raymond B. Cowles, in collaboration with Elna S. Bakker ; foreword by Robert C. Stebbins ; illustrations by Gerhard Bakker ; photographs by Raymond B. Cowles and Roy Pence. — Berkeley [etc.] ; London : University of California Press, 1977. — xv,263p : ill, map ; 23cm.
Ill. on lining papers. — Index.
ISBN 0-520-02879-1 : £8.25
(B77-23410)

574.9795 — Organisms. *Pacific Northwest*
Kozloff, Eugene Nicholas. Plants and animals of the Pacific Northwest : an illustrated guide to the natural history of Western Oregon, Washington and British Columbia / by Eugene N. Kozloff. — Seattle ; London : University of Washington Press, 1976. — ix,264p,48p of plates : ill(some col), map ; 26cm.
Bibl.: p.248-252. — Index.
ISBN 0-295-95449-3 : £12.00
(B77-04171)

574.999 — Extraterrestrial life
Collyns, Robin. Laser beams from star cities? / [by] Robin Collyns. — London : Sphere, 1977. — 144p,[12]p of plates : ill, port ; 18cm.
Originally published: London : Pelham, 1975. — Bibl.: p.141-144.
ISBN 0-7221-2457-0 Pbk : £0.75
(B77-20263)

Ridpath, Ian. Signs of life : the search for life in space / [by] Ian Ridpath. — Revised ed. — Harmondsworth [etc.] : Penguin, 1977. — 190p : ill, map, ports ; 20cm. — (Peacock books)
Also published: Harmondsworth : Kestrel Books, 1977. — Previous ed.: published as 'Worlds beyond'. London : Wildwood House, 1975. — Bibl.: p.181-182. — Index.
ISBN 0-14-047104-9 Pbk : £1.25
(B77-27860)

Shklovskiĭ, Iosif Samuilovich. Intelligent life in the universe / [by] I.S. Shklovskii and Carl Sagan ; authorized translation [from the Russian] by Paula Fern. — London : Pan Books, 1977. — xvi,509p : ill ; 20cm. — (Picador)
This translation originally published: San Francisco : Holden-Day, 1966. — Translation, extension and revision of: 'Vselennaia, zhizn' razum'. Moskva : Izd-vo Akademii nauk SSSR, 1962. — Bibl.: p.489-495. — Index.
ISBN 0-330-25125-2 Pbk : £1.75
(B77-28618)

Tomas, Andrew. On the shores of endless worlds : the search for cosmic life / [by] Andrew Tomas. — London : Sphere, 1975. — 175p ; 18cm.
Originally published: London : Souvenir Press, 1974. — Bibl.: p.168-171. — Index.
ISBN 0-7221-8556-1 Pbk : £0.85
(B77-31189)

574.999 — Extraterrestrial life. Theories
Jonas, Doris. Other senses, other worlds / [by] Doris Jonas and David Jonas. — London : Cassell, 1976. — 240p ; 22cm.
Also published: New York : Stein and Day, 1976. — Bibl.: p.231-234. — Index.
ISBN 0-304-29762-3 : £4.50
(B77-10367)

575 — EVOLUTION
Grzimek's encyclopedia of evolution / editor-in-chief Bernhard Grzimek. — English ed. / [general editor George M. Narita ; translator David R. Martinez]. — New York ; London [etc.] : Van Nostrand Reinhold, 1976. — 560p : ill(chiefly col), maps, ports ; 25cm.
Col. ill. on lining papers. — Previous ed.: published in German. Zürich : Kindler, 1972. — Bibl.: p.542-544. — Index.
ISBN 0-442-22963-1 : £32.50
(B77-02307)

McAlester, Arcie Lee. The history of life / [by] A. Lee McAlester. — 2nd ed. — Englewood Cliffs ; London [etc.] : Prentice-Hall, 1977. — [7],168p : ill, facsim, map, port ; 24cm. — (Prentice-Hall foundations of earth science series)
Previous ed.: 1968. — Bibl.: p.159-160. — Index.
ISBN 0-13-390146-7 : £7.15
ISBN 0-13-390120-3 Pbk : £3.15
(B77-23411)

Savage, Jay Mathers. Evolution / [by] Jay M. Savage. — 3rd ed. — New York ; London [etc.] : Holt, Rinehart and Winston, 1977. — viii,184p : ill, maps ; 24cm. — (Modern biology series)
Previous ed.: New York : Holt, Rinehart and Winston, 1969. — Bibl. — Index.
ISBN 0-03-089536-7 Pbk : £3.50
(B77-20264)

Stansfield, William D. The science of evolution / [by] William D. Stansfield. — New York : Macmillan ; London : Collier Macmillan, 1977. — viii,614p : ill, maps, ports ; 26cm.
Bibl.: p.580-588. — Index.
ISBN 0-02-415750-3 : £12.00
(B77-21127)

Stebbins, George Ledyard. Processes of organic evolution / [by] G. Ledyard Stebbins. — 3rd ed. — Englewood Cliffs ; London [etc.] : Prentice-Hall, 1977. — xiii,269p : ill, port ; 24cm. — (Concepts of modern biology series)
Previous ed.: 1971. — Bibl.: p.259-261. — Index.
ISBN 0-13-723452-x Pbk : £6.00
(B77-26315)

575 — Speciation
Endler, John A. Geographic variation, speciation, and clines / [by] John A. Endler. — Princeton ; Guildford : Princeton University Press, 1977. — ix,246p : ill, map ; 23cm. — (Monographs in population biology ; 10)
Bibl.: p.187-239. — Index.
ISBN 0-691-08187-5 : £12.00
ISBN 0-691-08192-1 Pbk : £5.45
(B77-29426)

575'.008 — Evolution. *Essays*
Mayr, Ernst. Evolution and the diversity of life : selected essays / [by] Ernst Mayr. — Cambridge, Mass. ; London : Belknap Press of Harvard University Press, 1976 [i.e. 1977]. — xi,721p : ill, maps ; 24cm.
Published in the United States: 1976. — Bibl. — Index.
ISBN 0-674-27104-1 : £14.95
(B77-11809)

575'.0092'4 — Evolution. Darwin, Charles. Sickness
Colp, Ralph. To be an invalid : the illness of Charles Darwin / [by] Ralph Colp, Jr. — Chicago ; London : University of Chicago Press, 1977. — xiii,285p,[15]p of plates : ill, ports ; 24cm.
Bibl.: p.171-173. — Index.
ISBN 0-226-11401-5 : £10.25
(B77-31190)

575.01 — Evolution. Theories
Gould, Stephen Jay. Ontogeny and phylogeny / [by] Stephen Jay Gould. — Cambridge, Mass. ; London : Belknap Press of Harvard University Press, 1977. — xv,501p : ill ; 24cm.
Bibl.: p.441-477. — Index.
ISBN 0-674-63940-5 : £12.65
(B77-27861)

Melling, Leonard. Anatomy of existence / by Leonard Melling. — London [etc.] : Torch Publishing Co., 1977. — 232p,[2]leaves of plates : ill ; 23cm.
£4.50
(B77-28619)

575.01'6 — Evolution. Theories, ca 1850-1975
Wolsky, Maria de Issekutz. The mechanism of evolution : a new look at old ideas / [by] Maria de Issekutz Wolsky and Alexander Wolsky. — Basel ; London [etc.] : Karger ; [Chichester] : [Distributed by Wiley], 1976. — vii,160p : 3 ill ; 23cm. — (Contributions to human development ; 4)
Bibl.: p.154-160.
Pbk : Unpriced
ISBN 3-8055-2347-5
(B77-03547)

575.01'66'0924 — Evolution. Theories of Lamarck, Jean Baptiste
Burkhardt, Richard W. The spirit of system : Lamarck and evolutionary biology / [by] Richard W. Burkhardt, Jr. — Cambridge, Mass. ; London : Harvard University Press, 1977. — [11],285p : ill, facsim, ports ; 25cm.
Bibl.: p.261-280. — Index.
ISBN 0-674-83317-1 : £11.55
(B77-27077)

575.1 — Evolution. Genetic factors
Chai, Chen Kang. Genetic evolution / [by] Chen Kang Chai. — Chicago ; London : University of Chicago Press, 1976. — xviii,341p : ill ; 25cm.
Bibl.: p.299-323. — Index.
ISBN 0-226-10066-9 : £13.60
(B77-00221)

Theories of plant and animal breeding ; [and], Ecological and evolutionary genetics / [prepared by a Course Team for the Open University]. — [Milton Keynes] : Open University Press, [1976]. — p555-615,plate : ill(some col), maps, col port ; 30cm. — (Science, a second level course : genetics ; 12, 13) (S299 ; 12, 13)
Cover title. — With answers to in-text and self-assessment questions. — Bibl.
Pbk : Unpriced
Also classified at 575.1; 631.5'3; 636.08'21
(B77-04172)

575.1 — Genetics
Baer, Adela Swenson. The genetic perspective / [by] Adela S. Baer. — Philadelphia ; London [etc.] : Saunders, 1977. — xi,279p : ill, ports ; 27cm.
Bibl. — Index.
ISBN 0-7216-1471-x : £10.50
(B77-24220)

Handbook of genetics / Robert C. King, editor. — New York ; London : Plenum Press.
Vol.3 : Invertebrates of genetic interest. — [1976]. — xiv,874p,[6]fold p of plates,[2]fold leaves of plates : ill, maps ; 26cm.
Published in the United States: 1975. — Bibl. — Index.
ISBN 0-306-37613-x : £31.19
(B77-00222)

Vol.4 : Vertebrates of genetic interest. — [1976] . — xiv,669p,fold leaf : ill ; 26cm.
Published in the United States: 1975. — Bibl. — Index.
ISBN 0-306-37614-8 : £31.19
(B77-04173)

Herskowitz, Irwin Herman. Principles of genetics / [by] Irwin H. Herskowitz. — 2nd ed. — New York : Macmillan ; London : Collier Macmillan, 1977. — xxiv,836p : ill, map, ports ; 26cm.
With answers to selected questions and problems. — Previous ed.: 1973. — Bibl. — Index.
ISBN 0-02-353930-5 : £12.75
(B77-27862)

Mackean, Donald Gordon. Introduction to genetics / [by] D.G. Mackean. — 3rd ed. — London : J. Murray, 1977. — [6],42p : ill ; 30cm.
Previous ed.: 1971. — Bibl.: p.41. — Index.
ISBN 0-7195-3346-5 Pbk : £1.40
(B77-18137)

Strickberger, Monroe Wolf. Genetics / by Monroe W. Strickberger. — 2nd ed. — New York : Macmillan ; London : Collier Macmillan.
Previous ed.: 1968.
Answer manual. — 1976. — viii,159p : ill ; 24cm.
ISBN 0-02-418110-2 Pbk : £0.95
(B77-12444)

575.1 — Genetics. *Reviews of research*
Advances in genetics. — New York [etc.] ; London : Academic Press.
Vol.19 / edited by E.W. Caspari. — 1977. — vii,585p : ill ; 24cm.
Bibl. — Index.
ISBN 0-12-017619-x : £31.60
(B77-22584)

575.1 — Genetics. *Secondary school texts*
Roberts, Michael Wyn. Genetics / [by] M.W. Roberts. — Plymouth : Macdonald and Evans, 1977. — vi,90p : ill ; 19cm. — (The M. & E. handbook series)
Bibl.: p.72. — Index.
ISBN 0-7121-0729-0 Pbk : £1.25
(B77-22585)

575.1 — Organisms. Adaptation. Genetic aspects
Ford, Edmund Brisco. Genetics and adaptation / [by] E.B. Ford. — London : Edward Arnold, 1976. — v,58p : ill ; 22cm. — (Institute of Biology. Studies in biology ; no.69)
Bibl.: p.57-58.
ISBN 0-7131-2562-4 : £2.60
ISBN 0-7131-2563-2 Pbk : £1.30
(B77-01447)

575.1 — Population genetics. *Study regions: Great Britain*
Berry, Robert James. Inheritance and natural history / [by] R.J. Berry ; with 12 colour photographs, 19 photographs in black and white and 110 line drawings. — London : Collins, 1977. — 350p,12p of plates : ill(some col), facsim, maps ; 23cm. — (The new naturalist ; [61])
Bibl.: p.311-338. — Index.
ISBN 0-00-219084-2 : £6.50
(B77-33797)

575.1 — Population genetics. Ecological aspects
Theories of plant and animal breeding ; [and], Ecological and evolutionary genetics / [prepared by a Course Team for the Open University]. — [Milton Keynes] : Open University Press, [1976]. — p555-615,plate : ill(some col), maps, col port ; 30cm. — (Science, a second level course : genetics ; 12, 13) (S299 ; 12, 13)
Cover title. — With answers to in-text and self-assessment questions. — Bibl.
Pbk : Unpriced
Primary classification 575.1
(B77-04172)

575.1 — Population genetics. Evolutionary aspects
Wright, Sewall. Evolution and the genetics of populations : a treatise in four volumes / [by] Sewall Wright. — Chicago ; London : University of Chicago Press.
Vol.3 : Experimental results and evolutionary deductions. — 1977. — [7],613p : ill ; 24cm.
Bibl.: p.563-597. — Index.
ISBN 0-226-91051-2 : £24.50
(B77-25627)

575.1'01'84 — Genetics. Mathematical models
Edwards, Anthony William Fairbank. Foundations of mathematical genetics / [by] A.W.F. Edwards. — Cambridge [etc.] : Cambridge University Press, 1977. — viii,119p : ill ; 23cm.
Bibl.: p.111-116. — Index.
ISBN 0-521-21325-8 : £5.80
(B77-09019)

575.2'1 — Gene expression. Regulation. *Conference proceedings*
Molecular Mechanisms in the Control of Gene Expression *(Conference), Keystone, 1976.* Molecular Mechanisms in the Control of Gene Expression / edited by Donald P. Nierlich, W.J. Rutter, C. Fred Fox. — New York [etc.] ; London : Academic Press, 1976 [i.e. 1977]. — xi,655p : ill ; 24cm. — (ICN-UCLA symposia on molecular and cellular biology ; vol.5)
'The ICN-UCLA conference on Molecular Mechanisms in the Control of Gene Expression, organized through the Molecular Biology Institute of UCLA, was held in Keystone, Colorado, March 21 to 26, 1976' - Preface. — Published in the United States: 1976. — Index.
ISBN 0-12-518550-2 : £20.25
(B77-13041)

575.2'1 — Genes. Recombination. Mechanisms
Catcheside, David Guthrie. The genetics of recombination / [by] D.G. Catcheside. — London : Edward Arnold, 1977. — x,172p : ill ; 23cm. — (Genetics, principles and perspectives ; 2)
Bibl.: p.161-168. — Index.
ISBN 0-7131-2612-4 : £11.50
ISBN 0-7131-2613-2 Pbk : £5.75
(B77-29427)

575.2'1 — Molecular genetics
Fincham, John Robert Stanley. Microbial and molecular genetics / [by] J.R.S. Fincham. — 2nd ed. — London [etc.] : Hodder and Stoughton [etc.], 1976. — viii,150p : ill ; 23cm.
Previous ed.: London : English Universities Press, 1965. — Bibl.: p.139-144. — Index.
ISBN 0-340-18067-6 : £3.95
ISBN 0-340-18068-4 Pbk : £2.45
(B77-01448)

575.2'1 — Organisms. Population. Chromosomes. Variation. Genetic aspects
John, Bernard. Population cytogenetics / [by] Bernard John. — London : Edward Arnold, 1976. — [4],76p : ill, maps ; 22cm. — (Institute of Biology. Studies in biology ; no.70)
Bibl.: p.75-76.
ISBN 0-7131-2596-9 : £3.00
ISBN 0-7131-2597-7 Pbk : £1.50
(B77-03548)

575.2'92'072 — Organisms. Mutation. Research, to 1975
Auerbach, Charlotte. Mutation research : problems, results and perspectives / [by] Charlotte Auerbach. — London : Chapman and Hall [etc.], 1976. — xxviii,504p : ill ; 24cm.
'A Halsted Press book'. — Bibl.: p.469-471. — Index.
ISBN 0-412-11280-9 : £10.50
(B77-07348)

576 — MICROORGANISMS
Carpenter, Philip Lewis. Microbiology / [by] Philip L. Carpenter. — 4th ed. — Philadelphia ; London [etc.] : Saunders, 1977. — ii-xi,512p,iv p of plates : ill(some col), map, ports ; 27cm.
Text on lining papers. — Previous ed.: 1972. — Bibl. — Index.
ISBN 0-7216-2438-3 : £10.00
(B77-24221)

Hunter, Peter. General microbiology : the student's textbook / [by] Peter Hunter. — Saint Louis : Mosby ; London : Distributed by Kimpton, 1977. — ix,366p : ill ; 26cm.
With answers. — Index.
ISBN 0-8016-2313-8 Pbk : £8.05
(B77-22586)

Stanier, Roger Yate. The microbial world. — 4th ed. / [by] Roger Y. Stanier, Edward A. Adelberg, John L. Ingraham. — Englewood Cliffs ; London [etc.] : Prentice-Hall, [1977]. — xix,871p : ill, ports ; 25cm.
This ed. published in the United States: 1976. — Previous ed.: / by Roger Y. Stanier, Michael Doudoroff, Edward A. Adelberg. 1970. — Bibl. — Index.
ISBN 0-13-581025-6 : £18.00
(B77-07908)

576 — Microbiology
Pelczar, Michael Joseph. Microbiology. — 4th ed. / [by] Michael J. Pelczar, Jr, Roger D. Reid, E.C.S. Chan. — New York ; London [etc.] : McGraw-Hill, 1977. — vii,952p,[8]p of plates : ill(some col), maps, ports ; 24cm.
Text, ill. on lining papers. — Previous ed.: / by Michael J. Pelczar, Jr, Roger D. Reid. 1972. — Bibl. — Index.
ISBN 0-07-049229-8 : £13.50
(B77-21866)

Stanier, Roger Yate. General microbiology. — 4th ed. / [by] Roger Y. Stanier, Edward A. Adelberg, John L. Ingraham. — London [etc.] : Macmillan, 1977. — xix,871p : ill, ports ; 24cm.
This ed. originally published: Englewood Cliffs : Prentice-Hall, 1976. — Previous ed.: / by Roger Y. Stanier, Michael Doudoroff, Edward A. Adelberg. 1971. — Bibl. — Index.
ISBN 0-333-22013-7 : £15.00
ISBN 0-333-22014-5 Pbk : £7.95
(B77-17494)

576 — Microorganisms. Cells. Ultrastructure
Society for Applied Bacteriology. *Autumn Demonstration Meeting, University College, London, 1974.* Microbial ultrastructure : the use of the electron microsope / edited by R. Fuller and D.W. Lovelock. — London [etc.] : Academic Press, 1976. — xv,340p : ill ; 24cm. — (Society for Applied Bacteriology. Technical series ; no.10)
' ... contributions made to the 1974 Autumn Demonstration Meeting of the Society for Applied Bacteriology ... [held at] University College, London' - Preface. — Bibl. — Index.
ISBN 0-12-269450-3 : £10.80
(B77-06083)

576 — Microorganisms. Protoplasts. *Conference proceedings*
International Symposium on Yeast and Other Protoplasts, *4th, University of Nottingham, 1975.* Microbial and plant protoplasts / edited by J.F. Peberdy ... [et al.]. — London [etc.] : Academic Press, 1976. — xii,370p : ill ; 24cm.
' ... Proceedings of the Fourth International Symposium on Yeast and Other Protoplasts held in the University of Nottingham, England in September 1974' - Preface. — Index.
ISBN 0-12-549050-x : £7.80
Primary classification 581.8'73
(B77-02309)

576 — Schools. Microorganisms used in teaching. *Great Britain*
Schools Council Educational Use of Living Organisms Project. Micro-organisms / Schools Council Educational Use of Living Organisms [Project] ; author Peter Fry, contributors B. Bainbridge, G. Holt. — London [etc.] : Hodder and Stoughton, 1977. — 64p : ill ; 25cm.
Bibl.: p.63-64.
ISBN 0-340-17052-2 Sd : £2.45
(B77-26316)

576'.028 — Microbiology. *Laboratory manuals*
Smith, Alice Lorraine. Microbiology : laboratory manual and workbook / [by] Alice Lorraine Smith. — 4th ed. — Saint Louis : Mosby ; London : Distributed by Kimpton, 1977. — ix, 179p : ill ; 27cm.
Pages perforated at inside edge. — Pierced for binder. — Previous ed.: 1973. — Bibl.: p.11-12.
ISBN 0-8016-4706-1 Pbk : £5.60
(B77-20265)

576'.028 — Microbiology. Laboratory techniques. *Reviews of research*
Methods in microbiology. — London [etc.] : Academic Press.
Vol.9 / edited by J.R. Norris. — 1976. — xv, 251p : ill ; 24cm.
Bibl. — Index.
ISBN 0-12-521509-6 : £9.00
(B77-04805)

576'.028 — Microorganisms. Continuous culture. *Conference proceedings*
International Symposium on Continuous Culture of Micro-organisms, *6th, St Catherine's College, Oxford, 1975.* Continuous culture 6 : applications and new fields / editors A.C.R. Dean ... [et al.]. — Chichester : Ellis Horwood for the Society of Chemical Industry : Distributed by Wiley, 1976. — xi,364p : ill ; 24cm.
'(This monograph has evolved from the 6th International Symposium on Continuous Culture of Micro-organisms, St Catherine's College, Oxford, July 1975.)'. — Bibl. — Index.
ISBN 0-85312-055-2 : £15.50
(B77-12445)

576'.028'53 — Microbiology. Laboratory techniques. Automation. *Conference proceedings*
International Symposium on Rapid Methods and Automation in Microbiology, *2nd, Cambridge, 1976.* 2nd International Symposium on Rapid Methods and Automation in Microbiology, Cambridge, England, September 19th-25th, 1976 / edited by H.H. Johnston, S.W.B. Newsom. — Oxford [etc.] (Woodside House, Hinksey Hill, Oxford) : Learned Information (Europe) Ltd, 1976. — xii,318p : ill ; 31cm.
Cover title: Rapid methods and automation in microbiology. — Bibl. — Index.
ISBN 0-904933-03-2 : Unpriced
(B77-27079)

576'.07'8 — Schools. Teaching. Use of microorganisms. *England*
Great Britain. *Department of Education and Science.* The use of micro-organisms in schools / Department of Education and Science. — London : H.M.S.O., 1977. — 35p ; 22cm. — (Education pamphlet ; no.61)
Bibl.: p.29-31. — Index.
ISBN 0-11-270391-7 Sd : £0.95
(B77-30260)

576'.09 — Microbiology, to 1975
Collard, Patrick. The development of microbiology / [by] Patrick Collard. — Cambridge [etc.] : Cambridge University Press, 1976. — vii,201p : ill, ports ; 24cm.
Bibl. — Index.
ISBN 0-521-21177-8 : £6.50
(B77-00762)

576'.11 — Microorganisms. Physiology. *Reviews of research*
Advances in microbial physiology. — London [etc.] : Academic Press.
Vol.14 / edited by A.H. Rose, D.W. Tempest. — 1976. — x,416p : ill ; 24cm.
Bibl. — Index.
ISBN 0-12-027714-x : £14.20
(B77-03549)

Vol.15 / edited by A.H. Rose, D.W. Tempest. — 1977. — x,445p : ill ; 24cm.
Bibl. — Index.
ISBN 0-12-027715-8 : £18.50
(B77-27080)

576'.11'9121 — Microorganisms. Bioenergetics. *Conference proceedings*
Microbial energetics / edited by B.A. Haddock and W.A. Hamilton. — Cambridge [etc.] : Cambridge University Press for the Society for General Microbiology, 1977. — ix,442p : ill ; 24cm. — (Society for General Microbiology. Symposia ; 27th)
'... held at Imperial College London March 1977'. — Bibl. — Index.
ISBN 0-521-21494-7 : £17.50
(B77-14236)

576'.15 — Microorganisms. Ecological communities
Campbell, Richard. Microbial ecology / [by] R. Campbell. — Oxford [etc.] : Blackwell Scientific, 1977. — vii,148p : ill ; 24cm. — (Basic microbiology ; vol.5)
Bibl. — Index.
ISBN 0-632-00389-8 Pbk : £4.25 : CIP rev.
(B77-10368)

576'.15 — States of matter. Interfaces. Adaptation of microorganisms
Marshall, K C. Interfaces in microbial ecology / [by] K.C. Marshall. — Cambridge, Mass. ; London : Harvard University Press, 1976. — xiii,156p : ill ; 24cm.
Bibl.: p.129-152. — Index.
ISBN 0-674-45822-2 : £9.40
(B77-05414)

576'.16 — Applied microbiology. *Reviews of research*
Advances in applied microbiology. — New York [etc.] ; London : Academic Press.
Vol.20 / edited by D. Perlman. — 1976 [i.e. 1977]. — ix,373p : ill ; 24cm.
Published in the United States: 1976. — Bibl. — Index.
ISBN 0-12-002620-1 : £20.95
(B77-09020)

Vol.21 / edited by D. Perlman. — 1977. — x, 292p : ill ; 24cm.
Bibl. — Index.
ISBN 0-12-002621-x : Unpriced
(B77-18138)

576'.163'028 — Food. Contaminants: Microorganisms. Identification. Laboratory techniques. *Manuals*
Harrigan, Wilkie Francis. Laboratory methods in food and dairy microbiology / [by] W.F. Harrigan and Margaret E. McCance. — Revised ed. / prepared by W.F. Harrigan. — London [etc.] : Academic Press, 1976. — xii, 452p : ill ; 24cm.
Previous ed.: published as 'Laboratory methods in microbiology'. 1966. — Bibl.: p.407-430. — Index.
ISBN 0-12-326040-x : £9.20
(B77-07349)

576'.19'0948 — Soil microorganisms
Alexander, Martin. Introduction to soil microbiology / [by] Martin Alexander. — 2nd ed. — New York ; London [etc.] : Wiley, 1977. — xi,467p : ill ; 24cm.
Previous ed.: 1961. — Bibl. — Index.
ISBN 0-471-02179-2 : £13.50
(B77-23412)

576'.19'2 — Aquatic microbiology. *Reviews of research*
Advances in aquatic microbiology. — London [etc.] : Academic Press.
Vol.1 / edited by M.R. Droop, H.W. Jannasch. — 1977. — ix,381p : ill ; 24cm.
Bibl. — Index.
ISBN 0-12-003001-2 : £14.50
ISSN 0140-2625
(B77-28620)

576'.64 — Viruses. *Reviews of research*
Advances in virus research. — New York [etc.] ; London : Academic Press.
Vol.21 / edited by Max A. Lauffer ... [et al.]. — 1977. — ix,409p : ill, maps ; 24cm.
Bibl. — Index.
ISBN 0-12-039821-4 : £20.95
(B77-20266)

576'.64 — Viruses. Reproduction. Control systems. *Conference proceedings*
Control processes in virus multiplication / edited by D.C. Burke and W.C. Russell. — Cambridge [etc.] : Cambridge University Press for the Society for General Microbiology, 1975. — ix,449p,4,2,4p of plates : ill ; 24cm. — (Society for General Microbiology. Symposia ; 25)
'Held at Imperial College London, April 1975'. — Bibl. — Index.
ISBN 0-521-20728-2 : £9.00
(B77-18764)

576'.6484 — Animals. Pathogens: Viruses
Animal virology / edited by David Baltimore, Alice S. Huang, C. Fred Fox. — New York [etc.] ; London : Academic Press, 1976. — xiii, 824p : ill ; 24cm. — (ICN-UCLA symposia on molecular and cellular biology ; vol.4) (Academic Press rapid manuscript reproduction)
Index.
ISBN 0-12-077350-3 : £18.00
(B77-05415)

576'.6484 — Insects. Parasites: Viruses
Smith, Kenneth Manley. Virus-insect relationships / [by] Kenneth M. Smith. — London [etc.] : Longman, 1976. — viii,291p : ill ; 24cm.
Bibl.: p.241-277. — Index.
ISBN 0-582-46612-1 : £11.00
(B77-04174)

578 — BIOLOGY. MICROSCOPY
578.4 — Microscopy. Quantitative methods. *For biology. Conference proceedings*
Analytical and quantitative methods in microscopy / edited by G.A. Meek and H.Y. Elder. — Cambridge [etc.] : Cambridge University Press, 1977. — vii,276p : ill ; 24cm. — (Society for Experimental Biology. Seminar series ; 3)
Proceedings of an SEB symposium. — Bibl. — Index.
ISBN 0-521-21404-1 : £12.00
ISBN 0-521-29141-0 Pbk : £4.75
(B77-25628)

578'.4'5 — Biology. Electron microscopy
Grimstone, Albert Victor. The electron microscope in biology / [by] A.V. Grimstone. — 2nd ed. — London : Edward Arnold, 1977. — [5],65p : ill ; 22cm. — (Institute of Biology. Studies in biology ; no.9)
Previous ed.: 1968. — Bibl.: p.64-65.
ISBN 0-7131-2610-8 : £3.00
ISBN 0-7131-2611-6 Pbk : £1.50
(B77-15290)

578'.4'5 — Biology. Scanning electron microscopy
Principles and techniques of electron microscopy : biological applications / edited by M.A. Hayat. — New York ; London [etc.] : Van Nostrand Reinhold.
Vol.7. — 1977. — xxi,383p : ill, ports ; 24cm.
Bibl. — Index.
ISBN 0-442-25691-4 : £22.30
(B77-21128)

579 — BIOLOGICAL SPECIMENS. COLLECTION AND PRESERVATION
579 — Dragonflies. Collecting. *Manuals*
Keen, David. Collecting and studying dragonflies (Odonata) / by David Keen. — Revised ed. — Hanworth : Amateur Entomologists' Society, 1977. — [7],24p : ill ; 22cm. — (Amateur Entomologists' Society. Leaflets ; no.12)
Appendix II. Folder ([2] leaves) as insert. — Previous ed.: published as 'Collecting dragonflies' / by A.F. O'Farrell. 1945. — Bibl.: p.22.
Sd : Unpriced
(B77-31905)

579'.4 — Birds. Taxidermy. *Manuals*
Harrison, James Maurice. Bird taxidermy / by James M. Harrison. — [1st ed. reprinted] ; [with addendum edited by Jeffery Harrison]. — Newton Abbot [etc.] : David and Charles, 1976. — xvii,67p,viii p of plates : ill ; 20cm.
Originally published: London : Marshall, 1964. — Bibl.: p.66. — Index.
ISBN 0-7153-7372-2 : £2.95
(B77-11217)

579'.4 — Museums. *West Sussex. Arundel. Potter's Museum of Curiosity. Exhibits. Catalogues*
Potter's Museum of Curiosity. Potter's Museum of Curiosity, 6 High Street, Arundel, Sussex / [text by Walter Potter, James Cartland and the 'Saturday book']. — Derby : English Life Publications, 1977. — [2],18p : ill(some col), port ; 20cm.
ISBN 0-85101-119-5 Sd : £0.25
(B77-11810)

580 — BOTANICAL SCIENCES
580'.744'42195 — Botanical gardens. *London. Richmond upon Thames (London Borough). Royal Botanic Gardens, Kew. Plants*
King, Ronald, *b.1914.* The world of Kew / [by] Ronald King. — London [etc.] : Macmillan, 1976. — 128p : ill(some col), facsims, 2 maps(1 col), ports(some col) ; 30cm.
Col. ill., col. map on lining papers. — Index.
ISBN 0-333-18572-2 : £6.95
(B77-02308)

581 — BOTANY
581 — Plants
Arnett, Ross Harold. Plant biology : a concise introduction. — 4th ed. / [by] Ross H. Arnett, Jr, George F. Bazinet, Jr. — Saint Louis : Mosby ; London : Distributed by Kimpton, 1977. — xii,553p : ill, facsim, maps ; 26cm.
Previous ed.: published as 'An introduction to plant biology' / by Ross H. Arnett, Dale C. Braungart. 1970. — Bibl. — Index.
ISBN 0-8016-0316-1 Pbk : £8.90
(B77-21867)

Bold, Harold Charles. The plant kingdom / [by] Harold C. Bold. — 4th ed. — Englewood Cliffs ; London [etc.] : Prentice-Hall, 1977. — x,310p : ill ; 23cm. — (Prentice-Hall foundations of modern biology series)
Previous ed.: 1970. — Bibl.: p.299-301. — Index.
ISBN 0-13-680389-x Pbk : £6.35
(B77-21129)

The **encyclopedia** of the plant kingdom / [botanical editor Anthony Huxley]. — London [etc.] : Hamlyn, 1977. — 240p : ill(chiefly col) ; 31cm. — (A salamander book)
Col. ill. on lining papers. — Bibl.: p.240. — Index.
ISBN 0-600-33134-2 : £4.95
(B77-31191)

Norstog, Knut. Plant biology / [by] Knut Norstog, Robert W. Long. — Philadelphia ; London [etc.] : Saunders, 1976. — vi,585p : ill, maps, ports ; 27cm.
Bibl. — Index.
ISBN 0-7216-6864-x : £5.00
(B77-01449)

Norstog, Knut. Plant biology / [by] Knut Norstog, Robert W. Long. — Philadelphia ; London [etc.] : Saunders.
A laboratory manual for elementary botany / [by] Robert W. Long, Knut Norstog. — 1976. — v,231p : ill, forms, maps ; 26cm.
Pages perforated at inside edge. — Bibl.: p.7.
ISBN 0-7216-5791-5 Pbk : £10.25
(B77-01450)

Skellern, Claire. Basic botany / [by] Claire Skellern and Paul Rogers. — Plymouth : Macdonald and Evans, 1977. — xii,192p : ill ; 19cm. — (The M. & E. handbook series)
Index.
ISBN 0-7121-0255-8 Pbk : £1.75
(B77-21130)

581 — Plants. *Juvenile literature*
Stonehouse, Bernard. A closer look at plant life / [by] Bernard Stonehouse ; illustrated by Richard Orr, Philip Weare, Gary Hincks. — London : Hamilton, 1977. — 32p : ill(chiefly col), col map ; 27cm. — (A closer look book ; 20)
Index.
ISBN 0-241-89556-1 : £1.75
(B77-27081)

581 — Plants. *Reviews of research*
Commentaries in plant science / edited by Harry Smith. — Oxford [etc.] : Pergamon, 1976. — ix,286p : ill ; 26cm.
'The articles were published originally in ... "Current Advances in Plant Science" between March 1973 and December 1975 ... ' - Preface. — Bibl. — Index.
ISBN 0-08-019759-0 : £9.00
(B77-04175)

581 — Plants. Aesthetic aspects
Bager, Bertel. Nature as designer : a botanical art study / [by] Bertel Bager ; [translated from the Swedish by Albert Read]. — London : F. Warne, 1976. — 3-176p : ill ; 26cm.
This translation originally published: 1967. — Translation of: 'Naturen som formgivare'. Stockholm : Nordisk Rotograyr, 1955.
ISBN 0-7232-0035-1 : £6.95
(B77-25629)

581 — Plants. Psychic powers
Bolton, Brett L. The secret powers of plants / [by] Brett L. Bolton. — London : Abacus, 1975. — 174p,[8]p of plates : ill, 2 ports ; 20cm.
Originally published: New York : Berkley Publishing, 1974. — Bibl.: p.167-170. — Index.
ISBN 0-349-10342-9 Pbk : £1.00
(B77-14732)

581'.01'2 — Plants. Classification by Tzeltal. *Mexico. Chiapas (State). Highlands*
Berlin, Brent. Principles of Tzeltal plant classification : an introduction to the botanical ethnography of a Mayan-speaking people of highland Chiapas / [by] Brent Berlin, Dennis E. Breedlove, Peter H. Raven. — New York ; London : Academic Press, 1974. — xxiii,660p : ill, maps, port ; 27cm. — (Language, thought and culture)
Bibl.: p.619-621. — Index.
ISBN 0-12-785047-3 : Unpriced
(B77-19377)

581'.092'2 — Botanists. *Great Britain, to 1977. Biographical dictionaries*
Desmond, Ray. Dictionary of British and Irish botanists and horticulturists : including plant collectors and botanical artists / by Ray Desmond ; with historical introduction by William T. Stearn. — London : Taylor and Francis, 1977. — xxvi,747p ; 26cm.
Bibl.: p.xv-xxiii. — Index.
ISBN 0-85066-089-0 : £40.00
Also classified at 635'.092'2
(B77-28621)

581'.092'4 — Botany. Henslow, John Stevens. *Biographies*
Russell-Gebbett, Jean P. Henslow of Hitcham : botanist, educationalist and clergyman / by Jean Russell-Gebbett. — Lavenham : T. Dalton, 1977. — 139p,[24]p of plates : ill, facsims, map(on lining papers), ports ; 23cm.
Index.
ISBN 0-900963-76-x : £4.40
(B77-33798)

581.1 — PLANTS. PHYSIOLOGY
Plant structure, function and adaptation / edited by M.A. Hall. — London [etc.] : Macmillan, 1976. — xii,443p : ill ; 24cm.
Bibl. — Index.
ISBN 0-333-14763-4 : £7.95
(B77-06683)

581'.1 — Plants. Physiology. Ecological aspects
Bannister, Peter. Introduction to physiological plant ecology / [by] P. Bannister. — Oxford [etc.] : Blackwell Scientific, 1976. — ix,273p : ill ; 22cm.
Bibl.: p.227-252. — Index.
ISBN 0-632-08980-6 Pbk : £4.75
(B77-03001)

581.1'028 — Plants. Physiology. Experiments. *Laboratory manuals*
Roberts, J. Practical plant physiology / [by] J. Roberts, D.G. Whitehouse. — London [etc.] : Longman, 1976. — xii,161p : ill ; 22cm.
Index.
ISBN 0-582-44127-7 Pbk : £4.95
(B77-04176)

581.1'33 — Plants. Nitrogen. Fixation
A **treatise** on dinitrogen fixation / general editor R.W.F. Hardy. — New York ; London [etc.] : Wiley.
Section 3 : Biology / section III editor W.S. Silver. — 1977. — xiii,675p : ill ; 24cm.
'A Wiley-Interscience publication'. — Index.
ISBN 0-471-35138-5 : £25.00
(B77-25630)

Section 4 : Agronomy and ecology / editor A.H. Gibson. — 1977. — xiii,527p : ill, maps ; 24cm.
'A Wiley-Interscience publication'. — Index.
ISBN 0-471-02343-4 : £23.00
(B77-25631)

581.1'3342 — Plants. Photosynthesis
Gregory, Richard Paul Fitzgerald. Biochemistry of photosynthesis / [by] R.P.F. Gregory. — 2nd ed. — London [etc.] : Wiley, 1977. — xiv, 221p : ill ; 24cm.
'A Wiley-Interscience Publication'. — With answers. — Previous ed.: 1971. — Bibl.: p.200-208. — Index.
ISBN 0-471-32676-3 : £8.50
(B77-08382)

Hall, David Oakley. Photosynthesis / [by] D.O. Hall and K.K. Rao. — 2nd ed. — London : Edward Arnold, 1977. — [4],71p,[4]p of plates : ill ; 22cm. — (Institute of Biology. Studies in biology ; no.37)
Previous ed.: 1972. — Bibl.: p.69-71.
ISBN 0-7131-2620-5 : £2.80
ISBN 0-7131-2621-3 Pbk : £1.40
(B77-17495)

581.1'5 — Plants. Gene expression
Molecular aspects of gene expression in plants / edited by J.A. Bryant. — London [etc.] : Academic Press, 1976. — ix,338p : ill ; 24cm. — (Experimental botany ; vol.11)
Bibl.: p.299-326. — Index.
ISBN 0-12-138150-1 : £9.60
(B77-09021)

581.1'5 — Plants. Genetic engineering. *Conference proceedings*
NATO Advanced Study Institute on Genetic Manipulations with Plant Material, *Liège, 1974.* Genetic manipulations with plant material / edited by Lucien Ledoux. — New York ; London : Plenum Press [for the] NATO Scientific Affairs Division, [1976]. — xiii,601p : ill ; 26cm. — (NATO Advanced Study Institutes : series A, life sciences ; vol.3)
'Lectures presented at the 1974 NATO Advanced Study Institute on Genetic Manipulations with Plant Material, held in Liège, Belgium, Summer 1974' - title page verso. — Published in the United States: 1975. — Bibl. — Index.
ISBN 0-306-35603-1 : £30.24
(B77-03550)

581.1'51 — Plants. Cells. Genetics
Moore, David Moresby. Plant cytogenetics / [by] D.M. Moore. — London : Chapman and Hall [etc.], 1976. — 64p : ill, maps ; 21cm. — (Outline studies in biology)
Bibl.: p.62-63. — Index.
ISBN 0-412-13440-3 Pbk : £1.30
(B77-00763)

581.1'9'12 — Plants. Transport phenomena. *Conference proceedings*
Transport and transfer processes in plants : proceedings of a symposium held under the auspices of the US-Australia Agreement for Scientific and Technical Cooperation, Canberra, Australia, December 1975 / edited by I.F. Wardlaw and J.B. Passioura. — New York [etc.] ; London : Academic Press, 1976. — xvii, 484p : ill ; 24cm.
Bibl. — Index.
ISBN 0-12-734850-6 : £11.90
(B77-07350)

581.1'9'2 — Plants. Biochemistry
Plant biochemistry / edited by James Bonner, Joseph E. Varner. — 3rd ed. — New York [etc.] ; London : Academic Press, [1977]. — xvii,925p : ill ; 24cm.
This ed. published in the United States: 1976. — Previous ed.: New York : Academic Press, 1965. — Bibl. — Index.
ISBN 0-12-114860-2 : £17.40
(B77-11811)

581.1'9'2 — Plants. Biochemistry. *Reviews of research*
Plant biochemistry II / edited by D.H. Northcote. — Baltimore ; London [etc.] : University Park Press, 1977. — ix,262p : ill ; 24cm. — (International review of biochemistry ; vol.13)
Index.
ISBN 0-8391-1077-4 : £21.25
(B77-29428)

Progress in phytochemistry. — Oxford [etc.] : Pergamon.
Vol.4 / edited by L. Reinhold, J.B. Harborne, T. Swain. — 1977. — vii,289p : ill ; 24cm.
Index.
ISBN 0-08-021004-x : £16.50
(B77-18765)

Recent advances in phytochemistry. — New York ; London : Plenum Press.
Vol.9 / edited by V.C. Runeckles. — [1976]. — ix,309p : ill ; 24cm.
'Proceedings of the Fourteenth Annual Meeting of the Phytochemical Society of North America held in August 1974 at Western Carolina University in Cullowhee, North Carolina' - title page verso. — Published in the United States: 1975. — Index.
ISBN 0-306-34709-1 : £17.33
(B77-03551)

581.1'9'245 — Plants. Proteins. Biochemistry. *Conference proceedings*
The **chemistry** and biochemistry of plant proteins : proceedings of the Phytochemical Society symposium, University of Ghent, Belgium, September, 1973 / edited by J.B. Harborne and C.F. van Sumere. — London [etc.] : Academic Press, 1975. — xiii,326p : ill ; 24cm. — (Phytochemical Society. Annual proceedings of the Phytochemical Society ; no.11) (Phytochemical Society. Symposia series ; no.11)
Bibl. — Index.
ISBN 0-12-324668-7 : £11.60
(B77-18766)

581.2 — PLANTS. DISEASES
581.2 — Plants. Diseases. *Reviews of research*
Plant disease : an advanced treatise. — New York [etc.] ; London : Academic Press.
In 5 vols.
Vol.1 : How disease is managed / edited by James G. Horsfall, Ellis B. Cowling. — 1977. — xxi,465p : ill ; 24cm.
Bibl. — Index.
ISBN 0-12-356401-8 : £20.60
(B77-27083)

581.2'3 — Plants. Diseases caused by microorganisms. Biochemical aspects. *Conference proceedings*
Biochemical Aspects of Plant Parasite Relationships *(Conference), University of Hull, 1975.* Biochemical aspects of plant-parasite relationships : proceedings of the Phytochemical Society symposium, University of Hull, England, April 1975 / edited by J. Friend and D.R. Threlfall. — London [etc.] : Academic Press, 1976. — xiv,354p : ill ; 24cm. — (Phytochemical Society. Annual proceedings of the Phytochemical Society ; no.13) (Phytochemical Society. Symposia series ; no.13)
'... Phytochemical Society Symposium held at Hull in April, 1975, on Biochemical Aspects of Plant Parasite Relationships ...' - Preface. — Bibl. — Index.
ISBN 0-12-267950-4 : £10.80
(B77-05416)

581.2'3 — Plants. Diseases caused by microorganisms. Specificity. *Conference proceedings*
NATO Advanced Study Institute on Specificity in Plant Diseases, *Alghero, 1975.* Specificity in plant diseases / edited by R.K.S. Wood and A. Graniti. — New York ; London : Plenum Press [for the] NATO Scientific Affairs Division, 1976. — ix,354p : ill ; 26cm. — (NATO Advanced Study Institutes : series A, life sciences ; vol.10)
'Lectures presented at the NATO Advanced Study Institute on Specificity in Plant Diseases, held in Porto Conte, nr. Alghero (Sardinia), Italy, May 4-17, 1975' - title page verso. — Bibl. — Index.
ISBN 0-306-35610-4 : £22.05
(B77-18767)

581.2'3 — Plants. Pathogens: Microorganisms
Dickinson, Colin Hedley. Plant pathology and plant pathogens / [by] C.H. Dickinson, J.A. Lucas. — Oxford [etc.] : Blackwell Scientific, 1977. — x,161p : ill ; 24cm. — (Basic microbiology ; vol.6)
Bibl. — Index.
ISBN 0-632-00399-5 Pbk : £4.25 : CIP rev.
(B77-10369)

581.2'32 — Plants. Resistance to bacteria & fungi
Deverall, Brian James. Defence mechanisms of plants / by Brian J. Deverall. — Cambridge [etc.] : Cambridge University Press, 1977. — vii,110p : ill ; 23cm. — (Cambridge monographs in experimental biology ; no.19)
Bibl.: p.89-105. — Index.
ISBN 0-521-21335-5 : £5.50
(B77-05417)

581.3 — PLANTS. DEVELOPMENT
581.3'1 — Plants. Growth. Effects of light. *Conference proceedings*
Easter School in Agricultural Science, *22nd, University of Nottingham, 1975.* Light and plant development / [edited by] H. Smith. — London [etc.] : Butterworth, 1976. — [12], 516p : ill ; 24cm.
'... proceedings of the 22nd University of Nottingham Easter School in Agricultural Science which was held at Sutton Bonington from April 7th to 10th, 1975' - Preface. — Bibl. — Index.
ISBN 0-408-70719-4 : Unpriced
(B77-00223)

581.3'1 — Plants. Growth. Effects of light. Role of phytochrome
Kendrick, Richard E. Phytocrome and plant growth / [by] Richard E. Kendrick, Barry Frankland. — London : Edward Arnold, 1976. — [4],68p : ill ; 22cm. — (Institute of Biology. Studies in biology ; no.68)
Bibl.: p.67-68.
ISBN 0-7131-2560-8 : £3.00
ISBN 0-7131-2561-6 Pbk : £1.50
(B77-01451)

581.3'1 — Plants. Roots. Growth. Role of soils
Russell, R Scott. Plant root systems : their function and interaction with the soil / [by] R. Scott Russell. — London [etc.] : McGraw-Hill, 1977. — xiii,298p : ill ; 24cm. — (European plant biology series)
Bibl. — Index.
ISBN 0-07-084068-7 : £10.00 : CIP rev.
(B77-08383)

581.3'34 — Vascular plants. Embryos. Development
Raghavan, V. Experimental embryogenesis in vascular plants / [by] V. Raghavan. — London [etc.] : Academic Press, 1976. — x,603p : ill ; 24cm. — (Experimental botany ; vol.10)
Bibl.: p.462-565. — Index.
ISBN 0-12-575450-7 : £21.00
(B77-09022)

581.5 — PLANTS. ECOLOGY
581.5'09794 — Plants. Ecology. *California*
Terrestrial vegetation of California / edited by Michael G. Barbour, Jack Major. — New York ; London [etc.] : Wiley, 1977. — xi, 1002p : ill, maps ; 26cm.
'A Wiley-Interscience publication'. — Text on lining paper. — Col. map (fold. sheet) in pocket. — Bibl. — Index.
ISBN 0-471-56536-9 : £35.65
(B77-25632)

581.5'24 — Plants. Interactions with insects. Evolutionary aspects
Bernays, Elizabeth A. Some evolutionary aspects of the insect-host plant relationship / [by] Elizabeth A. Bernays. — Ilford : Central Association of Bee-keepers, 1976. — [1],15p : ill ; 21cm. — (Central Association of Bee-keepers. Lectures)
'A lecture given to the Central Association of Bee-keepers on 12th February 1976' - note.
ISBN 0-900909-51-x Sd : £0.55
Primary classification 595.7'05'24
(B77-11223)

581.5'24 — Plants. Population
Harper, John Lander. Population biology of plants / [by] John L. Harper. — London [etc.] : Academic Press, 1977. — xxvi,892p : ill(some col) ; 24cm.
Bibl.: p.779-828. — Index.
ISBN 0-12-325850-2 : £30.00
(B77-25633)

581.5'24'09411 — Plants. Ecological communities. *Scotland. Lowland regions. Reports, surveys*
Birse, Eric Leslie. Plant communities and soils of the lowland and southern upland regions of Scotland / by E.L. Birse and J.S. Robertson ; with a chapter on post-glacial change in vegetation by S.E. Durno. — Aberdeen (Craigiebuckler, Aberdeen AB9 2QJ) : Macaulay Institute for Soil Research, 1976. — [9],226p : ill, maps ; 25cm. — (Soil Survey of Great Britain (Scotland). Monographs)
Bibl.: p.79-83.
ISBN 0-902701-05-3 Pbk : £6.00
Primary classification 631.4'9411
(B77-00812)

581.5'24'094137 — Plants. Ecological communities. *Scotland. Southern Uplands. Reports, surveys*
Birse, Eric Leslie. Plant communities and soils of the lowland and southern upland regions of Scotland / by E.L. Birse and J.S. Robertson ; with a chapter on post-glacial change in vegetation by S.E. Durno. — Aberdeen (Craigiebuckler, Aberdeen AB9 2QJ) : Macaulay Institute for Soil Research, 1976. — [9],226p : ill, maps ; 25cm. — (Soil Survey of Great Britain (Scotland). Monographs)
Bibl.: p.79-83.
ISBN 0-902701-05-3 Pbk : £6.00
Primary classification 631.4'9411
(B77-00812)

581.5'265 — Industrial waste land. Plants. Ecology. *Great Britain*
Gemmell, Raymond P. Colonization of industrial wasteland / [by] Raymond P. Gemmell. — London : Edward Arnold, 1977. — [4],75p : ill ; 22cm. — (Institute of Biology. Studies in biology ; no.80)
Bibl.: p.73-75.
ISBN 0-7131-2586-1 : £3.20
ISBN 0-7131-2587-x Pbk : £1.60
(B77-31906)

581.6 — ECONOMIC BOTANY
581.6'1 — Plants useful to man
Gordon, Lesley. Green magic : flowers, plants & herbs in lore & legend / [by] Lesley Gordon. — [London] : Ebury Press, 1977. — 200p : ill(some col), facsims(1 col), ports ; 25cm.
Bibl.: p.193-195. — Index.
ISBN 0-85223-117-2 : £6.95
Primary classification 398'.368
(B77-30162)

Mabey, Richard. Plants with a purpose : a guide to the everyday uses of wild plants / [by] Richard Mabey ; with 8 colour plates and 79 line drawings by Marjorie Blamey. — London : Collins, 1977. — 176p,8p of plates : ill(some col) ; 23cm.
Bibl.: p.166-170. — Index.
ISBN 0-00-219117-2 : £4.50
(B77-30261)

581.6'1'097 — Plants of use to man. *North America*
Saunders, Charles Francis. Edible and useful wild plants of the United States and Canada / [by] Charles Francis Saunders ; illustrated with photographs by the author and with drawings by Lucy Hamilton Aring. — Revised ed. — New York : Dover Publications [etc.] ; London : Constable, 1976. — v-xvi,275p,[16] leaves of plates : ill ; 21cm.
Facsimile reprint. — This ed. originally published: as 'Useful wild plants of the United States and Canada'. New York : McBride, 1934. — Index.
ISBN 0-486-23310-3 Pbk : £2.15
(B77-13042)

581.6'32'0941 — Edible plants. *Great Britain*
Ceres. Free for all : weeds and wild plants as a source of food / by Ceres ; drawings by Alison Ross. — Wellingborough : Thorsons, 1977. — 128p : ill ; 23cm.
Index.
ISBN 0-7225-0366-0 : £3.25
ISBN 0-7225-0349-0 Pbk : £1.75
(B77-30262)

Eley, Geoffrey. 101 wild plants for the kitchen / by Geoffrey Eley. — Wakefield : EP Publishing, 1977. — 71p : ill ; 24cm. — (Invest in living)
Bibl.: p.69. — Index.
ISBN 0-7158-0489-8 Pbk : £1.45
(B77-25634)

581.6'34 — Medicinal plants
Bianchini, Francesco. 'The kindly fruits' / [by] F. Bianchini and F. Corbetta ; English adaptation [i.e. translation] by M.A. Dejey ; illustrations by Marilena Pistoia. — London : Cassell, 1977. — 3-242p : col ill ; 31cm.
Translation of: 'Le piante della salute'. Milano : Mondadori, 1975. — Bibl.: p.235. — Index.
ISBN 0-304-29790-9 : £12.50
(B77-10370)

Le Strange, Richard. A history of herbal plants / [by] Richard le Strange ; illustrated by Derek Cork ; foreword by Anthony Huxley. — London [etc.] : Angus and Robertson, 1977. — xxi,304p : ill ; 25cm.
Ill. on lining papers. — Bibl.: p.283-287. — Index.
ISBN 0-207-95645-6 : £8.00
(B77-22587)

Schauenberg, Paul. Guide to medicinal plants / [by] Paul Schauenberg, Ferdinand Paris ; from a translation [from the French] by Maurice Pugh Jones ; colour illustrations by Violette Niestle, line illustrations by Paul Schauenberg. — Guildford [etc.] : Lutterworth Press, 1977. — 349p,39p of plates : ill(chiefly col) ; 21cm.
Translation of 'Guide des plantes médicinales'. 2. éd. revisé et augmentée. Neuchâtel : Delachaux et Niestlé, 1974. — Index.
ISBN 0-7188-2261-7 : £5.95
(B77-27863)

581.6'5 — Plants dangerous to man
Tampion, John. Dangerous plants / [by] John Tampion. — Newton Abbot [etc.] : David and Charles, 1977. — 176p : ill ; 24cm.
Bibl.: p.166-167. — Index.
ISBN 0-7153-7375-7 : £4.95
(B77-19378)

581.6'5 — Weeds
Hill, Thomas Anthony. The biology of weeds / [by] Thomas A. Hill. — London : Edward Arnold, 1977. — iv,64p : ill ; 23cm. — (Institute of Biology. Studies in biology ; no.79)
Bibl.: p.60-61.
ISBN 0-7131-2636-1 : £3.00
ISBN 0-7131-2637-x Pbk : £1.50
(B77-24222)

581.8 — PLANTS. HISTOLOGY AND CYTOLOGY

581.8'73 — Plants. Protoplasts. *Conference proceedings*
International Symposium on Yeast and Other Protoplasts, *4th, University of Nottingham, 1975.* Microbial and plant protoplasts / edited by J.F. Peberdy ... [et al.]. — London [etc.] : Academic Press, 1976. — xii,370p : ill ; 24cm.
' ... Proceedings of the Fourth International Symposium on Yeast and Other Protoplasts held in the University of Nottingham, England in September 1974' - Preface. — Index.
ISBN 0-12-549050-x : £7.80
Also classified at 576
(B77-02309)

581.8'733 — Plants. Cells. Chloroplasts
The **intact** chloroplast / edited by J. Barber. — Amsterdam [etc.] ; Oxford : Elsevier, 1976. — xi,476p : ill ; 25cm. — (Topics in photosynthesis ; vol.1)
Bibl. — Index.
ISBN 0-444-41451-7 : £32.79
(B77-16384)

581.8'733 — Plants. Cells. Chloroplasts. Biosynthesis & genetics. *Conference proceedings*
Interdisciplinary Conference on the Genetics and Biogenesis of Chloroplasts and Mitochondria, *Munich, 1976.* Genetics and biogenesis of chloroplasts and mitochondria : Interdisciplinary Conference on the Genetics and Biogenesis of Chloroplasts and Mitochondria, Munich, Germany, August 2-7, 1976, held under the auspices of the Bayerische Akademie der Wissenschaften, Mathematisch-Naturwissenschaftliche Klasse / editors Th. Bücher ... [et al.]. — Amsterdam [etc.] ; Oxford : North-Holland Publishing Co., 1976. — xiii,895p : ill ; 25cm.
Index.
ISBN 0-7204-0604-8 : £40.98
Also classified at 574.8'734
(B77-15850)

581.9 — BOTANY. GEOGRAPHICAL TREATMENT

581.9'4 — Botany. *Europe. Conference proceedings*
European floristic and taxonomic studies : [proceedings of] a conference held in Cambridge, 29 June to 2 July 1974 / edited by S.M. Walters, with the assistance of C.J. King. — Faringdon : Classey for the Botanical Society of the British Isles, 1975. — ix,144p,[4] p of plates : ill, maps ; 23cm. — (Botanical Society of the British Isles. Conference reports ; no.15)
Bibl.
ISBN 0-900848-90-1 Pbk : Unpriced
(B77-19379)

581.9'41 — Plants. *Great Britain*
Prime, Cecil Thomas. Plant life / [by] C.T. Prime ; with line drawings by Marjorie Blamey ; and diagrams by Diedre Yuill. — London : Collins, 1977. — 160p,24p of plates : ill, maps ; 22cm. — (Collins countryside series ; 4)
Bibl.: p.154. — Index.
ISBN 0-00-219111-3 : £2.50
(B77-17496)

581.9'4116'5 — Plants. *Scotland. Highland Region. Sutherland (District)*
Anthony, John, *b.1894.* John Anthony's flora of Sutherland / edited and compiled by J.B. Kenworthy. — [Edinburgh] ([c/o Royal Botanic Garden, Arboretum Row, Edinburgh 3]) : Botanical Society of Edinburgh, 1976. — ix,201p,[2]leaves of plates,4p of plates : ill, maps, ports ; 21cm.
Bibl.: p.38-41. — Index.
ISBN 0-903077-01-9 Pbk : £4.00
(B77-06084)

581.9'422'1 — Plants. *Surrey*
Lousley, Job Edward. Flora of Surrey : based on records collected by the Surrey Flora Committee, 1957-1974 / [by] J.E. Lousley ; with a chapter on 'Geology and soils' by A.J. Stevens. — Newton Abbot : David and Charles [etc.], 1976. — 475,[9]p : ill(some col), maps, port ; 23cm.
Bibl. — Index.
ISBN 0-7153-7048-0 : £12.50
(B77-00764)

581.9'425'3 — Plants. *Lincolnshire. Lists*
Gibbons, E Joan. The flora of Lincolnshire / [by] E. Joan Gibbons. — Lincoln ([Headquarters, City and County Museum, Lincoln]) : Lincolnshire Naturalists' Union, 1975. — xii, 351p,[8]p of plates : ill, charts, coat of arms, maps(1 col), ports ; 22cm. — (Lincolnshire natural history brochure ; no.6)
Bibl. — Index.
ISBN 0-9500353-4-3 Pbk : £4.20
(B77-09023)

581.9'627 — Plants. Distribution. *Sudan. Jebel Marra*
Wickens, G E. The flora of Jebel Marra (Sudan Republic) and its geographical affinities / [by] G.E. Wickens. — London : H.M.S.O., 1976. — [11],368p : ill, maps ; 30cm. — (Royal Botanic Gardens, Kew. Kew bulletins : additional series ; 5)
Spine title: Jebel Marra. — Two overlay maps in pocket. — Bibl.: p.194-198. — Index.
ISBN 0-11-241100-2 Pbk : £25.00
(B77-16877)

581.9'729 — Plants. *Caribbean region*
Adams, Charles Dennis. Caribbean flora / [by] C. Dennis Adams. — London [etc.] : Nelson Caribbean, 1976. — 61p : col ill ; 21cm.
ISBN 0-17-566186-3 Pbk : £1.30
(B77-08384)

581.9'73 — Plants. *North America. Illustrations. For visual arts*
Harlow, William Morehouse. Art forms from plant life / [by] William M. Harlow. — Revised and expanded [ed.]. — New York : Dover Publications [etc.] ; London : Constable, 1976. — xvii,121p : chiefly ill ; 28cm. — (Dover pictorial archive series)
Previous ed.: published as 'Patterns of life'. New York : Harper and Row, 1966. — Index.
ISBN 0-486-23262-x Pbk : £2.85
(B77-26317)

581.9'95 — Plants. *New Guinea*
New Guinea vegetation / K. Paijmans, editor. — Ansterdam ; Oxford [etc.] : Elsevier [etc.], 1976. — xvii,213p : ill, maps ; 26cm.
Bibl.: p.185-199. — Index.
ISBN 0-444-99827-6 : £19.91
(B77-14733)

582 — SPERMATOPHYTES

582'.01 — Seed plants. Physiology. *Conference proceedings*
Society for Experimental Biology. *Symposium, 31st, Durham, 1976.* Integration of activity in the higher plant : symposia of the Society for Experimental Biology, number XXXI / [edited by D.H. Jennings]. — Cambridge [etc.] : Cambridge University Press for the Society for Experimental Biology, 1977. — vii,539,leaf of plate,2p of plates : ill ; 24cm.
'... held from 7-9 September 1976, at the University of Durham' - Preface. — Bibl. — Index.
ISBN 0-521-21617-6 : £20.00
(B77-31192)

582'.04 — Seed plants. Anatomy
Esau, Katherine. Anatomy of seed plants / [by] Katherine Esau. — 2nd ed. — New York ; London [etc.] : Wiley, 1977. — xxi,550p : ill ; 24cm.
Previous ed.: New York : Wiley ; London : Chapman and Hall, 1960. — Bibl. — Index.
ISBN 0-471-24520-8 : £11.50
(B77-17497)

582'.0467 — Antiquities: Seeds. Excavation of remains. Techniques
Renfrew, Jane Margaret. First aid for seeds / [by] Jane M. Renfrew, M. Monk and P. Murphy. — Hertford (15a Bull Plain, Hertford, Herts.) : RESCUE, [1976]. — [1],35p : ill ; 21cm. — (RESCUE. Publications ; no.6)
Bibl.: p.34-35.
Sd : £0.80(£0.60 to members of RESCUE)
(B77-05419)

582'.13'012 — Flowering plants. Taxonomic groups
Faulks, Philip James. The descent of the flowering plants / by P.J. Faulks. — Aberdeen : Alex P. Reid, 1977. — 31p ; 22cm.
£2.00
(B77-27864)

582'.13'0222 — Flowering plants. *Illustrations. Juvenile literature*
Picture reference book of flowers / general editor Boswell Taylor ; illustrator Barry Raynor. — Leicester : Hodder and Stoughton Children's Books, 1977. — [1],40p : chiefly ill(some col), ports ; 25cm. — (Picture reference)
Cover title: Flowers, their world and ours. — Ill. on lining papers.
ISBN 0-340-20494-x : £2.25
(B77-22588)

582'.13'0433 — Flowering plants. Embryos. *For Indian students*
Bhojwani, S S. The embryology of angiosperms / [by] S.S. Bhojwani, S.P. Bhatnagar. — 2nd ed. — Delhi [etc.] : Vikas ; Hemel Hempstead (66 Wood Lane End, Hemel Hempstead, Herts.) : [Distributed by] International Book Distributors Ltd, 1975 [i.e. 1976]. — xiv,264p,[2]leaves of plates : ill(some col) ; 24cm.
This ed. published in India: 1975. — Previous ed.: 1974. — Bibl. — Index.
ISBN 0-7069-0335-8 Pbk : £1.15
(B77-03552)

582'.13'0438 — Flowering plants. Evolution
Good, Ronald. Features of evolution in the flowering plants / by Ronald Good ; illustrated by Marjorie E. Cunningham and the author. — [1st ed. reprinted] ; with a new preface by the author. — New York : Dover Publications [etc.] ; London : Constable, 1974 [i.e. 1976]. — x,405p : ill ; 22cm.
Published in the United States: 1974. — Originally published: London : Longmans, Green, 1956. — Index.
ISBN 0-486-61591-x Pbk : £2.95
(B77-01452)

582'.13'0438 — Flowering plants. Evolution. Natural selection. Theories of Darwin, Charles
Allan, Mea. Darwin and his flowers : the key to natural selection / [by] Mea Allan. — London : Faber, 1977. — 3-318p : ill(some col), facsims, map, ports ; 24cm.
Map on lining papers. — Bibl.: p.305-308. — Index.
ISBN 0-571-10783-4 : £6.95
(B77-21868)

582.13'09181'3 — Flowering plants. *Northern hemisphere*
Jordan, Michael. A guide to wild plants : the edible and poisonous species of the Northern Hemisphere / text and photographs by Michael Jordan. — Blandford : Millington, 1976. — 240p : ill(chiefly col) ; 23cm.
Bibl.: p.233-235. — Index.
ISBN 0-86000-063-x : £5.00
ISBN 0-86000-064-8 Pbk : £2.50
(B77-02310)

582'.13'094 — Flowering plants. *North-western Europe. Identification manuals*
Blamey, Marjorie. Wild flowers : the wild flowers of Britain and Northern Europe / [by] Marjorie Blamey, Richard Fitter, Alastair Fitter ; with a foreword by Geoffrey Grigson. — London : Collins, 1977. — xv,82p,126p of plates : ill(chiefly col), map ; 29cm.
Based on: 'The wild flowers of Britain and northern Europe' / text by Richard Fitter, Alastair Fitter ; illustrated by Marjorie Blamey. 1974. — Index.
ISBN 0-00-219757-x : £5.95
(B77-31193)

582'.13'0941 — Flowering plants. *Great Britain*
Greenoak, Francesca. Wild flowers / [by] Francesca Greenoak. — [London] : [Macdonald Educational], [1977]. — 96p : ill(some col), facsims, maps ; 21cm. — (Macdonald guidelines)
Bibl.: p.92. — Index.
ISBN 0-356-06011-x Pbk : £1.00
(B77-17498)

582'.13'0941 — Flowering plants. *Great Britain. Chalk regions & limestone regions*
Ellis, Edward Augustine. Wild flowers of chalk and limestone / with text and photographs by E.A. Ellis. — Norwich : Jarrold and Sons, 1977. — [33]p : col ill ; 20cm. — (Jarrold wild flowers series ; book 7)
Index.
ISBN 0-85306-717-1 Sd : £0.40
(B77-28624)

582'.13'0941 — Flowering plants. *Great Britain. Illustrations*
Phillips, Roger. Wild flowers of Britain / [by] Roger Phillips ; assisted by Sheila Grant ; edited by Tom Wellsted. — London : Pan Books, 1977. — 192p : col ill ; 30cm.
Bibl.: p.176. — Index.
ISBN 0-330-25183-x Pbk : £3.95
(B77-26318)

Phillips, Roger. Wild flowers of Britain / [by] Roger Phillips ; assisted by Sheila Grant ; edited by Tom Wellsted. — London : Ward Lock, 1977. — 192p : col ill ; 30cm.
Bibl.: p.176. — Index.
ISBN 0-7063-5580-6 : £6.50
(B77-26319)

582'.13'0941 — Flowering plants. *Great Britain. Juvenile literature*
Wild flowers. — St Ives, Cornwall : Pike, 1974. — 32p : ill, form ; 26cm. — (Look learn projects)
Fill-in book. — With answers. — '... with a merit award certificate'.
ISBN 0-85932-051-0 Sd : £0.30
(B77-18768)

582'.13'0941 — Waste land. Flowering plants. *Great Britain*
Imrie, Jean. Wild flowers of verges and waste land / [by] Jean Imrie. — London : A. and C. Black, 1977. — 3-56p : ill(some col) ; 21cm. — (Black's picture information books)
Bibl.: p.49. — Index.
ISBN 0-7136-1696-2 : £2.55
ISBN 0-7136-1697-0 Pbk : £1.45
(B77-21869)

582'.13'0941 — Wild flowering plants. *Great Britain. Towns*
Mabey, Richard. Street flowers / [by] Richard Mabey ; illustrated by Sarah Kensington. — Harmondsworth : Kestrel Books, 1976. — 77p : ill(some col) ; 25cm.
Index.
ISBN 0-7226-5151-1 : £3.25
(B77-02311)

582'.13'0941162 — Flowering plants. *Scotland. Highland Region. Caithness (District). Lists*
Caithness Field Club. The wild flowers of Caithness / [Caithness Field Club] ; [compiled] by E.R. Bullard ... [et al.] ; cover design by Sheila Butler. — Wick (c/o Mrs M. Gladstone, 11 Miller Ave., Wick [Caithness]) : The Club, 1977. — [32]p ; 21cm.
Sd : Unpriced
(B77-24939)

582'.13'094234 — Flowering plants. *Channel Islands*
Ellis, Edward Augustine. Wild flowers of the Channel Islands / text by E.A. Ellis. — Norwich : Jarrold and Sons. — (A Jarrold area guide)
In 2 vols.
Book 1. — 1977. — [33]p : col ill ; 20cm.
Index.
ISBN 0-85306-699-x Sd : £0.40
(B77-26320)

Book 2. — 1977. — [33]p : col ill ; 20cm.
Index.
ISBN 0-85306-700-7 Sd : £0.40
(B77-26321)

582'.13'09495 — Flowering plants. *Greece*
Huxley, Anthony Julian. Flowers of Greece and the Aegean / by Anthony Huxley and William Taylor ; ... line drawings by Victoria Gordon. — London : Chatto and Windus, 1977. — vi, 185p,[64]p of plates : ill(chiefly col), 2 maps ; 21cm.
Bibl.: p.57-58. — Index.
ISBN 0-7011-2190-4 : £6.50
ISBN 0-7011-2228-5 Pbk : £3.95
(B77-11812)

582'.13'09684 — Flowering plants. *South Africa. Natal*
Jeppe, Barbara. Natal wild flowers / [by] Barbara Jeppe. — Cape Town [etc.] ; London : Purnell, 1975. — xiii,118p,56p of plates : ill(chiefly col), map ; 29cm.
Ill. on lining papers. — Index.
ISBN 0-360-00203-x : £20.00
(B77-13043)

582'.13'096897 — Flowering plants. *Malawi*
Moriarty, Audrey. Wild flowers of Malawi / [by] Audrey Moriarty. — Cape Town [etc.] ; London : Purnell, 1975. — viii,166p : col ill ; 25cm.
Index.
ISBN 0-360-00174-2 : Unpriced
(B77-00765)

582'.13'097 — Flowering plants. *North America. Illustrations*
Ferguson, Mary. Wildflowers / [by] Mary Ferguson, Richard M. Saunders. — Toronto ; London [etc.] : Van Nostrand Reinhold, 1976. — 192p : col ill ; 25cm.
Index.
ISBN 0-442-29850-1 : £15.15
(B77-33230)

582'.13'0979 — Flowering plants. *United States. Great Basin*
Intermountain flora : vascular plants of the Intermountain West, USA / by Arthur Cronquist ... [et al.]. — New York ; Guildford : Columbia University Press for the New York Botanical Gardens.
Vol.6 : The monocotyledons. — 1977. — [11], 584p : ill ; 28cm.
Bibl. — Index.
ISBN 0-231-04120-9 : £29.40
(B77-25635)

582'.13'0994 — Flowering plants. *South-eastern Australia. Identification manuals*
Galbraith, Jean. A field guide to the wild flowers of South-east Australia / by Jean Galbraith. — Sydney ; London : Collins, 1977. — 450p,105p of plates : ill(some col), col maps(on lining papers) ; 20cm.
Bibl.: p.405-407. — Index.
ISBN 0-00-219246-2 : £6.50
(B77-15851)

582'.14 — Succulents
Bechtel, Helmut. Cactus identifier : including succulent plants / by Helmut Bechtel ; [translated from the German by Manly Banister ; adapted by E.W. Egan]. — New York : Sterling [etc.] ; London : Distributed by Ward Lock, 1977. — 256p : col ill ; 15cm.
Translation and adaptation of: 'Bunte Welt der Kakteen'. Stuttgart : Franckh'sche Verlagshandlung W. Keller, 1975. — Index.
ISBN 0-7061-2537-1 : £2.95
(B77-28625)

Innes, Clive. The complete handbook of cacti and succulents : a comprehensive guide to cacti and succulents in their habitats, to their care and cultivation in house and greenhouse and to the genera and their species / [by] Clive Innes. — London : Ward Lock, 1977. — 224p : ill(some col) ; 26cm.
Index.
ISBN 0-7063-1836-6 : £5.95 : CIP rev.
(B77-16385)

582'.16 — Trees
Leathart, Scott. Trees of the world / [by] Scott Leathart. — London [etc.] : Hamlyn, 1977. — 224p : ill(chiefly col), map ; 33cm.
Col. ill. on lining papers. — Index.
ISBN 0-600-38745-3 : £4.95
(B77-26322)

582'.16 — Trees. *Juvenile literature*
Selberg, Ingrid. The Nature Trail book of trees & leaves / [by] Ingrid Selberg ; [illustrated by John Barber et al.]. — London : Usborne, 1977. — 32p : chiefly col ill ; 28cm.
Spine title: Trees & leaves. — Bibl.: p.32. — Index.
£1.95
ISBN 0-86020-099-x Pbk : £0.95
(B77-28626)

582'.16'00222 — Trees. *Juvenile literature. Illustrations*
Mari, Iela. The tree / [by] Iela Mari. — London [etc.] : Dent, 1977. — [34]p : col ill ; 22cm.
Translation of: 'L'albero'. Milan : Elle, 1976.
ISBN 0-460-06847-4 : £1.95
(B77-30263)

582'.16'005 — Trees. *Yearbooks*
International Dendrology Society. International Dendrology Society year book. — London (c/o Mrs A.M. Eustace, Whistley Green Farmhouse, Hurst, Reading RG10 9DU) : The Society.
1976 / [editor Patrick M. Synge]. — 1977. — 97p : ill, map, port ; 22cm.
Bibl.: p.93-96.
Pbk : £2.00
ISSN 0307-322x
Also classified at 582'.17'05
(B77-20267)

582'.16'0941 — Trees. *Great Britain. Encyclopaedias*
Bean, William Jackson. Trees and shrubs hardy in the British Isles / [by] W.J. Bean. — London : J. Murray.
In 4 vols.
Vol.1 : A-C. — 8th ed. revised / chief editor D.L. Clarke ; general editor Sir George Taylor. — 1976. — xx,845p,[48]p of plates : ill ; 23cm.
This ed. originally published: 1970. — Bibl. — Index.
£15.00
ISBN 0-7195-1790-7
Also classified at 582'.17'0941
(B77-17499)

Vol.3 : N-Rh. — 8th ed. revised / chief editor D.L. Clarke ; general editor Sir George Taylor. — 1976. — xvi,973p,[64]p of plates : ill ; 23cm.

Previous ed.: 1950. — Index.
ISBN 0-7195-2427-x : £17.50
Also classified at 582'.17'0941
(B77-01453)

582'.16'0941 — Trees. *Great Britain. Identification manuals*
Yewlett, Gerry. Trees and timber / by Gerry Yewlett. — Wokingham (California Park, Nine Mile Ride, Finchampstead, Wokingham, Berks. [RG11 4HT]) : Jogger, 1977. — [24]p : chiefly ill ; 84mm x15cm. — (Waterproof outdoor pocketbooks)
Notebook format. — Originally published: 1976.
Sd : £0.55
(B77-24940)

582'.16'0941 — Trees. *Great Britain. Juvenile literature*
Trees. — St Ives, Cornwall : Pike, [1974]. — 30p : ill, form ; 26cm. — (Look learn projects)
Fill-in book. — With answers. — '... with a merit award certificate'.
ISBN 0-85932-049-9 Sd : £0.30
(B77-18769)

582'.16'0942574 — Universities. *Oxfordshire. Oxford. University of Oxford. Parks. Trees. Guidebooks*
Guide to the trees and shrubs in the University Parks, Oxford. — Oxford ([Keble College, Oxford OX1 3PG]) : Curators of the University Parks, 1977. — 111p,[4]p of plates,fold leaf of plate : ill, plans ; 22cm.
Ill. (incl. 1 col.) on covers. — Index.
Pbk : Unpriced
Also classified at 582'.17'0942574
(B77-30264)

582'.17'05 — Shrubs. *Yearbooks*
International Dendrology Society. International Dendrology Society year book. — London (c/o Mrs A.M. Eustace, Whistley Green Farmhouse, Hurst, Reading RG10 9DU) : The Society.
1976 / [editor Patrick M. Synge]. — 1977. — 97p : ill, map, port ; 22cm.
Bibl.: p.93-96.
Pbk : £2.00
ISSN 0307-322x
Primary classification 582'.16'005
(B77-20267)

582'.17'0941 — Shrubs. *Great Britain. Encyclopaedias*
Bean, William Jackson. Trees and shrubs hardy in the British Isles / [by] W.J. Bean. — London : J. Murray.
In 4 vols.
Vol.1 : A-C. — 8th ed. revised / chief editor D.L. Clarke ; general editor Sir George Taylor. — 1976. — xx,845p,[48]p of plates : ill ; 23cm.
This ed. originally published: 1970. — Bibl. — Index.
£15.00
ISBN 0-7195-1790-7
Primary classification 582'.16'0941
(B77-17499)

Vol.3 : N-Rh. — 8th ed. revised / chief editor D.L. Clarke ; general editor Sir George Taylor. — 1976. — xvi,973p,[64]p of plates : ill ; 23cm.

Previous ed.: 1950. — Index.
ISBN 0-7195-2427-x : £17.50
Primary classification 582'.16'0941
(B77-01453)

582'.17'0942574 — Universities. *Oxfordshire. Oxford. University of Oxford. Parks. Shrubs. Guidebooks*
Guide to the trees and shrubs in the University Parks, Oxford. — Oxford ([Keble College, Oxford OX1 3PG]) : Curators of the University Parks, 1977. — 111p,[4]p of plates,fold leaf of plate : ill, plans ; 22cm.
Ill. (incl. 1 col.) on covers. — Index.
Pbk : Unpriced
Primary classification 582'.16'0942574
(B77-30264)

583 — DICOTYLEDONS
583 — Insectivorous plants
Lloyd, Francis Ernest. The carnivorous plants / by Francis Ernest Lloyd. — New York : Dover Publications [etc.] ; London : Constable, 1976. — iii-xvi,352p : ill ; 22cm.
Originally published: Waltham, Mass. : Chronica Botanica Co., 1942. — Index.
ISBN 0-486-23321-9 Pbk : £3.20
(B77-13044)

583'.163 — Hypericum
Studies in the genus Hypericum L. (Guttiferae). — London : British Museum (Natural History).

1 : Infrageneric classification / by Norman Keith Bonner Robson. — 1977. — p291-355 : 2 ill(1 col), maps ; 25cm. — (British Museum (Natural History). Bulletins of the British Museum (Natural History) : botany ; vol.5, no.6 ISSN 0068-2292)
Bibl.: p.345-347. — Index.
Pbk : £7.25
(B77-21131)

583'.38 — Sedum. *North America*
Clausen, Robert T. Sedum of North America north of the Mexican Plateau / by Robert T. Clausen ; drawings by Elfriede Abbe. — Ithaca ; London : Cornell University Press, [1976]. — 742p : ill, maps ; 25cm.
'A Comstock book'. — Published in the United States: 1975. — Bibl.: p.711-721. — Index.
ISBN 0-8014-0950-0 : £52.00
(B77-05420)

583'.57 — Campanulaceae. *East Africa*
Thulin, Mats. Campanulaceae / by Mats Thulin. — Nairobi ; London [etc.] (P.O. Box 569, SE1 9NH) : Crown Agents for Oversea Governments and Administrations [for] the East African Community, 1976. — iv,40p : ill, map ; 26cm. — (Flora of tropical East Africa)
Index.
ISBN 0-85592-041-6 Sd : £0.68
(B77-04806)

583'.672 — Plumbaginaceae. *East Africa*
Wilmot-Dear, C M. Plumbaginaceae / by C.M. Wilmot-Dear. — Nairobi ; London [etc.] (P.O. Box 569, SE1 9NH) : Crown Agents for Oversea Governments and Administrations [for] the East African Community, 1976. — [iv], 12p : ill ; 26cm. — (Flora of tropical East Africa)
Index.
ISBN 0-85592-049-1 Sd : £0.33
(B77-04807)

583'.932'0968 — Proteaceae. *South Africa*
Rousseau, Frank. The Proteaceae of South Africa / [by] Frank Rousseau. — Cape Town [etc.] ; London : Purnell, 1976. — xvi,110p : ill(chiefly col) ; 29cm.
Originally published: Cape Town : Purnell, 1970. — Index.
ISBN 0-360-00106-8 : £15.00
(B77-14734)

583'.933 — Daphnes
Brickell, C D. Daphne : the genus in the wild and in cultivation / by C.D. Brickell and B. Mathew. — Woking (Lye End Link, St John's, Woking, Surrey GU21 1SW) : Alpine Garden Society, 1976. — [2],194p,leaf of plate,[4]p of plates : ill(some col) ; 22cm. — (Alpine Garden Society. Guides)
Bibl.: p.187. — Index.
Unpriced
(B77-30265)

584 — MONOCOTYLEDONS
584'.07'12 — Middle schools. Curriculum subjects: Biology. Teaching
Web of life / editor Max Blythe ; authors Max Blythe ... [et al.]. — London : Longman, 1977. — v,190p : ill(some col), map ; 25cm.
Bibl. — Lists of films. — Index.
ISBN 0-582-32288-x : £12.50
ISBN 0-582-32297-9 Pbk : £7.50
(B77-11218)

584'.15'0967 — Orchids. *Southern Central Africa*
Williamson, Graham. The orchids of South Central Africa / [by] Graham Williamson ; with the co-operation of R.B. Drummond and R. Grosvenor. — London : Dent, 1977. — 237p,[48]p of plates : ill(some col), maps ; 29cm.
Bibl.: p.16. — Index.
ISBN 0-460-04295-5 : £15.00
(B77-31907)

584'.15'0987 — Orchids. *Venezuela*
Dunsterville, Galfrid Clement Keyworth. Venezuelan orchids illustrated / [by] G.C.K. Dunsterville and Leslie A. Garay. — London : Deutsch.
Vol.6. — 1976. — 463p,plate : ill(incl 1 col), maps(on lining papers) ; 29cm.
English text, English and Spanish introduction and notes. — Index.
ISBN 0-233-96828-8 : £15.00
(B77-10807)

584'.84'09773 — Sedges. *Illinois*
Mohlenbrock, Robert H. Sedges / [by] Robert H. Mohlenbrock. — Carbondale [etc.] : Southern Illinois University Press ; London [etc.] : Feffer and Simons. — (The illustrated flora of Illinois)
In 2 vols.
Cyperus to Sclevia. — 1976. — xvi,192p : ill, maps ; 23cm.
Bibl.: p.187-190. — Index.
ISBN 0-8093-0604-2 : £12.00
(B77-01454)

584'.9'09667 — Grasses. *Ghana*
Innes, R Rose. A manual of Ghana grasses / [by] R. Rose Innes ; (with a key to species by W.D. Clayton). — Surbiton : Ministry of Overseas Development, Land Resources Division, 1977. — xxiv,261p,[3] leaves : ill, maps ; 25cm.
Bibl.: p.259-261.
ISBN 0-902409-44-1 Pbk : £1.50
(B77-16386)

585 — GYMNOSPERMS
585'.2 — Native pine trees. *Scotland. Conference proceedings*
Native pinewoods of Scotland : proceedings of Aviemore symposium, 1975 / edited by R.G.H. Bunce and J.N.R. Jeffers ; [for the] Natural Environment Research Council, Institute of Terrestrial Ecology. — Cambridge (68 Hills Rd, Cambridge CB2 1LA) : The Institute, 1977. — x,120p : ill, maps ; 30cm.
Bibl.
ISBN 0-904282-08-2 Pbk : £2.50
(B77-33231)

586 — CRYPTOGAMS
586'.001'2 — Cryptogams. Taxonomy. *Early works. Facsimiles. Latin texts*
Micheli, P. Nova plantarum genera : iuxta Tournefortii methodum disposita / by P. Micheli. — [1st ed. reprinted] ; new introduction by D.L. Hawksworth. — Richmond, Surrey : Richmond Publishing, 1976. — [32],232p,108 leaves of plates : ill ; 25cm.
Limited ed. of 200 numbered copies. — Facsimile reprint of: 1st ed. Florentiae : s.n., 1729. — Bibl.: p.[8]. — Index.
ISBN 0-85546-198-5 : £32.50
(B77-07351)

589 — THALLOPHYTES
589'.1'045222 — Lichens. Effects of atmospheric pollution
Hawksworth, David Leslie. Lichens as pollution monitors / [by] David L. Hawksworth, Francis Rose. — London : Edward Arnold, 1976. — [4],60p : ill, maps ; 22cm. — (Institute of Biology. Studies in biology ; no.66)
Bibl.: p.60.
ISBN 0-7131-2554-3 : £2.80
ISBN 0-7131-2555-1 Pbk : £1.40
(B77-03002)

589'.2 — Fungi
Burnett, John Harrison. Fundamentals of mycology / [by] J.H. Burnett. — 2nd ed. — London : Edward Arnold, 1976. — xiii,673p : ill, maps ; 24cm.
Previous ed.: 1968. — Bibl.: p.617-664. — Index.
ISBN 0-7131-2617-5 : £27.50
(B77-07909)

Kibby, Geoffrey. The love of mushrooms and toadstools / [by] Geoffrey Kibby. — London : Octopus Books, 1977. — 96p : col ill ; 33cm.
Col. ill. on lining papers. — Index.
ISBN 0-7064-0584-6 : £2.95
(B77-24223)

Pursey, Helen L. The wonderful world of mushrooms and other fungi / [by] Helen L. Pursey. — London [etc.] : Hamlyn, 1977. — 96p : col ill ; 33cm.
Col. ill. on lining papers. — Index.
ISBN 0-600-36248-5 : £2.95
(B77-18770)

589'.2'04524 — Fungi. Symbiosis
Cooke, Roderic. The biology of symbiotic fungi / [by] Roderic Cooke. — London [etc.] : Wiley, 1977. — xi,282p : ill ; 24cm.
Bibl. — Index.
ISBN 0-471-99467-7 : £10.75
(B77-21870)

589.2'0973 — Fungi. *United States. Early works*
Hard, Miron Elisha. Mushrooms, edible and otherwise : habitat and time of growth / [by] Miron Elisha Hard. — [1st ed., reprinted] ; with a new appendix on nomenclatural changes by Martina S. Gillian. — New York : Dover Publications [etc.] ; London : Constable, 1976. — ii-xii,623p : ill, port ; 24cm.
Facsimile reprint of: 1st ed., published as 'The mushroom, edible and otherwise'. Columbus, Ohio : The Ohio Library Co., 1908. — Bibl.: p.599. — Index.
ISBN 0-486-23309-x Pbk : £5.70
(B77-15852)

589'.24 — Aquatic hyphomycetes
Ingold, Cecil Terence. An illustrated guide to aquatic and water-borne hyphomycetes (fungi imperfecti) : with notes on their biology / by C.T. Ingold. — [Ambleside] ([The Ferry House, Ambleside, Cumbria LA22 0LP]) : Freshwater Biological Association, 1975. — 96p : ill ; 21cm. — (Freshwater Biological Association. Scientific publications ; no.30 ISSN 0367-1887)
Spine title: Aquatic hyphomycetes. — Cover title: Guide to aquatic hyphomycetes. — Bibl.: p.92-96.
ISBN 0-900386-22-3 Pbk : £1.00(£0.75 to members)
(B77-20268)

589'.24 — Cercospora
Deighton, Frederick Claude. Studies on Cercospora and allied genera / by F.C. Deighton. — Kew : Commonwealth Mycological Institute.
6 : Pseudocercospora speg., Pantospora cif. and Cercoseptoria petr. — 1976. — 168p,6p of plates : ill ; 25cm. — (Mycological papers ; no.140 ISSN 0027-5522)
Cover title. — Bibl.: p.167-168.
Pbk : £5.00
(B77-07352)

589'.24 — Dematiaceous hyphomycetes
Ellis, Martin Beazor. More dematiaceous hyphomycetes / by M.B. Ellis. — Kew : Commonwealth Mycological Institute, 1976. — 507p : ill ; 26cm.
Index.
ISBN 0-85198-365-0 : £15.00
(B77-02312)

589'.3'0724 — Algae. Culture
Fogg, Gordon Elliott. Algal cultures and phytoplankton ecology / [by] G.E. Fogg. — 2nd ed. — Madison ; London : University of Wisconsin Press, 1975. — xv,175,[1]p : ill ; 23cm.
Previous ed.: Madison : University of Wisconsin Press ; London : Athlone Press, 1965. — Bibl.: p.141-166. — Index.
ISBN 0-299-06760-2 : Unpriced
Also classified at 589'.4
(B77-19380)

589'.3'07402659 — Microbiology. Organisations. *Cambridgeshire. Cambridge. Culture Centre of Algae and Protozoa. Stock: Algae. Cultures. Catalogues*
Culture Centre of Algae and Protozoa. List of strains / Culture Centre of Algae and Protozoa ; edited by E.A. George. — [3rd ed.]. — [Cambridge] ([36 Storey's Way, Cambridge CB3 0DT]) : [The Centre], [1976]. — [3],ii, 120p ; 30cm.
Previous ed.: 1971. — Bibl.: p.119-120.
ISBN 0-904282-06-6 Pbk : £1.00
Also classified at 593'.1'07402659
(B77-23413)

589'.39'29 — Freshwater algae
Belcher, Hilary. A beginner's guide to freshwater algae / [by] Hilary Belcher & Erica Swale ; [for the] Institute of Terrestrial Ecology ... — London : H.M.S.O., 1976. — 47p : ill ; 21cm.
Index.
ISBN 0-11-881393-5 Sd : £0.85
(B77-09024)

589'.39'41 — Seaweeds. *Great Britain*
British Phycological Society. Seaweeds of the British Isles : a collaborative project of the British Phycological Society and the British Museum (Natural History). — London : The Museum.
Vol.1 : Rhodophyta. Part 1 : Introduction, Nemaliales, Gigartinales / [by] Peter S. Dixon & Linda M. Irvine. — 1977. — xi,252p : ill ; 21cm. — (British Museum (Natural History). Publications ; no.781)
Bibl. — Index.
ISBN 0-565-00781-5 Pbk : £10.00
(B77-13650)

589'.39'764122 — Marine algae. *Texas. Port Aransas region*
Edwards, Peter. Illustrated guide to the seaweeds and sea grasses in the vicinity of Port Aransas, Texas / by Peter Edwards. — Austin ; London : University of Texas Press, 1976. — [3],131p : ill(some col), map ; 26cm.
Spine title: Seaweeds and sea grasses. — 'Previously published as supplement to volume 15 of "Contributions in marine science" September 1970, by the University of Texas Marine Science Institute, Port Aransas, Texas' - title page verso. — Bibl.: p.50-52. — Index.
ISBN 0-292-77549-0 Pbk : £5.25
(B77-16387)

589'.4 — Phytoplankton. Ecology
Fogg, Gordon Elliott. Algal cultures and phytoplankton ecology / [by] G.E. Fogg. — 2nd ed. — Madison ; London : University of Wisconsin Press, 1975. — xv,175,[1]p : ill ; 23cm.
Previous ed.: Madison : University of Wisconsin Press ; London : Athlone Press, 1965. — Bibl.: p.141-166. — Index.
ISBN 0-299-06760-2 : Unpriced
Primary classification 589'.3'0724
(B77-19380)

589'.481 — Diatoms
The **biology** of diatoms / edited by Dietrich Werner. — Oxford [etc.] : Blackwell Scientific, 1977. — ix,498p : ill ; 25cm. — (Botanical monographs ; vol.13 ISSN 0068-0389)
Bibl. — Index.
ISBN 0-632-00067-8 : £17.00
(B77-24224)

589.9'01'88 — Vegetative bacteria. Inactivation & inhibition. *Conference proceedings*
Inhibition and Inactivation of Vegetative Microbes *(Conference), University of Nottingham, 1975.* Inhibition and inactivation of vegetative microbes / edited by F.A. Skinner and W.B. Hugo. — London [etc.] : Academic Press, 1976. — xiii,378p : ill ; 24cm. — (Society for Applied Bacteriology. Symposium series ; no.5)
'A symposium on the "Inhibition and Inactivation of Vegetative Microbes" was organized by the Society for Applied Bacteriology in collaboration with the North West European Microbiological Group and held during the Summer Conference of the Society in the University of Nottingham, July 1975' - Preface. — Bibl. — Index.
ISBN 0-12-648065-6 : £12.00
(B77-14238)

589.9'01'915 — Bacteria. Effects of radiation
Bridges, B A. Bacterial reaction to radiation / [by] B.A. Bridges. — Shildon (ISA Building, Shildon, Co. Durham) : Meadowfield Press Ltd, 1976. — [6],72p : ill ; 21cm. — (Patterns of progress : microbiology series)
Bibl.: p.63-70.
ISBN 0-904095-21-5 Pbk : £2.80
(B77-04177)

589.9'08'732 — Bacteria. Transfection & transformation
European Meeting on Bacterial Transformation and Transfection, *3rd, Granada, 1976.* Modern trends in bacterial transformation and transfection : proceedings of the Third European Meeting on Bacterial Transformation and Transfection, Granada, Spain, August 31-September 3, 1976 / editors A. Portolés, R. López, M. Espinosa. — Amsterdam [etc.] ; Oxford : North-Holland Publishing Co., 1977. — x,329p : ill ; 25cm.
Bibl. — Index.
ISBN 0-7204-0608-0 : £18.74
(B77-16388)

589.9'08'75 — Bacteria. Membranes. Formation
Membrane biogenesis : mitochondria, chloroplasts and bacteria / edited by Alexander Tzagoloff. — New York ; London : Plenum Press, [1976]. — xvii,460p : ill ; 24cm.
Published in the United States: 1975. — Index.
ISBN 0-306-30825-8 : £18.59
Primary classification 574.8'734
(B77-04167)

589.9'2 — Mycobacteria
Ratledge, Colin. The mycobacteria / [by] Colin Ratledge. — Shildon : Meadowfield Press, 1977. — [8],130p : ill ; 21cm. — (Patterns of progress : microbiology series)
Index.
ISBN 0-900541-95-4 Pbk : £3.20
(B77-20269)

589.9'2 — Nocardiae
The **biology** of the nocardiae / edited by M. Goodfellow, G.H. Brownell, and J.A. Serrano. — London [etc.] : Academic Press, 1976. — xvii,517p : ill ; 24cm.
Bibl. — Index.
ISBN 0-12-289650-5 : £15.00
(B77-01455)

590 — ZOOLOGICAL SCIENCES

590'.6'242132 — Zoology. Organisations. *London. Westminster (London Borough). Zoological Society of London, to 1976*
Zoological Society of London. The Zoological Society of London, 1826-1976. — [London] ([Regent's Park, NW1 4RY]) : The Society, 1976. — 8p : col ill, col port ; 16x22cm.
Sd : Unpriced
(B77-21132)

590'.6'242132 — Zoology. Organisations. *London. Westminster (London Borough). Zoological Society of London, to 1976. Conference proceedings*
The **Zoological** Society of London, 1826-1976 and beyond : (the proceedings of a symposium held at the Zoological Society of London on 25 and 26 March, 1976) / edited by Lord Zuckerman and staff of the publications department. — London : Academic Press for the Zoological Society of London, 1976. — xviii,353p,4p of plates : ill(some col), facsims, forms, maps, plan, ports(1 col) ; 24cm. — (Zoological Society of London. Symposia ; no.40)
Plans on lining papers. — Bibl. — Index.
ISBN 0-12-613340-9 : £9.80
(B77-04808)

590'.6'2427 — Zoology. Organisations. *North-west England. Lancashire and Cheshire Fauna Society. Reports, surveys. Serials*
Lancashire and Cheshire Fauna Society. Secretary's annual report ... / Lancashire and Cheshire Fauna Society. — [Manchester] ([c/o A. Brindle, Manchester Museum, Manchester M13 9PL]) : [The Society].
1976. — 1977. — [1],16p : port ; 22cm. — (Lancashire and Cheshire Fauna Society. Publications ; no.71 ISSN 0306-7599)
Sd : Unpriced
(B77-20270)

590'.744 — Zoos. Animals. *Juvenile literature*
Morris, Johnny. Johnny Morris looks at the zoo. — London [etc.] : Hamlyn, 1977. — 4-61p : col ill, col ports ; 28cm.
Col. ill. on lining papers. — Index.
ISBN 0-600-35526-8 : £1.50
(B77-31194)

590'.744'05 — Zoos. *Serials*
International zoo yearbook. — London (Regent's Park, NW1 4RY) : Zoological Society of London.
Vol.17 : 1977 / edited by P.J.S. Olney ; assistant editors Ruth Biegler, Pat Ellis. — 1977. — xii,392p,[24]p of plates : ill, maps, plans ; 25cm.
Text on lining papers. — Bibl. — Index. — Author index to vols 1-17. — Includes papers presented at the Second World Conference on Breeding Endangered Species in Captivity, held at the London Zoo on 6, 7 and 8 July 1976.
£12.00
ISSN 0074-9664
(B77-30266)

590'.744'415 — Zoos. *Ireland. Secondary school texts*
McCullagh, Marion. Irish zoos / text Marion McCullagh ; illustrations James McIntyre. — [Tallaght] : Folens, [1977]. — [1],p.97-128 : col ill ; 25cm. — (Irish environmental library series ; no.29)
Sd : £0.60
(B77-18771)

590'.744'42142 — Zoos. *London. Westminster (London Borough). London Zoo. Guidebooks*
Zoological Society of London. London Zoo guide / [Zoological Society of London]. — [London] ([Regent's Park, NW1 4RY]) : Zoological Society, 1977. — 60p : ill(some col), col map, 2 ports ; 23cm.
£0.40
(B77-29429)

Zoological Society of London. The London Zoo guide / [Zoological Society of London]. — [New ed.] / [photography by Michael Lyster]. — [London] ([Regents Park, NW1 4RY]) : The Society, 1975. — [1],60,[1]p : ill(some col), coat of arms, 2 col plans ; 23cm.
Previous ed.: 1973.
Sd : £0.30
(B77-21871)

Zoological Society of London. London Zoo guide / [Zoological Society of London]. — [New ed.] / [photography by Michael Lyster]. — [London] ([Regents Park, NW1 4RY]) : The Society, 1976. — [1],60,[1]p : ill(some col), col plan, ports ; 23cm.
Previous ed.: 1975.
Sd : £0.35
(B77-21872)

590'.744'42234 — Zoos. *Kent. Canterbury. Howletts Zoo Park, to 1976. Personal observations*
Aspinall, John. The best of friends / [by] John Aspinall. — London [etc.] : Macmillan, 1976. — 159p,[16]p of plates : ill(some col), ports(some col) ; 25cm.
Bibl.: p.157-158.
ISBN 0-333-19308-3 : £4.95
(B77-05421)

590'.744'42341 — Zoos. *Jersey. Jersey Zoo, to 1975. Personal observations*
Durrell, Gerald. The stationary ark / [by] Gerald Durrell. — [London] : Fontana, 1977. — 157p, 4p of plates : ill, plan ; 18cm.
Originally published: London : Collins, 1976.
ISBN 0-00-635000-3 Pbk : £0.75
(B77-29430)

590'.744'42565 — Zoos. *Bedfordshire. Whipsnade. Whipsnade Zoo. Guidebooks*
Zoological Society of London. Whipsnade Zoo guide / [Zoological Society of London]. — [London] ([Regent's Park, NW1 4RY]) : Zoological Society, 1976. — 19p : col ill, map ; 23cm.
Sd : £0.25
(B77-29431)

Zoological Society of London. Whipsnade Zoo guide / [Zoological Society of London]. — [New ed.]. — [London] ([Regent's Park, NW1 4RY]) : The Society, 1976. — 19p : col ill, map ; 23cm.
Sd : £0.25
(B77-21133)

590'.744'73 — Wildlife parks. *United States*
Straughan, Robert Paul Louis. Build a jungle zoo / [by] Robert P.L. Straughan. — South Brunswick [etc.] : Barnes ; London : Yoseloff, 1973. — 272p : ill, plans, ports ; 29cm.
Bibl.: p.267. — Index.
ISBN 0-498-07999-6 : £6.50
(B77-20271)

591 — ZOOLOGY
Principles of zoology / [by] Willis H. Johnson ... [et al.]. — 2nd ed. — New York ; London [etc.] : Holt, Rinehart and Winston, 1977. — xi,747p,[16]p of plates : ill(some col), maps ; 29cm.
Previous ed.: 1969. — Bibl. — Index.
ISBN 0-03-012046-2 : £12.00
(B77-21134)

591 — Animals
Weisz, Paul B. The science of zoology / [by] Paul B. Weisz. — 2nd ed. — New York ; London [etc.] : McGraw-Hill, 1973. — xvi, 727p,[16]p of plates : ill(some col) ; 24cm.
Previous ed.: 1966. — Bibl. — Index.
ISBN 0-07-069135-5 : £12.40
(B77-19381)

Wood, Gerald Lester. The Guinness book of animal facts and feats / by Gerald L. Wood. — 2nd ed. — Enfield : Guinness Superlatives, 1976. — 255p : ill(some col) ; 24cm.
Text on lining papers. — Previous ed.: 1972. — Bibl.: p.234-242. — Index.
ISBN 0-900424-60-5 : £6.50
(B77-11219)

591 — Animals. *Juvenile literature*
Barthelemy, Georgette. Animal secrets / [by] Georgette Barthelemy ; illustrations by J. Reschofsky ; [translated from the French by Richard Marsden]. — London : Marshall Cavendish, 1974. — 5-77p : col ill ; 27cm. — (A question and answer book) (A 'Golden hands' book)
Ill. on lining papers. — Translation of: 'Les animaux et leurs secrets' Paris : Nathan, 1973.
ISBN 0-85685-078-0 : £1.25
(B77-18772)

Forrest, Don. Creatures that look alike / written and illustrated by Don Forrest. — London [etc.] : F. Watts, 1977. — 32p : col ill ; 18x22cm. — (Wildlife books)
ISBN 0-85166-599-3 : £1.95
(B77-20272)

Ricciuti, Edward Raphael. An animal for Alan / by Edward R. Ricciuti ; pictures by Tom Eaton. — Tadworth : World's Work, 1976. — 64p : col ill ; 22cm. — (A science I can read book ; no.107)
Originally published: New York : Harper and Row, 1970.
ISBN 0-437-90107-6 : £1.90
(B77-11220)

Scarry, Richard. About animals / with illustrations by Richard Scarry. — London [etc.] : Hamlyn, 1977. — [24]p : col ill ; 21cm. — (A golden look-look book)
Originally published: as 'Richard Scarry's about animals'. New York : Golden Press, 1976.
ISBN 0-600-30353-5 Sd : £0.40
(B77-28627)

591 — Animals. *Stories, anecdotes*
Modern classic animal stories / collected and with a preface by Jeremy Mallinson ; drawings by William Oliver. — Newton Abbot [etc.] : David and Charles, 1977. — 190p : ill ; 23cm.
ISBN 0-7153-7433-8 : £3.95
(B77-24225)

591 — Animals. Asymmetry
Neville, Anthony Charles. Animal asymmetry / [by] A.C. Neville. — London : Edward Arnold, 1976. — [4],60p : ill ; 23cm. — (Institute of Biology. Studies in biology ; no.67)
Bibl.: p.60.
ISBN 0-7131-2556-x : £2.60
ISBN 0-7131-2557-8 Pbk : £1.30
(B77-04178)

591 — Animals which spend time upside-down. *Juvenile literature*
Gray, Patricia. Upside-down creatures / by Patricia Gray ; illustrated by Derick Bown. — London [etc.] : F. Watts, 1977. — 31p : col ill ; 18x22cm. — (Wildlife books)
ISBN 0-85166-640-x : £1.95
(B77-29432)

591'.01'41 — Animals. Communication with man. *Personal observations*
Boone, J Allen. Kinship with all life / by J. Allen Boone. — New York [etc.] ; London : Harper and Row, 1976. — 157p ; 21cm.
Originally published: New York : Harper and Row, 1954.
ISBN 0-06-060912-5 Pbk : £2.95
(B77-03553)

Boone, J Allen. The language of silence / [by] J. Allen Boone ; edited by Paul and Blanche Leonard. — New York [etc.] ; London : Harper and Row, 1976. — xv,139p ; 21cm.
Originally published: 1970.
ISBN 0-06-060913-3 Pbk : £2.95
(B77-02313)

591'.07'206694 — Zoological expeditions. *Nigeria. Enugu region & Ikom region. Birmingham Biological Expedition to Africa. Reports, surveys*
Birmingham Biological Expedition to Africa. Birmingham Biological Expedition to Africa report. — Birmingham (School of Biological Sciences, University of Birmingham, P.O. Box 363, Birmingham B15 2TT) : [The Expedition], 1976. — [4],72[i.e. 76]p,[12]p of plates : ill, form, maps, ports ; 30cm.
ISBN 0-7044-0243-2 Sp : £1.50
(B77-12446)

591'.072'4 — Animals. Tissues. Culture
Sharp, John Anthony. An introduction to animal tissue culture / [by] J.A. Sharp. — London : Edward Arnold, 1977. — iv,58p : ill ; 22cm. — (Institute of Biology. Studies in biology ; no.82)

Bibl.: p.58.
ISBN 0-7131-2644-2 : £3.00 : CIP rev.
ISBN 0-7131-2645-0 Pbk : £1.50
(B77-28628)

591'.092'4 — Animals. *Personal observations*
Burkett, Molly. Foxes, owls and all : lively, humorous tales of an animal-crazy household / [by] Molly Burkett. — London : Wingate, 1977. — 189p,4p of plates : ill, port ; 21cm. — (A Longbow book)
ISBN 0-85523-241-2 : £3.50
(B77-23414)

Durrell, Jacquie. Intimate relations / [by] Jacquie Durrell. — Large print [ed.]. — London : Prior [etc.], 1977. — [5],211p ; 24cm.
Originally published: New York : Stein and Day ; London : Collins, 1976.
ISBN 0-86043-050-2 : £4.50
(B77-33799)

Gillott, Jacky. Providence Place : animals in a landscape / [by] Jacky Gillott ; line drawings by Jane Percival. — London [etc.] : Hodder and Stoughton, 1977. — 190p : ill ; 23cm.
ISBN 0-340-22369-3 : £4.50
(B77-33800)

591'.092'4 — Zoology. Durrell, Gerald. *Autobiographies*
Durrell, Gerald. Birds, beasts and relatives / [by] Gerald Durrell. — Harmondsworth [etc.] : Penguin, 1976. — [7],248p ; 18cm.
Originally published: London : Collins, 1969.
ISBN 0-14-004385-3 Pbk : £0.75
(B77-20273)

Durrell, Gerald. Catch me a colobus / [by] Gerald Durrell ; illustrated by Edward Mortelmans. — Harmondsworth [etc.] : Penguin, 1976. — 221p : ill ; 18cm.
Originally published: London : Collins, 1972.
ISBN 0-14-004337-3 Pbk : £0.65
(B77-20274)

Durrell, Gerald. Fillets of plaice / [by] Gerald Durrell. — Harmondsworth [etc.] : Penguin, 1976. — xi,178p ; 18cm.
Originally published: London : Collins, 1971.
ISBN 0-14-004338-1 Pbk : £0.60
(B77-20275)

Durrell, Gerald. My family and other animals / [by] Gerald Durrell. — Large print ed. — Leicester : Ulverscroft, 1977. — [6],535p ; 23cm. — (Ulverscroft large print series : [non-fiction])
Originally published: London : Hart-Davis, 1956.
ISBN 0-85456-543-4 : Unpriced
(B77-19382)

Durrell, Gerald. A zoo in my luggage / [by] Gerald Durrell ; with illustrations by Ralph Thompson. — Large print ed. — Leicester : Ulverscroft, 1977. — [6],312p : ill ; 23cm. — (Ulverscroft large print series : [non-fiction])
Originally published: London : Hart-Davis, 1960.
ISBN 0-7089-0017-8 : £2.95
(B77-19383)

591.1 — ANIMALS. PHYSIOLOGY
Gordon, Malcolm Stephen. Animal physiology : principles and adaptations / [by] Malcolm S. Gordon in collaboration with ... [others]. — 3rd ed. — New York : Macmillan ; London : Collier Macmillan, 1977. — xx,669p : ill ; 26cm.
Previous ed.: 1972. — Bibl. — Index.
ISBN 0-02-345330-3 : £12.00
(B77-21873)

591.1 — Organisms. Physiology. Expounded by systems theory. *Study examples: Animals*
Basar, Erol. Biophysical and physiological systems analysis : based on lectures to graduate students / [by] Erol Basar. — Reading, Mass. ; London [etc.] : Addison-Wesley, 1976 [i.e. 1977]. — xvii,429p : ill ; 24cm.
Published in the United States: 1976. — Bibl. — Index.
ISBN 0-201-00846-7 : £20.85
ISBN 0-201-00847-5 Pbk : £10.00
(B77-12447)

591.1'09'04 — Animals. Physiology, 1876-1976. *Essays*
The **pursuit** of nature : informal essays on the history of physiology / [by] A.L. Hodgkin ... [et al.]. — Cambridge [etc.] : Cambridge University Press, 1977. — [6],180p,plate : ill ; 24cm.
'These essays were written as part of the celebrations of the Centenary of the Physiological Society in 1976'. — Bibl. — Index.
ISBN 0-521-21505-6 : £7.50
(B77-28629)

591.1'3 — Animals. Nutrition. *Comparative studies*
Carbohydrates, lipids and accessory growth factors / editor M. Rechcigl, Jr. — Basel ; London [etc.] : Karger ; [Chichester] : [Distributed by Wiley], 1976. — xii,223p : ill ; 23cm. — (Comparative animal nutrition ; vol.1)

Bibl. — Index.
Pbk : Unpriced
ISBN 3-8055-2268-1
(B77-04809)

591.1'3 — Animals. Nutrition. Biochemical aspects
Freedland, R A. A biochemical approach to nutrition / [by] R.A. Freedland and Stephanie Briggs. — London : Chapman and Hall [etc.], 1977. — 63p : ill ; 21cm. — (Outline studies in biology)
Bibl. — Index.
ISBN 0-412-13040-8 Pbk : £1.30
(B77-16878)

591.1'3'2 — Animals. Pancreas. Islets. Evolution. *Conference proceedings*
The **evolution** of pancreatic islets : proceedings of a symposium held at Leningrad, September 1975, under the auspices of the Academy of Sciences, Leningrad / edited by T. Adesanya I. Grillo, L. Leibson, A. Epple. — Oxford [etc.] : Pergamon, 1976. — xii,377p : ill ; 26cm.
Bibl. — Index.
ISBN 0-08-021257-3 : £12.50
(B77-14735)

591.1'33 — Animals. Nutrition. Trace elements
Underwood, Eric John. Trace elements in human and animal nutrition / [by] Eric J. Underwood. — 4th ed. — New York [etc.] ; London : Academic Press, 1977. — xiii,545p : ill ; 24cm.
Previous ed.: 1971. — Bibl. — Index.
ISBN 0-12-709065-7 : £20.95
Also classified at 612'.3924
(B77-21874)

591.1'5 — Animals. Variation
Fingerman, Milton. Animal diversity / [by] Milton Fingerman. — 2nd ed. — New York ; London [etc.] : Holt, Rinehart and Winston, 1976. — vi,250p : ill ; 24cm. — (Modern biology series)
Previous ed.: 1969. — Bibl. — Index.
ISBN 0-03-088405-5 Pbk : £3.75
(B77-04810)

591.1'5'1 — Animals. Embryos. Genes
Davidson, Eric H. Gene activity in early development / [by] Eric H. Davidson. — 2nd ed. — New York [etc.] ; London : Academic Press, 1976. — xvi,452p : ill ; 24cm.
Previous ed.: 1968. — Bibl.: p.383-431. — Index.
ISBN 0-12-205160-2 : £13.50
(B77-24226)

591.1'6 — Animals. Reproduction
Cohen, Jack, *b.1933.* Reproduction / [by] Jack Cohen. — London [etc.] : Butterworth, 1977. — xix,356p : ill ; 24cm.
Bibl.: p.293-308. — Index.
ISBN 0-408-70798-4 Pbk : £3.00
(B77-14736)

591.1'6 — Animals. Reproduction. *Secondary school texts*
Tribe, Philip. Reproduction and growth / [by] Philip Tribe. — London : Macdonald Educational, 1977. — [1],24,[1]p : ill(chiefly col), port ; 27cm. — (Biology colour units)
ISBN 0-356-05527-2 Sd : £0.85
(B77-15853)

591.1'66 — Animals. Viviparity
Hogarth, Peter J. Viviparity / [by] Peter J. Hogarth. — London : Edward Arnold, 1976. — iv,68p : ill ; 22cm. — (Institute of Biology. Studies in biology ; no.75)
Bibl.: p.68.
ISBN 0-7131-2592-6 : £2.60
ISBN 0-7131-2593-4 Pbk : £1.30
(B77-10371)

591.1'6'62 — Animals. Sexual intercourse
Sparks, John. The sexual connection : mating the wild way / [by] John Sparks ; with cartoons by ffolkes. — Newton Abbot [etc.] : David and Charles, 1977. — 192p : ill ; 22cm.
Bibl.: p.186-188. — Index.
ISBN 0-7153-7339-0 : £3.95
(B77-29433)

591.1'8 — Animals. Control systems. *Conference proceedings*
International Colloquium on Physical and Chemical Information Transfer in Regulation of Reproduction and Aging, *1st, Varna, 1974.* Physical and chemical bases of biological information transfer / edited by Julia G. Vassileva-Popova. — New York ; London : Plenum Press, [1976]. — xii,463p : ill ; 26cm.
'Proceedings of the First International Colloquium on Physical and Chemical Information Transfer in Regulation of Reproduction and Aging, October 7-14, 1974, Varna, Bulgaria' - title page verso. — Published in the United States: 1975. — Bibl. — Index.
ISBN 0-306-30862-2 : £22.05
(B77-06085)

591.1'82 — Animals. Sensory perception. Neurophysiological aspects. *Conference proceedings*
'OHOLO' Biological Conference on Sensory Physiology and Behavior, *19th, Ma'alot, 1974.* Sensory physiology and behavior / edited by Rachel Galun ... [et al.]. — New York ; London : Plenum Press, [1976]. — x,357p : ill ; 26cm. — (Advances in behavioral biology ; vol.15)
'Proceedings of the Nineteenth Annual "OHOLO" Biological Conference on Sensory Physiology and Behavior, held in Ma'alot, Israel, March 26-29, 1974' - title page verso. — Published in the United States: 1975. — Bibl. — Index.
ISBN 0-306-37915-5 : £15.44
(B77-06684)

591.1'852 — Animals. Flight & swimming. *Conference proceedings*
Symposium on Swimming and Flying in Nature, *California Institute of Technology, 1974.* Swimming and flying in nature / edited by Theodore Y. -T. Wu, Charles J. Brokaw and Christopher Brennen. — New York ; London : Plenum Press.
Published in the United States: 1975.
Vol.1. — [1976]. — 421,xxi p : ill ; 26cm.
'Proceedings of the first half of the Symposium on Swimming and Flying in Nature, held at the California Institute of Technology, Pasadena, California, July 8-12, 1974' - title page verso. — Bibl. — Index.
ISBN 0-306-37088-3 : £24.89
(B77-01456)

Vol.2. — [1976]. — xv p,p423-1005p : ill ; 26cm.
'Proceedings of the second half of the Symposium on Swimming and Flying in Nature held at the California Institute of Technology, Pasadena, California, July 8-12, 1974' - title page verso. — Bibl. — Index.
ISBN 0-306-37089-1 : £24.89
(B77-01457)

591.1'852 — Animals. Locomotion
Dagg, Anne Innis. Running, walking and jumping : the science of locomotion / [by] Anne Innis Dagg. — London [etc.] : Wykeham Publications, 1977. — x,143p : ill ; 23cm. — (Wykeham science series)
Bibl.: p.135. — Index.
ISBN 0-85109-570-4 : Unpriced
ISBN 0-85109-530-5 Pbk : £3.25
(B77-24227)

591.1'852 — Animals. Locomotion. *Secondary school texts*
Gray, Don. Movement / [by] Don Gray. — London : Macdonald Educational, 1977. — [1], 24,[1]p : ill(chiefly col), col chart ; 27cm. — (Biology colour units)
ISBN 0-356-05525-6 Pbk : £0.85
(B77-08385)

591.1'852 — Animals. Locomotion. Effects of size. *Conference proceedings*
Scale effects in animal locomotion : based on the proceedings of an international symposium held at Cambridge University, September 1975 / edited by T.J. Pedley. — London [etc.] : Academic Press, 1977. — xxi,545p : ill, port ; 24cm.
Bibl. — Index.
ISBN 0-12-549650-8 : £18.00
(B77-24228)

591.1'852 — Animals. Muscles
Wilkie, Douglas Robert. Muscle / [by] D.R. Wilkie. — 2nd ed. — London : Edward Arnold, 1976. — [4],68p : ill ; 22cm. — (Institute of Biology. Studies in biology ; no.11)
Previous ed.: 1968. — Bibl.: p.68.
ISBN 0-7131-2190-4 : £2.50
ISBN 0-7131-2191-2 Pbk : £1.25
(B77-01458)

591.1'852 — Animals. Muscles. Physiology. *Micrographs*
Uehara, Yasuo. Muscle and its innervation : an atlas of fine structure / [by] Yasuo Uehara, Gordon R. Campbell, Geoffrey Burnstock. — London : Edward Arnold, 1976. — x,526p ; 25cm.
Bibl. — Index.
ISBN 0-7131-2520-9 : £35.00
(B77-03003)

591.1'88 — Animals. Brain. Lateralisation
Lateralization in the nervous system / edited by Stevan Harnad ... [et al.]. — New York [etc.] ; London : Academic Press, 1977. — xlix,537p : ill ; 24cm.
Bibl. — Index.
ISBN 0-12-325750-6 : £15.25
(B77-24229)

591.1'88 — Animals. Conditioned reflexes. *Conference proceedings*
Operant-Pavlovian Interactions *(Conference), University of Guelph, 1975.* Operant-pavlovian interactions / edited by Hank Davis, Harry M.B. Hurwitz. — Hillsdale : Erlbaum ; New York ; London [etc.] : Distributed by Wiley, 1977. — xvii,327p : ill ; 24cm.
'On September 4,5, and 6, 1975 a conference entitled "Operant-Pavlovian Interactions" was held at the University of Guelph, in Ontario, Canada' - Preface. — Bibl. — Index.
ISBN 0-470-99026-0 : £14.20
(B77-27084)

591.1'88 — Animals. Muscles. Innervation. *Reviews of research*
Motor innervation of muscle / edited by S. Thesleff. — London [etc.] : Academic Press, 1976. — xiv,351p : ill ; 24cm.
Bibl. — Index.
ISBN 0-12-685950-7 : £9.80
(B77-09699)

591.1'88 — Animals. Nervous system. Evolution. Research. Methodology
Evolution, brain and behavior : persistent problems / edited by R.B. Masterton, William Hodos, Harry Jerison. — Hillsdale : Erlbaum ; New York ; London [etc.] : Distributed by Wiley, 1976. — ix,276p : ill ; 24cm.
Bibl. — Index.
ISBN 0-470-15046-7 : £11.20
Also classified at 591.5
(B77-14239)

591.1'88 — Animals. Nervous system. Signals. Analysis
Glaser, Edmund M. Principles of neurobiological signal analysis / [by] Edmund M. Glaser, Daniel S. Ruchkin. — New York [etc.] ; London : Academic Press, 1976 [i.e. 1977]. — xii,471p : ill ; 24cm.
Published in the United States: 1976. — Bibl. — Index.
ISBN 0-12-285950-2 : £15.25
(B77-13045)

591.1'88 — Animals. Nervous system. Synapses. *Conference proceedings*
Synapses : the proceedings of an International Symposium held under the auspices of the Scottish Electrophysiological Society, 29 March-2 April 1976 / general editors Glen A. Cottrell and Peter N.R. Usherwood. — Glasgow [etc.] : Blackie, 1977. — xix,384p : ill, facsims ; 24cm.
Bibl. — Index.
ISBN 0-216-90326-2 : £13.95
(B77-29434)

591.1'88 — Neurobiology. *Reviews of research*
Progress in neurobiology. — Oxford [etc.] : Pergamon.
Vol.6 / editors G.A. Kerkut, J.W. Phillis. — 1976. — vii,382p : ill ; 28cm.
Bibl. — Index.
ISBN 0-08-020319-1 : £25.00
(B77-00766)

Vol.7 / editors G.A. Kerkut, J.W. Phillis. — 1977. — vii,396p,[18]p of plates,leaf of plate : ill ; 28cm.
Bibl. — Index.
ISBN 0-08-020321-3 : Unpriced
(B77-18139)

591.1'88'0724 — Neurobiology. Research. Use of aneural organisms
Aneural organisms in neurobiology / edited by Edward M. Eisenstein. — New York ; London : Plenum Press, [1976]. — vii,145p : ill ; 26cm. — (Advances in behavioral biology ; vol.13)
'Based in part on the proceedings of the symposium "Aneural Organisms : Their Significance for Neurobiology" held at the Winter Conference on Brain Research in Vail, Colorado, in January, 1972' - title page verso. — Published in the United States: 1975. — Bibl. — Index.
ISBN 0-306-37913-9 : £10.35
(B77-04179)

591.1'9'1 — Animals. Physiology. Effects of environment
Environmental physiology of animals / editors J. Bligh, J.L. Cloudsley-Thompson, A.G. Macdonald. — Oxford [etc.] : Blackwell Scientific, 1976. — viii,456p : ill ; 24cm.
Bibl. — Index.
ISBN 0-632-00068-6 : £18.00
ISBN 0-632-00416-9 Pbk : £9.50
(B77-08386)

591.1'9'27 — Animals. Prostaglandins
Curtis-Prior, P B. Prostaglandins : an introduction to their biochemistry, physiology and pharmacology / [by] P.B. Curtis-Prior. — Amsterdam [etc.] ; Oxford : North-Holland Publishing Co., 1976. — xiii,159p : ill ; 25cm.
Index.
ISBN 0-7204-0588-2 : £10.50
(B77-03554)

591.2 — ANIMALS. DISEASES
591.2'1'823 — Animals. Eyes. Pathology
Saunders, L Z. Ophthalmic pathology of animals : an atlas and reference book / [by] L.Z. Saunders and L.F. Rubin. — Basel ; London [etc.] : Karger ; [Chichester] : [Distributed by Wiley], 1975. — xiv,258p : ill, facsims, ports ; 31cm.
Ill. on lining papers. — Index.
Unpriced
ISBN 3-8055-1580-4
(B77-24230)

591.2'3 — Animals. Parasitic diseases. *Reviews of research*
Advances in parasitology. — London [etc.] : Academic Press.
Vol.15 / edited by Ben Dawes. — 1977. — xx, 409p,plate : ill, 2 maps, ports ; 24cm.
Bibl. — Index.
ISBN 0-12-031715-x : Unpriced
(B77-18140)

591.2'3 — Animals. Pathogens: Microorganisms
Buxton, A. Animal microbiology / [by] A. Buxton and G. Fraser. — Oxford [etc.] : Blackwell Scientific.
In 2 vols.
Vol.1 : Immunology, bacteriology, mycology, disease of fish and laboratory methods. — 1977. — [1],357[i.e. 415],xxxv p,leaf of plate,[34]p of plates : ill(some col) ; 26cm.
Bibl. — Index.
ISBN 0-632-00690-0 : £20.00 : CIP rev.
(B77-14737)

Buxton, Anthony. Animal microbiology / [by] A. Buxton and G. Fraser. — Oxford [etc.] : Blackwell Scientific.
In 2 vols.
Vol.2 : Rickettsias and viruses. — 1977. — viii p,p358a-830[i.e.518p],[78]p of plates : ill(some col) ; 26cm.
Bibl. — Index.
ISBN 0-632-00941-1 : £25.00 : CIP rev.
(B77-14738)

591.2'9 — Animals. Immunology. Evolution. *Conference proceedings*
International Conference on Immunologic Phylogeny, *University of Hawaii, 1975.*
Immunologic phylogeny / edited by W.H. Hildemann and A.A. Benedict. — New York ; London : Plenum Press, 1975. — xiv,485p : ill ; 26cm. — (Advances in experimental medicine and biology ; vol.64)
'Proceedings of the International Conference on Immunologic Phylogeny held at the University of Hawaii Manoa and Hilo campuses, June 11-14, 1975' - title page verso. — Bibl.: p.124. — Index.
ISBN 0-306-39064-7 : £20.48
(B77-10808)

591.3 — ANIMALS. DEVELOPMENT
591.3'1 — Animals. Growth
Chevallier, F. Biodynamics and indicators / [by] F. Chevallier ; translated from the French by E. Drucker. — New York ; London [etc.] : Gordon and Breach, 1977. — xv,225p : ill ; 24cm.
Translation of: 'Biodynamique et indicateurs'. London : Gordon and Breach, 1972. — Bibl.: p.217-222. — Index.
ISBN 0-677-30440-4 : £13.00
(B77-27085)

591.3'2 — Animals. Spermatogenesis
Phillips, David M. Spermiogenesis / [by] David M. Phillips. — New York ; London : Academic Press, 1974. — [4],68p : ill ; 27cm. — (Ultrastructure of cells and organisms)
Bibl.: p.64-67. — Index.
ISBN 0-12-553650-x Sd : Unpriced
(B77-19384)

Roosen-Runge, Edward C. The process of spermatogenesis in animals / [by] Edward C. Roosen-Runge. — Cambridge [etc.] : Cambridge University Press, 1977. — viii,214p, [16]p of plates,leaf of plate : ill ; 24cm. — (Development and cell biology ; 5)
Bibl.: p.170-200. — Index.
ISBN 0-521-21233-2 : £15.50
(B77-18773)

591.3'8 — Animals. Evolution
Hanson, Earl Dorchester. The origin and early evolution of animals / by Earl D. Hanson. — Middletown, Conn. : Wesleyan University Press ; London [etc.] : Pitman, 1977. — x, 670p : ill ; 26cm.
Bibl.: p.594-637. — Index.
ISBN 0-273-01132-4 : £21.00 : CIP rev.
(B77-21875)

591.3'9 — Young animals. *Juvenile literature*
Roberts, David, *b.1926.* First book of baby animals / [by] David Roberts. — [London] ([59 Grosvenor St., W.1]) : Sundial Books Ltd, [1977]. — 5-156p : col ill ; 29cm.
Spine title: The St Michael first book of baby animals. — Col. ill. on lining papers.
ISBN 0-904230-50-3 : £1.99
(B77-28630)

591.4 — ANIMALS. ANATOMY
591.4'094 — Zoology. Comparative anatomy. *Europe, to ca 1800*
Cole, Francis Joseph. A history of comparative anatomy : from Aristotle to the eighteenth century / by F.J. Cole. — New York : Dover Publications [etc.] ; London : Constable, 1975 [i.e. 1976]. — viii,524p : ill, facsims, ports ; 22cm.
Published in the United States: 1975. — Originally published: London : Macmillan, 1944.
ISBN 0-486-60224-9 Pbk : £3.90
Bibl.: p.490-507. - Index
(B77-02314)

591.5 — ANIMALS. ECOLOGY
591.5 — Animals. Behaviour
Ardrey, Robert. The social contract : a personal inquiry into the evolutionary sources of order and disorder / [by] Robert Ardrey ; illustrated by Berdine Ardrey. — [London] : Fontana, 1977. — [9],405p : ill ; 19cm.
Originally published: London : Collins, 1970. — Bibl.: p.376-391. — Index.
ISBN 0-00-635042-9 Pbk : £1.25
(B77-27086)

Barash, David P. Sociobiology and behavior / [by] David P. Barash ; foreword by Edward O. Wilson. — New York ; Oxford [etc.] : Elsevier, 1977. — xvii,378p : ill ; 24cm.
Bibl.: p.333-365. — Index.
ISBN 0-444-99029-1 : £7.14
ISBN 0-444-99036-4 Pbk : Unpriced
Primary classification 301.1
(B77-22346)

Bleibtreu, John Nathan. The parable of the beast / [by] John Bleibtreu. — St Albans : Paladin, 1976. — 283p ; 20cm.
Originally published: New York : Macmillan ; London : Gollancz, 1968. — Index.
ISBN 0-586-08023-6 Pbk : £1.50
(B77-01459)

Burton, Maurice. Inside the animal world : an encyclopedia of animal behaviour / [by] Maurice & Robert Burton. — London [etc.] : Macmillan, 1977. — 5-316p : ill(some col), map ; 26cm.
Index.
ISBN 0-333-19213-3 : £6.95 : CIP rev.
(B77-07353)

591.5 — Animals. Behaviour. *Readings*
Readings in animal behavior / edited by Thomas E. McGill. — 3rd ed. — New York ; London [etc.] : Holt, Rinehart and Winston, 1977. — xiii,482p : ill ; 24cm.
Previous ed.: New York : Holt, Rinehart and Winston, 1973. — Bibl. — Index.
ISBN 0-03-089926-5 Pbk : £5.00
(B77-21135)

591.5 — Animals. Behaviour. *Reviews of research*
Advances in the study of behavior. — New York [etc.] ; London : Academic Press.
Vol.7 / edited by Jay S. Rosenblatt ... [et al.]. — 1976. — xv,395p : ill ; 24cm.
Bibl. — Index.
ISBN 0-12-004507-9 : £17.40
(B77-07910)

591.5 — Animals. Behaviour. Evolution. Ecological aspects
Evolutionary ecology / edited by Bernard Stonehouse and Christopher Perrins. — London [etc.] : Macmillan, 1977. — viii,310p : ill, maps ; 24cm. — (Biology and environment)
Bibl. — Index.
ISBN 0-333-19676-7 : £12.95
(B77-33801)

591.5 — Animals. Behaviour. Evolution. Research. Methodology
Evolution, brain and behavior : persistent problems / edited by R.B. Masterton, William Hodos, Harry Jerison. — Hillsdale : Erlbaum ; New York ; London [etc.] : Distributed by Wiley, 1976. — ix,276p : ill ; 24cm.
Bibl. — Index.
ISBN 0-470-15046-7 : £11.20
Primary classification 591.1'88
(B77-14239)

591.5 — Animals. Instincts
Tinbergen, Nikolaas. The study of instinct / by N. Tinbergen. — [1st ed. reprinted] ; with a new introduction. — New York ; Oxford : Oxford University Press, 1974 [i.e.1976]. — xxi, 228p,plate : ill ; 23cm.
Originally published: 1951. — Bibl. — Index.
ISBN 0-19-501371-9 Pbk : £2.90
(B77-05422)

591.5 — Animals. Instincts. *Stories, anecdotes*
Krachmalnicoff, Patrizia. The magic of the animals / [by] Patrizia Krachmalnicoff ; translated [from the Italian] by Sue Newson-Smith ; with illustrations by Pat Hannah. — London : Arlington Books, 1977. — x,259p : ill ; 23cm.
Translation of: 'Magia degli animali'. Milano : Sugarlo, 1975.
ISBN 0-85140-259-3 : £4.50
(B77-21136)

591.5 — Ethology
Grzimek's encyclopedia of ethology / editor-in-chief Bernhard Grzimek ; [edited by Klaus Immelmann ; translated from the German by Monica Baehr]. — New York ; London [etc.] : Van Nostrand Reinhold, 1977. — xx,705p : ill(some col), maps, ports ; 25cm.
Col. ill. on lining papers. — Originally published: in German. Zurich : Kindler Verlag, 1973. — Bibl.: p.681-684. — Index.
ISBN 0-442-22946-1 : Unpriced
(B77-27865)

591.5'092'4 — Ethology. Lorenz, Konrad. *Biographies*
Nisbett, Alec. Konrad Lorenz / [by] Alec Nisbett. — London : Dent, 1976. — xiv,240p, [16]p of plates : ill, ports ; 24cm.
Bibl.: p.225-230. — Index.
ISBN 0-460-04215-7 : £5.95
(B77-08387)

591.5'0967 — Animals. Ecology. *Africa. Tropical regions*
Owen, Denis Frank. Animal ecology in tropical Africa / [by] D.F. Owen. — 2nd ed. — London [etc.] : Longman, 1976. — 132p,[8]p of plates : ill(some col), maps ; 25cm. — (Tropical ecology series)
Previous ed.: Edinburgh : Oliver and Boyd, 1966. — Bibl.: p.124-126. — Index.
ISBN 0-582-44363-6 : £7.00
ISBN 0-582-44362-8 Pbk : £3.50
(B77-00224)

Reader, John. Pyramids of life : an investigation of nature's fearful symmetry / [by] John Reader, Harvey Croze. — London [etc.] : Collins, 1977. — 222p : ill ; 28cm.
Bibl.: p.219. — Index.
ISBN 0-00-219004-4 : £6.95
(B77-18141)

591.5'24 — Animals. Competition. Mathematical models
Hassell, Michael Patrick. The dynamics of competition and predation / [by] Michael P. Hassell. — London : Edward Arnold, 1976. — iv,68p : ill ; 23cm. — (Institute of Biology. Studies in biology ; no.72)
Bibl.: p.67-68.
ISBN 0-7131-2584-5 : £2.60
ISBN 0-7131-2585-3 Pbk : £1.30
Also classified at 591.5'3
(B77-11813)

591.5'2'4 — Animals. Parasites
Noble, Elmer Ray. Parasitology : the biology of animal parasites / [by] Elmer R. Noble, Glenn A. Noble. — 4th ed. — Philadelphia ; Lea and Febiger ; London : Kimpton, 1976. — ix,566, [6]p of plates,leaf of plate : ill(some col), map ; 27cm.
Previous ed.: 1971. — Bibl. — Index.
ISBN 0-8121-0543-5 : £14.60
(B77-05423)

Smyth, James Desmond. Introduction to animal parasitology / [by] J.D. Smyth. — 2nd ed. — London [etc.] : Hodder and Stoughton, 1976. — xiv,466p : ill ; 29cm. — (Biological science texts)
Previous ed.: London : English Universities Press, 1962. — Bibl. — Index.
ISBN 0-340-21259-4 : £15.00
ISBN 0-340-18232-6 Pbk : £9.75
(B77-03004)

591.5'2'4 — Animals. Parasites. *Secondary school texts*
Probert, A J. Parasites / [by] A.J. Probert. — Harmondsworth : Kestrel Books, 1976. — 96p : ill(some col), facsims, col maps, ports ; 23cm.
Originally published: Harmondsworth : Penguin, 1972. — Bibl.: p.90-91. — List of films: p.92. — Index.
ISBN 0-7226-5291-7 : £2.75
(B77-04811)

591.5'2'4 — Animals. Parasites. Population control
Regulation of parasite populations / edited by Gerald W. Esch ; with introductory remarks by Brent B. Nickol. — New York ; London [etc.] : Academic Press, 1977. — xi,253p : ill ; 24cm.
'In November, 1975, a symposium was jointly sponsored by the American Microscopial Society and the American Society of Parasitologists at their meeting in New Orleans, Louisiana' - Preface. — Bibl. — Index.
ISBN 0-12-241750-x : £9.25
(B77-28631)

591.5'2'4 — Parasites: Animals. Ecology
Ecological aspects of parasitology / editor C.R. Kennedy. — Amsterdam ; Oxford : North-Holland Publishing Co., 1976. — x, 474p : ill ; 25cm.
Bibl. — Index.
ISBN 0-7204-0602-1 : £33.96
(B77-16389)

591.5'2636 — Environment. Adaptation of marine animals
Adaptation to environment : essays on the physiology of marine animals / edited by R.C. Newell. — London [etc.] : Butterworth, 1976. — [13],539p : ill ; 24cm.
Bibl. — Index.
ISBN 0-408-70778-x : £25.00
(B77-02315)

591.5'2'64 — Animals. Ecology. *Soils*
Wallwork, John Anthony. The distribution and diversity of soil fauna / [by] John A. Wallwork. — London [etc.] : Academic Press, 1976. — xiv,355p : ill, map ; 24cm.
Bibl. — Index.
ISBN 0-12-733350-9 : £11.00
(B77-22589)

591.5'3 — Animals. Feeding behaviour. Evolutionary aspects
Cloudsley-Thompson, John Leonard. Dietary adaptations in animals / [by] J.L Cloudsley-Thompson. — Shildon (I.S.A. Building, Shildon, Co. Durham) : Meadowfield Press Ltd, 1976. — [6],69p : ill ; 21cm. — (Patterns of progress : zoology series)
Bibl.: p.62-63. — Index.
ISBN 0-900541-83-0 Pbk : £2.80
(B77-12448)

591.5'3 — Animals. Predatory behaviour. Mathematical models
Hassell, Michael Patrick. The dynamics of competition and predation / [by] Michael P. Hassell. — London : Edward Arnold, 1976. — iv,68p : ill ; 23cm. — (Institute of Biology. Studies in biology ; no.72)
Bibl.: p.67-68.
ISBN 0-7131-2584-5 : £2.60
ISBN 0-7131-2585-3 Pbk : £1.30
Primary classification 591.5'24
(B77-11813)

591.5'6 — Animals. Reproductive behaviour
Dröscher, Vitus Bernwand. They love and kill : sex, sympathy and aggression in courtship and mating / [by] Vitus B. Dröscher ; translated from the German by Jan van Heurck. — London : W.H. Allen, 1977. — xix,363p,[16]p of plates : ill(some col) ; 22cm.
Translation of: 'Sie töten und sie lieben sich'. Hamburg : Hoffman und Campe, 1974. — Index.
ISBN 0-491-01648-4 : £6.50
(B77-11814)

591.5'6 — Animals. Sexual behaviour
Burton, Robert, *b.1941.* The mating game / [by] Robert Burton. — Oxford : Elsevier [etc.], 1976. — 160p : ill(chiefly col) ; 29cm.
Index.
ISBN 0-7290-0039-7 : £4.50
(B77-00225)

591.5'7 — Animals. Behaviour. Role of colour
Street, Philip. Colour in animals / [by] Philip Street ; illustrated by Carol Lawson. — Harmondsworth : Kestrel Books, 1977. — 71p : ill(some col) ; 25cm.
Index.
ISBN 0-7226-5152-x : £3.50
(B77-27087)

591.5'9 — Animals. Communication. Role of pheromones
Shorey, H H. Animal communication by pheromones / [by] H.H. Shorey. — New York [etc.] ; London : Academic Press, 1976. — viii, 167p : ill ; 24cm.
Bibl.: p.123-157. — Index.
ISBN 0-12-640450-x : £10.05
(B77-06685)

591.5'9 — Animals. Optical communication
Hailman, Jack Parker. Optical signals : animal communication and light / [by] Jack P. Hailman. — Bloomington ; London : Indiana University Press, 1977. — xix,362p : ill ; 24cm.
Bibl.: p.317-335. — Index.
ISBN 0-253-34254-6 : £11.25
(B77-29435)

591.6 — ECONOMIC ZOOLOGY
591.6'9 — Venomous animals. *Juvenile literature*
Pope, Joyce. Deadly creatures / [by] Joyce Pope ; illustrated by Richard Orr. — London (90 Great Russell St., WC1B 3PT) : Scimitar, 1977. — [1],32p : col ill ; 14cm. — (Scatterbox)
ISBN 0-241-89714-9 Pbk : £0.40
(B77-31908)

591.6'9'0994 — Venomous animals. *Australia*
Worrell, Eric. Things that sting / [by] Eric Worrell ; drawings by Graham Bryce. — London [etc.] : Angus and Robertson, 1975. — [4],68p : ill ; 22cm.
'An A & R guide' - cover. — Index.
ISBN 0-207-13412-x Sd : Unpriced
Primary classification 615.9'42'0994
(B77-27122)

591.8 — ANIMALS. HISTOLOGY AND CYTOLOGY
591.8'76 — Animals. Cells. Cilia & flagella. *Reviews of research*
Cilia and flagella / edited by M.A. Sleigh. — London [etc.] : Academic Press, 1974. — xi, 500p : ill ; 24cm.
Bibl. — Index.
ISBN 0-12-648150-4 : £10.00
(B77-19385)

591.9 — ZOOLOGY. GEOGRAPHICAL TREATMENT
591.9'2 — Animals. *Oceans. Abyssal zone. Juvenile literature. Fill-in-books*
Knight, Dennis. Monsters of the deep / [by Dennis Knight]. — London ([Dept RWH], 100 Drayton Park, N5 1NA) : Royal Sovereign Group Ltd, 1976. — [2],18p,[2]leaves of plates : ill(chiefly col), port ; 15x21cm. — (Knight, Dennis. Activity books)
Contains Letraset instant pictures.
ISBN 0-900862-44-0 Sd : £0.50
(B77-06686)

591.9'2 — Marine animals dangerous to man
Ziliox, Marc. Dangerous animals of the sea / [by] Marc Ziliox. — Toronto [etc.] ; London : Bantam, 1977. — 159,[1]p : col ill ; 18cm. — (All-colour guide)
'A Ridge Press book'. — Index.
Pbk : £0.85
ISBN 0-553-11142-8
(B77-32631)

591.9'2'941 — Freshwater animals. *Great Britain. Lists*
Maitland, Peter Salisbury. A coded checklist of animals occurring in fresh water in the British Isles / [by] P.S. Maitland. — Edinburgh (12 Hope Terrace, Edinburgh EH9 2AS) : Institute of Terrestrial Ecology, 1977. — 76p ; 30cm.
Bibl.: p.74-76.
ISBN 0-904282-10-4 Sd : £1.50
(B77-18142)

591.9'41 — Animals. *Great Britain*
Thorburn, Archibald. Thorburn's naturalist's sketchbook. — [New ed.] ; with an introduction by Robert Dougall. — London : Joseph, 1977. — 136p : ill(some col) ; 27cm.
Previous ed.: published as 'A naturalist's sketchbook'. London : Longmans, 1919. — Index.
ISBN 0-7181-1567-8 : £6.50
Also classified at 759.2
(B77-15291)

591.9'4114 — Animals. *Scotland. Western Isles. North Uist. Juvenile literature*
Coxon, Philip. The world of an island / [by] Philip Coxon ; illustrated by Michèle Coxon. — London : Faber, 1977. — 3-102p : ill, maps ; 22cm.
Index.
ISBN 0-571-10999-3 : £3.25 : CIP rev.
(B77-23415)

591.9'429'63 — Animals. *Dyfed. Orielton, 1955-1965. Personal observations*
Lockley, Ronald Mathias. Orielton : the human and natural history of a Welsh manor / [by] Ronald Lockley ; illustrated by C.F. Tunnicliffe. — London : Deutsch, 1977. — 332p : ill ; 23cm.
ISBN 0-233-96928-4 : £5.95 : CIP rev.
(B77-24231)

591.9'68 — Animals. *Southern Africa. Personal observations*
Hart, Susanne. Back in the wild / [by] Sue Hart ; illustrated by Leigh Voigt ; with a foreword by George Adamson. — London [etc.] : Collins ; London : Harvill Press, 1977. — 158p : ill ; 26cm.
'The articles ... first appeared as weekly features in the "Rand daily mail" during 1974, 1975 and 1976' - Acknowledgements.
ISBN 0-00-262049-9 : £5.50
(B77-24941)

591.9'711 — Animals. *British Columbia. Personal observations*
Tomkies, Mike. Alone in the wilderness / [by] Mike Tomkies. — London : Macdonald and Jane's, 1977. — 215p ; 23cm.
Originally published: as 'A world of my own'. New York : Reader's Digest Press, 1976.
ISBN 0-354-04142-8 : £4.95
(B77-31195)

591.9'866'5 — Animals. *Galapagos Islands. Primary school texts*
McCullagh, Sheila Kathleen. Galapagos : the strangest islands in the world / [by] Sheila McCullagh and Lois Myers. — London : Longman, 1977. — [1],32p : ill(some col), maps ; 21cm. — (Whizz bang series : whizz bang adventures)
ISBN 0-582-19338-9 Sd : £0.70
(B77-31909)

592 — INVERTEBRATES
592'.01'42 — Invertebrates. Endocrine system
Highnam, Kenneth Charles. The comparative endocrinology of the invertebrates / [by] Kenneth C. Highnam and Leonard Hill. — 2nd ed. — London : Edward Arnold, 1977. — ix, 357p : ill ; 23cm. — (Contemporary biology)
Previous ed.: 1969. — Bibl.: p.308-345. — Index.
ISBN 0-7131-2598-5 : £16.00
ISBN 0-7131-2599-3 Pbk : £8.50
(B77-15292)

592'.09'2 — Marine zooplankton
Wickstead, John Horace. Marine zooplankton / [by] John H. Wickstead. — London : Edward Arnold, 1976. — [4],60p : ill, maps ; 22cm. — (Institute of Biology. Studies in biology ; no.62)
Bibl.: p.60.
ISBN 0-7131-2548-9 : £2.80
ISBN 0-7131-2549-7 Pbk : £1.40
(B77-02316)

592'.09'29 — Biology. Applications of statistical mathematics. *Study examples: Sampling of freshwater benthic invertebrates*
Elliott, John Malcolm. Some methods for the statistical analysis of samples of benthic invertebrates / by J.M. Elliott. — 2nd ed. — Ambleside (The Librarian, The Ferry House, Ambleside, Cumbria LA22 0LP) : Freshwater Biological Association, 1977. — 156p : ill ; 22cm. — (Freshwater Biological Association. Scientific publications ; no.25 ISSN 0367-1887)
Spine title: Statistical analysis. — Previous ed.: 1971. — Bibl.: p.139-142. — Index.
ISBN 0-900386-29-0 Pbk : £2.00
(B77-31196)

592'.09'2941 — Freshwater invertebrates. *Great Britain. Identification manuals*
Quigley, Michael. Invertebrates of streams and rivers : a key to identification / [by] Michael Quigley. — London : Edward Arnold, 1977. — [11],84p : ill ; 25cm.
Bibl.: p.79.
ISBN 0-7131-0091-5 Pbk : £2.95
(B77-21137)

593 — Lower animals. Behaviour. *Early works. Facsimiles*
Jennings, Herbert Spencer. Behavior of the lower organisms / by H.S. Jennings ; with a new foreword by Ching Kung. — Bloomington ; London : Indiana University Press, 1976. — xxix,366p : ill ; 22cm.
Originally published: New York : Columbia University Press ; Macmillan, 1906. — Bibl.: p.351-358. — Index.
ISBN 0-253-31135-7 : £8.70
ISBN 0-253-31136-5 Pbk : £4.90
(B77-00226)

593'.1 — Protozoa. *Festschriften*
Festschrift in honour of C.A. Hoare, FRS on the occasion of his 85th birthday / [edited by P.C.C. Garnham and R. Killick-Kendrick]. — [London] : London School of Hygiene and Tropical Medicine ; Folkestone : Distributed by Dawson, 1977. — [5],199p,[13]leaves of plates,[10]p of plates : ill(incl 1 col), map, ports ; 25cm. — (Protozoology ; vol.3 ISSN 0309-2607)
Includes some contributions in Russian with English summaries. — Bibl.
Pbk : £5.50
(B77-27088)

593'.1'04524 — Animals. Parasites: Protozoa
Parasitic protozoa / edited by Julius P. Kreier. — New York [etc.] ; London : Academic Press.

In 4 vols.
Vol.1 : Taxonomy, kinetoplastids and flagellates of fish. — 1977. — xv,441p : ill, maps ; 24cm.
Bibl. — Index.
ISBN 0-12-426001-2 : £24.85
(B77-23416)

Vol.4 : Babesia, Theileria, Myxosporida, Microsporida, Bartonellaceae, Anaplasmataceae, Ehrlichia and Pneumocystis. — 1977. — xv, 386p : ill ; 24cm.
Bibl. — Index.
ISBN 0-12-426004-7 : £23.50
(B77-31910)

593'.1'07402659 — Microbiology. Organisations. *Cambridgeshire. Cambridge. Culture Centre of Algae and Protozoa. Stock: Protozoa. Cultures. Catalogues*
Culture Centre of Algae and Protozoa. List of strains / Culture Centre of Algae and Protozoa ; edited by E.A. George. — [3rd ed.]. — [Cambridge] ([36 Storey's Way, Cambridge CB3 0DT]) : [The Centre], [1976]. — [3],ii, 120p ; 30cm.
Previous ed.: 1971. — Bibl.: p.119-120.
ISBN 0-904282-06-6 Pbk : £1.00
Primary classification 589'.3'07402659
(B77-23413)

593'.117 — Amoebas. *Secondary school texts*
Brocklehurst, Keith George. Amoeba for schools / [by] K.G. Brocklehurst, B. Joan Davies, assisted by M.I. Walker. — London [etc.] : Hodder and Stoughton, 1977. — 24p : ill ; 25cm. — (Photobiological studies ; no.1)
Bibl.: p.24.
ISBN 0-340-19075-2 Sd : £0.60
(B77-16390)

593'.117'09148 — Soil amoebas. *Identification manuals*
Page, F C. An illustrated key to freshwater and soil amoebae : with notes on cultivation and ecology / by F.C. Page. — Ambleside (The Ferry House, Ambleside, Cumbria LA22 0LP) : Freshwater Biological Association, 1976. — 155p : ill ; 22cm. — (Freshwater Biological Association. Scientific publications ; no.34 ISSN 0367-1887)
Bibl.: p.149-152. — Index.
ISBN 0-900386-26-6 Pbk : £2.50
Also classified at 593'.117'09169
(B77-01460)

593'.117'09169 — Freshwater amoebas. *Identification manuals*
Page, F C. An illustrated key to freshwater and soil amoebae : with notes on cultivation and ecology / by F.C. Page. — Ambleside (The Ferry House, Ambleside, Cumbria LA22 0LP) : Freshwater Biological Association, 1976. — 155p : ill ; 22cm. — (Freshwater Biological Association. Scientific publications ; no.34 ISSN 0367-1887)
Bibl.: p.149-152. — Index.
ISBN 0-900386-26-6 Pbk : £2.50
Primary classification 593'.117'09148
(B77-01460)

593'.12 — Foraminifera. *Reviews of research*
Foraminifera. — London [etc.] : Academic Press.

Vol.2 / edited by R.H. Hedley, C.G. Adams. — 1976. — x,265p,plate : ill, maps, port ; 24cm.
Bibl. — Index.
ISBN 0-12-336402-7 : £10.50
(B77-06687)

593'.9'0968 — Echinoderms. *Southern Africa. Coastal waters*
Clark, Ailsa McGown. The echinoderms of Southern Africa / by Ailsa M. Clark and Jane Courtman-Stock. — London : British Museum (Natural History), 1976. — [6],277p : ill, map ; 26cm. — (British Museum (Natural History). Publications ; no.776)
Bibl.: p.254-259. — Index.
ISBN 0-565-00776-9 : £20.00
(B77-00227)

594 — Molluscs
Purchon, Richard Denison. The biology of the mollusca / by R.D. Purchon. — 2nd ed. — Oxford [etc.] : Pergamon, 1977. — xxv,560p : ill, maps ; 24cm. — (International series of monographs in pure and applied biology : zoology division ; vol.57 ISSN 0074-8307)
Previous ed.: 1968. — Bibl. — Index.
ISBN 0-08-021028-7 : £17.50
(B77-08388)

594'.04'7 — Marine molluscs. Shells
Lindner, Gert. Seashells of the world / [by] Gert Lindner ; translated [from the German] and edited by Gwynne Vevers. — Poole : Blandford Press, 1977. — 271p : ill(chiefly col) ; 20cm.
Ill. on lining papers. — Translation of: 'Muscheln und Schnecken der Weltmeere'. München : BLV Verlagsgesellschaft, 1975. — Bibl.: p.252-254. — Index.
ISBN 0-7137-0844-1 : £4.75
(B77-33232)

594'.04'7 — Marine molluscs. Shells. *Collectors' guides*
Dance, Stanley Peter. The shell collector's guide : an introduction to the world of shells / [by] S. Peter Dance. — Newton Abbot [etc.] : David and Charles, 1976. — 192p : ill(some col), map ; 26cm.
Bibl.: p.183-184. — Index.
ISBN 0-7153-7304-8 : £4.95
(B77-03005)

594'.04'7 — Marine molluscs. Shells. *New Zealand*
Powell, Arthur William Baden. Shells of New Zealand : an illustrated handbook / by A.W.B. Powell. — 5th revised ed. — Christchurch, N.Z. [etc.] ; London : Whitcoulls, 1976. — 154p,[52]p of plates : ill(2 col), maps ; 25cm.
Previous ed.: Christchurch, N.Z. : Whitcombe and Tombs, 1961. — Bibl.: p.134-146. — Index.

ISBN 0-7233-0470-x : £9.20
(B77-21138)

594'.04'7 — Marine molluscs. Shells. *Texas*
Andrews, Jean. Shells and shores of Texas / by Jean Andrews. — [New ed.] ; foreword by William J. Clench. — Austin ; London : University of Texas Press, 1977. — iii-xx,365p, [4]p of plates : ill(some col), maps ; 29cm. — (Elma Dill Russell Spencer Foundation. Series ; no.5)
Previous ed.: published as 'Sea shells of the Texas coast'. 1971. — Bibl.: p.335-353. — Index.
ISBN 0-292-77519-9 : £15.00
(B77-33233)

594'.04'7 — Molluscs. Shells. Collecting. *Australia. Manuals*
Coleman, Neville. Shell collecting in Australia / [by] Neville Coleman. — Sydney [etc.] ; London : A.H. and A.W. Reed, 1976. — 176p : ill(some col), col map(on lining papers), ports ; 27cm.
Bibl.: p.172. — Index.
ISBN 0-589-07195-5 : £13.00
(B77-21139)

594'.11 — Mussels. Predation by oystercatchers. Ecological aspects. *Study regions: Devon. Exe Estuary region*
Goss-Custard, John. Oystercatchers and shellfish : predator-prey studies / [by] John Goss-Custard, Selwyn McGrorty and Chris Reading. — Cambridge (68 Hills Rd, Cambridge CB2 1LA) : Institute of Terrestrial Ecology, 1977. — [2],10p : ill, map ; 21cm.
ISBN 0-904282-12-0 Sd : £0.60
(B77-32632)

594'.3 — Snails. *Juvenile literature*
Zim, Herbert Spencer. Snails / [by] Herbert S. Zim, Lucretia Krantz ; illustrated by René Martin. — Tadworth : World's Work, 1977. — 64p : ill ; 22cm.
Originally published: New York : Morrow, 1975. — Index.
ISBN 0-437-89304-9 : £2.20
(B77-09025)

594'.32'0941 — Prosobranchiata. *Great Britain*
Fretter, Vera. The prosobranch molluscs of Britain and Denmark / by Vera Fretter and Alastair Graham. — Reading (35 Minster St., Reading RG1 2JB) : Angus Graham Associates.
Part 1 : Pleurotomariacea, fissurellacea and patellacea. — 1976. — [4],37,[2]p : ill ; 25cm.
'Supplement 1, The Journal of molluscan studies'. — Bibl.
ISBN 0-905991-00-1 Sd : £1.00
Also classified at 594'.32'09489
(B77-11221)

594'.32'09489 — Prosobranchiata. *Denmark*
Fretter, Vera. The prosobranch molluscs of Britain and Denmark / by Vera Fretter and Alastair Graham. — Reading (35 Minster St., Reading RG1 2JB) : Angus Graham Associates.
Part 1 : Pleurotomariacea, fissurellacea and patellacea. — 1976. — [4],37,[2]p : ill ; 25cm.
'Supplement 1, The Journal of molluscan studies'. — Bibl.
ISBN 0-905991-00-1 Sd : £1.00
Primary classification 594'.32'0941
(B77-11221)

594'.5 — Cephalopoda. *Conference proceedings*
The **biology** of cephalopods : the proceedings of a symposium held at the Zoological Society of London on 10 and 11 April 1975 / edited by Marion Nixon and J.B. Messenger. — London [etc.] : Academic Press for the Society, 1977. — xviii,615p : ill, maps, port ; 24cm. — (Zoological Society of London. Symposia ; no.38)
'The 38th Symposium ... was held in honour of ... J.Z. Young' - jacket. — Bibl. — Index.
ISBN 0-12-613338-7 : £21.00
(B77-23417)

594'.5 — Cephalopoda. *Juvenile literature*
Vevers, Gwynne. Octopus, cuttlefish & squid / [by] Gwynne Vevers ; illustrated by Joyce Bee. — London [etc.] : Bodley Head, 1977. — 48p : col ill ; 24cm. — (The Bodley Head new biologies)
Index.
ISBN 0-370-10806-x : £2.25
(B77-24942)

595'.182 — Longidorus & Xiphinema. Feeding systems. Tissues. Ultrastructure
Robertson, W M. Nematode ultrastructure : the feeding apparatus of Longidorus and Xiphinema / [by] W.M. Robertson and C.E. Taylor. — Dundee (Invergowrie, Dundee DD2 5DA) : Scottish Horticultural Research Institute, 1977. — 20p : ill ; 30cm. — (Scottish Horticultural Research Institute. Lecture notes)

Bibl.: p.20.
Sd : £2.00
(B77-15854)

595'.182 — Roundworms
Croll, Neil Argo. Biology of nematodes / [by] Neil A. Croll and Bernard E. Matthews. — Glasgow [etc.] : Blackie, 1977. — viii,201p : ill ; 21cm. — (Tertiary level biology)
Bibl.: p.185-193. — Index.
ISBN 0-216-90294-0 : £6.25
(B77-18774)

The **organization** of nematodes / edited by N.A. Croll. — London [etc.] : Academic Press, 1976. — viii,439p,fold plate : ill ; 24cm.
Bibl. — Index.
ISBN 0-12-196850-2 : £15.00
(B77-06688)

595'.182'012 — Roundworms. Taxonomy. Implications of evolution
Andrássy, I. Evolution as a basis for the systematization of nematodes / [by] I. Andrássy ; [translated from the Hungarian by I. Andrássy and L. Zombori]. — London [etc.] : Pitman, 1976. — 288p : ill ; 25cm.
Bibl.: p.232-239. — Index.
ISBN 0-273-00968-0 : £5.90
(B77-04180)

595'.182'041 — Roundworms. Physiology
Lee, Donald Lewis. Physiology of nematodes. — 2nd ed. / by D.L. Lee and H.J. Atkinson. — London [etc.] : Macmillan, 1976. — x,218p : ill ; 24cm.
Previous ed.: / by D.L. Lee. Edinburgh, etc. : Oliver and Boyd, 1965. — Index.
ISBN 0-333-18600-1 : £5.95
(B77-04181)

595'.182'04524 — Plants. Parasites: Roundworms
Commonwealth Institute of Helminthology. CIH descriptions of plant-parasitic nematodes / [Commonwealth Institute of Helminthology]. — Slough : Commonwealth Agricultural Bureaux.
Set 3 ; nos 31-45 / [editors Sheila Willmott et al.]. — 1974. — Portfolio : ill ; 34cm.
Nine folders ([33]p.), 8 sheets ([16]p.). — Bibl.
Unpriced
ISSN 0305-0351
(B77-10372)

Commonwealth Institute of Helminthology. CIH descriptions of plant-parasitic nematodes / Commonwealth Institute of Helminthology. — Slough : Commonwealth Agricultural Bureaux.
Set 5 : nos 61-75 / [editors Sheila Willmott et al.]. — 1975. — Portfolio : ill ; 34cm.
Thirteen folders ([48]p), 2 sheets ([4]p). — Bibl.
£4.00
(B77-09026)

Set 6 : nos 76-90 / [editors Sheila Willmott et al.]. — 1975. — Portfolio : ill ; 34cm.
Eleven folders ([37]p), 4 sheets ([8]p). — Bibl.
£4.00
(B77-09027)

595'.187'074094134 — Museums. *Edinburgh. Royal Scottish Museum. Stock: Tardigrada. Catalogues*
Royal Scottish Museum. An annotated catalogue of Tardigrada in the collections of the Royal Scottish Museum, Edinburgh / [compiled by] Clive I. Morgan. — Edinburgh (c/o The Librarian, Royal Scottish Museum, Chambers St., Edinburgh EH1 1JF) : The Museum, 1977. — [2],ii,29p ; 30cm. — (Royal Scottish Museum. Information series : natural history ; 5 ISSN 0307-5036)
Bibl.: p.24-27. — Index.
Sd : Unpriced
(B77-27089)

595.2'04'56 — Arthropoda. Mating behaviour. Evolutionary aspects
Cloudsley-Thompson, John Leonard. Evolutionary trends in the mating of arthropoda / [by] J.L. Cloudsley-Thompson. — Shildon (I.S.A. Building, Shildon, Co. Durham) : Meadowfield Press Ltd, 1976. — [5] ,85p : ill ; 21cm. — (Patterns of progress : zoology series)
Bibl.: p.80-81. — Index.
ISBN 0-900541-82-2 Pbk : £2.80
(B77-11815)

595'.34 — Oncaeidae. Taxonomy. *North-east Atlantic Ocean*
Boxshall, Geoffrey Allan. The planktonic copepods of the northeastern Atlantic Ocean : some taxonomic observations on the Oncaeidae (Cyclopoida) / by Geoffrey Allan Boxshall. — London : British Museum (Natural History), 1977. — [2]p,p103-155 : ill ; 25cm. — (British Museum (Natural History). Bulletins of the British Museum (Natural History) : zoology series ; vol.31, no.3 ISSN 0007-1498)
Bibl.: p.154-155.
Pbk : £4.75
(B77-17500)

595'.3842 — Crabs
Warner, G F. The biology of crabs / [by] G.F. Warner. — London : Elek, 1977. — xv,202p : ill ; 25cm.
Bibl.: p.179-194. — Index.
ISBN 0-236-40087-8 : £6.95
(B77-27090)

595'.3842 — Crabs. *Juvenile literature*
Piers, Helen. The crab / [by] Helen Piers. — London [etc.] : Angus and Robertson, 1977. — [32]p : ill(some col) ; 18x22cm. — (The young nature series)
ISBN 0-207-95674-x : £2.20
(B77-13651)

595'.4 — Arachnida
Savory, Theodore. Arachnida / [by] Theodore Savory. — 2nd ed. — London [etc.] : Academic Press, 1977. — xi,340p : ill, maps ; 24cm.
Previous ed.: 1964. — Bibl.: p.325-334. — Index.
ISBN 0-12-619660-5 : £10.80
(B77-23418)

595'.42'04650941 — Residences. Pests: Mites. Biology. *Great Britain*
Hughes, Agnes Margaret. The mites of stored food and houses / [by] A.M. Hughes. — 2nd ed. — London : H.M.S.O., 1976. — [6],400p, plate : ill ; 26cm. — (Great Britain. Ministry of Agriculture, Fisheries and Food. Technical bulletins ; 9)
Previous ed.: published as 'The mites of stored food'. 1961. — Bibl.: p.380-395. — Index.
ISBN 0-11-240909-1 : £12.00
Primary classification 595'.42'04650941
(B77-00767)

595'.42'04650941 — Stored food. Pests: Mites. Biology. *Great Britain*
Hughes, Agnes Margaret. The mites of stored food and houses / [by] A.M. Hughes. — 2nd ed. — London : H.M.S.O., 1976. — [6],400p, plate : ill ; 26cm. — (Great Britain. Ministry of Agriculture, Fisheries and Food. Technical bulletins ; 9)
Previous ed.: published as 'The mites of stored food'. 1961. — Bibl.: p.380-395. — Index.
ISBN 0-11-240909-1 : £12.00
Also classified at 595'.42'04650941
(B77-00767)

595'.44 — Black widow spiders
Thorp, Raymond W. The black widow spider / [by] Raymond W. Thorp and Weldon D. Woodson ; with a foreword by Emil Bogen. — New York : Dover Publications ; London : Constable, 1976. — iii-xi,222p,[12]p of plates : ill, facsims ; 22cm.
Originally published: as 'Black widow : America's most poisonous spider'. Chapel Hill : University of North Carolina Press, 1945. — Bibl.: p.195-208. — Index.
ISBN 0-486-23405-3 Pbk : £2.50
(B77-32633)

595'.44 — Spiders. *Juvenile literature*
Connell, Stephanie. Spiders / written by Stephanie Connell and Vivienne Driscoll. — London : Macdonald Educational, 1977. — [1], 32p : col ill ; 18cm. — (Readabout)
Adaptation of: 'Spiders'. 1971. — Index.
ISBN 0-356-05541-8 Sd : £0.35
(B77-11816)

595.7 — Entomology
Borror, Donald Joyce. An introduction to the study of insects. — 4th ed. / [by] Donald J. Borror, Dwight M. DeLong, Charles A. Triplehorn. — New York ; London [etc.] : Holt, Rinehart and Winston, 1976. — xii,852p : ill ; 25cm.
Previous ed.: / by Donald J. Borror, Dwight M. DeLong. 1971. — Bibl. — Index.
ISBN 0-03-088406-3 : £15.75
(B77-06689)

595.7 — Insects
Horn, David J. Biology of insects / [by] David J. Horn. — Philadelphia ; London [etc.] : Saunders, 1976. — vii,439p : ill, map ; 27cm.
Bibl.: p.403-417. — Index.
ISBN 0-7216-4780-4 : £11.25
(B77-06086)

Pain, Nesta. Grassblade jungle / by Nesta Pain ; illustrated by Rosamund Seymour. — Hornchurch : I. Henry, 1976. — 207p : ill ; 21cm.
Originally published: London : MacGibbon and Kee, 1957.
ISBN 0-86025-805-x : £3.75
(B77-03006)

Tweedie, Michael. Insect life / [by] Michael Tweedie ; line drawings by Denys Ovenden. — London : Collins, 1977. — 192p,24p of plates : ill ; 22cm. — (Collins countryside series)
Bibl.: p.178-179. — Index.
ISBN 0-00-219343-4 : £2.50
(B77-11222)

Zanetti, Adriano. The world of insects / [by] Adriano Zanetti. — Maidenhead : Sampson Low, 1977. — 256p : ill(chiefly col), col map ; 20cm. — (Sampson Low guides)
Bibl.: p.252-253. — Index.
ISBN 0-562-00061-5 : £3.95
(B77-16879)

595.7 — Insects. *Identification manuals*
Zahradník, Jiří. A field guide in colour to insects / by Jiří Zahradník ; illustrated by František Severa ; [translated from the Czech by Olga Kuthanová]. — London : Octopus Books, 1977. — 319p : ill(chiefly col) ; 22cm.
Spine title: Insects. — Bibl.: p.313. — Index.
ISBN 0-7064-0582-x : £2.95
(B77-31911)

595.7 — Insects. *Juvenile literature*
Manley, Deborah. Let's look at insects / written by Deborah Manley ; illustrated by Annabel Milne and Peter Stebbing ; edited by Jennifer Justice. — London : Ward Lock, 1977. — 3-30p : col ill ; 33cm.
Spine title: Insects. — Index.
ISBN 0-7063-5329-3 : £1.50
(B77-33802)

595.7'001'2 — Insects. Taxonomy. *Periodicals*
Systematic entomology. — Oxford [etc.] : Blackwell Scientific for the Royal Entomological Society of London.
Vol.1, no.1- ; Jan. 1976-. — [1976]. — ill, maps ; 25cm.
Quarterly. — Cover title. — 94p. in 1st issue. — Supersedes: Journal of entomology, series B. — Bibl.
Pbk : £15.00 yearly
ISSN 0307-6970
(B77-03008)

595.7'005 — Entomology. *Periodicals*
Antenna : bulletin of the Royal Entomological Society of London. — London : The Society.
Supersedes: Proceedings of the Royal Entomological Society of London.
Vol.1, no.1- ; July 1977-. — [1977]-. — ill(some col) ; 25cm.
Quarterly. — [1],32p., plate in 1st issue. — Bibl.
Sd : £4.00
ISSN 0140-1890
(B77-27091)

595.7'008 — Insects. *Essays*
Wigglesworth, *Sir* Vincent. Insects and the life of man : collected essays on pure science and applied biology / [by] Sir Vincent B. Wigglesworth. — London : Chapman and Hall [etc.], 1976. — vi,217p : ill ; 23cm.
'A Halsted Press Book'. — Bibl. — Index.
ISBN 0-412-14700-9 : £6.00
ISBN 0-412-14730-0 Pbk : £3.25
(B77-02317)

595.7'01 — Insects. Physiology
The **physiology** of insecta / edited by Morris Rockstein. — 2nd ed. — New York ; London : Academic Press.
In 6 vols. — Previous ed.: in 3 vols. 1964-65.
Vol.2. — 1974. — xix,568p : ill ; 24cm.
Bibl. — Index.
ISBN 0-12-591602-7 : Unpriced
(B77-19386)

Vol.5. — 1974. — xix,648p : ill ; 24cm.
Bibl. — Index.
ISBN 0-12-591605-1 : Unpriced
(B77-19387)

595.7'01 — Insects. Physiology. *Reviews of research*
Advances in insect physiology. — London [etc.] : Academic Press.
Vol.12 / edited by J.E. Treherne, M.J. Berridge and V.B. Wigglesworth. — 1976. — vii,348p : ill ; 24cm.
Bibl. — Index.
ISBN 0-12-024212-5 : £12.80
(B77-05424)

595.7'01'05 — Insects. Physiology. *Periodicals*
Physiological entomology. — Oxford [etc.] : Blackwell Scientific for the Royal Entomological Society of London.
Vol.1, no.1- ; Mar. 1976-. — [1976]-. — ill ; 25cm.
Quarterly. — Cover title. — 71p. in 1st issue. — Supersedes: Journal of entomology, series A. — Bibl.
Pbk : £15.00 yearly
ISSN 0307-6962
(B77-03007)

595.7'01'8 — Insects. Navigation. Role of infrared radiation
Callahan, Philip S. Tuning in to nature : solar energy, infrared radiation, and the insect communication system / [by] Philip S. Callahan ; photographs by the author ; line drawings by James Brogdon. — London [etc.] : Routledge and Kegan Paul, 1977. — xxviii, 240p : ill, ports ; 23cm.
Bibl.: p.223-225. — Index.
ISBN 0-7100-8694-6 : £4.95
Also classified at 595.7'05'9
(B77-27866)

595.7'01'92 — Insects. Biochemistry
Rees, H H. Insect biochemistry / [by] H.H. Rees. — London : Chapman and Hall [etc.], 1977. — 64p : ill ; 21cm. — (Outline studies in biology)
'A Halsted Press Book'. — Bibl. — Index.
ISBN 0-470-98987-4 Pbk : £1.50
(B77-26323)

595.7'01'927 — Insects. Juvenile hormones. *Conference proceedings*
International Symposium on the Chemistry, Metabolism, and Modes of Action of the Juvenile Hormones of Insects, *Lake Geneva, Wis., 1975.* The juvenile hormones / edited by Lawrence I. Gilbert. — New York ; London : Plenum Press, 1976. — x,572p : ill ; 26cm.
'Proceedings of an International Symposium on the Chemistry, Metabolism, and Modes of Action of the Juvenile Hormones of Insects held at Lake Geneva, Wisconsin, November, 1975' - title page verso. — Bibl. — Index.
ISBN 0-306-30959-9 : £28.35
(B77-18775)

595.7'01'9285 — Insects. Chemical analysis
Analytical biochemistry of insects / edited by Ralph B. Turner. — Amsterdam ; Oxford [etc.] : Elsevier, 1977. — vii,315p : ill ; 25cm.
Index.
ISBN 0-444-41539-4 : £17.33
(B77-17501)

595.7'05 — Insects. Behaviour
Passarin d'Entrèves, P. The secret life of insects / [by] P. Passarin d'Entrèves and M. Zunino ; [translation from the French by AGET (language services) Ltd]. — London : Orbis Books, 1976. — 384p : ill(chiefly col) ; 30cm.
'... based on the television series "Les insect[e]s, un monde étrange et méconnu"' - title page verso. — Ill. on lining papers. — Bibl.: p.380. — Index.
ISBN 0-85613-260-8 : £8.95
(B77-16880)

595.7'05 — Insects. Behaviour. Chemical control
Chemical control of insect behavior : theory and application / edited by H.H. Shorey, John J. McKelvey, Jr. — New York ; London [etc.] : Wiley, 1977. — xiii,414p : ill ; 24cm. — (Environmental science and technology)
'A Wiley-Interscience publication'. — Index.
ISBN 0-471-78840-6 : £14.65
(B77-24943)

595.7'05'05 — Insects. Ecological aspects. *Periodicals*
Ecological entomology. — Oxford [etc.] : Blackwell Scientific for the Royal Entomological Society of London.
Vol.1, no.1- ; Feb. 1976-. — [1976]-. — ill ; 25cm.
Quarterly. — Cover title. — 70p. in 1st issue. — Supersedes: Transactions of the Royal Entomological Society of London. — Bibl.
Pbk : £15.00 yearly
ISSN 0307-6946
(B77-03009)

595.7'05'0994 — Insects. Ecology. *Australia*
Matthews, E G. Insect ecology / [by] E.G. Matthews. — St Lucia : University of Queensland Press ; Hemel Hempstead : Distributed by Prentice-Hall, 1976. — xvii, 226p,[6]p of plates : ill(some col) ; 22cm. — (Australian ecology series)
Bibl.: p.186-208. — Index.
ISBN 0-7022-1250-4 : £8.70
ISBN 0-7022-1251-2 Pbk : £4.95
(B77-16391)

595.7'05'24 — Insects. Interactions with plants. Evolutionary aspects
Bernays, Elizabeth A. Some evolutionary aspects of the insect-host plant relationship / [by] Elizabeth A. Bernays. — Ilford : Central Association of Bee-keepers, 1976. — [1],15p : ill ; 21cm. — (Central Association of Bee-keepers. Lectures)
'A lecture given to the Central Association of Bee-keepers on 12th February 1976' - note.
ISBN 0-900909-51-x Sd : £0.55
Also classified at 581.5'24
(B77-11223)

595.7'05'9 — Insects. Communication. Role of infrared radiation
Callahan, Philip S. Tuning in to nature : solar energy, infrared radiation, and the insect communication system / [by] Philip S. Callahan ; photographs by the author ; line drawings by James Brogdon. — London [etc.] : Routledge and Kegan Paul, 1977. — xxviii, 240p : ill, ports ; 23cm.
Bibl.: p.223-225. — Index.
ISBN 0-7100-8694-6 : £4.95
Primary classification 595.7'01'8
(B77-27866)

595.7'0941 — Insects. *Great Britain*
Hyde, George Edward. Insects in Britain / text [and photographs] by George E. Hyde. — Norwich : Jarrold and Sons.
Book 3. — 1977. — [33]p : col ill ; 20cm. — (Jarrold insects series ; book 3)
ISBN 0-85306-686-8 Sd : £0.40
(B77-24232)

Book 4. — 1977. — [33]p : col ill ; 20cm. — (Jarrold insects series ; book 4)
ISBN 0-85306-687-6 Sd : £0.40
(B77-24233)

595.7'0941 — Insects. *Great Britain. Juvenile literature*
Thomson, Ruth. The Nature Trail book of insectwatching / [written by] Ruth Thomson ; [illustrated by John Barber et al.]. — London : Usborne, 1976. — 32p : col ill ; 28cm. — (The Nature Trail series)
Bibl.: p.32. — Index.
ISBN 0-86020-047-7 Sd : £0.75
(B77-11817)

595.7'0941 — Insects. *Great Britain. Lists*
Kloet, George Sidney. A check list of British insects / by George Sidney Kloet and the late Walter Douglas Hincks. — 2nd ed. (completely revised). — London : Royal Entomological Society of London.
Previous ed.: Stockport : Kloet and Hincks, 1945.
Part 3 : [Cleoptera and Strepsiptera] / [revised by R.D. Pope ; editor A. Watson]. — 1977. — xiv,105p ; 23cm. — (Handbook for the identification of British insects ; vol.11, part 3)
Index.
ISBN 0-901546-42-9 Pbk : £8.25
(B77-11818)

595.7'26 — Locusts
Chapman, Reginald Frederick. A biology of locusts / [by] R.F. Chapman. — London : Edward Arnold, 1976. — [4],67p : ill, maps ; 23cm. — (Institute of Biology. Studies in biology ; no.71)
Bibl.: p.66-67.
ISBN 0-7131-2618-3 : £2.80
ISBN 0-7131-2619-1 Pbk : £1.40
(B77-01461)

595.7'31'0941 — Thrips. *Great Britain. Identification manuals*
Thysanoptera / by L.A. Mound ... [et al.]. — London : Royal Entomological Society of London, 1976. — 79p : ill ; 23cm. — (Handbooks for the identification of British insects ; vol.1, part 11)
Bibl.: p.75. — Index.
ISBN 0-901546-40-2 Pbk : £5.30
(B77-07354)

595.7'35'0941 — Stoneflies. *Great Britain. Identification manuals*
Hynes, Hugh Bernard Noel. A key to the adults and nymphs of the British stoneflies (Plecoptera) : with notes on their ecology and distribution / by H.B.N. Hynes. — 3rd ed., with minor revision. — Ambleside [etc.] (The Ferry House, Ambleside, Cumbria LA22 0LP) : Freshwater Biological Association, 1977. — [3], 90,[2]p : ill, maps ; 22cm. — (Freshwater Biological Association. Scientific publications ; no.17 ISSN 0367-1887)
Previous ed.: i.e. 2nd revised ed., 1967. — Bibl.: p.88-90. — Index.
ISBN 0-900386-28-2 Sd : £1.00
(B77-17502)

595.7'4 — Megaloptera & Neuroptera. *Great Britain. Identification manuals*
Elliott, John Malcolm. A key to the larvae and adults of British freshwater Megaloptera and Neuroptera : with notes on their life cycles and ecology / by J.M. Elliott ; illustrated by D.E. Kimmins and C. Joan Worthington. — Ambleside [etc.] (The Ferry House, Ambleside, Cumbria LA22 0LP) : Freshwater Biological Association, 1977. — [1],52p,plate : ill ; 21cm. — (Freshwater Biological Association. Scientific publications ; no.35 ISSN 0367-1887)
Cover title: A key to British freshwater Megaloptera and Neuroptera. — Bibl.: p.48-51. — Index.
ISBN 0-900386-27-4 Sd : £1.00
(B77-17503)

595.7'52 — Callaphididae & Chaitophoridae. *Great Britain. Identification manuals*
Stroyan, Henry Lindsay Gray. Homoptera, Aphidoidea, Chaitophoridae & Callaphididae / by H.L.G. Stroyan. — London : Royal Entomological Society of London, 1977. — viii, 130p : ill ; 23cm. — (Handbooks for the identification of British insects ; Vol.2, part 4(a))
Bibl.: p.124. — Index.
ISBN 0-901546-41-0 Pbk : £9.75
(B77-13652)

595.7'52 — Plants. Virus diseases. Vectors: Aphids
Aphids as virus vectors / edited by Kerry F. Harris, Karl Maramorosch. — New York [etc.] ; London : Academic Press, 1977. — xvi, 559p : ill ; 24cm.
Bibl. — Index.
ISBN 0-12-327550-4 : £20.60
(B77-25636)

595.7'6 — Beetles
Evans, Glyn. The life of beetles / [by] Glyn Evans ; foreword by R.A. Crowson. — London : Allen and Unwin, 1977. — 232p : ill ; 24cm.
Originally published: 1975. — Bibl.: p.213-223. — Index.
ISBN 0-04-595012-1 Pbk : £2.95
(B77-27867)

595.7'6'094 — Beetles. *Europe*
Lyneborg, Leif. Beetles in colour / [by] Leif Lyneborg ; illustrations by Niels Jonsson. — English ed. / supervised [i.e. translated from the Danish and adapted] by Gwynne Vevers. — Poole : Blandford Press, 1977. — [4],187p : ill(chiefly col) ; 19cm. — ([Blandford colour series])
Previous ed: published in Danish. Copenhagen : Politikens, 1976. — Bibl.: p.180. — Index.
ISBN 0-7137-0827-1 : £3.25
(B77-16392)

595.7'6'0941 — Beetles. *Great Britain*
Joy, Norman Humbert. A practical handbook of British beetles / by Norman H. Joy. — Faringdon : Classey, 1976. — 2v.(xvii,622;[4], 194p) : ill ; 23cm.
Facsimile reprint of: 1st ed. London : H.F. and G. Witherby, 1932. — Index.
ISBN 0-900848-91-x : £30.00
(B77-09028)

595.7'74 — Houseflies. *Juvenile literature*
Benson, Barbara. The fly / [by Barbara Benson] ; [adapted from the Dutch of Francis Brewer ; illustrated by Jan van Wijngaarden]. — Cambridge [etc.] : Cambridge University Press, 1977. — [1],16,[2]p : chiefly ill(chiefly col), map ; 22cm. — (A pole star book)
ISBN 0-521-21435-1 Sd : £0.45(non-net)
(B77-07911)

595.7'8 — Butterflies & moths
Staněk, Václav Jan. The illustrated encyclopedia of butterflies & moths / by V.J. Staněk ; edited by Brian Turner ; [translated from the Czech by Vera Gissing]. — London : Octopus Books, 1977. — 352p : chiefly ill(chiefly col) ; 24cm.
Bibl.: p.345-346. — Index.
ISBN 0-7064-0547-1 : £3.95
(B77-33234)

595.7'8 — Lepidoptera
Goodden, Robert. The wonderful world of butterflies and moths / [by] Robert Goodden. — London [etc.] : Hamlyn, 1977. — 96p : col ill ; 33cm.
Col. ill. on lining papers. — Index.
ISBN 0-600-31392-1 : £2.95
(B77-20276)

595.7'8 — Lepidoptera. *Juvenile literature*
Whitlock, Ralph. A closer look at butterflies and moths / [by] Ralph Whitlock ; illustrated by Norman Weaver, Tony Swift, Philip Weare. — London : Hamilton, 1977. — 32p : ill(chiefly col), col maps ; 27cm. — (A closer look book ; 17)
Index.
ISBN 0-241-89557-x : £1.75
(B77-27092)

595.7'8'09415 — Butterflies & moths. *Ireland. Secondary school texts*
Goodhue, Derek. Irish butterflies and moths / text and illustrations Derek Goodhue. — [Tallaght] : Folens, [1977]. — [1],p.129-160 : col ill ; 25cm. — (Irish environmental library series ; no.30)
Sd : £0.60
(B77-18776)

595.7'81'097 — Moths. *North America*
The **moths** of America north of Mexico / [board of editors Richard B. Dominick et al.]. — London : Classey [etc.] [for the Wedge Entomological Research Foundation].
Fasc. 13.2B : Pyraloidea, Pyralidae, comprising the subfamily Pyraustinae, tribe Pyraustini (conclusion) / [by] Eugene Munroe. — 1976. — [18]p,p81-150,p xiii-xvii,[5]leaves of plates,[12]p of plates : ill(some col) ; 30cm.
Index.
ISBN 0-900848-96-0 Pbk : £19.70
(B77-07355)

595.7'89 — Butterflies. *Cut-out books*
Make and know butterflies / [main drawings by Anthony Colbert]. — [London] ([Wheatsheaf House, Carmelite St., E.C.4]) : GeminiScan Ltd, 1974. — [2],24,[1]p : ill(chiefly col), col map ; 33cm.
Six leaves, with versos blank, are perforated for making press-out models.
ISBN 0-85691-009-0 Sd : £0.85
(B77-20277)

595.7'89 — Butterflies. *Juvenile literature*
Sheehan, Angela. The butterfly / by Angela Sheehan ; illustrated by Maurice Pledger. — London [etc.] : Angus and Robertson, 1976. — [26]p : col ill ; 23cm. — (Eye-view library)
ISBN 0-207-95709-6 : £1.60
(B77-01462)

595.7'89 — Butterflies. Life cycle. *Study examples: Large white butterflies. Illustrations. Juvenile literature*
Cooke, John. The butterfly cycle / photography by John Cooke ; editorial consultants Oxford Scientific Films. — London : G. Whizzard Publications Ltd : [Distributed by] Deutsch, 1976. — [29]p : chiefly ill(chiefly col) ; 20x26cm. — (Nature's way ; no.2)
Ill. on lining papers.
ISBN 0-233-96766-4 : £1.75
(B77-03555)

595.7'89 — Hipparchiae. Taxonomy
Kudrna, Otakar. A revision of the genus Hipparchia Fabricius / [by] Otakar Kudrna. — Faringdon : Classey, 1977. — [4],300p : ill ; 21cm.
Bibl.: p.181-200. — Index.
ISBN 0-900848-97-9 Pbk : Unpriced
(B77-32634)

595.7'89'04390941 — Butterflies. Caterpillars. *Great Britain*
Hyde, George Edward. British caterpillars, butterflies / with text and photographs by George E. Hyde. — Norwich : Jarrold and Sons, 1977. — [33]p : col ill ; 20cm. — (Jarrold caterpillars series ; book 1)
Index.
ISBN 0-85306-720-1 Sd : £0.40
(B77-33803)

595.7'89'0941 — Butterflies. *Great Britain*
Newman, Leonard Hugh. Looking at butterflies / [by] L. Hugh Newman ; illustrated by Anthony Moore. — [New ed.] / edited by George E. Hyde. — London : Collins, 1977. — 144p,16p of plates : col ill, col maps ; 20cm.
Previous ed.: 1959. — Index.
ISBN 0-00-219688-3 : £3.95
(B77-29436)

595.7'89'094252 — Butterflies. *Nottinghamshire*
Measures, David G. Bright wings of summer : watching butterflies / [by] David G. Measures. — London [etc.] : Cassell, [1976]. — 160p : ill(some col), facsims ; 26cm.
Ill., text on lining papers. — Bibl.: p.155-156. — Index.
ISBN 0-304-29764-x : £5.00
(B77-09029)

595.7'9'0941 — Hymenoptera. *Great Britain. Identification manuals*
Richards, Owain Westmacott. Hymenoptera : introduction and key to families / by Owain Westmacott Richards. — 2nd ed. — London : Royal Entomological Society of London, 1977. — iv,100p : ill ; 23cm. — (Handbooks for the identification of British insects ; vol.6, part 1)
Previous ed.: 1956. — Bibl.: p.88-92. — Index.
Pbk : Unpriced
(B77-31912)

595.7'96 — Black ants. *Illustrations. Juvenile literature*
Knobler, Susan. The black ant / [by] Susan Knobler. — London : A. and C. Black, 1977. — [28]p : of col ill ; 22cm. — (Books without words)
Col. ill. on lining papers.
ISBN 0-7136-1692-x : £1.50
(B77-21876)

595.7'96'0941 — Ants. *Great Britain*
Brian, Michael Vaughan. Ants / [by] M.V. Brian. — London : Collins, 1977. — 223p,2 leaves of plates, 16p of plates : ill(some col), maps ; 23cm. — (The new naturalist ; [59])
Bibl.: p.201. — Index.
ISBN 0-00-219378-7 : £5.95
(B77-28632)

595.7'98 — Sphecidae. Taxonomic groups
Bohart, R M. Sphecid wasps of the world : a generic revision / [by] R.M. Bohart and A.S. Menke in collaboration with [others]. — Berkeley [etc.] ; London : University of California Press, 1976 [i.e. 1977]. — ix,695p, plate : ill(some col) ; 29cm.
Published in the United States: 1976. — Bibl.: p.593-625. — Index.
ISBN 0-520-02318-8 : £34.00
(B77-12449)

595.7'99 — Bees. *Juvenile literature*
Björk, Gun. Bees / text by Gun Björk ; illustrations by Ingvar Björk ; translated [from the Swedish] by Joan Tate. — London : Pelham, 1977. — 32p : col ill ; 23cm.
Translation of: 'Bin'. Stockholm : Bonniers, 1976. — Index.
ISBN 0-7207-0963-6 : £1.95
(B77-24235)

595.7'99 — Honey-bees
More, Daphne. The bee book : the history and natural history of the honeybee / [by] Daphne More. — Newton Abbot [etc.] : David and Charles, 1976. — 143p : ill, facsims, ports ; 24cm.
Bibl.: p.137. — Index.
ISBN 0-7153-7268-8 : £4.50
Also classified at 638'.1'09
(B77-03010)

595.7'99 — Honey-bees. *Juvenile literature. Illustrations*
Thompson, David, *b.1945.* Bees and honey / photography by David Thompson ; editorial consultants Oxford Scientific Films. — London : G. Whizzard Publications Ltd : [Distributed by] Deutsch, 1976. — [29]p : chiefly ill(chiefly col) ; 20x26cm. — (Nature's way ; no.3)
Ill. on lining papers.
ISBN 0-233-96768-0 : £1.75
(B77-03011)

595.7'99 — Honey-bees. Brain. Physiology
Pickard, Robert Stewart. The honeybee brain / [by] R.S. Pickard. — Ilford : Central Association of Bee-keepers, 1976. — [1],16p : ill ; 21cm. — (Central Association of Bee-keepers. Lectures)
' ... given ... on 27th September 1975' - p.1. — Bibl.: p.15-16.
ISBN 0-900909-48-x Sd : £0.60
(B77-01463)

595.7'99 — Honey-bees. Flight
Pringle, John William Sutton. The flight of the bee / [by] J.W.S. Pringle. — Ilford (8 Gloucester Gardens, Ilford, Essex) : Central Association of Bee-keepers, 1976. — [1],13p : ill ; 21cm. — (Central Association of Bee-keepers. Lectures)
'A lecture given to the Central Association of Bee-keepers on 5th November 1976' - p.1. — Bibl.: p.7.
ISBN 0-900909-52-8 Sd : £0.60
(B77-14240)

596 — VERTEBRATES
Orr, Robert Thomas. Vertebrate biology / [by] Robert T. Orr. — 4th ed. — Philadelphia ; London [etc.] : Saunders, 1976. — viii,472p : ill, maps ; 27cm.
Previous ed.: 1971. — Bibl. — Index.
ISBN 0-7216-7018-0 : £10.50
(B77-01464)

596 — Vertebrates. *Juvenile literature*
Another picture book of animals. — [London] ([26 Thornhill Rd, N1 1HW]) : [Ramboro Enterprises Ltd], [1977]. — [28]p : col ill ; 32cm.
Col. ill. on lining papers.
£0.70
(B77-15855)

My book of animals. — [London] ([26 Thornhill Rd, N1 1HW]) : [Ramboro Enterprises Ltd], [1977]. — [28]p : col ill ; 32cm.
Col. ill. on lining papers. — Not the same as B71-12012.
£0.70
(B77-15856)

596 — Vertebrates. *Primary school texts*
Fice, Robert Henry Charles. Animal world / [by R.H.C. Fice, with a contribution by Ruth Snell ; illustrated by John Francis]. — London [etc.] : Macmillan, 1977. — 1v. : ill(some col) ; 52x93cm fold. to 22x46cm. — (Young researchers project)
Two copies each of 7 booklets, 1 copy of 1 booklet, 6 fold. sheets ([6] sides), 18 cards ([36] sides), sound disc (2s. ; 7in. ; 33 1/3 rpm) all in plastic pockets. — Bibl.: p.6-10 (Teachers' resource book). — List of visual aids: p.11-12 (Teachers' resource book).
ISBN 0-333-18459-9 : Unpriced
(B77-17504)

596'.0022'2 — Vertebrates. *Colouring books*
Wild animals. — Maidenhead : Purnell, 1977. — [48]p : ill ; 28cm. — (Colour and learn)
Fill-in book.
Pbk : £0.15
(B77-09700)

596'.0022'2 — Vertebrates. *Illustrations*
Grassé, P P. Larousse animal portraits / [by] P.P. Grassé ; consultant editor Maurice Burton ; [translated from the French by John Bailie]. — London [etc.] : Hamlyn, 1977. — 174p : col ill ; 29cm.
Translation of: 'Le plus beau bestiaire du monde'. Paris : Librairie Larousse, 1970.
ISBN 0-600-35507-1 : £6.95
Primary classification 758'.3
(B77-25792)

596'.0074 — Zoos. Vertebrates. *Colouring books*
Zoo animals colour copy book. — Maidenhead : Purnell, 1977. — [20]p : of ill(some col) ; 28cm.

Sd : £0.15
(B77-09701)

596'.01 — Organisms. Comparative physiology. *Study examples: Vertebrates*
Introduction to comparative physiology / Leon Goldstein, editor ; contributors P.J. Bentley ... [et al.]. — New York ; London [etc.] : Holt, Rinehart and Winston, 1977. — ix,533p : ill ; 25cm.
Bibl. — Index.
ISBN 0-03-012411-5 : £7.50
(B77-22590)

596'.01'1 — Vertebrates. Microcirculatory system
Microcirculation / edited by Gabor Kaley and Burton M. Altura. — Baltimore ; London [etc.] : University Park Press.
In 3 vols. — '... a volume on microcirculation ... to honor Benjamin W. Zweifach' - Preface.
Vol.1. — 1977. — xiv,528p : ill, port ; 24cm.
Bibl. — Index.
ISBN 0-8391-0966-0 : £28.25
(B77-18777)

596'.01'42 — Vertebrates. Endocrine system
Turner, Clarence Donnell. General endocrinology / [by] C. Donnell Turner, Joseph T. Bagnara. — 6th ed. — Philadelphia ; London [etc.] : Saunders, 1976. — iii-x,596p : ill ; 26cm.
Previous ed.: 1971. — Bibl. — Index.
ISBN 0-7216-8933-7 : £13.00
(B77-03556)

596'.01'42 — Vertebrates. Pineal gland. *State-of-the-art reviews*
The **pineal.** — Montreal ; Lancaster : Eden Press ; [Edinburgh] : Distributed by Churchill Livingstone. — (Annual research reviews ISSN 0703-1629)
[Vol.1] : [1976] / [by] Richard Relkin. — 1976. — [9],187p ; 22cm.
Bibl.: p.80-181. — Index.
ISBN 0-904406-26-1 : £11.50
ISBN 0-443-01729-8 (Churchill Livingstone)
(B77-33804)

[Vol.2] : 1977 / [by] Russel J. Reiter. — 1977. — [8],184p ; 22cm.
Bibl.: p.151-177. — Index.
ISBN 0-88831-006-4 : £11.50
(B77-33805)

596'.01'852 — Vertebrates. Bones. Physiology
The **biochemistry** and physiology of bone / edited by Geoffrey H. Bourne. — 2nd ed. — New York [etc.] ; London : Academic Press.
In 4 vols.
Vol.4 : Calcification and physiology. — 1976. — xix,580p : ill ; 24cm.
Previous ed.: in 1 vol. New York : Academic Press, 1956. — Bibl. — Index.
ISBN 0-12-119204-0 : £27.45
(B77-08389)

596'.01'88 — Vertebrates. Nervous system. Evolution. Related to evolution of behaviour. *Conference proceedings*
Evolution of brain and behavior in vertebrates / edited by R.B. Masterton ... [et al.]. — Hillsdale : Erlbaum ; New York ; London [etc.] : Distributed by Wiley, 1976. — xiii, 482p : ill ; 24cm.
Based on a conference held in Tallahassee in February, 1973. — Bibl. — Index.
ISBN 0-470-15045-9 : £22.45
Also classified at 596'.05
(B77-14739)

596'.02 — Vertebrates. Diseases. *Conference proceedings*
International Wildlife Disease Conference, *3rd, University of Munich, 1975.* Wildlife diseases / edited by Leslie Andrew Page. — New York ; London : Plenum Press, 1976. — xv,686p : ill, maps ; 24cm.
'Proceedings of the Third International Wildlife Disease Conference held at the University of Munich's Institute for Zoology and Hydrobiology in Munich, 1975 and sponsored by the Wildlife Disease Association Inc.' - title page verso. — Includes some contributions in German. — Bibl. — Index.
ISBN 0-306-30922-x : £31.19
(B77-19388)

596'.02'2 — Vertebrates. Embryos. Teratology. Testing. *Conference proceedings*
International Conference on Tests of Teratogenicity in Vitro, *Woods Hole, 1975.* Tests of teratogenicity in vitro : proceedings of the International Conference on Tests of Teratogenicity in Vitro, Woods Hole, Mass., 1-4 April, 1975 / editors J.D. Ebert, M. Marois. — Amsterdam [etc.] ; Oxford : North-Holland Publishing Co., 1976. — 494,[3]p : ill, port ; 25cm.
At head of title: Institut de la Vie. — '... conference held ... in honor of Professor Etienne Wolff' - p.11. — English text, parallel French and English opening and closing addresses.
ISBN 0-7204-0476-2 : £35.13
(B77-15857)

596'.02'95 — Vertebrates. Immune reactions. Evolution
Marchalonis, John J. Immunity in evolution / [by] John J. Marchalonis. — London : Edward Arnold, 1977. — xx,316p : ill ; 24cm.
Originally published: Cambridge, Mass. : Harvard University Press, 1976. — Bibl.: p.265-309. — Index.
ISBN 0-7131-2657-4 : £10.00
(B77-23420)

596'.02'95 — Vertebrates. Immune reactions. Role of lymphocytes. Development. *Conference proceedings*
International Symposium on the Phylogeny of T and B Cells, *New Orleans, 1976.* Phylogeny of thymus and bone marrow-bursa cells : proceedings of an International Symposium on the Phylogeny of T and B Cells, New Orleans, Louisiana, 1-3 June 1976, organized by R.K. Wright under the auspices of the Division of Comparative Immunology, American Society of Zoologists / edited by Richard K. Wright and Edwin L. Cooper. — Amsterdam [etc.] ; Oxford : North-Holland Publishing Co., 1976. — xix,325p : ill ; 25cm.
Index.
ISBN 0-7204-0603-x : £15.93
(B77-18143)

596'.02'95 — Vertebrates. Immune reactions. Role of spleen. *Conference proceedings*
Conference on Immunodynamics, *1st, Cleveland, 1976.* Immuno-aspects of the spleen : proceedings of a Conference on Immunodynamics, Cleveland, Ohio, May 19 and 20, 1976 / editors Jack R. Battisto and J. Wayne Streilein. — Amsterdam [etc.] ; Oxford : North-Holland Publishing Co., 1976. — xii, 471p : ill ; 25cm.
'... First Conference on Immunodynamics' - Introduction. — Index.
ISBN 0-7204-0593-9 : £22.84
(B77-05425)

596'.03'8 — Vertebrates. Evolution. *Festschriften*
Problems in vertebrate evolution : essays presented to Professor T.S. Westoll, FRS, FLS / editors S. Mahala Andrews, R.S. Miles, A.D. Walker. — London [etc.] : Academic Press for the Linnean Society of London, 1977. — xi,411p,[6] leaves of plates,[20]p of plates : ill, port ; 27cm. — (Linnean Society of London. Symposium series ; no.4)
'This volume is associated with the symposium held on 8th January 1976 in the rooms of the Linnean Society at Burlington House, Piccadilly, London ...' - Preface. — Bibl. — Index.
ISBN 0-12-059950-3 : £18.50
(B77-17505)

596'.03'8 — Vertebrates. Evolution. Expounded by classification
Lovtrup, Soren. The phylogeny of vertebrata / [by] Soren Lovtrup. — London [etc.] : Wiley, 1977. — xii,330p : ill, maps ; 26cm.
'A Wiley-Interscience Publication'. — Bibl.: p.287-310. — Index.
ISBN 0-471-99412-x : £15.00
(B77-21140)

596'.04 — Chordates. Anatomy
Kluge, Arnold G. Chordate structure and function. — 2nd ed. / [by] Arnold G. Kluge in collaboration with ... [others]. — New York : Macmillan ; London : Collier Macmillan, 1977. — x,628p : ill ; 26cm.
Previous ed.: / by Allyn J. Waterman in collaboration with others. 1971. — Bibl. — Index.
ISBN 0-02-364800-7 : £12.00
(B77-31913)

596'.04 — Vertebrates. Anatomy
Romer, Alfred Sherwood. The vertebrate body. — 5th ed. / [by] Alfred Sherwood Romer, Thomas S. Parsons. — Philadelphia ; London [etc.] : Saunders, 1977. — viii,624p : ill(some col) ; 27cm.
Previous ed.: / by Alfred Sherwood Romer. 1970. — Bibl.: p.584-601. — Index.
ISBN 0-7216-7668-5 : £12.50
(B77-24944)

596'.05 — Vertebrates. Behaviour. Evolution. Related to evolution of nervous system. *Conference proceedings*
Evolution of brain and behavior in vertebrates / edited by R.B. Masterton ... [et al.]. — Hillsdale : Erlbaum ; New York ; London [etc.] : Distributed by Wiley, 1976. — xiii, 482p : ill ; 24cm.
Based on a conference held in Tallahassee in February, 1973. — Bibl. — Index.
ISBN 0-470-15045-9 : £22.45
Primary classification 596'.01'88
(B77-14739)

596'.05'24 — Vertebrates. Population. Statistical analysis
Caughley, Graeme. Analysis of vertebrate populations / [by] Graeme Caughley. — London [etc.] : Wiley, 1977. — ix,234p : ill ; 24cm.
'A Wiley-Interscience Publication'. — Bibl.: p.217-228. — Index.
ISBN 0-471-01705-1 : £8.75
(B77-12450)

596'.08'24 — Vertebrates. Nervous system. Tissues. Anatomy. Research. Freeze-etching
Sandri, C. Membrane morphology of the vertebrate nervous system : a study with freeze-etch technique / by C. Sandri, J.M. van Buren and K. Akert. — Amsterdam ; Oxford [etc.] : Elsevier, 1977. — ix,384p : ill ; 27cm. — (Progress in brain research ; vol.46)
Bibl.: p.363-380. — Index.
ISBN 0-444-41479-7 : £39.81
(B77-16393)

596'.0941 — Naturalised vertebrates. *Great Britain*
Lever, Christopher. The naturalized animals of the British Isles / [by] Christopher Lever ; foreword by Peter Scott ; drawings by Ann Thomson. — London : Hutchinson, 1977. — 600p : ill, maps ; 24cm.
Maps on lining papers. — Bibl.: p.521-558. — Index.
ISBN 0-09-127790-6 : £7.50
(B77-23421)

596'.0942 — Vertebrates. *England. Personal observations*
Drabble, Phil. A weasel in my meatsafe / [by] Phil Drabble ; with drawings by Ralph Thompson. — [Revised ed.]. — London : Joseph, 1977. — 187p : ill ; 21cm.
Previous ed.: London : Collins, 1957.
ISBN 0-7181-1635-6 : £3.95
(B77-25637)

596'.099 — Vertebrates. *Oceania. Juvenile literature*
Animals of Oceania / [text editors Rinaldo D. D'Ami, Mario Faustinelli, Antonio Aliperta ; illustrated by Andrew W. Allen et al.] ; translated [from the Italian] by Irene R. Anderson ; edited in Australia by Alec Chisholm. — London [etc.] : F. Warne, 1976. — 5-61p : col ill, col maps ; 31cm. — (The private lives of animals series)
Text on lining paper. — Originally published: in Italian. Milan : AMZ Editrice, 1970.
ISBN 0-7232-1859-5 : £2.50
(B77-00228)

597 — Fish
De Carli, Franco. The world of fishes / [by] Franco de Carli. — Maidenhead : Sampson Low, 1977. — 256p : ill(chiefly col), col maps ; 20cm. — (Sampson Low guides)
Bibl.: p.252-253. — Index.
ISBN 0-562-00060-7 : £3.95
(B77-29437)

Ichthyology / [by] Karl F. Lagler ... [et al.] ; illustrated by William L. Brudon. — 2nd ed. — New York ; London [etc.] : Wiley, 1977. — xvii,506p : ill, maps ; 24cm.
Previous ed.: / by K.F. Lagler, J.E. Bardach, and R.R. Miller. New York : Wiley, 1962. — Bibl. — Index.
ISBN 0-471-51166-8 : £13.50
(B77-33235)

597'.05'0913 — Fish. Ecology. *Tropical regions*
Lowe-McConnell, Rosemary Helen. Ecology of fishes in tropical waters / [by] R.H. Lowe-McConnell. — London : Edward Arnold, 1977. — iv,64p : ill, map ; 22cm. — (Institute of Biology. Studies in biology ; no.76)
Bibl.: p.63-64.
ISBN 0-7131-2594-2 : £3.60
ISBN 0-7131-2595-0 Pbk : £1.80
(B77-25638)

597'.05'24 — Fish. Population. Dynamics. *Reviews of research*
Fish population dynamics / edited by J.A. Gulland. — London [etc.] : Wiley, 1977. — xi, 372p : ill, charts, forms ; 24cm.
'A Wiley-Interscience publication'. — Bibl. — Index.
ISBN 0-471-01575-x : £13.50
(B77-22591)

597'.092 — Marine fish. *Australia. Coastal waters*
Coleman, Neville. Australian marine fishes in colour / [by] Neville Coleman. — Sydney [etc.] ; London : A.H. and A.W. Reed, 1974. — 108p : ill(chiefly col) ; 18x19cm.
Bibl.: p.11. — Index.
ISBN 0-589-07141-6 : £4.75
(B77-30267)

597'.0923'4 — Marine fish. *Gulf of Mexico*
Hoese, H Dickson. Fishes of the Gulf of Mexico : Texas, Louisiana and adjacent waters / by H. Dickson Hoese and Richard H. Moore ; underwater photography by Farley Sonnier ; drawings by Dinah Bowman. — College Station ; London ([c/o American University Publishers Group Ltd, 70 Great Russell St., WC1B 3BY]) : Texas A & M University Press, 1977. — xv,327p,plate : ill(some col), map ; 24cm. — (The W.L. Moody, Jr, natural history series ; no.1)
Bibl.: p.289-310. — Index.
ISBN 0-89096-027-5 : £8.05
ISBN 0-89096-028-3 Pbk : £5.95
(B77-30268)

597'.092'56 — Fish. *Western Pacific Ocean. Coral reefs*
Carcasson, Robert Herbert. A field guide to the coral reef fishes of the Indian and West Pacific Oceans / [by] R.H. Carcasson. — London : Collins, 1977. — 320p,48p of plates : ill(chiefly col), map ; 20cm.
Bibl.: p.284. — Index.
ISBN 0-00-219664-6 : £5.95
Also classified at 597'.0927
(B77-09030)

597'.0926'3 — Fish. *North America. Pacific coastal waters*
Somerton, David. Field guide to the fish of Puget Sound and the Northwest Coast / [by] David Somerton and Craig Murray ; foreword by Allan C. DeLacy. — Seattle ; London : University of Washington Press, 1976. — x, 70p : ill ; 22cm.
'A Washington Sea Grant publication'. — Index.
ISBN 0-295-95497-3 Sd : £4.00
(B77-08390)

597'.0926'32 — Marine fish. *California. Coastal waters*
Fitch, John Edgar. Tidepool and nearshore fishes of California / by John E. Fitch amd Robert J. Lavenberg ; illustrations by Evie Templeton. — Berkeley [etc.] ; London : University of California Press, 1975. — iv,156p,8p of plates : ill(some col), 2 maps ; 22cm. — (California natural history guides ; 38)
Bibl.: p.147-148. — Index.
ISBN 0-520-02844-9 : £6.70
ISBN 0-520-02845-7 Pbk : £3.50
(B77-27093)

597'.0927 — Fish. *Indian Ocean. Coral reefs*
Carcasson, Robert Herbert. A field guide to the coral reef fishes of the Indian and West Pacific Oceans / [by] R.H. Carcasson. — London : Collins, 1977. — 320p,48p of plates : ill(chiefly col), map ; 20cm.
Bibl.: p.284. — Index.
ISBN 0-00-219664-6 : £5.95
Primary classification 597'.092'56
(B77-09030)

597'.0929'4 — Freshwater fish. *Europe*
Cambridgeshire Libraries. *Peterborough Division. Technical Information Service.* Technical, commercial & scientific information : a directory of resources in the Peterborough area / compiled by [the] Technical Information Service [Cambridgeshire Libraries, Peterborough Division]. — 4th ed. — Peterborough (Reference Library, Central Library, Broadway, Peterborough PE1 1RX) : The Technical Information Service, 1977. — [3],15 leaves ; 21cm.
Previous ed.: 1976. — Index.
Pbk : £1.00
(B77-31197)

Maitland, Peter Salisbury. The Hamlyn guide to freshwater fishes of Britain and Europe / [by] Peter S. Maitland ; illustrated by Keith Linsell. — London [etc.] : Hamlyn, 1977. — 256p : ill(chiefly col), maps(chiefly col) ; 20cm.
Bibl.: p.248. — Index.
ISBN 0-600-33624-7 : £3.50
ISBN 0-600-33986-6 Pbk : £2.25
(B77-31198)

597'.0929'794 — Freshwater fish. *California*
Moyle, Peter B. Inland fishes of California / by Peter B. Moyle ; illustrated by Alan Marciochi and Chris van Dyck. — Berkeley [etc.] ; London : University of California Press, [1977]. — viii,405p : ill, maps ; 25cm.
Text, ill. on lining papers. — Published in the United States: 1976. — Bibl.: p.371-396. — Index.
ISBN 0-520-02975-5 : £16.00
(B77-13653)

597'.31 — Man. Attacks by sharks. *Reports, surveys*
Baldridge, Henry David. Shark attack / [by] H. David Baldridge. — London [etc.] : White Lion Publishers, 1977. — 278p,[20]p of plates : ill, ports ; 21cm.
Originally published: Sarasota : Mote Marine Laboratory, 1973 ; London : Everest Books, 1976.
ISBN 0-7274-0218-8 : £5.25
(B77-11224)

597'.31 — Sharks. *Juvenile literature*
Blumberg, Rhoda. Sharks / by Rhoda Blumberg. — New York ; London : F. Watts, 1976. — [4] ,68p : ill ; 23cm. — (A first book)
Index.
ISBN 0-85166-606-x : £1.95
(B77-00229)

Riedman, Sarah Regal. Sharks / by Sarah Riedman. — London [etc.] : F. Watts, 1977. — 48p : ill(chiefly col), map ; 22cm. — (A first look book)
Index.
ISBN 0-85166-654-x : £1.75
(B77-29438)

597'.53 — Sticklebacks
Wootton, Robin Jeremy. The biology of the sticklebacks / [by] R.J. Wootton. — London [etc.] : Academic Press, 1976. — x,387p : ill, maps ; 24cm.
Bibl.: p.346-370. — Index.
ISBN 0-12-763650-1 : £13.50
(B77-09031)

597'.53 — Sticklebacks. Life cycle. *Illustrations. Juvenile literature*
Thompson, David, *b.1945.* The life and times of a stickleback / photography by David Thompson ; editorial consultants Oxford Scientific Films. — London : G. Whizzard Publications Ltd : [Distributed by] Deutsch, 1976. — [30]p : chiefly ill(chiefly col) ; 20x26cm. — (Nature's way ; no.1)
Ill. on lining papers.
ISBN 0-233-96767-2 : £1.75
(B77-03557)

597'.55 — Salmon. *Juvenile literature*
The **salmon** / after an idea by Iliane Roels ; adapted from the text written by Claude Nicolas ; illustrated by Pauline Baynes. — Edinburgh : W. and R. Chambers, 1976. — [25]p : chiefly ill(chiefly col) ; 19x20cm. — (Questbooks : how life goes on)
ISBN 0-550-31915-8 : £1.40
(B77-14740)

597'.58 — Cod. Quality. Geographical factors & seasonal factors. *North Atlantic Ocean. For fish processing industries*
Love, Robert Malcolm. Processing cod : the influence of season and fishing ground / [by] R.M. Love. — Aberdeen (P.O. Box 31, 135 Abbey Rd, Aberdeen AB9 8DG) : Ministry of Agriculture, Fisheries and Food, Torry Research Station, [1977]. — 8p : ill ; 21cm. — (Torry Research Station. Torry advisory notes ; no.71)
Sd : Unpriced
(B77-09702)

597'.6'041 — Amphibians. Physiology
Physiology of the amphibia. — New York ; London : Academic Press.
In 3 vols.
Vol.2 / edited by Brian Lofts. — 1974. — xi, 592p,[4]p of plates : ill(some col) ; 24cm.
Bibl. — Index.
ISBN 0-12-455402-4 : £35.70
(B77-03558)

597'.6'041823 — Amphibians. Visual system
The **amphibian** visual system : a multidisciplinary approach / edited by Katherine V. Fite. — New York [etc.] ; London : Academic Press, 1976. — xiv,374p,[2]p of plates : ill(some col) ; 24cm.
Bibl.: p.327-366. — Index.
ISBN 0-12-257450-8 : £18.00
(B77-08391)

597'.8 — Frogs & toads. *Juvenile literature*
Piers, Helen. Frogs / [by] Helen Piers. — London [etc.] : Angus and Robertson, 1977. — [32]p : ill(some col) ; 18x22cm. — (The young nature series)
ISBN 0-207-95675-8 : £2.20
(B77-13654)

597'.8 — Frogs. Development. *Illustrations. Juvenile literature*
Sheehan, Angela. The frog / by Angela Sheehan ; illustrated by Maurice Pledger. — London [etc.] : Angus and Robertson, 1976. — [26]p : col ill ; 23cm. — (Eye-view library)
Col. ill. on lining papers.
ISBN 0-207-95708-8 : £1.60
(B77-06690)

598.1 — Reptiles
Biology of the Reptilia / edited by Carl Gans. — London [etc.] : Academic Press.
Vol.6 : Morphology E / coeditor for this volume Thomas S. Parsons. — 1977. — xiii, 505p : ill ; 24cm.
Bibl. — Index.
ISBN 0-12-274606-6 : £19.50
(B77-27094)

598.1 — Reptiles. *Conference proceedings*
Morphology and biology of reptiles / edited by A. d'A. Bellairs and C. Barry Cox. — London [etc.] : Academic Press for the Linnean Society of London, 1976. — xi,290p,[8]p of plates,leaf of plate : ill, maps ; 27cm. — (Linnean Society of London. Symposium series ; no.3)
'... papers given at the symposium on the morphology and biology of living and fossil reptiles held in the rooms of the Linnean Society at Burlington House, Piccadilly, London on 9 and 10 September 1975' - Foreword. — Bibl. — Index.
ISBN 0-12-085850-9 : £14.50
(B77-04812)

598.1 — Reptiles. *Juvenile literature*
Pitt, Valerie, *b.1939.* Reptiles / by Valerie Pitt ; illustrated by Jim Robins. — London [etc.] : F. Watts, 1977. — 48p : ill(chiefly col), 2 col maps ; 22cm. — (A first look book)
Index.
ISBN 0-85166-626-4 : £1.75
(B77-27868)

598.1 — Reptiles. *Juvenile literature. Welsh texts*
Tasnádi-Kubacska, András. Yr ymlusgiaid / ... gan András Tasnádi-Kubacska ; y darluniau gan László Réber ; [addaswyd i'r Gymraeg o'r Hwngareg gan Owain Owain]. — Pontypridd : Cyhoeddiadau Modern Cymreig, 1975. — [1], 33p : col ill ; 23cm.
Col. ill. on lining papers. — Translation of: 'Sárkányok unokái'. Budapest : Móra Kiadó, 1968.
£1.05
(B77-00768)

598.1 — Reptiles & amphibians
Echternacht, Arthur C. How reptiles and amphibians live / [by] Arthur C. Echternacht. — Oxford : Elsevier-Phaidon, 1977. — 142p : ill(chiefly col), col maps ; 29cm. — (How animals live ; vol.6)
Index.
ISBN 0-7290-0023-0 : £4.50
(B77-28633)

598.1'04'50994 — Reptiles. Ecology. *Australia*
Heatwole, Harold. Reptile ecology / [by] Harold Heatwole. — St Lucia : University of Queensland Press ; Hemel Hempstead : Distributed by Prentice-Hall, 1976. — xviii, 178p,vi p of plates : ill(some col), maps ; 22cm. — (Australian ecology series)
Bibl.: p.149-168. — Index.
ISBN 0-7022-1301-2 : £6.25
ISBN 0-7022-1220-2 Pbk : £3.15
(B77-15293)

598.1'094 — Reptiles & amphibians. *Europe*
Blum, Joachim. European reptiles and amphibians : a pocket identification guide / [by] Joachim Blum ; [translated from the German by K.M. James]. — Yeovil : Haynes, 1976. — 64p : ill(chiefly col) ; 17cm. — (Foulis spectrum books)
Translation of: 'Die Reptilien und Amphibien Europas'. Bern : Hallwag, 197-?. — Index.
ISBN 0-85429-525-9 Pbk : £0.85
(B77-03012)

598.1'0994 — Reptiles. *Australia*
Cogger, Harold George. Australian reptiles in colour / [by] Harold Cogger. — Sydney [etc.] ; London : A.H. and A.W. Reed, 1975. — 112p : col ill ; 18x19cm. — ([Reeds colourbook series])

Originally published: Sydney : A.H. and A.W. Reed, 1967. — Index.
ISBN 0-589-07012-6 : £4.75
(B77-23422)

598.1'0994 — Reptiles & amphibians. *Australia. Identification manuals*
Cogger, Harold George. Reptiles and amphibians of Australia / [by] Harold G. Cogger. — Sydney [etc.] ; London : A.H. and A.W. Reed, 1975. — 584p,[24]p of plates : ill(some col), maps ; 26cm.
Maps (1 col.) on lining papers. — Bibl.: p.568-573. — Index.
ISBN 0-589-07176-9 : £22.15
(B77-00769)

598.1'12'0994 — Lizards. *Australia*
Swanson, Stephen. Lizards of Australia / [by] Stephen Swanson. — Sydney ; London [etc.] : Angus and Robertson, 1976. — [7],80p,[64]p of plates : ill(chiefly col) ; 19cm.
Index.
ISBN 0-207-13073-6 : Unpriced
(B77-33236)

598.1'2 — Snakes
Parker, Hampton Wildman. Snakes : a natural history / [by] H.W. Parker. — 2nd ed. / revised and enlarged by A.G.C. Grandison ; illustrator B.C. Groombridge. — [London] : British Museum (Natural History) ; Ithaca ; London : Cornell University Press, 1977. — [4], 108p,16p of plates : ill(some col) ; 22cm.
Not the same as B63-9400. — Previous ed.: published as 'Natural history of snakes'. London : British Museum (Natural History), 1965. — Bibl.: p.98. — Index.
ISBN 0-8014-1095-9 : £4.95
ISBN 0-8014-9164-9 Pbk : Unpriced
(B77-24236)

598.1'2'0994 — Snakes. *Australia*
Gow, Graeme F. Snakes of Australia / [by] Graeme F. Gow. — Sydney ; London [etc.] : Angus and Robertson, 1976. — [7],88p,[45]p of plates : ill(chiefly col) ; 18cm.
Bibl.: p.83. — Index.
ISBN 0-207-12937-1 Pbk : Unpriced
(B77-33237)

598.2 — Birds
The **bird-watchers**' book. — Newton Abbot [etc.] : David and Charles.
3rd / compiled and edited by John Gooders. — 1976. — 160p : ill ; 23cm.
ISBN 0-7153-7250-5 : £3.95
(B77-00230)

Cruickshank, Allan D. 1001 questions answered about birds / by Allan D. Cruickshank and Helen G. Cruickshank ; with photographs by Allan D. Cruickshank and drawings by James MacDonald. — New York : Dover Publications [etc.] ; London : Constable, 1976. — iii-xi,291p, [16]p of plates : ill ; 21cm.
Originally published: New York : Dodd, Mead, 1958. — Bibl.: p.276-277. — Index.
ISBN 0-486-23315-4 Pbk : £2.50
(B77-12451)

Hanzák, Jan. The illustrated encyclopedia of birds / by Jan Hanzák and Jiří Formánek ; edited by Laura Steward ; [translated from the Czech by Olga Kuthanová]. — London : Octopus Books, 1977. — 352p : ill(some col), maps ; 24cm.
Bibl.: p.345. — Index.
ISBN 0-7064-0519-6 : £3.95
(B77-19389)

Perrins, Christopher. Birds / [by] Christopher Perrins. — London : Collins, 1976. — 176p,24p of plates : ill, maps ; 22cm. — (Collins countryside series)
Originally published: 1974. — Bibl.: p.167-168. — Index.
ISBN 0-00-219351-5 : £2.50
(B77-26324)

598.2 — Birds. *Cut-out books*
Make and know birds. — [London] ([Wheatsheaf House, Carmelite St., E.C.4]) : GeminiScan Ltd, 1974. — [2],24,[1]p : ill(chiefly col), col map ; 33cm.
Six leaves, with versos blank, are perforated for making press-out models.
ISBN 0-85691-008-2 Sd : £0.85
(B77-20278)

598.2 — Birds. *Juvenile literature*
Ardley, Neil. Birds / [by Neil Ardley]. — Maidenhead : Sampson Low, 1974. — 48p : ill(chiefly col) ; 29cm. — ([New horizon library])
Index.
ISBN 0-562-00005-4 : £1.50
(B77-19390)

Ardley, Neil. Let's look at birds / written by Neil Ardley ; illustrated by John Rignall, Richard Millington and Graham Allen ; edited by Jennifer Justice. — London : Ward Lock, 1977. — 4-29p : col ill, col map ; 33cm.
Spine title: Birds. — Col. ill. on lining papers. — Index.
ISBN 0-7063-5339-0 : £1.50
(B77-27869)

The **superbook** of birds. — London : Macdonald Educational, 1977. — 32p : col ill, col map ; 29cm.
Adaptation of: 'The life of birds' / by Maurice Burton, 1972. — Bibl.: p.32.
ISBN 0-356-05596-5 Sd : £0.50
(B77-27095)

598.2 — Flightless birds. *Juvenile literature*
Gray, Patricia. Flightless birds / by Patricia Gray ; illustrated by Frankie Coventry. — London [etc.] : F. Watts, 1976. — 32p : col ill ; 18x22cm. — (Wildlife books)
ISBN 0-85166-597-7 : £1.95
(B77-00231)

598.2'07'20729725 — Ornithological expeditions. *British Virgin Islands. Cambridge Ornithological Expedition to the British Virgin Islands 1976. Reports, surveys*
Cambridge Ornithological Expedition to the British Virgin Islands. Report of the Cambridge Ornithological Expedition to the British Virgin Islands, 1976. — Cambridge (c/o D.N. Mirecki, Churchill College, Cambridge) : [The Expedition], 1977. — 44p : maps ; 22cm.
Bibl.: p.42-43.
Sd : Unpriced
(B77-23423)

598.2'073'02541 — Birds. Observation. Sites. *Great Britain. Directories*
Gooders, John. Where to watch birds / [by] John Gooders ; illustrated by David Thelwell ; introduction by Roger Tory Peterson. — 2nd revised ed. — London [etc.] : Pan Books, 1977. — 343p : ill, maps ; 20cm.
This ed. originally published: London : Deutsch, 1974. — Index.
ISBN 0-330-25030-2 Pbk : £1.50
(B77-13655)

598.2'073'0941 — Birds. Observation. *Great Britain. Manuals*
Dobinson, Humphrey Mark. Bird count : a practical guide to bird surveys / [by] Humphrey M. Dobinson ; illustrated by Roy Wiltshire and Robert Micklewright. — Harmondsworth [etc.] : Penguin, 1976. — 192p : ill, chart, forms, maps ; 20cm. — (Peacock books)
Bibl.: p.183-189. — Index.
ISBN 0-14-047087-5 Pbk : £0.75
(B77-13046)

Dobinson, Humphrey Mark. Bird count : a practical guide to bird surveys / [by] Humphrey M. Dobinson ; illustrated by Roy Wiltshire and Robert Micklewright. — Harmondsworth : Kestrel Books, 1976. — 192p : ill, chart, forms, maps ; 21cm.
Bibl.: p.183-189. — Index.
ISBN 0-7226-5153-8 : £2.75
(B77-13047)

598.2'073'0941 — Gardens. Birds. Observation. *Great Britain. Manuals*
Gooders, John. How to watch birds / [by] John Gooders ; illustrated by David Thelwell. — London : Pan Books, 1977. — 155p : ill, maps ; 20cm.
Originally published: London : Deutsch, 1975. — Bibl.: p.149-151. — Index.
ISBN 0-330-25029-9 Pbk : £0.95
(B77-13656)

598.2'092'4 — Ornithology. Scott, Sir Peter, b.1909. *Autobiographies*
Scott, *Sir* Peter, *b.1909*. The eye of the wind / [by] Peter Scott. — Revised ed. — London [etc.] : Hodder and Stoughton, 1977. — 256p, [16]p of plates : ill, ports ; 23cm.
This ed. originally published: 1966. — Index.
ISBN 0-340-21515-1 : £4.95
(B77-18778)

598.2'5 — Birds. Behaviour
Broom, Donald. The wonderful world of birds and their behaviour / [by] Donald Broom. — London [etc.] : Hamlyn, 1977. — 96p : col ill ; 33cm.
Col. ill. on lining papers. — Index.
ISBN 0-600-31391-3 : £2.95
(B77-31200)

598.2'5'26360941 — Marine birds. Ecology. *Great Britain*
Natural Environment Research Council. The report of a working group on ecological research on seabirds / [Natural Environment Research Council]. — [London] : N.E.R.C., 1977. — iv,48p : ill, maps ; 30cm. — (Natural Environment Research Council. Publications : series C ; no.18)
Cover title: Ecological research on seabirds. — Bibl.: p.38-40.
ISBN 0-901875-50-3 Sd : Unpriced
(B77-16394)

598.2'5'6 — Birds. Nests. Construction
Goodfellow, Peter. Birds as builders / [by] Peter Goodfellow. — Newton Abbot [etc.] : David and Charles, [1977?]. — 168p : ill(some col) ; 24cm.
Bibl.: p.161-164. — Index.
ISBN 0-7153-7401-x : £4.95
(B77-28634)

598.2'5'9 — Birds. Songs
Armstrong, Edward Allworthy. Discovering bird song / [by] Edward A. Armstrong. — 2nd ed. — Aylesbury : Shire Publications, 1977. — 72p : ill, music ; 18cm. — (Discovering series ; no.202)
Previous ed.: 1975. — Bibl.: p.70. — Index.
ISBN 0-85263-395-5 Pbk : £0.70
(B77-28635)

598.2'91'822 — Birds. *Mediterranean region*
Handbook of the birds of Europe, the Middle East and North Africa : the birds of the Western Palearctic. — Oxford [etc.] : Oxford University Press.
Vol.1 : Ostrich to ducks / Stanley Cramp chief editor ... [with others]. — 1977. — [9],722p,[76] p of plates,[2] leaves of plates : ill(some col), maps(some col) ; 26cm.
Map on lining papers. — Bibl.: p.701-714. — Index.
ISBN 0-19-857358-8 : £25.00 : CIP rev.
Primary classification 598.2'94
(B77-07912)

598.2'924'05 — Marine birds. *Reports, surveys. Serials*
Seabird report / produced by the Seabird Group. — [Sandy] ([c/o Royal Society for the Protection of Birds, The Lodge, Sandy, Beds. SG19 2DL]) : [The Group].
1975-76. — [1977]. — [1],54p : ill, maps ; 21cm.
Bibl.
ISBN 0-903138-08-5 Sd : Unpriced
(B77-13048)

598.2'938 — Birds. *Ancient Greece*
Pollard, John. Birds in Greek life and myth / [by] John Pollard. — [London] : Thames and Hudson, 1977. — 224p,[16]p of plates : ill ; 23cm. — (Aspects of Greek and Roman life)
Bibl.: p.213-217. — Index.
ISBN 0-500-40032-6 : £8.50
(B77-33806)

598.2'94 — Birds. *Europe*
Giggisberg, Charles Albert Walter. Birds : a pocket identification guide / [by] C.A.W. Guggisberg ; [translated from the German by Ursula Lehrburger]. — Yeovil : Haynes, 1976. — 80p : ill(chiefly col) ; 17cm. — (Foulis spectrum books)
Translation of: 'Unsere Vogel'. Bern : Hallwag AG, 197-? - Originally published in 2 vols. — Index.
ISBN 0-85429-508-9 Pbk : £0.85
(B77-03013)

Handbook of the birds of Europe, the Middle East and North Africa : the birds of the Western Palearctic. — Oxford [etc.] : Oxford University Press.
Vol.1 : Ostrich to ducks / Stanley Cramp chief editor ... [with others]. — 1977. — [9],722p,[76] p of plates,[2] leaves of plates : ill(some col), maps(some col) ; 26cm.
Map on lining papers. — Bibl.: p.701-714. — Index.
ISBN 0-19-857358-8 : £25.00 : CIP rev.
Also classified at 598.2'91'822
(B77-07912)

598.2'94 — Birds. *Northern Europe. Coastal regions*
Campbell, Bruce, *b.1912*. Birds of coast and sea : Britain and Northern Europe / [by] Bruce Campbell ; illustrated by Raymond Watson. — Oxford [etc.] : Oxford University Press, 1977. — 151p : ill(chiefly col) ; 23cm.
Index.
ISBN 0-19-217661-7 : £3.75
(B77-14241)

598.2'941 — Birds. *Great Britain*
Soper, Tony. Everyday birds / [by] Tony Soper ; illustrations by Robert Gillmor. — Newton Abbot [etc.] : David and Charles, 1976. — 126p : ill ; 23cm.
Index.
ISBN 0-7153-7277-7 : £2.95
(B77-05426)

598.2'941 — Birds. *Great Britain. Juvenile literature*
Taunton, John. Birds of the countryside / edited [i.e. written] by John Taunton ; illustrated by A. Oxenham ; in association with Thames Television. — Revised ed. — Guildford [etc.] : Lutterworth Press, 1976. — [46]p : ill(chiefly col), map ; 11x14cm. — ('Magpie' pocket books)
Previous ed.: 1970.
ISBN 0-7188-2274-9 Pbk : £0.35
(B77-03559)

598.2'941 — Birds. *Great Britain. Serials*
Royal Society for the Protection of Birds. *Young Ornithologists' Club.* RSPB YOC bird life annual. — Maidenhead : Purnell.
[1976] / compiled by Linda Bennett. — 1976. — 2-79p : ill(some col), forms, col maps, plans ; 32cm.
Ill. on lining papers.
ISBN 0-361-03519-5 : £1.50
(B77-00770)

[1977] / compiled by Linda Bennett and Sylvia Sullivan. — 1977. — 2-79p : ill(some col), maps ; 31cm.
Ill. (some col.) on lining papers.
ISBN 0-361-03905-0 : £1.95
(B77-30269)

598.2'941 — Birds. Names. *Great Britain. Dictionaries. Facsimiles*
Swann, H Kirke. A dictionary of English and folk-names of British birds : with their history, meaning and first usage, and the folk-lore, weather-lore, legends, etc., relating to the more familiar species / by H. Kirke Swann. — Wakefield : EP Publishing, 1977. — xii,266p ; 23cm.
Facsimile reprint of: 1st ed. London : Witherby and Co., 1913. — Bibl.: p.ix-xii.
ISBN 0-7158-1239-4 : £5.95 : CIP rev.
(B77-25639)

598.2'941 — Gardens. Birds. *Great Britain*
Jones, Reginald. Birds in our gardens / with text by Reg Jones. — Norwich : Jarrold and Sons, 1976. — [33]p : chiefly col ill, port ; 19cm. — (Jarrold bird series)
ISBN 0-85306-662-0 Sd : £0.40
(B77-03014)

598.2'941 — Gardens. Birds. *Great Britain. Juvenile literature*
Firmin, Joe. Wonder why book of garden birds / [by] Joe Firmin ; illustrated by John Sibbick. — London : Transworld, 1977. — [2],32p : ill(chiefly col), maps(chiefly col) ; 29cm.
Index. — Previous control number ISBN 0-552-57007-9.
ISBN 0-552-98041-2 : £1.35
ISBN 0-552-57007-9 Sd : £0.50
(B77-13049)

598.2'941 — Marine birds. *Great Britain*
Cramp, Stanley. The seabirds of Britain and Ireland / [by] Stanley Cramp, W.R.P. Bourne, David Saunders. — 3rd ed. — London : Collins, 1976. — 288p,[12]p of plates : ill(some col), col charts, col maps ; 22cm.
Previous ed.: 1975. — Bibl.: p.266-284. — Index.
ISBN 0-00-219654-9 : £4.50
(B77-07356)

598.2'9411 — Birds. *Scotland*
Batten, Harry Mortimer. Tales of wild bird life / [by] H. Mortimer Batten ; illustrated by Len Fullerton. — Glasgow [etc.] : Blackie, 1976. — 190p : ill ; 20cm.
Originally published: 1948.
ISBN 0-216-90276-2 : £2.15
ISBN 0-216-90277-0 Pbk : £0.95
(B77-00771)

598.2'94113'5 — Birds. *Scotland. Shetland. Foula. Reports, surveys. Serials*
Ornithological studies on Foula / Brathay Exploration Group. — Ambleside ([Brathay Hall], Ambleside, Cumbria) : Brathay Hall Trust.
1974 / [by] R.W. Furness. — [1976]. — [4], 35p,[5] leaves of plates : maps ; 30cm. — (Brathay Exploration Group. Field studies reports ; no.28, 1976 ISSN 0307-966x)
Sp : Unpriced
(B77-16395)

598.2'9412'6 — Birds. *Scotland. Tayside Region. Angus (District)*
Crighton, George M. The birds of Angus, including South Kincardineshire / [by] George M. Crighton ; designed and illustrated by David G. Adams. — Brechin (23 Church St., Brechin, Angus) : The author, 1976. — [56]p : ill, map ; 21cm.
Sd : Unpriced
(B77-24945)

598.2'9413'95 — Birds. *Scotland. Borders Region. Berwickshire (District), ca 1917-1977. Personal observations*
Douglas-Home, Henry. The birdman : memories of birds / by Henry Douglas-Home ; with a foreword by The Lord Home of The Hirsel ; edited by John McEwen ; line drawings by Sir Peter Scott and Robert Gillmor. — London : Collins, 1977. — 175p,[16]p of plates : ill, ports ; 24cm.
Col. ill. on lining papers.
ISBN 0-00-219014-1 : £4.95
(B77-33807)

598.2'9415 — Birds. *Ireland*
Ruttledge, Robert Francis. A list of the birds of Ireland / by Robert F. Ruttledge. — [New ed.]. — Dublin (Government Publications Sale Office, G.P.O. Arcade, Dublin 1) : Stationery Office, 1975. — [7],146p ; 24cm.
'The present "List" contains all records and information available up to the end of 1972' - Introduction. — Previous ed.: published as 'A list of Irish birds' / compiled by P.G. Kennedy et al. 1961. — Bibl.: p.6-7. — Index.
ISBN 0-7076-0022-7 Pbk : £0.60
(B77-06087)

598.2'9417 — Birds. *Ireland (Republic). Reports, surveys. Serials*
Irish bird report. — Waringstown (c/o K. Perry, 11 Magherana Park, Waringstown, Craigavon) : Irish Wildbird Conservancy.
23rd : 1975 / editor K. Preston. — 1976. — 44p : ill ; 21cm.
Bibl.: p.44.
ISBN 0-9504454-1-x Sd : £0.75
(B77-07357)

598.2'9418'85 — Birds. *Wexford (County). Saltee Islands. Reports, surveys*
Perry, Kenneth W. The birds and flowers of the Saltee Islands / [by] Kenneth W. Perry & Stephen W. Warburton ; design & photography by Ken Perry. — [Northern Ireland] : [The authors], [1976?]. — viii,170p : ill, charts, maps, port ; 22cm.
Bibl.: p.v-vii.
ISBN 0-9505658-1-4 : £4.00
ISBN 0-9505658-0-6 Pbk : £3.25
(B77-12452)

598.2'942 — Water birds. *England. Seashore*
Jones, Reginald. Birds of the coast / text by Reg Jones. — Norwich : Jarrold and Sons. — (Jarrold bird series)
Book 2. — 1977. — [33]p : col ill, port ; 20cm.
ISBN 0-85306-688-4 Sd : £0.40
(B77-26325)

598.2'9421 — Royal parks. Birds. *London. Reports, surveys. Serials*
Bird life in the Royal parks : a report / by the Committee on Bird Sanctuaries in the Royal Parks. — London ([Gaywood House, 29 Great Peter St., SW1P 3LW]) : Department of the Environment.
1975. — 1977. — 14p ; 21cm.
ISBN 0-86056-005-8 Sd : £0.25
(B77-16396)

598.2'9422 — Birds. *England. Thames Estuary*
Harrison, Jeffery Graham. The Thames transformed : London's river and its waterfowl / [by] Jeffery Harrison and Peter Grant ; photographs by Pamela Harrison ; foreword by Prince Philip, Duke of Edinburgh. — London : Deutsch, 1976. — 240p,[12]p of plates : ill(some col), facsim, maps, plan, ports ; 25cm.
Maps on lining papers. — Bibl.: p.232-235. — Index.
ISBN 0-233-96840-7 : £5.95
Primary classification 639'.97'84109421
(B77-01608)

598.2'9422'1 — Birds. *Surrey. Reports, surveys. Serials*
Surrey bird report / [Surrey Bird Club]. — Egham (21 Simons Walk, Englefield Green, Egham, Surrey) : The Club.
1975 : No.23 / editor Derek Washington, assistant editor J.J. Wheatley. — 1976. — 88p, iv p of plates : ill, 2 maps ; 22cm.
Sd : £1.00
ISSN 0491-6255
(B77-21141)

598.2'9422'352 — Birds. *Kent. Sandwich Bay. Reports, surveys. Serials*
Sandwich Bay Bird Observatory. Sandwich Bay Bird Observatory report. — [Ramsgate] ([c/o The Secretary, 22 Royal Rd, Ramsgate, Kent]) : [The Observatory].
1975. — [1976]. — [1],57p : ill ; 21cm.
Sd : £0.60
(B77-20279)

598.2'9422'9 — Birds. *Berkshire. Reports, surveys. Serials*
The **birds** of Berkshire : an introduction and annual report based on county records / [the Reading Ornithological Club]. — South Ascot (c/o Peter Standley, 7 Llanvair Drive, South Ascot, Berks. SL5 9HS) : The Club.
1st : 1974 / edited by Peter Standley. — 1976. — 48,[1]p : 2 ill ; 21cm.
Sd : £0.75
ISSN 0140-3192
(B77-17506)

598.2'9423'7 — Birds. *Cornwall. Reports, surveys. Serials*
Cornwall Bird-Watching and Preservation Society. Annual report / Cornwall Bird-Watching and Preservation Society. — Redruth (c/o The Editor, Fourways, Tolcarne, St Day, Redruth, Cornwall) : [The Society].
1975 : Forty-fourth / [editor D.J. Barker]. — [1976]. — [1],90p ; 22cm.
Cover title: Birds in Cornwall, 1975 = Ydhyn yn Kernow.
Sd : £0.50
(B77-21142)

598.2'9423'79 — Birds. *Isles of Scilly. Reports, surveys. Serials*
Isles of Scilly bird report / Cornwall Bird-Watching and Preservation Society. — [Penzance] ([c/o H.P.K. Robinson, Carn View, Newbridge, Penzance, Cornwall]) : [The Society].
1975 / [edited by D.B. Hunt and H.P.K. Robinson]. — [1976]. — [2],45p : ill ; 22cm.
Sd : £0.50
(B77-21143)

598.2'9424'4 — Birds. *Hereford and Worcester. Herefordshire. Reports, surveys*
Walker, Charles William. Herefordshire birds. — [New ed.] / by C.W. Walker and A.J. Smith. — Hereford (c/o Hereford Library, Broad St., Hereford) : Woolhope Naturalists' Field Club, 1975. — 74p ; 22cm.
Previous ed.: / by H.A. Gilbert and C.W. Walker, 1954. — Bibl.: p.4.
Sd : £0.75
(B77-18779)

598.2'9425'47 — Country parks. *Leicestershire. Anstey. Bradgate Park. Birds*
Otter, Jack. The birds of Bradgate / written by Jack Otter ; illustrated by John Stacey. — [Leicester] ([Estate Office, County Hall, Glenfield, Leicester LE3 8RR]) : Bradgate Park Trust, 1976. — 45p : ill ; 21cm. — (The Bradgate books ; vol.5)
Sd : £0.35
(B77-07358)

598.2'9425'7 — Birds. *Oxfordshire. Reports, surveys. Serials*
Oxford Ornithological Society. Report of the Oxford Ornithological Society on the birds of Oxfordshire. — Oxford (c/o The Hon. Secretary, c/o Edward Grey Institute, Zoology Department, Oxford) : The Society.
1975 / edited by J.M. Campbell. — [1976]. — [3],56p : ill, map ; 21cm.
Sd : Unpriced
(B77-21877)

598.2'9426 — Birds. *East Anglia*
Tate, Peter, *b.1926.* East Anglia and its birds / [by] Peter Tate ; illustrated with drawings by John Last. — London : Witherby, 1977. — 288p : ill, maps, ports ; 24cm.
Bibl.: p.280-283. — Index.
ISBN 0-85493-123-6 : £6.50
(B77-22592)

598.2'9426'54 — Natural resources: Water. Reservoirs. *Cambridgeshire. Huntingdon (District). Grafham Water. Birds. Reports, surveys*
Cooke, Arnold. The birds of Grafham Water / [by] Arnold Cooke. — Huntingdon (The Education Office, Gazely House, Huntingdon, Cambridgeshire PE18 6NS) : Huntingdon Local Publications Group, 1977. — viii,38p : ill ; 21cm.
ISBN 0-904463-14-1 Sd : £1.00
(B77-13657)

598.2'9426'56 — Nature reserves. *Cambridgeshire. Wicken. Wicken Fen. Birds. Reports, surveys*
Wicken Fen Group. Wicken Fen Group report. — [Cambridge] ([c/o The Secretary, St Catharine's College, Cambridge]) : [The Group].
No.8 : 1976 / [editor Rhys Green]. — [1977]. — [1],36,[1]p : ill, maps ; 21cm.
Sd : £0.50
(B77-08392)

598.2'9426'7 — Birds. *Essex. Reports, surveys. Serials*
The **Essex** bird report / [Essex Bird Watching and Preservation Society]. — Chelmsford (c/o G.R. Ekins, 18 Arbour La., Chelmsford, [Essex]) : The Society.
1975. — [1976]. — 104p,[2]p of plates : ill, maps ; 22cm.
Sd : £1.25
(B77-06088)

598.2'9427'6 — Birds. *Lancashire. Reports, surveys. Serials*
Lancashire bird report ; [and] Lancashire bird ringing report. — [Manchester] (c/o A. Brindle, Manchester Museum, Manchester M13 9PL) : Lancashire and Cheshire Fauna Society.
1976 / by K.G. Spencer, D.R. Mirams. — 1977. — 23p ; 22cm. — (Lancashire and Cheshire Fauna Society. Publications ; no.72 ISSN 0306-7599)
Sd : £0.60
(B77-20280)

598.2'9428'1 — Birds. *Yorkshire. Reports, surveys. Serials*
Yorkshire Naturalists' Union. Ornithological report / Yorkshire Naturalists' Union. — [Knaresborough] ([c/o John R. Mather, 44 Aspin La., Knaresborough, N. Yorkshire]) : [Yorkshire Naturalists' Union, Ornithological Section].
1975 / compiled by John R. Mather. — [1976]. — [1],71p : ill ; 21cm.
Sd : £0.75
ISSN 0306-3925
(B77-17507)

598.2'9428'8 — Birds. *Northumberland. Reports, surveys. Serials*
Birds in Northumbria : Northumberland bird report. — [Morpeth] ([c/o J. Day, 2 Station House, Stannington, Morpeth, Northd]) : Tyneside Bird Club.
1975 / by B. Galloway, M.S. Hodgson and E.R. Meek ; illustrated by J.P. Deacon. — [1975]. — 97p : ill ; 22cm.
Index.
ISBN 0-9505527-0-4 Sd : £0.90
ISSN 0309-2208
(B77-04813)

598.2'9429 — Birds. *Wales. Coastal regions*
Jones, Reginald. Birds of the Welsh coast / written and compiled by Reg Jones. — Norwich : Jarrold and Sons, 1977. — [33]p : col ill, port ; 20cm. — (A Jarrold area guide ; [birds])
ISBN 0-85306-701-5 Sd : £0.40
(B77-30270)

598.2'9429'9 — Birds. *Gwent*
The **birds** of Gwent / edited and written by P.N. Ferns ... [et al.]. — [Pontypool] ([c/o Hon. Secretary, 'Andorra', Sunlea Cres., Pontypool, Gwent]) : Gwent Ornithological Society, 1977. — [1],xii,152p,leaf of plate,10p of plates : ill, maps ; 22cm.
Maps (1 col.) on lining papers. — Bibl.: p.150-152.
ISBN 0-9505760-0-x : £3.50
(B77-27870)

598.2'9491'2 — Birds. *South-eastern Iceland. Reports, surveys*
Brathay Exploration Group. Review of ornithological studies in South-east Iceland, 1973-1975 / Brathay Exploration Group ; [written by] R.V. Collier and M. Stott. — Ambleside (Brathay Hall Trust, Ambleside, Cumbria) : [The Group], 1976. — [2] leaves,27p,[4] leaves of plates,[2]p of plates : ill, 2 maps ; 30cm. — (Brathay Exploration Group. Field studies reports ; no.29 ISSN 0307-966x)
Bibl.: p.27.
ISBN 0-906015-02-2 Sp : £0.75
(B77-13050)

598.2'9595'1 — Birds. *West Malaysia*
The **birds** of the Malay peninsula : a general account of the birds inhabiting the region from the isthmus of Kra to Singapore with the adjacent islands. — London : Witherby [etc.].
Vol.5 : Conclusion, and survey of every species / by Lord Medway and David R. Wells ; with 25 colour plates by the late H. Grönvold. — 1976. — xxxi[i.e.xxv],448p,leaf of plate,24p of plates : ill(chiefly col), maps(1 col) ; 28cm.
Includes a chapter by Ian C.T. Nisbet. — Bibl.: p.409-424. — Index.
ISBN 0-85493-104-x : £25.00
(B77-32635)

598.2'966 — Birds. *West Africa*
Serle, William. A field guide to the birds of West Africa / [by] William Serle and Gérard J. Morel ; with 48 plates by Wolfgang Hartwig. — London : Collins, 1977. — 351p,48p of plates : ill(chiefly col), col map(on lining papers) ; 20cm.
Index.
ISBN 0-00-219204-7 : £5.95
(B77-14741)

598.2'968 — Birds. *South Africa*
Johnson, Peter, *b.1940.* As free as a bird / [by] Peter Johnson. — Cambridge : Stephens, 1977. — 208p : chiefly col ill ; 30cm.
Originally published: Cape Town : Struik, 1976. — Index.
ISBN 0-85059-280-1 : Unpriced
(B77-21144)

598.2'9728 — Birds. *Central America*
Blake, Emmet Reid. Manual of neotropical birds / [by] Emmet R. Blake. — Chicago ; London : University of Chicago Press.
Vol.1 : Spheniscidae (penguins) to laridae (gulls and allies). — 1977. — l,674p,[23]p of plates : ill(some col), maps ; 26cm.
Maps on lining papers. — Bibl.: p.xxiii. — Index.
ISBN 0-226-05641-4 : £30.00
Primary classification 598.2'98
(B77-33238)

598.2'98 — Birds. *South America. Tropical regions*
Blake, Emmet Reid. Manual of neotropical birds / [by] Emmet R. Blake. — Chicago ; London : University of Chicago Press.
Vol.1 : Spheniscidae (penguins) to laridae (gulls and allies). — 1977. — l,674p,[23]p of plates : ill(some col), maps ; 26cm.
Maps on lining papers. — Bibl.: p.xxiii. — Index.
ISBN 0-226-05641-4 : £30.00
Also classified at 598.2'9728
(B77-33238)

598.2'98 — Fruit-eating birds. *Latin America. Tropical regions*
Snow, David William. The web of adaptation : bird studies in the American tropics / by David W. Snow. — London [etc.] : Collins, 1976. — xiii,176p : ill ; 23cm.
'A Demeter Press book' - title page verso. — Originally published: New York : Quadrangle, 1976.
ISBN 0-00-219735-9 : £4.50
(B77-18144)

598.2'9931 — Birds. *New Zealand*
Marshall, Janet. The Fiat book of common birds in New Zealand / [paintings by] Janet Marshall ; [text by] F.C. Kinsky, C.J.R. Robertson. — Wellington [N.Z.] [etc.] ; London : A.H. and A.W. Reed.
In 3 vols.
[Vol.]3. — 1975. — 94p : col ill ; 19cm.
Vol.3 has title: 'The Fiat book of uncommon birds in New Zealand'. — Bibl.: p.94.
ISBN 0-589-00941-9 Sp : £2.10
(B77-06089)

Soper, Michael Fryer. New Zealand birds / [by] M.F. Soper. — 2nd ed. — Christchurch, N.Z. [etc.] ; London : Whitcoulls, 1976[i.e.1977]. — 251p,[160]p of plates : ill(some col), map ; 25cm.
Published in New Zealand: 1976. — Previous ed.: London : Hale, 1972. — Index.
ISBN 0-7233-0482-3 : £14.90
(B77-10373)

598.2'994 — Birds. *Australia*
Hindwood, Keith. Australian birds in colour / [by] Keith Hindwood. — Sydney [etc.] ; London : A.H. and A.W. Reed, 1976. — 112p : col ill ; 18x19cm. — (Reed colourbook series)
Originally published: 1966. — Index.
ISBN 0-589-07184-x : £4.75
(B77-18145)

598.2'9945 — Birds. *Australia. Bass Strait region*
Simpson, Ken. Birds in Bass Strait / [by] Ken Simpson. — Sydney ; London [etc.] : A.H. and A.W. Reed for Broken Hill Proprietary Co., 1972. — 112p : ill(some col), maps ; 30cm.
Bibl.: p.110. — Index.
ISBN 0-589-07108-4 : £6.05
(B77-03015)

598.4'1 — Swans. *Illustrations. Juvenile literature*
McTrusty, Ron. Swans / [by] Ron McTrusty. — London : A. and C. Black, 1977. — [28]p : of ill(chiefly col) ; 22cm. — (Books without words)
ISBN 0-7136-1693-8 : £1.75
(B77-21878)

598.4'1'045094 — Wildfowl. *Ecology. Europe*
Owen, Myrfyn. Wildfowl of Europe / [by] Myrfyn Owen ; foreword by Sir Peter Scott ; colour plates by Hilary Burn ; [line drawings by Joe Blossom]. — London [etc.] : Macmillan, 1977. — 256p : ill(some col), maps ; 31cm.
Bibl.: p.252-254. — Index.
ISBN 0-333-18701-6 : £15.00 : CIP rev.
(B77-07359)

598.7'1 — Lories
Low, Rosemary. Lories and lorikeets : the brush-tongued parrots / [by] Rosemary Low. — London : Elek, 1977. — xii,180p,[8]p of plates : ill(chiefly col), map(on lining paper) ; 26cm.
Text on lining paper. — Bibl.: p.175-176. — Index.
ISBN 0-236-40102-5 : £12.50
(B77-32636)

598.8'64 — Corvidae
Wilmore, Sylvia Bruce. Crows, jays, ravens and their relatives / [by] Sylvia Bruce Wilmore. — Newton Abbot [etc.] : David and Charles, 1977. — 208p : ill, maps ; 23cm.
Bibl.: p.198-200. — Index.
ISBN 0-7153-7428-1 : £5.95
(B77-33808)

598.8'64 — Jackdaws. *Juvenile literature*
Hansen, Elvig. A jackdaw in the chimney / [by] Elvig Hansen. — Hove : Firefly Books, 1977. — 63p : ill, maps ; 25cm.
Translation of: 'Gaester i skorstenen'. Tisvilde : Skarv, 1976.
ISBN 0-904724-28-x : £2.95
(B77-28636)

598.9'1 — Birds of prey
Brown, Leslie. Birds of prey : their biology and ecology / [by] Leslie Brown. — London [etc.] : Hamlyn, 1976. — 256p : ill(some col), maps ; 25cm.
Bibl.: p.251-253. — Index.
ISBN 0-600-31306-9 : £4.50
(B77-00772)

598.9'1 — Birds of prey. *Juvenile literature*
Law, Felicia. Birds of prey / written by Felicia Law ; illustrated by Richard Millington. — London [etc.] : Collins, 1977. — 32p : col ill, col map ; 22cm. — (Dandelions)
ISBN 0-00-651220-8 Sd : £0.50
(B77-30271)

598.9'1 — Eagles
Brown, Leslie. Eagles of the world / [by] Leslie Brown. — Newton Abbot [etc.] : David and Charles, 1976. — 224p : ill ; 24cm.
Bibl.: p.215-220. — Index.
ISBN 0-7153-7269-6 : £4.95
(B77-04814)

598.9'1 — Golden eagles. *Personal observations*
MacNally, Lea. The ways of an eagle / [by] Lea MacNally. — London : Collins : Harvill Press, 1977. — 143p,[24]p of plates : ill(some col) ; 25cm.
Bibl.: p.137. — Index.
ISBN 0-00-262208-4 : £5.95
(B77-24237)

Summers, Gerald, *b.1920.* Owned by an eagle / [by] Gerald Summers ; drawings by Eva Hülsmann. — London : Collins, 1976. — 223p : ill ; 24cm.
Ill. on lining papers.
ISBN 0-00-216710-7 : £3.95
(B77-02318)

Summers, Gerald, *b.1920.* Owned by an eagle / [by] Gerald Summers. — [London] : Fontana, 1977. — 190p ; 18cm.
Originally published: London : Collins, 1976.
ISBN 0-00-634853-x Pbk : £0.85
(B77-31201)

598.9'1 — Hen harriers
Watson, Donald, *b.1918.* The hen harrier / by Donald Watson. — Berkhamsted : Poyser, 1977. — 307p,4p of plates : ill(some col), maps ; 24cm.
Bibl.: p.273-280. — Index.
ISBN 0-85661-015-1 : £6.80
(B77-31202)

598.9'1'094 — Birds of prey. *Europe*
Bouchner, Miroslav. Birds of prey of Britain and Europe / by Miroslav Bouchner ; illustrated by Dan Bárta ; consultant editor D.M. Broom ; [translated from the Czech by Olga Kuthanová]. — London [etc.] : Hamlyn, 1976. — 235p : ill(chiefly col) ; 17cm. — (A concise guide in colour)
Index.
ISBN 0-600-31291-7 : £1.50
(B77-21145)

598.9'7 — Owls
Everett, Michael. A natural history of owls / [by] Michael Everett. — London [etc.] : Hamlyn, 1977. — 5-156p : ill(some col) ; 30cm.
Ill. on lining papers. — Bibl.: p.153. — Index.
ISBN 0-600-36575-1 : £3.50
ISBN 0-600-36585-9 Pbk : £1.95
(B77-18780)

598.9'7 — Tawny owls. *Juvenile literature*
Nyholm, Niels. Tawny owl / [by] Niels Nyholm ; [drawings Jon Fjeldsa]. — Hove : Firefly Books, 1977. — 64p : ill ; 25cm.
Translation of: 'Ojne i morket'. Tisvilde : Skarv, 1976.
ISBN 0-904724-29-8 : £2.95
(B77-27871)

599 — Mammals
Buckles, Mary Parker. Mammals of the world / [by] Mary Parker Buckles. — Toronto [etc.] ; London : Bantam, 1976. — 159p : col ill ; 18cm. — (All-colour guide)
'A Ridge Press book'. — Bibl.: p.157. — Index.
ISBN 0-552-60118-7 Pbk : £0.75
(B77-08393)

Buckles, Mary Parker. Mammals of the world / [by] Mary Parker Buckles. — London : Transworld, 1976. — 159,[1]p : col ill ; 19cm. — (All-color guide)
'A Ridge Press book'. — Originally published: Toronto ; London : Bantam, 1976. — Bibl.: p.157. — Index.
ISBN 0-552-98010-2 : £1.45
(B77-16881)

Duplaix-Hall, Nicole. World guide to mammals / by Nicole Duplaix and Noel Simon ; introduction by Prue and John Napier ; illustrations by Peter Barrett. — London : Octopus Books, 1977. — [2],283p : col ill, col maps ; 27cm.
Index.
ISBN 0-7064-0671-0 : £5.95
(B77-33809)

Gunderson, Harvey L. Mammalogy / [by] Harvey L. Gunderson. — New York ; London [etc.] : McGraw-Hill, 1976. — viii,483p : ill, facsim, maps ; 24cm. — (McGraw-Hill series in organismic biology)
Bibl.: p.402-445. — Index.
ISBN 0-07-025190-8 : £14.25
(B77-27872)

Hanák, Vladimír. A colour guide to familiar mammals / by Vladimír Hanák ; illustrated by Květoslav Hísek ; [translated from the Czech by Stanislava Pošustová]. — London : Octopus Books, 1977. — 184p : ill(chiefly col) ; 20cm.
Spine title: Mammals. — Originally published: in Czech. Prague : Artia, 1977. — Bibl.: p.180-181. — Index.
ISBN 0-7064-0609-5 : £1.25
(B77-13051)

599 — Mammals. *Juvenile literature*
Animals and their young. — London : Dean, 1977. — [28]p : chiefly col ill ; 32cm.
ISBN 0-603-08502-4 : £0.85
(B77-33239)

Civardi, Anne. How animals live / [by] Anne Civardi and Cathy Kilpatrick ; illustrated by George Thompson ; designed by Sally Burrough. — London : Usborne, 1976. — 2-47p : col ill, col map ; 29cm.
Col. ill., text on lining papers. — Index.
ISBN 0-86020-057-4 : £1.50
(B77-09703)

Long, J B. Gold star book of animals we know / illustrated by J.B. Long. — London : Dean, 1974. — [26]p : chiefly col ill ; 28cm.
ISBN 0-603-05775-6 : Unpriced
(B77-20281)

The **superbook** of wild animals. — London : Macdonald Educational, 1977. — 32p : col ill, col maps ; 29cm.
Adaptation of: 'The life of monkeys and apes' / by Michael Boorer, 1974, and 'The life of meat eaters' / by Maurice Burton and Robert Burton, 1973. — Bibl.: p.32.
ISBN 0-356-05599-x Sd : £0.50
(B77-27873)

599'.001'2 — Mammals. Taxonomy
Webb, Joseph Ernest. Guide to living mammals / [by] J.E. Webb, J.A. Wallwork, J.H. Elgood. — London [etc.] : Macmillan, 1977. — vii,152p : ill, maps ; 22cm.
Index.
ISBN 0-333-21696-2 Pbk : £2.95
(B77-15858)

599'.01'13 — Mammals. Blood. Platelets. *Conference proceedings*
Platelets : production, function, transfusion and storage / edited by Mario G. Baldini, Shirley Ebbe. — New York [etc.] ; London : Grune and Stratton, 1974. — xviii,418p : ill ; 26cm.
'This volume comprises the thirty-six contributions to a conference on blood platelets held at St. Elizabeth's Hospital in Boston in June, 1973' - Preface. — Index.
ISBN 0-8089-0845-6 : Unpriced
(B77-21146)

599'.01'16 — Mammals. Haematopoietic system
Weiss, Leon. The blood cells and hematopoietic tissues / [by] Leon Weiss. — New York ; London [etc.] : McGraw-Hill, 1977. — 253p in various pagings : ill ; 24cm.
'A Blakiston publication'. — '... consists entirely of chapters taken from Weiss and Greep's "Histology", Fourth Edition' - Preface. — Bibl. — Index.
ISBN 0-07-069101-0 Pbk : £7.50
(B77-30272)

599'.01'16 — Mammals. Heart. Muscles. Diseases. Biochemistry. *Conference proceedings*
International Study Group for Research in Cardiac Metabolism. *Annual Meeting, 6th, Freiburg, 1973.* Biochemistry and pharmacology of myocardial hypertrophy, hypoxia and infarction / edited by Peter Harris, Richard J. Bing and Albrecht Fleckenstein. — Baltimore ; London [etc.] : University Park Press, 1976. — xiii,491p : ill ; 25cm. — (Recent advances in studies on cardiac structure and metabolism ; vol.7)
'Proceedings of the Sixth Annual Meeting of the International Study Group for Research in Cardiac Metabolism, 25-28 September, 1973, Freiburg, Germany' - note. — Bibl. — Index.
ISBN 0-8391-0667-x : £24.75
(B77-00232)

599'.01'16 — Mammals. Heart. Muscles. Sarcolemma. *Conference proceedings*
International Study Group for Research in Cardiac Metabolism. *Annual Meeting, 7th, Quebec, 1974.* The sarcolemma / edited by Paul-Emile Roy and Naranjan S. Dhalla. — Baltimore ; London [etc.] : University Park Press, 1976. — xiii,490p : ill ; 25cm. — (Recent advances in studies on cardiac structure and metabolism ; vol.9)
'Proceedings of the Seventh Annual Meeting of the International Study Group for Research in Cardiac Metabolism, 18-21 June, 1974, Québec Canada ... Organized by the Department of Pathology and Medicine of Laval University and by the Institute of Cardiology of Laval Hospital' - note. — Bibl. — Index.
ISBN 0-8391-0669-6 : £24.75
(B77-01465)

599'.01'33 — Mammals. Foreign compounds. Metabolism. *Reviews of research*
Foreign compound metabolism in mammals. — London : Chemical Society. — (Chemical Society. Specialist periodical reports)
Vol.4 : a review of the literature published during 1974 and 1975 / senior reporter D.E. Hathway, reporters ... [others]. — 1977. — xiii, 411p : ill ; 23cm.
Index.
ISBN 0-85186-038-9 : £27.00
ISSN 0300-3493
(B77-20282)

599'.01'33 — Mammals. Purines & pyrimidines. Metabolism. *Conference proceedings*
Symposium on Purine and Pyrimidine Metabolism, *London, 1976.* Purine and pyrimidine metabolism. — Amsterdam ; Oxford [etc.] : Elsevier [etc.], 1977. — xi,369p : ill ; 25cm. — (Ciba Foundation. Symposia : new series ; 48)
'Symposium on Purine and Pyrimidine Metabolism held at the Ciba Foundation, London, 9-11th June, 1976' - Participants. — Bibl. — Index.
ISBN 0-444-15256-3 : Unpriced
(B77-24238)

599'.01'4 — Mammals. Lactation
Lactation : a comprehensive treatise / edited by Bruce L. Larson, Vearl R. Smith. — New York ; London : Academic Press.
Vol.1 : The mammary gland : development and maintenance. — 1974 [i.e. 1976]. — xii,516p : ill ; 24cm.
Published in the United States: 1974. — Bibl. — Index.
ISBN 0-12-436701-1 : £20.00
(B77-06090)

Vol.2 : Biosynthesis and secretion of milk, diseases. — 1974 [i.e. 1977]. — xiv,458p plate : ill(some col) ; 24cm.
Published in the United States: 1974. — Bibl. — Index.
ISBN 0-12-436702-x : £16.90
(B77-09704)

599'.01'42 — Mammals. Neuroendocrine system. Research, to 1974. *Personal observations. Collections*
Pioneers in neuroendocrinology / edited by Joseph Meites, Bernard T. Donovan and Samuel M. McCann. — New York ; London : Plenum Press, [1976]. — viii,327p : ill, facsims, ports ; 24cm. — (Perspectives in neuroendocrine research ; vol.1)
Published in the United States: 1975. — Bibl. — Index.
ISBN 0-306-34901-9 : £17.33
(B77-04182)

599.01'5'1 — Mammals. Genes. Molecular biology
The **molecular** biology of the mammalian genetic apparatus. — Amsterdam [etc.] ; Oxford : North-Holland Publishing Co.
Vol.1 / edited Paul O.P. Ts'o. — 1977. — xx, 444p : ill, port ; 25cm.
'... [Proceedings of] the "International Symposium on the Molecular Biology of the Mammalian Genetic Apparatus - Its Relationship to Cancer, Aging and Medical Genetics" ... held at the California Institute of Technology in December of 1975' - Preface. — Bibl. — Index.
ISBN 0-7204-0625-0 : £27.80
(B77-29439)

599'.01'6 — Mammals. Parturition. Role of foetuses. *Conference proceedings*
Fetus and Birth *(Conference), London, 1976.* The fetus and birth. — Amsterdam ; Oxford [etc.] : Elsevier [etc.], 1977. — viii,481p : ill ; 25cm. — (Ciba Foundation. Symposia : new series ; 47)
'Symposium on "The Fetus and Birth" held at the Ciba Foundation, London, 18-20th May, 1976' - p.vii. — Bibl. — Index.
ISBN 0-444-15255-5 : £19.80
(B77-25640)

599'.01'6 — Mammals. Reproduction
Reproduction in mammals / edited by C.R. Austin and R.V. Short ; illustrations by John R. Fuller. — Cambridge [etc.] : Cambridge University Press.
Book 6 : The evolution of reproduction / [contributors C.R. Austin et al.]. — 1976. — viii,189p : ill, maps ; 23cm.
Spine title: The evolution of reproduction. — Bibl. — Index.
ISBN 0-521-21286-3 : £6.50
ISBN 0-521-29085-6 Pbk : £2.50
(B77-04183)

599'.01'6 — Mammals. Reproduction. *Conference proceedings*
World Congress of Fertility and Sterility, *8th, Buenos Aires, 1974.* Biological and clinical aspects of reproduction : selected, updated papers presented at VIII World Congress on Fertility and Sterility, Buenos Aires, November 3-9, 1974 / editors F.J.G. Ebling, I.W. Henderson. — Amsterdam ; Oxford ([256 Banbury Rd, Oxford OX2 7DH]) : Excerpta Medica, 1976. — ix,476p : ill ; 25cm. — (International congress series ; no.394)
Bibl. — Index.
£42.15
ISBN 90-219-0324-5
(B77-16882)

599'.01'66 — Mammals. Sex hormones. Effects. Regulation. Mechanisms
Regulatory mechanisms affecting gonadal hormone action / edited by J.A. Thomas, R.L. Singhal. — Aylesbury : HM + M, 1977. — xi, 340p : ill ; 24cm. — (Advances in sex hormone research ; vol.3)
Also published: Baltimore : University Park Press, 1977. — Bibl. — Index.
ISBN 0-85602-066-4 : £19.50
(B77-14242)

599'.01'825 — Mammals. Hearing. *Conference proceedings*
Symposium on Sound Reception in Mammals, *Zoological Society of London, 1974.* Sound reception in mammals : the proceedings of a symposium organized jointly by the British Society of Audiology and the Zoological Society of London on 21 and 22 March, 1974 / edited by R.J. Bench, Ade Pye and J.D. Pye. — London [etc.] : Academic Press for the Zoological Society of London, 1975. — xviii, 357p : ill ; 24cm. — (Zoological Society of London. Symposia ; no.37)
'[Proceedings of the] Symposium on Sound Reception in Mammals ...' - Preface. — Bibl. — Index.
ISBN 0-12-613337-9 : £9.80
(B77-18781)

599'.01'826 — Mammals. Behaviour. Role of odours
Stoddart, D Michael. Mammalian odours and pheromones / [by] D. Michael Stoddart. — London : Edward Arnold, 1976. — iv,60p : ill ; 22cm. — (Institute of Biology. Studies in biology ; no.73)
Bibl.: p.60.
ISBN 0-7131-2590-x : £2.60
ISBN 0-7131-2591-8 Pbk : £1.30
(B77-10374)

599'.01'852 — Mammals. Running
Gambarian, P P. How mammals run : anatomical adaptations / [by] P.P. Gambaryan ; translated from Russian by Hilary Hardin. — New York [etc.] : Wiley ; Jerusalem ; London : Israel Program for Scientific Translations ; Chichester : Distributed by Wiley, [1977]. — xiv,367p : ill ; 25cm.
'A Halsted Press book'. — This translation published in the United States: 1974. — Translation of: 'Beg mlekopitaiushchikh'. Leningrad : Nauka, Leningradskoe Otdelenie, 1972. — Bibl.: p.357-362. — Index.
ISBN 0-470-29059-5 : £16.10
(B77-10809)

599'.01'88 — Mammals. Brain. Biochemistry
Bachelard, H S. Brain biochemistry / [by] H.S. Bachelard. — London : Chapman and Hall, 1976. — 71p : ill ; 21cm. — (Outline studies in biology)
Originally published: 1974. — Index.
Pbk : £1.50
ISBN 0-412-12760-1
(B77-30273)

Bachelard, Herman Stanton. Brain biochemistry / [by] H.S. Bachelard. — London : Chapman and Hall, 1974. — 71p : ill ; 21cm. — (Outline studies in biology)
Index.
ISBN 0-412-12760-1 Pbk : £0.95
(B77-18782)

599'.01'88 — Mammals. Brain. Chemical transmitters. Metabolic compartmentation. *Conference proceedings*
NATO Advanced Study Institute on Metabolic Compartmentation in Relation to Structure and Function of the Brain, *Oxford, 1974.* Metabolic compartmentation and neurotransmission : relation to brain structure and function / edited by Soll Berl, D.D. Clarke and Diana Schneider. — New York ; London : Plenum Press [for the] NATO Scientific Affairs Division, [1976]. — xxiii,721p : ill ; 26cm. — (NATO Advanced Study Institutes : series A, life sciences ; vol.6)
'Proceedings of the NATO Advanced Study Institute on Metabolic Compartmentation in Relation to Structure and Function of the Brain, held in Oxford, England, September 1-8, 1974' - title page verso. — Published in the United States: 1975. — Bibl. — Index.
ISBN 0-306-35606-6 : £31.19
(B77-03560)

599'.01'88 — Mammals. Central nervous system. Synapses. Chemical transmitters: Drugs. *Conference proceedings*
Use of Pharmacological Agents in the Elucidation of Central Synaptic Transmission *(Conference), Central Drug Research Institute, Lucknow, 1974.* Drugs and central synaptic transmission / edited by P.B. Bradley and B.N. Dhawan. — London [etc.] : Macmillan, 1976. — xiv,391p : ill ; 24cm.
'This book ... contains the material presented at this recent international symposium which was held at the Central Drug Research Institute in Lucknow from 28th to 30th October 1974, under the title "Use of Pharmacological Agents in the Elucidation of Central Synaptic Transmission"' - Preface. — Bibl. — Index.
ISBN 0-333-12735-8 : £15.00
(B77-03561)

599'.01'88 — Mammals. Nervous system. Neurons. Cells. Physiology
Peters, Alan, *b.1929.* The fine structure of the nervous system : the neurons and supporting cells / [by] Alan Peters, Sanford L. Palay, Henry de F. Webster. — Philadelphia ; London [etc.] : Saunders, 1976 [i.e. 1977]. — xxii,406p : ill ; 28cm.
Published in the United States: 1976. — ' ... an altogether new book rather than a revision of the old [New York: London : Harper and Row, 1970]' - Preface. — Bibl.: p.345-395. — Index.
ISBN 0-7216-7207-8 : £25.25
(B77-12453)

599'.01'9242 — Mammals. Effects of opiates. *Conference proceedings*
International Narcotics Research Club. *Conference, Aberdeen, 1976.* Opiates and endogenous opioid peptides : proceedings of the International Narcotics Research Club meeting, Aberdeen, United Kingdom, 19-22 July, 1976 / organizing committee, S. Archer ... H.W. Kosterlitz ... [et al.]. — Amsterdam [etc.] ; Oxford : North-Holland Publishing Co., 1976. — x,456p : ill ; 25cm.
Index.
ISBN 0-7204-0599-8 : £22.13
Primary classification 599'.01'9245
(B77-06091)

599'.01'9245 — Mammals. Effects of endogenous opioid peptides. *Conference proceedings*
International Narcotics Research Club. *Conference, Aberdeen, 1976.* Opiates and endogenous opioid peptides : proceedings of the International Narcotics Research Club meeting, Aberdeen, United Kingdom, 19-22 July, 1976 / organizing committee, S. Archer ... H.W. Kosterlitz ... [et al.]. — Amsterdam [etc.] ; Oxford : North-Holland Publishing Co., 1976. — x,456p : ill ; 25cm.
Index.
ISBN 0-7204-0599-8 : £22.13
Also classified at 599'.01'9242
(B77-06091)

599'.01'925 — Mammals. Enzymes. Regulation. *Reviews of research*
Advances in enzyme regulation. — Oxford [etc.] : Pergamon.
Vol.15 : Proceedings of the Fifteenth Symposium on Regulation of Enzyme Activity and Synthesis in Normal and Neoplastic Tissues, held at Indiana University School of Medicine, Indianapolis, Indiana, September 27 and 28, 1976 / edited by George Weber, technical editor Catherine E. Forrest Weber. — 1977. — xv,451p,[8] leaves of plates : ill, ports ; 24cm.
Ill. on lining papers. — Index.
ISBN 0-08-021507-6 : Unpriced
ISSN 0567-9915
(B77-21147)

599'.02 — Mammals. Communicable diseases. Epidemiology
Smith, C E Gordon. Epidemiology and infections / [by] C.E. Gordon Smith. — Shildon : Meadowfield Press, 1976. — [6],50p : ill, maps ; 21cm. — (Patterns of progress : microbiology series)
Bibl.: p.47-50.
ISBN 0-904095-19-3 Pbk : £1.90
(B77-20283)

599'.02'113 — Mammals. Haematology. *Comparative studies*
Comparative clinical haematology / edited by R.K. Archer and L.B. Jeffcott ; with a foreword by H. Lehmann. — Oxford [etc.] : Blackwell Scientific, 1977. — xi,737p : ill ; 25cm.
Bibl.: p.621-701. — Index.
ISBN 0-632-00289-1 : £25.00 : CIP rev.
(B77-15859)

599'.02'121 — Mammals. Lungs. Cells. Diseases. *Conference proceedings*
Brook Lodge Conference on Lung Cells in Disease, *Augusta, Mich., 1976.* Lung cells in disease : proceedings of a Brook Lodge Conference [held at] Augusta, Michigan, April 21-23, 1976 / editor Arend Bouhuys. — Amsterdam [etc.] ; Oxford : North-Holland Publishing Co., 1976. — xiv,350p : ill ; 25cm.
'The Brook Lodge Conference on Lung Cells in Disease ...' - Preface. — Index.
ISBN 0-7204-0589-0 : £18.11
(B77-06092)

599'.02'34 — Mammals. Rabies
Rabies : the facts / edited by Colin Kaplan. — Oxford [etc.] : Oxford University Press, 1977. — viii,116p,[8]p of plates : ill, map, port ; 23cm.
Index.
ISBN 0-19-264918-3 : £1.95
(B77-10810)

599'.02'9 — Mammals. Cellular immunity. Role of lymphocytes
Katz, David Harvey. Lymphocyte differentiation, recognition and regulation / [by] David H. Katz. — New York [etc.] ; London : Academic Press, 1977. — xii,749p : ill ; 24cm. — (Immunology)
Bibl.: p.684-740. — Index.
ISBN 0-12-401640-5 : £29.80
(B77-27874)

599'.03 — Mammals: Chimaeras
McLaren, Anne. Mammalian chimaeras / [by] Anne McLaren. — Cambridge [etc.] : Cambridge University Press, 1976. — vi,154p : ill ; 24cm. — (Developmental and cell biology series ; 4)
Bibl.: p.135-147. — Index.
ISBN 0-521-21183-2 : £8.00
(B77-03016)

599'.03 — Mammals. Development
Development in mammals. — Amsterdam [etc.] ; Oxford : North-Holland Publishing Co.
Vol.1 / editor Martin H. Johnson. — 1977. — vii,390p : ill ; 25cm.
Bibl. — Index.
ISBN 0-7204-0631-5 : £20.00
(B77-18146)

Vol.2 / editor Martin H. Johnson. — 1977. — vii,241p : ill ; 25cm.
Bibl. — Index.
ISBN 0-7204-0646-3 : Unpriced
(B77-22593)

599'.03'2 — Mammals. Gametes. Immunological aspects
Immunobiology of gametes / edited by M. Edidin, M.H. Johnson. — Cambridge [etc.] : Cambridge University Press, 1977. — x,310p : ill ; 24cm. — (Clinical and experimental immunoreproduction ; 4)
'[Proceedings of a] conference ... held in May ... 1976 in The Johns Hopkins University, Baltimore ... ' - Preface. — Bibl. — Index.
ISBN 0-521-21441-6 : £14.50
(B77-16883)

599'.03'2 — Mammals. Spermatogenesis. Role of hormones. *Conference proceedings*
Workshop on the Testis, *2nd, Chapel Hill, N.C., 1975.* Hormonal regulation of spermatogenesis / edited by Frank S. French ... [et al.]. — New York ; London : Plenum Press, [1976]. — xi, 526p : ill ; 26cm. — (Current topics in molecular endocrinology ; vol.2)
'Proceedings of the Second Annual Workshop on the Testis held in Chapel Hill, North Carolina, April 2, 1975' - title page verso. — Published in the United States: 1975. — Bibl. — Index.
ISBN 0-306-34002-x : £24.89
(B77-04815)

599'.03'33 — Mammals. Foetuses. Endocrine system. Physiology
Nathanielsz, Peter W. Fetal endocrinology : an experimental approach / [by] P.W. Nathanielsz. — Amsterdam [etc.] ; Oxford : North-Holland Publishing Co., 1976. — [2],xiii,261p : ill ; 25cm. — (Monographs in fetal physiology ; vol.1)
Bibl.: p.221-256. — Index.
ISBN 0-7204-0582-3 : Unpriced
(B77-16397)

599'.03'33 — Mammals. Ova. Implantation. *Conference proceedings*
Various Methods for the Study of Ovo-Implantation *(Conference), Washington, D.C., 1972.* Implantation of the ovum / edited by K. Yoshinaga, R.K. Meyer, R.O. Greep. — Cambridge, Mass. ; London : Harvard University Press, 1976 [i.e. 1977]. — xi,161p : ill ; 24cm.
'[Papers from] ... a workshop entitled "Various Methods for the Study of Ovo-Implantation "[held in connection with the Fourth International Congress of Endocrinology, Washington, D.C., 1972]' - Preface. — Published in the United States: 1976. — Bibl. — Index.
ISBN 0-674-44523-6 : £12.35
(B77-13658)

599'.05'6 — Mammals. Sexual behaviour. Effects of olfactory perception. *Reviews of research*
Mammalian olfaction, reproductive processes, and behavior / edited by Richard L. Doty. — New York [etc.] ; London : Academic Press, 1976 [i.e. 1977]. — xi,344p : ill ; 24cm.
Published in the United States: 1976. — Bibl. — Index.
ISBN 0-12-221250-9 : £16.70
(B77-14742)

599'.08'75 — Mammals. Cells. Membranes
Mammalian cell membranes / edited by G.A. Jamieson and D.M. Robinson. — London [etc.] : Butterworth.
In 5 vols.
Vol.2 : The diversity of membranes. — 1977. — xi,364p : ill ; 25cm.
Bibl. — Index.
ISBN 0-408-70723-2 : £18.00
(B77-04816)

Vol.3 : Surface membranes of specific cell types. — 1977. — ix,276p,[2]p of plates : ill(some col) ; 24cm.
Bibl. — Index.
ISBN 0-408-70773-9 : £18.00
(B77-04817)

Vol.4 : Membranes and cellular functions. — 1977. — xi,262p : ill ; 24cm.
Bibl. — Index.
ISBN 0-408-70774-7 : Unpriced
(B77-15294)

Vol.5 : Responses of plasma membranes. — 1977. — xi,316p : ill ; 24cm.
Bibl. — Index.
ISBN 0-408-70775-5 : Unpriced
(B77-15295)

599'.08'75 — Mammals. Lymphocytes. Membranes. Receptors. *Conference proceedings*
International Symposium on Membrane Receptors of Lymphocytes, *Paris, 1975.*
Membrane receptors of lymphocytes : proceedings of the International Symposium on Membrane Receptors of Lymphocytes, held in Paris, 22-24 May, 1975 : sponsored by Délégation générale à la recherche scientifique et technique, Institut national de la santé et de la recherche médicale and the World Health Organization / editors M. Seligmann, J.L. Preud'homme, F.M. Kourilsky. — Amsterdam ; Oxford : North-Holland Publishing Co. [etc.], 1975. — xvi,475p : ill ; 25cm. — (Institut national de la santé et de la médicale recherche. INSERM symposia ; no.1)
Bibl. — Index.
ISBN 0-7204-4528-0 : Unpriced
(B77-20284)

599'.08'765 — Mammals. Cells. Plasma membranes. Effects of non-oncogenic viruses. *Reviews of research*
Virus infection and the cell surface / edited by George Poste and Garth L. Nicolson. — Amsterdam [etc.] ; Oxford : North-Holland Publishing Co., 1977. — xix,342p : ill ; 25cm. — (Cell surface reviews ; vol.2)
Bibl.: p.320-329. — Index.
ISBN 0-7204-0598-x : £27.40
(B77-23424)

599'.09'2 — Marine mammals. *Encyclopaedias*
Coffey, David J. The encyclopedia of sea mammals / [by] David J. Coffey ; American consultant editors David K. Caldwell, Melba C. Caldwell. — London : Hart-Davis MacGibbon, 1977. — 223p : ill(some col), maps ; 25cm.
Index.
ISBN 0-246-10979-3 : £12.00
(B77-14743)

599'.094 — Mammals. *Europe*
Burton, Maurice. Guide to the mammals of Britain and Europe / [by] Maurice Burton ; illustrated by Rob van Assen, with additional illustrations by Bryon Harvey and Tony Morris ; text on the habitats of Europe by Christopher Barnard. — Oxford : Elsevier-Phaidon, 1976. — 256p : ill(chiefly col), 2 maps(1 col) ; 20cm.
Index.
ISBN 0-7290-0026-5 : £4.50
ISBN 0-7290-0027-3 Pbk : £1.95
(B77-15296)

599'.0941 — Mammals. *Great Britain*
The **handbook** of British mammals / edited by G.B. Corbet and H.N. Southern. — 2nd ed. — Oxford [etc.] : Blackwell Scientific for the Mammal Society, 1977. — xxxii,520p : ill, maps ; 23cm.
Previous ed.: 1964. — Bibl.: p.465-515. — Index.
ISBN 0-632-09080-4 : £9.75 : CIP rev.
(B77-06093)

Jennings, Terry John. Mammals in Britain and Ireland / [by] Terry Jennings. — London : A. and C. Black, 1977. — 56p : ill(some col) ; 21cm. — (Black's picture information books)
Bibl.: p.54. — Index.
ISBN 0-7136-1694-6 : £2.55
ISBN 0-7136-1695-4 Pbk : £1.45
(B77-21879)

599'.0941 — Mammals. *Great Britain. Juvenile literature*
Harris, Roy Andrew. Rolf Harris animal quiz book : animals of the British Isles / compiled by Roy Harris ; illustrated by Tony Morris. — London : Independent Television Books Ltd : Arrow Books, 1977. — 110p : ill ; 20cm. — (Look-in books)
Bibl.: p.110.
ISBN 0-09-915440-4 Pbk : £0.65
(B77-33240)

599'.2 — Marsupials
The **biology** of marsupials / edited by Don Hunsaker II. — New York [etc.] ; London : Academic Press, 1977. — xvii,537p : ill, map ; 24cm.
Bibl. — Index.
ISBN 0-12-362250-6 : £25.55
(B77-26326)

The **biology** of marsupials / edited by Bernard Stonehouse and Desmond Gilmore. — London [etc.] : Macmillan, 1977. — viii,486p : ill, maps ; 24cm. — (Biology and environment)
Bibl. — Index.
ISBN 0-333-18795-4 : £19.50
(B77-08394)

599'.31 — Three-toed sloths. *Personal observations. Juvenile literature*
Hoke, John. Discovering the world of the three-toed sloth / by John Hoke ; photographs by the author. — New York ; London : F. Watts, 1976. — [8],88p : ill, ports ; 23cm.
Bibl.: p.84-85. — Index.
ISBN 0-531-00339-6 : £1.95
(B77-18147)

599'.322 — Rabbits & hares. *Juvenile literature*
Whitehead, Robert. Rabbits and hares / by Robert Whitehead. — New York ; London : F. Watts, 1977. — [8],62p : ill ; 23cm. — (A first book)
Originally published: New York : F. Watts, 1976. — Index.
ISBN 0-85166-610-8 : £1.95
(B77-15860)

599'.3232 — Beavers. *Juvenile literature*
Benson, Barbara. The beaver / [by Barbara Benson] ; [adapted from the Dutch of Francis Brewer ; illustrations by Kees de Kiefte]. — Cambridge [etc.] : Cambridge University Press, 1977. — [1],16,[2]p : chiefly ill(chiefly col), map ; 22cm. — (A pole star book)
ISBN 0-521-21436-x Sd : £0.45(non-net)
(B77-07913)

599'.3232 — Prairie dogs. *Juvenile literature*
Alston, Eugenia. Come visit a prairie dog town / by Eugenia Alston ; illustrated by St. Tamara. — New York ; London : Harcourt Brace Jovanovich, 1976. — 63,[1]p : ill ; 22cm. — (Let me read books)
ISBN 0-15-219480-0 : £3.05
ISBN 0-15-219481-9 Pbk : £1.20
(B77-18148)

599'.3232 — Squirrels. *Juvenile literature*
Sheehan, Angela. The squirrel / by Angela Sheehan ; illustrated by Maurice Pledger. — London [etc.] : Angus and Robertson, 1976. — [26]p : col ill ; 23cm. — (Eye-view library)
Col. ill. on lining papers.
ISBN 0-207-95710-x : £1.60
(B77-00773)

599'.3233 — Mice. Life cycle. *Illustrations. Juvenile literature*
Thompson, David, *b.1945.* House mouse / photographs by David Thompson. — London : G. Whizzard Publications Ltd : [Distributed by] Deutsch, 1977. — [30]p : col ill ; 20x26cm. — (Nature's way ; no.4)
ISBN 0-233-96891-1 : £1.75
(B77-31203)

599'.3233 — Mice. Nervous system. Scrapie
Kimberlin, Richard Henry. Scrapie in the mouse : a model slow disease / [by] Richard H. Kimberlin. — Shildon (ISA Building, Shildon, Co. Durham) : Meadowfield Press Ltd, 1976. — [8],77p : ill ; 21cm. — (Patterns of progress : microbiology series)
Bibl.: p.71-77.
ISBN 0-900541-96-2 Pbk : £2.80
(B77-04184)

599'.3233 — Wood mice. *Juvenile literature*
Sheehan, Angela. The mouse / by Angela Sheehan ; illustrated by Maurice Pledger. — London : Angus and Robertson, 1977. — [26] p : col ill ; 23cm. — (Eye-view library)
ISBN 0-207-95773-8 : £1.80
(B77-33241)

599'.33 — Shrews. *Juvenile literature*
Björk, Gun. Shrews / text by Gun Björk ; illustrations by Ingvar Björk ; translated [from the Swedish] by Joan Tate. — London : Pelham, 1977. — 32p : col ill ; 23cm.
Translation of: 'Näbbmöss'. Stockholm : Bonniers, 1976. — Index.
ISBN 0-7207-0964-4 : £1.95
(B77-24946)

599'.4 — Bats
Pitt, Valerie, *b.1939.* Bats / by Valerie Pitt. — New York ; London : F. Watts, 1977. — [8], 63p : ill ; 23cm. — (A first book)
Originally published: New York : F. Watts, 1976. — Bibl.: p.61. — Index.
ISBN 0-85166-609-4 : £1.95
(B77-16884)

599'.53 — Dolphins. *Juvenile literature*
The **dolphin** / after an idea by Iliane Roels ; adapted from the text written by Claude Nicolas ; illustrated by Pauline Baynes. — Edinburgh : W. and R. Chambers, 1977. — [26]p : chiefly col ill ; 19x20cm. — (Questbooks : how life goes on)
ISBN 0-550-31916-6 : £1.40
(B77-14744)

599'.53 — Young dolphins. *Juvenile literature*
Morris, Robert Ada. Dolphin / by Robert A. Morris ; pictures by Mamoru Funai. — Tadworth : World's Work, 1976. — 62,[1]p : col ill ; 22cm. — (A science I can read book ; no.104)
Originally published: New York : Harper and Row, 1975.
ISBN 0-437-90104-1 : £2.10
(B77-04185)

599'.725 — Equines
Willoughby, David Patrick. The empire of Equus / [by] David P. Willoughby. — South Brunswick [etc.] : Barnes ; London : Yoseloff, 1974. — 475p : ill, maps, ports ; 27cm.
Bibl.: p.446-449. — Index.
ISBN 0-498-01047-3 : £6.00
(B77-27875)

599'.725 — Horses. *Juvenile literature*
Thomson, Neil. A closer look at horses / [by] Neil Thomson ; illustrated by Peter Barrett. — London : Hamilton, 1977. — 3-30p : ill(chiefly col), col maps ; 27cm. — (A closer look book ; 15)
Col. ill., text on lining papers.
ISBN 0-241-89559-6 : £1.75
(B77-19391)

599'.735'04132 — Ruminants. Rumen. Microflora
Hobson, P N. The microflora of the rumen / [by] P.N. Hobson. — Shildon (I.S.A. Building, Shildon, Co. Durham) : Meadowfield Press Ltd, 1976. — [6],49p : ill ; 21cm. — (Patterns of progress : microbiology series)
Bibl.: p.49.
ISBN 0-900541-94-6 Pbk : £1.90
(B77-11819)

599'.7357 — Deer
Chaplin, Raymond Edwin. Deer / [by] Raymond E. Chaplin. — Poole : Blandford Press, 1977. — ix,218p,[16]p of plates : ill(some col), map ; 23cm. — (Blandford mammal series)
Bibl.: p.203-205. — Index.
ISBN 0-7137-0796-8 : £5.75
(B77-20285)

599'.7357 — Deer. *Essex. Reports, surveys*
Chapman, D I. Deer of Essex / compiled by D.I. Chapman. — London (Passmore Edwards Museum, Romford Rd, E.15) : Essex Field Club, 1977. — 50p : ill, maps ; 21cm. — (Essex naturalist : new series ; no.1)
Bibl.: p.39-41.
Sd : Unpriced
(B77-31916)

599'.7357 — Deer. *Great Britain, to 1964*
Prior, Richard. Living with deer / [by] Richard Prior. — London [etc.] : White Lion Publishers, 1976. — 150p,[12]p of plates : ill(some col), maps ; 22cm. — (Survival books)
Originally published: London : Deutsch, 1965. — Index.
ISBN 0-7274-0117-3 : £3.95
(B77-02319)

599'.7357 — Deer. *Hampshire. New Forest*
Jackson, John. Deer in the New Forest / [by] John Jackson. — Bradford-on-Avon : Moonraker Press, 1977. — [3],25p,[16]p of plates : ill, map ; 22cm.
Bibl.: p.24-25.
ISBN 0-239-00170-2 Pbk : £1.25
(B77-18783)

599'.7357 — Fallow deer. *Great Britain. Juvenile literature*
Taylor Page, Jim. Fallow deer / [author Jim Taylor Page] ; [illustrators John Barber, Michael Clark, Victor Ross]. — Warminster (Riverside House, Heytesbury, Warminster, Wilts. BA12 0HF) : British Deer Society, [1977]. — Folder([12]p) : ill(some col), col map ; 22cm. — (The deer of Britain ; no.2)
Bibl.
ISBN 0-905476-01-8 : £0.18
(B77-12454)

599'.7357 — Red deer. *Great Britain. Juvenile literature*
Taylor Page, Jim. Red deer / [author Jim Taylor Page] ; [illustrators Michael Clark, Victor Ross]. — Warminster (Riverside House, Heytesbury, Warminster, Wilts. BA12 0HF) : British Deer Society, [1977]. — Folder([12]p) : ill(some col), col map ; 22cm. — (The deer of Britain ; no.1)
Bibl.
ISBN 0-905476-00-x : £0.18
(B77-12455)

599'.7357 — Roe deer. *Juvenile literature*
The **roe** deer / after an idea by Iliane Roels ; adapted from the text written by Claude Nicolas ; illustrated by Pauline Baynes. — Edinburgh : W. and R. Chambers, 1977. — [26]p : col ill ; 19x20cm. — (Questbooks : how life goes on)
ISBN 0-550-31917-4 : £1.40
(B77-32637)

599'.736 — Camels. *Juvenile literature*
Benson, Barbara. The camel / [by Barbara Benson] ; [adapted from the Dutch of Francis Brewer ; illustrated by W.P. Hessels]. — Cambridge [etc.] : Cambridge University Press, 1977. — [1],16,[2]p : chiefly ill(chiefly col), map ; 22cm. — (A pole star book)
ISBN 0-521-21482-3 Sd : £0.45(non-net)
(B77-07914)

599'.74428 — Leopards. *Juvenile literature*
Benson, Barbara. The leopard / [by Barbara Benson] ; [adapted from the Dutch of Francis Brewer ; illustrated by The Tjong Khing]. — Cambridge [etc.] : Cambridge University Press, 1977. — [1],16,[2]p : chiefly ill(chiefly col), map ; 22cm. — (A pole star book)
ISBN 0-521-21510-2 Sd : £0.45(non-net)
(B77-07915)

599'.74428 — Lions. *Juvenile literature*
Law, Felicia. Lions / written by Felicia Law ; illustrated by Caroline Webbe. — Glasgow [etc.] : Collins, 1977. — 32p : ill(chiefly col), col coat of arms, col map ; 22cm. — (Dandelions)
ISBN 0-00-106013-9 : £1.50
(B77-33242)

599'.74442 — Foxes. *Cumbria. Lake District. Juvenile literature*
More stories of the wild. — London [etc.] : E. Benn, 1977. — [4],96,96p : ill ; 22cm.
Contents: Vix : the story of a fox cub / by A. Windsor-Richards ; illustrated by D.J. Watkins-Pitchford. Originally published: 1960 - The badgers of Bearshanks / by 'BB' ; illustrated by D.J. Watkins-Pitchford. Originally published: 1961.
ISBN 0-510-15502-2 : £2.25
Also classified at 599'.74447
(B77-14745)

599'.74442 — Foxes. *Great Britain. Juvenile literature*
Dudley, Ernest. The fox / by Ernest Dudley. — London : Muller, 1976. — 5p : ill ; 24cm. — (Our unknown wildlife)
Bibl.: pz6.
ISBN 0-584-63739-x : £2.50
(B77-00774)

599'.74442 — Foxes. *Juvenile literature*
Sheehan, Angela. The fox / by Angela Sheehan ; illustrated by Bernard Robinson. — London : Angus and Robertson, 1977. — [26]p : col ill ; 23cm. — (Eye-view library)
ISBN 0-207-95772-x : £1.80
(B77-32638)

599'.74442 — Wolves. *British Columbia. Personal observations*
Leslie, Robert Franklin. Queen Wolf : the true story of a friendship between man and wolf / [by] Robert Franklin Leslie. — London : Pan Books, 1977. — 156p ; 18cm.
Originally published: as 'In the shadow of a rainbow', New York : Norton, 1974 ; and as 'Queen Wolf', London : Macmillan, 1975.
ISBN 0-330-25084-1 Pbk : £0.70
(B77-20286)

599'.74447 — Badgers
Neal, Ernest Gordon. Badgers / [by] Ernest G. Neal. — Poole : Blandford Press, 1977. — x, 321p,[16]p of plates : ill(some col), maps ; 23cm. — (Blandford mammal series)
Not the same as B62-5059. — Bibl.: p.307-314. — Index.
ISBN 0-7137-0816-6 : £7.25
(B77-28637)

599'.74447 — Badgers. *Northamptonshire. Kettering. Juvenile literature*
More stories of the wild. — London [etc.] : E. Benn, 1977. — [4],96,96p : ill ; 22cm.
Contents: Vix : the story of a fox cub / by A. Windsor-Richards ; illustrated by D.J. Watkins-Pitchford. Originally published: 1960 - The badgers of Bearshanks / by 'BB' ; illustrated by D.J. Watkins-Pitchford. Originally published: 1961.
ISBN 0-510-15502-2 : £2.25
Primary classification 599'.74442
(B77-14745)

599'.74447 — Badgers. *Personal observations*
Drabble, Phil. Badgers at my window / [by] Phil Drabble ; illustrated by Stanley Porter. — [London] : Fontana, 1976. — 160p,[8]p of plates : ill, port ; 18cm.
Originally published: London : Pelham, 1969. — Index.
ISBN 0-00-634110-1 Pbk : £0.70
(B77-03017)

Lewis, Ralph. Mister Badger : a study of badgers / by Ralph Lewis ; illustrated by T.A.S. Gibson. — London : Research Publishing Co., 1976. — 107p : ill ; 22cm.
ISBN 0-7050-0042-7 : £2.00
(B77-05427)

599'.74447 — Badgers. Behaviour. *Great Britain. Reviews of research*
Kruuk, Hans. Behaviour of badgers / [by] Hans Kruuk and Timothy Parish. — Cambridge (68 Hills Rd, Cambridge CB2 1LA) : Institute of Terrestrial Ecology, 1977. — [2],16p : ill, map ; 21cm.
ISBN 0-904282-11-2 Sd : £0.60
(B77-18149)

599'.74447 — Otters. *Great Britain. Juvenile literature*
Dudley, Ernest. The otter / by Ernest Dudley. — London : Muller, 1976. — 55p : ill ; 24cm. — (Our unknown wildlife)
Bibl.: p.55.
ISBN 0-584-63740-3 : £2.50
(B77-00775)

599'.74447 — Otters. *Juvenile literature*
Maxwell, Gavin. The otters' tale / [by] Gavin Maxwell. — Harmondsworth [etc.] : Puffin Books, 1977. — 91,[1]p,[16]p of plates : ill, ports ; 19cm. — (Puffin books)
Originally published: London : Longman, 1962.
ISBN 0-14-030915-2 Pbk : £0.50
(B77-16398)

599'.74447 — Otters. *Personal observations*
Wayre, Philip. The river people / [by] Philip Wayre. — [London] : Fontana, 1977. — 186p, [8]p of plates : ill ; 18cm.
Originally published: London : Collins : Harvill Press, 1976.
ISBN 0-00-634851-3 Pbk : £0.80
(B77-31204)

599'.748 — Common seals. *Maine. Penobscot Bay. Personal observations*
Goodridge, Harry. A seal called Andre / [by] Harry Goodridge & Lew Dietz. — Large print [ed.]. — London : Prior [etc.], 1977. — xiii, 275p ; 25cm.
Originally published: New York : Praeger, 1975.
ISBN 0-86043-030-8 : £4.50
(B77-13659)

599'.748 — Grey seal sanctuaries. *Cornwall. Gweek Seal Sanctuary. Grey seals. Personal observations*
Jones, Ken, *b.1926.* Orphans of the sea / [by] Ken Jones. — [London] : Fontana, 1976. — 96p,[16]p of plates : ill ; 18cm.
Originally published: London : Harvill Press, 1970.
ISBN 0-00-634323-6 Pbk : £0.60
(B77-02320)

599'.748 — Grey seals & common seals. *Great Britain*
Lockley, Ronald Mathias. Grey seal, common seal : an account of the life histories of British seals / [by] R.M. Lockley. — London [etc.] : White Lion Publishers, 1977. — 175p,[12]p of plates : ill(some col), maps ; 23cm. — (A 'Survival' book)
Originally published: London : Deutsch, 1966. — Index.
ISBN 0-7274-0122-x : £3.95
(B77-15861)

599'.8 — Primates
Annixter, Jane. Monkeys and apes / by Jane and Paul Annixter. — New York ; London : F. Watts, 1977. — [6],65p : ill ; 23cm. — (A first book)
Originally published: New York : F. Watts, 1976. — Index.
ISBN 0-85166-611-6 : £1.95
(B77-16885)

Freeman, Dan. The love of monkeys and apes / [by] Dan Freeman. — [London] : Octopus Books, [1977]. — 96p : col ill ; 33cm.
Ill. on lining papers. — Index.
ISBN 0-7064-0612-5 : £2.95
(B77-31205)

599'.8 — Primates. *Conference proceedings*
International Congress of Primatology, *5th, Nagoya, 1974.* Contemporary primatology : proceedings of the Fifth International Congress of Primatology, Nagoya, August 21-24, 1974 / editors S. Kondo, M. Kawai and A. Ehara. — Basel ; London [etc.] : Karger ; [Chichester] : [Distributed by Wiley], 1975. — x,522p : ill, maps ; 25cm.
Bibl. — Index.
Unpriced
ISBN 3-8055-2165-0
(B77-07360)

599'.8'04182 — Primates. Skin. Sensory perception. *Conference proceedings*
International Symposium on Sensory Functions of the Skin in Primates, *Stockholm, 1976.* Sensory functions of the skin in primates, with special reference to man : proceedings of the International Symposium held at the Wenner-Gren Center, Stockholm, January 1976 / edited by Yngve Zotterman. — Oxford [etc.] : Pergamon, 1976. — xii,607p : ill, ports ; 26cm. — (Wenner-Gren Center. International symposium series ; vol.27)
'International Symposium on Sensory Functions of the Skin in Primates held at Wenner-Gren Center, Stockholm January 13-15 1976' - title page verso. — Bibl.
ISBN 0-08-021208-5 : £15.00
(B77-04186)

599'.8'0438 — Primates. Evolution
Phylogeny of the primates : a multidisciplinary approach / edited by W. Patrick Luckett and Frederick S. Szalay. — New York ; London : Plenum Press, [1976]. — xiv,483p : ill ; 26cm.
'Proceedings of the Wenner Gren Symposium No.61 in Burg Wartenstein, Austria, July 6-14, 1974' - title page verso. — Published in the United States: 1975. — Bibl. — Index.
ISBN 0-306-30852-5 : £24.89
(B77-07916)

599.8'04'5 — Primates. Behaviour
Primate ecology : studies of feeding and ranging behaviour in lemurs, monkeys and apes / edited by T.H. Clutton-Brock. — London [etc.] : Academic Press, 1977. — xxii,631p : ill, maps ; 24cm.
Bibl.: p.603-624. — Index.
ISBN 0-12-176850-3 : £25.00
(B77-29440)

599'.8'04524 — Primates. Aggression
Primate aggression, territoriality and xenophobia : a comparative perspective / edited by Ralph L. Holloway. — New York ; London : Academic Press, 1974. — xiv,513p : ill, maps ; 24cm.
Bibl. — Index.
ISBN 0-12-352850-x : Unpriced
(B77-18784)

599'.81 — Lemurs
Lemur biology / edited by Ian Tattersall and Robert W. Sussman. — New York ; London : Plenum Press, [1976]. — xiii,365p : ill, maps ; 24cm.
Bibl. — Index.
ISBN 0-306-30817-7 : £14.49
(B77-03562)

599'.81 — Prosimii. *Juvenile literature*
Napier, Prudence Hero. Lemurs, lorises & bushbabies / [by] Prue Napier ; illustrated by Colin Threadgall. — London [etc.] : Bodley Head, 1977. — 48p : col ill ; 24cm. — (A Bodley Head new biology)
Index.
ISBN 0-370-10836-1 : £2.50
(B77-33810)

599'.884 — Mountain gorillas. *Uganda. Kisoro. Personal observations*
Baumgartel, Walter. Up among the mountain gorillas / [by] Walter Baumgartel. — New York : Hawthorn Books ; London : Hale, 1977. — viii,164p,[4]p of plates : ill(some col), ports ; 24cm.
Index.
ISBN 0-7091-6107-7 : £4.95
(B77-22594)

600 — TECHNOLOGY
Open University. *Technology for Teachers Course Team.* Selected technology topics / by the Open University [Technology for Teachers Course Team]. — Milton Keynes : Open University Press.
1a : Structures and materials. — 1977. — 58p : ill(some col) ; 30cm. — (Educational studies/technology, a post-experience and second level course : technology for teachers ; block 3, unit 7) (PET271 ; block 3(7))
With answers. — Originally published: in 'Selected technology topics.1'. 1975. — Bibl.: p.56-57. — List of films: p.57-58.
ISBN 0-335-02811-x Pbk : Unpriced
(B77-27876)

600 — Alternative technology. *Readings*
Alternative technology. — Brighton : Noyce.
Vol.2 / edited by Horace Herring ; contributions by Robin Cooper ... [et al.]. — 1977. — 98p in various pagings : ill ; 30cm.
Bibl.
Sd : £3.25
(B77-28638)

600 — Alternative technology. Organisations. *Powys. Machynlleth. National Centre for Alternative Technology. Guidebooks*
National Centre for Alternative Technology. Centre for Alternative Technology : visitors' guide / [National Centre for Alternative Technology]. — Machynlleth (Llwynwern Quarry, Machynlleth, Powys) : The Centre, 1976. — [1],16,[1]p : ill, map ; 22cm.
ISBN 0-9505632-0-x Sd : £0.20
(B77-12456)

600 — Technology. *Middle school texts*
Kincaid, Doug. Science in a topic / [by] Doug Kincaid and Peter S. Coles. — London : Hulton.
Food / illustrated by Chris Hoggett. — 1977. — 64p : ill(some col), port ; 25cm.
ISBN 0-7175-0769-6 Pbk : £1.50
Primary classification 500
(B77-22532)

602'.75 — Companies. Trade names. *Great Britain. Lists. Serials*
UK trade names. — Haywards Heath : Kompass.

1977 : [5th ed.]. — 1977. — [4],540p : ill ; 31cm.
ISBN 0-611-00619-7 : £20.00
(B77-23425)

602'.75 — Trade marks. *United States, to 1976. Illustrations*
American trademark designs : a survey with 732 marks logos and corporate-identity symbols / [compiled] by Barbara Baer Capitman. — New York : Dover Publications [etc.] ; London : Constable, 1976. — iii-xv,160p : chiefly ill, facsims ; 28cm.
Bibl.: p.xiv. — Index.
ISBN 0-486-23259-x Pbk : £2.85
(B77-20287)

602'.8'5 — Technology. Data processing. *Conference proceedings*
International CODATA Conference, *5th, University of Colorado, 1976.* The proceedings of the Fifth Biennial International CODATA Conference, June 28-July 1, 1976, held at the University of Colorado, Boulder, Colorado, USA at the invitation of the National Academy of Sciences / edited by Bertrand Dreyfus. — Oxford [etc.] : Pergamon, 1977. — xxvi,642p : ill, forms, maps ; 31cm.
Bibl. — Index.
ISBN 0-08-021291-3 : £27.75
ISBN 0-08-021290-5 Pbk : Unpriced
Primary classification 502.8'5
(B77-29377)

603 — Technology. *Encyclopaedias*
McGraw-Hill encyclopedia of science and technology : an international reference work ... — New York ; London [etc.] : McGraw-Hill.
Reader's guide / compiled by the editorial staff of the 'Encyclopedia of science and technology'. — [2nd ed.]. — 1977. — [5],33p : ill ; 28cm.
Previous ed.: New York : McGraw-Hill, 1971.
ISBN 0-07-045336-5 Sd : Unpriced
Primary classification 503
(B77-24167)

Study guide / compiled by the editorial staff of the 'Encyclopedia of science and technology'. — [2nd ed.]. — 1977. — [4],50p : ill ; 28cm.
Previous ed.: New York : McGraw-Hill, 1971.
ISBN 0-07-045337-3 Sd : Unpriced
Primary classification 503
(B77-24168)

McGraw-Hill encyclopedia of science and technology : an international reference work ... — [4th ed.]. — New York ; London [etc.] : McGraw-Hill, 1977. — 15v. : ill(chiefly col), charts(chiefly col), maps(chiefly col), plans(chiefly col) ; 29cm.
Previous ed.: New York : McGraw-Hill, 1971. — Bibl. — Index.
ISBN 0-07-079590-8 : £295.00 the set
Primary classification 503
(B77-24169)

Van Nostrand's scientific encyclopedia. — 5th ed. / edited by Douglas M. Considine. — New York ; London [etc.] : Van Nostrand Reinhold, 1976. — xi,2370p : ill, maps ; 31cm.
Previous ed.: Princeton ; London : Van Nostrand, 1968. — Bibl.
ISBN 0-442-21629-7 : £55.00
Primary classification 503
(B77-05377)

603 — Technology. *French-English dictionaries*
De Vries, Louis. French-English science and technology dictionary / [by] Louis DeVries. — 4th ed. / revised and enlarged by Stanley Hochman. — New York ; London [etc.] : McGraw-Hill, 1976. — xiii,683p ; 21cm.
Previous ed.: published as 'French-English science dictionary'. 1962.
ISBN 0-07-016629-3 : £11.20
Primary classification 503
(B77-01391)

604'.2'01516 — Technical drawings. Geometric aspects. *For Irish students. Secondary school texts*
Clarke, Michael Gerard. Exercises in plane and solid geometry : technical drawing for Leaving Certificate / [by] Michael G. Clarke. — Tallaght : Folens, 1976. — 183p : ill ; 25cm.
Pbk : £1.80
(B77-19392)

604'.2'4 — Technical drawings. Draftsmanship. *For Commonwealth students. Secondary school texts*
Driscoll, Terence. Technical drawing for today / [by] Terence Driscoll. — London [etc.] : Macmillan.
In 2 vols.
Book 2. — 1977. — 191p : ill ; 22x28cm.
ISBN 0-333-18965-5 Pbk : £1.75
(B77-27877)

Book 2. — 1977. — 191p : chiefly ill ; 22x28cm.
Pbk : £1.75
(B77-23426)

604'.2'4 — Freehand technical drawings. Draftsmanship
Knowlton, Kenneth W. Technical freehand drawing and sketching / [by] Kenneth W. Knowlton, Robert A. Beauchemin, Patrick J. Quinn. — New York ; London [etc.] : McGraw-Hill, 1977. — v,314p : ill ; 28cm.
Index.
ISBN 0-07-035207-0 Pbk : £7.45
(B77-13052)

604'.2'4 — Technical drawings. Draftsmanship
Bethune, James D. Essentials of drafting / [by] James D. Bethune. — Englewood Cliffs ; London [etc.] : Prentice-Hall, 1977. — xiii, 386p : ill ; 29cm.
Text on lining paper. — Bibl.: p.381. — Index.
ISBN 0-13-284430-3 : £11.95
(B77-15297)

Mott, Leslie Charles. Engineering drawing and construction / [by] L.C. Mott. — 2nd ed. — Oxford [etc.] : Oxford University Press, 1976. — x,244p : ill ; 25cm.
Previous ed.: in 2 vols. London : Oxford University Press, 1965. — Index.
ISBN 0-19-859114-4 Pbk : £3.95
(B77-09032)

604'.2'4 — Technical drawings. Draftsmanship. *Secondary school texts*
Mullins, Raymond Kenneth. Programmed technical drawing / [by] R.K. Mullins, D.A. Cooper. — Revised ed. — London : Hutchinson.
Book 1. — 1977. — 140p : ill(some col) ; 24cm.
Previous ed.: Wellington, N.Z. : Reed International, 1972.
ISBN 0-09-129931-4 Pbk : £1.95
(B77-31917)

Book 2. — 1977. — 224p : ill(some col), col maps, plans ; 25cm.
'SI units' - cover. — Originally published: Sydney ; London : Reed Education, 1974.
ISBN 0-09-129321-9 Pbk : £2.25
(B77-31920)

Workbook 1. — 1977. — [2],48p : chiefly ill, maps ; 30cm.
Fill-in book. — Previous ed.: Wellington, N.Z. : Reed International, 1972.
ISBN 0-09-129971-3 Sd : £0.70
(B77-31918)

Workbook 2. — 1977. — [2],48p : chiefly ill, maps, plans ; 30cm.
Previous ed.: Wellington, N.Z. : Reed International, 1974.
ISBN 0-09-129981-0 Sd : £0.70
(B77-31919)

Parkinson, Kenneth. Technical drawing for post-primary schools / by Kenneth Parkinson. — Revised and enlarged [ed.]. — Tallaght : Folens, [1977]. — 256p : ill(some col) ; 25cm.
Pbk : Unpriced
(B77-31921)

Twyford, John. Technical graphics for schools / by John Twyford. — Ely (Back Hill, Ely, Cambridgeshire) : Ely Resource and Technology Centre.
'A trial production published by EARO'.
Book 1 : Two-dimensional illustrations. — 1977. — 45p : chiefly ill ; 21x30cm.
ISBN 0-904463-17-6 Sd : £0.60
(B77-13660)

Yarwood, Alfred. An introduction to technical drawing / [by] A. Yarwood. — Sunbury-on-Thames [etc.] : Nelson.
Book 1. — 1976. — 64p : ill, 2 plans ; 25cm.
ISBN 0-17-431201-6 Pbk : £0.80
(B77-04187)

Book 2. — 1976. — 64p : ill ; 25cm.
ISBN 0-17-431202-4 Pbk : £0.80
(B77-04188)

604'.2'4076 — Technical drawings. Draftsmanship. *Exercises, worked examples. Secondary school texts*
Rolfe, John. Design drawing / [by] John Rolfe. — London [etc.] : Hodder and Stoughton.
2. — 1977. — [64]p : chiefly ill, plans ; 28cm.
ISBN 0-340-19258-5 Sd : £0.95
(B77-15862)

604'.2'621381 — Electronic equipment. Technical drawings. Draftsmanship
Raskhodoff, Nicholas Michael. Electronic drafting and design / [by] Nicholas M. Raskhodoff. — 3rd ed. — Englewood Cliffs ; London [etc.] : Prentice-Hall, 1977. — xix, 555p : ill ; 24cm.
Previous ed.: 1972. — Bibl.: p.524-526. — Index.
ISBN 0-13-250613-0 : £13.55
(B77-27096)

604'.2'6292 — Motor vehicles. Technical drawings. Draftsmanship
Zammit, Saviour J. Geometrical and engineering drawing for motor vehicle students / [by] Saviour J. Zammit. — London [etc.] : Longman, 1977. — iii,132p : ill ; 29cm.
Notebook format. — Index.
ISBN 0-582-41081-9 : £5.95
ISBN 0-582-41082-7 Pbk : £3.95
(B77-12457)

604'.2'6900148 — Buildings. Construction. Technical drawings. Symbols. *Standards*
British Standards Institution. Recommendations for symbols and other graphic conventions for building production drawings = Recommendations pour les symboles et d'autres conventions graphiques pour les dessins de bâtiment = Empfehlungen für Symbole und andere üblichen Zeichen zur Verwendung auf Bauzeichnungen / British Standards Institution. — London : B.S.I., 1976. — [2],79p : ill ; 30cm. — (PD6479 : 1976)
Pierced for binder. — Index.
ISBN 0-580-09395-6 Sd : £7.50
(B77-09705)

604'.6'05 — Waste materials. *Periodicals*
Waste. — London : IPC Industrial Press.
[No.1]- ; [May 1976]-. — [1976]-. — ill, facsims, ports ; 29cm.
Six issues a year. — 24p. in May 1976 issue.
Sd : £0.60(£5.00 yearly)
ISSN 0309-2623
(B77-06691)

604'.6'05 — Waste materials. Recycling. *Periodicals*
Conservation & recycling. — Oxford [etc.] : Pergamon.
Vol.1, no.1- ; 1976-. — 1976-. — ill, maps ; 25cm.
Quarterly. — [2],167p. in 1st issue. — Bibl.
Pbk : £20.41
ISSN 0361-3658
(B77-04818)

604'.6'0941 — Industrial waste materials. *Great Britain. Serials*
'Materials reclamation weekly' handbook & buyer's guide. — Croydon : Maclaren [for] Distinctive Publications Ltd.
1977. — 1977. — 360p : ill ; 25cm.
ISBN 0-903072-10-6 Pbk : £5.00
(B77-14746)

604'.7 — Blasting. *Manuals*
Nobel's Explosives Company. Blasting practice / [Nobel's Explosives Company]. — 4th ed. — Stevenson ([Nobel House, Stevenson, Ayrshire]) : Nobel's Explosives Co. Ltd, [1977]. — vii,284p : ill ; 20cm.
This ed. originally published: 1972.
Unpriced
(B77-29441)

604'.7 — Dangerous materials
Meyer, Eugene. Chemistry of hazardous materials / [by] Eugene Meyer. — Englewood Cliffs ; London [etc.] : Prentice-Hall, 1977. — xiv,370p : ill, facsims, map ; 25cm.
Bibl. — Index.
ISBN 0-13-129239-0 : £11.95
(B77-32639)

Schieler, Leroy. Hazardous materials / [by] Schieler [and] Pauzé. — New York ; London [etc.] : Van Nostrand Reinhold, 1976. — vi, 249p : ill(some col), map ; 27cm.
Index.
ISBN 0-442-27394-0 : £7.50
(B77-18785)

605 — Technology. *Serials*
Yearbook of science and the future. — Chicago ; London[etc.] : Encyclopaedia Britannica.
1976 / [editor Dave Calhoun]. — 1975. — 447, [1]p : ill(some col), col charts, map, ports(some col) ; 29cm.
Bibl. — Index.
ISBN 0-85229-307-0 : £10.50
Primary classification 505
(B77-13001)

1977 / [editor David Calhoun]. — 1976. — 447,[1]p : ill(some col), maps(some col), ports ; 29cm.
Bibl. — Index.
ISBN 0-85229-319-4 : £13.00
Primary classification 505
(B77-13002)

605 — Technology. *Yearbooks*
McGraw-Hill yearbook of science and technology / compiled by the staff of the 'McGraw-Hill encyclopedia of science and technology'. — New York ; London [etc.] : McGraw-Hill.
1976 : comprehensive coverage of the important events of the year. — 1977. — [10],454[i.e.450] p : ill, maps, ports ; 29cm.
Bibl. — Index.
ISBN 0-07-045344-6 : £22.15
Primary classification 505
(B77-32609)

605 — Technology. Conferences. *Reports, surveys. Serials*
Conference reports, engineering, technology and applied sciences. — London : Applied Science Publishers.
Vol.1, [no.1]- ; 1977-. — 1977-. — 24cm.
Quarterly. — [1],80p. in 1st issue. — Index.
Pbk : £16.00(yearly)
ISSN 0309-5908
(B77-15863)

606'.025 — Technology. Organisations. *Directories*
Commonwealth Science Council. International activities in science and technology : register of organisations of interest to Commonwealth countries / Commonwealth Science Council. — London : Commonwealth Secretariat, 1976. — [4],58p ; 29cm.
Index.
ISBN 0-85092-119-8 Pbk : £2.00
Primary classification 506'.025
(B77-02255)

607 — Technology. European information sources. *Lists*
Guide to European sources of technical information / editor Ann Pernet. — 4th ed. — Guernsey : Hodgson, 1976. — 416p ; 26cm.
Previous ed.: Paris : O.E.C.D., 1965. — Index.
ISBN 0-85280-161-0 : Unpriced
(B77-28640)

607'.11'41 — Technical colleges. *Great Britain. Directories*
United Kingdom technical colleges / [Data Research Group]. — Amersham (Hill House, [Hill Ave.,] Amersham, Bucks.) : The Group.
[1976]. — 1976. — 79 leaves in various pagings ; 30cm.
ISBN 0-905570-58-8 Sp : £12.00
(B77-07361)

1977. — [1977]. — 76 leaves in various pagings ; 30cm.
ISBN 0-86099-036-2 Sp : £14.00
(B77-23427)

607'.2 — Industrial testing. Results. Statistical analysis. Presentation. *Standards*
British Standards Institution. Guide to statistical interpretation of data = Guide pour l'interprétation statistique des données = Hinweise für die statistische Auswertung von Daten / British Standards Institution. — London : B.S.I.
Part 5 = Partie 5 = Teil 5 : Power of tests relating to means and variances = Efficacité des tests portant sur des moyennes et des variances = Schärfe von Prüfungen mit Bezug auf Durchschnittswerte und Variante. — 1977. — [2],44,[2]p(8 fold) : ill ; 30cm. — (BS2846 : Part 5 : 1977) (ISO3494 - 1976)
'ISO title: Statistical interpretation of data - Power of tests relating to means and variances'. — Pierced for binder.
ISBN 0-580-09920-2 Sd : £6.60
(B77-33811)

607'.2 — Technological innovation. *Reviews of research*
Science fact / edited by Frank George. — Great Missenden (67 High St., Great Missenden, Bucks.) : Topaz Records Ltd, 1977. — [4],540p, [16]p of plates : ill ; 19cm.
Bibl.
ISBN 0-905553-01-2 Pbk : £1.50
(B77-24947)

607'.2'41 — Consultant scientists. Organisations. *Great Britain. Association of Consulting Scientists. Directories*
Association of Consulting Scientists. List of members, including the Testing Laboratories Group [and] services offered / the Association of Consulting Scientists. — Buntingford (Owles Hall, Buntingford, Herts.) : The Association.
1977-1978. — [1977]. — [1],52p ; 21cm.
Previously published: as 'List of members and services offered'. — Index.
Sd : Unpriced
(B77-26327)

607'.2'41 — Research & development by Great Britain. Department of Industry. *Great Britain. Reports, surveys. Serials*
Great Britain. *Department of Industry.* Report on research and development / Department of Industry. — London : H.M.S.O.
1974-76. — 1977. — iii,60p ; 21cm.
Bibl.: p.42-43.
ISBN 0-11-512033-5 Sd : £1.25
ISSN 0308-5309
(B77-15864)

607'.2'41 — Research & development by Great Britain. Department of the Environment. *Great Britain. Reports, surveys. Serials*
Great Britain. *Department of the Environment.* Report on research and development / Department of the Environment. — London : H.M.S.O.
1976. — 1977. — iv,58p ; 21cm.
Bibl.: p.47-48.
ISBN 0-11-751227-3 Sd : £1.00
(B77-31922)

607'.2'41 — Research & development by Great Britain. Ministry of Overseas Development. *Reports, surveys. Serials*
Great Britain. *Ministry of Overseas Development.* Report on research and development / Ministry of Overseas Development. — London : H.M.S.O.
1976. — 1976. — v,72p ; 30cm.
ISBN 0-11-580206-1 Sd : £1.60
(B77-09033)

607'.2'41 — Research & development financed by government. Information sources. *Great Britain. Lists*
Government research and development : a guide to sources of information / Cabinet Office. — London : H.M.S.O.
1976. — 1976. — iv,36p ; 21cm.
Index.
ISBN 0-11-630154-6 Sd : £0.60
(B77-07362)

607'.2'41 — Technology. Research & development. Evaluation. Organisations. *Great Britain. Programmes Analysis Unit, 1971-1976. Reports, surveys*
Programmes Analysis Unit. The Programmes Analysis Unit : the second five years, 1971-1976. — Didcot (Chilton, Didcot, Oxon. OX11 0RF) : The Unit, 1976. — [7],80p ; 30cm.
Sp : Unpriced
(B77-20288)

607'.2'41 — Technology. Research by British institutions. *Directories*
Industrial research in Britain. — 8th ed. / editor Trevor I. Williams, associate editor Stella E.L. Wheeler. — [St Peter Port] : Hodgson, 1976. — 884p ; 26cm.
Previous ed.: 1972. — Bibl.: p.745-811. — Index.
ISBN 0-85280-171-8 : Unpriced
(B77-23428)

607'.34'41 — Museums. *London. Kensington and Chelsea (London Borough). Victoria and Albert Museum. Exhibits: Items associated with Festival of Britain. Exhibitions: Tonic to the Nation*
Victoria and Albert Museum. A tonic to the nation / [Victoria and Albert Museum]. — [London] : [The Museum], [1976]. — [8]p : ill ; 21cm.
Not the exhibition catalogue.
ISBN 0-901486-97-3 Sd : £0.10
(B77-08395)

607'.5 — Technical education. *Asia. Commonwealth countries. Reports, surveys*
Dasgupta, R. A survey of technician training in Commonwealth countries of Asia / [by] R. Dasgupta. — London : Commonwealth Secretariat, 1976. — [3],104p ; 29cm. — (Education in the Commonwealth series ; no.12 ISSN 0306-1833)
ISBN 0-85092-115-5 Pbk : £1.00
(B77-02321)

607'.9 — Technologists. Awards. *Ireland (Republic). Directories*
Murphy, Diarmuid. Fellowships and scholarships available to Irish scientists and technologists / compiled by Diarmuid Murphy and Michael Fitzgerald (with the assistance of Rachel Brew) ; [for the] National Science Council = An Chomhairle Eolaíochta. — Dublin (Government Publications Sales Office, GPO, Dublin 1) : Stationery Office, 1976. — 85p ; 24cm.
Index.
ISBN 0-7076-0023-5 Pbk : £0.45
Primary classification 507'.9
(B77-08350)

608'.7 — Invention. *Manuals*
Thring, Meredith Wooldridge. How to invent / [by] M.W. Thring and E.R. Laithwaite. — London [etc.] : Macmillan, 1977. — vii,173p : ill ; 24cm.
Index.
ISBN 0-333-22026-9 : £7.95
ISBN 0-333-17794-0 Pbk : £3.95
(B77-09706)

608'.7 — Patented products. Manufacture. Licensing. *Periodicals*
Product licensing intelligence. — London (Stone Buildings, Lincoln's Inn, WC2A 3XT) : N.P.M. Product Licensing Intelligence.
Continues: PLI licensing know how.
[No.] 157- ; May 1977-. — 1977-. — ill ; 30cm.

Monthly. — 32p. in issue no.157.
Sd : £2.00(£15.00 yearly)
ISSN 0309-9385
(B77-20289)

608'.7'41 — Inventions. Development. *Great Britain. Periodicals*
National Research Development Corporation.
Bulletin of the National Research Development Corporation. — London (Kingsgate House, 66 Victoria St., SW1E 6SL) : The Corporation.
No.44- ; Summer 1976-. — [1976]-. — ill(some col), ports(some col) ; 30cm.
Two issues a year. — 36p. in Summer 1976 issue. — Continues: Inventions for Industry.
Sd : Unpriced
ISSN 0308-9576
(B77-03018)

609 — TECHNOLOGY. HISTORICAL AND GEOGRAPHICAL TREATMENT

609 — Industrial archaeology. *Periodicals*
Industrial archaeology review. — [London] : Oxford University Press ; [Telford] : Association for Industrial Archaeology.
Vol.1, no.1- ; Autumn 1976-. — 1976-. — ill, maps, plans, ports ; 25cm.
Three issues a year. — 97p. in 1st issue. — Bibl.
Pbk : £3.50(£10.00 yearly)
ISSN 0309-0728
(B77-03563)

609 — Inventions, to 1976
Hornsby, Jeremy. The story of inventions / [by] Jeremy Hornsby. — London : Weidenfeld and Nicolson, 1977. — 142p : ill(chiefly col), facsims(some col), col map, ports(some col) ; 31cm.
Col. ill. on lining papers. — Index.
ISBN 0-297-77372-0 : £4.95
(B77-28641)

609 — Inventions, to 1976. *Juvenile literature*
Curry, Jennifer. How did it start? / [by] Jennifer Curry ; illustrated by Alan Saunders. — London [etc.] : Hamlyn, 1977. — 4-61p : col ill ; 31cm.
ISBN 0-600-34879-2 : £1.95
(B77-22595)

609 — Inventions, to ca 1750. *Juvenile literature*
Sauvain, Philip Arthur. Discoveries and inventions before the age of steam / by Philip Sauvain ; illustrated by Jim Robins. — London [etc.] : F. Watts, 1977. — 48p : ill(chiefly col) ; 22cm. — (A first look book)
Index.
ISBN 0-85166-624-8 : £1.75
(B77-13661)

609 — Inventions, to ca 1950
Hooper, Meredith. More everyday inventions / [by] Meredith Hooper. — London [etc.] : Angus and Robertson, 1976. — 127p : ill(some col), facsims, ports ; 26cm.
Ill. on lining papers. — Index.
ISBN 0-207-95606-5 : £3.20
(B77-01467)

609 — Technology. *History. Readings. Serials*
History of technology. — London : Mansell Information Publishing.
2nd annual vol. : 1977 / edited by A. Rupert Hall and Norman Smith. — 1977. — vii,261p : ill, plans ; 24cm.
ISBN 0-7201-0716-4 : £12.50 : CIP rev.
ISSN 0307-5451
(B77-27097)

609 — Technology, 1700-1930. *Juvenile literature*
Roberts, David, *b.1926.* The age of machines / [written by David Roberts] ; compiled and edited by Kenneth Bailey. — Glasgow [etc.] : Collins, 1977. — 3-63p : col ill, col ports ; 31cm. — (Collins wide world encyclopedias)
Text on lining papers. — Selection from: 'Science and invention'. 1974. — Index.
ISBN 0-00-106303-0 : £1.50
Primary classification 509
(B77-26275)

609'.03 — Inventions, 1691-1971
Baker, Ronald. New and improved - : inventors and inventions that have changed the modern world / [by] R. Baker. — London : British Museum Publications Ltd for the British Library, 1976. — 168p : ill, facsims ; 25cm.
At head of title: The Science Reference Library. — Bibl.: p.28-29. — Index.
ISBN 0-7141-0380-2 : £3.50
(B77-02322)

609'.04 — Technology. *Forecasts for 1976-1999*
Rosen, Stephen. Future facts : a forecast of the world as we will know it before the end of the century / by Stephen Rosen ; illustrations by the Chartmakers, Inc. — London [etc.] : Heinemann, 1976. — viii,535p : ill, maps, plan ; 23cm.
Originally published: New York : Simon and Schuster, 1975. — Index.
ISBN 0-434-64959-7 : £4.90
(B77-22596)

609'.41 — Industrial antiquities. *Great Britain*
Burton, Anthony. Remains of a revolution / [by] Anthony Burton ; photographs by Clive Coote. — London : Cardinal, 1975. — 255p,[88]p of plates : ill(some col), maps ; 25cm.
Also published: London : Deutsch, 1975. — Bibl.: p.249-250. — Index.
ISBN 0-351-15441-8 Pbk : £2.25
(B77-16886)

609'.41 — Industrial antiquities. *Great Britain. Guidebooks*
TIP handbook : transport & industrial preservation : a guide to what, where & when in the preservation world. — Crawley (8 Brock Rd, Langley Green, Crawley, W. Sussex RH11 7PP) : The compiler.
76-77 / compiled ... by Derek Baines. — 1976. — 3-115p,[8]p of plates : ill, maps ; 21cm.
Index.
ISBN 0-9505668-1-0 Pbk : £0.75
ISSN 0309-4553
(B77-11820)

609'.41 — Industrial antiquities. Description & travel. *Great Britain*
Burton, Anthony. Industrial archaeological sites of Britain / [by] Anthony Burton ; photographs by Clive Coote. — London : Weidenfeld and Nicolson, 1977. — 160p : ill ; 24cm.
Bibl.: p.153. — Index.
ISBN 0-297-77373-9 : £5.50
(B77-27878)

609'.41 — Inventions & technological innovation. *Great Britain, 1877-1977*
Taylor, Gordon Rattray. A salute to British genius / by Gordon Rattray Taylor. — London : Secker and Warburg, 1977. — 160p : ill(some col), facsims(some col), map, plans, ports(some col) ; 26cm.
Official souvenir book of the British Genius Exhibition. — Index.
ISBN 0-436-51639-x : £5.90
ISBN 0-436-51637-3 Pbk : £2.95
(B77-22597)

609'.41 — Technology. *Great Britain. Reports, surveys. Serials*
Great Britain. *Parliament. House of Commons. Select Committee on Science and Technology.*
Special report from the Select Committee on Science and Technology, session 1976-77. — London : H.M.S.O.
1st. — [1977]. — v p ; 25cm. — ([1976-77 H.C.] 88)
ISBN 0-10-208877-2 Sd : £0.25
Primary classification 509'.41
(B77-08351)

2nd. — [1977]. — Folder(iv p) ; 25cm. — ([1976-77 H.C.] 269)
ISBN 0-10-226977-7 : £0.15
Primary classification 509'.41
(B77-11773)

609'.411 — Industrial antiquities. *Scotland. Guidebooks*
The **industrial** archaeology of Scotland. — London : Batsford. — (The industrial archaeology of the British Isles)
1 : The Lowlands and Borders / [by] John R. Hume. — 1976. — 279p : ill, maps ; 23cm.
Bibl.: p.272-274. — Index.
ISBN 0-7134-3234-9 : £5.95
(B77-00776)

609'.422'1 — Industrial antiquities. *Surrey. Guidebooks*
Payne, Gordon A. Surrey industrial archaeology : a field guide / compiled by Gordon A. Payne. — London [etc.] : Phillimore, 1977. — 64p : ill, map, port ; 22cm.
Port, text on inside covers. — Bibl.: p.64.
ISBN 0-85033-277-x Pbk : £1.25
(B77-30274)

609'.424'56 — Industrial antiquities. *Salop. Coalbrookdale. Guidebooks*
Ironbridge Gorge Museum Trust. Coalbrookdale museum and furnace site : a guide to the site and exhibits / Ironbridge Gorge Museum Trust ; [text by Barrie Trinder ; illustrations by Pat Read and Peter Stoddart]. — [Ironbridge] (Ironbridge, Telford, Salop TF8 7AW) : The Trust, 1977. — 12p : ill(incl 1 col), facsim, geneal table, plan ; 25cm.
Sd : £0.15
(B77-29442)

609'.424'56 — Industrial antiquities. *Salop. Ironbridge Gorge region*
Cossons, Neil. Ironbridge : landscape of industry / text by Neil Cossons ; photographs by Harry Sowden. — London : Cassell, 1977. — 160p : ill(some col), facsim, maps ; 26cm.
Ill. on lining papers. — Index.
ISBN 0-304-29693-7 : £15.00
(B77-28642)

610 — MEDICINE
Davies, Ieuan John Treharne. Postgraduate medicine / [by] I.J.T. Davies. — 3rd ed. — London : Lloyd-Luke, 1977. — xi,467p,[2]p of plates : ill ; 22cm.
Previous ed.: 1972. — Bibl. — Index.
ISBN 0-85324-123-6 : £8.00
(B77-08396)

Harrison, Richard John. Textbook of medicine with relevant physiology and anatomy / [by] R.J. Harrison. — London [etc.] : Hodder and Stoughton, 1977. — xxii,442p : ill ; 22cm. — (Modern nursing series)
Index.
ISBN 0-340-20834-1 : £6.95
ISBN 0-340-20835-x Pbk : £3.95
(B77-05428)

Roper, Nancy. Man's anatomy, physiology, health and environment / [by] Nancy Roper. — 5th ed. — Edinburgh [etc.] : Churchill Livingstone, 1976. — viii,520p : ill(some col) ; 24cm.
Previous ed.: 1973. — Index.
ISBN 0-443-01497-3 Pbk : £4.95
(B77-08397)

610 — Medicine. *Reviews of research*
Advanced medicine. — Tunbridge Wells : Pitman Medical.
13 / edited by Michael Besser. — 1977. — xiii, 497p : ill ; 24cm.
Bibl. — Index.
ISBN 0-272-79423-6 : £8.50
ISSN 0308-3888
(B77-27098)

The **medical** annual : the year-book of treatment. — Bristol : J. Wright.
[1977-8] : 95th year / editors Sir Ronald Bodley Scott, Sir James Fraser. — 1977. — xxxii,381p : ill ; 23cm.
Bibl. — Index.
ISBN 0-7236-0469-x : £11.00
(B77-33812)

610 — Medicine. Information systems. *Periodicals*
Medical informatics = Médecine et informatique. — London : Taylor and Francis.
Vol.1, no.1- ; Apr. 1976-. — 1976-. — ill ; 26cm.
Quarterly. — [2],74p. in 1st issue. — English text, English and French abstracts.
Pbk : £4.50(£16.00 yearly)
ISSN 0307-7640
(B77-27099)

610 — Medicine. Measurement. Système International d'Unités. Symbols & abbreviations. *Dictionaries*
Units, symbols, and abbreviations : a guide for biological and medical editors and authors / editor D.N. Baron. — 3rd ed. — London (Publications Office, 2 Queen Anne St., W1M 0BR) : Royal Society of Medicine, 1977. — 48p ; 23cm.
Previous ed.: 1972.
ISBN 0-905958-00-4 Sd : £2.00
Primary classification 574
(B77-21859)

610'.1'4 — Medicine. Terminology
Dirckx, John H. The language of medicine : its evolution, structure and dynamics / [by] John H. Dirckx. — Hagerstown [etc.] ; London : Harper and Row, 1976. — ix,170p ; 21cm.
Bibl.: p.145-146. — Index.
ISBN 0-06-140689-9 Pbk : £3.70
(B77-04819)

610'.1'4 — Medicine. Terminology. *Exercises, worked examples*
Radcliff, Ruth K. Nursing and medical terminology : a workbook / [by] Ruth K. Radcliff, Sheila J. Ogden. — Saint Louis : Mosby ; London : Distributed by Kimpton, 1977. — vii,203p : ill, forms ; 27cm.
Pierced for binder. — Pages perforated at inside edge. — Fill-in book. — With answers. — '784 separately packaged flash cards' (99 perforated sheets, ([198] sides)). — Index.
ISBN 0-8016-3714-7 Pbk : £8.55
(B77-19393)

610'.1'41 — Medicine. Communication
The **communication** interface : reports of fourteen meetings / edited by T. Andrew Quilliam. — London (Gower St., WC1E 6BT) : University College, London, [1976]. — [1],43p ; 30cm. — (Communication in medicine)
Originally published: 1974. — Bibl.
ISBN 0-902137-19-0 Sd : £0.50
(B77-03019)

Instinct and intellect in human communication : reports of eleven further meetings / edited by T. Andrew Quilliam. — London (Gower St., WC1E 6BT) : University College, London, [1976]. — [4],41p ; 30cm. — (Communication in medicine)
Originally published: 1975. — Bibl.
ISBN 0-902137-21-2 Sd : £0.50
(B77-03020)

610'.1'82 — Medicine. Decision making. Statistical methods. *Conference proceedings*
IFIP Working Conference on Decision Making and Medical Care, *Dijon, 1976.* Decision making and medical care : can information science help? : proceedings of the IFIP Working Conference on Decision Making and Medical Care / edited by F.T. de Dombal and F. Grémy ; ... [organized by IFIP Technical Committee 4]. — Amsterdam [etc.] ; Oxford : North-Holland Publishing Co., 1976. — xviii, 603p : ill ; 23cm.
'... [held in] Dijon, France, 24-29 May 1976' - Prelims. — Bibl. — Index.
ISBN 0-7204-0464-9 : £35.00
Primary classification 610'.28'54044
(B77-05431)

610'.1'9 — Medicine. Psychological aspects
Contributions to medical psychology. — Oxford [etc.] : Pergamon.
Vol.1 / edited by S. Rachman. — 1977. — viii, 243p : ill ; 26cm.
Bibl. — Index.
ISBN 0-08-020511-9 : £8.00
(B77-29443)

610'.28 — Bioengineering. *Conference proceedings*
New England Bioengineering Conference, *5th, University of New Hampshire, 1977.*
Proceedings of the Fifth New England Bioengineering Conference, April 14-15, 1977, University of New Hampshire, Durham, New Hampshire / editor Michael R. Cannon. — New York ; Oxford [etc.] : Pergamon, 1977. — xv,283p : ill ; 28cm.
Bibl. — Index.
ISBN 0-08-021937-3 Pbk : £19.50
(B77-21880)

610'.28 — Bioengineering. *Periodicals*
Journal of bioengineering. — New York ; Oxford : Pergamon.
Vol.1, no.1- ; Nov. 1976-. — 1976-. — ill ; 26cm.
Six issues a year. — [2],53p. in 1st issue.
Pbk : Unpriced
ISSN 0145-3068
(B77-16399)

Journal of medical engineering & technology. — London : United Trade Press.
Vol.1, no.1- ; Jan. 1977-. — 1977-. — ill ; 29cm.
Six issues a year. — [2],68p. in 1st issue. — Supersedes: Biomedical engineering.
Pbk : £11.90
ISSN 0309-1902
(B77-07917)

Medical & biological engineering & computing : journal of the International Federation for Medical & Biological Engineering. — Stevenage : Peregrinus.
Continues: Medical & biological engineering.
Vol.15, no.3- ; May 1977-. — 1977-. — ill ; 25cm.
Six issues a year. — Cover title. — p.209-334 in vol.15, no.3. — 'MBEC news' (18p. in issue no.3) bound in. — English text, French and German summaries.
Pbk : £40.00 yearly(£6.00 yearly to members)
ISSN 0140-0118
(B77-20290)

610'.28 — Bioengineering. *Reviews of research*
Physical techniques in medicine. — London [etc.] : Wiley.
Vol.1 / edited by J.T. McMullan. — 1977. — x,318p : ill ; 24cm.
'A Wiley-Interscience Publication'. — Bibl. — Index.
ISBN 0-471-99468-5 : £12.75
(B77-27100)

610'.28 — Bioengineering. Applications of biochemistry
Applied biochemistry and bioengineering / edited by Lemuel B. Wingard, Jr, Ephraim Katchalski-Katzir, Leon Goldstein. — New York [etc.] ; London : Academic Press.
Vol.1 : Immobilized enzyme principles. — 1976 [i.e. 1977]. — xi,364p : ill ; 24cm.
Published in the United States: 1976. — Bibl. — Index.
ISBN 0-12-041101-6 : £28.05
(B77-14747)

610'.28 — Electronic medical equipment. *Reviews of research*
Institution of Electrical Engineers. IEE medical electronics monographs / edited by D.W. Hill, B.W. Watson. — Stevenage : Peregrinus [for] the Institution of Electrical Engineers.
18-22. — 1976. — vii,160p : ill ; 23cm.
Bibl. — Index.
ISBN 0-901223-84-0 : £10.90
ISSN 0305-9596
(B77-05429)

610'.28 — Medical equipment
Welkowitz, Walter. Biomedical instruments : theory and design / [by] Walter Welkowitz, Sid Deutsch. — New York [etc.] ; London : Academic Press, 1976 [i.e. 1977]. — xv,279p : ill ; 24cm.
Published in the United States: 1976. — Index.
ISBN 0-12-744150-6 : £13.85
(B77-14243)

610'.28 — Medical equipment. *Reviews of research*
Advances in biomedical engineering. — New York [etc.] ; London : Academic Press.
Vol.6 / edited by J.H.U. Brown, James F. Dickson, III. — 1976. — xiii,269p : ill ; 24cm.
'Published under the auspices of The Biomedical Engineering Society'. — Bibl. — Index.
ISBN 0-12-004906-6 : £19.90
(B77-05430)

610'.28 — Medical technology. *Periodicals*
Medical laboratory world. — London : United Trade Press.
Vol.1, no.1- ; Sept. 1977-. — 1977-. — ill ; 22cm.
Monthly. — 84p. in 1st issue. — 'Directory of suppliers' ([28]p.) as insert in 1st issue. — Bibl.

Pbk : £14.00 yearly
ISSN 0140-3028
(B77-27879)

610'.28 — Medicine. Laboratory techniques. *Manuals*
Lynch, Matthew Joseph. Lynch's medical laboratory technology. — 3rd ed. — Philadelphia ; London [etc.] : Saunders.
Previous ed.: in 1 vol. as 'Medical laboratory technology and clinical pathology / by Matthew J. Lynch and others. 1969.
Vol.1 / senior author Stanley S. Raphael [with] ... [others]. — 1976. — 928p in various pagings : ill, ports ; 27cm.
Bibl. — Index.
ISBN 0-7216-7463-1 : £20.75
(B77-02323)

Vol.2 / senior author Stanley S. Raphael [with] ... [others]. — 1976. — ii-xiip,p875-1485,xxii p : ill, forms, port ; 27cm.
Bibl. — Index.
ISBN 0-7216-7464-x : £16.00
(B77-06094)

610'.28 — Medicine. Use of polymers. *Conference proceedings*
Polymers in medicine and surgery / edited by Richard L. Kronenthal, Zale Oser and E. Martin. — New York ; London : Plenum Press, [1976]. — x,335p : ill ; 26cm. — (Polymer science and technology ; vol.8)
'Proceedings of the Johnson & Johnson Symposium held in Morristown, New Jersey, July 11-12, 1974' - title page verso. — Published in the United States: 1975. — Index.
ISBN 0-306-36408-5 : £17.33
(B77-02324)

610'.28 — Medicine. Use of ultrasonic waves
Wells, Peter Neil Temple. Biomedical ultrasonics / [by] P.N.T. Wells. — London [etc.] : Academic Press, 1977. — x,635p : ill ; 24cm. — (Medical physics series)
Bibl.: p.511-594. — Index.
ISBN 0-12-742940-9 : £24.00
Also classified at 574'.028
(B77-23429)

610'.28 — Patients. Care. Use of medical equipment
Bronzino, Joseph D. Technology for patient care : applications for today, implications for tomorrow / [by] Joseph D. Bronzino. — Saint Louis : Mosby ; London : Distributed by Kimpton, 1977. — xiii,255p : ill, forms ; 26cm.
Bibl. — Index.
ISBN 0-8016-0790-6 Pbk : £7.60
(B77-31206)

610'.28'54 — Medicine. Applications of computer systems. *Conference proceedings*
Medical computing : proceedings of an international symposium, Toulouse, 22-25 March 1977, organized by IRIA, Institut de recherche d'informatique et d'automatique / edited by M. Laudet, J. Anderson, F. Begon. — London : Taylor and Francis, 1977. — xii, 602p : ill, forms ; 26cm.
Contributions in English and French, English and French abstracts. — Index.
ISBN 0-85066-131-5 : £30.00
Primary classification 362.1'028'54
(B77-31792)

Medical data processing : proceedings of an international symposium, Toulouse, 2-5 March 1976, organized by IRIA Institut de recherche d'informatique et d'automatique / edited by M. Laudet, J. Anderson, F. Begon. — London : Taylor and Francis, 1976. — xi,775p : ill, facsims, forms ; 26cm.
Contributions in English and French. — Bibl. — Index.
ISBN 0-85066-106-4 : £25.00
Primary classification 362.1'028'54
(B77-04054)

610'.28'54044 — Medicine. Applications of digital computer systems
Biomedical computing / edited by W.J. Perkins. — Tunbridge Wells : Pitman Medical, 1977. — ix,362p : ill, form ; 26cm.
Index.
ISBN 0-272-79401-5 : £20.00
(B77-18786)

610'.28'54044 — Medicine. Decision making. Applications of digital computer systems. *Conference proceedings*
IFIP Working Conference on Decision Making and Medical Care, *Dijon, 1976.* Decision making and medical care : can information science help? : proceedings of the IFIP Working Conference on Decision Making and Medical Care / edited by F.T. de Dombal and F. Grémy ; ... [organized by IFIP Technical Committee 4]. — Amsterdam [etc.] ; Oxford : North-Holland Publishing Co., 1976. — xviii, 603p : ill ; 23cm.
'... [held in] Dijon, France, 24-29 May 1976' - Prelims. — Bibl. — Index.
ISBN 0-7204-0464-9 : £35.00
Also classified at 610'.1'82
(B77-05431)

610'.3 — Medicine. *Dictionaries*
Dorland, William Alexander Newman. Dorland's pocket medical dictionary. — 22nd ed. — Philadelphia ; London [etc.] : Saunders, 1977. — xxi,741p,xvi p of plates : col ill ; 19cm.
Previous ed.: 1968. — 'Abridged from "Dorland's illustrated medical dictionary"'.
ISBN 0-7216-3163-0 Pbk : £5.00
ISBN 0-7216-3162-2 Tab indexed ed. : £7.50
(B77-25645)

610'.3 — Medicine. *Dictionaries. For medical secretaries*
Roberton, Jo. Basic medical vocabulary / [by] Jo Roberton. — London [etc.] : McGraw-Hill, 1977. — vii,244p ; 19cm.
ISBN 0-07-084220-5 Pbk : £2.15 : CIP rev.
(B77-15865)

610'.3 — Medicine. *Encyclopaedias*
Brown, James Alexander Campbell. Pears medical encyclopaedia / [by] J.A.C. Brown. — [New ed.] / revised by A.M. Hastin Bennett. — London : Sphere, 1977. — 784p ; 18cm.
This ed. originally published: as 'Pears medical encyalopedia, illustrated'. London : Pelham, 1971.
ISBN 0-7221-1908-9 Pbk : £2.95
(B77-09707)

Brown, James Alexander Campbell. Pears medical encyclopedia, illustrated / [by] J.A.C. Brown. — Revised ed. / revised by A.M. Hastin Bennett ; with drawings by Margot Cooper. — London : Pelham, 1977. — 3-462p : ill(some col), map, ports ; 25cm.
Previous ed.: 1971.
ISBN 0-7207-0992-x : £7.95
(B77-24948)

610'.5 — Medicine. *Periodicals*
Galway medical annual. — [Galway] ([College Rd, Galway, Republic of Ireland]) : [University College].
No.1- ; 1970-. — [1970]-. — ill, ports ; 25cm.
Annual. — [1],72p. in 7th issue.
Sd : £0.60
(B77-24239)

Nucleus : the journal of audio-visual medicine. — Harrow (Hanover House, Lyon Rd, Harrow, Middx) : I.R.F.A. (U.K.) Ltd.
No.1- ; [1977]-. — [1977]-. — col ill ; 27cm.
Quarterly. — 14p. in 1st issue.
Sd : Unpriced
ISSN 0309-5819
(B77-11821)

610'.5 — Medicine. Conferences. *Reports, surveys. Serials*
Conference reports, medicine. — London : Applied Science Publishers.
Vol.1, [no.1]- ; 1977-. — 1977-. — 24cm.
Quarterly. — [1],83p. in 1st issue. — Index.
Pbk : £16.00(yearly)
ISSN 0309-5878
(B77-15866)

610'.6'24134 — Physicians. Organisations. *Scotland. Royal College of Physicians of Edinburgh, to 1975*
Craig, William Stuart. History of the Royal College of Physicians of Edinburgh / [by] W.S. Craig. — Oxford [etc.] : Blackwell Scientific, 1976. — xxix,1127p,[10] leaves of plates,[52]p of plates : ill, col coat of arms, facsims, map(on lining papers), ports ; 26cm.
Ill. on lining papers. — Index.
ISBN 0-632-00088-0 : £35.00
(B77-10811)

610.69 — Doctors. Professional competence. *Great Britain. Inquiry reports*
Committee of Enquiry into Competence to Practise. Competence to practise : the report of a Committee of Enquiry set up for the medical profession in the United Kingdom / [Committee of Enquiry into Competence to Practise]. — London (27 Sussex Place, Regents Park, NW1 4RG) : The Committee, 1976. — [3],74p ; 24cm.
Chairman: E.A.J. Alment.
ISBN 0-9505287-0-6 Pbk : £1.00
(B77-05432)

610.69'52'02541 — Medical profession. *Great Britain. Directories*
The **medical** register / [General Medical Council]. — London (44 Hallam St., W1N 6AE) : The Council.
1977. — 1977. — 2v.(xxiii,3349p) ; 26cm.
£22.00
(B77-18150)

610.69'52'062421 — Physicians. Organisations. *England. Royal College of Physicians of London. Directories*
Royal College of Physicians of London. List of the Fellows and Members of the Royal College of Physicians of London. — London : The College.
1976. Annual supplement. 1st. — 1977. — 64p : coat of arms ; 21cm.
Index.
ISBN 0-900596-35-x Sd : Supplement free with 1976 list
ISSN 0307-8841
(B77-06692)

610.69'53'02541 — Medical laboratory technicians. *Great Britain. Directories*
The **medical** laboratory technicians register. — [London] ([York House, Westminster Bridge Rd, SE1 7UH]) : Medical Laboratory Technicians Board.
1977. — [1977]. — 15 leaves,17-251p ; 21x30cm.
Pbk : £2.00
ISSN 0306-4328
(B77-16887)

610.69'6 — Doctors. Communication with patients. *For general practice*
Language and communication in general practice / edited by B.A. Tanner. — London [etc.] : Hodder and Stoughton, 1976. — vi, 202p,8p of plates : ill ; 23cm.
Bibl. — Index.
ISBN 0-340-20749-3 : £4.95
ISBN 0-340-20750-7 Pbk : £2.95
(B77-14748)

610.69'6 — General practitioners. Verbal communication with patients. *Great Britain. Reports, surveys*
Byrne, Patrick Sarsfield. Doctors talking to patients : a study of the verbal behaviour of general practitioners consulting in their surgeries / [by] Patrick S. Byrne and Barrie E.L. Long. — London : H.M.S.O., 1976. — 195p : ill, forms ; 25cm.
At head of title: Department of Health and Social Security.
ISBN 0-11-320652-6 Pbk : £2.45
(B77-02325)

610.69'6 — Hospitals. Doctors. Communication with patients with cancer
McIntosh, Jim. Communication and awareness in a cancer ward / [by] Jim McIntosh. — London : Croom Helm [etc.], 1977. — 3-210p ; 23cm.
Bibl.: p.205-208. — Index.
ISBN 0-85664-407-2 : £6.95
(B77-23430)

610.69'6 — Hospitals. Patients: Children. Communication with medical personnel
Klinzing, Dennis R. The hospitalized child : communication techniques for health personnel / [by] Dennis R. Klinzing, Dene G. Klinzing. — Englewood Cliffs ; London [etc.] : Prentice-Hall, 1977. — vii,168p : ill ; 23cm.
Bibl. — Index.
ISBN 0-13-394817-x Pbk : £4.75
(B77-16888)

610'.7'11 — General practitioners. Professional education. *Reports, surveys*
Kuenssberg, E V. An opportunity to learn : an international study of learning and teaching in general practice / [by] E.V. Kuenssberg. — London (14 Princes Gate, Hyde Park, SW7 1PU) : 'Journal of the Royal College of General Practitioners', 1976. — [4],78p : ill, plan ; 25cm. — (Royal College of General Practitioners. 'Journal of the Royal College of General Practitioners' occasional papers ; 2 ISSN 0309-6300)
Bibl.: p.77-78.
ISBN 0-85084-059-7 Sd : £2.25
(B77-14244)

610'.7'1141 — Doctors. Lifelong professional education. *Great Britain. Conference proceedings*
Anglo-American Conference on Continuing Medical Education, *University of North Carolina School of Medicine, 1974.*
Anglo-American Conference on Continuing Medical Education : proceedings of a Conference sponsored jointly by the Royal Society of Medicine Foundation Inc., the Royal Society of Medicine and the University of North Carolina School of Medicine held at Berryhill Hall, University of North Carolina School of Medicine, Chapel Hill, U.S.A., 8-10 April, 1974 / editors Charles L. Joiner, G. Edward Paget. — London (1 Wimpole St., W1M 8AE) : Royal Society of Medicine, 1974. — vi,126p : ill, map ; 25cm.
Bibl.
ISBN 0-9501555-7-8 Pbk : £2.00
Also classified at 610'.7'1173
(B77-19394)

610'.7'1141 — Doctors. Professional education. *Great Britain*
Webb-Peploe, M M. The challenge of medical education / [by] M.M. Webb-Peploe. — London : [Christian Medical Fellowship], [1976]. — [4],14,[1]p ; 22cm. — (Barnardo lecture ; 6th)
'The Sixth Lecture was given at a Conference on the Christian Medical Fellowship at Cambridge on Saturday, March 27th, 1976 ... ' - note.
ISBN 0-85111-958-1 Sd : £0.20
(B77-11822)

610'.7'11411 — General practitioners. Professional education. Vocational courses. *Scotland*
Scottish Council for Postgraduate Medical Education. Training in general practice / [by Alastair G. Donald ; for the Scottish Council for Postgraduate Medical Education]. — Edinburgh (8 Queen St., Edinburgh EH2 1JE) : The Council, 1977. — [2],22p ; 21cm.
ISBN 0-905830-00-8 Sd : Unpriced
(B77-15298)

610'.7'114134 — Universities. Medical schools. *Edinburgh. Edinburgh Medical School, to ca 1790. Conference proceedings*
The **early** years of the Edinburgh Medical School : a symposium jointly organised by the Royal Scottish Museum and the Scottish Society of the History of Medicine in connection with the special exhibition 'Edinburgh and Medicine' and the 250th anniversary of the foundation of the Faculty of Medicine of the University of Edinburgh, held in the Royal Scottish Museum, Chambers Street, Edinburgh, on 26th June 1976 / edited by R.G.W. Anderson and A.D.C. Simpson. — Edinburgh (Chambers St., Edinburgh EH1 1JF) : Royal Scottish Museum, 1976. — viii, 124p ; 30cm.
ISBN 0-900733-10-1 Pbk : £3.00
(B77-00233)

610'.7'1142132 — Universities. Medical schools. *London. Westminster (London Borough). Middlesex Hospital Medical School. Yearbooks*
Middlesex Hospital Medical School. Calendar / Middlesex Hospital Medical School, University of London. — [London] ([c/o The Secretary, Middlesex Hospital Medical School, W1P 7PN]) : [The School].
1976-77. — [1976]. — [2],100p,[8]p of plates : ill, map ; 22cm.
Index.
Sd : Unpriced
ISSN 0305-117x
(B77-17508)

610'.7'1143613 — Universities. Medical schools. *Austria. Vienna. Universität Wien. Medizinische Fakultät, 1800-1900*
Lesky, Erna. The Vienna Medical School of the 19th century / [by] Erna Lesky ; [translated from the German by L. Williams and I.S. Levij]. — Baltimore ; London : Johns Hopkins University Press, 1976. — xv,604p,[56]p of plates,leaf of plate : ill, facsims, plans, ports ; 25cm.
Translation of 'Die Wiener Medizinische Schule im 19. Jahrhundert'. Köln : Graz, 1965. — Bibl.: p.xiii-xv. — Index.
ISBN 0-8018-1908-3 : Unpriced
(B77-25646)

610'.7'1173 — Doctors. Lifelong professional education. *United States. Conference proceedings*
Anglo-American Conference on Continuing Medical Education, *University of North Carolina School of Medicine, 1974.*
Anglo-American Conference on Continuing Medical Education : proceedings of a Conference sponsored jointly by the Royal Society of Medicine Foundation Inc., the Royal Society of Medicine and the University of North Carolina School of Medicine held at Berryhill Hall, University of North Carolina School of Medicine, Chapel Hill, U.S.A., 8-10 April, 1974 / editors Charles L. Joiner, G. Edward Paget. — London (1 Wimpole St., W1M 8AE) : Royal Society of Medicine, 1974. — vi,126p : ill, map ; 25cm.
Bibl.
ISBN 0-9501555-7-8 Pbk : £2.00
Primary classification 610'.7'1141
(B77-19394)

610'.7'1173 — Doctors. Professional education. *United States, 1765-1910*
Kaufman, Martin. American medical education : the formative years, 1765-1910 / [by] Martin Kaufman. — Westport, Conn. ; London : Greenwood Press, 1976. — x,208,[1]p ; 22cm.
Bibl.: p.183-197. — Index.
ISBN 0-8371-8590-4 : £10.50
(B77-17509)

610'.7'1173 — Doctors. Professional education. *United States. Reports, surveys*
Carnegie Council on Policy Studies in Higher Education. Progress and problems in medical and dental education : federal support versus federal control : a report of the Carnegie Council on Policy Studies in Higher Education. — San Francisco [etc.] ; London : Jossey-Bass, 1976. — xiii,178p : ill, maps ; 24cm. — (Carnegie Council on Policy Studies in Higher Education. Series)
Bibl.: p.169-174. — Index.
ISBN 0-87589-295-7 : £5.65
Also classified at 617.6'007'1173
(B77-05433)

610'.72 — Medicine. Research
Coleman, Vernon. Paper doctors : a critical assessment of medical research / [by] Vernon Coleman. — London : Temple Smith, 1977. — 170p ; 23cm.
Bibl.: p.162-164. — Index.
ISBN 0-85117-109-5 : £4.50
(B77-07363)

610'.72 — Medicine. Research. Financial assistance. Organisations. *Scotland. Scottish Hospital Endowments Research Trust. Reports, surveys*
Scottish Hospital Endowments Research Trust. Annual report and accounts for the year ended 31st July / Scottish Hospital Endowments Research Trust. — Edinburgh : H.M.S.O. [1975]-1976. — [1977]. — iv,18p ; 25cm. — ([1976-77 H.C.]403)
Bibl.: p.12-18.
ISBN 0-10-240377-5 Sd : £0.60
(B77-22598)

610'.72 — Medicine. Research. Methodology
Cuschieri, A. Introduction to research in medical sciences / [by] A. Cuschieri, P.R. Baker. — Edinburgh [etc.] : Churchill Livingstone, 1977. — [7],216p : ill ; 22cm.
Bibl. — Index.
ISBN 0-443-01466-3 Pbk : £3.95
(B77-09034)

610'.72'073 — Medicine. Research. *United States*
The **horizons** of health / edited by Henry Wechsler, Joel Gurin, George F. Cahill, Jr. — Cambridge, Mass. ; London : Harvard University Press, 1977. — xvi,412p : ill ; 24cm.
Bibl.: p.393-398. — Index.
ISBN 0-674-40630-3 : £10.25
(B77-30275)

610'.72'081 — Medicine. Research. *Brazil, to 1920*
Stepan, Nancy. Beginnings of Brazilian science : Oswaldo Cruz, medical research and policy, 1890-1920 / [by] Nancy Stepan. — New York : Science History Publications ; Folkestone : [Distributed by] Dawson, 1976. — xi,225p : ill, ports ; 24cm.
Bibl.: p.187-207. — Index.
ISBN 0-88202-032-3 : £9.00
(B77-33243)

610.73 — Medicine. Nursing
Barber, Janet Miller. Adult and child care : a client approach to nursing / [by] Janet Miller Barber, Lillian Gatlin Stokes, Diane McGovern Billings. — 2nd ed. — Saint Louis : Mosby ; London : Distributed by Kimpton, 1977. — xiv, 1036p : ill, forms ; 27cm.
Previous ed.: 1973. — Bibl. — Index.
ISBN 0-8016-0444-3 : £14.55
(B77-27101)

Bendall, Eve Rosemarie Duffield. Basic nursing / by Eve R.D. Bendall and Elizabeth Raybould. — 4th ed. / revised by Maureen J. Wray. — London : H.K. Lewis, 1977. — viii,224p : ill, map ; 22cm.
Previous ed.: 1970. — Bibl. — Index.
ISBN 0-7186-0428-8 : £5.00
(B77-16889)

Bower, Fay Louise. The process of planning nursing care : a model for practice / [by] Fay Louise Bower. — 2nd ed. — Saint Louis : Mosby ; London : Distributed by Kimpton, 1977. — xiii,153p : ill ; 23cm.
Previous ed.: 1972. — Bibl.: p.140-143. — Index.
ISBN 0-8016-0728-0 Pbk : £4.70
(B77-31207)

Chapman, Christine Muriel. Medical nursing. — 9th ed. / revised by Christine M. Chapman. — London : Baillière Tindall, 1977. — viii,390p : ill, form ; 19cm. — (Nurses' aids series)
Previous ed.: / by Marjorie Houghton. 1972. — Index.
ISBN 0-7020-0616-5 Pbk : £1.80
(B77-15299)

Du Gas, Beverly Witter. Introduction to patient care : a comprehensive approach to nursing. — 3rd ed. / [by] Beverly Witter du Gas, with Barbara Marie du Gas. — Philadelphia ; London [etc.] : Saunders, 1977. — xix,686p : ill, forms ; 27cm.
Previous ed.: published as 'Kozier, Du Gas introduction to patient care' / by B.B. Kozier, Beverly Witter du Gas. 1972. — Bibl. — Index.

ISBN 0-7216-3226-2 : £9.00
(B77-33813)

Johnson, R Winifred Heyward. Introduction to nursing care / [by] R. Winifred Heyward Johnson, Douglass W. Johnson. — New York ; London [etc.] : McGraw-Hill, 1976. — xi, 212p : ill, forms ; 24cm. — (Nursing and allied health series)
Index.
ISBN 0-07-032595-2 Pbk : £5.15
(B77-02326)

Mosby's comprehensive review of nursing. — 9th ed. / [editor Dolores F. Saxton, assistant editors Patricia M. Nugent, Phyllis K. Pelikan]. — Saint Louis : Mosby ; London : Distributed by Kimpton, 1977. — xiii,609p : ill(some col) ; 28cm.
'Test papers and answer book' (39p.;sd) as insert. — Previous ed.: 1973. — Bibl.: p.561-565. — Index.
ISBN 0-8016-3529-2 : £10.10
(B77-17510)

Nursing care of the patient with medical-surgical disorders / edited by Harriet Coston Moidel, Elizabeth C. Giblin, Berniece M. Wagner. — 2nd ed. — New York ; London [etc.] : McGraw-Hill, 1976. — xvii,1193p : ill ; 25cm.
'A Blakiston Publication'. — Text, col. ill. on lining paper. — Previous ed.: New York : McGraw-Hill, 1971. — Index.
ISBN 0-07-042655-4 : £15.75
(B77-04820)

610.73 — Medicine. Nursing. *For student nurses*
Concepts basic to nursing / [edited by] Pamela Holsclaw Mitchell. — 2nd ed. — New York ; London [etc.] : McGraw-Hill, 1977. — xiii, 575p : ill ; 25cm.
'A Blakiston Publication'. — Previous ed.: New York : McGraw-Hill, 1973. — Bibl. — Index.
ISBN 0-07-042581-7 : £8.95
(B77-24949)

Hector, Winifred. The role of the nurse / by Winifred Hector. — London : British Broadcasting Corporation, 1977. — 64p : ill ; 21cm.
'Published to accompany the BBC-TV series "The Role of the Nurse"' - title page verso. — Bibl.
ISBN 0-563-16135-3 Sd : £1.10
(B77-16890)

Readey, Helen. Introduction to nursing essentials : a handbook / [by] Helen Readey, Mary Teague, William Readey III. — Saint Louis : Mosby ; London : Distributed by Kimpton, 1977. — ix,197p : ill, forms ; 27cm.
With answers. — Bibl. — Index.
ISBN 0-8016-4099-7 Pbk : £4.80
(B77-31923)

610.73 — Medicine. Nursing. *Manuals*
Brunner, Lillian Sholtis. Textbook of medical-surgical nursing. — 3rd ed. / [by] Lillian Sholtis Brunner, Doris Smith Suddarth, contributors ... [others]. — Philadelphia [etc.] : Lippincott ; Oxford [etc.] : Distributed by Blackwell Scientific, 1975. — xix,1156p : ill(some col), forms, map ; 28cm.
Previous ed.: / by Lillian Sholtis Brunner et al. 1970. — Bibl. — Index.
ISBN 0-397-54161-9 : £15.80
(B77-01468)

King, Eunice M. Illustrated manual of nursing techniques / [by] Eunice M. King, Lynn Wieck, Marilyn Dyer. — Philadelphia [etc.] : Lippincott ; London [etc.] : Distributed by Blackwell Scientific, 1977. — xi,432p : ill ; 24cm.
Bibl.: p.423-424. — Index.
ISBN 0-397-54183-x : Unpriced
(B77-18151)

610.73 — Medicine. Nursing. Leadership
Claus, Karen Emily. Power and influence in health care : a new approach to leadership / [by] Karen E. Claus, June T. Bailey. — Saint Louis : Mosby ; London : Distributed by Kimpton, 1977. — xii,191p : ill ; 26cm.
Bibl.: p.173-183. — Index.
ISBN 0-8016-0417-6 Pbk : £5.30
(B77-20291)

Kron, Thora. The management of patient care : putting leadership skills to work / [by] Thora Kron. — 4th ed. — Philadelphia ; London [etc.] : Saunders, 1976. — viii,247p : ill, form ; 24cm.
Previous ed.: 1971. — Bibl. — Index.
ISBN 0-7216-5528-9 Pbk : £3.75
(B77-07364)

Yura, Helen. Nursing leadership : theory and process / [by] Helen Yura, Dorothy Ozimek, Mary B. Walsh. — New York : Appleton-Century-Crofts ; London [etc.] : Prentice-Hall, 1976. — xiii,237p : 4 ill ; 23cm.
Bibl.: p.215-232. — Index.
ISBN 0-8385-7027-5 Pbk : £6.85
(B77-04189)

610.73 — Medicine. Nursing. Leadership. *United States*
Douglass, Laura Mae. Review of leadership in nursing / [by] Laura Mae Douglass. — 2nd ed. — Saint Louis : Mosby ; London : Distributed by Kimpton, 1977. — ix,173p ; 22cm. — (Mosby's review series)
Previous ed.: published as 'Review of team nursing'. 1973. — Bibl. — Index.
ISBN 0-8016-1442-2 Pbk : £5.85
(B77-27102)

610.73 — Medicine. Nursing. Problem oriented systems. *Manuals*
Dynamics of problem-oriented approaches : patient care and documentation / edited by Judith Bloom Walter, Geraldine P. Pardee, Doris M. Molbo. — Philadelphia [etc.] : J.B. Lippincott ; Oxford [etc.] : Distributed by Blackwell Scientific, 1976. — x,206p : ill, form ; 23cm.
Bibl. — Index.
ISBN 0-397-54187-2 Pbk : £5.60
(B77-03021)

610.73 — Medicine. Practical nursing
Clarke, Margaret. Practical nursing. — 12th ed. / [by] Margaret Clarke ; foreword by H. Marjorie Simpson. — London : Baillière Tindall, 1977. — xi,384p : ill ; 19cm. — (Nurses' aids series)
Previous ed.: 1971. — Bibl.: p.368. — Index.
ISBN 0-7020-0607-6 Pbk : £1.60
(B77-15300)

Story, Donna Ketchum. Principles and practices of nursing care / [by] Donna Ketchum Story. — New York ; London [etc.] : McGraw-Hill, 1976. — x,358p : ill, ports ; 25cm. — (Nursing and allied health series)
Index.
ISBN 0-07-061770-8 : £9.90
(B77-04821)

610.73 — Nursing. *Manuals*
Dickie, Helen McEwen. Trays, trolleys and treatments : a nurse's guide / [by] Helen M. Dickie. — 6th ed. — Edinburgh [etc.] : Churchill Livingstone, 1977. — [9],184p : ill ; 19cm.
Previous ed.: published as 'Pocket book on tray and trolley setting'. Edinburgh : E. & S. Livingstone, 1970. — Index.
ISBN 0-443-01619-4 Pbk : £1.50
Primary classification 610.73'028
(B77-31208)

610.73 — Patients. Lifting & carrying. *Manuals*
Rantz, Marilyn J. Lifting, moving and transferring patients : a manual / [by] Marilyn J. Rantz, Donald Courtial ; with 250 illustrations by Richard Pearce. — St Louis : Mosby ; London : Distributed by Kimpton, 1977. — ix,138p : ill ; 26cm.
Index.
ISBN 0-8016-4086-5 Sp : £5.60
(B77-19395)

610.73'01'51 — Medicine. Calculations. *For nursing*
Watchorn, George Wright. Medical calculations for nurses / [by] G.W. Watchorn ; with a foreword by B.A. Young. — 2nd ed. — London : Faber, 1976. — [5],11-84p : ill ; 14cm.
With answers. — Previous ed.: 1973.
ISBN 0-571-04915-x Pbk : £0.95
(B77-02327)

610.73'028 — Nursing. Equipment. *Manuals*
Dickie, Helen McEwen. Trays, trolleys and treatments : a nurse's guide / [by] Helen M. Dickie. — 6th ed. — Edinburgh [etc.] : Churchill Livingstone, 1977. — [9],184p : ill ; 19cm.
Previous ed.: published as 'Pocket book on tray and trolley setting'. Edinburgh : E. & S. Livingstone, 1970. — Index.
ISBN 0-443-01619-4 Pbk : £1.50
Also classified at 610.73
(B77-31208)

610.73'05 — Medicine. Nursing. *Periodicals*
Journal of advanced nursing. — Oxford [etc.] : Blackwell Scientific.
Vol.1, no.1- ; Jan. 1976-. — 1976-. — ill, forms ; 25cm.
Six issues a year. — Cover title. — [2],iv,98p. in 1st issue. — Bibl.
Pbk : £12.00 yearly
ISSN 0309-2402
(B77-23431)

610.73'069 — Nurses. Interpersonal relationships with patients. Communication
Collins, Mattie. Communication in health care : understanding and implementing effective human relationships / [by] Mattie Collins. — Saint Louis : Mosby ; London : Distributed by Kimpton, 1977. — xiii,261p : ill ; 25cm.
Bibl.: p.250-251. — Index.
ISBN 0-8016-1021-4 Pbk : Unpriced
(B77-26328)

610.73'07'1141 — Nurses. Professional education. Schools of nursing. *Great Britain. Directories*
Directory of schools of nursing : with pre-basic, basic and post-basic nursing and midwifery training schemes, and educational and career opportunities. — London : H.M.S.O.
[3rd ed. : 1977] / Department of Health & Social Security. — 1977. — vii,374p : maps ; 30cm.
Previously published: as 'Schools of nursing directory' by King Edward's Hospital Fund for London. — Index.
ISBN 0-11-320658-5 Pbk : £6.75
(B77-18152)

610.73'07'15 — Nurses. Lifelong education. *United States*
Nursing and the process of continuing education / edited by Elda S. Popiel. — 2nd ed. — Saint Louis : Mosby ; London : Distributed by Kimpton, 1977. — xxii,249p : ill, forms, map ; 25cm.
Previous ed.: 1973. — Bibl.: p.246-249.
ISBN 0-8016-3969-7 Pbk : £6.20
(B77-31209)

610.73'07'2 — Medicine. Nursing. Research. Methodology
Treece, Eleanor Walters. Elements of research in nursing / [by] Eleanor Walters Treece, James William Treece, Jr. — 2nd ed. — St Louis : Mosby ; London : Distributed by Kimpton, 1977. — x,349p : ill, forms, plan ; 26cm.
Previous ed.: 1973. — Bibl. — Index.
ISBN 0-8016-5104-2 Pbk : £6.45
(B77-19396)

610.73'09 — Medicine. Nursing, to 1976
Deloughery, Grace L. History and trends of professional nursing. — 8th ed. / [by] Grace L. Deloughery ; with a special unit on legal aspects by Eileen A. O'Neil. — Saint Louis : Mosby ; London : Distributed by Kimpton, 1977. — vii,277p : ill, map, ports ; 26cm.
Previous ed.: / by Gerald Joseph Griffin, Joanne King Griffin. 1973. — Bibl. — Index.
ISBN 0-8016-1974-2 Pbk : £6.80
(B77-31210)

610.73'092'4 — Medicine. District nursing. Jordan, Patricia. *Autobiographies*
Jordan, Patricia. District nurse / [by] Patricia Jordan. — London : Weidenfeld and Nicolson, 1977. — 176p ; 23cm.
ISBN 0-297-77355-0 : £3.95
(B77-22599)

610.73'092'4 — Medicine. Nursing. *Personal observations*
Holford, Ida M. But the nights are long / [by] Ida M. Holford. — London : Hale, 1977. — 3-205p ; 23cm.
ISBN 0-7091-6222-7 : £3.95
(B77-24240)

610.73'092'4 — Medicine. Nursing. Hill, Judy. *Canada. Arctic. Biographies*
McDougall, Jim. Angel of the snow / [by] Jim McDougall. — London : Muller, 1977. — 174p,[14]p of plates : ill, ports ; 24cm.
ISBN 0-584-10317-4 : £4.95 : CIP rev.
(B77-23432)

610.73'092'4 — Medicine. Nursing. Nightingale, Florence. *Biographies*
Woodham-Smith, Cecil. Florence Nightingale, 1820-1910 / [by] Cecil Woodham-Smith. — [London] : Fontana, 1977. — 445p ; 18cm.
Originally published: London : Constable, 1950. — Bibl.: p.430-436. — Index.
ISBN 0-00-634860-2 Pbk : £1.50
(B77-15867)

610.73'092'4 — Medicine. Nursing. Pattison, Dora. *Biographies*
Manton, Jo. Sister Dora : the life of Dorothy Pattison / [by] Jo Manton. — London [etc.] : Quartet Books, 1977. — 3-380p : facsim ; 20cm.
Originally published: London : Methuen, 1971. — Bibl.: p.367-371. — Index.
ISBN 0-7043-3161-6 Pbk : £2.25
(B77-22600)

610.73'0973 — Medicine. Nursing. *United States, ca 1940-ca 1970. Transcripts of interviews*
Safier, Gwendolyn. Contemporary American leaders in nursing : an oral history / [by] Gwendolyn Safier. — New York ; London [etc.] : McGraw-Hill, 1977. — vii,392p : ports ; 24cm.
'A Blakiston Publication'.
ISBN 0-07-054412-3 : £8.65
(B77-23433)

610.73'43'0941 — Medicine. District nursing. *Great Britain*
Keywood, Olive. Nursing in the community / [by] Olive Keywood. — London [etc.] : Baillière Tindall, 1977. — xii,212p ; 19cm.
Bibl. — Index.
ISBN 0-7020-0620-3 Pbk : £2.50
(B77-23434)

610.73'43'0941 — Medicine. District nursing. *Great Britain. Periodicals*
Journal of community nursing. — London (295 Balham High Rd, SW17 7BA) : PTM Publishers Ltd.
Vol.1, no.1- ; July 1977-. — [1977]-. — ill, ports ; 30cm.
Monthly. — 36p. in 1st issue.
Sd : £0.35(£4.00 yearly ; free to regional health authorities, area health authorities, health districts and to all district nurses and district nurse/midwives in England and Wales)
ISSN 0140-0908
(B77-24241)

610.73'43'0973 — Medicine. District nursing. *United States*
Current practice in family-centered community nursing. — Saint Louis : Mosby ; London : Distributed by Kimpton.
Vol.1 / edited by Adina M. Reinhardt, Mildred D. Quinn. — 1977. — xx,355p : ill, forms, maps ; 25cm. — (Mosby's current practice and perspectives in nursing series)
Bibl.
ISBN 0-8016-4107-1 Pbk : £7.00
(B77-21148)

Tinkham, Catherine W. Community health nursing : evolution and process / [by] Catherine W. Tinkham, Eleanor F. Voorhies. — 2nd ed. — New York : Appleton-Century-Crofts ; London [etc.] : Prentice-Hall, 1977. — xv, 299p : forms ; 24cm.
Previous ed.: New York : Appleton-Century-Crofts, 1972. — Bibl. — Index.
ISBN 0-8385-1188-0 : £10.00
(B77-31924)

610.73'6 — Chronically ill patients. Nursing
Gillies, Dee Ann. Patient assessment and management by the nurse practitioner / [by] Dee Ann Gillies, Irene B. Alyn. — Philadelphia ; London [etc.] : Saunders, 1976. — viii,236p : ill ; 27cm.
Bibl. — Index.
ISBN 0-7216-4133-4 : £8.25
Also classified at 616.07'5'024613
(B77-04190)

610.73'6 — Patients. Rehabilitation. Nursing
Boroch, Rose Marie. Elements of rehabilitation in nursing : an introduction / [by] Rose Marie Boroch. — Saint Louis : Mosby ; London : Distributed by Kimpton, 1976. — xi,316p : ill, forms ; 26cm.
Bibl. — Index.
ISBN 0-8016-1425-2 Pbk : £6.90
(B77-04822)

610.73'6 — Patients with cancer. Nursing. Psychosocial aspects
Smith, Elizabeth A. Psychosocial aspects of cancer patient care : a self-instructional text / [by] Elizabeth A. Smith. — New York ; London [etc.] : McGraw-Hill, 1976 [i.e. 1977]. — x,182p : 1 ill ; 24cm.
'A Blakiston Publication'. — With answers. — Originally published: 1975. — Bibl.
ISBN 0-07-058493-1 Pbk : £4.10
(B77-12458)

610.73'6 — Patients with skin diseases. Nursing
Huckbody, Eileen. Nursing procedures for skin diseases / [by] Eileen Huckbody. — Edinburgh [etc.] : Churchill Livingstone, 1977. — [15], 135p : ill ; 24cm.
ISBN 0-443-01538-4 Sp : £2.95
(B77-13053)

610.73'6 — Patients with terminal illnesses. Nursing. Psychological aspects
The **nurse** as a caregiver for the terminal patient and his family / edited by Ann M. Earle, Nina T. Argondizzo and Austin H. Kutscher ; with the editorial assistance of Lillian G. Kutscher. — New York ; Guildford : Columbia University Press, 1976. — x,255p ; 24cm.
'The twenty-two papers which make up this volume are the result of a symposium ... sponsored by the Foundation of Thanatology and the nursing schools of Columbia, Cornell and Maryland' - jacket. — Bibl. — Index.
ISBN 0-231-04020-2 : £13.25
(B77-11823)

610.73'6 — Patients with urogenital diseases. Nursing
Winter, Chester Caldwell. Nursing care of patients with urologic diseases. — 4th ed. / [by] Chester C. Winter, Alice Morel. — St Louis : Mosby ; London : Distributed by Kimpton, 1977. — ix,366p : ill, forms ; 25cm.
Previous ed.: / by Chester C. Winter, Marilyn Roehm Barker. 1972. — Bibl. — Index.
ISBN 0-8016-5607-9 Pbk : £8.55
(B77-18153)

610.73'6'071141 — Post-graduate courses for nursing specialists. Foreign applicants. Admission standards. *Great Britain*
Joint Board of Clinical Nursing Studies. Post-basic, postgraduate courses in specialist aspects of clinical nursing : a guidance document for centres accepting nurses from overseas / Joint Board of Clinical Nursing Studies. — London (178 Great Portland St., W1N 5TB) : The Board, 1977. — [6]p ; 21cm.
Sd : Unpriced
(B77-25647)

610.73'6'0941 — Nursing specialists. Role. *Great Britain. Conference proceedings*
New horizons in clinical nursing : the report of a seminar held at Leeds Castle, Kent, 14-17 October 1975 under the auspices of the Royal College of Nursing of the United Kingdom. — [London] ([1 Henrietta Place, W.1]) : [The College], [1976]. — iv,53p ; 21cm.
Bibl.: p.47-50.
ISBN 0-902606-48-4 Sd : £1.00
(B77-02328)

610.73'62 — Children. Nursing
Brown, Marie Scott. Ambulatory pediatrics for nurses / [by] Marie Scott Brown, Mary Alexander Murphy. — New York ; London [etc.] : McGraw-Hill, [1977]. — xi,468p : ill, forms ; 24cm.
'A Blakiston publication'. — Published in the United States: 1975. — Bibl. — List of films: p.411-416. — Index.
ISBN 0-07-008290-1 : £9.70
(B77-14245)

Leifer, Gloria. Principles and techniques in pediatric nursing / [by] Gloria Leifer. — 3rd ed. — Philadelphia ; London [etc.] : Saunders, 1977. — xxvii,321p : ill, form ; 27cm.
Previous ed.: 1972. — Bibl. — Index.
ISBN 0-7216-5713-3 : £7.50
ISBN 0-7216-5719-2 Pbk : Unpriced
(B77-28644)

Pediatric nursing. — 3rd ed. / [by] Helen C. Latham ... [et al.]. — Saint Louis : Mosby ; London : Distributed by Kimpton, 1977. — xv, 605p,plate : ill(incl 2 col), forms ; 27cm.
Previous ed.: / by Helen C. Latham, Robert V. Heckel. 1972. — Bibl. — Index.
ISBN 0-8016-2877-6 : £11.15
(B77-28645)

610.73'65 — Old persons. Nursing
Stevens, Marion Keith. Geriatric nursing for practical nurses / [by] Marion Keith Stevens. — 2nd ed. — Philadelphia ; London [etc.] : Saunders, [1977]. — xi,244p : ill, forms ; 24cm.

Published in the United States: 1975. — Previous ed.: 1965. — Bibl.: p.235. — Index.
ISBN 0-7216-8594-3 Pbk : £4.50
(B77-09708)

610.73′677 — Medicine. Orthopaedics. Nursing
Webb, Jane T. Notes on orthopaedic nursing / [by] Jane T. Webb ; foreword by Charles W. Manning. — Edinburgh [etc.] : Churchill Livingstone, 1977. — viii,64p : ill ; 19cm.
Bibl.: p.viii. — Index.
ISBN 0-443-01518-x Pbk : £1.00
(B77-23435)

610.73′677 — Medicine. Surgery. Nursing
Broadwell, Lucile. Medical-surgical nursing procedures / [by] Lucile Broadwell, Barbara Milutinovic. — New York [etc.] ; London : Van Nostrand Reinhold, 1977. — vi,457p : ill, forms ; 27cm.
With answers to review questions. — Index.
ISBN 0-442-21062-0 : £9.70
(B77-25648)

Taylor, Selwyn. Principles of surgery and surgical nursing / [by] Selwyn Taylor. — 3rd ed. — London [etc.] : Hodder and Stoughton, 1977. — x,309p : ill, forms ; 23cm. — (Modern nursing series)
Previous ed.: London : English Universities Press, 1969. — Index.
ISBN 0-340-21122-9 : £4.25
ISBN 0-340-21123-7 Pbk : £1.95
(B77-07918)

610.73′677 — Medicine. Surgery. Operations. Nursing
The **surgical** patient : behavioral concepts for the operating room nurse / [by] Barbara J. Gruendemann ... [et al.]. — 2nd ed. — Saint Louis : Mosby ; London : Distributed by Kimpton, 1977. — xv,190p : ill, forms ; 26cm.
Previous ed.: 1973. — Bibl. — Index.
ISBN 0-8016-1981-5 Pbk : £5.60
(B77-23436)

610.73′678 — Midwives. *England. Directories*
The **roll** of practising midwives / Central Midwives Board. — [London] : [The Board]. 1975-76. Vol.2. — [1976]. — [1]p,p321-630 ; 34cm.
Pbk : £15.00
(B77-03564)

Roll of practising midwives / Central Midwives Board. — [London] : [The Board]. 1976-77. — [1977]. — 2v.([4],614p) ; 34cm.
Pbk : Unpriced
(B77-27880)

610.73′678 — Obstetrics. Nursing
Jensen, Margaret Duncan. Maternity care : the nurse & the family / [by] Margaret Duncan Jensen, Ralph C. Benson, Irene M. Bobak. — St Louis : Mosby ; London : Distributed by Kimpton, 1977. — xx,764p : ill, forms ; 29cm.
Bibl. — Index.
ISBN 0-8016-2489-4 : £14.25
(B77-24950)

610.73′68 — Mentally retarded persons. Nursing
Gibson, John, *b.1907.* Nursing the mentally retarded / [by] John Gibson and Thomas French. — 4th ed. — London : Faber, 1977. — 3-185p ; 20cm.
Previous ed.: 1971. — Index.
ISBN 0-571-04959-1 : £4.50 : CIP rev.
ISBN 0-571-04941-9 Pbk : £2.25
(B77-25649)

610.73′68 — Patients with mental disorders. Interpersonal relationships with nurses. *For nursing*
Simmons, Janet A. The nurse-client relationship in mental health nursing : workbook guides to understanding and management / [by] Janet A. Simmons. — 2nd ed. — Philadelphia ; London [etc.] : Saunders, 1976. — xii,248p : forms ; 26cm.
Previous ed.: Philadelphia : Saunders, 1969. — Bibl.: p.241-248.
ISBN 0-7216-8286-3 : £5.50
(B77-21149)

610.73′68 — Patients with mental disorders. Nursing
Aguilera, Donna Conant. Review of psychiatric nursing / [by] Donna Conant Aguilera. — Saint Louis : Mosby ; London : Distributed by Kimpton, 1977. — xi,159p ; 23cm.
Bibl.: p.136. — Index.
ISBN 0-8016-0090-1 Pbk : £4.50
(B77-16891)

Altschul, Annie. Psychiatric nursing. — 5th ed. / [by] Annie Altschul, Ruth Simpson. — London : Baillière Tindall, 1977. — viii,375p ; 19cm. — (Nurses' aids series)
Previous ed.: / by Annie Altschul, 1973. — Bibl. — Index.
ISBN 0-7020-0610-6 Pbk : £1.60
(B77-12459)

Robinson, Lisa. Psychiatric nursing as a human experience / [by] Lisa Robinson. — 2nd ed. — Philadelphia ; London [etc.] : Saunders, 1977. — x,459p ; 24cm.
Previous ed.: 1972. — Bibl. — Index.
ISBN 0-7216-7621-9 : £8.25
(B77-24951)

610.73′68 — Patients with mental disorders. Nursing. *Eastern Scotland. Case studies*
Cormack, Desmond. Psychiatric nursing observed : a descriptive study of the work of the charge nurse in acute admission wards of psychiatric hospitals / [by] Desmond Cormack. — London (Henrietta Place, Cavendish Sq., W1M 0AB) : Royal College of Nursing, 1976. — 117p : ill, form ; 22cm. — (Royal College of Nursing. Research series)
Bibl.: p.111-117.
ISBN 0-902606-49-2 Pbk : £1.80
(B77-11225)

610′.76 — Educational institutions. Curriculum subjects: Medicine. Academic achievement of students. Assessment. Multiple-choice tests
Anderson, John, *b.1921.* The multiple choice question in medicine / [by] John Anderson. — Tunbridge Wells [etc.] : Pitman Medical, 1976. — viii,152p : forms ; 22cm.
Bibl.: p.57-58. — Index.
ISBN 0-272-79376-0 Pbk : £3.00
(B77-16400)

610′.76 — Medicine. *Exercises, worked examples. For student nurses*
Morgan, Wendy. Pupil nurse's workbook / [by] Wendy Morgan and Brysson Whyte. — London [etc.] : McGraw-Hill, 1975. — vii,69p : ill ; 28cm.
Fill-in book.
ISBN 0-07-084209-4 Pbk : Unpriced
(B77-19397)

610′.7′8 — Educational institutions. Curriculum subjects: Medicine. Audio-visual aids
Communication media in medicine : eight reports. — 3rd ed. / edited by T. Andrew Quilliam. — London (Gower St., WC1E 6BT) : University College, London, 1975. — [4],24p ; 30cm. — (Communication in medicine)
Bibl.
ISBN 0-902137-20-4 Sd : £0.50
(B77-03022)

610′.8 — Medicine. *Essays*
Alvarez, Walter Clement. Walter C. Alvarez : American man of medicine / compiled by David H. Scott. — New York ; London [etc.] : Van Nostrand Reinhold, 1976. — 380p ; 22cm.

'The articles ... have been reprinted from "Modern Medicine"' - title page verso.
ISBN 0-442-20326-8 : £6.85
(B77-21150)

610′.8 — Medicine. *Lectures, speeches. Serials*
The **Harvey** lectures : delivered under the auspices of the Harvey Society of New York. — New York [etc.] ; London : Academic Press.

1974-1975 : series 70 / by David Baltimore ... [et al.]. — 1976 [i.e. 1977]. — xvii,202p : ill, port ; 21cm.
Published in the United States: 1976. — Bibl. — Index.
ISBN 0-12-312070-5 : £10.65
(B77-09035)

610′.9 — Medicine, to 1976. *Essays*
Temkin, Owsei. The double face of Janus, and other essays in the history of medicine / [by] Owsei Temkin. — Baltimore ; London : Johns Hopkins University Press, 1977. — x,543p ; 25cm.
Index.
ISBN 0-8018-1859-1 : £16.90
(B77-25650)

610′.9 — Medicine, to 1976. *Readings*
Essays on the history of medicine : selected from the Bulletin of the New York Academy of Medicine / edited by Saul Jarcho. — New York : Science History Publications ; Folkestone : [Distributed by] Dawson, 1976. — xi,446p : ill, facsims, ports ; 27cm. — (The history of medicine series ; no.49)
Bibl. — Index.
ISBN 0-88202-066-8 : £10.50
(B77-33814)

610′.9172′4 — Medicine. *Developing countries. For primary health workers*
World Health Organization. The primary health worker : working guide, guidelines for training, guidelines for adaptation / [World Health Organization]. — Experimental ed. — Geneva : W.H.O. ; [London] : [H.M.S.O.], 1977. — iv, 337p : ill ; 21cm.
Previous ed.: 1976.
Pbk : £5.60
ISBN 92-4-154122-9
(B77-17511)

610′.9181′2 — Medicine. *Western world*
Davies, Hywel. Modern medicine : a doctor's dissent / [by] Hywel Davies. — London : Abelard-Schuman, 1977. — x,133p ; 23cm.
Index.
ISBN 0-200-72454-1 : £4.50
(B77-16401)

610′.92′4 — Medicine. *North Africa, 1924-1943. Personal observations*
Denti di Pirajno, Alberto, *duca.* A cure for serpents : the life and adventures of a doctor in Africa / [by] Alberto Denti di Pirajno ; translated [from the Italian] by Kathleen Naylor. — London [etc.] : White Lion Publishers, 1977. — [7],277p,[16]p of plates : ill, 2 maps, ports ; 23cm.
This translation originally published: London : Deutsch, 1955. — Index.
ISBN 0-85617-808-x : £4.75
(B77-24952)

610′.92′4 — Medicine. *Somerset. Rural regions. Personal observations*
Clifford, Robert D. Just here, Doctor / [by] Robert D. Clifford. — London [etc.] : White Lion Publishers, 1977. — 160p ; 23cm.
ISBN 0-7285-0097-3 : £4.75
(B77-22601)

610′.92′4 — Medicine. Cassidy, Sheila. *Chile, 1971-1975. Autobiographies*
Cassidy, Sheila. Audacity to believe / [by] Sheila Cassidy. — London : Collins, 1977. — xiv, 335p,[12]p of plates : ill, facsims, ports ; 23cm.
ISBN 0-00-211858-0 : £4.50
(B77-27881)

610′.92′4 — Medicine. Linacre, Thomas
Essays on the life and work of Thomas Linacre, c.1460-1524 / edited by Francis Maddison, Margaret Pelling and Charles Webster. — Oxford : Clarendon Press, 1977. — liii,416p,xx p of plates : ill, facsims, ports ; 23cm. — (Linacre studies)
Includes Greek and Latin texts. — Bibl.: p.306-353. — Index.
ISBN 0-19-858150-5 : £12.00
(B77-11824)

610′.92′4 — Medicine. Russell, Richard, b.1687. *East Sussex. Brighton*
Garratt, Jean. The man who invented the seaside / by Jean Garratt. — Brighton ([North Gate House, Church St., Brighton BN1 1UE]) : Royal Pavilion, Art Gallery and Museums, Brighton, [1977?]. — Folder([4]p) : ill, map, ports ; 30cm. — (Royal Pavilion, Art Gallery and Museums, Brighton. Information sheets ; 1)

Unpriced
(B77-27103)

610′.941 — Medicine. *Great Britain. Conference proceedings*
Medical Education and Medical Care *(Conference), Edinburgh, 1976.* Medical education and medical care : a Scottish-American symposium arranged by the Nuffield Provincial Hospitals Trust and the Josiah Macy Jr Foundation to commemorate the 250th anniversary of the founding of the University of Edinburgh Medical School and the bicentennial of the Declaration of Independence and founding of the United States of America / papers by Alexander Bearn ... [et al.] ; edited by Gordon McLachlan. — London [etc.] : Oxford University Press for the Trust, 1977. — xiv,215p,[2]p of plates : ill ; 23cm.
'The Macy/Nuffield Symposium "Medical Education and Medical Care" ... was held in Edinburgh in September 1976 ...' - jacket. — Bibl.: p.42.
ISBN 0-19-721394-4 : £6.00
Also classified at 610′.973
(B77-23437)

610'.9413'4 — Museums. *Edinburgh. Royal Scottish Museum. Exhibits: Items associated with medicine in Edinburgh, to ca 1900. Catalogues*
Anderson, Robert Geoffrey William. Edinburgh & medicine : a commemorative catalogue of the exhibition held at the Royal Scottish Museum, Edinburgh, June 1976-January 1977 to mark the 250th anniversary of the foundation of the Faculty of Medicine of the University of Edinburgh, 1726-1976 / compiled by R.G.W. Anderson and A.D.C. Simpson ; with a foreword by H.R.H. Prince Philip. — Edinburgh ([Chambers St., Edinburgh EH1 1JF]) : Royal Scottish Museum, 1976. — vii, 72p,[16]p of plates : ill, facsims, map, plans, ports ; 20x25cm.
Bibl.: p.24-25.
ISBN 0-900733-11-x Pbk : £1.75
(B77-00234)

610'.942 — Medicine. *England, ca 1800-1900*
Health care and popular medicine in nineteenth century England : essays in the social history of medicine / edited by John Woodward and David Richards. — London : Croom Helm, 1977. — [5],195p ; 23cm.
Index.
ISBN 0-85664-321-1 : £7.95
(B77-21151)

610'.96 — Medicine. *Africa. Periodicals*
African journal of medicine and medical sciences. — Oxford [etc.] : Blackwell Scientific.
Continues : African journal of medical sciences.

Vol.5, no.1- ; Mar. 1976-. — [1976]-. — ill ; 25cm.
Quarterly. — [1], 100p. in 1st issue. — Bibl. — Includes a contribution in French.
Pbk : £16.00 yearly
ISSN 0309-3913
(B77-32641)

610'.973 — Medicine. *United States, 1700-1800. Essays*
Bell, Whitfield J. The colonial physician, & other essays / [by] Whitfield J. Bell, Jr. — New York : Science History Publications ; Folkestone : [Distributed by] Dawson, 1975. — iii-viii,229,[1]p : ill, facsims, ports ; 24cm.
ISBN 0-88202-024-2 : £5.00
(B77-33244)

610'.973 — Medicine. *United States, 1776-1976*
Bordley, James. Two centuries of American medicine, 1776-1976 / [by] James Bordley, III, A. McGehee Harvey. — Philadelphia ; London [etc.] : Saunders, 1976. — ii-xv,844p : ill(incl 1 col), facsim, ports ; 27cm.
Bibl.: p.799-826. — Index.
ISBN 0-7216-1873-1 : £16.25
(B77-03023)

610'.973 — Medicine. *United States. Conference proceedings*
Medical Education and Medical Care *(Conference), Edinburgh, 1976.* Medical education and medical care : a Scottish-American symposium arranged by the Nuffield Provincial Hospitals Trust and the Josiah Macy Jr Foundation to commemorate the 250th anniversary of the founding of the University of Edinburgh Medical School and the bicentennial of the Declaration of Independence and founding of the United States of America / papers by Alexander Bearn ... [et al.] ; edited by Gordon McLachlan. — London [etc.] : Oxford University Press for the Trust, 1977. — xiv,215p,[2]p of plates : ill ; 23cm.
'The Macy/Nuffield Symposium "Medical Education and Medical Care" ... was held in Edinburgh in September 1976 ...' - jacket. — Bibl.: p.42.
ISBN 0-19-721394-4 : £6.00
Primary classification 610'.941
(B77-23437)

611 — MEDICINE. ANATOMY
Cunningham, Daniel John. Cunningham's manual of practical anatomy. — 14th ed. / [by] G.J. Romanes. — Oxford [etc.] : Oxford University Press. — (Oxford medical publications)
Vol.2 : Thorax and abdomen. — 1977. — vi, 232p : ill(some col) ; 25cm.
Previous ed.: 1968. — Index.
ISBN 0-19-263135-7 Pbk : £3.25 : CIP rev.
(B77-06095)

Gardner, Ernest. Anatomy : a regional study of human structure / [by] Ernest Gardner, Donald J. Gray, Ronan O'Rahilly ; illustrations by Caspar Henselmann. — 4th ed. — Philadelphia ; London [etc.] : Saunders, [1977]. — ix,821p,plate : ill(some col), port ; 27cm.
Text, ill. on lining papers. — This ed. published in the United States: 1975. — Previous ed.: 1969. — Bibl. — Index.
ISBN 0-7216-4018-4 : £17.00
(B77-10812)

Grobler, N J. Textbook of clinical anatomy / [by] N.J. Grobler. — Amsterdam [etc.] ; Oxford : Elsevier.
In 2 vols.
Vol.1. — 1977. — xii,663p,iv p of plates : ill ; 25cm.
Index.
ISBN 0-444-41581-5 : £57.14
ISBN 0-444-80002-6 Pbk : £21.00
(B77-27104)

Johns Hopkins University. *School of Medicine.* The Johns Hopkins atlas of human functional anatomy / [written by the faculty of the Johns Hopkins University School of Medicine] ; original illustrations, with descriptive legends, by Leon Schlossberg ; text edited by George D. Zuidema. — London : Baillière Tindall, 1977. — xi,108p : ill(chiefly col) ; 29cm.
Originally published: Baltimore : Johns Hopkins University Press, 1976. — Index.
ISBN 0-7020-0641-6 : £9.50
ISBN 0-7020-0639-4 Pbk : £4.95
(B77-12460)

Langebartel, David Augustus. The anatomical primer : an embryological explanation of human gross morphology / [by] David A. Langebartel ; illustrated by Robert H. Ullrich, Jr. — Baltimore ; London [etc.] : University Park Press, 1977. — ix,510p : ill(chiefly col) ; 29cm.
Bibl.: p.499-502. — Index.
ISBN 0-8391-0625-4 : £16.25
(B77-17512)

Textbook of human anatomy / edited by the late W.J. Hamilton. — 2nd ed. — London [etc.] : Macmillan, 1976. — [11],753p : ill(some col) ; 32cm.
Previous ed.: 1956. — Index.
ISBN 0-333-18115-8 : £14.50
(B77-04191)

Tortora, Gerard Joseph. Principles of human anatomy / [by] Gerard J. Tortora. — San Francisco : Canfield Press ; New York [etc.] ; London : Harper and Row, 1977. — xii,532p : ill(some col) ; 29cm.
Bibl. — Index.
ISBN 0-06-388775-4 : Unpriced
(B77-21152)

611'.0022'2 — Man. Anatomy. *Illustrations*
Cross-sectional anatomy : computed tomography and ultrasound correlation / [by] Barbara L. Carter ... [et al.]. — New York : Appleton-Century-Crofts ; London [etc.] : Prentice-Hall, 1977. — [219]p : chiefly ill ; 24x31cm.
Index.
ISBN 0-8385-1255-0 : Unpriced
(B77-28646)

McMinn, Robert Matthew Hay. A colour atlas of human anatomy / [by] R.M.H. McMinn, R.T. Hutchings. — London : Wolfe Medical, 1977. — 352p : chiefly col ill ; 32cm. — ([Wolfe medical atlases ISSN 0302-0711])
Index.
ISBN 0-7234-0709-6 : £15.00
(B77-23438)

Pauchet, Victor. Pocket atlas of anatomy / by Victor Pauchet and S. Dupret. — 3rd ed. — London [etc.] : Oxford University Press, 1976. — xv,368p : of ill(some col) ; 19cm. — (Oxford medical publications)
This ed. originally published: 1937. — Index.
Pbk : £2.50
ISBN 0-19-263131-4
(B77-29444)

611'.002'4613 — Man. Anatomy. *For nursing*
Riddle, Janet Thomson Elliot. Elementary textbook of anatomy and physiology applied to nursing / [by] Janet T.E. Riddle ; illustrated by Kathleen B. Nicoll. — 5th ed. — Edinburgh [etc.] : Churchill Livingstone, 1977. — [7], 151p : ill ; 22cm. — (Livingstone nursing texts)

Cover title: Anatomy and physiology applied to nursing. — Previous ed.: Edinburgh : Livingstone, 1974. — Index.
ISBN 0-443-01614-3 Pbk : Unpriced
Primary classification 612'.002'4613
(B77-30278)

611'.002'4617 — Man. Anatomy. *For anaesthesia*
Ellis, Harold, *b.1926.* Anatomy for anaesthetists. — 3rd ed. / [by] Harold Ellis and Stanley Feldman. — Oxford [etc.] : Blackwell Scientific, 1977. — viii,397p : ill(some col) ; 23cm.
Previous ed.: / by Harold Ellis and Margaret McLarty. 1969. — Bibl. — Index.
ISBN 0-632-00196-8 : £10.75 : CIP rev.
(B77-04823)

611'.018 — Man. Cells & tissues. Structure
Amenta, Peter S. Review of medical histology / [by] Jacques Poirier, Jean-Louis Ribadeau Dumas ; translated [from the French] by Ursula Taube ; edited and adapted by Peter S. Amenta. — Philadelphia ; London [etc.] : Saunders, 1977. — xiii,227p : ill(some col) ; 24cm.
Bibl.: p.217-218. — Index.
ISBN 0-7216-7273-6 Pbk : £6.00
(B77-27882)

Beresford, William Anthony. Lecture notes on histology / [by] William A. Beresford. — 2nd ed. — Oxford [etc.] : Blackwell Scientific, 1977. — x,243p : ill ; 22cm.
Previous ed.: 1969. — Index.
ISBN 0-632-00269-7 Pbk : £4.50
(B77-17513)

Gardner, Dugald Lindsay. Human histology : an introduction to the study of histopathology / foreword to the first edition by the late J.D. Boyd. — 3rd ed. / by Dugald L. Gardner and the late T.C. Dodds. — Edinburgh [etc.] : Churchill Livingstone, 1976. — xi,432p : ill(some col) ; 25cm.
Previous ed.: / by Bruce Cruickshank, T.C. Dodds, Dugald L. Gardner. Edinburgh : E. and S. Livingstone, 1968. — Bibl.: p.404-408. — Index.
ISBN 0-443-01174-5 : £15.50
ISBN 0-443-01444-2 Pbk : £11.50
(B77-01469)

Leeson, Charles Roland. Histology / [by] C. Roland Leeson, Thomas S. Leeson. — 3rd ed. — Philadelphia ; London [etc.] : Saunders, 1976. — ix,605p : ill(some col) ; 26cm.
Text on lining papers. — Supplementary filmstrip available. — Previous ed.: 1970. — Bibl. — Index.
ISBN 0-7216-5708-7 : £9.75
(B77-06096)

Reith, Edward John. Atlas of descriptive histology / [by] Edward J. Reith, Michael H. Ross. — 3rd ed. — New York [etc.] ; London : Harper and Row, 1977. — xiii,287p : ill ; 26cm.
Previous ed.: 1970. — Index.
ISBN 0-06-045368-0 Pbk : £6.50
(B77-32642)

Windle, William Frederick. Textbook of histology / [by] William F. Windle. — 5th ed. — New York ; London [etc.] : McGraw-Hill, 1976. — xiii,561p : ill ; 24cm.
Previous ed.: 1970. — Bibl. — Index.
ISBN 0-07-070977-7 : £14.95
(B77-04192)

611'.018 — Man. Tissues. Specimens. Preparation. Staining. *Manuals*
Smith, Arthur, *b.1924.* A colour atlas of histological staining techniques / [by] Arthur Smith, John Bruton. — London : Wolfe Medical, 1977. — 192p : ill(chiefly col) ; 20cm. — (Wolfe medical atlases ; 18 ISSN 0302-0711)

Bibl.: p.186. — Index.
ISBN 0-7234-0721-5 : £5.00
(B77-31212)

611'.018 — Medicine. Histopathology. *Periodicals*
Histopathology : official journal of the British Division of the International Academy of Pathology. — Oxford : Blackwell Scientific.
Vol.1, no.1- ; Jan. 1977-. — 1977-. — ill ; 25cm.
Six issues a year. — Cover title. — 86p. in 1st issue. — Bibl.
Pbk : £27.00 yearly
ISSN 0309-0167
(B77-12461)

611'.0181 — Women. Reproductive system. Cells. Diseases. *Micrographs*
Grubb, Chandra. Colour atlas of gynaecological cytopathology / [by] Chandra Grubb ; foreword by Charles P. Douglas. — Aylesbury : HM + M, 1977. — 72p : col ill ; 32cm.
Index.
ISBN 0-85602-039-7 : £15.00
(B77-11825)

611'.0182 — Man. Connective tissues. Polymers. Dynamics. *Conference proceedings*
Dynamics of Connective Tissue Macromolecules *(Conference), Strangeways Research Laboratory, 1974.* Dynamics of Connective Tissue Macromolecules / edited by P.M.C. Burleigh and A.R. Poole. — Amsterdam ; Oxford : North-Holland Publishing Co. [etc.], 1975. — xxv,434p : ill, ports ; 23cm.
'This Symposium, on "Dynamics of Connective Tissue Macromolecules", was held in the Strangeways Research Laboratory in July 1974 ...' - Preface. — Bibl. — Index.
ISBN 0-7204-4515-9 : Unpriced
(B77-18787)

611'.02'4616 — Man. Anatomy. *For radiology*
Meschan, Isadore. An atlas of anatomy basic to radiology / [by] Isadore Meschan. — Philadelphia ; London [etc.] : Saunders, [1976]. — x,1131p : ill, forms ; 28x29cm.
Also published in 2 vols. — Published in the United States: 1975. — Bibl. — Index.
ISBN 0-7216-6310-9 : £38.00
(B77-06693)

611.3 — ANATOMY. DIGESTIVE SYSTEM
611'.314 — Man. Teeth. Anatomy
Scott, James Henderson. Introduction to dental anatomy / [by] the late James Henderson Scott and Norman Barrington Bray Symons. — 8th ed. — Edinburgh [etc.] : Churchill Livingstone, 1977. — [11],464p : ill ; 23cm.
Previous ed.: 1974. — Bibl. — Index.
ISBN 0-443-01618-6 : £11.50 : CIP rev.
ISBN 0-443-01620-8 Pbk : £8.00
(B77-22602)

611'.314 — Man. Teeth. Pulp cavities. Anatomy
Wheeler, Russell Charles. Pulp cavities of the permanent teeth : an anatomical guide to manipulative endodontics / [by] Russell C. Wheeler. — Philadelphia ; London [etc.] : Saunders, 1976. — vi,211p : ill ; 27cm.
Index.
ISBN 0-7216-9280-x : £11.50
(B77-01470)

611'.314'0222 — Man. Teeth. Anatomy. *Illustrations*
Kasle, Myron J. An atlas of dental radiographic anatomy / [by] Myron J. Kasle. — Philadelphia ; London [etc.] : Saunders, 1977. — ii-xiii,150p : chiefly ill ; 27cm.
Index.
ISBN 0-7216-5294-8 : £9.50
(B77-24953)

611.8 — ANATOMY. NERVOUS SYSTEM
611'.8 — Man. Nervous system. Anatomy
Ingram, Walter Robinson. A review of anatomical neurology / by Walter Robinson Ingram. — Baltimore ; London [etc.] : University Park Press, 1976. — ix,428p : ill ; 24cm.
Bibl. — Index.
ISBN 0-8391-0961-x : £13.95
(B77-14749)

611'.84 — Man. Eyes. Anatomy
Wolff, Eugene. Eugene Wolff's anatomy of the eye and orbit : including the central connexions, development and comparative anatomy of the visual apparatus. — 7th ed. / revised by Roger Warwick. — London : H.K. Lewis, 1976. — vii,545p,[20]leaves of plates,[16]p of plates : ill(some col) ; 26cm.
Previous ed.: / revised by R.J. Last. 1968. — Bibl.: p.517-532. — Index.
ISBN 0-7186-0426-1 : £13.00
(B77-02329)

611.9 — MEDICINE. REGIONAL ANATOMY
611'.9 — Man. Back & limbs. Anatomy
Hollinshead, William Henry. Functional anatomy of the limbs and back : a text for students of the locomotor apparatus / [by] W. Henry Hollinshead. — 4th ed. — Philadelphia ; London [etc.] : Saunders, 1976. — vii,428p : ill ; 25cm.
Previous ed.: 1969. — Index.
ISBN 0-7216-4757-x : £11.00
(B77-02330)

611'.91'0246176 — Man. Head & neck. Anatomy. *Programmed texts. For dentistry*
Reed, Gretchen Mayo. Basic structures of the head and neck : a programed instruction in clinical anatomy for dental professionals / [by] Gretchen Mayo Reed, Vincent F. Sheppard. — Philadelphia ; London [etc.] : Saunders, 1976. — xii,716p : ill ; 26cm.
Index.
ISBN 0-7216-7516-6 Pbk : £15.75
(B77-02331)

611'.91'0246176 — Man. Head & neck. Anatomy. *Questions & answers. For dentistry*
Berkovitz, B K B. Multiple choice questions in the anatomical sciences : for students of dentistry / [by] B.K.B. Berkovitz and B.J. Moxham. — Bristol : J. Wright, 1977. — [108] p([2]fold) ; 22cm.
With answers.
ISBN 0-7236-0451-7 Pbk : £2.50 : CIP rev.
(B77-10375)

612 — MEDICINE. PHYSIOLOGY
Anderson, Paul D. Clinical anatomy and physiology for allied health sciences / [by] Paul D. Anderson ; illustrated by Gayanne DeVry. — Philadelphia ; London [etc.] : Saunders, 1976. — vi,485p : ill ; 27cm.
Index.
ISBN 0-7216-1234-2 : £9.50
(B77-01471)

British Museum (Natural History). Human biology : an exhibition of ourselves / [British Museum (Natural History)]. — London : The Museum ; Cambridge [etc.] : Cambridge University Press, 1977. — 120p : ill(some col) ; 23cm.
'... produced in conjunction with an exhibition of the same name which opened at the British Museum (Natural History) in May 1977' Preface. — Index.
ISBN 0-521-21589-7 : £5.50
ISBN 0-521-29193-3 Pbk : £1.95
(B77-26329)

Fitch, Kenneth Leonard. Human life science / [by] Kenneth L. Fitch, Perry B. Johnson. — New York ; London [etc.] : Holt, Rinehart and Winston, 1977. — xxii,617p : ill ; 25cm.
'"Human life science" follows in most respects the theme and content of its predecessor, "Life Science and Man"' - Preface. — Bibl. — Index.
ISBN 0-03-018876-8 : £8.50
(B77-22603)

Guyton, Arthur Clifton. Basic human physiology : normal function and mechanisms of disease / [by] Arthur C. Guyton. — 2nd ed. — Philadelphia ; London [etc.] : Saunders, 1977. — xi,931p : ill ; 26cm.
Previous ed.: 1971. — Bibl. — Index.
ISBN 0-7216-4383-3 : £9.50
(B77-24242)

Guyton, Arthur Clifton. Textbook of medical physiology / [by] Arthur C. Guyton. — 5th ed. — Philadelphia ; London [etc.] : Saunders, 1976. — xxxvi,1194p : ill ; 27cm.
Previous ed.: 1971. — Bibl. — Index.
ISBN 0-7216-4393-0 : £18.00
(B77-01472)

Hartenstein, Roy. Human anatomy and physiology : principles and applications / [by] Roy Hartenstein. — New York ; London [etc.] : Van Nostrand, [1977]. — ix,726p : ill(some col) ; 24cm.
Text on lining papers. — Bibl.: p.686-693. — Index.
ISBN 0-442-23183-0 : £13.35
(B77-07919)

Human biology : an introduction to human evolution, variation, growth and ecology / by G.A. Harrison ... [et al.]. — 2nd ed. / with a chapter ... by V. Reynolds. — Oxford [etc.] : Oxford University Press, 1977. — xiv,499p,[4] leaves of plates : ill, maps ; 24cm.
Previous ed.: 1964. — Bibl. — Index.
ISBN 0-19-857164-x : £10.00
ISBN 0-19-857165-8 Pbk : £5.50
(B77-12462)

Human physiology / [by] Thomas F. Morrison ... [et al.]. — [Revised ed.]. — New York [etc.] ; London : Holt, Rinehart and Winston, 1972. — xii,497p,[8]p of plates : ill(some col) ; 25cm.
Previous ed.: New York : Holt, Rinehart and Winston, 1967. — Index.
ISBN 0-03-084990-x : £3.50
(B77-21153)

Jacob, Stanley Wallace. Elements of anatomy and physiology / [by] Stanley W. Jacob, Clarice Ashworth Francone. — Philadelphia ; London [etc.] : Saunders, 1976. — x,251p : ill(some col) ; 26cm.
Index.
ISBN 0-7216-5088-0 Pbk : £6.00
(B77-01473)

Levine, Louis, *b.1921.* Biology for a modern society / [by] Louis Levine. — St Louis : Mosby ; London : Distributed by Kimpton, 1977. — xviii,452p : ill, facsims, maps ; 26cm.
Bibl. — Index.
ISBN 0-8016-2990-x Pbk : £8.05
(B77-24954)

McNaught, Ann Boyce. Companion to 'Illustrated physiology' / by Ann B. McNaught. — 3rd ed. — Edinburgh [etc.] : Churchill Livingstone, 1976. — xi,248p ; 19cm.
'While the subject matter has been arranged to parallel the fuller treatment of "Illustrated Physiology" the text can also be used with the diagrams of "Nurses' Illustrated Physiology"' - Preface. — Previous ed.: Edinburgh : Livingstone, 1970. — Index.
ISBN 0-443-01392-6 Pbk : £2.23
(B77-02332)

Memmler, Ruth Lundeen. The human body in health and disease. — 4th ed. / by Ruth Lundeen Memmler, Dena Lin Wood. — Philadelphia : Lippincott ; Oxford [etc.] : Distributed by Blackwell Scientific, 1977. — viii,328p : col ill ; 26cm.
Previous ed.: / by Ruth Lundeen Memmler and Ruth Byers Rada. Philadelphia : Lippincott, 1970. — Bibl.: p.289-290. — Index.
ISBN 0-397-54202-x : £8.00
ISBN 0-397-54193-7 Pbk : £5.30
(B77-24243)

Memmler, Ruth Lundeen. Structure and function of the human body. — 2nd ed. / [by] Ruth Lundeen Memmler, Dena Lin Wood ; illustrated by Anthony Ravielli. — Philadelphia [etc.] : Lippincott ; Oxford [etc.] : Distributed by Blackwell Scientific, 1977. — viii,211p : col ill ; 27cm.
Previous ed.: / by Ruth Lundeen Memmler and Ruth Byers Rada. Philadelphia : Lippincott, 1970. — Bibl.: p.191-192. — Index.
ISBN 0-397-54203-8 : £6.50
(B77-23439)

Usher, George, *b.1930.* Human and social biology / [by] George Usher. — Plymouth : Macdonald and Evans, 1977. — ix,246p : ill ; 19cm. — (The M. & E. handbook series)
With answers to multiple-choice questions. — Index.
ISBN 0-7121-0808-4 Pbk : £1.95
(B77-21881)

Vander, Arthur Jerome. Human physiology : the mechanisms of body function / [by] Arthur J. Vander, James H. Sherman, Dorothy S. Luciano. — 2nd ed. — New York ; London [etc.] : McGraw-Hill, [1976]. — ix,614p,[2]p of plates : ill(chiefly col) ; 24cm.
This ed. published in the United States: 1975. — Previous ed.: New York : McGraw-Hill, 1970. — Bibl.: p.571-581. — Index.
ISBN 0-07-066954-6 : £11.85
(B77-00235)

Wittman, Karl S. Basic sciences for health careers / [by] Karl S. Wittman. — New York ; London [etc.] : McGraw-Hill, 1976. — vii, 375p : ill ; 25cm. — (Nursing and allied health series)
Bibl. — Index.
ISBN 0-07-071195-x : £9.90
(B77-03565)

612 — Man. Biofeedback. *State-of-the-art reviews*
Biofeedback : research and therapy. — Montreal ; Lancaster : Eden Press ; [Edinburgh] : Distributed by Churchill Livingstone. — (Annual research reviews ISSN 0703-1629)
[Vol.1] : [1976] / [by] Wilfrid I. Hume. — 1976. — [7],75p ; 22cm.
Bibl.: p.62-73. — Index.
ISBN 0-904406-46-6 : £6.50
ISBN 0-443-01730-1 (Churchill Livingstone)
(B77-33815)

612 — Man. Physiology. *Juvenile literature. Welsh texts*
Kaufman, Joe. A wyddoch chi sut mae'ch corff yn gweithio? / testun a lluniau gan Joe Kaufman newn yngynghoriad â Marshall Kaufman, Ellen Kaufman ac Arthur Kaufman ; ymgynghorwr i'r addasiad Cymraeg R. Elwyn Hughes. — Caerdydd[i.e. Cardiff] : Gwasg y Dref Wen, 1977. — 3-94p : col ill ; 31cm.
Col. ill. on lining papers. — Originally published: as 'Joe Kaufman's how we are born, how we grow, how our bodies work and how we learn'. New York : Golden Press, 1975.
ISBN 0-904910-28-8 : £2.95
(B77-15868)

612 — Man. Physiology. *Reviews of research*
International review of physiology / [consultant editor Arthur C. Guyton]. — Baltimore ; London [etc.] : University Park Press.
Vol.11 : Kidney and urinary tract physiology II / edited by Klaus Thurau. — [1977]. — ix, 326p : ill ; 24cm.
Published in the United States: 1976. — Index.
ISBN 0-8391-1060-x : £17.50
(B77-10813)

Vol.12 : Gastrointestinal physiology II / edited by Robert K. Crane. — 1977. — ix,371p : ill ; 24cm.
Index.
ISBN 0-8391-1061-8 : £1.25
(B77-16892)

Vol.13 : Reproductive physiology II / edited by Roy O. Greep. — 1977. — xi,284p : ill ; 24cm.
Index.
ISBN 0-8391-1062-6 : £17.50
(B77-24955)

Vol.14 : Respiratory physiology II / edited by John G. Widdicombe. — 1977. — xi,321p : ill ; 24cm.
Index.
ISBN 0-8391-1063-4 : Unpriced
(B77-30277)

Vol.15 : Environmental physiology II / edited by David Robertshaw. — 1977. — viii,264p : ill ; 24cm.
Index.
ISBN 0-8391-1065-0 : Unpriced
(B77-29445)

612 — Man. Physiology. *Secondary school texts*
Wallis, Cyril James. Human biology : a text book of human anatomy, physiology and hygiene, covering the syllabuses in human biology of the General Certificate of Education and other examinations of similar standard / by C.J. Wallis. — 2nd ed. — London : Heinemann Medical, 1976. — xii,452p : ill ; 23cm.
Previous ed.: 1969. — Index.
ISBN 0-433-34705-8 : £3.95
(B77-15869)

612 — Man. Physiology. Measurement. *For anaesthesia*
Sykes, Malcolm Keith. Principles of measurement for anaesthetists / [by] M.K. Sykes, M.D. Vickers. — Oxford [etc.] : Blackwell Scientific, 1977. — x,316p : ill ; 22cm.
Originally published: 1970. — Bibl. — Index.
Pbk : £5.50
ISBN 0-632-06910-4
(B77-23440)

612′.002′4613 — Man. Physiology. *For nursing*
Riddle, Janet Thomson Elliot. Elementary textbook of anatomy and physiology applied to nursing / [by] Janet T.E. Riddle ; illustrated by Kathleen B. Nicoll. — 5th ed. — Edinburgh [etc.] : Churchill Livingstone, 1977. — [7], 151p : ill ; 22cm. — (Livingstone nursing texts)
Cover title: Anatomy and physiology applied to nursing. — Previous ed.: Edinburgh : Livingstone, 1974. — Index.
ISBN 0-443-01614-3 Pbk : Unpriced
Also classified at 611′.002′4613
(B77-30278)

612′.002′4616 — Man. Physiology. *For radiography*
Warrick, Charles Kay. Anatomy and physiology for radiographers / [by] C.K. Warrick. — 5th ed. — London : Edward Arnold, 1976. — x, 294p : ill ; 22cm.
Previous ed.: 1973. — Index.
ISBN 0-7131-4267-7 Pbk : £6.75
(B77-01474)

612′.0028 — Man. Physiology. Telemetry. *Conference proceedings*
International Symposium on Biotelemetry, *3rd, Pacific Grove, 1976.* Biotelemetry III / edited by Thomas B. Fryer, Harry A. Miller, Harold Sandler ; associate editors ... [others]. — New York [etc.] ; London : Academic Press, 1976 [i.e. 1977]. — xxi,381p : ill ; 24cm.
'Proceedings of the Third International Symposium on Biotelemetry, Asilomar, Pacific Grove, California, May 1976' - half title page verso. — Published in the United States: 1976. — Bibl.
ISBN 0-12-269250-0 : £13.50
(B77-12463)

612′.0076 — Man. Physiology. *Exercises, worked examples*
Rickards, Ralph. Anatomy and physiology : a self-instructional course / [by] Ralph Rickards, David F. Chapman. — Edinburgh [etc.] : Churchill Livingstone.
In 5 vols.
1 : Introduction & the reproductive system. — 1977. — [2],82p : ill ; 30cm.
With answers.
ISBN 0-443-01666-6 Pbk : £0.95
(B77-32644)

2 : The endocrine glands & the nervous system. — 1977. — [2],82p : ill ; 30cm.
With answers.
ISBN 0-443-01667-4 Pbk : £0.95
(B77-32645)

3 : The locomotor system & the special senses. — 1977. — [2],78p : ill ; 30cm.
With answers.
ISBN 0-443-01668-2 Pbk : £0.95
(B77-32646)

4 : The respiratory system & the cardiovascular system. — 1977. — [2],75p : ill ; 30cm.
With answers.
ISBN 0-443-01669-0 Pbk : £0.95
(B77-32647)

5 : The urinary system & the digestive system. — 1977. — [2],73p : ill ; 30cm.
With answers.
ISBN 0-443-01670-4 Pbk : £0.95
(B77-32648)

612′.0076 — Man. Physiology. *Questions & answers. Secondary school texts*
Lyth, Mike. Biology of man / [by] Mike Lyth. — St Albans : Hart-Davis Educational, 1976. — [1],47p : ill ; 25cm. — (Science testers)
ISBN 0-247-12603-9 Sd : £0.95
(B77-16403)

612′.014 — Man. Biological rhythms
Gittelson, Bernard. Biorhythm : a personal science / by Bernard Gittelson. — London : Futura Publications, 1976. — [8],183p : ill ; 26cm.
Originally published: New York : Arco Publishing Company, 1975. — Bibl.: p.67-68.
ISBN 0-86007-361-0 Pbk : £1.95
(B77-07365)

612′.01426 — Man. Temperature. Regulation during exercise
Problems with temperature regulation during exercise / edited by Ethan R. Nadel. — New York [etc.] ; London : Academic Press, 1977. — x,141p : ill ; 24cm.
'... summaries of the topics of a symposium entitled Problems of Temperature Regulation during Exercise, which was held in conjunction with the American College of Sports Medicine meeting in Anaheim, California, May 1976' - Preface. — Index.
ISBN 0-12-513550-5 : £6.50
(B77-31213)

612′.0144 — Environment. Adaptation of human physiology. Research. *Directories*
International Biological Programme. Human adaptability : a history and compendium of research in the International Biological Programme / [by] K.J. Collins and J.S. Weiner. — London : Taylor and Francis, 1977. — ix, 356p : ill, maps ; 26cm.
Index. — Includes a history of the Human Adaptability Section.
ISBN 0-85066-087-4 : £15.00
(B77-07366)

612′.01446 — Cryonics
Cryonics : solid state human hypothermia / edited by Brian Blair-Giles. — Surbiton (40 Claremont Rd, Surbiton, Surrey KT6 4RF) : The editor.
Vol.1 : Administrative preparations. — 1977. — [120]p in various pagings : ill, facsims, ports ; 30cm.
Includes one article in Russian. — Page height varies.
ISBN 0-904904-04-0 Pbk : £7.00
(B77-07367)

Vol.2 : Medical practice. — 1977. — [159]p in various pagings : ill, facsims, ports ; 30cm.
Page height varies.
ISBN 0-904904-03-2 Pbk : £7.00
(B77-07368)

612′.01448′6 — Man. Effects of ionising radiation
Hall, Eric John. Radiation and life / by Eric J. Hall. — Oxford [etc.] : Pergamon, 1976. — x, 201p : ill, map, ports ; 22cm.
Index.
ISBN 0-08-020599-2 : £6.50
ISBN 0-08-020598-4 Pbk : £3.50
(B77-06097)

612′.0145 — Astronauts. Physiology. Effects of space flight. *Conference proceedings*
International Symposium on Basic Environmental Problems of Man in Space, *5th, Washington, D.C., 1973.* Proceedings of Fifth International Symposium on Basic Environmental Problems of Man in Space, [held] Washington, D.C., 27-30 November 1973 / editor Ashton Graybiel. — New York ; Oxford [etc.] : Pergamon, 1976. — xxxiii,365p : ill ; 26cm.
Cover title: Basic environmental problem of man in space. — English text, English, French and Russian tables of contents and Russian summaries at the end of 3 chapters. — Originally published: in 'Acta astronautica' Vol.2, Issues 1/2 and 3/4.
ISBN 0-08-021067-8 : £17.50
(B77-04824)

612′.015 — Medicine. Biochemistry
Brown, J M M. Elementary medical biochemistry / by J.M.M. Brown and G.G. Járos. — Durban ; London [etc.] : Butterworth, 1977. — 100p in various pagings : ill ; 24cm.
ISBN 0-409-08268-6 Pbk : Unpriced
(B77-25651)

612′.015 — Medicine. Biochemistry. *Reviews of research*
Essays in medical biochemistry. — London (7 Warwick Court, WC1R 5DP) : Biochemical Society : Association of Clinical Biochemists.
Vol.2 / edited by V. Marks and C.N. Hales. — 1976. — ix,187p,3[i.e.4]p of plates : ill ; 23cm.
ISBN 0-904498-02-6 Pbk : £4.00
ISSN 0306-2872
(B77-06694)

612′.015′06241 — Medicine. Biochemistry. Organisations. *Great Britain. Association of Clinical Biochemists. Yearbooks*
Association of Clinical Biochemists. Members' handbook / Association of Clinical Biochemists. — London (30 Russell Sq., WC1B 5DT) : The Association.
[1977]. — 1976. — 94p ; 22cm.
Previously published: as 'List of members'.
Sd : Unpriced(free to members)
ISSN 0140-2404
(B77-25652)

612′.015′0913 — Man. Biochemistry. *Tropical regions*
Candlish, John K. A medical biochemistry for the tropics / [by] John K. Candlish. — London : Baillière Tindall, 1977. — x,254p : ill ; 22cm.
Bibl.: p.244. — Index.
ISBN 0-7020-0619-x Pbk : £5.50
(B77-31214)

612′.01522 — Man. Body fluids. Electrolytes. Regulation. *Programmed texts*
Reed, Gretchen Mayo. Regulation of fluid and electrolyte balance : a programmed instruction in clinical physiology / [by] Gretchen Mayo Reed and Vincent F. Sheppard. — 2nd ed. — Philadelphia ; London [etc.] : Saunders, 1977. — ii-xi,322p : ill ; 26cm.
Fill-in book. — With answers to questions. — Previous ed.: 1971.
ISBN 0-7216-7513-1 Pbk : £6.50
(B77-27883)

612′.01522 — Man. Body fluids. Proteins. *Conference proceedings*
Protides of the biological fluids. — Oxford [etc.] : Pergamon.
Proceedings of the twenty-fourth Colloquium, Brugge, 1976 / edited by H. Peeters. — 1976. — xix,836p : ill, maps ; 26cm. — (Proteins and related subjects ; vol.24)
'... this XXIVth Colloquium on Protides of the Biological Fluids ...' - Preface. — Bibl. — Index.
ISBN 0-08-020359-0 : £37.50
(B77-06695)

612′.0157′5 — Man. Trytophan. Metabolites
Oliver, Ronald William Alfred. The aromatic tryptophan metabolites : an evaluated collection of thin layer chromatographic, chromogenic, electronic and mass spectral data : together with a bibliography of reports of their chromatographic separations for the period 1955-1976 / by R.W.A. Oliver and M. Corrie. — Salford (Peel Park, Salford, Lancs. M5 4WT) : Biological Materials Analysis Unit, Department of Chemistry and Applied Chemistry, University of Salford, 1977. — [3], viii leaves,62p : ill ; 30cm. — (University of Salford. Biological Materials Analysis Unit. Publications ; no.21 ISSN 0309-8060)
Bibl.: p.45-58.
Sp : £2.50
(B77-20293)

612'.02'4613 — Man. Physiology. *For physical education*
Perrott, John William. Structural and functional anatomy for students and teachers of physical education / [by] J.W. Perrott. — 3rd ed. — London : Edward Arnold, 1977. — v,346p : ill, port ; 23cm.
Previous ed.: published as 'Anatomy for students and teachers of physical education'. 1970. — Index.
ISBN 0-7131-4292-8 Pbk : £6.95 : CIP rev.
(B77-11226)

612'.04 — Man. Physiology. Effects of underwater diving. *For ergonomics*
The **underwater** hand book : a guide to physiology and performance for the engineer / edited by Charles W. Shilling, Margaret F. Werts and Nancy R. Schandelmeier. — London [etc.] : Wiley, 1976. — xxvii,912p : ill, chart, map ; 26cm.
Bibl. — Index.
ISBN 0-471-99453-7 : £40.00
Primary classification 616.9'8022
(B77-24978)

612'.042 — Man. Work. Kinetics. *Conference proceedings*
Physical Work and Effort *(Conference), 1st, Wenner-Gren Center, 1975.* Physical Work and Effort : proceedings of the first international symposium held at the Wenner-Gren Center, Stockholm, December 2-4, 1975 / edited by Gunnar Borg. — Oxford [etc.] : Pergamon Press, 1977. — xiii,439p : ill ; 26cm. — (Wenner-Gren Center. International symposium series ; vol.28)
'... this symposium on "Physical Work and Effort"' - p.xiii. — Bibl.
ISBN 0-08-021373-1 : £13.00
(B77-18154)

612'.044 — Sports & games. Physiological aspects
Exercise and sport sciences reviews. — New York ; London : Academic Press.
Vol.2 / edited by Jack H. Wilmore. — 1974. — xiii,381p : ill ; 24cm.
Bibl. — Index.
ISBN 0-12-227402-4 : Unpriced
(B77-19398)

Mathews, Donald Kenneth. The physiological basis of physical education and athletics / [by] Donald K. Mathews, Edward L. Fox ; illustrated by Nancy Allison Close. — 2nd ed. — Philadelphia ; London [etc.] : Saunders, 1976. — xvi,577p : ill ; 25cm.
Text on lining papers. — Previous ed.: 1971. — Bibl. — Index.
ISBN 0-7216-6184-x : £10.00
(B77-01475)

612.1 — PHYSIOLOGY. CIRCULATORY SYSTEM

612'.1 — Man. Blood. Circulation. *Early works*
Harvey, William, *b.1578.* [De motu cordis. English]. An anatomical disputation concerning the movement of the heart and blood in living creatures / by William Harvey ; translated [from the Latin] with introduction and notes by Gweneth Whitteridge. — Oxford [etc.] : Blackwell Scientific, 1976. — lxii,142p,[1],2 leaves of plates : ill, port ; 23cm.
Spine title: The movement of the heart and blood. — Bibl.: p.lxi-lxii. — Index.
ISBN 0-632-00059-7 : £9.75
(B77-13662)

612'.1 — Man. Cardiovascular system
Rushmer, Robert Fraser. Cardiovascular dynamics / [by] Robert F. Rushmer. — 4th ed. — Philadelphia ; London [etc.] : Saunders, 1976. — xv,584p : ill ; 26cm.
Previous ed.: 1970. — Index.
ISBN 0-7216-7847-5 : £16.25
(B77-14750)

Rushmer, Robert Fraser. Structure and function of the cardiovascular system / [by] Robert F. Rushmer. — 2nd ed. — Philadelphia ; London [etc.] : Saunders, 1976. — xiv,360p : ill ; 25cm. — (Organ physiology)
Previous ed.: 1972. — Index.
ISBN 0-7216-7852-1 Pbk : £8.25
(B77-01476)

612'.1 — Man. Cardiovascular system. Physiology
Berne, Robert Matthew. Cardiovascular physiology / [by] Robert M. Berne, Matthew N. Levy. — 3rd ed. — Saint Louis : Mosby ; London : Distributed by Kimpton, 1977. — ix, 282p : ill ; 26cm.
Previous ed.: 1972. — Bibl. — Index.
ISBN 0-8016-0653-5 Pbk : £8.05
(B77-18788)

Kelman, George Richard. Applied cardiovascular physiology / [by] G.R. Kelman. — 2nd ed. — London [etc.] : Butterworth, 1977. — xi,321p : ill ; 24cm.
Previous ed.: 1971. — Bibl.: p.283-310. — Index.
ISBN 0-407-10881-5 : £10.50
(B77-18155)

McLaughlin, Arthur J. Essentials of physiology for advanced respiratory therapy / [by] Arthur J. McLaughlin, Jr. — Saint Louis : Mosby ; London : Distributed by Kimpton, 1977. — xii, 223p : ill ; 23cm.
With answers to self-evaluations. — Bibl. — Index. — Contains chapters on the renal system.
ISBN 0-8016-3314-1 Pbk : £6.70
Also classified at 612'.2
(B77-22604)

612'.1'0924 — Man. Blood. Circulation. Harvey, William, b.1578
Pagel, Walter. New light on William Harvey / [by] Walter Pagel. — Basel ; London [etc.] : Karger ; [Chichester] : [Distributed by Wiley], 1976. — ix,189p : ill, facsims, port ; 23cm.
Bibl.: p.175-177. — Index.
Pbk : £27.85
ISBN 3-8055-0962-6
(B77-04193)

612'.111 — Man. Blood. Red cells. *Conference proceedings*
American National Red Cross. *Annual Scientific Symposium, 5th, Washington, D.C., 1973.* The human red cell in vitro / edited by Tibor J. Greenwalt & Graham A. Jamieson. — New York ; London : Grune and Stratton, 1974. — xii,363p : ill, port ; 24cm.
'The American National Red Cross Fifth Annual Scientific Symposium Washington, D.C., 7-8 May, 1973 ... honored Professor Alfred Chanutin ...' - note. — Index.
ISBN 0-8089-0828-6 : Unpriced
(B77-19399)

612'.111 — Man. Blood. Red cells. Physiology. *Conference proceedings*
International Conference on Red Cell Metabolism and Function, *3rd, University of Michigan, 1974.* Erythrocyte structure and function : proceedings of the Third International Conference on Red Cell Metabolism and Function held at the University of Michigan, Ann Arbor, October 16-19, 1974 / editor George J. Brewer. — New York : Liss ; Amsterdam ; Oxford : Elsevier, [1976]. — [4], xxvi,784p : ill, port ; 24cm. — (Progress in clinical and biological research ; vol.1)
Published in the United States : 1975. — Bibl. — Index.
ISBN 0-444-99842-x : £34.85
(B77-06696)

612'.1111 — Man. Blood. Haemoglobins
Bunn, H Franklin. Human hemoglobins / [by] H. Franklin Bunn, Bernard G. Forget, Helen M. Ranney. — Philadelphia ; London [etc.] : Saunders, 1977. — x,432p : ill ; 25cm.
Bibl.: p.351-410. — Index.
ISBN 0-7216-2178-3 : £17.00
(B77-32649)

612'.112 — Man. Blood. Neutrophils
Murphy, Patrick. The neutrophil / [by] Patrick Murphy. — New York ; London : Plenum Medical, 1976. — xii,217p : ill ; 24cm.
Index.
ISBN 0-306-30951-3 : Unpriced
(B77-33816)

612'.1181 — Man. Blood. Flow
The **mechanics** of the circulation / [by] C.G. Caro ... [et al.]. — Oxford [etc.] : Oxford University Press, 1978. — xiv,527p : ill ; 25cm. — (Oxford medical publications)
Text on lining paper. — Bibl. — Index.
ISBN 0-19-263323-6 : £22.00 : CIP rev.
(B77-11227)

612'.1181 — Man. Blood. Flow. *Conference proceedings*
NATO Advanced Study Institute on Cardiovascular Flow Dynamics, *Houston, 1975.* Cardiovascular flow dynamics and measurements / edited by Ned H.C. Hwang and Nils A. Norman. — Baltimore ; London [etc.] : University Park Press, 1977. — xvii, 970p : ill(some col) ; 24cm.
'... lectures presented at the 1975 NATO Advanced Study Institute on Cardiovascular Flow Dynamics, jointly sponsored by the NATO Scientific Affairs Division and the U.S. National Science Foundation ... held in Houston, Texas, October 6-17 ...' - p.xiii. — Bibl. — Index.
ISBN 0-8391-0972-5 : £32.25
(B77-22605)

612'.11822 — Man. Blood. Immunological properties
Bryant, Neville J. An introduction to immunohematology / [by] Neville J. Bryant. — Philadelphia ; London [etc.] : Saunders, 1976. — xxi,255p : ill ; 27cm.
Text on lining papers. — Bibl. — Index.
ISBN 0-7216-2170-8 : £10.75
(B77-03024)

612'.12 — Man. Blood. Albumin
Albumin structure, function and uses / edited by Victor M. Rosenoer, Murray Oratz, Marcus A. Rothschild. — Oxford [etc.] : Pergamon, 1977. — xiii,397p,[3]leaves of plates,[8]p of plates : ill, port ; 26cm.
Index.
ISBN 0-08-019603-9 : £25.00
(B77-27105)

612'.12 — Man. Blood. Angiotensin. Formation. Role of renin. *State-of-the-art reviews*
Renin. — Montreal ; Lancaster : Eden Press ; [Edinburgh] : Distributed by Churchill Livingstone. — (Annual research reviews ISSN 0703-1629)
[Vol.1] : 1976 / [by] Suzanne Oparil. — [1976]. — [7],251p ; 22cm.
Bibl.: p.196-245. — Index.
ISBN 0-88831-000-5 : £14.00
ISBN 0-443-01713-1 (Churchill Livingstone)
(B77-33817)

612'.12 — Man. Blood. Gases. Chemistry
Davenport, Horace Willard. The ABC of acid-base chemistry : the elements of physiological blood-gas chemistry for medical students and physicians / [by] Horace W. Davenport. — 6th ed., revised. — Chicago ; London : University of Chicago Press, 1974. — vii,124p : ill ; 24cm.
Previous ed.: 1969. — Bibl.: p.123-124.
ISBN 0-226-13705-8 : Unpriced
ISBN 0-226-13703-1 Pbk : Unpriced
(B77-18789)

612'.12 — Man. Blood plasma. Proteins. *Conference proceedings*
American National Red Cross. *Annual Scientific Symposium, 7th, Washington, D.C., 1975.* Trace components of plasma : isolation and clinical significance / edited by G.A. Jamieson and Tibor J. Greenwalt. — New York : Alan R. Liss ; Amsterdam ; Oxford : Elsevier, 1976. — xii,428p : ill ; 24cm. — (Progress in clinical and biological research ; vol.5)
'The American National Red Cross Seventh Annual Scientific Symposium, Washington, D.C. 6-7 May 1975' - note. — Index.
ISBN 0-8451-0005-x : £26.25
(B77-04825)

612'.171 — Man. Heart. Mitral valve. *Conference proceedings*
International Symposium on the Mitral Valve, *1st, Paris, 1975.* The mitral valve : a pluridisciplinary approach / Daniel Kalmanson, editor. — London : Edward Arnold, 1976. — xx,576p : ill ; 24cm.
'Proceedings of the First International Symposium on the Mitral Valve, Paris, May 26-28, 1975, under the auspices of the Foundation Adolphe de Rothschild, Department of Cardiology. Sponsored by the French Cardiac Society and the European Cardiac Society' - title page verso. — Bibl.
ISBN 0-7131-4283-9 : £19.50
(B77-02333)

612.2 — PHYSIOLOGY. RESPIRATORY SYSTEM
Bouhuys, Arend. Breathing : physiology, environment and lung disease / [by] Arend Bouhuys. — New York ; London : Grune and Stratton, 1974. — xii,511p : ill ; 26cm.
Bibl. — Index.
ISBN 0-8089-0758-1 : Unpriced
Also classified at 616.2'4'071
(B77-19400)

McLaughlin, Arthur J. Essentials of physiology for advanced respiratory therapy / [by] Arthur J. McLaughlin, Jr. — Saint Louis : Mosby ; London : Distributed by Kimpton, 1977. — xii, 223p : ill ; 23cm.
With answers to self-evaluations. — Bibl. — Index. — Contains chapters on the renal system.
ISBN 0-8016-3314-1 Pbk : £6.70
Primary classification 612'.1
(B77-22604)

612'.2 — Man. Lungs. Blood. Circulation
Harris, Peter, *b.1923 (May).* The human pulmonary circulation : its form and function in healeh and disease / [by] Peter Harris, Donald Heath ; foreword by Sir Melville Arnott. — 2nd ed. — Edinburgh [etc.] : Churchill Livingstone, 1977. — xii,712p : ill ; 26cm.
Previous ed.: 1962. — Index.
ISBN 0-443-01177-x : £28.00 : CIP rev.
(B77-16893)

612'.2 — Man. Lungs. Physiology
Murray, John F. The normal lung : the basis for diagnosis and treatment of pulmonary disease / [by] John F. Murray. — Philadelphia ; London [etc.] : Saunders, 1976. — xi,334p : ill(some col) ; 26cm.
Index.
ISBN 0-7216-6612-4 : £10.50
(B77-01477)

Regional differences in the lung / edited by John B. West. — New York [etc.] ; London : Academic Press, 1977. — xiv,488p : ill, facsim ; 24cm.
Bibl. — Index.
ISBN 0-12-744550-1 : £26.25
(B77-16894)

612'.2'0184 — Man. Respiratory system. Mathematical models. Applications of digital computer systems
Dickinson, C J. A computer model of human respiration : ventilation, blood gas transport and exchange, hydrogen regulation : for teaching, research and clinical use, 'MacPuf' / C.J. Dickinson. — Lancaster : M.T.P. Press, 1977. — xii,256p : ill ; 24cm.
Bibl.: p.181-184. — Index.
ISBN 0-85200-173-8 : £14.95
(B77-22606)

612'.2'024617 — Man. Respiratory system. Physiology. ***For anaesthesia***
Nunn, John Francis. Applied respiratory physiology / [by] J.F. Nunn. — 2nd ed. — London [etc.] : Butterworth, 1977. — xiii,524p, leaf of plate,[2]p of plates : ill(some col) ; 24cm.
Previous ed.: published as 'Applied respiratory physiology with special reference to anaesthesia'. 1969. — Bibl.: p.473-506. — Index.
ISBN 0-407-00060-7 : £17.50
(B77-19401)

612'.21 — Man. Breathing. Physiology
Bouhuys, Arend. The physiology of breathing : a textbook for medical students / [by] Arend Bouhuys. — New York [etc.] ; London : Grune and Stratton, 1977. — xvi,352p : ill ; 26cm.
Bibl. — Index.
ISBN 0-8089-0984-3 Pbk : £8.85
(B77-19402)

612'.22 — Man. Respiration. Gas exchange. Influence of inequality of blood flow & ventilation
West, John Burnard. Ventilation - blood flow and gas exchange / [by] John B. West. — 3rd ed. — Oxford [etc.] : Blackwell Scientific, 1977. — xi,113p : ill ; 22cm.
Previous ed.: 1970. — Bibl.: p.107-110. — Index.
ISBN 0-632-00188-7 Pbk : £2.50
(B77-26330)

612.3 — PHYSIOLOGY. DIGESTIVE SYSTEM
612'.3 — Adolescents. Nutrition. Physiology. *Conference proceedings*
Nutrient Requirements in Adolescence *(Conference), Airlie House, Va., 1973.* Nutrient Requirements in Adolescence / edited by John I. McKigney and Hamish N. Munro. — Cambridge, Mass. ; London : M.I.T. Press, 1976. — xviii,365p : ill ; 24cm.
'Proceedings of a conference held at Airlie House, Virginia, June 3-6, 1973 entitled "Nutrient Requirements in Adolescence" sponsored by the National Institute of Child Health and Human Development, National Institutes of Health' - half title page verso. — Index.
ISBN 0-262-13119-6 : £7.50
(B77-18790)

612'.3 — Man. Diet. Medical aspects
Burton, Benjamin T. Human nutrition : a textbook of nutrition in health and disease / [by] Benjamin T. Burton ; [edited by Floyd S. Doft et al.]. — 3rd ed. — New York ; London [etc.] : McGraw-Hill for H.J. Heinz Company, [1977]. — xiii,530p : ill ; 25cm.
'A Blakiston Publication'. — This ed. published in the United States: 1976. — Previous ed.: published as 'The Heinz handbook of nutrition'. New York : McGraw-Hill, 1965. — Index.
ISBN 0-07-009282-6 : £10.40
ISBN 0-07-009281-8 Pbk : £7.45
(B77-12464)

612'.3 — Pregnant women & lactating women. Nutrition. Physiology
Worthington, Bonnie S. Nutrition in pregnancy and lactation / [by] Bonnie S. Worthington, Joyce Vermeersch, Sue Rodwell Williams. — Saint Louis : Mosby ; London : Distributed by Kimpton, 1977. — ix,223p : ill ; 26cm.
Bibl. — Index.
ISBN 0-8016-5237-5 Pbk : £5.55
(B77-30279)

612'.3 — Women. Nutrition. Physiology
Nutritional impacts on women : throughout life with emphasis on reproduction / edited by Kamran S. Moghissi, Tommy N. Evans ; with 25 contributors. — Hagerstown [etc.] ; London : Harper and Row, 1977. — xvii,254p : ill ; 24cm.
Bibl. — Index.
ISBN 0-06-141793-9 : £11.20
(B77-25653)

612'.31 — Man. Mouth. Biochemistry
Dental biochemistry / Eugene P. Lazzari, editor. — 2nd ed. — Philadelphia : Lea and Febiger ; London : Kimpton, 1976. — ix,390p,fold leaf : ill ; 25cm.
Previous ed.: 1968. — Bibl. — Index.
ISBN 0-8121-0552-4 : £10.75
(B77-04194)

612'.33 — Man. Duodenum. Oddi's muscle. *Conference proceedings*
Gastroenterological Symposium, *3rd, Nice, 1976.* The sphincter of Oddi : proceedings of the Third Gastroenterological Symposium, Nice, June 8-9, 1976 / editor J. Delmont. — Basel ; London [etc.] : Karger ; [London] : [Distributed by Wiley], 1977. — xii,259p,v leaves of plates : ill(some col) ; 25cm.
Bibl. — Index.
Unpriced
ISBN 3-8055-1490-5
(B77-32650)

612'.33 — Man. Intestines. Permeation. *Conference proceedings*
Workshop Conference Hoechst, *4th, Schloss Reisensburg, 1975.* Intestinal permeation : proceedings of the Fourth Workshop Conference Hoechst, Schloss Reisensburg, 19-22 October, 1975 / editor M. Kramer, F. Lauterbach. — Amsterdam ; Oxford [etc.] ([256 Banbury Rd, Oxford OX2 7DH]) : Excerpta Medica [etc.], 1977. — xii,449p : ill(some col) ; 25cm. — (Workshop Conferences Hoechst ; vol.4) (International congress series ; no.391)
Bibl. — Index.
£38.10
ISBN 90-219-0321-0
(B77-26331)

612'.35 — Man. Bile acids. Metabolism. *Conference proceedings*
Bile Acid Meeting, *4th, Basel, 1976.* Bile acid metabolism in health and disease : proceedings of the IV Bile Acid Meeting, held at the Hilton Hotel, Basel, Switzerland, October 11-12, 1976 / edited by G. Paumgartner, A. Stiehl. — Lancaster : M.T.P. Press, 1977. — xix,297p : ill ; 24cm. — (Falk symposium ; 24)
Index.
ISBN 0-85200-169-x : £13.95
(B77-24244)

612'.35 — Man. Biliary tract. Physiology. *Conference proceedings*
NATO Advanced Study Institute on the Biliary System, *2nd, Aalborg, 1975.* The hepatobiliary system : fundamental and pathological mechanisms / edited by W. Taylor. — New York ; London : Plenum Press [for] NATO Scientific Affairs Division, 1976. — xvii,654p : ill ; 26cm. — (NATO Advanced Study Institutes : series A, life sciences ; vol.7)
'Proceedings of the Second NATO Advanced Study Institute on the Biliary System, held in Aalborg, Denmark, August 24-30, 1975' - title page verso. — Bibl. — Index.
ISBN 0-306-35607-4 : £31.19
(B77-07921)

612'.39 — Man. Metabolism
McMurray, W C. Essentials of human metabolism : the relationship of biochemistry to human physiology and disease / [by] W.C. McMurray. — Hagerstown [etc.] ; London : Harper and Row, 1977. — xi,308p : ill ; 24cm.
Bibl. — Index.
ISBN 0-06-141641-x Pbk : £11.20
(B77-15870)

612'.3924 — Man. Nutrition. Trace elements
Underwood, Eric John. Trace elements in human and animal nutrition / [by] Eric J. Underwood. — 4th ed. — New York [etc.] ; London : Academic Press, 1977. — xiii,545p : ill ; 24cm.
Previous ed.: 1971. — Bibl. — Index.
ISBN 0-12-709065-7 : £20.95
Primary classification 591.1'33
(B77-21874)

612'.3924 — Man. Trace elements
Schroeder, Henry Alfred. The trace elements and nutrition : some positive and negative aspects / [by] Henry A. Schroeder. — London : Faber, 1976. — 3-151p : ill ; 23cm.
Originally published: as 'The trace elements and man'. Old Greenwich, Conn. : Devin-Adair, 1973. — Index.
ISBN 0-571-10838-5 : £4.95
(B77-01478)

612'.3924 — Man. Trace elements. *Conference proceedings*
International Symposium on Trace Elements and Human Disease, *Wayne State University School of Medicine, 1974.* Trace elements in human health and disease / editor Ananda S. Prasad, associate editor Donald Oberleas. — New York [etc.] ; London : Academic Press. — (Nutrition Foundation. Monograph series)
Vol.2 : Essential and toxic elements. — 1976. — xviii,525p : ill ; 24cm.
'... based on papers presented at an International Symposium on Trace Elements and Human Disease held at Wayne State University School of Medicine, Detroit, Michigan, July 10-12, 1974' - Preface. — Bibl. — Index.
ISBN 0-12-564202-4 : £22.90
(B77-03566)

612.4 — PHYSIOLOGY. LYMPHATIC, ENDOCRINE, EXOCRINE SYSTEMS
612'.4 — Pregnant women. Endocrine system. Related to reproductive system
Endocrinology of pregnancy / edited by Fritz Fuchs, Arnold Klopper, with 16 contributors. — 2nd ed. — Hagerstown [etc.] ; London : Harper and Row, 1977. — xi,387p : ill ; 24cm.
Previous ed.: New York : Harper and Row, 1971. — Bibl. — Index.
ISBN 0-06-140841-7 : £16.90
Also classified at 612.6'2
(B77-16404)

612'.405 — Man. Blood. Hormones. Assay. Techniques
Hormones in human blood / detection and assay ; edited by Harry N. Antoniades. — Cambridge, Mass. ; London : Harvard University Press, 1976. — xvii,810p : ill ; 25cm.
Bibl. — Index.
ISBN 0-674-40635-4 : £37.15
(B77-04826)

612'.405'0154582 — Man. Hormones. Radioimmunoassay. Methods
Methods of hormone radioimmunoassay / edited by Bernard M. Jaffe, Harold R. Behrman. — New York [etc.] ; London : Academic Press, 1974. — xxi,520p : ill ; 24cm.
Bibl. — Index.
ISBN 0-12-379250-9 : Unpriced
(B77-18791)

612'.44 — Man. Thyroid hormones
Thyroid hormones : biosynthesis, physiological effects, and mechanisms of action / [by] Ya. Kh. Turakulov ... [et al.] ; edited by Ya. Kh. Turakulov ; translated from Russian by Basil Haigh ; translation editor Donald H. Ford. — New York ; London (8 Scrubs La., Harlesden, NW10 6SE) : Consultants Bureau, [1976]. — xii,317p : ill ; 24cm. — (Studies in Soviet science : life sciences)
This translation published in the United States: 1975. — Translation of 'Tireoidnye gormony'. Tashkent : Fan, 1972. — Bibl.
ISBN 0-306-10919-0 : £26.78
(B77-04195)

612'.44 — Man. Thyroid hormones. Metabolism. *State-of-the-art reviews*
Peripheral metabolism and action of thyroid hormones. — Montreal ; Lancaster : Eden Press ; [Edinburgh] : Distributed by Churchill Livingstone. — (Annual research reviews ISSN 0703-1629)
[Vol.1] : [1977] / [by] D.B. Ramsden. — [1977] . — [7],210[i.e.228]p,plate : 2 ill ; 22cm.
Bibl.: p.161-203. — Index.
ISBN 0-904406-54-7 : £10.25
ISSN 0703-1645
ISBN 0-443-01712-3 (Churchill Livingstone)
(B77-33818)

612'.461 — Man. Anti-diuretic hormones. *State-of-the-art reviews*
Anti-diuretic hormone. — Montreal ; Lancaster : Eden Press ; [Edinburgh] : Distributed by Churchill Livingstone. — (Annual research reviews ISSN 0703-1629)
[Vol.1] : [1977] / [by] Mary L. Forsling. — [1977]. — [7],158p,[2]leaves of plates : 4 ill ; 22cm.
Bibl.: p.122-153. — Index.
ISBN 0-904406-51-2 : £7.75
ISSN 0703-1750
ISBN 0-443-01707-7 (Churchill Livingstone)
(B77-33819)

612'.463 — Man. Kidneys
The **kidney** / edited by Barry M. Brenner, Floyd C. Rector, Jr ; with a foreword by Robert W. Berliner. — Philadelphia ; London [etc.] : Saunders.
In 2 vols.
Vol.1. — 1976. — xxvi,762,xxxv p : ill ; 27cm.
Index.
ISBN 0-7216-1965-7 : £60.50(for the 2 vols)
(B77-01479)

Vol.2. — 1976. — xxi,p,p765-1948,xxxv p : ill(some col) ; 27cm.
Index.
ISBN 0-7216-1966-5 : £60.50(for the 2 vols)
(B77-01480)

612'.463 — Man. Kidneys. Physiology
Koushanpour, Esmail. Renal physiology : principles and functions: an integrated analysis of renal-body fluid regulating systems / [by] Esmail Koushanpour. — Philadelphia ; London [etc.] : Saunders, 1976. — viii,581p : ill ; 27cm.
With answers to problems. — Bibl. — Index.
ISBN 0-7216-5493-2 : £10.00
(B77-01481)

612.6 — PHYSIOLOGY. REPRODUCTIVE SYSTEM AND DEVELOPMENT

612.6 — Man. Reproduction
Page, Ernest Winslow. Human reproduction : the core content of obstetrics and gynecology and perinatal medicine / [by] Ernest W. Page, Claude A. Villee, Dorothy B. Villee. — 2nd ed. — Philadelphia ; London [etc.] : Saunders, 1976 [i.e. 1977]. — xvii,471p : ill ; 25cm.
This ed. published in the United States: 1976. — Previous ed.: 1972. — Bibl. — Index.
ISBN 0-7216-7042-3 : £12.00
Primary classification 618
(B77-09730)

612.6 — Man. Reproduction. *Juvenile literature*
Chovil, Claire. How did I grow? / written by Claire Chovil ; drawings by Cheryl Drower. — London : British Broadcasting Corporation, 1977. — 64p : ill(some col) ; 21cm.
'Children's questions answered' - cover. — 'Based on three programmes in the school television series "Merry-go-round"'.
ISBN 0-563-16125-6 Sd : Unpriced
(B77-18792)

Jones, Eurfron Gwynne. How did I grow? / written by Eurfron Gwynne Jones ; drawings by Cheryl Drower. — London : British Broadcasting Corporation, 1977. — 64p : ill ; 21cm.
'A Parent's Guide to Children's Questions ... written and planned in the same order as the children's book ["How did I grow?" / by Claire Chovil]' - cover.
ISBN 0-563-16126-4 Sd : Unpriced
(B77-18793)

Shapp, Martha. Let's find out about babies / by Martha and Charles Shapp and Sylvia Shepard. — [New ed.] / [with] pictures by Jenny Williams. — London [etc.] : F. Watts, 1977. — [2],43p : col ill ; 23cm.
Col. ill. on lining paper. — Previous ed.: / pictures by Carol Wilde. New York : F. Watts, 1969.
ISBN 0-85166-580-2 : £1.75
(B77-23441)

612.6 — Man. Reproduction. Immunological aspects
Immunology of human reproduction / edited by James S. Scott and Warren R. Jones. — London : Academic Press [etc.], 1976. — xxii, 476p : ill ; 24cm.
Bibl. — Index.
ISBN 0-12-634050-1 : £15.00
(B77-01482)

612.6 — Man. Reproduction. Role of prolactin. *Conference proceedings*
Prolactin and human reproduction / edited by P.G. Crosignani, C. Robyn. — London [etc.] : Academic Press, 1977. — vii,305p : ill ; 24cm. — (Proceedings of the Serono symposia ; vol.11)
Bibl. — Index.
ISBN 0-12-198345-5 : £10.50
(B77-24958)

612.6 — Man. Sex
Steen, Edwin Benzel. Human sex and sexuality : with a dictionary of sexual terms / [by] Edwin B. Steen, James H. Price. — New York ; London [etc.] : Wiley, 1977. — xiii,338p : ill ; 23cm.
Bibl.: p.251-262. — Index.
ISBN 0-471-82101-2 Pbk : £7.00
(B77-20294)

612.6 — Man. Sexual intercourse
Rainer, Jerome. Sexual pleasure in marriage / [by] Jerome and Julia Rainer ; introduction by Harold T. Hyman. — St Albans : Mayflower, 1977. — 223p ; 18cm.
Originally published: London : Souvenir Press, 1959.
ISBN 0-583-12773-8 Pbk : £0.75
(B77-24959)

612.6 — Man. Sexual intercourse. *Manuals*
Brown, Paul. Treat yourself to sex : a guide for good loving / [by] Paul Brown & Carolyn Faulder. — London [etc.] : Dent : [for] the National Marriage Guidance Council, 1977. — 188p ; 23cm.
Index.
ISBN 0-460-04271-8 : £4.95 : CIP rev.
(B77-22607)

More joy : a lovemaking companion to 'The joy of sex' / edited by Alex Comfort. — [Illustrated and revised ed.] / illustrated by Charles Raymond and Christopher Foss. — London : Quartet Books, [1977]. — 220,[2]p : ill(some col) ; 27cm.
Cover title: More joy of sex. — This ed. originally published: New York : Crown Publishers, 1974 ; London : Mitchell Beazley, 1975. — Index.
ISBN 0-7043-3132-2 Pbk : £2.50
(B77-11228)

612.6 — Man. Sexual intercourse. Theories of Taoism
Chang, Jolan. The tao of love and sex : the Ancient Chinese way to ecstasy / by Jolan Chang ; foreword and postscript by Joseph Needham. — London : Wildwood House, 1977. — 136p : ill ; 26cm.
Bibl.: p.131-134. — Index.
ISBN 0-7045-0172-4 : £5.50
ISBN 0-7045-0188-0 Pbk : £2.95
(B77-21154)

612.6 — Man. Sexuality
Handbook of sexology / edited by John Money and Herman Musaph. — Amsterdam ; London [etc.] ([256 Banbury Rd, Oxford OX2 7DH]) : Excerpta Medica, 1977. — xxxvii,1402p : ill ; 25cm.
Bibl. — Index.
Unpriced
(B77-21155)

Human sexuality in four perspectives / Frank A. Beach editor ; [contributors] Milton Diamond ... [et al.]. — Baltimore ; London : Johns Hopkins University Press, 1977. — [5],330p : ill ; 24cm.
Published in the United States: 1976. — Bibl. — Index.
ISBN 0-8018-1845-1 : Unpriced
(B77-23442)

612.6 — Women. Sex relations. Orgasms. *Manuals*
Heiman, Julia. Becoming orgasmic : a sexual growth program for women / [by] Julia Heiman, Leslie LoPiccolo, Joseph LoPiccolo. — Englewood Cliffs ; London [etc.] : Prentice-Hall, [1977]. — xiii,219p : ill ; 21cm.
Published in the United States: 1976. — Bibl.: p.205-211. — Index.
ISBN 0-13-072652-4 : £7.20
ISBN 0-13-072645-1 Pbk : £3.20
(B77-13054)

612.6'007'2 — Man. Reproduction. Research
Greep, Roy Orval. Reproduction and human welfare : a challenge to research : a review of the reproductive sciences and contraceptive development / [by] Roy O. Greep, Marjorie A. Koblinsky, Frederick S. Jaffe. — Cambridge, Mass. ; London : M.I.T. Press, 1976. — xxi, 622p : ill ; 24cm.
Bibl. — Index.
ISBN 0-262-07067-7 : £7.50
Primary classification 613.9'4'072
(B77-18797)

612.6'03 — Man. Sexual intercourse. *Glossaries*
Jerrard, Veronica. Dictionary of sex terms / written by Veronica Jerrard & David Stern. — London (BCM Problems, WC1V 6XX) : Problem Books, 1976. — [1],31p ; 30cm.
Sd : £1.00
(B77-03025)

612.6'1 — Men. Reproductive system
Human semen and fertility regulation in men / edited by E.S.E. Hafez. — Saint Louis : Mosby ; London : Distributed by Kimpton, 1976. — xviii,615p : ill ; 28cm.
Bibl. — Index.
ISBN 0-8016-2008-2 : £38.60
(B77-07369)

612.6'2 — Pregnant women. Reproductive system. Related to endocrine system
Endocrinology of pregnancy / edited by Fritz Fuchs, Arnold Klopper, with 16 contributors. — 2nd ed. — Hagerstown [etc.] ; London : Harper and Row, 1977. — xi,387p : ill ; 24cm.
Previous ed.: New York : Harper and Row, 1971. — Bibl. — Index.
ISBN 0-06-140841-7 : £16.90
Primary classification 612'.4
(B77-16404)

612.6'2 — Women. Ovulation. *Conference proceedings*
Ovulation in the human / edited by P.G. Crosignani, D.R. Mishell. — London [etc.] : Academic Press, 1976. — xiv,317p : ill ; 24cm. — (Proceedings of the Serono symposia ; vol.8)

Held in Freiburg. — Bibl. — Index.
ISBN 0-12-198340-4 : £8.80
(B77-08398)

612.6'2 — Women. Reproductive system
Lanson, Lucienne. From woman to woman : a gynaecologist answers questions about you and your body / [by] Lucienne Lanson ; illustrations by Anita Karl. — Revised ed. — Harmondsworth [etc.] : Penguin, 1977. — 411p : ill ; 19cm. — (Pelican books)
Revised ed. also published: New York : Knopf, 1977. — Previous ed.: New York : Knopf, 1975.
ISBN 0-14-022002-x Pbk : £0.95
(B77-25654)

612.6'2 — Women. Uterus. Cervix
The **cervix** / edited by Joseph A. Jordan and Albert Singer. — London [etc.] : Saunders, 1976. — xviii,529p : ill ; 27cm.
Bibl. — Index.
ISBN 0-7216-5227-1 : £20.00
(B77-01483)

612.6'3 — Women. Pregnancy & childbirth. *Juvenile literature*
Caveney, Sylvia. Inside mum : an illustrated account of conception, pregnancy and childbirth / by Sylvia Caveney ; pictures by Simon Stern. — London : Sidgwick and Jackson, 1976. — 93p : ill(some col) ; 23cm.
Index.
ISBN 0-283-98247-0 : £2.95
(B77-01484)

Jarner, Bo. My new sister / [photographs by] Bo Jarner ; [translated from the Danish]. — London : A. and C. Black, 1977. — [21]p : chiefly ill ; 22cm.
Translation of: 'Sille far en lille-soster'. Copenhagen : Borgens, 1973?.
ISBN 0-7136-1708-x : £1.25
Also classified at 649'.122
(B77-14751)

612.6'3 — Women. Pregnancy & childbirth. *Manuals*
Brant, Margaret. Having a baby / [by] Margaret Brant. — London : Macdonald Educational, 1977. — 96p : ill(some col), form ; 21cm. — (Macdonald guidelines ; 14)
Bibl.: p.93. — Index.
ISBN 0-356-06014-4 Pbk : £1.00
Also classified at 649'.122
(B77-21156)

Lennane, Jean. Hard labour : a realists' guide to having a baby by Jean and John Lennane. — London : Gollancz, 1977. — 3-242p ; 23cm.
Bibl.: p.234-235. — Index.
ISBN 0-575-02180-2 : £5.95
Also classified at 649'.122
(B77-10376)

Rayner, Claire. Claire Rayner answers your 100 questions on pregnancy. — London : British Broadcasting Corporation, 1977. — 96p : ill ; 22cm.
'... accompanies the BBC TV "Parents and children" series of programmes "Having a baby" ... First broadcast on BBC-2 ... from 24 March 1977' - note. — Index.
ISBN 0-563-16109-4 Sd : £0.95
(B77-16895)

You and your baby / executive editor Evelyn Brown. — London : British Medical Association. — (A 'Family doctor' publication)
In 2 vols.
Part 1 : Pregnancy and birth. — 1977. — 95p : ill(chiefly col) ; 20cm.
Sd : Unpriced
Also classified at 649'.122
(B77-27884)

612.6'3 — Women. Pregnancy & childbirth. *Secondary school texts*
Fox, Dennis. Facts for life : family matters / [by] Dennis Fox, Jack Smith. — London : Macdonald Educational, 1977. — 32p : ill(some col) ; 22cm.
'... designed to accompany the Granada television series "Facts for Life, Family Matters" ...' - Cover. — Bibl.: p.30-31. — Index.
ISBN 0-356-05581-7 Sd : £0.75
(B77-08399)

612.6'3 — Women. Pregnancy & childbirth. Health aspects
Great Britain. *Department of Health and Social Security.* Prevention and health, reducing the risk : safer pregnancy and childbirth : a discussion paper / prepared jointly by the Health Departments of Great Britain and Northern Ireland. — London : H.M.S.O., 1977. — 55p : ill, map ; 21cm.
ISBN 0-11-320664-x Sd : £0.75
(B77-33245)

612.6'3'019 — Women. Pregnancy. Psychological aspects
Macfarlane, Aidan. The psychology of childbirth / [by] Aidan Macfarlane. — [London] : Fontana, 1977. — 128p ; 18cm. — (The developing child)
Also published: London : Open Books, 1977. — Bibl.: p.123-124. — Index.
ISBN 0-00-634857-2 Pbk : £1.00
(B77-18794)

Macfarlane, Aidan. The psychology of childbirth / [by] Aidan Macfarlane. — London : Open Books, 1977. — 128p ; 23cm. — (The developing child)
Also published: London : Fontana, 1977. — Bibl.: p.123-124. — Index.
ISBN 0-7291-0017-0 : £3.50
(B77-21882)

612.6'3'02403036 — Women. Pregnancy & childbirth. *For negro parents*
McLaughlin, Clara J. The black parents' handbook : a guide to healthy pregnancy, birth and child care / [by] Clara J. McLaughlin with Donald R. Frisby ... [et al.]. — New York ; London : Harcourt Brace Jovanovich, 1976. — xx,220p : ill ; 22cm.
Index.
ISBN 0-15-113185-6 : Unpriced
ISBN 0-15-613100-5 Pbk : Unpriced
Primary classification 649'.102'403036
(B77-10438)

612.6'3'02406947 — Women. Pregnancy & childbirth. *Manuals. For young unmarried mothers*
Gibb, Jennifer. Is this pregnancy? : what to do next, 3 stages of pregnancy, what to eat, what to wear, how a baby is born / [by Jennifer Gibb] ; [drawings by Judith Coney]. — Edinburgh (44 Albany St., Edinburgh EH1 3QR) : Scottish Council for Single Parents, [1977]. — [2],16,[1]p : ill ; 24cm.
Sd : £0.20
(B77-29446)

612.6'4 — Man. Embryos & foetuses. Development
Illustrated human embryology / [by H. Tuchmann-Duplessis et al.] ; translated [from the French] by Lucille S. Hurley. — New York : Springer Verlag ; London : Chapman and Hall [etc.].
In 3 vols.
Vol.3 : Nervous system and endocrine glands / by H. Tuchmann-Duplessis, M. Auroux, P. Haegel. — 1974. — xii[i.e.viii],143p : chiefly ill(some col) ; 27cm.
Translation of: 'Embryologie. Fasc. 3'. 3.éd. Paris : Masson, 1974. — Index.
ISBN 0-412-12160-3 Pbk : Unpriced
(B77-20295)

Patten, Bradley Merrill. Patten's human embryology : elements of clinical development. — [4th ed.] / [revised by] Clark Edward Corliss. — New York ; London [etc.] : McGraw-Hill, 1976. — ix,470p : ill(some col), port ; 25cm.
'A Blakiston publication'. — Col. ill. on lining papers. — Previous ed.: published as 'Human embryology'. New York ; Maidenhead : McGraw-Hill, 1968. — Bibl. — Index.
ISBN 0-07-013150-3 : £12.40
(B77-00236)

612.6'47 — Man. Foetuses. Physiology
Fetal physiology and medicine : the basis of perinatology / edited by Richard W. Beard and Peter W. Nathanielsz. — London [etc.] : Saunders, 1976. — xii,542p : ill ; 26cm.
Bibl. — Index.
ISBN 0-7216-1600-3 : £15.00
Also classified at 618.3'2
(B77-05434)

612.6'5 — Babies. Physical development. Screening
Illingworth, Ronald Stanley. Basic developmental screening : O-2 years / by Ronald S. Illingworth. — 2nd ed. — Oxford [etc.] : Blackwell Scientific, 1977. — v,58p : ill ; 17cm.
Text on inside back cover. — Previous ed.: 1973.
ISBN 0-632-00035-x Pbk : £1.40 : CIP rev.
(B77-06698)

612.6'5 — Children. Growth. Variation. *Comparative studies*
Eveleth, Phyllis B. Worldwide variation in human growth / [by] Phyllis B. Eveleth and J.M. Tanner ; foreword by W.H. Chang. — Cambridge [etc.] : Cambridge University Press, 1976. — xiv,498p : ill, map(on lining papers) ; 24cm.
'International Biological Programme 8'. — Bibl. : p.434-491. — Index.
ISBN 0-521-20806-8 : £20.00
(B77-06699)

612.6'5 — Children. Physical development
Holt, Kenneth Sunderland. Developmental paediatrics : perspectives and practice / [by] K.S. Holt. — London [etc.] : Butterworth, 1977. — ix,311p : ill ; 23cm. — (Postgraduate paediatrics series)
Bibl. — Index.
ISBN 0-407-00065-8 : Unpriced
(B77-15301)

612.6'5 — Children. Physical development. Effects of neonatal nutrition
Early nutrition and later development / edited by A.W. Wilkinson. — Tunbridge Wells : Pitman Medical, 1976. — x,236p ; 24cm.
Bibl.
ISBN 0-272-79411-2 : £8.00
(B77-08400)

612.6'62 — Women. Oestrous cycle
Vollman, Rudolf F. The menstrual cycle / [by] Rudolf F. Vollman. — Philadelphia ; London [etc.] : Saunders, 1977. — ii-xiii,193p : ill ; 25cm. — (Major problems in obstetrics and gynecology ; vol.7)
Bibl. — Index.
ISBN 0-7216-9075-0 : £11.50
(B77-29447)

612.6'64 — Mothers. Effects of breast feeding. *Conference proceedings*
Symposium on Breast-feeding and the Mother, *London, 1976.* Breast-feeding and the mother / [editors Katherine Elliott and David W. Fitzsimons]. — Amsterdam ; Oxford [etc.] : Elsevier [etc.], 1976. — viii,280p : ill ; 25cm. — (Ciba Foundation. Symposia : new series ; 45)
'Symposium on Breast-feeding and the Mother held at the Ciba Foundation, London, 2nd-4th March 1976' - note. — Bibl. — Index.
ISBN 0-444-15238-5 : £12.65
(B77-16405)

612.6'64 — White nursing mothers. Milk. Analysis. *Great Britain. Reports, surveys*
Committee on Medical Aspects of Food Policy. *Working Party on the Composition of Foods for Infants and Young Children.* The composition of mature human milk : report of a working party of the Committee on Medical Aspects of Food Policy [i.e. the Working Party on the Composition of Foods for Infants and Young Children]. — London : H.M.S.O., 1977. — xi,47p : ill ; 25cm. — (Report on health and social subjects ; 12)
Bibl.: p.30-32.
ISBN 0-11-320244-x Sd : £1.10
(B77-15871)

612.6'65 — Men. Menopause. Theories
Bowskill, Derek. The 'male' menopause / [by] Derek Bowskill, Anthea Linacre. — London : Muller, 1976. — 195p ; 23cm.
Bibl.: p.195.
ISBN 0-584-10202-x : £3.95
(B77-02334)

612.6'65 — Women. Menopause
Fielding, Jean. Change of life / [by] Jean Fielding. — Havant : K. Mason, 1977. — [1], 32p ; 15cm.
ISBN 0-85937-097-6 Sd : £0.30 : CIP rev.
(B77-20296)

Philipp, Elliot Elias. The change / by Elliot Philipp. — London : British Medical Association, [1977]. — 31p : ill ; 19cm. — (A 'Family doctor' booklet)
Sd : £0.30
(B77-32651)

612.6'65 — Women. Menopause. *Conference proceedings*
International Congress on the Menopause, *1st, La Grande Motte, 1976.* Consensus on menopause research : a summary of international opinion : the proceedings of the First International Congress on the Menopause held at La Grande Motte, France, in June 1976 under the auspices of the American Geriatric Society and the Medical Faculty of the University of Montpellier / edited by P.A. van Keep, R.B. Greenblatt & M. Albeaux-Fernet. — Lancaster : M.T.P. Press, 1976. — xii,183, [1]p : ill ; 24cm.
Index.
ISBN 0-85200-166-5 : £6.95
(B77-05435)

612.6'7 — Adults. Ageing
The **handbooks** of aging / editor-in-chief James E. Birren. — [New York] ; [London etc.] : [Van Nostrand Reinhold].
In 3 vols.
[Handbook of aging and the social sciences] / [editors Robert H. Binstock, Ethel Shanas, with the assistance of associate editors Vern L. Bengtson et al.]. — [1976]. — xvi,684p : ill ; 26cm.
Bibl. — Index.
ISBN 0-442-20798-0 : £26.35
(B77-21883)

[Handbook of the biology of aging] / [editors Caleb E. Finch, Leonard Hayflick, with the assistance of associate editors Harold Brody et al.]. — [1977]. — xvi,771p : ill ; 27cm.
Bibl. — Index.
ISBN 0-442-20796-4 : £26.35
(B77-21884)

[Handbook of the psychology of aging] / [editors James E. Birren, K. Warner Schaie, with the assistance of associate editors Jack Botwinick et al.]. — [1977]. — vii,787p : ill ; 26cm.
Bibl. — Index.
ISBN 0-442-20797-2 : £26.35
(B77-21885)

612.6'7 — Adults. Ageing. *Conference proceedings*
Philadelphia Symposium on Aging, *1974.* Explorations in aging / edited by Vincent J. Cristofalo, Jay Roberts and Richard C. Adelman. — New York ; London : Plenum Press, 1975. — ix,307p : ill ; 26cm. — (Advances in experimental medicine and biology ; vol.61)
'Proceedings of the Philadelphia Symposium on Aging held in Philadelphia, Pennsylvania, September 30-October 2 1974' - title page verso. — Bibl. — Index.
ISBN 0-306-39061-2 : £12.29
(B77-11229)

612.6'7 — Man. Ageing. *Conference proceedings*
Action on Ageing *(Conference), Basle, 1976.*
Action on ageing : proceedings of a symposium held at Basle, 20th/21st May, 1976 / editors A.N. Davison, N.A. Hood. — Tunbridge Wells (P.O. Box 14, Tunbridge Wells, Kent TN3 0BA) : MCS Consultants for Sandoz, 1976. — 60p : 1 ill ; 24cm.
'The title of the symposium is "Action on ageing" ... ' - Introduction. — Bibl.
ISBN 0-9505367-1-7 Pbk : Free
(B77-00777)

612.6'7 — Man. Ageing. Role of diet. *Conference proceedings*
Nutrition, Longevity and Aging *(Conference), University of Miami School of Medicine, 1976.*
Nutrition, longevity and aging / edited by Morris Rockstein, Marvin L. Sussman. — New York [etc.] ; London : Academic Press, 1976. — xi,284p : ill ; 24cm.
'Papers ... presented ... in an Symposium on "Nutrition, Longevity, and Aging" held on February 26 and 27, 1976 at the University of Miami School of Medicine, Miami, Florida' - Preface. — Bibl.
ISBN 0-12-591656-6 : £9.45
(B77-06700)

612.6'8 — Man. Longevity. Effects of auto-suggestion
Sage, J A S. Live to be 100 / [by] J.A.S. Sage. — London : Star Books, 1975. — 128p : ill ; 18cm.
Originally published: London : W.H. Allen, 1963.
ISBN 0-352-30045-0 Pbk : £0.40
(B77-19403)

612.6'8 — Man. Longevity. Effects of Pollen-B
Lyall, Neil. The secret of staying young : pollen-B and how it can prolong your youth / [by] Neil Lyall and Robert Chapman. — London [etc.] : Pan Books, 1976. — 159,[1]p,8p of plates : ill, maps, ports ; 18cm.
Bibl.: p.157-158.
ISBN 0-330-24781-6 Pbk : £0.60
(B77-00237)

612.7 — PHYSIOLOGY. MOTOR AND INTEGUMENTARY SYSTEMS

612'.7 — Man. Hands. *Juvenile literature*
Tourneur, Dina Kathelyn. Caspar's hands / [by] Dina-Kathelyn Tourneur ; [translated from the French]. — London [etc.] : Burke, 1977. — [19]p : col ill ; 21cm. — (Caspar books)
Translation of: 'La main de Marmouset'. Tournai : Casterman, 1975.
ISBN 0-222-00448-7 : £1.00
ISBN 0-222-00448-1 Pbk : £0.80
(B77-14246)

612'.7 — Man. Motor system. *Juvenile literature*
Backhouse, Kenneth Morley. Muscles and movement / by K.M. Backhouse. — St Albans : Hart-Davis Educational, 1976. — 48p : ill(some col) ; 22cm. — (Finding out about the living body)
ISBN 0-298-78901-9 : £1.75
(B77-17514)

612'.741 — Man. Stretch reflexes. *Conference proceedings*
Understanding the Stretch Reflex *(Conference), Tokyo, 1975.* Understanding the Stretch Reflex / edited by S. Homma. — Amsterdam ; Oxford [etc.] : Elsevier, 1976. — xiii,507p : ill ; 27cm. — (Progress in brain research ; vol.44)
'... lectures and presentations given at an international symposium : Understanding the Stretch Reflex, November 7-11, 1975, held at the Saskawa Hall, Mita, Tokyo' - Preface. — Bibl. — Index.
ISBN 0-444-41456-8 : £33.96
(B77-17515)

612'.744 — Man. Smooth muscles. Biochemistry. *Conference proceedings*
Biochemistry of Smooth Muscle *(Conference), Winnipeg, 1975.* The Biochemistry of Smooth Muscle / edited by Newman L. Stephens. — Baltimore ; London [etc.] : University Park Press, 1977. — xv,733p : ill ; 24cm.
'Proceedings of the symposium "The Biochemistry of Smooth Muscle" held in Winnipeg, Manitoba, Canada on August 27-29, 1975' - title page verso. — Bibl. — Index.
ISBN 0-8391-0848-6 : £24.75
(B77-18156)

612'.75 — Man. Face. Bones. Growth
Enlow, Donald Hugh. Handbook of facial growth / [by] Donald H. Enlow with contributions by Robert E. Moyers and William W. Merow ; illustrations by William Roger Poston II. — Philadelphia ; London [etc.] : Saunders, 1975[i.e.1976]. — xiii,423p : ill ; 27cm.
Published in the United States: 1975. — Bibl.: p.391-412. — Index.
ISBN 0-7216-3385-4 : £13.50
(B77-03026)

612'.76 — Children. Motor skills. Development. Physiological aspects
Wickstrom, Ralph Lee. Fundamental motor patterns / [by] Ralph L. Wickstrom. — 2nd ed. — Philadelphia : Lea and Febiger ; London : Kimpton, 1977. — ix,209p : ill ; 25cm. — (Health, human movement and leisure studies)
Previous ed.: 1970. — Bibl. — Index.
ISBN 0-8121-0583-4 : £7.10
(B77-31216)

612'.76 — Man. Exercise. Bioenergetics & biomechanics
Margaria, Rodolfo. Biomechanics and energetics of muscular exercise / by Rodolfo Margaria. — Oxford : Clarendon Press, 1976. — x,146p : ill ; 23cm.
Bibl.: p.140-144. — Index.
ISBN 0-19-857397-9 : £7.00
(B77-00778)

612'.76 — Man. Exercise. Physiological aspects
Neuromuscular mechanisms for therapeutic and conditioning exercise / edited by Howard G. Knottgen. — Baltimore ; London [etc.] : University Park Press, [1977]. — xiii,141p : ill ; 23cm.
Published in the United States: 1976. — Bibl.: p.135. — Index.
ISBN 0-8391-0954-7 Pbk : £5.75
(B77-12465)

612'.76 — Man. Exercise. Physiological aspects. *For physical education*
Sharkey, Brian J. Physiology and physical activity / [by] Brian J. Sharkey. — New York [etc.] ; London : Harper and Row, [1976]. — xvii,220p : ill ; 21cm. — (Harper's series on scientific perspectives of physical education)
Published in the United States: 1975. — Bibl.: p.199-211. — Index.
ISBN 0-06-045965-4 Pbk : £3.40
(B77-02335)

612'.76 — Man. Feet. *Juvenile literature*
Tourneur, Dina Kathelyn. Caspar's feet / [by] Dina-Kathelyn Tourneur ; [translated from the French]. — London [etc.] : Burke, 1977. — [19]p : col ill ; 21cm. — (Caspar books)
Translation of: 'Le pied de Marmouset'. Tournai : Casterman, 1975.
ISBN 0-222-00447-9 : £1.00
ISBN 0-222-00453-3 Pbk : £0.80
(B77-14247)

612'.76 — Man. Movement
Higgins, Joseph R. Human movement : an integrated approach / [by] Joseph R. Higgins. — Saint Louis : Mosby ; London : Distributed by Kimpton, 1977. — xv,154p : ill, forms ; 23cm.
Bibl.: p.144-147. — Index.
ISBN 0-8016-2181-x Pbk : £5.60
(B77-20297)

Thompson, Clem Wheelock. Manual of structural kinesiology / [by] Clem W. Thompson. — 8th ed. — Saint Louis : Mosby ; London : Distributed by Kimpton, 1977. — vii,167p : ill(some col) ; 27cm.
Previous ed.: 1973. — Bibl.: p.134. — Index.
ISBN 0-8016-4939-0 Pbk : £5.85
(B77-31925)

Wells, Katharine Fuller. Kinesiology : scientific basis of human motion. — 6th ed. / [by] Katharine F. Wells, Kathryn Luttgens. — Philadelphia ; London [etc.] : Saunders, [1977]. — xv,591p : ill, forms ; 26cm.
This ed. published in the United States: 1976. — Previous ed.: / by Katharine F. Wells. 1971. — Bibl. — Index.
ISBN 0-7216-9218-4 : £9.75
(B77-11826)

612'.76 — Man. Movement. Aesthetics. *For teaching*
Foster, Ruth. Knowing in my bones / [by] Ruth Foster ; with a preface by Sir Alec Clegg. — London : A. and C. Black, 1976. — ix,131p : ill ; 22cm.
Bibl.: p.131.
ISBN 0-7136-1653-9 : £2.50
ISBN 0-7136-1664-4 Pbk : £1.50
(B77-00779)

612'.76 — Man. Movement. Mechanics
Williams, Marian. Williams and Lissner biomechanics of human motion. — 2nd ed. / [by] Barney Le Veau. — Philadelphia ; London [etc.] : Saunders, 1977. — ix,230p : ill ; 27cm.
Previous ed.: / by Marian Williams, Herbert R. Lissner. 1962. — Bibl. — Index.
ISBN 0-7216-5773-7 : £11.25
(B77-22608)

612'.76'05 — Man. Movement. *Periodicals*
Momentum : a journal of human movement studies. — Edinburgh (Cramond Rd North, Edinburgh EH4 6JD) : Dunfermline College of Physical Education.
Supersedes: Journal of psycho-social aspects.
Vol.1, no.1- ; Feb. 1976-. — 1976-. — ill ; 30cm.
Three issues a year. — [3],76p. in 1st issue. — English text, French and German summaries. — Bibl.
Sd : £1.25(£3.00 yearly)
ISSN 0309-6637
(B77-19404)

612'.78 — Man. Speech. Production
Hardcastle, W J. Physiology of speech production : an introduction for speech scientists / [by] W.J. Hardcastle. — London [etc.] : Academic Press, 1976. — xviii,157p : ill ; 24cm.
Bibl.: p.139-149. — Index.
ISBN 0-12-324950-3 : £4.50
(B77-09036)

612'.78 — Man. Speech. Production & acoustics
Contemporary issues in experimental phonetics / edited by Norman J. Lass. — New York [etc.] ; London : Academic Press, 1976. — xiii,498p : ill ; 25cm. — (Perspectives in neurolinguistics and psycholinguistics)
Bibl. — Index.
ISBN 0-12-437150-7 : £10.70
Also classified at 152.1'5
(B77-00780)

612'.79 — Man. Skin. Physiology
The **physiology** and pathophysiology of the skin / edited by A. Jarrett. — London [etc.] : Academic Press.
Vol.4 : The hair follicle. — 1977. — xix p,p1237-1540,xxi p,plate : ill(incl 1 col) ; 24cm.
Index.
ISBN 0-12-380604-6 : £18.50
(B77-30280)

612.8 — PHYSIOLOGY. NERVOUS SYSTEM

Guyton, Arthur Clifton. Structure and function of the nervous system / [by] Arthur C. Guyton. — 2nd ed. — Philadelphia ; London [etc.] : Saunders, 1976. — xiv,312p : ill(some col) ; 26cm. — (Organ physiology)
'This text ... is derived almost entirely from my "Textbook of Medical Physiology", 5th Edition ...' - Preface. — Previous ed.: 1972. — Bibl. — Index.
ISBN 0-7216-4366-3 Pbk : £8.25
(B77-00781)

Noback, Charles Robert. The nervous system : introduction and review / [by] Charles R. Noback, Robert J. Demarest. — 2nd ed. — New York ; London [etc.] : McGraw-Hill, 1977. — ix,225p : ill ; 23cm.
'A Blakiston Publication'. — Previous ed.: 1972. — Index.
ISBN 0-07-046849-4 Pbk : £5.20
(B77-22609)

Willis, William Darrell. Medical neurobiology : neuroanatomical and neurophysiological principles basic to clinical neuroscience / [by] William D. Willis, Robert G. Grossman. — 2nd ed. — Saint Louis : Mosby ; London : Distributed by Kimpton, 1977. — ix,515p : ill ; 29cm.
Previous ed.: 1973. — Bibl. — Index.
ISBN 0-8016-5583-8 : £19.95
(B77-20298)

612'.8 — Babies. Nervous system. Development
Touwen, Bert Christian Louis. Neurological development in infancy / [by] Bert Touwen. — London : Heinemann [etc. for] Spastics International Medical Publications, 1976. — ix, 150p(2 fold) : ill ; 25cm. — (Clinics in developmental medicine ; no.58)
Bibl.: p.137-141.
ISBN 0-433-32621-2 : £5.00
(B77-05436)

612.8 — Language. Neurophysiological aspects
Studies in neurolinguistics. — New York [etc.] ; London : Academic Press. — (Perspectives in neurolinguistics and psycholinguistics)
Vol.3 / edited by Haiganoosh Whitaker, Harry A. Whitaker. — 1977. — xiv,322p : ill ; 24cm.
Bibl. — Index.
ISBN 0-12-746303-8 : £13.15
Primary classification 616.8'552
(B77-27897)

612'.8 — Man. Behaviour. Neurophysiological aspects
Behavior control and modification of physiological activity / David I. Mostofsky, editor. — Englewood Cliffs ; London [etc.] : Prentice-Hall, [1977]. — viii,504p : ill ; 24cm. — (Century psychology series)
Published in the United States: 1976. — Bibl. -Index.
ISBN 0-13-073908-1 : £14.35
(B77-12466)

Thompson, Richard Frederick. Introduction to physiological psychology / [by] Richard F. Thompson. — New York ; London [etc.] : Harper and Row, [1976]. — xv,669p : ill ; 24cm.
Published in the United States: 1975. — Bibl.: p.609-643. — Index.
ISBN 0-06-046604-9 Pbk : £8.25
(B77-04197)

612'.8 — Medicine. Physiological psychology. Models: Animal behaviour. *Conference proceedings*
Workshop on Animal Models in Psychiatry and Neurology, *Rockville, 1977.* Animal models in psychiatry and neurology / edited by I. Hanin and E. Usdin. — Oxford [etc.] : Pergamon, 1977. — xiv,499p : ill ; 28cm.
Proceedings of the Workshop on Animal Models in Psychiatry and Neurology, held in Rockville on June 6-8, 1977. — Bibl.
ISBN 0-08-021556-4 : £22.25 : CIP rev.
(B77-21886)

612'.8 — Medicine. Physiological psychology. Research. Methodology
Bureš, Jan. Techniques and basic experiments for the study of brain and behavior / by Jan Bureš and Olga Burešová and Joseph P. Huston. — Amsterdam [etc.] ; Oxford : Elsevier, 1976. — xi,277p : ill ; 25cm.
Bibl. — Index.
ISBN 0-444-41502-5 : £14.05
(B77-16406)

612'.8042 — Man. Behaviour. Neurochemical aspects. *Conference proceedings*
Behavioral neurochemistry / edited by J.M.R. Delgado and F.V. DeFeudis. — New York : Spectrum ; New York ; London [etc.] : Distributed by Wiley, 1977. — [13],270p : ill ; 24cm.
'... as part of the Fifth International Meeting of the International Society for Neurochemistry, ... a satellite symposium on Behavioral Neurochemistry [was] held at the new Autonomous Medical School in Madrid ... This book [contains] expanded versions of the presentations of contributors to this meeting as well as the work of [others] who were unable to participate' - Preface. — Bibl. — Index.
ISBN 0-470-15179-x : £15.00
(B77-25655)

612'.8042 — Medicine. Neurochemistry. *Reviews of research*
Essays in neurochemistry and neuropharmacology. — London [etc.] : Wiley.
Vol.1 / edited by M.B.H. Youdim ... [et al.]. — 1977. — xi,195p : ill ; 24cm.
'A Wiley-Interscience Publication'. — Bibl.
ISBN 0-471-99424-3 : £9.90
Also classified at 615'.78
(B77-08401)

612'.8'043 — Man. Nervous system. Membranes. Transport phenomena. *Conference proceedings*
International Society for Neurochemistry. *Satellite Symposium, Padua, 1975.* Transport phenomena in the nervous system : physiological and pathological aspects / edited by Giulio Levi, Leontino Battistin and Abel Lajtha. — New York ; London : Plenum Press, 1976. — xxii,541p : ill ; 26cm. — (Advances in experimental medicine and biology ; vol.69)
'Proceedings of the Satellite Symposium of the International Society for Neurochemistry held in Padua, Italy, September 9-11, 1975' - title page verso. — Bibl. — Index.
ISBN 0-306-39069-8 : £24.89
(B77-20299)

612'.81 — Man. Nervous system. Synapses. Neuronal recognition
Neuronal recognition / edited by Samuel H. Barondes. — London : Chapman and Hall, 1976. — xvi,367p : ill ; 24cm. — ([Current topics in neurology ; vol.2])
Also published: New York : Plenum Press, 1976. — Bibl. — Index.
ISBN 0-412-21430-x : £18.00
(B77-01485)

612'.813 — Man. Nervous system. Neurons. Impulses. Transmission. Electrical activity
Brazier, Mary Agnes Burniston. Electrical activity of the nervous system / [by] Mary A.B. Brazier. — 4th ed. — Tunbridge Wells : Pitman Medical, 1977. — viii,248p : ill, port ; 23cm.
Previous ed.: 1968. — Bibl. — Index.
ISBN 0-272-79403-1 : £8.00
(B77-04827)

612'.814 — Man. Nervous system. Neurons. Gangliosides. Biochemistry. *Conference proceedings*
International Satellite Meeting on Biochemical and Pharmacological Implications of Ganglioside Function, *Cortona, 1975.* Ganglioside function : biochemical and pharmacological implications / edited by Giuseppe Porcellati and Bruno Ceccarelli and Guido Tettamanti. — New York ; London : Plenum Press, 1976. — ix,306p : ill ; 26cm. — (Advances in experimental medicine and biology ; vol.71)
'... the International Satellite Meeting on Biochemical and Pharmacological Implications of Ganglioside Function [of the International Society for Neurochemistry] held at Cortona, Tuscany, Italy from 28 to 31 August, 1975' - Preface. — Bibl. — Index.
ISBN 0-306-39071-x : £18.59
(B77-20300)

612'.82 — Man. Brain. *Conference proceedings*
International Summer School of Brain Research, *9th, Amsterdam, 1975.* Perspectives in brain research : proceedings of the 9th International Summer School of Brain Research, organized by the Netherlands Central Institute for Brain Research, Amsterdam, and held at the Royal Netherlands Academy of Arts and Sciences at Amsterdam, the Netherlands on July 28-August 1, 1975 / edited by M.A. Comer and D.F. Swaab, (J. Sels assistant editor). — Amsterdam [etc.] ; Oxford : Elsevier, 1976. — xii,489p : ill ; 27cm. — (Progress in brain research ; vol.45)
Bibl. — Index.
ISBN 0-444-41457-6 : £40.98
(B77-15872)

612'.82 — Man. Memory. Neurophysiological aspects. Related to neurophysiological aspects of sleep. *Conference proceedings*
Neurobiology of sleep and memory / editors René R. Drucker-Colín, James L. McGaugh ; associate editors ... [others]. — New York [etc.] ; London : Academic Press, 1977. — xiii, 456p : ill ; 24cm.
'Proceedings of a conference held in Mexico City in March 1975' - half-title page verso. — Bibl.
ISBN 0-12-222350-0 : £13.85
Primary classification 612'.821
(B77-27106)

612'.82'072 — Man. Brain. Research, to 1976
Blakemore, Colin. Mechanics of the mind / [by] Colin Blakemore. — Cambridge [etc.] : Cambridge University Press, 1977. — x,208p : ill(some col), facsims, ports ; 26cm. — (BBC Reith lectures ; 1976)
Bibl.: p.197-204. — Index.
ISBN 0-521-21559-5 : £10.50
ISBN 0-521-29185-2 Pbk : £3.95
(B77-21157)

612'.821 — Man. Sleep
Copen, Bruce. Vital facts about sleep / by Bruce Copen. — Revised and enlarged [ed.]. — Haywards Heath : Academic Publications, 1977. — [4],62p : ill ; 20cm.
Previous ed.: 1973. — Bibl.: p.62.
Pbk : Unpriced
(B77-29448)

Paupst, James C. The sleep book / by James C. Paupst, with Toni Robinson. — London : Sphere, 1977. — 174p : forms ; 18cm.
Originally published: Toronto : Macmillan of Canada, 1975. — Bibl.: p.170-172.
ISBN 0-7221-6735-0 Pbk : £0.75
(B77-23443)

612'.821 — Man. Sleep. Effects of drugs. *Reviews of research*
Pharmacology of sleep / edited by Robert L. Williams, Ismet Karacan ; foreword by Jules H. Masserman. — New York ; London [etc.] : Wiley, [1977]. — xiii,354p : ill ; 27cm.
'A Wiley Medical publication'. — Published in the United States: 1976. — Bibl. — Index.
ISBN 0-471-94856-x : £19.30
(B77-11827)

612'.821 — Man. Sleep. Neurophysiological aspects. Related to neurophysiological aspects of memory. *Conference proceedings*
Neurobiology of sleep and memory / editors René R. Drucker-Colín, James L. McGaugh ; associate editors ... [others]. — New York [etc.] ; London : Academic Press, 1977. — xiii, 456p : ill ; 24cm.
'Proceedings of a conference held in Mexico City in March 1975' - half-title page verso. — Bibl.
ISBN 0-12-222350-0 : £13.85
Also classified at 612'.82
(B77-27106)

612'.821'01 — Man. Sleep. Theories
Meddis, Ray. The sleep instinct / [by] Ray Meddis. — London [etc.] : Routledge and Kegan Paul, 1977. — [8],148p : ill ; 23cm.
Index.
ISBN 0-7100-8545-1 : £4.50
(B77-22610)

612'.822 — Man. Brain. Biochemistry
Biochemical correlates of brain structure and function / edited by A.N. Davison. — London [etc.] : Academic Press, 1977. — xiii,345p : ill ; 24cm.
Bibl. — Index.
ISBN 0-12-206650-2 : £14.00
(B77-19405)

612'.822 — Man. Brain. Electrical activity. Effects of behaviour
Symposium on Behavior and Brain Electrical Activity, *7th, Texas Research Institute of Mental Sciences, 1973.* Behavior and brain electrical activity / edited by Neil Burch and H.L. Altshuler. — New York ; London : Plenum Press, [1976]. — xix,563p : ill ; 26cm.
'Proceedings of the Seventh Annual Symposium on Behavior and Brain Electrical Activity held at the Texas Research Institute of Mental Sciences, Texas Medical Center, Houston, Texas, November 28-30, 1973' - title page verso. — Published in the United States: 1975. — Bibl. — Index.
ISBN 0-306-30868-1 : £20.48
(B77-04198)

612'.825 — Man. Hippocampus. *Reviews of research*
The **hippocampus** / edited by Robert L. Isaacson and Karl H. Pribram. — New York ; London : Plenum Press.
In 2 vols.
Vol.1 : Structure and development. — [1976]. — xviii,418p : ill ; 26cm.
Published in the United States: 1975. — Bibl. — Index.
ISBN 0-306-37535-4 : £15.44
(B77-03567)

Vol.2 : Neurophysiology and behavior. — [1976]. — xviii,445p : ill ; 26cm.
Published in the United States: 1975. — Bibl. — Index.
ISBN 0-306-37536-2 : £15.44
(B77-04828)

612'.826 — Man. Brain. Corpus striatum. Psychophysiological aspects
Psychobiology of the Striatum *(Conference), University of Nijmegen, 1976.* Psychobiology of the striatum / edited by A.R. Cools, A.H.M. Lohman and J.H.L. van den Bercken. — Amsterdam [etc.] ; Oxford : North-Holland Publishing Co., 1977. — xii,197p : ill ; 25cm.
'... papers presented at the symposium on "Psychobiology of the Striatum", organized on the occasion of the 25th anniversary of the School of Medicine at the University of Nijmegen, The Netherlands, from October 27 to 30, 1976' - Preface. — Bibl.: p.26-30. — Index.
ISBN 0-7204-0633-1 : Unpriced
(B77-27107)

612'.826 — Man. Hypothalamus. Hormones. *Conference proceedings*
International Symposium on Hypothalamus and Endocrine Functions, *Quebec, 1975.* Hypothalamus and endocrine functions / edited by Fernand Labrie, Joseph Meites and Georges Pelletier. — New York ; London : Plenum Press, 1976. — xi,508p : ill ; 26cm. — (Current topics in molecular endocrinology ; vol.3)
'Proceedings of the International Symposium on Hypothalamus and Endocrine Functions held in Quebec City, September 21-24, 1975' - title page verso. — Bibl. — Index.
ISBN 0-306-34003-8 : £23.63
(B77-18795)

612'.84 — Man. Sight
Freese, Arthur S. The miracle of vision / [by] Arthur S. Freese. — New York [etc.] ; London : Harper and Row, 1977. — x,181p : ill ; 22cm.
Bibl.: p.171-173. — Index.
ISBN 0-06-011371-5 : £4.50
(B77-30281)

612'.84 — Man. Sight. Theories, to 1630
Lindberg, David C. Theories of vision from al-Kindi to Kepler / [by] David C. Lindberg. — Chicago ; London : University of Chicago Press, 1976. — xii,324p : ill ; 24cm. — ([The Chicago history of science and medicine])
Bibl.: p.285-309. — Index.
ISBN 0-226-48234-0 : £14.95
(B77-00238)

612'.85 — Man. Hearing
Green, David Marvin. An introduction to hearing / [by] David M. Green. — Hillsdale : Erlbaum ; New York ; London [etc.] : Distributed by Wiley, 1976. — xi,353p : ill ; 24cm.
With answers. — Bibl. — Index.
ISBN 0-470-15188-9 : £12.70
(B77-00239)

612'.86 — Man. Nose. *Juvenile literature*
Tourneur, Dina Kathelyn. Caspar's nose / [by] Dina-Kathelyn Tourneur ; [translated from the French]. — London [etc.] : Burke, 1977. — [19]p : col ill ; 21cm. — (Caspar books)
Translation of: 'Le nez de Marmouset'. Tournai : Casterman, 1975.
ISBN 0-222-00449-5 : £1.00
ISBN 0-222-00455-x Pbk : £0.80
(B77-14248)

612'.86 — Smell. *Juvenile literature*
Pluckrose, Henry. Things to smell / by Henry Pluckrose ; photographs by G.W. Hales. — London [etc.] : F. Watts, 1977. — 32p : chiefly ill ; 18x22cm.
ISBN 0-85166-633-7 : £1.45
(B77-24245)

612'.87 — Taste. *Juvenile literature*
Pluckrose, Henry. Things to taste / by Henry Pluckrose ; photographs by G.W. Hales. — London [etc.] : F. Watts, 1977. — 32p : chiefly ill ; 18x22cm.
ISBN 0-85166-634-5 : £1.45
(B77-22611)

613 — HYGIENE
613 — Executives. Health
Wright, Henry Beric. Executive ease and dis-ease / [by] H. Beric Wright. — Revised ed. — London [etc.] : Pan Books, 1977. — 254p : ill ; 18cm.
Previous ed.: Epping : Gower Press, 1975. — Index.
ISBN 0-330-25181-3 Pbk : £0.90
Also classified at 616
(B77-33246)

613 — Man. Health
Family health. — London : Sphere, 1975. — 159p : ill(some col) ; 22cm. — ('Good housekeeping' family library)
Originally published: London : Ebury Press, 1973. — Index.
ISBN 0-7221-3947-0 Pbk : £0.95
(B77-19406)

Fassbender, William. You and your health / [by] William Fassbender. — New York ; London [etc.] : Wiley, 1977. — xvii,438p : ill(some col), facsims ; 26cm.
Bibl. — Index.
ISBN 0-471-60503-4 Pbk : £7.00
(B77-17516)

Positive health : designs for action. — 2nd ed. / [by] Mary K. Beyrer ... [et al.]. — Philadelphia : Lea and Febiger ; London : Kimpton, 1977. — ix,185p ; 24cm. — (Health education, physical education and recreation series)
Previous ed.: / by W.P. Cushman and others. Columbus, Ohio : C.E. Merrill Books, 1965. — Bibl. — Index.
ISBN 0-8121-0572-9 Pbk : £4.45
(B77-16896)

Taking care of your health. — London : Reader's Digest Association, 1976. — 40p : ill(some col) ; 27cm. — ('Reader's digest' basic guide)
'The text and illustrations in this book are taken from "'Reader's Digest' family health guide" ...', London : Reader's Digest Association, 1972.
ISBN 0-276-00134-6 Sd : £0.65
(B77-18157)

613 — Man. Health. *For West African students. Secondary school texts*
Ademuwagun, Z A. Certificate health science / [by] Z.A. Ademuwagun, D.T.D. Hughes, P.T. Marshall. — Cambridge [etc.] : Cambridge University Press, 1976. — iv,156p : ill, plan ; 25cm.
ISBN 0-521-21148-4 Pbk : £1.95
(B77-04829)

613 — Man. Health. *Secondary school texts*
Taylor, Ron. World health / by Ron Taylor. — London : Macdonald Educational, 1977. — [1], 24p : ill(chiefly col), facsim, col maps, ports(1 col) ; 27cm. — (Macdonald Educational colour units : world topics)
ISBN 0-356-05419-5 Sd : £0.75
(B77-24960)

613 — Man. Health. Variation. Social factors
Eugenics Society. *Annual Symposium, 12th, London, 1975.* Equalities and inequalities in health : proceedings of the Twelfth Annual Symposium of the Eugenics Society, London, 1975 / edited by C.O. Carter, John Peel. — London [etc.] : Academic Press, 1976. — x, 170p : ill, maps ; 24cm.
Bibl. — Index.
ISBN 0-12-161850-1 : £4.80
(B77-16897)

613 — Tribal societies. Health. Influence of Western civilization. *Conference proceedings*
Symposium on Health and Disease in Tribal Societies, *Ciba Foundation, 1976.* Health and disease in tribal societies / [editors Katherine Elliott and Julie Whelan]. — Amsterdam ; Oxford [etc.] : Elsevier [etc.], 1977. — viii, 344p : ill, maps ; 25cm. — (Ciba Foundation. Symposia : new series ; 49)
'Symposium on Health and Disease in Tribal Societies, held at the Ciba Foundation, London, 28th-30th September 1976' - p.vii. — Bibl. — Index.
ISBN 0-444-15271-7 : £16.71
Primary classification 614.4
(B77-30283)

613'.02'4613 — Man. Health. *For nursing*
Priest, Margery Alice. Modern textbook of personal and communal health for nurses : including bacteriology and the principles of asepsis / by M.A. Priest. — 5th ed. — London : Heinemann Medical, 1977. — x, 289p : ill, map ; 22cm.
Previous ed.: 1972. — Index.
ISBN 0-433-26204-4 Pbk : £3.50
(B77-31217)

613'.02'4613 — Man. Health & hygiene. *For nursing*
Diekelmann, Nancy. Primary health care of the well adult / [by] Nancy Diekelmann. — New York ; London [etc.] : McGraw-Hill, 1977. — xi,243p : ill, forms ; 23cm.
'A Blakiston publication'. — Bibl. — Index.
ISBN 0-07-016879-2 Pbk : £5.20
(B77-27885)

613'.04234 — Men. Health & hygiene
Diagram Group. Man's body : an owner's manual / by the Diagram Group. — London : Corgi, 1977. — [396]p : ill ; 18cm.
Editor: David Heidenstam. — Originally published: New York ; London : Paddington Press, 1976. — Index.
ISBN 0-552-10515-5 Pbk : £1.35
(B77-21887)

613'.04244 — Women. Health & hygiene
Diagram Group. Woman's body : an owner's manual / by the Diagram Group ; [editor Ann Kramer]. — New York ; London : Paddington Press, 1977. — [256]p : ill, maps ; 28cm.
Bibl.(1p.). — Index.
ISBN 0-448-22180-2 Pbk : £3.50
(B77-24246)

613'.0432 — Children, 2-5 years. Health. *Manuals. For parents*
Macdougall, Jean. People want healthy toddlers / [text by Jean Macdougall and William Thomson ; designed and illustrated by Pat McNeill]. — Hamilton (14 Beckford St., Hamilton ML3 0TA) : Lanarkshire Health Board, [1977]. — [16]p : chiefly ill(chiefly col) ; 21cm.
ISBN 0-905453-03-4 Sd : Unpriced
(B77-11828)

613'.0437 — Middle aged persons. Health. *Manuals*
Burkitt, Ann. Life begins at forty : how to make sure you enjoy middle age / [by] Ann Burkitt ; illustrated by Val Biro. — London : Hutchinson [for] the Health Education Council, 1977. — 109p : ill(chiefly col) ; 19cm.
ISBN 0-09-129101-1 Pbk : £0.70
(B77-21888)

613'.0438 — Old persons. Health
Gardner, Mary. People 'live' longer / [text by Mary Gardner and Bill Fulton ; designed and illustrated by Roy Petrie]. — Hamilton [Lanarkshire] (14 Beckford St., Hamilton, [Lanarkshire] ML3 0TA) : Lanarkshire Health Board, [1977]. — [12]p : chiefly ill ; 21cm.
Sd : £0.06
(B77-18158)

613'.07 — Health education. *Great Britain*
Tones, B K. Effectiveness and efficiency in health education : a review of theory and practice / [by] B.K. Tones. — [Leeds] ([James Graham College, Lawns House, Chapel La., Farnley, Leeds LS12 5ET]) : Leeds Polytechnic [for] the Department of Community Medicine and General Practice, University of Leeds, [1977]. — [2],100,4 leaves,plate : ill ; 30cm. — (Leeds health education ISSN 0305-6074)
'Consultative Paper produced for the Scottish Health Education Unit'. — Bibl.: leaves 1-4 (3rd sequence).
Sd : £2.65
(B77-18159)

613'.07 — Health education. Organisations. *Great Britain. Health Education Council. Reports, surveys. Serials*
Health Education Council. Annual report / the Health Education Council. — [London] : [The Council].
1976-7. — [1977]. — [1],29p : ill(some col), facsim, map ; 30cm.
Sd : Unpriced
(B77-27108)

613'.07'1073 — Schools. Health education. Teaching methods. *United States*
Kime, Robert E. Health instruction : an action approach / [by] Robert E. Kime, Richard G. Schlaadt, Leonard E. Tritsch. — Englewood Cliffs ; London [etc.] : Prentice-Hall, 1977. — xiv,365p : ill, forms ; 24cm.
Index.
ISBN 0-13-385252-0 : £9.55
(B77-17517)

613'.07'1241 — Secondary schools. Health education. *Great Britain. Reports, surveys*
Schools Council Working Party on Health Education. Health education in secondary schools : an account of current practice / prepared by the Schools Council Working Party on Health Education and its teachers' study group ; with the support of the Health Education Council. — London : Evans Bros : Methuen, 1976. — 83p ; 21cm. — (Schools Council. Working papers ; 57 ISSN 0533-1668)
ISBN 0-423-50370-7 Pbk : £1.60
(B77-29449)

613'.07'1273 — Secondary schools. Health education. Teaching methods. *United States*
Willgoose, Carl Edward. Health teaching in secondary schools / [by] Carl E. Willgoose. — 2nd ed. — Philadelphia ; London [etc.] : Saunders, 1977. — ii-xii,457p : ill, facsims, forms, maps ; 27cm.
Previous ed.: 1972. — Bibl. — List of teaching aids: p.379-406. — Index.
ISBN 0-7216-9370-9 : £11.25
(B77-14249)

613.1 — HYGIENE. NATURAL ENVIRONMENTS
613.1'2 — Spas. *England, to ca 1900*
Searle, Muriel Vivienne. Spas and watering places / [by] Muriel V. Searle. — Tunbridge Wells : Midas Books, 1977. — 160p : ill, facsims, port ; 26cm. — (Heritage of the past)
Ill. on lining papers. — Index.
ISBN 0-85936-072-5 : £6.50
(B77-21889)

613.1'9 — Man. Health. Effects of ultraviolet radiation of sun
Giese, Arthur Charles. Living with our sun's ultraviolet rays / [by] Arthur C. Giese. — New York ; London : Plenum Press, 1976. — xii, 185p : ill ; 24cm.
Bibl. — Index.
ISBN 0-306-30883-5 : £12.29
(B77-20301)

613.2 — HYGIENE. DIETETICS
613.2 — Babies. Diet
Mac Keith, Ronald Charles. Infant feeding and feeding difficulties. — 5th ed. / [by] Ronald Mac Keith, Christopher Wood ; with the editorial assistance of the late Sydney Woodward. — Edinburgh [etc.] : Churchill Livingstone, 1977. — xii,330p : ill ; 22cm.
Previous ed.: London : Churchill, 1971. — Bibl. — Index.
ISBN 0-443-01474-4 Pbk : £5.95
(B77-15873)

613.2 — Fasting. *Manuals*
Cott, Alan. Fasting as a way of life / by Alan Cott with Jerome Agel and Eugene Boe. — Toronto ; London [etc.] : Bantam, 1977. — ix, 131p ; 18cm.
Bibl.: p.117-130.
ISBN 0-553-10865-4 Pbk : £0.65
(B77-27109)

613.2 — Man. Diet
Durrant, Merril. Eat well and keep healthy / [by] Merril Durrant. — London : Macdonald Educational, 1977. — 96p : ill(some col), 2 maps, 2 ports(1 col) ; 21cm. — (Macdonald guidelines)
Bibl.: p.90-91. — Index.
ISBN 0-356-06015-2 Pbk : £1.00
(B77-20302)

MacAdie, Diana. Healthy eating / [by] Diana MacAdie. — London : Paul, 1977. — 200p,[4]p of plates : ill(some col) ; 23cm.
'Based on the Tyne Tees Television series'. — Bibl.: p.198. — Index.
ISBN 0-09-131260-4 : £4.95
ISBN 0-09-131261-2 Pbk : £1.95
(B77-30282)

613.2 — Man. Health. Effects of diet
Williams, Roger John. The wonderful world within you : your inner nutritional environment / [by] Roger J. Williams. — Toronto [etc.] ; London : Bantam, 1977. — xi, 239p : ill ; 18cm.
Index.
ISBN 0-553-10411-x Pbk : £0.75
(B77-26332)

613.2 — Man. Health. Effects of diet. *Vegetarian viewpoints*
Mellor, Constance. How to be healthy, wealthy and wise / by Constance Mellor. — London : Daniel, 1977. — 116p : port ; 22cm.
Bibl.: p.115-116.
ISBN 0-85207-138-8 Pbk : £1.98
(B77-11230)

613.2 — Man. Health. Role of diet. *For adolescent girls*
Gillett, Cynthia. Eating for health and pleasure / [by] Cynthia Gillett. — Glasgow [etc.] : Blackie, 1977. — [2],36,[1]p : ill ; 22cm. — (Home economics topic books)
ISBN 0-216-90181-2 Sd : Unpriced
(B77-24247)

613.2'025'41 — Dietitians. *Great Britain. Directories*
The **dietitians** register. — [London] ([York House, Westminster Bridge Rd, SE1 7UH]) : [Council for Professions Supplementary to Medicine for] the Dietitians Board.
1977. — [1977]. — 79 leaves ; 21x30cm.
Sd : £1.00
ISSN 0305-3989
(B77-33820)

613.2'5 — Children. Physical fitness. Slimming. Diet. *For parents*
Mortimer, Phyllis. Overweight children / by Phyllis Mortimer. — London : British Medical Association, [1976]. — 30p : ill(some col) ; 19cm. — (A 'Family doctor' booklet)
ISBN 0-7279-0020-x Sd : £0.25
(B77-01486)

613.2'5 — Physical fitness. Slimming
Let's start to slim / by the editors of 'Slimmer magazine'. — London : Ward Lock, 1977. — 96p : ill(chiefly col) ; 24cm.
Index.
ISBN 0-7063-5286-6 Pbk : £1.50
(B77-15874)

613.2'5 — Physical fitness. Slimming. *Reports, surveys*
'Which?' slimming guide. — 3rd revised impression. — [Hertford] : Consumers' Association, 1977. — [1],76,[1]p : ill(some col) ; 23cm.
This ed. originally published: 1976.
Pbk : £1.95
ISBN 0-85202-122-4
(B77-17518)

613.2'5 — Physical fitness. Slimming. Diet
Maislen, Ruth. Eat, think & be thinner : the 'Weigh of Life' way / by Ruth Maislen, Thelma Kadish & Nan Lerner. — New York : Bold Face Books [etc.] ; London : Distributed by Ward Lock, 1976. — 190p : 2 ill, form ; 23cm.
Text on lining paper. — Index.
ISBN 0-7061-2513-4 : £3.95
(B77-11829)

Yudkin, John. A-Z of slimming / [by] John Yudkin ; with drawings by Scoular Anderson. — London : Davis-Poynter, 1977. — 166p : ill ; 23cm.
'... an expansion of a series of articles ... [written] for "Slimming and nutrition"' - Preface.
ISBN 0-7067-0213-1 : £3.50
(B77-33247)

613.2'5 — Women. Physical fitness. Slimming. *Periodicals*
Slim with beauty. — [London] ([12 Paul St., E.C.2]) : [Illustrated Publications Co. Ltd].
No.1- ; June 1976-. — [1976]-. — ill(some col), ports(some col) ; 21cm.
Monthly. — 78p. in 1st issue.
Sd : £0.30
ISSN 0309-5002
(B77-09037)

613.2'5'05 — Physical fitness. Slimming. *Periodicals*
Successful slimming. — London : IPC Magazine.
[No.1]- ; [1976]-. — 1976-. — ill(some col), ports ; 28cm.
Six issues a year. — Cover title: 'Woman's own' successful slimming. — 78p. in Feb./Mar. 1977 issue.
Sd : £0.30
ISSN 0309-6297
(B77-15302)

Weight watchers magazine. — London (Morgan-Grampian Ltd, 30 Calderwood St., SE18 0QH) : 'Weight Watchers Magazine'.
Issue 1- ; May 1977-. — [1977]-. — ill(some col), ports ; 30cm.
Monthly. — 64p. in 1st issue.
Sd : £0.35
ISSN 0309-8095
(B77-24248)

613.2'6 — Man. Diet. Role of honey
Cartland, Barbara. The magic of honey / [by] Barbara Cartland. — New and revised ed. — London : Corgi, 1976. — 140p ; 18cm.
Previous ed. 1970. — Index.
ISBN 0-552-10336-5 Pbk : £0.65
(B77-05437)

613.2'6 — Man. Health. Effects of natural foods
Wheatley, Michael. A way of living as a means of survival : an encyclopaedia of natural health / [by] Michael Wheatley. — London : Corgi, 1977. — 380p ; 18cm.
Index.
ISBN 0-552-10337-3 Pbk : £1.00
(B77-15303)

613.2'6 — Vegetarianism. *Periodicals*
New vegetarian. — [Altrincham] ([Parkdale, Dunham Rd, Altrincham, Cheshire WA14 4QG]) : [Vegetarian Society (UK) Ltd].
Supersedes: The vegetarian.
Revised series, no.1- ; Jan. 1977-. — 1977-. — ill, ports ; 30cm.
Monthly. — 36p. in 6th issue.
Sd : £0.15
ISSN 0309-9253
(B77-33821)

613.2'6 — Vegetarianism. Organisations. *Directories*
The **international** vegetarian health food handbook. — Altrincham (Parkdale, Dunham Rd, Altrincham, Cheshire WA14 4QG) : Vegetarian Society of the United Kingdom.
1977-78 / edited by Joanna Lawton. — [1976]. — 232p : ill ; 19cm.
Previously published: as 'The vegetarian health food handbook'. — Bibl.: p.17-19. — Index.
ISBN 0-900774-12-6 Pbk : £0.90
(B77-04199)

613.2'8 — Physical fitness. Slimming. High-protein diet. *Manuals*
Moyle, Alan. Slimming naturally with the high protein diet / by Alan Moyle. — Wellingborough : Thorsons, 1977. — 95p ; 18cm. — (Nature's way)
ISBN 0-7225-0384-9 Pbk : £0.75
(B77-33248)

613.2'8 — Physical fitness. Slimming. Low carbohydrate diet. *Manuals*
Manley, Derek. The diet book for diet haters / [by] Derek Manley. — New and revised ed. — London : Corgi, 1976. — 109p ; 18cm.
Previous ed.: London : Transworld, 1967.
ISBN 0-552-10339-x Pbk : £0.50
(B77-05438)

West, Ruth. Stop dieting! start losing! / [by] Ruth West. — Revised ed. — Toronto [etc.] ; London : Bantam, 1977. — xiii,191p ; 18cm.
Previous ed.: New York : Dutton, 1956. — Index.
ISBN 0-552-67242-4 Pbk : £0.75
(B77-24249)

613.5/6 — HYGIENE. ARTIFICIAL ENVIRONMENTS
613.6'2 — Enzymatic detergents industries. Personnel. Health. *Great Britain. Reports, surveys*
Soap and Detergent Industry Association. The medical review of workers in the enzymatic washing product industry in the United Kingdom, 1969 to July 1975 / the Soap and Detergent Industry Association. — [Hayes, Middx] ([P.O. Box 9, Hayes Gate House, Hayes, Middx UB4 OJD]) : [The Association], 1976. — [3],19,[8]leaves : 2 ill ; 30cm.
ISBN 0-905755-00-6 Sp : £10.00
(B77-01487)

613.6'2 — Industrial health. Hazards
Peterson, Jack E. Industrial health / [by] Jack E. Peterson. — Englewood Cliffs ; London [etc.] : Prentice-Hall, 1977. — xvii,347p : ill ; 25cm.
Index.
ISBN 0-13-459552-1 : £17.55
(B77-21890)

613.6'2 — Slaughterhouses. Industrial health. *Great Britain*
Baylis-Stranks, J W. Occupational health and safety in slaughter houses / by J.W. Baylis-Stranks. — [London] ([19 Grosvenor Place, SW1X 7HU]) : Environmental Health Officers Association], [1976]. — [1],61[i.e.63]p ; 31cm. — (Environmental Health Officers Association. Monograph series)
Pbk : Unpriced
Also classified at 614.8'52
(B77-31218)

613.6'2'0941 — Industrial health. *Great Britain. Periodicals*
Hazards bulletin. — London : British Society for Social Responsibility in Science [Work Hazards Group].
[No.] 1-. — [1976]-. — ill ; 30cm.
Five issues a year. — 12p. in issue no.6.
Sd : £0.20
ISSN 0140-0525
Primary classification 614.8'52'0941
(B77-26335)

613.6'2'0941 — Industrial health. *Great Britain. Reports, surveys. Serials*
Great Britain. *Factory Inspectorate.* Annual report [of] HM Chief Inspector of Factories. — London : H.M.S.O.
1974. — [1975]. — xiii,133p,[8]p of plates : ill ; 25cm. — (Cmnd.6322)
Bibl.: p.129-130.
ISBN 0-10-163220-7 Pbk : £2.05
Also classified at 614.8'52'0941
(B77-04830)

Industry & services : health and safety : a report of the work of the HM Factory Inspectorate / Health and Safety Executive. — London : H.M.S.O.
1975 : incorporating the annual reports of HM Inspector of Railways and HM Inspector of Explosives. — 1977. — 92p,[2]p of plates : ill ; 30cm.
Supersedes: Annual report of HM Chief Inspector of Factories.
ISBN 0-11-881112-6 Pbk : £2.00
Also classified at 614.8'52'0941
(B77-10377)

613.6'2'09416 — Industrial health. *Northern Ireland. Reports, surveys. Serials*
Northern Ireland. *Chief Inspector of Factories.* Report of the Chief Inspector [of Factories] ... — Belfast : H.M.S.O.
1974. — 1976. — 49p,fold leaf : ill ; 25cm.
ISBN 0-337-07118-7 Sd : £0.75
Also classified at 614.8'52'09416
(B77-25659)

613.6'6 — Self-defence by women. *Manuals*
Conroy, Mary. Common sense self-defense : a practical manual for students and teachers / [by] Mary Conroy, Edward R. Ritvo. — Saint Louis : Mosby ; London : Distributed by Kimpton, 1977. — xiii,146p : ill, forms ; 24cm.
ISBN 0-8016-1027-3 Pbk : £4.80
(B77-20303)

Hudson, Kathleen. Every woman's guide to self defence / [by] Kathleen Hudson. — Glasgow [etc.] : Collins, 1977. — 3-93p : ill ; 22cm.
ISBN 0-00-435003-0 : £2.95
ISBN 0-00-435002-2 Pbk : £1.25
(B77-20304)

613.6'9 — Aeroplanes. Accidents. Survival
Barker, Ralph. Survival in the sky / [by] Ralph Barker. — London [etc.] : Pan Books, 1977. — 206p,[8]p of plates : ill, map, ports ; 18cm.
Originally published: London : Kimber, 1976.
ISBN 0-330-25109-0 Pbk : £0.60
(B77-21159)

613.69 — Survival. *Juvenile literature*
Survival / [planned and edited by Beverley Birch]. — London : Macdonald Educational, 1977. — 47p : ill(some col) ; 29cm. — (Conquests of nature)
Index.
ISBN 0-356-05555-8 : £2.00
(B77-27110)

613.6'9'0247965 — Survival. Techniques. *For mountaineering. Manuals*
Brown, Terence Henry Charles. The Spur book of survival and rescue / by Terry Brown and Rob Hunter. — Bourne End : Spurbooks, 1977. — 63p : ill, chart, map ; 19cm. — (A Spur book venture guide)
ISBN 0-904978-72-9 Pbk : £0.90
(B77-27111)

613.7 — PHYSICAL FITNESS
Morehouse, Laurence Englemohr. Total fitness in 30 minutes a week / [by] Laurence E. Morehouse and Leonard Gross. — St Albans : Mayflower, 1977. — 189p ; 18cm.
Originally published: as 'Total fitness in 30 minutes a week', New York : Simon and Schuster, 1975 ; and as 'Total fitness in thiry minutes a week', London : Hart-Davis MacGibbon, 1976.
ISBN 0-583-12584-0 Pbk : £0.75
(B77-20305)

613.7 — Physical education
Barrow, Harold Marion. Man and movement : principles of physical education / [by] Harold M. Barrow. — 2nd ed. — Philadelphia : Lea and Febiger ; London : Kimpton, 1977. — xii, 396p : ill ; 27cm.
Previous ed.: published as 'Man and his movement'. 1971. — Bibl. — Index.
ISBN 0-8121-0599-0 : £9.80
(B77-33249)

Encyclopedia of physical education, fitness and sports / Thomas K. Cureton, Jr, series editor. — Reading, Mass. ; London [etc.] : Addison-Wesley.
In 5 vols.
[Vol.1] : Sports, dance, and related activities / volume editor Reuben B. Frost. — 1977. — xvii,973p : ill ; 24cm.
'Sponsored by the American Alliance for Health, Physical Education and Recreation'. — Bibl. — Index.
ISBN 0-201-01077-1 : £20.00
(B77-26333)

613.7 — Physical education. *Philosophical perspectives*
Zeigler, Earle Frederick. Physical education and sport philosophy / [by] Earle F. Zeigler. — [New ed.]. — Englewood Cliffs ; London [etc.] : Prentice-Hall, 1977. — xii,260p : ill ; 24cm. — (The Prentice-Hall foundations of physical education and sport series)
Previous ed.: published as 'Problems in the history and philosophy of physical education and sport'. 1968. — Bibl.: p.241-255. — Index.
ISBN 0-13-668731-8 : £7.95
(B77-12467)

613.7 — Physical education. *Soviet Union. Reports, surveys*
Speak, Michael Arthur. Physical education, recreation and sport in the USSR / by M.A. Speak and V.H. Ambler. — Lancaster (Bailrigg, Lancaster LA1 4YW) : Centre for Physical Education, University of Lancaster, 1976. — [3] ,92,xxi,[1]p : ill, form ; 21cm.
Bibl.: p.xiii-xviii.
ISBN 0-901699-37-3 Pbk : £1.50
Also classified at 796'.0947
(B77-02336)

613.7 — Physical fitness. *Manuals*
Balaskas, Arthur. Bodylife / [by] Arthur Balaskas ; foreword by R.D. Laing. — London : Sidgwick and Jackson, 1977. — 192p : ill ; 26cm.
Index.
ISBN 0-283-98309-4 : £6.50
ISBN 0-283-98368-x Pbk : £3.50
(B77-18160)

Hockey, Robert Victor. Physical fitness : the pathway to healthful living / [by] Robert V. Hockey. — 3rd ed. — Saint Louis : Mosby ; London : Distributed by Kimpton, 1977. — ix, 198p : ill, forms ; 23cm.
Fill-in book. — Pages perforated at inside edge. — Previous ed.: 1973. — Bibl. — Index.
ISBN 0-8016-2215-8 Pbk : £5.00
(B77-33822)

Shepro, David. Complete conditioning : the no-nonsense guide to fitness and good health / [by] David Shepro, Howard G. Knuttgen. — Reading, Mass. ; London [etc.] : Addison-Wesley, [1977]. — iii-xv,172p : ill ; 22cm.
Published in the United States: 1975. — Bibl.: p.162-165. — Index.
ISBN 0-201-03786-6 : £4.75
(B77-11830)

613.7 — Physical fitness. Ch'i kung. *Manuals*
Siou, Lily. Ch'i Kung : the art of mastering the unseen life force / [by] Lily Siou. — Rutland, Vt : Tuttle ; London : [Distributed by] Prentice-Hall, 1975. — [16],173p : ill ; 26cm.
Originally published: Honolulu : Lily Siou's School of the Six Chinese Arts, 1973.
ISBN 0-8048-1169-5 : Unpriced
(B77-11831)

613.7 — Physical fitness. Hatha-yoga
Folan, Lilias M. Lilias, yoga and you / by Lilias M. Folan. — Toronto [etc.] ; London : Bantam, 1976. — [8],136p : ill, ports ; 18cm.
Originally published: Cincinnati : WCET-TV, 1972. — Bibl.: p.25-26.
ISBN 0-552-62305-9 Pbk : £0.50
(B77-06098)

Gibbs, John, *b.1917.* Simple yoga / [by] John Gibbs. — Sittingbourne (4 Merlin Close, Sittingbourne, Kent ME10 4TY) : The author, [1976]. — [2],29,[1]p : ill ; 21cm.
Sd : £0.30
(B77-27886)

Hoare, Sophy. Yoga / [by] Sophy Hoare. — London : Macdonald Educational, 1977. — 96p : ill(some col), ports ; 21cm. — (Macdonald guidelines)
Bibl.: p.89-90. — Index.
ISBN 0-356-06012-8 Pbk : £1.00
(B77-15304)

Kirschner, M J. Yoga for health and vitality / [by] M.J. Kirschner ; translated from the German by Lilian K. Donat. — London : Allen and Unwin, 1977. — 3-175p : ill ; 21cm.
Translation of: 'Die Kunst sich selbst zu verjüngen'. Krefeld : Agis, 1956. — Index.
ISBN 0-04-149042-8 : £4.50
ISBN 0-04-149043-6 Pbk : Unpriced
(B77-06099)

Volin, Michael. Yoga over forty / [by] Michael Volin and Nancy Phelan. — London : Sphere, 1977. — 158p,[16]p of plates : ill ; 18cm.
Originally published: London : Pelham, 1965.
ISBN 0-7221-8742-4 Pbk : £0.75
(B77-29450)

Volin, Michael. Yoga over forty / [by] Michael Volin and Nancy Phelan. — London : Sphere, 1976. — 158p,[16]p of plates : ill ; 18cm.
Originally published: London : Pelham, 1965.
ISBN 0-7221-8750-5 Pbk : £0.65
(B77-00240)

Zorn, William. Easy yoga exercises / [by] William Zorn. — London : Sphere, 1977. — 95p : ill ; 18cm.
Originally published: as 'The easy yoga exercise book'. London : Pelham, 1971.
ISBN 0-7221-9435-8 Pbk : £0.65
(B77-31219)

613.7 — Physical fitness. Hatha-yoga. *Manuals*
Netscher, Brian. Yoga : the happy way to live / [by] Brian Netscher ; drawings by Max Lenvers. — [London] ([40 Tavistock St., WC2E 7PB]) : Chancerel Publishers Ltd ; [London] : Barrie and Jenkins, 1977. — 2-91p : ill, 2 ports ; 21cm. — (Action books)
Ill. on lining papers.
ISBN 0-905703-05-7 : £1.75
(B77-24250)

613.7'042 — Boys. Physical fitness. *Manuals*
Challenger, Robert. Boy of tomorrow / by Robert Challenger. — Boscastle (Boscastle, Cornwall) : North Wind Books, 1974. — 32p ; 19cm.
ISBN 0-905817-00-1 Sd : £0.60
(B77-04200)

613.7'045 — Pregnant women. Physical fitness. Hatha-yoga
Crisp, Tony. Yoga and childbirth / [by] Tony Crisp. — London : Sphere, 1976. — 142p : ill ; 18cm.
Originally published: Wellingborough: Thorsons, 1975. — Index.
ISBN 0-7221-2686-7 Pbk : £0.65
(B77-01488)

613.7'07 — Education. Role of physical education. *France & Great Britain. Conference proceedings*
The **place** of sport in education : report of an Anglo-French Symposium held at the Crystal Palace National Sports Centre, September 6th-10th 1976 in conjunction with the French State Department for Youth and Sport. — London (10 Nottingham Place, W1M 4AX) : Physical Education Association of Great Britain and Northern Ireland, 1976. — [2],182p : forms ; 30cm.
'Comparative studies in physical education : France'. — Bibl.
ISBN 0-900985-13-5 Sp : £3.00
Primary classification 796'.07
(B77-14867)

613.7'07 — Educational institutions. Curriculum subjects: Physical education. *United States. For teaching*
Physical education : foundations / Robert N. Singer, editor. — New York ; London [etc.] : Holt, Rinehart and Winston, 1976. — xiv, 481p : ill ; 25cm.
Bibl.: p.465-471. — Index.
ISBN 0-03-010386-x : £6.75
(B77-02337)

613.7'07 — Physical education. *United States. Forecasts*
Physical education : a view toward the future / edited by Raymond Welsh. — Saint Louis : Mosby ; London : Distributed by Kimpton, 1977. — xvii,222p : ill ; 23cm.
Bibl. — Index.
ISBN 0-8016-5379-7 Pbk : £6.10
(B77-21891)

613.7'07 — Teachers. Professional education. Curriculum subjects: Physical education. Evaluation. *Great Britain. Conference proceedings*
National Association of Teachers in Further and Higher Education. *Physical Education Section. Conference, Madeley College, 1976.* Evaluation in physical education : report of the NATFHE (formerly ATCDE) Physical Education Section 1976 conference held at Madeley College, nr Crewe / edited by Irene K. Glaister. — Milton-under-Wychwood (c/o Mrs I.K. Glaister, Fardon House, Frog La., Milton-under-Wychwood, Oxon) : The Section, [1977]. — [1],90p : ill, forms ; 21cm.
ISBN 0-904707-04-0 Sd : £2.20
(B77-13055)

613.7'07'101812 — Schools. Curriculum subjects: Physical education. *Western world. Sociological perspectives*
Saunders, E D. Social investigation in physical education and sport / [by] E.D. Saunders, G.B. White. — London : Lepus Books, 1977. — 103p : ill, forms ; 26cm.
Bibl.: p.96-99. — Index.
ISBN 0-86019-030-7 : £5.00
(B77-12468)

613.7'07'1041 — Schools. Curriculum subjects: Physical education. *Great Britain. For teaching*
Movement studies and physical education : a handbook for teachers / edited by J.E. Kane. — London [etc.] : Routledge and Kegan Paul, 1977. — xii,222p ; 22cm.
Bibl. — Index.
ISBN 0-7100-8775-6 : £5.75 : CIP rev.
ISBN 0-7100-8684-9 Pbk : £2.95
(B77-23444)

613.7'07'1073 — Educational institutions. Curriculum subjects: Physical education. Administration. *United States*
Daughtrey, Greyson. Physical education and intramural programs : organization and administration / [by] Greyson Daughtrey, John B. Woods. — 2nd ed. — Philadelphia ; London [etc.] : Saunders, 1976. — ii-xii,547p : ill, facsims, forms, plans ; 27cm.
Previous ed.: 1971. — Bibl. — Index.
ISBN 0-7216-2884-2 : £11.50
(B77-05439)

613.7'07'1273 — Secondary schools. Curriculum subjects: Physical education. Teaching. *United States. Urban regions*
Ridini, Leonard M. Physical education for inner city secondary schools / [by] Leonard M. Ridini, John E. Madden. — New York [etc.] ; London : Harper and Row, [1976]. — xi,174p : ill, forms ; 21cm. — (Issues in contemporary physical education)
Published in the United States: 1975. — Bibl. — Index.
ISBN 0-06-045406-7 Pbk : £4.15
(B77-02338)

613.7'1 — Physical fitness. Exercises
Carruthers, Malcolm. F-40 fitness on 40 minutes a week / [by] Malcolm Carruthers and Alistair Murray. — London : Futura Publications, 1976. — 128p : ill ; 18cm.
ISBN 0-86007-324-6 Pbk : £0.50
(B77-09038)

The **complete** head to toe exercise book : get fitter, feel better / [edited by Linda Fox]. — London [etc.] : Marshall Cavendish, 1977. — 184p : col ill ; 29cm.
'This material was first published by Marshall Cavendish Limited in the publication "Come Alive"' - title page verso.
ISBN 0-85685-252-x : £4.95
(B77-33823)

Walsh, Barry. Fitness the footballers' way / [by] Barry Walsh & Peter Douglas. — London ([17 Oakley Rd, N.1]) : Pierrot Publishing Ltd, 1976. — 125p : ill, forms ; 20cm.
Index.
ISBN 0-905310-00-4 Pbk : £1.25
(B77-01489)

Willis, Norman. The Spur book of fitness for the family / by Norman Willis. — Bourne End : Spurbooks, 1977. — 63p : ill ; 19cm. — (A Spur book venture guide)
ISBN 0-904978-66-4 Pbk : £0.90
(B77-21160)

613.7'1 — Physical fitness. Isometrics. Exercises
Johns, Edgar. Isometrics for muscle power / by Edgar Johns. — Hove ([P.O. Box 422, Valance Rd, Hove, E. Sussex BN3 2DU]) : Valldaro Publications, 1974. — 29p : ill, form ; 21cm.
ISBN 0-86077-006-0 : £0.75
(B77-00241)

613.7'1 — Physical fitness. Water exercises. Use of inflatable armbands
Kent, Allegra. Allegra Kent's water beauty book / text and captions by Allegra Kent ; introduction by Edward Villella ; exercise photos by Hank O'Neal, ballet photos by Martha Swope. — New York : St Martin's Press ; London : St James Press, 1976. — ii-xii, 163p : chiefly ill, ports ; 25cm.
ISBN 0-900997-82-6 : £5.50
(B77-02339)

613.7'9 — Physical fitness. Massage. *Manuals*
Inkeles, Gordon. The art of sensual massage / by Gordon Inkeles & Murray Todris ; with photographs by Robert Foothorap. — London : Mandala Books, 1977. — [11],162p : ill, port ; 25cm.
Originally published: San Francisco : Straight Arrow Books, 1972 ; London : Allen and Unwin, 1973.
ISBN 0-04-613032-2 Pbk : £2.95
(B77-19407)

613.7'9 — Physical fitness. Relaxation. Exercises
Mitchell, Laura. Simple relaxation : the physiological method for easing tension / [by] Laura Mitchell ; with drawings by Michael Bartlett. — London : J. Murray, 1977. — 126p : ill, ports ; 23cm.
Bibl.: p.124. — Index.
ISBN 0-7195-3425-9 : £3.95
ISBN 0-7195-3373-2 Pbk : £1.95
(B77-19408)

613.8 — ADDICTIONS AND HEALTH
613.8'1 — Alcoholic drinks. Consumption. Health aspects
Teachers' Advisory Council on Alcohol and Drug Education. Alcohol : basic facts / [script by TACADE staff]. — Manchester (2 Mount St., Manchester M2 5NG) : Teachers' Advisory Council on Alcohol and Drug Education, [1977]. — Folder([10]p) : ill ; 22x10cm.
ISBN 0-905954-01-7 : Unpriced
(B77-11832)

613.8'5 — Cigarette smoking. Stopping. *Manuals*
Gillie, Oliver. How to stop smoking or at least smoke less / [by] Oliver Gillie ; foreword by Charles Fletcher. — London [etc.] : Pan Books, 1977. — 3-129p : ill ; 18cm.
ISBN 0-330-25255-0 Pbk : £0.70
(B77-28647)

Olshavsky, Richard W. No more butts : a psychologist's approach to quitting cigarettes / [by] Richard W. Olshavsky ; drawings by Jim Hull. — Bloomington ; London : Indiana University Press, 1977. — ix,181p : ill ; 24cm.
Bibl.: p.169. — Index.
ISBN 0-253-15832-x : £7.50
(B77-28648)

613.9 — BIRTH CONTROL AND SEX HYGIENE
613.9'4 — Contraceptives. *Conference proceedings*
Contraceptives of the Future *(Conference), Royal Society, 1976.* Contraceptives of the future : a Royal Society discussion organized by R.V. Short, F.R.S. and D.T. Baird, held on 18 and 19 February 1976. — London : Royal Society, 1976. — [4],224p,plate : ill, map ; 26cm.
'... Royal Society Discussion Meeting on "Contraceptives of the Future" ...' - jacket. — 'First published in "Proceedings of the Royal Society of London", series B, volume 195 (no.1118), pages 1-224' - title page verso. — Bibl.
ISBN 0-85403-087-5 : £5.25
(B77-07922)

613.9'4 — Man. Contraception
Barnes, *Dame* **Josephine.** Essentials of family planning / [by] Josephine Barnes. — Oxford [etc.] : Blackwell Scientific, 1976. — xi,139p : ill ; 19cm.
Bibl. — Index.
ISBN 0-632-00348-0 Pbk : £2.50
(B77-01490)

Hubbard, Charles William. Family planning education / [by] Charles William Hubbard. — 2nd ed. — Saint Louis : Mosby ; London : Distributed by Kimpton, 1977. — xv,241p : ill ; 23cm.
Previous ed.: 1973. — Index.
ISBN 0-8016-2298-0 Pbk : £4.80
(B77-17519)

613.9'4 — Man. Contraception. *For general practice*
Oldershaw, K Leslie. Contraception, abortion and sterilization in general practice / [by] K. Leslie Oldershaw. — London : Kimpton, 1975. — 288p : ill ; 24cm.
Bibl. — Index.
ISBN 0-85313-790-0 : £6.50
(B77-18796)

613.9'4 — Man. Contraception. *Manuals*
Family Planning Association. Straight facts about sex and birth control / [Family Planning Association]. — London : The Association, [1976]. — Folder(10[i.e.12]p) : ill ; 22cm.
ISBN 0-903289-08-3 : £1.30
(B77-03027)

613.9'4 — Man. Eugenics. Organisations. *Germany. Lebensborn Eingetragener Verein, to 1945*
Henry, Clarissa. Children of the SS / [by] Clarissa Henry & Marc Hillel ; translated from the French by Eric Mosbacher. — London : Hutchinson, 1976. — 256p,[16]p of plates : ill, ports ; 23cm.
Translation of: 'Au nom de la race'. Paris : Fayard, 1975. — Bibl.: p.245-248. — Index.
ISBN 0-09-127960-7 : £4.75
(B77-18161)

613.9'4'05 — Man. Contraception. *Periodicals*
Fertility and contraception. — London (27 Mortimer St., W1N 7RJ) : Family Planning Information Service.
Quarterly. — 23p. in 1st issue.
Vol.1, no.1- ; Jan. 1977-. — 1977-. — ill ; 21cm.
Sd : £2.00 yearly
ISSN 0309-4545
(B77-11231)

613.9'4'072 — Man. Contraception. Research
Greep, Roy Orval. Reproduction and human welfare : a challenge to research : a review of the reproductive sciences and contraceptive development / [by] Roy O. Greep, Marjorie A. Koblinsky, Frederick S. Jaffe. — Cambridge, Mass. ; London : M.I.T. Press, 1976. — xxi, 622p : ill ; 24cm.
Bibl. — Index.
ISBN 0-262-07067-7 : £7.50
Also classified at 612.6'007'2
(B77-18797)

613.9'4'0924 — Man. Contraception. Stopes, Marie. *Biographies*
Hall, Ruth. Marie Stopes : a biography / [by] Ruth Hall. — London : Deutsch, 1977. — 351p,[12]p of plates : facsims, ports ; 25cm.
Bibl.: p.341-344. — Index.
ISBN 0-233-96879-2 : £5.95
(B77-24251)

613.9'42 — Man. Sterilisation
Morris, Norman, *b.1920.* Sterilization as a means of birth control in men and women / [by] Norman Morris and Humphrey Arthure. — London : Owen, 1976. — 125p,[4]p of plates : ill ; 22cm.
Index.
ISBN 0-7206-0363-3 : £4.50
(B77-06100)

613.9'42 — Women. Sterilisation. Techniques. *Conference proceedings*
Workshop on Advances in Female Sterilization Techniques, *Minneapolis, 1975.* Advances in female sterilization techniques : proceedings of a Workshop on Advances in Female Sterilization Techniques held in Minneapolis, Minnesota, United States of America, sponsored by the Program for Applied Research on Fertility Regulation, Northwestern University / edited by John J. Sciarra, William Droegemueller, J. Joseph Speidel. — Hagerstown [etc.] ; London : Harper and Row, 1976. — xx,284p : ill ; 24cm. — (Program for Applied Research on Fertility Regulation. PARFR series on fertility regulation)
Index.
ISBN 0-06-142366-1 : £8.75
(B77-28649)

613.9'432 — Oral contraceptives. *State-of-the-art reviews*
Oral contraceptives. — Montreal ; Lancaster : Eden Press ; [Edinburgh] : Distributed by Churchill Livingstone. — (Annual research reviews ISSN 0703-1629)
[Vol.1] : [1977] / by Michael Briggs and Maxine Briggs. — 1977. — [8],109[i.e.111]p ; 22cm.
Bibl.: p.81-102. — Index.
ISBN 0-88831-005-6 : £9.00
ISBN 0-443-01705-0 (Churchill Livingstone)
(B77-33824)

613.9'432 — Oral contraceptives. Availability. Proposals. *Great Britain. Conference proceedings*
The **pill** : on or off prescription? : a conference organised by the Family Planning Association at the Royal Commonwealth Society, London, Tuesday 23 March 1976. — London : F.P.A., [1976]. — [4],45[i.e.55]p ; 30cm.
ISBN 0-903289-07-5 Pbk : £0.50
(B77-02340)

613.9'432 — Oral contraceptives. Availability. Proposals. *Great Britain. Inquiry reports*
Joint Working Group on Oral Contraceptives. Report of the Joint Working Group on Oral Contraceptives / [for the] Department of Health and Social Security. — London : H.M.S.O., 1976. — viii,34p ; 25cm.
'... Working Group ... set up by the Central Health Services Council, the Medicines Commission and the Committee on Safety of Medicines ... ' - Foreword.
ISBN 0-11-320238-5 Sd : £0.65
(B77-02341)

613.9'432'0973 — Oral contraceptives. Social aspects. *United States*
Merkin, Donald H. Pregnancy as a disease : the pill in society / [by] Donald H. Merkin. — Port Washington, N.Y. ; London : Kennikat Press, 1976. — xv,134p ; 23cm. — (Kennikat Press national university publications)
Bibl.: p.119-131. — Index.
ISBN 0-8046-9138-x : £8.45
(B77-19409)

613.9'434 — Man. Contraception. Billings method. *Manuals*
Quinlan, Jane. Natural family planning : the Billings method / [by Jane Quinlan]. — [Cork] ([c/o Family Life Centre (Billings), 65B North Main St., Cork]) : [The author], 1976. — [4], 43p : ill(chiefly col) ; 22cm.
Folder ([4]p.),[3] sheets of adhesives (2 col.) as insert. — Bibl.: p.41.
Sd : £1.30
(B77-18798)

613.9'435 — Intrauterine devices
Snowden, Robert. The IUD : a practical guide / [by] Robert Snowdon, Margaret Williams, Denis Hawkins. — London : Croom Helm, 1977. — 117p : ill ; 22cm.
Bibl.: p.112. — Index.
ISBN 0-85664-439-0 : £6.95 : CIP rev.
(B77-24252)

613.9'5 — Sex relations. Effects of yoga
Volin, Michael. Yoga and sex / [by] Michael Volin and Nancy Phelan. — London : Sphere, 1977. — 144p,[8]p of plates : ill ; 18cm.
Originally published: as 'Sex and yoga'. London : Pelham, 1967.
ISBN 0-7221-8745-9 Pbk : £0.65
(B77-27887)

614 — PUBLIC HEALTH
McKeown, Thomas. An introduction to social medicine / [by] Thomas McKeown, C.R. Lowe. — 2nd ed. — Oxford [etc.] : Blackwell Scientific, 1977. — xii,356p : ill ; 22cm.
This ed. originally published: 1974. — Bibl. — Index. — Previous control number 0-632-09310-2.
Pbk : £5.00
ISBN 0-632-09310-2
(B77-21161)

614 — Public health. *Manuals*
Clay, Henry Hurrell. Clay's handbook of environmental health. — 14th ed. / revised by F.G. Davies with the assistance of W.H. Bassett. — London : H.K. Lewis, 1977. — x, 1020p,fold plate : ill, plans ; 23cm.
Previous ed.: published as 'Clay's public health inspector's handbook' / revised by F.G. Davies. 1972. — Bibl. — Index.
ISBN 0-7186-0425-3 : £12.50
(B77-06101)

614'.0941 — Public health. *Great Britain. Periodicals*
Health and hygiene : (the official journal of the Royal Institute of Public Health and Hygiene). — London (28 Portland Place, W1N 4DE) : The Institute.
Vol.1, no.1- ; July-Sept. 1977-. — 1977-. — ill ; 25cm.
Quarterly. — [2],58p. in 1st issue. — Bibl.
Sd : £1.50(£6.00 yearly)
ISSN 0140-2986
(B77-27112)

614'.0941 — Public health. *Great Britain. Reports, surveys. Serials*
Environmental health report / Environmental Health Officers Association. — London (19 Grosvenor Place, SW1X 7HU) : The Association.
1975. — [1976]. — 66p : ill, coat of arms ; 25cm.
ISBN 0-900103-14-0 Sd : £0.60
ISSN 0305-4004
(B77-00242)

614.3 — PUBLIC HEALTH. ADULTERATION AND CONTAMINATION CONTROL
614.3'1 — Chicken meat. Production. Public health aspects
Bremner, A S. Poultry meat hygiene and inspection / [by] A.S. Bremner. — London : Baillière Tindall, 1977. — vi,186p : ill, form, plans ; 22cm.
Bibl. — Index.
ISBN 0-7020-0654-8 Pbk : £2.95
(B77-27113)

614.3'1 — Food. Contaminants: Pesticides. *Conference proceedings*
Evaluations of some pesticide residues in food : the monographs. — Geneva : World Health Organization ; [London] : [H.M.S.O.].
1975 / ... prepared by the Joint Meeting of the FAO Working Party of Experts on Pesticide Residues and the WHO Expert Committee on Pesticide Residues that met in Geneva from 24 November to 3 December 1975. — 1976. — viii,409p ; 24cm. — (World Health Organization. Pesticide residues series ; no.5)
Bibl.
Pbk : £9.06
ISBN 92-4-166505-x
(B77-17520)

Pesticide residues in food : report of the 1975 Joint Meeting of the FAO Working Party of Experts on Pesticide Residues and the WHO Expert Committee on Pesticide Residues. — Geneva : World Health Organization ; [London] : [H.M.S.O.], 1976. — 45p ; 20cm. — (World Health Organization. Technical report series ; no.592) (Food and Agriculture Organization. Plant production and protection series ; no.1)
'1975 Joint Meeting ... Geneva, 24 November-3rd December 1975' - note.
Sd : Unpriced
ISBN 92-4-120592-x
(B77-04831)

614.3'1 — Food. Hygiene
Christie, Andrew Barnett. Food hygiene and food hazards for all who handle food / [by] A.B. Christie and Mary C. Christie. — 2nd ed. — London : Faber, 1977. — 3-232p : ill ; 21cm.
Previous ed.: 1971. — Bibl.: p.220-221. — Index.
ISBN 0-571-04949-4 : £4.95
ISBN 0-571-10902-0 Pbk : £2.50
(B77-20306)

614.3'3 — Food. Additives. Regulation. Role of United States. Food and Drug Administration. *United States. Reports, surveys*
The **chemical** feast : the Ralph Nader study group report on food protection and the food and drug administration / James S. Turner, project director. — Harmondsworth [etc.] : Penguin, 1976. — xiii,273p ; 19cm.
Originally published: New York : Grossman, 1970. — Index.
ISBN 0-14-004376-4 Pbk : Unpriced
(B77-11833)

614.3'5'0941 — Drugs. Regulation. *Great Britain. Reports, surveys. Serials*
Medicines Commission. Annual report of the Medicines Commission ... together with annual reports of standing committees appointed under section 4 of the Medicines Act 1968, Committee on Safety of Medicines, Veterinary Products Committee, British Pharmacopoeia Commission, Committee on the Review of Medicines, Committee on Dental and Surgical Materials, and with a memorandum prepared by the Medicines Division of the Department of Health and Social Security. — London : H.M.S.O.
1976. — [1977]. — 95p ; 25cm. — ([1976-77 H.C.]428)
ISBN 0-10-242877-8 Sd : £1.60
(B77-28650)

614.4 — PUBLIC HEALTH. INCIDENCE, DISTRIBUTION AND CONTROL OF DISEASE
614.4 — Man. Diseases. Epidemiology
Roberts, C J. Epidemiology for clinicians / [by] C.J. Roberts. — Tunbridge Wells : Pitman Medical, 1977. — [9],198p : ill ; 22cm.
Bibl.: p.191-192. — Index.
ISBN 0-272-79407-4 Pbk : £3.50 : CIP rev.
(B77-17521)

614.4 — Man. Diseases. Epidemiology. *Conference proceedings*
Symposium on Health and Disease in Tribal Societies, *Ciba Foundation, 1976.* Health and disease in tribal societies / [editors Katherine Elliott and Julie Whelan]. — Amsterdam ; Oxford [etc.] : Elsevier [etc.], 1977. — viii, 344p : ill, maps ; 25cm. — (Ciba Foundation. Symposia : new series ; 49)
'Symposium on Health and Disease in Tribal Societies, held at the Ciba Foundation, London, 28th-30th September 1976' - p.vii. — Bibl. — Index.
ISBN 0-444-15271-7 : £16.71
Also classified at 613
(B77-30283)

614.4 — Man. Epidemics
Sinnecker, Herbert. General epidemiology / [by] Herbert Sinnecker ; translated from the German by N. Walker. — London [etc.] : Wiley, 1976. — 228p : ill, maps ; 25cm.
'A Wiley-Interscience publication'. — Translation of 'Allgemeine Epidemiologie'. Jena : Fisher, 1971. — Bibl.: p.217-222. — Index.
ISBN 0-471-79318-3 : £8.50
(B77-09709)

614.4'07'2041 — Public health laboratories. *Great Britain. Public Health Laboratory Service Board. Accounts*
Public Health Laboratory Service Board. Accounts ... for the year ended 31st March, together with the report of the Comptroller and Auditor General thereon ... / Public Health Laboratory Service Board. — London : H.M.S.O.
1975-76. — [1977]. — 5p ; 25cm. — ([1975-76 H.C.] 363)
ISBN 0-10-236377-3 Sd : £0.25
(B77-21162)

614.4'07'2041 — Public health laboratories. *Great Britain. Public Health Laboratory Service Board. Reports, surveys. Serials*
Public health laboratory service annual report. — [London] ([Lower Entrance, Colindale Hospital, Colindale Ave., NW9 5EQ]) : [Public Health Laboratory Service Board].
1975. — 1976. — [3],62p : ill, 2 maps ; 25cm.
Bibl.: p.37-56.
ISBN 0-901144-07-x Sd : Unpriced
(B77-05440)

614.4'0913 — Man. Diseases. Epidemiology & public health measures. *Developing countries. Subtropical regions & tropical regions*
Epidemiology and community health in warm climate countries / [edited by] the late Robert Cruickshank, Kenneth L. Standard, Hugh B.L. Russell ; foreword by E.K. Cruickshank. — Edinburgh [etc.] : Churchill Livingstone, 1976. — xv,492p : ill, maps ; 24cm. — (Medicine in the tropics)
Bibl. — Index.
ISBN 0-443-01303-9 : £11.50
ISBN 0-443-01145-1 Pbk : £8.00
(B77-02342)

614.4'241 — Man. Diseases. Epidemiology. *Great Britain. Secondary school texts*
Burkitt, Ann. Patterns of health / [by] Ann Burkitt. — Sunbury on Thames [etc.] : Nelson, 1977. — 79p : ill, maps, ports ; 25cm. — (Nelson health education)
Bibl.: p.78.
ISBN 0-17-438221-9 Pbk : £1.10
(B77-22612)

614.4'242 — Morbidity. England, 1955-1956. Compared with morbidity, 1970-1971
Royal College of General Practitioners. *Birmingham Research Unit.* Trends in national morbidity : a comparison of two successive national morbidity surveys / from the Birmingham Research Unit of the Royal College of General Practitioners. — London (14 Princes Gate, Hyde Park, SW7 1PU) : 'Journal of the Royal College of General Practitioners', 1976. — [1],iv,41p : forms ; 25cm. — (Royal College of General Practitioners. 'Journal of the Royal College of General Practitioners' occasional papers ; 3 ISSN 0309-6300)
Bibl.: p.40-41.
ISBN 0-85084-060-0 Sd : Unpriced
(B77-14251)

614.4'3 — Man. Vectors. Control. Equipment. *Reports, surveys*
World Health Organization. *Expert Committee on Vector Biology and Control.* Engineering aspects of vector control operations : first report of the WHO Expert Committee on Vector Biology and Control. — Geneva : W.H.O. ; [London] : [H.M.S.O.], 1977. — 40p : 1 ill ; 21cm. — (World Health Organization. Technical report series ; 603)
Sd : Unpriced
ISBN 92-4-120603-9
(B77-16407)

614.4'322 — Man. Vectors: Tsetse flies. Control measures. *Africa, to 1972*
McKelvey, John J. Man against tsetse : struggle for Africa / [by] John J. McKelvey. — Ithaca ; London : Cornell University Press, 1975. — xvii,306p : ill, facsims, maps, plans, ports ; 21cm.
Originally published: 1973. — Bibl.: p.239-292. — Index.
£10.80
ISBN 0-8014-0768-0
Also classified at 636.089'44'322
(B77-27114)

McKelvey, John J. Man against tsetse : struggle for Africa / [by] John J. McKelvey, Jr. — Ithaca ; London : Cornell University Press, 1973. — xvii,306p : ill, facsims, maps, plan, ports ; 21cm.
Bibl.: p.239-245. — Index.
ISBN 0-8014-0768-0 : Unpriced
Also classified at 636.089'44'322
(B77-18799)

614.4'4 — Man. Diseases. Control measures
Brander, George C. The control of disease / [by] George C. Brander, Peter R. Ellis ; foreword by Sir Michael Swann. — London [etc.] : Baillière Tindall, 1976. — [8],136p ; 20cm. — (Animal and human health)
Bibl.: p.127-129. — Index.
ISBN 0-7020-0634-3 Pbk : £2.50
Also classified at 636.089'44'4
(B77-09710)

614.4'4'0941 — Preventive medicine. *Great Britain. Inquiry reports*
Great Britain. *Parliament. House of Commons. Expenditure Committee.* Preventive medicine : first report from the Expenditure Committee, session 1976-77, together with the minutes of evidence taken before the Social Services and Employment Sub-committee in sessions 1975-76 and 1976-77, appendices and index. — London : H.M.S.O.
In 3 vols.
Vol.1 : Report. — [1977]. — xcvii p ; 25cm. — ([1976-77 H.C.] 169-i)
ISBN 0-10-216977-2 Sd : £1.60
(B77-12469)

Vol.2 : Minutes of evidence, 10th December 1975-28th April 1976. — [1977]. — xiv,346p ; 25cm. — ([1976-77 H.C.] 169-ii)
ISBN 0-10-277677-6 Pbk : £6.85
(B77-12470)

Vol.3 : Minutes of evidence, 5th May-15th July 1976, appendices and index. — [1977]. — xiv p,p347-741 : ill ; 25cm. — ([1976-77 H.C.] 169-iii)
Index.
ISBN 0-10-277777-2 Pbk : £7.50
(B77-12471)

614.4'9 — Civilization. Effects of epidemics, to 1975
McNeill, William Hardy. Plagues and peoples / [by] William H. McNeill. — Oxford : Blackwell, 1977. — ix,371p : map ; 23cm.
Originally published: Garden City, N.Y. : Anchor Press, 1976. — Index.
ISBN 0-631-17880-5 : £4.95 : CIP rev.
(B77-04832)

614.5'14'096 — Man. Cholera. Epidemiological aspects. *Africa, 1970-1975. Reports, surveys*
Stock, Robert F. Cholera in Africa : diffusion of the disease, 1970-1975 with particular emphasis on West Africa / [by] Robert F. Stock. — London : International African Institute [for] the Environment Training Programme, 1976. — vii,127p : ill, maps ; 24cm. — (African environment special report ; 3 ISSN 0309-345x)
Bibl.: p.119-127.
ISBN 0-85302-050-7 Pbk : £2.00(£1.75 to members of the Institute)
(B77-09711)

614.5'18 — Man. Influenza. Public health measures. *Conference proceedings*
Influenza : virus, vaccines and strategy : proceedings of a Working Group on Pandemic Influenza, Rougemont, 26-28 January 1976 / edited by Philip Selby. — London [etc.] : Academic Press for Sandoz Institute for Health and Socio-Economic Studies, 1976. — 3-353p : ill, maps ; 21cm. — (Sandoz Institute for Health and Socio-Economic Studies. Publications ; no.5)
Bibl.
ISBN 0-12-635950-4 Pbk : £9.00
(B77-05441)

614.5'18'0973 — Man. Influenza. Epidemics. *United States, 1918-1919*
Crosby, Alfred W. Epidemic and peace, 1918 / [by] Alfred W. Crosby, Jr. — Westport, Conn. ; London : Greenwood Press, 1976. — vi,337p : ill, map ; 22cm.
Index.
ISBN 0-8371-8376-6 : £14.25
(B77-15875)

614.5'43 — Children. Whooping cough. Vaccination. *Great Britain. Inquiry reports*
Joint Committee on Vaccination and Immunization. Whooping cough vaccination : review of the evidence on whooping cough vaccination / by the Joint Committee on Vaccination and Immunization of the Central Health Services Council and the Scottish Health Service Planning Council. — London : H.M.S.O., 1977. — viii,38p : ill ; 25cm.
Bibl.: p.37-38.
ISBN 0-11-320318-7 Sd : £0.85
(B77-22613)

614.5'46 — Man. Leprosy. Control measures. *Developing countries. Periodicals. For auxiliary personnel in health services*
Partners : magazine for paramedical workers in leprosy. — London : Leprosy Mission.
No.1- ; [197-]-. — [197-]-. — ill, ports ; 21cm.
Two issues a year. — 24p. in 1st issue.
Sd : Unpriced
ISSN 0308-745x
(B77-11834)

614.5'46 — Man. Leprosy. Public health measures
Browne, Stanley George. Memorandum on leprosy control / by Stanley G. Browne ; [issued jointly by Oxfam, Lepra and the Leprosy Mission]. — Revised ed. — [London] ([50 Portland Place, W.1]) : [Leprosy Mission], 1976. — [1],31p ; 18cm.
Previous ed.: 1972. — Bibl.: p.29-30. — List of films: p.30.
Sd : Unpriced
(B77-31221)

614.5'46'0942 — Man. Leprosy. Public health measures. *England. Proposals*
Great Britain. *Department of Health and Social Security.* Memorandum on leprosy / Department of Health and Social Security and the Welsh Office. — London : H.M.S.O., 1977. — 15,[1]p ; 25cm.
ISBN 0-11-320196-6 Sd : £0.35
(B77-29451)

614.5'5'52 — Man. Onchocerciasis. Epidemiology. *Reports, surveys*
World Health Organization. *Expert Committee on Epidemiology of Onchocerciasis.* Epidemiology of onchocerciasis : report of a WHO Expert Committee / [WHO Expert Committee on Epidemiology of Onchocerciasis]. — Geneva : W.H.O. ; [London] : [H.M.S.O.], 1976. — 94p : ill, maps ; 20cm. — (World Health Organization. Technical report series ; no.597)
Pbk : £2.35
ISBN 92-4-120597-0
(B77-06102)

614.5'63'0942 — Man. Rabies. Public health measures. *England. Proposals*
Great Britain. *Department of Health and Social Security.* Memorandum on rabies / Department of Health and Social Security and the Welsh Office. — London : H.M.S.O., 1977. — 37p ; 25cm.
ISBN 0-11-320197-4 Sd : £0.60
(B77-29452)

614.5'7 — Man. Lassa fever. Public health measures. *England. Proposals*
Great Britain. *Department of Health and Social Security.* Memorandum on Lassa fever / Department of Health and Social Security and the Welsh Office. — London : H.M.S.O., 1976. — 29p : forms ; 25cm.
Bibl.: p.29.
ISBN 0-11-320195-8 Sd : £0.45
(B77-04833)

614.5'7 — Man. Virus diseases. Epidemiology & control measures
Viral infections of humans : epidemiology and control / edited by Alfred S. Evans. — London [etc.] : Wiley, 1976. — xxxi,584p,plate : ill(incl 1 col), maps ; 25cm.
Bibl. — Index.
ISBN 0-471-99435-9 : £23.00
(B77-08402)

614.5'73'2 — Man. Bubonic plague. Public health measures. *Manuals*
Bahmanyar, M. Plague manual / [by] M. Bahmanyar, D.C. Cavanaugh. — Geneva : World Health Organization ; [London] : [H.M.S.O.], 1976. — [6],76p,plate : ill ; 28cm.
Bibl.: p.63-65.
Pbk : £5.00
ISBN 92-4-154051-6
(B77-04834)

614.5'73'209421 — Man. Bubonic plague. Epidemics. *London, 1625. Christian viewpoints. Early works. Facsimiles*
Spencer, Benjamin. Vox civitatis / by Benjamin Spencer. — Exeter ([Amory Building, Rennes Drive, Exeter EX4 RJ]) : The Rota, 1977. — [12],41p ; 22cm.
Facsimile reprint of: 1st ed. London : Nicholas Bourne, 1625.
ISBN 0-904617-02-5 Sd : Unpriced
(B77-27115)

614.5'73'20956 — Man. Black Death. Epidemics. *Middle East, ca 1340-ca 1400*
Dols, Michael W. The Black Death in the Middle East / [by] Michael W. Dols. — Princeton ; Guildford : Princeton University Press, 1977. — xvii,390p : ill, maps ; 23cm.
Bibl.: p.337-373. — Index.
ISBN 0-691-03107-x : £15.80
(B77-16408)

614.5'93'9 — Population. Nutrition. Surveillance. Methodology. *Reports, surveys*
Joint FAO/UNICEF/WHO Expert Committee on the Methodology of Nutritional Surveillance. Methodology of nutritional surveillance : report of a Joint FAO/UNICEF/WHO Expert Committee / [Joint FAO/UNICEF/WHO Expert Committee on the Methodology of Nutritional Surveillance]. — Geneva : World Health Organization ; [London] : [H.M.S.O.], 1976. — 66p : ill ; 20cm. — (World Health Organization. Technical report series ; no.593)
Pbk : £1.75
ISBN 92-4-120593-8
(B77-01491)

614.5'93'9 — Preventive medicine. Role of nutrition
Nutrition in preventive medicine : the major deficiency syndromes, epidemiology and approaches to control / edited by G.H. Beaton & J.M. Bengoa. — Geneva : World Health Organization ; [London] : [H.M.S.O.], 1976. — 590p : ill(some col), forms, map ; 25cm. — (World Health Organization. Monograph series ; no.62 ISSN 0512-3038)
Bibl. — Index.
Pbk : £23.24
ISBN 92-4-140062-5
(B77-04835)

614.5'97'2 — Man. Rheumatic diseases. Epidemiology
Lawrence, John Stewart. Rheumatism in populations / [by] J.S. Lawrence. — London : Heinemann Medical, 1977. — xiii,572p : ill, forms, maps ; 24cm.
Bibl.: p.527-563. — Index.
ISBN 0-433-19070-1 : £22.00
(B77-03028)

614.5'996'0723 — Man. Dental health. Surveys. Methodology
World Health Organization. Oral health surveys : basic methods / [World Health Organization]. — 2nd ed. — Geneva : W.H.O. ; [London] : [H.M.S.O.], 1977. — 68p : facsims, forms ; 24cm.
Previous ed.: 1971.
Pbk : Unpriced
ISBN 92-4-154120-2
(B77-16409)

614.5'999 — Man. Cancer. Registration. *Manuals*
World Health Organization. WHO handbook for standardized cancer registries. — Geneva : W.H.O. ; [London] : [H.M.S.O.], 1976. — [2], 94p ; 21cm. — (World Health Organization. Offset publications ; no.25)
Sp : £2.50
ISBN 92-4-170025-4
(B77-01492)

614.5'999 — Man. Cancer. Vaccination. BCG vaccine. *Conference proceedings*
BCG in cancer immunotherapy / edited by Gilles Lamoureux, Raymond Turcotte, Vincent Portelance. — New York [etc.] ; London : Grune and Stratton ; London : Distributed by Academic Press, [1977]. — xxiv,392p : ill ; 26cm.
'Proceedings of the international symposium held i[n] honour of Professor Armand Frappier April 22-23, 1976' - half title page verso. — Published in the United States: 1976. — Index.
ISBN 0-8089-0995-9 : £12.80
(B77-13056)

614.6 — PUBLIC HEALTH. DISPOSAL OF THE DEAD
614.6'0941 — Disposal of the dead. *Great Britain*
Consumers' Association. What to do when someone dies / [Consumers' Association] ; [edited by Edith Rudinger]. — Revised ed. — London : The Association, 1977. — [4],122p : ill ; 19cm. — (A consumer publication)
This ed. originally published: 1976. — Index.
Pbk : £1.75
ISBN 0-85202-117-8
(B77-26334)

614'.62 — Cremation. *Conference proceedings*
Cremation Society. *Annual Conference, 126th, Torquay, 1976.* Verbatim report of the 1976 Annual Conference organised by the Cremation Society of Great Britain on Tuesday, Wednesday & Thursday, 6th, 7th & 8th July at the Imperial Hotel, Torquay. — Maidstone (Woodcut House, Ashford Rd, Hollingbourne, Maidstone, Kent ME17 1XH) : Pharos Press, [1976]. — 76,[1]p : ill, ports ; 25cm.
ISBN 0-905541-01-4 Sd : £4.00
(B77-09039)

614.7 — PUBLIC HEALTH. ENVIRONMENTAL SANITATION

614.7 — Environment. Pollution by mercury
D'Itri, Patricia A. Mercury contamination : a human tragedy / [by] Patricia A. D'Itri, Frank M. D'Itri. — New York ; London [etc.] : Wiley, 1977. — xxiii,311p : ill, facsims, maps ; 24cm. — (Environmental science and technology)
Text on lining paper. — 'A Wiley-Interscience publication'. — Bibl.: p.269-300. — Index.
ISBN 0-471-02654-9 : £13.45
(B77-24961)

614.7 — Environment. Pollution by trace elements
Purves, David. Trace-element contamination of the environment / [by] David Purves. — Amsterdam ; Oxford [etc.] : Elsevier, 1977. — xi,260p : ill ; 24cm. — (Fundamental aspects of pollution and environmental science ; 1)
Index.
ISBN 0-444-41570-x : Unpriced
(B77-25656)

614.7 — European Community countries. Environment. Pollution by asbestos. Public health aspects
Public health risks of exposure to asbestos : report of a Working Group of Experts prepared for the Commission of European Communities, Directorate-General for Social Affairs, Health and Safety Directorate / rapporteur R.L. Zielhuis. — Oxford [etc.] : Pergamon for the Commission of the European Communities, 1977. — [4],149p : ill ; 24cm. — (EUR5653e)
Bibl.: p.134-142.
ISBN 0-08-021580-7 Pbk : £6.75
(B77-18162)

614.7 — Great Britain. Environment. Pollutants: Airborne dust. *Micrographs*
Hamilton, Ernest Marcel. The identification of atmospheric dust by use of the microscope / by E.M. Hamilton and W.D. Jarvis. — London : Central Electricity Generating Board, 1976. — 32,[1]p : ill(some col) ; 29cm. — (Central Electricity Generating Board. Research and Development Department. Monographs)
Originally published: 1963.
Sd : Unpriced
(B77-28651)

614.7 — Great Britain. Environment. Pollution by combustion. *Reviews of research*
Pollution formation and destruction in flames / edited by N.A. Chigier. — Oxford [etc.] : Pergamon, 1976. — [5],219p : ill ; 28cm. — (Progress in energy and combustion science ; vol.1)
Bibl. — Index.
ISBN 0-08-020307-8 : £6.25
(B77-07370)

614.7 — Great Britain. Environment. Pollution by mercury. *Reports, surveys*
Great Britain. *Inter-Departmental Working Group on Heavy Metals.* Environmental mercury and man : a report of an Inter-Departmental Working Group on Heavy Metals. — London : H.M.S.O., 1976. — viii, 92p ; 25cm. — (Pollution paper ; no.10)
Bibl.: p.84-92.
ISBN 0-11-751118-8 Pbk : £1.40
(B77-09712)

614.7 — Japan. Environment. Pollution by polychlorinated biphenyls
PCB poisoning and pollution / edited by Kentaro Higuchi. — Tokyo : Kodansha ; New York [etc.] ; London : Academic Press, 1976. — x, 184p,plate : ill(incl 1 col), maps ; 23cm. — (Kodansha scientific books)
Index.
ISBN 0-12-347850-2 : £12.40
Primary classification 615.9'51'1
(B77-14754)

614.7 — London. Environment. Monitoring. Organisations: Greater London Council. Scientific Branch. *Reports, surveys. Serials*
Greater London Council. *Scientific Branch.* Annual report of the Scientific Adviser, Greater London Council, Scientific Branch ... — London : G.L.C.
1975 / Scientific Adviser R.T. Kelly ... — 1975. — [3],132p ; 30cm.
ISBN 0-7168-0891-9 Sd : £1.60
(B77-20307)

614.7 — Man. Adverse reactions to chemical pollutants of environment
Study Group on Functional Toxicity. Adverse effects of environmental chemicals and psychotropic drugs / Study Group on Functional Toxicity (Permanent Commission and International Association on Occupational Health). — Amsterdam ; Oxford [etc.] : Elsevier.
Vol.2 : Neurophysiological and behavioral tests / edited by Milan Horváth in collaboration with Emil Frantík. — 1976. — xv,334p : ill ; 25cm.
' ... the Second Workshop on Functional Toxicity Evaluation, [held in Prague] ... convened by the Subcommittee for the Study of Higher Nervous Functions of the International Association of Occupational Health' - Introductory address. — Bibl.
ISBN 0-444-41498-3 : £25.12
Also classified at 615'.78
(B77-07371)

614.7 — Urban regions. Social life. Medical aspects
Man in urban environments / edited by G.A. Harrison and J.B. Gibson. — Oxford [etc.] : Oxford University Press, 1976. — ix,367p : ill, chart, maps ; 23cm.
Bibl.
ISBN 0-19-857140-2 : £7.50
(B77-07923)

614.7'1 — Atmosphere. Pollution
Air pollution / edited by Arthur C. Stern. — 3rd ed. — New York [etc.] ; London : Academic Press. — (Environmental sciences)
In 5 vols. — Previous ed.: in 3 vols. 1968.
Vol.3 : Measuring, monitoring and surveillance of air pollution. — 1976. — xx,799p : ill, forms, maps ; 24cm.
Index.
ISBN 0-12-666603-2 : £30.15
(B77-15305)

Vol.4 : Engineering control of air pollution. — 1977. — xxii,946p : ill ; 24cm.
Index.
ISBN 0-12-666604-0 : £35.15
(B77-20308)

Perkins, Henry C. Air pollution / [by] Henry C. Perkins. — New York ; London [etc.] : McGraw-Hill, 1974. — xv,407p : ill, maps ; 24cm.
Bibl. — Index.
ISBN 0-07-049302-2 : £15.00
(B77-18800)

614.7'1 — Atmosphere. Pollution. *Conference proceedings*
Atmospheric pollution : proceedings of the 12th international colloquium, Paris, France, May 5-7, 1976 : organized by the Institut National de Recherche Chimique Appliquée, B.P.1, 91710 Vert-le-Petit, France / edited by Michel M. Benarie. — Amsterdam ; Oxford [etc.] : Elsevier, 1976. — x,649p : ill, maps ; 25cm.
Includes 10 papers in French, English summaries. — Bibl.
ISBN 0-444-41497-5 : £31.25
(B77-04201)

614.7'1'0941 — Great Britain. Atmosphere. Pollution. *Reports, surveys. Serials*
Industrial air pollution / [HM Alkali and Clean Air Inspectorate, HM Industrial Pollution Inspectorate for Scotland] ; [for the] Health & Safety Executive. — London : H.M.S.O.
1975. — 1977. — iii,71p,[2]p of plates : ill ; 30cm.
At head of title: Health and safety.
ISBN 0-11-883002-3 Pbk : £2.00
(B77-27116)

614.7'12 — Air. Pollutants: Aerosols. Physical properties
Friedlander, S K. Smoke, dust and haze : fundamentals of aerosol behavior / [by] S.K. Friedlander. — New York ; London [etc.] : Wiley, 1977. — xix,317p : ill, map ; 24cm.
'A Wiley-Interscience publication'. — Bibl. — Index.
ISBN 0-471-01468-0 : £11.35
(B77-21893)

614.7'12 — Great Britain. Atmosphere. Pollution by asbestos. Public health aspects
Selected written evidence submitted to the Advisory Committee on Asbestos, 1976-77... — London : H.M.S.O., 1977. — v,152p : ill ; 30cm.
Bibl.
ISBN 0-11-883004-x Pbk : £5.00
(B77-18163)

614.7'12'09421 — London. Atmosphere. Pollution by smoke, 1661. *Early works. Facsimiles*
Evelyn, John, *b.1620.* Fumifugium / by John Evelyn. — Exeter ([Amory Building, Rennes Drive, Exeter EX4 4RJ]) : 'The Rota', 1976. — [16],26p ; 20cm.
Facsimile reprint of: 1st ed. London : W. Godbid for Gabriel Bedel and Thomas Collins, 1661.
ISBN 0-904617-06-8 Sd : £0.75
(B77-02343)

614.7'72 — Drinking water. Contaminants: Lead. Public health aspects. *Great Britain. Reports, surveys*
Lead in drinking water : a survey in Great Britain, 1975-1976 : report of an interdepartmental working group. — London : H.M.S.O., 1977. — ix,47p : form ; 25cm. — (Pollution paper ; no.12)
ISBN 0-11-751230-3 Sd : £1.15
(B77-29453)

614.7'72 — Drinking water. Surveillance. Methodology. *Reports, surveys*
World Health Organization. Surveillance of drinking-water quality / [World Health Organization]. — Geneva : W.H.O. ; [London] : [H.M.S.O.], 1976. — 135p : ill, forms ; 24cm. — (World Health Organization. Monograph series ; no.63 ISSN 0512-3038)
Index.
Pbk : Unpriced
ISBN 92-4-140063-3
(B77-04836)

614.7'72 — England. Drought. Control. Role of National Water Council, 1976
Andrews, C D. "We didn't wait for the rain" / [by] C.D. Andrews. — London (1 Queen Anne's Gate, SW1H 9BT) : National Water Council, 1976. — [2],49p : ill(chiefly col) ; 30cm.
ISBN 0-904561-18-6 Pbk : £1.50
(B77-15306)

614.7'72 — Inhabitants. Blood. Contaminants: Lead. Sources: Drinking water. *Dyfed. Ceredigion. Reports, surveys*
Elwood, P C. Report on lead in water and in the blood of residents in North West Wales / by P.C. Elwood. — [Cardiff] ([Cathays Park, Cardiff]) : Welsh Office, [1977]. — [5],11p, plate : 1 ill ; 30cm.
Cover title: Lead in domestic water and in the blood of residents in North West Wales.
Sd : Unpriced
Also classified at 614.7'72
(B77-18164)

614.7'72 — Inhabitants. Blood. Contaminants: Lead. Sources: Drinking water. *Gwynedd. Caernarvonshire. Reports, surveys*
Elwood, P C. Report on lead in water and in the blood of residents in North West Wales / by P.C. Elwood. — [Cardiff] ([Cathays Park, Cardiff]) : Welsh Office, [1977]. — [5],11p, plate : 1 ill ; 30cm.
Cover title: Lead in domestic water and in the blood of residents in North West Wales.
Sd : Unpriced
Primary classification 614.7'72
(B77-18164)

614.7'8 — Aircraft. Noise. Control measures. *Great Britain*
Great Britain. *Department of Trade.* Action against aircraft noise / [prepared by the Department of Trade and the Central Office of Information]. — [London] ([1 Victoria St., SW1H 0ET]) : The Department, 1976. — [2], 25,[1]p : ill(some col), col maps ; 15x21cm.
ISBN 0-85605-290-6 Sd : Unpriced
(B77-15307)

614.7′8 — Airports. *London. Hillingdon (London Borough). London Airport (Heathrow). Concorde aeroplanes. Noise, 1976-1977. Reports, surveys*
Civil Aviation Authority. *Directorate of Operational Research and Analysis.* Noise data from the first year of scheduled Concorde operations at Heathrow Airport, London : a report prepared for the Department of Trade / Directorate of Operational Research and Analysis [Civil Aviation Authority]. — London : C.A.A., 1977. — v,10,[51]p : ill, col maps ; 30cm. — (Civil Aviation Authority. Directorate of Operational Research and Analysis. Reports ; 7703) (Civil Aviation Authority. Papers ; 77007)
ISBN 0-86039-040-3 Sd : £5.00
(B77-15876)

614.7′8 — Airports. Aircraft. Noise at night. *London. Reports, surveys*
Great Britain. *Department of Trade.* Night disturbance from aircraft noise at Heathrow and Gatwick : a consultation document / Department of Trade. — London ([1 Victoria St., SW1H 0ET]) : [The Department], 1977. — [2],ii,18,[2]p,[38]p of plates(18 fold),fold leaf of plate : col ill, col maps ; 30cm.
Sd : Unpriced
(B77-12472)

614.7′8 — Concorde aeroplanes. Noise. Measurement. *London. Reports, surveys*
Noise Advisory Council. *Working Group on Noise from Air Traffic.* Concorde noise levels : report / by a working group of the [Noise Advisory] Council [i.e. the Working Group on Noise from Air Traffic]. — London : H.M.S.O., 1977. — [3],9p : ill ; 25cm.
ISBN 0-11-751145-5 Sd : £0.50
(B77-15877)

614.7′8 — Low frequency vibration. Environmental aspects
Infrasound and low frequency vibration / edited by W. Tempest. — London [etc.] : Academic Press, 1976. — xi,364p : ill ; 24cm.
Bibl. — Index.
ISBN 0-12-685450-5 : £13.50
(B77-09040)

614.7′8 — Noise. Environmental aspects
Cunniff, Patrick F. Environmental noise pollution / [by] Patrick F. Cunniff. — New York ; London [etc.] : Wiley, 1977. — xii, 210p ; 24cm.
With answers to even-numbered problems. — Index.
ISBN 0-471-18943-x : £2.50
(B77-22614)

614.8 — PUBLIC SAFETY

614.8 — Accidents & natural disasters. Causes & safety measures
Thygerson, Alton Luie. Accidents & disasters : causes and countermeasures / [by] Alton L. Thygerson. — Englewood Cliffs ; London [etc.] : Prentice-Hall, 1977. — xix,411p : ill, maps ; 24cm.
Index. — Includes: Safety. 2nd ed. Originally published : Englewood Cliffs : Prentice-Hall, 1976.
ISBN 0-13-000968-7 : £9.55
(B77-12473)

614.8 — Children. Accidents. Causes & safety measures. *Great Britain. Conference proceedings*
Children, the environment and accidents / edited by R.H. Jackson. — Tunbridge : Pitman Medical, 1977. — [11],164p : ill ; 23cm.
Proceedings of a conference held at the University of Newcastle under the aegis of the Medical Commission on Accident Prevention and the Newcastle Department of Child Health. — Bibl. — Index.
ISBN 0-272-79406-6 Pbk : £2.95
(B77-27117)

614.8 — Emergencies. *Amateurs' manuals*
Winter, Ruth. Keep calm! : don't panic - here's what to do and what not to do in family emergencies / by Ruth Winter ; drawings by Roy Doty. — UK ed. — London : Associated Newspapers Group, [1977]. — 213p : ill, form ; 25cm.
'A Harmsworth Publication'. — Previous ed.: New York : Golden Press, 1975. — Index.
ISBN 0-85144-145-9 Pbk : £1.95
(B77-13663)

614.8 — Rescues. *Primary school texts*
Ramsbottom, Edward. Rescue / [by] Edward Ramsbottom and Joan Redmayne ; illustrated by Neil Rogers. — London [etc.] : Macmillan, 1977. — 16p : chiefly col ill ; 30cm. — (Bright ideas)
ISBN 0-333-19637-6 Sd : £0.48
(B77-24253)

614.8 — Safety. *Juvenile literature*
Safety first. — St Ives, Cornwall : Pike, 1974. — 31p : col ill ; 26cm. — (Look learn projects)
Fill-in book. — With answers. — '... with a merit award certificate'.
ISBN 0-85932-054-5 Sd : £0.30
(B77-18801)

614.8′1 — Beaches. Recreations. Safety measures. *Australia. Reports, surveys*
Sheen, Brian. To live or let die : a report on beach safety / by Brian Sheen. — Par (92 Par Green, Par, Cornwall PL24 2AG) : The author, [1976]. — [1],37,[1]p : ill, form ; 21cm.
ISBN 0-9505357-0-2 Sd : Unpriced
(B77-00782)

614.8′3 — Dangerous goods for transport by sea. Safety measures. *Standards*
Chamber of Shipping of the United Kingdom. Code of practice for the safe carriage of dangerous goods in freight containers / [Chamber of Shipping of the United Kingdom and Chemical Industries Association]. — London (30 St Mary Axe, EC3A 8ET) : The Chamber of Shipping ; London : The Association, 1973. — [5],iii,17p ; 21cm.
ISBN 0-900623-32-2 Sd : £0.50
(B77-08403)

614.8′3 — Dangerous industrial chemicals. Exposure of personnel. Permissible levels. Determination. Methodology
World Health Organization. *Expert Committee on Methods Used in Establishing Permissible Levels in Occupational Exposure to Harmful Agents.* Methods used in establishing permissible levels in occupational exposure to harmful agents : report of a WHO expert committee / [WHO Expert Committee on Methods Used in Establishing Permissible Levels in Occupational Exposure to Harmful Agents] ; with the participation of ILO. — Geneva : W.H.O. ; [London] : [H.M.S.O.], 1977. — 68p ; 20cm. — (World Health Organization. Technical report series ; 601)
Pbk : £2.24
ISBN 92-4-120601-2
(B77-11835)

614.8′3 — Vinyl chloride monomer. Safety aspects
British Chemical Industry Safety Council. Vinyl chloride monomer : advisory notes for PVC processors / [British Chemical Industry Safety Council]. — London (93 Albert Embankment, SE1 7TU) : The Council, 1975. — [2],4p ; 25cm.
Originally published: 1974.
ISBN 0-900623-19-5 Sd : £0.50
(B77-09713)

614.8′31 — Textile products. Inflammability. Safety measures. *Organisation for Economic Co-operation and Development countries. Reports, surveys*
Organisation for Economic Co-operation and Development. *Committee on Consumer Policy.* Safety requirements concerning the flammability of textile products : report / by the Committee on Consumer Policy [Organisation for Economic Co-operation and Development]. — Paris : O.E.C.D. ; [London] : [H.M.S.O.], 1977. — 49p ; 27cm.
Pbk : £2.00
ISBN 92-64-11616-8
(B77-11232)

614.8′312 — Chemical industries. Personnel exposed to dangerous gases. First aid. *Manuals*
Chemical Industries Association. Exposure to gases and vapours : notes on treatment / [Chemical Industries Association]. — [Revised ed.]. — London (93 Albert Embankment, S.E.1) : The Association, 1971. — [50]p : of forms ; 31cm.
In binder. — Previous ed.: published as 'Gassing casualties'. 1957. — Index.
ISBN 0-900623-26-8 Ls : £3.00
(B77-06103)

614.8′312 — Chemistry laboratories. Safety measures. *Manuals*
Hazards in the chemical laboratory / edited by G.D. Muir. — 2nd ed. — London : Chemical Society, 1977. — ii-xvii,473[i.e.475]p : ill ; 22cm.
Previous ed.: London : Royal Institute of Chemistry, 1971. — Index.
ISBN 0-85186-699-9 Pbk : £7.00
(B77-15878)

614.8′312 — Dangerous industrial chemicals. Freight transport. *Conference proceedings*
Chemical Industries Association. *Distribution Conference, Harrogate, 1975.* The Distribution Conference [held at] Harrogate, 12/13 February 1975, proceedings. — London (93 Albert Embankment, SE1 7TU) : C.I.A., [1976]. — [3] ,77p : ill(some col), forms(1 col) ; 30cm.
ISBN 0-900623-12-8 Sd : Unpriced
(B77-04202)

614.8′312 — Dangerous industrial chemicals. Freight transport. Emergencies. *Manuals*
Chemical Industries Association. Chemsafe : a manual of the chemical industry scheme for assistance in freight emergencies / [Chemical Industries Association]. — 2nd ed. — London (93 Albert Embankment, SE1 7TU) : C.I.A., 1976. — [3],33p : forms ; 21cm.
Pierced for binder. — Previous ed.: 1973.
ISBN 0-900623-07-1 Pbk : Unpriced
(B77-04203)

614.8′312 — Dangerous industrial chemicals. Road freight transport. Accidents. Emergency action. *Europe. Manuals*
European Council of Chemical Manufacturers' Federations. Transport emergency cards / [prepared by CEFIC]. — London (93 Albert Embankment, S.E.1) : Chemical Industries Association.
[Vol.1]. — [197-]. — [3],3,[4]p,[100] leaves ; 32cm.
In binder. — Index.
Ls : £8.50
(B77-06104)

Vol.2. — 1973. — [3],3,[4]p,[100] leaves ; 32cm.
In binder. — Index.
ISBN 0-900623-23-3 Ls : £8.50
(B77-06105)

Vol.3. — 1974. — [3],3,[16]p,[100] leaves ; 32cm.
In binder. — Index.
ISBN 0-900623-24-1 Ls : £8.50
(B77-06106)

Vol.4. — 1976. — [3],3,[20]p,[100] leaves ; 32cm.
In binder. — Index.
ISBN 0-900623-25-x Ls : £8.50
(B77-06107)

614.8′312 — Dangerous industrial chemicals. Road freight transport. Safety measures. *Manuals*
Road transport of hazardous chemicals : a manual of principal safety requirements / [prepared and updated by a working party of the Distribution Committee of the Chemical Industries Association]. — [1973 ed. reprinted with minor alterations]. — London ([93 Albert Embankment, SE1 7TU]) : Chemical Industries Association, 1976. — [9],49 : ill(some col), forms(some col) ; 21cm.
Pierced for binder. — Originally published: 1973. — Bibl.: p.26-28.
ISBN 0-900623-08-x Pbk : Unpriced
(B77-04204)

614.8′312 — Hydraulic power equipment. Fluids. Fire resistance. *Tables*
Association of Hydraulic Equipment Manufacturers. Fire resistant fluids data sheets / [Association of Hydraulic Equipment Manufacturers]. — London (54 Warwick Sq., SW1V 2AW) : The Association, 1976. — 11p, [5]fold leaves : 1 ill ; 30cm.
Sd : Unpriced
(B77-30284)

614.8′312 — Industrial chemicals: Anhydrous ammonia. Rail freight transport. Safety measures. *Great Britain. Manuals*
Code of practice for the safe handling and transport of anhydrous ammonia in bulk by rail in the UK / [prepared by a study group appointed by the Joint Working Party on Liquid Ammonia]. — London (93 Albert Embankment, SE1 7TU) : Chemical Industries Association, 1975. — [8],34p : 2 ill ; 22cm.
Bibl.: p.29-31.
ISBN 0-900623-05-5 Sd : £0.60
(B77-04205)

614.8'312 — Industrial chemicals: Anhydrous ammonia. Refrigerated storage. Safety measures. *Great Britain*
Chemical Industries Association. Code of practice for the large scale storage of fully refrigerated anhydrous ammonia in the United Kingdom / [Chemical Industries Association]. — London (93 Albert Embankment, SE1 7TU) : The Association, 1975. — [8],39p : ill ; 30cm.
ISBN 0-900623-10-1 Sd : £2.50
(B77-06108)

614.8'312 — Industrial chemicals: Anhydrous ammonia. Road freight transport. Safety measures. *Great Britain. Manuals*
Code of practice for the safe handling and transport of anhydrous ammonia in bulk by road in the UK / [prepared by a working party]. — London (93 Albert Embankment, SE1 7TU) : Chemical Industries Association, 1972. — [7],30p : col form ; 22cm.
Bibl.: p.27-29.
ISBN 0-900623-06-3 Sd : £0.30
(B77-04206)

614.8'312 — Industrial chemicals: Anhydrous hydrogen chloride. Accidents. Prevention. *Manuals. For management*
BP Chemicals International. Hydrogen chloride (anhydrous) / prepared by BP Chemicals International Ltd [and] Imperial Chemical Industries Ltd. — London (93 Albert Embankment, SE1 7TU) : British Chemical Industry Safety Council of the Chemical Industries Association, 1975. — [5],20p : 1 ill ; 24cm. — (Codes of practice for chemicals with major hazards) (CPP2)
ISBN 0-900623-17-9 Sp : £1.25
(B77-04207)

614.8'312 — Industrial chemicals: Chlorine. Accidents. Prevention. *Manuals. For management*
Chlorine / prepared by the Associated Octel Co. Ltd ... [et al.]. — London (93 Albert Embankment, SE1 7TU) : British Chemical Industry Safety Council, 1975. — [5],23p : 1 ill ; 25cm. — (Codes of practice for chemicals with major hazards) (CPP1)
ISBN 0-900623-33-0 Sp : £1.25
(B77-06109)

614.8'312 — Industrial chemicals: Ethylene dichloride. Accidents. Prevention. *Manuals. For management*
BP Chemicals International. Ethylene dichloride / prepared by BP Chemical International Ltd, Imperial Chemical Industries Ltd. — London (93 Albert Embankment, SE1 7TU) : British Chemical Industry Safety Council, 1975. — [4],16p : 1 ill ; 25cm. — (Codes of practice for chemicals with major hazards)
ISBN 0-900623-31-4 Sd : £1.25
(B77-06110)

614.8'312 — Industrial chemicals: Ethylene oxide. Accidents. Prevention. *Manuals. For management*
Imperial Chemical Industries. The handling and storage of ethylene oxide / prepared by Imperial Chemical Industries Ltd, Shell Chemicals UK Ltd, Union Carbide UK Ltd. — London (93 Albert Embankment, SE1 7TU) : Chemical Industry Safety and Health Council, 1975. — [5],18p : 1 ill ; 25cm. — (Codes of practice for chemicals with major hazards) (CPP4)
ISBN 0-900623-30-6 Sd : £1.50
(B77-06111)

614.8'312 — Industrial chemicals: Phosgene. Accidents. Prevention. *Manuals. For management*
Imperial Chemical Industries. *Organics Division.* Phosgene / prepared by Organics and Mond Divisions of Imperial Chemical Industries Ltd. — London (93 Albert Embankment, SE1 7TU) : Chemical Industry Safety and Health Council of the Chemical Industries Association, 1975. — [8],32p : 1 ill ; 25cm. — (Codes of practice for chemicals with major hazards) (CPP5)
ISBN 0-900623-18-7 Sd : Unpriced
(B77-04208)

614.8'312 — Petroleum products. Use. Health aspects & safety aspects
Shell UK Oil *(Firm).* Shell petroleum products guide to health and safety / [Shell UK Oil]. — [London] ([P.O. Box No.148, Shell-Mex House, WC2R 0DX]) : [Shell U.K. Oil], [1976]. — [1], 18p ; 30cm.
Sd : Unpriced
(B77-06112)

614.8'312 — Serious gas explosions. *Great Britain. Inquiry reports*
King, P J. Report of the inquiry into serious gas explosions / from P.J. King, G.T. Clegg and W.J. Walters ; to Anthony Wedgwood Benn, Secretary of State for Energy, Department of Energy and Sir Denis Rooke, Chairman, British Gas Corporation. — London : H.M.S.O., 1977. — iv,104p : ill ; 25cm.
ISBN 0-11-410608-8 Pbk : £1.75
(B77-22615)

614.8'312 — Ships carrying cargoes of liquefied gases. Safety measures. *Standards*
Inter-Governmental Maritime Consultative Organization. Code for existing ships carrying liquefied gases in bulk / Inter-Governmental Maritime Consultative Organization. — London : I.M.C.O., 1976. — 77,[1]p : 1 ill, forms ; 24cm.
Spine title: Gas carrier code for existing ships.
Pbk : £1.50
ISBN 92-801-1051-9
(B77-11836)

614.8'312 — Tank vehicles for transporting dangerous industrial chemicals. Marking codes
Hazard identification : a voluntary scheme for the marking of tank vehicles conveying dangerous substances by road and rail. — [Revised ed.]. — London (93 Albert Embankment, SE1 7TU) : Chemical Industries Association, 1976. — [1],12p : ill(some col) ; 30cm.
Previous ed.: 1975.
ISBN 0-900623-11-x Sd : £1.50
(B77-04209)

614.8'36 — Hospitals. Electric laboratory equipment. Safety measures. *Great Britain. Proposals*
Electrical safety code for hospital laboratory equipment / Department of Health and Social Security ... [et al.]. — London : H.M.S.O., 1977. — [2],39p : ill ; 30cm.
Bibl.: p.32-33. — Index.
ISBN 0-11-320674-7 Sd : £1.50
(B77-33251)

614.8'36'0942 — Residences. Fatal electrical accidents. *England. Reports, surveys. Serials*
A **commentary** on electrical fatalities in the home / Department of Prices and Consumer Protection. — London ([1 Victoria St., SW1H 0ET]) : [The Department].
1974-75. — 1976. — [4],51p : ill ; 30cm.
ISBN 0-86058-003-2 Sd : Unpriced
(B77-04210)

614.8'39 — Hospitals. Radioisotope departments. Safety measures. *Great Britain*
Hospital Physicists' Association. Notes for the guidance of radiological protection advisers and radiological safety officers in departments where radioisotopes are used / [Hospital Physicists' Association]. — London (47 Belgrave Sq., S.W.1) : The Association, 1975. — [2],42p ; 21cm. — (Hospital Physicists' Association. Report series ; no.14)
'... the H.P.A. Topic Groups on Radiation Protection and Radioisotopes jointly set up a Working Party to prepare ... [this] document' - Introduction.
Sd : £2.00(£0.50 to members)
(B77-20309)

614.8'39 — Ionising radiation. Safety measures. *Manuals*
Robertson, J Craig. A guide to radiation protection / [by] J. Craig Robertson. — London [etc.] : Macmillan, 1976. — vii,86p : ill ; 23cm.
Bibl.: p.82-84. — Index.
ISBN 0-333-19278-8 : £4.95
(B77-07372)

614.8'39 — Radioprotective agents: Sulphur compounds
Sulfur-containing radioprotective agents / [editor Z.M. Bacq] ; contributors ... [others]. — Oxford [etc.] : Pergamon, 1975. — vii,345p : ill ; 24cm. — (International encyclopedia of pharmacology and therapeutics ; section 79)
Bibl. — Index.
ISBN 0-08-016298-3 : £25.00
(B77-06701)

614.8'39'05 — Man. Protection from ionising radiation. *Periodicals*
International Commission on Radiological Protection. Annals of the ICRP. — Oxford [etc.] : Pergamon. — (International Commission on Radiological Protection. Publications ISSN 0074-2740)
Vol.1, no.1- ; 1977-. — [1977]-. — 25cm.
Four issues a year. — [5],iii,28p. in 1st issue. — Bibl.
Sd : £18.75 yearly
ISSN 0146-6453
(B77-27118)

614.8'39'06141 — Ionising radiation. Safety measures. Organisations. *Great Britain. National Radiological Protection Board, 1974-1976*
National Radiological Protection Board. The work of the NRPB, 1974-76 / National Radiological Protection Board. — [Didcot] : [The Board] ; [London] : Distributed by H.M.S.O., 1977. — [5],73p,[4]p of plates : col ill, col ports ; 25cm.
Bibl.: p.58-68. — Index.
ISBN 0-85951-059-x Pbk : £2.00
(B77-12474)

614.8'39'06141 — Ionising radiation. Safety measures. Organisations. *Great Britain. National Radiological Protection Board. Accounts*
National Radiological Protection Board. Account ... for the year ended 31st March, together with the report of the Comptroller and Auditor General thereon ... / National Radiological Protection Board. — London : H.M.S.O.
1975-76. — [1977]. — Folder(4p) ; 25cm. — ([1976-77 H.C.]273)
ISBN 0-10-227377-4 : £0.15
(B77-13057)

614.8'39'072041 — Ionising radiation. Safety measures. Research & development by National Radiological Protection Board. *Great Britain. Reports, surveys. Serials*
National Radiological Protection Board. Annual research and development report / National Radiological Protection Board. — Harwell : [The Board] ; [London] : [Distributed by H.M.S.O.].
1976. — 1977. — 152p : ill ; 30cm.
Bibl.
ISBN 0-85951-060-3 Pbk : £1.75
ISSN 0140-3362
(B77-25657)

614.8'5 — Domestic & industrial safety. *School texts*
National Safety Council. Making safety work / National Safety Council. — New York ; London [etc.] : Gregg Division, McGraw-Hill, 1976. — viii,72p : ill ; 28cm.
ISBN 0-07-046085-x Sd : £2.90
(B77-07924)

614.8'52 — Chemical industries. Industrial safety. *United States. Reports, surveys*
Safe and sound : report of a working party on US safety practices. — London (93 Albert Embankment, SE1 7TU) : British Chemical Industry Safety Council of the Chemical Industries Association, [1975]. — [2],51p : forms ; 25cm.
'Summary for managements' (4p.) as insert. — Originally published: 1969.
ISBN 0-900623-15-2 Sp : £1.25
(B77-04211)

614.8'52 — Factories. Accidents. Causes & prevention. *Great Britain. Conference proceedings*
Safety at work : recent research into the causes and prevention of industrial accidents : papers presented to a conference in Oxford in March 1977 / edited by Jennifer Phillips. — Oxford : Centre for Socio-Legal Studies, Wolfson College ; [London] : Social Science Research Council, 1977. — [2],iv,86p : ill ; 30cm. — (Wolfson College. Centre for Socio-Legal Studies. Conference papers ; no.1 ISSN 0140-5489)
ISBN 0-900296-65-8 Pbk : Unpriced
(B77-31927)

614.8'52 — Factories. Accidents. Prevention. *Great Britain. Reports, surveys*
Accident Prevention Advisory Unit. Success and failure in accident prevention : studies undertaken by the Accident Prevention Advisory Unit of the Health and Safety Executive. — London : H.M.S.O., 1976. — [3], 44p : ill ; 25cm.
Bibl.: p.43-44.
ISBN 0-11-880330-1 Sd : £0.80
(B77-06113)

614.8'52 — Factories. Immigrant personnel. Accidents. *Great Britain. Reports, surveys*
Lee, G L. Accidents are colour-blind : industrial accidents and the immigrant worker : a pilot study / [by] G.L. Lee, K.J. Wrench. — [London] : Community Relations Commission for the Birmingham Community Relations Council, 1977. — 24p : ill ; 21cm.
Bibl.: p.20.
Sd : Unpriced
(B77-18802)

614.8'52 — Slaughterhouses. Industrial safety. *Great Britain*
Baylis-Stranks, J W. Occupational health and safety in slaughter houses / by J.W. Baylis-Stranks. — [London] ([19 Grosvenor Place, SW1X 7HU]) : Environmental Health Officers Association], [1976]. — [1],61[i.e.63]p ; 31cm. — (Environmental Health Officers Association. Monograph series)
Pbk : Unpriced
Primary classification 613.6'2
(B77-31218)

614.8'52'02541 — Industrial safety. *Great Britain. Directories*
The **protection** directory of industrial and environmental safety personnel. — London (Unit 5, Seager Buildings, Brookmill Rd, S.E.8) : Alan Osborne and Associates (Books) Ltd.
1976-77 ed. — [1977]. — 104p : ill ; 21cm.
Index.
ISBN 0-904657-11-6 Pbk : £2.50
(B77-11837)

614.8'52'06141 — Great Britain. Health and Safety Commission. *Reports, surveys. Serials*
Great Britain. *Health and Safety Commission.* Report / Health and Safety Commission. — London : H.M.S.O.
1974-76. — 1977. — iv,51p : 2 ill ; 30cm.
Bibl.: p.41.
ISBN 0-11-883011-2 Sd : £2.00
ISSN 0140-5969
(B77-33252)

614.8'52'06141 — Great Britain. Health and Safety Executive. *Accounts*
Great Britain. *Health and Safety Commission.* Accounts for the period ended 31 March ... / Health and Safety Commission [and] Health and Safety Executive. — London : H.M.S.O.
1976. — [1977]. — 11p ; 25cm. — ([1976-77 H.C.]348)
ISBN 0-10-234877-4 Sd : £0.25
(B77-23445)

614.8'52'072041 — Great Britain. Health and Safety Executive. Research and Laboratory Services Division. *Reports, surveys. Serials*
Health and safety research : an account of the Executive's research testing and laboratory services. — London : H.M.S.O.
1975. — 1976. — v,52p,[2]p of plates : ill ; 30cm.
'incorporating the Annual report of the Safety in Mines Research Establishment'. — Bibl.: p.52.
ISBN 0-11-881110-x Sd : £1.75
(B77-08404)

614.8'52'0941 — Industrial safety. *Great Britain*
Industrial safety handbook / editor William Handley. — 2nd ed. — London [etc.] : McGraw-Hill, 1977. — x,480p,plate : ill(some col), forms, 2 plans ; 24cm.
Previous ed.: 1969. — Bibl. — Index.
ISBN 0-07-084481-x : £8.50
(B77-25658)

614.8'52'0941 — Industrial safety. *Great Britain. Periodicals*
Hazards bulletin. — London : British Society for Social Responsibility in Science [Work Hazards Group].
[No.] 1-. — [1976]-. — ill ; 30cm.
Five issues a year. — 12p. in issue no.6.
Sd : £0.20
ISSN 0140-0525
Also classified at 613.6'2'0941
(B77-26335)

614.8'52'0941 — Industrial safety. *Great Britain. Reports, surveys. Serials*
Great Britain. *Factory Inspectorate.* Annual report [of] HM Chief Inspector of Factories. — London : H.M.S.O.
1974. — [1975]. — xiii,133p,[8]p of plates : ill ; 25cm. — (Cmnd.6322)
Bibl.: p.129-130.
ISBN 0-10-163220-7 Pbk : £2.05
Primary classification 613.6'2'0941
(B77-04830)

Industry & services : health and safety : a report of the work of the HM Factory Inspectorate / Health and Safety Executive. — London : H.M.S.O.
1975 : incorporating the annual reports of HM Inspector of Railways and HM Inspector of Explosives. — 1977. — 92p,[2]p of plates : ill ; 30cm.
Supersedes: Annual report of HM Chief Inspector of Factories.
ISBN 0-11-881112-6 Pbk : £2.00
Primary classification 613.6'2'0941
(B77-10377)

614.8'52'09416 — Industrial safety. *Northern Ireland. Reports, surveys. Serials*
Northern Ireland. *Chief Inspector of Factories.* Report of the Chief Inspector [of Factories] ... — Belfast : H.M.S.O.
1974. — 1976. — 49p,fold leaf : ill ; 25cm.
ISBN 0-337-07118-7 Sd : £0.75
Primary classification 613.6'2'09416
(B77-25659)

614.8'53'072 — Residences. Accidents. Research. *Conference proceedings*
Social, Economic, and Legal Aspects of Accidents in the Home *(Conference), Wolfson College, 1976.* Accidents in the home / edited by Sandra Burman and Hazel Genn. — London : Croom Helm for [the] Centre for Socio-Legal Studies, 1977. — 140p : ill ; 23cm.
'... papers ... given at a ... conference organised by the Social Science Research Council's Centre for Socio-Legal Studies in [Wolfson College] Oxford in June 1976 to discuss the "Social Economic and Legal Aspects of Accidents in the Home"' - Preface. — Bibl. — Index.
ISBN 0-85664-452-8 : £5.95
(B77-21163)

614.8'6 — Expeditions. Medical equipment. *Practical information*
Illingworth, R N. Expedition medicine : a planning guide / by R.N. Illingworth ; [for the] Brathay Exploration Group. — Ambleside ([Brathay Hall], Ambleside, Cumbria) : Brathay Hall Trust, 1976. — [5],27p ; 21cm.
1 Table 4 'Summary of drugs contained in medical kits' (fold. sheet) as insert. — Bibl.: p.25-27.
ISBN 0-906015-03-0 Sp : £0.50
(B77-16410)

614.8'62 — Motor vehicles. Driving in poor visibility. Safety measures. *Organisation for Economic Co-operation and Development countries*
Organisation for Economic Co-operation and Development. *Road Research Group on Driving in Reduced Visibility Conditions due to Adverse Weather.* Adverse weather, reduced visibility and road safety : driving in reduced visibility conditions due to adverse weather : a report / prepared by an OECD Road Research Group [i.e. the Road Research Group on Driving in Reduced Visibility Conditions due to Adverse Weather]. — Paris : O.E.C.D. ; [London] : [H.M.S.O.], 1976. — [2],v,85p : ill, map ; 27cm. — (Road research)
Pbk : £2.20
ISBN 92-64-11553-6
(B77-00783)

614.8'62 — Road safety. *Juvenile literature*
Collingridge, Richard. Road sense / by R. Collingridge ; illustrated by B.H. Robinson. — Loughborough : Ladybird Books, 1977. — 2-51p : col ill ; 18cm. — (Early learning)
'RoSPA approved'.
ISBN 0-7214-0410-3 : £0.24
(B77-33825)

614.8'62 — Road traffic. Accidents. Effects of dangerous road locations. *Organisation for Economic Co-operation and Development countries. Reports, surveys*
Organisation for Economic Co-operation and Development. *Road Research Group on Hazardous Road Locations : Identification and countermeasures.* Hazardous road locations : identification and counter measures : a report / prepared by an OECD Road Research Group [i.e. the Road Research Group on Hazardous Road Locations : Identification and countermeasures]. — Paris : O.E.C.D. ; [London] : [H.M.S.O.], 1976. — [2],v,107p : ill, form ; 27cm. — (Road research)
Pbk : £2.20
ISBN 92-64-11570-6
(B77-00784)

614.8'62'0941 — Road safety. *Great Britain. Proposals*
Boaks, Bill. Road safety : the narrative of 'Josephine' : synopsis / by Bill Boaks. — London (Beggar's Roost Airstation, Merton Park, 188 Kingston Rd, Wimbledon, S.W.19) : The author, 1977. — [23]leaves : ill, facsims ; 33cm.
ISBN 0-9505569-0-4 Sd : £100.00
(B77-09714)

614.8'64 — Boating. Safety measures. *Great Britain. Coastal waters*
Desoutter, Denis Marcel. The small-boat skipper's safety book / [by] Denny Desoutter ; illustrations by David Jenkins. — 2nd ed., revised. — London [etc.] : Hollis and Carter, 1977. — 221p : ill ; 21cm.
Previous ed.: 1972. — Bibl.: p.215-216. — Index.
ISBN 0-370-30010-6 : £3.95
ISBN 0-370-30011-4 Pbk : £1.95
(B77-09715)

614.8'64 — Dangerous materials. Freight transport. Shipping. Safety aspects. *Conference proceedings*
International Symposium on the Transport of Hazardous Cargoes by Sea, *2nd, York, 1971.* Proceedings of the Second International Symposium on the Transport of Hazardous Cargoes by Sea : sponsored by Chamber of Shipping of the United Kingdom, Chemical Industries Association, London, Dock and Harbour Authorities' Association, London, York, England, 11-14 May, 1971. — [London] ([30 St Mary Axe, E.C.3]) : [Chamber of Shipping of the United Kingdom], 1972. — 446p in various pagings : ill, maps, plans ; 30cm.
Bibl.
ISBN 0-900623-21-7 Pbd : Unpriced
(B77-05442)

614.8'64 — Shipping. Safety aspects. *Conference proceedings*
Safety at Sea Symposium, *London, 1975.* Safety at Sea Symposium, the Waldorf Hotel, Aldwych, London WC2, May 14th and 15th 1975. — Redhill : Industrial Newspapers, [1977]. — [111]leaves : ill ; 30cm.
Symposium organised by 'Safety at sea international' and the Nautical Institute. — 12 fascicles. — Bibl.
Sd : £25.00
(B77-20310)

614.8'64 — Shipping. Safety measures
Safety in shipping. — Colchester [etc.] (Fairfax House, Colchester CO1 1RJ) : Seatrade Publications Ltd, 1976. — 48p : ill(some col), map, port ; 30cm. — (A 'Seatrade' study)
Sd : Free to subscribers to 'Seatrade'
(B77-04837)

614.8'64 — Shipping. Safety measures. *Regulations*
Derrett, Daniel Raymond. The mariners' highway code / [by] D.R. Derrett. — 4th ed. — London : Stanford Maritime, 1977. — 190p,[2]p of plates,leaf of plate : ill(some col), maps ; 23cm.
Self-testing coloured discs for practical work in envelope as insert. — Previous ed.: 1973. — Includes the text of the International Regulations for Preventing Collisions at Sea 1972 and extracts from official publications.
ISBN 0-540-07287-7 : £4.50
(B77-21164)

614.8'64 — Water traffic: Ships carrying dangerous cargoes. Control measures. *Scotland. Firth of Forth. Proposals*
National Ports Council. Hazardous cargoes in port approaches : a hazard rating assessment for ships carrying chemical cargoes : a report to the Forth Ports Authority / by the National Ports Council. — London : The Council, 1976. — [2],39leaves,[3]leaves of plates : ill ; 30cm.
Bibl.: leaf 38-39.
ISBN 0-901058-87-4 Sp : £10.00
(B77-04212)

614.8'69 — Air traffic. Control. Safety aspects
Brooker, P. Target levels of safety for controlled airspace / [by] P. Brooker, T. Ingham. — London : Civil Aviation Authority, 1977. — v, 27,[9]p : 1 ill ; 30cm. — (Civil Aviation Authority. Directorate of Operational Research and Analysis. Research papers ; no.7509) (Civil Aviation Authority. Papers ; 77002)
ISBN 0-86039-032-2 Sd : £1.80
(B77-09041)

614.8'69 — American civil aircraft. Accidents. Investigations by United States. Bureau of Aviation Safety. *Juvenile literature*
Dorman, Michael. Detectives of the sky : investigating aviation tragedies / by Michael Dorman. — New York ; London : F. Watts, 1976. — [9],106,[1]p : ill ; 24cm.
Bibl.: p.97. — Index.
ISBN 0-531-00342-6 : £2.50
(B77-18803)

614.8'69 — Civil aeroplanes. Mid-air collisions. Risks. Mathematical models. *Reports, surveys*
Brooker, P. Collision risk in air traffic systems : the derivation of the longitudinal-vertical overlap factor Pxz for parallel tracks / [by] P. Brooker, T. Ingham. — London : Civil Aviation Authority, 1977. — v,21p,[7]p of plates : ill ; 30cm. — (Civil Aviation Authority. Directorate of Operational Research and Analysis. Research papers ; 7510) (Civil Aviation Authority. Papers ; 77004)
ISBN 0-86039-038-1 Sd : £4.00
(B77-23446)

614.8'69 — Commercial aircraft. All weather operations. Safety measures. *Great Britain. Standards*
Civil Aviation Authority. United Kingdom operating requirements for all weather operations, categories II, IIIA and IIIB / [Civil Aviation Authority]. — London : C.A.A., 1976. — v,18,[2]p : ill ; 31cm. — (CAP ; 359)
ISBN 0-86039-011-x Sp : £1.00
(B77-04838)

614.8'69 — Restricted articles. Air transport. Safety measures. *Manuals*
Chemical Industries Association. Guide to the safe carriage of restricted articles by air / [prepared by the] Chemical Industries Association [with assistance from the] British Shippers' Council. — London (93 Albert Embankment, SE1 7TU) : C.I.A. : British Shippers' Council, [1976]. — [5],iii,20p ; 22cm.
Bibl.: p.20.
ISBN 0-900623-13-6 Sd : £1.20
(B77-04213)

614.8'69'0722 — Aircraft. Safety aspects. *Case studies. Periodicals*
General aviation safety information. — Redhill : Civil Authority, Safety Data Unit ; [Cheltenham] : [Distributed by C.A.A.].
1/77- ; 21 Jan. 1977-. — [1977]-. — 30cm.
Monthly. — 6,[1]p. in 1st issue.
Sd : £3.00 yearly
ISSN 0309-667x
(B77-16411)

614.8'7 — Nuclear warfare. Safety measures. *Manuals. For households*
Great Britain. *Home Office.* Protect and survive / [prepared for the Home Office by the Central Office of Information]. — [London] ([Whitehall, S.W.1]) : [Home Office], [1976]. — 31p : chiefly ill(some col) ; 21cm.
ISBN 0-903723-12-3 Sd : Unpriced
(B77-00785)

614.8'77 — First aid. *Manuals. For mountaineering*
Mitchell, Dick. Mountaineering first aid : a guide to accident response and first aid care / text by Dick Mitchell ; illustrations by Bruce Becker. — 2nd ed. — Seattle : The Mountaineers ; Leicester (249 Knighton Church Rd, Leicester) : Cordee Publishing, 1975 [i.e. 1977]. — 101p : ill, form ; 22cm.
This ed. originally published: Seattle : The Mountaineers, 1975. — Bibl.: p.100-101. — Previous control number ISBN 0-916890-06-6.
ISBN 0-916890-33-3 Sd : £1.80
(B77-11838)

614.8'77 — Mountain rescue. *Manuals. Serials*
Mountain and cave rescue, with lists of official rescue teams and posts : the handbook of the Mountain Rescue Committee. — Buxton (The Secretary, 9 Milldale Ave., Temple Meads, Buxton, Derbyshire SK17 9BE) : Mountain Rescue Committee.
1977. — 1977. — [2],97p : ill, maps(2 col) ; 19cm.
Sd : £0.40
(B77-32652)

614.8'77 — Mountain rescue. *Scotland. Personal observations*
MacInnes, Hamish. Call out : mountain rescue / [by] Hamish McInnes [i.e. MacInnes]. — Harmondsworth [etc.] : Penguin, 1977. — 238p, [16]p of plates : ill(some col), map, ports ; 19cm.
Originally published: London : Hodder and Stoughton, 1973. — Index.
ISBN 0-14-004298-9 Pbk : £0.95
(B77-24254)

614.8'77 — Outdoor recreations. Safety measures. *Manuals*
Great Britain. *Department of Education and Science.* Safety in outdoor pursuits / Department of Education and Science. — 2nd ed. — London : H.M.S.O., 1977. — iv,48p ; 21cm. — (DES safety series ; no.1)
Previous ed.: 1972. — Bibl.: p.14-15.
ISBN 0-11-270378-x Sd : £0.90
(B77-21165)

614.8'77 — Playgrounds. Equipment. Safety aspects. *Great Britain. Reports, surveys*
Great Britain. *Department of the Environment. Housing Development Directorate.* Children's playgrounds / Department of the Environment, Housing Development Directorate. — London (Room 1107, 1 Lambeth Palace Rd, SE1 7ER) : [The Directorate], [1976]. — [2],7p : ill ; 30cm. — (Great Britain. Department of the Environment. Housing Development Directorate. Occasional papers ; 2/76)
'... originally appeared in the August 1976 issue of Which? magazine ...' - title page verso.
ISBN 0-7184-0079-8 Sd : Unpriced
(B77-12475)

614.8'8 — First aid. *Manuals*
Cumann Croise Deirge na hÉireann. First aid manual / Cumann Croise Deirge na hÉireann. — Dublin (16 Merrion Sq., Dublin 2) : Irish Red Cross Society, [1977]. — 223p : ill(chiefly col) ; 21cm.
Index.
Pbk : £0.75
(B77-17522)

Gardner, Archibald Ward. New advanced first-aid / [by] A. Ward Gardner, with Peter J. Roylance ; illustrations by Michael Stokes. — 2nd ed. — Bristol : J. Wright, 1977. — ix, 262p : ill, forms ; 19cm.
Previous ed.: London : Butterworth, 1969. — Bibl.: p.253. — Index.
ISBN 0-7236-0472-x Pbk : £2.75 : CIP rev.
(B77-10378)

Parcel, Guy S. First aid in emergency care / [by] Guy S. Parcel. — Saint Louis : Mosby ; London : Distributed by Kimpton, 1977. — xxi, 312p : ill ; 25cm.
Bibl. — Index.
ISBN 0-8016-3400-8 : £10.00
ISBN 0-8016-3757-0 Pbk : £5.55
(B77-29454)

Proctor, Henry. Principles for first aid for the injured / [by] H. Proctor, P.S. London. — 3rd ed. — London [etc.] : Butterworth, 1977. — xiv,284p : ill, forms ; 23cm.
Previous ed.: 1968. — Bibl.: p.271-272. — Index.
ISBN 0-407-36441-2 : £6.25
(B77-11233)

614.8'8 — First aid. *Manuals. For outdoor activities*
Brown, Terence Henry Charles. The Spur book of outdoor first aid / by Terry Brown and Rob Hunter. — Bourne End, Bucks. : Spurbooks, 1976. — 64p : ill ; 19cm. — (A Spurbook venture guide)
ISBN 0-904978-10-9 Pbk : £0.75
(B77-04214)

614.8'8 — First aid. Homeopathic techniques
Chavanon, Paul. Emergency homoeopathic first-aid : a quick reference handbook / by Paul Chavanon and René Levannier ; translated from the French by Geoffrey A. Dudley. — Wellingborough : Thorsons, 1977. — 159p : 1 ill ; 22cm.
Spine title: Homoeopathic first-aid. — Translation of: 'Mémento homoeopathique d'urgence'. 4. éd. Paris : Editions Dangles, 1973.
ISBN 0-7225-0354-7 Pbk : £2.00
(B77-11839)

615.1 — DRUGS
Essentials of pharmacology : introduction to the principles of drug action / edited by John A. Bevan. — 2nd ed. / with 32 contributors. — Hagerstown [etc.] ; London : Harper and Row, 1976. — xix,649p,[2]p of plates : ill(some col) ; 27cm.
Text on lining papers. — Previous ed.: New York ; London : Hoeber, 1969. — Bibl. — Index.
ISBN 0-06-140464-0 : £15.75
(B77-21894)

Turner, Paul, *b.1933.* Clinical pharmacology / [by] Paul Turner, Alan Richens. — 2nd ed. — Edinburgh [etc.] : Churchill Livingstone, 1975. — vii,256p : ill ; 19cm. — (Livingstone medical text)
Previous ed.: 1973. — Index.
ISBN 0-443-01304-7 Pbk : £2.50
(B77-13664)

615'.1 — Drugs. *Conference proceedings*
International Symposium on Medicinal Chemistry, *5th, Paris, 1976.* Medicinal chemistry V : proceedings of the 5th International Symposium on Medicinal Chemistry, Paris, July 19-22, 1976 / editor J. Mathieu. — Amsterdam ; Oxford [etc.] : Elsevier, 1977. — vii,456p : ill ; 25cm.
ISBN 0-444-41594-7 : Unpriced
(B77-24255)

615'.1 — Drugs. *Reviews of research*
Progress in medicinal chemistry. — Amsterdam ; Oxford : North-Holland Publishing Co. [etc.].
13 / edited by G.P. Ellis and G.B. West. — 1976[i.e.1977]. — x,357p : ill ; 22cm.
Published in the Netherlands: 1976. — Index.
ISBN 0-7204-0650-1 : £19.47
(B77-11840)

615'.1 — Drugs. Design
Drug design / edited by E.J. Ariëns. — New York [etc.] ; London : Academic Press. — (Medicinal chemistry ; vol.11)
Vol.7. — 1976 [i.e. 1977]. — xv,295p : ill ; 24cm.
Published in the United States: 1976. — Bibl. — Index.
ISBN 0-12-060307-1 : £21.30
(B77-11234)

615'.1 — Pharmacology. *Conference proceedings*
Clinical pharmacy and clinical pharmacology : proceedings of an international symposium held in Boston, Mass., USA, September 17-19 1975 / editors William A. Gouveia, Gianni Tognoni, Eppo van der Kleijn. — Amsterdam [etc.] ; Oxford : North-Holland Publishing Co., 1976. — xviii,463p : ill ; 25cm.
Bibl. — Index.
ISBN 0-7204-0596-3 : £31.85
Also classified at 615'.4
(B77-16412)

International Congress of Pharmacology, *6th, Helsinki, 1975.* Abstracts [of the] Sixth International Congress of Pharmacology. — Oxford [etc.] : Pergamon, 1977. — [2],693p : ill ; 22cm.
Held in Helsinki, 1975. — 'Organised by the Finnish Pharmacological Society' - half title page. — Bibl. — Index.
ISBN 0-08-021308-1 : £12.50
(B77-15308)

615'.1 — Pharmacology. *For respiratory therapy*
Mathewson, Hugh S. Pharmacology for respiratory therapists / [by] Hugh S. Mathewson. — Saint Louis : Mosby ; London : Distributed by Kimpton, 1977. — ix,93p : ill ; 22cm.
Bibl. — Index.
ISBN 0-8016-3160-2 Pbk : £4.40
(B77-30285)

615'.1'0216 — Pharmaceutical products. Non-proprietary names. *Lists. Serials*
International nonproprietary names (INN) for pharmaceutical substances = Dénominations communes internationales (DCI) pour les substances pharmaceutiques / [World Health Organization]. — Genève : W.H.O. ; [London] : [H.M.S.O.].
1976 : Cumulative list no.4 = Liste récapitulative no 4 : Lists 1-35 of proposed INN and lists 1-15 of recommended INN = Listes 1-35 de DCI proposées et listes 1-15 de DCI recommandées. — 1976. — xvii,314p : ill ; 24cm.
Parallel English and French introductions, contents and explanatory notes. Computer printout in Latin, English, French, Russian and Spanish. — Spine title: INN for pharmaceutical substances = DCI pour les substances pharmaceutiques.
Pbk : Unpriced
ISBN 92-4-056009-2
(B77-04839)

615'.1'024613 — Drug therapy. *For nursing*
Asperheim, Mary Kaye. The pharmacologic basic of patient care / [by] Mary K. Asperheim, Laurel A. Eisenhauer. — 3rd ed. — Philadelphia ; London [etc.] : Saunders, 1977. — viii,565p : ill ; 27cm.
Previous ed.: 1973. — Bibl. — Index.
ISBN 0-7216-1437-x : £9.00
(B77-27119)

615'.1'024613 — Drugs. *For nursing*
Gibson, John, *b.1907.* The nurse's materia medica / [by] John Gibson. — 4th ed. — Oxford [etc.] : Blackwell Scientific, 1976. — xxi,295p ; 17cm.
Previous ed.: 1973. — Index.
ISBN 0-632-00069-4 Pbk : £2.50
(B77-06114)

Squire, Jessie Elma. Basic pharmacology for nurses. — 6th ed. / [by] Jessie E. Squire, Jean M. Welch. — Saint Louis : Mosby ; London : Distributed by Kimpton, 1977. — [1],x,383p : ill ; 27cm.
Previous ed.: 1973. — Bibl.: p.359-364. — Index.
ISBN 0-8016-4740-1 Pbk : £5.60
(B77-19410)

615'.1'0246176 — Pharmacology. *For dentistry*
Pennington, George Williams. Dental pharmacology. — 3rd ed. / [by] George W. Pennington, T.N. Calvey, T.C.A. O'Neil. — Oxford [etc.] : Blackwell Scientific, 1977. — ix, 206p : ill ; 22cm.
Previous ed.: / by George W. Pennington and T.N. Calvey, 1969. — Index.
ISBN 0-632-00249-2 Pbk : £6.75
(B77-13665)

615'.1'03 — Drugs. *Dictionaries*
Hopkins, Sidney John. Principal drugs : an alphabetical guide / [by] S.J. Hopkins ; with a foreword by C.A. Keele. — 5th ed. — London : Faber, 1977. — 3-157p ; 16cm.
Previous ed.: 1973.
ISBN 0-571-04938-9 Pbk : £1.50
(B77-30286)

Marler, E E J. Pharmacological and chemical synonyms : a collection of names of drugs, pesticides and other compounds drawn from the medical literature of the world / compiled by E.E.J. Marler. — 6th ed. — Amsterdam ; Oxford : Excerpta Medica, 1976. — [8],472p ; 25cm.
Previous ed.: Amsterdam : Excerpta Medica, 1973.
£48.75
ISBN 90-219-0298-2 (Excerpta Medica)
Also classified at 668'.6'03
(B77-04840)

615'.1'05 — Pharmacology. *Periodicals*
Pharmacology & therapeutics. Part C : Clinical pharmacology and therapeutics. — Oxford [etc.] : Pergamon.
Vol.1, no.1-2- ; 1976-. — 1976-. — ill ; 28cm.
Published at irregular intervals. — [2],257p. in Vol.1, no.1-2. — Bibl. — Previous control number ISBN 0-08-020269-1.
Pbk : Unpriced
ISSN 0362-5486
Also classified at 615'.58'05
(B77-09042)

615'.1'091724 — Pharmaceutical products. *Developing countries*
Two papers on pharmaceuticals in developing countries. — Brighton : Institute of Development Studies at the University of Sussex, [1976]. — [2],23p ; 30cm. — (Institute of Development Studies. Communications ; 119 ISSN 0308-5856)
Bibl.: p.15-16. — Contents: Pharmaceuticals and health planning in developing countries / by Malcolm Segall - Pharmaceutical production in a less developed country / by Carol Barker.
ISBN 0-903354-31-4 Sd : £1.50
(B77-01493)

615'.1'096 — Prescription drugs. *Africa. Lists. Periodicals*
Mims Africa. — Ewell (172 Kingston Rd, Ewell, Surrey) : A.E. Morgan Publications Ltd.
Continues: African mims.
Vol.16, no.1- ; [Jan.-Feb.] 1976-. — [1976]-. — ill ; 22cm.
Six issues a year. — 163p. in Vol.17, no.4.
Pbk : £1.20(£7.50 yearly)
ISSN 0140-4415
(B77-30287)

615'.11'41 — Drugs. *British pharmacopoeias*
British Pharmacopoeia 1973 : published on the recommendation of the Medicines Commission pursuant to the Medicines Act 1968. — London : H.M.S.O.
Addendum 1977. — 1977. — xix,51,A21p : ill ; 30cm.
'Effective date: 1 December 1977'. — Index.
ISBN 0-11-320228-8 Pbk : £6.00
(B77-31222)

British Pharmacopoeia (veterinary) 1977. — 1977. — xxi,171,A34p ; 31cm.
'Effective date: 1 December 1977'. — Index.
ISBN 0-11-320624-0 : £10.00
(B77-29455)

Martindale, William. The extra pharmacopoeia : incorporating Squire's 'Companion' / [by] Martindale. — 27th ed. / edited by Ainley Wade, assistant editor James E.F. Reynolds ; published by direction of the Council of the Pharmaceutical Society of Great Britain and produced in the Society's Department of Pharmaceutical Sciences. — London : Pharmaceutical Press, 1977. — xxxii,2077p ; 26cm.
Previous ed.: / edited by Norman W. Blacow, assistant editor Ainley Wade. 1972. — Index.
ISBN 0-85369-114-2 : £30.00
(B77-20311)

615'.11'41 — Pharmaceutical industries. Proprietary drugs. *Great Britain. Lists*
Wyatt, Alan G. Chemicals 77 : a directory giving information on chemicals and allied products marketed by member firms of the Chemical Industries Association / [technical compilation by Alan G. Wyatt and Moira T. Damer ...]. — London (93 Albert Embankment, SE1 7TU) : The Association, 1976. — xii,211p,fold leaf : ill ; 21cm.
English text, English, German, Spanish and French introductions. — Index.
Pbk : £8.00
Primary classification 661'.00941
(B77-09129)

615'.18 — Drugs. Storage. Temperatures. *Lists*
Cleveland Area Health Authority. *Pharmaceutical Service.* The storage of drugs under controlled temperature conditions / [Cleveland Area Health Authority, Pharmaceutical Service]. — Stockton-on-Tees (Pharmaceutical Department, North Tees General Hospital, Hardwick Estate, Stockton-on-Tees, Cleveland TS19 8PE) : [The Service], 1976. — [3],50p : 1 ill ; 21cm.
Sd : £1.50
(B77-19411)

615'.19 — Drugs. Quality control. *Conference proceedings*
International Congress of Pharmaceutical Sciences, *35th, Dublin, 1975.* The quality control of medicines : proceedings of the 35th International Congress of Pharmaceutical Sciences, Dublin 1975 / P.B. Deasy & R.F. Timoney, editors. — Amsterdam [etc.] ; Oxford : Elsevier, 1976. — xiii,398p : ill ; 25cm.
Index.
ISBN 0-444-41454-1 : £25.00
(B77-05443)

615'.19 — Drugs. Testing
Clinical trials / edited by F. Neil Johnson and Susan Johnson ; foreword by Lord Cohen of Birkenhead. — Oxford [etc.] : Blackwell Scientific, 1977. — xvi,212p : ill ; 23cm.
Bibl. — Index.
ISBN 0-632-00306-5 Pbk : £8.25 : CIP rev.
(B77-16898)

615'.19 — Pharmaceutics
Bentley, Arthur Owen. Bentley's textbook of pharmaceutics. — 8th ed. / edited by E.A. Rawlins. — London : Baillière Tindall, 1977. — x,725p : ill ; 26cm.
Previous ed.: published as 'Textbook of pharmaceutics' / by Harold Davis et al., 1961. — Bibl. — Index.
ISBN 0-7020-0391-3 : £12.50
(B77-07373)

615'.1901 — Drugs. Analysis
Berman, Eleanor. Analysis of drugs of abuse / [by] Eleanor Berman. — London [etc.] : Heyden, 1977. — x,80p : ill ; 24cm. — (Heyden international topics in science)
Index.
ISBN 0-85501-226-9 : £5.50
(B77-21895)

615'.19015 — Pharmaceutics. Quantitative methods
Jenkins, Glenn Llewellyn. Jenkins' quantitative pharmaceutical chemistry. — 7th ed. / [by] Adelbert M. Knevel, Frank E. Di Gangi, with a chapter on biomedical analytical chemistry by Stephen R. Byrn. — New York ; London [etc.] : McGraw-Hill, 1977. — xxiii,518p : ill ; 25cm.
'A Blakiston publication'. — With answers to selected problems. — Previous ed.: published as 'Quantitative pharmaceutical chemistry' / by Glenn L. Jenkins, Adelbert M. Knevel, Frank E. Di Gangi. New York : McGraw-Hill, 1967. — Bibl.: p.xiii-xx. — Index.
ISBN 0-07-035087-6 : £14.95
(B77-24963)

615'.19018 — Man. Body fluids. Impurities: Drugs. Assay
Assay of drugs and other trace compounds in biological fluids / edited by Eric Reid. — Amsterdam [etc.] ; Oxford : North-Holland Publishing Co., 1976. — x,254p : ill ; 25cm. — (Methodological developments in biochemistry ; vol.5)
Index.
ISBN 0-7204-0584-x : £15.12
(B77-00786)

615'.191'0941 — Pharmaceutical products. Manufacture. *Great Britain. Standards*
Guide to good pharmaceutical manufacturing practice / Department of Health and Social Security ... [et al.]. — 2nd ed. — London : H.M.S.O., 1977. — [3],52p ; 21cm.
Previous ed.: 1971.
ISBN 0-11-320662-3 Sd : £0.90
(B77-18165)

615.3 — ORGANIC DRUGS
615'.3 — Biological medicinal products. Manufacture. *Standards*
Compendium of licensing requirements for the manufacture of biological medicinal products / issued by the Department of Health and Social Security, Medicines Division. — London : H.M.S.O.
Issue 1 : 1977. — 1977. — [3],76p ; 25cm.
ISBN 0-11-320500-7 Sd : £1.75
(B77-16899)

615'.3 — Organic drugs. Synthesis
Lednicer, Daniel. The organic chemistry of drug synthesis / [by] Daniel Lednicer, Lester A. Mitscher ; with a glossary by Philip F. vonVoigtlander. — New York ; London [etc.] : Wiley, 1977. — xix,471p : ill ; 24cm.
'A Wiley-Interscience publication'. — Index.
ISBN 0-471-52141-8 : £16.90
(B77-14752)

615'.31'42 — Cimetidine. *Conference proceedings*
International Symposium on Histamine H2-Receptor Antagonists, *2nd, London, 1976.* Cimetidine : proceedings of the Second International Symposium on Histamine H2-Receptor Antagonists, Royal College of Physicians, London, October 26 and 27, 1976 / editors W.L. Burland and M. Alison Simkins ; chairmen J.J. Misiewicz ... [et al.]. — Amsterdam ; Oxford ([256 Banbury Rd, Oxford OX2 7DH]) : Excerpta-Medica, 1977. — xiv, 392p : ill ; 24cm. — (International congress series ; no.416)
Bibl. — Index.
Pbk : £23.81
ISBN 90-219-0347-4
(B77-22616)

615'.32 — Drugs obtained from plants
Lewis, Walter H. Medical botany : plants affecting man's health / [by] Walter H. Lewis, Memory P.F. Elvin-Lewis. — New York ; London [etc.] : Wiley, 1977. — xvii,515p : ill, maps ; 26cm.
'A Wiley-Interscience publication'. — Bibl.: p.456-465. — Index.
ISBN 0-471-53320-3 : £18.00
(B77-20312)

Ross, Malcolm Stewart Frank. An introduction to phytopharmacy / [by] M.S.F. Ross, K.R. Brain. — Tunbridge Wells : Pitman Medical, 1977 [i.e.1976]. — [7],305p : ill ; 23cm.
Bibl. — Index.
ISBN 0-272-00467-7 : £7.00
(B77-03029)

615'.32 — Medicine. Natural remedies: Propolis
Hill, Ray. Propolis : the natural antibiotic / by Ray Hill. — Wellingborough : Thorsons, 1977. — 64p ; 18cm. — (Nature's way)
Index.
ISBN 0-7225-0353-9 Pbk : £0.60
(B77-13058)

615'.32 — Medicine. Natural remedies: Raw juices
Charmine, Susan E. The complete raw juice therapy / by Susan E. Charmine. — Wellingborough : Thorsons, 1977. — 128p : ill ; 22cm.
Index.
ISBN 0-7225-0361-x Pbk : £1.95
(B77-23447)

615'.321 — Medicine. Herbal remedies
Beedell, Suzanne. Herbs for health and beauty / [by] Suzanne Beedell. — London : Sphere, 1977. — 174p : ill ; 18cm.
Originally published: 1972. — Bibl.: p.158-159. — Index.
ISBN 0-7221-1528-8 Pbk : £0.75
ISBN 0-7221-1531-8
Also classified at 668'.55
(B77-10379)

Copen, Bruce. Simplified botanic medicine / by Bruce Copen. — [Enlarged and revised ed.]. — Haywards Heath : Academic Publications, [1976]. — [4],65p ; 20cm.
Previous ed.: i.e. 2nd ed. Balcombe : Copen, 1968.
ISBN 0-900307-55-2 Sd : £1.50
(B77-02344)

Smith, William, *b.1910.* Wonders in weeds / by William Smith ; illustrations by Beryl Smith. — Holsworthy : Health Science Press, 1977. — 187p : ill ; 23cm. — (Health master)
Index.
ISBN 0-85032-151-4 : £4.95
(B77-25660)

615'.321 — Medicine. Herbal remedies. *Manuals*
Tisserand, Robert. The art of aromatherapy / by Robert Tisserand. — London : Daniel, 1977. — 320p : ill ; 23cm.
Bibl.: p.316-318.
ISBN 0-85207-140-x : £6.00
(B77-20313)

Yewlett, Gerry. Wild herbs for health and happiness : a particular selection of effective healing herbs / by Gerry Yewlett. — [Wokingham] ([20 California Park, Nine Mile Ride, Finchampstead, Wokingham, Berks. RG11 4HT]) : Jogger, 1977. — [28]p : ill ; 84mm x15cm. — (Waterproof outdoor pocketbooks)
Notebook format.
Sd : £0.60
Primary classification 641.3'5'7
(B77-25039)

615'.321 — Pharmacognosy
Tyler, Varro Eugene. Pharmacognosy. — 7th ed. / by Varro E. Tyler, Lynn R. Brady, James E. Robbers. — Philadelphia : Lea and Febiger ; London : Kimpton, 1976. — x,537p : ill ; 27cm.
Previous ed.: / by E.P. Claus, Varro E. Tyler, Lynn R. Brady. 1970. — Bibl. — Index.
ISBN 0-8121-0568-0 : £16.10
(B77-17523)

615'.323'55 — Medicine. Homeopathy. Use of arnica
Speight, Phyllis. Arnica, the wonder herb : the remedy that should be in every home / by Phyllis Speight ; drawing by Jill Fry. — Holsworthy : Health Science Press, 1977. — 45p : ill ; 19cm. — (Health in the home series)
ISBN 0-85032-138-7 Pbk : 0.85p
(B77-26336)

615'.329 — Antibiotics. Chemical properties. *Reviews of research*
Topics in antibiotic chemistry. — Chichester : Ellis Horwood ; New York ; London [etc.] : [Distributed by] Wiley.
Vol.1 : Aminoglycosides and ansamycins / edited by P.G. Sammes. — 1977. — [6],217p : ill ; 24cm.
Index.
ISBN 0-85312-059-5 : £12.50
ISSN 0140-0843
(B77-22617)

615'.329 — Antimicrobials
Pharmaceutical microbiology / edited by W.B. Hugo, A.D. Russell. — Oxford [etc.] : Blackwell Scientific, 1977. — xi,352p : ill ; 24cm.
Bibl. — Index.
ISBN 0-632-00499-1 Pbk : £8.50 : CIP rev.
(B77-06115)

615'.329 — Antimicrobials. Susceptibility tests
Barry, Arthur L. The antimicrobic susceptibility test : principles and practices / [by] Arthur L. Barry, with chapters contributed by Paul D. Hoeprich ..., Michael A. Saubolle ... — Philadelphia : Lea and Febiger ; London : Kimpton, 1976 [i.e. 1977]. — xii,236p : ill ; 24cm.
Published in the United States: 1976. — Bibl. — Index.
ISBN 0-8121-0530-3 : £8.25
(B77-14252)

615'.329 — Antimicrobials. Susceptibility tests. Techniques. *Conference proceedings*
American Society for Microbiology. *Eastern Pennsylvania Branch. Annual Symposium, 7th, Philadelphia, 1975.* The clinical laboratory as an aid in chemotherapy of infectious disease : proceedings of the Seventh Annual Symposium of the Eastern Pennsylvania Branch of the American Society for Microbiology, Philadelphia, 20-21 November 1975 / edited by Amedeo Bondi, Josephine T. Bartola, James E. Prier. — Baltimore ; London [etc.] : University Park Press, 1977. — xiii,183p : ill ; 24cm.
Bibl. — Index.
ISBN 0-8391-0967-9 : £11.95
(B77-27120)

615'.329 — Beta-lactam antibiotics. Chemical properties. *Conference proceedings*
Recent Advances in the Chemistry of Beta-Lactam Antibiotics *(Conference), Cambridge, 1976.* Recent Advances in the Chemistry of [beta]...-Lactam Antibiotics, Cambridge, England, 28-30 June, 1976 : the proceedings of an international symposium arranged by the Fine Chemicals and Medicinals Group of the Industrial Division of the Chemical Society / edited by J. Elks. — London : The Society, 1977. — vi,313p : ill ; 23cm. — (Chemical Society. Special publications ; no.28 ISSN 0577-618x)
'The Symposium on "Recent Advances in the Chemistry of [beta]...-Lactam Antibiotics" ...' - Preface.
ISBN 0-85186-198-9 : £14.50
(B77-31928)

615'.329 — Medicine. Drug therapy. Antibiotics
Noone, Paul. A clinician's guide to antibiotic therapy / [by] Paul Noone. — Oxford [etc.] : Blackwell Scientific, 1977. — ix,106p ; 22cm.
Index.
ISBN 0-632-00016-3 Pbk : £3.25 : CIP rev.
(B77-07374)

Smith, Hillas. Antibiotics in clinical practice / [by] Hillas Smith. — 3rd ed. — Tunbridge Wells [etc.] : Pitman Medical, 1977. — x,413p, [2]p of plates,leaf of plate : ill ; 23cm.
Previous ed.: 1972. — Bibl. — Index.
ISBN 0-272-79418-x : £8.00
(B77-13666)

615'.329 — Medicine. Drug therapy. Antimicrobials
Braude, Abraham I. Antimicrobial drug therapy / [by] Abraham I. Braude. — Philadelphia ; London [etc.] : Saunders, 1976. — ii-ix,218p : ill ; 24cm. — (Major problems in internal medicine ; vol.8)
Bibl. — Index.
ISBN 0-7216-1918-5 : £9.00
(B77-00243)

615'.329'03 — Antibiotics. *Encyclopaedias*
Glasby, John Stephen. Encyclopaedia of antibiotics / [by] John S. Glasby. — London [etc.] : Wiley, [1977]. — [5],372p : ill ; 19x26cm.
'A Wiley-Interscience publication'. — Bibl.
ISBN 0-471-01818-x : £17.50
(B77-09716)

615'.329'23 — Medicine. Drug therapy. Bromocriptine. *Conference proceedings*
Pharmacological and clinical aspects of bromocriptine (Parlodel) : proceedings of a symposium held at the Royal College of Physicians, London, 14 May, 1976 / editors R.I.S. Bayliss, P. Turner, W.P. Maclay. — Tunbridge Wells (PO Box 14, Tunbridge Wells, Kent TN3 0DX) : Medical Congresses and Symposia Consultants, 1976. — 117p : ill ; 25cm.
Bibl.
Pbk : Unpriced
(B77-17524)

615'.36 — Adjuvants. *Reports, surveys*
World Health Organization. *Scientific Group on Immunological Adjuvants.* Immunological adjuvants : report of a WHO Scientific Group / [WHO Scientific Group on Immunological Adjuvants]. — Geneva : W.H.O. ; [London] : [H.M.S.O.], 1976. — 40p ; 20cm. — (World Health Organization. Technical report series ; no.595)
Bibl.: p.39-40.
Sd : £1.50
ISBN 92-4-120595-4
(B77-01494)

615'.366 — Man. Physiology. Effects of drugs: Sex hormones
Brotherton, Janet. Sex hormone pharmacology / [by] J. Brotherton. — London [etc.] : Academic Press, 1976. — x,511p : ill ; 24cm.
Index.
ISBN 0-12-137250-2 : £16.00
(B77-08405)

615'.37 — Medicine. Drug therapy. Antivirals
Bauer, Denis John. The specific treatment of virus diseases / by D.J. Bauer. — Lancaster : M.T.P. Press, 1977. — viii,194p : ill ; 24cm.
Bibl.: p.161-188. — Index.
ISBN 0-85200-138-x : £8.95
(B77-21896)

615'.37 — Medicine. Drug therapy. Antivirals. *Conference proceedings*
Antivirals with clinical potential / edited by Thomas C. Merigan. — Chicago ; London : University of Chicago Press, [1977]. — [7], 292p : ill ; 29cm.
'Based on a symposium on antivirals held at Stanford University in August 1975' - half title page verso. — Published in the United States: 1976. — '... originally appeared as a supplement to the June 1976 issue of the "Journal of Infectious Diseases"' - title page verso. — Index.
ISBN 0-226-52027-7 : £12.00
(B77-11235)

615'.37 — Serology
Delaat, Adrian N C. Primer of serology / [by] Adrian N.C. Delaat. — Hagerstown [etc.] ; London : Harper and Row, Medical Department, 1976. — xi,148p : ill ; 24cm.
Bibl. — Index.
ISBN 0-06-140686-4 Pbk : £7.45
(B77-05444)

615.4 — PHARMACY
615'.4 — Drugs. Dispensing
Ansel, Howard Carl. Introduction to pharmaceutical dosage forms / [by] Howard C. Ansel. — 2nd ed. — Philadelphia : Lea and Febiger ; London : Kimpton, 1976. — viii, 415p : ill ; 27cm.
Ill. on lining papers. — Previous ed.: 1969. — Bibl. — Index.
ISBN 0-8121-0561-3 : £9.75
(B77-04841)

615'.4 — Pharmacy. *Conference proceedings*
Clinical pharmacy and clinical pharmacology : proceedings of an international symposium held in Boston, Mass., USA, September 17-19 1975 / editors William A. Gouveia, Gianni Tognoni, Eppo van der Kleijn. — Amsterdam [etc.] ; Oxford : North-Holland Publishing Co., 1976. — xviii,463p : ill ; 25cm.
Bibl. — Index.
ISBN 0-7204-0596-3 : £31.85
Primary classification 615'.1
(B77-16412)

615'.4'01513 — Drugs. Dosage. Arithmetical calculations. *Exercises, worked examples. For nursing*
Anderson, Ellen Marie. Workbook of solutions and dosage of drugs, including arithmetic. — 10th ed. / [by] Ellen M. Anderson, Thora M. Vervoren. — Saint Louis : Mosby ; London : Distributed by Kimpton, 1976. — vii,167p : ill ; 27cm.
Pages perforated at inside edge and pierced for binder. — Previous ed.: 1972. — Bibl.: p.167.
Pbk : £3.45
(B77-02345)

Radcliff, Ruth K. Calculation of drug dosages : workbook / [by] Ruth K. Radcliff, Sheila J. Ogden. — Saint Louis : Mosby ; London : Distributed by Kimpton, 1977. — ix,262p ; 27cm.
Pierced for binder. — Pages perforated at inside edge. — Fill-in book. — With answers. — 'With 202 separately packaged flash cards' (26 perforated sheets ([52] sides)).
ISBN 0-8016-3713-9 Pbk : £7.00
(B77-18166)

Richardson, Lloyd I. The mathematics of drugs and solutions with clinical applications / [by] Lloyd I. Richardson, Jr, Judith Knight Richardson. — New York ; London [etc.] : McGraw-Hill, 1976. — vi,153p : ill ; 26cm.
'A Blakiston publication'. — With answers.
ISBN 0-07-052309-6 Pbk : £4.95
(B77-04842)

615'.4'01513 — Drugs. Dosage. Arithmetical calculations. *For nursing. Programmed texts*
Hart, Laura Katherine. The arithmetic of dosages and solutions : a programmed presentation / [by] Laura K. Hart. — 4th ed. — St Louis : Mosby ; London : Distributed by Kimpton, 1977. — vii,74p : ill ; 26cm.
With answers. — Template in pocket. — Previous ed.: St Louis : Mosby, 1973.
ISBN 0-8016-2085-6 Sp : £4.70
(B77-19412)

Saxton, Dolores Frances. Programmed instruction in arithmetic, dosages and solutions. — 4th ed. / [by] Dolores F. Saxton, Norma H. Ercolano, John F. Walter. — Saint Louis : Mosby ; London : Distributed by Kimpton, 1977. — ix,64p : 1 ill ; 26cm.
Template in pocket. — Previous ed.: / by Dolores F. Saxton, John F. Walter. 1974.
ISBN 0-8016-4329-5 Sp : Unpriced
(B77-24257)

615'.4'02541 — Pharmaceutical chemists. *Great Britain. Directories*
Annual register of pharmaceutical chemists ; [and], List of bodies corporate and their superintendents ; [and], Register of premises / Pharmaceutical Society of Great Britain. — London (1 Lambeth High St., SE1 7JN) : The Society.
1976. — 1976. — 865p in various pagings ; 17x23cm.
Spine title: Register of pharmaceutical chemists ...
ISBN 0-85369-110-x Pbk : £18.00
(B77-04215)

615'.4'06241 — Pharmacy. Organisations. *Great Britain. Pharmaceutical Society of Great Britain. Yearbooks*
Pharmaceutical Society of Great Britain. Calendar / Pharmaceutical Society of Great Britain. — London [etc.] (1 Lambeth High St., SE1 7JN) : The Society.
1976-7. — 1976. — 135p : forms ; 22cm.
Index.
ISBN 0-85369-112-6 Pbk : £2.00
ISSN 0307-8094
(B77-09717)

615'.4'0942615 — Pharmaceutical chemists. *Norfolk. Norwich region, 1800-1975*
Coleman, W L B. The chemists and pharmacists of Norwich and district : from circa 1800 to 1975 / [by W.L.B. Coleman]. — [Norwich] ([59 Charles Close, Wroxham, Norwich NR12 8TT]) : [The author], [1977]. — [1],22p ; 21cm.
ISBN 0-9505623-0-0 Pbd : Unpriced
(B77-11236)

615'.43 — Drugs. Capsules & tablets. Preparation
Carstensen, Jens Thuro. Pharmaceutics of solids and solid dosage forms / [by] Jens T. Carstensen. — New York ; London [etc.] : Wiley, 1977. — xv,256p : ill ; 24cm.
'A Wiley-Interscience Publication'. — Index.
ISBN 0-471-13726-x : £12.40
(B77-20314)

615.5 — MEDICINE. THERAPY

615'.5 — Medicine. Therapy. *Comparative studies*
Forbes, Alec. Try being healthy / by Alec Forbes. — Wembury (The Old Laundry, Langdon, Wembury, Plymouth) : Langdon Books, 1976. — [3],188p ; 20cm. — (Health master)
Bibl.: p.172-184. — Index.
ISBN 0-85032-140-9 Pbk : £2.25
(B77-04216)

615'.5 — Medicine. Therapy. *Reviews of research*
Current therapy : latest approved methods of treatment for the practicing physician. — Philadelphia ; London [etc.] : Saunders.
1976 / edited by Howard F. Conn. — 1976. — xli,916,8p,[2] fold : ill, forms ; 27cm.
Text on lining papers. — Index.
ISBN 0-7216-2661-0 : £17.75
(B77-00244)

1977 / edited by Howard F. Conn. — 1977. — xli,986p : ill, form ; 27cm.
Index.
ISBN 0-7216-2662-9 : £19.50
(B77-20315)

Topics in therapeutics. — Tunbridge Wells : Pitman Medical.
3 / edited by R.G. Shanks. — 1977. — x, 251p : ill ; 24cm. — (Advanced medicine ISSN 0308-9630)
Bibl. — Index.
ISBN 0-272-79420-1 : £6.50
(B77-16900)

615'.5 — Therapeutic regimens. Compliance of patients. *Conference proceedings*
Workshop/Symposium on Compliance with Therapeutic Regimens, *McMaster University Medical Centre, 1974.* Compliance with therapeutic regimens / David L. Sackett and R. Brian Haynes, editors. — Baltimore ; London : Johns Hopkins University Press, [1977]. — xvii, 293,[1]p : ill, facsim ; 24cm.
' ... the Workshop/Symposium on Compliance with Therapeutic Regimens, held at the McMaster University Medical Centre in May 1974' - Preface. — Published in the United States : 1976. — Bibl.: p.193-287. — Index.
ISBN 0-8018-1783-8 : £12.00
(B77-14253)

615'.5'08 — Medicine. Therapy. *Readings. Serials*
Today's treatment. — London : British Medical Association.
2. — 1977. — [10],221p : 1 ill ; 22cm.
'Articles published in the "British Medical Journal"'. — Bibl. — Index.
ISBN 0-7279-0025-0 Pbk : £4.00
(B77-23448)

615'.532 — Medicine. Homeopathy
Puddephatt, Noel. Puddephatt's primers / revised by Phyllis Speight. — Holsworthy : Health Science Press, 1976. — 68p ; 19cm.
Bibl.: p.66-68. — Contents: First steps to homoeopathy. New ed. Originally published: London : Homoeopathic Publishing Co., 1950 - How to find the correct remedy. Originally published: London : Homoeopathic Publishing Co., 1945 - The homoeopathic materia medica. New ed. Originally published: 1972.
ISBN 0-85032-136-0 Pbk : £1.25
(B77-11841)

Stephenson, James H. A doctor's guide to helping yourself with homeopathic remedies / by James H. Stephenson. — Wellingborough : Thorsons, 1977. — 7-197p ; 22cm.
Originally published: West Nyack, N.Y. : Parker, 1976.
ISBN 0-7225-0372-5 Pbk : £2.00
(B77-11842)

615'.532 — Medicine. Homeopathy. Prescription. *Manuals*
Ross, Andrew Christie Gordon. Arnica, the amazing healer : and a dozen other homoeopathic remedies for aches, pains and strains / by A.C. Gordon Ross. — Wellingborough : Thorsons, 1977. — 96p ; 18cm.
ISBN 0-7225-0374-1 Pbk : £0.90
(B77-31929)

Voegeli, Adolf. Homoeopathic prescribing : remedies for home and surgery / by Adolf Voegeli ; translated from the German by Geoffrey Dudley. — Wellingborough : Thorsons, 1976. — 94p ; 22cm.
Translation of: 'Die korrecte homöopathische Behandlung in der täglichen Praxis'. Ulm : Haug, 1964.
ISBN 0-7225-0343-1 Pbk : £1.75
(B77-07375)

615'.533 — Medicine. Osteopathy
Chaitow, Leon. Osteopathy : head-to-toe health through manipulation / by Leon Chaitow ; drawings by Troy Fox. — Wellingborough : Thorsons, 1977. — 92p : ill ; 18cm.
Originally published: 1974.
ISBN 0-7225-0378-4 Pbk : £0.90
(B77-11843)

615'.533'02541 — Osteopaths. *Great Britain. Directories. For judo*
Members of the Register of Osteopaths ; and, Directory of practitioners of the London & Counties Society of Physiologists / J. Milom Ltd. — Manchester (68 Great Ducie St., Manchester M3 1ND) : J. Milom Ltd.
[1976]. — 1976. — 11,7p ; 33cm.
Sd : Unpriced
(B77-16901)

615'.533'06241 — Medicine. Osteopathy. Organisations: British Naturopathic and Osteopathic Association. *Great Britain. Directories*
British Naturopathic and Osteopathic Association. Official register of practitioner members ; and, Manifesto of the Association / British Naturopathic and Osteopathic Association. — London (6 Netherhall Gardens, NW3 5RR) : [The Association].
1977. — [1977]. — [2],35p ; 22cm.
Sd : £0.40
Also classified at 615'.535'06241
(B77-26337)

615'.535 — Medicine. Natural remedies
Moyle, Alan. Natural healing : an introduction to nature cure with advice on diet, fasting, hydrotherapy and osteopathy / by Alan Moyle. — Wellingborough : Athene Publishing Co., 1977. — [2],62p ; 18cm.
Originally published: as 'About nature cure'. London : Thorsons, 1965.
ISBN 0-7225-0397-0 Pbk : £0.60
(B77-22618)

615'.535 — Medicine. Naturopathy
Ledermann, Erich Kurt. Good health through natural therapy / [by] E.K. Ledermann. — London : Kogan Page, 1976. — [8],147p : ill ; 23cm.
Index.
ISBN 0-85038-141-x : £3.95
(B77-04843)

615'.535'06241 — Medicine. Naturopathy. Organisations: British Naturopathic and Osteopathic Association. *Great Britain. Directories*
British Naturopathic and Osteopathic Association. Official register of practitioner members ; and, Manifesto of the Association / British Naturopathic and Osteopathic Association. — London (6 Netherhall Gardens, NW3 5RR) : [The Association].
1977. — [1977]. — [2],35p ; 22cm.
Sd : £0.40
Primary classification 615'.533'06241
(B77-26337)

615'.542 — Children. Therapy
Current pediatric therapy. — Philadelphia ; London [etc.] : Saunders.
7 / [edited by] Sydney S. Gellis and Benjamin M. Kagan. — [1977]. — xxx,781p ; 27cm.
Published in the United States: 1976. — Index.
ISBN 0-7216-4090-7 : £21.00
(B77-08406)

615'.58 — Man. Drug therapy. *Conference proceedings*
International Congress of Chemotherapy, *9th, London, 1975.* Chemotherapy. — New York ; London : Plenum Press.
'Proceedings of the Ninth International Congress of Chemotherapy held in London, July, 1975' - title page verso. — In 8 vols.
Vol.5 : Penicillins and cephalosporins / edited by J.D. Williams and A.M. Geddes. — [1977]. — xiv,420p : ill ; 26cm.
Published in the United States: 1976. — Bibl.
ISBN 0-306-38225-3 : £22.05
(B77-09719)

Vol.6 : Parasites, fungi and viruses / edited by J.D. Williams and A.M. Geddes. — [1977]. — xiv,434p : ill ; 26cm.
Published in the United States: 1976. — Bibl.
ISBN 0-306-38226-1 : £22.05
(B77-09720)

615'.58 — Medicine. Drug therapy. *Conference proceedings*
International Congress of Chemotherapy, *9th, London, 1975.* Chemotherapy. — New York ; London : Plenum Press.
'Proceedings of the Ninth International Congress of Chemotherapy held in London, July, 1975' - title page verso. — In 8 vols.
Vol.1 : Clinical aspects of infections / edited by J.D. Williams and A.M. Geddes. — [1977]. — xiv,438p : ill ; 26cm.
Published in the United States: 1976. — Bibl.
ISBN 0-306-38221-0 : £22.05
(B77-09718)

Vol.2 : Laboratory aspects of infections / edited by J.D. Williams and A.M. Geddes. — [1977]. — xiv,462p : ill ; 26cm.
Published in the United States: 1976. — Bibl.
ISBN 0-306-38222-9 : £22.05
(B77-09043)

Vol.3 : Special problems in chemotherapy / edited by J.D. Williams and A.M. Geddes. — 1976. — xiv,442p : ill ; 26cm.
Bibl.
ISBN 0-306-38223-7 : £22.05
(B77-16902)

Vol.4 : Pharmacology of antibiotics / edited by J.D. Williams and A.M. Geddes. — 1976. — xiv,436p : ill ; 26cm.
Bibl.
ISBN 0-306-38224-5 : £22.05
(B77-16903)

Vol.7 : Cancer chemotherapy. 1 / edited by K. Hellmann and T.A. Connors. — 1976. — xii, 364p : ill ; 26cm.
Bibl.
ISBN 0-306-38227-x : £22.05
(B77-16904)

615'.58 — Medicine. Drug therapy. *Reviews of research*
Advances in pharmacology and chemotherapy. — New York [etc.] ; London : Academic Press. Vol.14 / edited by Silvio Garattini ... [et al.]. — 1977. — x,421p : ill ; 24cm.
Bibl. — Index.
ISBN 0-12-032914-x : £27.00
(B77-22619)

615'.58'024613 — Medicine. Drug therapy. *For nursing*
Falconer, Mary Waring. Patient studies in pharmacology : a guidebook / [by] Mary W. Falconer. — Philadelphia ; London [etc.] : Saunders, 1976. — xi,147p ; 26cm.
Fill-in book. — Bibl.
ISBN 0-7216-3545-8 Pbk : £4.25
(B77-18804)

Foundations of pharmacologic therapy / consultant Joan Thiele. — New York ; London [etc.] : Wiley, 1977. — xi,167p : ill, forms ; 28cm. — (Wiley nursing concept modules)
'A Wiley medical publication'. — With answers. — Pages perforated at inside edge and pierced for binder. — Fill-in book. — Bibl.
ISBN 0-471-02168-7 Pbk : £5.20
(B77-26338)

615'.58'05 — Medicine. Drug therapy. *Periodicals*
Pharmacology & therapeutics. Part A : Chemotherapy, toxicology and metabolic inhibitors. — Oxford [etc.] : Pergamon.
Vol.1, no.1- ; 1976-. — [1976]-. — ill ; 28cm.
Quarterly. — [2]p.,p.231-348 in Vol.1, no.3. — Bibl.
Pbk : £50.00 yearly
ISSN 0362-5478
(B77-29456)

Pharmacology & therapeutics. Part C : Clinical pharmacology and therapeutics. — Oxford [etc.] : Pergamon.
Vol.1, no.1-2- ; 1976-. — 1976-. — ill ; 28cm.
Published at irregular intervals. — [2],257p. in Vol.1, no.1-2. — Bibl. — Previous control number ISBN 0-08-020269-1.
Pbk : Unpriced
ISSN 0362-5486
Primary classification 615'.1'05
(B77-09042)

615.6 — DRUG THERAPY. MEDICATION
615'.6 — Prescribed drugs. Self-administration. *United States. Manuals*
Smith, Dorothy L. Medication guide for patient counseling / [by] Dorothy L. Smith. — Philadelphia : Lea and Febiger ; London : Kimpton, 1977. — xiii,442p : ill, forms ; 24cm.
Bibl.: p.422. — Index.
ISBN 0-8121-0586-9 Pbk : £8.40
(B77-32653)

615'.63 — Medicine. Intravenous therapy. Fluids. Contaminants. *Conference proceedings*
Microbiological hazards of infusion therapy : proceedings of an international symposium held at the University of Sussex, England, March 1976 / edited by I. Phillips, P.D. Meers, P.F. D'Arcy. — Lancaster : M.T.P. Press, 1976. — x,186p : ill ; 24cm.
Index.
ISBN 0-85200-162-2 : £6.95
(B77-13059)

615'.65 — Man. Blood. Transfusion
Wallace, John, *b.1916.* Blood transfusion for clinicians / [by] John Wallace ; foreword by Cyril A. Clarke. — Edinburgh [etc.] : Churchill Livingstone, 1977. — ix,351p : ill ; 25cm.
Bibl. — Index.
ISBN 0-443-01537-6 : £10.00
(B77-15879)

615.7 — PHARMACODYNAMICS
615'.7 — Drugs. Action
Basic pharmacology in medicine / Joseph R. DiPalma, editor. — New York ; London [etc.] : McGraw-Hill, 1976. — xii,420p : ill ; 25cm.
'A Blakiston Publication'. — 'Based on the 4th ed. of V.A. Drill's "Pharmacology in medicine"' - Library of Congress Cataloging in Publication Data. — Bibl.: p.397-406. — Index.
ISBN 0-07-017010-x : £10.90
(B77-16905)

Curry, Stephen Henry. Drug disposition and pharmacokinetics : with a consideration of pharmacological and clinical relationships / [by] Stephen H. Curry. — 2nd ed. — Oxford [etc.] : Blackwell Scientific, 1977. — xi,275p, fold leaf : ill ; 24cm.
Previous ed.: 1974. — Bibl.: p.269-270. — Index.
ISBN 0-632-00476-2 Pbk : £6.25 : CIP rev.
(B77-04844)

Gibaldi, Milo. Biopharmaceutics and clinical pharmacokinetics / [by] Milo Gibaldi. — 2nd ed. — Philadelphia : Lea and Febiger ; London : Kimpton, 1977. — ix,181p : ill ; 26cm.
Previous ed.: 197-. — Index.
ISBN 0-8121-0584-2 Pbk : £5.95
(B77-29457)

Ryan, Sheila A. Handbook of practical pharmacology / [by] Sheila A. Ryan, Bruce D. Clayton. — Saint Louis : Mosby ; London : Distributed by Kimpton, 1977. — xv,235p ; 22cm.
Bibl.: p.227. — Index.
ISBN 0-8016-0978-x Sp : £5.60
(B77-18805)

615'.7 — Drugs. Action. *Reviews of research*
Advances in general and cellular pharmacology. — New York ; London : Plenum Press.
Vol.1 / edited by Toshio Narahashi and C. Paul Bianchi. — 1976. — xi,252p : ill ; 24cm.
Bibl. — Index.
ISBN 0-306-35071-8 : £15.44
(B77-04845)

615'.7 — Man. Adverse reactions to drugs
Textbook of adverse drug reactions / edited by D.M. Davies. — Oxford [etc.] : Oxford University Press, 1977. — xvi,503p : ill ; 26cm. — (Oxford medical publications)
Bibl. — Index.
ISBN 0-19-263206-x : £14.00
(B77-31930)

615'.7 — Man. Drugs. Metabolism. *Reviews of research*
Progress in drug-metabolism. — London [etc.] : Wiley.
Bibl. — Index.
Vol.2 / edited by J.W. Bridges, L.F. Chasseaud. — 1977. — ix,348p : ill ; 24cm.
'A Wiley-Interscience Publication'.
ISBN 0-471-99442-1 : £13.50
(B77-18167)

615'.7 — Man. Drugs. Oxidation. Role of microsomes. *Conference proceedings*
International Symposium on Microsomes and Drug Oxidations, *3rd, Berlin, 1976.*
Microsomes and drug oxidations : proceedings of the Third International Symposium, Berlin, July 1976 / editors Volker Ullrich ... [et al.]. — Oxford [etc.] : Pergamon, 1977. — xxxiv,768p, plate : ill, port ; 26cm.
'... [Proceedings of the] Third International Symposium on Microsomes and Drug Oxidations ...' - Preface. — 'Published as a Supplement to "Biochemical Pharmacology"'. — Index. — Includes abstracts to some papers.
ISBN 0-08-021523-8 : £25.00
(B77-28653)

615'.7 — Man. Effects of drugs
Teachers' Advisory Council on Alcohol and Drug Education. Drugs : basic facts / [script by TACADE staff]. — Manchester (2 Mount St., Manchester M2 5NG) : Teachers' Advisory Council on Alcohol and Drug Education, [1977]. — Folder([1],9p) : ill ; 21x10cm.
ISBN 0-905954-02-5 : Unpriced
(B77-09721)

615'.7 — Medicine. Drug therapy. Effectiveness. Assessment by clinical trials. *Conference proceedings*
International Colloquium on Prospective Biology, *3rd, Pont-à-Mousson, 1975.* Drug interference and drug measurement in clinical chemistry : proceedings of the Third International Colloquium on Prospective Biology, Pont-à-Mousson, October 6-10, 1975 / editors G. Siest and D.S. Young ; co-editors C. Heusghem, G. Olive and J.R. Royer. — Basel ; London [etc.] : Karger ; [London] : [Distributed by Wiley], 1976. — viii,207p : ill ; 25cm.
Bibl.
Unpriced
ISBN 3-8055-2360-2
(B77-31224)

The **principles** and practice of clinical trials : based on a symposium organised by the Association of Medical Advisers in the Pharmaceutical Industry / edited by C.S. Good ; foreword by Sir Cyril Clarke. — Edinburgh [etc.] : Churchill Livingstone, 1976. — xii,201p : ill, facsim, forms ; 25cm. — ([A Churchill Livingstone symposium])
'... symposium ... held ... at the Royal College of Physicians, on 6th and 7th May 1976 ...' - Preface. — Bibl. — Index.
ISBN 0-443-01525-2 : £6.50
(B77-24258)

615'.704 — Drugs. Interactions. *Conference proceedings*
Drug interactions / edited by D.G. Grahame-Smith ; [for the] Biological Council, the Co-ordinating Committee for Symposia on Drug Action. — London [etc.] : Macmillan, 1977. — x,310p : ill, forms ; 24cm.
'On March 24 and 25 1975 the Co-ordinating Committee for Symposia on Drug Action of the Biological Council held a symposium entitled "Drug Interactions" at the Middlesex Hospital Medical School, London' - Foreword. — Bibl. — Index.
ISBN 0-333-21283-5 : £15.00
(B77-12476)

615'.704 — Drugs. Interactions & ocular side effects
Fraunfelder, F T. Drug-induced ocular side effects and drug interaction / [by] F.T. Fraunfelder. — Philadelphia : Lea and Febiger ; London : Kimpton, 1976. — xix, 370p ; 25cm.
Bibl. — Index.
ISBN 0-8121-0551-6 : £12.00
(B77-07926)

615'.704 — Drugs. Interactions & side effects
Beeley, Linda. Safer prescribing : a guide to some problems in the use of drugs / [by] Linda Beeley. — Oxford [etc.] : Blackwell Scientific, 1976. — vi,42p ; 19cm.
Index.
ISBN 0-632-00146-1 Sd : £0.90
(B77-07925)

615'.7042'05 — Drugs. Side effects. *Serials*
Side effects of drugs annual : a worldwide yearly survey of new data and trends. — Amsterdam ; Oxford ([256 Banbury Rd, Oxford OX2 7DH]) : Excerpta Medica.
'"Meyler's side effects of drugs" ... and the "Side effects of drugs annual" are designed to complement one another... ' - half title page verso.
1 : 1977 / edited by M.N.G. Dukes. — 1977. — xvii,420p ; 25cm.
Bibl. — Index.
£20.00
ISBN 90-219-3038-2
(B77-19413)

615'.71 — Anti-hypertensive drugs. *Conference proceedings*
Richards (A.N.) Symposium, *17th, King of Prussia, Pa, 1975.* New antihypertensive drugs / edited by Alexander Scriabine and Charles S. Sweet. — New York : Spectrum Publications ; New York ; London [etc.] : Distributed by Wiley, 1976. — [19],608p : ill ; 24cm. — (Physiological Society of Philadelphia. Monographs ; vol.2)
'Proceedings of the A.N. Richards Symposium, King of Prussia, Pennsylvania, May 19-20, 1975' - half-title page verso. — Bibl. — Index.
ISBN 0-470-15181-1 : £28.95
Also classified at 616.1'32'061
(B77-12477)

615'.739 — Man. Lipids. Metabolism. Effects of drugs. *Conference proceedings*
International Symposium on Drugs Affecting Lipid Metabolism, *5th, Milan, 1974.* Lipids, lipoproteins and drugs / edited by David Kritchevsky, Rodolfo Paoletti and William L. Holmes. — New York ; London : Plenum Press, [1976]. — xii,515p : ill ; 26cm. — (Advances in experimental medicine and biology ; vol.63)
'Proceedings of the Fifth International Symposium on Drugs Affecting Lipid Metabolism held in Milan, Italy, September 9-12, 1974' - title page verso. — Published in the United States: 1975. — Index.
ISBN 0-306-39063-9 : £24.89
(B77-02346)

615'.739 — Man. Lipids. Metabolism. Effects of drugs. *Reviews of research*
Lipid pharmacology. — New York [etc.] ; London : Academic Press. — (Medicinal chemistry ; vol.2 ISSN 0076-6054)
Vol.2 / edited by Rodolfo Paoletti and Charles J. Glueck. — 1976. — xv,326p : ill ; 24cm.
Bibl. — Index.
ISBN 0-12-544952-6 : £15.95
(B77-03030)

615'.78 — Man. Adverse reactions to psychotropic drugs
Study Group on Functional Toxicity. Adverse effects of environmental chemicals and psychotropic drugs / Study Group on Functional Toxicity (Permanent Commission and International Association on Occupational Health). — Amsterdam ; Oxford [etc.] : Elsevier.
Vol.2 : Neurophysiological and behavioral tests / edited by Milan Horváth in collaboration with Emil Franták. — 1976. — xv,334p : ill ; 25cm.
' ... the Second Workshop on Functional Toxicity Evaluation, [held in Prague] ... convened by the Subcommittee for the Study of Higher Nervous Functions of the International Association of Occupational Health' - Introductory address. — Bibl.
ISBN 0-444-41498-3 : £25.12
Primary classification 614.7
(B77-07371)

615'.78 — Man. Behaviour. Effects of drugs
Behavioral pharmacology / edited by Stanley D. Glick, Joseph Goldfarb. — Saint Louis : Mosby ; London : Distributed by Kimpton, 1976. — xvii,379p : ill ; 27cm.
Bibl. — Index.
ISBN 0-8016-1851-7 : £13.75
(B77-03031)

Seiden, Lewis S. Psychopharmacology : a biochemical and behavioral approach / [by] Lewis S. Seiden, Linda A. Dykstra. — New York ; London [etc.] : Van Nostrand Reinhold, 1977. — xi,451p : ill ; 24cm.
Bibl. — Index.
ISBN 0-442-27481-5 : £16.15
(B77-21897)

615'.78 — Man. Brain. Effects of drugs
Jones, Hardin B. Sensual drugs : deprivation and rehabilitation of the mind / [by] Hardin B. Jones and Helen C. Jones. — Cambridge [etc.] : Cambridge University Press, 1977. — x,373p : ill ; 22cm.
Bibl.: p.333-354. — Index.
ISBN 0-521-21247-2 : £7.40
ISBN 0-521-29077-5 Pbk : £2.25
(B77-10814)

615'.78 — Man. Eyes. Effects of drugs. *Conference proceedings*
International Society for Eye Research. *Meeting, 2nd, Jerusalem, 1976.* Drug and ocular tissues / editor S. Dikstein. — Basel ; London [etc.] : Karger ; [London] : [Distributed by Wiley], 1977. — xx,661p : ill ; 22cm.
'Second meeting of the International Society for Eye Research, Jerusalem, 1976' - cover. — Bibl. — Index.
Pbk : Unpriced
ISBN 3-8055-2637-7
(B77-31225)

615'.78 — Man. Nervous system. Synapses. Effects of drugs
Triggle, David John. Chemical pharmacology of the synapse / [by] D.J. Triggle and C.R. Triggle. — London [etc.] : Academic Press, 1976. — ix,654p : ill ; 24cm.
Bibl. — Index.
ISBN 0-12-700340-1 : £20.00
(B77-09044)

615'.78 — Neuropharmacology. *Reviews of research*
Essays in neurochemistry and neuropharmacology. — London [etc.] : Wiley.
Vol.1 / edited by M.B.H. Youdim ... [et al.]. — 1977. — xi,195p : ill ; 24cm.
'A Wiley-Interscience Publication'. — Bibl.
ISBN 0-471-99424-3 : £9.90
Primary classification 612'.8042
(B77-08401)

615'.78 — Neuropsychopharmacology. *Reviews of research*
Progress in neuro-psychopharmacology. — Oxford [etc.] : Pergamon.
Vol.1, no.1- ; [Jan.] 1977-. — 1977-. — ill ; 25cm.
Quarterly. — Cover title. — 230p. in 1st issue. — Bibl.
Pbk : Unpriced
ISSN 0364-7722
(B77-18168)

615'.78 — Psychopharmacology
Handbook of psychopharmacology / edited by Leslie L. Iversen, Susan D. Iversen and Solomon H. Snyder. — New York ; London : Plenum Press.
Vol.1 : Biochemical principles and techniques in neuropharmacology. — [1976]. — xiii,298p : ill ; 26cm.
Published in the United States: 1975. — Bibl. — Index.
ISBN 0-306-38921-5 : £14.18
(B77-01495)

Vol.2 : Principles of receptor research. — [1976]. — xii,288p : ill ; 26cm.
Published in the United States: 1975. — Bibl. — Index.
ISBN 0-306-38922-3 : £14.18
(B77-01496)

Vol.3 : Biochemistry of biogenic amines. — [1976]. — xii,486p : ill ; 26cm.
Published in the United States: 1975. — Bibl. — Index.
ISBN 0-306-38923-1 : £22.05
(B77-01497)

Vol.4 : Amino acid neurotransmitters. — [1976] . — xi,317p : ill ; 26cm.
Published in the United States: 1975. — Bibl. — Index.
ISBN 0-306-38924-x : £15.75
(B77-01498)

Vol.5 : Synaptic modulators. — [1976]. — xii, 381p : ill ; 26cm.
Published in the United States: 1975. — Bibl. — Index.
ISBN 0-306-38925-8 : £18.59
(B77-01499)

Vol.6 : Biogenic amine receptors. — [1977]. — xii,307p : ill ; 26cm.
Published in the United States: 1975. — Bibl. — Index.
ISBN 0-306-38926-6 : Unpriced
(B77-09722)

Psychopharmacology in the practice of medicine / edited by Murray E. Jarvik ; foreword by Louis Jolyon West. — New York : Appleton-Century-Crofts ; London [etc.] : Prentice-Hall, 1977. — xvii,553p : ill ; 24cm.
Bibl. — Index.
ISBN 0-8385-7950-7 : £16.40
(B77-31226)

615'.78 — Psychopharmacology. *Reviews of research*
Advances in behavioral pharmacology. — New York [etc.] ; London : Academic Press.
Vol.1 / edited by Travis Thompson and Peter B. Dews. — 1977. — x,267p : ill ; 24cm.
Bibl. — Index.
ISBN 0-12-004701-2 : £11.70
(B77-21898)

Current developments in psychopharmacology. — New York : Spectrum Publications ; New York ; London [etc.] : Distributed by Wiley.
Vol.1 / editors Walter B. Essman, L. Valzelli. — 1975. — [12],345p : ill ; 24cm.
Bibl. — Index.
ISBN 0-470-24567-0 : £18.85
(B77-10380)

Vol.3 / editors Walter B. Essman, L. Valzelli. — 1976. — [14],303p : ill ; 24cm.
Bibl. — Index.
ISBN 0-470-99002-3 : £18.75
(B77-15309)

615'.78'05 — Psychopharmacology. *Periodicals*
Communications in psychopharmacology. — Oxford [etc.] : Pergamon.
Vol.1, no.1- ; 1977-. — 1977-. — ill ; 23cm.
Six issues a year. — Cover title. — 87,[3]p. in 1st issue.
Pbk : £22.92
ISSN 0145-5699
(B77-18806)

615'.782 — Depressants. Addiction potential. Evaluation. *Conference proceedings*
Conference on Prediction of Abuse Liability of Stimulant and Depressant Drugs, *Washington, D.C., 1976.* Predicting dependence liability of stimulant and depressant drugs / edited by Travis Thompson and Klaus R. Unna. — Baltimore ; London [etc.] : University Park Press, 1977. — xv,328p : ill ; 24cm.
'Proceedings of the "Conference on Prediction of Abuse Liability of Stimulant and Depressant Drugs", held April 19-21, 1976, at the National Academy of Sciences, Washington, D.C.' - p.v.. — Index.
ISBN 0-8391-1147-9 : £13.95
Also classified at 615'.785
(B77-30288)

615'.782 — Man. Effects of ethanol & opiates. *Reviews of research*
Neurochemical and Behavioral Mechanisms of Alcohol and Opiate Dependence *(Conference), New York, 1976.* Alcohol and opiates : neurochemical and behavioral mechanisms / edited by Kenneth Blum, associate editors Diana L. Bard and Murray G. Hamilton. — New York [etc.] ; London : Academic Press, 1977. — xxiii,403p : ill ; 24cm.
'Proceedings of a conference entitled "The Neurochemical and Behavioral Mechanisms of Alcohol and Opiate Dependence", New York, March 26-28, 1976' - half title page verso.
ISBN 0-12-108450-7 : £12.40
(B77-31931)

615'.782 — Man. Tissues. Effects of addictive narcotics. *Conference proceedings*
Tissue Responses to Addictive Drugs *(Conference), State University of New York, 1975.* Tissue responses to addictive drugs : proceedings of a workshop session for the International Society for [Psycho]neuroendocrinology, Downstate Medical Center, State University of New York, June 1975 / edited by Donald H. Ford and Doris H. Clouet. — New York : Spectrum ; New York ; London [etc.] : Distributed by Wiley, [1977]. — [19],704p : ill ; 24cm.
'... conference on "Tissue Responses to Addictive Drugs" ...' - Preface. — Published in the United States: 1976. — Bibl. — Index.
ISBN 0-470-15192-7 : £37.50
(B77-13060)

615'.785 — Stimulants. Addiction potential. Evaluation. *Conference proceedings*
Conference on Prediction of Abuse Liability of Stimulant and Depressant Drugs, *Washington, D.C., 1976.* Predicting dependence liability of stimulant and depressant drugs / edited by Travis Thompson and Klaus R. Unna. — Baltimore ; London [etc.] : University Park Press, 1977. — xv,328p : ill ; 24cm.
'Proceedings of the "Conference on Prediction of Abuse Liability of Stimulant and Depressant Drugs", held April 19-21, 1976, at the National Academy of Sciences, Washington, D.C.' - p.v.. — Index.
ISBN 0-8391-1147-9 : £13.95
Primary classification 615'.782
(B77-30288)

615'.788 — Psychotropic drugs
The price of tranquillity : the manufacture and use of psychotropic drugs : two papers / given by Sanjaya Lall and Peter A. Parish. — London : MIND, [1977]. — [14],8,[1]p ; 30cm. — (MIND. Occasional papers ; 4 ISSN 0306-8625)
'These two papers are the substance of presentations given by Peter Parish and Sanjaya Lall at a conference organised by MIND and the Medical Practitioners Union in November 1974 on "Inequalities in the Distribution and Inadequacies in the Treatment of Mental Illness"' - Foreword. — Contents: The family doctor's role in psychotropic drug use / by Peter A. Parish - The international pharmaceutical industry, with special reference to psychotropic drugs / by S. Lall.
Sd : £0.55
(B77-17525)

615'.7883'0924 — Man. Mental processes. Effects of hallucinogenic drugs. *Personal observations*
Huxley, Aldous. The doors of perception ; and, Heaven and hell / [by] Aldous Huxley. — St Albans : Triad, 1977. — 143p ; 18cm.
This collection originally published: London : Chatto and Windus, 1961. — 'The doors of perception' originally published: London : Chatto and Windus, 1954. — 'Heaven and hell' originally published: London : Chatto and Windus, 1956.
ISBN 0-586-04437-x Pbk : £0.60
(B77-10381)

615.8 — PHYSICAL AND OTHER THERAPIES
615'.82 — Medicine. Physiotherapy. Exercises
Hollis, Margaret. Practical exercise therapy / [by] Margaret Hollis, with contributions by Barbara Sanford, Patricia J. Waddington. — Oxford [etc.] : Blackwell Scientific, 1976. — ix, 244p : ill ; 24cm.
Bibl.: p.239. — Index.
ISBN 0-632-00189-5 Pbk : £9.50
(B77-03032)

615'.82'023 — Medicine. Physiotherapy. *Great Britain. Career guides*
Employment Service Agency. *Careers and Occupational Information Centre.* The remedial professions. — 6th ed. / [prepared by the Careers and Occupational Information Centre of the Employment Service Agency in association with the Careers Service Branch of the Department of Employment, and by the Central Office of Information]. — [London] : H.M.S.O., 1976. — [2],41p : ill ; 22cm. — (Choice of careers : new series ; 52)
ISBN 0-11-880903-2 Sd : £0.30
(B77-14753)

615'.822 — Man. Spine. Manipulation
Maitland, Geoffrey Douglas. Vertebral manipulation / [by] G.D. Maitland ; with a contribution by D.A. Brewerton. — 4th ed. — London [etc.] : Butterworth, 1977. — xii,338p : ill ; 23cm.
Previous ed.: 1973. — Index.
ISBN 0-407-43504-2 : £7.50
(B77-18169)

615'.822 — Shiatzu. *Manuals*
Irwin, Yukiko. Shiatzu : Japanese finger pressure for energy, sexual vitality and relief from tension and pain / by Yukiko Irwin with James Wagenvoord ; foreword by M. Dorothea Kerr ; illustrations by Raymond Burns. — London [etc.] : Routledge and Kegan Paul, 1977. — 239,[1]p : ill(chiefly col) ; 16x24cm.
Originally published: Philadelphia : Lippincott, 1976.
ISBN 0-7100-8612-1 : £6.50
ISBN 0-7100-8507-9 Pbk : £3.25
(B77-19414)

Ohashi, Wataru. Do-it-yourself shiatsu : how to perform the ancient Japanese art of acupuncture without needles / by Wataru Ohashi ; edited by Vicki Lindner. — London : Mandala Books, 1977. — 144p : ill ; 28cm.
Originally published: New York : Dutton, 1976.
ISBN 0-04-613033-0 Pbk : £3.50
(B77-24259)

615'.824 — Medicine. Physiotherapy. Exercises
Daniels, Lucille. Therapeutic exercise for body alignment and function / [by] Lucille Daniels, Catherine Worthingham ; illustrations by Harold Black, Lorene Sigal and Phyllis Hedberg. — 2nd ed. — Philadelphia ; London [etc.] : Saunders, 1977. — viii,117p : ill ; 27cm.
Previous ed.: 1957. — Bibl.: p.109-111. — Index.
ISBN 0-7216-2873-7 Sp : £8.50
(B77-28654)

615'.824'02541 — Remedial gymnasts. *Great Britain. Directories*
The **remedial** gymnasts register. — [London] ([York House, Westminster Bridge Rd, SE1 7UH]) : Remedial Gymnasts Board.
1977. — [1977]. — 41 leaves ; 21x30cm.
Pbk : £1.00
(B77-29458)

615'.836 — Critically ill patients. Intensive care. Respiratory therapy
Mathewson, Hugh S. Respiratory therapy in critical care / [by] Hugh S. Mathewson. — Saint Louis : Mosby ; London : Distributed by Kimpton, 1976. — ix,133p : ill ; 22cm.
Bibl. — Index.
ISBN 0-8016-3158-0 Pbk : £5.30
(B77-20316)

615'.836 — Respiratory therapy equipment
McPherson, Steven P. Respiratory therapy equipment / [by] Steven P. McPherson. — Saint Louis : Mosby ; London : Distributed by Kimpton, 1977. — xiii,382p : ill ; 26cm.
Index.
ISBN 0-8016-3319-2 : £11.95
(B77-30289)

615'.837 — Medicine. Music therapy. *Conference proceedings*
Music therapy in the clinical and remedial team : papers read at the one day conference held at St Michael's School, Graham Terrace, London, S.W.1, 13th October 1973. — London (48 Lanchester Rd, N6 4TA) : British Society for Music Therapy, [1973?]. — [3],49p : ill ; 26cm.
ISBN 0-85513-010-5 Sd : £1.00
(B77-16415)

615'.845 — Medicine. Electron dosimetry below 5 MeV. *For radiotherapy*
Hospital Physicists' Association. *Electron Beam Working Party.* A practical guide to electron dosimetry below 5 MeV for radiotherapy purposes / the Hospital Physicists' Association, Radiotherapy Physics Committee, Electron Beam Working Party. — [London] ([47 Belgrave Sq., S.W.1]) : [The Association], [1975]. — [2],16,[2]p : 1 ill ; 21cm. — (Hospital Physicists' Association. Report series ; no.13)
Bibl.: p.16.
Sd : £0.20
(B77-20317)

615'.85 — Medicine. Orgonomy. *Essays*
Reich, Wilhelm. Selected writings : an introduction to orgonomy / [by] Wilhelm Reich. — [New revised ed.]. — London : Vision Press, 1973. — xxv,560p : ill ; 21cm.
Previous ed.: 1961. — Bibl.: p.545-553. — Index.
ISBN 0-85478-093-9 : £6.40
(B77-19415)

615'.8512 — Medicine. Hypnotherapy
Gibson, H B. Hypnosis : its nature and therapeutic uses / [by] H.B. Gibson. — London : Owen, 1977. — 191p,[4]p of plates : ill ; 22cm.
Index.
ISBN 0-7206-0334-x : £6.00
(B77-14254)

615'.8512 — Medicine. Hypnotherapy. *Manuals*
Erickson, Milton H. Hypnotic realities : the induction of clinical hypnosis and forms of indirect suggestion / by Milton H. Erickson, Ernest L. Rossi, Sheila I. Rossi ; with a foreword by André M. Weitzenhoffer. — New York : Irvington ; New York ; London [etc.] : Distributed by Wiley, 1976. — xxi,326p ; 24cm & sound cassette.
Bibl.: p.315-318. — Index.
ISBN 0-470-15169-2 : £17.65
(B77-13667)

615'.8515 — Medicine. Occupational therapy
Jones, Mary Senior. An approach to occupational therapy / [by] Mary S. Jones. — 3rd ed. / revised by Peggy Jay. — London [etc.] : Butterworth, 1977. — [11],451p : ill, form, plans ; 23cm.
Previous ed.: 1964. — Bibl. — List of films: p.347. — Index.
ISBN 0-407-00053-4 : £14.50 : CIP rev.
(B77-24964)

615'.852 — Atlanteans. Spiritual healing. *Manuals*
Atlanteans. A practical course on Atlantean healing / [Atlanteans]. — Cheltenham (42 St George's St., Cheltenham GL50 4AF) : The Atlanteans, 1976. — [1],19p ; 33cm.
ISBN 0-900112-10-7 Sd : £0.50
(B77-04217)

615'.852 — Christianity. Spiritual healing
Scanlan, Michael. Inner healing / [by] Michael Scanlan. — Dublin : Veritas Publications, 1977. — vi,85p ; 19cm.
Originally published: New York : Paulist Press, 1974. — Bibl.: p.83-85.
ISBN 0-905092-16-3 : Unpriced
(B77-18170)

615'.852 — Christianity. Spiritual healing. *Personal observations*
Dearing, Trevor. Exit the Devil / by Trevor Dearing ; with Dan Wooding. — Ongar ('Ashlings', Moreton Rd, Ongar, Essex) : Logos Publishing International Ltd, 1976. — [7], 117p ; 18cm.
ISBN 0-905156-03-x Pbk : £0.60
(B77-12478)

Stapleton, Ruth Carter. The gift of inner healing / [by] Ruth Carter Stapleton. — London [etc.] : Hodder and Stoughton, 1977. — 126p ; 18cm. — (Hodder Christian paperbacks)
Originally published: Waco, Tex. : Word Books, 1976.
ISBN 0-340-21600-x Pbk : £0.75
(B77-12479)

615'.852 — Christianity. Spiritual healing, 1971-1972. *Personal observations*
Stanbury, Ralph. Elizabeth : journey to a miracle / by Ralph Stanbury. — London [etc.] : Hodder and Stoughton, 1976. — 160p ; 21cm.
Bibl.: p.159-160.
ISBN 0-340-20993-3 : £3.50
(B77-03568)

615'.852 — Christianity. Spiritual healing. Kuhlman, Kathryn. *Biographies*
Hosier, Helen Kooiman. Kathryn Kuhlman : the life she led, the legacy she left / [by] Helen Kooiman Hosier. — London : Lakeland, 1977. — 152p,[8]p of plates : ill, ports ; 18cm.
Originally published: Old Tappan, N.J. : Revell, 1976.
ISBN 0-551-00599-8 Pbk : £0.75
(B77-16416)

615'.852 — Christianity. Spiritual healing. Sikorzyna, Waleria. *Biographies*
Noell, Nell Halina. The queen of goodness : Sikorzyna / [by] Nell Halina Noell. — London ([27 The Drive, Wembley Park, Middx]) : Garby Publications, 1977. — 48p : 1 ill, ports ; 21cm.
Pbk : £1.00
(B77-31227)

615'.852 — Spiritual healing, 1944-1975. *Personal observations*
Sadgrove, Michael. How I became a healer : an autobiography / [by] Michael Sadgrove. — King's Lynn (99 Wootton Rd, King's Lynn, Norfolk) : The Healing Centre, 1976. — 85p ; 18cm.
ISBN 0-9500632-2-3 Sd : £1.00
(B77-27121)

615'.852 — Spiritual healing, 1949-1976. *Personal observations*
Fricker, E G. God is my witness : the story of the world-famous healer / [by] E.G. Fricker. — London : A. Barker, 1977. — 190p ; 23cm.
ISBN 0-213-16648-8 : £4.50
(B77-22620)

615'.852 — Spiritual healing. White Eagle methods
Cooke, Ivan. Healing by the spirit / [by] Ivan Cooke. — Revised ed., with new matter. — Liss : White Eagle Publishing Trust, 1976. — [6],196p ; 23cm.
Previous ed.: published as 'Healing'. 1955. — Index.
ISBN 0-85487-039-3 : £3.50
(B77-01500)

615'.853 — Medicine. Hydrotherapy. *Manuals*
Sneddon, James Russell. Healing yourself with water : how you can use hydrotherapy for gaining and maintaining health / by J. Russell Sneddon. — Completely revised and reset ed. — Wellingborough : Thorsons, 1977. — 64p ; 18cm. — (Nature's way)
Previous ed.: published as 'About the water cure'. 1965. — Index.
ISBN 0-7225-0309-1 Pbk : £0.60
(B77-13668)

615'.853 — Medicine. Hydrotherapy. Exercises
Exercise in water / edited by M.H. Duffield. — 2nd ed. — London : Baillière Tindall, 1976. — ix,135p,[8]p of plates : ill, plan ; 22cm.
Previous ed.: London : Baillière Tindall and Cassell, 1969. — Index.
ISBN 0-7020-0600-9 Pbk : £2.50
(B77-01501)

615'.854 — Critically ill patients. Therapy. Role of nutrition. *Conference proceedings*
Nutritional aspects of care in the critically ill / edited by J.R. Richards, J.M. Kinney ; foreword by L.H. Blumgart. — Edinburgh [etc.] : Churchill Livingstone, 1977. — xvii, 678p : ill ; 25cm.
'... a record of the proceedings of a conference organised by the University [of Glasgow] Department of Surgery, Glasgow Royal Infirmary ...' - Foreword. — Bibl. — Index.
ISBN 0-443-01578-3 : £12.00 : CIP rev.
(B77-15310)

615'.854 — Medicine. Therapy. Diet
Robinson, Corinne Hogden. Normal and therapeutic nutrition. — 15th ed. / [by] Corinne H. Robinson and Marilyn R. Lawler. — New York : Macmillan ; London : Collier Macmillan, 1977. — x,739p : ill, forms ; 25cm.
Text on lining paper. — Previous ed.: / by Corinne H. Robinson with the assistance of Marilyn R. Lawler. 1972. — Bibl. — Index.
ISBN 0-02-402300-0 : £9.75
Primary classification 641.1
(B77-33897)

Williams, Sue Rodwell. Nutrition and diet therapy / [by] Sue Rodwell Williams. — 3rd ed. — Saint Louis : Mosby ; London : Distributed by Kimpton, 1977. — xviii,723p : ill, forms ; 27cm.
Previous ed.: 1973. — Bibl. — Index.
ISBN 0-8016-5560-9 : £10.35
Primary classification 641.1
(B77-33898)

615'.854 — Medicine. Therapy. Role of nutrition
Nutritional support of medical practice / editors Howard A. Schneider, Carl E. Anderson, David B. Coursin, with 45 contributors. — Hagerstown [etc.] ; London : Harper and Row, 1977. — xxv,555p : ill, forms ; 27cm.
Bibl. — Index.
ISBN 0-06-140259-1 : £18.75
(B77-28655)

615'.854'024613 — Medicine. Therapy. Diet. *For nursing*
Beck, Mary Elizabeth. Nutrition and dietetics for nurses / [by] Mary E. Beck ; foreword by H.E. Magee. — 5th ed. / illustrations by Rowel Friers. — Edinburgh [etc.] : Churchill Livingstone, 1977. — [10],228p : ill, forms ; 22cm. — (Livingstone nursing texts)
Previous ed.: 1975. — Bibl.: p.223-224. — Index.
ISBN 0-443-01557-0 Pbk : £2.95
(B77-23449)

615'.892 — Acupuncture
Warren, Frank Z. Handbook of medical acupuncture / [by] Frank Z. Warren. — New York ; London [etc.] : Van Nostrand Reinhold, 1976. — [11],273p : ill ; 24cm.
Index.
ISBN 0-442-29198-1 : £11.00
(B77-03033)

615'.892'06241 — Acupuncture. Organisations. *Great Britain. Acupuncture Association. Directories*
Acupuncture Association. The register and year book / the Acupuncture Association. — [London] ([34 Alderney St., SW1V 4EU]) : [The Association].
Bibl.: p.18-20.
1976. — [1977]. — [1],44p ; 21cm.
ISBN 0-9504160-2-9 Sd : £0.50
ISSN 0306-669x
(B77-06702)

615.9 — TOXICOLOGY
Current approaches in toxicology / edited by Bryan Ballantyne. — Bristol : J. Wright, 1977. — viii,310p : ill ; 22cm.
Bibl. — Index.
ISBN 0-7236-0437-1 Pbk : £8.50
(B77-08407)

615.9 — Children. Poisoning by household products. *England. Reports, surveys*
Great Britain. *Department of Prices and Consumer Protection.* Child poisoning from household products : a report based on a detailed investigation into suspected child poisoning in the home / Department of Prices and Consumer Protection. — London (1 Victoria St., SW1H 0ET) : Consumer Safety Unit, D.P.C.P., 1976. — [4],25p : ill ; 30cm.
Bibl.: p.25.
ISBN 0-86058-002-4 Sd : Unpriced
(B77-01502)

Great Britain. *Department of Prices and Consumer Protection.* Child poisoning from household products : a report based on a detailed investigation into suspected child poisoning in the home / Department of Prices and Consumer Protection. — Revised [ed.]. — London (1 Victoria St., SW1H 0ET) : Consumer Safety Unit, D.P.C.P., 1977. — [5], 25p : ill ; 30cm.
Previous ed.: 1976. — Bibl.: p.25.
Sd : Unpriced
(B77-31932)

615.9 — Medicine. Toxicology. *Conference proceedings*
Clinical toxicology : proceedings of the meeting held at Edinburgh, June 1976 / editors W.A.M. Duncan, B.J. Leonard. — Amsterdam ; Oxford : Excerpta Medica, 1977. — ix,348p : ill ; 25cm. — (European Society of Toxicology. Proceedings ; vol.18) (International congress series ; no.417)
Includes two chapters in French. — Bibl. — Index.
Pbk : £17.50
ISBN 90-219-0333-4
(B77-21899)

615.9 — Medicine. Toxicology. *Reviews of research*
Advances in modern toxicology / [editor Myron A. Mehlman]. — Washington, D.C. ; London : Hemisphere ; New York ; London [etc.] : Wiley.
Vol.1, part 1 : New concepts in safety evaluation / edited by Myron A. Mehlman, Raymond E. Shapiro, Herbert Blumenthal. — 1976. — xix,455p : ill, port ; 24cm.
'A Halsted Press book'. — Bibl. — Index.
ISBN 0-470-98919-x : £19.50
(B77-07377)

Vol.4 : Dermatotoxicology and pharmacology / edited by Francis N. Marzulli, Howard I. Maibach. — 1977. — xix,567p,[4]p of plates : ill(some col) ; 24cm.
'A Halsted Press book'. — Bibl. — Index.
ISBN 0-470-99063-5 : £26.00
(B77-23450)

615.9'0028 — Medicine. Toxicology. Laboratory techniques. Quality control. *Conference proceedings*
Quality Control in Toxicology *(Conference), 1977?.* Quality control in toxicology / edited by G.E. Paget. — Lancaster : M.T.P. Press, 1977. — xiii,128p : ill ; 23cm.
'Quality Control in Toxicology was sponsored and organized by Inveresk Research International. The meeting was the second in their series "Topics in Toxicology" ...' - p.vi. — Index.
ISBN 0-85200-184-3 : £8.50
(B77-33827)

615.9'02 — Industrial medicine. Toxicology
Plunkett, E R. Handbook of industrial toxicology / by E.R. Plunkett. — [New ed.]. — London : Heyden, 1976. — [3],552p : ill, form ; 23cm.
This ed. originally published: New York : Chemical Publishing Co., 1976. — Bibl.: p.532-536. — Index.
ISBN 0-85501-214-5 : £17.50
(B77-02347)

615.9'25'3 — Man. Toxic effects of metallic powders
Brakhnova, Irina Tikhonovna. Environmental hazards of metals : toxicity of powdered metals and metal compounds / [by] I.T. Brakhnova ; translated from Russian by J.H. Slep. — New York ; London (8 Scrubs La., Harlesden, NW10 6SE) : Consultants Bureau, [1976]. — xiii,277p : ill ; 24cm. — (Studies in Soviet science : physical sciences)
This translation published in the United States : 1975. — Translation and revision of: 'Toksichnost' poroshkov metallov i ikh soedinenii'. Kiev : Nauka Dumka, 1971. — Bibl.: p.255-277.
ISBN 0-306-10897-6 : £18.59
(B77-01503)

615.9'25'663095215 — Inhabitants. Poisoning by mercury. *Japan. Niigata*
Minamata disease : methylmercury poisoning in Minamata and Niigata, Japan / edited by Tadao Tsubaki, Katsuro Irukayama. — Tokyo : Kodansha ; Amsterdam ; Oxford [etc.] : Elsevier, 1977. — [9],317p : ill, maps ; 24cm. — (Kodansha scientific books)
Index.
ISBN 0-444-99816-0 : Unpriced
Primary classification 615.9'25'66309522
(B77-22621)

615.9'25'66309522 — Inhabitants. Poisoning by mercury. *Japan. Minimata*
Minamata disease : methylmercury poisoning in Minamata and Niigata, Japan / edited by Tadao Tsubaki, Katsuro Irukayama. — Tokyo : Kodansha ; Amsterdam ; Oxford [etc.] : Elsevier, 1977. — [9],317p : ill, maps ; 24cm. — (Kodansha scientific books)
Index.
ISBN 0-444-99816-0 : Unpriced
Also classified at 615.9'25'663095215
(B77-22621)

615.9'25'663097131 — Inhabitants. Poisoning by mercury. *Ontario. Grassy Narrows region*
Hutchison, George. Grassy Narrows / text by George Hutchison ; photos by Dick Wallace ; foreword by Philippe Cousteau. — Toronto ; London [etc.] : Van Nostrand Reinhold, 1977. — xiv,178p : ill, maps, ports ; 20cm.
ISBN 0-442-29877-3 Pbk : £6.80
(B77-32654)

615.9'42 — Venoms
Tu, Anthony T. Venoms : chemistry and molecular biology / [by] Anthony T. Tu. — New York ; London [etc.] : Wiley, 1977. — xi, 560,[2]p(2 fold) : ill ; 26cm.
'A Wiley-Interscience publication'. — Bibl. — Index.
ISBN 0-471-89229-7 : £25.90
(B77-25662)

615.9'42'0994 — Man. Animal stings. First aid. *Australia*
Worrell, Eric. Things that sting / [by] Eric Worrell ; drawings by Graham Bryce. — London [etc.] : Angus and Robertson, 1975. — [4],68p : ill ; 22cm.
'An A & R guide' - cover. — Index.
ISBN 0-207-13412-x Sd : Unpriced
Also classified at 591.6'9'0994
(B77-27122)

615.9'5 — Naturally occurring toxins. *Conference proceedings*
International Symposium on Animal, Plant and Microbial Toxins, *4th, Tokyo, 1974.* Animal, plant and microbial toxins. — New York ; London : Plenum Press.
In 2 vols.
Vol.1 : Biochemistry / edited by Akira Ohsaka, Kyozo Hayashi and Yoshio Sawai, associate editors ... [others]. — 1976. — xxvi,555p : ill ; 24cm.
'Proceedings of the first half of The Fourth International Symposium on Animal, Plant, and Microbial Toxins, organized by the International Society on Toxinology, held in Tokyo, Japan, September 8-13, 1974' - title page verso. — Bibl. — Index.
ISBN 0-306-37065-4 : £37.49
(B77-21900)

615.9'51'1 — Polychlorinated biphenyls. Toxic effects
PCB poisoning and pollution / edited by Kentaro Higuchi. — Tokyo : Kodansha ; New York [etc.] ; London : Academic Press, 1976. — x, 184p,plate : ill(incl 1 col), maps ; 23cm. — (Kodansha scientific books)
Index.
ISBN 0-12-347850-2 : £12.40
Also classified at 614.7
(B77-14754)

615.9'51'31 — Man. Poisons: Alcohol. Biochemistry
Metabolic aspects of alcoholism / edited by Charles S. Lieber. — Lancaster : M.T.P. Press, 1977. — ix,308p : ill ; 24cm.
Index.
ISBN 0-85200-129-0 : £11.50
(B77-05445)

616 — DISEASES
Boyd, William, *b.1885.* An introduction to the study of disease. — 7th ed. / [by] William Boyd, Huntington Sheldon. — Philadelphia : Lea and Febiger ; London : Kimpton, 1977. — xxiii,492p : ill ; 26cm.
Previous ed.: / by William Boyd. 1971. — Bibl. — Index.
ISBN 0-8121-0600-8 : £9.45
(B77-33254)

Charles, Simon. Home medical handbook / [by] Simon Charles. — London : Sphere, 1975. — 160p : ill(some col) ; 22cm. — ('Good housekeeping' family library)
Originally published: London : Ebury Press, 1973.
ISBN 0-7221-3953-5 Pbk : £0.95
(B77-19416)

Connon, J J. An introductory textbook of medicine / by J.J. Connon. — London : Lloyd-Luke, 1977. — ix,373p : ill ; 21cm.
Index.
ISBN 0-85324-110-4 Pbk : £4.75
(B77-13061)

Jacobson, Bertil. Medicine and clinical engineering. — American ed. / [by] Bertil Jacobson, John G. Webster. — Englewood Cliffs ; London [etc.] : Prentice-Hall, 1977. — xiv,674p : ill ; 24cm.
Previous ed.: published in Swedish as 'Medicin och teknik' / by Bertil Jacobson. Lund : Studentlitteratur, 1975. — Bibl. — Index.
ISBN 0-13-572966-1 : £20.00
(B77-15311)

Rubenstein, David. Lecture notes on clinical medicine / [by] David Rubenstein, David Wayne. — Oxford [etc.] : Blackwell Scientific, 1977. — x,277p : ill ; 24cm.
Originally published: 1976. — Bibl.: p.256-258. — Index.
Pbk : £4.00
ISBN 0-632-09620-9
(B77-21902)

Vickery, Donald M. Take care of yourself : a consumer's guide to medical care / [by] Donald M. Vickery, James F. Fries. — Reading, Mass. ; London [etc.] : Addison-Wesley, [1977]. — xvi,269p : ill, forms ; 27cm.
Published in the United States: 1976. — Index.
ISBN 0-201-02401-2 : £7.00
ISBN 0-201-02402-0 Pbk : £3.90
(B77-11844)

616 — Adolescent medicine. *Reviews of research*
Adolescent medicine topics. — New York : Spectrum Publications ; New York ; London [etc.] : Distributed by Wiley.
Vol.1 / [edited by] Ralph I. Lopez. — [1976]. — [11],260p : ill ; 24cm.
Bibl. — Index.
ISBN 0-470-15151-x : £16.75
(B77-08408)

616 — Executives. Diseases
Wright, Henry Beric. Executive ease and dis-ease / [by] H. Beric Wright. — Revised ed. — London [etc.] : Pan Books, 1977. — 254p : ill ; 18cm.
Previous ed.: Epping : Gower Press, 1975. — Index.
ISBN 0-330-25181-3 Pbk : £0.90
Primary classification 613
(B77-33246)

616 — Hospitals. House physicians. Duties. *Great Britain. Manuals*
Birch, Charles Allan. The house physician's handbook / [by] C. Allan Birch. — 4th ed. — Edinburgh [etc.] : Churchill Livingstone, 1977. — xv,320p : ill ; 19cm.
Previous ed.: 1972. — Index.
ISBN 0-443-01536-8 Pbk : £3.75
(B77-11237)

616 — Man. Diseases. *For African students*
Principles of medicine in Africa / edited by E.H.O. Parry. — Oxford [etc.] : Oxford University Press, 1976. — xi,604p : ill, maps ; 25cm. — (Oxford medical publications)
Bibl. — Index.
ISBN 0-19-264223-5 : £12.00
(B77-27123)

616 — Man. Diseases. *For general practice*
General practice medicine / edited by J.H. Barber, F.A. Boddy ; foreword by E.V. Kuenssberg. — Edinburgh [etc.] : Churchill Livingstone, 1975. — xii,352p : ill, forms, plan ; 24cm.
Bibl. — Index.
ISBN 0-443-01143-5 Pbk : £4.95
(B77-11238)

A **textbook** of medical practice / edited by J. Fry, P.S. Byrne and S. Johnson. — Lancaster : M.T.P. Press, 1976. — x,665p ; 23cm.
Bibl.: p.75. — Index.
ISBN 0-85200-130-4 : £9.95
(B77-11239)

616 — Medicine. Intensive care
Burrell, Zeb Lee. Critical care / [by] Zeb L. Burrell, Jr, Lenette Owens Burrell. — 3rd ed. — Saint Louis : Mosby ; London : Distributed by Kimpton, 1977. — xii,427p : ill, form, plan ; 27cm.
Previous ed.: published as 'Intensive nursing care' / by Lenette Owens Burrell, Zeb L. Burrell, Jr. 1973. — Bibl.: p.415-417. — Index.
ISBN 0-8016-0914-3 : £9.55
(B77-21166)

616 — Medicine. Intensive care. *Reviews of research*
Recent advances in intensive therapy. — Edinburgh [etc.] : Churchill Livingstone.
No.1 / edited by I. McA. Ledingham. — 1977. — xi,257p : ill ; 25cm.
Bibl. — Index.
ISBN 0-443-01432-9 : £12.00 : CIP rev.
(B77-24966)

616 — Negroes. Diseases
Textbook of Black-related diseases / edited by Richard Allen Williams. — New York ; London [etc.] : McGraw-Hill, [1976]. — xxii, 805p : ill, facsim, maps, port ; 24cm.
Col. ill. on lining papers. — Published in the United States : 1975. — Bibl. — Index.
ISBN 0-07-070560-7 : £29.05
(B77-03034)

616'.002'4613 — Man. Diseases. *For nursing*
Cooke, Ralph Gordon. A summary of medicine for nurses and medical auxiliaries / [by] R. Gordon Cooke. — 7th ed. / revised by Ann C. Miller. — London : Faber, 1977. — 3-156p ; 19cm.
Previous ed.: 1973. — Index.
ISBN 0-571-04942-7 Pbk : £1.50 : CIP rev.
(B77-25663)

Fream, William Charles. Notes on medical nursing / [by] William C. Fream. — 2nd ed. — Edinburgh [etc.] : Churchill Livingstone, 1977. — vii,206p : 2 ill ; 19cm.
Previous ed.: 1971. — Index.
ISBN 0-443-01612-7 Pbk : £2.25
(B77-22622)

Morris, John Frederick, *b.1913.* Medicine / [by] John F. Morris, John C. Small. — London : Heinemann Medical.
1. — 1976. — v,155p : ill ; 25cm. — (Revision notes for senior nurses)
Index.
ISBN 0-433-30431-6 Pbk : £2.75
(B77-06703)

616'.002'4616 — Man. Diseases. *For physiotherapy*
A **textbook** of medical conditions for physiotherapists. — 5th ed. / edited by Joan E. Cash. — London : Faber, 1976. — xx,291p : ill ; 23cm.
Previous ed.: / by Joan E. Cash and others. 1971. — Bibl. — Index.
ISBN 0-571-04893-5 : £6.50
ISBN 0-571-04894-3 Pbk : £4.25
(B77-01504)

616'.002'4617 — Man. Diseases. *For anaesthesia*
Medicine for anaesthetists / edited by M.D. Vickers ; foreword by William W. Mushin. — Oxford [etc.] : Blackwell Scientific, 1977. — xii, 571p : ill ; 26cm.
Bibl. — Index.
ISBN 0-632-00156-9 : £21.50 : CIP rev.
(B77-06704)

616'.002'46176 — Man. Diseases & injuries. *For dentistry*
Ford, Peter Michael. Lecture notes on clinical medicine and surgery for dental students / [by] P.M. Ford, D. Maclean. — 2nd ed. — Oxford [etc.] : Blackwell Scientific, 1977. — viii,237p : ill ; 22cm.
Previous ed.: 1972. — Index.
ISBN 0-632-00466-5 Pbk : £4.75 : CIP rev.
(B77-05446)

Kennedy, Arthur Colville. Essentials of medicine and surgery for dental students. — [3rd ed.] / [by] A.C. Kennedy, L.H. Blumgart. — Edinburgh [etc.] : Churchill Livingstone, 1977. — vii,271p : ill ; 22cm.
Previous ed.: published as 'Essentials of medicine for dental students' / by A.C. Colville. 1970. — Index.
ISBN 0-443-01643-7 Pbk : £5.00 : CIP rev.
(B77-22623)

616'.007'2 — Man. Diseases. Research. *Periodicals*
European journal of clinical investigation. — Berlin ; New York : Springer.
Supersedes: Archiv für klinische Medizin.
Vol.1, no.1- ; Mar. 1970-. — 1970-. — ill ; 28cm.
Six issues a year. — Cover title. — From Vol.7, no.1 published: Oxford, etc. : Blackwell Scientific for the European Society for Clinical Investigation. — 76p. in vol.7, no.1. — Bibl.
Pbk : £26.00 yearly
ISSN 0014-2972
(B77-17527)

616.01 — Medicine. Microbiology
Smith, Alice Lorraine. Principles of microbiology / [by] Alice Lorraine Smith. — 8th ed. — Saint Louis : Mosby ; London : Distributed by Kimpton, 1977. — xiii,773p : ill(some col), forms ; 26cm.
Previous ed.: 1973. — Bibl. — Index.
ISBN 0-8016-4681-2 : £12.10
(B77-21167)

Stewart, Frederick Stanley. Bacteriology, virology and immunity for students of medicine. — 10th ed. / [by] F.S. Stewart, T.S.L. Beswick. — London : Baillière Tindall, 1977. — vii,486p, ii p of plates : ill(some col) ; 25cm.
Previous ed.: published as 'Bacteriology and immunology for students of medicine' / by F.S. Stewart. London : Baillière, Tindall and Cassell, 1968. — Index.
ISBN 0-7020-0637-8 Pbk : £9.75
(B77-27888)

Stratford, Bryan C. An atlas of medical microbiology : common human pathogens / [by] Bryan C. Stratford. — Oxford [etc.] : Blackwell Scientific, 1977. — xvi,202p : ill(chiefly col) ; 25cm.
Index.
ISBN 0-632-00398-7 : £5.50
(B77-11845)

616.01'4 — Man. Pathogens: Anaerobic bacteria
Finegold, Sydney M. Anaerobic bacteria in human disease / [by] Sydney M. Finegold. — New York [etc.] ; London : Academic Press, 1977. — xxii,710p : ill, maps ; 24cm.
Index.
ISBN 0-12-256750-1 : £34.80
(B77-31229)

616.01'4 — Man. Pathogens: Bacteria. *Identification manuals*
Larone, Davise Honig. Medically important fungi : a guide to identification / [by] Davise Honig Larone ; illustrated by the author. — Hagerstown [etc.] ; London : Harper and Row, 1976. — xvii,156p : ill ; 24cm.
Bibl.: p.146. — Index.
ISBN 0-06-141513-8 Pbk : £7.45
(B77-31230)

616.01'4 — Medicine. Anaerobic bacteriology
Willis, Allan Trevor. Anaerobic bacteriology : clinical and laboratory practice / [by] A. Trevor Willis. — 3rd ed. — London [etc.] : Butterworth, 1977. — x,360p : ill ; 23cm.
Previous ed.: 1964. — Bibl. — Index.
ISBN 0-407-00081-x : Unpriced : CIP rev.
(B77-22624)

616.01'4 — Medicine. Bacteriology
Selected topics in clinical bacteriology / edited by J. de Louvois. — London : Baillière Tindall, 1976. — ix,262p : ill ; 23cm.
Bibl. — Index.
ISBN 0-7020-0601-7 : £6.50
(B77-04218)

616.01'5'0212 — Man. Pathogens: Fungi. *Lists*
British Society for Mycopathology.
Nomenclature of fungi pathogenic to man and animals / [compiled by a subcommittee of the British Society for Mycopathology]. — 4th ed. — London : H.M.S.O., 1977. — v,26p ; 25cm. — (Medical Research Council. Memoranda ; no.23)
Previous ed.: issued by Medical Research Council, Medical Mycology Committee. 1967. — Bibl.: p.24-26.
ISBN 0-11-450037-1 Sd : £0.75
(B77-28656)

616.01'94 — Medical virological specimens. Collecting & transport. *Manuals*
Madeley, Charles Richard. Guide to the collection and transport of virological specimens : (including Chlamydial and rickettsial specimens) / [by] C.R. Madeley. — Geneva : World Health Organization ; [London] : [H.M.S.O.], 1977. — 40p : 2 ill ; 24cm.
Sd : Unpriced
ISBN 92-4-154055-9
(B77-15312)

616.01'94 — Medicine. Virology. *Reviews of research*
Progress in medical virology. — Basel ; London [etc.] : Karger ; [Chichester] : [Distributed by Wiley].
Vol.22 / editor J.L Melnick ; contributors ... [others]. — 1976. — ix,230p : ill ; 25cm.
Bibl. — Index.
Unpriced
ISBN 3-8055-2315-7
(B77-03569)

Recent advances in clinical virology. — Edinburgh [etc.] : Churchill Livingstone.
No.1 / edited by A.P. Waterson. — 1977. — ix,200p : ill ; 24cm.
Bibl. — Index.
ISBN 0-443-01542-2 : £9.75
Also classified at 636.089'601'94
(B77-06116)

616.01'94'09 — Medicine. Virology, to 1976
Hughes, Sally Smith. The virus : a history of the concept / [by] Sally Smith Hughes. — London : Heinemann Educational [etc.], 1977. — xix,140p : ill, ports ; 24cm.
Bibl.: p.121-136. — Index.
ISBN 0-435-54755-0 : £3.90
(B77-28657)

616'.025 — Medicine. Emergency treatment
Emergencies in medical practice / edited by C. Allan Birch. — 10th ed. — Edinburgh [etc.] : Churchill Livingstone, 1976. — xx,864p,fold leaf,[6] leaves of plates,[34]p of plates : ill(some col), map ; 23cm.
Previous ed.: 1971. — Bibl. — Index.
ISBN 0-443-01169-9 : £15.00
(B77-03035)

616'.025 — Medicine. Emergency treatment. *For general practice*
Vakil, Rustom Jal. Diagnosis and management of medical emergencies / by Rustom Jal Vakil and Farokh Erach Udwadia [et al.]. — 2nd ed. reprinted with corrections. — Delhi ; London [etc.] : Oxford University Press, [1977]. — xxii, 750p : ill ; 25cm. — ([Oxford medical publications])
This corrected ed. published in India: 1976. — Previous ed.: 1972. — Index.
ISBN 0-19-261118-6 : £10.00
(B77-07927)

616'.025 — Medicine. Emergency treatment. *Manuals*

Hardy, R H. Accidents and emergencies : a practical handbook for personal use / [by] R.H. Hardy. — Oxford (Wolfson College, Oxford OX2 6UD) : R. Dugdale, 1976. — viiip,62 leaves : ill ; 22cm.
Bibl.: leaves 58-60. — Index.
ISBN 0-9503880-1-7 Sp : £1.50
(B77-06117)

Robinson, Richard Oakley. Medical emergencies : diagnosis and management. — 2nd ed. / by Richard Robinson and Robin Stott. — London : Heinemann Medical, 1976. — x, 214p : ill ; 19cm.
Previous ed.: / by R.O. Robinson. 1970. — Bibl.: p.194-205. — Index.
ISBN 0-433-28103-0 Pbk : £3.00
(B77-16417)

616'.025 — Medicine. Emergency treatment. *Manuals. For paramedics*

Wasserberger, Jonathan. Advanced paramedic procedures : a practical approach / [by] Jonathan Wasserberger, David H. Eubanks. — Saint Louis : Mosby ; London : Distributed by Kimpton, 1977. — xv,154p : ill ; 26cm.
Bibl.: p.143-144. — Index.
ISBN 0-8016-5351-7 Pbk : £5.30
(B77-21903)

616'.025 — Victims of accidents. Emergency treatment

Rescue emergency care / edited by Ken Easton ; with a foreword by the late Norman Capener. — London : Heinemann Medical, 1977. — xix, 490p : ill, forms, map, plan ; 23cm.
Bibl. — Index.
ISBN 0-433-08000-0 : £9.95
(B77-21168)

616'.026 — Internal medicine

Harrison, Tinsley Randolph. Harrison's principles of internal medicine. — 8th ed. / editors George W. Thorn ... [et al.]. — Tokyo ; London [etc.] : McGraw-Hill, 1977. — xxxi, 2088,6,102p,10p of plates : ill(some col) ; 27cm.

'A Blakiston publication'. — Previous ed.: / editors Maxwell M. Wintrobe et al. New York : McGraw-Hill, 1974. — Bibl. — Index.
ISBN 0-07-064518-3 : £30.70
(B77-24261)

616'.026'076 — Internal medicine. *Questions & answers*

The **practice** of medicine : a self-assessment guide / edited by Simeon Margolis ; co-editors A. McCrehee Harvey ... [et al.]. — New York : Appleton-Century-Crofts ; London [etc.] : Prentice-Hall, 1976. — xv,397p ; 26cm.
With answers. — '... aims to help readers assess and as a consequence sharpen their knowledge and understanding of major points of patient management encompassed by "The Principles and Practice of Medicine, 19th Edition"' - Preface.
ISBN 0-8385-7876-4 Pbk : £9.20
(B77-06705)

616'.042 — Adolescents. Genetic disorders

Endocrine and genetic diseases of childhood and adolescence / edited by Lytt I. Gardner. — 2nd ed. — Philadelphia ; London [etc.] : Saunders, 1975 [i.e. 1976]. — xxx,1404p : ill ; 27cm.
This ed. published in the United States: 1975. — Previous ed.: published as 'Endocrine and genetic diseases of childhood'. 1969. — Bibl. — Index.
ISBN 0-7216-3991-7 : £51.25
Primary classification 618.9'24
(B77-06722)

616'.042 — Man. Diseases. Genetic factors. *For counselling in general practice*

Stevenson, Alan Carruth. Genetic counselling / [by] Alan Carruth Stevenson and B.C. Clare Davison with assistance from Michael W. Oakes. — 2nd ed. — London : Heinemann Medical, 1976. — ix,357p : ill ; 23cm.
Previous ed.: 1970. — Bibl. — Index.
ISBN 0-433-31591-1 : £5.50
(B77-05447)

616'.042 — Man. Genetic disorders. Pathogens: Chemicals. Testing. *Conference proceedings*

Symposium on the Role of Metabolic Activation in Producing Mutagenic and Carcinogenic Environmental Chemicals, *Research Triangle Park, N.C., 1976.* 'In vitro' metabolic activation in mutagenesis testing : proceedings of the Symposium on the Role of Metabolic Activation in Producing Mutagenic and Carcinogenic Environmental Chemicals, Research Triangle Park, North Carolina, February 9-11, 1976 / editors Frederick J. de Serres ... [et al.]. — Amsterdam [etc.] ; Oxford : North-Holland Publishing Co., 1976. — vii,363p : ill ; 25cm.
Bibl.
ISBN 0-7204-0612-9 : £17.56
Primary classification 616.9'94'071
(B77-18817)

616'.042 — Man. Genetic disorders. Syndromes: Face manifestations

Goodman, Richard Merle. Atlas of the face in genetic disorders / [by] Richard M. Goodman, Robert J. Gorlin. — 2nd ed. — St Louis : Mosby ; London : Distributed by Kimpton, 1977. — xiii,586p : ill(some col) ; 32cm.
Previous ed.: published as 'The face in genetic disorders'. 1970. — Bibl. — Index.
ISBN 0-8016-1895-9 : £46.75
(B77-32655)

616'.042 — Man. Genetics. Medical aspects. *Reviews of research*

Progress in medical genetics. — New [ed.]. — Philadelphia ; London [etc.] : Saunders.
Vol.1 / edited by Arthur G. Steinberg ... [et al.]. — 1976. — ii-ix,297p : ill ; 24cm.
Previous ed.: New York : Grune and Stratton, 1961. — Bibl. — Index.
ISBN 0-7216-8586-2 : £18.25
(B77-00245)

616'.043 — Man. Congenital abnormalities. Syndromes

Smith, David Weyhe. Recognizable patterns of human malformation : genetic, embryologic and clinical aspects / by David W. Smith. — 2nd ed. — Philadelphia ; London [etc.] : Saunders, 1976. — xvii,504p : ill ; 27cm. — (Major problems in clinical pediatrics ; vol.7)
Col. ill. on lining papers. — Previous ed.: 1970. — Index.
ISBN 0-7216-8376-2 : £15.50
(B77-15313)

616'.047 — Man. Pain. Relief

Persistent pain : modern methods of treatment. — London : Academic Press [etc.].
Vol.1 / edited by Sampson Lipton. — 1977. — ix,272p : ill ; 24cm.
Bibl. — Index.
ISBN 0-12-451701-3 : £10.50
(B77-22625)

Villaverde, Manuel M. Pain : from symptom to treatment / [by] Manuel M. Villaverde, C. Wright MacMillan. — New York ; London [etc.] : Van Nostrand Reinhold, 1977. — vi, 346p : ill ; 24cm.
Index.
ISBN 0-442-25107-6 : £18.25
(B77-21169)

616'.047 — Man. Pain. Relief. Use of acupuncture. *Manuals*

Chaitow, Leon. The acupuncture treatment of pain / by Leon Chaitow ; drawings by Ken Morling. — Wellingborough : Thorsons, 1976. — 160p : ill(chiefly col) ; 29cm.
Index.
ISBN 0-7225-0356-3 Pbk : £5.95
ISBN 0-7225-0334-2 Pbk : £3.95
(B77-05448)

616.07 — Medicine. Pathology

Burton, John Lloyd. Aids to undergraduate medicine / [by] J.L. Burton. — 2nd ed. — Edinburgh [etc.] : Churchill Livingstone, 1976. — vii,128p : ill ; 22cm.
Previous ed.: 1973. — Index.
ISBN 0-443-01502-3 Pbk : £1.75
(B77-13062)

Damjanov, Ivan. General pathology / by Ivan Damjanov ; illustrations by Michael Capobianco. — London : Kimpton, 1976. — 263p : ill ; 22cm. — (Medical outline series)
Also published: Flushing, N.Y. : Medical Examination Publishing Co., 1976. — Index.
ISBN 0-87488-628-7 Sp : £6.50
(B77-05449)

Muir, *Sir* **Robert.** Muir's textbook of pathology. — 10th ed. / edited by J.R. Anderson. — London : Edward Arnold, 1976. — xiii,1046p : ill ; 25cm.
Previous ed.: / revised by D.F. Cappell and J.R. Anderson. 1971. — Bibl.: p.1016-1019. — Index.
ISBN 0-7131-4268-5 Pbk : £13.75
(B77-01505)

Pathology / edited by W.A.D. Anderson, John M. Kissane. — 7th ed. — Saint Louis : Mosby ; London : Distributed by Kimpton, 1977. — 2v.(xv,2148,39p,[4]leaves of plates,[2]p of plates) : ill(some col), maps ; 28cm.
Previous ed.: 1971. — Bibl. — Index.
ISBN 0-8016-0186-x : £30.00
(B77-30290)

Principles of pathobiology / edited by Mariano F. La Via and Rolla B. Hill, Jr. — 2nd ed. — New York ; London [etc.] : Oxford University Press, 1975 [i.e. 1976]. — xvii,259p : ill ; 24cm.

This ed. published in the United States: 1975. — Previous ed.: published as 'Principles of pathobiology'. New York : Oxford University Press, 1971 ; and as 'Principles of pathology'. London : Oxford University Press, 1971. — Bibl. — Index.
ISBN 0-19-501852-4 Pbk : £5.00
(B77-08409)

Robbins, Stanley Leonard. Basic pathology / [by] Stanley L. Robbins, Marcia Angell. — 2nd ed. — Philadelphia ; London [etc.] : Saunders, [1977]. — xii,705p : ill ; 27cm.
This ed. published in the United States: 1976. — Previous ed.: 1971. — Bibl. — Index.
ISBN 0-7216-7599-9 : £14.75
(B77-11846)

Spector, Walter Graham. An introduction to general pathology / [by] W.G. Spector. — Edinburgh [etc.] : Churchill Livingstone, 1977. — viii,316p : ill ; 18cm.
Bibl. — Index.
ISBN 0-443-01490-6 Pbk : £3.25
(B77-06706)

Systemic pathology / by thirty-eight authors. — 2nd ed. — Edinburgh [etc.] : Churchill Livingstone.
In 5 vols. — Previous ed.: in 2 vols / edited by G.P. Wright and W. St C. Symmers. London : Longmans, 1966.
Vol.1 : Cardiovascular system, respiratory system / [editor W. St C. Symmers]. — 1976. — xii,428,56p : ill, port ; 26cm.
Index.
ISBN 0-443-01330-6 : £19.50
(B77-13063)

Walter, John Brian. An introduction to the principles of disease / [by] John B. Walter. — Philadelphia ; London [etc.] : Saunders, 1977. — xii,739p : ill ; 26cm.
Bibl. — Index.
ISBN 0-7216-9114-5 : £12.00
(B77-24262)

Young, Clara Gene. Introduction to medical science / [by] Clara Gene Young, James D. Barger. — 3rd ed. — Saint Louis : Mosby ; London : Distributed by Kimpton, 1977. — vii, 395p : ill ; 27cm.
Previous ed.: 1973. — Bibl. — Index.
ISBN 0-8016-5657-5 : £8.05
(B77-16907)

616.07 — Medicine. Pathology. *Conference proceedings*

World Congress of Anatomic and Clinical Pathology, *9th, Sydney, 1975.* The effects of environment on cells and tissues : proceedings of the 9th World Congress of Anatomic and Clinical Pathology, Sydney, 13-17 October, 1975 / editor E.S. Finckh ; co-editor E. Clayton-Jones. — Amsterdam ; Oxford : Excerpta Medica, 1976. — xvii,305p : ill ; 25cm. — (International congress series ; no.384)
Bibl. — Index.
£23.75
ISBN 90-219-0316-4 (Excerpta Medica)
(B77-04846)

616.07 — Medicine. Pathology. *Reviews of research*

International review of experimental pathology. — New York [etc.] ; London : Academic Press.

Vol.17 : 1977 / edited by G.W. Richter, M.A. Epstein. — 1977. — ix,244p : ill ; 24cm.
Bibl. — Index.
ISBN 0-12-364917-x : £18.10
(B77-17528)

Progress in clinical pathology. — New York ; London : Grune and Stratton.
Vol.2 / editor Mario Stefanini. — 1969. — ix, 385p : ill, form ; 26cm.
Bibl. — Index.
ISBN 0-8089-0476-0 : £23.80
(B77-04847)

Vol.3 / editor Mario Stefanini. — 1970. — xi, 426p : ill, plan ; 26cm.
Bibl. — Index.
ISBN 0-8089-0477-9 : £23.80
(B77-04848)

616.07 — Pathology laboratories. Quality control
Dharan, Murali. Total quality control in the clinical laboratory / [by] Murali Dharan. — Saint Louis : Mosby ; London : Distributed by Kimpton, 1977. — ix,242p : ill, facsims, forms ; 25cm.
Bibl. — Index.
ISBN 0-8016-1290-x Pbk : £7.15
(B77-30291)

616.07'2 — Man. Diseases. Haematological aspects
Haematological aspects of systemic disease / edited by M.C.G. Israëls and I.W. Delamore. — London [etc.] : Saunders, 1976. — ix,545p : ill ; 26cm.
Bibl. — Index.
ISBN 0-7216-5047-3 : £17.50
(B77-04219)

616.07'2 — Man. Diseases. Syndromes: Head & neck manifestations
Gorlin, Robert James. Syndromes of the head and neck. — 2nd ed. / [by] Robert J. Gorlin, Jens J. Pindborg, M. Michael Cohen. — New York ; London [etc.] : McGraw-Hill, 1977. — xx,812p : ill ; 25cm.
'A Blakiston Publication'. — Previous ed.: / by Robert J. Gorlin, Jens J. Pindborg. 1964. — Bibl. — Index.
ISBN 0-07-023790-5 : £31.90
(B77-19417)

616.07'2 — Man. Diseases. Syndromes: Oral manifestations
Shklar, Gerald. The oral manifestations of systemic disease / [by] Gerald Shklar, Philip L. McCarthy. — Boston [Mass.] ; London : Butterworth, 1976. — x,336p,8p of plates : ill(some col) ; 24cm.
Bibl.: p.311-327. — Index.
ISBN 0-409-95002-5 : £12.75
(B77-04220)

616.07'2 — Man. Tissues. Inflammation. *Conference proceedings*
International Meeting on Future Trends in Inflammation, *3rd, London, 1977.* Perspectives in inflammation : future trends and developments : the proceedings of the Third International Meeting on Future Trends in Inflammation, organized by the European Biological Research Association and held in London, February 14th-18th, 1977 / edited by D.A. Willoughby, J.P. Giroud, G.P. Velo. — Lancaster : M.I.T. Press, 1977. — xii,638p : ill ; 24cm.
ISBN 0-85200-185-1 : £15.95
(B77-31934)

616.07'5 — Man. Diagnosis. Imaging systems. *Conference proceedings*
Gray (L.H.) Conference, *7th, University of Leeds, 1976.* Medical images : formation, perception and measurement : proceedings of the Seventh L.H. Gray Conference, held at the University of Leeds, 13-15 April 1976 / edited by George A. Hay. — [Bristol] : Institute of Physics ; [Chichester] : Wiley, 1976. — ix,368p, [2]leaves of plates,[2]p of plates : ill(some col) ; 24cm.
Bibl. — Index.
ISBN 0-471-99447-2 : £12.50
(B77-23451)

616.07'5 — Man. Diseases. Symptoms. Diagnosis
Davis, Alan Edward. Symptom analysis and physical diagnosis in medicine / [by] A.E. Davis, T.D. Bolin, with the assistance of N.M. Wilton. — Rushcutters Bay ; Oxford [etc.] : Pergamon Press, 1977. — [8],281p : ill ; 20cm.
Index.
ISBN 0-08-021245-x : Unpriced
ISBN 0-08-021244-1 Pbk : £4.85
(B77-27124)

616.07'5 — Medicine. Diagnosis
Clinical skills : a system of clinical examination / edited by Ian A.D. Bouchier and John S. Morris. — London [etc.] : Saunders, 1976. — xix,654p : ill ; 18cm.
Bibl. — Index.
ISBN 0-7216-1892-8 Pbk : £6.25
(B77-01506)

616.07'5 — Medicine. Diagnosis. *Manuals*
Clinical methods : the history, physical and laboratory examinations / editors H. Kenneth Walker, W. Dallas Hall, J. Willis Hurst, with the assistance of ... [others]. — Boston [Mass.] ; London : Butterworth, 1976. — xix,1098p : ill, forms ; 23cm.
Parts I-IV originally published: in 1 vol. 1976. — Bibl. — Index.
ISBN 0-409-95006-8 : £8.00
(B77-27125)

Clinical methods : the history, physical and laboratory examinations. — Boston [Mass.] ; London : Butterworth.
Vol.1 / editors H. Kenneth Walker, W. Dallas Hall, J. Willis Hurst. — 1976. — xix,420p : ill, forms ; 23cm.
Bibl.
ISBN 0-409-95003-3 Sp : £8.00
(B77-07928)

Vol.2 / editors H. Kenneth Walker, W. Dallas Hall, J. Willis Hurst with the assistance of ... [others]. — 1976. — xix,421-1098p : ill ; 23cm.
Index.
ISBN 0-409-95004-1 Sp : £8.00
(B77-11240)

616.07'5 — Medicine. Diagnosis. Laboratory techniques
The **laboratory** in clinical medicine : interpretation and application / edited by James A. Halsted. — Philadelphia ; London [etc.] : Saunders, 1976. — xxiv,866p : ill ; 27cm.
Bibl. — Index.
ISBN 0-7216-4478-3 : £26.75
(B77-01508)

616.07'5'024613 — Medicine. Diagnosis. *For nursing*
French, Ruth Marie. Guide to diagnostic procedures / [by] Ruth M. French. — 4th ed. — New York ; London [etc.] : McGraw-Hill, [1976]. — xiii,369p : ill ; 21cm.
'A Blakiston Publication'. — Previous ed.: published as 'The nurse's guide to diagnostic procedures'. 1971. — Bibl. — Index.
ISBN 0-07-022141-3 : £7.45
ISBN 0-07-022140-5 Pbk : £5.95
(B77-01507)

Gillies, Dee Ann. Patient assessment and management by the nurse practitioner / [by] Dee Ann Gillies, Irene B. Alyn. — Philadelphia ; London [etc.] : Saunders, 1976. — viii,236p : ill ; 27cm.
Bibl. — Index.
ISBN 0-7216-4133-4 : £8.25
Primary classification 610.73'6
(B77-04190)

Nursing assessment / consultant Robinetta Wheeler. — New York ; London [etc.] : Wiley, 1977. — xi,167p : ill ; 28cm. — (Wiley nursing concept modules)
'A Wiley medical publication'. — With answers. — Pages perforated at inside edge. — Pierced for binder. — Fill-in book. — Bibl.
ISBN 0-471-02167-9 Pbk : £4.95
(B77-23452)

616.07'54 — Man. Diagnosis. Endoscopy
Endoscopy / edited by George Berci ; with 58 coauthors ; foreword by Maurice R. Ewing. — New York : Appleton-Century-Crofts ; London [etc.] : Prentice-Hall, 1976. — xxv,[16],805p, [14]p of plates,leaf of plate : ill(some col) ; 26cm.
Bibl. — Index.
ISBN 0-8385-2216-5 : £62.85
(B77-07929)

616.07'54 — Man. Diagnosis. Physical examination
Introduction to clinical examination / [edited by] John Macleod, E.B. French, J.F. Munro. — 2nd ed. — Edinburgh [etc.] : Churchill Livingstone, 1977. — vii,112p : ill ; 19cm.
Previous ed.: 1974. — Bibl.: p.106. — Index.
ISBN 0-443-01582-1 Pbk : £1.50
(B77-16908)

Wolf, George A. Collecting data from patients / by George A. Wolf, Jr. — Baltimore ; London [etc.] : University Park Press, 1977. — xi,275p : ill, form ; 23cm.
Bibl.: p.265-267. — Index.
ISBN 0-8391-0983-0 Pbk : £9.25
(B77-26339)

616.07'54 — Man. Diagnosis. Physical examination. *For East African students*
Essex, B J. Diagnostic pathways in clinical medicine : an epidemiological approach to clinical problems / [by] B.J. Essex ; foreword by W.J. Makene ; illustrations by A. Barrett. — Edinburgh [etc.] : Churchill Livingstone, 1977. — [11],173p : ill ; 28cm. — (Medicine in the tropics)
Index.
ISBN 0-443-01514-7 Pbk : £4.00
(B77-09724)

616.07'54 — Man. Diagnosis. Use of ultrasonic waves
Gosink, Barbara Bowling. Diagnostic ultrasound / [by] Barbara Bowling Gosink, Lucy Frank Squire. — Philadelphia ; London [etc.] : Saunders, 1976. — [12],183p : ill(some col) ; 26cm. — (Exercises in diagnostic radiology ; 8)
With answers. — Bibl.: p.[4]. — Index.
ISBN 0-7216-4176-8 Pbk : £6.75
(B77-03036)

Ultrasonics in clinical diagnosis / edited by P.N.T. Wells. — 2nd ed. — Edinburgh [etc.] : Churchill Livingstone, 1977. — xiv,195p : ill ; 24cm.
Previous ed.: 1972. — Bibl. — Index.
ISBN 0-443-01644-5 : £8.00
ISBN 0-443-01369-1 Pbk : £5.50
(B77-26340)

616.07'54 — Man. Diagnosis. Use of ultrasonic waves. *Conference proceedings*
Present and future of diagnostic ultrasound : proceedings of the third symposium of the Fondation pour la recherche en endocrinologie sexuelle et l'étude de la reproduction humaine (FRESERH), held at Brussels, Belgium, 9-10 May 1975, under the patronage of Royal Highness the Grand Duchess Josephine Charlotte / edited by Ian Donald & Salvator Levi. — Rotterdam : Kooyker Scientific Publications ; New York ; London [etc.] : Distributed by Wiley, 1976. — xii,211p : ill ; 25cm. — (Kooyker symposia series ; no.002)
Bibl.
ISBN 0-471-01621-7 : £21.25
(B77-13669)

616.07'56 — Medicine. Diagnosis. Chemical analysis
Alberti, K G M M. Chemical pathology : medicine's cuckoo / by K.G.M.M. Alberti. — [Southampton] : University of Southampton, 1976. — 14p ; 21cm. — (University of Southampton. Inaugural lectures)
'... delivered at the University 3rd February, 1976'.
ISBN 0-85432-164-0 Sd : £0.50
(B77-13670)

Fundamentals of clinical chemistry / edited by Norbert W. Tietz ; editorial committee Wendell T. Caraway ... [et al.]. — [New ed.]. — Philadelphia ; London [etc.] : Saunders, 1976. — ii-xxvi,1263p : ill ; 27cm.
Text on lining papers. — Previous ed.: 1970. — Bibl. — Index.
ISBN 0-7216-8866-7 : Unpriced
(B77-17529)

Gray, Charles Horace. Clinical chemical pathology. — 8th ed. / [by] C.H. Gray and P.J.N. Howorth. — London : Edward Arnold, 1977. — vii,245p : ill ; 21cm.
Previous ed.: / by C.H. Gray. 1974. — Bibl. — Index.
ISBN 0-7131-4290-1 : £6.00 : CIP rev.
ISBN 0-7131-4291-x Pbk : £3.50
(B77-11241)

Varley, Harold. Practical clinical biochemistry. — 5th ed. / by Harold Varley, Alan H. Gowenlock, Maurice Bell. — London : Heinemann Medical.
In 2 vols. — Previous ed.: in one vol. / by Harold Varley. 1967.
Vol.2 : Hormones, vitamins, drugs and poisons. — 1976. — xii,402p : ill ; 24cm.
Bibl. — Index.
ISBN 0-433-33803-2 : £8.00
(B77-06707)

616.07'56 — Medicine. Diagnosis. Chemical analysis. *Reviews of research*
Advances in clinical chemistry. — New York [etc.] ; London : Academic Press.
Vol.19 : 1977 / edited by Oscar Bodansky, A.L. Latner. — 1977. — x,263p : ill ; 24cm.
Bibl. — Index.
ISBN 0-12-010319-2 : £18.45
(B77-17530)

616.07'56 — Medicine. Diagnosis. Chemical analysis. Quality control

Whitehead, Thomas Patterson. Quality control in clinical chemistry / [by] T.P. Whitehead ; foreword by Morton K. Schwartz. — New York ; London [etc.] : Wiley, 1977. — xiv, 130p : ill ; 26cm. — (Quality control methods in the clinical laboratory)
'A Wiley medical publication'. — Bibl. — Index.
ISBN 0-471-94075-5 : £11.00
(B77-22626)

616.07'56'0151 — Medicine. Diagnosis. Chemical analysis. Laboratory techniques. Applications of mathematics

Routh, Joseph Isaac. Mathematical preparation for the health sciences / [by] Joseph I. Routh. — 2nd ed. — Philadelphia ; London [etc.] : Saunders, 1976. — ix,157p : ill ; 24cm.
With answers. — Previous ed.: published as 'Mathematical preparation for laboratory technicians'. 1971. — Index.
ISBN 0-7216-7736-3 Pbk : £5.25
(B77-07378)

616.07'56'0711 — Clinical chemists. Professional education

Education and training for clinical chemistry / prepared for publication [i.e. edited] by Martin Rubin, Per Lous. — Lancaster : M.T.P. Press for the International Federation of Clinical Chemistry, Committee on Education and Training in Clinical Chemistry, 1977. — [10], 196p ; 23cm.
ISBN 0-85200-161-4 : £6.50
(B77-25664)

616.07'57 — Man. Diagnosis. Radiography

Clifford, Margaret Anne. Radiographic techniques related to pathology / by Margaret A. Clifford and Anne E. Drummond ; with a foreword by T.H. Hills. — 2nd ed. — Bristol : J. Wright, 1977. — [8],77p ; 17cm.
Previous ed.: 1968. — Bibl.: p.76-77.
ISBN 0-7236-0467-3 Pbk : £2.00 : CIP rev.
(B77-21904)

Sprawls, Perry. The physical principles of diagnostic radiology / by Perry Sprawls. — Baltimore ; London [etc.] : University Park Press, 1977. — xi,365p : ill ; 24cm.
Index.
ISBN 0-8391-0968-7 : £17.50
(B77-27889)

Sutton, David, *b.1917.* Radiology for medical students / [by] David Sutton. — 3rd ed. — Edinburgh [etc.] : Churchill Livingstone, 1977. — vii,153p : ill ; 24cm.
Previous ed.: published as 'Radiology for general practitioners and medical students'. 1971. — Index.
ISBN 0-443-01606-2 Pbk : £4.95
(B77-23453)

Teplick, Joseph George. Roentgenologic diagnosis : a complement in radiology to the Beeson and McDermott 'Textbook of medicine' / [by] J. George Teplick, Marvin E. Haskin. — 3rd ed. — Philadelphia ; London [etc.] : Saunders, 1976[i.e.1977]. — 2v.(1714 p in various pagings) : ill ; 27cm.
This ed. published in the United States: 1976. — Previous ed.: 1971. — Index.
ISBN 0-7216-8789-x : £48.75
(B77-13064)

616.07'57 — Man. Diagnosis. Radiography. Complications

Complications in diagnostic radiology / edited by G. Ansell. — Oxford [etc.] : Blackwell Scientific, 1976. — ix,509p : ill ; 24cm.
Index.
ISBN 0-632-00039-2 : £18.00
(B77-02348)

616.07'57 — Man. Diagnosis. Radiography. Safety measures

Frankel, Robert. Radiation protection for radiologic technologists / [by] Robert Frankel. — New York ; London [etc.] : McGraw-Hill, 1976. — x,150p : ill ; 24cm.
'A Blakiston Publication'. — With answers. — Index.
ISBN 0-07-021875-7 : £8.20
(B77-31231)

616.07'57 — Medicine. Radiology

Jacobi, Charles Arnold. Textbook of radiologic technology / [by] Charles A. Jacobi, Don Q. Paris. — 6th ed. — Saint Louis : Mosby ; London : Distributed by Kimpton, 1977. — xi, 559p,plate : ill(incl 1 col), forms ; 26cm.
Previous ed.: 1972. — Bibl. — Index.
ISBN 0-8016-2385-5 : £14.25
(B77-33256)

Meredith, William John. Fundamental physics of radiology / by W.J. Meredith and J.B. Massey. — 3rd ed. — Bristol : J. Wright, 1977. — viii, 710p : ill(some col) ; 24cm.
Previous ed.: 1972. — Index.
ISBN 0-7236-0450-9 : £12.50 : CIP rev.
(B77-07379)

Stevens, Matthew. Comprehensive review for the radiologic technologist / [by] Matthew Stevens, Robert I. Phillips. — 3rd ed. — Saint Louis : Mosby ; London : Distributed by Kimpton, 1977. — ix,243p : ill ; 26cm.
With answers to simulated registry examinations. — Previous ed.: 1972. — Index.
ISBN 0-8016-4789-4 Pbk : £6.10
(B77-18171)

616.07'57 — Medicine. Radiology. *Reviews of research*

Current concepts in radiology. — Saint Louis : Mosby ; London : Distributed by Kimpton.
Vol.3 / edited by E. James Potchen. — 1977. — xvii,453p : ill ; 26cm.
Bibl. — Index.
ISBN 0-8016-3987-5 : Unpriced
(B77-31935)

616.07'572 — Man. Diagnosis. Radiography. Use of x-rays

Meschan, Isadore. Synopsis of 'Analysis of roentgen signs in general radiology' / [by] Isadore Meschan with the assistance of R.M.F. Farrer-Meschan [and] with the assistance in selection of materials from the three-volume text and editing by Anne G. Osborn. — Philadelphia ; London [etc.] : Saunders, 1976. — ii-xiii,677p : ill ; 27cm.
'Analysis of roentgen signs in general radiology' originally published: in 3 vols. 1973. — Index.
ISBN 0-7216-6301-x : £18.75
(B77-02349)

Roentgen diagnosis / edited by H.R. Schinz ... [et al.]. — 2nd American ed. / arranged and edited by Leo. G. Rigler. — New York ; London : Grune and Stratton.
Vol.4. Part 2 : Pleura, mediastinum and lungs / translators D. Adler ... [et al.]. — 1975 [i.e. 1976]. — xvi,940p : ill(some col) ; 26cm.
This ed. published in the United States: 1975. — Translation of: 'Lehrbuch der Röntgendiagnostik. Bund IV. Teil II'. Stuttgart : Georg Thieme, 1973. — Bibl. — Index.
ISBN 0-8089-0702-6 : £90.40
(B77-01509)

616.07'572 — Man. Diagnosis. Radiography. Use of x-rays. Techniques

Snopek, Albert Michael. Fundamentals of special radiographic procedures / [by] Albert Michael Snopek. — New York ; London [etc.] : McGraw-Hill, [1976]. — x,326p : ill ; 24cm.
'A Blakiston publication'. — Published in the United States: 1975. — Bibl. — Index.
ISBN 0-07-059515-1 : £13.25
(B77-05450)

616.07'572 — Man. Diagnosis. Tomography. *Conference proceedings*

Symposium Actualitatis Tomographiae, *Genoa, 1975.* The new image in tomography : proceedings of the Symposium Actualitatis Tomographiae, Genoa, Italy, September 11-13, 1975 / editor L. Oliva, co-editor R.J. Berry. — Amsterdam ; Oxford ([256 Banbury Rd, Oxford OX2 7DH]) : Excerpta Medica, 1976. — viii, 351p : ill ; 25cm. — (International congress series ; no.392)
Bibl. — Index.
Pbk : £31.62
ISBN 90-219-0320-2
(B77-16418)

616.07'572'02854044 — Man. Diagnosis. Tomography. Applications of digital computer systems. *Periodicals*

Computerized tomography : the international journal of radiological diagnosis using ct scanners. — Oxford [etc.] : Pergamon.
Vol.1, no.1- ; Jan. 1977-. — 1977-. — ill(some col) ; 28cm.
Quarterly. — [2],130p. in 1st issue.
Pbk : Unpriced
ISSN 0363-8235
(B77-10815)

616.07'575 — Man. Diagnosis. Radiography. Use of radioisotope scanning

Spencer, Richard Paul. Nuclear medicine : focus on clinical diagnosis / by Richard P. Spencer. — London : Kimpton, 1977. — 249p : ill ; 22cm.
Bibl.: p.241-242. — Index.
ISBN 0-87488-825-5 Sp : £9.00
(B77-21905)

616.07'575 — Nuclear medicine. *Conference proceedings*

Quality control in nuclear medicine : radiopharmaceuticals, instrumentation, and in vitro assays / editor Buck A. Rhodes. — Saint Louis : Mosby ; London : Distributed by Kimpton, 1977. — xvii,508p : ill, facsims, forms ; 26cm.
'... outgrowth of a meeting held at the National Bureau of Standards in June 1975' - Preface. — Bibl. — Index.
ISBN 0-8016-4115-2 : £31.60
(B77-30293)

616.07'583 — Medicine. Diagnosis. Histology

Theory and practice of histological techniques / editors John D. Bancroft, Alan Stevens ; foreword by I.M.P. Dawson. — Edinburgh [etc.] : Churchill Livingstone, 1977. — [9],436p, [8]leaves of plates : ill(some col) ; 26cm.
Bibl. — Index.
ISBN 0-443-01534-1 : £13.00
(B77-22627)

616.07'583 — Medicine. Diagnosis. Histopathology. Laboratory techniques

Kennedy, Alexander. Basic techniques in diagnostic histopathology / [by] Alexander Kennedy. — Edinburgh [etc.] : Churchill Livingstone, 1977. — x,117p : ill ; 23cm.
Bibl.: p.111-114. — Index.
ISBN 0-443-01464-7 : £4.00
(B77-30294)

Lillie, R D. Histopathologic technic and practical histochemistry. — 4th ed. / [by] R.D. Lillie, Harold M. Fullmer. — New York ; London [etc.] : McGraw-Hill, 1976. — xvii,942p : ill ; 24cm.
'A Blakiston publication'. — Previous ed.: / by R.D. Lillie. New York : McGraw-Hill, 1965. — Bibl.: p.xv-xvii. — Index.
ISBN 0-07-037862-2 : £31.50
(B77-31232)

616.07'9 — Man. Diseases. Role of immune complexes

World Health Organization. *Scientific Group on the Role of Immune Complexes in Disease.* The role of immune complexes in disease : report of a WHO scientific group / [WHO Scientific Group on the Role of Immune Complexes in Disease]. — Geneva : W.H.O. ; [London] : [H.M.S.O], 1977. — 58p ; 20cm. — (World Health Organization. Technical report series ; 606)
Bibl.: p.53-58.
Sd : Unpriced
ISBN 92-4-120606-3
(B77-18172)

616.07'9 — Man. Immunological deficiency

Hayward, Anthony R. Immunodeficiency / [by] Anthony R. Hayward. — London : Edward Arnold, 1977. — xiii,125p : ill ; 23cm. — (Current topics in immunology series ; no.6)
Bibl.: p.105-122. — Index.
ISBN 0-7131-4278-2 Pbk : £5.50
(B77-15314)

616.07'9 — Medicine. Immunology

Barber, Hugh R K. Immunobiology for the clinician / [by] Hugh R.K. Barber ; foreword by Philip J. DiSaia. — New York ; London [etc.] : Wiley, 1977. — ix,310p : ill ; 26cm.
'A Wiley medical publication'. — Bibl. — Index.
ISBN 0-471-04785-6 : £14.65
(B77-11847)

Clinical immunobiology. — New York ; London : Academic Press.
Vol.2 / edited by Fritz H. Bach, Robert A. Good. — 1974. — xvii,312p : ill ; 24cm.
Bibl. — Index.
ISBN 0-12-070002-6 : Unpriced
(B77-18807)

Vol.3 / edited by Fritz H. Bach, Robert A. Good. — 1976 [i.e. 1977]. — xx,442p : ill ; 24cm.
Published in the United States: 1976. — Bibl. — Index.
ISBN 0-12-070003-4 : £17.40
(B77-11848)

Clinical immunology. — 2nd ed. / editors Samuel O. Freedman, Phil Gold with 12 contributors. — Hagerstown [etc.] ; London : Harper and Row, Medical Department, 1976. — xi,665p : ill ; 26cm.
Previous ed.: / by Samuel O. Freedman. 1971. — Bibl. — Index.
ISBN 0-06-140834-4 : £24.35
(B77-06118)

Immunology in medicine : a comprehensive guide to clinical immunology / edited by E.J. Holborow and W.G. Reeves. — London : Academic Press [etc.], 1977. — xix,1185p : ill, map ; 24cm.
Bibl. — Index.
ISBN 0-12-352250-1 : £25.00
(B77-27890)

Textbook of immunopathology / edited by Peter A. Miescher and Hans J. Müller-Eberhard. — 2nd ed. — New York [etc.] ; London : Grune and Stratton.
Previous ed.: New York : Grune and Stratton, 1968-69.
Vol.1. — 1976. — 554p,xlviii p : ill ; 28cm.
Bibl. — Index.
ISBN 0-8089-0931-2 : £30.20
(B77-06119)

Vol.2. — 1976. — p555-1118,xlvii p : ill(some col) ; 28cm.
Bibl. — Index.
ISBN 0-8089-0932-0 : £30.20
(B77-06120)

616.07'9 — Medicine. Immunology. *Reviews of research*
Progress in clinical immunology. — New York [etc.] ; London : Grune and Stratton.
Vol.3 / edited by Robert S. Schwartz. — 1977. — x,208p : ill ; 26cm.
Index.
ISBN 0-8089-0997-5 : £15.95
(B77-17531)

Recent advances in clinical immunology. — Edinburgh [etc.] : Churchill Livingstone.
No.1 / edited by R.A. Thompson. — 1977. — ix,299p : ill ; 25cm.
Bibl. — Index.
ISBN 0-443-01388-8 : £10.00 : CIP rev.
ISSN 0140-6957
(B77-20319)

616.07'9 — Medicine. Radioimmunoassay
Parker, Charles W. Radioimmunoassay of biologically active compounds / [by] Charles W. Parker. — Englewood Cliffs ; London [etc.] : Prentice-Hall, 1976. — xiv,239p : ill ; 24cm. — (Prentice-Hall foundations of immunology series)
Bibl.: p.215-228. — Index.
ISBN 0-13-750505-1 : £14.75
(B77-06121)

Practical radioimmunoassay / [edited by] A.J. Moss, Jr, Glenn V. Dalrymple, Charles M. Boyd. — Saint Louis : Mosby ; London : Distributed by Kimpton, 1976. — ix,158p : ill ; 26cm.
Bibl. — Index.
ISBN 0-8016-3561-6 : £9.70
(B77-04221)

616.07'9'028 — Man. Cells. Diseases. Immunology. Laboratory techniques: In vitro methods
In vitro methods in cell-mediated and tumor immunity / edited by Barry R. Bloom and John R. David, with the editorial assistance of ... [others]. — New York [etc.] ; London : Academic Press, 1976 [i.e. 1977]. — xxxi,748p : ill, form ; 24cm.
Published in the United States: 1976.
ISBN 0-12-107760-8 : £24.50
Also classified at 616.9'92'079028
(B77-14755)

616.07'9'028 — Medicine. Immunology. Laboratory techniques
Techniques in clinical immunology / edited by R.A. Thompson. — Oxford [etc.] : Blackwell Scientific, 1977. — ix,241p,ii p of plates : ill(incl 2 col) ; 24cm.
Bibl. — Index.
ISBN 0-632-00076-7 Pbk : £6.25 : CIP rev.
(B77-06122)

616.07'9'09 — Medicine. Immunology, to 1976
Glasser, Ronald Joel. The body is the hero / [by] Ronald J. Glasser. — London : Collins, 1977. — [5],248,[1]p ; 24cm.
Originally published: New York : Random House, 1976.
ISBN 0-00-216077-3 : £4.95
(B77-28658)

616.07'9'5 — Man. Immune reactions. *Conference proceedings*
Irwin Strasburger Memorial Seminar on Immunology, *3rd, Cornell University Medical College, 1976.* Clinical evaluation of immune function in man : proceedings of the Third Irwin Strasburger Memorial Seminar on Immunology, held at Cornell University Medical College, New York City on February 29, 1976 / edited by Stephen D. Litwin, Charles L. Christian, Gregory W. Siskind ; sponsored by the Department of Medicine, Cornell University Medical College ... — New York [etc.] ; London : Grune and Stratton, [1977]. — xiv,236p : ill ; 24cm.
'Grune & Stratton rapid manuscript reproduction'. — Published in the United States: 1976.
ISBN 0-8089-0971-1 : £8.15
(B77-13671)

616.07'9'5 — Man. Immune reactions. Role of lymphocytes. *Conference proceedings*
International Conference on Lymphatic Tissue and Germinal Centers in Immune Reactions, *5th, Tiberias, 1975.* Immune reactivity of lymphocytes : development, expression and control / edited by Michael Feldman and Amiela Globerson. — New York ; London : Plenum Press, [1977]. — xix,732p : ill ; 26cm. — (Advances in experimental medicine and biology ; vol.66)
'Proceedings of the Fifth International Conference on Lymphatic Tissue and Germinal Centers in Immune Reactions held in Tiberias, Israel, June 24-30, 1975' - title page verso. — Published in the United States: 1976. — Bibl. — Index.
ISBN 0-306-39066-3 : £31.19
(B77-09725)

616.08 — Man. Psychosomatic diseases. Therapy
Psychosomatic medicine : its clinical applications / edited by Eric D. Wittkower, Hector Warnes. — Hagerstown [etc.] ; London : Harper and Row, 1977. — xxiii, 356p : ill ; 25cm.
Bibl. — Index.
ISBN 0-06-142768-3 : £14.95
(B77-23454)

616.08'07'24 — Man. Psychosomatic diseases. Simulations: Experimentally induced psychosomatic diseases of primates. *Reviews of research*
Startsev, Valentin Georgievich. Primate models of human neurogenic disorders / [by] V.G. Startsev ; translated [from the Russian] by Marienne Schweinler, Vadim Pahn ; editor of the English translation Douglas M. Bowden. — Hillsdale : Erlbaum ; New York ; London [etc.] : Distributed by Wiley, 1976. — x,198p : ill ; 24cm.
'A Halsted Press book'. — Translation of: 'Modelirovanie nevrogennykh zabolevaniĭ cheloveka v eksperimente na obez'ianakh'. Moscow : Meditsina Press, 1971. — Bibl.: p.183-191. — Index.
ISBN 0-470-15193-5 : £15.00
(B77-03037)

616.1 — DISEASES OF CARDIOVASCULAR SYSTEM

616.1'002'4613 — Man. Cardiovascular system. Diseases. *For nursing*
Turner, P P. The cardiovascular system / [by] P.P. Turner. — Edinburgh : Churchill Livingstone, 1976. — 208p : ill, form, plan ; 20cm. — (Penguin library of nursing)
Bibl.: p.191-200. — Index.
ISBN 0-443-01526-0 Pbk : £2.25
(B77-02350)

616.1'06'36 — Man. Blood. Artificial circulation. Oxygenators. Design. *Conference proceedings*
Advances in Oxygenator Design *(Conference), Copenhagen, 1975.* Physiological and clinical aspects of oxygenator design : proceedings of the seminar on Advances in Oxygenator Design, Copenhagen, June 15-20, 1975 : sponsored by the Commission of the European Communities with the assistance of the Committee on Medical Research and Public Health of the Scientific and Technical Research Committee / editors S.G. Dawids and H.C. Engell. — Amsterdam ; Oxford [etc.] : Elsevier for the Commission of the European Communities, 1976. — xvii,330p : ill ; 25cm.
Bibl. — Index.
ISBN 0-444-41453-3 : £22.48
(B77-17532)

616.1'07'1 — Man. Cardiovascular system. Diseases. Role of diet
Nutrition and cardiovascular disease / edited by Elaine B. Feldman ; foreword by William Dock. — New York : Appleton Century Crofts ; London [etc.] : Prentice-Hall, 1976. — xxi,326p : ill ; 24cm.
Bibl. — Index.
ISBN 0-8385-7071-2 : £15.50
(B77-12480)

616.1'2 — Man. Heart. Diseases
Clinical cardiology / edited by James T. Willerson, Charles A. Sanders. — New York [etc.] ; London : Grune and Stratton, 1977. — xiv,660p : ill ; 29cm. — (The science and practice of clinical medicine ; vol.3)
Bibl. — Index.
ISBN 0-8089-0992-4 : £28.50
(B77-27891)

Fleming, James Samuel. Lecture notes on cardiology / [by] J.S. Fleming and M.V. Brainbridge. — 2nd ed. — Oxford [etc.] : Blackwell Scientific, 1977. — xiii,326p : ill ; 22cm.
This ed. originally published: 1974. — Index.
Pbk : £4.25
ISBN 0-632-08600-9
(B77-21906)

Ross, John, *b.1928.* Understanding the heart & its diseases / [by] John Ross Jr, Robert A. O'Rourke. — New York ; London [etc.] : McGraw-Hill, 1976. — x,182p : ill ; 21cm. — (McGraw-Hill series in health education)
Bibl. — Index.
ISBN 0-07-053861-1 : £6.25
ISBN 0-07-053862-x Pbk : £3.75
(B77-03570)

616.1'2 — Man. Heart. Diseases. *Reviews of research*
Advances in heart disease. — New York [etc.] ; London : Grune and Stratton.
Vol.1 / edited by Dean T. Mason. — 1977. — xxi,548p : ill ; 24cm. — (Clinical cardiology monographs)
Index.
ISBN 0-8089-1003-5 : £24.50
(B77-20320)

Progress in cardiology. — Philadelphia : Lea and Febiger ; London : [Distributed by] Kimpton.
5 / edited by Paul N. Yu and John F. Goodwin. — 1976 [i.e. 1977]. — xvii,357p : ill ; 27cm.
Published in the United States: 1976. — Bibl.
ISBN 0-8121-0578-8 : £14.60
(B77-09045)

616.1'2 — Man. Heart. Heart failure
Bradley, Ronald D. Studies in acute heart failure / [by] Ronald D. Bradley. — London : Edward Arnold, 1977. — x,78p : ill ; 22cm.
Index.
ISBN 0-7131-4295-2 Pbk : £2.95 : CIP rev.
(B77-17533)

616.1'2 — Medicine. Cardiology. *Reviews of research*
Recent advances in cardiology. — Edinburgh [etc.] : Churchill Livingstone.
No.7 / edited by John Hamer. — 1977. — ix, 511p : ill ; 24cm.
Bibl. — Index.
ISBN 0-443-01560-0 : £17.00
(B77-24967)

616.1'2'070222 — Man. Heart. Pathology. *Illustrations*
Farrer-Brown, Geoffrey. A colour atlas of cardiac pathology / [by] Geoffrey Farrer-Brown. — London : Wolfe Medical, 1977. — 158p : ill(chiefly col) ; 27cm.
Spine title: Cardiac pathology. — Index.
ISBN 0-7234-0703-7 : £13.00
(B77-30295)

616.1'2'0754 — Man. Heart. Diagnosis. Echocardiography
Feigenbaum, Harvey. Echocardiography / [by] Harvey Feigenbaum. — 2nd ed. — Philadelphia : Lea and Febiger ; London : Kimpton, 1976. — xii,512p : ill ; 27cm.
Previous ed.: / with the assistance of Sonia Chang. 1972. — Bibl.: p.473-495. — Index.
ISBN 0-8121-0571-0 : £14.60
(B77-13065)

Felner, Joel M. Echocardiography : a teaching atlas / [by] Joel M. Felner, Robert C. Schlant. — New York [etc.] ; London : Grune and Stratton, [1977]. — [7],562p : ill, forms ; 19x26cm. — (Clinical cardiology monographs)
Published in the United States: 1976. — Bibl.: p.531-547. — Index.
ISBN 0-8089-0965-7 : £27.35
(B77-13066)

Friedewald, Vincent E. Textbook of echocardiography / [by] Vincent E. Friedewald, Jr. — Philadelphia ; London [etc.] : Saunders, 1977. — xii,317p : ill, form ; 27cm.
Index.
ISBN 0-7216-3919-4 : £14.50
(B77-13067)

Kra, Siegfried J. Basic correlative echocardiography technique and interpretation / by Siegfried J. Kra. — London : Kimpton, 1977. — 270p : ill ; 22cm.
Originally published: Flushing, N.Y. : Medical Examination Publishing Co., 1976. — Bibl. — Index.
ISBN 0-87488-978-2 Sp : £10.50
(B77-17534)

616.1'2'0754 — Man. Heart. Diagnosis. Echocardiography. *Case studies*
Clark, Ralph D. Case studies in echocardiography : a diagnostic workbook / [by] Ralph D. Clark ; with the assistance of John S. Edelen. — Philadelphia ; London [etc.] : Saunders, 1977. — x,334p : ill ; 27cm.
With answers. — Index.
ISBN 0-7216-2594-0 Pbk : £12.25
(B77-27128)

616.1'2'0754 — Man. Heart. Diagnosis. Echocardiography. *Manuals*
Miskovits, Christine. Echocardiography : a manual for technicians / by Christine Miskovits ; with special consultant Ernest Federici. — London : Kimpton, 1977. — 224p : ill ; 22cm.
Index.
ISBN 0-87488-987-1 Sp : £9.00
(B77-27129)

616.1'2'0754 — Man. Heart. Diagnosis. Electrocardiograms. Interpretation. *Manuals*
Passman, Jerome. The EKG : basic techniques for interpretation : a practical guide for interpreting and analyzing the electrocardiogram / by Jerome Passman and Constance D. Drummond ; foreword by Alvin H. Freiman. — New York ; London [etc.] : McGraw-Hill, 1976. — xv,316p : ill ; 24cm.
'A Blakiston publication'. — Bibl.: p.306. — Index.
ISBN 0-07-048715-4 Pbk : £9.90
(B77-04849)

616.1'2'0754 — Man. Heart. Diagnosis. Electrocardiography
Schamroth, Leo. An introduction to electrocardiography / [by] L. Schamroth. — 5th ed. — Oxford [etc.] : Blackwell Scientific, 1976. — xii,240p : ill, form ; 24cm.
Previous ed.: 1971. — Bibl. — Index.
ISBN 0-632-00426-6 Pbk : £3.50
(B77-10817)

Stein, Emanuel. The electrocardiogram : a self-study course in clinical electrocardiography / [by] Emanuel Stein. — Philadelphia ; London [etc.] : Saunders, 1976. — ix,405p : ill ; 27cm.
Bibl.: p.399. — Index.
ISBN 0-7216-8585-4 : £11.00
(B77-00787)

616.1'2'0754 — Man. Heart. Diagnosis. Non-invasive mechanical techniques. *Conference proceedings*
World Congress on Ballistocardiography and Cardiovascular Dynamics, *4th, Amsterdam, 1975.* Non-invasive mechanical methods in cardiology and cardiovascular dynamics : proceedings of the 4th World Congress on Ballistocardiography and Cardiovascular Dynamics, Amsterdam, April 1975 / editor W.J.A. Goedhard. — Basel ; London [etc.] : Karger ; [Chichester] : [Distributed by Wiley], 1976. — xx,271p : ill, port ; 25cm. — (Bibliotheca cardiologica ; no.35)
Bibl. — Index.
Pbk : Unpriced
ISBN 3-8055-2295-9
(B77-23455)

616.1'2'09 — Man. Heart. Diseases. *Case studies*
Goyette, Richert E. Cardiopulmonary pathology and pathophysiology case studies : case histories with related questions and discussion / by Robert E. Goyette in consultation with Harlan J. Spjut. — London : Kimpton, 1976. — 218p : ill ; 22cm.
'I am indebted beyond words to Harlan Spjut for several years of constructive criticism, careful attention to the smallest detail, and many of the illustrations' - Acknowledgements. — Also published: Flushing, N.Y. : Medical Examination Publishing Co., 1976. — Bibl. — Index.
ISBN 0-87488-075-0 Sp : £6.50
Also classified at 616.2'4'09
(B77-07380)

616.1'23 — Man. Heart. Coronary diseases
Gorlin, Richard. Coronary artery disease / [by] Richard Gorlin. — Philadelphia ; London [etc.] : Saunders, 1976. — ii-xiii,317p : ill(incl 1 col) ; 25cm. — (Major problems in internal medicine ; vol.11)
Index.
ISBN 0-7216-4165-2 : £13.50
(B77-06123)

616.1'23'025024613 — Man. Heart. Coronary diseases. Emergency treatment. *For nursing*
Foster, William T. Principles of acute coronary care / [by] William T. Foster. — New York : Appleton-Century-Crofts ; London [etc.] : Prentice-Hall, 1976. — [7],263p : ill ; 24cm.
Index.
ISBN 0-8385-7918-3 : Unpriced
ISBN 0-8385-7916-7 Pbk : £7.95
(B77-22628)

616.1'23'05 — Man. Heart. Coronary diseases. Prevention. *Reports, surveys*
Joint Working Party of the Royal College of Physicians of London and the British Cardiac Society. Prevention of coronary heart disease : report of a Joint Working Party of the Royal College of Physicians of London and the British Cardiac Society. — [London] : [R.C.P.L.], [1976]. — 63p : ill ; 21cm.
Reprinted from the Journal of the Royal College of Physicians of London, Vol.10, no.3; April 1976. — Bibl.: p.54-58.
ISBN 0-900596-39-2 Sd : Unpriced
(B77-06708)

616.1'23'05 — Man. Heart. Coronary diseases. Prevention. Role of exercise
Kavanagh, Terence. Heart attack? counter-attack! : a practical plan for a healthy heart / [by] Terence Kavanagh. — Toronto [etc.] ; London : Van Nostrand Reinhold, 1976. — viii,232p : ill, form, ports ; 23cm.
Bibl.: p.217-228. — Index.
ISBN 0-442-29927-3 : £7.10
(B77-01510)

616.1'23'06 — Man. Heart. Coronary diseases. Therapy
Coronary care in the community / edited by Aubrey Colling. — London : Croom Helm, 1977. — 3-226p : ill ; 23cm.
Index.
ISBN 0-85664-481-1 : £12.95 : CIP rev.
(B77-23456)

616.1'23'061 — Man. Heart. Coronary diseases. Drug therapy: Nifedipine. *Conference proceedings*
International Adalat Symposium, *3rd, Rio de Janeiro, 1975.* New therapy of ischemic heart disease : proceedings of the symposium held at Rio de Janeiro, October 10-11, 1975 / edited by Adib Domingos Jatene and Paul R. Lichtlen. — Amsterdam ; Oxford ([256 Banbury Rd, Oxford OX2 7DH]) : Excerpta Medica, 1976. — xiii,313p : ill ; 24cm. — (International congress series ; no.388)
'3rd International Adalat Symposium'. — Bibl. — Index.
Pbk : £21.74
(B77-04222)

616.1'23'07 — Man. Heart. Coronary diseases. Pathology
Crawford, *Sir* **Theo.** Pathology of ischaemic heart disease / [by] Sir Theo Crawford. — London [etc.] : Butterworth, 1977. — x,170p : ill ; 25cm. — (Postgraduate pathology series)
Bibl. — Index.
ISBN 0-407-00091-7 : £10.50 : CIP rev.
(B77-24968)

616.1'25 — Man. Heart. Persistent common atrioventricular canal
Atrioventricular canal defects / editor Robert H. Feldt, associate editors ... [others]. — Philadelphia ; London [etc.] : Saunders, 1976. — ii-xii, 145p : ill, port ; 27cm.
Bibl. — Index.
ISBN 0-7216-3615-2 : £18.00
(B77-09726)

616.1'26 — Man. Heart. Muscles. Acute infarction. *For nursing*
Acute myocardial infarction : reaction and recovery / [by] Rue L. Cromwell ... [et al.]. — Saint Louis : Mosby ; London : Distributed by Kimpton, 1977. — xvi,224p : ill ; 26cm.
Index.
ISBN 0-8016-1079-6 : £8.55
(B77-29460)

616.1'26 — Man. Heart. Muscles. Infarction. Role of shock
Shock in myocardial infarction / edited by Rolf M. Gunnar, Henry S. Loeb, Shahbudin H. Rahimtoola. — New York ; London : Grune and Stratton, 1974. — xiii,295p : ill ; 24cm. — (Clinical cardiology monographs)
Index.
ISBN 0-8089-0830-8 : Unpriced
(B77-19418)

616.1'28 — Man. Heart. Arrhythmia
Cardiac arrhythmias : diagnosis and treatment / edited by Noble O. Fowler. — 2nd ed. — Hagerstown [etc.] ; London : Harper and Row, 1977. — xiii,236p : ill ; 24cm.
Previous ed.: published as 'Treatment of cardiac arrhythmias'. New York : Harper and Row, 1970. — Bibl. — Index.
ISBN 0-06-140826-3 : £11.20
(B77-17535)

616.1'28 — Man. Heart. Arrhythmia. *Conference proceedings*
Re-entrant arrhythmias : mechanisms and treatment / edited by Henri E. Kulbertus. — Lancaster : M.T.P. Press, 1977. — xviii,372p : ill ; 24cm.
'... based on a Symposium ... held in Liège, in September 1976' - jacket. — Index.
ISBN 0-85200-113-4 : £14.50
(B77-24969)

616.1'3 — Man. Blood vessels. Diseases
Ryan, Terence John. Microvascular injury : vasculitis, stasis and ischaemia / [by] T.J. Ryan with contributions by M.W. Kanan, G.W. Cherry. — London [etc.] : Saunders, 1976. — xvi,418p : ill, facsims ; 26cm. — (Major problems in dermatology ; vol.7)
Bibl. — Index.
ISBN 0-7216-7858-0 : £17.75
(B77-02351)

616.1'3 — Man. Blood vessels. Thrombosis. *Reviews of research*
Progress in hemostasis and thrombosis. — New York ; London : Grune and Stratton.
Vol.1 / edited by Theodore H. Spaet. — 1972. — xi,257p : ill ; 26cm.
Index.
ISBN 0-8089-0760-3 : £15.45
Also classified at 616.1'57
(B77-04850)

616.1'3 — Man. Ischaemia. *Conference proceedings*
Hypoxia and ischaemia : symposium organized by the Royal College of Pathologists, delivered in London in February 1977 / edited by Basil C. Morson. — London (BMA House, Tavistock Sq., WC1H 9JR) : 'Journal of clinical pathology' for the College, 1977. — [5],190p : ill ; 25cm.
Bibl. — Index.
Pbk : £5.00
Also classified at 616.1'5
(B77-28659)

616.1'32 — Man. Blood. Essential hypertension. Pathogenesis
Birkenhäger, W H. Control mechanisms in essential hypertension / [by] W.H. Birkenhäger and M.A.D.H. Schalekamp. — Amsterdam ; Oxford [etc.] : Elsevier, 1976. — xiv,181p : ill ; 23cm.
Bibl. — Index.
ISBN 0-444-41452-5 : £15.85
(B77-07381)

616.1'32 — Man. Blood. Hypertension
Hypertension : physiopathology and treatment / editors Jaques Genest, Erich Koiw, Otto Kuchel ; associate editors Roger Boucher ... [et al.]. — New York ; London [etc.] : McGraw-Hill, 1977. — xvii,1208p : ill ; 27cm.
'A Blakiston publication'. — Index.
ISBN 0-07-023060-9 : £32.25
(B77-21907)

616.1'32 — Man. Blood. Hypertension. *Conference proceedings*
WHO Meeting on the Control of Hypertension and Stroke in the Community, *Tokyo, 1974.* Hypertension and stroke control in the community : proceedings of a WHO meeting held in Tokyo, 11-13 March 1974 / edited by S. Hatano, I. Shigematsu, T. Strasser. — Geneva : World Health Organization ; [London] : [H.M.S.O.], 1976. — 362p : ill, forms, map ; 24cm.
' ... WHO Meeting on the Control of Hypertension and Stroke in the Community ... ' - Preface.
ISBN 0-11-950808-7 Pbk : £7.50
Also classified at 616.8'1
(B77-06124)

616.1'32 — Man. Blood. Hypertension. Regulation by brain. *Conference proceedings*
Hypertension and Brain Mechanisms *(Conference), Utrecht, 1976.* Hypertension and brain mechanisms / edited by W. de Jong and A.P. Provoost and A.P. Shapiro. — Amsterdam ; Oxford [etc.] : Elsevier, 1977. — xvi,432p : ill ; 27cm. — (Progress in brain research ; vol.47)
'... the result of a workshop held in Utrecht in June 1976' - jacket. — '... the workshop "Hypertension and Brain Mechanisms"' - Acknowledgements. — Bibl. — Index.
ISBN 0-444-41534-3 : Unpriced
(B77-27892)

616.1'32 — Man. Blood. Hypertension. Regulation by central nervous system. *Conference proceedings*
Hahnemann International Symposium on Hypertension, *4th, Philadelphia, 1975.* Regulation of blood pressure by the central nervous system / editors Gaddo Onesti, Michael Fernandes, Kwan Eun Kim. — New York [etc.] ; London : Grune and Stratton, 1976. — xix,484p : ill ; 26cm.
'The Fourth Hahnemann International Symposium on Hypertension, [Philadelphia, 1975]'. — Index.
ISBN 0-8089-0936-3 : £22.25
(B77-00788)

616.1'32'05 — Man. Blood. Hypertension. Prevention & control. Use of relaxation
Benson, Herbert. The relaxation response / [by] Herbert Benson with Miriam Z. Klipper. — London (14 St James's Place, S.W.1) : Fountain Books, 1977. — 3-158p : ill, form ; 19cm.
Originally published: New York : Morrow, 1975 ; London : Collins, 1976. — Bibl.: p.129-150. — Index.
ISBN 0-00-624439-4 Pbk : £0.75
(B77-10818)

616.1'32'061 — Man. Blood. Hypertension. Drug therapy. *Conference proceedings*
Richards (A.N.) Symposium, *17th, King of Prussia, Pa, 1975.* New antihypertensive drugs / edited by Alexander Scriabine and Charles S. Sweet. — New York : Spectrum Publications ; New York ; London [etc.] : Distributed by Wiley, 1976. — [19],608p : ill ; 24cm. — (Physiological Society of Philadelphia. Monographs ; vol.2)
'Proceedings of the A.N. Richards Symposium, King of Prussia, Pennsylvania, May 19-20, 1975' - half-title page verso. — Bibl. — Index.
ISBN 0-470-15181-1 : £28.95
Primary classification 615'.71
(B77-12477)

616.1'35'061 — Man. Thrombolysis. Role of urokinase. *Conference proceedings*
Thrombosis and urokinase / edited by R. Paoletti, S. Sherry. — London [etc.] : Academic Press, 1977. — viii,257p : ill ; 24cm. — (Proceedings of the Serono symposia ; vol.9)
'This monograph represents an edited version of the proceedings of an international symposium on urokinase which was held in the Istituto Superiore de Sanita in Rome on October 30-November 1, 1975' - Preface. — Bibl. — Index.
ISBN 0-12-544960-7 : £8.20
(B77-22629)

616.1'36 — Man. Arteries. Atherosclerosis
Duguid, John B. The dynamics of atherosclerosis / [by] John B. Duguid. — [Aberdeen] : Aberdeen University Press, 1976. — xi,78p,[2]p of plates : ill(some col) ; 21cm.
Bibl.: p.71-75. — Index.
ISBN 0-900015-36-5 Pbk : £3.00
(B77-06709)

616.1'36'061 — Man. Arteries. Atherosclerosis. Drug therapy. Drugs. Evaluation. *Conference proceedings*
Brook Lodge Symposium on Anti-Atherosclerosis Drug Discovery, *1st, Augusta, 1975.* Atherosclerosis drug discovery / edited by Charles E. Day. — New York ; London : Plenum Press, 1976. — x,467p : ill ; 26cm. — (Advances in experimental medicine and biology ; vol.67)
'Proceedings of the First Brook Lodge Symposium on Anti-Atherosclerosis Drug Discovery held at Brook Lodge in Augusta, Michigan, August 13-15, 1975' - title page verso. — Index.
ISBN 0-306-39067-1 : £23.63
(B77-21170)

616.1'4 — Man. Legs. Veins. Diseases
Johnson, Harold Daintree. The swollen leg : causes and treatment / [by] H. Daintree Johnson, Joseph Pflug ; with foreword by Karl A. Lofgren. — London : Heinemann Medical, 1975. — xvii,284p, plate : ill(incl 2 col) ; 23cm.
Bibl. — Index.
ISBN 0-433-07042-0 : £4.75
Also classified at 616.4'2
(B77-09046)

The **treatment** of venous disorders : a comprehensive review of current practice in the management of varicose veins and the post-thrombotic syndrome / edited by John T. Hobbs. — Lancaster : M.T.P. Press, 1977. — xvi,438p : ill, 2 forms ; 24cm.
Bibl. — Index.
ISBN 0-85200-084-7 : £12.50
(B77-17536)

616.1'43'065 — Man. Veins. Varicose veins. Naturopathy
Sneddon, James Russell. The nature cure treatment of varicose veins and ulcers / [by] J. Russell Sneddon. — 2nd ed. — Wellingborough : Thorsons, 1975. — 63p ; 19cm. — (The self-help series)
Spine title: Varicose veins and ulcers. — This ed. originally published: 1974.
ISBN 0-7225-0269-9 Pbk : £1.25
(B77-11849)

616.1'45'05 — Man. Veins. Thromboembolism. Prevention
Venous thromboembolism : prevention and treatment / edited by John L. Madden, Michael Hume. — New York : Appleton-Century-Crofts ; London [etc.] : Prentice-Hall, 1976. — xiii,240p : ill ; 24cm.
Bibl. — Index.
ISBN 0-8385-9406-9 : £13.20
Also classified at 616.1'45'06
(B77-29461)

616.1'45'06 — Man. Veins. Thromboembolism. Therapy
Venous thromboembolism : prevention and treatment / edited by John L. Madden, Michael Hume. — New York : Appleton-Century-Crofts ; London [etc.] : Prentice-Hall, 1976. — xiii,240p : ill ; 24cm.
Bibl. — Index.
ISBN 0-8385-9406-9 : £13.20
Primary classification 616.1'45'05
(B77-29461)

616.1'5 — Man. Anoxia. *Conference proceedings*
Hypoxia and ischaemia : symposium organized by the Royal College of Pathologists, delivered in London in February 1977 / edited by Basil C. Morson. — London (BMA House, Tavistock Sq., WC1H 9JR) : 'Journal of clinical pathology' for the College, 1977. — [5],190p : ill ; 25cm.
Bibl. — Index.
Pbk : £5.00
Primary classification 616.1'3
(B77-28659)

616.1'5 — Man. Blood. Diseases
Block, Matthew H. Text-atlas of hematology / [by] Matthew H. Block. — Philadelphia : Lea and Febiger ; London : Kimpton, 1976. — ix, 651p,lxiv p of plates : ill(some col), ports ; 27cm.
Bibl. — Index.
ISBN 0-8121-0014-x : £57.35
(B77-05451)

Eastham, Robert Duncan. Clinical haematology / by R.D. Eastham. — 5th ed. — Bristol : J. Wright, 1977. — [7],326p : ill ; 18cm.
Previous ed.: 1974. — Index.
ISBN 0-7236-0456-8 Pbk : £3.00 : CIP rev.
(B77-06710)

Goldstone, A H. Examination haematology / [by] A.H. Goldstone ; [with a chapter entitled] 'Blood coagulation' [by] B.A. McVerry. — London [etc.] : Saunders, 1977. — vi,206p : ill ; 23cm.
With answers. — Index.
ISBN 0-7216-4148-2 Pbk : £4.95
(B77-27893)

Hematology / edited by William S. Beck. — 2nd ed. — Cambridge, Mass. ; London : M.I.T. Press, 1977. — xiii,589p : ill ; 26cm.
Previous ed.: 1973. — Bibl. — Index.
ISBN 0-262-02124-2 : £14.00
ISBN 0-262-52038-9 Pbk : £7.00
(B77-33834)

Leavell, Byrd Stuart. Fundamentals of clinical hematology. — 4th ed. / [by] Byrd Stuart Leavell, Oscar Andreas Thorup, Jr, with the assistance of ... [others]. — Philadelphia ; London [etc.] : Saunders, 1976. — xiii,755p : ill(incl 1 col) ; 26cm.
Previous ed.: / by Byrd S. Leavell, Oscar A. Thorup, Jr. 1971. — Bibl. — Index.
ISBN 0-7216-5678-1 : £20.00
(B77-01511)

616.1'5'09 — Man. Blood. Diseases. *Case studies*
Goyette, Richert E. Hematologic and reticuloendothelial pathology and pathophysiology case studies : case histories with related questions and discussion / by Richert E. Goyette in consultation with Harlan J. Spjut. — London : Kimpton, 1976. — 192p : ill ; 22cm.
'I am indebted beyond words to Harlan Spjut for several years of constructive criticism, careful attention to the smallest detail, and many of the illustrations' - Acknowledgments. — Also published: Flushing, N.Y. : Medical Examination Publishing, 1976. — Bibl. — Index.
ISBN 0-87488-076-9 Sp : £6.50
Primary classification 616.4'2'09
(B77-07384)

616.1'52 — Man. Blood. Haemoglobins. Abnormalities
Bunn, H Franklin. Hemoglobinopathies / by H. Franklin Bunn, Bernard G. Forget, Helen M. Ranney. — Philadelphia ; London [etc.] : Saunders, 1977. — ix,308p : ill ; 25cm. — (Major problems in internal medicine ; vol.12)
Bibl.: p.251-291. — Index.
ISBN 0-7216-2179-1 : £13.50
(B77-21171)

616.1'52 — Man. Pernicious anaemia
Kass, Lawrence. Pernicious anemia / [by] Lawrence Kass. — Philadelphia ; London [etc.] : Saunders, 1976 [i.e. 1977]. — ii-xiv, 247p : ill(some col), facsims, ports ; 25cm. — (Major problems in internal medicine ; vol.7)
Published in the United States: 1976. — Bibl.: p.220-237. — Index.
ISBN 0-7216-5295-6 : £12.50
(B77-12481)

616.1'55 — Man. Blood. Leukaemia. *Reviews of research*
Leukemia research. — Oxford [etc.] : Pergamon. Vol.1, no.1- ; [Jan.] 1977-. — 1977-. — ill ; 25cm.
Quarterly. — Cover title: - 73p. in 1st issue.
Pbk : Unpriced
ISSN 0145-2126
(B77-18173)

616.1'55 — Man. Blood. Leukaemia. Lymphoid cells. Membranes. Use in classification of leukaemia lymphoid cells
Seligmann, Maxime. Lymphocyte membrane markers in human leukaemias and lymphomas / by Maxime Seligmann. — London (43 Great Ormond St., WC1N 3JJ) : Leukaemia Research Fund, 1976. — 27p ; 22cm. — (Leukaemia Research Fund. Annual guest lectures ; 11th ISSN 0459-1666)
'... delivered on 27th August, 1975 at the Queen Elizabeth Hall, London'. — Bibl.: p.23-27.
ISBN 0-9502230-2-6 Sd : £1.00
Also classified at 616.4'2
(B77-02352)

616.1'57 — Man. Blood. Coagulation disorders. *Reviews of research*
Recent advances in blood coagulation / edited by L. Poller. — Edinburgh [etc.] : Churchill Livingstone.
No.2. — 1977. — ix,388p : ill ; 25cm.
Bibl. — Index.
ISBN 0-443-01559-7 : £15.00
(B77-14255)

616.1'57 — Man. Blood. Haemostatic disorders
Zieve, Philip D. Disorders of hemostasis / [by] Philip D. Zieve, Jack Levin. — Philadelphia ; London [etc.] : Saunders, 1976. — ii-xvi,97p : ill(some col) ; 25cm. — (Major problems in internal medicine ; vol.10)
Bibl. — Index.
ISBN 0-7216-9685-6 : £12.75
(B77-07382)

616.1'57 — Man. Blood. Haemostatic disorders. *Reviews of research*
Progress in hemostasis and thrombosis. — New York ; London : Grune and Stratton.
Vol.1 / edited by Theodore H. Spaet. — 1972. — xi,257p : ill ; 26cm.
Index.
ISBN 0-8089-0760-3 : £15.45
Primary classification 616.1'3
(B77-04850)

616.2 — DISEASES OF RESPIRATORY SYSTEM
Brewis, Robert Alistair Livingston. Lecture notes on respiratory disease / written and illustrated by R.A.L. Brewis. — Oxford [etc.] : Blackwell Scientific, 1977. — vii,242p : ill ; 22cm.
Originally published: 1975. — Bibl.: p.233-236. — Index.
Pbk : £3.75
ISBN 0-632-00651-x
(B77-21908)

Respiratory disease / edited by D.J. Lane. — London : Heinemann Medical, 1976. — xvi, 565p : ill ; 22cm. — (Tutorials in postgraduate medicine ; vol.5)
Bibl. — Index.
ISBN 0-433-19055-8 : £12.50
(B77-14256)

616.2'002'4613 — Man. Respiratory system. Diseases. *For nursing*
Grenville-Mathers, Ronald. The respiratory system / [by] R. Grenville-Mathers. — Harmondsworth [etc.] : Penguin ; [Edinburgh] : [Distributed by Churchill Livingstone], 1973 [i.e. 1976]. — 140p : ill ; 20cm. — (Penguin education) (Penguin library of nursing)
Originally published: 1973. — Bibl.: p.127-133. — Index.
ISBN 0-443-01545-7 Pbk : £1.25
(B77-02353)

Wade, Jacqueline Fiona. Respiratory nursing care : physiology and technique / [by] Jacqueline F. Wade. — 2nd ed. — Saint Louis : Mosby ; London : Distributed by Kimpton, 1977. — xi,231p : ill ; 24cm.
Previous ed.: 1973. — Bibl. — Index.
ISBN 0-8016-5281-2 Pbk : £6.10
(B77-21172)

616.2'004'71 — Man. Respiratory system. Pathogens: Atmospheric particles. *Conference proceedings*
Inhaled particles. — Oxford [etc.] : Pergamon.
4 : Proceedings of an international symposium organized by the British Occupational Hygiene Society, Edinburgh, 22-26 September 1975 / edited by W.H. Walton assisted by Brenda McGovern. — 1977. — 2v.(xii,838p) : ill ; 26cm.
Bibl. — Index.
ISBN 0-08-020560-7 : £52.00
(B77-18174)

616.2'004'9 — Man. Respiratory system. Diseases. *Case studies*
DeKornfeld, Thomas J. Respiratory care case studies / by Thomas J. DeKornfeld and Jay S. Finch. — 2nd ed. — London : Kimpton.
Vol.1. — 1976. — 189p : ill ; 22cm.
Previous ed.: Flushing, N.Y. : Medical Examination Pub. Co., 1971. — Bibl. — Index.
ISBN 0-87488-019-x Sp : £6.50
(B77-02354)

616.2'03 — Man. Influenza
Stuart-Harris, *Sir* Charles Herbert. Influenza : the viruses and the disease / [by] Sir Charles H. Stuart-Harris, Geoffrey C. Schild. — Littleton : Publishing Sciences Group ; [London] : Edward Arnold, 1976. — x,242p : ill, map ; 24cm.
Bibl. — Index.
ISBN 0-88416-124-2 : £12.00
(B77-07930)

616.2'03'009 — Man. Influenza, to 1976
Beveridge, William Ian Beardmore. Influenza : the last great plague : an unfinished story of discovery / [by] W.I.B. Beveridge. — London : Heinemann, 1977. — xii,124p : ill, maps, ports ; 20cm.
Index.
ISBN 0-435-62065-7 : £2.95
(B77-07931)

616.2'03'061 — Man. Influenza. Herbal remedies
Gosling, Nalda. Herbs for colds and 'flu / by Nalda Gosling ; drawings by A.R. Gosling. — Wellingborough : Thorsons, 1976. — 64p : ill ; 18cm. — (Everybody's home herbal)
ISBN 0-7225-0344-x Pbk : £0.50
Also classified at 616.2'05'061
(B77-04223)

616.2'05'061 — Man. Colds. Herbal remedies
Gosling, Nalda. Herbs for colds and 'flu / by Nalda Gosling ; drawings by A.R. Gosling. — Wellingborough : Thorsons, 1976. — 64p : ill ; 18cm. — (Everybody's home herbal)
ISBN 0-7225-0344-x Pbk : £0.50
Primary classification 616.2'03'061
(B77-04223)

616.2'1 — Man. Ears, eyes, nose & throat. Diseases. *For nursing*
Casey, Thomas Aquinas. The special senses / [by] T.A. Casey, H.N. Waller. — Edinburgh [etc.] : Churchill Livingstone, 1976. — 168p : ill ; 20cm. — (Penguin library of nursing)
Bibl.: p.151-160. — Index.
ISBN 0-443-01495-7 Pbk : £1.75
(B77-03038)

616.2'1 — Man. Ears, nose & throat. Diseases
Foxen, Eric Harry Miles. Lecture notes on diseases of the ear, nose and throat / [by] E.H. Miles Foxen. — 4th ed. — Oxford [etc.] : Blackwell Scientific, 1976. — x,226p : ill ; 19cm.
Previous ed.: 1972. — Bibl.: p.217. — Index.
ISBN 0-632-00129-1 Pbk : £3.25
(B77-00246)

Hall, Ion Simson. Diseases of the nose, throat and ear : a handbook for students and practitioners / [by] I. Simson Hall, Bernard H. Colman. — 11th ed. — Edinburgh [etc.] : Churchill Livingstone, 1977. — [9],352p : ill ; 22cm.
This ed. originally published: 1975. — Index.
ISBN 0-443-01313-6 Pbk : £3.95
(B77-28660)

Logan Turner's diseases of the nose, throat and ear. — 8th ed. / edited by J.F. Birrell ; assisted by ... [others]. — Bristol : J. Wright, 1977. — xii,435p,[10]p of plates,leaf of plate : ill(some col) ; 22cm.
Previous ed.: / edited by John P. Stewart ; assisted by J.F. Birrell. 1968. — Index.
ISBN 0-7236-0434-7 Pbk : £6.50
(B77-05452)

616.2'1'061 — Man. Ears, nose & throat. Drug therapy
Saunders, William Howerton. Pharmacotherapy in otolaryngology / [by] William H. Saunders, Robert W. Gardier. — Saint Louis : Mosby ; London : Distributed by Kimpton, 1976. — xi, 296p : ill ; 25cm.
Bibl.: p.271. — Index.
ISBN 0-8016-4310-4 : £15.00
(B77-11850)

616.2'2 — Otolaryngology
English, Gerald M. Otolaryngology : a textbook / [by] Gerald M. English, with 17 contributors. — Hagerstown [etc.] ; London : Harper and Row, [1977]. — xv,815p : ill ; 24cm.
Published in the United States: 1976. — Bibl. — Index.
ISBN 0-06-140783-6 : £31.90
(B77-10384)

616.2'3 — Man. Bronchi. Asthma
Office of Health Economics. Asthma / Office of Health Economics. — London : O.H.E., 1976. — 47p : col ill ; 21cm. — (Studies of current health problems ; no.57 ISSN 0473-8837)
Bibl.: p.44-47.
Sd : £0.35
(B77-01512)

616.2'3 — Man. Bronchi. Asthma. *Reviews of research*
Asthma / edited by T.J.H. Clark and S. Godfrey. — London : Chapman and Hall, 1977. — xii, 409p : ill ; 24cm.
Bibl. — Index.
ISBN 0-412-13330-x : £11.00
(B77-23457)

616.2'3'0754 — Man. Bronchi. Diagnosis. Bronchoscopy
Stradling, Peter. Diagnostic bronchoscopy : an introduction / [by] Peter Stradling. — 3rd ed. — Edinburgh [etc.] : Churchill Livingstone, 1976. — x,150p : ill(some col) ; 26cm.
Previous ed.: 1973. — Index.
ISBN 0-443-01355-1 : £15.00
(B77-06125)

616.2'4 — Man. Blood. Pulmonary hypertension. Pathology
Wagenvoort, C A. Pathology of pulmonary hypertension / [by] C.A. Wagenvoort and Noeke Wagenvoort ; foreword by Jesse E. Edwards. — New York ; London [etc.] : Wiley, 1977. — xiii,345p : ill ; 26cm.
'A Wiley Medical Publication'. — Bibl. — Index.
ISBN 0-471-91355-3 : £16.50
(B77-23458)

616.2'4 — Man. Lungs. Chronic obstructive diseases
Thurlbeck, William M. Chronic airflow obstruction in lung disease / [by] William M. Thurlbeck. — Philadelphia ; London [etc.] : Saunders, 1976. — xiii,456p : ill, facsims, maps ; 25cm. — (Major problems in pathology ; vol.5)
Index.
ISBN 0-7216-8859-4 : £13.50
(B77-01513)

616.2'4'07 — Man. Lungs. Diseases. Physiological aspects
Saunders, Kenneth B. Clinical physiology of the lung / [by] Kenneth B. Saunders. — Oxford [etc.] : Blackwell Scientific, 1977. — [5],255p : ill ; 24cm.
Index.
ISBN 0-632-00046-5 : £9.75 : CIP rev.
(B77-18175)

616.2'4'07 — Man. Lungs. Pathology
Spencer, Herbert, *b.1915.* Pathology of the lung (excluding pulmonary tuberculosis) / [by] H. Spencer ; with a foreword by Averill A. Liebow. — 3rd ed. — Oxford [etc.] : Pergamon, 1977. — 2v.(xv,1099p) : ill ; 25cm.
Previous ed.: 1968. — Bibl.: p.1021-1070. — Index.
ISBN 0-08-021021-x : £47.50
(B77-25665)

616.2'4'071 — Man. Lungs. Diseases. Environmental factors
Bouhuys, Arend. Breathing : physiology, environment and lung disease / [by] Arend Bouhuys. — New York ; London : Grune and Stratton, 1974. — xii,511p : ill ; 26cm.
Bibl. — Index.
ISBN 0-8089-0758-1 : Unpriced
Primary classification 612'.2
(B77-19400)

616.2'4'07575 — Man. Lungs. Diagnosis. Scintiphotographs. Interpretation
Mandell, Charles H. Scintillation camera lung imaging : an anatomic atlas and guide / [by] Charles H. Mandell with the assistance of Herta M. Houle. — New York [etc.] ; London : Grune and Stratton, 1976. — xi, 191p : chiefly ill ; 29cm.
Bibl.: p.187-191.
ISBN 0-8089-0960-6 : £17.10
(B77-04851)

616.2'4'09 — Man. Lungs. Diseases. *Case studies*
Goyette, Richert E. Cardiopulmonary pathology and pathophysiology case studies : case histories with related questions and discussion / by Robert E. Goyette in consultation with Harlan J. Spjut. — London : Kimpton, 1976. — 218p : ill ; 22cm.
'I am indebted beyond words to Harlan Spjut for several years of constructive criticism, careful attention to the smallest detail, and many of the illustrations' - Acknowledgements. — Also published: Flushing, N.Y. : Medical Examination Publishing Co., 1976. — Bibl. — Index.
ISBN 0-87488-075-0 Sp : £6.50
Primary classification 616.1'2'09
(B77-07380)

616.2'44'00941 — Mechanised iron foundries. Personnel. Lungs. Pneumoconiosis. *Great Britain. Reports, surveys*
Joint Standing Committee on Health, Safety and Welfare in Foundries. *Sub-committee on Dust and Fume.* Some aspects of pneumoconiosis in a group of mechanised iron foundries : third report of the Sub-committee on Dust and Fume, Joint Standing Committee on Health, Safety and Welfare in Foundries / [for the] Health and Safety Executive. — London : H.M.S.O., 1977. — 72p : ill ; 25cm.
ISBN 0-11-883005-8 Sd : £2.50
(B77-26341)

616.2'5 — Man. Pleura. Pleural effusions
Lowell, James R. Pleural effusions : a comprehensive review / by James R. Lowell. — Baltimore ; London [etc.] : University Park Press, 1977. — xiii,177p : ill ; 24cm.
Bibl.: p.147-171. — Index.
ISBN 0-8391-0985-7 : £10.50
(B77-16420)

616.3 — DISEASES OF DIGESTIVE SYSTEM
Bouchier, Ian Arthur Dennis. Gastroenterology / [by] Ian A.D. Bouchier. — 2nd ed. — London : Baillière Tindall, 1977. — x,374p,[16] p of plates : ill ; 20cm. — (Concise medical textbooks)
Previous ed.: 1973. — Bibl. — Index.
ISBN 0-7020-0659-9 Pbk : £4.50
(B77-29462)

Gastroenterology : an integrated course / editors Iain E. Gillespie, T.J. Thomson. — 2nd ed. — Edinburgh [etc.] : Churchill Livingstone, 1977. — [9],294p : ill ; 22cm.
Previous ed.: 1972. — Bibl. — Index.
ISBN 0-443-01457-4 Pbk : £2.75
(B77-28661)

Gastroenterology / edited by Henry L. Bockus ... [et al.]. — 3rd ed. — Philadelphia ; London [etc.] : Saunders.
In 4 vols.
Vol.2. — 1976. — ii-xxv,1171p : ill(some col) ; 27cm.
Previous ed.: 1963. — Bibl. — Index.
ISBN 0-7216-1774-3 : £29.25
(B77-00247)

Vol.3 : The liver, gallbladder, bile ducts and pancreas. — 1976. — ii-xxvii,1211p : ill(some col) ; 27cm.
Previous ed.: 1966. — Bibl. — Index.
ISBN 0-7216-1775-1 : £24.75
(B77-01514)

Vol.4 : [Peritoneum, parasitic diseases, system interrelationships]. — 1976. — ii-xxv,795p : ill(some col) ; 27cm.
Previous ed.: 1963. — Bibl. — Index.
ISBN 0-7216-1776-x : £28.50
(B77-11851)

Spiro, Howard Marget. Clinical gastroenterology / [by] Howard M. Spiro. — 2nd ed. — New York : Macmillan [etc.] ; London : Baillière Tindall, 1977. — xxi,1289p : ill ; 27cm.
Previous ed.: New York : Macmillan ; London : Collier-Macmillan, 1970. — Bibl. — Index.
ISBN 0-7020-0626-2 : £33.75
(B77-19419)

Topics in gastroenterology. — Oxford [etc.] : Blackwell Scientific.
2 / edited by S.C. Truelove and Joan Trowell. — 1975. — x,373p : ill ; 24cm.
Bibl. — Index.
ISBN 0-632-00461-4 Pbk : £10.00
(B77-27130)

4 / edited by S.C. Truelove and J.A. Ritchie. — 1976. — x,384p : ill ; 24cm.
Bibl. — Index.
ISBN 0-632-00229-8 Pbk : £11.00
(B77-01515)

616.3 — Man. Intestines. Malabsorption syndromes
Sleisenger, Marvin Herbert. Malabsorption / [by] Marvin H. Sleisenger, Lloyd L. Brandborg. — Philadelphia ; London [etc.] : Saunders, 1977. — x,261p : ill ; 25cm. — (Major problems in internal medicine ; vol.13)
Index.
ISBN 0-7216-8361-4 : £11.50
(B77-24971)

616.3 — Medicine. Gastroenterology. *Reviews of research*
Recent advances in gastroenterology. — Edinburgh [etc.] : Churchill Livingstone.
No.3 / edited by Ian A.D. Bouchier. — 1976. — ix,338p : ill ; 24cm.
Bibl. — Index.
ISBN 0-443-01319-5 : £13.00
(B77-03571)

616.3'002'4613 — Man. Digestive system. Diseases. *For nursing*
Gribble, Helen E. Gastroenterological nursing / [by] Helen E. Gribble. — London : Baillière Tindall, 1977. — viii,309p : ill ; 20cm. — (Nurses' aids series : special interest text)
Index.
ISBN 0-7020-0605-x Pbk : £3.75
(B77-14257)

616.3'025 — Man. Digestive system. Acute disorders. Emergency treatment. *Conference proceedings*
International Symposium on Gastrointestinal Emergencies, *1st, Stockholm, 1975.* Gastrointestinal emergencies : proceedings of the First International Symposium held at the Wenner-Gren Center, Stockholm, September 1975 / edited by Franz R. Bárány and Aldo Torsoli. — Oxford [etc.] : Pergamon, 1977. — xvii,428p : ill, plan ; 26cm. — (Wenner-Gren Center. International symposium series ; vol.26)

'The First International Symposium on Gastrointestinal Emergencies, held in Stockholm on the 15th-18th September 1975 ...' - Editors' Preface. — Bibl. — Index.
ISBN 0-08-020494-5 : £16.00
(B77-14258)

616.3'09 — Man. Digestive system. Diseases. *Case studies*
Goyette, Richert E. Digestive and hepatobiliary pathology and pathophysiology case studies : case histories with related questions and discussion / by Richert E. Goyette ; in consultation with Harlan J. Spjut. — London : Kimpton, 1977. — 201p : ill ; 22cm.
Also published: Flushing, N.Y. : Medical Examination Publishing Co., 1977. — Bibl. — Index.
ISBN 0-87488-078-5 Sp : £6.50
(B77-14259)

616.3'1 — Man. Salivary glands. Diseases
Diseases of the salivary glands / [edited by] Robin M. Rankow, Irving M. Polayes. — Philadelphia ; London [etc.] : Saunders, 1976. — x,379p,[2]leaves of plates : ill(some col), facsims ; 27cm.
Bibl. — Index.
ISBN 0-7216-7453-4 : £24.00
(B77-12482)

616.3'3 — Man. Gastrointestinal tract. Diseases
Salter, Robin Hugh. Common gastroenterological problems / [by] R.H. Salter. — Bristol : J. Wright, 1977. — [5],108p : ill ; 19cm.
Bibl. — Index.
ISBN 0-7236-0470-3 Pbk : £2.50 : CIP rev.
(B77-21909)

616.3'3 — Man. Gastrointestinal tract. Haemorrhages
Balint, John A. Gastrointestinal bleeding : diagnosis and management / [by] John A. Balint, I. James Sarfeh, Martin B. Fried. — New York ; London [etc.] : Wiley, 1977. — xv, 101p : ill ; 26cm. — (Clinical gastroenterology monograph series)
'A Wiley medical publication'. — Index.
ISBN 0-471-04607-8 : £9.50
(B77-29463)

616.3'4 — Man. Colon. Diverticular disease. *State-of-the-art reviews*
Painter, Neil Stamford. Diverticular disease of the colon / by N.S. Painter. — 6th ed. — London (59 High Holborn, WC1V 6EB) : Norgine Ltd, 1977. — [1],31p : ill ; 21cm. — (The present state of knowledge ; no.1)
Previous ed.: 1974?. — Bibl.: p.30-31.
ISBN 0-901210-14-5 Sd : £0.75
(B77-30297)

616.3'4 — Man. Intestines. Blood vessels. Ischaemia
Marston, Adrian. Intestinal ischaemia / [by] Adrian Marston ; with illustrations by Peter Drury. — London : Edward Arnold, 1977. — x,190p : ill(incl 2 col) ; 24cm.
Bibl. — Index.
ISBN 0-7131-4264-2 : £10.95
(B77-21910)

616.3'4'0757 — Man. Small intestine. Radiology
Marshak, Richard Harvey. Radiology of the small intestine / [by] Richard H. Marshak and Arthur E. Lindner. — 2nd ed. — Philadelphia ; London [etc.] : Saunders, 1976. — ii-xiv,620p : ill ; 29cm.
Previous ed.: 1970. — Index. — Includes contributions from other writers.
ISBN 0-7216-6127-0 : £31.25
(B77-00248)

616.3'4'079 — Man. Intestines. Diseases. Immunological aspects. *Conference proceedings*
Symposium on Immunology of the Gut, *Ciba Foundation, 1976.* Immunology of the gut : in memory of the late Joseph Heremans. — Amsterdam ; Oxford [etc.] : Elsevier [etc.], 1977. — viii,376p : ill ; 25cm. — (Ciba Foundation. Symposia : new series ; 46)
'Symposium on Immunology of the Gut, held at the Ciba Foundation, London, 26th-28th April 1976' - p.vii. — Bibl. — Index.
ISBN 0-444-15246-6 : £16.67
(B77-22630)

616.3'42 — Man. Large intestine. Disorders
Naish, John Michael. Understanding your bowels / [by] John M. Naish. — London : Heinemann Health, 1975. — [6],87p : ill ; 20cm.
ISBN 0-433-23050-9 Pbk : £1.75
(B77-20321)

616.3'433 — Man. Duodenum. Ulcers. *State-of-the-art reviews*
Duodenal ulcer. — Montreal ; Lancaster : Eden Press ; [Edinburgh] : Distributed by Churchill Livingstone. — (Annual research reviews ISSN 0703-1629)
[Vol.1] : [1977] / [by] K.G. Wormsley. — [1977]. — [7],100p ; 22cm.
Bibl.: p.70-97. — Index.
ISBN 0-904406-53-9 : £7.75
ISSN 0703-1637
ISBN 0-443-01709-3 (Churchill Livingstone)
(B77-33837)

616.3'44 — Man. Colon. Crohn's disease
Crohn's disease : aetiology, clinical manifestations and management / [by] Bryan N. Brooke ... [et al.]. — London [etc.] : Macmillan, 1977. — x, 113p,[4]p of plates : ill(some col), port ; 25cm.
Bibl.: p.94-110. — Index.
ISBN 0-333-21560-5 : £9.75
(B77-20322)

616.3'5 — Man. Haemorrhoids. *State-of-the-art reviews*
Thomson, Hamish. Haemorrhoids / by Hamish Thomson. — London (59 High Holborn, WC1V 6EB) : Norgine Limited, 1977. — 13p : ill ; 21cm. — (The present state of knowledge ; no.8)
ISBN 0-901210-16-1 Sd : £0.75
(B77-31233)

616.3'6 — Man. Biliary tract. Diseases
White, Thomas Taylor. Liver, bile ducts, and pancreas / by Thomas Taylor White, Henri Sarles, Jean-Pierre Benhamou ; illustrations by Phyllis Wood. — New York [etc.] ; London : Grune and Stratton, 1977. — viii,440p : ill ; 24cm.
Translation and revision: of 'Foie, pancreas, voies 'biliares' / by Henri Sarles, Jean-Pierre Benhamou. Paris : Flammarion Medecine Sciences, 1972. — Bibl. — Index.
ISBN 0-8089-1002-7 : £23.05
(B77-27894)

616.3'6 — Man. Biliary tract. Diseases. *Conference proceedings*
International Association for the Study of the Liver. *Quadrennial Meeting, 5th, Acapulco, 1974.* Diseases of the liver and biliary tract : with a standardization of nomenclature, diagnostic criteria and diagnostic methodology : proceedings of the Fifth Quadrennial Meeting of the International Association for the Study of the Liver, Acapulco, 1974 / editor Carroll M. Leevy. — Basel ; London [etc.] : Karger, 1976. — ix,187p : ill ; 26cm.
'Standardization of nomenclature, diagnostic criteria and diagnostic methodology for diseases of the liver and biliary tract' / by Carroll M. Leevy and Niels Tygstrup, (vi,60p. : Pbk) as insert. — Bibl.
Pbk : Unpriced
ISBN 3-8055-2276-2
(B77-27131)

616.3'6'07572 — Man. Biliary tract. Diagnosis. Radiography. Use of x-rays
Roentgenology of the gallbladder and biliary tract / edited by Benjamin Felson. — New York [etc.] ; London : Grune and Stratton, [1977]. — vii,150p : ill ; 29cm. — (A "Seminars in roentgenology" reprint)
Published in the United States: 1976. — 'The chapters of this book appeared originally in the July and October 1976 issues (Vol.XI. No.8). 3 and 4 of "Seminars in Roentgenology" - title page verso. — Bibl. — Index.
ISBN 0-8089-0999-1 : £10.30
(B77-13672)

616.3'62 — Man. Liver. Diseases
Chen, Thomas S. Essential hepatology / [by] Thomas S. Chen, Peter S. Chen. — Massachusetts [etc.] ; London : Butterworth, 1977. — viii,360p : ill ; 24cm.
Bibl.: p.345. — Index.
ISBN 0-409-95005-x : £17.90
(B77-32657)

616.3'62'06 — Man. Liver. Therapy
International Symposium on New Trends in the Therapy of Liver Diseases, *Tirrenia, 1974.* New trends in the therapy of liver diseases : proceedings of the International Symposium on New Trends in the Therapy of Liver Diseases, Tirrenia, June 6-7, 1974 / editor Aldo Bertelli. — Basel ; London [etc.] : Karger ; [London] : [Distributed by Wiley], 1975. — vi,209p : ill ; 25cm.
Bibl. — Index.
Unpriced
ISBN 3-8055-2118-9
(B77-30298)

616.3'623 — Man. Liver. Viral hepatitis
World Health Organization. *Expert Committee on Viral Hepatitis.* Advances in viral hepatitis : report of the WHO Expert Committee on Viral Hepatitis. — Geneva : W.H.O. ; [London] : [H.M.S.O.], 1977. — 62p : map ; 20cm. — (World Health Organization. Technical report series ; 602)
Sd : £2.24
ISBN 92-4-120602-0
(B77-11242)

616.3'65 — Man. Gall bladder. Cholecystitis
Levine, Talya. Chronic cholecystitis : its pathology and the role of vascular factors in its pathogenesis / [by] Talya Levine. — New York [etc.] ; Chichester : Wiley [etc.], 1975. — ix, 270p : ill ; 25cm.
'A Halsted Press book'. — Bibl.: p.233-270.
ISBN 0-470-53122-3 : £10.00
(B77-10385)

616.3'65'065 — Man. Gall bladder. Naturopathy
Newman Turner, Roger. Self-help for gall-bladder troubles / [by] Roger Newman Turner. — Wellingborough : Thorsons, 1977. — 64p : ill ; 18cm. — (Self help series)
ISBN 0-7225-0369-5 Pbk : £0.50
(B77-33257)

616.3'9 — Indians. Nutritional disorders. Ethnic factors. *Great Britain*
Van den Berghs and Jurgens Limited. Asians in Britain : a study of their dietary patterns in relation to their cultural and religious backgrounds / [Van den Berghs and Jurgens Limited]. — Burgess Hill (Sussex House, Civic Way, Burgess Hill, Sussex RH15 9AW) : Van den Berghs and Jurgens Ltd, [1976]. — 22p : ill, 2 maps ; 20x21cm. — (A Van den Berghs & Jurgens nutrition publication)
Bibl.: p.22.
ISBN 0-901874-14-0 Sd : Unpriced
(B77-02355)

616.3'9 — Man. Acid-base balance & electrolyte balance. Disorders
Acid-base and electrolyte balance : normal regulation and clinical disorders / edited by Allan B. Schwartz, Harvey Lyons. — New York [etc.] ; London : Grune and Stratton, 1977. — xv,320p : ill ; 24cm.
'Much of the material presented herein is adapted from our annual Acid-Base and Electrolyte Seminar and Workshop' - Foreword. — With answers. — Bibl. — Index.
ISBN 0-8089-0991-6 : £13.35
(B77-33838)

616.3'9 — Man. Acid-base balance, electrolyte balance & fluid balance. Disorders
Fluid, electrolyte and acid-base disturbances : a practical guide for interns / edited by R.H. Loblay, D.J. Tiller, W.J. Hensley. — Aylesbury : HM+M, 1976. — [6],136p : ill ; 18cm.
Also published: Brookvale : Australia and New Zealand Book Co., 1976. — Index.
ISBN 0-85602-065-6 Pbk : £2.50
(B77-09727)

Rose, Burton David. Clinical physiology of acid-base and electrolyte disorders / [by] Burton David Rose. — New York ; London [etc.] : McGraw-Hill, 1977. — viii,548p : ill ; 24cm.
'A Blakiston publication'. — With answers to problems. — Index.
ISBN 0-07-053621-x Pbk : £8.95
(B77-26342)

616.3'9'042 — Man. Genetic metabolic disorders. Early diagnosis. *Great Britain. Conference proceedings*
Medico-social management of inherited metabolic disease : a monograph derived from the proceedings of the Thirteenth Symposium of the Society for the Study of Inborn Errors of Metabolism / edited and enlarged by D.N. Raine. — Lancaster : M.T.P. Press, 1977. — x, 310p : ill, forms, map, plan, port ; 24cm. — (Society for the Study of Inborn Errors of Metabolism. Symposia ; 13)
Index.
ISBN 0-85200-160-6 : £9.95
(B77-13068)

616.3'95 — Man. Osteomalacia
Darke, S J. Vitamin D deficiency and osteomalacia / by S.J. Darke and J.M.L. Stephen. — [London] : [H.M.S.O.], [1976]. — [1],vi,18p : ill ; 21cm. — (Topics of our time ; 1)
ISBN 0-11-320240-7 Sd : £0.75
(B77-11243)

616.3'98 — Man. Obesity
Bray, George A. The obese patient / [by] George A. Bray. — Philadelphia ; London [etc.] : Saunders, 1976. — xiv,450p : ill ; 25cm. — (Major problems in internal medicine ; vol.9)
Bibl. — Index.
ISBN 0-7216-1931-2 : £12.00
(B77-16421)

616.3'98'00941 — Man. Obesity. *Great Britain. Reports, surveys*
DHSS/MRC Group on Obesity Research. Research on obesity : a report of the DHSS/MRC group / [DHSS/MRC Group on Obesity Research] ; compiled by W.P.T. James ; [for the] Department of Health and Social Security [and the] Medical Research Council. — London : H.M.S.O., 1976. — ix, 94p : ill ; 25cm.
Chairman: J.C. Waterlow. — Index.
ISBN 0-11-450034-7 Pbk : £3.90
(B77-11244)

616.3'98'0651 — Man. Obesity. Behaviour therapy
Behavioral treatments of obesity / edited by John Paul Foreyt. — Oxford [etc.] : Pergamon, 1977. — xv,512p : ill ; 24cm. — (Pergamon international library) (Pergamon general psychology series ; vol.61)
Bibl. — Index.
ISBN 0-08-019902-x : £13.00
Pbk : £9.00
(B77-27132)

616.3'99 — Man. Amyloidosis. *Conference proceedings*
International Symposium on Amyloidosis, *Helsinki, 1974.* Amyloidosis : proceedings of the Fifth Sigrid Jusélius Foundation Symposium / edited by Otto Wegelius and Amos Pasternack. — London [etc.] : Academic Press, 1976. — xvi,605p : ill, map ; 24cm.
'... [proceedings of] the International Symposium on Amyloidosis [held] in Helsinki in August 1974' - Preface. — Bibl. — Index.
ISBN 0-12-741350-2 : £18.00
(B77-18808)

616.3'99 — Man. Calcium metabolic disorders. Complications of renal failure
Calcium metabolism in renal failure and nephrolithiasis / edited by David S. David ; with a foreword by Claude D. Arnaud. — New York ; London [etc.] : Wiley, 1977. — xiii, 402p : ill ; 26cm. — (Perspectives in nephrology and hypertension)
'A Wiley medical publication'. — Index.
ISBN 0-471-19673-8 : £25.50
Primary classification 616.6'1
(B77-27895)

616.3'99 — Man. Gout & hyperuricemia
Wyngaarden, James B. Gout and hyperuricemia / [by] James B. Wyngaarden, William N. Kelley. — New York [etc.] ; London : Grune and Stratton, 1976. — xiv, 512p,72p of plates : ill(some col), facsims, ports ; 26cm.
Index.
ISBN 0-8089-0946-0 : £24.10
(B77-09047)

616.3'99 — Man. Sphingolipidoses. *Conference proceedings*
Symposium on the Current Trends in Sphingolipidoses and Allied Disorders, 5th, *Downstate Medical Center, 1975.* Current trends in sphingolipidoses and allied disorders / edited by Bruno W. Volk and Larry Schneck. — New York ; London : Plenum Press, 1976. — xi,612p : ill ; 26cm. — (Advances in experimental medicine and biology ; vol.68)
'Proceedings of the Symposium on the Current Trends in Sphingolipidoses and Allied Disorders held at the Downstate Medical Center, State University of New York, Brooklyn, N.Y., October 20-21, 1975' - title page verso. — Bibl.: - Index.
ISBN 0-306-39068-x : £28.35
(B77-18809)

616.4 — DISEASES OF BLOOD-FORMING, LYMPHATIC, ENDOCRINE SYSTEMS

616.4 — Adolescents. Endocrine system. Diseases
Endocrine and genetic diseases of childhood and adolescence / edited by Lytt I. Gardner. — 2nd ed. — Philadelphia ; London [etc.] : Saunders, 1975 [i.e. 1976]. — xxx,1404p : ill ; 27cm.
This ed. published in the United States: 1975. — Previous ed.: published as 'Endocrine and genetic diseases of childhood'. 1969. — Bibl. — Index.
ISBN 0-7216-3991-7 : £51.25
Primary classification 618.9'24
(B77-06722)

616.4 — Man. Endocrine system. Diseases
Bolinger, Robert E. Endocrinology : new directions in therapy / by Robert E. Bolinger. — London : Kimpton, 1977. — 275p : ill ; 22cm.
Also published: Flushing, N.Y. : Medical Examination Publishing Co., 1977. — Index.
ISBN 0-87488-678-3 Sp : £9.00
(B77-11852)

Thomson, John A. An introduction to clinical endocrinology / [by] John A. Thomson. — Edinburgh [etc.] : Churchill Livingstone, 1976. — vii,197p : ill ; 19cm. — (Livingstone medical texts)
Bibl. — Index.
ISBN 0-443-01499-x Pbk : £2.50
(B77-06711)

616.4 — Man. Endocrine system. Diseases. *Reviews of research*
Recent advances in endocrinology and metabolism. — Edinburgh [etc.] : Churchill Livingstone.
No.1 / edited by J.L.H. O'Riordan. — 1978. — xi,282p : ill ; 25cm.
Bibl. — Index.
ISBN 0-443-01651-8 : £12.00 : CIP rev.
ISSN 0140-9123
(B77-25666)

616.4 — Medicine. Endocrinology. *Conference proceedings*
International Congress of Endocrinology, 5th, *Hamburg, 1976.* Endocrinology : proceedings of the Vth International Congress of Endocrinology, Hamburg, July 18-24, 1976 / editor V.H.T. James. — Amsterdam ; Oxford (256 Banbury Rd, Oxford OX2 2DH) : Excerpta Medica.
In 2 vols.
Vol.1. — 1977. — [15],603p : ill ; 25cm.
Index.
£38.00
ISBN 90-219-0331-8
(B77-25667)

Vol.2. — 1977. — [15],616p : ill ; 25cm.
Index.
£39.00
ISBN 90-219-0349-0
(B77-25668)

616.4'002'4613 — Man. Endocrine system. Diseases. *For nursing*
Krueger, Judith Amerkan. Endocrine problems in nursing : a physiologic approach / [by] Judith Amerkan Krueger, Janis Compton Ray. — Saint Louis : Mosby ; London : Distributed by Kimpton, 1976. — x,165p ; 24cm.
Bibl. — Index.
ISBN 0-8016-2784-2 Pbk : £5.00
(B77-04852)

616.4'2 — Man. Hodgkin's disease. *Personal observations*
Lee, Laurel. Walking through the fire : a hospital journal / [by] Laurel Lee ; illustrated with drawings by the author. — London [etc.] : Macmillan, 1977. — [7],113p : ill ; 23cm.
Originally published: New York : Dutton, 1977.

ISBN 0-333-22562-7 : £3.95
(B77-32658)

616.4'2 — Man. Legs. Lymphatic vessels. Diseases
Johnson, Harold Daintree. The swollen leg : causes and treatment / [by] H. Daintree Johnson, Joseph Pflug ; with foreword by Karl A. Lofgren. — London : Heinemann Medical, 1975. — xvii,284p, plate : ill(incl 2 col) ; 23cm.
Bibl. — Index.
ISBN 0-433-07042-0 : £4.75
Primary classification 616.1'4
(B77-09046)

616.4'2 — Man. Lymphomas. *State-of-the-art reviews*
Hodgkin's disease and the lymphomas. — Montreal ; Lancaster : Eden Press ; [Edinburgh] : Distributed by Churchill Livingstone. — (Annual research reviews ISSN 0703-1629)
[Vol.1] : [1977] / [by] C.R. Taylor. — [1977]. — [8],254p : 4 ill ; 22cm.
Bibl.: p.183-247. — Index.
ISBN 0-904406-48-2 : £12.75
ISSN 0703-1653
ISBN 0-443-01708-5 (Churchill Livingstone)
(B77-33839)

616.4'2 — Man. Lymphomas. Lymphoid cells. Membranes. Use in classification of lymphoma lymphoid cells
Seligmann, Maxime. Lymphocyte membrane markers in human leukaemias and lymphomas / by Maxime Seligmann. — London (43 Great Ormond St., WC1N 3JJ) : Leukaemia Research Fund, 1976. — 27p ; 22cm. — (Leukaemia Research Fund. Annual guest lectures ; 11th ISSN 0459-1666)
'... delivered on 27th August, 1975 at the Queen Elizabeth Hall, London'. — Bibl.: p.23-27.
ISBN 0-9502230-2-6 Sd : £1.00
Primary classification 616.1'55
(B77-02352)

616.4'2 — Man. Reticuloendothelial system. Diseases
Lymphoreticular disease : an introduction for the pathologist and oncologist / by I. Carr ... [et al.] ; illustrated by A. Sylvester ; and edited by I. Carr. — Oxford [etc.] : Blackwell Scientific, 1977. — [14],214p : ill, form ; 24cm.
Bibl. — Index.
ISBN 0-632-00238-7 Pbk : £9.25 : CIP rev.
(B77-07383)

616.4'2'09 — Man. Reticuloendothelial system. Diseases. *Case studies*
Goyette, Richert E. Hematologic and reticuloendothelial pathology and pathophysiology case studies : case histories with related questions and discussion / by Richert E. Goyette in consultation with Harlan J. Spjut. — London : Kimpton, 1976. — 192p : ill ; 22cm.
'I am indebted beyond words to Harlan Spjut for several years of constructive criticism, careful attention to the smallest detail, and many of the illustrations' - Acknowledgments. — Also published: Flushing, N.Y. : Medical Examination Publishing, 1976. — Bibl. — Index.
ISBN 0-87488-076-9 Sp : £6.50
Also classified at 616.1'5'09
(B77-07384)

616.4'62 — Man. Diabetes
Bacchus, Habeeb. Rational management of diabetes / [by] Habeeb Bacchus. — Baltimore ; London [etc.] : University Park Press, 1977. — xiii,221p : ill ; 24cm.
Index.
ISBN 0-8391-1106-1 : £11.95
(B77-21173)

Bonar, Jeanne R. Diabetes : a clinical guide / by Jeanne R. Bonar. — London : Kimpton, 1977. — 354p : ill ; 22cm.
Also published: Flushing, N.Y. : Medical Examination Publishing Co., 1977. — Bibl. — Index.
ISBN 0-87488-710-0 Sp : £7.50
(B77-16911)

Insulin and metabolism / edited by Jasbir S. Bajaj. — Amsterdam ; London [etc.] ([256 Banbury Rd, Oxford OX2 7DH]) : Excerpta Medica, 1977. — xii,296p,plate : ill(incl 1 col) ; 25cm.
Bibl. — Index.
£23.81
ISBN 90-219-2105-7
(B77-27133)

616.4'62 — Man. Diabetes. *Conference proceedings*
International Diabetes Federation. *Congress, 9th, New Delhi, 1976.* Current topics in diabetes research : abstracts [of the] 9th Congress of the International Diabetes Federation, New Delhi, India, October 31-November 5, 1976 / [editor J.S. Bajaj]. — Amsterdam ; Oxford ([256 Banbury Rd, Oxford OX2 7DH]) : Excerpta Medica, 1976. — viii,207p ; 24cm. — (International congress series ; no.400)
Index.
Pbk : £16.25
ISBN 90-219-1227-9 (Excerpta Medica)
(B77-05453)

Totts Gap Colloquium on Diabetes Mellitus, *1974.* Dilemmas in diabetes / edited by Stewart Wolf and Beatrice Bishop Berle. — New York ; London : Plenum Press, [1977]. — xi,166p : ill ; 26cm. — (Advances in experimental medicine and biology ; vol.65)
'Proceedings of the Totts Gap Colloquium on Diabetes Mellitus, held in Totts Gap, Pennsylvania, May 9-11, 1974' - title page verso. — Published in the United States: 1975. — Bibl.: p.147-158. — Index.
ISBN 0-306-39065-5 : £12.29
(B77-09048)

616.5 — DISEASES OF SKIN, HAIR, NAILS

616.5 — Man. Integumentary system. Diseases
Dermatology / edited by R. Marks and P.D. Samman. — London : Heinemann Medical, 1977. — xi,507p : ill ; 23cm. — (Tutorials in postgraduate medicine ; vol.6)
Bibl. — Index.
ISBN 0-433-29035-8 : £11.00
(B77-15880)

616.5 — Man. Skin. Diseases
Solomons, Bethel. Lecture notes on dermatology / [by] Bethel Solomons. — 4th ed. — Oxford [etc.] : Blackwell Scientific, 1977. — vii,271p,[20]p of plates : ill(some col) ; 17cm.
Previous ed.: 1973. — Bibl.: p.262. — Index.
ISBN 0-632-00145-3 Pbk : £4.50 : CIP rev.
(B77-18176)

616.5 — Man. Skin. Disorders. Manifestations of virus diseases
Nasemann, Theodor. Viral diseases of the skin, mucous membranes and genitals : clinical features, differential diagnosis and therapy, with basic principles of virology / by Theodor Nasemann with the collaboration of Gertrud Schaeg and Otto Schultka ; translated [from the German] by Peter J. Frosch. — Philadelphia ; London [etc.] : Saunders [etc.], 1977. — xii, 217p,12p of plates : ill(some col), map ; 25cm.
Translation of: 'Viruskrankheiten der Haut, der Schleimhäute und des Genitales'. Stuttgart : Thieme, 1974. — Bibl.: p.207-208. — Index.
ISBN 0-7216-6655-8 : £24.75
Primary classification 616.9'2
(B77-16426)

616.5 — Medicine. Dermatology. *Reviews of research*
Recent advances in dermatology. — Edinburgh [etc.] : Churchill Livingstone.
No.4 / edited by Arthur Rook. — 1977. — ix, 395p : ill, maps ; 24cm.
Bibl. — Index.
ISBN 0-443-01318-7 : £12.50
(B77-19420)

616.5'002'4613 — Man. Skin. Diseases. *For nursing*
Wilkinson, Darrell Sheldon. The nursing and management of skin diseases : a guide to practical dermatology for doctors and nurses / [by] D.S. Wilkinson. — 4th ed. — London : Faber, 1977. — 403p,[32]p of plates : ill ; 21cm.
Previous ed.: 1969. — Bibl.: p.393-394. — Index.
ISBN 0-571-04875-7 : £8.50
ISBN 0-571-04876-5 Pbk : £5.95
(B77-23460)

616.5'075 — Man. Skin. Differential diagnosis
Korting, Günter Waldemar. Differential diagnosis in dermatology / by G.W. Korting, R. Denk ; translated and adapted [i.e. translated from the German, with footnotes] by Helen O. Curth, William Curth. — Philadelphia ; London [etc.] : Saunders, 1976. — xiii,767p : ill(chiefly col) ; 27cm.
Translation of: 'Dermatologische Differentialdiagnose'. Stuttgart : F.K. Schattauer, 1974. — Bibl. — Index.
ISBN 0-7216-5488-6 : £69.50
(B77-01516)

616.5'08 — Man. Skin. Diseases. Psychophysiological aspects
Whitlock, Francis Antony. Psychophysiological aspects of skin disease / [by] F.A. Whitlock. — London [etc.] : Saunders, 1976. — ix,248p : ill, ports ; 24cm. — (Major problems in dermatology ; vol.8)
Bibl. — Index.
ISBN 0-7216-9301-6 : £8.50
(B77-04224)

616.5'22'065 — Man. Shingles. Naturopathy
Clements, Harry, *b.1893.* Nature cure for shingles and cold sores / [by] Harry Clements. — Wellingborough : Thorsons, 1977. — 64p ; 18cm. — (Self-help series)
ISBN 0-7225-0405-5 Pbk : £0.50
(B77-32659)

616.5'45 — Man. Skin. Pressure sores. *For nursing*
Miller, Marian E. About bedsores : what you need to know to help prevent and treat them / [by] Marian E. Miller, Marvin L. Sachs. — New York [etc.] : Lippincott ; London [etc.] : Distributed by Blackwell Scientific, 1974. — [10],45,[1]p : ill(chiefly col) ; 28cm.
ISBN 0-397-54186-4 : Unpriced
ISBN 0-397-54156-2 Pbk : Unpriced
(B77-27134)

616.6 — DISEASES OF UROGENITAL SYSTEM

Rous, Stephen N. Urology in primary care / [by] Stephen N. Rous ; with an evaluation protocol by Donna Edison and Sarah A. Sprafka ; line drawings by Brian Coleman. — Saint Louis : Mosby ; London : Distributed by Kimpton, 1976. — xv,278p : ill ; 25cm.
Bibl - Index.
ISBN 0-8016-4205-1 Pbk : £9.55
(B77-03572)

616.6 — Andrology
Hellinga, G. Clinical andrology : a systematic approach, with a chapter on intersexuality / by G. Hellinga. — London : Heinemann Medical, 1976. — x,294p : ill ; 25cm.
Bibl. — Index.
ISBN 0-433-14330-4 : £13.75
(B77-11853)

616.6 — Man. Hermaphroditism
Simpson, Joe Leigh. Disorders of sexual differentiation : etiology and clinical delineation / [by] Joe Leigh Simpson, with contributions by ... [others]. — New York [etc.] ; London : Academic Press, 1976. — xiii, 466p : ill ; 24cm.
Bibl.: p.389-441. — Index.
ISBN 0-12-644450-1 : £28.05
(B77-16912)

616.6 — Medicine. Urology
Fundamentals of urology / [edited by] Jack Lapides. — Philadelphia ; London [etc.] : Saunders, 1976. — xvi,593p : ill ; 26cm.
Based on: 'Fundamentals of urology' / by R.M. Nesbit, J. Lapides and W.C. Baum. 4th rev. ed. Ann Arbor : J.W. Edwards, 1953. — Bibl. — Index.
ISBN 0-7216-5629-3 : £14.50
(B77-02356)

616.6'07 — Man. Urogenital system. Pathology
Scientific foundations of urology / edited by David Innes Williams and Geoffrey D. Chisholm. — London : Heinemann Medical.
Vol.2 : Urogenital tract, oncology and the urological armamentarium. — 1976. — xvi, 474p : ill ; 29cm.
Bibl. — Index.
ISBN 0-433-16551-0 : £20.00
(B77-03039)

616.6'09 — Man. Urogenital system. Diseases. *Case studies*
Goyette, Richert E. Renal, genitourinary and breast pathology and pathophysiology case studies : case histories with related questions and discussion / by Richert E. Goyette in consultation with Harlan J. Spjut. — London : Kimpton, 1976. — 204p : ill ; 22cm.
'I am indebted beyond words to Harlan Spjut for several years of constructive criticism, careful attention to the smallest detail, and many of the illustrations' - Acknowledgements. — Also published: Flushing, N.Y. : Medical Examination Publishing, 1976. — Bibl. — Index.
ISBN 0-87488-077-7 Sp : £6.50
Also classified at 618.1'9'09
(B77-07385)

616.6′1 — Man. Blood. Renovascular hypertension. *Conference proceedings*
Medical and surgical aspects of renovascular hypertension : International Symposium, May 30-31, 1976, Günzburg / volume editors J. Rosenthal and H.E. Franz. — Basel ; London [etc.] : Karger ; [Chichester] : [Distributed by Wiley], 1976. — vii,172p : ill ; 23cm. — (Contributions to nephrology ; vol.3)
Bibl. — Index.
Pbk : Unpriced
ISBN 3-8055-2341-6
(B77-03573)

616.6′1 — Man. Kidneys. Diseases
Dunnill, M S. Pathological basis of renal disease / [by] M.S. Dunnill. — London [etc.] : Saunders, 1976. — vii,473p : ill ; 26cm.
Bibl. — Index.
ISBN 0-7216-3230-0 : £15.00
(B77-01517)

Gabriel, Roger. Renal medicine / [by] Roger Gabriel. — London [etc.] : Baillière Tindall, 1977. — viii,280p : ill ; 20cm. — (Concise medical textbooks)
Bibl.: p.269. — Index.
ISBN 0-7020-0645-9 Pbk : £3.50
(B77-24974)

Nephrology : a review of clinical nephrology / edited by Marvin Forland. — London : Kimpton, 1977. — 457p : ill ; 22cm.
Index.
ISBN 0-87488-622-8 Sp : £10.50
(B77-33258)

Seminars in nephrology / edited by E. Lovell Becker. — New York ; London [etc.] : Wiley, 1977. — xii,194p : ill ; 24cm. — (Perspectives in nephrology and hypertension)
'A Wiley medical publication'. — '... a compilation of lectures ... given at the Rogosin Kidney Center of the New York Hospital - Cornell Medical Center ...' - Preface. — Index.
ISBN 0-471-01804-x : £12.00
(B77-18177)

616.6′1 — Man. Kidneys. Renal failure. Complications: Calcium metabolic disorders
Calcium metabolism in renal failure and nephrolithiasis / edited by David S. David ; with a foreword by Claude D. Arnaud. — New York ; London [etc.] : Wiley, 1977. — xiii, 402p : ill ; 26cm. — (Perspectives in nephrology and hypertension)
'A Wiley medical publication'. — Index.
ISBN 0-471-19673-8 : £25.50
Also classified at 616.3′99
(B77-27895)

616.6′1′0024613 — Man. Kidneys. Diseases. *For nursing*
Cameron, John Stewart. Nephrology for nurses : a modern approach to the kidney. — 2nd ed. / [by] J. Stewart Cameron, Alison M.E. Russell, Diana N.T. Sale. — London : Heinemann Medical, 1976. — vi,330p : ill ; 22cm.
Previous ed.: / by J.S. Cameron, Alison M.E. Russell. 1970. — Bibl. — Index.
ISBN 0-433-05111-6 Pbk : £3.60
(B77-04853)

616.6′1′0757 — Man. Kidneys. Radiology
Griffiths, Harry J. Radiology of renal failure / [by] Harry J. Griffiths. — Philadelphia ; London [etc.] : Saunders, 1976. — ii-xi,296p : ill ; 27cm. — (Saunders monographs in clinical radiology ; vol.9)
Index.
ISBN 0-7216-4283-7 : £16.25
(B77-00249)

616.6′3 — Man. Incontinence
Health Education Council. Incontinence : a very common complaint / the Health Education Council. — London : The Council, [1977]. — Folder ([6]p) ; 21cm.
ISBN 0-903652-03-x : Unpriced
(B77-16422)

616.6′3 — Women. Enuresis
Stanton, Stuart L. Female urinary incontinence / [by] Stuart L. Stanton. — London : Lloyd-Luke, 1977. — ix,118p : ill ; 23cm.
Bibl. — Index.
ISBN 0-85324-129-5 : £4.00
(B77-24263)

616.6′5 — Men. Prostate gland. Diseases. *Conference proceedings*
Prostatic disease : proceedings of the American-European Symposium held in Vienna, November 3-5, 1975 sponsored by Physicians Associated for Continuing Education in cooperation with the Johns Hopkins University, the University of Vienna and the University of Innsbruck / edited by H. Marberger ... [et al.]. — New York : Alan R. Liss ; Amsterdam ; Oxford : Elsevier, 1976. — xi,421p : ill ; 24cm. — (Progress in clinical and biological research ; vol.6)
Bibl. — Index.
ISBN 0-444-99826-8 : £21.25
(B77-04854)

616.6′92 — Man. Sexual disorders
Sex and the life cycle / edited by Wilbur W. Oaks, Gerald A. Melchiode, Ilda Ficher. — New York [etc.] ; London : Grune and Stratton, 1976. — x,223p : ill ; 26cm. — (Hahnemann symposium ; 35)
Bibl. — Index.
ISBN 0-8089-0822-7 : £10.65
(B77-04855)

616.6′92 — Men. Infertility. *Conference proceedings*
Winfield W. Scott Symposium, *2nd, University of Rochester, School of Medicine and Dentistry, 1976.* Male infertility : workup, treatment and research / edited by A.T.K. Cockett, Ronald L. Urry. — New York [etc.] ; London : Grune and Stratton ; London : Distributed by Academic Press, 1977. — xv,328p : ill, form ; 24cm.
'Proceedings of the Second Winfield W. Scott Symposium at the University of Rochester School of Medicine and Dentistry sponsored by the Division of Urology Rochester, New York April 22-24, 1976' - half title page verso. — Bibl. — Index.
ISBN 0-8089-0987-8 : £10.30
(B77-21911)

616.6′92′0651 — Man. Sexual disorders. Behaviour therapy
Annon, Jack S. Behavioral treatment of sexual problems : brief therapy / [by] Jack S. Annon. — New York [etc.] ; London : Harper and Row, 1976. — xvii,166p : ill ; 24cm.
Bibl. — Index.
ISBN 0-06-140265-6 Pbk : £8.95
(B77-16423)

Caird, William. Sex therapy : a behavioral approach / [by] William Caird, John P. Wincze. — Hagerstown [etc.] ; London : Harper and Row, Medical Department, 1977. — xiii,197p : ill ; 24cm.
Bibl.: p.175-180. — Index.
ISBN 0-06-140595-7 : £9.70
(B77-33259)

616.6′92′075 — Men. Sexual disorders. Diagnosis. Methodology. *Conference proceedings*
C.S. Mott Symposium on Andrology, *2nd, Detroit, 1976.* Techniques of human andrology / editor E.S.E. Hafez. — Amsterdam [etc.] ; Oxford : North-Holland Publishing Co., 1977. — xviii,536p,[2] leaves of plates : ill(some col), forms ; 25cm. — (Human reproductive medicine ; vol.1)
'... represents the Second C.S. Mott Symposium on Andrology ... held in Detroit, Mich. on 6 and 7 May 1976 ...' - Preface. — Bibl. — Index.
ISBN 0-7204-0614-5 : Unpriced
(B77-27135)

616.7 — DISEASES OF MUSCULOSKELETAL SYSTEM

616.7′1 — Man. Bones. Diseases
Bone and joint diseases : articles published in the 'British medical journal'. — London : British Medical Association, 1977. — [8],131p : ill ; 22cm.
Index.
ISBN 0-7279-0026-9 Pbk : £3.00
Also classified at 616.7′2
(B77-30300)

616.7′1 — Man. Bones. Hyperostosis corticalis generalisata
Buchem, F S P van. Hyperostosis corticalis generalisata familiaris (Van Buchem's disease) / ... by F.S.P. van Buchem ... J.J.G. Prick and H.H.J. Jaspar. — Amsterdam ; Oxford : Excerpta Medica [etc.], 1976. — ix,205p : ill ; 25cm.
Bibl. — Index. — Contents: Part A: Considered from the internal medical viewpoint / F.S.P. van Buchem - Part B: Seen from various aspects of neurological science / by J.J.G. Prick and H.H.J. Jaspar.
£18.03
ISBN 90-219-2070-0
(B77-07932)

616.7′1′0757 — Man. Skeletal system. Diagnosis. Radiography
Murray, Ronald Ormiston. The radiology of skeletal disorders : exercises in diagnosis / [by] Ronald O. Murray, Harold G. Jacobson. — 2nd ed. — Edinburgh [etc.] : Churchill Livingstone, 1977. — 4v. : ill ; 29cm.
With answers. — Previous ed.: in 1 vol. 1971. — Bibl. — Index.
ISBN 0-443-01267-9 : £95.00
(B77-11854)

616.7′2 — Man. Joints. Diseases
Bone and joint diseases : articles published in the 'British medical journal'. — London : British Medical Association, 1977. — [8],131p : ill ; 22cm.
Index.
ISBN 0-7279-0026-9 Pbk : £3.00
Primary classification 616.7′1
(B77-30300)

616.7′2 — Man. Joints. Rheumatoid arthritis. *State-of-the-art reviews*
Rheumatoid arthritis and related conditions. — Montreal ; Lancaster : Eden Press ; [Edinburgh] : Distributed by Churchill Livingstone. — (Annual research reviews ISSN 0703-1629)
[Vol.1] : [1977] / [by] G.S. Panayi. — [1977]. — [7],113p ; 22cm.
Bibl.: p.81-110. — Index.
ISBN 0-88831-003-x : £7.75
ISBN 0-443-01715-8 (Churchill Livingstone)
(B77-33840)

616.7′2 — Man. Knees. Joints. Diagnosis. Arthroscopy
Jackson, Robert W. Arthroscopy of the knee / [by] Robert W. Jackson, David J. Dandy. — New York [etc.] ; London : Grune and Stratton, 1976. — xvii,102p,16p of plates : ill(some col), ports ; 24cm. — (Modern orthopedic monographs)
Bibl.: p.93-97. — Index.
ISBN 0-8089-0947-9 : £10.65
(B77-07386)

616.7′2 — Man. Rheumatic diseases
Wright, Verna. Rheumatism for nurses and remedial therapists / [by] V. Wright and Ian Haslock with the collaboration of B. Champney. — London : Heinemann Medical, 1977. — ix,243p : ill ; 22cm.
Index.
ISBN 0-433-37020-3 Pbk : £4.25
(B77-28662)

616.7′2′005 — Man. Rheumatic diseases. *Periodicals*
Clinics in rheumatic diseases. — London [etc.] : Saunders.
Vol.1, no.1- ; Apr. 1975-. — 1975-. — ill, port ; 24cm.
Three issues a year. — viii,213p. in 1st issue. — Bibl. — Index.
£15.00 yearly
ISSN 0307-742x
(B77-04856)

616.7′2′06 — Man. Joints. Arthritis. Therapy
MacFarlane, Helen Beverley. Arthritis : help in your own hands / by Helen B. MacFarlane. — 2nd ed., revised. — Wellingborough : Thorsons, 1976. — 94p ; 18cm. — (Nature's way)
Previous ed.: 1970.
ISBN 0-7225-0345-8 Pbk : £0.75
(B77-11855)

616.7′2′060941 — Man. Joints. Arthritis & rheumatic diseases. Therapy. *Great Britain. Reports, surveys*
The **challenge** of arthritis and rheumatism : a report on problems and progress in health care for rheumatic disorders and with special reference to rehabilitation services (based on evidence collected for presentation to the Royal Commission on the National Health Service) / edited by Philip H.N. Wood ; for a Working Party of the British League against Rheumatism. — London (c/o The Arthritis and Rheumatism Council, 8 Charing Cross Rd, W.C.2) : The League, 1977. — vi,94p : facsims, forms ; 30cm.
Bibl.: p.71-72.
Sd : £0.50
(B77-21174)

616.7′2′0622 — Man. Joints. Manipulation
Maitland, Geoffrey Douglas. Peripheral manipulation / [by] G.D. Maitland. — 2nd ed. — London [etc.] : Butterworth, 1977. — [15], 363p : ill ; 23cm.
Previous ed.: 1970. — Index.
ISBN 0-407-35671-1 : £13.50 : CIP rev.
(B77-17538)

616.7′2′065 — Man. Joints. Arthritis & rheumatic diseases. Naturopathy
Warmbrand, Max. Overcoming arthritis and other rheumatic diseases / [by] Max Warmbrand. — London : Bachman and Turner, 1977. — xv,220p ; 23cm.
Originally published: Old Greenwich, Conn. : Devin-Adair, 1976.
ISBN 0-85974-057-9 : £3.95
(B77-17537)

616.7′2′07 — Man. Joints. Pathology
Huskisson, Edward Cameron. Joint disease : all the arthropathies / [by] E.C. Huskisson, F. Dudley Hart. — 2nd ed. — Bristol : J. Wright, 1975. — xiii,152p ; 24cm.
Previous ed.: 1973. — Index.
ISBN 0-7236-0408-8 Pbk : £3.75
(B77-01518)

616.7′2′075 — Man. Rheumatic diseases. Diagnosis. *German texts*
Pararheumatische Erkrankungen / herausgegeben von G. Kaganas, W. Müller, F. Wagenhäuser. — Basel ; London [etc.] : Karger ; [Chichester] : [Distributed by Wiley], 1974. — v,216p : ill ; 23cm. — (Fortbildungskurse für Rheumatologie ; 3)
Bibl.
Pbk : Unpriced
(B77-21912)

616.7′2′079 — Man. Rheumatic diseases. Immunological aspects
Maini, R N. Immunology of the rheumatic diseases : aspects of autoimmunity / [by] R.N. Maini, D.N. Glass, J.T. Scott. — London : Edward Arnold, 1977. — xiii,146p : ill ; 23cm. — (Current topics in immunology series ; no.7)
Bibl. — Index.
ISBN 0-7131-4279-0 Pbk : £5.95
(B77-15316)

616.7′3 — Man. Back. Backache
Delvin, David. You and your back / by David Delvin ; ... edited by Helene Grahame ; for the Back Pain Association. — Revised ed. — London [etc.] : Pan Books, 1977. — 93p : ill ; 18cm.
Previous ed.: Teddington? : Back Pain Association, 1975.
ISBN 0-330-25065-5 Pbk : £0.60
(B77-32660)

Health Education Council. Mind your back / the Health Education Council. — London : The Council, [1977]. — [8]p : col ill ; 21cm.
ISBN 0-903652-04-8 Sd : Unpriced
(B77-16424)

616.7′3 — Man. Spine. Diseases
Spinal disorders : diagnosis and treatment / edited by Daniel Ruge and Leon L. Wiltse. — Philadelphia ; Lea and Febiger ; London : Kimpton, 1977. — [13],444p : ill ; 29cm.
Bibl. — Index.
ISBN 0-8121-0452-8 : £29.75
(B77-29464)

616.7′3′065 — Man. Back. Backache. Naturopathy
Clements, Harry, *b.1893.* Banishing backache and disc troubles / [by] Harry Clements. — 2nd ed., revised. — Wellingborough : Thorsons, 1975. — 64p ; 19cm. — (Self help series)
This ed. originally published: 1974.
ISBN 0-7225-0258-3 Pbk : £1.25
(B77-12484)

616.7′3′0754 — Man. Spine. Diagnosis. Use of physical examination of sensorimotor activities
Conesa, Salvador Hernández. A visual aid to the examination of nerve roots / [by] Salvador Hernández Conesa and M.L. Argote. — London : Baillière Tindall, 1976. — vii,24p : ill(some col) ; 19x25cm.
Notebook format.
ISBN 0-7020-0622-x Sp : £2.50
(B77-08410)

616.7′4 — Man. Muscles. Diseases
Bethlem, Jaap. Myopathies / [by] Jaap Bethlem. — Amsterdam [etc.] ; Oxford : North-Holland Publishing Co., 1977. — [11],281p : ill ; 25cm.
Bibl. — Index.
ISBN 0-7204-0641-2 : £22.48
(B77-33841)

616.7′4 — Man. Muscles. Nerves. Diseases
McComas, Alan J. Neuromuscular function and disorders / [by] Alan J. McComas. — London [etc.] : Butterworth, 1977. — x,364p : ill ; 26cm.
Bibl.: p.319-350. — Index.
ISBN 0-407-00058-5 : £17.50
(B77-16425)

616.7′4 — Man. Muscles. Nerves. Electroneuromyography
Cohen, Hyman Lewis. Manual of electroneuromyography / [by] Hyman L. Cohen, Joel Brumlik. — 2nd ed. — Hagerstown [etc.] ; London : Harper and Row, Medical Department, [1977]. — xvii,179p : ill ; 24cm.
This ed. published in the United States: 1976. — Previous ed.: New York : London : Hoeber Medical, 1968. — Bibl. — Index.
ISBN 0-06-140644-9 : £10.45
(B77-12485)

616.7′4 — Young persons. Muscles. Diseases
Siegel, Irwin M. The clinical management of muscle disease : a practical manual of diagnosis and treatment / [by] Irwin M. Siegel. — London : Heinemann Medical, 1977. — xii, 162p : ill ; 22cm.
Bibl. — Index.
ISBN 0-433-30275-5 Pbk : £3.75
(B77-19421)

616.7′4′0754 — Man. Muscles. Electromyography
Lenman, John Andrew Reginald. Clinical electromyography / [by] J.A.R. Lenman, A.E. Ritchie ; with a foreword by J.A. Simpson. — 2nd ed. — Tunbridge Wells [etc.] : Pitman Medical, 1977. — xvi,214p : ill ; 23cm.
Previous ed.: London : Pitman Medical, 1970. — Bibl.: p.185-208. — Index.
ISBN 0-272-79391-4 : £7.50
(B77-07387)

Smorto, Mario P. Electrodiagnosis : a handbook for neurologists / [by] Mario P. Smorto, John V. Basmajian. — Hagerstown [etc.] ; London : Harper and Row, 1977. — ix,163p : ill ; 27cm.
Bibl. — Index.
ISBN 0-06-142410-2 : £12.70
(B77-15881)

616.7′7 — Man. Connective tissues. Diseases
Hughes, Graham Robert Vivian. Connective tissue diseases / [by] Graham R.V. Hughes. — Oxford [etc.] : Blackwell Scientific, 1977. — vi, 266p : ill ; 24cm.
Bibl. — Index.
ISBN 0-632-00821-0 Pbk : £9.00 : CIP rev.
(B77-14260)

616.8 — DISEASES OF NERVOUS SYSTEM
Adams, Raymond Delacy. Principles of neurology / [by] Raymond D. Adams, Maurice Victor. — New York ; London [etc.] : McGraw-Hill, 1977. — xiii,1041p : ill ; 25cm.
'A Blakiston publication'. — Bibl. — Index.
ISBN 0-07-000293-2 : £19.50
(B77-21913)

Ashworth, Bryan. Management of neurological disorders / [by] Bryan Ashworth, Michael Saunders ; foreword by John N. Walton. — Tunbridge Wells : Pitman Medical, 1977. — x, 278p ; 23cm.
Bibl.: p.260-262. — Index.
ISBN 0-272-79421-x : £7.50 : CIP rev.
(B77-24264)

Brain, Walter Russell, *Baron Brain.* Brain's diseases of the nervous system. — 8th ed. / revised by John N. Watton. — Oxford [etc.] : Oxford University Press, 1977. — xv,1277p,2p of plates : ill(some col), port ; 25cm. — (Oxford medical publications)
Previous ed.: / revised by the late Lord Brain and John N. Walton. 1969. — Bibl. — Index.
ISBN 0-19-261309-x : £17.50 : CIP rev.
(B77-08411)

Introduction to basic neurology / [by] Harry D. Patton ... [et al.]. — Philadelphia ; London [etc.] : Saunders, 1976. — xi,440p : ill ; 27cm.
Bibl. — Index.
ISBN 0-7216-7113-6 : £13.25
(B77-03040)

616.8 — Man. Nervous system. Deficiency diseases & metabolic disorders
Metabolic and deficiency diseases of the nervous system. — Amsterdam [etc.] ; Oxford : North-Holland Publishing Co.
Part 2 / edited by P.J. Vinken and G.W. Bruyn in collaboration with Harold L. Klawans. — 1976. — [2],xii,613p : ill, port ; 27cm. — (Handbook of clinical neurology ; vol.28)
Bibl. — Index.
ISBN 0-7204-7228-8 : £50.00
(B77-04857)

Part 3 / edited by P.J. Vinken and G.W. Bruyn in collaboration with Harold L. Klawans. — 1977. — xii,562p : ill ; 27cm. — (Handbook of clinical neurology ; vol.29)
Bibl. — Index.
ISBN 0-7204-7229-6 : Unpriced
(B77-33842)

616.8 — Man. Nervous system. Diseases. *Reviews of research*
Progress in neuropathology. — New York [etc.] ; London : Grune and Stratton.
Vol.3 / edited by H.M. Zimmerman. — [1977]. — xii,495p : ill ; 26cm.
Published in the United States : 1976. — Bibl.: p.288-295. — Index.
ISBN 0-8089-0957-6 : £29.95
(B77-09049)

616.8 — Man. Nervous system. Diseases. Related to mental disorders
Pincus, Jonathan H. Behavioral neurology / [by] Jonathan H. Pincus, Gary J. Tucker. — New York ; London [etc.] : Oxford University Press, 1974 [i.e. 1975]. — xvii,205p : ill ; 21cm.
Originally published: 1974. — Bibl. — Index.
ISBN 0-19-501802-8 Pbk : £3.00
Also classified at 616.8′9
(B77-21175)

616.8′0092′4 — Neurology. Miller, Henry, b.1913. *Biographies*
Remembering Henry / edited by Stephen Lock and Heather Windle. — London : British Medical Association, 1977. — iii-xii,166p,[4]p of plates : ports ; 22cm.
Bibl.: p.161-166.
ISBN 0-7279-0027-7 Pbk : £3.00
(B77-30301)

616.8′02′4613 — Man. Nervous system. Diseases. *For nursing*
Kocen, R S. The neuromuscular system / [by] R.S. Kocen. — Edinburgh [etc.] : Churchill Livingstone, 1976. — 127p : ill ; 20cm. — (Penguin library of nursing)
Bibl.: p.111-122. — Index.
ISBN 0-443-01496-5 Pbk : £1.50
(B77-02357)

Purchese, Gillian. Neuromedical and neurosurgical nursing / [by] Gillian Purchese with the assistance of John Pilling ; foreword by Michael Kremar. — London : Baillière Tindall, 1977. — x,342p : ill ; 20cm. — (Nurses' aids series : special interest texts)
Index.
ISBN 0-7020-0621-1 Pbk : £3.75
(B77-12486)

616.8′04′25 — Man. Nervous system. Diseases & injuries. Emergency treatment
O'Doherty, Desmond S. Handbook of neurologic emergencies / by Desmond S. O'Doherty and Joseph L. Fermaglich. — London : Kimpton, 1977. — 344p : ill ; 22cm.
Index.
ISBN 0-87488-643-0 Sp : £7.50
(B77-27896)

616.8′04′5 — Man. Nervous system. Diseases. Prevention & control. Use of relaxation
Jacobson, Edmund. You must relax / [by] Edmund Jacobson. — 5th ed., revised and enlarged. — London : Souvenir Press, 1977. — xix,270p,[12]p of plates : ill ; 23cm.
This ed. originally published: New York : McGraw-Hill, 1976. — Bibl.: p.254-264. — Index.
ISBN 0-285-62299-4 : £4.50 : CIP rev.
(B77-17539)

616.8′04′7 — Man. Nervous system. Diseases. Physiological aspects
Physiological Aspects of Clinical Neurology *(Conference), Charing Cross Hospital, 1976?.* Physiological aspects of clinical neurology / edited by F. Clifford Rose. — Oxford [etc.] : Blackwell Scientific, 1977. — viii,343p : ill, 2 ports ; 24cm.
'On the occasion of the centenary of his [i.e. Sir Gordon Holmes'] birth, a Symposium based on the theme "The Physiological Aspects of Clinical Neurology" was held at Charing Cross Hospital ...' - Preface. — Bibl. — Index.
ISBN 0-632-00336-7 : £16.00 : CIP rev.
(B77-06712)

616.8′04′75 — Man. Nervous system. Diagnosis
Clinical examinations in neurology / by members of the Department of Neurology and the Department of Physiology and Biophysics, Mayo Clinic and Mayo Foundation for Medical Education and Research, Graduate School, University of Minnesota, Rochester, Minnesota. — 4th ed. — Philadelphia ; London [etc.] : Saunders, 1976. — ii-xvi,385p : ill ; 24cm.
Previous ed.: 1971. — Index.
ISBN 0-7216-6228-5 : £12.50
(B77-01519)

616.8'04'75 — Man. Nervous system. Differential diagnosis
Heilman, Kenneth M. Handbook for differential diagnosis of neurologic signs and symptoms / [by] Kenneth M. Heilman, Robert T. Watson, Melvin Greer. — New York : Appleton-Century-Crofts ; London [etc.] : Prentice-Hall, 1977. — xiii,231p : ill ; 23cm.
ISBN 0-8385-3617-4 Pbk : £7.15
(B77-29465)

616.8'04'757202854 — Man. Brain. Diagnosis. Tomography. Applications of computer systems
Gonzalez, Carlos F. Computed brain and orbital tomography : technique and interpretation / [by] Carlos F. Gonzalez, Charles B. Grossman, Enrique Palacios ; contributor and consultant in anatomy and pathology Justin L. Parr. — New York ; London [etc.] : Wiley, 1976. — xii, 276p : chiefly ill ; 29cm.
'A Wiley Medical Publication'. — Bibl.: p.267-268. — Index.
ISBN 0-471-01692-6 : £21.75
(B77-19422)

616.8'04'757202854044 — Man. Brain. Diagnosis. Tomography. Applications of digital computer systems
Ramsey, Ruth G. Computed tomography of the brain : with clinical, angiographic, and radionuclide correlation / [by] Ruth G. Ramsey. — Philadelphia ; London [etc.] : Saunders, 1977. — ii-xiv,239p : ill ; 26cm. — (Advanced exercises in diagnostic radiology ; 9)
Index.
ISBN 0-7216-7452-6 Pbk : £8.25
(B77-15882)

616.8'04'7582 — Man. Central nervous system. Diagnosis. Use of cerebrospinal fluid cytology
Oehmichen, Manfred. Cerebrospinal fluid cytology : an introduction and atlas / by Manfred Oehmichen ; [translated from the German MS by M.M. Clarkson]. — Philadelphia ; London [etc.] : Saunders [etc.], 1976. — vii,208p : ill(some col) ; 24cm.
Bibl.: p.181-199. — Index.
ISBN 0-7216-6948-4 : £30.75
(B77-17540)

616.8'1 — Man. Brain. Blood vessels. Diseases
McCormick, William Frederick. Atlas of cerebrovascular disease / [by] William F. McCormick, Sydney S. Schochet, Jr. — Philadelphia ; London [etc.] : Saunders, 1976. — vi,422p : ill ; 27cm.
Index.
ISBN 0-7216-5896-2 : £23.25
(B77-14756)

616.8'1 — Man. Brain. Blood vessels. Ischaemia. Sequelae of surgery of carotid arteries
Jennett, Bryan. Effect of carotid artery surgery on cerebral blood flow : clinical and experimental studies / [by] Bryan Jennett, J. Douglas Miller, A. Murray Harper. — Amsterdam ; London [etc.] (256 Banbury Rd, Oxford OX2 7DH) : Excerpta Medica, 1976. — vii,170p : ill ; 25cm.
Bibl. — Index.
£17.56
ISBN 90-219-2106-5 (Excerpta Medica)
Primary classification 617'.413
(B77-16430)

616.8'1 — Man. Brain. Strokes. *Conference proceedings*
WHO Meeting on the Control of Hypertension and Stroke in the Community, *Tokyo, 1974.* Hypertension and stroke control in the community : proceedings of a WHO meeting held in Tokyo, 11-13 March 1974 / edited by S. Hatano, I. Shigematsu, T. Strasser. — Geneva : World Health Organization ; [London] : [H.M.S.O.], 1976. — 362p : ill, forms, map ; 24cm.
' ... WHO Meeting on the Control of Hypertension and Stroke in the Community ... ' - Preface.
ISBN 0-11-950808-7 Pbk : £7.50
Primary classification 616.1'32
(B77-06124)

616.8'1 — Man. Brain. Strokes. Therapy
Johnstone, Margaret. The stroke patient : principles of rehabilitation / [by] Margaret Johnstone ; illustrated by Estrid Barton ; foreword by Bernard Isaacs. — Edinburgh [etc.] : Churchill Livingstone, 1976. — ix,84p : ill(chiefly col) ; 24cm.
Index.
ISBN 0-443-01487-6 Sp : £2.25
(B77-06126)

616.8'3 — Fore. Central nervous system. Kuru. *Papua New Guinea. Okapa region. Readings*
Essays on kuru / R.W. Hornabrook, editor. — Faringdon : Classey, 1976. — 150p : ill, maps ; 25cm. — (Institute of Human Biology. Monograph series ; 3)
Bibl. — Index.
ISBN 0-900848-95-2 : £8.50
(B77-17541)

616.8'3 — Man. Amyotrophic lateral sclerosis. *Conference proceedings*
Research Trends in Amyotrophic Lateral Sclerosis *(Conference), Pacific Palisades, 1975.* Amyotrophic lateral sclerosis : recent research trends : proceedings of a Conference on Research Trends in Amyotrophic Lateral Sclerosis held October 18-20, 1975, in Pacific Palisades, California / edited by John M. Andrews, Richard T. Johnson, Mary A.B. Brazier. — New York [etc.] ; London : Academic Press, 1976. — xiii,298p : ill ; 26cm. — (University of California at Los Angeles. Forums in medical sciences ; no.19)
Bibl. — Index.
ISBN 0-12-059750-0 : £12.05
(B77-18179)

616.8'3 — Man. Paralysis
Roaf, Robert. The paralysed patient / [by] Robert Roaf and Leonard J. Hodkinson. — Oxford [etc.] : Blackwell Scientific, 1977. — [5], 293p : ill, 2 forms ; 24cm.
Index.
ISBN 0-632-09470-2 Pbk : £6.75
(B77-21176)

616.8'34 — Man. Multiple sclerosis
Multiple sclerosis : a critical conspectus / edited by E.J. Field. — Lancaster : M.T.P. Press, 1977. — xi,265p : ill, maps ; 24cm.
Index.
ISBN 0-85200-149-5 : £9.95
(B77-20323)

616.8'34'06 — Man. Multiple sclerosis. Therapy. *Case studies*
Russell, William Ritchie. Multiple sclerosis : control of the disease / [by] W. Ritchie Russell. — Oxford [etc.] : Pergamon, 1976. — vi,77p : form ; 22cm.
Index.
ISBN 0-08-021003-1 Pbk : £3.95
ISBN 0-08-021002-3 Pbk : £2.50
(B77-31234)

616.8'49 — Man. Insomnia. *Readings*
Rubinstein, Hilary, *b.1926.* The complete insomniac : a bedside book / written and edited by Hilary Rubinstein. — London : Coronet, 1976. — 217p ; 21cm.
Originally published: London : Cape, 1974.
ISBN 0-340-20815-5 Pbk : £1.00
(B77-04858)

616.8'5 — Man. Brain. Brain damage. Neuropsychological aspects
Gardner, Howard. The shattered mind : the person after brain damage / [by] Howard Gardner. — London [etc.] : Routledge and Kegan Paul, 1977. — xiv,481,viii p : ill, ports ; 23cm.
Ill., text on lining papers. — Originally published: New York : Knopf, 1975. — Index.
ISBN 0-7100-8641-5 : £9.75 : CIP rev.
(B77-13673)

616.8'5 — Man. Neuroses. Behaviour therapy
Eysenck, Hans Jürgen. You and neurosis / [by] H.J. Eysenck. — London : Temple Smith, 1977. — 224p : ill ; 23cm.
Bibl.: p.211-214. — Index.
ISBN 0-85117-127-3 : £4.00
(B77-18180)

616.8'51 — Man. Nervous system. Huntington's chorea
Stevens, David Lawrence. Huntington's chorea : a booklet for the families and friends of patients with the disease / [by David L. Stevens]. — London (2 Widecombe Court, Lyttelton Rd, N2 0HN) : Association to Combat Huntington's Chorea, 1975. — [3],8p ; 21cm.
ISBN 0-9505364-0-7 Sd : £0.20
(B77-00250)

616.8'522 — Man. Agoraphobia. Therapy
Weekes, Claire. Agoraphobia : simple, effective treatment / [by] Claire Weekes. — London : Angus and Robertson, 1977. — x,178p ; 23cm.
Index.
ISBN 0-207-95723-1 : £3.20
(B77-15317)

616.8'522 — Man. Neuroses: Anxiety. *Reviews of research*
Emotions and anxiety : new concepts, methods and applications / edited by Marvin Zuckerman, Charles D. Spielberger. — Hillsdale : Erlbaum ; New York ; London [etc.] : Distributed by Wiley, 1976. — x,362p : ill ; 24cm.
Bibl. — Index.
ISBN 0-470-15148-x : £18.75
(B77-03041)

616.8'522 — Man. Neuroses: Obsession. Behaviour therapy. *Conference proceedings*
European Association of Behaviour Therapy. *Annual Meeting, 6th, Spetsae, 1976.* The treatment of phobic and obsessive compulsive disorders : selected papers from the Sixth Annual Meeting of the European Association of Behaviour Therapy, Spetsae, Greece, September 1976 / edited by J.C. Boulougouris and A.D. Rabavilas. — Oxford [etc.] : Pergamon, 1977. — xii,147p : ill ; 26cm.
Bibl. — Index.
ISBN 0-08-021472-x : £7.50
Also classified at 616.8'522
(B77-29466)

616.8'522 — Man. Phobias
Melville, Joy. Phobias and obsessions : their understanding and treatment / [by] Joy Melville. — London : Allen and Unwin, 1977. — 3-190p ; 21cm.
Bibl.: p.187-190.
ISBN 0-04-150063-6 : £4.50
ISBN 0-04-150064-4 Pbk : £2.25
(B77-24265)

616.8'522 — Man. Phobias. Behaviour therapy. *Conference proceedings*
European Association of Behaviour Therapy. *Annual Meeting, 6th, Spetsae, 1976.* The treatment of phobic and obsessive compulsive disorders : selected papers from the Sixth Annual Meeting of the European Association of Behaviour Therapy, Spetsae, Greece, September 1976 / edited by J.C. Boulougouris and A.D. Rabavilas. — Oxford [etc.] : Pergamon, 1977. — xii,147p : ill ; 26cm.
Bibl. — Index.
ISBN 0-08-021472-x : £7.50
Primary classification 616.8'522
(B77-29466)

616.8'523 — Man. Amnesia
Amnesia : clinical, psychological and medicolegal aspects / edited by C.W.M. Whitty and O.L. Zangwill. — 2nd ed. — London [etc.] : Butterworth, 1977. — xvi,306p : ill ; 23cm.
Previous ed.: 1966. — Bibl.: p.265-289. — Index.
ISBN 0-407-00056-9 : £9.50 : CIP rev.
(B77-20324)

616.8'523 — Man. Memory disorders. Neurophysiological aspects. *Case studies*
Luriia, Aleksandr Romanovich. The neuropsychology of memory / [by] Alexander R. Luria ; [translated from the Russian by Basil Haigh]. — Washington, D.C. : Winston ; New York [etc.] ; London : Distributed by Wiley, 1976. — xvi,372p : ill ; 24cm.
'A Halsted Press Book'. — Translation of: 'Neĭropsikhologiia pamiati'. Moskva : Pedagogika, 1974-1976. — Bibl.: p.347-363. — Index.
ISBN 0-470-15107-2 : £17.50
(B77-03042)

616.8'53 — Man. Petit-mal epilepsy. Aetiology. Role of wave-spike activity
Myslobodsky, Michael. Petit mal epilepsy : a search for the precursors of wave-spike activity / [by] Michael Myslobodsky. — New York [etc.] ; London : Academic Press, 1976 [i.e. 1977]. — xi,218p : ill ; 24cm.
Published in the United States: 1976. — Bibl.: p.191-208. — Index.
ISBN 0-12-511950-x : £13.50
(B77-12487)

616.8'53 — Man. Seizures
Solomon, Gail E. Clinical management of seizures : a guide for the physician / [by] Gail E. Solomon, Fred Plum. — Philadelphia ; London [etc.] : Saunders, 1976. — vii,152p : ill ; 24cm.
Bibl.: p.131-137. — Index.
ISBN 0-7216-8495-5 Pbk : £5.50
(B77-03043)

616.8'53 — Man. Severe epilepsy. Therapy. *Conference proceedings*
International Symposium on Epilepsy, *6th, William Lennox Centre, 1974.* Total care in severe epilepsy : proceedings of the Sixth International Symposium on Epilepsy, held in Belgium from 15th to 18th September 1974 / edited by M.J. Parsonage. — London (44 Gray's Inn Rd, W.C.1) : International Bureau for Epilepsy, [1977?]. — [3],117p : ill ; 30cm.
Bibl.
Sd : £6.00
(B77-25670)

616.8'53'061 — Man. Epilepsy. Drug therapy. Anticonvulsants. Monitoring. *Conference proceedings*
International Workshop on the Determination of Antiepileptic Drugs in Body Fluids, *3rd, Exeter, 1976.* Antiepileptic drug monitoring / edited by C. Gardner-Thorpe ... [et al.]. — Tunbridge Wells : Pitman Medical, 1977. — [7],388p : ill ; 24cm.
'... proceedings of the Third International Workshop on the Determination of Antiepileptic Drugs in Body Fluids ... held in Exeter, England, in August 1976' - Introduction. — Bibl. — Index.
ISBN 0-272-79396-5 : £16.00
(B77-29467)

616.8'53'061 — Man. Epilepsy. Drug therapy. Sodium valproate. *Conference proceedings*
Clinical and pharmacological aspects of sodium valproate (Epilim) in the treatment of epilepsy : proceedings of a symposium held at Nottingham University, 23-24 September, 1975 / editor N.J. Legg. — Tunbridge Wells (P.O. Box 14, Tunbridge Wells, Kent TN3 0BA) : MCS Consultants for Reckitt-Labaz, 1976. — 175p : ill ; 24cm.
Bibl.
Pbk : Unpriced
(B77-19423)

616.8'55 — Fluency disorders
Dalton, Peggy. Disorders of fluency and their effects on communication / [by] Peggy Dalton, W.J. Hardcastle. — London : Edward Arnold, 1977. — x,161p ; 25cm. — (Studies in language disability and remediation ; 3)
Bibl.: p.145-157. — Index.
ISBN 0-7131-5906-5 : £9.50
ISBN 0-7131-5907-3 Pbk : £4.50
(B77-21914)

616.8'55 — Man. Communication disorders
Byrne, Margaret C. Introduction to communicative disorders / [by] Margaret C. Byrne, Chris C. Shervanian. — New York [etc.] ; London : Harper and Row, 1977. — ix, 291p : ill, form ; 24cm.
Bibl. — Index.
ISBN 0-06-041116-3 : £8.95
(B77-16913)

Hardy, William George, *b.1910.* Essays on communication and communicative disorders / [by] William G. Hardy, Miriam Pauls Hardy. — New York [etc.] ; London : Grune and Stratton, 1977. — xii,161p : ill ; 24cm.
Bibl.: p.147-155. — Index.
ISBN 0-8089-1012-4 : £9.60
(B77-29468)

616.8'55 — Man. Speech disorders
Espir, Michael Lucien Ernest. The basic neurology of speech / [by] Michael L.E. Espir and F. Clifford Rose. — 2nd ed. — Oxford [etc.] : Blackwell Scientific, 1976. — vii,150p : ill ; 22cm.
Previous ed.: 1970. — Bibl.: p.139-143. — Index.
ISBN 0-632-00259-x Pbk : £4.25
(B77-03574)

Perkins, William Hughes. Speech pathology : an applied behavioral science / [by] William H. Perkins. — 2nd ed. — Saint Louis : Mosby ; London : Distributed by Kimpton, 1977. — x, 459p : ill ; 27cm.
Previous ed.: 1971. — Bibl. — Index.
ISBN 0-8016-3785-6 : £12.10
(B77-17542)

616.8'55 — Man. Speech disorders. Effects of diseases of nervous system
Darley, Frederic L. Motor speech disorders / [by] Frederic L. Darley, Arnold E. Aronson, Joe R. Brown. — Philadelphia ; London [etc.] : Saunders, 1975. — viii,304p : ill ; 25cm.
Bibl. — Index.
ISBN 0-7216-2878-8 : £11.00
(B77-31235)

616.8'55'0072 — Man. Communication disorders. Research. Methodology
Silverman, Franklin H. Research design in speech pathology and audiology : asking and answering questions / [by] Franklin H. Silverman. — Englewood Cliffs ; London [etc.] : Prentice-Hall, 1977. — xiv,353p : ill ; 24cm.
Bibl. — Index.
ISBN 0-13-774117-0 : £11.95
(B77-29469)

616.8'55'071173 — Speech pathologists. Professional education. In-service training. Supervision. *United States*
Oratio, Albert R. Supervision in speech pathology : a handbook for supervisors and clinicians / [by] Albert R. Oratio. — Baltimore ; London [etc.] : University Park Press, 1977. — xvii,148p : ill ; 23cm.
Bibl. — Index.
ISBN 0-8391-1113-4 Pbk : £5.75
(B77-24976)

616.8'55'075 — Man. Speech & language disorders. Diagnosis
Nation, James E. Diagnosis of speech and language disorders / [by] James E. Nation, Dorothy M. Aram. — Saint Louis : Mosby ; London : Distributed by Kimpton, 1977. — xii, 453p : ill, forms ; 27cm.
Bibl. — Index.
ISBN 0-8016-3631-0 : £11.80
(B77-18811)

616.8'552 — Language disorders
Studies in neurolinguistics. — New York [etc.] ; London : Academic Press. — (Perspectives in neurolinguistics and psycholinguistics)
Vol.3 / edited by Haiganoosh Whitaker, Harry A. Whitaker. — 1977. — xiv,322p : ill ; 24cm.
Bibl. — Index.
ISBN 0-12-746303-8 : £13.15
Also classified at 612.8
(B77-27897)

616.8'552 — Man. Aphasia. Psycholinguistic aspects
Psycholinguistics and aphasia / [edited by] Harold Goodglass and Sheila Blumstein. — Baltimore ; London : Johns Hopkins University Press, 1973. — vi,346p : ill ; 24cm.
Bibl.: p.331-338. — Index.
ISBN 0-8018-1437-5 : Unpriced
(B77-19424)

616.8'554 — Man. Stuttering
Wingate, Marcel Edward. Stuttering : theory and treatment / [by] Marcel E. Wingate. — New York : Irvington Publishers ; New York ; London [etc.] : Distributed by Wiley, 1976. — xx,364p : ill, facsims ; 25cm. — (The Irvington speech and hearing series)
Bibl. — Index.
ISBN 0-470-15171-4 : £13.20
(B77-11245)

616.8'57 — Man. Migraine
Wilkinson, Marcia. Living with migraine / [by] Marcia Wilkinson. — London : Heinemann Health, 1976. — [5],82p ; 19cm.
ISBN 0-433-36350-9 Pbk : £1.50
(B77-18812)

616.8'58 — Man. Personality disorders. Effects of childhood
Saul, Leon Joseph. The childhood emotional pattern : the key to personality, its disorders and therapy / [by] Leon J. Saul. — New York ; London [etc.] : Van Nostrand Reinhold, 1977. — xxiii,323p : 1 ill ; 24cm.
Bibl. — Index.
ISBN 0-442-27360-6 : £12.90
(B77-22631)

616.8'583 — Man. Sexual deviance
Stoller, Robert Jesse. Perversion : the erotic form of hatred / [by] Robert J. Stoller. — London [etc.] : Quartet Books, 1977. — iii-xviii, 240p : 1 ill ; 20cm.
Originally published: New York : Pantheon Books ; Hassocks : Harvester Press, 1976. — Bibl.: p.221-231. — Index.
ISBN 0-7043-3166-7 Pbk : £2.50
(B77-29470)

616.8'583 — Men. Psychosexual disorders
Bowskill, Derek. Men, the sensitive sex / [by] Derek Bowskill, Anthea Linacre. — London : Muller, 1977. — vii,150p ; 23cm.
ISBN 0-584-10252-6 : £3.95 : CIP rev.
(B77-10386)

616.8'583'06 — Man. Psychosexual disorders. Therapy
Psychosexual problems : psychotherapy, counselling and behavioural modification / edited by Sidney Crown. — London : Academic Press [etc.], 1976. — xiii,471p ; 24cm.
Bibl. — Index.
ISBN 0-12-199350-7 : £5.80
(B77-01520)

616.8'5844 — Suicide. Medical aspects
Suicide : assessment and intervention / [edited by] Corrine Loing Hatton, Sharon McBride Valente, Alice Rink ; foreword by Edwin S. Schneidman. — New York : Appleton-Century-Crofts ; London [etc.] : Prentice-Hall, 1977. — xix,220p : ill, forms ; 23cm.
Bibl. — Index.
ISBN 0-8385-8697-x Pbk : £7.80
(B77-23461)

616.8'588 — Man. Mental retardation. *Conference proceedings*
International Association for the Scientific Study of Mental Deficiency. *Congress, 4th, Washington, 1976.* Research to practice in mental retardation : [proceedings of the] Fourth Congress of the International Association for the Scientific Study of Mental Deficiency, [Washington, D.C., 22-27 August 1976, the American University]. — Baltimore ; London [etc.] : University Park Press.
In 3 vols.
Vol.1 : Code and intervention / edited by Peter Mittler ; technical editor Jean M. de Jong. — 1977. — xxv,A1-A30,472p : ill, forms ; 24cm.
Bibl. — Index.
ISBN 0-8391-1122-3 : £17.50
(B77-32661)

616.8'588 — Man. Mental retardation. *Reviews of research*
International review of research in mental retardation. — New York [etc.] ; London : Academic Press.
Vol.8 / edited by Norman R. Ellis ; [consulting editors for this volume Alfred A. Baumeister et al.]. — 1976 [i.e. 1977]. — xvii,259p : ill ; 24cm.
Published in the United States: 1976. — Bibl. — Index.
ISBN 0-12-366208-7 : £13.85
(B77-13674)

616.8'58842 — Man. Down's syndrome. *Reviews of research*
Smith, George Franklin. Down's anomaly. — 2nd ed. / [by] G.F. Smith, J.M. Berg. — Edinburgh [etc.] : Churchill Livingstone, 1976. — ix,348p : ill, port ; 23cm.
Previous ed.: / by Lionel Sharples Penrose and George Franklin Smith. 1966. — Bibl.: p.279-334. — Index.
ISBN 0-443-01398-5 : £12.50
(B77-10387)

616.8'61 — Alcoholism. Medical aspects
Hore, Brian David. Alcohol dependence / [by] Brian D. Hore. — London [etc.] : Butterworth, 1976. — xiii,153p : ill ; 23cm. — (Postgraduate psychiatry series)
Bibl. — Index.
ISBN 0-407-00082-8 : £4.95
(B77-01521)

616.8'61 — Alcoholism. Medical aspects. *Conference proceedings*
International Magnus Huss Symposium, *1st, Stockholm, 1976.* Recent advances in the study of alcoholism : proceedings of the First International Magnus Huss Symposium, Stockholm, 2-3 September 1976, organized by the Department of Clinical Alcohol and Drug Research, Karolinska institutet / editor Carl-Magnus Ideström. — Amsterdam ; Oxford ([256 Banbury Rd, Oxford OX2 7DH]) : Excerpta Medica, 1977. — vii,135p : ill ; 24cm. — (International congress series ; no.407)
Bibl. — Index.
ISBN 0-444-15247-4 Pbk : £11.90
ISBN 90-219-0332-6
(B77-21915)

616.8'61 — Alcoholism. Medical aspects. *State-of-the-art reviews*
Alcohol and alcoholism. — Montreal ; Lancaster : Eden Press ; [Edinburgh] : Distributed by Churchill Livingstone. — (Annual research reviews ISSN 0703-1629)
[Vol.1] : [1977] / [by] Keith J.B. Rix. — [1977] . — [10],251p ; 22cm.
Bibl.: p.175-240. — Index.
ISBN 0-88831-004-8 : £12.75
ISBN 0-443-01704-2 (Churchill Livingstone)
(B77-33844)

616.8'61 — Women. Alcoholism. Medical aspects
Alcoholism problems in women and children / edited by Milton Greenblatt, Marc A. Schuckit. — New York [etc.] ; London : Grune and Stratton, [1977]. — xi,287p : ill ; 24cm. — (Seminars in psychiatry)
Published in the United States: 1976. — Bibl. — Index.
ISBN 0-8089-0972-x : £13.85
Also classified at 618.9'28'61
(B77-13069)

616.8'61'005 — Alcoholism. Medical aspects. *Periodicals*
British journal on alcohol and alcoholism. — London (36 Eccleston Sq., SW1V 1PF) : B. Edsall.
Continues: Journal of alcoholism.
Vol.12, [no.]1- ; [Spring] 1977-. — 1977-. — ill ; 22cm.
Quarterly. — At head of title: Medical Council on Alcoholism. — [2],45p. in 1st issue. — Bibl.
Sd : £4.50 yearly
ISSN 0309-1635
(B77-23462)

616.8'61'05 — Alcoholic drinks. Consumption. Self-limitation. *Manuals*
MacLochlainn, P. How to stop drinking / [by] P. MacLochlainn. — [London] ([82 Eaton Sq., S.W.1]) : [The author], 1977. — [8]p ; 22cm.
Sd : Unpriced
(B77-33260)

Miller, William R. How to control your drinking / [by] William R. Miller, Ricardo F. Muñoz. — Englewood Cliffs ; London [etc.] : Prentice-Hall, 1976. — x,246p : forms ; 21cm. — (The self-management psychology series)
Bibl. — Index.
ISBN 0-13-404392-8 : £7.15
ISBN 0-13-404384-7 Pbk : £3.15
(B77-18181)

616.8'63 — Drug abuse. Medical aspects
Cohen, Sidney. The drug dilemma / [by] Sidney Cohen. — 2nd ed. — New York ; London [etc.] : McGraw-Hill, 1976. — xiv,103p ; 21cm. — (McGraw-Hill series in health education)
Previous ed.: New York : McGraw-Hill, 1969. — Bibl.: p.93-97.
ISBN 0-07-011587-7 : £6.25
ISBN 0-07-011588-5 Pbk : £3.75
(B77-04859)

Drug dependence : current problems and issues / edited by M.M. Glatt. — Lancaster : M.T.P. Press, 1977. — viii,332p : ill ; 23cm.
Bibl. — Index.
ISBN 0-85200-112-6 : £11.50
(B77-21177)

616.8'63'025 — Man. Acute diseases caused by drug abuse. Emergency treatment. *Manuals*
Acute drug abuse emergencies : a treatment manual / edited by Peter G. Bourne. — New York [etc.] ; London : Academic Press, 1976 [i.e. 1977]. — xx,361p : ill ; 22cm.
Published in the United States: 1976. — Bibl. — Index.
ISBN 0-12-119560-0 : £11.70
(B77-13675)

Acute drug abuse emergencies : a treatment manual / edited by Peter G. Bourne. — New York [etc.] ; London : Academic Press, 1976. — xx,361p : ill ; 22cm.
Bibl. — Index.
ISBN 0-12-119565-1 Pbk : £5.70
(B77-15883)

616.8'7 — Man. Peripheral nervous system. Diseases
Weller, Roy O. Pathology of peripheral nerves / [by] Roy O. Weller, Jorge Cervós-Navarro. — London [etc.] : Butterworth, 1977. — vii,225p : ill ; 24cm.
Bibl. — Index.
ISBN 0-407-00073-9 : £13.50
(B77-13676)

616.8'8 — Man. Autonomic nervous system. Diseases
Appenzeller, Otto. The autonomic nervous system : an introduction to basic and clinical concepts / [by] Otto Appenzeller. — 2nd revised and enlarged ed. — Amsterdam ; Oxford : North-Holland Publishing Co. [etc.], 1976. — xviii,403p : ill ; 25cm.
Previous ed.: 1970. — Bibl.: p.309-355. — Index.
ISBN 0-7204-0670-6 : £30.19
(B77-03575)

616.8'9 — Man. Mental disorders
Abnormality : experimental and clinical approaches / [by] Steven Reiss ... [et al.]. — New York : Macmillan ; London : Collier Macmillan, 1977. — xvi,662p : ill, ports ; 24cm.
Bibl.: p.599-638. — Index.
ISBN 0-02-399300-6 : £10.50
(B77-21916)

Kisker, George W. The disorganized personality / [by] George W. Kisker. — 3rd ed. — New York ; London [etc.] : McGraw-Hill, 1977. — xvi,476p : ill, facsim, form, ports ; 25cm.
Previous ed.: New York : McGraw-Hill, 1972. — Bibl.: p.440-458. — Index.
ISBN 0-07-034878-2 : £11.20
(B77-21178)

Snyder, Solomon Halbert. The troubled mind : a guide to release from distress / [by] Solomon H. Snyder. — New York ; London [etc.] : McGraw-Hill, 1976. — [7],243p ; 22cm.
Bibl.: p.230-236. — Index.
ISBN 0-07-059523-2 : £7.45
(B77-04225)

616.8'9 — Man. Mental disorders. Effects of ego development
Ausubel, David Paul. Ego psychology and mental disorder : a developmental approach to psychopathology / [by] David P. Ausubel, Daniel Kirk. — New York [etc.] ; London : Grune and Stratton, 1977. — xiii,348p ; 24cm.
Bibl.: p.299-330. — Index.
ISBN 0-8089-1004-3 : £13.85
(B77-23463)

616.8'9 — Man. Mental disorders. Related to diseases of the nervous system
Pincus, Jonathan H. Behavioral neurology / [by] Jonathan H. Pincus, Gary J. Tucker. — New York ; London [etc.] : Oxford University Press, 1974 [i.e. 1975]. — xvii,205p : ill ; 21cm.
Originally published: 1974. — Bibl. — Index.
ISBN 0-19-501802-8 Pbk : £3.00
Primary classification 616.8
(B77-21175)

616.8'9 — Man. Nervous breakdowns
Mitchell, Alexander Ross Kerr. What is a nervous breakdown? / by A.R.K. Mitchell. — London : British Medical Association, [1977]. — 31p : ill ; 19cm. — (A 'Family doctor' booklet)
Bibl.: p.31.
Sd : £0.30
(B77-30302)

616.8'9 — Man. Psychoses. Role of ego
Federn, Paul. Ego psychology and the psychoses / [by] Paul Federn ; edited and with an introduction by Edoardo Weiss. — London (c/o H. Karnac (Books) Ltd, 58 Gloucester Rd, S.W.7) : Maresfield Reprints, 1977. — [7], 375p ; 22cm.
Originally published: London : Imago Publishing Co., 1953. — Bibl.: p.365-369. — Index.
ISBN 0-9501647-3-9 : £6.50
(B77-18813)

616.8'9 — Medicine. Psychiatry
Eaton, Merrill Thomas. Psychiatry. — 3rd ed. / by Merrill T. Eaton, Margaret H. Peterson, James A. Davis. — [Flushing, N.Y.] : Medical Examination Publishing Co. ; London : Kimpton [etc.], 1976. — 510p ; 22cm. — (Medical outline series)
With answers. — Previous ed.: Flushing, N.Y. : Medical Examination Publishing Co., 1969. — Bibl. — Index.
ISBN 0-87488-621-x : £6.75
(B77-11246)

Encyclopaedic handbook of medical psychology / edited by Stephen Krauss ; honorary editorial consultants ... [others]. — London [etc.] : Butterworth, 1976. — xvii,585p : ill ; 29cm.
Bibl. — Index.
ISBN 0-407-00044-5 : £13.50
(B77-01522)

Laing, Ronald David. The facts of life / [by] R.D. Laing. — Harmondsworth [etc.] : Penguin, 1977. — 143p : ill ; 18cm.
Originally published: New York : Pantheon Books ; London : Allen Lane, 1976.
ISBN 0-14-004423-x Pbk : £0.65
(B77-30304)

Menninger, Karl, *b.1893*. The vital balance : the life process in mental health and illness / [by] Karl Menninger, with Martin Mayman and Paul Pruyser. — Harmondsworth [etc.] : Penguin, 1977. — [9],531p ; 20cm.
Originally published: New York : Viking Press, 1963. — Index.
ISBN 0-14-004530-9 Pbk : £2.75
(B77-27138)

New dimensions in psychiatry : a world view / [edited by] Silvano Arieti and Gerard Chrzanowski. — New York ; London [etc.] : Wiley.
Vol.2. — 1977. — xiii,509p ; 24cm.
'A Wiley-Interscience Publication'. — Bibl. — Index.
ISBN 0-471-03318-9 : £20.20
(B77-21179)

Rees, William Linford Llewelyn. A short textbook of psychiatry / [by] W.L. Linford Rees. — 2nd ed. — London [etc.] : Hodder and Stoughton, 1976. — viii,332p : ill ; 22cm. — (University medical texts)
Previous ed.: 1967. — Bibl. — Index.
ISBN 0-340-20044-8 : £4.95
ISBN 0-340-20051-0 Pbk : £2.65
(B77-00251)

Renewal in psychiatry : a critical rational perspective / with a foreword by Leon Eisenberg ; edited by Theo C. Manschreck, Arthur K. Kleinman. — Washington ; London : Hemisphere Publishing Corporation ; New York ; London [etc.] : Wiley, 1977. — xxi,346p ; 24cm. — (The series in clinical and community psychology)
'A Halsted Press book'. — Bibl. — Index.
ISBN 0-470-99108-9 : £17.65
(B77-27139)

Sainsbury, Maurice J. Key to psychiatry : a textbook for students / [by] Maurice J. Sainsbury. — 2nd ed. — Aylesbury : HM + M, 1976. — xiii,415p : ill ; 24cm.
This ed. also published: Brookvale : Australia and New Zealand Book Co., 1976. — Previous ed.: 1974. — Bibl.: p.399-402. — Index.
ISBN 0-85602-058-3 Pbk : £5.95
(B77-05454)

Smythies, John Raymond. Psychiatry for students of medicine / [by] John R. Smythies and Lionel Corbett. — London : Heinemann Medical, 1976. — [7],321p : ill, form ; 21cm.
With answers. — Index.
ISBN 0-433-30761-7 Pbk : £3.50
(B77-08412)

Szasz, Thomas Stephen. The myth of mental illness : foundations of a theory of personal conduct / by Thomas S. Szasz. — Revised ed. — New York [etc.] ; London : Harper and Row, [1976]. — xviii,297,[1]p ; 18cm. — (Perennial library)
This ed., i.e. 2nd revised ed. originally published: 1974. — Bibl.: p.281-289. — Index.
ISBN 0-06-080330-4 Pbk : £1.45
(B77-01523)

616.8'9 — Medicine. Psychiatry. *Reviews of research*
Developments in psychiatric research : essays based on the Sir Geoffrey Vickers lectures of the Mental Health Foundation (formerly Mental Health Research Fund) / edited by J.M. Tanner ; for the Mental Health Foundation. — London [etc.] : Hodder and Stoughton, 1977. — x,294p : ill ; 24cm.
Index.
ISBN 0-340-20977-1 : £7.95
(B77-27898)

The **world** biennial of psychiatry and psychotherapy / edited by Silvano Arieti. — New York ; London : Basic Books.
Vol.1. — 1971. — xiii,622p : ill ; 25cm.
Bibl. — Index.
ISBN 0-465-09221-7 : £16.50
(B77-18182)

616.8'9 — Medicine. Psychiatry. Applications of biochemistry
Foundations of biochemical psychiatry / [edited by] David S. Segal, Joel Yager, John L. Sullivan. — Boston [Mass.] ; London : Butterworth, 1976. — xii,346p : ill ; 26cm.
Bibl. — Index.
ISBN 0-409-95001-7 : £12.50
(B77-15884)

616.8'9'0024613 — Man. Mental disorders. *For nursing*
Koshy, K T. Revision notes on psychiatry / [by] K.T. Koshy ; foreword by M.S. Perinpanayagam. — London [etc.] : Hodder and Stoughton, 1977. — xi,148p ; 22cm. — (Modern nursing series)
Bibl.: p.148.
ISBN 0-340-19067-1 Pbk : £1.45
(B77-21917)

Snell, H. Mental disorder : an introductory textbook for nurses / [by] H. Snell. — London : Allen and Unwin, 1977. — 3-200p : ill ; 22cm.
Index.
ISBN 0-04-610005-9 Pbk : £2.95
(B77-11247)

616.8'9'003 — Man. Mental disorders. *United States. Encyclopaedias*
Fann, William E. The language of mental health / [by] William E. Fann, Charles E. Goshen. — 2nd ed. — Saint Louis : Mosby ; London : Distributed by Kimpton, 1977. — x, 165p ; 26cm.
Previous ed.: 1973. — Index.
ISBN 0-8016-1548-8 Pbk : £7.00
(B77-31236)

616.8'9'003 — Psychiatry. *Encyclopaedias*
A **concise** encyclopaedia of psychiatry / edited by Denis Leigh, C.M.B. Pare, John Marks. — Lancaster : M.T.P. Press, 1977. — [7],400p : ill, ports ; 24cm.
'... based upon a series of publications originally sponsored and issued under the Roche Continuing Medical Education Campaign' - title page verso.
ISBN 0-85200-144-4 : £6.95
(B77-24977)

616.8'9'009 — Man. Mental disorders. Theories, to 1976
Altschule, Mark David. Origins of concepts in human behavior : social and cultural factors / [by] Mark D. Altschule. — Washington, D.C. ; London : Hemisphere ; New York ; London [etc.] : Wiley, 1977. — iv,204p : ill, facsims, plan, ports ; 24cm.
'A Halsted Press book'. — Index.
ISBN 0-470-99001-5 : £13.50
(B77-22632)

616.8'9'00924 — Psychiatry. Laing, Ronald David. *Critical studies*
Howarth-Williams, Martin. R.D. Laing : his work and its relevance for sociology / [by] Martin Howarth-Williams. — London [etc.] : Routledge and Kegan Paul, 1977. — viii,219p : 1 ill ; 24cm.
'Routledge direct editions'. — Bibl.: p.206-216. — Index.
ISBN 0-7100-8624-5 Pbk : £4.50 : CIP rev.
(B77-21180)

616.8'9'025 — Man. Mental disorders. Emergency treatment. *Manuals*
Psychiatric emergencies / edited by Robert A. Glick ... [et al.]. — New York [etc.] ; London : Grune and Stratton, 1976. — ix,300p : ill ; 24cm.
Bibl. — Index.
ISBN 0-8089-0948-7 : £9.75
(B77-06127)

616.8'9'027 — Medicine. Psychiatry. Applications of psychobiology. *Conference proceedings*
Relevance of the Animal Psychopathological Model to the Human *(Conference), New York, 1974.* Animal models in human psychobiology / edited by George Serban and Arthur Kling ; with a foreword by José M.R. Delgado. — New York ; London : Plenum Press, [1977]. — xiv, 297p : ill ; 24cm.
'In March 1974, an International Symposium was held at the Harmonie Club in New York to discuss ... the "Relevance of the Animal Psychopathological Model to the Human". This meeting was sponsored [i.e. organised] by the Kittay Foundation' - Foreword. — Published in the United States: 1976. — Bibl. — Index.
ISBN 0-306-30864-9 : £14.18
(B77-11248)

616.8'9'075 — Man. Mental disorders. Diagnosis. *State-of-the-art reviews*
Frank, George. Psychiatric diagnosis : a review of research / [by] George Frank. — Oxford [etc.] : Pergamon, 1975. — viii,140p ; 22cm. — (International series of monographs in experimental psychology ; vol.19)
Bibl.: p.83-125. — Index.
ISBN 0-08-017712-3 : £12.50
(B77-02358)

616.8'9'075 — Medicine. Psychiatry. Interviewing. *Manuals*
Pustan, R. Taking the psychiatric case history : a collection of sample questions to put to the patient / [by R. Pustan]. — London ([82 Hawksley Rd, N.16]) : [The author], 1976. — [4],10[i.e.12]p : ill ; 16cm.
Bibl.: p.[12].
ISBN 0-9505472-0-4 Sd : Unpriced
(B77-04860)

616.8'91 — Man. Mental disorders. Therapy
Berke, Joseph. Butterfly man : madness, degradation and redemption / [by] Joseph H. Berke. — London [etc.] : Hutchinson, 1977. — 168p ; 22cm.
Index.
ISBN 0-09-129440-1 : £4.95
(B77-33262)

616.8'91 — Man. Mental disorders. Therapy. *Reviews of research*
Current psychiatric therapies. — New York [etc.] ; London : Grune and Stratton.
Vol.16 : 1976 / edited by Jules H. Masserman. — [1977]. — xiii,351p : ill ; 24cm.
Published in the United States: 1976. — Bibl. — Index.
ISBN 0-8089-0978-9 : £20.25
(B77-13070)

616.8'91 — Man. Mental disorders. Therapy. Diet
Cheraskin, Emanuel. Psychodietetics : food as the key to emotional health / by E. Cheraskin and W.M. Ringsdorf, Jr, with Arline Brecher. — Toronto [etc.] ; London : Bantam, 1976. — xi, 239,[1]p ; 18cm.
Originally published: New York : Stein and Day, 1974. — Bibl. — Index.
ISBN 0-553-02125-7 Pbk : £0.75
(B77-06713)

616.8'91 — Man. Mental disorders. Therapy. Use of Problem Oriented Psychiatric Index
Meldman, Monte Jay. The problem-oriented psychiatric index and treatment plans / [by] Monte J. Meldman, Gertrude McFarland, Edith Johnson. — Saint Louis : Mosby ; London : Distributed by Kimpton, 1976. — ix,202p : forms ; 26cm.
Index.
ISBN 0-8016-3393-1 Pbk : £6.10
(B77-03576)

616.8'912 — Man. Mental disorders. Electroconvulsive therapy. Neurophysiological aspects. *Conference proceedings*
Psychobiology of Convulsive Therapy *(Conference), Dorado Beach Hotel, Puerto Rico, 1972.* Psychobiology of convulsive therapy / edited by Max Fink ... [et al.]. — Washington, D.C. : V.E. Winston ; New York ; London [etc.] : Distributed by Wiley, 1974. — xii,312p : ill ; 24cm.
'This volume presents the reports at the Conference, "Psychobiology of Convulsive Therapy", held at Dorado Beach, Puerto Rico, April 22-24, 1972' - Introduction. — Bibl. — Index.
ISBN 0-470-25901-9 : £9.55
(B77-11249)

616.8'914 — Man. Mental disorders. Psychotherapy: Emotional flooding
Emotional flooding / edited by Paul Olsen with [others]. — Harmondsworth [etc.] : Penguin, 1977. — [1],270p : ill ; 19cm.
'A publication of the National Institute for the Psychotherapies'. — "This book developed from the second annual professional conference and workshop of the National Institute for the Psychotherapies' - Preface. — Originally published: New York : Human Sciences Press, 1976. — Bibl.: p.251-257. — Index.
ISBN 0-14-004350-0 Pbk : Unpriced
(B77-14261)

616.8'914 — Medicine. Gestalt psychotherapy
San Francisco Gestalt Institute. Gestalt awareness : papers from the San Francisco Gestalt Institute / edited and with an introduction by Jack Downing. — New York [etc.] ; London : Harper and Row, 1976. — xiv, 161p : ill ; 18cm. — (Perennial library)
ISBN 0-06-080373-8 Pbk : £1.45
(B77-08413)

616.8'914 — Medicine. Psychotherapy
Brammer, Lawrence Martin. Therapeutic psychology : fundamentals of counseling and psychotherapy / [by] Lawrence M. Brammer, Everett L. Shostrom. — 3rd ed. — Englewood Cliffs ; London [etc.] : Prentice-Hall, 1977. — xi,476p : ill ; 24cm. — (Prentice-Hall psychology series)
Previous ed.: 1968. — Bibl.: p.442-466. — Index.
ISBN 0-13-914622-9 : £11.15
(B77-17543)

Carkhuff, Robert Rolf. Beyond counseling and therapy / [by] Robert R. Carkhuff, Bernard G. Berenson. — 2nd ed. — New York ; London [etc.] : Holt, Rinehart and Winston, 1977. — xviii,295p : ill ; 24cm.
Previous ed.: 1967. — Bibl. — Index.
ISBN 0-03-089812-9 : £10.00
(B77-22633)

Kovel, Joel. A complete guide to therapy : from psychoanalysis to behavior modification / [by] Joel Kovel. — Hassocks : Harvester Press, 1977. — xviii,284p ; 24cm.
Originally published: New York : Pantheon Books, 1976. — Index.
ISBN 0-85527-929-x : £5.95 : CIP rev.
(B77-05455)

Modern therapies / edited by Virginia Binder, Arnold Binder, Bernard Rimland. — Englewood Cliffs ; London [etc.] : Prentice-Hall, 1976. — ix,230p : ill ; 21cm.
'A spectrum book'. — Bibl. — Index. — Includes chapters on the therapeutic use of psychedelics and megavitamins.
ISBN 0-13-599001-7 : £6.95
ISBN 0-13-598995-7 Pbk : £3.05
(B77-07388)

616.8'914 — Medicine. Psychotherapy: Bioenergetics
Lowen, Alexander. Bioenergetics / [by] Alexander Lowen. — Harmondsworth [etc.] : Penguin, 1976. — 352p : ill ; 20cm.
Originally published: New York : Coward, McCann and Geoghegan, 1975. — Index.
ISBN 0-14-004322-5 Pbk : Unpriced
(B77-01524)

Lowen, Alexander. Bioenergetics / [by] Alexander Lowen. — London : Coventure, 1976[i.e.1977]. — 352p : ill ; 23cm.
Originally published: New York : Coward, McCann and Geoghegan, 1975. — Index.
ISBN 0-904576-28-0 : £4.95
(B77-03044)

616.8'914 — Medicine. Psychotherapy: Reality therapy
Glasser, William. Reality therapy : a new approach to psychiatry / [by] William Glasser ; with a foreword by O.H. Mowrer. — New York [etc.] ; London : Harper and Row, 1975. — xxix,207p ; 18cm. — (Perennial library)
Originally published: 1965.
ISBN 0-06-080348-7 Pbk : Unpriced
(B77-33845)

616.8'914 — Medicine. Psychotherapy. Reality therapy. *Readings*
The **reality** therapy reader : a survey of the work of William Glasser, M.D. / editors Alexander Bassin, Thomas Edward Bratter, Richard L. Rachin. — New York [etc.] ; London : Harper and Row, 1976. — xii,691p ; 22cm.
Includes essays by William Glasser. — Bibl. — Index.
ISBN 0-06-010238-1 : £11.25
(B77-03045)

616.8'914 — Medicine. Psychotherapy: Relationship Enhancement therapy
Guerney, Bernard Guilbert. Relationship enhancement / [by] Bernard G. Guerney, Jr, with chapters contributed by Jerry D. Collins ... [et al.]. — San Francisco [etc.] ; London : Jossey-Bass, 1977. — xxiii,400p ; 24cm. — (The Jossey-Bass behavioral science series)
Bibl.: p.381-391. — Index.
ISBN 0-87589-310-4 : Unpriced
(B77-23464)

616.8'914 — Medicine. Psychotherapy. Transactional analysis. *United States. Personal observations*
Abell, Richard G. Own your own life / [by] Richard G. Abell with Corlis Wilber Abell. — Toronto [etc.] ; London : Bantam, 1977. — xxiii,260,[1]p : ill ; 18cm.
'A Quicksilver book'. — Originally published: New York : D. McKay, 1976. — Index.
ISBN 0-552-60219-1 Pbk : £0.85
(B77-24266)

616.8'914 — Medicine. Psychotherapy. Use of conversation
Labov, William. Therapeutic discourse : psychotherapy as conversation / [by] William Labov, David Fanshel. — New York [etc.] ; London : Academic Press, 1977. — x,392p : ill ; 24cm.
Text on lining papers. — Bibl.: p.373-377. — Index.
ISBN 0-12-432050-3 : £10.65
(B77-30305)

616.8'914'071173 — Psychotherapists. Professional education. Group methods. ***United States***
Rioch, Margaret J. Dialogues for therapists / [by] Margaret J. Rioch, Winifred R. Coulter, David M. Weinberger. — San Francisco [etc.] ; London : Jossey-Bass, 1976. — xv,239p ; 24cm. — (The Jossey-Bass behavioral science series)
Index.
ISBN 0-87589-283-3 : £10.60
(B77-07389)

616.8'914'0926 — Medicine. Psychotherapy. ***Case studies***
Kapelovitz, Leonard H. To love and to work : a demonstration and discussion of psychotherapy / [by] Leonard H. Kapelovitz. — New York [etc.] ; London : Grune and Stratton, [1977]. — xv,256p : ill ; 24cm.
Published in the United States: 1976. — Index.
ISBN 0-8089-0975-4 : £11.00
(B77-13071)

Psychotherapies : a comparative casebook / edited by Stephen J. Morse and Robert I. Watson, Jr. — New York ; London [etc.] : Holt, Rinehart and Winston, 1977. — x,421p : ill ; 25cm.
Bibl. — Index.
ISBN 0-03-017826-6 : £11.50
(B77-21918)

616.8'915 — Medicine. Family therapy
Haley, Jay. Problem-solving therapy / [by] Jay Haley. — San Francisco [etc.] ; London : Jossey-Bass, 1976. — xv,275p ; 24cm. — (The Jossey-Bass behavioral science series)
Index.
ISBN 0-87589-300-7 : £11.50
(B77-04861)

616.8'915 — Medicine. Group therapy
How to begin a psychotherapy group : six approaches / edited by Herbert M. Rabin and Max Rosenbaum. — London [etc.] : Gordon and Breach, 1976. — [4],139p ; 24cm.
Bibl.
ISBN 0-677-15800-9 : £7.10
(B77-04862)

Rose, Sheldon D. Group therapy : a behavioral approach / [by] Sheldon D. Rose. — Englewood Cliffs ; London [etc.] : Prentice-Hall, 1977. — xi,308p : ill ; 24cm.
Bibl.: p.274-291. — Index.
ISBN 0-13-365239-4 : £7.95
(B77-15885)

616.8'915'08 — Medicine. Group therapy. ***Readings***
From group dynamics to group psychoanalysis : therapeutic applications of group dynamic understanding / edited by Morton Kissen. — Washington, D.C. ; London : Hemisphere ; New York ; London [etc.] : Wiley, 1976. — xv, 362p ; 24cm. — (Series in clinical and community psychology)
'A Halsted Press book'. — Bibl.: p.345-352. — Index.
ISBN 0-470-15132-3 : £15.50
(B77-22634)

616.8'916 — Medicine. Behaviour therapy
Goldfried, Marvin R. Clinical behavior therapy / [by] Marvin R. Goldfried, Gerald C. Davison. — New York ; London [etc.] : Holt, Rinehart and Winston, 1976. — xiii,301p : forms, ports ; 24cm.
Bibl.: p.279-292. — Index.
ISBN 0-03-008151-3 : £10.00
(B77-02359)

616.8'916 — Medicine. Behaviour therapy. ***Case studies***
Behavior therapy in psychiatric practice : the use of behavioral procedures by psychiatrists. — New York ; Oxford [etc.] : Pergamon.
Vol.1 : Selections from 'The journal of behaviour therapy and experimental psychiatry' (1970-1975) / editors Joseph Wolpe and Leo J. Reyna. — 1976. — xi,230p : ill ; 26cm.
Bibl.
ISBN 0-08-021148-8 : £6.25
ISBN 0-08-021147-x Pbk : £4.75
(B77-03046)

Wolpe, Joseph. Theme and variations : a behavior therapy casebook / [by] Joseph Wolpe. — New York ; Oxford [etc.] : Pergamon, 1976. — xi,257p : ill ; 24cm. — (Pergamon international library) (Pergamon general psychology series ; vol.51)
Bibl.: p.245-252. — Index.
ISBN 0-08-020422-8 : £6.25
ISBN 0-08-020421-x Pbk : £5.00
(B77-03047)

616.8'916 — Medicine. Primal therapy
Janov, Arthur. The primal revolution / [by] Arthur Janov. — London : Abacus Press, 1975. — 246p ; 20cm.
Originally published: New York : Simon and Schuster, 1972 ; London : Garnstone Press, 1974.
ISBN 0-349-11830-2 Pbk : £0.90
(B77-08414)

616.8'916 — Patients with mental disorders. Behaviour therapy by nurses
Nursing in behavioural psychotherapy : an advanced clinical role for nurses / [by] I.M. Marks ... [et al.]. — London (Henrietta Place, Cavendish Sq., W1M 0AB) : Royal College of Nursing of the United Kingdom, 1977. — 149p : ill, forms ; 22cm. — (Royal College of Nursing. Research series)
Bibl.: p.146-149.
ISBN 0-902606-50-6 Pbk : £2.00
(B77-11856)

616.8'916'2 — Man. Mental disorders. Hypnotherapy
Frankel, Fred H. Hypnosis : trance as a coping mechanism / [by] Fred H. Frankel. — New York ; London : Plenum Press, [1977]. — xii, 185p ; 24cm. — (Topics in general psychiatry)
Published in the United States: 1976. — Bibl.: p.173-179. — Index.
ISBN 0-306-30932-7 : £9.45
(B77-10819)

616.8'916'5 — Man. Mental disorders. Therapy. Role of arts
Therapy and the arts : tools of consciousness / edited by Walt Anderson. — New York [etc.] ; London : Harper and Row, 1977. — xv,203p ; 21cm. — (Harper colophon books)
ISBN 0-06-090429-1 Pbk : £3.70
(B77-17544)

616.8'917 — Medicine. Psychoanalysis
Nichols, Michael P. Catharsis in psychotherapy / [by] Michael P. Nichols, Melvin Zax. — New York : Gardner Press ; New York ; London [etc.] : Distributed by Wiley, 1977. — xi,258p ; 25cm.
Index.
ISBN 0-470-99064-3 : £13.15
(B77-21181)

616.8'917'08 — Medicine. Psychoanalysis. ***Essays***
Groddeck, Georg. The meaning of illness : selected psychoanalytic writings, including his correspondence with Sigmund Freud / by Georg Groddeck ; selected, and with an introduction by Lore Schacht ; translated [from the German] by Gertrud Mander. — London : Hogarth Press : Institute of Psycho-Analysis, 1977. — [5],270p ; 23cm. — (The international psycho-analytical library ; no.105)
Bibl.: p.265-266. — Index.
ISBN 0-7012-0422-2 : £7.50 : CIP rev.
(B77-05456)

616.8'918 — Man. Mental disorders. Drug therapy. ***Conference proceedings***
Symposium on Advances in the Drug Therapy of Mental Illness, ***Geneva, 1973.*** Advances in the drug therapy of mental illness : based on the proceedings of a symposium jointly sponsored by the World Health Organization and the International Task Force on World Health Manpower, Geneva, 21-23 November 1973. — Geneva : W.H.O ; [London] : [H.M.S.O.], 1976. — 170p : ill ; 24cm.
' ... WHO, jointly with the International Task Force on World Health manpower ... [convened] a Symposium on Advances in the Drug Therapy of Mental Illness' - p.8. — Bibl.
Pbk : £7.50
ISBN 92-4-156051-7
(B77-01525)

616.8'918 — Man. Mental disorders. Drug therapy. Lithium carbonate. ***State-of-the-art reviews***
Fieve, Ronald Robert. The practical uses of lithium carbonate / by Ronald R. Fieve. — 2nd ed. — London (59 High Holborn, WC1V 6EB) : Norgine Ltd, 1976. — [1],16p ; 21cm. — (The present state of knowledge ; no.5)
Previous ed.: 1976. — Bibl.: p.14-16.
ISBN 0-901210-10-2 Sd : £0.50(free to members of medical and allied professions)
(B77-18814)

616.8'918 — Man. Mental disorders. Emergency treatment. Drug therapy. ***Manuals***
Pustan, Regina. What the house physician prescribes for some common emergency psychiatric admissions : based on the practice at Tooting Bec Hospital, London. — [London] ([2A St Paul's Rd, N.1]) : [The author], 1976. — [8]p : ill, facsims ; 21cm.
Author: Regina Pustan.
ISBN 0-9505472-1-2 Sd : Unpriced
(B77-06714)

616.8'95 — Man. Depression. Psychotherapy. Use of anger
Birnbaum, Jack. How to stop hating and start loving / [by] Jack Birnbaum. — London : Pan Books, 1977. — [1],188p : ill ; 18cm.
Originally published: as 'Cry anger'. Don Mills, Ont. : General Publishing Co., 1973 ; and as 'How to stop hating and start loving', London : Heinemann, 1975. — Bibl.: p.184. — Index.
ISBN 0-330-25064-7 Pbk : £0.70
(B77-15886)

616.8'982 — Man. Schizophrenia. ***Conference proceedings***
Schizophrenia Workshop, ***Capri, 1975.***
Schizophrenia today / edited by D. Kemali, G. Bartholini and D. Richter. — Oxford [etc.] : Pergamon, 1976. — xv,282p : ill ; 26cm.
'... "Schizophrenia Workshop" arranged at Capri in October 1975' - Foreword. — Bibl. — Index.
ISBN 0-08-020928-9 : £9.00
(B77-04226)

616.8'982'009 — Man. Schizophrenia. Theories, to 1975
Szasz, Thomas Stephen. Paresis and plunder : the models of madness in psychiatry and anti-psychiatry / [by] Thomas Szasz. — [Colchester] ([Wivenhoe Park, Colchester, Essex CO4 3SQ]) : University of Essex, [1977]. — [2], 17p ; 21cm. — (Noel Buxton lecture ; 11th : 1975)
'Adapted from ... "Schizophrenia : the sacred symbol of psychiatry", New York : Basic Books, 1976' - title page verso.
ISBN 0-901726-13-3 Sd : £0.50
(B77-13072)

616.8'982'06 — Man. Schizophrenia. Therapy. ***Reviews of research***
Treatment of schizophrenia : progress and prospects / edited by Louis Jolyon West, Don E. Flinn. — New York [etc.] ; London : Grune and Stratton, [1977]. — xvii,291p : ill ; 24cm.
'... outgrowth of a conference on the treatment of schizophrenia held at UCLA in 1972' - Preface. — Published in the United States: 1976. — Bibl. — Index.
ISBN 0-8089-0970-3 : £15.95
(B77-13073)

616.9 — GENERAL DISEASES
616.9 — Man. Communicable diseases
Infectious diseases : a modern treatise of infectious processes / edited by Paul D. Hoeprich ; with 97 contributors. — 2nd ed. — Hagerstown [etc.] ; London : Harper and Row, 1977. — xxxi,1258p,[9]leaves of plates : ill(some col), maps ; 27cm.
Previous ed.: published as 'Infectious diseases : a guide to the understanding and management of infectious processes'. 1972. — Bibl. — Index.
ISBN 0-06-141196-5 : Unpriced
(B77-29471)

Recent Advances in Infectious Diseases ***(Conference), 3rd, Charlottesville, 1976.*** Current concepts of infectious diseases / edited by Edward W. Hook ... [et al.]. — New York ; London [etc.] : Wiley, 1977. — x,277p : ill ; 26cm.
'The Division of Infectious Diseases of the Department of Medicine of the University of Virginia School of Medicine has presented a course entitled "Recent Advances in Infectious Diseases" every two years since 1971 ... [This book is] based on presentations made at the third conference held in Charlottesville in April, 1976' - Preface. — 'A Wiley Medical Publication'. — Bibl. — Index.
ISBN 0-471-01598-9 : £16.50
(B77-27141)

Youmans, Guy P. The biologic and clinical basis of infectious diseases / [by] Guy P. Youmans, Philip Y. Paterson, Herbert M. Sommers [et al.]. — Philadelphia ; London [etc.] : Saunders, 1975. — xiii,813p : ill ; 26cm.
Bibl. — Index.
ISBN 0-7216-9650-3 : £14.75
ISBN 0-7216-9649-x Pbk : £11.00
(B77-21919)

616.9 — Man. Diseases caused by microorganisms
Communicable and infectious diseases. — 8th ed. / edited by Franklin H. Top, Sr, Paul F. Wehrle. — Saint Louis : Mosby ; London : Distributed by Kimpton, 1976. — xvii,807p,[98] leaves of plates,[6]p of plates : ill(some col), maps ; 28cm.
Previous ed.: 1972. — Index.
ISBN 0-8016-5007-0 : £32.10
(B77-18183)

616.9 — Man. Diseases caused by microorganisms. *Conference proceedings*
Infections and Infestations *(Conference), Edinburgh, 1975.* Symposium, infections and infestations : held on 4th and 5th December 1975 in the Hall of the Royal College of Physicians of Edinburgh / editor A.T. Proudfoot. — [Edinburgh] : Royal College of Physicians of Edinburgh, 1976. — 124p,[4]p of plates : ill ; 22cm. — (Royal College of Physicians of Edinburgh. Publications ; no.48 ISSN 0537-3947)
Bibl.
Pbk : £3.00
(B77-09050)

616.9 — Man. Diseases caused by microorganisms. Pathogenesis
Mims, Cedric Arthur. The pathogenesis of infectious disease / [by] Cedric A. Mims. — London : Academic Press [etc.], 1976. — x, 246p : ill ; 24cm.
Bibl. — Index.
ISBN 0-12-498250-6 : £6.80
(B77-02360)

616.9'2 — Man. Slow virus diseases
Adams, David H. Slow viruses / [by] David H. Adams, Thomas M. Bell. — Reading, Mass. ; London [etc.] : Addison-Wesley, 1976. — x, 214p : ill ; 25cm.
Bibl.: p.201-208. — Index.
ISBN 0-201-00042-3 : £15.60
ISBN 0-201-00043-1 Pbk : £6.00
(B77-15318)

616.9'2 — Man. Virus diseases. Manifestations: Skin disorders
Nasemann, Theodor. Viral diseases of the skin, mucous membranes and genitals : clinical features, differential diagnosis and therapy, with basic principles of virology / by Theodor Nasemann with the collaboration of Gertrud Schaeg and Otto Schultka ; translated [from the German] by Peter J. Frosch. — Philadelphia ; London [etc.] : Saunders [etc.], 1977. — xii, 217p,12p of plates : ill(some col), map ; 25cm.
Translation of: 'Viruskrankheiten der Haut, der Schleimhäute und des Genitales'. Stuttgart : Thieme, 1974. — Bibl.: p.207-208. — Index.
ISBN 0-7216-6655-8 : £24.75
Also classified at 616.5
(B77-16426)

616.9'26 — Man. Fevers
Lawson, James Howat. A synopsis of fevers and their treatment. — 12th ed. / [by] James H. Lawson. — London : Lloyd-Luke, 1977. — xiii, 328p ; 22cm.
Previous ed.: 1965. — Index.
ISBN 0-85324-115-5 Pbk : £6.00
(B77-07933)

616.9'5 — Man. Zoonoses
Andrewes, *Sir* **Christopher.** Viral and bacterial zoonoses / [by] Sir Christopher Andrewes, John R. Walton ; foreword by Sir Michael Swann. — London [etc.] : Baillière Tindall, 1977. — xiv, 161p,[4]p of plates : ill ; 20cm. — (Animal and human health)
Bibl.: p.152-153. — Index.
ISBN 0-7020-0632-7 Pbk : £2.50
Also classified at 636.089'69'5
(B77-09051)

616.9'51'09 — Man. Venereal diseases. *Case studies*
Sava, George. Crusader's clinic / [by] George Sava. — London : Kimber, 1977. — 206p ; 23cm.
ISBN 0-7183-0075-0 : £3.25
(B77-22635)

616.9'515 — Man. Gonorrhoea
Morton, Robert Steel. Gonorrhoea / [by] R.S. Morton. — London [etc.] : Saunders, 1977. — ix,292p : ill, 2 forms ; 25cm. — (Major problems in dermatology ; vol.9)
Bibl. — Index.
ISBN 0-7216-6563-2 : £12.00
(B77-29472)

616.9'6 — Man. Parasitic diseases
Markell, Edward Kingsmill. Medical parasitology / [by] Edward K. Markell, Marietta Voge. — 4th ed. — Philadelphia ; London [etc.] : Saunders, 1976. — viii,393p : ill(some col) ; 25cm.
Text on lining papers. — Previous ed.: 1971. — Bibl. — Index.
ISBN 0-7216-6083-5 : £11.50
(B77-06128)

616.9'64 — Man. Hydatid disease. Surgery
Saidi, Farrokh. Surgery of hydatid disease / [by] Farrokh Saidi. — London [etc.] : Saunders, 1976. — x,396p : ill ; 26cm.
Bibl. — Index.
ISBN 0-7216-7900-5 : £24.00
(B77-01526)

616.9'68 — Man. Skin. Parasites: Arthropoda, to 1975
Busvine, James Ronald. Insects, hygiene and history / by J.R. Busvine. — London : Athlone Press, 1976. — [7],262p : ill, facsim ; 23cm.
Bibl.: p.243-255. — Index.
ISBN 0-485-11160-8 : £6.95
(B77-04227)

616.9'69 — Man. Mycoses
Medical mycology. — 3rd ed. / [by] Chester W. Emmons ... [et al.]. — Philadelphia : Lea and Febiger ; London : Kimpton, 1977. — xi,592p,ii leaves of plates : ill(incl 2 col) ; 27cm.
Previous ed.: / by Chester W. Emmons, Chapman H. Binford, John P. Utz. 1970. — Bibl. — Index.
ISBN 0-8121-0566-4 : £14.60
(B77-16427)

616.9'7 — Man. Allergies
Criep, Leo Hermann. Allergy and clinical immunology / [by] Leo H. Criep. — New York [etc.] ; London : Grune and Stratton, 1976. — xi,641p : ill ; 26cm.
Bibl. — Index.
ISBN 0-8089-0823-5 : £27.45
(B77-00252)

616.9'7 — Man. Allergies. *Reviews of research*
Annual review of allergy. — London : Kimpton.
1975-1976 / edited by Claude Albee Frazier. — 1977. — 474p : ill, map ; 22cm.
Index.
ISBN 0-87488-328-8 Sp : £13.50
(B77-27142)

Progress in allergy. — Basel ; London [etc.] : Karger ; [Chichester] : [Distributed by Wiley].
Vol.19 / editors Paul Kallós, Byron H. Waksman and Alain de Weck ; contributors P.E. Bigazzi ... [et al.]. — 1975. — xx,312p : ill ; 25cm.
Bibl.
Unpriced
ISBN 3-8055-2033-6
(B77-10388)

616.9'7'079 — Man. Allergies. Immunological aspects
Immunological aspects of allergy and allergic diseases / edited by E. Rajka and S. Korossy. — London [etc.] : Plenum Press.
In 8 vols.
Vol.3 : Clinical aspects of autoimmune diseases. — 1975. — vii,261p : ill ; 25cm.
Also published: Budapest : Akadémiai Kiadó, 1975. — Bibl. — Index.
ISBN 0-306-37753-5 : £22.05
(B77-18184)

Vol.4 : Clinical aspects of immune pathology. — 1975. — vii,200p : ill ; 25cm.
Also published: Budapest : Akadémiai Kiadó, 1975. — Bibl. — Index.
ISBN 0-306-37754-3 : £22.05
(B77-18185)

616.9'7'08 — Man. Allergies. Psychosomatic aspects
Frazier, Claude A. Psychosomatic aspects of allergy / [by] Claude A. Frazier. — New York ; London [etc.] : Van Nostrand Reinhold, 1977. — xi,257p : ill, form ; 24cm.
Bibl.: p.243-244. — Index.
ISBN 0-442-21685-8 : £12.10
(B77-21182)

616.9'8022 — Underwater diving. Medical aspects. *For ergonomics*
The **underwater** hand book : a guide to physiology and performance for the engineer / edited by Charles W. Shilling, Margaret F. Werts and Nancy R. Schandelmeier. — London [etc.] : Wiley, 1976. — xxvii,912p : ill, chart, map ; 26cm.
Bibl. — Index.
ISBN 0-471-99453-7 : £40.00
Also classified at 612'.04
(B77-24978)

616.9'88 — Man. Hypothermia
Maclean, Derek. Accidental hypothermia / [by] Derek Maclean, Donald Emslie-Smith. — Oxford [etc.] : Blackwell Scientific, 1977. — ix, 476p : ill, charts, maps ; 25cm.
Bibl.: p.411-456. — Index.
ISBN 0-632-00831-8 : £18.50 : CIP rev.
(B77-13677)

616.9'88'3 — Tropical medicine
Hunter, George William. Tropical medicine. — 5th ed. / [by] George W. Hunter III, J. Clyde Swartzwelder, David F. Clyde. — Philadelphia ; London [etc.] : Saunders, 1976. — ii-xxx,900p : ill ; 27cm.
Previous ed.: published as 'A manual of tropical medicine' / by George W. Hunter, William F. Frye and J. Clyde Swartzwelder. 1966. — Index.
ISBN 0-7216-4847-9 : £21.50
(B77-00253)

616.9'88'30222 — Man. Diseases. *Tropical regions. Illustrations*
Peters, Wallace, *b.1924.* A colour atlas of tropical medicine and parasitology / [by] Wallace Peters, Herbert M. Gilles. — London : Wolfe Medical, 1977. — 416p : ill(chiefly col), maps ; 20cm. — (Wolfe medical atlases ; 17 ISSN 0302-0711)
Bibl.: p.402. — Index.
ISBN 0-7234-0176-4 : £18.00
(B77-01527)

616.9'88'306241 — Tropical medicine. Organisations: Royal Society of Tropical Medicine and Hygiene. *Directories*
Royal Society of Tropical Medicine and Hygiene. Yearbook of the Royal Society of Tropical Medicine and Hygiene. — [London] ([26 Portland Place, W1N 4EY]) : [The Society].
1976. — [1976]. — [2],100p : ill, ports ; 21cm.
ISBN 0-902271-05-9 Sd : £2.00
ISSN 0080-4711
(B77-05457)

616.9'893'07 — Man. Disorders caused by high altitudes. Physiological aspects
Heath, Donald. Man at high altitude : the pathophysiology of acclimatization and adaptation / [by] Donald Heath, David Reid Williams ; foreword by Sir Cyril Astley Clarke. — Edinburgh [etc.] : Churchill Livingstone, 1977. — xii,292p : ill, map, ports ; 25cm.
Bibl. — Index.
ISBN 0-443-01555-4 : £12.50
(B77-13678)

616.9'92 — Oncology
Scientific foundations of oncology / edited by T. Symington and R.L. Carter. — London : Heinemann Medical, 1976. — xx,690p : ill, maps ; 29cm.
Bibl. — Index.
ISBN 0-433-31950-x : £25.00
(B77-30306)

616.9'92'079028 — Man. Tumours. Immunology. Laboratory techniques: In vitro methods
In vitro methods in cell-mediated and tumor immunity / edited by Barry R. Bloom and John R. David, with the editorial assistance of ... [others]. — New York [etc.] ; London : Academic Press, 1976 [i.e. 1977]. — xxxi,748p : ill, form ; 24cm.
Published in the United States: 1976.
ISBN 0-12-107760-8 : £24.50
Primary classification 616.07'9'028
(B77-14755)

616.9'92'31 — Man. Mouth. Tumours
Lucas, Raleigh Barclay. Pathology of tumours of the oral tissues / [by] R.B. Lucas. — 3rd ed. — Edinburgh [etc.] : Churchill Livingstone, 1976. — x,426p : ill ; 25cm.
Previous ed.: 1972. — Bibl. — Index.
ISBN 0-443-01397-7 : £16.50
(B77-01528)

616.9'92'36 — Man. Liver. Solid tumours
Foster, James H. Solid liver tumors / by James H. Foster and Martin M. Berman. — Philadelphia ; London [etc.] : Saunders, 1977. — ii-xii,342p : ill ; 25cm. — (Major problems in clinical surgery ; vol.22)
Bibl. — Index.
ISBN 0-7216-3824-4 : £14.75
(B77-23465)

616.9'92'47 — Man. Pituitary gland. Tumours
Hankinson, John, *b.1919.* Pituitary and parapituitary tumours / [by] John Hankinson, M. Banna with contributions by ... [others]. — Philadelphia ; London [etc.] : Saunders, 1976. — ix,217p : ill ; 26cm. — (Major problems in neurology ; vol.6)
Bibl. — Index.
ISBN 0-7216-4495-3 : £17.50
(B77-01529)

616.9'92'8 — Man. Nervous systems. Tumours. Pathology
Russell, Dorothy Stuart. Pathology of tumours of the nervous system / [by] Dorothy S. Russell, Lucien J. Rubinstein. — 4th ed. — London : Edward Arnold, 1977. — vii,448p : ill ; 26cm.
Previous ed.: 1971. — Bibl. — Index.
ISBN 0-7131-4287-1 : £25.00
(B77-25671)

616.9'92'81 — Man. Brain. Tumours. Syndromes: Eye manifestations
Huber, Alfred. Eye signs and symptoms in brain tumors / [by] Alfred Huber ; English translation [from the German] ... by Stefan van Wien ; foreword by H. Krayenbühl ; foreword to the first English translation by Derrick Vail. — 3rd ed. / edited and newly written material translated [from the German] by Frederick C. Blodi. — Saint Louis : Mosby ; London : Distributed by Kimpton, 1976. — xvi,424p : ill ; 26cm.
Translation of: 'Augensymptome bei Hirntumoren'. 3.Aufl. Bern : Hans Huber, 1976? - Previous ed. of this translation: 1971. — Bibl.: p.341-401. — Index.
ISBN 0-8016-2302-2 : £30.50
(B77-12488)

616.9'92'81 — Man. Cerebellum. Tumours
Amici, R. Cerebellar tumors : clinical analysis and physiopathologic correlations / [by] R. Amici, G. Avanzini, and L. Pacini. — Basel ; London [etc.] : Karger, 1976. — viii,136p : ill ; 23cm. — (Monographs in neural sciences ; vol.4)
Bibl.: p.112-132. — Index.
Pbk : £16.35
ISBN 3-8055-2358-0
(B77-25672)

616.9'92'84 — Man. Eyes. Tumours
Reese, Algernon Beverly. Tumors of the eye / [by] Algernon B. Reese [and others]. — 3rd ed. — Hagerstown [etc.] ; London : Harper and Row, Medical Department, 1976. — xiii,477p : ill(some col) ; 27cm.
Previous ed.: 1963. — Bibl. — Index.
ISBN 0-06-142241-x : £37.50
(B77-06715)

616.9'94 — Man. Cancer
Cancer : a comprehensive treatise / Frederick F. Becker, editor. — New York ; London : Plenum Press.
2 : Etiology : viral carcinogenesis. — [1976]. — xvi,439p : ill ; 26cm.
Published in the United States: 1975. — Bibl. — Index.
ISBN 0-306-35202-8 : £23.63
(B77-03577)

4 : Biology of tumors : surfaces, immunology and comparative pathology. — [1976]. — xv, 439p : ill ; 26cm.
Published in the United States: 1975. — Bibl. — Index.
ISBN 0-306-35204-4 : £23.63
(B77-04228)

Understanding cancer : a guide for the caring professions / [edited] by Ian Burn, Roger Ll. Meyrick ; [for the] Department of Health and Social Security. — London : H.M.S.O., 1977. — 99p : ill ; 21cm.
ISBN 0-11-320511-2 Pbk : £2.00
(B77-29473)

616.9'94 — Man. Cancer. *Reviews of research*
Advances in cancer research. — New York [etc.] ; London : Academic Press.
Vol.24 / edited by George Klein, Sidney Weinhouse. — 1977. — xiii,343p : ill ; 24cm.
Bibl. — Index.
ISBN 0-12-006624-6 : £20.95
(B77-11857)

Vol.25 / edited by George Klein, Sidney Weinhouse. — 1977. — ix,394p : ill ; 24cm.
Bibl. — Index.
ISBN 0-12-006625-4 : £20.95
(B77-23466)

Methods in cancer research. — New York [etc.] ; London : Academic Press.
Vol.13 / edited by Harris Busch. — 1976. — xxi,355p : ill ; 24cm.
Bibl. — Index.
ISBN 0-12-147673-1 : £16.40
(B77-04863)

616.9'94 — Man. Cancer. *State-of-the-art reviews*
Maugh, Thomas H. Seeds of destruction : the science report on cancer research / [by] Thomas H. Maugh II and Jean L. Marx. — New York ; London : Plenum Press [for the] American Association for the Advancement of Science, [1976]. — xii,251p : ill, map ; 24cm.
'Part of the material in this book originally appeared as a series in the "Research News" section of "Science", the Journal of the Americn Association for the Advancement of Science' - title page verso. — Published in the United States: 1975. — Bibl.: p.239-240. — Index.
ISBN 0-306-30836-3 : £11.34
(B77-01530)

616.9'94 — Man. Cancer. Cells. Growth. Regulation. *Conference proceedings*
Control processes in neoplasia / edited by Myron A. Mehlman, Richard W. Hanson. — New York ; London : Academic Press, 1974. — xiii, 223p : ill, port ; 24cm. — (Symposia on metabolic regulation)
'Proceedings of a Symposium held at the University of Nebraska Medical Center Omaha, Nebraska, June 11-12, 1973'. — Index.
ISBN 0-12-487860-1 : Unpriced
(B77-18815)

616.9'94 — Man. Cancer. Therapy. Applications of Corynebacterium parvum
International Conference on the Effects of 'Corynebacterium parvum' in Experimental and Clinical Oncology, *1st, Paris, 1974.* Corynebacterium parvum : applications in experimental and clinical oncology / edited by Bernard Halpern. — New York ; London : Plenum Press, 1976. — xiv,444p : ill ; 24cm.
'Proceedings of the First International Conference on the Effects of Corynebacterium parvum in Experimental and Clinical Oncology held in Paris, May 9-10, 1974' - title page verso. — Published in the United States: 1975. — Bibl. — Index.
ISBN 0-306-30837-1 : £23.63
(B77-04229)

616.9'94'0028 — Man. Cancer. Cells. Separation. *Conference proceedings*
Cell separation methods : workshop on methods in cancer research held in Lunteren, the Netherlands on November 11-12 1976, organized under the auspices of the Scientific Council of the Netherlands Cancer Society (Koningin Wilhelmina Fonds) / editor Hans Bloemendal. — Amsterdam [etc.] ; Oxford : North-Holland Publishing Co., 1977. — v, 177p : ill ; 25cm.
Bibl. — Index.
ISBN 0-7204-0649-8 : Unpriced
(B77-25673)

616.9'94'00720427 — Man. Cancer. Research organisations. *North-west England. North Western Regional Cancer Organisation. Periodicals*
Cancer newsletter. — [Manchester] ([c/o Mrs E. Barrett, Department of Social Research, Christie Hospital, Kinnaird Rd, Manchester 20]) : North Western Regional Cancer Organisation.
No.1- ; 1977-. — [1977]-. — 30cm.
Quarterly. — 8p. in 1st issue.
Sd : Unpriced
ISSN 0309-6106
(B77-13679)

616.9'94'0077 — Man. Cancer. *Programmed texts*
Sherman, Charles D. Clinical concepts in cancer management : a self-instructional manual / [by] Charles D. Sherman, Jr. ; editors Margot L. Fass, William Preston. — New York ; London [etc.] : McGraw-Hill, 1976. — xviii,413p : ill, forms ; 24cm.
'A Blakiston publication'. — Originally published: in separate units. New York : University of Rochester School of Medicine and Dentistry, 1969. — Bibl.
ISBN 0-07-056580-5 Pbk : £11.50
(B77-02361)

616.9'94'05 — Man. Cancer. Prevention. *Conference proceedings*
Princess Takamatsu Cancer Research Fund. *International Symposium, 6th, Tokyo, 1975.* Fundamentals in cancer prevention : proceedings of the 6th International Symposium of the Princess Takamatsu Cancer Research Fund, Tokyo, 1975 / edited by Peter N. Magee ... [et al.]. — Baltimore ; London [etc.] : University Park Press, [1977]. — xvii,433p,2 leaves of plates : ill(incl 1 col), col port ; 27cm.

Originally published: Tokyo : University of Tokyo Press, 1976. — Bibl.
ISBN 0-8391-0965-2 : £28.25
(B77-14757)

616.9'94'06 — Man. Cancer. Therapy
Management of the patient with cancer / edited by Thomas F. Nealon, Jr. — 2nd ed. / with contributions by 71 authorities. — Philadelphia ; London [etc.] : Saunders, 1976. — xvi,1012p : ill ; 27cm.
Previous ed.: 1966. — Bibl. — Index.
ISBN 0-7216-6702-3 : £36.75
(B77-03048)

616.9'94'06 — Man. Cancer. Therapy. Use of immune RNA. *Conference proceedings*
Immune RNA in neoplasia / edited by Mary A. Fink. — New York [etc.] ; London : Academic Press, 1976 [i.e. 1977]. — xxiii,316p : ill ; 24cm.
'... the conference ... was held at the Marine Biological Laboratory, Woods Hole, Massachusetts, October 8-11, 1975' - Preface. — Published in the United States: 1976.
ISBN 0-12-256940-7 : £10.65
(B77-14262)

616.9'94'061 — Man. Cancer. Drug therapy
Priestman, T J. Cancer chemotherapy : an introduction / by T.J. Priestman. — Barnet (Kingmaker House, Station Rd, Barnet, Herts.) : Montedison Pharmaceuticals Ltd, 1977. — 214p : ill ; 21cm.
Bibl. — Index.
ISBN 0-9505545-0-2 Pbk : £4.50
(B77-18186)

616.9'94'061 — Man. Cancer. Drug therapy. *Conference proceedings*
International Conference on the Adjuvant Therapy of Cancer, *1st, Tucson, 1977.* Adjuvant therapy of cancer : proceedings of the International Conference on the Adjuvant Therapy of Cancer, held in Tucson, Arizona, USA, March 2-5, 1977 / editors Sydney E. Salmon and Stephen E. Jones. — Amsterdam ; Oxford [etc.] : North-Holland Publishing Co., 1977. — xii,646p : ill ; 25cm.
'... organized by the Section of Hematology and Oncology and the Cancer Center of the University of Arizona ...' - Preface. — Bibl. — Index.
ISBN 0-7204-0642-0 : Unpriced
(B77-23467)

616.9'94'061 — Man. Cancer. Drug therapy. Bleomycin
Fundamental and clinical studies of bleomycin / edited by Stephen K. Carter ... [et al.]. — Baltimore ; London : University Park Press, [1976]. — viii,320p : ill(some col) ; 27cm. — (Gann monograph on cancer research ; no.19)
Also published: Tokyo : University of Tokyo Press, 1976. — Bibl. — Index.
ISBN 0-8391-0962-8 : £31.95
(B77-16428)

616.9'94'0642 — Man. Cancer. Radiobiology
Duncan, William, *b.1930.* Clinical radiobiology / [by] W. Duncan, A.H.W. Nias. — Edinburgh [etc.] : Churchill Livingstone, 1977. — [7], 226p : ill ; 24cm.
Bibl. — Index.
ISBN 0-443-01147-8 : £12.50
(B77-22636)

616.9'94'0642 — Man. Cancer. Radiotherapy
Walter, Joseph. Cancer and radiotherapy : a short guide for nurses and medical students / [by] J. Walter. — 2nd ed. — Edinburgh [etc.] : Churchill Livingstone, 1977. — [11],271p : ill ; 22cm.
Previous ed.: London : Churchill, 1971. — Bibl. : p.265-266. — Index.
ISBN 0-443-01533-3 Pbk : £3.95
(B77-30307)

616.9'94'07 — Man. Cancer. Cells. Population. Kinetics
Steel, G Gordon. Growth kinetics of tumours : cell population kinetics in relation to the growth and treatment of cancer / [by] G. Gordon Steel. — Oxford : Clarendon Press, 1977. — xi,351p : ill ; 24cm.
Bibl.: p.309-341. — Index.
ISBN 0-19-857388-x : £15.00 : CIP rev.
(B77-15319)

616.9'94'071 — Man. Cancer. Pathogens: Chemicals
Arcos, Joseph Charles. Chemical induction of cancer : structural bases and biological mechanisms / [by] Joseph C. Arcos, Mary F. Argus, George Wolf. — New York ; London : Academic Press.
Revision of: 'Chemical induction of cancer' / by George Wolf. Cambridge, Mass. : Harvard University Press ; London : Cassell, 1952.
Vol.2A / [by] Joseph C. Arcos, Mary F. Argus. — 1974. — xvii,386p : ill ; 24cm.
Index.
ISBN 0-12-059302-5 : Unpriced
(B77-18816)

International Agency for Research on Cancer. IARC monographs on the evaluation of the carcinogenic risk of chemicals to man. — Lyon : I.A.R.C ; [London] : [H.M.S.O].
Vol.11 : Cadmium, nickel, some epoxides, miscellaneous industrial chemicals and general considerations on volatile anaesthetics : ... the views of two IARC Working Groups on the Evaluation of the Carcinogenic Risk of Chemicals to Man which met in Lyon, 9-11 December 1975 and 3-9 February 1976. — 1976. — 306p : ill ; 24cm.
Bibl. — Index to vols 1-11.
ISBN 0-11-950815-x Pbk : £8.50
(B77-01531)

International Agency for Research on Cancer. IARC monographs on the evaluation of the carcinogenic risk of chemicals to man. — Lyon : I.A.R.C. ; [London] : [H.M.S.O.].
Vol.12 : Some carbamates, thiocarbamates and carbazides : ... the views of an IARC Working Group on the Evaluation of the Carcinogenic Risk of Chemicals to Man which met in Lyon, 9-15 June 1976. — 1976. — 282p ; 24cm.
Bibl. — Index to vols 1-12.
ISBN 0-11-950834-6 Pbk : £9.52
(B77-09052)

616.9'94'071 — Man. Cancer. Pathogens: Chemicals. Testing. *Conference proceedings*
Symposium on the Role of Metabolic Activation in Producing Mutagenic and Carcinogenic Environmental Chemicals, *Research Triangle Park, N.C., 1976.* 'In vitro' metabolic activation in mutagenesis testing : proceedings of the Symposium on the Role of Metabolic Activation in Producing Mutagenic and Carcinogenic Environmental Chemicals, Research Triangle Park, North Carolina, February 9-11, 1976 / editors Frederick J. de Serres ... [et al.]. — Amsterdam [etc.] ; Oxford : North-Holland Publishing Co., 1976. — vii,363p : ill ; 25cm.
Bibl.
ISBN 0-7204-0612-9 : £17.56
Also classified at 616'.042
(B77-18817)

616.9'94'071 — Man. Cells. Effects of oncogenic viruses. *Conference proceedings*
NATO Advanced Study Institute on Tumor Virus-Host Cell Interaction, *Monte Carlo, 1973.* Tumor virus-host cell interaction / edited by Alan Kolber. — New York ; London : Plenum Press, [1976]. — x,461p : ill ; 26cm. — (NATO Advanced Study Institutes : series A, life sciences ; vol.5)
'Lectures presented at the 1973 NATO Advanced Study Institute on Tumor Virus-Host Cell Interaction, held in Monte Carlo, Monaco, September, 1973' - title page verso. — Published in the United States: 1975. — Bibl. — Index.
ISBN 0-306-35605-8 : £22.68
(B77-02362)

616.9'94'075 — Man. Melanoma. Diagnosis
McGovern, Vincent J. Malignant melanoma : clinical and histological diagnosis / [by] Vincent J. McGovern. — New York ; London [etc.] : Wiley, 1976. — xiv,178p : ill ; 26cm.
'A Wiley medical publication'. — Bibl. — Index.
ISBN 0-471-58417-7 : £16.60
(B77-24267)

616.9'94'0757 — Man. Cancer. Diagnosis. Radiography
Diagnosis and staging of cancer : a radiologic approach / [edited by] Richard J. Steckel, A. Robert Kagan ; foreword by Leo G. Rigler. — Philadelphia ; London [etc.] : Saunders, 1976 [i.e. 1977]. — xx,376p : ill ; 27cm.
Published in the United States: 1976. — Index.
ISBN 0-7216-8579-x : £20.75
(B77-10820)

616.9'94'079 — Man. Cancer. Immunological aspects
Harris, Jules E. The immunology of malignant disease / [by] Jules E. Harris, Joseph G. Sinkovics. — 2nd ed. — Saint Louis : Mosby ; London : Distributed by Kimpton, 1976. — xv, 606p,plate : ill(incl 1 col) ; 26cm.
Previous ed.: 1970. — Index.
ISBN 0-8016-2067-8 : £35.35
(B77-03578)

Mechanisms of tumor immunity / edited by Ira Green, Stanley Cohen, Robert T. McCluskey. — New York ; London [etc.] : Wiley, 1977. — xi,320p : ill ; 26cm. — (Basic and clinical immunology)
'A Wiley medical publication'. — Index.
ISBN 0-471-32481-7 : £16.50
(B77-30308)

616.9'94'079 — Man. Malignant tumours. Resistance. Role of macrophages. *Conference proceedings*
The **macrophage** in neoplasia / edited by Mary A. Fink. — New York [etc.] ; London : Academic Press, 1976. — ix,265p : ill ; 24cm.
'... [papers from] a workshop ... held at the Marine Biological Laboratory, Woods Hole, Massachusetts, October 8-11, 1975 ...' - Preface. — 'Academic Press rapid manuscript reproduction' - half title page verso.
ISBN 0-12-256950-4 : £8.85
(B77-10389)

616.9'94'0792 — Man. Cancer related antigens. *Conference proceedings*
Cancer related antigens : proceedings of the European Economic Communities Symposium held at Liège on 3rd and 4th May 1976 / edited by Paul Franchimont. — Amsterdam [etc.] ; Oxford : North-Holland Publishing Co., 1976. — ix,266p : ill ; 25cm.
Index.
ISBN 0-7204-0609-9 : £14.99
(B77-17545)

616.9'94'0792 — Man. Cancer. Role of gene expression. *Conference proceedings*
San Diego Conference on Onco-developmental Gene Expression, *1976.* Onco-developmental gene expression / edited by William H. Fishman, Stewart Sell. — New York [etc.] ; London : Academic Press, 1976 [i.e. 1977]. — xxxix,788p : ill, ports ; 24cm.
'... the fourth international meeting organized by the International Research Group for Carcinoembryonic Proteins ... the San Diego Conference on Onco-Developmental Gene Expression [May 29-June 1, 1976]' - Opening remarks. — Published in the United States: 1976. — Index. — Includes contributions from the Soviet-American Conference on Fetal and Tumor Antigens, Moscow, May 17-19, 1976.
ISBN 0-12-257660-8 : £15.90
(B77-09728)

616.9'94'24 — Man. Lungs. Cancer
Lung cancer : natural history, prognosis and therapy / edited by Lucien Israel, A. Philippe Chahinian. — New York [etc.] ; London : Academic Press, 1976. — xiv,316p : ill ; 24cm.
Bibl. — Index.
ISBN 0-12-375050-4 : £16.15
(B77-04864)

Lung cancer : clinical diagnosis and treatment / edited by Marc J. Straus. — New York [etc.] ; London : Grune and Stratton, 1977. — xv, 295p : ill ; 26cm.
Index.
ISBN 0-8089-0998-3 : £20.25
(B77-28663)

616.9'94'36 — Man. Liver. Cancer
Hepatocellular carcinoma / edited by Kunio Okuda, Robert L. Peters. — New York ; London [etc.] : Wiley, 1976. — xi,499p,plate : ill(some col) ; 26cm. — (Wiley series on diseases of the liver)
'A Wiley medical publication'. — Index.
ISBN 0-471-65316-0 : £27.60
(B77-24268)

Liver cell cancer / edited by H.M. Cameron, D.A. Linsell and G.P. Warwick. — Amsterdam [etc.] ; Oxford : Elsevier, 1976. — xv,292p : ill ; 25cm.
Bibl. — Index.
ISBN 0-444-41542-4 : £25.53
(B77-15887)

616.9'94'4 — Man. Haematopoietic system. Cancer. *Case studies*
Goldstone, A H. Leukaemias, lymphomas and allied disorders : case studies, the Cambridge experience / [by] A.H. Goldstone, J.C. Cawley, F.G.J. Hayhoe. — London [etc.] : Saunders, 1976. — lx,314p : ill ; 24cm.
Bibl. — Index.
ISBN 0-7216-4149-0 : £6.50
(B77-01532)

616.9'94'49 — Women. Breasts. Cancer
Kushner, Rose. Breast cancer : a personal history and an investigative report / [by] Rose Kushner ; foreword by Thomas L. Dao. — New York ; London : Harcourt Brace Jovanovich, [1976]. — xiii,400p : ill ; 22cm.
Published in the United States: 1975. — Bibl.: p.359-376. — Index.
ISBN 0-15-122569-9 : £6.70
(B77-08415)

616.9'94'49 — Women. Breasts. Cancer. Diagnosis
Breast cancer diagnosis / [edited by] Gerald S. Johnston and A. Eric Jones. — New York ; London (Davis House (4th Floor), 8 Scrubs La., Harlesden, NW10 6SE) : Plenum Medical Book Co., [1976]. — ix,168p : ill ; 26cm.
Published in the United States: 1975. — Bibl.: p.viii. — Index.
ISBN 0-306-30893-2 : £11.97
(B77-05458)

616.9'94'62 — Chemical industries. Personnel. Bladder. Cancer
Tumours of the bladder in the chemical industry : a study of their cause and prevention. — [New ed.]. — London ([93 Albert Embankment, SE1 7TU]) : Chemical Industries Association, [1976]. — [1],39p ; 22cm.
Previous ed.: published as 'Papilloma of the bladder in the chemical industry'. London : Association of British Chemical Manufacturers, 1953.
ISBN 0-900623-09-8 Sd : Unpriced
(B77-04230)

616.9'94'63 — Men. Prostate gland. Cancer
Urologic pathology : the prostate / [edited by] Myron Tannenbaum. — Philadelphia ; Lea and Febiger ; London : Kimpton, 1977. — xii, 419p : ill, facsims ; 27cm.
Index.
ISBN 0-8121-0546-x : £22.10
(B77-30309)

616.9'94'74 — Man. Nonepithelial malignant tumours
Hajdu, Steven Istvan. Cytopathology of sarcomas and other nonepithelial malignant tumors / [by] Steven I. Hajdu, Eva O. Hajdu. — Philadelphia ; London [etc.] : Saunders, 1976. — xiv,416p : ill(some col) ; 27cm.
Index.
ISBN 0-7216-4451-1 : £22.00
(B77-00254)

616.9'94'77 — Man. Skin. Cancer
Cancer of the skin : biology-diagnosis-management / edited by Rafael Andrade ... [et al.]. — Philadelphia ; London [etc.] : Saunders, 1976 [i.e. 1977]. — 2v.([139],1661p,xii,xii p of plates) : ill(some col), forms ; 27cm.
Published in the United States: 1976. — Bibl. — Index.
£75.00
ISBN 0-7216-1245-8 (Vol.1). ISBN 0-7216-1246-6 (Vol.2)
(B77-12489)

616.9'94'77 — Man. Skin. Melanoma
Milton, G W. Malignant melanoma of the skin and mucous membrane / [by] G.W. Milton ; with chapters by V.J. McGovern, Martin G. Lewis. — Edinburgh [etc.] : Churchill Livingstone, 1977. — vii,174p,[4]p of plates : ill(some col) ; 26cm.
Bibl. — Index.
ISBN 0-443-01422-1 : £12.00
(B77-27899)

616.9′94′91 — Man. Head. Cancer. Surgery
Surgical treatment of head and neck tumors / edited by Jorge Fairbanks Barbosa ; illustrations by José Gonçalves ; translation [from the Portuguese MSS.] by Rosemarie von Becker Froon. — New York ; London : Grune and Stratton, 1974. — xiii,311p : ill ; 29cm.
Index.
ISBN 0-8089-0811-1 : Unpriced
Also classified at 616.9′94′93
(B77-19425)

616.9′94′93 — Man. Neck. Cancer. Surgery
Surgical treatment of head and neck tumors / edited by Jorge Fairbanks Barbosa ; illustrations by José Gonçalves ; translation [from the Portuguese MSS.] by Rosemarie von Becker Froon. — New York ; London : Grune and Stratton, 1974. — xiii,311p : ill ; 29cm.
Index.
ISBN 0-8089-0811-1 : Unpriced
Primary classification 616.9′94′91
(B77-19425)

616.9′98 — Man. Leprosy
Browne, Stanley George. Leprosy : new hope and continuing challenge / by Stanley G. Browne. — Revised ed. — London : Leprosy Mission, 1977. — 82p,[4]p of plates : ill, map ; 19cm.
Previous ed.: 1966.
Sd : £0.35
(B77-26345)

617 — SURGERY
Bailey, Hamilton. Bailey & Love's short practice of surgery. — 17th ed. / revised by A.J. Harding Rains and H. David Ritchie. — London : H.K. Lewis, 1977. — x,1352p : ill(some col), port ; 26cm.
Previous ed.: 1975. — Index.
ISBN 0-7186-0431-8 : £17.50
(B77-31237)

Brief textbook of surgery / [edited by] Curtis P. Artz, Isidore Cohn, Jr, John H. Davis. — Philadelphia ; London [etc.] : Saunders, 1976. — xvi,694p : ill ; 26cm.
Bibl. — Index.
ISBN 0-7216-1415-9 : £13.00
(B77-01533)

Controversy in surgery / edited by Richard L. Varco and John P. Delaney. — Philadelphia ; London [etc.] : Saunders, 1976. — xxvi,713p : ill ; 26cm.
Index.
ISBN 0-7216-9016-5 : £23.75
(B77-03049)

Davis, Loyal. Davis-Christopher textbook of surgery : the biological basis of modern surgical practice. — Philadelphia ; London [etc.] : Saunders.
In 2 vols. — Previous ed.: 1972. — Index.
Vol.1. — 11th ed. / edited by David C. Sabiston, Jr. — 1977. — xlv,1360,cxiii p : ill, ports ; 28cm.
Bibl.
ISBN 0-7216-7869-6 : £15.00
(B77-33846)

Vol.2. — 11th ed. / edited by David C. Sabiston, Jr. — 1977. — xxi,1361-2465,cxiii p : ill ; 28cm.
Bibl. — Index.
ISBN 0-7216-7870-x : £15.00
(B77-33847)

Pye, Walter. Pye's surgical handicraft. — 20th ed. / edited by James Kyle. — Bristol : J. Wright, 1977. — xii,744p : ill(some col) ; 22cm.
Previous ed.: 1969. — Index.
ISBN 0-7236-0432-0 Pbk : £10.50 : CIP rev.
(B77-18187)

Smiddy, Francis Geoffrey. Tutorials in surgery / by F.G. Smiddy. — Tunbridge Wells [etc.] : Pitman Medical.
1. — 1977. — ix,331p ; 22cm.
ISBN 0-272-79417-1 Pbk : £3.95
(B77-30310)

Taylor, Selwyn. A short textbook of surgery / [by] Selwyn Taylor, Leonard Cotton. — 4th ed. — London [etc.] : Hodder and Stoughton, 1977. — vi,634p : ill ; 23cm. — ([University medical texts])
Previous ed.: London : English Universities Press, 1973. — Bibl. — Index.
ISBN 0-340-21543-7 : £7.45
ISBN 0-340-21544-5 Pbk : £1.15
(B77-19426)

Textbook of surgery / edited by David A. Macfarlane, Lewis P. Thomas ; foreword by Norman C. Tanner. — 4th ed. — Edinburgh : Churchill Livingstone, 1977. — xi,787p : ill ; 22cm.
Previous ed.: 1972. — Bibl. — Index.
ISBN 0-443-01607-0 Pbk : £8.50 : CIP rev.
(B77-22637)

Thomas, Meirion. Aids to postgraduate surgery / [by] Meirion Thomas, John S. Belstead. — Edinburgh [etc.] : Churchill Livingstone, 1976. — viii,140p ; 22cm.
Bibl.
ISBN 0-443-01511-2 Pbk : £2.25
(B77-01534)

617 — Medicine. Surgery. *Conference proceedings*
Controversial Opinions in Surgery *(Conference), Amsterdam, 1975.* General surgery, orthopaedics, plastic surgery controversial opinions : selected proceedings of the IX European Federation Congress, June 29-July 4, 1975, organized by the International College of Surgeons and the Collegium Chirurgicum Amstelodamense / editors J.M. Greep, H.H.M. de Boer, G. den Otter. — Amsterdam ; Oxford : Excerpta Medica [etc.], 1976. — [11], 311p : ill ; 24cm.
'After the successful conference on Controversial Opinions in Surgery held in Amsterdam in 1975 ...' - Foreword. — Bibl. — Index.
Pbk : £26.79
ISBN 90-219-0308-3
(B77-06129)

617 — Medicine. Surgery. *Reviews of research*
Current surgical practice. — London : Edward Arnold.
Vol.1 / edited on behalf of the Royal College of Surgeons of England by John Hadfield and Michael Hobsley ; with a foreword by Sir Rodney Smith. — 1976. — xii,268p : ill ; 24cm.
Bibl. — Index.
ISBN 0-7131-4281-2 : £14.00
ISBN 0-7131-4282-0 Pbk : £6.95
(B77-07934)

Recent advances in surgery. — Edinburgh [etc.] : Churchill Livingstone.
No.9 / edited by Selwyn Taylor. — 1977. — xii,450p : ill ; 24cm.
Bibl. — Index.
ISBN 0-443-01506-6 : £11.00
(B77-10390)

Surgery annual. — New York : Appleton-Century-Crofts ; London [etc.] : Prentice-Hall.
Vol.9 : 1977 / series editor Lloyd M. Nyhus. — 1977. — xv,427p,[4]p of plates : ill(some col) ; 25cm.
Bibl. — Index.
ISBN 0-8385-8710-0 : £21.20
(B77-31238)

617 — Medicine. Surgery. *State-of-the-art reviews*
Illingworth, ***Sir*** **Charles.** The sanguine mystery : 'this bloody and butcherly department of the healing art' / [by] Sir Charles Illingworth. — London : Nuffield Provincial Hospitals Trust, 1970. — ix,72p ; 23cm. — (The Rock Carling Fellowship ; 1970 ISSN ISSN 0305-0688)
ISBN 0-900574-25-9 : £0.80
(B77-02363)

617′.002′4613 — Medicine. Surgery. *For nursing*
Ellis, Harold, *b.1926.* General surgery for nurses / [by] Harold Ellis, Christopher Wastell ; including contributions by Paul Aichroth on fractures and orthopaedics, E.H. Miles Foxen on ear, nose and throat, Patrick D. Trevor-Roper on ophthalmology. — Oxford [etc.] : Blackwell Scientific, 1976. — ix,584p : ill, forms ; 23cm.
Index.
ISBN 0-632-09500-8 : £5.80
(B77-05459)

617′.006′24134 — Medicine. Surgery. Organisations. *Edinburgh. Royal College of Surgeons of Edinburgh. Fellows. Directories*
Royal College of Surgeons of Edinburgh. List of fellows at 31st December / the Royal College of Surgeons of Edinburgh. — [Edinburgh] ([18 Nicolson St., Edinburgh EH8 9DW]) : [R.C.S.E.].
1969. — [1971]. — xix,113p ; 26cm.
ISBN 0-9503620-1-8 : Unpriced
(B77-04231)

Royal College of Surgeons of Edinburgh. List of subscribing fellows at 31st December / the Royal College of Surgeons of Edinburgh. — [Edinburgh] ([18 Nicolson St., Edinburgh EH8 9DW]) : [The College].
1974. — [1976]. — iii-xx,159p ; 24cm.
Previously published: as 'List of fellows'.
Pbk : Unpriced
(B77-08416)

1974. Supplementary list. 1975. — [1976]. — 43p ; 24cm.
Sd : Unpriced
(B77-08417)

617′.0076 — Medicine. Surgery. *Questions & answers*
Craven, John Leonard. Surgical MCQs for undergraduates / [by] J.L. Craven, J.S.P. Lumley. — Edinburgh [etc.] : Churchill Livingstone, 1976. — xv,221p ; 22cm.
ISBN 0-443-01463-9 Pbk : £3.75
(B77-06717)

Fleming, Peter Robert. Multiple choice questions on 'Lecture notes on general surgery' / [by] P.R. Fleming, J.F. Stokes ; foreword by Harold Ellis. — Oxford [etc.] : Blackwell Scientific, 1977. — [4],60p ; 19cm.
With answers.
ISBN 0-632-00419-3 Sd : £1.25 : CIP rev.
(B77-04865)

617′.01 — Man. Surgery. Nosocomial infections. Control
Hospital-acquired infections in surgery / editors Hiram C. Polk, Jr, and H. Harlan Stone. — Baltimore ; London [etc.] : University Park Press, 1977. — ix,158p : ill ; 24cm.
Index.
ISBN 0-8391-1102-9 : £11.95
(B77-29474)

617′.026 — Medicine. Surgery. Emergency treatment
Bailey, Hamilton. Hamilton Bailey's emergency surgery. — 10th ed. / edited by Hugh A.F. Dudley. — Bristol : J. Wright, 1977. — xiv, 1017p : ill(some col) ; 25cm.
Previous ed.: / edited by T.J. McNair. 1972. — Index.
ISBN 0-7236-0448-7 : £25.00 : CIP rev.
(B77-10391)

Sharp, Edward H. Handbook of general surgical emergencies : a guide to the diagnosis and management of general surgical emergencies / [by] Edward H. Sharp. — London : Kimpton, 1977. — 174p : ill ; 22cm.
Also published: Flushing, N.Y. : Medical Examination Publishing Co., 1977. — Index.
ISBN 0-87488-632-5 Sp : £7.50
(B77-16914)

617′.07 — Medicine. Surgery. Immunology
Immunology for surgeons / edited by J.E. Castro. — Lancaster : M.T.P. Press, 1976. — ix,401p : ill ; 23cm.
Bibl. — Index.
ISBN 0-85200-135-5 : £12.50
(B77-03050)

Surgical immunology / edited by Andrew M. Munster. — New York [etc.] ; London : Grune and Stratton, 1976. — vii,327p : ill, ports ; 24cm.
Index.
ISBN 0-8089-0943-6 : £13.70
(B77-03051)

617′.075 — Medicine. Surgery. Diagnosis
Qvist, George. Surgical diagnosis / [by] George Qvist ; medical photography C.C. Gilson. — London : H.K. Lewis, 1977. — [8],699p : ill ; 26cm.
Index.
ISBN 0-7186-0427-x : £15.00
(B77-06130)

617′.092′4 — Medicine. Surgery. Lister, Joseph, 1st Baron Lister. *Great Britain. Biographies*
Fisher, Richard Bernard. Joseph Lister, 1827-1912 / [by] Richard B. Fisher. — London : Macdonald and Jane's, 1977. — 351p, 16p of plates : ill, facsim, ports ; 25cm.
Bibl.: p.326-331. — Index.
ISBN 0-354-04145-2 : £7.95
(B77-23468)

617'.092'4 — Medicine. Surgery. Short, Arthur Rendle. *Autobiographies*
Short, Arthur Rendle. The faith of a surgeon : belief and experience in the life of Arthur Rendle Short / edited by W.M. Capper and D. Johnson. — Exeter : Paternoster Press, 1976. — iv,156p ; 22cm.
Bibl.: p.154-156.
ISBN 0-85364-198-6 Pbk : £1.80
(B77-07391)

617.1 — WOUNDS AND INJURIES
617'.1 — Man. Head. Injuries. *Conference proceedings*
Chicago Symposium on Neural Trauma, *2nd, 1975.* Head injuries : proceedings of the Second Chicago Symposium on Neural Trauma / edited by Robert L. McLaurin. — New York [etc.] ; London : Grune and Stratton, 1976. — xv,301p : ill ; 26cm.
Bibl. — Index.
ISBN 0-8089-0938-x : £7.60
(B77-07392)

617'.1 — Man. Injuries
Aston, John Nevile. A short textbook of orthopaedics and traumatology / [by] J.N. Aston. — 2nd ed. / revised by Sean Hughes. — London [etc.] : Hodder and Stoughton, 1976. — ix,302p : ill ; 23cm. — (University medical texts)
Previous ed.: Sevenoaks : English Universities Press, 1967. — Index.
ISBN 0-340-11839-3 : £4.75
ISBN 0-340-08367-0 Unibook : £1.85
Also classified at 617'.3
(B77-04232)

617'.1 — Man. Injuries. Therapy
American College of Surgeons. *Committee on Trauma.* Early care of the injured patient / by the Committee on Trauma, American College of Surgeons. — 2nd ed. — Philadelphia ; London [etc.] : Saunders, 1976. — xi,443p : ill ; 24cm.
Text on lining papers. — Previous ed.: 1972. — Index.
ISBN 0-7216-1161-3 : £10.50
(B77-07393)

Initial management of the trauma patient / edited by Charles F. Frey. — Philadelphia : Lea and Febiger ; London : Kimpton, 1976. — xiv,498p : ill ; 24cm.
Bibl. — Index.
ISBN 0-8121-0519-2 : £15.00
(B77-06131)

617'.1 — Man. Spine & spinal cord. Injuries
Injuries of the spine and spinal cord / edited by P.J. Vinken and G.W. Bruyn in collaboration with R. Braakman. — Amsterdam ; Oxford : North-Holland Publishing Co. [etc.].
Part 2 / associate editor Harold L. Klawans, Jr. — 1976. — xii,550p : ill ; 27cm. — (Handbook of clinical neurology ; vol.26)
Bibl. — Index.
ISBN 0-7204-7226-1 : Unpriced
(B77-00255)

617'.1 — Man. Spine. Injuries. Aggravation. Prevention. *Manuals*
Whitaker, Heather Elizabeth. Your back and you : help yourself to help your back / [compiled by Heather E. Whitaker ; illustrations by Arthur Blood]. — Plymouth (c/o P.D.S. Printers, Faraday Rd, Prince Rock, Plymouth, PL4 0ST) : The compiler, [1976]. — [16]p : ill ; 14cm.
ISBN 0-9505373-0-6 Sd : £0.25
(B77-00256)

617'.1 — Man. Spine. Injuries. Therapy
Guttmann, *Sir* **Ludwig.** Spinal cord injuries : comprehensive management and research / by Sir Ludwig Guttmann. — 2nd ed. — Oxford [etc.] : Blackwell Scientific, 1976. — xv,731p : ill ; 26cm.
Previous ed.: 1973. — Bibl.: p.679-724. — Index.
ISBN 0-632-00079-1 : £21.00
(B77-08418)

617'.1 — Man. Thorax. Injuries. *Conference proceedings*
Trauma of the Chest *(Conference), Coventry, 1977.* Trauma of the chest : the Coventry Conference / edited by W.G. Williams and R.E. Smith. — Bristol : J. Wright, 1977. — xi, 266p : ill ; 22cm.
'"Trauma of the Chest", the subject of the fourth Coventry Conference' - Foreword. — Bibl. — Index.
ISBN 0-7236-0484-3 Pbk : £9.50 : CIP rev.
(B77-25675)

617'.1027 — Association footballers. Injuries. Therapy
Harris, Harry, *b.1952.* The treatment of football injuries / [by] Harry Harris & Mike Varney. — London : Macdonald and Jane's, 1977. — 159p : ill, ports ; 21cm.
ISBN 0-354-08510-7 Pbk : £2.95
(B77-30311)

617'.1027 — Man. Muscles. Injuries sustained during sports & games. Cryotherapy
O'Connell, Bob. The ice treatment of muscle injuries in sport : the application of cold with combined exercise ; precautions and contra indications ; timetable of muscle treatment / by T.J.C. "Bob" O'Connell. — [Dublin?] : [s.n.] ; Dublin (16 Clare St, Dublin 2) : [Distributed by] Greene's Book Shop, [1977]. — [20]p : ill ; 21cm.
Bibl.: p.20.
Sd : £0.44
(B77-18818)

617'.1027 — Mountaineering. Medical aspects
Medicine for mountaineering / edited by James A. Wilkerson. — 2nd ed. — Seattle : The Mountaineers ; Leicester (249 Knighton Church Rd, Leicester) : Cordee Publishing, 1975. — 368p : ill ; 20cm.
Previous ed.: Seattle : The Mountaineers, 1967. — Index. — Previous control number B7716429.
ISBN 0-916890-06-6 Pbk : £4.80
(B77-16429)

617'.1027 — Sports & games. Injuries
O'Donoghue, Don Horatio. Treatment of injuries to athletes / [by] Don H. O'Donoghue. — 3rd ed. — Philadelphia ; London [etc.] : Saunders, 1976. — ii-xviii,834p : ill ; 26cm.
Previous ed.: 1970. — Index.
ISBN 0-7216-6927-1 : £22.50
(B77-03052)

617'.11 — Man. Arms. Burns
Salisbury, Roger E. Burns of the upper extremity / by Roger E. Salisbury and Basil A. Pruitt. — Philadelphia ; London [etc.] : Saunders, 1976. — xii,180p : ill ; 25cm. — (Major problems in clinical surgery ; vol.19)
Index.
ISBN 0-7216-7902-1 : £10.00
(B77-01535)

617'.14 — Man. Wounds. Healing
Peacock, Erle Ewart. Wound repair / [by] Erle E. Peacock, Jr, Walton Van Winkle, Jr. — 2nd ed. — Philadelphia ; London [etc.] : Saunders, 1976. — xiv,699p : ill ; 25cm.
Previous ed.: published as 'Surgery and biology of wound repair'. 1970. — Bibl. — Index.
ISBN 0-7216-7124-1 : £24.00
(B77-06132)

617'.15'6 — Man. Face. Middle third. Bones. Fractures. *For dentistry*
Killey, Homer Charles. Fractures of the middle third of the facial skeleton / [by] H.C. Killey. — 2nd ed. revised reprint. — Bristol : J. Wright, 1974. — 84p : ill ; 23cm. — ('Dental practitioner' handbooks ; no.3)
Previous ed.: i.e. 2nd ed., 1971. — Bibl.: p.77-84.
ISBN 0-7236-0394-4 Pbk : £1.60
(B77-20325)

617'.15'6 — Man. Maxillofacial region. Bones. Fractures. *For dentistry*
Killey, Homer Charles. Fractures of the middle third of the facial skeleton / [by] H.C. Killey. — 3rd ed. — Bristol : J. Wright, 1977. — 87p : ill ; 22cm. — (A 'Dental practitioner' handbook ; no.3)
Previous ed.: i.e. 2nd ed. revised reprint, 1974. — Bibl.: .77-84. — Index.
ISBN 0-7236-0459-2 Pbk : £2.50
(B77-10821)

617'.21 — Man. Shock. Cell therapy. *Reviews of research*
Shock : pathology, metabolism, shock cell, treatment / [by] Iuliu Suteu ... [et al.] ; [translated from the Romanian by Ioana Sturza]. — Revised, up-dated English [ed.]. — Tunbridge Wells : Abacus Press, 1977. — xxiii, 447p,[28]p of plates : ill(some col) ; 25cm.
Previous ed.: published as 'Socul'. Bucharest : Editura Militară, 1973. — Bibl. — Index.
ISBN 0-85626-091-6 : £18.85
(B77-27144)

617.3 — MEDICINE. ORTHOPAEDICS
Adams, John Crawford. Outline of orthopaedics / by John Crawford Adams. — 8th ed. — Edinburgh [etc.] : Churchill Livingstone, 1976. — vii,472p : ill ; 22cm.
Previous ed.: 1971. — Bibl.: p.436-459. — Index.
ISBN 0-443-01472-8 : £8.75
ISBN 0-443-01167-2 Pbk : £4.75
(B77-06718)

Apley, Alan Graham. System of orthopaedics and fractures / [by] A. Graham Apley. — 5th ed. — London [etc.] : Butterworth, 1977. — x, 477p,plate : ill(some col) ; 26cm.
Previous ed.: 1973. — Bibl. — Index.
ISBN 0-407-40653-0 : £15.95
(B77-31936)

Aston, John Nevile. A short textbook of orthopaedics and traumatology / [by] J.N. Aston. — 2nd ed. / revised by Sean Hughes. — London [etc.] : Hodder and Stoughton, 1976. — ix,302p : ill ; 23cm. — (University medical texts)
Previous ed.: Sevenoaks : English Universities Press, 1967. — Index.
ISBN 0-340-11839-3 : £4.75
ISBN 0-340-08367-0 Unibook : £1.85
Primary classification 617'.1
(B77-04232)

Care of the orthopaedic patient / edited by Joyce W. Rowe, Lois Dyer. — Oxford [etc.] : Blackwell Scientific, 1977. — ix,421p : ill ; 24cm.
Bibl. — Index.
ISBN 0-632-00861-x : £10.00 : CIP rev.
(B77-06133)

Cyriax, James. Textbook of orthopaedic medicine. — London : Baillière Tindall.
Vol.2 : Treatment by manipulation, massage and injection. — 9th ed. / [by] James Cyriax and Gillean Russell. — 1977. — xiv,462p : ill ; 23cm.
Previous ed.: / by James Cyriax. London : Baillière, Tindall and Cassell, 1971. — Bibl.: p.454. — Index.
ISBN 0-7020-0638-6 : £7.50
(B77-15888)

Schneider, Franz Richard. Handbook for the orthopaedic assistant / [by] F. Richard Schneider ; with 135 illustrations by Roger Stringham. — 2nd ed. — Saint Louis : Mosby ; London : Distributed by Kimpton, 1976. — xi, 232p : ill ; 27cm.
Previous ed.: 1972. — Index.
ISBN 0-8016-4351-1 : £9.70
(B77-03579)

617'.3 — Medicine. Orthopaedics. Diagnosis. Physical examination
McRae, Ronald. Clinical orthopaedic examination / [by] Ronald McRae ; with original drawings by the author. — Edinburgh [etc.] : Churchill Livingstone, 1976. — vii, 219p : chiefly ill ; 25cm.
With answers.
ISBN 0-443-01512-0 Pbk : £5.00
(B77-04866)

617'.3'0076 — Medicine. Orthopaedics. *Questions and answers*
Questions and answers in orthopaedics for students, interns, residents, and board aspirants / edited by Floyd G. Goodman, George R. Schoedinger III. — 3rd ed. — Saint Louis : Mosby ; London : Distributed by Kimpton, 1977. — xi,293[i.e.296]p ; 25cm. — (Mosby's review series)
Previous ed.: 1971. — Bibl.: p.257-262.
ISBN 0-8016-1900-9 Pbk : £12.40
(B77-29475)

617'.3'008 — Medicine. Orthopaedics. *Lectures, speeches*
American Academy of Orthopaedic Surgeons. Instructional course lectures / American Academy of Orthopaedic Surgeons. — Saint Louis : Mosby ; London : Distributed by Kimpton.
Vol.25 : 1976. — 1976. — xi,247p : ill, facsim, form, map ; 29cm.
Bibl. — Index.
ISBN 0-8016-0014-6 : £28.05
(B77-06134)

617'.307 — Medicine. Orthotics
Bunch, Wilton H. Principles of orthotic treatment / [by] Wilton H. Bunch, Robert D. Keagy. — Saint Louis : Mosby ; London : Distributed by Kimpton, 1976. — vii,144p : ill, forms ; 26cm.
Bibl. — Index.
ISBN 0-8016-0880-5 : £14.25
(B77-04233)

617'.307 — Medicine. Orthotics. *Conference proceedings*
The advance in orthotics / edited by George Murdoch ; with a foreword by R.M. Kenedi. — London : Edward Arnold, 1976. — xiii,602p : ill, form ; 24cm.
Proceedings of a conference held in Dundee. — Bibl. — Index.
ISBN 0-7131-4214-6 : £27.50
(B77-07394)

617'.307 — Surgical appliances. Attitudes of patients
Jay, Peggy Elizabeth. The patients' viewpoint : a study of people's experience of and feelings about their special footwear, lumbar supports and long-leg calipers / by Peggy Jay and Michael Dunne. — [London] ([Vincent House, Vincent Sq., S.W.1]) : [National Fund for Research into Crippling Diseases], [1976]. — [1],38p : ill ; 30cm. — (Action research for the crippled child monograph)
'... a project carried out for the National Fund for Research into Crippling Diseases by the Research Institute for Consumer Affairs'.
Sp : £2.00
(B77-27145)

617'.307'05 — Medicine. Orthotics. *Periodicals*
Prosthetics and orthotics international. — Hellerup : International Society for Prosthetics and Orthotics ; Glasgow (University of Strathclyde, 73 Rottenrow, Glasgow G4 0NG) : 'Prosthetics and orthotics international'.
[Vol.1, no.1]- ; [Apr. 1977]-. — [1977]-. — ill ; 25cm.
Three issues a year. — iv,70p. in 1st issue. — Bibl.
Pbk : Unpriced
ISSN 0309-3646
Also classified at 617.95'005
(B77-16915)

617'.375 — Man. Spine. Disorders
Consumers' Association. Avoiding back trouble / [Consumers' Association] ; [edited by Edith Rudinger]. — London : The Association, 1977. — [5],153p : ill ; 18cm. — (A Consumer publication)
Originally published: 1975. — Index.
Pbk : £1.75
ISBN 0-85202-103-8
(B77-14758)

617'.375 — Man. Spine. Scoliosis
Roaf, Robert. Spinal deformities / [by] Robert Roaf. — Tunbridge Wells [etc.] : Pitman Medical, 1977. — viii,256p : ill ; 26cm.
Bibl. — Index.
ISBN 0-272-79379-5 : £10.00
(B77-13074)

617'.398 — Man. Toes. Deformities. Correction. Use of silicone orthoses
Coates, Ian S. Silicone orthodigita and shielding / [by] Ian S. Coates. — Bebington (c/o Reprography Dept, UML Ltd, Lever House, Bebington, Wirral, Merseyside) : The author, [1977]. — [3],33,[1]p : ill ; 21cm.
Reprinted from 'Journal of the American Podiatry Association', Vol.66, Aug.-Dec. 1976.
ISBN 0-903544-06-7 Sd : £1.50
(B77-11859)

617.4 — SURGICAL OPERATIONS BY SYSTEM
617'.41 — Man. Cardiovascular system. Surgery. Artificial circulation. *Conference proceedings*
Mechanical support of the failing heart and lungs / edited by David Bregman. — New York : Appleton-Century-Crofts ; London [etc.] : Prentice-Hall, 1977. — xiii,210p : ill, form ; 24cm.
'... papers presented at a conference on ... June 5th, 1976' - Foreword. — Bibl. — Index.
ISBN 0-8385-6196-9 : £12.00
(B77-23469)

617'.41 — Man. Microvascular system. Plastic surgery. Microsurgery
O'Brien, Bernard McC. Microvascular reconstructive surgery / [by] Bernard McC. O'Brien. — Edinburgh [etc.] : Churchill Livingstone, 1977. — [11],359p : ill, map, port ; 24cm.
Bibl. — Index.
ISBN 0-443-01443-4 : £14.00
(B77-18819)

617'.412 — Man. Heart. Cardiac pacemakers. *Conference proceedings*
International Symposium on Cardiac Pacing, *5th, Tokyo, 1976.* Cardiac pacing : proceedings of the Vth International Symposium, Tokyo, March 14-18, 1976 / editor Yoshio Watanabe. — Amsterdam ; Oxford ([256 Banbury Rd, Oxford OX2 7DH]) : Excerpta Medica, 1977. — xvi,601p : ill, port ; 25cm. — (International congress series ; no.395)
'Fifth International Symposium on Cardiac Pacing ...' - Preface. — Bibl. — Index.
£49.00
ISBN 90-219-0326-1
(B77-24979)

617'.412 — Man. Heart. Surgery
Surgery of the Heart *(Conference), Coventry, 1975.* Surgery of the Heart : the Coventry conference / edited by J.A. Dyde and R.E. Smith. — New York ; London ([8 Scrubs La., NW10 6SE]) : Plenum Medical Book Co., 1976. — xi,209p : ill ; 26cm.
'... this conference on Surgery of the Heart' - Prologue. — 'Proceedings of a Conference organized by the Warwickshire Postgraduate Medical Centre held in Coventry, England, September 11-12, 1975' - title page verso. — Bibl. — Index.
ISBN 0-306-30944-0 : £12.29
(B77-16916)

617'.412 — Man. Heart. Vascular grafts & implantation of artificial valves. Sequelae. *Conference proceedings*
Infections of Prosthetic Valves and Vascular Grafts *(Conference), Medical College of Virginia, 1976.* Infections of prosthetic heart valves and vascular grafts : prevention, diagnosis and treatment / edited by Richard J. Duma. — Baltimore ; London [etc.] : University Park Press, 1977. — xvi,352p : ill ; 24cm.
'On March 22 and 23, 1976, at the Medical College of Virginia, Richmond, Virginia, a conference entitled 'Infections of Prosthetic Valves and Vascular Grafts' was held ...' - Preface. — Index.
ISBN 0-8391-0973-3 : £18.95
(B77-29476)

617'.413 — Man. Blood vessels. Surgery
Haimovici, Henry. Vascular surgery : principles & techniques / [by] Henry Haimovici. — New York ; London [etc.] : McGraw-Hill, 1976. — xiii,967p : ill ; 25cm.
'A Blakiston publication'. — Bibl. — Index. — Includes contributions by others.
ISBN 0-07-025514-8 : £45.00
(B77-27146)

617'.413 — Man. Carotid arteries. Surgery. Sequelae: Ischaemia of blood vessels of brain
Jennett, Bryan. Effect of carotid artery surgery on cerebral blood flow : clinical and experimental studies / [by] Bryan Jennett, J. Douglas Miller, A. Murray Harper. — Amsterdam ; London [etc.] (256 Banbury Rd, Oxford OX2 7DH) : Excerpta Medica, 1976. — vii,170p : ill ; 25cm.
Bibl. — Index.
£17.56
ISBN 90-219-2106-5 (Excerpta Medica)
Also classified at 616.8'1
(B77-16430)

617'.43 — Man. Digestive system. Surgery. Preoperative & postoperative care. *Manuals*
Vukovich, Virginia C. Care of the ostomy patient / [by] Virginia C. Vukovich, Reba Douglass Grubb ; drawings by Travis L. Mayhall. — 2nd ed. — Saint Louis : Mosby ; London : Distributed by Kimpton, 1977. — xiii,150p : ill, 2 forms, plan ; 23cm.
Previous ed.: 1973. — Bibl.: p.137-139. — Index.
ISBN 0-8016-5276-6 Pbk : £5.30
(B77-21920)

617'.46'01 — Man. Urogenital system. Surgery. Sequelae
Complications of urologic surgery : prevention and management / edited by Robert B. Smith, Donald G. Skinner ; with contributions by 27 authorities. — Philadelphia ; London [etc.] : Saunders, 1976. — ii-xiii,520p : ill ; 26cm.
Bibl. — Index.
ISBN 0-7216-8418-1 : £24.25
(B77-04234)

617'.461 — Man. Kidneys. Dialysis & transplantation. *Conference proceedings*
European Dialysis and Transplant Association. *Congress, 13th, Hamburg, 1976.* Dialysis, transplantation, nephrology : proceedings of the Thirteenth Congress of the European Dialysis and Transplant Association held in Hamburg, Germany, 1976 / editor B.H.B. Robinson, associate editors P. Vereerstraeten, J.B. Hawkins. — Tunbridge Wells : Pitman Medical, 1976. — xvi,655p : ill, map ; 24cm. — (European Dialysis and Transplant Association. Proceedings ; vol.13 ISSN 0308-9401)
Bibl. — Index.
ISBN 0-272-79408-2 : £17.50
(B77-06135)

617'.461 — Man. Kidneys. Transplantation. *Case studies*
Corry, Robert J. Renal transplantation case studies : 37 case studies related to problems of clinical renal transplantation / by Robert J. Corry and John S. Thompson. — London : Kimpton, 1977. — 168p : ill ; 22cm.
Also published: Flushing, N.Y. : Medical Examination Publishing Co., 1977. — Bibl. — Index.
ISBN 0-87488-015-7 Sp : £9.00
(B77-28664)

617'.47 — Man. Hair. Transplants. *Personal observations*
Davies, David, *b.1939.* I've had a hair transplant : gain from my experiences / [by] David Davies. — London (101 Tarnwood Park, SE9 5PE) : The author, [1977?]. — 40p : ill, ports ; 21cm.
ISBN 0-9502815-1-4 Pbk : £0.75
(B77-11858)

617'.471 — Man. Bone marrow. Transplantation. Immunological aspects. *Conference proceedings*
International Symposium on Bone Marrow Transplantation, *1st, United States?, 1975.* Immunobiology of bone marrow transplantation / edited by Bo Dupont and Robert A. Good. — New York [etc.] ; London : Grune and Stratton, 1976. — xvi, 346p : ill, port ; 26cm.
'... First International Symposium on Bone Marrow Transplantation ...' - p.xiv. — Reprint of: 'Transplantation proceedings'. Vol. VIII, nos 3 and 4, Sept. and Dec. 1976. — Index.
ISBN 0-8089-0982-7 : £20.45
(B77-30313)

617'.472 — Man. Joints. Arthritis. Surgery
Marmor, Leonard. Arthritis surgery / [by] Leonard Marmor. — Philadelphia : Lea and Febiger ; London : Kimpton, 1976. — xi,548p : ill(some col) ; 26cm.
Originally published: as 'Surgery of rheumatoid arthritis'. 1967. — Bibl. — Index.
ISBN 0-8121-0537-0 : £31.55
(B77-01536)

617'.48 — Man. Central nervous system. Surgery
Jennett, Bryan. An introduction to neurosurgery / [by] Bryan Jennett ; foreword by Charles Wells. — 3rd ed. — London : Heinemann Medical, 1977. — xvii,366p : ill, forms ; 23cm.
Previous ed.: 1970. — Bibl. — Index.
ISBN 0-433-17302-5 : £9.95
(B77-21183)

617'.48 — Man. Nervous system. Surgery
Current controversies in neurosurgery / edited by T.P. Morley. — Philadelphia ; London [etc.] : Saunders, 1976. — xxviii,853p : ill ; 26cm.
Index.
ISBN 0-7216-6557-8 : £25.00
(B77-04235)

617'.48 — Man. Nervous system. Surgery. *Conference proceedings*
International Congress of Neurological Surgery, *6th, Sao Paulo, 1977.* Sixth International Congress of Neurological Surgery, Sao Paulo, Brazil, 19-25 June, 1977 : abstracts of papers, special lectures, scientific exhibits and films / editor Raul Carrea. — Amsterdam ; Oxford ([256 Banbury Rd, Oxford OX2 7DH]) : Excerpta-Medica, 1977. — xii,262p ; 24cm. — (International congress series ; no.418)
'Organized by the World Federation of Neurological Societies' p.v. — Index.
Pbk : Unpriced
ISBN 90-219-1224-4
(B77-25676)

617'.481 — Medicine. Psychosurgery. *Conference proceedings*
World Congress of Psychiatric Surgery, *4th, Madrid, 1975.* Neurosurgical treatment in psychiatry, pain and epilepsy / edited by William H. Sweet, Sixto Obrador, José Martín-Rodríguez. — Baltimore ; London [etc.] : University Park Press, 1977. — xxxi, 768p : ill ; 24cm.
'Proceedings of the Fourth World Congress of Psychiatric Surgery, September 7-10, 1975, Madrid, Spain' - p.v. — Bibl. — Index.
ISBN 0-8391-0881-8 : £30.50
(B77-15889)

617.5 — REGIONAL SURGERY
617'.51 — Man. Head & neck. Plastic surgery. *Conference proceedings*
International Symposium on Plastic and Reconstructive Surgery of the Face and Neck, *2nd, Chicago, 1975.* Plastic and reconstructive surgery of the face and neck : proceedings of the Second International Symposium / edited by George A. Sisson, M. Eugene Tardy, Jr. — New York [etc.] ; London : Grune and Stratton.
'Second International Symposium on Plastic and Reconstructive Surgery of the Face and Neck' - Preface. — In 2 vols.
Vol.1 : Aesthetic surgery. — 1977. — xi,236p : ill, form ; 29cm.
Index.
ISBN 0-8089-0941-x : £25.90
(B77-23470)

617'.51 — Man. Head & neck. Plastic surgery. Regional flaps
Conley, John, *b.1912 (June).* Regional flaps of the head and neck / by John Conley ; with contributions by ... [others]. — Philadelphia ; London [etc.] : Saunders [etc.], 1976. — viii, 268p : ill ; 29cm.
Index.
ISBN 0-7216-2647-5 : £50.00
(B77-09053)

617'.52 — Man. Face. Pain
Facial pain. — 2nd ed. / edited by Charles C. Alling III, Parker E. Mahan. — Philadelphia : Lea and Febiger ; London : Kimpton, 1977. — xii,286p : ill ; 27cm.
Previous ed.: published as the proceedings of the International Conference on Facial Pain, 1967 / edited by Charles C. Alling. 1968. — Bibl. — Index.
ISBN 0-8121-0577-x : £16.50
(B77-29477)

617'.522 — Man. Mouth. Surgery
Moore, Joseph Reginald. Principles of oral surgery / [by] J.R. Moore. — 2nd ed. — Manchester : Manchester University Press, 1976. — viii,255p : ill, form ; 22cm.
Previous ed.: Oxford : Pergamon Press, 1965. — Bibl. — Index.
ISBN 0-7190-0650-3 Pbk : £4.75
(B77-00789)

Oral surgery and anesthesia / [edited by] Robert B. Steiner, Robert D. Thompson. — Philadelphia ; London [etc.] : Saunders, 1977. — xvii,560p : ill, form ; 27cm.
Bibl. — Index.
ISBN 0-7216-8589-7 : £27.50
(B77-24980)

617'.522 — Man. Oral region. Diseases. Genetic aspects
Oral facial genetics / edited by Ray E. Stewart, Gerald H. Prescott. — Saint Louis : Mosby ; London : Distributed by Kimpton, 1976. — xiii,680p : ill, ports ; 27cm.
Bibl. — Index.
ISBN 0-8016-4810-6 : £38.60
(B77-24269)

617'.522'07 — Man. Oral region. Pathology
Bhaskar, Surinder Nath. Synopsis of oral pathology / [by] S.N. Bhaskar. — 5th ed. — Saint Louis : Mosby ; London : Distributed by Kimpton, 1977. — xi,684p : ill ; 20cm.
Previous ed.: 1973. — Bibl. — Index.
ISBN 0-8016-0689-6 : £12.80
(B77-30314)

617'.523 — Man. Nose. Surgery. *Conference proceedings*
Symposium on corrective rhinoplasty : proceedings of the Symposium of the Educational Foundation of the American Society of Plastic and Reconstructive Surgeons Inc., held at Miami, Florida January 15-18, 1975 / editor D. Ralph Millard, Jr. — Saint Louis ; Mosby ; London : Distributed by Kimpton, 1976. — x,316p,[2]p of plates,leaf of plate : ill(some col), facsims, forms, ports ; 29cm. — (American Society of Plastic and Reconstructive Surgeons. Educational Foundation. Symposia ; vol.13)
Bibl. — Index.
ISBN 0-8016-3413-x : £34.55
(B77-07935)

617'.533 — Man. Trachea. Intubation
Applebaum, Edward L. Tracheal intubation / by Edward L. Applebaum and David L. Bruce. — Philadelphia ; London [etc.] : Saunders, 1976. — [5],97p : ill ; 27cm.
Index.
ISBN 0-7216-1311-x : £7.00
(B77-00257)

617'.54 — Man. Thorax. Physiotherapy
Gaskell, Diana Vaughan. The Brompton Hospital guide to chest physiotherapy / compiled by D.V. Gaskell and B.A. Webber. — 3rd ed. — Oxford [etc.] : Blackwell Scientific, 1977. — vii, 99p : ill ; 22cm.
Previous ed.: 1973. — Index.
ISBN 0-632-00005-8 Pbk : £2.25 : CIP rev.
(B77-06136)

617'.54 — Man. Thorax. Surgery
Gibbon, John Heysham. Gibbon's surgery of the chest. — 3rd ed. by David C. Sabiston, Jr, Frank C. Spencer. — Philadelphia ; London [etc.] : Saunders, 1976. — xxi,1592p : ill, port ; 27cm.
Previous ed.: published as 'Surgery of the chest'. 1969. — Bibl. — Index.
ISBN 0-7216-7872-6 : £54.50
(B77-01537)

617'.54'0757 — Man. Thorax. Diagnosis. Radiography
Sagel, Stuart S. Special procedures in chest radiology / [by] Stuart S. Sagel. — Philadelphia ; London [etc.] : Saunders, 1976. — ii-xv,219p : ill ; 27cm. — (Saunders monographs in clinical radiology ; vol.8)
Bibl. — Index.
ISBN 0-7216-7897-1 : £14.25
(B77-00258)

617'.542 — Man. Respiratory system. Acute respiratory failure. Therapy. Use of artificial lungs. *Conference proceedings*
International Conference on Membrane Lung Technology and Prolonged Extracorporeal Perfusion, *Rungstedgaard, 1975.* Artificial lungs for acute respiratory failure : theory and practice / edited by Warren M. Zapol and Jesper Qvist. — New York [etc.] ; London : Academic Press ; Washington ; London : Hemisphere Publishing Corporation, 1976. — xii,557p : ill ; 24cm.
'The meeting, International Conference on Membrane Lung Technology and Prolonged Extracorporeal Perfusion, was held in June 1975 at Rungstedgaard, Denmark' - Foreword. — Bibl. — Index.
ISBN 0-12-775450-4 : £28.95
(B77-08419)

617'.55'075 — Man. Abdomen. Acute abdomen. Diagnosis
Botsford, Thomas Winston. The acute abdomen : an approach to diagnosis and management / [by] Thomas W. Botsford, Richard E. Wilson. — 2nd ed. — Philadelphia ; London [etc.] : Saunders, 1977. — xvi,325p : ill ; 18cm.
Previous ed.: 1969. — Bibl.: p.313-315. — Index.
ISBN 0-7216-1886-3 Pbk : £7.00
(B77-25677)

617'.55'0757 — Man. Abdomen. Diagnosis. Radiography. Anatomical aspects
Whalen, Joseph P. Radiology of the abdomen : anatomic basis / [by] Joseph P. Whalen. — Philadelphia : Lea and Febiger ; London : Kimpton, 1976. — xv,310p : ill ; 29cm.
Bibl.: p.285-286. — Index.
ISBN 0-8121-0569-9 : £22.10
(B77-13680)

617'.553'01 — Man. Stomach. Ulcers. Surgery. Sequelae
Bushkin, Frederic L. Postgastrectomy syndromes / by Frederic L. Bushkin and Edward R. Woodward. — Philadelphia ; London [etc.] : Saunders, 1976. — ii-xv,167p : ill ; 24cm. — (Major problems in clinical surgery ; vol.20)
Index.
ISBN 0-7216-2208-9 : £8.00
(B77-04236)

617'.5541 — Man. Gastrointestinal tract. Peptic ulcers. Surgery
Menguy, René. Surgery of peptic ulcer / by René Menguy. — Philadelphia ; London [etc.] : Saunders, 1976. — ii-x,297p : ill ; 25cm. — (Major problems in clinical surgery ; vol.18)
Bibl. — Index.
ISBN 0-7216-6248-x : £12.00
(B77-01538)

617'.575'075 — Man. Hands. Diagnosis. *For surgery*
Lister, Graham. The hand : diagnosis and indications / [by] Graham Lister ; foreword by Adrian E. Flatt. — Edinburgh [etc.] : Churchill Livingstone, 1977. — xi,224p : ill ; 25cm.
Ill. on lining papers. — Bibl.: p.189-199. — Index.
ISBN 0-443-01482-5 : £12.00
(B77-18820)

617'.58 — Man. Hips. Diagnosis. Arthrography
Grech, Paul. Hip arthrography / [by] Paul Grech. — London : Chapman and Hall, 1977. — xii,106p : ill ; 24cm.
Bibl. — Index.
ISBN 0-412-15090-5 : £8.50
(B77-32664)

617'.58 — Man. Hips. Joints. Surgery. *Conference proceedings*
The **hip,** proceedings of the fourth open scientific meeting of the Hip Society, 1976. — Saint Louis : Mosby ; London : Distributed by Kimpton, 1976. — xiii,270p : ill ; 26cm.
'... held in New Orleans, Louisiana ...' - Preface. — Bibl. — Index.
ISBN 0-8016-0036-7 : £24.00
(B77-17546)

617'.58 — Man. Joints. Prostheses. Engineering aspects
The **scientific** basis of joint replacement / edited by S.A.V. Swanson and M.A.R. Freeman. — Tunbridge Wells [etc.] : Pitman Medical, 1977. — viii,182p : ill ; 26cm.
Bibl. — Index.
ISBN 0-272-79380-9 : £10.50
(B77-18188)

617'.584 — Man. Ankles. Therapy. *Conference proceedings*
Foot science : a selection of papers from the proceedings of the American Orthopaedic Foot Society Inc., 1974 and 1975 / edited by James E. Bateman. — Philadelphia ; London [etc.] : Saunders, 1976. — xvi,290p : ill ; 25cm.
Bibl. — Index.
ISBN 0-7216-1580-5 : £24.75
Primary classification 617'.585
(B77-01539)

617'.585 — Man. Feet. Therapy. *Conference proceedings*
Foot science : a selection of papers from the proceedings of the American Orthopaedic Foot Society Inc., 1974 and 1975 / edited by James E. Bateman. — Philadelphia ; London [etc.] : Saunders, 1976. — xvi,290p : ill ; 25cm.
Bibl. — Index.
ISBN 0-7216-1580-5 : £24.75
Also classified at 617'.584
(B77-01539)

617.6 — DENTISTRY
617.6 — Dentistry. *For dental assistants*
Gelbier, Stanley. Handbook for dental surgery assistants and other ancilliary workers / by Stanley Gelbier and Margaret A.H. Copley ; with a foreword by H.M. Pickard. — 2nd ed. — Bristol : J. Wright, 1977. — xi,244p : ill ; 22cm.
Previous ed.: 1972. — Index.
ISBN 0-7236-0464-9 Pbk : £4.50 : CIP rev.
(B77-25678)

617.6 — Dentistry. Surgery
Operative dentistry. — 3rd ed. / [by] William H. Gilmore ... [et al.]. — Saint Louis : Mosby ; London : Distributed by Kimpton, 1977. — ix, 380p : ill ; 27cm.
Previous ed.: / by William H. Gilmore, Melvin R. Lund. 1973. — Bibl. — Index.
ISBN 0-8016-1822-3 : £18.80
(B77-28665)

617.6 — Dentistry. Surgery. Sequelae
Killey, Homer Charles. The prevention of complications in dental surgery / [by] H.C. Killey, L.W. Kay. — 2nd ed. — Edinburgh [etc.] : Churchill Livingstone, 1977. — vii, 210p : ill ; 22cm.
Previous ed.: 1969. — Index.
ISBN 0-443-01462-0 Pbk : £4.50
(B77-22638)

617.6 — Handicapped persons. Dentistry
Dentistry for the handicapped patient / [edited by] Arthur J. Nowak. — Saint Louis : Mosby ; London : Distributed by Kimpton, 1976. — xii, 419p : ill ; 26cm.
Bibl. — Index.
ISBN 0-8016-3671-x : £24.00
(B77-19428)

617.6'001'4 — Dentistry. Terminology. *Programmed texts*
Ashley, Ruth. Dental anatomy and terminology / [by] Ruth Ashley, Tess Kirby, in consultation with Harry R. Pape. — New York ; London [etc.] : Wiley, 1977. — xi,235p : ill ; 26cm. — (Self-teaching guides)
Fill-in book. — With answers. — Index.
ISBN 0-471-01348-x Pbk : £3.75
(B77-21184)

617.6'0025'41 — Dentists. *Great Britain. Directories*
The **dentists** register : comprising the names and addresses of dental practitioners ... on 31 January 1977 ... — London : General Dental Council.
1977. — [1977]. — 43,641p ; 25cm.
Pbk : £7.50
(B77-21185)

617.6'006'241 — Dentistry. Christian organisations. *Great Britain. Christian Dental Fellowship, to 1976*
Christian Dental Fellowship. Christian Dental Fellowship : the first twenty-five years. — Godalming ('Rosemead', Petworth Rd, Milford, Godalming, Surrey GU8 5BY) : [The Fellowship], [1977]. — [1],52,[1]p : ill, col map, ports ; 21cm.
Index.
Sd : Unpriced
(B77-20326)

617.6'007'1173 — Dentists. Professional education. *United States. Reports, surveys*
Carnegie Council on Policy Studies in Higher Education. Progress and problems in medical and dental education : federal support versus federal control : a report of the Carnegie Council on Policy Studies in Higher Education. — San Francisco [etc.] ; London : Jossey-Bass, 1976. — xiii,178p : ill, maps ; 24cm. — (Carnegie Council on Policy Studies in Higher Education. Series)
Bibl.: p.169-174. — Index.
ISBN 0-87589-295-7 : £5.65
Primary classification 610'.7'1173
(B77-05433)

617.6'01 — Dental hygiene
Current concepts in dental hygiene / edited by Suzanne Styers Boundy, Nancy J. Reynolds. — Saint Louis : Mosby ; London : Distributed by Kimpton, 1977. — xi,243p : ill, forms ; 25cm.
Bibl. — Index.
ISBN 0-8016-0735-3 : £10.35
(B77-18189)

Fulton, Bill. People want good teeth / [text by Bill Fulton] ; [designed and illustrated by Roy Petrie]. — Hamilton [Lanarkshire] ([14 Beckford St., Hamilton [Lanarkshire] ML3 0TA) : Lanarkshire Health Board, [1976]. — [8]p : chiefly ill ; 21cm.
ISBN 0-905453-02-6 Sd : £0.03
(B77-01540)

617.6'01 — Preventive dentistry
A **textbook** of preventive dentistry / [edited by] Robert C. Caldwell, Richard E. Stallard. — Philadelphia ; London [etc.] : Saunders, 1977. — xii,403p : ill, form, map ; 27cm.
Bibl. — Index.
ISBN 0-7216-2239-9 : £16.50
(B77-19429)

617.6'01'07 — Dental health education
Stoll, Frances Agnes. Dental health education : principles and methods for the education of individuals during dental treatment in the dental office, public health dental programs, school health curriculums. — 5th ed. / [by] Frances A. Stoll. — Philadelphia : Lea and Febiger ; London : Kimpton, 1977. — xvi, 235p : ill, facsims, forms, 2 maps, plan ; 27cm.
Previous ed.: / by Frances A. Stoll, Joan L. Catherman. 1972. — Bibl. — Index.
ISBN 0-8121-0579-6 : £8.25
(B77-16431)

617.6'07'57 — Dentistry. Diagnosis. Radiography
Mason, Rita A. A guide to dental radiography / [by] Rita A. Mason. — Bristol : J. Wright, 1977. — vii,136p : ill ; 22cm. — (A 'Dental practitioner' handbook ; no.27)
Bibl.: p.131. — Index.
ISBN 0-7236-0478-9 Pbk : £5.00 : CIP rev.
(B77-21921)

617.6'07'572 — Dentistry. Diagnosis. Radiography. Use of x-rays
O'Brien, Richard C. Dental radiography : an introduction for dental hygienists and assistants / [by] Richard C. O'Brien. — 3rd ed. — Philadelphia ; London [etc.] : Saunders, 1977. — viii,257p : ill ; 25cm.
Previous ed.: 1972. — Index.
ISBN 0-7216-6892-5 : £8.75
(B77-14759)

Wuehrmann, Arthur H. Dental radiology / [by] Arthur H. Wuehrmann, Lincoln R. Manson-Hing. — 4th ed. — Saint Louis : Mosby ; London : Distributed by Kimpton, 1977. — xiii,497p : ill ; 26cm.
Bibl.: p.474-485. — Index.
ISBN 0-8016-5642-7 : £18.70
(B77-19430)

617.6'32 — Man. Gums. Gingivitis
Cross, William George. Gingivitis / [by] W.G. Cross. — 2nd ed. — Bristol : J. Wright, 1977. — [7],44p,[8]p of plates : ill(some col) ; 22cm. — ('Dental practitioner' handbooks ; no.2)
Previous ed.: 1965. — Index.
ISBN 0-7236-0452-5 Pbk : £3.25
(B77-11250)

617.6'32 — Man. Periodontal diseases
Pawlak, Elizabeth A. Essentials of periodontics / [by] Elizabeth A. Pawlak, Philip M. Hoag ; with 132 illustrations by Christo M. Popoff. — Saint Louis : Mosby ; London : Distributed by Kimpton, 1976. — xi,153p : ill, forms ; 26cm.
Index.
ISBN 0-8016-3765-1 Sp : £6.95
(B77-03053)

Schluger, Saul. Periodontal disease : basic phenomena, clinical management, and occlusal and restorative interrelationships / [by] Saul Schluger, Ralph A. Yuodelis, Roy C. Page. — Philadelphia : Lea and Febiger ; London : Kimpton, 1977. — [12],737p : ill, port ; 29cm.
Bibl. — Index.
ISBN 0-8121-0558-3 : £36.35
(B77-30315)

617.6'34 — Dentistry. Endodontics
Ingle, John Ide. Endodontics. — 2nd ed. / [by] John Ide Ingle, Edward Edgerton Beveridge ; plates by Virginia E. Brooks ; 23 contributors. — Philadelphia : Lea and Febiger ; London : Kimpton, 1976. — xxiii,811p : ill, forms, port ; 29cm.
Text on lining paper. — Previous ed.: / by John Ide Ingle, 22 contributors ; plates by Virginia E. Brooks. Philadelphia : Lea and Febiger, 1965 ; London : Kimpton, 1966. — Index.
ISBN 0-8121-0542-7 : £24.40
(B77-01541)

Nicholls, Edward. Endodontics / [by] E. Nicholls. — 2nd ed. — Bristol : J. Wright, 1977. — [7],360p : ill ; 24cm.
Previous ed.: 1967. — Bibl. — Index.
ISBN 0-7236-0427-4 : £15.00 : CIP rev.
(B77-21922)

617.6'43 — Children. Teeth. Malocclusion. Therapy
Cohen, Meyer Michael. Minor tooth movement in the growing child / [by] M. Michael Cohen, with contributions by John R. Orr and Gerald Borell. — Philadelphia ; London [etc.] : Saunders, 1977. — xvi,143p : ill ; 27cm.
Bibl.: p.137-140. — Index.
ISBN 0-7216-2632-7 : £12.50
(B77-13681)

617.6'43 — Dentistry. Orthodontics
Begg, Percy Raymond. Begg orthodontic theory and technique. — 3rd ed. / [by] P.R. Begg, Peter C. Kesling. — Philadelphia ; London [etc.] : Saunders, 1977. — ii-xii,705p : ill ; 27cm.
Previous ed.: 1971. — Bibl. — Index.
ISBN 0-7216-1670-4 : £35.00
(B77-24981)

Current orthodontic concepts and techniques. — 2nd ed. / [edited by] T.M. Graber, Brainerd F. Swain. — Philadelphia ; London [etc.] : Saunders.
In 2 vols. — This ed. published in the United States: 1975. — Previous ed.: / edited by T.M. Graber. 1969.
Vol.1. — 1975 [i.e. 1976]. — ii-xvi,664,xxxvi p : ill, forms ; 27cm.
Index.
ISBN 0-7216-4187-3 : £49.50(set of 2 vols)
(B77-04237)

Vol.2. — 1975 [i.e. 1976]. — vi p,p665-1137,xxxvi p : ill ; 27cm.
Bibl.: p.1090-1094. — Index. — Index.
ISBN 0-7216-4188-1 : £49.50(set of 2 vols)
(B77-04238)

White, Thomas Cyril. Orthodontics for dental students / [by] T.C. White, J.H. Gardiner, B.C. Leighton. — 3rd ed. — London [etc.] : Macmillan, 1976. — ix,345p : ill ; 23cm.
Previous ed.: London : Staples Press, 1967. — Bibl.: p.321-333. — Index.
ISBN 0-333-19713-5 : £10.00
ISBN 0-333-19714-3 Pbk : £4.95
(B77-00790)

617.6'43 — Man. Teeth. Malocclusion. Myofunctional therapy
Myofunctional therapy / [edited by] Daniel Garliner. — Philadelphia ; London [etc.] : Saunders, 1976. — viii,443p : ill ; 27cm.
Bibl. — Index.
ISBN 0-7216-4055-9 : £24.00
(B77-15320)

617.6'43'0028 — Man. Removable orthodontic appliances. Design & construction
Houston, William John Ballantyne. Orthodontic treatment with removable appliances / [by] W.J.B. Houston and K.G. Isaacson. — Bristol : J. Wright, 1977. — vii,144p : ill ; 22cm. — (A 'Dental practitioner' handbook ; no.25)
Bibl. — Index.
ISBN 0-7236-0461-4 Pbk : £5.00 : CIP rev.
(B77-18190)

617.6'75 — Man. Teeth. Cavities. Fillings: Silver amalgams
Gainsford, Ian Derek. Silver amalgam in clinical practice / [by] I.D. Gainsford. — 2nd ed. — Bristol : J. Wright, 1976. — [7],111p : ill ; 23cm. — ('Dental practitioner' handbooks ; no.1)
Previous ed.: 1965. — Bibl.: p.99-105. — Index.
ISBN 0-7236-0372-3 Pbk : £4.25
(B77-01542)

617.6'9 — Prosthetic dentistry
Basker, R M. Prosthetic treatment of the edentulous patient / [by] R.M. Basker, J.C. Davenport, H.R. Tomlin. — London [etc.] : Macmillan, 1976. — xiii,193p : ill ; 24cm.
Bibl. — Index.
ISBN 0-333-19715-1 : £10.00
ISBN 0-333-19717-8 Pbk : £4.95
(B77-04239)

617.6'9'028 — Prosthetic dentistry. Laboratory techniques
Hudis, Morris Mac. Dental laboratory prosthodontics / [by] Morris Mac Hudis. — Philadelphia ; London [etc.] : Saunders, 1977. — xv,425p : ill ; 26cm.
Bibl. — Index.
ISBN 0-7216-4794-4 : £16.00
(B77-14760)

617.6'92 — Man. Fixed dentures. Bridges & crowns. *Manuals*
Horn, Harold R. Practical considerations for successful crown and bridge therapy : biologic considerations, psychologic considerations, preventive factors / [by] Harold R. Horn. — Philadelphia ; London [etc.] : Saunders, 1976. — xiv,312p : ill ; 27cm.
Index.
ISBN 0-7216-4783-9 : £20.00
(B77-13682)

617.6'92 — Man. Full dentures. Design
Watt, David M. Designing complete dentures / [by] David M. Watt, A.R. MacGregor. — Philadelphia ; London [etc.] : Saunders, 1976. — x,414p : ill ; 26cm.
Index.
ISBN 0-7216-9137-4 : £18.00
(B77-04240)

617.6'92 — Man. Partial dentures
McCracken, William Lionel. McCracken's removable partial prosthodontics. — 5th ed. / [by] Davis Henderson, Victor L. Steffel. — Saint Louis : Mosby ; London : Distributed by Kimpton, 1977. — xvii,457p : ill, forms ; 27cm.

Previous ed.: 1973. — Bibl.: p.427-443. — Index.
ISBN 0-8016-2141-0 : £17.05
(B77-21186)

617.6'92 — Man. Partial dentures. Construction. *Laboratory manuals*
Neill, Derrick James. Partial denture prosthetics / [by] D.J. Neill, J.D. Walter. — Oxford [etc.] : Blackwell Scientific, 1977. — vii, 111p : ill ; 22cm.
Bibl.: p.107-108. — Index.
ISBN 0-632-00006-6 Pbk : £4.75 : CIP rev.
(B77-06137)

617.6'95 — Dental materials
Anderson, John Neil. Applied dental materials / [by] John N. Anderson. — 5th ed. — Oxford [etc.] : Blackwell Scientific, 1976. — ix,425p : ill ; 23cm.
Previous ed.: 1972. — Bibl.: p.416. — Index.
ISBN 0-632-00028-7 : £11.00
(B77-06138)

Phillips, Ralph Wilbur. Elements of dental materials for dental hygienists and assistants / [by] Ralph W. Phillips. — 3rd ed. — Philadelphia ; London [etc.] : Saunders, 1977. — xi,376p : ill ; 25cm.
Previous ed.: 1971. — Bibl. — Index.
ISBN 0-7216-7232-9 : £8.50
(B77-33263)

617.7 — OPHTHALMOLOGY
Scheie, Harold Glendon. Textbook of ophthalmology. — 9th ed. / [by] Harold G. Scheie, Daniel M. Albert. — Philadelphia ; London [etc.] : Saunders, 1977. — ii-xv,616p : ill(some col) ; 27cm.
Previous ed.: published as 'Adler's textbook of ophthalmology'. 1969. — Bibl. — Index.
ISBN 0-7216-7951-x : £19.50
(B77-24270)

Scientific foundations of ophthalmology / edited by Edward S. Perkins and David W. Hill. — London : Heinemann Medical, 1977. — xiv, 337p : ill ; 29cm.
Bibl. — Index.
ISBN 0-433-25015-1 : £25.00
(B77-33849)

617.7 — Man. Eyes. Xerophthalmia. Effects of vitamin A deficiency. *Reports, surveys*
Meeting on Vitamin A Deficiency and Xerophthalmia. Vitamin A deficiency and xerophthalmia : report of a joint WHO/USAID meeting. — Geneva : World Health Organization ; [London] : [H.M.S.O.], 1976. — 88p,4p of plates : ill(some col) ; 20cm. — (World Health Organization. Technical report series ; no.590)
'A Meeting on Vitamin A Deficiency and Xerophthalmia was convened jointly by WHO and USAID ...' - page 5.
Pbk : £2.50
ISBN 92-4-120590-3
(B77-01543)

617.7 — Ophthalmology. *Reviews of research*
Current concepts in ophthalmology. — Saint Louis : Mosby ; London : Distributed by Kimpton.
Vol.5 / editors Herbert E. Kaufman, Thom J. Zimmerman. — 1976. — xi,297p,plate : ill(some col) ; 26cm.
Bibl. — Index.
ISBN 0-8016-2627-7 : £28.05
(B77-03580)

617.7'026 — Man. Eyes. Diseases & injuries. Emergency treatment
Handbook of ophthalmologic emergencies : a guide for emergencies in ophthalmology / [edited] by George M. Gombos. — 2nd ed. — London : Kimpton, 1977. — 291p : ill ; 22cm.
Previous ed.: 1973. — Bibl. — Index.
ISBN 0-87488-633-3 : £8.25
(B77-27900)

617.7'06 — Man. Eyes. Diseases. Natural remedies
Bates, William H. The Bates method for better eyesight without glasses / by William H. Bates. — [New and revised ed.]. — London : Souvenir Press, 1977. — [7],200p,fold plate : ill ; 23cm.
This ed. originally published: New York : H. Holt, 1968.
ISBN 0-285-62302-8 : £3.50
(B77-27901)

617.7'06 — Man. Eyes. Therapy
Gordon's medical management of ocular disease. — 2nd ed. / editor Edward A. Dunlap. — Hagerstown [etc.] ; London : Harper and Row, Medical Department, 1976. — xvii,345p,plate : ill(some col) ; 26cm.
Previous ed.: published as 'Medical management of ocular disease' / edited by Daniel Morris Gordon. New York : Harper and Row, 1964. — Bibl. — Index.
ISBN 0-06-140730-5 : £26.35
(B77-21187)

617.7'1 — Man. Eyes. Diagnosis
Keeney, Arthur Hail. Ocular examination : basis and technique / [by] Arthur H. Keeney. — 2nd ed. — Saint Louis ; Mosby ; London : Distributed by Kimpton, 1976. — xiii,322p : ill, forms ; 27cm.
Previous ed.: 1970. — Bibl. — Index.
ISBN 0-8016-2632-3 : £17.50
(B77-04867)

617.7'1 — Man. Eyes. Diagnosis. Radiography. Use of radioisotopes
Nuclear ophthalmology / edited by Millard N. Croll ... [et al.]. — New York ; London [etc.] : Wiley, 1976. — xvii,284p : ill ; 27cm. — (Wiley series in diagnostic and therapeutic radiology)
'A Wiley Medical publication'. — Index.
ISBN 0-471-01388-9 : £19.25
(B77-00259)

O'Rourke, James. Nuclear ophthalmology : dynamic function studies in intraocular disease / [by] J. O'Rourke. — Philadelphia ; London [etc.] : Saunders, 1976. — xi,156p : ill ; 24cm.
Bibl. — Index.
ISBN 0-7216-7009-1 : £11.75
(B77-00260)

617.7'1 — Man. Eyes. Histoplasmosis
Schlaegel, Theodore F. Ocular histoplasmosis / by T.F. Schlaegel, Jr. — New York [etc.] ; London : Grune and Stratton, 1977. — xv, 301p : ill, form, maps, ports ; 24cm. — (Current ophthalmology monographs)
Index.
ISBN 0-8089-0994-0 : £20.95
(B77-30316)

617.7'1 — Ophthalmology. Plastic surgery. Techniques
Fox, Sydney A. Ophthalmic plastic surgery / [by] Sydney A. Fox. — 5th ed. — New York [etc.] ; London : Grune and Stratton, 1976. — xviii,666p : ill ; 26cm.
Previous ed.: New York : Grune and Stratton, 1970. — Bibl. — Index.
ISBN 0-8089-0966-5 : £25.65
(B77-06139)

617.7'13 — Man. Eyes. Injuries. Therapy
Paton, David. Management of ocular injuries / [by] David Paton, Morton F. Goldberg. — [Expanded ed.]. — Philadelphia ; London [etc.] : Saunders, 1976. — xiv,381p : ill ; 21cm.
Previous ed.: published as 'Injuries of the eye, the lids and the orbit'. Philadelphia : Saunders, 1968. — Bibl.: p.347-360. — Index.
ISBN 0-7216-7106-3 : £13.25
(B77-01544)

617.7'19 — Man. Eyes. Scleritis
Watson, Peter Gordon. The sclera and systemic disorders / [by] Peter G. Watson, Brian L. Hazleman. — London [etc.] : Saunders, 1976. — xii,458p,[2]p of plates : ill(some col) ; 24cm. — (Major problems in ophthalmology ; vol.2)
Bibl. — Index.
ISBN 0-7216-9134-x : £15.00
(B77-04868)

617.7'2 — Man. Eyes. Choroids. Genetic disorders
Krill, Alex E. Hereditary retinal and choroidal diseases / [by] Alex E. Krill. — Hagerstown [etc.] ; London : Harper and Row.
In 2 vols.
Vol.2 : chapters 8-25 : Clinical characteristics / [by] Alex E. Krill with the special assistance of Desmond B. Archer with 13 contributors. — 1977. — xv p,p355-1371,[2]p of plates : ill(some col), port ; 25cm.
Vol.2 has title: Krill's hereditary retinal and choroidal diseases. — Bibl. — Index.
ISBN 0-06-141491-3 : Unpriced
Primary classification 617.7'3
(B77-20327)

617.7'2 — Man. Eyes. Choroids. Photocoagulation. *Conference proceedings*
International Photocoagulation Congress, *New York, 1975.* Current diagnosis and management of chorioretinal diseases / edited by Francis A. L'Esperance, Jr. — Saint Louis : Mosby ; London : Distributed by Kimpton, 1977. — xix, 573p,plate : ill(some col) ; 27cm.
'[Proceedings of] ... the International Photocoagulation Congress - convened from September 28 to October 1, 1975, at the Waldorf-Astoria Hotel in New York City' - Preface. — Bibl. — Index.
ISBN 0-8016-2949-7 : £50.80
Also classified at 617.7'3
(B77-25679)

617.7'3 — Man. Eyes. Macular region. Diseases
Gass, John Donald MacIntyre. Stereoscopic atlas of macular diseases : diagnosis and treatment / [by] J. Donald M. Gass. — 2nd ed. — Saint Louis : Mosby ; London : Distributed by Kimpton, 1977. — xi,411p : ill ; 29cm.
Text on lining paper. — 19 'View-master' reels (col. ill.) in pockets. — Previous ed.: 1970. — Bibl. — Index.
ISBN 0-8016-1754-5 : £52.00
(B77-23471)

617.7'3 — Man. Eyes. Retinas. Diseases
Tolentino, Felipe I. Vitreoretinal disorders : diagnosis and management / by Felipe I. Tolentino, Charles L. Schepens, H. Mackenzie Freeman ; illustrated by David A. Tilden. — Philadelphia ; London [etc.] : Saunders, 1976 [i.e. 1977]. — ii-xvii,659p : ill(some col) ; 27cm.

Published in the United States: 1976. — Index.
ISBN 0-7216-8870-5 : £48.00
Primary classification 617.7'46
(B77-07395)

617.7'3 — Man. Eyes. Retinas. Genetic disorders
Krill, Alex E. Hereditary retinal and choroidal diseases / [by] Alex E. Krill. — Hagerstown [etc.] ; London : Harper and Row.
In 2 vols.
Vol.2 : chapters 8-25 : Clinical characteristics / [by] Alex E. Krill with the special assistance of Desmond B. Archer with 13 contributors. — 1977. — xv p,p355-1371,[2]p of plates : ill(some col), port ; 25cm.
Vol.2 has title: Krill's hereditary retinal and choroidal diseases. — Bibl. — Index.
ISBN 0-06-141491-3 : Unpriced
Also classified at 617.7'2
(B77-20327)

617.7'3 — Man. Eyes. Retinas. Photocoagulation. *Conference proceedings*
International Photocoagulation Congress, *New York, 1975.* Current diagnosis and management of chorioretinal diseases / edited by Francis A. L'Esperance, Jr. — Saint Louis : Mosby ; London : Distributed by Kimpton, 1977. — xix, 573p,plate : ill(some col) ; 27cm.
'[Proceedings of] ... the International Photocoagulation Congress - convened from September 28 to October 1, 1975, at the Waldorf-Astoria Hotel in New York City' - Preface. — Bibl. — Index.
ISBN 0-8016-2949-7 : £50.80
Primary classification 617.7'2
(B77-25679)

617.7'3 — Man. Eyes. Retinas. Photocoagulation. Use of argon lasers
Zweng, H Christian. Argon laser photocoagulation / [by] H. Christian Zweng, Hunter L. Little in collaboration with Arthur Vassiliadis. — Saint Louis : Mosby ; London : Distributed by Kimpton, 1977. — xi,319p : ill ; 26cm.
Index.
ISBN 0-8016-5706-7 : £34.00
(B77-30317)

617.7'3 — Man. Eyes. Retinas. Surgery. *Conference proceedings*
New and controversial aspects of vitreoretinal surgery / editor Alice McPherson. — Saint Louis : Mosby ; London : Distributed by Kimpton, 1977. — xviii,455p : ill(some col) ; 27cm.
Proceedings of an international symposium on vitreous surgery, held at the Texas Medical Center, Houston, April 10-12, 1975. — Bibl. — Index.
ISBN 0-8016-3321-4 : £39.60
Also classified at 617.7'46
(B77-29478)

617.7'41 — Man. Eyes. Glaucoma. Diagnosis & therapy

Becker, Bernard. Becker-Shaffer's diagnosis and therapy of the glaucomas. — 4th ed. / [by] Allan E. Kolker, John Hetherington, Jr. — Saint Louis : Mosby ; London : Distributed by Kimpton, 1976. — ix,526p,[5]leaves of plates,[4]p of plates : ill(some col) ; 26cm.
Three Viewmaster reels in pockets. — Previous ed.: 1970. — Bibl. — Index.
ISBN 0-8016-2720-6 : £37.50
(B77-06140)

617.7'42 — Man. Eyes. Cataracts. Surgery

Jaffe, Norman S. Cataract surgery and its complications / [by] Norman S. Jaffe. — 2nd ed. — Saint Louis : Mosby ; London : Distributed by Kimpton, 1976. — xii,503p : ill ; 27cm.
Previous ed.: Saint Louis : Mosby, 1972. — Index.
ISBN 0-8016-2403-7 : £39.45
(B77-03054)

617.7'46 — Man. Eyes. Vitreous bodies. Diseases

Tolentino, Felipe I. Vitreoretinal disorders : diagnosis and management / by Felipe I. Tolentino, Charles L. Schepens, H. Mackenzie Freeman ; illustrated by David A. Tilden. — Philadelphia ; London [etc.] : Saunders, 1976 [i.e. 1977]. — ii-xvii,659p : ill(some col) ; 27cm.

Published in the United States: 1976. — Index.
ISBN 0-7216-8870-5 : £48.00
Also classified at 617.7'3
(B77-07395)

617.7'46 — Man. Eyes. Vitreous bodies. Surgery. *Conference proceedings*

New and controversial aspects of vitreoretinal surgery / editor Alice McPherson. — Saint Louis : Mosby ; London : Distributed by Kimpton, 1977. — xviii,455p : ill(some col) ; 27cm.
Proceedings of an international symposium on vitreous surgery, held at the Texas Medical Center, Houston, April 10-12, 1975. — Bibl. — Index.
ISBN 0-8016-3321-4 : £39.60
Primary classification 617.7'3
(B77-29478)

617.7'523 — Man. Contact lenses

Bier, Norman. Contact lens correction. — [New ed.] / [by] Norman Bier and Gerald E. Lowther. — London [etc.] : Butterworth, 1977. — viii,520p,leaf of plate,[14]p of plates : ill(some col) ; 26cm.
Previous ed.: i.e. 2nd ed., published as 'Contact lens routine and practice' / by Norman Bier. 1957. — Bibl. — Index.
ISBN 0-407-00101-8 : £28.00
(B77-14761)

617.7'55 — Man. Eyes. Refraction disorders. Therapy. Use of ophthalmic lenses, to 1976

Levene, John Reuben. Clinical refraction and visual science / [by] John R. Levene. — London [etc.] : Butterworth, 1977. — xiv,346p : ill, facsims, geneal table, ports ; 23cm.
Bibl.: p.317-321. — Index.
ISBN 0-407-00043-7 : £12.00
(B77-13075)

617.7'62 — Man. Eyes. Strabismus. Surgery

Helveston, Eugene McGillis. Atlas of strabismus surgery / [by] Eugene M. Helveston. — 2nd ed. — Saint Louis : Mosby ; London : Distributed by Kimpton, 1977. — xvii,262p : ill ; 29cm.
Previous ed.: 1973. — Bibl.: p.247-249. — Index.
ISBN 0-8016-2138-0 : £28.40
(B77-29479)

617.7'64 — Man. Eyes. Lacrimal apparatus. Diseases

Veirs, Everett R. Lacrimal disorders : diagnosis and treatment / [by] Everett R. Veirs. — Saint Louis : Mosby ; London : Distributed by Kimpton, 1976. — ix,179p : ill ; 26cm.
Bibl. — Index.
ISBN 0-8016-5233-2 : Unpriced
(B77-03581)

617.7'71 — Man. Eyes. Eyelids. Plastic surgery. *Conference proceedings*

Orbital Plastic Surgery Symposium, *Dallas, 1974.* Symposium on plastic surgery in the orbital region : proceedings of the symposium of the Educational Foundation of the American Society of Plastic and Reconstructive Surgeons, Inc. held at Dallas, Texas, March 18-20, 1974 / editors Paul Tessier ... [et al.]. — Saint Louis : Mosby ; London : Distributed by Kimpton, 1976. — xiii,480p : ill ; 29cm. — (American Society of Plastic and Reconstructive Surgeons. Educational Foundation. Symposia ; vol.12)
'... the Orbital Plastic Surgery Symposium held in Dallas in 1974 ...' - Preface. — Bibl. — Index.
ISBN 0-8016-4871-8 : £46.75
Primary classification 617.7'8
(B77-06719)

617.7'71 — Man. Eyes. Eyelids. Ptosis. Surgery

Beard, Crowell. Ptosis / [by] Crowell Beard ; medical illustrations Joan Esperson Weddell. — 2nd ed. — Saint Louis : Mosby ; London : Distributed by Kimpton, 1976. — xi,288p : ill ; 29cm.
Previous ed.: 1969. — Bibl. — Index.
ISBN 0-8016-0531-8 : £26.40
(B77-18821)

617.7'8 — Man. Eyes. Orbits. Plastic surgery. *Conference proceedings*

Orbital Plastic Surgery Symposium, *Dallas, 1974.* Symposium on plastic surgery in the orbital region : proceedings of the symposium of the Educational Foundation of the American Society of Plastic and Reconstructive Surgeons, Inc. held at Dallas, Texas, March 18-20, 1974 / editors Paul Tessier ... [et al.]. — Saint Louis : Mosby ; London : Distributed by Kimpton, 1976. — xiii,480p : ill ; 29cm. — (American Society of Plastic and Reconstructive Surgeons. Educational Foundation. Symposia ; vol.12)
'... the Orbital Plastic Surgery Symposium held in Dallas in 1974 ...' - Preface. — Bibl. — Index.
ISBN 0-8016-4871-8 : £46.75
Also classified at 617.7'71
(B77-06719)

617.8 — DISEASES OF THE EAR

617'.8 — Man. Deafness

Ballantyne, John. Deafness / [by] John Ballantyne. — 3rd ed. — Edinburgh [etc.] : Churchill Livingstone, 1977. — [12],250p : ill ; 22cm.
Previous ed.: London : Churchill, 1970. — Bibl. : p.236-240. — Index.
ISBN 0-443-01602-x Pbk : £3.75
(B77-24982)

617.8 — Man. Genetic deafness

Konigsmark, Bruce W. Genetic and metabolic deafness / [by] Bruce W. Konigsmark, Robert J. Gorlin. — Philadelphia ; London [etc.] : Saunders, 1976. — ii-xx,419p : ill, port ; 27cm.
Bibl. — Index.
ISBN 0-7216-5489-4 : £26.50
(B77-01545)

617.8 — Man. Hearing disorders. *Conference proceedings*

British Society of Audiology. *Conference, 2nd, University of Southampton, 1975.* Disorders of the auditory function II : proceedings of the British Society of Audiology Second Conference, held at the University of Southampton, from 16-18 July 1975 / edited by S.D.G. Stephens. — London [etc.] : Academic Press, 1976. — xi,311p,[114]p of plates,[13]leaves of plates : ill ; 24cm.
Bibl. — Index.
ISBN 0-12-665750-5 : £9.60
(B77-05462)

617.8'8 — Man. Cochlea. Electrocochleography. *Conference proceedings*

Electrocochleography / edited by Robert J. Ruben, Claus Elberling, Gerhard Salomon. — Baltimore ; London [etc.] : University Park Press, [1977]. — xvii,506p : ill, ports ; 24cm.
'Proceedings of a symposium on electrocochleography held June 12-14, 1974 at the Department of Otorhinolaryngology, Albert Einstein College of Medicine, Yeshiva University, Bronx, New York' - Library of Congress Cataloging in Publication data. — Published in the United States: 1976. — Bibl. — Index.
ISBN 0-8391-0846-x : £17.50
(B77-11860)

617.8'8'075 — Man. Inner ears. Diagnosis

Neuro-otological examination : with special reference to equilibrium function tests / [by] Takuya Uemura ... [et al.]. — Baltimore ; London : University Park Press [etc.], 1977. — x,178p : ill ; 27cm.
Bibl.: p.161-174. — Index.
ISBN 0-8391-0887-7 : £28.25
(B77-21188)

617.8'9'028 — Man. Hearing. Testing. Instrumentation

McPherson, David L. Instrumentation in the hearing sciences / [by] David L. McPherson, John W. Thatcher ; illustrations by Diane McPherson. — New York [etc.] ; London : Grune and Stratton, 1977. — ix,181p : ill ; 24cm.
Index.
ISBN 0-8089-1005-1 : £10.30
(B77-29480)

617.9 — SURGICAL TECHNIQUES AND SPECIALITIES

617'.91 — Medicine. Surgery. Operations

Operative surgery : fundamental international techniques / under the general editorship of Charles Rob and Sir Rodney Smith ; associate editor Hugh Dudley. — 3rd ed. — London [etc.] : Butterworth.
In 18 vols. — Previous ed.: published in 14 vols, 1969-1971.
[Colon, rectum and anus] / [edited by Ian P. Todd]. — 1977. — xv,412p : ill ; 29cm.
Index.
ISBN 0-407-00606-0 : £23.00
(B77-15890)

[Gynaecology and obstetrics] / [edited by D.W.T. Roberts]. — 1977. — xiii,212p : ill ; 29cm.
Index.
ISBN 0-407-00615-x : £14.00
(B77-15891)

[The hand] / [edited by R. Guy Pulvertaft]. — 1977. — xiii,407p,plate : ill(some col) ; 29cm.
Bibl. — Index.
ISBN 0-407-00618-4 : £25.00
(B77-11861)

[Urology] / edited by D. Innes Williams]. — 1977. — xvii,468p : ill ; 29cm.
ISBN 0-407-00612-5 : £28.00 : CIP rev.
(B77-13683)

[Vascular surgery] / [edited by Charles Rob]. — 1976. — xiv,354p,plate : ill(some col) ; 29cm.
Bibl. — Index.
ISBN 0-407-00644-3 : £25.00
(B77-00791)

Shipman, John Jeffrey. Operative surgery revision / [by] John J. Shipman. — 3rd ed. — London : H.K. Lewis, 1977. — vii,183p ; 23cm.

Previous ed.: 1969. — Index.
ISBN 0-7186-0429-6 : £5.00
(B77-18822)

617'.91 — Medicine. Surgery. Operations by spiritualist mediums

Stelter, Alfred. Psi-healing / [by] Alfred Stelter ; translated from the German by Ruth Hein. — Toronto [etc.] ; London : Bantam, 1976. — ix, 308,[1]p ; 18cm.
Originally published: in German. München : Scherz, 1976. — Bibl.: p.281-299. — Index.
ISBN 0-552-62505-1 Pbk : £0.75
(B77-15321)

617'.91 — Medicine. Surgery. Operations by spiritualist mediums. Arigo, José. *Brazil. Biographies*

Fuller, John Grant. Arigo : surgeon of the rusty knife / [by] John G. Fuller ; afterword by Henry K. Puharich. — St Albans : Panther, 1977. — 253,[16]p of plates : ill, facsims, ports ; 18cm.
Originally published: New York : Crowell, 1974 ; London : Hart-Davis MacGibbon, 1975. — Bibl.: p.241-243. — Index.
ISBN 0-586-04253-9 Pbk : £0.75
(B77-09729)

617'.917 — Hospitals. Operating theatres. Safety measures

Safety in the operating theatre / collating editors J.F. Mainland, H.A.F. Dudley ; [for] the Royal Australasian College of Surgeons. — London [etc.] : Edward Arnold, 1976. — vii,167p : ill, forms, plans ; 25cm.
Bibl. — Index.
ISBN 0-7131-4263-4 : £29.50
(B77-02364)

617'.919 — Medicine. Surgery. Physiotherapy
Cash, Joan Elizabeth. Physiotherapy in some surgical conditions / [by] Joan E. Cash. — 5th ed. — London : Faber, 1977. — 318p,[16]p of plates : ill ; 23cm.
Previous ed.: 1971. — Bibl. — Index.
ISBN 0-571-04910-9 : £7.25
ISBN 0-571-04911-7 Pbk : £4.95
(B77-15892)

617'.95 — Man. Artificial organs
Rorvik, David Michael. As man becomes machine : the evolution of the cyborg / [by] David M. Rorvik. — London : Abacus, 1975. — 205p ; 20cm.
Originally published: Garden City, N.Y. : Doubleday, 1971 ; London : Souvenir Press, 1973. — Index.
ISBN 0-349-13035-3 Pbk : £1.00
(B77-18823)

617'.95 — Man. Organs & tissues. Transplantation. Immunological aspects. *Conference proceedings*
Humoral Factors in Transplantation *(Conference), New York, 1975.* Humoral aspects of transplantation / edited by Albert L. Rubin and Kurt H. Stenzel. — New York [etc.] ; London : Grune and Stratton, 1976. — [8],152p : ill ; 26cm.
'Proceedings of the Second Rogosin Kidney Center Symposium, Humoral Factors in Transplantation, The New York Hospital - Cornell Medical Center, New York, N.Y., September 26-27, 1975' - note. — '"Humoral Aspects of Transplantation" is the hardcover edition of the June 1976 issue (Volume VIII, Number 2) of the quarterly journal "Transplantation Proceedings" ...' - title page verso. — Bibl. — Index.
ISBN 0-8089-0963-0 : £9.45
(B77-03055)

617'.95 — Medicine. Plastic surgery. *Conference proceedings*
Symposium on Basic Science in Plastic Surgery, *New Haven, 1975.* Symposium on Basic Science in Plastic Surgery : proceedings of the Symposium of the Educational Foundation of the American Society of Plastic and Reconstructive Surgeons, Inc., held at New Haven, Connecticut, April 7-9, 1975 / editors Thomas J. Krizek, John E. Hoopes. — Saint Louis : Mosby ; London : Distributed by Kimpton, 1976. — xii,293p : ill, facsims, maps, ports ; 29cm. — (American Society of Plastic and Reconstructive Surgeons. Educational Foundation. [Symposia] ; vol.15)
Bibl. — Index.
ISBN 0-8016-2746-x : £34.55
(B77-08420)

617'.95 — Medicine. Plastic surgery. Microsurgery. *Conference proceedings*
International Symposium on Microsurgery, *New York City, 1974.* Symposium on microsurgery : proceedings of the Symposium of the Educational Foundation of the American Society of Plastic and Reconstructive Surgeons Inc., held in New York City, October 14-18, 1974 / eeitors Avron I. Daniller, Berish Strauch. — Saint Louis : Mosby ; London : Distributed by Kimpton, 1976. — x,257p : ill ; 29cm. — (American Society of Plastic and Reconstructive Surgeons. Educational Foundation. Symposia ; vol.14)
'... the first large International Symposium on Microsurgery ...' - Preface. — Bibl. — Index.
ISBN 0-8016-1202-0 : £30.50
(B77-07936)

617.95'005 — Medicine. Prosthetics. *Periodicals*
Prosthetics and orthotics international. — Hellerup : International Society for Prosthetics and Orthotics ; Glasgow (University of Strathclyde, 73 Rottenrow, Glasgow G4 0NG) : 'Prosthetics and orthotics international'.
[Vol.1, no.1]- ; [Apr. 1977]-. — [1977]-. — ill ; 25cm.
Three issues a year. — iv,70p. in 1st issue. — Bibl.
Pbk : Unpriced
ISSN 0309-3646
Primary classification 617'.307'05
(B77-16915)

617'.96 — Medicine. Anaesthesia
Atkinson, Richard Stuart. A synopsis of anaesthesia. — 8th ed. / [by] R.S. Atkinson and G.B. Rushman ; contributing editor J. Alfred Lee. — Bristol : J. Wright, 1977. — viii, 986p : ill ; 19cm.
Spine title: Anaesthesia. — Index.
ISBN 0-7236-0442-8 : £9.25
(B77-24985)

Catron, Donald G. The anesthesiologist's handbook / [by] Donald G. Catron. — 2nd ed. — Baltimore ; London [etc.] : University Park Press, 1976. — ix,201p : ill ; 18cm.
Previous ed.: 1972. — Index.
ISBN 0-8391-0956-3 Sp : £6.50
(B77-14263)

617'.96 — Medicine. Anaesthesiology. *Conference proceedings*
World Congress of Anaesthesiology, *6th, Mexico City, 1976.* Anaesthesiology : proceedings of the VI World Congress of Anaesthesiology, Mexico City, April 24-30, 1976 / editors Enrique Hülsz ... [et al.]. — Amsterdam ; Oxford ([256 Banbury Rd, Oxford OX2 7DH]) : Excerpta Medica, 1977. — xvi,564p : ill, forms, map ; 25cm.
Bibl. — Index.
£42.00
ISBN 90-219-0327-x
(B77-23472)

617'.96'024613 — Medicine. Anaesthesia. *For nursing*
Norris, Walter. A nurse's guide to anaesthetics, resuscitation and intensive care / [by] the late Walter Norris, Donald Campbell ; foreword by Margaret C.N. Lamb. — 6th ed. — Edinburgh [etc.] : Churchill Livingstone, 1975. — ix,159p : ill ; 22cm. — (Livingstone nursing texts)
Previous ed.: 1972. — Index.
ISBN 0-443-01345-4 Pbk : £2.75
(B77-10822)

617'.967'412 — Man. Heart. Anaesthesia
Branthwaite, Margaret Annie. Anaesthesia for cardiac surgery and allied procedures / [by] M.A. Branthwaite ; with a contribution by D.J. Hatch ; foreword by M.K. Sykes. — Oxford [etc.] : Blackwell Scientific, 1977. — xi,203p : ill ; 24cm.
Bibl. — Index.
ISBN 0-632-00369-3 : £8.25 : CIP rev.
(B77-15893)

617'.967'461 — Man. Kidneys. Effects of anaesthesia
Bastron, R Dennis. Anesthesia and the kidney / [by] R. Dennis Bastron, Stanley Deutsch. — New York [etc.] ; London : Grune and Stratton, [1977]. — xiii,98p : ill ; 24cm. — (The scientific basis of clinical anesthesia)
Published in the United States: 1976. — Index.
ISBN 0-8089-0974-6 : £7.15
(B77-13684)

617'.967'6 — Dentistry. Analgesia. Use of nitrous oxide
Langa, Harry. Relative analgesia in dental practice : inhalation analgesia and sedation with nitrous oxide / [by] Harry Langa with contributions by Harold Diner ... [et al.]. — 2nd ed. — Philadelphia ; London [etc.] : Saunders, 1976. — xv,419p : ill, forms, port ; 26cm.
Previous ed.: 1968. — Bibl. — Index.
ISBN 0-7216-5621-8 : £15.50
(B77-14762)

617'.9682 — Childbirth. Labour. Anaesthesia & analgesia
Moir, Donald Dundas. Obstetric anaesthesia and analgesia / [by] Donald D. Moir ; with a contribution by Matthew J. Carty. — London : Baillière Tindall, 1976. — x,293p : ill ; 24cm.
Bibl. — Index.
ISBN 0-7020-0608-4 : £8.00
(B77-06141)

617'.97 — Old persons. Surgery
The **aged** and high risk surgical patient : medical, surgical, and anesthetic management / edited by John H. Siegel, Peter Chodoff. — New York [etc.] ; London : Grune and Stratton, 1976. — xix,920p ; 26cm. — (Modern surgical monographs)
Bibl. — Index.
ISBN 0-8089-0935-5 : Unpriced
(B77-08421)

Surgery in the aged / [edited] by Lazar J. Greenfield. — Philadelphia ; London [etc.] : Saunders, 1975 [i.e. 1977]. — ii-xii,151p : ill ; 25cm. — (Major problems in clinical surgery ; vol.17)
Cover title: Surgery of the aged. — Published in the United States: 1975. — Bibl. — Index.
ISBN 0-7216-4250-0 : £10.50
(B77-10392)

617'.98 — Babies, to 6 months. Surgery
Redo, S Frank. Principles of surgery in the first six months of life / [by] S. Frank Redo ; with a contribution by Alfred N. Krauss. — Hagerstown, Md [etc.] ; London : Harper and Row, 1976. — xi,180p : ill, facsim ; 26cm.
Bibl. — Index.
ISBN 0-06-142238-x : £16.85
(B77-08422)

617'.98 — Children. Surgery
Royal Children's Hospital, *Melbourne.* Clinical paediatric surgery : diagnosis and management / by the staff of the Royal Children's Hospital, Melbourne ; compiled and edited by Peter G. Jones. — 2nd ed. — Oxford [etc.] : Blackwell Scientific, 1976. — xiv,586p : ill(some col), forms ; 24cm.
Previous ed.: Bristol : J. Wright, 1970. — Bibl. — Index.
ISBN 0-632-00436-3 : £10.00
(B77-08423)

618 — GYNAECOLOGY AND OBSTETRICS
Chamberlain, Geoffrey. A practice of obstetrics and gynaecology / [by] Geoffrey Chamberlain, C.J. Dewhurst ; with a contribution on the social and community aspects of obstetrics and gynaecology by Mark McCarthy. — Tunbridge Wells : Pitman Medical, 1977. — [6],271p : ill ; 23cm.
Bibl.: p.257. — Index.
ISBN 0-272-79388-4 : £6.00
(B77-07396)

Gynecology and obstetrics : the health care of women / [edited by] Seymour L. Romney ... [et al.]. — New York ; London [etc.] : McGraw-Hill, 1975. — xix,1163p : ill ; 27cm.
'A Blakiston publication'. — Bibl. — Index.
ISBN 0-07-053581-7 : £17.40
(B77-00792)

Llewellyn-Jones, Derek. Fundamentals of obstetrics and gynaecology / [by] Derek Llewellyn-Jones. — 2nd ed. — London : Faber.

Previous ed.: 1969.
Vol.1 : Obstetrics. — 1977. — 3-471p : ill(some col), map ; 26cm.
Bibl.: p.451-453. — Index.
ISBN 0-571-04913-3 : £12.00
ISBN 0-571-04914-1 Pbk : Unpriced
(B77-25681)

Obstetrics and gynecology / with 73 authors ; editor David N. Danforth ; associate editor ... [others]. — 3rd ed. — New York [etc.] ; London : Harper and Row, 1977. — xxv, 1206p : ill ; 26cm.
Previous ed.: published as 'Textbook of obstetrics and gynecology'. 1971. — Bibl. — Index.
ISBN 0-06-140684-8 : £31.00
(B77-25682)

Page, Ernest Winslow. Human reproduction : the core content of obstetrics and gynecology and perinatal medicine / [by] Ernest W. Page, Claude A. Villee, Dorothy B. Villee. — 2nd ed. — Philadelphia ; London [etc.] : Saunders, 1976 [i.e. 1977]. — xvii,471p : ill ; 25cm.
This ed. published in the United States: 1976. — Previous ed.: 1972. — Bibl. — Index.
ISBN 0-7216-7042-3 : £12.00
Also classified at 612.6
(B77-09730)

Scientific foundations of obstetrics and gynaecology / edited by Elliot E. Philipp, Josephine Barnes and Michael Newton. — 2nd ed. — London : Heinemann Medical, 1977. — xx,922p,[2]leaves of plates, 4p of plates : ill(some col), maps ; 29cm.
Previous ed.: 1970. — Bibl. — Index.
ISBN 0-433-25101-8 : £37.50
(B77-33850)

618 — Gynaecology & obstetrics. *Reviews of research*
Recent advances in obstetrics and gynaecology. — Edinburgh [etc.] : Churchill Livingstone.
No.12 / edited by John Stallworthy, Gordon Bourne. — 1977. — xi,368p : ill ; 24cm.
Bibl. — Index.
ISBN 0-443-01020-x : £12.00
(B77-10823)

618 — Gynaecology & obstetrics. Applications of physical sciences
Physical science techniques in obstetrics and gynaecology / edited by Martin Black and Michael English. — Tunbridge Wells : Pitman Medical [for the] Biological Engineering Society, 1977. — viii,184p,plate : ill(some col) ; 26cm.
Index.
ISBN 0-272-79405-8 : £10.00
(B77-27147)

618'.092'2 — Gynaecology & obstetrics. Organisations. *Great Britain. Royal College of Obstetricians and Gynaecologists. Fellows, to 1969. Biographies*

Peel, *Sir* **John,** *b.1912.* The lives of the Fellows of the Royal College of Obstetricians and Gynaecologists, 1929-1969 / compiled by Sir John Peel. — London : Heinemann Medical, 1976. — xviii,390p,plate : 1 ill ; 23cm.
ISBN 0-433-25002-x : £15.00
(B77-08424)

618.1 — GYNAECOLOGY

Beacham, Daniel Winston. Synopsis of gynecology. — 9th ed. / [by] Daniel Winston Beacham, Woodard Davis Beacham. — Saint Louis : Mosby ; London : Distributed by Kimpton, 1977. — xi,444p,plate : ill(some col) ; 20cm.
Previous ed.: 1972. — Bibl. — Index.
ISBN 0-8016-0525-3 Pbk : £9.55
(B77-29481)

Textbook of gynecology / edited by Russell Ramon de Alvarez. — Philadelphia : Lea and Febiger ; London : Kimpton, 1977. — xvi,546p, ii leaves of plates : ill(incl 2 col) ; 27cm.
Bibl. — Index.
ISBN 0-8121-0515-x : £31.85
(B77-16433)

618.1 — Women. Reproductive system. Diseases

Barnes, *Dame* **Josephine.** Lecture notes on gynaecology / [by] Josephine Barnes. — 3rd ed. — Oxford [etc.] : Blackwell Scientific, 1977. — viii,255p,leaf of plate,[6]p of plates : ill ; 19cm.
This ed. originally published: 1975. — Index. — Previous control number ISBN 0-632-08470-7.
Pbk : £3.25
ISBN 0-632-08470-7
(B77-22639)

618.1 — Women. Reproductive system. Diseases caused by microorganisms

Ledger, William J. Infection in the female / [by] William J. Ledger. — Philadelphia : Lea and Febiger ; London : Kimpton, 1977. — ix,240p : ill ; 24cm. — (Current concepts in obstetrics and gynecology)
Index.
ISBN 0-8121-0560-5 : £9.00
(B77-22640)

618.1'07'54 — Women. Reproductive system. Diagnosis. Laparoscopy

Semm, K. Atlas of gynecologic laparoscopy and hysteroscopy / by K. Semm ; introduction by Raoul Palmer ; translated [from the German] by Allan Lake Rice ; edited by Lawrence Stephen Borow. — Philadelphia ; London [etc.] : Saunders, 1977. — x,329p(2 fold) : ill(chiefly col) ; 26cm.
Originally published: in German. Stuttgart : F.K. Schattaner, 1975?. — Bibl.: p.295-323. — List of films: p.323-324. — Index.
ISBN 0-7216-8063-1 : £47.25
Also classified at 618.1'4'0754
(B77-27148)

618.1'1 — Women. Ovaries. Disorders

Tacchi, Derek. Ovarian gynaecology / [by] Derek Tacchi. — London [etc.] : Saunders, 1976. — x, 168p : ill ; 24cm.
Bibl. — Index.
ISBN 0-7216-8725-3 : £8.50
(B77-04241)

618.1'4'00222 — Women. Uterus. Cervix. Lesions. *Illustrations. For colposcopy*

Kolstad, Per. Atlas of colposcopy / [by] Per Kolstad, Adolf Stafl. — 2nd ed revised ed. — Oslo ; London : Universitetsforlaget [etc.] ; [Henley-on-Thames] ([37 Queen St., Henley-on-Thames, Oxon.]) : [Distributed by Global Books Resources], 1977. — 152p,x leaves of plates : chiefly ill(some col) ; 29cm.
'Scandinavian university books' - half title verso. — Previous ed.: Baltimore : University Park Press, 1972. — Bibl.: p.149-152.
£27.50
ISBN 82-00-02395-8
(B77-27149)

618.1'4'0754 — Women. Uterus. Diagnosis. Hysteroscopy

Semm, K. Atlas of gynecologic laparoscopy and hysteroscopy / by K. Semm ; introduction by Raoul Palmer ; translated [from the German] by Allan Lake Rice ; edited by Lawrence Stephen Borow. — Philadelphia ; London [etc.] : Saunders, 1977. — x,329p(2 fold) : ill(chiefly col) ; 26cm.
Originally published: in German. Stuttgart : F.K. Schattaner, 1975?. — Bibl.: p.295-323. — List of films: p.323-324. — Index.
ISBN 0-7216-8063-1 : £47.25
Primary classification 618.1'07'54
(B77-27148)

618.1'5'01 — Women. Vagina. Pathogens: Microorganisms

Schnell, Johannes D. Cytology and microbiology of the vagina : a brief atlas for doctors and medical students / [by] Johannes D. Schnell. — Basel [etc.] ; London : Karger ; [Chichester] : [Distributed by Wiley], 1975. — [2],89,[1]p : ill(chiefly col) ; 25cm.
Bibl.: p.88-89. — Index.
Unpriced
ISBN 3-8055-2179-0
(B77-12490)

618.1'6 — Women. Vulva. Diseases

Friedrich, Eduard G. Vulvar disease / [by] Eduard G. Friedrich, Jr. — Philadelphia ; London [etc.] : Saunders, 1976. — ii-xiii,217p : ill(chiefly col) ; 27cm. — (Major problems in obstetrics and gynecology ; vol.9)
Bibl. — Index.
ISBN 0-7216-3918-6 : £31.00
(B77-18191)

618.1'78 — Man. Infertility

Harrison, Ronald George. Sex and infertility / [by] R.G. Harrison, C.H. de Boer. — London [etc.] : Academic Press, 1977. — xii,122p : ill ; 23cm. — (Monographs for students of medicine)
Bibl.: p.117. — Index.
ISBN 0-12-327850-3 Pbk : £2.80
(B77-20328)

618.1'9 — Women. Breasts. Plastic surgery

Reconstructive breast surgery / edited by Nicholas G. Georgiade. — Saint Louis : Mosby ; London : Distributed by Kimpton, 1976. — xi,333p : ill, facsim ; 26cm.
Bibl. — Index.
ISBN 0-8016-1802-9 : £32.10
(B77-03582)

618.1'9 — Women. Breasts. Surgery. *For patients*

Robinson, Nancy. Mastectomy : a patient's guide to coping with breast surgery / by Nancy Robinson and Ian Swash ; with a foreword by Katie Boyle ; afterword by Gilbert H. Collier. — Wellingborough : Thorsons, 1977. — 128p : ill, form, ports ; 22cm.
Bibl.: p.123-124. — Index.
ISBN 0-7225-0365-2 : £3.95
ISBN 0-7225-0348-2 Pbk : £2.50
(B77-12491)

618.1'9'09 — Women. Breasts. Diseases. *Case studies*

Goyette, Richert E. Renal, genitourinary and breast pathology and pathophysiology case studies : case histories with related questions and discussion / by Richert E. Goyette in consultation with Harlan J. Spjut. — London : Kimpton, 1976. — 204p : ill ; 22cm.
'I am indebted beyond words to Harlan Spjut for several years of constructive criticism, careful attention to the smallest detail, and many of the illustrations' - Acknowledgements. — Also published: Flushing, N.Y. : Medical Examination Publishing, 1976. — Bibl. — Index.
ISBN 0-87488-077-7 Sp : £6.50
Primary classification 616.6'09
(B77-07385)

618.2 — OBSTETRICS

Beischer, Norman A. Obstetrics and the newborn : for midwives and medical students / [by] Norman A. Beischer, Eric V. Mackay. — Sydney [etc.] ; London : Saunders, 1976. — [11],532p,[16]p of plates : ill(some col) ; 28cm.
Index.
ISBN 0-03-900051-6 : £15.00
Also classified at 618.9'201
(B77-24271)

Williams, John Whitridge. Williams' obstetrics. — 15th ed. / [by] Jack A. Pritchard, Paul C. MacDonald. — New York : Appleton-Century-Crofts ; London [etc.] : Prentice-Hall, 1976. — xv,1003p,[8]p of plates : ill(some col), form ; 26cm.
Previous ed.: published as 'Obstetrics' / by Louis M. Helman, Jack A. Pritchard with the collaboration of Ralph M. Wynn. New York : Appleton-Century-Crofts ; London : Butterworth, 1971. — Bibl. — Index.
ISBN 0-8385-9730-0 : £26.00
(B77-19431)

618.2 — Obstetrics. *For midwifery*

Hallum, Jean Lilian. Midwifery / [by] Jean L. Hallum. — 2nd ed. — London [etc.] : Hodder and Stoughton, 1976. — iv,156p : ill ; 23cm.
Previous ed.: London : English Universities Press, 1972. — Index.
ISBN 0-340-21124-5 : £3.95
ISBN 0-340-21125-3 Pbk : £1.75
(B77-11862)

Mayes, Mary. Mayes' midwifery : a textbook for midwives. — 9th ed. / by Rosemary E. Bailey. — London : Baillière Tindall, 1976. — vii, 543p : ill ; 22cm.
Previous ed.: 1972. — Bibl. — Index.
ISBN 0-7020-0603-3 Pbk : £3.75
(B77-05463)

618.2 — Perinatal medicine. *Reviews of research*

Perinatal medicine : review and comments. — Saint Louis : Mosby ; London : Distributed by Kimpton.
Vol.1 / edited by Frederick C. Battaglia, Giacomo Meschia, E.J. Quilligan. — 1976. — xi,146p : ill ; 26cm.
Index.
ISBN 0-8016-0511-3 : £15.00
(B77-01546)

618.2'002'4613 — Obstetrics. *For nursing*

Fream, William Charles. Notes on obstetrics / [by] William C. Fream. — Edinburgh [etc.] : Churchill Livingstone, 1977. — [11],179p : ill ; 19cm. — (Livingstone nursing notes)
Index.
ISBN 0-443-01451-5 Pbk : £2.25
(B77-16434)

618.2'0076 — Obstetrics. *Exercises, worked examples. For midwifery*

CMB questions and how to answer them / [compiled by] Vera da Cruz. — 5th ed. — London : Faber, 1977. — 3-197p : ill ; 19cm.
Previous ed.: 1969.
ISBN 0-571-04919-2 Pbk : £1.25
(B77-16435)

618.2'00913 — Obstetrics. *Tropical regions. For midwifery*

Ojo, O A. A textbook for midwives in the tropics / [by] O.A. Ojo and Enang Bassey Briggs. — London : Edward Arnold, 1976. — xi,441p : ill ; 22cm.
Index.
ISBN 0-7131-4258-8 Pbk : £5.95
(B77-11251)

618.2'06 — Obstetrics. Therapy. *Conference proceedings*

Therapeutic problems in pregnancy / edited by P.J. Lewis. — Lancaster : M.T.P. Press, 1977. — xi,165p : ill ; 23cm.
'[Based on proceedings] of a recent symposium in the Institute of Obstetrics and Gynaecology' - Foreword. — Bibl. — Index.
ISBN 0-85200-183-5 : £8.95
(B77-24272)

618.2'4 — Childbirth. Preparation

Consumers' Association. Pregnancy month by month / [Consumers' Association] ; [edited by Edith Rudinger]. — 4th ed. (newly revised). — London : The Association, 1977. — [6],116p : ill ; 18cm. — (A consumer publication)
Previous ed.: i.e. Revised ed. 1974. — Index.
ISBN 0-85202-131-3 Pbk : £1.75
(B77-17547)

618.2'4 — Natural childbirth. Preparation. *Manuals*

Brook, Danaë. Naturebirth : preparing for natural birth in an age of technology / [by] Danaë Brook ; foreword by Peter J. Huntingford. — Harmondsworth [etc.] : Penguin, 1976. — ix,292p : ill ; 20cm.
Also published: London : Heinemann, 1976. — Bibl.: p.282-284. — Index.
ISBN 0-14-046247-3 Pbk : £0.90
(B77-06142)

618.2'4 — Women. Pregnancy & childbirth. Counselling
Kitzinger, Sheila. Education and counselling for childbirth / [by] Sheila Kitzinger. — London [etc.] : Cassell and Collier Macmillan, 1977. — xiv,303p ; 20cm.
Bibl.: p.287-293. — Index.
ISBN 0-7020-0642-4 Pbk : £2.95
(B77-18192)

618.3 — Pregnant women. Blood. Hypertension. *Conference proceedings*
Invitational Symposium on Hypertension in Pregnancy, *University of Chicago, Center for Continuing Education, 1975.* Hypertension in pregnancy / edited by Marshall D. Lindheimer, Adrian I. Katz, Frederick P. Zuspan. — New York ; London [etc.] : Wiley, [1977]. — xiii, 443p : ill ; 26cm. — (Perspectives in nephrology and hypertension ; 5)
'A Wiley medical publication'. — ' ... the proceedings of an "Invitational Symposium on Hypertension in Pregnancy" held at the University of Chicago's Center for Continuing Education, September 25-27, 1975' - Preface. — Published in the United States: 1976. — Index.
ISBN 0-471-53783-7 : £23.20
(B77-12492)

618.3 — Pregnant women. Diseases. *Conference proceedings*
The **pathology** of pregnancy : symposium organized by the Royal College of Pathologists delivered in London in February 1976 / edited by Rosalinde Hurley. — London (BMA House, Tavistock Sq., WC1H 9JR) : 'Journal of clinical pathology' for the College, 1976. — [4],179p : ill ; 25cm. — ('Journal of clinical pathology' supplement : Royal College of Pathologists ; 10)

Bibl. — Index.
Pbk : £5.00
(B77-22641)

618.3 — Pregnant women. Kidneys. Diseases
The **kidney** in pregnancy / [edited by] Russell Ramon de Alvarez. — New York ; London [etc.] : Wiley, [1977]. — xv,235p : ill ; 27cm. — (Clinical monographs in obstetrics and gynecology)
'A Wiley medical publication'. — Published in the United States: 1976. — Bibl. — Index.
ISBN 0-471-20030-1 : £13.75
(B77-12483)

618.3 — Pregnant women. Toxemia. *Conference proceedings*
International Workshop on the Diagnostic Criteria of Toxemia of Pregnancy, *1st, Bethesda, 1975?.* Blood pressure, edema and proteinuria in pregnancy : Task Force on Toxemia, the collaborative perinatal project of the National Institute of Neurological and Communicative Disorders and Stroke : sponsored by Perinatal Research Branch, NINCDS [and] John E. Fogarty International Center ... / editorial committee Emanuel A. Friedman with ... [others]. — New York : Alan R. Liss ; Amsterdam ; Oxford : Elsevier, 1976. — [4],292p : ill, map ; 24cm. — (Progress in clinical and biological research ; vol.7)
'... report of the First International Workshop on the Diagnostic Criteria of "Toxemia" of Pregnancy, held in Bethesda, Maryland [1975?]' - Foreword. — Bibl. — Index.
ISBN 0-444-99825-x : £16.86
(B77-16436)

618.3'2 — Man. Foetuses & newborn babies. Injuries. *Conference proceedings*
Preventability of perinatal injury : proceedings of a symposium held in New York City, March 1974, sponsored jointly by the Mount Sinai School of Medicine and the National Foundation-March of Dimes / edited by Karlis Adamsons, Howard A. Fox. — New York : Liss ; Amsterdam ; Oxford : Elsevier, 1975[i.e.1976]. — x,229p : ill ; 24cm. — (Progress in clinical and biological research ; vol.2)
Published in the United States: 1975. — Bibl. — Index.
ISBN 0-444-99841-1 : £12.74
(B77-05464)

618.3'2 — Man. Foetuses. Diagnosis. Research, 1955-1975
Reid, Robert William. My children, my children : life before and after birth : an account of some recent developments / [by] Robert Reid. — London : British Broadcasting Corporation, 1977. — [5],186p ; 24cm.
Based on the BBC TV series. — Bibl.: p.181-183. — Index.
ISBN 0-563-12857-7 : £3.50
(B77-22642)

618.3'2 — Man. Foetuses. Diseases
Fetal physiology and medicine : the basis of perinatology / edited by Richard W. Beard and Peter W. Nathanielsz. — London [etc.] : Saunders, 1976. — xii,542p : ill ; 26cm.
Bibl. — Index.
ISBN 0-7216-1600-3 : £15.00
Primary classification 612.6'47
(B77-05434)

Infections of the fetus and the newborn infant : proceedings of a symposium held in New York City, March 1975 / edited by Saul Krugman, Anne A. Gershon. — New York : Liss ; Amsterdam ; Oxford : Elsevier, 1975 [i.e. 1976]. — ix,193p : ill ; 24cm. — (Progress in clinical and biological research ; vol.3)
'Presented by New York University Medical Center. Sponsored by the National Foundation - March of Dimes'. — Published in the United States: 1975. — Bibl. — Index.
ISBN 0-444-99840-3 : £59.00
Also classified at 618.9'201
(B77-04242)

Perinatal intensive care / edited by Silvio Aladjem, Audrey K. Brown. — Saint Louis : Mosby ; London : Distributed by Kimpton, 1977. — xiii,447p : ill ; 26cm.
Bibl. — Index.
ISBN 0-8016-0105-3 : £23.60
(B77-28666)

618.3'2 — Man. Foetuses. Diseases caused by microorganisms
Infectious diseases of the fetus and newborn infant / edited by Jack S. Remington and Jerome O. Klein. — Philadelphia ; London [etc.] : Saunders, 1976. — xvii,1121p : ill ; 26cm.
Index.
ISBN 0-7216-7547-6 : £36.50
Also classified at 618.9'201
(B77-16437)

618.4 — Childbirth
Leboyer, Frédérick. Birth without violence / [by] Frédérick Leboyer ; [translated from the French]. — [London] : Fontana, 1977. — [5], 105p : ill ; 19x24cm.
This translation originally published: Adelaide : Rigby ; London : Wildwood House, 1975. — Translation of: 'Pour une naissance sans violence'. Paris : Seuil, 1974.
ISBN 0-00-634305-8 Pbk : £1.50
(B77-18193)

618.8 — Obstetrics. Surgery
Kerr, John Martin Munro. Munro Kerr's operative obstetrics. — 9th ed. / [by] P.R. Myerscough. — London : Baillière Tindall, 1977. — ix,882p,leaf of plate,ii-ix p of plates : ill(some col) ; 24cm.
Previous ed.: / by J. Chassar Moir and P.R. Myerscough. 1971. — Index.
ISBN 0-7020-0612-2 : £15.00
ISBN 0-7020-0636-x Pbk : Unpriced
(B77-10824)

618.8'8 — Abortion: Menstrual regulation
International Planned Parenthood Federation. *Central Medical Committee.* Menstrual regulation / edited for the IPPF Central Medical Committee by R.L. Kleinman. — London : International Planned Parenthood Federation, 1976. — 34p : ill ; 21cm.
Bibl.: p.33-34.
ISBN 0-900924-81-0 Sd : £0.80
(B77-03056)

618.92 — PAEDIATRICS
Carne, Stuart. Paediatric care : child health in family practice / by Stuart Carne. — Lancaster : M.T.P. Press, 1976. — xiii,259p : ill, forms ; 23cm.
Index.
ISBN 0-85200-153-3 : £6.50
(B77-06143)

Catzel, Pincus. A short textbook of paediatrics / [by] Pincus Catzel. — London [etc.] : Hodder and Stoughton, 1976. — ix,446p : ill ; 23cm. — (University medical texts)
Bibl. — Index.
ISBN 0-340-05108-6 : £6.25
ISBN 0-340-05109-4 Pbk : £3.45
(B77-17548)

A **paediatric** vade-mecum / edited by Ben Wood. — 9th ed. — London : Lloyd-Luke, 1977. — xi,203p : ill ; 19cm.
Previous ed.: 1974. — Index.
ISBN 0-85324-126-0 Pbk : £3.50
(B77-29482)

618.9'2 — Children. Developmental disorders. Assessment. *United States*
Detection of developmental problems in children : a reference guide for community nurses and other health care professionals / edited by Marilyn J. Krajicek, Alice I. Tearney. — Baltimore ; London [etc.] : University Park Press, 1977. — xv,204p : ill, form ; 23cm.
Bibl. — Index.
ISBN 0-8391-0949-0 Pbk : £4.95
(B77-16438)

618.9'2 — Children. Diseases
Allen, John E. Practical points in pediatrics / by John E. Allen, Vymutt J. Gururaj, Raymond M. Russo. — 2nd ed. — London : Kimpton, 1977. — 324p : ill, forms ; 22cm.
Previous ed.: Flushing, N.Y. : Medical Examination Publishing, 1973. — Index.
ISBN 0-87488-702-x Sp : £7.50
(B77-11252)

The **critically** ill child : diagnosis and management / edited by Clement A. Smith. — 2nd ed. — Philadelphia ; London [etc.] : Saunders, 1977. — xvii,363p : ill ; 25cm.
'Based on articles appearing in "Pediatrics", the Journal of the American Academy of Pediatrics'. — Previous ed.: Philadelphia : Saunders, 1972. — Index.
ISBN 0-7216-8385-1 : £10.75
(B77-20329)

Moll, Helmut. Atlas of pediatric diseases / [by] Helmut Moll ; translated [from the German] by Walter Kleindienst. — Philadelphia ; London [etc.] : Saunders [etc.], 1976. — vii,275p : ill(chiefly col) ; 25cm.
Translation of: 'Pädiatrische Krankheitsbilder'. Stuttgart : Thieme, 1975. — Index.
ISBN 0-7216-6430-x : £32.50
(B77-19432)

618.9'2 — Children. Diseases. *For general practice*
Child care in general practice / edited by Cyril Hart. — Edinburgh [etc.] : Churchill Livingstone, 1977. — xii,442p : 2 ill ; 24cm.
Bibl. — Index.
ISBN 0-443-01575-9 Pbk : £5.50
(B77-23473)

618.9'2 — Children. Gross lesions
Koop, Charles Everett. Visible & palpable lesions in children / [by] C. Everett Koop. — New York [etc.] ; London : Grune and Stratton, 1976. — xi,123p : ill ; 24cm.
Index.
ISBN 0-8089-0958-4 : £8.40
(B77-07937)

618.9'2 — Children. Medical aspects. *For teaching*
Willis, M. Medical care in schools / [by] M. Willis, M. McLachlan. — London : Edward Arnold, 1977. — vii,216p : ill ; 22cm.
Index.
ISBN 0-7131-0108-3 Pbk : £3.25
(B77-21189)

618.9'2 — Handicapped children. Diagnosis & therapy. Social aspects
Early management of handicapping disorders / edited by T.E. Oppé and F. Peter Woodford. — Amsterdam ; Oxford [etc.] : Elsevier [etc.], 1976. — [6],139p : ill ; 25cm. — (Institute for Research into Mental and Multiple Handicap. Reviews of research and practice ; 19)
'... based on papers delivered at meetings held in Liverpool, Cardiff, Wolverhampton, Exeter and London between October 1975 and April 1976' - Preface. — Bibl. — Index.
ISBN 0-444-15242-3 : £8.89
(B77-06720)

618.9'2'00024613 — Children. Diseases. *For nursing*
Kessel, Israel. The essentials of paediatrics for nurses / [by] I. Kessel. — 5th ed. — Edinburgh [etc.] : Churchill Livingstone, 1976. — xiv,306p : ill ; 22cm. — (Livingstone nursing texts)
Previous ed.: 1972. — Index.
ISBN 0-443-01420-5 Pbk : £4.75
(B77-00261)

618.9'2'00024613 — Paediatrics. *For nursing*
Thompson, Eleanor Dumont. Pediatrics for practical nurses / [by] Eleanor Dumont Thompson. — 3rd ed. — Philadelphia ; London [etc.] : Saunders, 1976. — ii-x,378p : ill, ports ; 25cm.
Previous ed.: 1970. — Bibl. — Index.
ISBN 0-7216-8842-x Pbk : £5.25
(B77-02365)

618.9'2'0008 — Paediatrics. *Readings*
Problems of childhood : articles published in the 'British medical journal'. — London : British Medical Association, 1976. — [8],149p : ill ; 22cm.
Bibl. — Index.
ISBN 0-7279-0019-6 Pbk : £2.50
(B77-09054)

618.9'2002'5 — Children. Emergency treatment
Valman, Hyman Bernard. Accident and emergency paediatrics / [by] H.B. Valman ; foreword by Harold Ellis. — Oxford [etc.] : Blackwell Scientific, 1976. — x,97p : ill ; 22cm.
Bibl.: p.90. — Index.
ISBN 0-632-00169-0 Pbk : £3.75
(B77-03057)

618.9'2004'2 — Children. Genetic disorders
Endocrine and genetic diseases of childhood and adolescence / edited by Lytt I. Gardner. — 2nd ed. — Philadelphia ; London [etc.] : Saunders, 1975 [i.e. 1976]. — xxx,1404p : ill ; 27cm.
This ed. published in the United States: 1975. — Previous ed.: published as 'Endocrine and genetic diseases of childhood'. 1969. — Bibl. — Index.
ISBN 0-7216-3991-7 : £51.25
Primary classification 618.9'24
(B77-06722)

618.9'2006'37 — Handicapped children. Music therapy. *Conference proceedings*
The **nature** and scope of music therapy with handicapped children : papers read at the conferences held in Manchester and Birmingham, 8th February 1975 and 26th October 1974. — London (48 Lanchester Rd, N6 4TA) : British Society for Music Therapy, [1975?]. — [2],42p ; 26cm.
ISBN 0-85513-011-3 Sd : £1.00
(B77-16414)

618.9'2006'515 — Hospitals. Patients: Children. Play therapy
Lindquist, Ivonny. Therapy through play / [by] Ivonny Lindquist ; [translated from the Swedish]. — London : Arlington Books, 1977. — xx,90p : ill, facsims ; 19cm.
Translation of: 'Terapi genom lek'. Stockholm : Läromedelsförlaget, 1970. — Bibl.: p.89-90.
ISBN 0-85140-264-x Pbk : £1.95
(B77-33264)

618.9'2007'54 — Children. Diagnosis. Exercise testing
Godfrey, Simon. Exercise testing in children : applications in health and disease / [by] Simon Godfrey. — London [etc.] : Saunders, 1974. — xi,168p : ill ; 24cm.
Bibl.: p.155-164. — Index.
ISBN 0-7216-4142-3 : £5.00
(B77-11253)

618.9'2007'54024613 — Children. Diagnosis. Physical examination. *For nursing*
Alexander, Mary M. Pediatric physical diagnosis for nurses / [by] Mary M. Alexander, Marie Scott Brown. — New York ; London [etc.] : McGraw-Hill, [1977]. — x,275p : ill ; 24cm.
'A Blakiston publication'. — Published in the United States: 1974. — Bibl. — Index.
ISBN 0-07-001016-1 : £18.20
ISBN 0-07-001017-x Pbk : £6.00
(B77-14763)

618.9'2007'57 — Children. Diagnosis. Radiography
Gordon, I R S. Diagnostic radiology in paediatrics / [by] I.R.S. Gordon, F.G.M. Ross. — London [etc.] : Butterworth, 1977. — xii, 384p : ill ; 29cm. — (Postgraduate paediatrics series)
Bibl. — Index.
ISBN 0-407-00121-2 : £25.00
(B77-16439)

618.9'2007'572 — Children. Diagnosis. Radiography. Use of X-rays. *Manuals*
Gyll, Catherine. A handbook of paediatric radiography / [by] Catherine Gyll ; illustrations by Susan Cleaver. — Oxford [etc.] : Blackwell Scientific, 1977. — viii,162p : ill ; 22cm.
Index.
ISBN 0-632-00489-4 Pbk : £3.75
(B77-16918)

618.9'201 — High risk newborn babies
Lubchenco, Lula O. The high risk infant / by Lula O. Lubchenco. — Philadelphia ; London [etc.] : Saunders, 1976. — ii-xii,294p : ill ; 25cm. — (Major problems in clinical pediatrics ; vol.14)
Bibl. — Index.
ISBN 0-7216-5800-8 : £15.00
(B77-06721)

618.9'201 — Newborn babies. Communicable diseases
Infectious diseases of the fetus and newborn infant / edited by Jack S. Remington and Jerome O. Klein. — Philadelphia ; London [etc.] : Saunders, 1976. — xvii,1121p : ill ; 26cm.
Index.
ISBN 0-7216-7547-6 : £36.50
Primary classification 618.3'2
(B77-16437)

618.9'201 — Newborn babies. Diseases
Infections of the fetus and the newborn infant : proceedings of a symposium held in New York City, March 1975 / edited by Saul Krugman, Anne A. Gershon. — New York : Liss ; Amsterdam ; Oxford : Elsevier, 1975 [i.e. 1976]. — ix,193p : ill ; 24cm. — (Progress in clinical and biological research ; vol.3)
'Presented by New York University Medical Center. Sponsored by the National Foundation - March of Dimes'. — Published in the United States: 1975. — Bibl. — Index.
ISBN 0-444-99840-3 : £59.00
Primary classification 618.3'2
(B77-04242)

Pierog, Sophie Helen. Medical care of the sick newborn / [by] Sophie H. Pierog, Angelo Ferrara. — 2nd ed. — Saint Louis : Mosby ; London : Distributed by Kimpton, 1976. — xiv, 368p : ill, forms ; 24cm.
Previous ed.: published as 'Approach to the medical care of the sick newborn'. 1971. — Bibl. — Index.
ISBN 0-8016-3936-0 : £11.80
(B77-17549)

Schaffer, Alexander John. Diseases of the newborn. — 4th ed. / [by] Alexander J. Schaffer, Mary Ellen Avery. — Philadelphia ; London [etc.] : Saunders, 1977. — ii-xxviii, 1116p : ill(incl 1 col) ; 27cm.
Previous ed.: 1971. — Bibl. — Index.
ISBN 0-7216-7947-1 : £25.00
(B77-28667)

Vulliamy, David Gibb. The newborn child / [by] David G. Vulliamy. — 4th ed. — Edinburgh [etc.] : Churchill Livingstone, 1977. — vii, 223p : ill ; 22cm.
Previous ed.: 1972. — Index.
ISBN 0-443-01396-9 Pbk : £3.25
(B77-32666)

618.9'201 — Newborn babies. Intensive care. *Conference proceedings*
Intensive care in the newborn / [edited by] Leo Stern, Bent Friis-Hansen, Poul Kildeberg. — Lancaster : M.T.P. Press, [1977]. — xiv,283p : ill ; 26cm.
'... conference held [August 25th-30th, 1975] in Stavrby Skov, Denmark' - Foreword. — Originally published: New York : Masson, 1976. — Index.
ISBN 0-85200-175-4 : £19.50
(B77-15894)

618.9'201 — Newborn babies. Medical aspects
Beischer, Norman A. Obstetrics and the newborn : for midwives and medical students / [by] Norman A. Beischer, Eric V. Mackay. — Sydney [etc.] ; London : Saunders, 1976. — [11],532p,[16]p of plates : ill(some col) ; 28cm.
Index.
ISBN 0-03-900051-6 : £15.00
Primary classification 618.2
(B77-24271)

618.9'201 — Newborn babies. Pathology
Larroche, Jeanne Claudie. Developmental pathology of the neonate / [by] Jeanne-Claudie Larroche. — Amsterdam ; London [etc.] ([256 Banbury Rd, Oxford OX2 7DH]) : Excerpta Medica, 1977. — xviii,525p,plate : ill(incl 2 col), forms ; 27cm.
Bibl. — Index.
£42.15
ISBN 90-219-2107-3
(B77-16440)

618.9'209'75140757 — Children. Skull. Diagnosis. Radiography
Harwood-Nash, Derek C. Neuroradiology in infants and children / [by] Derek C. Harwood-Nash with the assistance of Charles R. Fitz. — Saint Louis : Mosby ; London : Distributed by Kimpton, 1976. — 3v.(xv,1227, 28p) : ill ; 29cm.
Bibl. — Index.
ISBN 0-8016-2086-4 : £132.00
Primary classification 618.9'28'04757
(B77-08426)

618.9'209'7585 — Children. Feet. Care
Health Education Council. Care of young feet : and a few tips for mothers too / [Health Education Council in association with the Society of Chiropodists]. — London : The Council, [1976]. — [12]p : ill ; 15x21cm.
ISBN 0-903652-02-1 Sd : Unpriced
(B77-02366)

618.9'209'78 — Children, 1-7 years. Hearing disorders. Diagnosis. Tests: Stycar Hearing Tests. *Manuals*
Sheridan, Mary Dorothy. Manual for the Stycar Hearing Tests / [by] Mary D. Sheridan. — Revised ed. — [Windsor] : NFER, 1976. — 60p : ill ; 22cm.
Previous ed.: 1968. — Bibl.: p.59-60.
Sd : £1.55
(B77-03058)

618.9'209'78 — Children. Deafness. Aetiology
Fraser, George Robert. The causes of profound deafness in childhood : a study of 3,535 individuals with severe hearing loss present at birth or of childhood onset / [by] George R. Fraser. — London : Baillière Tindall, 1976. — xv,410p ; 26cm.
Bibl.: p.357-390. — Index.
ISBN 0-7020-0640-8 : £17.00
(B77-08425)

618.9'209'78 — Children. Hearing disorders
Hearing loss in children : a comprehensive text / edited by Burton F. Jaffe. — Baltimore ; London [etc.] : University Park Press, 1977. — xxiii,784p : ill ; 24cm.
Index.
ISBN 0-8391-0824-9 : £21.25
(B77-23474)

618.9'21'20754 — Children. Heart. Diagnosis. Echocardiography
Meyer, Richard A. Pediatric echocardiography / [by] Richard A. Meyer, with chapters by Russell L. Uphoff and with the assistance of Joan Korfhagen. — Philadelphia : Lea and Febiger ; London : Kimpton, 1977. — xi,303p : ill ; 25cm.
Index.
ISBN 0-8121-0589-3 : £12.75
(B77-31240)

618.9'21'307572 — Children. Blood vessels. Diagnosis. Angiography
Angiography in infants and children / edited by Michael T. Gyepes. — New York ; London : Grune and Stratton, 1974. — xiv,378p : ill ; 26cm.
Bibl. — Index.
ISBN 0-8089-0827-8 : Unpriced
(B77-20330)

618.9'21'5 — Children. Blood. Diseases
Willoughby, Michael L N. Paediatric haematology / [by] Michael L.N. Willoughby. — Edinburgh [etc.] : Churchill Livingstone, 1977. — xv,434p,plate : ill(incl 1 col), map ; 26cm.
Bibl. — Index.
ISBN 0-443-01442-6 : £18.00
(B77-13685)

618.9'22 — Children. Respiratory system. Diseases. Intensive care. *Manuals*
Levin, Richard M. Pediatric respiratory intensive care handbook / by Richard M. Levin. — London : Kimpton, 1976. — 333p : ill ; 22cm.
Also published: Flushing, N.Y. : Medical Examination Publishing Co., 1976. — Index.
ISBN 0-87488-649-x Sp : £6.50
(B77-06145)

618.9'23'30757 — Children. Gastrointestinal tract. Diagnosis. Radiography
Singleton, Edward B. Radiology of the alimentary tract in infants and children. — 2nd ed. / [by] Edward B. Singleton, Milton L. Wagner, Robert V. Dutton. — Philadelphia ; London [etc.] : Saunders, 1977. — ii-xiv,461p : ill ; 27cm. — (Saunders monographs in clinical radiology ; vol.10)
Previous ed.: published as 'X-ray diagnosis of the alimentary tract in infants and children' / by Edward B. Singleton. Chicago : Year Book Publishers, 1959. — Bibl. — Index.
ISBN 0-7216-8314-2 : £21.50
(B77-27150)

618.9'23'6 — Children. Biliary tract. Biliary atresias & neonatal hepatitis
Pérez-Soler, A. The inflammatory and atresia-inducing disease of the liver and bile ducts / [by] A. Pérez-Soler. — Basel ; London [etc.] : Karger ; [London] : [Distributed by Wiley], 1976. — x,245p,[16]p of plates : ill(some col) ; 23cm. — (Monographs in paediatrics ; vol.8)
Bibl. — Index.
Pbk : £21.85
ISBN 3-8055-2257-6
(B77-04869)

618.9'23'99 — Babies. Carbohydrate metabolic disorders
Cornblath, Marvin. Disorders of carbohydrate metabolism in infancy / by Marvin Cornblath and Robert Schwartz. — 2nd ed. — Philadelphia ; London [etc.] : Saunders, 1976. — ii-xvi,501p : ill(some col) ; 25cm. — (Major problems in clinical pediatrics ; vol.3)
Previous ed.: Philadelphia : Saunders, 1966. — Index.
ISBN 0-7216-2721-8 : £17.25
(B77-01547)

618.9'23'99 — Children. Protein-calorie malnutrition
Protein-energy malnutrition / [by] G.A.O. Alleyne ... [et al.]. — London : Edward Arnold, 1977. — x,244p,[8]p of plates : ill ; 24cm.
Bibl.: p.196-219. — Index.
ISBN 0-7131-4285-5 : £8.50
(B77-15895)

618.9'24 — Children. Endocrine system. Diseases
Endocrine and genetic diseases of childhood and adolescence / edited by Lytt I. Gardner. — 2nd ed. — Philadelphia ; London [etc.] : Saunders, 1975 [i.e. 1976]. — xxx,1404p : ill ; 27cm.
This ed. published in the United States: 1975. — Previous ed.: published as 'Endocrine and genetic diseases of childhood'. 1969. — Bibl. — Index.
ISBN 0-7216-3991-7 : £51.25
Also classified at 616.4; 618.9'2004'2; 616'.042
(B77-06722)

618.9'24'5 — Children. Adrenal glands. Congenital adrenal hyperplasia. *Conference proceedings*
Treatment of Congenital Adrenal Hyperplasia : A Quarter of a Century Later *(Conference), Johns Hopkins Hospital, 1975.* Congenital adrenal hyperplasia / edited by Peter A. Lee ... [et al.]. — Baltimore ; London [etc.] : University Park Press, 1977. — xxiii,532p : ill, ports ; 24cm.
'Proceedings of "Treatment of Congenital Adrenal Hyperplasia : A Quarter of a Century Later", an international symposium held at the Johns Hopkins Hospital, Baltimore, Maryland, October 20-24, 1975' - title page verso. — Bibl. — Index.
ISBN 0-8391-0974-1 : £26.95
(B77-27902)

618.9'24'62 — Children. Diabetes
Craig, Oman. Childhood diabetes and its management / [by] Oman Craig. — London [etc.] : Butterworth, 1977. — xiii,265p : ill ; 23cm. — (Postgraduate paediatrics series)
Bibl. — Index.
ISBN 0-407-00126-3 : £7.95
(B77-16441)

618.9'24'62 — Children. Diabetes. *Conference proceedings*
International Beilinson Symposium on the Various Faces of Diabetes in Juveniles, *2nd, Jerusalem, 1972.* Diabetes in juveniles : medical and rehabilitation aspects : International Beilinson Symposium on the Various Faces of Diabetes in Juveniles, Jerusalem, Israel, 1972 / editor Zvi Laron ; assistant Moshe Karp. — 2nd, unchanged ed. [i.e. 1st ed. reprinted]. — Basel ; London [etc.] : Karger ; [London] : [Distributed by Wiley], 1977. — xiv,418p : ill ; 23cm.
Originally published: 1975. — Bibl.
Pbk : Unpriced
(B77-29483)

618.9'24'66075 — Children. Hypoglycaemia. Diagnosis
Zuppinger, Klaus A. Hypoglycemia in childhood : evaluation of diagnostic procedures / [by] Klaus A. Zuppinger. — Basel ; London [etc.] : Karger ; [Chichester] : [Distributed by Wiley], 1975. — vi,135p : ill ; 23cm. — (Monographs in paediatrics ; vol.4)
Bibl.: p.122-135.
Pbk : Unpriced
ISBN 3-8055-2061-1
(B77-07397)

618.9'26 — Children. Urogenital system. Diseases
Clinical pediatric urology / [editors] Panayotis P. Kelalis, Lowell R. King ; associate editor, A. Barry Belman. — Philadelphia ; London [etc.] : Saunders, 1976. — 2v.(1107,[77]p) : ill ; 27cm.
Bibl. — Index.
ISBN 0-7216-5350-2 : £50.25
Vol.1 ISBN 0-7216-5350-2
Vol.2 ISBN 0-7216-5351-0
(B77-13686)

618.9'26'1 — Children. Kidneys. Diseases
James, John Alexander. Renal disease in childhood / [by] John A. James. — 3rd ed. / contributing authors Ellin Lieberman, Richard N. Fine. — Saint Louis : Mosby ; London : Distributed by Kimpton, 1976. — ix,402p : ill ; 26cm.
Previous ed.: 1973. — Bibl.: p.390. — Index.
ISBN 0-8016-2414-2 : £20.75
(B77-06146)

618.9'27'2 — Children. Joints. Still's disease. *Conference proceedings*
International Symposium on Still's Disease, *1st, Bristol, 1975.* Still's disease : juvenile chronic polyarthritis / edited by Malcolm I.V. Jayson. — London [etc.] : Academic Press, 1976. — xiii,289p : ill ; 24cm.
'... proceedings of the 1st International Symposium on Still's Disease which was held in Bristol in 1975' - jacket. — Bibl. — Index.
ISBN 0-12-381250-x : £6.50
(B77-02367)

618.9'27'3043 — Children. Spine. Spina bifida
Stark, Gordon David. Spina bifida : problems and management / [by] G.D. Stark. — Oxford [etc.] : Blackwell Scientific, 1977. — xi,192p : ill ; 24cm.
Bibl.: p.173-185. — Index.
ISBN 0-632-00158-5 Pbk : £6.00
(B77-11863)

618.9'27'3043 — Children. Spine. Spina bifida. *Conference proceedings*
Studies in hydrocephalus and spina bifida. — London : Spastics International Medical Publications ; Tadworth : [Distributed by] Heinemann Medical [etc.].
[1976] : Proceedings of the Society for Research into Hydrocephalus and Spina Bifida, Berne, 23rd-26th June 1976 / edited by Gordon Stark. — 1976. — [4],172p : ill ; 25cm. — ('Developmental medicine and child neurology' supplement ; no.37 ISSN 0419-0238)
English text, English, French, German and Spanish summaries. — Bibl.
ISBN 0-901260-21-5 Pbk : £5.25
Also classified at 618.9'28'58843
(B77-16442)

618.9'27'30757 — Children. Spine. Diagnosis. Radiography
Harwood-Nash, Derek C. Neuroradiology in infants and children / [by] Derek C. Harwood-Nash with the assistance of Charles R. Fitz. — Saint Louis : Mosby ; London : Distributed by Kimpton, 1976. — 3v.(xv,1227, 28p) : ill ; 29cm.
Bibl. — Index.
ISBN 0-8016-2086-4 : £132.00
Primary classification 618.9'28'04757
(B77-08426)

618.9'28 — Children. Abnormal development. *Conference proceedings*
Gatlinburg (Tennessee) Conference on Research and Theory in Mental Retardation, *7th, 1974.* Aberrant development in infancy : human and animal studies / edited by Norman R. Ellis. — Hillsdale : Erlbaum ; New York ; London [etc.] : Distributed by Wiley, 1975 [i.e. 1977]. — viii,287p : ill ; 25cm.
'[Papers presented] ... at the seventh annual "Gatlinburg (Tennessee) Conference on Research and Theory in Mental Retardation" ...' - Preface. — Published in the United States: 1975. — Bibl. — Index.
ISBN 0-470-23859-3 : £11.70
(B77-11864)

618.9'28 — Children. Motor delay. Therapy
Levitt, Sophie. Treatment of cerebral palsy and motor delay. — Oxford : Blackwell Scientific, 1977. — 1v..
Previous control number ISBN 0-632-08480-4.
ISBN 0-632-00931-4 Pbk : £5.00 : CIP entry
Primary classification 618.9'28'3606
(B77-09055)

618.9'28 — Children. Nervous system. Diseases
Gordon, Neil. Paediatric neurology for the clinician / [by] Neil Gordon. — London : Heinemann [etc. for] Spastics International Medical Publications, 1976. — viii,280p : ill ; 25cm. — (Clinics in developmental medicine ; nos. 59, 60)
Bibl. — Index.
ISBN 0-433-12410-5 : £7.50
(B77-05465)

618.9'28'024613 — Children. Nervous system. Diseases. *For nursing*
Conway, Barbara Lang. Pediatric neurologic nursing / [by] Barbara Lang Conway. — Saint Louis : Mosby ; London : Distributed by Kimpton, 1977. — xiii,361p : ill ; 26cm.
Index.
ISBN 0-8016-1029-x : £11.80
(B77-22643)

618.9'28'04754 — Newborn babies. Nervous system. Diagnosis. Physical examination. *Manuals*
Prechtl, Heinz. The neurological examination of the full term newborn infant / [by] Heinz F.R. Prechtl. — 2nd ed. — London : Heinemann Medical [etc.] [for] Spastics International Medical Publications, 1977. — viii,68p : ill, form ; 25cm. — (Clinics in developmental medicine ; no.63)
Booklet (8p.) in pocket. — Previous ed.: / by Heinz Prechtl and David Beintema. London : Spastics Society, 1964. — Bibl.: p.66. — Index.
£4.25
(B77-30319)

618.9'28'04757 — Children. Central nervous system. Diagnosis. Radiography
Harwood-Nash, Derek C. Neuroradiology in infants and children / [by] Derek C. Harwood-Nash with the assistance of Charles R. Fitz. — Saint Louis : Mosby ; London : Distributed by Kimpton, 1976. — 3v.(xv,1227, 28p) : ill ; 29cm.
Bibl. — Index.
ISBN 0-8016-2086-4 : £132.00
Also classified at 618.9'209'75140757; 618.9'27'30757
(B77-08426)

618.9'28'04757202854 — Children. Brain. Diagnosis. Tomography. Applications of computer systems
Jabbour, J T. Atlas of CT scans in pediatric neurology / by J.T. Jabbour, D. Randolph Ramey, Steve Roach. — Singapore : Toppan ; London : Kimpton [etc.], 1977. — 256p : ill ; 27cm.
Cover title: Atlas of computerized tomography scans in pediatric neurology. — Bibl.: p.240-248. — Index.
ISBN 0-87488-979-0 : £22.50
(B77-29484)

618.9'28'3606 — Children. Cerebral palsy. Therapy
Levitt, Sophie. Treatment of cerebral palsy and motor delay. — Oxford : Blackwell Scientific, 1977. — 1v..
Previous control number ISBN 0-632-08480-4.
ISBN 0-632-00931-4 Pbk : £5.00 : CIP entry
Also classified at 618.9'28
(B77-09055)

618.9'28'5 — Children. Hyperactivity. Therapy. Use of stimulating agents
The **hyperactive** child and stimulant drugs / edited by James J. Bosco and Stanley S. Robin. — Chicago ; London : University of Chicago Press, 1977. — vii,191p ; 24cm.
'The contents of this volume originally appeared as the November 1976 issue of "School Review"' - title page verso. — Bibl. — Index.
ISBN 0-226-06661-4 : £7.00
(B77-23475)

618.9'28'522 — Children. Neuroses. *For parents*
Janov, Arthur. The feeling child / [by] Arthur Janov. — London : Abacus, 1977. — 286,[1]p ; 20cm.
Originally published: New York : Simon and Schuster, 1973.
ISBN 0-349-11832-9 Pbk : £1.50
(B77-09056)

618.9'28'55 — Children. Communication disorders. Assessment & therapy. Techniques
Weiss, Curtis E. Communicative disorders : a handbook for prevention and early intervention / [by] Curtis E. Weiss, Harold S. Lillywhite. — Saint Louis : C.V. Mosby ; London : Distributed by Kimpton, 1976. — ix, 289p : ill, forms ; 22cm.
Bibl. — Index.
ISBN 0-8016-5386-x Pbk : £5.60
(B77-03583)

618.9'28'58 — Juvenile delinquents. Personality disorders

Lewis, Dorothy Otnow. Delinquency and psychopathology / by Dorothy Otnow Lewis and David A. Balla ; with the assistance of Shelley S. Shanok ; forewords by Justine Wise Polier and Dennis P. Cantwell. — New York [etc.] ; London : Grune and Stratton, [1977]. — xxv,209p(4 fold) ; 24cm.
Published in the United States: 1976. — Bibl.: p.181-199. — Index.
ISBN 0-8089-0976-2 : £10.50
(B77-13076)

618.9'28'588 — Children. Mental retardation

Mackay, R I. Mental handicap in child health practice / [by] R.I. Mackay. — London [etc.] : Butterworth, 1976. — xiv,322p : ill, port ; 23cm. — (Postgraduate paediatrics series)
Bibl.: p.295-297. — Index.
ISBN 0-407-00113-1 : £8.00
(B77-07398)

Robinson, Halbert Benefiel. The mentally retarded child : a psychological approach. — 2nd ed. / [by] Nancy M. Robinson, Halbert B. Robinson, with contributions by Gilbert S. Omenn ... [et al.]. — New York ; London [etc.] : McGraw-Hill, 1976. — xvi,592p : ill ; 25cm. — (McGraw-Hill series in psychology)
Previous ed.: / Halbert B. Robinson, Nancy M. Robinson. 1965. — Bibl.: p.475-565. — Index.
ISBN 0-07-053202-8 : £12.00
(B77-16919)

618.9'28'58806515 — Mentally handicapped children. Art therapy

Williams, Geraldine H. Developmental art therapy / by Geraldine H. Williams and Mary M. Wood. — Baltimore ; London [etc.] : University Park Press, 1977. — ix,198p : ill, form ; 28cm.
Bibl.: p.195-196. — Index.
ISBN 0-8391-1140-1 Pbk : £6.95
(B77-31241)

618.9'28'58843 — Children. Hydrocephalus. *Conference proceedings*

Studies in hydrocephalus and spina bifida. — London : Spastics International Medical Publications ; Tadworth : [Distributed by] Heinemann Medical [etc.].
[1976] : Proceedings of the Society for Research into Hydrocephalus and Spina Bifida, Berne, 23rd-26th June 1976 / edited by Gordon Stark. — 1976. — [4],172p : ill ; 25cm. — ('Developmental medicine and child neurology' supplement ; no.37 ISSN 0419-0238)
English text, English, French, German and Spanish summaries. — Bibl.
ISBN 0-901260-21-5 Pbk : £5.25
Primary classification 618.9'27'3043
(B77-16442)

618.9'28'61 — Children. Alcoholism. Medical aspects

Alcoholism problems in women and children / edited by Milton Greenblatt, Marc A. Schuckit. — New York [etc.] ; London : Grune and Stratton, [1977]. — xi,287p : ill ; 24cm. — (Seminars in psychiatry)
Published in the United States: 1976. — Bibl. — Index.
ISBN 0-8089-0972-x : £13.85
Primary classification 616.8'61
(B77-13069)

618.9'28'9 — Children. Behavioural disorders

Child psychiatry : modern approaches / edited by Michael Rutter, Lionel Hersov. — Oxford [etc.] : Blackwell Scientific, 1977. — xv,1024p : ill ; 24cm.
Bibl. — Index.
ISBN 0-632-00151-8 : £21.50
(B77-13687)

618.9'28'9 — Children. Psychiatry

Duffy, John C. Child psychiatry / by John C. Duffy. — 2nd ed. — London : Kimpton, 1977. — 252p : 1 ill, forms ; 22cm. — (Medical outline series)
This ed. also published: Flushing, N.Y. : Medical Examination Publishing Co., 1977. — Previous ed.: Flushing, N.Y. : Medical Examination Publishing Co., 1971. — Bibl. — Index.
ISBN 0-87488-613-9 Sp : £9.00
(B77-21924)

Stone, Frederick Hope. Psychiatry and the paediatrician / [by] Frederick H. Stone. — London [etc.] : Butterworth, 1976. — x,175p ; 23cm. — (Postgraduate paediatrics series)
Bibl. — Index.
ISBN 0-407-00074-7 : £6.00
(B77-05466)

618.9'28'9 — Children. Psychiatry. *Conference proceedings*

Three clinical faces of childhood / edited by E. James Anthony and Doris C. Gilpin. — New York : Spectrum ; New York ; London [etc.] : Distributed by Wiley, [1977]. — [13],255p : ill ; 24cm.
Proceedings of 3 workshops organized and held annually by the Washington University Child Guidance Clinic, St Louis, Missouri. — Published in the United States: 1976. — Bibl. — Index.
ISBN 0-470-15150-1 : £11.25
(B77-14764)

618.9'28'9 — Children. Psychiatry. *Reviews of research*

Child personality and psychopathology : current topics. — New York ; London [etc.] : Wiley.
Vol.3 / edited by Anthony Davids. — [1977]. — xi,299p : ill ; 24cm.
'A Wiley-Interscience publication'. — Published in the United States: 1976. — Bibl. — Index.
ISBN 0-471-19702-5 : £14.00
(B77-10393)

618.9'28'914 — Children. Psychotherapy

The **child** psychotherapist : and problems of young people / edited by Mary Boston and Dilys Daws. — London : Wildwood House, 1977. — 3-322p : ill ; 23cm.
Bibl.: p.315-320. — Index.
ISBN 0-7045-0273-9 : £8.50
(B77-21190)

618.9'28'9140926 — Maladjusted children. Psychotherapy. *Case studies*

MacCracken, Mary. Lovey, a child reclaimed / [by] Mary MacCracken. — London : Deutsch, 1977. — 189p ; 23cm.
Originally published as 'Lovey, a very special child'. Philadelphia : Lippincott, 1976.
ISBN 0-233-96886-5 : £3.95
(B77-27151)

618.9'28'917 — Children. Psychoanalysis

Handbook of child psychoanalysis : research, theory and practice / edited by Benjamin B. Wolman in collaboration with ... [others] ; foreword by Peter Blos ; Susan Knapp, editorial assistant. — New York ; London [etc.] : Van Nostrand Reinhold, 1972. — xii,643p ; 24cm.
Bibl. — Index.
ISBN 0-442-78288-8 : Unpriced
(B77-19433)

618.9'28'9170926 — Children. Psychoanalysis. *Case studies. Serials*

The **psychoanalytic** study of the child. — London : Hogarth Press [for] the Institute of Psycho-analysis.
Vol.31. — 1976. — vii,573p ; 24cm.
Bibl. — Index.
ISBN 0-7012-0428-1 : £12.00
(B77-08427)

618.9'28'9820651 — Children. Schizophrenia. Psychotherapy

Yudkovitz, Elaine. Communication therapy in childhood schizophrenia : an auditory monitoring approach / [by] Elaine Yudkovitz, Nancy Lewison, Judy Rottersman. — New York [etc.] ; London : Grune and Stratton, [1977]. — xiii,209p ; 24cm.
A 'Psychosocial process' reprint. — This ed. published in the United States: 1976. — '... the hard cover edition of the Spring 1975 issue (volume IV, Number 1) of the semiannual journal "Psychosocial Process" ...' - title page verso. — Bibl.: p.170-175. — Index.
ISBN 0-8089-0993-2 : £6.05
(B77-14264)

618.9'29 — Children. Communicable diseases

Krugman, Saul. Infectious diseases of children. — 6th ed. / [by] Saul Krugman, Robert Ward, Samuel L. Katz. — Saint Louis : Mosby ; London : Distributed by Kimpton, 1977. — xiii,539p,[5]leaves of plates,[6]p of plates : ill(some col) ; 26cm.
Previous ed.: published as 'Infectious diseases of children and adults' / by Saul Krugman, Robert Ward. 1973. — Bibl. — Index.
ISBN 0-8016-2800-8 : £24.00
(B77-23476)

618.9'29'7 — Children. Allergies

Sly, R Michael. Pediatric allergy / by R. Michael Sly ; illustrated by Don Alvarado. — London : Kimpton, 1977. — 334p : ill, maps ; 22cm. — (Medical outline series)
Also published: Flushing, N.Y. : Medical Examination Publishing Co., 1977. — Index.
ISBN 0-87488-624-4 Sp : £9.00
(B77-13077)

618.9'29'94 — Children. Cancer. *Conference proceedings*

Trends in childhood cancer : proceedings of the Fifth Annual Symposium of the Division of Oncology of the Children's Hospital of Philadelphia and the Department of Radiation Therapy of the American Oncologic Hospital of the Fox Chase Cancer Center / edited by Milton H. Donaldson, H. Gunter Seydel. — New York ; London [etc.] : Wiley, [1977]. — xiii,144p : ill ; 26cm. — (Wiley series in diagnostic and therapeutic radiology)
'A Wiley Medical Publication'. — Published in the United States: 1976. — Index.
ISBN 0-471-21782-4 : £12.40
(B77-13078)

618.9'29'9406 — Children with cancer. Therapy. *Conference proceedings*

The **truly** cured child : the new challenge in pediatric cancer care / edited by Jan van Eys. — Baltimore ; London [etc.] : University Park Press, 1977. — xiii,177p ; 23cm.
'Proceedings of a workshop held by the Department of Pediatrics, the University of Texas System Cancer Center, M.D. Anderson Hospital and Tumor Institute, Houston, Texas, on March 13 and 14, 1976' - title page verso. — Index.
ISBN 0-8391-1108-8 Pbk : £5.50
(B77-27904)

618.9'29'948 — Children. Nervous system. Neuroblastomas. *Reviews of research*

Neuroblastoma / [edited by] Carl Pochedly. — London : Edward Arnold, 1977. — viii,314p : ill ; 24cm.
Originally published: Acton, Mass. : Publishing Sciences Group, 1976. — Index.
ISBN 0-7131-4286-3 : £16.50
(B77-10394)

618.97 — GERIATRICS

Adams, George Fowler. Essentials of geriatric medicine / [by] George Adams. — Oxford [etc.] : Oxford University Press, 1977. — xiii, 98p ; 24cm. — (Oxford medical publications)
Bibl.: p.89-91. — Index.
ISBN 0-19-261216-6 Pbk : £1.95 : CIP rev.
(B77-21925)

Coni, Nicholas. Lecture notes on geriatrics / [by] Nicholas Coni, William Davison, Stephen Webster ; foreword by W.J.H. Butterfield. — Oxford [etc.] : Blackwell Scientific, 1977. — xiii,332p : ill ; 22cm.
Index.
ISBN 0-632-00266-2 Pbk : £6.75 : CIP rev.
(B77-04870)

618.9'7'0024613 — Old persons. Medical aspects. *For nursing*

Nursing and the aged / edited by Irene Mortenson Burnside. — New York ; London [etc.] : McGraw-Hill, 1976. — xvii,654p : ill, plan, ports ; 25cm.
'A Blakiston Publication'. — Bibl. — List of films: p.630. — Index.
ISBN 0-07-009209-5 : £11.60
(B77-05467)

618.9'7'061 — Old persons. Drug therapy

Judge, Thomas Grieve. Drug treatment of the elderly patient / [by] T.G. Judge, F.I. Caird. — Tunbridge Wells : Pitman Medical, 1978. — 117p ; 22cm.
Index.
ISBN 0-272-79383-3 Pbk : £2.50 : CIP rev.
(B77-18825)

618.9'7'0756 — Old persons. Diagnosis. Chemical analysis. Laboratory techniques

Hodkinson, Henry Malcolm. Biochemical diagnosis of the elderly / [by] H.M. Hodkinson. — London : Chapman and Hall, 1977. — xii, 111p : ill ; 25cm.
Bibl.: p.95-100. — Index.
ISBN 0-412-13720-8 : £5.50
(B77-32667)

618.9'76'12 — Old persons. Heart. Diseases

Cardiology in old age / edited by F.I. Caird, J.L.C. Dall and R.D. Kennedy. — New York ; London : Plenum Press, 1976. — xvi,412p : ill ; 24cm.
Bibl. — Index.
ISBN 0-306-30927-0 : £20.48
(B77-29485)

618.9'76'63 — Old persons. Incontinence

Incontinence in the elderly / edited by F.L. Willington. — London [etc.] : Academic Press, 1976. — xiv,265p : ill, forms ; 24cm.
Bibl. — Index.
ISBN 0-12-757050-0 : £7.80
(B77-01548)

618.9'76'89 — Old persons. Mental disorders
Butler, Robert Neil. Aging and mental health : positive psychosocial approaches / [by] Robert N. Butler, Myrna I. Lewis. — 2nd ed. — Saint Louis : Mosby ; London : Distributed by Kimpton, 1977. — xiv,365p : ill, forms, port ; 26cm.
Previous ed.: 1973. — Bibl. — Index.
ISBN 0-8016-0921-6 Pbk : £7.00
(B77-22644)

618.9'76'89 — Old persons. Psychiatry
Geriatric psychiatry : a handbook for psychiatrists and primary care physicians / edited by Leopold Bellak, Toksoz B. Karasu with the assistance of Caroline Birenbaum. — New York [etc.] ; London : Grune and Stratton, [1977]. — viii,312p : ill, forms ; 24cm.
Published in the United States: 1976. — Index.
ISBN 0-8089-0967-3 : £10.65
(B77-13079)

619 — EXPERIMENTAL MEDICINE
619 — Medicine. Research. Use of laboratory animals. *National Anti-Vivisection Society viewpoints. Conference proceedings*
Moral, Scientific and Economic Aspects of Research Techniques not involving the Use of Living Animals *(Conference), Brighton, 1976.* 'The Moral, Scientific and Economic Aspects of Research Techniques not involving the Use of Living Animals' : text of speeches given at Brighton conference, March 1976. — London (51 Harley St., W1N 1DD) : National Anti-Vivisection Society, [1977]. — x,80p,[5] leaves of plates : ill, facsim, ports ; 21cm.
Pbk : £1.50
(B77-23477)

620 — ENGINEERING
620 — Engineering. Technological development. *Reports, surveys*
Advancing technologies / edited by E.G. Semler. — London [etc.] : Mechanical Engineering Publications, 1977. — ix,182p : ill ; 23cm.
Bibl. — Index.
ISBN 0-85298-346-8 : £6.00
(B77-21926)

620 — Jet cutting. *Conference proceedings*
International Symposium on Jet Cutting Technology, *3rd, Chicago, 1976.* Proceedings of the Third International Symposium on Jet Cutting Technology, Chicago U.S.A., 1976 / [editors H.S. Stephens, N.G. Coles, C.A. Stapleton]. — Cranfield (Cranfield, Bedford MK43 0AJ) : BHRA Fluid Engineering, 1976. — 552p in various pagings : ill, plans ; 31cm.
'... organised by BHRA Fluid Engineering in conjunction with IIT Research Institute, Chicago, ... [and] ... held at IIT Research Institute from May 11th to the 13th, 1976' - note. — Bibl. — Index.
ISBN 0-900983-55-8 : Unpriced
(B77-30320)

620 — Self piloting boring & drilling. *Conference proceedings*
International Conference on Deep Hole Drilling and Boring, *2nd, Brunel University, 1977.* Proceedings of the Second International Conference on Deep Hole Drilling and Boring, 25, 26, 27 May 1977, organised by the Department of Production Technology, Brunel University / edited by R.J. Grieve, B.J. Griffiths. — [Uxbridge] ([Uxbridge, Middx UB8 3PH]) : [The Department], [1977]. — 153 leaves in various pagings,[156]leaves of plates : ill ; 30cm.
ISBN 0-902215-36-1 Pbk : £20.00
(B77-31242)

620'.001'51535 — Engineering. Nonlinear dynamical processes
Distéfano, Néstor. Nonlinear processes in engineering : dynamic programming, invariant imbedding, quasilinearization, finite elements, system identification, optimization / [by] Néstor Distéfano. — New York ; London : Academic Press, 1974. — xvii,366p : ill ; 24cm. — (Mathematics in science and engineering ; vol.110)
Bibl. — Index.
ISBN 0-12-218050-x : Unpriced
(B77-20331)

620'.001'515353 — Engineering. Mathematics. Finite element methods
Zienkiewicz, Olgierd Cecil. The finite element method / [by] O.C. Zienkiewicz. — 3rd expanded and revised ed. — London [etc.] : McGraw-Hill, 1977. — xv,787p : ill ; 24cm.
Previous ed.: i.e. 2nd. expanded and revised ed., published as 'The finite element method in engineering science'. 1971. — Index.
ISBN 0-07-084072-5 : £13.50 : CIP rev.
(B77-16443)

620'.001'515353 — Engineering. Mathematics. Finite element methods. *Periodicals*
FEN : finite element news. — Wimborne (Horton Rd, Woodlands, Wimborne, Dorset BH21 6NB) : Robinson and Associates.
Issue [no.1]- ; Jan. 1976-. — [1976]-. — ill, ports ; 31cm.
Quarterly. — 32p. in 5th issue.
Sd : £8.50 yearly
ISSN 0309-6688
(B77-19434)

620'.0021'2 — Engineering. Foreign standards. *Periodicals. For British exporters*
Technical export news / Technical Help to Exporters. — Hemel Hempstead (Maylands Ave., Hemel Hempstead, Herts. HP2 4SQ) : T.H.E., British Standards Institution.
Supersedes: THE quarterly bulletin.
No.1- ; Sept. 1977-. — [1977]-. — ill ; 30cm.
Quarterly. — [8]p. in 1st issue.
Sd : Unpriced (free to members)
ISSN 0140-4474
(B77-31937)

620'.0022'8 — Engineering models. Design
Stansfield, Frank Melvin. Models / [by] F.M. Stansfield. — [Oxford] : Oxford University Press for the Design Council, the British Standards Institution and the Council of Engineering Institutions, 1976. — [2],26p : ill ; 30cm. — (Engineering design guides ; 16)
ISBN 0-19-859149-7 Sd : £1.50
(B77-11865)

620'.0022'8 — Engineering models. Making. *Manuals*
Evans, Martin. Model engineering / [by] Martin Evans. — London : Pitman, 1977. — xiv,210p : ill, ports ; 26cm.
Index.
ISBN 0-273-00380-1 : £7.95 : CIP rev.
(B77-16444)

620'.0022'8 — Engineering scale models
Schuring, Dieterich J. Scale models in engineering : fundamentals and applications / [by] Dieterich J. Schuring. — Oxford [etc.] : Pergamon, 1977. — xii,299p ; 26cm. — (Pergamon international library)
With answers to problems. — Bibl. — Index.
ISBN 0-08-020861-4 Pbk : Unpriced
ISBN 0-08-020860-6 Pbk : £7.00
(B77-27905)

620'.0022'8 — Radio controlled models. Radio controls
Butcher, Norman. Radio control guide / by Norman Butcher ; artwork Peter Holland ; photographs Dave Hughes ; additional contributions by Peter Chinn ... [et al.]. — Teddington (84 High St., Teddington, Middx TW11 8JD) : Radio Control Publishing Co. Ltd, 1976. — 250p,plate : ill, ports ; 21cm.
ISBN 0-903676-07-9 Pbk : Unpriced
(B77-01549)

Warring, Ronald Horace. Radio control for models / [by] R.H. Warring. — 2nd, revised ed. — London [etc.] : Pitman, 1976. — [5], 213p : ill, facsim ; 26cm.
Previous ed.: 1974. — Index.
ISBN 0-273-00204-x : £6.95
(B77-11254)

620'.0023 — Engineering. *Career guides*
Employment Service Agency. *Careers and Occupational Information Centre.* Professional engineers. — 5th ed. / Careers and Occupational Information Centre of the Employment Service Agency. — London : H.M.S.O., 1976. — [2],36,[1]p : ill ; 22cm. — (Choice of careers : new series ; 92)
Previous ed.: / prepared by the Central Youth Employment Executive. 1971.
ISBN 0-11-880906-7 Sd : £0.30
(B77-09057)

620'.0042 — Engineering. Design
Stephenson, John. Engineering design / [by] John Stephenson, R.A. Callander. — Sydney ; London [etc.] : Wiley, 1974. — xiii,705p : ill ; 28cm.
Bibl. — Index.
ISBN 0-471-82210-8 : £18.00
(B77-09731)

620'.0042 — Engineering. Design. *Conference proceedings*
Engineering Design Conference, *London, 1977.* Engineering Design Conference, 1977 : organised by Fairs & Exhibitions Limited ... — London : Fairs and Exhibitions Ltd.
[Spring : Part 1] : Mount Royal Hotel, Marble Arch, London ... 21-24 February 1977. — 1977. — 309p,(2 fold)in various pagings : ill, forms, ports ; 30cm.
Sp : £20.00
(B77-18194)

620'.0042 — Engineering. Design. Information systems. *Conference proceedings*
Information systems for designers : third international symposium : the proceedings of the meeting held at the University [of Southampton] 23-25 March 1977 / [editor G. Pitts]. — Worthing (33 Foxley La., High Salvington, Worthing, Sussex BN13 3AD) : Publication Services [for] Design Group, Department of Mechanical Engineering, University of Southampton, 1977. — [5],159p : ill, forms, map ; 30cm.
Bibl.
Pbk : £14.85
(B77-21191)

620'.0042 — Engineering. Design. Management aspects
Flurscheim, Cedric Harald. Engineering design interfaces : a management philosophy / [by] Charles H. Flurscheim. — London : Design Council, 1977. — 138p : ill ; 23cm.
ISBN 0-85072-051-6 : £4.95
(B77-23478)

620'.0042'02854 — Engineering. Design. Applications of computer systems. *Conference proceedings*
IFIP Working Conference on Computer-Aided Design Systems, *Austin, Texas, 1976.* CAD systems : proceedings of the IFIP Working Conference on Computer-Aided Design Systems / edited by John J. Allan III. — Amsterdam [etc.] ; Oxford : North-Holland Publishing Co., 1977. — xiii,457p : ill ; 23cm.
'... Conference [held] 12-14 February 1976 ... Organized by IFIP Technical Committee 5 ...' - half title page verso. — Index.
ISBN 0-7204-0472-x : £19.91
(B77-16920)

620'.0044 — Engineering components. Roundness. Measurement. Techniques
Dagnall, Henry. Let's talk roundness / [by] H. Dagnall. — Leicester (P.O. Box 36, Guthlaxton St., Leicester LE2 0SP) : Rank Taylor Hobson, 1976. — iv,77p : ill ; 21cm.
Index.
ISBN 0-901920-02-9 Pbk : £2.50
(B77-12493)

620'.0044 — Engineering. Measuring instruments
Gray, Bernard Francis. Measurements, instrumentation, and data transmission : a text for the OND in technology (engineering) / [by] B.F. Gray. — London [etc.] : Longman, 1977. — vi,169p : ill ; 22cm.
Index.
ISBN 0-582-41065-7 : £4.95
ISBN 0-582-41066-5 Pbk : £2.95
Also classified at 621.381
(B77-15322)

620'.0044 — Engineering. Measuring instruments. Accuracy. Testing
Hayward, A T J. Repeatability and accuracy : an introduction to the subject, and a proposed standard procedure for measuring the repeatability and estimating the accuracy of industrial measuring instruments / [by] A.T.J. Hayward. — London [etc.] : Mechanical Engineering Publications, 1977. — 63p : ill ; 21cm.
Bibl.: p.56. — Index.
ISBN 0-85298-351-4 Sd : Unpriced
(B77-27153)

620'.0044 — Instrumentation
Jones, Barry E. Instrumentation, measurement and feedback / [by] Barry E. Jones. — London [etc.] : McGraw-Hill, 1977. — xvi,283p : ill ; 24cm.
Bibl.: p.269-271. — Index.
ISBN 0-07-084069-5 : £6.25
(B77-18826)

620'.0044 — Instrumentation systems. *Readings*
Instrumentation / edited by J.J. Hunter, D.I. Crecraft ; [for the Open University, Instrumentation Course Team]. — Edinburgh : Holmes-McDougall [for] the Open University Press, 1973. — 178p : ill ; 30cm. — (Open University. Set books) (T291)
ISBN 0-7157-1294-2 Pbk : Unpriced
(B77-20332)

620'.0044 — Instrumentation systems. Operation. Effects of adverse environments. *Conference proceedings*
Operation of Instruments in Adverse Environments *(Conference), London, 1976.* Operation of instruments in adverse environments, 1976 : invited and contributed papers from the conference on the Operation of Instruments in Adverse Environments, held in London on 4 and 5 October 1976 / edited by J. Knight. — Bristol [etc.] : Institute of Physics, 1977. — vii,134p : ill ; 25cm. — (Institute of Physics. Conference series ; no.34 ISSN 0305-2346)
'... papers given at the conference on "The Operation of Instruments in Adverse Environments" ...' - Preface. — organized jointly by the Materials and Testing Group of the Institute of Physics, the Institute of Measurement and Control, and Professional Group C7 (Measuring and Control Equipment) of the Institution of Electrical Engineers' - title page verso. — Bibl.
ISBN 0-85498-125-x : £16.00 : CIP rev.
(B77-07938)

620'.0045 — Engineering equipment. Reliability
Smith, Charles Oliver. Introduction to reliability in design / [by] Charles O. Smith. — New York ; London [etc.] : McGraw-Hill, 1976. — xiv,269p : ill ; 25cm.
Bibl.: p.203-204. — Index.
ISBN 0-07-059083-4 : £13.70
(B77-04871)

620'.005 — Engineering. *Juvenile literature. Serials*
The '**Look** and learn' book of speed & power. — London : IPC Magazines.
1978. — 1977. — 2-79p : ill(some col), col map, plan ; 28cm. — (A Fleetway annual)
ISBN 0-85037-369-7 : £1.45
ISSN 0140-7163
(B77-33265)

620'.005 — Engineering. *Serials*
Kempe's engineers year-book. — London : Morgan-Grampian.
1977 : 82nd ed. / edited by C.E. Prockter. — 1977. — 2v.(ca 2760p) : ill, maps, plans ; 19cm.
In slip case. — Bibl. — Index.
Unpriced
ISBN 0-900865-61-x Vol.1
ISBN 0-900865-57-1 Vol.2
(B77-05468)

620'.005 — Periodicals on engineering: Periodicals with British imprints: 'Engineer'. Articles, to 1976. *Reports, surveys*
'The **engineer**' : highlights of 120 years / editor John Mortimer ; associate editor Ralph Taphouse ; writers Cedric Beaton ... [et al.]. — London : Morgan-Grampian, 1976. — 242p,[5] fold leaves of plates : ill(some col), facsims, plans, ports ; 31cm.
Pbk : £5.00
(B77-25683)

620'.006'241 — Consulting engineering. Organisations. *Great Britain. Association of Consulting Engineers. Directories*
Association of Consulting Engineers. List of members of the Association of Consulting Engineers. — London (87 Vincent Sq., SW1P 2PH) : The Association.
[1977] : corrected to 1st September, 1976. — [1977]. — [1],132p : coat of arms ; 21cm.
ISBN 0-903397-07-2 Pbk : £1.50
(B77-06545)

The **consulting** engineers who's who & year book / [Association of Consulting Engineers]. — London (Elm House, Elm St., WC1X 0BP) : Northwood Publications Ltd [for] the Association.
1976. — [1976]. — 472,xliv p : ill ; 22cm.
£4.00
(B77-20333)

1977. — [1977]. — 488,xlvi p : ill ; 22cm.
£4.95
ISBN 0-7198-2590-3
(B77-18195)

620'.007 — Engineering. Information sources
Mount, Ellis. Guide to basic information sources in engineering / by Ellis Mount. — New York ; London [etc.] : Wiley, 1976. — viii, 196p : facsims ; 22cm. — (Information resources series)
'A Halsted Press Book'. — Index.
ISBN 0-470-15013-0 : £9.50
(B77-08428)

620'.007'1141 — Engineers. Professional education. *Great Britain*
Wearne, Stephen Hugh. The white heat of technology with a human face / [by] Stephen Wearne. — [Bradford] ([Bradford, W. Yorkshire BD7 1DP]) : University of Bradford, [1975]. — [5],7p ; 21cm. — (University of Bradford. Inaugural lectures)
'Edited version of inaugural lecture delivered at the University of Bradford on 25 November 1975' - p.[3].
Sd : Unpriced
(B77-20334)

620'.007'22 — Engineering. *Case studies*
Vesper, Karl H. Engineers at work : a casebook / [by] Karl H. Vesper. — Boston [Mass.] [etc.] ; London : Houghton Mifflin, 1975. — ix,226p : ill, forms, maps ; 28cm.
ISBN 0-395-18407-x Pbk : £5.00
(B77-20335)

620'.007'22 — Engineering, 1800-1977. *Case studies*
Low, Michael. Making things work : great achievements in engineering / [by] Michael Low, Frank McKim, Kevin Walton ; with a foreword by the Duke of Edinburgh. — [London] ([2 Queens Drive, W3 0HA]) : Peter Lowe, 1977. — 5-115p : ill(chiefly col), maps(chiefly col) ; 28cm.
Bibl.: p.112. — Index.
ISBN 0-85654-020-x : £3.25
(B77-33266)

620'.0076 — Engineering science. *Exercises, worked examples. Secondary school texts*
Engineering Science Project. Problems book / Engineering Science Project. — Basingstoke [etc.] : Macmillan for the Schools Council, 1977. — vii,104p : ill ; 30cm.
With answers. — Index.
ISBN 0-333-15641-2 Pbk : £2.95 : CIP rev.
(B77-04872)

620'.009 — Engineering, to 1975
Thompson, Hugh. Engineers and engineering / [by] Hugh Thompson. — London : Batsford, 1976. — 95p : ill, facsim, ports ; 26cm. — (Past-into-present series)
Bibl.: p.94. — Index.
ISBN 0-7134-3241-1 : £2.95
(B77-00793)

620'.0092'4 — Engineering. Rolt, Lionel Thomas Caswall. *Autobiographies*
Rolt, Lionel Thomas Caswall. Landscape with canals / [by] L.T.C. Rolt. — London : Allen Lane, 1977. — 188p,[8]p of plates : ill, maps, ports ; 23cm.
'Being the second volume of "Landscape with machines" an autobiography'.
ISBN 0-7139-0799-1 : £5.50
(B77-16921)

620.1 — ENGINEERING MECHANICS AND MATERIALS
620.1 — Applied mechanics
Bacon, Dennis Henry. Mechanical technology / [by] D.H. Bacon and R.C. Stephens. — London [etc.] : Newnes-Butterworths, 1977. — [11], 412p : ill ; 24cm.
ISBN 0-408-00280-8 Pbk : Unpriced
(B77-18827)

Hughes, J H. Basic engineering mechanics / [by] J.H. Hughes, K.F. Martin. — London [etc.] : Macmillan, 1977. — x,364p : ill ; 23cm.
With answers. — Index.
ISBN 0-333-17721-5 Pbk : £5.95
(B77-19435)

Parker, Harry, *b.1887.* Simplified mechanics and strength of materials / [by] the late Harry Parker. — 3rd ed. / prepared by Harold D. Hauf. — New York ; London [etc.] : Wiley, 1977. — xvii,325p : ill ; 22cm.
'A Wiley-Interscience Publication'. — With answers to selected problems. — Text on lining paper. — Previous ed.: 1961. — Index.
ISBN 0-471-66562-2 : £11.25
(B77-30321)

Smith, Charles Edward, *b.1932.* Applied mechanics / [by] Charles E. Smith. — New York ; London [etc.] : Wiley.
In 3 vols.
[Vol.1] : Statics. — [1977]. — xiii,200p : ill(chiefly col) ; 24cm.
Text, col. ill. on lining papers. — Published in the United States: 1976. — Bibl.: p.195. — Index.
ISBN 0-471-80460-6 : £7.80
(B77-09732)

[Vol.2] : Dynamics. — [1977]. — xi,184p : ill(chiefly col) ; 24cm.
Text, col. ill. on lining papers. — Published in the United States: 1976. — Bibl.: p.179. — Index.
ISBN 0-471-80178-x : £7.80
(B77-09733)

[Vol.3] : More dynamics. — 1976. — xii,244p : ill ; 24cm.
Ill. on lining papers. — Bibl.: p.239. — Index.
ISBN 0-471-79996-3 : £11.00
(B77-00262)

620.1 — Applied mechanics. *Reviews of research*
Advances in applied mechanics. — New York [etc.] ; London : Academic Press.
Vol.16 / edited by Chia-Shun Yih. — 1976. — xii,433p : ill, port ; 24cm.
Bibl. — Index.
ISBN 0-12-002016-5 : £28.05
(B77-09734)

Mechanics today. — New York ; Oxford [etc.] : Pergamon [for] the American Academy of Mechanics. — (Pergamon mechanics today series)
Vol.3 / edited by S. Nemat-Nasser. — 1976. — xxii,306p : ill ; 24cm.
Index.
ISBN 0-08-019882-1 : £15.00
(B77-01550)

620.1'001'51563 — Applied mechanics. Vector analysis
Beer, Ferdinand Pierre. Vector mechanics for engineers : statics and dynamics / [by] Ferdinand P. Beer, E. Russell Johnston, Jr. — 3rd ed. — New York ; London [etc.] : McGraw-Hill, 1977. — xxv,957p : col ill ; 25cm.
With answers to even-numbered problems. — Text, ill. on lining papers. — Previous ed. New York : McGraw-Hill, 1972. — Index.
ISBN 0-07-004277-2 : £18.40
(B77-22645)

620.1'03 — Applied statics
Ginsberg, Jerry H. Statics / [by] Jerry H. Ginsberg, Joseph Genin. — New York ; London [etc.] : Wiley, 1977. — xiii,439p : ill(chiefly col) ; 25cm.
Text on lining papers. — With answers to odd-numbered problems. — Index.
ISBN 0-471-29607-4 : Unpriced
(B77-22646)

620.1'06 — Fluid power equipment
Goodwin, A B. Fluid power systems : theory, worked examples and problems / [by] A.B. Goodwin. — London [etc.] : Macmillan, 1976. — ix,212p : ill ; 24cm.
ISBN 0-333-19368-7 Pbk : £3.25
(B77-05469)

620.1'06 — Fluids. Applied mechanics
Duckworth, R A. Mechanics of fluids / by R.A. Duckworth. — London [etc.] : Longman, 1977. — ix,275p : ill ; 22cm. — (Introductory engineering series)
With answers to problems. — Bibl.: p.269-270. — Index.
ISBN 0-582-44139-0 : £8.50
ISBN 0-582-44138-2 Pbk : £4.95
(B77-14265)

620.1'06 — Fluids. Applied mechanics. *Conference proceedings*
International Conference on Hydraulics, Pneumatics and Fluidics in Control and Automation, *Toronto, 1976.* Proceedings of the conference on fluids in control and automation : International Conference on Hydraulics, Pneumatics and Fluidics in Control and Automation, Toronto, Canada, 1976, organised and sponsored by BHRA [i.e. British Hydromechanics Research Association] Fluid Engineering in conjunction with Ontario Ministry of Industry and Tourism / [edited by H.S. Stephens, J.A.G. Hemmings]. — Cranfield (Cranfield, Bedford MK43 0AJ) : BHRA Fluid Engineering, 1977. — 478p in various pagings : ill ; 31cm.
ISBN 0-900983-53-1 : £20.00 : CIP rev.
(B77-07399)

620.1'06'0212 — Fluid power. *Technical data*
Brater, Ernest Frederick. Handbook of hydraulics for the solution of hydraulic engineering problems. — 6th ed. / [by] Ernest F. Brater, Horace Williams King. — New York ; London [etc.] : McGraw-Hill, 1976. — 600p in various pagings : ill ; 20cm.
Previous ed.: published as 'Handbook of hydraulics for the solution of hydrostatic and fluid-flow problems' / by Horace Williams King and Ernest Frederick Brater. 1963. — Index.
ISBN 0-07-007243-4 : £22.00
(B77-02368)

620.1'064 — Fluids. Drag. Reduction. *Conference proceedings*
International Conference on Drag Reduction, *2nd, University of Cambridge, 1977.* Drag reduction : papers presented at the Second International Conference on Drag Reduction / [editors H.S. Stephens, J.A. Clarke]. — Cranfield (Cranfield, Bedford MK43 0AJ) : BHRA Fluid Engineering, 1977. — 374p in various pagings : ill ; 30cm.
'Conference held at University of Cambridge, August 31-September 2, 1977'. — Bibl.
ISBN 0-900983-71-x Pbk : Unpriced
(B77-30322)

620.1'064 — Fluids. Flow. Separation. Control
Chang, Paul Keuk. Control of flow separation : energy conservation, operational efficiency and safety / [by] Paul K. Chang. — Washington ; London : Hemisphere Publishing Corporation ; New York ; London [etc.] : McGraw-Hill, 1976. — xvii,523p : ill ; 24cm. — (Series in thermal and fluids engineering)
Bibl. — Index.
ISBN 0-07-010513-8 : £29.20
(B77-25684)

620.1'1 — Materials
Smith, Charles Oliver. The science of engineering materials / [by] Charles O. Smith. — 2nd ed. — Englewood Cliffs ; London [etc.] : Prentice-Hall, 1977. — xix,491p : ill ; 24cm.
Ill. on lining papers. — Previous ed.: 1969. — Bibl.: p.467-480. — Index.
ISBN 0-13-794990-1 : £14.35
(B77-15897)

620.1'1 — Materials. *For craftwork. School texts*
Stokes, Peter. Looking at materials / [by] Peter Stokes. — Sunbury-on-Thames [etc.] : Nelson, 1976. — 64p : ill(chiefly col), forms ; 18x26cm. — (Nelson integrated craft ; 1)
ISBN 0-17-431060-9 Pbk : £0.95
(B77-05470)

620.1'1 — Materials. *Reviews of research*
Progress in materials science. — Oxford [etc.] : Pergamon.
Vol.21 / edited by Bruce Chalmers, J.W. Christian and T.B. Massalski. — 1976. — [5], 461p : ill ; 26cm. — (International series on materials science and technology)
Index.
ISBN 0-08-018171-6 : £28.00
ISSN 0079-6425
(B77-10825)

620.1'1'03 — Materials. *Encyclopaedias*
Brady, George Stuart. Materials handbook : an encyclopedia for managers, technical professionals, purchasing and production managers, technicians, supervisors, and foremen. — 11th ed. / [by] George S. Brady, Henry R. Clauser. — New York ; London [etc.] : McGraw-Hill, 1977. — xi,1011p ; 24cm.

Previous ed.: published as 'Materials handbook : an encyclopedia for purchasing managers, engineers, executives and foremen' / by George S. Brady. New York : McGraw-Hill, 1971. — Index.
ISBN 0-07-007069-5 : £21.40
(B77-25685)

620.1'12 — Materials. Mechanics
Ford, *Sir* Hugh, *b.1913.* Advanced mechanics of materials / [by] Sir Hugh Ford ... with the collaboration of J.M. Alexander. — 2nd ed. — Chichester : Ellis Horwood ; New York ; London [etc.] : Distributed by Wiley, 1977. — x,672p : ill ; 24cm. — ([Ellis Horwood series in engineering science])
Previous ed.: London : Longman, 1963. — Bibl. — Index.
ISBN 0-85312-056-0 : £12.50
(B77-21927)

Shigley, Joseph Edward. Applied mechanics of materials / [by] Joseph Edward Shigley. — New York ; London [etc.] : McGraw-Hill, 1976. — ix,371p : ill ; 25cm.
Text on lining papers. — With answers to selected problems. — Index.
ISBN 0-07-056845-6 : £14.55
(B77-04873)

620.1'12 — Materials. Physical properties
Chong, C V Y. Properties of materials / [by] C.V.Y. Chong. — Plymouth : Macdonald and Evans, 1977. — xviii,318p : ill ; 19cm. — (The M. & E. handbook series)
Bibl. — Index.
ISBN 0-7121-1659-1 Pbk : £3.00
(B77-10395)

620.1'12 — Materials. Structure & physical properties
Brick, Robert Maynard. Structure and properties of engineering materials. — 4th ed. / [by] Robert M. Brick, Alan W. Pense, Robert B. Gordon. — New York ; London [etc.] : McGraw-Hill, 1977. — xii,500p : ill ; 25cm. — (McGraw-Hill series in materials science and engineering)
Text on lining papers. — Previous ed.: published as 'Structure and properties of alloys' / by Robert M. Brick, Robert B. Gordon, Arthur Phillips. 1965. — Index.
ISBN 0-07-007721-5 : £17.65
(B77-24273)

Guy, Albert Glasgow. Essentials of materials science / [by] A.G. Guy. — New York ; London [etc.] : McGraw-Hill, 1976. — x,468p : ill ; 24cm.
Text, ill. on lining papers. — With answers to review questions and selected problems. — Bibl. — Index.
ISBN 0-07-025351-x : £14.55
(B77-00263)

Treatise on materials science and technology / edited by Herbert Herman. — New York [etc.] ; London : Academic Press.
Vol.7 : Microstructures of irradiated materials / [by] H.S. Rosenbaum. — 1975. — xiii,173p : ill ; 24cm.
Bibl.: p.160-168. — Index.
ISBN 0-12-341807-0 : Unpriced
(B77-19436)

620.1'12 — Materials. Structure & properties
Harris, Bryan, *b.1935.* Structure and properties of engineering materials / [by] B. Harris and A.R. Bunsell. — London [etc.] : Longman, 1977. — xv,347p : ill ; 23cm. — (Introductory engineering series)
Bibl. — Index.
ISBN 0-582-44000-9 : £10.95
ISBN 0-582-44001-7 Pbk : £7.95
(B77-29486)

Higgins, Raymond Aurelius. The properties of engineering materials / [by] Raymond A. Higgins. — London [etc.] : Hodder and Stoughton, 1977. — [6],441p : ill ; 23cm.
Index.
ISBN 0-340-17908-2 : £8.45
ISBN 0-340-17909-0 Pbk : £4.95
(B77-29487)

620.1'12 — Solid materials. Strength
Open University. *Introduction to Materials Course Team.* Strong materials ; [and], Electrons and waves / prepared by the [Open University, Introduction to Materials] Course Team. — 3rd ed. — Milton Keynes : Open University Press, 1977. — [9],31,61p : ill(chiefly col) ; 30cm. — (A second level course : an introduction to materials ; units 1A and 1B) (TS251 ; 1A and 1B)
With answers. — Previous ed.: 1974.
Pbk : Unpriced
Also classified at 531'.1133
(B77-26349)

620.1'1217 — Materials. Effects of high temperatures
Open University. *Materials under Stress Course Team.* Survival at high temperature / prepared by the [Open University, Materials under Stress] Course Team. — Milton Keynes : Open University Press.
Compendium of your reference and instructional literature. — 1976. — 57p : ill(some col) ; 30cm. — (Technology, a third level course : materials under stress ; units 13B-15B) (T351 ; 13B-15B CYRIL)
With answers. — Pierced for binder. — Bibl.: p.53.
ISBN 0-335-06159-1 Pbk : Unpriced
(B77-14765)

620.1'1223 — Corrosion. Control
Pludek, V R. Design and corrosion control / [by] V.R. Pludek. — London [etc.] : Macmillan, 1977. — ix,383p : ill ; 24cm.
Index.
ISBN 0-333-19139-0 : £15.00
(B77-09058)

620.11'223 — Corrosion. Control. Use of metallic coatings
Carter, V E. Metallic coatings for corrosion control / [by] V.E. Carter. — London [etc.] : Newnes-Butterworths, 1977. — [8],183p : ill ; 23cm. — (Corrosion control series)
Bibl.: p.179. — Index.
ISBN 0-408-00270-0 : £9.00
(B77-18197)

620.1'123 — Materials. Dimensional stability
Marschall, Charles W. Dimensional instability : an introduction / by Charles W. Marschall and Robert E. Maringer. — Oxford [etc.] : Pergamon, 1977. — viii,323p : ill ; 26cm. — (Pergamon international library : international series on materials science and technology ; vol.22)
Bibl. — Index.
ISBN 0-08-021305-7 : £12.50
(B77-32668)

620.1'123 — Materials. Fatigue. Effects of environment. *Conference proceedings*
The **influence** of environment on fatigue : [papers read at a] conference sponsored [i.e. organised] by the Applied Mechanics Group of the Institution of Mechanical Engineers and the Society of Environmental Engineers, London, 18-19 May 1977. — London [etc.] : Mechanical Engineering Publications Limited for the Institution, 1977. — xiv,169p : ill ; 31cm. — (Institution of Mechanical Engineers. Conference publications ; 1977-4)
ISBN 0-85298-376-x : Unpriced
(B77-28668)

620.1'123 — Materials. Stresses & strains. Measurement
British Society for Strain Measurement. Methods and practice for stress and strain measurement / British Society for Strain Measurement. — [London] ([20 Peel St., W.8]) : [The Society].
Part 1 : Measurement of strain, load and temperature / editor I.M. Allison. — 1977. — 25p : ill ; 25cm.
Sd : Unpriced
(B77-28669)

620.1'123 — Stress analysis
Budynas, Richard G. Advanced strength and applied stress analysis / [by] Richard G. Budynas. — New York ; London [etc.] : McGraw-Hill, 1977. — xvii,508p : ill, facsim ; 25cm.
With answers to selected problems. — Index.
ISBN 0-07-008828-4 : £15.75
(B77-32669)

Hendry, Arnold William. Elements of experimental stress analysis / by A.W. Hendry. — SI ed. — Oxford [etc.] : Pergamon, 1977. — viii,193p : ill ; 22cm. — (Pergamon international library : structures and solid body mechanics division)
Previous ed.: 1964. — Bibl. — Index.
ISBN 0-08-021301-4 : £5.50
ISBN 0-08-021300-6 Pbk : £3.00
(B77-15898)

620.1'1233 — Nonlinear viscoelastic materials. Deformation. Mathematics
Findley, William N. Creep and relaxation of nonlinear viscoelastic materials : with an introduction to linear viscoelasticity / by William N. Findley, James S. Lai and Kasif Onaran. — Amsterdam [etc.] ; Oxford : North-Holland publishing Co. [etc.], 1976. — xiii,367p : ill ; 23cm. — (North-Holland series in applied mathematics and mechanics)
Index.
ISBN 0-7204-2369-4 : £19.80
(B77-06147)

620.1'126 — Solid materials. Fracture
Institute of Physics. *Stress Analysis Group. Annual Conference, University of Sheffield, 1976.* Fracture mechanics in engineering practice / edited by P. Stanley. — London : Applied Science Publishers, 1977. — xiii,419p : ill ; 23cm.
'Papers presented at the 1976 Annual Conference of the Stress Analysis Group of the Institute of Physics held at the University of Sheffield ...' - half title page verso. — Index.
ISBN 0-85334-723-9 : £25.00
(B77-31938)

620.1'126 — Universities. *Great Britain. Open University. Curriculum subjects: Solid materials. Fracture. Courses: 'Materials under stress'*
Open University. *Materials under Stress Course Team.* Course guide / prepared by the [Open University, Materials under Stress] Course Team. — Milton Keynes : Open University Press, 1976. — 15p ; 30cm. — (Technology, a third level course : materials under stress) (T351 ; CG)
Sd : Unpriced
(B77-04243)

620.1'1299 — Crystalline materials. Stereographic projections. *Collections*
Clarke, P T. Standard stereograms for materials science / [by] P.T. Clarke ; [for the] National Physical Laboratory, Department of Industry. — London : H.M.S.O., 1976. — [11],223p : ill ; 29cm.
Two plastic sheets in pocket. — Bibl.: p.[7].
ISBN 0-11-480038-3 : .00
(B77-08429)

620.1'2 — Timber. *Identification manuals*
Edlin, Herbert Leeson. What wood is that? : a manual of wood identification / [by] Herbert L. Edlin. — London (67 Worship St., EC2A 2EL) : Stobart and Son Ltd, 1977. — 160p : ill, samples ; 23cm.
Fold. leaf of 40 wood samples attached to inside cover. — Originally published: London : Thames and Hudson, 1969.
ISBN 0-85442-008-8 : £6.95
(B77-23479)

620.1'36'03 — Materials: Concrete. *Polyglot dictionaries*
Fédération internationale de la précontrainte. Multilingual dictionary of concrete : a compilation of terms in English, French, German, Spanish, Dutch and Russian / compiled under the auspices of Fédération internationale de la précontrainte. — Amsterdam ; Oxford [etc.] : Elsevier, 1976. — [7],201p ; 22cm.
Indexes.
ISBN 0-444-41237-9 : £16.88
(B77-03584)

620.1'36'2 — Concrete. Effects of alkalies. *Conference proceedings*
The **effect** of alkalies on the properties of concrete : proceedings of a symposium held in London, September 1976 / editor A.B. Poole ; sponsored by Concrete-International Group on Alkali Reactions ... [et al.]. — Slough : Cement and Concrete Association, [1977]. — vi,374p : ill, maps ; 21cm.
'... Symposium held at the Cement and Concrete Association, Wexham Springs ...' - Foreword.
ISBN 0-7210-1070-9 Pbk : Private circulation
(B77-21928)

620.1'37 — Materials: Reinforced concrete
Faber, John. Reinforced concrete simply explained. — 6th ed. / [by] John Faber and David Alsop. — London [etc.] : Oxford University Press, 1976. — vii,148p : ill ; 23cm.
Previous ed.: / by Oscar Faber ; revised by John Faber. 1959.
ISBN 0-19-859514-x : £4.95
(B77-02369)

620.1'4 — Materials: Ceramics. Electrical properties & optical properties
Electrical and optical properties of glasses and ceramics : a joint meeting of the Basic Science Section of the British Ceramic Society and the Technology Section of the Society of Glass Technology. — [Stoke-on-Trent] ([Shelton House, Stoke-on-Trent, Staffs.]) : British Ceramic Society, 1976. — 48p in various pagings : ill ; 30cm.
'Extended Abstracts (unrefereed) of papers to be presented at the Convention 1976' - cover. — '[held at] St Andrews, 6-8th April 1976' - cover.
Sd : Unpriced
(B77-20336)

620.1'6'23 — Cathodic protection
Baeckmann, W von. Handbook of cathodic protection : the theory and practice of electrochemical corrosion protection techniques / [by] W. v. Baeckmann and W. Schwenk ; with contributions by ... [others] ; [translated from the German by E. Neufeld and P. Neufeld]. — Redhill (2 Queensway, Redhill, Surrey) : Portcullis Press, 1975. — xix,396p : ill ; 25cm.
Translation of: 'Handbuch des kathodischen Korrosionsschutzes'. Weinheim : Verlag Chemie, 1971. — Index.
ISBN 0-901994-57-x : £20.00
(B77-10396)

620.1'6'23 — Metals. Corrosion
British Steel Corporation. Corrosion : attack and defence / [British Steel Corporation and NCST Trent Polytechnic] ; material collected and arranged by Cyril Gorham. — [Sheffield] ([P.O. Box 64, The Mount, Sheffield S10 2PZ]) : Market Promotion Department, British Steel Corporation, Special Steels Division, 1975. — 70p : ill ; 30cm.
Bibl.: p.68-69. — Index.
ISBN 0-9500451-2-8 Pbk : £1.50
(B77-15900)

620.1'6'3 — Engineering equipment. Metal components. Fatigue
Harris, William John. The significance of fatigue / [by] W.J. Harris. — [London] : Oxford University Press for the Design Council, the British Standards Institution and the Council of Engineering Institutions, 1976. — [2],23p : ill ; 30cm. — (Engineering design guides ; 14)
Bibl.: p.23.
ISBN 0-19-859146-2 Sd : £1.40
(B77-14766)

620.1'6'3 — Metal components. Fatigue. *For design*
Duggan, Terance Vincent. Fatigue as a design criterion / [by] Terance V. Duggan and James Byrne. — London [etc.] : Macmillan, 1977. — xii,164p : ill ; 24cm.
Index.
ISBN 0-333-21488-9 : £10.50
(B77-32670)

620.1'6'33 — Metals. Plasticity
Slater, R A C. Engineering plasticity : theory and application to metal forming processes / [by] R.A.C. Slater. — London [etc.] : Macmillan, 1977. — x,422p : ill ; 25cm.
Index.
ISBN 0-333-15709-5 : £21.00
(B77-23480)

620.1'6'6 — Metals. Dynamic fracture toughness. Measurement. *Conference proceedings*
Dynamic fracture toughness : an international conference arranged by the Welding Institute and the American Society for Metals, London, 5-7 July 1976 / conference technical director, M.G. Dawes. — Cambridge : Welding Institute.
Vol.1 : Papers. — 1977. — [4],349p : ill ; 30cm.
ISBN 0-85300-107-3 Pbk : £16.50
(B77-18198)

620.1'6'6 — Metals. Plane strain fracture toughness. Measurement. *Standards*
British Standards Institution. Methods of test for plane strain fracture toughness (KIC) of metallic materials = Méthodes d'essais de la ténacité a rupture sous des efforts planaires (KIC) des matériaux métalliques = Prüfverfahren für die Planbeanspruchungsbruchzähigkeit (KIC) metallischer Werkstoffe / British Standards Institution. — London : B.S.I., 1977. — [2],11, [2]p : ill ; 30cm. — (BS5447 : 1977)
Pierced for binder.
ISBN 0-580-09429-4 Sd : £3.60
(B77-17550)

620.1'92 — Materials: Organolithic polymers
Wilson, Alan D. Organolithic macromolecular materials / [by] Alan D. Wilson, Stephen Crisp. — London : Applied Science Publishers, 1977. — ix,298p : ill ; 23cm.
Bibl. — Index.
ISBN 0-85334-699-2 : £16.00
(B77-20337)

620.1'92 — Polymer composite materials. Structure & mechanical properties
Polymer engineering composites / edited by M.O.W. Richardson. — London : Applied Science Publishers, 1977. — xii,568p : ill ; 23cm. — (Materials science series)
Index.
ISBN 0-85334-722-0 : £30.00
(B77-24986)

620.1'923 — Materials: Plastics. Physical properties
Ogorkiewicz, Richard Marian. The engineering properties of plastics / [by] R.M. Ogorkiewicz. — [Oxford] : Oxford University Press for the Design Council, the British Standards Institution and the Council of Engineering Institutions, 1977. — [2],22p : ill ; 30cm. — (Engineering design guides ; 17)
Bibl.: p.22.
ISBN 0-19-859152-7 Sd : £1.50
(B77-09735)

620.1'923'3 — Plastics. Stresses & strains. Testing. *For design*
Open University. *Materials under Stress Course Team.* Designing with plastics / prepared by the [Open University, Materials under Stress] Course Team. — Milton Keynes : Open University Press.
Compendium of your reference and instructional literature. — 1976. — 31p : ill(some col) ; 30cm. — (Technology, a third level course : materials under stress ; unit 12B [CYRIL]) (T351 ; 12B CYRIL)
With answers. — Pierced for binder. — Bibl.: p.28.
ISBN 0-335-06163-x Pbk : Unpriced
(B77-02370)

620.2 — ENGINEERING. SOUND AND RELATED VIBRATIONS

620.2'05 — Acoustic engineering. *Periodicals*
MOA : IEE journal on microwaves, optics and acoustics. — Stevenage (c/o P.O. Box 8, Southgate House, Stevenage, Herts. SG1 1HO) : Institution of Electrical Engineers.
Vol.1, no.1- ; Sept. 1976-. — 1976-. — ill ; 30cm.
Three issues a year. — 40, 3p. in 1st issue.
Sd : £7.50
ISSN 0308-6976
Primary classification 621.381'3'05
(B77-12499)

620.2'3 — Machinery. Noise. Control measures. *Conference proceedings*
Industrial noise and its reduction : edited proceedings of the seminar, Leamington Spa, October 1975 / edited by D. Boxall. — Wantage (Grove Laboratories, Denchworth Rd, Wantage, Oxon. OX12 9BJ) : BNF Metals Technology Centre : International Environmental Bureau, 1976. — [8],200p : ill ; 30cm.
Bibl.: p.193-194.
Pbk : Unpriced
(B77-21193)

620.2'3'071141 — Higher education institutions. Curriculum subjects: Noise. Teaching. *Great Britain. Conference proceedings*
British Conference on the Teaching of Vibration and Noise in Higher Education, *1st, Sheffield, 1975.* Proceedings of the First British Conference on the Teaching of Vibration and Noise in Higher Education, held in Sheffield City Polytechnic, 8-10 July 1975 / edited by G.J. McNulty ... [et al.]. — Sheffield (Halfords House, 16 Fitzalan Sq., Sheffield S1 2BZ) : Industrial Liaison Centre, Sheffield City Polytechnic, 1976. — [5],7,762[i.e.804]p : ill ; 31cm.
ISBN 0-903761-03-3 : Unpriced
Also classified at 620.3'07'1141
(B77-30323)

620.3 — ENGINEERING. MECHANICAL VIBRATION

620.3 — Mechanical vibration & shock. Engineering aspects
Shock and vibration handbook / edited by Cyril M. Harris and Charles E. Crede. — 2nd ed. — New York ; London [etc.] : McGraw-Hill, [1977]. — 1332p in various pagings : ill ; 24cm. — (McGraw-Hill handbooks)
This ed. published in the United States: 1976. — Previous ed.: in 3 vols. 1961. — Bibl. — Index.
ISBN 0-07-026799-5 : £27.00
(B77-09736)

620.3 — Resonance oscillations. Engineering aspects
Evan-Iwanowski, R M. Resonance oscillations in mechanical systems / by R.M. Evan-Iwanowski. — Amsterdam ; Oxford [etc.] : Elsevier, 1976. — xiii,292p : ill ; 25cm.
Index.
ISBN 0-444-41474-6 : £17.94
(B77-06148)

620.3'03 — Mechanical vibration & shock. Engineering aspects. *Glossaries*
British Standards Institution. Glossary of terms relating to mechanical vibration and shock = Vocabulaire des termes relatifs aux vibrations et chocs mécaniques = Verzeichnis von Begriffen in Verbindung mit mechanischer Schwingung und Erschütterung / British Standards Institution. — 1st revision. — London : B.S.I., 1976. — [2],30p ; 30cm. — (BS.3015 : 1976)
Pierced for binder. — Index.
ISBN 0-580-09142-2 Sd : £4.00
(B77-03059)

620.3'07'1141 — Higher education institutions. Curriculum subjects: Engineering aspects of mechanical vibration. Teaching. *Great Britain. Conference proceedings*
British Conference on the Teaching of Vibration and Noise in Higher Education, *1st, Sheffield, 1975.* Proceedings of the First British Conference on the Teaching of Vibration and Noise in Higher Education, held in Sheffield City Polytechnic, 8-10 July 1975 / edited by G.J. McNulty ... [et al.]. — Sheffield (Halfords House, 16 Fitzalan Sq., Sheffield S1 2BZ) : Industrial Liaison Centre, Sheffield City Polytechnic, 1976. — [5],7,762[i.e.804]p : ill ; 31cm.
ISBN 0-903761-03-3 : Unpriced
Primary classification 620.2'3'071141
(B77-30323)

620.4 — ENGINEERING TECHNOLOGIES
620'.416'2 — Fixed marine structures. Dynamics
Hallam, M G. Dynamics of marine structures : methods of calculating the dynamic response of fixed structures subject to wave and current action / [by] M.G. Hallam, N.J. Heaf, L.R. Wootton ; [for Atkins Research and Development]. — London (6 Storey's Gate, SW1P 3AU) : Construction Industry Research and Information Association, Underwater Engineering Group, 1977. — 315p : ill ; 30cm. — (Construction Industry Research and Information Association. Underwater Engineering Group. Reports ; UR8 ISSN 0305-4055)
Bibl.: p.296-305.
ISBN 0-86017-023-3 Pbk : £36.00(£12.00 to members)
(B77-20338)

620'.416'2 — Marine structures. Corrosion
Rowlands, J C. Corrosion for marine and offshore engineers / by J.C. Rowlands and B. Angell. — London (76 Mark La., EC3R 7JN) : Marine Media Management Ltd for the Institute of Marine Engineers, 1976. — [5], 66p : ill ; 21cm. — (Marine engineering practice ; vol.2, part 11)
Bibl.
ISBN 0-900976-55-1 Sd : £3.95
(B77-14266)

620'.416'2025 — Ocean engineering. *Directories*
Jane's ocean technology. — London : Jane's Yearbooks.
1976-77 : second year of issue / edited by Robert L. Trillo. — 1976. — 52,679p : ill, plans ; 33cm.
Index.
ISBN 0-354-00530-8 : £25.00
ISSN 0307-3149
(B77-03060)

620'.416'207 — Ocean engineering. Information sources
Heriot-Watt University. *Institute of Offshore Engineering.* Guide to information services in marine technology / [Institute of Offshore Engineering, Heriot-Watt University]. — 2nd ed. / compiled by Arnold Myers. — Edinburgh (Riccarton, Edinburgh EH14 4AS) : The Institute, 1976. — 107p ; 21cm.
Previous ed.: / compiled by Martran Limited. 1973. — Bibl.: p.96-102. — Index.
ISBN 0-904046-02-8 Sp : £2.00
(B77-12494)

620'.416'2071141 — Ocean engineers. Professional education. *Great Britain. Conference proceedings*
Symposium on Education and Training for Naval Architecture and Ocean Engineering, *Royal Institution of Naval Architects, 1976.* Proceedings of the Symposium on Education and Training for Naval Architecture and Ocean Engineering : held at the Royal Institution of Naval Architects ... 9th April, 1976. — London (10 Upper Belgrave St., SW1X 8BQ) : Royal Institution of Naval Architects, 1976. — [5], 88p : ill ; 30cm.
ISBN 0-903055-10-4 Pbk : £10.00
Also classified at 623.8'1'071141
(B77-04874)

620'.46 — Telecommunication systems: Remote control systems. *Conference proceedings*
Remscon 77 Conference, *London, 1977.*
Conference proceedings, 27th, 28th, 29th April 1977 [at the] Wembley Conference Centre, London, England. — [Newport Pagnell] ([84 High St., Newport Pagnell, Bucks. MK16 8EG]) : [Network].
'... Proceedings of the Remscon 77 Conference' - p.[3]. — In 6 vols.
Session no.4. — [1977]. — [7],93p : ill, maps ; 30cm.
Sd : £7.00
(B77-17553)

Session no.1. — [1977]. — [9],45p : ill ; 30cm.
Sd : £7.00
(B77-17554)

Session no.6. — [1977]. — [9],79p : ill ; 30cm.
Sd : £7.00
(B77-17557)

Session no.3. — [1977]. — [9],74p : ill ; 30cm.
Sd : £7.00
(B77-17555)

Session no.5. — [1977]. — [9],77p : ill ; 30cm.
Sd : £7.00
(B77-17556)

Session no.2. — [1977]. — [7],67p : ill, map ; 30cm.
Sd : £7.00
(B77-17552)

620.7 — SYSTEMS ENGINEERING
620'.7 — Engineering systems. *Conference proceedings*
International Symposium on Large Engineering Systems, *University of Manitoba, 1976.* Large engineering systems : proceedings of the International Symposium held at the University of Manitoba, Winnipeg, Manitoba, Canada, August 9-12, 1976 / editor Alvin Wexler. — Oxford [etc.] : Pergamon, 1977. — xi,710p : ill ; 26cm.
'... the International Symposium on Large Engineering Systems' - Acknowledgements. — Index.
ISBN 0-08-021295-6 : £33.00
(B77-30324)

620'.72 — Systems engineering. Design
Ostrofsky, Benjamin. Design, planning and development methodology / [by] Benjamin Ostrofsky. — Englewood Cliffs ; London [etc.] : Prentice-Hall, 1977. — xiv,401p : ill, forms ; 24cm.
Bibl. — Index.
ISBN 0-13-200246-9 : £13.55
(B77-17558)

620.8 — ENVIRONMENT ENGINEERING
McCormick, Ernest James. Human factors in engineering and design / [by] Ernest J. McCormick. — 4th ed. — New York ; London [etc.] : McGraw-Hill, 1976. — xi,491p : ill ; 25cm.
Previous ed.: published as 'Human factors engineering'. 1970. — Bibl.: p.480-481. — Index.
ISBN 0-07-044886-8 : £16.20
(B77-05471)

620.8'2 — Man-machine systems. Failure involving loss of life. *Great Britain, 1966-1972. Case studies*
Bignell, Victor. Catastrophic failures / by Victor Bignell, Geoff Peters and Christopher Pym ; with bibliographies by Caryl Hunter-Brown. — Milton Keynes : Open University Press, 1977. — 274p : ill, maps, plans ; 21cm. — (Open University. Set books)
Bibl.
ISBN 0-335-00038-x Pbk : £5.50
(B77-13688)

620.8'2 — Man-machine systems. Human factors
Human aspects of man-made systems : readings on conceptual models, practical strategies, design situations / [compiled by] the Open University Systems Group in consultation with ... [others] ; edited by Stephen C. Brown, John N.T. Martin. — [Milton Keynes] : Open University Press, 1977. — vi,355p : ill ; 21cm. — (Open University. Set books)
Bibl. — Index.
ISBN 0-335-00047-9 Pbk : £5.95
(B77-23481)

620.8'2 — Man-machine systems. Monitoring & control. *Conference proceedings*
International Symposium on Monitoring Behavior and Supervisory Control, *Berchtesgaden, 1976.* Monitoring behavior and supervisory control / edited by Thomas B. Sheridan and Gunnar Johannsen. — New York ; London : Plenum Press [for] NATO Scientific Affairs Division, 1976. — x,527p : ill ; 26cm. — (North Atlantic Treaty Organisation. NATO conference series : 3, human factors ; vol.1)
'Proceedings of an International Symposium on Monitoring Behavior and Supervisory Control held at Berchtesgaden, Federal Republic of Germany, March 8-12, 1976, which was sponsored by the NATO Special Program Panel on Human Factors' - title page verso. — Bibl. — Index.
ISBN 0-306-32881-x : Unpriced
(B77-26350)

620.8'2'0722 — Ergonomics. *Case studies*
Human factors in work, design and production / contributions by R.C. [i.e. R.G.] Sell ... [et al.]. — London : Taylor and Francis, 1977. — xviii, 138p : ill ; 26cm. — (Case studies in ergonomics practice ; vol.1)
Index.
ISBN 0-85066-076-9 : £7.00
(B77-21194)

620.8'6 — Industrial safety. Engineering aspects
Warner, *Sir* **Frederick.** Engineering safety and the environment / by Sir Frederick Warner. — [London] : Exchange Publications ; [Egham] ([c/o R.P. Peter, P-E Consulting Group Ltd, Park House, Wick Rd, Egham, Surrey TW20 0HW]) : [Distributed by the Maurice Lubbock Memorial Fund], 1976. — 16p : ill ; 21cm. — (Maurice Lubbock memorial lecture ; 11)
'[Delivered] 6 May 1976' - cover.
ISBN 0-905766-00-8 Sd : £0.20
(B77-01551)

620.8'6 — Rescue equipment. *Juvenile literature*
Milsome, John. Machines and rescue / [by] John Milsome ; illustrated by Harry Sheldon. — London [etc.] : Blake, 1977. — 32p : col ill ; 22cm. — (The world of machines)
ISBN 0-222-00504-1 : £1.60
ISBN 0-222-00506-8 Pbk : £1.00
(B77-25686)

621 — MECHANICAL ENGINEERING
General power mechanics. — 2nd ed. / [by] William H. Crouse ... [et al.]. — New York ; London [etc.] : McGraw-Hill, 1976. — xiii, 529p : ill(some col), col map ; 25cm. — (McGraw-Hill publications in industrial education)
Previous ed.: / by Robert M. Worthington, Morton Margules, William H. Crouse. New York : McGraw-Hill, 1968. — Index.
ISBN 0-07-014697-7 : £9.85
(B77-04244)

Savage, Terry Edward. Mechanical engineering for link courses / [by] T.E. Savage, D.W.G. Hall. — London [etc.] : Macmillan, 1977. — vii,101p : ill ; 24cm.
ISBN 0-333-19242-7 Pbk : £1.95
(B77-20339)

621 — Applied physics. *Conference proceedings*
Physics in Industry *(Conference), Dublin, 1976.*
Physics in industry : proceedings of the international conference held in Dublin, March 9-13, 1976 / edited by E. O'Mongain and C.P. O'Toole. — Oxford [etc.] : Pergamon, 1976. — xvi,595p : ill ; 26cm.
Conference on the theme 'Physics in Industry'. — 'Organised by the National Committee for Physics of the Royal Irish Academy' - title page verso. — Bibl. — Index.
ISBN 0-08-020922-x : £17.00
(B77-06149)

621 — Engineering. Nonlinear networks. Applications of Hilbert spaces
Dolezal, Vaclav. Nonlinear networks / [by] Vaclav Dolezal. — Amsterdam [etc.] ; Oxford : Elsevier Scientific, 1977. — ix,156p : ill ; 25cm.
With answers. — Bibl.: p.154-155. — Index.
ISBN 0-444-41571-8 : £14.60
(B77-23482)

621 — Mechanical engineering. *Manuals*
Greer, Alec. Mechanical engineering craft studies / [by] A. Greer, W.H. Howell. — London : Edward Arnold.
Part 3 / [by] A. Greer. — 2nd ed. — 1977. — [6],132p : ill ; 25cm.
With answers. — Previous ed.: 1973. — Index.
ISBN 0-7131-3390-2 Pbk : £3.65
(B77-29488)

621'.07'114281 — Further education institutions. Curriculum subjects: Mechanical engineering. Courses. *Yorkshire*
Yorkshire and Humberside Council for Further Education. *Examinations Board.* Mechanical trades principles : a TRADEC (trade education) course / [by a working party of the Yorkshire and Humberside Council for Further Education's Examinations Board]. — Leeds (Bowling Green Terrace, Leeds LS11 9SX) : The Council, 1977. — [6],117p : 1 ill ; 21cm.
ISBN 0-9502705-2-0 Pbk : £0.75
(B77-14767)

621'.08 — Applied physics. *Essays*
Laithwaite, Eric Roberts. All things are possible : an engineer looks at research and development / [by] E.R. Laithwaite. — London (Dorset House, Stamford St., SE1 9LU) : IPC Electrical-Electronic Press Ltd, 1976. — [1], 88p : ill, port ; 30cm.
'Each chapter in this book has previously appeared as an article in "Electrical Review" - Introduction.
ISBN 0-617-00165-0 Pbk : £2.85
(B77-04875)

621.1 — STEAM ENGINEERING
621.1'84 — Boilers
Higgins, Alex. Boiler room questions and answers. — 2nd ed. / [by] Alex Higgins, Stephen Michael Elonka. — New York ; London [etc.] : McGraw-Hill, 1976. — xi, 403p : ill ; 21cm.
Previous ed.: / by Alex Higgins. 1945. — Bibl. — Index.
ISBN 0-07-028754-6 : £10.60
(B77-06723)

621.1'84 — Boilers. Accidents: Explosions. *Great Britain. Reports, surveys. Serials*
Boiler explosions : report on the working of the Boiler Explosion Acts 1882 and 1890 / Department of Trade. — London : H.M.S.O.
1973-4 : for the two years ended 31 December 1974. — 1976. — 16p ; 22cm.
ISBN 0-11-511741-5 Sd : £0.28
(B77-00794)

621.1'84 — Boilers. Feed water. Supply. Use of steam condensates. *Manuals*
Great Britain. *Department of Energy.* How to make the best use of condensate / Department of Energy. — London (Library, Thames House South, Millbank, SW1P 4QJ) : The Department, [1977]. — [1],16p : ill(some col) ; 21cm. — (Fuel efficiency booklet ; 9)
Sd : Unpriced
(B77-18199)

621.2 — HYDRAULIC POWER
621.2'0422 — Wave power. Development. *Great Britain. Reports, surveys*
Leishman, J M. The development of wave power : a techno-economic study / [by] J.M. Leishman and G. Scobie. — East Kilbride (East Kilbride, Glasgow) : National Engineering Laboratory, 1976. — [1],x,80p,[34]p of plates,leaf of plate : ill, maps ; 30cm. — (EAU M25)
Based on a report prepared by the National Engineering Laboratory for the Department of Energy, in 1975. — 'The text has not been revised to take account of developments which have taken place since February 1975' - Preface.
Sp : £5.00
(B77-29489)

621.2'1 — Watermills. *Great Britain, 1856-1916. Illustrations*
Victorian and Edwardian windmills and watermills from old photographs / introduction and commentaries by J. Kenneth Major, Martin Watts. — London : Batsford, 1977. — [96]p : chiefly ill ; 26cm.
ISBN 0-7134-0621-6 : £3.95
Primary classification 621.4'5
(B77-24283)

621.2'1 — Watermills. *Kent, to 1930. Early works*
Finch, William Coles. Watermills & windmills : a historical survey of their rise, decline and fall as portrayed by those of Kent / [by] William Coles Finch. — Sheerness [31 Broadway, Sheerness, Kent ME12 1AB] : Arthur J. Cassell Ltd, 1976. — 336p,leaf of plate,[98]p of plates : ill, facsims, maps, port ; 25cm.
Facsimile reprint of: 1st ed. London : Daniel, 1933. — Index.
ISBN 0-903253-02-x : £10.00
Primary classification 621.4'5
(B77-09745)

621.2'1 — Watermills. *Leicestershire*
Ashton, N D. In search of Leicestershire watermills : a record of visits made during 1975 to old Leicestershire watermill sites / by N.D. Ashton. — [Leicester] ([18 Walker Rd, Birstall, Leicester LE4 3BN]) : The author, 1976. — [9], 81[i.e.83]p,[12]p of plates : ill, facsim, maps, ports ; 26cm.
Spine title: Leicestershire watermills.
ISBN 0-9505194-0-5 : £3.00
ISBN 0-9505194-1-3 Pbk : Unpriced
(B77-23483)

621.2'1 — Watermills. *West Midlands (Metropolitan County). Black Country, to ca 1900*
Dilworth, Douglas. The Tame mills of Staffordshire / by D. Dilworth. — London [etc.] : Phillimore, 1976. — x,212p,[8]p of plates, leaf of plates : ill, geneal tables, maps ; 23cm.
Bibl.: p.199. — Index.
ISBN 0-85033-216-8 : £4.75
(B77-01552)

621.3 — ELECTRICAL, ELECTRONIC, ELECTROMAGNETIC ENGINEERING
621.3 — Electrical engineering
Bell, Ernest Clifford. Basic electrical engineering and instrumentation for engineers / [by] E.C. Bell, R.W. Whitehead. — London : Crosby Lockwood Staples, 1977. — [8],487p : ill ; 24cm.
Index.
ISBN 0-258-97051-0 Pbk : £4.95
(B77-24275)

Boylestad, Robert. Electricity, electronics, and electromagnetics : principles and applications / [by] Robert Boylestad, Louis Nashelsky. — Englewood Cliffs ; London [etc.] : Prentice-Hall, 1977. — xi,516p : ill ; 24cm.
With answers to odd-numbered problems. — Index.
ISBN 0-13-248310-6 : £12.80
(B77-18200)

Constance, John Dennis. Electrical engineering for professional engineers' examinations / [by] John D. Constance. — 3rd ed. — New York ; London [etc.] : McGraw-Hill, [1976]. — xxxiii, 537p : ill ; 21cm.
With answers. — This ed. published in the United States: 1975. — Previous ed.: 1969. — Bibl.: p.503-507. — Index.
ISBN 0-07-012448-5 : £14.10
(B77-04876)

Electrical engineering handbook. — English ed. / [translated from the German ; edited by Reginald Gill]. — Berlin [etc.] : Siemens ; London [etc.] : Heyden, 1976. — xii,750p : ill ; 22cm.
Previous ed. published as: 'Handbuch der Elektrotechnik'. Berlin : Siemens, 1969?. — Index.
ISBN 0-85501-231-5 : £16.50
(B77-07400)

Klayton, Marvin H. Fundamental electrical technology / [by] Marvin H. Klayton. — Reading, Mass. ; London [etc.] : Addison-Wesley, 1977. — xv,710p : ill ; 25cm.
With answers to selected problems. — Index.
ISBN 0-201-03830-7 : £13.60
(B77-17559)

Laycock, C H. Applied electrotechnology for engineers / [by] C.H. Laycock. — London [etc.] : Macmillan, 1976. — x,293p : ill ; 25cm.
With answers. — Bibl.: p.286. — Index.
ISBN 0-333-17684-7 : £10.00
ISBN 0-333-19378-4 Pbk : £4.95
(B77-01553)

Watson, William Golightly. Electrical and electronic engineering / [by] W.G. Watson. — London : Longman, 1977. — [4],232p : ill ; 27cm. — (Longman craft studies series)
Notebook format. — Index.
ISBN 0-582-41606-x Pbk : £4.95
(B77-16446)

621.3 — Electrical engineering. *For maintenance & repair of American household equipment*
Basics of electric appliance servicing : fundamentals of circuits, motors, and heat / edited by Robert Scharff. — New York ; London [etc.] : McGraw-Hill, 1976. — ix, 229p : ill, form ; 29cm. — ([Practical appliance servicing and repair course ; book 1])
Index.
ISBN 0-07-055141-3 : £9.55
(B77-06150)

621.3 — Electrical engineering. *For technicians*
Shrader, Robert Louis. Electrical fundamentals for technicians / [by] Robert L. Shrader. — 2nd ed. — New York ; London [etc.] : McGraw-Hill, 1977. — xiii,465p : ill ; 25cm.
With answers to check-up quizzes and test questions. — Previous ed.: New York : McGraw-Hill, 1969. — Index.
ISBN 0-07-057141-4 : £10.90
(B77-24987)

621.3 — Electrical engineering. *Juvenile literature*
Chapman, Philip. The young scientist book of electricity / [written by Philip Chapman ; art and editorial direction David Jefferis ; illustrators Roland Berry et al.]. — London : Usborne, 1976. — 32p : col ill, col map, col ports ; 29cm.
ISBN 0-86020-077-9 : £1.40
(B77-10827)

621.3 — Electricity. Conservation
Efficient electricity use : a practical handbook for an energy constrained world / Craig B. Smith, editor. — New York ; Oxford [etc.] : Pergamon, 1976. — xxvii,960p : ill ; 29cm.
'Applied Nucleonics Company, Inc., Santa Monica, California, was selected by the Electric Power Research Institute to conduct a research program to compile efficient methods of using energy, particularly electricity' - Preface. — Index.
ISBN 0-08-020869-x : £22.50
ISBN 0-08-020868-1 Pbk : £10.00
(B77-00264)

621.3'02'46238 — Electrical engineering. *For marine engineering*
Kraal, Edmund George R. Reed's advanced electrotechnology for engineers / by Edmund G.R. Kraal. — 2nd ed., (in SI units). — Sunderland [etc.] : T. Reed, 1977. — [13], 669p : ill ; 22cm. — (Reed's practical mathematics series ; vol.7)
Cover title: Advanced electrotechnology for engineers. — With answers. — Previous ed.: published as 'Reed's advanced electrotechnology for marine engineers'. 1970. — Index.
ISBN 0-900335-41-6 Pbd : £7.80
(B77-16922)

621.3'028 — Electrical engineering. Experiments. *Laboratory manuals*
Zbar, Paul Bernard. Electricity-electronics fundamentals : a text-lab manual. — 2nd ed. / [by] Paul B. Zbar, Joseph G. Sloop. — New York ; London [etc.] : McGraw-Hill, 1977. — xiv,370p : ill ; 28cm.
With answers to self-tests. — Previous ed.: / by Paul B. Zbar. New York : McGraw-Hill, 1969.
ISBN 0-07-072748-1 Pbk : £7.45
(B77-32672)

621.3'03 — Electrical engineering. *Glossaries*
British Standards Institution. Glossary of electrotechnical, power, telecommunication, electronics, lighting and colour terms = Glossaire des termes relatifs à l'électrotechnique, à l'électricité, aux télécommunications, à l'électronique, à l'éclairage et à la couleur = Glossarium von Begriffen aus der Elektrotechnik, Fernmeldetechnik, Elektronik und Lichttechnik, sowie dem Energie- und Farbwesen / British Standards Institution. — London : B.S.I.
Part 3 = Partie 3 = Teil 3 : Terms particular to telecommunications and electronics = Termes specialisés des télécommunications et de l'électronique = Bestimmung von Begriffen der Fernmeldetechnik und Elektronik. Group 04 = Group 04 = Gruppe 04 : Broadcasting and television terminology = Terminologie de radiodiffusion et de télévision = Rundfunk- und Fernsehterminologie. — 1st revision. — 1976. — [2],33,[1]p : 1 ill ; 30cm. — (BS4727 : Part 3 : Group 04 : 1976)
Pierced for binder. — Index.
ISBN 0-580-09157-0 Sd : £5.80
(B77-07939)

621.3'06'241 — Electrical engineering. Organisations. *Great Britain. Institution of Electrical Engineers. Directories*
Institution of Electrical Engineers. Year book & list of members / the Institution of Electrical Engineers. — London : The Institution.
1976-77. — 1976. — xxii,601p : ports ; 30cm.
ISBN 0-85296-170-7 Pbk : Unpriced
(B77-07940)

621.3'07'2041 — Electrical engineering. Research organisations. *Great Britain. Electrical Research Association. Yearbooks*
Electrical Research Association. ERA handbook. — Leatherhead : E.R.A.
1977-78. — 1977. — iii-x,401p : ill ; 21cm.
Bibl.
ISBN 0-7008-0116-2 Pbk : £2.50
(B77-10397)

621.3'092'2 — Electrical engineering. *Great Britain. Biographical dictionaries*
Who's who and guide to the electrical industry : brief biographies of leading members of the professional and industrial branches of the electrical and electronic industries / compiled in collaboration with 'Electrical review'. — London (Dorset House, Stamford St., SE1 9LU) : IPC Electrical-Electronic Press Ltd. 1977-78 / edited by Kenneth Ellmore. — 1977. — 255p : ill ; 23cm.
Previously published: as 'Electrical who's who'. £10.00
(B77-26351)

621.3'092'4 — Electrical engineering. Bain, Alexander, b.1810. *Biographies*
Gunn, Robert P. Alexander Bain of Watten : genius of the North / by Robert P. Gunn ; illustrated by J. Saxon and J.R. Vandecasteele. — Wick (c/o Mrs M. Gladstone, 11 Miller Ave., Wick) : Caithness Field Club, 1976. — [3],19p : ill, port ; 21cm.
ISBN 0-9505550-1-0 Sd : £0.50
(B77-09059)

621.3'092'4 — Electrical engineering. Edison, Thomas. *Biographies*
Clark, Ronald William. Edison : the man who made the future / [by] Ronald W. Clark. — London : Macdonald and Jane's, 1977. — 256p : ill, facsim, ports ; 25cm.
Bibl.: p.244-245. — Index.
ISBN 0-354-04093-6 : £6.95
(B77-30325)

621.3'092'4 — Electrical engineering. Page, Charles Grafton. *United States. Biographies*
Post, Robert C. Physics, patents, and politics : a biography of Charles Grafton Page / [by] Robert C. Post. — New York : Science History Publications ; [Folkestone] : [Distributed by Dawson], 1976. — [5],227p,[12]p of plates : ill, facsims, ports ; 24cm.
Bibl.: p.206-213. — Index.
ISBN 0-88202-046-3 : £11.25
(B77-33267)

621.31'042 — Electric equipment. Certification. *West Germany. For British businessmen*
British Standards Institution. *Technical Help to Exporters Section.* Electrical equipment certification in the Federal Republic of Germany : a survey of the procedures for the certification of electrical equipment (excluding hazardous atmosphere equipment) / [British Standards Institution, Technical Help to Exporters Section]. — Hemel Hempstead (Maylands Ave., Hemel Hempstead, Herts. HP2 4SQ) : T.H.E., 1977. — iii,53p : ill, facsims ; 21cm.
ISBN 0-903886-22-7 Pbk : Unpriced
(B77-28670)

621.31'042 — Electric equipment. Reliability
Simpson, Arnold. Testing methods and reliability, power / [by] A. Simpson. — London [etc.] : Macmillan, 1976. — vii,176p : ill ; 24cm. — (Macmillan basis books in electronics)
With answers. — Index.
ISBN 0-333-18407-6 Pbk : £3.95
Primary classification 621.31'042
(B77-06151)

621.31'042 — Electric equipment. Testing. Techniques
Simpson, Arnold. Testing methods and reliability, power / [by] A. Simpson. — London [etc.] : Macmillan, 1976. — vii,176p : ill ; 24cm. — (Macmillan basis books in electronics)
With answers. — Index.
ISBN 0-333-18407-6 Pbk : £3.95
Also classified at 621.31'042
(B77-06151)

621.31'042 — Electric industrial processing equipment. Energy. Conservation. *Conference proceedings*
Electricity for Materials Processing and Conservation *(Conference), London, 1977.* Conference on Electricity for Materials Processing and Conservation (EMPAC), 8-9 March 1977 : organised by the Power and Science, Education and Management Divisions of the Institution of Electrical Engineers in association with ... [others], venue the Institution of Electrical Engineers, Savoy Place, London WC2. — Stevenage : The Institution, 1977. — v,116p : ill ; 30cm. — (Institution of Electrical Engineers. Conference publications ; no.149 ISSN 0537-9989)
Cover title: Electricity for materials processing & conservation.
ISBN 0-85296-171-5 Pbk : £7.50
(B77-16923)

621.31'042 — Electric machinery
Daniels, A R. Introduction to electrical machines / [by] A.R. Daniels. — London [etc.] : Macmillan, 1976. — viii,187p : ill ; 24cm.
Index.
ISBN 0-333-19626-0 : £7.95
ISBN 0-333-19627-9 Pbk : £3.95
(B77-03585)

Hindmarsh, John. Electrical machines and their applications / [by] J. Hindmarsh. — 3rd ed. — Oxford [etc.] : Pergamon, 1977. — xxi,655p,leaf of plate,[10]p of plates : ill(incl 1 col) ; 22cm. — (Pergamon international library)
With answers. — Previous ed.: 1970. — Index.
ISBN 0-08-021165-8 : £12.50
ISBN 0-08-021164-x Pbk : £7.50
(B77-14267)

621.31'042 — Rotating electric machinery. *Standards*
British Standards Institution. Specification for general requirements for rotating electrical machines = Exigences générales relatives aux machines électriques tournantes = Allgemeine Anforderungen bezüglish auf elektrische umlaufende Maschinen / British Standards Institution. — London : B.S.I.
Part 61 = Partie 61 = Teil 61 : Test of the insulation of bars and coils of high voltage machines = Essai de l'isolation des barres et des bobines des machines à haute tension = Prüfung der Isolation von Stäben und Spulen von Hochspannungsmaschinen. — 1977. — [2], 3,[2]p : 1 ill ; 30cm. — (BS4999 : Part 61 : 1977)
Pierced for binder.
ISBN 0-580-09940-7 Sd : £1.60
(B77-13080)

621.31'042'0212 — British electrical products. Certification by Underwriters' Laboratories Inc.. *For British businessmen*
British Standards Institution. *Technical Help to Exporters Section.* Underwriters' Laboratories Inc. (UL) : a guide to the UL approval of electrical equipment in the USA for first time submittors / [British Standards Institution, Technical Help for Exporters Section]. — 2nd (revised) ed. — Hemel Hempstead (Maylands Ave., Hemel Hempstead, Herts. HP2 4SQ) : The Section, 1977. — [2],9p ; 21cm.
Previous ed.: 1975.
Sd : Unpriced
(B77-19438)

621.31'042'028 — Electric equipment. Experiments. *Laboratory manuals*
Zbar, Paul Bernard. Basic electricity : a text-lab manual / [by] Paul B. Zbar. — 4th ed. — New York ; London [etc.] : McGraw-Hill, 1974. — xvi,352p : ill ; 28cm.
With answers to self-tests. — Previous ed.: New York : McGraw-Hill, 1966.
ISBN 0-07-072787-2 Pbk : Unpriced
(B77-18828)

621.31'0941 — Electricity supply. *Great Britain. Statistics*
Handbook of electricity supply statistics / Electricity Council. — London : The Council.
1976. — [1976]. — vii,124p ; 20cm.
Index.
ISBN 0-85188-047-9 Pbk : Unpriced
ISSN 0440-1905
(B77-00265)

1977. — 1977. — viii,133p : ill ; 20cm.
Index.
ISBN 0-85188-068-1 Pbk : Unpriced
ISSN 0440-1905
(B77-30326)

621.312 — Electricity. Generation. *Amateurs' manuals*
McLaughlin, Terence. Make your own electricity / [by] Terence McLaughlin. — Newton Abbot [etc.] : David and Charles, 1977. — 128p : ill ; 22cm.
Index.
ISBN 0-7153-7418-4 : £3.95
(B77-16924)

621.312'134 — Hydroelectric power stations. Hydraulic power equipment. Fluids. Transients
Jaeger, Charles. Fluid transients in hydro-electric engineering practice / [by] Charles Jaeger. — Glasgow [etc.] : Blackie, 1977. — xvii,413p : ill ; 24cm.
Bibl.: p.381-398. — Index.
ISBN 0-216-90225-8 : £18.50
(B77-30327)

621.312'136'0941 — Electricity supply. Generation by wind power. *Great Britain*
Atomic Energy Research Establishment. *Energy Technology Support Unit.* The prospects for the generation of electricity from wind energy in the United Kingdom : a report prepared for the Department of Energy / [written] by J. Allen and R.A. Bird ; [for the] Energy Technology Support Unit, Harwell. — London : H.M.S.O., 1977. — viii,67p : ill, charts ; 25cm. — (Energy papers ; no.21)
Bibl.: p.67.
ISBN 0-11-410604-5 Sd : £2.25
(B77-21195)

621.312'4 — Direct power generation
Angrist, Stanley Wolff. Direct energy conversion / [by] Stanley W. Angrist. — 3rd ed. — Boston, Mass. ; London [etc.] : Allyn and Bacon, 1976. — x,518p : ill ; 24cm. — (Allyn and Bacon series in mechanical engineering and applied mechanics)
With answers. — Previous ed.: Boston, Mass. : Allyn and Bacon, 1971. — Index.
ISBN 0-205-05581-8 : £19.95
(B77-02371)

621.313'2 — Direct current machines
Mychael, Arthur. DC machines / [by] Arthur Mychael. — Sydney ; London [etc.] : McGraw-Hill, 1977. — x,177p : ill ; 24cm. — (McGraw-Hill Australian series in electrical technology)
With answers. — Index.
ISBN 0-07-093409-6 Pbk : £6.20
(B77-31940)

621.313'7 — Electric equipment: Converters. Control devices: Diode circuits & thyristor circuits
Davis, Rex Mountford. Power diode and thyristor circuits / [by] Rex M. Davis. — Stevenage : Peregrinus [for] the Institution of Electrical Engineers, 1976. — xiv,265p,plate : ill ; 22cm. — (Institution of Electrical Engineers. IEE monograph series ; 7 ISSN 0806-8269)
Originally published: London : Cambridge University Press for the Institution of Electrical Engineers, 1971. — Bibl.: p.253-260. — Index.
ISBN 0-901223-90-5 Pbk : £3.50
(B77-01554)

621.31'7 — Electric equipment. Circuits. Switches. *Standards*
British Standards Institution. Specification for control switches = Spécification des auxiliaires de commande = Spezifikation für Hilfsstromschalter : (switching devices, including contactor relays, for control and auxiliary circuits, for voltages up to and including 1000V ac and 1200V dc) = (appareils de connexion, y compris les contacteurs auxiliaires, pour des circuits de commande et des circuits auxiliaires, pour les tensions inférieures et égales à 1000V en courant alternatif et 1200V en courant continu) / British Standards Institution. — London : B.S.I.
Part 2 = Partie 2. Special requirements for specific types of control switches = Prescriptions particulières pour des types déterminés d'auxiliaires de commande. Section 2.1 = Section 2.1 : Push-buttons and related control switches = Boutons-poussoirs et auxiliaires de commande analogues. — 1977. — [2],9,[1]p : ill ; 30cm. — (BS4794 : Part 2 : Section 2.1 : 1977) (IEC337-2 : 1972)
Pierced for binder.
ISBN 0-580-09169-4 Sd : £2.70
(B77-14769)

British Standards Institution. Specification for control switches = Spécification des auxiliaires de commande = Spezifikation für Hilfsstromschalter : (switching devices, including contactor relays, for control and auxiliary circuits, for voltages up to and including 1000 V ac and 1200 V dc) = (appareils de connexion, y compris les contacteurs auxiliaires, pour des circuits de commande et des circuits auxiliaires, pour les tensions inférieures et égales à 1000 V en courant alternatif et 1200 V en courant continu) / British Standards Institution. — London : B.S.I.
Part 2 = Partie 2. Special requirements for specific types of control switches = Prescriptions particulières pour des types déterminés d'auxiliaires de commande. Section 2.2 = Section 2.2 : Additional requirements for rotary control switches = Prescriptions supplémentaires pour les commutateurs rotatifs de commande. — 1977. — [2],6,[1]p : 1 ill ; 30cm. — (BS4794 : Part 2 : Section 2.2 : 1977) (IEC337-2A : 1973)
Pierced for binder.
ISBN 0-580-09179-1 Sd : £2.70
(B77-14768)

621.31'7 — Electric equipment. Control devices. *Standards*
British Standards Institution. Specification for controlgear for voltages up to and including 1000V ac and 1200V dc = Spécification de l'appareillage de commande pour les tensions inférieures et égales à 1000V en courant alternatif et 1200V en courant continu = Spezifikation für Befehlschaltgeräte bis und einschliesslich 1000V Wechselstrom und 1200V Gleichstrom / British Standards Institution. — London : B.S.I.
Part 1 = Partie 1 = Teil 1 : Contactors = Contacteurs = Schütze. — 1977. — [2],41,[1] p : ill ; 30cm. — (BS5424 : Part 1 : 1977) (IEC 158-1 : 1970) (IEC 158-1A : 1975)
Pierced for binder.
ISBN 0-580-09139-2 Sd : £6.60
(B77-14770)

621.31'7 — Electric equipment. Indicator lights, push buttons, annunciators & digital readouts. Colours. *Standards*
British Standards Institution. Specification for colours of indicator lights, push buttons, annunciators and digital readouts = Spécification des couleurs des voyants lumineux de signalisation, des boutons-pressoirs, des avertisseurs et des lectures numériques = Spezifikation für die Farben von Aufleuchtlampen, Druckknöpfen, Signalfallscheiben und Zahlenbildern / British Standards Institution. — London : B.S.I.
Part 1 = Partie 1 = Teil 1 : Colours of indicator lights and push buttons = Couleurs des voyants lumineux de signalisation et des boutons-pressoirs = Farben von Aufleuchtlampen und Druckknöpfen. — 1st revision. — 1976. — [2],10,[1]p ; 30cm. — (BS4099 : Part 1 : 1976) (IEC73 : 1975)
Pierced for binder.
ISBN 0-580-09037-x Sd : £3.10
(B77-03586)

621.31'7 — Electric equipment. Low voltage air-break disconnectors, low voltage air-break switches & low voltage fuse-combination units. *Standards*
British Standards Institution. Specification for air-break switches, air-break disconnectors, air-break switch disconnectors and fuse-combination units for voltages up to and including 1000 V ac and 1200 V dc = Spécification des interrupteurs dans l'air, sélectionneurs dans l'air, interrupteurs-sélectionneurs dans l'air et combinés à fusibles pour les tensions inférieures et égales à 1000 V en courant alternatif et 1200 V en courant continu = Spezifikation für Lastschalter in Luft, Trennschalter in Luft, Lasttrennschalter in Luft und Schalter-Sicherungseinheiten für Spannungen bis und einschliesslich 1000 V Wechselstrom und 1200 V Gleichstrom / British Standards Institution. — London : B.S.I., 1977. — [2],42, [1]p : ill ; 30cm. — (BS5419 : 1977) (IEC 408 : 1972)
Pierced for binder.
ISBN 0-580-09099-x Sd : £6.60
(B77-15323)

621.31'7 — Electric equipment. Low voltage controlgear. *Standards*
British Standards Institution. Specification for switchgear and controlgear for voltages up to and including 1000V ac and 1200V dc = Spécification de l'appareillage de connexion et de commande pour les tensions inférieures et égales à 1000V en courant alternatif et 1200V en courant continu = Spezifikation für Verteilungsschaltgeräte für Spannungen bis und einschliesslich 1000V Wechselstrom und 1200V Gleichstrom / British Standards Institution. — London : B.S.I.
Part 1 = Partie 1 = Teil 1 : Circuit-breakers = Disjoncteurs = Leistungsschalter. — 1977. — [2],59,[1]p : ill ; 30cm. — (BS4752 : Part 1 : 1977) (IEC 157-1 : 1973) (IEC 157-1A : 1976)
Pierced for binder.
ISBN 0-580-09189-9 Sd : £8.20
(B77-15324)

621.31'7 — Electric equipment. Low voltage controlgear. Protection. *Standards*
British Standards Institution. Specification for degrees of protection of enclosures of switchgear and controlgear for voltages up to and including 1000V ac and 1200V dc = Spécification des degrés de protection des enveloppes de l'appareillage de connexion et de commande pour les tensions inférieures et égales à 1000V en courant alternatif et 1200V en courant continu = Spezifikation für die Schutzgrade der Mäntel von Schalt- und Steuergeräten für Spannungen bis und einschliesslich 1000V Wechselstrom und 1200V Gleichstrom / British Standards Institution. — London : B.S.I., 1977. — [2],12,[1]p : ill ; 30cm. — (BS5420 : 1977) (IEC 144 : 1963)
Pierced for binder.
ISBN 0-580-09199-6 Sd : £3.60
(B77-15325)

621.31'7 — Electric equipment. Switchgear & controlgear. *Manuals*
Switchgear and control handbook / Robert W. Smeaton, editor. — New York ; London [etc.] : McGraw-Hill, 1977. — 987p in various pagings : ill, forms ; 24cm.
Index.
ISBN 0-07-058439-7 : £27.00
(B77-32673)

621.31'7 — Electric equipment: Switchgear for voltages up to 145kV. *Standards*
British Standards Institution. Code of practice for the maintenance of electrical switchgear for voltages up to and including 145kv = Code de tonne pratique relatif à l'entretien de l'appareillage de connexion électrique pour les tensions inférieures et égales à 145kv = Richtlinie für die Wattung von elecktrischen Schaltgerälten für Spannungen bis auf und einschliesslich von 145 kv / British Standards Institution. — 1st revision. — London : B.S.I., 1976. — [2],44,[2]p : 1 ill, forms ; 30cm. — (BS5405 : 1976)
Pierced for binder. — '(formerly CP 1008)'.
ISBN 0-580-09347-6 Sd : £6.60
(B77-12495)

621.319 — Electricity distribution equipment. *Conference proceedings*
International Conference on Electricity Distribution, *London, 1977.* International Conference on Electricity Distribution, 23-27 May 1977 : venue Royal Lancaster Hotel, London. — [English version]. — [London] : Institution of Electrical Engineers. — (Institution of Electrical Engineers. Conference publications ; no.151 ISSN 0537-9989)
Part 1 : Full texts of contributions included in the programme. — 1977. — viii,234p : ill, maps ; 30cm.
At head of title: CIRED 1977.
ISBN 0-85296-174-x Pbk : £10.90
(B77-33853)

621.319 — Electricity distribution equipment. Installation. Standard costs. *Great Britain. Lists*
Great Britain. *Department of the Environment. Directorate of Engineering Services Development.* Schedule of rates for electrical distribution systems external to buildings, 1976 / Department of the Environment, Property Services Agency [Directorate of Engineering Services Development, Directorate of Quantity Surveying Development]. — 2nd ed. — London : H.M.S.O., 1976. — [1],vi,81p ; 30cm. — (Schedule ; 6)
Previous ed.: published as 'Schedule of rates for electrical distribution systems external to buildings'. London : Ministry of Public Building and Works, 1970.
ISBN 0-11-670566-3 Pbk : £3.25
(B77-15901)

621.319 — Electricity supply. Transmission
Chard, Frederic de la Court. Electricity supply : transmission and distribution / [by] F. de la C. Chard. — London [etc.] : Longman, 1976. — xiv,390p : ill ; 24cm. — (Electrical engineering series)
Bibl. — Index.
ISBN 0-582-44462-4 Pbk : £5.95
(B77-09737)

621.319'1 — Electric power transmission systems
Guile, Alan Elliott. Electrical power systems / [by] A.E. Guile, the late W. Paterson. — 2nd ed. (SI-metric units). — Oxford [etc.] : Pergamon. — (Pergamon international library)

In 2 vols.
Vol.1. — 1977. — xvi,405p : ill ; 22cm.
Previous ed.: Edinburgh : Oliver and Boyd, 1969. — Bibl. — Index.
ISBN 0-08-021728-1 : £9.00
ISBN 0-08-021729-x Pbk : £5.50
(B77-33854)

Vol.2. — 1977. — xvi,354p : ill ; 22cm.
Previous ed.: Edinburgh : Oliver and Boyd, 1972. — Bibl. — Index.
ISBN 0-08-021730-3 : £7.50
ISBN 0-08-021731-1 Pbk : £4.50
(B77-33855)

621.319'1 — Electricity supply systems. Reliability. *Conference proceedings*
International Conference on Reliability of Power Supply Systems, *Institution of Electrical Engineers, 1977.* International Conference on Reliability of Power Supply Systems, 21-23 February 1977 : organised by the Power and Control and Automation Divisions of the Institution of Electrical Engineers in association with the Institute of Electrical and Electronics Engineers (United Kingdom and Republic of Ireland Section) : venue, The Institution of Electrical Engineers ... — London : The Institution, 1977. — viii,161p : ill ; 30cm. — (Institution of Electrical Engineers. Conference publications ; no.148 ISSN 0537-9989)
ISBN 0-85296-169-3 Pbk : £8.80
(B77-19439)

621.319'12 — Electric equipment. Direct current circuits
Kosow, Irving Lionel. Study guide in direct current circuits : a personalized system of instruction / [by] Irving L. Kosow. — New York ; London [etc.] : Wiley, 1977. — xv, 383p : ill ; 28cm. — (Electronic technology series)
Pierced for binder. — With answers. — Index.
ISBN 0-471-01664-0 Pbk : £3.95
(B77-33268)

621.319'13 — Electric equipment. Alternating current circuits
Cutler, Phillip Cutler. AC circuit analysis : with illustrative problems / [by] Phillip Cutler. — New York ; London [etc.] : McGraw-Hill, 1974. — xiii,184p : ill ; 28cm.
With answers. — Index.
ISBN 0-07-014996-8 Pbk : Unpriced
(B77-20340)

Lockhart, Noble L. AC circuit analysis / [by] Noble L. Lockhart, Ora E. Rice. — New York ; London [etc.] : Van Nostrand Reinhold, [1977]. — ix,172p : ill ; 27cm. — (Electronics technology series)
With answers. — Published in the United States: 1976. — Index.
ISBN 0-442-24831-8 : £6.35
(B77-09738)

621.319'2 — Electric equipment. Circuits
Churchman, Lee W. Introduction to circuits / [by] Lee W. Churchman. — New York : Holt, Rinehart and Winston, 1976. — xv,600p : ill ; 25cm.
With answers to odd-numbered problems. — Index.
ISBN 0-03-091198-2 : £10.75
(B77-14268)

Kubala, Thomas S. Circuit concepts : direct and alternating current / [by] Thomas S. Kubala. — New York ; London [etc.] : Van Nostrand Reinhold, 1976. — viii,207p : ill ; 27cm. — (Electronics technology series)
Index.
ISBN 0-442-23129-6 : £16.15
(B77-28671)

Leach, Donald P. Basic electric circuits / [by] Donald P. Leach. — 2nd ed. — New York ; London [etc.] : Wiley, 1976. — xiii,637p : ill ; 26cm.
With answers to review questions and selected problems. — Previous ed.: 1969. — Index.
ISBN 0-471-52003-9 : Unpriced
(B77-21929)

Ridsdale, R E. Electric circuits for engineering technology / [by] R.E. Ridsdale. — New York ; London [etc.] : McGraw-Hill, 1976. — vi,762p : ill ; 25cm.
Bibl.: p.730. — Index.
ISBN 0-07-052937-x : £14.05
(B77-04877)

Temes, Gabor Charles. Introduction to circuit synthesis and design / [by] Gabor C. Temes, Jack W. LaPatra. — New York ; London [etc.] : McGraw-Hill, 1977. — ix,598p : ill ; 25cm.
Index.
ISBN 0-07-063489-0 : Unpriced
(B77-27907)

Tuttle, David F. Circuits / [by] David F. Tuttle, Jr. — New York ; London [etc.] : McGraw-Hill, 1977. — xi,820p : ill ; 25cm. — (McGraw-Hill series on the fundamentals of electronic science)
Bibl.: p.759-760. — Index.
ISBN 0-07-065591-x : £15.40
(B77-21930)

621.319'2 — Electric equipment. Circuits. Analysis
Ng, K C. Electrical network theory / [by] K.C. Ng. — London : Pitman, 1977. — x,350p : ill ; 23cm. — (A Pitman international text)
Bibl.: p.347-348. — Index.
ISBN 0-273-00458-1 Pbk : £4.75 : CIP rev.
(B77-07941)

621.319'2 — Electric equipment. Linear circuits
Kerr, Robert B. Electrical network science / [by] Robert B. Kerr. — Englewood Cliffs ; London [etc.] : Prentice-Hall, 1977. — xv,352p : ill ; 24cm. — (Prentice-Hall electrical engineering series)
Index.
ISBN 0-13-247627-4 : £14.35
(B77-15902)

621.319'2 — Electric equipment. Resistive circuits. Theories
Spence, Robert, *b.1933.* Resistive circuit theory / [by] Robert Spence. — New York ; London [etc.] : McGraw-Hill, 1974. — [8],279p : ill ; 28cm.
Index.
ISBN 0-07-060130-5 Pbk : Unpriced
(B77-19440)

621.319'2'01512943 — Electric equipment. Circuits. Analysis. Applications of matrices
Shipley, R Bruce. Introduction to matrices and power systems / [by] R. Bruce Shipley. — New York ; London [etc.] : Wiley, 1976. — xiii, 274p : ill ; 24cm.
'A Wiley-Interscience Publication'. — Bibl. — Index.
ISBN 0-471-78642-x : £15.00
(B77-03587)

621.319'21 — Electric power transmission systems. Transient voltages. Mathematical models
Bickford, J P. Computation of power system transients / [by] J.P. Bickford, N. Mullineux, J.R. Reed. — Stevenage : Peregrinus [for] the Institution of Electrical Engineers, 1976. — ix, 176p : ill ; 23cm. — (Institution of Electrical Engineers. IEE monograph series ; 18 ISSN 0306-8269)
Bibl.: p.167-171. — Index.
ISBN 0-901223-85-9 : £10.00
(B77-07401)

621.319'21 — Transmission lines. Effects of external electromagnetic fields
Smith, Albert A. Coupling of external electromagnetic fields to transmission lines / [by] Albert A. Smith, Jr. — New York ; London [etc.] : Wiley, 1977. — xi,132p : ill ; 24cm.
'A Wiley-Interscience Publication'. — Bibl.: p.126-127. — Index.
ISBN 0-471-01995-x : £10.25
(B77-23484)

621.319'24 — Buildings. Electric equipment. Installation
Neidle, Michael. Basic electrical installations / [by] Michael Neidle. — London [etc.] : Macmillan, 1977. — x,69p : ill, form ; 26cm.
With answers. — Index.
ISBN 0-333-19404-7 Pbk : £2.50
(B77-24276)

621.319'24 — Buildings. Electric equipment. Installation. Regulations: Institution of Electrical Engineers. Regulations for the electrical equipment of buildings
Miller, Henry Arthur. Guide to the 'IEE wiring regulations' / by H.A. Miller. — 2nd ed. — Stevenage : Peregrinus, 1976. — viii,116p : ill ; 21cm.
This ed. originally published: 1972. — Index.
ISBN 0-901223-74-3 Pbk : Unpriced
(B77-31243)

621.319'24 — Buildings. Electric equipment. Installation. Standard costs. *Great Britain. Lists*
Great Britain. *Department of the Environment. Directorate of Mechanical and Electrical Engineering Services.* Schedule of rates for electrical installations, 1976 / Department of the Environment, Property Services Agency [Directorate of Mechanical and Electrical Engineering Services, Directorate of Quantity Surveying Services]. — 2nd ed. — London : H.M.S.O., 1977. — [5],ii,126p ; 30cm. — (Schedule ; 5)
Previous ed.: published as 'Schedule of rates for electrical installations'. London : Ministry of Public Building and Works, 1970.
ISBN 0-11-670565-5 Pbk : £5.00
(B77-15903)

621.319'24 — Buildings. Electric equipment. Safety aspects. *Manuals*
Kinloch, C D. Electrical installation snags and solutions : recommendations on the application of the 14th edition of the IEE 'Regulations for the electrical equipment of buildings' / [by] C.D. Kinloch, D.M. Williams. — London : IPC Electrical-Electronic Press [for] the National Inspection Council for Electrical Installation Contracting and [the] 'Electrical Times', 1976. — 72p ; 21cm.
Spine title: Snags and solutions. — Index.
ISBN 0-617-00185-5 Pbk : £1.50
(B77-10398)

621.319'24 — Buildings. Electric wiring systems. Installation. *Great Britain. Questions & answers*
Lewis, M L. Multiple-choice questions in electrical installation work / [by] M.L. Lewis. — London : Hutchinson, 1977. — 103p : ill ; 22cm.
With answers.
ISBN 0-09-129561-0 Pbk : £1.75
(B77-33856)

621.319'24 — Buildings. Electric wiring systems. Installation. *United States*
Richter, Herbert P. Practical electrical wiring : residential, farm and industrial / [by] H.P. Richter. — 10th ed. — New York ; London [etc.] : McGraw-Hill, 1976. — x,645p : ill, facsims ; 21cm.
'Based on the 1975 National Electrical Code'. — Previous ed.: New York : McGraw-Hill, 1972. — Bibl.: p.587. — Index.
ISBN 0-07-052387-8 : £12.40
(B77-03061)

621.319'24 — Electric equipment. Installation. Safety measures. *United States. Standards. Texts with commentaries*
NFPA handbook of the national electrical code. — 4th ed. / edited by Wilford I. Summers ; [for] the National Fire Protection Association. — New York ; London [etc.] : McGraw-Hill, [1976]. — xliii,797p : ill ; 21cm.
'Based on the current 1975 code'. — This ed. published in the United States: 1975. — Previous ed.: / edited by John H. Watt. New York : McGraw-Hill, 1972. — Index. — Includes the text of the code.
ISBN 0-07-068586-x : £13.25
(B77-05472)

621.319'24 — Electric equipment: Plugs & sockets. *Reports, surveys*
British Standards Institution. *Technical Help to Exporters Section.* Electrical plugs : an international survey / [Technical Help to Exporters, British Standards Institution]. — 2nd (revised) ed. — Hemel Hempstead (Maylands Ave., Hemel Hempstead, Herts. HP2 4SQ) : Technical Help to Exporters, British Standards Institution, 1977. — 28p(4fold) : ill ; 21x31cm.
Previous ed.: 1973.
ISBN 0-903886-42-1 Sd : £13.00(£10.00 to members)
(B77-18829)

621.319'24 — Industrial buildings. Electric wiring systems. *Manuals*
Smith, Robert L. Electrical wiring, industrial : code, theory, plans, specifications, installation methods / [by] Robert L. Smith. — New York ; London [etc.] : Van Nostrand Reinhold, 1977. — [6],135p : ill ; 27cm.
Two fold. sheets ([4]sides: ill.,plan) in pocket. — Index.
ISBN 0-442-22388-9 : Unpriced
(B77-26352)

621.319'24 — Residences. Electric wiring systems. *Amateurs' manuals*
Day, Roy. All about home electrics / [by] Roy Day. — London [etc.] : Hamlyn, 1976. — 112p : ill(chiefly col) ; 29cm.
With answers. — Index.
ISBN 0-600-30253-9 : £2.95
ISBN 0-600-30299-7 Pbk : £1.95
(B77-06724)

621.319'24 — Residences. Electric wiring systems. *United States. Manuals*
Mullin, Ray C. Electrical wiring, residential : code, theory, plans, specifications, installation methods / [by] Ray C. Mullin. — 5th ed. — New York ; London [etc.] : Van Nostrand Reinhold, [1976]. — vi,242p : ill, plans ; 27cm.
Five fold. sheets (ill., plans) in pocket. — This ed. published in the United States: 1975. — Previous ed.: Albany, N.Y. : Delmar Publishers, 1973. — Index.
ISBN 0-442-25594-2 : £6.80
(B77-03062)

621.319'24 — Structures. Electric equipment. *Irish standards*
Electro-technical Council of Ireland. National rules for electrical installations / [Electro-technical Council of Ireland]. — Dublin (Ballymun Rd, Dublin 9) : The Council.

Part 1 : General requirements. — 1976. — ii-xi, 76p : ill, forms ; 30cm.
Pierced for binder. — 'Provisional part 2:1 : Particular requirements for domestic premises' (Folder ([4]p.) as insert. — Index.
ISBN 0-9505651-0-5 Pbk : £3.90
(B77-14269)

621.319'34 — Electric equipment. Underwater cables
Barnes, Cyril Charles. Submarine telecommunication and power cables / [by] C.C. Barnes. — Stevenage : Peregrinus [for] the Institution of Electrical Engineers, 1977. — xii, 206p : ill, maps ; 23cm. — (Institution of Electrical Engineers. IEE monograph series ; 20 ISSN 0306-8269)
Index.
ISBN 0-901223-87-5 : Unpriced
Also classified at 621.387'84
(B77-32674)

621.32'2 — Agricultural industries. Farms. Electric lighting. Installation. *Great Britain. Manuals*
Electricity Council. Farm lighting : a guide to the practical design of installations / [Electricity Council]. — Revised [ed.]. — London (1 Charing Cross, SW1A 2DS) : The Council, 1970. — 103p : ill(some col) ; 18cm. — (Farmelectric handbook ; no.12 ISSN 0309-247x)
Bibl.: p.103.
ISBN 0-85188-057-6 Sd : £0.50
(B77-07402)

621.32'3 — Ancient Roman lamps. *Romania. Sarmizegetusa. Reports, surveys*
Alicu, Dorin. Roman lamps from Ulpia Traiana Sarmizegetusa / [by] Dorin Alicu and Emil Nemeş. — Oxford : British Archaeological Reports, 1977. — [14],119p,[24],lxv p of plates : ill, map, plans ; 30cm. — (British archaeological reports : supplementary series ; 18)
Spine and cover title: Roman lamps from Sarmizegetusa. — Bibl.: p.[11]-[14].
ISBN 0-904531-62-7 Pbk : £4.50
(B77-22647)

621.35'3 — Primary batteries & primary cells. *Standards*
British Standards Institution. Specification for primary cells and batteries = Spécification pour piles électriques = Spezifikation fur elektrochemische Zellen / British Standards Institution. — 4th revision. — London : B.S.I., 1976. — 130p in various pagings : ill ; 31cm. — (BS397 : 1976)
In binder.
ISBN 0-580-09209-7 Ls : £7.50
(B77-09739)

621.35'9 — Fuel cells
McDougall, Angus. Fuel cells / by Angus McDougall. — London [etc.] : Macmillan, 1976. — xii,147p : ill ; 25cm. — (Energy alternatives series)
Bibl.: p.140-141. — Index.
ISBN 0-333-18408-4 : £7.95
ISBN 0-333-18409-2 Pbk : Unpriced
(B77-04878)

621.36 — Applied optics
Carlson, F Paul. Introduction to applied optics for engineers / [by] F. Paul Carlson. — New York [etc.] ; London : Academic Press, 1977. — xiii,277p : ill ; 24cm.
Index.
ISBN 0-12-160050-5 : £11.70
(B77-31941)

621.36 — Electro-optical equipment. *Conference proceedings*
British electro-optics : proceedings of a conference at the British Export Marketing Centre, Tokyo, in December 1975 / edited by L.R. Baker. — London : Taylor and Francis, 1977. — vii,142p : ill, map ; 26cm.
'... organized by Sira' - jacket. — Index.
ISBN 0-85066-101-3 : £8.00
(B77-27155)

Electro-Optics Conference, *4th, Brighton, 1976.* Electro-Optics/Laser International '76 UK, Brighton, 9-11 March 1976 : conference proceedings / edited by H.G. Jerrard. — Guildford : IPC Science and Technology Press, 1976. — vii,244p : ill ; 31cm.
'... the Fourth Electro-Optics Conference' - Foreword. — '... organized by Kiver Communications Ltd'. — Bibl.
ISBN 0-902852-63-9 : Unpriced
(B77-07942)

621.36 — Optical information processing. Engineering aspects. *Conference proceedings*
US-USSR Science Cooperation Seminar on Optical Information Processing, *1st, Washington, D.C., 1975.* Optical information processing / edited by Yu. E. Nesterikhin, George W. Stroke and Winston E. Kock. — New York ; London : Plenum Press, 1976. — xiv,401p : ill ; 26cm.
'Proceedings of the [First] US-USSR Science Cooperation Seminar on Optical Information Processing, sponsored by The National Science Foundation, held in Washington, D.C., June 16-20, 1975' - title page verso. — Bibl.: p.344-346. — Index.
ISBN 0-306-30899-1 : £20.48
(B77-18831)

621.36'05 — Optical engineering. *Periodicals*
MOA : IEE journal on microwaves, optics and acoustics. — Stevenage (c/o P.O. Box 8, Southgate House, Stevenage, Herts. SG1 1HO) : Institution of Electrical Engineers.
Vol.1, no.1- ; Sept. 1976-. — 1976-. — ill ; 30cm.
Three issues a year. — 40, 3p. in 1st issue.
Sd : £7.50
ISSN 0308-6976
Primary classification 621.381'3'05
(B77-12499)

621.36'08 — Electro-optical equipment. *Readings*
Kaminow, Ivan P. An introduction to electrooptic devices : selected reprints and introductory text / by Ivan P. Kaminow [et al.]. — New York ; London : Academic Press, 1974. — xiv,409p : ill ; 25cm.
Index. — Includes facsimile reprints of readings.
ISBN 0-12-395050-3 : Unpriced
(B77-18830)

621.36'6 — Chemical lasers. *Reviews of research*
Handbook of chemical lasers / edited by R.W.F. Gross, J.F. Bott. — New York ; London [etc.] : Wiley, 1976. — xi,744p : ill ; 24cm.
'A Wiley-Interscience publication'. — Index.
ISBN 0-471-32804-9 : £31.00
(B77-05473)

621.36'6 — Electronic transition lasers. *Conference proceedings*
Summer Colloquium on Electronic Transition Lasers, *2nd, Woods Hole, Mass., 1975.* Electronic transition lasers : proceedings of the second Summer Colloquium on Electronic Transition Lasers held at the Marine Biology Laboratory Conference Center, Woods Hole, Massachusetts, September 17 to 19, 1975 / edited by Jeffrey I. Steinfeld. — Cambridge, Mass. ; London : M.I.T. Press, 1976. — xi, 311p : ill ; 24cm.
Index.
ISBN 0-262-19146-6 : £11.25
(B77-06152)

621.36'6 — Lasers. *Conference proceedings*
Orbis Scientiae *(Conference), 2nd, University of Miami, 1975.* Progress in lasers and laser fusion / ... editors Arnold Perlmutter, Susan M. Widmayer ... — New York ; London : Plenum Press, [1976]. — viii,416p : ill, ports ; 26cm. — (Studies in the natural sciences ; vol.8)
'Part of the Proceedings of Orbis Scientiae held by the Center for Theoretical Studies, University of Miami, January 20-24, 1975' - title page verso. — Published in the United States: 1975. — Bibl. — Index.
ISBN 0-306-36908-7 : £22.05
(B77-03588)

621.36'6 — Lasers. *Juvenile literature*
Burroughs, William, *b.1942.* Lasers / [by] William Burroughs. — Hove : Priory Press, 1976. — 88p : ill, ports ; 24cm. — (Science in action)
Bibl.: p.84. — Index.
ISBN 0-85078-225-2 : £3.25
(B77-05474)

621.36'6 — Lasers. *Reviews of research*
Laser applications. — New York [etc.] ; London : Academic Press.
Vol.3 / edited by Monte Ross. — 1977. — xiii, 238p : ill ; 24cm.
Bibl. — Index.
ISBN 0-12-431903-3 : £16.35
(B77-23485)

621.36'6 — Lasers. Applications
Kock, Winston Edward. Engineering applications of lasers and holography / [by] Winston E. Kock. — New York ; London : Plenum Press, [1976]. — xv,400p : ill, ports ; 24cm. — (Optical physics and engineering)
Published in the United States: 1975. — Bibl.: p.389-390. — Index.
ISBN 0-306-30849-5 : £15.75
Also classified at 774
(B77-05475)

621.36'63 — Carbon dioxide lasers. Applications
Duley, Walter Winston. CO2 lasers : effects and applications / [by] W.W. Duley. — New York [etc.] ; London : Academic Press, 1976. — xv, 427p : ill ; 24cm. — (Quantum electronics, principles and applications)
Bibl.: p.391-417. — Index.
ISBN 0-12-223350-6 : £18.40
(B77-00795)

621.36'63 — High energy gas lasers. Applications
Summer School on the Physics and Technology of High-power Gas Lasers, *Capri, 1975.* High-power gas lasers, 1975 : lectures given at a Summer School, organized by the International College of Applied Physics, on the Physics and Technology of High-power Gas Lasers. The School was held in Capri from 22 September to 4th October 1975 / edited by E.R. Pike. — Bristol [etc.] : Institute of Physics, 1976. — x,333p : ill ; 24cm. — (Institute of Physics. Conference series ; no.29 ISSN 0305-4632)
Bibl.
ISBN 0-85498-119-5 : £19.00
ISBN 0-85498-219-1 Pbk : Unpriced
(B77-01555)

621.36'7 — Acoustic imaging
Acoustic imaging : cameras, microscopes, phased arrays and holographic systems / edited by Glen Wade. — New York ; London : Plenum Press, 1976. — xiv,325p : ill ; 24cm.
'Lectures ... presented at the University of California in Santa Barbara, California, March 1975' - title page verso. — Index.
ISBN 0-306-30914-9 : £15.75
(B77-20341)

621.36'7 — Remote sensing. Data processing
Remote sensing data processing / edited by J.L. van Genderen and W.G. Collins ; [for] the Remote Sensing Society. — [Sheffield] : University of Sheffield ; Reading (c/o The General Secretary, Department of Geography, University of Reading, Whiteknights, Reading RG6 2AF) : [Distributed by] the Society, 1975. — [3] leaves,142p ; 30cm.
Bibl.
Pbk : £4.50
(B77-16447)

621.36'7 — Remote sensing systems. *Conference proceedings*
Symposium of the Colston Research Society, *28th, University of Bristol, 1976.* Remote sensing of the terrestrial environment : proceedings of the 28th Symposium of the Colston Research Society, held in the University of Bristol, April 5th-9th, 1976 / edited by R.F. Peel, L.F. Curtis and E.C. Barrett. — London [etc.] : Butterworth, 1977. — xx,275p,[2]p of plates : ill(some col), charts, maps, port ; 26cm. — (Colston papers ; vol.28)
ISBN 0-408-70805-0 : £12.00 : CIP rev.
(B77-11866)

621.36'7 — Remote sensing systems. *For environmental studies*
Barrett, Eric Charles. Introduction to environmental remote sensing / [by] E.C. Barrett and L.F. Curtis. — London : Chapman and Hall [etc.], 1976. — xi,336p,[8]p of plates : ill(some col), charts, maps ; 26cm.
'A Halsted Press Book'. — Bibl. — Index.
ISBN 0-412-12460-2 : £11.00
(B77-09740)

Remote sensing of environment / edited by Joseph Lintz, Jr and David S. Simonett. — Reading, Mass. ; London [etc.] : Addison-Wesley, 1976. — xix,694[i.e. 704]p,viii p of plates : ill(some col), maps ; 24cm.
Bibl.: p.627-674. — Index.
ISBN 0-201-04245-2 : £22.00
(B77-14270)

621.36'7 — Remote sensing. Techniques. *Conference proceedings*
Remote Sensing Society. *Technical Session, 1st, London, 1974.* Fundamentals of remote sensing : proceedings of the First Technical Session of the Remote Sensing Society, London, February 13th 1974 / edited by W.G. Collins and J.L. van Genderen. — [Reading] ([c/o The General Secretary, Department of Geography, University of Reading, Whiteknights, Reading RG6 2AF]) : The Society, [1974]. — [3] leaves,149p : ill, maps ; 30cm.
Bibl.
ISBN 0-9505798-0-7 Pbk : £4.50
(B77-16448)

621.37 — Electric measuring instruments. Accuracy. Effects of electrical noise
Van der Ziel, Aldert. Noise in measurements / [by] Aldert van der Ziel. — New York ; London [etc.] : Wiley, 1976. — xi,228p : ill ; 24cm.
'A Wiley-Interscience publication'. — Index.
ISBN 0-471-89895-3 : £10.80
(B77-21196)

621.38 — ELECTRONIC AND COMMUNICATIONS ENGINEERING

621.38 — Communication systems. Control devices
Morris, David J. Introduction to communication command and control systems / by David J. Morris. — Oxford [etc.] : Pergamon, 1977. — ix,308p : ill ; 26cm.
Index.
ISBN 0-08-020378-7 : £15.00
(B77-25687)

621.38 — Telecommunication systems
Brown, John, *b.1923.* Telecommunications / [by] J. Brown and E.V.D. Glazier. — 2nd ed. / this ed. revised by J. Brown. — London : Chapman and Hall, 1975. — xiv,382p : ill ; 24cm. — (Science paperbacks)
This ed. originally published: 1974. — Bibl.: p.377-378. — Index.
Pbk : £3.95
ISBN 0-412-12220-0
(B77-27156)

Kennedy, George, *b.1937.* Electronic communication systems / [by] George Kennedy. — 2nd ed. — New York ; London [etc.] : McGraw-Hill, Gregg Division, 1977. — xxv,774p : ill, map ; 24cm.
With answers to self-testing questions. — Previous ed.: New York : McGraw-Hill, 1970. — Index.
ISBN 0-07-034052-8 : £12.70
(B77-25688)

Peebles, Peyton Z. Communication system principles / [by] Peyton Z. Peebles, Jr. — Reading, Mass. ; London [etc.] : Addison-Wesley, 1976 [i.e. 1977]. — xx,488p : ill ; 27cm.
Published in the United States: 1976. — Index.
ISBN 0-201-05758-1 : £18.40
(B77-10829)

621.38'0412 — Interdigital surface acoustic wave devices. *Readings*
Key papers on surface-acoustic-wave passive interdigital devices / edited by David P. Morgan. — Stevenage : Peregrinus [for] the Institution of Electrical Engineers, 1976. — xi, 372p : ill, port ; 30cm. — (Institution of Electrical Engineers. IEE reprint series ; 2)
Reprints of 74 articles, originally published between 1965 and 1975. — Bibl.: p.347-370. — Index.
ISBN 0-901223-82-4 Pbk : Unpriced
(B77-04245)

621.38'0413 — Computer-telecommunication systems
Martin, James, *b.1933.* Telecommunications and the computer / [by] James Martin. — 2nd ed. — Englewood Cliffs, N.J. ; London [etc.] : Prentice-Hall, [1977]. — xviii,670p : ill(some col), maps ; 24cm. — (Prentice-Hall series in automatic computation)
Ill. on lining paper. — This ed. published in the United States: 1976. — Previous ed.: 1969. — Bibl. — Index.
ISBN 0-13-902494-8 : £22.40
(B77-11867)

621.38'0414 — Electronic visual displays. *Conference proceedings*
Electronic Displays '76 *(Conference), London, 1976.* Electronic Displays '76, Mount Royal Hotel, London, England, 30 Nov., 1, 2 Dec. : conference proceedings. — [Newport Pagnell] ([84 High St., Newport Pagnell, Bucks. MK16 8EG]) : [Network].
In 6 vols.
Session no.1 : [Communication with machine and systems (man-machine interfaces)]. — [1976]. — [4],27 leaves : ill ; 30cm.
Bibl.: leaves 13-14.
Sd : £7.00
(B77-18835)

Session no.2 : [Display techniques]. — [1976]. — [4],63 leaves : ill ; 30cm.
Sd : £7.00
(B77-18836)

Session no.3 : [Graphics and interactive displays]. — [1976]. — [4],47 leaves : ill ; 30cm.
Bibl.
Sd : £7.00
(B77-18837)

Session no.4 : [Display components]. — [1976]. — [4],34 leaves : ill ; 30cm.
Sd : £7.00
(B77-18838)

Session no.5 : [Displays in avionics and defence]. — [1976]. — [4],35 leaves : ill ; 30cm.
Sd : £7.00
(B77-18839)

Session no.6 : [Future developments]. — [1976]. — [4],49 leaves : ill ; 30cm.
Sd : £7.00
(B77-18840)

International Conference on Displays for Man-Machine Systems, *University of Lancaster, 1977.* International Conference on Displays for Man-Machine Systems, 4-7 April 1977 : organised by the Control of Automation, and Electronics Divisions of the Institution of Electrical Engineers in association with ... [others] : venue, University of Lancaster, Bailrigg, Lancaster. — [London] : [Institution of Electrical Engineers], [1977]. — vii,141p : ill ; 30cm. — (Institution of Electrical Engineers. Conference publications ; no.150 ISSN 0537-9989)
Cover title: Displays for man-machine systems.
ISBN 0-85296-173-1 Pbk : Unpriced
(B77-17561)

621.38'0414 — Image processing
Andrews, Harry Charles. Digital image restoration / [by] H.C. Andrews, B.R. Hunt. — Englewood Cliffs ; London [etc.] : Prentice-Hall, 1977. — xviii,238p : ill ; 24cm. — (Prentice-Hall signal processing series)
Bibl.: p.225-232. — Index.
ISBN 0-13-214213-9 : £19.95
(B77-24277)

Rosenfeld, Azriel. Digital picture processing / [by] Azriel Rosenfeld, Avinash C. Kak. — New York [etc.] ; London : Academic Press, 1976. — xii,457p : ill ; 24cm. — (Computer science and applied mathematics)
'The book supersedes an earlier book by one of us, (A.R.), "Picture Processing by Computer" (Academic Press, 1969 ...)' - Preface. — Bibl. — Index.
ISBN 0-12-597360-8 : £17.40
(B77-00266)

621.38'0414 — Nonemissive electronic visual displays. *Conference proceedings*
Brown Boveri Symposium on Nonemissive Electrooptic Displays, *4th, Baden, 1975.* Nonemissive electrooptic displays / edited by A.R. Kmetz and F.K. von Willisen. — New York ; London : Plenum Press, 1976. — xxi, 360p : ill ; 26cm.
'Proceedings of the Fourth Brown Boveri Symposium on Nonemissive Electrooptic Displays held at the Brown Boveri Research Center, Baden, Switzerland, September 29-30, 1975' - title page verso. — Index.
ISBN 0-306-30957-2 : £22.05
(B77-21931)

621.38'0414'01 — Optical communication systems. Information theory
Yu, Francis T S. Optics and information theory / [by] Francis T.S. Yu. — New York ; London [etc.] : Wiley, [1977]. — xiii,203p : ill ; 24cm.
'A Wiley-Interscience publication'. — Published in the United States: 1976. — Index.
ISBN 0-471-01682-9 : £11.50
(B77-12496)

621.38'043 — Communication systems. Signals
Stremler, Ferrel G. Introduction to communication systems / [by] Ferrel G. Stremler. — Reading, Mass. ; London [etc.] : Addison-Wesley, 1977. — xii,562p : ill ; 25cm. — (Addison-Wesley series in electrical engineering)
Bibl. — Index.
ISBN 0-201-07244-0 : £16.80
(B77-25689)

621.38'043 — Discrete time systems. Signals. Processing
Tretter, Steven A. Introduction to discrete-time signal processing / [by] Steven A. Tretter. — New York ; London [etc.] : Wiley, 1976. — xv, 460p : ill ; 24cm.
Bibl.: p.445-451. — Index.
ISBN 0-471-88760-9 : £18.25
(B77-07943)

621.38'043 — Signals. Processing
Papoulis, Athanasios. Signal analysis / [by] Athanasios Papoulis. — New York ; London [etc.] : McGraw-Hill, 1977. — xi,431p : ill ; 25cm.
With answers. — Index.
ISBN 0-07-048460-0 : £16.15
(B77-31942)

621.38'043 — Telecommunication systems. Digital signals. Transmission
Clark, A P. Principles of digital data transmission / [by] A.P. Clark. — London [etc.] (Estover Rd, Plymouth PL6 7PZ) : Pentech Press Ltd, 1976. — [10],246p : ill ; 23cm.
Index.
ISBN 0-7273-1603-6 : £7.50
ISBN 0-7273-1604-4 Pbk : £4.25
(B77-04246)

621.38'043 — Telecommunication systems. Signals. Processing. *Conference proceedings*
Impact of New Technologies in Signal Processing *(Conference), Aviemore, 1976.* International specialist seminar on The Impact of New Technologies in Signal Processing, 20-24 September 1976 : organised by the Electronics Division of the Institution of Electrical Engineers, venue Coylumbridge Hotel, Aviemore, Scotland / proceedings editor Peter M. Grant. — [Stevenage] : I.E.E., 1976. — vii, 176p : ill, ports ; 30cm. — (Institution of Electrical Engineers. Conference publications ; no.144 ISSN 0537-9989)
Cover title: The impact of new technologies in signal processing.
ISBN 0-85296-168-5 Pbk : £9.20
(B77-12497)

621.38'043 — Telecommunication systems. Signals. Sequency theory
Harmuth, Henning F. Sequency theory : foundations and applications / [by] Henning F. Harmuth. — New York [etc.] ; London : Academic Press, 1977. — xiv,505p : ill ; 24cm. — (Advances in electronics and electron physics, supplements ; 9)
Bibl.: p.483-497. — Index.
ISBN 0-12-014569-3 : £28.05
(B77-14271)

621.38'07'1141 — Universities. *Great Britain. Open University. Curriculum subjects: Telecommunication systems. Courses: 'Telecommunication systems'*
Open University. *Telecommunication Systems Course Team.* Introductory handbook / prepared by the [Open University, Telecommunication Systems] Course Team. — Milton Keynes (Walton Hall, Milton Keynes MK7 6AA) : Open University, 1976. — 8p ; 30cm. — (Technology, a third level course : telecommunication systems) (T321 ; IH)
Sd : Unpriced
(B77-14272)

621.38'08 — Telecommunication systems. *Readings*
Telecommunication systems / edited by M.P.R. Hamer, G. Smol. — Edinburgh : Holmes-McDougall ; Milton Keynes : Open University Press, 1977. — 219p : ill, maps ; 30cm. — (Open University. Set books)
ISBN 0-7157-1596-8 Pbk : £4.20
(B77-14771)

621.38'09'04 — Telecommunication systems, to 1976
Larsen, Egon. Telecommunications : a history / [by] Egon Larsen ; illustrations by Peter Bridgewater. — London : Muller, 1977. — 86p, [8]p of plates : ill, chart, map, ports ; 23cm.
Index.
ISBN 0-584-10298-4 : £2.95 : CIP rev.
(B77-07403)

621.381 — ELECTRONIC ENGINEERING
621.381 — Electronic equipment
Brophy, James John. Basic electronics for scientists / [by] James J. Brophy. — 3rd ed. — New York ; London [etc.] : McGraw-Hill, 1977. — xv,430p : ill ; 25cm.
Previous ed.: 1972. — Bibl. — Index.
ISBN 0-07-008107-7 : £13.90
(B77-31244)

Electronics designers' handbook. — 2nd ed. / completely revised and edited by L.J. Giacoletto. — New York [etc.] ; London : McGraw-Hill, 1977. — 2351p in various pagings : ill ; 24cm.
Previous ed.: / by Robert W. Landee, Donovan C. Davis, Albert P. Albrecht. 1957. — Bibl. — Index.
ISBN 0-07-023149-4 : £35.65
(B77-21932)

Fisher, Jack Edward. Electronics : from theory into practice / by J.E. Fisher and H.B. Gatland. — 2nd ed. — Oxford [etc.] : Pergamon. — (Pergamon international library)
In 2 vols. — Previous ed.: in one vol. 1966.
Vol.2 : Operational amplifiers, oscillators and digital techniques. — 1976. — p 211-445,xlix p : ill ; 21cm. — (Applied electricity and electronics division)
Index.
ISBN 0-08-019856-2 Pbk : £4.75
ISBN 0-08-019857-0 Set of 2 vols : £8.75
(B77-01556)

Gray, Bernard Francis. Measurements, instrumentation, and data transmission : a text for the OND in technology (engineering) / [by] B.F. Gray. — London [etc.] : Longman, 1977. — vi,169p : ill ; 22cm.
Index.
ISBN 0-582-41065-7 : £4.95
ISBN 0-582-41066-5 Pbk : £2.95
Primary classification 620'.0044
(B77-15322)

Grob, Bernard. Basic electronics / [by] Bernard Grob. — 4th ed. — New York ; London [etc.] : McGraw-Hill, 1977. — xv,768p : ill(some col) ; 25cm.
With answers. — Previous ed.: 1971. — Bibl.: p.713-716. — Index.
ISBN 0-07-024923-7 : £11.20
(B77-27908)

Handbook for electronics engineering technicians / editors Milton Kaufman, Arthur H. Seidman ; Perry J. Sheneman, associate editor. — New York ; London [etc.] : McGraw-Hill, 1976. — 538p in various pagings : ill ; 24cm.
Index.
ISBN 0-07-033401-3 : £16.20
(B77-00796)

Harris, Douglas James. The physical basis of electronics : an introductory course / [by] D.J. Harris and P.N. Robson. — 2nd ed. — Oxford [etc.] : Pergamon, 1974. — xii,266p : ill ; 22cm. — (Applied electricity and electronics) ([Pergamon international library])
With answers. — Previous ed.: published as 'Vacuum and solid state electronics'. 1963. — Bibl.: p.240. — Index.
ISBN 0-08-017900-2 : £6.15
ISBN 0-08-017901-0 Pbk : £3.15
(B77-00797)

Millman, Jacob. Electronic fundamentals and applications for engineers and scientists / [by] Jacob Millman, Christos C. Halkias. — New York ; London [etc.] : McGraw-Hill, [1977]. — xv,482p : ill ; 25cm.
Answer book ([2],15p. : sd) as insert. — Published in the United States: 1976. — '... a simplification, rearrangement, and condensation of the material in [the authors'] I[ntegrated] E[lectronics] ... [New York : Maidenhead : McGraw-Hill, 1972]' - Preface. — Index.
ISBN 0-07-042310-5 : £13.25
(B77-11868)

Morris, Noel Malcolm. Electronics for works electricians / [by] Noel M. Morris. — London [etc.] : McGraw-Hill, 1976. — xi,268p : ill ; 23cm.
Bibl.: p.262. — Index.
ISBN 0-07-084476-3 Pbk : £6.00
(B77-01557)

Olsen, George Henry. Modern electronics made simple / [by] George H. Olsen. — London : W.H. Allen, 1977. — xi,306p : ill ; 23cm. — (Made simple books ISSN 0464-2902)
Bibl. — Index.
ISBN 0-491-01758-8 : £2.95
ISBN 0-491-01768-5 Pbk : £1.75
(B77-17560)

Rubaroe, G T. Essential theory for the electronics hobbyist / by G.T. Rubaroe. — London : Bernards, 1977. — 118p : ill ; 18cm. — (Bernards & Babani Press radio and electronics books ; no.228)
ISBN 0-900162-69-4 Pbk : £1.25
(B77-28672)

Ryder, John Douglas. Electronic fundamentals and applications : integrated and discrete systems / [by] John D. Ryder. — 5th ed. — London : Pitman, 1977. — xvii,538p : ill ; 23cm. — (A Pitman international text)
This ed. originally published: Englewood Cliffs : Prentice-Hall, 1976. — Bibl. — Index.
ISBN 0-273-01057-3 Pbk : £4.95 : CIP rev.
(B77-06725)

621.381 — Electronic equipment. *For technicians*
Bishop, Graham Dudley. Electronics II / [by] G.D. Bishop. — London [etc.] : Macmillan, 1977. — viii,76p : ill ; 21x24cm. — (Macmillan technician series)
With answers. — '... follows the syllabus of the Standard TEC Unit Electronics II' - Preface.
ISBN 0-333-21390-4 Pbk : £2.95 : CIP rev.
(B77-18202)

621.381 — Electronic equipment. Projects. *Amateurs' manuals*
Penfold, R A. Beginner's guide to building electronic projects / by R.A. Penfold. — London : Bernards, 1977. — 107p : ill ; 18cm. — (Bernards & Babani Press radio and electronics books ; no. 227)
ISBN 0-900162-68-6 Pbk : £1.25
(B77-27909)

621.381 — Electronic equipment. Safety measures. *United States*
Lacy, Edward A. Handbook of electronic safety procedures / [by] Edward A. Lacy. — Englewood Cliffs ; London [etc.] : Prentice-Hall, 1977. — xv,269p : ill, maps ; 24cm.
Bibl.: p.255-256. — Index.
ISBN 0-13-377341-8 : £11.95
(B77-30328)

621.381'01'51 — Electronic engineering. Mathematics
Clifford, Jerrold R. Modern electronic maths / [by] Jerrold R. Clifford, Martin Clifford ; with a specially written chapter for the guidance of the English reader by W. Oliver. — Slough : Foulsham-Tab, 1977. — viii,3-684p : ill ; 21cm.
With answers. — Originally published: as 'Modern electronics math'. Blue Ridge Summit, Pa. : Tab Books, 1976. — Index.
ISBN 0-7042-0178-x Pbk : £5.95
(B77-27157)

621.381'028 — Electronic equipment. Experiments. *Laboratory manuals*
Zbar, Paul Bernard. Basic electronics : a text-lab manual / [by] Paul B. Zbar. — 4th ed. — New York ; London [etc.] : McGraw-Hill, 1976. — xiv,305p : ill ; 28cm.
With answers to self-tests. — Previous ed.: New York : McGraw-Hill, 1967.
ISBN 0-07-072761-9 Pbk : £7.45
(B77-04247)

621.381'028 — Electronic equipment. Maintenance & repair. *Manuals*
Lenk, John D. Handbook of basic electronic troubleshooting / [by] John D. Lenk. — Englewood Cliffs ; London [etc.] : Prentice-Hall, 1977. — xv,239p : ill ; 24cm.
Index.
ISBN 0-13-372482-4 : £12.80
(B77-12498)

621.381'042 — Electronic equipment. Design. Implications of effects of electromagnetic pulse radiation
Ricketts, L W. EMP radiation and protective techniques / [by] L.W. Ricketts, J.E. Bridges, J. Miletta. — New York ; London [etc.] : Wiley, 1976. — xv,380p : ill, maps ; 24cm.
'A Wiley-Interscience publication'. — Index.
ISBN 0-471-01403-6 : £21.20
(B77-09060)

621.381'042 — Electronic equipment. Reliability
British Standards Institution. Guide on the reliability of electronic equipment and parts used therein = Guide sur la fiabilité des équipements électroniques et de leurs parties composantes = Hinweisblatt über die Zuverlässigkeit von elektronischen Geräten und deren Teile / British Standards Institution. — London : B.S.I.
Part 8 = Partie 8 = Teil 8 : The screening (sorting) of electronic equipment and parts = Triage des équipements et composantes électroniques = Kontrolle von elektronischen Geräten und Teilen. — 1976. — [2],4,[2]p : ill ; 30cm. — (BS4200 : Part 8 : 1976)
Pierced for binder.
ISBN 0-580-09078-7 Sd : £1.50
(B77-07944)

621.381'05 — Electronic equipment. *Periodicals*
Institution of Electrical Engineers. IEE journal on electronic circuits and systems. — London : I.E.E.
Vol.1, no.1- ; Sept. 1976-. — 1976-. — ill, ports ; 30cm.
Quarterly. — 2,48p. in 1st issue.
Sd : £7.50(£25.00 yearly)
ISSN 0308-6984
(B77-13081)

621.381'05 — Electronic equipment. *Serials*
Allen Clark Research Centre. Annual review / Allen Clark Research Centre. — Towcester (Caswell, Towcester, Northants.) : The Centre. 76. — [1976]. — [1],80,[1]p : ill(some col), map ; 26cm.
Previously published: as 'Newsletter' / Allen Clark Research Centre. — Bibl.: p.68-77.
ISBN 0-9505642-0-6 Sd : Private circulation
ISSN 0308-7549
(B77-11870)

621.381'076 — Electronic equipment. *Exercises, worked examples*
Benson, Frank Atkinson. Problems in electronics with solutions / [by] F.A. Benson. — 5th ed. — London : Chapman and Hall, 1976. — x, 380p : ill ; 22cm.
Previous ed.: London : Spon, 1965. — Index.
ISBN 0-412-14770-x Pbk : £3.95
(B77-03589)

621.381'07'7 — Electronic equipment. *Programmed texts*
New York Institute of Technology. A programmed course in basic electronics. — 2nd ed. / New York Institute of Technology ; Alexander Schure, project director. — New York ; London [etc.] : McGraw-Hill, 1976. — xiii,561p : ill ; 24cm.
With answers to criterion check tests. — Previous ed.: / by staff of Electrical Technology Department, New York Institute of Technology. 1964. — Index.
ISBN 0-07-046391-3 : £8.25
(B77-04248)

621.381'09'03 — Electronic equipment. Inventions. *Western world, 1745-1976*
Dummer, Geoffrey William Arnold. Electronic inventions, 1745-1976 / by G.W.A. Dummer. — Oxford [etc.] : Pergamon, 1977. — v,158p : ill ; 28cm.
Bibl.: p.149-151. — Index.
ISBN 0-08-020982-3 : £4.00
(B77-09061)

621.381'1 — Digital communication systems
Clark, A P. Advanced data-transmission systems / [by] A.P. Clark. — London [etc.] : Pentech Press, 1977. — xii,427p : ill ; 23cm.
Index.
ISBN 0-7273-0101-2 : £12.50
(B77-20342)

621.381'3'05 — Microwave equipment. *Periodicals*
MOA : IEE journal on microwaves, optics and acoustics. — Stevenage (c/o P.O. Box 8, Southgate House, Stevenage, Herts. SG1 1HO) : Institution of Electrical Engineers.
Vol.1, no.1- ; Sept. 1976-. — 1976-. — ill ; 30cm.
Three issues a year. — 40, 3p. in 1st issue.
Sd : £7.50
ISSN 0308-6976
Also classified at 621.36'05; 620.2'05
(B77-12499)

621.381'33 — Microwave equipment: Antennas. Design
Cornbleet, S. Microwave optics : the optics of microwave antenna design / [by] S. Cornbleet. — London [etc.] : Academic Press, 1976. — xvii,416p : ill ; 24cm. — (Pure and applied physics ; vol.41)
Bibl. — Index.
ISBN 0-12-189650-1 : £15.80
(B77-09741)

621.381'331 — Telecommunication systems. Millimetric waveguides. *Conference proceedings*
International Conference on Millimetric Waveguide Systems, *Institution of Electrical Engineers, 1976.* International Conference on Millimetric Waveguide Systems, 9-12 November 1976 [held at the] Institution of Electrical Engineers, Savoy Place, London W.C.2, organised by the Electronics Division of the Institution of Electrical Engineers in association with ... [others]. — [London] : [The Institution], [1976]. — xv,250p : ill, maps ; 30cm. — (Institution of Electrical Engineers. Conference publications ; no.146 ISSN 0537-9989)
Cover title: Millimetric waveguide systems.
ISBN 0-85296-166-9 Pbk : Unpriced
(B77-04249)

621.3815 — Digital electronic equipment
Tocci, Ronald J. Digital systems : principles and applications / [by] Ronald J. Tocci. — Englewood Cliffs ; London [etc.] : Prentice-Hall, 1977. — xvi,479p : ill ; 24cm.
With answers to selected problems. — Index.
ISBN 0-13-212266-9 : £12.80
(B77-18203)

621.3815 — Digital electronic equipment. Design. Applications of digital computer systems
Digital system design automation : languages, simulation & data base / edited by Melvin A. Breuer ; contributing authors M.H. MacDougall ... [et al.]. — London [etc.] : Pitman, 1977. — xiii,417p : ill ; 24cm. — (Digital system design series)
Originally published: Woodland Hills : Computer Science Press, 1975. — Bibl. — Index.
ISBN 0-273-01072-7 : £13.95
(B77-25690)

621.3815 — Digital electronic equipment. Design. Testing
Breuer, Melvin A. Diagnosis & reliable design of digital systems / [by] Melvin A. Breuer, Arthur D. Friedman. — London [etc.] : Pitman, 1977. — ix,308p : ill ; 24cm. — (Digital system design series)
Originally published: Woodland Hills : Computer Science Press, 1976. — Bibl.: p.301-303. — Index.
ISBN 0-273-01071-9 : £13.95
(B77-25691)

621.3815 — Digital electronic equipment. Experiments
Leach, Donald P. Experiments in digital principles / [by] Donald P. Leach. — New York ; London [etc.] : McGraw-Hill, 1976. — vii,136p : ill, forms ; 28cm.
Pages perforated at inside edge and pierced for binder.
ISBN 0-07-036915-1 Pbk : £8.25
(B77-04250)

621.3815'1 — Digital electronic equipment. Transducers
Woolvet, G A. Transducers in digital systems / [by] G.A. Woolvet. — Stevenage : Peregrinus [for] the Institution of Electrical Engineers, 1977. — viii,193p : ill ; 23cm. — (Institution of Electrical Engineers. IEE control engineering series ; 3)
Bibl. — Index.
ISBN 0-901223-70-0 : Unpriced
(B77-30329)

621.3815'1 — Electronic equipment. Components. *Manuals*
Handbook of components for electronics / Charles A. Harper, editor-in-chief. — New York [etc.] ; London : McGraw-Hill, 1977. — 1103p in various pagings : ill ; 24cm.
Index.
ISBN 0-07-026682-4 : £27.40
(B77-27910)

621.3815'1 — Electronic equipment. Custom-built inductors & custom-built transformers. Testing. *Standards*
British Standards Institution. Specification for custom-built transformers and inductors of assessed quality, generic data and methods of test = Spécification pour transformateurs et inducteurs fait sur commande et de qualité assurée, données génériques et méthodes d'essai = Spezifikation für gütebestätigte Transformatoren und Induktoren nach Kundenspezifikation, allgemeine Daten und Prüfmethoden / British Standards Institution. — London : B.S.I., 1976. — [40]p : ill ; 30cm. — (BS9720 : 1976)
Pierced for binder.
ISBN 0-580-09464-2 Sd : £5.80
(B77-03063)

621.3815'1 — Electronic equipment. Inductors & transformers. Nickel-iron laminated cores. *Standards*
British Standards Institution. Specification for nickel-iron transformer and choke laminations = Spécification pour lamelles en fer au nickel pour transformateurs et bobines d'arrêt = Spezifikation für Laminierungen aus Nickel-Eisen für Transformatoren und Drosseln / British Standards Institution. — 1st revision. — London : B.S.I., 1976. — [2],26,[2] p : ill ; 30cm. — (BS2857 : 1976)
Pierced for binder.
ISBN 0-580-09672-6 Sd : £4.00
(B77-03064)

621.3815'1 — Long life electronic components. *Standards*
British Standards Institution. Requirements for the manufacture of electronic components of assessed quality intended for long life applications / British Standards Institution. — London : B.S.I., 1977. — [2],8,[1]p ; 30cm. — (BS9003 : 1977)
Pierced for binder.
ISBN 0-580-09319-0 Sd : £2.70
(B77-11871)

621.3815'2 — Semiconductor devices
Deboo, Gordon J. Integrated circuits and semiconductor devices : theory and application / [by] Gordon J. Deboo, Clifford N. Burrous. — 2nd ed. — New York ; London [etc.] : McGraw-Hill, 1977. — xiii,479p : ill ; 24cm.
With answers to selected problems. — Previous ed.: New York : McGraw-Hill, 1971. — Index.
ISBN 0-07-016246-8 : £12.00
Primary classification 621.381'73
(B77-21934)

Electronic power control and digital techniques / edited by Bryan Norris. — New York ; London [etc.] : McGraw-Hill, [1977]. — [7],216p : ill ; 26cm. — (Texas Instruments. Electronics series)
Published in the United States: 1976. — Index.
ISBN 0-07-063752-0 : £13.70
(B77-11872)

Tedeschi, Frank P. Solid-state electronics / [by] Frank P. Tedeschi, Margaret R. Taber. — New York ; London [etc.] : Van Nostrand Reinhold, 1976. — vii,204p : ill ; 27cm. — (Electronics technology series)
With answers to student review questions. — Also published: Albany, N.Y. : Delmar Publishers, 1976. — Index.
ISBN 0-442-28460-8 : £6.80
(B77-01558)

621.3815'2 — Semiconductor devices. *Conference proceedings*
European Solid State Device Research Conference, *6th, Technische Universität München, 1976*. Solid state devices, 1976 : seven invited papers presented at the Sixth European Solid State Device Research Conference (ESSDERC) held at Technische Universität, München, 13-16 September 1976 / edited by R. Müller and E. Lange. — Bristol [etc.] : Institute of Physics, 1977. — vii,140p : ill ; 24cm. — (Institute of Physics. Conference series ; no.32 ISSN 0305-2346)
Bibl.
ISBN 0-85498-122-5 : £13.00 : CIP rev.
(B77-06726)

621.381'52 — Semiconductor devices. *Reviews of research*
Applied solid state science : advances in materials and device research. — New York [etc.] ; London : Academic Press.
Vol.6 / edited by Raymond Wolfe. — 1976 [i.e. 1977]. — xi,263p : ill ; 24cm.
Published in the United States: 1976. — Index.
ISBN 0-12-002906-5 : £19.20
(B77-12500)

621.3815'2 — Unipolar semiconductor devices
Dascălu, Dan. Electronic processes in unipolar solid-state devices / [by] Dan Dascălu. — Bucureşti [i.e. Bucharest] : Editura Academiei ; Tunbridge Wells : Abacus Press, 1977. — 624p : ill ; 25cm.
Text on lining paper. — Index.
ISBN 0-85626-025-8 : £18.50
(B77-18832)

621.3815'2'05 — Semiconductor devices. *Periodicals*
Institution of Electrical Engineers. IEE journal on solid-state and electron devices. — London : I.E.E.
Vol.1, no.1- ; Sept. 1976-. — 1976-. — ill ; 30cm.
Quarterly. — 2,36p. in 1st issue.
Sd : £7.50(£25.00 yearly)
ISSN 0308-6968
(B77-13082)

621.3815'22 — Negative resistance semiconductor devices
Roy, D K. Tunnelling and negative resistance phenomena in semiconductors / by D.K. Roy ; edited by B.R. Pamplin. — Oxford [etc.] : Pergamon Press, 1977. — xv,213p : ill ; 26cm. — (International series in the science of the solid state ; vol.11)
Bibl.: p.177-209. — Index.
ISBN 0-08-021044-9 : £9.75
Also classified at 537.6'22
(B77-15326)

621.3815'22 — Semiconductor devices: Epitaxial planar switching diodes
Kocsis, Miklós. High-speed silicon planar-epitaxial switching diodes / by Miklós Kocsis ; [translated from the Hungarian by Imre Zólomi]. — London : Hilger, 1976. — 177p : ill ; 24cm.
Originally published: in Hungarian. Budapest : Akadémiai Kiadó, 1976. — Bibl.: p.173-175. — Index.
ISBN 0-85274-206-1 : £10.00
(B77-15327)

621.3815'28 — Field effect transistors. *Technical data*
Towers, Thomas Dundas. Towers' international fet selector : specification data for the identification, selection and substitution of fet's / by T.D. Towers and N.S. Towers. — London [etc.] : Foulsham, 1977. — 57p : ill ; 26cm.
ISBN 0-572-00938-0 Pbk : £3.50
(B77-32675)

621.3815'28 — Field effect transistors. Projects. *Amateurs' manuals*
Rayer, Francis George. 50 (FET) field effect transistor projects / by F.G. Rayer. — London : Babani Press, 1977. — 104p : ill ; 18cm.
ISBN 0-85934-042-2 Pbk : £1.25
(B77-33857)

621.3815'28 — Transistor equipment. Projects. *Amateurs' manuals*
Torrens, R. 28 tested transistor projects / by R. Torrens. — London : Bernards, 1976. — 85p : ill ; 18cm. — (Bernards & Babani Press radio and electronics books ; no.221)
ISBN 0-900162-63-5 Pbk : £0.95
(B77-02372)

621.3815'28'0212 — Transistors. *Technical data*
Towers, Thomas Dundas. Towers' international transistor selector : specification data for the identification, selection and substitution of transistors / by T.D. Towers. — Revised ed. update one. — London [etc.] : Foulsham, 1977. — 196p : ill ; 26cm.
Previous ed.: 1974.
ISBN 0-572-00955-0 Pbk : £4.50
(B77-18833)

621.3815'3 — Analogue function circuits
Wong, Yu Jen. Function circuits : design and applications / [by] Yu Jen Wong, William E. Ott. — New York ; London [etc.] : McGraw-Hill, 1976. — xii,291p : ill ; 24cm. — (The BB electronics series)
Index.
ISBN 0-07-071570-x : £13.90
(B77-32676)

621.3815'3 — Digital circuits
Gothmann, William H. Digital electronics : an introduction to theory and practice / [by] William H. Gothmann. — Englewood Cliffs ; London [etc.] : Prentice-Hall, 1977. — xiii, 386p : ill ; 24cm. — (Prentice-Hall series in electronic technology)
With answers to selected problems. — Bibl.: p.368-369. — Index.
ISBN 0-13-212217-0 : £11.95
(B77-28673)

621.3815'3 — Digital circuits. Design. Applications of digital computer systems
Lewin, Douglas. Computer-aided design of digital systems / [by] Douglas Lewin. — New York : Crane Russak ; London : Edward Arnold, 1977. — x,313p : ill ; 24cm. — (Computer systems engineering series)
Index.
ISBN 0-7131-2633-7 : £15.00
(B77-22649)

621.3815'3 — Digital circuits. Logic design
Friedman, Arthur Daniel. Logical design of digital systems / [by] Arthur D. Friedman. — London [etc.] : Pitman, 1977. — x,278p : ill ; 23cm. — (Digital system design series) (A Pitman international text)
Originally published: Woodland Hills : Computer Science Press, 1975. — Bibl. — Index.
ISBN 0-273-01061-1 Pbk : £3.95 : CIP rev.
(B77-06727)

Mowle, Frederic J. A systematic approach to digital logic design / [by] Frederic J. Mowle. — Reading, Mass. ; London [etc.] : Addison-Wesley, [1977]. — xiv,543p : ill ; 25cm. — (Addison-Wesley series in electrical engineering)
Published in the United States: 1976. — Bibl. — Index.
ISBN 0-201-04920-1 : £15.30
(B77-13083)

United Technical Publications. Modern guide to digital logic : processors, memories & interfaces / United Technical Publications Inc. ; with a specially written chapter for the guidance of the English reader by W. Oliver. — Slough : Foulsham-Tab, 1977. — xi,11-290p : ill ; 21cm.
Originally published: Blue Ridge Summit, Pa. : Tab Books, 1976. — Index.
ISBN 0-7042-0179-8 Pbk : £3.60
(B77-25692)

621.3815'3 — Electronic equipment. Circuits
Jones, Martin Hartley. A practical introduction to electronic circuits / [by] Martin Hartley Jones. — Cambridge [etc.] : Cambridge University Press, 1977. — xii,237p : ill ; 26cm.
Bibl.: p.232. — Index.
ISBN 0-521-21291-x : £9.50
ISBN 0-521-29087-2 Pbk : £3.95
(B77-24988)

Lowenberg, Edwin C. Schaum's outline of theory and problems of electronic circuits / by Edwin C. Lowenberg. — SI (metric) ed. — New York ; London [etc.] : McGraw-Hill, 1976. — [6],274p : ill ; 28cm. — (Schaum's outline series)
Cover title: Theory and problems of electronic circuits. — Spine title: Electronic circuits. — With answers to supplementary problems. — Previous ed.: New York : McGraw-Hill, 1967. — Index.
ISBN 0-07-084367-8 Pbk : £3.75
(B77-16449)

Malvino, Albert Paul. Resistive and reactive circuits / [by] Albert Paul Malvino. — New York ; London [etc.] : McGraw-Hill, 1974. — xiv,592p : ill ; 25cm.
With answers to odd numbered problems. — Text on lining paper. — Index.
ISBN 0-07-039856-9 : Unpriced
(B77-19441)

Temes, Lloyd. Electronic circuits for technicians / [by] Lloyd Temes. — 2nd ed. — New York ; London [etc.] : McGraw-Hill, 1977. — xx,427p : ill ; 25cm.
With answers to selected problems. — Previous ed.: New York : McGraw-Hill, 1970. — Index.
ISBN 0-07-063492-0 : £9.70
(B77-29490)

Zanger, Henry. Electronic systems : theory and applications / [by] Henry Zanger. — Englewood Cliffs ; London [etc.] : Prentice-Hall, 1977. — xii,340p : ill ; 24cm.
Bibl.: p.332-333. — Index.
ISBN 0-13-252155-5 : Unpriced
(B77-26353)

621.3815'3 — Electronic equipment. Circuits. Construction. *Amateurs' manuals*

Capel, Vivian. How to build electronic kits / [by] Vivian Capel. — Kings Langley : Fountain Press, 1975. — vii,87p : ill ; 22cm.
Index.
ISBN 0-85242-437-x Pbk : £1.75
(B77-18204)

Dobbs, George Christopher. Practical electronic projects / by G.C. Dobbs ; illustrations by David Gibby. — [Nottingham] ([8] Redgates Court, Calverton, [Nottingham NG14 6LR]) : Calverton Publications Ltd, 1976. — 64p : ill ; 18cm.
ISBN 0-905148-10-x Pbk : £0.75
(B77-02373)

621.3815'3 — Electronic equipment. Circuits. Design

Circuit designs : collected circards / [by] P. Williams ... [et al.]. — London : IPC Business Press, 1975. — 2v.(168; 168p) : ill ; 30cm. — (A 'Wireless world' publication)
'First published as "Wireless world" Circards in card format in 1972 and 1973 by IPC Electrical-Electronic Press Ltd. ... Introductory articles were first published in "Wireless world"' - title page verso.
Unpriced
(B77-24278)

621.3815'3 — Electronic equipment. Nonlinear circuits

Van der Ziel, Aldert. Nonlinear electronic circuits / [by] Aldert van der Ziel. — New York ; London [etc.] : Wiley, 1977. — xi,267p : ill ; 24cm.
'A Wiley-Interscience publication'. — With solutions to selected problems. — Bibl.: p.264. — Index.
ISBN 0-471-02227-6 : £10.50
(B77-26354)

621.3815'3 — Sequential digital circuits

Lind, L F. Analysis and design of sequential digital systems / [by] L.F. Lind, J.C.C. Nelson. — London [etc.] : Macmillan, 1977. — viii, 146p : ill ; 24cm. — (Electrical and electronic engineering)
Bibl. — Index.
ISBN 0-333-19266-4 : £8.95
ISBN 0-333-19267-2 Pbk : £4.50
(B77-23486)

621.3815'3042 — Semiconductor circuits

MOS and special-purpose bipolar integrated circuits and R-F power transistor circuit design / edited by Bryan Norris. — New York ; London [etc.] : McGraw-Hill, [1977]. — [11],228p : ill ; 26cm. — (Texas Instruments. Electronics series)
Published in the United States: 1976. — Index.
ISBN 0-07-063751-2 : £13.70
(B77-11873)

621.3815'3042 — Semiconductor circuits. Design

Manasse, Fred Kurt. Semiconductor electronics design. — [Revised ed.] / [by] Fred K. Manasse. — Englewood Cliffs ; London [etc.] : Prentice-Hall, 1977. — xiv,562p : ill ; 24cm.
Previous ed.: published as 'Modern transistor electronics analysis and design' / by Fred K. Manasse, John A. Ekiss, Charles R. Gray. 1967. — Index.
ISBN 0-13-806273-0 : £15.15
(B77-18205)

621.3815'30422 — Transistor circuits

Veatch, Henry Charles. Transistor circuit action / [by] Henry C. Veatch. — 2nd ed. — New York ; London [etc.] : McGraw-Hill, 1977. — vii,392p : ill ; 24cm.
With answers. — Previous ed.: 1968. — Bibl.: p.380. — Index.
ISBN 0-07-067383-7 : Unpriced
(B77-28674)

621.3815'32 — Active filters. Design

Daryanani, Gobind. Principles of active network synthesis and design / [by] Gobind Daryanani. — New York ; London [etc.] : Wiley, 1976. — xv,495p : ill ; 24cm.
With answers to selected problems. — Bibl. — Index.
ISBN 0-471-19545-6 : £13.45
(B77-06728)

621.3815'32 — Digital filters

Hamming, Richard Wesley. Digital filters / [by] R.W. Hamming. — Englewood Cliffs ; London [etc.] : Prentice-Hall, 1977. — xiii,226p : ill ; 24cm. — (Prentice-Hall signal processing series)

Bibl.: p.219-221. — Index.
ISBN 0-13-212571-4 : £14.35
(B77-25693)

621.3815'33 — Electronic equipment. Quartz crystal oscillators. Crystals. *Standards*

British Standards Institution. Specification for quartz crystal units of assessed quality for oscillator application = Spécification des quartz de qualité assurée pour les oscillateurs = Spezifikation für Quarzkristalle bestätigter Güte für Oszillatoren : generic data and methods of test = données génériques et méthodes d'essais = generische Daten und Prüfverfahren / British Standards Institution. — 1st revision. — London : B.S.I., 1977. — [34]p : ill, form ; 30cm. — (BS9610 : 1977)
Pierced for binder.
ISBN 0-580-09880-x Sd : £6.60
(B77-15328)

621.3815'35 — Electronic equipment. Operational amplifiers

Carr, Joseph. Op-amp circuit design & applications / [by] Joseph Carr ; with a specially written chapter for the guidance of the English reader by W. Oliver. — Slough : Foulsham-Tab, 1977. — vii,7-282p : ill ; 21cm.
Originally published: Blue Ridge Summit : G/L Books, 1976. — Index.
ISBN 0-7042-0173-9 Pbk : £3.50
(B77-18834)

Digital integrated circuits and operational-amplifier and optoelectronic circuit design / edited by Bryan Norris. — New York ; London [etc.] : McGraw-Hill, 1976. — [11],206p : ill ; 26cm. — (Texas Instruments. Electronics series)
Index.
ISBN 0-07-063753-9 : £13.70
Primary classification 621.381'73'7
(B77-13689)

Faulkenberry, Lucas M. An introduction to operational amplifiers / [by] Lucas M. Faulkenberry. — New York ; London [etc.] : Wiley, 1977. — xi,257p : ill ; 25cm. — (Electronic technology series)
With answers to self test questions. — Index.
ISBN 0-471-01548-2 : £10.00
(B77-20343)

621.3815'37 — Logic circuits

Lee, Samuel C. Digital circuits and logic design / [by] Samuel C. Lee. — Englewood Cliffs ; London [etc.] : Prentice-Hall, 1976. — xii, 594p : ill ; 24cm.
Bibl. — Index.
ISBN 0-13-212225-1 : £19.65
(B77-00798)

621.3815'37 — Switching circuits

Friedman, Arthur Daniel. Theory & design of switching circuits / [by] Arthur D. Friedman, Premachandran R. Menon. — London : Pitman, 1977. — xii,581p : ill ; 24cm. — (Digital system design series)
Originally published: Woodland Hills : Computer Science Press, 1975. — Bibl. — Index.
ISBN 0-273-01111-1 : £15.00 : CIP rev.
(B77-21933)

621.3815'37 — Ternary switching functions

Thelliez, S. Introduction to the study of ternary switching structures / [by] S. Thelliez ; translated from the French by W.G. Stripp. — London [etc.] : Gordon and Breach, 1975. — xii,186p : ill ; 24cm. — (Information and systems theory ; vol.4)
Translation of: 'Introduction à l'étude des structures ternaires de commutation'. Paris : Gordon and Breach, 1973. — Bibl.: p.171-186.
ISBN 0-677-30330-0 : £7.60
(B77-11874)

621.3815'42 — Electronic equipment: Imaging devices. *Reviews of research*

Advances in image pickup and display. — New York [etc.] ; London : Academic Press.
Vol.3 / edited by B. Kazan. — 1977. — xiii, 302p : ill ; 24cm.
Bibl. — Index.
ISBN 0-12-022103-9 : £22.00
(B77-27158)

621.3815'48 — Cathode ray oscilloscopes. Use. *Manuals*

Sinclair, Ian Robertson. The oscilcoscope in use / [by] Ian R. Sinclair. — Watford : Fountain Press, 1976. — [7],129p : ill ; 22cm.
Index. — Previous control number ISBN 0-85242-471-x.
ISBN 0-85242-489-2 Pbk : £2.50
(B77-11875)

621.3815'48 — Miniature electronic measuring instruments. Construction. *Amateurs' manuals*

Haviland, Robert Paul. Build-it book of miniature test & measurement instruments / [by] Robert P. Haviland ; with a specially written chapter for the guidance of the English reader by W. Oliver. — Slough : Foulsham-Tab, 1976. — viii,5-238p : ill ; 21cm.

Also published: Blue Ridge Summit, Pa : GL Tab Books, 1976. — Bibl.: p.233-234. — Index.

ISBN 0-7042-0170-4 Pbk : £2.95
(B77-09742)

621.381'73 — Charge coupled devices. *Conference proceedings*

International Conference on Technology and Applications of Charge-Coupled Devices, *3rd, University of Edinburgh, 1976.* The technology and applications of charge coupled devices : [proceedings of the] 3rd international conference, organised by University of Edinburgh Centre for Industrial Consultancy and Liaison in association with the Electronics Division of the Institution of Electrical Engineers and the Royal Signals and Radar Establishment / [edited by John Mavor. — Edinburgh (16 George Sq., EH8 9LD) : The Centre, 1976. — [7],380,[64]p : ill ; 29cm.
'CCD '76 is the third International Conference devoted entirely to the Technology and Applications of Charge-Coupled Devices' - Foreword. — Name taken from previous conferences in the series.
ISBN 0-903042-05-3 Pbk : £14.00
(B77-03065)

621.381'73 — Electronic equipment. Complementary symmetry metal oxide silicon integrated circuits. Projects. *Amateurs' manuals*

Penfold, R A. 50 CMOS IC projects / by R.A. Penfold. — London : Bernards, 1977. — [6], 102p : ill ; 18cm. — (Bernards & Babani Press radio and electronics books ; no.224)
ISBN 0-900162-64-3 Pbk : £0.95
(B77-15904)

621.381'73 — Electronic equipment. Integrated circuits

Deboo, Gordon J. Integrated circuits and semiconductor devices : theory and application / [by] Gordon J. Deboo, Clifford N. Burrous. — 2nd ed. — New York ; London [etc.] : McGraw-Hill, 1977. — xiii,479p : ill ; 24cm.
With answers to selected problems. — Previous ed.: New York : McGraw-Hill, 1971. — Index.
ISBN 0-07-016246-8 : £12.00
Also classified at 621.3815'2
(B77-21934)

Grinich, Victor H. Introduction to integrated circuits / [by] Victor H. Grinich, Horace G. Jackson. — New York ; London [etc.] : McGraw-Hill, [1976]. — xxxiv,638p : ill ; 25cm. — (McGraw-Hill series on the fundamentals of electronic science)
Text, ill. on lining papers. — With answers. — Published in the United States: 1975. — Index.
ISBN 0-07-024875-3 : £15.75
(B77-03590)

Hallmark, Clayton. Microelectronics / [by] Clayton L. Hallmark ; with a specially written chapter for the guidance of the English reader by W. Oliver. — Slough : Foulsham-Tab, 1977. — viii p,p5-265 : ill ; 21cm.
Originally published: Blue Ridge Summit : G/L Tab Books, 1976. — Index.
ISBN 0-7042-0172-0 Pbk : £3.40
(B77-18206)

Hibberd, Robert Guy. Integrated circuit pocket book / [by] R.G. Hibberd. — London : Newnes Technical Books, 1976. — [7],274p : ill ; 19cm.
Originally published: London : Newnes-Butterworths, 1972. — Index.
ISBN 0-408-00255-7 Pbk : £3.90
(B77-18207)

Muller, Richard S. Device electronics for integrated circuits / [by] Richard S. Muller, Theodore I. Kamins. — New York ; London [etc.] : Wiley, 1977. — xii,404p : ill ; 24cm.
Text on lining paper. — Index.
ISBN 0-471-62364-4 : £14.70
(B77-27159)

Sinclair, Ian Robertson. Beginner's guide to integrated circuits / [by] I.R. Sinclair. — London [etc.] : Newnes Technical Books, 1977. — [6],185p : ill ; 19cm.
Index.
ISBN 0-408-00278-6 Pbk : £2.75
(B77-21197)

621.381'73 — Electronic equipment. Large scale integrated circuits. *Readings*
Large and medium scale integration : devices and applications / edited by Samuel Weber. — New York ; London [etc.] : McGraw-Hill, 1974. — vi,314p : ill ; 29cm.
Bibl. — Index.
ISBN 0-07-068815-x : Unpriced
(B77-20344)

621.381'73 — Electronic equipment. Linear integrated circuits
Hamilton, T D S. Handbook of linear integrated electronics for research / [by] T.D.S. Hamilton. — London [etc.] : McGraw-Hill, 1977. — xviii, 469p : ill ; 26cm.
Bibl.: p.445-446. — Index.
ISBN 0-07-084483-6 : £14.50 : CIP rev.
(B77-08430)

621.381'73'5 — Electronic equipment. Amplifiers using integrated circuits. Construction. *Amateurs' manuals*
Rayer, Francis George. Handbook of IC audio preamplifier and power amplifier construction / by F.G. Rayer. — London : Babani Press, 1976. — 106p : ill ; 18cm. — (Bernards & Babani Press radio and electronics books)
ISBN 0-85934-038-4 Pbk : £0.95
(B77-06729)

621.381'73'5 — Electronic equipment: Linear integrated circuits. Operational amplifiers
Coughlin, Robert Francis. Operational amplifiers and linear integrated circuits / [by] Robert F. Coughlin and Frederick F. Driscoll. — Englewood Cliffs ; London [etc.] : Prentice-Hall, 1977. — xxiii,312p : ill ; 24cm.
Bibl.: p.264-266. — Index.
ISBN 0-13-637850-1 : £12.75
(B77-14772)

621.381'73'7 — Digital integrated circuits
Dempsey, John A. Basic digital electronics with MSI applications / [by] John A. Dempsey. — Reading, Mass. ; London [etc.] : Addison-Wesley, 1977. — xv,415p : ill ; 25cm.
Text on lining paper. — With answers to selected problems. — Index.
ISBN 0-201-01478-5 : £11.20
(B77-15905)

Digital integrated circuits and operational-amplifier and optoelectronic circuit design / edited by Bryan Norris. — New York ; London [etc.] : McGraw-Hill, 1976. — [11],206p : ill ; 26cm. — (Texas Instruments. Electronics series)
Index.
ISBN 0-07-063753-9 : £13.70
Also classified at 621.3815'35
(B77-13689)

Taub, Herbert. Digital integrated electronics / [by] Herbert Taub, Donald Schilling. — New York ; London [etc.] : McGraw-Hill, 1977. — xxi,650p : ill ; 25cm.
Index.
ISBN 0-07-062921-8 : £16.45
(B77-30330)

621.381'73'7 — Digital integrated circuits. *Amateurs' manuals*
Easterling, Dennis William. A practical introduction to digital IC's / by D.W. Easterling. — London : Bernards, 1977. — 76p : ill ; 18cm. — (Bernards & Babani Press radio and electronics books ; no.225)
ISBN 0-900162-66-x Pbk : £0.95
(B77-23487)

621.381'73'7 — Digital integrated circuits. Design
Greenfield, Joseph D. Practical digital design using ICs / [by] Joseph D. Greenfield. — New York ; London [etc.] : Wiley, 1977. — xiii, 569p : ill ; 25cm. — (Electronic technology series)
Bibl. — Index.
ISBN 0-471-32505-8 : £11.35
(B77-24279)

621.381'74 — Printed wiring. *Standards*
British Standards Institution. Guide to printed wiring (design, manufacture and repair) = Guide pour la filerie imprimée (calcul, fabrication et réparation) = Richtlinien für gedruckte Drähte (Berechnung, Herstellung und Repartur) / British Standards Institution. — London : B.S.I., 1976. — [2],30,[2]p : ill ; 30cm. — (BS5370 : 1976)
Pierced for binder.
ISBN 0-580-09365-4 Sd : £5.80
(B77-02374)

621.3819'58 — Digital computers
Boyce, Jefferson C. Digital computer fundamentals / [by] Jefferson C. Boyce. — Englewood Cliffs ; London [etc.] : Prentice-Hall, 1977. — xv,430p : ill ; 24cm.
Bibl.: p.423-424. — Index.
ISBN 0-13-214114-0 : £12.80
(B77-11255)

Nashelsky, Louis. Introduction to digital computer technology / [by] Louis Nashelsky. — 2nd ed. — New York ; London [etc.] : Wiley, 1977. — xiv,529p : ill ; 24cm.
With answers to selected odd numbered exercises and problems. — Previous ed.: 1973. — Index.
ISBN 0-471-02094-x : £10.70
(B77-17562)

Sloan, Martha Evans. Computer hardware and organization : an introduction / [by] M.E. Sloan. — Chicago ; Henley-on-Thames [etc.] : Science Research Associates.
Instructor's guide. — [1977]. — [2],125p : ill ; 24cm.
With answers. — Published in the United States: 1976.
Pbk : Unpriced
(B77-09062)

621.3819'58 — Interactive computers
Nichols, Kenneth Graham. A time for interaction / by K.G. Nichols. — [Southampton] : University of Southampton, 1976. — 28p : ill ; 21cm. — (University of Southampton. Inaugural lectures)
'... Delivered at the University, 13th May 1976'.
ISBN 0-85432-162-4 Sd : £0.50
(B77-15329)

621.3819'58'2 — Digital computers. Design
Foster, Caxton Croxford. Computer architecture / [by] Caxton C. Foster. — 2nd ed. — New York ; London [etc.] : Van Nostrand-Reinhold, 1976. — xix,300p : ill ; 24cm. — (Computer science series)
Previous ed.: 1970. — Index.
ISBN 0-442-22434-6 : £10.60
(B77-19442)

Kline, Raymond M. Digital computer design / [by] Raymond M. Kline. — Englewood Cliffs ; London [etc.] : Prentice-Hall, 1977. — xiii, 429p : ill ; 24cm. — (Prentice-Hall computer applications in electrical engineering series)
Bibl. — Index.
ISBN 0-13-214205-8 : £15.60
(B77-10830)

621.3819'58'2 — Digital computers. Logic design
Langdon, Glen G. Logic design : a review of theory and practice / [by] Glen G. Langdon, Jr. — New York [etc.] ; London : Academic Press, 1974. — ix,179p : ill ; 24cm. — (Association for Computing Machinery. Monograph series)
Index.
ISBN 0-12-436550-7 : Unpriced
(B77-20345)

621.3819'58'2 — Digital computers. Multiple-valued logic design. Mathematical aspects
Computer science and multiple-valued logic : theory and applications / edited by David C. Rine. — Amsterdam [etc.] ; Oxford : North-Holland Publishing Co., 1977. — xiv, 548p : ill ; 23cm.
Bibl.
ISBN 0-7204-0406-1 : £29.27
(B77-15330)

621.3819'58'3 — Digital computers. Hardware
Cripps, Martin. An introduction to computer hardware / [by] Martin Cripps. — London : Edward Arnold, 1977. — vi,130p : ill ; 25cm.
Index.
ISBN 0-7131-2572-1 Pbk : £3.50
(B77-19443)

621.3819'58'3 — Digital computers. Hardware. *Buyers' guides. Periodicals*
Computer hardware record / the National Computing Centre. — [Manchester] : [The Centre].
Vol.1, issue 1- ; Jan. 1977-. — [1977]-. — 22x30cm.
Monthly. — [11],45 [i.e.47]p. in 1st issue.
Pbk : £120.00 yearly
ISSN 0309-9083
(B77-18208)

621.3819'58'320216 — Digital computers. Peripheral equipment. *Lists. Serials*
'Systems' product guide. — Dartford ([106 Church Rd, London SE19 2UB]) : Gershire Ltd.
1976. — 1976. — 2-101,[2]p,(2 fold) : ill ; 29cm.
Pbk : £1.00
ISSN 0140-2412
(B77-31943)

[1977]. — 1977. — 2-103p : ill ; 29cm.
Pbk : £2.00
ISSN 0140-2412
(B77-31944)

621.3819'58'35 — Digital computers. Circuits. Analysis
Ilardi, Frank A. Computer circuit analysis : theory and applications / [by] Frank A. Ilardi. — Englewood Cliffs ; London [etc.] : Prentice-Hall, 1976. — x,406p : ill ; 24cm.
Index.
ISBN 0-13-165357-1 : £14.05
(B77-24989)

621.3819'58'35 — Microprocessors
Introduction to microprocessors / edited by D. Aspinall and E.L. Dagless. — London : Pitman [etc.], 1977. — vii,162p : ill ; 23cm.
Bibl.: p.138. — Index.
ISBN 0-273-01060-3 Pbk : £4.95
Also classified at 001.6'4044
(B77-21935)

Microprocessor systems : development and application. — Guildford : IPC Science and Technology Press [for] 'Microprocessors', 1977. — vi,90p : ill ; 24cm.
ISBN 0-902852-75-2 Pbk : Unpriced
(B77-24280)

621.3819'58'35 — Microprocessors. *Periodicals*
Microprocessors. — Guildford : IPC Science and Technology Press.
Vol.1, no.1- ; Sept. 76-. — 1976-. — ill, ports ; 30cm.
Quarterly. — 76p. in 1st issue.
Pbk : £6.50(£20.00 yearly)
ISSN 0308-5953
(B77-03591)

621.3819'58'35 — Microprocessors. *Periodicals. For marketing*
Mini-market micro-market monitor : news and analysis of minicomputer and microprocessor market directions. — London (140 Camden St., NW1 9PF) : IDC Europa Ltd.
Vol.1, no.1- ; Aug. 24, 1976-. — 1976-. — 30cm.
Twenty issues a year. — 12p. in 1st issue.
Sd : £1.75(£30.00 yearly)
ISSN 0308-9371
Primary classification 001.6'4044
(B77-03310)

621.3819'58'35 — Microprocessors. Applications. *Conference proceedings*
A symposium on microprocessors at work, University of Sussex, September 26-29, 1976 : organised by the Society of Electronic and Radio Technicians. — London (8 Charing Cross Rd, WC2H 0HP) : [The Society], [1977]. — [3],228p : ill ; 30cm.
Pbk : Unpriced
(B77-17563)

621.3819'58'35 — Microprocessors. Design
Klingman, Edwin E. Microprocessor systems design / [by] Edwin E. Klingman. — Englewood Cliffs ; London [etc.] : Prentice-Hall, 1977. — xv,480p : ill, facsims ; 25cm.
Bibl.: p.467-469. — Index.
ISBN 0-13-581413-8 : £15.60
(B77-23488)

621.382 — TELEGRAPHY
621.382 — Morse code. *For amateur radio*
Mills, Margaret. The morse code for radio amateurs / compiled by Margaret Mills. — 6th ed. — London : Radio Society of Great Britain, 1977. — 19p : 1 ill ; 25cm.
Previous ed.: 1969.
Sd : £0.35
(B77-27160)

621.384 — RADIO
621.3841 — Digital radio equipment. *Conference proceedings*
Digital techniques in broadcasting. — [Winchester] ([Crawley Court, Winchester, Hants. SO21 2QA]) : Independent Broadcasting Authority, Engineering Information Service, [1977]. — 197p in various pagings : ill ; 30cm.
Papers presented at a conference held, 27, 28, 29 April 1976 at Crawley Court, Winchester.
Sp : Unpriced
Primary classification 621.388
(B77-17564)

621.3841 — Radio equipment
King, Gordon John. Beginner's guide to radio / [by] Gordon J. King. — 8th ed. — London [etc.] : Newnes Technical Books, 1977. — [7], 232p : ill ; 19cm.
Previous ed.: London : Newnes-Butterworths, 1970. — Index.
ISBN 0-408-00275-1 Pbk : £2.75
(B77-28675)

Radio, TV & audio technical reference book / edited by S.W. Amos, with specialist contributors. — London [etc.] : Newnes-Butterworths, 1977. — 1157p in various pagings,[2]p of plates : ill(incl 2 col), plans ; 23cm.
Bibl. — Index.
ISBN 0-408-00259-x : £25.00
Also classified at 621.388; 621.389'3
(B77-21936)

621.3841'3 — Amateur radio equipment. Construction. *Manuals*
Hawker, John Patrick. Amateur radio techniques / by Pat Hawker. — 5th ed. — London : Radio Society of Great Britain, 1976. — 304p : ill ; 25cm.
This ed. originally published: 1974. — Index.
Pbk : £2.85
(B77-21937)

621.3841'33 — Radio equipment. Crystal filters. *Standards*
British Standards Institution. Specification for piezoelectric crystal filters of assessed quality = Spécification des filtres à cristal piézo-électrique de qualité assurée = Spezifikation für piezoelektrische Kristallfilter bestätigter Güte : generic data and methods of test = données génériques et méthodes d'essais = generische Daten und Prüfverfahren / British Standards Institution. — London : B.S.I., 1977. — [24]p : ill, form ; 30cm. — (BS9600 : 1977)
Pierced for binder.
ISBN 0-580-09840-0 Sd : £4.70
(B77-15906)

621.3841'366 — Radio equipment: Crystal receivers, 1922-1927
Bussey, Gordon. Vintage crystal sets, 1922-1927 / [by] Gordon Bussey. — London (Dorset House, Stamford St., SE1 9LU) : IPC Electrical-Electronic Press Ltd, 1976. — 128p : ill,facsims ; 25cm. — (A 'Wireless world' publication)
ISBN 0-617-00171-5 Pbk : £2.50
(B77-07404)

621.3841'366 — Radio equipment: Crystal receivers. Projects. *Amateurs' manuals*
Warring, Ronald Horace. Modern crystal sets : fully illustrated step-by-step / by R.H. Warring. — Guildford [etc.] : Lutterworth Press, 1976. — 32p : ill(chiefly col) ; 20x25cm. — (See and make series ; 1)
ISBN 0-7188-2159-9 : £1.95
(B77-04251)

621.3841'366 — Radio equipment: Transistor receivers. Projects. *Amateurs' manuals*
Warring, Ronald Horace. Modern transistor radios : fully illustrated step-by-step / by R.H. Warring. — Guildford [etc.] : Lutterworth Press, 1976. — 32p : ill(chiefly col) ; 20x25cm. — (See and make series ; 2)
ISBN 0-7188-2160-2 : £1.95
(B77-04252)

621.3841'366 — Shortwave radio equipment: Receivers. Construction. *Amateurs' manuals*
Penfold, R A. How to build advanced short wave receivers / by R.A. Penfold. — London : Bernards, 1977. — 117p : ill ; 18cm. — (Bernards & Babani Press radio and electronics books ; no.226)
ISBN 0-900162-67-8 Pbk : £1.20
(B77-23489)

621.3841'366 — Shortwave radio equipment: Receivers. Semiconductor circuits. Projects. *Amateurs' manuals*
Penfold, R A. Solid state short wave receivers for beginners / by R.A. Penfold. — London : Bernards, 1976. — 92p : ill ; 18cm. — (Bernards & Babani Press radio and electronics books ; no.222)
ISBN 0-900162-62-7 Pbk : £0.95
(B77-03066)

621.3841'51 — Amateur radio equipment
Radio Society of Great Britain. Radio communication handbook / [Radio Society of Great Britain]. — 5th ed. — London : R.S.G.B.
In 2 vols. — Previous ed.: in 1 vol. 1968.
Vol.1. — 1976. — 475p in various pagings : ill ; 26cm.
Index.
ISBN 0-900612-29-0 : Unpriced
(B77-05476)

Radio Society of Great Britain. Radio communication handbook. — 5th ed. — London : R.S.G.B.
In 2 vols. — Previous ed.: in 1 vol. 1968.
Vol.2. — 1977. — 306p in various pagings : chart, 2 maps ; 26cm.
Index.
ISBN 0-900612-30-4 : £7.20
(B77-24281)

621.3841'51 — Shortwave radio links
Wiesner, Lothar. Telegraph and data transmission over shortwave radio links : fundamental principles and networks / by Lothar Wiesner ; [translated from the German]. — Berlin [etc.] : Siemens ; London [etc.] : Heyden, 1977. — 163p : ill ; 21cm.
Translation of: 'Fernschreib- und Datenübertragung über Kurzwelle'. Berlin, etc. : Siemens, 1975. — Index.
ISBN 0-85501-243-9 Pbk : £7.00
(B77-09743)

621.3841'51 — Very high frequency radio equipment & ultra high frequency radio equipment
Evans, Dain Stedman. VHF-UHF manual. — 3rd ed. / by D.S. Evans and G.R. Jessop ; edited by R.A. Staton. — London : Radio Society of Great Britain, 1977. — 416p in various pagings : ill, maps ; 26cm.
This ed. originally published: 1976. — Previous ed. / by G.R. Jessop. 1972. — Index.
ISBN 0-900612-31-2 : Unpriced
(B77-30331)

621.3841'66 — Amateur radio communication. *Manuals*
Ullyett, Kenneth. Ham radio : a practical guide and handbook / [by] Kenneth Ullyett. — Newton Abbot [etc.] : David and Charles, 1976. — 163p : ill, facsim, form, ports ; 23cm.
Index.
ISBN 0-7153-7247-5 : £4.50
(B77-16925)

621.3841'66'02541 — Amateur radio stations. *Great Britain. Directories*
Radio Society of Great Britain. RSGB amateur radio call book. — 1976 ed. / compiled by the RSGB editorial staff. — London : R.S.G.B., 1975. — 168p : map ; 25cm.
Text and ill. on inside covers. — Previous ed.: i.e. 1974 ed., 1973.
Pbk : £1.20
(B77-32677)

Radio Society of Great Britain. RSGB amateur radio call book. — London : R.S.G.B.
1977 ed. / compiled by the RSGB editorial staff. — 1976. — 176p : ill, map(on back cover) ; 24cm.
Ill., text on inside covers.
ISBN 0-900612-27-4 Pbk : £2.01
(B77-30332)

621.3841'66'0941 — Amateur radio communication. *Great Britain. Exercises, worked examples*
Radio Society of Great Britain. *Education Committee.* Radio amateurs' examination questions and answers / compiled by the RSGB Education Committee. — London : Radio Society of Great Britain, 1977. — [118]p : ill ; 25cm.
ISBN 0-900612-33-9 Sp : £1.70
(B77-32678)

621.3841'87 — Radio equipment: Receivers. Servicing. *Manuals*
Hicks, Bernard William. Fundamentals of radio servicing / [by] Bernard W. Hicks. — 2nd ed. — London [etc.] : Hutchinson.
In 2 vols.
1 : Basic principles. — 1976. — [7],120p : ill ; 25cm.
Previous ed.: 1971.
ISBN 0-09-126190-2 : Unpriced
ISBN 0-09-126191-0 Pbk : £2.25
(B77-06153)

Patchett, Gerald Norman. Radio servicing / [by] G.N. Patchett. — London : Price.
Vol.2 : Electronic devices and AM receivers. — 5th ed. — 1977. — xii,156p : ill ; 22cm.
Previous ed.: 1966. — Index.
ISBN 0-85380-058-8 Pbk : £2.25
(B77-21198)

Vol.1 : Basic electrotechnology. — 6th ed. — 1977. — vii,88p : ill ; 22cm.
Previous ed.: 1963. — Index.
ISBN 0-85380-057-x Pbk : £1.25
(B77-25694)

Radio and television servicing. — London : Macdonald and Jane's.
1969-70 models / editor J. Harris ; assistant editors C.M. Ferrier, R.N. Wainwright. — 1976. — 679p : ill ; 23cm.
Originally published: London : International Learning Systems Corporation, 1970. — Index.
ISBN 0-356-03735-5 : £6.00
Also classified at 621.3888'7
(B77-06154)

621.3841'87'05 — Radio equipment: Receivers. Servicing. *Manuals. Serials*
Radio and television servicing. — London : Macdonald and Jane's.
1976-77 models / editor R.N. Wainwright. — 1977. — 865p : ill ; 24cm.
Index.
ISBN 0-354-04063-4 : £9.50
ISSN 0307-3165
Also classified at 621.3888'7'05
(B77-24282)

621.3848 — Radar. *Conference proceedings*
Radar 77 *(Conference), Institution of Electrical Engineers, 1977.* International conference Radar 77, 25-28 October 1977 : organised by the Electronics Division of the Institution of Electrical Engineers in association with the IEEE Aerospace and Electronic Systems Society, with the support of ... [others], venue the Institution of Electrical Engineers, Savoy Place, London WC2. — [London] : I.E.E., 1977. — xv,568p : ill, maps ; 30cm. — (Institution of Electrical Engineers. Conference publications ; no.155 ISSN 0537-9989)
ISBN 0-85296-181-2 Pbk : £20.60
(B77-33858)

621.3848 — Secondary radar
Honold, Peter. Secondary radar : fundamentals and instrumentation / by Peter Honold ; [translated from the German]. — Berlin [etc.] : Siemens ; London [etc.] : Heyden, 1976. — 224p : ill ; 22cm.
Translation of: 'Sekundär-Radar'. Berlin, etc. : Siemens, 1971. — Index.
ISBN 0-85501-248-x : £9.50
(B77-09063)

621.385 — TELEPHONY
621.385'4 — Telephone exchanges
Flowers, Thomas Harold. Introduction to exchange systems / [by] T.H. Flowers. — London [etc.] : Wiley, 1976. — xvii,326p : ill ; 24cm.
'A Wiley-Interscience Publication'. — Index.
ISBN 0-471-01865-1 : £13.00
(B77-02375)

621.387'84 — Telephone equipment. Underwater cables
Barnes, Cyril Charles. Submarine telecommunication and power cables / [by] C.C. Barnes. — Stevenage : Peregrinus [for] the Institution of Electrical Engineers, 1977. — xii, 206p : ill, maps ; 23cm. — (Institution of Electrical Engineers. IEE monograph series ; 20 ISSN 0306-8269)
Index.
ISBN 0-901223-87-5 : Unpriced
Primary classification 621.319'34
(B77-32674)

621.388 — TELEVISION
621.388 — Digital television equipment. *Conference proceedings*
Digital techniques in broadcasting. — [Winchester] ([Crawley Court, Winchester, Hants. SO21 2QA]) : Independent Broadcasting Authority, Engineering Information Service, [1977]. — 197p in various pagings : ill ; 30cm.
Papers presented at a conference held, 27, 28, 29 April 1976 at Crawley Court, Winchester.
Sp : Unpriced
Also classified at 621.3841
(B77-17564)

621.388 — Small television studios. Television equipment. Design & maintenance
Knecht, Kenneth. Designing and maintaining the CATV and small TV studio / [by] Kenneth Knecht ; with a specially written chapter for the guidance of the English reader by W. Oliver. — Slough : Foulsham-Tab, 1977. — xii, 11-281p : ill, plans ; 22cm.
Originally published: Blue Ridge Summit, Pa. : G/L Tab Books, 1972. — Index.
ISBN 0-7042-0177-1 Pbk : £3.95
(B77-27161)

621.388 — Television. *Juvenile literature*
Beal, George. See inside a television studio / [author George Beal] ; [illustrations John Berry, John Marshall, Tudor Art]. — London : Hutchinson, 1977. — 4-29p : ill(chiefly col), 2 ports ; 29cm. — (See inside)
Bibl.: p.28. — Index.
ISBN 0-09-131490-9 : £1.50
(B77-31245)

621.388 — Television equipment
Independent Broadcasting Authority. Technical reference book / [Independent Broadcasting Authority]. — 3rd ed. / technical editor C.W.B. Reis. — London (c/o I.B.A. Engineering Information Service, Crawley Court, Winchester, Hants. SO21 2QA) : I.B.A., 1977. — 95p : ill(chiefly col), col forms, port ; 23cm. — (Independent Broadcasting Authority. IBA technical reviews ; 2 ISSN 0308-423x)
English text, French, German and Spanish summaries. — Previous ed.: 1974.
Pbk : Unpriced
(B77-25695)

Independent Broadcasting Authority. Technical reference book / [Independent Broadcasting Authority]. — Revised ed. — London (70 Brompton Rd, SW3 1EY) : I.B.A., 1974. — 64p : ill(chiefly col), col forms ; 23cm. — (Independent Broadcasting Authority. IBA technical reviews ; 2 ISSN 0308-423x)
Previous ed.: 1972.
Pbk : Unpriced
(B77-25696)

Open University. *Telecommunication Systems Course Team.* Television systems : study supplement / prepared by the [Open University, Telecommunication Systems] Course Team. — Milton Keynes : Open University Press, 1976. — 48p : ill ; 30cm. — (Technology, a third level course : telecommunication systems ; units 11, 12, 13 and 14) (T321 ; 11, 12, 13 and 14)
With answers.
ISBN 0-335-06105-2 Pbk : Unpriced
(B77-13690)

Radio, TV & audio technical reference book / edited by S.W. Amos, with specialist contributors. — London [etc.] : Newnes-Butterworths, 1977. — 1157p in various pagings,[2]p of plates : ill(incl 2 col), plans ; 23cm.
Bibl. — Index.
ISBN 0-408-00259-x : £25.00
Primary classification 621.3841
(B77-21936)

621.388 — Television equipment: ORACLE system. Performance. *Great Britain. Reports, surveys*
Sherry, L A. An assessment of Teletext data transmission over the UHF television network / [by] L.A. Sherry. — Winchester (Crawley Court, Winchester, Hants. SO21 2QA) : Engineering Division, Independent Broadcasting Authority, [1977]. — [5],17p : ill ; 30cm. — (Teletext Transmission Working Group. Notes ; 10)
Sd : Unpriced
(B77-17565)

621.388 — Television equipment: Teletext systems. *Great Britain. Standards*
British Broadcasting Corporation. Broadcast Teletext specification / [British Broadcasting Corporation, Independent Broadcasting Authority, British Radio Equipment Manufacturers' Association]. — [London] : B.B.C. : I.B.A. : B.R.E.M.A., 1976. — [4],20p : ill(some col) ; 30cm.
ISBN 0-563-17261-4 Sd : £1.00
(B77-07405)

621.388'0021'2 — Television equipment. *Standards*
Guild of Television Cameramen. Outline specifications for standard studio & OB camera, portable camera, earphones, portable video recorder / the Guild of Television Cameramen. — [Leeds] ([c/o Hon. Secretary, 25 Carrholm Rd, Leeds LS7 2NQ]) : [The Guild], [1976]. — [25]leaves ; 30cm.
ISBN 0-9505576-0-9 Pbk : Unpriced
(B77-09744)

621.388'0021'2 — Television equipment. *Technical data. Serials*
Video yearbook. — Poole (Link House, West St., Poole, Dorset) : Dolphin Press.
1977 / edited by Angus Robertson. — 1976. — 286p : ill ; 23cm.
ISBN 0-85642-064-6 : £4.75
ISSN 0140-2277
(B77-01559)

1978 / edited by Angus Robertson. — 1977. — 440p : ill ; 23cm.
Index.
ISBN 0-85642-066-2 : £7.95
ISSN 0140-2277
(B77-33859)

621.388'092'4 — Television. Baird, John Logie. *Biographies*
Exwood, Maurice. John Logie Baird : 50 years of television / by Maurice Exwood. — London (8 Bedford Sq., WC1B 3RG) : Institution of Electronic and Radio Engineers, 1976. — 31p : ill, facsims, ports ; 21cm. — (Institution of Electronic and Radio Engineers. IERE history of technology monographs)
Bibl.: p.30-31.
ISBN 0-903748-29-0 Sd : Unpriced
(B77-31246)

621.388'36 — Long-distance television equipment: Receivers. *Amateurs' manuals*
Bunney, Roger W. Long distance television / [by] Roger W. Bunney. — 3rd ed. — [Romsey] ([33 Cherville St., Romsey, Hants. SO5 8FB]) : Weston Publishing, 1976. — [3],58,[1]p : ill ; 21cm.
Previous ed.: 197-.
Sd : £1.11
(B77-26355)

621.388'36 — Schools. Audio-visual aids: Television equipment: Receivers. *Standards*
British Standards Institution. Specification for school television receivers and stands / British Standards Institution. — London : B.S.I.
Supplement No.1 : Colour television receivers. — 1976. — [2],3,[2]p ; 30cm. — (Supplement No.1 (1976) to BS4958 : 1973)
Pierced for binder.
ISBN 0-580-09028-0 Sd : £1.50
(B77-03067)

621.388'62 — Commercial broadcasting services. *Great Britain. Independent Broadcasting Authority. Television transmitting stations, to 1974*
Independent Broadcasting Authority. *Station Design and Construction Department.* Television transmitting stations / ... by members of the IBA's Station Design and Construction Department. — London (c/o I.B.A. Engineering Information Service, Crawley Court, Winchester, Hants. SO21 2QA) : I.B.A., 1974. — 71p : ill(some col), plans(some col) ; 23cm. — (Independent Broadcasting Authority. IBA technical reviews ; 4 ISSN 0308-423x)
Pbk : Unpriced
(B77-25697)

621.3888'7 — Colour television equipment: Receivers. Maintenance & repair. *Amateurs' manuals*
Miller, Chas Edward. Practical repair and renovation of colour TVs / by Chas E. Miller. — London : Babani Press, 1976. — 79p : ill ; 19cm. — (Bernards & Babani Press radio and electronics books ; 34)
ISBN 0-85934-037-6 Pbk : £0.95
(B77-05477)

621.3888'7 — Television equipment: Receivers. Servicing. *Manuals*
Radio and television servicing. — London : Macdonald and Jane's.
1969-70 models / editor J. Harris ; assistant editors C.M. Ferrier, R.N. Wainwright. — 1976. — 679p : ill ; 23cm.
Originally published: London : International Learning Systems Corporation, 1970. — Index.
ISBN 0-356-03735-5 : £6.00
Primary classification 621.3841'87
(B77-06154)

621.3888'7'05 — Television equipment: Receivers. Servicing. *Manuals. Serials*
Radio and television servicing. — London : Macdonald and Jane's.
1976-77 models / editor R.N. Wainwright. — 1977. — 865p : ill ; 24cm.
Index.
ISBN 0-354-04063-4 : £9.50
ISSN 0307-3165
Primary classification 621.3841'87'05
(B77-24282)

621.389 — PUBLIC ADDRESS SYSTEMS, SOUND RECORDING, ETC.
621.389'2 — Electronic equipment: Alarm circuits. Projects
Marston, Raymond Michael. 110 electronic alarm projects for the home constructor / [by] R.M. Marston. — London [etc.] : Newnes Technical Books, 1977. — [7],112p : ill ; 22cm.
Index.
ISBN 0-408-00269-7 Pbk : £2.95
(B77-00267)

621.389'3 — High-fidelity sound recording & reproduction equipment
Borwick, John. Living with hi-fi / by John Borwick. — 2nd ed. — Harrow (117 Kenton Rd, Harrow, Middx HA3 0HA) : General Gramophone Publications Ltd, 1976. — [3], 150p : ill ; 22cm.
Previous ed.: 1972. — Bibl.: p.148. — Index.
Pbk : £1.40
(B77-31247)

Everard, Dan. The Bang & Olufsen book of hi-fi : how hi-fi works & how to get the best from it / [by] Dan Everard. — Cambridge : Woodhead-Faulkner, 1977. — 134p : ill ; 19cm.
ISBN 0-85941-065-x Pbk : £1.25
(B77-33270)

Gayford, Michael Lawrence. Hi-fi for the enthusiast / [by] M.L. Gayford. — 2nd (enlarged) ed. — London [etc.] : Pitman, 1976 [i.e. 1977]. — xv,235p : ill, facsim ; 22cm.
This ed. originally published: 1975. — Index.
ISBN 0-273-00722-x Pbk : £2.25
(B77-10399)

Wasley, John. A guide to hi-fi / [by] John Wasley and Ron Hill. — London : Pelham, 1977. — 192p,[8]p of plates : ill, port ; 22cm.
Index.
ISBN 0-7207-0906-7 : £4.25
(B77-09064)

621.389'3 — High-fidelity sound recording & reproduction equipment. *Great Britain. Buyers' guides*
Hifi yearbook. — London (Dorset House, Stamford St., SE1 9LU) : IPC Electrical-Electronic Press Ltd.
1978 / edited by Kenneth Ellmore. — 1978. — 464p : ill ; 23cm.
£3.00
ISSN 0073-2060
(B77-29491)

621.389'3 — High-fidelity sound recording & reproduction equipment. *Great Britain. Periodicals*
What hi-fi?. — London : Haymarket Publishing.
Supersedes : Popular hi-fi.
Vol.1, no.1- ; Oct. 1976-. — 1976-. — ill(some col), maps, ports ; 30cm.
Monthly. — 217p. in 1st issue.
Pbk : £0.35
ISSN 0309-3336
(B77-09065)

621.389'3 — Sound recording & reproduction equipment
Radio, TV & audio technical reference book / edited by S.W. Amos, with specialist contributors. — London [etc.] : Newnes-Butterworths, 1977. — 1157p in various pagings,[2]p of plates : ill(incl 2 col), plans ; 23cm.
Bibl. — Index.
ISBN 0-408-00259-x : £25.00
Primary classification 621.3841
(B77-21936)

Sinclair, Ian Robertson. Beginner's guide to audio / [by] Ian R. Sinclair. — London [etc.] : Newnes Technical Books, 1977. — [6],184p : ill ; 19cm. — (Beginner's guides)
Index.
ISBN 0-408-00274-3 Pbk : £2.50
(B77-19444)

621.389'3 — Sound recording & reproduction equipment. *Standards*
British Standards Institution. Methods for specifying and measuring the characteristics of sound system equipment = Méthodes de spécification et de mesure des caractéristiques des équipments pour systèmes électroacoustiques = Verfahren zur Bestimmung und Messung der Eigenschaften von Schall-Aufnahme und- Wiedergabegeräten / British Standards Institution. — London : B.S.I.
Part 1 = Partie = Teil 1 : General = Général = Allgemein. — 1977. — [2],9,[2]p : ill ; 30cm. — (BS5428 : Part 1 : 1977)
Pierced for binder.
ISBN 0-580-09079-5 Sd : £3.60
(B77-11256)

621.389'3 — Sound recording & reproduction equipment. Amplifiers. Construction. *Amateurs' manuals*
Sinclair, Ian Robertson. Audio amplifiers for the home constructor / [by] Ian R. Sinclair. — Watford : Fountain Press, 1976. — iv,107p : ill ; 22cm.
Index.
ISBN 0-85242-472-8 Pbk : £2.25
(B77-14273)

621.389'32 — Animals. Sound recording. *Manuals*
Fisher, John B. Wildlife sound recording / [by] John B. Fisher ; foreword by Robert Dougall. — London : Pelham, 1977. — 173p,[8]p of plates : ill ; 23cm.
Index.
ISBN 0-7207-1017-0 : £5.95
(B77-29492)

621.389'32 — Cassette tape recorders
Earl, John. Cassette tape recorders / [by] John Earl. — Watford : Fountain Press, 1977. — 168p : ill ; 23cm.
Index.
ISBN 0-85242-510-4 : £4.75
(B77-27911)

621.389'32 — Stereophonic cassette tape recorders. *Buyers' guides*
McKenzie, Angus. Cassette decks and tapes : a unique consumer guide / by Angus McKenzie ; [edited by Sally Peberdy]. — [New ed.]. — [London] ([26 Parkway, N.W.1]) : [Aquarius Books Ltd], [1977]. — 226p : ill(some col) ; 20cm. — (Hi-fi choice ; no.4)
Cover title. — Previous ed.: published as 'Cassette decks' / edited by Richard Howell. 1975. — Index.
Pbk : £1.50
(B77-21938)

621.389'32 — Stereophonic cassette tape recording. *Manuals*
Sinclair, Ian Robertson. Master stereo cassette recording / [by] I.R. Sinclair. — Sevenoaks : Newnes Technical Books [etc.], 1976. — [7], 112p : ill(chiefly col) ; 22cm.
Index.
ISBN 0-408-00238-7 : £2.50
(B77-04879)

621.389'32 — Tape recorders. Maintenance & repair. *Manuals*
Gardner, John, *b.1937.* Newnes tape recorder servicing manual. — 2nd ed. / [by] John Gardner. — London [etc.] : Newnes-Butterworths.
In 2 vols. — Previous ed.: published in 1 vol. as 'Tape recorder servicing manual' / by H.W. Hellyer. London : Newnes, 1965.
Vol.1 : covering models from 1968 to 1970. — 1977. — [6],207p : ill ; 26cm.
Index.
ISBN 0-408-00252-2 : £7.80
(B77-19445)

Vol.2 : covering models from 1971 to 1974. — 1977. — [6],207p : ill ; 26cm.
Index.
ISBN 0-408-00253-0 : £7.80
(B77-19446)

621.389'32 — Tape recording. *Manuals*
Gardner, John, *b.1937.* Master creative tape recordings / [by] John Gardner. — [London] : Newnes Technical Books [etc.], 1977. — [7], 136p : col ill ; 22cm.
Bibl.: p.131. — Index.
ISBN 0-408-00244-1 Pbk : £2.50
(B77-31248)

621.389'32 — Videorecording. *Standards*
Consultative Committee International Radio. *National Study Group 11. Sub-Group 11c.* Broadcast video-tape recording handbook / prepared by Sub-Group 11c of the UK National Study Group 11 of the CCIR. — Winchester (c/o G.G.E. Blagdon, Engineering Information Service, Independent Broadcasting Authority, Crawley Court, Winchester, Hants. SO21 2QA) : [The Sub-Group], [1976]. — 232p in various pagings : ill ; 30cm.
Bibl. — Index.
Sp : Unpriced
(B77-17566)

621.389'32 — Videorecording. Techniques. *Manuals*
Robinson, Joseph Frederick. Using videotape / [by] J.F. Robinson, P.H. Beards. — London [etc.] : Focal Press, 1976. — 163p : col ill, facsims, forms ; 22cm. — (Media manuals)
Bibl.: p.156.
ISBN 0-240-50859-9 Pbk : £2.75
(B77-01560)

621.389'33 — Juke boxes, to 1975
Krivine, J. Juke-box Saturday night / [by] J. Krivine. — London : New English Library, 1977. — 160p : ill(some col), facsims(some col), ports ; 35cm.
Index.
ISBN 0-450-02963-8 : £7.50
(B77-10400)

621.389'33 — Quadraphonic sound reproduction equipment
Borwick, John. Quadraphony now / by John Borwick. — [Harrow] ([177 Kenton Rd, Harrow, Middx HA3 0HA]) : General Gramophone Publications, [1977]. — 40p : ill ; 30cm.
A 'Gramophone' publication.
ISBN 0-902470-09-4 Sd : £0.40
(B77-14773)

621.389'33 — Record players, to 1925
Trigg, David L. Clockwork music hall / [by] David L. Trigg ; illustrated by the author. — Ilfracombe : Stockwell, 1976. — 63p : ill, ports ; 14x21cm.
ISBN 0-7223-0934-1 Pbk : £1.50
(B77-13084)

621.389'33 — Record players, to 1930
Jewell, Brian. Veteran talking machines : history and collectors' guide / [by Brian Jewell]. — Tunbridge Wells : Midas Books, 1977. — 128p : ill, facsims, ports ; 21cm.
Bibl.: p.128.
ISBN 0-85936-085-7 : £3.25
(B77-22651)

621.4 — HEAT ENGINEERING AND PRIME MOVERS
621.4 — Alternative energy sources. Development. *Great Britain. Inquiry reports*
Great Britain. *Parliament. House of Commons. Select Committee on Science and Technology.* The development of alternative sources of energy for the United Kingdom : third report from the Select Committee on Science and Technology, session 1976-77. — London : H.M.S.O.
Vol.1 : Report and minutes of proceedings. — [1977]. — lxi p ; 25cm. — ([1976-77 H.C.]534-I)
ISBN 0-10-297377-6 Sd : £1.10
(B77-29493)

Vol.2 : Minutes of evidence taken before the Energy Resources Sub-committee in session 1975-76. — [1977]. — xii,507p : ill, map ; 25cm. — ([1976-77 H.C.]534-ii)
ISBN 0-10-295777-0 Pbk : £9.60
(B77-29494)

Vol.3 : Appendices to the minutes of evidence taken before the Energy Resources Sub-committee in session 1975-76 and memoranda laid before the Sub-committee in session 1976-77. — [1977]. — xi p,p509-632 : ill ; 25cm. — ([1976-77 H.C.]534-iii)
ISBN 0-10-295877-7 Pbk : £2.10
(B77-29495)

621.4 — Energy compression. *Conference proceedings*
International Conference on Energy Storage, Compression and Switching, *Asti-Torino, 1974.* Energy storage, compression and switching / edited by W.H. Bostick, V. Nardi, O.S.F. Zucker. — New York ; London : Plenum Press, 1976. — xiii,537p : ill ; 28cm.
'Proceedings of the International Conference on Energy Storage, Compression, and Switching held in Asti-Torino, Italy, November 5-7, 1974' - title page verso. — Index.
ISBN 0-306-30892-4 : £22.05
(B77-04880)

621.4 — Energy conversion
Tyldesley, John Richard. An introduction to applied thermodynamics and energy conversion / [by] John R. Tyldesley. — London [etc.] : Longman, 1977. — viii,178p : ill ; 23cm.
Spine title: Applied thermodynamics and energy conversion. — With answers. — Index.
ISBN 0-582-44066-1 : £7.75
ISBN 0-582-44067-x Pbk : £3.50
(B77-33860)

621.4 — Energy conversion. Role of microorganisms. *Conference proceedings*
Microbial energy conversion : the proceedings of a seminar sponsored by the UN Institute for Training and Research (UNITAR) and the Ministry for Research and Technology of the Federal Republic of Germany held in Göttingen, October 1976 / edited by H.G. Schlegel and J. Barnea. — Oxford [etc.] : Pergamon, 1977. — 643p : ill ; 24cm.
'Published as a supplement to "Solar Energy" ...' - title page verso. — Bibl. — Index.
ISBN 0-08-021791-5 Pbk : £27.00
(B77-28676)

621.4 — Energy engineering
Sheahan, Richard T. Fueling the future : an environmental and energy primer / [by] Richard T. Sheahan. — New York : St Martin's Press ; London : St James Press, 1976. — xv,127p : ill ; 24cm.
Bibl.: p.115-117. — Index.
ISBN 0-86066-002-8 : £4.50
Also classified at 628
(B77-21939)

621.4 — Energy engineering. *Periodicals*
International journal of energy research. — London [etc.] : Wiley.
Vol.1, no.1- ; Jan.-Mar. 1977-. — 1977-. — ill, plans ; 26cm.
Quarterly. — [2],96p. in 1st issue. — Bibl.
Sd : £22.50 yearly
ISSN 0363-907x
(B77-21199)

621.4 — Energy engineering. Environmental aspects
Priest, Joseph. Problems of our physical environment : energy, transportation, pollution / [by] Joseph Priest. — Reading, Mass. ; London [etc.] : Addison-Wesley, 1973. — [18],389p : ill, facsim, maps ; 24cm. — (Addison-Wesley series in physics)
With answers to selected exercises. — Bibl. — Index.
ISBN 0-201-05972-x : Unpriced
(B77-21200)

621.4 — Energy sources
Energy technology handbook / prepared by 142 specialists ; Douglas M. Considine, editor-in-chief. — New York [etc.] ; London : McGraw-Hill, 1977. — 1887p in various pagings : ill, maps ; 24cm.
Bibl. — Index.
ISBN 0-07-012430-2 : £37.15
(B77-23490)

621.4 — Energy sources. Heat transfer & mass transfer. *Conference proceedings*
Future Energy Production - Heat and Mass Transfer Problems *(Conference), Dubrovnik, 1975.* Future energy production systems : heat and mass transfer processes / edited by Jessie C. Denton, Naim H. Afgan. — New York [etc.] ; London : Academic Press [etc.].
In 2 vols. — '... volumes grew out of the lectures and papers presented at the 1975 International Seminar on "Future Energy Production - Heat and Mass Transfer Problems" which was organized by the International Centre for Heat and Mass Transfer and held at Dubrovnik, Yugoslavia, August 25-30, 1975' - Preface.
Vol.1. — 1976. — xi,378p : ill ; 25cm.
Bibl.
ISBN 0-12-210001-8 : £23.20
(B77-06155)

Future Energy Production - Heat and Mass Transfer Problems *(Conference), Dubrovnik, 1975.* Future energy production systems : heat and mass transfer processes / edited by Jesse C. Denton, Naim H. Afgan. — New York [etc.] ; London : Academic Press [etc.].
In 2 vols. — ' ... volumes grew out of the lectures and papers presented at the 1975 International Seminar on "Future Energy Production - Heat and Mass Transfer Problems" which was organized by the International Centre for Heat and Mass Transfer and held at Dubrovnik, Yugoslavia, August 25-30, 1975' - Preface.
Vol.2. — 1976. — iii-xi p,p381-866 : ill, maps ; 24cm.
Bibl.
ISBN 0-12-210002-6 : £23.20
(B77-03592)

621.4 — Perpetual motion machines. *Proposals*
Plunkett, Oliver J B. Dynamic gravity / by Olliver Plunkett. — London (30 Mountfield Rd, Finchley, N.3) : The author, 1977. — Sheet([1]p) : 1 ill ; 30x21cm.
Unpriced
(B77-33861)

621.4 — Perpetual motion machines, to 1976
Ord-Hume, Arthur Wolfgang Julius Gerald. Perpetual motion : the history of an obsession / [by] Arthur W.J.G. Ord-Hume. — London : Allen and Unwin, 1977. — 3-235p : ill, facsim, port ; 23cm.
Bibl.: p.224-227. — Index.
ISBN 0-04-621024-5 : £5.50
(B77-22652)

621.4'0028 — Energy engineering equipment. Materials
Critical materials problems in energy production / edited by Charles Stein. — New York [etc.] ; London : Academic Press, 1976. — xii,915p : ill ; 24cm.
'This volume is the result of a series of Distinguished Lectures sponsored [i.e. organised] by the Joint Center for Materials Science in New Mexico' - Preface. — Bibl. — Index.
ISBN 0-12-665050-0 : £20.95
(B77-18209)

621.4'009 — Energy sources, to 1976. *Secondary school texts*
Bainbridge, Jack. Power / [by] Jack Bainbridge ; design by Ellis Iddon. — Oxford : Blackwell, 1977. — 64p : ill(some col), 2 col maps ; 30cm. — (Land marks)
Index.
ISBN 0-631-93940-7 Sd : £1.60
(B77-23491)

621.4'021 — Heat engineering. Thermodynamics
Balzhiser, Richard E. Engineering thermo-dynamics / [by] Richard E. Balzhiser, Michael R. Samuels. — Englewood Cliffs ; London [etc.] : Prentice-Hall, 1977. — xii, 612p : ill ; 24cm.
Index.
ISBN 0-13-279570-1 : £15.95
(B77-16926)

Benson, Rowland Seider. Advanced engineering thermodynamics / by Rowland S. Benson. — 2nd ed. — Oxford [etc.] : Pergamon, 1977. — xi,345p : ill ; 26cm. — (Pergamon international library) (Thermodynamics and fluid mechanics series)
With answers. — Previous ed.: 1967. — Index.
ISBN 0-08-020719-7 : £8.00
ISBN 0-08-020718-9 Pbk : £4.50
(B77-18210)

Reynolds, William Craig. Engineering thermodynamics / [by] William C. Reynolds, Henry C. Perkins. — 2nd ed. — New York ; London [etc.] : McGraw-Hill, 1977. — xiii, 690p : ill ; 25cm.
With answers to selected problems. — Text on lining papers. — Previous ed.: New York : McGraw-Hill, 1970. — Bibl. — Index.
ISBN 0-07-052046-1 : £14.60
(B77-22653)

621.4'021'076 — Heat engineering. Thermodynamics. *Exercises, worked examples*
Boxer, George. Engineering thermodynamics : theory, worked examples and problems / [by] G. Boxer. — London [etc.] : Macmillan, 1976. — xxv,149p : ill ; 24cm.
ISBN 0-333-19226-5 Pbk : £2.95
(B77-04253)

621.4'023 — Fuels. Fluidised combustion. *Conference proceedings*
Conference on Fluidised Combustion, *Imperial College of Science and Technology, 1975.* Fluidised combustion : an international conference held at Imperial College, London, UK, 16-17 September 1975. — London (18 Devonshire., W1N 2AU) : Institute of Fuel [etc.], 1975. — 305p in various pagings : ill ; 30cm. — (Institute of Fuel. Symposium series ; no.1)
'Also available in 2 vols'.
ISBN 0-902597-07-8 Pbk : £15.00
(B77-18841)

621.4'023'0151 — Fuels. Combustion. Calculations
Goodger, Eric Martin. Combustion calculations : theory, worked examples and problems / [by] E.M. Goodger. — London [etc.] : Macmillan, 1977. — xiv,106p : ill ; 24cm.
Bibl.: p.100-101. — Index.
ISBN 0-333-21801-9 Pbk : £2.95
(B77-26356)

621.4'023'028 — Combustion engineering. Measurement. *Conference proceedings*
Project Squid Workshop on Combustion Measurements in Jet Propulsion Systems, *Purdue University, 1975.* Combustion measurements : modern techniques and instrumentation / edited by R. Goulard. — New York [etc.] ; London : Academic Press [etc.], 1976. — xii,483p : ill ; 25cm.
'Proceedings of the Project Squid Workshop on Combustion Measurements in Jet Propulsion Systems, held at Purdue University, West Lafayette, Indiana, May 22-23, 1975 ...' - title page verso. — Bibl.: p.463-470. — Index.
ISBN 0-12-294150-0 : £21.50
(B77-08431)

621.4'025 — Furnaces
Gilchrist, James Duncan. Fuels, furnaces and refractories / by J.D. Gilchrist. — Oxford [etc.] : Pergamon, 1977. — xiii,353p : ill ; 22cm. — (Pergamon international library) (International series on materials science and technology ; vol.21)
'A combined revision of the author's "Fuels and refractories" and "Furnaces"' - Library of Congress Cataloging in Publication Data. — Bibl.: p.344-345. — Index.
ISBN 0-08-020430-9 : £7.80
ISBN 0-08-020429-5 Pbk : £4.50
Also classified at 662'.6; 666'.72
(B77-16450)

621.4'025 — Heat pumps
Sumner, John Arthur. An introduction to heat pumps / by John A. Sumner. — Dorchester, Dorset (Stable Court, Chalmington, Dorchester, Dorset DT2 0HB) : Prism Press, 1976. — 54p : ill ; 23cm. — (Conservation Tools and Technology Limited. Series ; no.4)
ISBN 0-904727-38-6 : £3.50
ISBN 0-904727-39-4 Pbk : £1.25
(B77-05478)

621.43 — INTERNAL COMBUSTION ENGINES
621.43 — Internal combustion engines. Alternative fuels. *Conference proceedings*
Power plants and future fuels : conference sponsored by the Combustion Engines Group and the Automobile Division of the Institution of Mechanical Engineers, London, 21-22 January 1975. — London [etc.] : Mechanical Engineering Publications for the Institution of Mechanical Engineers, 1976. — ix,229p : ill ; 31cm. — (Institution of Mechanical Engineers. Conference publications ; 1-1975)
Index.
ISBN 0-85298-336-0 : £18.60
(B77-27162)

621.43'3 — Industries. Gas turbines. Fuels. Handling
British Petroleum Company. Gas turbines in industry, fuel handling / BP. — [London] ([Britannic House, Moor La., E.C.2]) : [British Petroleum Co.], 1977. — 12p : ill ; 30cm.
Sd : Unpriced
(B77-18211)

621.43'4 — Stratified charge engines
Stratified charge engines. — London : Gordon and Breach.
Vol.2 / edited by Frediano V. Bracco. — 1976. — [2],111,[2]p : ill ; 27cm.
'A collection of papers published in "Combustion Science and Technology" (Volume 12, Nos. 1/2/3) ... '. — Bibl.
ISBN 0-677-05355-x Sd : £19.70
(B77-11877)

621.43'4 — Stratified charge engines. *Conference proceedings*
Stratified charge engines : [proceedings of a] conference sponsored [i.e. organized] by the Automobile Division and the Combustion Engines Group [of the Institution of Mechanical Engineers] ; London, 23-25 November 1976. — London [etc.] : Mechanical Engineering Publications for the Institution, 1977. — [5],240p : ill ; 31cm. — (Institution of Mechanical Engineers. Conference publications ; 1976-11)
ISBN 0-85298-355-7 : £21.00
(B77-32679)

621.43'7 — High speed internal combustion engines. Valves
Smith, Philip Hubert. Valve mechanisms for high-speed engines : their design and development / [by] Philip H. Smith. — 2nd ed. / edited and revised by L.J.K. Setright. — Henley-on-Thames : Foulis, [1976]. — xvi,237p, [36]p of plates : ill ; 22cm.
This ed. originally published: 1971. — Bibl.: p.xiii. — Index.
ISBN 0-85429-214-4 Pbk : £3.95
(B77-08432)

621.43'7 — Reciprocating internal combustion engines. Piston rings up to 200mm diameter. *Standards*
British Standards Institution. Specification for piston rings up to 200mm diameter for reciprocating and internal combustion engines = Spécification des segments de pistons jusqu'à 200mm de diamètre pour moteurs alternatifs à combustion interne = Spezifikation für Kolbenringe mit Durchmessern bis 200mm für Kobenmotoren / British Standards Institution. — London : B.S.I.
Part 3 = Partie 3 = Teil 3 : Quality requirements = Exigences de qualité = Qualitätsvorschrift. — 1976. — [2],8,[2]p : ill ; 30cm. — (BS5341 : Part 3 : 1976)
Pierced for binder.
ISBN 0-580-09296-8 Sd : £2.40
(B77-00799)

British Standards Institution. Specification for piston rings up to 200mm diameter for reciprocating internal combustion engines = Spécification des segments de pistons jusqu'à 200mm de diamètre pours moteurs alternatifs à combustion interne = Spezifikation für Kolbenringe mit Durchmesser bis 200mm für Kolbenmotoren / British Standards Institution. — London : B.S.I.
Part 5 = Partie 5 = Teil 5 : Ring grooves = Rainures de segments = Kolbennuten. — 1976. — [2],15,[2]p : ill ; 30cm. — (BS5341 : Part 5 : 1976)
Pierced for binder.
ISBN 0-580-09218-6 Sd : £4.00
(B77-07945)

British Standards Institution. Specification for piston rings up to 200mm diameter for reciprocating internal combustion engines = Spécification des segments de pistons jusqu'à 200mm de diamètre pour moteurs alternatifs à combustion interne = Spezifikation für Kolbenmotoren / British Standards Institution. — London : B.S.I.
Part 2 = Partie 2 = Teil 2 : Designs, dimensions, materials and designations for multi-piece oil control rings = Calculs, dimensions matérieux et désignations des segments racleurs d'huile en plusieures pièces = Ausführingen, Masse, Werkstoffe und Benennungen für mehrteilige Ölabstreifringe. — 1977. — [2],6,[2]p : ill ; 30cm. — (BS5341 : Part 2 : 1977)
Pierced for binder.
ISBN 0-580-09844-3 Sd : £2.70
(B77-33271)

621.45 — WIND POWER
621.4'5 — Windmills. *Cambridgeshire. Huntingdon (District) & Peterborough (District). Reports, surveys*
Smith, Arthur Carlton. Windmills in Huntingdon and Peterborough : a contemporary survey / [by] Arthur C. Smith. — Stevenage ([Lytton Way, Stevenage, Herts. SG1 1XR]) : Stevenage Museum, 1977. — [1],20p : ill, map ; 30cm.
Bibl.: p.19.
ISBN 0-9504239-4-7 Sd : £0.70
(B77-15907)

621.4'5 — Windmills. *Devon. Reports, surveys*
Minchinton, Walter Edward. Windmills of Devon / [by] Walter Minchinton. — [Exeter] (Department of Economic History, University of Exeter [Exeter EX4 4RJ]) : Exeter Industrial Archaeology Group, 1977. — 56p : ill, facsim, maps, plans ; 21cm. — (Exeter papers in industrial archaeology ; 7)
Bibl.: p.56.
ISBN 0-9501778-6-5 Sd : £0.60
(B77-28677)

621.4'5 — Windmills. *England*
Vince, John. Discovering windmills / [by] John Vince ; line drawings by the author. — [4th ed.]. — Aylesbury : Shire Publications, 1977. — 56p : ill, plans ; 18cm. — (Discovering series ; 13)
Previous ed.: 1973. — Bibl.: p.56.
ISBN 0-85263-373-4 Pbk : £0.50
(B77-31249)

621.4'5 — Windmills. *England, to ca 1945*
Wailes, Rex. Windmills in England : a study of their origin, development and future / by Rex Wailes. — London : Skilton, 1975. — viii,48p : ill, map, ports ; 28cm.
Originally published: London : Architectural Press, 1948. — Index.
ISBN 0-284-40007-6 : £2.90
(B77-31945)

621.4'5 — Windmills. *Great Britain, 1856-1916. Illustrations*
Victorian and Edwardian windmills and watermills from old photographs / introduction and commentaries by J. Kenneth Major, Martin Watts. — London : Batsford, 1977. — [96]p : chiefly ill ; 26cm.
ISBN 0-7134-0621-6 : £3.95
Also classified at 621.2'1
(B77-24283)

621.4'5 — Windmills. *Kent, to 1930. Early works*
Finch, William Coles. Watermills & windmills : a historical survey of their rise, decline and fall as portrayed by those of Kent / [by] William Coles Finch. — Sheerness [31 Broadway, Sheerness, Kent ME12 1AB] : Arthur J. Cassell Ltd, 1976. — 336p,leaf of plate,[98]p of plates : ill, facsims, maps, port ; 25cm.
Facsimile reprint of: 1st ed. London : Daniel, 1933. — Index.
ISBN 0-903253-02-x : £10.00
Also classified at 621.2'1
(B77-09745)

621.4'5 — Windmills. *London. Merton (London Borough). Wimbledon Windmill, to 1976*
Plastow, Norman. Wimbledon windmill / [written by Norman Plastow]. — London (Ranger's Office, Wimbledon Common [S.W.19]) : Wimbledon and Putney Commons Conservators, 1977. — [1],12p : ill(some col), plan ; 21cm.
Sd : £0.30
(B77-31250)

621.4'5'05 — Wind engineering. *Periodicals*
Wind engineering. — London (The Old Mill, Dorset Place, E15 1DJ) : Multi-Science Publishing Co. Ltd.
Vol.1, no.1- ; [Jan?] 1977-. — [1977]-. — ill, maps ; 25cm.
Quarterly. — [3],90p. in 1st issue.
Pbk : £20.00 per year
ISSN 0309-524x
(B77-12501)

621.46 — ELECTRIC MOTORS, ION MOTORS, PLASMA MOTORS

621.46'2 — Direct current electric motors. Control devices
Electro-craft Corporation. DC motors, speed controls, servo systems : an engineering handbook / prepared by Electro-craft Corporation, USA. — [Expanded 3rd ed.]. — Oxford [etc.] : Pergamon, 1977. — 524p in various pagings : ill ; 23cm.
Previous ed.: i.e. 2nd ed. United States : s.n., 1973. — Index.
ISBN 0-08-021714-1 : Unpriced
ISBN 0-08-021715-x Pbk : £5.50
(B77-21201)

621.46'2 — Electric motors. Starters. *Standards*
British Standards Institution. Specification for motor starters for voltages up to and including 1000V ac and 1200V dc = Spécification des démarreurs de moteur pour les tensions inférieures et égales à 1000V en courant alternatif et 1200V en courant continu = Spezifikation für Motorstarter für Spannungen bis und einschliesslich 1000V Wechselstrom und 1200V Gleichstrom / British Standards Institution. — London : B.S.I.
Part 2 = Partie 2 = Teil 2 : Reduced voltage ac starters, star delta starters = Démarreurs sous tension réduite en courant alternatif, démarreurs étoile-triangle = Motorstarter zum Einschalten unter verminderter Spannung, Sterndreiecksanlasser. — 1977. — [2],18,[1]p : ill ; 30cm. — (BS4941 : Part 2 : 1977) (IEC 292-2 : 1970)
Pierced for binder.
ISBN 0-580-09149-x Sd : £4.70
(B77-14774)

Part 3 = Partie 3 = Teil 3 : Rheostatic rotor starters = Démarreurs rotoriques à résistances = Widerstandsanlasser für Schleifringläufermotoren. — 1977. — [2],32,[1] p : ill ; 30cm. — (BS4941 : Part 3 : 1977) (IEC 292-3 : 1973)
Pierced for binder.
ISBN 0-580-09159-7 Sd : £6.60
(B77-14775)

621.46'2 — Electronic frequency changer fed electric motors
Jong, H C J de. AC motor design with conventional and converter supplies / [by] H.C.J. de Jong. — Oxford : Clarendon Press, 1976. — xi,108p : ill ; 24cm. — (Monographs in electrical and electronic engineering)
With answers. — Index.
ISBN 0-19-859321-x : £5.00
(B77-10401)

621.46'2 — Induction electric motors. Parasitic phenomena. Mathematical aspects
Heller, Bedřich. Harmonic field effects in induction machines / [by] Bedřich Heller and Václav Hamata ; [translated from the Czech by Rudolf Major]. — Amsterdam ; Oxford [etc.] : Elsevier, 1977. — 330p : ill ; 25cm.
Translation and revision of: 'Přídavná pole, síly a ztráty v asynchronním stroji'. Praha : Nakl. Československé akademie věd, 1961. — Bibl.: p.312-328. — Index.
ISBN 0-444-99856-x : Unpriced
ISBN 0-485-12206-5 Pbk : £2.50
(B77-27912)

621.47 — SOLAR ENERGY ENGINEERING

621.47 — Solar energy. Applications
McVeigh, J C. Sun power : an introduction to the applications of solar energy / by J.C. McVeigh. — Oxford [etc.] : Pergamon, 1977. — x,208p : ill, chart ; 26cm. — (Pergamon international library)
Bibl.: p.193-195. — Index.
ISBN 0-08-020863-0 : £6.00
ISBN 0-08-020862-2 Pbk : £2.75
(B77-27163)

Meinel, Aden B. Applied solar energy : an introduction / [by] Aden B. Meinel and Marjorie P. Meinel. — Reading, Mass. ; London [etc.] : Addison-Wesley, [1977]. — [1], xvi,651p : ill, facsims, form, maps ; 24cm. — (Addison-Wesley series in physics)
Published in the United States: 1976. — Bibl.: p.629-639. — Index.
ISBN 0-201-04719-5 : £14.20
(B77-11257)

621.47'05 — Solar energy. *Periodicals*
Solar news international. — Croydon (111 St James's Rd, Croydon, Surrey CR9 2TH) : Heating and Ventilating Publications Ltd.
Vol.1, no.01- ; Apr. 1977-. — 1977-. — 30cm.
Two issues a month. — 10p. in 1st issue. — 'Published simultaneously in English, French and German'.
Sd : £60.00 yearly
ISSN 0309-801x
(B77-18212)

621.47'0941 — Solar energy. *Great Britain. Reports, surveys*
Long, Geoffrey. Solar energy : its potential contribution within the United Kingdom : a report / prepared for the Department of Energy by G. Long, with contributions from J.D. Garnish ... [et al.]. — London : H.M.S.O., 1976. — viii,81p : ill, maps ; 25cm. — (Energy paper ; no.16)
Bibl.: p.79-81.
ISBN 0-11-410294-5 Pbk : £3.00
(B77-10831)

621.48 — NUCLEAR ENGINEERING
Foster, Arthur R. Basic nuclear engineering / [by] Arthur R. Foster, Robert L. Wright, Jr. — 3rd ed. — Boston [Mass.] ; London [etc.] : Allyn and Bacon, 1977. — xii,548p : ill ; 24cm. — (Allyn and Bacon series in mechanical engineering and applied mechanics)
With answers to selected problems. — Previous ed.: Boston, Mass. : Allyn and Bacon, 1973. — Index.
ISBN 0-205-05697-0 : Unpriced
(B77-07946)

621.48 — Nuclear engineering. *Reviews of research*
Advances in nuclear science and technology. — New York [etc.] ; London : Academic Press.
Vol.9 / edited by Ernest J. Henley, Jeffery Lewins. — 1976. — xvii,359p : ill ; 24cm.
Index.
ISBN 0-12-029309-9 : £21.15
(B77-04881)

621.48 — Nuclear power. *Conference proceedings*
Hearing on Nuclear Energy, *Sigtuna, 1975.*
Facing up to nuclear power : a contribution to the debate on the risks and potentialities of the large-scale use of nuclear energy / edited by John Francis and Paul Abrecht. — Edinburgh : St Andrew Press, 1976. — x,244p : ill ; 20cm.
'... [the] Hearing on Nuclear Energy ... was held at Sigtuna, Sweden, June 24-29, 1975' - Foreword.
ISBN 0-7152-0340-1 Pbk : £1.50
(B77-05479)

621.48'06'11 — Nuclear Energy Agency. *Reports, surveys. Serials*
Nuclear Energy Agency. Activity report / Nuclear Energy Agency. — Paris : N.E.A. ; [London] : [H.M.S.O.].
4th : [1975]. — 1976. — 77p : 3 ill ; 27cm.
Pbk : Unpriced
(B77-04882)

621.48'06'141 — Nuclear engineering. Organisations. *Great Britain. United Kingdom Atomic Energy Authority. Reports, surveys. Serials*
United Kingdom Atomic Energy Authority.
Report and accounts of the United Kingdom Atomic Energy Authority for the year ended 31 March ... — London (Information Services Branch, 11 Charles II St., SW1Y 4QP) : U.K.A.E.A.
[1976]-1977. — [1977]. — 75,[1]p(2 fold) : ill(some col) ; 30cm.
Index.
ISBN 0-7058-0168-3 Pbk : £2.00
(B77-29496)

621.48'0942 — Nuclear power. *England*
Central Electricity Generating Board. Nuclear power : a report on progress by Mr Glyn England, chairman of the Central Electricity Generating Board, addressing staff at the Oldbury-on-Severn nuclear power station in Gloucestershire on 24 August 1977. — London (Press and Publicity Office, 15 Newgate St., EC1A 7AU) : The Board, 1977. — [10]p : port ; 21cm.
Sd : Unpriced
(B77-31946)

621.48'1 — Nuclear power stations. Safety aspects. *Great Britain. Reports, surveys*
Great Britain. *Health and Safety Executive.* Some aspects of the safety of nuclear installations in Great Britain : replies to questions submitted by the Secretary of State for Energy to the Nuclear Installations Inspectorate in October 1976 / Health & Safety Executive. — London : H.M.S.O., 1977. — v,48p ; 30cm.
ISBN 0-11-883001-5 Sd : £1.00
(B77-15331)

621.48'1 — Steam generating heavy water reactors. Policies of British government. *Inquiry reports*
Great Britain. *Parliament. House of Commons. Select Committee on Science and Technology.*
The SGHWR programme : first report from the Select Committee on Science and Technology, session 1976-77, together with memoranda submitted to the General Purposes Sub-committee. — London : H.M.S.O, [1976]. — xxx,40p ; 25cm. — ([1976-77 H.C.] 89)
ISBN 0-10-208977-9 Sd : £1.35
(B77-07406)

621.48'32 — Nuclear reactors. Design
Elements of nuclear reactor design / edited by Joel Weisman. — Amsterdam ; Oxford [etc.] : Elsevier, 1977. — xii,466p : ill ; 25cm.
Index.
ISBN 0-444-41509-2 : £29.04
(B77-16451)

621.48'32 — Nuclear reactors. Prestressed concrete pressure vessels & prestressed concrete containments. *Conference proceedings*
Experience in the design, construction and operation of prestressed concrete pressure vessels and containments for nuclear reactors : conference sponsored by the Institution of Mechanical Engineers ... [et al., held at the] University of York, 8-12 September 1975. — London [etc.] : Mechanical Engineering Publications for the Institution, 1976. — vii, 659p : ill ; 31cm.
Spine title: Prestressed concrete pressure vessels. — Bibl.
ISBN 0-85298-339-5 : £37.00
(B77-11878)

621.48'33 — Nuclear materials. Irradiation creep. Measurement. *Conference proceedings*
International Colloquium on the Measurement of Irradiation Enhanced Creep in Nuclear Materials, *Petten, 1976.* Measurement of irradiation-enhanced creep in nuclear materials : proceedings of an international conference organized by the Commission of the European Communities at the Joint Research Centre, Pette, the Netherlands, May 5-6, 1976 / editors M.R. Cundy, P. von der Hardt, R.H. Loelgen. — Amsterdam ; Oxford [etc.] : North-Holland Publishing Co., 1977. — iii-xii,337p : ill ; 27cm.

'The International Colloquium on the Measurement of Irradiation Enhanced Creep in Nuclear Materials ...' - Introduction/Preface. — English, French and German abstracts. — 'Reprinted from "Journal of nuclear materials" Vol.65' - title page verso. — Index.
ISBN 0-7204-0572-6 : £50.00
(B77-27913)

621.48'332 — Nuclear reactors. Steel components. Corrosion by coolants: Carbon dioxide. *Conference proceedings*
BNES International Conference on Corrosion of Steels in CO2, *University of Reading, 1974.* Corrosion of steels in CO2 : proceedings of the British Nuclear Energy Society international conference at Reading University, 23-24 September 1974 / edited by D.R. Holmes, R.B. Hill, L.M. Wyatt. — [London] : B.N.E.S., 1974. — 391[i.e.405],xxv p : ill ; 30cm.
At head of papers: B.N.E.S. International Conference on Corrosion of Steels in CO2 (Sept. 1974).
ISBN 0-7277-0020-0 Pbk : £15.00
(B77-13691)

621.48'336 — Liquid metal fast breeder reactors. Coolants: Sodium
Sodium-NaK engineering handbook / O.J. Foust, editor. — New York ; London [etc.] : Gordon and Breach.
In 5 vols.
Vol.2 : Sodium flow, heat transfer, intermediate heat exchangers and steam generators. — 1976. — xii,390p : ill ; 29cm.
Index.
ISBN 0-677-03030-4 : £22.30
(B77-00800)

621.48'34 — Nuclear power stations. Fast breeder reactors. *Conference proceedings*
Pugwash Debate on Fast Breeder Reactors, *Royal Society, 1976.* Nuclear reactors : to breed or not to breed : a Pugwash Debate on Fast Breeder Reactors held at the Royal Society, London, on 28 September 1976 under the chairmanship of Sir Alec Merrison / edited by J. Rotblat. — London : Taylor and Francis, 1977. — 124p : ill ; 22cm.
ISBN 0-85066-117-x Pbk : £1.00
(B77-07407)

621.48'35 — Nuclear engineering. Safety aspects
Nuclear power safety / edited by James H. Rust and Lynn E. Weaver. — New York ; Oxford [etc.] : Pergamon, 1976. — viii,410p : ill ; 29cm. — (Georgia Institute of Technology. Series in nuclear engineering)
'The material in this book is derived from the notes for a short course on Nuclear Power Safety offered at Georgia Tech ... ' - Preface. — Index.
ISBN 0-08-021417-7 : £12.50
ISBN 0-08-021744-3 Pbk : £8.50
(B77-14776)

621.48'38 — Nuclear reactors. Spent fuels. Reprocessing. *Organisation for Economic Co-operation and Development countries. Reports, surveys*
Nuclear Energy Agency. *Expert Group on Oxide Fuel Reprocessing.* Reprocessing of spent nuclear fuels in OECD countries : a report / by an Expert Group of the OECD Nuclear Energy Agency [Expert Group on Oxide Fuel Reprocessing]. — Paris : Organisation for Economic Co-operation and Development ; [London] : [H.M.S.O.], 1977. — 47p : ill ; 27cm.
Pbk : £2.50
ISBN 92-64-11615-x
(B77-11258)

621.48'38 — Radioactive waste materials. Bituminisation. *Organisation for Economic Co-operation and Development countries. Conference proceedings*
Seminar on the Bituminization of Low and Medium Level Radioactive Wastes, *Antwerp, 1976.* Seminar on the Bituminization of Low and Medium Level Radioactive Wastes = Séminaire sur le Conditionnement dans le Bitume des Déchets Radioactifs de Faible et Moyenne Activité : proceedings of a seminar organised jointly by the OECD Nuclear Energy Agency and the Eurochemic Company, Antwerp, 18-19 May 1976 = Compte rendu du séminaire organisé conjointement par l'Agence de l'OCDE pour L'Energie Nucléaire et la Société Eurochemic, Anvers, 18-19 Mai 1976. — Paris : Organisation for Economic Co-operation and Development ; [London] : [H.M.S.O.], 1976. — [2],246p : ill, plans ; 24cm.
English and French text. — Bibl.
Pbk : £4.70
ISBN 92-64-01509-4
(B77-01561)

621.48'4 — Nuclear fusion technology. *Conference proceedings*
Symposium on Fusion Technology, *9th, Garmisch-Partenkirchen, 1976.* Proceedings of the 9th Symposium on Fusion Technology, Garmisch-Partenkirchen (FRG), June 14-18, 1976 : organized by IPP-Institut für Plasmaphysik, Garching (FRG). — Oxford [etc.] : Pergamon for the Commission of the European Communities, 1976. — xxi,925p : ill ; 30cm.
Spine title: Fusion technology. — At head of title: Association European Atomic Energy Community - EURATOM, Max-Planck-Institut für Plasmaphysik - IPP'. — Index.
ISBN 0-08-021369-3 Pbk : £22.50
(B77-09746)

621.5 — PNEUMATIC, VACUUM, LOW TEMPERATURE TECHNOLOGY

621.5 — Hydro-pneumatic energy sources
Groom, A O. Energy : (hydro-pneumatics) / inventions and illustrations by A.O. Groom. — Sturminster Newton (Sturminster Newton, Dorset DT10 1AN) : The author, 1976. — 56p : ill, plans ; 21x30cm.
ISBN 0-9504855-0-0 Sd : £1.50
(B77-05480)

621.5'1 — Compressed air equipment. Safety fittings. *Standards*
British Standards Institution. Specification for safety valves, gauges and other safety fittings for air receivers and compressed air installations = Spécification des soupapes, jauges et autres accessoires de sécurité pour les récipients à air et les installations à air comprimé = Spezifikation für Sicherheitsventile, Messer und andere Sicherheitszubehörteile für Luftbehälter und Druckluftanlagen / British Standards Institution. — 3rd revision. — London : B.S.I., 1976. — [2],7,[2]p : ill ; 30cm. — (BS1123 : 1976)
Pierced for binder.
ISBN 0-580-09126-0 Sd : £2.40
(B77-03068)

621.5'9 — Cryogenic engineering. *Conference proceedings*
International Cryogenic Engineering Conference, *6th, Grenoble, 1976.* Proceedings of the Sixth International Cryogenic Engineering Conference, Grenoble, 11-14 May 1976 / edited by K. Mendelssohn. — Guildford : IPC Science and Technology Press, 1976. — [8],527p : ill ; 31cm. — (International cryogenic engineering conferences ; vol.6 ISSN 0308-5422)
Index.
ISBN 0-902852-58-2 : Unpriced
(B77-01562)

621.5'9 — Cryogenic liquids. Small-scale storage. Safety measures. *Standards*
British Standards Institution. Code of practice for safe operation of small-scale storage facilities for cryogenic liquids = Code de bonne pratique pour le fonctionnement sans danger des facilités de stockage sur une petite échelle des liquides cryogéniques = Richtlinie für den gefahrlosen Betrieb von kleinen Lagerungsmöglichkeiten für kryogene Flüssigkeiten / British Standards Institution. — London : B.S.I., 1976. — [2],6,[1]p ; 30cm. — (BS5429 : 1976)
Pierced for binder.
ISBN 0-580-09109-0 Sd : £2.70
(B77-11259)

621.5'9 — Double-walled welded vertical cylindrical cryogenic storage tanks. *Standards*
British Standards Institution. Specification for vertical cylindrical welded storage tanks for low-temperature service, double-wall tanks for temperatures down to -196°C = Spécification des récipients de stockage cylindriques verticaux soudés en acier pour usage à basses températures, récipients à paroi double pour les températures jusqu'à -196°C = Spezifikation für senkrechte, zylindrische Lagerbehälter aus geschweisstem Stahl zur Verwendung bei niedrigen Temperaturen, doppelwändige Behälter für Temperaturen bis -196°C / British Standards Institution. — London : B.S.I., 1976. — [2],53,[2]p : ill ; 30cm. — (BS5387 : 1976)
Pierced for binder.
ISBN 0-580-09416-2 Sd : £5.80
(B77-04254)

621.6 — ENGINEERING. FANS, BLOWERS, PUMPS

621.6 — Pumps
Pump handbook / edited by Igor J. Karassik ... [et al.]. — New York ; London [etc.] : McGraw-Hill, 1976. — 1118p in various pagings : ill, forms ; 24cm.
Bibl.: p.9/97. — Index.
ISBN 0-07-033301-7 : £28.65
(B77-03069)

621.6'5 — Pumping stations. *London. Hounslow (London Borough). Kew Bridge Pumping Station. Beam engines*
Yates, John, *b.1946.* A guide to Kew Bridge engines / by John Yates. — [Andover] (Penton Manor, Penton Mewsey Andover, Hants.) : Kew Bridge Engines Trust, [1976]. — [1],8p : 1 ill ; 25cm.
Sd : Unpriced
(B77-17567)

621.7 — PRODUCTION ENGINEERING

621.7'5 — Materials. Chemical machining
Harris, William T. Chemical milling : the technology of cutting materials by etching / [by] William T. Harris. — Oxford : Clarendon Press, 1976. — xv,371p : ill ; 24cm. — (Oxford series on advanced manufacturing)
Bibl. — Index.
ISBN 0-19-859115-2 : £16.00
(B77-12502)

621.7'5 — Workshop practice
Lindberg, Roy Alfred. Processes and materials of manufacture / [by] Roy A. Lindberg. — 2nd ed. — Boston, Mass. ; London [etc.] : Allyn and Bacon, 1977. — [11],714p : ill ; 24cm.
Previous ed.: Boston, Mass. : Allyn and Bacon, 1964. — Bibl. — Index.
ISBN 0-205-05414-5 : Unpriced
(B77-11879)

National Coal Board. *Industrial Training Branch.* Basic mechanical engineering / prepared by NCB Industrial Training Branch. — London [etc.] : Hodder and Stoughton, 1977. — [5], 153p : ill(some col) ; 22cm.
ISBN 0-340-19585-1 Pbk : £1.95
(B77-13692)

Roberts, Arthur D. Manufacturing processes / [by] Arthur D. Roberts, Samuel C. Lapidge. — New York ; London [etc.] : McGraw-Hill, 1977. — x,454p : ill ; 28cm.
Bibl. — Index.
ISBN 0-07-053151-x Pbk : £13.45
(B77-24990)

621.7'5 — Workshop practice. *Manuals*
Machine tools and machining practices / [by] Warren T. White ... [et al.]. — New York ; London [etc.] : Wiley. — (Manufacturing technology series)
In 2 vols.
Vol.1. — 1977. — xvii,781p : ill, facsims ; 29cm.
With answers to self-tests. — Index.
ISBN 0-471-94035-6 : £15.00
(B77-18842)

Vol.2. — 1977. — xix,619p : ill ; 29cm.
With answers to self-tests. — Index.
ISBN 0-471-94036-4 : £14.95
(B77-31251)

621.7'57 — Containers & packaging materials
The **packaging** media / general editor F.A. Paine. — Glasgow [etc.] : Blackie [for] the Council of the Institute of Packaging, 1977. — 548p in various pagings : ill ; 24cm.
Index.
ISBN 0-216-90191-x : £15.95
(B77-08433)

621.7'57 — Prepacked consumer goods. Quantity control. *Great Britain. Inquiry reports*
Working Party on Metrological Control Systems. Metrological control systems : report of the Working Party on Metrological Control Systems ... / chairman E.N. Eden. — London : H.M.S.O., [1977]. — xi,146p : ill ; 25cm. — (Cmnd.6805)
Index.
ISBN 0-10-168050-3 Pbk : £2.35
(B77-22655)

621.7'8 — Industries. Process control. Digital control systems
Blaschke, W S. The control of industrial processes by digital techniques : the organisation, design and construction of digital control systems / [by] W.S. Blaschke and J. McGill. — Amsterdam ; Oxford [etc.] : Elsevier, 1976. — viii,185p(4 fold) : ill ; 25cm.
Bibl.: p.181. — Index.
ISBN 0-444-41493-2 : £18.79
(B77-06731)

621.7'8 — Industries. Process control. Instrumentation
Johnson, Curtis D. Process control instrumentation technology / [by] Curtis D. Johnson. — New York ; London [etc.] : Wiley, 1977. — xv,428p : ill ; 25cm. — (Electronic technology series)
With answers. — Bibl.: p.417. — Index.
ISBN 0-471-44614-9 : £11.50
(B77-18213)

621.7'8 — Industries. Process control. Remote control systems
Young, Robert Eric. Supervisory remote control systems / [by] R.E. Young. — Stevenage : Peregrinus [for] the Institution of Electrical Engineers, 1977. — ix,195p : ill ; 23cm. — (Institution of Electrical Engineers. IEE control engineering series ; [4])
Index.
ISBN 0-901223-94-8 : £10.00(overseas including Americas £11.70)
(B77-24991)

621.8 — MACHINERY, FASTENINGS, ETC
621.8 — Industrial machinery. *Ireland, ca 1750-1900*
McCutcheon, Alan. Wheel and spindle : aspects of Irish industrial history / [by] Alan McCutcheon. — Belfast : Blackstaff Press, 1977. — viii,83,[1]p : ill, facsims, map, ports ; 20cm.
Bibl.: p.80. — Index.
ISBN 0-85640-098-x Pbk : £3.60
(B77-26357)

621.8 — Machinery. *Juvenile literature*
Ardley, Neil. The amazing world of machines / [author Neil Ardley] ; [editor Deborah Manley]. — London [etc.] : Angus and Robertson, 1977. — 32p : ill(chiefly col) ; 33cm.
Spine title: Machines. — Index.
ISBN 0-207-95756-8 : £1.95
(B77-30334)

Milsome, John. Machines and leisure / [by] John Milsome ; illustrated by Harry Sheldon. — London [etc.] : Burke, 1977. — 32p : col ill ; 22cm. — (The world of machines)
ISBN 0-222-00505-x : £1.60
ISBN 0-222-00507-6 Pbk : £1.00
(B77-22656)

Rawson, Christopher. How machines work / [by] Christopher Rawson ; illustrated by Colin King. — London : Usborne, 1976. — 2-47p : col ill ; 29cm.
Col. ill., text on lining papers. — Index.
ISBN 0-86020-056-6 : £1.50
(B77-09747)

621.8 — Mechanisms. *Conference proceedings*
Mechanisms *(Conference), University of Newcastle upon Tyne, 1973.* Mechanisms 1973 : a conference arranged by the University of Newcastle upon Tyne and co-sponsored by the Mechanisms Section of the Applied Mechanics Group of the Institution of Mechanical Engineers, 11th September 1973. — London : The Institution, 1977. — vii,75p : ill ; 31cm.
Index. — Previous control number ISBN 0-85298-316-6.
Unpriced
ISBN 0-85298-316-6
(B77-27164)

621.8'09'031 — Machinery, ca 1590. *Early works*
Ramelli, Agostino. [Le diverse et artificiose machine. English]. The various and ingenious machines of Agostino Ramelli / translated from the Italian and French with a biographical study of the author by Martha Teach Gnudi ; technical annotations and a pictorial glossary by Eugene S. Ferguson. — [Baltimore] : Johns Hopkins University Press ; London : Scolar Press, 1976. — 604p : ill, port ; 36cm.
'Le diverse et artificiose machine' originally published: Paris : Agostino Ramelli, 1588. — Bibl.: p.583-589. — Index.
ISBN 0-85967-247-6 : £50.00
(B77-06156)

621.8'11 — Machinery. Dynamics
Holmes, Roy, *b.1931.* The characteristics of mechanical engineering systems / [by] R. Holmes. — Oxford [etc.] : Pergamon, 1977. — vii,157p : ill ; 26cm. — (Pergamon international library)
Index.
ISBN 0-08-021033-3 : £6.25
ISBN 0-08-021032-5 Pbk : £3.00
(B77-23492)

621.8'11 — Machinery. Mechanics. *Juvenile literature*
Ladyman, Phyllis. How machines work / [text and illustrations] by Phyllis Ladyman. — London [etc.] : Hodder and Stoughton, 1977. — 32p : col ill ; 25cm. — (A picture science book)
Index.
ISBN 0-340-20481-8 : £2.10
(B77-00801)

621.8'16 — Machinery. Maintenance & repair. Techniques
Collacott, Ralph Albert. Mechanical fault diagnosis, and condition monitoring / by R.A. Collacott. — London : Chapman and Hall [etc.], 1977. — ix,496p : ill ; 24cm.
Index.
ISBN 0-412-12930-2 : £20.00
(B77-20347)

621.8'22 — Ball bearings & roller bearings
Houghton, Philip Stephen. Ball and roller bearings / [by] P.S. Houghton. — London : Applied Science Publishers, 1976. — viii,427p : ill ; 23cm.
Bibl.: p.416-420. — Index.
ISBN 0-85334-598-8 : £25.00
(B77-02376)

621.8'22 — Bearings. Design & fitting. *Amateurs' manuals*
Bradley, Ian, *b.1900.* Bearing design & fitting / [by] Ian Bradley. — New revised ed. — Kings Langley : Model and Allied Publications, 1976. — viii,72p : ill ; 19cm. — (Technical publication)
Previous ed.: / published under the name 'Duplex', now known as Ian Bradley and Norman Hallows. Hemel Hempstead : Model Aeronautical Press, 1967.
ISBN 0-85242-463-9 Pbk : £1.25
(B77-07408)

621.8'22 — Bearings. Rusting. Protection by lubricating greases. Testing. *Standards*
British Standards Institution. Method for the IP dynamic anti-rust test for lubricating greases = Méthode de l'Institut du pétrole pour l'essai dynamique des propriétés antirouille des graisses lubrifiantes = Verfahren des Petroleuminstituts für die dynamische Rostschutzprüfung von Schmierfetten / [British Standards Institution]. — London : B.S.I., 1976. — 11p : ill ; 21cm. — (BS5299 : 1976)
'(Identical with IP 220/67)'.
ISBN 0-580-09061-2 Sd : £1.60
(B77-13693)

621.8'33'03 — Gears. *Glossaries*
British Standards Institution. Glossary for gears = Vocabulaire des engrenages = Lexikon für Zahnräder / British Standards Institution. — London : B.S.I.
Part 1 = Partie 1 = Teil 1 : Geometrical definitions = Définitions géométriques = Geometrische Definitionen. — 1st revision. — 1976. — [2],37,[2]p : ill ; 30cm. — (BS2519 : Part 1 : 1976) (ISO/R 1122-1969)
ISO title: Glossary of gears - Geometrical definitions. — Pierced for binder.
ISBN 0-580-09039-6 Sd : £6.60
(B77-11260)

Part 2 = Partie 2 = Teil 2 : Notation = Notation = Bezeichnungen. — 1st revision. — 1976. — [2],5,[1]p ; 30cm. — (BS2519 : Part 2 : 1976) (ISO701-1976)
ISO title: International gear notation - Symbols for geometrical data. — Pierced for binder.
ISBN 0-580-09069-8 Sd : £1.60
(B77-11261)

621.8'4 — Industrial valves. *Standards*
British Standards Institution. Testing of general purpose industrial valves = Essais des appareils de robinetterie industrielle d'usage courant = Prüfung von Industriearmaturen für allgemeine Verwendung / British Standards Institution. — London : B.S.I., 1976. — [2],3,[2]p ; 30cm. — (BS5417 : 1976) (EN 17)
Pierced for binder.
ISBN 0-580-09178-3 Sd : £1.50
(B77-02377)

621.8'52 — Power transmission equipment. Rubber belting, balata belting & plastics belting. *Standards*
British Standards Institution. Specification for rubber, balata or plastics flat transmission belting of textile construction for general use = Spécification pour courroies plates de transmission en caoutchouc, balata ou matières plastiques de construction textile à usage général = Spezifikation für Flache Treibriemen aus Gummi, Balata oder Kunststoffen von Textilherstellung für allgemeine Zwecke / British Standards Institution. — 3rd revision. — London : B.S.I., 1976. — [2],9,[2]p : ill ; 30cm. — (BS351 : 1976)
Pierced for binder.
ISBN 0-580-09456-1 Sd : £3.10
(B77-04255)

621.8'6 — Grocery trades. Unit load mechanical handling equipment: Cage pallets. Use. *Great Britain. Reports, surveys*
Cranfield School of Management. *Marketing and Logistics Systems Research Centre.* Cage palletisation in the UK grocery industry : an evaluation of total system costs and benefits : a study / commissioned by the Institute of Grocery Distribution ; produced by Martin Christopher ... [et al.] ; for the Marketing & Logistics Systems Research Centre [and the] Retailing Development Centre, Cranfield School of Management. — [Watford] ([Letchmore Heath, Watford WD2 8DQ]) : [Institute of Grocery Distribution], 1977. — [1],ii,209 leaves : ill ; 30cm.
Pbk : £75.00
(B77-33862)

621.8'672 — Acrylonitrile-butadiene-styrene pressure pipes. *Standards*
British Standards Institution. Specification for acrylonitrile-butadiene-styrene (ABS) pressure pipe = Spécification des tubes en butadiène-styrène-acrylonitrile (ABS) pour utilisation avec pression = Spezifikation für Akrylonitril-Butadien-Styren-(ABS) -Druckrohre / British Standards Institution. — London : B.S.I.
Part 1 = Partie 1 = Teil 1 : Pipe for industrial uses = Tubes à usage industriel = Rohre zur industriellen Verwendung. — 1976. — [2],6,[2] p : ill ; 30cm. — (BS5391 : Part 1 : 1976)
Pierced for binder.
ISBN 0-580-09486-3 Sd : £2.40
(B77-05481)

621.8'672 — Acrylonitrile-butadiene-styrene pressure pipes. Acrylonitrile-butadiene-styrene fittings. *Standards*
British Standards Institution. Specification for acrylonitrile-butadiene-styrene (ABS) fittings for use with ABS pressure pipe = Spécification des raccords en butadiène-styrène-acrylonitrile (ABS) utilisés avec les tubes en ABS avec pression = Spezifikation für Anschlussstüke aus Akrylonitril-Butadien-Styren (ABS) zur Verwendung mit ABS-Druckrohren / British Standards Institution. — London : B.S.I.
Part 1 = Partie 1 = Teil 1 : Fittings for use with pipe for industrial use = Raccords utilisés avec les tubes à usage industriel = Anschlussstücke für Industrierohre. — 1976. — [2],3,[2]p : ill ; 30cm. — (BS5392 : Part 1 : 1976)
Pierced for binder.
ISBN 0-580-09496-0 Sd : £1.50
(B77-05482)

621.8'672 — Seamless steel pressure pipes, seamless steel pressure tubes, welded steel pressure pipes & welded steel pressure tubes. Dimensions & mass. *Standards*
British Standards Institution. Specification for dimensions and masses per unit length of welded and seamless steel pipes and tubes for pressure purposes = Spécification des dimensions et des masses par unité de longueur des tubes en acier soudés et sans soudure pour usage sous pression = Spezifikation für die Masse und Massen je Langeneinheit von geschweissten und nahtlosen Druckrohren aus Stahl / British Standards Institution. — 1st revision. — London : B.S.I., 1976. — [2],7,[2] p ; 30cm. — (BS3600 : 1976)
Pierced for binder.
ISBN 0-580-09288-7 Sd : £2.40
(B77-09748)

621.8'672 — Solids. Hydraulic transport in pipes. *Conference proceedings*
International Conference on the Hydraulic Transport of Solids in Pipes, *4th, Banff, Alta, 1976.* Proceedings of Hydrotransport 4, 1976 : 4th International Conference on th Hydraulic Transport of Solids in Pipes / [edited by H.S. Stephens et al.]. — Bedford (Cranfield, Bedford MK43 0AJ) : BHRA Fluid Engineering, [1977]. — 594p in various pagings : ill, maps, port ; 31cm.
'Hydrotransport 4 was sponsored and organised by BHRA Fluid Engineering, U.K., in conjunction with the Alberta Research Council, Canada and was held at Banff, Alberta, Canada from May 18th-21st, 1976' - p.iii. — Bibl. — Index.
ISBN 0-900983-56-6 : £20.00 : CIP rev.
(B77-15909)

621.8'672'0212 — Piping systems. *Technical data*
Williamson, E H. Data book for pipe fitters and pipe welders / [by] E.H. Williamson. — [Folkestone] : Bailey and Swinfen, 1977. — [2], v,154p : ill ; 16cm.
ISBN 0-561-00291-6 Pbk : Unpriced
(B77-10402)

621.8'73'0212 — Lifting equipment: Cranes. *Technical data. Serials*
Cranes annual. — London : Morgan Grampian.
1976 : construction plant & equipment / plant editor Chris Barlow ... — 1976. — 99p : ill ; 29cm.
ISBN 0-900865-56-3 Pbk : £3.50
ISSN 0305-523x
(B77-03070)

621.8'77 — Passenger lifts. Control systems
Barney, G C. Lift traffic analysis, design and control / [by] G.C. Barney, S.M. dos Santos. — Stevenage : Peregrinus [for] the Institution of Electrical Engineers, 1977. — xiii,317p : ill, forms ; 23cm. — (Institution of Electrical Engineers. IEE control engineering series ; 2)
Bibl.: p.310-312. — Index.
ISBN 0-901223-86-7 : £15.00
(B77-15332)

621.8'77'05 — High-rise access equipment. *Periodicals*
Access today. — Edgware (290A Hale La., Edgware, Middx HA8 8NP) : MW Publishers.
Issue no.1- ; Apr. 1977-. — 1977-. — ill, ports ; 29cm.
Quarterly. — 32p. in 1st issue.
Sd : £1.50
ISSN 0309-7870
(B77-20348)

621.8'8 — Engineering components: Fastenings
Standard handbook of fastening and joining / Robert O. Parmley, editor in chief. — New York ; London [etc.] : McGraw-Hill, 1977. — 651p in various pagings : ill ; 24cm.
Index.
ISBN 0-07-048511-9 : £17.80
(B77-24285)

621.8'8 — Spring retaining rings. *Standards*
British Standards Institution. Specification for spring retaining rings, metric series = Spécification des bagues à retenir les ressorts, série métrique = Spezifikation für Federhalteringe, metrische Serie / British Standards Institution. — London : B.S.I.
Part 4 = Partie 4 = Teil 4 : Carbon steel circlips = Circlips en acier au carbone = Sprengringe aus unlegiertem Stahl. — 1977. — [2],19,[2]p : ill ; 30cm. — (BS3673 : Part 4 : 1977)
Pierced for binder.
ISBN 0-580-95215-0 Sd : £4.70
(B77-17569)

621.8'85 — Engineering components: Fluid seals. *Conference proceedings*
International Conference on Fluid Sealing, *7th, University of Nottingham, 1975.* Proceedings of the Seventh International Conference on Fluid Sealing, Nottingham, England, 1975 / [editors H.S. Stephens, N.G. Coles, N.G. Guy]. — Cranfield (Cranfield, Bedford MK43 0AJ) : British Hydromechanics Research Association Fluid Engineering, 1976. — 615p in various pagings : ill ; 31cm.
'The 7th International Conference on Fluid Sealing was sponsored and organized by BHRA Fluid Engineering and was held at the University of Nottingham, England from 24th-26th September 1975' - p. iii. — Index.
ISBN 0-900983-48-5 : £17.50
(B77-09066)

621.8'85 — Engineering components: Mechanical seals
Mayer, Ehrhard. Mechanical seals / [by] E. Mayer ; English translation [from the German] prepared by the Motor Industry Research Association, and edited by B.S. Nau. — 3rd ed. — London [etc.] : Newnes-Butterworth, 1977. — [12],291p : ill ; 23cm.
Translation of: 'Axiale Gleitringdichtungen'. 5.Aufl. Düsseldorf : VDI-Verlag, 1974. — Previous English ed. London : Iliffe, 1972. — Bibl.: p.261-282. — Index.
ISBN 0-408-00307-3 : £9.50
(B77-33863)

621.8'85 — Engineering components: Seals. Design
Fern, A G. Seals / [by] A.G. Fern and B.S. Nau. — [Oxford] : Oxford University Press for the Design Council, the British Standards Institution and the Council of Engineering Institutions, 1976. — [2],36p : ill ; 30cm. — (Engineering design guides ; 15)
Bibl.: p.35. — Index.
ISBN 0-19-859148-9 Sd : £1.80
(B77-11880)

621.8'9 — Elastohydrodynamic lubrication
Dowson, Duncan. Elasto-hydrodynamic lubrication / [by] D. Dowson and G.R. Higginson ; chapters 9 and 10 by J.F. Archard and A.W. Crook. — [2nd], SI ed. — Oxford [etc.] : Pergamon, 1977. — xiv,235p,[2]leaves of plates : ill ; 22cm. — (Pergamon international library : international series on materials science and technology ; vol.23)
Previous ed.: 1966. — Bibl.: p.224-230. — Index.
ISBN 0-08-021303-0 : £6.50
ISBN 0-08-021302-2 Pbk : £3.75
(B77-24992)

621.8'9 — Lubrication
Cameron, Alastair, *b.1917.* Basic lubrication theory / by A. Cameron. — 2nd ed. — Chichester : Ellis Horwood ; New York ; London [etc.] : Distributed by Wiley, 1976. — xx,195p : ill ; 24cm. — ([Ellis Horwood series in engineering science])
Previous ed.: Harlow : Longman, 1971. — Bibl. : p.190-192. — Index.
ISBN 0-85312-057-9 : £6.75
(B77-13085)

621.8'9 — Materials. Wear by impact
Engel, Peter A. Impact wear of materials / [by] Peter A. Engel. — Amsterdam ; Oxford [etc.] : Elsevier, 1976. — xv,339p : ill ; 25cm.
Bibl. — Index.
ISBN 0-444-41533-5 : £24.12
(B77-17570)

621.8'9'071241 — Secondary schools. Curriculum subjects: Tribology. *Great Britain. For teaching*
Great Britain. *Department of Trade and Industry.* Tribology for schools / Department of Trade and Industry. — London (c/o Industrial Technology Secretariat, Room 539, Abell House, John Islip St., SW1P 4LN) : [The Department], 1972. — [5],49,[1]p : ill ; 25cm.
'... produced under the auspices of the Education and Training Committee of the Department of Trade and Industry's Committee on Tribology ...' - Foreword.
Sd : Unpriced
(B77-31947)

621.9 — WORKSHOP TOOLS

621.9 — Small tools. Sharpening. *Amateurs' manuals*
Bradley, Ian, *b.1900.* Sharpening small tools and some domestic appliances / [by] Ian Bradley. — Completely revised ed. — Kings Langley : Model and Allied Publications, 1976. — [5], 106p : ill ; 19cm. — (Technical publication)
Previous ed.: / published under the name 'Duplex', now known as Ian Bradley and Norman Hallows. London : P. Marshall, 1948. — Index.
ISBN 0-85242-459-0 Pbk : £1.25
(B77-05483)

621.9 — Tools. *Juvenile literature*
Kerrod, Robin. Tools / by Robin Kerrod ; illustrated by Robert Geary. — London [etc.] : F. Watts, 1977. — 48p : ill(chiefly col) ; 22cm. — (A first look book)
Index.
ISBN 0-85166-630-2 : £1.75
(B77-30335)

621.9'02 — Machine tools. Accuracy. *Standards*
British Standards Institution. Specification for the accuracy of machine tools and methods of test = Spécification de la précision des machines-outils et méthodes d'essai = Spezifikation für die Genauigkeit von Werkzeugmaschinen und Prüfverfahren / British Standards Institution. — London : B.S.I.
Part 20 = Partie 20 = Teil 20 : Machining centres, vertical spindle type = Pointes d'usinage, type à broche verticale = Bearbeitungszentren mit senkrechtem Spindel. — 1976. — [2],9.[2]p : ill ; 30cm. — (BS4656 C Part 20 : 1976)
Pierced for binder.
ISBN 0-580-09467-7 Sd : £3.10
(B77-00802)

621.9'02 — Machine tools. Components. *Standards*
British Standards Institution. British Standard specification for machine tool components = Specification pour organes de machines outils = Spezifikation für Werkzeugmaschinenelemente / British Standards Institution. — London : B.S.I.
Part 12 = Partie 12 = Teil 12 : Ball screws = Vis à billes = Kugelschrauben : nominal diameters and basic leads = diamètres nominaux et pas hélicoïdaux = Nenndurchmesser und grundsätzliche Gewindesteigungen. — 1976. — Folder ([4]p) ; 30cm. — (BS4185 : Part 12 : 1976)
Pierced for binder.
ISBN 0-580-09138-4 : £1.15
(B77-07948)

621.9'02 — Machine tools. Design. *Conference proceedings*
International Machine Tool Design and Research Conference, *17th, Birmingham, 1976.* Proceedings of the Seventeenth International Machine Tool Design and Research Conference held in Birmingham 20th-24th September, 1976 / edited by S.A. Tobias. — Birmingham : Department of Mechanical Engineering, University of Birmingham ; London [etc.] : Macmillan, 1977. — xii,671p : ill ; 31cm.
Index.
ISBN 0-333-21777-2 : Unpriced
(B77-27165)

621.9'02 — Machine tools. Numerical control. Applications of digital computer systems
Pressman, Roger S. Numerical control and computer-aided manufacturing / [by] Roger S. Pressman, John E. Williams. — New York ; London [etc.] : Wiley, 1977. — xvii,310p : ill, 2 facsims ; 24cm.
Index.
ISBN 0-471-01555-5 : £13.00
(B77-20349)

621.9'02 — Portable power woodworking tools. *Manuals*
McDonnell, Leo P. The use of portable power tools / [by] Leo P. McDonnell, with the assistance of Donald M. Kidd and Louis J. Siy. — New York ; London [etc.] : Van Nostrand Reinhold, [1977]. — vii,214p : ill, facsims ; 27cm.
Originally published: as 'Portable power tools'. Albany : Delmar, 1962. — Index.
ISBN 0-442-25272-2 : £6.45
(B77-27166)

621.9'02'072041 — Machine tools. Research in British institutions. *Directories*
Register of research on machine tools and related production engineering ... / compiled by the Machine Tool Industry Research Association. — Macclesfield (Hulley Rd, Macclesfield, Cheshire SK10 2NE) : [M.T.I.R.A.]. 1976. — 1976. — [2],viii,166p ; 30cm.
Previously published: as 'Register of research on machine tools and production engineering'. — Index.
Sd : Unpriced
(B77-03071)

621.9'02'0941 — Machine tools. *Great Britain. Buyers' guides*
Machine Tool Trades Association. British machine tools and equipment = Machines-outils britanniques et equipements = Britische Werkzeugmaschinen und Zubehör / Machine Tool Trades Association. — [New ed.]. — London (62 Bayswater Rd, W2 3PH) : The Association, 1977. — 315p : ill ; 30cm.
English, French and German texts. — Previous ed.: 1973. — Index.
Pbk : £8.00
(B77-33864)

621.9'04 — Hand-held pneumatic percussive tools & hand-held pneumatic rotary tools: Acceptance testing. *Standards*
British Standards Institution. Methods for acceptance tests for rotary and percussive pneumatic tools = Essais de réception pour des outils pneumatiques rotatifs et percutants = Abnahmeprüfungen für rotierende und schlagende Pressluftwerkzeuge / British Standards Institution. — London : B.S.I., 1976. — [2],15,[2]p : ill ; 30cm. — (BS5344 : 1976)
Pierced for binder.
ISBN 0-580-09382-4 Sd : £4.70
(B77-12503)

621.9'08 — Hand woodworking tools. *Manuals*
McDonnell, Leo P. The use of hand woodworking tools / [by] Leo P. McDonnell, with the assistance of Donald M. Kidd and Louis J. Siy. — New York ; London [etc.] : Van Nostrand Reinhold, [1977]. — vii,294p : ill, facsim ; 27cm.
Originally published: as 'Hand woodworking tools'. Albany : Delmar, 1962. — Index.
ISBN 0-442-25271-4 : Unpriced
(B77-25698)

621.9'08'0246213 — Hand tools. *Manuals. For electronics*
Kitchens, Harry Thomas. Hand tools for the electronics workshop / [by] Harry T. Kitchens. — Watford : Fountain Press, 1976. — viii, 115p : ill ; 22cm.
ISBN 0-85242-475-2 Pbk : £2.25
(B77-26358)

621.9'12 — Shaping machines. Cutting tools
Bradley, Ian, *b.1900.* Shaping machine and lathe tools / [by] Ian Bradley. — Revised ed. — Watford : Model and Allied Publications, 1976. — [6],74p,xvi p of plates : ill ; 19cm.
Previous ed.: published as 'Lathe and shaping machine tools'. s.l. : s.n., 1949. — Index.
ISBN 0-85242-485-x Pbk : £1.50
Also classified at 621.9'42
(B77-14274)

621.9'2 — Grinding wheels. *Standards*
British Standards Institution. Specification for bonded abrasive products = Spécification pour produits abrasifs agglomérés = Spezifikation für verbundene Schleifprodukte / British Standards Institution. — London : B.S.I.
Part 2 = Partie 2 = Teil 2 [i.e.2] : Dimensions of grinding wheels and segments = Dimensions des meules et des segments = Masse der Schleifräder und Teile. — 1st revision. — 1976. — [2],35,[2]p : ill ; 30cm. — (BS4481 : Part 2 : 1976)
Pierced for binder.
ISBN 0-580-09448-0 Sd : £6.60
(B77-11262)

621.9'3 — Neolithic flint axes. *England. Cotswolds*
Tyler, Alan. Neolithic flint axes from the Cotswold Hills / [by] Alan Tyler. — Oxford : British Archaeological Reports, 1976. — [8], 98p(2 fold) : ill, maps ; 30cm. — (British archaeological reports ; 25 ISSN 0306-1205)
Bibl.: p.86-89.
ISBN 0-904531-28-7 Sd : £1.90
(B77-03072)

621.9'42 — Lathes. Cutting tools
Bradley, Ian, *b.1900.* Shaping machine and lathe tools / [by] Ian Bradley. — Revised ed. — Watford : Model and Allied Publications, 1976. — [6],74p,xvi p of plates : ill ; 19cm.
Previous ed.: published as 'Lathe and shaping machine tools'. s.l. : s.n., 1949. — Index.
ISBN 0-85242-485-x Pbk : £1.50
Primary classification 621.9'12
(B77-14274)

621.9'42 — Screwcutting lathes. *Manuals*
Boxford Machine Tools Ltd. Know your lathe : a screwcutting lathe manual / produced by Boxford Machine Tools Ltd. — Watford : Model and Allied Publications, 1977. — [2], 102p : ill ; 22cm.
Index.
ISBN 0-85242-557-0 Pbk : £2.50
(B77-31948)

621.9'52 — Electric hand drilling tools. Armatures. Rewinding. *Amateurs' manuals*
Banner, E C. Rewinding armatures and repairing vac cleaners and power tools / by E.C. Banner. — Manchester ([c/o Magnum Associates, Brinksway Trading Estate, Brinksway, Stockport, Cheshire]) : Magnum Publications, [1976]. — [3],129p : ill ; 26cm.
ISBN 0-900144-03-3 Sp : £4.00
Also classified at 683'.83
(B77-15333)

621.9'55 — Screwing taps. *Standards*
British Standards Institution. Specification for screwing taps = Spécification des tarauds de filetage = Richtlinien für Innengewinde / British Standards Institution. — London : B.S.I.
Part 1 = Partie 1 = Teil 1 : Taps for ISO metric threads = Tarauds pour filetages métriques ISO = Innengewinde des ISO metrischen Gewinde. — 1976. — [2],36,[2]p : ill ; 30cm. — (BS949 : Part 1 : 1976)
Pierced for binder.
ISBN 0-580-09314-x Sd : £5.80
(B77-09749)

621.9'92 — Machine tools. Jigs. Bushes. *Standards*
British Standards Institution. Specification for jig bushes = Spécification des guides de perçage = Spezifikation für Bohrbuchsen / British Standards Institution. — London : B.S.I.
Part 2 = Partie 2 = Teil 2 : Metric units = Unités métriques = Metrische Einheiten. — 1976. — [2],8,[2]p : ill ; 30cm. — (BS1098 : Part 2 : 1977)
Pierced for binder.
ISBN 0-580-09650-5 Sd : £2.70
(B77-11263)

622 — MINING

622 — Mining. Environmental aspects
Down, Christopher Gordon. Environmental impact of mining / [by] C.G. Down and J. Stocks. — London : Applied Science Publishers, 1977. — ix,371p : ill, maps ; 23cm.
Index.
ISBN 0-85334-716-6 : £19.00
(B77-15910)

622'.028 — Mining equipment. *Great Britain. Buyers' guides*
Association of British Mining Equipment Exporters. ABMEX buyers' guide ... — Sheffield (P.O. Box 121, 301 Glossop Rd, Sheffield S10 2HN) : A.B.M.E.X.
[1977]. — [1977]. — 140p ; 22cm.
English, French, German and Spanish text.
Pbk : Unpriced
(B77-31949)

622'.06'241 — Mining. Organisations: Institution of Mining and Metallurgy. *Great Britain. Periodicals*
Institution of Mining and Metallurgy. IMM bulletin : bulletin of the Institution of Mining and Metallurgy. — London (44 Portland Place, W1N 4BR) : I.M.M.
No.830- ; Jan. 1976-. — 1976-. — 30cm.
Monthly. — 8p. in Jan. 1976 issue. — Continues: Institution of Mining and Metallurgy. Bulletin.
Sd : £6.00 yearly
ISSN 0308-9789
Also classified at 669'.006'241
(B77-04256)

622'.09425'13 — Mines. *Derbyshire. Matlock Bath, to 1975*
The caverns and mines of Matlock Bath. — Buxton (The Market Place, Hartington, Buxton, Derbyshire SK17 0AL) : Moorland Publishing Company.
1 : The Nestus Mines : Rutland and Masson Caverns / [by] Roger Flindall, Andrew Hayes. — 1976. — 72p : ill, maps, plans ; 22cm.
Index.
ISBN 0-903485-19-2 Pbk : £1.10
(B77-11881)

622'.1 — Mineral deposits. Prospecting. *Glaciated regions. Conference proceedings*
Prospecting in areas of glaciated terrain, 1977 : papers presented at a symposium organized by the Institution of Mining and Metallurgy, with the cooperation of the Geological Survey of Finland and held in Helsinki, Finland, on 15-17 August, 1977. — London (44 Portland Place, W1N 4BR) : The Institution, 1977. — vi,140p : ill, maps ; 30cm.
Bibl.
ISBN 0-900488-38-7 Pbk : £16.00
(B77-30336)

622'.13'015195 — Mineral deposits. Estimation. Use of statistical mathematics
David, Michel. Geostatistical ore reserve estimation / by Michel David. — Amsterdam ; Oxford [etc.] : Elsevier, 1977. — xx,364p : ill ; 25cm. — (Developments in geomathematics ; 2)
Bibl.: p.347-356. — Index.
ISBN 0-444-41532-7 : Unpriced
(B77-27167)

622'.14 — Industrial regions. Disused mines. Shafts. Location. *Great Britain. Manuals. For reclamation of derelict land*
Ove Arup and Partners. Procedure for locating abandoned mine shafts / prepared by Ove Arup & Partners ... — London ([1 Lambeth Palace Rd, SE1 7ER]) : Planning, Regional and Minerals Directorate, Department of the Environment, 1976. — [3],i,88p,[2] leaves : ill, maps ; 30cm. — (Reclamation of derelict land)
Bibl.: p.80-88.
Sp : £1.50
(B77-13694)

622'.15 — Mineral deposits. Prospecting. Applications of geophysics
Dobrin, Milton Burnett. Introduction to geophysical prospecting / [by] Milton B. Dobrin. — 3rd ed. — New York ; London [etc.] : McGraw-Hill, 1976. — ix,630p : ill, maps ; 24cm.
Previous ed.: 1960. — Index.
ISBN 0-07-017195-5 : £16.50
(B77-18214)

622'.15'02854044 — Mineral deposits. Prospecting. Applications of geophysics. Applications of digital computer systems
Claerbout, Jon F. Fundamentals of geophysical data processing : with applications to petroleum prospecting / [by] Jon F. Claerbout. — New York ; London [etc.] : McGraw-Hill, 1976. — xiii,274p : ill ; 25cm. — (McGraw-Hill international series in the earth and planetary sciences)
Index.
ISBN 0-07-011117-0 : £15.75
(B77-21202)

622'.154 — Mineral deposits. Prospecting. Applications of induced polarisation techniques
Sumner, J S. Principles of induced polarization for geophysical exploration / [by] J.S. Sumner. — Amsterdam ; Oxford [etc.] : Elsevier, 1976. — xiv,277p : ill, forms ; 25cm. — (Developments in economic geology ; 5)
Bibl.: p.257-262. — Index.
ISBN 0-444-41481-9 : £16.39
(B77-17571)

622'.18'282 — Petroleum deposits. Prospecting. Applications of probabilities
Harbaugh, John Warvelle. Probability methods in oil exploration / [by] John W. Harbaugh, John H. Doveton, John C. Davis. — New York ; London [etc.] : Wiley, 1977. — xiii,269p : ill, charts, maps ; 24cm.
'A Wiley-Interscience Publication'. — Bibl.: p.253-261. — Index.
ISBN 0-471-35129-6 : £12.70
(B77-29498)

622'.18'282 — Petroleum. Prospecting. Applications of geophysics
Nettleton, L L. Gravity and magnetics in oil prospecting / [by] L.L. Nettleton. — New York ; London [etc.] : McGraw-Hill, 1976. — xvi,464p : ill, maps ; 25cm. — (McGraw-Hill international series in the earth and planetary sciences)
Bibl. — Index.
ISBN 0-07-046303-4 : £20.75
(B77-04883)

622'.19 — Refuse dumps. Excavation of remains. *Great Britain, 1837-1901. Amateurs' manuals*
Fletcher, Edward. Where to dig up antiques / [by] E. Fletcher ; photographs M.J. Coffin ; illustrations A. Payne. — Southampton (7 Maple Rd, Bitterne, Southampton [Hants.]) : Southern Collectors Publications, 1976. — [3], 55p : ill ; 21cm.
ISBN 0-905438-04-3 Sd : £1.35
(B77-09067)

622'.19 — Treasure hunting. *Great Britain. Manuals*
Hill, Cuthbert William. Treasure hunting : Britain's fastest growing hobby / by C.W. Hill. — Brentwood : NPC ; Watford : [Distributed by] Argus books, 1977. — 3-62p : ill(some col), ports ; 28cm.
Bibl.: p.61. — Index.
ISBN 0-901265-07-1 Sd : £0.70
(B77-25699)

622'.19'0941 — Treasure hunting. *Great Britain. Periodicals*
Treasure hunting. — Brentwood (Sovereign House, High St., Brentwood, Essex CM14 4SE) : NPC.
Vol.1, no.1- ; Aug. 1977-. — 1977-. — ill, ports ; 28cm.
Monthly. — 60p. in 1st issue.
Sd : £0.45(£5.40 yearly)
ISSN 0140-4539
(B77-30337)

622'.33 — Coal. Production. *Conference proceedings*
International Conference on Coal Research, *2nd, London, 1974.* Proceedings [of] the Second International Conference on Coal Research, Mayfair Hotel, London, 8-9 October 1974. — Cheltenham (Stoke Orchard, Cheltenham, Glos.) : National Coal Board, Coal Research Establishment [for] the International Committee for Coal Research, [1976]. — 301p in various pagings : ill, maps ; 30cm.
Includes 6 papers in German and 3 in French.
ISBN 0-901429-95-3 Pbk : Unpriced
(B77-02378)

622'.33'028 — Coal mining equipment. *Great Britain. Reviews of research*
Ministry Research and Development Establishment. MRDE projects. — Burton-on-Trent (Ashby Rd, Stanhope Bretby, Burton-on-Trent, Staffs. DE15 0QD) : M.R.D.E.
1974-5. — [1975]. — [4],41p : ill ; 30cm.
Previously published: as MRDE report. — Bibl. : p.41.
Sd : Unpriced
ISSN 0140-4393
(B77-30338)

622'.33'0941 — Coal. Mining. *Great Britain*
Coal : technology for Britain's future. — London [etc.] : Macmillan, 1976. — 144p : ill(some col), facsim, maps(1 col), plans ; 26cm.
Index.
ISBN 0-333-19418-7 : £4.95
(B77-06157)

622'.33'8072041 — Natural gas & petroleum. Production. Research projects. *Great Britain. Periodicals*
Offshore research focus. — London (6 Storey's Gate, SW1P 3AU) : Construction Industry Research and Information Association for the Department of Energy.
No.1- ; Mar. 1977-. — 1977-. — ill, ports ; 30cm.
Quarterly. — 8p. in 1st issue.
Sd : Unpriced
ISSN 0309-4189
(B77-18843)

622'.33'82 — Petroleum deposits. Extraction. *Juvenile literature*
Law, Felicia. Oil rigs / written by Felicia Law ; illustrated by Stephen Cartwright. — Glasgow [etc.] : Collins, 1977. — 32p : col ill ; 22cm. — (Dandelions)
Originally published: 1976.
ISBN 0-00-106003-1 : £1.50
(B77-28680)

622'.33'8201576 — Petroleum deposits. Extraction. Applications of microbiology. *Conference proceedings*
The **genesis** of petroleum and microbiological means for its recovery : papers presented at the [Institute of Petroleum] Microbiology Group symposium on 6th October 1976. — [London] : Institute of Petroleum, [1977]. — [4],82p : ill ; 30cm.
Sd : £3.50
(B77-30339)

622'.33'820184 — Petroleum reservoir engineering. Mathematical models
Crichlow, Henry B. Modern reservoir engineering : a simulation approach / [by] Henry B. Crichlow. — Englewood Cliffs ; London [etc.] : Prentice-Hall, 1977. — xiv, 354p : ill, maps ; 24cm.
Bibl. — Index.
ISBN 0-13-597468-2 : £20.00
(B77-16927)

622'.33'82023 — Petroleum offshore drilling rigs industries. Personnel. *North Sea. Career guides*
Potter, Neil. Oil rig / [by] Neil Potter. — London : Macdonald Educational, 1977. — 48p : ill(some col), 2 col maps ; 29cm. — (Macdonald insiders)
Bibl.: p.47. — List of films: p.47. — Index.
ISBN 0-356-05584-1 : £1.95
(B77-26359)

622'.33'820916336 — Petroleum deposits. Extraction. Floating production platforms. *North Sea. Argyll field*
Bluston, H S. Argyll, the first floating production platform : a critical study / [by] H.S. Bluston. — Bedford ([24 Elm Close, Bedford MK41 8BZ]) : Energy Consultancy, 1977. — [2]p,10,[2]leaves ; 30cm.
ISBN 0-9505736-0-4 Sd : £3.10
(B77-16452)

622'.34'0941 — Metals mines. Industrial antiquities. *Great Britain, to 1976. Illustrations*
Bird, R H. Yesterday's Golcondas : notable British metal mines / [by] R.H. Bird. — Hartington (The Market Place, Hartington, Buxton, Derbyshire SK17 0AL) : Moorland Publishing Co., 1977. — [112]p : chiefly ill, maps ; 25cm.
Bibl.: p.138-140. — Index.
ISBN 0-903485-37-0 : £3.95
(B77-33865)

622'.35'3 — Firestone mines. Industrial antiquities. *Surrey. Merstham. Reports, surveys*
Croydon Caving Club. Merstham firestone quarries : an interim account / by members of Croydon Caving Club. — Carshalton (44 Culvers Way, Carshalton, Surrey) : The Club, 1976. — [3],27,ii p,[15]leaves of plates : ill, map, plans ; 30cm.
Bibl.: p.i-ii.
ISBN 0-9505649-0-7 Sd : £0.50
(B77-14777)

622'.35'4094292 — Slate quarries. *Gwynedd, to 1976. Illustrations. Welsh-English parallel texts*
Llechi = Slate / [compilation and text by] M.J.T. Lewis. — [Caernarfon] ([County Offices, Caernarfon, Gwynedd]) : Gwynedd Archives Service, 1976. — [62]p : ill, facsims, ports ; 21cm.
Parallel Welsh and English text.
ISBN 0-901337-17-x Sd : £1.50
(B77-27168)

622'.473 — Coal miners' flame safety lamps. Use. *Programmed texts*
National Coal Board. *Industrial Training Branch.* Flame safety lamps / [National Coal Board, Industrial Training Branch]. — [London] ([Hobart House, Grosvenor Place, S.W.1]) : The Branch.
Part 2. — 1976. — [3],59 leaves : ill ; 18cm. — (Programmed text ; 6)
Eleven leaves printed on both sides. — 'Test answers' (Sheet ([1]p.)) as insert.
ISBN 0-901429-96-1 Pbk : £1.95
(B77-12504)

622'.48 — Coal mines. Electric equipment. Flameproof gate-end boxes. *Standards*
British Standards Institution. Specification for mining type flameproof supply and control units for use on systems up to 1100v = Spécification des dispositifs d'approvisionnement et de commande antidéflagrants du type minier pour les systèmes jusqu'à 1100v = Spezifikation für flammenbeständige Versorgungs-und Stevergeräte zur Verwendung in Anlagen bis auf 1100v im Bergbau / British Standards Institution. — London : B.S.I.
Part 2 = Partie 2 = Teil 2 : 300A circuit breaker units = Dispositifs disjoncteurs de 300A = 300A Stromunterbrecher. — 1976. — [2],14,[2]p : ill ; 30cm. — (BS5126 : Part 2 : 1976)
Pierced for binder.
ISBN 0-580-09208-9 Sd : £4.00
(B77-09750)

622'.67 — Mines. Winding equipment. Safety measures. *Great Britain. Reports, surveys*
National Committee for Safety of Manriding in Shafts and Unwalkable Outlets. Safe manriding in mines : first report of the National Committee for Safety of Manriding in Shafts and Unwalkable Outlets [to the] Health and Safety Executive. — London : H.M.S.O., 1976. — ix,177p : ill, forms ; 30cm.
ISBN 0-11-880491-x Pbk : £5.00
(B77-03073)

622'.8 — Coal mines. Air. Pollutants: Gases. *Programmed texts*
National Coal Board. *Industrial Training Branch.* More pit gases / [National Coal Board, Industrial Training Branch]. — [London] : The Branch, 1977. — [5],61p ; 18cm. — (Programmed text ; 11)
Two-way paging. — 'Test questions' and 'Test answers' (2 sheets ([3]p.)) as inserts.
Sd : Unpriced
(B77-23493)

622'.8 — Mines. Air. Contaminants: Radon. Monitoring. *Conference proceedings*
Specialist Meeting on Personal Dosimetry and Area Monitoring Suitable for Radon and Daughter Products, *Elliot Lake, Ont., 1976.* Proceedings of the Specialist Meeting on Personal Dosimetry and Area Monitoring Suitable for Radon and Daughter Products = Compte rendu d'une réunion de spécialistes sur la dosimétrie individuelle en ce qui concerne le radon et ses produits de filiation, Elliot Lake, Canada, 4-8 Oct. 1976. — Paris : Nuclear Energy Agency, Organisation for Economic Co-operation and Development ; [London] : [H.M.S.O.], 1977. — 314p : ill, maps ; 24cm.
Cover title: Personal dosimetry and area monitoring suitable for radon and daughter products = La dosimétrie individuelle et la surveillance de l'atmosphère en ce qui concerne le radon et ses produits de filiation. — Includes 4 papers in French, English and French preliminaries. — Bibl.
Pbk : £6.80
ISBN 92-64-01603-1
(B77-11882)

622'.8'0941 — Mining & quarrying. Safety measures. *Great Britain. Reports, surveys. Serials*
Great Britain. *Mines Inspectorate.* Reports of HM Inspectors of Mines and Quarries. — London : H.M.S.O.
1975. North and South Midlands Districts : report / by G.H. Thomas and F. Tootle. — 1976. — iii,62p,[2]p of plates : ill ; 25cm.
ISBN 0-11-880507-x Sd : £1.25
ISSN 0307-7454
(B77-07409)

1975. North and South Yorkshire Districts : report / by E.J.H. Nicholas & G.W. Taylor. — 1976. — iv,45p,fold leaf,[4]p of plates : ill ; 25cm.
ISBN 0-11-880495-2 Sd : £1.25
ISSN 0307-7454
(B77-07410)

1975. Scottish District : report / by M.G. Thomas. — 1976. — iii,44p,fold leaf,[4]p of plates : ill ; 25cm.
Previously issued by the Mines Inspectorate.
ISBN 0-11-880496-0 Sd : £1.25
ISSN 0307-7454
(B77-03593)

1975. South Wales District / report by A.W. Davies. — 1976. — iii,55p(2 fold),ii p of plates,leaf of plate : ill ; 25cm.
ISBN 0-11-880494-4 Sd : £1.25
ISSN 0307-7454
(B77-06158)

1975. Southern District : report / by J.D. Tankard. — 1976. — v,56p,[4]p of plates : ill ; 24cm.
ISBN 0-11-880497-9 Sd : £1.25
ISSN 0307-7454
(B77-01563)

1975. The North of England District : report / by D. Richards. — 1976. — iv,48p,fold leaf,iv p of plates : ill ; 25cm.
ISBN 0-11-880498-7 Sd : £1.25
ISSN 0307-7454
(B77-00803)

1975. West Midlands and North Western District : report / by E.J. Raine. — 1976. — iv,58p,fold leaf,[4]p of plates : ill ; 25cm.
ISBN 0-11-880499-5 Sd : £1.25
ISSN 0307-7454
(B77-00804)

Mines & quarries : health and safety / Health and Safety Executive [Mines Inspectorate]. — London : H.M.S.O.
1975. — 1976. — v,57p,[2]p of plates : ill ; 30cm.
ISBN 0-11-881107-x Sd : £1.75
ISSN 0309-1686
(B77-03594)

Mines & quarries : health and safety / Health & Safety Executive [Mines Inspectorate]. — London : H.M.S.O.
1976. North & South Yorkshire District. — [1977]. — [7],42p(2 fold),[4]p of plates : ill ; 21cm.
ISBN 0-11-882004-4 Sd : £1.50
(B77-32680)

1976. Scottish District. — [1977]. — [7],46p(2 fold),[2]p of plates : ill, plan ; 21cm.
ISBN 0-11-882005-2 Sd : £1.50
(B77-32681)

1976. South Wales District. — [1977]. — [7], 58p,[2]p of plates : ill ; 21cm.
ISBN 0-11-882003-6 Sd : £1.50
(B77-33272)

1976. Southern District. — [1977]. — [8],51p, [4]p of plates : ill ; 21cm.
ISBN 0-11-882001-x Sd : £1.50
(B77-32682)

623 — MILITARY ENGINEERING

623'.0943 — Germany. Heer. Assault engineer units. Army equipment 1939-1945
Ellis, Chris. German infantry and assault engineer equipment, 1939-1945 / [by] Chris Ellis. — Kings Langley : Argus Books, 1976. — 64p : ill ; 21cm. — (Bellona publications)
ISBN 0-85242-456-6 Pbk : £1.50
Primary classification 623.4'0943
(B77-09068)

623'.1'094 — German coastal defences. *Western Europe. Atlantic Wall, 1940-1944*
Partridge, Colin. Hitler's Atlantic Wall / [by] Colin Partridge. — Guernsey (Les Goddards, Rue des Goddards, Castel, Guernsey, Channel Islands) : D.I. Publications, 1976. — 144p : ill, maps, plans ; 25cm.
Bibl.: p.141-142. — Index.
ISBN 0-9504729-0-5 Pbk : £3.50
(B77-07411)

623'.1'0941 — Fortifications & fortified buildings. *Great Britain*
Forde-Johnston, James. Castles and fortifications of Britain and Ireland / [by] J. Forde-Johnston. — London [etc.] : Dent, 1977. — 192p : ill, maps, plans ; 25cm.
Bibl.: p.188. — Index.
ISBN 0-460-04195-9 : £5.95 : CIP rev.
(B77-11883)

623'.1'09416 — Fortified buildings. *Northern Ireland, to 1976. Secondary school texts*
British Broadcasting Corporation. Ulster castles & defensive buildings : BBC Irish history for schools. — London : British Broadcasting Corporation [for] the School Broadcasting Council for the United Kingdom, 1977. — 40p : ill, maps, plans ; 30cm. — (Modern Irish history ; 116PA)
Bibl.: p.40.
ISBN 0-563-30069-8 Sd : Unpriced
(B77-31950)

623'.1'0942 — Fortifications. *England. Coastal regions, 1509-1547*
Morley, B M. Henry VIII and the development of coastal defence / [by] B.M. Morley. — London : H.M.S.O., 1976. — [1],44,[2]p : ill(incl 2 col), maps, plans, ports ; 16x26cm. — (Great Britain. Department of the Environment. Souvenir guidebooks) (Ancient monuments and historic buildings)
ISBN 0-11-670777-1 Sd : £0.60
(B77-15334)

623'.12'09361 — Ancient Roman forts. Fortifications. *Great Britain, to 117*
Jones, Michael John, *b.1947.* Roman fort-defences to AD 117, with special reference to Britain / [by] Michael J. Jones. — Oxford : British Archaeological Reports, 1975. — [23], 192,[1]p,fold plate : ill, maps, plans ; 30cm. — (British archaeological reports ; 21 ISSN 0306-1205)
Bibl.: p.[13]-[23].
ISBN 0-904531-24-4 Pbk : £3.90
(B77-00268)

623'.19'362881 — Ancient Roman fortifications. *Northern England. Hadrian's Wall. Conservation. Proposals*
Dartington Amenity Research Trust. Hadrian's Wall : a strategy for conservation and visitor services / prepared for the Countryside Commission by Dartington Amenity Research Trust. — [Cheltenham] : [The Commission], 1976. — [2],151p : ill, maps ; 21x30cm. — (DART publication ; no.25) (CCP 98)
ISBN 0-902590-38-3 Pbk : £2.20
Also classified at 333.7'8'0942881
(B77-04884)

623.4 — Armies. Infantry. Military equipment: Weapons
Foss, Christopher Frank. Infantry weapons of the world / [by] Christopher F. Foss & T.J. Gander. — London : Allan, 1977. — 141p : ill ; 23cm.
Index.
ISBN 0-7110-0734-9 : £3.50
(B77-10403)

623.4 — Armies. Infantry. Military equipment: Weapons. *Serials*
Jane's infantry weapons. — London : Jane's Yearbooks.
1977 : 3rd ed. / edited by Denis H.R. Archer. — 1977. — 736p : ill ; 33cm.
Index.
ISBN 0-354-00549-9 : £25.00
ISSN 0306-3410
(B77-16928)

623.4'05 — Weapon systems. *Serials*
Jane's weapon systems. — London : Jane's Yearbooks.
1977 : 8th ed. / edited by R.T. Pretty. — 1976. — 99,872p : ill(some col) ; 33cm.
Index.
ISBN 0-354-00541-3 : £25.00
(B77-07412)

623.4'09 — Weapons, to 1975
Reid, William, *b.1926.* The lore of arms / [by] William Reid. — London : Mitchell Beazley, 1976. — 280p : ill(some col), col coat of arms, facsims, plans(1 col) ; 31cm.
Bibl.: p.269-270. — Index.
ISBN 0-85533-082-1 : £13.95
(B77-00269)

623.4'09'034 — Military equipment: Weapons, ca 1850-ca 1975
Weapons & warfare of the 20th century : a comprehensive and historical survey of modern military methods and machines / [by] Eric Morris ... [et al.]. — [London] : Octopus Books, [1976]. — 480p : ill(some col), maps(some col), plans(some col), ports(some col) ; 33cm.
Ill. on lining papers. — Index.
ISBN 0-7064-0534-x : £7.95
(B77-00805)

623.4'09'04 — Military equipment: Weapons, 1914-1975
How weapons work / edited by Christopher Chant. — London [etc.] : Marshall Cavendish, 1976. — chiefly ill(some col), ports ; 28cm.
Col. ill. on lining papers. — 'Some of this material was previously published in "How it works" and 'War monthly"' - title page verso. — Index.
ISBN 0-85685-196-5 : £4.95
(B77-15911)

623.4'09'043 — Armies. Military equipment: Weapons, 1939-1945
Batchelor, John. Weapons & war machines / [illustrated by John Batchelor ; compiled by Andrew Kershaw and Ian Close]. — London : Phoebus, 1976. — 256p : ill(some col), col maps ; 31cm.
Ill. on lining papers. — Index.
ISBN 0-7026-0008-3 : £4.95
(B77-33866)

623.4'092'2 — Weapons manufacturers. *Scotland, ca 1400-1870. Biographical dictionaries*
Whitelaw, Charles E. Scottish arms makers : a biographical dictionary of makers of firearms, edged weapons and armour, working in Scotland from the 15th century to 1870 / [by] Charles E. Whitelaw ; edited by Sarah Barter ; foreword by William Reid. — [London] : Arms and Armour Press, [1977]. — 5-339p : ill ; 26cm.
Index.
ISBN 0-85368-201-1 : £11.50
(B77-23494)

623'.4'094 — European armies. Military equipment: Weapons, 1700-1800
Funcken, Liliane. The lace wars / [by] Liliane and Fred Funcken ; [translated from the French]. — London : Ward Lock. — (Arms and uniforms)
Translation of: 'L'uniforme et les armes des soldats de la guerre en dentelle'. Tournai : Casterman, 1976.
Part 2 : 1700-1800 : French, British and Prussian cavalry and artillery, other countries : infantry, cavalry and artillery. — 1977. — 5-158p : col ill ; 25cm.
Col. ill. on lining papers. — Index.
ISBN 0-7063-5566-0 : £5.95 : CIP rev.
Primary classification 355.1'4'094
(B77-21026)

623.4'0943 — Germany. Heer. Infantry. Military equipment: Weapons, 1939-1945
Ellis, Chris. German infantry and assault engineer equipment, 1939-1945 / [by] Chris Ellis. — Kings Langley : Argus Books, 1976. — 64p : ill ; 21cm. — (Bellona publications)
ISBN 0-85242-456-6 Pbk : £1.50
Also classified at 623'.0943
(B77-09068)

623.4'1'0212 — Artillery. *Technical data*
Brassey's artillery of the world : guns, howitzers, mortars, guided weapons, rockets and ancillary equipment in service with the regular and reserve forces of all nations / editor Shelford Bidwell ; co-authors, compilers and consultants Brian Blunt, Tolley Taylor. — London (15 Cavendish Sq., W1M 0HT) : Brassey's Publishers Ltd, 1977. — 274p : ill ; 32cm.
Index.
ISBN 0-904609-04-9 : £18.50
(B77-13086)

623.4'1'0904 — Artillery, ca 1940-1975
Foss, Christopher Frank. Artillery of the world / [by] Christopher F. Foss. — [2nd ed.]. — London : I. Allan, 1976. — 202p : ill ; 23cm.
Previous ed.: 1974. — Bibl.: p.198. — Index.
ISBN 0-7110-0719-5 : £2.95
(B77-29499)

623.4'41 — Bronze Age spearheads. *England. South Midlands*
Ehrenberg, Margaret R. Bronze Age spearheads from Berkshire, Buckinghamshire and Oxfordshire / [by] Margaret R. Ehrenberg. — Oxford : British Archaeological Reports, 1977. — [10],95p : ill, maps ; 30cm. — (British archaeological reports ; 34 ISSN 0306-1205)
Bibl.: p.61-66.
ISBN 0-904531-61-9 Sd : £1.90
(B77-23495)

623.4'41 — Weapons, to 1500
Cowper, H S. The art of attack : being a study in the development of weapons and appliances of offence, from the earliest times to the age of gunpowder / by H.S. Cowper. — Wakefield : EP Publishing, 1977. — xix,312p,plate : ill ; 23cm.
Facsimile reprint of: 1st ed. Ulverston : W. Holmes, 1906. — Bibl.: p.299-301. — Index.
ISBN 0-7158-1212-2 : £5.75
(B77-17572)

623.4'42 — Military equipment: Rifles. *Technical data*
Jane's pocket book of rifles and light machine guns / edited by Denis Archer. — London : Macdonald and Jane's, 1977. — 231p : ill ; 12x19cm. — (Jane's pocket book ; 17)
Index.
ISBN 0-354-01014-x : Unpriced
ISBN 0-354-01015-8 Pbk : £2.75
Primary classification 623.4'424
(B77-27169)

623.4'424 — Light machine guns. *Technical data*
Jane's pocket book of rifles and light machine guns / edited by Denis Archer. — London : Macdonald and Jane's, 1977. — 231p : ill ; 12x19cm. — (Jane's pocket book ; 17)
Index.
ISBN 0-354-01014-x : Unpriced
ISBN 0-354-01015-8 Pbk : £2.75
Also classified at 623.4'42
(B77-27169)

623.4'424 — Military equipment: Self loading rifles & sub-machine guns, 1939-1945
Chamberlain, Peter. Sub-machine guns and automatic rifles / [by] Peter Chamberlain and Terry Gander. — London : Macdonald and Jane's, 1976. — [2],64p : ill ; 28cm. — (World War 2 fact files)
Includes details of flame-throwers.
ISBN 0-354-01006-9 : £2.95
(B77-04257)

623.4'424 — Sub-machine guns
Jane's pocket book of pistols and sub-machine guns / edited by Denis Archer. — London : Macdonald and Jane's, 1976. — 237p : ill ; 13x19cm. — ([Jane's pocket book ; 16])
Index.
ISBN 0-354-01012-3 : £3.75
ISBN 0-354-01013-1 Pbk : £2.75
Primary classification 683'.43
(B77-08463)

623.4'424 — Sub-machine guns. *History*
Nelson, Thomas B. The world's submachine guns (machine pistols) / by Thomas B. Nelson ; with the assistance of Hans B. Lockhoven. — London : Arms and Armour Press.
Vol.1 : Developments from 1915-1963 : containing data, history and photographs of over 300 weapons ... — 1977. — iii-xi,741[i.e. 753]p : ill ; 29cm.
English text, technical guide in 22 languages. — Originally published: Cologne : International Small Arms Publishers, 1963. — Bibl.: p.741. — Index.
ISBN 0-85368-481-2 : £10.95
(B77-28681)

623.4'425 — Allied forces. Military equipment: Rifles, 1939-1945
Chamberlain, Peter. Allied pistols, rifles and grenades / [by] Peter Chamberlain and Terry Gander. — London : Macdonald and Jane's, 1976. — 64p : chiefly ill ; 27cm. — (World War 2 fact files)
Cover title.
ISBN 0-354-01005-0 Pbk : £1.75
Also classified at 623.4'43
(B77-04258)

623.4'425 — Axis forces. Military equipment: Rifles, 1939-1945
Chamberlain, Peter. Axis pistols, rifles and grenades / [by] Peter Chamberlain and Terry Gander. — London : Macdonald and Jane's, 1976. — 64p : chiefly ill ; 27cm. — (World War 2 fact files)
Cover title.
ISBN 0-354-01031-x Pbk : £1.75
Also classified at 623.4'43
(B77-04259)

623.4'43 — Allied forces. Military equipment: Pistols, 1939-1945
Chamberlain, Peter. Allied pistols, rifles and grenades / [by] Peter Chamberlain and Terry Gander. — London : Macdonald and Jane's, 1976. — 64p : chiefly ill ; 27cm. — (World War 2 fact files)
Cover title.
ISBN 0-354-01005-0 Pbk : £1.75
Primary classification 623.4'425
(B77-04258)

623.4'43 — Axis forces. Military equipment: Pistols, 1939-1945
Chamberlain, Peter. Axis pistols, rifles and grenades / [by] Peter Chamberlain and Terry Gander. — London : Macdonald and Jane's, 1976. — 64p : chiefly ill ; 27cm. — (World War 2 fact files)
Cover title.
ISBN 0-354-01031-x Pbk : £1.75
Primary classification 623.4'425
(B77-04259)

623.4'44 — German ersatz bayonets, 1914-1918
Carter, Anthony. German ersatz bayonets / [by] Anthony Carter. — Brighton (111 Lowther Rd, Brighton BN1 6LH) : Lyon Press.
1 : A concise illustrated history of the emergency all-metal designs, 1914-18. — 1976. — 64p : ill, port ; 30cm.
ISBN 0-904256-10-3 : £3.45
(B77-19447)

623.4'44 — Germany. Heer. Bayonets, 1871-1945
Walter, John. The German bayonet : a comprehensive illustrated history of the regulation patterns, 1871-1945 / [by] John Walter. — London : Arms and Armour Press [etc.], 1976. — 128p : ill, facsims, ports ; 26cm.

Bibl.: p.128.
ISBN 0-85368-211-9 : £5.75
(B77-16929)

623.4'44'09 — Edged weapons, to 1940
Wilkinson-Latham, Robert John. Swords in colour : including other edged weapons / [by] Robert Wilkinson-Latham ; special photography John Searle Austin ; colour drawings by Peter Sarson and Tony Bryan. — Poole : Blandford Press, 1977. — 227p : ill(chiefly col), facsims ; 20cm.
Index.
ISBN 0-7137-0818-2 : £3.50
(B77-21203)

623.4'5 — Underground nuclear explosions. Monitoring
Dahlman, Ola. Monitoring underground nuclear explosions / by Ola Dahlman and Hans Israelson. — Amsterdam ; Oxford [etc.] : Elsevier, 1977. — x,440p : ill(some col), maps ; 25cm.
Bibl.: p.406-431. — Index.
ISBN 0-444-41604-8 : Unpriced
(B77-24993)

623.4'519 — Guided missiles. Control systems
Garnell, P. Guided weapon control systems / by P. Garnell and D.J. East. — Oxford [etc.] : Pergamon, 1977. — viii,282p : ill ; 26cm.
Index.
ISBN 0-08-019691-8 : £7.50
(B77-23496)

623.4'519'0212 — Guided missiles. *Technical data*
Taylor, Michael John Haddrick. Missiles of the world / [by] Michael J.H. Taylor and John W.R. Taylor. — 2nd ed. — London : Allan, 1976. — 159p : ill(some col) ; 23cm.
Previous ed.: 1972. — Index.
ISBN 0-7110-0712-8 : £3.30
(B77-01564)

623.6'4 — Prefabricated harbours: Mulberry. Design & construction, 1941-1944
Hartcup, Guy. Code name Mulberry : the planning, building and operation of the Normandy harbours / [by] Guy Hartcup. — Newton Abbot [etc.] : David and Charles [etc.], 1977. — 160p : ill, plans ; 22cm.
Bibl.: p.143-144. — Index. — Previous control number B7726360.
ISBN 0-7153-7388-9 : £4.95
(B77-26360)

623.7'3'072042339 — Military communication systems. Research organisations. *Dorset. Christchurch. Signals Research and Development Establishment, to 1973*
Jones, Eric Gwynne. SRDE, 1903-1973 / [by E. Gwynne Jones]. — [Christchurch] ([Somerford, Christchurch, Dorset BH23 4JB]) : [Signals Research and Development Establishment], 1975. — [2],vii,46p : ill, facsims, map, ports ; 30cm.
Sd : Unpriced
(B77-00270)

623.74'6 — Military aircraft
Gunston, Bill. The illustrated encyclopedia of the world's modern military aircraft / [by] Bill Gunston. — London (27 Old Gloucester St., WC1N 3AF) : Salamander Books, 1977. — 256p : ill(chiefly col) ; 32cm.
Spine title: Modern military aircraft. — Col. ill. on lining papers. — Index.
ISBN 0-86101-010-8 : £5.95
(B77-32683)

623.74'6 — Military gliders, 1939-1945
Mrazek, James Edward. Fighting gliders of World War II / [by] James E. Mrazek. — London : Hale [etc.], 1977. — 207p : ill ; 25cm.

Index.
ISBN 0-7091-5083-0 : £6.50
(B77-22657)

623.74'6 — Naval aircraft, to 1945
Casey, Louis S. Naval aircraft / [by Louis S. Casey] ; [illustrated by John Batchelor]. — London [etc.] : Hamlyn, 1977. — 127p : ill(chiefly col) ; 31cm.
Ill. on lining papers. — 'Part published in "Naval Aircraft, 1939-1945" - title page verso.
ISBN 0-600-36583-2 : £2.95
(B77-19448)

623.74'6047 — Military helicopters, to 1976
Gunston, Bill. Helicopters at war / [by Bill Gunston] ; [illustrated by John Batchelor]. — London [etc.] : Hamlyn, 1977. — 127p : ill(chiefly col), ports ; 31cm.
Ill. on lining papers.
ISBN 0-600-34530-0 : £2.95
(B77-19449)

623.74'6'09044 — Military aircraft, 1939-1945. *Technical data*
Weal, Elke C. Combat aircraft of World War Two / compiled by Elke C. Weal ; colour plates by John A. Weal ; line drawings by Richard F. Barker ; editorial consultant J.M. Bruce. — London : Arms and Armour Press, 1977. — 238p : ill(some col) ; 32cm.
Bibl.: p.227-231. — Index.
ISBN 0-85368-191-0 : £9.95 : CIP rev.
(B77-07949)

623.74'6'0941 — Great Britain. Royal Air Force. Military aircraft, 1918-1975
Thetford, Owen. Aircraft of the Royal Air Force since 1918 / [by] Owen Thetford. — 6th ed. — London : Putnam, 1976. — 640p : ill ; 23cm.
Previous ed.: 1971. — Index.
ISBN 0-370-10056-5 : £8.50
(B77-06159)

623.74'6'0941 — Military aeroplanes. *Great Britain, 1914-1918. Technical data. Facsimiles*
Great Britain. *Air Ministry.* British military aircraft of World War One : the official technical and rigging notes for RFC and RNAS fighting and training aeroplanes, 1914-1918. — London : Arms and Armour Press [etc.], 1976. — 313p : ill ; 23x24cm. — (Royal Air Force Museum. RAF Museum series ; vol.4)
Facsimile reprints. — '... originally appeared as RAF Technical Notes, Aeroplanes A-L and RAF Technical Notes, Aeroplanes M-Z. Both were produced for official use and internal purposes by the Air Ministry' - title page verso.

ISBN 0-85368-261-5 : £7.50
(B77-02379)

623.74'6'0943 — Germany. Luftwaffe. Military aeroplanes, 1939-1945
Brown, Eric, *b.1919.* Wings of the Luftwaffe : flying German aircraft of the Second World War / [by] Eric Brown ; edited by William Green and Gordon Swanborough ; illustrated ... by John Weal. — London : Macdonald and Jane's, 1977. — 176p : ill, ports ; 29cm.
ISBN 0-354-01075-1 : £5.95
(B77-26361)

623.74'6'0973 — United States. Navy. Military aircraft, 1911-1975
Swanborough, Gordon. United States navy aircraft since 1911 / [by] Gordon Swanborough & Peter M. Bowers. — 2nd ed. — London : Putnam, 1976. — x,546p : ill ; 23cm.
Previous ed.: 1968. — Index.
ISBN 0-370-10054-9 : £10.50
(B77-06160)

623.74'63 — De Havilland Mosquito aeroplanes, to 1955
Hardy, Michael John. The de Havilland Mosquito / [by] M.J. Hardy. — Newton Abbot [etc.] : David and Charles, 1977. — 128p : ill, ports ; 26cm. — (David and Charles aircraft family monographs)
Bibl.: p.122. — Index.
ISBN 0-7153-7367-6 : £4.95
(B77-15912)

623.74'63 — Model Junkers JU87 aeroplanes. Making. *Manuals*
Robertson, Bruce. JU87 Stuka / [by] Bruce Robertson and Gerald Scarborough. — Cambridge : Stephens [for] Airfix Products Ltd, 1977. — 96p : ill ; 26cm. — (Classic aircraft ; no.5)
ISBN 0-85059-193-7 : £2.95
Primary classification 940.54'49'43
(B77-23873)

623.74'64 — Focke-Wulf Fw 190 aeroplanes, 1941-1945
Green, William. The Focke-Wulf Fw 190 / [by] William Green and Gordon Swanborough. — Newton Abbot [etc.] : David and Charles, 1976. — 152p : ill ; 26cm.
ISBN 0-7153-7084-7 : £4.95
(B77-04260)

623.74'64 — McDonnell Douglas Phantom aeroplanes, to 1976
Gunston, Bill. F-4 Phantom / [by] Bill Gunston. — London : I. Allan, 1977. — 112p : ill(some col), ports ; 25cm. — (Modern combat aircraft ; 1)
ISBN 0-7110-0727-6 : £3.95
(B77-33867)

623.74'64 — Night fighter aeroplanes, to 1975
Gunston, Bill. Night fighters : a development & combat history / [by] Bill Gunston ; foreword by John Cunningham. — Cambridge : Stephens, 1976. — 192p,[16]p of plates : ill, ports ; 25cm.
ISBN 0-85059-236-4 : £4.50
(B77-00271)

623.74'64'0228 — Plastics model fighter aeroplanes, 1939-1945. Construction. *Manuals*
Philpott, Bryan. Modelling World War 2 fighters / [by] Bryan Philpott. — Cambridge : Stephens [for] Airfix Products Ltd, 1977. — 64p : ill ; 23cm. — ('Airfix magazine' guide ; 25)
ISBN 0-85059-262-3 : £1.60
(B77-25700)

623.74'64'0943 — Germany. Luftwaffe. Fighter aeroplanes, 1939-1945
Philpott, Bryan. German fighters of World War 2 / [by] Bryan Philpott. — Cambridge : Stephens [for] Airfix Products Ltd, 1977. — 64p : ill ; 23cm. — ('Airfix magazine' guide ; 23)
Bibl.: p.64.
ISBN 0-85059-257-7 : £1.60
(B77-27170)

623.74'64'0952 — Japan. Army Air Force. Fighter aeroplanes, 1940-1945
Green, William. Japanese Army fighters / [by] William Green and Gordon Swanborough. — London : Macdonald and Jane's. — (World War 2 fact files : [aircraft])
In 2 vols.
Part 1. — 1976. — [2],58p : ill(some col) ; 28cm.
ISBN 0-356-08223-7 : £2.95
(B77-04885)
Part 2. — 1977. — [2],68p : ill(some col) ; 28cm.
ISBN 0-354-01067-0 : £2.95
(B77-31252)

623.74'64'0973 — United States. Army Air Force. Fighter aeroplanes, 1941-1945
Green, William. US Army Air Force fighters / [by] William Green and Gordon Swanborough. — London : Macdonald and Jane's.
In 2 vols.
Part 1. — 1977. — [1],76p : ill(some col) ; 27cm. — (World War 2 fact files)
ISBN 0-356-08218-0 Pbk : £1.75
(B77-24286)

623.74'64'0973 — United States. Navy. Fighter aeroplanes, 1941-1945
Green, William. US Navy and Marine Corps fighters / [by] William Green and Gordon Swanborough. — London : Macdonald and Jane's, 1976. — [2],68p : ill(some col) ; 28cm. — (World War 2 fact files : [aircraft])
ISBN 0-356-08221-0 : £2.95
(B77-04886)

623.74'75 — Armoured combat vehicles: Allied tanks, 1933-1945
Ross, G MacLeod. The business of tanks, 1933 to 1945 / by G. MacLeod Ross in collaboration with Sir Campbell Clarke. — Ilfracombe : Stockwell, 1976. — 338p,[32]p of plates : ill, facsims, ports ; 22cm.
Bibl.: p.334.
ISBN 0-7223-0870-1 : £4.00
(B77-12505)

623.74'75 — Germany. Heer. Armoured combat vehicles: Tanks, 1933-1945
Ellis, Chris. Panzerkampfwagen : German combat tanks, 1933-1945 / [by] Chris Ellis and Hilary Doyle. — Kings Langley : Argus Books, 1976. — 160p : ill ; 21cm. — (Bellona publications)
ISBN 0-85242-453-1 Pbk : £2.75
(B77-04887)

623.74'75 — Plastics model armoured cars. Construction. *Manuals*
Scarborough, Gerald. Modelling armoured cars / [by] Gerald Scarborough. — Cambridge : Stephens [for] Airfix Products Ltd, 1977. — 64p : ill ; 23cm. — ('Airfix magazine' guide ; 21)
ISBN 0-85059-249-6 : £1.60
(B77-15335)

623.74'75 — Union of Soviet Socialist Republics. Armiia. Armoured combat vehicles: Tanks, 1917-1945
Milsom, John. Russian tanks of World War 2 / [by] John Milsom and Steve Zaloga. — Cambridge : Stephens [for] Airfix Products Ltd, 1977. — 64p : ill, facsims ; 23cm. — ('Airfix magazine' guide ; 22)
ISBN 0-85059-250-x : £1.60
(B77-15336)

623.74'75 — United States. Army. Armoured combat vehicles: Tanks, 1939-1945
Gander, Terence John. American tanks of World War 2 / [by] Terry Gander and Peter Chamberlain. — Cambridge : Stephens [for] Airfix Products Ltd, 1977. — 64p : ill ; 23cm. — ('Airfix magazine' guide ; 26)
ISBN 0-85059-260-7 : £1.60
(B77-25701)

623.74'75'0212 — Armoured combat vehicles. *Technical data*
Foss, Christopher Frank. Armoured fighting vehicles of the world / [by] Christopher F. Foss. — 3rd ed. — London : I. Allan, 1977. — 192p,[8]p of plates : ill(some col) ; 23cm.
Previous ed.: 1974. — Index.
ISBN 0-7110-0778-0 : £3.95
(B77-28682)

Foss, Christopher Frank. Jane's world armoured fighting vehicles / [by] Christopher F. Foss. — London : Macdonald and Jane's, 1976. — 437p : ill ; 26cm.
Index.
ISBN 0-354-01022-0 : £7.95
(B77-04888)

623.74'75'0904 — Armoured combat vehicles, to 1976
Foss, Christopher Frank. The illustrated encyclopedia of the world's tanks and fighting vehicles : a technical directory of major combat vehicles from World War 1 to the present day / [by] Christopher F. Foss. — London (27 Old Gloucester St., WC1N 3AF) : Salamander Books, 1977. — 248p : ill(chiefly col) ; 32cm.
Spine title: Tanks and fighting vehicles. — Ill. on lining papers. — Index.
ISBN 0-86101-003-5 : £5.95
(B77-33868)

623.8 — SHIPS, SHIPBUILDING AND SEAMANSHIP

623.8'1 — Ships. Design
Baxter, Brian. Naval architecture / [by] Brian Baxter. — 2nd ed. — London : Teach Yourself Books, 1976. — viii,256p : ill ; 18cm. — (Teach yourself books)
With answers. — Previous ed.: published as 'Teach yourself naval architecture'. London : English Universities Press, 1960. — Bibl.: p.245-246. — Index.
ISBN 0-340-17883-3 Pbk : £1.95
(B77-21940)

623.8'1'071141 — Naval architects. Professional education. *Great Britain. Conference proceedings*
Symposium on Education and Training for Naval Architecture and Ocean Engineering, *Royal Institution of Naval Architects, 1976.* Proceedings of the Symposium on Education and Training for Naval Architecture and Ocean Engineering : held at the Royal Institution of Naval Architects ... 9th April, 1976. — London (10 Upper Belgrave St., SW1X 8BQ) : Royal Institution of Naval Architects, 1976. — [5], 88p : ill ; 30cm.
ISBN 0-903055-10-4 Pbk : £10.00
Primary classification 620'.416'2071141
(B77-04874)

623.8'1'0924 — Naval architecture. Russell, John Scott. *Great Britain. Biographies*
Emmerson, George Sinclair. John Scott Russell : a great Victorian engineer and naval architect / [by] George S. Emmerson. — London : J. Murray, 1977. — x,342p,[12]p of plates : ill, plans, ports ; 24cm.
Index.
ISBN 0-7195-3393-7 : £6.50
(B77-27171)

623.8'12'2 — Sailing catamarans. Design
Amateur Yacht Research Society. Cruising catamarans : history, design principles, examples / by members of the AYRS. — 2nd ed. — Newbury (Hermitage, Newbury, Berks.) : The Society, 1977. — 319p : ill, plans ; 21cm.
Previous ed. 1972. — Index.
Pbk : £6.00
(B77-25702)

623.8'17'1 — Ships. Stability. *Conference proceedings*
International Conference on Stability of Ships and Ocean Vehicles, *University of Strathclyde, 1975.* Proceedings of the International Conference on Stability of Ships and Ocean Vehicles, March 1975, [organized by] University of Strathclyde [Department of Shipbuilding and Naval Architecture], Glasgow, Scotland in collaboration with UK Departments of Industry and Trade / edited by C. Kuo. — Glasgow ([26 Richmond St.], Glasgow G1 1XH) : [University of Strathclyde, Department of Shipbuilding and Naval Architecture], [1976]. — 511p in various pagings : ill, forms, maps ; 31cm.
Spine title: Stability conference. — Bibl. — Index.
ISBN 0-902013-19-x : £22.00
(B77-05484)

623.82 — Boats. *Teaching kits*
Porter, Caroline. Boats / illustrated by Caroline Porter. — London : Jackdaw [for] Thames Television [etc.], 1977. — 1v. : chiefly col ill ; 22x26cm. — (Rainbows)
Twelve sheets (6 fold.) in plastic envelope. — 'Playpacks from ITV's "Rainbow" programme'.
ISBN 0-305-62130-0 : £0.99(non-net)
(B77-22658)

623.82 — Boats & ships. *Juvenile literature*
Milsome, John. Machines and the sea / [by] John Milsome ; illustrated by Harry Sheldon. — London [etc.] : Burke, 1976. — 32p : col ill ; 22cm. — (The world of machines)
ISBN 0-222-00500-9 : £1.50
ISBN 0-222-00502-5 Pbk : £1.00
(B77-02380)

623.82 — Inland waterways boats. *Great Britain, to 1977*
Smith, Donald John. Discovering craft of the inland waterways / [by] D.J. Smith. — Aylesbury : Shire Publications, 1977. — 87p : ill ; 18cm. — (Discovering series ; no.227)
Bibl.: p.85. — Index.
ISBN 0-85263-368-8 Pbk : £0.60
(B77-33273)

623.82 — Ships. *Juvenile literature*
The **super** book of ships. — London : Macdonald Educational, 1977. — 32p : ill(some col), col ports ; 28cm.
Adaptation of: 'Ships'. 1970.
ISBN 0-356-05594-9 Sd : £0.50
(B77-18215)

623.82 — Ships. Components & fittings. Dimensions. *Standards*
British Standards Institution. Recommendations for the co-ordination of dimensions in shipbuilding = Recommandations concernant la coordination dimensionelle dans la construction navale = Empfehlungen für die Koordination von Abmessungen im Schiffsbau : co-ordinating sizes for services = dimensions de coordination des services = Koordination von Grössen für Versorgungsdienste / British Standards Institution. — London : B.S.I., 1976. — 9,[1]p : ill ; 30cm. — (British Standard marine series = Série maritime = Marinen Serie) (BS MA77 : 1976)
Pierced for binder.
ISBN 0-580-09860-5 Sd : £3.60
(B77-13695)

623.82 — Ships registered in Great Britain. Accidents. *Statistics*
Casualties to vessels and accidents to men : vessels registered in the United Kingdom : returns / Department of Trade. — London : H.M.S.O.
1975. — 1977. — [5],46p : ill ; 30cm.
ISBN 0-11-511710-5 Sd : £1.75
(B77-15913)

623.82'0028'54 — Ships. Design & construction. Applications of computer systems. *Conference proceedings*
Computer applications in shipping and shipbuilding. — Amsterdam [etc.] ; Oxford : North-Holland Publishing Co.
Vol.3 : Automation in offshore oil field operation : proceedings of the IFAC/IFIP Symposium, Bergen, Norway, June 14-17, 1976 / edited by Frode L. Galtung, Kare Rosandhaug, Theodore J. Williams. — 1976. — ix,439p : ill, maps ; 31cm.
'The Proceedings of the IFAC/IFIP Symposium on Automation in Offshore Oil Field Operation held in Bergen, Norway, June 14-17, 1976 ...' - Foreword. — Index.
ISBN 0-7204-0516-5 : £31.62
Also classified at 623.85'04
(B77-15337)

Vol.4 : Computer applications in the automation of shipyard operation and ship design, II : proceedings of the IFIP-IFAC-SSI-City of Gothenburg Scandinavian joint conference, Gothenburg, Sweden, June 8-11, 1976 / edited by Ake Jacobsson, Folke Borgström, Theodore J. Williams. — 1976. — xiii,447p : ill ; 31cm.
'The second International Conference on Computer Applications in the Automation of Shipyard Operation and Ship Design was held in Gothenburg, Sweden, June 8-11, 1976' - Foreword. — Index.
ISBN 0-7204-0530-0 : £37.50
Also classified at 623.85'04
(B77-04889)

Vol.5 : Ship operation automation, II : proceedings of the 2nd IFAC/IFIP Symposium, Washington, DC, USA, August 30-September 2, 1976 / edited by Marvin Pitkin, John J. Roche, Theodore J. Williams. — 1976. — xxvi,587p : ill, charts, forms, maps, plans ; 31cm.
Bibl. — Index.
ISBN 0-7204-0542-4 : £20.24
Also classified at 623.85'04
(B77-20350)

623.82'009 — Boats & ships, to 1967. *Illustrations. Juvenile literature*
Ships / general editor Boswell Taylor ; ... designer and illustrator Roy M. Schofield. — Leicester : Knight Books, 1977. — [1],32p : of ill, maps, plans, ports ; 21cm. — (Picture teach yourself : project books)
Originally published: as 'Picture reference book of ships'. Leicester, Brockhampton Press, 1969.
ISBN 0-340-21555-0 Pbk : £0.50
(B77-06734)

623.82'01 — Model steam boats & model steamships. Construction. *Manuals*
Model steamer building : a practical handbook on the design and construction of model steamer hulls, deck fittings, and other details / edited by Percival Marshall. — [New ed.] / [revised by V.W. Delves-Broughton]. — Watford : Model and Allied Publications, 1976. — 50p : ill, plans ; 19cm. — (MAP technical publication)
First published as no.12 in the 'Model engineer' series. London : Dawbarn and Ward, 1903.
ISBN 0-85242-478-7 Pbk : £1.50
(B77-13696)

623.82'01'2 — Model four-masted barques. Construction. *Manuals*
Bowness, Edward. The four-masted barque / by Edward Bowness. — Revised ed. — Kings Langley : Model and Allied Publications, 1976. — viii,128p,[4]fold leaves of plates : ill, plans ; 23cm.
Previous ed.: London : P. Marshall, 1955.
ISBN 0-85242-461-2 : £5.00
(B77-07413)

623.82'01'2 — Universities. *Texas. College Station.* **Texas A & M University. Exhibits:** *Model Chinese junks. Collections: Spencer Collection*
Texas A & M University. Junks of Central China : the Spencer Collection of models at Texas A & M University / text by J.E. Spencer ; photographs by Jim Bones Jr ; foreword by Edwin Doran Jr. — College Station ; London (c/o American University Publishers, 70 Gt Russell St., WC1B 3BY) : Texas A & M University Press, 1976. — 104p : ill, map ; 27cm.
Bibl.: p.99. — Index.
ISBN 0-89096-015-1 : £7.50
(B77-15338)

623.82'02 — Boats. Construction. Carpentry
Smith, Hervey Garrett. Boat carpentry : repairs, alterations, construction / [by] Hervey Garrett Smith. — 2nd ed. — New York ; London [etc.] : Van Nostrand Reinhold, [1977]. — vii, 178p : ill ; 22cm.
This ed. originally published: 1965. — Index.
ISBN 0-442-37784-3 : £6.85
ISBN 0-442-27794-6 Pbk : £3.75
(B77-22659)

623.82'03'09 — Sailing ships, to 1900. *Juvenile literature*
Drew, Stephen. Sailing ships / [written by Stephen Drew]. — Glasgow [etc.] : Collins, 1977. — 3-62p : ill(chiefly col), col maps, col port ; 30cm. — (Collins transport series)
Index.
ISBN 0-00-106240-9 : £1.50
(B77-24287)

623.82'07'33 — Ferrocement boats. Fitting out. *Manuals*
Tucker, Robert. Fitting out ferrocement hulls / [by] Robert Tucker. — St Albans [etc.] : Coles, 1977. — vi,187p : ill ; 25cm.
Index.
ISBN 0-229-11512-8 : £11.50
(B77-14778)

623.82'07'34 — Concrete ships. *Conference proceedings*
Concrete afloat : proceedings of the conference on concrete ships and floating structures organized by The Concrete Society in association with the Royal Institution of Naval Architects and held in London on 3 and 4 March, 1977. — London : Telford, 1977. — [4] ,204p : ill ; 24cm.
Bibl.
ISBN 0-7277-0048-0 : £10.00
(B77-30340)

623.82'07'38 — Glass fibre reinforced plastics boats. Construction. *Amateurs' manuals*
Making glassfibre boats. — Revised, expanded ed. — Watford : Model and Allied Publications, 1976. — 60p : ill ; 21cm. — (MAP technical publication)
Previous ed.: Hemel Hempstead : Model and Allied Publications, 1972.
ISBN 0-85242-541-4 Pbk : £1.50
(B77-24994)

623.82'07'4 — Wooden boats. Repair. *Amateurs' manuals*
Lewis, John, *b.1912.* Repair of wooden boats / [by] John Lewis. — Newton Abbot [etc.] : David and Charles, 1977. — 96p : ill, 2 plans, ports ; 26cm.
ISBN 0-7153-7378-1 : £4.95
(B77-20351)

623.82'08 — Small boats. Maintenance & repair. *Amateurs' manuals*
Sleightholme, John Desmond. Fitting out : maintenance and repair of small craft / [by] J.D. Sleightholme. — 3rd ed. — London [etc.] : Coles, 1977. — [5],130p : ill, plan ; 21cm.
Previous ed.: 1972.
ISBN 0-229-11590-x : £4.25
(B77-31253)

623.82'1 — Oared warships, to ca 1850
Anderson, Roger Charles. Oared fighting ships : from Classical times to the coming of steam / by R.C. Anderson. — New ed. — Kings Langley : Model and Allied Publications : Argus Books, 1976. — xiv,102p,[2]leaves of plates,[24]p of plates : ill ; 23cm.
Previous ed.: London : Percival Marshall, 1962. — Bibl.: p.xii-xiv. — Index. — Previous control number B7713697.
ISBN 0-85242-471-x : £3.50
(B77-13697)

623.82'1 — Viking longships
From Viking ship to 'Victory'. — London : H.M.S.O. for the National Maritime Museum, 1977. — [1],49p : ill(chiefly col), map, plan, port ; 15x21cm.
The recto of each page contains text by Roger Finch ; the verso contains a section (translated from the Danish by J.R. McCormack) from 'Traeskibet' by Ole Crumlin-Pedersen. Kobenhavn : D.B.K., 1968. — Bibl.: p.49.
ISBN 0-11-880759-5 Sd : £0.75
Primary classification 623.82'2
(B77-16453)

623.82'2 — Dhows
Howarth, David. Dhows / [by] David Howarth ; photographs by Robin Constable. — London [etc.] : Quartet Books, 1977. — 159p : ill(some col) ; 32cm.
ISBN 0-7043-2148-3 : £8.50
(B77-33274)

623.82'2 — Dhows, to 1976
Hawkins, Clifford W. The dhow : an illustrated history of the dhow and its world / [by] Clifford W. Hawkins. — Lymington : Nautical Publishing Co., 1977. — [2],144p : ill(some col), chart, facsim, map, plans ; 31cm. — (Nautical historical record series)
Bibl.: p.142-143.
ISBN 0-245-52655-2 : £18.50
(B77-24857)

623.82'2 — Great Britain. Royal Navy. Warships. Sailing ships: Victory (Ship)
From Viking ship to 'Victory'. — London : H.M.S.O. for the National Maritime Museum, 1977. — [1],49p : ill(chiefly col), map, plan, port ; 15x21cm.
The recto of each page contains text by Roger Finch ; the verso contains a section (translated from the Danish by J.R. McCormack) from 'Traeskibet' by Ole Crumlin-Pedersen. Kobenhavn : D.B.K., 1968. — Bibl.: p.49.
ISBN 0-11-880759-5 Sd : £0.75
Also classified at 623.82'1
(B77-16453)

623.82'2 — Sailing boats
Fairley, Gordon. The observer's book of small craft / [by] Gordon Fairley. — London [etc.] : F. Warne, 1976. — 192p,[8]p of plates : ill(some col) ; 15cm. — (The observer's pocket series ; [64])
Index.
ISBN 0-7232-1559-6 : £0.90
(B77-02381)

623.82'2 — Sailing boats. *Great Britain, to 1976*
Glasspool, John. Boats of the longshoremen / [by] John Glasspool ; illustrations by Jane Michaelis. — Lymington : Nautical Publishing Co., 1977. — 136p : ill ; 26cm.
ISBN 0-245-53111-4 : £5.50
(B77-26362)

623.82'2 — Sailing cruisers
Nixon, W M. The sailing cruiser / [by] W.M. Nixon ; illustrated by Peter A.G. Milne. — Lymington : Nautical Publishing Co., 1977. — 256p : ill, plans ; 24cm.
Index.
ISBN 0-245-52681-1 : £9.95
(B77-32684)

623.82'2 — Sailing dinghies. Construction. *Amateurs' manuals*
Creagh-Osborne, Richard. Dinghy building / [by] Richard Creagh-Osborne. — London : Coles, 1976. — 240p : ill ; 23cm.
Previous ed.: 1963. — Index.
ISBN 0-229-11574-8 : £5.50
(B77-02382)

623.82'2 — Yachts. *Buyers' guides*
Bristow, Philip. Bristow's book of yachts. — Tonbridge (47 High St., Tonbridge, Kent) : Weald of Kent Publications.
1977. — 1977. — 208p : ill ; 21cm.
Supersedes: 'Bristow's book of sailing cruisers' and 'Bristow's book of motor cruisers'.
ISBN 0-904238-07-5 Pbk : £3.95
ISSN 0309-1252
(B77-30341)

623.82'2 — Yachts. Maintenance & repair. *Manuals*
Goring, Loris. Modern yacht maintenance / [by] Loris Goring. — London : Stanford Maritime, 1977. — [9],148p : ill ; 22cm.
Index.
ISBN 0-540-07268-0 Pbk : £2.25 : CIP rev.
(B77-24288)

623.82'2'0941 — Sailing vessels. *Great Britain, ca 1700-ca 1950*
Finch, Roger. Sailing craft of the British Isles / [by] Roger Finch ; with illustrations by the author. — London [etc.] : Collins, 1976. — 160p : ill(some col), col maps ; 25cm.
Bibl.: p.157-158. — Index.
ISBN 0-00-219710-3 : £4.95
(B77-00806)

623.82'3 — Hydrofoil boats. *Conference proceedings*
International Hovering Craft, Hydrofoil and Advanced Transit Systems Conference, *2nd, Amsterdam, 1976.* Second International Hovering Craft, Hydrofoil and Advanced Transit Systems Conference, 17-20 May 1976 Amsterdam : conference papers : the conference is sponsored and organised by the journal 'Hovering craft and hydrofoil'. — London (51 Welbeck St., W1M 7HE) : Kalerghi Publications [for] 'Hovering craft and hydrofoil', [1977]. — [5],391p : ill, charts, maps, plans ; 30cm.
'... [held at the] RAI Exhibition and Congress Centre, Amsterdam ...' - cover. — Bibl.
ISBN 0-903238-01-2 Pbk : £30.75
Primary classification 629.3
(B77-14791)

623.82'3 — Hydrofoil boats. *Serials*
Jane's surface skimmers : hovercraft and hydrofoils. — London : Jane's Yearbooks.
1976-77 : tenth ed. / compiled and edited by Roy McLeavy. — 1977. — iv,28,424,iii p : ill, plans ; 33cm.
Bibl.: p.361-366. — Index.
ISBN 0-354-00540-5 : £16.50
ISSN 0075-305x
Primary classification 629.3'05
(B77-13100)

623.82'31 — Motorboats
Mudie, Rosemary. Power yachts / [by] Rosemary and Colin Mudie. — London [etc.] : Granada, 1977. — [6],286p : ill, plans ; 29cm.
Index.
ISBN 0-229-98663-3 : £15.00
(B77-24289)

623.82'314 — Motorsailers
Pike, Dag. Motorsailers / [by] Dag Pike. — London : Stanford Maritime, 1976. — 224p : ill, plans ; 24cm.
ISBN 0-540-07143-9 : £4.95
(B77-10404)

623.82'32 — Tugs. *Conference proceedings*
International Tug Convention, *5th, Rotterdam, 1976?.* The Fifth International Tug Convention : organised by Thomas Reed Publications Limited / edited by Kenneth D. Troup. — London : T. Reed, 1977. — xx, 259p : ill, coat of arms, form, maps, plans ; 31cm.
'... held in Rotterdam, Holland' - title page verso.
£25.00
(B77-31254)

623.82'4 — Offshore natural gas & petroleum industries. Safety measures: Standby ships. Surveying. *Great Britain. Manuals*
Great Britain. *Department of Trade.* Assessment of the suitability of stand-by safety vessels attending offshore installations : instructions for the guidance of surveyors / Department of Trade. — Revised ed. — London ([c/o Marine Division, Offshore Safety Section, Room 723, Chancery House, Chancery La., WC2A 1QU]) : [The Department], 1977. — [2],22p : forms, map ; 30cm.
Sd : £1.00
(B77-18216)

623.82'4 — Offshore natural gas & petroleum industries. Support ships. *Conference proceedings*
International Offshore Craft Conference, *2nd, London, 1976.* The Second International Offshore Craft Conference : organised by Thomas Reed Publications Limited / edited by Kenneth D. Troup. — London : T. Reed, 1977. — xv,205p : ill, form, map ; 31cm.
'The complete proceedings of the second conference held in London in September 1976' - title page verso.
£25.00
(B77-16930)

623.82'5 — Warships. Underwater noise
Ross, Donald. Mechanics of underwater noise / [by] Donald Ross. — New York ; Oxford [etc.] : Pergamon, [1977]. — xiv,375p : ill ; 25cm.
Published in the United States: 1976. — Bibl. — Index.
ISBN 0-08-021182-8 : £14.00
ISBN 0-08-021181-x Pbk : £8.00
(B77-11884)

623.82'5'0212 — Warships. *Technical data*
Ireland, Bernard. Warships of the world / [by] Bernard Ireland. — London : Allan.
In 3 vols.
Major classes. — 1976. — 128p,[4]p of plates : ill(some col) ; 23cm.
Index.
ISBN 0-7110-0687-3 : £3.50
(B77-02383)

623.82'5'0212 — Warships. *Technical data. Serials*
Jane's fighting ships. — London : Jane's Yearbooks.
1977-78 / edited by John E. Moore. — 1977. — 158,829p : ill ; 33cm.
Index.
ISBN 0-354-00550-2 : £27.50
(B77-24290)

623.82'5'09 — Warships, to 1974
MacIntyre, Donald, *b.1904.* Man-of-war : a history of the fighting vessel / [by] Donald MacIntyre, Basil W. Bathe. — Revised ed. ; preface by Edward L. Beach. — London : Jupiter Books, 1975. — 280p : ill(some col), facsim, col map, plans(some col), ports ; 26x27cm.
Ill. on lining papers. — Previous ed.: London : Methuen, 1968. — Bibl.: p.270-271. — Index.
ISBN 0-904041-07-7 : £4.50
(B77-04261)

623.82'5'0904 — Warships, 1900-1977
Janitch, Michael. A source book of twentieth-century warships / written and compiled by Michael Janitch. — London : Ward Lock, 1977. — 128p : ill ; 12x18cm.
Index.
ISBN 0-7063-1819-6 : £2.50
(B77-16454)

623.82'5'09044 — Warships, 1939-1945
Ellis, Chris. Famous ships of World War 2, in colour / by Chris Ellis ; illustrated by John W. Wood ... [et al.]. — Poole : Blandford Press, 1976. — [5],210p : ill(chiefly col) ; 20cm. — ([Blandford colour series])
Index.
ISBN 0-7137-0786-0 : £2.95
(B77-03595)

623.82'5'0941 — Great Britain. Royal Navy. Warships. *Identification manuals*
Goss, James. Spot the warships : includes details of the Spithead Jubilee Review / by James Goss. — Havant : K. Mason, 1977. — [1],32p : ill ; 15cm.
ISBN 0-85937-092-5 Sd : £0.25 : CIP rev.
(B77-12506)

623.82'5'0947 — Union of Soviet Socialist Republics. Voenno-morskoĭ flot. Warships, 1939-1945. *Technical data*
Meister, Jürg. Soviet warships of the Second World War / [by] Jürg Meister. — London : Macdonald and Jane's, 1977. — [6],348p : ill ; 26cm.
ISBN 0-356-08402-7 : £7.95
(B77-17573)

623.82'52'0941 — Great Britain. Royal Navy. Battleships, 1911-1945
Raven, Alan. British battleships of World War 2 : the development and technical history of the Royal Navy's battleships and battlecruisers from 1911 to 1946 / by Alan Raven and John Roberts. — London : Arms and Armour Press, 1976. — 436p(16 fold) : ill(some col), plans ; 26cm.
Bibl.: p.431-432. — Index.
ISBN 0-85368-141-4 : £19.95
Also classified at 623.82'53'0941
(B77-06161)

623.82'52'0943 — Germany. Kriegsmarine. Battleships: Tirpitz (Ship), to 1944
Brown, David, *b.1938 (Sept.).* 'Tirpitz', the floating fortress / [text by] David Brown. — London : Arms and Armour Press, 1977. — 160p,[2]leaves of plates : chiefly ill, map, plans, ports ; 26cm.
ISBN 0-85368-341-7 : £6.95 : CIP rev.
(B77-21941)

623.82'53'0941 — Great Britain. Royal Navy. Battle cruisers, 1911-1945
Raven, Alan. British battleships of World War 2 : the development and technical history of the Royal Navy's battleships and battlecruisers from 1911 to 1946 / by Alan Raven and John Roberts. — London : Arms and Armour Press, 1976. — 436p(16 fold) : ill(some col), plans ; 26cm.
Bibl.: p.431-432. — Index.
ISBN 0-85368-141-4 : £19.95
Primary classification 623.82'52'0941
(B77-06161)

623.82'55'0904 — Aircraft carriers, to 1977. *Illustrations*
Watts, Anthony John. A source book of aircraft carriers and their aircraft / written and compiled by Anthony J. Watts. — London : Ward Lock, 1977. — 128p : ill ; 12x18cm.
Index.
ISBN 0-7063-5538-5 : £2.50
(B77-27172)

623.82'57 — Submarines. *Juvenile literature*
Icenhower, Joseph Bryan. Submarines / by Joseph B. Icenhower. — Revised ed. — London [etc.] : F. Watts, 1977. — 78p : ill ; 23cm. — (A first book)
Previous ed.: published as 'The first book of submarines', New York : F. Watts ; London : Bailey and Swinfen, 1957 ; and as 'Submarines', London : F. Watts, 1972. — Index.
ISBN 0-85166-676-0 : £2.25
(B77-33869)

623.82'572'09044 — Allied forces. Submarines, 1939-1945
Watts, Anthony John. Allied submarines / [by] Anthony J. Watts. — London : Macdonald and Jane's, 1977. — [1],64p : ill ; 27cm. — (World War 2 fact files)
ISBN 0-354-01011-5 Pbk : £1.75
(B77-14275)

623.82'572'09044 — Axis forces. Submarines, 1939-1945
Watts, Anthony John. Axis submarines / [by] Anthony J. Watts. — London : Macdonald and Jane's, 1977. — [1],63p : ill ; 27cm. — (World War 2 fact files)
ISBN 0-354-01059-x Pbk : £1.75
(B77-14276)

623.82'58 — Motor torpedo boats, to 1976
Phelan, Keiren. Fast attack craft : the evolution of design and tactics / [by] Keiren Phelan & Martin H. Brice. — London : Macdonald and Jane's, 1977. — 224p : ill, plans, ports ; 28cm.
Bibl.: p.212-216. — Index.
ISBN 0-356-04912-4 : £8.50
(B77-30342)

623.84'8 — Ships. Hulls. Corrosion. Prevention. *Conference proceedings*
Corrosion in marine environment. — Washington, D.C. ; London : Hemisphere ; New York ; London [etc.] : Distributed by Wiley.
International sourcebook 1 : Ship painting and corrosion / edited by Derek H. Deere. — 1977. — xii,259p,11p of plates : ill(some col) ; 29cm.
'... based on the first Interantional [i.e. International] Ship Painting and Corrosion Conference held in London, May 1974' - title page verso. — 'A Halsted Press book'. — Index.
ISBN 0-470-15203-6 : £50.00
(B77-22660)

623.85'01 — Marine piping systems. Valves. *Standards*
British Standards Institution. Specification for general purpose and petroleum industry valves for use in marine pipework systems, summary and application = Spécification de la robinetterie à usage général et pour l'industrie pétrolière pour utilisation dans les canalisations maritimes, resumé et application = Spezifikation für Ventile für allgemeine Zwecke und die Petroleumindustrie zum Einsatz in den Leitungssystemen von Schiffen, Zusammenfassung und Anwendung / British Standards Institution. — London : B.S.I.
Part 2 = Partie 2 = Teil 2 : Steel gate valves = Robinets-vannes en acier = Absperrschieber aus Stahl. — 1976. — 8,[1]p ; 30cm. — (British Standard marine series = Série maritime = Marine Serie) (BA MA 65 : Part 2 : 1976)
Pierced for binder.
ISBN 0-580-09089-2 Sd : £2.70
(B77-12507)

British Standards Institution. Specification for general purpose and petroleum industry valves for use in marine pipework systems, summary and application = Spécification de la robinetterie à usage général et pour l'industrie pétrolière destinée aux canalisations maritimes, exposé et application = Spezifikation für Ventile für allgemeine Anwendung und für die Petroleumindustrie zum Einsatz in Seerohrleitungssystemen, Zusammenfassung und Anwendung / British Standards Institution. — London : B.S.I.
Part 3 = Partie 3 = Teil 3 : Cast iron parallel slide valves = Robinets à sièges parallèl enfonte = Absperrschieber aus Gusseisen. — 1976. — 6,[1]p ; 30cm. — (British Standard marine series = Série maritime = Marinenserie) (BS MA 65 : Part 3 : 1976)
Pierced for binder.
ISBN 0-580-09048-5 Sd : £1.60
(B77-12509)

British Standards Institution. Specification for general purpose and petroleum industry valves for use in marine pipework systems, summary and application = Spécification de la robinetterie à usage général et pour l'industrie pétrolière destinée aux canalisations maritimes, exposé et application = Spezifikation für Ventile für allegemeine Anwendung und für die Petroleumindustrie zum Einsatz in Seerohrleitungssystemen, Zusammenfassung und Anwendung / British Standards Institution. — London : B.S.I.
Part 4 = Partie 4 = Teil 4 : Steel parallel slide valves = Robinets à sièges parallèles en acier = Absperrchieber aus Stahl. — 1976. — 10,[1] p : ill ; 30cm. — (British Standard marine series = Série maritime = Marinenserie) (BS MA 65 : Part 4 : 1976)
Pierced for binder.
ISBN 0-580-09357-3 Sd : £2.20
(B77-12508)

British Standards Institution. Specification for general purpose and petroleum industry valves for use in marine pipework systems, summary and application = Spécification des soupapes à usage général pour l'industrie pétrolière destinées aux canalisations maritimes, exposé et application = Spezifikation für Ventile für allgemeine Verwendung und für die Erdölindustrie zum Einsatz in Seerohrleitungssystemen, Zusammenfassung und Anwendung / British Standards Institution. — London : B.S.I. — (British Standard marine series = Série maritime = Schiffbauserie)
Part 7 = Partie 7 = Teil 7 : Cast iron check valves = Clapets de non retour en fonde = Rückflussverhinderer aus Gusseisen. — 1976. — 8p : 2 ill ; 30cm. — (BS MA 65 : Part 7 : 1976)
Pierced for binder.
ISBN 0-580-09017-5 Sd : £1.50
(B77-03074)

623.85'04 — Ships. Computer systems. *Conference proceedings*

Computer applications in shipping and shipbuilding. — Amsterdam [etc.] ; Oxford : North-Holland Publishing Co.
Vol.3 : Automation in offshore oil field operation : proceedings of the IFAC/IFIP Symposium, Bergen, Norway, June 14-17, 1976 / edited by Frode L. Galtung, Kare Rosandhaug, Theodore J. Williams. — 1976. — ix,439p : ill, maps ; 31cm.
'The Proceedings of the IFAC/IFIP Symposium on Automation in Offshore Oil Field Operation held in Bergen, Norway, June 14-17, 1976 ...' - Foreword. — Index.
ISBN 0-7204-0516-5 : £31.62
Primary classification 623.82'0028'54
(B77-15337)

Vol.4 : Computer applications in the automation of shipyard operation and ship design, II : proceedings of the IFIP-IFAC-SSI-City of Gothenburg Scandinavian joint conference, Gothenburg, Sweden, June 8-11, 1976 / edited by Ake Jacobsson, Folke Borgström, Theodore J. Williams. — 1976. — xiii,447p : ill ; 31cm.
'The second International Conference on Computer Applications in the Automation of Shipyard Operation and Ship Design was held in Gothenburg, Sweden, June 8-11, 1976' - Foreword. — Index.
ISBN 0-7204-0530-0 : £37.50
Primary classification 623.82'0028'54
(B77-04889)

Vol.5 : Ship operation automation, II : proceedings of the 2nd IFAC/IFIP Symposium, Washington, DC, USA, August 30-September 2, 1976 / edited by Marvin Pitkin, John J. Roche, Theodore J. Williams. — 1976. — xxvi,587p : ill, charts, forms, maps, plans ; 31cm.
Bibl. — Index.
ISBN 0-7204-0542-4 : £20.24
Primary classification 623.82'0028'54
(B77-20350)

623.85'04 — Ships. Electronic equipment. *Conference proceedings*

Marine Electronics *(Conference), University of Southampton, 1976.* Marine electronics, University of Southampton, 5-8 July 1976 : a symposium organised by the Society of Electronic and Radio Technicians in association with the Institution of Electrical and Electronics Technician Engineers. — [Stevenage] ([P.O. Box 8, Southgate House, Stevenage, Herts.]) : [The Institution], [1976?]. — [3],161p : ill, maps ; 30cm.
Cover title.
Pbk : Unpriced
(B77-27173)

623.85'6 — Ships. Lights & signalling equipment. Surveying. *Great Britain. Manuals*

Great Britain. *Department of Trade.* Survey of lights and signalling equipment : instructions for the guidance of surveyors / Department of Trade. — London : H.M.S.O., 1977. — [2],iv, 40p : ill ; 30cm.
Index.
ISBN 0-11-512030-0 Sd : £3.25
(B77-18217)

623.86'05 — Yachting equipment. *Buyers' guides. Periodicals*

Geartest. — Havant : K. Mason.
No.1- ; [June] 1976-. — 1976-. — ill, facsim, port ; 30cm.
Four issues a year. — 36p. in 1st issue.
Sd : £8.00 yearly
ISSN 0308-6437
(B77-06735)

623.86'2 — Sailing boats. Gear & rigging. Making, maintenance & repair. *Amateurs' manuals*

Rosenow, Frank. The ditty bag book / [by] Frank Rosenow ; illustrated by the author. — St Albans [etc.] : Coles, 1976. — 127,[1]p : ill ; 23cm.
Also published: Boston, Mass. : Sail Books, 1976. — Index.
ISBN 0-229-11581-0 : £3.95
(B77-03596)

623.86'5 — Ships. Life saving equipment. Surveying. *Manuals*

Great Britain. *Department of Trade.* Survey of life-saving appliances : instructions for the guidance of surveyors / Department of Trade. — Revised ed. — London : H.M.S.O., 1976. — [2],xix,244p : ill, forms ; 30cm.
'Publication of Instructions to surveyors on life-saving appliances in a loose leaf binder (uniform with other volumes of Instructions to surveyors) has been deferred until any amendments arising from the 1974 SOLAS Convention can be incorporated. This revised edition of the current Instructions is published as an interim measure'. — Index.
ISBN 0-11-511739-3 Pbk : £9.00
(B77-00272)

623.87'23'4 — Motorboats. Outboard motors. *Manuals*

Warren, Nigel. Outboard motor handbook / [by] Nigel Warren. — London : Stanford Maritime, 1977. — vii,159p : ill ; 23cm.
ISBN 0-540-07152-8 : £3.50
(B77-24291)

623.87'3 — Ships. Pumping systems

Sterling, Leslie. Pumping systems and their ancillary equipment / by L. Sterling. — London (76 Mark La., EC3R 7JN) : Marine Media Management for the Institute of Marine Engineers, 1976. — [4],74p : ill ; 21cm. — (Marine engineering design and installation series)
ISBN 0-900976-43-8 Sd : £2.85
(B77-07414)

623.88 — Seamanship

Knight, Austin Melvin. Knight's modern seamanship. — 16th ed. / revised by John V. Noel, Jr, assisted by Frank E. Bassett. — New York ; London [etc.] : Van Nostrand Reinhold, 1977. — xiii,676p : ill(some col), charts, maps ; 24cm.
Previous ed.: published as 'Modern seamanship'. 1972. — Index.
ISBN 0-442-26049-0 : £12.75
(B77-16931)

623.88'2'2 — Sailing boats. Sailing. Seamanship. *Manuals*

Lewis, Geoff. The small-boat skipper's handbook / [by] Geoff Lewis ; illustrations by Geoff Page. — London [etc.] : Hollis and Carter, 1977. — 310p : ill(some col), charts, forms, plans ; 21cm.
Bibl.: p.296-300. — Index.
ISBN 0-370-10319-x : £3.95
(B77-19450)

623.88'2'2 — Sailing dinghies. Sailing. Seamanship. *Manuals*

Colgate, Stephen. Colgate's basic sailing theory / illustrations John Tubb Associates. — New York ; London [etc.] : Van Nostrand Reinhold, [1977]. — [4],123p : ill, plans ; 23cm.
Originally published: 1973.
ISBN 0-442-21627-0 Pbk : £2.95
(B77-07950)

623.88'2'2 — Sailing ships. Sailing. Seamanship. *Manuals*

Rouse, Alan. Sail the tall ships / by Alan Rouse. — London [etc.] ([2 Westferry Rd, E.14]) : Seafarers Books, 1976. — xv,141p : ill ; 23cm.
£3.95
(B77-16932)

623.88'2'2 — Seamanship. *For yachting*

Russell, John, *b.1920.* Yachtmaster offshore : the art of seamanship / [by] John Russell ; preface by James Myatt ; with seven drawings by Seachase and diagrams by the author. — Newton Abbot [etc.] : David and Charles [for the] Royal Yachting Association, 1977. — 136p : ill ; 23cm.
ISBN 0-7153-7465-6 : £3.95
(B77-31255)

623.88'2'4 — Seamanship. *For merchant shipping. Manuals*

Nicholls, Alfred Edward. Nicholls's seamanship and nautical knowledge. — 23rd ed. / by Charles H. Brown ; revised by A.N. Cockcroft. — Glasgow : Brown and Ferguson, 1977. — [11],443p,[5]leaves of plates,[6]p of plates : ill(some col), charts ; 22cm.
Previous ed.: published as 'Seamanship and nautical knowledge' / by Charles H. Brown ; revised by H.H. Brown. 1966. — Index.
ISBN 0-85174-269-6 : £8.00
(B77-24995)

623.88'2'4023 — Merchant shipping. Deck officers. Professional competence. Certification. *Great Britain*

Great Britain. *Department of Trade.* Certificates of competency in the Merchant Navy, Deck Officer requirements / Department of Trade. — London : H.M.S.O., 1977. — iv,79p : form ; 21cm.
Index.
ISBN 0-11-512066-1 Pbk : £1.50
(B77-26363)

623.88'82 — Knots. *Juvenile literature*

Hinton, Ronald A L. Knots / by Ronald A.L. Hinton ; illustrations by Eric Winter and Frank Humphris ; photographs by John Moyes and Tim Clark. — Loughborough : Ladybird Books, 1977. — 52p : col ill ; 18cm. — (Learnabout)
Text, col. ill. on lining papers. — Index.
ISBN 0-7214-0467-7 : £0.24
(B77-24996)

623.88'82 — Knots. *Manuals*

Burgess, J Tom. Knots, ties and splices : a handbook for seafarers, travellers and all who use cordage, with special notes on wire and wire splicing, angler's knots, etc. / originally written by J. Tom Burgess ; revised and rewritten by Commander J. Irving. — Revised ed. / further revised by Crab Searl. — London [etc.] : Routledge and Kegan Paul, 1977. — vii, 129p : ill ; 19cm.
Previous ed.: i.e. revised ed. / revised and rewritten by J. Irving. 1934. — Index.
ISBN 0-7100-8671-7 Pbk : £1.25 : CIP rev.
Also classified at 623.88'82
(B77-21942)

Fry, Eric Cyril. The Shell book of knots and ropework / [by] Eric C. Fry ; photographs by Peter Wilson. — Newton Abbot [etc.] : David and Charles, 1977. — [96]p : ill ; 26cm.
ISBN 0-7153-7350-1 : £3.50
(B77-19451)

623.88'82 — Ropes. Splicing. *Manuals*

Blandford, Percy W. Rope splicing / by Percy W. Blandford. — 3rd ed. — Glasgow : Brown and Ferguson, 1976. — 3-105p : ill ; 18cm.
Previous ed.: 1969. — Index.
ISBN 0-85174-268-8 Pbk : £2.85
(B77-13698)

Burgess, J Tom. Knots, ties and splices : a handbook for seafarers, travellers and all who use cordage, with special notes on wire and wire splicing, angler's knots, etc. / originally written by J. Tom Burgess ; revised and rewritten by Commander J. Irving. — Revised ed. / further revised by Crab Searl. — London [etc.] : Routledge and Kegan Paul, 1977. — vii, 129p : ill ; 19cm.
Previous ed.: i.e. revised ed. / revised and rewritten by J. Irving. 1934. — Index.
ISBN 0-7100-8671-7 Pbk : £1.25 : CIP rev.
Primary classification 623.88'82
(B77-21942)

623.88'87'09162 — Rescues. *Oceans, 1835-1966*

Garrett, Richard. Famous rescues at sea / [by] Richard Garrett. — London : Barker, 1977. — viii,171p ; 23cm.
ISBN 0-213-16607-0 : £3.95
(B77-08434)

623.88'87'0942 — Rescues. *England. Coastal waters, 1796-1975*
Great sea rescues. — Tavistock : Heritage Publications ; London : New English Library.
Vol.2 / [by] E.W. Middleton. — 1976. — 143p ; 18cm.
Vol.1 published: as 'Great sea rescues of the SW / by R.L Elliott ; plus, The story of the Plymouth lifeboats / by J.P. Morris'. 1974.
ISBN 0-903975-31-9 Pbk : £0.50
(B77-01565)

623.89'02'46392 — Seamanship. Navigation. *Manuals. For fishing*
Howell, F S. Navigation primer for fishermen / [by] F.S. Howell. — Farnham : Fishing News, 1977. — xv,180p : ill(some col), facsims, maps ; 23cm.
Bibl.: p.153. — Index.
ISBN 0-85238-081-x Pbk : £5.75
(B77-25703)

623.89'02'47971 — Seamanship. Navigation. *For yachting*
Dixon, Conrad. Start to navigate / [by] Conrad Dixon. — St Albans : Coles, 1977. — 125p : ill, charts ; 21cm.
With answers. — Bibl.: p.121. — Index.
ISBN 0-229-11573-x : £2.95
(B77-31256)

623.89'05 — Seamanship. Navigation. *Serials*
Great Britain. *Hydrographic Department.* Annual summary of Admiralty notices to mariners / Hydrographic Department. — [Taunton] : [Hydrographer of the Navy].
1977, in force on 1st January. — [1977]. — [6], 167p,[11]leaves of plates(7 fold),[4]p of plates : ill(chiefly col), col maps ; 25cm.
ISBN 0-7077-0113-9 Sd : Unpriced
(B77-13699)

623.89'0941 — Great Britain. Royal Navy. Navigation. Techniques, 1900-1976
Schofield, Brian Betham. Navigation and direction : the story of HMS 'Dryad' / by B.B. Schofield. — Havant : K. Mason, 1977. — 199p : ill, ports ; 22cm.
Index.
ISBN 0-85937-087-9 : £5.95 : CIP rev.
(B77-20352)

623.89'22 — Yachts. Pilotage. *Manuals*
Howard-Williams, Jeremy. Practical pilotage for yachtsmen / [by] Jeremy Howard-Williams. — London : Coles, 1977. — [4],60p : ill(some col), charts, forms, maps ; 22cm.
With answers. — Index.
ISBN 0-229-11580-2 Sp : £2.50
(B77-24292)

623.89'29 — Coastal waters. Navigation. *Manuals*
Budlong, John Perry. Shoreline and sextant : practical coastal navigation / [by] John P. Budlong. — New York ; London [etc.] : Van Nostrand Reinhold, 1977. — vi,214p,fold plate : ill(some col), charts(1 col), facsim, form ; 26cm.
With answers. — Bibl. — Index.
ISBN 0-442-21142-2 : £9.60
(B77-25704)

623.89'29 — Seamanship. Navigation. *Coastal waters. For yachting*
Watkins, Gordon Geoffrey. Coastwise navigation : notes for yachtsmen / [by] G.G. Watkins. — 3rd ed. — London : Stanford Maritime, 1977. — [4],124p : ill, charts, facsims, maps ; 22cm.
Previous ed.: 1974. — Index.
ISBN 0-540-07266-4 Pbk : £1.95
(B77-23497)

623.89'29 — Seamanship. Navigation. *Coastal waters. Manuals*
Duxbury, Ken. Basic coastal navigation / by Ken Duxbury ; with illustrations by the author. — Wakefield : EP Publishing, 1977. — 48,[2]p : ill(some col), charts, maps ; 14x21cm. — (Know the game)
'Produced in collaboration with the Royal Yachting Association'.
ISBN 0-7158-0538-x Sd : £0.50
(B77-31257)

623.89'29'077 — Seamanship. Navigation. *Coastal waters. Programmed texts*
Smith, Gerry. Coastal navigation : a programmed learning course / [by] Gerry Smith. — London : Elek, 1977. — vii,182p : ill, charts, facsims, maps ; 25cm.
With answers. — Bibl.: p.181. — Index.
ISBN 0-236-40112-2 Sp : £4.95
(B77-31258)

623.89'29'1632 — Arctic Ocean. Coastal waters. *Pilots' guides*
Great Britain. *Hydrographic Department.* Arctic pilot / [Hydrographic Department]. — [Taunton] : Hydrographer of the Navy.
Vol.3 : Davis Strait and Baffin Bay with west and north-west coasts of Greenland, the north coast of Canada including Hudson Bay and the Arctic Archipelago. — 6th ed. — 1976. — xvi, 552p,[30]p of plates,leaf of plate : ill(some col), charts(some col) ; 31cm. — (NP12)
Previous ed.: London : Admiralty (Hydrographic Department), 1959. — Index.
ISBN 0-7077-0110-4 : £6.00
(B77-13700)

623.89'29'16334 — Baltic Sea area. *Pilots' guides*
Great Britain. *Hydrographic Department.* Baltic pilot / [Hydrographic Department]. — [Taunton] : Hydrographer of the Navy.
Vol.3 : Gulf of Finland, Gulf of Bothnia and Aland Islands. — 6th ed. / [prepared by H.C.J. Shand and A.V. Clark]. — 1976. — xviii,357p, [24]p of plates : ill(some col), charts(some col) ; 31cm. — (NP20)
Previous ed.: 1965. — Bibl.: p.iii. — Index.
Unpriced
(B77-27914)

623.89'29'16336 — Harbours. *Western English Channel. Pilots' guides. For yachting*
Coles, Kaines Adlard. Channel harbours and anchorages / [by] K. Adlard Coles. — 5th ed. / with assistance of A.N. Black and the Royal Cruising Club. — Lymington : Nautical Publishing Co., 1977. — 199p : ill, charts, maps, plans ; 26cm.
Charts, map, text on lining papers. — Previous ed.: 1974.
ISBN 0-245-52064-3 : £7.50
(B77-24293)

623.89'29'1638 — Mediterranean Sea. Coastal waters. *Pilots' guides*
Great Britain. *Hydrographic Department.* Mediterranean pilot / [Hydrographic Department]. — [Taunton] : Hydrographer of the Navy.
Vol.5 : The coasts of Libya, Egypt, Syria, Lebanon and Israel ; the southern coast of Turkey and the Island of Cyprus. — 6th ed. — 1976. — xvii,171p,[18]p of plates : ill, charts(incl 2 col), maps ; 31cm. — (N.P.49)
Previous ed.: 1961. — Index.
ISBN 0-7077-0109-0 : £6.00
(B77-09751)

623.89'29'16472 — South China Sea. *Pilots' guides*
Great Britain. *Hydrographic Department.* China sea pilot / [Hydrographic Department]. — [Taunton] : Hydrographer of the Navy.
Vol. 2 : The western and north-western coasts of Borneo, the Philippine Islands from Balabac Island to Cape Bojeador in Luzon, and the outlying islands and dangers in the southern and eastern parts of the China Sea. — 4th ed. — 1975. — xii,195,[i.e.197]p,[20]p of plates,leaf of plate : ill(some col), charts(some col) ; 31cm. — (N.P. 31)
Previous ed.: 1961. — Index.
ISBN 0-7077-0107-4 : £6.30
(B77-09069)

623.89'29'422 — Harbours. *Southern England. Pilots' guides. For sailing*
Coles, Kaines Adlard. The Shell pilot to the South Coast harbours / [by] K. Adlard Coles ; with plans by Alan H. Irving. — 5th, completely new and revised ed. — London : Faber, 1977. — 3-192p,[39]p of plates : ill, charts(chiefly col) ; 16x22cm. — (A Shell guide)
Text, ill., map on lining papers. — Previous ed.: i.e. Interim new ed., 1973.
ISBN 0-571-04937-0 : £6.95 : CIP rev.
(B77-07415)

623.89'29'4234 — Channel Islands. Coastal waters. *Pilots' guides. For yachting*
Robson, John Malcolm. Channel Islands pilot / [by] Malcolm Robson. — Lymington : Nautical Publishing Co., 1976. — 173p : ill, charts ; 26cm.
Index.
ISBN 0-245-52870-9 : £7.50
(B77-01591)

623.89'29'46 — Northern Spain. Coastal waters. Navigation. *For yachting*
Brandon, Robin. South Biscay pilot : the Gironde estuary to La Coruña / [by] Robin Brandon. — 2nd ed. — London : Coles, 1977. — xii,388p : ill, charts, map ; 26cm.
Previous ed.: 1971. — Bibl.: p.33-34. — Index.
ISBN 0-229-11572-1 : £17.50
(B77-11885)

623.89'29'481 — Norway. Coastal waters. *Pilots' guides*
Great Britain. *Hydrographic Department.* Norway pilot / [Hydrographic Department]. — [Taunton] : Hydrographer of the Navy.
Vol.1 : South coast of Norway eastward from Lindesnes, and the west coast of Sweden southward to Marstrardsfjorden. — 9th ed. — 1975. — xv,245p,[4] leaves of plates,[6]p of plates : ill(some col), charts(1 col) ; 31cm. — (NP56)
Previous ed.: London : Hydrographic Department, 1960. — Index.
ISBN 0-7077-0100-7 : £6.00
(B77-00273)

623.89'29'598 — Indonesia. Coastal waters. *Pilots' guides*
Great Britain. *Hydrographic Department.* Indonesia pilot / [Hydrographic Department]. — [Taunton] : Hydrographer of the Navy.
Vol.1 : The western end of Jawa, the southern and eastern coasts of Sumatera, Sunda Strait, Selat Bangka, Selat Gelasa, Karimata Strait, the southern and western coasts of Borneo from Tanjung Puting to Pulau Pontijanak, Kepulauan Badas and Tambelan, Kepulauan Riau and Lingga, with the various routes leading to Singapore and the China Sea. — 1975. — xiii,198[i.e. 202]p,[4]leaves of plates,[8]p of plates : ill(some col), charts(some col) ; 31cm. — (N.P. 36)
Index.
ISBN 0-7077-0108-2 : £6.30
(B77-09070)

Vol.2 : South coast of Jawa, north coast of Jawa east of Tanjung Awarawar, east coast of Jawa, Nasa Tegngara, south coast of Kalinantan east of Tanjung Puting, east coast of Kalinantan south of the parallel of 4°10'N, Sulawesi and the west part of Kepulauan Sula. — 1976. — xiii,407,[1]p,[16]p of plates,[3]leaves of plates : ill(some col), charts, col maps ; 31cm. — (N.P.34)
Index.
ISBN 0-7077-0114-7 : £6.00
(B77-13087)

623.89'29'711 — British Columbia. Coastal waters. *Pilots' guides*
Great Britain. *Hydrographic Department.* British Columbia pilot / [Hydrographic Department]. — 6th ed. — [Taunton] : Hydrographer of the Navy.
Vol.2 : The coast of British Columbia from Cape Caution to Portland Inlet with Queen Charlotte Islands and from Sitklan Island to Cape Fox, Alaska. — 1976. — viii,180,[1]p,[2] leaves of plates,[14]p of plates : ill(some col), charts(1 col) ; 31cm. — (NP 26)
Previous ed.: 1960. — Index.
Unpriced
(B77-20353)

623.89'29'72 — Western Central America & western Mexico. Coastal waters. *Pilots' guides*
Great Britain. *Hydrographic Department.* Pacific coasts of Central America and United States pilot : Pacific coasts of Panama (west of Punta Mariato), Costa Rica including Isla del Coco, Nicaragua, Honduras, El Salvador, Guatemala, Mexico and United States of America ; off-lying islands between latitudes 4°N and 48°25'N / [Hydrographic Department]. — 8th ed. / [prepared by G.A. French]. — [Taunton] : Hydrographer of the Navy, 1975. — xiii,341p, [20]p of plates,[2] leaves of plates : ill(some col), charts(some col) ; 31cm. — (NP8)
Previous ed.: published as 'West coasts of Central America and United States pilot'. London : Admiralty, Hydrographic Department, 1961. — Bibl.: p.iii. — Index.
ISBN 0-7077-0104-x : £6.00
Primary classification 623.89'29'79
(B77-05485)

623.89'29'79 — South-western United States. Coastal waters. *Pilots' guides*
Great Britain. *Hydrographic Department.* Pacific coasts of Central America and United States pilot : Pacific coasts of Panama (west of Punta Mariato), Costa Rica including Isla del Coco, Nicaragua, Honduras, El Salvador, Guatemala, Mexico and United States of America ; off-lying islands between latitudes 4°N and 48°25'N / [Hydrographic Department]. — 8th ed. / [prepared by G.A. French]. — [Taunton] : Hydrographer of the Navy, 1975. — xiii,341p, [20]p of plates,[2] leaves of plates : ill(some col), charts(some col) ; 31cm. — (NP8)
Previous ed.: published as 'West coasts of Central America and United States pilot'. London : Admiralty, Hydrographic Department, 1961. — Bibl.: p.iii. — Index.
ISBN 0-7077-0104-x : £6.00
Also classified at 623.89'29'72
(B77-05485)

623.89'32 — Shipping. Navigational aids: Radio signals. *Lists*
Admiralty list of radio signals / [Hydrographic Department]. — Taunton : Hydrographer of the Navy.
1977. Vol.2 : Radio direction-finding stations, radiobeacons, radar beacons. — 1977. — 302 leaves ; 21cm.
Bibl.: leaf 10. — Index.
Pbk : £4.10
(B77-16455)

623.89'33 — Small boats. Radar equipment. Use
French, John, *b.1936.* Small craft radar / [by] John French. — London : Stanford Maritime, 1977. — 207p : ill, maps ; 23cm.
Bibl.: p.204. — Index.
ISBN 0-540-07150-1 : £4.50
(B77-13701)

623.89'4 — Seamanship. Signalling. *Manuals*
Russell, Percy John. Sea signalling simplified : a manual of instruction for the new International Code of Signals / [by] P.J. Russell. — 5th ed. — London : Coles, 1976. — [4],108p : ill(some col) ; 20cm.
Col. ill. on lining papers. — Previous ed.: St Albans : Coles, 1976. — Index. — Previous control number ISBN 0-229-11554-3.
£2.95
ISBN 0-229-11554-3
(B77-05486)

623.89'4 — Shipping. Navigational aids: Weather bulletins. *Great Britain*
Meteorological Office. Meteorological Office services : weather bulletins and gale warnings for shipping including fishing vessels. — Bracknell (Eastern Rd, Bracknell, Berks. RG12 2UR) : Meteorological Office, 1976. — 12p,[2] fold p of plates : maps ; 21cm. — (Met. O. leaflet ; no.3)
Sd : Unpriced
(B77-05487)

623.89'4 — Shipping. Signals. *Standards*
Moore, Dennis Alan. International light, shape and sound signals / by D.A. Moore. — London : Stanford Maritime, 1976. — 143p : ill(chiefly col) ; 26cm.
With answers to self-examination questions.
ISBN 0-540-07271-0 : £3.00
(B77-18218)

623.89'44 — Shipping. Navigational aids: Buoyage systems: IALA Maritime Buoyage System 'A'. *Manuals*
International Association of Lighthouse Authorities. IALA maritime buoyage system 'A' : combined cardinal and lateral system (red to port). — Taunton : Hydrographer of the Navy, 1976. — i,10p,[6]p of plates : ill(chiefly col), col charts ; 30cm. — (NP735)
ISBN 0-7077-0101-5 Sd : £0.60
(B77-03075)

623.89'45 — Shipping. Navigational aids: Lights. *Lists*
Admiralty list of lights and fog signals / [Hydrographic Department]. — [Taunton] : [Hydrographer of the Navy].
Vol.A 1977 : British Isles and north coast of France from Dunkerque to entrance to Goulet de Brest including North Sea oil & gas production installations : corrected to ANM weekly edition no. 1/77 dated 15th January 1977. — 1977. — 462p : ill ; 25cm. — (NP 74)
Index.
ISBN 0-7077-0111-2 Pbk : £3.00
(B77-11264)

Admiralty list of lights and fog signals / [Hydrographic Department]. — [Taunton] : Hydrographer of the Navy.
Vol.C 1977 : Baltic Sea, with Kattegat, Belts and Sound corrected to ... 28th May 1977. — 1977. — 771p : ill ; 25cm. — (NP76)
Index.
Pbk : £5.25
(B77-21943)

Vol.D 1977 : Eastern side of Atlantic Ocean, from Goulet de Brest southward, including off-lying islands : corrected to 27th August 1977. — 1977. — 276p : ill, map(on back cover) ; 25cm. — (NP 77)
Index.
Pbk : £1.85
(B77-33275)

Admiralty list of lights and fog signals / [Hydrographic Department]. — Taunton : [Hydrographer of the Navy].
Vol.E 1977 : Mediterranean, Black and Red Seas : corrected to ANM weekly edition no.26-77 dated 9th July 1977. — 1977. — 596p : ill, map(on back cover) ; 25cm. — (NP78)
Index.
Pbk : £4.50
(B77-28683)

Admiralty list of lights and fog signals / [Hydrographic Department]. — [Taunton] : Hydrographer of the Navy.
Vol.K 1976 : Indian and Pacific Oceans south of the Equator : corrected to 23rd October 1976. — 1976. — [2],495p : ill ; 25cm. — (NP83)
Notebook format. — Index.
Pbk : £3.45
(B77-03076)

624 — CIVIL ENGINEERING

624 — Civil engineering. *Manuals*
Standard handbook for civil engineers / Frederick S. Merritt, editor. — 2nd ed. — New York [etc.] ; London : McGraw-Hill, 1976. — 1335p in various pagings : ill, maps, plans ; 24cm.
Previous ed.: 1968. — Bibl. — Index.
ISBN 0-07-041510-2 : £29.95
(B77-26364)

624 — Civil engineering. Measurement
Seeley, Ivor Hugh. Civil engineering quantities / [by] Ivor H. Seeley. — 3rd ed. — London [etc.] : Macmillan, 1977. — xii,242p : ill, forms, plans ; 24cm.
Previous ed.: 1971. — Index.
ISBN 0-333-22775-1 : £5.95
(B77-31951)

624 — Civil engineering. Measurement. Standards: Institution of Civil Engineers. Civil engineering standard method of measurement. Use. *Manuals*
Barnes, Martin. Measurement in contract control : a guide to the financial control of contracts using the Civil Engineering Standard Method of Measurement / [by] Martin Barnes. — London : Institution of Civil Engineers, 1977. — [8],296p : ill, forms ; 22cm.
Index.
ISBN 0-7277-0040-5 : £7.00
(B77-29500)

624 — Construction industries. Information systems
Paterson, John. Information methods for design and construction / [by] John Paterson ; illustrations by Pamela Paterson. — London [etc.] : Wiley, 1977. — viii,200p : ill ; 27cm.
'A Wiley-Interscience publication'. — Text on lining papers. — Bibl.: p.191-192. — Index.
ISBN 0-471-99449-9 : £7.95
(B77-24294)

624 — Construction industries. Overseas work. Information sources. *Great Britain. Lists*
A guide to government information and advice for construction exporters. — [London] ([2 Marsham St., SW1P 3EB]) : Department of the Environment, [1976]. — [1],23p ; 21cm.
'... prepared at the instigation of the Working Group on Exports of the National Consultative Council of the Building and Civil Engineering Industries ...' - Introduction.
ISBN 0-7184-0070-4 Sd : Unpriced
(B77-02384)

624 — Construction. Standard costs. *United States. Lists. Serials*
Heavy construction cost file : unit prices. — New York ; London [etc.] : Van Nostrand Reinhold.

1977 / [compiled by] Coert Engelsman. — 1977. — vi,182p ; 28cm.
'A Construction Publishing Company Book'. — Index.
ISBN 0-442-12188-1 Pbk : £16.20
(B77-32686)

624 — Pneumatic structures
Herzog, Thomas. Pneumatic structures : a handbook for the architect and engineer / [by] Thomas Herzog ; with contributions by Gernot Minke and Hans Eggers ; [translated from the German by Sheila Bacon]. — St Albans : Crosby Lockwood Staples, 1977. — 192p : ill, facsims, plans ; 26cm.
Originally published: in German. Stuttgart : Verlag Gerd Hatje, 1976. — Bibl.: p.186-189.
ISBN 0-258-97049-9 : £15.00
(B77-07951)

624'.01'84 — Civil engineering. Environmental aspects. Mathematical models. *Conference proceedings*
Mathematical models for environmental problems : proceedings of the international conference held at the University of Southampton, England, September 8-12, 1975 / edited by C.A. Brebbia. — London (8 John St., WC1N 2HY) : Pentech Press Ltd, 1976. — [8], 537p : ill, maps ; 24cm.
Bibl.
ISBN 0-7273-1301-0 : £12.50
(B77-00807)

624'.021'2 — Civil engineering. Specifications. Preparation. *Manuals*
Seeley, Ivor Hugh. Civil engineering specification / [by] Ivor H. Seeley. — 2nd ed. — London [etc.] : Macmillan, 1976. — viii, 247p ; 24cm.
Previous ed.: 1968. — Index.
ISBN 0-333-04227-1 : £4.95
ISBN 0-333-19870-0 Printed case : £5.95
(B77-07416)

624'.021'2 — Civil engineering. Specifications. Writing. *United States*
Ayers, Chesley. Specifications : for architecture, engineering and construction / [by] Chesley Ayers. — New York ; London [etc.] : McGraw-Hill, [1976]. — xi,430p : forms ; 25cm.
Published in the United States: 1975. — Index. — Includes sample specifications in the appendix.
ISBN 0-07-002638-6 : £12.40
(B77-07417)

624'.06'241 — Civil engineering. Organisations. *Great Britain. Institution of Civil Engineers. Yearbooks*
Institution of Civil Engineers. Yearbook / the Institution of Civil Engineers. — London (Great George St., SW1P 3AA) : [Telford for] the Institution.
1977. — 1977. — [4],xxxii,666p : ill ; 25cm.
ISBN 0-7277-0037-5 Pbk : £12.50
ISSN 0308-4159
(B77-10832)

624'.07'1141 — Civil engineers. Professional education. *Conference proceedings*
Civil engineering education and training 1976 : proceedings of a conference organized by the Institution of Civil Engineers and held in Swansea on 23 and 24 September, 1976 / [production editor Thelma Darwent]. — London : Telford for the Institution, 1977. — [4],186p : ill, form ; 22cm.
ISBN 0-7277-0042-1 Pbk : £4.00
(B77-27174)

624'.09 — Civil engineering, to ca 1970
Pannell, John Percival Masterman. Man the builder : an illustrated history of engineering / [by] J.P.M. Pannell. — London : Thames and Hudson, 1977. — 256p : ill, facsims, maps, ports ; 21cm.
Originally published: as 'An illustrated history of civil engineering'. 1964. — Bibl.: p.251-252. — Index.
ISBN 0-500-01180-x : £4.95
(B77-14277)

624'.092'4 — Civil engineering. Fairbairn, Sir William, bart. *Biographies*
Hayward, Ronald Arthur. Sir William Fairbairn / by R.A. Hayward. — [Manchester] ([97 Grosvenor St., Manchester M1 7HF]) : North Western Museum of Science & Industry, [1977?]. — [1],20p : ill, port ; 22cm.
Bibl.: p.20.
Sd : Unpriced
(B77-27175)

624'.092'4 — Civil engineering. Telford, Thomas. *Biographies. Juvenile literature*
Althea. Thomas Telford, man of iron / by Althea ; illustrated by Tim Hunkin. — Cambridge : Dinosaur Publications for the Ironbridge Gorge Museum Trust and Telford Development Corporation, 1977. — [32]p : col ill, col map on back cover ; 23cm.
ISBN 0-85122-131-9 Sd : £0.50
(B77-28684)

624.1 — STRUCTURAL ENGINEERING

624'.1 — Structures. Demolition
Pledger, David M. A complete guide to demolition / [by] David M. Pledger. — Lancaster : Construction Press, 1977. — 104p : ill ; 31cm.
Bibl.: p.101. — Index.
ISBN 0-904406-22-9 : £6.50
(B77-31259)

624.1'06'241 — Structural engineering. Organisations. Great Britain. *Institution of Structural Engineers. Directories*
Institution of Structural Engineers. Year book and directory of members / the Institution of Structural Engineers. — London : Morris.
1977 : (corrected to 1st September 1976). — [1976]. — A20,5-220p,B4p : ill ; 25cm.
Index.
Pbk : £5.00(£2.50 to members)
(B77-03077)

624'.15 — Structures. Foundations. Design. *Manuals*
Bowles, Joseph Esmond. Foundation analysis and design / [by] Joseph E. Bowles. — 2nd ed. — New York ; London [etc.] : McGraw-Hill, 1977. — xv,750p : ill ; 25cm.
Previous ed.: 1968. — Bibl.: p.723-739. — Index.
ISBN 0-07-006750-3 : £18.75
(B77-21944)

624'.151 — Civil engineering. Geological aspects. Numerical methods. *Periodicals*
International journal for numerical and analytical methods in geomechanics. — London [etc.] : Wiley.
Vol.1, no.1- ; Jan.-Mar. 1977-. — 1977-. — ill ; 26cm.
Quarterly. — Cover title. — Spine title: Numerical and analytical methods in geomechanics. — 'A Wiley-Interscience Publication'. — 103p. in 1st issue. — Bibl.
Pbk : £22.50 yearly
ISSN 0363-9061
(B77-18845)

624'.151 — Civil engineering. Geological factors
Roberts, Albert. Geotechnology : an introductory text for students and engineers / by A. Roberts. — Oxford [etc.] : Pergamon, 1977. — xvii, 347p : ill ; 26cm.
Bibl. — Index.
ISBN 0-08-019602-0 : £19.50
ISBN 0-08-021594-7 Pbk : £9.75
(B77-27176)

624'.151 — Civil engineering. Geological factors. *Conference proceedings*
Structural and Geotechnical Mechanics *(Conference), University of Illinois, 1975.*
Structural and geotechnical mechanics : a volume honoring Nathan M. Newmark / editor W.J. Hall. — Englewood Cliffs ; London [etc.] : Prentice-Hall, 1977. — vi,442p : ill, port ; 24cm.
'On October 2 and 3, 1975, a symposium on Structural and Geotechnical Mechanics ... was held at the University of Illinois, Urbana, Illinois' - Preface. — Bibl.
ISBN 0-13-853804-2 : £22.00
Also classified at 624'.171
(B77-19452)

624'.151'0285424 — Sediments. Cores. Geotechnical properties. Analysis. Applications of programs written in Basic & Fortran languages
Parker, Andrew. The computation and display of geotechnical properties for sediment cores using BASIC and FORTRAN / by Andrew Parker and Roger Till ; (with programs by Margaret Moss). — Reading (Reading RG6 2AB) : Geology Department, University of Reading, 1977. — [4],63p : ill ; 30cm. — (University of Reading. Department of Geology. Geological reports ; no.10) (Computer-based packages for teaching earth science report ; no.4)
ISBN 0-7049-0280-x Sp : £0.75
(B77-18846)

624'.151'0722 — Civil engineering. Geological factors. *Case studies*
Anderson, John Graham Comrie. Case-histories in engineering geology / [by] J.G.C. Anderson and C.F. Trigg. — London : Elek, 1976. — viii, 264p : ill, maps, plans ; 22cm.
Bibl. — Index.
ISBN 0-236-40049-5 : £12.50
(B77-02385)

624'.1513 — Frozen soils. Mechanics
TSytovich, N A. The mechanics of frozen ground / [by] N.A. Tsytovich ; [translated from the Russian by Scripta Technica, Inc.] ; edited by George K. Swinzow ; Gregory P. Tschebotarioff, advisory editor. — Washington, D.C. : Scripta Book Company ; New York ; London [etc.] : McGraw-Hill, [1976]. — xix, 426p : ill, maps ; 24cm. — (McGraw-Hill series in modern structures)
This translation published in the United States: 1975. — Translation of 'Mekhanika merzlykh gruntov'. Moscow : Vysshaia Shkola, 1973. — Bibl.: p.413-421. — Index.
ISBN 0-07-065410-7 : £31.95
(B77-03078)

624'.1513 — Oceans. Bed. Soils. Mechanics
Offshore soil mechanics : a course of lectures and practical exercises held at Cambridge University, 29 March-2 April 1976 / edited by Philip George, David Wood. — [Cambridge] : Cambridge University Engineering Department ; [London] : Lloyd's Register of Shipping, 1976. — x,468p : ill, maps ; 30cm.
Bibl.
ISBN 0-900528-83-4 Pbk : £8.50
(B77-11886)

624'.1513 — Soils. Mechanics
Singh, Alam. Soil engineering in theory and practice / [by] Alam Singh. — 2nd revised and enlarged ed. — London : Asia Publishing House.
In 3 vols. — Previous ed.: in 1 vol. 1967.
Vol.1 : Fundamentals and general principles. — 1976. — xix,813p,plate : ill ; 25cm.
Index.
ISBN 0-210-22552-1 : £8.00
(B77-09752)

624'.1513'05 — Soils. Mechanics. *Periodicals*
Géotechnique. — London : Geotechnical Society, 1948.
Cumulative index 1948-1974. Part 1, vols 1-14 1948-64. Part 2 / compiled by J. Edwin Holmstrom. Vols 15-24 1965-74. — London : Institution of Civil Engineers, 1975. — [3],49p ; 26cm.
£12.00
(B77-08435)

624'.154 — Structures. Foundations. Piles in weak rock
Piles in weak rock. — London (26 Old St., EC1V 9AD) : Thomas Telford Ltd for the Institution of Civil Engineers, 1977. — [3], 233p : ill, maps, plans ; 26cm.
' ... first published as a Symposium in Print in "Géotechnique" March 1976' - title page verso. — Bibl.
ISBN 0-7277-0034-0 : £5.50
(B77-12510)

624'.16 — Rock slopes. Design
Hoek, Evert. Rock slope engineering / [by] Evert Hoek, John Bray. — Revised 2nd ed. — London ([44 Portland Place, W1N 4BR]) : Institution of Mining and Metallurgy, 1977. — [3],402p : ill ; 31cm.
Previous ed.: 1974.
ISBN 0-900488-36-0 : £10.00
(B77-27915)

624'.16 — Structures. Retaining walls. Design. *Manuals*
Newman, Morton. Standard cantilever retaining walls / [by] Morton Newman. — New York ; London [etc.] : McGraw-Hill, 1976. — xxi, 648p : ill ; 29cm.
Bibl.: p.645-646. — Index.
ISBN 0-07-046347-6 : £20.65
(B77-30343)

624'.171 — Structures. Analysis
Beaufait, Fred William. Basic concepts of structural analysis / [by] Fred W. Beaufait. — Englewood Cliffs ; London [etc.] : Prentice-Hall, 1977. — xiii,591p : ill ; 24cm. — (Civil engineering and engineering mechanics series)
Bibl.: p.583. — Index.
ISBN 0-13-058347-2 : £19.15
(B77-22661)

Charlton, Thomas Malcolm. Principles of structural analysis / [by] T.M. Charlton. — Revised ed. — Aberdeen ([Marischal College, Aberdeen AB9 1AS]) : Department of Engineering, University of Aberdeen, 1977. — viii,188p : ill ; 21cm.
Previous ed.: Harlow : Longmans, 1969. — Bibl.: p.184. — Index.
ISBN 0-9505890-0-4 Pbk : Unpriced
(B77-33870)

Marshall, William Thomas. Structures : SI units / [by] the late W.T. Marshall, H.M. Nelson. — 2nd ed. — London : Pitman, 1977. — xiii,455p : ill ; 22cm. — (A Pitman international text)
Previous ed.: 1969. — Bibl. — Index. — Previous control number ISBN 0-273-00846-3.
ISBN 0-273-00827-7 Pbk : £3.95 : CIP rev.
(B77-09071)

Norris, Charles Head. Elementary structural analysis. — 3rd ed. / by Charles Head Norris, John Benson Wilbur, Senol Utku. — Tokyo ; London [etc.] : McGraw-Hill, 1976. — xxv, 673p : ill ; 21cm.
With answers. — Previous ed.: / by Charles Head Norris and John Benson Wilbur. 1960. — Index.
ISBN 0-07-047256-4 Pbk : £7.60
(B77-24997)

624'.171 — Structures. Dynamics. Applications of digital computer systems
Levy, Samuel. The component element method in dynamics : with application to earthquake and vehicle engineering / [by] Samuel Levy and John P.D. Wilkinson. — New York ; London [etc.] : McGraw-Hill, 1976. — xiv,363p : ill ; 24cm.
Index.
ISBN 0-07-037398-1 : £17.35
(B77-21204)

624'.171 — Structures. Mechanics
Tauchert, Theodore R. Energy principles in structural mechanics / [by] Theodore R. Tauchert. — New York ; London [etc.] : McGraw-Hill, 1974. — xiii,380p : ill ; 24cm.
With answers to selected problems. — Index.
ISBN 0-07-062925-0 : Unpriced
(B77-21205)

624'.171 — Structures. Mechanics. *Conference proceedings*
Structural and Geotechnical Mechanics *(Conference), University of Illinois, 1975.*
Structural and geotechnical mechanics : a volume honoring Nathan M. Newmark / editor W.J. Hall. — Englewood Cliffs ; London [etc.] : Prentice-Hall, 1977. — vi,442p : ill, port ; 24cm.
'On October 2 and 3, 1975, a symposium on Structural and Geotechnical Mechanics ... was held at the University of Illinois, Urbana, Illinois' - Preface. — Bibl.
ISBN 0-13-853804-2 : £22.00
Primary classification 624'.151
(B77-19452)

624'.171 — Structures. Vibration
Vibrations of engineering structures / by C.A. Brebbia ... [et al.]. — Southampton (18 Spring Cres., Southampton [SO2 1GA]) : Computational Mechanics Ltd, 1976. — vii, 387p : ill ; 23cm.
Bibl.
ISBN 0-905451-00-7 : £12.00
(B77-00808)

624'.171 — Structures. Vibration induced by fluid flow
Blevins, Robert D. Flow-induced vibration / [by] Robert D. Blevins. — New York ; London [etc.] : Van Nostrand Reinhold, 1977. — xv, 363p : ill, charts ; 24cm.
Index.
ISBN 0-442-20828-6 : £13.75
(B77-24998)

624'.171'01515353 — Structures. Mechanics. Mathematics. Finite element methods. *Conference proceedings*
World Congress on Finite Element Methods in Structural Mechanics, *Bournemouth, 1975.*
World Congress on Finite Element Methods in Structural Mechanics, Bournemouth, Dorset, England, 12-17 October 1975. — [Verwood] ([c/o Robinson and Associates, Vicarage Rd, Verwood, Dorset]) : [John Robinson], [1976?]. — 4v. : ill ; 30cm.
Cover title. — Bibl.
Pbk : £40.00
(B77-29501)

624'.176 — Earthquake engineering
Seismic risk and engineering decisions / by C. Lomnitz and E. Rosenblueth (editors). — Amsterdam ; Oxford [etc.] : Elsevier, 1976. — ix,425p : ill, maps ; 25cm. — (Developments in geotechnical engineering ; 15)
Bibl. — Index.
ISBN 0-444-41494-0 : £28.75
(B77-09072)

624'.176 — Earthquake resistant structures. Design. *Manuals*
Dowrick, D J. Earthquake resistant design : a manual for engineers and architects / [by] D.J. Dowrick. — London [etc.] : Wiley, 1977. — x, 374p : ill, maps ; 24cm.
'A Wiley-Interscience Publication'. — Index.
ISBN 0-471-99433-2 : £12.50
(B77-20354)

624'.176 — Structures. Effects of winds. *Conference proceedings*
International Conference on Wind Effects on Buildings and Structures, *4th, Heathrow, 1975.*
Proceedings of the Fourth International Conference on Wind Effects on Buildings and Structures, Heathrow, 1975 / edited by Keith J. Eaton. — Cambridge [etc.] : Cambridge University Press, 1977. — xiii,845p : ill, maps, port ; 29cm.
'The Conference was organised by the Building Research Establishment' - Foreword. — Bibl. — Index.
ISBN 0-521-20801-7 : £25.00
(B77-03079)

624'.176 — Structures. Fatigue & fracture
Rolfe, Stanley T. Fracture and fatigue control in structures : applications of fracture mechanics / [by] Stanley T. Rolfe, John M. Barsom. — Englewood Cliffs ; London [etc.] : Prentice-Hall, 1977. — xiv,562p : ill ; 24cm. — (Civil engineering and engineering mechanics series)
Index.
ISBN 0-13-329953-8 : £22.10
(B77-12511)

624'.176 — Structures. Stresses & strains
Roark, Raymond Jefferson. Formulas for stress and strain. — 5th ed. / [by] Raymond J. Roark, Warren C. Young. — New York ; London [etc.] : McGraw-Hill, [1976]. — xvi, 624p : ill ; 24cm.
This ed. originally published in the United States: 1975. — Previous ed.: / by Raymond J. Roark. 1965. — Index.
ISBN 0-07-053031-9 : £16.20
(B77-01566)

624'.1771 — Model tensegrity systems. Making. *Manuals*
Pugh, Anthony. An introduction to tensegrity / by Anthony Pugh. — Berkeley [etc.] ; London : University of California Press, 1976. — x,122p : ill ; 23cm.
Bibl.: p.122.
ISBN 0-520-02996-8 : £10.00
ISBN 0-520-03055-9 Pbk : £3.50
(B77-14278)

624'.1772 — Structural components: Beams
Donnell, Lloyd Hamilton. Beams, plates, and shells / [by] Lloyd Hamilton Donnell. — New York ; London [etc.] : McGraw-Hill, 1976. — xiii,453p : ill ; 25cm. — (Engineering societies monographs)
Index.
ISBN 0-07-017593-4 : £16.45
Also classified at 624'.1776
(B77-25705)

624'.1772 — Structures. Beam-columns
Chen, Wai-Fah. Theory of beam-columns / [by] Wai-Fah Chen, Toshio Atsuta. — New York ; London [etc.] : McGraw-Hill.
In 2 vols.
Vol.1 : In-plane behavior and design. — 1976. — xv,513p : ill ; 25cm.
With answers to some selected problems. — Bibl. — Index.
ISBN 0-07-010754-8 : £22.10
(B77-23498)

624'.1776 — Geodesic structures. Mathematics
Kenner, Hugh. Geodesic math and how to use it / by Hugh Kenner. — Berkeley [etc.] ; London : University of California Press, 1976. — xi,172p : ill ; 23cm.
ISBN 0-520-02924-0 : £10.00
(B77-14279)

624'.1776 — Shell structures. Statics. Analysis
Heyman, Jacques. Equilibrium of shell structures / by Jacques Heyman. — Oxford : Clarendon Press, 1977. — [7],134p : ill ; 24cm. — (The Oxford engineering science series)
Index.
ISBN 0-19-856139-3 : £5.50
(B77-22662)

624'.1776 — Structural components: Plates & shells
Donnell, Lloyd Hamilton. Beams, plates, and shells / [by] Lloyd Hamilton Donnell. — New York ; London [etc.] : McGraw-Hill, 1976. — xiii,453p : ill ; 25cm. — (Engineering societies monographs)
Index.
ISBN 0-07-017593-4 : £16.45
Primary classification 624'.1772
(B77-25705)

624'.18 — Composite construction materials
Nicholls, Robert Lee. Composite construction materials handbook / [by] Robert Nicholls. — Englewood Cliffs ; London [etc.] : Prentice-Hall, 1976. — xii,580p : ill ; 24cm.
Index.
ISBN 0-13-164889-6 : £18.70
(B77-09073)

624'.18 — Structures. Composite materials. Use
Cook, John Philip. Composite construction methods / [by] John P. Cook. — New York ; London [etc.] : Wiley, 1977. — xv,330p : ill ; 24cm. — (Wiley series of practical construction guides)
'A Wiley-Interscience publication'. — Index.
ISBN 0-471-16905-6 : £16.50
(B77-22663)

624'.1821 — Steel plated structures. Mechanics. *Conference proceedings*
International Conference on Steel Plated Structures, *Imperial College of Science and Technology, 1976.* Steel plated structures : an international symposium / edited by P.J. Dowling, J.E. Harding, P.A. Frieze. — London : Crosby Lockwood Staples, 1977. — [10],902p : ill ; 24cm.
'Proceedings of the International Conference on Steel Plated Structures [held at Imperial College, London in July, 1976] ... organised by Imperial College and Constrado' - Introduction.
ISBN 0-258-97076-6 : £16.00
(B77-21948)

624'.1821 — Steel structural components. Design
Knowles, Peter Reginald. Design of structural steelwork / [by] Peter Knowles. — London : Surrey University Press : International Textbook Co., 1977. — x,198p : ill ; 24cm.
Bibl.: p.195. — Index.
ISBN 0-903384-16-7 : Unpriced
(B77-30344)

Kuzmanović, Bogdan O. Steel design for structural engineers / [by] Bogdan O. Kuzmanović, Nicholas Willems. — Englewood Cliffs ; London [etc.] : Prentice-Hall, 1977. — xvii,509p : ill ; 24cm. — (Civil engineering and engineering mechanics series)
Index.
ISBN 0-13-846352-2 : £17.60
(B77-11265)

624'.1826 — Structural components: Extruded aluminium alloy sections. *Standards*
British Standards Institution. Specification for aluminium alloy sections for structural purposes = Spécification des profilés en alliages d'aluminium de construction = Spezifikation für Profile aus Alulegierung für Bauzwecke / British Standards Institution. — 2nd revision. — London : B.S.I., 1977. — [2],13,[1]p : ill ; 30cm. — (BS1161 : 1977)
Pierced for binder.
ISBN 0-580-09870-2 Sd : £3.60
(B77-14780)

624'.1834 — Concrete. Formwork. Design & construction
Peurifoy, Robert Leroy. Formwork for concrete structures / [by] R.L. Peurifoy. — 2nd ed. — New York ; London [etc.] : McGraw-Hill, 1976. — xiii,333p : ill ; 24cm.
Previous ed.: 1964. — Bibl. — Index.
ISBN 0-07-049754-0 : £12.70
(B77-20355)

624'.1834 — Concrete structural components. Use. Standards. Council for Codes of Practice. Code of practice for the structural use of concrete. Use. *Manuals*
Wilby, Charles Bryan. Concrete for structural engineers : a text to CP 110 / [by] C.B. Wilby. — London [etc.] : Newnes-Butterworths, 1977. — xii,212p : ill ; 23cm.
Index.
ISBN 0-408-00256-5 : £10.00
(B77-15914)

624'.1834 — Construction materials: Concrete. *Dutch standards*
Nederlands Normalisatie-Instituut. Regulations for concrete, 1974 / prepared ... by Nederlands Normalisatie-Instituut ; translated [from the Dutch] by British Standards Institution, Technical Help to Exporters. — Hemel Hempstead (Maylands Ave., Hemel Hempstead, Herts. HP2 4SQ) : Technical Help to Exporters, British Standards Institution.
Part F : Prestressed concrete, additional requirements. — 1977. — 47p : ill ; 30cm.
Translation of: Netherlands Standard NEN 3866. — Originally published: in Dutch. Rijswijk : Nederlands Normalisatie-Instituut, 1976.
ISBN 0-903886-31-6 Pbk : Unpriced
(B77-17574)

624'.1834 — Construction. Use of ready-mixed concrete. *Conference proceedings*
International Conference on Ready-Mixed Concrete, *1st, University of Dundee, 1975.* Advances in ready mixed concrete technology / edited by Ravindra K. Dhir. — Oxford [etc.] : Pergamon, 1976. — xxiv,492p : ill ; 26cm.
'Proceedings of the First International Conference on Ready-Mixed Concrete held at Dundee University 29th September-1st October 1975 organised by Civil Engineering Department, Dundee University in collaboration with ... [others]'. — Index.
ISBN 0-08-020415-5 : £15.00
Primary classification 666'.89
(B77-01639)

624'.1834 — Prestressed concrete structures. Design
Ramaswamy, G S. Modern prestressed concrete design / [by] G.S. Ramaswamy. — London [etc.] : Pitman, 1976. — iii-x,175p : ill ; 24cm. — (A Pitman international text)
Index.
ISBN 0-273-00434-4 : £7.50
ISBN 0-273-00455-7 Pbk : £3.95
(B77-01567)

624'.1834 — Reinforced concrete structural components. Design
Morrell, P J B. Design of reinforced concrete elements / [by] P.J.B. Morrell. — London : Crosby Lockwood Staples, 1977. — xvi,214p : ill ; 24cm.
Index.
ISBN 0-258-97018-9 Pbk : £6.00
(B77-14781)

624'.1834 — Reinforced concrete structural components. Design. *Manuals*
Hassoun, M Nadim. Ultimate-load design of reinforced concrete : a practical handbook / by M. Nadim Hassoun. — Slough : Cement and Concrete Association, 1976. — xvii,191p : ill ; 30cm. — (A viewpoint publication)
Index.
ISBN 0-7210-1046-6 Pbk : £12.00
(B77-32687)

624'.1834 — Reinforced concrete structures. Repair
Perkins, Philip Harold. Concrete structures : repair, waterproofing and protection / [by] Philip H. Perkins. — London : Applied Science Publishers, 1976. — x,302p : ill ; 23cm.
Bibl. — Index.
ISBN 0-85334-697-6 : £16.00
(B77-16456)

624'.1836 — Structures. Brickwork. *England, to 1976*
Brunskill, Ronald William. English brickwork / [by] Ronald Brunskill and Alec Clifton-Taylor. — London : Ward Lock, 1977. — 160p : ill ; 23cm. — (A Hyperion book)
Bibl.: p.154. — Index.
ISBN 0-7063-5087-1 : £6.95
(B77-27177)

624'.1836 — Structures. Reinforced clay brickwork & prestressed clay brickwork. Design. *Standards*
Structural Ceramics Advisory Group. Design guide for reinforced and prestressed clay brickwork / drafted by the Structural Ceramics Advisory Group of the Structural Ceramics Research Panel. — Stoke-on-Trent (Queens Rd, Penkhull, Stoke-on-Trent ST4 7LQ) : British Ceramic Research Association, [1977]. — [1],vi, 28,[1]p : ill ; 30cm. — (British Ceramic Research Association. Special publications ; no.91)
ISBN 0-900910-27-5 Sd : £6.00
(B77-15915)

624'.19 — Tunnels. Construction. *Conference proceedings*
Tunnelling '76 : proceedings of an international symposium, organized by the Institution of Mining and Metallurgy, with the cooperation of ... [others], held in London from 1 to 5 March, 1976 / edited by M.J. Jones. — [London] ([44 Portland Place, W1N 4BR]) : The Institution, 1976. — xx,455p : ill, maps, plans ; 31cm.
Bibl. — Index.
ISBN 0-900488-34-4 : £28.00
(B77-33276)

624'.19 — Vehicle tunnels. Aerodynamics & ventilation. *Conference proceedings*
International Symposium on the Aerodynamics and Ventilation of Vehicle Tunnels, *2nd, Cambridge, 1976.* Proceedings of the Second International Symposium on the Aerodynamics and Ventilation of Vehicle Tunnels, Cambridge, 1976 / [edited by H.S. Stephens et al.]. — [Bedford] ([Cranfield, Bedford MK43 0AJ]) : British Hydromechanics Research Association, Fluid Engineering, [1977]. — 611p in various pagings : ill ; 31cm.
Index.
ISBN 0-900983-51-5 : £20.00 : CIP rev.
(B77-04890)

624.2 — BRIDGES
624.2 — Road bridges. *Gwent. Chepstow, to 1976*
Waters, Ivor. Chepstow road bridges / by Ivor Waters. — [Chepstow] ([c/o Ivor Waters, 41 Hardwick Ave., Chepstow, Gwent NP6 5DS]) : Moss Rose Press, 1977. — 19p,[8]p of plates : ill ; 22cm.
Limited ed. of 180 numbered copies.
ISBN 0-906134-00-5 Sd : Unpriced
(B77-29502)

624.2'09 — Bridges, to 1976
Hayden, Martin. The book of bridges / [by] Martin Hayden ; [edited by Linda Doeser]. — London [etc.] : Marshall Cavendish, 1976. — 153p : ill, plans, ports ; 30cm.
Ill. on lining papers. — Index.
ISBN 0-85685-192-2 : £3.95
(B77-27178)

624.2'8 — Bridges. Construction. Bills of quantities. *Great Britain. Standards*
Great Britain. *Department of Transport.* Method of measurement for road and bridge works / Department of Transport [and] Scottish Development Department [and] Welsh Office. — 2nd ed. — London : H.M.S.O., 1977. — v, 120p ; 21cm.
Previous ed.: issued by the Department of the Environment and Scottish Development Department and Welsh Office. 1971.
ISBN 0-11-550439-7 Pbk : £4.50
Primary classification 625.7
(B77-21951)

624.2'8 — Road bridges. Inspection. *Organisation for Economic Co-operation and Development countries. Reports, surveys*
Organisation for Economic Co-operation and Development. *Road Research Group on Bridge Inspection.* Bridge inspection : a report / prepared by an OECD Road Research Group [the Road Research Group on Bridge Inspection]. — Paris : O.E.C.D. ; [London] : [H.M.S.O.], 1976. — 132p : ill, forms ; 27cm. — (Road research)
Pbk : £2.70
ISBN 92-64-11540-4
(B77-01568)

624.5'5 — Cable-stayed bridges. Design
Troitsky, M S. Cable-stayed bridges : theory and design / [by] M.S. Troitsky. — London : Crosby Lockwood Staples, 1977. — xi,385p : ill ; 26cm.
Index.
ISBN 0-258-97034-0 : £20.00
(B77-05488)

624.5'5'09563 — Road bridges. *Turkey. Bosporus. Bosporus Bridge. Design & construction*
Brown, W C. Bosporus bridge : design and construction / [by] W.C. Brown, M.F. Parsons and H.S.G. Knox. — London : Institution of Civil Engineers, 1976. — [4],92p : ill, maps, plans ; 22cm.
Originally published: in 'Proceedings of the Institution of Civil Engineers', Part 1, 1975, 58, Nov., 505-557 ; 1976, 60, Aug., 503-530.
ISBN 0-7277-0039-1 Pbk : £2.00
(B77-11888)

624.8'2'094215 — Road bridges. *London. Tower Bridge. Maintenance & repair. Workshops*
Greater London Industrial Archaeology Society. Tower Bridge Workshops : a GLIAS report. — [Bromley] ([c/o The Secretary, 9A Upper Park Rd, Bromley, Kent]) : The Society, 1976. — [3] ,16[i.e.23]p : ill, plans ; 21x30cm.
ISBN 0-905042-07-7 Sd : £0.50(£0.35 to members)
(B77-20356)

625.1 — RAILWAY ENGINEERING
625.1 — China clay mining industries. Industrial railway services. *Devon. Redlake. Redlake Tramway. Industrial antiquities*
Stabb, I. The Redlake Tramway and the china clay industry / edited and compiled [i.e. written] by I. Stabb & T. Downing. — [Bittaford] ([15 Hillside, Bittaford, Devon]) : [I. Stabb] ; [Ivybridge] : [T. Downing], 1977. — [12]p : ill, map ; 21cm.
Sd : Unpriced
(B77-19453)

625.1 — Railways. Accidents. *Great Britain. Inquiry reports*
Great Britain. *Railway Inspectorate.* Railway accident, report on the accident that occurred on 20th June 1976 at Kilnwick public level crossing in the Eastern Region, British Railways / Department of the Environment [Railway Inspectorate]. — London : H.M.S.O., 1977. — [2],4,[1]p : map, plan ; 34cm.
ISBN 0-11-550435-4 Sd : £0.25
(B77-10405)

Great Britain. *Railway Inspectorate.* Railway accident, report on the collision that occurred on 19th July 1976 between Merkland Street and Govan Cross on the underground railway of the Greater Glasgow Passenger Transport Executive / Department of Transport [Railway Inspectorate]. — London : H.M.S.O., 1977. — 12p,fold plate : ill, map ; 34cm.
ISBN 0-11-550446-x Sd : £0.85
(B77-31952)

Great Britain. *Railway Inspectorate.* Railway accident, report on the derailment that occurred on 6th June 1975 at Nuneaton in the London Midland Region, British Railways / Department of Transport [Railway Inspectorate]. — London : H.M.S.O., 1976. — 19p,[2]fold leaves of plates : ill, map, plan ; 35cm.
ISBN 0-11-550416-8 Sd : £1.60
(B77-09753)

Great Britain. *Railway Inspectorate.* Railway accident, report on the derailment that occurred on 12th February 1976 at Shortlands Junction in the Southern Region, British Railways / Department of Transport [Railway Inspectorate]. — London : H.M.S.O., 1977. — [2],8p : maps, plans ; 34cm.
ISBN 0-11-550438-9 Sd : £0.35
(B77-14280)

Great Britain. *Railway Inspectorate.* Railway accident, report on the derailment that occurred on 15th June 1976 at Southerham Junction in the Southern Region, British Railways / Department of Transport [Railway Inspectorate]. — London : H.M.S.O., 1977. — 9,[1]p : 1 ill, map, plan ; 33cm.
ISBN 0-11-550444-3 Sd : £0.40
(B77-27179)

Great Britain. *Railway Inspectorate.* Railway accident, report on the electrical fusing that occurred on 6th February 1976 between Finsbury Park and Arsenal Stations on the Piccadilly Line of London Transport Railways / Department of Transport [Railway Inspectorate]. — London : H.M.S.O., 1977. — 18p,2 fold leaves of plates : 2 ill, 2 maps, plans ; 34cm.
ISBN 0-11-550441-9 Sd : £1.10
(B77-21949)

625.1 — Railways. Accidents. *Great Britain. Reports, surveys. Serials*
Railway accidents : report to the Secretary of State for Transport on the safety record of the railways in Great Britain during the year / [Railway Inspectorate]. — London : H.M.S.O. 1975. — 1976. — [5],102p : ill ; 25cm.
ISBN 0-11-550414-1 Pbk : £1.35
(B77-07418)

625.1 — Railways. Accidents. *Great Britain, to 1975*
Rolt, Lionel Thomas Caswall. Red for danger : a history of railway accidents and railway safety / by L.T.C. Rolt. — 3rd ed. / revised and with additional material by Geoffrey Kichenside. — Newton Abbot [etc.] : David and Charles, 1976. — 5-297p,12p of plates : ill ; 23cm.
Previous ed.: 1966. — Bibl.: p.293. — Index.
ISBN 0-7153-7292-0 : £4.95
(B77-08436)

625.1 — Railways. Engineering aspects. *Conference proceedings*
International Engineering Conference, *London, 1975.* Rail engineering - the way ahead : papers presented at the International Engineering Conference held to mark the 150th anniversary of passenger railways, organized by the Institution of Mechanical Engineers and sponsored by the Institution of Civil Engineers, the Institution of Electrical Engineers and the Institution of Railway Signal Engineers, London, 22-26 September 1975. — London [etc.] : Mechanical Engineering Publications for the Institution of Mechanical Engineers, 1976. — 2v.(viii,311;[5],76p) : ill, maps ; 31cm. — (Institution of Mechanical Engineers. Conference publications ; CP10-1975)
ISBN 0-85298-340-9 : £30.00
(B77-20357)

625.1'005 — Railways. Engineering aspects. *Periodicals*
Rail international. — [Chelmsford] ([Little Leighs, Chelmsford, Essex CM3 1PF]) : [Broadfields (Technical Publishers) Ltd]. '76. — [1976]. — 52p : ill, ports ; 30cm.
Cover title. — 'A "Rail engineering international" associated publication'.
Pbk : Unpriced
(B77-24999)

625.1'0092'4 — Railways. Stephenson, George, b.1781. *Great Britain. Biographies*
Davies, Hunter. George Stephenson : a biographical study of the father of the railways / [by] Hunter Davies. — London [etc.] : Quartet Books, 1977. — xiii,337p,[8]p of plates : ill, ports ; 20cm.
Originally published: as 'A biographical study of the father of railways, George Stephenson ...'. London : Weidenfeld and Nicolson, 1975. — Bibl.: p.325-328. — Index.
ISBN 0-7043-3168-3 Pbk : £2.50
(B77-28685)

625.1'65'0942 — Railway services. *England. British Rail. Western Region. Signalling systems & telecommunications systems, to 1976. Engineering aspects*
Signalling : from mechanics to modules. — Bristol (9 Poplar Ave., Westbury-on-Trym, Bristol BS9 2BE) : Avon-AngliA Publications and Services, [1977]. — [1],24p : ill ; 30cm. — (Specialist monographs and reprints)
'... first appeared in "Western Management News" ...' - note.
Sd : £0.60
(B77-21206)

625.1'65'09422 — Railway services. *Southern England. Southern Railway. Signalling systems, to 1976. Engineering aspects. Illustrations*
Pryer, G A. A pictorial record of Southern signals / by G.A. Pryer. — Oxford : Oxford Publishing, 1977. — viii,200p : ill, facsims, plans ; 28cm.
Ill. on lining papers. — Bibl.: p.vi. — Index.
ISBN 0-902888-81-1 : £5.95
(B77-24295)

625.1'9 — Miniature railways & model railways
Model & miniature railways / [general editors J.H.L. Adams and P.B. Whitehouse]. — London [etc.] : Hamlyn : New English Library, 1976. — 512p : ill(chiefly col), col facsims, plans, ports(chiefly col) ; 35cm.
Bibl.: p.506-507. — Index.
ISBN 0-600-36241-8 : £6.95
(B77-01569)

625.1'9 — Model railways. Baseboards. Making. *Manuals*
Laughton, Ralph. Baseboard techniques / by Ralph Laughton. — New Malden : Almark Publishing, 1977. — 24p : ill ; 20x22cm. — (Focus on railway modelling ; no.1)
ISBN 0-85524-277-9 Sd : £0.70
(B77-18847)

625.1'9 — Model railways. Scenery. Making. *Manuals*
Andress, Michael. Scenic railway modelling / by Michael Andress. — London : Almark Publishing, 1977. — 72p : ill(some col) ; 21x22cm.
ISBN 0-85524-274-4 : £2.75
(B77-10406)

Laughton, Ralph. Landscape techniques / by Ralph Laughton. — London : Almark Publishing, 1977. — 24p : ill ; 20x21cm. — (Focus on railway modelling ; no.4)
ISBN 0-85524-286-8 Sd : £0.70
(B77-30345)

625.1'9 — Model steam locomotives. Boilers. Construction. *Manuals*
Evans, Martin. Model locomotive boilers : their design and construction / [by] Martin Evans ; foreword by D.H. Chaddock. — Revised ed. — Watford : Model and Allied Publications, 1976. — 144p,[36]p of plates : ill, ports ; 21cm.
Previous ed.: 1969.
ISBN 0-85242-483-3 Pbk : £2.50
(B77-09754)

625.1'9 — 'N' gauge model railways. Construction. *Manuals*
Andress, Michael. 'N' gauge model railways / by Michael Andress. — London : Almark Publishing, 1977. — 48p : ill, plans ; 20x21cm.
Cover title: An illustrated guide to 'N' gauge model railways. — Not the same as B72-12629.

ISBN 0-85524-285-x Pbk : £1.75
(B77-30346)

625.1'9'0223 — Model railways. Track layouts. *Plans*
Laughton, Ralph. Trackplans for all gauges / by Ralph Laughton. — New Malden [etc.] : Almark Publishing, 1977. — 24p : ill ; 20x22cm. — (Focus on railway modelling ; no.2)
ISBN 0-85524-278-7 Sd : £0.70
(B77-18219)

625.1′9′09042 — Model railways, 1925. *Periodicals. Facsimiles*
[The **model** railway news. Vol.1]. The model railway news : clockwork steam and electric : Vol.1, January-December, 1925. — Watford : Model and Allied Publications, 1977. — [12], 384p : ill, plans, ports ; 23cm.
Facsimile reprint. — Originally published: London : Percival Marshall. — Index.
ISBN 0-85242-518-x : £6.95
(B77-28686)

625.1′9′0924 — Model railways. Construction. Roberts, Frank. *New Zealand. Biographies*
Roberts, Joyce. Steam in miniature : Frank Roberts and his garden railway / [by] Joyce Roberts. — Wellington [N.Z.] [etc.] ; London : A.H. and A.W. Reed, 1976. — 88p : ill, ports ; 27cm.
Col. plan on back cover verso.
ISBN 0-589-00948-6 Pbk : £3.00
(B77-24296)

625.2′09422 — Railway services. *South-east England. London, Brighton and South Coast Railway. Rolling stock, 1846-1925. Technical data*
Newbury, Peter James. Carriage stock of the LB & SCR / [by] P.J. Newbury. — Blandford : Oakwood Press, 1976. — [2],80p,[12]p of plates : ill ; 25cm.
ISBN 0-85361-195-5 Pbk : £3.00
(B77-01570)

625.2′4 — Privately owned goods wagons. Engineering aspects. *England, 1892-1939. Illustrations*
Private owner wagons / [compiled] by Bill Hudson. — Oxford : Oxford Publishing.
Vol.1. — 1976. — x,118p : chiefly ill, maps ; 28cm.
All but six of the plates come from the records of Charles Roberts and Company. — Bibl.: p.118.
ISBN 0-902888-70-6 Pbk : £2.95
(B77-00274)

625.2′4′0941 — Railway services. *Great Britain. British Rail. Goods wagons, 1948-1976. Engineering aspects. Illustrations*
Pre-nationalisation freight wagons on British railways : a pictorial survey / [compiled by] David Larkin. — Truro : Barton, 1977. — 64p : chiefly ill ; 21cm.
ISBN 0-85153-302-7 Sd : £1.95
(B77-06736)

625.2′4′0941 — Railway services. *Great Britain. London and North Eastern Railway. Freight rolling stock. Engineering aspects. Illustrations. For modelling*
A pictorial record of LNER wagons / [compiled] by Peter Tatlow. — Oxford : Oxford Publishing, 1976. — vi,180p : chiefly ill, plans ; 29cm.
Spine title: LNER wagons. — Bibl.: p.170. — Index.
ISBN 0-902888-92-7 : £4.80
(B77-04262)

625.2′4′0941 — Railway services. *Great Britain. London. Midland and Scottish Railway. Goods wagons. Engineering aspects*
Essery, Robert John. The LMS wagon / [by] R.J. Essery and K.R. Morgan. — Newton Abbot [etc.] : David and Charles, 1977. — 128p : ill, plans ; 26cm.
Index.
ISBN 0-7153-7357-9 : £4.95
(B77-16933)

625.2′4′0942 — Railway services. *England. Great Western Railway. Goods wagons, 1870-1947. Engineering aspects*
A history of GWR goods wagons / [by] A.G. Atkins ... [et al.]. — Newton Abbot [etc.] : David and Charles.
Vol.2 : Wagon types in detail. — 1976. — 128p : ill ; 26cm.
Bibl.: p.126. — Index.
ISBN 0-7153-7290-4 : £4.50
(B77-06737)

625.2′6′0941 — Preserved locomotives. Engineering aspects. *Great Britain*
Casserley, Henry Cyril. Preserved locomotives / [by] H.C. Casserley. — 4th ed. — London : Allan, 1976. — 368p : ill ; 19cm.
Previous ed.: 1973. — Index.
ISBN 0-7110-0725-x : £3.95
(B77-01571)

625.2′61 — Fireless locomotives. Engineering aspects. *Great Britain, to 1967*
Civil, Allen. Fireless locomotives : being a history of all British built examples with notes on the general history of the type and its principles of operation / [by] Allen Civil, Allan Baker. — Blandford : Oakwood Press, 1976. — 94p,[20]p of plates : ill ; 22cm. — (Locomotion papers ; no.97 ISSN 0305-5493)
Index.
ISBN 0-85361-193-9 Pbk : £2.70
(B77-04263)

625.2′61 — Railway services. *Great Britain. British Rail. Steam locomotives. Operation. Manuals*
British Transport Commission. Handbook for railway steam locomotive enginemen / British Transport Commission. — London : I. Allan, 1977. — 196p : ill(some col) ; 23cm.
Originally published: London? : British Transport Commission, 1957. — Index.
ISBN 0-7110-0628-8 : £4.95
(B77-19454)

625.2′61 — Steam locomotives. Preservation. *Personal observations*
Latham, J B. Railways and preservation / by J.B. Latham. — Woking (5 Church Path, Woking, Surrey) : The author, 1975. — 70p : ill ; 19x23cm.
ISBN 0-9505743-0-9 Pbk : £1.50
(B77-16457)

625.2′61′0904 — High-powered steam locomotives, to 1975. Engineering aspects. *Illustrations*
Evans, R K. Steam superpower around the world / [by] R.K. Evans. — Truro : Barton, 1976. — 96p : of ill ; 23cm.
ISBN 0-85153-209-8 : £3.75
(B77-00809)

625.2′61′0924 — Railway services. *England. London and North Western Railway. Steam locomotives designed by Bowen Cooke, Charles John, 1909-1931. Engineering aspects*
Nock, Oswald Stevens. LNWR locomotives of C.J. Bowen Cooke / [by] O.S. Nock. — Truro : Barton, 1977. — 112p : ill, ports ; 22cm.
Index.
ISBN 0-85153-285-3 : £3.95
(B77-33871)

625.2′61′0924 — Railway services. *Great Britain. London, Midland and Scottish Railway. 4-6-0 steam locomotives designed by Stanier, William Arthur, to 1975. Engineering aspects*
Rowledge, John Westbury Peter. The Stanier 4-6-0s of the LMS : (the Jubilees, Class 5s and the BR Standard Class 5s) / [by] J.W.P. Rowledge and Brian Reed. — Newton Abbot [etc.] : David and Charles, 1977. — 96p : ill, plans ; 25cm. — (David and Charles locomotive studies)
Index.
ISBN 0-7153-7385-4 : £4.95
(B77-21950)

625.2′61′0924 — Steam locomotives. Design. Bulleid, Oliver Vaughan Snell. *Great Britain. Biographies*
Bulleid, H A V. Bulleid of the Southern / [by] H.A.V. Bulleid. — London : Allan, 1977. — 229p,[48]p of plates : ill, ports ; 23cm.
Bibl.: p.222. — Index.
ISBN 0-7110-0689-x : £5.95
(B77-10407)

Day-Lewis, Sean. Bulleid : last giant of steam / [by] Sean Day-Lewis. — Revised 2nd ed. — London : Allen and Unwin, 1968 [i.e. 1977]. — 3-303p,[2],34p of plates : ill, ports ; 22cm.
This ed. originally published: 1968. — Index.
ISBN 0-04-923068-9 Pbk : £3.50
(B77-10408)

625.2′61′0924 — Steam locomotives. Design. Hackworth, Timothy. *Great Britain. Biographies*
Young, Robert, *b.1860.* Timothy Hackworth and the locomotive / by Robert Young. — Shildon ([c/o D. Swan, Park House, Windlestone, Ferryhill, Co. Durham DL17 0NF]) : Shildon 'Stockton and Darlington Railway' Jubilee Committee, 1975. — [1],406,xxxii p,[36]leaves of plates,[6]p of plates : ill, facsims, map, plan, ports(1 col) ; 23cm.
In slip case. — Facsimile reprint of: 1st ed. London : Locomotive Publishing Co., 1923. — Index.
Unpriced
Pbk : Unpriced
(B77-20358)

625.2′61′0924 — Steam locomotives designed by Bulleid, Oliver Vaughan Snell. Engineering aspects. *Great Britain, to 1967*
Bulleid locomotives : a pictorial history / [compiled] by Brian Haresnape. — London : I. Allan, 1977. — 112p : chiefly ill ; 25cm.
Bibl.: p.112.
ISBN 0-7110-0794-2 : £3.95
(B77-25000)

625.2′61′0924 — Steam locomotives designed by Churchward, George Jackson. Engineering aspects. *Great Britain*
Churchward locomotives : a pictorial history / [compiled by] Brian Haresnape, Alec Swain. — London : I. Allan, 1976. — 112p : ill ; 24cm.
Bibl.: p.112.
ISBN 0-7110-0697-0 : £3.30
(B77-32689)

625.2′61′0924 — Steam locomotives designed by Maunsell, Richard Edward Lloyd. Engineering aspects. *Great Britain, to 1965*
Maunsell locomotives : a pictorial history / [compiled by] Brian Haresnape. — London : I. Allan, 1977. — 128p : chiefly ill ; 25cm.
Bibl.: p.128.
ISBN 0-7110-0743-8 : £3.75
(B77-20359)

625.2′61′09411 — 4-6-0 steam locomotives. Engineering aspects. *Scotland, to ca 1930*
Atkins, C P. The Scottish 4-6-0 classes / [by] C.P. Atkins. — London : Allan, 1976. — 123p, [48]p of plates : ill, port ; 23cm.
Bibl.: p.123.
ISBN 0-7110-0700-4 : £3.25
(B77-04264)

625.2′61′09414 — Railway services. *South-west Scotland. Glasgow and South Western Railway. Steam locomotives, to 1923. Engineering aspects*
Smith, David Larmer. Locomotives of the Glasgow and South Western Railway / [by] David L. Smith. — Newton Abbot [etc.] : David and Charles, 1976. — 192p : ill, map ; 23cm.
Index.
ISBN 0-7153-6960-1 : £5.25
(B77-03597)

625.2′61′0942 — Railway services. *England. Great Western Railway. Steam locomotives, to 1962. Engineering aspects. Illustrations*
Freezer, Cyril John. Locomotives in outline, GWR / [by] C.J. Freezer. — Seaton : Peco, 1977. — [2],38p : chiefly ill ; 22x30cm.
ISBN 0-900586-46-x : £1.95
(B77-30347)

625.2′61′09422 — Railway services. *Southern England. London and South Western Railway. Greyhound class locomotives, 1895-1923. Engineering aspects*
Bradley, Donald Laurence. The Drummond Greyhounds of the LSWR / [by] D.L. Bradley. — Newton Abbot [etc.] : David and Charles, 1977. — 96p : ill, plans ; 26cm. — (David and Charles locomotive studies)
Bibl.: p.95. — Index.
ISBN 0-7153-7329-3 : £4.95
(B77-27916)

625.6′6′07402835 — Museums. *Humberside. Sandtoft. Sandtoft Transport Centre. Exhibits: Trolleybuses. Catalogues*
Sandtoft Transport Centre. The Sandtoft guide : a guide and history of the museum and its exhibits / compiled by P.A. Goddard and J.R. Whitehead. — Completely revised 2nd ed. — Reading (c/o F.R. Whitehead, 68 Albert Rd, Caversham, Reading, Berks. RG4 7PF) : Sandtoft Transport Centre Association, 1976. — 34p : ill, plan ; 21cm.
At head of title: The Sandtoft Transport Centre presents ...
ISBN 0-904235-03-3 Sd : Unpriced
(B77-28687)

625.7 — ROADS. CONSTRUCTION

625.7 — Roads. Construction. Bills of quantities. *Great Britain. Standards*

Great Britain. *Department of Transport.* Method of measurement for road and bridge works / Department of Transport [and] Scottish Development Department [and] Welsh Office. — 2nd ed. — London : H.M.S.O., 1977. — v, 120p ; 21cm.
Previous ed.: issued by the Department of the Environment and Scottish Development Department and Welsh Office. 1971.
ISBN 0-11-550439-7 Pbk : £4.50
Also classified at 624.2'8
(B77-21951)

625.7'042 — National Primary Routes. Surfaces. Resistance to skids. *Ireland (Republic). Reports, surveys*

Crowley, Finbarr. Friction characteristics of road surfaces / [by] F. Crowley. — Dublin : Foras Forbartha, 1976. — v,33p : form ; 30cm. — (RS 195)
Cover title: Friction characteristics of road surfaces = Áiríona cuimilteacha dromchlaí bóthair.
Sd : £1.00
(B77-10409)

625.7'2 — Roads. Geometric aspects. Design. Standards. *Organisation for Economic Co-operation and Development countries. Conference proceedings*

Symposium on Methods for Determining Geometric Road Design Standards, *Elsinore, 1976.* Geometric road design standards : proceedings of the Symposium on Methods for Determining Geometric Road Design Standards, organized by the Road Directorate of the Ministry for Public Works and the Danish Council for Road Safety Research and held in Elsinore, Denmark on 10th, 11th and 12th May 1976. — Paris : Organisation for Economic Co-operation and Development ; [London] : [H.M.S.O.], 1977. — 209p : ill ; 27cm. — (Road research)
Pbk : £3.90
ISBN 92-64-11640-0
(B77-17575)

625.7'34 — Roads. Drainage systems. Manhole covers, gully gratings & frames. *Standards*

British Standards Institution. Specification for manhole covers, road gully gratings and frames for drainage purposes = Spécification concernant les cadres et tampons de voirie pour trous d'homme utilisés pour le drainage = Schachtabdeckungen, Strassenabläufe-Roste und Rahmen (für Entwässerungszwecke) / British Standards Institution. — London : B.S.I.
Part 1 = Partie 1 = Teil 1 : Cast iron and cast steel = Fonte de fer et fonte d'acier = Gusseisen und Stahlguss. — 4th revision. — 1976. — [2],8,[2]p : ill ; 30cm. — (BS497 : Part 1 : 1976)
Pierced for binder.
ISBN 0-580-09580-0 Sd : £2.40
(B77-03598)

625.7'6 — Roads. Reinforcement. *Organisation for Economic Co-operation and Development countries. Reports, surveys*

Organisation for Economic Co-operation and Development. *Road Research Group on Road Strengthening.* Road strengthening : a report / prepared by an OECD Road Research Group [i.e. the Road Research Group on Road Strengthening]. — Paris : O.E.C.D. ; [London] : [H.M.S.O.], 1976. — 155p : ill ; 27cm.
Pbk : £2.90
ISBN 92-64-11557-9
(B77-00810)

625.7'6'0941 — Roads. Maintenance. *Great Britain. Standards*

Preferred methods for highway maintenance / [prepared by an assessment team formed from representatives of central and local government for the] Department of the Environment [and the] Scottish Development Department [and the] Welsh Office. — London : H.M.S.O.
Part 2 : Kerb-laying. — 1976. — iii,19p : 1 ill ; 30cm.
Cover title: Preferred methods of construction. Part 2 : Kerb laying.
ISBN 0-11-550382-x Sd : £0.80
(B77-09755)

Part 3 : Drain-laying. — 1976. — [3],10p : 2 ill ; 30cm.
Cover title: Preferred methods of construction. Part 3 : Drain laying.
ISBN 0-11-550383-8 Sd : £0.80
(B77-09756)

625.7'94 — Signal-controlled road traffic control systems. Traffic assignment & signal timings

Charlesworth, J A. Mutually consistent traffic assignment and signal timings for a signal-controlled road network / [by] J.A. Charlesworth. — Newcastle upon Tyne : Transport Operations Research Group, University of Newcastle upon Tyne, 1977. — 41p : ill ; 30cm. — (University of Newcastle upon Tyne. Transport Operations Research Group. Working papers ; no.24 ISSN 0306-3402)
Bibl.: p.31-32.
Sd : £2.50
(B77-13088)

625.7'94 — Vehicle actuated traffic lights. *Ireland (Republic). Rural regions. Reports, surveys*

Staunton, M M. Vehicle actuated signal controls for isolated locations / [by] M.M. Staunton. — Dublin : Foras Forbartha, 1976. — [8],100p : ill, form ; 30cm. — (RT159)
Cover title: Vehicle actuated signal controls for isolated locations = Rialaitheorí comharthaíochta feithicil ghníomhaithe d'áiteanna seoite. — Bibl.: p.79-84.
ISBN 0-900115-89-0 Sd : £2.00
(B77-06738)

625.8'5 — Bitumen-surfaced roads. Design. *Tropical regions & sub-tropical regions*

Transport and Road Research Laboratory. A guide to the structural design of bitumen-surfaced roads in tropical and sub-tropical countries / Transport and Road Research Laboratory, Department of the Environment, Department of Transport. — 3rd ed. — London : H.M.S.O., 1977. — 26p : ill ; 30cm. — (Road note ; 31)
Previous ed.: 1966.
ISBN 0-11-550162-2 Sd : £1.00
(B77-11266)

627 — HYDRAULIC ENGINEERING

627 — Hydraulic engineering. *Reviews of research*

Hydraulics research : report of the Hydraulics Research Station. — London : H.M.S.O.
1976 / with an introduction by the Director of Hydraulics Research. — 1977. — ix,83p,[4]p of plates : ill, maps, plans ; 30cm.
Bibl.: p.76-79.
ISBN 0-11-470562-3 Pbk : £2.15
ISSN 0073-4187
(B77-23499)

627.1'0941 — Inland waterways. Structures. *Great Britain. Guidebooks*

Hadfield, Charles. Waterways sights to see / [by] Charles Hadfield ; with plates, plans by Richard Dean and text illustrations by Robert Cox. — Newton Abbot [etc.] : David and Charles, 1976. — [144]p : ill, maps ; 21cm.
Bibl.: p.[139]-[142]. — Index.
ISBN 0-7153-7303-x : £2.95
(B77-08437)

627'.32 — Ships: Oil tankers. Terminals. Single-point moorings. *Reports, surveys*

Single-point moorings : an appraisal of the position at 31 January 1975, and an assessment of the feasibility of a computer-based design-analysis system / compiled by A.R. Halliwell ... [et al.]. — Edinburgh (Research Park, Riccarton, Currie, Edinburgh EH14 4AS) : Institute of Offshore Engineering, Heriot-Watt University, 1977. — xi,182p,[4] leaves of plates : ill ; 30cm.
'IOE project no.77/41'. — Bibl.: p.167-182.
ISBN 0-904046-04-4 Sp : £12.50
(B77-31260)

627'.34 — Freight transport. Shipping. Terminals. *London. Greenwich (London Borough). Victoria Deep Water Terminal. Container handling equipment: Gantry cranes. Ergonomic aspects. Reports, surveys*

Ritchie, John. A human factors evaluation of the container gantry cranes at Victoria Deep Water Terminal / by John Ritchie and John Cross and William Lucas ; edited by Andrew West. — London : National Ports Council, 1976. — [3],53 leaves : ill ; 30cm.
Bibl.: leaf 53.
ISBN 0-901058-94-7 Sp : £7.50
(B77-02386)

627'.34 — Ports. Clark van carriers. Automatic electronic guidance equipment. Performance. *Great Britain. Reports, surveys*

National Ports Council. Performance of automatic electronic guidance equipment fitted to Clark van carrier / [National Ports Council]. — London : The Council, 1977. — [8],97[i.e. 98]p : ill ; 30cm.
ISBN 0-901058-99-8 Sp : £8.00
(B77-13702)

627'.38 — Marinas. Design. *Manuals*

Adie, Donald Woodrow. Marinas : a working guide to their development and design / [by] Donald W. Adie. — 2nd ed. — London : Architectural Press [etc.], 1977. — 352p : ill, maps, plans ; 31cm.
Previous ed.: 1975. — Bibl. — Index.
ISBN 0-85139-381-0 : £22.00
(B77-33872)

627.7'03 — Marine salvage

Forsberg, Gerald. Salvage from the sea / [by] Gerald Forsberg. — London [etc.] : Routledge and Kegan Paul, 1977. — xviii,179p,[12]p of plates : ill ; 22cm.
Index.
ISBN 0-7100-8698-9 : £4.95 : CIP rev.
(B77-21952)

627.7'2 — Mixed gas underwater diving. Training. *Manuals*

Training Services Agency. Mixed gas diving / [Training Services Agency]. — London (162 Regent St., W1R 6DE) : The Agency, 1976. — 22p : form ; 30cm. — (A TSA training standard)
Bibl.: p.22.
ISBN 0-9504011-3-7 Sd : £1.50
(B77-17576)

627.7'2'0924 — Underwater diving. Falco, Albert. *Biographies*

Diolé, Philippe. The memoirs of Falco chief diver of the Calypso / by Philippe Diolé and Albert Falco ; translated from the French by Joseph Harriss. — London : Cassell, 1977. — 296p : ill(chiefly col), maps, ports(some col) ; 27cm.
Cover title: Falco chief diver of the Calypso. — Translation of: 'Les mémoires de Falco, chef plongeur de la Calypso'. Paris : Flammarion, 1976. — Index.
ISBN 0-304-29898-0 : £7.50
(B77-26365)

627'.8 — Tidal power barrages. *England. Severn Estuary. Reports, surveys*

Great Britain. *Department of Energy.* Tidal power barrages in the Severn Estuary : recent evidence on their feasibility / Department of Energy. — London : H.M.S.O., 1977. — iv, 19p : maps, plans ; 25cm. — (Energy papers ; no.23)
Bibl.: p.13.
ISBN 0-11-410607-x Sd : £1.50
(B77-21207)

627'.81'015194 — Dams. Design. Applications of numerical analysis. *Conference proceedings*

International Symposium on Criteria and Assumptions for Numerical Analysis of Dams, *Swansea, 1975.* Criteria and assumptions for numerical analysis of dams / [edited by] D.J. Naylor, K.G. Stagg, [and] O.C. Zienkiewicz. — Swansea (Singleton Park, Swansea SA2 8PP) : University College of Swansea, 1975. — [9], 1206p : ill ; 22cm.
'The International Symposium on Criteria and Assumptions for Numerical Analysis of Dams ...' - p.2. — 'Proceedings of an International Symposium held at Swansea ... 8-11 September, 1975, organised by Department of Civil Engineering of the University College, Swansea in collaboration with the British National Committee on Large Dams and the Laboratorio Nacional de Engenharia Civil, Lisbon under the patronage of the International Commission on Large Dams ...' - title page verso.
Unpriced
(B77-28688)

627'.883 — Water supply systems. Siphons. Design. *Conference proceedings*

Symposium on Design and Operation of Siphons and Siphon Spillways, *London, 1975.* Proceedings of the Symposium on Design and Operation of Siphons and Siphon Spillways, London, 1975 / [edited by Susan K. Hemmings]. — Cranfield (Cranfield, Bedford MK43 0AJ) : BHRA Fluid Engineering, 1976. — 416p in various pagings : ill, maps, ports ; 31cm.
'The Symposium on Design and Operation of Siphons and Siphon Spillways was sponsored and organised by BHRA Fluid Engineering and was held at the Scientific Societies, Lecture Theatre, Savile Row, London, W.1. England, 13-14th May, 1975' - p.iii. — Index.
ISBN 0-900983-44-2 : £15.00
(B77-02387)

627'.98 — Offshore structures. Corrosion. Control. *Conference proceedings*
Long service from offshore structures : a two day joint conference held on Thursday and Friday, 19 and 20 February, 1976 : [sponsored by] the Institute of Marine Engineers ... [et al.]. — London (76 Mark La., EC3R 7JN) : Marine Media Management Ltd for the Institute of Marine Engineers, 1976. — [3],86,[1]p : ill ; 30cm. — (Institute of Marine Engineers. Transactions : series C)
'European Federation of Corrosion event no.86'.
ISBN 0-900976-63-2 Sd : £21.00
(B77-17577)

627'.98 — Offshore structures. Fouling
Freeman, J H. The marine fouling of fixed offshore installations / [by] J.H. Freeman. — London (6 Storey's Gate, SW1P 3AU) : Construction Industry Research and Information Association for the Department of Energy, 1977. — 19[i.e. 21]p ; 30cm. — (Offshore technology paper ; 1 ISSN 0309-8184)
Pbk : Unpriced
(B77-20360)

628 — SANITARY ENGINEERING
Sheahan, Richard T. Fueling the future : an environmental and energy primer / [by] Richard T. Sheahan. — New York : St Martin's Press ; London : St James Press, 1976. — xv,127p : ill ; 24cm.
Bibl.: p.115-117. — Index.
ISBN 0-86066-002-8 : £4.50
Primary classification 621.4
(B77-21939)

628 — Hospitals. Sanitary engineering. *Great Britain. Conference proceedings*
Public Health Engineering for Hospitals - Some Current Developments *(Conference), Brunel University?, 1975.* Symposium, Public Health Engineering for Hospitals - Some Current Developments : report of proceedings, 25th-26th September 1975 : organised by the Institution of Public Health Engineers in conjunction with Department of Health and Social Security. — [London] ([32 Eccleston Sq., S.W.1]) : [Institution of Public Health Engineers], [1977]. — 162p in various pagings : ill, maps ; 30cm.
'The theme of this Conference is "Public Health Engineering for Hospitals - Some Current Developments"' - p.A-1.
Pbk : £10.00
(B77-20361)

628 — Urban regions. Ecology. Sanitary engineering aspects. *For West African students. Secondary school texts*
Gadd, P. The ecology of urbanisation and industrialisation / [by] P. Gadd ; general editor, O.F. Esuruoso. — London [etc.] : Macmillan, 1976. — [3],30,[1]p : ill, maps ; 22cm. — (Advanced readers in tropical biology)
Sd : £0.35
(B77-09074)

628'.07'1141 — Sanitary engineers. Professional education. *Great Britain. Conference proceedings*
Public Health Engineering Conference, *7th, Loughborough University of Technology, 1974.* Education and training for public health engineering and environmental management : proceedings [of the] Seventh Public Health Engineering Conference, held in the Department of Civil Engineering, Loughborough University of Technology, January 1974 / edited by John Pickford. — [Loughborough] ([Loughborough, Leics. LE11 3TU]) : [The Department], [1976]. — [1],67p : ill ; 30cm.
Pbk : Unpriced
(B77-01572)

628'.0913 — Sanitary engineering. *Tropical regions*
Water, wastes and health in hot climates / edited by Richard Feachem, Michael McGarry, Duncan Mara. — London [etc.] : Wiley, 1977. — xvi,399p : ill ; 24cm.
'A Wiley-Interscience publication'. — Bibl. — Index.
ISBN 0-471-99410-3 : £10.75
(B77-18848)

628'.0913 — Sanitary engineering. Planning. *Tropical regions. Developing countries. Conference proceedings*
International Conference on Environmental Health Engineering in Hot Climates and Developing Countries, *3rd, Loughborough University of Technology, 1976.* Planning for water and waste in hot countries : proceedings [of the] Third International Conference on Environmental Health Engineering in Hot Climates & Developing Countries, Loughborough University of Technology Department of Civil Engineering, 26th-28th September 1976 / edited by John Pickford. — Loughborough (Department of Civil Engineering, [Loughborough] University of Technology, Loughborough, Leics. LE11 3TU) : Water and Waste Engineering for Developing Countries Group, 1977. — 110p : ill ; 30cm.
£5.00
(B77-21208)

628'.0941 — Sanitary engineering. *Great Britain. Serials*
The **public** health engineering data book. — London (86 Edgware Rd, W2 2YW) : Sterling Professional Publications Ltd.
1977-78 / editor Ronald E. Bartlett. — [1977]. — 308p : ill ; 22cm.
Index.
Pbk : Unpriced
ISSN 0140-5411
(B77-30348)

628.1 — WATER SUPPLY
Overman, Michael. Water : solutions to a problem of supply and demand / [by] Michael Overman. — Revised ed. — Milton Keynes : Open University Press, 1976. — 204p : ill(chiefly col), col maps ; 22cm. — (Open University. Set books)
Previous ed.: London : Aldus Books, 1968. — Bibl.: p.199. — Index.
ISBN 0-335-00046-0 Pbk : £4.50
(B77-13089)

628.1'06'241 — Water supply. Organisations. *Great Britain. Institution of Water Engineers and Scientists. Directories*
Institution of Water Engineers and Scientists. Year book and list of members / the Institution of Water Engineers and Scientists. — London (6 Sackville St., W1X 1DD) : [The Institution]. 1976 : corrected to 1st May. — [1976]. — 32, xxiv,104p : ill ; 21cm.
Pbk : £6.00
(B77-17578)

628.1'09429'3 — Water supply. Projects: Dee Abstraction Scheme. *Clwyd*
Welsh National Water Development Authority. *Dee and Clwyd Water Division.* Dee abstraction scheme / Welsh National Water Development Authority, Dee and Clwyd Water Division = Awdurdod Cenedlaethol Datblygu Dŵr Cymru, Dee and Clwyd Water Division. — [Rhyl] ([91 Russell Rd, Rhyl, Clwyd LL18 3EA]) : The Division, [1977]. — Folder([6]p) : col ill, col map ; 30cm.
ISBN 0-86097-010-8 : Unpriced
(B77-12512)

628.1'09429'31 — Water supply systems. *Clwyd. Glascoed region*
Welsh National Water Development Authority. *Dee and Clwyd Water Division.* Glascoed supply system / Welsh National Water Development Authority, Dee and Clwyd Water Division = Awdurdod Cenedlaethol Datblygu Dŵr Cymru, Dee and Clwyd Water Division. — Rhyl (91 Russell Rd, Rhyl, Clwyd LL18 3EA) : The Division, 1975. — [2],3,[2]leaves : 1 ill, map, plan ; 21x30cm.
ISBN 0-86097-011-6 Sd : Unpriced
(B77-12513)

628.1'1 — Water supply. Wells. *Hampshire. Aldershot region. Lists*
Flatt, Arthur G. Records of wells in the area around Aldershot : inventory for one-inch geological sheet 285, new series / [by] Arthur G. Flatt, P.G. Hearsum and others. — London : H.M.S.O., 1977. — v,123p : maps ; 30cm. — (Well inventory series (metric units))
ISBN 0-11-884001-0 Pbk : £5.00
Primary classification 628.1'1
(B77-14782)

628.1'1 — Water supply. Wells. *Surrey. Farnham region. Lists*
Flatt, Arthur G. Records of wells in the area around Aldershot : inventory for one-inch geological sheet 285, new series / [by] Arthur G. Flatt, P.G. Hearsum and others. — London : H.M.S.O., 1977. — v,123p : maps ; 30cm. — (Well inventory series (metric units))
ISBN 0-11-884001-0 Pbk : £5.00
Also classified at 628.1'1
(B77-14782)

628.1'1 — Water supply. Wells. Construction by hand. *Tropical regions. Manuals*
Watt, Simon B. Hand dug wells and their construction / [by] S.B. Watt, W.E. Wood. — London : Intermediate Technology Publications, 1976. — 234p : ill ; 21cm.
ISBN 0-903031-27-2 Pbk : £3.50
(B77-18849)

628.1'6 — Water. Purification. *Conference proceedings*
Towards absolute water : a survey of current water purification : proceedings of the international symposium held at the Lorch Foundation, Lane End, England in May 1976 / edited by John B. Goodall. — High Wycombe (Lane End, High Wycombe, Bucks. HP14 3JH) : The Elga Group, [1977]. — [4],152p : ill, map, ports ; 30cm.
Pbk : £5.00
(B77-20362)

628.1'6 — Water. Purification. *European Community countries. State-of-the-art reviews*
Water Research Centre. Water purification in the EEC : a state-of-the-art review : a report / prepared for the Directorate-General for Research, Science and Education and the Environment and Consumer Protection Service of the Commission of the European Communities by the Water Research Centre. — Oxford [etc.] : Pergamon for the Commission, 1977. — vii,467p : ill, maps ; 24cm.
ISBN 0-08-021225-5 Pbk : £21.00
(B77-30349)

628.1'61 — Water. Quality. *Conference proceedings*
International Water Quality Forum, *Washington, D.C., 1975.* Water quality : proceedings of an international forum / edited by Frederick Coulston, Emil Mrak. — New York [etc.] ; London : Academic Press, 1977. — xiii,295p : ill ; 24cm. — (Ecotoxicology and environmental quality ; vol.1)
The International Water Quality Forum was held at the National Wildlife Federation's Hall of Fame, Washington, D.C., September 22-24, 1975. — Index.
ISBN 0-12-193150-1 : £10.30
(B77-23500)

628.1'61 — Water. Quality. *England. Severn River Basin & Trent River Basin. Reports, surveys. Serials*
Water quality : a report by the Water Quality Advisory Panel of the quality of water supplied, the quality of effluents discharged and the quality of rivers within the Severn-Trent Water Authority's area. — [Birmingham] (2297 Coventry Rd, Sheldon, Birmingham) : The Authority.
1975-76. — [1976]. — xi,479p : ill, maps ; 30cm.
Two fold. sheets (col. maps) in pocket.
ISBN 0-904891-03-8 Pbk : £15.00
(B77-04265)

628.1'61 — Water. Quality control
Tebbutt, Thomas Hugh Yelland. Principles of water quality control / by T.H.Y. Tebbutt. — 2nd ed. — Oxford [etc.] : Pergamon, 1977. — x,201p : ill ; 22cm. — (Pergamon international library)
Previous ed.: 1971. — Bibl. — Index.
ISBN 0-08-021297-2 : £7.50
ISBN 0-08-021296-4 Pbk : £3.75
(B77-23501)

628.1'61 — Water. Quality. Forecasting. Effects of irregular recording of data. Mathematical models. *Great Britain. Reports, surveys*
London School of Economics and Political Science. *Geography Department.* Non-sequential Water Quality Project / [Department of Geography, London School of Economics and Political Science]. — London : The Department.
[Working] paper 7 : Patching by simple interpolation / [by] John Thornes and Malcolm W. Clark. — 1976. — [3],37p : ill ; 30cm.
Working paper 7 has title: Non-sequential Water Quality Records Project. — Bibl.: p.37.
Sd : Unpriced
(B77-15339)

628.1'61'01515353 — Natural resources: Water. Analysis. Applications of finite element methods
International Conference on Finite Elements in Water Resources, *1st, Princeton University, 1976.* Finite elements in water resources : proceedings of the First International Conference on Finite Elements in Water Resources, held at Princeton University, USA, in July, 1976 / edited by W.G. Gray and G.F. Pinder and C.A. Brebbia. — London [etc.] : Pentech Press, 1977. — 1017p in various pagings : ill, maps ; 24cm.
Bibl.
ISBN 0-7273-0601-4 : £22.50
(B77-27180)

628.1'67 — Water. Desalination. Use of membranes. *Conference proceedings*
Biological and artificial membranes and desalination of water : proceedings of the study week at the Pontifical Academy of Sciences, April 14th-19th, 1975 / edited by Roberto Passino. — Amsterdam ; Oxford [etc.] : Elsevier, 1976. — iii-xxxi,901p : ill ; 25cm. — (Pontificia Academia Scientiarum. Scripta varia ; 40)
Second title page has French title: Semaine d'étude sur le thème Membranes biologiques et artificielles et la desalinisation de l'eau, 14-19 avril 1975. — Bibl.
ISBN 0-444-99822-5 : £60.66
(B77-16458)

628.1'68'062429 — Natural resources: Water. Pollution. Control. Organisations. *Wales. Welsh National Water Development Authority. Water Quality Panel. Reports, surveys. Serials*
Welsh National Water Development Authority. *Water Quality Panel.* Annual report of the Water Quality Panel, Welsh National Water Development Authority = Awdurdod Cenedlaethol Datblygu Dwr Cymru for the year ended 31st March. — [Brecon] ([Cambrian Way, Brecon, Powys]) : [The Authority].
2nd : [1975]-1976. — 1976. — [48]p ; 30cm.
Cover title.
Pbk : Unpriced
ISSN 0309-4596
(B77-13090)

628.1'68'0941 — Natural resources: Water. Pollution. Control. *Great Britain. Glossaries*
Institute of Water Pollution Control. Glossary of terms used in water pollution control / [Institute of Water Pollution Control]. — Maidstone (53 London Rd, Maidstone, Kent ME16 8JH) : The Institute, 1975. — [3],152p ; 25cm. — (Manuals of British practice in water pollution control)
£6.00
Pbk : £3.50
(B77-18220)

628.1'68'0973 — Natural resources: Water. Pollution. Control. *United States*
Luken, Ralph Andrew. Water pollution control : assessing the impacts and costs of environmental standards / [by] Ralph A. Luken, Edward H. Pechan. — New York ; London : Praeger, 1977. — xv,182p : ill, maps ; 25cm. — (Praeger special studies : design - environmental planning series)
Bibl.
ISBN 0-275-24470-9 : £12.40
(B77-31261)

628.1'683'0916336 — North Sea. Pollution by petroleum discharged by North Sea petroleum industries. Treatment. *Conference proceedings*
Separation of Oil from Water for North Sea Operations *(Conference), Heriot-Watt University, 1976.* The separation of oil from water for North Sea operations : proceedings of seminar, 22 and 23 June 1976. — Edinburgh (Research Park, Riccarton, Edinburgh EH14 4AS) : Institute of Offshore Engineering, Heriot-Watt University, 1977. — [3],124[i.e.168] p : ill, chart, maps, plans ; 30cm.
'With the backing and encouragement of the Department of Energy and the Department of the Environment (CUEP), the Institute of Offshore Engineering organised the technical seminar entitled "The Separation of Oil from Water for North Sea Operations" held at Riccarton ...' - Introduction. — Bibl.
ISBN 0-904046-03-6 Sp : Unpriced
(B77-11267)

628.1'686'162 — Oceans. Pollution
Marine pollution / edited by R. Johnston. — London [etc.] : Academic Press, 1976. — xiv, 729p : ill ; 24cm.
Bibl. — Index.
ISBN 0-12-387650-8 : £23.40
(B77-06162)

628.1'686'162 — Oceans. Pollution by petroleum
The **control** of oil pollution on the sea and inland waters : the effect of oil spills on the marine environment and methods of dealing with them / edited by J. Wardley-Smith. — London : Graham and Trotman, 1976. — 251p : ill, maps ; 24cm.
Index.
ISBN 0-86010-021-9 : £9.75
(B77-01573)

628.1'686'162 — Oceans. Pollution. Monitoring. *Reports, surveys*
Strategies for marine pollution monitoring / [edited by] Edward D. Goldberg. — New York ; London [etc.] : Wiley, 1976. — x,310p : ill, port ; 24cm.
'A Wiley-Interscience publication'. — Bibl. — Index.
ISBN 0-471-31070-0 : £16.50
(B77-02388)

628.1'686'1698 — Ground water. Pollution. Mathematical models
Fried, Jean J. Groundwater pollution : theory, methodology, modelling and practical rules / [by] Jean J. Fried. — Amsterdam ; Oxford [etc.] : Elsevier, 1975. — xvi,330p : ill, maps ; 25cm. — (Developments in water science ; 4)
Bibl.: p.313-325. — Index.
ISBN 0-444-41316-2 : Unpriced
(B77-06739)

628.1'688'162 — Oceans. Pollution by petroleum. Control measures
Inter-Governmental Maritime Consultative Organization. Manual on oil pollution / Inter-Governmental Maritime Consultative Organization. — London : I.M.C.O.
In 4 sections.
Section 1 (Prevention). — 1976. — 27p : ill ; 24cm.
Sd : £1.25
ISBN 92-801-1053-5
(B77-11268)

628.1'688'42753 — Coastal waters. Pollution by petroleum. Safety measures. *Merseyside (Metropolitan County). Liverpool. Proposals*
Great Britain. *Department of Trade.* Oil pollution contingency plan, Liverpool district / Department of Trade. — Liverpool (Marine Survey Office, Graeme House, Derby Sq., Liverpool L2 7SQ) : The Department, 1976. — [7],67p : map, plan ; 30cm.
Pbk : Unpriced
(B77-12514)

628.2 — DRAINAGE
628'.21 — Storm drainage systems. *Scotland. Reports, surveys*
Working Party on Storm Sewage (Scotland). Storm sewage : separation and disposal : report of the Working Party on Storm Sewage (Scotland). — Edinburgh : H.M.S.O., 1977. — 3-121p,leaf of plate,[6]p of plates : ill, plans ; 30cm.
ISBN 0-11-491485-0 Pbk : £4.25
(B77-28689)

628'.3 — Sewage. Constituents: Synthetic detergents. *Great Britain. Reports, surveys. Serials*
Standing Technical Committee on Synthetic Detergents. Progress report of the Standing Technical Committee on Synthetic Detergents. — London : H.M.S.O.
17th. — [1977]. — [1],v,25p ; 25cm.
ISBN 0-11-751132-3 Sd : £0.90
(B77-15340)

628'.3 — Waste water. Recycling
Water renovation and reuse / edited by Hillel I. Shuval. — New York [etc.] ; London : Academic Press, 1977. — xiii,463p : ill, 2 maps ; 24cm. — (Water pollution)
Bibl. — Index.
ISBN 0-12-641250-2 : £20.95
(B77-32690)

628'.3 — Waste water. Treatment
Ramalho, R S. Introduction to wastewater treatment processes / [by] R.S. Ramalho. — New York [etc.] ; London : Academic Press, 1977. — ix,409p : ill ; 24cm.
Bibl. — Index.
ISBN 0-12-576550-9 : £15.95
(B77-25001)

628'.3'02541 — Sewage treatment works. *Great Britain. Directories*
Institute of Water Pollution Control. Directory of municipal wastewater treatment plants / the Institute of Water Pollution Control. — [New ed.]. — [Maidstone] ([53 London Rd, Maidstone, Kent]) : [The Institute].
Previous ed.: published in 1 vol. as 'Directory of sewage works' / by the Institute of Sewage Purification. London : C.R. Books, 1963.
Vol.1 : County boroughs and Scottish authorities. — [1972]. — [3],315 leaves ; 30cm.
ISBN 0-904178-05-6 Sp : Unpriced
(B77-09757)

Vol.2 : Borough councils. — [1972]. — [2],100 leaves ; 30cm.
ISBN 0-904178-06-4 Sp : Unpriced
(B77-09758)

Vol.3 : Urban district councils. — [1972]. — [2] ,132 leaves ; 30cm.
ISBN 0-904178-07-2 Sp : Unpriced
(B77-09759)

Vol.4 : Rural district councils, joint sewerage boards and development corporations. — [1972] . — [3],209 leaves ; 30cm.
ISBN 0-904178-08-0 Sp : Unpriced
(B77-09760)

628'.3'0942971 — Sewage treatment works. *Mid Glamorgan. Merthyr Mawr. Penybont Sewage Treatment Works*
Welsh National Water Development Authority. *Morgannwg Sewage Division.* Inauguration of the Penybont Sewage Treatment Works and sewerage scheme by T. Alec Jones, M.P., Parliamentary Under-Secretary of State for Wales, 24th September 1976 / Welsh National Water Development Authority, Morgannwg Sewage Division = Awdurdod Cenedlaethol Datblygu Dŵr Cymru, Morgannwg Sewage Division. — [Brecon] ([Cambrian Way, Brecon, Powys]) : The Authority, [1977]. — [17]p : 1 col ill, map, plan ; 15x21cm.
Cover title: Penybont Sewage Treatment Works & sewerage scheme.
ISBN 0-86097-007-8 Sd : Unpriced
(B77-13091)

628.4 — PUBLIC CLEANSING AND SANITATION
628'.44 — Solid waste materials. Collection, treatment & disposal
Tchobanoglous, George. Solid wastes : engineering principles and management issues / [by] George Tchobanoglous, Hilary Theisen, Rolf Eliassen. — New York ; London [etc.] : McGraw-Hill, 1977. — xvii,621p : ill, maps, plans ; 25cm. — (McGraw-Hill series in water resources and environmental engineering)
Bibl. — Index.
ISBN 0-07-063235-9 : £16.50
(B77-33873)

628'.442 — Waste materials for recycling. Collection. *Great Britain. Manuals. For voluntary organisations*
Save and recycle : a guide to voluntary waste collection / [prepared by the Central Office of Information ; for the National Anti-Waste Programme]. — [London] : H.M.S.O., [1977]. — [2],22p : ill ; 30cm.
Sd : Unpriced
(B77-27181)

628'.442 — Waste paper. Collection by local authorities. *Great Britain. Reports, surveys*
Working Party on Local Authority Collections. Report on waste paper collection by local authorities / [Working Party on Local Authority Collections] ; [for the] Waste Management Advisory Council. — London : H.M.S.O., 1976. — vi,25p ; 21cm. — (Waste Management Advisory Council. Papers ; no.2)
'... Working Party set up by the Advisory Group on Waste Paper Recycling' - Foreword.
ISBN 0-11-751008-4 Sd : £0.60
(B77-04892)

628'.442'028 — Refuse storage containers. Rubber components. *Standards*
British Standards Institution. British Standard specification for rubber components for refuse containers = Spécification pour les éléments en caoutchouc pour les récipients aux ordures = Spezifikation für Gummibestandteile für Abfallbehälter / British Standards Institution. — 1st revision. — London : B.S.I, 1976. — Folder (4p) ; 30cm. — (BS3735 : 1976)
Pierced for binder.
ISBN 0-580-09487-1 Sd : £1.15
(B77-03599)

628'.442'0924 — Refuse. Collection. *South Yorkshire (Metropolitan County). Barnsley, 1969-1970. Personal observations*
Marshall, David, *b.1948.* The man in the street / [by] David Marshall. — London : Davis-Poynter, 1976. — 147p ; 23cm.
ISBN 0-7067-0209-3 : £3.75
(B77-01574)

628'.445 — Hospitals. Incinerators. Multi-flue chimneys. Design
Great Britain. *Department of the Environment. Directorate of Civil Engineering Development.* Design of multi-flue chimneys / [Department of the Environment, Directorate of Civil Engineering Development]. — [London] : [The Directorate], [1977]. — vii,96p : ill ; 30cm.
Cover title: Multi flue chimneys : a design guide.
Sp : £5.00
Primary classification 697'.8
(B77-32027)

628'.445'0941 — Waste materials. Disposal. Planning by local authorities. *Great Britain. Manuals*
Great Britain. *Department of the Environment.* Guideline for the preparation of a waste disposal plan / Department of the Environment. — London : H.M.S.O., [1976]. — v,22p(2 fold) : 1 ill, map ; 21cm. — (Waste management paper ; no.3)
Bibl.: p.23-24.
ISBN 0-11-751124-2 Sd : £0.70
(B77-09075)

628'.445'094225 — Solid waste materials. Disposal. *East Sussex. Reports, surveys. For structure plan making*
East Sussex *(County). Planning Department.* County structure plan, report of survey, 1977 review, solid waste disposal / East Sussex County Council [Planning Department]. — Lewes (Southover House, Southover Rd, Lewes, E. Sussex BN7 1YA) : [The Department], 1976. — [3],25p,[3]fold leaves of plates : maps ; 30cm.
'This report will form a new chapter 11 of the County Structure Plan Report of Survey ...'.
ISBN 0-900348-54-2 Sd : £0.55
(B77-13703)

628'.445'0973 — Solid waste materials. Treatment & disposal. *United States*
General Electric Company. Solid waste management : technology assessment / by General Electric Company. — [New ed.]. — New York ; London [etc.] : Van Nostrand Reinhold, 1975. — [1],xix,350[i.e.352]p : ill ; 29cm. — (Van Nostrand Reinhold-General Electric series)
Previous ed.: 1973. — Bibl.: p.341-348. — Index.
ISBN 0-442-22648-9 : £20.25
(B77-27182)

628.5 — INDUSTRIAL SANITATION

628.5 — Environment. Pollution. Control measures
Berthouex, P Mac. Strategy of pollution control / [by] P. Mac Berthouex, Dale F. Rudd. — New York ; London [etc.] : Wiley, 1977. — ix,579p : ill, maps ; 24cm.
Bibl. — Index.
ISBN 0-471-74449-2 : £14.20
(B77-19455)

Hodges, Laurent. Environmental pollution / [by] Laurent Hodges. — 2nd ed. — New York ; London [etc.] : Holt, Rinehart and Winston, 1977. — xvi,496p : ill, facsims, maps, port ; 25cm.
Previous ed.: 1973. — Bibl.: p.471-479. — Index.
ISBN 0-03-089878-1 : £9.00
(B77-20363)

628.5 — Environment. Pollution. Control measures. *Reviews of research*
Advances in environmental science and technology. — New York ; London [etc.] : Wiley.
Vol.8 : Fate of pollutants in the air and water environments. Part 1 : Mechanism of interaction between environments and mathematical modeling and the physical fate of pollutants / edited by I.H. Suffet. — 1977. — xxi,484p : ill, charts, maps ; 24cm.
'A Wiley-Interscience publication'. — 'From paper[s] presented in part at the symposium on "Fate of Pollutants in the Air and Water Environments" at the 165th National American Chemical Society Meeting in the Environmental Chemistry Division held in April 1975 in Philadelphia, Pennsylvania'. — Bibl. — Index.
ISBN 0-471-83539-0 : £18.70
(B77-26366)

628.5 — Environment. Pollution. Control. Use of microorganisms
Dart, R K. Microbiological aspects of pollution control / [by] R.K. Dart and R.J. Stretton. — Amsterdam ; Oxford [etc.] : Elsevier, 1977. — vii,215p : ill ; 24cm. — (Fundamental aspects of pollution control and environmental science ; 2)
ISBN 0-444-41589-0 : £20.00
(B77-31263)

628.5 — European Community countries. Environment. Pollution by iron & steel industries. Control measures. *Conference proceedings*
Quality of the Environment and the Iron and Steel Industry, Results and Prospects *(Conference), Luxembourg, 1974.* Quality of the environment and the iron and steel industry, results and prospects : proceedings of a conference organized by the Commission of the European Communities Directorate-General for Social Affairs, Luxembourg 25-26 September 1974. — Oxford [etc.] : Pergamon for the C.E.C., 1977. — viii,847p : ill, chart, maps, plans ; 24cm. — (EUR 5482 d,e,f)
'... Conference on "The Quality of the Environment and the Iron and Steel Industry - Results and Prospects" ...' - Introductory address.
ISBN 0-08-020915-7 Pbk : £30.00
(B77-13092)

628.5 — European Community countries. Environment. Pollution by iron & steel industries. Control measures. *Conference proceedings. French texts*
Quality of the Environment and the Iron and Steel Industry, Results and Prospects *(Conference), Luxembourg, 1974.* Qualité de l'environnement et sidérurgie, résultats et perspectives : compte rendu d'une conférence organisée par la Commission des communautés européennes, Direction générale 'Affaires sociales', Luxembourg, 24-26 septembre 1974. — Oxford [etc.] : Pergamon pour la C.C.E., 1977. — viii,852p : ill, chart, maps, plans ; 24cm. — (EUR 5482 d,e,f)
Heading supplied from English edition. — French text.
ISBN 0-08-020916-5 Pbk : £30.00
(B77-12515)

628.5 — Great Britain. Environment. Pollution. Control measures. Policies of government. Decision making. Participation of professionals & public
Pollution : the professionals and the public / compiled by Keith Attenborough, Christopher Pollitt and Andrew Porteous at the Open University. — Milton Keynes : Open University Press, 1977. — 212p : ill, maps ; 21cm. — (Open University. Set books)
Bibl.
ISBN 0-335-00037-1 Pbk : £2.85
(B77-16934)

628.5'1 — Factories. Pollutants: Vinyl chloride. Measurement. *Manuals*
Analytical Methods and Monitoring Procedures Group. The determination of vinyl chloride : a plant manual : analytical methods required for the control of vinyl chloride concentrations in and around manufacturing and process plants / compiled by specialists convened by the Vinyl Chloride Committee of the Chemical Industries Association Ltd [i.e. the Analytical Methods and Monitoring Procedures Group] and edited by W. Thain. — 2nd ed. — London (93 Albert Embankment SE1 7TU) : Chemical Industries Association, 1975. — [7],122[i.e. 124]p,[18]leaves of plates : ill ; 30cm.
Previous ed.: 1974.
Pbk : Unpriced
(B77-04266)

628.5'3 — Atmosphere pollution control equipment
Parker, Homer W. Air pollution / [by] Homer W. Parker. — Englewood Cliffs ; London [etc.] : Prentice-Hall, 1977. — xiii,287p : ill ; 25cm.
Index.
ISBN 0-13-021006-4 : £15.15
(B77-21953)

628.5'3 — Atmosphere. Pollution. Control measures
Open University. *Environmental Control and Public Health Course Team.* Air pollution control / prepared by the Course Team [i.e. The Environmental Control and Public Health Course Team]. — Milton Keynes : Open University Press, 1975. — 87p : ill(some col), col maps, port ; 30cm. — (PT272 ; 15) (Technology, a second level and post-experience course : environmental control and public health ; unit 15)
With answers to self-assessment questions.
ISBN 0-335-06008-0 Pbk : £2.40
(B77-25706)

628.5'3 — Atmosphere. Pollution. Control measures. Technical aspects
Crawford, Martin. Air pollution control theory / [by] Martin Crawford. — New York ; London [etc.] : McGraw-Hill, 1976. — xv,624p : ill ; 25cm.
With answers. — Index.
ISBN 0-07-013490-1 : £17.65
(B77-27917)

628.5'3 — Dust extraction equipment
Batel, Wilhelm. Dust extraction technology : principles, methods, measurement technique / [by] Wilhelm Batel ; English translation [from the German] by R. Hardbottle. — Stonehouse (66 High St., Stonehouse, Glos. GL10 2NA) : Technicopy Ltd, 1976. — xvi,272p : ill ; 22cm.
Translation of: 'Entstaubungstechnik : Grundlagen, Verfahren, Messwesen'. Berlin : Springer, 1972. — Index.
ISBN 0-905228-02-2 : £12.50
(B77-01575)

628.5'3 — Factories. Air. Pollutants. Assessment & control. *Conference proceedings*
Airborne hazards at work : assessment and control : a one-day symposium organised by QMC Industrial Research Ltd, 20 December 1976. — [London] ([229 Mile End Rd, E1 4AA]) : [QMC Industrial Research Ltd], [1977]. — 206leaves in various pagings : ill ; 30cm.
Includes: 'Threshold limit values for 1975' / American Conference of Governmental Industrial Hygienists. Originally published: London : H.M. Factory Inspectorate, 1976 - 'Hygiene standards for airborne asbestos dust concentrations for use with the Asbestos Regulations 1969'. Originally published: London : H.M. Factory Inspectorate, 1974.
Sp : £10.00
(B77-26367)

628.5'3'024658 — Atmosphere. Pollution. Control measures. *For management*
Air pollution control : guidebook for management / edited by August T. Rossano, Jr. — New York ; London [etc.] : McGraw-Hill, 1974[i.e.1976]. — ix,214p : ill ; 24cm.
Originally published: New York : McGraw-Hill, 1969. — Bibl.: p.212-213.
ISBN 0-07-053879-4 : £11.50
(B77-02389)

628.5'3'094273 — Atmosphere. Pollution. Control measures. *Greater Manchester (Metropolitan County), 1956-1976. Reports, surveys*
Manchester Area Council for Clean Air and Noise Control. Twenty years review of air pollution control in the area of the Council / Manchester Area Council for Clean Air and Noise Control. — Manchester (Town Hall, Manchester M60 2JS) : The Council, [1976]. — 64p : ill, maps ; 30cm.
Sheet (1 side, col. map) as insert. — Bibl.: p.64.
ISBN 0-9505506-0-4 Sd : £1.00
(B77-05489)

628.5'3'2 — Atmosphere. Pollutants: Industrial boilers. Flue gases. Solid materials. Measurement. *Manuals*
Hawksley, P G W. Measurement of solids in flue gases / [by] P.G.W. Hawksley, S. Badzioch, J.H. Blackett. — 2nd ed. / edited by P.G.W. Hawksley. — London (18 Devonshire St., W1N 2AU) : Institute of Fuel, 1977. — xi,248p : ill ; 21cm.
Previous ed.: Leatherhead : British Coal Utilisation Research Association, 1961. — Index.
ISBN 0-902597-13-2 Pbk : £15.00
(B77-11269)

628.5'3'2 — Factories. Air. Pollutants: Cyclohexanone & methylcyclohexanone. Measurement
Great Britain. *Factory Inspectorate.* Cyclohexanone and methylcyclohexanone / Health & Safety Executive, HM Factory Inspectorate. — 2nd ed. — London : H.M.S.O., 1977. — 10p : 1 ill ; 21cm. — (Methods for the detection of toxic substances in air ; booklet no.26)
Previous ed.: 1972.
ISBN 0-11-881454-0 Sd : £0.35
(B77-11889)

628.5'3'2 — Quarries. Airborne dust. Control measures. *Great Britain*
Great Britain. *Health and Safety Executive.* Airborne dust in quarries : health precautions : guidance note / from the Health & Safety Executive. — London : H.M.S.O., 1976. — [2], 21p : ill ; 22cm.
ISBN 0-11-880500-2 Sd : £0.50
(B77-04893)

628.5'4 — Industrial effluents. Treatment
Treatment of industrial effluents / edited by A.G. Callely, C.F. Forster, D.A. Stafford. — London [etc.] : Hodder and Stoughton, 1977. — xiii, 378p : ill, maps ; 22cm.
Index.
ISBN 0-340-19799-4 : £7.95
(B77-22664)

628.5'4 — Ports. Facilities for collection of residues from petroleum products carrying ships. *Reports, surveys*
Inter-Governmental Maritime Consultative Organization. Facilities in ports for the reception of oil residues : results of an enquiry made in 1972 / Inter-Governmental Maritime Consultative Organization. — London ([101 Piccadilly, W.1]) : I.M.C.O.
Supplement : 1976. — 1976. — 20p : forms ; 30cm.
ISBN 0-900496-38-x Sd : £1.00
ISBN 92-801-1049-7
(B77-05490)

628.5'4'0973 — Industrial waste materials. Treatment & disposal. *United States*
Besselievre, Edmund Bulkley. The treatment of industrial wastes. — 2nd ed. / [by] Edmund B. Besselievre and Max Schwartz. — New York ; London [etc.] : McGraw-Hill, 1976. — ix, 386p : ill, forms, map ; 24cm.
Previous ed.: / by Edmund B. Besselievre. New York : McGraw-Hill, 1968. — Bibl.: p.371-376. — Index.
ISBN 0-07-005047-3 : £15.75
(B77-06740)

628.7 — RURAL SANITARY ENGINEERING
628.7 — Agricultural waste materials. Treatment. *Great Britain*
Hobson, P N. Waste treatment in agriculture / [by] P.N. Hobson and A.M. Robertson. — London : Applied Science Publishers, 1977. — x,257p : ill, plans ; 23cm.
Bibl.: p.243-249. — Index.
ISBN 0-85334-736-0 : £14.00
(B77-31262)

628.7 — Agricultural waste materials. Treatment. *United States*
Loehr, Raymond C. Pollution control for agriculture / [by] Raymond C. Loehr. — New York [etc.] ; London : Academic Press, 1977. — xiii,383p : ill ; 24cm.
Originally published: as 'Agricultural waste management'. New York : Academic Press, 1974. — Index.
ISBN 0-12-455260-9 : £12.05
(B77-17579)

628.7 — Agricultural waste materials. Treatment & disposal. *Great Britain*
Weller, John Brian. Farm wastes management / [by] John B. Weller, Stephen L. Willetts. — London : Crosby Lockwood Staples, 1977. — 235p : ill, 2 facsims, map, plans ; 23cm.
Bibl.: p.221-227. — Index.
ISBN 0-258-96928-8 : £15.00
(B77-29504)

628'.7 — Livestock. Waste materials. Management. *Conference proceedings*
Seminar on Animal Wastes, *Czechoslovak Research and Development Centre for Environmental Pollution Control, 1976?.* Animal wastes / edited by E. Paul Taiganides. — London : Applied Science Publishers, 1977. — xvi,429p : ill, map ; 23cm.
'... revised material based upon papers presented at the Seminar on Animal Wastes organized by the Regional Office for Europe of the World Health Organization and the Government of the Czechoslovak Socialist Republic, in cooperation with the United Nations Development Programme and held at the Czechoslovak Research and Development Centre for Environmental Pollution Control, Bratislava' - half title page verso. — Bibl. — Index.
ISBN 0-85334-721-2 : £25.00
(B77-31264)

628'.7 — Livestock. Waste materials: Slurry. Treatment & utilisation. *Manuals*
Agricultural Development and Advisory Service. Farm waste management, general information / [Agricultural Development and Advisory Service] ; [compiled by C.V. Nielsen]. — Pinner : Ministry of Agriculture, Fisheries and Food, 1977. — [2],iii,34p ; 21cm. — (Short term leaflet ; 67)
Sd : Unpriced
(B77-16935)

628'.742 — Small scale sewage treatment works. Operation. *Manuals*
Barnes, D. The design and operation of small sewage works / [by] D. Barnes and F. Wilson. — London : Spon [etc.], 1976. — xvi,180p : ill, form ; 24cm.
Bibl. — Index.
ISBN 0-419-10980-3 : £6.75
(B77-05491)

628.92 — FIRE FIGHTING TECHNOLOGY
628.9'2'03 — Fire protection & fire fighting. *Dictionaries*
Kuvshinoff, B W. Fire science dictionary / B.W. Kuvshinoff compiler, chief editor ; editors ... [others]. — New York ; London [etc.] : Wiley, 1977. — viii,439p ; 26cm.
'A Wiley-Interscience publication'.
ISBN 0-471-51113-7 : £11.00
(B77-31265)

628.9'2'03 — Fire protection & fire fighting. *Glossaries*
British Standards Institution. Glossary of terms associated with fire = Lexique des termes associés avec le feu = Lexikon der Begriffe von Brand und Feuer / British Standards Institution. — London : B.S.I.
Part 5 = Partie 5 = Teil 5 : Miscellaneous terms = Termes divers = Verschiedene Begriffe. — 1976. — [2],6,[2]p ; 30cm. — (BS4422 : Part 5 : 1976)
Pierced for binder.
ISBN 0-580-09338-7 Sd : £2.40
(B77-09076)

628.9'22 — Automatic fire alarms. *Programmed texts*
Great Britain. *Home Office. Unit for Educational Methods.* Automatic fire detection and alarm systems / prepared by the Home Office Unit for Educational Methods ; for the Home Office Fire Department ... — Moreton-in-Marsh (Moreton-in-Marsh, Glos. GL56 0RH) : The Unit, 1976. — [2],97,[1]p : ill(some col), facsim, forms ; 30cm.
With answers to revision tests. — Accompanied by student's workbook (29p.: ill.: Sd.). — '... designed to be worked through in conjunction with Book 9 of the Manual of Firemanship "Fire Protection of Buildings"' - Introduction.
ISBN 0-903727-45-5 Sp : Unpriced
(B77-13093)

628.9'22 — Printing industries. Fire protection. *Manuals*
British Printing Industries Federation. Planning programme for the prevention and control of fire in the printing industry / [British Printing Industries Federation and the Fire Protection Association]. — London (11 Bedford Row, WC1R 4DX) : The Federation : The Association, 1976. — 20p : ill, forms, plans ; 30cm.
ISBN 0-85168-098-4 Sd : £1.75(£1.25 to members of the Federation)
(B77-09761)

628.9'22 — Residences. Automatic fire alarms. *Standards*
British Standards Institution. Specification for components of automatic fire alarm systems for residential premises = Spécification des eléments des systèmes automatiques d'avertissement d'incendie pour les habitations = Spezifikation für Bestandteile von automatischen Feuermelderanlagen für Wohnbauten / British Standards Institution. — London : B.S.I.
Part 1 = Partie 1 = Teil 1 : Point-type smoke detectors = Détecteurs de fumée du type ponctuel = Punktförmige Rauchmelder. — 1977. — [2],9,[1]p : ill ; 30cm. — (BS5446 : Part 1 : 1977)
Pierced for binder.
ISBN 0-580-09631-9 Sd : £2.70
(B77-14783)

628.9'22'0973 — Fire protection. *United States. Manuals*
Bare, William K. Fundamentals of fire prevention / [by] William K. Bare. — New York ; London [etc.] : Wiley, 1977. — x, 2-213p : ill, forms ; 24cm. — (Wiley series in fire science)
Bibl. — Index.
ISBN 0-471-04835-6 : £9.20
(B77-10410)

628.9'25 — Fire fighting. *Juvenile literature*
Law, Felicia. Fighting fire / written by Felicia Law ; illustrated by Jenny Parsons. — Glasgow [etc.] : Collins, 1977. — 32p : col ill ; 22cm. — (Dandelions)
ISBN 0-00-106005-8 : £0.50
(B77-31266)

628.9'25 — Fire fighting. *Manuals*
Great Britain. *Home Office. Fire Department.* Manual of firemanship : a survey of the science of fire-fighting / Home Office (Fire Department). — [New ed.]. — London : H.M.S.O.
Previously published: in 9 parts. 1943-.
Book 3 : Fire extinguishing equipment. — 1976. — x,127p : col ill ; 22cm.
ISBN 0-11-340583-9 Pbk : £2.00
(B77-14784)

Walsh, Charles Vincent. Firefighting strategy and leadership. — 2nd ed. / [by] Charles V. Walsh, Leonard G. Marks. — New York ; London [etc.] : Gregg Division, McGraw-Hill, 1977. — vi,378p : ill, facsims, forms ; 24cm.
Previous ed.: / by Charles V. Walsh. 1963. — Index.
ISBN 0-07-068026-4 : £9.70
(B77-24298)

628.9'25'076 — Fire fighting. Examinations set by Fire Services Central Examinations Board for England and Wales. *England. Reports, surveys*
Working Party to Review Statutory Promotion Examinations in the Fire Service. Report / Central Fire Brigades Advisory Councils for England and Wales and for Scotland Joint Training Committee, Working Party to Review Statutory Promotion Examinations in the Fire Service. — [London] ([c/o A.R. Boddy (Working Party Secretary), Home Office Fire Department, Horseferry Rd, Dean Ryle St., SW1P 2AW]) : [The Joint Training Committee], [1976]. — [2]leaves,56[i.e.61]p(4 fold) ; 30cm.
Sd : Unpriced
(B77-31953)

628.9'25'0941 — Fire fighting. *Great Britain, to 1976*
Butcher, Thomas Kennedy. The fire-fighters / [by] T.K. Butcher. — London : Batsford, 1977. — 95p : ill, facsims, ports ; 26cm. — (Past-into-present series)
Bibl.: p.94. — Index.
ISBN 0-7134-3279-9 : £2.95
(B77-09762)

628.9'25'0942132 — Hotels. *London. Westminster (London Borough). Worsley Hotel. Fire fighting, 1974*
Honeycombe, Gordon. Red Watch / [by] Gordon Honeycombe. — London : Arrow Books, 1977. — 304p,[8]p of plates : ill, map, plans, ports ; 18cm.
Originally published: London : Hutchinson, 1976.
ISBN 0-09-914230-9 Pbk : £0.85
(B77-30350)

629 — TRANSPORT ENGINEERING, AUTOMATIC CONTROL SYSTEMS, ETC
629.04 — Guided land transport. Engineering aspects
Transport without wheels / edited by E.R. Laithwaite. — London : Elek, 1977. — ix, 322p : ill, 2 maps, plan ; 24cm.
Index.
ISBN 0-236-40066-5 : £15.00
(B77-27918)

629.04 — Steam powered vehicles. *England, ca 1900-1920. Illustrations*
Steam on farms and roads. — [Chelmsford] ([c/o M. Rayce, Hankins Farm, Waltham Rd, Terling, Chelmsford, Essex CM3 2RA]) : [East Anglian Traction Engine Club].
Part 1 / [edited and compiled by R.A. Harding]. — [1977]. — [57]p : ill, ports ; 13x18cm.
'A book of vintage prints presented to the East Anglian Traction Engine Club by B.M. Taylor to commemorate the 21st anniversary of the club in steam 1955-1976' - note.
Sd : Unpriced
(B77-26368)

629.04 — Transport engineering
The **encyclopedia** of transport / [edited by Donald Clarke]. — London [etc.] : Marshall Cavendish, 1976. — 249p : ill(chiefly col), facsims, col map, ports ; 30cm.
Ill. on lining papers. — '... first published ... in "How it works". [1974-1976]' - title page verso. — Index.
ISBN 0-85685-176-0 : £4.95
(B77-27183)

629.04 — Vehicles. *Juvenile literature*
Wrigley, Denis. Wonder why book of moving machines / written and illustrated by Denis Wrigley. — London : Transworld, 1977. — [2], 32p : col ill ; 29cm.
Index. — Previous control number ISBN 0-552-57005-2.
ISBN 0-552-98039-0 : £1.35
ISBN 0-552-57005-2 Sd : £0.50
(B77-11270)

629.04 — Vehicles. Engines. Testing. Automation. *Conference proceedings*
International Symposium on Engine Testing Automation, *4th, Naples, 1975.* Fourth International Symposium on Engine Testing Automation : performance, emission & diagnostics : Naples 29 Sept.-3 Oct. 1975. — Croydon (62 High St., Croydon CR0 1NA) : Automotive Automation Ltd.
[Vol.2]. — [1977?]. — 584p in various pagings : ill, form ; 30cm.
Cover title. — Vol.2 has address: 42 Lloyd Park Ave., Croydon CR0 5SB. — '... organized ... by the Istituto Motori' - Introduction.
Pbk : Unpriced
(B77-33277)

629.04 — Vehicles, to ca 1940. *Periodicals*
Three on the floor. — Shottesbrooke (Smewins, Shottesbrooke, Maidenhead, Berks. SL6 3SR) : Independent Shottesbrooke Press.
[No.1]-. — [1972]-. — ill ; 21cm.
Published at irregular intervals. — 48p. in issue no.27.
Sd : £3.00 for 6 issues
ISSN 0140-3257
(B77-25002)

629.04'022'2 — Vehicles. *Colouring books*
Things that go. — Maidenhead : Purnell, 1977. — [48]p : ill ; 28cm. — (Colour and learn)
Fill-in book.
Pbk : £0.15
(B77-09077)

629.1 — AEROSPACE ENGINEERING
629.1 — 0.5% nickel-chromium-molybdenum steel bars for forged nuts & bolts of aerospace vehicles. *Standards*
British Standards Institution. Specification for 0.5% nickel-chromium-molybdenum steel bars for the manufacture of forged bolts and forged nuts = Spécification, barres en acier à 0.5% de nickel-chrome-molybdène pour la fabrication des vis forgées et écrous forgés = Spezifikation, Stahlstäbe mit einem 0.5% Nickel-Chrom-Molybdän-Gehalt für die Herstellung von geschmiedeten Schrauben und Muttern / British Standards Institution. — London : B.S.I., 1976. — Sheet ([2]p) ; 30x21cm. — (British Standard aerospace series = Série aérospatiale = Luftraumserie) (2S 147 : 1976)
Pierced for binder. — '(Superseding British Standard S 147)'.
ISBN 0-580-09500-2 : £0.80
(B77-14281)

629.1 — 1.75% nickel-chromium-molybdenum steel bars for forged nuts & bolts of aerospace vehicles. *Standards*
British Standards Institution. Specification for 1.75% nickel-chromium-molybdenum steel bars for the manufacture of forged bolts and forged nuts = Spécification, barres en acier à 1.75% de nickel-chrome-molybdène pour la fabrication des vis forgées et écrous forgés = Spezifikation, Stahlstäbe mit einem 1.75% Nickel-Chrom-Molybdän-Gehalt für die Herstellung von geschmiedeten Schrauben und Muttern / British Standards Institution. — London : B.S.I., 1976. — Sheet ([2]p) ; 31x21cm. — (British Standard aerospace series = Série aérospatiale = Luftraumserie) (2S 149 : 1976)
Pierced for binder. — '(Superseding British Standard S 149)'.
ISBN 0-580-09510-x : £0.80
(B77-14282)

629.1 — Aerospace vehicles. Engines. Pistons. Centrifugally cast chromium alloy cast iron ring pots for piston rings up to 400mm diameter. *Standards*
British Standards Institution. Specification for high chromium alloy cast iron ring pots (centrifugally cast) = Spécification des pots en fonte alliée à haute teneur en chrome (coulés par centrifugation) = Spezifikation für Kolbengehaüse aus legiertem Gusseisen mit hohem Chromgehalt (zentrifugalgegossen) : (suitable for piston rings up to 400 mm in diameter) = (applicables aux segments de piston jusqu'à 400 mm de diamètre) = geeignet für Kolbenringe mit Durchmesser bis 400 mm) / British Standards Institution. — London : B.S.I., 1977. — Folder (4p) : ill ; 30cm. — (British Standard aerospace series = Série aérospatiale = Luftraumserie) (HC 403 : 1977)
Pierced for binder. — '(Superseding Ministry of Defence specification DTD 485A)'.
ISBN 0-580-09690-4 : £1.20
(B77-14283)

629.1 — Aerospace vehicles. Engines. Pistons. Centrifugally cast iron ring pots for piston rings up to 200mm diameter. *Standards*
British Standards Institution. Specification for cast iron ring pots (centrifugally cast) = Spécification des pots en fonte (coulés par centrifugation) = Spezifikation für Kolbengehaüse aus Gusseisen (zentrifugalgegossen) : (suitable for piston rings up to 200mm in diameter) = (applicables aux segments de piston jusqu'à 200mm de diamètre) = (beeignet für Kolbenringe mit Durchmesser bis 200mm) / British Standards Institution. — London : B.S.I., 1977. — Folder (4p) : ill ; 30cm. — (British Standard aerospace series = Série aérospatiale = Luftraumserie) (HC 402 : 1977)
Pierced for binder. — '(Superseding Ministry of Defence specification DTD 233A)'.
ISBN 0-580-09680-7 : £1.20
(B77-14284)

629.1 — Aerospace vehicles. Engines. Pistons. Chromium-molybdenum alloy cast iron ring pots. *Standards*
British Standards Institution. Specification for chromium-molybdenum alloy cast iron ring pots = Spécification des pots en fonte alliée au chrome-molybdène = Spezifikation für Kolbengehäuse aus legiertem Gusseisen mit Chrom-Molybdän-Behalt : (suitable for centrifugally cast and sand cast sealing rings, piston rings and cylinder liners) = (applicables aux anneaux de joint, segments de piston et fourrures de cylindre coulés par centrifugation et en sable) = (beeignet für zentrifugalgegossene und sandgegossene Dichtringe, Kolbenringe und Zylinderfutter) / British Standards Institution. — London : B.S.I., 1977. — Folder (4p) : ill ; 30cm. — (British Standard aerospace series = Série aérospatiale = Luftraumserie) (HC 404 : 1977)
Pierced for binder. — '(Superseding Ministry of Defence specification DTD 719)'.
ISBN 0-580-09700-5 : £1.20
(B77-14285)

629.13 — AERONAUTICS
629.13 — Aircraft. Accidents. *Inquiry reports*
Great Britain. *Department of Trade. Accidents Investigation Branch.* Beechcraft 95-B55(Baron) G-AZUJ, report on the accident at Birmingham Airport, England, on 29 November 1975 / Department of Trade, Accidents Investigation Branch. — London : H.M.S.O., 1977. — v,16, [1]p ; 30cm. — (Aircraft accident report ; 18-76)
ISBN 0-11-511804-7 Sd : £0.85
(B77-14785)

Great Britain. *Department of Trade. Accidents Investigation Branch.* Bell 47G Helicopter G-BBKP, report on the accident at Grange Farm, Kingswood, near Wotton-under-Edge, Gloucestershire on 20 March 1975 / Department of Trade, Accidents Investigation Branch. — London : H.M.S.O., 1977. — [5],9, [1]p ; 30cm. — (Aircraft accident report ; 17-76)
ISBN 0-11-511803-9 Sd : £0.65
(B77-13704)

Great Britain. *Department of Trade. Accidents Investigation Branch.* Cessna 310 G-BCKL, report on the accident at Black Hill, Perthshire, Scotland on 4 March 1976 / Department of Trade, Accidents Investigation Branch. — London : H.M.S.O., 1977. — iii,12p : map ; 30cm. — (Aircraft accident report ; 2-77)
ISBN 0-11-511806-3 Sd : £0.70
(B77-20364)

Great Britain. *Department of Trade. Accidents Investigation Branch.* Cessna F150 H G-AVSS and Cessna F150 G G-AVAB, report on the accident near Guildtown, Perthshire, on 22 November 1975 / Department of Trade, Accidents Investigation Branch. — London : H.M.S.O., 1977. — v,17,[1]p ; 30cm. — (Aircraft accident report ; 16-76)
ISBN 0-11-511802-0 Sd : £0.85
(B77-14786)

Great Britain. *Department of Trade. Accidents Investigation Branch.* Handley Page Dart Herald 203 G-BBXJ, report on the accident at Jersey Airport, Jersey, Channel Islands on 24 December 1974 : including the review before Gerald A. Draycott, Captain J.H. Montgomery, Pilot Assessor and Mr R.F. Franklin, Engineer Assessor / Department of Trade, Accidents Investigation Branch. — London : H.M.S.O., 1977. — vi,34,[1]p : ill ; 30cm. — (Aircraft accident report ; 4-76)
ISBN 0-11-511436-x Sd : £1.25
(B77-30351)

Great Britain. *Department of Trade. Accidents Investigation Branch.* Hawker Siddeley HS 125 series 600B G-BCUX, report on the accident near Dunsfold Aerodrome, Surrey, 20 November 1975 / Department of Trade, Accidents Investigation Branch. — London : H.M.S.O., 1977. — v,16,[1]p,[2]leaves of plates(1 fold) : 2 maps ; 30cm. — (Aircraft accident report ; 1-77)
ISBN 0-11-511805-5 Sd : £0.95
(B77-14787)

Great Britain. *Department of Trade. Accidents Investigation Branch.* Piper PA-31 model 350 G-BBPV, report on the accident at Little Sandhurst, Berkshire, on 19 October 1975 / Department of Trade, Accidents Investigation Branch. — London : H.M.S.O., 1977. — [5],12, [1]p ; 30cm. — (Aircraft accident report ; 15-76)
ISBN 0-11-511801-2 Sd : £0.70
(B77-13705)

629.13 — Aircraft. Noise. Engineering aspects
AIAA Aero-acoustics Conference, *2nd, Hampton, Va, 1975.* Aeroacoustics, acoustic wave propagation, aircraft noise prediction, aeroacoustic instrumentation : technical papers from AIAA 2nd Aero-acoustics Conference, March 1975, subsequently revised for this volume / edited by Ira R. Schwartz ; assistant editors Henry T. Nagamatsu, Warren C. Strahle. — New York : American Institute of Aeronautics and Astronautics ; Cambridge, Mass. ; London : M.I.T. Press, 1976. — xxxiv, 307p : ill ; 24cm. — (Progress in astronautics and aeronautics ; vol.46)
Index.
ISBN 0-915928-10-8 : £13.60
(B77-04267)

629.13 — Aviation
The **international** encyclopedia of aviation / general editor David Mondey ; foreword by Juan Trippe. — London : Octopus Books, 1977. — 480p : ill(some col), ports ; 33cm.
Col. ill. on lining papers. — Index.
ISBN 0-7064-0603-6 : £12.95
(B77-33874)

629.13 — British registered aircraft. Accidents. *Reports, surveys. Serials*
Accidents to aircraft on the British register : a survey including statistics of airmiss incidents involving civil aircraft in United Kingdom airspace / Civil Aviation Authority. — London : The Authority.
1975. — 1976. — viii,62p : ill ; 21x30cm. — (CAP389)
ISBN 0-86039-015-2 Pbk : £2.00
ISSN 0306-3550
(B77-03080)

629.13'03 — Aviation. *Encyclopaedias*
Wings / executive editor, Anthony Robinson. — London : Orbis Books.
Vol.1 ; Part 1-. — 1977-. — ill(some col) ; 30cm.
In 120 weekly parts. — [1],20p.,fold. sheet in 1st issue. — Binders available at £3.00 each.
Sd : £0.40
(B77-15341)

629.13'09 — Aircraft. Flights, to 1975. *Juvenile literature*
Shephard, Peter. Flight / [by] Peter Shephard. — London : Ward Lock, 1976. — 92p : ill(chiefly col), ports ; 29cm.
With answers to quiz. — Index.
ISBN 0-7063-1860-9 : £1.95
(B77-03600)

629.13'09 — Aircraft. Flights, to 1977. *Records of achievement*

The **Guinness** book of air facts and feats. — 3rd ed. / edited by John W.R. Taylor, Michael J.H. Taylor, David Mondey ; artwork by Mike Roffe. — Enfield : Guinness Superlatives, 1977. — 240p,[16]p of plates : ill(some col), ports ; 25cm.
Previous ed.: 1973. — Bibl.: p.223-225. — Index.
ISBN 0-900424-34-6 : £6.50
(B77-33278)

629.13'09 — Aviation, to 1976

Ellis, Chris. The world of aviation / [by] Chris Ellis. — London [etc.] : Hamlyn, 1977. — 192p : ill(some col), port ; 31cm.
Col. ill. on lining papers. — Index.
ISBN 0-600-30318-7 : £3.95
(B77-30352)

629.13'091'1 — Flights across North Atlantic Ocean, 1919

Rowe, Percy. The great Atlantic air race / [by] Percy Rowe. — London [etc.] : Angus and Robertson, 1977. — 224p : ill ; 24cm.
Bibl.: p.223-224.
ISBN 0-207-95766-5 : £6.00
(B77-28690)

629.13'091'1 — Flights across North Atlantic Ocean, to 1975

Beaty, David. The water jump : the story of transatlantic flight / [by] David Beaty. — London : Secker and Warburg, 1976. — xv, 304p : ill, chart, maps, ports ; 24cm.
Bibl.: p.291-292. — Index.
ISBN 0-436-03913-3 : £4.50
(B77-02390)

629.13'092'4 — Aeroplanes. Flying. Doolittle, James Harold. *Biographies*

Thomas, Lowell, *b.1892.* Bomber commander : the life of James H. Doolittle / [by] Lowell Thomas and Edward Jablonski. — London : Sidgwick and Jackson, 1977. — xvi,368p,[32]p of plates : ill, ports ; 23cm.
Also published: as 'Doolittle'. Garden City, N.Y. : Doubleday, 1977. — Bibl.: p.350-351. — Index.
ISBN 0-283-98382-5 : £6.95
(B77-27919)

629.13'092'4 — Aeroplanes. Flying. Jackson, Archibald Stewart. *Autobiographies*

Jackson, Archibald Stewart. Both feet in the air : an airline pilot's story / by A.S. Jackson. — Lavenham : T. Dalton, 1977. — 123p : ill, facsim, ports ; 24cm.
ISBN 0-900963-73-5 : £4.80
(B77-31954)

629.13'092'4 — Aeroplanes. Flying. Johnson, Amy. *Biographies*

Babington Smith, Constance. Amy Johnson / [by] Constance Babington Smith. — London [etc.] : White Lion Publishers, 1977. — 384p, [24]p of plates,[2] leaves of plates : ill, 2 facsims, map, ports ; 23cm.
Originally published: London : Collins, 1967. — Index.
ISBN 0-7274-0264-1 : £5.75
(B77-22665)

629.13'092'4 — Aeroplanes. Flying. Zumbach, Jean, 1935-1967. *Autobiographies*

Zumbach, Jean. On wings of war : my life as a pilot adventurer / [by] Jean Zumbach ; translated from the French by Steve Cox. — London : Corgi, 1977. — 285p ; 18cm.
This translation originally published: London : Deutsch, 1975. — Translation of: 'Mister Brown'. Paris : R. Laffont, 1973.
ISBN 0-552-10521-x Pbk : £0.85
(B77-27920)

629.13'092'4 — Aircraft. Flying. Piggott, Derek. *Autobiographies*

Piggott, Derek. Delta papa : a life of flying / [by] Derek Piggott ; with line illustrations by the author ; and a foreword by Sir Peter Scott. — London : Pelham, 1977. — xii,179p,[16]p of plates : ill, ports ; 23cm.
ISBN 0-7207-0979-2 : £4.50
(B77-21209)

629.13'09411 — Aircraft: Balloons. Flights. *Scotland, 1745-1746. Correspondence. Facsimiles*

Lunardi, Vincenzo. An account of five aerial voyages in Scotland / [by] Vincent Lunardi. — [1st ed. reprinted] ; with an introduction by Alexander Law. — Edinburgh ([Edinburgh University Library, George Sq., Edinburgh EH8 9LJ]) : Friends of Edinburgh University Library, 1976. — [12],3-6,114p : port ; 22cm. — (The Drummond books ; no.1)
Limited ed. of 420 copies, of which 400 are numbered and 20 are lettered. — Facsimile reprint of: 1st ed. London : Printed for the author, 1786.
£6.00
ISBN 0-905152-00-x Lettered ed.: £6.00
(B77-09078)

629.13'09426 — Aviation. *East Anglia, 1937-1976*

Kinsey, Gordon. Aviation : flight over the Eastern counties since 1937 / by Gordon Kinsey. — Lavenham : T. Dalton, 1977. — 268p : ill, map, ports ; 24cm.
Map, text on lining papers. — Index.
ISBN 0-900963-29-8 : £5.80
(B77-30353)

629.13'09427'3 — Aviation. *Greater Manchester (Metropolitan County), to 1976*

Robinson, Brian R. Aviation in Manchester : a short history / by Brian R. Robinson. — Stockport (c/o M.J. Taylor, c/o Flight Development Department, Hawker Siddeley Aviation Ltd, Woodford, Stockport, Cheshire SK7 1QR) : Manchester Branch of the Royal Aeronautical Society, 1977. — 97p : ill, facsims ; 21cm.
ISBN 0-9505515-0-3 Sd : £0.80
(B77-16936)

629.132 — Flight

Dalton, Stephen. The miracle of flight / [by] Stephen Dalton. — Maidenhead : Sampson Low, 1977. — 168p : ill(chiefly col), facsims ; 27cm.
Bibl.: p.163. — Index.
ISBN 0-562-00070-4 : £5.95
(B77-33279)

629.132 — Flight. *Primary school texts*

Ramsbottom, Edward. In the air / [by] Edward Ramsbottom and Joan Redmayne ; illustrated by John Dyke. — London [etc.] : Macmillan, 1977. — 16p : chiefly col ill ; 30cm. — (Bright ideas)
ISBN 0-333-19638-4 Sd : £0.48
(B77-24299)

629.132'076 — Flight. *Questions & answers. Juvenile literature*

Thompson, James Edgar. Air quiz / [by] J.E. Thompson ; illustrated by John Batchelor. — London [etc.] : Beaver Books, 1977. — 126p : ill ; 18cm.
With answers.
ISBN 0-600-30322-5 Pbk : £0.45
(B77-27184)

629.1325 — AIRCRAFT. FLYING

629.132'51 — Aeronautics. Navigation

Canner, W H P. Air navigation : 'for GCE candidates and those looking for a thorough grounding in the theory and practice of air navigation' / by W.H.P. Canner. — Glasgow : Brown and Ferguson, 1976. — [9],334p : ill, chart, maps ; 22cm.
Index.
ISBN 0-85174-243-2 : £9.00
(B77-01576)

629.132'5216 — Passenger aeroplanes. Flying. *Technical data*

Civil Aviation Authority. Specimen performance charts for aeroplanes certificated in performance group A / [Civil Aviation Authority]. — London : The Authority, 1976. — v,37p,[20] leaves of plates(17 fold),[6]p of plates : ill ; 30cm. — (Civil Aviation Authority. Papers ; 385)
Previous ed.: / issued by the Air Registration Board. 1959.
ISBN 0-86039-008-x Sp : £2.30
(B77-11890)

629.132'523 — Gliding. *Manuals*

Piggott, Derek. Understanding gliding : the principles of soaring flight / [by] Derek Piggott ; with illustrations by the author. — London : A. and C. Black, 1977. — 259p : ill, charts, map ; 26cm.
Index.
ISBN 0-7136-1640-7 : £7.25
(B77-14286)

629.132'524 — Aeroplanes. Flying

Gilbert, James. The flier's world / by James Gilbert. — Walton-on-Thames (25 Bridge St., Walton-on-Thames, Surrey) : M. and J. Hobbs ; London : Joseph, 1977. — 252p : ill(chiefly col), map, ports(1 col) ; 28cm.
Originally published: New York : Random House, 1976. — Index.
ISBN 0-7181-1655-0 : £10.50
(B77-29505)

629.133 — AIRCRAFT. SPECIAL TYPES

629.133 — Aircraft. *Juvenile literature*

The **super** book of aircraft. — London : Macdonald Educational, 1977. — 32p : ill(some col), maps(1 col), ports ; 28cm.
Adaptation of: 'Aircraft'. London : Macdonald, 1969.
ISBN 0-356-05592-2 Sd : £0.50
(B77-18221)

629.133'021'2 — Aircraft. *Technical data. Serials*

Jane's all the world's aircraft. — London : Jane's Yearbooks.
1976-77 : [67th year] / compiled and edited by John W.R. Taylor ; assistant editor Kenneth Munson. — 1976. — 72,860p : ill ; 33cm.
Index.
ISBN 0-354-00538-3 : £25.00
ISSN 0075-3017
(B77-06741)

The **observer's** book of aircraft. — London : F. Warne. — (The observer's pocket series ; [11])
1977 ed. : 26th ed. / compiled by William Green ; with silhouettes by Dennis Punnett. — 1977. — 254p : ill ; 15cm.
Index.
ISBN 0-7232-1562-6 : £1.10
(B77-15916)

629.133'07'2 — Aircraft, to 1976. Research. *Manuals*

Robertson, Bruce. Aviation archaeology : a collectors guide to aeronautical relics / [by] Bruce Robertson. — Cambridge : Stephens, 1977. — 152p : ill, facsim, maps, ports ; 25cm.
ISBN 0-85059-255-0 : £4.50
(B77-29506)

629.133'074'0941 — Museums. Exhibits: Aircraft. *Great Britain. Catalogues*

Ellis, Ken. British museum aircraft : 39 museums and the histories of their exhibits / compiled by Ken Ellis and Phil Butler ; photos edited by Martin Chell. — Liverpool (Room 14, Hangar No.2, Liverpool Airport, Merseyside L24 8QE) : Merseyside Aviation Society Limited, 1977. — 166p : ill, map ; 21cm.
Bibl.: p.158-160. — Index.
ISBN 0-902420-15-1 Pbk : Unpriced
(B77-30354)

629.133'09'04 — Aircraft, to 1939

Allward, Maurice. Early aircraft / [written by Maurice Allward] ; [illustrated by Mike Atkinson et al.]. — Glasgow [etc.] : Collins, 1977. — 3-62p : ill(chiefly col), col map, ports(chiefly col) ; 30cm. — (Collins transport series)
'Collins all colour transport books' - cover. — Index.
ISBN 0-00-106241-7 : £1.50
(B77-23502)

629.133'09'04 — Aircraft, to 1970. *Illustrations. Juvenile literature*

Aircraft / general editor Boswell Taylor ; ... illustrator John Young. — Leicester : Knight Books, 1977. — [1],32p : of ill, facsims, 2 maps, plan, ports ; 21cm. — (Picture teach yourself : project books)
Originally published: Leicester : Brockhampton Press, 1967.
ISBN 0-340-21554-2 Pbk : £0.50
(B77-06742)

629.133'09'04 — Aircraft, to 1976. *Juvenile literature*

Kerrod, Robin. Aircraft / by Robin Kerrod. — London [etc.] : F. Watts, 1977. — 48p : ill(chiefly col) ; 22cm. — (A first look book)
Index.
ISBN 0-85166-636-1 : £1.75
(B77-30355)

629.133'09'04 — Aircraft, to 1977

Andrews, Allen. Back to the drawing board : the evolution of flying machines / [by] Allen Andrews. — Newton Abbot [etc.] : David and Charles, 1977. — 168p : ill, facsim, port ; 26cm.
Index.
ISBN 0-7153-7342-0 : £4.95
(B77-30356)

629.133'1'34 — Model aeroplanes. Construction. *Manuals*
Warring, Ronald Horace. Basic aeromodelling / [by] R.H. Warring. — Watford : Model and Allied Publications, 1976. — [5],176p : ill, ports ; 21cm. — (MAP technical publication)
Index.
ISBN 0-85242-396-9 Pbk : £2.95
(B77-21954)

629.133'3 — Man-powered flight, to 1975
Haining, Peter. The compleat birdman : an illustrated history of man-powered flight / [by] Peter Haining. — London : Hale [etc.], 1976. — 160p,[64]p of plates : ill, facsims, ports ; 23cm.
Index.
ISBN 0-7091-5758-4 : £5.00
(B77-01577)

629.133'3'07402412 — Museums. *Gloucestershire. Staverton. Skyfame Aircraft Museum. Guidebooks*
Skyfame Aircraft Museum. The Skyfame aircraft story : an official guide to the Skyfame Aircraft Museum / compiled by Geoffrey Body in conjunction with Peter M. Thomas. — Bristol (9 Poplar Ave., Bristol BS9 2BE) : Avon-Anglia Publications and Services, 1976. — 28p : ill ; 21cm.
Cover title: Your AAA guide to the Skyfame aircraft story.
Sd : £0.40
(B77-19456)

629.133'3'0904 — Heavier than air aircraft, 1920-1975. *Illustrations*
Aviation workhorses around the world / [compiled by] G.R. Duval. — Truro : Barton, 1977. — 96p : chiefly ill ; 22cm.
ISBN 0-85153-304-3 : £3.50
(B77-33875)

629.133'32 — Kites
Lloyd, Ambrose. Making and flying kites / [by] Ambrose Lloyd, Charles Mitchell and Nicolette Thomas. — London [etc.] : Beaver Books, 1977. — 110p : ill, map ; 20cm.
Originally published: London : J. Murray, 1975.
ISBN 0-600-35336-2 Pbk : £0.50
(B77-20365)

Pelham, David. The Penguin book of kites / [by] David Pelham. — Harmondsworth [etc.] : Penguin, 1977. — 226,[1]p : ill(some col), facsims, ports ; 20cm.
Spine title: Kites. — Originally published: London : Allen Lane, 1976. — Bibl.: p.224-225. — Index.
ISBN 0-14-004117-6 Pbk : £2.75
(B77-04894)

629.133'32 — Kites. *Juvenile literature*
Rutland, Jonathan Patrick. Kites and gliders / by J.P. Rutland ; illustrated by Jim Russell. — London [etc.] : F. Watts, 1977. — 48p : ill(chiefly col) ; 22cm. — (A first look book)
Index.
ISBN 0-85166-627-2 : £1.75
Also classified at 629.133'33
(B77-30357)

629.133'32 — Kites. Construction. *Manuals. Juvenile literature*
Newnham, Jack. Kites to make and fly / written, illustrated and produced by Jack Newnham. — Harmondsworth [etc.] : Puffin Books, 1977. — [33]p : chiefly ill(chiefly col) ; 20cm. — (Practical puffins)
ISBN 0-14-049139-2 Sd : £0.50
(B77-25707)

Wood, Chris. Making simple kites / [by] Chris Wood. — London : Studio Vista, 1977. — 44p : ill ; 26cm. — (Something to do)
Index.
ISBN 0-289-70688-2 : £2.25
(B77-18850)

629.133'33 — Gliders. *Juvenile literature*
Rutland, Jonathan Patrick. Kites and gliders / by J.P. Rutland ; illustrated by Jim Russell. — London [etc.] : F. Watts, 1977. — 48p : ill(chiefly col) ; 22cm. — (A first look book)
Index.
ISBN 0-85166-627-2 : £1.75
Primary classification 629.133'32
(B77-30357)

629.133'34 — Aeroplanes. *Teaching kits*
Petty, Mike. The airport / by Mike Petty ; illustrated by Steve Forster ... [et al.]. — London : Jackdaw [for] Thames Television, 1977. — Portfolio : ill(some col) ; 23x27cm. — (Magpies)
Eleven sheets (8 fold.)([21] sides). — Bibl.: (1p.).
ISBN 0-305-62135-1 : £0.99(non-net)
Primary classification 387.7'36
(B77-25542)

629.133'34'02541 — Aeroplanes. *Great Britain, to 1951. Directories*
Riley, Gordon, *b.1950.* Vintage aircraft directory / by Gordon Riley. — [London] : The author ; London (3 New Plaistow Rd, E15 3JA) : Distributed by Battle of Britain Prints International Ltd.
Includes some helicopters.
[1976] : 4th ed. — 1976. — [1],65p : ill ; 18cm.
ISBN 0-9504482-1-4 Sd : £0.85
(B77-08438)

629.133'340422 — Home-built aircraft. *Technical data*
Jane's pocket book of home-built aircraft / compiled by Michael J.H. Taylor ; edited by John W.R. Taylor. — London : Macdonald and Jane's, 1977. — 261p : ill ; 13x19cm. — ([Jane's pocket book ; 14])
Index.
ISBN 0-356-08420-5 : £3.75
ISBN 0-356-08421-3 Lp : £2.75
(B77-17580)

629.133'340423 — Passenger aeroplanes. Mid-air collisions, 1946-1975. *Statistics*
Belcher, B W. A statistical study of mid-air collisions involving public transport and executive jet aircraft, 1946-1975, world wide / [by] B.W. Belcher, D.M. Penna. — London : Civil Aviation Authority, 1976. — iii,19p : ill ; 30cm. — (Civil Aviation Authority. Directorate of Operational Research and Analysis. Research papers ; no.7508) (Civil Aviation Authority. Papers ; 76041)
ISBN 0-86039-028-4 Sd : £2.50
(B77-09079)

629.133'34'09034 — Aeroplanes, to 1975
Munson, Kenneth George. Famous aircraft of all time / [by] Kenneth Munson ; illustrated by John W. Wood ... [et al.]. — Poole : Blandford Press, 1976. — vii,189p : ill(chiefly col), col maps ; 20cm. — ([Blandford colour series])
Index.
ISBN 0-7137-0785-2 : £2.95
(B77-04268)

629.133'343 — Handley Page Jetstream aeroplanes, to 1976
Pardoe, Alan John. The HP137 Jetstream : a production history / [by Alan J. Pardoe]. — Glasgow (23 Southview Drive, Bearsden, Glasgow G61 4HQ) : Central Scotland Aviation Group, 1977. — 56p : ill ; 22cm.
Bibl.: p.4.
ISBN 0-9503891-2-9 Sd : Unpriced
(B77-33876)

629.133'343 — Vickers Armstrong Viking aeroplanes, Vickers Armstrong Valetta aeroplanes & Vickers Armstrong Varsity aeroplanes
Martin, Bernard, *b.1941.* Viking, Valetta, Varsity / compiled by Bernard Martin, assisted by E.B. Morgan, P.G. Smith et al.. — Tonbridge : Air-Britain, 1975. — 46p,[28]p of plates : ill ; 24cm.
ISBN 0-85130-038-3 Sd : Unpriced
(B77-20366)

629.133'347'0904 — Float seaplanes, to 1976. *Illustrations*
World float planes : a pictorial survey / [compiled by] G.R. Duval. — Truro : Barton, 1977. — 96p : of ill, ports ; 22cm.
ISBN 0-85153-254-3 : £3.50
(B77-21210)

629.133'349 — Concorde aeroplanes. *Humorous texts*
The **Mach** 2 smile : the British Airways book of good humour and concorde. — [London] ([West End House, Hills Place, W1]) : Thomas Tudor Organisation for British Airways, [1976]. — 30p : ill(some col) ; 23cm.
'... we present a selection of the cartoons Concorde has inspired, contrasting them with the reality of the world's most advanced passenger transport' - introduction.
ISBN 0-9505513-0-9 : Unpriced
(B77-06743)

629.133'349 — Concorde aeroplanes, to 1976
Clark, Francis Graham. Concorde / by F.G. Clark and Arthur Gibson. — London : Phoebus : B.P.C. Publishing [etc.], 1976. — 64p : ill(chiefly col), facsim, col ports ; 31cm.
ISBN 0-7026-0013-x : £1.95
(B77-31955)

629.133'349 — Jet aeroplanes. *Juvenile literature*
Hewish, Mark. The young scientist book of jets / [written by Mark Hewish] ; [illustrators Derek Bunce et al.]. — London : Usborne, 1976. — 32p : ill(chiefly col), col map ; 28cm.
ISBN 0-86020-051-5 Pbk : £0.75
(B77-12518)

629.133'349 — Jet aeroplanes. Noise. Engineering aspects. *Conference proceedings*
AIAA Aero-acoustics Conference, *2nd, Hampton, Va, 1975.* Aeroacoustics, STOL noise, airframe and airfoil noise : technical papers from AIAA 2nd Aero-acoustics Conference, March 1975, subsequently revised for this volume / edited by Ira R. Schwartz ; assistant editors Henry T. Nagamatsu, Warren C. Strahle. — New York : American Institute of Aeronautics and Astronautics ; Cambridge, Mass. ; London : M.I.T. Press, 1976. — xxxiv,445p : ill ; 24cm. — (Progress in astronautics and aeronautics ; vol.45)
Index.
ISBN 0-915928-08-6 : £13.60
(B77-04269)

629.133'35 — Helicopters
Fay, John. The helicopter : history, piloting and how it flies / by John Fay ; illustrated by Lucy Raymond, David Gibbings, Dulcie Legg. — 3rd ed., revised ; and with additional chapter. — Newton Abbot [etc.] : David and Charles, 1976. — xiii,194p,[8]p of plates : ill, 2 ports ; 23cm.
Previous ed.: i.e. 2nd ed. published as 'The helicopter and how it flies'. London : Pitman, 1967. — Bibl.: p.187-188. — Index.
ISBN 0-7153-7249-1 : £4.95
(B77-15342)

629.133'35 — Helicopters. *Technical data*
AIAA Aero-acoustics Conference, *2nd, Hampton, Va, 1975.* Aeroacoustics, fan noise and control, duct acoustics, rotor noise : technical papers from AIAA 2nd Aero-acoustics Conference, March 1975, subsequently revised for this volume / edited by Ira R. Schwartz ; assistant editors Henry T. Nagamatsu, Warren C. Strahle. — New York : American Institute of Aeronautics and Astronautics ; Cambridge, Mass. ; London : M.I.T. Press, 1976. — xxxiv, 635p : ill ; 24cm. — (Progress in astronautics and aeronautics ; vol.44)
Index.
ISBN 0-915928-09-4 : £13.60
Also classified at 629.134'36
(B77-04270)

Taylor, Michael John Haddrick. Helicopters of the world / [by] Michael J. H. Taylor & John W.R. Taylor. — London : Allan, 1976. — 128p : ill(some col) ; 23cm.
Index.
ISBN 0-7110-0685-7 : £2.95
(B77-01578)

629.133'35 — Helicopters. Specialised operations. *Conference proceedings*
Problems of specialised helicopter operations, 9 February 1977 : [papers] presented [to a conference] at the Royal Aeronautical Society ... — London (4 Hamilton Place, W1V 0BQ) : The Society, [1977]. — 69p in various pagings : ill ; 30cm.
Pbk : £4.50
(B77-32691)

629.133'35 — Helicopters, to 1975
Gregory, Hollingsworth Franklin. The helicopter / [by] Hollingsworth Franklin Gregory. — [New ed.]. — South Brunswick ; New York : Barnes ; London : Yoseloff, 1976. — 223p : ill, ports ; 32cm.
Previous ed.: published as '- Anything a horse can do'. New York : Reynal and Hitchcock, 1944. — Index.
ISBN 0-498-01670-6 : £6.50
(B77-30358)

629.134 — AIRCRAFT CONSTRUCTION
629.134'32'0228 — Flying model aeroplanes. Aerofoils. Construction. *Manuals*
Pressnell, Martyn. Aerofoils for aeromodellers / [by] Martyn Pressnell. — London [etc.] : Pitman, 1977. — 207p : ill, ports ; 28cm.
ISBN 0-273-01015-8 Pbk : £4.95 : CIP rev.
(B77-08439)

629.134'353 — Jet aeroplanes. Engines. Noise. Engineering aspects. *Conference proceedings*
AIAA Aero-acoustics Conference, *2nd, Hampton, Va, 1975.* Aeroacoustics, jet noise, combustion and core engine noise : technical papers from AIAA 2nd Aero-acoustics Conference, March 1975, subsequently revised for this volume / edited by Ira R. Schwartz ; assistant editors Henry T. Nagamatsu, Warren C. Strahle. — New York : American Institute of Aeronautics and Astronautics ; Cambridge, Mass. ; London : M.I.T. Press, 1976. — xxxiv,613p : ill ; 24cm. — (Progress in aeronautics and astronautics ; vol.43)
Index.
ISBN 0-915928-07-8 : £13.60
(B77-04271)

629.134'36 — Helicopters. Rotors. Noise. Engineering aspects. *Conference proceedings*
AIAA Aero-acoustics Conference, *2nd, Hampton, Va, 1975.* Aeroacoustics, fan noise and control, duct acoustics, rotor noise : technical papers from AIAA 2nd Aero-acoustics Conference, March 1975, subsequently revised for this volume / edited by Ira R. Schwartz ; assistant editors Henry T. Nagamatsu, Warren C. Strahle. — New York : American Institute of Aeronautics and Astronautics ; Cambridge, Mass. ; London : M.I.T. Press, 1976. — xxxiv, 635p : ill ; 24cm. — (Progress in astronautics and aeronautics ; vol.44)
Index.
ISBN 0-915928-09-4 : £13.60
Primary classification 629.133'35
(B77-04270)

629.134'6 — Light aircraft. Maintenance & repair. *Amateurs' manuals*
Heywood, J E. Light aircraft inspection / [by] J.E. Heywood. — Berkhamsted : Poyser, 1977. — 135p : ill, plans ; 23cm.
Bibl.: p.131-132. — Index.
ISBN 0-85661-016-x : £4.00
(B77-33280)

629.135'1 — Aeroplanes. All-weather systems. *Conference proceedings*
International Conference on the Future of Aircraft All-weather Operations?, *Institution of Electrical Engineers, 1976.* International Conference on the Future of Aircraft All-weather Operations?, 23-26 November 1976, organised by the Electronics Division of the Institution of Electrical Engineers in association with ... [others], venue, Institution of Electrical Engineers, Savoy Place, London WC2. — [London] : [The Institution], [1976]. — viii, 183p : ill ; 30cm. — (Institution of Electrical Engineers. Conference publications ; no.147 ISSN 0537-9989)
Cover title: The future of aircraft all-weather operations?.
ISBN 0-85296-167-7 Pbk : Unpriced
Primary classification 629.136'6
(B77-05492)

629.135'4 — Aeroplanes. Electrical systems
Pallett, Edwin Henry John. Aircraft electrical systems / [by] E.H.J. Pallett. — London [etc.] : Pitman, 1976. — vii,159p : ill ; 26cm. — (Introduction to aeronautical engineering series)
Index.
ISBN 0-273-36159-7 : £6.50
(B77-02391)

629.135'4 — Aircraft. Screened electric cables. Screens. Terminations. *Standards*
British Standards Institution. Specification for screen terminating devices for aircraft electric cables = Spécification des dispositifs de terminaison du blindage des câbles électriques pour usage à bord des aéronefs = Spezifikation für Abschirmungsendverschlüsse für Flugzeug-Leitungskabel / British Standards Institution. — London : B.S.I., 1977. — 7,[1]p : ill ; 30cm. — (British Standard aerospace series = Série aérospatiale = Luftraumserie) (G223 : 1977)
Pierced for binder.
ISBN 0-580-09279-8 Sd : £2.70
(B77-14788)

629.136 — AIRPORTS
629.136'6 — Aerodromes. Birds. Control measures. *Great Britain*
Civil Aviation Authority. *Directorate of Aerodrome Standards.* Bird control on aerodromes / [Civil Aviation Authority] Directorate of Aerodrome Standards. — London : C.A.A., 1976. — [3],28p : ill, form ; 30cm. — (CAP ; 384)
'... supersedes DAT Paper 14 ... issued by the Department of Trade and Industry, Aerodromes Technical Directorate' - title page verso. — Bibl.: p.11.
ISBN 0-86039-017-9 Sd : £1.50
(B77-04895)

629.136'6 — Airports. All-weather systems. *Conference proceedings*
International Conference on the Future of Aircraft All-weather Operations?, *Institution of Electrical Engineers, 1976.* International Conference on the Future of Aircraft All-weather Operations?, 23-26 November 1976, organised by the Electronics Division of the Institution of Electrical Engineers in association with ... [others], venue, Institution of Electrical Engineers, Savoy Place, London WC2. — [London] : [The Institution], [1976]. — viii, 183p : ill ; 30cm. — (Institution of Electrical Engineers. Conference publications ; no.147 ISSN 0537-9989)
Cover title: The future of aircraft all-weather operations?.
ISBN 0-85296-167-7 Pbk : Unpriced
Also classified at 629.135'1
(B77-05492)

629.136'6'076 — Air traffic controllers. Licensing. Examinations. *Great Britain*
Civil Aviation Authority. The air traffic controller's licence and student air traffic controller's licence / [Civil Aviation Authority]. — 9th ed. — London : C.A.A., 1977. — viii, 71p ; 21cm. — (CAP 160)
Previous ed.: 1975.
ISBN 0-86039-026-8 Sd : £1.50
(B77-18222)

629.136'6'0941 — Air traffic. Control. *Great Britain. Manuals*
Civil Aviation Authority. Air traffic control training manual / [Civil Aviation Authority]. — 2nd ed. — London : C.A.A.
Section 3 : Air navigation. — 1977. — vi,118p : ill ; 21cm. — (CAP ; 390)
Previous ed.: / prepared by the Directorate of Air Traffic Planning of the Civil Aviation Authority for the National Air Traffic Services. London : H.M.S.O., 1972. — Index.
ISBN 0-86039-042-x Sd : £4.25
(B77-28691)

Section 4 : Radar theory. — 1977. — vii,90p : ill ; 21cm. — (CAP ; 390)
Previous ed.: i.e. Revised ed., 1971. — Index.
ISBN 0-86039-006-3 Sd : £2.45
(B77-07419)

Section 5 : Approach radar control. — 1977. — vi,42p : ill, map ; 21cm. — (CAP 390)
Previous ed.: i.e. Revised ed. 1969. — Index.
ISBN 0-86039-034-9 Sd : £1.50
(B77-18223)

629.2 — MOTOR VEHICLES
Hillier, Victor Albert Walter. Motor vehicle basic principles / [by] V.A.W. Hillier. — London : Hutchinson, 1976. — 112p : ill ; 25cm.
Index.
ISBN 0-09-127050-2 : £4.00
ISBN 0-09-127051-0 Pbk : £2.25
(B77-04896)

629.2 — Motor vehicles. *Juvenile literature*
Things that go. — Maidenhead : Purnell, 1977. — [12]p : chiefly col ill ; 22cm.
Pbd : £0.45
(B77-17581)

629.2'021'2 — Motor vehicles. *Technical data. Serials*
Technical service data : private cars, commercial vans, trucks & tractors. — Chertsey (25 Windsor St., Chertsey, Surrey KT16 8AX) : Palgrave Publishing Co. Ltd.
1977 ed.: 40th year. — 1977. — 248p ; 28cm.
Pbk : £4.20
(B77-20367)

629.2'0941 — Motor vehicles. *Great Britain, to 1976*
Baldwin, Nick. A motoring heritage / [by] Nick Baldwin, Peter Hull, John McLellan ; editor John McLellan. — Edinburgh : J. Bartholomew [for] Leyland Historic Vehicles Ltd, 1976. — 60p,[4]p of plates : ill(some col), ports ; 28cm.
Index.
ISBN 0-7028-1065-7 : £1.75
(B77-23503)

629.22 — MOTOR VEHICLES. SPECIAL TYPES
629.22'1 — Model motor vehicles. Making. *Manuals*
Fairhurst, Peter. Making model transport vehicles / [by] Peter Fairhurst ; illustrated by the author. — London : Carousel, 1977. — 112p : ill ; 20cm.
ISBN 0-552-54122-2 Pbk : £0.45
(B77-29507)

629.22'22 — Allard cars, to 1975
Kinsella, David. Allard / [by] David Kinsella. — Yeovil : Haynes, 1977. — 3-199p : ill, facsims, ports ; 24cm.
Index.
ISBN 0-85429-173-3 : £4.95
(B77-15343)

629.22'22 — BMW cars, to 1975
Frostick, Michael. BMW, the Bavarian Motor Works / [by] Michael Frostick. — London : Dalton Watson, 1976. — 207p : ill(some col), ports ; 26cm.
Ill. on lining papers.
ISBN 0-901564-20-6 : £7.50
Also classified at 629.22'75
(B77-21955)

629.22'22 — Cars
Automobile Association. AA book of the car. — 3rd ed. — London : Drive Publications for the Automobile Association, 1976. — 408p : ill(chiefly col), facsims, col maps, ports ; 27cm.
Previous ed.: 1970. — Index.
ISBN 0-903356-21-x : £8.95
(B77-16459)

Automobile Association. AA book of the car. — 3rd ed., 1st revise. — London : Drive Publications, 1977. — 408p : ill(chiefly col), facsims, col maps ; 27cm.
Previous ed.: i.e. 3rd ed. 1976. — Index.
£8.95
(B77-33281)

Cutting the cost of motoring. — London : Reader's Digest Association, 1976. — 63p : ill(some col) ; 27cm. — ('Reader's digest' basic guide)
'The text and illustrations are based on ... "Money-saving motoring" ...' London : Drive Publications Ltd for the Automobile Association, 1974.
ISBN 0-276-00144-3 Sd : £0.75
(B77-18851)

Johnstone, Roy. Understanding your car / [by] Roy Johnstone. — London : Macdonald Educational, 1977. — 96p : ill(some col), port ; 21cm. — (Macdonald guidelines)
Bibl.: p.91. — Index.
ISBN 0-356-06016-0 Pbk : £1.00
(B77-27185)

629.22'22 — Cars. *Juvenile literature*
The **super** book of cars. — London : Macdonald Educational, 1977. — 32p : ill(some col), col plan, ports ; 28cm.
Adaptation of: 'Cars'. London : Macdonald, 1971.
ISBN 0-356-05593-0 : £0.50
(B77-18224)

629.22'22 — Cars. *Manuals*
Dyson, John. Know your car / [by] John Dyson ; illustrated by Peter Gregory. — London : Severn House : [Distributed by Hutchinson], [1976]. — 96p : ill ; 18x23cm. — (Severn House 'TV times' family books)
Originally published: London : Independent Television Books, 1975.
ISBN 0-7278-0203-8 : £3.95
(B77-06163)

629.22'22 — Daimler cars used by British royal families, to 1975
Smith, Brian Ernest. Royal Daimlers / [by] Brian E. Smith. — Brentford : Transport Bookman Publications, 1976. — [10],469p : ill, facsims, maps, ports ; 25cm.
Bibl.: p.457-458. — Index.
ISBN 0-85184-019-1 : £10.00
(B77-24301)

629.22'22 — Ford Fiesta cars. Manufacture, 1973-1976
Seidler, Edouard. Let's call it Fiesta : the auto-biography of Ford's project Bobcat / [by] Edouard Seidler. — [Cambridge] : Stephens [etc.], 1976. — 240p : ill(some col), ports(some col) ; 23cm.
ISBN 0-85059-272-0 : £4.95
(B77-04897)

629.22'22 — Healey & Austin-Healey cars, to 1975
Browning, Peter. Healeys and Austin-Healeys, including Jensen-Healey : an illustrated history of the marque with specifications and tuning data / [by] Peter Browning and Les Needham. — 2nd ed. — Yeovil : Haynes : Foulis, 1976. — xii,316p : ill, ports ; 24cm.
Previous ed.: 1970. — Index.
ISBN 0-85429-209-8 : £5.95
(B77-09080)

629.22'22 — Jaguar E-type cars, to 1976
Harvey, Chris. E type : end of an era / [by] Chris Harvey. — Oxford : Oxford Illustrated Press, 1977. — [7],236p : ill(some col), ports(some col) ; 26cm.
Index.
ISBN 0-902280-42-2 : £12.00
(B77-31267)

629.22'22 — Morgan cars, to 1976
More Morgan : a pictorial history of the Morgan sports car / [compiled by] Gregory Houston Bowden. — London : Wilton House Gentry, 1976. — 223p,[8]p of plates : chiefly ill(some col), facsims, ports ; 25cm.
Ill. on lining papers. — Index.
ISBN 0-905064-11-9 : £5.95
(B77-23504)

629.22'22 — Touring cars, 1945-1976
Robson, Graham. The post war touring car / [by] Graham Robson. — Yeovil : Haynes, 1977. — 2-129p : ill, ports ; 24cm. — (A Foulis motoring book)
ISBN 0-85429-225-x : £5.95
(B77-24302)

629.22'22'0207 — Cars. *Manuals. Humorous texts. Early works*
Robinson, William Heath. How to be a motorist / by Heath Robinson and K.R.G. Browne. — London : Duckworth, 1977. — iii-x,116p : ill ; 23cm.
Facsimile reprint of: 1st ed. London : Hutchinson, 1936.
ISBN 0-7156-1180-1 : £3.50
(B77-30359)

629.22'22'0212 — Cars. *Technical data*
The **observer's** book of automobiles. — 20th ed. / compiled by the Olyslager Organisation ; edited by Michael Turner. — London : F. Warne, 1977. — 177p : ill ; 15cm. — (The observer's pocket series ; [21])
Previous ed.: 1975.
ISBN 0-7232-1563-4 : £1.10
(B77-15917)

629.22'22'0212 — Cars. *Technical data. Serials*
Stone and Cox motor specifications and prices : (private cars, motor cycles, motor scooters, mo-peds, and index marks). — London : Stone and Cox.
1977 ed. — [1977]. — xiv,401p ; 19cm.
Spine title: Motor specifications and prices. — Index.
ISBN 0-85443-073-3 Pbk : £3.80
(B77-13094)

629.22'22'0904 — Cars, 1896-1936
Bampton, Daphne. Rare and exciting cars / by Daphne Bampton. — Melksham : Venton, 1977. — 190p,[18]p of plates : ill, facsim ; 22cm.
Index.
ISBN 0-85475-118-1 : £5.95
(B77-31268)

629.22'22'0904 — Cars, 1903-1976
Georgano, George Nicholas. A source book of classic cars / written and compiled by G.N. Georgano. — London : Ward Lock, 1977. — 128p : ill ; 12x17cm.
Index.
ISBN 0-7063-5039-1 : £2.50
(B77-15918)

629.22'22'0904 — Cars, to 1976
Bishop, George, *b.1917.* The age of the automobile / [by] George Bishop. — London [etc.] : Hamlyn, 1977. — 192p : ill(some col), ports ; 31cm.
Col. ill. on lining papers. — Index.
ISBN 0-600-30319-5 : £3.95
(B77-31269)

Wise, David Burgess. The motor car : an illustrated international history / by David Burgess Wise ; special photography by J. Spencer Smith. — London : Orbis Books, 1977. — viii,316p : ill(some col), facsims, ports(1 col) ; 31cm.
Ill. on lining papers. — Index.
ISBN 0-85613-267-5 : £7.95
(B77-30360)

629.22'22'0904 — Cars, to 1976. *Encyclopaedias*
Robson, Graham. The encyclopedia of the world's classic cars / [by] Graham Robson ; [editor Ray Bonds ; colour drawings by Gordon Davies et al.]. — London (27 Old Gloucester St., WC1N 3AF) : Salamander Books Ltd, 1977. — 248p : ill(chiefly col) ; 32cm.
Spine title: Classic cars. — Ill. on lining papers. — Index.
ISBN 0-86101-001-9 : £5.95
(B77-33877)

629.22'22'0904 — Cars, to 1977
Roberts, Peter, *b.1925.* Pictorial history of cars / [by] Peter Roberts. — London (59 Grosvenor St., W.1) : Sundial Books Ltd, [1977]. — 128p : ill(chiefly col), facsims, col port ; 33cm.
Spine title: The St Michael pictorial history of cars. — Col. ill. on lining papers. — Index.
ISBN 0-904230-26-0 : Unpriced
(B77-31270)

629.22'22'0904 — Cars, to 1977. *Illustrations*
Roberts, Peter, *b.1925.* A pictorial history of the motor car / by Peter Roberts. — New York ; London : F. and S. Publications ; [Leicester] ([Euston St., Freemen's Common, Aylestone Rd, Leicester LE2 7SS]) : Distributed by WHS Distributors, 1977. — 416p,[32]p of plates : ill(some col), facsims(some col), ports ; 29cm.
£3.95
ISBN 1-448-02169-3
(B77-22666)

629.22'22'09041 — Cars, to 1930
Posthumus, Cyril. The story of veteran & vintage cars / by Cyril Posthumus. — London [etc.] : Hamlyn, [1977]. — 128p : ill(some col), facsims(some col), ports ; 31cm.
Ill. on lining papers. — 'This material first appeared in "First Cars"' - note. — Index.
ISBN 0-600-39155-8 : £2.25
(B77-19457)

629.22'22'09042 — Cars, 1920-1930
Hull, Peter. A vintage car casebook / [by] Peter Hull & Nigel Arnold-Forster. — London : Batsford, 1976. — 192p,[16]p of plates : ill, ports ; 23cm.
Index.
ISBN 0-7134-3231-4 : £4.50
(B77-06164)

629.22'22'0945 — Italian cars. *Technical data. Italian texts*
Società italiana additivi per carburanti. Dati tecnici delle autovetture italiane / Società italiana additivi per carburanti. — Milano : [S.I.A.C.] ; London : Associated Octel Company.
1977. — 1977. — viii,35p,[2]leaves(1 fold) : ill ; 21cm.
Bibl.
Sp : Unpriced
(B77-33878)

629.22'22'0994 — Cars. *Australia, 1903-1929*
Grant, Malcolm. Veteran & vintage cars of Australia / [by] Malcolm Grant. — Sydney ; London [etc.] : A.H. and A.W. Reed, 1976. — 102p : col ill ; 18x19cm. — ([Reed colourbook series])
Originally published: 1972. — Index.
ISBN 0-589-07114-9 : £5.15
(B77-19458)

629.22'233 — Buses & motor coaches manufactured by Duple Coachbuilders Ltd, to 1976. *Illustrations*
Duple / [compiled by] Eric Ogden. — Glossop (22 Longmoor Rd, Glossop, Derbyshire) : Transport Publishing Co., 1976. — 136p : chiefly ill(some col), facsims, ports ; 21x30cm.
Cover title: Duple : a pictorial survey of their activities from the 'twenties with a brief history. — Text, ill. on lining papers. — Index.
ISBN 0-903839-12-1 : £4.50
(B77-06165)

629.22'233 — Buses manufactured by British Leyland Motor Corporation, to 1976
Jack, Doug. The Leyland bus / by Doug Jack. — Glossop (Glossop, Derbyshire) : Transport Publishing Co., 1977. — 440p : ill(incl 2 col), port ; 29cm.
ISBN 0-903839-13-x : £13.50
(B77-23505)

629.22'233'0941 — Buses & motor coaches. *Great Britain, 1945-1965*
Gillham, John Charles. Buses and coaches, 1945-1965 / by John C. Gillham. — London : Almark Publishing, 1976. — 96p : ill(some col) ; 21x22cm.
ISBN 0-85524-270-1 : £3.50
(B77-06744)

629.22'233'0941 — Buses & motor coaches. *Great Britain, 1976*
Booth, Gavin. The British motor bus : an illustrated history / by Gavin Booth. — London : I. Allan, 1977. — 112p : ill, facsims ; 30cm.
ISBN 0-7110-0817-5 : £4.95
(B77-32692)

629.22'233'09421 — Buses. *London. Serials*
London buses. — London : Allan.
[1976 : 32nd ed.] / [revised by] London Country Bus Services Ltd [and] London Transport Executive. — 1977. — 80p : ill ; 19cm.
ISBN 0-7110-0816-7 Sd : £0.85
(B77-17582)

629.22'3'09042 — Light commercial motor vans, 1919-1939. *Illustrations*
Light vans and trucks, 1919-1939 / [compiled] by Nick Baldwin and Arthur Ingram. — London : Almark Publishing, 1977. — 96p : chiefly ill, facsims ; 21x22cm.
Index.
ISBN 0-85524-262-0 : £3.50
(B77-25708)

629.22'4 — British Leyland commercial vehicles, to 1975
Licensed to carry : Leyland's 80 years in commercial transport / [compiled by Alan Thomas and John Aldridge]. — London : IPC Transport Press, 1976. — [2],100p : chiefly ill(some col), facsims(1 col) ; 30cm. — (A 'Motor transport' special)
'... compiled from original photographs and material in the archives of 'Motor transport'.
Sd : £1.25
(B77-18225)

629.22'4 — Commercial vehicles. *Buyers' guides*
Commercial vehicle buyer's guide. — London : Kogan Page.
1 / [compiled by] Christopher Mann & David Lowe. — 1977. — 288p : ill ; 28cm.
Index.
ISBN 0-85038-142-8 Pbk : £4.95
(B77-29508)

629.22'4 — Ford commercial vehicles, to 1975
Task Force / contributors Les Geary ... [et al.] ; special photography Ken Denyer and John Wright. — London : IPC Transport Press, 1976. — [1],68p : ill(some col) ; 30cm. — (A 'Motor transport' special)
ISBN 0-617-00178-2 Sd : £1.25
(B77-03601)

629.22'4'09042 — Heavy commercial vehicles, 1919-1939
Heavy goods vehicles, 1919-1939 / [compiled] by Nick Baldwin. — New Malden : Almark Publishing, 1976. — 96p : ill ; 21x22cm.
Index.
ISBN 0-85524-266-3 : £3.25
(B77-01579)

629.22'5 — Agricultural tractors, to 1946
Vigzol Oil Refining Company (London). Farm tractors : the history of their development with notes on their proper maintenance / Vigzol Oil Refining Co. (London). — Hinckley (216 Coventry Rd, Hinckley, Leics. LE10 0NG) : Traction Engine Enterprises, 1976. — 63p : ill ; 23cm.
Facsimile reprint of: 1st ed. London : Vigzol Oil Refining Co., 1946.
ISBN 0-905100-07-7 Sd : £1.95
(B77-13706)

629.22'5 — Crawler-loaders manufactured by JCB & Co Limited. Design. Terotechnological factors
Committee for Terotechnology. Designing earth-moving equipment for minimum life-cycle cost / Department of Industry, Committee for Terotechnology. — London (Industrial Technology Secretariat, Room 539, Abell House, John Islip St., SW1P 4LN) : [The Committee], 1977. — [2],i,13p : 1 ill, form ; 30cm. — (Terotechnology case history ; no.7 ISSN 0306-7777)
Sd : Unpriced
(B77-27921)

629.22'6'05 — Caravans. *Serials*
Caravan factfinder. — London : Link House Publications.
1977 / editor Tony Bradford. — 1977. — 96p : ill ; 22cm. — (A Link House Group annual)
Pbk : £0.70
(B77-33282)

629.22'72 — Bicycles. *Juvenile literature*
Ballantine, Richard. The Piccolo bicycle book / [by] Richard Ballantine. — London : Pan Books, 1977. — 191p : ill, facsims, map ; 20cm. — (Piccolo)
Index.
ISBN 0-330-25017-5 Pbk : £0.60
(B77-26369)

629.22'75 — BMW motorcycles, to 1974
Frostick, Michael. BMW, the Bavarian Motor Works / [by] Michael Frostick. — London : Dalton Watson, 1976. — 207p : ill(some col), ports ; 26cm.
Ill. on lining papers.
ISBN 0-901564-20-6 : £7.50
Primary classification 629.22'22
(B77-21955)

629.22'75 — Motorcycles
Dandy, Roy. Motor cycle knowledge / [by] R. Dandy. — London : Cassell.
Part 2 : [Workbook]. — 1977. — 32p : ill ; 22cm.
ISBN 0-304-29672-4 Sd : £0.50
(B77-33283)

629.22'75 — Motorcycles. *Buyers' guides*
'Daily mail' Motorcycle Show review. — London : Associated Newspapers Group.
1977. — [1977]. — 64p : ill, ports ; 30cm.
Sd : £0.50
ISSN 0140-4954
(B77-30361)

629.22'75 — Motorcycles. *Manuals*
Bacon, Roy Hunt. The motorcycle manual / [by] Roy H. Bacon. — London [etc.] : Newnes-Butterworths, 1976. — [7],180p : ill ; 22cm.
Index.
ISBN 0-408-00260-3 Pbk : £3.25
(B77-31956)

Dandy, Roy. Motorcyclist's handbook : a guide to the use and maintenance of motorbikes and scooters / [by] R. Dandy. — London : Cassell, 1977. — 158p : ill ; 22cm.
ISBN 0-304-29745-3 Pbk : £2.75
(B77-29509)

Dyson, John. The motorcycling book / [by] John Dyson ; illustrated by Lionel Willis. — Harmondsworth [etc.] : Penguin, 1977. — 178[i.e.176]p : ill ; 20cm. — (Peacock books)
Also published: Harmondsworth : Kestrel Books, 1977. — Index.
ISBN 0-14-047098-0 Pbk : £0.75
(B77-21211)

Dyson, John. The motorcycling book / [by] John Dyson ; illustrated by Lionel Willis. — Harmondsworth : Kestrel Books, 1977. — 3-178p : ill ; 21cm.
Also published: Harmondsworth : Penguin, 1977. — Index.
ISBN 0-7226-5293-3 : £2.75
(B77-25003)

629.22'75 — Vincent HRD motorcycles, to 1966
Harper, Roy. The Vincent HRD story / [by] Roy Harper. — [s.l.] : Vincent Publishing Company ; Spalding (41 High St., Spalding, Lincs.) : Distributed by Turnpike Bookshop, 1975. — 220p : ill, facsims, ports ; 23cm. — (The authorised record of the HRD and Vincent era ; vol.2)
Bibl.: p.vi. — Index.
ISBN 0-9504186-5-x : £5.75
(B77-02392)

629.22'75'0904 — Motorcycles, 1884-1960
Crowley, Terence Eldon. Discovering old motorcycles / [by] T.E. Crowley. — 2nd ed. — Aylesbury : Shire Publications, 1977. — 54p : ill, facsim, port ; 18cm. — (Discovering series ; no.160)
Previous ed.: 1973. — Bibl.: p.52. — Index.
ISBN 0-85263-390-4 Pbk : £0.50
(B77-29510)

629.22'75'0904 — Motorcycles, to 1950
The **classic** motorcycles / edited by Harry Louis and Bob Currie ; drawings by Carlo Demand. — Cambridge : Stephens, 1977. — 126,[1]p : ill(some col), facsims, ports ; 31cm.
ISBN 0-85059-284-4 : £14.95
(B77-19459)

629.22'8'0904 — Racing cars, 1906-1976
Posthumus, Cyril. Classic racing cars / [by] Cyril Posthumus. — London [etc.] : Hamlyn, 1977. — 160p : ill(some col), ports(some col) ; 31cm.
ISBN 0-600-31909-1 : £4.95
(B77-25004)

629.22'92 — Steam powered road vehicles. Rallies. *Dorset. Stourpaine. Stourpaine Gathering. Illustrations*
Case, Malcolm. The Stourpaine Gathering : a pictorial souvenir of the world's largest steam working / by Malcolm Case. — Shaftesbury (Donhead St Andrew, Shaftesbury, Dorset) : The author, 1976. — 80p : of ill(incl 2 col), ports ; 15x21cm.
ISBN 0-9505184-0-9 Pbk : £1.00
(B77-13707)

629.22'92'0941 — Preserved traction engines. *Great Britain, 1974-. Illustrations*
Blenkinsop, Richard James. The steam scene / by R.J. Blenkinsop. — Leamington Spa (78 Southam Rd, Radford Semele, Leamington Spa, Warwickshire) : Steam Engine Publications.
Vol.2. — 1976. — [2],95-188p : of ill ; 30cm.
Notebook format.
ISBN 0-905271-01-7 Pbk : £2.95
(B77-13095)

Vol.3. — 1977. — [2],189-282p : of ill, ports ; 30cm.
Notebook format.
ISBN 0-905271-02-5 Pbk : £3.30
(B77-13096)

629.22'92'0941 — Traction engines. *Great Britain, to 1975*
Lane, Michael Ross. Pride of the road : the pictorial story of traction engines / [by] Michael R. Lane. — London : New English Library, 1976. — 160p : ill(some col), col coat of arms, facsims, ports(some col) ; 32cm.
Bibl.: p.158. — Index. — Previous control number ISBN 0-450-03277-9.
ISBN 0-450-02837-2 : £8.50
ISBN 0-450-03277-9 Pbk : £3.95
(B77-04898)

629.22'93 — Battery operated buses. Projects. *Great Britain, 1972-1974. Reports, surveys*
Saunders, David Anthony. Battery electric bus project, final report / by D.A. Saunders ; [for the] Department of Industry. — London (Abell House, John Islip St., SW1P 4LN) : Vehicles Division, Department of Industry, 1976. — [5], 43p : ill ; 30cm.
'... supersedes the Interim Report issued in 1973' - Introduction.
Sd : Unpriced
(B77-02393)

629.22'93 — Battery operated road vehicles, to 1976
Battelec. Battery road vehicles : an outline history and development / by 'Battelec'. — Sherborne (71 Ridgeway, Sherborne, Dorset) : Battery Vehicle Society, 1977. — [1],29p : ill ; 21cm.
ISBN 0-9504881-1-9 Sd : £0.50
(B77-25709)

629.23 — MOTOR VEHICLES. CONSTRUCTION
629.2'32 — Cars. Manufacture. Metallurgical aspects. *Conference proceedings*
Metals and the Motor Car *(Conference), Bickenhill, 1976.* Metals & the Motor Car : the future outlook : [proceedings of the conference held] Friday 12th March 1976, [at the] National Exhibition Centre, Bickenhill, Warwickshire. — [Birmingham] ([c/o Leyland Cars, Woodcocks Lane North, Acocks Green, Birmingham B27 6SG]) : Birmingham Metallurgical Association, [1977]. — 144p in various pagings,[65] leaves of plates : ill, maps ; 30cm.
Pbk : £10.00
(B77-19460)

629.2'34 — Motor vehicles. Production line automatic testing. *Conference proceedings*
International Symposium on Automotive Technology and Automation, *Rome, 1976.* ISATA 76 : proceedings [of the] International Symposium on Automotive Technology & Automation, automation of component & product testing, Rome, 27 Sept.-1 Oct. 1976. — Croydon (42 Lloyd Park Ave., Croydon CR0 5SB) : Automotive Automation Ltd, [1977]. — 2v.(1191p in various pagings) : ill, form ; 30cm.
Cover title.
Pbk : Unpriced
(B77-29511)

629.24/7 — MOTOR VEHICLES. PARTS
629.2'4 — Cars. Chassis
Crouse, William Harry. Automotive chassis and body : suspension, steering, alignment, brakes, tires, air conditioning. — 5th ed. / [by] William H. Crouse, Donald L. Anglin. — New York [etc.] ; London : McGraw-Hill, 1976. — xi, 340p : ill ; 28cm. — ([McGraw-Hill automobile technology series])
With answers. — Previous ed.: / by William H. Crouse. 1971. — Index.
ISBN 0-07-014653-5 Pbk : £10.75
(B77-04899)

629.2'44 — Cars. Transmission systems
Crouse, William Harry. Automotive transmissions and power trains : construction, operation and maintenance. — 5th ed. / [by] William H. Crouse, Donald L. Anglin. — New York ; London [etc.] : McGraw-Hill, 1976. — xvi,381p : ill(some col) ; 28cm. — (McGraw-Hill automotive technology series)
With answers. — 'Color plates of automatic-transmission hydraulic circuits' ([32]p.) as insert. — Previous ed.: / by William H. Crouse. New York : McGraw-Hill, 1971. — Index.
ISBN 0-07-014637-3 Pbk : £10.75
(B77-06166)

629.2'46 — Cars. Braking systems
Newcomb, Thomas Peter. Automobile brakes & braking / [by] T.P. Newcomb, R.T. Spurr. — Sevenoaks : Newnes Technical Books, 1977. — [10],92,[1]p : ill ; 17cm. — (Questions and answers series)
Index.
ISBN 0-408-00265-4 Pbk : Unpriced
(B77-21212)

629.2'46 — Commercial vehicles. Compressed air braking systems
Homewood, M N. Air brake technology / by M.N. Homewood. — Bexleyheath (6 Eskdale Rd, Bexleyheath, Kent DA7 5DL) : The author, 1977. — 151p : ill(some col) ; 25cm.
Index.
ISBN 0-9505410-0-1 Pbk : £3.50
(B77-23506)

629.2'46 — Motor vehicles. Braking systems. *Conference proceedings*
Braking of road vehicles : [papers read at a] conference sponsored [i.e. organised] by the Automobile Division of the Institution of Mechanical Engineers in association with the Institute of Road Transport Engineers, Loughborough University of Technology, 23-25 March 1976. — London [etc.] : Mechanical Engineering Publications Limited for the Institution, 1977. — [6],392p : ill, maps ; 31cm. — (Institution of Mechanical Engineers. Conference publications ; 1976-5)
ISBN 0-85298-356-5 : Unpriced
(B77-28692)

629.2'48 — Motor vehicles. Tyres & wheels. *Standards*
British Standards Institution. Specification for tyres and wheels = Spécification des pneus et des roues = Spezifikation für Reifen und Räder / British Standards Institution. — London : B.S.I. — (British Standard automobile series = Série automobile = Kraftfahrzeugserie)
Part 1 = Partie 1 = Teil 1 : Tyres = Pneus = Reifen. Section 3 = Section 3 = Abschnitt 3 : Off-the-road tyres = Pneus tout-terrain = Geländereifen. — 1977. — 33,[1]p(4 fold) ; 30cm. — (BS AU50 : Part 1 : Section 3b : 1977)
Pierced for binder. — 'Superseding BS AU50 : Part 1 : Section 3a : 1974'.
ISBN 0-580-09713-7 Sd : £6.60
(B77-32693)

629.2'504 — Cars. Engines
Crouse, William Harry. Automotive engines : construction, operation and maintenance. — 5th ed. / [by] William H. Crouse, Donald L. Anglin. — New York ; London [etc.] : McGraw-Hill, [1977]. — xi,420p : ill ; 28cm. — (McGraw-Hill automotive technology series)
With answers. — This ed. published in the United States: 1976. — Previous ed.: / by William H. Crouse. 1971. — Index.
ISBN 0-07-014602-0 Pbk : £10.75
(B77-13097)

629.2'504 — Cars. Engines. Maintenance & repair. *Manuals*
Crouse, William Harry. Automotive tuneup / [by] William H. Crouse, Donald L. Anglin. — New York ; London [etc.] : McGraw-Hill, 1977. — x,406p : ill, facsims, form ; 28cm.
With answers. — Index.
ISBN 0-07-014810-4 Pbk : £9.70
(B77-27922)

Johnson, James A. Automotive diagnosis and tune-up / [by] James A. Johnson. — 2nd ed. — New York ; London [etc.] : McGraw-Hill, 1977. — vi,394p : ill ; 28cm.
Pages perforated at inside edge. — Pierced for binder. — Previous ed.: New York : McGraw-Hill, 1972.
ISBN 0-07-032593-6 Pbk : £9.40
(B77-27923)

629.2'504 — Cars. Engines. Tuning. *Amateurs' manuals*
Smith, Philip Hubert. The theory of tuning and the choice of conversion equipment / by Philip H. Smith. — 3rd ed. / edited and revised by Peter W. Browning. — [Brentford] : [Speedsport Motorbooks], [1972]. — 135p : ill ; 22cm.
This ed. originally published: Henley-on-Thames : Foulis, 1972. — Index.
ISBN 0-85113-089-5 Pbk : £1.50
(B77-19461)

629.2'504 — Motor vehicles. Blown engines
Setright, Leonard John Kensell. Turbocharging and supercharging for maximum power and torque / [by] L.J.K. Setright. — Yeovil : Haynes, 1976. — 2-127p : ill, ports ; 24cm.
'A Foulis motoring book'.
ISBN 0-85429-184-9 : £3.95
(B77-02394)

629.2'506 — Motor vehicles. Diesel engines. Maintenance & repair. *Manuals*
Schulz, Erich J. Diesel mechanics / [by] Erich J. Schulz. — New York ; London [etc.] : McGraw-Hill, 1977. — ix,420p : ill ; 28cm.
Index.
ISBN 0-07-055664-4 Pbk : £13.45
(B77-30362)

629.2'52 — Cars. Engines. Exhaust systems
Crouse, William Henry. Automotive emission control. — 2nd ed. / by William H. Crouse, Donald L. Anglin. — New York ; London [etc.] : McGraw-Hill, Gregg Division, 1977. — x,278p : ill, facsims, forms ; 28cm.
With answers. — Previous ed.: / by William H. Crouse. New York : McGraw-Hill, 1971. — Index.
ISBN 0-07-014640-3 Pbk : £8.95
(B77-27186)

629.2'52 — Cars. Engines. Exhaust systems. Design
Smith, Philip Hubert. The scientific design of exhaust and intake systems / [by] Philip H. Smith in collaboration with John C. Morrison. — 3rd ed. / edited and revised by John C. Morrison. — Henley-on-Thames : Foulis, 1971 [i.e. 1976]. — [2],274p,[16]p of plates : ill ; 23cm.
This ed. originally published: 1971. — Index.
ISBN 0-85429-213-6 Pbk : £3.95
(B77-09081)

629.2'53 — Cars. Engines. Stromberg CD carburettors. Maintenance & repair. *Amateurs' manuals*
Peers, Don. Stromberg CD carburettors owners workshop manual / by Don Peers. — Yeovil : Haynes, 1976. — 56,[19]p : ill ; 27cm. — (Haynes owners workshop manuals ISSN 0305-4446)
ISBN 0-85696-300-3 Pbk : £1.95
(B77-07420)

629.2'53 — Cars. Engines. SU carburettors. Maintenance & repair. *Amateurs' manuals*
Peers, Don. SU carburettors owners workshop manual / by Don Peers. — Yeovil : Haynes, 1976. — 62,[25]p : ill ; 27cm. — (Haynes owners workshop manuals ISSN 0305-4446)
ISBN 0-85696-299-6 Pbk : £1.95
(B77-06745)

629.2'53 — Cars. Fuel supply systems
Crouse, William Harry. Automotive fuel, lubricating and cooling systems : construction, operation and maintenance. — 5th ed. / [by] William H. Crouse, Donald L. Anglin. — New York ; London [etc.] : McGraw-Hill, 1976. — x,294p : ill ; 28cm. — ([McGraw-Hill automotive technology series])
With answers. — Previous ed.: / by William H. Crouse. 1971. — Index.
ISBN 0-07-014648-9 Pbk : £8.30
(B77-05493)

629.2'53 — Motor vehicles. Engines. Solex carburettors. Maintenance & repair. *Amateurs' manuals*
British Solex carburetters. — [Brentford] : [Speedsport Motobooks], [1976]. — 218p : ill, port ; 21cm.
ISBN 0-903192-70-5 Pbk : £2.75
(B77-14287)

629.2'53 — Motor vehicles. Petrol. Consumption. Reduction. Effects of design. *Great Britain*
Road Vehicle and Engine Design Working Group. Road vehicle and engine design : short and medium term energy considerations / [Road Vehicle and Engine Design Working Group]. — London : H.M.S.O., 1977. — v, 38p : ill ; 25cm. — (Advisory Council on Energy Conservation. Papers ; no.5) (Energy paper ; no.18)
Chairman: Sir Ieuan Maddock.
ISBN 0-11-410297-x Sd : £1.75
(B77-12519)

629.2'54 — Cars. Electric equipment
Crouse, William Harry. Automotive electrical equipment : construction, operation and maintenance / [by] William H. Crouse. — 8th ed. — New York ; London [etc.] : McGraw-Hill, [1977]. — xix,295p : ill ; 28cm. — (McGraw-Hill automotive technology series)
With answers. — This ed. published in the United States: 1976. — Previous ed.: 1971. — Index.
ISBN 0-07-014666-7 Pbk : £8.30
(B77-14288)

629.2'54 — Cars. Electrical systems
Bacon, Roy Hunt. Electricity in cars / by R.H. Bacon. — 2nd ed. — London [etc.] : Macmillan, 1976. — viii,180p : ill ; 24cm. — (Philips technical library)
Previous ed.: 1967. — Index.
ISBN 0-333-21378-5 Pbk : £3.95
(B77-30363)

629.2'54 — Cars. Electrical systems. Maintenance & repair. *Amateurs' manuals*
Macdonald, Bowman Cruickshank. Trace and repair your car electrical faults / by B.C. Macdonald. — Kingswood : Elliot Right Way Books, 1976. — 142p : ill ; 18cm. — (Paperfronts)
Index.
ISBN 0-7160-0626-x Pbk : £0.40
(B77-00275)

629.2'6 — Cars. Bodywork. Design, to 1976
Beattie, Ian. The complete book of automobile body design / [by] Ian Beattie. — Yeovil : Haynes, 1977. — 3-143p : ill ; 24cm.
'a Foulis motoring book' - title page verso. — Index.
ISBN 0-85429-217-9 : £4.50
(B77-15919)

629.2'6 — Cars. Bodywork. Maintenance & repair. *Amateurs' manuals*
Joselyn, Joss. Car body care & repair / [by] Joss Joselyn. — Borough Green : Newnes Technical Books, 1977. — [7],84p : ill ; 17cm. — (Questions and answers series)
Index.
ISBN 0-408-00281-6 Pbk : £1.35
(B77-23507)

629.2'6 — Cars. Spraying. *Amateurs' manuals*
Revere, Paul. Do your own car spraying / by Paul Revere. — London [etc.] : Foulsham, 1977. — 95p : ill ; 23cm.
ISBN 0-572-00904-6 : £2.95
(B77-18227)

629.2'6 — Rolls-Royce cars. Bodywork. *United States, 1906-1974*
De Campi, John Webb. Rolls-Royce in America / [by] John Webb de Campi. — London (76 Wardour St., W1V 4AN) : Dalton Watson Ltd, 1975. — 256p : ill(incl 1 col), ports ; 26cm.
Ill. on lining papers. — Index.
ISBN 0-901564-14-1 : Unpriced
(B77-02395)

629.2'6'06241 — Commercial vehicles. Bodywork. Building & repair. Organisations. *Great Britain. Vehicle Builders and Repairers Association. Directories*
Vehicle Builders and Repairers Association. Directory / Vehicle Builders and Repairers Association. — Leeds (102 Finkle La., Gildersome, Leeds LS27 7TW) : The Association.
1977 / editor Robert Hadfield. — [1977]. — 191p : ill ; 21cm.
Cover title: Directory of members : incorporating buyers guide.
ISBN 0-901593-05-2 Pbk : £3.00
(B77-11271)

629.2'71 — Motor vehicles. Polarised headlamps. *Organisation for Economic Co-operation and Development countries. Reports, surveys*
Organisation for Economic Co-operation and Development. *Committee on the Application of Polarized Headlights.* Polarized light for vehicle headlamps : proposal for its public evaluation, the technical and behavioural problems involved : a report / prepared by an OECD Road Research Group [i.e. the Committee on the Application of Polarized Headlights]. — Paris : O.E.C.D. ; [London] : [H.M.S.O.], 1976. — 95p : ill, maps ; 27cm. — (Road research)
'On the initiative of the Road Research Group on Lighting, Visibility and Accidents, an ad hoc Committee on the Application of Polarized Headlights (CAP) was appointed ...' - Foreword.
Pbk : £2.70
ISBN 92-64-11476-9
(B77-01580)

629.2'76 — Agricultural tractors. Seat belts. Anchorages. *Standards*
British Standards Institution. Specification for anchorages for seat belts in protective cabs and frames on agricultural tractors = Spécification des ancrages pour ceintures de sécurité dans les cabines et cadres de protection sur des tracteurs agricoles = Spezifikation für Befestigungen für Anschnallgurte in Schutz-Fahrerhäusern und - Gestellen auf Ackerschleppern / British Standards Institution. — London : B.S.I., 1977. — [2],3,[1]p : ill ; 30cm. — (BS5453 : 1977) (ISO 3776-1976)
ISO title: Agricultural tractors - Anchorages for seat belts. — Pierced for binder.
ISBN 0-580-09711-0 Sd : £1.60
(B77-17583)

629.2'77 — Caravans. Fittings. Installation. *Amateurs' manuals*
Fowler, Eric. Customise your caravan / by Eric Fowler. — London (50a Sheen La., SW14 8LP) : Continental Leisure Publications, 1976. — 96p : ill ; 21cm.
ISBN 0-905136-06-3 Pbk : £0.95
(B77-24303)

629.28 — MOTOR VEHICLES. OPERATION AND MAINTENANCE

629.28'24 — Cars. Road tests. *Reports, surveys*
'Motor' road test annual. — Sutton : IPC Specialist and Professional Press : Distributed by IPC Business Press.
1977. — [1977]. — 285p : ill ; 32cm.
Pbk : £2.75
ISSN 0307-7020
(B77-31957)

629.28'24 — Morgan cars. Road tests, 1912-1965. *Collections*
Morgan sports : sixth in a series of portfolios of contemporary road tests, descriptions, drawings and photographs from the pages of 'Autocar' (and, in this case, 'Motor cycle') through the years / edited and compiled by Peter Garnier. — London : IPC Transport Press, 1977. — 80p,[4]p of plates : ill(some col), ports ; 30cm. — (An 'Autocar' = 'Motor cycle' special)
Sd : £1.50
(B77-27187)

629.28'24 — Rolls-Royce cars. Road tests, 1904-1977. *Collections*
Rolls-Royce : fifth in a series of portfolios of contemporary road tests, descriptions, drawings and photographs from the pages of 'Autocar' through the years / edited and compiled by Peter Garnier with assistance from Warren Allport. — London : IPC Transport Press, 1977. — 240p,[8]p of plates : ill(some col), ports ; 30cm.
'An "Autocar" special'.
Pbk : £3.25
(B77-18228)

629.28'25'0941 — Motor vehicles. Testing. *Great Britain. Manuals. For MOT tests*
Great Britain. *Department of Transport.* Vehicle testing, the MOT tester's manual : including explanatory notes on the statutory provisions & regulations for testing of motor vehicles (except motor cycles) and light goods vehicles, under section 43 of the Road Traffic Act 1972 / Department of Transport. — London : H.M.S.O., 1976. — iv,56p : ill, form ; 22x30cm.
ISBN 0-11-550406-0 Sd : £2.00
(B77-11892)

629.28′25′0941 — Motor vehicles. Testing: MOT test. *Great Britain*
Toyne, Clifford Clarke. Motor vehicle testing and plating : for transport managers, fleet engineers, supervisors, vehicle inspectors, students and apprentices / by C.C. Toyne. — 3rd ed. — Northwood (Evington House, The Avenue, Northwood, Middx HA6 2NL) : Liffon Engineering Services, 1977. — 120p : ill ; 21cm.

Previous ed.: 1972.
ISBN 0-9500679-4-6 Sd : £2.00
(B77-13708)

629.28′25′0941 — Motor vehicles. Testing: MOT test. *Great Britain. Manuals*
Great Britain. *Department of Transport.* Vehicle testing, a guide to the operation of the MOT test / Department of Transport. — London : H.M.S.O., 1976. — [2],26p(4 fold) : forms ; 25cm.
ISBN 0-11-550407-9 Sd : £0.85
(B77-10411)

629.28′3′07 — Motor vehicles. Driving. Teaching. Assessment. *Organisation for Economic Co-operation and Development countries. Reports, surveys*
Organisation for Economic Co-operation and Development. *Road Research Group on Driver Education and Training.* Driver instruction : a report / prepared by an OECD Road Research Group [the Road Research Group on Driver Education and Training]. — Paris : O.E.C.D. ; [London] : [H.M.S.O.], 1976. — [2],vi,93p : ill ; 27cm. — (Road research)
Bibl.: p.82-90.
Pbk : £2.40
ISBN 92-64-11514-5
(B77-01581)

629.28′3′2 — Cars. Driving. *Manuals*
Giles, W E. Pass first time / [by] W.E. Giles. — St Ives, Cornwall : United Writers Publications, 1976. — 55p : col ill, forms ; 22cm.
ISBN 0-901976-38-5 Pbk : £0.60
(B77-13709)

Johnstone, Roy. Lucas make the 'L' Test easy / by Roy Johnstone ; photography Tony Timmington ; foreword by Noel Edmonds. — London [etc.] : Foulsham, 1976. — [2],142p : ill, facsims ; 22cm.
With answers.
ISBN 0-572-00956-9 Pbk : £0.95
(B77-06746)

Miles, John. Expert driving the police way / [by] John Miles ; diagrams by Ronald Morley ; photographs by Carl Bruin. — New ed. — London : P. Davies, 1977. — 156p,[8]p of plates : ill ; 21cm.
Previous ed.: 1970. — Index.
£3.50
ISBN 0-432-09390-7
(B77-11272)

629.28′3′2076 — Road safety. Great Britain. Ministry of Transport. Highway Code. *Questions & answers. For learner drivers*
Whitehead, Geoffrey. Test yourself on the Highway Code / by Geoffrey Whitehead. — London : Shaw and Sons, 1976. — [4],45p : ill(some col) ; 22cm.
'A Shaway publication'. — With answers.
ISBN 0-7219-0690-7 Sd : £0.65
(B77-15344)

629.28′4′4 — Commercial vehicles. Driving. *Manuals*
Thompson, Bertram Albert, *b.1911.* Professional driver's guide / by B.A. Thompson. — 4th ed. — New Malden (46 Coombe Rd, New Malden, Surrey KT3 4QL) : Croner Publications Ltd, 1977. — 167p : ill ; 17cm.
Previous ed.: 1975.
Lp : £2.20
ISBN 0-900319-17-8
(B77-16937)

629.28′4′75 — Motorcycles. Riding. *Manuals*
Institute of Advanced Motorists. Advanced motorcycling : the art of better motorcycle riding and advanced motorcycling techniques / compiled by the Institute of Advanced Motorists ; [edited by Ian Webb]. — London : Macdonald and Jane's, [1977]. — [7],140,[3] leaves of plates,[8]p of plates : ill(some col), forms.
ISBN 0-354-08517-4 Pbk : £2.95
(B77-30364)

629.28′7′22 — Cars. Maintenance & repair. Equipment. *Manuals*
Hill, Harry G. Automotive service and repair tools / [by] Harry G. Hill. — New York ; London [etc.] : Van Nostrand Reinhold, 1975. — vi,344p : ill ; 27cm.
Index.
ISBN 0-442-23415-5 : £7.25
(B77-01582)

629.28′7′4 — Diesel commercial vehicles. Maintenance & repair. *Manuals*
Tempest, Clifford Morley. Diesel and mobile plant service technology / [by] Clifford M. Tempest. — Sydney ; London [etc.] : McGraw-Hill, 1976. — xi,452p : ill ; 25cm.
Index.
ISBN 0-07-093275-1 : £11.20
(B77-26370)

629.28′7′4 — Motor vehicles: Heavy trucks. Recovery. *Great Britain. Manuals*
Grice, R J. Vehicle recovery : a practical manual for the heavy-vehicle driver, fleet operator and recovery specialist / [by] R.J. Grice ; with illustrations by Steve Palmer. — London [etc.] : Newnes-Butterworth, 1977. — [8],108p : ill ; 23cm.
Index.
ISBN 0-408-00264-6 : £5.00
(B77-13098)

629.28′8′22 — Alfa Romeo Alfasud cars. Maintenance & repair. *Amateurs' manuals*
Ball, Kenneth. Alfasud 1972-77 autobook ... / by Kenneth Ball and the Autobooks team of technical writers. — [2nd ed., fully revised]. — Brighton : Autobooks, 1977. — 129p : ill ; 26cm. — (The autobook series of workshop manuals)
Previous ed: published as 'Alfasud 1972-76 autobook'. 1976. — Index.
ISBN 0-85147-696-1 : £3.75
(B77-29512)

Haynes, John Harold. Alfasud owners workshop manual / by J.H. Haynes and Tim Parker. — Yeovil [etc.] : Haynes, 1977. — 134p : ill ; 28cm. — (Haynes owners workshop manuals ISSN 0305-4446)
Cover title: Alfa Romeo Alfasud, 1974 to 1976. — Index.
ISBN 0-85696-292-9 : £3.75
(B77-12520)

629.28′8′22 — Alfa Romeo Giulia cars. Maintenance & repair. *Amateurs' manuals*
Ball, Kenneth. Giulia, 1750, 2000 1962-76 autobook ... / by Kenneth Ball and the Autobooks team of technical writers. — [7th ed., fully revised]. — Brighton : Autobooks, 1976. — 163p : ill ; 26cm. — (The autobook series of workshop manuals)
Spine title: Alfa Romeo Giulia, 1750, 2000 1962-76. — Previous ed.: 1975. — Index.
ISBN 0-85147-664-3 : £3.75
(B77-30365)

629.28′8′22 — Audi 100 cars. Maintenance & repair. *Amateurs' manuals*
Ball, Kenneth. Audi 100 1969-76 autobook ... / by Kenneth Ball and the Autobooks team of technical writers. — [4th ed., fully revised]. — Brighton : Autobooks, [1976]. — 184p : ill ; 26cm. — (The autobook series of workshop manuals)
Previous ed.: published as 'Audi 100 1969-73 autobook ...'. Brighton : Autopress, 1973. — Index.
ISBN 0-85147-644-9 : £3.75
(B77-17584)

629.28′8′22 — Audi 80 cars. Maintenance & repair. *Amateurs' manuals*
Ball, Kenneth. Audi 80, Fox 1973-77 autobook ... / by Kenneth Ball and the Autobooks team of technical writers. — Brighton : Autobooks, [1977]. — 171p : ill ; 26cm. — (The autobook series of workshop manuals)
Index.
ISBN 0-85147-648-1 : £3.75
(B77-23508)

629.28′8′22 — Austin Allegro 1500 & 1750 cars. Maintenance & repair. *Amateurs' manuals*
Abbey, Staton. All-in-one book of the Austin Allegro 1500/1750 and Vanden Plas 1500 : a maintenance, fault-tracing and home workshop manual / [by] Staton Abbey. — London [etc.] : Pitman, 1976. — 111p : ill(some col) ; 25cm.
Spine title: All-in-one book of the Allegro 1500 & 1750. — Index.
ISBN 0-273-00966-4 Pbk : £1.95
(B77-01583)

629.28′8′22 — Austin-Healey Sprite cars. Maintenance & repair. *Amateurs' manuals*
Haynes, John Harold. Midget, Sprite owners workshop manual. — [New ed.] / by J.H. Haynes and I.M. Coomber. — Yeovil : Haynes, 1977. — 214p : ill(some col) ; 28cm. — (Haynes owners workshop manuals ISSN 0305-4446)
Cover title: MG Midget & AH Sprite Mk I, II, III & IV. — Previous ed.: / by John Harold Haynes. 1974. — Index.
ISBN 0-85696-265-1 : £3.75
Also classified at 629.28′8′22
(B77-21956)

629.28′8′22 — BMW 2000 & 2002 cars. Maintenance & repair. *Amateurs' manuals*
Ball, Kenneth. BMW 2000, 2002, 1966-76 autobook ... / by Kenneth Ball and the Autobooks team of technical writers. — 6th ed., fully revised. — Brighton : Autobooks, 1976. — 179p : ill ; 26cm. — (The autobook series of workshop manuals)
Previous ed.: published as 'BMW 2000, 2002 1966-75 autobook'. 1975. — Index.
ISBN 0-85147-639-2 : £3.75
(B77-05494)

629.28′8′22 — BMW 2500, 2800, 3.0 & 3.3 cars & BMW Bavaria cars. Maintenance & repair. *Amateurs' manuals*
Ball, Kenneth. BMW 2500, 2800, 3.0, 3.3, Bavaria 1968-77 autobook ... / by Kenneth Ball and Mary Ball and the Autobooks team of technical writers. — Brighton : Autobooks, [1977]. — [1],170p : ill, port ; 26cm. — (The autobook series of workshop manuals)
Index.
ISBN 0-85147-661-9 : £3.75
(B77-33879)

629.28′8′22 — British Chrysler cars. Maintenance & repair. *Amateurs' manuals*
Ball, Kenneth. Imp 1969-76 autobook ... / by Kenneth Ball and the Autobooks team of technical writers. — [4th ed., fully revised]. — Brighton : Autobooks, [1976]. — 167p : ill ; 26cm. — (The autobook series of workshop manuals)
Spine title: Hillman Imp, Singer, Chamois, Sunbeam Stiletto 1969-76. — Previous ed.: published as 'Hillman Imp 1969-73 autobook'. 1973. — Index.
ISBN 0-85147-660-0 : £3.75
(B77-09763)

629.28′8′22 — British Leyland 1100 & 1300 cars. Maintenance & repair. *Amateurs' manuals*
Haynes, John Harold. BLMC 1100 & 1300 owners workshop manual ... — 2nd ed. / by J.H. Haynes and B.L. Chalmers-Hunt. — Yeovil : Haynes, 1977. — 251p : ill(some col) ; 28cm. — (Haynes owners workshop manuals ISSN 0305-4446)
Cover title: BLMC 1100 & 1300 Mk I, II & III. — Previous ed.: published as 'BLMC 1100-1300, all models 1961 to 1971' / by B.L. Chalmers-Hunt. 1971. — Index.
ISBN 0-85696-260-0 : £3.75
(B77-20368)

629.28′8′22 — Cars. Maintenance & repair. *Amateurs' manuals*
Twite, Mike. Motorcars : maintenance and minor repairs / text by Mike Twite ; drawings by R. Deynis. — London : Chancerel : Barrie and Jenkins, 1977. — 2-91p : chiefly ill, ports ; 21cm. — (Action books)
Ill. on lining papers.
ISBN 0-905703-07-3 : £1.75
(B77-22667)

629.28′8′22 — Citroën 2CV/6 & 2CV/4 cars. Maintenance & repair. *Amateurs' manuals*
Russek, Peter. Repair guide, Citroën 2CV/6, 2CV/4 from February 1970 : another workshop manual / by Peter Russek. — Marlow : Russek, 1975. — 190,[12]p : ill ; 20cm. — (Peter Russek glove-box series)
Cover title: Citroën 2CV/6 and 2CV/4. — Fold. sheet ([2]p.:ill.) as insert.
ISBN 0-904509-13-3 Pbk : Unpriced
(B77-33284)

629.28'8'22 — Citroën cars. Maintenance & repair. *Amateurs' manuals*
Ball, Kenneth. Citroen 2CV, Dyane, Ami 1964-76 autobook ... / by Kenneth Ball and the Autobooks team of technical writers. — [3rd ed., fully revised]. — Brighton : Autobooks, [1976]. — 144p : ill ; 26cm. — (The autobook series of workship manuals)
Previous ed.: published as 'Citroen Dyane, Ami 1964-75 autobook'. 1975. — Index.
ISBN 0-85147-659-7 : £3.75
(B77-09764)

629.28'8'22 — Citroën GS cars. Maintenance & repair. *Amateurs' manuals*
Haynes, John Harold. Citroen GS owners workshop manual / by J.H. Haynes and B. Gilmour. — Yeovil : Haynes, 1977. — 131p : ill ; 28cm. — (Haynes owners workshop manuals ISSN 0305-4446)
Cover title: Citroen GS, 1971 to 1976. — Index.
ISBN 0-85696-290-2 : £3.75
(B77-21213)

629.28'8'22 — Daf 31, 32, 33, 44 & 46 cars. Maintenance & repair. *Amateurs' manuals*
Ball, Kenneth. DAF 31, 32, 33, 44, 46 1961-76 autobook / by Kenneth Ball and the Autobooks team of technical writers. — [4th ed., fully revised]. — Brighton : Autobooks, [1977]. — 175p : ill ; 26cm. — (The autobook series of workshop manuals)
Previous ed.: 1976. — Index.
ISBN 0-85147-697-x : £3.75
(B77-33880)

629.28'8'22 — Datsun 1000 & 1200 cars. Maintenance & repair. *Amateurs' manuals*
Ball, Kenneth. Datsun 1000, 1200, 120Y 1968-76 autobook .. / by Kenneth Ball and the Autobooks team of technical writers. — [7th ed., fully revised]. — Brighton : Autobooks, [1976]. — 172p : ill ; 26cm. — (The autobook series of workshop manuals)
Previous ed.: published as 'Datsun 1000, 1200, 120Y 1968-74 autobook ... '. Brighton : Autopress, 1974. — Index.
ISBN 0-85147-627-9 : £3.75
(B77-01584)

629.28'8'22 — Datsun 100A cars. Maintenance & repair. *Amateurs' manuals*
Russek, Peter. Repair guide, Datsun Cherry / by Peter Russek. — Revised [ed.]. — Marlow : Russek, 1974. — 166p : ill ; 21cm. — (Peter Russek glovebox series)
Two ill. on fold. sheet in pocket. — Previous ed.: 1972.
Unpriced
ISBN 0-903168-55-3
(B77-18229)

629.28'8'22 — Datsun 140J, 160J & 710 cars. Maintenance & repair. *Amateurs' manuals*
Ball, Kenneth. Datsun 140J, 160J, 710 1973-76 autobook / by Kenneth Ball and John Plummer. — Brighton : Autobooks, [1976]. — 176p : ill ; 26cm. — (The autobook series of workshop manuals)
Index.
ISBN 0-85147-637-6 : £3.75
(B77-09765)

629.28'8'22 — Datsun Cherry cars. Maintenance & repair. *Amateurs' manuals*
Ball, Kenneth. Datsun 100A, 120A, 1971-76 autobook : Datsun 100A Cherry-1971-76, Datsun 120A Cherry 1973-76 / by Kenneth Ball and the Autobook team of technical writers. — [4th ed., fully revised]. — Brighton : Autobooks, [1976]. — 150p : ill ; 26cm. — (The autobook series of workshop manuals)
Cover title: Cherry owners workshop manual. — Previous ed.: published as 'Datsun 100A, 120A 1971-75 autobook'. Brighton : Autopress, 1975. — Index.
ISBN 0-85147-640-6 : £3.75
(B77-17585)

629.28'8'22 — Fiat 124 cars. Maintenance & repair. *Amateurs' manuals*
Ball, Kenneth. Fiat 124 1966-74 autobook / by Kenneth Ball and the Autobooks team of technical writers. — [7th ed., fully revised]. — Brighton : Autobooks, [1976]. — 185p : ill ; 26cm. — (The autobook series of workshop manuals)
Spine title: 'Fiat 124, Special, Special T, 1966-74'. — Previous ed.: Brighton : Autopress, 1974. — Index.
ISBN 0-85147-647-3 : £3.75
(B77-31958)

629.28'8'22 — Fiat 126 cars. Maintenance & repair. *Amateurs' manuals*
Haynes, John Harold. Fiat 126 owners workshop manual ... / by J.H. Haynes ; and P.G. Strasman. — Yeovil : Haynes, 1977. — 123p : ill(some col) ; 28cm. — (Haynes owners workshop manuals ISSN 0305-4446)
Index.
ISBN 0-85696-305-4 : £3.75
(B77-20369)

629.28'8'22 — Fiat 131 cars. Maintenance & repair. *Amateurs' manuals*
Ball, Kenneth. Fiat 131 1975-77 autobook ... / by Kenneth Ball and the Autobooks team of technical writers. — Brighton : Autobooks, [1977]. — 150p : ill ; 26cm. — (The autobook series of workshop manuals)
Cover title: Fiat 131 owners workshop manual. — Spine title: Fiat 131 Mirafiori 1975-77. — Index.
ISBN 0-85147-651-1 : £3.75
(B77-20370)

629.28'8'22 — Fiat 850 cars. Maintenance & repair. *Amateurs' manuals*
Ball, Kenneth. Fiat 850, 1964-74 autobook ... / by Kenneth Ball and the Autopress team of technical writers. — [5th ed., fully revised]. — Brighton : Autopress, [1974]. — 175p : ill ; 26cm. — (The autobook series of workshop manuals)
Previous ed.: published as 'Fiat 850, 1964-72 autobook'. 1972. — Index.
ISBN 0-85147-531-0 : £3.75
(B77-03081)

629.28'8'22 — Ford Capri 1300 & 1600 OHV cars. Maintenance & repair. *Amateurs' manuals*
Ball, Kenneth. Ford Capri 1300 OHV, 1600 OHV 1968-77 autobook ... / by Kenneth Ball and the Autobooks team of technical writers. — [7th ed., fully revised]. — Brighton : Autobooks, 1977. — 173p : ill ; 26cm. — (The autobook series of workshop manuals)
Cover title: Capri 1300, 1600. — Previous ed.: published as 'Ford Capri 1300 OHV, 1600 OHV 1968-76 autobook'. 1975. — Index.
ISBN 0-85147-698-8 : £3.75
(B77-33285)

629.28'8'22 — Ford Capri 2000 & 3000 cars. Maintenance & repair. *Amateurs' manuals*
Ball, Kenneth. Ford Capri 2000 V4, 3000 V6 1969-76 autobook ... / by Kenneth Ball and the Autobooks team of technical writers. — [5th ed., fully revised]. — Brighton : Autobooks, [1976]. — 190p : ill ; 26cm. — (The autobook series of workshop manuals)
Previous ed.: published as 'Ford Capri 2000 V4, 3000 V6 1969-75 autobook'. 1974. — Index.
ISBN 0-85147-628-7 : £3.75
(B77-10412)

629.28'8'22 — Ford Capri 2600 & 2800 cars. Maintenance & repair. *Amateurs' manuals*
Ball, Kenneth. Capri 2600, 2800, 1972-76 autobook ... / by Kenneth Ball and the Autobooks team of technical writers. — [2nd ed., fully revised]. — Brighton : Autobooks, [1976]. — 154p : ill ; 26cm. — (The autobook series of workshop manuals)
Spine title: 'Ford Capri 2600, 2800, 1972-76'. — Previous ed.: 1975. — Index.
ISBN 0-85147-645-7 : £3.75
(B77-33881)

629.28'8'22 — Ford Capri II 1600 & 2000 cars. Maintenance & repair. *Amateurs' manuals*
Haynes, John Harold. Capri II owners workshop manual / by J.H. Haynes and Peter Ward. — Yeovil [etc.] : Haynes, 1976. — 256p : ill ; 28cm. — (Haynes owners workshop manuals ISSN 0305-4446)
Cover title: Ford 1600 & 2000 Capri II. — Index.
ISBN 0-85696-283-x : £3.75
(B77-00276)

629.28'8'22 — Ford Consul cars & Ford Granada cars. Maintenance & repair. *Amateurs' manuals*
Abbey, Staton. All-in-one book of the Ford Granada and Consul : a maintenance, fault-tracing and home workshop manual / [by] Staton Abbey. — London : Pitman, 1977. — 112p : ill(some col), port ; 25cm.
Cover title: Pitman's all-in-one book of the Granada & Consul. — Spine title: All-in-one book of the Granada & Consul. — Index.
ISBN 0-273-01011-5 Pbk : £1.95
(B77-19462)

629.28'8'22 — Ford Cortina Mk 2 cars. Maintenance & repair. *Amateurs' manuals*
Abbey, Staton. All-in-one book of the Ford Cortina Mk 2 : a maintenance, fault-tracing and home workshop manual / [by] Staton Abbey. — London : Pitman, 1977. — 112p : ill(some col), port ; 25cm.
Cover title: Pitman's all-in-one book of the Cortina Mk 2. — Spine title: All-in-one book of the Cortina Mk 2. — Index.
ISBN 0-273-01068-9 Pbk : £1.95
(B77-19463)

629.28'8'22 — Ford Cortina Mk4 1600 & 2000 cars. Maintenance & repair. *Amateurs' manuals*
Haynes, John Harold. Ford Cortina IV 1600 and 2000 ohc owners workshop manual ... / by J.H. Haynes. — Yeovil : Haynes, 1977. — 207p : ill(some col) ; 28cm. — (Haynes owners workshop manuals ISSN 0305-4446)
Index.
ISBN 0-85696-343-7 : £3.75
(B77-24304)

629.28'8'22 — Hillman Avenger cars. Maintenance & repair. *Amateurs' manuals*
Ball, Kenneth. Chrysler Hillman Avenger 1970-77 autobook : Chrysler Avenger, S, GLS, GT 1976-77, Hillman Avenger, GL, GLS, GT 1970-76, Sunbeam 1250, 1500 1970-74, Sunbeam 1300, 1600 1974-77, Plymouth Cricket 1971-72 / by Kenneth Ball and the Autobooks team of technical writers. — [5th ed., fully revised]. — Brighton : Autobooks, [1977]. — 172p : ill ; 26cm. — (The autobook series of workshop manuals)
Cover title: Avenger owners workshop manual. — Previous ed.: published as 'Hillman Avenger 1970-76 autobook ...'. 1976. — Index.
ISBN 0-85147-685-6 : Unpriced
(B77-31959)

Ball, Kenneth. Hillman Avenger 1970-76 autobook ... / by Kenneth Ball and the Autobooks team of technical writers. — [4th ed., fully revised]. — Brighton : Autobooks, 1976. — 170p : ill ; 26cm. — (The autobook series of workshop manuals)
Previous ed.: published as 'Hillman Avenger 1970-73 autobook ... '. Brighton : Autopress, 1973. — Index. — Includes other Chrysler cars of the same type.
ISBN 0-85147-641-4 : £3.75
(B77-04900)

629.28'8'22 — Hillman Hunter cars. Maintenance & repair. *Amateurs' manuals*
Ball, Kenneth. Hillman Hunter 1966-76 autobook ... / by Kenneth Ball and the Autobooks team of technical writers. — [5th ed., fully revised]. — Brighton : Autobooks, [1976]. — 158p : ill ; 26cm. — (The autobook series of workshop manuals)
Previous ed.: published as 'Hillman Hunter 1966-73 autobook ... '. Brighton : Autopress, 1973. — Index. — Includes other Chrysler cars of the same type.
ISBN 0-85147-642-2 : £3.75
(B77-04901)

Ball, Kenneth. Hillman Hunter 1966-77 autobook ... / by Kenneth Ball and the Autobooks team of technical writers. — [6th ed., fully revised]. — Brighton : Autobooks, [1977]. — 158p : ill ; 26cm. — (The autobook series of workshop manuals)
Cover title: Hunter owners workshop manual. — Previous ed.: published as 'Hillman Hunter 1966-76 autobook'. 1976. — Index.
ISBN 0-85147-680-5 : £3.75
(B77-20371)

629.28'8'22 — Honda Civic cars. Maintenance & repair. *Amateurs' manuals*
Ball, Kenneth. Civic 1973-76 autobook : Honda Civic 1200 1973-76, Honda Civic 1500 1975-76, Honda Civic CVCC 1975-76 / by Kenneth Ball and John Plummer. — Brighton : Autobooks, [1976]. — 164p : ill ; 26cm. — (The autobook series of workshop manuals)
Index.
ISBN 0-85147-528-0 : £3.75
(B77-04902)

629.28'8'22 — Jaguar XJ6 cars & Jaguar XJ cars. Maintenance & repair. *Amateurs' manuals*
Haynes, John Harold. Jaguar XJ6 & XJ owners workshop manual / by J.H. Haynes and Peter Strasman. — Yeovil : Haynes, 1976. — 204p : ill ; 28cm. — (Haynes owners workshop manuals)
Index.
ISBN 0-85696-242-2 : £3.75
(B77-05495)

629.28'8'22 — Landrover cars. Maintenance & repair. *Amateurs' manuals*
Ball, Kenneth. Land-Rover 2, 2A, 3 1959-77 autobook ... / by Kenneth Ball and the Autobooks team of technical writers. — [8th ed., fully revised]. — Brighton : Autobooks, [1976]. — 210p : ill ; 26cm. — (The autobook series of workshop manuals)
Previous ed.: published as 'Land-Rover 2, 2A, 3 1959-76 autobook'. 1976. — Index.
ISBN 0-85147-663-5 : £3.75
(B77-13099)

Haynes, John Harold. Land Rover owners workshop manual / by J.H. Haynes and M.S. Daniels. — Yeovil : Haynes, 1977. — 184p : ill ; 28cm. — (Haynes owners workshop manuals ISSN 0305-4446)
Index.
ISBN 0-85696-314-3 : Unpriced
(B77-32694)

629.28'8'22 — MG Midget cars. Maintenance & repair. *Amateurs' manuals*
Haynes, John Harold. Midget, Sprite owners workshop manual. — [New ed.] / by J.H. Haynes and I.M. Coomber. — Yeovil : Haynes, 1977. — 214p : ill(some col) ; 28cm. — (Haynes owners workshop manuals ISSN 0305-4446)
Cover title: MG Midget & AH Sprite Mk I, II, III & IV. — Previous ed.: / by John Harold Haynes. 1974. — Index.
ISBN 0-85696-265-1 : £3.75
Primary classification 629.28'8'22
(B77-21956)

629.28'8'22 — Opel Ascona cars & Opel Manta cars. Maintenance & repair. *Amateurs' manuals*
Ball, Kenneth. Ascona, Manta 1975-77 autobook ... / by Kenneth Ball and the Autobooks team of technical writers. — Brighton : Autobooks, [1977]. — 156p : ill ; 26cm. — (The autobook series of workshop manuals)
Spine title: Opel Ascona, Manta 1975-77. — Index.
ISBN 0-85147-650-3 : £3.75
(B77-16938)

Haynes, John Harold. Opel Ascona & Manta owners workshop manual / by J.H. Haynes and Marcus Daniels. — Yeovil : Haynes, 1977. — 195p : ill ; 28cm. — (Haynes owners workshop manuals ISSN 0305-4446)
Index.
ISBN 0-85696-316-x : £3.75
(B77-18852)

629.28'8'22 — Peugeot 204 cars. Maintenance & repair. *Amateurs' manuals*
Ball, Kenneth. Peugeot 204 1965-76 autobook ... / by Kenneth Ball and the Autobooks team of technical writers. — [4th ed., fully revised]. — Brighton : Autobooks, [1977]. — 138p : ill ; 26cm. — (The autobook series of workshop manuals)
Previous ed.: published as 'Peugeot 204 1965-75 autobook ...'. 1975. — Index.
ISBN 0-85147-668-6 : £3.75
(B77-32695)

629.28'8'22 — Porsche 911 cars. Maintenance & repair. *Amateurs' manuals*
Ball, Kenneth. Porsche 911 1964-73 autobook ... / by Kenneth Ball and the Autopress team of technical writers. — [2nd ed., fully revised]. — Brighton : Autopress, [1974]. — [7],166p : ill ; 26cm. — (The autobook series of workshop manuals)
'Mechanical changes from 1969 to 1973 in supplement form'. — Previous ed.: published as 'Porsche 911 1964-69 autobook'. 1971. — Index.
ISBN 0-85147-493-4 : £3.75
(B77-03082)

Haynes, John Harold. Porsche 911 owners workshop manual / by J.H. Haynes and Peter Ward. — Yeovil [etc.] : Haynes, 1977. — 254p : ill ; 28cm. — (Haynes owners workshop manuals ISSN 0305-4446)
Index.
ISBN 0-85696-264-3 : £3.75
(B77-11273)

629.28'8'22 — Porsche 914 cars. Maintenance & repair. *Amateurs' manuals*
Haynes, John Harold. Porsche 914 owners workshop manual / by J.H. Haynes and Peter Ward. — Yeovil : Haynes, 1976. — 214p : ill ; 28cm. — (Haynes owners workshop manuals)
Index.
ISBN 0-85696-239-2 : £3.75
(B77-05496)

629.28'8'22 — Renault 12 cars. Maintenance & repair. *Amateurs' manuals*
Abbey, Staton. All-in-one book of the Renault 12 : a maintenance, fault-tracing and home workshop manual : covering Renault 12 synchromesh-gearbox and automatic-transmission models ... / [by] Staton Abbey. — London [etc.] : Pitman, 1977. — 112p : ill(some col), port ; 25cm.
Cover title: Pitman's all-in-one book of the Renault 12. — Text, ill. on back cover. — Index.
ISBN 0-273-01070-0 Pbk : £1.95
(B77-33882)

Ball, Kenneth. Renault 12 1969-77 autobook ... / by Kenneth Ball and the Autobooks team of technical writers. — [6th ed. fully revised]. — Brighton : Autobooks, 1977. — 179p : ill ; 26cm. — (The autobook series of workshop manuals)
Previous ed.: published as 'Renault 12 1969-76 autobook'. 1976. — Index.
ISBN 0-85147-702-x : £3.75
(B77-31960)

Russek, Peter. Repair guide, Renault 12 / by Peter Russek. — [New ed.]. — Marlow : Russek, 1974. — 168p : ill ; 21cm. — (Peter Russek glovebox series)
Previous ed.: 1972.
Unpriced
ISBN 0-903168-06-5
(B77-18230)

629.28'8'22 — Renault 15 & 17 cars. Maintenance & repair. *Amateurs' manuals*
Ball, Kenneth. Renault 15, 17 1971-76 autobook ... / by Kenneth Ball and the Autobooks team of technical writers. — [2nd ed., fully revised]. — Brighton : Autobooks, [1976]. — 189p : ill ; 26cm. — (The autobook series of workshop manuals)
Previous ed.: published as 'Renault 15, 17 1971-74 autobook ...' Brighton : Autopress, 1974. — Index.
ISBN 0-85147-634-1 : £3.75
(B77-01585)

629.28'8'22 — Renault 4 cars. Maintenance & repair. *Amateurs' manuals*
Abbey, Staton. All-in-one book of the Renault 4 : maintenance, fault-tracing and home workshop manual : covering the Renault 4 from October 1965 onwards, R1123 : de Luxe, L and TL models / [by] Staton Abbey. — London [etc.] : Pitman, 1976 [i.e. 1977]. — 110p : ill(some col), port ; 25cm.
Cover title: Pitman's all-in-one book of the Renault 4. — Index.
ISBN 0-273-01003-4 Pbk : £1.95
(B77-05497)

629.28'8'22 — Rover 2000 & 2200 cars. Maintenance & repair. *Amateurs' manuals*
Ball, Kenneth. Rover 2000, 2200 1963-77 autobook ... / by Kenneth Ball and the Autobooks team of technical writers. — [8th ed., fully revised]. — Brighton : Autobooks, [1977]. — 161p : ill ; 26cm. — (The autobook series of workshop manuals)
Cover title: Rover 2000, 2200 owners workshop manual. — Previous ed.: published as 'Rover 2000, 2200 1963-76 autobook'. 1975. — Index.
ISBN 0-85147-679-1 : £3.75
(B77-21214)

629.28'8'22 — Saab 99 cars. Maintenance & repair. *Amateurs' manuals*
Haynes, John Harold. Saab 99 owners workshop manual / by J.H. Haynes and P.G. Strasman. — Yeovil : Haynes, 1976. — 239p : ill ; 28cm. — (Haynes owners workshop manuals ISSN 0305-4446)
Index.
ISBN 0-85696-247-3 : £3.75
(B77-01586)

629.28'8'22 — Saab V4 cars. Maintenance & repair. *Amateurs' manuals*
Ball, Kenneth. Saab V4 1966-76 autobook : Saab 96 V4 1966-76, Saab 95 V4 1967-76 ... / by Kenneth Ball and the Autobooks team of technical writers. — [4th ed., fully revised]. — Brighton : Autobooks, [1976]. — 178p : ill ; 26cm. — (The autobook series of workshop manuals)
Previous ed.: i.e. 3rd ed., published as 'Saab V4 1966-75 autobook'. Brighton : Autopress, 1975. — Index.
ISBN 0-85147-638-4 : £3.75
(B77-14789)

629.28'8'22 — Simca 1100 cars. Maintenance & repair. *Amateurs' manuals*
Ball, Kenneth. Simca 1100 1967-76 autobook / by Kenneth Ball and the Autobooks team of technical writers. — [4th ed., fully revised]. — Brighton : Autobooks, [1977]. — 178p : ill ; 26cm. — (The autobook series of workshop manuals)
Cover title: Simca 1100 owners workshop manual. — Previous ed.: published as 'Simca 1100 1967-73 autobook'. Brighton : Autopress, 1973. — Index.
ISBN 0-85147-506-x : £3.75
(B77-21215)

629.28'8'22 — Skoda 1000 & 1100 cars. Maintenance & repair. *Amateurs' manuals*
Haynes, John Harold. Skoda 1000 & 1100 owners workshop manual / by J.H. Haynes and I.M. Coomber. — Yeovil [etc.] : Haynes, 1977. — 161p : ill ; 28cm. — (Haynes owners workshop manuals ISSN 0305-4446)
Index.
ISBN 0-85696-303-8 : £3.75
(B77-15920)

629.28'8'22 — Toyota 1000 cars. Maintenance & repair. *Amateurs' manuals*
Haynes, John Harold. Toyota 1000 owners workshop manual / by J.H. Haynes and M.S. Daniels. — Yeovil [etc.] : Haynes, 1977. — 159p : ill ; 28cm. — (Haynes owners workshop manuals ISSN 0305-4446)
Index.
ISBN 0-85696-323-2 : £3.75
(B77-11893)

629.28'8'22 — Toyota Corolla cars. Maintenance & repair. *Amateurs' manuals*
Russek, Peter. Repair guide, Toyota Corolla / by Peter Russek. — [Revised ed.]. — Marlow : Russek, 1976. — 203p : ill ; 20cm. — (Peter Russek glove-box series)
Cover title: Toyota Corolla 1100, 1200E, 30SR & 1400. — Fold. sheet ([2]p. : ill.) as insert. — Previous ed.: 1975.
ISBN 0-904509-17-6 Pbk : Unpriced
(B77-32696)

629.28'8'22 — Toyota Land Cruiser cars. Maintenance & repair. *Amateurs' manuals*
Haynes, John Harold. Toyota Land Cruiser owners workshop manual ... / by J.H. Haynes and Peter Ward. — Yeovil : Haynes, 1977. — 268p : ill(some col) ; 28cm. — (Haynes owners workshop manuals ISSN 0305-4446)
Cover title: Toyota Land Cruiser 1975 to 1977. — Index.
ISBN 0-85696-313-5 : £3.75
(B77-25005)

629.28'8'22 — Triumph 1500 cars. Maintenance & repair. *Amateurs' manuals*
Abbey, Staton. All-in-one book of the Triumph 1500, 1500TC and Toledo : a maintenance, fault-tracing and home workshop manual / [by] Staton Abbey. — London [etc.] : Pitman, 1976. — 112p : ill(some col) ; 25cm.
Spine title: All-in-one-book of the Triumph 1500 & Toledo. — Index.
ISBN 0-273-00726-2 Pbk : £1.95
Also classified at 629.28'8'22
(B77-01587)

629.28'8'22 — Triumph Dolomite 1300 & 1500 cars. Maintenance & repair. *Amateurs' manuals*
Ball, Kenneth. Dolomite 1300, 1500 1976-77 autobook ... / by Kenneth Ball and the Autobooks team of technical writers. — Brighton : Autobooks, [1977]. — 177p : ill ; 26cm. — (The autobook series of workshop manuals)
Spine title: Triumph Dolomite 1300, 1500 1976-77. — Index.
ISBN 0-85147-677-5 : £3.75
(B77-22668)

629.28'8'22 — Triumph Dolomite cars. Maintenance & repair. *Amateurs' manuals*
Ball, Kenneth. Triumph Dolomite 1850 1972-76 autobook : Triumph Dolomite 1854cc 1972-76 / by Kenneth Ball and the Autobooks team of technical writers. — [3rd ed., fully revised]. — Brighton : Autobooks, 1976. — 203p : ill ; 26cm. — (The autobook series of workshop manuals)
Previous ed.: published as 'Triumph Dolomite 1972-75 autobook'. Brighton : Autopress, 1975. — Index.
ISBN 0-85147-635-x : £3.75
(B77-01588)

629.28'8'22 — Triumph Toledo cars. Maintenance & repair. *Amateurs' manuals*
Abbey, Staton. All-in-one book of the Triumph 1500, 1500TC and Toledo : a maintenance, fault-tracing and home workshop manual / [by] Staton Abbey. — London [etc.] : Pitman, 1976. — 112p : ill(some col) ; 25cm.
Spine title: All-in-one-book of the Triumph 1500 & Toledo. — Index.
ISBN 0-273-00726-2 Pbk : £1.95
Primary classification 629.28'8'22
(B77-01587)

Ball, Kenneth. Triumph Toledo 1500 TC 1970-76 autobook ... / by Kenneth Ball and the Autobooks team of technical writers. — [4th ed., fully revised]. — Brighton : Autobooks, [1976]. — 191p : ill ; 26cm. — (The autobook series of workshop manuals)
Previous ed.: published as 'Triumph Toledo 1970-75 autobook'. 1975. — Index.
ISBN 0-85147-636-8 : £3.75
(B77-31271)

629.28'8'22 — Triumph TR7 cars. Maintenance & repair. *Amateurs' manuals*
Ball, Kenneth. TR7 1975-76 autobook : Triumph TR7 1975-76 / by Kenneth Ball and John Plummer. — Brighton : Autobooks, [1976]. — 161p : ill ; 26cm. — (The autobook series of workshop manuals)
Index.
ISBN 0-85147-646-5 : £3.75
(B77-03602)

Haynes, John Harold. Triumph TR 7 owners workshop manual / by J.H. Haynes and Peter Ward. — Yeovil [etc.] : Haynes, 1977. — 160p : ill ; 28cm. — (Haynes owners workshop manuals ISSN 0305-4446)
Index.
ISBN 0-85696-322-4 : £3.75
(B77-15921)

629.28'8'22 — Vauxhall Cavalier cars. Maintenance & repair. *Amateurs' manuals*
Ball, Kenneth. Cavalier 1975-77 autobook ... / by Kenneth Ball and the Autobooks team of technical writers. — Brighton : Autobooks, [1977]. — 156p : ill ; 26cm. — (The autobook series of workshop manuals)
Cover title: Cavalier owners workshop manual. — Spine title: Vauxhall Cavalier 1975-77. — Index.
ISBN 0-85147-649-x : £3.75
(B77-16460)

Haynes, John Harold. Vauxhall Cavalier owners workshop manual / by J.H. Haynes and Marcus Daniels. — Yeovil : Haynes, 1977. — 195p : ill ; 28cm. — (Haynes owners workshop manuals ISSN 0305-4446)
Cover title: Vauxhall Cavalier saloon & coupé. — Index.
ISBN 0-85696-315-1 : £3.75
(B77-18853)

629.28'8'22 — Vauxhall Chevette cars. Maintenance & repair. *Amateurs' manuals*
Abbey, Staton. All-in-one book of the Vauxhall Chevette : a maintenance, fault-tracing and home workshop manual, covering the 1256cc Hatchback Saloon estate car / [by] Staton Abbey. — London : Pitman, 1977. — 112p : ill(some col), port ; 25cm.
Spine title: All-in-one book of the Chevette. — Index.
ISBN 0-273-01010-7 Pbk : £1.95
(B77-21216)

Vauxhall Chevette : with specifications, repair and maintenance data. — Sydney ; London [etc.] : Scientific Publications ; [London] : [Distributed by Muller], 1976. — 157p : ill ; 28cm. — (Scientific Publications' workshop manual series ; no.114)
Index.
ISBN 0-85566-202-6 Pbk : £2.95
(B77-02396)

629.28'8'22 — Vauxhall Victor cars & Vauxhall VX cars. Maintenance & repair. *Amateurs' manuals*
Abbey, Staton. All-in-one book of the Vauxhall Victor and VX : a maintenance, fault-tracing and home workshop manual : covering models from October 1967 ... / [by] Staton Abbey. — London [etc.] : Pitman, 1977. — 112p : ill(some col), port ; 25cm.
Cover title: Pitman's all-in-one book of the Vauxhall Victor & VX. — Index.
ISBN 0-273-00487-5 Pbk : £1.95
(B77-14790)

629.28'8'22 — Vauxhall Victor FE cars & Vauxhall Ventora cars. Maintenance & repair. *Amateurs' manuals*
Ball, Kenneth. Victor FE, Ventora 1972-76 autobook ... / by Kenneth Ball and the Autobooks team of technical writers. — [2nd ed., fully revised]. — Brighton : Autobooks, [1976]. — 193p : ill ; 26cm. — (The autobook series of workshop manuals)
Spine title: Vauxhall Victor FE, Ventora 1972-76. — Previous ed.: published as 'Vauxhall Victor FE, Ventora 1972-73 autobook'. Brighton : Autopress, 1973. — Index.
ISBN 0-85147-658-9 : £3.75
(B77-15345)

629.28'8'22 — Vauxhall Viva OHV cars & Vauxhall Firenza cars. Maintenance & repair. *Amateurs' manuals*
Vauxhall Viva Firenza OHV 1159cc, 1256cc : with specifications, repair and maintenance data. — Sydney ; London [etc.] : Scientific Publications ; London : Distributed by Muller, 1976. — 188,4p : ill ; 28cm. — (Scientific Publications' workshop manual series ; no.57)
Cover title: Viva OHV.
ISBN 0-85566-195-x Pbk : £2.95
(B77-14289)

629.28'8'22 — Volkswagen Golf cars, Volkswagen Rabbit cars & Volkswagen Scirocco cars. Maintenance & repair. *Amateurs' manuals*
Russek, Peter. Volkswagen Golf, Rabbit, Scirocco (1100, 1500 and 1600 cc) : repair guide / by Peter Russek. — [Revised ed.]. — Marlow : Russek, 1976. — 192,[12]p : ill ; 20cm. — (Peter Russek glove-box series)
Wiring diagram as insert. — Previous ed.: 1975. — Index.
ISBN 0-904509-12-5 Pbk : Unpriced
(B77-31961)

629.28'8'22 — Volkswagen Passat cars & Volkswagen Dasher cars. Maintenance & repair. *Amateurs' manuals*
Ball, Kenneth. Passat, Dasher 1973-77 autobook ... / by [Kenneth Ball and] the Autobooks team of technical writers. — [2nd ed., fully revised]. — Brighton : Autobooks, [1977]. — 179p : ill ; 26cm. — (The autobook series of workshop manuals)
Cover title: Passat, Dasher owners workshop manual. — Spine title: Volkswagen Passat, Dasher 1973-77. — Previous ed.: 1975. — Index.
ISBN 0-85147-671-6 : £3.75
(B77-20372)

629.28'8'22 — Volkswagen Polo cars. Maintenance & repair. *Amateurs' manuals*
Ball, Kenneth. Polo 1975-77 autobook ... / by Kenneth Ball and the Autobooks team of technical writers. — [2nd ed., fully revised]. — Brighton : Autobooks, [1977]. — 139p : ill ; 26cm. — (The autobook series of workshop manuals)
Previous ed.: published as 'Polo 1975-76 autobook ...' 1976. — Index.
ISBN 0-85147-674-0 : Unpriced
(B77-32697)

Haynes, John Harold. VW Polo owners workshop manual ... / by J.H. Haynes and K.F. Kinchin. — Yeovil : Haynes, 1977. — 206p : ill(some col) ; 28cm. — (Haynes owners workshop manuals ISSN 0305-4446)
Index.
ISBN 0-85696-335-6 : £3.75
(B77-24305)

629.28'8'22 — Volvo 164 cars. Maintenance & repair. *Amateurs' manuals*
Ball, Kenneth. Volvo 160 series 1968-74 autobook ... / by Kenneth Ball and the Autobooks team of technical writers. — [2nd ed., fully revised]. — Brighton : Autobooks, [1975]. — 152p : ill ; 26cm. — (The autobook series of workshop manuals)
Previous ed.: published as 'Volvo 160 series 1968-72 autobook'. Brighton : Autopress, 1972. — Index.
ISBN 0-85147-565-5 : £3.75
(B77-24306)

Haynes, John Harold. Volvo 164 owners workshop manual / by J.H. Haynes and P.G. Strasman. — Yeovil : Haynes, 1976. — 165p : ill ; 28cm. — (Haynes owners workshop manuals ISSN 0305-4446)
Index.
ISBN 0-85696-244-9 : £3.75
(B77-09766)

629.28'8'22 — Volvo 240 cars. Maintenance & repair. *Amateurs' manuals*
Haynes, John Harold. Volvo 240 series owners workshop manual ... / by J.H. Haynes and B. Gilmour. — Yeovil : Haynes, 1977. — 200p : ill(some col) ; 28cm. — (Haynes owners workshop manuals ISSN 0305-4446)
Index.
ISBN 0-85696-270-8 : £3.75
(B77-21217)

629.28'8'3 — Bedford Beagle HA motor vans. Maintenance & repair. *Amateurs' manuals*
Ball, Kenneth. Beagle, HA van 1964-76 autobook ... / by Kenneth Ball and the Autobooks team of technical writers. — [3rd ed., fully revised]. — Brighton : Autobooks, [1976]. — 184p : ill ; 26cm. — (The autobook series of workshop manuals)
Spine title: Bedford Beagle, HA van 1964-76. — Previous ed.: published as 'Bedford Beagle and HA vans 1964-74 autobook'. Brighton : Autopress, 1974. — Index.
ISBN 0-85147-665-1 : £3.75
(B77-13710)

629.28'8'3 — Bedford CF motor vans. Maintenance & repair. *Amateurs' manuals*
Ball, Kenneth. Bedford CF 1969-1977 autobook ... / by Kenneth Ball and the Autobooks team of technical writers. — [4th ed., fully revised]. — Brighton : Autobooks, [1977]. — 167p : ill ; 26cm. — (The autobook series of workshop manuals)
Previous ed.: published as 'Bedford CF vans 1969-76 autobook ...'. 1976. — Index.
ISBN 0-85147-673-2 : £3.75
(B77-31272)

629.28'8'3 — Datsun 620 pick-up trucks. Maintenance & repair. *Amateurs' manuals*
Haynes, John Harold. Datsun pick-up owners workshop manual / by J.H. Haynes and Peter Ward. — Yeovil : Haynes, 1976. — 194p : ill ; 28cm. — (Haynes owners workshop manuals ISSN 0305-4446)
Index.
ISBN 0-85696-277-5 : £3.75
(B77-01589)

629.28'8'3 — Ford Transit motor vans. Maintenance & repair. *Amateurs' manuals*
Ball, Kenneth. Ford Transit V4 1965-77 autobook ... / by Kenneth Ball and the Autobooks team of technical writers. — [5th ed., fully revised]. — Brighton : Autobooks, [1977]. — 170p : ill ; 26cm. — (The autobook series of workshop manuals)
Previous ed.: published as 'Ford Transit V4 1965-76 autobook ...' 1975. — Index.
ISBN 0-85147-675-9 : £3.75
(B77-29513)

629.28'8'3 — Toyota Hi-Lux pick-up trucks & Toyota Hi-Ace pick-up trucks. Maintenance & repair. *Amateurs' manuals*
Haynes, John Harold. Toyota Hi-Lux and Hi-Ace owners workshop manual ... / by J.H. Haynes and P.G. Strasman. — Yeovil : Haynes, 1977. — 240p : ill ; 28cm. — (Haynes owners workshop manuals ISSN 0305-4446)
Index.
ISBN 0-85696-304-6 : £3.75
(B77-24307)

629.28'8'5 — Field Marshall series 3 diesel agricultural tractors. Maintenance & repair. *Amateurs' manuals*
Marshall Sons and Company. Field Marshall diesel tractor series 3 : instruction manual / [Marshall Sons and Company]. — Hinckley (216 Coventry Rd, Hinckley, Leicestershire LE10 0NG) : Traction Engine Enterprises, 1976. — [1],48p : ill ; 19x23cm.
Facsimile reprint of: 1st ed. Gainsborough : Marshall Sons & Co., 1928?. — Index.
ISBN 0-905100-08-5 Sd : £1.75
(B77-14290)

629.28'8'72 — Fantic Motor mopeds. Maintenance & repair. *Amateurs' manuals*
Darlington, Mansur. Fantic Motor mopeds owners workshop manual / by Mansur Darlington. — Yeovil : Haynes, 1976. — 99p : ill ; 27cm. — (Haynes owners workshop manuals for motorcycles)
Index.
ISBN 0-85696-320-8 Pbk : £2.50
(B77-09767)

629.28′8′72 — Honda 4-stroke mopeds. Maintenance & repair. *Amateurs' manuals*
Bleach, Mervyn. Honda 4-stroke mopeds owners workshop manual / by Mervyn Bleach. — Yeovil [etc.] : Haynes, 1977. — 92p : ill ; 28cm. — (Haynes owners workshop manuals for motorcycles)
Index.
ISBN 0-85696-317-8 Pbk : £2.50
(B77-15922)

629.28′8′72 — Puch MS, MV, M2, M3 & VS mopeds. Maintenance & repair. *Amateurs' manuals*
Bleach, Mervyn. Puch MS, MV, M2, M3 and VS mopeds owners workshop manual / by Mervyn Bleach. — Yeovil : Haynes, 1976. — 83p : ill ; 28cm. — (Haynes owners workshop manuals for motorcycles)
Index.
ISBN 0-85696-255-4 Pbk : £2.50
(B77-02397)

629.28′8′72 — Puch sports mopeds. Maintenance & repair. *Amateurs' manuals*
Bleach, Mervyn. Puch sports mopeds owners workshop manual / by Mervyn Bleach. — Yeovil : Haynes, 1976. — 120p : ill ; 27cm. — (Haynes owners workshop manuals for motorcycles)
Index.
ISBN 0-85696-318-6 Pbk : £2.50
(B77-07421)

629.28′8′72 — Suzuki A50 mopeds. Maintenance & repair. *Amateurs' manuals*
Hammond, Jim. Suzuki A50P mopeds owners workshop manual ... / by Jim Hammond. — Yeovil : Haynes, 1977. — 98p : ill ; 27cm. — (Haynes owners workshop manuals for motorcycles)
Cover title: Suzuki A50P, A50 & AS50. — Index.
ISBN 0-85696-328-3 Pbk : £2.50
(B77-23509)

629.28′8′75 — BSA 350, 500 & 600 pre-unit single cylinder motorcycles. Maintenance & repair. *Amateurs' manuals*
Darlington, Mansur. BSA 350, 500 and 600 pre-unit singles owners workshop manual ... / by Mansur Darlington. — Yeovil : Haynes, 1977. — 144p : ill(some col) ; 27cm. — (Haynes owners workshop manuals for motorcycles)
Cover title: BSA pre-unit singles. — Index.
ISBN 0-85696-326-7 Pbk : £2.50
(B77-25006)

629.28′8′75 — Gilera 50 motorcycles. *Maintenance & repair. Amateurs' manuals*
Darlington, Mansur. Gilera 50 owners workshop manual ... / by Mansur Darlington. — Yeovil : Haynes, 1976. — 88p : ill ; 27cm. — (Haynes owners workshop manuals for motorcycles)
Index.
ISBN 0-85696-257-0 Pbk : £2.50
(B77-22669)

629.28′8′75 — Harley-Davidson Sportster motorcycles. Maintenance & repair. *Amateurs' manuals*
Clew, Jeff. Harley-Davidson sportsters owners workshop manual / by Jeff Clew. — Yeovil : Haynes, 1976. — 125p : ill ; 27cm. — (Haynes owners workshop manuals for motorcycles ; 250)
Index.
ISBN 0-85696-250-3 Pbk : £2.50
(B77-01590)

629.28′8′75 — Honda 125 & 175 Elsinore motorcycles. Maintenance & repair. *Amateurs' manuals*
Darlington, Mansur. Honda 125 and 175 Elsinore owners workshop manual / by Mansur Darlington. — Yeovil [etc.] : Haynes, 1977. — 116p : ill ; 28cm. — (Haynes owners workshop manuals for motorcycles)
Index.
ISBN 0-85696-312-7 Pbk : £2.50
(B77-12521)

629.28′8′75 — Honda C50, C70 & C90 motorcycles. Maintenance & repair. *Amateurs' manuals*
Darlington, Mansur. Honda C50, C70 and C90 owners workshop manual ... / by Mansur Darlington. — Yeovil : Haynes, 1977. — 120p : ill ; 27cm. — (Haynes owners workshop manuals for motorcycles)
Index.
ISBN 0-85696-324-0 Pbk : £2.50
(B77-22670)

629.28′8′75 — Honda CB 500 & 550 four cylinder motorcycles. Maintenance & repair. *Amateurs' manuals*
Thorpe, John, *b.1928.* Bikebook of the Honda CB500-550 four : a guide to maintenance, service and overhaul / [by] John Thorpe. — London : Pitman, 1977. — iv,91p : ill ; 23cm. — (Pitman bikebooks)
Cover title: Honda CB500-550 four. — Index.
ISBN 0-273-01098-0 Pbk : £1.25
(B77-21218)

629.28′8′75 — Honda CB175 & CD175 motorcycles. Maintenance & repair. *Amateurs' manuals*
Thorpe, John, *b.1928.* Bikebook of the Honda CB-CD 175 : a guide to maintenance, service and overhaul / [by] John Thorpe. — London [etc.] : Pitman, 1976 [i.e. 1977]. — [5],72p : ill ; 23cm. — (Pitman bikebooks)
Cover title: Honda CB-CD 175. — Index.
ISBN 0-273-00280-5 Pbk : £1.25
(B77-10413)

629.28′8′75 — Honda CB250, CB350 & CB360 motorcycles. Maintenance & repair. *Amateurs' manuals*
Thorpe, John, *b.1928.* Bikebook of the Honda CB 250-350-360 : a guide to maintenance, service and overhaul / [by] John Thorpe. — London [etc.] : Pitman, 1976 [i.e. 1977]. — vi,81p : ill ; 23cm. — (Pitman bikebooks)
Cover title: Honda CB 250-350-360. — Index.
ISBN 0-273-00281-3 Pbk : £1.25
(B77-10414)

629.28′8′75 — Honda Gold Wing motorcycles. Maintenance & repair. *Amateurs' manuals*
Darlington, Mansur. Honda Gold Wing owners workshop manual / by Mansur Darlington. — Yeovil : Haynes, 1976. — 157p : ill ; 27cm. — (Haynes owners workshop manuals for motorcycles)
Index.
ISBN 0-85696-309-7 Pbk : £2.50
(B77-06167)

629.28′8′75 — Kawasaki 500 & 750 three cylinder motorcycles. Maintenance & repair. *Amateurs' manuals*
Wilkins, Stewart Wallace. Kawasaki 500 and 750 3 cylinder models owners workshop manual ... / by Stewart W. Wilkins. — Yeovil : Haynes, 1977. — 119p : ill(some col) ; 28cm. — (Haynes owners workshop manuals for motorcycles)
Index.
ISBN 0-85696-325-9 Pbk : £2.50
(B77-25007)

629.28′8′75 — Motorcycles, ca 1915-ca 1950. Restoration. *Amateurs' manuals*
Clew, Jeff. The restoration of vintage & thoroughbred motorcycles / [by] Jeff Clew. — Yeovil : Haynes, 1976. — 2-208p : ill, port ; 26cm.
'A Foulis motorcycle book' - title page verso. — Bibl.: p.205-206.
ISBN 0-85429-185-7 : £6.95
(B77-07422)

629.28′8′75 — Motorcycles. Maintenance & repair. *Amateurs' manuals*
Robinson, John. The motorcycle doctor / by John Robinson. — Kingswood : Elliot Right Way Books, 1977. — 160p : ill ; 18cm. — (Paperfronts)
ISBN 0-7160-0633-2 Pbk : £0.50
(B77-32698)

629.28′8′75 — Sunbeam four stroke single cylinder motorcycles. Maintenance & repair. *Amateurs' manuals*
Heathcote, Leslie K. The book of the Sunbeam single-cylinder four-stroke motorcycles, 1928-1939 / originally written by Leslie K. Heathcote. — [New ed.]. — Leatherhead (P.O. Box 20, Leatherhead, Surrey) : Bruce Main-Smith & Co., 1977. — [2],69p : ill, facsims, map, port ; 21x28cm. — (Bruce Main-Smith and Company. Service series)
Cover title: Sunbeam four-stroke singles, 1928-1939. — Previous ed.: / revised by W.C. Haycraft. London : Pitman, 1932.
ISBN 0-904365-14-x Sd : Unpriced
(B77-13711)

629.28′8′75 — Suzuki 50 motorcycles. Maintenance & repair. *Amateurs' manuals*
Thorpe, John, *b.1928.* Bikebook of the Suzuki 50 : a guide to maintenance, service and overhaul / [by] John Thorpe. — London [etc.] : Pitman, 1976 [i.e. 1977]. — viii,63p : ill ; 23cm. — (Pitman bikebooks)
Cover title: Suzuki 50. — Index.
ISBN 0-273-00271-6 Pbk : £1.25
(B77-10415)

629.28′8′75 — Suzuki B100P & Student motorcycles. Maintenance & repair. *Amateurs' manuals*
Wilkins, Stewart Wallace. Suzuki Student owners workshop manual / by Stewart W. Wilkins. — Yeovil [etc.] : Haynes, 1976. — 90p : ill ; 28cm. — (Haynes owners workshop manuals for motorcycles)
Cover title: Suzuki Student & B100P. — Index.
ISBN 0-85696-298-8 Pbk : £2.50
(B77-00277)

629.28′8′75 — Suzuki GT 125 & GT 185 motorcycles. Maintenance & repair. *Amateurs' manuals*
Wilkins, Stewart Wallace. Suzuki GT 125 and GT 185 owners workshop manual / [by] Stewart W. Wilkins. — Yeovil [etc.] : Haynes, 1976. — 97p : ill ; 28cm. — (Haynes owners workshop manuals for motorcycles)
Index.
ISBN 0-85696-301-1 Pbk : £2.50
(B77-00278)

629.28′8′75 — Suzuki GT 750 motorcycles. Maintenance & repair. *Amateurs' manuals*
Darlington, Mansur. Suzuki GT 750 owners workshop manual / by Mansur Darlington. — Yeovil [etc.] : Haynes, 1976. — 149p : ill ; 27cm. — (Haynes owners workshop manuals for motorcycles)
Cover title: Suzuki 750 3 cylinder models. — Index.
ISBN 0-85696-302-x Pbk : £2.50
(B77-13712)

629.28′8′75 — Suzuki TS 125 motorcycles. Maintenance & repair. *Amateurs' manuals*
Thorpe, John, *b.1928.* Bikebook of the Suzuki TS 125 : a guide to maintenance, service and overhaul / [by] John Thorpe. — London [etc.] : Pitman, 1976 [i.e. 1977]. — viii,66p : ill ; 23cm. — (Pitman bikebooks)
Cover title: Suzuki TS 125. — Index.
ISBN 0-273-00822-6 Pbk : £1.25
(B77-10416)

629.28′8′75 — Triumph 350, 500 & 650 twin cylinder motorcycles. Maintenance & repair. *Amateurs' manuals*
Haycraft, William Clifford. Bikebook of the Triumph twins : a guide to maintenance, service and overhaul of 1956-69 twin-cylinder spring frame models except 1967-69 models T100T, T120R and T150 (Trident) / [by] W.C. Haycraft. — 13th ed. — London [etc.] : Pitman, 1976. — vi,106p : ill ; 23cm. — (Pitman bikebooks)
Cover title: Triumph twins. — This ed. originally published: as 'Book of the Triumph twins'. 1969. — Index.
ISBN 0-273-01009-3 Pbk : £1.25
(B77-11274)

629.28′8′75 — Yamaha 500 twin cylinder motorcycles. Maintenance & repair. *Amateurs' manuals*
Clew, Jeff. Yamaha 500 twin owners workshop manual / by Jeff Clew. — Yeovil : Haynes, 1976. — 139p : ill ; 27cm. — (Haynes owners workshop manuals for motorcycles ISSN 0305-4446)
Index.
ISBN 0-85696-308-9 Pbk : £2.50
(B77-10417)

629.28′8′75 — Yamaha FS1-E motorcycles. Maintenance & repair. *Amateurs' manuals*
Thorpe, John, *b.1928.* Bikebook of the Yamaha FS1-E : a guide to maintenance, service and overhaul / [by] John Thorpe. — London [etc.] : Pitman, 1977. — viii,60p : ill ; 23cm. — (Pitman bikebooks)
Cover title: Yamaha FS1-E. — Index.
ISBN 0-273-01019-0 Pbk : £1.25
(B77-10418)

629.28′8′75 — Yamaha RD400 twin cylinder motorcycles. Maintenance & repair. *Amateurs' manuals*
Darlington, Mansur. Yamaha RD 400 twin, owners workshop manual / by Mansur Darlington. — Yeovil [etc.] : Haynes, 1977. — 119p : ill ; 28cm. — (Haynes owners workshop manuals for motorcycles)
Index.
ISBN 0-85696-333-x Pbk : £2.50
(B77-18854)

629.28'8'750222 — Motorcycles. Maintenance & repair. *Amateurs' manuals. Illustrations*
Bettiol, Guido. Motorcycles : maintain your own machine / by Guido Bettiol ; adapted [i.e. translated from the French] by Vic Willoughby ; drawings by George Domenech. — London : Chancerel Publishers Ltd : Barrie and Jenkins, 1977. — 2-91p : ill, ports ; 21cm. — (Action books)
'Published with co-operation and assistance of Leslie Nichol'. — Ill. on lining papers. — Translation of: 'La moto'. Paris : Chancerel, 1976.
ISBN 0-905703-03-0 : £1.75
(B77-26371)

629.3 — HOVERCRAFT
629.3 — Hovercraft. *Conference proceedings*
International Hovering Craft, Hydrofoil and Advanced Transit Systems Conference, 2nd, *Amsterdam, 1976.* Second International Hovering Craft, Hydrofoil and Advanced Transit Systems Conference, 17-20 May 1976 Amsterdam : conference papers : the conference is sponsored and organised by the journal 'Hovering craft and hydrofoil'. — London (51 Welbeck St., W1M 7HE) : Kalerghi Publications [for] 'Hovering craft and hydrofoil', [1977]. — [5],391p : ill, charts, maps, plans ; 30cm.
'... [held at the] RAI Exhibition and Congress Centre, Amsterdam ...' - cover. — Bibl.
ISBN 0-903238-01-2 Pbk : £30.75
Also classified at 623.82'3
(B77-14791)

629.3'05 — Hovercraft. *Serials*
Jane's surface skimmers : hovercraft and hydrofoils. — London : Jane's Yearbooks.
1976-77 : tenth ed. / compiled and edited by Roy McLeavy. — 1977. — iv,28,424,iii p : ill, plans ; 33cm.
Bibl.: p.361-366. — Index.
ISBN 0-354-00540-5 : £16.50
ISSN 0075-305x
Also classified at 623.82'3
(B77-13100)

629.4 — ASTRONAUTICS
629.4 — Astronautics. *Conference proceedings*
International Astronautical Congress, 26th, *Lisbon, 1975.* Selected papers from the 26th International Astronautical Congress, Lisbon, Portugal, 21-27 September 1975 / editor Luigi G. Napolitano. — Oxford [etc.] : Pergamon, 1976. — viii p,p317-470,5-16p : ill, map ; 27cm.
'Published as a special issue of the Journal "Acta Astronautica", Volume 3, Number 5-6 ...' - title page verso. — Bibl.
ISBN 0-08-021286-7 : £15.00
(B77-04903)

International Astronautical Congress, 26th, *Lisbon, 1975.* Space and energy : proceedings of the XXVIth International Astronautical Congress, Lisbon, 21-27 September 1975 / edited by L.G. Napolitano. — Oxford [etc.] : Pergamon, 1977. — viii,487p : ill, charts, maps ; 26cm.
'Together with a special issue of the journal "Acta Astronautica" it constitutes the Proceedings of the Congress itself' - Preface. — Includes two chapters in French and one chapter in German. — Bibl.
ISBN 0-08-021053-8 : £27.50
(B77-15923)

629.4 — Astronautics. *Juvenile literature*
Taylor, Ron. The space age / [text by Ron Taylor] ; [planned and edited by Dale Gunthorp]. — London : Macdonald Educational, 1977. — 3-47p : ill(chiefly col), ports(some col) ; 25cm. — (Action world)
Col. ill. on lining paper. — Index.
ISBN 0-356-05563-9 : £1.25
(B77-16461)

629.4 — Instantaneous interstellar space flight. Use of black holes & iron stars
Berry, Adrian. The iron sun : crossing the universe through black holes / [by] Adrian Berry. — London : Cape, 1977. — 176p : ill ; 23cm.
Bibl.: p.161-165. — Index.
ISBN 0-224-01357-2 : £3.95 : CIP rev.
(B77-05498)

629.4'09'04 — Astronautics, to 1975. *Readings*
Space science and astronomy : escape from earth / edited by Thornton Page and Lou Williams Page. — New York : Macmillan ; London : Collier Macmillan, 1976. — xix, 467p : ill, charts, map, ports ; 24cm. — ('Sky and telescope' library of astronomy ; vol.9)
'... articles that first appeared in ... "Sky and Telescope", "The Sky", and "The Telescope"' - half title page verso. — Bibl.: p.450-452. — Index.
ISBN 0-02-594310-3 : £10.50
Primary classification 520'.8
(B77-11786)

629.41 — Space vehicles. Control
Kaplan, Marshall H. Modern spacecraft dynamics & control / [by] Marshall H. Kaplan. — New York ; London [etc.] : Wiley, 1976. — xii,415p : ill ; 24cm.
With answers to selected exercises. — Bibl. — Index.
ISBN 0-471-45703-5 : £15.85
(B77-04904)

629.41'09'046 — Space flight, to 1975. *Juvenile literature. Fill-in books*
Knight, Dennis. Space flight / [by Dennis Knight] ; [illustrations by Dan Escott]. — London ([Dept. RWH], 100 Drayton Park, N5 1NA) : Royal Sovereign Group Ltd, 1976. — [2],18,[2]p,[2]leaves of plates : ill(chiefly col), ports(1 col) ; 15x21cm. — (Knight, Dennis. Activity books)
Contains Letraset instant pictures.
ISBN 0-900862-45-9 Sd : Unpriced
(B77-06168)

629.44'5 — Outer space. Manned space flight. Skylab, 1973-1974
Cooper, Henry S F. A house in space / [by] Henry S.F. Cooper, Jr. — London [etc.] : Angus and Robertson, 1977. — [7],184p,[2] leaves of plates : ill, 2 plans(1 col), ports ; 22cm.
Originally published: New York : Holt, Rinehart and Winston, 1976.
ISBN 0-207-95722-3 : £4.20
(B77-10419)

629.47 — Artificial satellites
Porter, Richard W. The versatile satellite / [by] Richard W. Porter. — Oxford [etc.] : Oxford University Press, 1977. — viii,173p,[2]leaves of plates : ill(incl 2 col), maps ; 24cm.
Index.
ISBN 0-19-885104-9 : £4.95
(B77-25008)

629.8 — AUTOMATIC CONTROL SYSTEMS
Phelan, Richard Magruder. Automatic control systems / [by] Richard M. Phelan. — Ithaca ; London : Cornell University Press, 1977. — 280,[3]p : ill ; 23cm.
Index.
ISBN 0-8014-1033-9 : £11.25
(B77-26372)

629.8 — Automatic control systems. *Reviews of research*
Control and dynamic systems : advances in theory and applications. — New York [etc.] ; London : Academic Press.
Vol.13 : 1977 / edited by C.T. Leondes. — 1977. — xviii,365p : ill ; 24cm.
Index.
ISBN 0-12-012713-x : £18.10
(B77-20373)

629.8 — Control systems
DiStefano, Joseph J. Schaum's outline of theory and problems of feedback and control systems / by Joseph J. DiStefano, III, Allen R. Stubberud, Ivan J. Williams. — SI (metric) ed. — New York ; London [etc.] : McGraw-Hill, 1976. — [7],371p : ill ; 28cm. — (Schaum's outline series)
Cover title: Theory and problems of feedback and control systems. — Spine title: Feedback and control systems. — Previous ed.: New York : McGraw-Hill, 1967. — Bibl.: p.365. — Index.
ISBN 0-07-084369-4 Pbk : £3.75
(B77-09768)

629.8'042 — Automatic control systems. Hydraulic equipment
Prokeš, Josef. Hydraulic mechanisms in automation / [by] Josef Prokeš ; [translated from the Czech by Julius Freundlich]. — Amsterdam ; Oxford [etc.] : Elsevier, 1977. — 334p : ill ; 25cm.
Translation of: 'Hydraulické machanismy y automatizaci'. Praha : SNTL, t.Mír 1, 1973. — Bibl.: p.330. — Index.
ISBN 0-444-99829-2 : £23.07
(B77-17586)

629.8'312 — Control systems. Mathematics
Buckley, Ruth Victoria. Control engineering : theory, worked examples and problems / [by] Ruth V. Buckley. — London [etc.] : Macmillan, 1976. — vii,112p : ill ; 24cm.
Bibl.: p.112.
ISBN 0-333-19776-3 Pbk : £2.50
(B77-07423)

629.8'312 — Control systems. States. Analysis. State space methods
Blackman, P F. Introduction to state-variable analysis / [by] P.F. Blackman. — London [etc.] : Macmillan, 1977. — vi,257p : ill ; 24cm.
Bibl. — Index.
ISBN 0-333-14680-8 : £10.00
(B77-25710)

629.8'312 — Multivariable control systems
Layton, J M. Multivariable control theory / [by] J.M. Layton. — Stevenage : Peregrinus [for] the Institution of Electrical Engineers, 1976. — x, 236p : ill ; 23cm. — (Institution of Electrical Engineers. IEE control engineering series ; 1)
Index.
ISBN 0-901223-89-1 : £11.00
(B77-09082)

629.8'312 — Optimal control theory
Bryson, Arthur E. Applied optimal control : optimization, estimation and control / [by] Arthur E. Bryson, Jr, Yu-Chi Ho. — Revised [ed.]. — Washington, D.C. : Hemisphere ; New York ; London [etc.] : Wiley, 1975. — [14], 481p : ill ; 24cm.
'A Halsted Press book'. — Previous ed.: Waltham, Mass. : Blaisdell, 1969. — Index.
ISBN 0-470-11481-9 : £13.80
(B77-13101)

Sage, Andrew Patrick. Optimum systems control. — 2nd ed. / [by] Andrew P. Sage, Chelsea C. White, III. — Englewood Cliffs ; London [etc.] : Prentice-Hall, 1977. — xv,413p : ill ; 24cm.
Previous ed.: / by Andrew P. Sage. 1968. — Index.
ISBN 0-13-638296-7 : £18.00
(B77-20374)

629.8'32 — Linear control systems. Analysis & design
D'Azzo, John J. Linear control system analysis and design : conventional and modern / [by] John J. d'Azzo, Constantine H. Houpis. — Tokyo ; London [etc.] : McGraw-Hill, 1975. — xix,636p : ill ; 21cm. — (McGraw-Hill electrical and electronic engineering series)
With answers to selected problems. — Index.
ISBN 0-07-016179-8 Pbk : £7.60
(B77-25711)

629.8'92 — Electronic robots. Construction. *Amateurs' manuals*
Heiserman, David L. Build your own working robot / [by] David L. Heiserman ; with a specially written chapter for the guidance of the English reader by W. Oliver. — Slough : Foulsham-Tab, 1976. — viii,3-234p : ill ; 21cm.
Also published: Blue Ridge Summit : Tab Books, 1976. — Index.
ISBN 0-7042-0171-2 Pbk : £3.25
(B77-05499)

629.8'92 — Industrial robots. *Conference proceedings*
Conference on Industrial Robot Technology, 3rd, *University of Nottingham, 1976.* Proceedings [of the] 3rd Conference on Industrial Robot Technology and 6th International Symposium on Industrial Robots, University of Nottingham, UK, March 24th-26th, 1976 / [edited by T. E. Brock]. — Kempston (35 High St., Kempston, Beds.) : International Fluidics Services Ltd, 1976. — 562p in various pagings : ill ; 31cm.
Index.
ISBN 0-903608-05-7 : £22.00
(B77-04905)

629.8'92'01 — Automata theory
Hopkin, David. Automata / [by] David Hopkin, Barbara Moss. — London [etc.] : Macmillan, 1976. — vi,170p : ill ; 24cm. — (Macmillan computer science series)
Bibl.: p.165-167. — Index.
ISBN 0-333-15398-7 : £8.95
ISBN 0-333-21217-7 Pbk : £3.95
(B77-04906)

630 — AGRICULTURE

630 — Agriculture. *For Caribbean students. Middle school texts*

Persad, Ralph Sakaldip. Agricultural science for the Caribbean / [by] Ralph S. Persad. — Sunbury-on-Thames [etc.] : Nelson.
In 3 vols.
2. — 1977. — 176p : ill ; 25cm.
Index.
ISBN 0-17-566167-7 Pbk : £1.90
(B77-27188)

630 — Agriculture. *For West African students. Secondary school texts*

Fakorede, M A B. Agricultural science / [by] M.A.B. Fakorede. — London [etc.] : Macmillan, 1977. — [8],104p : ill, chart, map ; 22cm. — (School Certificate revision course)
ISBN 0-333-21229-0 Sd : £1.00
(B77-13102)

630 — Agriculture. *Juvenile literature*

Baker, Susan. Farms / [written and planned by Susan Baker]. — [London] : Macdonald Educational, [1977]. — 3-46p : ill(chiefly col) ; 29cm. — (Topic books)
Col. ill., text on lining papers. — Index.
ISBN 0-356-05448-9 : £1.60
(B77-27189)

Scarry, Richard. On the farm / with illustrations by Richard Scarry. — London [etc.] : Hamlyn, 1977. — [24]p : col ill ; 21cm. — (A golden look-look book)
Originally published: as 'Richard Scarry's on the farm'. New York : Golden Press, 1976.
ISBN 0-600-33629-8 Sd : £0.40
(B77-28693)

630 — Agriculture. *Reviews of research*

Advances in agronomy / prepared under the auspices of the American Society of Agronomy. — New York [etc.] ; London : Academic Press.

Vol.28 / edited by N.C. Brady. — 1976. — xii, 411p : ill ; 24cm.
Bibl. — Index.
ISBN 0-12-000728-2 : £24.15
(B77-05500)

Applied biology. — London [etc.] : Academic Press.
Vol.2 / edited by T.H. Coaker. — 1977. — x, 272p : ill ; 24cm.
Bibl. — Index.
ISBN 0-12-040902-x : £9.80
(B77-23510)

630 — Applied biology. *Reviews of research*

Applied biology. — London [etc.] : Academic Press.
Vol.1 / edited by T.H. Coaker. — 1976. — x, 358p : ill, maps ; 24cm.
Bibl. — Index.
ISBN 0-12-040901-1 : £10.50
(B77-09083)

630 — Food. Production. *Amateurs' manuals*

Allaby, Michael. Home farm : complete food self-sufficiency / [by] Michael Allaby with Colin Tudge. — London : Macmillan, 1977. — 224p : ill, maps, plans ; 26cm.
Bibl. — Index.
ISBN 0-333-22090-0 : £5.50 : CIP rev.
(B77-19464)

630 — Smallholdings. Agriculture. *Manuals*

Smith, Joanna. Farm your garden / [by] Joanna Smith. — London : Sidgwick and Jackson, 1977. — 176p,[12]p of plates : ill, 2 ports ; 23cm.
Bibl. — Index.
ISBN 0-283-98311-6 : £4.95
(B77-27924)

630'.2012'2 — Agriculture. *Illustrations. Juvenile literature*

Blanco, Josette. On the farm / by Josette Blanco ; illustrated by Claude d'Ham. — Purton (Restrop Manor, Purton, Wilts.) : Child's Play (International) Ltd, [1977]. — [20] p : chiefly col ill ; 22cm. — (Child's Play moments ; book 2)
Page width varies.
ISBN 0-85953-040-x : £0.90
ISBN 0-85953-036-1 Pbk : £0.45
(B77-13103)

630'.5 — Agriculture. Conferences. *Reports, surveys. Serials*

Conference reports, agriculture, food and biology. — London : Applied Science Publishers.
Vol.1, [no.1]- ; 1977-. — 1977-. — 24cm.
Quarterly. — [1],79p. in 1st issue. — Index.
Pbk : £16.00(yearly)
ISSN 0309-5886
Also classified at 664'.005; 574'.05
(B77-15924)

630'.7'104 — Educational institutions. Curriculum subjects: Agriculture. *Western Europe. Reports, surveys*

Agricultural education in Europe. — London : British Council ; Slough : Distributed [by] Commonwealth Agricultural Bureaux, 1977. — iii,135p : ill ; 30cm.
Contains reports on visits to 11 European countries by teams of agricultural educationists in 1975 and 1976 and the proceedings of a symposium organised by the British Council entitled 'Agricultural Education and Europe', held at the Royal Society, 9 February 1977.
ISBN 0-900229-28-4 Pbk : £4.50
(B77-21219)

630'.711'171241 — Further education institutions & higher education institutions. Curriculum subjects: Agriculture. Courses. *Commonwealth countries. Directories*

Commonwealth Secretariat. *Food Production and Rural Development Division.* Training for agricultural development : directory of resources in the Commonwealth / [Food Production and Rural Development Division, Commonwealth Secretariat]. — London : The Division, 1976. — x,360p ; 30cm.
Bibl.: p.340. — Index.
ISBN 0-85092-112-0 Pbk : £3.00
(B77-02398)

630'.7'1141235 — Agricultural colleges. *Scotland. Grampian Region. Aberdeen. North of Scotland College of Agriculture. Reports, surveys. Serials*

North of Scotland College of Agriculture. Annual report / the North of Scotland College of Agriculture. — [Aberdeen] ([581 King St., Aberdeen AB9 1UD]) : [The College].
1975-76. — [1976]. — v,134p ; 21cm.
ISBN 0-901766-59-3 Pbk : Unpriced
ISSN 0550-8525
(B77-11275)

630'.711'422392 — Universities. Agricultural colleges. *Kent. Wye. Wye College. Serials*

Wye College. The report of the principal to the governing body / Wye College (University of London). — [Wye] : [Wye College].
1975-76. — 1977. — 137p ; 21cm.
Bibl.
ISBN 0-900830-08-5 Pbk : £0.40
(B77-15925)

630'.7'2 — Agriculture. Research. *Reports, surveys. Serials*

Rothamsted Experimental Station. Report / Rothamsted Experimental Station. — Harpenden (Harpenden, Herts. AL5 2JQ) : Lawes Agricultural Trust.
1976. — 1977. — 2v.(379p,fold plate;234p,2,2p of plates,fold leaf of plate) : ill, maps, plans ; 25cm.
Bibl. — Index.
Pbk : £5.00
(B77-20375)

630'.72 — Agriculture. Research. Pattern analysis

Pattern analysis in agricultural science / edited by W.T. Williams. — Melbourne : CSIRO ; Amsterdam ; Oxford [etc.] : Elsevier, 1976. — xii,331p : ill, maps ; 24cm.
'... arose out of a course organized by members of the Davies Laboratory of the CSIRO Division of Tropical Agronomy ... The course was ... held in the James Cook University of North Queensland ...' - Preface. — Bibl. — Index.
ISBN 0-444-99844-6 : £23.57
(B77-23511)

630'.7'2041 — Agriculture. Research & development financed by government. Coordination. Organisations: Joint Consultative Organisation for Research and Development in Agriculture and Food. *Great Britain. Reports, surveys. Serials*

Joint Consultative Organisation for Research and Development in Agriculture and Food. Reports of the Boards of the Joint Consultative Organisation for Research and Development in Agriculture and Food. — London : H.M.S.O.
'Sponsors of the Joint Consultative Organisation, Agricultural Research Council, Department of Agriculture and Fisheries for Scotland, Ministry of Agriculture, Fisheries and Food'.
2nd. — 1975. — [3],135p ; 25cm.
ISBN 0-11-240625-4 Pbk : £1.70
(B77-06169)

630'.7'2041 — Research & development by Great Britain. Ministry of Agriculture, Fisheries and Food. *Great Britain. Reports, surveys. Serials*

Great Britain. *Ministry of Agriculture, Fisheries and Food.* Research and development report / Ministry of Agriculture, Fisheries and Food. — London : H.M.S.O.
1975. — 1976. — [3],50p : 1 ill ; 25cm.
Cover title: Report on research and development 1975. — Bibl.: p.46-50.
ISBN 0-11-241098-7 Sd : £0.90
(B77-13713)

630'.7'20411 — Agriculture. Research. *Scotland. Reports, surveys. Serials*

North of Scotland College of Agriculture. Research investigations and field trials / North of Scotland College of Agriculture. — [Aberdeen] : [The College].
1975-76. — [1977]. — vi,241p(14 fold) : ill ; 21cm.
Cover title.
Pbk : Unpriced
(B77-21220)

630'.7'20416 — Agriculture. Research by Northern Ireland. Department of Agriculture. *Reports, surveys. Serials*

Northern Ireland. *Department of Agriculture.* Annual report on research and technical work of the Department of Agriculture for Northern Ireland. — [Belfast] ([Dundonald House, Upper Newtownards Rd, Belfast BT4 3SB]) : [The Department].
1975. — [1977]. — [21],244p : ill ; 25cm.
Previously published: as 'Annual report on research and technical work of the Ministry of Agriculture for Northern Ireland'. — Bibl.
Pbk : £7.00
ISSN 0309-5665
(B77-13714)

630'.7'20416 — Agriculture. Research organisations. *Northern Ireland. Agricultural Research Institute of Northern Ireland, to 1976*

Agricultural Research Institute of Northern Ireland. Jubilee report, 1926-1977 / Agricultural Research Institute of Northern Ireland. — Hillsborough (Hillsborough, Co. Down) : [The Institute], [1976]. — 86p : 1 ill ; 25cm.
Bibl.
Pbk : Unpriced
(B77-31962)

630'.7'20416 — Agriculture. Research organisations. *Northern Ireland. Northern Ireland Agricultural Trust. Reports, surveys. Serials*

Northern Ireland Agricultural Trust. Annual report of the Northern Ireland Agricultural Trust for the year ended 31 March ... — Belfast : H.M.S.O.
8th : [1974]-1975. — [1976]. — 25p ; 25cm.
At head of title: Department of Agriculture for Northern Ireland.
ISBN 0-337-05168-2 Sd : £0.40
(B77-20376)

630'.7'2042 — Agriculture. Research organisations. *England. Agricultural Development and Advisory Service. Reports, surveys. Serials*

Agriculture service annual report / Agricultural Development and Advisory Service. — London : H.M.S.O.
1975-76. — 1977. — 117p,[4]p of plates : ill, facsims, maps, port ; 21cm.
ISBN 0-11-241132-0 Pbk : £2.75
(B77-21957)

630'.7'2042 — Agriculture. Research organisations. *England. Agricultural Development and Advisory Service. Science Arm. Reports, surveys. Serials*

Agricultural Development and Advisory Service. *Science Service.* Agricultural Development and Advisory Service Science Service annual report. — London : H.M.S.O.
1975. — 1976. — ii-xxi,308p,iv p of plates : ill, map ; 21cm.
Bibl.
ISBN 0-11-241094-4 Pbk : £9.00
(B77-04272)

630.9 — AGRICULTURE. HISTORICAL AND GEOGRAPHICAL TREATMENT

630'.9'01 — Prehistoric agriculture. *Conference proceedings*

The **early** history of agriculture : a joint symposium of the Royal Society and the British Academy, organized by Sir Joseph Hutchinson ... [et al.]. — Oxford [etc.] : Oxford University Press for the British Academy, 1977. — [4], 213p,5p of plates : ill, maps ; 31cm.
'Discussion held 9 and 10 April 1975 ...' - p.1. — '... also published in a paper-bound edition by the Royal Society in its series "Philosophical Transactions" B vol. 275, no.1-213' - title page verso. — Bibl.
ISBN 0-19-725967-7 : £13.00
(B77-09084)

630'.913 — Agriculture. *Tropical regions*

Ruthenberg, Hans. Farming systems in the tropics / [by] Hans Ruthenberg. — 2nd ed. — Oxford : Clarendon Press, 1976. — xviii,366p, [20]p of plates : ill(some col), maps ; 24cm.
Previous ed.: 1971. — Bibl.: p.336-356. — Index. — Includes 2 chapters by J.D. MacArthur.
ISBN 0-19-859458-5 : £10.00
ISBN 0-19-859461-5 Pbk : £4.95
(B77-18231)

630'.913 — Agriculture. *Tropical regions. Programmed texts. For cooperative officers*

Yeo, Peter. An initial course in tropical agriculture for the staff of co-operatives / by Peter Yeo. — London (9 King St., WC2E 8HN) : Intermediate Technology Development Group [for] the Co-operative Educational Materials Advisory Service of the International Co-operative Alliance, 1976. — [5],54p ; 15x22cm.
With answers.
ISBN 0-903031-39-6 Sp : £1.25
(B77-03603)

630'.9162 — Aquaculture. Use of water pollutants. *Conference proceedings*

Harvesting polluted waters : waste heat and nutrient-loaded effluents in the aquaculture / edited by O. Devik. — New York ; London : Plenum Press, 1976. — xi,324p : ill, maps ; 24cm. — (Environmental science research ; vol.8)
'... [proceedings of] a meeting of experts on "Waste Heat and Nutrient-Loaded Effluents in Aquaculture" ...' - Preface. — Bibl. — Index.
ISBN 0-306-36308-9 : £18.59
(B77-07953)

630'.92'4 — Agriculture. *Derbyshire. Chapel-en-le-Frith region, 1914-1969. Personal observations*

Virtue, Alan. Memoirs of a Derbyshire hill farmer / by Alan Virtue. — London [etc.] : Virtue and Co., 1976. — ix,129p : ill, ports ; 23cm.
Limited ed. of 226 copies.
ISBN 0-900778-09-1 : £8.00
(B77-00279)

630'.92'4 — Agriculture. *Wales. Personal observations*

Cragoe, Elizabeth. Cowslips and clover / [by] Elizabeth Cragoe. — London : Hamilton, 1977. — [4],172p ; 23cm.
ISBN 0-241-89761-0 : £4.50
(B77-29515)

630'.92'4 — Agriculture. *Welsh Marches. Personal observations*

Holgate, John, *b.1924.* Make a cow laugh : a first year in farming / [by] John Holgate. — London : P. Davies, 1977. — [6],234p ; 23cm.
ISBN 0-432-06740-x : £3.90
(B77-30366)

630'.933 — Agriculture. *Ancient Palestine. School texts*

Pitman, Brian Dyett. Getting to know about farming and fishing in the lands of the Bible / [by] Brian D. Pitman ; artist Anne Farncombe. — Redhill : Denholm House Press, 1976. — 32p : ill(chiefly col), col maps ; 25cm. — (Getting to know about ; book 7)
Index.
ISBN 0-85213-148-8 Sd : £0.75
Also classified at 639'.2'00933
(B77-09769)

630'.941 — Agriculture. *Great Britain, ca 1750-ca 1950*

Niall, Ian. To speed the plough : mechanisation comes to the farm / [by] Ian Niall. — London : Heinemann, 1977. — [7],231p : ill ; 23cm.
ISBN 0-434-51024-6 : £4.90
(B77-23512)

630'.941 — Agriculture. *Great Britain, to 1934. Early works*

Hennell, Thomas. Change in the farm / by T. Hennell ; with illustrations by the author. — Wakefield : EP Publishing, 1977. — x.201p,[8]p of plates : ill ; 23cm.
Facsimile reprint of: 2nd enlarged ed. Cambridge : Cambridge University Press, 1936.
ISBN 0-7158-1220-3 : £5.75 : CIP rev.
(B77-09770)

630'.942 — Agriculture. *England*

Harvey, Nigel. Farms and farming / [by] Nigel Harvey. — Aylesbury : Shire Publications, 1977. — 33p : ill ; 21cm. — (Shire album ; 26)
Bibl.: p.33.
ISBN 0-85263-382-3 Sd : £0.50
(B77-31273)

630'.9422'3 — Agriculture. *Kent. Weald. Humorous texts*

Creaton, David. The beasts of my fields / by David Creaton. — London [etc.] : Hodder and Stoughton, 1977. — 3-254p : map(on lining papers) ; 23cm.
ISBN 0-340-21267-5 : £4.50
(B77-16462)

630'.9669 — Agriculture. *Nigeria. Manuals*

Phillips, Tom Alan. An agricultural notebook : (with special reference to Nigeria) / compiled by T.A. Phillips. — Metric ed. — London : Longman, 1977. — [8],312p : ill ; 19cm.
Previous ed.: London : Longmans, Green for the Government of the Federation of Nigeria, 1956. — Index.
ISBN 0-582-60768-x Pbk : £1.50
(B77-25712)

631 — CROPS, AGRICULTURAL EQUIPMENT AND OPERATIONS

631 — Agricultural industries. Smallholdings. Self-sufficiency. *Manuals*

Soil Association. Self-sufficient small holding / [Soil Association]. — Stowmarket (Walnut Tree Manor, Haughley, Stowmarket, Suffolk IP14 3RS) : The Association, 1976. — [2],14p(6 fold) ; 21cm.
Originally published: 1976.
ISBN 0-905200-05-5 Sd : £0.50
(B77-00811)

631 — Crops. Botanical aspects

Berrie, Alex M M. An introduction to the botany of the major crop plants / [by] Alex M.M. Berrie. — London [etc.] : Heyden, 1977. — x,220p : ill ; 25cm. — (Botanical sciences series)
Bibl.: p.187-189. — Index.
ISBN 0-85501-220-x : £9.50
(B77-21221)

631 — Schools. Plants used in teaching. *Great Britain*

Schools Council Educational Use of Living Organisms Project. Plants / Schools Council Educational Use of Living Organisms [Project] ; author C.D. Bingham, contributor J.D. Wray. — Sevenoaks : Hodder and Stoughton, 1977. — ii,77p : ill ; 25cm.
Bibl.: p.74-77.
ISBN 0-340-17053-0 Pbk : £2.45
(B77-09771)

631'.0913 — Tropical crops

Cobley, Leslie Samuel. An introduction to the botany of tropical crops / [by] Leslie S. Cobley. — 2nd ed. / revised by W.M. Steele. — London [etc.] : Longman, 1976. — xvi,371p : ill ; 22cm.
Previous ed.: / by Leslie S. Cobley. London : Longmans, Green, 1956. — Bibl. — Index.
ISBN 0-582-44153-6 Pbk : £6.00
ISBN 0-582-44185-4 ELBS ed. : £2.10
(B77-04907)

631'.0966 — Crops. *Lowland tropical regions. Study regions: West Africa. Reviews of research*

Food crops of the lowland tropics / edited by C.L.A. Leakey and J.B. Wills. — Oxford [etc.] : Oxford University Press, 1977. — xiv, 345p : ill, maps ; 26cm.
Bibl. — Index.
ISBN 0-19-854517-7 : £9.00
(B77-21222)

631.2 — FARM BUILDINGS AND STRUCTURES

631.2'3 — Ancient Roman forts. Stone granaries. *Great Britain. Reports, surveys*

Gentry, Anne Patricia. Roman military stone-built granaries in Britain / [by] Anne P. Gentry. — Oxford : British Archaeological Reports, 1976. — [18],95[i.e. 96]p,[2]p of plates : ill, maps, plans ; 29cm. — (British archaeological reports ; 32 ISSN 0306-1205)
Bibl.: p.[11]-[18]. — Index.
ISBN 0-904531-45-7 Pbk : £1.95
(B77-01592)

631.2'3 — Silos. *Western Scotland*

West of Scotland Agricultural College. Silos, choice and construction / the West of Scotland Agricultural College. — [Auchincruive] : [The College], [1977?]. — [1],7p ; 21cm. — (Advisory publication ; no.9 ISSN 0309-6734)
Sd : Unpriced
(B77-32699)

631.2'7 — Agricultural industries. Farms. Electric fences. *Great Britain*

Agricultural Development and Advisory Service. Electric fencing. — 5th ed. / Ministry of Agriculture, Fisheries and Food, [Agricultural Development and Advisory Service]. — London : H.M.S.O., 1976. — iv,37p,3p of plates : ill, plans ; 25cm. — (Great Britain. Ministry of Agriculture, Fisheries and Food. Bulletins ; 147)
Previous ed.: / issued by the Ministry of Agriculture, Fisheries and Food. 1966. — Bibl.: p.28.
ISBN 0-11-240656-4 Sd : £0.80
(B77-09085)

631.2'7 — Agricultural land. Trees. Shelter belts. Use

Agricultural Development and Advisory Service. Shelter belts for farmland / Ministry of Agriculture, Fisheries and Food, ADAS. — London : H.M.S.O., 1977. — [1],26p,[8]p of plates : ill ; 25cm. — (Fixed equipment of the farm ; leaflet 15)
Bibl.: p.26.
ISBN 0-11-240611-4 Sd : £0.85
(B77-12522)

631.3 — AGRICULTURAL MACHINERY AND IMPLEMENTS

631.3 — Agricultural machinery

Stone, Archie Augustus. Machines for power farming / [by] Archie A. Stone, Harold E. Gulvin. — 3rd ed. — New York ; London [etc.] : Wiley, 1977. — ix,533p : ill ; 24cm.
Previous ed.: 1967. — Index.
ISBN 0-471-82556-5 : £12.70
(B77-24308)

631.3 — Agricultural machinery. *Juvenile literature*

Milsome, John. Machines and farms / [by] John Milsome ; illustrated by Harry Sheldon. — London [etc.] : Burke, 1977. — 32p : col ill ; 22cm. — (The world of machines)
ISBN 0-222-00414-2 : £1.60
ISBN 0-222-00418-5 Pbk : £1.00
(B77-30367)

631.3'09426'4 — Agricultural equipment. Use. *Suffolk, 1800-1950*

The **farming** year in Suffolk : the use of some of the agricultural tools at the Museum of East Anglian Life, Stowmarket : an introduction for teachers / [compiled by S. Bowell et al. ; edited by J.G. Fairclough]. — Ely (Back Hill, Ely, Cambs.) : EARO, The Resource and Technology Centre, [1977]. — vi,54p : ill, facsims ; 24cm.
Bibl.: p.54.
ISBN 0-904463-16-8 Sd : £1.10
(B77-25713)

631.3'09429 — Agricultural equipment. Use. *Wales, to ca 1945. Welsh texts*

Welsh Folk Museum. Yr Oriel Amaethyddiaeth, Amgueddfa Werin Cymru / [gan] Elfyn Scourfield, Is-Geidwad, Adran Diwylliant Materol. — [Cardiff] ([St Fagan's Castle, St Fagan's, Cardiff CF5 6XB]) : Amgueddfa Werin Cymru, 1976. — [1],42p : ill, port ; 15x21cm.
ISBN 0-85485-038-4 Sd : £0.50
(B77-04273)

631.3'0973 — Agricultural machinery. *United States*

Smith, Harris Pearson. Farm machinery and equipment. — 6th ed. / [by] Harris Pearson Smith, Lambert Henry Wilkes. — New York ; London [etc.] : McGraw-Hill, [1977]. — viii, 488p : ill ; 25cm. — (McGraw-Hill publications in the agricultural sciences)
This ed. published in the United States: 1976. — Previous ed.: / by Harris Pearson Smith. 1964. — Bibl. — Index.
ISBN 0-07-058957-7 : £12.60
(B77-12523)

631.3'1 — Agricultural machinery: Steam diggers. *Great Britain, to ca 1900*
Tyler, Colin. Digging by steam : a history of steam cultivation by means of the application of steam power to the fork, mattock and similar implements / by Colin Tyler. — Watford : Model and Allied Publications, 1977. — 173p : ill ; 25cm. — ([MAP technical publication])
Bibl.: p.169. — Index.
ISBN 0-85242-522-8 : £5.00
(B77-25714)

631.3'71 — Agricultural industries. Farms. Automation. Use of electric equipment. *Great Britain. Manuals*
Electricity Council. Automation : a guide to the practical design of installations / [Electricity Council]. — London (1 Charing Cross, SW1A 2DS) : The Council, 1970. — [8],91p : ill ; 18cm. — (Farmelectric handbooks ; no.18 ISSN 0309-247x)
ISBN 0-85188-060-6 Sd : £0.50
(B77-09772)

631.3'71 — Agricultural industries. Farms. Electric pumps. Installation. *Great Britain. Manuals*
Electricity Council. Pumping : a guide to the practical design of installations / [Electricity Council]. — Revised ed. — London (1 Charing Cross, SW1A 2DS) : The Council, 1969. — 77p : ill ; 18cm. — (Farmelectric handbook ; no.11 ISSN 0309-247x)
ISBN 0-85188-056-8 Sd : £0.50
(B77-07424)

631.3'71 — Agricultural machinery powered by steam engines, to 1976
Williams, Michael, *b.1935 (Nov.).* Steam power in agriculture / [by] Michael Williams ; drawings by Denis Bishop. — Poole : Blandford Press, 1977. — 184p : ill(chiefly col) ; 20cm. — ([Blandford colour series])
Index.
ISBN 0-7137-0819-0 : £3.75
(B77-22671)

631.3'73 — Agricultural vehicles: British carts & wagons, 1800-1950
Arnold, James. Farm waggons and carts / [by] James Arnold. — Newton Abbot [etc.] : David and Charles, 1977. — 144p : ill, maps ; 24x27cm.
Index.
ISBN 0-7153-7330-7 : £6.50
(B77-22672)

631.4 — AGRICULTURE. SOILS
Briggs, David John. Soils / [by] David Briggs. — London [etc.] : Butterworth, 1977. — 192p : ill ; 15x21cm. — (Sources and methods in geography)
Bibl.: p.184-187. — Index.
ISBN 0-408-70911-1 Pbk : £1.95 : CIP rev.
(B77-16940)

Donahue, Roy Luther. Soils : an introduction to soils and plant growth. — 4th ed. / [by] Roy L. Donahue, Raymond W. Miller, John C. Shickluna ; editorial assistance Joyce U. Miller. — Englewood Cliffs ; London [etc.] : Prentice-Hall, 1977. — xiii,626p,[2]p of plates,fold leaf of plate : ill(some col), facsims, form, maps ; 25cm.
Previous ed.: / by Roy L. Donahue, John C. Shickluna, Lynn S. Robertson. 1971. — Index.
ISBN 0-13-821918-4 : £13.55
(B77-21223)

631.4'02'493 — Soils. *For archaeology*
Limbrey, Susan. Soil science and archaeology / [by] Susan Limbrey. — London [etc.] : Academic Press, 1975. — xv,384p : ill ; 24cm. — (Studies in archaeological science)
Bibl.: p.343-351. — Index.
ISBN 0-12-785477-0 : £8.40
(B77-09086)

631.4'2 — Soils. Fertility
Howard, *Sir* **Albert.** An agricultural testament / by Sir Albert Howard. — [Berkhamsted] : Rodale Press, 1976. — xvii,253p,13p of plates : ill, plans ; 22cm.
Originally published: London [etc.] : Oxford University Press, 1940. — Bibl. — Index.
Unpriced
(B77-30368)

631.4'3 — Soils. Density. *England*
Water retention, porosity and density of field soils / [by] D.G.M. Hall ... [et al.]. — Harpenden (Rothamsted Experimental Station, Harpenden, Herts. AL5 2JQ) : Soil Survey of England and Wales, 1977. — viii,75p,[2]p of plates : ill, 2 maps ; 21cm. — (Soil Survey of Great Britain (England and Wales). Technical monographs ; no.9)
Bibl.: p.71-73.
Pbk : £1.00
Also classified at 631.4'32; 631.4'32
(B77-26373)

631.4'32 — Soils. Moisture tension. Determination. Statistical models
Lai, Pong-wai. Empirical evaluation of soil tension, with emphasis on variations during a drying period / [by] Pong-wai Lai. — [London] : London School of Economics and Political Science, Graduate Geography Department, 1976. — [4],15,[12]p,plate : ill ; 30cm. — (London School of Economics and Political Science. Graduate School of Geography. Discussion papers ; no.58 ISSN 0307-1960)
Bibl.: p.14-15.
ISBN 0-85328-055-x Sd : Unpriced
(B77-02399)

631.4'32 — Soils. Porosity. *England*
Water retention, porosity and density of field soils / [by] D.G.M. Hall ... [et al.]. — Harpenden (Rothamsted Experimental Station, Harpenden, Herts. AL5 2JQ) : Soil Survey of England and Wales, 1977. — viii,75p,[2]p of plates : ill, 2 maps ; 21cm. — (Soil Survey of Great Britain (England and Wales). Technical monographs ; no.9)
Bibl.: p.71-73.
Pbk : £1.00
Primary classification 631.4'3
(B77-26373)

631.4'32 — Water. Retention by soils. *England*
Water retention, porosity and density of field soils / [by] D.G.M. Hall ... [et al.]. — Harpenden (Rothamsted Experimental Station, Harpenden, Herts. AL5 2JQ) : Soil Survey of England and Wales, 1977. — viii,75p,[2]p of plates : ill, 2 maps ; 21cm. — (Soil Survey of Great Britain (England and Wales). Technical monographs ; no.9)
Bibl.: p.71-73.
Pbk : £1.00
Primary classification 631.4'3
(B77-26373)

631.4'4 — England. Clay soils. Minerals. Taxonomic aspects. *Reports, surveys*
Avery, Brian William. Mineralogy of clayey soils in relation to soil classification / [by] B.W. Avery and P. Bullock. — Harpenden (Rothamsted Experimental Station, Harpenden, Herts. AL5 2JQ) : Soil Survey of Great Britain (England and Wales), 1977. — viii,64p : ill, maps ; 21cm. — (Soil Survey of Great Britain (England and Wales). Technical monographs ; no.10)
Bibl.: p.57-60. — Index.
Pbk : £0.80
(B77-25009)

631.4'4'09429 — Forests. Soils. Classification. Site-types. *Wales*
Pyatt, David Graham. Guide to site types in forests of North and Mid Wales. — 2nd ed. / [by] D.G. Pyatt. — London [etc.] : H.M.S.O., 1977. — 51,[1]p : col ill, map ; 21cm. — (Forest record ; 69)
Previous ed.: / by D.G. Pyatt, D. Harrison & A.S. Ford. 1969. — Bibl.: p.50-51.
ISBN 0-11-710182-6 Sd : £1.75
(B77-23513)

631.4'7 — Soils. Mapping. Applications of aerial photography
Carroll, Douglas Michael. Air photo-interpretation for soil mapping / [by] D.M. Carroll, R. Evans and V.C. Bendelow. — Harpenden (Rothamsted Experimental Station, Harpenden, Herts.) : Soil Survey, 1977. — vi, 85p : ill, maps ; 30cm. — (Soil Survey of Great Britain (England and Wales). Technical monographs ; no.8)
Bibl.: p.82-83. — Index.
Sd : £2.00
(B77-26374)

631.4'7 — Soils. Surveying. Applications of remote sensing
White, Leslie Paul. Aerial photography and remote sensing for soil survey / [by] L.P. White. — Oxford : Clarendon Press, 1977. — viii,104p,[8]p of plates : ill(some col), map ; 23cm. — (Monographs on soil survey)
Bibl.: p.94-96. — Index.
ISBN 0-19-854509-6 : £6.00 : CIP rev.
(B77-10420)

631.4'7'41 — Soils. Surveys. Applications. *Great Britain*
Welsh Soils Discussion Group. Soil survey interpretation and use / Welsh Soils Discussion Group = Cylch Cymreig Trafod Priddoedd ; edited by Donald A. Davidson. — Swansea (c/o P.S. Wright, Soil Survey of England and Wales, University College, Singleton Park, Swansea SA2 8PP) : [The Group], 1976. — [3], viii,215p : ill, maps ; 30cm. — (Report ; no.17 ISSN 0083-7938)
Bibl.
Pbk : Unpriced
(B77-30369)

631.4'9 — Soils. Exploitation, to ca 1950
Hyams, Edward. Soil and civilization / [by] Edward Hyams. — London : J. Murray, 1976. — vii,312p : 5 maps ; 21cm.
Originally published: London : Thames and Hudson, 1952. — Index.
ISBN 0-7195-3311-2 Pbk : £2.50
(B77-09774)

631.4'913 — Tropical regions. Soils
Sanchez, Pedro A. Properties and management of soils in the tropics / [by] Pedro A. Sanchez. — New York ; London [etc.] : Wiley, 1976. — xi, 618p : ill, maps ; 24cm.
'A Wiley-Interscience publication'. — Bibl. — Index.
ISBN 0-471-75200-2 : £22.50
(B77-18232)

Young, Anthony. Tropical soils and soil survey / [by] Anthony Young. — Cambridge [etc.] : Cambridge University Press, 1976. — viii,468p : ill ; 24cm. — (Cambridge geographical studies ; 9)
Bibl.: p.436-457. — Index.
ISBN 0-521-21054-2 : £15.00
(B77-04274)

631.4'9411 — Scotland. Lowland regions. Soils. *Reports, surveys*
Birse, Eric Leslie. Plant communities and soils of the lowland and southern upland regions of Scotland / by E.L. Birse and J.S. Robertson ; with a chapter on post-glacial change in vegetation by S.E. Durno. — Aberdeen (Craigiebuckler, Aberdeen AB9 2QJ) : Macaulay Institute for Soil Research, 1976. — [9],226p : ill, maps ; 25cm. — (Soil Survey of Great Britain (Scotland). Monographs)
Bibl.: p.79-83.
ISBN 0-902701-05-3 Pbk : £6.00
Also classified at 631.4'9413'7; 581.5'24'09411; 581.5'24'094137
(B77-00812)

631.4'94116'2 — Scotland. Highland Region. Caithness (District). Soils. *Reports, surveys*
Futty, D W. The soils of the country round Wick (Sheets 110, 116 and part 117) / by D.W. Futty and F.T. Dry ; with an account of the vegetation by E.L. Birse and J.S. Robertson. — Aberdeen (Craigiebuckler, Aberdeen AB9 2QJ) : Macaulay Institute for Soil Research, 1977. — [10],288p,fold leaf,[16]p of plates : ill(some col), maps ; 26cm. — (Soil Survey of Great Britain (Scotland). Memoirs)
Two fold. sheets(col. maps) in pocket. — Bibl.: p.164-166. — Index.
ISBN 0-902701-06-1 : £9.00
(B77-33286)

631.4'9413'7 — Scotland. Southern Uplands. Soils. *Reports, surveys*
Birse, Eric Leslie. Plant communities and soils of the lowland and southern upland regions of Scotland / by E.L. Birse and J.S. Robertson ; with a chapter on post-glacial change in vegetation by S.E. Durno. — Aberdeen (Craigiebuckler, Aberdeen AB9 2QJ) : Macaulay Institute for Soil Research, 1976. — [9],226p : ill, maps ; 25cm. — (Soil Survey of Great Britain (Scotland). Monographs)
Bibl.: p.79-83.
ISBN 0-902701-05-3 Pbk : £6.00
Primary classification 631.4'9411
(B77-00812)

631.4'9422'3 — Kent. Soils. *Reports, surveys*
Soils in Kent. — Harpenden (Rothamsted Experimental Station, Harpenden, Herts. AL5 2JQ) : Soil Survey of England and Wales.
3 : Sheet TQ86(Rainham) / [by] S.J. Fordham and R.D. Green. — 1976. — 1v. : ill, maps(1 col) ; 21cm. — (Soil Survey of Great Britain (England and Wales). Survey records ; no.37)
Book (x,166p., leaf of plate,[4]p. of plates) and 2 fold. sheets (col. maps) in plastic envelope. — Also available without maps. — Bibl.: p.152-154. — Index.
ISBN 0-7086-0022-0 : £1.00
ISBN 0-7086-0023-9 Without maps : £0.50
(B77-02400)

631.4'9423'5 — Devon. Soils. *Reports, surveys*
Soils in Devon. — Harpenden (Rothamsted Experimental Station, Harpenden, Herts. [AL5 2JQ]) : Soil Survey of England and Wales.
2 : Sheet SX65 (Ivybridge) / [by] T.R. Harrod, D.V. Hogan and S.J. Staines. — 1976. — 1v. : ill(some col), map ; 21cm. — (Soil Survey of Great Britain (England and Wales). Survey records ; no.39)
Book (viii,136p.) and 2 fold. sheets (col. maps) in plastic envelope. — Also available without maps. — Bibl.: p.132-133. — Index.
ISBN 0-7086-0024-7 : £1.00
ISBN 0-7086-0025-5 Without maps : £0.50
(B77-06747)

631.4'9426'1 — Norfolk. Soils. *Reports, surveys*
Soils in Norfolk. — Harpenden (Rothamsted Experimental Station, Harpenden, Herts. AL5 2JQ) : Soil Survey of England and Wales.
3 : Sheet TG31 (Horning) / [by] W. Tatler and W.M. Corbett. — 1977. — 1v. : ill, maps(some col) ; 25cm. — (Soil Survey of Great Britain (England and Wales). Survey records ; no.41)
Book (viii, 117p.), 2 fold. sheets ([2]p.: col. maps) in plastic envelope. — Also available without maps. — Bibl.: p.105-106. — Index.
£1.00
Without maps : £0.50
(B77-32700)

631.4'9427'1 — Cheshire. Soils. *Reports, surveys*
Soils in Cheshire. — Harpenden (Rothamsted Experimental Station, Harpenden, Herts. AL5 2JQ) : Soil Survey of Great Britain (England and Wales).
3 : Sheet SJ 45E/55W (Burwardsley) / [by] S.J. King. — 1977. — 1v. : ill(incl 1 col), maps(chiefly col) ; 22cm. — (Soil Survey of Great Britain (England and Wales). Survey records ; no.43)
Pbk book (viii,156p.,[2] leaves of plates(1 fold),[4]p. of plates) and fold. sheet (col. map) in plastic envelope. — Also available without map. — Bibl.: p.127-129. — Index.
£1.25
Without map : £1.00
(B77-23514)

631.4'9428'2 — South Yorkshire (Metropolitan County). Soils. *Reports, surveys*
Soils in South Yorkshire. — Harpenden (Rothamsted Experimental Station, Harpenden, Herts. AL5 2SQ) : Soil Survey of England and Wales.
1 : Sheet SK59 (Maltby) / [by] R. Hartnup. — 1977. — 1v. : ill(incl 1 col), maps ; 22cm. — (Soil Survey of Great Britain (England and Wales). Survey records ; no.42)
Pbk book (viii,160p,plate) and 2 fold. sheets (col. maps) in plastic envelope. — Also available without maps. — Bibl.: p.137-138. — Index.
£3.00
Without maps: £1.00
(B77-24310)

631.4'9428'4 — North Yorkshire. Soils. *Reports, surveys*
Soils in North Yorkshire. — Harpenden (Rothamsted Experimental Station, Harpenden, Herts. AL5 2JQ) : Soil Survey of England and Wales.
3 : Parts of sheets SE79, 88, 89, 98, 99 (Pickering Moor and Troutsdale) / [by] V.C. Bendelow and D.M. Carroll. — 1976. — 1v. : ill, maps ; 21cm. — (Soil Survey of Great Britain (England and Wales). Survey records ; no.35)
Book (x,155p., leaf of plate,ii p. of plates) and 4 fold. sheets(col. maps) in plastic envelope. — Also available without maps. — Bibl.: p.139-140. — Index.
ISBN 0-7086-0020-4 : £1.50
ISBN 0-7086-0021-2 Without maps : £0.50
(B77-02401)

631.4'9428'81 — Northumberland. Hexham region. Soils. *Reports, surveys*
Jarvis, Ronald Arthur. Soils of the Hexham district (Sheet 19) / [by] R.A. Jarvis ; incorporating material by G.D. Ashley. — Harpenden (Rothamsted Experimental Station, Harpenden, Herts.) : Soil Survey of England and Wales, 1977. — vii,72p,[2] leaves of plates,[4]p of plates : ill, maps(1 col) ; 25cm. — (Soil Survey of Great Britain (England and Wales). Memoirs)
Fold. sheet (col. map) in pocket. — Bibl.: p.68-69. — Index.
ISBN 0-7086-0028-x : £4.00
(B77-14792)

631.4'9669'2 — Nigeria. Western states. Savanna regions. Soils. *Reports, surveys*
Great Britain. *Ministry of Overseas Development. Land Resources Division.* Soils of the Western State savanna in Nigeria / Land Resources Division. — Surbiton : The Division. — (Land resource study ; 23 ISSN 0305-6554)
In 3 vols.
Maps. — 1976. — Portfolio : of col maps ; 30x22cm.
Fifteen fold. sheets ([15] sides).
ISBN 0-902409-48-4 : £7.50
(B77-09087)

Vol.1 : The environment / [by] G. Murdoch ... [et al.]. — 1976. — xiv,102p(12 fold),[2]leaves : ill(incl 1 col), maps(chiefly col) ; 30cm.
Bibl.: p.89-96.
ISBN 0-902409-49-2 Pbk : £7.50
(B77-09088)

Vol.2 : Descriptions of basement complex soil series / [by] G. Murdoch ... [et al.]. — 1976. — xi,145p(2 fold),leaf : 2 ill(1 col) ; 30cm.
Bibl.: p.137-144.
ISBN 0-902409-50-6 Pbk : £7.50
(B77-09089)

Vol.3 : Atlas of sample blocks mapped during the survey / [by] G. Colborne ... [et al.]. — 1976. — vi p,27 leaves : ill, col maps ; 30x42cm.
English and French text.
ISBN 0-902409-47-6 Sd : £7.50
(B77-09090)

631.4'9775 — Wisconsin. Soils
Hole, Francis D. Soils of Wisconsin / [by] Francis D. Hole, with contributions by Marvin T. Beatty, Gerhard B. Lee ; illustrations by R.D. Sale ... [et al.]. — Madison ; London : University of Wisconsin Press for the Geological and Natural History Survey, University of Wisconsin-Extension, 1976. — xvi,223,[1]p,8p of plates : ill(some col), maps(some col) ; 29cm. — (University of Wisconsin Extension. Geological and Natural History Survey. Bulletins ; 87) (University of Wisconsin Extension. Geological and Natural History Survey. Soil series ; 62)
Fold. sheet (col. map) in pocket. — Bibl.: p.207-213. — Index.
ISBN 0-299-06830-7 : £11.25
(B77-21958)

631.4'9931 — New Zealand. Soils. Conservation, to 1972
McCaskill, Lance W. Hold this land : a history of soil conservation in New Zealand / [by] L.W. McCaskill. — Wellington, N.Z. [etc.] ; London : A.H. and A.W. Reed, 1973. — xi, 274p : ill, maps, ports ; 25cm.
Ill., maps on lining papers. — Index.
ISBN 0-589-00708-4 : £8.25
(B77-19465)

631.5 — FARM OPERATIONS
631.5 — Crops. Biochemistry
Draper, Simon R. Biochemical analysis in crop science / [by] Simon R. Draper. — Oxford [etc.] : Oxford University Press, 1976. — ix, 130p : ill ; 23cm.
Bibl. — Index.
ISBN 0-19-854128-7 : £5.50
ISBN 0-19-854132-5 Pbk : £2.75
(B77-09091)

631.5 — Crops. Physiology. Effects of environment. *Conference proceedings*
Long Ashton Symposium, *5th, 1975.*
Environmental effects on crop physiology : proceedings of a symposium held at Long Ashton Research Station, University of Bristol, 13-16 April 1975 / edited by J.J. Landsberg and C.V. Cutting. — London [etc.] : Academic Press, 1977. — xvii,388p : ill, map ; 24cm.
Head of title: Fifth Long Ashton Symposium, 1975. — Bibl. — Index.
ISBN 0-12-435050-x : £14.50
(B77-32701)

631.5'094 — Crops. Production. *Western Europe*
Eddowes, Maurice. Crop production in Europe / [by] Maurice Eddowes. — London [etc.] : Oxford University Press, 1976. — ix,318p,[4]p of plates : ill ; 23cm.
Bibl. — Index.
ISBN 0-19-859444-5 : £8.00
ISBN 0-19-859460-7 Pbk : £4.00
(B77-09092)

631.5'09415 — Crops. Production. *Ireland. Secondary school texts*
Murphy, Desmond. Crops in Ireland / text Desmond Murphy ; illustrations Mary O'Connell. — [Tallaght] : Folens, [1977]. — [1] ,p.33-64 : col ill, col map ; 25cm. — (Irish environmental library series ; no.22)
Sd : £0.60
(B77-18233)

631.5'21 — Crops. Seeds. Quality
National Institute of Agricultural Botany. Seed quality / NIAB. — Cambridge (Huntingdon Rd, Cambridge CB3 0LE) : N.I.A.B., 1977. — 14,[1]p : 1 ill ; 21cm. — (Technical leaflet ; no.1 ISSN 0140-4199)
Sd : £0.15
(B77-30370)

631.5'3 — Crops. Breeding. Genetic aspects
Theories of plant and animal breeding ; [and], Ecological and evolutionary genetics / [prepared by a Course Team for the Open University]. — [Milton Keynes] : Open University Press, [1976]. — p555-615,plate : ill(some col), maps, col port ; 30cm. — (Science, a second level course : genetics ; 12, 13) (S299 ; 12, 13)
Cover title. — With answers to in-text and self-assessment questions. — Bibl.
Pbk : Unpriced
Primary classification 575.1
(B77-04172)

631.5'3 — Crops. Breeding. Heterosis. *Conference proceedings*
Eucarpia. *Congress, 7th, Budapest, 1974.*
Heterosis in plant breeding : proceedings of the Seventh Congress of Eucarpia, the European Association for Research in Plant Breeding ..., Budapest, 24-29 June 1974 / editors A. Jánossy and F.G.H. Lupton. — Amsterdam ; Oxford [etc.] : Elsevier, 1976. — 366p : ill, port ; 25cm.
Bibl.
ISBN 0-444-99835-7 : £23.42
(B77-16941)

631.5'3 — Crops. Planting times. Astrological aspects. *Calendars*
Thun, Maria. Working with the stars : a bio-dynamic sowing and planting calendar / by Maria Thun ; [translated from the German]. — East Grinstead (Peredur, East Grinstead, Sussex) : Lanthorn Press.
[1977] / foreword by Siegfried Rudel ; introduction to the 1977 calendar by M. Thun. — 1977. — 37p ; 22cm.
Translation of: 'Aussaat-Tage 1977'. Germany : s.n., 1976?.
Sd : £0.80
(B77-30371)

631.5'3'072042659 — Crops. Breeding. Research organisations. *Cambridgeshire. Cambridge. Plant Breeding Institute. Reports, surveys. Serials*
Plant Breeding Institute. Annual report / Plant Breeding Institute. — Cambridge (Cambridge CB2 2LQ) : The Institute.
1976. — 1977. — 153p,plate : ill ; 25cm.
Bibl.: p.147-152.
Pbk : £1.50
(B77-25010)

631.5'44 — Greenhouses. Crops. Liquid fertilisers. *Western Scotland*
West of Scotland Agricultural College. Liquid feeds for glasshouse crops / the West of Scotland Agricultural College. — [Auchincruive] : [The College], [1977]. — [1],6, [1]p ; 21cm. — (Advisory publications ; no.19 ISSN 0306-7165)
Sd : Unpriced
(B77-20377)

631.5'8 — Crops. Organic cultivation
Soil Association. Farming organically / [Soil Association] ; edited by Sam Mayall. — Stowmarket (Walnut Tree Manor, Haughley, Stowmarket, Suffolk IP14 3RS) : Soil Association, 1976. — [2],16,[1]p,[3]p of plates : ill ; 21cm.
ISBN 0-905200-06-3 Sd : £0.30
(B77-00813)

631.5'85 — Hydroponics. *Manuals*
Harris, Dudley. Hydroponics : growing plants without soil / [by] Dudley Harris. — [Revised] ed. / revised for temporate zones by A.M.M. Berrie and Ian G. Walls. — London : Sphere, 1977. — 191p,[16]p of plates : ill ; 18cm.
This ed. originally published: Newton Abbot : David and Charles, 1975. — Bibl.: p.182-184. — Index.
ISBN 0-7221-4340-0 Pbk : £0.95
(B77-15926)

631.6 — AGRICULTURE. LAND RECLAMATION AND DRAINAGE

631.6'2'03 — Agricultural land. Drainage. *Dictionaries*

Rees, Tom, *b.1925.* 'There's a word for it' : a glossary of land drainage terms / [compiled by Tom Rees]. — Stroud (Brimscombe, Stroud, Glos. GL5 2TH) : Critchley Bros Ltd, [1977]. — [3],42,[1]p ; 22cm.
Sd : £0.60
(B77-27190)

631.7 — AGRICULTURE. IRRIGATION

631.7 — Water for irrigation of agricultural land. Storage. *Great Britain. Reports, surveys*

Land Drainage Service. Water for irrigation : supply and storage / Ministry of Agriculture, Fisheries and Food, Land Drainage Service. — 2nd ed. — London : H.M.S.O., 1977. — viii, 100p,viii p of plates : ill, forms, map ; 25cm. — (Great Britain. Ministry of Agriculture, Fisheries and Food. Bulletins ; no.202)
Previous ed.: 1967. — Index.
ISBN 0-11-241519-9 Pbk : £2.25
(B77-18234)

631.7'0915'4 — Agricultural land. Irrigation. *Arid regions. Reviews of research*

Arid zone irrigation / edited by B. Yaron, E. Danfors and Y. Vaadia. — London : Chapman and Hall [etc.], 1973. — x,434p : ill, maps ; 25cm. — (Ecological studies ; vol.5)
Bibl. — Index.
ISBN 0-412-12570-6 : Unpriced
(B77-19466)

631.7'0942 — Agricultural land. Irrigation. *England. Manuals*

Agricultural Development and Advisory Service. Thinking irrigation / ADAS, Ministry of Agriculture, Fisheries and Food. — Revised [ed.]. — Pinner : The Ministry, 1976. — [2], 18p : 1 ill, 2 maps(1 col) ; 22cm. — (Farm water supply ; leaflet no.2)
ISBN 0-85521-188-1 Sd : Unpriced
(B77-11894)

631.7'0968'1 — Eastern Botswana. Soils. Irrigation. *Feasibility studies*

Mitchell, A J B. The irrigation potential of soils along the main rivers of Eastern Botswana : a reconnaissance assessment / [by] A.J.B. Mitchell. — Surbiton : Land Resources Division, Ministry of Overseas Development, 1976. — xii,216,[2]p(4 fold) : ill, maps(chiefly col) ; 30cm. — (Land resource study ; 7 ISSN 0305-6554)
'... an amplified version of preliminary reports already submitted to the Government of Botswana'. — Bibl.: p.177-184.
Pbk : £2.50
(B77-09093)

Mitchell, A J B. The irrigation potential of soils along the main rivers of Eastern Botswana : a reconnaissance assessment / [by] A.J.B. Mitchell. — Surbiton : Land Resources Division, Ministry of Overseas Development. — (Land resource study ; 7 ISSN 0305-6554)
'... an amplified version of preliminary reports already submitted to the Government of Botswana'.
Maps. — 1976. — Portfolio : of ill, col maps ; 30x22cm.
Eleven fold. sheets ([11] sides).
£2.50
(B77-09094)

631.8 — AGRICULTURE. FERTILISERS

631.81'09411 — Agricultural land. Use of fertilisers. *Western Scotland. Manuals*

West of Scotland Agricultural College. Farm fertiliser recommendations / the West of Scotland Agricultural College. — [Auchincruive] : The College, [1975?]. — [1], 11p ; 21cm. — (Advisory publication ; no.1)
Sd : Unpriced
(B77-18235)

631.8'21 — Soil conditioners: Lime. Use. *Manuals*

Agricultural Development and Advisory Service. Lime in agriculture / Ministry of Agriculture, Fisheries and Food, ADAS. — Revised [ed.] / [revised by N.W. Whinham]. — Pinner : The Ministry, 1976. — 7p ; 22cm. — (Advisory leaflet ; 542)
Previous ed.: / issued by the Ministry of Agriculture, Fisheries and Food. London : H.M.S.O., 1965.
ISBN 0-85521-194-6 Sd : Unpriced
(B77-11895)

631.8'5 — Fertilisers: Phosphates. Use. *Manuals*

Agricultural Development and Advisory Service. Phosphatic fertilizers / Ministry of Agriculture, Fisheries and Food, ADAS. — Revised [ed.] / [revised by G.R. Davies]. — Pinner : The Ministry, 1976. — Folder (6)p : 2 col ill ; 22cm. — (Advisory leaflet ; 442)
Previous ed.: published as 'Phosphate fertilizers for farm crops' / issued by the Ministry of Agriculture, Fisheries and Food. London : H.M.S.O., 1956.
ISBN 0-85521-192-x Sd : Unpriced
(B77-11896)

631.8'61 — Farmyard manure. Use. *Manuals*

Agricultural Development and Advisory Service. Making the most of farmyard manure / Ministry of Agriculture, Fisheries and Food, ADAS. — Revised [ed.] / [revised by H.T. Davies]. — Pinner : The Ministry, 1976. — Folder ([3]p) ; 22cm. — (Advisory leaflet ; 435)

Previous ed.: / issued by the Ministry of Agriculture, Fisheries and Food. London : H.M.S.O., 1960.
ISBN 0-85521-193-8 Sd : Unpriced
(B77-11897)

632 — AGRICULTURE. PLANT INJURIES, DISEASES, PESTS

632 — Crops. Diseases, pests & weeds. Origins. Ecological aspects. *Conference proceedings*

Origins of pest, parasite, disease and weed problems : the 18th Symposium of the British Ecological Society, Bangor, 12-14 April 1976 / edited by J.M. Cherrett and G.R. Sagar. — Oxford [etc.] : Blackwell Scientific, 1977. — x, 413p : ill, maps ; 24cm. — (British Ecological Society. Symposia ; 18th)
Bibl. — Index.
ISBN 0-632-00226-3 : £14.00 : CIP rev.
Also classified at 636.089'6
(B77-06170)

632'.07'11 — Higher education institutions. Curriculum subjects: Crop protection. *Conference proceedings*

British Crop Protection Council. Proceedings of a symposium on syllabuses and course content for crop protection courses : 7th to 10th September 1976, held at the University of Stirling, Central Region, Scotland / British Crop Protection Council ; edited by W. Fletcher & D. Martin. — Droitwich (Clacks Farm, Boreley, Ombersley, Droitwich, Worcs. WR9 0HX) : The Council, 1976. — ix,126p : ill ; 21cm. — (British Crop Protection Council. Monographs ; no.20)
Cover title: Symposium on syllabuses and course content for crop protection courses. — Bibl. — List of films: p.125-126.
Pbk : £3.50
(B77-25715)

632.5 — AGRICULTURE. HARMFUL PLANTS

632'.58 — Crops. Weeds. Control measures. *Conference proceedings*

British Crop Protection Conference, Weeds, *Brighton, 1976.* Proceedings of the 1976 British Crop Protection Conference, Weeds (13th British Weed Control Conference), 15th-18th November 1976, [held at] Hotel Metropole, Brighton ... organised by the British Crop Protection Council / [compiled by the ARC Weed Research Organization]. — [London] (c/o A.W. Billitt, Clacks Farm, Boreley, Ombersley, Droitwich WR9 0HX) : [British Crop Protection Council], [1977]. — 3v.([39], 1051p) : ill, maps ; 21cm.
'The conferences at Brighton organised ... as the Weed Control Conference and the Insecticide and Fungicide Conference have been unified and are being referred to as the British Crop Protection Conference' - Preface. — Bibl.
Pbd : Unpriced
(B77-12524)

632'.58'0941 — Weeds. Control measures. *Great Britain. Manuals*

British Crop Protection Council. Weed control handbook / issued by the British Crop Protection Council. — Oxford [etc.] : Blackwell Scientific.
In 2 vols.
Vol.1 : Principles, including plant growth regulators. — 6th ed. / ... edited by J.D. Fryer and R.J. Makepeace ; editorial assistant J.H. Fearon. — 1977. — xvii,510p : ill ; 23cm.
Previous ed.: / edited by J.D. Fryer and S.A. Evans. 1968. — Bibl. — Index.
ISBN 0-632-00209-3 : £13.50 : CIP rev.
(B77-06171)

632.6 — AGRICULTURE. ANIMAL PESTS

632'.6'542 — Greenhouses. Crops. Pests: Red spider mites. Control measures

Agricultural Development and Advisory Service. Red spider mites on glasshouse crops / Ministry of Agriculture, Fisheries and Food, Agricultural Development and Advisory Service. — Revised [ed.] / [revised by the Entomology Department, Glasshouse Crops Research Institute]. — Pinner : The Ministry, 1976. — 9p : col ill ; 22cm. — (Advisory leaflet ; 224)
Previous ed.: published as 'Red spider mite on glasshouse crops' / issued by the Ministry of Agriculture, Fisheries and Food. London : H.M.S.O., 1960.
ISBN 0-85521-191-1 Sd : Unpriced
(B77-12525)

632'.6'865 — Pests: Feral pigeons. Control measures

Agricultural Development and Advisory Service. The feral pigeon / Ministry of Agriculture, Fisheries and Food, ADAS. — Pinner : The Ministry, 1976. — Folder (6p) : 3 ill(2 col) ; 22cm. — (Advisory leaflet ; 601)
ISBN 0-85521-200-4 : Unpriced
(B77-13104)

632'.6'865 — Pests: Woodpigeons. Control. *Great Britain. Manuals*

Agricultural Development and Advisory Service. The woodpigeon / ADAS, Ministry of Agriculture, Fisheries and Food. — Revised [ed.]. — Pinner : The Ministry, 1976. — 7p : 1 col ill ; 21cm. — (Advisory leaflet ; 165)
Previous ed.: / issued by the Ministry of Agriculture, Fisheries and Food. London : H.M.S.O., 1959.
Sd : Unpriced
(B77-19467)

632'.6'9323 — Pests: Rodents

Barnett, Samuel Anthony. Rodents of economic importance / [by] S.A. Barnett and Ishwar Prakash. — London [etc.] : Heinemann Educational, 1976. — 175p,[8]leaves of plates : ill, 2 plans ; 23cm.
Bibl.: p.153-168. — Index.
ISBN 0-435-62048-7 : £5.00
(B77-12526)

632.7 — AGRICULTURE. INSECT PESTS

632'.7 — Crops. Pests: Insects. Biological control. Compared with use of insecticides

Winfield, Arthur Leslie. Insecticides and beneficial insects / [by] A.L. Winfield. — Ilford : Central Association of Bee-keepers, 1976. — [1],10p ; 21cm. — (Central Association of Bee-keepers. Lectures)
' ... given ... on 1st March 1976' - p.1.
ISBN 0-900909-50-1 Sd : £0.50
Also classified at 632'.951
(B77-03604)

632'.7 — Crops. Pests: Insects. Control. *State-of-the-art reviews*

Coaker, Thomas Henry. Future prospects for insect pest control / [by] T.H. Coaker. — Ilford : Central Association of Bee-keepers, 1976. — [1],8p ; 21cm. — (Central Association of Bee-keepers. Lectures)
'... given ... on October 10th 1975 at Caxton Hall, London' - p.1. — Bibl.: p.8.
Sd : £0.40
(B77-02402)

632'.7'072042134 — Pests: Insects. Research organisations. *London. Kensington and Chelsea (London Borough). Commonwealth Institute of Entomology. Conference proceedings*

Commonwealth Entomological Conference, *10th, London, 1975.* Report of the Tenth Commonwealth Entomological Conference, 2nd-4th July, 1975 / issued by the Commonwealth Institute of Entomology, 56 Queen's Gate, London SW7 5JR. — Farnham Royal : Commonwealth Agricultural Bureaux, 1976. — [3],58p ; 24cm.
ISBN 0-85198-371-5 Sd : £1.00
Also classified at 632'.96'072072983
(B77-01593)

632.8 — AGRICULTURE. VIRAL AND RICKETTSIAL DISEASES

632'.8 — Crops. Pathogens: Viruses

Smith, Kenneth Manley. Plant viruses / [by] Kenneth M. Smith. — 6th ed. — London : Chapman and Hall [etc.], 1977. — ix,241p,20p of plates : ill ; 23cm.
Previous ed.: 1974. — Bibl. — Index.
ISBN 0-412-14710-6 : £5.50
ISBN 0-412-14740-8 Pbk : £3.25
(B77-17587)

632'.8 — Crops. Virus diseases. *Conference proceedings*
Beltsville Symposium in Agricultural Research, *1st, 1976.* Virology in agriculture : invited papers presented at a symposium held May 10-12, 1976, at the Beltsville Agricultural Research Center (BARC), Beltsville, Maryland 20705, organized by the BARC Science Seminar Committee, T.O. Diener, Chairman, sponsored by the Beltsville Agricultural Research Center, Northeastern Region, Agricultural Research Service, United States Department of Agriculture / [general editor John A. Romberger, associate editors James D. Anderson, Rex L. Powell]. — Tunbridge Wells : Abacus Press, 1977. — xiv,293p : ill ; 25cm.
'... the first Beltsville Symposium in Agriculture Research' - Preface to this volume. — Bibl. — Index.
ISBN 0-85626-137-8 : Unpriced : CIP rev.
Also classified at 636.089'69'2
(B77-06748)

632.9 — AGRICULTURE. PEST CONTROL
632'.9'072 — Pests. Control. Research. *Reports, surveys. Serials*
Centre for Overseas Pest Research. Report of the Centre for Overseas Pest Research. — London : The Centre.
1975. — 1976. — vi,142p : ill, ports ; 21cm.
Bibl.: p.115-120.
ISBN 0-85135-085-2 Pbk : £2.75
(B77-07425)

632'.95'0212 — Crops. Pesticides. Constituents. *Technical data*
British Crop Protection Council. Pesticide manual : basic information on the chemicals used as active components of pesticides / [British Crop Protection Council] ; edited by Hubert Martin and Charles R. Worthing. — 5th ed. — [Droitwich] ([c/o Mr A.W. Billitt, Clacks Farm, Boreley, Ombersley, Droitwich, Worcs. WR9 0HX]) : The Council, 1977. — vii,593p ; 24cm.
Previous ed.: 1974. — Index.
£15.00
(B77-22673)

632'.95'0941 — Crops. Pesticides approved under Agricultural Chemicals Approval Scheme. *Great Britain. Lists. Serials*
List of approved products and their uses for farmers and growers / [Agricultural Chemicals Approval Organisation for the] Ministry of Agriculture, Fisheries and Food. — [Pinner] : [The Ministry].
1976. — [1976]. — 190p ; 21cm.
Cover title: Approved products for farmers and growers. — Index.
Pbk : Unpriced
(B77-03083)

List of approved products and their uses for farmers and growers / [Agricultural Chemicals Approval Organisation for the] Ministry of Agriculture, Fisheries and Food. — [London] : H.M.S.O.
1977. — 1977. — 200p ; 21cm.
Cover title: Approved products for farmers and growers. — Previously issued by the Ministry of Agriculture, Fisheries and Food. — Index.
ISBN 0-11-241079-0 Pbk : £2.00
(B77-09775)

632'.951 — Crops. Insecticides. Use. *Manuals*
British Crop Protection Council. Insecticide and fungicide handbook for crop protection / issued by the British Crop Protection Council. — 5th ed. / edited by Hubert Martin and Charles R. Worthing. — Oxford [etc.] : Blackwell Scientific, 1976. — xvi,427p ; 23cm.
Previous ed.: / edited by Hubert Martin. 1972. — Index.
ISBN 0-632-00109-7 : £12.50 : CIP rev.
Also classified at 632'.952
(B77-06172)

632'.951 — Crops. Insecticides. Use. Compared with biological control of insects
Winfield, Arthur Leslie. Insecticides and beneficial insects / [by] A.L. Winfield. — Ilford : Central Association of Bee-keepers, 1976. — [1],10p ; 21cm. — (Central Association of Bee-keepers. Lectures)
' ... given ... on 1st March 1976' - p.1.
ISBN 0-900909-50-1 Sd : £0.50
Primary classification 632'.7
(B77-03604)

632'.951 — Insecticides. Toxic effects
Insecticide biochemistry and physiology / edited by C.F. Wilkinson. — London [etc.] : Heyden, 1976. — xxii,768p : ill ; 24cm.
Bibl. — Index.
ISBN 0-85501-216-1 : £32.00
(B77-00814)

632'.952 — Crops. Fungicides. Use. *Manuals*
British Crop Protection Council. Insecticide and fungicide handbook for crop protection / issued by the British Crop Protection Council. — 5th ed. / edited by Hubert Martin and Charles R. Worthing. — Oxford [etc.] : Blackwell Scientific, 1976. — xvi,427p ; 23cm.
Previous ed.: / edited by Hubert Martin. 1972. — Index.
ISBN 0-632-00109-7 : £12.50 : CIP rev.
Primary classification 632'.951
(B77-06172)

632'.952 — Fungicides. *Conference proceedings*
Herbicides and fungicides, factors affecting their activity : the proceedings of a symposium arranged jointly by the Fine Chemicals and Medicinals Group of the Industrial Division, the Chemical Society and the Pesticides Group of the Society of Chemical Industry, [held at] Bangor, Wales, 15-17 September, 1976 / edited by N.R. McFarlane. — London : Chemical Society, 1977. — xi,141p : ill ; 22cm. — (Chemical Society. Special publications ; no.29 ISSN 0577-618x)
Pbk : Unpriced
Primary classification 632'.954
(B77-25011)

632'.952 — Systemic fungicides
Systemic fungicides / edited by R.W. Marsh, with the assistance of R.J.W. Byrde and D. Woodcock. — 2nd ed. — London [etc.] : Longman, 1977. — xiv,401p : ill ; 23cm.
Previous ed.: Harlow : Longman, 1972. — Bibl. : p.320-388. — Index.
ISBN 0-582-44167-6 : £12.00
(B77-16942)

632'.954 — Herbicides
Herbicides : physiology, biochemistry, ecology / edited by L.J. Audus. — 2nd ed. — London [etc.] : Academic Press.
In 2 vols. — Previous ed.: published in 1 vol. as 'The physiology and biochemistry of herbicides'. 1964.
Vol.2. — 1976. — xx,564,[4]p of plates(4 fold) : ill ; 24cm.
Bibl. — Index.
ISBN 0-12-067702-4 : £17.50
(B77-03605)

632'.954 — Herbicides. *Conference proceedings*
Herbicides and fungicides, factors affecting their activity : the proceedings of a symposium arranged jointly by the Fine Chemicals and Medicinals Group of the Industrial Division, the Chemical Society and the Pesticides Group of the Society of Chemical Industry, [held at] Bangor, Wales, 15-17 September, 1976 / edited by N.R. McFarlane. — London : Chemical Society, 1977. — xi,141p : ill ; 22cm. — (Chemical Society. Special publications ; no.29 ISSN 0577-618x)
Pbk : Unpriced
Also classified at 632'.952
(B77-25011)

632'.954 — Herbicides: 2,4-dichlorophenoxyacetic acid & 2,4,5-trichlorophenoxyacetic acid. Safety. *Reports, surveys*
Turner, D J. The safety of the herbicides 2,4-D and 2,4,5-T / [by] D.J. Turner. — London : H.M.S.O., 1977. — [1],56p : 3 ill ; 25cm. — (Forestry Commission. Bulletins ; 57)
ISBN 0-11-710149-4 Sd : £1.20
(B77-32702)

632'.96 — Pests. Biological control
Theory and practice of biological control / edited by C.B. Huffaker, P.S. Messenger. — New York [etc.] ; London : Academic Press, 1976. — xxi,788p : ill ; 24cm.
Bibl. — Index.
ISBN 0-12-360350-1 : £30.15
(B77-17588)

632'.96'072072983 — Pests. Biological control. Research organisations. *Trinidad and Tobago. Trinidad. Curepe. Commonwealth Institute of Biological Control. Conference proceedings*
Commonwealth Entomological Conference, *10th, London, 1975.* Report of the Tenth Commonwealth Entomological Conference, 2nd-4th July, 1975 / issued by the Commonwealth Institute of Entomology, 56 Queen's Gate, London SW7 5JR. — Farnham Royal : Commonwealth Agricultural Bureaux, 1976. — [3],58p ; 24cm.
ISBN 0-85198-371-5 Sd : £1.00
Primary classification 632'.7'072042134
(B77-01593)

633 — AGRICULTURE. FIELD CROPS
633 — Field crops. Cultivation. Use of fertilisers. Chemical aspects. *India (Republic)*
Mariakulandai, A. Chemistry of fertilizers and manures : a textbook for students of agriculture / [by] A. Mariakulandai and T.S. Manickam. — London : Asia Publishing House, 1975. — xv,399p : ill ; 22cm.
Bibl. — Index.
ISBN 0-210-22249-2 Pbk : £6.50
(B77-10421)

633'.08'2 — Crops. Pollination by insects. *Tropical regions*
Free, John Brand. Insect pollination of tropical crops / [by] J.B. Free. — Ilford : Central Association of Bee-keepers, 1976. — [1],10p ; 21cm. — (Central Association of Bee-keepers. Lectures)
'... given ... on 28th September 1974' - p.1. — Bibl.: p.8.
ISBN 0-900909-49-8 Sd : £0.50
(B77-01594)

633.1 — AGRICULTURE. CEREAL CROPS
633'.104'46 — Cereals. Cultivation. Tramline systems. *Great Britain*
Agricultural Development and Advisory Service. Tramline systems for cereal production / Ministry of Agriculture, Fisheries and Food, ADAS. — Pinner : The Ministry, 1977. — [1], 14,[1]p : ill ; 21cm. — (Short term leaflet ; 189)
Sd : Unpriced
(B77-25012)

633'.104'6 — Cereals. Threshing. Mills. *Scotland. Orkney, to 1976*
Leith, Peter. Orkney threshing mills / [by] Peter Leith & Sheila Spence. — Dundee [etc.] ([149 Strathern Rd, West Ferry, Dundee DD5 1BR]) : Scottish Vernacular Buildings Working Group, 1977. — 16p : ill, facsim ; 21cm.
ISBN 0-9505084-1-1 Sd : £0.50
(B77-15346)

633'.104'6 — Electric cereals drying & cereals storage equipment. Use. *Great Britain. Manuals*
Electricity Council. *Farm-electric Centre.* Grain drying and storage : a guide to the practical design of installations / [Electricity Council, Farm-electric Centre]. — Kenilworth (National Agricultural Centre, Kenilworth, Warwickshire CV8 2LS) : The Centre, 1975. — iv,123p : ill(some col) ; 21cm. — (Farmelectric handbook ; no.21 ISSN 0309-247x)
Originally published: 1974.
ISBN 0-85188-063-0 Pbk : £0.75
(B77-07426)

633.1'04'943 — Cereals. Mildews. Control measures. *Western Scotland. Manuals*
West of Scotland Agricultural College. Mildew control in cereals / the West of Scotland Agricultural College. — [Auchincruive] : [The College], [1976?]. — Folder([4]p) ; 21cm. — (Advisory publication ; no.6)
Unpriced
(B77-18236)

633'.104'958 — Cereals. Weeds. Control measures. *Manuals*
Agricultural Development and Advisory Service. Weed control in cereals, 1977 / Ministry of Agriculture, Fisheries and Food, Agricultural Development and Advisory Service. — Revised [ed.]. — Pinner : The Ministry, 1976. — [1],33, [1]p : 1 ill ; 21cm. — (Short term leaflet ; 19)
Previous ed.: published as 'Weed control in cereals, 1976'. 1975.
ISBN 0-85521-206-3 Sd : Unpriced
(B77-11898)

633'.1'0941 — Cereals. Production. *Great Britain. Conference proceedings*
Cereal production in times of change : crop conference, Cambridge, 15-17 December 1976 ... — Cambridge (Huntingdon Rd, Cambridge CB3 9LE) : National Institute of Agricultural Botany, [1977]. — [2],56p : ill ; 24cm.
Bibl.: p.54-55.
Sd : £2.00
(B77-18237)

633'.1'0941 — Cereals. Production. *Great Britain. Manuals*
Fisons Limited. *Agrochemical Division.* Cereals : a manual for farmers and advisors / [Fisons Agrochemical Division]. — Harston (Harston, Cambridge CB2 5HU) : The Division, [1977]. — 157p : ill(chiefly col) ; 21cm.
Bibl.
Pbk : Unpriced
(B77-15347)

633'.1'09411 — Cereals. Cultivation. *Scotland. Reports, surveys*
East of Scotland College of Agriculture. Cereal husbandry for higher yields : ESCA-RHAS regional demonstration 1976, Tues. 27th and Wed. 28th July 1976, Clifton Mains, Newbridge, Midlothian ... / the East of Scotland College of Agriculture and the Royal Highland & Agricultural Society of Scotland. — [Edinburgh] ([West Mains Rd, Edinburgh EH9 3JG]) : [E.S.C.A.] ; [s.l.] : [R.H.A.S.], 1976. — [4],ii,39p : plans ; 21cm.
ISBN 0-902164-24-4 Sd : Unpriced
(B77-14291)

633'.11'7 — Winter wheat. Varieties. Trials. *Western Europe*
University College, *Dublin. Department of Farm Management.* Winter wheat varietal trials, 1973-1975 : field data, yield, quality / University College Dublin, Department of Farm Management, Lyons. — [Lyons, Co. Dublin] ([Lyons, Newcastle, Co. Dublin]) : [The Department], [1977]. — [1],13 leaves ; 33cm. — (Wheat bulletin ; no.15)
'Cereals trials, Lyons, 1976' ([1],23 leaves ; sd) as insert.
Sd : Unpriced
(B77-17589)

633'.14'0941 — Winter rye. Production. *Great Britain. Manuals*
Agricultural Development and Advisory Service. Winter rye for grazing and grain / Ministry of Agriculture, Fisheries and Food [Agricultural Development and Advisory Service]. — Pinner : The Ministry, 1976. — Folder ([4]p) ; 21cm. — (Advisory leaflet ; 501)
ISBN 0-85521-208-x : Unpriced
(B77-13105)

633'.15 — Maize. Cultivation. Use of fertilisers
Greenwood, Duncan Joseph. Fertiliser requirements of vegetable crops / by D.J. Greenwood, T.J. Cleaver and Mary K. Turner. Maize and its fertilisation / by R. Gervy. — London (93 Albert Embankment, SE1 7TU) : Fertiliser Society, [1974]. — [1],56p : ill, maps ; 22cm. — (Fertiliser Society. Proceedings ; no.145)
'Presented to The Fertiliser Society of London on 19th December, 1974'. — Bibl.
Sd : £4.50
Primary classification 635
(B77-13717)

633'.15'0942 — Maize. Production. *England. Manuals*
Agricultural Development and Advisory Service. Maize production for silage and grain / Ministry of Agriculture, Fisheries and Food, ADAS. — Revised [ed.]. — Pinner : The Ministry, 1977. — [1],23,[1]p : map ; 22cm. — (Short term leaflet ; 93)
Sd : Unpriced
(B77-25013)

633.2/3 — AGRICULTURE. FORAGE CROPS
633'.2 — Grassland. Fertilisers: Phosphates. Use. *Manuals*
Agricultural Development and Advisory Service. Phosphate on grassland / Ministry of Agriculture, Fisheries and Food, ADAS. — Amended [ed.]. — Pinner : The Ministry, 1976. — [1],6p ; 22cm. — (Grassland practice ; no.5) (Short term leaflet ; 101)
ISBN 0-85521-199-7 Sd : Unpriced
(B77-12527)

633.2 — Pastures. Management
Heady, Harold Franklin. Rangeland management / [by] Harold F. Heady. — New York ; London [etc.] : McGraw-Hill, [1976]. — xiii,460p : ill ; 24cm. — (McGraw-Hill series in forest resources)
Published in the United States: 1975. — Bibl. — Index.
ISBN 0-07-027693-5 : £13.30
(B77-02403)

633'.2 — Recreation facilities: Grassland. Maintenance. *Ireland. Conference proceedings*
Next Decade in Amenity Grassland *(Conference), Queen's University of Belfast, 1976.* Proceedings of a symposium on The Next Decade in Amenity Grassland, 25th and 26th March 1976 held in the Faculty of Agriculture and Food Science, the Queen's University of Belfast, [organised by the] Institute of Biology, Northern Ireland Branch and Department of Extra-Mural Studies, Queen's University / edited by C.E. Wright. — [Belfast] ([c/o Institute of Biology, Northern Ireland Branch, Newforge La., Belfast BT9 5PX]) : [The editor], [1976]. — [3],112p,plate : ill ; 30cm.
Bibl.
ISBN 0-905874-00-5 Sp : £1.00
(B77-07427)

633'.2'0072013 — Agriculture. Research. *Tropical regions. Pastures. Manuals. For developing countries*
Tropical pasture research : principles and methods / edited by N.H. Shaw and W.W. Bryan. — Farnham Royal : Commonwealth Agricultural Bureaux, 1976. — xiv,454p : ill, maps ; 24cm. — (Commonwealth Bureau of Pastures and Field Crops. Bulletins ; 51)
Bibl.: p.393-442. — Index.
ISBN 0-85198-358-8 : £12.00
(B77-04275)

633'.2'00913 — Crops: Grasses. Production. *Tropical regions*
Bogdan, A V. Tropical pasture and fodder plants : (grasses and legumes) / [by] A.V. Bogdan. — London [etc.] : Longman, 1977. — xiii,475p : ill, 3 maps ; 23cm. — (Tropical agriculture series)
Bibl.: p.432-461. — Index.
ISBN 0-582-46676-8 : £17.00
Also classified at 633'.3'0913
(B77-14793)

633'.2'00941 — Crops: Grasses. Production. *Great Britain*
Craven, F W. Grass : a profitable crop / by F.W. Craven and J.T. Parry. — Grimsby (Field House, Grimsby, Lincs.) : Nickerson Seed Organisation, [1977]. — [3],43p : ill ; 21cm.
Pbk : £0.75
(B77-24311)

633'.2'00941 — Grassland. Cultivation. *Great Britain. Manuals*
Cooper, Malcolm McGregor. Grass farming. — 4th ed. (revised) / by M.McG. Cooper and David W. Morris. — Ipswich : Farming Press, 1977. — 252p,[16]p of plates : ill ; 23cm.
Previous ed.: / by M.McG. Cooper and David W. Morris. 1973. — Index.
ISBN 0-85236-076-2 : £4.00
(B77-30372)

633'.2'009411 — Grasslands. Management. *Western Scotland*
West of Scotland Agricultural College. Grassland management : problem/action checklist / the West of Scotland College of Agriculture. — [Auchincruive] : [The College], [1977]. — [1], 6p ; 21cm. — (Advisory publication ; no.10 ISSN 0309-6734)
Sd : Unpriced
(B77-33883)

633'.208'6 — Electric hay drying equipment. Use. *Great Britain. Manuals*
Electricity Council. *Farm-electric Centre.* Hay drying : a guide to the practical design of installations / [Electricity Council, Farm-electric Centre]. — Kenilworth (National Agricultural Centre, Stoneleigh, Kenilworth, Warwickshire CV8 2LS) : The Centre, 1975. — v,66p : ill ; 21cm. — (Farmelectric handbook ; no.22 ISSN 0309-247x)
ISBN 0-85188-064-9 Pbk : £0.75
(B77-07428)

633'.208'7 — Forage crops. Varieties suitable for storage
National Institute for Agricultural Botany. Grasses and legumes for conservation, 1977-78 / NIAB. — Cambridge (Huntingdon Rd, Cambridge CB3 0LE) : N.I.A.B., [1977]. — 6,[2]p(2 fold) : col ill ; 21cm. — (Technical leaflet ; no.2 ISSN 0140-4199)
Sd : £0.15
(B77-30373)

633'.208'9 — Crops: Grasses. Diseases. *Ireland (Republic)*
O'Rourke, C J. Diseases of grasses and forage legumes in Ireland / by C.J. O'Rourke. — Dublin (19 Sandymount Ave., Dublin 4) : Foras Talúntais, 1976. — vi,115p,12p of plates,2 leaves of plates : ill(some col) ; 21cm.
Bibl.: p.83-104. — Index.
ISBN 0-905442-07-5 Pbk : £3.00
Also classified at 633'.3
(B77-07429)

633'.25'509417 — Forage crops: Maize. *Ireland (Republic). Reports, surveys*
Report on fodder maize in Ireland, 1971-1975 / compiled and edited by M. Neenan. — Dublin (19 Sandymount Ave., Ballsbridge, Dublin 4) : An Foras Talúntais, 1976. — [3],41p : ill, charts, map ; 29cm.
ISBN 0-905442-06-7 Sd : £1.75
(B77-05501)

633'.3 — Crops: Legumes. Diseases. *Ireland (Republic)*
O'Rourke, C J. Diseases of grasses and forage legumes in Ireland / by C.J. O'Rourke. — Dublin (19 Sandymount Ave., Dublin 4) : Foras Talúntais, 1976. — vi,115p,12p of plates,2 leaves of plates : ill(some col) ; 21cm.
Bibl.: p.83-104. — Index.
ISBN 0-905442-07-5 Pbk : £3.00
Primary classification 633'.208'9
(B77-07429)

633'.3'0913 — Crops: Legumes. Production. *Tropical regions*
Bogdan, A V. Tropical pasture and fodder plants : (grasses and legumes) / [by] A.V. Bogdan. — London [etc.] : Longman, 1977. — xiii,475p : ill, 3 maps ; 23cm. — (Tropical agriculture series)
Bibl.: p.432-461. — Index.
ISBN 0-582-46676-8 : £17.00
Primary classification 633'.2'00913
(B77-14793)

633'.31 — Lucerne. Production. *Conference proceedings*
Lucerne for use on the farm / edited by R.D. Sheldrick, J. Johnson ; [for the] Grassland Research Institute and [the] Agricultural Development and Advisory Service. — Hurley ([Hurley, Maidenhead, Berks. SL6 5LR]) : The Institute, [1977]. — [2],ii leaves,44p : ill, map ; 30cm.
'[Proceedings of] ... a meeting ... held at Hurley in November 1976 ...' - Foreword.
Sd : £0.75
(B77-20378)

633.4 — AGRICULTURE. ROOT AND TUBER CROPS
633'.4 — Feedingstuffs: Root crops. Weeds. Control measures: Herbicides. *Manuals*
Agricultural Development and Advisory Service. Chemical weed control in fodder roots, kale and fodder rape, 1977 / Ministry of Agriculture, Fisheries and Food, Agricultural Development and Advisory Service. — Pinner : The Ministry, 1977. — [1],ii,26p ; 22cm. — (Short term leaflet ; 163)
ISBN 0-85521-186-5 Sd : Unpriced
Also classified at 635'.34
(B77-11899)

633'.43'9752 — Carrots. Pests: Willow-carrot aphids. *Great Britain*
Agricultural Development and Advisory Service. Willow-carrot aphid / Ministry of Agriculture, Fisheries and Food, ADAS. — Pinner : The Ministry, 1976. — Folder (6p) : 3 col ill ; 21cm. — (Advisory leaflet ; 603)
Includes a section on parsley.
Unpriced
(B77-25014)

633'.491'50941 — Potatoes. Harvesting. *Great Britain. Manuals*
Potato Marketing Board. Advice on the harvesting and storage of the 1976 crop / Potato Marketing Board. — London (50 Hans Cres., SW1X 0NB) : The Board, [1976]. — Folder([4]p) : 1 ill ; 21cm.
ISBN 0-903623-15-3 Sd : Unpriced
Also classified at 633'.491'6
(B77-00280)

633'.491'6 — Potatoes. Indoor storage. Handling equipment. *Great Britain*
Agricultural Development and Advisory Service. Handling equipment for indoor potato storage / Ministry of Agriculture, Fisheries and Food, Agricultural Development and Advisory Service. — Revised [ed.]. — Pinner : The Ministry, 1977. — [1],15,[1]p : ill, plan ; 21cm. — (Short term leaflet ; 128)
Sd : Unpriced
(B77-17590)

633'.491'6 — Potatoes. Storage. *Great Britain. Manuals*
Potato Marketing Board. Advice on the harvesting and storage of the 1976 crop / Potato Marketing Board. — London (50 Hans Cres., SW1X 0NB) : The Board, [1976]. — Folder([4]p) : 1 ill ; 21cm.
ISBN 0-903623-15-3 Sd : Unpriced
Primary classification 633'.491'50941
(B77-00280)

633'.491'70941 — Potatoes. Varieties. Grading. *Great Britain. Standards*
Potato Marketing Board. Potatoes : a guide to the Potato Marketing Board's minimum standard of grading / containing a damage and disease identification chart. — [London] ([50 Hans Cres., SW1X 0NB]) : [The Board], [1976]. — Folder([4]p) : ill(chiefly col) ; 21x26cm.
ISBN 0-903623-17-x : Unpriced
(B77-02404)

633'.491'9752 — Potatoes. Pests. Aphids. Control measures. *Eastern Scotland. Manuals*
East of Scotland College of Agriculture. Control of aphids on potatoes / the East of Scotland College of Agriculture. — Edinburgh (Edinburgh School of Agriculture, West Mains Rd, Edinburgh EH9 3JG) : Crop Protection Department, The College, 1977. — [1],7p ; 21cm. — (Advisory leaflet ; 102 ISSN 0308-8278)
Sd : Unpriced
(B77-18238)

633'.491'9752 — Potatoes. Virus diseases. Vectors: Aphids. Control measures. *Western Scotland*
West of Scotland Agricultural College. Aphid control on potatoes / the West of Scotland Agricultural College. — [Auchincruive] : [The College], [1977]. — [1],7p ; 21cm. — (Advisory publication ; no.22 ISSN 0309-6734)
Sd : Unpriced
(B77-32703)

633'.491'9954 — Potatoes. Weeds. Control measures: Herbicides. *Manuals*
Agricultural Development and Advisory Service. Chemical weed control in potato, 1977 / Ministry of Agriculture, Fisheries and Food, ADAS. — [Revised ed.]. — Pinner : The Ministry, 1977. — [1],ii,28p ; 22cm. — (Short term leaflet ; 167)
Previous ed.: published as 'Chemical weed control in potato, 1976'. 1975.
ISBN 0-85521-185-7 Sd : Unpriced
(B77-11900)

633.6 — AGRICULTURE. SUGAR AND STARCH PLANTS
633'.63'965182 — Sugar beet. Docking disorder. *England*
Agricultural Development and Advisory Service. Docking disorder of sugar beet / ADAS, Ministry of Agriculture, Fisheries and Food. — Revised [ed.] / by R.A. Dunning and D.A. Cooke, with the help of M.F. Harrod. — Pinner : The Ministry, 1977. — Folder (6p) : 4 ill(2 col) ; 22cm. — (Advisory leaflet ; 582)
Unpriced
(B77-27191)

633'.63'9954 — Sugar beet. Weeds. Control measures: Herbicides. *Manuals*
Agricultural Development and Advisory Service. Chemical weed control in sugar beet, 1977 / [Agricultural Development and Advisory Service]. — Revised [ed.]. — Pinner : Ministry of Agriculture, Fisheries and Food, 1976. — [1],24,[1]p ; 21cm. — (Short term leaflet ; 166)
Previous ed.: 1975.
ISBN 0-85521-204-7 Sd : Unpriced
(B77-12528)

633.7 — AGRICULTURE. ALKALOIDAL CROPS
633'.71'310941 — Gardens. Tobacco. Cultivation from seeds. *Great Britain. Manuals*
Smith, Guy Newman. Tobacco culture : a DIY guide / by Guy N. Smith. — Liss : Spur Publications, 1977. — xi,114p : ill, forms ; 23cm.
ISBN 0-904558-28-2 : £3.30
(B77-20379)

633.8 — AGRICULTURE. PLANTS FOR PERFUMES, FLAVOURINGS, MEDICINAL PURPOSES, ETC
633'.82 — Hop-gardens. Wirework systems. Use. *England. Manuals*
Agricultural Development and Advisory Service. Wirework systems for hop growing / [Agricultural Development and Advisory Service]. — Revised [ed.]. — Pinner : Ministry of Agriculture, Fisheries and Food, 1976. — [1],17,[1]p : ill ; 30cm. — (Short term leaflet ; 58)
ISBN 0-85521-207-1 Sd : Unpriced
(B77-12529)

633'.82 — Hops. Pests. Control measures
Agricultural Development and Advisory Service. Hops, control of pests / Ministry of Agriculture, Fisheries and Food, ADAS ; [written by P. Carden et al.]. — Pinner : The Ministry, 1976. — [2],10,[1]p ; 22cm. — (Short term leaflet ; 193)
ISBN 0-85521-196-2 Sd : Unpriced
(B77-11901)

633'.85 — Oil palms. Cultivation
Hartley, Charles William Stewart. The oil palm (Elaeis guineensis Jacq.) / [by] C.W.S. Hartley. — 2nd ed. — London [etc.] : Longman, 1977. — xviii,806p,[8]p of plates : ill(some col), forms, map ; 23cm. — (Tropical agriculture series)
Previous ed.: 1967. — Index.
ISBN 0-582-46809-4 : £25.00
(B77-24312)

634 — FRUIT. CULTIVATION
634 — Gardens. Fruit. Cultivation
Encyclopedia of vegetable gardening : the complete growing, cooking & freezing guide to vegetables, herbs & fruit / [by A.G. Biggs et al.]. — London : Octopus Books, 1977. — 255p : col ill ; 31cm.
Col. ill. on lining papers. — Index.
ISBN 0-7064-0616-8 : £4.95
Primary classification 635
(B77-31963)

Furner, Brian George. Food crops from your garden or allotment / [by] Brian Furner ; plates from photographs taken by the author. — London [etc.] : Pan Books, 1976. — 192p,[8]p of plates : ill ; 18cm. — (Small garden series)
Bibl.: p.170. — Index.
ISBN 0-330-24785-9 Pbk : £0.60
Primary classification 635
(B77-00281)

Furner, Brian George. Food crops from your garden or allotment / [by] Brian Furner. — London : Hale, 1977. — 192p,[8]p of plates : ill ; 23cm.
Originally published: London : Pan Books, 1976. — Bibl.: p.170. — Index.
ISBN 0-7091-6270-7 : £3.95
Primary classification 635
(B77-22676)

Grow your own : the step-by-step guide to successful vegetable and fruit growing. — [London] : Marshall Cavendish.
Part 1-. — [1977]-. — ill(chiefly col) ; 23cm.
Weekly. — In 52 parts. — [2],28p. in 1st issue.

Sd : £0.30
Also classified at 635
(B77-24313)

Grow your own vegetables, fruit & herbs / [editor Susan Joiner, assistant editor Pamela Hunter]. — London : Phoebus, 1977. — 96p : ill(chiefly col), col maps ; 29cm.
Ill. on lining papers. — Originally published: as 'Grow your own vegetables'. 1976. — Index.
ISBN 0-7026-0030-x : £2.50
Primary classification 635
(B77-09778)

Mossman, Keith. Home grown : a harvest of information about growing, cooking and preserving food from your garden / [by] Keith Mossman and Mary Norwak. — London : Spectator Publications for Stanley Garden Tools Ltd, 1977. — 2-126p : ill(some col) ; 28cm.
Cover title.
ISBN 0-900869-31-3 Pbk : £2.80
Primary classification 635
(B77-24316)

Oldale, Adrienne. Growing fruit / [by] Adrienne & Peter Oldale. — Newton Abbot [etc.] : David and Charles, 1977. — 118p : ill ; 22cm. — (1001 questions answered)
ISBN 0-7153-7144-4 : £3.50
(B77-10422)

Seabrook, Peter. Fruit guide / by Peter Seabrook. — London : British Broadcasting Corporation ; Nottingham : Floraprint Ltd, 1977. — 2-63p : ill(chiefly col) ; 22cm.
Based on 'Dig this!' BBC TV series.
ISBN 0-563-17280-0 Sd : £0.60
ISBN 0-903001-12-8 (Floraprint) : £0.60
(B77-16463)

Smith, Geoffrey. Mr Smith's fruit garden / by Geoffrey Smith ; illustrated by Colin Gray ; edited by Brian Davies. — London : British Broadcasting Corporation, 1977. — 48p : ill ; 21cm.
'Published to accompany the BBC-tv series "Mr Smith's fruit garden" produced by Peter Reding and Brian Davies and first broadcast on BBC-2 on Fridays at 7.05 p.m. 9th September-7th October 1977. Published to accompany a series of programmes prepared in consultation with the BBC Further Education Advisory Council' - title page verso.
ISBN 0-563-16111-6 Sd : £0.60
(B77-14794)

Thrower, Percy. Percy Thrower's how to grow vegetables and fruit. — London [etc.] : Hamlyn, 1977. — 5-125p : ill(some col) ; 31cm.
Col. ill. on lining papers. — Index.
ISBN 0-600-38756-9 : £2.95
Primary classification 635
(B77-18855)

634 — Town gardens. Fruit. Cultivation
Mossman, Keith. The kitchen garden / [by] Keith Mossman. — London : Sphere, 1977. — 156p : ill ; 18cm.
Originally published: 1972. — Bibl.: p.149-150. — Index.
ISBN 0-7221-6252-9 Pbk : £0.65
Primary classification 635
(B77-09782)

Wickers, David. The complete urban farmer : growing your own fruit and vegetables in town / by David Wickers ; with drawings by Sharon Finmark. — [London] : Fontana, 1977. — [8],174p : ill, plan ; 22cm.
Originally published: London : Friedmann, 1976. — Bibl.: p.169-172. — Index.
ISBN 0-00-634472-0 Pbk : £1.50
Primary classification 635
(B77-16946)

634'.04'30913 — Fruit trees. Propagation. *Tropical regions. Manuals*
Garner, Robert John. The propagation of tropical fruit trees / by R.J. Garner, Saeed Ahmed Chaudhri and the staff of the Commonwealth Bureau of Horticulture and Plantation Crops. — [Rome] : Food and Agriculture Organization of the United Nations ; Slough : Commonwealth Agricultural Bureaux, 1976. — xv,566p : ill ; 21cm. — (Horticultural review ; no.4 ISSN 0069-6986)
Bibl.
ISBN 0-85198-351-0 Pbk : £8.00
(B77-04908)

634'.04'6 — Fruit. Quality. *Standards. Collections. Texts with commentaries*
Organisation for Economic Co-operation and Development. International standardisation of fruit and vegetables / [Organisation for Economic Co-operation and Development]. — Paris : O.E.C.D. ; [London] : [H.M.S.O.], 1976. — x p,p651-805(2 fold) : ill(chiefly col), facsims ; 24cm.
Contents: Apples and pears (limited revision) - Tomatoes (revision) - Citrus fruit (limited revision) - Shelling peas - Beans - Carrots.
Sd : £12.00
ISBN 92-64-11578-1
Also classified at 635'.04'6
(B77-12530)

634'.04'70941 — Fruit. Varieties. Trials. *Great Britain. Serials*
National Fruit Trials. Annual report / National Fruit Trials. — Faversham (Brogdale Farm, Faversham, Kent ME13 8XZ) : [National Fruit Trials].
1975 : fourth. — [1976]. — vi,79p,[4]p of plates : col ill ; 21cm.
ISBN 0-85521-205-5 Pbk : Unpriced
(B77-12531)

634'.04'70941 — Gardens. Fruit trees. Varieties. *Great Britain*
Hills, Lawrence Donegan. The fruit finder / by Lawrence D. Hills. — [Braintree] : Henry Doubleday Research Association, 1977. — [2], 33p : map ; 21cm.
Sd : £0.50
(B77-24314)

634'.04'8 — Gardens. Fruit. Organic cultivation
Alth, Max. How to farm your backyard the mulch-organic way / [by] Max Alth. — New York ; London [etc.] : McGraw-Hill, 1977. — xi,272p : ill, maps, ports ; 24cm.
Index.
ISBN 0-07-001128-1 : Unpriced
Primary classification 635'.04'8
(B77-25718)

634'.04'943 — Fruit. Pests: Brown rot fungi
Byrde, Robert Jocelyn Walter. The brown rot fungi of fruit : their biology and control / by R.J.W. Byrde and H.J. Willetts. — Oxford [etc.] : Pergamon, 1977. — xv,171p : ill ; 26cm.

Bibl.: p.145-161. — Index.
ISBN 0-08-019740-x : £6.50
(B77-22674)

634'.04'994 — Fruit. Pests. Control measures: Spraying. *Great Britain. Manuals*
Fruit grower's guide to the use of chemical sprays / Agricultural Development and Advisory Service, Ministry of Agriculture, Fisheries and Food. — [Pinner] : [The Ministry].
1977. — [1976]. — [1],iii,83p : ill ; 21cm.
ISBN 0-85521-180-6 Pbk : Unpriced
(B77-13715)

634'.11'9752 — Apple trees. Parasites: Apple suckers. Control measures
Agricultural Development and Advisory Service. Apple and pear suckers / Ministry of Agriculture, Fisheries and Food, Agricultural Development and Advisory Service. — Revised [ed.] / [revised by G.H.L. Dicker]. — Pinner : The Ministry, 1976. — 7p : 4 ill(2 col) ; 22cm. — (Advisory leaflet ; 96)
Previous ed.: / issued by the Ministry of Agriculture, Fisheries and Food. London : H.M.S.O., 1974.
ISBN 0-85521-201-2 Sd : Unpriced
Also classified at 634'.13'9752
(B77-11902)

634'.13'9752 — Pear trees. Parasites: Pear suckers. Control measures
Agricultural Development and Advisory Service. Apple and pear suckers / Ministry of Agriculture, Fisheries and Food, Agricultural Development and Advisory Service. — Revised [ed.] / [revised by G.H.L. Dicker]. — Pinner : The Ministry, 1976. — 7p : 4 ill(2 col) ; 22cm. — (Advisory leaflet ; 96)
Previous ed.: / issued by the Ministry of Agriculture, Fisheries and Food. London : H.M.S.O., 1974.
ISBN 0-85521-201-2 Sd : Unpriced
Primary classification 634'.11'9752
(B77-11902)

634'.7 — Bush fruit. Weeds. Control measures: Herbicides. *Great Britain. Manuals*
Agricultural Development and Advisory Service. Chemical weed control in bush and cane fruit / ADAS, Ministry of Agriculture, Fisheries and Food. — Revised [ed.]. — Pinner : The Ministry, 1977. — [2],[i],18p ; 21cm. — (Short term leaflet ; 14)
Sd : Unpriced
Also classified at 634'.71
(B77-29516)

634'.7 — Gardens. Soft fruit. Cultivation
Genders, Roy. Growing soft fruit / [by] Roy Genders. — London : Pelham, 1977. — 128p : ill ; 21cm. — (Garden farming series)
Index.
ISBN 0-7207-0951-2 : £3.25
(B77-09095)

634'.71 — Cane fruit. Weeds. Control measures: Herbicides. *Great Britain. Manuals*
Agricultural Development and Advisory Service. Chemical weed control in bush and cane fruit / ADAS, Ministry of Agriculture, Fisheries and Food. — Revised [ed.]. — Pinner : The Ministry, 1977. — [2],[i],18p ; 21cm. — (Short term leaflet ; 14)
Sd : Unpriced
Primary classification 634'.7
(B77-29516)

634'.72'0941 — Bush fruit. Cultivation. *Great Britain. Manuals*
Agricultural Development and Advisory Service. Bush fruits. — [New ed.] / [Agricultural Development and Advisory Service]. — London : H.M.S.O., 1977. — viii,103p,viii p of plates : ill(some col) ; 25cm. — (Great Britain. Ministry of Agriculture, Fisheries and Food. Bulletins ; 4)
Previous ed.: i.e. 8th ed. / prepared by the Ministry of Agriculture, Fisheries and Food. 1965. — Bibl.: p.98-99. — Index.
ISBN 0-11-240527-4 Pbk : £3.00
(B77-22675)

634'.75 — Strawberries. *European Economic Community standards*
Great Britain. ***Ministry of Agriculture, Fisheries and Food.*** EEC standards for fresh strawberries / Ministry of Agriculture, Fisheries and Food [and] Department of Agriculture and Fisheries for Scotland [and] Department of Agriculture for Northern Ireland. — Pinner : The Ministry, 1975. — [3],12p ; 21cm.
ISBN 0-85521-174-1 Sd : Free
(B77-00815)

634'.75 — Strawberries. Red core disease. Control
Montgomerie, Isabel G. Red core disease of strawberry / by Isabel G. Montgomerie. — Slough : Commonwealth Agricultural Bureaux, 1977. — [2],47p ; 25cm. — (Horticultural reviews ; no.5 ISSN 0069-6986)
Bibl.: p.33-47.
ISBN 0-85198-375-8 Sd : £2.00
(B77-15348)

634'.75 — Strawberries. Weeds. Control measures: Herbicides. *Manuals*
Agricultural Development and Advisory Service. Chemical weed control in strawberries / Ministry of Agriculture, Fisheries and Food, ADAS. — Revised [ed.] / [revised by A.G. Jones]. — Pinner : The Ministry, 1977. — [2],i, 24p ; 22cm. — (Short term leaflet ; 23)
ISBN 0-85521-184-9 Sd : Unpriced
(B77-11903)

634'.8'0924 — Vineyards. Grapes. Cultivation. *Cambridgeshire. Wilburton. Personal observations*
Sneesby, Norman. A vineyard in England : the story of the planning, planting and bringing to fruition of an estate of vines on an island in the fens / [by] Norman Sneesby. — London : Hale, 1977. — 223p,[8]p of plates : ill, 2 plans, ports ; 23cm.
Index.
ISBN 0-7091-5943-9 : £4.50
(B77-09776)

634'.8'0941 — Grapes. Cultivation. *Great Britain. Amateurs' manuals. For winemaking*
Turner, Ben. Growing your own wine / [by] Ben Turner. — London : Pelham, 1977. — 96p : ill ; 21cm. — (Garden farming series)
Index.
ISBN 0-7207-0945-8 : £3.25
(B77-09096)

634'.8'0942 — Vineyards. Grapes. Cultivation. *England*
Ordish, George. Vineyards in England and Wales / [by] George Ordish. — London : Faber, 1977. — 186p : map ; 23cm.
Bibl.: p.177-182. — Index.
ISBN 0-571-10928-4 : £6.95 : CIP rev.
(B77-23515)

634'.8'09794 — Vineyards. Grapes. Cultivation. *Study regions: California*
Weaver, Robert J. Grape growing / [by] Robert J. Weaver. — New York ; London [etc.] : Wiley, [1977]. — xii,371p : ill, map ; 24cm.
'A Wiley-Interscience publication'. — Published in the United States: 1976. — Bibl.: p.335-345. — Index.
ISBN 0-471-92324-9 : £11.40
(B77-09777)

634.9 — FORESTRY

634.9'06'141 — Forestry. Organisations. *Great Britain. Forestry Commission. Reports, surveys. Serials*
Forestry Commission. Annual report and accounts of the Forestry Commission for the year ended 31st March, together with the Comptroller and Auditor General's report on the accounts. — London : H.M.S.O.
[1975]-1976 : [56th]. — [1976]. — 94p,leaf,8p of plates : ill(some col), maps, col ports ; 25cm. — ([1976-77 H.C.]1)
Bibl.: p.42.
ISBN 0-10-200177-4 Pbk : £2.00
(B77-06173)

634.9'06'173 — Forestry. Organisations. *United States. Forest Service, to 1975*
Steen, Harold K. The US Forest Service : a history / [by] Harold K. Steen. — Seattle ; London : University of Washington Press, 1976. — xvi,356p,[16]p of plates : ill, map, ports ; 25cm.
Index.
ISBN 0-295-95523-6 : £12.00
(B77-07430)

634.9'07'2041 — Forestry. Research in British institutions. *Reports, surveys. Serials*
Report on forest research for the year ended March / Forestry Commission. — London : H.M.S.O.
[1976]-1977. — 1977. — viii,90p,4p of plates : ill, map ; 25cm.
Bibl. — Index.
ISBN 0-11-710116-8 Pbk : £1.90
ISSN 0436-4120
(B77-33287)

634.9'07'2041 — Forestry. Research organisations. *Great Britain. Commonwealth Forestry Institute. Reports, surveys. Serials*
Commonwealth Forestry Institute. Annual report / the Commonwealth Forestry Institute, University of Oxford. — Oxford ([9 Alfred St., High St., Oxford]) : Holywell Press Ltd.
52nd : 1975-76. — 1976. — 44p ; 21cm.
ISBN 0-85074-017-7 Sd : Unpriced
(B77-07431)

634.9'0973 — Forestry. *United States*
Sharpe, Grant William. Introduction to forestry. — 4th ed. / [by] Grant W. Sharpe, Clare W. Hendee, Shirley W. Allen. — New York ; London [etc.] : McGraw-Hill, 1976. — xiii, 544p : ill, facsim, maps, ports ; 24cm. — (McGraw-Hill series in forest resources)
Previous ed.: published as 'An introduction to American forestry' / by Shirley Walter Allen and Grant William Sharpe. 1960. — Bibl. — Index.
ISBN 0-07-056480-9 : £11.05
(B77-03084)

634.9'5 — Forests. Timber trees. Yields. Improvement. Physiological aspects
Physiological Genetics of Forest Tree Yield *(Conference), Gorebridge, 1975.* Tree physiology and yield improvement : a compendium of papers given at a meeting held near Edinburgh in July 1975 / edited by M.G.R. Cannell and F.T. Last. — London [etc.] : Academic Press, 1976. — xvii,567p : ill ; 24cm.
'... proceedings of a conference on "Physiological Genetics of Forest Tree Yield" held at Middleton Hall Conference Centre, Gorebridge, Scotland, from 13th to 21st July 1975, under the auspices of the International Union of Forest Research Organisations ...' - Preface. — Bibl. — Index.
ISBN 0-12-158750-9 : £15.00
(B77-07432)

634.9'5 — Trees. Planting by local authorities. Organisation. *England. Rural regions*
Countryside Commission. Local authority tree planting programmes in the countryside : a guide to their organisation / prepared by Peter Downing and Dartington Amenity Research Trust for the Countryside Commission. — Cheltenham : The Commission, 1977. — [1], 18p ; 21cm. — (Advisory series ; no.1 ISSN 0140-5357)
Bibl.: p.17-18.
Sd : Unpriced
(B77-32704)

634.9'53 — Trees. Pruning
Brown, George Ernest. The pruning of trees, shrubs and conifers / by George E. Brown. — London : Faber, 1977. — xix,351p,[32]p of plates : ill ; 22cm.
Originally published: 1972. — Index.
ISBN 0-571-11084-3 Pbk : £3.95
Also classified at 635.9'76
(B77-13716)

634.9'56 — Timber trees. Species & provenance. Research. *Tropical regions. Manuals*
Burley, Jeffery. A manual on species and provenance research with particular reference to the tropics / compiled by J. Burley and P.J. Wood ; from contributions by P.G. Adlard ... [et al.]. — [Oxford] ([South Park Rd, Oxford]) : [Commonwealth Forestry Institute], [1976]. — [1],viii,226p : ill, forms ; 30cm. — (Tropical forestry papers ; no.10)
'... rewritten from an original draft which was submitted to the Tenth Commonwealth Forestry Conference ...' - Preface. — Bibl.: p.158-167.
ISBN 0-85074-016-9 Pbk : £4.00
(B77-07955)

634.9'6 — Broad-leaved trees. Diseases of foreign origin. *Great Britain*
Burdekin, David Armstrong. Some important foreign diseases of broadleaved trees / by D.A. Burdekin and D.H. Phillips. — [London] : H.M.S.O., 1977. — 3-11,[1]p : col ill ; 21cm. — (Forest record ; 111)
ISBN 0-11-710181-8 Sd : £0.40
(B77-20380)

634.9'6'180994 — Bushfires. Prevention & control. *Australia*
Foster, Ted. Bushfire : history, prevention, control / [by] Ted Foster. — Sydney [etc.] ; London : A.H. and A.W. Reed, 1976. — 247p : ill, facsims, maps, plans ; 27cm.
Ill. on lining papers. — Bibl.: p.243. — Index.
ISBN 0-589-07177-7 : £15.60
(B77-20381)

634.9'6'4 — Trees. Damage by fungi. Symptoms
Young, Charles William Tone. External signs of decay in trees / [by] C.W.T. Young ; prepared for the Department of the Environment by the Forestry Commission. — [London] : H.M.S.O., 1977. — 8p : col ill ; 21cm. — (Arboricultural leaflet ; 1 ISSN 0309-9318)
ISBN 0-11-751153-6 Sd : £0.40
(B77-18239)

634.9'6'688630941 — Woodlands. Pests: Starlings. Roosts. Dispersal. *Great Britain. Manuals*

Currie, F A. Starling roost dispersal from woodlands / [by] F.A. Currie, D. Elgy, S.J. Petty. — [London] : H.M.S.O., 1977. — 8p : ill(incl 1 col) ; 21cm. — (Forestry Commission. Leaflets ; 69)
Bibl.: p.8.
ISBN 0-11-710218-0 Sd : £0.30
(B77-29517)

634.9'6'69322 — Woodlands. Pests: Rabbits. Control. *Great Britain. Manuals*

Pepper, Harry William. Rabbit management in woodlands / by H.W. Pepper. — [London] : H.M.S.O., 1976. — 16p : ill(incl 1 col) ; 21cm. — (Forestry Commission. Leaflets ; 67)
Bibl.: p.15.
ISBN 0-11-710216-4 Sd : £0.50
(B77-11277)

634.9'7 — Timber trees. *Juvenile literature*

Ellis, Rosemary. Trees for use and delight / [by] Rosemary and Penelope Ellis. — London [etc.] : Bodley Head, 1976. — 48p : ill ; 26cm. — (Outlooks and insights series)
Index.
ISBN 0-370-10860-4 : £2.00
(B77-01595)

634.9'7'09429 — Timber trees. *Wales*

Hyde, Harold Augustus. Welsh timber trees : native and introduced / by H.A. Hyde. — 4th ed. / revised by S.G. Harrison. — Cardiff : National Museum of Wales, 1977. — xi,165p, xxviii p of plates : ill, maps ; 22cm.
Previous ed.: 1961. — Bibl.: p.151-157. — Index.
ISBN 0-7200-0202-8 : £3.00
(B77-16943)

634.9'728'643 — Elm trees. Dutch elm disease. *Great Britain*

Gibbs, John Newton. Dutch elm disease / by J.N. Gibbs, D.A. Burdekin, C.M. Brasier. — [London] : H.M.S.O., 1977. — 12,[1]p : ill(incl 1 col) ; 21cm. — (Forest record ; 115)
'... a revision of Forest Record 94 (The Biology of Dutch Elm Disease) and Leaflet 54 (The Control of Dutch Elm Disease) ...'. — Bibl.: p.11-12.
ISBN 0-11-710237-7 Sd : £0.50
(B77-31274)

634.9'728'643 — Elm trees. Dutch elm disease. Control. Policies of East Sussex (County). Council. *East Sussex. Reports, surveys*

East Sussex *(County). Planning Department.* A report on the East Sussex County Council campaign to control Dutch elm disease / [East Sussex County Planning Department]. — Lewes (47 St Anne's Cres., Lewes, East Sussex) : [The Department], 1977. — 16,[1]p : map ; 30cm.
Cover title: Dutch elm disease control.
Sd : £1.50
(B77-20382)

634.9'75 — Forests. Timber trees: Conifers. Weeds: Heather. Control measures: Herbicides: 2,4-dichlorophenoxyacetic esters. *Great Britain. Manuals*

MacKenzie, John Murdoch. Control of heather by 2,4-D / by J.M. MacKenzie, J.H. Thomson and K.E. Wallis. — [Edinburgh] : H.M.S.O., 1976. — 20p : ill(chiefly col) ; 21cm. — (Forestry Commission. Leaflets ; 64)
Bibl.: p.17.
ISBN 0-11-710213-x Sd : £0.70
(B77-01596)

635 — GARDENING

The **AZ** of gardening / edited by Martin Parsons. — London : Octopus, 1977. — 128p : ill(chiefly col) ; 31cm.
Index.
ISBN 0-7064-0631-1 : £2.50
(B77-27193)

Barratt, Michael, *b.1928.* Michael Barratt's complete gardening guide / with 280 line-drawings by Mary I. French and Maggie Read. — London : Weidenfeld and Nicolson, 1977. — 224p,[24]p of plates : ill(some col) ; 26cm.
Bibl.: p.216. — Index.
ISBN 0-297-77380-1 : £5.25
(B77-26375)

Bradley, John. Gardening encyclopedia / [by] John Bradley. — London : Octopus Books, 1977. — 336p : ill ; 22cm.
Index.
ISBN 0-7064-0634-6 : £1.99
(B77-27194)

Bristow, Alec. The easy garden / [by] Alec Bristow. — London : Mitchell Beazley, 1977. — [6],154p : ill, plan ; 22cm. — ([Home reference library])
Index.
ISBN 0-85533-124-0 : £3.95
(B77-31275)

Davidson, Max. The 'Sunday express' weekend gardening book / by Maxwell Davidson ; cartoons by Bill Martin. — [London] : Beaverbrook Newspapers, 1977. — [5],169p : ill ; 21cm.
Originally published: London : White Lion Publishers, 1976.
ISBN 0-85079-081-6 Pbk : £1.75
(B77-15927)

Gammidge, Ian. Mr Digwell's everyday gardening book / written by Ian Gammidge ; illustrated by Jack Dunkley. — London : Mirror Group Books, 1977. — 160p : ill ; 14x22cm.
Index.
ISBN 0-85939-078-0 Pbk : £0.60
(B77-17591)

Hellyer, Arthur George Lee. Your garden week by week / [by] A.G.L. Hellyer. — 4th ed. — London [etc.] : Hamlyn, 1977. — 303p : ill ; 16cm.
Previous ed.: 1967?. — Index.
ISBN 0-600-39519-7 : £1.95
(B77-31276)

The **practical** gardener's encyclopedia / edited by Alan Gemmell. — London [etc.] : Collins, 1977. — 256p : ill(chiefly col), plans ; 32cm.
Text on lining papers. — Index. — Previous control number ISBN 0-00-435007-3.
£5.95
ISBN 0-00-435007-3
(B77-27195)

The **practical** gardening encyclopedia / edited by Roger Davies ; advisory editor Roy Hay. — London : Ward Lock, 1977. — 352p : ill(chiefly col), plans(some col) ; 27cm.
Index.
ISBN 0-7063-5066-9 : £6.95 : CIP rev.
(B77-21224)

'Reader's digest' complete book of the garden / [consultant editor Roy Hay, revisions editor Lizzie Boyd]. — London [etc.] : Reader's Digest Association, 1977. — 3v.(256p;256p; 255p) : ill(some col) ; 21cm.
In slip case. — '... based on "The 'Reader's Digest' Complete Library of the Garden" (published in 1963) which has been extensively revised and updated' - Acknowledgements. — Indexes.
Pbk : £4.95
(B77-25716)

Smith, Geoffrey. The craft of gardening / [by] Geoffrey Smith. — London : Paul, 1977. — 96p : ill, plans ; 23cm. — (The craftsman's art series)
Index.
ISBN 0-09-128920-3 : £2.95
ISBN 0-09-128921-1 Pbk : £1.75
(B77-25717)

Streeter, Fred. Fred Streeter's gardening year : a month by month guide / [compiled by] Frank Hennig. — London [etc.] : Angus and Robertson, 1977. — 136p : ill ; 21cm.
Index.
ISBN 0-207-95765-7 : £2.95
(B77-30374)

The **Sunday** gardener / edited and with an introduction by Alan Gemmell. — Revised ed. — [London] : Fontana, 1977. — 256p : ill ; 19cm.
Previous ed.: London : Elm Tree Books, 1973. — Index.
ISBN 0-00-634868-8 Pbk : £0.80
(B77-15928)

635 — Gardening. *Juvenile literature*

Kelly, Mary. The Puffin book of gardening / by Mary Kelly ; illustrated by Vera Croxford. — Harmondsworth [etc.] : Puffin Books, 1977. — 96p : ill(some col) ; 20cm.
Also published: London : Kestrel Books, 1977. — Bibl.: p.94. — Index.
ISBN 0-14-030922-5 Pbk : £0.60
(B77-24315)

Simmons, Diana. Gardening is easy : when you know how / [author Diana Simmons] ; [illustrations Marilyn Day]. — London : Marshall Cavendish, 1974. — 48p : col ill ; 32cm. — (A 'Golden hands' book)
ISBN 0-85685-073-x : £0.99
(B77-19468)

635 — Gardening. Use of beneficial plants

Soil Association. Make your plants work for you / [the Soil Association]. — 2nd enlarged and illustrated ed. / research by Joy Griffith-Jones ; illustrations by Dominic Poelsma, Roger Bunce. — Stowmarket (Walnut Tree Manor, Haughley, Stowmarket, Suffolk IP14 3RS) : The Association, 1976. — [2],18p : ill ; 21cm.
Previous ed.: 1975.
ISBN 0-905200-04-7 Sd : £0.30
(B77-01597)

635 — Gardens. Plants. Cultivation. Use of compost

Shewell-Cooper, Wilfred Edward. Compost gardening / [by] W.E. Shewell-Cooper. — Revised ed. — London : Sphere, 1977. — 158p ; 18cm.
This ed. i.e. 2nd ed., originally published: Newton Abbot : David and Charles, 1974. — Index.
ISBN 0-7221-7803-4 Pbk : £0.75
(B77-10423)

635 — Gardens. Vegetables. Cultivation

Bristow, Alec. Grow your own / [by] Alec Bristow. — London : Mitchell Beazley, 1977. — 160p : ill ; 22cm. — ([Home reference library])
Index.
ISBN 0-85533-123-2 : £3.95
(B77-31277)

Conran, Terence. The vegetable book : how to grow and cook your own vegetables / [by] Terence Conran and Maria Kroll ; paintings by Faith Shannon. — Glasgow [etc.] : Collins, 1977. — 96p : ill(some col) ; 28cm.
Originally published: 1976. — Index.
£3.95
ISBN 0-00-435183-5
Also classified at 641.6'5
(B77-23516)

Davidson, Max. Basic vegetable gardening / by Max Davidson. — London [etc.] : Marshall Cavendish, 1977. — 64p : ill(chiefly col) ; 30cm.
Index.
ISBN 0-85685-254-6 : £1.99
(B77-27196)

Encyclopedia of vegetable gardening : the complete growing, cooking & freezing guide to vegetables, herbs & fruit / [by A.G. Biggs et al.]. — London : Octopus Books, 1977. — 255p : col ill ; 31cm.
Col. ill. on lining papers. — Index.
ISBN 0-7064-0616-8 : £4.95
Also classified at 634; 641.6'5; 641.6'4
(B77-31963)

Fordyce, Keith. More kitchen garden / [by] Keith Fordyce & Claire Rayner ; illustrated by Norman Barber. — London (247 Tottenham Court Rd, W1P 0AU) : Independent Television Publications Ltd for Independent Television Books Ltd, 1977. — 64p : ill ; 20cm. — (A 'TV times' book)
'... based on the Thames Television programme "Kitchen Garden" (1977)'. — Index.
ISBN 0-900727-64-0 Pbk : £0.50
Also classified at 641.6'5
(B77-14795)

Furner, Brian George. Food crops from your garden or allotment / [by] Brian Furner ; plates from photographs taken by the author. — London [etc.] : Pan Books, 1976. — 192p,[8]p of plates : ill ; 18cm. — (Small garden series)
Bibl.: p.170. — Index.
ISBN 0-330-24785-9 Pbk : £0.60
Also classified at 634
(B77-00281)

Furner, Brian George. Food crops from your garden or allotment / [by] Brian Furner. — London : Hale, 1977. — 192p,[8]p of plates : ill ; 23cm.
Originally published: London : Pan Books, 1976. — Bibl.: p.170. — Index.
ISBN 0-7091-6270-7 : £3.95
Also classified at 634
(B77-22676)

Grange, Cyril, *b.1900.* The right way to grow fresh vegetables all year round / by Cyril Grange ; with illustrations drawn by Christine Bousfield. — Kingswood : Elliot Right Way Books, 1977. — 240p : ill ; 18cm. — (Paperfronts)
Index.
ISBN 0-7160-0629-4 Pbk : £0.50
(B77-16945)

Grounds, Roger. Growing vegetables and herbs / [by] Roger Grounds. — London : Ward Lock, 1977. — 104p : ill(some col) ; 21cm. — (Concorde books)
Index.
ISBN 0-7063-5361-7 Pbd : £2.75
ISBN 0-7063-5363-3 Pbk : £1.50
(B77-31278)

Grow your own : the step-by-step guide to successful vegetable and fruit growing. — [London] : Marshall Cavendish.
Part 1-. — [1977]-. — ill(chiefly col) ; 23cm.
Weekly. — In 52 parts. — [2],28p. in 1st issue.

Sd : £0.30
Primary classification 634
(B77-24313)

Grow your own vegetables, fruit & herbs / [editor Susan Joiner, assistant editor Pamela Hunter]. — London : Phoebus, 1977. — 96p : ill(chiefly col), col maps ; 29cm.
Ill. on lining papers. — Originally published: as 'Grow your own vegetables'. 1976. — Index.
ISBN 0-7026-0030-x : £2.50
Also classified at 634
(B77-09778)

Hessayon, David Gerald. Vegetable plotter / by D.G. Hessayon. — Waltham Cross : Pan Britannica, 1976. — 36p : ill(chiefly col) ; 24cm.
ISBN 0-903505-06-1 Sd : £0.35
(B77-09779)

Jephcott, C T. Nuttall's vegetable year : home production of vegetables from seed to store / by C.T. Jephcott. — London [etc.] : F. Warne, 1976. — 48p : ill ; 15cm.
ISBN 0-7232-1879-x Sd : £0.25
(B77-01598)

Mossman, Keith. Home grown : a harvest of information about growing, cooking and preserving food from your garden / [by] Keith Mossman and Mary Norwak. — London : Spectator Publications for Stanley Garden Tools Ltd, 1977. — 2-126p : ill(some col) ; 28cm.
Cover title.
ISBN 0-900869-31-3 Pbk : £2.80
Also classified at 634; 641.6'5; 641.6'4
(B77-24316)

Oldale, Adrienne. Growing vegetables : 1001 questions answered / [by] Adrienne and Peter Oldale. — London : Sphere, 1977. — 157p ; 18cm.
Originally published: Newton Abbot : David and Charles, 1976.
ISBN 0-7221-6523-4 Pbk : £0.65
(B77-09780)

Seabrook, Peter. Peter Seabrook's complete vegetable gardener / written by Peter Seabrook ; illustrated by Brian Edwards, Andrew Farmer and Martin Holbrook ... — London : Cassell, 1976. — 128p : ill(chiefly col) ; 30cm.
Col. ill. on lining papers. — Index.
ISBN 0-304-29738-0 : £2.95
(B77-08441)

Shewell-Cooper, Wilfred Edward. Basic book of vegetable growing / [by] W.E. Shewell-Cooper. — 2nd ed. — London : Barrie and Jenkins, 1977. — 144p,[4]leaves of plates : ill(some col) ; 23cm. — (Shewell-Cooper, Wilfred Edward. Basic books of gardening)
Spine title: Dr Shewell-Cooper's basic book of vegetable growing. — This ed. originally published: 1976. — Index.
ISBN 0-214-20300-x : £3.95
(B77-13106)

Thrower, Percy. Percy Thrower's how to grow vegetables and fruit. — London [etc.] : Hamlyn, 1977. — 5-125p : ill(some col) ; 31cm.
Col. ill. on lining papers. — Index.
ISBN 0-600-38756-9 : £2.95
Also classified at 634
(B77-18855)

Wellsted, Tom. Vegetable and herb growing / [by] Tom Wellsted. — London : Sphere, 1977. — 144p : ill ; 18cm.
ISBN 0-7221-8974-5 Pbk : £0.95
Also classified at 635'.7
(B77-09781)

635 — Horticulture

Fundamentals of horticulture. — 4th ed. / [by] J.B. Edmond ... [et al.]. — New York ; London [etc.] : McGraw-Hill, [1976]. — xiii,560p : ill, maps, plans ; 24cm.
This ed. published in the United States: 1975. — Previous ed.: / by J.B. Edmond, T.L. Senn, F.S. Andrews, 1964. — Bibl. — Index.
ISBN 0-07-018985-4 : £11.85
(B77-01599)

635 — Horticulture. Soil conditioners: Lime. Use. *Manuals*

Agricultural Development and Advisory Service. Lime in horticulture / Ministry of Agriculture, Fisheries and Food, ADAS. — Revised [ed.]. — Pinner : The Ministry, 1976. — Folder (6)p ; 22cm. — (Advisory leaflet ; 518)
Previous ed.: / issued by the Ministry of Agriculture, Fisheries and Food. London : H.M.S.O., 1963?.
ISBN 0-85521-195-4 Sd : Unpriced
(B77-11904)

635 — Plants. Cultivation. *Juvenile literature*

Patterson, Allen. Wonder why book of growing plants / [by] Allen Paterson ; illustrated by Elsie Wrigley. — London : Transworld, 1977. — [2],32p : col ill ; 29cm.
Index. — Previous control number ISBN 0-552-57004-4.
ISBN 0-552-98038-2 : £1.35
ISBN 0-552-57004-4 Sd : £0.50
(B77-12532)

635 — Small gardens. Cultivation

Evans, Hazel, *b.1928.* 'Good housekeeping' small space gardening / [by] Hazel Evans ; illustrations by Chris Evans. — Sevenoaks : Coronet, 1977. — 189p : ill ; 18cm.
Originally published: London : Ebury Press, 1974. — Index.
ISBN 0-340-21239-x Pbk : £0.60
(B77-13107)

635 — Town gardens. Vegetables. Cultivation

Mossman, Keith. The kitchen garden / [by] Keith Mossman. — London : Sphere, 1977. — 156p : ill ; 18cm.
Originally published: 1972. — Bibl.: p.149-150. — Index.
ISBN 0-7221-6252-9 Pbk : £0.65
Also classified at 634
(B77-09782)

Wickers, David. The complete urban farmer : growing your own fruit and vegetables in town / by David Wickers ; with drawings by Sharon Finmark. — [London] : Fontana, 1977. — [8],174p : ill, plan ; 22cm.
Originally published: London : Friedmann, 1976. — Bibl.: p.169-172. — Index.
ISBN 0-00-634472-0 Pbk : £1.50
Also classified at 634
(B77-16946)

635 — Vegetables. Cultivation

Antill, David N. Home vegetable production / by David N. Antill. — Wakefield : EP Publishing, 1976. — 72p : ill ; 24cm. — (Invest in living)
ISBN 0-7158-0455-3 Pbk : £1.25
(B77-05502)

Jackson, Allan A. The observer's book of vegetables / [by] Allan A. Jackson. — London : F. Warne, 1977. — 184p,8p of plates : ill(some col) ; 15cm. — (The observer's pocket series ; [67])
Ill. on lining papers. — Bibl.: p.177. — Index.
ISBN 0-7232-1557-x : £1.10
(B77-15929)

635 — Vegetables. Cultivation. Use of fertilisers

Greenwood, Duncan Joseph. Fertiliser requirements of vegetable crops / by D.J. Greenwood, T.J. Cleaver and Mary K. Turner. Maize and its fertilisation / by R. Gervy. — London (93 Albert Embankment, SE1 7TU) : Fertiliser Society, [1974]. — [1],56p : ill, maps ; 22cm. — (Fertiliser Society. Proceedings ; no.145)
'Presented to The Fertiliser Society of London on 19th December, 1974'. — Bibl.
Sd : £4.50
Also classified at 633'.15
(B77-13717)

635'.028 — Electric horticultural equipment. Use. *Manuals*

Electricity Council. Electric growing / [Electricity Council]. — Revised [ed.]. — London : The Council, 1972. — vi,90p : ill, plan ; 21cm.
Previous ed.: 1970.
ISBN 0-85188-055-x Pbk : £0.25
(B77-07433)

635'.04'310973 — Gardens. Vegetables. Cultivation from seeds. *United States*

Barr, Stringfellow. The kitchen garden book : vegetables from seed to table / by Stringfellow Barr and Stella Standard. — Harmondsworth [etc.] : Penguin, 1977. — xi,372p ; 20cm. — (Penguin handbooks)
Originally published: New York : Viking Press, 1956. — Index.
ISBN 0-14-046257-0 Pbk : Unpriced
Primary classification 641.6'5
(B77-27219)

635'.04'44 — Gardening in greenhouses

Fogg, Harry George Witham. The small greenhouse / [by] H.G. Witham Fogg. — Revised ed. — London [etc.] : Pan Books, 1977. — 144p,[12]p of plates : ill(some col) ; 18cm. — (Small garden series)
Previous ed.: i.e. Revised ed. 1972. — Index.
ISBN 0-330-23089-1 Pbk : £0.75
(B77-10424)

Grounds, Roger. How to grow and save with your greenhouse / [by] Roger Grounds. — Revised [ed.]. — London : Ward Lock, 1977. — 63p : col ill ; 21cm.
Previous ed.: published as 'Your greenhouse'. 1975.
Sd : £0.45
ISBN 0-7063-5078-2
(B77-11278)

Menage, Ronald Herbert. Greenhouse gardening / [by] Ronald H. Menage. — Revised ed. — Harmondsworth [etc.] : Penguin, 1977. — 255p : ill ; 20cm. — (Penguin handbooks)
Previous ed.: published as 'Woolman's greenhouse gardening'. London : Hamilton, 1974. — Index.
ISBN 0-14-046241-4 Pbk : £0.90
(B77-11905)

635'.04'44 — Greenhouses. Crops. Cultivation. Use of fertilisers. *Scotland. Manuals*

East of Scotland College of Agriculture. Lime and fertiliser recommendations for glasshouse crops / the Scottish agricultural colleges [i.e. East of Scotland College of Agriculture, North of Scotland College of Agriculture, West of Scotland Agricultural College]. — [Edinburgh] ([c/o Edinburgh School of Agriculture, West Mians Rd, Edinburgh EH9 3JG]) : [Council of the Scottish Agricultural Colleges], 1976. — [1], 15p ; 21cm. — (Scottish agricultural colleges publication ; no.14 ISSN 0308-5708)
Sd : Unpriced
(B77-15930)

635'.04'44 — Greenhouses. Vegetables. Cultivation

Mather, Jim. The easy greenhouse, vegetables / [by] Jim Mather. — London [etc.] : Foulsham, 1977. — 62p : ill ; 22cm.
ISBN 0-572-00967-4 Pbk : £1.00
(B77-18240)

Shepherd, Frederick William. Early garden crops / [by] F.W. Shepherd. — London : Royal Horticultural Society, 1977. — 39p : ill ; 21cm. — (Wisley handbook ; 30)
ISBN 0-900629-87-8 Sd : £0.65
(B77-24317)

635'.04'44 — Growing rooms. Design

Electricity Council. *Farm-electric Centre.* Growing rooms : a guide to the practical design of installations / [Electricity Council, Farm-electric Centre]. — Revised [ed.]. — Kenilworth (National Agricultural Centre, Kenilworth, Warwickshire CV8 2LS) : Electricity Council, Farm-electric Centre, 1975. — ii,77p : ill ; 21cm. — (Grow electric handbook ; no.1)
Previous ed.: 1972.
ISBN 0-85188-052-5 Pbk : £0.75
(B77-03606)

635'.04'44 — Heated greenhouses. Heating systems. *Manuals*

Agricultural Development and Advisory Service. Greenhouse heating systems / Ministry of Agriculture, Fisheries and Food, Agricultural Development and Advisory Service. — [London] : H.M.S.O., 1976. — 10,[1]p : ill ; 26cm. — (Mechanization leaflets ; 27)
ISBN 0-11-240727-7 Sd : £0.18
(B77-14292)

635'.04'44 — Heated greenhouses. Heating systems. Pumps & piping systems. *Manuals*
Agricultural Development and Advisory Service. Pumps and pipework for greenhouse heating systems / Ministry of Agriculture, Fisheries and Food, Agricultural Development and Advisory Service. — Revised [ed.]. — London [etc.] : H.M.S.O., 1976. — 12p : ill(incl 1 col) ; 25cm. — (Mechanization leaflet ; 3)
Previous ed.: i.e. new ed., published as 'Pumps and pipework for heating systems'. 1965.
ISBN 0-11-240703-x Sd : £0.35
(B77-14293)

635'.04'44 — Horticultural greenhouses. Ventilation. *Manuals*
Electricity Council. *Farm-electric Centre.* Ventilation for greenhouses : a guide to the practical design of installations / [Electricity Council, Farm-electric Centre]. — Kenilworth (National Agricultural Centre, Kenilworth, Warwickshire CV8 2LS) : The Centre, 1975. — v,82p : ill(some col), plans ; 21cm. — (Growelectric handbook ; no.3)
ISBN 0-85188-054-1 Pbk : £0.75
(B77-07434)

635'.04'440973 — Gardening in greenhouses. *United States*
Kramer, Jack, *b.1927.* Greenhouse gardening made easy / [by] Jack Kramer. — Toronto [etc.] ; London : Bantam, 1976. — xii,18cm.
Bibl.: p.181-182. — Index.
ISBN 0-552-62960-x Pbk : £0.75
(B77-17592)

635'.04'6 — Electric vegetable storage equipment. Use. *Great Britain. Manuals*
Electricity Council. *Farm-electric Centre.* Vegetable storage : a guide to the practical design of installations / [the Electricity Council, Farm-electric Centre]. — Kenilworth (National Agricultural Centre, Kenilworth, Warwickshire CV8 2LS) : The Centre, 1975. — vii,118p : ill(some col), plans(chiefly col) ; 21cm. — (Farmelectric handbook ; no.23 ISSN 0309-247x)
Originally published: 1974.
Pbk : £0.75
(B77-07435)

635'.04'6 — Vegetables. Quality. *Standards. Collections. Texts with commentaries*
Organisation for Economic Co-operation and Development. International standardisation of fruit and vegetables / [Organisation for Economic Co-operation and Development]. — Paris : O.E.C.D. ; [London] : [H.M.S.O.], 1976. — x p,p651-805(2 fold) : ill(chiefly col), facsims ; 24cm.
Contents: Apples and pears (limited revision) - Tomatoes (revision) - Citrus fruit (limited revision) - Shelling peas - Beans - Carrots.
Sd : £12.00
ISBN 92-64-11578-1
Primary classification 634'.04'6
(B77-12530)

635'.04'70941 — Gardens. Vegetables. Varieties. *Great Britain*
Hills, Lawrence Donegan. The vegetable finder / by Lawrence D. Hills. — [Braintree] : Henry Doubleday Research Association, 1977. — [2], 49p ; 21cm.
Sd : £0.50
(B77-24318)

635'.04'8 — Gardens. Organic cultivation
The **good** food growing guide : gardening and living nature's way / John Bond, editor ... [et al.]. — Newton Abbot [etc.] : David and Charles, 1976. — 144p : ill ; 25cm.
'A Thompson & Morgan, 'Mother Earth' production'. — Bibl.: p.134-136. — Index.
ISBN 0-7153-7174-6 : £3.95
(B77-06749)

Hills, Lawrence Donegan. Organic gardening / [by] Lawrence D. Hills ; illustrated by Christine Robins. — Harmondsworth [etc.] : Penguin, 1977. — 240p : ill ; 20cm. — (Penguin handbooks)
Bibl.: p.234. — Index.
ISBN 0-14-046246-5 Pbk : £0.90
(B77-21225)

635'.04'8 — Gardens. Vegetables. Organic cultivation
Alth, Max. How to farm your backyard the mulch-organic way / [by] Max Alth. — New York ; London [etc.] : McGraw-Hill, 1977. — xi,272p : ill, maps, ports ; 24cm.
Index.
ISBN 0-07-001128-1 : Unpriced
Also classified at 634'.04'8
(B77-25718)

635'.04'8 — Vegetables. Cultivation in containers
Wickers, David. Indoor farming / by David Wickers ; with drawings by Sharon Finmark. — London : Friedmann, 1977. — 202p : ill ; 23cm.
Bibl.: p.193-197. — Index.
ISBN 0-904014-22-3 : £3.95
(B77-21226)

635'.04'85 — Plants. Cultivation. Nutrient film
Cooper, Allen. Nutrient film technique of growing crops / [by] Allen Cooper. — London (49 Doughty St., WC1N 2LP) : Grower Books, 1976. — viii,33p : ill, port ; 21cm.
'First published in "The Grower" 1975' - title page verso.
ISBN 0-901361-19-4 Sd : £0.75
(B77-07956)

635'.04'9 — Gardens. Vegetables. Diseases & pests
Brooks, Audrey. Vegetable pests, diseases and disorders / [by] Audrey Brooks and Andrew Halstead. — London : Royal Horticultural Society, 1977. — 48p : ill ; 21cm. — (Wisley handbook ; 28)
Index.
ISBN 0-900629-86-x Sd : £0.65
(B77-21959)

635'.04'950941 — Gardens. Pesticides. *Great Britain*
British Agrochemicals Association. Directory of garden chemicals / British Agrochemicals Association. — 2nd ed. — London (93 Albert Embankment, SE1 7TU) : The Association, 1977. — 40p ; 21cm.
Previous ed.: 1976.
ISBN 0-905598-01-6 Sd : £0.50
(B77-15931)

635'.04'9752 — Greenhouses. Crops. Pests: Whiteflies. Biological control. Use of parasites: Encarsia formosa. *Western Scotland. Manuals*
West of Scotland Agricultural College. Biocontrol of whitefly / the West of Scotland Agricultural College. — [Auchincruive] : [The College], [1976?]. — [1],7p ; 22cm. — (Advisory publication ; no.7)
Sd : Unpriced
(B77-18241)

635'.06'242823 — Horticultural societies. *South Yorkshire (Metropolitan County). Treeton. Treeton Horticultural Society, to 1977*
Treeton Horticultural Society. 25 years on : Treeton Horticultural Society silver jubilee, 1952-1977 / compiled by Eddie Hinchliffe. — [Rotherham] ([c/o L.E. Hinchliffe, 26 Stag Cres., Broom, Rotherham, S. Yorkshire]) : The Society, 1977. — 111p : ill, facsims, ports ; 30cm.
Sd : Unpriced
(B77-33289)

635'.07'204127 — Horticulture. Research organisations. *Scotland. Tayside Region. Dundee. Scottish Horticultural Research Institute. Reports, surveys. Serials*
Scottish Horticultural Research Institute. Annual report for the year / the Scottish Horticultural Research Institute. — Dundee (Invergowrie, Dundee DD2 5DA) : The Institute.
1975 : 22nd. — 1976. — 111p : ill ; 24cm.
Bibl.: p.105-108.
ISBN 0-905875-00-1 Pbk : £1.25
ISSN 0559-1961
(B77-04276)

635'.07'20422372 — Horticulture. Research organisations. *Kent. East Malling. East Malling Research Station. Reports, surveys. Serials*
East Malling Research Station. Report / East Malling Research Station. — Maidstone (Maidstone, Kent ME19 6BJ) : The Station.
[1975]-1976 : 1st October 1975 to 30th September 1976. — 1977. — 220p : ill ; 25cm.
Bibl. — Index.
Pbk : £2.50
ISSN 0306-6398
(B77-20383)

635'.092'2 — Horticulturists. *Great Britain, to 1977. Biographical dictionaries*
Desmond, Ray. Dictionary of British and Irish botanists and horticulturists : including plant collectors and botanical artists / by Ray Desmond ; with historical introduction by William T. Stearn. — London : Taylor and Francis, 1977. — xxvi,747p ; 26cm.
Bibl.: p.xv-xxiii. — Index.
ISBN 0-85066-089-0 : £40.00
Primary classification 581'.092'2
(B77-28621)

635'.092'4 — Gardening. Thrower, Percy. *Great Britain. Autobiographies*
Thrower, Percy. My lifetime of gardening / [by] Percy Thrower ; with Ronald Webber. — London [etc.] : Hamlyn, [1977]. — 176p : ill(some col), facsim, plan, ports(some col) ; 25cm.
ISBN 0-600-35519-5 : £3.95
(B77-21227)

635'.0973 — Gardens. Plants mentioned in Bible. *United States*
King, Eleanor Anthony. Bible plants for American gardens / by Eleanor Anthony King. — New York : Dover Publications [etc.] ; London : Constable, 1975 [i.e. 1976]. — iii-xii, 204p,leaf of plate,[8]p of plates : ill ; 21cm.
Originally published: New York : Macmillan, 1941. — Index.
ISBN 0-486-23188-7 Pbk : £1.95
Primary classification 220.8'581
(B77-02012)

635'.25'0941 — Onions. Production. *Great Britain. Manuals*
Agricultural Development and Advisory Service. Dry bulb onions : production and marketing of bulb onions for the ware market and for processing, excluding silverskin types / Agricultural Development and Advisory Service, Ministry of Agriculture, Fisheries and Food. — 3rd ed. / [editor P.B. Tatham]. — Pinner : The Ministry, 1975. — iv,67p : ill ; 21cm. — (Horticultural enterprises ; booklet 1)
Bibl.: p.66. — Index.
ISBN 0-85521-209-8 Pbk : Unpriced
(B77-14294)

635'.3 — Crops: Brassica. Pests: Turnip gall weevils. Control. *Great Britain. Manuals*
Agricultural Development and Advisory Service. Turnip gall weevil / ADAS, Ministry of Agriculture, Fisheries and Food. — Revised [ed.]. — Pinner : The Ministry, 1976. — Folder([4]p) : 3 ill(1 col) ; 22cm. — (Advisory leaflet ; 196)
Previous ed.: / issued by the Ministry of Agriculture, Fisheries and Food. London : H.M.S.O., 1963.
Unpriced
(B77-19469)

635'.3 — Crops: Brassica. Weeds. Control measures: Herbicides. *Manuals*
Agricultural Development and Advisory Service. Weed control in horticultural Brassicas / Ministry of Agriculture, Fisheries and Food, ADAS. — Revised [ed.]. — Pinner : The Ministry, 1977. — [1],iii,30,[1]p ; 21cm. — (Short term leaflet ; 72)
Sd : Unpriced
(B77-25015)

635'.34 — Feedingstuffs: Kale & rape. Weeds. Control measures: Herbicides. *Manuals*
Agricultural Development and Advisory Service. Chemical weed control in fodder roots, kale and fodder rape, 1977 / Ministry of Agriculture, Fisheries and Food, Agricultural Development and Advisory Service. — Pinner : The Ministry, 1977. — [1],ii,26p ; 22cm. — (Short term leaflet ; 163)
ISBN 0-85521-186-5 Sd : Unpriced
Primary classification 633'.4
(B77-11899)

635'.63'4 — Cucumbers. Cultivation. Use of straw bales. *Western Scotland*
West of Scotland Agricultural College. Modified straw bale method for cucumbers / the West of Scotland Agricultural College. — [Auchincruive] : [The College], [1977]. — Folder([1],3p) ; 21cm. — (Advisory publications ; no.18 ISSN 0306-7165)
Unpriced
(B77-20384)

635'.642 — Tomatoes. Cultivation in peat. *Western Scotland*
West of Scotland Agricultural College. Peat culture of tomatoes / the West of Scotland Agricultural College. — [Auchincruive] : [The College], [1977?]. — [1],24p ; 21cm. — (Advisory publication ; no.20 ISSN 0306-7165)
Sd : Unpriced
(B77-33290)

635'.655 — Gardens. Soya beans. Cultivation
Whisker, R G. The soybean grow-and-cook book / [by] R.G. Whisker and Pamela Dixon. — London : Duckworth, 1977. — 64p ; 23cm.
ISBN 0-7156-1260-3 : £3.95
ISBN 0-7156-1163-1 Pbk : £1.00
Also classified at 641.6'5'655
(B77-32705)

635'.656 — Peas. Physiology
The **physiology** of the garden pea / edited by J.F. Sutcliffe and J.S. Pate. — London [etc.] : Academic Press, 1977. — xii,500p : ill ; 24cm. — (Experimental botany ; vol.12)
Bibl. — Index.
ISBN 0-12-677550-8 : £18.50
(B77-29518)

635'.7 — Gardens. Herbs. Cultivation
Back, Philippa. Profitable herbs / [by] Philippa Back ; illustrated by Linda Diggins. — London : Darton, Longman and Todd, 1977. — 94p,[4]p of plates : ill(some col) ; 18cm. — (Herbwise ; 2)
Bibl.: p.94.
ISBN 0-232-51345-7 Pbk : £0.95
(B77-09097)

Wellsted, Tom. Vegetable and herb growing / [by] Tom Wellsted. — London : Sphere, 1977. — 144p : ill ; 18cm.
ISBN 0-7221-8974-5 Pbk : £0.95
Primary classification 635
(B77-09781)

635.9 — GARDENING. FLOWERS AND ORNAMENTAL PLANTS

635.9'022'2 — Gardens. Flowering plants. *Colouring books*
Flowers colour copy book. — Maidenhead : Purnell, 1977. — [20]p : of ill(some col) ; 28cm.
Sd : £0.15
(B77-09098)

635.9'02'4745 — Gardens. Flowering plants. *For flower arrangement*
Macqueen, Sheila. Flower arranging from your garden / [by] Sheila Macqueen. — London : Ward Lock, 1977. — 159p : ill(some col) ; 27cm.
'A Hyperion book'. — Index.
ISBN 0-7063-5303-x : £4.95
(B77-22677)

635.9'09 — Gardens. Plants, to 1975
Fogg, Harry George Witham. History of popular garden plants from A to Z / [by] H.G. Witham Fogg. — London : Kaye and Ward [etc.], 1976. — [7],153p : ill ; 23cm.
Bibl.: p.153.
ISBN 0-7182-1140-5 : £3.50
(B77-09783)

635.9'097 — Gardens. Plants. *North America. Lists*
Bailey, Liberty Hyde. Hortus third : a concise dictionary of plants cultivated in the United States and Canada / initially compiled by Liberty Hyde Bailey and Ethel Zoe Bailey. — [New ed.] / revised and expanded by the staff of the Liberty Hyde Bailey Hortorium. — New York : Macmillan ; London : Collier Macmillan, 1976. — xv,1290p : ill, map(on lining papers) ; 29cm.
Previous ed.: published as 'Hortus second'. New York : Macmillan, 1941.
Unpriced
(B77-33884)

635.9'0994 — Gardens. Plants. *Australia*
Maloney, Betty. More about bush gardens / by Betty Maloney and Jean Walker ; edited by Barbara Mullins. — Sydney [etc.] ; London : A.H. and A.W. Reed, 1975. — 124p : ill ; 20cm.
Originally published: Sydney : Horwitz, 1967. — Index.
ISBN 0-589-07174-2 Pbk : Unpriced
(B77-30375)

635.9'31 — Gardens. Annual flowering plants. Cultivation
Robbins, Ann Roe. How to grow annuals / [by] Ann Roe Robbins ; illustrated by L.J. Robbins. — Revised ed. — New York : Dover Publications [etc.] ; London : Constable, 1977. — [1],ix,297p : ill, 2 maps ; 22cm.
Previous ed.: New York : Macmillan, 1949. — Index.
ISBN 0-486-23272-7 Pbk : £2.50
(B77-32706)

635.9'31 — Gardens. Annual flowering plants. Cultivation from seeds
Genders, Roy. Annuals from seed / by Roy Genders. — Large print ed. — Litton : Magna Print Books, 1974. — 231p ; 20cm.
Originally published: London : Foyle, 1956.
ISBN 0-86009-021-3 : Unpriced
(B77-18856)

635.9'32 — Gardens. Island flower beds. Hardy perennial plants. Cultivation
Bloom, Alan. Perennials in island beds : a selection of the best hardy plants / [by] Alan Bloom. — London : Faber, 1977. — 3-94p,[16] p of plates : ill ; 21cm.
Index.
ISBN 0-571-10892-x : £3.95 : CIP rev.
(B77-08442)

635.9'32'024745 — Gardens. Perennial flowering plants. Cultivation. *For flower arrangement*
Jeffreys, John. Perennials for cutting / [by] John Jeffreys ; with line drawings by Yvonne Skargon. — London : Faber, 1977. — 224p : ill ; 21cm.
Index.
ISBN 0-571-10916-0 : £4.95 : CIP rev.
(B77-07436)

635.9'33'111 — Gardens. Clematis
Lloyd, Christopher, *b.1921.* Clematis / [by] Christopher Lloyd ; illustrated by Marjorie Blamey. — London : Collins, 1977. — 280p, 16p of plates : ill(chiefly col) ; 23cm.
Index.
ISBN 0-00-219588-7 : £4.95
(B77-14796)

635.9'33'15 — Gardens. Carnations. *Yearbooks*
Carnation year book / [British National Carnation Society]. — Hassocks (Roman Ridge, Brighton Rd, Hassocks, Sussex) : The Society.
1977 / edited by H.E. Palmer. — [1977]. — 64p : ill, port ; 22cm.
Sd : Unpriced
ISSN 0069-0627
(B77-25016)

635.9'33'216 — Gardens. Pelargoniums
Key, Hazel. Pelargoniums / [by] Hazel Key. — London : Royal Horticultural Society, 1974. — 31p : ill ; 21cm. — (Wisley handbook ; 18)
ISBN 0-900629-65-7 Sd : £0.40
(B77-19470)

635.9'33'322 — Gardens. Sweet peas. Cultivation
Jones, Bernard Rees. The complete guide to sweet peas / [by] Bernard Jones ; with a foreword by Kenneth Colledge. — Revised ed. — London : Gifford, 1975. — 192p,[24]p of plates : ill(some col) ; 23cm.
Previous ed.: 1965. — Index.
£3.50
(B77-15932)

635.9'33'37206241 — Gardens. Roses. Organisations. *Great Britain. Royal National Rose Society. Yearbooks*
The **rose** annual / [Royal National Rose Society]. — St Albans (Bone Hill, Chiswell Green La., St Albans, Herts.) : The Society.
1977 : international conference ed. / edited by Ken Lemmon. — 1977. — 196p,[32]p of plates : ill(some col), ports ; 21cm.
ISBN 0-901558-08-7 Pbk : Unpriced
(B77-15349)

635.9'33'3720941 — Roses. Cultivation. *Great Britain, 1800-1837*
Beales, Peter. Georgian and Regency roses / with text by Peter Beales and photographs by Keith Money. — Norwich : Jarrold and Son, 1977. — [33]p : col ill ; 20cm. — (A Jarrold book of roses ; no.1)
ISBN 0-85306-737-6 Sd : £0.45
(B77-31279)

635.9'33'3720941 — Roses. Cultivation. *Great Britain, 1837-1870*
Beales, Peter. Early Victorian roses / with text by Peter Beales and photographs by Keith Money. — Norwich : Jarrold and Son, 1977. — [33]p : col ill ; 20cm. — (A Jarrold book of roses ; no.2)
ISBN 0-85306-738-4 Sd : £0.45
(B77-31280)

635.9'33'44 — Gardens. Fuchsias. Organisations. *Great Britain. British Fuchsia Society. Yearbooks*
The **fuchsia** annual : the official publication of the British Fuchsia Society. — [Brookwood] ([c/o The Secretary, The Bungalow, Brookwood Military Cemetery, Brookwood, Surrey GU24 0BL]) : The Society.
1977 : thirty-ninth year / editor Susan Travis-Powell. — 1977. — 96p : ill ; 24cm.
Sd : Unpriced
(B77-17593)

635.9'33'46 — Indoor plants: Begonias
Kramer, Jack, *b.1927.* Begonias as house plants / [by] Jack Kramer ; drawings by Andrew Roy Addkison. — New York ; London [etc.] : Van Nostrand Reinhold, [1977]. — 128p : ill ; 21cm.
Originally published: as 'Begonias, indoors and out'. New York : Dutton, 1967. — Bibl.: p.22. — Index.
ISBN 0-442-24517-3 Pbk : £2.80
(B77-11906)

635.9'33'47 — Indoor plants. Cacti. *Manuals*
Cutak, Ladislaus. Cactus guide / [by] Ladislaus Cutak. — New York ; London [etc.] : Van Nostrand Reinhold, 1976 [i.e. 1977]. — vii, 144p : ill ; 21cm.
Originally published: Princeton, N.J. : Van Nostrand ; London : Macmillan, 1956. — Bibl.: p.129-134. — Index.
ISBN 0-442-21819-2 Pbk : £2.95
(B77-12533)

635.9'33'55 — Chrysanthemums. Pests: Chrysanthemum leaf miners
Agricultural Development and Advisory Service. Chrysanthemum leaf miner / ADAS, Ministry of Agriculture, Fisheries and Food. — Revised [ed.] / by N.W. Hussey. — Pinner : The Ministry, 1977. — Folder([4]p) : 2 col ill ; 22cm. — (Advisory leaflet ; 550)
Unpriced
(B77-27197)

635.9'33'55 — Gardens. Chrysanthemums. *Yearbooks*
The **chrysanthemum** year book / [National Chrysanthemum Society]. — London (65 St Margaret's Ave., N20 9HT) : The Society.
1977 / edited by Stanley Gosling, assistant editor Harry Randall. — [1977]. — 119,[1]p : ill(some col), port ; 22cm.
Pbk : Unpriced
(B77-20385)

635.9'33'55 — Gardens. Dahlias. Organisations. *Great Britain. National Dahlia Society. Yearbooks*
The **dahlia** annual / [National Dahlia Society]. — Leamington Spa (26 Burns Rd, Lillington, Leamington Spa, Warwickshire) : National Dahlia Society.
1977 / editor ... Philip Damp, deputy editors L.F. White, E.K. Pitt. — [1977]. — 92,iv p : ill(some col), ports ; 22cm.
Pbk : £2.00(free to members)
(B77-20386)

635.9'33'55 — Greenhouses. Chrysanthemums. Pests. Control. *Manuals*
Agricultural Development and Advisory Service. Chrysanthemum pests under glass and their control / [Agricultural Development and Advisory Service]. — Revised [ed.] / by H.J. Gould and M. Brock. — Pinner : ADAS, 1976. — [2],13p ; 22cm. — (Short term leaflet ; 122)
Previous ed.: 1971.
Sd : Unpriced
(B77-09784)

635.9'33'62 — Gardens. Rhododendrons. *Yearbooks*
Rhododendrons : with magnolias and camellias / [Royal Horticultural Society]. — London : The Society.
1974 / [editors Elspeth Napier, James Platt]. — 1974. — 127p : ill, map ; 22cm.
Index.
ISBN 0-900629-68-1 Sd : £0.25
(B77-04909)

1975 / [editors Elspeth Napier, James Platt, honorary assistant editor E.W.M. Magor]. — 1975. — 115p : ill, map, port ; 22cm.
Index.
ISBN 0-900629-75-4 Sd : £1.25
(B77-04910)

635.9'33'672 — Gardens. Rock plants: Asiatic primulas. *Great Britain. Lists*
Green, Roy. Asiatic primulas : a gardeners' guide / by Roy Green. — Woking (Lye End Link, St John's, Woking, Surrey) : Alpine Garden Society, 1976. — viii,163p,[24]p of plates : ill ; 23cm.
Index.
ISBN 0-900048-21-2 : £3.00
(B77-07437)

635.9'34'15 — Gardens. Hybrid orchids. *Lists*
Messrs David Sander's Orchids Ltd. Sander's list of orchid hybrids. — London : The Society.
Addendum 1971-1975 : containing the names and parentage of all orchid hybrids registered from 1st January 1971 to 31st December 1975 / compiled and listed in tabular alphabetical form by the Royal Horticultural Society as International Authority for the Registration of Orchid Hybrids. — [1977]. — lxvii,460p ; 25cm.
'... the Society has agreed to publish, from time to time, a list of all registrations accepted after December 31st, 1960. In order to maintain continuity, the title "Sander's List of Orchid Hybrids" is retained' - Introduction.
ISBN 0-900629-85-1 : Unpriced
(B77-27925)

635.9'34'15012 — Cultivated orchids. Genera. Names
Gilmour, J S L. Handbook on orchid nomenclature and registration. — 2nd ed. / prepared by the Handbook Committee, J.S.L. Gilmour, J. Greatwood, P.F. Hunt ; at the authorization of the International Orchid Commission. — London (Royal Horticultural Society, Vincent Sq., SW1P 2PE) : The Commission, 1976. — x,149p ; 23cm.
Previous ed.: 1969. — Bibl.: p.88-89. — Index.
ISBN 0-900629-81-9 Pbk : £2.25
(B77-29519)

635.9'34'22 — Indoor plants: Bromeliads
Kramer, Jack, *b.1927.* Bromeliads : the colourful house plants / [by] Jack Kramer ; drawings and photographs, Andrew R. Addkison. — New York ; London [etc.] : Van Nostrand Reinhold, 1976[i.e.1977]. — x,113p : ill ; 21cm.
Originally published: Princeton, N.J. : D. Van Nostrand, 1965. — Index.
ISBN 0-442-24518-1 Pbk : £2.80
(B77-11907)

635.9'34'24 — Gardens. Gladioli
Park, R. A handbook of the world's gladioli / compiled by R. Park ; foreword by Anthony Hamilton. — Shepperton (65 Gaston Way, Shepperton, Middx TW17 8EZ) : De Be Miniglads, 1976. — 48p : ill, ports ; 21cm.
'Issued to commemorate the Golden Jubilee of The British Gladiolus Society'.
ISBN 0-9505246-0-3 Sd : £0.75
(B77-11908)

635.9'34'2405 — Gardens. Irises. *Serials*
The **iris** year book / British Iris Society. — [Wokingham] ([c/o Miss M.C.O. Fowler, 53 Barkham Rd, Wokingham, Berks. RG11 2RG]) : The Society.
1976. — 1976. — 136p,leaf of plate,[8]p of plates : ill ; 21cm.
Index.
ISBN 0-901483-16-8 Pbk : £2.50
(B77-09099)

635.9'34'25 — Crops: Narcissi. Pests. Control measures: Hot water treatment. *Great Britain. Manuals*
Agricultural Development and Advisory Service. Hot water treatment of narcissus bulbs / Ministry of Agriculture, Fisheries and Food, ADAS. — Revised [ed.] / [revised by A.A. Tompsett and J.S. Robertson ; edited by L.W. Wallis]. — Pinner : The Ministry, 1977. — [1], i,20,[1]p : ill ; 21cm. — (Short term leaflet ; 21)
Sd : Unpriced
(B77-25017)

635.9'34'25 — Crops: Narcissi. Pests: Stem eelworms. *Great Britain*
Agricultural Development and Advisory Service. Stem eelworm on narcissus / Ministry of Agriculture, Fisheries and Food, ADAS. — Revised [ed.] / [revised with the help of G. Murdoch]. — Pinner : The Ministry, 1976. — 8p : 4 ill(incl 3 col) ; 22cm. — (Advisory leaflet ; 460)
Previous ed.: 1974. — Previous control number ISBN 0-85521-082-6.
Sd : Unpriced
ISBN 0-85521-082-6
(B77-11909)

635.9'34'25 — Gardens. Daffodils. *Yearbooks*
Daffodils : an annual for amateurs & specialists / Royal Horticultural Society. — London : The Society.
1977. — 1977. — 73p : ill(incl 1 col) ; 23cm.
'Newly registered daffodil names'. Folder ([4]p.) as insert. — Index.
ISBN 0-900629-89-4 Sd : £1.50
(B77-29520)

635.9'34'324 — Tulips. Cultivation. *Western Europe, to 1976*
Blunt, Wilfrid. Tulips & tulipomania / by Wilfrid Blunt. — Fully revised ed. / with sixteen plates from paintings by Rory McEwen. — London ([32 Englands La., N.W.3]) : Basilisk Press, 1977. — 100p : ill(some col), facsim, port ; 30cm.
Limited ed. of 515 signed copies, of which 500 are for sale and numbered, the remainder being lettered. — Quarter leather. — Col. ill. tipped in. — Accompanied by 8 sheets (col. ill.;59x52cm) all in box (62cm). — Previous ed.: published as 'Tulipomania'. Harmondsworth : Penguin, 1950. — Bibl.: p.95-96. — Index.
£314.60
Also classified at 759.9411
(B77-25018)

635.9'42 — Gardens. Flowering plants. Cultivation from seeds
Prucha, Jaroslav. Flowers from seed / by Jaroslav Prucha ; illustrated by František Severa ; [translated from the Czech by O. Kuthanová]. — London [etc.] : Hamlyn, 1976. — 252p : ill(chiefly col) ; 18cm. — (A concise guide in colour)
Index.
ISBN 0-600-33580-1 : £1.25
(B77-00816)

635.9'44 — Gardens. Flowering bulbs
Miles, Bebe. The complete guide to bulbs / [by] Bebe Miles ; illustrations by Judy Singer. — London : Octopus Books, 1977. — 208p : ill(chiefly col) ; 29cm.
Ill. on lining papers. — Originally published: as 'Bulbs for the home gardener'. New York : Grosset and Dunlap, 1976. — Index.
ISBN 0-7064-0556-0 : £4.95
(B77-30376)

635.9'53 — Gardens. Summer flowering plants
Summer flowers / edited by Anthony du Gard Pasley. — London : Allen Lane, 1977. — vii, 103p : ill(chiefly col) ; 22cm.
ISBN 0-7139-1006-2 : £2.50
(B77-11279)

635.9'54 — Plants. Cultivation. Use of artificial light
Kranz, Frederick H. Gardening indoors under lights / [by] Frederick H. Kranz and Jacqueline L. Kranz ; foreword by R.J. Downs. — New revised ed. — Harmondsworth [etc.] : Penguin, 1976. — xii,242p,[16]p : ill ; 20cm. — (Penguin handbooks)
This ed. originally published: New York : Viking Press, 1971. — Bibl.: p.232-233. — Index.
ISBN 0-14-046258-9 Pbk : Unpriced
(B77-00282)

635.9'54 — Plants. Cultivation. Use of artificial light. *Research reports*
Canham, Allan Ernest. Supplementary artificial light for plant production / by A.E. Canham. — Stoneleigh, Warwickshire (Farm Electric Centre, Stoneleigh, Warwickshire CV8 2LS) : Electricity Council, 1974. — [2],23leaves,[6] leaves of plates : ill ; 30cm. — (Electricity Council. Research ; 838)
Cover title. — Bibl.: leaf 20.
Sp : Unpriced
(B77-05503)

635.9'55 — Gardens. Succulents. Cultivation
Glass, Charles. Cacti and succulents for the amateur / [by] Charles Glass and Robert Foster. — Poole : Blandford Press, 1977. — 80p : ill ; 26cm.
Also published: New York : Van Nostrand Reinhold, 1977. — Index.
ISBN 0-7137-0834-4 Pbk : £1.95
(B77-15933)

635.9'55 — Gardens with alkaline soils. Plants. Cultivation
Dyson, Ronald. Gardening on chalk and lime / [by] Ronald Dyson. — London : Dent, 1977. — 256p,[4]p of plates : ill(some col), map ; 24cm.
Bibl.: p.240. — Index.
ISBN 0-460-04267-x : £7.95 : CIP rev.
(B77-04911)

635.9'55 — Succulents. Cultivation
Martin, Margaret Joan. Succulents and their cultivation / [by] Margaret J. Martin and Peter R. Chapman. — London : Faber, 1977. — 5-300p,[16]p of plates : ill(some col), map ; 23cm.
Bibl.: p.284. — Index.
ISBN 0-571-10221-2 : £9.50 : CIP rev.
(B77-25719)

635.9'64 — Gardens. Ground cover plants
Van Der Spuy, Una. Gardening with ground covers : ground covers of the world for gardens in the Southern Hemisphere and other temperate regions / [by] Una Van Der Spuy. — Wellington [N.Z.] ; London [etc.] : A.H. and A.W. Reed, 1976. — 112p : col ill ; 29cm.
Index.
ISBN 0-589-00967-2 : £9.10
(B77-24319)

635.9'64 — Sports grounds. Grass playing areas. Construction & maintenance. *Manuals*
Dawson, Robert Brian. Dawson's practical lawncraft. — 7th ed. / revised by R. Hawthorn. — London : Crosby Lockwood Staples, 1977. — ix,313p : ill, map ; 24cm.
Previous ed.: published as 'Practical lawn craft and management of sports turf'. 1969. — Bibl.: p.289. — Index.
ISBN 0-258-97029-4 : £8.00
(B77-08443)

635.9'64'0973 — Gardens. Lawns. Cultivation. *United States. Amateurs' manuals*
Schery, Robert Walter. Lawn keeping / [by] Robert W. Schery. — Englewood Cliffs ; London [etc.] : Prentice-Hall, 1976. — viii, 232p : ill, maps ; 24cm.
'A Spectrum book'. — Index.
ISBN 0-13-526889-3 : £9.45
ISBN 0-13-526863-x Pbk : £4.35
(B77-01600)

635.9'65 — Indoor plants
Blashfield, Jean F. Apartment greenery : growing plants in unpromising places / [by] Jean F. Blashfield ; illustrations by Mary Purcell. — Large print ed. — London : Prior [etc.], 1977. — [2],384p : ill ; 24cm.
Originally published: Boston, Mass. : Little, Brown, 1975. — Index.
ISBN 0-86043-051-0 : £4.95
(B77-12534)

Rapp, Lynn. Easy indoor plants / [by] Lynn and Joel Rapp ; illustrated by Marvin Rubin. — Revised ed. — Harmondsworth [etc.] : Penguin, 1977. — 110p : ill ; 20cm. — (Penguin handbooks)
Previous ed.: published as 'Mother Earth's hassle-free indoor plant book'. Los Angeles : J.P. Tarcher, 1973. — Index.
ISBN 0-14-046235-x Pbk : £0.70
(B77-17594)

Seddon, George. Your indoor garden : the comprehensive guide to living with plants / [by] George Seddon. — London : Mitchell Beazley, 1976. — 208p : ill(chiefly col), facsim ; 29cm. — (The joy of living library)
Index.
ISBN 0-85533-094-5 : £7.95
ISBN 0-85533-090-2 Pbk : £4.95
(B77-07957)

Stevenson, Violet. Flower arranging & house-plants / [by] Violet Stevenson. — London : Sphere, 1975. — 160p : ill(chiefly col) ; 22cm. — ('Good housekeeping' family library)
Originally published: London : Ebury Press, 1973. — Index.
ISBN 0-7221-3949-7 Pbk : £0.95
Primary classification 745.92
(B77-19533)

635.9'65 — Indoor plants. *Identification manuals*
Hessayon, David Gerald. Be your own house plant spotter / by D.G. & J.P. Hessayon. — Waltham Cross : Pan Britannica, 1977. — 36p : chiefly col ill ; 24cm.
Index.
ISBN 0-903505-07-x Sd : £0.35
(B77-12535)

635.9'65 — Indoor plants. Cultivation
The **A-Z** of house plants / [editor Susan Joiner ; assistant editors Pamela Hunter, Sarie Forster ; translated from the German by Hugh Young]. — London [etc.] : Hamlyn, 1977. — 160p : col ill ; 29cm.
Ill. on lining papers. — Translation of: 'Der Zimmergärtner'. Hamburg : s.n., 1976.
ISBN 0-600-34529-7 : £3.95
(B77-31281)

Bonar, Ann. The guide to houseplants / [by] Ann Bonar. — [London] ([59 Grosvenor St., W.1]) : [Sundial Books Ltd], [1977]. — 4-157p : col ill ; 29cm.
Spine title: The St Michael guide to houseplants. — Index.
ISBN 0-904230-36-8 : £1.99
(B77-32707)

Collins book of house plants / edited by Leslie Johns ; [translated from the Italian by Caroline Bidwell]. — Glasgow [etc.] : Collins, 1977. — [1],125p : col ill ; 28cm.
Translation of: 'Angolo verde'. Milan : Fratelli Fabbri Edition, 1974. — Index.
ISBN 0-00-435401-x : £3.25
ISBN 0-00-435402-8 Pbk : £1.95
(B77-27198)

Herwig, Rob. House plants in colour / [by] Rob Herwig. — Newton Abbot [etc.] : David and Charles, 1977. — 192p : col ill ; 25cm.
Index.
ISBN 0-7153-7464-8 : £3.95
(B77-31965)

Indoor gardening. — London [etc.] : Reader's Digest Association, 1977. — [1],48p : ill ; 27cm. — ('Reader's digest' basic guides)
'The text and illustrations ... are taken from "'Reader's digest' illustrated guide to gardening" [London : Reader's Digest Association, 1975]'. — Index.
ISBN 0-276-00159-1 Sd : £0.75
(B77-27199)

Oplt, Jaroslaw. Decorative house plants / by Jaroslaw Oplt ; illustrated by Jiřina Kaplická ; [translated from the Czech by Olga Kuthanová]. — London [etc.] : Hamlyn, 1976. — 231p : ill(chiefly col) ; 17cm. — (A concise guide in colour)
Index.
ISBN 0-600-34481-9 : £1.25
(B77-00283)

Ward, Brian. Indoor plants / [by] Brian Ward and Tom Wellsted. — London : Macdonald Educational, 1977. — 96p : ill(some col) ; 21cm. — (Macdonald guidelines)
Bibl.: p.91-92. — Index.
ISBN 0-356-06017-9 Pbk : £1.00
(B77-31966)

635.9'65 — Indoor plants. Cultivation. *Juvenile literature*
Griffin-King, June. Indoor gardening / by J. Griffin-King ; with illustrations by B.H. Robinson. — Loughborough : Ladybird Books, 1977. — 52p ; ol ill ; 18cm. — (Learnabout)
Text, ill. on lining papers. — Originally published: Loughborough : Wills and Hepworth, 1969. — Index.
£0.24
ISBN 0-7214-0232-1
(B77-33885)

635.9'65 — Indoor plants. Propagation
Crayson, Suzanne. Plants from plants : how to grow new houseplants for next to nothing / by Suzanne Crayson ; illustrated by the author. — London : Thames and Hudson, 1976. — vii, 120p : ill ; 28cm.
Also published: as 'Parents in pots : new houseplants for next to nothing'. Philadelphia : Lippincott, 1976. — Bibl.: p.116. — Index.
ISBN 0-500-27091-0 Pbk : £2.95
(B77-00284)

Nehrling, Arno. Propagating house plants / [by] Arno and Irene Nehrling ; drawings by Charlotte E. Bowden. — Toronto [etc.] ; London : Bantam, 1976 [i.e. 1977]. — xii,307, [1]p : ill ; 18cm.
Originally published: New York : Hearthside Press, 1962. — Index.
ISBN 0-553-02903-7 Pbk : £0.75
(B77-09785)

635.9'65 — Pot plants. Cultivation from pips, seeds & stones
Mossman, Keith. The pip book / [by] Keith Mossman ; line drawings by Marion Bagshawe. — Harmondsworth [etc.] : Penguin, 1977. — viii,118p : ill ; 20cm. — (Penguin handbooks)
Originally published: London : Witherby, 1973. — Index.
ISBN 0-14-046255-4 Pbk : £0.70
(B77-33886)

635.9'65 — Window boxes. Plants. Cultivation
Hieke, Karel. Window-box, balcony and patio gardening / by Karel Hieke ; illustrated by Jiřina Kaplická ; [translated from the Czech by Olga Kuthanová]. — London [etc.] : Hamlyn, 1976. — 248p : ill(chiefly col) ; 18cm. — (A concise guide in colour)
Index.
ISBN 0-600-31366-2 : £1.25
Primary classification 635.9'671
(B77-20387)

635.9'67 — Miniature gardens. *Manuals*
Ashberry, Anne. Miniature gardens / [by] Anne Ashberry ; illustrated by Creina Glegg. — Newton Abbot [etc.] : David and Charles, 1977. — 135p : ill, plans ; 23cm.
'Some of the material in this book has been revised from my earlier books ...' - half-title page verso.
ISBN 0-7153-7289-0 : £3.95
(B77-18857)

635.9'671 — Balconies & patios. Plants. Cultivation
Hieke, Karel. Window-box, balcony and patio gardening / by Karel Hieke ; illustrated by Jiřina Kaplická ; [translated from the Czech by Olga Kuthanová]. — London [etc.] : Hamlyn, 1976. — 248p : ill(chiefly col) ; 18cm. — (A concise guide in colour)
Index.
ISBN 0-600-31366-2 : £1.25
Also classified at 635.9'65
(B77-20387)

635.9'671 — Garden features: Patios & terraces. Plants. Cultivation
Nightingale, Gay. ABC of patio and terrace gardening / [by] Gay Nightingale. — London [etc.] : J. Bartholomew, 1977. — 5-89p : ill(chiefly col) ; 26cm.
Index.
ISBN 0-7028-1093-2 : £3.95
(B77-23517)

635.9'672'06241 — Gardens. Rock plants. Organisations. *Great Britain. Alpine Garden Society. Yearbooks*
Alpine Garden Society. Year book / Alpine Garden Society. — Woking (Lye End Link, St John's, Woking, Surrey) : The Society.
1977. — 1977. — 51p ; 21cm.
ISBN 0-900048-22-0 Sd : £0.50(free to members)
(B77-06750)

635.9'672'0941 — Rock gardens. Plants. Cultivation. *Great Britain*
Farrer, Reginald. My rock garden / by Reginald Farrer. — Wakefield : EP Publishing, 1977. — xii,303p,[16]leaves of plates : ill ; 20cm.
Facsimile reprint of: 1920 ed. London : Edward Arnold, 1920. — Index.
ISBN 0-7158-1222-x : £6.75 : CIP rev.
(B77-08444)

635.9'674 — Aquariums. Water plants
Rataj, Karel. Aquarium plants : their identification, cultivation and ecology / by Karel Rataj and Thomas J. Horeman. — Hong Kong : T.F.H. Publications ; Reigate : Distributed by T.F.H., 1977. — 448p : ill(some col) ; 21cm.
Index.
ISBN 0-87666-455-9 : £10.60
(B77-23518)

635.9'674 — Water gardens
Aslet, Ken. Water gardens / [by] Ken Aslet. — London : Royal Horticultural Society, 1977. — 40p : ill ; 21cm. — (Wisley handbook ; 29)
ISBN 0-900629-88-6 Sd : £0.65
(B77-20388)

635.9'674 — Water gardens. *Manuals*
Dutta, Reginald. Water gardening indoors and out / [by] Reginald Dutta ; drawings by Rosanne McConachie. — London : Batsford, 1977. — 128p : ill(some col) ; 26cm.
Bibl.: p.126. — Index.
ISBN 0-7134-0886-3 : £4.50
(B77-27926)

635.9'676 — Gardens. Wild flowering plants. Cultivation
Genders, Roy. The wild-flower garden / [by] Roy Genders. — Newton Abbot [etc.] : David and Charles, 1976. — 155p : ill ; 23cm.
Index.
ISBN 0-7153-7154-1 : £4.50
(B77-03607)

635.9'676 — Gardens. Wild flowers. Cultivation
Dealler, Stephen. Wild flowers for the garden / [by] Stephen Dealler ; drawings by Anne Baikie. — London : Batsford, 1977. — 136p : ill, plans ; 26cm.
Ill. on lining papers. — Index.
ISBN 0-7134-0089-7 : £4.95
ISBN 0-7134-0090-0 Pbk : £3.25
(B77-24320)

635.9'76 — Gardens. Shrubs
Lloyd, Christopher, *b.1921.* Shrubs and trees for small gardens / [by] Christopher Lloyd. — Revised ed. — London [etc.] : Pan Books, 1977. — 144p,[12]p of plates : ill(some col) ; 18cm. — (Small garden series)
Previous ed.: i.e. Revised ed. 1972. — Index.
ISBN 0-330-23078-6 Pbk : £0.75
Also classified at 635.9'77
(B77-10425)

635.9'76 — Gardens. Shrubs. Pruning
Brown, George Ernest. The pruning of trees, shrubs and conifers / by George E. Brown. — London : Faber, 1977. — xix,351p,[32]p of plates : ill ; 22cm.
Originally published: 1972. — Index.
ISBN 0-571-11084-3 Pbk : £3.95
Primary classification 634.9'53
(B77-13716)

635.9'76 — Hedges. Maintenance
Merton *(London Borough). Parks Department.* Hedge care / [prepared by London Borough of Merton Parks Department]. — [London] ([Camzaro West Side, S.W.19]) : [The Department], [1976]. — [4]leaves : ill ; 21cm.
ISBN 0-905174-01-1 Sd : Unpriced
(B77-00817)

635.9'77 — Gardens. Trees
Lloyd, Christopher, *b.1921.* Shrubs and trees for small gardens / [by] Christopher Lloyd. — Revised ed. — London [etc.] : Pan Books, 1977. — 144p,[12]p of plates : ill(some col) ; 18cm. — (Small garden series)
Previous ed.: i.e. Revised ed. 1972. — Index.
ISBN 0-330-23078-6 Pbk : £0.75
Primary classification 635.9'76
(B77-10425)

635.9'77 — Kamuti
Bollmann, Willi E. Kamuti : a new way in bonsai / by Willi E. Bollmann. — London : Faber, 1977. — 3-106p : ill ; 21cm.
Originally published: 1974. — Index.
ISBN 0-571-11060-6 Pbk : £1.75 : CIP rev.
(B77-22679)

636 — LIVESTOCK, PETS
636 — Agricultural industries. Farms. Livestock
Campbell, John Roy. The science of animals that serve mankind / [by] John R. Campbell, John F. Lasley. — 2nd ed. — New York ; London [etc.] : McGraw-Hill, [1977]. — xix,732p : ill, map ; 24cm. — (McGraw-Hill publications in the agricultural sciences)
This ed. published in the United States: 1975. — Previous ed.: New York : McGraw-Hill, 1969. — Index.
ISBN 0-07-009696-1 : £13.70
(B77-13108)

636 — Agricultural industries. Farms. Livestock. *Illustrations. Juvenile literature*
Hay, Dean. On the farm / photographs by Dean Hay. — London [etc.] : Collins, 1977. — [16] leaves : chiefly col ill ; 21cm.
One leaf printed on both sides.
ISBN 0-00-195618-3 : £1.25
(B77-33887)

Youngs, Betty. Farm animals / [by] Betty Youngs. — London : Bodley Head, 1976. — [8] p : of col ill ; 15x21cm.
ISBN 0-370-11500-7 Pbd : £0.85
(B77-04912)

636 — Animals. Use by man
Bowman, John Christopher. Animals for man / [by] John C. Bowman. — London : Edward Arnold, 1977. — iv,70p : ill, map ; 23cm. — (Institute of Biology. Studies in biology ; no.78)

Bibl.: p.70.
ISBN 0-7131-2628-0 : £3.20
ISBN 0-7131-2629-9 Pbk : £1.60
(B77-25019)

636 — Livestock. Behaviour
Kiley-Worthington, M. Behavioural problems of farm animals / by M. Kiley-Worthington. — Stocksfield [etc.] : Oriel Press, 1977. — vii, 134p ; 23cm.
Bibl.: p.117-134.
ISBN 0-85362-163-2 Pbk : £4.00
(B77-21960)

636'.0092'4 — Animals. Care. Fitt, J A N. *Autobiographies*
Fitt, J A N. The 'Bob' man : a life with animals / [by] J.A.N. Fitt. — Bradford-on-Avon : Moonraker Press, 1977. — 123p,[8]p of plates : ill, ports ; 22cm.
Index.
ISBN 0-239-00173-7 : £4.75
(B77-24321)

636'.01'0942763 — Agricultural industries. Experimental livestock farms. *Lancashire. Helmshore. Great House Experimental Husbandry Farm. Reports, surveys*
Agricultural Development and Advisory Service. Great House EHF, 1977 / ADAS, Ministry of Agriculture, Fisheries and Food. — [London] ([Great Westminster House, Horseferry Rd, SW1P 2AE]) : A.D.A.S., [1977]. — [2],25,[1]p : ill, maps ; 21cm.
ISBN 0-85521-197-0 Sd : Unpriced
(B77-11910)

636'.01'0942763 — Agricultural industries. Experimental livestock farms. *Lancashire. Helmshore. Great House Experimental Husbandry Farm. Reports, surveys. Serials*
Great House Experimental Husbandry Farm, annual review / [ADAS, Ministry of Agriculture, Fisheries and Food]. — [London] ([Great Westminster House, Horseferry Rd, SW1P 2AE]) : A.D.A.S.
1977. — [1977]. — [2],ii,58p : ill, maps, plan ; 21cm.
ISBN 0-85521-198-9 Pbk : Unpriced
(B77-11911)

636.08'2'0941 — Livestock. Breeding. *Great Britain. Reviews of research*
Animal Breeding Research Organisation. Report / Animal Breeding Research Organisation. — Edinburgh : Agricultural Research Council : [Distributed by H.M.S.O.]. 1977. — [1977]. — [1],48p : ill, port ; 25cm.
Bibl.: p.43-45.
ISBN 0-7084-0052-3 Sd : £1.00
(B77-15350)

636.08'21 — Livestock. Breeding. Genetic aspects
Theories of plant and animal breeding ; [and], Ecological and evolutionary genetics / [prepared by a Course Team for the Open University]. — [Milton Keynes] : Open University Press, [1976]. — p555-615,plate : ill(some col), maps, col port ; 30cm. — (Science, a second level course : genetics ; 12, 13) (S299 ; 12, 13)
Cover title. — With answers to in-text and self-assessment questions. — Bibl.
Pbk : Unpriced
Primary classification 575.1
(B77-04172)

636.08'3'05 — Livestock. Management. *Periodicals*
Masstock Systems Limited. Masstock digest : modern livestock management. — London (151 Great Portland St., W1N 5FB) : Graham Cherry Organisation.
No.1- ; Winter 1977-. — [1977]-. — 30cm.
Quarterly. — [10]p. in 1st issue.
Sd : Unpriced
ISSN 0309-5916
(B77-12536)

636.08'4 — Agricultural industries. Farms. Electric feedingstuffs preparation equipment. Installation. *Great Britain. Manuals*
Electricity Council. Feed preparation : a guide to the practical design of installations / [Electricity Council]. — Revised [ed.]. — London (1 Charing Cross, SW1A 2DS) : The Council, 1971. — [4],108p : ill ; 18cm. — (Farmelectric handbook ; no.14 ISSN 0309-247x)
Previous ed.: 1970.
ISBN 0-85188-058-4 Sd : £0.50
(B77-07438)

636.08'52 — Livestock. Nutrition. Effects of climate. *Conference proceedings*
Nutrition Conference for Feed Manufacturers, *10th, University of Nottingham, 1976.* Nutrition and the climatic environment / [edited by] William Haresign, Henry Swan and Dyfed Lewis. — London [etc.] : Butterworth, 1977. — [8],200p : ill ; 25cm. — (Studies in the agricultural and food sciences)
'The tenth Conference was held at the School of Agriculture, Sutton Bonington, from 4th to 6th January, 1976 ...' -p.183. — Bibl. — Index.
ISBN 0-408-70819-0 : £6.00
(B77-06751)

636.08'55 — Feedingstuffs. Supplements: Drugs. *Lists*
Great Britain. *Ministry of Agriculture, Fisheries and Food.* Compendium of medicinal feed additives / [Ministry of Agriculture, Fisheries and Food]. — Pinner : The Ministry, 1976. — [108]p ; 18cm.
Index.
ISBN 0-85521-179-2 Sp : £1.00
(B77-11280)

636.08'552 — Grass silage. Nutritional values. Effects of cutting dates. *Western Scotland*
West of Scotland Agricultural College. Silage : plan for quality / the West of Scotland Agricultural College. — [Auchincruive] : [The College], [1975?]. — [1],6p : 1 ill ; 21cm. — (Advisory publication ; no.2)
Sd : Unpriced
(B77-25020)

636.08'552 — Grass silage. Production. *Western Scotland. Manuals*
West of Scotland Agricultural College. Making good silage / the West of Scotland Agricultural College. — [Auchincruive] : [The College], [1975?]. — [1],6p ; 21cm. — (Advisory publication ; no.3)
Sd : Unpriced
(B77-18242)

636.08'6 — Feedingstuffs: Sugar beet pulp
Agricultural Development and Advisory Service. Sugar beet pulp for feeding / Ministry of Agriculture, Fisheries and Food, ADAS. — Revised [ed.]. — Pinner : The Ministry, 1976. — Folder (4)p ; 22cm. — (Advisory leaflet ; 363)
Previous ed.: / issued by the Ministry of Agriculture, Fisheries and Food. London : H.M.S.O., 1958.
ISBN 0-85521-189-x Sd : Unpriced
(B77-11912)

636.08'83 — Livestock: Animals reared for meat. Growth. Related to efficiency in meat production. *Conference proceedings*
Symposium on Growth and Productivity of Meat Animals, *Prestbury, 1974.* Meat animals : growth and productivity / edited by D. Lister ... [et al.]. — New York ; London : Plenum Press [for] NATO Scientific Affairs Division, 1976. — xii,541p : ill ; 26cm. — (NATO Advanced Study Institutes : series A, life sciences ; vol.8)
'Proceedings of a Symposium on Growth and Productivity of Meat Animals held at Mottram Hall, Prestbury, Cheshire, England, December 2-6, 1974' - title page verso. — Index.
ISBN 0-306-35608-2 : £26.78
(B77-07439)

636.08'83'072041 — Meat. Production. Research in British institutions. *Lists*
Meat and Livestock Commission. Index of research supported by MLC : with reports and references. — Bletchley (Queensway House, Queensway, Bletchley, Milton Keynes MK2 2EF) : The Commission.
1977. — [1977]. — [3],iv,92p ; 30cm.
Bibl.: p.86-87. — Index.
ISBN 0-904650-06-5 Sd : Unpriced
(B77-10833)

636.08'85 — Laboratory animals
Williams, Christine S F. Practical guide to laboratory animals / [by] Christine S.F. Williams. — Saint Louis : Mosby ; London : Distributed by Kimpton, 1976. — vii,207p : ill ; 25cm.
Bibl.: p.198. — Index.
ISBN 0-8016-5574-9 Pbk : £8.05
(B77-04913)

636.08'85 — Laboratory animals. Behaviour. *Exercises, worked examples*
Hansell, Michael H. Experimental animal behaviour : a selection of laboratory exercises / [by] Michael H. Hansell and John J. Aitken ; illustrated by Norma Aird. — Glasgow [etc.] : Blackie, 1977. — 186p : ill ; 25cm.
Bibl. — Index.
ISBN 0-216-90325-4 : £8.25
(B77-25021)

636.08'85 — Laboratory animals. Care
The **UFAW** handbook on the care and management of laboratory animals / edited by UFAW ; foreword by C.W. Hume. — 5th ed. — Edinburgh [etc.] : Churchill Livingstone, 1976. — x,635p : ill ; 26cm.
Previous ed.: 1972. — Bibl. — Index.
ISBN 0-443-01404-3 : £15.00
(B77-02405)

636.08'85 — Laboratory animals. Care. *Secondary school texts*
Orlans, F Barbara. Animal care from protozoa to small mammals / [by] F. Barbara Orlans. — Menlo Park ; London [etc.] : Addison-Wesley, 1977. — viii,374p : ill ; 24cm. — (Addison-Wesley innovative series)
Bibl. — Index.
ISBN 0-201-05484-1 Pbk : £4.95
(B77-21228)

636.08'85 — Schools. Laboratory animals
Animals in schools. — London [etc.] : Heinemann Educational.
Vol.1 : Vertebrates / [by] Margaret E. Hogg. — 1977. — xii,100p : ill ; 22cm.
Bibl.: p.97. — Index.
ISBN 0-435-57402-7 Pbk : £1.95
(B77-32708)

636.08'85'094 — Laboratory animals. *European Community countries. Buyers' guides*
'**Laboratory** animals' buyers guide. — [Buckden] ([38 Mill Rd, Buckden, Huntingdon PE18 9SS]) : [Laboratory Animals Ltd].
1977-78. — 1977. — 41p : ill ; 25cm.
Sd : Unpriced
ISSN 0309-7382
(B77-18243)

636.08'86 — Working animals. *Juvenile literature*
Ramsbottom, Edward. Animals at work / [by] Edward Ramsbottom and Joan Redmayne ; illustrated by John Francis. — London [etc.] : Macmillan, 1977. — 16p : col ill ; 30cm. — (Bright ideas)
ISBN 0-333-19636-8 Sd : £0.48
(B77-23519)

636.08'87 — Pets. *Juvenile literature*
Pets. — Maidenhead : Purnell, 1977. — [12]p : chiefly col ill ; 22cm.
Pbd : £0.45
(B77-16948)

Potter, Angela. The how and why wonder book of pets / written by Angela Potter ; illustrated by Ann Baum. — London : Transworld, 1977. — 48p : ill(some col) ; 28cm.
Index.
ISBN 0-552-86589-3 Pbk : £0.50
(B77-33292)

636.08'87 — Pets. Care
Drabble, Phil. Phil Drabble's book of pets. — [London] : Fontana, 1976. — 251p,[8]p of plates : ill ; 18cm.
Originally published as: 'Pleasing pets'. London : Luscombe, 1975. — Index.
ISBN 0-00-634108-x Pbk : £0.85
(B77-02406)

636.08'87 — Pets. Care. *Juvenile literature*
Caras, Roger. A zoo in your room / [by] Roger Caras ; illustrations by Pamela Johnson. — New York ; London : Harcourt Brace Jovanovich, 1975. — 96p : ill ; 24cm.
Bibl.: p.91-92. — Index.
ISBN 0-15-299968-x : £1.65
(B77-19471)

636.08'87'0222 — Pets. *Colouring books*
Pets colour copy book. — Maidenhead : Purnell, 1977. — [20]p : of ill(some col) ; 28cm.
Sd : £0.15
(B77-09786)

636.08'899'0924 — Zoos. *Bedfordshire. Whipsnade. Whipsnade Zoo. Animals. Care. Personal observations*
Durrell, Gerald. Beasts in my belfry / [by] Gerald Durrell ; drawings by Edward Mortelmans. — [London] : Fontana, 1976. — 189p : ill ; 18cm.
Originally published: London : Collins, 1973.
ISBN 0-00-634161-6 Pbk : £0.70
(B77-13718)

636.089 — VETERINARY MEDICINE
Aspinall, K W. First steps in veterinary science / [by] K.W. Aspinall. — London : Baillière Tindall, 1976. — vii,213p : ill ; 24cm.
Index.
ISBN 0-7020-0635-1 Pbk : £2.95
(B77-03085)

636.089 — Veterinary medicine. *Manuals*
Kirk, Robert Warren. Handbook of veterinary procedures and emergency treatment / [by] Robert W. Kirk, Stephen I. Bistner. — 2nd ed. — Philadelphia ; London [etc.] : Saunders, [1976]. — xvii,716p : ill, forms ; 19cm.
Text on lining paper. — Published in the United States: 1975. — Previous ed.: 1969. — Bibl. — Index.
ISBN 0-7216-5473-8 : £13.50
(B77-03086)

636.089 — Veterinary medicine. *Reviews of research*
The **veterinary** annual. — Bristol : Wright-Scientechnica.
[1976] : seventeenth issue / editors C.S.G. Grunsell, F.W.G. Hill. — 1977. — xx,319p : ill, forms ; 26cm.
Bibl. — Index.
ISBN 0-85608-019-5 : £11.50
ISSN 0083-5870
(B77-07958)

636.089'03 — Veterinary medicine. *Dictionaries*
Black's veterinary dictionary. — 12th ed. / edited by Geoffrey P. West. — London : A. and C. Black, 1976. — [7],867p : ill, maps ; 23cm.
Previous ed.: 1975.
ISBN 0-7136-1699-7 : £6.75
(B77-01601)

636.089'06'241 — Veterinary medicine. Organisations. *Great Britain. British Small Animal Veterinary Association. Directories*
British Small Animal Veterinary Association. Annual handbook / the British Small Animal Veterinary Association. — Melton Mowbray (c/o A.T.B. Edney, Animal Studies Centre, Waltham-on-the-Wolds, Freeby, Melton Mowbray, Leics. LE14 4RT) : The Association.
1976-1977 / (compiled June 1976). — [1976]. — 101,[1]p : ill, map, ports ; 21cm.
ISBN 0-905214-01-3 Sd : Unpriced
(B77-05504)

636.089'092'4 — Veterinary medicine. *Cornwall, ca 1900. Personal observations*
Smythe, Reginald Harrison. Healers on horseback : the reminiscences of an English veterinary surgeon / by R.H. Smythe. — London : J.A. Allen, 1977. — x,135p ; 22cm.
Originally published: Springfield, Ill. : Thomas, 1963.
ISBN 0-85131-282-9 Pbk : £2.50 : CIP rev.
(B77-25022)

636.089'092'4 — Veterinary medicine. Herriot, James. *Autobiographies*
Herriot, James. Vet in a spin / [by] James Herriot ; drawings by Larry. — London : Joseph, 1977. — 256p : ill ; 23cm.
ISBN 0-7181-1645-3 : £4.25
(B77-27927)

Herriot, James. Vet in harness / [by] James Herriot ; drawings by Larry. — Large print ed. — Leicester : Ulverscroft, 1976. — [5],499p : ill ; 23cm. — (Ulverscroft large print series : [non-fiction])
Originally published: London : Joseph, 1974.
ISBN 0-85456-487-x : £2.65
(B77-00285)

Herriot, James. Vets might fly / [by] James Herriot. — London [etc.] : Pan Books, 1977. — 240p ; 18cm.
Originally published: London : Joseph, 1976.
ISBN 0-330-25221-6 Pbk : £0.70
(B77-31967)

Herriot, James. Vets might fly / [by] James Herriot ; drawings by Larry. — Large print ed. — Leicester : Ulverscroft, 1977. — [7],462p : ill ; 23cm. — (Ulverscroft large print series : [non-fiction])
Originally published: London : Joseph, 1976.
ISBN 0-7089-0028-3 : £2.95
(B77-20389)

636.089'0941 — Veterinary medicine. *Great Britain. Reports, surveys. Serials*
Animal health : report of the Chief Veterinary Officer / [for the] Ministry of Agriculture, Fisheries and Food [and] Department of Agriculture and Fisheries for Scotland. — London : H.M.S.O.
1975. — 1977. — iv,168p ; 21cm.
Bibl. — Index.
ISBN 0-11-241506-7 Pbk : £2.75
(B77-15934)

636.089'26 — Livestock. Reproduction
Reproduction in domestic animals / edited by H.H. Cole, P.T. Cupps. — 3rd ed. — New York [etc.] ; London : Academic Press, 1977. — xvi,665p : ill ; 24cm.
Previous ed.: 1969. — Bibl. — Index.
ISBN 0-12-179252-8 : £28.05
(B77-26377)

636.089'44'322 — Livestock. Vectors: Tsetse flies. Control measures. *Africa, to 1972*
McKelvey, John J. Man against tsetse : struggle for Africa / [by] John J. McKelvey. — Ithaca ; London : Cornell University Press, 1975. — xvii,306p : ill, facsims, maps, plans, ports ; 21cm.
Originally published: 1973. — Bibl.: p.239-292. — Index.
£10.80
ISBN 0-8014-0768-0
Primary classification 614.4'322
(B77-27114)

McKelvey, John J. Man against tsetse : struggle for Africa / [by] John J. McKelvey, Jr. — Ithaca ; London : Cornell University Press, 1973. — xvii,306p : ill, facsims, maps, plan, ports ; 21cm.
Bibl.: p.239-245. — Index.
ISBN 0-8014-0768-0 : Unpriced
Primary classification 614.4'322
(B77-18799)

636.089'44'4 — Livestock. Diseases. Control measures
Brander, George C. The control of disease / [by] George C. Brander, Peter R. Ellis ; foreword by Sir Michael Swann. — London [etc.] : Baillière Tindall, 1976. — [8],136p ; 20cm. — (Animal and human health)
Bibl.: p.127-129. — Index.
ISBN 0-7020-0634-3 Pbk : £2.50
Primary classification 614.4'4
(B77-09710)

636.089'5'1 — Veterinary medicine. Pharmacology
Alexander, Frank. An introduction to veterinary pharmacology / by Frank Alexander. — 3rd ed. — Edinburgh [etc.] : Churchill Livingstone, 1976. — x,382p : ill ; 22cm.
Previous ed.: Edinburgh : Livingstone, 1969. — Bibl. — Index.
ISBN 0-443-01168-0 Pbk : £7.50
(B77-02407)

636.089'6 — Livestock. Diseases. *Reviews of research*
Advances in veterinary science and comparative medicine. — New York [etc.] ; London : Academic Press.
Vol.20 / edited by C.A. Brandly, Charles E. Cornelius, guest editor W.I.B. Beveridge. — 1976 [i.e. 1977]. — xii,316p : ill ; 24cm.
Published in the United States: 1976. — Bibl. — Index.
ISBN 0-12-039220-8 : £23.80
(B77-09100)

Current veterinary therapy : small animal practice. — Philadelphia ; London [etc.] : Saunders.
6 / edited by Robert W. Kirk. — 1977. — ii-xlv,1418p : ill ; 27cm.
Text on lining paper. — Bibl. — Index.
ISBN 0-7216-5470-3 : £29.50
(B77-25720)

636.089'6 — Livestock. Diseases. Origins. Ecological aspects. *Conference proceedings*
Origins of pest, parasite, disease and weed problems : the 18th Symposium of the British Ecological Society, Bangor, 12-14 April 1976 / edited by J.M. Cherrett and G.R. Sagar. — Oxford [etc.] : Blackwell Scientific, 1977. — x, 413p : ill, maps ; 24cm. — (British Ecological Society. Symposia ; 18th)
Bibl. — Index.
ISBN 0-632-00226-3 : £14.00 : CIP rev.
Primary classification 632
(B77-06170)

636.089'6'00941 — Livestock. Diseases. *Great Britain. Reports, surveys. Periodicals*
Animal disease report : a quarterly report on animal disease in Great Britain ... / compiled by the Epidemiology Unit, Central Veterinary Laboratory ... — New Haw (New Haw, Surrey KT15 3NB) : The Unit.
Vol.1, no.1- ; Mar. 1977-. — [1977]-. — ill, maps ; 30cm.
[2],13p. in 1st issue.
Sd : Unpriced
ISSN 0140-4180
(B77-31968)

636.089'6'00941 — Livestock. Diseases. *Great Britain. Reports, surveys. Serials*
Return of proceedings under the Diseases of Animals Act, 1950 / Ministry of Agriculture, Fisheries and Food [and the] Department of Agriculture and Fisheries for Scotland. — London : H.M.S.O.
1976. — 1977. — 12p ; 25cm.
ISBN 0-11-241067-7 Sd : £0.25
(B77-15351)

636.089'601'94 — Veterinary medicine. Virology. *Reviews of research*
Recent advances in clinical virology. — Edinburgh [etc.] : Churchill Livingstone.
No.1 / edited by A.P. Waterson. — 1977. — ix,200p : ill ; 24cm.
Bibl. — Index.
ISBN 0-443-01542-2 : £9.75
Primary classification 616.01'94
(B77-06116)

636.089'65 — Livestock: Small mammals. Skin. Diseases
Muller, George H. Small animal dermatology / [by] George H. Muller, Robert W. Kirk. — 2nd ed. — Philadelphia ; London [etc.] : Saunders, 1976. — ii-xxiv,809p : ill(some col), forms, ports ; 27cm.
Previous ed.: Philadelphia : Saunders, 1969. — Bibl. — Index.
ISBN 0-7216-6606-x : £38.50
(B77-01602)

636.089'68 — Livestock: Mammals. Nervous system. Diseases
Palmer, Anthony Claude. Introduction to animal neurology / [by] A.C. Palmer. — 2nd ed. — Oxford [etc.] : Blackwell Scientific, 1976. — xvi,272p,12p of plates : ill ; 22cm.
Previous ed.: 1965. — Bibl.: p.225-260. — Index.
ISBN 0-632-00139-9 Pbk : £7.80
(B77-05505)

636.089'69'2 — Livestock. Virus diseases. *Conference proceedings*
Beltsville Symposium in Agricultural Research, *1st, 1976.* Virology in agriculture : invited papers presented at a symposium held May 10-12, 1976, at the Beltsville Agricultural Research Center (BARC), Beltsville, Maryland 20705, organized by the BARC Science Seminar Committee, T.O. Diener, Chairman, sponsored by the Beltsville Agricultural Research Center, Northeastern Region, Agricultural Research Service, United States Department of Agriculture / [general editor John A. Romberger, associate editors James D. Anderson, Rex L. Powell]. — Tunbridge Wells : Abacus Press, 1977. — xiv,293p : ill ; 25cm.
'... the first Beltsville Symposium in Agriculture Research' - Preface to this volume. — Bibl. — Index.
ISBN 0-85626-137-8 : Unpriced : CIP rev.
Primary classification 632'.8
(B77-06748)

636.089'69'5 — Livestock. Zoonoses
Andrewes, *Sir* **Christopher.** Viral and bacterial zoonoses / [by] Sir Christopher Andrewes, John R. Walton ; foreword by Sir Michael Swann. — London [etc.] : Baillière Tindall, 1977. — xiv, 161p,[4]p of plates : ill ; 20cm. — (Animal and human health)
Bibl.: p.152-153. — Index.
ISBN 0-7020-0632-7 Pbk : £2.50
Primary classification 616.9'5
(B77-09051)

636.089'69'607 — Livestock. Parasitic diseases. Physiological aspects. *Conference proceedings*
World Association for the Advancement of Veterinary Parasitology. *International Conference, 7th, Thessaloniki, 1975.* Pathophysiology of parasitic infection / edited by E.J.L. Soulsby. — New York [etc.] ; London : Academic Press, 1976[i.e.1977]. — xvii,258p : ill ; 24cm.
The Seventh International Conference of the World Association for the Advancement of Veterinary Parasitology on which this volume is based was held in Thessaloniki, Greece on July 14-16, 1975. — Published in the United States: 1976. — Bibl. — Index.
ISBN 0-12-655365-3 : £9.60
(B77-14797)

636.089'69'69 — Livestock. Pathogens: Mycotoxins. *Conference proceedings*
Mycotoxins in Animal Disease *(Conference), 2nd, University of Aberdeen, King's College, 1976.* Proceedings of a second meeting on mycotoxins in animal disease held at the University of Aberdeen, King's College 7-8 April 1976 / D.S.P. Patterson, G.A. Pepin and B.J. Shreeve editors ; [for the] Ministry of Agriculture, Fisheries and Food Agricultural Development and Advisory Service. — Pinner : Ministry of Agriculture Fisheries and Food, 1977. — [1],iv, 65,[1]p : ill ; 30cm.
'... the second in what is hoped to be a continuing series of occasional discussions on "Mycotoxins in Animal Disease"' - Introduction. — Bibl.
Sd : £2.00
(B77-27200)

636.089'69'883 — Livestock. Diseases. *Tropical regions*
British Veterinary Association. Handbook on animal diseases in the tropics / [British Veterinary Association]. — 3rd ed. / revised and edited by Sir Alexander Robertson. — London (7 Mansfield St., W1M 0AT) : The Association, 1976. — vii,304p ; 22cm.
Previous ed.: / revised by the staff of the Centre for Tropical Veterinary Medicine, Edinburgh University. 1968. — Bibl. — Index.
ISBN 0-901028-10-x : £6.00
(B77-28694)

Hall, H T B. Diseases and parasites of livestock in the tropics / [by] H.T.B. Hall. — London : Longman, 1977. — xv,288p : ill, map ; 22cm. — (Intermediate tropical agriculture series)
Bibl. — Index.
ISBN 0-582-60618-7 Pbk : £2.50
(B77-26378)

636.089'7 — Veterinary medicine. Surgery
Fundamental techniques in veterinary surgery / [by] Charles D. Knecht ... [et al.]. — Philadelphia ; London [etc.] : Saunders, 1975 [i.e. 1976]. — ii-xii,194p : ill ; 27cm.
Published in the United States: 1975. — Bibl. — Index.
ISBN 0-7216-5482-7 : £11.00
(B77-06174)

636.1 — LIVESTOCK. HORSES
Encyclopaedia of the horse / edited by Elwyn Hartley Edwards. — [London] : Octopus Books, [1977]. — 256p : ill(chiefly col), col plan, ports(chiefly col) ; 31cm.
Col. ill. on lining papers. — Index.
ISBN 0-7064-0606-0 : £4.95
(B77-33889)

Goodall, Daphne Machin. Horses and their world / [by] Daphne Machin Goodall. — Newton Abbot [etc.] : David and Charles, 1976. — 168p : chiefly ill(some col), ports ; 26cm.
ISBN 0-7153-7259-9 : £3.95
(B77-00286)

Skelton, Betty. Purnell's pictorial encyclopedia of horses and riding / [by] Betty Skelton. — Maidenhead : Purnell, 1977. — 224p : ill(some col) ; 31cm.
Index.
ISBN 0-361-03885-2 : £3.50
(B77-29521)

Vavra, Robert. Equus : the creation of a horse / [by] Robert Vavra ; foreword by James A. Michener. — London [etc.] : Collins, 1977. — 224p : ill(chiefly col) ; 29cm.
Originally published in Spanish as: 'El noble bruto'. Sevilla : Editorial Olivo, 1976.
ISBN 0-00-216206-7 : £15.00
(B77-27928)

636.1 — Livestock: Horses. *Juvenile literature*
Pajot, Anne Marie. Trojan the horse / by Anne-Marie Pajot ; translated [from the French] by Anna L. Ponder ; photographs by A. and R. Gibel-Causse ... [et al.]. — London : Schlesinger, 1974. — [16]p : ill(some col) ; 23cm. — (My animal friends)
Translation of : 'Figaro le cheval'. Paris : Hatier, 1972.
ISBN 0-85093-171-1 : £0.50
(B77-19472)

Pullen, George. Horses / [by] Werner Kirst and [translated from the German and adapted by] George Pullen. — St Albans : Hart-Davis, 1977. — 2-47p : ill(some col), ports(chiefly col) ; 23x25cm. — (Reporter books)
Originally published: in German. Stuttgart : Deutsche Verlags-Anstalt, 1974.
ISBN 0-247-12725-6 : £1.95
(B77-10426)

The **superbook** of horses. — London : Macdonald Educational, 1977. — 32p : ill(chiefly col), maps(chiefly col), port ; 29cm.
Adaptation of: 'Horses' / by Toni Webber, 1975. — Bibl.: p.32.
ISBN 0-356-05598-1 Sd : £0.50
(B77-27201)

636.1 — Livestock: Horses. Behaviour. *For training*
Blake, Henry Norman. Thinking with horses / by Henry Blake. — London : Souvenir Press, 1977. — 199p,[16]p of plates : ill, ports ; 23cm.
ISBN 0-285-62241-2 : £4.25 : CIP rev.
(B77-13109)

636.1 — Livestock: Horses. Behaviour. *Stories, anecdotes*
Haley, Neale. Understanding your horse : equine character and psychology / [by] Neale Haley ; with drawings by Margery Reeves Kinley. — South Brunswick ; New York : Barnes ; London : Yoseloff, 1973. — 204p : ill ; 27cm.
ISBN 0-498-01163-1 : £3.25
(B77-20391)

636.1'003 — Livestock: Horses. *Encyclopaedias*
Kidd, Jane. The complete horse encyclopedia / [by Jane Kidd and others]. — London [etc.] : Hamlyn, 1976. — 256p : ill(chiefly col), col map ; 31cm.
'A Salamander book'. — Col. ill. on lining papers. — Bibl.: p.250. — Index.
ISBN 0-600-34897-0 : £4.95
(B77-07440)

636.1'005 — Livestock: Horses. *Juvenile literature. Annuals*
'**Princess** Tina' pony book. — London : IPC Magazines.
1978. — 1977. — 2-79p : ill(some col), col port ; 28cm. — (A Fleetway annual)
ISBN 0-85037-348-4 : £1.35
(B77-32709)

'**Riding**' annual. — [London] : [IPC Magazines].
1978. — [1977]. — 79p : ill(some col), map, ports(some col) ; 28cm. — (A Fleetway annual)
Cover title.
ISBN 0-85037-349-2 : £1.65
(B77-32710)

636.1'008 — Livestock: Horses. *Anthologies. Juvenile literature*
True horse & pony stories / compiled by Diana Pullein-Thompson. — London : Armada, 1976. — 128p,[4]p of plates : ill, ports ; 18cm.
ISBN 0-00-691082-3 Pbk : £0.40
(B77-02408)

636.1'009415 — Livestock: Horses. *Ireland. Secondary school texts*
Minch, Janet. Horses and ponies in Ireland / text and illustrations Janet Minch. — [Tallaght] : Folens, [1977]. — [1]p,p129-160 : col ill ; 25cm. — (Irish environmental library series ; no.25)
Sd : £0.60
(B77-18858)

636.1'08 — Livestock: Horses. Breeding, training & care
Murray, Robbie. The gentle art of horse-breaking / [by] Robbie Murray ; photography by Stella Curtin. — London : Hale [etc.], 1976. — 93p : ill ; 25cm.
ISBN 0-7091-6049-6 : £4.25
(B77-18244)

The **Salamander** horse and pony manual : a comprehensive guide to caring for, training and riding your horse / compiled by Jane Kidd ; foreword by Alison Oliver. — London (27 Old Gloucester St., WC1N 3AF) : Salamander Books Ltd, 1977. — [2],209p : ill(chiefly col), col ports ; 25x27cm.
Col. ill. on lining papers. — Spine title: Horse and pony manual. — Index.
ISBN 0-86101-002-7 : £4.95
(B77-33890)

636.1'08'209 — Livestock: Horses. Breeding, to 1974
Goodall, Daphne Machin. A history of horse breeding / [by] Daphne Machin Goodall. — London : Hale, 1977. — 270p : ill, 3 maps, ports ; 25cm.
Bibl.: p.252-256. — Index.
ISBN 0-7091-5593-x : £6.95
(B77-24322)

636.1'08'21 — Livestock: Horses. Hair. Colour. Genetic factors
Geurts, Reiner. Hair colour in the horse / [by] R. Geurts ; translated [from the Dutch] by Anthony Dent. — London : J.A. Allen, 1977. — 108p : ill ; 20cm.
Translation of: 'De haarkleur bij het paard'. Wageningen : Centrum voor Landbouwpublikaties en Landbouwdocumentatie, 1973. — Bibl.: p.105-108.
ISBN 0-85131-290-x Pbk : £2.50 : CIP rev.
(B77-20392)

636.1'08'22 — Livestock: Horses : Hunters: Stallions. *Great Britain. Registers*
Hunter stallion directory. — Newport, Salop (National Foaling Bank, Meretown Stud, Newport, Salop) : Vardon Publications.
1973 : 3rd ed. / edited by Johanna Vardon ; secretary Clare Wilson. — [1973]. — 47p : ill ; 25cm.
Sd : Unpriced
ISSN 0309-3379
(B77-09101)

Hunter stallion guide. — Newport, Salop (National Foaling Bank, Meretown Stud, Newport, Salop) : Vardon Publications.
1974 : 4th ed. / edited by Johanna Vardon ; secretary Clare Wilson. — [1974]. — 51p : ill ; 25cm.
Continues: Hunter stallion directory.
Pbk : Unpriced
ISSN 0309-3360
(B77-09102)

1975 : 5th ed. / edited by Johanna Vardon ; secretary Clare Wilson. — [1975]. — 41p : ill ; 25cm.
Pbk : Unpriced
ISSN 0309-3360
(B77-09103)

1976 : 6th ed. / edited by Johanna Vardon and Clare Wilson. — [1976]. — 58p : ill ; 24cm.
Pbk : £2.00
ISSN 0309-3360
(B77-09104)

636.1'08'3 — Livestock: Horses. Care. *Manuals*
Parsons, Derrick. Do your own horse / by Derrick Parsons ; illustrated by Vincent Haddelsey. — London [etc.] : J.A. Allen, 1977. — 95p : ill ; 20x23cm.
Bibl.: p.89. — Index.
ISBN 0-85131-280-2 : £3.50 : CIP rev.
(B77-12537)

Rose, Mary. The horsemaster's notebook / [by] Mary Rose ; foreword by Michael Simons ; illustrated by D. Diane Lent. — Revised ed. — London : Harrap, 1977. — x,230p : ill ; 23cm.
Previous ed.: published with 'An anatomy of the horse' / by R.N. Smith. London : Peter Barker, 1972. — Bibl.: p.225-226. — Index.
ISBN 0-245-53181-5 : £4.95
(B77-33293)

Tuke, Diana. Getting your horse fit / [by] Diana R. Tuke. — London : J.A. Allen, 1977. — 48p : ill ; 22cm.
ISBN 0-85131-255-1 Sd : £1.25 : CIP rev.
(B77-07441)

636.1'08'3 — Livestock: Horses. Lungeing. *Manuals*
Inderwick, Sheila. Lungeing the horse and rider / [by] Sheila Inderwick ; illustrations by 'Tiptaft'. — Newton Abbot [etc.] : David and Charles, 1977. — 91p : ill ; 23cm.
Index.
ISBN 0-7153-7370-6 : £4.95
(B77-24323)

636.1'08'3 — Livestock: Horses. Training. *Manuals*
Edwards, Elwyn Hartley. From paddock to saddle / [by] Elwyn Hartley Edwards. — London : Pelham, 1977. — 215p : ill ; 26cm.
Originally published: London : Nelson, 1972. — Index.
ISBN 0-7207-1006-5 : £5.95
(B77-30377)

Rose, Mary. Training your own horse / [by] Mary Rose. — London : Harrap, 1977. — xiii, 217p,[16]p of plates : ill, ports ; 23cm.
Index.
ISBN 0-245-53151-3 : £4.95
(B77-31282)

636.1'08'3 — Stables. Outdoor manèges. Construction & maintenance. *Manuals*
Chandler, Geoffrey. The construction and maintenance of an outdoor manège / by Geoffrey Chandler. — Chislehurst (1 Tahoma Lodge, Lubbock Rd, Chislehurst, Kent BR7 5JS) : 'Stable management', 1974. — 8p : ill ; 19cm. — (A 'Stable management' handbook)
'... first appeared in print in the April/May issue of "Stable Management"' - p.1.
ISBN 0-905769-01-5 Sd : £0.30
(B77-02409)

636.1'08'30924 — Livestock: Horses. Training. White, Freda, b.1909. *New Zealand. Autobiographies*
White, Freda, *b.1909.* Horses, people & fun / by Freda White. — Wellington [N.Z.] [etc.] ; London : A.H. and A.W. Reed, 1976. — ix, 112p : ill, ports ; 23cm.
ISBN 0-589-00974-5 : £4.75
(B77-25721)

636.1'08'31 — Stables. Management
Green, Carol. Stable management explained / [by] Carol Green. — London : Ward Lock, 1977. — 96p : ill(some col) ; 21cm. — (Horseman's handbooks) (Concorde books)
ISBN 0-7063-5554-7 : £2.95
ISBN 0-7063-1963-x Pbk : £1.50
(B77-25722)

636.1'08'33 — Livestock: Horses. Manes. Plaiting. *Manuals*
A **photographic** guide to mane plaiting / [photographs by Clive Hiles]. — [Chislehurst] ([1 Tahoma Lodge, Lubbock Rd, Chislehurst, Kent BR7 5JS]) : Riding School and Stable Management Ltd, 1975. — 11,[1]p : chiefly ill ; 15x21cm. — (A 'Stable management' handbook)
'... originally published in "Stable Management"' - note.
ISBN 0-905769-00-7 Sd : £0.40
(B77-02410)

636.1'08'33 — Livestock: Horses. Tails. Plaiting. *Manuals. Illustrations*
De Beaumont, Marguerite. A photographic guide to tail plaiting / [photographic sequence arranged, with text, by Marguerite de Beaumont ; photographs by Guy Wilmot]. — Chislehurst (1 Tahoma Lodge, Lubbock Rd, Chislehurst, Kent BR7 5JS) : 'Stable management', 1976. — 11p : ill ; 15x21cm. — (A 'Stable management' handbook)
ISBN 0-905769-02-3 Sd : £0.40
(B77-02411)

636.1'08'4 — Livestock: Horses. Feeding
Leighton Hardman, Ann Catharine. A guide to feeding horses and ponies / [by] A.C. Leighton Hardman. — London : Pelham, 1977. — 163p : ill ; 23cm.
Bibl.: p.154. — Index.
ISBN 0-7207-0944-x : £4.50
(B77-20393)

636.1'08'86 — Dressage. *Amateurs' manuals*
ffrench Blake, Robert Lifford Valentine. Elementary dressage / [by] R.L.V. ffrench Blake. — London : Seeley Service, 1976. — 75p : ill ; 23cm.
ISBN 0-85422-127-1 : £2.95
(B77-03087)

Oliveira, Nuno. Reflections on equestrian art / [by] Nuno Oliveira ; translated [from the French] by Phyllis Field. — London : J.A. Allen, 1976. — 106p : ill ; 22cm.
Translation and revision of: 'Réflexions sur l'art équestre'. 2. éd. Paris : Crépin-Leblond, 1969.
ISBN 0-85131-250-0 : £3.50
(B77-14295)

636.1'08'96 — Livestock: Horses. Diseases
Serth, Geoffrey Walter. The horse owner's guide to common ailments / [by] G.W. Serth. — London : Pelham, 1977. — x,97p,[8]p of plates : ill ; 21cm. — (Pelham horsemaster series)
Originally published: London : Nelson, 1971. — Index.
ISBN 0-7207-1010-3 : £3.95
(B77-25023)

636.1'08'984 — Livestock: Horses. Parturition. *Juvenile literature*
Isenbart, Hans-Heinrich. A foal is born / text by Hans-Heinrich Isenbart ; [translated from the German] ; photos by Hanns-Jörg Anders. — London [etc.] : Angus and Robertson, 1977. — [40p] : ill ; 24cm.
Translation of: 'Ein Fohlen kommt zur Welt'. Lucerne : Reich, 1975.
ISBN 0-207-95689-8 : £2.50
(B77-14798)

636.1'0941 — Great Britain. Master of the Horse, to 1975
Reese, Max Meredith. The Royal office of Master of the Horse / [by] M.M. Reese. — London (20 Buckingham Palace Rd, S.W.1) : Threshold Books Ltd, 1976. — 360p : ill(some col), coats of arms(some col), facsims(some col), map, plan, ports(some col) ; 28cm.
Cover title: Master of the Horse. — Index.
ISBN 0-901366-90-0 : £16.50
(B77-10834)

636.1'1 — Stud farms. Anglo-Arab stallions & Arab stallions. *Great Britain. Registers*
Directory of pure Arabian studs in the British Isles : including a list of Anglo Arabs standing at stud. — Cranbrook (Goddards Green, Cranbrook, Kent) : Arab Horse Society.
1977-1978. — [1977]. — 187p ; 21cm.
Index.
Pbk : £2.50
(B77-30378)

636.1'2 — Flat racing racehorses. Breeding & training, 1965-1968. *Great Britain. Personal observations*
Silver, Caroline. Classic lives / [by] Caroline Silver. — St Albans : Paladin, 1974. — 202p, [16]p of plates : ill, ports ; 20cm.
Originally published: London : Cape, 1973.
ISBN 0-586-08187-9 Pbk : £0.75
(B77-19473)

636.1'2 — Racehorses. Breeding. *Manuals*
Hislop, John. Breeding for racing / [by] John Hislop. — London : Secker and Warburg, 1976. — xv,192p : ill, ports ; 23cm.
Bibl.: p.182-185. — Index.
ISBN 0-436-19701-4 : £4.50
(B77-01603)

636.1'2 — Racehorses. Breeding. Theories
Napier, Miles. Blood will tell : orthodox breeding theories examined / [by] Miles Napier. — London : J.A. Allen, 1977. — 160p ; 22cm.
ISBN 0-85131-254-3 Pbk : £2.50
(B77-10835)

636.1'2 — Racehorses: Stallions. *Registers*
The **stallion** review. — London (26 Charing Cross Rd, WC2H 0DJ) : Review Publications.
1976 season / compiled by Alan Yuill Walker. — [1976]. — 268p : ill(chiefly col) ; 30cm.
'Produced in conjunction with the "Bloodstock breeders' annual review"'. — Index.
Pbk : £4.25
(B77-22680)

1977 season / compiled by Alan Yuill Walker. — 1977. — 276p : ill(chiefly col) ; 30cm.
'Produced in conjunction with the "Bloodstock breeders' annual review"'.
Pbk : £4.25
(B77-18245)

636.1'2'0922 — Racehorses. Trainers. *Great Britain. Biographies*
Herbert, Ivor. Six at the top / [by] Ivor Herbert. — London : Heinemann, 1977. — xiv,210p : ill, ports ; 25cm.
Index.
ISBN 0-434-32640-2 : £5.95
(B77-32713)

636.1'2'0922 — Racehorses. Training. Rimell, Fred & Rimell, Mercy. *Autobiographies*
Rimell, Fred. Aintree iron : the autobiography of Fred and Mercy Rimell. — London : W.H. Allen, 1977. — [6],154p,[16]p of plates : ill, ports ; 23cm.
Index.
ISBN 0-491-02350-2 : £4.95
(B77-32714)

636.1'2'0924 — Racehorses. Training. Budgett, Arthur. *Great Britain. Biographies*
Curling, Bill. Derby double : the unique story of racehorse trainer Arthur Budgett / by Bill Curling. — London : Luscombe, 1977. — [7], 152p,[8]p of plates : ill, ports ; 23cm.
Index.
ISBN 0-86002-164-5 : £4.95
(B77-22681)

636.1'2'0941 — Racehorses in training. *Great Britain. Registers*
'**Sporting** chronicle' horses in training. — Manchester [etc.] (Thomson House, Manchester M60 4BJ) : 'Sporting Chronicle' Publications Ltd.
1977 : 84th year of publication. — [1977]. — 544p : ill, map ; 17cm.
Cover title: Horses in training. — Index.
Pbk : £2.00
(B77-24324)

636.1'3 — Appaloosa horses
Haddle, Jan. The complete book of the Appaloosa / [by] Jan Haddle. — South Brunswick ; New York : Barnes ; London : Yoseloff, 1975. — 371p : ill, ports ; 26cm.
Bibl.: p.352-353. — Index.
ISBN 0-498-01420-7 : £6.00
(B77-30379)

636.1'3 — British thoroughbred horses. *Yearbooks*
The **bloodstock** breeders' annual review : an illustrated world-wide survey of the British thoroughbred. — London (26 Charing Cross Rd, WC2H 0DJ) : Review Publications.
Vol.64 : 1975 / [edited by Tony Morris]. — [1976]. — 774p in various pagings : ill(some col), ports ; 31cm.
Quarter leather. — Index. — Includes: The stallion review, 1976 season / compiled by Alan Yuill Walker.
£22.00
(B77-25024)

636.1'3 — Lipizzaner horses: Henry
Quicke, Kenneth. Immortal Henry : the story of a Lipizzaner stallion / [by] Kenneth Quicke. — London : Elek, 1977. — 142p,[8]p of plates : ill, ports ; 23cm.
ISBN 0-236-40096-7 : £3.95
(B77-24325)

636.1'3 — Quarter horses
Porter, Willard H. How to enjoy the quarter horse / [by] Willard H. Porter. — South Brunswick ; New York : Barnes ; London : Yoseloff, 1973. — 200p : ill, ports ; 27cm.
Index.
ISBN 0-498-01215-8 : £4.75
(B77-20394)

636.1'4 — Harness horses. *Great Britain*
Rider, Bevan. Horses in harness today / [by] Bevan Rider. — London : Kaye and Ward, 1977. — 128p,plate : ill(incl 1 col) ; 23cm.
ISBN 0-7182-1148-0 : £3.50
Also classified at 741.9'42
(B77-28695)

636.1'4'05 — Carriage horses & carthorses. *Periodicals*
Heavy horse & driving. — Bradford (Idle, Bradford, W. Yorkshire BD10 8NL) : Watmoughs Ltd.
1st year, no.1- ; Spring 1977-. — 1977-. — ill, facsims, ports ; 30cm.
Quarterly. — 96p. in 1st issue.
Pbk : £1.25
ISSN 0309-7099
(B77-19474)

636.1'4'0941 — Carriage horses. *Great Britain, to 1975*
Gilbey, *Sir* Walter, *bart.* The harness horse / by Sir Walter Gilbey, bart. — 5th ed. / revised by Sanders Watney ; foreword by Walter Gilbey. — Liss (Hill Brow, Liss, Hants. GU33 7PU) : Spur Publications Co., 1976. — x,100p : ill ; 23cm. — (Sir Walter Gilbey series)
Previous ed.: London : Vinton, 1905.
ISBN 0-904558-21-5 : £3.30
(B77-04277)

636.1'5'0941 — British carthorses
Whitlock, Ralph. Gentle giants : the past, present and future of the heavy horse / [by] Ralph Whitlock. — Guildford [etc.] : Lutterworth Press, 1976. — 176p,[16]p of plates : ill(some col), facsim, ports ; 26cm.
Bibl.: p.172. — Index.
ISBN 0-7188-2257-9 : £6.50
(B77-03088)

636.1'6 — Livestock: Ponies. Care. *Manuals*
Petrie-Hay, Victoria. So your children want a pony / [by] Victoria Petrie-Hay ; illustrated by Eve Littleton. — London [etc.] : White Lion Publishers, 1976. — 147p : ill ; 23cm.
Index.
ISBN 0-7274-0188-2 : £3.75
ISBN 0-7285-0014-0 Pbk : £1.95
(B77-33891)

636.1'6 — Livestock: Ponies. Care. *Manuals. Juvenile literature*
Geddes, Candida. Making friends with your pony / [by] Candida Geddes. — London : Ward Lock, 1976. — 80p : ill ; 27cm.
ISBN 0-7063-5204-1 : £1.95
(B77-03089)

636.1'6 — Livestock: Ponies. Foals. *Illustrations. Juvenile literature*
Miller, Jane. Birth of a foal / [by] Jane Miller. — London : Dent, 1977. — [44]p : ill ; 25cm.
Ill. on lining papers.
ISBN 0-460-06746-x : £1.75
(B77-08445)

636.1'6 — Livestock: Ponies: Stallions. *Great Britain. Registers*
Pony stallion guide. — Newport, Salop (National Foaling Bank, Meretown Stud, Newport, Salop) : Vardon Publications.
1973 : 4th ed. / edited by Johanna Vardon ; secretary Clare Wilson. — [1973]. — 71,[1], 58p : ill ; 25cm.
Index.
Pbk : £1.00
ISSN 0309-3387
(B77-06753)

1974 : 5th ed. / edited by Johanna Vardon ; secretary Clare Wilson. — [1974]. — 78,67p : ill ; 25cm.
Index.
Pbk : £1.00
ISSN 0309-3387
(B77-06754)

1975 : 6th ed. / edited by Johanna Vardon ; secretary Clare Wilson. — [1975]. — 85,27p : ill ; 25cm.
Index.
Pbk : £1.50
ISSN 0309-3387
(B77-06755)

636.1'6 — Livestock: Shetland ponies. Breeding. *Scotland. Shetland, to 1975*
Cox, Maurice, *b.1899.* The ponies of Shetland / by Maurice Cox. — Lerwick ([77 Commercial St., Lerwick, Shetland ZE1 9AJ]) : The Shetland Times Ltd, 1976. — [16]p : ill ; 22cm.
Sd : Unpriced
(B77-04914)

636.1'6'0207 — Livestock: Ponies. *Humorous texts*
Tickner, John. Tickner's ponies / written and illustrated by John Tickner ; with a foreword by Sir Michael Ansell. — Revised [ed.]. — Saul (Saul, Glos.) : The Standfast Press, 1976. — 78p : ill ; 23cm.
Previous ed.: i.e. 1st ed. London : Putnam, 1966.
ISBN 0-904602-03-6 : £2.50
(B77-16464)

636.1'8 — Livestock: Donkeys. *Anthologies*
Enamoured of an ass : a donkey anthology / compiled by Stella Walker ; with illustrations by Michael Lyne. — London [etc.] : Angus and Robertson, 1977. — [11],196p : ill ; 25cm.
Ill. on lining papers. — Index.
ISBN 0-207-95688-x : £6.50
(B77-22682)

636.1'8 — Livestock: Donkeys. Training. *Manuals*
Dunkels, Marjorie. Donkey wrinkles and tales / [by] Marjorie Dunkels. — London [etc.] : J.A. Allen, 1977. — 80p : ill ; 16cm.
ISBN 0-85131-274-8 Pbk : £1.25 : CIP rev.
(B77-15353)

636.1'8 — Pets: Donkeys
Lewis, Colin Andrew. Donkeys : care, choice, training / by Colin A. Lewis. — Dublin (11 Talbot St., Dublin 1) : Actis, 1976. — 104p : ill ; 19cm.
ISBN 0-9505302-0-4 Pbk : £1.50
(B77-25026)

636.2 — LIVESTOCK. RUMINANTS, CATTLE

636.2'007'24 — Livestock: Cattle. Experiments. *Conference proceedings*
Consideration for the design and interpretation of cattle experiments : proceedings of a symposium on cattle experiments, British Society of Animal Production, 8 December 1975 / editor P.D.P. Wood. — [Milton Keynes] ([c/o J.R. Southgate, Meat and Livestock Commission, P.O. Box 44, Queensway House, Milton Keynes MK2 2EF]) : [British Society of Animal Production], [1977]. — [1],80[i.e.82]p : ill ; 21cm.
Bibl.
Sd : Unpriced
(B77-27202)

636.2'08'1 — Livestock: Cattle. Condition. Assessment. *Manuals*
East of Scotland College of Agriculture. *Animal Production, Advisory and Development Department.* Condition scoring of cattle / the East of Scotland College of Agriculture, Animal Production, Advisory and Development Department ; [written by] B.G. Lowman, N.A. Scott, S.H. Somerville. — Revised ed. — Edinburgh (West Mains Rd, Edinburgh EH9 3JG) : Edinburgh School of Agriculture, 1976. — iv,31p : ill ; 22cm. — (East of Scotland College of Agriculture. Bulletins ; no.6 ISSN 0306-8668)
Previous ed.: 1973.
ISBN 0-902164-23-6 Sd : £0.80
(B77-04915)

636.2'08'12 — Livestock: Cattle: Cows. Identification marking. *Manuals*
Agricultural Development and Advisory Service. Cow identification / Ministry of Agriculture, Fisheries and Food, ADAS. — Pinner : The Ministry, 1976. — Folder (6p) : ill ; 22cm. — (Advisory leaflet ; 600)
ISBN 0-85521-187-3 Sd : Unpriced
(B77-11913)

636.2'08'31 — Bull housing. Design. *Great Britain. Manuals*
Agricultural Development and Advisory Service. The bull pen / Ministry of Agriculture, Fisheries and Food, ADAS. — London : H.M.S.O., 1977. — [1],14p : ill, plans ; 25cm. — (Fixed equipment of the farm ; leaflet no.16)
ISBN 0-11-240612-2 Sd : £0.35
(B77-17596)

636.2'08'4 — Automatic electric cattle feeding equipment. Use. *Great Britain. Manuals*
Electricity Council. *Farm-electric Centre.* Automatic feeding of cattle : a guide to the practical design of installations / [Electricity Council, Farm-electric Centre]. — Kenilworth (National Agricultural Centre, Kenilworth, Warwickshire CV8 2LS) : The Centre, 1975. — vi,81p : ill(some col) ; 21cm. — (Farmelectric handbook ; no.19 ISSN 0309-247x)
Originally published: 1974.
ISBN 0-85188-061-4 Pbk : £0.75
(B77-07442)

636.2'08'52 — Livestock: Ruminants. Feedingstuffs. Requirements. Estimation. Applications of metabolisable energy requirements. *Great Britain*
Agricultural Development and Advisory Service. The metabolisable energy system and its use in ration calculations for ruminant livestock / Ministry of Agriculture, Fisheries and Food, Agricultural Development and Advisory Service. — Pinner : The Ministry, 1977. — [1], 14,[1]p ; 21cm. — (Short term leaflet ; 195)
Sd : Unpriced
(B77-17597)

636.2'08'552 — Livestock: Cattle. Feedingstuffs: Silage. Use. *Western Scotland. Manuals*
West of Scotland Agricultural College. Silage for cattle / the West of Scotland Agricultural College. — [Auchincruive] : [The College], [1975?]. — [1],7p ; 21cm. — (Advisory publication ; no.5)
Sd : Unpriced
(B77-18246)

West of Scotland Agricultural College. Silage handling : cutting to feeding / the West of Scotland Agricultural College. — [Auchincruive] : [The College], [1977]. — [1], 7p ; 21cm. — (Advisory publication ; no.8 ISSN 0309-6734)
Sd : Unpriced
(B77-31284)

636.2'08'94565 — Livestock: Cattle. Brucellosis. Veterinary health measures. *Great Britain. Manuals*
Great Britain. *Ministry of Agriculture, Fisheries and Food.* Brucellosis eradication : advice to herd owners outside eradication areas / Ministry of Agriculture, Fisheries and Food [and] Department of Agriculture and Fisheries for Scotland. — [Pinner] : The Ministry ; [Edinburgh] : The Department, 1975. — [2],13, [1]p ; 21cm.
ISBN 0-903386-03-8 Sd : Unpriced
(B77-01604)

636.2'08'96 — Livestock: Cattle. Diseases
TV Vet. The TV Vet book for stock farmers / by the TV Vet. — 4th ed. — Ipswich : Farming Press.
No.1 : Recognition and treatment of common cattle ailments. — 1976. — 176p : ill ; 25cm.
Previous ed.: 1972. — Index.
ISBN 0-85236-072-x : £3.75
(B77-03608)

636.2'1'3 — Cowboys. *United States. Juvenile literature*
Connell, Stephanie. Cowboys / written by Stephanie Connell and Vivienne Driscoll. — London : Macdonald Educational, 1977. — [1], 32p : col ill, col port ; 18cm. — (Readabout)
Adaptation of: 'Cowboys'. 1971. — Index.
ISBN 0-356-05545-0 Sd : £0.35
(B77-11914)

636.2'1'3 — Cowboys. *United States, to 1973*
Hassrick, Royal Brown. Cowboys : the real story of cowboys and cattlemen / [by] Royal B. Hassrick. — London : Octopus Books, 1975. — 144p : ill(some col), facsims, map, ports(1 col) ; 28cm.
Originally published: 1974. — Bibl.: p.141. — Index.
ISBN 0-7064-0487-4 Pbk : £1.50
(B77-20395)

636.2'1'3 — Livestock: Beef cattle. Production
Goodwin, Derek Harry. Beef management and production : a practical guide for farmers and students / [by] Derek H. Goodwin. — London : Hutchinson, 1977. — 198p : ill ; 23cm.
Bibl.: p.195-198.
ISBN 0-09-127060-x : £4.95
ISBN 0-09-127061-8 Pbk : £2.95
(B77-09105)

636.2'1'3091724 — Livestock: Beef cattle. Production. *Developing countries. Conference proceedings*
Conference on Beef Cattle Production in Developing Countries, *Edinburgh, 1974.* Beef cattle production in developing countries : proceedings of the conference held in Edinburgh from the 1st to 6th September 1974 organized by the Centre for Tropical Veterinary Medicine / edited by A.J. Smith. — [Roslin] ([Easter Bush, Roslin, Midlothian]) : University of Edinburgh, Centre for Tropical Veterinary Medicine, 1976. — xvi,487p : ill, maps ; 24cm.
'... the Conference on Beef Cattle Production in Developing Countries' - Foreword. — Bibl. — Index.
ISBN 0-85224-294-8 : £15.00
(B77-18247)

636.2'1'30973 — Livestock: Beef cattle. Production. *United States*
Neumann, Alvin Ludwig. Beef cattle. — 7th ed. / [by] A.L. Neumann. — New York ; London [etc.] : Wiley, 1977. — xii,883p : ill, form, maps ; 24cm.
Previous ed.: / by A.L. Neumann, Roscoe R. Snapp. 1969. — Index.
ISBN 0-471-63236-8 : £12.70
(B77-21232)

636.2'1'4 — Livestock: Dairy cattle. Cubicles. Design & construction. *Western Scotland. Manuals*
West of Scotland Agricultural College. Cubicle design / the West of Scotland Agricultural College. — [Auchincruive] : [The College], [1975?]. — [8]p : ill ; 30cm. — (Advisory publication ; no.4)
Sd : Unpriced
(B77-18248)

636.2'1'4 — Livestock: Dairy cattle. Judging. *Manuals*
Trimberger, George William. Dairy cattle judging techniques / [by] George W. Trimberger. — 2nd ed. — Englewood Cliffs ; London [etc.] : Prentice-Hall, 1977. — xi,338p : ill, ports ; 24cm.
Previous ed.: Englewood Cliffs : Prentice-Hall ; London : Bailey and Swinfen, 1958. — Index.
ISBN 0-13-197020-8 : £10.35
(B77-08446)

636.2'1'4 — Livestock: Dairy cattle. Yields. *England. Statistics*
National Milk Records. Report for the year ended September / National Milk Records. — Thames Ditton : Milk Marketing Board.
[1975]-1976. England and Wales. [Areas 1] : [Far Northern area, Mid Northern area edition]. — [1977]. — 24,104p : ill, ports ; 25cm.
Pbk : £2.00
Set of 4 vols : £7.00
(B77-25027)

[1975]-1976. England and Wales. [Areas 2] : [North Midland area, West Midland area, North Wales area, South Wales area edition]. — [1977]. — 24,182p : ill, ports ; 25cm.
Pbk : £2.00
Set of 4 vols : £7.00
(B77-25028)

[1975]-1976. England and Wales. [Areas 3] : [Eastern area, East Midland area, South Eastern area edition]. — [1977]. — 24,170p : ill, ports ; 25cm.
Pbk : £2.00
Set of 4 vols : £7.00
(B77-25029)

[1975]-1976. England and Wales. [Areas 4] : [Southern area, Mid Western area, Far Western area edition]. — [1977]. — 24,224p : ill, ports ; 25cm.
Pbk : £2.00
Set of 4 vols: £7.00
(B77-25030)

636.2'1'409411 — Dairy farming. *Scotland. Periodicals*
Scottish Milk Marketing Board. SMMB milk bulletin. — Paisley (Underwood Rd, Paisley) : Scottish Milk Marketing Board.
Supersedes: SMMB bulletin.
[No.1]- ; Jan. 1975-. — [1975]-. — ill, maps, ports ; 22cm.
Monthly. — Cover title: Milk bulletin. — 23p. in Oct. 1976 issue.
Sd : Unpriced
ISSN 0309-0809
(B77-04278)

636.2′22 — Livestock: Lincoln Red cattle. Herds. *Great Britain. Registers*
Lincoln Red herd book / Lincoln Red Cattle Society. — [Woodhall Spa] ([Agriculture House, Woodhall Spa, Lincs.]) : The Society.
Vol.76. — 1976. — 143p ; 23cm.
ISBN 0-9502204-6-9 : £3.24
(B77-06756)

636.2′22 — Livestock: Shorthorn cattle. Herds. *Great Britain. Registers*
Coates's herd book. — Market Harborough (Green Lodge, Great Bowden, Market Harborough, Leics. LE16 7HP) : Shorthorn Society of the United Kingdom of Great Britain and Ireland.
Vol.122, containing the pedigrees of beef shorthorn cattle ... — [1976]. — xxx,38p ; 22cm.
£5.60
(B77-21963)

636.2′23 — Livestock: Aberdeen-Angus cattle. Herds. *Great Britain. Registers*
The **Aberdeen-Angus** herd book / the Aberdeen-Angus Cattle Society. — Perth (6 King's Place, Perth [PH2 8AD]) : The Society.
Vol.100. — 1976. — [4],282p,[2]p of plates : 1 ill, port ; 21cm.
Unpriced
(B77-20396)

The **Aberdeen-Angus** herd book. — Perth (6 King's Place, Perth) : Aberdeen-Angus Cattle Society.
Vol.101 : [entries to June 1, 1976]. — 1977. — [4],288p,[2]p of plates : 1 ill, port ; 21cm.
Unpriced
(B77-17598)

636.2′23 — Livestock: Galloway cattle. Herds. *Great Britain. Registers*
The **Galloway** herd book : containing pedigrees of Galloway bulls which have, for the first time produced registered progeny since publication of the last herd book / [Galloway Cattle Society of Great Britain and Ireland]. — [Castle Douglas] ([Normandale, Castle Douglas, Kirkcudbright]) : The Society.
[Vol.94 : 1975-1976] : [Bulls, index nos. 384-487]. — [1977]. — 93p ; 22cm.
Index.
Unpriced
(B77-18249)

636.2′24 — Livestock: Guernsey cattle. *Personal observations*
Jee, Nigel. Guernsey cow / [by] Nigel Jee. — London [etc.] : Elek, 1977. — 169p ; 22cm.
ISBN 0-236-40104-1 : £3.95
(B77-30380)

636.2′24 — Livestock: Jersey cattle. *Great Britain*
Jersey Cattle Society of the United Kingdom. The Jersey : a guide to the breed in the United Kingdom / [Jersey Cattle Society of the United Kingdom]. — Reading (154 Castle Hill, Reading RG1 7RP) : The Society, [1977]. — [38]p : ill, form ; 30cm.
Bibl.: p.[20].
Pbk : Unpriced
(B77-18859)

636.2′3 — Livestock: Simmental bulls. *Great Britain. Reports, surveys*
Limousin and Simmental Tests Steering Committee. Report of the evaluation of the first importation into Great Britain in 1970-71 of Limousin bulls from France and Simmental bulls from Germany and Switzerland, 27 July 1976 / Limousin and Simmental Tests Steering Committee. — London : H.M.S.O., 1977. — 101p,[8]p of plates : col ill ; 21cm.
Cover title: An evaluation of Limousin and Simmental bulls in Britain. — Bibl.: p.99-100.
ISBN 0-11-241520-2 Pbk : £3.50
Also classified at 636.2′4
(B77-21233)

636.2′36 — Great Britain. Imports: Livestock: Simmental cattle. Herds. *Registers*
British Simmental Cattle Society. Register of imported cattle / British Simmental Cattle Society. — [Kenilworth] ([c/o A. Wrinch, National Agricultural Centre, Kenilworth, Warwickshire CV8 2LR]) : [The Society].
Vol.6 : 1975 importations. — [1976]. — [3], 35p ; 21cm.
Sd : Unpriced
(B77-21964)

636.2′4 — Livestock: Limousin bulls. *Great Britain. Reports, surveys*
Limousin and Simmental Tests Steering Committee. Report of the evaluation of the first importation into Great Britain in 1970-71 of Limousin bulls from France and Simmental bulls from Germany and Switzerland, 27 July 1976 / Limousin and Simmental Tests Steering Committee. — London : H.M.S.O., 1977. — 101p,[8]p of plates : col ill ; 21cm.
Cover title: An evaluation of Limousin and Simmental bulls in Britain. — Bibl.: p.99-100.
ISBN 0-11-241520-2 Pbk : £3.50
Primary classification 636.2′3
(B77-21233)

636.3 — LIVESTOCK. SHEEP AND GOATS
636.3′0092′4 — Shepherds: Nixon, David B. *Great Britain. Autobiographies*
Nixon, David B. Walk soft in the fold / [by] David B. Nixon ; illustrated by Mary Williams. — London : Chatto and Windus, 1977. — 235p : ill ; 21cm.
ISBN 0-7011-2216-1 : £3.95 : CIP rev.
(B77-06757)

636.3′08′3 — English shepherding equipment, 1738-1906
Ingram, Arthur. Shepherding tools and customs / [by] Arthur Ingram. — Aylesbury : Shire Publications, 1977. — 33p : ill, port ; 21cm. — (Shire album ; 23)
Bibl.: p.33.
ISBN 0-85263-379-3 Sd : £0.50
(B77-31285)

636.3′08′33 — Livestock: Sheep. Sheep scab. Control measures: Dipping. *Scotland. Manuals*
East of Scotland College of Agriculture. Dipping for sheep scab / the East of Scotland College of Agriculture. — Edinburgh (West Mains Rd, Edinburgh EH9 3JG) : Farm Buildings Advisory and Development Dept, the East of Scotland College of Agriculture, 1976. — [8]p : ill ; 21cm. — (Advisory leaflet ; 97 ISSN 0308-8278)
ISBN 0-902164-20-1 Sd : Unpriced
(B77-03090)

636.3′08′96968 — Livestock: Sheep. Sheep scab. Control measures. *Great Britain*
Great Britain. *Ministry of Agriculture, Fisheries and Food.* Sheep scab / Ministry of Agriculture, Fisheries and Food, Department of Agriculture and Fisheries for Scotland. — Amended [ed.]. — Pinner : The Ministry ; Edinburgh : The Department, 1976. — Folder([4]p) : 1 ill ; 21cm. — (Advisory leaflet ; 593)
ISBN 0-85521-190-3 Sd : Unpriced
(B77-12538)

636.3′08′982 — Livestock: Ewes. Lambing
Speedy, Andrew. Management at lambing / [by Andrew Speedy]. — [Edinburgh] ([c/o East of Scotland College of Agriculture, West Mains Rd, Edinburgh EH9 3TG]) : [Council of the Scottish Agricultural Colleges], 1976. — 21p : ill ; 21cm. — (Scottish agricultural colleges publication ; no.22 ISSN 0308-5708)
'In February 1975 a symposium for workers from research institutes, universities and Scottish Colleges was held at Stirling University. The author has attempted to combine the results and conclusions of this meeting ...' - Foreword.
ISBN 0-905084-17-9 Sd : Unpriced
(B77-09787)

636.3′2 — Livestock: Cheviot sheep. Flocks. *Registers*
Cheviot sheep flock book / compiled by the Cheviot Sheep Society. — Hawick ([c/o Mr G.H. Armstrong, 5 Tower Knowe, Hawick, Roxburghshire]) : The Society.
Vol.86 : [1977] : [Rams nos 9002-9119]. — 1977. — xvi,28p,[2] leaves of plates : 2 ill ; 17cm.
Pbk : £2.00
ISSN 0305-1617
(B77-20397)

636.3′2 — Livestock: Devon closewool sheep. Flocks. *Registers*
Devon Closewool Sheep Breeders' Society. The flock book of the Devon Closewool Sheep Breeders' Society (Incorporated). — [Barnstaple] (4 Cross St., Barnstaple, Devon) : The Society.
Vol.53 : Flocks 1 to 326. — 1976. — xxi,51p, plate : port ; 22cm.
Index.
Sd : £1.00(free to members)
(B77-18250)

636.3′2 — Livestock: Dorset Down sheep. Flocks. *Registers*
The **Dorset** Down flock book / [Dorset Down Sheep Breeders' Association]. — Bath (c/o The Secretary, Brierley House, Summer La., Combe Down, Bath [BA2 5LE]) : The Association.
Vol.68 : [1976]. — [1976]. — 38p : ill, ports ; 21cm.
Sd : £2.00(free to members)
(B77-01605)

The **Dorset** Down flock book / [Dorset Down Sheep Breeders' Association]. — Bath (c/o The Secretary, Brierley House, Summer La., Combe Down, Bath [BA2 5LE]) : Dorset Down Sheep Breeders' Association.
Vol.69 : [1977]. — [1977]. — 51p : ill, port ; 21cm.
Sd : £2.00 (free to members)
(B77-18860)

636.3′2 — Livestock: Dorset Horn sheep. Flocks. *Registers*
The **flock** book of Dorset Horn sheep : (incorporating the Poll Dorset Horn sheep) / [Dorset Horn Sheep Breeders' Association]. — Dorchester (The Secretary, 3 High West St., Dorchester, Dorset) : The Association.
Vol.84 : [1975]. — [1975]. — 105p,plate : port ; 23cm.
Spine title: Dorset Horn flock book.
£1.00(free to members)
ISSN 0305-2400
(B77-25031)

Vol.85 : [1976]. — [1976]. — 72p,plate : port ; 22cm.
Spine title: Dorset Horn flock book.
£1.00(free to members)
ISSN 0305-2400
(B77-25032)

Vol.86 : [1977]. — [1977]. — 84p,plate : port ; 22cm.
Spine title: Dorset Horn flock book.
£3.00(free to members)
ISSN 0305-2400
(B77-25033)

636.3′2 — Livestock: Exmoor Horn sheep. Flocks. *Registers*
Exmoor Horn Sheep Breeders' Society. The flock book of Exmoor Horn Sheep Breeders' Society. — [Minehead] ([c/o The Editor and Secretary, 32 The Avenue, Minehead, Somerset]) : The Society.
Vol.66 : Flocks 1 to 197 / [edited by T.W. Rook]. — 1972. — xvii,65p ; 21cm.
Index.
Pbk : £0.50(free to members)
(B77-24326)

Vol.67 : Flocks 1 to 197 / [edited by T.W. Rook]. — 1973. — xvii,64p ; 21cm.
Index.
Pbk : £0.50(free to members)
(B77-24327)

Vol.68 : Flocks 1 to 197 / [edited by T.W. Rook]. — 1974. — xviii,63p ; 21cm.
Index.
Sd : £1.00(free to members)
(B77-24328)

Vol.69 : Flocks 1 to 197 / [edited by T.W. Rook]. — 1975. — xviii,65p ; 21cm.
Index.
Sd : £1.00(free to members)
(B77-24329)

636.3′2 — Livestock: North Country Cheviot sheep. Flocks. *Registers*
Flock book of North Country Cheviot Sheep / [North Country Cheviot Sheep Society]. — [Inverness] ([37 Bellfield Rd, Kessock, Inverness 1V1 1XU]) : The Society.
Vol.31 : [1976-77] : [Ram nos. 3102 to 3388] / [editor Alex Murray]. — 1977. — 142p : ill ; 22cm.
Index.
Pbk : £2.50(free to members)
(B77-18251)

636.3′2 — Livestock: Suffolk sheep. Flocks. *Registers*
The **flock** book of Suffolk sheep / [Suffolk Sheep Society]. — Ipswich (Suffolk Showground, Bucklesham Rd, Ipswich) : Suffolk Sheep Society.
Vol.91 : Rams no.48155 to 49121]. — 1977. — 377p,plate : 1 ill, port ; 21cm.
Spine title: Suffolk flock book. — Index.
Unpriced
(B77-23520)

636.3'908'3 — Livestock: Goats. Care & management. *Amateurs' manuals*
Hetherington, Lois. All about goats / [by] Lois Hetherington. — Ipswich : Farming Press, 1977. — 196p : ill, plans ; 23cm.
Bibl.: p.191-192. — Index.
ISBN 0-85236-067-3 : £4.65
(B77-16949)

636.4 — LIVESTOCK. PIGS
636.4'08 — Livestock: Pigs. Production. *Manuals*
Johnson, Geoffrey, *b.1909.* Profitable pig farming / by Geoffrey Johnson. — 5th (revised) ed. — Ipswich : Farming Press, 1976. — 208p, [24]p of plates : ill, facsim ; 23cm.
Previous ed.: 1973. — Index.
ISBN 0-85236-071-1 : £4.00
(B77-05506)

636.4'08'22 — Livestock: Pigs. Herds. *Great Britain. Registers*
National Pig Breeders' Association. Herd book of the National Pig Breeders' Association. — Watford (49 Clarendon Rd, Watford, Herts. WD1 1HT) : The Association.
1976 : containing entries of Berkshire (vol.92), British Saddleback (vol.9), Gloucestershire Old Spots (vol.41), Hampshire (vol.2), Large Black (vol.69), Middle White (vol.92), also Tamworth (vol.92) and Welsh Pigs (vol.28) : pigs born before 1st January 1976 ... — [1977]. — 152p : ill ; 24cm.
£1.50
(B77-20398)

636.4'08'4 — Automatic electric pig feeding equipment. Use. *Great Britain. Manuals*
Electricity Council. *Farm-electric Centre.* Automatic feeding of poultry and pigs : a guide to the practical design of installations / [Electricity Council, Farm-electric Centre]. — [Kenilworth] (National Agricultural Centre, [Kenilworth], Warwickshire CV8 2LD) : The Centre, 1974. — iv,57p : ill(some col) ; 21cm. — (Farmelectric handbook ; no.20 ISSN 0309-247x)
ISBN 0-85188-062-2 Pbk : £0.75
Also classified at 636.5'08'4
(B77-07443)

636.4'08'96 — Livestock: Pigs. Diseases
Barron, Norman. The pig farmer's veterinary book / [by] Norman Barron. — 9th ed. (revised). — Ipswich : Farming Press, 1976. — 182p,[26]p of plates(2 fold) : ill(incl 1 col) ; 23cm.
Previous ed.: 1974. — Index.
ISBN 0-85236-069-x : £4.00
(B77-00819)

TV Vet. The TV Vet book for pig farmers : how to recognise and treat common pig ailments / by the TV Vet. — 4th ed. — Ipswich : Farming Press, 1976. — 160p : ill ; 25cm.
Previous ed.: 1973. — Index.
ISBN 0-85236-073-8 : £3.75
(B77-03091)

636.4'11'0941 — Livestock: Pigs: Breeding stock. *Great Britain. Reports, surveys. Serials*
Meat and Livestock Commission. *Pig Improvement Services.* Second test results / MLC Pig Improvement Services. — Bletchley (Queensway House, Bletchley, Milton Keynes MK2 2EF) : The Commission.
1976 : pigs purchased 1973-74. — [1976]. — [6],58p : ill ; 30cm. — (Commercial product evaluation report)
Sd : Unpriced
(B77-08447)

636.5 — LIVESTOCK. POULTRY
636.5'002'22 — Poultry. Breeds. *Illustrations*
Batty, Joseph. Poultry colour guide : covering large fowl, natural bantams, ducks, geese, turkeys and guinea fowl / [by] J. Batty, Charles Francis ; illustrations based on the paintings by Charles Francis. — Liss : Spur Publications, 1977. — 79p : ill(chiefly col) ; 31cm. — (Spur Publications poultry fanciers' library)
ISBN 0-904558-19-3 : £7.50
(B77-12539)

636.5'08'072041 — Poultry. Production. Research. Organisations. *Great Britain. Agricultural Research Council. Poultry Research Centre. Reports, surveys. Serials*
Agricultural Research Council. *Poultry Research Centre.* Summary of research reports published in the year ended 31st March / Poultry Research Centre, Agricultural Research Council. — Edinburgh ; [London etc.] : [Distributed by H.M.S.O.].
1977. — [1977]. — xx,90p ; 22cm.
Index.
ISBN 0-7084-0051-5 Sd : £1.15
(B77-15354)

636.5'08'3 — Poultry. Care & management. *Amateurs' manuals*
Eley, Geoffrey. Home poultry keeping / by Geoffrey Eley. — Wakefield : EP Publishing, 1976. — 72p : ill ; 24cm. — (Invest in living)
Bibl.: p.72.
ISBN 0-7158-0456-1 Pbk : £1.25
(B77-15355)

Kay, David. Poultry keeping for beginners / [by] David Kay. — Newton Abbot [etc.] : David and Charles, 1977. — 104p : ill, port ; 23cm.
Index.
ISBN 0-7153-7395-1 : £3.50
(B77-21234)

Singer, Andrew. The backyard poultry book / by Andrew Singer. — Dorchester (Stable Court, Chalmington, Dorchester, Dorset DT2 0HB) : Prism Press, 1976. — [9],110p : ill, plan ; 23cm.
Bibl.: p.107-110.
ISBN 0-904727-17-3 : £3.50
ISBN 0-904727-18-1 Pbk : £1.50
(B77-00820)

Walters, John, *b.1944.* Keeping ducks, geese and turkeys / [by] John Walters and Michael Parker. — London : Pelham, 1976. — 128p : ill, plan ; 21cm. — (Garden farming series)
Bibl.: p.123. — Index.
ISBN 0-7207-0932-6 : £2.90
Also classified at 636.5'9208'3; 636.5'97; 636.5'98
(B77-02412)

636.5'08'4 — Automatic electric poultry feeding equipment. Use. *Great Britain. Manuals*
Electricity Council. *Farm-electric Centre.* Automatic feeding of poultry and pigs : a guide to the practical design of installations / [Electricity Council, Farm-electric Centre]. — [Kenilworth] (National Agricultural Centre, [Kenilworth], Warwickshire CV8 2LD) : The Centre, 1974. — iv,57p : ill(some col) ; 21cm. — (Farmelectric handbook ; no.20 ISSN 0309-247x)
ISBN 0-85188-062-2 Pbk : £0.75
Primary classification 636.4'08'4
(B77-07443)

636.5'08'9444 — Poultry. Cannibalism & feather pecking. Control measures
Agricultural Development and Advisory Service. Cannibalism and feather pecking in poultry / Ministry of Agriculture, Fisheries and Food, Agricultural Development and Advisory Service. — Revised [ed.]. — Pinner : The Ministry, 1976. — Folder([4]p) ; 22cm. — (Advisory leaflet ; 480)
Previous ed.: published as 'Cannibalism and feather picking in poultry' / issued by the Ministry of Agriculture, Fisheries and Food. London : H.M.S.O., 1960.
ISBN 0-85521-183-0 Sd : Unpriced
(B77-12540)

636.5'08'96 — Poultry. Diseases
Poultry diseases / edited by R.F. Gordon. — London : Baillière Tindall, 1977. — xii,352p,ii p of plates : ill(some col) ; 24cm.
Bibl. — Index.
ISBN 0-7020-0602-5 : £9.00
(B77-14296)

636.5'1'3 — Livestock: Broilers. Production. *Manuals*
Agricultural Development and Advisory Service. Broiler production / Ministry of Agriculture, Fisheries and Food, ADAS. — Revised [ed.]. — Pinner : The Ministry, 1977. — Folder (6p) : 1 ill ; 21cm. — (Advisory leaflet ; 430)
Previous ed.: published as 'Production of small roasting chicken (broilers)'. London : H.M.S.O., 1965.
Unpriced
(B77-25034)

636.5'1'4 — Poultry. Eggs. Intensive production. *Manuals*
Great Britain. *Ministry of Agriculture, Fisheries and Food.* Intensive poultry management for egg production / Ministry of Agriculture, Fisheries and Food. — 5th ed. — London : H.M.S.O., 1976. — iv,88p,viii p of plates : ill, forms, plans ; 25cm. — (Bulletin ; 152)
Previous ed.: 1970. — Index.
ISBN 0-11-241115-0 Sd : £1.75
(B77-11915)

636.5'1'4 — Poultry. Eggs. Small scale production. *Manuals*
Agricultural Development and Advisory Service. Domestic poultry keeping : notes on the small scale production of eggs / Ministry of Agriculture, Fisheries and Food, Agricultural Development & Advisory Service. — [Pinner] : [The Ministry], [1976]. — [1],15p : ill, plans ; 22cm.
ISBN 0-85521-177-6 Sd : Unpriced
(B77-05507)

636.5'2 — Old English Game poultry
Batty, Joseph. Understanding Old English Game : large and bantams / [by] J. Batty ; colour plates based on paintings by Charles Francis ; drawings by Ann Hutchings from birds kept by the author. — 2nd ed. — Liss : Spur Publications, 1976. — [10],65p,[2]leaves of plates : ill(some col) ; 23cm. — (Spur Publications poultry fanciers' library)
Previous ed.: 1973. — Bibl.: p.65.
ISBN 0-904558-18-5 : £3.30
(B77-16950)

636.5'9208'3 — Livestock: Turkeys. Care & management. *Amateurs' manuals*
Walters, John, *b.1944.* Keeping ducks, geese and turkeys / [by] John Walters and Michael Parker. — London : Pelham, 1976. — 128p : ill, plan ; 21cm. — (Garden farming series)
Bibl.: p.123. — Index.
ISBN 0-7207-0932-6 : £2.90
Primary classification 636.5'08'3
(B77-02412)

636.5'94 — Livestock: Pheasants
Roles, D Grenville. Rare pheasants of the world : a study of birds in captivity / by D. Grenville Roles ; with drawings by the author. — Liss (Hill Brow, Liss, Hants. GU33 7PU) : Spur Publications Co., 1976. — v,106p,[2]leaves of plates : ill(some col) ; 31cm.
ISBN 0-904558-20-7 : £7.50
(B77-03092)

636.5'94 — Livestock: Pheasants. Production. Artificial incubation. *Manuals*
Agricultural Development and Advisory Service. Pheasant incubation / ADAS, Ministry of Agriculture, Fisheries and Food. — Pinner : The Ministry, 1977. — Folder(6p) : form ; 22cm. — (Advisory leaflet ; 604)
Unpriced
(B77-27203)

636.5'96 — Pets: Pigeons
McNeillie, Andrew. Guide to the pigeons of the world / [by] Andrew McNeillie ; illustrated by Johan Lentink ; with additional illustrations by Stephen Cocking and Graham Smith. — Oxford : Elsevier-Phaidon, 1976. — 160p : ill(chiefly col) ; 20cm.
Bibl.: p.154-155. — Index.
ISBN 0-7290-0030-3 : £3.50
ISBN 0-7290-0031-1 Pbk : £1.95
(B77-14799)

636.5'96 — Racing pigeons. *Yearbooks*
'Homing world' stud book. — Cheltenham (The Reddings, Cheltenham, Glos. GL51 6RN) : Royal Pigeon Racing Association.
1977 : 15th olympiad ed. — [1977]. — 416p : ill, forms, ports ; 20cm.
ISBN 0-900204-08-7 Pbk : £1.40
Also classified at 798'.8
(B77-10427)

636.5'97 — Livestock: Ducks. Care & management. *Amateurs' manuals*
Walters, John, *b.1944.* Keeping ducks, geese and turkeys / [by] John Walters and Michael Parker. — London : Pelham, 1976. — 128p : ill, plan ; 21cm. — (Garden farming series)
Bibl.: p.123. — Index.
ISBN 0-7207-0932-6 : £2.90
Primary classification 636.5'08'3
(B77-02412)

636.5'98 — Livestock: Geese. Care & management. *Amateurs' manuals*
Walters, John, *b.1944.* Keeping ducks, geese and turkeys / [by] John Walters and Michael Parker. — London : Pelham, 1976. — 128p : ill, plan ; 21cm. — (Garden farming series)
Bibl.: p.123. — Index.
ISBN 0-7207-0932-6 : £2.90
Primary classification 636.5'08'3
(B77-02412)

636.6 — LIVESTOCK. BIRDS (OTHER THAN POULTRY)

636.6 — Livestock: Birds

Encyclopaedia of aviculture / edited by A. Rutgers and K.A. Norris. — Poole : Blandford Press.
In 3 vols. — Revised translation of the Dutch 'Encyclopedie voor de vogelliefhebber'. Gorssel : Uitg. 'Littera Scripta Manet', 1964-1968.
Vol.3 / edited by A. Rutgers and K.A. Norris with Cyril H. Rogers ; contributors include J.L. Albrecht-Moller ... [et al.]. — English language ed. — 1977. — xii,241p,[45]leaves of plates : ill(some col) ; 31cm.
Bibl.: p.225-227. — Index.
ISBN 0-7137-0802-6 : £12.00
(B77-18252)

636.6'86 — Cage birds & aviary birds. *Manuals*

Rogers, Cyril Harold. Foreign birds : their care and breeding / [by] Cyril H. Rogers. — Leicester ([1487 Melton Rd], Queniborough, Leicester) : K and R Books Ltd, 1976. — 79p : ill ; 19cm. — (A K & R handbook)
Not the same as B54-10572. — Bibl.: p.77. — Index.
ISBN 0-903264-12-9 : £1.00
(B77-31970)

636.6'862 — Pets: Canaries

Dodwell, Gordon Terence. Canaries / [by] G.T. Dodwell. — Edinburgh [etc.] : J. Bartholomew, 1976. — 3-94p : col ill, col maps ; 19cm.
Index.
ISBN 0-7028-1071-1 Pbk : £0.95
(B77-11281)

636.6'862 — Pets: Coloured canaries

Walker, G B R. Coloured canaries / [by] G.B.R. Walker ; photographs and illustrations by Dennis Avon & Tony Tilford. — Poole : Blandford Press, 1976. — 140p : ill(chiefly col) ; 23cm.
Index.
ISBN 0-7137-0804-2 : £4.25
(B77-03093)

636.6'862 — Pets: Zebra finches

Rogers, Cyril. Zebra finches / [by] Cyril Rogers. — Edinburgh [etc.] : J. Bartholomew, 1977. — 94p : col ill, col map, col plan ; 19cm.
Index.
ISBN 0-7028-1085-1 Pbk : £0.95
(B77-22683)

636.6'864 — Pets: Budgerigars. Breeding & care

Rogers, Cyril Harold. Budgerigars : their care and breeding / [by] Cyril H. Rogers. — Leicester (Queniborough, Leicester) : K. and R. Books, 1976. — 72p : ill ; 18cm. — (A K and R handbook)
Bibl.: p.69. — Index.
ISBN 0-903264-13-7 : Unpriced
(B77-30381)

636.6'865 — Livestock: Parrots. Breeding. *Great Britain. Registers*

Parrot Society. A register of parrots bred by some British members of the Parrot Society. — Bedford (17 De Parys Ave., Bedford) : The Society.
1976 / collated and presented by N.D. Cooper & E.A. Dracup. — 1977. — [31]p : 1 ill ; 21cm.
Cover title: Breeding register.
Sd : Unpriced
(B77-25723)

636.6'865 — Pets: Cockatiels. *Personal observations*

Moon, *Mrs* E L. Experiences with my cockatiels / by Mrs E.L. Moon. — Revised ed. — Neptune City, N.J. ; Reigate : T.F.H., 1976. — 128p : ill(some col), port ; 21cm.
Previous ed.: Fond du Lac, Wis. : All-Pets Books, 1962. — Index.
ISBN 0-87666-954-2 Pbk : £2.03
(B77-04279)

636.6'869 — Pets: Mynah birds. Care

Low, Rosemary. Mynah birds / [by] Rosemary Low. — Edinburgh [etc.] : J. Bartholomew, 1976. — 93p : col ill, col map ; 19cm.
Index.
ISBN 0-7028-1002-9 Pbk : £0.95
(B77-11916)

636.6'869 — Pets: Ravens. *South Africa. Personal observations*

Von Kirchhoff, F. Two ravens came tapping / [by] F. Von Kirchhoff ; [photographs by the author and Zelda Wahl]. — London : Hale, 1976. — 91p,[24]p of plates : ill, ports ; 22cm.
ISBN 0-7091-5827-0 : £3.95
(B77-06175)

636.7 — LIVESTOCK. DOGS

Dogs & puppies / edited by Douglas James ; with contributions from Wendy Boorer ... [et al.]. — [London] : Octopus Books, [1977]. — 160p : ill(some col) ; 29cm.
Col. ill. on lining papers. — Index.
ISBN 0-7064-0630-3 : £2.95
(B77-33296)

Méry, Fernand. The life, history and magic of the dog / by Fernand Mery ; [translated from the French]. — New York : Grosset and Dunlap ; [Leicester] ([Euston St., Freemen's Common, Aylestone Rd, Leicester LE2 7SS]) : Distributed by WHS Distributors, [1977]. — 5-235p,[10]leaves of plates : ill(some col), 3 col facsims, ports(some col) ; 27cm.
'A Madison Square Press book' - title page verso. — Ill. on lining papers. — This translation originally published: as 'The life, history and magic of the dog', New York : Grosset and Dunlap ; and as 'The dog', London : Cassell, 1970. — Translation of: 'Le chien'. Paris : Laffont, 1968.
ISBN 0-448-02144-7 : Unpriced
(B77-23521)

636.7 — Livestock: Dogs. *Juvenile literature*

The **superbook** of dogs. — London : Macdonald Educational, 1977. — 32p : ill(chiefly col), col maps, ports ; 29cm.
Adaptation of: 'Dogs' / by Rex Marchant, 1974. — Bibl.: p.32.
ISBN 0-356-05597-3 Sd : £0.50
(B77-27204)

636.7 — Livestock: Dogs. Behaviour

Fox, Michael Wilson. Understanding your dog / by Michael W. Fox. — Toronto [etc.] ; London : Bantam, 1977. — x,212,[1]p : ill ; 18cm.
Originally published: New York : Coward, McCann and Geoghegan, 1972 ; London : Blond and Briggs, 1974. — Bibl.: p.207. — Index.
ISBN 0-552-62341-5 Pbk : £0.75
(B77-31286)

636.7 — Livestock: Dogs. Behaviour. *Stories, anecdotes*

Millard, Adele. Dogs in fact & legend / by Adele Millard ; illustrations by Minn. — New York : Sterling [etc.] ; London : Distributed by Ward Lock, 1977. — 96p : ill ; 21cm.
Index.
ISBN 0-7061-2547-9 : £2.50
(B77-22684)

636.7'005 — Livestock: Dogs. *Periodicals*

Dog news and family pets. — [Lee-on-Solent] ([92 High St., Lee-on-Solent, Hants.]) : 'Dog news'.
Continues: New dog news.
Vol.2, no.2- ; October-November 1976-. — [1976]-. — ill, ports ; 28cm.
Six issues a year. — [2],16,[2]p. in Vol.2, no.2 ; Oct.-Nov. 1976.
Sd : £0.25
ISSN 0309-1031
(B77-03094)

636.7'005 — Livestock: Dogs. *Serials*

'**Our** dogs' Christmas annual. — [Manchester] ([Oxford Rd, Station Approach, Manchester M60 1SX]) : ['Our dogs' Publishing Co.].
[1976-77]. — [1976]. — 268p : ill, ports ; 30cm.
Cover title. — Index.
ISBN 0-903034-05-0 Pbk : £2.00
(B77-09788)

636.7'008 — Livestock: Dogs. *Anthologies*

In praise of dogs / compiled by Daniel Farson ; illustrated by Barbara Howes. — London : Harrap, 1976. — [8],119p : ill ; 24cm.
ISBN 0-245-53006-1 : £3.95
(B77-01606)

636.7'00941 — Livestock: Dogs. *Great Britain. Yearbooks*

'**Dog** world' annual. — Ashford, Kent ([32 New St.], Ashford, Kent) : Dog World Ltd.
1977. — [1977]. — 298,civ p : ill, ports ; 28cm.
Cover title. — Index.
ISBN 0-9500418-8-2 Pbk : £2.00
(B77-06758)

636.7'08'2 — Livestock: Dogs. Breeding

Portman-Graham, Reginald. The mating and whelping of dogs / [by] R. Portman-Graham. — 9th ed. — London : Popular Dogs Publishing Co., 1975. — 162p : ill ; 20cm.
Previous ed.: 1973. — Index.
ISBN 0-09-035061-8 : £2.25
(B77-06176)

636.7'08'3 — Livestock: Dogs. Training. *Manuals*

Griffiths, Peter, *b.1944.* Understanding your dog : a new approach to training / [by] Peter Griffiths. — Newton Abbot [etc.] : David and Charles, 1977. — 109p : ill ; 22cm.
Index.
ISBN 0-7153-7353-6 : £3.50
(B77-10428)

Howell, Jack. Good dog! : the basic training book for all breeds / [by] Jack Howell. — Ipswich : Farming Press, 1977. — 102p : ill, port ; 25cm.
Index.
ISBN 0-85236-078-9 : £3.85
(B77-29522)

Martin, Robert J. Toward the Ph.D for dogs : obedience training from novice through utility / [by] Robert J. Martin and Napoleon A. Chagnon. — New York ; London : Harcourt Brace Jovanovich, [1976]. — xiii,382p : ill, forms, plans ; 24cm.
Published in the United States: 1975. — Index.
ISBN 0-15-190911-3 : £10.05
(B77-06177)

636.7'08'86 — Guide dogs. *Research reports*

Guide dogs for the blind : their selection, development, and training / [by] Clarence J. Pfaffenberger ... [et al.] ; with the editorial assistance of Sarah F. Scott. — Amsterdam ; Oxford [etc.] : Elsevier, 1976. — xi,225p : ill, forms, ports ; 25cm. — (Developments in animal and veterinary sciences ; 1)
Bibl. — Index.
ISBN 0-444-41520-3 : £15.61
(B77-05508)

636.7'08'87 — Pets: Dogs. Care

Gordon, John, *b.1916.* Dogs / [by] John Gordon. — Edinburgh [etc.] : J. Bartholomew, 1976. — 95p : ill(chiefly col) ; 19cm.
'Bartholomew pet books' - note. — Index.
ISBN 0-7028-1023-1 Pbk : £0.95
(B77-11917)

636.7'08'87 — Pets: Dogs. Care. *Juvenile literature*

Creek, Rosemary. Dogs / by Rosemary Creek ; illustrated by Veronica Barge. — Cambridge : Dinosaur Publications, 1977. — 23p : col ill ; 16x18cm. — (Althea's pet series)
ISBN 0-85122-125-4 Sd : £0.35
(B77-30382)

636.7'08'96 — Livestock: Dogs. Diseases

Textbook of veterinary internal medicine : diseases of the dog and cat / edited by Stephen J. Ettinger. — Philadelphia ; London [etc.] : Saunders, [1976]. — 2v.(xxiii,1767,lxxvii p) : ill(some col) ; 27cm.
Published in the United States: 1975. — Bibl. — Index.
ISBN 0-7216-3424-9 : £53.50
Also classified at 636.8'08'96
(B77-04916)

636.7'08'96120754 — Livestock: Dogs. Heart. Electrocardiography. *Manuals*

Bolton, Gary R. Handbook of canine electrocardiography / [by] Gary R. Bolton. — Philadelphia ; London [etc.] : Saunders, [1976]. — x,370p ; 27cm.
Published in the United States: 1975. — Bibl. — Index.
ISBN 0-7216-1838-3 : £16.25
(B77-06178)

636.7'1 — Livestock: Dogs. Breeds

Bengtson, Bo. The dogs of the world / [by] Bo Bengtson, Ake Wintzell ; [translated from the Swedish by Kristina Husberg]. — Newton Abbot [etc.] : David and Charles, 1977. — 288p : ill(chiefly col) ; 24cm.
Translation of: 'All världens Hundar'. Västeräs : ICA-förlaget, 1973. — Index.
ISBN 0-7153-7466-4 : £4.50
(B77-31971)

Novotný, J. A field guide in colour to dogs / by J. Novotný and J. Najman ; [translated from the Czech by Ruth Shepherd] ; photographs by Z. Humpál. — London : Octopus Books, 1977. — 175p : ill(chiefly col) ; 22cm.
Spine title: Dogs. — Originally published: in Czech. Prague : Artia, 1977?. — Bibl.: p.172. — Index.
ISBN 0-7064-0611-7 : £2.50
(B77-23522)

Troy, Suzanne. Dogs : pets of pedigree / text & photography by Suzanne Troy. — Newton Abbot [etc.] : David and Charles, 1976. — 192p : ill(chiefly col) ; 29cm.
Index.
ISBN 0-7153-7219-x : £3.95
(B77-00821)

636.7'2 — Chow chows
Draper, Samuel. The book of the chow chow / by Samuel Draper and Joan McDonald Brearley. — Neptune City ; Reigate [etc.] : T.F.H., 1977. — 576p : ill(some col), ports ; 29cm.
Index.
ISBN 0-87666-653-5 : £12.10
(B77-24330)

636.7'2 — Poodles
Walne, Shirley. The poodle / [by] Shirley Walne. — Edinburgh [etc.] : J. Bartholomew, 1977. — 94p : ill(chiefly col) ; 19cm.
Bibl.: p.90. — Index.
ISBN 0-7028-1064-9 Pbk : £0.95
(B77-21235)

Walne, Shirley. The standard poodle / by Shirley Walne. — Leicester ([55 Kings Rd], Leicester) : K and R Books Ltd, 1976[i.e.1977]. — 144p,[4] p of plates : ill(some col), ports(some col) ; 20cm. — (The dog owner's library)
Ill. on lining papers. — Bibl.: p.131-132. — Index.
ISBN 0-903264-18-8 : £2.95
(B77-13719)

636.7'3 — Alsatian dogs
Ixer, Joyce. The alsatian : (the German shepherd dog) / [by] Joyce Ixer. — Edinburgh [etc.] : J. Bartholomew, 1977. — 96p : col ill, form, col plans ; 19cm.
Bibl.: p.93. — Index.
ISBN 0-7028-1044-4 Pbk : £0.95
(B77-21966)

636.7'3 — Boxer dogs
Royle, Jo. The boxer / by Jo Royle. — Leicester ([55 King Richards Rd] Leicester [LE3 5QG]) : K and R Books Ltd, 1976 [i.e. 1977]. — 149p : ill(some col), geneal tables, ports ; 20cm. — (The dog owner's library)
Bibl.: p.145. — Index.
ISBN 0-903264-17-x : £2.95
(B77-15356)

Somerfield, Elizabeth. The boxer / [by] Elizabeth Somerfield. — 10th ed., revised. — London : Popular Dogs Publishing Co., 1977. — 186p, [20]p of plates : ill ; 23cm. — (Popular Dog's breed series)
Previous ed.: 1974. — Index.
ISBN 0-09-128030-3 : £4.45
(B77-24331)

White, Kay. The boxer / [by] Kay White. — Edinburgh [etc.] : J. Bartholomew, 1977. — 96p : col ill ; 19cm.
Bibl.: p.94. — Index.
ISBN 0-7028-1035-5 Pbk : £0.95
(B77-21236)

636.7'3 — Dobermanns
Curnow, Fred. The dobermann / [by] Fred Curnow and Jean Faulks. — 3rd ed., revised. — London : Popular Dogs Publishing Co., 1976. — 205p,16p of plates : ill ; 23cm. — (Popular Dogs' breed series)
Previous ed.: 1975. — Bibl.: p.197. — Index.
ISBN 0-09-127720-5 : £4.45
(B77-09789)

636.7'3 — Great Danes
Lanning, Jean. The great dane / [by] Jean Lanning. — 3rd ed., revised. — London : Popular Dogs Publishing Co., 1977. — 196p, [16]p of plates : ill, plan, 2 ports ; 23cm. — (Popular Dogs' breed series)
Previous ed.: i.e. 2nd ed., revised, 1974. — Bibl. : p.189. — Index.
ISBN 0-09-128040-0 : £4.45
(B77-29524)

636.7'3 — Great Danes. ***Personal observations***
Woodhouse, Barbara. Almost human / [by] Barbara Woodhouse. — Rickmansworth (Campions, Croxley Green, Rickmansworth, [Herts.]) : The author, 1976. — 136p,leaf of plate,[58]p of plates : ill(some col), ports ; 22cm.
ISBN 0-900819-11-1 : £2.95
(B77-06759)

636.7'3 — Old English sheepdogs
Davis, Ann. The Old English sheepdog / [by] Ann Davis. — 3rd ed. — London : Popular Dogs Publishing Co., 1977. — 176p,[16]p of plates : ill, port ; 23cm. — (Popular Dogs' breed series)
Previous ed.: 1974. — Bibl.: p.169. — Index.
ISBN 0-09-128100-8 : £4.45
(B77-21237)

636.7'3 — Shetland sheepdogs
Osborne, Margaret. The Shetland sheepdog / [by] Margaret Osborne. — 6th ed. revised. — London : Popular Dogs Publishing Co., 1977. — 221p,[16]p of plates : ill, forms ; 23cm. — (Popular Dogs' breed series)
Previous ed.: 1973. — Index.
ISBN 0-09-127730-2 : £4.45
(B77-07444)

Shiel. The Shetland sheepdog / [by] Shiel. — Edinburgh [etc.] : J. Bartholomew, 1977. — 96p : col ill, col plan ; 19cm.
Bibl.: p.93. — Index.
ISBN 0-7028-1005-3 Pbk : £0.95
(B77-33892)

636.7'52 — Cocker spaniels
Lucas-Lucas, Veronica. The cocker spaniel / [by] Veronica Lucas-Lucas. — 8th ed. revised. — London : Popular Dogs Publishing Co., 1976. — 162p,[16]p of plates : ill, ports ; 23cm. — (Popular Dogs' breed series)
Previous ed.: 1974. — Index.
ISBN 0-09-127710-8 : £4.45
(B77-04280)

636.7'52 — Golden retrievers
Tudor, Joan. The golden retriever / [by] Joan Tudor. — 6th ed., revised. — London : Popular Dogs Publishing Co., 1977. — 247p,[16]p of plates : ill, ports ; 23cm. — (Popular Dogs' breed series)
Previous ed.: 1974. — Bibl.: p.238. — Index.
ISBN 0-09-129360-x : £4.45
(B77-29525)

636.7'52 — Gordon setters
Gompertz, Godfrey St George Montague. The Gordon setter : history and character / by G. St G.M. Gompertz. — [Reading] ([Four Points Cottage, Aldworth, Reading]) : [The author], 1976. — xv,247p,[4]leaves of plates,32p of plates : ill(some col), ports ; 26cm.
Bibl.: p.241-244. — Index.
ISBN 0-9505578-0-3 : £7.50
(B77-09790)

636.7'52 — Gun dogs. Training. ***Manuals***
Kersley, Jack Anthony. Training the mind of your gun dog / [by] J.A. Kersley and F. Haworth ; illustrated by James Croft. — London : Pelham, 1977. — 143p : ill ; 23cm.
Index.
ISBN 0-7207-0948-2 : £4.50
(B77-09791)

636.7'52 — Labradors
Darlington, Katya. The Labrador retriever / [by] Katya Darlington. — Edinburgh [etc.] : J. Bartholomew, 1977. — 95p : col ill, col plan ; 19cm.
Bibl.: p.92. — Index.
ISBN 0-7028-1094-0 Pbk : £0.95
(B77-33893)

636.7'52 — Retrievers. Training. ***Manuals***
Scales, Susan. Retriever training : the modern way / by Susan Scales. — Newton Abbot [etc.] : David and Charles, 1976. — 157p : ill ; 22cm.
Cover title: 'The Field' retriever training. — Index.
ISBN 0-7153-7246-7 : £4.50
(B77-06760)

636.75'3 — Afghan hounds
McCarthy, Dennis. The Afghan hound / [by] Dennis McCarthy. — Edinburgh [etc.] : J. Bartholomew, 1977. — 96p : ill(chiefly col), col map, col plans ; 19cm.
Bibl.: p.94. — Index.
ISBN 0-7028-1054-1 Pbk : £0.98
(B77-21238)

636.7'53 — Beagles
Sutton, Catherine. The beagle / [by] Catherine Sutton. — Edinburgh [etc.] : J. Bartholomew, 1977. — 96p : col ill ; 19cm.
Bibl.: p.94. — Index.
ISBN 0-7028-1045-2 Pbk : £0.95
(B77-24332)

636.7'53 — Dachshunds
Harrap, Elizabeth. The dachshund / [by] Elizabeth Harrap. — Edinburgh [etc.] : J. Bartholomew, 1977. — 95p : ill(chiefly col), col plan ; 19cm.
Bibl.: p.92. — Index.
ISBN 0-7028-1025-8 Pbk : £0.95
(B77-33894)

636.7'53 — Gazehounds
Russell, Joanna. All about gazehounds / [by] Joanna Russell. — London : Pelham, 1976. — 160p,[12]p of plates : ill ; 23cm.
Bibl.: p.156-157. — Index.
ISBN 0-7207-0926-1 : £3.95
(B77-00822)

636.7'53 — Greyhounds, to 1973
Genders, Roy. The greyhound and greyhound racing : a history of the greyhound in Britain from earliest times to the present day / by Roy Genders. — London : Sporting Handbooks, 1975. — xi,345p,[24]p of plates,leaf of plate : ill, facsim, forms, ports ; 23cm.
Bibl.: p.303-305. — Index.
ISBN 0-85020-047-4 : £5.25
(B77-33297)

636.7'53 — Hounds for coursing
Walsh, Edward Geoffrey. Lurchers and longdogs / by E.G. Walsh. — Saul (Saul, Glos.) : Standfast Press, 1977. — [23],150p : ill ; 25cm.
ISBN 0-904602-09-5 : £5.25
(B77-25035)

636.7'53 — Whippets
Douglas-Todd, Charles Henry. The whippet / [by] C.H. Douglas-Todd. — 3rd ed. / revised by Kay Douglas-Todd. — London : Popular Dogs Publishing Co., 1976. — 232p,[16]p of plates : ill, ports ; 23cm. — (Popular Dogs' breed series)
Previous ed.: 1973. — Index.
ISBN 0-09-127360-9 : £4.45
(B77-10429)

636.7'55 — American pit bull terriers
Stratton, Richard F. This is the American pit bull terrier / [by] Richard F. Stratton. — Neptune, N.J. : T.F.H. Publications ; Reigate : Distributed by T.F.H. (Gt Britain) [etc.], [1977]. — 176p : ill, ports ; 21cm.
Spine title: American pit bull terrier. — Published in the United States: 1976. — Index.
ISBN 0-87666-660-8 : £7.85
(B77-11282)

636.7'55 — Border terriers
Roslin-Williams, Anne. The border terrier / by Anne Roslin-Williams. — London : Witherby, 1976. — xi,196p,[16]p of plates : ill, map ; 21cm.
Bibl.: p.194.
ISBN 0-85493-118-x : £3.50
(B77-11918)

636.7'55 — Staffordshire bull terriers. ***Encyclopaedias***
Gordon, John Frazer. The Staffordshire Bull Terrier owner's encyclopaedia / [by] John F. Gordon. — 2nd ed. — London : Pelham, 1977. — 240p,[8]p of plates : ill, ports ; 23cm.
Previous ed.: 1967.
ISBN 0-7207-0943-1 : £4.95
(B77-13111)

636.7'55 — West Highland white terriers
Hands, Barbara. The West Highland white terrier / [by] Barbara Hands. — Edinburgh [etc.] : J. Bartholomew, 1977. — 96p : col ill, col plans ; 19cm.
Bibl.: p.93. — Index.
ISBN 0-7028-1074-6 Pbk : £0.95
(B77-22685)

636.7'6 — Yorkshire terriers
Bulgin, Gwen. The Yorkshire terrier / [by] Gwen Bulgin. — Edinburgh [etc.] : J. Bartholomew, 1977. — 96p : col ill ; 19cm.
Bibl.: p.90. — Index.
ISBN 0-7028-1084-3 Pbk : £0.95
(B77-24333)

Munday, Ethel. The Yorkshire terrier / [by] Ethel Munday. — 7th ed. revised. — London : Popular Dogs Publishing Co., 1976. — 173p, [12]p of plates : ill, port ; 23cm. — (Popular Dogs' breed series)
Previous ed.: 1974. — Index.
ISBN 0-09-127580-6 : £4.45
(B77-17599)

636.7'6'09 — Toy dogs, to 1976
Glover, Harry. Toydogs / [by] Harry Glover ; paintings by the author ; photography Diane Pearce. — Newton Abbot [etc.] : David and Charles, 1977. — 110p : ill ; 18x24cm.
Index.
ISBN 0-7153-7338-2 : £4.95
(B77-21239)

636.8 — PETS. CATS
Beadle, Muriel. The cat : history, biology, and behaviour / [by] Muriel Beadle ; drawings by E. John Pfiffner. — London : Collins : Harvill Press, 1977. — 3-251p : ill ; 25cm.
Also published: New York : Simon and Schuster, 1977. — Bibl.: p.235-242. — Index.
ISBN 0-00-262109-6 : £4.95
(B77-27930)

The **great** all-picture cat show / [compiled by] Alexandra Artley. — London : Astragal Books, 1977. — [10],134p,[16]p of plates : ill(some col), facsims ; 26cm.
ISBN 0-85139-254-7 : £5.95
(B77-30383)

Nichols, Beverley. Beverley Nichols' cats' A-Z / illustrated by Derrick Sayer. — London : W.H. Allen, 1977. — 248p : ill ; 24cm.
'... made up of two previously published books : "Beverley Nichols' cats' A.B.C". [London : Cape, 1960 ; and,] "Beverley Nichols' cats' X.Y.Z". [London : Cape, 1961]' - title page verso.
ISBN 0-491-02351-0 : £5.00
(B77-33298)

Pond, Grace. The observer's book of cats : describing all recognised breeds and varieties / [by] Grace Pond. — 2nd revised ed. — London [etc.] : F. Warne, 1975. — 157,[3]p,[32]p of plates : ill(some col) ; 15cm. — (Observer's pocket series ; [30])
Ill. on lining paper. — Previous ed.: 1959. — Index.
ISBN 0-7232-1548-0 : £0.90
(B77-00287)

Warner, Matt. Cats of the world / [by] Matt Warner. — Toronto [etc.] ; London : Bantam, 1976. — 160p : ill(chiefly col) ; 18cm. — (All-color guide)
'A Ridge Press Book'. — Bibl.: p.157. — Index.
ISBN 0-552-60117-9 Pbk : £0.75
(B77-07959)

Warner, Matt. Cats of the world / [by] Matt Warner. — London : Transworld, 1976. — 159, [1]p : ill(chiefly col) ; 19cm. — (All-color guide)
'A Ridge Press Book'. — Originally published: Toronto ; London : Bantam, 1976. — Bibl.: p.157. — Index.
ISBN 0-552-98011-0 : £1.45
(B77-16465)

636.8 — Pets: Cats. Behaviour

Fox, Michael Wilson. Understanding your cat / by Michael W. Fox. — Toronto [etc.] ; London : Bantam, 1977. — xii,193p : ill ; 18cm.
Originally published: London : Blond and Briggs, 1974. — Bibl.: p.185. — Index.
ISBN 0-552-62371-7 Pbk : £0.75
(B77-31972)

Pond, Grace. The intelligent cat / [by] Grace Pond and Angela Sayer. — London : Davis-Poynter, 1977. — 120p,[8]p of plates : ill ; 23cm.
Index.
ISBN 0-7067-0204-2 : £3.95
(B77-31973)

636.8 — Pets: Cats. Behaviour. ***Stories, anecdotes***

Millard, Adele. Cats in fact & legend / by Adele Millard ; drawings by Minn. — New York : Sterling [etc.] ; London : Distributed by Ward Lock, 1976. — 128p ; 21cm.
Index.
ISBN 0-7061-2151-1 : £1.95
(B77-00288)

636.8'008 — Pets: Cats. ***Anthologies***

The **book** of cats / edited by George MacBeth and Martin Booth. — London : Secker and Warburg, 1976. — ix,288p,[16]p of plates : ill(some col), ports(some col) ; 29cm.
Index.
ISBN 0-436-27019-6 : £8.50
(B77-03095)

636.8'009 — Pets: Cats, to 1976

Kirk, Mildred. The everlasting cat / [by] Mildred Kirk. — London : Faber, 1977. — 3-207p,[8]p of plates : ill, facsim ; 23cm.
Index.
ISBN 0-571-11112-2 : £4.95 : CIP rev.
(B77-09106)

636.8'0092'4 — Pets: Cats. ***Cornwall. Personal observations***

Tangye, Derek. A cat affair / [by] Derek Tangye. — London : Sphere, 1976. — 159p ; 18cm.
Originally published: London : Joseph, 1974.
ISBN 0-7221-8365-8 Pbk : £0.50
(B77-15935)

Tangye, Derek. Somewhere a cat is waiting / [by] Derek Tangye ; drawings by Jean Nicol Tangye. — London : Joseph, 1977. — 368p : ill, ports ; 23cm.
'This volume is a revised, abridged and edited version of three separate books entitled "A cat in the window" (1962), "Lama" (1966), and "A cat affair" (1974), all published ... by Michael Joseph' - title page verso.
ISBN 0-7181-1628-3 : £4.95
(B77-21967)

636.8'08 — Pets: Cats. Breeding & care

TV Vet. Cats, their health and care : owner's guide to cat ailments and conditions / by the TV Vet. — Ipswich : Farming Press, 1977. — 128p : ill ; 25cm.
Index.
ISBN 0-85236-068-1 : £3.75
(B77-07445)

636.8'08'21 — Pets: Cats. Breeding. Genetic factors

Robinson, Roy. Genetics for cat breeders / by Roy Robinson. — 2nd ed. — Oxford [etc.] : Pergamon, 1977. — viii,202p,8p of plates : ill, form ; 22cm. — (International series in pure and applied biology : division zoology ; vol.58 ISSN 0074-8307)
Previous ed.: 1971. — Bibl.: p.194-198. — Index.
ISBN 0-08-021209-3 : £6.00
(B77-28696)

636.8'08'241 — Pets: Cats. Pure breeds. Breeding. ***Manuals***

Richards, Dorothy Silkstone. A handbook of pedigree cat breeding / [by] Dorothy Silkstone Richards. — London : Batsford, 1977. — 143p, [16]p of plates : ill, forms, plans ; 22cm.
Index.
ISBN 0-7134-0421-3 : £4.95
ISBN 0-7134-0422-1 Pbk : £2.95
(B77-27205)

636.8'08'3 — Pets: Cats. Care. ***Juvenile literature***

Alexander, Rosemary. A cat of your own / [by] Rosemary Alexander ; illustrated by Nikki Keep. — London : Carousel Books, 1977. — 61p : ill ; 20cm. — (Carousel books) (Pet books)
ISBN 0-552-54117-6 Pbk : £0.40
(B77-16951)

636.8'08'96 — Pets: Cats. Diseases

Textbook of veterinary internal medicine : diseases of the dog and cat / edited by Stephen J. Ettinger. — Philadelphia ; London [etc.] : Saunders, [1976]. — 2v.(xxiii,1767,lxxvii p) : ill(some col) ; 27cm.
Published in the United States: 1975. — Bibl. — Index.
ISBN 0-7216-3424-9 : £53.50
Primary classification 636.7'08'96
(B77-04916)

636.9 — LIVESTOCK. RABBITS, GUINEA PIGS, ETC

636'.93'22 — Livestock: Rabbits. Breeds. ***Great Britain. Standards***

British Rabbit Council. Breed standards & show rules / [British Rabbit Council]. — [Newark] ([7 Kirkgate, Newark, Notts. NG24 1AD]) : [The Council].
1976-1980. — [1976]. — [1],61p ; 19cm.
ISBN 0-901556-07-6 Sd : £0.50(free to members)
(B77-16952)

636'.93'22 — Livestock: Rabbits. Care & management. ***Amateurs' manuals***

Downing, Elisabeth. Keeping rabbits / [by] Elisabeth Downing. — London : Pelham, 1977. — 144p : ill ; 21cm. — (Garden farming series)
Bibl.: p.142. — Index.
ISBN 0-7207-0938-5 : £3.25
(B77-21240)

Netherway, Marjorie Edith Pamela. Home rabbit keeping / by Marjorie E.P. Netherway. — Wakefield : EP Publishing, 1976. — 71p : ill, 2 forms ; 24cm. — (Invest in living)
Bibl.: p.71.
ISBN 0-7158-0458-8 Pbk : £1.25
(B77-15936)

636'.93'22 — Livestock: Rabbits. Production. ***Developing countries. Research reports***

Owen, John Edward. The rabbit as a producer of meat and skins in developing countries / [by] J.E. Owen, D.J. Morgan and J. Barlow. — London : Tropical Products Institute, 1977. — v,30,[1]p : ill ; 30cm. — (G108)
English text ; summary and conclusions in French and Spanish. — Bibl.: p.28-30.
ISBN 0-85954-062-6 Sd : £0.90
(B77-18253)

636'.93'22 — Pets: Rabbits. Care. ***Juvenile literature***

Creek, Rosemary. Rabbits / by Rosemary Creek ; illustrated by Nita Sowter. — Cambridge : Dinosaur Publications, 1977. — 23p : col ill ; 16x18cm. — (Althea's pet series)
ISBN 0-85122-127-0 Sd : £0.35
(B77-30384)

636'.93'233 — Laboratory animals: Mice. Anatomy

Cook, Margaret Jean. The anatomy of the laboratory mouse / [by] Margaret J. Cook. — London [etc.] : Academic Press, 1976. — vii, 143p : ill(some col) ; 25cm.
Originally published: London : Academic Press, 1965. — Index.
ISBN 0-12-186956-3 Pbk : £6.00
(B77-01466)

636'.93'233 — Pets: Gerbils. Care. ***Juvenile literature***

Creek, Rosemary. Gerbils / by Rosemary Creek ; illustrated by Veronica Barge. — Cambridge : Dinosaur Publications, 1977. — 23p : col ill ; 16x18cm. — (Althea's pet series)
ISBN 0-85122-126-2 Sd : £0.35
(B77-30385)

636'.93'233 — Pets: Mice & rats. Care

Smith, K W. Mice & rats / [by] K.W. Smith. — Edinburgh [etc.] : J. Bartholomew, 1976. — 62p : col ill, col form ; 19cm.
Index.
ISBN 0-7028-1095-9 Pbk : £0.95
(B77-11283)

636'.93'234 — Exhibition guinea pigs. ***Manuals***

Turner, Isabel. Exhibition and pet cavies / by Isabel Turner. — Liss : Spur Publications, 1977. — vii,148p,4 leaves plates : ill(some col), forms ; 23cm. — (Exhibition and family pets series)
Bibl.: p.148.
ISBN 0-904558-22-3 : £3.30
(B77-11919)

636'.93'234 — Pets: Chinchillas & guinea pigs

Denham, Ken. Guinea pigs and chinchillas / [by] Ken Denham. — Edinburgh [etc.] : J. Bartholomew, 1977. — 5-93p : col ill ; 19cm.
Index.
ISBN 0-7028-1075-4 Pbk : £0.95
(B77-22686)

636'.93'234 — Pets: Guinea pigs. Care. ***Juvenile literature***

Creek, Rosemary. Guinea pigs / by Rosemary Creek ; illustrated by Nita Sowter. — Cambridge : Dinosaur Publications, 1977. — 23p : col ill ; 16x18cm. — (Althea's pet series)
ISBN 0-85122-128-9 Sd : £0.35
(B77-30386)

636'.93'234 — Pets: Hamsters. ***Juvenile literature***

Runte, Mathilde. My hamster / text by Mathilde Runte ; [translated from the German] ; photos by Ulrich Thomas. — London [etc.] : Angus and Robertson, 1977. — [41p] : ill ; 24cm.
Translation of: Meine kleinen Hamster'. Lucerne : Reich Verlag, 1975.
ISBN 0-207-95690-1 : £2.50
(B77-14297)

636'.97'4447 — Livestock: Ferrets. Care. ***Manuals***

Samuel, Ernest, *b.1890.* Rabbiting and ferreting / by E. Samuel and J. Ivester Lloyd ; photographs by K.H. Purkiss and Oliver Pike. — 7th ed. — London (26 Caxton St., SW1H 0RG) : British Fields Sports Society, 1976. — 67p : ill ; 22cm. — (British Field Sports Society. Booklets)
Previous ed.: 1974.
ISBN 0-903549-09-3 Sd : £0.30
Also classified at 799.2'59'322
(B77-04917)

637 — DAIRY PRODUCTS

637 — Dairy products. Making. ***Manuals***

Black, Maggie. Home-made butter, cheese and yoghurt / by Maggie Black. — Wakefield : EP Publishing, 1977. — 72p : ill ; 24cm. — (Invest in living)
Bibl.: p.72.
ISBN 0-7158-0453-7 Pbk : £1.25
(B77-14298)

637'.028 — English dairy equipment, 1850-1920

Ingram, Arthur. Dairying bygones / [by] Arthur Ingram. — Aylesbury : Shire Publications, 1977. — 33p : ill ; 21cm. — (Shire album ; 29)
Bibl.: p.33.
ISBN 0-85263-393-9 Sd : £0.50
(B77-32716)

637'.125 — Electric milk production equipment. Use. *Great Britain. Manuals*
Electricity Council. *Farm-electric Centre.* Milk production : a guide to the practical design of installations / [Electricity Council, Farm-electric Centre]. — Kenilworth (National Agricultural Centre, Kenilworth, Warwickshire CV8 2LS) : The Centre, 1972. — v,68p : ill ; 21cm. — (Farmelectric handbook ; no.17 ISSN 0309-247x)
ISBN 0-85188-059-2 Pbk : £0.50
(B77-07446)

637'.125 — Milking equipment. Use. *Manuals*
East of Scotland College of Agriculture. Modern milking equipment and its use / Scottish agricultural colleges [i.e. East of Scotland College of Agriculture, North of Scotland College of Agriculture, West of Scotland Agricultural College]. — [Edinburgh, etc.] ([c/o Edinburgh School of Agriculture, West Mains Rd, Edinburgh EH9 3TG]) : [Council of the Scottish Agricultural Colleges], 1976. — [4], 40p : ill ; 21cm. — (Scottish agricultural colleges publication ; no.14 ISSN 0308-5708)
ISBN 0-905084-16-0 Sd : Unpriced
(B77-04918)

637'.3 — Cheeses. Manufacture
Davis, John Gilbert. Cheese / by J.G. Davis. — Edinburgh [etc.] : Churchill Livingstone.
Vol.3 : Manufacturing methods. — 1976. — [9] p,p465-1032 : ill, maps, port ; 26cm.
Index.
ISBN 0-443-01067-6 : £17.00
(B77-03096)

637'.356 — Cream cheeses. Manufacture on farms. *Manuals*
Agricultural Development and Advisory Service. Farmhouse production of cream cheese / Ministry of Agriculture, Fisheries and Food, ADAS. — Revised [ed.]. — Pinner : The Ministry, 1977. — Folder([4]p) : 1 ill ; 21cm. — (Advisory leaflet ; 222)
Previous ed.: published as 'Cream cheese' / issued by the Ministry of Agriculture, Fisheries and Food. London : H.M.S.O., 1966.
Unpriced
(B77-25036)

638 — INSECT CULTURE
638'.1 — Bee-keeping. *Manuals*
Beckley, Peter. Keeping bees / [by] Peter Beckley. — London : Pelham, 1977. — 125p : ill ; 21cm. — (Garden farming series)
Index.
ISBN 0-7207-0942-3 : £3.50
(B77-26379)

Mace, Herbert. Practical bee-keeping / [by] Herbert Mace ; edited in consultation with Karl Showler. — London : Ward Lock, 1977. — 96p : ill ; 20cm. — (Concorde books)
'... based on Herbert Mace's "The Complete Handbook of Bee-keeping", which has been printed in several editions, the first of which appeared in 1952' - Introduction. — Bibl.: p.93-94. — Index.
ISBN 0-7063-5391-9 Pbk : £1.50
(B77-21968)

More, Daphne. Discovering beekeeping / [by] Daphne More. — [Aylesbury] : Shire Publications, [1977]. — 48p : ill ; 18cm. — (Discovering series ; 226)
Bibl.: p.47. — Index.
ISBN 0-85263-367-x Pbk : £0.50
(B77-31287)

Sechrist, Edward Lloyd. Amateur beekeeping / by Edward Lloyd Sechrist ; edited by A.C. Brown. — 2nd ed. — London : Hale, 1976. — 156p : ill ; 22cm.
Previous ed.: New York : Devin Adair, 1955 ; London : Hale, 1958. — Bibl.: p.151-152. — Index.
ISBN 0-7091-5661-8 : £3.50
(B77-06761)

Shida, John. Beekeeping / by John Shida. — Gloucester : Thornhill Press, 1976. — 30p : ill ; 20cm. — (A Thornhill guide ; 4)
ISBN 0-904110-39-7 Sd : £0.40
(B77-11284)

Vernon, Frank George. Beekeeping / [by] Frank Vernon. — Sevenoaks : Teach Yourself Books, 1977. — xii,212p,4p of plates : ill ; 18cm. — (Teach yourself books)
Originally published: 1976. — Bibl.: p.206. — Index.
Pbk : £1.25
ISBN 0-340-20382-x
(B77-27206)

638'.1'09 — Bee-keeping, to 1975
More, Daphne. The bee book : the history and natural history of the honeybee / [by] Daphne More. — Newton Abbot [etc.] : David and Charles, 1976. — 143p : ill, facsims, ports ; 24cm.
Bibl.: p.137. — Index.
ISBN 0-7153-7268-8 : £4.50
Primary classification 595.7'99
(B77-03010)

638'.1'0913 — Bee-keeping. *Tropical regions. Conference proceedings*
Conference on Apiculture in Tropical Climates, *1st, London, 1976.* Apiculture in tropical climates : full report of the First Conference on Apiculture in Tropical Climates / edited by Eva Crane. — London (Hill House, Gerrards Cross, Bucks. SL9 0NR) : International Bee Research Association, 1976. — x,208p : ill, maps, plans ; 30cm.
'... Conference ... held on 18-20 October 1976, at the Penta Hotel London ...' - title page verso. — Bibl. — Index.
ISBN 0-900149-85-x Pbk : Unpriced
(B77-27207)

638'.1'0924 — Bee-keeping. Langstroth, Lorenzo Lorraine. *United States. Biographies*
Naile, Florence. America's master of bee culture : the life of L.L. Langstroth / by Florence Naile ; edited, with a foreword and an introduction, by Everett Franklin Phillips. — [1st ed. reprinted] ; [with] a new foreword by Roger A. Morse. — Ithaca ; London : Cornell University Press, 1976. — 215,[1]p : 1 ill, facsim, port ; 23cm.
Originally published: as 'The life of Langstroth'. Ithaca : Cornell University Press, 1942. — Index. — Includes a catalogue of the library of L.L. Langstroth.
ISBN 0-8014-1053-3 : £6.75
(B77-14299)

638'.145 — Queen honey-bees. Rearing. Punched cell methods. *Manuals*
Smailes, Richard. Raise your own queens by the punched cell method / by Richard Smailes. — 2nd ed. — Derby (Whitegates, Thulston, Derby DE7 3EW) : The British Isles Bee Breeders' Association, 1977. — [1],32p : ill, port ; 21cm. — (British Isles Bee Breeders' Association. Leaflets ; 10)
Previous ed.: 1970.
ISBN 0-905369-10-6 Sd : Unpriced
(B77-25724)

638'.16 — Honey. Making. *Manuals*
Bielby, W B. Home honey production / by W.B. Bielby. — Wakefield : EP Publishing, 1977. — 72p : ill ; 24cm. — (Invest in living)
Bibl.: p.71-72.
ISBN 0-7158-0452-9 Pbk : £1.25
(B77-13720)

638'.16 — Honey. Standards
Wix, Paul. The concept and development of honey standards / [by] Paul Wix. — Ilford : Central Association of Bee-keepers, 1976. — [1] ,13p : ill ; 21cm. — (Central Association of Bee-keepers. Lectures)
'... given ... on March 12th 1975 at Caxton Hall, London' - p.1.
Sd : £0.40
(B77-02413)

639.1 — HUNTING AND TRAPPING
639'.11'74446 — Grizzly bears. Commercial hunting. *Early works*
Wright, William Henry. The grizzly bear : the narrative of a hunter-naturalist / by William H. Wright. — [1913 ed. reprinted] ; foreword by Frank C. Craighead, Jr. — Lincoln [Neb.] ; London : University of Nebraska Press, 1977. — xii,274p,[23]leaves of plates : ill ; 21cm.
Facsimile reprint of: 1913 ed. New York : Scribner, 1913. — Index.
ISBN 0-8032-0927-4 : £10.15
ISBN 0-8032-5865-8 Pbk : £3.00
(B77-31288)

639.2 — FISHING, WHALING, SEALING
639'.2 — Fishing equipment: Nets. Materials: Netting. Yarns. Elongation. Measurement. *Standards*
British Standards Institution. Method of test for determination of elongation of netting yarns for fishing nets = Méthode d'essai pour la détermination de l'allongement des fils pour filets de pêche = Prüfverfahren für die Bestimmung der Dehnung von Netzgarnen für Fisehfangnetze / British Standards Institution. — London : B.S.I., 1976. — [2],4,[1]p : 1 ill ; 30cm. — (Bs. 5414 : 1976) (ISO 3790-1976)
ISO title: Fishing nets - determination of elongation of netting yarns. — Pierced for binder.
ISBN 0-580-09038-8 Sd : £1.50
(B77-03097)

639.2 — Trawling. *Illustrations. Juvenile literature*
Claxton, John. Fish and ships / photographs John Claxton ; story Sally Doganis. — London : Hamilton, 1977. — [32]p : chiefly ill ; 26cm. — (All-in-a-day books)
ISBN 0-241-89370-4 : £2.50
(B77-27208)

639'.2'00933 — Fishing. *Ancient Palestine. School texts*
Pitman, Brian Dyett. Getting to know about farming and fishing in the lands of the Bible / [by] Brian D. Pitman ; artist Anne Farncombe. — Redhill : Denholm House Press, 1976. — 32p : ill(chiefly col), col maps ; 25cm. — (Getting to know about ; book 7)
Index.
ISBN 0-85213-148-8 Sd : £0.75
Primary classification 630'.933
(B77-09769)

639'.2'028 — Commercial fishing equipment. *Essays*
Baranov, F I. Selected works on fishing gear / [by] F.I. Baranov ; translated from [the] Russian by E. Velim ; edited by P. Greenberg. — Jerusalem : Israel Program for Scientific Translations ; [London] : [Distributed by Wiley].
Translation of: 'Izbrannye trudy'. Moskva : Pishchevaia Promyshlennost', 1969.
Vol.1 : Commercial fishing techniques. — 1976. — xx,631p : ill, port ; 25cm.
ISBN 0-7065-1561-7 : £47.60
(B77-31289)

Vol.2 : Theory and practice of commercial fishing. — 1976. — iii,261p : ill ; 25cm.
ISBN 0-7065-1574-9 : £19.45
(B77-31290)

639'.2'028 — Fish. Stowage. Use of chilled seawater
Kelman, J H. Stowage of fish in chilled sea water / [by] J.H. Kelman. — [Aberdeen] ([135 Abbey Rd, Aberdeen AB9 8DG]) : Ministry of Agriculture, Fisheries and Food, Torry Research Station, [1977]. — 10p : ill ; 21cm. — (Torry Research Station. Torry advisory notes ; no.73)
Sd : Unpriced
(B77-19475)

639'.21 — Angling waters. Management. *Great Britain. Manuals*
Behrendt, Alex. The management of angling waters / [by] Alex Behrendt ; sketches by Katharine Behrendt. — London : Deutsch, 1977. — 205p,[12]p of plates : ill, plans ; 23cm.
Index.
ISBN 0-233-96857-1 : £6.50 : CIP rev.
(B77-24334)

639'.22 — Sea fishing
Barrett, Harry. Seafood / [by] Harry Barrett. — Hove : Priory Press [etc.], 1977. — 89p : ill, map(on lining papers) ; 20x23cm. — (World resources)
Ill. on lining papers. — Bibl.: p.86. — Index.
ISBN 0-85078-239-2 : £2.95
(B77-21241)

639'.22'028 — Deep sea trawling equipment
Garner, John. Modern deep sea trawling gear / [by] John Garner. — 2nd ed. — Farnham, Surrey : Fishing News, 1977. — 83p : ill, chart, plans ; 26cm.
Ill. on lining papers. — Previous ed.: 1967.
ISBN 0-85238-085-2 : £6.25
(B77-33895)

639'.22'05 — Sea fishing. *Serials*
Olsen's fisherman's nautical almanack : containing tide tables and directory of British fishing vessels. — Tonbridge (1 Bank St., Tonbridge, Kent TN9 1BL) : Pearce Publications Ltd.
1975 : 99th year. — [1975]. — 2-661p : ill, charts ; 19cm.
Diary on alternate pages from p.34-56. — Index.
ISBN 0-903406-04-7 Pbd : £3.75
(B77-13721)

1976 : [100th year] : centenary ed. / [edited by H.G. Johannesen]. — [1976]. — 700p : ill, charts ; 19cm.
Diary on p.683-694. — Index.
ISBN 0-903406-05-5 Pbd : £4.75
(B77-13722)

639'.27'58 — Tunny. Fishing. *France. Brittany. Personal observations*
Millar, Ronald, *b.1928.* A time of cherries : sailing with the Breton tunnymen / [by] Ronald Millar. — London : Cassell, 1977. — [10],214p, [8]p of plates : ill, ports ; 22cm.
ISBN 0-304-29842-5 : £5.75
(B77-21242)

639'.28'0924 — Whaling. *Antarctic. Coastal waters. Personal observations*
McLaughlin, William Raffan Davidson. Call to the South : a story of British whaling in Antarctica / [by] W.R.D. McLaughlin. — London [etc.] : White Lion Publishers, 1976. — 188p,[8]p of plates : ill, map ; 23cm.
Originally published: London : Harrap, 1962. — Index.
ISBN 0-7274-0114-9 : £4.95
(B77-07447)

639'.28'0924 — Whaling. *Arctic. Coastal waters, 1866-1867. Personal observations*
Smith, Charles Edward, *b.1838.* From the deep of the sea : the diary of Charles Edward Smith, surgeon of the whaleship 'Diana' of Hull / edited by his son Charles Edward Smith Harris. — Edinburgh : P. Harris, 1977. — xii,288p,[4]p of plates : ill, maps ; 23cm.
Facsimile reprint of: 1st ed. London : A. and C. Black, 1922. — Index.
ISBN 0-904505-29-4 : £4.50
(B77-25725)

639.3 — FISH CULTURE, FISH AS PETS
639'.3 — Aquatic animals. Culture
Bardach, John. Aquaculture : the farming and husbandry of freshwater and marine organisms / [by] John E. Bardach, John H. Ryther and William O. McLarney. — New York ; London [etc.] : Wiley, [1977]. — xiii, 868p : ill, ports ; 23cm.
Originally published: New York : Chichester : Wiley-Interscience, 1972. — Bibl. — Index.
ISBN 0-471-04826-7 Pbk : £12.35
(B77-10836)

639'.3 — Marine animals. Culture. *Coastal waters*
Iversen, Edwin Severin. Farming the edge of the sea / [by] E.S. Iversen. — [2nd ed.]. — Farnham (1 Long Garden Walk, Farnham, Surrey) : Fishing News, 1976. — [3],434p : ill, map ; 22cm.
Previous ed.: 1968. — Bibl.: p.372-411. — Index.
ISBN 0-85238-079-8 : £13.50
(B77-14800)

639'.34 — Aquariums. *Amateurs' manuals*
Simister, William. The home aquarium book / [by] W. Simister. — Newton Abbot [etc.] : David and Charles, 1976. — 127p : ill ; 22cm.
Index.
ISBN 0-7153-7255-6 : £2.95
(B77-03609)

639'.34 — Aquariums. Tropical fish
Wainwright, Neil. The observer's book of tropical fishes / [by] Neil Wainwright. — London [etc.] : F. Warne, 1976. — 160p,16p of plates : ill(chiefly col) ; 15cm. — (The observer's pocket series ; [65])
Bibl.: p.150-151. — Index.
ISBN 0-7232-1560-x : £0.90
(B77-01607)

639'.34 — Marine aquariums. Fish. Diseases
Dulin, Mark P. Diseases of marine aquarium fishes / [by] Mark P. Dulin. — Neptune, N.J. : T.F.H. Publications ; Reigate : Distributed by T.F.H. (Gt Britain), 1976. — 128p : ill(chiefly col) ; 21cm.
Bibl.: p.126. — Index.
ISBN 0-87666-099-5 Pbk : £5.06
(B77-03098)

639'.34 — Marine aquariums. Tropical fish. *Amateurs' manuals*
Campbell, Gail. Salt-water tropical fish in your home / by Gail Campbell. — New York : Sterling [etc.] ; London : Distributed by Ward Lock, 1976. — 144p : ill(chiefly col) ; 22cm.
Index.
ISBN 0-7061-2167-8 : £3.50
(B77-00289)

Denham, Ken. Marine tropical fish : plus some coldwater fishes for home aquariums / [by] Ken Denham. — Edinburgh [etc.] : J. Bartholomew, 1977. — 3-96p : ill(chiefly col) ; 19cm.
Index.
ISBN 0-7028-1076-2 Pbk : £0.95
(B77-21969)

639'.34'03 — Aquariums. Fish. *Encyclopaedias*
Coffey, David J. The encyclopedia of aquarium fish / [by] David J. Coffey ; photographs taken by Heather Angel. — London : Pelham, 1977. — 224p : ill(some col) ; 25cm.
Ill. on lining papers.
ISBN 0-7207-0895-8 : £6.75
(B77-21243)

639'.375'3 — Pets: Guppies. Showing. *Manuals*
Wasserman, Lou. How to raise show guppies / by Lou Wasserman. — Neptune City ; Reigate [etc.] : T.F.H., 1977. — 112p : ill(some col), ports ; 21cm.
Index.
ISBN 0-87666-453-2 Pbk : £2.40
(B77-24335)

639.39 — CULTURE OF REPTILES
639'.39 — Pets: Reptiles. Care
Foden, John. Reptiles, including crocodilians, chelonians, snakes and lizards / [by] John Foden & Michael Sutton. — Edinburgh [etc.] : J. Bartholomew, 1976. — 94,[1]p : col ill, col map ; 19cm.
Index.
ISBN 0-7028-1081-9 Pbk : £0.95
(B77-11286)

639'.39'12 — Pets: Anoles. *Manuals*
White, William, *b.1934.* The American chameleon / [by] William White, Jr. — New York : Sterling [etc.] ; London : Distributed by Ward Lock, 1977. — 80p : ill ; 21cm. — (Sterling nature series)
Index.
ISBN 0-7061-2539-8 : £2.50
(B77-29526)

639'.39'12 — Pets: Anoles & chameleons. *Manuals*
Roberts, Mervin Francis. All about chameleons and anoles / by Mervin F. Roberts. — Neptune City ; Reigate [etc.] : T.F.H., 1977. — 80p : ill(some col) ; 21cm.
Index.
ISBN 0-87666-902-x Pbk : £1.20
(B77-26380)

639'.39'3 — Pets: Tortoises, turtles & terrapins. Care
Robinson, David, *b.1947.* Tortoises, including turtles and terrapins / [by] David Robinson. — Edinburgh [etc.] : J. Bartholomew, 1976. — 94, [1]p : col ill, col maps ; 19cm.
Index.
ISBN 0-7028-1003-7 Pbk : £0.95
(B77-11920)

639.4/7 — CULTURE OF INVERTEBRATES (OTHER THAN MOLLUSCS AND CRUSTACEANS)
639'.54'1 — Crayfish. Fishing. *New Zealand. Coastal waters. For New Zealand students. Secondary school texts*
Locke, Elsie. Crayfishermen and the sea : interaction of man and environment / [by] Elsie Locke. — Christchurch, N.Z. [etc.] ; London : Whitcoulls, 1976. — 32p : ill, facsim, maps, ports ; 24cm. — (A social studies resource book)
Bibl.: p.32.
ISBN 0-7233-0479-3 Sd : £1.54
(B77-05509)

639'.54'1 — Lobster fishing. *New Zealand. Fiordland. Personal observations*
Powell, Paul, *b.1917.* Fisherman of Fiordland / [by] Paul Powell. — Wellington [N.Z.] [etc.] ; London : A.H. and A.W. Reed, 1976. — xii, 119p : ill(some col), 2 maps(on lining paper), 4 plans(on lining paper), ports(some col) ; 25cm.
ISBN 0-589-00938-9 : £6.90
(B77-21244)

639'.54'4 — Pets: Land hermit crabs. Care. *Manuals*
Nash, Paul J. Land hermit crabs / by Paul J. Nash. — Hong Kong : T.F.H. Publications ; Reigate : Distributed by T.F.H., [1977]. — 32p : ill(chiefly col) ; 21cm.
Published in Hong Kong : 1976.
ISBN 0-87666-907-0 Sd : £0.50
(B77-11921)

639.9 — WILDLIFE CONSERVATION
The **world** of wildlife / edited by Nigel Sitwell. — London [etc.] : Hamlyn : World Wildlife Fund, 1977. — 144p : ill(chiefly col), col maps, ports ; 27cm.
'... yearbook of the World Wildlife Fund' - jacket. — Index.
ISBN 0-600-39391-7 : £2.95
(B77-33299)

639'.9 — Marine organisms. Conservation. *Dorset. Reports, surveys*
Dorset Naturalists' Trust. *Marine Sub-committee.* Marine wildlife conservation in Dorset : a report to the officers and council of the Dorset Naturalists' Trust / compiled by a Marine Sub-committee ... — [Poole] ([c/o Col. F.D.M. Warm, 58 Pearce Ave., Parkstone, Poole, Dorset]) : The Trust, 1974. — [1],32 leaves : ill, charts, maps ; 30cm. — (Dorset Naturalists' Trust. Conservation studies ; 1 ISSN 0309-5681)
Bibl.: leaf 16.
Sd : Unpriced
(B77-13112)

639'.9'06141 — Nature conservation. Organisations. *Great Britain. Nature Conservancy Council. Accounts*
Nature Conservancy Council. Account ... for the year ended 31st March ..., together with the report of the Comptroller and Auditor General thereon ... / Nature Conservancy Council. — London : H.M.S.O.
1975-76. — [1977]. — 7p ; 25cm. — ([1976-77 H.C.]251)
ISBN 0-10-225177-0 Sd : £0.25
(B77-13723)

639'.9'06141 — Nature conservation. Organisations. *Great Britain. Nature Conservancy Council. Reports, surveys. Serials*
Nature Conservancy Council. Nature Conservancy Council report ... — London : H.M.S.O.
2nd : covering the period 1 April 1975-31 March 1976. — 1976. — vi,126p,[16]p of plates : ill, map ; 25cm. — ([1975-76] H.C.44)
Bibl.: p.122-125.
ISBN 0-10-204477-5 Pbk : £2.75
ISSN 0309-3190
(B77-06762)

639'.9'061416 — Northern Ireland. Nature Reserves Committee. *Reports, surveys. Serials*
Northern Ireland. *Nature Reserves Committee.* Report of the Nature Reserves Committee for the year ended 14 August ... — Belfast : H.M.S.O.
9th : 1975. — 1975 [i.e. 1976]. — 32p : ill(some col) ; 25cm.
ISBN 0-337-08069-0 Sd : £0.65
(B77-04281)

Northern Ireland. *Nature Reserves Committee.* Report of the Nature Reserves Committee for the year ended 14th August ... — Belfast : H.M.S.O.
10th : 1976. — 1976. — 31p : ill(some col) ; 25cm.
ISBN 0-337-08085-2 Sd : £1.00
(B77-07448)

639'.9'0624233 — Wildlife. Conservation. Organisations. *Dorset. Dorset Naturalists' Trust, to 1971*
Dorset Naturalists' Trust. DNT 10 : the first ten years of the Dorset Naturalists' Trust. — Poole (c/o Mrs H.J. Brotherton, 58 Pearce Ave., Parkstone, Poole [Dorset]) : [The Trust], [1977]. — [20]p : ill(incl 1 col), map ; 22cm.
ISBN 0-901871-01-x Sd : £0.50
(B77-16466)

639'.9'0624235 — Nature conservation. Organisations. *Devon. Devon Trust for Nature Conservation. Periodicals*
Devon Trust for Nature Conservation. Newsletter / Devon Trust for Nature Conservation. — [Exeter] ([75 Queen St., Exeter EX4 4RX]) : [The Trust].
[No.1]- ; Sept. 1974-. — 1974-. — 26cm.
Published at irregular intervals. — 9p. in 1st issue.
Sd : Unpriced
ISSN 0309-8702
(B77-17600)

639'.9'09146 — Natural resources. Management. Technical aspects. *Coastal regions. Manuals*
Clark, John R. Coastal ecosystem management : a technical manual for the conservation of coastal zone resources / [by] John R. Clark ; [for] the Conservation Foundation. — New York ; London [etc.] : Wiley, 1977. — xi,928p : ill, maps ; 26cm.
'A Wiley-Interscience publication'. — Index.
ISBN 0-471-15854-2 : £28.90
(B77-23523)

639'.9'0924 — Wildlife. Conservation. *Falkland Islands, 1960-1972. Personal observations*
Strange, Ian John. The bird man : an autobiography / [by] Ian Strange. — London (34 Seymour Rd, N8 0BE) : Gordon and Cremonesi, 1976. — 182p,[28]p of plates : ill(some col), map(on lining papers), port ; 27cm.
Index.
ISBN 0-86033-015-x : £6.90
(B77-04282)

639.9'0941 — Agricultural land. Nature conservation. *Great Britain. Reports, surveys*
Nature Conservancy Council. Nature conservation and agriculture : appraisal and proposals / by the Nature Conservancy Council. — London [etc.] : The Council, 1977. — [2],40p : ill, maps ; 30cm.
Bibl.: p.36.
Sd : £1.00
(B77-16467)

639'.9'0941 — Nature conservation. Scientific factors. *Great Britain*
Scientific aspects of nature conservation in Great Britain : a Royal Society discussion organized by J.E. Smith, A.R. Clapham and D.A. Ratcliffe, held on 10 June 1976. — London : Royal Society, 1977. — iii-ix,103p : ill, 3 maps ; 26cm.
'First published in "Proceedings of the Royal Society of London", series B, volume 197 (no.1126), pages 1-103' - title page verso. — Bibl.
ISBN 0-85403-089-1 : £3.50
(B77-23524)

639'.9'0941 — Nature conservation. Sites. *Great Britain. Reports, surveys*
A **nature** conservation review : the selection of biological sites of national importance to nature conservation in Britain / editor Derek Ratcliffe. — Cambridge [etc.] : Cambridge University Press [for the Nature Conservancy Council and the Natural Environment Research Council].
In 2 vols.
Vol.1. — 1977. — xvi,401p,[2]leaves of plates(1 fold),24,8p of plates : ill(incl 1 col), maps ; 29cm.
Bibl.: p.389-391. — Index.
ISBN 0-521-21159-x : £35.00
(B77-20399)

Vol.2 : Site accounts. — 1977. — viii,320p ; 29cm.
Index.
ISBN 0-521-21403-3 : £25.00
(B77-20400)

639'.9'094233 — Wildlife. Conservation. *Dorset. Reports, surveys*
Wise, A J. Wildlife conservation in the Avon Valley, Bournemouth and Christchurch / by A.J. Wise. — [Poole] ([c/o Col. F.D.M. Warm, 58 Pearce Ave., Parkstone, Poole, Dorset]) : Dorset Naturalists' Trust, 1975. — [27]p ; 30cm. — (Dorset Naturalists' Trust. Conservation studies ; 3 ISSN 0309-5681)
Bibl.: p.[27].
Sd : Unpriced
(B77-13113)

639'.9'0942337 — Wildlife. Conservation. *Dorset. Poole (District). Reports, surveys*
Copland, W O. Wildlife conservation in the Poole District and Poole Harbour / prepared by W.O. Copland (Part 1) and W.G. Teagle (Part II) ; edited by W.G. Teagle. — [Poole] ([c/o Col. F.D.M. Warm, 58 Pearce Ave., Parkstone, Poole, Dorset]) : Dorset Naturalists' Trust, 1974. — [4],38[i.e.53]p : 2 maps ; 29cm. — (Dorset Naturalists' Trust. Conservation studies ; 2 ISSN 0309-5681)
Bibl.: p.38.
Sd : Unpriced
(B77-13114)

639'.9'0942357 — Nature reserves. *Devon. East Devon (District). Axmouth to Lyme Regis Undercliffs National Nature Reserve*
Nature Conservancy Council. Axmouth to Lyme Regis Undercliffs National Nature Reserve / Nature Conservancy Council. — Banbury : The Council, 1977. — Folder ([8]p) : ill(some col), col map ; 22cm.
ISBN 0-901204-39-0 : £0.05
(B77-30387)

639'.9'0944 — Wildlife. Conservation. *France. Secondary school texts*
Walling, James Jonas. Wildlife in France / [by] J.J. Walling. — London : Harrap, 1977. — [1], 16,[1]p : ill, facsims, maps ; 14x22cm. — ([Destination France] : life French style)
ISBN 0-245-53054-1 Sd : £0.35
(B77-15357)

639'.95 — Heathland. Gamekeeping. *Great Britain*
Spottiswoode, Joseph. The moorland gamekeeper / [by] J. Spottiswoode ; with photographs by John Marchington. — Newton Abbot [etc.] : David and Charles, 1977. — 184p : ill ; 23cm.
Index.
ISBN 0-7153-7384-6 : £4.95
(B77-24336)

639'.95'0924 — Gamekeeping. *England, 1829-1891. Personal observations*
Wilkins, John, *b.1816?.* The autobiography of an English gamekeeper / by John Wilkins. — [2nd and revised ed.] / edited by Arthur H. Byng and Stephen M. Stephens ; illustrated by Sidney Starr. — Chesham ([Lee Farm House, Botley, Chesham, Bucks.]) : Sporting and Leisure Press, 1976. — [8],441p,leaf of plate,[4]p of plates : ill, maps(on lining papers), port ; 20cm. — (Country classic)
Spine title: An English gamekeeper. — Facsimile reprint of: 2nd and revised ed. London : J. Fisher Unwin, 1892.
ISBN 0-86023-025-2 : £6.95
(B77-16468)

639'.95'0941 — Gamekeeping. *Great Britain. Amateurs' manuals*
Smith, Guy Newman. Gamekeeping and shooting for amateurs / by Guy N. Smith. — Liss (Hill Brow, Liss, Hants. GU33 7PU) : The Spur Publications Co., 1976. — viii,166p : ill ; 23cm. — (Field sports library)
ISBN 0-904558-17-7 : £3.90
Primary classification 799.2'13'0941
(B77-05588)

639'.97'6 — Vertebrates. Conservation. *Juvenile literature*
Constant, Anne Marie. Animals / written and illustrated by Anne-Marie Constant. — London [etc.] : Burke, 1977. — 31,[1]p : ill(chiefly col) ; 18x19cm. — (Waste not want not)
ISBN 0-222-00518-1 : £0.95
ISBN 0-222-00522-x Pbk : £0.80
ISBN 0-222-00514-9 Library ed. : £1.50
(B77-20401)

639'.97'709294 — Inland fisheries. Water. Pollution. Biological monitoring. *Europe. Conference proceedings*
Symposium on the Nature and Extent of Water Pollution Problems affecting Inland Fisheries in Europe, *Helsinki, 1976.* Biological monitoring of inland fisheries / edited by John S. Alabaster. — London : Applied Science Publishers, 1977. — xvi,226p : ill, maps ; 23cm.

'... to help it in forward planning the Fifth Session of EIFAC ... recommended that a Symposium on the Nature and Extent of Water Pollution Problems affecting Inland Fisheries in Europe be held' - Foreword. — 'Proceedings of a Symposium of the European Inland Fisheries Advisory Commission, Helsinki, Finland, 7-8 June 1976' - half title page verso. — English and French summaries. — Bibl. — Index.
ISBN 0-85334-719-0 : £15.00
(B77-21245)

639'.97'82094 — Birds. Conservation. *Europe. Reports, surveys*
Cramp, Stanley. Bird conservation in Europe : a report / prepared for the Environment and Consumer Protection Service, Commission of the European Communities [by] Stanley Cramp. — London : H.M.S.O., 1977. — vi,58p : ill ; 25cm.
At head of title: Nature Conservancy Council. — Bibl.: p.57-58. — Index.
ISBN 0-11-700258-5 : £2.25
(B77-14801)

639'.97'82924 — Water birds. Conservation. *Conference proceedings*
International Conference on the Conservation of Wetlands and Waterfowl, *Heiligenhafen, 1974.* Proceedings [of the] International Conference on the Conservation of Wetlands and Waterfowl, Heiligenhafen, Federal Republic of Germany, 2-6 December 1974 / edited by M. Smart. — Slimbridge ([Slimbridge, Glos., GL1 7BX]) : International Waterfowl Research Bureau, 1976. — [5],v,492p : ill, maps ; 25cm.
Spine title: Conservation of wetlands and waterfowl. — Bibl.
ISBN 0-9505731-0-8 Pbk : £8.50
Primary classification 333.9'5
(B77-15738)

639'.97'82942646 — Bird sanctuaries. *Suffolk. Suffolk Coastal (District). Minsmere*
Axell, Herbert. Minsmere : portrait of a bird reserve / [by] Herbert Axell ; photographs by Eric Hosking ; foreword by Prince Philip, Duke of Edinburgh. — London : Hutchinson, 1977. — 256p,[16]p of plates : ill(some col), maps, plan, ports ; 24cm.
Map on lining papers. — Bibl.: p.247-248. — Index.
ISBN 0-09-128840-1 : £7.50
(B77-27209)

639'.97'84109421 — Wildfowl. Conservation. *London. Thames River, 1960-1975*
Harrison, Jeffery Graham. The Thames transformed : London's river and its waterfowl / [by] Jeffery Harrison and Peter Grant ; photographs by Pamela Harrison ; foreword by Prince Philip, Duke of Edinburgh. — London : Deutsch, 1976. — 240p,[12]p of plates : ill(some col), facsim, maps, plan, ports ; 25cm.
Maps on lining papers. — Bibl.: p.232-235. — Index.
ISBN 0-233-96840-7 : £5.95
Also classified at 598.2'9422
(B77-01608)

639'.97'8410942613 — Wildfowl reserves. *Norfolk. Welney. Welney Wildfowl Refuge, to 1976*
Mason, H J. Welney Wildfowl Refuge / by H.J. Mason ; with a foreword by Sir Peter Scott. — Ely (Providence Place, Wardy Hill, Ely, Cambs.) : Providence Press [for] the Wildfowl Trust, 1976. — 16,[1]p : ill(chiefly col), 2 maps(1 col) ; 19cm.
ISBN 0-903803-02-x Sd : £0.30
(B77-05510)

639'.97'84109426715 — Wildfowl farms. *Essex. Lamarsh. Daw's Hall Wildfowl Farm, to 1976*
Grahame, Iain. Flying feathers / [by] Iain Grahame ; foreword by Gerald Durrell ; illustrations by Timothy Greenwood. — London : Macdonald and Jane's, 1977. — [8], 148p : ill, map(on lining papers) ; 23cm.
ISBN 0-354-04084-7 : £3.75
(B77-15358)

639'.97'8842 — Bluebirds. Conservation. *United States. Amateurs' manuals*
Zeleny, Lawrence. The bluebird : how you can help its fight for survival / [by] Lawrence Zeleny. — Bloomington ; London : Indiana University Press, 1976. — xxi,170p,[4]p of plates : ill(some col), map, plans ; 22cm. — (The Audubon naturalist library)
Bibl.: p.161-167. — Index.
ISBN 0-253-10750-4 : £6.00
(B77-24337)

639'.97'97357 — Red deer. Conservation. Organisations. *Scotland. Red Deer Commission. Reports, surveys. Serials*
Red Deer Commission. Annual report ... / the Red Deer Commission. — Edinburgh : H.M.S.O.
1976. — [1977]. — 18p : 1 ill, map ; 25cm.
ISBN 0-11-491466-4 Sd : £0.35
(B77-15359)

639'.97'974447 — Otters. Conservation. *Great Britain*
King, Angela. The declining otter : a guide to its conservation / by Angela King, John Ottaway and Angela Potter on behalf of the Friends of the Earth Otter Campaign. — Chard (Yew Tree Cottage, Chaffcombe, Chard, Somerset TA20 4AW) : The Campaign, 1976. — [6], 63p ; 21cm.
Bibl.: p.60-62.
Sd : Unpriced
(B77-25726)

639'.99 — Plants. Conservation. *Juvenile literature*
Constant, Anne Marie. Plants / written and illustrated by Anne-Marie Constant. — London [etc.] : Burke, 1977. — 32p : col ill ; 18x19cm. — (Waste not want not)
ISBN 0-222-00521-1 : £1.50
ISBN 0-222-00517-3 Library ed. : £0.90
ISBN 0-222-00525-4 Pbk : £0.85
(B77-20402)

640 — HOUSEHOLD MANAGEMENT
640 — Home economics
Griggs, Barbara. Nouveau poor, or, how to live better on less / by Barbara Griggs & Shirley Lowe ; illustrated by Tom Barling. — London [etc.] : Hodder and Stoughton, 1976. — 158p : ill ; 25cm.
ISBN 0-340-21272-1 : £3.25
(B77-10430)

Griggs, Barbara. Nouveau poor, or, How to live better on less / by Barbara Griggs and Shirley Lowe ; illustrated by Tom Barling. — Revised ed. — London : Sphere, 1977. — 176p : ill ; 18cm.
Previous ed.: London : Hodder and Stoughton, 1976.
ISBN 0-7221-4081-9 Pbk : £0.95
(B77-31291)

640 — Home economics. *For Irish students. Secondary school texts*
Murphy, Eileen. Post primary home economics / [by] Eileen Murphy. — Dublin : Educational Company of Ireland.
In 2 vols.
1 / [illustrations Bob Rogan]. — 1977. — [12], 356p : ill, plans ; 21cm.
Index.
Pbk : £3.19
(B77-27210)

640 — Home economics. *Secondary school texts*
Moloney, Angela. Junior home economics / [by] Angela Moloney. — Metric ed. — Dublin : Gill and Macmillan, 1976. — x,198p : ill ; 22cm.
Previous ed.: Dublin : Gill and Macmillan ; London : Macmillan, 1971. — Index.
ISBN 0-7171-0759-0 Pbk : £1.95
(B77-26381)

Ruth, Beryl. Learning home economics / [by] Beryl Ruth. — London : Heinemann Educational.
Book 4 : You and the community / illustrated by David Farris. — 2nd ed. (metricated). — 1977. — [6],42p : ill ; 23cm.
Previous ed.: 1970.
ISBN 0-435-42249-9 Sd : £0.60
(B77-10837)

640 — Household management. *Manuals*
Conran, Shirley. Superwoman : everywoman's book of household management / [by] Shirley Conran ; illustrations by Jan Mitchener. — Harmondsworth [etc.] : Penguin, 1977. — xiii, 209p : ill, forms ; 20cm.
Originally published: London : Sidgwick and Jackson, 1975. — Index.
ISBN 0-14-004218-0 Pbk : £0.80
(B77-25037)

Evans, Hazel, *b.1928.* How to cheat at housekeeping / [by] Hazel Evans ; illustrations by Vanessa Pancheri. — Sevenoaks : Coronet, 1977. — 142p : ill ; 18cm.
Index.
ISBN 0-340-21253-5 Pbk : £0.70
(B77-28697)

Hatcher, Jo. Home-making on a budget / by Jo Hatcher. — Wellingborough : Thorsons, 1977. — 96p : ill ; 22cm. — (Pauperbacks)
Index.
ISBN 0-7225-0399-7 Pbk : £1.25
(B77-30388)

'Reader's digest' household manual / [edited and designed by the Reader's Digest Association ; consultant editors Elizabeth Gundrey, Barty Phillips]. — London [etc.] : Reader's Digest Association, 1977. — 432p : ill(some col) ; 23x28cm.
Text on lining papers. — Index.
£9.95
(B77-33896)

640 — Household management. *Practical information*
Boyle, Katie. Dear Katie / [by] Katie Boyle. — London : Severn House : [Distributed by Hutchinson], 1976. — 141p : ill ; 21cm. — ('TV times' family books)
Originally published: London : Independent Television Books Ltd, 1975.
ISBN 0-7278-0310-7 : £3.95
(B77-06179)

Make ends meet with David Hamilton / edited by Susannah Head ; illustrated by Alison Swan ; additional research by Elizabeth Stanley. — London : Everest, 1976. — 176p : ill ; 18cm.
Index.
ISBN 0-905018-11-7 Pbk : £0.60
(B77-13115)

640 — Household management. *Secondary school texts*
Grice, Rosalie. A life of your own / [by] Rosalie Grice ; illustrated by John Grice. — London [etc.] : Cassell and Collier Macmillan.
Assignment cards. — 1975. — lv. : ill, plans ; 27cm.
Twenty-eight cards ([28]sides), sheet in plastic envelope.
ISBN 0-304-29786-0 : £3.50
(B77-03099)

Cookery cards. — 1975. — lv. : ill(chiefly col) ; 27cm.
Twenty-three cards ([56]sides), sheet in plastic envelope.
ISBN 0-304-29785-2 : £7.00
(B77-03100)

640 — Households. Self-sufficiency. *Great Britain. Manuals*
Allaby, Michael. The survival handbook : self-sufficiency for everyone / by Michael Allaby with ... [others]. — London : Pan Books, 1977. — 320p : ill, chart, plans ; 20cm.
Originally published: London : Macmillan, 1975. — Bibl.: p.305-311. — Index.
ISBN 0-330-24813-8 Pbk : £1.25
(B77-09792)

Hinde, Thomas. On next to nothing : a guide to survival today / [by] Thomas and Susan Hinde. — London : Sphere, 1977. — 286p : ill ; 18cm.
Originally published: London : Weidenfeld and Nicolson, 1976. — Bibl.: p.275-276. — Index.
ISBN 0-7221-4558-6 Pbk : £1.25
(B77-28698)

640 — Households. Self-sufficiency. *Great Britain. Periodicals*
Practical self sufficiency. — Saffron Walden (Widdington, Saffron Walden, Essex CB11 3SP) : Broad Leys Publishing Co.
No.1- ; Nov.-Dec. 1975-. — 1975-. — ill, ports ; 30cm.
Six issues a year. — 2-36p. in 1st issue.
Sd : £0.60
ISSN 0309-510x
(B77-20403)

640 — Households. Self-sufficiency. *Rural regions. Manuals*
Massacrier, Jacques. Another way of living / written and drawn by Jacques Massacrier ; translated from the French by Carol Martin-Sperry. — London : Turnstone Books, 1977. — 191p : ill(chiefly col), col charts, form, col plan ; 23cm.
Translation of: 'Savoir revivre'. Paris : A. Michel, 1973. — Bibl.: p.184-187. — Index.
ISBN 0-85500-039-2 Pbk : £2.95
(B77-21246)

640 — Households. Self-sufficiency. *Western Europe*
Rivers, Patrick. Living better on less / [by] Patrick Rivers. — London : Turnstone Books, 1977. — [4],197p : ill ; 21cm.
Bibl.: p.192-193.
ISBN 0-85500-074-0 : £3.95
ISBN 0-85500-064-3 Pbk : £1.95
(B77-21247)

640'.1'5 — Household management. Scientific aspects. *Juvenile literature*
Kilgour, Owen Frederick George. At home with science / [by] O.F.G. Kilgour ; illustrated by Geoff Salter. — London [etc.] : Heinemann Educational, 1976. — iv,125p : ill(some col) ; 25cm.
Index.
ISBN 0-435-42231-6 Pbk : £1.95
(B77-07449)

640'.2'4055 — Home economics. *United States. For adolescents*
Brinkley, Jeanne Hayden. Teen guide to homemaking. — 4th ed. / [by] Jeanne Hayden Brinkley, Valerie M. Chamberlain, Frances Champion. — New York ; London [etc.] : Webster Division, McGraw-Hill, 1977. — 528p : ill(some col) ; 22cm.
Previous ed.: / by Marion S. Barclay et al. 1971. — Index.
ISBN 0-07-007840-8 : £9.45
(B77-04283)

640'.2'4055 — Household management. *Manuals. For adolescents*
Paterson, Barbara. Help! : starting out on your own / [by] Barbara Paterson ; illustrated by Graham Round. — Harmondsworth [etc.] : Penguin, 1977. — 378p : ill ; 20cm. — (Peacock books)
Index.
ISBN 0-14-047088-3 Pbk : £1.00
(B77-13724)

640'.2'436 — Household management. *For cub scouting*
Handyman & home help. — [New ed.]. — Glasgow : Brown and Ferguson, 1976. — 33p : ill ; 16cm. — (Cub Scout badge series ; no.5)
Previous ed.: published as 'Handyman' / by V.B. 1968.
ISBN 0-85174-034-0 Sd : £0.35
(B77-03101)

640'.46'0922 — Men domestic servants. *England, ca 1920-ca 1970. Biographies*
Gentlemen's gentlemen : my friends in service / [compiled] by Rosina Harrison. — London : Arlington Books, 1976. — x,245p,[32]p of plates : ill, ports ; 23cm.
ISBN 0-85140-258-5 : £3.95
(B77-02414)

640'.46'0924 — Domestic service. Rennie, Jean. *Autobiographies*
Rennie, Jean. Every other Sunday / [by] Jean Rennie. — Revised and updated ed. — Sevenoaks : Coronet, 1977. — 217p ; 18cm.
Previous ed.: London : Barker, 1955.
ISBN 0-340-21837-1 Pbk : £0.95
(B77-31974)

640'.46'0942 — Domestic service. *England, 1837-1918*
Huggett, Frank Edward. Life below stairs : domestic servants in England from Victorian times / [by] Frank E. Huggett. — London : J. Murray, 1977. — 186p : ill, facsims, ports ; 26cm.
Index.
ISBN 0-7195-3381-3 : £4.95
(B77-21970)

640'.46'0942 — Domestic service. *England, 1871-1914*
Ebery, Mark. Domestic service in late Victorian and Edwardian England, 1871-1914 / [by] Mark Ebery, Brian Preston. — Reading (Whiteknights, Reading RG6 2AB) : Department of Geography, University of Reading, 1976. — [2],i,117p : ill, maps ; 21cm. — (Geographical papers ; no.42 ISSN 0305-5914)
ISBN 0-7049-0458-6 Sd : £1.30
(B77-06763)

640'.5 — Household management. *Serials*
Conran, Shirley. Superwoman yearbook : a home notebook / [by] Shirley Conran. — London : Sidgwick and Jackson.
[1978] : including the Superwoman diary for 1978 and Patric Walker's guide to your future in the stars. — 1977. — 223p : ill, map, ports ; 21cm.
ISBN 0-283-98419-8 Pbk : £1.25
(B77-32717)

640'.7'24 — Home economics. Experiments
Kilgour, Owen Frederick George. Experimental science for catering and homecraft students / [by] O.F.G. Kilgour and Aileen L'Amie ; drawings by Oxford Illustrators. — London : Heinemann, 1977. — xv,142p : ill ; 14x22cm.
Index.
ISBN 0-434-90264-0 Pbk : £2.50
(B77-03610)

640.73 — Consumer goods. *Great Britain. Consumers' guides*
Black, Sheila P. The Black book : a selective shopping tour with - Sheila P. Black. — London (3rd Floor, 29 Great Marlborough St., W1V 1DB) : Cole Black and Partners Ltd, 1976. — 254p : ill(some col) ; 21cm.
Index.
ISBN 0-905616-00-6 Pbk : £2.75
(B77-16469)

640.73 — Consumer goods. After sales service. *European Community countries. Reports, surveys*
Bureau européen des unions de consommateurs. After sales service in the EEC : a report prepared for the Environment and Consumer Protection Service of the Commission of the European Communities / by the Bureau européen des unions de consommateurs. — London : Graham and Trotman for the Commission of the European Communities, 1976. — vii,271p ; 30cm.
ISBN 0-86010-056-1 Pbk : £15.00
(B77-30389)

640.73'02'4372 — Consumer education. *For teaching*
Williams, Alma. Reading and the consumer : a practical guide / [by] Alma Williams. — London : Hodder and Stoughton [for] the United Kingdom Reading Association, 1976. — 110p ; 22cm. — (Open University. Set books) (Teaching of reading monographs)
Bibl.: p.96-99. — Index.
ISBN 0-340-21027-3 Pbk : £1.25
(B77-07450)

640.73'0941 — Consumer protection. *Great Britain*
Great Britain. *Central Office of Information. Reference Division.* Fair trading and consumer protection in Britain / [prepared by the Reference Division, Central Office of Information]. — London : H.M.S.O., 1976. — [4],60p ; 24cm. — (Central Office of Information reference pamphlet ; 144)
Bibl.: p.59-60.
ISBN 0-11-700801-x Sd : £1.00
(B77-00823)

Turner, Helen. Consumerwise / [by] Helen Turner. — London : Harrap, 1977. — 38p : ill, facsims ; 28cm.
ISBN 0-245-52965-9 Sd : £0.95
(B77-20404)

640.73'0942 — Consumer protection. *England*
Wraith, Ronald Edward. The consumer cause : a short account of its organization, power and importance / [by] Ronald Wraith. — London : Royal Institute of Public Administration, 1976. — 80p ; 22cm. — (Royal Institute of Public Administration. Research booklets)
Bibl.: p.80.
ISBN 0-900628-14-6 Pbk : £1.50
(B77-00824)

640'.76 — Home economics. *Exercises, worked examples. For Irish students. Secondary school texts*
Rodgers, Angela. Intermediate Certificate domestic science / [by] Angela Rodgers. — Dublin : Helicon, 1977. — [4],103p : ill, map ; 21cm. — (Study assessment series)
Fill-in book.
Sd : £1.10
(B77-16953)

640'.92'4 — Household management. Beeton, Isabella. *Great Britain. Biographies*
Freeman, Sarah. Isabella and Sam : the story of Mrs Beeton / by Sarah Freeman. — London : Gollancz, 1977. — 336p,[8]p of plates : ill, facsim, geneal table, ports ; 23cm.
Bibl.: p.325-327. — Index.
ISBN 0-575-01835-6 : £6.95
(B77-33300)

640'.941 — Home economics. *Great Britain. Periodicals*
Journal of consumer studies and home economics. — Oxford [etc.] : Blackwell Scientific.
Vol.1, no.1- ; Mar. 1977-. — 1977-. — ill ; 24cm.
Quarterly. — [2],91p.,plate in 1st issue.
Pbk : £12.00 yearly
ISSN 0309-3891
(B77-22687)

641 — FOOD AND DRINK, NUTRITION
641'.09415 — Food & drinks. *Ireland, to 1976. Secondary school texts*
Mahon, Bríd. Irish food / text Bríd Mahon ; illustrations Mary O'Connell. — [Tallaght] : Folens, [1977]. — [1]p,p65-96 : col ill ; 25cm. — (Irish environmental library series ; no.23)
Sd : £0.60
(B77-18861)

641.1 — Children. Nutrition
Pipes, Peggy L. Nutrition in infancy and childhood / [by] Peggy L. Pipes [et al.]. — Saint Louis : Mosby ; London : Distributed by Kimpton, 1977. — xi,205p : ill, forms ; 26cm.
Bibl. — Index.
ISBN 0-8016-3940-9 Pbk : £5.30
(B77-23525)

641.1 — Food. Chemical constituents & properties
Fox, Brian Anthony. Food science : a chemical approach / [by] Brian A. Fox, Allan G. Cameron. — 3rd ed. — London [etc.] : Hodder and Stoughton, 1977. — 380p : ill ; 23cm.
Previous ed.: London : University of London Press, 1970. — Bibl. — Index.
ISBN 0-340-21366-3 : £4.75
ISBN 0-340-20962-3 Pbk : £2.45
(B77-21248)

Gaman, P M. The science of food : an introduction to food science, nutrition and microbiology / by P.M. Gaman and K.B. Sherrington. — Oxford [etc.] : Pergamon, 1977. — xi,300p : ill ; 21cm. — (Pergamon international library)
Bibl.: p.290. — Index.
ISBN 0-08-019948-8 : £8.25
ISBN 0-08-019947-x Pbk : £4.95
(B77-21249)

641.1 — Food. Constituents. Nutritional values
Stare, Frederick John. Living nutrition / [by] Frederick J. Stare, Margaret McWilliams. — 2nd ed. — New York ; London [etc.] : Wiley, 1977. — xi,497p : ill(some col) ; 25cm.
Previous ed.: 1973. — Bibl. — Index.
ISBN 0-471-82081-4 : £8.70
(B77-11922)

641.1 — Man. Nutrition
Birch, Gordon Gerard. Food science / [by] Gordon G. Birch, Michael Spencer, Allan G. Cameron. — 2nd ed. — Oxford [etc.] : Pergamon, 1977. — viii,191p : ill ; 22cm. — (Pergamon international library)
Previous ed.: 1972. — Bibl. — Index.
ISBN 0-08-021347-2 : £6.95
ISBN 0-08-021346-4 Pbk : £3.95
(B77-23526)

Fremes, Ruth. NutriScore : the rate-yourself plan for better nutrition / [by] Ruth Fremes and Zak Sabry. — London : Eyre Methuen, 1977. — [8],261p : ill ; 24cm.
Originally published: Agincourt, Ont. : Methuen, 1976. — Index.
ISBN 0-413-10000-6 Pbk : £2.95
(B77-21971)

Howe, Phyllis Sullivan. Basic nutrition in health and disease : including selection and care of food / [by] Phyllis Sullivan Howe. — 6th ed. — Philadelphia ; London [etc.] : Saunders, 1976. — xi,454p : ill, facsims ; 24cm.
Previous ed.: 1971. — Bibl.: p.436-439. — Index.
ISBN 0-7216-4788-x Pbk : £6.50
(B77-25727)

McLaren, Donald Stewart. Nutrition and its disorders / [by] Donald S. McLaren. — 2nd ed. — Edinburgh [etc.] : Churchill Livingstone, 1976. — [7],293p : ill ; 19cm. — (Livingstone medical text)
Previous ed.: 1972. — Bibl. — Index.
ISBN 0-443-01521-x Pbk : £3.25
(B77-01609)

Rankin, William Munn. Foods and nutrition / by W. Munn Rankin and E.M. Hildreth. — 12th (revised) ed. / [revised by] Barbara Lake, Mary Waterworth. — London : Mills and Boon ; [London] : Allman, 1976. — 383p : ill ; 22cm.
Previous ed.: / revised by M. Andross. London : Mills and Boon, 1972. — Index.
ISBN 0-263-06231-7 Pbk : £2.95
(B77-25038)

Robinson, Corinne Hogden. Normal and therapeutic nutrition. — 15th ed. / [by] Corinne H. Robinson and Marilyn R. Lawler. — New York : Macmillan ; London : Collier Macmillan, 1977. — x,739p : ill, forms ; 25cm.
Text on lining paper. — Previous ed.: / by Corinne H. Robinson with the assistance of Marilyn R. Lawler. 1972. — Bibl. — Index.
ISBN 0-02-402300-0 : £9.75
Also classified at 615'.854
(B77-33897)

Williams, Sue Rodwell. Nutrition and diet therapy / [by] Sue Rodwell Williams. — 3rd ed. — Saint Louis : Mosby ; London : Distributed by Kimpton, 1977. — xviii,723p : ill, forms ; 27cm.
Previous ed.: 1973. — Bibl. — Index.
ISBN 0-8016-5560-9 : £10.35
Also classified at 615'.854
(B77-33898)

Williams, Sue Rodwell. Nutrition and diet therapy / [by] Sue Rodwell Williams ; with 134 ill., including original drawings by George Straus. — 3rd ed. — Saint Louis : Mosby ; London : Distributed by Kimpton.
A learning guide for students. — 1977. — x, 186p : ill ; 27cm.
Fill in book. — Pages perforated at inside edge and pierced for binder. — Previous ed.: 1973. — Bibl. — Index.
ISBN 0-8016-5565-x Pbk : £5.50
(B77-31975)

641.1'021'2 — Food. Constituents. Nutritional values. *Tables*
Watt, Bernice K. Handbook of the nutritional contents of foods / prepared by Bernice K. Watt and Annabel L. Merrill with the assistance of ... [others] ; for the United States Department of Agriculture. — New York : Dover Publications [etc.] ; London : Constable, 1975 [i.e. 1976]. — [2],190p ; 31cm.
Originally published: as 'Composition of foods'. Washington, D.C. : Consumer and Food Economics Research Division, Agricultural Research Service, U.S. Dept. of Agriculture, 1964. — Bibl.: p.190.
ISBN 0-486-21342-0 Pbk : £2.60
(B77-00825)

641.1'03 — Man. Nutrition. *Dictionaries*
Bingham, Sheila. Dictionary of nutrition : a consumer's guide to the facts of food / [by] Sheila Bingham. — London : Barrie and Jenkins, 1977. — 319p ; 23cm.
Bibl.: p.317-319.
ISBN 0-214-20177-5 : £5.95
(B77-10838)

641.1'05 — Man. Nutrition. *Periodicals*
Nutritional services quarterly review. — London : National Dairy Council.
[No.1]- ; 1975-. — 1975-. — 21cm.
14p. in Jan. 1977 issue.
Sd : Unpriced
ISSN 0309-7749
(B77-17601)

641.1'076 — Food. Nutritional values. *Questions & answers. Secondary school texts*
Kilgour, Owen Frederick George. Multiple choice questions in food and nutrition / [by] O.F.G. Kilgour. — London : Heinemann Educational, 1976. — [2],71p : ill ; 25cm.
With answers.
ISBN 0-435-42520-x Sd : £0.90
(B77-04284)

641.1'09172'4 — Man. Nutrition. *Developing countries*
Sai, Fred T. Food, population and politics / by Fred T. Sai ; with editorial assistance from Penny Kane. — London : International Planned Parenthood Federation, 1977. — 35p : ill ; 21cm. — (Sai, Fred T. Occasional essays ; no.3)
ISBN 0-900924-95-0 Sd : £0.85
(B77-27211)

641.1'3 — Food. Carbohydrates. *Reviews of research*
Developments in food carbohydrate. — London : Applied Science Publishers. — (Developments series)
1 / edited by G.G. Birch and R.S. Shallenberger. — 1977. — x,189p : ill ; 23cm.
'Most of the chapters in this book were presented at an American Chemical Society Symposium organized by the Divisions of Carbohydrate Chemistry (primary sponsor) and Agricultural and Food Chemistry' - Preface. — Index.
ISBN 0-85334-733-6 : £12.50
(B77-23527)

641.1'3 — Food. Carbohydrates. Quantitative analysis
Southgate, D A T. Determination of food carbohydrates / [by] D.A.T. Southgate. — London : Applied Science Publishers, 1976. — ix,178p : ill ; 23cm.
Bibl.: p.167-171. — Index.
ISBN 0-85334-693-3 : £10.00
(B77-05511)

641.1'3'0212 — Food. Carbohydrates. *Tables*
Keating, Leslie. Check your carbohydrates / [by] Leslie Keating. — Revised ed. — Havant : K. Mason, 1976. — [1],32p ; 11cm. — ([Handbag books])
Previous ed.: 1974.
ISBN 0-85937-084-4 Sd : £0.15
(B77-02415)

641.2 — Alcoholic drinks
Amis, Kingsley. On drink / [by] Kingsley Amis ; Nicolas Bentley drew the pictures. — St Albans : Panther, 1974. — 109p : ill ; 18cm.
Originally published: London : Cape, 1972.
ISBN 0-586-04076-5 Pbk : £0.60
(B77-19476)

641.2'02'4642 — Alcoholic drinks. *For waiters*
Tuor, Conrad. Wine and food handbook = Aide-mémoire du Sommelier / [by] Conrad Tuor ; [translated from the French]. — London [etc.] : Hodder and Stoughton, 1977. — 255p : ill, maps ; 16cm.
Translation of: 'Aide-mémoire du Sommelier'. 5. éd. Lausanne : The author, 1970.
ISBN 0-340-17906-6 : £3.50
ISBN 0-340-17907-4 Pbk : £1.75
Primary classification 641.3'002'4642
(B77-25729)

641.2'2 — English wines. Judging. *Manuals*
Andrews, Sidney Whiston. Be a wine and beer judge : a guide for the lover of wines and beers, both amateur and commercial / by S.W. Andrews. — Andover : Amateur Winemaking Publications Ltd, 1977. — [9],116p,[4]p of plates : ill, form, ports ; 18cm. — (An 'Amateur winemaker' publication)
Bibl.: p.111. — Index.
ISBN 0-900841-47-8 Pbk : £0.75
(B77-19477)

641.2′2 — Wines
Don, Robin. Wine / [by] R.S. Don. — 2nd ed. — Sevenoaks : Teach Yourself Books, 1977. — [7],197p : ill, maps ; 18cm. — (Teach yourself books)
Previous ed.: London : English Universities Press, 1968. — Index.
ISBN 0-340-17884-1 Pbk : £1.50
(B77-27931)

Sharp, William J. Wine : how to develop your taste & get your money's worth / [by] William J. Sharp, Joseph Martin ; illustrations by Charles C. Pitcher. — Englewood Cliffs ; London [etc.] : Prentice-Hall, 1976. — xv, 176p : ill, forms, maps ; 22cm.
'A spectrum book'. — Bibl. — Index.
ISBN 0-13-957746-7 : £7.20
ISBN 0-13-957738-6 Pbk : £2.15
(B77-01610)

641.2′2 — Wines. Selection & serving
Price, Pamela Vandyke. Entertaining with wine / [by] Pamela Vandyke Price ; [illustrations by John Hopkins]. — London ([93 Goswell Rd, EC1V 7QA]) : Northwood Publications Ltd, 1976. — xii,196p : ill ; 23cm.
Index.
ISBN 0-7198-2613-6 : £3.95
(B77-12541)

641.2′2 — Wines. Tasting. *Manuals*
Amerine, Maynard Andrew. Wines : their sensory evaluation / [by] Maynard A. Amerine, Edward B. Roessler. — San Francisco ; [Reading] : W.H. Freeman, 1976. — xv,230p, [8]p of plates : ill, forms, ports ; 22cm.
Bibl.: p.207-214. — Index.
ISBN 0-7167-0553-2 : £6.20
(B77-02416)

641.2′2′03 — Wines. *Encyclopaedias*
Baldwinson, John. Plonk and super-plonk / [by] John Baldwinson. — Revised ed. / illustrations by Nick Baker. — Sevenoaks : Coronet, 1977. — 141p : ill ; 18cm.
Previous ed.: London : Joseph, 1975.
ISBN 0-340-21808-8 Pbk : £0.75
(B77-27212)

Morris, Denis. ABC of wine / [by] Denis Morris ; drawings by Holland. — London : 'Daily Telegraph', 1977. — 116p : ill ; 18cm.
Bibl.: p.114.
Pbk : £1.00
(B77-20405)

Schoonmaker, Frank. Frank Schoonmaker's encyclopedia of wine. — 2nd ed. — London : A. and C. Black, 1977. — viii,452p : ill, facsims, maps ; 22cm.
Previous British ed.: i.e. 5th American ed. revised, 1975.
ISBN 0-7136-1804-3 : £7.50
(B77-25728)

641.2′2′0943 — German wines
Ray, Cyril. The wines of Germany / [by] Cyril Ray. — London : Allen Lane, 1977. — 224p : maps ; 21cm.
Bibl.: p.218-219. — Index.
ISBN 0-7139-1033-x : £4.25
(B77-31292)

641.2′2′0944 — French wines
Wildman, Frederick S. A wine tour of France : a convivial wine guide & travel guide to French vintages & vineyards / [by] Frederick S. Wildman. — [New ed.]. — London [etc.] : Cassell, 1976. — xv,335p : maps ; 23cm.
Previous ed.: New York : Morrow, 1972. — Index.
ISBN 0-304-29776-3 : £4.50
(B77-08448)

641.2′2′09444 — Burgundies
Chidgey, Graham. Guide to the wines of Burgundy / [by] Graham Chidgey. — London : Pitman, 1977. — [4],123p : ill, maps ; 23cm.
Bibl.: p.112. — Index.
ISBN 0-273-01043-3 Pbk : £1.95
(B77-31293)

641.2′2′094471 — Bordeaux wines
Price, Pamela Vandyke. Guide to the wines of Bordeaux / [by] Pamela Vandyke Price. — London : Pitman, 1977. — [5],121p : ill, map ; 23cm.
Bibl.: p.110-111. — Index.
ISBN 0-273-00936-2 Pbk : £1.95
(B77-31977)

641.2′2′0946 — Spanish wines
Read, Jan. Guide to the wines of Spain and Portugal / [by] Jan Read. — London : Pitman, 1977. — [2],126p : ill, maps ; 23cm.
Bibl.: p.120-121. — Index.
ISBN 0-273-01024-7 Pbk : £1.95
Also classified at 641.2′2′09469
(B77-30390)

641.2′2′09469 — Portuguese wines
Read, Jan. Guide to the wines of Spain and Portugal / [by] Jan Read. — London : Pitman, 1977. — [2],126p : ill, maps ; 23cm.
Bibl.: p.120-121. — Index.
ISBN 0-273-01024-7 Pbk : £1.95
Primary classification 641.2′2′0946
(B77-30390)

641.2′2′0968 — South African wines. *Encyclopaedias*
De Jongh, S J. Encyclopaedia of South African wine / [by] S.J. De Jongh. — Düsseldorf ; London [etc.] : McGraw-Hill, 1976. — [13], 130p,[2] leaves,[12]p of plates : col maps ; 28cm.
ISBN 0-07-091307-2 : Unpriced
(B77-21250)

641.2′3 — Beers. *Great Britain*
Boston, Richard. Beer and skittles / [by] Richard Boston. — [London] : Fontana, 1977. — 221p : ill ; 19cm.
Originally published: London : Collins, 1976. — Bibl.: p.211-213. — Index.
ISBN 0-00-634846-7 Pbk : £0.85
(B77-17602)

Hardman, Michael. Beer naturally / written by Michael Hardman ; photographs by Theo Bergström. — London (22 Maddox St., London W1R 9PG) : Bergström and Boyle Books Ltd ; St Albans : The Campaign for Real Ale, 1976. — [88]p : ill(some col), map, ports ; 26cm.
ISBN 0-903767-13-9 : £3.75
ISBN 0-903767-09-0 Pbk : £2.50
(B77-03611)

641.2′3 — Beers. *Yorkshire. Poems. Facsimiles*
Meriton, George. The praise of Yorkshire ale / [by] George Meriton. — York ([70 Micklegate, York]) : Ken Spelman Booksellers, 1975. — [132]p in various pagings ; 16cm.
Includes original paging. — Facsimile reprint of: 1st ed. York : J. White for Francis Hilyard, 1685.
Pbk : £0.75
(B77-12542)

641.2′5 — Liqueurs & spirits
White, Francesca. Cheers! : a spirited guide to liquors and liqueurs / distilled, blended and bottled by Francesca White. — New York ; London : Paddington Press, 1977. — 160p : ill, facsims, maps, ports ; 26cm.
Index.
ISBN 0-448-23165-4 : £3.50
(B77-22688)

641.2′52 — Scotch whiskies
Brander, Michael. A guide to Scotch whisky / [by] Michael Brander. — Edinburgh [etc.] : Johnston and Bacon, 1977. — 96p : ill, facsims, maps ; 18cm.
Originally published: London : Collier Macmillan, 1975.
ISBN 0-7179-4561-8 Pbk : £1.35
(B77-13116)

641.2′52 — Scotch whiskies, to 1934
Gunn, Neil Miller. Whisky & Scotland : a practical and spiritual survey / by Neil M. Gunn. — London : Souvenir Press, 1977. — [8] ,198p ; 20cm.
Originally published: London : Routledge, 1935.

£3.00
ISBN 0-285-62289-7 Pbk : £1.60
(B77-20406)

641.2′52 — Scotch whiskies, to 1975
Daiches, David. Scotch whisky : its past and present / [by] David Daiches. — Revised ed. — [London] : Fontana, 1977. — 192p,[8]p of plates : ill, maps, port ; 18cm.
This ed. originally published: 1976. — Bibl.: p.186. — Index.
ISBN 0-00-634902-1 Pbk : £0.80
(B77-21972)

641.3 — Food. *Secondary school texts*
Gray, Don. What is food? / [by] Don Gray. — London : Macdonald Educational, 1977. — [1], 24,[1]p : ill(chiefly col), col map, col port ; 27cm. — (Biology colour units)
ISBN 0-356-05520-5 Sd : £0.85
(B77-15360)

Moore, Wilfred George. Food / [by] W.G. Moore ; [maps and diagrams by A.G. Hodgkiss]. — Amersham : Hulton. — (Man and his world)
Work book. — 1976. — [31]p ; 21cm.
Index.
ISBN 0-7175-0767-x Sd : £0.25
(B77-03612)

641.3′002′4642 — Food. *Dictionaries. For waiters*
Tuor, Conrad. Wine and food handbook = Aide-mémoire du Sommelier / [by] Conrad Tuor ; [translated from the French]. — London [etc.] : Hodder and Stoughton, 1977. — 255p : ill, maps ; 16cm.
Translation of: 'Aide-mémoire du Sommelier'. 5. éd. Lausanne : The author, 1970.
ISBN 0-340-17906-6 : £3.50
ISBN 0-340-17907-4 Pbk : £1.75
Also classified at 641.2′02′4642; 642′.6
(B77-25729)

641.3′009 — Food, to 1976
Larsen, Egon. Food : past, present and future / [by] Egon Larsen ; illustrations by David Armitage. — London : Muller, 1977. — 112p : ill, facsim, maps, ports ; 23cm.
Bibl.: p.107. — Index.
ISBN 0-584-10293-3 : £3.25 : CIP rev.
(B77-23528)

641.3′009′01 — Food, to 500. *Early works. Facsimiles*
Soyer, Alexis. The pantropheon, or, A history of food and its preparation in ancient times : embellished with forty-one engravings illustrating the greatest gastronomic marvels of antiquity / by Alexis Soyer. — New York ; London : Paddington Press, 1977. — [2],xvi, 3-469,[1]p,[26] leaves of plates,[16]p of plates : ill, ports ; 25cm.
Facsimile reprint of: 1st ed. London : Simpkin Marshall, 1853. — Index.
ISBN 0-448-22976-5 : £6.95
(B77-14802)

641.3′00932 — Food. Cultural aspects. *Ancient Egypt*
Darby, William Jefferson. Food : the gift of Osiris / [by] William J. Darby, Paul Ghalioungui, Louis Grivetti. — London [etc.] : Academic Press.
In 2 vols. — Ill. on lining papers. — In slip case.
Vol.1. — 1977. — xxxiii,452,xlii p,[7] leaves of plates : ill(some col) ; 24cm.
Index.
ISBN 0-12-203401-5 : £12.50
(B77-28699)

Vol.2. — 1977. — xxxiii p,p453-877,xlii p,[3] leaves of plates : ill(some col), maps ; 24cm.
Bibl.: p.845-877. — Index.
ISBN 0-12-203402-3 : £12.50
(B77-28700)

641.3′009361 — Food. *Great Britain, ca 200*
Woodman, Marian. Food and cooking in Roman Britain / [by] Marian Woodman ; illustrated by Alison Howard-Drake ; photographs W.J. Barrett ; design and typography R.M. Bryant. — Cirencester ([Park St., Cirencester, Glos. GL7 2BX]) : Corinium Museum, 1976. — 16, [1]p : ill ; 15x21cm. — (Corinium Museum. Brief guides)
Bibl.: p.16.
Sd : £0.35
(B77-17603)

641.3′00941 — Food. *Great Britain, 1870-1975*
Johnston, James P. A hundred years eating : food, drink and the daily diet in Britain since the late nineteenth century / [by] James P. Johnston. — Dublin : Gill and Macmillan [etc.], 1977. — xii,148p,[16]p of plates : ill, facsims, ports ; 23cm.
Bibl.: p.138-142. — Index.
ISBN 0-7171-0747-7 : £4.95
(B77-29527)

641.3′00941 — Food. *Great Britain, ca 1920-ca 1970*
Food in 'Vogue' : six decades of cooking and entertaining / edited by Barbara Tims. — London : Harrap [etc.], 1976. — 255p,[16]p of plates : ill(some col), facsims, ports ; 29cm.
Index.
ISBN 0-245-52945-4 : £12.50
(B77-00826)

641.3'00941 — Food. *Great Britain, to ca 2000. Juvenile literature*
Ellis, Audrey. The 'Magpie' history of food / [by] Audrey Ellis ; text illustrations by Maggie Read and Juliet Stanwell-Smith ; cover illustration by Sandy Nightingale. — London : Pan Books [for] Thames Television's 'Magpie', 1977. — 191p : ill ; 20cm. — (Piccolo)
ISBN 0-330-25138-4 Pbk : £0.50
(B77-13725)

Ellis, Audrey. The 'Magpie' history of food / [by] Audrey Ellis ; text illustrations by Maggie Read and Juliet Stanwell-Smith ; cover illustration by Sandy Nightingale. — London : Severn House : [Distributed by Hutchinson], 1977. — 191p : ill ; 21cm.
Also published: London : Pan Books, 1977.
ISBN 0-7278-0285-2 : £3.25
(B77-31294)

641.3'0094113 — Locally produced food. *Scotland. Orkney & Shetland*
Fenton, Alexander. Traditional elements in the diet of the northern isles of Scotland / [by] A. Fenton. — Edinburgh (c/o Shetland Times Limited, Lerwick, Shetland) : Scottish Country Life Museums Trust, 1976. — [1],16,[1]p ; 26cm.
Reprinted from 'Ethnological food research : reports from the Second International Symposium for Ethnological Food Research, Helsinki, August 1973'. Helsinki, 1975. — Bibl.: p.15-16.
ISBN 0-9505583-0-3 Sd : £0.40
(B77-11287)

641.3'00944 — Food. *France. Secondary school texts*
Carré, Gérard Francis. Food in France / [by] G.F. Carré. — London : Harrap, 1977. — [1], 16,[1]p : ill, map ; 14x22cm. — ([Destination France] : life French style)
ISBN 0-245-53053-3 Sd : £0.35
(B77-15361)

641.3'31 — Bread. *Juvenile literature*
Roscoe, P B. Bread / by P.B. Roscoe ; with illustrations by Jennifer Moore and Gerald Witcomb and photographs by John Moyes. — Loughborough : Ladybird Books, 1977. — 52p : col ill ; 18cm. — (Ladybird leaders ; 31)
Text, col. ill. on lining papers. — Index.
ISBN 0-7214-0459-6 : £0.24
(B77-12543)

641.3'31 — Bread, to 1977
David, Elizabeth, *b.1913.* English bread and yeast cookery / [by] Elizabeth David ; with illustrations by Wendy Jones. — London : Allen Lane, 1977. — xxii,591p,[8]p of plates : ill, facsims ; 23cm.
Ill. on lining papers. — Bibl.: p.549-556. — Index.
ISBN 0-7139-1026-7 : £6.50
(B77-33899)

641.3'37'309 — Coffee, to 1976
Roden, Claudia. Coffee / [by] Claudia Roden. — London : Faber, 1977. — 3-136p,[8]p of plates : ill, facsim, map(on lining papers) ; 23cm.
Bibl.: p.130. — Index.
ISBN 0-571-10932-2 : £4.50
(B77-23529)

641.3'37'309 — Coffee, to 1976. *Juvenile literature*
Smith, Michael, *b.1929.* Coffee / by Michael Smith ; with illustrations by David Palmer. — Loughborough : Ladybird Books, 1977. — 52p : col ill, col maps ; 18cm. — (Ladybird leaders ; 28)
Text, col. ill. on lining papers. — Index.
ISBN 0-7214-0432-4 : £0.24
(B77-08449)

641.3'37'4 — Chocolate & cocoa. *Juvenile literature*
Smith, Michael, *b.1929.* Chocolate and cocoa / by Michael Smith ; with illustrations by B.H. Robinson. — Loughborough : Ladybird Books, 1977. — 52p : col ill, col maps ; 18cm. — (Ladybird leaders ; 30)
Text, col. ill. on lining papers. — Index.
ISBN 0-7214-0433-2 : £0.24
(B77-13726)

641.3'38 — Food. Flavourings. *Stories for children*
Owen, Dilys. Mr Munch - salt & spices / [by] Dilys Owen ; illustrated by Angela Lewer. — London : Muller, 1976. — 64p : ill, map ; 24cm.
ISBN 0-584-63716-0 : £2.25
(B77-07960)

641.3'38'203 — Food. Flavourings. *Encyclopaedias*
Stobart, Tom. Herbs, spices and flavourings / [by] Tom Stobart ; illustrations by Ian Garrard. — Harmondsworth [etc.] : Penguin, 1977. — 320p,[8]p of plates : ill(some col) ; 20cm.
Originally published: as 'The International Wine and Food Society's guide to herbs, spices and flavourings'. London : International Wine and Food Publishing Co. ; Newton Abbot : David and Charles, 1970. — Index.
ISBN 0-14-046261-9 Pbk : £1.25
Also classified at 641.3'5'703
(B77-28701)

641.3'38'3 — Spices. *Juvenile literature*
Spices / adapted from the text written by Joseph Philippe ; illustrated by Louis Joos. — Edinburgh : W. and R. Chambers, 1977. — [27]p : chiefly ill(chiefly col) ; 19x21cm. — (Questbooks : where do things come from?)
ISBN 0-550-31928-x : £1.40
(B77-15362)

641.3'4 — Fruit. *For deep freezing*
Howarth, Sheila. Grow, freeze and cook : your garden on a plate / [by] Sheila Howarth. — St Albans : Mayflower, 1977. — 158p,[8]p of plates : ill ; 18cm.
Originally published: London : Pelham, 1974. — Index.
ISBN 0-583-12701-0 Pbk : £0.75
Also classified at 641.3'5
(B77-22689)

Stevenson, Violet. All about growing for your freezer / [by] Violet Stevenson, Mary Norwak. — London [etc.] : Hamlyn, 1977. — 80p : ill(some col) ; 25cm.
ISBN 0-600-33618-2 Pbk : £1.25
Also classified at 641.3'5
(B77-19478)

641.3'5 — Vegetables. *For deep freezing*
Howarth, Sheila. Grow, freeze and cook : your garden on a plate / [by] Sheila Howarth. — St Albans : Mayflower, 1977. — 158p,[8]p of plates : ill ; 18cm.
Originally published: London : Pelham, 1974. — Index.
ISBN 0-583-12701-0 Pbk : £0.75
Primary classification 641.3'4
(B77-22689)

Stevenson, Violet. All about growing for your freezer / [by] Violet Stevenson, Mary Norwak. — London [etc.] : Hamlyn, 1977. — 80p : ill(some col) ; 25cm.
ISBN 0-600-33618-2 Pbk : £1.25
Primary classification 641.3'4
(B77-19478)

641.3'5'7 — Herbs
Angeloglou, Maggie. All about herbs / by Maggie Angeloglou. — Wakefield : EP Publishing, 1977. — 72p : ill ; 24cm. — (Invest in living)
ISBN 0-7158-0480-4 Pbk : £1.45
(B77-22690)

Back, Philippa. Herbs about the house / [by] Philippa Back ; illustrated by Linda Diggins. — London : Darton, Longman and Todd, 1977. — 94p,[4]p of plates : ill(some col) ; 18cm. — (Herbwise ; 6)
Index.
ISBN 0-232-51389-9 Pbk : £0.99
(B77-30391)

Bylsma-Vriens, Joanne. A spicy and opinionated herb book / by Joanne Bylsma-Vriens ; illustrations by Ko van den Broecke ; [translated from the Dutch]. — Wellingborough : Thorsons, 1977. — 96p : ill ; 18cm. — (Nature's way)
Translation of: 'Een kruid-ig en eigen-wijs boekje'. Helmond : 'Helmond', 1972.
ISBN 0-7225-0385-7 Pbk : £0.90
(B77-22691)

Howarth, Sheila. Herbs with everything : how to grow, preserve and cook them / [by] Sheila Howarth ; with drawings by Yvonne Skargon. — London : Sphere, 1977. — 128p : col ill ; 21cm.
Originally published: London : Pelham, 1976. — Index.
ISBN 0-7221-4720-1 Pbk : £1.75
(B77-13727)

Huson, Paul. Mastering herbalism : a practical guide / [by] Paul Huson ; illustrated by the author. — London : Abacus, 1977. — 330p : ill ; 20cm.
Originally published: New York : Stein and Day, 1974. — Bibl.: p.304-308. — Index.
ISBN 0-349-11803-5 Pbk : £1.95
(B77-20407)

Sherborne House book of herbs. — Sherborne, Glos. : Coombe Springs Press, [1977]. — xi, 71p : ill ; 29cm.
Bibl.: p.71.
ISBN 0-900306-22-x Pbk : £0.90
(B77-09107)

Taylor, Gordon, *b.1935.* A handfull of herbs / gathered by Gordon Taylor. — London [etc.] : Blond and Briggs, 1976. — [48]p : ill ; 22cm.
Bibl.: p.[48].
ISBN 0-85634-058-8 Pbk : £0.95
(B77-03102)

Yewlett, Gerry. Wild herbs for health and happiness : a particular selection of effective healing herbs / by Gerry Yewlett. — [Wokingham] ([20 California Park, Nine Mile Ride, Finchampstead, Wokingham, Berks. RG11 4HT]) : Jogger, 1977. — [28]p : ill ; 84mm x15cm. — (Waterproof outdoor pocketbooks)
Notebook format.
Sd : £0.60
Also classified at 615'.321
(B77-25039)

641.3'5'703 — Herbs. *Encyclopaedias*
Stobart, Tom. Herbs, spices and flavourings / [by] Tom Stobart ; illustrations by Ian Garrard. — Harmondsworth [etc.] : Penguin, 1977. — 320p,[8]p of plates : ill(some col) ; 20cm.
Originally published: as 'The International Wine and Food Society's guide to herbs, spices and flavourings'. London : International Wine and Food Publishing Co. ; Newton Abbot : David and Charles, 1970. — Index.
ISBN 0-14-046261-9 Pbk : £1.25
Primary classification 641.3'38'203
(B77-28701)

641.3'6 — Meat
The **complete** book of meat / edited by Frank Gerrard and F.J. Mallion ; assistant editor Mabel Quin. — London [etc.] : Virtue and Co., 1977. — xv,635p,[72]p of plates : ill(some col), coat of arms, maps, plans ; 27cm.
Index.
£15.50
(B77-25040)

641.3'6 — Meat. *Stories for children*
Owen, Dilys. Mr Munch - meat / [by] Dilys Owen ; illustrated by Angela Lewer. — London : Muller, 1976. — 64p : ill, map ; 24cm.
ISBN 0-584-63715-2 : £2.25
(B77-07961)

641.3'6 — Meat. Properties. *Periodicals*
Meat science. — London : Applied Science Publishers.
Vol.1, [no.1]- ; [Jan.] 1977-. — [1977]-. — ill ; 24cm.
Quarterly. — [3],85p. in 1st issue. — Bibl.
Pbk : £25.00
ISSN 0309-1740
(B77-01611)

641.3'6'2 — Beef. *Juvenile literature*
Wilson, Granville. Beef / by Granville Wilson ; illustrated by Lorraine Calaora. — London [etc.] : F. Watts, 1977. — 47p : col ill, col map ; 22cm. — (A first look book)
Index.
ISBN 0-85166-621-3 : £1.75
(B77-16954)

641.3'7'2 — Butter. *Juvenile literature*
Hinds, Lorna. Butter and margarine / by Lorna Hinds ; illustrated by Lorraine Calaora. — London [etc.] : F. Watts, 1977. — 48p : ill(some col), 2 col ports ; 22cm. — (A first look book)
Index.
ISBN 0-85166-637-x : £1.75
Also classified at 664'.32
(B77-30392)

641.3'7'3 — Cheeses
Eekhof-Stork, Nancy. The world atlas of cheese / by Nancy Eekhof-Stork. — English language ed. / edited by Adrian Bailey. — [London] : Paddington Press [etc.], 1976. — 240p : ill(chiefly col), facsims(some col), col maps, port ; 30cm.
Originally published: in Dutch. Amsterdam : Spectrum International, 1976. — Bibl.: p.233. — Index.
ISBN 0-8467-0133-2 : £12.95
(B77-16955)

641.3'7'350944 — French cheeses. *Encyclopaedias*
Androuet, Pierre. Encyclopedia of cheese / by Pierre Androuet with the help of N. Roche and G. Lambert ; translated from the French by John Githens. — New York ; London [etc.] : Omnibus Press, 1976. — [5],545p : maps ; 21cm.
This translation originally published: as 'The complete encyclopedia of French cheese', New York : Harper's Magazine Press, 1973 ; and as 'Guide du fromage', Henley-on-Thames : Aidan Ellis, 1974. — Translation of: 'Guide du fromage'. Paris : Stock, 1971.
ISBN 0-86001-293-x Pbk : £3.50
(B77-16470)

641.3'7'354 — Wensleydale cheeses, to 1976
Calvert, Kit. Wensleydale cheese / by Kit Calvert. — Enlarged ed. — Clapham, N. Yorkshire : Dalesman, 1977. — 47p : ill ; 19cm. — (A Dalesman mini-book)
Previous ed.: 1946.
ISBN 0-85206-381-4 Pbk : £0.50
(B77-14803)

641.3'8 — Honey. *Juvenile literature*
Munro, Sarah. Honey / by Sarah Munro ; illustrated by Alan Male. — London [etc.] : F. Watts, 1977. — 48p : ill(some col) ; 22cm. — (A first look book)
Index.
ISBN 0-85166-625-6 : £1.75
(B77-21251)

641.3'92 — Food: Fish. *Stories for children*
Owen, Dilys. Mr Munch - fish / [by] Dilys Owen ; illustrated by Angela Lewer. — London : Muller, 1976. — 64p : ill, map ; 24cm.
ISBN 0-584-63714-4 : £2.25
(B77-07962)

641.3'92'0941 — Food: Fish. *Great Britain*
Cullen, Margaret. Fish / [by] Margaret Cullen ; illustrated by Maurice Hutchings. — London : Heinemann Educational, 1977. — [4],107p : ill, map ; 25cm. — (Food for today ; 2)
ISBN 0-435-42466-1 Pbk : £1.50
(B77-25730)

641.4 — Food. Preservation. *Amateurs' manuals*
Cameron-Smith, Marye. The complete book of preserving / [by] Marye Cameron-Smith. — London [etc.] : Marshall Cavendish, 1976. — [2],248,[2]p : ill(chiefly col), facsim ; 30cm.
Ill. on lining papers. — Index.
ISBN 0-85685-174-4 : £6.95
Also classified at 641.6'1
(B77-12544)

Dotter, Pamela. Preserving food / [by] Pamela Dotter. — London : Macdonald Educational, 1977. — 96p : ill(some col) ; 21cm. — (Macdonald guidelines ; 19)
Bibl.: p.91-92. — List of films: p.92. — Index.
ISBN 0-356-06019-5 Pbk : £1.00
(B77-30393)

641.4'53 — Food. Deep freezing
The **complete** encyclopedia of home freezing / general editor Jeni Wright. — London : Octopus Books, 1977. — 256p : ill(chiefly col) ; 31cm.
Col. ill. on lining papers. — Index.
ISBN 0-7064-0594-3 : £4.95
(B77-31295)

641.4'53 — Food. Deep freezing. *Amateurs' manuals*
Cox, Pat Mary. The home book of food freezing / by Pat M. Cox. — Revised ed. — London : Faber, 1977. — 3-352p : ill ; 20cm.
Previous ed.: 1972. — Index.
ISBN 0-571-11104-1 Pbk : £2.50 : CIP rev.
(B77-16956)

Ellis, Audrey. The Hamlyn encyclopedia of freezing / [by] Audrey Ellis. — London [etc.] : Hamlyn, 1977. — 272p : ill(some col), plan, port ; 29cm.
Index.
ISBN 0-600-33146-6 : £4.95
(B77-32718)

McCulloch, Norma. Deep freeze cookery / [by] Norma McCulloch ; editor Anne Marshall ; photographer Svend Bendtsen ; designer Hugh McLeod. — Sydney ; London [etc.] : Hamlyn, 1975. — 120p,[16]p of plates : ill(some col), forms ; 23cm.
Originally published: Sydney : Hamlyn, 1971. — Index.
ISBN 0-600-07086-7 Pbk : Unpriced
(B77-18862)

641.4'53 — Food. Deep freezing. Use of small freezers. *Amateurs' manuals*
Atterbury, Stella. The smallest freezers : and how to make the most of them / [by] Stella Atterbury. — London : Faber, 1977. — 3-192p : ill ; 21cm.
Index.
ISBN 0-571-10888-1 : £4.95 : CIP rev.
ISBN 0-571-11176-9 Pbk : £2.50
(B77-23530)

641.4'6 — Food. Smoke curing. *Amateurs' manuals*
Erlandson, Keith. Home smoking and curing : how you can smoke cure, salt and preserve fish, meat and game / [by] Keith Erlandson. — London : Barrie and Jenkins, 1977. — [7], 118p : ill ; 23cm.
ISBN 0-214-20322-0 : Unpriced
(B77-29528)

641.4'9 — Meat. Preservation. *Amateurs' manuals*
Black, Maggie. Meat preserving at home / by Maggie Black. — Wakefield : EP Publishing, 1976. — 72p : ill ; 24cm. — (Invest in living)
Bibl.: p.72.
ISBN 0-7158-0454-5 Pbk : £1.25
(B77-25041)

641.4'92'53 — Butchery. *Amateurs' manuals. For deep freezing*
Richards, Michael Edward. Meat for your freezer : how to buy and prepare it / [by] Michael E. Richards. — London : Sphere, 1977. — 135p : ill ; 18cm.
Originally published: London : Faber, 1974. — Index.
ISBN 0-7221-7336-9 Pbk : £0.75
(B77-21973)

641.5 — COOKERY
641.5 — Cookery. *Manuals*
Fitzsimmons, Muriel. Cooking for absolute beginners / [by] Muriel Fitzsimmons, Cortland Fitzsimmons. — New York : Dover Publications [etc.] ; London : Constable, 1976 [i.e. 1977]. — iii-xii,364p ; 22cm.
Originally published: as 'You can cook if you can read'. New York : Viking Press, 1946. — Index.
ISBN 0-486-23311-1 Pbk : £2.80
(B77-10431)

Pajot, Anne Marie. Cookery : skills of French cuisine / [by] Anne-Marie Pajot and Elizabeth Pomeroy ; drawings by Roland Garel. — London : Chancerel : Barrie and Jenkins, 1977. — 2-91p : ill, ports ; 21cm. — (Action books)
Ill. on lining papers.
ISBN 0-905703-09-x : £1.75
(B77-27932)

641.5 — Cookery. Techniques. *Manuals*
Nuttall's food facts / compiled by Helen Perrin. — London : F. Warne, 1977. — 48p ; 15cm.
ISBN 0-7232-2022-0 Sd : £0.25
(B77-27213)

641.5 — Food. *Recipes*
Abeles, Kim Victoria. Crafts, cookery, and country living / [by] Kim Victoria Abeles. — New York ; London [etc.] : Van Nostrand Reinhold, 1976. — [9],165p : ill ; 28cm.
Bibl.: p.160-161. — Index.
ISBN 0-442-20236-9 Pbk : £5.65
Primary classification 745.5
(B77-01672)

Adair, Hazel. The Crossroads cookbook / [by] Hazel Adair and Peter Ling. — London : Star Books, 1977. — 189p ; 18cm.
Also published: London : W.H. Allen, 1977. — Index.
ISBN 0-352-39561-3 Pbk : £0.70
(B77-21252)

Beeby, Bruce. Father in the kitchen / [by] Bruce Beeby ; illustrations by Ingrid Johnson. — London : Joseph, 1977. — 143p : ill ; 23cm.
Index.
ISBN 0-7181-1543-0 : £3.95
(B77-12545)

Bond, Jean. Time to stir : a personal collection of home-made recipes / by Jean Bond ; illustrated by John A. Rushton. — Nelson : Hendon Publishing Co., 1977. — 64p : ill ; 24cm.
Index.
ISBN 0-902907-99-9 Pbk : £1.40
(B77-33900)

The **busy** woman's cookbook / Ellen Sinclair, food editor. — London : Souvenir Press, 1977. — 3-45p : col ill ; 27cm.
Text, col. ill. on lining papers. — Originally published: Sydney : Golden Press, 1972.
ISBN 0-285-62266-8 : £1.95
(B77-12546)

Carrier, Robert. Entertaining / [by] Robert Carrier. — London : Sidgwick and Jackson, 1977. — 256p : ill(chiefly col) ; 26cm.
Col. ill. on lining papers. — Index.
ISBN 0-283-98348-5 : £6.95
(B77-27933)

Cartland, Barbara. Recipes for lovers / [by] Barbara Cartland [and Nigel Gordon]. — London : Corgi, 1977. — 128p ; 18cm.
Index.
ISBN 0-552-10510-4 Pbk : £0.65
(B77-21253)

The **complete** colour cookbook / edited by Gill Edden. — London : Octopus Books, 1977. — 256p : col ill ; 31cm.
Col. ill. on lining papers. — Index.
ISBN 0-7064-0635-4 : £3.99
(B77-27934)

The **cooks'** catalogue : a critical selection of the best, the necessary and the special in kitchen equipment and utensils : over 4000 items including 200 extraordinary recipes plus cooking folklore and 1700 illustrations produced with the assistance of the world's leading food authorities / introduction by James Beard ; edited by James Beard ... [et al.]. — New York [etc.] ; London : Harper and Row, [1976]. — x,566p : ill, facsims, port ; 29cm.
Published in the United States: 1975. — Bibl.: p.530-536. — Index.
ISBN 0-06-011563-7 : £11.95
Primary classification 683'.82
(B77-07491)

Everett, Lee. The Lee and Kenny Everett cookery book. — London : Duckworth, 1976. — 62p : ill ; 23cm.
ISBN 0-7156-1137-2 : £2.95
ISBN 0-7156-1138-0 Pbk : £1.95
(B77-00827)

Family cookery / [compiled and edited by Brenda Holroyd]. — London : Sphere, 1975. — 160p : col ill ; 22cm. — ('Good housekeeping' family library)
Originally published: London : Ebury Press, 1973. — Index.
ISBN 0-7221-3948-9 Pbk : £0.95
(B77-19479)

Farmhouse kitchen / edited by Rosemary Heesom. — Leeds (Television Centre, Leeds LS3 1JS) : Yorkshire Television, 1975. — 183p : ill ; 22cm.
'Based on the Independent Television series, presented by Dorothy Sleightholme'. — Index.
ISBN 0-9501113-1-7 Pbk : £1.35
(B77-08450)

Favourite foods of the famous / compiled by Freda Riseman. — London : Coronet, 1976. — 144p : ill, facsims ; 21cm.
Originally published: London : Robson Books, 1974. — Index.
ISBN 0-340-19986-5 Pbk : £1.00
(B77-03103)

Ferguson, Louis G. Advanced cookery / [by] Louis G. Ferguson ; illustrated by Alison J. Marshall. — Carlton, Victoria ; London [etc.] : Pitman, 1974. — [7],279p : ill ; 25cm.
Index.
ISBN 0-85896-249-7 Sp : £3.70
(B77-03104)

'Good housekeeping' cookery for all occasions. — [Revised, up-dated and metricated ed.]. — [London] : Octopus Books, [1976]. — 128p : col ill ; 31cm.
Col. ill. on lining papers. — Previous ed.: published as '"Good housekeeping" cooking for today'. 1973. — Index.
ISBN 0-7064-0577-3 : £2.95
(B77-25731)

Good Housekeeping Institute. 'Good housekeeping' cooking is fun / compiled by Good Housekeeping Institute. — Metric ed. — London : Ebury Press, 1977. — 256p : ill ; 20cm.
Previous ed.: i.e. Revised ed. 1976. — Index.
ISBN 0-85223-121-0 Pbk : £1.95
(B77-31978)

Good Housekeeping Institute. 'Good housekeeping' cooking is fun / compiled by the Good Housekeeping Institute. — Revised ed. — London : Ebury Press, 1976. — 256p : ill ; 20cm.
Previous ed.: 1970. — Index.
ISBN 0-85223-101-6 Pbk : £1.10
(B77-06180)

Graham, Susan. Simple family meals / [by] Susan Graham. — London [etc.] : Collins, 1977. — 104p : ill(some col) ; 28cm. — (Collins cheerful cooking)
Originally published: 1973. — Index.
Pbk : £1.25
ISBN 0-00-435270-x
(B77-28702)

Great dishes of the world in colour / [edited by Jennifer Feller]. — London [etc.] : Hamlyn, 1976. — 320p : ill(some col) ; 29cm.
Ill. on lining papers. — Index.
ISBN 0-600-31927-x : £3.95
(B77-00290)

Kerr, Graham. The new seasoning / [by] Graham Kerr. — Berkhamsted : Lion Publishing, 1977. — 238p : ill ; 21cm.
Originally published: New York : Simon and Schuster, 1976. — Index.
ISBN 0-85648-072-x : £1.95
(B77-17604)

Krüger, Arne. The best of cooking / [by] Arne Krüger & Annette Wolter ; photography by Christian Teubner ; [translated from the German]. — London [etc.] : Hamlyn, 1977. — 336p : col ill ; 29cm.
Translation of: 'Koch vergnügen wie noch nie'. München : Gräfe und Unzer, 1977?. — Index.
ISBN 0-600-31979-2 : £4.95
(B77-30394)

McKee, Alma. Mrs McKee's royal cookery book / decorated by David Hutter. — Jubilee ed. [i.e. 1st ed. reprinted]. — London : Arlington Books, 1977. — x,206p : ill ; 26cm.
This ed. originally published: 1964.
ISBN 0-85140-261-5 : £4.95
(B77-27214)

Mortimer, J C. Presents from the kitchen / [recipes J.C. Mortimer] ; [editor Philippa Davenport ; photographer Melvin Grey]. — London [etc.] : Marshall Cavendish, 1976. — [4],64p : ill(some col) ; 30cm.
'This material has previously appeared in the publication "101 presents to cook"' - title page verso.
ISBN 0-85685-195-7 : £1.50
(B77-07451)

O'Leary, Helen. Career girl's cook book / [by] Helen O'Leary ; illustrated by Peter Davis. — London : Harrap, 1976. — [7],145p : ill ; 21cm.
Bibl.: p.141. — Index.
ISBN 0-245-53028-2 : £3.50
ISBN 0-245-52970-5 Pbk : £1.90
(B77-00828)

Patten, Marguerite. Colourful family cooking / [by] Marguerite Patten. — London : Octopus Books, 1977. — 128p : ill(chiefly col) ; 31cm.
Index.
ISBN 0-7064-0651-6 : £1.99
(B77-20408)

Patten, Marguerite. Marguerite Patten's 100 great menus. — London : Octopus Books, 1976. — 128p : col ill ; 33cm.
Originally published: as 'Marguerite Patten's menu maker'. 1973. — Index.
£3.95
ISBN 0-7064-0250-2
(B77-03105)

Pelton, Robert Wayne. Natural cooking the old-fashioned way / [by] Robert W. Pelton. — South Brunswick ; New York : Barnes ; London : Yoseloff, 1975. — 271p ; 22cm.
Index.
ISBN 0-498-01274-3 : £3.75
(B77-29529)

'Reader's digest' good cook book / [edited and designed by the Reader's Digest Association]. — London [etc.] : The Association, 1977. — 224p : ill(some col), form ; 28cm.
Ill. on lining papers. — Based on: 'The cookery year' / edited and designed by the Reader's Digest Association. London : Reader's Digest Association, 1973. — Index.
£4.95
(B77-20409)

Recipes from a village then and now / compiled and edited by Pauline Sondheim ; illustrated by Ann Wren. — Brightling (Becket House, Brightling, Sussex) : Pauline Sondheim, 1976. — [4],60p : ill, facsims ; 22cm.
Index.
Sp : £1.50
(B77-20410)

Sherborne House cook book. — Sherborne [Glos.] : Coombe Springs Press, [1977]. — [10], 103p : ill ; 29cm.
ISBN 0-900306-00-9 Pbk : £0.95
(B77-09108)

Supercookery! / [edited by Isabel Moore]. — London [etc.] : Marshall Cavendish, 1976. — [8],384p : col ill ; 30cm.
'This material was first published ... in the partwork "Supercook"' - title page verso.
ISBN 0-85685-122-1 : £3.95
(B77-13117)

True blue cookery book : a volume of recipes contributed by various Conservative Members of Parliament and their wives. — Kingswood : Elliot Right Way Books, 1977. — 123p : ill ; 18cm. — (Paperfronts)
Index.
ISBN 0-7160-0630-8 Pbk : £0.50
(B77-16957)

Westland, Pamela. The everyday gourmet : new ideas with basic ingredients / [by] Pamela Westland. — St Albans : Mayflower, 1977. — [1],154p : ill ; 20cm.
Originally published: London : Elm Tree Books, 1976. — Index.
ISBN 0-583-12753-3 Pbk : £0.75
(B77-27215)

Willan, Anne. Great cooks and their recipes, from Taillevent to Escoffier / by Anne Willan. — London : Elm Tree Books, 1977. — 199p : ill(some col), facsims, ports ; 28cm.
Also published: New York : McGraw-Hill, 1977. — Bibl.: p.195-197. — Index.
ISBN 0-241-89587-1 : £8.50
(B77-30395)

'Woman's weekly' popular cook book. — London : IPC Magazines, [1976]. — 192p : ill ; 18cm.
Index.
Pbk : £0.30
(B77-01612)

'Woman's weekly' popular cook book. — London : IPC Magazines, 1977. — 192p : ill ; 17cm.
Originally published: 1976. — Index.
Pbk : £0.30
(B77-18863)

641.5 — Food. *Recipes. For astrology*

Deacon, Eileen. Astrological cook-book / [by] Eileen Deacon. — London : Muller, 1977. — 112p : ill ; 23cm.
Index.
ISBN 0-584-10204-6 : £3.95 : CIP rev.
(B77-22692)

641.5 — Food. *Recipes. For primary school teaching*

Philip, Mary. Who wants to cook? : in playgroup, nursery, infant or junior school / [by] Mary Philip. — London : Heinemann Educational, 1977. — [6],81p ; 22cm.
Index.
ISBN 0-435-42650-8 Pbk : £1.50
(B77-33901)

641.5 — Food. *Recipes. Juvenile literature*

Bakhle, Jill. The first look cook book / by Jill Bakhle ; illustrated by Suzanna Rust. — London [etc.] : F. Watts, 1977. — 48p : ill(some col) ; 22cm.
Index.
ISBN 0-85166-588-8 : £1.75
(B77-12547)

Barrett, Isabelle. Cooking is easy : when you know how / [author Isabelle Barrett] ; [illustrations Joy Simpson]. — London : Marshall Cavendish, 1974. — 48p : col ill ; 32cm. — (A 'Golden hands' book)
ISBN 0-85685-072-1 : £0.99
(B77-19480)

Jarvis, Deborah. Kitchen wizard / by Deborah Jarvis ; illustrated by Arthur Robins. — London : Fontana, 1977. — 129p : ill ; 20cm. — (Lions original)
ISBN 0-00-671209-6 Pbk : £0.50
(B77-25732)

Newman, Nanette. The fun food factory / by Nanette Newman ; illustrated by Alan Cracknell. — [London] : G. Whizzard Publications Ltd ; London : [Distributed by] Deutsch, 1976. — [41]p : ill(chiefly col) ; 30cm.
ISBN 0-233-96821-0 : £1.95
(B77-07452)

Peebles, Lynne. Cooking / by Lynne Peebles ; photographs by John Moyes. — Loughborough : Ladybird Books, 1977. — 53p : col ill ; 18cm. — (Learnabout)
Text, col. ill. on lining papers. — Index.
ISBN 0-7214-0444-8 : £0.24
(B77-14804)

Peebles, Lynne. Cooking with mother / by Lynne Peebles ; photographs by John Moyes ; and illustrations by Roger Hall. — Loughborough : Ladybird Books, 1977. — 53p : chiefly col ill ; 18cm. — (Early learning)
Text, col. ill. on lining papers.
ISBN 0-7214-0413-8 : £0.24
(B77-14805)

Reid, David, *b.1938.* Just William's cookin' book / written by David Reid ; compiled by Brenda Leys ; designed by Terry Griffiths ; illustrated by Pat Gavin. — London : Armada, 1977. — 95p : ill ; 20cm.
Index.
ISBN 0-00-691357-1 Pbk : £0.50
(B77-29530)

Stewart, Katie. 'The Times' calendar cookbook / [by] Katie Stewart. — London [etc.] : Pan Books, 1977. — [4],364p : ill ; 20cm.
Originally published: London : Hamlyn, 1975. — Index.
ISBN 0-330-25200-3 Pbk : £1.50
(B77-28703)

Stewart, Katie. 'The Times' cookery book / [by] Katie Stewart ; illustrated by Pauline Baynes. — London : Pan Books, 1977. — [11],397p : ill ; 20cm.
Originally published: London : Collins, 1972. — 'This book contains a selection of recipes carefully chosen from those that have been published in "The Times" over the last few years' - Introduction. — Index.
ISBN 0-330-25234-8 Pbk : £1.50
(B77-28704)

Travers, Pamela Lyndon. Mary Poppins in the kitchen / [by] P.L. Travers ; Maurice Moore-Betty, culinary consultant ; illustrated by Mary Shepard. — London : Collins, 1977. — [6],122p : ill ; 21cm.
Originally published: New York : Harcourt Brace Jovanovich, 1975. — Index.
ISBN 0-00-195524-1 : £2.25
(B77-10432)

Webber, Kathie. Kathie Webber's New World young cooks' book. — Slough : Foulsham, 1972. — [2],113p : ill(chiefly col), col map ; 25cm.
Index.
ISBN 0-572-00960-7 Sp : £1.95
(B77-07453)

641.5 — Food: Dishes associated with the sea. *Recipes*

Fitzgibbon, Theodora. A taste of the sea in food and pictures / [by] Theodora Fitzgibbon ; period photographs specially prepared by George Morrison. — Newton Abbot [etc.] : David and Charles, 1977. — 105p : ill, facsim, 2 ports ; 18x25cm.
Ill. on lining papers. — Index. — Includes photographs of and notes on life aboard ship.
ISBN 0-7153-7337-4 : £3.95
(B77-20411)

641.5 — Food: Dishes prepared using ovens. *Recipes*

Ellis, Audrey. Oven to table cooking / [by] Audrey Ellis ; illustrated by Kate Simunek. — London : Hutchinson, 1977. — 128p : ill(some col) ; 27cm.
Index.
ISBN 0-09-131570-0 : £3.95
(B77-33301)

641.5 — Food: Dishes using raw food. *Recipes*

Reekie, Jennie. No need to cook : recipes for raw food / by Jennie Reekie ; with illustrations by Yvonne Skargon. — London : Pelham, 1977. — 128p : col ill ; 22cm.
Index.
ISBN 0-7207-1025-1 : £3.75
(B77-32719)

641.5 — Food: Seasonal dishes. *Recipes*

Brady, Christine. Cooking in season / by Christine Brady. — London : Elm Tree Books, 1977. — ix,158p : ill ; 24cm.
Index.
ISBN 0-241-89451-4 : £4.50
(B77-19481)

Ellis, Audrey. Cookery for all seasons / [by] Audrey Ellis ; drawings by Marilyn Day. — Maidenhead : Sampson Low, 1977. — 320p : ill(some col) ; 27cm.
'Much of the contents of this edition previously published in the series Four Seasons Cookery Books' - half title page verso. — Index.
ISBN 0-562-00088-7 : £5.95
(B77-33902)

641.5 — Food: Seasonal dishes. *Recipes. Juvenile literature*
Stewart, Katie. A young cook's calendar / [by] Katie Stewart ; cover illustrations by Jannat Houston, text illustrations by Julia Fryer. — London : Severn House : [Distributed by Hutchinson], 1976. — 144p : ill ; 21cm.
ISBN 0-7278-0278-x : £2.75
(B77-25043)

641.5'02'436 — Food. *Recipes. For Brownie Guides*
Anderson, Verily. Brownie cook-book / [by] Verily Anderson ; illustrated by Ted Draper. — Leicester : Knight Books, 1977. — [2],121p : ill ; 18cm.
Originally published: Leicester : Brockhampton Press, 1972. — Index.
Pbk : £0.50
ISBN 0-340-19112-0
(B77-16471)

641.5'03 — Cookery. *Dictionaries*
Allison, Sonia. The cooks dictionary / [by] Sonia Allison. — Glasgow [etc.] : Collins, 1976. — 3-223p : ill ; 26cm.
Bibl.: p.220-221.
ISBN 0-00-435103-7 : £5.95
(B77-09793)

King, Aileen. Dictionary of cooking terms / [by] Aileen King ; including a section on wines and spirits contributed by John Doxat. — London (Hartree House, Queensway, W2 4SH) : Forbes Publications Ltd, 1976. — vi,165p : ill, maps ; 22cm.
ISBN 0-901762-22-9 : £5.95
(B77-11288)

641.5'07'24 — Cookery. Experiments. *Secondary school texts*
Brown, Margaret A. Experimental cooking / [by] Margaret A. Brown, Allan G. Cameron. — London : Edward Arnold, 1977. — 79p : ill ; 28cm.
Bibl.: p.76.
ISBN 0-7131-0058-3 Sd : £1.95
(B77-27216)

641.5'3 — Suppers. *Recipes*
Cooking lively suppers. — Bishop's Stortford (Elsenham, Bishop's Stortford, Herts.) : Penday Publishing Ltd, 1977. — 24p : ill ; 17cm. — (Family meals)
ISBN 0-86090-010-x Sd : £0.40
(B77-31979)

641.5'52 — Food: Dishes using leftovers. *Recipes*
Keen, Liane. Make a meal of it : recipes for when you 'haven't a thing in the fridge' / by Liane Keen. — London : Deutsch, 1977. — 238p ; 23cm.
Index.
ISBN 0-233-96877-6 : £4.50
(B77-33904)

641.5'52 — Food: Inexpensive dishes. *Recipes*
Ardley, Bridget. The austerity cookbook / [by] Bridget Ardley ; illustrated by Ros Forster. — London : Arrow Books, 1977. — 192p : ill ; 21cm.
Originally published: London : Latimer New Dimensions, 1975. — Index.
ISBN 0-09-914770-x Pbk : £1.50
(B77-30396)

Black, Maggie. Waste not, eat well / [by] Maggie Black. — London : Joseph, 1976. — 293p ; 23cm.
Index.
ISBN 0-7181-1549-x : £4.95
(B77-23531)

Campbell, Susan. Family cook : more fabulous food for next to nothing / by Susan Campbell & Caroline Conran. — [London] : Sphere, 1974. — 191p : ill ; 18cm.
Originally published: London : Macmillan, 1972. — Index.
ISBN 0-7221-2197-0 Pbk : £0.90
(B77-28705)

Ellis, Audrey. The all colour budget cookery book / [by] Audrey Ellis. — [London] ([59 Grosvenor St., W.1]) : Sundial Books Ltd, [1977]. — 5-156p : col ill ; 29cm.
Cover title: The St Michael all colour budget cookery book. — Col. ill. on lining papers.
ISBN 0-904230-35-x : £1.99
(B77-33905)

'Good housekeeping' budget cookbook. — [London] : Octopus Books, [1977]. — 127p : col ill ; 31cm.
Col. ill. on lining papers. — Index.
ISBN 0-7064-0597-8 : £2.95
(B77-25733)

Hopcraft, Jan. Entertaining on a budget / [by] Jan Hopcraft. — London : Eyre Methuen, 1976. — 158p,[8]p of plates : col ill ; 23cm.
Index.
ISBN 0-413-31980-6 : £2.95
ISBN 0-413-31990-3 Pbk : Unpriced
(B77-03106)

Wright, Carol. Budget recipes / [by] Carol Wright. — London [etc.] : Collins, 1977. — 104p : ill(some col) ; 28cm. — (Collins cheerful cooking)
Originally published: 1973. — Index.
Pbk : £1.25
ISBN 0-00-435269-6
(B77-28706)

641.5'55 — Food: Dishes for deep freezing. *Recipes*
Berry, Mary, *b.1935.* Cooking for your freezer / [by] Mary Berry. — [London] ([59 Grosvenor St., W.1]) : Sundial Books Ltd, [1977]. — 96p : col ill ; 28cm. — (St Michael cookery library)
Index.
ISBN 0-904230-46-5 Pbk : £0.99
(B77-30397)

Berry, Mary, *b.1935.* Freezer cookery / [by] Mary Berry. — London : Octopus Books, 1977. — 4-93p : col ill ; 27cm.
Jacket title: The colour book of freezer cookery. — Index.
ISBN 0-7064-0662-1 : £1.99
(B77-27217)

Ellis, Audrey. Easy freeze cooking / [by] Audrey Ellis. — New and revised ed. — London : Corgi, 1976. — 127p : ill ; 18cm.
Previous ed.: 1973. — Index.
ISBN 0-552-10362-4 Pbk : £0.60
(B77-09109)

Maynard, Moya. Hamlyn's all-colour book of freezer cookery / [recipes created by Moya Maynard ; photography by John Lee]. — London [etc.] : Hamlyn, 1977. — 3-63p : ill(chiefly col) ; 29cm.
Spine title: Freezer cookery. — Index.
ISBN 0-600-33611-5 : £1.50
(B77-24338)

Norwak, Mary. Complete freezer recipes / [by] Mary Norwak. — London : Ward Lock, 1977. — 512p,[14]p of plates : ill(some col) ; 23cm.
Originally published: in 4 vols. London : Futura Publications, 1976. — Index.
ISBN 0-7063-5282-3 : £4.95
(B77-31980)

Norwak, Mary. Deep freezing menus and recipes / [by] Mary Norwak. — New ed. — London : Sphere, 1976. — 164p : ill ; 18cm.
Previous ed.: 1970. — Index.
ISBN 0-7221-6431-9 Pbk : £0.60
(B77-27935)

Rennie, Caroline. Simple freezer cookery / [by] Caroline Rennie. — [London] : Fontana, 1977. — 189p ; 18cm.
Originally published: Glasgow : Collins, 1973. — Index.
ISBN 0-00-634990-0 Pbk : £0.75
(B77-22693)

641.5'55 — Food: Dishes prepared in advance. *Recipes*
Marshall, Anne. Night before cookery / [by] Anne Marshall. — [New ed.]. — London : Octopus Books, 1977. — 4-93p : ill(chiefly col) ; 27cm.
Cover title: The colour book of night before cookery. — Ill. on lining papers. — Previous ed.: 1973. — Index.
ISBN 0-7064-0643-5 : £1.99
(B77-25042)

641.5'55 — Food: French dishes for deep freezing. *Recipes*
Hume, Rosemary. Cordon Bleu cookbook : recipes for freezing and entertaining / by Rosemary Hume and Muriel Downes. — London [etc.] : Hamlyn, 1977. — 128p : col ill ; 32cm.
'This material first appeared in two special issues of "Cordon Bleu monthly cookery course", the first published in 1975, the second in 1976' - title-page verso. — Index.
ISBN 0-600-31959-8 : £2.95
(B77-21974)

641.5'55 — Food: Time-saving dishes. *Recipes*
Barry, Michael, *b.1941.* Crafty cooking with Michael Barry. — London (27 Chancery La., W.C.2) : Foxwood Publishing Ltd, 1977. — 63p : col ill ; 23cm.
Adaptation of: 'The crafty cook'. 1975.
ISBN 0-904897-90-7 : £0.95
ISBN 0-904897-30-3 Pbk : £0.95
(B77-24339)

Cooking from your storecupboard. — Bishop's Stortford (Elsenham, Bishop's Stortford, Herts.) : Penday Publishing Ltd, 1977. — 24p : ill ; 17cm. — (Family meals)
ISBN 0-86090-011-8 Sd : £0.40
(B77-31981)

Maynard, Moya. Hamlyn's all colour book of quick dishes / [recipes created by Moya Maynard ; photography by John Lee]. — London [etc.] : Hamlyn, 1977. — 3-63p : ill(chiefly col) ; 29cm.
Spine title: Quick dishes. — Index.
ISBN 0-600-37417-3 : £1.50
(B77-21975)

Norwak, Mary. A calendar of home freezing / [by] Mary Norwak. — Revised ed. — London : Sphere, 1976. — 176p ; 18cm.
Previous ed.: 1972. — Index.
ISBN 0-7221-6450-5 Pbk : £0.60
(B77-06764)

Patten, Marguerite. Cooking in a hurry / [by] Marguerite Patten. — London : Octopus Books, 1977. — 4-93p : col ill ; 28cm.
Originally published: 1973. — Index.
ISBN 0-7064-0645-1 : £1.99
(B77-17605)

Rennie, Caroline. Simple freezer cookery / [by] Caroline Rennie. — Glasgow [etc.] : Collins, 1976. — 3-95p : col ill ; 29cm.
Originally published: 1973. — Index.
ISBN 0-00-435171-1 : £1.95
(B77-06181)

641.5'61 — Food: Dishes for two persons. *Recipes*
'Better homes and gardens' cooking for two. — Toronto [etc.] ; London : Bantam, 1976. — [5], 167p ; 18cm.
Originally published: New York : Meredith Press, 1968. — Index.
ISBN 0-552-66499-5 Pbk : £0.50
(B77-03107)

Castle, Coralie. The art of cooking for two / [by] Coralie Castle, Astrid Newton ; illustrations by Sara Raffetto. — London : Pitman, 1977. — iv, 188p : ill ; 21cm.
Originally published: San Francisco : 101 Productions, 1976. — Index.
ISBN 0-273-01041-7 Pbk : £1.95 : CIP rev.
(B77-08451)

Russell, Sue. Cooking for two / [by] Sue Russell. — [New] ed.. — London : Octopus Books, 1977. — 4-93p : ill(chiefly col) ; 28cm.
Previous ed.: 1974. — Index.
ISBN 0-7064-0644-3 : £1.99
(B77-15937)

641.5'622 — Babies. Food. *Recipes*
Hull, Sylvia. Cooking for a baby / [by] Sylvia Hull ; cartoons [by] Jon. — London (12 Paul St., EC2A 4JS) : Illustrated Publications Co. Ltd, 1976. — 96p : ill ; 21cm. — (A 'Mother & baby' publication)
ISBN 0-901446-15-7 Pbk : £0.60
(B77-00829)

641.5'622 — Children. Food. *Recipes*
Cooking to excite children. — Bishop's Stortford (Elsenham, Bishop's Stortford, Herts.) : Penday Publishing Ltd, 1977. — 24p : ill ; 17cm. — (Family meals)
ISBN 0-86090-009-6 Sd : £0.40
(B77-31982)

Firth, Gay. What's for lunch, Mum? / [by] Gay Firth and Jane Donald. — London : Pan Books, 1977. — 160p : ill ; 20cm.
Originally published: London : Heinemann, 1976. — Index.
ISBN 0-330-25031-0 Pbk : £0.80
(B77-12548)

641.5'622 — Children, to 5 years. Food. *Recipes*
Lansky, Vicki. Feed me! I'm yours : a recipe book for mothers : delicious, nutritious & fun things to cook up for your kids / by Vicki Lansky with ... [others] ; illustrations by Pat Seitz. — Toronto [etc.] ; London : Bantam, 1977. — xiii,153,[3]p : ill ; 18cm.
Originally published: Wayzata : Meadowbook Press, 1974. — Index.
ISBN 0-552-60496-8 Pbk : £0.75
(B77-31296)

641.5'63 — Diabetics. Food. *Recipes*
Beer, Gretel. The diabetic gourmet / [by] Gretel Beer and Paula Davies. — St Albans : Mayflower, 1977. — 173p ; 18cm.
Originally published: London : Pelham, 1974. — Index.
ISBN 0-583-12579-4 Pbk : £0.75
(B77-20412)

641.5'63 — Food: Dishes using natural foods. *Recipes*
Deadman, Peter. Nature's foods / by Peter Deadman & Karen Betteridge ; scripts & drawings by Karen Betteridge. — London : Rider, 1977. — 126p : ill ; 26cm.
Originally published: Llanfynydd : Unicorn Bookshops, 1973. — Index.
ISBN 0-09-128741-3 Pbk : £2.95
(B77-18254)

Munro, Nina. I care cook book / [by] Nina & Jim Munro. — Christchurch [N.Z.] [etc.] ; London : Whitcoulls, 1976. — 56p : ill ; 21x27cm.
Index.
ISBN 0-7233-0452-1 Sp : £3.46
(B77-03108)

641.5'63 — Food: Gluten free dishes, milkless dishes & eggless dishes. *Recipes*
Shattuck, Ruth R. Creative cooking without wheat, milk and eggs / [by] Ruth R. Shattuck. — South Brunswick ; New York : Barnes ; London : Yoseloff, 1976. — 188p ; 22cm.
Originally published: South Brunswick : Barnes, 1974. — Index.
ISBN 0-498-01157-7 : £2.75
(B77-31297)

641.5'63 — Food: Low cholesterol dishes. *Recipes*
Good Housekeeping Institute. Good Housekeeping eating for a healthy heart / by Good Housekeeping Institute ; [editor Amanda Atha ; photographs by Melvin Grey ; line drawings by C.R. Evans]. — London : Ebury Press, 1976. — 128p,[8]p of plates : ill(some col) ; 25cm.
Index.
ISBN 0-85223-105-9 Pbk : £1.50
(B77-00291)

Havenstein, Nathalie. The anti-coronary cookbook : how to achieve weight reduction and cholesterol control / by Nathalie Havenstein and Elizabeth Richardson. — 3rd ed. — Guildford : Lutterworth Press, 1976. — 144p ; 21cm.
Previous ed.: Sydney : Ure Smith, 1975. — Index.
ISBN 0-7188-7005-0 Pbk : £1.50
(B77-01613)

The **low** cholesterol cookbook / [edited by] Jean Walsh. — London : Octopus Books, 1977. — 5-93p : col ill ; 28cm.
Index.
ISBN 0-7064-0589-7 : £1.99
(B77-28707)

MacFarlane, Helen Beverley. The cholesterol control cookbook : dozens of recipes for a healthy heart / by Helen B. MacFarlane. — Wellingborough : Thorsons, 1977. — 96p ; 18cm. — (Nature's way)
Index.
ISBN 0-7225-0382-2 Pbk : £0.90
(B77-31983)

641.5'63 — Health food dishes. *Recipes*
Good Housekeeping Institute. 'Good housekeeping' wholefoods cook book / text by Pamela Dixon ; recipes by Good Housekeeping Institute. — London : Sphere, 1974 [i.e. 1977]. — 192p,[8]p of plates : ill(some col) ; 25cm.
Originally published: as '"Good housekeeping" whole foods cook book'. London : Ebury Press, 1971. — Index.
ISBN 0-7221-2991-2 Pbk : £1.40
(B77-13118)

Mulliss, Christine. Goodness! eating healthily / by Christine Mulliss. — Holsworthy : Health Science Press, 1977. — 63p : ill ; 19cm. — (Health master)
Index.
ISBN 0-85032-157-3 Pbk : £1.25
(B77-29531)

641.5'63 — Persons with ulcers. Food. *Recipes*
Liddell, Caroline. Ulcer superdiet : delicious dishes for sensitive stomachs / [by] Caroline Liddell and Nickey Ross. — London [etc.] : Pitman, 1977. — [4],124p : ill ; 15x23cm. — (The Pitman superdiet series)
Index.
ISBN 0-273-00110-8 : £2.50 : CIP rev.
(B77-08452)

641.5'63 — Pregnant women & nursing mothers. Food. *Recipes*
Liddell, Caroline. Mother's superdiet : healthy eating for you and your baby / [by] Caroline Liddell and Nickey Ross. — London [etc.] : Pitman, 1977. — [5],122p : ill ; 15x23cm. — (The Pitman superdiet series)
Index.
ISBN 0-273-00109-4 : £2.50 : CIP rev.
(B77-09110)

641.5'632 — Food: Low salt dishes. *Recipes*
Brown, William Jann. Cook to your heart's content on a low-fat, low-salt diet. — Revised ed. / [by] W. Jann Brown, Daniel Liebowitz, Marlene Olness. — New York ; London [etc.] : Van Nostrand Reinhold, 1976 [i.e. 1977]. — ix, 150p : ill ; 28cm.
This ed. published in the United States: 1976. — Previous ed.: / by D. Liebowitz, W.J. Brown and M. Olness. Menlo Park : Pacific Coast Publishers, 1969. — Bibl.: p.146. — Index.
ISBN 0-442-24812-1 Pbk : £4.25
Primary classification 641.5'638
(B77-11289)

641.5'632 — Food: Salt-free dishes. *Recipes*
Lloyd, Nancy Doreen. Salt free recipes to save your life / by Nancy D. Lloyd. — 2nd ed. — Wellingborough : Thorsons, 1977. — 64p ; 18cm. — (Nature's way)
Previous ed.: published as 'About salt-free recipes'. London : Thorsons, 1967. — Index.
ISBN 0-7225-0404-7 Pbk : £0.65
(B77-31984)

641.5'635 — Slimmers. Food. *Recipes*
Bowen, Carol. Cooking for slimmers / [by] Carol Bowen. — London ([59 Grosvenor St., W1]) : Sundial Books Ltd [for Marks and Spencer Ltd], 1977. — 96p : col ill ; 28cm. — (St Michael cookery library)
Index.
ISBN 0-904230-47-3 Pbk : £0.99
(B77-27936)

Evans, Michele. Cuisine minceur cookbook / [by] Michele Evans. — London : Sphere, 1978 [i.e. 1977]. — 222p ; 18cm.
Index.
ISBN 0-7221-3378-2 Pbk : £0.75
(B77-31298)

Gibbons, Barbara. The slim gourmet cook book / [by] Barbara Gibbons. — New York [etc.] ; London : Harper and Row, 1976. — vii,401p ; 24cm.
Index.
ISBN 0-06-011517-3 : £6.95
(B77-27937)

Good Housekeeping Institute. 'Good housekeeping' slimmers' cook book / compiled by Good Housekeeping Institute ; [photographs by Gina Harris]. — Revised ed. / [edited by Gill Edden]. — London : Ebury Press, 1977. — 240p,[24]p of plates : ill(some col) ; 25cm.
Previous ed.: 1975. — Index.
ISBN 0-85223-127-x Pbk : £3.25
(B77-30398)

Pappas, Lou Seibert. Gourmet cooking, the slim way / [by] Lou Seibert Pappas. — Reading, Mass. ; London [etc.] : Addison-Wesley, 1977. — ix,198p : ill ; 24cm.
Index.
ISBN 0-201-05670-4 : £5.95
ISBN 0-201-05671-2 Pbk : £3.30
(B77-20413)

641.5'636 — Vegetarians. Food. *Recipes*
Batt, Eva. What's cooking? : a guide to good eating / by Eva Batt. — Revised ed. — Enfield (123 Baker St., Enfield, Middx EN1 3HA) : Vegan Society, 1976. — [2],xxxii,100p,plate : ports ; 21cm.
Previous ed.: 1973. — Index.
ISBN 0-9503393-7-7 Sp : £1.95
(B77-06182)

Elliot, Rose. Simply delicious / [by] Rose Elliot. — [Revised ed.]. — [London] : Fontana, 1977. — ix,165p ; 18cm.
This ed. originally published: Liss : White Eagle Publishing Trust, 1974. — Index.
ISBN 0-00-634991-9 Pbk : £0.80
(B77-22694)

From a monastery kitchen / [compiled by] Elise Boulding, with the assistance of Victor Antonio Avila and Jean-Marie Pearse ; illustrations by Daniel Marshall. — Glasgow [etc.] : Collins, 1977. — 3-127p : ill ; 24x26cm.
Originally published: New York : Harper and Row, 1976. — Index.
ISBN 0-00-435208-4 : £4.95
(B77-29532)

Hunt, Janet. A vegetarian in the family : meatless recipes for the odd one out / by Janet Hunt ; drawings by Dinah Cohen. — Wellingborough : Thorsons, 1977. — 96p : ill ; 18cm. — (Nature's way)
Index.
ISBN 0-7225-0368-7 Pbk : £0.90
(B77-22695)

James, Isabel. Vegetarian cuisine / [by] Isabel James. — 3rd ed. — Altrincham (Parkdale, Dunham Rd, Altrincham, Cheshire WA14 4QG) : Vegetarian Society (UK) Ltd, 1976. — [1],98p ; 22cm.
Previous ed.: 1972. — Index.
ISBN 0-900774-09-6 : £2.50
ISBN 0-900774-10-x Sp : £1.25
(B77-13728)

641.5'638 — Food: Cuisine minceur dishes. *Recipes*
Guérard, Michel. Michel Guérard's cuisine minceur / translated [from the French] and adapted [i.e. with an introduction] by Caroline Conran. — London [etc.] : Macmillan, 1977. — 413p,[8]p of plates : ill(some col) ; 24cm.
Translation of: 'La grande cuisine minceur'. Paris : Éditions Robert Laffont, 1976. — Index.
ISBN 0-333-21907-4 : £5.95
(B77-22696)

641.5'638 — Food: Fatless dishes. *Recipes*
Lampen, Nevada. Fat-free recipes / [by] Nevada Lampen. — London : Faber, 1977. — 95p ; 19cm.
Index.
ISBN 0-571-11026-6 Pbk : £1.50
(B77-16958)

641.5'638 — Food: Low saturated fat dishes. *Recipes*
Brown, William Jann. Cook to your heart's content on a low-fat, low-salt diet. — Revised ed. / [by] W. Jann Brown, Daniel Liebowitz, Marlene Olness. — New York ; London [etc.] : Van Nostrand Reinhold, 1976 [i.e. 1977]. — ix, 150p : ill ; 28cm.
This ed. published in the United States: 1976. — Previous ed.: / by D. Liebowitz, W.J. Brown and M. Olness. Menlo Park : Pacific Coast Publishers, 1969. — Bibl.: p.146. — Index.
ISBN 0-442-24812-1 Pbk : £4.25
Also classified at 641.5'632
(B77-11289)

641.5'67'6 — Jews. Food. *Recipes*
More ways to a man's heart / compiled by the Helpful '8' ; edited by Gillian Burr, assisted by Susan Stone. — London : Vallentine, Mitchell, 1976. — 217p : ill ; 26cm.
Index.
ISBN 0-85303-190-8 Sp : £3.95
(B77-17606)

641.5'68 — Food: Christmas dishes. *Recipes*
Boxer, *Lady* **Arabella.** Christmas food and drink / [by] Arabella Boxer. — London : Sphere, 1975. — 128p : ill ; 20cm.
ISBN 0-7221-1797-3 Pbk : £0.65
(B77-18864)

Parker, Audrey. Cooking for Christmas / [by] Audrey Parker ; with illustrations by Peter Branfield. — London : Faber, 1977. — 3-111p : ill ; 20cm.
Originally published: 1970. — Index.
ISBN 0-571-11043-6 Pbk : £1.30 : CIP rev.
(B77-19482)

641.5'68 — Food: Dishes for dinner parties & dishes for supper parties. *Recipes*
Hamlyn's all-colour book of dinner and supper parties. — London [etc.] : Hamlyn, 1977. — 3-63p : ill(chiefly col) ; 29cm.
Spine title: Dinner and supper parties. — Index on lining paper.
ISBN 0-600-32936-4 : £1.50
(B77-31985)

641.5'68 — Food: Dishes for seasonal festivals. *Recipes*
Gordon, Victor. Feasts / by Victor Gordon. — Ipswich : Boydell Press for Justin de Blank Provisions Ltd, 1975. — 48p : ill ; 22cm.
ISBN 0-85115-051-9 Pbk : £1.45
(B77-03613)

641.5'68 — Food: Party dishes. *Recipes*
Jeeves, Peter. 'Supercook's' party book / [text by Peter Jeeves ; recipes by Lisa Anderson]. — London [etc.] : Marshall Cavendish, 1976. — [4],65p : ill(chiefly col) ; 30cm.
Originally published: as 'Supercook party book'. 1973.
ISBN 0-85685-197-3 : £1.50
(B77-12549)

Wilkinson, Alison. Food for drinks parties / by Alison Wilkinson. — London : Faber, 1977. — 3-191p ; 21cm.
Index.
ISBN 0-571-11056-8 : £4.95 : CIP rev.
ISBN 0-571-11177-7 Pbk : £2.75
(B77-22697)

641.5′68 — Food: Party dishes for deep freezing. *Recipes*
Good Housekeeping Institute. 'Good housekeeping' parties from your freezer / by Good Housekeeping Institute ; illustrated by Vanessa Luff ; [editor Amanda Atha]. — London : Ebury Press, 1977. — 96p : ill ; 25cm.
Adaptation of: '"Good housekeeping" freezer recipes'. London : Ebury Press, 1974. — Index.
ISBN 0-85223-112-1 Pbk : £0.95
(B77-18255)

641.5′7 — Cookery. *Manuals. For chefs*
Wolfe, Kenneth C. Cooking for the professional chef / [by] Kenneth C. Wolfe. — New York ; London [etc.] : Van Nostrand Reinhold, 1976. — vi,256p : ill ; 31cm.
Index.
ISBN 0-442-29505-7 : £8.50
(B77-14300)

641.5′7 — Food: Dishes for twenty or more persons. *Recipes*
Miles, Darrell. Quantity cooking : tested recipes for twenty or more / [by] Darrell Miles and William Bigley. — New York : Dover Publications ; London : Constable, 1976. — [5], 56p ; 24cm.
Originally published: as 'Dare to excel in cooking'. Washington, D.C. : United States Government Printing Office, 1966. — Index.
ISBN 0-486-23318-9 Pbk : £1.05
(B77-28708)

641.5′78 — Barbecues. *Manuals*
Marks, James F. Barbecues / [by] James F. Marks ; illustrated by Tony Odell. — Harmondsworth [etc.] : Penguin, 1977. — 160p : ill ; 18cm. — (Penguin handbooks)
Index.
ISBN 0-14-046264-3 Pbk : £0.65
(B77-22698)

641.5′78 — Food: Dishes for barbecues. *Recipes*
Norwak, Mary. The complete book of barbecues / [by] Mary Norwak. — London : Futura Publications, 1975. — ix,134p : ill ; 20cm.
Originally published: London : Pelham, 1974. — Index.
ISBN 0-86007-209-6 Pbk : £0.60
(B77-18865)

641.5′78 — Outdoor cookery. *Manuals*
Cox, Jack. The outdoor cookbook / [by] Jack Cox ; illustrated with line drawings by Ian McAdam. — Guildford [etc.] : Lutterworth Press, 1976. — 208p,[8]p of plates : ill ; 23cm.
Bibl.: p.201. — Index.
ISBN 0-7188-2012-6 : £3.90
(B77-01614)

Martin, George Winston. The complete book of outdoor cooking / [by] George W. Martin. — [New ed.]. — South Brunswick ; New York : Barnes ; London : Yoseloff, 1975. — xix,200p : ill ; 22cm.
Previous ed.: published as 'Come and get it!'. New York : Barnes, 1942. — Index.
ISBN 0-498-01352-9 : £2.75
(B77-29533)

641.5′8 — Food: Dishes using tabletop equipment. *Recipes*
Howells, Marion. Fondue and table top cookery / [by] Marion Howells. — London : Octopus Books, 1977. — 4-93p : col ill ; 27cm.
Originally published: 1971. — Index.
ISBN 0-7064-0647-8 : £1.99
Also classified at 641.8
(B77-18256)

Nilson, Bee. Fondue, flambé and side table cooking / [by] Bee Nilson. — St Albans : Mayflower, 1974. — 238p : ill ; 18cm.
Originally published: London : Pelham, 1972. — Index.
ISBN 0-583-19749-3 Pbk : £0.60
(B77-19483)

641.5′87 — Food: Dishes prepared using pressure cookers. *Recipes*
Broughton, Kathleen Frances. Pressure cooking day by day / [by] Kathleen Broughton. — Revised ed. — London [etc.] : Pan Books, 1977. — 288p : ill ; 20cm.
Previous ed.: i.e. 1st ed., London : Kaye and Ward, 1970. — Index.
ISBN 0-330-25067-1 Pbk : £0.95
(B77-14806)

Cox, Helen M. Cooking under pressure / [by] Helen M. Cox. — London : Faber, 1977. — 3-217p ; 21cm.
Index.
ISBN 0-571-10825-3 : £3.95
ISBN 0-571-11103-3 Pbk : £1.75
(B77-21254)

Patten, Marguerite. Marguerite Patten's pressure cookery. — Glasgow [etc.] : Collins, 1977. — 96p : ill(chiefly col) ; 29cm.
Index.
ISBN 0-00-435153-3 : £2.95
ISBN 0-00-435153-3 Pbk : £1.50
(B77-26382)

Todd, Jane. The Hamlyn pressure cookbook / [by] Jane Todd. — London [etc.] : Hamlyn, 1977. — 128p : ill(some col) ; 23cm.
Originally published: 1976. — Index.
ISBN 0-600-37131-x : £1.75
(B77-20414)

641.5′88 — Catering establishments. Cookery. Use of microwave ovens
Napleton, Lewis. A guide to microwave catering / [by] Lewis Napleton. — Revised ed. — London (93 Goswell Rd, EC1V 7QA) : Northwood Publications Ltd, 1976. — 109p,[6] leaves of plates,[2]p of plates : ill, plans ; 21cm. — (A 'Catering times' book)
Previous ed.: i.e. Revised ed., 1971.
Pbk : £1.75
ISBN 0-7198-2523-7
(B77-12550)

641.5′88 — Food: Dishes for slow cooking. *Recipes*
Cutts, Sue. The Prestige book of crock-pot cookery / [by] Sue Cutts. — London : Octopus Books, 1977. — 128p : col ill ; 29cm.
Col. ill. on lining papers. — Index.
ISBN 0-7064-0595-1 : £2.95
(B77-27938)

641.5′88 — Food: Dishes prepared using microwave ovens. *Recipes*
Litton Microwave Cooking Center. Exciting world of microwave cooking from Litton. — New York ; London [etc.] : Van Nostrand Reinhold, [1977]. — 168p : ill(chiefly col) ; 26cm.
Originally published: as 'An exciting new world of microwave cooking from Litton'. Minneapolis : Pilisbury Publications, 1971. — Index.
ISBN 0-442-84832-3 Pbk : £3.70
(B77-07963)

Norman, Cecilia. Microwave cookery for the housewife / [by] Cecilia Norman. — London : Pitman, 1976. — vi,137p : ill ; 22cm.
Originally published: 1974. — Index.
ISBN 0-273-01008-5 Pbk : £1.95
(B77-04919)

641.5′89 — Food: Dishes cooked in one utensil. *Recipes*
Gin, Margaret. One pot meals / [by] Margaret Gin ; drawings by Rik Olson. — London : Pitman, 1977. — 160p : ill ; 21cm.
Originally published: San Francisco : 101 Publications, 1976. — Index.
ISBN 0-273-01101-4 Pbk : £2.50 : CIP rev.
(B77-09794)

641.5′89 — Food: Dishes prepared using blenders & dishes prepared using food mixers. *Recipes*
Hamlyn's all-colour book of mixer and blender cookery. — London [etc.] : Hamlyn, 1977. — 3-63p : ill(chiefly col) ; 29cm.
Spine title: Mixer and blender cookery. — Index on lining paper.
ISBN 0-600-36265-5 : £1.50
(B77-28709)

Norwak, Mary. The complete mixer and blender / [by] Mary Norwak. — London : Ward Lock, 1977. — 176p : col ill ; 26cm.
Index.
ISBN 0-7063-5534-2 : £4.95 : CIP rev.
(B77-18866)

641.5′9 — Food: Foreign dishes. *Recipes*
The **anthropologists'** cookbook / edited by Jessica Kuper ; illustrated by Joan Koster. — London [etc.] : Routledge and Kegan Paul, 1977. — ix, 230p : ill ; 24cm.
Bibl.
ISBN 0-7100-8583-4 : £4.75 : CIP rev.
(B77-25044)

641.593/9 — COOKERY AND RECIPES OF SPECIAL COUNTRIES

641.5′94 — Food: European dishes. *Recipes*
Allison, Sonia. European cooking / [by] Sonia Allison. — Glasgow [etc.] : Collins, 1977. — 256p : col ill ; 30cm.
Index.
ISBN 0-00-435180-0 : £4.95
(B77-28710)

Conil, Jean. European cookery / [by] Jean Conil, Lida Hansley ; photography by Rob Matheson. — London : Croom Helm, 1977. — 442p,[12]p of plates, 2 leaves of plates : col ill ; 26cm.
Index.
ISBN 0-85664-505-2 : £7.95 : CIP rev.
(B77-24340)

641.5′9411 — Food: Scottish dishes, ca 1710. *Recipes*
Castlehill, Martha Lockhart, *Baroness.* Lady Castlehill's receipt book : a selection of 18th century Scottish fare : original recipes from a collection made in 1712 / by Martha Lockhart, the Lady Castlehill ; edited and with an introduction by Hamish Whyte. — Glasgow : Molendinar Press, 1976. — xvi,84p : ill, facsims, geneal table ; 20x25cm.
Bibl.: p.xv. — Index.
ISBN 0-904002-20-9 Pbk : £2.75
(B77-05513)

641.5′942 — Food: English dishes. *Recipes*
Grigson, Jane. English food : an anthology / chosen [and written] by Jane Grigson ; with illustrations by Gillian Zeiner. — Harmondsworth [etc.] : Penguin, 1977. — [8], 322p : ill ; 20cm. — (Penguin handbooks)
Originally published: London : Macmillan, 1974. — Bibl.: p.311-312. — Index.
ISBN 0-14-046243-0 Pbk : £0.90
(B77-29534)

Smith, Michael, *b.1927.* Fine English cookery / [by] Michael Smith ; with a foreword by the Earl of Harewood. — London : Faber, 1977. — 3-286p ; 22cm.
Originally published: 1973. — Index.
ISBN 0-571-11128-9 Pbk : £2.50
(B77-16472)

Smith, Michael, *b.1927.* Grace and flavour / [by] Michael Smith. — London : British Broadcasting Corporation, 1977. — 32p ; 18cm.
'from Pebble Mill' - cover.
ISBN 0-563-17266-5 Sd : £0.40
(B77-09111)

Smith, Michael, *b.1927.* More grace and flavour / [by] Michael Smith. — London : British Broadcasting Corporation, 1977. — 64p ; 18cm.
ISBN 0-563-17406-4 Sd : £0.45
(B77-33303)

Troake, Gwen. Gwen Troake's country cookbook. — London : Macdonald and Jane's, 1977. — 3-112p : ill ; 23cm.
Index.
ISBN 0-354-08513-1 : £3.25
(B77-31299)

Woodford, Martha. The Archers' country cookbook / [by] Martha Woodford ; with decorations by Val Biro. — London : Hutchinson, 1977. — 222p : ill ; 21cm.
ISBN 0-09-131430-5 : £3.50
(B77-31300)

641.5′942 — Food: English dishes, 1714-1830. *Recipes*
Black, Maggie. Georgian menus and meals / [by] Maggie Black. — Bath : Kingsmead, 1977. — xiv,111p : ill ; 22cm.
Bibl.: p.105. — Index.
ISBN 0-901571-82-2 : £2.50
(B77-25734)

641.5′942 — Food: English dishes, 1800-1900. *Recipes*
Cradock, Fanny. The Sherlock Holmes cookbook / by Mrs Hudson ; compiled by Fanny Cradock ; illustrations by Val Biro. — London : W.H. Allen, 1976. — 254p : ill ; 24cm.
Includes recipes by Agnes Bertha Marshall (the original of Mrs Hudson). — Index.
ISBN 0-491-01947-5 : £5.95
(B77-01615)

641.5'942 — Food: English dishes, ca 1400-1973. *Recipes*

Ayrton, Elisabeth. The cookery of England : being a collection of recipes for traditional dishes of all kinds from the fifteenth century to the present day, with notes on their social and culinary background / [by] Elisabeth Ayrton. — Harmondsworth [etc.] : Penguin, 1977. — [7],547p : ill ; 20cm. — (Penguin handbooks)
Originally published: London : Deutsch, 1974. — Bibl.: p.533-536. — Index.
ISBN 0-14-046188-4 Pbk : £1.25
(B77-11923)

641.5'942 — Food: English dishes, ca 1550-1900. *Recipes*

Black, Maggie. A heritage of British cooking / [by] Maggie Black. — London [etc.] : Letts, 1977. — viii,184p : ill(some col), facsims, ports ; 27cm. — (Letts guides)
Ill. on lining papers. — Bibl.: p.179-180. — Index.
ISBN 0-85097-236-1 : £3.95
(B77-21255)

641.5'9422 — Food: Thames Valley dishes. *Recipes*

Poulson, Joan. Old Thames Valley recipes / by Joan Poulson. — Nelson : Hendon Publishing Co., 1977. — 48p : ill, port ; 14x22cm.
ISBN 0-86067-015-5 Sd : £0.70
(B77-23532)

641.5'9425'1 — Food: Derbyshire dishes. *Recipes*

Douglas, Joyce. Old Derbyshire recipes and customs / by Joyce Douglas. — Nelson : Hendon Publishing Co., 1976. — 48,[1]p : ill, facsim ; 15x22cm.
ISBN 0-86067-002-3 Sd : £0.70
(B77-00830)

641.5'9425'2 — Food: Nottinghamshire dishes. *Recipes*

Martin, Joan. The Nottinghamshire taste / compiled by Joan Martin ; illustrated by Margaret Hollins. — Newark (Trent Bridge House, Newark, Notts.) : Nottinghamshire Federation of Women's Institutes, 1977. — 50, [14]p : ill ; 21cm.
Tab indexed.
Sp : Unpriced
(B77-32720)

641.5'9425'45 — Food: Rutland dishes. *Recipes*

Ruddle, Rosemary. Rosemary Ruddle's Rutland recipes. — [Leicester] ([Clarence St., at Lee Circle, Leicester LE1 3RW]) : Leicestershire Libraries and Information Service, 1976. — [8], 43p : ill, map ; 14x22cm.
ISBN 0-85022-007-6 Sd : £0.75
(B77-06183)

641.5'9436'13 — Food: Viennese dishes. *Recipes*

Johnston, Trude. The home book of Viennese cookery / by Trude Johnston. — London : Faber, 1977. — 190p ; 21cm.
Index.
ISBN 0-571-10923-3 : £4.95 : CIP rev.
ISBN 0-571-11178-5 Pbk : £2.95
(B77-18257)

641.5'944 — Food: French dishes. *Recipes*

Beck, Simone. Mastering the art of French cooking / by Simone Beck, Louisette Bertholle, Julia Child. — London : Joseph.
Vol.2 / [by] Julia Child, Simone Beck ; illustrated by Sidonie Coryn ; based on photographs by Paul Child who also contributed 36 of his own drawings. — 1977. — 762p : ill ; 24cm.
Originally published: New York : Knopf, 1970. — Index.
ISBN 0-7181-1403-5 : £12.00
(B77-07454)

Bernard, Françoise. Secrets from my French kitchen / [by] Françoise Bernard ; [translated from the French]. — London : Macdonald and Jane's, 1977. — viii,216p : ill ; 23cm.
Translation of: 'Mes secrets de cuisine'. Paris : Hachette, 1972. — Index.
ISBN 0-354-04085-5 : £5.95
(B77-33907)

Berry, Mary, *b.1935.* Popular French cookbook / [by] Mary Berry. — [New ed.]. — London : Octopus Books, 1977. — 96p : col ill ; 28cm.
Ill. on lining papers. — Previous ed.: published as 'Popular French cookery'. 1972. — Index.
ISBN 0-7064-0627-3 : £1.99
(B77-16473)

David, Elizabeth, *b.1913.* French provincial cooking / [by] Elizabeth David ; illustrated by Juliet Renny. — 2nd ed. (revised). — London : Joseph, 1977. — 519p : ill ; 24cm.
This ed. originally published: 1965. — Bibl.: p.462-475. — Index.
ISBN 0-7181-0149-9 : £10.00
(B77-31987)

Délu, Christian Roland. The Guinness guide to French country cooking / [by] Christian Roland Délu ; [translated from the French by Michael and Pamela Hopf]. — Enfield : Guinness Superlatives, 1976. — 173,[2]p : col ill, col port ; 30cm.
Translation of: 'La cuisine des Français'. Paris : Editions Denoël, 1976. — Index.
ISBN 0-900424-59-1 : £7.95
(B77-11290)

Francine. 'Vogue' French cookery / by Francine. — [New ed.] / edited by Mary Reynolds ; drawings by David Gentleman. — Glasgow [etc.] : Collins ; [London] : Condé Nast, 1976. — 160p : ill ; 26cm.
Ill. on lining papers. — Previous ed.: published as 'Vogue's French cookery book'. London : Vogue, 1961. — Index.
ISBN 0-00-435054-5 : £5.95
(B77-09112)

Seaver, Jeannette. Jeannette's secrets of everyday good cooking / [by] Jeannette Seaver ; illustrated by Nathalie Seaver. — Toronto [etc.] ; London : Bantam, 1976. — [7],403,[1]p : ill ; 18cm.
Originally published: New York : Knopf, 1975. — Index.
ISBN 0-552-62892-1 Pbk : £0.75
(B77-17607)

641.5'944 — Restaurants. Food: French dishes. *France. Recipes*

Secrets of the great French restaurants : nearly 400 recipes from famous restaurants starred in the Michelin Guide / selected and edited by Louisette Bertholle, author of the introduction, appendices and glossary ; translated [from the French] by Carole Fahy and Bud MacLennan. — London : Sphere, 1975. — [4],375p : ill, maps ; 24cm.
This translation originally published: London : Weidenfeld and Nicolson, 1973. — Translation of: 'Les Recettes secrètes des meilleurs restaurants de France'. Paris : Editions Albin Michel, 1972. — Index.
ISBN 0-7221-1613-6 Pbk : £2.15
(B77-10433)

641.5'945 — Food: Italian dishes. *Recipes*

David, Elizabeth, *b.1913.* Italian food / [by] Elizabeth David ; drawings by Renato Gutuso. — Revised ed. — London : Allen Lane, 1977. — 368p : ill ; 23cm.
This ed. originally published: Harmondsworth : Penguin, 1963. — Bibl.: p.323-325. — Index.
ISBN 0-7139-1098-4 : £6.95
(B77-31988)

Howells, Marion. Popular Italian cookbook / [by] Marion Howells. — [New ed.]. — London : Octopus Books, 1977. — 96p : col ill ; 28cm.
Ill. on lining papers. — Previous ed.: published as 'Popular Italian cookery'. 1972. — Index.
ISBN 0-7064-0628-1 : £1.99
(B77-16474)

Romagnoli, Margaret. The Romagnolis' table : Italian family recipes / [by] Margaret and G. Franco Romagnoli ; photographs by G. Franco Romagnoli. — Toronto [etc.] ; London : Bantam, 1977. — xv,332,[1]p,[8]p of plates : ill ; 18cm.
Originally published: Boston, Mass. : Little, Brown, 1975. — Index.
ISBN 0-552-62965-0 Pbk : £0.85
(B77-31989)

641.5'947'9 — Food: Transcaucasian dishes. *Recipes*

Uvezian, Sonia. The best foods of Russia / [by] Sonia Uvezian. — New York ; London : Harcourt Brace Jovanovich, 1976. — [8],280p : map ; 22cm.
Index.
ISBN 0-15-111905-8 : £6.35
(B77-21256)

641.5'9494 — Food: Swiss dishes. *Recipes*

Mason, Anne. Swiss cooking / [by] Anne Mason. — Revised [ed.]. — London : Deutsch, 1977. — 3-162p ; 21cm.
Previous ed.: 1964. — Index.
ISBN 0-233-96257-3 : £2.95
(B77-29535)

641.5'9495 — Food: Greek dishes. *Recipes*

Mallos, Tess. Greek cookbook / [by] Tess Mallos ; food photography by Howard Jones. — London [etc.] : Hamlyn, 1976. — 128p : col ill, col map(on lining papers) ; 25cm.
Bibl.: p.126. — Index.
ISBN 0-600-34060-0 : £2.75
(B77-18867)

641.5'95 — Food: Oriental dishes. *Recipes*

Leong, Yee Soo. Art of oriental cooking / by Leong Yee Soo. — London : Deutsch, 1977. — 208p : ill(chiefly col) ; 21x28cm.
Originally published: Singapore : Eastern University Press, 1976. — Index.
ISBN 0-233-96907-1 : £7.50
(B77-23533)

641.5'951 — Food: Chinese dishes. *Recipes*

Burt, Alison. Popular Chinese cookbook / [by] Alison Burt. — [New ed.]. — London : Octopus Books, 1977. — 96p : col ill ; 28cm.
Ill. on lining papers. — Previous ed.: published as 'Popular Chinese cookery'. 1972. — Index.
ISBN 0-7064-0629-x : £1.99
(B77-16475)

Lo, Kenneth. Cheap chow : Chinese cooking on next to nothing / [by] Kenneth Lo ; illustrated by Delia Delderfield. — London [etc.] : Pan Books, 1977. — 159p : ill ; 20cm.
Originally published: London : Elm Tree Books, 1976. — Index.
ISBN 0-330-25199-6 Pbk : £0.80
(B77-29536)

Lo, Kenneth. The love of Chinese cooking / [by] Kenneth Lo. — [London] : Octopus Books, [1977]. — 96p : col ill, col map ; 33cm.
Col. ill. on lining papers. — Index.
ISBN 0-7064-0593-5 : £2.95
(B77-23534)

Miller, Gloria Bley. Learn Chinese cooking in your own kitchen / by Gloria Bley Miller. — Toronto [etc.] ; London : Bantam, 1977. — xi, 174,[1]p ; 18cm.
Originally published: New York : Grosset and Dunlap, 1976. — Index.
ISBN 0-552-60088-1 Pbk : £0.75
(B77-22699)

Spunt, Georges. The step-by-step Chinese cookbook / [by] Georges Spunt ; illustrations by Halcyon Cowles. — London : Cape, 1977. — xviii,424p : ill ; 24cm.
Originally published: New York : Crowell, 1973. — Index.
ISBN 0-224-01176-6 : £6.95 : CIP rev.
(B77-05514)

Wong, Ella-mei. The commonsense Chinese cookery book / [by] Ella-mei Wong. — London [etc.] : Angus and Robertson, 1977. — ix,125p, [16]p of plates : col ill ; 26cm.
Originally published: 1976. — Index.
ISBN 0-207-13317-4 : £3.80
(B77-27218)

641.5'954 — Food: Indian dishes. *Recipes*

Mathews, Sara. The commonsense Indian cookery book / [by] Sara Mathews. — London [etc.] : Angus and Robertson, 1977. — x,108p, [16]p of plates : col ill ; 26cm.
Index.
ISBN 0-207-13450-2 : £4.20
(B77-31301)

641.5'9564'5 — Food: Cypriot dishes. *Recipes*

Pourounas, Andreas. Aphrodite's cookbook / by Andreas Pourounas ; compiled and edited by Helene Grosvenor. — St Helier : Spearman, 1977. — 174p : ill ; 23cm.
Bibl.: p.171. — Index.
ISBN 0-85978-028-7 : £2.95
(B77-29537)

641.5'9599 — Food: Filipino dishes. *Recipes*

Dayrit, Pat Limjuco. Favorite Filipino recipes / [by] Pat Limjuco Dayrit ; photography by Ben Laxina. — Manila ; London [etc.] : Tradewinds ; [London] : [Distributed by Hamlyn], 1975. — 128p : ill(some col) ; 25cm.
Index.
ISBN 0-600-07193-6 Pbk : Unpriced
(B77-18258)

641.5'96 — Food: African dishes

Van der Post, Laurens. First catch your eland : a taste of Africa / [by] Laurens van der Post. — London : Hogarth Press, 1977. — x,211p ; 22cm.
ISBN 0-7012-0413-3 : £4.95 : CIP rev.
(B77-21257)

641.5'972 — Food: Mexican dishes. *Recipes*

Booth, George C. The food and drink of Mexico / [by] George C. Booth ; illustrated by Cas Duchow. — New York : Dover Publications [etc.] ; London : Constable, 1976. — [2],190p : ill ; 22cm.
Originally published: Los Angeles : Ward Ritchie Press, 1964. — Spanish and English index.
ISBN 0-486-23314-6 Pbk : £2.00
(B77-11924)

641.5'9729 — Food: Caribbean dishes. *Recipes*
Ortiz, Elisabeth Lambert. Caribbean cooking / [by] Elisabeth Lambert Ortiz. — Revised ed. — Harmondsworth [etc.] : Penguin, 1977. — xv, 323p ; 20cm. — (Penguin handbooks)
Spine title: Caribbean cookery. — This ed. originally published: London : Deutsch, 1975. — Index.
ISBN 0-14-046215-5 Pbk : £0.90
(B77-11925)

641.5'9729 — Food: West Indian dishes. *Recipes*
Clark, E Phyllis. West Indian cookery / [by] E. Phyllis Clark. — Revised ed. — Sunbury-on-Thames [etc.] : Nelson, 1976. — [4] ,196p ; 18cm.
Previous ed.: 1945. — Index.
ISBN 0-17-566185-5 Pbk : £1.25
(B77-13729)

641.5'973 — Food: American dishes. *Recipes*
Turgeon, Charlotte. 'The Saturday evening post' all American cookbook : 500 all-American recipes / by Charlotte Turgeon ; with a light-hearted history of eating in America by Frederic A. Birmingham. — London : Elm Tree Books, 1977. — 320p : ill(some col), facsims(some col) ; 27cm.
Spine title: All American cookbook. — Originally published: Indianapolis : Curtis Publishing Co., 1976. — Index.
ISBN 0-241-89590-1 : £5.95
(B77-10840)

641.5'973 — Food: American dishes. *Recipes. Facsimiles*
Nichols, Nell B. The farm cook & rule book / [by] Nell B. Nichols. — Golden anniversary ed. — New York ; London : Harcourt Brace Jovanovich, 1976. — x,303p ; 29cm.
Previous ed.: i.e. 1st ed., New York : Macmillan, 1923. — Index. — Includes a section of miscellaneous household tips.
ISBN 0-15-130406-8 : £7.90
ISBN 0-15-130407-6 Pbk : £4.25
(B77-14301)

641.5'9772 — Food: Indiana dishes. *Recipes*
The **Hoosier** cookbook / edited by Elaine Lumbra ; illustrated by Jackie Lacy. — Bloomington ; London : Indiana University Press, 1976. — xii,330p : ill ; 25cm.
Index.
ISBN 0-253-13865-5 : £8.00
(B77-03614)

641.5'9773 — Food: Illinois dishes, 1800-1900. *Recipes*
Linsenmeyer, Helen Walker. Cooking plain : a treasury of century-old family recipes, with a selection of natural foods and wild game cookery, and with sections on preserving foods and on household hints - from the Illinois country / [by] Helen Walker Linsenmeyer. — Carbondale [etc.] : Southern Illinois University Press ; London [etc.] : Feffer and Simons, 1976. — x,275p ; 24cm.
Index.
ISBN 0-8093-0782-0 : Unpriced
(B77-00292)

641.5'9931 — Food: New Zealand dishes. *Recipes*
The **New Zealand** radio & television cookbook / edited by Alison Holst ; photography by Richard Silcock. — Auckland ; London [etc.] : Hamlyn, 1976. — 384p : ill(chiefly col) ; 29cm.
Originally published: 1974. — Index.
ISBN 0-600-07270-3 : Unpriced
(B77-24341)

641.6 — COOKERY AND RECIPES BASED ON SPECIAL MATERIALS

641.6 — Food: Dishes using olive oil. *Recipes*
The **pure** gold of Spain / contains contributions by Marguerite Patten and Madame Simone Prunier and over 80 recipes with nutritional analysis. — [London] : [Jupiter Books], [1975]. — 125p : ill(some col), ports(some col) ; 28cm.
Cover title. — Col. ill. on lining papers. — Index.
ISBN 0-904041-39-5 : £1.95
(B77-04920)

641.6'1 — Preserved food. *Recipes*
Cameron-Smith, Marye. The complete book of preserving / [by] Marye Cameron-Smith. — London [etc.] : Marshall Cavendish, 1976. — [2],248,[2]p : ill(chiefly col), facsim ; 30cm.
Ill. on lining papers. — Index.
ISBN 0-85685-174-4 : £6.95
Primary classification 641.4
(B77-12544)

641.6'2 — Food: Dishes using cider. *Recipes*
Berry, Mary, *b.1935.* Cider for all seasons : Mary Berry's cider recipes and drinks. — Cambridge : Woodhead-Faulkner [for] H.P. Bulmer Limited, 1977. — 96p : ill(some col) ; 19cm.
ISBN 0-85941-036-6 Pbk : £0.99
(B77-33304)

641.6'2 — Food: Dishes using wine & dishes using spirits. *Recipes*
Meek, Joanne. Sip and stir / [by] Joanne Meek and Shirley Woolley ; illustrations by Linda Jordan. — South Brunswick [etc.] : Barnes ; London : Yoseloff, 1973. — 195p : ill ; 22cm.
Index.
ISBN 0-498-01165-8 : £3.00
(B77-18868)

641.6'3'11 — Food: Dishes using wholemeal flour. *Recipes*
The **wholemeal** kitchen / edited by Miriam Polunin ... [et al.] ; drawings by Eric Rose ; cover design by Cecilia Northcott. — London : Heinemann, 1977. — [5],122p : ill ; 22cm.
Index.
ISBN 0-434-59219-6 Sp : £1.90
(B77-28711)

641.6'3'18 — Food: Rice dishes. *Recipes*
Cooking with rice. — Bishop's Stortford (Elsenham, Bishop's Stortford, Herts.) : Penday Publishing Ltd, 1977. — 24p : ill ; 17cm. — (Family meals)
ISBN 0-86090-004-5 Sd : £0.40
(B77-31990)

Tracy, Marian. The east-west book of rice cookery / by Marian Tracy ; illustrated by Marguerite Burgess. — New York : Dover Publications ; London : Constable, 1976. — xi, 148p : ill ; 22cm.
Originally published: New York : Viking Press, 1952. — Index.
ISBN 0-486-23413-4 Pbk : £1.60
(B77-31991)

641.6'3'83 — Food: Dishes using ginger. *Recipes*
Ager, Anne. The ginger cookbook / [by] Anne Ager. — [Pinner] : Vantage Books ; London : Distributed by Hale, 1976. — 144p : ill ; 23cm.
Index.
ISBN 0-904545-03-2 : £3.95
(B77-31302)

Ginger up your cookery / edited by Charles Seely ; decorations by Kate Simunek. — London : Hutchinson, 1977. — 96p,[4]p of plates : ill(some col) ; 22cm.
Index.
ISBN 0-09-128721-9 Pbk : £0.95
(B77-10434)

641.6'3'83 — Food: Dishes using spices. *Recipes*
Claiborne, Craig. Cooking with herbs & spices / by Craig Claiborne ; drawings by Alice Golden. — New revised and enlarged ed. — Toronto [etc.] ; London : Bantam, 1977. — xix,383p : ill ; 18cm.
This ed. originally published: New York : Harper and Row, 1970. — Previous ed.: published as 'An herb and spice cook book'. New York ; London : Harper and Row, 1963 ; London : Faber, 1965. — Index.
ISBN 0-552-68390-6 Pbk : £0.95
Primary classification 641.6'5'7
(B77-29538)

641.6'3'84 — Food: Curried dishes. *Recipes*
Ady, Doris. Curries from the Sultan's kitchen : curries from India, Pakistan, Burma and Ceylon / by Doris Ady ; illustrations by Inge Fernando. — Sydney [etc.] ; London : A.H. and A.W. Reed, 1976. — 126,[1]p : ill ; 22cm.
Originally published: Sydney : Reed, 1968. — Index.
ISBN 0-589-00030-6 Sp : £3.00
(B77-23535)

641.6'4 — Food: Dishes using seasonal fruit. *Recipes*
Duff, Gail. Fresh all the year / [by] Gail Duff ; illustrated by Gillian Zeiner. — London : Pan Books, 1977. — 286p : ill ; 20cm.
Originally published: London : Macmillan, 1976. — Index.
ISBN 0-330-25002-7 Pbk : £0.95
Also classified at 641.6'5
(B77-13119)

Harris, Marion. Fresh fruit dishes / by Marion Harris. — London : Barrie and Jenkins, 1977. — 95p : ill ; 20cm. — (Good cook)
Index.
ISBN 0-214-20318-2 : £1.25
(B77-27939)

641.6'4 — Food: Dishes using wild fruit. *Recipes*
Eley, Geoffrey. Wild fruits and nuts / by Geoffrey Eley. — Wakefield : EP Publishing, 1976. — 72p : ill ; 24cm. — (Invest in living)
Bibl.: p.72.
ISBN 0-7158-0457-x Pbk : £1.25
Also classified at 641.6'4'5
(B77-15938)

641.6'4 — Food: Fruit dishes. *Recipes*
Encyclopedia of vegetable gardening : the complete growing, cooking & freezing guide to vegetables, herbs & fruit / [by A.G. Biggs et al.]. — London : Octopus Books, 1977. — 255p : col ill ; 31cm.
Col. ill. on lining papers. — Index.
ISBN 0-7064-0616-8 : £4.95
Primary classification 635
(B77-31963)

Mossman, Keith. Home grown : a harvest of information about growing, cooking and preserving food from your garden / [by] Keith Mossman and Mary Norwak. — London : Spectator Publications for Stanley Garden Tools Ltd, 1977. — 2-126p : ill(some col) ; 28cm.
Cover title.
ISBN 0-900869-31-3 Pbk : £2.80
Primary classification 635
(B77-24316)

Norwak, Mary. From garden to table / [by] Mary Norwak. — London : Elm Tree Books, 1977. — ix,176p : ill ; 24cm.
Index.
ISBN 0-241-89593-6 : £5.50
Also classified at 641.6'5
(B77-33305)

641.6'4 — Food: Fruit dishes. *Recipes. Juvenile literature*
Smithson, Sheila. Playing with fruit and vegetables / [by] Sheila Smithson. — London : Studio Vista, 1976. — 44p : ill ; 26cm. — (Something to do)
Index.
ISBN 0-289-70692-0 : £2.25
Primary classification 745.5
(B77-19530)

641.6'4'5 — Food: Dishes using nuts. *Recipes*
Eley, Geoffrey. Wild fruits and nuts / by Geoffrey Eley. — Wakefield : EP Publishing, 1976. — 72p : ill ; 24cm. — (Invest in living)
Bibl.: p.72.
ISBN 0-7158-0457-x Pbk : £1.25
Primary classification 641.6'4
(B77-15938)

641.6'5 — Food: Dishes using seasonal vegetables. *Recipes*
Duff, Gail. Fresh all the year / [by] Gail Duff ; illustrated by Gillian Zeiner. — London : Pan Books, 1977. — 286p : ill ; 20cm.
Originally published: London : Macmillan, 1976. — Index.
ISBN 0-330-25002-7 Pbk : £0.95
Primary classification 641.6'4
(B77-13119)

641.6'5 — Food: Vegetable dishes. *Recipes*
Barr, Stringfellow. The kitchen garden book : vegetables from seed to table / by Stringfellow Barr and Stella Standard. — Harmondsworth [etc.] : Penguin, 1977. — xi,372p ; 20cm. — (Penguin handbooks)
Originally published: New York : Viking Press, 1956. — Index.
ISBN 0-14-046257-0 Pbk : Unpriced
Also classified at 635'.04'310973
(B77-27219)

Boxer, *Lady* **Arabella.** Arabella Boxer's garden cookbook. — London : Sphere, 1977. — 303p ; 18cm.
Originally published: London : Weidenfeld and Nicolson, 1974. — Index.
ISBN 0-7221-1798-1 Pbk : £0.95
(B77-09795)

Burrows, Lois M. Too many tomatoes, squash, beans, and other good things : a cookbook for when your garden explodes / [by] Lois M. Burrows & Laura G. Myers. — New York [etc.] ; London : Harper and Row, 1976. — xv, 287p : ill ; 21cm.
Index.
ISBN 0-06-013132-2 : £4.95
(B77-26383)

Conran, Terence. The vegetable book : how to grow and cook your own vegetables / [by] Terence Conran and Maria Kroll ; paintings by Faith Shannon. — Glasgow [etc.] : Collins, 1976. — 96p : ill(some col) ; 28cm.
Index.
ISBN 0-00-435183-5 : £3.95
(B77-14302)

Conran, Terence. The vegetable book : how to grow and cook your own vegetables / [by] Terence Conran and Maria Kroll ; paintings by Faith Shannon. — Glasgow [etc.] : Collins, 1977. — 96p : ill(some col) ; 28cm.
Originally published: 1976. — Index.
£3.95
ISBN 0-00-435183-5
Primary classification 635
(B77-23516)

Cullen, Margaret. Vegetables / [by] Margaret Cullen ; illustrated by Maurice Hutchings. — London : Heinemann Educational, 1977. — viii, 86p : ill ; 25cm. — (Food for today ; 1)
ISBN 0-435-42465-3 Pbk : £1.30
(B77-15939)

Encyclopedia of vegetable gardening : the complete growing, cooking & freezing guide to vegetables, herbs & fruit / [by A.G. Biggs et al.]. — London : Octopus Books, 1977. — 255p : col ill ; 31cm.
Col. ill. on lining papers. — Index.
ISBN 0-7064-0616-8 : £4.95
Primary classification 635
(B77-31963)

Fordyce, Keith. More kitchen garden / [by] Keith Fordyce & Claire Rayner ; illustrated by Norman Barber. — London (247 Tottenham Court Rd, W1P 0AU) : Independent Television Publications Ltd for Independent Television Books Ltd, 1977. — 64p : ill ; 20cm. — (A 'TV times' book)
'... based on the Thames Television programme "Kitchen Garden" (1977)'. — Index.
ISBN 0-900727-64-0 Pbk : £0.50
Primary classification 635
(B77-14795)

Mossman, Keith. Home grown : a harvest of information about growing, cooking and preserving food from your garden / [by] Keith Mossman and Mary Norwak. — London : Spectator Publications for Stanley Garden Tools Ltd, 1977. — 2-126p : ill(some col) ; 28cm.
Cover title.
ISBN 0-900869-31-3 Pbk : £2.80
Primary classification 635
(B77-24316)

Norwak, Mary. From garden to table / [by] Mary Norwak. — London : Elm Tree Books, 1977. — ix,176p : ill ; 24cm.
Index.
ISBN 0-241-89593-6 : £5.50
Primary classification 641.6'4
(B77-33305)

641.6'5 — Food: Vegetable dishes. *Recipes. Juvenile literature*

Smithson, Sheila. Playing with fruit and vegetables / [by] Sheila Smithson. — London : Studio Vista, 1976. — 44p : ill ; 26cm. — (Something to do)
Index.
ISBN 0-289-70692-0 : £2.25
Primary classification 745.5
(B77-19530)

641.6'5'09455 — Food: Tuscan vegetable dishes. *Recipes*

Ross, Janet, *b.1842.* Leaves from our Tuscan kitchen, or, How to cook vegetables / by Janet Ross ... — [Revised ed.] / [by] Michael Waterfield ; line drawings by Michael Waterfield. — Harmondsworth [etc.] : Penguin, 1977. — 200p : ill ; 20cm. — (Penguin handbooks)
This ed. originally published: London : J. Murray, 1973.
ISBN 0-14-046253-8 Pbk : £0.80
(B77-13120)

641.6'5'21 — Food: Potato dishes. *Recipes*

Smart, Lyn. Country collection : a book of country foods and facts with over 200 potato recipes / [by] Lyn Smart. — London : Spectator Publications for the Popato Marketing Board, 1977. — 111p : ill(some col) ; 29cm.
Index. — Previous control number ISBN 0-900869-29-1.
ISBN 0-900869-33-x : Unpriced
ISBN 0-900869-29-1 Pbk : £0.60
(B77-07455)

641.6'5'21 — Food: Potato dishes. *Recipes. For school meals services*

Potato Marketing Board. Potatoes in school meals / Potato Marketing Board. — London (50 Hans Cres., SW1X 0NB) : The Board, [1977]. — 20p : col ill ; 28cm.
Index.
ISBN 0-903623-19-6 Sd : Free
(B77-09796)

641.6'5'21 — Food: Potato dishes. *Recipes. For small scale catering*

Potato Marketing Board. Potatoes and the five to twenty-five plus caterer / Potato Marketing Board. — London (50 Hans Cres., SW1X 0NB) : The Board, [1977]. — 12p : ill(chiefly col), port ; 28cm.
ISBN 0-903623-18-8 Sd : Unpriced
(B77-10435)

641.6'5'25 — Food: Dishes using onions. *Recipes*

Bothwell, Jean. The onion cookbook / [by] Jean Bothwell ; with illustrations by Margaret Ayer. — New York : Dover Publications [etc.] ; London : Constable, [1977]. — xii,166p : ill ; 22cm.
Originally published: as 'Onions without tears'. New York : Hastings House, 1950. — Index.
ISBN 0-486-23312-x Pbk : £2.00
(B77-11291)

641.6'5'65 — Food: Dishes using beans. *Recipes*

White, Beverly. Bean cuisine : a culinary guide for the ecogourmet / by Beverly White ; illustrated by Julie Maas. — London [etc.] : Routledge and Kegan Paul, 1977. — xvi,142p : ill ; 20cm.
Also published: Boston, Mass. : Beacon Press, 1977. — Index.
ISBN 0-7100-8759-4 Pbk : £2.50 : CIP rev.
(B77-25045)

641.6'5'655 — Food: Dishes using soya beans. *Recipes*

Whisker, R G. The soybean grow-and-cook book / [by] R.G. Whisker and Pamela Dixon. — London : Duckworth, 1977. — 64p ; 23cm.
ISBN 0-7156-1260-3 : £3.95
ISBN 0-7156-1163-1 Pbk : £1.00
Primary classification 635'.655
(B77-32705)

641.6'5'7 — Food: Dishes using herbs. *Recipes*

Claiborne, Craig. Cooking with herbs & spices / by Craig Claiborne ; drawings by Alice Golden. — New revised and enlarged ed. — Toronto [etc.] ; London : Bantam, 1977. — xix,383p : ill ; 18cm.
This ed. originally published: New York : Harper and Row, 1970. — Previous ed.: published as 'An herb and spice cook book'. New York ; London : Harper and Row, 1963 ; London : Faber, 1965. — Index.
ISBN 0-552-68390-6 Pbk : £0.95
Also classified at 641.6'3'83
(B77-29538)

Loewenfeld, Claire. Herbs for health and cookery / [by] Claire Loewenfeld and Philippa Back. — London [etc.] : Pan Books, 1977. — 336p ; 20cm.
Originally published: 1965. — Index.
ISBN 0-330-25336-0 Pbk : £1.00
(B77-28712)

641.6'5'8 — Food: Dishes using mushrooms. *Recipes*

Nelson, Kay Shaw. Cooking with mushrooms / [by] Kay Shaw Nelson ; with illustrations by Wendy Cortesi. — New York : Dover Publications [etc.] ; London : Constable, 1976. — 5-226p : ill ; 22cm.
Originally published: as 'The magic of mushroom cookery'. Washington, D.C. : R.B. Luce, 1971. — Index.
ISBN 0-486-23414-2 Pbk : £2.15
(B77-27220)

641.6'6 — Food: Fish dishes, game dishes & poultry dishes. *Recipes*

The **best** of fish, poultry and game. — London : Reader's Digest Association, 1976. — 64p : ill(chiefly col) ; 27cm. — ('Reader's digest' basic guide)
'The text and illustrations in this book are taken from "The cookery year" ...', 3rd revision. London : Reader's Digest Association, 1976. — Index.
ISBN 0-276-00146-x Sd : £0.75
(B77-18259)

641.6'6 — Food: Meat dishes. *Recipes*

Hutchings, Ken. Pebble Mill good meat guide / [by] Ken Hutchings. — London : British Broadcasting Corporation, 1977. — 48p : ill ; 18cm.
ISBN 0-563-17252-5 Sd : £0.45
(B77-18869)

Squire, D. Getting the best from meat / compiled by D. Squire & P. McHoy. — Wakefield : EP Publishing, 1976. — 72p : ill ; 24cm. — (Invest in living)
ISBN 0-7158-0459-6 Pbk : £1.25
(B77-20416)

Wadey, Rosemary. Meat cooking / [by] Rosemary Wadey. — [London] ([59 Grosvenor St., W.1]) : Sundial Books Ltd, [1977]. — 96p : col ill ; 28cm. — (St Michael cookery library)
Index.
ISBN 0-904230-41-4 Pbk : £0.99
(B77-29539)

641.6'6 — Food: Sausage dishes. *Recipes*

Cooking with sausages. — Bishop's Stortford (Elsenham, Bishop's Stortford, Herts.) : Penday Publishing Ltd, 1977. — 24p : ill ; 17cm. — (Family meals)
ISBN 0-86090-005-3 Sd : £0.40
(B77-33306)

641.6'6'0954 — Food: Indian meat dishes. *Recipes*

Santa Maria, Jack. Indian meat and fish cookery / [by] Jack Santa Maria ; illustrated by Carmen Miranda. — London : Rider, 1977. — 175p : ill ; 24cm.
Bibl.: p.175.
ISBN 0-09-129251-4 Pbk : £2.50
Also classified at 641.6'9'20954
(B77-29540)

641.6'62 — Food: Minced beef dishes. *Recipes*

Cooking with mince. — Bishop's Stortford (Elsenham, Bishop's Stortford, Herts.) : Penday Publishing Ltd, 1977. — 24p : ill ; 17cm. — (Family meals)
ISBN 0-86090-008-8 Sd : Unpriced
(B77-33307)

641.6'6'3 — Food: Lamb dishes. *Recipes*

Cooking with lamb. — Bishop's Stortford (Elsenham, Bishop's Stortford, Herts.) : Penday Publishing Ltd, 1977. — 24p : ill ; 17cm. — (Family meals)
ISBN 0-86090-000-2 Sd : £0.40
(B77-31992)

641.6'6'4 — Food: Bacon dishes, ham dishes & pork dishes. *Recipes*

McCallum, Norma. The crackling cookbook : pork, bacon and ham / [by] Norma McCallum. — Wellington [N.Z.] [etc.] ; London : A.H. and A.W. Reed, 1975 [i.e. 1976]. — [7],72p : ill ; 22cm. — (A Reedway cookbook)
Published in New Zealand: 1975. — Index.
ISBN 0-589-00906-0 Sp : £2.05
(B77-01616)

641.6'6'4 — Food: Pork dishes. *Recipes*

Cooking with pork. — Bishop's Stortford (Elsenham, Bishop's Stortford, Herts.) : Penday Publishing Ltd, 1977. — 24p : ill ; 17cm. — (Family meals)
ISBN 0-86090-002-9 Sd : Unpriced
(B77-33308)

641.6'6'5 — Food: Chicken dishes. *Recipes*

Cooking with chicken. — Bishop's Stortford (Elsenham, Bishop's Stortford, Herts.) : Penday Publishing Ltd, 1977. — 24p : ill ; 17cm. — (Family meals)
ISBN 0-86090-001-0 Sd : £0.40
(B77-31993)

Lyren, Carl. 365 ways to cook chicken / [by] Carl Lyren. — Revised ed. — London : Hale, 1977. — [5],192p ; 23cm.
Previous ed.: Garden City, N.Y. : Doubleday, 1974. — Index.
ISBN 0-7091-5999-4 : £3.95
(B77-18260)

641.6'7'3 — Cheesecakes. *Recipes*

100 fabulous cheesecakes / Ellen Sinclair, food editor. — London : Souvenir Press, 1977. — 2-45p : ill(chiefly col) ; 27cm.
Col. ill. on lining papers.
ISBN 0-285-62263-3 : £1.95
(B77-13730)

641.6'7'3 — Food: Cheese dishes. *Recipes*

Cooking with cheese. — Bishop's Stortford (Elsenham, Bishop's Stortford, Herts.) : Penday Publishing Ltd, 1977. — 24p : ill ; 17cm. — (Family meals)
ISBN 0-86090-006-1 Sd : £0.40
(B77-31994)

641.6'7'5 — Food: Egg dishes. *Recipes*

Cooking with eggs. — Bishop's Stortford (Elsenham, Bishop's Stortford, Herts.) : Penday Publishing, 1977. — 24p : ill ; 17cm. — (Family meals)
ISBN 0-86090-007-x Sd : £0.40
(B77-31995)

641.6'8 — Food: Dishes using honey. *Recipes*
Mary Workman's honey recipes / compiled by Clara A. Furness from Mary Workman's diaries and illustrated by Margaret Hawkes ... — Derby (Whitegates, Thurlston, Derby DE7 3EW) : British Isles Bee Breeders' Association, 1974. — [56]p : ill, port ; 21cm.
Sp : Unpriced
(B77-05515)

641.6'9 — Food: Seafood dishes. *Recipes*
Hill, Paul J. The edible sea / [by] Paul J. and Mavis A. Hill. — South Brunswick ; New York : Barnes ; London : Yoseloff, 1975. — 276p,[4]p of plates : ill(some col), ports ; 26cm.
Index.
ISBN 0-498-01550-5 : £7.00
(B77-29541)

641.6'9'1 — Food: American game bird dishes. *Recipes*
Youel, Milo A. Cook the wild bird : an erudite treatise on the joy of hunting, cooking and eating game birds, containing a galaxy of modern recipes on game bird cookery in America with significant information on the various game birds plus hints on how they are hunted / [by] Milo A. Youel ; illustrations by Bob Stevens. — South Brunswick ; New York : Barnes ; London : Yoseloff, 1975. — 452p,[4] leaves of plates : ill(some col) ; 26cm.
Index.
ISBN 0-498-01193-3 : £6.00
(B77-31303)

641.6'9'1 — Food: Game dishes. *Recipes*
Gore, Lilli. Game cooking / [by] Lilli Gore ; illustrated by M.J. Mott. — Harmondsworth [etc.] : Penguin, 1976. — 184p : ill ; 20cm. — (Penguin handbooks)
Originally published: London : Weidenfeld and Nicolson, 1974. — Index.
ISBN 0-14-046248-1 Pbk : £0.75
(B77-02417)

641.6'9'2 — Food: Fish dishes. *Recipes*
Ager, Anne. 100 ways with fish / [by] Anne Ager. — London [etc.] : Letts, 1977. — 64p : ill ; 21cm. — (Letts guides)
Index.
ISBN 0-85097-235-3 Pbk : £0.65
(B77-17608)

Froud, Nina. International fish dishes / [by] Nina Froud and Tamara Lo. — London : Sphere, 1976. — 240p ; 18cm.
Originally published: London : Pelham Books, 1974. — Index.
ISBN 0-7221-3693-5 Pbk : £0.65
(B77-06184)

Lassalle, George. The adventurous fish cook / [by] George Lassalle. — London [etc.] : Macmillan, 1976. — 224p : ill ; 23cm.
Index.
ISBN 0-333-19530-2 : £3.95
(B77-00831)

Squire, D. Getting the best from fish / compiled by D. Squire and P. McHoy. — Wakefield : EP Publishing, 1977. — 70p : ill ; 24cm. — (Invest in living)
ISBN 0-7158-0460-x Pbk : £1.45
(B77-17609)

641.6'9'20954 — Food: Indian fish dishes. *Recipes*
Santa Maria, Jack. Indian meat and fish cookery / [by] Jack Santa Maria ; illustrated by Carmen Miranda. — London : Rider, 1977. — 175p : ill ; 24cm.
Bibl.: p.175.
ISBN 0-09-129251-4 Pbk : £2.50
Primary classification 641.6'6'0954
(B77-29540)

641.6'94 — Food: Mussel dishes. *Recipes*
Hurlburt, Sarah. The mussel cookbook / [by] Sarah Hurlburt ; drawings by Edith Allard. — Cambridge, Mass. ; London : Harvard University Press, 1977. — xiv,169p : ill, ports ; 21cm.
Index.
ISBN 0-674-59535-1 : £6.30
(B77-24342)

641.7 — COOKERY. SPECIAL PROCESSES AND TECHNIQUES
641.7'1 — Dishes using natural foods. Baking. *Recipes*
Pelton, Robert Wayne. Natural baking the old-fashioned way / [by] Robert W. Pelton. — South Brunswick [etc.] : Barnes ; London : Yoseloff, 1973. — 156p ; 22cm.
Index.
ISBN 0-498-01250-6 : £2.50
(B77-28713)

641.7'9 — Food: Cold dishes. *Recipes*
MacDonald, Kim. Light meals / [by] Kim MacDonald. — [New] ed. — London : Octopus Books, 1977. — 4-93p : ill(chiefly col) ; 28cm.
Previous ed.: 1971. — Index.
ISBN 0-7064-0642-7 : £1.99
(B77-15940)

641.8 — COOKERY. COMPOSITE DISHES
641.8 — Food: Fondue dishes. *Recipes*
Burt, Alison. Fondue cookery / [by] Alison Burt. — London [etc.] : Hamlyn, 1975. — 114,[5]p, [16]p of plates : ill(some col) ; 23cm.
Ill. on lining papers. — Originally published: Sydney : Hamlyn, 1970 ; Feltham : Hamlyn, 1971. — Index.
£1.50
ISBN 0-600-33457-0
(B77-17610)

Howells, Marion. Fondue and table top cookery / [by] Marion Howells. — London : Octopus Books, 1977. — 4-93p : col ill ; 27cm.
Originally published: 1971. — Index.
ISBN 0-7064-0647-8 : £1.99
Primary classification 641.5'8
(B77-18256)

641.8'12 — Food: Starters. *Recipes*
The **best** of starters and puddings. — London : Reader's Digest Association, 1976. — 48p : ill(chiefly col) ; 27cm. — ('Reader's digest' basic guides)
'The text and illustrations in this book are taken from "The cookery year" ...', 3rd version. London : Reader's Digest Association, 1976. — Index.
ISBN 0-276-00147-8 Sd : £0.75
Also classified at 641.8'6
(B77-16959)

Wadey, Rosemary. Hamlyn's all colour book of soups and starters / [recipes created by Rosemary Wadey ; photography by John Lee]. — London [etc.] : Hamlyn, 1977. — 3-63p : ill(chiefly col) ; 29cm.
Spine title: Soups and starters. — Index.
ISBN 0-600-38229-x : £1.50
Also classified at 641.8'13
(B77-23536)

641.8'13 — Soups. *Recipes*
Heath, Ambrose. Soups and soup garnishes / by Ambrose Heath. — London : Barrie and Jenkins, 1977. — 93p : ill ; 19cm. — (Good cook)
Originally published: 1957. — Index.
ISBN 0-214-20319-0 : £1.25
(B77-30399)

Norman, Ursel. Soup, beautiful soup : a collection of soup recipes / [text] by Ursel Norman ; designed and illustrated by Derek Norman. — Glasgow [etc.] : Collins, 1976. — 63p : ill(chiefly col) ; 28cm. — ([Look and cook])
Index.
ISBN 0-00-435189-4 : £2.95
(B77-19484)

Norman, Ursel. Soup, beautiful soup : a collection of soup recipes / [compiled and edited] by Ursel Norman ; designed and illustrated by Derek Norman. — [London] : Fontana, 1977. — 64p : ill(chiefly col) ; 27cm.
Originally published: London : Collins, 1976. — Index.
ISBN 0-00-635039-9 Pbk : £1.50
(B77-27221)

Wadey, Rosemary. Hamlyn's all colour book of soups and starters / [recipes created by Rosemary Wadey ; photography by John Lee]. — London [etc.] : Hamlyn, 1977. — 3-63p : ill(chiefly col) ; 29cm.
Spine title: Soups and starters. — Index.
ISBN 0-600-38229-x : £1.50
Primary classification 641.8'12
(B77-23536)

641.8'14 — Sauces. *Recipes*
Beckwith, *Lady* **Muriel.** Sauces, sweet and savoury / by Lady Muriel Beckwith. — London : Barrie and Jenkins, 1977. — 96p : ill ; 19cm. — (Good cook)
Originally published: 1953. — Index.
ISBN 0-214-20303-4 : £1.25
(B77-31304)

641.8'15 — Bread. *Recipes*
Eno, David. The little brown bread book / text & illustrations [by] David Eno ; calligraphy [by] Jenny Ivermee. — Winchester : Juniper Press, 1976. — 31p : ill ; 15cm.
ISBN 0-903981-06-8 Sd : £0.45
(B77-14807)

Good Housekeeping Institute. 'Good housekeeping' home baking / by Good Housekeeping Institute ; illustrated by Hilary Evans ; [editor Amanda Atha]. — London : Ebury Press, 1977. — 128p,[8]p of plates : ill(some col) ; 25cm.
Index.
ISBN 0-85223-113-x : £3.50
Also classified at 641.8'65
(B77-30400)

Honey, Babs. Home-baked breads & scones / by Babs Honey. — Wakefield : EP Publishing, 1977. — 72p : ill ; 24cm. — (Invest in living)
Index.
ISBN 0-7158-0541-x Pbk : £1.45
Also classified at 641.8'65
(B77-31305)

Norman, Ursel. Use your loaf : a book of bread recipes / compiled and edited by Ursel Norman ; with drawings and step-by-step illustrations by Derek Norman. — [London] : Fontana, 1976. — 63p : ill(chiefly col) ; 27cm.
Originally published: Glasgow : Collins, 1974. — Index.
ISBN 0-00-634432-1 Pbk : £1.25
(B77-04285)

Sherborne House bread book. — Sherborne, Glos. : Coombe Springs Press, [1977]. — v,64, [2],[2]leaves of plates : ill ; 29cm.
ISBN 0-900306-37-8 Pbk : £0.90
(B77-09113)

Walker, Lorna. The complete bread book / [by] Lorna Walker & Joyce Hughes. — London [etc.] : Hamlyn, 1977. — 185p : ill(chiefly col) ; 31cm.
Col. ill. on lining papers. — Index.
ISBN 0-600-31414-6 : £4.95
(B77-30401)

641.8'15 — Bread. *Recipes. Juvenile literature*
Hinde, Cecilia. Your book of breadmaking / [by] Cecilia H. Hinde ; illustrated by Jean H. Hinde. — London : Faber, 1977. — 79p : ill ; 22cm. — (The 'Your book' series)
Index.
ISBN 0-571-10641-2 : £2.20 : CIP rev.
Also classified at 641.8'65
(B77-09114)

641.8'2 — Food: Tortilla dishes. *Recipes*
Kennedy, Diana. The tortilla book / [by] Diana Kennedy ; drawings by Sidonie Coryn. — New York [etc.] ; London : Harper and Row, 1975. — 158p : ill ; 28cm.
Bibl.: p.153. — Index.
ISBN 0-06-012347-8 Pbk : £3.20
(B77-16960)

641.8'21 — Food: Casserole dishes. *Recipes*
Brunner, Lousene Rousseau. New casserole treasury / [by] Lousene Rousseau Brunner. — London [etc.] : Pan Books, 1977. — 320p ; 20cm.
Originally published: New York : Harper and Row ; London : Collins, 1970. — Index.
ISBN 0-330-25335-2 Pbk : £1.00
(B77-28714)

Roles, Julia. Hamlyn's all-colour book of casserole cookery / [recipes created by Julia Roles ; photography by John Lee]. — London [etc.] : Hamlyn, 1977. — 3-63p : ill(chiefly col) ; 29cm.
Spine title: Casserole cookery. — Index.
ISBN 0-600-31941-5 : £1.50
(B77-24343)

Street, Myra. Casserole cooking / [by] Myra Street. — London ([59 Grosvenor St., W1]) : Sundial Books Ltd [for Marks and Spencer Ltd], 1977. — 96p : col ill ; 28cm. — (St Michael cookery library)
Index.
ISBN 0-904230-43-0 Pbk : £0.99
(B77-27940)

641.8'22 — Food: Pasta dishes. *Recipes*
Buonassisi, Vincenzo. Pasta / [by] Vincenzo Buonassisi ; translated [from the Italian] by Elisabeth Evans. — London : Macdonald and Jane's, 1977. — 3-371p : ill(chiefly col) ; 26cm.
Spine title: The classic book of pasta. — Translation of: 'Il codice della pasta'. Milano : Rizzoli, 1973. — Index.
ISBN 0-356-08430-2 : £7.95
(B77-14808)

Cooking with pasta. — Bishop's Stortford (Elsenham, Bishop's Stortford, Herts.) : Penday Publishing Ltd, 1977. — 24p : ill ; 17cm. — (Family meals)
ISBN 0-86090-003-7 Sd : £0.40
(B77-31996)

Norman, Ursel. Pasta! pasta! : a collection of pasta recipes / compiled and edited by Ursel Norman ; designed and illustrated by Derek Norman. — [London] : Fontana, 1977. — 64p : ill(chiefly col) ; 27cm.
Originally published: as 'Pasta & oodles of noodles'. Glasgow : Collins, 1975.
ISBN 0-00-635038-0 Pbk : £1.50
(B77-27941)

641.8'4 — Sandwiches. *Recipes*
Beer, Gretel. Sandwiches for parties and picnics / by Gretel Beer. — London : Barrie and Jenkins, 1977. — 94p : ill ; 19cm. — (Good cook)
Originally published: 1953. — Index.
ISBN 0-214-20304-2 : £1.25
(B77-31306)

Dodd, Ken. Ken Dodd's butty book / in collaboration with Dave Dutton and Hal Dootson ; illustrated by Bill Tidy. — London [etc.] : Macmillan, 1977. — 95p : ill ; 25cm.
Index.
ISBN 0-333-23282-8 Pbk : £1.95
(B77-32721)

641.8'52 — Preserves. *Recipes*
Jams & preserves / [compiled and edited by Brenda Holroyd]. — London : Sphere, 1975. — 160p : ill(chiefly col) ; 22cm. — ('Good housekeeping' family library)
Originally published: London : Ebury Press, 1973. — Index.
ISBN 0-7221-3951-9 Pbk : £0.95
(B77-19485)

Norwak, Mary. Mary Norwak's book of jams, marmalades and sweet preserves. — London : Sphere, 1977. — 208p : ill ; 18cm.
Originally published: as 'Mary Norwak's book on jams, marmalades and sweet preserves'. 1973. — Index.
ISBN 0-7221-6452-1 Pbk : £0.75
(B77-23537)

641.8'53 — Confectionery: Sweets. *Recipes*
Graham, Winifred. Chocolates and candies for pleasure and profit / [by] Winifred Graham. — London [etc.] : White Lion Publishers, 1977. — 159p : ill ; 22cm.
£3.95
ISBN 0-7285-0012-5
ISBN 0-7285-0029-9 Pbk : £1.95
(B77-21976)

Norwak, Mary. Toffees, fudges, chocolates and sweets / [by] Mary Norwak. — London : Pelham, 1977. — 144p ; 23cm.
Index.
ISBN 0-7207-0956-3 : £3.95
(B77-08453)

641.8'53 — Confectionery: Sweets. *Recipes. Juvenile literature*
Powell, Margaret. Sweetmaking for children / [by] Margaret Powell ; illustrations by Karen Heywood. — London : Severn House : [Distributed by Hutchinson], 1976. — [6],121p : ill ; 21cm.
Originally published: London : Pan Books, 1972. — Index.
ISBN 0-7278-0220-8 : £2.50
(B77-02418)

641.8'6 — Desserts. *Recipes*
The **best** of starters and puddings. — London : Reader's Digest Association, 1976. — 48p : ill(chiefly col) ; 27cm. — ('Reader's digest' basic guides)
'The text and illustrations in this book are taken from "The cookery year" ...', 3rd version. London : Reader's Digest Association, 1976. — Index.
ISBN 0-276-00147-8 Sd : £0.75
Primary classification 641.8'12
(B77-16959)

The **great** dessert cookbook / Ellen Sinclair, food editor. — London : Souvenir Press, 1977. — 3-45p : col ill ; 27cm.
Text, col. ill. on lining papers. — Originally published: Sydney : Golden Press, 197-?. — Index.
ISBN 0-285-62267-6 : £1.95
(B77-12551)

Pomeroy, Elizabeth. Puddings and desserts / [by] Elizabeth Pomeroy. — [London] ([59 Grosvenor St., W.1]) : Sundial Books Ltd, [1977]. — 96p : col ill ; 28cm. — (St Michael cookery library)
Index.
ISBN 0-904230-42-2 Pbk : £0.99
(B77-29542)

641.8'62 — Ice cream. *Recipes*
Rubinstein, Helge. Ices galore / [by] Helge Rubinstein and Sheila Bush ; with decorations by Susan Neale. — London : Deutsch, 1977. — 128p : ill ; 23cm.
Index.
ISBN 0-233-96831-8 : £2.95
(B77-13121)

641.8'65 — Pastries. *Recipes*
Crocker, Betty. Betty Crocker's pie and pastry cookbook. — Toronto [etc.] ; London : Bantam, 1976. — [5],218p : ill ; 18cm.
Originally published: New York : Golden Press, 1968. — Index.
ISBN 0-553-02769-7 Pbk : £0.65
(B77-23538)

Fearon, Ethelind. Fancy cakes and pastries / by Ethelind Fearon. — London : Barrie and Jenkins, 1977. — 96p : ill ; 19cm. — (Good cook)
Originally published: 1954. — Index.
ISBN 0-214-20323-9 : £1.25
Primary classification 641.8'653
(B77-33909)

Good Housekeeping Institute. 'Good housekeeping' home baking / by Good Housekeeping Institute ; illustrated by Hilary Evans ; [editor Amanda Atha]. — London : Ebury Press, 1977. — 128p,[8]p of plates : ill(some col) ; 25cm.
Index.
ISBN 0-85223-113-x : £3.50
Primary classification 641.8'15
(B77-30400)

Powell, Phyllis. Teatime cookery / [by] Phyllis Powell. — London [etc.] : Collins, 1977. — 104p : ill(some col) ; 28cm. — (Collins cheerful cooking)
Originally published: 1973. — Index.
Pbk : £1.25
ISBN 0-00-435267-x
(B77-28715)

641.8'65 — Pastries. *Recipes. Juvenile literature*
Hinde, Cecilia. Your book of breadmaking / [by] Cecilia H. Hinde ; illustrated by Jean H. Hinde. — London : Faber, 1977. — 79p : ill ; 22cm. — (The 'Your book' series)
Index.
ISBN 0-571-10641-2 : £2.20 : CIP rev.
Primary classification 641.8'15
(B77-09114)

641.8'65 — Scones. *Recipes*
Honey, Babs. Home-baked breads & scones / by Babs Honey. — Wakefield : EP Publishing, 1977. — 72p : ill ; 24cm. — (Invest in living)
Index.
ISBN 0-7158-0541-x Pbk : £1.45
Primary classification 641.8'15
(B77-31305)

641.8'653 — Cakes. *Recipes*
100 favourite cakes / Ellen Sinclair, food editor. — London : Souvenir Press, 1977. — 3-46p : col ill ; 27cm.
Text, col ill. on lining papers. — Originally published: Sydney : Golden Press, 1972. — Index.
ISBN 0-285-62265-x : £1.95
(B77-12552)

Smith, Delia. Delia Smith's book of cakes. — London [etc.] : Hodder and Stoughton, 1977. — 221p,[8]p of plates : ill(some col) ; 23cm.
Index.
ISBN 0-340-22376-6 : £4.95
(B77-33908)

641.8'653 — Cakes. Decoration
Vercoe, Bernice. Cake decorating / [by] Bernice Vercoe, Dorothy Evans. — London : Souvenir Press, 1976. — 160p : ill(some col) ; 30cm.
Originally published: as 'Australian book of cake decorating', Sydney : Hamlyn, 1973. — Index.
ISBN 0-285-62259-5 : £3.50
(B77-00832)

641.8'653 — Fancy cakes. *Recipes*
Fearon, Ethelind. Fancy cakes and pastries / by Ethelind Fearon. — London : Barrie and Jenkins, 1977. — 96p : ill ; 19cm. — (Good cook)
Originally published: 1954. — Index.
ISBN 0-214-20323-9 : £1.25
Also classified at 641.8'65
(B77-33909)

641.8'654 — Biscuits. *Recipes*
100 delicious biscuits and slices / Ellen Sinclair, food editor. — London : Souvenir Press, 1977. — 3-44,[1]p : col ill ; 27cm.
Text, col. ill. on lining papers. — Originally published: as 'The "Australian women's weekly", 100 delicious biscuits and slices'. Sydney : Golden Press, 1972. — Index.
ISBN 0-285-62264-1 : £1.95
(B77-12553)

Priestley, Florence. The biscuit book / [by] Florence Priestley. — Havant : K. Mason, 1977. — [1],32p ; 15cm.
ISBN 0-85937-088-7 Sd : £0.35 : CIP rev.
(B77-10436)

641.87 — PREPARATION OF BEVERAGES
641.8'72 — Wines. Making. *Amateurs' manuals*
Beedell, Suzanne. Winemaking and home brewing : a complete guide / [by] Suzanne Beedell ; flowers drawn by Pat Moody. — London : Sphere, 1977. — 189p : ill ; 18cm.
Originally published: 1969. — Index.
ISBN 0-7221-1529-6 Pbk : £0.75
Also classified at 641.8'73
(B77-30402)

Bravery, Harold Edwin. The complete book of home winemaking / [by] H.E. Bravery. — London [etc.] : Pan Books, 1977. — 175p : ill ; 18cm.
Originally published: London : Arco, 1970. — Index.
Pbk : £0.75
ISBN 0-330-23503-6
(B77-27222)

Hanssen, Maurice. Wines, beers and spirits : the secrets of successful home production / by Maurice Hanssen and Jacqueline Dineen. — Wellingborough : Thorsons, 1977. — 96p ; 22cm.
Index.
ISBN 0-7225-0414-4 : £1.50
Also classified at 641.8'73
(B77-31307)

Turner, Bernard Charles Arthur. The winemaker's companion : a handbook for those who make wine at home / by B.C.A. Turner, C.J.J. Berry. — [New ed.] with amendments. — London : Mills and Boon, 1975. — 5-221p,[8]p of plates : ill, forms ; 22cm.
Previous ed.: i.e. 2nd ed. revised, 1971. — Index.
ISBN 0-263-06115-9 : £2.70
(B77-27942)

641.8'72 — Wines. Making. *Amateurs' manuals. Welsh texts*
Jones, Elsi Wyn. Gwin a diodydd eraill : 80 o risetau ar gyfer pob math o ddiodydd a'u defnydd newn bwyd / gan Elsi Wyn Jones. — Penygroes, Gwynedd ([Bryn Mair, Dolydd Y Groeslon, Caernarfon, Gwynedd]) : Cyhoeddiadau Mei, 1977. — 64p : ill, facsims ; 12x19cm.
ISBN 0-905775-04-x Pbk : £0.60
(B77-29543)

641.8'73 — Brewing. *Amateurs' manuals*
Beedell, Suzanne. Winemaking and home brewing : a complete guide / [by] Suzanne Beedell ; flowers drawn by Pat Moody. — London : Sphere, 1977. — 189p : ill ; 18cm.
Originally published: 1969. — Index.
ISBN 0-7221-1529-6 Pbk : £0.75
Primary classification 641.8'72
(B77-30402)

Hanssen, Maurice. Wines, beers and spirits : the secrets of successful home production / by Maurice Hanssen and Jacqueline Dineen. — Wellingborough : Thorsons, 1977. — 96p ; 22cm.
Index.
ISBN 0-7225-0414-4 : £1.50
Primary classification 641.8'72
(B77-31307)

Laing, Dave. Beer and brewing / [by] Dave Laing and John Hendra. — [London] : [Macdonald Educational], [1977]. — 96p : ill(some col), 2 maps(1 col) ; 21cm. — (Macdonald guidelines)
Bibl.: p.91. — Index.
ISBN 0-356-06009-8 Pbk : £1.00
(B77-15363)

641.8'73 — Cider. Making. *Amateurs' manuals*
Deal, Josephine. Making cider / by Jo Deal. — Andover : 'Amateur winemaker', 1976. — 64,[6]p,[4]p of plates : ill ; 18cm.
Index.
ISBN 0-900841-45-1 Pbk : £0.60
(B77-18261)

641.8'74 — Cocktails. *Recipes*
Doxat, John. Booth's handbook of cocktails and mixed drinks / [by] John Doxat. — [New and revised ed.]. — London [etc.] : Pan Books, 1977. — 191p ; 18cm.
Previous ed.: London : Barker, 1967. — Bibl.: p.180-182. — Index.
ISBN 0-330-10593-0 Pbk : £0.70
(B77-32722)

642 — FOOD AND MEAL SERVICE
642'.3 — Expeditions by school parties. Food. Planning. *Manuals*
Young Explorers' Trust. Expedition food and rations planning manual / Young Explorers' Trust. — [Stockport] ([238 Wellington Rd South, Stockport, Cheshire SK2 6NW]) : [The Trust], [1976]. — [1],17,[24]p,[4]p of plates : ill ; 21cm.
ISBN 0-905965-01-9 Pbk : £0.75
(B77-13122)

642'.47'0924 — Catering. Lewis, Rosa. *London. Biographies*
Harrison, Michael. Rosa / [by] Michael Harrison. — London : Corgi, 1977. — 302p,[8] p of plates : ill, facsim, ports ; 18cm.
Originally published: London : P. Davies, 1962. — Bibl.: p.295-297. — Index.
ISBN 0-552-10582-1 Pbk : £0.85
(B77-32723)

Masters, Anthony. Rosa Lewis : an exceptional Edwardian / [by] Anthony Masters. — London : Weidenfeld and Nicolson, 1977. — xi, 210p,[8]p of plates : ill, facsim, ports ; 23cm.
Bibl.: p.202-204. — Index.
ISBN 0-297-77358-5 : £5.95
(B77-26385)

642'.5 — Catering equipment. Choice. *Manuals*
Kotschevar, Lendal Henry. Foodservice planning : layout and equipment / [by] Lendal H. Kotschevar, Margaret E. Terrell. — 2nd ed. — New York ; London [etc.] : Wiley, 1977. — xv,601p : ill, forms, plans ; 24cm.
Previous ed.: 1961. — Bibl.: p.589-593. — Index.
ISBN 0-471-50491-2 : £13.75
Primary classification 642'.5
(B77-21258)

642'.5 — Catering industries. Food preparation areas. Planning. *Manuals*
Kotschevar, Lendal Henry. Foodservice planning : layout and equipment / [by] Lendal H. Kotschevar, Margaret E. Terrell. — 2nd ed. — New York ; London [etc.] : Wiley, 1977. — xv,601p : ill, forms, plans ; 24cm.
Previous ed.: 1961. — Bibl.: p.589-593. — Index.
ISBN 0-471-50491-2 : £13.75
Also classified at 642'.5
(B77-21258)

642'.5 — Institutions. Food services. *United States*
Food service in institutions / [by] Bessie Brooks West ... [et al.]. — 5th ed. — New York ; London [etc.] : Wiley, 1977. — viii,839p : ill, facsim, forms, plans ; 24cm.
Previous ed.: 1966. — Bibl. — Index.
ISBN 0-471-93393-7 : £13.50
(B77-24344)

642'.56'09421 — Restaurants. Menus. *London. Collections. Facsimiles*
The **London** book of menus : the menus from a selection of the finest restaurants in London. — London (P.O. Box 184, SW1P 2PZ) : Brombacher Publishing Co., 1976. — 229p : chiefly facsims(some col), maps ; 30cm.
ISBN 0-905401-00-x Pbk : £4.00
(B77-04286)

642'.6 — Cafés. Waitressing. *Personal observations*
Stuart-Knill, Eve, *Lady.* One of the world's workers / by Eve, Lady Knill. — London (Crawford House, Willow St., E4 7EQ) : E.G. Ellis and Sons, [1977]. — 15p ; 21cm.
Sd : £1.00
(B77-18262)

642'.6 — Catering. Waitering. *Manuals*
Tuor, Conrad. Wine and food handbook = Aide-mémoire du Sommelier / [by] Conrad Tuor ; [translated from the French]. — London [etc.] : Hodder and Stoughton, 1977. — 255p : ill, maps ; 16cm.
Translation of: 'Aide-mémoire du Sommelier'. 5. éd. Lausanne : The author, 1970.
ISBN 0-340-17906-6 : £3.50
ISBN 0-340-17907-4 Pbk : £1.75
Primary classification 641.3'002'4642
(B77-25729)

642'.6 — Catering. Waitering. *United States. Manuals*
Aikin, Brenton R. The waiter-waitress manual / [by] Brenton R. Aikin. — New York ; London [etc.] : McGraw-Hill, 1976. — [6],122p : ill, forms ; 28cm. — (A job skill manual in marketing)
Pages perforated at inside edge.
ISBN 0-07-000742-x Sd : £3.95
(B77-06185)

642'.6 — Meat. Carving. *Amateurs' manuals*
Cullen, M O. How to carve meat, game and poultry / by M.O. Cullen. — New York : Dover Publications [etc.] ; London : Constable, 1976. — ix,209p,leaf of plate,[2]p of plates : ill ; 22cm.
Originally published: New York : McGraw-Hill, 1941. — Index.
ISBN 0-486-23313-8 Pbk : £2.00
(B77-11926)

643 — THE HOME AND ITS EQUIPMENT
643 — Homes. *Juvenile literature*
Scarry, Richard. My house / with illustrations by Richard Scarry. — London [etc.] : Hamlyn, 1977. — [24]p : col ill ; 21cm. — (A golden look-look book)
Originally published as: 'Richard Scarry's my house'. New York : Golden Press, 1976.
ISBN 0-600-34538-6 Sd : £0.40
(B77-28716)

643 — Homes. *Secondary school texts*
Dixon, Joan. Houses and housing / [by] Joan Dixon ; illustrated by Peter Kesteven. — 3rd ed. — London : Longman, 1977. — xiii,163p : ill, plans ; 21cm. — (Longman housecraft series)
Previous ed.: Harlow : Longman, 1971. — Bibl.
ISBN 0-582-22077-7 Pbk : £1.20
(B77-32724)

Jordan, M R. Houses and homes / [by] M.R. Jordan, R.E. Hosking. — London : Longman, 1977. — 160p : ill, form, plans ; 20x26cm. — (Practical)
Accompanied by 'Workbook' (31 leaves: Sd). — Bibl.: p.159. — List of films: p.158. — Index.
ISBN 0-582-23393-3 Pbk : £1.95
ISBN 0-582-23394-1 Replacement workbooks : Unpriced
(B77-31997)

643 — Houses. Purchase & sale. *United States. Practical information*
Irwin, Robert, *b.1941.* Protect yourself in real estate / [by] Robert Irwin. — New York ; London [etc.] : McGraw-Hill, 1977. — viii, 312p ; 24cm.
Index.
ISBN 0-07-032064-0 : £9.70
(B77-26386)

643 — Residences. *Juvenile literature*
Hogarth, Elizabeth. Wigwams, igloos and bungalows / [by] Elizabeth Hogarth ; illustrated by Rowan Barnes-Murphy. — London : Pan Books, 1977. — 93p : ill ; 20cm. — (Piccolo original)
Also published: London : Severn House, 1977.
ISBN 0-330-25116-3 Pbk : £0.45
(B77-22373)

Hogarth, Elizabeth. Wigwams, igloos and bungalows / [by] Elizabeth Hogarth ; illustrated by Rowan Barnes-Murphy. — London : Severn House : [Distributed by Hutchinson], 1977. — 93p : ill ; 21cm.
Also published: London : Pan Books, 1977.
ISBN 0-7278-0335-2 : £2.75 : CIP rev.
(B77-25772)

643 — Residences. Burglary. Prevention. *United States. Manuals*
Keogh, James Edward. Burglarproof : a complete guide to home security / [by] James Edward Keogh, John Koster. — New York ; London [etc.] : McGraw-Hill, 1977. — vi,170p : ill ; 21cm.
Index.
ISBN 0-07-034146-x : £7.45
(B77-25736)

643 — Residences. Removal. *Great Britain. Personal observations. Humorous texts*
Boothroyd, Basil. Let's move house / [by] Basil Boothroyd. — London [etc.] : Allen and Unwin, 1977. — 3-158p : ill ; 21cm.
ISBN 0-04-827015-6 : £3.50
(B77-27943)

643'.3 — Residences. Kitchens. Improvement. *Amateurs' manuals*
Smith, Piera. The economy kitchen / by Piera Smith. — Wellingborough : Thorsons, 1977. — 93p : ill ; 22cm. — (Pauperbacks)
Index.
ISBN 0-7225-0398-9 Pbk : £1.25
(B77-32725)

643'.6 — Household electric equipment. Maintenance & repair. *Amateurs' manuals*
Burdett, Geoffrey Arnold Thomas. Repair your own home electrical appliance / [by] Geoffrey Burdett and John Mattick. — London [etc.] : Foulsham, 1977. — 313p : ill ; 23cm.
ISBN 0-572-00832-5 : £5.50
(B77-27944)

643'.6 — Household equipment. *Juvenile literature*
Things. — Maidenhead : Purnell, 1977. — [12]p : chiefly col ill ; 22cm.
Pbd : £0.45
(B77-16476)

643'.6 — Household equipment for physically handicapped persons
Consumers' Association. Coping with disablement / [Consumers' Association]. — Revised ed. / [written by Peggy Jay] ; [edited by Edith Rudinger]. — London : The Association, 1976. — [6],229p : ill ; 21cm. — (Open University. Set books) (A consumer publication)
Previous ed.: i.e. Amended ed., 1974. — Index.
ISBN 0-85202-120-8 Pbk : £1.75
(B77-07456)

643'.6 — Household equipment. Maintenance & repair. *Amateurs' manuals*
Johnson, Lorraine. How to restore and repair practically everything / [by] Lorraine Johnson. — London : Joseph, 1977. — 192p : ill ; 27cm.
Bibl.: p.184-187. — Index.
ISBN 0-7181-1629-1 : £5.50
(B77-30403)

643'.7 — Houses. Extension & improvement. *Amateurs' manuals*
Goodson, Bill. Home building work / [by] Bill Goodson. — London [etc.] : Newnes Technical Books, 1977. — [8],104p : ill(chiefly col), plans ; 25cm. — (Do it yourself)
Text on inside covers. — Index.
ISBN 0-408-00276-x Pbk : Unpriced
(B77-31308)

Home improvements. — [London] ([30 Old Burlington St., W1X 2AE]) : [Troup Publications Ltd for the National Federation of Builders' and Plumbers' Merchants].
'77 / [editors Sonia Roberts, Neville Davis]. — [1977]. — 64p : chiefly col ill, ports ; 28cm.
Cover title.
Pbk : £0.35
ISSN 0140-251x
(B77-27945)

643'.7 — Residences. Decorating. *Amateurs' manuals*
Home decorating. — London : IPC Magazines, [1977]. — 63p : ill(some col) ; 21cm.
'A "Homemaker" do-it-yourself booklet'. — Index.
Sd : £0.40
(B77-14809)

Wilkins, Tony. Home decorating / [by] Tony Wilkins. — London [etc.] : Newnes Technical Books, 1977. — [7],96,[8]p : ill(some col) ; 25cm. — (Do it yourself)
Index.
ISBN 0-408-00243-3 Pbk : £2.90
(B77-16477)

643'.7 — Residences. Improvement. *Amateurs' manuals*
Scharff, Robert. The complete book of home remodeling / [by] Robert Scharff. — New York ; London [etc.] : McGraw-Hill, [1976]. — xi,496p : ill, plans ; 25cm.
Published in the United States: 1975. — Index.
ISBN 0-07-055167-7 : £12.40
(B77-00833)

643'.7 — Residences. Interiors. Decorating. *Amateurs' manuals*
Grime, Kitty. Let's decorate - together! / [by] Kitty Grime. — Guildford : Lutterworth Press ; [s.l.] : Richard Smart Publishing, 1977. — 72p : ill ; 21cm. — (Leisure series)
ISBN 0-7188-7013-1 Pbk : £1.95
(B77-28718)

643'.7 — Residences. Maintenance & repair. *Amateurs' manuals*
Jackson, Albert. 'Good housekeeping' do-it-yourself book / [by] Albert Jackson & David Day. — London : Ebury Press, 1977. — 256p : col ill ; 29cm.
Index.
ISBN 0-85223-119-9 : £6.95
(B77-31998)

King, Harold, *b.1927.* The A-Z of do-it-yourself in the home / by Harold and Elizabeth King ; illustrations by Stanton Phillips. — Kingswood : Elliot Right Way Books, 1977. — 192p : ill ; 18cm. — (Paperfronts)
Index.
ISBN 0-7160-0634-0 Pbk : £0.50
(B77-33309)

Limon, Alec C. House & garden maintenance / by Alec C. Limon. — Wellingborough : Thorsons, 1977. — 93p : ill ; 22cm. — (Pauperbacks)
Index.
ISBN 0-7225-0401-2 Pbk : £1.25
(B77-30404)

Pettit, Tom. Home maintenance & outdoor repairs / by Tom Pettit. — Wakefield : EP Publishing, 1977. — 72p : ill, plan ; 24cm. — (Invest in living)
Bibl.: p.72.
ISBN 0-7158-0490-1 Pbk : £1.45
(B77-31309)

Phillips, Barty. Wonder worker : Barty Phillips' book of repairs and renovations / illustrations by Susan Finch. — London : Sidgwick and Jackson, 1977. — x,236p : ill ; 24cm.
Bibl.: p.225-228. — Index.
ISBN 0-283-98381-7 : £5.50
(B77-27223)

'**Reader's** digest' book of do-it-yourself skills and techniques / [edited and designed by the Reader's Digest Association]. — London [etc.] : The Association, 1977. — 240p : ill(some col), col map ; 28cm.
'"The Reader's Digest Book of Do-It-Yourself Skills and Techniques" draws its text and illustrations from "The Reader's Digest Complete Do-It-Yourself Manual", first published in 1968 ...' - Introduction. — Index.
ISBN 0-276-00152-4 : £4.95
(B77-16478)

'**Reader's** digest' concise repair manual / [edited and designed by the Reader's Digest Association]. — London [etc.] : Reader's Digest Association, 1977. — 264p : ill(chiefly col) ; 28cm.
'The "Reader's digest concise repair manual" draws its text and illustrations from the "Reader's digest repair manual", first published in 1972' - Preface. — Index.
£4.95
(B77-30405)

'**Reader's** digest' repair manual : the complete guide to home maintenance / [edited and designed by the Reader's Digest Association]. — 1st ed., 7th revise. — London [etc.] : Reader's Digest Association, 1976. — 704p : ill(chiefly col) ; 20x28cm.
First ed. originally published: 1972. — Index.
£7.95
(B77-09797)

'**Reader's** digest' repair manual : the complete guide to home maintenance / [edited and designed by the Reader's Digest Association]. — 1st ed., 8th revise. — London [etc.] : Reader's Digest Association, 1976. — 704p : ill(chiefly col) ; 20x27cm.
First ed. originally published: 1972. — Index.
ISBN 0-276-00153-2 : £9.95
(B77-03615)

Stilgoe, Richard. Oddjob / [by] Richard Stilgoe and Tom Gutteridge. — London : British Broadcasting Corporation, 1977. — 64p : ill(some col) ; 21cm.
ISBN 0-563-17405-6 Sd : £0.95
(B77-30406)

The '**Sunday** times' book of do-it-yourself / edited by Bill Cater and Shirley Crabtree. — Hornby : Construction Press, 1976. — 125p : ill(chiefly col) ; 31cm.
'... compiled from material originally published by the "Sunday Times" in the weekly colour magazine' - jacket. — Index.
ISBN 0-904406-13-x : £4.95
(B77-01617)

Whitman, Roger C. More first aid for the ailing house : money-saving ways to improve your home and property / [by] Roger C. Whitman ; edited by Robert Scharff. — New York ; London [etc.] : McGraw-Hill, 1977. — ix, 370p : ill ; 24cm.
Index.
ISBN 0-07-069985-2 : £11.20
(B77-22700)

Wilkins, Tony. Beginners guide to do-it-yourself / [by] Tony Wilkins and Ron Grace. — London : Sphere, 1975. — 158p : ill ; 18cm. — (Sphere's beginners guides series)
Originally published: London : Pelham, 1974. — Index.
ISBN 0-7221-9142-1 Pbk : £0.50
(B77-18870)

Wilkins, Tony. Home repair and maintenance / [by] Tony Wilkins. — London [etc.] : Newnes Technical Books, 1977. — [7],102p : ill(some col) ; 25cm. — (Do it yourself)
Text on inside covers. — Index.
ISBN 0-408-00242-5 Pbk : Unpriced
(B77-31999)

643'.7 — Residences. Maintenance, repair & improvement. *Amateurs' manuals*
The **complete** home handywoman / edited by Dawn Marsden and Alan Morgan. — London : Octopus Books, 1977. — 256p : ill(chiefly col) ; 31cm.
Index.
ISBN 0-7064-0533-1 : £4.95
(B77-14810)

Schuler, Stanley. 5,000 questions answered about maintaining, repairing and improving your home / [by] Stanley Schuler. — New York : Collier Books ; London : Collier Macmillan, 1976. — ix,416p : ill ; 28cm.
Index.
ISBN 0-02-081840-8 Pbk : £7.50
(B77-12554)

643'.7 — Timber framed houses. Improvement. *United States. Amateurs' manuals*
Sherwood, Gerald E. How to select and renovate an older house / [by] Gerald E. Sherwood. — New York : Dover Publications [etc.] ; London : Constable, 1976. — [2],94p : ill, 2 maps, plans ; 28cm.
Originally published: as 'New life for old dwellings'. Washington, D.C. : U.S. Dept of Agriculture, Forest Service, 1975. — Index.
ISBN 0-486-23374-x Pbk : £1.80
(B77-25759)

643'.7'09417 — Residences. Maintenance, repair & improvement. *Ireland (Republic). Amateurs' manuals. Periodicals*
The **Irish** home improver. — Dublin (175 North Strand Rd, Dublin 1) : Construction and Property News Ltd.
Feb. 1977-. — [1977]-. — ill ; 45cm.
Monthly. — 16p. in 1st issue. — Size varies.
Sd : £0.15
ISSN 0332-0790
(B77-32726)

645 — HOUSEHOLD FURNISHINGS
645 — Household furnishings. Making. *Manuals*
Muter, Penny. Furnishing on a shoe-string / by Penny Muter. — Wellingborough : Thorsons, 1977. — 94p : ill ; 22cm. — (Pauperbacks)
Index.
ISBN 0-7225-0400-4 Pbk : £1.25
(B77-30407)

645'.2 — Residences. Internal walls. Maintenance & repair. *Amateurs' manuals*
Beedell, Suzanne. The wall handbook : a guide to the maintenance, repair and decoration of your inside walls / [by] Suzanne Beedell. — London : Macdonald and Jane's, 1976. — 142p : ill ; 26cm.
Index.
ISBN 0-354-04020-0 : £4.95
(B77-00834)

646 — CLOTHING
646 — Clothing. *For slow learning adolescents*
McCarthy, M L. Clothes / [text by M.L. McCarthy] ; [planned and edited by Dale Gunthorp]. — London : Macdonald Educational, 1977. — 3-46p : ill(chiefly col), ports(some col) ; 25cm. — (Action world)
Text, col. ill. on lining papers. — Index.
ISBN 0-356-05561-2 : £1.25
(B77-28719)

646.1'5 — Clothing. Making. Use of leather. *Manuals*
Goldsworthy, Maureen. Dressmaking with leather / [by] Maureen Goldsworthy. — London : Batsford, 1976. — 119p,[4]p of plates : ill(some col) ; 26cm.
Index.
ISBN 0-7134-3240-3 : £5.50
(B77-23539)

646.2 — Sewing. *Amateurs' manuals*
Kinmond, Jean. Sewing / [by] Jean Kinmond. — Leicester : Knight Books, 1975. — [4],91p : ill(some col) ; 21cm. — (Illustrated teach yourself)
Originally published: Leicester : Brockhampton Press, 1970. — Index.
ISBN 0-340-19609-2 Pbk : £0.95
(B77-02419)

646.2 — Sewing. *Juvenile literature*
Barber, Janet. Have fun with sewing / [by] Janet Barber. — London : Severn House : [Distributed by Hutchinson], 1977. — 128p : ill ; 21cm. — (Severn House 'TV times' look-in books)
Originally published: London : Independent Television Books, 1975. — Index.
ISBN 0-7278-0241-0 : £2.75
(B77-15941)

646.2'1 — Sewing machines. *Amateurs' manuals*
Perkins, Margaret. Using the sewing machine / [by] Margaret Perkins ; illustrated by Jane Lewington. — London : Heinemann Educational, 1977. — v,73p : ill(chiefly col) ; 25cm.
ISBN 0-435-42840-3 Pbk : £1.70
(B77-24345)

646.2'12 — Soft furnishings. Making. *Manuals*
Collins encyclopedia of home sewing / edited by Jean Kinmond. — Glasgow [etc.] : Collins, 1976. — 223p : ill(chiefly col) ; 31cm.
Index.
ISBN 0-00-434603-3 : £4.95
(B77-20417)

'**Sewing** & knitting' book of soft furnishings. — London : IPC Magazines, 1977. — 3-62p : ill(some col) ; 22cm.
Sd : £0.40
(B77-16479)

646'.34 — Women's clothing. Selection. *For adolescent girls*
Jeans, Heather. Yourself and your clothes / [by] Heather Jeans. — Glasgow [etc.] : Blackie, 1977. — [2],36,[1]p : ill ; 22cm. — (Home economics topic books)
ISBN 0-216-90182-0 Sd : Unpriced
Also classified at 646.6'2
(B77-23540)

646.4 — Clothing. Making. *Manuals*
Christensen, Olive. Concise needlecraft / [by] Olive Christensen. — Exeter : Wheaton, 1977. — vii,71p : ill(chiefly col) ; 30cm.
Index.
ISBN 0-08-018306-9 Pbk : £1.75
(B77-14303)

646.4 — Clothing. Repair. *Amateurs' manuals*
Foote, Estelle. The mender's manual : repairing and preserving garments and bedding / [by] Estelle Foote. — New York ; London : Harcourt Brace Jovanovich, [1977]. — 180p : ill ; 19cm.
Published in the United States: 1976. — Index.
ISBN 0-15-159150-4 : Unpriced
(B77-11927)

646.4'04 — Women's clothing. Decoration by hand. *Amateurs' manuals*
Robinson, Renée. Fashion sewing / [by] Renée Robinson. — London : Studio Vista, 1977. — 112p : ill ; 26cm.
ISBN 0-289-70724-2 : £3.25
(B77-19486)

646.4'04 — Women's clothing. Making. *Manuals*
Boutique attire / by the editors of Time-Life Books. — [London] ([42 Conduit St., W.1]) : Time Life Books [etc.], 1976. — 184p : chiefly col ill ; 30cm. — (The art of sewing)
Originally published: New York : Time Inc., 1975. — Index.
ISBN 0-7054-0363-7 : £5.95
Also classified at 746.9'2
(B77-15942)

646.4'04 — Women's clothing. Making. *Secondary school texts*
Nelms, Ivy. Fashion and clothing technology / [by] Ivy Nelms. — Amersham : Hulton, 1976. — [4],159p : ill(some col) ; 25cm.
ISBN 0-7175-0682-7 Pbk : £2.80
Also classified at 746.9'2
(B77-09798)

646.4'04 — Women's clothing. Remodelling. *Amateurs' manuals*
Corrigan, Barbara. How to make something out of practically nothing : new fashions from old clothes / [by] Barbara Corrigan. — Revised ed. — Stevenage (15 Leyden Rd, Stevenage, Herts. SG1 2BW) : Robin Clark Ltd, 1977. — 104p : ill ; 18cm.
Previous ed.: Garden City, N.Y. : Doubleday ; London : Muller, 1976.
ISBN 0-86072-005-5 Pbk : £0.75
(B77-32000)

646.4'04'05 — Women's clothing. Making. Patterns. *Periodicals*
'**Weekend**' patterns for sewing, knitting and crochet. — [London] : [Associated Newspapers Group].
[No.1]-. — [197-?]-. — ill(some col) ; 30cm.
64p. in 1977 spring and summer edition.
Sd : £0.40
ISBN 0-85144-146-7
Also classified at 746.9'2
(B77-14811)

646.4'06 — Children's clothing. Making. *Manuals*
Larter, Vera. Sewing children's clothes made easy / by Vera Larter ; illustrated by Marta Cone. — London : Muller, 1977. — vii,230p : ill ; 25cm.
Originally published: Garden City, N.Y. : Doubleday, 1971. — Index.
ISBN 0-584-10292-5 : £3.50
(B77-18263)

Lecko, Marie. Making clothes for the kids / [by] Marie Lecko. — Guildford : Lutterworth Press ; [s.l.] : Richard Smart Publishing, 1977. — 72p : ill ; 21cm. — (Leisure series)
ISBN 0-7188-7014-x Pbk : £1.95
(B77-28720)

Mordle-Barnes, Mollie. 'Good housekeeping' making children's clothes / by Mollie Mordle-Barnes. — London : Ebury Press, 1977. — 160p : ill ; 25cm.
Index.
ISBN 0-85223-103-2 : £2.95
(B77-12555)

646.4'3 — Tailoring. *Amateurs' manuals*
Milani, Lucille. Tailoring the easy way / [by] Lucille Milani. — Englewood Cliffs ; London [etc.] : Prentice-Hall, 1976. — x,197p : ill ; 24cm. — (The creative handicrafts series)
'A spectrum book'. — Index.
ISBN 0-13-882183-6 : £9.30
ISBN 0-13-882175-5 Pbk : £3.85
(B77-08454)

646.4'3'04 — Dressmaking. *Manuals*
'**Golden** hands' encyclopedia of dressmaking. — Completely revised, new metric ed. — Glasgow [etc.] : Collins, 1977. — 224p : ill(chiefly col) ; 31cm.
Card ([2] sides) 'Conversion chart' as insert. — Previous ed.: London : Collins, 1972. — Index.
ISBN 0-00-435040-5 : £4.95
(B77-25046)

Hayden, Peggie. The complete dressmaker / [by] Peggie Hayden. — London : Book Club Associates, 1977. — [1],232p : ill(chiefly col) ; 28cm.
Ill. on lining papers. — '... first published in ... "Fashionmaker"' - title page verso. — Index.
ISBN 0-85685-194-9 : £4.95
(B77-07964)

Horner, Isabel. Dressmaking / [by] Isabel Horner ... — 4th ed. / revised by Eileen Wainwright. — Sevenoaks : Teach Yourself Books, 1977. — xii,236p : ill ; 18cm. — (Teach yourself books)
Previous ed.: / revised by Carol Underwood. 1970. — Index.
ISBN 0-340-21279-9 Pbk : £1.50
(B77-15943)

646.4'3'04 — Dressmaking. *Patterns*
The '**Women** only' pattern book / compiled by Mij Evans ; patterns and instructions by Katy Dunscombe ; illustrations by Janet Haigh ; patterns drawn by Michael Head. — London (247 Tottenham Court Rd, W1P 0AU) : Independent Television Publications Ltd, 1977. — 48p : ill ; 20cm. — (A 'TV times' book)
'From the HTV programme' - cover. — Index.
ISBN 0-900727-54-3 Sd : £0.50
(B77-30408)

646.4'3'04 — Dressmaking. *Secondary school texts*
Moloney, Angela. Dressmaking / [by] Angela Moloney. — Metric ed. — Dublin : Gill and Macmillan, 1976. — [6],121p : ill ; 24cm.
Index.
ISBN 0-7171-0760-4 Pbk : £1.95
(B77-32727)

646.4'3'04 — Dressmaking. Patterns. Adaptation. *Manuals*
Jacobi, Gaby. Pattern adaptations / by Gaby Jacobi and Kitty Todor. — London (Hartree House, Queensway, W2 4SH) : Forbes Publications Ltd, 1976. — vi,87p : ill ; 21x30cm.
Index.
ISBN 0-901762-24-5 Pbk : £3.50
(B77-14304)

646.4'3'04 — Dressmaking. Techniques. *Amateurs' manuals*
Ladbury, Ann. Making things do sewing book / by Ann Ladbury ; fashion drawings by Rosalyn Toohig, sewing drawings by Terry Russell. — London (247 Tottenham Court Rd, W1P 0AU) : Independent Television Publications Ltd for Independent Television Books Ltd, 1976. — 64p : ill ; 20cm. — (A 'TV times' book)
Cover title: Ann Ladbury's making things do sewing book. — 'Based on the Southern Television programme'. — Index.
ISBN 0-900727-63-2 Pbk : £0.50
(B77-09115)

Warburton, Agnes. Dressmaking in pictures / by Agnes Warburton. — 3rd ed. — Kingswood : Elliot Right Way Books, 1974. — 128p : ill ; 18cm. — (Paperfronts)
Previous ed.: 1972. — Index.
ISBN 0-7160-0606-5 Pbk : £0.35
(B77-18871)

646.4'7 — Theatre. Costumes. Design & making. *Manuals*
Peters, Joan. Making costumes for plays / [by] Joan Peters and Anna Sutcliffe. — New ed. — London : Batsford, 1977. — 96p : ill ; 26cm.
Previous ed.: published as 'Making costumes for school plays'. 1970.
ISBN 0-7134-0029-3 : £2.95
(B77-18264)

646.4'7 — Theatre. Costumes. Making. *Manuals. Juvenile literature*
Bruun-Rasmussen, Ole. Make-up, costumes and masks : for the stage / by Ole Bruun-Rasmussen and Grete Petersen ; [translated from the Danish by Kathleen Margaret Brondal]. — New York : Sterling [etc.] ; London : Distributed by Ward Lock, [1977]. — 96p : ill ; 21cm.
Published in the United States: 1976. — Translation of: 'Sjove masker af papir'. Copenhagen : Host, 1972 ; and 'Sminkning og maskering'. Copenhagen : Host, 1975. — Index.
ISBN 0-7061-2519-3 : £3.50
Primary classification 792'.027
(B77-13190)

646.4'7'06 — Children's fancy dress. Making. *Juvenile literature*
Haley, Gail Einhart. Costumes for plays and playing / written and illustrated by Gail E. Haley. — London : Methuen, 1977. — [8], 136p : ill ; 26cm.
Bibl.: p.134. — Index.
ISBN 0-416-83900-2 : £3.75
(B77-21259)

646.6'2 — Women's clothing. Cleaning. *For adolescent girls*
Jeans, Heather. Yourself and your clothes / [by] Heather Jeans. — Glasgow [etc.] : Blackie, 1977. — [2],36,[1]p : ill ; 22cm. — (Home economics topic books)
ISBN 0-216-90182-0 Sd : Unpriced
Primary classification 646'.34
(B77-23540)

646.7 — CARE OF BODY AND PERSONAL APPEARANCE

646.7'02'4055 — Adolescent girls. Cleanliness & personal appearance. *Manuals*
Saunders, Rubie. Good grooming for girls / by Rubie Saunders ; illustrated by Carolyn Bentley. — New York ; London : F. Watts, 1977. — [4],60p : ill ; 24cm. — (A concise guide)
Published in the United States: 1976. — Index.
ISBN 0-85166-614-0 : £1.95
(B77-13731)

646.7'2 — Women. Beauty care. *Manuals*
David Hamilton's beauty tips for women / [compiled by Doreen Davies]. — London : Everest, 1974. — 3-119p ; 18cm.
ISBN 0-903925-20-6 Pbk : £0.40
(B77-19487)

Meredith, Bronwen. Vogue body and beauty book / [by] Bronwen Meredith. — London : Allen Lane, 1977. — 352p,[16]p of plates : ill(some col), facsims(some col), ports ; 26cm.
Index.
ISBN 0-7139-1036-4 : £6.95
(B77-29544)

The **Prentice-Hall** textbook of cosmetology : a professional guide to the theory and practice of beauty culture / [by] Olive P. Scott ... [et al.]. — Englewood Cliffs ; London [etc.] : Prentice-Hall, 1976. — xviii,462p,[2] leaves of plates : ill(some col), ports ; 29cm.
Index.
ISBN 0-13-695312-3 : £7.45
(B77-00293)

646.7'24 — Hairdressing. Colouring
Galvin, Daniel. The world of hair colour : the art and techniques of modern hair colour / [by] Daniel Galvin. — London [etc.] : Macmillan [for] the Hairdressing Council, 1977. — x,67p, [20]p of plates : ill(some col), form, col port ; 24cm.
ISBN 0-333-23350-6 : £10.00 : CIP rev.
ISBN 0-333-23351-4 Pbk : £3.95
(B77-22701)

646.7'24 — Hairdressing. Cutting. *Amateurs' manuals*
Leighton, Harold. Haircutting for everyone / [by] Harold Leighton ; photography Bill Ling ; make-up Celia Hunter and Sara. — London : A. Barker, 1977. — 96p : ill, ports ; 24cm.
ISBN 0-213-16654-2 : £2.95
ISBN 0-213-16659-3 Pbk : £1.75
(B77-25737)

646.7'24 — Hairdressing. Cutting. *Manuals. For adolescents*
Brent, Patricia Jenkins. Haircutting / by Patricia Jenkins Brent ; illustrated by Terry Fehr. — New York ; London : F. Watts, 1977. — [4], 60p : ill ; 24cm. — (A concise guide)
Published in the United States: 1976. — Index.
ISBN 0-85166-615-9 : £1.95
(B77-14305)

646.7'24 — Hairdressing. Techniques. *Amateurs' manuals*
Bent, Bob. How to cut hair, including your own / by Bob Bent ; illustrations by Jack Bozzi. — London : Hale, 1977. — 140p : ill ; 20cm.
Originally published: as 'How to cut your own or anybody else's hair'. New York : Simon and Schuster, 1975.
ISBN 0-7091-6094-1 Sp : £1.95
(B77-20418)

646.7'24 — Man. Hair. Care
Thomson, James Charles. Healthy hair : care and restoration by natural methods. — New ed. revised and enlarged / by James C. Thomson and C. Leslie Thomson. — Wellingborough : Thorsons, 1974. — 95p : ill ; 22cm.
This ed. originally published: 1967.
ISBN 0-7225-0203-6 Pbk : £0.75
(B77-14306)

646.7'24 — Man. Hair. Care. *Early works*
Hair and beauty secrets of Queen Victoria's reign / edited by J. Stevens Cox. — St Peter Port : Toucan Press, 1977. — [16]p ; 16cm.
Sd : £0.60
(B77-32728)

647.94 — HOTELS, INNS, VACATION ACCOMMODATION

647'.94 — Hotel industries. Receptionists. *Manuals*
Paige, Grace. The hotel receptionist / [by] Grace & Jane Paige. — London : Cassell, 1977. — 188p : ill, facsims, forms ; 22cm.
Index.
ISBN 0-304-29757-7 Pbk : £4.25
(B77-23541)

647'.94 — Hotels. *Directories*
'The **financial** times' world hotel directory. — London : Financial times.
1977-78 / editors John Greig, Deborah Greig. — 1977. — 2-655p : ill, maps ; 22cm.
Index.
ISBN 0-900671-81-5 : £9.00
ISSN 0308-8464
(B77-25047)

647'.944 — Camping & caravanning. Sites. *Europe. Directories*
Automobile Association. AA guide to camping and caravanning on the Continent. — München : ADAC Verlag GmbH ; London : Distributed by Hutchinson.
[1976]. — 1976. — 528p : ill(some col), col maps ; 22cm.
Index.
ISBN 0-09-125851-0 Pbk : £2.50
(B77-01618)

Automobile Association. AA guide to camping and caravanning on the Continent. — Basingstoke : A.A. ; London : Distributed by Hutchinson.
[1977]. — 1977. — 368p : ill(some col), col maps ; 23cm.
ISBN 0-09-128181-4 Pbk : £2.95
(B77-33310)

Continental camping and caravan sites : (incorporating continental camping sites). — Croydon : Link House Publications.
1977 / editor Heather Salter. — 1977. — 200p : ill, maps ; 22cm.
Pbk : £0.85
(B77-25048)

Guide to British and Continental camping and caravanning sites / Royal Automobile Club. — London : Rand McNally for the RAC.
[1977]. — 1977. — 352p : col ill, col maps ; 28cm.
English, French, German and Italian parallel text. — Index.
ISBN 0-902628-12-7 Pbk : £2.50 to members of the RAC
ISSN 0146-3470
(B77-16962)

647'.944 — Camping & caravanning. Sites. *Western Europe. Directories*
Rogers, Alan, *b.1918.* Alan Rogers' selected sites for caravanning and camping in Europe. — Brighton : Deneway Guides and Travel Ltd ; London : Distributed by Independent Magazines Ltd.
1977. — 1976. — 200p : ill, form, maps ; 22cm.
Index.
ISBN 0-901586-11-0 Pbk : £0.95
(B77-13123)

647'.944 — Hotels. *Europe. Cities. Directories*
The **agent's** hotel gazetteer, tourist cities. — Beaconsfield : C.H.G. Travel Publications ; London (50 Sheen La., S.W.14) : [Distributed by] B.A.S. Overseas Publications Ltd.
[1977] / compiled by R.A. Isaacs. — [1977]. — 208p : ill, maps ; 28cm.
Previously published: as 'The agent's hotel gazetteer, tourist cities of Europe'. — Index.
Pbk : £10.00
(B77-32729)

647'.944 — Hotels. *Europe. Directories*
The **agent's** hotel gazetteer, resorts of Europe. — Beaconsfield : C.H.G. Travel Publications ; London (50 Sheen La., S.W.14) : [Distributed by] B.A.S. Overseas Publications Ltd.
[1977] / compiled by R.A. Isaacs. — [1977]. — 288p : ill, maps ; 28cm.
Index.
Pbk : £10.00
(B77-31310)

647'.944 — Vacation accommodation. *Western Europe. Directories*
Automobile Association. AA budget guide to Europe. — Basingstoke : A.A.
[1976]. — 1975. — 239p : ill, form, col maps ; 23cm.
ISBN 0-09-126691-2 Pbk : £1.95
(B77-07457)

647'.944 — Vacation accommodation: Villas. *Europe. Directories*
Guide to overseas holiday villas and apartments. — [London] : [BAS Overseas Publications Ltd] ; [London] ([181 Queen Victoria St., EC4V 4DD]) : [Distributed by Independent Magazines Ltd].
1977 / [compiled & edited by Francesca Roe]. — [1977]. — 144p : ill(chiefly col), forms, col map, plan ; 21cm.
ISBN 0-904959-03-1 Sd : £0.50
(B77-10437)

647'.9441 — Camping & caravanning. Sites. *Great Britain. Directories*
Automobile Association. AA guide to camping and caravanning. — [Basingstoke] : A.A. ; London : Distributed by Hutchinson.
[1977] / [editors Gillian McWilliam, Roger McWilliam]. — [1976]. — 236p,53p of plates : ill(some col), forms, col maps ; 23cm.
ISBN 0-09-128121-0 Pbk : £1.95
(B77-04921)

Britain, camping & caravan sites / British Tourist Authority. — [London] : B.T.A.
1977. — [1977]. — [1],104,[2]p(2 fold),24p of plates : ill, maps(chiefly col) ; 21cm.
Cover title. — English text, English, French, German, Dutch, Italian, Spanish and Portuguese introduction and keys.
ISBN 0-85630-304-6 Pbk : £1.00
(B77-10841)

Caravan and campsites in Britain. — London [etc.] : Letts. — (Letts guides)
'77 / compiled and edited by Nancy and Frederick Tingey. — 1977. — 183p : maps ; 21cm.
Previously published: as 'Campsites in Britain'.
ISBN 0-85097-231-0 Pbk : £0.95
(B77-11928)

The **guide** to camping caravan sites in the UK. — [London] ([54 Wilton Rd, S.W.1]) : ['Camping caravan monthly'].
1976 / author Maggie Scott. — [1976]. — 100p : ill ; 21cm.
Sd : £0.70
(B77-18872)

1977. — [1977]. — 112p : ill, map ; 21cm.
Index.
Sd : £0.80
(B77-18873)

647'.9441 — Camping. Sites. *Great Britain. Directories*
Rogers, Alan, *b.1918.* Good camps guide : a guide to recommended British camping sites for the touring caravanner and camper / by Alan Rogers. — Brighton : Deneway Guides and Travel Ltd ; London (181 Queen Victoria St., E.C.4) : Distributed by Independent Magazines Ltd.
1977. — 1976. — [2],72p : ill, map ; 22cm.
Index.
ISBN 0-901586-12-9 Sd : £0.70
(B77-13732)

647'.9441 — Caravanning. Sites. *Great Britain. Directories*
Caravan Club. Sites directory and handbook / the Caravan Club. — [East Grinstead] ([East Grinstead House, East Grinstead, W. Sussex RH19 1UA]) : [The Club].
1977-8. — [1977]. — 304p : forms, maps ; 25cm.
Cover title. — 'Stop press' (folder ([4]p.)), fold. sheet (2 sides; col. maps) as inserts. — Index.
Pbk : Unpriced
(B77-20419)

647'.9441 — Conferences. Meeting-places. *Great Britain. Directories*
British Tourist Authority. Britain, the meeting place / [British Tourist Authority]. — London : B.T.A., 1977. — 44p : col ill, col map, ports ; 21cm.
ISBN 0-85630-479-4 Sd : Unpriced
(B77-31311)

647'.9441 — Hotels. *Great Britain. Directories*
Automobile Association. AA guide to hotels and restaurants. — [Basingstoke] : A.A. ; London : Distributed by Hutchinson.
[1977] / [editor Jean Heselden]. — 1976. — [1], 624,52,[1]p : ill(some col), col maps, ports ; 23cm.
ISBN 0-09-128151-2 : £3.25
Also classified at 647'.9541
(B77-18265)

Michelin et Cie. Great Britain and Ireland / Michelin. — London (81 Fulham Rd, SW3 6RD) : Michelin Tyre Co.
1977. — 1977. — 2-558[i.e.552]p(2 fold) : ill(chiefly col), col maps ; 21cm.
£3.05
ISBN 2-06-006577-1
Also classified at 647'.9541
(B77-16963)

The **official** guide to hotels & restaurants in Great Britain, Ireland and overseas. — [London] : [British Hotels, Restaurants and Caterers Association].
1977 : forty-ninth ed. : (with sections for party and function catering, trade members, motorway service areas, affiliated hotel associations and the International Hotel Association). — [1977]. — xxxii,639,24p : ill, col maps ; 21cm.
Spine title: British hotels & restaurants 1977.
ISBN 0-900202-08-4 Pbk : £2.00
ISSN 0307-062x
Also classified at 647'.9541
(B77-27946)

United Kingdom group owners / [Data Research Group]. — Amersham (Hill House, [Hill Ave.], Amersham, Bucks.) : The Group.
[1977]. — 1977. — 191 leaves in various pagings ; 30cm.
ISBN 0-86099-060-5 Pbk : £18.00
(B77-30409)

647'.9441 — Hotels & inns. *Great Britain. Directories*
Courtenay, Ashley. Let's halt awhile in Great Britain and Ireland : the pioneer and authoritative guide to the best hotels and inns in England, Wales, Scotland, Isles of Scilly, the Channel Islands, and Ireland, which are personally recommended by the author and his colleagues for the high standards they offer in their respective spheres / [by] Ashley Courtenay. — London : Distributed by Joseph.
1977 : 44th ed. — 1976. — 608p : ill, maps ; 21cm.
Index.
ISBN 0-7181-1563-5 Pbk : £3.10
(B77-04922)

Egon Ronay's Lucas guide to hotels, restaurants, inns in Great Britain and Ireland. — London : Ronay.
1977 : including economy evening meals in London and bargain winter weekends. — 1976. — 768,32p : ill, forms, maps(some col) ; 21cm.
Previously published: as 'Egon Ronay's Dunlop guide to hotels, restaurants, inns in Great Britain and Ireland'.
ISBN 0-900624-21-3 Pbk : £3.50
Also classified at 647'.9541
(B77-26387)

647'.9441 — Residential conference centres. *Great Britain. Directories*
Hulke, Malcolm. Bring your own towel : a guide to residential conference centres / devised and compiled by Malcolm Hulke. — London : Bedford Square Press, 1977. — 88p : ill ; 21cm.
ISBN 0-7199-0928-7 Pbk : £2.00
(B77-30410)

647'.9441 — Self-catering vacation accommodation. *Great Britain. Directories*
Automobile Association. AA guide to self-catering holiday accommodation / [editor Jean Heselden]. — Basingstoke : A.A. ; London : Distributed by Hutchinson, 1976. — [1],190p,50p of plates : ill, col maps ; 23cm.
ISBN 0-09-128161-x Pbk : £1.95
(B77-00835)

Britain, holiday homes / [British Tourist Authority]. — London : B.T.A.
1976/77. — 1976. — [2],76p : map ; 21cm. — (British Tourist Authority. Information sheets ; no.344/76/183)
English text, French, German, Dutch, Italian and Spanish introduction. — Bibl.: p.76.
Sd : £0.30
ISBN 0-85630-109-4
(B77-07458)

647'.9441 — Vacation accommodation. *Great Britain. Directories*
Automobile Association. AA guide to guesthouses, farmhouses and inns. — [Basingstoke] : A.A. ; London : Distributed by Hutchinson.
[1977]. — [1976]. — 236,52p : ill, col maps ; 23cm.
ISBN 0-09-128141-5 Pbk : £1.95
(B77-07459)

Britain, commended country hotels, guest houses and restaurants / [British Tourist Authority]. — London : B.T.A.
[1977]. — 1977. — [2],80p : ill, col maps ; 21cm.
English text, French, German, Italian and Spanish explanatory note and key. — Index.
ISBN 0-85630-371-2 Sd : Unpriced
(B77-21260)

Holiday haunts in Great Britain. — London (42 Gerrard St., W1V 7LP) : Dickens Press.
'77 / editor Robert Redman. — [1976]. — 474p : ill, maps(chiefly col) ; 22cm.
Pbk : £0.50
ISSN 0073-3016
(B77-30411)

Ramblers' Association. The Ramblers' Association bed, breakfast and bus guide. — London : The Association.
1977. — [1977]. — 107p : ill ; 18cm.
Cover title: Bed and breakfast guide, and bus guide. — Index.
ISBN 0-900613-35-1 Sd : £0.35
(B77-12556)

647'.9441 — Vacation accommodation. *Great Britain. Directories. For families*
Family holiday guide. — Kingston-upon-Thames : J. Lewis.
[1977]. — 1976. — 160p : ill, maps, ports ; 25cm.
ISBN 0-901449-08-3 Pbk : £0.45
(B77-09799)

647'.94411 — Camping & caravanning. Sites. *Scotland. Directories*
Camping and caravan sites in Scotland = Terrains de camping et caravaning en Écosse = Selt-und Wohnwagenplätze in Schottland / [Scottish Tourist Board]. — Edinburgh : The Board.
1977. — [1977]. — 63p,8p of plates : ill, col maps ; 21cm.
English text, French and German introduction. — Previously published: as 'Scotland, caravan & camping sites'.
Sd : £0.45
(B77-17611)

647'.94411 — Christmas vacation accommodation. *Scotland. Directories*
Christmas and New Year entertainment / Scottish Tourist Board. — Edinburgh : The Board. — (Scottish Tourist Board. Information booklets)
1976-77. — [1976]. — 36p : 1 ill ; 21x10cm.
Sd : Unpriced
(B77-23542)

647'.94411 — Hotels. *Scotland. Directories. For angling*
Watson, Graham, *b.1913.* A guide to the fishing inns of Scotland / [by] Graham Watson. — [Revised ed.]. — London : Constable, 1977. — 141p : ill ; 18cm. — ([A Constable guide])
Previous ed.: / compiled by R. Crombie Saunders. London : Kaye, 1951. — Index.
ISBN 0-09-461190-4 : £2.50
(B77-16964)

647'.94411 — Self-catering vacation accommodation. *Scotland. Directories*
Self catering accommodation in Scotland = Pensions avec kitchenette en Écosse = Unterkünfte mit Selbstverpflegung in Schottland : cottages, flats, chalets, houses and caravans for hire / [Scottish Tourist Board]. — Edinburgh : The Board.
1977. — 1977. — 163p : ill, maps ; 21cm.
English text, French and German introduction. — Bibl.: p.5. — Index.
Pbk : £0.45
(B77-19488)

647'.94411 — Vacation accommodation. *Scotland. Directories*
Scottish Tourist Board. Spring holiday bargains in Scotland, 1977 / [Scottish Tourist Board]. — Edinburgh : The Board, [1977]. — 47,[1]p : ill(some col) ; 21cm.
Bibl.: p.47.
Sd : Unpriced
(B77-19489)

Where to stay in Scotland = Où se loger en Écosse = Wo übernachtet man in Schottland / [Scottish Tourist Board]. — Edinburgh : The Board.
1977. — [1977]. — 544p : ill, maps ; 21cm.
English text, French and German introduction.
Pbk : £0.75
(B77-16965)

647'.94411 — Vacation accommodation. *Scotland. Directories. For old persons*
Accommodation with facilities for elderly visitors / Scottish Tourist Board. — Edinburgh : The Board. — (Scottish Tourist Board. Information booklets)
1977. — [1976]. — 64p : 1 ill ; 21x10cm.
Sd : Unpriced
(B77-22702)

647'.94411 — Vacation accommodation. *Scotland. Directories. For physically handicapped persons*
Accommodation with facilities for disabled visitors / Scottish Tourist Board. — Edinburgh : The Board. — (Scottish Tourist Board. Information booklets)
1977. — [1976]. — 48p : 1 ill ; 21x10cm.
Sd : Unpriced
(B77-22703)

647'.94411 — Vacation accommodation: Farmhouses. *Scotland. Directories*
Farmhouse accommodation / Scottish Tourist Board. — Edinburgh : The Board. — (Scottish Tourist Board. Information booklets)
1977. — [1976]. — 48p : 1 ill ; 21x10cm.
Sd : Unpriced
(B77-21261)

647'.94411 — Youth hostels. *Scotland. Directories*
Scottish Youth Hostels Association. Handbook / Scottish Youth Hostels Association. — Stirling (7 Glebe Cres., Stirling FK8 2JA) : S.Y.H.A.
1976. — [1976]. — 132p : ill, maps ; 20cm.
Cover title.
Pbk : £0.25
(B77-28723)

647'.944111 — Self-catering vacation accommodation. *Scotland. Highlands & Islands. Directories*
Self catering accommodation, the Scottish Highlands and Islands = Locations en meublés dans les Highlands et les Iles d'Ecosse = Unterkunft mit Selbstverpflegung im Hochland und auf den Inseln Schottlands / [Highlands and Islands Development Board]. — Inverness : The Board.
1977. — [1977]. — [150]p(2 fold) : ill, col maps ; 21cm.
English, German and French text.
Sd : £0.25
(B77-11929)

647'.944111 — Vacation accommodation. *Scotland. Highlands & Islands. Directories*
Hotels, guest houses, b & b accommodation. — Inverness : Highlands and Islands Development Board.
1977. — [1977]. — [152]p(2 fold) : ill, col maps ; 22cm.
English, German and French text.
Sd : £0.25
(B77-15364)

647'.9442 — Self-catering vacation accommodation. *England. Directories*
Where to stay / English Tourist Board. — London : The Board.
'77. Self-catering accommodation in England. — 1977. — vi,242p(6 fold) : ill(some col), maps(1 col) ; 21cm.
ISBN 0-903265-62-1 Pbk : £0.95
(B77-08455)

647'.9442 — Vacation accommodation. *England. Directories*
Where to stay / English Tourist Board. — London : The Board.
'76. Hotels in England : hotels, motels, bed & breakfast, inns, guest houses, farmhouses. — [1976]. — [2],vi,514,[1]p(6 fold) : ill, forms, maps(1 col) ; 22cm.
Cover title. — Spine title: Hotels in England. — Index.
ISBN 0-903265-44-3 Pbk : £1.60
(B77-00294)

'77. East Anglia : Cambridgeshire, Essex, Norfolk, Suffolk. — 1977. — vi,82p(6 fold) : ill(some col), maps(1 col) ; 21cm.
ISBN 0-903265-56-7 Pbk : £0.40
(B77-07460)

'77. East Midlands : Derbyshire, Leicestershire, Lincolnshire, Northamptonshire, Nottinghamshire. — 1977. — vi,66p(6 fold) : ill(some col), maps(1 col) ; 21cm.
ISBN 0-903265-54-0 Pbk : £0.40
(B77-07461)

'77. English Lakeland : Cumbria. — 1977. — vi,130p(6 fold) : ill(some col), maps(1 col) ; 21cm.
ISBN 0-903265-49-4 Pbk : £0.40
(B77-07462)

'77. Heart of England : Gloucestershire, Hereford and Worcester, Shropshire, Staffordshire, Warwickshire, West Midlands. — 1977. — vi,82p(6 fold) : ill(some col), maps(1 col) ; 21cm.
ISBN 0-903265-53-2 Pbk : £0.40
(B77-07463)

'77 : Hotels in England : hotels, motels, guesthouses, hostels, bed & breakfast, inns, farmhouses. — [1977]. — vi,[i.e. ii],554p(2 fold) : ill, forms, maps(1 col) ; 21cm.
Cover title. — Spine title: Hotels in England. — Index.
ISBN 0-903265-61-3 Pbk : £1.95
(B77-07464)

'77. London : Greater London. — 1977. — vi, 82p(6 fold) : ill(some col), maps(1 col) ; 21cm.
ISBN 0-903265-57-5 Pbk : £0.40
(B77-07465)

'77. North west England : Cheshire, Greater Manchester, Lancashire, Merseyside. — 1977. — vi,66p(6 fold) : ill(some col), maps(1 col) ; 21cm.
ISBN 0-903265-51-6 Pbk : £0.40
(B77-07466)

'77. Northumbria : Cleveland, Durham, Northumberland, Tyne & Wear. — 1977. — vi, 66p(6 fold) : ill(some col), maps(1 col) ; 21cm.
ISBN 0-903265-50-8 Pbk : £0.40
(B77-07467)

'77. South east England : East Sussex, Kent, Surrey, West Sussex. — 1977. — vi,74p(6 fold) : ill(some col), maps(1 col) ; 21cm.
ISBN 0-903265-59-1 Pbk : £0.40
(B77-07468)

'77. South of England : East Dorset, Hampshire and the Isle of Wight. — 1977. — vi,66p(6 fold) : ill(some col), maps(1 col) ; 21cm.
ISBN 0-903265-60-5 Pbk : £0.40
(B77-07469)

'77. Thames and Chilterns : Bedfordshire, Berkshire, Buckinghamshire, Hertfordshire, Oxfordshire. — 1977. — vi,66p(6 fold) : ill(some col), maps(1 col) ; 21cm.
ISBN 0-903265-55-9 Pbk : £0.40
(B77-07470)

'77. West Country : Avon, Cornwall, Devon, North and West Dorset, Somerset, Wiltshire and the Isles of Scilly. — 1977. — vi,194p(6 fold) : ill(some col), maps(1 col) ; 21cm.
ISBN 0-903265-58-3 Pbk : £0.50
(B77-07471)

'77. Yorkshire and Humberside : North, South and West Yorkshire, and Humberside. — 1977. — vi,66p(6 fold) : ill(some col), maps(1 col) ; 21cm.
ISBN 0-903265-52-4 Pbk : £0.40
(B77-07472)

647'.94421 — Hotels. *London. Directories*
Michelin et Cie. Greater London / Michelin. — London (81 Fulham Rd, SW3 6RD) : Michelin Tyre Co. Ltd.
1977. — [1977]. — xiv,68[i.e.62]p(2 fold) : col ill, col maps ; 20cm.
English, French, Italian and German text. — Index.
Sd : £0.75
ISBN 2-06-006677-8
Also classified at 647'.95421
(B77-16966)

647'.94421 — Vacation accommodation. *London. Directories*
Britain, London, hotels & restaurants including budget accommodation / [produced by the British Tourist Authority in co-operation with the English Tourist Board and the London Tourist Board]. — [London] : The Authority. [1977]. — 1977. — [2],95p(2 fold) : ill, forms, map ; 21cm.
Previously published: as 'Britain, hotels & restaurants in London'. — '... brings together the broad selection of hotels and restaurants appearing in the British Tourist Authority's guide "Britain : Hotels & Restaurants 1977" and the wide range of accommodation listed in the English Tourist Board's "Where to Stay' '77 : London"'. — Index.
ISBN 0-85630-485-9 Pbk : £0.45
Also classified at 647'.95421
(B77-20420)

647'.94422 — Hotels. *South-east England. Directories*
British Tourist Authority. Hotels in London's country : hotels within easy reach of London / [British Tourist Authority]. — London : B.T.A., 1977. — 32p : 2 maps(1 col) ; 21cm.
Cover title: Britain, hotels in London's country. — English text, French and German introduction and notes.
ISBN 0-85630-523-5 Sd : Unpriced
(B77-20421)

647'.94422'57 — Inns. *East Sussex. Lewes, to 1976*
Davey, Leslie Stuart. The inns of Lewes past and present / by L.S. Davey. — Lewes (212 High St., Lewes, E. Sussex BN7 2NH) : Friends of Lewes, 1977. — [7],51p : ill, 2 facsims ; 19cm.
Index.
Sd : Unpriced
(B77-31312)

647'.94425'24 — Inns. *Nottinghamshire. Newark, to 1976*
Cousins, P R. Newark inns & public houses / [by P.R. Cousins]. — Newark on Trent (27 Spring Gardens, Newark on Trent [Notts.]) : The author, 1977. — [2],42p : ill, maps, plan ; 21cm.
Sd : £0.50
Also classified at 647'.95425'24
(B77-14812)

647'.94426'5 — Inns. *Cambridgeshire. Guidebooks*
Old English inns of Cambridgeshire / photography by Anthony D. Thomson. — [Taplow] ([Briarbank, Ellington Rd, Taplow, Bucks.]) : [Daric Enterprises], [1977]. — [19]p : ill, map ; 12x15cm.
Sd : £0.17
(B77-26388)

647'.94428'1 — Inns. *Yorkshire. Guidebooks*
Boyes, Malcolm. Yorkshire inns / by Malcolm Boyes. — Clapham, N. Yorkshire : Dalesman, 1977. — 63p : ill ; 19cm. — (A Dalesman mini-book)
Index.
ISBN 0-85206-373-3 Pbk : £0.60
(B77-14813)

647'.94429 — Vacation accommodation. *Wales. Directories*
Where to stay in Wales / [Wales Tourist Board]. — Cardiff : The Board.
1977. — [1977]. — 256p : ill, maps ; 22cm.
English text, English, French and German preliminaries.
ISBN 0-900784-55-5 Pbk : £0.45
(B77-33911)

647'.94429'56 — National parks. *South Wales. Brecon Beacons National Park. Camping & caravanning. Sites. Directories*
Brecon Beacons National Park Committee. Camping and caravan sites / [Brecon Beacons National Park Committee]. — [Brecon] ([Glamorgan St., Brecon, Powys]) : The Committee, 1977. — Folder([6]p) : map ; 21cm. — (Information sheet ; no.17)
£0.03
(B77-18874)

647'.94429'56 — National parks. *South Wales. Brecon Beacons National Park. Vacation accommodation. Directories*
Brecon Beacons National Park Committee. Holiday accommodation / [Brecon Beacons National Park Committee]. — [Brecon] ([Glamorgan St., Brecon, Powys]) : The Committee.
1977. — 1977. — [16]p ; 22cm. — (Information sheet ; no.14)
Sd : £0.06
(B77-18266)

647'.9444 — Camping & caravanning. Sites. *France. Directories*
Caravanning and camping through France. — London [etc.] : Letts.
'77 / [by] Nancy and Frederick Tingey. — 1977. — 128p : ill, maps ; 21cm. — (Letts guides)
Previously published: as 'Camping through France'. — Index.
ISBN 0-85097-232-9 Pbk : £0.90
(B77-11930)

The **guide** to camping caravan sites in France & Spain. — [London] ([54 Wilton Rd, S.W.1]) : ['Camping caravan monthly'].
1977. — [1977]. — 144p : ill, maps ; 21cm.
Index.
Sd : £0.80
(B77-26389)

Where to camp in France. — London (94 Alton Rd, SW15 4NS) : Continental Leisure Publications Ltd.
[1976] : over 400 of the best camp & caravan sites in France / [edited by Eric Fowler]. — 1976. — 128p : ill, 2 forms, maps ; 22cm.
Index.
ISBN 0-905136-03-9 Pbk : £0.95
(B77-07473)

Where to camp in France / the Camping Club of Great Britain and Ireland. — London (50a Sheen La., SW14 8LP) : Continental Leisure Publications Ltd.
[1977] / [edited by Eric Fowler]. — 1977. — 136p : ill, form, maps ; 21cm.
ISBN 0-905136-08-x Pbk : £0.95
(B77-23543)

647'.9446 — Camping & caravanning. Sites. *Spain. Directories*
Where to camp in Spain? : a detailed guide to Spain's best camp and caravan sites. — London (94 Alton Rd, SW15 4NS) : Continental Leisure Publications Ltd.
[1976]. — 1976. — 144p : ill(some col), maps ; 22cm.
Previously published: as 'Which site in Spain?'.
ISBN 0-905136-02-0 Pbk : £0.95
(B77-08456)

647'.9446 — Paradores. *Spain, to 1976*
Read, Jan. Paradores of Spain : their history, cooking and wines / [by] Jan Read & Maite Manjon. — London [etc.] : Macmillan, 1977. — 224p : ill(some col), facsim, col form, maps(some col), ports ; 25cm.
Map on lining papers. — Index.
ISBN 0-333-21937-6 : £6.95 : CIP rev.
(B77-07965)

647.95 — CATERING, RESTAURANTS
647'.95 — Catering establishments. Kitchens. Management
Fuller, John, *b.1916.* Chef's manual of kitchen management / [by] John Fuller. — 3rd ed. — London : Batsford, 1977. — xvi,335p : ill, forms, 2 plans ; 22cm.
This ed. originally published: 1974. — Index.
ISBN 0-7134-0551-1 Pbk : £4.95
(B77-25049)

647'.95'028 — Catering equipment. Design. *Conference proceedings*
Catering equipment and systems design / edited by G. Glew. — London : Applied Science Publishers, 1977. — xiii,481p : ill, plan ; 23cm.
'Proceedings of a Symposium organised by the Catering Research Unit of Leeds University' - half title page verso. — Bibl. — Index.
ISBN 0-85334-730-1 : £30.00
(B77-29545)

647'.954 — Relais Routiers. *Western Europe. Directories. French texts*
Guide des relais routiers. — London (354 Fulham Rd, SW10 9UH) : Routiers (British Isles and Commonwealth) Limited.
1977. — [1977]. — 353p,[28]p of plates : ill, forms, maps(chiefly col) ; 21cm.
Cover title. — Directory in French, introductory section in English.
Pbk : £3.45
(B77-33912)

647'.9541 — Public houses & restaurants. *Great Britain. Directories*
The **best** of British pubs : and other places to eat and drink / edited and compiled by Peter Earle. — London [etc.] : Letts, 1977. — 160p : maps ; 21cm. — (Letts guides)
ISBN 0-85097-261-2 Pbk : £1.25
(B77-16967)

647'.9541 — Public houses selling unpressurised beers. *Great Britain. Directories*
Good beer guide / Campaign for Real Ale. — St Albans (34 Alma Rd, St Albans, Herts. AL1 3BW) : CAMRA ; London : Arrow Books.
1977 / [editor Michael Hardman]. — 1977. — 256p : ill(some col), col maps ; 23cm.
ISBN 0-09-914510-3 Pbk : £1.60
(B77-12557)

647'.9541 — Restaurants. *Great Britain. Directories*
Automobile Association. AA guide to hotels and restaurants. — [Basingstoke] : A.A. ; London : Distributed by Hutchinson.
[1977] / [editor Jean Heselden]. — 1976. — [1], 624,52,[1]p : ill(some col), col maps, ports ; 23cm.
ISBN 0-09-128151-2 : £3.25
Primary classification 647'.9441
(B77-18265)

Egon Ronay's Lucas guide to hotels, restaurants, inns in Great Britain and Ireland. — London : Ronay.
1977 : including economy evening meals in London and bargain winter weekends. — 1976. — 768,32p : ill, forms, maps(some col) ; 21cm.
Previously published: as 'Egon Ronay's Dunlop guide to hotels, restaurants, inns in Great Britain and Ireland'.
ISBN 0-900624-21-3 Pbk : £3.50
Primary classification 647'.9441
(B77-26387)

The **good** food guide. — [London] : Consumers' Association : Hodder and Stoughton.
1977 / edited by Christopher Driver. — 1977. — xvi,503,[32]p : maps(chiefly col) ; 21cm.
ISBN 0-340-21924-6 Pbk : £3.95
(B77-13733)

Michelin et Cie. Great Britain and Ireland / Michelin. — London (81 Fulham Rd, SW3 6RD) : Michelin Tyre Co.
1977. — 1977. — 2-558[i.e.552]p(2 fold) : ill(chiefly col), col maps ; 21cm.
£3.05
ISBN 2-06-006577-1
Primary classification 647'.9441
(B77-16963)

The **official** guide to hotels & restaurants in Great Britain, Ireland and overseas. — [London] : [British Hotels, Restaurants and Caterers Association].
1977 : forty-ninth ed. : (with sections for party and function catering, trade members, motorway service areas, affiliated hotel associations and the International Hotel Association). — [1977]. — xxxii,639,24p : ill, col maps ; 21cm.
Spine title: British hotels & restaurants 1977.
ISBN 0-900202-08-4 Pbk : £2.00
ISSN 0307-062x
Primary classification 647'.9441
(B77-27946)

United Kingdom restaurants / [Data Research Group]. — Amersham (Hill House [Hill Ave.] Amersham, Bucks.) : The Group.
[1975]. — 1975. — 289 leaves in various pagings ; 30cm.
ISBN 0-905570-86-3 Pbk : Unpriced
(B77-11292)

[1977]. — 1977. — 301 leaves in various pagings ; 30cm.
ISBN 0-86099-033-8 Pbk : £22.00
(B77-33913)

647'.9541 — Transport cafés. *Great Britain. Directories*
Egon Ronay's Lucas guide to transport cafés and accommodation. — London : Ronay : Distributed by Seymour Press.
1977. — 1976. — 112p : ill ; 19cm.
Previously published: as 'Crane Fruehauf's Egon Ronay guide to transport cafés'. — Index.
ISBN 0-900624-23-x Pbk : £0.95
(B77-23544)

647'.9542 — Public houses. *England*
Jackson, Michael, *b.1942.* The English pub / [edited and written by] Michael Jackson [and Frank Smyth ; original photography by Ian Howes et al.]. — London : Collins, 1976. — [1] ,170p : ill(some col), facsims(1 col), ports(incl 2 col) ; 30cm. — (A quarto book)
Ill. on lining papers. — Index.
ISBN 0-00-216210-5 : £6.00
(B77-09116)

647'.9542 — Restaurants serving English dishes. *England. Directories*
A **taste** of England : 750 restaurants offering English food prepared in the traditional way. — London : English Tourist Board, 1977. — [2], 137p : ill, maps ; 21x10cm.
Pbk : £0.10
(B77-22704)

647'.95421 — Restaurants. *London. Directories*
Britain, London, hotels & restaurants including budget accommodation / [produced by the British Tourist Authority in co-operation with the English Tourist Board and the London Tourist Board]. — [London] : The Authority.
[1977]. — 1977. — [2],95p(2 fold) : ill, forms, map ; 21cm.
Previously published: as 'Britain, hotels & restaurants in London'. — '... brings together the broad selection of hotels and restaurants appearing in the British Tourist Authority's guide "Britain : Hotels & Restaurants 1977" and the wide range of accommodation listed in the English Tourist Board's "Where to Stay' '77 : London"'. — Index.
ISBN 0-85630-485-9 Pbk : £0.45
Primary classification 647'.94421
(B77-20420)

Michelin et Cie. Greater London / Michelin. — London (81 Fulham Rd, SW3 6RD) : Michelin Tyre Co. Ltd.
1977. — [1977]. — xiv,68[i.e.62]p(2 fold) : col ill, col maps ; 20cm.
English, French, Italian and German text. — Index.
Sd : £0.75
ISBN 2-06-006677-8
Primary classification 647'.94421
(B77-16966)

Sherwood, James. James Sherwood's discriminating guide [to] London : fine dining and shopping, with a special section on museums and art galleries. — London : Heinemann.
[1977] / edited by Susan Blackburn ; illustrations by Rodney Shackell. — 1977. — viii,419,[15]p : ill, col maps ; 20cm.
Index.
ISBN 0-448-14057-8 : £4.50
Also classified at 381'.025'421
(B77-21977)

647'.95422 — Public houses. *Central Southern England. Guidebooks*
Dunning, James. Pubbing, eating & sleeping in the South : the guide to value for money / by James Dunning. — 2nd revised ed. — Tavistock (Merchants House, Barley Market St., Tavistock, Devon) : Heritage Publications ; [London] : New English Library, 1977. — 206p : ill, 2 maps ; 18cm.
Previous ed.: 1975. — Index.
ISBN 0-903975-66-1 Pbk : £0.60
(B77-15365)

647'.95422 — Public houses. *South-east England. Guidebooks*
Elliott, Ronald London. Pubbing, eating & sleeping in the South East : the guide to value for money / by R.L. Elliott & S.P. Farley. — Tavistock (Merchant's House, Barley Market St., Tavistock, Devon) : Heritage Publications ; [London] : New English Library, 1977. — 141p : ill, 2 maps ; 18cm.
Index.
ISBN 0-903975-71-8 Pbk : £0.60
(B77-15366)

647'.95422 — Public houses. *Southern England. Directories*
Thirkell, John. Pubs for pleasure / [compiled by] John Thirkell. — London (145 North End Rd, NW11 7HT) : Imprint Company, 1977. — vi, 305p : ill, ports ; 21cm.
Index.
ISBN 0-9502708-4-9 Pbk : £1.25
(B77-24346)

647'.95422'7 — Public houses. *Hampshire. Guidebooks*
Alka-Seltzer guide to the pubs of Hampshire and the Isle of Wight / edited by R.M. Smith ; introduction by John Arlott ; illustrated by Myerscough. — London (24 Highbury Cres., N5 1RX) : Bayard Books, 1975. — 127p : ill, 2 maps ; 22cm.
Spine title: Pubs of Hampshire and the Isle of Wight. — Index.
ISBN 0-220-66656-3 Pbk : £0.75
Also classified at 647'.95422'8
(B77-18875)

647'.95422'8 — Public houses. *Isle of Wight. Guidebooks*
Alka-Seltzer guide to the pubs of Hampshire and the Isle of Wight / edited by R.M. Smith ; introduction by John Arlott ; illustrated by Myerscough. — London (24 Highbury Cres., N5 1RX) : Bayard Books, 1975. — 127p : ill, 2 maps ; 22cm.
Spine title: Pubs of Hampshire and the Isle of Wight. — Index.
ISBN 0-220-66656-3 Pbk : £0.75
Primary classification 647'.95422'7
(B77-18875)

647'.95423'8 — Public houses. *Somerset*
Better pubs in old Somerset / [edited by Jimmy Young]. — Crediton (Red Cross House, Crediton, Devon) : Better Pubs Ltd, 1977. — 96p : ill, maps ; 21cm.
Cover title: The history of old Somerset pubs. — Bibl.: p.96.
ISBN 0-9504285-1-5 Sd : £0.75
Also classified at 647'.95423'9
(B77-15944)

647'.95423'9 — Public houses. *Avon*
Better pubs in old Somerset / [edited by Jimmy Young]. — Crediton (Red Cross House, Crediton, Devon) : Better Pubs Ltd, 1977. — 96p : ill, maps ; 21cm.
Cover title: The history of old Somerset pubs. — Bibl.: p.96.
ISBN 0-9504285-1-5 Sd : £0.75
Primary classification 647'.95423'8
(B77-15944)

647'.95425'24 — Public houses. *Nottinghamshire, Newark, to 1976*
Cousins, P R. Newark inns & public houses / [by P.R. Cousins]. — Newark on Trent (27 Spring Gardens, Newark on Trent [Notts.]) : The author, 1977. — [2],42p : ill, maps, plan ; 21cm.
Sd : £0.50
Primary classification 647'.94425'24
(B77-14812)

647'.95426'5 — Public houses selling unpressurised beers. *Cambridgeshire. Directories*
Campaign for Real Ale. *Cambridge and District Branch.* Real ale in Cambridgeshire / [compiled by the three Cambridgeshire branches, Cambridge and District Branch, Peterborough Branch, and St Neots Branch, of the Campaign for Real Ale ; edited by Bill Noblett]. — [Huntington] ([8 Rookery Way, Fenstanton, Huntington, Cambs.]) : [CAMRA], 1976. — [2],32p : ill, maps ; 21cm.
ISBN 0-9505687-1-6 Sd : £0.25
(B77-14307)

647'.95426'74 — Catering establishments: Retreats. *Essex. Epping Forest, 1870-1920*
Ward, Bernard. The retreats of Epping Forest / by Bernard Ward. — [Loughton] ([The Warren, Loughton, Essex]) : Conservators of Epping Forest, [1977]. — [2],31p : ill ; 21cm.
Sd : £0.35
(B77-30412)

647'.95428 — Public houses selling unpressurised beers. *North-east England. Directories*
Campaign for Real Ale. *Cleveland Branch.* Real beer in North East England : a guide for the discerning drinker / prepared jointly by the Cleveland, Durham and Tyneside branches of CAMRA]. — 2nd ed. (enlarged). — St Albans : CAMRA ([Durham]) ([50 Saddler St., Durham City DH1 3NU]) : [Distributed by ADAB Books], 1976. — [1],iii[i.e.iv],44p : ill, maps ; 22cm.
ISBN 0-9505205-1-9 Sd : £0.45
(B77-04923)

648 — LAUNDERING, CLEANING, ETC

648.1 — Fabrics. Laundering
Nuttall's fabric facts / compiled by Helen Perrin. — London [etc.] : F. Warne, 1976. — 48p : ill ; 15cm.
ISBN 0-7232-1991-5 Sd : £0.25
(B77-00836)

648'.1 — Laundering. *Secondary school texts*
Lamb, Barbara. Care & clean / [by] Barbara Lamb ; illustrated by David Lamb. — London : Edward Arnold, 1976. — [4],50p : ill ; 19x25cm.
ISBN 0-7131-0057-5 Sd : £1.00
(B77-03109)

649.1 — HOME CARE OF CHILDREN

649'.1 — Children. Home care
Thomson, Jessie Robertson. Natural and healthy childhood / by Jessie R. Thomson. — Completely revised [ed.] / revised by C. Leslie Thomson. — London : Daniel, 1976 [i.e. 1977]. — 117p ; 22cm.
Previous ed.: published as 'Healthy childhood'. London : Thorsons, 1952. — Index.
ISBN 0-85207-139-6 Pbk : £1.98
(B77-11293)

649'.1 — Children. Home care. *Manuals*
Spock, Benjamin. Bringing up children in a difficult time : a philosophy of parental leadership and high ideals / [by] Benjamin Spock. — London : New English Library, 1977. — 253p ; 18cm.
Originally published: New York : Norton ; London : Bodley Head, 1974. — Index.
ISBN 0-450-03088-1 Pbk : £0.90
(B77-06186)

Spock, Benjamin. Bringing up children in a difficult time : a philosophy of parental leadership and high ideals / [by] Benjamin Spock. — London : New English Library, 1977. — 253p ; 18cm.
Originally published: New York : Norton ; London : Bodley Head, 1974. — Index.
ISBN 0-450-03426-7 Pbk : £0.95
(B77-20422)

649'.1'019 — Children, to 5 years. Behaviour modification
Erickson, Marcene L. Assessment and management of developmental changes in children / [by] Marcene L. Erickson ; chapter 9 contributed by Peggy L. Pipes ; original photographs by Janis K. Smith ; original drawings by Mary K. Shrader ; original cover art by Greg Owen. — Saint Louis : Mosby ; London : Distributed by Kimpton, 1976. — xi, 268p : ill, forms ; 26cm.
Bibl. — Index.
ISBN 0-8016-1526-7 Pbk : £6.95
Primary classification 155.4'22
(B77-05852)

649'.102'403036 — Children, to 6 years. Home care. *For negro parents*
McLaughlin, Clara J. The black parents' handbook : a guide to healthy pregnancy, birth and child care / [by] Clara J. McLaughlin with Donald R. Frisby ... [et al.]. — New York ; London : Harcourt Brace Jovanovich, 1976. — xx,220p : ill ; 22cm.
Index.
ISBN 0-15-113185-6 : Unpriced
ISBN 0-15-613100-5 Pbk : Unpriced
Also classified at 612.6'3'02403036
(B77-10438)

649'.102'4613 — Children. Home care. *For nursery nursing*
Nursery nursing / edited by P.J. Cunningham for the British Association for Early Childhood Education ; with 17 line drawings by Audrey Besterman. — 3rd ed. — London : Faber, 1977. — 214p : ill ; 20cm.
Previous ed.: 1974. — Bibl.: p.206-207. — Index.
ISBN 0-571-04940-0 Pbk : £2.50 : CIP rev.
(B77-25050)

649'.10248 — Childminding. *Manuals*
Jackson, Sonia. Other people's children / written by Sonia Jackson, Joyce Moseley, Barbara Wheeler ; edited by David Allen and Sonia Jackson ; cartoons by 'Larry' and Quentin Blake. — London : British Broadcasting Corporation, 1976. — 84p : ill, forms, ports ; 24cm.
'Published to accompany a series of programmes prepared in consultation with the BBC Further Education Advisory Council' - title page verso. — Bibl.
ISBN 0-563-16107-8 Sd : £1.00
(B77-07966)

649'.12 — Children, to 6 years. Home care. *Manuals*
Chess, Stella. Your child is a person : a psychological approach to parenthood without guilt / [by]Stella Chess, Alexander Thomas, Herbert G. Birch. — Harmondsworth [etc.] : Penguin, 1976. — x,213p ; 20cm.
Originally published: New York : Viking Press, 1965 ; London : P. Davies, 1966. — Bibl.: p.205-207. — Index.
ISBN 0-14-004439-6 Pbk : £1.20
(B77-13124)

649'.122 — Babies. Home care
You and your baby / executive editor Evelyn Brown. — London : British Medical Association. — (A 'Family doctor' publication)

In 2 vols.
Part 1 : Pregnancy and birth. — 1977. — 95p : ill(chiefly col) ; 20cm.
Sd : Unpriced
Primary classification 612.6'3
(B77-27884)

649'.122 — Children, to 3 years. Home care
Stoppard, Miriam. Miriam Stoppard's book of babycare. — London : Weidenfeld and Nicolson, 1977. — 160p : ill ; 26cm.
Index.
ISBN 0-297-77211-2 : £4.50
(B77-20423)

649'.122 — Children, to 5 years. Home care. *Manuals*
Leach, Penelope. Baby and child / [by] Penelope Leach ; photography by Camilla Jessel. — London : Joseph, 1977. — 512p : ill(some col) ; 25cm.
Index.
ISBN 0-7181-1648-8 : £6.95
(B77-30413)

The **open** home / [edited by Iris Grender and Catherine Munnion based on material originated by Sara Stein]. — Kenley : Three Four Five, 1976. — 128p : ill(some col) ; 27cm.

Based on a series published in 'Mother'. — Index.
ISBN 0-903016-40-0 : £2.95
(B77-11294)

649'.122 — Newborn babies. Home care. *Juvenile literature*
Jarner, Bo. My new sister / [photographs by] Bo Jarner ; [translated from the Danish]. — London : A. and C. Black, 1977. — [21]p : chiefly ill ; 22cm.
Translation of: 'Sille far en lille-soster'. Copenhagen : Borgens, 1973?.
ISBN 0-7136-1708-x : £1.25
Primary classification 612.6'3
(B77-14751)

649'.122 — Newborn babies. Home care. *Manuals*
Brant, Margaret. Having a baby / [by] Margaret Brant. — London : Macdonald Educational, 1977. — 96p : ill(some col), form ; 21cm. — (Macdonald guidelines ; 14)
Bibl.: p.93. — Index.
ISBN 0-356-06014-4 Pbk : £1.00
Primary classification 612.6'3
(B77-21156)

Lennane, Jean. Hard labour : a realists' guide to having a baby by Jean and John Lennane. — London : Gollancz, 1977. — 3-242p ; 23cm.
Bibl.: p.234-235. — Index.
ISBN 0-575-02180-2 : £5.95
Primary classification 612.6'3
(B77-10376)

649'.122'019 — Babies. Home care. Psychological aspects. *Manuals. For parents*
Lehane, Stephen. Help your baby learn : 100 Piaget-based activities for the first two years of life / [by] Stephen Lehane. — Englewood Cliffs ; London [etc.] : Prentice-Hall, 1976. — xvii,205p : ill ; 21cm. — (Psychology of living books)
Bibl.: p.202-205.
ISBN 0-13-386326-3 : £7.15
ISBN 0-13-386318-2 Pbk : £2.35
(B77-02420)

649'.123 — Children, 4 years. Home care. *England. Sociological perspectives. Study regions: Nottinghamshire. Nottingham. Reports, surveys*
Newson, John. Four years old in an urban community / [by] John and Elizabeth Newson. — Harmondsworth [etc.] : Penguin, 1976. — 606p ; 19cm. — (Pelican books)
Originally published: London : Allen and Unwin, 1968. — Bibl.: p.593-597. — Index.
Pbk : £1.25
ISBN 0-14-021206-x
(B77-04287)

649'.3 — Babies. Breast feeding
Buckinghamshire Area Health Authority. What's so special about breast feeding? / [Buckinghamshire Area Health Authority]. — [Aylesbury] ([Peveral Court, Portway Rd, Stone, Aylesbury HP20]) : Buckinghamshire Area Health Authority, [1976]. — [1],3p ; 21cm.
ISBN 0-902805-53-3 Sd : Unpriced
(B77-00295)

649'.4 — Babies. Massage. *Manuals*
Leboyer, Frédérick. Loving hands / [by] Frederick Leboyer. — London : Collins, 1977. — 137p : ill ; 28cm.
This translation originally published: New York : Knopf, 1976. — Translation of: 'Shantala'. Paris : Seuil, 1976.
ISBN 0-00-216486-8 Pbk : £2.50
(B77-13734)

649'.5 — Activities for children, 4-7 years. *For parents & teaching*
Presland, John, *b.1935.* How many? / devised by John Presland ; illustrated by Pam Adams. — Purton (Restrop Manor, Purton, Wilts.) : Child's Play (International) Ltd, 1975. — [14]p, [2]leaves of plates : chiefly col ill ; 21cm. — (Child's Play motivation books ; 3)
Leaves of plates perforated to form press-out cards.
ISBN 0-85953-045-0 Sd : £0.45
(B77-14335)

Presland, John, *b.1935.* Letters and words / devised by John Presland ; illustrated by Pam Adams. — Purton (Restrop Manor, Purton, Wilts.) : Child's Play (International) Ltd, 1975. — [14]p,[2]leaves of plates : chiefly col ill ; 21cm. — (Child's Play motivation books ; 4)
Leaves of plates perforated to form press-out cards.
ISBN 0-85953-046-9 Sd : £0.45
(B77-14336)

Presland, John, *b.1935.* Same and different / devised by John Presland ; illustrated by Pam Adams. — Purton (Restrop Manor, Purton, Wilts.) : Child's Play (International) Ltd, 1975. — [14]p,[2]leaves of plates : chiefly col ill ; 21cm. — (Child's Play motivation books ; 1)
Leaves of plates perforated to form press-out cards.
ISBN 0-85953-043-4 Sd : £0.45
(B77-14337)

Presland, John, *b.1935.* What is it? / devised by John Presland ; illustrated by Pam Adams. — Purton (Restrop Manor, Purton, Wilts.) : Child's Play (International) Ltd, 1975. — [14]p, [2] leaves of plates : chiefly col ill ; 21cm. — (Child's Play motivation books ; 2)
Leaves of plates perforated to form press-out cards.
ISBN 0-85953-044-2 Sd : £0.45
(B77-14338)

649'.5 — Activities for children, to 5 years. *For parents*
What to do when 'there's nothing to do' / [by] members of the staff of the Boston Children's Medical Center and Elizabeth M. Gregg ; foreword by Philip Evans ; illustrations by Marc Simont. — London : Arrow Books, 1976. — 189p : ill ; 19cm.
Originally published: New York : Dial Press, 1968 ; London : Hutchinson, 1969. — Bibl.: p.157-170. — List of sound discs: p.171-179. — Index.
Pbk : £0.70
ISBN 0-09-004490-8
(B77-21978)

649'.5 — Activities for children, to 9 years. *Manuals. Secondary school texts*
Chetwood, Doreen. Where shall we go today? / [by] Doreen Chetwood ; designed and illustrated by Christopher Neal. — Edinburgh : Oliver and Boyd, 1976. — 32p : ill(some col) ; 25cm. — (You at home)
Bibl.
ISBN 0-05-003007-8 Sd : £0.70
(B77-09117)

649'.5 — Activities for handicapped children. *Manuals. For parents*
Lear, Roma. Play helps : toys and activities for handicapped children / [by] Roma Lear ; illustrated by Gillian Hunter. — London : Heinemann Medical, 1977. — xi,158p : ill ; 25cm. — (Heinemann health books)
Bibl. — Index.
ISBN 0-433-19085-x Pbk : £2.50
Also classified at 649'.552
(B77-11931)

649'.5 — Children, to 5 years. Play. *Manuals. For parents*
Marzollo, Jean. Learning through play / by Jean Marzollo and Janice Lloyd ; illustrated by Irene Trivas. — Harmondsworth [etc.] : Penguin, 1977. — [11],211p : ill ; 13x20cm.
Originally published: New York : Harper and Row, 1972 ; London : Allen and Unwin, 1974. — Index.
ISBN 0-14-046251-1 Pbk : £0.80
(B77-23545)

649'.5'0222 — Children. Play. *Illustrations. Juvenile literature*
Blanco, Josette. Playtime / by Josette Blanco ; illustrated by Claude d'Ham. — Purton (Restrop Manor, Purton, Wilts.) : Child's Play (International) Ltd, [1977]. — [20]p : chiefly col ill ; 22cm. — (Child's Play moments ; book 4)
Page width varies.
ISBN 0-85953-042-6 : £0.90
ISBN 0-85953-038-8 Pbk : £0.45
(B77-13125)

649'.552 — Toys for handicapped children. *Manuals. For parents*
Lear, Roma. Play helps : toys and activities for handicapped children / [by] Roma Lear ; illustrated by Gillian Hunter. — London : Heinemann Medical, 1977. — xi,158p : ill ; 25cm. — (Heinemann health books)
Bibl. — Index.
ISBN 0-433-19085-x Pbk : £2.50
Primary classification 649'.5
(B77-11931)

649'.6 — Children. Toilet training. *Manuals*
Azrin, Nathan. Toilet training in less than a day / [by] N. Azrin and R. Foxx. — London : Pan Books, 1977. — 155p : ill, form ; 18cm.
Originally published: New York : Simon and Schuster, 1974 ; London : Macmillan, 1975. — Bibl.: p.149. — Index.
ISBN 0-330-25032-9 Pbk : £0.70
(B77-12558)

649.8 — HOME NURSING
649.8 — Children with terminal illness. Home care
Home care for the dying child : professional and family perspectives / edited by Ida Marie Martinson. — New York : Appleton-Century-Crofts ; London [etc.] : Prentice-Hall, 1976. — xiii,332p : ill ; 23cm.
Index.
ISBN 0-8385-3824-x Pbk : £7.80
(B77-16480)

649.8 — Home nursing. *Manuals*
Home nursing. — London [etc.] : Reader's Digest Association, 1976. — 40p : ill(some col) ; 27cm. — ('Reader's digest' basic guide)
'The text and illustrations in this book are taken from "'Reader's Digest' family health guide"'. London : Reader's Digest Association, 1972.
ISBN 0-276-00133-8 Sd : £0.65
(B77-15367)

650 — BUSINESS PRACTICES
650'.0971 — Business practices. *Canada*
Business fundamentals. — 3rd ed. / [by] Graham Bruce ... [et al.]. — Toronto ; London [etc.] : McGraw-Hill, 1977. — [7],200p : ill, facsims, forms, map, ports ; 24cm.
Previous ed.: / by Graham Bruce, Robert H. Heywood, William T. Abercrombie. Toronto : McGraw-Hill, 1969. — Index.
ISBN 0-07-082472-x : £5.00
(B77-23546)

650'.1 — Business enterprise. Success. *Manuals*
Cerney, J V. Dynamic law of thinking rich / [by] J.V. Cerney. — London : Heron Books, [1977]. — 218p : forms ; 24cm. — (A business leader's book)
Originally published: West Nyack : Parker Pub. Co., 1967.
ISBN 0-900948-85-x : Unpriced
(B77-10439)

651 — OFFICE PRACTICES
Bunting, Ernest. Clerical duties / by E. Bunting. — 4th (one-volume) ed. — London : Cassell, 1977. — v,266p : ill, forms ; 22cm.
Previous ed.: in 2 vols. 1973. — Index.
ISBN 0-304-29782-8 Pbk : £3.40
(B77-30414)

Whitehead, Geoffrey. Office practice made simple / [by] Geoffrey Whitehead. — 2nd ed. — London : W.H. Allen, 1976. — xv,327p,[16] p of plates : ill, forms ; 22cm. — (Made simple books ISSN 0464-2902)
Previous ed.: 1973. — Bibl.: p.300-306. — Index.
ISBN 0-491-01791-x Pbk : £1.50
(B77-19490)

651 — Office practices. *For African students*
Burton, Mabel. Secretarial and office practice / [by] Mabel Burton. — London : Longman, 1977. — [7],127p : ill, forms ; 21cm. — (Longman commercial studies)
ISBN 0-582-60898-8 Pbk : £1.15
(B77-26390)

651'.023 — Office work. *Career guides*
Peterson, Marla P. Exploring business and office occupations / [by] Marla P. Peterson ; consulting editor Charles S. Winn. — New York ; London [etc.] : McGraw-Hill, 1976. — [8],152p : ill(some col), forms(some col), col plan ; 28cm. — (Careers in focus)
Worksheet booklet also available.
ISBN 0-07-071037-6 Pbk : £3.45
(B77-05516)

651'.02'40816 — Office work. *Manuals. For physically handicapped persons*
Mara, Henry. Get yourself going the work-easy way : an action handbook for the handicapped office worker / by Henry Mara & Penny Thrift. — [London] : Central Council for the Disabled] ; [London] ([c/o Disablement in the City, 40 Etherly Rd, N15 3AJ]) : [Distributed by the author], [1977]. — 3-104p : ill ; 21cm.
Cover title.
Pbk : £1.00
(B77-30415)

651'.076 — Office practices. *Questions & answers*
MacDonald, Muriel. Office practice : multiple choice questions and general knowledge / [by] Muriel MacDonald. — Glasgow [etc.] : Blackie, 1976. — [7],117p ; 19cm.
With answers.
ISBN 0-216-90183-9 Pbk : £1.40
(B77-03616)

651'.07'7 — Office practices. *Programmed texts*
Foster, Thelma J. Revise your office practice / [by] Thelma J. Foster. — London : Pitman, 1977. — vi,150p ; 22cm.
Index.
ISBN 0-273-01002-6 Pbk : £1.45 : CIP rev.
(B77-09800)

651'.2 — Office equipment. Selection. *Manuals*
Chambers, Harry Thomas. Office equipment selection handbook / [by] Harry T. Chambers. — London : Business Books, 1976. — vi,278p, [16]p of plates : ill, plans ; 24cm.
Index.
ISBN 0-220-66303-3 : £10.00
(B77-29546)

651'.32 — Offices. Layout
Palmer, Alvin E. Planning the office landscape / [by] Alvin E. Palmer, M. Susan Lewis. — New York ; London [etc.] : McGraw-Hill, 1977. — xiv,188p : ill, forms, plans ; 25cm.
Bibl.: p.181-182. — Index.
ISBN 0-07-048415-5 : £13.15
(B77-22705)

651'.32 — Offices. Management
Institute of Administrative Management. Office administration / edited for the Institute of Administrative Management [by] Geoffrey Mills and Oliver Standingford. — 3rd ed. — London [etc.] : Pitman, 1977. — vii,235p : ill, forms ; 23cm. — (A Pitman international text)
Previous ed.: / edited for the Institute of Office Management. 1966. — Bibl.: p.231-232. — Index.
ISBN 0-273-00793-9 : £3.25
(B77-16968)

651'.3741 — Legal secretaryship. *England. Manuals*
Parry, Annette K. A secretary's guide to the legal office / [by] Annette K. Parry. — New Era ed. — London [etc.] : Pitman, 1976. — vii,70p : ill, facsims, forms ; 30cm.
ISBN 0-273-00706-8 Pbk : £2.40
(B77-06187)

Parry, Annette K. A secretary's guide to the legal office / [by] Annette K. Parry. — Pitman 2000 ed. — London [etc.] : Pitman, 1976. — vii, 70p : ill, facsims, forms ; 30cm.
ISBN 0-273-00704-1 Pbk : £2.40
(B77-06188)

651'.3741 — Secretaryship. *Manuals*
Lee, Dorothy E. Secretarial office procedures / [by] Dorothy E. Lee, Walter A. Brower. — New York ; London [etc.] : McGraw-Hill, 1976. — ix,194,169p : ill, facsims, forms ; 28cm. — (McGraw-Hill college series)
Originally published: as 'Secretarial practice for colleges' / by Dorothy E. Lee, Tilly S. Dickinson, Walter A. Brower. 1960. — Bibl.: p.14-16. — Index.
ISBN 0-07-037035-4 Pbk : £8.25
(B77-03617)

651.5 — Hospitals. *New York (City). Beth Israel Hospital. Outpatients. Medical records. Records management. Problem-Oriented Medical Records*
Vorzimer, Jefferson J. Coordinated ambulatory care : the POMR / by Jefferson J. Vorzimer. — New York : Appleton-Century-Crofts ; London [etc.] : Prentice-Hall, 1976. — xiii, 128p : ill, facsim, forms ; 23cm.
Bibl. — Index.
ISBN 0-8385-1203-8 Pbk : £6.00
(B77-20424)

651.5 — Medical records. Records management. Applications of digital computer systems. *Conference proceedings*
IFIP Working Conference on Information Systems for Patient Care : Review, Analysis and Evaluation, *Amsterdam, 1976.* Informtion systems for patient care : proceedings of the IFIP Working Conference on Information Systems for Patient care : Review, Analysis and Evaluation / edited by J. van Egmond, P.F. de Vries Robbé and A.H. Levy. — Amsterdam [etc.] ; Oxford : North-Holland Publishing Co., 1976. — xii,479p : ill, forms, map ; 23cm.
'... [held] Amsterdam, The Netherlands, 27-31 October 1976 organized by IFIP Technical Committee 4, Information Processing in Medicine International Federation for Information Processing' - half title page verso. — Bibl. — Index. — Previous control number B7717612.
ISBN 0-7204-0463-0 : £25.76
(B77-17612)

651.5 — Medical records. Records management. Implications of right to privacy. *Conference proceedings*
IFIP-WG 4.2 Working Conference on Realization of Data Protection in Health Information Systems, *Kiel, 1976.* Realization of data protection in health information systems : proceedings of the IFIP-WG 4.2 Working Conference on Realization of Date [i.e. Data] Protection in Health Information Systems, Kiel, 23-25 June 1976 / edited by G. Griesser, in collaboration with ... [others]. — Amsterdam [etc.] ; Oxford : North-Holland Publishing Co., 1977. — xvi,214p : ill ; 23cm.
'organized by IFIP Technical Committee 4 ...' - half title page verso. — Bibl. — Index.
ISBN 0-7204-0462-2 : £14.29
(B77-27224)

651.5 — Offices. Records. Records management
Leafe, Margaret. Workbook on office records / [by] Margaret Leafe. — London : Cassell, 1977. — [5],58p : ill, forms ; 22cm. — (Cassell's office practice series)
With numerical answers.
ISBN 0-304-29834-4 Sd : £1.20
(B77-25738)

651.5'9 — Fire brigades. Personnel. Records. Records management. Applications of digital computer systems. *Great Britain*
Local Authorities Management Services and Computer Committee. *Computer Panel.* Fire service personnel records by computer : report of the Computer Panel of LAMSAC. — London : LAMSAC, 1976. — 33p ; 30cm.
ISBN 0-85497-091-6 Sd : £2.00
(B77-02421)

651.7 — Business practices. Communication. *Manuals*
Murphy, Herta A. Effective business communications / [by] Herta A. Murphy, Charles E. Peck. — 2nd ed. — New York ; London [etc.] : McGraw-Hill, [1977]. — xv, 703p : ill, facsims, forms, map ; 25cm.
This ed. published in the United States: 1976. — Previous ed.: New York : McGraw-Hill, 1972. — Bibl.: p.5. — Index.
ISBN 0-07-044061-1 : £11.60
(B77-11932)

Phillips, Bonnie D. Effective business communications / [by] Bonnie D. Phillips. — New York ; London [etc.] : Van Nostrand Reinhold, 1977. — v,247p : ill, forms ; 27cm.
Index.
ISBN 0-442-26552-2 : £8.05
(B77-21262)

651.7'076 — Business practices. Communication. *Exercises, worked examples*
Parsons, Christopher James. Problems in business communication / [by] C.J. Parsons. — London : Edward Arnold, 1977. — 96p : 1 ill, form ; 22cm.
With solutions to selected problems. — Bibl.: p.95-96.
ISBN 0-7131-0107-5 Sd : £1.35
(B77-27947)

651.7'3 — Business firms. Telephones. Use. *Manuals*
Roman, Eva. How to use the telephone effectively and economically / by Eva Roman. — London : Business Books, 1976. — viii,160p : ill ; 23cm.
ISBN 0-220-66300-9 : £6.00
(B77-26391)

651.7'4 — Business practices. Written communication. *Manuals*
Weaver, Patricia C. Persuasive writing : a manager's guide to effective letters and reports / by Patricia C. Weaver, Robert G. Weaver. — New York : Free Press ; London : Collier Macmillan, 1977. — xi,239p : facsims ; 25cm.
Index.
ISBN 0-02-934020-9 : £7.50
(B77-22706)

651.7'4 — Business practices. Written communication. *Manuals. For data processing*
Smith, Rändi Sigmund. Written communication for data processing / [by] Rändi Sigmund Smith. — New York ; London [etc.] : Van Nostrand Reinhold, 1976. — vii,199p : ill, form ; 24cm.
Index.
ISBN 0-442-27793-8 : £10.35
(B77-18267)

651.7'4 — English language. Business English. *For non-English speaking students*
Yates, C St J. State your case / [by C. St J. Yates]. — London [etc.] : Oxford University Press.
Teacher's kit. — 1976. — [309] leaves : ill, forms, maps ; 32cm.
In binder. — 'Catalogue' (18p.; sd), 120 cards ([129] sides) in plastic pockets also in binder.
ISBN 0-19-457150-5 Ls : £40.00
(B77-17613)

651.7'5 — Business correspondence. *Manuals*
Fruehling, Rosemary T. Business correspondence/30 / [by] Rosemary T. Fruehling, Sharon Bouchard. — 2nd ed. — New York ; London [etc.] : McGraw-Hill, 1976. — vi,170p : ill ; 24cm.
Pages perforated at inside edge and pierced for binder. — Previous ed.: New York : McGraw-Hill, 1971.
ISBN 0-07-022342-4 Pbk : £4.10
(B77-06189)

Gartside, Leonard. Modern business correspondence : a practical course for use in schools and by all who would write better business letters / [by] L. Gartside. — 3rd ed. — Plymouth : Macdonald and Evans, 1976. — xiii,465p : ill, facsims ; 22cm.
Previous ed.: 1967. — Index.
ISBN 0-7121-1392-4 Pbk : £2.50
(B77-06190)

651.8 — Business practices. Applications of data processing systems
Robichaud, Beryl. Introduction to data processing. — 2nd ed. / [by] Beryl Robichaud, Eugene Muscat, Alix-Marie Hall. — New York ; London [etc.] : Gregg Division of McGraw-Hill, 1977. — vii,2-345p : ill, forms ; 25cm.
With answers. — Previous ed.: published as 'Understanding modern business data processing' / by Beryl Robichaud. 1966. — Index.
ISBN 0-07-053190-0 : £7.10
(B77-11933)

651.8'4 — Business firms. Digital computer systems. *Great Britain. Buyers' guides. Periodicals*
Which computer?. — [London] ([51 Colney Hatch La., N.10]) : ['Which Computer' Ltd]. Vol.1, issue 1- ; Sept. 1977-. — [1977]-. — ill ; 30cm.
Monthly. — 66p. in 1st issue. — Index.
Sd : £2.00(£18.00 yearly)
ISSN 0140-3435
(B77-27225)

652.3 — TYPING
652.3'003 — Typing. *Encyclopaedias*
Mackay, Edith. The typewriting dictionary / [by] Edith Mackay. — London [etc.] : Pitman, 1977. — [4],269p : ill, forms, port ; 23cm.
ISBN 0-273-31721-0 : £5.00
(B77-17614)

652.3'024 — Numbers. Typing. *Exercises, worked examples*
Bloomquist, Roger. Number-key practice : for use on typewriter, ten-key and keypunch keyboards / [by] Roger Bloomquist, George P. Grill, John L. Rowe. — New York ; London [etc.] : McGraw-Hill, [1976]. — [5],90p : ill ; 23cm.
Notebook format. — Published in the United States: 1975.
ISBN 0-07-006105-x Sp : £3.60
(B77-05517)

652.3'024 — Typing. *Exercises, worked examples*
Gregg typing, series six. — [New ed.] / [by] Alan C. Lloyd ... [et al.]. — New York ; London [etc.] : McGraw-Hill.
Typing 2 : Advanced course. — 1977. — vii, 281p : forms, maps, plans ; 22x28cm.
Notebook format. — Two-way paging. — Previous ed.: published as 'Typing 300. Vol.2' / by John L. Rowe, Alan C. Lloyd and Fred E. Winger. New York : McGraw-Hill, 1973. — Index.
ISBN 0-07-038244-1 : £6.50
(B77-32001)

Holt, Gordon Henry. Typing fluency and accuracy practice. — Revised ed. / by Gordon H. Holt ... [et al.]. — London [etc.] : McGraw-Hill, 1977. — ix,55p ; 23cm.
Two-way paging. — Previous ed.: / by Gordon Henry Holt and Alan Chester Lloyd. 1964.
ISBN 0-07-084218-3 Sp : £1.35
(B77-17615)

Robinson, Mary Thorpe. Exercises for elementary typewriting examinations / by Mary T. Robinson. — 3rd ed. — London : Cassell, 1977. — iv,124p : forms ; 20x26cm.
Notebook format. — Two-way paging. — Previous ed.: i.e. Decimal currency ed., 1970.
ISBN 0-304-29831-x Pbk : Unpriced
(B77-23547)

Rowe, John L. Typewriting drills for speed and accuracy / [by] John L. Rowe, Faborn Etier. — 4th ed. — New York ; London [etc.] : Gregg Division, McGraw-Hill, 1977. — vi,90p ; 22x29cm.
Notebook format. — Two-way paging. — Previous ed.: New York : Gregg Division, McGraw-Hill, 1966.
ISBN 0-07-054151-5 Sp : £3.15
(B77-21263)

Stanwell, Sheila Toft. 'Typewell' typewriting course / [by S.T. Stanwell, J. Shaw, M.K. Swift]. — London : Edward Arnold.
In 5 vols.
Book 4 : Advanced display / [by] Sheila T. Stanwell, Josephine Shaw. — 1977. — iv,124p : ill ; 21x31cm.
Notebook format. — Two-way paging.
ISBN 0-7131-1842-3 Sp : £3.75
(B77-32002)

652.3'024 — Typing. *Manuals*

Drummond, Archibald Manson. Typing, first course / [by] A.M. Drummond, I.E. Scattergood. — 3rd ed. — London [etc.] : McGraw-Hill.
Handbook and solutions. — 1977. — v,201p : forms ; 27cm.
Pierced for binder. — Previous ed.: published as 'Gregg typing, first course. Handbook and solutions'. Maidenhead : McGraw-Hill, 1971.
ISBN 0-07-084217-5 Ls : £3.95
(B77-28724)

Drummond, Archibald Manson. Typing, first course / [by] A.M. Drummond, I.E. Scattergood. — 3rd ed. — London [etc.] : McGraw-Hill, 1977. — vii,169p : col ill ; 23x28cm.
Notebook format. — Two-way paging. — Previous ed.: published as 'Gregg typing, first course'. 1970. — Index.
ISBN 0-07-084212-4 : £1.95
(B77-15945)

Walmsley, William. Walmsley's commercial typewriting / [by William and Elizabeth Walmsley]. — 8th ed. / by Aileen M. Prince. — London [etc.] : Pitman.
In 2 vols. — Previous ed.: published in 1 vol as 'Pitman commercial typewriting'. 1970.
Horizontal method. — 1977. — vi,170p : ill(some col), facsims ; 21x30cm.
Notebook format. Printed tête-bêche. — Index.
ISBN 0-273-01014-x Sp : £1.95 : CIP rev.
(B77-06766)

Vertical method. — 1977. — vi,170p : ill(some col), forms ; 21x30cm.
Notebook format. — Two-way paging. — Index.
ISBN 0-273-01018-2 Sp : £1.95
(B77-33311)

652.3'07 — Timed typing. *Exercises, worked examples*

Axelrod, Marshall. Creative timed writings / [by] Marshall Axelrod ; in collaboration with a multiethnic board of contributors and consultants. — New York ; London [etc.] : McGraw-Hill, [1976]. — vi,90p : ill ; 19x24cm.
Notebook format. — Two-way paging. — Published in the United States: 1975.
ISBN 0-07-002610-6 Sp : £3.95
(B77-06767)

Jonsson, Allan S. Timed writings / [by] Allan S. Jonsson. — SI metric [ed.]. — Toronto ; London [etc.] : McGraw-Hill Ryerson, 1977. — [1],iv,108p : 1 ill ; 24x18cm.
Notebook format.
ISBN 0-07-082534-3 Sp : £4.30
(B77-28725)

653 — SHORTHAND

653'.09 — Shorthand, to 1975

As fast as speech : an outline history of shorthand from 2400 BC. — London : Pitman, 1977. — [2],21p : ill, facsims, map, port ; 15x21cm.
ISBN 0-273-01075-1 Sd : £0.30
(B77-27226)

653'.18 — Shorthand. Dictation. *Exercises, worked examples. For medical shorthand typists*

Cross, Walter Ray. Dictation passages for medical secretaries / [by] W.R. Cross. — London : Edward Arnold, 1977. — [10],181p ; 22cm.
ISBN 0-7131-0109-1 Pbk : £2.35
(B77-21264)

653'.4242 — Pitman 2000 shorthand. Speed reading. *Exercises, worked examples*

Coombs, Bryan. Pitman 2000 shorthand speedbuilder / [by] Bryan Coombs. — London [etc.] : Pitman, 1976. — iii,139p ; 22cm.
ISBN 0-273-00879-x Pbk : £1.70
(B77-00837)

653'.4242'076 — Pitman 2000 shorthand. *Exercises, worked examples*

Coombs, Bryan. Pitman 2000 shorthand, first course graded exercises / [by] Bryan Coombs. — London [etc.] : Pitman, 1977. — vi,72p ; 22cm.
With answers. — Index.
ISBN 0-273-00962-1 Pbk : £1.00
(B77-15368)

653'.428 — Teeline. *Exercises, worked examples*

Hill, Ivy Constance. First Teeline workbook / [by] I.C. Hill. — London : Heinemann Educational, 1977. — [3],52,27,viii p ; 21cm.
With answers. — '... intended to be used with the textbook, "Teeline" by I.C. Hill' - Introduction.
ISBN 0-435-45341-6 Pbk : £1.25
(B77-29547)

653'.43'1 — Pitman German shorthand. *Exercises, worked examples*

Tarl, Dorothy. Pitman German shorthand / by Dorothy Tarl. — Pinner (23 Latimer Close, Pinner, Middx) : The author, [1976]. — [3],ii, 42p ; 22cm.
'With key to exercises' - cover. — Originally published: 1972.
ISBN 0-903371-03-0 Sd : £1.50
(B77-00838)

657 — ACCOUNTING

Barton, A D. The anatomy of accounting / [by] A.D. Barton. — 2nd ed. — St Lucia : University of Queensland Press ; Hemel Hempstead : Distributed by Prentice-Hall, 1977. — xv,593p : ill ; 24cm.
With answers to selected problems. — Previous ed.: St Lucia : University of Queensland Press, 1975. — Bibl. — Index.
ISBN 0-7022-1482-5 : £9.95
ISBN 0-7022-1460-4 Pbk : Unpriced
(B77-31313)

Callam, A A. A foundation in business accounting / [by] A.A. Callam and M.J. Ryder. — London [etc.] : Macmillan, 1977. — viii, 403p : ill ; 24cm.
Index.
ISBN 0-333-18452-1 Pbk : £6.95
(B77-21265)

Corbett, Peter. Accounting and decision making / [by] Peter Corbett. — London : Longman, 1977. — xi,207p : ill ; 24cm. — (Understanding business)
Index.
ISBN 0-582-35542-7 Pbk : £2.75
(B77-14814)

Dixon, Robert Livingston. The McGraw-Hill 36-hour accounting course / [by] Robert L. Dixon. — New York ; London [etc.] : McGraw-Hill, 1976. — xxiii,344p ; 25cm.
Previous ed.: published as 'The executive's accounting primer'. 1971.
ISBN 0-07-017090-8 : £24.85
(B77-03110)

Foundation in accounting. — London [etc.] : Prentice-Hall.
2 / [by] Richard Lewis, Michael Firth. — 1977. — xvi,511p : ill ; 22cm.
Bibl.: p.505-506. — Index.
ISBN 0-13-329672-5 Pbk : £4.95
(B77-25051)

Hindmarch, Arthur. Accounting : an introduction / [by] Arthur Hindmarch, Miles Atchison, Richard Marke. — London [etc.] : Macmillan, 1977. — xvii,314p : ill ; 24cm. — ([Macmillan business management and administration series])
Bibl. — Index.
ISBN 0-333-15023-6 : £12.00
ISBN 0-333-19167-6 Pbk : £5.95
(B77-20425)

McKechnie, John. Rational book-keeping and accounting / [by] John McKechnie. — 14th ed. / fully revised by L.G. Pepper. — London : Cassell.
In 2 vols. — Previous ed.: published in 1 vol. as 'Rational book-keeping for commercial students'. 1969.
Part 2. — 1977. — [5],289p : ill ; 22cm.
With answers to exercises.
ISBN 0-304-29301-6 Pbk : £5.15
(B77-29548)

Meigs, Walter Berkeley. Accounting : the basis for business decisions. — 4th ed. / [by] Walter B. Meigs, Charles E. Johnson, Robert F. Meigs. — New York ; London [etc.] : McGraw-Hill, 1977. — xix,1034p : ill(chiefly col), forms(some col) ; 24cm.
Text on lining papers. — Previous ed.: / by Walter B. Meigs, A.N. Mosich and Charles E. Johnson. New York : McGraw-Hill, 1972. — Index.
ISBN 0-07-041241-3 : £11.20
(B77-31314)

Metcalf, Richard W. Principles of accounting / [by] Richard W. Metcalf, Pierre L. Titard. — Philadelphia ; London [etc.] : Saunders, 1976. — xxvi,1023p : ill(some col), forms(some col) ; 26cm.
Index.
ISBN 0-7216-6313-3 : £11.00
(B77-01619)

Palmer, Alfred. Palmer's examination notebook for accountancy and secretarial students. — 13th ed. / by Emile Woolf. — London : Gee and Co., 1977. — [7],208p ; 22cm. — (A Gee's study book)
Interleaved. — Previous ed.: 1970. — Index.
ISBN 0-85258-152-1 Pbk : £3.75
(B77-13735)

Rowland, Stanley William. Rowland and Magee's accounting. — 9th ed. / by Charles Magee. — London : Gee and Co., 1977. — xiii,390p : 2 ill ; 22cm. — (A Gee's study book)
Previous ed.: / by Brian Magee. 1971. — Index.
ISBN 0-85258-158-0 Pbk : £4.50
(B77-32003)

Rundle, Cyril. Accountancy for everyone / [by] Cyril Rundle. — Newton Abbot [etc.] : David and Charles, 1977. — 173p : ill, forms ; 23cm.
Index.
ISBN 0-7153-6864-8 : £3.95
(B77-24347)

Stott, John Randall. Basic accounts / [by] J. Randall Stott. — London : Edward Arnold, 1977. — 167p ; 24cm.
Originally published: London : Dent, 1973.
ISBN 0-7131-0166-0 Pbk : £1.95 : CIP rev.
(B77-09118)

657 — Accountancy. *For Irish students. Secondary school texts*

Dowling, Noel. Leaving Certificate accountancy / [by] Noel Dowling. — Dublin : Helicon, 1977. — [4],337p ; 21cm. — (Study assessment series)

Pbk : £2.64
(B77-29549)

657 — Accounting. *Comparative studies. Tables*

Price Waterhouse International. Accounting principles and reporting practices : a survey in 46 countries / [Price Waterhouse International]. — [New ed.]. — [London] ([32 London Bridge St., SE1 9SY]) : Price Waterhouse [International], 1975. — [91],264,[13]p ; 23cm.
Parallel English, French, German and Spanish text. — Previous ed.: published as 'Survey of accounting principles and reporting practice in 38 countries'. London : Institute of Chartered Accountants in England and Wales, Chartered Accountants' Trust for Educational Research, 1974. — Index.
ISBN 0-9502558-1-5 Pbk : £5.95
(B77-00296)

Price Waterhouse International. A survey in 46 countries : accounting principles and reporting practices / [Price Waterhouse International]. — [New ed.]. — London : Institute of Chartered Accountants in England and Wales, 1976. — [91],264,[13]p ; 23cm.
Parallel English, French, German and Spanish texts. — This ed. originally published: as 'Accounting principles and reporting practices : a survey in 46 countries'. London : Price Waterhouse International, 1975. — Index.
ISBN 0-85291-159-9 Pbk : £5.95
(B77-07474)

657 — Accounting. *Manuals*

Handbook of modern accounting / Sidney Davidson, editor ; Roman L. Weil, associate editor. — 2nd ed. — New York [etc.] ; London : McGraw-Hill, 1977. — 1408p in various pagings : ill, forms ; 24cm.
Previous ed.: 1970. — Bibl. — Index.
ISBN 0-07-015451-1 : £22.45
(B77-27227)

657 — Accounting. *Secondary school texts*

Thomas, David John. That's the way the money goes! : accounts in everyday life / [by] D.J. Thomas ; cartoons by Larry. — London [etc.] : Pitman, 1976. — iii,115p : ill, forms ; 25cm.
ISBN 0-273-00329-1 Sd : £1.45
(B77-07967)

657 — Accounting. Information systems

Cushing, Barry E. Accounting information systems and business organizations / [by] Barry E. Cushing. — Reading, Mass. ; London [etc.] : Addison-Wesley, 1974. — x,469p : ill, forms ; 25cm.
Index.
ISBN 0-201-01263-4 : Unpriced
(B77-19491)

657 — International accounting
Rueschhoff, Norlin G. International accounting and financial reporting / [by] Norlin G. Rueschhoff. — New York [etc.] ; London : Praeger, 1976. — xi,173p : ill ; 25cm. — (Praeger special studies in international business, finance and trade)
Bibl.: p.164-167. — Index.
ISBN 0-275-23110-0 : £12.25
(B77-07968)

657′.01′51952 — Accounting. Statistical mathematics. Sampling
Vanasse, Robert W. Statistical sampling for auditing and accounting decisions : a simulation / [by] Robert W. Vanasse. — 2nd ed. — New York ; London [etc.] : McGraw-Hill, 1976. — viii,108p : ill, forms ; 28cm.
Previous ed.: New York : McGraw-Hill, 1968. — Bibl.: p.59-60.
ISBN 0-07-066851-5 Pbk : £3.65
(B77-03618)

657′.02′4332 — Accounting. *For banking*
Egginton, Don Albert. Accounting for the banker / [by] Don A. Egginton. — London ; New York : Longman, 1977. — x,272p : ill, form ; 24cm.
Includes facsimile reprints. — Index.
ISBN 0-582-45055-1 : £7.95
ISBN 0-582-45056-x Pbk : £4.50
(B77-21981)

657′.02′4658 — Accounting. *For management*
Slater, H W. Accounting for managers / [by] H.W. Slater. — Henley ([Greenlands, Henley-on-Thames, Oxon. RG9 3AU]) : Administrative Staff College, 1977. — [5], 105p(4 fold) : ill ; 31cm.
Sp : £1.50
(B77-29550)

657′.028′54044 — Accounting. Applications of digital computer systems
McRae, Thomas Watson. Computers and accounting / [by] T.W. McRae. — London [etc.] : Wiley, 1976. — xi,167p : ill, forms ; 24cm.
'A Wiley-Interscience publication'. — Bibl. — Index.
ISBN 0-471-58985-3 : £4.95
(B77-19492)

657′.042 — Accounting. *Introductions, primers*
Chahin, Mekerdich. Accounting for first examinations / [by] M. Chahin. — London : University Tutorial Press, 1977. — [6],337p : forms ; 25cm.
With answers.
ISBN 0-7231-0747-5 Pbk : £2.85
(B77-21266)

657′.044 — Accounting. *Intermediate texts*
Cashin, James A. Schaum's outline of theory and problems of intermediate accounting / by James A. Cashin, Saul Feldman and Joel J. Lerner. — New York ; London [etc.] : McGraw-Hill. — (Schaum's outline series)
1. — [1976]. — [9],306p : ill ; 28cm.
Cover title: Theory and problems of intermediate accounting. — Spine title : Intermediate accounting. — With answers. — Published in the United States: 1975. — Index.
ISBN 0-07-010202-3 Pbk : £3.75
(B77-06191)

Kieso, Donald Ervin. Intermediate accounting / [by] Donald E. Kieso, Jerry J. Weygandt. — 2nd ed. — Santa Barbara ; London [etc.] : Wiley, 1977. — xvii,1165p : ill ; 24cm.
'A Wiley/Hamilton Publication' - Text on lining papers. — Previous ed.: 1974. — Index.
ISBN 0-471-47466-5 : £11.35
(B77-18268)

657′.06′21 — Accountancy. Organisations: Association of Certified Accountants. *Directories*
Association of Certified Accountants. List of members / the Association of Certified Accountants. — London : The Association.
1977-78. — 1977. — xv,748p ; 25cm.
ISBN 0-900094-34-6 Pbk : £5.00
(B77-30416)

657′.06′241 — Accountancy. Organisations. *Great Britain. Institute of Cost and Management Accountants. Directories*
Institute of Cost and Management Accountants. List of members / Institute of Cost and Management Accountants. — [London] : [The Institute].
1976-1977, as at 1st October, 1976. — [1977]. — xvii,542p ; 25cm.
ISBN 0-901308-37-4 Pbk : £8.00
ISSN 0306-6711
(B77-09802)

657′.06′2411 — Accountancy. Organisations. *Scotland. Institute of Chartered Accounts of Scotland. Directories*
Institute of Chartered Accountants of Scotland. Official directory / Institute of Chartered Accountants of Scotland. — Edinburgh : The Institute.
1976-77 : (corrected to 8th October 1976). — [1977]. — 817p in various pagings ; 19cm.
Pbk : Unpriced
(B77-09803)

657′.06′242 — Accountancy. Organisations. *England. Institute of Chartered Accountants in England and Wales. Directories*
Institute of Chartered Accountants in England and Wales. List of members / [Institute of Chartered Accountants in England and Wales]. — London : The Institute.
1976-77 : as at 9 June, 1976 (addresses revised to 1 May, 1976). — [1976]. — xxxvii,1002p : map ; 26cm.
ISBN 0-85291-150-5 : £8.80(£4.50 to members)
(B77-01620)

657′.07′11489 — Accountants. Professional education. *Denmark. Reports, surveys*
Institute of Chartered Accountants in England and Wales. Requirements for qualification as a statsautoriseret revisor in Denmark / [Institute of Chartered Accountants in England and Wales and Foreningen af Statsautoriserede Revisorer]. — London : The Institute, 1976. — [6],20p ; 30cm.
ISBN 0-85291-170-x Sp : Unpriced
(B77-00297)

657′.076 — Accounting. *Exercises, worked examples*
Kaluza, Henry J. Accounting projects and simulations / [by] Henry J. Kaluza. — Toronto ; London [etc.] : McGraw-Hill, 1977. — iii,161p : forms ; 28cm.
Pages perforated at inside edge. — Pierced for binder. — Fill-in book. — 'The chapter numbers mentioned at the beginning of each project refer to "Accounting : A Systems Approach" by Henry Kaluza. [Toronto ; New York : McGraw-Hill Ryerson, 1976]' - Preface.
ISBN 0-07-082470-3 Pbk : £2.80
(B77-25739)

657′.07′7 — Accounting. *Programmed texts*
Anthony, Robert Newton. Essentials of accounting / [by] Robert N. Anthony ; programmed by Matthew L. Israel ; tested by Teaching Systems Corporation. — 2nd ed. — Reading, Mass. ; London [etc.] : Addison-Wesley, 1976. — v,175[i.e.176],[54]p : facsim ; 28cm.
Two-way paging. — Some pages perforated at inside edge. — Previous ed.: Reading, Mass. : Addison-Wesley, 1964.
ISBN 0-201-00252-3 Pbk : £4.95
(B77-15369)

657′.09172′4 — Accountancy. *Developing countries*
Enthoven, Adolf Jan Henri. Accounting systems in Third World economies ... / by Adolf J.H. Enthoven ; with a foreword by Jan Tinbergen. — Amsterdam [etc.] ; Oxford : North-Holland Publishing Co., 1977. — viii,359p,[5]leaves ; 25cm.
Index.
ISBN 0-7204-0721-4 : Unpriced
(B77-25740)

657′.094 — Accounting. *Europe. Comparative studies*
Price Waterhouse and Company. Accounting principles and practices in European countries / Price Waterhouse. — Revised [ed.]. — [London] ([32 London Bridge St., SE1 9SY]) : Price Waterhouse and Co., 1976. — [2],104p ; 22cm.
Cover title. — Previous ed.: 1972.
Pbk : Unpriced
(B77-10440)

657′.0941 — Accountancy. *Great Britain*
Institute of Chartered Accountants in England and Wales. You need a chartered accountant / [Institute of Chartered Accountants in England and Wales]. — New ed. — London : The Institute, 1976. — 15,[1]p ; 21cm.
Previous. ed.: published as 'See a chartered accountant'. 1968.
ISBN 0-85291-169-6 Sd : £0.15
(B77-01621)

657′.0941 — Accounting. Implications of variation in foreign exchange rates. *Great Britain. Reports, surveys*
Flower, John, *b.1934.* Accounting treatment of overseas currencies : a background study / by John Flower (in conjunction with Arthur Andersen & Co.) ; [revised by P. Raymond Hinton]. — London : Institute of Chartered Accountants in England and Wales, 1976. — ix,99p ; 30cm.
Bibl.: p.73-74.
ISBN 0-85291-161-0 Sp : £5.95
(B77-07475)

657′.09493 — Accountancy. *Belgium*
Anglo-Belgian Liaison Committee of the Institute of Chartered Accountants in England and Wales, Collège National des Experts Comptables de Belgique, Institut des Reviseurs d'Entreprises. Some of the main services provided by practising accountants in Belgium : a study / undertaken by the Anglo-Belgian Liaison Committee of the Institute of Chartered Accountants in England and Wales, Collège National des Experts Comptables de Belgique, Institut des Reviseurs d'Entreprises. — [London] : The Institute, [1976]. — [8],23p ; 30cm.
ISBN 0-85291-171-8 Sp : Unpriced
(B77-02422)

657′.0973 — Accounting. *United States*
Granof, Michael H. Financial accounting : principles and issues / [by] Michael H. Granof. — Englewood Cliffs ; London [etc.] : Prentice-Hall, 1977. — xi,643p : ill, facsims, forms ; 25cm.
Index.
ISBN 0-13-314724-x : £11.95
(B77-25052)

657′.2 — Book-keeping
Accounting 10/12. — 3rd ed. / [by] David H. Weaver ... [et al.]. — New York ; London [etc.] : McGraw-Hill, 1977. — xvi,592p : ill(some col), forms ; 24cm.
Previous ed.: / by M. Herbert Freeman and others. New York : McGraw-Hill, 1973. — Index.
ISBN 0-07-068900-8 : £7.45
(B77-22707)

Cousins, Donald. Book-keeping / [by] Donald Cousins. — 7th ed. / revised by A.G. Piper and E.C. Turner. — London : Teach Yourself Books, 1976. — vii,257p : forms ; 18cm. — (Teach yourself books)
With answers. — Previous ed.: / revised by A.G. Piper and E.C. Turner. London : English Universities Press, 1970. — Index. — Previous control number ISBN 0-340-05527-8.
Pbk : £0.75
ISBN 0-340-05527-8
(B77-21267)

Huffman, Harry. General recordkeeping. — 7th ed. / [by] Harry Huffman, Jeffrey R. Stewart, Jr. — New York ; London [etc.] : McGraw-Hill, 1976. — ix,2-536p : ill, facsims, forms, ports ; 25cm.
Previous ed.: / by Harry Huffman, Jeffrey R. Stewart and Arnold E. Schneider. New York : McGraw-Hill, 1971. — Index.
ISBN 0-07-031030-0 : £8.55
(B77-04924)

657′.3 — Companies. Consolidated accounts. *Exercises, worked examples*
Jaeger, H K. The structure of consolidated accounting / [by] H.K. Jaeger. — London [etc.] : Macmillan [for] the Institute of Cost and Management Accountants, 1976. — viii, 218p ; 23cm.
Index.
ISBN 0-333-19802-6 : £10.00
ISBN 0-333-19803-4 Pbk : £4.95
(B77-04288)

657′.3 — Companies. Price-level accounting. *Great Britain*
Inflation Accounting Steering Group. The Inflation Accounting Steering Group's background papers to the exposure draft on current cost accounting. — Croydon : Tolley ; London : Institute of Chartered Accountants in England and Wales, Publications Department, 1976. — [5],58p ; 30cm.
ISBN 0-510-49361-0 Pbk : £3.95
(B77-07476)

Inflation Accounting Steering Group. The Inflation Accounting Steering Group's guidance manual on current cost accounting, including the exposure draft / [written by David Gilbert]. — Croydon : Tolley ; London : Publications Department of the Institute of Chartered Accountants in England and Wales, 1976. — [4],278,[133]p ; 24cm.
Index.
ISBN 0-510-49349-1 Pbk : £6.25
(B77-16969)

657'.3 — Price-level accounting
Davidson, Sidney. Inflation accounting : a guide for the accountant and the financial analyst / [by] Sidney Davidson, Clyde P. Stickney, Roman L. Weil. — New York ; London [etc.] : McGraw-Hill, 1976. — ix,242p ; 24cm.
Bibl.: p.227-232. — Index.
ISBN 0-07-015478-3 : £10.40
(B77-00298)

Scapens, Robert William. Accounting in an inflationary environment / [by] Robert W. Scapens. — London [etc.] : Macmillan, 1977. — xii,163p : ill ; 23cm. — (Studies in finance and accounting)
Index.
ISBN 0-333-17790-8 : £8.95
ISBN 0-333-22626-7 Pbk : £3.95
(B77-32004)

657'.3 — Price-level accounting. *Manuals*
Cox, Bernard. Management accounting in inflationary conditions / [by] Bernard Cox, J.C.R. Hewgill. — London : Institute of Cost and Management Accountants, 1976. — xi, 177p : ill, forms ; 21cm.
Bibl.: p.157-173.
ISBN 0-901308-35-8 Pbk : £3.00
(B77-04925)

657'.3'0941 — Companies. Published accounts. *Great Britain. Reports, surveys. Serials*
Survey of published accounts : methods of financial reporting used by 300 major British industrial companies and by major property companies and investment trusts / [Institute of Chartered Accountants in England and Wales]. — London : The Institute.
1976. — 1977. — 200p ; 24cm.
Index.
ISBN 0-85291-162-9 Pbk : £6.95
ISSN 0308-1761
(B77-10842)

657'.42 — Cost accounting
Tubb, A J. Cost accounting / [by] A.J. Tubb ; editorial adviser Ronald Chappell. — London : Hodder and Stoughton, 1977. — xi,414p : ill, forms ; 18cm. — (Business & management studies) (Teach yourself books)
Bibl.: p.404. — Index.
ISBN 0-340-21904-1 Pbk : £2.95
(B77-24348)

657'.42 — Variance accounting
Laidler, Ernest. Variance accounting / [by] Ernest Laidler. — London [etc.] : Macmillan [for] the Institute of Cost and Management Accountants, 1976. — xiv,135p : ill ; 23cm.
Index.
ISBN 0-333-19608-2 : £7.95
ISBN 0-333-19609-0 Pbk : £2.95
(B77-03619)

657'.45 — Auditing
Arens, Alvin A. Auditing : an integrated approach / [by] Alvin A. Arens, James K. Loebbecke. — Englewood Cliffs ; London [etc.] : Prentice-Hall, 1976. — xv,688p : ill, forms ; 24cm.
Index.
ISBN 0-13-051698-8 : £12.80
(B77-01622)

Howard, Leslie Reginald. Auditing / [by] Leslie R. Howard. — 5th ed. — Plymouth : Macdonald and Evans, 1976. — xii,294p ; 19cm. — (The M. & E. handbook series)
Previous ed.: 1974. — Index.
ISBN 0-7121-0162-4 Pbk : £1.50
(B77-16482)

Stettler, Howard Frederic. Auditing principles / [by] Howard F. Stettler. — 4th ed. — Englewood Cliffs ; London [etc.] : Prentice-Hall, 1977. — xvii,845p : ill, forms ; 24cm.
Previous ed.: 1970. — Index.
ISBN 0-13-051706-2 : £13.55
(B77-21268)

657'.45 — Auditing. Implications of price-level accounting. *Great Britain*
Auditing Practices Committee. The audit implications of ED 18 'Current cost accounting' : a preliminary view / by the Auditing Practices Committee. — London (P.O. Box 443, Chartered Accountants' Hall, Moorgate Place, EC2P 2BJ) : The Committee, 1977. — [2],48p ; 21cm.
Sd : £1.50
(B77-14815)

657'.48 — Financial accounting
Corbett, Peter. Accounting and decision making / [by] Peter Corbett. — London : Longman. — (Understanding business)
Teachers guide. — 1977. — [2],32,[1]p ; 30cm.
Bibl.: p.2-3.
ISBN 0-582-35549-4 Sp : £0.75
(B77-15370)

657'.48'0182 — Financial accounting. Estimates. Statistical methods. Applications of digital computer systems
Newman, Maurice S. Financial accounting estimates through statistical sampling by computer / [by] Maurice S. Newman. — New York ; London [etc.] : Wiley, 1976. — xv, 247p : ill, forms ; 24cm. — (Wiley series on systems and controls for financial management)

'A Wiley-Interscience publication'. — Bibl.: p.225-226. — Index.
ISBN 0-471-01567-9 : £12.30
(B77-11934)

657'.72 — Business firms. Cash forecasting. *Programmed texts*
Construction Industry Training Board. *Building Sector.* The principles of cash forecasting : a learning guide for (non-accountant) proprietors and managers of small and medium-sized building firms to enable them to appreciate the principles used in cash forecasting / [Construction Industry Training Board Building Sector]. — [London] ([Radnor House, London Rd, SW16 4EL]) : C.I.T.B., 1976. — [7],43p(2 fold),[4]leaves of plates(3 fold) : forms ; 30cm. — (CITB training aid ; B/13)
ISBN 0-902029-26-6 Sp : £2.25
(B77-03111)

657'.73 — Companies. Assets. Valuation. *Great Britain. Manuals*
Royal Institution of Chartered Surveyors. *Assets Valuation Standards Committee.* Guidance notes on the valuation of assets / prepared by the Assets Valuation Standards Committee [of] the Royal Institution of Chartered Surveyors. — London : The Institution, 1976. — [35]p : form ; 32cm.
In binder.
ISBN 0-85406-074-x Ls : £5.00(includes supplements up to end 1977)
(B77-03620)

657'.73 — Depreciation accounting. *International standards*
International Accounting Standards Committee. International accounting standard, depreciation accounting / International Accounting Standards Committee. — London (3 St Helen's Place, EC3A 6DN) : The Committee, 1976. — [11]p ; 21cm. — (International accounting standard ; no.4)
ISBN 0-905625-01-3 Sd : £0.45
(B77-14816)

657'.75 — Research & development by companies. Accounting. *International standards. Proposals*
International Accounting Standards Committee. International accounting standard, proposed statement, accounting for research and development costs / issued for comment by the International Accounting Standards Committee. — London : Institute of Chartered Accountants in England and Wales, 1977. — [11]p ; 21cm. — (Exposure draft ; 9)
ISBN 0-905625-02-1 Sd : £0.45
(B77-14817)

657'.833 — Housing associations. Published accounts. Presentation. *Great Britain*
Housing Corporation. Recommended form of published accounts for Housing Associations / the Housing Corporation. — London (Sloane Square House, SW1W 8NT) : The Corporation, 1976. — [2],iii,41[i.e.44]p(6 fold) : forms ; 21cm.
Index.
Sd : £1.00
(B77-21982)

657'.869 — Construction industries. Accounting
Coombs, William E. Construction accounting and financial management. — 2nd ed. / [by] William E. Coombs, William J. Palmer. — New York ; London [etc.] : McGraw-Hill, 1977. — ix,558p : ill, forms, plans ; 24cm. — (McGraw-Hill series in modern structures)
Previous ed.: / by William E. Coombs. New York : F.W. Dodge Corp., 1958. — Index.
ISBN 0-07-012610-0 : £16.15
(B77-25741)

657'.95 — Companies. Accounting. *Great Britain. Proposals*
Bradbury, Farel. Accountability & company administration : MMRS : notes / [by] Farel Bradbury. — Ross-on-Wye : Hydatum ; London (P.O. Box 752, W6 0EF) : Distributed by Bradbury Controls Ltd, 1976. — [2],9p ; 25cm.
ISBN 0-905682-02-5 Sd : £1.00(£0.25 to Business Bureau full members)
(B77-05518)

657'.95 — Companies. Accounting. *Western Europe*
European financial reporting. — London : Institute of Chartered Accountants in England and Wales, Research Committee.
3 : Italy / by M.I. Stillwell. — 1976. — [13], 237p ; 30cm.
Bibl.: p.172. — Index.
ISBN 0-85291-167-x Pbk : £6.00
(B77-09119)

657'.95'0941 — Companies. Accounts. *Great Britain*
Jones, Frank Horace. Guide to company balance sheets and profit & loss accounts : for directors, secretaries, accountants, bankers, investors and students / by Frank H. Jones. — 8th ed., revised. — Bournemouth : Barkeley Book Co., 1977. — xxii,640p : facsims ; 23cm.
Previous ed.: i.e. 7th ed. Cambridge : Heffer, 1970. — Index.
ISBN 0-900132-08-6 : £8.75
(B77-15371)

658 — MANAGEMENT
The **director's** handbook / edited by George Bull. — 2nd ed. — London [etc.] : McGraw-Hill, 1977. — xxviii,773p : ill ; 26cm.
Previous ed.: New York ; Maidenhead : McGraw-Hill, 1969. — Index.
ISBN 0-07-084487-9 : £14.95 : CIP rev.
(B77-14818)

Wild, Ray. The principles of modern management / by Ray Wild, Bryan Lowes ... [et al.]. — Revised [ed.]. — London [etc.] : Holt, Rinehart and Winston, 1977. — xi,356p : ill ; 26cm.
Previous ed.: 1972. — Index. — Previous control number ISBN 0-03-910132-0.
£6.50
ISBN 0-03-910132-0
(B77-20427)

658 — Business firms. Management
Company administration handbook. — 3rd ed. — Farnborough, Hants. : Gower Press, 1977. — xxiv,738p : ill, forms, plans ; 24cm. — (A Gower Press handbook)
Previous ed.: i.e. Revised 2nd ed. 1973. — Index.
ISBN 0-566-02011-4 : £15.00
(B77-22708)

658 — Management. *Reviews of research*
Management bibliographies & reviews. — Bradford : MCB.
Vol.1 / edited by Ken Elliott. — 1975. — x, 306p : ill ; 25cm.
ISBN 0-903763-32-x : Unpriced
(B77-33313)

Vol.2 / edited by David Ashton. — [1976]. — x,294p : ill ; 25cm.
ISBN 0-905440-20-x : Unpriced
(B77-33314)

658'.002'4613 — Management. *For nursing*
Lemin, Brian. First line nursing management / [by] Brian Lemin. — Tunbridge Wells : Pitman Medical, 1977. — viii,262p : ill, facsim, forms ; 22cm.
Bibl. — Index.
ISBN 0-272-79355-8 Pbk : £3.95 : CIP rev.
(B77-16483)

658'.003 — Management. *Dictionaries*
French, Derek. Dictionary of management / [by] Derek French & Heather Saward. — London [etc.] : Pan Books, 1977. — xiii,447p ; 20cm. — (Pan reference books)
Originally published: Epping : Gower Press, 1975.
ISBN 0-330-25066-3 Pbk : £1.50
(B77-14308)

658'.003 — Management. *Encyclopaedias*
Johannsen, Hano. International dictionary of management : a practical guide / [by] Hano Johannsen, G. Terry Page. — London : Kogan Page, 1975 [i.e. 1977]. — 416p : ill, maps ; 23cm.
Originally published: 1975.
ISBN 0-85038-122-3 Pbk : £4.95
(B77-32730)

658'.003 — Management. *German-English, English-German dictionaries*
Coveney, James. Glossary of German and English management terms = Taschenwörterbuch englischer und deutscher Handelsausdrücke / by = von James Coveney and = und Christina Degens. — Harlow [etc.] : Longman, 1977. — vii,160p ; 20x9cm.
ISBN 0-582-55525-6 Pbk : £1.50
(B77-26393)

658'.005 — Management. *Periodicals*
The **specialist** (international). — Leamington Spa (2 Hamilton Terrace, Leamington Spa, Warwickshire) : Institute of Management Specialists.
Continues: The specialist.
Vol.1, paper no.4- ; Mar.-Apr. 1976-. — [1976] -. — ill ; 30cm.
Two issues a year. — [3],18p. in Vol.1, paper no.5.
Sd : £0.50(free to members)
ISSN 0308-1559
(B77-32005)

658'.007'1141 — Librarians. Post-experience training. Curriculum subjects: Management. *Great Britain. Reports, surveys*
Anderson, Ursula. Management training for librarians : report of an investigation into post-experience management training for librarians and information scientists - evaluation of courses and summary of perceived needs / by Ursula Anderson. — London : Library Association, 1977. — 82p ; 21cm. — (Library Association. Research publications ; no.18)
ISBN 0-85365-329-1 Sd : £1.50(£1.20 to members) : CIP rev.
(B77-06768)

658'.007'1141 — Universities. Business schools. *Great Britain, to 1975. Personal observations*
Wills, Gordon. Business school graffiti : a decennial transcript / by Gordon Wills. — Bradford (200 Keighley Rd, Bradford, W. Yorkshire BD9 4JZ) : MCB Books, 1976. — [7],135p : ill ; 25cm.
ISBN 0-903763-99-0 Pbk : £9.95
(B77-13736)

658'.007'1142 — Further education institutions. Curriculum subjects: Business studies. Organisations. *England. Business Education Council. Periodicals*
Business Education Council. BEC news. — London (76 Portland Place, W1N 4AA) : The Council.
No.1- ; Dec. 1976-. — [1976]-. — ports ; 30cm.

Published at irregular intervals. — Folder (6p.) as 1st issue.
Unpriced
ISSN 0309-3697
(B77-10843)

658'.007'1142 — Further education institutions. Curriculum subjects: Business studies. Organisations. *England. Business Education Council. Policies. Implementation*
Business Education Council. Initial guidelines on the implementation of policy / Business Education Council. — London (76 Portland Place, W1N 4AA) : [The Council], 1977. — [3] ,39p ; 21cm.
Sd : Unpriced
(B77-32731)

Business Education Council. Initial guidelines on the implementation of policy / Business Education Council. — London (76 Portland Place, W1N 4AA) : B.E.C., 1977. — [3],39p ; 21cm.
Sd : Unpriced
(B77-26394)

658'.007'11422 — Higher education institutions. Curriculum subjects: Management. Organisations. *England. Thames Valley. Thames Valley Regional Management Centre*
Thames Valley Regional Management Centre. A guide to the Centre and its services / Thames Valley Regional Management Centre. — [Slough] ([Office of the Dean, Slough College of Higher Education, Wellington St., Slough, Berks. SL1 1YG]) : [The Centre], [1976]. — [4] ,8,[1]p ; 22cm.
Sd : Unpriced
(B77-10441)

658'.007'11424 — Educational institutions. Curriculum subjects: Management & business studies. Courses. *England. South Midlands. Calendars*
Thames Valley Regional Management Centre. Management and business education in the Thames Valley, 1977-78 : a quick reference guide to courses, consultancy and research offered by further education colleges, universities and independent and commercial establishments in the Berkshire, Buckinghamshire & Oxfordshire regions / [Thames Valley Regional Management Centre]. — Slough (Wellington St., Slough SL1 1YG) : The Centre, [1977]. — 92p : col map ; 22cm.
ISBN 0-902805-67-3 Sd : £1.30
(B77-15946)

658'.007'11931 — Higher education institutions. Curriculum subjects: International business studies. Courses. *New Zealand. Directories*
International business education : a curriculum survey of Australia and New Zealand / edited by Michael T. Skully. — Sydney : Dryden Press ; Catterham [i.e. Caterham] (26 Manor Ave., Caterham, Surrey) : Australiana Publications, 1977. — iv,63[i.e.65]leaves : maps ; 30cm.
Index.
Sd : Unpriced
ISBN 0-909162-01-8
Primary classification 658'.007'1194
(B77-31315)

658'.007'1194 — Higher education institutions. Curriculum subjects: International business studies. Courses. *Australia. Directories*
International business education : a curriculum survey of Australia and New Zealand / edited by Michael T. Skully. — Sydney : Dryden Press ; Catterham [i.e. Caterham] (26 Manor Ave., Caterham, Surrey) : Australiana Publications, 1977. — iv,63[i.e.65]leaves : maps ; 30cm.
Index.
Sd : Unpriced
ISBN 0-909162-01-8
Also classified at 658'.007'11931
(B77-31315)

658'.007'2 — Management. Research projects: Glacier Project. *Readings*
The **Glacier** Project, concepts and critiques : selected readings on the Glacier theories of organization and management / edited by Jerry L. Gray. — New York : Crane, Russak ; London : Heinemann Educational, 1976. — xv, 452p : ill ; 24cm.
Bibl.: p.437-442. — Index.
ISBN 0-435-85280-9 : £12.00
(B77-02423)

658'.008 — Management. *Essays*
Eilon, Samuel. Aspects of management / by Samuel Eilon. — Oxford [etc.] : Pergamon, 1977. — viii,162p : ill ; 22cm. — (Omega management science) (Pergamon international library)
Bibl. — Index.
ISBN 0-08-020969-6 : £5.00
ISBN 0-08-020968-8 Pbk : Unpriced
(B77-22709)

658'.00941 — Factories. Management. *Great Britain. Manuals*
Lock, Dennis. Factory administration handbook / [by] Dennis Lock. — Epping : Gower Press, 1976. — xvi,496p : ill, forms ; 24cm. — (A Gower Press handbook)
Index.
ISBN 0-7161-0323-0 : £12.50
(B77-00299)

658'.00941 — Management. *Great Britain. Periodicals*
Anglian management review. — Romford (c/o The Editor, Asta House, High Rd, Chadwell Heath, Romford, Essex RM6 6LX) : Nelpress [for the] Anglian Regional Management Centre.

Vol.1, no.1- ; Summer 1977-. — 1977-. — ill, maps ; 22cm.
Two issues a year. — [1],39p. in 1st issue.
Sd : £0.50
ISSN 0140-0282
(B77-33316)

658'.00973 — Management. *United States*
Hodgetts, Richard Michael. Introduction to business / [by] Richard M. Hodgetts. — Reading, Mass. ; London [etc.] : Addison-Wesley, 1977. — xvi,557p : ill(some col), facsims, forms, col maps, ports ; 24cm.
Index.
ISBN 0-201-02897-2 : £11.20
(B77-24349)

658'.022 — Home-based small firms. Management. *United States. Manuals*
The **'Mother** earth news' handbook of home business ideas and plans / by the staff of the 'Mother earth news'. — Toronto [etc.] ; London : Bantam, 1976. — xi,372p : ill, forms ; 18cm.
Index.
ISBN 0-553-10155-2 Pbk : £0.85
(B77-11935)

658'.022'0941 — Small firms. Organisation. *Great Britain. Manuals*
Knightley, M. How to set up a business of your own : basic information for the man or woman starting up in business for the first time / [by] M. Knightley. — 3rd ed. — London (P.O. Box 265, N.3) : Malcolm Stewart Books Ltd, 1977. — 48p ; 22cm. — (Bee's business guides)
Previous ed.: London : Kingfisher Booksellers, 1976. — Index.
ISBN 0-904132-29-3 Sd : £0.95
(B77-25743)

Knightley, M. Your own first business : the wise way / [by] M. Knightley. — London (P.O. Box 265, N22 4UP) : Kingfisher Books, 1976. — 55p ; 25cm. — (A Kingfisher business guide)
Index.
ISBN 0-904132-27-7 Pbk : £1.50
(B77-01623)

658'.022'0973 — Small firms. Management. *United States*
Hosmer, LaRue T. The entrepreneurial function : text and cases on smaller firms / [by] LaRue T. Hosmer, Arnold C. Cooper, Karl H. Vesper. — Englewood Cliffs ; London [etc.] : Prentice-Hall, 1977. — xi,484p : ill, facsims, map, 2 plans ; 24cm.
Includes facsimile reprints.
ISBN 0-13-283093-0 : £12.75
(B77-25053)

658'.022'0973 — Small firms. Management. *United States. Manuals*
Hailes, William D. Small business management : planning and operation / [by] William D. Hailes, Jr, Raymond T. Hubbard. — New York ; London [etc.] : Van Nostrand Reinhold, 1977. — [8],240p : ill, facsims, forms ; 27cm.
Bibl.: p.230. — Index.
ISBN 0-442-23020-6 : £7.25
(B77-25744)

Macfarlane, William N. Principles of small business management / [by] William N. Macfarlane. — New York ; London [etc.] : McGraw-Hill, 1977. — ix,534p : ill, facsims, forms ; 25cm.
With answers. — Bibl.: p.524-525. — Index.
ISBN 0-07-044380-7 : £10.45
(B77-30417)

Young, Jerrald F. Decision making for small business management / [by] Jerrald F. Young. — New York ; London [etc.] : Wiley, 1977. — vii,248p : ill, facsims, forms ; 26cm.
Index.
ISBN 0-471-97938-4 : £9.35
(B77-20428)

658'.05 — Business firms. Management. Applications of data processing
Orilia, Lawrence. Business data processing systems / [by] Lawrence S. Orilia, Nancy B. Stern, Robert A. Stern. — 2nd ed. — Santa Barbara ; London [etc.] : Wiley, 1977. — xi, 404p : ill, forms ; 25cm.
'A Wiley-Hamilton publication'. — Previous ed.: in 2 vols. 1972. — Index.
ISBN 0-471-65700-x : £10.70
(B77-24350)

658'.05'4 — Business firms. Management. Applications of computer systems
Awad, Elias Michael. Introduction to computers in business / [by] Elias M. Awad. — Englewood Cliffs ; London [etc.] : Prentice-Hall, 1977. — xiii,496p : ill, forms ; 24cm.
Index.
ISBN 0-13-479378-1 : £11.15
(B77-21983)

658'.05'4044 — Management. Applications of digital computer systems
Fuori, William Michael. Introduction to the computer : the tool of business / [by] William M. Fuori. — 2nd ed. — Englewood Cliffs ; London [etc.] : Prentice-Hall, 1977. — xv, 688p : ill(chiefly col), facsims(chiefly col), forms ; 24cm.
With answers to selected exercises. — Previous ed.: 1973. — Bibl.: p.674-676. — Index.
ISBN 0-13-480103-2 : £12.75
(B77-20429)

658'.05'4044 — Small firms. Management. Applications of digital computer systems. *Manuals*
Munyan, Jack. So you're going to automate : an EDP guide to automation for small businesses / [by] Jack Munyan. — New York : Petrocelli/Charter ; London : Mason/Charter ; [Chichester] ([Unit 3, Bognor Rd, Chichester, W. Sussex]) : [Distributed by Ian Allan], 1975 [i.e. 1977]. — viii,160p : ill, forms ; 25cm.
Published in the United States: 1975. — Index.
ISBN 0-88405-317-2 : Unpriced
(B77-11936)

658'.05'4404 — Management. Applications of time-sharing computer systems
Haidinger, Timothy P. A manager's guide to computer timesharing / [by] Timothy P. Haidinger, Dana R. Richardson. — New York ; London [etc.] : Wiley, [1977]. — xv, 182p : ill ; 22cm. — (Manager's guide series)
'A Wiley-Interscinece publication'. — Published in the United States: 1975. — Bibl.: p.162-166. — Index.
ISBN 0-471-33925-3 : £8.55
(B77-10442)

658.1 — COMPANY ORGANISATION AND FINANCE

658.1'5 — Business firms. Financial management
Pritchard, Robert E. Operational financial management / [by] Robert E. Pritchard. — Englewood Cliffs ; London [etc.] : Prentice-Hall, 1977. — xii,436p : ill, facsims ; 25cm.
With answers. — Bibl.: p.419-432. — Index.
ISBN 0-13-637827-7 : £11.15
(B77-16970)

658.1'5 — Business firms. Financial management. Analysis. *United States*
Schwartzman, Sylvan D. Elements of financial analysis / [by] Sylvan D. Schwartzman, Richard E. Ball. — New York ; London [etc.] : Van Nostrand Reinhold, 1977. — x,133p ; 24cm.
Bibl.: p.86-88. — Index.
ISBN 0-442-27469-6 : £3.20
(B77-27228)

658.1'5 — Companies. Financial management
Boudreaux, Kenneth J. The basic theory of corporate finance / [by] Kenneth J. Boudreaux, Hugh W. Long. — Englewood Cliffs ; London [etc.] : Prentice-Hall, 1977. — xv,415p : ill ; 25cm.
Text, ill. on lining papers. — Bibl. — Index.
ISBN 0-13-069435-5 : £11.95
(B77-24351)

Franks, Julian Ralph. Corporate financial management / [by] Julian R. Franks and Harry H. Scholefield. — 2nd ed. — Farnborough, Hants. : Gower Press, 1977. — xii,310p : ill ; 24cm.
Previous ed.: 1974. — Bibl. — Index.
ISBN 0-566-02054-8 : £8.50 : CIP rev.
ISBN 0-566-02055-6 Pbk : £3.95
(B77-18876)

Van Horne, James Carter. Fundamentals of financial management / [by] James C. Van Horne. — 3rd ed. — Englewood Cliffs ; London [etc.] : Prentice-Hall, 1977. — ix,630p : ill, forms ; 24cm.
Previous ed.: 1974. — Bibl. — Index.
ISBN 0-13-339341-0 : £11.95
(B77-15947)

658.1'5 — Financial management
Jones, Griffith Leonard. Financial measurement for managers / [by] G.L. Jones. — London : Edward Arnold, 1976. — vii,146p : ill ; 22cm.
Index.
ISBN 0-7131-3366-x : £7.00
ISBN 0-7131-3367-8 Pbk : £3.50
(B77-10443)

Schall, Lawrence Delano. Introduction to financial management / [by] Lawrence D. Schall, Charles W. Haley. — New York ; London [etc.] : McGraw-Hill, 1977. — xv, 810p : ill ; 24cm. — (McGraw-Hill series in finance)
Bibl.: p.779-785. — Index.
ISBN 0-07-055097-2 : £12.40
(B77-22710)

Spiro, Herbert T. Finance for the nonfinancial manager / [by] Herbert T. Spiro. — New York ; London [etc.] : Wiley, 1977. — xvi, 255p : ill, facsims ; 27cm.
'A Wiley-Interscience publication'. — Index.
ISBN 0-471-01788-4 : £11.50
(B77-18877)

Van Horne, James Carter. Financial management and policy / [by] James C. Van Horne. — 4th ed. — London : Prentice-Hall, 1977. — xii, 756p : ill(chiefly col), facsims, forms ; 23cm.
Previous ed.: 1974. — Bibl. — Index.
ISBN 0-13-315796-2 Pbk : £6.50
(B77-16971)

658.1'5 — Financial management. *For company directors*
Wright, Maurice Gordon. The director's guide to accounting and finance / [by] M.G. Wright. — London [etc.] : McGraw-Hill, 1976. — xii, 199p : ill ; 24cm.
Index.
ISBN 0-07-084479-8 : £6.00
(B77-04926)

658.1'5 — Financial management. Implications of inflation
Gee, Kenneth Philip. Management planning and control in inflation / [by] Kenneth P. Gee. — London [etc.] : Macmillan, 1977. — ix,122p : ill ; 23cm.
Bibl.: p.114-118. — Index.
ISBN 0-333-22070-6 : £10.00 : CIP rev.
(B77-24352)

658.1'5'02462 — Financial management. *For engineering*
Tarquin, Anthony Joseph. Engineering economy : a behavioral approach / [by] Anthony J. Tarquin, Leland T. Blank. — New York ; London [etc.] : McGraw-Hill, 1976. — xvii, 431p : ill ; 25cm.
With answers. — Bibl. — Index.
ISBN 0-07-062934-x : £12.20
(B77-03621)

658.1'5'0973 — Companies. Financial management. *United States. Case studies*
Cases in finance / [by] David F. Scott, Jr ... [et al.]. — Englewood Cliffs ; London [etc.] : Prentice-Hall, 1977. — iii-xvii,219p : 2 ill ; 23cm.
ISBN 0-13-115337-4 Pbk : £6.35
(B77-22711)

658.1'51 — Business firms. Financial management. Forecasting
Belew, Richard C. How to negotiate a business loan / [by] Richard C. Belew. — New York ; London [etc.] : Van Nostrand Reinhold, [1976]. — xv,176p : ill, forms ; 28cm.
Originally published: as 'How to win profits and influence bankers'. 1973. — Index.
ISBN 0-442-20666-6 Pbk : £5.30
(B77-04290)

658.1'511 — Financial management. Use of accounts
Gray, Jack, *b.1931.* Accounting and management action / [by] Jack Gray, Kenneth S. Johnston. — 2nd ed. — New York ; London [etc.] : McGraw-Hill, 1977. — xviii,749p : ill ; 25cm.
Previous ed.: New York : McGraw-Hill, 1973. — Bibl.: p.739. — Index.
ISBN 0-07-024216-x : £12.70
(B77-27948)

658.1'512 — Companies. Financial statements. Analysed information. Disclosure. Requirements. *Reports, surveys*
Coopers and Lybrand Associates Limited. Analysed reporting : a research study paper / by the United Kingdom firm of Coopers & Lybrand for the Research Committee of the Institute of Chartered Accountants in England and Wales. — London : I.C.A.E.W., 1977. — 211p : 1 ill, forms ; 25cm.
Bibl.: p.75-76.
ISBN 0-85291-166-1 Pbk : Unpriced
(B77-23548)

658.1'513 — Financial management. Ratios. *Programmed texts*
Construction Industry Training Board. *Building Sector.* Financial ratios, an aid to profitability : a guide for proprietors and non-accountant managers of construction companies who produce or use information from company accounts in managing their businesses / produced by the Construction Industry Training Board, Building Sector. — [London] ([Radnor House, London Rd, SW16 4EL]) : C.I.T.B., 1977. — 109,[8]p,[2]fold leaves : ill(incl 1 col) ; 30cm. — (CITB training aid ; B/14)
'The use of financial ratios : review exercise' (12 leaves (1 fold.)) ; and, 'Supplement' ([1],6,4 leaves) as inserts. — Notebook format.
ISBN 0-902029-28-2 Sp : £4.50(£3.00 to members)
(B77-15948)

658.1'514 — Financial management. Decision making
Davies, Roger, *b.1946.* Financial decisions / [by] Roger Davies. — London : Longman. — (Understanding business)
Teachers guide. — 1976. — [2],33p ; 30cm.
With answers. — Bibl.
ISBN 0-582-35548-6 Sp : £0.75
(B77-03112)

Lynch, Richard Martin. Accounting for management : planning and control. — 2nd ed. / [by] Richard M. Lynch, Robert W. Williamson. — New York ; London [etc.] : McGraw-Hill, 1976. — xiii,509p : ill, forms ; 25cm.
With answers to selected problems. — Previous ed.: / by Richard M. Lynch. 1967. — Index.
ISBN 0-07-039217-x : £11.60
(B77-04291)

658.1'514'0973 — Companies. Financial management. Decision making. *United States*
Bierman, Harold. Decision making and planning for the corporate treasurer / [by] Harold Bierman, Jr ; with verse contributions by Florence M. Kelso. — New York ; London [etc.] : Wiley, 1977. — xi,195p : ill ; 24cm. — (Wiley series on systems and controls for financial management)
'A Wiley-Interscience Publication'. — Bibl.: p.vii. — Index.
ISBN 0-471-07238-9 : £12.40
(B77-23549)

658.1'522'0941 — Companies. Financing. *Great Britain. Manuals*
Aydon, Cyril. How to finance your company / by Cyril Aydon. — London : Business Books, 1976. — x,206p : ill ; 23cm.
Index.
ISBN 0-220-66309-2 : £6.00
(B77-29551)

658.1'5242 — Industrial equipment. Leasing. *Periodicals*
Leasing digest. — Coggeshall (7 Bridge St., Coggeshall, Essex CO6 1NP) : Hawkins Publishers Ltd.
No.1- ; Nov. 1976-. — [1976]-. — ill ; 30cm.
Monthly. — 8p. in 1st issue.
Sd : £30.00 yearly
ISSN 0309-5258
(B77-16485)

658.1'5244 — Financial management. Working capital
Firth, Michael Arthur. Management of working capital / [by] Michael Firth. — London [etc.] : Macmillan, 1976. — viii,148p : ill ; 23cm. — (Studies in finance and accounting)
Index.
ISBN 0-333-18709-1 : £7.95
ISBN 0-333-18710-5 Pbk : £3.95
(B77-03113)

658.1'527 — Capital investment by business firms. Decision making. Discounted cash flow techniques
Heukensfeldt Jansen, H P J. Project evaluation and discounted cash flow : a reassessment and an alternative suggestion / by H.P.J. Heukensfeldt Jansen. — Amsterdam [etc.] ; Oxford : North-Holland Publishing Co., 1977. — xi,208p : ill ; 23cm.
Bibl.: p.197-198. — Index.
ISBN 0-7204-0480-0 : Unpriced
(B77-25745)

658.1'527 — Capital investment. Decision making. Discounted cash flow techniques. *For surveying*
Wood, Ernest. Discounted cash flow and the surveyor / [by] E. Wood, N.D. Schofield. — Revised [ed.]. — Liverpool (Clarence St., Liverpool L3 5UG) : Department of Surveying, Liverpool Polytechnic, 1977. — 41p : ill ; 21cm.
'Transcript of a one day course held at Liverpool Polytechnic Faculty of Construction Department of Surveying 13th February, 1974. Organised by the Liverpool Polytechnic Department of Surveying in association with the Lancashire Cheshire and Isle of Man Branch of the Royal Institution of Chartered Surveyors' - p.3.
ISBN 0-905008-04-9 Sd : £1.25
(B77-26395)

658.1'527 — Capital investment. Planning. Applications of dynamic programming
Dore, M H I. Dynamic investment planning / [by] M.H.I. Dore. — London : Croom Helm, 1977. — 5-163p : ill ; 23cm.
Bibl.: p.156-160. — Index.
ISBN 0-85664-415-3 : £9.95 : CIP rev.
(B77-09120)

658.1'53 — Charities. Donations. Policies of companies. *Great Britain. Conference proceedings*
Seminar on Company Charitable Giving, *British Institute of Management, 1976.* Company charitable giving : seminar report. — Tonbridge (48 Pembury Rd, Tonbridge, Kent) : Charities Aid Foundation, [1976]. — 24p ; 22cm.
'... Seminar on Company Charitable Giving' - Opening address. — Held at the British Institute of Management, 27th May 1976.
ISBN 0-904757-03-x Sd : Unpriced
(B77-06192)

658.1'53 — Companies. Tax avoidance. *Great Britain. Manuals*
Carrell, John. Tax strategy for private companies and their shareholders / [by] John Carrell and Stanton Marcus. — Woking ([P.O. Box 3, Woking, Surrey]) : Financial Techniques, 1976. — [3],iii,170p : ill ; 21cm.
Index.
ISBN 0-903583-00-3 : £5.50
(B77-09121)

658.1'53 — Occupational superannuation schemes. Financial aspects. *Great Britain*
Tutt, Sylvia. Private pension scheme finance / by Sylvia Tutt and Leslie Tutt. — [1st ed. reprinted] ; new appendix added. — London : Stone and Cox, 1976. — xi,316p ; 23cm.
Originally published: 1971. — Index.
£5.75
(B77-18878)

658.1'53 — Partnerships. Tax avoidance. *Great Britain. Manuals*
Marcus, Stanton. Partnership taxation : a practical guide / [by] Stanton Marcus. — Woking ([P.O. Box 3], Woking, Surrey) : Financial Techniques Ltd, 1976. — [2],iv,170p : ill ; 21cm.
Index.
ISBN 0-903583-01-1 : £5.50
(B77-09122)

658.1'54 — Business firms. Financial management. Budgeting
Holland, Ron. Get out of debt and into the money / by Ron Holland. — [Westgate] ([c/o Pronate Company Services, 75 Sea Rd, Westgate, Kent]) : [The author], [1977]. — [2] leaves,i,110p : 1 ill ; 21cm.
Cover title.
Pbk : £4.00
(B77-32006)

Matthews, Lawrence Millbourne. Practical operating budgeting / [by] Lawrence M. Matthews. — New York ; London [etc.] : McGraw-Hill, 1977. — xiii,238p : ill, forms ; 24cm.
Index.
ISBN 0-07-040950-1 : £11.20
(B77-23550)

658.1'54 — Capital expenditure. Budgeting. Techniques
Wilkes, Francis Michael. Capital budgeting techniques / [by] F.M. Wilkes. — London [etc.] : Wiley, 1977. — xiv,424p : ill ; 24cm.
'A Wiley-Interscience publication'. — Bibl. — Index.
ISBN 0-471-99416-2 : £13.00
(B77-14819)

658.1'54 — Financial management. Budgeting
McAlpine, Thomas Somerville. The basic arts of budgeting / [by] T.S. McAlpine. — London : Business Books, 1976. — xiv,223p : ill, forms ; 22cm.
Index.
ISBN 0-220-66269-x : £6.00
(B77-09804)

658.1'552 — Buildings. Construction. Cost planning. *Great Britain*
Junior Organisation Quantity Surveyors. *Standing Committee.* An introduction to cost planning / the Royal Institution of Chartered Surveyors (Junior Organisation Quantity Surveyors Standing Committee). — London : R.I.C.S., 1976. — [2],v,103p : 2 ill ; 30cm.
Bibl.
ISBN 0-85406-077-4 Pbk : £4.00
(B77-09805)

658.1'552 — Buildings. Construction. Costing
Seeley, Ivor Hugh. Building economics : appraisal and control of building design cost and efficiency / by Ivor H. Seeley. — 2nd ed. — London [etc.] : Macmillan, 1976. — xiv, 332p : ill, plans ; 27cm.
Previous ed.: 1972. — Index.
ISBN 0-333-19869-7 : £7.95
(B77-09806)

658.1'552 — Catering industries. Costs. Control. *Manuals*
Kotas, Richard. Food cost control / [by] Richard Kotas and Bernard Davis. — Revised ed. — London : International Textbook Co., 1976. — vii,152p : ill ; 23cm.
Previous ed.: Aylesbury : Intertext, 1973. — Index.
ISBN 0-7002-0271-4 : £4.50
(B77-07477)

Paige, Grace. Catering costs and control / [by] Grace Paige. — London : Cassell, 1977. — 222p : ill, forms ; 22cm.
ISBN 0-304-29758-5 Pbk : £4.95
(B77-32007)

658.1'552 — Hospitals. Costs. Reduction by reduction in length of stay of in-patients. *England*
Hurst, J W. Saving hospital expenditure by reducing in-patient stay / [by] J.W. Hurst. — London : H.M.S.O., 1977. — iii,14p : ill ; 30cm. — (Government Economic Service occasional papers ; 14)
Bibl.: p.12.
ISBN 0-11-630290-9 Sd : £2.50
(B77-13737)

658.1'552 — Industries. Costs. Control. *Manuals*
Gittus, John Frederick. Croner's guide to cost control / by J.F. Gittus. — New Malden (46 Coombe Rd, New Malden, Surrey KT3 4QL) : Croner Publications Ltd, 1976. — [1],vi,155 leaves ; 23cm.
One leaf printed on both sides. — In binder. — Originally published: 1974.
Ls : £6.50
ISBN 0-900319-14-3
(B77-16486)

658.1'552 — Plastics mouldings industries. Costing. *Great Britain*
British plastics Federation. Key factors for costing and extimating in plastics moulding for 1977 / [British Plastics Federation]. — London : The Federation, 1977. — [6],35p : form ; 30cm.
ISBN 0-900213-45-0 Sp : £8.00(£5.00 to members of the Federation)
(B77-15949)

658.1'552 — Printing industries. Small firms. Costing. *Great Britain. Manuals*
British Printing Industries Federation. Costing for the smaller printing business / British Printing Industries Federation. — London (11 Bedford Row, WC1R 4DX) : The Federation, 1976. — 28p : forms ; 21cm.
ISBN 0-85168-105-0 Sd : £2.00
(B77-09123)

658.1'552 — Social surveys. Costing. *Great Britain*
Levens, G E. The use of survey research : organisations and the costing of survey research. — 1975 [revised] ed. / by G.E. Levens. — London (Regent House, Fifth floor, 89 Kingsway, W.C.2) : Social Science Research Council, Survey Unit, [1976]. — [1],iii leaves,44p : 2 ill ; 30cm. — (Occasional papers in survey research ; 1)
Previous ed.: / by Donald Monk. 1972.
ISBN 0-900296-60-7 Pbk : £0.50
(B77-04927)

658.1'552'0182 — Industries. Costs. Analysis. Statistical methods
Dean, Joel. Statistical cost estimation / [by] Joel Dean. — Bloomington ; London : Indiana University Press, 1976. — xi,499p : ill ; 25cm.
Index.
ISBN 0-253-35445-5 : £15.00
(B77-23551)

658.1'552'03 — Industries. Costs. Control. *Encyclopaedias*
Higgins, Lindley R. Cost reduction from A to Z / [by] Lindley R. Higgins, Ruth W. Stidger. — New York ; London [etc.] : McGraw-Hill, 1976. — [4],507p : ill ; 25cm.
Index.
ISBN 0-07-028765-1 : £16.90
(B77-22712)

658.1'553 — Buildings. Costs. Management
Great Britain. *Department of Industry.* The management of physical resources : buildings and services / [produced by the Department of Industry in collaboration with the Building Terotechnology Group and the Property Services Agency of the Department of Industry, Committee for Terotechnology [and the] National Terotechnology Centre. — London (Industrial Technology Secretariat, Room 539, Abell House, John Islip St., SW1P 4LN) : [The Committee] ; [Leatherhead] : [The Centre], 1977. — [2],12p : ill(incl 2 col) ; 30cm. — (Building aspects of terotechnology ; 1)
Sd : Unpriced
(B77-27949)

658.1'553 — Catering services. Food. Costs. Control. *Programmed texts*
Riley, Michael. Understanding food cost control : a programmed approach / [by] Michael Riley. — London : Edward Arnold, 1976. — 167p : forms ; 12x19cm.
Notebook format. — Two-way paging. — With answers. — Index.
ISBN 0-7131-0085-0 Sp : £2.25
(B77-10444)

658.1'553 — Engineering equipment. Financial management. Use of accounts
Committee for Terotechnology. Management accounting / Department of Industry, Committee for Terotechnology [and] National Terotechnology Centre. — London (Industrial Technology Secretariat, Room 539, Abell House, John Islip St., SW1P 4LN) : [The Committee] ; [Leatherhead] : [The Centre], 1976. — [2],10p : 2 col ill, col form ; 30cm. — (Management aspects of terotechnology ; 2)
Sd : Unpriced
(B77-27950)

658.1'553 — Industries. Personnel-related costs. Control
Brearley, Arthur. The control of staff-related overhead / [by] Arthur Brearley. — London [etc.] : Macmillan, 1976. — ix,181p ; 22cm.
Bibl.: p.171-176. — Index.
ISBN 0-333-18593-5 : £10.00
(B77-09807)

658.1'553 — Materials handling. Costs. Control. *Great Britain. Reports, surveys*
Materials-handling costs : a new look at manufacture : report of a pilot study into the costs of storage and materials handling in manufacturing (engineering) industries / Department of Industry, Committee for Materials Handling (Management and Technology), Working party on materials-handling costs. — London : H.M.S.O., 1976. — iv,59p : ill, plans ; 25cm.
ISBN 0-11-511745-8 Sd : £2.10
(B77-01624)

658.1'554 — Construction industries. Applications of value engineering
O'Brien, James Jerome. Value analysis in design and construction / [by] James J. O'Brien. — New York ; London [etc.] : McGraw-Hill, 1976. — xiii,301p : ill, facsims, forms, maps ; 24cm.
Index.
ISBN 0-07-047566-0 : £13.70
(B77-06769)

658.1'554 — Industrial buildings. Heating systems. Hot pipes. Thermal insulation. Cost effectiveness

Great Britain. *Department of Energy.* The economic thickness of insulation for hot pipes / [Department of Energy]. — [London] ([Library, Thames House South, Millbank SW1P 4QJ]) : The Department, [1977]. — [1],40p : ill ; 21cm. — (Fuel efficiency booklet ; 8)
ISBN 0-904552-18-7 Sd : Unpriced
(B77-15950)

658.1'5904 — Small firms. Financial management

Price, A St J. Profit from figures : financial control for small businesses / [by] A. St J. Price. — York (28 Blossom St., York YO2 2AJ) : Lynxplan (Sheffield) Ltd, 1976. — [93] p : ill ; 30cm.
ISBN 0-905859-01-4 Sp : £15.00
(B77-08457)

658.1'5932 — World Health Organization. Financial management

Hoole, Francis W. Politics and budgeting in the World Health Organization / by Francis W. Hoole. — Bloomington ; London : Indiana University Press, 1976. — xiii,226p : ill ; 24cm. — (Indiana University. International Development Research Center. Studies in development ; no.11)
Bibl.: p.201-222. — Index.
ISBN 0-253-39611-5 : £7.50
(B77-13738)

658.1'5933 — Financial institutions. Financial management. *United States*

Hempel, George H. Financial management of financial institutions / [by] George H. Hempel, Jess B. Yawitz. — Englewood Cliffs ; London [etc.] : Prentice-Hall, 1977. — xxiii,263p : ill ; 24cm. — (Prentice-Hall foundations of finance series)
Bibl. — Index.
ISBN 0-13-315978-7 : Unpriced
ISBN 0-13-315960-4 Pbk : £7.15
(B77-18269)

658.1'5934 — Solicitorship. Private practice. Financial management. *England. Manuals*

Porter, David S. Profitable management of a solicitor's practice / [by] David S. Porter. — London : Oyez Publishing, 1976. — xii,127p : ill, forms ; 22cm.
Index.
ISBN 0-85120-303-5 Pbk : £3.25
(B77-10844)

658.1'5937 — Hotel industries & catering industries. Financial management

Kotas, Richard. Management accounting for hotels and restaurants : a revenue accounting approach / [by] Richard Kotas. — London : Surrey University Press : [Distributed by] International Textbook Company, 1977. — vii, 271p : ill, forms ; 24cm.
Index.
ISBN 0-903384-17-5 : £7.25
(B77-09808)

658.1'596 — Engineering industries. Financial management

Riggs, James Lear. Engineering economics / [by] James L. Riggs. — New York ; London [etc.] : McGraw-Hill, 1977. — xix,617p : ill, forms, map ; 25cm. — (McGraw-Hill series in industrial engineering and management science)
Bibl.: p.581-582. — Index.
ISBN 0-07-052860-8 : £14.60
(B77-23552)

Thuesen, Holger George. Engineering economy / [by] H.G. Thuesen, W.J. Fabrycky, G.J. Thuesen. — 5th ed. — Englewood Cliffs ; London [etc.] : Prentice-Hall, 1977. — xv, 589p : ill ; 24cm. — (Prentice-Hall international series in industrial and systems engineering)
Previous ed.: 1971. — Bibl.: p.578-580. — Index.
ISBN 0-13-277491-7 : £13.55
(B77-16487)

658.1'5963 — Crop production industries. Financial management

Rae, Allan N. Crop management economics / [by] Allan N. Rae. — London : Crosby Lockwood Staples, 1977. — xii,525p : ill ; 24cm.
Bibl.: p.505-515. — Index.
ISBN 0-258-97013-8 : £12.50
(B77-15951)

658.2 — PLANT MANAGEMENT

658.2'02 — Container handling industries. *Great Britain. Containerbase Federation Limited. Container handling equipment. Planned maintenance*

Committee for Terotechnology. Planned maintenance improves Containerbase efficiency / Department of Industry, Committee for Terotechnology. — London (Industrial Technology Secretariat, Room 539, Abell House, John Islip St., SW1P 4LN) : [The Committee], 1975. — [2],15p : 1 ill ; 30cm. — (Terotechnology case history ; no.5 ISSN 0306-7777)
Sd : Unpriced
(B77-27951)

658.2'02 — Industries. Maintenance. Management

Heintzelman, John E. The complete handbook of maintenance management / [by] John E. Heintzelman. — Englewood Cliffs ; London [etc.] : Prentice-Hall, 1976. — 335p : ill, forms ; 29cm.
Index.
ISBN 0-13-160994-7 : £19.95
(B77-21269)

Husband, Thomas Mutrie. Maintenance management and terotechnology / [by] T.M. Husband. — Farnborough : Saxon House, 1976. — xii,167,[1]p : ill ; 24cm.
Bibl.: p.157-163. — Index.
ISBN 0-566-00146-2 : £8.25
(B77-01625)

658.2'02 — Mining industries. Planned maintenance. *Great Britain. Case studies*

Kelly, Anthony, *b.1939.* A study of plant availability / [by Anthony Kelly] ; [for the] Department of Industry, Committee for Terotechnology. — London (Industrial Technology Secretariat, Room 539, Abell House, John Islip St., SW1P 4LN) : [Department of Industry, Committee for Terotechnology], 1975. — [2],23a[1]p : ill ; 30cm. — (Terotechnology case history ; no.4 ISSN 0306-7777)
Sd : Unpriced
(B77-27952)

658.2'02 — Ships. Planned maintenance

Shields, S. Ship maintenance : a quantitative approach / [by] S. Shields, K.J. Sparshott, E.A. Cameron. — London (76 Mark La., EC3R 7JN) : Marine Media Management Ltd for the Institute of Marine Engineers, [1977]. — [5], 157p : ill, forms ; 22cm.
ISBN 0-900976-51-9 Pbk : £5.75
(B77-13739)

658.2'02 — Terotechnology

Joint Advisory Committee for the Industrial Technologies. Guidelines on terotechnology ; and, Terotechnology 'A' / produced by the Joint Advisory Committee for the Industrial Technologies of the Technician Education Council and the Industrial Technologies Education & Training Committee of the Department of Industry. — London (Room 539, Abell House, John Islip St., SW1P 4LN) : Industrial Technology Secretariat, 1977. — [4], 3,[1],4p ; 30cm.
Sd : Unpriced
(B77-33914)

658.2'02'0141 — Terotechnology. Communication

Great Britain. *Department of Industry.* Technical communication / [produced by the Department of Industry and the Society of Technical Presentation and Communication] ; [for the] Department of Industry, Committee for Terotechnology [and the] National Terotechnology Centre. — London (Industrial Technology Secretariat, Room 539, Abell House, John Islip St., SW1P 4LN) : [The Committee] ; [Leatherhead] : [The Centre], 1976. — [2],16p : col ill ; 30cm. — (Communication aspects of terotechnology ; 1)
Sd : Unpriced
(B77-27953)

658.2'02'0184 — Preventive maintenance. Mathematical models

Gertsbakh, I B. Models of preventive maintenance / [by] I.B. Gertsbakh ; [translated from the Russian]. — Amsterdam [etc.] ; Oxford : North-Holland Publishing Co., 1977. — xiv,257p : ill ; 23cm. — (Studies in mathematical and managerial economics ; vol.23)
Translation of: 'Modeli profilaktiki'. Moscow : Sov. Radio, 1969. — Bibl.: p.249-252. — Index.
ISBN 0-7204-0465-7 : £21.25
(B77-07478)

658.2'1'0973 — Business firms. Location. Planning. Effects of telecommunication systems. *United States*

The **telecommunications-transportation** tradeoff : options for tomorrow / by Jack M. Nilles and ... [others]. — New York ; London [etc.] : Wiley, 1976. — xi,196p : ill, forms, maps ; 24cm.
'A Wiley-Interscience Publication'. — Bibl. — Index.
ISBN 0-471-01507-5 : £17.50
(B77-03622)

658.2'6 — Fuel. Consumption by industries. Reduction. *Great Britain. Manuals*

Questions and answers on cutting fuel costs / [by] W. Short ... [et al.]. — London : Graham and Trotman, 1975. — [7],104p : ill ; 21cm.
Index.
ISBN 0-86010-019-7 Sp : £4.95
(B77-04292)

658.2'6 — Industries. Energy. Conservation. Management. *Great Britain. Manuals*

Payne, Gordon A. The energy managers' handbook / [by] Gordon A. Payne. — Guildford : IPC Science and Technology Press, 1977. — x,147p : ill, forms ; 22cm.
Bibl.: p.135-141. — Index.
ISBN 0-902852-73-6 : £7.50 : CIP rev.
ISBN 0-902852-59-0 Pbk : £4.75
(B77-07969)

658.2'6 — Industries. Energy. Conservation. Policies of governments. *International Energy Agency countries. Reports, surveys. Serials*

International Energy Agency. Energy conservation in the International Energy Agency : review. — Paris : Organisation for Economic Co-operation and Development ; [London] : [H.M.S.O.].
1976. — 1976. — 55p(2 fold) ; 24cm.
Pbk : £2.70
ISBN 92-64-11554-4
(B77-00839)

658.3 — PERSONNEL MANAGEMENT

Beach, Dale Stuart. Personnel : the management of people at work / [by] Dale S. Beach. — 3rd ed. — New York : Macmillan ; London : Collier Macmillan, 1975. — xvi,811p : ill, forms ; 24cm.
Previous ed.: 1970. — Bibl. — Index.
ISBN 0-02-979940-6 Pbk : £6.30
(B77-29552)

Flippo, Edwin Bly. Principles of personnel management / [by] Edwin B. Flippo. — 4th ed. — New York ; London [etc.] : McGraw-Hill, 1976. — xvi,592p : ill ; 25cm. — (McGraw-Hill series in management)
Previous ed.: 1971. — Bibl. — Index.
ISBN 0-07-021316-x : £11.60
(B77-04293)

Industrial Society. A guide to employment practices / the Industrial Society. — Revised [ed.]. — London : Industrial Society, 1974. — [4],25p ; 21cm. — (Notes for managers ; no.8)
Previous ed.: i.e. New ed., 1969.
ISBN 0-85290-096-1 Sd : £0.50
(B77-18879)

Ingalls, John D. Human energy : the critical factor for individuals and organizations / [by] John D. Ingalls. — Reading, Mass. ; London [etc.] : Addison-Wesley, 1976. — xviii,285p : ill, form ; 25cm.
Bibl.: p.271-277. — Index.
ISBN 0-201-03202-3 : £11.90
(B77-16972)

Miner, John Burnham. Personnel and industrial relations : a managerial approach. — 3rd ed. / [by] John B. Miner, Mary Green Miner. — New York : Macmillan ; London : Collier Macmillan, 1977. — x,613p : ill, forms ; 24cm.
Previous ed.: 1974. — Bibl. — Index.
ISBN 0-02-381660-0 Pbk : £6.30
(B77-21984)

Pigors, Paul. Personnel administration : a point of view and a method / [by] Paul Pigors, Charles A. Myers. — 8th ed. — Tokyo ; London [etc.] : McGraw-Hill, 1977. — xiii, 546p : ill, forms ; 24cm.
Previous ed.: New York ; London : McGraw-Hill, 1973. — Bibl. — Index.
ISBN 0-07-050001-0 Pbk : £6.85
(B77-21985)

Sayles, Leonard Robert. Managing human resources / [by] Leonard R. Sayles, George Strauss. — Englewood Cliffs ; London [etc.] : Prentice-Hall, 1977. — xv,528p : ill, forms ; 24cm.
Ill. on lining papers. — Index.
ISBN 0-13-550442-2 : £11.15
(B77-16973)

Sikula, Andrew Frank. Personnel management : a short course for professionals / [by] Andrew F. Sikula. — New York ; London [etc.] : Wiley, 1977. — Case : ill ; 27x22x5cm. — (Wiley professional development programs)
Ten booklets. — With answers.
ISBN 0-471-01931-3 : £21.00
(B77-30418)

Thomason, George Frederick. A textbook of personnel management / [by] George F. Thomason. — Revised ed. — London : Institute of Personnel Management, 1976. — 534p : ill, forms ; 23cm.
Previous ed.: 1975. — Bibl.: p.495-524. — Index.
ISBN 0-85292-140-3 : £5.50
ISBN 0-85292-139-x Pbk : £3.95
(B77-00840)

658.3 — Multinational companies. Personnel management
Desatnick, R L. Human resource management in the multinational company / [by] R.L. Desatnick & M.L. Bennett ; edited by Raymond Maddison. — Farnborough, Hants. : Gower Press, 1977. — xii,411p : ill, forms ; 23cm.
Index.
ISBN 0-566-02003-3 : £12.50
(B77-31317)

658.3 — Personnel management. *Manuals*
Armstrong, Michael, *b.1928.* A handbook of personnel management practice / [by] Michael Armstrong. — London : Kogan Page, 1977. — 408p : ill, forms ; 23cm.
Index.
ISBN 0-85038-111-8 : £12.00
ISBN 0-85038-082-0 Pbk : £6.95
(B77-29553)

658.3'001'9 — Organisations. Personnel. Behaviour. Management aspects. *Case studies & readings*
Critical incidents in organizational behavior and administration : with selected readings / [edited by] Francis J. Bridges, James E. Chapman. — Englewood Cliffs ; London [etc.] : Prentice-Hall, 1977. — v,282p : ill, forms ; 28cm.
Pages perforated at inside edge. — Bibl.
ISBN 0-13-193896-7 Pbk : £7.95
(B77-26396)

658.3'001'9 — Personnel management. Applications of transactional analysis. *Manuals*
Albano, Charles. TA on the job / [by] Charles Albano. — New York [etc.] ; London : Harper and Row, 1976. — 89p : ill ; 18cm. — (Perennial library)
'... originally appeared as a series of four articles in "Supervisory Management", January-April, 1974' - title page verso. — Bibl.: p.27.
ISBN 0-06-080385-1 Pbk : £0.95
(B77-33317)

James, Muriel. The OK boss / [by] Muriel James. — Reading, Mass. ; London [etc.] : Addison-Wesley, [1976]. — xii,163p : ill(chiefly col) ; 23cm.
Published in the United States: 1975.
ISBN 0-201-03272-4 : £4.75
(B77-06770)

658.3'001'9 — Personnel management. Psychological factors. *Readings*
Readings in managerial psychology / edited by Harold J. Leavitt and Louis R. Pondy. — 2nd ed. — Chicago ; London : University of Chicago Press, 1973. — xii,787p : ill ; 24cm.
Previous ed.: 1964.
ISBN 0-226-46984-0 : Unpriced
(B77-19493)

658.3'007'22 — Personnel management. *Case studies*
Chilver, Joseph. The human aspects of management : a case study approach / by Joseph Chilver. — Oxford [etc.] : Pergamon, 1976. — xiv,103p ; 22cm. — (Pergamon international library)
ISBN 0-08-021048-1 : £4.50
ISBN 0-08-021047-3 Pbk : £2.25
(B77-05519)

658.3'008 — Personnel management. *Readings*
Policy issues in contemporary personnel and industrial relations / [edited by] Mary Green Miner, John B. Miner. — New York : Macmillan ; London : Collier Macmillan, 1977. — xi,580p : ill ; 24cm.
Bibl.
ISBN 0-02-381640-6 Pbk : £10.50
(B77-23553)

658.3'00941 — Industries. Personnel management. *Great Britain. Manuals*
Boyce-Martin, Jane. Personnel management / [by] Jane Boyce-Martin. — Plymouth : Macdonald and Evans, 1977. — xiii,98p : ill, forms ; 22cm. — (Essentials of management)
Bibl. — Index.
ISBN 0-7121-0563-8 Pbk : £1.50
(B77-33318)

658.3'00941 — Personnel management. *Great Britain*
Betts, Peter Wilfred. Staff management / [by] P.W. Betts. — Plymouth : Macdonald and Evans, 1977. — viii,152p : ill, forms ; 22cm. — (Essentials of management)
Index.
ISBN 0-7121-1954-x Pbk : £1.50
(B77-29554)

658.3'00941 — Personnel management. *Great Britain. Yearbooks*
Personnel and training management yearbook and directory. — London : Kogan Page.
1977 / edited by G. Terry Page with Michael Armstrong. — 1976. — 480p : ill, maps ; 23cm.
Index.
ISBN 0-85038-451-6 : £10.00
ISSN 0306-6673
Also classified at 658.31'24'0941
(B77-05520)

658.3'00954 — Personnel management. *India (Republic)*
Davar, Rustom S. Personnel management and industrial relations in India / [by] Rustom S. Davar. — Delhi [etc.] : Vikas ; Hemel Hempstead (66 Wood Lane End, Hemel Hempstead, Herts.) : Distributed by International Book Distributors Ltd, 1976. — xvi,369p,[2]fold leaves of plates : ill, forms ; 22cm.
Index.
ISBN 0-7069-0392-7 : Unpriced
(B77-16974)

658.3'00973 — Personnel management. *United States. Manuals*
Harris, Orville Jeff. How to manage people at work : a short course for professionals / [by] O. Jeff Harris, Jr. — New York ; London [etc.] : Wiley, 1977. — Case : ill ; 27cm. — (Wiley professional development programs)
Twelve booklets. — With answers. — Text on case.
ISBN 0-471-01930-5 : £22.00
(B77-27229)

658.3'02 — Management. Supervision
Bittel, Lester Robert. Improving supervisory performance / [by] Lester R. Bittel. — New York ; London [etc.] : McGraw-Hill, 1976. — xi,404p : ill, forms ; 25cm.
Bibl. — Index.
ISBN 0-07-005451-7 : £7.35
(B77-00300)

658.3'02 — Management. Supervision. *Manuals*
Bittel, Lester Robert. What every supervisor should know / [by] Lester R. Bittel ; cartoons by Al Ross. — 3rd ed. — New York ; London [etc.] : McGraw-Hill, 1974. — xi,722p : ill, forms ; 24cm.
Previous ed.: 1968. — Bibl. — Index.
ISBN 0-07-005460-6 : Unpriced
(B77-19494)

Broadwell, Martin Mason. The practice of supervising : making experience pay / [by] Martin M. Broadwell ; cartoons by Johnny Sajem. — Reading [Mass.] ; London [etc.] : Addison-Wesley, 1977. — [6],169p : ill ; 21cm.
Index.
ISBN 0-201-00789-4 Pbk : £5.20
(B77-17616)

658.3'06 — Data processing services. Personnel. Job analysis
Hansen, Peter. Job descriptions in data processing / by P. Hansen. — Manchester : NCC Publications, 1977. — 205p in various pagings : ill ; 30cm.
Pierced for binder. — Bibl.: p.205.
ISBN 0-85012-171-x Ls : £9.00 : CIP rev.
(B77-17617)

658.3'06 — Medicine. District nursing. Job evaluation. *Scotland. Reports, surveys*
McIntosh, Jean B. Work study of district nursing staff / [by] Jean B. McIntosh, I.M. Richardson. — [Edinburgh] ([New St Andrew's House, St James Centre, Edinburgh EH1 3TF]) : Scottish Home and Health Department, 1976. — iii,26p : 1 ill, form ; 30cm. — (Scottish Health Service studies ; no.37)
Bibl.: p.25.
Sd : £0.70
(B77-12559)

658.3'06'0941 — Job evaluation. *Great Britain*
Great Britain. *Advisory, Conciliation and Arbitration Service.* Job evaluation / Advisory, Conciliation and Arbitration aService. — London (Cleland House, Page St., SW1P 4ND) : The Service, [1975]. — [2],12p ; 21cm. — (ACAS guide ; no.1 ISSN 0309-7153)
Bibl.: p.12.
Sd : Unpriced
(B77-15952)

658.31'1 — Personnel. Recruitment & selection. *Manuals*
Agrell, Tina. Recruitment techniques : for modern managers / [by] Tina Agrell. — Wellingborough : Thorsons, 1977. — 127p : ill, form ; 23cm. — ([Business success series])
Bibl.: p.123. — Index.
ISBN 0-7225-0371-7 : £2.95
(B77-23554)

Courtis, John. Cost effective recruitment / [by] John Courtis. — London : Institute of Personnel Management, 1976. — 91p ; 21cm.
ISBN 0-85292-136-5 Pbk : £0.95
(B77-00841)

658.31'11 — Great Britain. Local Government Staff Commission for England, to 1976. *Reports, surveys*
Great Britain. *Local Government Staff Commission for England.* The report of the Local Government Staff Commission for England. — London : H.M.S.O., 1977. — v, 160p : 1 ill, forms ; 25cm.
ISBN 0-11-751138-2 Pbk : £1.00
(B77-29555)

658.31'12 — Coloured personnel. Selection. *Great Britain. Manuals*
Pearn, M A. Selecting and training coloured workers / [by] M.A. Pearn. — London : H.M.S.O., 1977. — [3],46p : ill ; 21cm. — (Training information paper ; 9)
Bibl.: p.44.
ISBN 0-11-885601-4 Sd : £1.00
Also classified at 658.31'24
(B77-21986)

658.31'12 — Personnel. Selection. Applications of psychological tests. *Great Britain. Reports, surveys*
Sneath, Frank. Testing people at work / [by] Frank Sneath, Manab Thakur and Bruce Medjuck. — London : Institute of Personnel Management, 1976. — [5],105p : forms ; 30cm. — (Institute of Personnel Management. Information reports : new series ; 24)
ISBN 0-85292-137-3 Pbk : £5.00
(B77-13126)

658.31'12 — Personnel. Selection. Interviewing. *Manuals*
Rogers, Jean L. Fair employment interviewing / [by] Jean L. Rogers, Walter L. Fortson. — Reading, Mass. ; London [etc.] : Addison-Wesley, [1977]. — vii,152p : forms ; 22cm.
Published in the United States: 1976.
ISBN 0-201-06469-3 Pbk : £4.80
(B77-10845)

658.31'24 — Coloured personnel. Industrial training. *Great Britain. Manuals*
Pearn, M A. Selecting and training coloured workers / [by] M.A. Pearn. — London : H.M.S.O., 1977. — [3],46p : ill ; 21cm. — (Training information paper ; 9)
Bibl.: p.44.
ISBN 0-11-885601-4 Sd : £1.00
Primary classification 658.31'12
(B77-21986)

658.31'24 — Industrial training. Cost-benefit analysis
Hall, Nigel. Cost-benefit analysis in industrial training / [by] Nigel Hall. — [Manchester] : Department of Adult Education, University of Manchester, 1976. — vi,76p : ill ; 21cm. — (Manchester monographs ; 6 ISSN 0305-4152)
ISBN 0-903717-11-5 Pbk : £1.90
(B77-04294)

658.31'24 — Iron & steel industries. Personnel. Training. *Great Britain. Periodicals*
Iron and steel training. — London (4 Little Essex St., WC2R 3LH) : Iron and Steel Industry Training Board.
'... replaces the Iron and Steel Industry Training Board's Information Bulletins'.
No.1- ; June 1977-. — 1977-. — ill, ports ; 42cm.
Folder (4p.) as 1st issue.
Sd : Unpriced
ISSN 0309-7536
(B77-27954)

658.31'24 — Personnel. Training. Applications of behaviour analysis
Rackham, Neil. Behaviour analysis in training / [by] Neil Rackham and Terry Morgan. — London [etc.] : McGraw-Hill, 1977. — xiv, 327p : ill, forms ; 24cm.
Bibl.: p.314-315. — Index.
ISBN 0-07-084480-1 : £8.25
(B77-14820)

658.31'24 — Ports. Personnel. Training. Courses. *Great Britain. Serials*
National Ports Council. Training schemes for the port transport industry / [National Ports Council]. — London : The Council.
1977. — [1977]. — 21p ; 21cm.
ISBN 0-86073-000-x Sd : Unpriced
(B77-15953)

658.31'24 — Small firms. Personnel. Training. *Manuals*
Paper and Paper Products Industry Training Board. Training in small establishments : practical guide to planning your training, with special emphasis on managers, supervisors and specialist staff / [Paper and Paper Products Industry Training Board]. — Potters Bar (Star House, Potters Bar, Herts EN6 2PG) : The Board, [1976]. — [2],8p : forms ; 30cm.
Booklet ([8]p.) (forms) ; 8 fold. sheets ([16] sides) (forms) in pocket.
ISBN 0-902929-13-5 Sd : Unpriced
(B77-02424)

658.31'2404 — Industrial training. Decision making. Use of CRAMP system. *Great Britain. Manuals*
Industrial Training Research Unit. CRAMP : a guide to training decisions : a user's manual / [Industrial Training Research Unit] ; [written by Michael Pearn]. — Revised ed. — Cambridge (32 Trumpington St., Cambridge) : The Unit, 1977. — [3],43p,[2]fold leaves of plates : ill ; 24cm. — (Industrial Training Research Unit. Publications ; TR1) (Industrial Training Research Unit. Research papers ; TR1)
Previous ed.: 1972. — Bibl.
Sd : Unpriced
(B77-27955)

658.31'2404 — Industrial training. Programmes. Design. Use of CRAMP system. *Great Britain. Study examples: London Transport*
Industrial Training Research Unit. Using the CRAMP system to design a training programme : a study at London Transport / [Industrial Training Research Unit]. — Cambridge (32 Trumpington St., Cambridge) : ITRU, (University College London), 1977. — [4],31p,fold plate : ill ; 24cm. — (Industrial Training Research Unit. Research papers ; TR8)
ISBN 0-905308-04-2 Sd : £2.50
(B77-14821)

658.31'2404 — Printing & publishing industries. Industrial training officers. Industrial training. *Great Britain. Proposals*
Printing and Publishing Industry Training Board. Training of trainers / Printing and Publishing Industry Training Board. — Revised [ed.]. — London (Merit House, Edgware Rd, NW9 5AG) : P.P.I.T.B., 1976. — [2],8,[1]p ; 30cm. — (Training recommendation ; 5)
Previous ed.: 1972.
ISBN 0-7032-0031-3 Sd : £0.75
(B77-00301)

658.31'24'0941 — Industrial training. Management aspects. *Great Britain. Case studies*
Case studies for practical training / edited by Richard Ayres. — London : British Association for Commercial and Industrial Education, 1977. — 143p : ill ; 25cm.
Index.
ISBN 0-85171-064-6 Pbk : Unpriced
(B77-21270)

658.31'24'0941 — Industrial training. Management aspects. *Great Britain. Yearbooks*
Personnel and training management yearbook and directory. — London : Kogan Page.
1977 / edited by G. Terry Page with Michael Armstrong. — 1976. — 480p : ill, maps ; 23cm.

Index.
ISBN 0-85038-451-6 : £10.00
ISSN 0306-6673
Primary classification 658.3'00941
(B77-05520)

658.31'24'0941 — Personnel. Training. *Great Britain*
Johnson, Ron. Meeting needs - training in context / by Ron Johnson. — London : Association of Colleges for Further and Higher Education, [1977]. — [1],11,[1]p ; 21cm.
Address delivered at the Annual General Meeting of the Association of Colleges for Further and Higher Education held on Thursday and Friday, 24th and 25th February 1977, at the Institution of Electrical Engineers, Savoy Place, London W.C.2.
Sd : £0.50
(B77-27956)

658.31'242'094254 — School leavers. First employment. Induction training. *Leicestershire. Reports, surveys*
Keil, E T. The induction of school-leavers into work in Leicestershire / by E.T. Keil. — [Leicester] : [Leicestershire Committee for Education and Industry], 1976. — 283p in various pagings : forms ; 30cm.
Cover title: Becoming a worker.
Sp : Unpriced
Also classified at 373.1'4'25094254
(B77-27957)

658.31'244 — Chemical industries. Safety measures. Industrial training. *Great Britain. Manuals*
British Chemical Industry Safety Council. Safety training : a guide for the chemical industry / British Chemical Industry Safety Council of the Chemical Industries Association Limited. — London (93 Albert Embankment, SE1 7TU) : The Council, 1972. — [3],17p : form ; 30cm.
Bibl.: p.15-17.
Sd : £0.10
(B77-07479)

658.31'244 — Motor vehicle repair industries. Safety measures. Industrial training. *Great Britain. Manuals*
Road Transport Industry Training Board. Basic safety training in motor vehicle workshops, stores and forecourts / [Road Transport Industry Training Board]. — Revised [ed.]. — Wembley (Capitol House, Empire Way, Wembley, Middx) : The Board, 1975. — 64p : ill ; 30cm.
Previous ed.: published as 'Basic safety training in vehicle repair premises'. 1971. — Bibl.: p.62-63. — List of films: p.64.
Sd : Unpriced
(B77-17618)

658.31'25 — Nurses. Appraisal. *Great Britain. Reports, surveys*
Jones, Deborah. Nursing staff appraisal in the Health Service : a study of the system : final report to the National Staff Committee for Nurses and Midwives, April 1976 / [by] Deborah Jones, Anne Rogers. — [London] ([76 Mortimer St., W1N 7DE]) : Polytechnic of Central London, [1975]. — xi[i.e.xiii],58[i.e.62] p,14p of plates : ill, forms ; 30cm. — (PCL research)
Cover title. — Bibl.: p.38-39.
ISBN 0-905526-01-5 Pbk : Unpriced
(B77-03623)

658.31'25 — Personnel. Performance. Appraisal. *Manuals*
Universal Training Systems Company. How to review and evaluate employee performance : new appraisal techniques for better motivation / prepared by the staff of Universal Training Systems Company. — Chicago [etc.] ; London : Dartnell ; [Epsom] : [Distributed by Leviathan House], 1976. — [5],251p(4 fold) : ill, forms ; 30cm. — (A Dartnell management guide)
In binder. — Tab-indexed.
ISBN 0-85013-073-5 Ls : £38.50
(B77-16975)

658.31'4 — Personnel. Motivation. Management
Hersey, Paul. Management of organizational behavior : utilizing human resources / [by] Paul Hersey, Kenneth H. Blanchard. — 3rd ed. — Englewood Cliffs ; London [etc.] : Prentice-Hall, 1977. — xvii,360p : ill ; 24cm.
Previous ed.: 1972. — Bibl.: p.325-351. — Index.
ISBN 0-13-548875-3 : £9.55
ISBN 0-13-548867-2 Pbk : £5.55
(B77-24353)

Todes, Jay L. Management and motivation : an introduction to supervision / [by] Jay L. Todes, John McKinney, Wendell Ferguson, Jr. — New York [etc.] ; London : Harper and Row, 1977. — x,444p : ill, form, map ; 24cm.
Index.
ISBN 0-06-046636-7 : £8.95
(B77-32008)

658.31'4 — Personnel. Productivity. Role of job satisfaction. *United States*
People and productivity / [edited by] Robert A. Sutermeister. — 3rd ed. — New York [etc.] ; London : McGraw-Hill, 1976. — xvii,475p : ill ; 24cm. — (McGraw-Hill series in management)
Previous ed.: 1969. — Bibl.: p.109-113. — Index.
ISBN 0-07-062367-8 : £9.10
ISBN 0-07-062371-6 Pbk : £6.60
(B77-05521)

658.31'4 — Personnel. Self-actualisation. *Manuals*
Sperry, Len. You can make it happen : a guide to self-actualization and organizational change / [by] Len Sperry, Douglas J. Mickelson, Phillip L. Hunsaker. — Reading, Mass. ; London [etc.] : Addison-Wesley, 1977. — xiv,210p ; 21cm.
Bibl.: p.206-208. — Index.
ISBN 0-201-07129-0 Pbk : £5.60
(B77-24354)

658.31'4'0941 — Personnel. Discipline. *Great Britain. Manuals*
Great Britain. *Advisory, Conciliation and Arbitration Service.* Disciplinary practice and procedures in employment / [prepared by the] Advisory, Conciliation and Arbitration Service [and the Central Office of Information]. — London : H.M.S.O., 1977. — [2],5,[1]p ; 21cm. — (Code of practice ; 1 ISSN 0140-007x)
ISBN 0-11-885000-8 Sd : £0.15
(B77-19495)

658.31'42 — Industries. Productivity. Effects of improvement of working conditions of personnel. Management aspects
Cummings, Thomas G. Improving productivity and the quality of work life / [by] Thomas G. Cummings, Edmund S. Molloy. — New York ; London : Praeger, 1977. — xvii,307p : ill ; 24cm. — (Praeger special studies in US economic, social and political issues)
Bibl.: p.292-305.
ISBN 0-275-56870-9 : Unpriced
ISBN 0-03-022601-5 Pbk : £5.25
(B77-33915)

Glaser, Edward M. Productivity gains through worklife improvements [i.e. improvement] / [by] Edward M. Glaser. — New York ; London : Harcourt Brace Jovanovich, [1977]. — x,342p : ill, forms ; 22cm.
Published in the United States: 1976. — Bibl.: p.327-335. — Index.
ISBN 0-15-800095-1 : £10.95
(B77-11937)

658.31'42 — Personnel. Job satisfaction
Humanising the workplace : new proposals and perspectives / edited by Richard N. Ottaway. — London : Croom Helm, 1977. — 175p : ill ; 23cm.
Bibl. — Index.
ISBN 0-85664-345-9 : £7.95 : CIP rev.
(B77-11295)

658.31'42 — Personnel. Job satisfaction. *Great Britain. Readings*
Job satisfaction : challenge and response in modern Britain / edited by Mary Weir. — [London] : Fontana, 1976. — 288p : ill ; 18cm. — (The modern Britain series)
Bibl. — Index.
ISBN 0-00-633541-1 Pbk : £1.75
(B77-00302)

658.31'42 — Personnel. Job satisfaction. Surveys. *Organisation for Economic Co-operation and Development countries. Critical studies*
Barbash, Jack. Job satisfaction attitudes surveys / by Jack Barbash. — Paris : Organisation for Economic Co-operation and Development : [H.M.S.O.], 1976. — 36p ; 24cm. — (Organisation for Economic Co-operation and Development. OECD Industrial Relations Programme special studies)
Bibl.: p.34-36.
Pbk : £0.90
ISBN 92-64-11537-4
(B77-01626)

658.3'142 — Personnel. Status. *Great Britain*
Institute of Personnel Management. *National Committee on Payment and Employment Conditions.* Staff status for all / ... prepared by the Institute of Personnel Management's National Committee on Payment and Employment Conditions. — London : The Institute, 1977. — [4],70p ; 30cm.
ISBN 0-85292-150-0 Pbk : £6.50
(B77-26397)

658.31'45 — Companies. Managers. Communication with personnel. *Great Britain. Manuals*
Confederation of British Industry. Communication with people at work / [Confederation of British Industry]. — London : C.B.I., 1977. — [1],32p : 2 ill ; 22cm.
Sd : £1.00
(B77-30421)

658.31'45 — Companies. Performance. Communication between managers & personnel. *Great Britain. Manuals*
Stuart, John, *b.1924.* Explaining the financial facts / [by] John Stuart and Jenny Davenport. — London : Industrial Society, 1976. — [4], 40p : ill ; 21cm.
ISBN 0-85290-132-1 Sd : £1.00
(B77-00303)

658.31'5 — Companies. Financial statements. Disclosure to personnel. *Great Britain. Reports, surveys*
Goodlad, John Brian. Disclosure of financial information to employees : a general survey of the current practice of six large UK organisations / [by] J.B. Goodlad. — London : Institute of Cost and Management Accountants, 1976. — 45p ; 21cm.
ISBN 0-901308-36-6 Pbk : £1.25
(B77-05522)

658.31'5 — Company information. Disclosure to personnel. *Great Britain. Reports, surveys*
Arthur Young Management Services. Sharing the facts : current law and practice on disclosure of information / prepared by Arthur Young Management Services. — London (Moor House, London Wall, EC2Y 5HP) : [Arthur Young Management Services], 1976. — 74 leaves in various pagings ; 31cm.
Sp : Unpriced
(B77-16976)

Norkett, P. Disclosure of information to employees : a summary of research results sent to questionnaire respondents / [by] P. Norkett. — [Enfield] ([Queensway, Enfield, Middx]) : Middlesex Polytechnic, 1976. — [2],26,[5] leaves : form ; 30cm.
'Business Studies and Management. Research Summary'.
ISBN 0-904804-01-1 Sp : Unpriced
(B77-21271)

658.31'52 — Higher education institutions. Libraries. Management. Participation of personnel. *United States*
Marchant, Maurice P. Participative management in academic libraries / [by] Maurice P. Marchant. — Westport, Conn. ; London : Greenwood Press, 1976. — xix,260p : ill ; 22cm. — (Contributions in librarianship and information science ; no.16)
Bibl.: p.247-251. — Index.
ISBN 0-8371-8935-7 : £13.95
(B77-31318)

658.31'52 — Small firms. Management. Control by personnel. *Study examples: Computer services*
Hill, Mike. Proposal for a self-managed computing firm / [by] Mike Hill. — Brighton : Smoothie Publications, 1976. — [2],15p ; 30cm. — (Alternative technology)
Bibl.: p.15.
ISBN 0-903612-39-9 Sd : £1.00
(B77-02425)

658.31'52'094 — Industries. Management. Participation of personnel. *Europe*
Carby-Hall, Joseph Roger. Worker participation in Europe / [by] J.R. Carby-Hall. — London : Croom Helm [etc.], 1977. — 5-271p ; 23cm.
Index.
ISBN 0-85664-337-8 : £9.95 : CIP rev
(B77-18270)

658.31'52'094 — Industries. Management. Participation of personnel. *Western Europe, 1976. Reports, surveys*
Harrison, Roger, *b.1949.* Workers' participation in Western Europe, 1976 / [by] Roger Harrison. — London : Institute of Personnel Management, 1976. — 89p ; 30cm.
Bibl.: p.85-87.
ISBN 0-85292-144-6 Pbk : £5.00
(B77-04295)

658.31'52'094 — Industries. Management. Participation of personnel. *Western Europe, ca 1960-1976*
Worker self-management in industry : the West European experience / edited by G. David Garson. — New York ; London : Praeger, 1977. — vii,231p : ill ; 25cm. — (Praeger special studies in international business, finance and trade)
Bibl.: p.146-151.
ISBN 0-03-022406-3 : £13.40
(B77-31319)

658.31'52'0941 — Companies. Management. Participation of personnel. *Great Britain. Proposals*
Chiplin, Brian. Can workers manage? : post-Bullock essays in the economics of the inter-relationships between ownership, control and risk-taking in industry, with special reference to participation by employees / [by] Brian Chiplin and John Coyne, Ljubo Sirc ... [et al.]. — London : Institute of Economic Affairs, 1977. — 109p ; 22cm. — (Hobart paper ; 77 ISSN 0073-2818)
Bibl.: 108-109.
ISBN 0-255-36103-3 Pbk : £1.50
(B77-33916)

658.31'52'0941 — Industries. Management. Participation of personnel. *Great Britain*
Wall, Toby. Worker participation : a critique of the literature and some fresh evidence / [by] Toby D. Wall and Joseph A. Lischeron. — London [etc.] : McGraw-Hill, 1977. — ix, 162p ; 23cm.
Bibl.: p.154-160. — Index.
ISBN 0-07-084071-7 Pbk : £4.50
(B77-15954)

658.31'52'0941 — Industries. Management. Participation of personnel. *Great Britain. Proposals*
British Institute of Management. Employee participation : the way ahead : incorporating a guide to participative practice / British Institute of Management. — [London] : B.I.M., [1977]. — [1],v,10p ; 21cm.
Sd : £1.00
(B77-33917)

658.31'52'0941 — Industries. Management. Participation of personnel. *Great Britain, to 1976. Liberal Party viewpoints*
Smith, Cyril, *b.1928.* Industrial participation / [by] Cyril Smith. — London [etc.] : McGraw-Hill, 1977. — viii,174p : 1 ill ; 24cm.
Index.
ISBN 0-07-084496-8 : £5.50 : CIP rev.
(B77-15372)

658.31'52'09497 — Industries. Management. Participation of personnel. *Study regions: Yugoslavia. Readings*
Vanek, Jaroslav. The labor-managed economy : essays / by Jaroslav Vanek. — Ithaca ; London : Cornell University Press, 1977. — 288p : ill ; 23cm.
Bibl. — Index.
ISBN 0-8014-0955-1 : £12.50
(B77-28729)

658.31'53 — Trade unions. Disclosure of financial information: Disclosure by employers
Foley, B J. Accounting information disclosure and collective bargaining / [by] B.J. Foley and K.T. Maunders. — London [etc.] : Macmillan, 1977. — x,210p : ill ; 23cm.
Bibl. — Index.
ISBN 0-333-16693-0 : £10.00
(B77-21987)

658.31'53 — Trade unions. Disclosure of information: Disclosure by employers. *Great Britain. Codes of conduct*
Great Britain. *Advisory, Conciliation and Arbitration Service.* Disclosure of information to trade unions for collective bargaining purposes / [prepared by the Advisory, Conciliation and Arbitration Service and the Central Office of Information]. — [London] : H.M.S.O., 1977. — [2],6p ; 21cm. — (Code of practice ; 2)
ISBN 0-11-885001-6 Sd : £0.15
(B77-21272)

658.31'54 — Collective bargaining. Negotiation. Simulation games. *Collections*
Sisson, Keith. Negotiating in practice : role-playing for managers and shop stewards / by Keith Sisson. — London : Institute of Personnel Management, 1977. — [7],127p ; 30cm.
ISBN 0-85292-153-5 Sp : £6.00
(B77-32009)

658.32 — Remuneration. Management aspects
McBeath, Gordon. Salary administration / [by] G. McBeath and D.N. Rands. — 3rd ed. — London : Business Books, 1976. — ix,374p : ill, forms ; 23cm.
Previous ed.: 1969. — Index.
ISBN 0-220-66285-1 : Unpriced
(B77-32010)

658.32'0973 — Remuneration. Management aspects. *United States*
Patten, Thomas Henry. Pay : employee compensation and incentive plans / [by] Thomas H. Patten, Jr. — New York : Free Press ; London : Collier Macmillan, 1977. — xv,607p : ill, forms ; 24cm.
Bibl.: p.597-600. — Index.
ISBN 0-02-924920-1 : £12.00
(B77-21988)

658.32'22 — Solicitors. Remuneration. Costing. *England*
The **expense** of time. — 2nd ed. — [London] : [Law Society], [1976]. — [1],17p ; 21cm.
Previous ed.: 1972.
ISBN 0-901064-73-4 Sd : £0.50
(B77-12560)

658.32'53 — Superannuation schemes. Trusteeship. *England. Manuals*
Metropolitan Pensions Association Limited. Pension scheme trusteeship / Metropolitan Pensions Association Limited. — Croydon (Prudential House, Wellesley Rd, Croydon CR0 2AD) : National Association of Pension Funds, 1976. — [2],29p ; 21cm. — (Notes on pensions ; no.2 ISSN 0309-006x)
Originally published: as 'The pension scheme trustee'. London : Metropolitan Pensions Association Ltd, 1975.
ISBN 0-905796-01-2 Sd : £1.25
(B77-01627)

658.3'7'64794 — Hotel industries. Personnel management. *Manuals*
Magurn, J Philip. A manual of staff management in the hotel and catering industry / [by] J. Philip Magurn. — London : Heinemann, 1977. — xiv,336p : ill, forms, map ; 22cm.
Bibl. — Index.
ISBN 0-434-91198-4 Pbk : £4.90
Also classified at 658.3'7'64795
(B77-30422)

658.3'7'64795 — Catering industries. Personnel management. *Manuals*
Magurn, J Philip. A manual of staff management in the hotel and catering industry / [by] J. Philip Magurn. — London : Heinemann, 1977. — xiv,336p : ill, forms, map ; 22cm.
Bibl. — Index.
ISBN 0-434-91198-4 Pbk : £4.90
Primary classification 658.3'7'64794
(B77-30422)

658.38 — Lead mining industries. *Great Britain. London Lead Company. Welfare services, 1692-1905*
Raistrick, Arthur. Two centuries of industrial welfare : the London (Quaker) Lead Company, 1692-1905 : the social policy and work of the 'Governor and Company for Smelting down Lead with Pit Coal and Sea Coal', mainly in Alston Moor and the Pennines / by Arthur Raistrick. — Revised 2nd ed. — Buxton (The Market Place, Hartington, Buxton, Derbyshire SK17 0AL) : Moorland Publishing Co., 1977. — 168p,[8]p of plates : ill, facsim, geneal tables, maps, plan ; 22cm.
Previous ed.: i.e. 1st ed. London : 'Journal of the Friends Historical Society', 1938. — Bibl.: p.16. — Index.
ISBN 0-903485-13-3 : £3.95
(B77-30423)

658.38'2 — Chemical industries. Emergencies. *Manuals. For management*
British Chemical Industry Safety Council. Recommended procedures for handling major emergencies / British Chemicals Industry Safety Council of the Chemical Industries Association Limited. — London (93 Albert Embankment, SE1 7TU) : The Council, 1974. — [2],16p : 2 ill ; 20cm.
Originally published: 1970.
ISBN 0-900623-16-0 Sd : £0.50
(B77-04296)

658.38'2 — Industrial safety. Management aspects
Petersen, Dan. Techniques of safety management / [by] Dan Petersen. — New York ; London [etc.] : McGraw-Hill, 1971. — xv,250p : ill, facsims, forms, plan ; 24cm.
Bibl. — Index.
ISBN 0-07-049595-5 : £15.00
(B77-20430)

658.38'2'0941 — Industrial health & industrial safety. Management aspects. *Great Britain. For iron & steel industries*
Iron and Steel Industry Training Board. Management of health and safety / Iron and Steel Industry Training Board. — London (4 Little Essex St., WC2R 3LH) : The Training Board, [1976]. — [2],16,[1]p : ill(incl 1 col) ; 21cm.
Thumb indexed.
Sd : Unpriced
(B77-16977)

Iron and Steel Industry Training Board. Management of health and safety - training of management / Iron and Steel Industry Training Board. — London (4 Little Essex St., WC2R 3LH) : The Training Board, [1976]. — [2],40, [1]p : 2 col ill, forms ; 30cm.
Thumb indexed.
Sd : Unpriced
(B77-16978)

658.38'5'0941 — Personnel. Counselling. *Great Britain. Conference proceedings*
Counselling at work : papers presented by a working party of the Standing Conference for the Advancement of Counselling / edited by A.G. Watts. — London : Bedford Square Press, 1977. — 92p ; 23cm.
Bibl.: p.91-92.
ISBN 0-7199-0925-2 : £2.95
ISBN 0-7199-0924-4 Pbk : £1.75
(B77-21273)

658.4 — EXECUTIVE MANAGEMENT
658.4 — Business firms. Management. *Manuals*
Cron, Rodney L. Survival and success in a shrinking economy / [by] Rodney L. Cron. — New York ; London [etc.] : Van Nostrand Reinhold, 1976. — ix,326p : ill, forms ; 24cm.
Index.
ISBN 0-442-21756-0 : £11.95
(B77-19496)

658.4 — Business firms. Management. Techniques
Glueck, William F. Business policy : strategy formation and management action / [by] William F. Glueck [et al.]. — 2nd ed. — New York ; London [etc.] : McGraw-Hill, 1976. — viii,687p : ill, facsims, maps, plan, port ; 25cm. — (McGraw-Hill series in management)
Previous ed.: 1972. — Bibl.
ISBN 0-07-023514-7 : £12.40
(B77-04297)

658.4 — Industries. Management. Leadership. *Great Britain*
Prior, Peter J. Leadership is not a bowler hat / [by] Peter J. Prior. — Newton Abbot [etc.] : David and Charles, 1977. — 64p : ill, facsim, ports ; 23cm.
ISBN 0-7153-7487-7 : £1.95
(B77-30424)

658.4 — Management. Applications of behavioural sciences
Boot, R L. Behavioural sciences for managers / [by] R.L. Boot, A.G. Cowling and M.J.K. Stanworth. — London : Edward Arnold, 1977. — viii,232p : ill ; 23cm.
Index.
ISBN 0-7131-3382-1 : £10.00 : CIP rev.
ISBN 0-7131-3383-x Pbk : £4.95
(B77-29556)

658.4 — Management by objectives
Morrisey, George Lewis. Management by objectives and results / [by] George L. Morrisey. — Reading, Mass. ; London [etc.] : Addison-Wesley, [1977]. — xii,164p : ill, forms ; 21cm.
Originally published: Reading, Mass. : Addison-Wesley, 1970. — Bibl.: p.146-148.
ISBN 0-201-04837-x Pbk : Unpriced
(B77-12561)

Morrisey, George Lewis. Management by objectives and results for business and industry / [by] George L. Morrisey. — 2nd ed. — Reading, Mass. ; London [etc.] : Addison-Wesley, 1977. — iii-xviii,252p : ill, forms ; 21cm.
Previous ed.: published as 'Management by objectives and results'. Reading, Mass. : Addison-Wesley, 1970. — Bibl.: p.222-230.
ISBN 0-201-04906-6 Pbk : £5.20
(B77-21989)

658.4 — Management. Cultural aspects. *Readings*
Culture and management : selected readings / edited by Theodore D. Weinshall. — Harmondsworth [etc.] : Penguin, 1977. — 447p : ill ; 19cm. — (Penguin education) (Penguin modern management readings)
Bibl. — Index.
ISBN 0-14-080923-6 Pbk : £1.75
(B77-17619)

658.4 — Management. Forecasting
Firth, Michael Arthur. Forecasting methods in business and management / [by] Michael Firth. — London : Edward Arnold, 1977. — xi,264p : ill ; 23cm.
Bibl. — Index.
ISBN 0-7131-3371-6 : £8.00
ISBN 0-7131-3372-4 Pbk : £4.95
(B77-14822)

Wheelwright, Steven Charles. Forecasting methods for management / [by] Steven C. Wheelwright, Spyros Makridakis. — 2nd ed. — New York ; London [etc.] : Wiley, 1977. — xvii,266p : ill ; 24cm. — (Wiley series on systems and controls for financial management)
'A Wiley-Interscience Publication'. — Previous ed.: 1973. — Bibl. — Index.
ISBN 0-471-02225-x : £13.35
(B77-17620)

658.4 — Management. Leadership. *Manuals*
Fiore, Michael V. How to develop dynamic leadership : a short course for professionals / [by] Michael V. Fiore, Paul S. Strauss. — New York ; London [etc.] : Wiley, 1977. — Case : ill ; 27x22x5cm. — (Wiley professional development programs)
Six booklets.
ISBN 0-471-02314-0 : £19.75
(B77-32732)

658.4 — Management. Quantitative methods
Godfrey, Arthur. Quantitative methods for managers / [by] Arthur Godfrey. — London : Edward Arnold, 1977. — viii,265p : ill ; 23cm.
Index.
ISBN 0-7131-3348-1 : £8.00
ISBN 0-7131-3349-x Pbk : £4.95
(B77-24355)

658.4 — Management. Techniques
Deverell, Cyril Spencer. Management techniques in administration and finance : aids to decision-making / by C.S. Deverell. — London : Gee and Co., 1976. — 328p : ill ; 22cm. — (A Gee's study book)
Bibl.: p.323-324. — Index.
ISBN 0-85258-154-8 Pbk : £3.95
(B77-06193)

Falk, *Sir* Roger. The business of management : art or craft? / [by] Roger Falk. — 5th ed. — Harmondsworth [etc.] : Penguin, 1976. — 265p ; 18cm. — (Pelican books)
Previous ed.: 1970. — Index.
Pbk : £0.85
ISBN 0-14-020528-4
(B77-27958)

Gruber, William H. The new management : line executive and staff professional in the future firm / [by] William H. Gruber, John S. Niles. — New York ; London [etc.] : McGraw-Hill, 1976. — xiv,242p : ill ; 24cm.
Index.
ISBN 0-07-025073-1 : £10.75
(B77-04298)

Koontz, Harold. Essentials of management / [by] Harold Koontz, Cyril O'Donnell. — New York ; London [etc.] : McGraw-Hill, 1974. — xi,482p : ill ; 23cm.
Index.
ISBN 0-07-035371-9 Pbk : Unpriced
(B77-19497)

Koontz, Harold. Management : a systems and contingency analysis of managerial functions / [by] Harold Koontz, Cyril O'Donnell. — 6th ed. — New York ; London [etc.] : McGraw-Hill, 1976. — xv,824p : col ill ; 25cm. — (McGraw-Hill series in management)
Previous ed.: published as 'Principles of management'. 1972. — Index.
ISBN 0-07-035356-5 : £11.60
(B77-04299)

Koontz, Harold. Management : a systems and contingency analysis of managerial functions / [by] Harold Koontz & Cyril J. O'Donnell. — 6th ed. — New York ; London [etc.] : McGraw-Hill. — (McGraw-Hill series in management)
Previous ed.: published as 'Principles of management'. New York : McGraw-Hill, 1972.
Study guide / [by] John Halff. — 1976. — [2], 325,[11]p : ill ; 26cm.
With answers.
ISBN 0-07-035358-1 Pbk : £4.10
(B77-04289)

Massie, Joseph Logan. Managing : a contemporary introduction / [by] Joseph L. Massie, John Douglas. — 2nd ed. — Englewood Cliffs ; London [etc.] : Prentice-Hall, 1977. — xix,554p : col ill ; 24cm.
Previous ed.: 1973. — Index.
ISBN 0-13-548545-2 : £11.95
(B77-17621)

Newman, William Herman. The process of management : concepts, behavior, and practice / [by] William H. Newman, E. Kirby Warren. — 4th ed. — Englewood Cliffs ; London [etc.] : Prentice-Hall, 1977. — xv, 670p : ill(some col) ; 24cm.
Previous ed.: 1972. — Bibl. — Index.
ISBN 0-13-723429-5 : £11.95
(B77-16488)

658.4 — Management. Techniques. *Manuals*
Finch, Frederic E. Managing for organizational effectiveness : an experiential approach / [by] Frederic E. Finch, Halsey R. Jones, Joseph A. Litterer. — New York ; London [etc.] : McGraw-Hill, [1977]. — xiii,282p : ill, forms, plan ; 28cm. — (McGraw-Hill series in management)
Published in the United States: 1976. — Bibl.
ISBN 0-07-020899-9 Pbk : £7.45
(B77-11938)

Luthans, Fred. Organizational behavior / [by] Fred Luthans. — 2nd ed. — New York ; London [etc.] : McGraw-Hill, 1977. — xviii, 588p : ill, form ; 25cm. — (McGraw-Hill series in management)
Previous ed.: 1973. — Bibl. — Index.
ISBN 0-07-039130-0 : £11.20
(B77-27230)

Merry, Uri. Developing teams and organizations : a practical handbook for managers and consultants / [by] Uri Merry, Melvin E. Allerhand. — Reading, Mass. ; London [etc.] : Addison-Wesley, 1977. — x, 422p : ill, forms ; 25cm.
Index.
ISBN 0-201-04531-1 : £13.60
(B77-25746)

658.4 — Management. Theories
Child, John. Organization : a guide to problems and practice / [by] John Child. — London [etc.] : Harper and Row, 1977. — 243p : ill ; 22cm.
Bibl.: p.236-240. — Index.
ISBN 0-06-318040-5 : £4.95 : CIP rev.
ISBN 0-06-318036-7 Pbk : £2.95
(B77-07970)

Thierauf, Robert James. Management principles and practices : a contingency and questionnaire approach / [by] Robert J. Thierauf, Robert C. Klekamp, Daniel W. Geeding. — Santa Barbara ; London [etc.] : Wiley, 1977. — xv, 819p : ill, forms ; 25cm. — (Wiley/Hamilton series in management and administration)
'A Wiley/Hamilton publication'. — Index.
ISBN 0-471-29504-3 : £11.25
(B77-23556)

658.4 — Management. Time factors
Mackenzie, R Alec. The time trap / [by] R. Alec Mackenzie. — New York [etc.] ; London : McGraw-Hill, 1975 [i.e. 1976]. — xi,195p : ill, forms ; 21cm.
Published in the United States: 1975. — Originally published: New York : AMACOM, 1972. — Index.
ISBN 0-07-044650-4 Pbk : £2.45
(B77-01628)

Webber, Ross Arkell. Time and management / [by] Ross A. Webber. — New York ; London [etc.] : Van Nostrand Reinhold, [1977]. — xi, 167p : ill ; 23cm. — (Frontiers in management series)
Originally published: 1972. — Index.
ISBN 0-442-29236-8 Pbk : £5.65
(B77-28732)

658.4 — Managers. Leadership. Self-appraisal. *Programmed texts*
Fiedler, Fred Edward. Improving leadership effectiveness : the leader match concept / [by] Fred E. Fiedler, Martin M. Chemers with Linda Mahar. — New York ; London [etc.] : Wiley, 1976. — viii,229p : ill ; 26cm. — (Self-teaching guides)
Bibl.: p.215. — Index.
ISBN 0-471-25811-3 Pbk : £5.30
(B77-02426)

658.4 — Organisations. Design. Management
Prescriptive models of organizations / edited by Paul C. Mystrom and William H. Starbuck. — Amsterdam [etc.] ; Oxford : North-Holland Publishing Co., 1977. — [5],189p : ill ; 24cm. — (North-Holland/TIMS studies in the management sciences ; vol.5)
Bibl.
ISBN 0-7204-0573-4 Pbk : Unpriced
(B77-28733)

658.4 — Organisations. Design. Management. *Conference proceedings*
The **management** of organization design / edited by Ralph H. Kilmann, Louis R. Pondy, Dennis P. Slevin. — New York ; Oxford [etc.] : North-Holland Publishing Co.
In 2 vols. — '... papers ... originally presented at a conference on organization design held at the University of Pittsburgh in October of 1974' - Preface.
Vol.1 : Research and methodology. — 1976. — xiii,312p : ill, plan ; 24cm.
Bibl. — Index.
ISBN 0-7204-8609-2 : £14.05
(B77-16979)

658.4 — Organisations. Management
Hicks, Herbert Gosa. The management of organizations. — 3rd ed. / [by] Herbert G. Hicks, C. Ray Gullett. — New York ; London [etc.] : McGraw-Hill, [1977]. — xxi,602p : ill ; 25cm. — (McGraw-Hill series in management)
This ed. published in the United States: 1976. — Previous ed.: / by Herbert G. Hicks. New York : Maidenhead : McGraw-Hill, 1972. — Bibl. — Index.
ISBN 0-07-028721-x : £11.60
(B77-11939)

Roy, Robert Hall. The cultures of management / [by] Robert H. Roy. — Baltimore ; London : Johns Hopkins University Press, 1977. — xvi, 431,[1]p : ill, forms ; 26cm.
Index.
ISBN 0-8018-1875-3 : £14.95
(B77-24356)

658.4 — Organisations. Social conflict. Management
Likert, Rensis. New ways of managing conflict / [by] Rensis Likert, Jane Gibson Likert. — New York [etc.] ; London : McGraw-Hill, 1976. — vii,375p : ill ; 24cm.
Bibl.: p.347-363. — Index.
ISBN 0-07-037842-8 : £12.05
(B77-03624)

658.4'001'9 — Executive management. Psychological aspects
Fox, Joseph M. Executive qualities / [by] Joseph M. Fox. — Reading, Mass. ; London [etc.] : Addison-Wesley, 1976. — xiv,256p : ill ; 23cm.
Pbk : £6.40
ISBN 0-201-02437-0
(B77-16980)

658.4'001'9 — Organisations. Management. Transactional analysis
Jongeward, Dorothy. Everybody wins : transactional analysis applied to organizations / [by] Dorothy Jongeward and contributors. — Revised ed. — Reading, Mass. ; London [etc.] : Addison-Wesley, 1976. — viii,326p : ill ; 25cm.
Previous ed.: i.e. 1st ed., Reading, Mass. : Addison-Wesley, 1973. — Bibl.: p.318-319. — List of audiovisuals: p.317.
ISBN 0-201-03271-6 : £7.70
(B77-14309)

658.4'002'07 — Management. Theories. *Humorous texts*
Martin, Thomas L. Malice in blunderland / by Thomas L. Martin, Jr. — New York ; London [etc.] : McGraw-Hill, [1976]. — xi,143p : 1 ill ; 24cm.
Published in the United States: 1973. — Index.
ISBN 0-07-040617-0 : £5.75
(B77-04928)

658.4'0028'54044 — Organisations. Management. Applications of digital computer systems
Couger, James Daniel. A first course in data processing / [by] J. Daniel Couger, Fred R. McFadden. — Santa Barbara ; London [etc.] : Wiley, 1977. — xiv,557p : ill(some col), forms ; 28cm.
'A Wiley/Hamilton Publication'. — With answers. — Index.
ISBN 0-471-17738-5 Pbk : £9.00
(B77-33319)

658.4'008 — Management. Techniques. *Essays*
Drucker, Peter Ferdinand. People and performance : the best of Peter Drucker on management / how to use this book [and] definitions of key terms by Oscar Tivis Nelson, Jr. — London : Heinemann, 1977. — xviii, 366p ; 24cm.
Also published: New York : Harper and Row, 1977. — Index.
ISBN 0-434-90400-7 Pbk : £3.95
(B77-17622)

658.4'008 — Management. Techniques. *Readings*
Management : a book of readings / [edited by] Harold Koontz, Cyril O'Donnell. — 4th ed. — New York ; London [etc.] : McGraw-Hill, 1976. — xiii,642p : ill ; 26cm. — (McGraw-Hill series in management)
Previous ed.: 1972. — Bibl.
ISBN 0-07-035353-0 : Unpriced
ISBN 0-07-035352-2 Pbk : £7.45
(B77-04300)

The **management** process : cases and readings / [edited by] Stephen J. Carroll, Jr, Frank T. Paine, John B. Miner. — 2nd ed. — New York : Macmillan ; London : Collier Macmillan, 1977. — xiii,477p : ill ; 24cm.
Previous ed.: 1973.
ISBN 0-02-319520-7 Pbk : £5.25
(B77-22713)

658.4'00941 — Executive management. *Great Britain, to 1976*
Mant, Alistair. The rise and fall of the British manager / [by] Alistair Mant ; illustrations by the author. — London [etc.] : Macmillan, 1977. — viii,142p : ill, map ; 23cm.
Bibl.: p.137-139. — Index.
ISBN 0-333-19865-4 : £5.95 : CIP rev.
(B77-19498)

658.4'00951'249 — Industries. Executive management. *Taiwan*
Silin, Robert H. Leadership and values : the organization of large-scale Taiwanese enterprises / by Robert H. Silin. — [Cambridge, Mass.] : East Asian Research Center, Harvard University ; Cambridge, Mass. ; London : Distributed by Harvard University Press, 1976. — xvii,226p ; 24cm. — (Harvard East Asian monographs ; 62)
Bibl.: p.203-215. — Index.
ISBN 0-674-51857-8 : £11.25
(B77-04929)

658.4'00973 — Business firms. Executive management. *United States. Case studies*
McNichols, Thomas Joseph. Policy-making and executive action / [by] Thomas J. McNichols. — 5th ed. — New York ; London [etc.] : McGraw-Hill, 1977. — xv,928p : ill, facsims, maps ; 25cm. — (McGraw-Hill series in management)
Previous ed.: 1972.
ISBN 0-07-045678-x : £13.45
(B77-24357)

658.4'01 — Business firms. Management. Long-range planning
Strategic planning systems / [edited by] Peter Lorange and Richard F. Vancil. — Englewood Cliffs ; London [etc.] : Prentice-Hall, 1977. — xvii,364p : ill, forms ; 24cm.
Bibl.: p.362-364.
ISBN 0-13-851006-7 : £11.95
(B77-21990)

658.4'01 — Business firms. Planning
Eliasson, Gunnar. Business economic planning : theory, practice and comparison / [by] Gunnar Eliasson. — Stockholm : Swedish Industrial Publications ; London [etc.] : Wiley, 1976. — 324p : ill, forms ; 24cm.
Bibl.: p.313-321. — Index.
ISBN 0-471-01813-9 : £7.00
(B77-02427)

658.4'01 — Corporate planning
Rogers, David Charles Drummond. Business policy and planning : text and cases / [by] David C.D. Rogers. — Englewood Cliffs ; London [etc.] : Prentice-Hall, 1977. — xi,544p : ill, facsims, forms, map ; 25cm.
Includes facsimile reprints. — Bibl.: p.530-531.
ISBN 0-13-107409-1 : £13.55
(B77-25055)

658.4'01 — Management. Planning. Applications of digital computer systems
Boulden, James B. Computer-assisted planning systems : management concept, application, and implementation / [by] James B. Boulden. — New York ; London [etc.] : McGraw-Hill, [1976]. — xiv,286p : ill ; 24cm.
Published in the United States: 1975. — Index.
ISBN 0-07-006657-4 : £12.45
(B77-06771)

658.4'01 — Management. Policies
Steiner, George Albert. Management policy and strategy : text, readings, and cases / [by] George A. Steiner, John B. Miner. — New York : Macmillan ; London : Collier Macmillan, 1977. — x,1014p : ill, forms, map ; 25cm.
Includes facsimile reprints. — Bibl.: p.965-996. — Index.
ISBN 0-02-416750-9 : £12.00
(B77-25056)

658.4'01'0973 — Business firms. Corporate planning. *United States*
McNichols, Thomas Joseph. Executive policy and strategic planning / [by] Thomas J. McNichols. — New York ; London [etc.] : McGraw-Hill, 1977. — xvii,189p : 1 ill ; 23cm.
Bibl.
ISBN 0-07-045683-6 Pbk : £5.65
(B77-24358)

658.4'02 — Business firms. Internal organisation structure
O'Shaughnessy, John. Patterns of business organization / [by] J. O'Shaughnessy. — London : Allen and Unwin, 1976. — 3-316p : ill ; 23cm.
Bibl.: p.292-300. — Index.
ISBN 0-04-658222-3 : £7.25
ISBN 0-04-658223-1 Pbk : £3.95
(B77-01629)

658.4'02 — Management. Delegation
Steinmetz, Lawrence Leo. The art and skill of delegation / [by] Lawrence L. Steinmetz. — Reading, Mass. ; London [etc.] : Addison-Wesley, 1976. — iii-xvii,204p : ill ; 21cm.
Index.
ISBN 0-201-07269-6 Pbk : £5.60
(B77-13740)

658.4'02 — Matrix management
Matrix management / edited by Kenneth Knight. — Farnborough, Hants. : Gower Press, 1977. — ix,233p : ill ; 24cm. — (Gower Press special study)
Bibl.: p.218-225. — Index.
ISBN 0-566-02076-9 : £8.50 : CIP rev.
(B77-21991)

658.4'03 — Business firms. Management. Decision making
Clifford, Jim. Decision making in organisations / [by] Jim Clifford. — London : Longman, 1976. — xi,273p : ill ; 24cm. — (Understanding business)
Index.
ISBN 0-582-35539-7 Pbk : £2.95
(B77-03625)

Clifford, Jim. Decision making in organisations / [by] Jim Clifford. — London : Longman. — (Understanding business)
Teachers guide. — 1976. — [2],67,[1]p : ill ; 30cm.
ISBN 0-582-35554-0 Sp : £1.25
(B77-06772)

658.4'03 — Business firms. Management. Information systems
Kanter, Jerome. Management-oriented management information systems / [by] Jerome Kanter. — 2nd ed. — Englewood Cliffs ; London [etc.] : Prentice-Hall, 1977. — xxvii, 484p : ill ; 24cm.
Previous ed.: 1972. — Bibl.: p.474-476. — Index. — Includes the text of the Privacy Act 1974.
ISBN 0-13-548818-4 : £13.55
(B77-17623)

658.4'03 — Decision analysis
Keeney, Ralph L. Decisions with multiple objectives : preferences and value tradeoffs / [by] Ralph L. Keeney and Howard Raiffa ; with a contribution by Richard F. Meyer. — New York ; London [etc.] : Wiley, 1976. — xxix,569p : ill ; 24cm. — (Wiley series in probability and mathematical statistics)
Bibl.: p.549-560. — Index.
ISBN 0-471-46510-0 : £15.85
(B77-03114)

658.4'03 — Decision analysis. *Readings*
Modern decision analysis : selected readings / edited by Gordon M. Kaufman and Howard Thomas. — Harmondsworth [etc.] : Penguin, 1977. — 508p : ill, map ; 19cm. — (Penguin education) (Penguin modern management readings)
Bibl.
ISBN 0-14-080925-2 Pbk : £2.25
(B77-16981)

658.4'03 — Higher education institutions. Management. Information systems. *Organisation for Economic Co-operation and Development countries*
Management information systems for higher education / edited by K.M. Hussain. — Paris : Organisation for Economic Co-operation and Development ; [London] : [H.M.S.O.], 1977. — 353p : ill, forms ; 24cm. — (Studies in institutional management in higher education)
'Based on presentations made at a Professional Seminar organised by CERI's Programme on Institutional Management in Higher Education in June 1975'. — Bibl.
Pbk : £6.60
(B77-18880)

658.4'03 — Management. Decision making
Adair, John, *b.1934.* Training for decisions, a tutor's manual : a course in decision making, problem solving, creative thinking / by John Adair. — London : British Association for Commercial and Industrial Education : Chemical and Allied Products Industry Training Board, 1976. — 119p,[11]leaves of plates : ill, facsims, forms, map ; 32cm.
Tab indexed. — In binder. — Bibl.: p.107.
ISBN 0-85171-062-x Ls : £30.00(£20.00 to members)
(B77-01630)

658.4'03 — Management. Decision making. *Manuals*
Easton, Allan. Decision making : a short course in problem solving for professionals / [by] Allan Easton. — [London] : Wiley, 1976. — Box : ill, forms ; 27cm. — (Wiley professional development programs)
Contains 7 booklets.
ISBN 0-471-01700-0 : £21.00
(B77-00842)

658.4'03 — Management. Decision making. Applications of estimation of probabilities
Binder Hamlyn Fry and Company. Forecasts for decision-making on sales targets, budgets, prices, production capacity, capital investment and stock levels / [Binder Hamlyn Fry & Co.]. — London (76 Shoe La., EC4A 3JB) : Binder Hamlyn Fry and Co., [1977]. — 472p in various pagings : ill, forms ; 31cm.
With answers. — Bibl.(3p.).
ISBN 0-9503033-2-1 Sp : £25.00
(B77-16489)

658.4'03 — Management. Decision making. Economic aspects
Kierulff, Herbert E. The economics of decision : a practical decision system for business and management / [by] Herbert E. Kierulff, Jr. — Port Washington ; London : Kennikat Press, 1976. — x,118p : ill, forms ; 23cm.
'A Dunellen Publishing Company Book'.
ISBN 0-8046-7107-9 : £10.15
(B77-00304)

658.4'03 — Management. Decision making. Multiple criteria methods
Multiple criteria decision making / edited by Martin K. Starr and Milan Zeleny. — Amsterdam [etc.] ; Oxford : North-Holland Publishing Co., 1977. — vi,326p : ill ; 25cm. — (Institute of Management Sciences. TIMS studies in the management sciences ; vol.6)
Bibl.
ISBN 0-7204-0764-8 Pbk : £14.12
(B77-32011)

658.4'03 — Management. Decision making. Quantitative methods
Johnson, Rodney D. Quantitative techniques for business decisions / [by] Rodney D. Johnson, Bernard R. Siskin. — Englewood Cliffs ; London [etc.] : Prentice-Hall, 1976. — ix,485p : ill ; 24cm.
Index.
ISBN 0-13-746990-x : £11.65
(B77-16982)

658.4'03 — Management. Information systems
Higgins, John Christopher. Information systems for planning and control : concepts and cases / [by] J.C. Higgins. — London : Edward Arnold, 1976. — vii,247p : ill, maps ; 22cm.
Index.
ISBN 0-7131-3375-9 : £10.00
ISBN 0-7131-3376-7 Pbk : £4.95
(B77-10445)

Lucas, Henry Cameron. Why information systems fail / [by] Henry C. Lucas, Jr. — New York ; London : Columbia University Press, 1975[i.e.1977]. — xi,130p : ill ; 24cm.
Published in the United States: 1975. — Bibl.: p.125-127. — Index.
ISBN 0-231-03792-9 : £13.75
(B77-10446)

658.4'03 — Management. Information systems. *Manuals*
Lucey, Terence. Management information systems : an instructional manual for business and accountancy students / [by] T. Lucey. — Winchester (4 Amport Close, Harestock, Winchester, Hants. [SO22 6LP]) : D.P. Publications, 1976. — [3],45p : ill ; 21cm.
With answers. — Index.
ISBN 0-905435-01-x Sd : £0.75
(B77-04930)

Samuelson, K. Information systems and networks : design and planning guidelines of informatics for managers, decision makers and systems analysts / [by] K. Samuelson, H. Borko, G.X. Amey. — Amsterdam [etc.] ; Oxford : North-Holland Publishing Co., 1977. — x,148p : ill ; 23cm.
Bibl.: p.121-128. — Index.
ISBN 0-7204-0407-x : £11.90
(B77-20431)

658.4'03 — Management. Information systems. *Readings*
Readings in management information systems / edited by Gordon B. Davis and Gordon C. Everest. — New York ; London [etc.] : McGraw-Hill, 1976. — xii,284p : ill, form, ports ; 28cm. — (McGraw-Hill series in management information systems)
Facsimile reprints. — Bibl.
ISBN 0-07-015835-5 Pbk : £4.80
(B77-02428)

658.4'03 — Management. Information systems. Applications of digital computer systems
Lucas, Henry Cameron. The analysis, design and implementation of information systems / [by] Henry C. Lucas, Jr. — New York ; London [etc.] : McGraw-Hill, 1976. — xi,255p : ill ; 24cm. — (McGraw-Hill series in management information systems)
Bibl.: p.245-247. — Index.
ISBN 0-07-038920-9 : £11.60
(B77-04931)

658.4'03 — Management. Information systems: Digital computer systems. Long-range planning. *Conference proceedings*
Long-Range Planning for Information Systems *(Conference), University of California at Los Angeles, 1974.* Strategic planning for MIS / [edited by] Ephraim R. McLean, John V. Soden ; with a special contribution by George A. Steiner. — New York ; London [etc.] : Wiley, 1977. — xix,489p : ill, forms ; 24cm.
'A Wiley-Interscience publication'. — 'In the spring of 1974 an invitational conference was held at the University of California, Los Angeles' - p.4. — '... [The] title for the conference [was] - "Long-Range Planning for Information Systems"' - p.7. — Bibl.: p.29-30. — Index.
ISBN 0-471-58562-9 : £16.90
(B77-23557)

658.4'03 — Management. Information systems: Digital computer systems. Machine readable files
Infotech Information Limited. Data base systems / [Infotech Information Limited] ; [C.J. Bunyan, editor]. — Maidenhead (Nicholson House, Maidenhead, Berks.) : Infotech Information Ltd, 1975. — x,722p(2 fold) : ill, forms ; 31cm. — (Infotech state of the art report)
Bibl.: p.649-672. — Index.
ISBN 0-85539-250-9 : Unpriced
(B77-20432)

658.4'03 — Retailing. Management. Information systems. Applications of data processing systems
Jones, Gilbert Thomas. Data capture in the retail environment / by G.T. Jones. — Manchester : NCC Publications, 1977. — vii,152p : ill, 2 facsims ; 30cm.
Bibl.: p.145-152.
ISBN 0-85012-168-x Pbk : £6.00 : CIP rev.
(B77-06194)

658.4'03'02854044 — Management. Decision making. Applications of digital computer systems
Simon, Herbert Alexander. The new science of management decision / [by] Herbert A. Simon. — Revised ed. — Englewood Cliffs ; London [etc.] : Prentice-Hall, 1977. — xiii,175p ; 24cm.
Previous ed.: i.e. 2nd ed. published as 'The shape of automation for men and management'. New York : Harper and Row, 1965. — Index.
ISBN 0-13-616144-8 : £8.75
ISBN 0-13-616136-7 Pbk : £4.75
(B77-21992)

658.4'032 — Building industries. Management. Critical path analysis. *Great Britain*
Roderick, I F. Examination of the use of critical path methods in building / [by] I.F. Roderick. — Watford : Building Research Establishment, [1977]. — [1]p,p16-19 : ill ; 30cm. — (Building Research Establishment. Current papers ; 12/77)
'Reprinted from "Building technology and management", 1977, 15(3) 16-19'.
Sd : Unpriced
(B77-19499)

658.4'032 — Critical path analysis
Lang, Douglas Wallace. Critical path analysis / [by] Douglas W. Lang. — 2nd ed. — [Sevenoaks] : Teach Yourself Books, 1977. — xi,217p : ill ; 18cm. — (Teach yourself books) (Business & management studies)
Previous ed.: 1970. — Bibl.: p.213-214. — Index.
ISBN 0-340-21278-0 Pbk : £1.75
(B77-15955)

658.4'032 — Health services. Management. Systems analysis
World Health Organization. *Expert Committee on the Application of Systems Analysis to Health Management.* Application of systems analysis to health management : report of a WHO Expert Committee / [WHO Expert Committee on the Application of Systems Analysis to Health Management]. — Geneva : W.H.O. ; [London] : [H.M.S.O.], 1976. — 69p : ill ; 20cm. — (World Health Organization. Technical report series ; no.596)
Pbk : £1.96
ISBN 92-4-120596-2
(B77-06195)

658.4'032 — Management. Decision making. Applications of systems analysis
Ramalingam, P. Systems analysis for managerial decisions : a computer approach / [by] P. Ramalingam. — New York ; London [etc.] : Wiley, 1976. — xv,607p : ill ; 24cm.
Bibl. — Index.
ISBN 0-471-70710-4 : £12.40
(B77-00305)

658.4'032 — Management. Systems analysis
Coyle, Robert Geoffrey. Management system dynamics / [by] R.G. Coyle. — London [etc.] : Wiley, 1977. — xii,463p : ill ; 24cm.
'A Wiley-Interscience Publication'. — Bibl.: p.441-446. — Index.
ISBN 0-471-99444-8 : £16.95
ISBN 0-471-99451-0 Pbk : £6.95
(B77-21274)

Neuschel, Richard F. Management systems for profit and growth / [by] Richard F. Neuschel. — [New ed.]. — New York ; London [etc.] : McGraw-Hill, 1976. — xiii,365p : ill, forms, plans ; 25cm.
Previous ed.: i.e. 2nd ed. published as 'Management by system'. 1960. — Index.
ISBN 0-07-046323-9 : £10.75
(B77-04301)

658.4'032 — Management. Systems theory. *Reviews of research*
Systems and management annual. — New York : Petrocelli Books ; London ([3 Henrietta St., WC23 8LU]) : Mason and Lipscomb.
1974 ; first ed. / Russell L. Ackoff, editor. — 1974. — xx,620p : ill ; 24cm.
Bibl. — Index.
ISBN 0-88405-280-x : Unpriced
(B77-19500)

658.4'032 — Manufacturing industries. Systems design. *Great Britain*
Parnaby, J. Eclecticism, change and dilemma in manufacturing / by J. Parnaby. — [Bradford] ([Bradford, W. Yorkshire BD7 1DP]) : [University of Bradford], [1976]. — [5],30p : ill ; 21cm. — (University of Bradford. Inaugural lectures)
'... delivered ... on 2 March 1976'. — Bibl.: p.29-30.
Sd : Unpriced
(B77-22714)

658.4'032 — Planning. Networks. Analysis
Offler, F. Networks explained / by F. Offler. — Manchester : NCC Publications, 1976. — 529p(32 fold) : ill, forms ; 32cm.
'Prepared as a set of lecture notes for use in the Civil Service College ...' - p.1. — In binder. — Tab indexed.
ISBN 0-85012-174-4 Ls : Unpriced
(B77-27231)

658.4'032 — Planning. Networks. Analysis. *Manuals*
Wiest, Jerome Douglas. A management guide to PERT-CPM : with GERT-PDM-DCPM and other networks / [by] Jerome D. Wiest, Ferdinand K. Levy. — 2nd ed. — Englewood Cliffs ; London [etc.] : Prentice-Hall, 1977. — x,229p : ill ; 24cm.
With answers. — Previous ed.: 1969. — Bibl.: p.178-196. — Index.
ISBN 0-13-549113-4 : Unpriced
ISBN 0-13-549105-3 Pbk : £5.20
(B77-25747)

658.4'032 — Work study
Currie, Russell Mackenzie. Work study / [by] R.M. Currie. — 4th ed. / revised by Joseph E. Faraday. — London : Pitman for the British Institute of Management, 1977. — ix,326p : ill, facsims ; 22cm. — (A Pitman international text)
Previous ed.: 1972. — Index.
ISBN 0-273-00959-1 Pbk : £3.50 : CIP rev.
(B77-10846)

Whitmore, Dennis Ainsworth. Work study and related management services / [by] Dennis A. Whitmore. — 3rd ed. — London : Heinemann, 1976. — xiv,338p : ill, forms ; 22cm. — (The Heinemann accountancy and administration series)
Previous ed.: 1970. — Bibl.: p.329-330. — Index.
ISBN 0-434-92255-2 Pbk : £3.50
(B77-03626)

658.4'033 — Industries. Management. Mathematical models
Smith, David Eugene. Quantitative business analysis / [by] David Eugene Smith. — Santa Barbara ; London [etc.] : Wiley, 1977. — [2], xiii,654p : ill ; 25cm. — (The Wiley/Hamilton series in management and administration)
'A Wiley/Hamilton publication'. — Bibl. — Index.
ISBN 0-471-80405-3 : £12.50
(B77-23558)

658.4'034 — Management. Decision making. Applications of operations research
Shamblin, James E. Operations research : a fundamental approach / [by] James E. Shamblin, G.T. Stevens, Jr. — New York ; London [etc.] : McGraw-Hill, 1974. — xi, 404p : ill ; 24cm.
Bibl. — Index.
ISBN 0-07-056378-0 : Unpriced
(B77-19501)

658.4'034 — Management. Operations research
Operational research for managers / edited by S.C. Littlechild. — Deddington : P. Allan, 1977. — x,246p : ill ; 23cm. — (Philip Allan textbooks in business studies)
Bibl. — Index.
ISBN 0-86003-504-2 : £7.50
ISBN 0-86003-604-9 Pbk : £3.75
(B77-10847)

Riggs, James Lear. Introduction to operations research and management science : a general systems approach / [by] James L. Riggs, Michael S. Inoue. — New York ; London [etc.] : McGraw-Hill, [1976]. — xiii,497p : ill ; 24cm. — (McGraw-Hill series in industrial engineering and management science)
Published in the United States: 1975. — Bibl.: p.485-491. — Index.
ISBN 0-07-052870-5 : £14.10
(B77-04302)

Whitehouse, Gary E. Applied operations research : a survey / [by] Gary E. Whitehouse, Ben L. Wechsler. — New York ; London [etc.] : Wiley, 1976. — xi,434p : ill ; 24cm.
Bibl. — Index.
ISBN 0-471-94077-1 : £11.90
(B77-05523)

658.4'034 — Organisation & methods
Breadmore, Robert George. Organisation and methods / [by] R.G. Breadmore. — [New ed.]. — London : Teach Yourself Books, 1976. — 248p : ill ; 18cm. — (Business & management studies) (Teach yourself books)
Previous ed.: published as 'O & M'. 1971. — Bibl.: p.245. — Index.
ISBN 0-340-20767-1 Pbk : £1.25
(B77-00306)

658.4'034'0184 — Management. Operations research. Mathematical models
Buffa, Elwood Spencer. Management science, operations research : model formulation and solution methods / [by] Elwood S. Buffa, James S. Dyer. — Santa Barbara ; London [etc.] : Wiley, 1977. — x,725p : ill(chiefly col), forms ; 24cm. — (The Wiley-Hamilton series in management and administration)
'A Wiley-Hamilton Publication'. — Bibl. — Index.
ISBN 0-471-11915-6 : £12.00
(B77-18881)

658.4'034'0184 — Management. Operations research. Mathematical models. Use of digital computer systems
Harris, Roy Duane. Computer models in operations management : a computer-augmented system / [by] Roy D. Harris, Michael J. Maggard. — 2nd ed. — New York [etc.] ; London : Harper and Row, 1977. — ix,230p : ill ; 28cm.
Previous ed.: 1972. — Index.
ISBN 0-06-042664-0 Pbk : £6.70
(B77-27232)

658.4'04 — Engineering industries. Project management
Hajek, Victor G. Management of engineering projects / [by] Victor G. Hajek. — [New ed.]. — New York ; London [etc.] : McGraw-Hill, 1977. — xvi,264p : ill ; 24cm.
Previous ed.: published as 'Project engineering'. 1965. — Index.
ISBN 0-07-025534-2 : £11.95
(B77-23559)

Snowdon, Maurice. Management of engineering projects / [by] Maurice Snowdon. — London [etc.] : Newnes-Butterworths, 1977. — [7], 134p : ill, forms, plan ; 23cm. — (Newnes-Butterworths management library)
Bibl.: p.131-132. — Index.
ISBN 0-408-00273-5 : £5.00
(B77-26398)

658.4'04 — Housing. Improvement areas. Projects. Programming. *England. Algorithms*
Great Britain. *Department of the Environment.* Networks for house and area improvement / Department of the Environment, Welsh Office. — London : H.M.S.O., 1977. — [4]p ; 30cm. — (Area improvement note ; 11)
Ten fold. sheets ([20] sides : ill.) in pocket.
ISBN 0-11-751115-3 Sd : £1.50
(B77-09809)

658.4'04 — Project management
Archibald, Russell Dean. Managing high-technology programs and projects / [by] Russell D. Archibald. — New York ; London [etc.] : Wiley, [1977]. — x,278p,fold plate : ill, forms ; 24cm.
'A Wiley-Interscience publication'. — Published in the United States: 1976. — Bibl.: p.271-273. — Index.
ISBN 0-471-03308-1 : £14.65
(B77-09810)

Silverman, Melvin. Project management : a short course for professionals / [by] Melvin Silverman. — New York ; London [etc.] : Wiley, 1976. — Case : ill, forms ; 27cm. — (Wiley professional development programs)
Ten booklets. — With answers.
ISBN 0-471-79163-6 : £17.95
(B77-09124)

658.4'04 — Project management. *Conference proceedings*
Internet *(Organization). World Congress, 5th, Birmingham, 1976.* Internet 76 : [proceedings of the] Fifth Internet World Congress, Project Implementation and Management : Bridging the Gap, [held at the] Metropole Hotel at the National Exhibition Centre, Birmingham, UK, September 13th to 17th 1976. — [Manchester] : [NCC Publications], [1976]. — 5v. : ill, forms, map, plan ; 30cm.
'... held ... under the auspices of INTERNET (UK) and the National Computing Centre Ltd' - Foreword. — Bibl. — Index.
ISBN 0-85012-182-5 Pbk : £45.00
(B77-10447)

658.4'06 — Companies. Changes. Management. *Manuals*
Marlow, Hugh. Managing change : a strategy for our time / [by] Hugh Marlow. — London : Institute of Personnel Management. — (Management information)
Key questions and working papers. — 1975. — 67p ; 30cm.
Fill-in book.
ISBN 0-85292-123-3 Sp : Unpriced
(B77-20433)

658.4'06 — Metal industries. Innovation. Management. *Conference proceedings*
Institution of Metallurgists. *Autumn Review Course, Bristol, 1975.* Innovation management in metallurgy : Autumn Review Course, November 1975. — London (Northway House, Whetstone, N20 9LW) : The Institution, [1975]. — 88p7.b ill ; 30cm. — (Series 3 ; no.4)
'papers ... presented at the Autumn Review Course of the Institution of Metallurgists held at the Grand Hotel, Bristol from 31 October to 2 November 1975' - title page verso.
ISBN 0-901462-02-0 Pbk : £10.00(£7.00 to members)
(B77-15956)

658.4'06'0722 — Organisational change. Management aspects. *Case studies*
Guest, Robert H. Organizational change through effective leadership / [by] Robert H. Guest, Paul Hersey, Kenneth H. Blanchard. — Englewood Cliffs ; London [etc.] : Prentice-Hall, 1977. — viii,184p ; 24cm.
Bibl.: p.177-183. — Index.
ISBN 0-13-641316-1 : £7.95
ISBN 0-13-641308-0 Pbk : £4.80
(B77-22715)

658.4'07'111 — Executives. Recruitment. Role of executive search firms
Executive search : a guide for recruiting outstanding executives / Richard R. Conarroe editor-in-chief. — New York ; London [etc.] : Van Nostrand Reinhold, 1976. — xv,108p : ill ; 22cm.
Index.
ISBN 0-442-21452-9 : £9.70
(B77-23560)

658.4'07'124 — Companies. Managers. Professional education. Courses. *Study examples: General Electric Company*
More than management development : action learning at GEC / edited by David Casey & David Pearce. — Farnborough, Hants. : Gower Press, 1977. — xii,146p : ill ; 23cm.
ISBN 0-566-02005-x : £6.00
(B77-19502)

658.4'07'124 — Executives. Development. *Manuals*
Farnsworth, Terry. Developing executive talent : a practical guide / [by] Terry Farnsworth. — London [etc.] : McGraw-Hill, [1975]. — ix, 162p ; 24cm.
Index.
ISBN 0-07-084457-7 : £4.50
(B77-09125)

658.4'07'124 — Managers. Professional education. Great Britain. Related to work
Stewart, Rosemary. Management education and managerial work / based on the first management research lecture given by Rosemary Stewart, 2 February 1977. — [Slough] ([Wellington St., Slough SL1 1YG]) : Thames Valley Regional Management Centre, [1977]. — [1],i,10 leaves ; 31cm. — (Thames Valley Regional Management Centre. Occasional papers ; no.1 ISSN 0309-8788)
Sd : £0.50
(B77-31320)

658.4'07'124 — Small firms. Consultants. Training. *Developing countries. Manuals*
Harper, Malcolm. Consultancy for small businesses : the concept, training the consultants / [by] Malcolm Harper. — London : Intermediate Technology Publications, [1976]. — ix,254p : ill, forms, plan ; 30cm.
ISBN 0-903031-42-6 Pbk : £5.95
(B77-29557)

658.4'07'1240941 — Managers. Professional education. *Great Britain*
Pearce, S D. Management education by objectives / by S.D. Pearce. — Henley-on-Thames (Publications Secretary, The Library, The Administrative Staff College, Greenlands, Henley-on-Thames RG9 3AU) : Administrative Staff College, 1977. — 30p ; 23cm. — (Administrative Staff College, Henley. College papers)
Sd : £1.50
(B77-30426)

658.4'07'1244 — Managers. Training. Curriculum subjects: Industrial relations. *Great Britain. Reports, surveys*
Southern Regional Council for Further Education. Industrial relations training and education for management : a policy for development / Southern Regional Council for Further Education. — [Reading] ([26 Bath Rd, Reading RG1 6NT]) : [The Council], 1976. — 52p in various pagings ; 30cm.
'Report of the Advisory Committee for Management Studies and its Sub-Committee for Industrial Relations Training' - note.
£0.50
(B77-07480)

658.4'07'1244 — Managers. Training. Curriculum subjects: Industrial relations. Teaching. *Manuals*
Food, Drink and Tobacco Industry Training Board. Industrial relations training, methods guide / [Food, Drink and Tobacco Industry Training Board]. — Gloucester (Barton House, Barton St., Gloucester GL1 1QQ) : The Board, [1976]. — [2],31p : ill ; 21x30cm.
Bibl.
Sd : £2.00
(B77-22716)

658.4'08 — Broadcasting services. *Northern Ireland. British Broadcasting Corporation. Northern Ireland Region. Social responsibility, 1964-1976*
Francis, Richard, *b.1934.* Broadcasting to a community in conflict : the experience in Northern Ireland : a lecture given by Richard Francis at the Royal Institute of International Affairs, Chatham House, Tuesday 22 February 1977. — London : British Broadcasting Corporation, [1977]. — 16,[1]p ; 21cm.
ISBN 0-563-17292-4 Sd : Unpriced
(B77-28734)

658.4'08 — Chemical industries. Safety auditing. *Manuals. For management*
Chemical Industry Safety and Health Council. Safety audits : a guide for the chemical industry / Chemical Industry Safety and Health Council of the Chemical Industries Association Limited. — London (93 Albert Embankment, SE1 7TU) : The Council, 1975. — [2],46p : ill, forms ; 25cm.
'Summary for managements' (folder ([3]p.)) as insert. — Originally issued by the British Chemical Industry Safety Council. 1973.
ISBN 0-900623-20-9 Sd : £1.50
(B77-04303)

658.4'08 — Industries. Disasters. Prevention. Management aspects. *Study regions: Italy. Seveso, 1976*
Temple, C J. Seveso : the issues and the lessons / by C.J. Temple. — London (5th Floor, Adelaide House, London Bridge, EC4R 9DS) : 'Foresight', 1976. — [4],39p ; 29cm. — ('Foresight' special ; no.1 ISSN 0309-4847)
Bibl.: p.39.
Sd : £1.20
(B77-15957)

658.4'08'0973 — Business firms. Social responsibility. *United States*
Jacoby, Neil Herman. Corporate power and social responsibility / [by] Neil H. Jacoby ; foreword by Arthur F. Burns. — New York : Macmillan ; London : Collier Macmillan, 1977. — xix,282,[1]p : ill ; 21cm. — (Studies of the modern corporation)
Originally published: New York : Macmillan, 1973. — Index.
ISBN 0-02-915950-4 Pbk : £3.75
(B77-25057)

658.4'08'0973 — Companies. Social auditing. *United States*
Blake, David Haven. Social auditing : evaluating the impact of corporate programs / [by] David H. Blake, William C. Frederick, Mildred S. Myers, with the assistance of Rogene A. Bucholz, Donald E. Wygal. — New York [etc.] ; London : Praeger, 1976. — vi,169p : ill ; 25cm. — (Praeger special studies in US economic, social and political issues)
Bibl.: p.166. — Index.
ISBN 0-275-56700-1 : £12.20
ISBN 0-275-85710-7 Student ed. : £4.00
(B77-09811)

658.4'08'0973 — Companies. Social responsibility. *United States*
Harper, John D. A view of the corporate role in society / [by] John D. Harper. — Pittsburgh : Carnegie-Mellon University Press ; New York ; Guildford : Distributed by Columbia University Press, 1977. — 57p : ill, ports ; 23cm. — (Benjamin F. Fairless memorial lectures ; 1976)
ISBN 0-915604-11-6 : £4.40
(B77-27233)

658.4'2 — Companies. Boards of directors. *United States*
Brown, Courtney C. Putting the corporate board to work / [by] Courtney C. Brown. — New York : Macmillan ; London : Collier Macmillan, 1976. — xxix,159,[1]p ; 24cm. — (Studies of the modern corporation)
Bibl.: p.147-151. — Index.
ISBN 0-02-904760-9 : £8.25
(B77-13741)

658.4'2'09046 — Managers, 1966-1976. *Reports, surveys*
Heller, Robert. The once and future manager / [by] Robert Heller in association with the partners of Berndtson International. — London : Associated Business Programmes, 1976. — viii,181p ; 23cm.
Index.
ISBN 0-85227-058-5 : £7.95
(B77-06773)

658.4'5 — Business firms. Management. Communication. *Manuals*
Rosenblatt, S Bernard. Communication in business / [by] S. Bernard Rosenblatt, T. Richard Cheatham, James T. Watt. — Englewood Cliffs ; London [etc.] : Prentice-Hall, 1977. — xiv,370p : ill, facsims, map ; 24cm. — (Prentice-Hall series in speech communication)
Bibl. — Index.
ISBN 0-13-153262-6 : £9.55
(B77-23561)

658.4'5 — Management. Communication
Allen, Richard K. Organizational management through communication / [by] Richard K. Allen. — New York [etc.] ; London : Harper and Row, 1977. — x,309p : ill ; 24cm.
Bibl.: p.301-306. — Index.
ISBN 0-06-040206-7 : £8.20
(B77-16490)

Downs, Cal W. The organizational communicator / [by] Cal W. Downs, David M. Berg, Wil A. Linkugel. — New York [etc.] ; London : Harper and Row, 1977. — x,286p : ill, forms ; 24cm.
Index.
ISBN 0-06-041734-x : £8.20
(B77-16491)

Farace, Richard V. Communicating and organizing / [by] Richard V. Farace, Peter R. Monge, Hamish M. Russell. — Reading, Mass. ; London [etc.] : Addison-Wesley, 1977. — xvii,281p : ill ; 24cm.
Bibl.: p.261-269. — Index.
ISBN 0-201-01980-9 : £8.80
(B77-16492)

Hargreaves, Basil John Alexander. Good communications : what every manager should need to know / [by] John Hargreaves. — London : Associated Business Programmes, 1977. — xi,116p : ill ; 23cm.
Index.
ISBN 0-85227-048-8 : £5.95
(B77-06196)

658.4'5 — Organisations. Management. Communication
Koehler, Jerry W. Organizational communication : behavioral perspectives / [by] Jerry W. Koehler, Karl W.E. Anatol, Ronald L. Applbaum. — New York ; London [etc.] : Holt, Rinehart and Winston, 1976. — xiii, 274p : ill ; 25cm.
Bibl.: p.263-268. — Index.
ISBN 0-03-013251-7 : £6.75
(B77-04304)

Wofford, Jerry C. Organizational communication : the keystone to managerial effectiveness / [by] Jerry C. Wofford, Edwin A. Gerloff, Robert C. Cummins. — New York ; London [etc.] : McGraw-Hill, 1977. — xvi, 477p : ill ; 25cm. — (McGraw-Hill series in management)
Bibl. — Index.
ISBN 0-07-070230-6 : £10.45
(B77-22717)

658.4'5'08 — Organisations. Management. Communication. *Readings*
Communication in organizations : selected readings / edited by Lyman W. Porter and Karlene H. Roberts. — Harmondsworth [etc.] : Penguin, 1977. — 442p : ill ; 19cm. — (Penguin education) (Penguin modern management readings)
Bibl. — Index.
ISBN 0-14-080368-8 Pbk : £1.75
(B77-09812)

658.4'52 — Management. Oral communication
Mambert, W A. Effective presentation : a short course for professionals / [by] W.A. Mambert. — New York ; London [etc.] : Wiley, 1976. — Case : ill, forms ; 27cm. — (Wiley professional development programs)
Ten booklets. — With answers.
ISBN 0-471-56630-6 : Unpriced
(B77-09126)

658.4'55 — Organisations. Manuals. Production. *Manuals*
Morrell, J C. Preparing an organisation manual / [by] J.C. Morrell. — London : British Institute of Management Foundation, 1977. — vii,120p : ill, facsim, forms ; 21cm.
Bibl.: p.116-117. — Index.
ISBN 0-85946-076-2 Pbk : Unpriced
(B77-26399)

658.4'56 — Meetings. Procedure. *Manuals. For management*
Gray, Henry Lewis. On the conduct of meetings / [by] H.L. Gray. — Chadwell Heath : Nelpress, 1976. — [34]p ; 21cm. — (Management series ISSN 0309-3794)
Bibl.: p.[29].
Sd : £0.50
(B77-28735)

658.4'6'06241 — Consultants. Organisations. *Great Britain. British Consultants Bureau. Directories*
British Consultants Bureau. British Consultants Bureau directory. — [London] ([55 Pall Mall, SW1Y 5LH]) : [The Bureau].
[1976]. — [1976]. — xxvii,336p,[12] leaves ; 30cm.
English text, English, French, Spanish and Arabic preliminaries.
ISBN 0-9505621-0-6 Pbk : £7.50
(B77-13742)

658.4'6'06241 — Management consultants. Organisations. *Great Britain. Institute of Management Consultants. Directories*
Institute of Management Consultants. List of members / Institute of Management Consultants. — [London] ([86 Edgware Rd, W2 2HP]) : [Sterling Professional Publications Ltd].
1976-77. — [1977]. — 164p : ill, port ; 21cm.
Cover title.
ISBN 0-904133-04-4 Pbk : £3.00
(B77-10848)

658.4'7 — Business firms. Security measures. Management
Warne, A E. Industrial security / [by] A.E. Warne, D.G. Brown. — Chichester [etc.] : Rose, 1977. — x,274p ; 23cm.
Index.
ISBN 0-85992-090-9 : £6.95 : CIP rev.
(B77-16493)

658.4'7 — Computer systems. Risks. Management
Wong, Kenneth Kiu. Risk analysis and control : a guide for DP managers / by Kenneth K. Wong. — Manchester : NCC Publications [etc.], 1977. — viii,144p : ill ; 22cm. — (Computer security series)
Bibl.: p.143-144.
ISBN 0-85012-179-5 : £6.00 : CIP rev.
(B77-18882)

658.4'7 — Computer systems. Security measures
Becker, Robert S. The data processing security game : safeguarding against the real dangers of computer abuse / [by] Robert S. Becker. — New York ; Oxford [etc.] : Pergamon, 1977. — [8],103p : ill, facsim, forms, plan ; 22cm.
Bibl.: p.100. — Index.
ISBN 0-08-021790-7 : £3.25
(B77-22718)

658.4'7 — Computer systems. Security measures: Standby facilities. *Great Britain. Reports, surveys*
National Computing Centre. *South West and South Wales Regional Association. Working Party on Standby.* Planning for standby : a report of the NCC South West & South Wales Regional Association Working Party on Standby / edited by L.P. Waring. — Manchester : NCC Publications, 1976. — [2], 109p ; 30cm.
Bibl.: p.91-93.
ISBN 0-85012-183-3 Pbk : £5.00
(B77-06774)

658.4'7 — Hospitals. Security measures. *United States*
Burstein, Harvey. Hospital security management / [by] Harvey Burstein. — New York [etc.] ; London : Praeger, 1977. — xii, 130p ; 25cm. — (Praeger special studies in US economic, social and political issues)
Bibl.: p.124-126. — Index.
ISBN 0-275-23680-3 : £11.10
(B77-16494)

658.4'7 — Industrial espionage. Martin, Charles Albert de Louis. *Biographies*
Gregg, Gillian R. The 'Precis historique' of Charles Albert : (a story of industrial espionage in the 18th century) / translated [from the French] and edited [i.e. retold] by Gillian R. Gregg. — [Lancaster] ([Old Town Hall, Market Sq., Lancaster]) : [Lancaster Museum], [1977]. — [1],5p ; 30cm. — (City of Lancaster Museum and Art Gallery. Monographs)
Adaptation of: 'Mémoire pour le citoyen Boyer-Fonfrède contre le citoyen Albert'. Paris : s.n., 1796?.
ISBN 0-905665-01-5 Sd : £0.10
(B77-14823)

658.4'7 — Local authorities. Computer systems. Security measures. *Great Britain. Reports, surveys*
Local Authorities Management Services and Computer Committee. *Computer Privacy Working Party.* Computers and privacy - the evidence of local government : a joint submission to the Data Protection Committee by Association of Metropolitan Authorities ... [et al.] / [prepared by the Computer Privacy Working Party of] LAMSAC. — London : Local Authorities Management Services and Computer Committee, 1977. — [1],15p ; 30cm.
ISBN 0-85497-096-7 Sd : £2.00
(B77-13743)

658.4'7 — Organisations. Fraud. Prevention
Comer, Michael J. Corporate fraud / [by] Michael J. Comer. — London [etc.] : McGraw-Hill, 1977. — ix,393p : ill, forms, plan ; 24cm.
Bibl.: p.384-385. — Index.
ISBN 0-07-084494-1 : £8.95 : CIP rev.
(B77-10448)

658.4'7 — Retail trades. Security measures
Byrne, Denis E. Retail security : a management function / by Denis E. Byrne and Peter H. Jones. — Leatherhead (293 Kingston Rd, Leatherhead, Surrey KT22 7NJ) : 20th Century Security Education Ltd, 1977. — [10],242p : ill, forms ; 23cm.
Index.
ISBN 0-905961-00-5 : Unpriced
(B77-32734)

658.4'7 — Security equipment. *Serials*
Securitech : the international guide to security equipment. — Tunbridge Wells (32 Dudley Rd, Tunbridge Wells, Kent TN1 1LH) : Unisaf Publications.
1977 / editor-in-chief Harry Klopper. — [1977] . — 348,[2]p(2 fold) : ill ; 29cm.
English, French, German, Spanish and Arabic text. — Index.
Pbk : £5.50
ISSN 0307-7780
(B77-12562)

658.5 — PRODUCTION MANAGEMENT
Buffa, Elwood Spencer. Modern production management : managing the operations function / [by] Elwood S. Buffa. — 5th ed. — Santa Barbara ; London [etc.] : Wiley, 1977. — xii,743p : ill(some col), col maps ; 25cm. — (The Wiley/Hamilton series in management and administration)
'A Wiley/Hamilton publication'. — Previous ed.: New York : London : Wiley, 1973. — Bibl. — Index.
ISBN 0-471-11829-x : £12.70
(B77-12563)

Monks, Joseph G. Operations management : theory and problems / [by] Joseph G. Monks. — New York ; London [etc.] : McGraw-Hill, 1977. — xiii,671p : ill, form ; 25cm. — (McGraw-Hill series in management)
With answers to odd-numbered problems. — Bibl. — Index.
ISBN 0-07-042718-6 : £11.20
(B77-21994)

Radford, John Dennis. The management of manufacturing systems / [by] J.D. Radford, D.B. Richardson. — London [etc.] : Macmillan, 1977. — vii,224p : ill, plan ; 24cm.
Index.
ISBN 0-333-19521-3 : £10.00
ISBN 0-333-19522-1 Pbk : £4.95
(B77-20434)

658.5 — Canned food industries. Production development
Philip, Maxwell. Recipe and process development for canners / by Maxwell Philip. — Orpington (29 High St., Green Street Green, Orpington, Kent BR6 6LS) : Food Trade Press, 1976. — [7],163p : ill, port ; 23cm.
Index.
ISBN 0-900379-21-9 : £9.00
(B77-09127)

658.5 — Industrial engineering
Hicks, Philip E. Introduction to industrial engineering and management science / [by] Philip E. Hicks. — New York ; London [etc.] : McGraw-Hill, 1977. — xv,336p : ill, forms, plans ; 25cm. — (McGraw-Hill series in industrial engineering and management science)
Bibl. — Index.
ISBN 0-07-028767-8 : £12.40
(B77-23562)

658.5 — Production control
Corke, Dennis Kingsley. Production control in engineering / [by] D.K. Corke. — [New ed.]. — London : Edward Arnold, 1977. — vii, 257p : ill, forms ; 23cm.
Previous ed.: published as 'Production control in management'. 1969. — Index.
ISBN 0-7131-3380-5 : £7.95
(B77-21995)

658.5'001'84 — Production management. Operations research. *Conference proceedings*
International Conference on Production Research, *3rd, Amherst, 1975.* The production system : an efficient integration of resources : proceedings of the Third International Conference on Production Research held at Amherst, Maryland [i.e. Massachusetts], USA, 4-7 August 1975 / editors R.H. Hollier and J.M. Moore. — London : Taylor and Francis, 1977. — xiv,752,[1]p : ill ; 26cm.
Bibl. — Index.
ISBN 0-85066-103-x : £30.00
(B77-30427)

658.5'03 — Production management. Planning. Applications of information systems
Verzijl, J J. Production planning and information systems / [by] J.J. Verzijl ; [translated from the Dutch MS.]. — London [etc.] : Macmillan, 1976. — vii,124p : ill ; 23cm.
Index.
ISBN 0-333-19210-9 : £10.00
(B77-06775)

658.5'6 — Nursing services. Quality control. *United States*
Froebe, Doris J. Quality assurance programs and controls in nursing / [by] Doris J. Froebe, R. Joyce Bain. — Saint Louis : Mosby ; London : Distributed by Kimpton, 1976. — xiii,161p : ill ; 25cm.
Bibl. — Index.
ISBN 0-8016-1695-6 Pbk : £5.00
(B77-04932)

Phaneuf, Maria C. The nursing audit : self-regulation in nursing practice / [by] Maria C. Phaneuf [et al.]. — 2nd ed. — New York : Appleton-Century-Crofts ; London [etc.] : Prentice-Hall, 1976. — xix,204p,[8] fold leaves : ill, forms ; 23cm.
Previous ed.: New York : Appleton-Century-Crofts, 1972. — Index.
ISBN 0-8385-7005-4 Pbk : £6.80
(B77-19503)

658.5'6 — Quality control. Sampling inspection
Wetherill, George Barrie. Sampling inspection and quality control / [by] G. Barrie Wetherill. — 2nd ed. — London : Chapman and Hall [etc.], 1977. — viii,146p : ill ; 22cm. — (Science paperbacks)
'A Halsted Press book'. — Previous ed.: London : Methuen, 1969. — Bibl.: p.137-143. — Index.
ISBN 0-412-14960-5 Pbk : £2.95
(B77-23563)

658.5'6'0182 — Quality control. Statistical methods
Ott, Ellis R. Process quality control : troubleshooting and interpretation of data / [by] Ellis R. Ott. — New York ; London [etc.] : McGraw-Hill, [1976]. — xvii,379p : ill ; 24cm.
Published in the United States: 1975. — Bibl.: p.369-372. — Index.
ISBN 0-07-047923-2 : £12.40
(B77-04933)

658.5'6'02854044 — Production control. Applications of digital computer systems. *Manuals*
Green, Antony Hugh. Production control implementation / by A.H. Green and P.E. Hall. — Manchester : NCC Publications, 1977. — vi, 42p : ill, form ; 21cm. — (Computerguide ; 13)
ISBN 0-85012-165-5 Sd : £3.50
(B77-29558)

658.5'68 — Quality assurance. *Periodicals*
Quality assurance news. — London (54 Princes Gate, SW7 2PG) : Institute of Quality Assurance.
Vol.1, no.1- ; Jan. 1975-. — 1975-. — ill ; 30cm.
Monthly. — p.113-124 in Sept. 1976 issue. — Supersedes : Quality engineer.
Sd : Free to members
ISSN 0309-0116
(B77-03115)

658.5'7 — Research & development. Management. *Conference proceedings*
Whither R & D?. — London (47 Belgrave Sq., SW1X 8QX) : Research and Development Society, 1976. — [3],73p : ill, map ; 30cm.
'Proceedings of the 1976 symposium held on 27th April at the Royal Society, London' - cover.
ISBN 0-901336-05-x Sp : £6.00(£3.00 to members of the Society)
(B77-03627)

658.5'75 — New products. Management
Hanan, Mack. Venture management : a game plan for corporate growth and diversification / [by] Mack Hanan. — New York ; London [etc.] : McGraw-Hill, 1976. — viii,392p : ill ; 24cm.
Index. — Previous control number ISBN 0-07-037060-5.
ISBN 0-07-025970-4 : £12.40
(B77-04934)

Pessemier, Edgar A. Product management : strategy and organization / [by] Edgar A. Pessemier. — Santa Barbara ; London [etc.] : Wiley, 1977. — xiv,478p : ill, forms ; 24cm. — (Wiley-Hamilton series in marketing)
Bibl. — Index.
ISBN 0-471-68235-7 : £10.75
(B77-22719)

Stone, Merlin, *b.1948.* Product planning : an integrated approach / [by] Merlin Stone. — London [etc.] : Macmillan, 1976. — xii,142p : ill ; 23cm.
Bibl.: p.137-139. — Index.
ISBN 0-333-16674-4 : £7.95
(B77-01631)

658.7 — MATERIALS MANAGEMENT
658.7'2 — Purchasing by organisations
Hill, Roy Wells. Organisational buying behaviour : the key to more effective selling to industrial markets / [by] Roy W. Hill and Terry J. Hillier. — London [etc.] : Macmillan, 1977. — xii,212p : ill, form ; 23cm. — (Macmillan studies in marketing management)
Bibl.: p.186-208. — Index.
ISBN 0-333-21510-9 : £10.00
ISBN 0-333-21511-7 Pbk : Unpriced
(B77-21996)

658.7'2 — Stock control. Purchasing
Baily, Peter John Hartwell. Purchasing principles and techniques : a management approach / [by] Peter Baily, David Farmer. — 3rd ed. — London : Pitman, 1977. — xi,353p : ill, forms ; 23cm.
Previous ed.: 1974. — Bibl. — Index.
ISBN 0-273-01028-x Pbk : £5.95 : CIP rev.
(B77-10849)

658.7'2'05 — Stock control. Purchasing. *Periodicals*
Buyers & buying : journal of the Institution of Buyers. — Royal Leamington Spa (24 Warwick New Rd, Royal Leamington Spa, Warwickshire) : ISE Publications Ltd for the Institution of Buyers.
Feb. 1975-. — 1975-. — ill, ports ; 29cm.
Ten issues a year. — 31p. in 1st issue.
Sd : Unpriced(free to members)
ISSN 0140-2528
(B77-33321)

658.7'2'0941 — Stock control. Purchasing. *Great Britain. Periodicals*
Purchasing and supply : journal of the Institute of Purchasing and Supply. — [London] : [The Institute].
Supersedes: Procurement.
Oct. 1976-. — 1976-. — ill, ports ; 30cm.
Monthly. — Cover title. — 56p. in Apr. 1977 issue.
Pbk : £1.50(£15.00 yearly)
ISSN 0309-7242
(B77-25748)

658.7'85 — Warehousing
Powell, Victor G. Warehousing : analysis for effective operations / [by] Victor G. Powell. — London : Business Books, 1976. — x,240p : ill ; 24cm.
Bibl.: p.235-236. — Index.
ISBN 0-220-66301-7 : £10.00
(B77-28736)

658.7'88 — Products. Delivery. Punctuality. *Manuals. For manufacturing industries*
Paulden, Sydney. How to deliver on time / [by] Sydney Paulden. — Farnborough : Gower Press, Aug. 1977. — vii,120p : ill, forms ; 23cm.
Bibl.: p.116. — Index.
ISBN 0-566-02075-0 : £6.00 : CIP rev.
(B77-17624)

658.7'882 — Goods. Distribution. Management
Christopher, Martin. Distribution planning and control : a corporate approach / [by] Martin Christopher, David Walters with John Gattorna. — Farnborough, Hants. : Gower Press, 1977. — ix,161p : ill, forms ; 24cm. — (A Gower Press special study)
Index.
ISBN 0-566-02013-0 : £8.50 : CIP rev.
(B77-19504)

658.7'882'0941 — Goods. Distribution. *Great Britain. Conference proceedings*
Distribution - Is There a Better Way? *(Conference), London, 1976.* Conference, Distribution - is there a better way? : [held on] Wed. 22nd September 1976 at the Hyde Park Hotel, London. — [Cranfield] ([Cranfield Institute of Technology, Cranfield, Bedford MK43 0AL]) : National Materials Handling Centre, [1976]. — 106 leaves in various pagings : ill ; 30cm.
Bibl.: leaf 74.
ISBN 0-902937-27-8 Pbk : £5.00
(B77-04305)

658.8 — MARKETING
Crissy, W J E. Selling : the personal force in marketing / [by] W.J.E. Crissy, William H. Cunningham, Isabella C.M. Cunningham. — Santa Barbara ; London [etc.] : Wiley, 1977. — [12],491p : ill, facsim, maps ; 24cm. — (Wiley/Hamilton series in marketing)
'A Wiley/Hamilton publication'. — Bibl. — Index.
ISBN 0-471-18757-7 : £10.00
(B77-11296)

Dodge, H Robert. Industrial marketing / [by] H. Robert Dodge. — New York ; London [etc.] : McGraw-Hill, 1970. — x,467p : ill ; 24cm.
Bibl. — Index.
ISBN 0-07-017301-x : Unpriced
(B77-19505)

Marketing : theory and practice / edited by Michael J. Baker. — London [etc.] : Macmillan, 1976. — xii,177p : ill ; 22cm. — (Macmillan studies in marketing management)
Index.
ISBN 0-333-19820-4 : Unpriced
ISBN 0-333-19821-2 Pbk : £2.95
(B77-04306)

Peterson, Robin. Marketing : a contemporary introduction / [by] Robin Peterson. — Santa Barbara ; London [etc.] : Wiley, 1977. — [10], 675p : ill(some col), forms(some col), col maps ; 24cm. — (Wiley/Hamilton series in marketing)
'A Wiley/Hamilton publication'. — Bibl. — Index.
ISBN 0-471-68331-0 : £10.50
(B77-17625)

Willsmer, Ray Leonard. The basic arts of marketing / [by] Ray L. Willsmer. — London : Business Books, 1976. — xii,230p : ill ; 23cm. — ('Basic arts' series)
Index.
ISBN 0-220-66307-6 : £6.95
(B77-27959)

658.8 — Exporting. *Great Britain. Manuals*
Deschampsneufs, Henry. Export made simple / [by] Henry Deschampsneufs. — London : W.H. Allen, 1977. — xii,242p : ill, forms ; 23cm. — (Made simple books ISSN 0464-2902)
Bibl.: p.232-237. — Index.
ISBN 0-491-01908-4 : £2.95
ISBN 0-491-01918-1 Pbk : £1.75
(B77-18884)

Walker, Alexander George. Export practice and documentation / [by] A.G. Walker. — 2nd ed. — London [etc.] : Newnes-Butterworths, 1977. — [8],244p : ill, forms ; 23cm.
Previous ed.: London : Butterworth, 1970. — Bibl.: p.237-238. — Index.
ISBN 0-408-00271-9 : £7.00
(B77-16983)

658.8 — Exporting. *Manuals*
Day, Arthur J. Exporting for profit : the practical handbook for improving export sales / [by] Arthur J. Day. — London : Graham and Trotman, 1976. — x,377p : ill, forms ; 23cm.
Bibl.: p.361-363. — Index.
ISBN 0-86010-054-5 : Unpriced
ISBN 0-86010-055-3 Pbk : Unpriced
(B77-25058)

658.8 — Exporting by plastics industries. *Great Britain. Conference proceedings*
Plastics, an Export Success *(Conference), London?, 1977.* Plastics, an export success. — London : British Plastics Federation, 1977. — [3],51p ; 30cm. — (British Plastics Federation. Publications ; no.168/1)
'The British Plastics Federation's European and International Trade Committee held a seminar "Plastics - an export success" on 23 March 1977' - Introduction.
Sp : £12.00(£8.00 to members)
(B77-29559)

658.8 — Exporting. Marketing. *United States*
Alexandrides, C G. Export marketing management / [by] C.G. Alexandrides, George P. Moschis. — New York ; London : Praeger, 1977. — xvii,181p : ill ; 25cm. — (Praeger special studies in international business, finance and trade)
Bibl.: p.175-179.
ISBN 0-275-23610-2 : £10.50
(B77-25749)

658.8 — Exports. Direct-mail marketing. *Manuals*
Handbook of international direct marketing / edited by John Dillon. — London [etc.] : McGraw-Hill, 1976. — xvii,428p : ill, forms ; 24cm.
Bibl.: p.401-412. — Index.
ISBN 0-07-084473-9 : £11.00
(B77-04935)

658.8 — Exports. Marketing
Majaro, Simon. International marketing : a strategic approach to world markets / [by] Simon Majaro. — London : Allen and Unwin, 1977. — 3-303p : ill, forms, maps ; 25cm.
Bibl.: p.295-297. — Index.
ISBN 0-04-658224-x : £11.50
(B77-07481)

658.8 — Great Britain. Exports to developing countries. Marketing. *Periodicals*
New markets report, the Middle East, Latin America, Asia, Africa : export opportunities advance information. — London (7 Bell Yard, Temple Bar, WC2A 2JR) : Market Information Publishing.
Issue no.1- ; Mid-June 1976-. — 1976-. — 30cm.
Monthly. — 8p. in 4th issue.
Sd : Private circulation
ISSN 0309-0124
(B77-06197)

658.8 — Industrial marketing
Chisnall, Peter Michael. Effective industrial marketing / [by] Peter M. Chisnall. — London [etc.] : Longman, 1977. — xii,302p : ill ; 23cm.
Index.
ISBN 0-582-45067-5 : £6.25
(B77-32012)

658.8 — Marketing. Communication
DeLozier, M Wayne. The marketing communications process / [by] M. Wayne DeLozier. — New York ; London [etc.] : McGraw-Hill, 1976. — xii,324p : ill, facsims ; 25cm.
Index.
ISBN 0-07-016302-2 : £10.75
(B77-07971)

658.8 — Plastics products. Exporting. *Great Britain. Manuals*
British Plastics Federation. Instant guide to exporting / [British Plastics Federation]. — London : The Federation.
In 2 vols.
Part 1. — [1977]. — [3],28p ; 30cm. — (British Plastics Federation. Publications ; no.165/1)
Sp : £10.00(£5.00 to members)
(B77-29560)

658.8'005 — Marketing. *Periodicals*
Worldwide marketing opportunities digest. — Harrogate (17 Victoria Ave., Harrogate, N. Yorkshire) : International Commercial Network.
Supersedes: Worldwide marketing horizons.
[No.1]- ; Feb./Mar. 1977-. — [1977]-. — ill, ports ; 30cm.
Six issues a year. — 16p. in 1st issue.
Sd : £7.50
ISSN 0309-4960
(B77-14824)

658.8'007'22 — Marketing. *Case studies*
Problems in marketing. — 5th ed. / [by] Steven H. Star ... [et al.]. — New York ; London [etc.] : McGraw-Hill, 1977. — xii,857p : ill, facsims, form, maps ; 25cm. — (McGraw-Hill series in marketing)
Previous ed.: / by Milton P. Brown and others. 1968.
ISBN 0-07-060835-0 : £11.95
(B77-29561)

658.8'008 — Marketing. *Readings*
Fundamentals of marketing, additional dimensions : selections from the literature / edited by Jack L. Taylor, Jr, and James F. Robb. — 2nd ed. — New York ; London [etc.] : McGraw-Hill, 1975. — xvii,485p : ill ; 24cm.
Previous ed.: 1971. — Bibl.: p.xii-xv. — Index.
ISBN 0-07-063116-6 Pbk : £4.70
(B77-00843)

Marketing classics : a selection of influential articles / [edited by] Ben M. Enis, Keith K. Cox. — 3rd ed. — Boston [Mass.] ; London [etc.] : Allyn and Bacon, 1977. — xvii,2-461p : ill ; 24cm.
Previous ed.: Boston, Mass. : Allyn and Bacon, 1973. — Index.
ISBN 0-205-05715-2 Pbk : Unpriced
(B77-14310)

658.8'009172'4 — Marketing. *Developing countries. Conference proceedings*
International Conference on Marketing Systems for Developing Countries, *Tel-Aviv University, 1974.* Proceedings of International Conference on Marketing Systems for Developing Countries (INCOMAS), Tel-Aviv University, January 6-10, 1974 / edited by Dov Izraeli and Dafna N. Izraeli, Frank Meissner. — New York [etc.] : Wiley [etc.] ; Chichester : Distributed by Wiley.
In 2 vols.
Vol.1 : Marketing systems for developing countries. — 1976. — xv,200p : ill ; 25cm.
'A Halsted Press book'. — Bibl.
£16.40
(B77-26400)

Vol.2 : Agricultural marketing for developing countries. — 1976. — xv,202p : ill ; 25cm.
'A Halsted Press book'. — Bibl.
ISBN 0-470-15095-5 : £14.00
(B77-27235)

658.8'0094 — Industrial marketing. Information sources. *Europe*
Industrial Aids Limited. Published data on European industrial markets / Industrial Aids Limited. — [3rd revised and enlarged ed.]. — London (52 Grosvenor Gardens, SW1W 0AU) : Industrial Aids Ltd, [1976]. — [2],190p ; 30cm.

Cover title. — Previous ed.: 1974. — Index.
Pbk : £20.00
(B77-00844)

658.8'09'687120973 — Women's clothing. Marketing. *United States*
Troxell, Mary D. Fashion merchandising. — 2nd ed. / [by] Mary D. Troxell. — New York ; London [etc.] : Gregg Division, McGraw-Hill, 1976. — x,422p : ill, facsims, forms, ports ; 25cm. — (The Gregg-McGraw-Hill marketing series)
Previous ed.: / by Mary D. Troxell, Beatrice Judelle. 1971. — Bibl.: p.410-414. — Index. — Includes a chapter on men's fashions.
ISBN 0-07-065278-3 : £11.60
(B77-04936)

658.8'09'74544973 — Design services. Marketing. *United States. Manuals*
Bachner, John Philip. Marketing and promotion for design professionals / [by] John Philip Bachner and Naresh Kumar Khosla. — New York ; London [etc.] : Van Nostrand Reinhold, 1977. — xiv,354p : ill, facsims, forms ; 24cm.
Index.
ISBN 0-442-20478-7 : £14.55
(B77-22720)

658.8'09'91 — Tourism. Marketing
Schmoll, G A. Tourism promotion : marketing background, promotion techniques and promotion planning methods / [by] G.A. Schmoll. — London (154 Cromwell Rd, S.W.7) : Tourism International Press, 1977. — 136p : ill ; 22cm.
Cover title: Schmoll on tourism promotion. — Bibl.: p.135-136.
ISBN 0-904873-07-2 Pbk : Unpriced
(B77-21998)

Wahab, Salah. Tourism marketing : a destination-orientated programme for the marketing of international tourism / [by] Salah Wahab, L.J. Crampon, L.M. Rothfield. — London (154 Cromwell Rd, S.W.7) : Tourism International Press, 1976. — 273p : ill, form ; 22cm.
Bibl.: p.260-262.
ISBN 0-904873-03-x Pbk : Unpriced
(B77-02429)

658.81 — SALES MANAGEMENT
658.8'12 — Marketing. Policies of companies. Influence of consumers. *United States. Reports, surveys*
Fornell, Claes. Consumer input for marketing decisions : a study of corporate departments for consumer affairs / [by] Claes Fornell. — New York [etc.] ; London : Praeger, 1976. — xxi, 165p : ill ; 25cm. — (Praeger special studies in US economic, social and political issues)
Bibl.: p.151-164.
ISBN 0-275-23480-0 : £11.10
(B77-07972)

658.8'12 — Professional personnel. Relations with clients. *United States*
May, Judith V. Professionals and clients : a constitutional struggle / [by] Judith V. May. — Beverly Hills ; London : Sage Publications, 1976. — 43p ; 22cm. — (Sage professional papers in administrative and policy studies ; vol.3, no.03-036)
Bibl.: p.39-42.
ISBN 0-8039-0630-7 Pbk : £1.75
(B77-14311)

658.82 — SALES PROMOTION
Stanley, Richard E. Promotion : advertising, publicity, personal selling, sales promotion / [by] Richard E. Stanley. — Englewood Cliffs ; London [etc.] : Prentice-Hall, 1977. — xxii, 394p : ill, facsims, forms ; 24cm.
Index.
ISBN 0-13-999997-3 : £11.15
(B77-18271)

658.8'2 — Bookselling. Promotion. *Great Britain. Manuals*
Selling the book : a bookshop promotion manual / edited by Sydney Hyde. — London : Bingley, 1977. — 127p,16p of plates : ill ; 23cm.
ISBN 0-85157-513-7 : £3.75
(B77-10449)

658.83 — MARKET RESEARCH AND ANALYSIS
658.8'3 — Marketing. Research
Livingstone, James McCardle. A management guide to market research / [by] James M. Livingstone. — London [etc.] : Macmillan, 1977. — vii,173p : ill ; 23cm. — (Macmillan studies in marketing management)
Bibl.: p.168-170. — Index.
ISBN 0-333-22676-3 : £8.95 : CIP rev.
ISBN 0-333-22677-1 Pbk : £3.95
(B77-21275)

Tull, Donald Stanley. Marketing research : meaning, measurement and method : a text with cases / [by] Donald S. Tull, Del I. Hawkins. — New York : Macmillan ; London : Collier Macmillan, 1976. — xv,736p : ill, forms ; 24cm.
Bibl. — Index.
ISBN 0-02-421740-9 : £10.15
(B77-11941)

658.8'3 — Marketing. Research. *Manuals*
Breen, George Edward. Do-it-yourself marketing research / [by] George Edward Breen ; illustrated by Howard Munce. — New York [etc.] ; London : McGraw-Hill, 1977. — xi, 258p : ill, facsims, forms ; 24cm.
Index.
ISBN 0-07-007445-3 : £11.20
(B77-24360)

658.8'3 — New products. Marketing
Midgley, David. Innovation and new product marketing / [by] David F. Midgley. — London : Croom Helm, 1977. — 3-296p : ill ; 23cm.
Bibl.: p.281-290. — Index.
ISBN 0-85664-260-6 : £9.95
ISBN 0-85664-265-7 Pbk : £5.50
(B77-11942)

658.8'34 — Children. Consumer behaviour. Development. *Information processing perspectives*
Ward, Scott. How children learn to buy : the development of consumer information-processing skills / [by] Scott Ward, Daniel B. Wackman, Ellen Wartella. — Beverly Hills ; London : Sage Publications, 1977. — 271p : forms ; 23cm. — (People and communication ; vol.1)
Bibl.: p.193-197. — Index.
ISBN 0-8039-0424-x : Unpriced
ISBN 0-8039-0744-3 Pbk : £4.95
(B77-28737)

658.8'34 — Complaints by consumers. Role of Great Britain. Office of Fair Trading. *Great Britain*
Methven, John. The Office of Fair Trading - our vital statistics / by M.J. Methven. — Stockport (c/o Aldersyde, Maynestone Rd, Chinley, Stockport, Cheshire SK12 6AH) : Manchester Statistical Society, [1976]. — 11p ; 20cm.
Text of a paper read before the Society on 2nd December, 1975.
ISBN 0-85336-031-6 Sd : £1.20
(B77-10450)

658.8'34 — Consumer behaviour. Psychological aspects
Blum, Milton L. Psychology and consumer affairs / [by] Milton L. Blum. — New York [etc.] ; London : Harper and Row, 1977. — xiii,317p : ill ; 24cm.
Index.
ISBN 0-06-040782-4 Pbk : £6.70
(B77-16495)

658.8'34 — National health services. Complaints by public. *Great Britain. Reports, surveys. Serials*
Great Britain. *Health Service Commissioner.* Annual report : report of the Health Service Commissioner. — London : H.M.S.O.
1975-76 : 1st, session 1975-76. — [1976]. — 59p ; 25cm. — ([1975-76 H.C.] 528)
ISBN 0-10-252876-4 Sd : £0.75
(B77-05311)

1976-77 : 4th, Session 1976-77. — [1977]. — 16p ; 25cm. — ([1976-77 H.C.] 322)
ISBN 0-10-232277-5 Sd : £0.45
(B77-17626)

Great Britain. *Health Service Commissioner.* Report of the Health Service Commissioner, session 1976-77 ... — London : H.M.S.O.
3rd : investigations completed, December 1976 to March 1977. — [1977]. — 139p ; 25cm. — ([1976-77 H.C.] 321)
ISBN 0-10-232177-9 Pbk : £2.10
(B77-17627)

Great Britain. *Health Service Commissioner.* Report of the Health Service Commissioner, session 1976-77. — London : H.M.S.O.
1st. — [1976]. — 131p ; 25cm. — ([1976-77 H.C.]21)
ISBN 0-10-202177-5 Pbk : £2.25
(B77-07233)

Great Britain. *Health Services Commission.* Report of the Health Services Commission, session 1976-77 ... — London : H.M.S.O.
5th : investigations completed - April to July 1977. — [1977]. — 137p ; 25cm. — ([1976-77 H.C.] 505)
ISBN 0-10-250577-2 Pbk : £2.10
(B77-32013)

658.8'34 — Social services. Complaints by public. Administration. Procedure. *Great Britain. Reports, surveys*
Personal Social Services Council. Complaints procedures in the personal social services : a discussion paper / [Personal Social Services Council]. — London (2 Torrington Place, WC1E 7HN) : The Council, 1976. — [2],17,[1] p ; 30cm.
ISBN 0-905250-03-6 Sd : £0.80
(B77-09128)

658.85 — SALESMANSHIP
658.85 — Industrial salesmanship. *Manuals*
Seltz, David D. Industrial selling : gateway to the million dollar sale! / [by] David D. Seltz. — New York ; London [etc.] : McGraw-Hill, 1976. — ix,212p : ill, facsims, forms ; 25cm.
Index.
ISBN 0-07-056209-1 : £11.05
(B77-01632)

658.85 — Industrial salesmanship. *United States. Manuals*
Clark, L H. How to get and hold key accounts : the complete guide for the manufacturer's rep / [by] L.H. Clark. — New York ; London [etc.] : McGraw-Hill, [1976]. — xvii,165p ; 24cm.
Published in the United States: 1975. — Index.
ISBN 0-07-011160-x : £11.60
(B77-07482)

658.85 — Manufacturers' agents. *Great Britain. Directories*
United Kingdom manufacturers agents / [Data Research Group]. — Amersham (Hill House, [Hill Ave.], Amersham, Bucks.) : The Group. [1975]. — 1975. — 130 leaves in various pagings ; 30cm.
ISBN 0-905570-56-1 Sp : £12.00
(B77-07483)

[1977]. — 1977. — 126 leaves in various pagings ; 30cm.
Sp : £13.00
(B77-28738)

658.85 — Salesmanship. *Manuals*
Anderson, B Robert. Professional selling / [by] B. Robert Anderson. — Englewood Cliffs ; London [etc.] : Prentice-Hall, 1977. — xi,356p : ill, form ; 24cm.
Bibl.: p.351-352. — Index.
ISBN 0-13-725937-9 : £10.35
(B77-20435)

Lidstone, John, *b.1929.* Negotiating profitable sales / [by] John Lidstone. — Farnborough, Hants. : Gower Press, 1977. — xiv,221p : ill ; 23cm.
Bibl.: p.217. — Index.
ISBN 0-566-02006-8 : £7.50 : CIP rev.
(B77-18885)

658.85'0973 — Salesmanship. *United States. Manuals*
Bodle, Yvonne Gallegos. Retail selling / [by] Yvonne Gallegos Bodle, Joseph A. Corey. — 2nd ed. — New York ; London [etc.] : McGraw-Hill, 1977. — viii,424p : ill, facsims, forms ; 25cm.
Previous ed.: New York : McGraw-Hill, 1972. — Index.
ISBN 0-07-006371-0 : £8.05
(B77-25750)

658.87 — RETAILING
Pintel, Gerald. Retailing / [by] Gerald Pintel, Jay Diamond. — 2nd ed. — Englewood Cliffs ; London [etc.] : Prentice-Hall, 1977. — vi,408p : ill, facsims, forms, plan ; 25cm.
Previous ed.: 1971. — Bibl. — Index.
ISBN 0-13-777532-6 : £11.20
(B77-19506)

658.8'7 — Retailing. Management
Gillespie, Karen R. Retail business management / [by] Karen R. Gillespie, Joseph C. Hecht. — 2nd ed. — New York ; London [etc.] : Gregg Division, McGraw-Hill, 1977. — ix,470p : ill, facsims, forms ; 25cm. — (The Gregg-McGraw-Hill marketing series)
Previous ed.: New York : Gregg Division, McGraw-Hill, 1970. — Index.
ISBN 0-07-023232-6 : £9.40
(B77-21276)

Redinbaugh, Larry D. Retailing management : a planning approach / [by] Larry D. Redinbaugh. — New York ; London [etc.] : McGraw-Hill, [1977]. — xviii,429p ; 25cm.
Published in the United States: 1976. — Index.
ISBN 0-07-051366-x : £10.40
(B77-11943)

658.8'7 — Shops. Purchase. *Great Britain. Manuals*
Price, A St J. Buying a shop? : questions you should ask / [by] A. St J. Price. — York (Prudential House, Blossom St., York YO2 2AJ) : Lynxplan (Sheffield) Ltd, 1976. — 33p in various pagings ; 30cm.
ISBN 0-905859-02-2 Pbk : £2.50
(B77-07484)

658.8'7'007 — Retailing. Information sources. *Great Britain*
Smith, Janet, *b.1949.* Retailing and retail planning : a guide to sources of information / compiled by Janet Smith. — London [etc.] (2 Birling Rd, Tunbridge Wells, Kent TN2 5LX) : Capital Planning Information Ltd, 1977. — [5], 53p ; 30cm. — (Capital Planning Information. CPI information reviews ; no.1 ISSN 0140-3087)
Index.
ISBN 0-906011-00-0 Pbk : £4.00
(B77-30428)

658.8'7'00941 — Retailing. *Great Britain. Periodicals*
Unit for Retail Planning Information. Information brief / [Unit for Retail Price Information]. — Reading (229 King's Rd, Reading RG1 4LS) : The Unit.
[No.] 1- ; Feb. 1976-. — 1976-. — 30cm.
Published at irregular intervals. — [3]p. in 1st issue.
Sd : £1.00(free to members)
ISSN 0309-2909
(B77-08458)

Unit for Retail Planning Information. Newsletter / [Unit for Retail Planning Information]. — Reading (229 King's Rd, Reading RG1 4LS) : The Unit.
[No.] 1- ; Autumn 1975-. — 1975-. — 30cm.
Quarterly. — Folder ([4]p.) as 1st issue.
£1.00(free to members)
ISSN 0390-2852
(B77-08459)

658.8'78'0973 — Supermarkets. Procedures. *United States*
Peak, Hugh S. Supermarket merchandising and management / [by] Hugh S. Peak, Ellen F. Peak. — Englewood Cliffs ; London [etc.] : Prentice-Hall, 1977. — xi,372p : ill, facsims, forms, maps, plans ; 24cm.
Bibl. — Index.
ISBN 0-13-876037-3 : £11.20
(B77-16985)

658.8'8'0941 — Credit management. *Great Britain*
Credit management handbook / editor Herbert Edwards. — Epping : Gower Press, 1976. — xxv,477p : ill, forms ; 23cm. — (A Gower Press handbook)
Bibl.: p.453-455. — Index.
ISBN 0-7161-0325-7 : £8.50
(B77-22721)

658.89'0705'73 — Antiquarian bookselling. *Manuals*
Ginsberg, Louis. An open letter to a beginner bookseller / [by] Louis Ginsberg. — [Wormley, Surrey] ([Dr A.S. Osley, 'The Glade', Brook Rd, Sandhills, Witley, Godalming, Surrey]) : Glade Press, 1973. — [1],8,[1]p ; 21cm.
Limited ed. of 100 copies. — Originally published: 1972.
Sd : Unpriced
(B77-20436)

Ginsberg, Louis. Open letter two to a beginner bookseller / [by] Louis Ginsberg. — Wormley [Surrey] ([Dr A.S. Osley, 'The Glade', Brook Rd, Sandhills, Witley, Godalming, Surrey]) : Glade Press, 1973. — [1],9p ; 21cm.
Limited ed. of 50 copies.
Sd : Unpriced
(B77-20437)

658.89'0705'730941 — Bookselling. *Great Britain. Manuals*
Booksellers Association. Opening a bookshop : some of your questions answered / [Booksellers Association]. — 2nd ed. — London : The Association, 1977. — 12p ; 22cm.
Previous ed.: 1975. — Bibl.: p.12.
ISBN 0-901690-45-7 Sd : £0.75
(B77-32014)

Booksellers Association. Trade reference book / the Booksellers Association of Great Britain and Ireland. — 3rd ed. — London : Booksellers Association, 1976. — [8],76p : forms ; 21cm.
Previous ed.: 1970. — Index.
ISBN 0-901690-41-4 Pbk : £2.00
(B77-03628)

658.9 — MANAGEMENT OF SPECIAL KINDS OF ORGANISATIONS

658'.91'0016425 — Computer systems. Software. Production. Management
Buckle, J K. Managing software projects / [by] J.K. Buckle. — London : Macdonald and Jane's [etc.], 1977. — [8],116p : ill ; 23cm. — (Computer monographs)
Index.
ISBN 0-354-04067-7 : £3.95
(B77-18886)

658'.91'02 — Information services & libraries. Management. Research. *Conference proceedings*
European Conference on the Application of Research in Information Services and Libraries, *Amsterdam, 1976.* EURIM II : a European Conference on the Application of Research in Information Services and Libraries, presented by Aslib in association with ... [others], 23-25 March 1976, RAI International Congrescentrum, Amsterdam, Netherlands. — London : Aslib, 1977. — [6],226p : ill, form, map ; 30cm.
Includes one paper in French and one in German. — EURIM I published as 'EURIM : a European Conference on Research into the Management of Information Services and Libraries'. 1974. — Bibl.
ISBN 0-85142-091-5 Pbk : £12.00(£10.00 to Aslib members)
(B77-27960)

658'.91'021 — Libraries. Management
Studies in library management. — London : Bingley [etc.].
Vol.4 / edited by Gileon Holroyd. — 1977. — 178p ; 23cm.
Bibl.
ISBN 0-85157-240-5 : £4.50
ISSN 0307-0808
(B77-25751)

658'.91'021071141 — Librarians. Professional education. Curriculum subjects: Library management. Simulation games. *Great Britain. Reports, surveys*
Eastcott, C N. Evaluation of the Lancaster University Library management game : a report of a research project commissioned by the British Library Research and Development Department (formerly O.S.T.I.) / [by] C.N. Eastcott. — [Leeds] ([28 Park Place, Leeds LS1 2SY]) : Leeds Polytechnic, Department of Librarianship, 1974. — [4],128p : ill ; 26cm. — (British Library. Research and Development Department. Reports ; no.5279)
ISBN 0-900738-07-3 Sd : £2.00
(B77-25752)

658'.91'26 — Christian church. Management
Rudge, Peter Frederick. Management in the Church / [by] Peter F. Rudge. — London [etc.] : McGraw-Hill, 1976. — xvi,172p ; 24cm.
Bibl. — Index.
ISBN 0-07-084478-x : £5.25
(B77-04307)

658'.91'3015409411 — Housing. Management. *Scotland. Proposals*
Scottish Housing Advisory Committee. Training for tomorrow : an action plan for Scottish housing : report / by a sub-committee of the Scottish Housing Advisory Committee. — Edinburgh : H.M.S.O., 1977. — v,64p : 2 ill ; 21cm.
ISBN 0-11-491458-3 Sd : £1.50
(B77-28739)

658'.91'36210941 — National health services. Management. Participation of public. *Great Britain. Proposals*
Co-operative auxiliaries branch programme theme. — Loughborough (Stanford Hall, Loughborough, Leics.) : Education Department, Co-operative Union.
1976-77 : NHS. — 1976. — [3],37p : map ; 22cm.
Sd : £0.20
(B77-02430)

658'.91'36211 — Hospitals. Management
Grant, Colin. Hospital management / [by] Colin Grant. — Edinburgh [etc.] : Churchill Livingstone, 1977. — ix,259p ; 22cm.
Originally published: 1973. — Index.
ISBN 0-443-01677-1 Pbk : £3.50
(B77-29562)

658'.91'362110973 — Hospitals. Management. *United States*
Schulz, Rockwell. Management of hospitals / [by] Rockwell Schulz, Alton C. Johnson. — New York ; London [etc.] : McGraw-Hill, 1976. — xii,299p : ill ; 25cm.
'A Blakiston Publication'. — Bibl. — Index.
ISBN 0-07-055651-2 : £11.60
(B77-04937)

Sloane, Robert Malcolm. A guide to health facilities : personnel and management / [by] Robert M. Sloane, Beverly LeBov Sloane. — 2nd ed. / with 65 illustrations prepared by Kurt Smolen. — Saint Louis : Mosby ; London : Distributed by Kimpton, 1977. — xii, 209p : ill ; 25cm.
Previous ed.: 1971. — Bibl. — Index.
ISBN 0-8016-4653-7 Pbk : £5.60
(B77-21999)

658'.91'368 — Insurance companies. Management. *Manuals*
Bertschinger, P P. Know how in insurance and reinsurance / by P.P. Bertschinger. — London : Witherby, 1977. — xiii,152p ; 22cm. — (Monument series)
ISBN 0-900886-15-3 : £6.00
(B77-20438)

658'.91'37873 — Higher education institutions. Management. Techniques. *United States*
Handbook of institutional advancement / A. Westley Rowland general editor. — San Francisco [etc.] ; London : Jossey-Bass, 1977. — xxv,577p : ill ; 24cm. — (The Jossey-Bass series in higher education)
Bibl.: p.539-563. — Index.
ISBN 0-87589-313-9 : £15.00
(B77-25753)

658'.91'37873 — Universities. Management. *United States*
Balderston, Frederick E. Managing today's university / [by] Frederick E. Balderston. — San Francisco [etc.] ; London : Jossey-Bass, 1975. — xvii,307p : ill ; 24cm. — (The Jossey-Bass series in higher education)
Originally published: 1974. — Bibl.: p.293-299. — Index.
Unpriced
ISBN 0-87589-236-1
(B77-27961)

Balderston, Frederick E. Managing today's university / [by] Frederick E. Balderston. — San Francisco [etc.] ; London : Jossey-Bass, 1974 [i.e. 1975]. — xvii,307p : ill ; 24cm. — (The Jossey-Bass series in higher education)
Published in the United States: 1974. — Bibl.: p.293-299. — Index.
ISBN 0-87589-236-1 : Unpriced
(B77-18887)

658'.91'61073 — Medicine. Nursing. Management
A guide for nurse managers / edited by Elizabeth Raybould ; foreword by I.C.S. Brown. — Oxford [etc.] : Blackwell Scientific, 1977. — ix, 225p : ill, map ; 25cm.
Bibl. — Index.
ISBN 0-632-00095-3 Pbk : £7.75 : CIP rev.
(B77-25059)

658'.91'61540941 — Pharmacies. Management. *Great Britain*
Tomski, Heinz Werner. A textbook of pharmacy management : for students and practising pharmacists / [by] H.W. Tomski. — London : Kogan Page, 1976. — 256p : ill, facsims, forms, plans ; 23cm.
Bibl.: p.249-251. — Index.
ISBN 0-85038-421-4 : £4.95
(B77-00845)

658'.91'61607575 — Nuclear medicine laboratories. Management. *Conference proceedings*
Financial operation and management concepts in nuclear medicine / edited by James L. Bennington, Hirsch Handmaker, Gerald S. Freedman. — Baltimore ; London [etc.] : University Park Press, 1977. — xiii,232p : ill, forms ; 24cm.
'... based on a symposium held in New York City on October 9-11, 1975, entitled "Financial Operation and Management Concepts in Nuclear Medicine" ... Original presentations have been augmented and rewritten ... Material has been included that was not presented at the symposium' - Acknowledgements. — Bibl. — Index.
ISBN 0-8391-0953-9 : £11.95
(B77-15959)

658'.91'6425 — Catering services. Management. *United States. Manuals*
Knoll, Anne Powell. Food service management : a human relations approach / [by] Anne Powell Knoll. — New York ; London [etc.] : McGraw-Hill, 1976. — viii,200p : ill, forms, plan ; 24cm.
Index.
ISBN 0-07-035183-x Pbk : £5.75
(B77-07973)

658'.91'64795 — Catering industries. Management. *Manuals*
Steel, James. Control in catering / by James Steel. — 2nd ed. — London : Barrie and Jenkins, 1977. — 198p : ill, forms ; 23cm.
Previous ed.: London : Barrie and Rockliff, 1968. — Index.
ISBN 0-214-20225-9 : £6.00
(B77-11297)

658'.91'64795 — Recreation centres & social clubs. Bars. Management. *England. Conference proceedings*
The **management** of licensed bars in leisure centres and clubs : report of a conference held at Kelham Hall, Newark, Thursday 29th April 1976, jointly arranged by Newark District Council and the Sports Council (E.M. Region). — [Nottingham] ([26 Musters Rd, West Bridgford, Nottingham NG2 7PL]) : [Sports Council (East Midland Region)], [1976]. — [1], 83[i.e. 92p] : ill, forms ; 30cm.
Cover title.
ISBN 0-905163-06-0 Pbk : £1.75
(B77-03116)

658'.91'7900973 — Recreation services. Administration. *United States*
Kraus, Richard Gordon. Creative administration in recreation and parks / [by] Richard G. Kraus, Joseph E. Curtis. — 2nd ed. — Saint Louis : Mosby ; London : Distributed by Kimpton, 1977. — xiii,331p : ill, facsims, forms, map ; 26cm.
Previous ed.: 1973. — Bibl.: p.322-324. — Index.
ISBN 0-8016-2739-7 : £10.10
(B77-22000)

658'.91'796071273 — Secondary schools. Activities: Sports & games. Management. *United States*
Fuoss, Donald E. Creative management techniques in interscholastic athletics / [by] Donald E. Fuoss, Robert J. Troppmann. — New York ; London [etc.] : Wiley, 1977. — xviii,494p : ill, forms ; 24cm.
Bibl. — Index.
ISBN 0-471-28815-2 : £10.45
(B77-22722)

658'.91'7984010941 — Betting industries. Management. *Great Britain. Manuals*
Woolley, Richard Alexander. The comprehensive guide to betting and bookmaking : settling and betting shop management / by Richard Alexander Woolley. — Sheffield (Grenoside, Sheffield, S. Yorkshire) : Securi-Pen Co., 1976. — [3],ii,146p : ill ; 21cm.
ISBN 0-905959-00-0 Sd : £7.00
(B77-28740)

658'.92'07 — Systems engineering. Management
Coutinho, John de S. Advanced systems development management / [by] John de S. Coutinho. — New York ; London [etc.] : Wiley, 1977. — xvii,433p : ill ; 24cm. — (Wiley series on systems engineering and analysis)
'A Wiley-Interscience publication'. — Index.
ISBN 0-471-01487-7 : £17.25
(B77-33323)

658.92'13 — Electrical engineering industries. Management
Centre for Interfirm Comparison. 'What's happening?' : a management ratio kit / prepared for the Electrical Contractors' Association of Scotland [by the Centre for Interfirm Comparison]. — [London] ([Radnor House, London Rd, Norbury, SW16 4EL]) : [Construction Industry Training Board], 1977. — [2],73p : ill ; 21x30cm.
Sp : £7.00
(B77-27236)

658'.92'4 — Construction industries. Management
Harris, Frank, *b.1944.* Modern construction management / [by] Frank Harris and Ronald McCaffer. — London : Crosby Lockwood Staples, 1977. — [7],363p : ill, forms ; 24cm.
Index.
ISBN 0-258-97064-2 : £8.50
(B77-23564)

658'.92'40184 — Construction. Sites. Management. Mathematical models
Halpin, Daniel W. Design of construction and process operations / [by] Daniel W. Halpin, Ronald W. Woodhead. — New York ; London [etc.] : Wiley, 1976. — xiii,539p : ill ; 24cm.
Bibl.: p.445-449. — Index.
ISBN 0-471-34565-2 : £13.95
(B77-02431)

658'.92'40941 — Construction industries. *Great Britain. Case studies. For management*
Construction Industry Training Board. 'J.N., Contractors & Company Limited' : a total business case study / [produced by the Construction Industry Training Board and the Ashridge Management Research Unit]. — [London] ([Radnor House, London Rd, SW16 4EL]) : [C.I.T.B.], [1976]. — [1],iii,44 leaves(11 fold),p45-84(2 fold) : ill(some col), maps ; 30cm.
Index.
ISBN 0-902029-27-4 Sp : £4.42
(B77-07485)

658'.92'40973 — Construction industries. Management. *United States*
Goldhaber, Stanley. Construction management : principles and practices / [by] Stanley Goldhaber, Chandra K. Jha, Manuel C. Macedo, Jr. — New York ; London [etc.] : Wiley, 1977. — xix,312p,fold plate : ill, facsims ; 24cm. — (Construction management and engineering)
Bibl.: p.304-307. — Index.
ISBN 0-471-44270-4 : Unpriced
(B77-25060)

658'.92'41834 — Construction. Sites. Construction materials: Concrete. Use. Management aspects
Thursby, Harry. Controlling concrete on the site / [by] Harry Thursby. — Slough : Cement and Concrete Association, 1976. — viii,88p : ill ; 24cm. — (Viewpoint publications)
Index.
ISBN 0-7210-1008-3 Pbk : Unpriced
(B77-03629)

658'.92'920941 — Motor vehicle industries & trades. Management. *Great Britain*
Shier, Alan. Motor trade management / by Alan Shier. — Oxford [etc.] : Oxford University Press, 1977. — [5],104p : ill, facsims, forms ; 24cm.
Bibl.: p.103. — Index.
ISBN 0-19-859150-0 Pbk : £1.95 : CIP rev.
(B77-07486)

658'.93'0184 — Agricultural industries. Management. Simulation games. *Collections. Secondary school texts*
Minshull, Roger Michael. Factors in farming : twenty geographical games / [by] Roger Minshull. — Sunbury-on-Thames [etc.] : Nelson, 1976. — 30p : ill, form ; 28cm.
ISBN 0-17-434202-0 Sd : £0.45
(B77-00307)

Minshull, Roger Michael. Factors in farming : twenty geographical games / [by] Roger Minshull. — Sunbury-on-Thames [etc.] : Nelson.
Teachers' book, including printed spirit duplicating masters. — 1976. — 38p : ill, maps ; 28cm.
Map pages perforated on inside edge and interleaved with tissue. — Bibl.: p.12.
ISBN 0-17-434201-2 Pbk : £5.00
(B77-00308)

658'.93'096894 — Small scale agricultural industries. Management. *Zambia. Reports, surveys*
Bessell, James Edward. Farmer operating efficiency and credit-worthiness / by J.E. Bessell and M.J. Iles. — Sutton Bonington : University of Nottingham, Department of Agriculture and Horticulture, 1976. — ix,123p : 1 ill, forms, 2 maps ; 21cm. — (University of Nottingham's Farm Management Investigations for Zambia. Bulletins ; no.2)
Pbk : £2.50
(B77-29563)

658'.96'972206541172 — Aluminium smelting industries. *Scotland. Highland Region. Invergordon. British Aluminium Company. Aluminium smelters. Management, to 1972*
Drummond, George Gordon. The Invergordon smelter : a case study in management / [by] G. Gordon Drummond. — London (3 Fitzroy Sq., W.1) : Hutchinson Benham, 1977. — 158p ; 22cm.
Bibl.: p.154. — Index.
ISBN 0-09-129871-7 Pbk : £3.00
(B77-30430)

658'.98 — Craft workshops. Organisation. *Manuals*
Setting up a workshop. — 2nd ed. — London (12 Waterloo Place, SW1Y 4AU) : Crafts Advisory Committee, 1976. — 39,[1]p ; 21cm.
'Much of the material ... was first presented at a seminar ... organised by the Crafts Advisory Committee' - Introduction. — Previous ed.: 1975.
ISBN 0-903798-12-3 Sd : £0.50
(B77-11944)

659.1 — ADVERTISING
Advertising. — 4th ed. / [by] John S. Wright ... [et al.]. — New York ; London [etc.] : McGraw-Hill, 1977. — xiii,769p,[8]p of plates : ill(some col), facsims ; 25cm.
Previous ed.: / by John S. Wright, Daniel S. Warner, Willis L. Winter. 1971. — Bibl. — Index.
ISBN 0-07-072067-3 : £11.20
(B77-23565)

Institute of Practitioners in Advertising. What advertising does / [Institute of Practitioners in Advertising]. — 3rd ed. — London : I.P.A., 1976. — [2],9p ; 21cm.
Previous ed.: 1966. — Bibl.: p.9.
Sd : Unpriced
(B77-32735)

Jefkins, Frank William. Advertising today / [by] Frank Jefkins. — 2nd ed. — London : International Textbook Co., 1977. — viii,312p : ill ; 23cm.
Previous ed.: 1971. — Bibl.: p.302. — Index.
ISBN 0-7002-0263-3 : £8.50
ISBN 0-7002-0265-x Pbk : £4.50
(B77-10850)

659.1 — Women. Portrayal by advertising media. *Conference proceedings*
The **packaging** of women : how women are portrayed in advertisements / ... report ... produced by members of Women in Media ... — London (37 Brondesbury Rd, N.W.6) : W.I.M., 1976. — [2],26,v p ; 21cm.
'Report of Women in Media seminar held on March 27, 1976 at Conway Hall' - Introduction.
ISBN 0-9505435-0-0 Sd : £1.00
(B77-03117)

659.1'0941 — Advertising. *Great Britain*
Great Britain. *Central Office of Information. Reference Division.* Advertising and public relations in Britain / [prepared by the Reference Division, Central Office of Information]. — London : H.M.S.O., 1976. — [3],30p ; 24cm. — (Central Office of Information reference pamphlet ; 146)
Bibl.: p.30.
ISBN 0-11-700803-6 Sd : £0.65
Also classified at 659.2'0941
(B77-06776)

Institute of Practitioners in Advertising. Advertising conditions in the United Kingdom / [Institute of Practitioners in Advertising]. — 2nd ed. — London : I.P.A., 1976. — 22p ; 21cm.
Previous ed.: 1973.
Sd : £0.75
(B77-25061)

659.1'125'0941 — Advertising agencies. *Great Britain, to 1939*
Treasure, John. The history of British advertising agencies, 1875-1939 / [by] J.A.P. Treasure. — Edinburgh : Scottish Academic Press, 1977. — [2],20p ; 22cm. — (University of Edinburgh. Commerce Graduates' Association. Jubilee lectures ; 1976)
ISBN 0-7073-0134-3 Sd : £0.50
(B77-24361)

659.13 — Pictorial advertising. *Great Britain. Illustrations. Serials*
D & AD / [Designers and Art Directors Association of London]. — London : Designers and Art Directors Association of London : [Distributed by] Deutsch.
'76 : the 14th annual of British advertising ... / [executive editor Edward Booth-Clibborn, assistant editor Jo Jones]. — 1976. — [287]p : chiefly ill(some col), facsims(some col), ports ; 30cm & sound disc(1 s. ; 7in. 33 1/3 rpm).
Index.
ISBN 0-233-96823-7 : £15.00
(B77-04308)

659.13 — Pictorial advertising. *Illustrations. Serials*
Advertisement parade annual. — Worthing (32 Liverpool Rd, Worthing, Sussex) : Visual Publications Ltd.
English, French and German parallel introductions.
1977. [A]. : [Home products = Pour le foyer = Das Heim]. — 1977. — 6p,132 leaves : chiefly ill, facsims ; 21x27cm.
Cover title: Home products publicity annual. — Index.
ISBN 0-903887-44-4 Pbk : £18.00
(B77-10851)

1977. [B] : [Food & drink = Alimentation & boissons = Ernahrung & Getränke]. — 1977. — 7p,132 leaves : chiefly ill, facsims ; 21x27cm.

Cover title: Food & drink publicity annual. — Index.
ISBN 0-903887-45-2 Pbk : £18.00
(B77-10852)

1977. [C] : [Fashion & footwear = Vêtements & chaussures = Bekleidung & Schuhe]. — 1977. — 6p,132 leaves : chiefly ill, facsims ; 21x27cm.
Cover title: Fashion & footwear publicity annual. — Index.
ISBN 0-903887-46-0 Pbk : £18.00
(B77-10853)

1977. [D] : [Beauty & hygiene = Beauté & hygiène = Kosmetik & Hygiene]. — 1977. — 6p,132 leaves : chiefly ill, facsims ; 21x27cm.
Cover title: Beauty & hygiene publicity annual. — Index.
ISBN 0-903887-47-9 Pbk : £18.00
(B77-10854)

1977. [M] : [Automobile = Autos & produits associés = Kraftfahrzeuge & Zubehör]. — 1977. — 6p,132 leaves : chiefly ill, facsims ; 21x27cm.
Cover title: Automobile publicity annual. — Index.
ISBN 0-903887-48-7 Pbk : £18.00
(B77-10855)

659.13'2 — Promotional literature: Brochures. Design. *Manuals*
Jones, Gerre. How to prepare professional design brochures / [by] Gerre Jones. — New York ; London [etc.] : McGraw-Hill, 1976. — ix, 277p : ill, facsims, forms, plan ; 25cm.
Bibl.: p.271-272. — Index.
ISBN 0-07-032801-3 : £13.70
(B77-03630)

659.13'22 — Newspapers & periodicals. Advertisements. Writing. Techniques
Jefkins, Frank William. Advertisement writing / [by] Frank Jefkins. — Plymouth : Macdonald and Evans, 1976. — vii,248p,[8]p plates : ill, facsims ; 22cm.
Index.
ISBN 0-7121-0138-1 Pbk : £3.50
(B77-07487)

659.14'3 — Public service television advertising. Political aspects. *United States*
Paletz, David L. Politics in public service advertising on television / [by] David L. Paletz, Roberta E. Pearson, Donald L. Willis. — New York ; London : Praeger, 1977. — xiii,125p ; 25cm. — (Praeger special studies in US economic, social and political issues)
Index.
ISBN 0-275-23880-6 : £10.05
(B77-26401)

659.1'52 — Bookselling. Exhibitions. Organisation. *Manuals*
Booksellers Association. Go meet your market : a simple guide to book exhibitions. — [2nd ed.] / [Booksellers Association of Great Britain and Ireland ; text by Ernest Hochland ; drawings by Michael Turner]. — London : The Association, [1976]. — [3],16p : ill ; 21cm.
Previous ed.: i.e. New ed. / Booksellers Association, Charter Group ; text Ernest Hochland ; drawings Michael Turner. 1975?.
ISBN 0-901690-38-4 Sd : £0.70
(B77-11945)

659.1'52 — Fashion. Modelling, to 1976
Castle, Charles, *b.1939.* Model girl / [by] Charles Castle. — Newton Abbot [etc.] : David and Charles, 1977. — 208p : ill(some col), facsims(2 col), ports(some col) ; 30cm.
Index.
ISBN 0-7153-7412-5 : £6.95
(B77-33918)

659.1'7 — Trade competitions. *Manuals*
Kendal, Robert. Competitors handbook / [by] Robert Kendal. — London : Elek, 1977. — [7], 171p ; 16cm.
Bibl.: p.147-156. — Index.
ISBN 0-236-31083-6 : £3.95
(B77-33324)

659.1'9'62922220904 — Cars. Advertising, to ca 1939
Roberts, Peter, *b.1925.* Any color so long as it's black - : the first fifty years of automobile advertising / [by] Peter Roberts. — Newton Abbot [etc.] : David and Charles, 1976. — 144p : ill(some col), facsims(some col) ; 32cm.
Index.
ISBN 0-7153-7239-4 : £5.95
(B77-04309)

659.2 — PUBLIC RELATIONS
659.2 — Public relations. *Manuals*
Bowman, Pat. Manual of public relations / [by] Pat Bowman and Nigel Ellis. — 2nd ed. ; forewords by Peter Earl, Norman A. Hart, Alec Newman. — London : Heinemann [for] Communication, Advertising and Marketing Education Foundation, 1977. — x,290p ; 22cm.

Previous ed.: 1969. — Index.
ISBN 0-434-90171-7 Pbk : £3.50
(B77-21277)

Jefkins, Frank. Planned press and public relations / [by] Frank Jefkins. — London : International Textbook Co., 1977. — viii,334p : 2 ill, 2 forms ; 24cm.
Index.
ISBN 0-7002-0264-1 : £8.75
ISBN 0-7002-0272-2 Pbk : £4.75
(B77-22723)

659.2'0941 — Public relations. *Great Britain*
Great Britain. *Central Office of Information. Reference Division.* Advertising and public relations in Britain / [prepared by the Reference Division, Central Office of Information]. — London : H.M.S.O., 1976. — [3],30p ; 24cm. — (Central Office of Information reference pamphlet ; 146)
Bibl.: p.30.
ISBN 0-11-700803-6 Sd : £0.65
Primary classification 659.1'0941
(B77-06776)

659.2'8'70941 — Cooperatives. Promotion. Organisations. *Great Britain. Proposals*
Great Britain. *Working Group on a Co-operative Development Agency.* Report of the Working Group on a Co-operative Development Agency ... — London : H.M.S.O., [1977]. — iv,43p ; 25cm. — (Cmnd.6972)
Chairman: Dennis Lawrence.
ISBN 0-10-169720-1 Sd : £0.75
(B77-33325)

659.2'9'61510973 — Prescription drugs. Promotion by pharmaceutical industries. United States. Compared with promotion of prescription drugs by pharmaceutical industries in Latin America
Silverman, Milton. The drugging of the Americas : how multinational drug companies say one thing about their products to physicians in the United States, and another thing to physicians in Latin America / by Milton Silverman. — Berkeley [etc.] ; London : University of California Press, 1976. — xv, 147p ; 25cm.
Index.
ISBN 0-520-03122-9 : £6.40
Also classified at 659.2'9'6151098
(B77-01633)

659.2'9'6151098 — Prescription drugs. Promotion by pharmaceutical industries. Latin America. Compared with promotion of prescription drugs by pharmaceutical industries in United States
Silverman, Milton. The drugging of the Americas : how multinational drug companies say one thing about their products to physicians in the United States, and another thing to physicians in Latin America / by Milton Silverman. — Berkeley [etc.] ; London : University of California Press, 1976. — xv, 147p ; 25cm.
Index.
ISBN 0-520-03122-9 : £6.40
Primary classification 659.2'9'61510973
(B77-01633)

659.2'9'6600941 — Chemical industries. Public relations. *Great Britain. Manuals*
Chemical Industries Association. Members' guide to public relations / Chemical Industries Association. — London : [C.I.A.], [1976]. — [175]p(2 fold) : ill(some col), maps(some col), ports ; 32cm.
Tab indexed. — In binder. — Contains 7 pamphlets in plastic bags. — Bibl.: p.[175].
ISBN 0-900623-22-5 Ls : Unpriced
(B77-06777)

659.2'9'720941 — Architects. Public relations. *Great Britain. Conference proceedings*
Architects and public relations / edited by Kate Wharton. — London : Transcripta Books, 1974. — [1],55p : ill ; 28cm.
'Verbatim report of a Conference arranged by IPC Business and Industrial Training Limited and held at the Cafe Royal, London on 2 May 1974' - title page verso.
ISBN 0-903012-29-4 Pbk : £3.50
(B77-02432)

659.2'9'7694071073 — Educational institutions. Activities: Athletics. Public relations. *United States*
Bronzan, Robert T. Public relations, promotions, and fund-raising for athletic and physical education programs / [by] Robert T. Bronzan. — New York ; London [etc.] : Wiley, 1977. — xiv,268p : ill, facsims, ports ; 24cm.
Bibl.: p.259-262. — Index.
ISBN 0-471-01540-7 : £10.00
Also classified at 796.4'07'1073
(B77-11946)

659.2'9'91411 — Tourism. Promotion. Organisations. *Scotland. Scottish Tourist Board. Reports, surveys. Serials*
Scottish Tourist Board. Report / the Scottish Tourist Board. — Edinburgh : The Board.
7th : 1st April 1975-31st March 1976. — 1976. — 69p : ill(some col), col maps, ports ; 30cm.
ISBN 0-85419-112-7 Sd : £0.60
ISSN 0306-9125
(B77-02433)

659.2'9'9142 — Tourism. Promotion. Organisations. *England. English Tourist Board. Reports, surveys. Serials*
English Tourist Board. English Tourist Board annual report and accounts for the year ended 31 March ... — London : The Board.
[1976]-1977. — [1977]. — 56p : ill(chiefly col), col maps, ports ; 21cm.
Pbk : Unpriced
(B77-22001)

659.2'9'91423 — Tourism. Promotion. Organisations. *South-west England. West Country Tourist Board. Reports, surveys. Serials*
West Country Tourist Board. Annual report of the West Country Tourist Board for the year ended 31 March. — [Exeter] ([Trinity Court, Southerhay East, Exeter EX1 1QS]) : The Board.
1977. — [1977]. — [2],48p : ill, ports ; 21cm.
Sd : £0.50
(B77-18888)

660 — CHEMICAL TECHNOLOGY
660 — Applied chemistry. *Reviews of research*
Reports on the progress of applied chemistry. — Oxford [etc.] : Blackwell Scientific for the Society of Chemical Industry.
1975 : Vol.60. — 1976. — viii,696p : ill ; 21cm.

Bibl. — Index.
ISBN 0-632-00179-8 : £25.00
ISSN 0370-6648
(B77-00846)

660'.05 — Chemical technology. Conferences. *Reports, surveys. Serials*
Conference reports, physical and chemical sciences. — London : Applied Science Publishers.
Vol.1, [no.1]- ; 1977-. — 1977-. — 24cm.
Quarterly. — [1],83p. in 1st issue. — Index.
Pbk : £16.00(yearly)
ISSN 0309-5894
Primary classification 500.2'05
(B77-15822)

660.2 — CHEMICAL ENGINEERING
Chemical engineering. — 3rd ed. (SI units). — Oxford [etc.] : Pergamon.
Vol.1 : Fluid flow, heat transfer and mass transfer / [by] J.M. Coulson and J.F. Richardson ; with editorial assistance from J.R. Backhurst and J.H. Harker. — 1977. — xiii, 449p,[6]leaves of plate(1 fold),[16]p of plates : ill ; 26cm.
Previous ed.: 1964. — Bibl. — Index.
ISBN 0-08-020614-x : Unpriced
ISBN 0-08-021015-5 Pbk : £7.50
(B77-18272)

Thompson, Edward V. Introduction to chemical engineering / [by] Edward V. Thompson, William H. Ceckler. — New York ; London [etc.] : McGraw-Hill, 1977. — xi,401p : ill ; 25cm. — (McGraw-Hill chemical engineering series)
Index.
ISBN 0-07-064396-2 : £14.65
(B77-20439)

660.2 — Chemical engineering. *Conference proceedings*
Design Congress, *University of Aston in Birmingham, 1976.* Design developments related to safety, costs and solids systems : selected papers from Design Congress '76, University of Aston in Birmingham 9 and 10 September 1976, organised by the Institution of Chemical Engineers (Midlands Branch). — Rugby (165 Railway Terrace, Rugby, Warwickshire CV21 3HQ) : I.Chem.E. Services for the Institution of Chemical Engineers, 1977. — 193p in various pagings : ill, maps ; 30cm. — (Institution of Chemical Engineers. Symposium series ; no.45 ISSN 0307-0492)
Bibl.
ISBN 0-85295-104-3 Pbk : Unpriced
(B77-25062)

World Congress on Chemical Engineering, *1st, Amsterdam, 1976.* Chemical engineering in a changing world : proceedings of the plenary sessions of the First World Congress on Chemical Engineering, Amsterdam, June 28-July 1, 1976 / edited by Wicher T. Koetsier. — Amsterdam ; Oxford [etc.] : Elsevier, 1976. — xxii,550p : ill, maps ; 25cm.
'Organized under the auspices of the Koninklijke Nederlandse Chemische Vereniging and the Koninklijk Instituut van Ingenieurs' - half title page verso. — Bibl.
ISBN 0-444-41543-2 : £34.89
(B77-15960)

660.2'028'54 — Chemical engineering. Applications of computer systems. *Periodicals*
Computers & chemical engineering. — Oxford [etc.] : Pergamon.
Vol.1, no.1- ; 1977-. — 1977-. — ill ; 28cm.
Quarterly. — [2],102p. in 1st issue.
Pbk : Unpriced
ISSN 0098-1354
(B77-15961)

660.2'08 — Chemical engineering. *Readings*
Krevelen, Dirk Willem van. Selected papers on chemical engineering science / [by] Dirk Willem van Krevelen. — Amsterdam ; Oxford [etc.] : Elsevier, 1976. — xii,385p : ill, 2 ports ; 28cm.
Includes original pagings, 6 papers in German and 3 in French. — Bibl.
ISBN 0-444-41529-7 : £25.76
(B77-16496)

660.2'804 — Chemical engineering. Hazards. *Conference proceedings*
Symposium on Chemical Process Hazards with Special Reference to Plant Design, *6th, University of Manchester Institute of Science and Technology, 1977.* Papers of the Symposium on Chemical Process Hazards with Special Reference to Plant Design, VI : a symposium organised by the North Western Branch of the Institution of Chemical Engineers at the University of Manchester Institute of Science and Technology, 5-7 April 1977, symposium organisers J.H. Burgoyne ... [et al.]. — Rugby : I. Chem. E. Services for the Institution of Chemical Engineers, 1977. — [8], 152p : ill ; 30cm. — (Institution of Chemical Engineers. Symposium series ; no.49 ISSN 0307-0492)
'180th event of the European Federation of Chemical Engineering' - cover. — Cover title: Chemical process hazards with special reference to plant design, VI.
ISBN 0-85295-100-0 Pbk : £12.50
(B77-19507)

660.2'804 — Chemical engineering plants. Accidents. Explosions. *Great Britain. Inquiry reports*
Great Britain. *Factory Inspectorate.* The explosion at Laporte Industries Ltd, Ilford, 5 April 1975 : a report / by HM Factory Inspectorate, Health & Safety Executive. — [London] : H.M.S.O., 1976. — 24p : ill, plan ; 30cm.
ISBN 0-11-880333-6 Sd : £1.25
(B77-03118)

660.2'804 — Chemical engineering plants. Extension. Safety aspects. *Great Britain. For management*
Major hazards : memorandum of guidance on extensions to existing chemical plant introducing a major hazard / [prepared by a working party of the British Chemical Industry Safety Council]. — London (93 Albert Embankment, SE1 7TU) : The Council, 1972. — [2],11[i.e.12]p ; 30cm.
Includes: Development involving the use or storage in bulk of hazardous material : joint circular from the Department of the Environment ... and Welsh Office ... London : The Department : The Office, 1972.
ISBN 0-900623-29-2 Sd : £1.00
(B77-06778)

660.2'83 — Mechanical draught cooling towers
Cooling Water Association. Guide to mechanical draught evaporative cooling towers / Cooling Water Association. — London (74 Queensway, W2 3RW) : The Association, 1975. — 124 leaves in various pagings : ill, chart, forms ; 31cm.
In binder.
ISBN 0-905832-01-9 Ls : £11.50
(B77-01634)

660.2'83 — Welded chemical engineering components. *Conference proceedings*
Fabrication and reliability of welded process plant : an international conference, London, 16-18 November 1976. — Cambridge : Welding Institute.
In 2 vols.
Vol.1 : Papers. — 1977. — [4],236p : ill ; 30cm.

ISBN 0-85300-110-3 Pbk : £16.50(set of 2 vols)
(B77-33326)

660.2'842 — Chemical engineering. Mass transfer
Sherwood, Thomas Kilgore. Mass transfer. — [3rd ed.] / [by] Thomas K. Sherwood, Robert L. Pigford, Charles R. Wilke. — New York ; London [etc.] : McGraw-Hill, [1976]. — xi, 677p : ill ; 25cm. — (McGraw-Hill chemical engineering series)
This ed. published in the United States: 1975. — Previous ed.: published as 'Absorption and extraction' / by T.K. Sherwood and R.L. Pigford. 1952. — Bibl. — Index.
ISBN 0-07-056692-5 : £18.70
(B77-04938)

660.2'842 — Chemical engineering. Unit operations
McCabe, Warren Lee. Unit operations of chemical engineering / [by] Warren L. McCabe, Julian C. Smith. — 3rd ed. — New York ; London [etc.] : McGraw-Hill, 1976. — ix, 1028p ; 25cm.
Previous ed.: 1967. — Index.
ISBN 0-07-044825-6 : £18.70
(B77-05524)

660.2'8426 — Spray drying
Masters, Keith. Spray drying : an introduction to principles, operational practice and applications / [by] K. Masters. — 2nd ed. — London : Godwin [etc.], 1976. — xxxv,684p : ill ; 23cm.
Previous ed.: London : L. Hill, 1972. — Index.
ISBN 0-7114-4921-x : £18.00
(B77-02434)

660.2'8427 — Recirculation cooling systems. Water. Treatment. *Manuals*
Cooling Water Association. Cooling water treatment : a code of practice / [Cooling Water Association]. — London (74 Queensway, W2 3RW) : The Association, 1973. — [3],45p : ill ; 31cm.
In binder.
ISBN 0-905832-00-0 Ls : £11.50
(B77-01635)

660.2'84298 — Industrial chemicals. Crystallisation. *Conference proceedings*
Symposium on Industrial Crystallization, *6th, Ústí nad Labem, 1975.* Industrial crystallization / edited by J.W. Mullin. — New York ; London : Plenum Press, 1976. — x, 473p : ill ; 26cm.
'Proceedings of the Sixth Symposium on Industrial Crystallization held at Usti nad Labem, Czechoslovakia, September 1-3, 1975' - title page verso. — '... organized by the Crystallization Research Group ... jointly with the European Federation of Chemical Engineering Working Party on Crystallization ...' - Preface. — Bibl. — Index.
ISBN 0-306-30945-9 : Unpriced
(B77-26402)

660.2'9'8 — Chemical engineering. Applications of ionising radiation. *Conference proceedings*
International Meeting on Radiation Processing, *1st, Dorado Beach, 1976.* Radiation processing : transactions of the First International Meeting on Radiation Processing : a conference jointly sponsored by Polymer Chemistry Division, American Chemical Society, Isotopes and Radiation Division, American Nuclear Society, Electronics Division, Society of Plastics Engineers, held at Dorado Beach, Puerto Rico, 9-13 May 1976 / editors Joseph Silverman and A.R. van Dyken. — Oxford [etc.] : Pergamon, 1977. — 2v.(xxvi,885p) : ill, maps ; 26cm.
'Published as a special issue of the journal "Radiation physics and chemistry", Volume 9, Numbers 1-3 ...' - title page verso. — Index.
ISBN 0-08-021640-4 : £55.00
(B77-32736)

660.2'9'92 — Industrial chemicals: Carbon. Chemical reactions with hydrogen & oxygen. Equilibria. *Technical data*
Baron, Robert E. Chemical equilibria in carbon-hydrogen-oxygen systems / [by] Robert E. Baron, James H. Porter and Ogden H. Hammond, Jr. — Cambridge, Mass. ; London : M.I.T. Press, 1976. — xii,110p : ill ; 26cm. — (The MIT Press energy laboratory series ; 1)
ISBN 0-262-02121-8 Sp : £7.50
(B77-06779)

660.2'9'93 — Chemical engineering. Heterogeneous chemical reactions
Carberry, James J. Chemical and catalytic reaction engineering / [by] James J. Carberry. — New York ; London [etc.] : McGraw-Hill, 1976. — xxiii,642p : ill ; 25cm. — (McGraw-Hill chemical engineering series)
Bibl. — Index.
ISBN 0-07-009790-9 : £18.70
(B77-04310)

660.6 — INDUSTRIAL BIOLOGY
660'.62 — Industrial microbiology. *Reviews of research*
Industrial microbiology / [edited by] Brinton M. Miller, Warren Litsky. — New York ; London [etc.] : McGraw-Hill, 1976. — xiii,465p : ill ; 25cm.
Bibl. — Index.
ISBN 0-07-042142-0 : £16.15
(B77-27962)

660'.63 — Industrial biochemistry
Bailey, James E. Biochemical engineering fundamentals / [by] James E. Bailey, David F. Ollis. — New York ; London [etc.] : McGraw-Hill, 1977. — xiv,753p : ill ; 24cm. — (McGraw-Hill chemical engineering series) (McGraw-Hill series in water resources and environmental engineering)
Index.
ISBN 0-07-003210-6 : £18.75
(B77-27237)

661 — INDUSTRIAL CHEMICALS
661 — Industrial chemicals: Inorganic materials. High temperature reactions. *Conference proceedings*
High temperature chemistry of inorganic and ceramic materials, Keele University, September 1976 : the proceedings of a conference organized jointly by the Inorganic Chemicals Group of the Industrial Division of the Chemical Society and the Basic Science Section of the British Ceramic Society / edited by F.P. Glasser and P.E. Potter. — London : Chemical Society, 1977. — [10],240p : ill ; 23cm. — (Chemical Society. Special publications ; no.30 ISSN 0577-618x)
ISBN 0-85186-168-7 : £11.00
(B77-32015)

661'.00941 — Proprietary industrial chemicals. *Great Britain. Lists*
Wyatt, Alan G. Chemicals 77 : a directory giving information on chemicals and allied products marketed by member firms of the Chemical Industries Association / [technical compilation by Alan G. Wyatt and Moira T. Damer ...]. — London (93 Albert Embankment, SE1 7TU) : The Association, 1976. — xii,211p,fold leaf : ill ; 21cm.
English text, English, German, Spanish and French introductions. — Index.
Pbk : £8.00
Also classified at 615'.11'41
(B77-09129)

661'.06'83 — Pyrogenic silica. Manufacture from fluosilicic acid
Flemmert, G L. Hydrogen fluoride and pyrogenic silica from fluosilicic acid / by G.L. Flemmert. — London (93 Albert Embankment, SE1 7TU) : Fertiliser Society, [1977]. — [1],23p ; 21cm. — (Fertiliser Society. Proceedings ; no.163)
'Paper read before The Fertiliser Society of London on 14th April, 1977'.
Sd : £1.50
Primary classification 661'.08
(B77-13744)

661'.08 — Hydrogen fluoride. Manufacture from fluosilicic acid
Flemmert, G L. Hydrogen fluoride and pyrogenic silica from fluosilicic acid / by G.L. Flemmert. — London (93 Albert Embankment, SE1 7TU) : Fertiliser Society, [1977]. — [1],23p ; 21cm. — (Fertiliser Society. Proceedings ; no.163)
'Paper read before The Fertiliser Society of London on 14th April, 1977'.
Sd : £1.50
Also classified at 661'.06'83
(B77-13744)

661'.8 — Industrial chemicals: Enzymes. *Reviews of research*
Topics in enzyme and fermentation biotechnology. — Chichester : Ellis Horwood [etc.].
1 / editor Alan Wiseman. — 1977. — 191p : ill ; 24cm.
Bibl. — Index.
ISBN 0-85312-051-x : £10.50
(B77-08460)

661'.8 — Industrial chemicals: Starch. Manufacture
Starch production technology / edited by J.A. Radley. — London : Applied Science Publishers, 1976. — viii,587p : ill ; 23cm.
Index.
ISBN 0-85334-662-3 : £35.00
(B77-02435)

661'.806 — Essential oils. Testing. *Standards*
British Standards Institution. Methods of test for essential oils = Méthodes d'essai des huiles essentielles = Verfahren zur Prüfung von ätherischen Ölen / British Standards Institution. — 2nd revision. — London : B.S.I., 1976. — [2],26,[2]p : ill ; 30cm. — (BS2073 : 1976)
Pierced for binder.
ISBN 0-580-09215-1 Sd : £4.00
(B77-01636)

661'.807 — Mineral solvents. *Standards*
British Standards Institution. Specification for mineral solvents (white spirit and related hydrocarbon solvents) for paints and other purposes = Spécification pour solvants d'origine minérale ('white spirit' et hydrocarbures analogues) pour peintures et d'autres applications = Spezifikation für Minerallösungsmittel ('white spirit' und ähnliche Kohlenwasserstofflösungsmittel) für Anstrichstoff und andere Zwecke / British Standards Institution. — 3rd revision. — London : B.S.I., 1976. — [2],4,[2]p ; 30cm. — (BS245 : 1976)
Pierced for binder.
ISBN 0-580-09530-4 Sd : £1.50
(B77-10451)

661'.808 — Sensitometry. *Programmed texts*
Todd, Hollis Nelson. Photographic sensitometry : a self-teaching text / [by] Hollis N. Todd. — New York ; London [etc.] : Wiley, 1976. — xi, 225p : ill ; 29cm. — (Wiley series on photographic science and technology and the graphic arts)
'A Wiley-Interscience publication'. — With answers to self-tests. — Transparent sheet, 2 card strips in pocket. — Bibl.: p.219. — Index.
ISBN 0-471-87649-6 : £10.60
(B77-06780)

661'.815 — Nucleosides & nucleotides. Manufacture. Use of microorganisms
Microbial production of nucleic acid-related substances / edited by the Association of Amino Acid and Nucleic Acid ; [by] Koichi Ogata ... [et al.]. — Tokyo : Kodansha ; New York ; London [etc.] : Wiley, 1976. — xviii, 348p : ill ; 23cm.
'A Halsted Press book'. — Index.
ISBN 0-470-15167-6 : £19.50
(B77-01637)

662.2 — EXPLOSIVES
662'.2'0216 — Authorised explosives. *Great Britain. Lists. Serials*
List of authorised explosives / Health and Safety Executive. — London : H.M.S.O.
1977. January / [by] F.W. Ireland, HM Chief Inspector of Explosives. — 1977. — 30p ; 21cm.
ISBN 0-11-883000-7 Sd : £0.80
(B77-11298)

662.6 — FUELS
Gilchrist, James Duncan. Fuels, furnaces and refractories / by J.D. Gilchrist. — Oxford [etc.] : Pergamon, 1977. — xiii,353p : ill ; 22cm. — (Pergamon international library) (International series on materials science and technology ; vol.21)
'A combined revision of the author's "Fuels and refractories" and "Furnaces"' - Library of Congress Cataloging in Publication Data. — Bibl.: p.344-345. — Index.
ISBN 0-08-020430-9 : £7.80
ISBN 0-08-020429-5 Pbk : £4.50
Primary classification 621.4'025
(B77-16450)

662.6 — Fuels: Carbohydrates & lignins. Thermal properties. *Conference proceedings*
Symposium on Thermal Uses and Properties of Carbohydrates and Lignins, *San Francisco, 1976.* Thermal uses and properties of carbohydrates and lignins : Symposium on Thermal Uses and Properties of Carbohydrates and Lignins, 172nd National Meeting of the American Chemical Society, San Francisco, September, 1976 / edited by Fred Shafizadeh, Kyosti V. Sarkanen, David A. Tillman. — New York [etc.] ; London : Academic Press, 1976. — xi,320p : ill ; 24cm.
Index.
ISBN 0-12-637750-2 : £10.65
(B77-14825)

662.6'021'2 — Fuels. *Technical data*
Technical data on fuel. — 7th ed. completely revised in SI units / edited by J.W. Rose and J.R. Cooper. — London : British National Committee, World Energy Conference ; Edinburgh : Distributed by Scottish Academic Press, 1977. — xi,343p : ill ; 29cm.
Previous ed.: / World Power Conference, British National Committee, Technical Data on Fuel Committee. 1961. — Index.
ISBN 0-7073-0129-7 : £30.00
(B77-30431)

662'.6'06241 — Fuel technology. Organisations. *Great Britain. Institute of Fuel, to 1976*
Hayman, Roy. The Institute of Fuel : the first 50 years / by Roy Hayman. — London (18 Devonshire St., W1N 2AU) : The Institute, 1977. — [6],112p ; 21cm.
ISBN 0-902597-14-0 Pbk : £5.00
(B77-23566)

662'.622 — Coal. Testing. *Standards*
British Standards Institution. Methods for analysis and testing of coal and coke = Méthodes d'analyse et d'essai du charbon et du coke = Verfahren für Analyse und Prüfung von Kohle und Koks / British Standards Institution. — 4th revision. — London : B.S.I.
Part 5 = Partie 5 = Teil 5 : Gross colorific value of coal and coke = Pouvoir colorifique supérieur du charbon et du coke = Verbrennungswärme von Kohle und Koks. — 1977. — [2],8,[2]p ; 30cm. — (BS1016 : Part 5 : 1977)
Pierced for binder.
ISBN 0-580-09043-4 Sd : £2.70
Also classified at 662'.72
(B77-16986)

662'.6622 — Coal. Liquefaction. *Conference proceedings*
American Chemical Society. *National Meeting, 172nd, San Francisco, 1976.* Liquid fuels from coal / edited by Rex T. Ellington. — New York [etc.] ; London : Academic Press, 1977. — xvii,273p : ill ; 24cm.
Proceedings of the 172nd National Meeting of the American Chemical Society held in San Francisco, August 29-September 3, 1976. — Index.
ISBN 0-12-237250-6 : £10.30
(B77-23567)

662'.666 — Aerospace vehicles: Rockets. Propellants. Quantitative analysis. *Laboratory manuals*
Malone, Hugh Edward. The analysis of rocket propellants / [by] Hugh E. Malone. — London [etc.] : Academic Press, 1976. — x,148p : ill ; 24cm. — (The analysis of organic materials ; vol.12)
Bibl. — Index.
ISBN 0-12-466750-3 : £6.50
(B77-10452)

662'.72 — Coke. Testing. *Standards*
British Standards Institution. Methods for analysis and testing of coal and coke = Méthodes d'analyse et d'essai du charbon et du coke = Verfahren für Analyse und Prüfung von Kohle und Koks / British Standards Institution. — 4th revision. — London : B.S.I.
Part 5 = Partie 5 = Teil 5 : Gross colorific value of coal and coke = Pouvoir colorifique supérieur du charbon et du coke = Verbrennungswärme von Kohle und Koks. — 1977. — [2],8,[2]p ; 30cm. — (BS1016 : Part 5 : 1977)
Pierced for binder.
ISBN 0-580-09043-4 Sd : £2.70
Primary classification 662'.622
(B77-16986)

663 — BEVERAGE MANUFACTURES
663'.1'01576 — Alcoholic drinks. Production. Microbiological aspects
Alcoholic beverages / edited by A.H. Rose. — London [etc.] : Academic Press, 1977. — xiv, 760p : ill ; 24cm. — (Economic microbiology ; vol.1)
Bibl. — Index.
ISBN 0-12-596550-8 : £25.00
(B77-23568)

663'.19 — Wine & spirits bottles. Metrication
United Glass. UG packaging forum, guide to metrication - a rational approach, wines & spirits / [editor P.W. Nelson]. — Staines (Kingston Rd, Staines, Middx TW18 1AD) : United Glass, 1976. — [1],13p : col ill ; 30cm.
Supplements 1-5 ([19] leaves; ill.) bound in.
ISBN 0-9505407-0-6 Sd : Unpriced
(B77-02436)

663'.19'05 — Drinks. Bottling. *Serials*
The **bottlers'** year book. — Purley (7 Higher Drive, Purley, Surrey CR2 2HP) : B.Y.B. Ltd.
1977. — [1977]. — 383p in various pagings : ill ; 19cm.
Index.
Pbk : £3.50
(B77-33919)

663'.3'06241 — Brewing. Organisations. *Great Britain. Institute of Brewing. Directories*
Institute of Brewing. List of members / Institute of Brewing. — London (30 Clarges St., W1Y 8EE) : [The Institute].
1976 : (corrected to 30.6.76). — [1976]. — 102p ; 23cm.
ISBN 0-900489-04-9 Pbk : Private circulation
(B77-06781)

663'.42 — Industrial antiquities: Hop warehouses. *London. Southwark (London Borough). Bermondsey*
Greater London Industrial Archaeology Society. A hop merchant's warehouse, 24 Melior Street, London SE1 / [Greater London Industrial Archaeology Society]. — London (c/o A. Tayler, 28 Tower Hamlets Rd, E17 4RH) : GLIAS, 1977. — [4]p : ill, map, plan ; 30cm.
ISBN 0-905042-08-5 Sd : £0.12(free to members)
(B77-23569)

664 — FOOD MANUFACTURES
664 — Food technology. *Secondary school texts*
Tooley, Peter. Food and technology / by Peter Tooley. — St Albans : Hart-Davis Educational, 1977. — [2],70,[1]p : ill, facsim ; 21x24cm. — (Technology around us)
Bibl.: p.69. — Index.
ISBN 0-247-12592-x Sd : £1.45
(B77-11947)

664 — Green crops. Fractionation. *Conference proceedings*
Green crop fractionation : proceedings of a symposium organised by the British Grassland Society and the British Society of Animal Production, 25-26 November, 1976 held at Harrogate, Yorkshire / editor R.J. Wilkins. — Maidenhead (c/o Grassland Research Institute, Hurley, Maidenhead, Berks. SL6 5LR) : British Grassland Society, 1977. — vii,189p : ill ; 24cm. — (British Grassland Society. Occasional symposia ; no.9)
Bibl.
ISBN 0-905944-00-3 Pbk : £5.00
(B77-32016)

664'.005 — Food technology. *Periodicals*
Irish journal of food science and technology. — Dublin : An Foras Talúntais.
Vol.1, no.1- ; 1977-. — 1977-. — ill ; 24cm.
Two issues a year. — Cover title. — 70p. in 1st issue.
Pbk : £1.00
(B77-18273)

664'.005 — Food technology. Conferences. *Reports, surveys. Serials*
Conference reports, agriculture, food and biology. — London : Applied Science Publishers.
Vol.1, [no.1]- ; 1977-. — 1977-. — 24cm.
Quarterly. — [1],79p. in 1st issue. — Index.
Pbk : £16.00(yearly)
ISSN 0309-5886
Primary classification 630'.5
(B77-15924)

664'.0284 — Intermediate moisture food. *Conference proceedings*
Intermediate moisture foods / edited by R. Davies, G.G. Birch and K.J. Parker. — London : Applied Science Publishers, 1976. — xii,306p : ill ; 23cm.
'An industry-university co-operation Symposium organised under the auspices of the National College of Food Technology, University of Reading' - half title verso. — Index.
ISBN 0-85334-702-6 : £15.00
(B77-03119)

664'.02842 — Food. Effects of preservative thermal processing
Physical, chemical and biological changes in food caused by thermal processing / edited by Tore Hoyem and Oskar Kvale. — London : Applied Science Publishers, 1977. — xi,398p : ill ; 23cm.
'Proceedings of an international symposium sponsored by the International Union of Food Science and Technology, the Scandinavian Association of Agricultural Scientists and the Norwegian Agricultural Food Research Society, held in Oslo, Norway' - half title page verso. — Index.
ISBN 0-85334-729-8 : £25.00
(B77-29564)

664'.0285 — Food. Refrigeration
Cooling technology in the food industry / [by] Aurel Ciobanu ... [et al.] ; [translated from the Romanian by C. Sturza and A. Ciobanu ; translation editor John Hammel]. — Revised English ed. — Tunbridge Wells : Abacus Press, 1976. — 500,[1]p,[2]fold leaves of plates : ill ; 25cm.
Translation and revision of: 'Frigul artificial in fabricarea si conservarea produselor alimentare'. Bucureşti : Editura technică, 1971.
ISBN 0-85626-018-5 : £16.50
(B77-09814)

664'.02852'05 — Food. Cold storage. *Periodicals*
Temperature controlled storage & distribution. — Redhill (2 Queensway, Redhill RH1 1QS) : Retail Journals Ltd.
No.1- ; Sept. 1977-. — [1977]-. — ill(some col), ports ; 30cm.
48p. in preview issue.
Sd : Unpriced
Also classified at 380.5'2
(B77-21278)

664'.02852'06241 — Food. Cold storage. Organisations. *Great Britain. National Cold Storage Federation. Yearbooks*
National Cold Storage Federation. Year book of the National Cold Storage Federation. — Wallington (272 London Rd, Wallington, Surrey SM6 7DJ) : [The Federation].
1977. — [1977]. — 136p : ill, maps, ports ; 22cm.
ISBN 0-900555-05-x Pbk : £1.50
(B77-06782)

664'.0288 — Food. Irradiation. *Reports, surveys*
Joint FAO/IAEA/WHO Expert Committee on the Wholesomeness of Irradiated Food. Wholesomeness of irradiated food : report of a Joint FAO/IAEA/WHO Expert Committee [on the Wholesomeness of Irradiated Food]. — Geneva : World Health Organization ; [London] : [H.M.S.O.], 1977. — 44p ; 20cm. — (World Health Organization. Technical report series ; 604) (Food and Agriculture Organization. Food and nutrition series ; 6)
'A Joint FAO/IAEA/WHO Expert Committee on the Wholesomeness of Irradiated Food met in Geneva from 31 August to 7 September 1976' - p.7. — Bibl.: p.40-41.
Sd : Unpriced
ISBN 92-4-120604-7
(B77-17628)

664'.0288 — Food. Preservation. Applications of irradiation. *Reviews of research*
Radiation chemistry of major food components : its relevance to the assessement [i.e. assessment] of the wholesomeness of irradiated foods / editors P.S. Elias and A.J. Cohen. — Amsterdam ; Oxford [etc.] : Elsevier, 1977. — xii,220p : ill ; 25cm.
'... commissioned by the International Project in the Field of Food Irradiation ...' - Foreword. — Foreword in English and French.
ISBN 0-444-41587-4 : £12.60
(B77-23570)

664'.06 — Food. Additives
Why additives? : the safety of foods / devised and edited by the British Nutrition Foundation. — London (Hartree House, Queensway, W2 4SH) : Forbes Publications, 1977. — xvi,75p ; 19cm.
Index.
ISBN 0-901762-09-1 : £1.50
(B77-21279)

664'.07 — Food. Chemical analysis
Pearson, David, *b.1919.* The chemical analysis of foods / [by] David Pearson. — 7th ed. — Edinburgh [etc.] : Churchill Livingstone, 1976. — xii,575p : ill ; 24cm.
Previous ed.: 1970. — Bibl. — Index.
ISBN 0-443-01411-6 : £13.50
(B77-05525)

664'.07 — Food. Gas chromatography
Dickes, Geoffrey James. Gas chromatography in food analysis / [by] G.J. Dickes and P.V. Nicholas. — London [etc.] : Butterworth, 1976. — [12],393p : ill ; 24cm.
Index.
ISBN 0-408-70781-x : Unpriced
(B77-00847)

664'.122 — Cane sugar. Processing. *Manuals*
Meade, George Peterkin. Meade-Chen cane sugar handbook : a manual for cane sugar manufacturers and their chemists. — 10th ed. / by the late George P. Meade and James C.P. Chen. — New York ; London [etc.] : Wiley, 1977. — xix,947p : ill ; 22cm.
'A Wiley-Interscience publication'. — Text on lining papers. — Previous ed.: published as 'Cane sugar handbook' / by Guilford Lawson Spencer and George Peterkin Meade. 1963. — Bibl.: p.xv-xvii. — Index.
ISBN 0-471-58995-0 : £35.00
(B77-23571)

664'.123 — Sugar beet. Physical properties & chemical properties
Vukov, Konstantin. Physics and chemistry of sugar-beet in sugar manufacture / [by] Konstantin Vukov ; [translated from the German by Alfred Falvay]. — Amsterdam ; Oxford [etc.] : Elsevier, 1977. — 595p : ill ; 25cm.
Translation, revision and enlargement of: 'Physik und Chemie der Zuckerrübe als Grundlage der Verarbeitungsverfahren'. Budapest : Akadémiai Kiadó, 1972. — Index.
ISBN 0-444-99836-5 : £29.00
(B77-21280)

664'.26 — Gelatine
The science and technology of gelatin / edited by A.G. Ward, A. Courts. — London [etc.] : Academic Press, 1977. — xvi,564p : ill ; 24cm. — (Food science and technology)
Bibl. — Index.
ISBN 0-12-735050-0 : £18.00
(B77-27238)

664'.26 — Gelatine. Sampling & testing. *Standards*
British Standards Institution. British Standard methods for microbiological examination of gelatine = Méthodes pour l'examen microbiologique de la gélatine = Mikrobiologische Untersuchungsverfahren für Gelatin / British Standards Institution. — London : B.S.I.
Part 6 = Partie 6 = Teil 6 : Detection of sulphite-reducing organisms = Détection des organismes réducteurs des sulfites = Nachweis von sulfitreduzierenden Organismen. — 1976. — Sheet ([2]p) ; 30x21cm. — (BS5349 : Part 6 : 1976)
Pierced for binder. — Previous control number ISBN 0-580-09273-9.
ISBN 0-580-09794-3 : £0.75
(B77-07974)

British Standards Institution. British Standard methods for microbiological examination of gelatine = Méthodes pour l'examen microbiologique de la gélatine = Verfahren für die mikrobiologische Untersudiung von Gelatine / British Standards Institution. — London : B.S.I.
Part 9 = Partie 9 = Teil 9 : Detection of Staphylococcus aureus m Détection du Staphylococcus aureus m Nachweis von Staphylococcus aureus. — 1976. — Folder (4p) ; 30cm. — (BS5349 : Part 9 : 1976)
Pierced for binder.
ISBN 0-580-09478-2 : £1.15
(B77-07975)

664'.32 — Margarine. *Juvenile literature*
Hinds, Lorna. Butter and margarine / by Lorna Hinds ; illustrated by Lorraine Calaora. — London [etc.] : F. Watts, 1977. — 48p : ill(some col), 2 col ports ; 22cm. — (A first look book)
Index.
ISBN 0-85166-637-x : £1.75
Primary classification 641.3'7'2
(B77-30392)

664'.52 — Food: Vanilla. *Standards*
British Standards Institution. British Standard specification for vanilla = Spécification de la vanille = Spezifikation für Vanille / British Standards Institution. — London : B.S.I.
Part 1 = Partie 1 = Teil 1 : Vocabulary = Vocabulaire = Wortschatz. — 1976. — Folder (4p) ; 30cm. — (BS5432 : Part 1 : 1976) (ISO 3493-1976)
Pierced for binder.
ISBN 0-580-09600-9 : £1.60
(B77-11948)

664'.7207 — Flour milling mills. *Surrey. Sunbury-on-Thames, to 1950*
Heselton, Kenneth Yeaman. Sunbury mills and fire services / [by] Kenneth Y. Heselton. — Sunbury-on-Thames (12 Heathcroft Ave., Sunbury-on-Thames, [Middx]) : Sunbury and Shepperton Local History Society, 1977. — [2], 12p ; 26cm. — (Sunbury and Shepperton Local History Society. Occasional publications ; no.4 ISSN 0309-2070)
Sd : £0.20
Primary classification 363.3'7'0942212
(B77-15770)

664'.7207 — Museums. *South Glamorgan. St Fagans. Welsh Folk Museum. Exhibits: Flour milling watermills: Melin Bompren Corn Mill. Guidebooks*
Welsh Folk Museum. Melin Bompren Corn Mill : at the Welsh Folk Museum, St Fagans, Cardiff / [written by] Eurwyn William. — [Cardiff] : Welsh Folk Museum, 1977. — 27p : ill, plans, port ; 15x22cm.
Bibl.: p.23.
ISBN 0-85485-042-2 Sd : Unpriced
(B77-26403)

664'.7207 — Museums. *South Glamorgan. St Fagans. Welsh Folk Museum. Exhibits: Flour milling watermills: Melin Bompren Corn Mill. Guidebooks. Welsh texts*

Welsh Folk Museum. Melin Bompren : yn Amgueddfa Werin Cymru, Sain Ffagan, Caerdydd / [gan] Eurwyn Wiliam. — [Cardiff] : Amgueddfa Werin Cymru, [1977]. — 27p : ill, plans, port ; 15x22cm.
Bibl.: p.23.
ISBN 0-85485-041-4 Sd : Unpriced
(B77-26404)

664'.8 — Quick-frozen trimmed Brussels sprouts. *Standards*

Campden Food Preservation Research Association. Specifications for raw materials and final product for quick frozen trimmed brussels sprouts / ... prepared [by the Campden Food Preservation Research Association] in collaboration with participating members of the British Frozen Food Federation and the Processed Vegetable Growers Association. — Chipping Campden (Chipping Campden, Glos. GL55 6LD) : The Association, 1977. — [2],7, 12p : ill ; 26cm.
ISBN 0-905942-03-5 Sd : Unpriced
(B77-14312)

664'.9 — Meat & meat products. Processing. *Conference proceedings*

European Meeting of Meat Research Workers, *20th, Dublin, 1974.* The 20th European Meeting of Meat Research Workers, Dublin, September 15-20, 1974. — [Dublin] ([19 Sandymount Ave., Dublin 4]) : An Foras Talúntais.
Abstracts & communications. — [1976]. — 278p : ill ; 30cm.
Includes papers in German, Russian and French. — English, French, German and Russian summaries. — Bibl.
Pbk : Unpriced
(B77-02437)

Rapporteurs' papers. — [1976]. — [4],224p : ill ; 30cm.
Includes 3 contributions in German and 1 in French. — Bibl.
Pbk : £3.00
(B77-02438)

664'.9 — Meat. Transport. *Reports, surveys*

The **transportation** and handling of meat and meat products : the first report of an international study group. — London (15 Wilton Rd, SW1V 1LX) : International Cargo Handling Co-ordination Association, 1976. — [1],52p : ill ; 30cm.
Bibl.: p.49-51.
Sp : £25.06
(B77-17629)

664'.907 — Animal products. Processing. Odours. Control. *Manuals*

Great Britain. *Department of the Environment.* The prevention and abatement of smells from animal wastes : a code of practice / Department of the Environment. — London : H.M.S.O., 1977. — [2],i,13p ; 21cm.
ISBN 0-11-751140-4 Sd : £0.35
(B77-16497)

664'.94 — Fish meal production industries. Odours. Control measures. *Proposals*

Torry Research Station. Reducing odour in fish meal production / Ministry of Agriculture, Fisheries and Food, Torry Research Station. — [Aberdeen] ([135 Abbey Rd, Aberdeen AB9 8DG]) : [The Station], [1977]. — 8p : 1 ill ; 21cm. — (Torry Research Station. Torry advisory notes ; no.72)
Sd : Unpriced
(B77-19508)

665 — INDUSTRIAL OILS, FATS, WAXES, GASES

665'.0288 — Industrial chemicals: Fats & fatty oils. Chemical analysis. *Standards*

British Standards Institution. British Standard methods of analysis of fats and fatty oils = Méthodes d'analyse des graisses et huiles fixes = Untersuchungsverfahren für Fette und Fettöle / British Standards Institution. — London : B.S.I.
Part 1 = Partie 1 = Teil 1 : Physical methods = Méthodes physiques = Physische Verfahren. Section 1.12 = Section 1.12 = Abschnitt 1.12 : Determination of the dilatation of fats = Détermination de la dilatation des graisses = Bestimmung der Schmelzausdehnung von Fetten. — 1976. — 8p : 1 ill, form ; 30cm. — (BS684 : Section 1.12 : 1976)
Pierced for binder.
ISBN 0-580-09485-5 Sd : £1.50
(B77-03653)

Part 2 = Partie 2 = Teil 2 : Other methods = Autres méthodes = Andere Verfahren. Section 2.20 = Section 2.20 = Abschnitt 2.20 : Determination of carotene in vegetable oils = Détermination du carotène dans les huiles végétales = Bestimmung des Karotengehaltes in Pflanzenölen. — 1977. — Sheet ([2]p) ; 30x21cm. — (BS684 : Section 2.20 : 1977)
Pierced for binder.
ISBN 0-580-09750-1 : £0.80
(B77-10857)

Part 1 = Partie 1 = Teil 1 : Physical methods = Méthodes physiques = Physische Verfahren. Section 1.9 = Section 1.9 = Abschnitt 1.9 : Determination of water-insoluble solvents = Détermination des solvents insolubles dans l'eau = Bestimmung der wasserunlöslichen Lösungsmittel. — 1976. — 4p : ill ; 30cm. — (BS684 : Section 1.9 : 1976)
Pierced for binder.
ISBN 0-580-09475-8 Sd : £1.15
(B77-03642)

Part 2 = Partie 2 = Teil 2 : Other methods = Autres méthodes = Andere Verfahren. Section 2.23 = Section 2.23 = Abschnitt 2.23 : Determination of Bömer value = Détermination de l'indice de Bömer = Bestimmung der Bömer-Zahl. — 1977. — 4p ; 30cm. — (BS684 : Section 2.23 : 1977) (ISO3577-1976)
ISO title : Animal fats - Determination of Bömer value. — Pierced for binder.
ISBN 0-580-09820-6 Sd : £1.20
(B77-10856)

Part 1 = Partie 1 = Teil 1 : Physical methods = Méthodes physiques = Physische Verfahren. Section 1.13 = Section 1.13 = Abschnitt 1.13 : Determination of cooling curve = Détermination de la courbe de refroidissement = Bestimmung der Kühlungskurve. — 1976. — 4p : 2 ill ; 30cm. — (BS684 : Section 1.13 : 1976)
Pierced for binder.
ISBN 0-580-09495-2 Sd : £1.15
(B77-03644)

Part 1 = Partie 1 = Teil 1 : Physical methods = Méthodes physiques = Physische Verfahren. Section 1.8 = Section 1.8 = Abschnitt 1.8 : Determination of smoke point = Détermination du point du fumée = Bestimmung des Rauchpunktes. — 1976. — 4p : ill ; 30cm. — (BS684 : Section 1.8 : 1976)
Pierced for binder.
ISBN 0-580-09045-0 Sd : £1.15
(B77-03641)

Part 1 = Partie 1 = Teil 1 : Physical methods = Méthodes physiques = Physische Verfahren. Section 1.1 = Section 1.1 = Abschnitt 1.1 : Determination of relative density at t/20°C in air and apparent density (g/ml) in air of fats = Détermination de la masse volumique rélative à t/20°C dans l'air et la masse volumique apparente (g/ml) dans l'air des graisses = Bestimmung der relativen Dichte bei t/20°C in Luft und der scheinbaren Dichte (g/ml) in Luft von Fetten. — 1976. — 4p ; 30cm. — (BS684 : Section 1.1 : 1976)
Pierced for binder.
ISBN 0-580-09005-1 Sd : £1.15
(B77-03643)

Part 1 = Partie 1 = Teil 1 : Physical methods = Méthodes physiques = Physische Verfahren. Section 1.3 = Section 1.3 = Abschnitt 1.3 : Determination of melting point (slip point) = Détermination du point de fusion = Bestimmung des Schmelzpunktes. — 1976. — 4p : 1 ill ; 30cm. — (BS684 : Section 1.3 : 1976)
Pierced for binder.
ISBN 0-580-09015-9 Sd : £1.15
(B77-03639)

Part 1 = Partie 1 = Teil 1 : Physical methods = Méthodes physiques = Physische Verfahren. Section 1.5 = Section 1.5 = Abschnitt 1.5 : Determination of cloud point = Détermination du point de trouble = Bestimmung des Trübungspunktes. — 1976. — 4p : 1 ill ; 30cm. — (BS684 : Section 1.5 : 1976)
Pierced for binder.
ISBN 0-580-09035-3 Sd : £1.15
(B77-03645)

Part 1 = Partie 1 = Teil 1 : Physical methods = Méthodes physiques = Physische Verfahren. Section 1.4 = Section 1.4 = Abschnitt 1.4 : Determination of flow and drop points = Détermination du point d'écoulement et du point de goutte = Bestimmung des Fliepunktes und des Tropfpunktes. — 1976. — Sheet([2]p) ; 30x21cm. — (BS684 : Section 1.4 : 1976)
Pierced for binder.
ISBN 0-580-09025-6 : £0.75
(B77-03634)

Part 2 = Partie 2 = Teil 2 : Other methods = Autres méthodes = Andere Verfahren. Section 2.4 = Section 2.4 = Abschnitt 2.4 : Calculation of total fatty matter = Calcul de la teneur en matière grasse totale = Berechnung des gesamten Fettstoffes. — 1976. — Sheet([2] p) ; 30x21cm. — (BS684 : Section 2.4 : 1976)
Pierced for binder.
ISBN 0-580-09046-9 : £0.75
(B77-03650)

Part 2 = Partie 2 = Teil 2 : Other methods = Autres méthodes = Andere Verfahren. Section 2.14 = Section 2.14 = Abschnitt 2.14 : Determination of peroxide value = Détermination de l'indice de peroxyde = Bestimmung des Peroxidzahl. — 1976. — Sheet([2]p) ; 30x21cm. — (BS684 : Section 2.14 : 1976)
Pierced for binder.
ISBN 0-580-09235-6 : £1.15
(B77-03647)

Part 1 = Partie 1 = Teil 1 : Physical methods = Méthodes physiques = Physische Verfahren. Section 1.16 = Section 1.16 = Abschnitt 1.16 : Determination of water (Azeotropic distillation method) = Détermination de la teneur en eau (méthode par distillation az eotrope) = Bestimmung des Wassergehaltes (azeotrope Destillationsverfahren). — 1976. — 4p : 2 ill ; 30cm. — (BS684 : Section 1.16 : 1976)
Pierced for binder.
ISBN 0-580-09305-0 Sd : £1.15
(B77-03633)

Part 1 = Partie 1 = Teil 1 : Physical methods = Méthodes physiques = Physische Verfahren. Section 1.11 = Section 1.11 = Abschnitt 1.11 : Determination of penetration value = Détermination de l'indice de pénétration = Bestimmung des Eindringungswertes. — 1976. — 4p : 2 ill ; 30cm. — (BS684 : Section 1.11 : 1976)
Pierced for binder.
ISBN 0-580-09165-1 Sd : £1.15
(B77-03636)

Part 2 = Partie 2 = Teil 2 : Other methods = Autres méthodes = Andere Verfahren. Section 2.13 = Section 2.13 = Abschnitt 2.13 : Determination of iodine value = Détermination de l'indice d'iode = Bestimmung des Jodwertes. — 1976. — Sheet([2]p) ; 30x21cm. — (BS684 : Part 2 : Section 2.13 : 1976)
Pierced for binder.
ISBN 0-580-09278-x : £0.75
(B77-09130)

Part 1 = Partie 1 = Teil 1 : Physical methods = Méthodes physiques = Physische Verfahren. Section 1.10 = Abschnitt 1.10 : Determination of moisture and volatile matter = Détermination de la teneur en eau et en matières volatiles = Bestimmung des Feuchtigkeitsgehaltes und des Gehaltes an flüchtigen Stoffen. — 1976. — 4p : 1 ill ; 30cm. — (BS684 : Section 1.10 : 1976)
Pierced for binder.
ISBN 0-580-09375-1 Sd : £1.15
(B77-03652)

Part 1 = Partie 1 = Teil 1 : Physical methods = Méthodes physiques = Physische Verfahren. Section 1.6 = Section 1.6 = Abschnitt 1.6 : Determination of titre = Détermination du titre = Bestimmung des Titers. — 1976. — Sheet ([2]p) ; 20x21cm. — (BS684 : Section 1.6 : 1976)
Pierced for binder.
ISBN 0-580-09125-2 : £0.75
(B77-03651)

Part 2 = Partie 2 = Teil 2 : Other methods = Autres méthodes = Andere Verfahren. Section 2.10 = Section 2.10 = Abschnitt 2.10 : Determination of acidity, acid value and mineral acidity = Détermination de l'acidité, de l'indice d'acide et de l'acidite minérale = Bestimmung des Säuregehaltes, der Säurezahl und des Mineralsäuregghaltes. — 1976. — 4p ; 30cm. — (BS684 : Section 2.10 : 1976)
Pierced for binder.
ISBN 0-580-09245-3 Sd : £1.15
(B77-03638)

Part 2 = Partie 2 = Teil 2 : Other methods = Autres méthodes = Andere Verfahren. Section 2.1 = Section 2.1 = Abschnitt 2.1 : Determination of water by the Karl Fischer method = Détermination de la teneur en eau par la méthode Karl Fischer = Bestimmung des Wassergehaltes nach dem Karl-Fischer-Verfahren. — 1976. — 6p : ill ; 30cm. — (BS684 : Section 2.1 : 1976)
Pierced for binder.
ISBN 0-580-09155-4 Sd : £1.50
(B77-03631)

Part 2 = Partie 2 = Teil 2 : Other methods = Autres méthodes = Andere Verfahren. Section 2.16 = Section 2.16 = Abschnitt 2.16 : Determination of copper - colorimetric method = Dosage du cuivre - méthode colorimétrique = Bestimmung des Kupfergehaltes - Farbenmessverfahren. — 1976. — Sheet([2]p) ; 30x21cm. — (BS684 : Section 2.16 : 1976)
Pierced for binder.
ISBN 0-580-09405-7 : £0.75
(B77-03637)

Part 1 = Partie 1 = Teil 1 : Physical methods = Méthodes physiques = Physische Verfahren. Section 1.7 = Section 1.7 = Abschnitt 1.7 : Determination of surface-drying time = Détermination de la durée de sechage en surface = Bestimmung der Oberflächen-trocknungsperiode. — 1976. — Sheet([2]p) ; 30x21cm. — (BS684 : Section 1.7 : 1976)
Pierced for binder.
ISBN 0-580-09135-x : £0.75
(B77-03632)

Part 2 = Partie 2 = Teil 2 : Other methods = Autres méthodes = Andere Verfahren. Section 2.11 = Section 2.11 = Abschnitt 2.11 : Determination of volatile acids (Reichert, Polenske and Kirschner values) = Détermination des acides volatils (Indices Reichert, Polenske et Kirschner) = Bestimmung von fluchtigen Sauren (Reichertsche, Polenskische und Kirschnersche Werte). — 1976. — 4p : 2 ill ; 30cm. — (BS684 : Section 2.11 : 1976)
Pierced for binder.
ISBN 0-580-09145-7 Sd : £1.15
(B77-03649)

Part 1 = Partie 1 = Teil 1 : Physical methods = Méthodes physiques = Physische Verfahren. Section 1.14 = Section 1.14 = Abschnitt 1.14 : Determination of colour = Détermination de la couleur = Bestimmung der Farbe. — 1976. — Sheet([2]p) ; 30x21cm. — (BS684 : Section 1.14 : 1976)
Pierced for binder.
ISBN 0-580-09285-2 : £0.75
(B77-03635)

Part 2 = Partie 2 = Teil 2 : Other methods = Autres méthodes = Andere Verfahren. Section 2.3 = Section 2.3 = Abschnitt 2.3 : Determination of impurities = Détermination de la teneur en impuretés = Bestimmung des Unreinigkeitsgehaltes. — 1976. — 4p ; 30cm. — (BS684 : Section 2.3 : 1976)
Pierced for binder.
ISBN 0-580-09425-1 Sd : £1.15
(B77-03646)

Part 2 = Partie 2 = Teil 2 : Other methods = Autres méthodes = Andere Verfahren. Section 2.2 = Section 2.2 = Abschnitt 2.2 : Determination of ash = Détermination des cendres = Aschebestimmung. — 1976. — Sheet([2]p) ; 30x21cm. — (BS684 : Section 2.2 : 1976)
Pierced for binder.
ISBN 0-580-09435-9 : £0.75
(B77-03640)

Part 2 = Partie 2 = Teil 2 : Other methods = Autres méthodes = Andere Verfahren. Section 2.17 = Section 2.17 = Abschnitt 2.17 : Determination of iron - colorimetric method = Dosage du fer - méthode colorimétrique = Bestimmung des Eisengehaltes - Farbenmessverfahren. — 1976. — Sheet([2]p) ; 30x21cm. — (BS684 : Section 2.17 : 1976)
Pierced for binder.
ISBN 0-580-09445-6 : £0.75
(B77-03648)

British Standards Institution. Methods of analysis of fats and fatty oils = Méthodes d'analyse des graisses et huiles fixes = Untersuchungsverfahren für Fette und Fettöle / British Standards Institution. — London : B.S.I.
General introduction = Introduction générale = Allgemeine Einführung. — 3rd revision. — 1976. — [2],6,[2]p ; 30cm. — (BS684 : Introduction : 1976)
Pierced for binder. — Index.
ISBN 0-580-09444-8 Sd : £2.00
(B77-03654)

665.4 — MINERAL OILS AND WAXES
665'.4 — Cut-back asphaltic products. Testing. Fractional distillation. *Standards*
British Standards Institution. Method for the determination of distillation of cut-back asphaltic (bituminous) products = Méthode de déterminer la distillation des produits d'asphalte (bitumen) fluidifié = Verfahren für die Bestimmung des Destillationsverhalten von Verschnittasphalt-bzw. Verschnittbitumenprodukten / [British Standards Institution]. — London : B.S.I., 1976. — 13p : ill ; 21cm. — (BS4453 : 1976)
'(Identical with ASTMD 403-73 : IP27/74)'.
ISBN 0-580-09021-3 Sd : £1.60
(B77-11949)

665'.4 — Mineral insulating oils. Oxidation. Resistance. Measurement. *Standards*
British Standards Institution. Method for the determination of oxidation stability of mineral insulating oils = Méthode de déterminer la stabilité à l'oxydation des huiles minérales isolantes = Verfahren zur Bestimmung der Oxydationsbeständigkeit von Mineralisolieröl / [British Standards Institution]. — London : B.S.I., 1976. — 6p ; 21cm. — (BS5302 : 1976)
'(Identical with IP307/75) (Technically identical with IEC Publication 74)'.
ISBN 0-580-09091-4 Sd : £1.20
(B77-11950)

665'.4 — Straight mineral oils. Oxidation. Resistance. Measurement. *Standards*
British Standards Institution. Method for the determination of oxidation stability of straight mineral oil = Méthode de déterminer la stabilité à l'oxydation des huiles minérales sans additif = Verfahren für die Bestimmung der Oxydationsbeständigkeit von Blankwalzöl / [British Standards Institution]. — London : B.S.I., 1976. — 7p ; 21cm. — (BS5301 : 1976)
'(Identical with IP306/75)'.
ISBN 0-580-09081-7 Sd : £1.20
(B77-11951)

665.5 — PETROLEUM
665'.5'028 — Petroleum industries. Safety measures
Institute of Petroleum. Model code of safe practice in the petroleum industry / Institute of Petroleum. — London : Heyden.
Part 12 : Pressure vessel inspection safety code. — 1976. — viii,24p ; 25cm.
ISBN 0-85501-302-8 : Unpriced
(B77-04311)

665'.53825 — Aircraft. Fuels. Anti-knock additives: Lead. Gravimetric analysis. *Standards*
British Standards Institution. Method for the determination of lead in gasoline (gravimetric method) = Méthode de déterminer le plomb dans les carburants (méthode gravimétrique) = Verfahren zur Bestimmung des Bleigehalts von Benzin (Masseverfahren) / [British Standards Institution]. — 2nd revision. — London : B.S.I., 1976. — 10p : 1 ill ; 21cm. — (BS2878 : 1976)
'(Identical with ASTM D526-70 : IP96/70)'.
ISBN 0-580-09011-6 Sd : £1.60
Also classified at 665'.53827
(B77-11952)

665'.53827 — Motor vehicles. Petrol. Anti-knock additives: Lead. Gravimetric analysis. *Standards*
British Standards Institution. Method for the determination of lead in gasoline (gravimetric method) = Méthode de déterminer le plomb dans les carburants (méthode gravimétrique) = Verfahren zur Bestimmung des Bleigehalts von Benzin (Masseverfahren) / [British Standards Institution]. — 2nd revision. — London : B.S.I., 1976. — 10p : 1 ill ; 21cm. — (BS2878 : 1976)
'(Identical with ASTM D526-70 : IP96/70)'.
ISBN 0-580-09011-6 Sd : £1.60
Primary classification 665'.53825
(B77-11952)

665'.5384 — Fuel oils. Pumpability. Determination. *Standards*
British Standards Institution. Method for the determination of pumpability of industrial fuel oils = Méthode de déterminer l'aptitude au pompage des fuel-oils industriels = Verfahren zur Bestimmung der Pumpfähigkeit von Industrieheizöl / [British Standards Institution]. — London : B.S.I., 1976. — 12p : ill ; 21cm. — (BS5300 : 1976)
'(Identical with IP230/74)'.
ISBN 0-580-09071-x Sd : £1.60
(B77-11953)

665'.5385 — Lubricating greases. Consistency. Measurement. Penetration by standard cones. *Standards*
British Standards Institution. Method for the determination of cone penetration of lubricating greases = Méthode de déterminer la pénétrabilité au cône des graisses lubrifiantes = Verfahren zur Bestimmung der Kegeleindringtiefe in Schmierfelt / [British Standards Institution]. — London : B.S.I., 1976. — 22p : ill ; 21cm. — (BS5296 : 1976)
'(Identical with ASTMD 217-68 : IP50/69) (Technically identical with ISO 2137 : 1972)'.
ISBN 0-580-09031-0 Sd : £2.70
(B77-11954)

665'.5385 — Lubricating greases. Drop point. Measurement. *Standards*
British Standards Institution. Method for the determination of dropping point of lubricating grease = Méthode de déterminer le point de goutte des graisses lubrifiantes = Verfahren zur Bestimmung des Tropfpunkts von Schmierfett / [British Standards Institution]. — 1st revision. — London : B.S.I., 1976. — 11p : ill ; 21cm. — (BS2877 : 1976)
'(Identical with ASTM D566-64 : IP132/65) (Technically identical with ISO2176 : 1972)'.
ISBN 0-580-09001-9 Sd : £1.60
(B77-11955)

665'.5385 — Lubricating oils. Air release value. Determination. *Standards*
British Standards Institution. Method for the determination of air release value of industrial oils = Méthode de déterminer l'indice de liberation d'air des huiles industrielles = Verfahren zur Bestimmung des Luftaustrittswerts von industriellen Ölen / [British Standards Institution]. — London : B.S.I., 1976. — 10p : ill ; 21cm. — (BS5303 : 1976)
'(Identical with IP313/75T)'.
ISBN 0-580-09101-5 Sd : £1.60
(B77-11956)

665'.5385 — Stored lubricating greases. Oxidation. Resistance. Measurement. Oxygen bomb method. *Standards*
British Standards Institution. Method of determination of oxidation stability of lubricating greases by the oxygen bomb method = Méthode de déterminer la stabilité à l'oxydation des graisses lubrifiantes au moyen d'une bombe d'oxygène = Verfahren zur Bestimmung der Oxydationsbeständigkeit von Schmierfetten-Sauerstoffbombenverfahren / [British Standards Institution]. — London : B.S.I., 1976. — 11p : ill ; 21cm. — (BS5298 : 1976)
'(Identical with ASTM D 942-70:IP 142/74)'.
ISBN 0-580-09051-5 Sd : £1.60
(B77-11957)

665'.5385 — Stored lubricating greases. Separation of oils. Measurement. *Standards*
British Standards Institution. Method for the determination of oil separation on storage of grease = Méthode de déterminer la separation de l'huile pendant stockage des graisses = Verfahren zur Bestimmung der Ölabscheidung bei der Lagerung von Fett / [British Standards Institution]. — London : B.S.I., 1976. — 7p : 1 ill ; 21cm. — (BS5297 : 1976)
'(Identical with IP121/75)'.
ISBN 0-580-09041-8 Sd : £1.20
(B77-11958)

665.7/8 — INDUSTRIAL GASES
665'.73 — Gas filters. Fibrous materials. *Conference proceedings*
Fibrous and related materials for the filtration of gases : papers presented at a Shirley Institute Conference held on 29-30 June 1977. — Manchester : The Institute, 1977. — [3],81p : ill ; 30cm. — (Shirley Institute. Publications ; S27 ISSN 0306-5154)
Pbk : £10.00(£7.00 to members)
(B77-31322)

665'.74 — Liquefied natural gas & liquefied petroleum gas. Storage & transport. *Conference proceedings*

Gastech 76 : [proceedings of the] Gastech 76 LNG & LPG conference, New York, October 5-8 1976. — Rickmansworth (2 Station Rd, Rickmansworth, Herts. WD3 1QP) : Gastech Exhibitions Ltd, 1977. — vi,306p : ill, maps, plans ; 30cm.
'The fifth meeting on LNG and LPG organised by Gastech ...' - Foreword.
ISBN 0-904930-04-1 Pbk : Unpriced
(B77-16498)

665'.74 — Transportable gas containers. *Standards*

British Standards Institution. Specification for transportable gas containers = Spécification des récipients à gaz transportables = Spezifikation für Transportfähige Gasbehälter / British Standards Institution. — London : B.S.I.
Part 1 = Partie 1 = Teil 1 : Seamless steel containers = Récipients en acier sans soudure = Nahtlose Stahlbbehälter. — 1976. — [2],23,[2]p : ill, forms ; 30cm. — (BS5045 : Part 1 : 1976)
Pierced for binder.
ISBN 0-580-09396-4 Sd : £4.00
(B77-01638)

665'.75'0941 — Natural gas & town gas. Use. *Great Britain. Practical information. Serials*

Gas marketing pocket book. — London : Benn Bros.
1977. — [1976]. — 160,[32]p : ill ; 18cm.
Diary: p.[1]-[32].
ISBN 0-510-49665-2 : £2.00
(B77-06783)

665'.81 — Fuels: Hydrogen. *Conference proceedings*

World Hydrogen Energy Conference, *1st, Miami Beach, 1976.* Conference proceedings : 1st World Hydrogen Energy Conference 1-3 March 1976, Miami Beach, Florida presented by International Association for Hydrogen Energy, Clean Energy Research Institute, University of Miami ; sponsored by Energy Research and Development Administration, the School of Continuing Studies, University of Miami / edited by T. Nejat Veziroğlu. — Coral Gables : University of Miami ; Oxford [etc.] : Distributed by Pergamon, [1977]. — 3v.(2310p in various pagings) : ill, facsims, maps, plans ; 28cm.
Bibl.
ISBN 0-08-021561-0 Pbk : £75.00
(B77-10453)

666 — CERAMICS AND RELATED TECHNOLOGIES

666'.06'241 — Ceramics. Organisations. *Great Britain. British Ceramic Society. Directories*

British Ceramic Society. List of members / the British Ceramic Society. — Stoke-on-Trent (Shelton House, Stoke-on-Trent, [Staffs.]) : [The Society].
1976, Jan. — [1976]. — [1],42p ; 30cm.
ISBN 0-901092-31-2 Sd : Unpriced
(B77-05526)

666'.1 — Glass. Colouring

Bamford, C R. Colour generation and control in glass / [by] C.R. Bamford. — Amsterdam ; Oxford [etc.] : Elsevier, 1977. — xiii,224p : ill ; 25cm. — (Glass science and technology ; vol.2)

Index.
ISBN 0-444-41614-5 : £20.00
(B77-33920)

666'.1 — Glass. Manufacture

Babcock, Clarence L. Silicate glass technology methods / [by] Clarence L. Babcock. — New York ; London [etc.] : Wiley, 1977. — x,326p : ill ; 24cm. — (Wiley series in pure and applied optics)
Bibl.: p.319-321. — Index.
ISBN 0-471-03965-9 : £16.45
(B77-22724)

666'.1042 — Glass. Physical properties

Leadbetter, A J. Solid liquids and liquid crystals / [by] A.J. Leadbetter. — [Exeter] : University of Exeter, 1976. — 35p : ill ; 21cm. — (University of Exeter. Inaugural lectures)
'... delivered in the University of Exeter on 20 November, 1975'.
ISBN 0-85989-081-3 Sd : £0.50
Also classified at 548'.9
(B77-15373)

666'.1042 — Vitreous state. Physical chemistry. *Study examples: Glass*

Baltă, P. Introduction to the physical chemistry of the vitreous state / [by] P. Baltă and E. Baltă ; [translated from the Romanian by Tatiana Nichitin ; translation editor John Hammel]. — 2nd ed. — Bucureşti [i.e. Bucharest] : Editura Academiei ; Tunbridge Wells : Abacus Press, 1976. — 287p : ill ; 25cm.
Translation and revision of: 'Introducere în chimia fizică a stării vitroase'. Bucureşti : Editura Academiei Republicii Socialiste România, 1971.
ISBN 0-85626-088-6 : £14.65
(B77-10454)

666'.157 — Synthetic resin bonded woven glass fabric laminated sheets. *Standards*

British Standards Institution. Specification for synthetic resin bonded woven glass fabric laminated sheet = Spécification des plaques stratifiées en tissus à base de verre textile liés au moyen des résines synthétiques = Spezifikation Glasgewebe / British Standards Institution. — 1st revision. — London : B.S.I., 1976. — [2],16,[2]p : ill ; 30cm. — (BS3953 : 1976)
Pierced for binder.
ISBN 0-580-09195-3 Sd : £4.00
(B77-03655)

666'.19 — English glass soft drinks bottles, to ca 1930

Morgan, Roy. Mainly Codd's wallop : the story of the Great British pop bottle / by Roy Morgan. — Revised ed. — Wellingborough (63 Torrington Rd, Wellingborough, Northants.) : Kollectarama, 1977. — [2],26p : ill, facsims ; 22cm.
Previous ed.: 1974.
Sd : £0.95
Also classified at 666'.68
(B77-17630)

666'.19 — Glass containers. Re-use & recycling. *Proposals*

Bate, Richard. Many happy returns : glass containers and the environment / by Richard Bate. — London (9 Poland St., W1V 3DG) : Friends of the Earth Ltd, 1976. — vi,82p : ill ; 22cm.
Bibl.: p.81-82.
Pbk : £1.20
(B77-12564)

666'.3 — Pottery & porcelain tableware. Manufacture. *Illustrations*

Statham, Claire. Making ceramic tableware : an illustrated guide to the basic processes / [devised and drawn by Claire Statham]. — [Cheddleton] ([c/o Wood, Mitchell & Co. Ltd (Printers), Hanley, Staffs.]) : Cheddleton Flint Mill Industrial Heritage Trust, 1976. — [1],9,[1]p : chiefly ill ; 21cm.
'Based on the booklet "Spode-Never out of fashion"' - cover. — Bibl.: p.9.
ISBN 0-9502668-1-7 Sd : £0.20
(B77-11959)

666'.58 — Porcelain tableware. Translucency. Measurement. *Standards*

British Standards Institution. British Standard specification for water absorption and translucency of china or porcelain table-ware = Spécification sur absorption d'eau et la translucidité des articles de table en faience ou en porcelaine = Spezifikation für die Wasseraufnahme und Durchsichtigkeit von Tischwaren aus Keramik / British Standards Institution. — London : B.S.I., 1976. — Folder (4p) ; 30cm. — (BS5416 : 1976)
Pierced for binder.
ISBN 0-580-09108-2 : £1.15
Primary classification 666'.58
(B77-03656)

666'.58 — Water. Absorption by porcelain tableware. Measurement. *Standards*

British Standards Institution. British Standard specification for water absorption and translucency of china or porcelain table-ware = Spécification sur absorption d'eau et la translucidité des articles de table en faience ou en porcelaine = Spezifikation für die Wasseraufnahme und Durchsichtigkeit von Tischwaren aus Keramik / British Standards Institution. — London : B.S.I., 1976. — Folder (4p) ; 30cm. — (BS5416 : 1976)
Pierced for binder.
ISBN 0-580-09108-2 : £1.15
Also classified at 666'.58
(B77-03656)

666'.68 — English stoneware soft drinks bottles, to ca 1930

Morgan, Roy. Mainly Codd's wallop : the story of the Great British pop bottle / by Roy Morgan. — Revised ed. — Wellingborough (63 Torrington Rd, Wellingborough, Northants.) : Kollectarama, 1977. — [2],26p : ill, facsims ; 22cm.
Previous ed.: 1974.
Sd : £0.95
Primary classification 666'.19
(B77-17630)

666'.72 — Refractories

Gilchrist, James Duncan. Fuels, furnaces and refractories / by J.D. Gilchrist. — Oxford [etc.] : Pergamon, 1977. — xiii,353p : ill ; 22cm. — (Pergamon international library) (International series on materials science and technology ; vol.21)
'A combined revision of the author's "Fuels and refractories" and "Furnaces"' - Library of Congress Cataloging in Publication Data. — Bibl.: p.344-345. — Index.
ISBN 0-08-020430-9 : £7.80
ISBN 0-08-020429-5 Pbk : £4.50
Primary classification 621.4'025
(B77-16450)

666'.89 — Concrete

White, George R. Concrete technology. — [3rd ed.] / [by] George R. White. — New York ; London [etc.] : Van Nostrand Reinhold, 1977. — viii,136p : ill, forms ; 27cm.
Previous ed.: / issued by the Portland Cement Association. Chicago : Portland Cement Association, 196-?. — Index.
ISBN 0-442-29406-9 : Unpriced
(B77-25754)

666'.89 — Ready-mixed concrete. Production. *Conference proceedings*

International Conference on Ready-Mixed Concrete, *1st, University of Dundee, 1975.* Advances in ready mixed concrete technology / edited by Ravindra K. Dhir. — Oxford [etc.] : Pergamon, 1976. — xxiv,492p : ill ; 26cm.
'Proceedings of the First International Conference on Ready-Mixed Concrete held at Dundee University 29th September-1st October 1975 organised by Civil Engineering Department, Dundee University in collaboration with ... [others]'. — Index.
ISBN 0-08-020415-5 : £15.00
Also classified at 624'.1834
(B77-01639)

666'.894 — Concrete. Lightweight aggregates. *Standards*

British Standards Institution. Specification for lightweight aggregates for concrete = Spécification pour granulats légers pour le béton = Spezifikation für Leichtaggregate für Beton / British Standards Institution. — London : B.S.I.
Part 2 = Partie 2 = Teil 2 : Metric units = Unités métriques = Metrische Einheiten. — 1976. — [2],2,[2]p ; 30cm. — (BS3797 : Part 2 : 1976)
Pierced for binder.
ISBN 0-580-09198-8 Sd : £1.50
(B77-09815)

667 — CLEANING, DYEING, INKS, COATINGS

667'.2'0212 — Dyes. *Technical data*

Society of Dyers and Colourists. Colour index / [prepared by the Society of Dyers and Colourists] and the American Association of Textile Chemists and Colorists. — Bradford (P.O. Box 244, 82 Gratton Rd, Bradford, W. Yorkshire BD1 2JB) : The Society.
Previous ed.: i.e. 3rd ed., in 5 vols. 1971.
Vol.5. — Revised 3rd ed. — 1976. — xvip, p5001-5814 ; 28cm.
ISBN 0-901956-26-0 : Unpriced
(B77-06198)

Vol.6 : First supplement to volumes 1-4. — Revised 3rd ed. — 1975. — vp,p6001-6411 ; 28cm.
Bibl.
ISBN 0-901956-27-9 : Unpriced
(B77-06199)

667'.6 — Paint technology

Boxall, John. Concise paint technology / [by] J. Boxall, J.A. von Fraunhofer. — London : Elek, 1977. — [10],214p : ill ; 23cm.
Bibl. — Index.
ISBN 0-236-40086-x : £4.95
(B77-27239)

Oil and Colour Chemists' Association.
Introduction to paint technology / [Oil and Colour Chemists' Association]. — 4th ed. / revised by W.M. Morgans and J.R. Taylor. — Wembley (Priory House, 967 Harrow Rd, Wembley, Middlesex HA0 2SF) : The Association, 1976. — [2],219p,[8]p of plates : ill ; 18cm.
Previous ed.: 1967. — Bibl.: p.212. — Index.
ISBN 0-903809-03-6 Pbk : £5.00
(B77-02439)

667'.6 — Paints. Safety measures
O'Neill, L A. Health and safety, environmental pollution and the paint industry : a survey covering legislation, standards, codes of practice and toxicology / by L.A. O'Neill. — [Teddington] ([Waldegrave Rd, Teddington, Middx TW11 8LD]) : Paint Research Association], 1977. — [1],v,52leaves ; 30cm.
ISBN 0-9505319-1-x Pbk : £25.00
(B77-10858)

667'.6'072041 — Paints. Manufacture. Research organisations. *Great Britain. Paint Research Association. Periodicals*
Paint Research Association. PRA newsletter. — Teddington (Waldegrave Rd, Teddington, Middx TW11 8LD) : The Association.
[No.1]- ; Aug. 1976-. — [1976]-. — ill, ports ; 30cm.
Quarterly. — Folder ([4]p.) as 1st issue.
Unpriced
ISSN 0309-250x
(B77-06785)

667'.9 — Finishing. *Periodicals*
Finishing industries : incorporating 'Industrial finishing', 'Surface coatings', 'Electroplating & metal finishing', 'Metal finishing journal', 'Corrosion'. — Watford : Wheatland Journals.
[Vol.1, no.1]- ; Jan. 1977-. — [1977]-. — ill, ports ; 30cm.
Monthly. — 64p. in 1st issue.
Sd : £10.45 yearly(including yearly 'Manual')
ISSN 0309-3018
(B77-10455)

667'.9 — Metallic coatings. Testing. *Standards*
British Standards Institution. British Standard methods of test for metallic and related coatings = Méthodes d'essai des revêtements métalliques et similaires = Prüfverfahren für metallische und ähnliche Überzüge / British Standards Institution. — London : B.S.I.
Part 5 = Partie 5 = Teil 5 : Measurement of the local thickness of metal and oxide coatings by the microscopical examination of cross sections = Mesurage de l'épaisseur locale des revêtements métalliques et couches d'oxyde par coupe micrographique = Messung der Ortsdicke von Metall- und Oxydüberzügen durch die mikroskopische Untersuchung von Querschnitten. — 1976. — Folder(4p) ; 30cm. — (BS5411 : Part 5 : 1976)
Pierced for binder.
ISBN 0-580-09640-8 : £1.20
(B77-10860)

Part 1 = Partie 1 = Teil 1 : Definitions and conventions concerning the measurement of thickness = Définitions et conventions concernant le mesurage de l'épaisseur = Definitionen und Übereinkomnen zur Messung der Dicke. — 1976. — Folder(4p) ; 30cm. — (BS5411 : Part 1 : 1976)
Pierced for binder.
ISBN 0-580-09620-3 : £1.20
(B77-10859)

Part 3 = Partie 3 = Teil 3 : Eddy current mehtod for measurement of coating thickness of non-conductive coatings on non-magnetic basis metals = Méthode des courants de Foucault pour le mesurage de l'épaisseur des revetements non-conducteurs sur métal de base non magnétique = Wirbelstromverfahren zur Messung der Dicke der Auftragsschicht bei nichtleitfähigen Überzügen auf Metallen mit nichtmagnetischer Basis. — 1976. — Folder (4)p ; 30cm. — (BS5411 : Part 3 : 1976)
Pierced for binder.
ISBN 0-580-09520-7 : £1.15
(B77-09816)

British Standards Institution. Methods of test for metallic and related coatings = Méthodes d'essai des revêtements métalliques et similaires = Prüfverfahren für metallische und ähnliche Überzuge / British Standards Institution. — London : B.S.I.
Part 8 = Partie 8 = Teil 8 : Measurement of coating thickness of metallic coatings, X-ray spectrometric methods = Mesurage de l'épaisseur des revêtements métalliques - méthodes par spectrométrie de rayons X = Messung der Dicke von Metallüberzügen - Röntgenspektrometrische Verfahren. — 1976. — [2],7,[1]p : 2 ill ; 30cm. — (BS5411 : Part 8 : 1976) (ISO 3497-1976)
Pierced for binder.
ISBN 0-580-09437-5 Sd : £2.40
(B77-03120)

British Standards Institution. Methods of test for metallic and related coatings = Méthodes d'essai des revêtements métalliques et similaires = Prüfverfahren für metallische und ähnliche Überzüge / British Standards Institution. — London : B.S.I.
Part 9 = Partie 9 = Teil 9 : Measurement of coating thickness of electrodeposited nickel coatings on magnetic and non-magnetic substrates, magnetic method = Mesurage de l'épaisseur des revêtements électrolytiques de nickel sur métal de base magnétique et non magnétique, méthode magnétique = Messung der Dicke der Auftragsschicht von galvanischen Nickelüberzügen auf magnetischen und nichtmagnetischen Substraten, magnetisches Verfahren. — 1977. — [2],3,[1]p ; 30cm. — (BS5411 : Part 9 : 1977) (ISO 2361-1972)
Pierced for binder.
ISBN 0-580-09379-4 Sd : £1.60
(B77-14313)

Part 11 = Partie 11 = Teil 11 : Measurement of coating thickness of non-magnetic metallic and vitreous or porcelain enamel coatings on magnetic basis metals, magnetic method = Mesurage de l'épaisseur des revêtements métalliques non-magnétiques et émaux vitrifiés sur métal de base magnétique, méthode magnétique = Messung der Dicke der Auftragsschicht von nichtmagnetischen, metallischen und Glas- oder Porzellanemailleüberzügen auf magnetischen Basismetallen, magnetisches Verfahren. — 1977. — [2],3,[1]p ; 30cm. — (BS5411 : Part 11 : 1977) (ISO 2178-1972)
Pierced for binder.
ISBN 0-580-09890-7 Sd : £1.60
(B77-14314)

667'.9 — Powder coatings
Harris, S T. The technology of powder coatings / by S.T. Harris ; edited by E.C. Roberson. — London (2 Queensway, Redhill, Surrey RH1 1QS) : Portcullis Press, 1976. — x, 304p : ill, form ; 24cm.
Index.
ISBN 0-901994-93-6 : £20.00
(B77-03657)

667'.9 — Powder coatings. *Conference proceedings*
Powder for Profit *(Conference), Sutton Coldfield, 1975.* Written papers submitted for presentation at 'Powder for Profit' : 3 day Conference on Powder Coatings at the Penns Hall Hotel, Sutton Coldfield, West Midlands, 28th, 29th & 30th October 1975. — Croydon (Prudential House, Wellesley Rd, Croydon CR9 2ET) : Paint Makers Association of Great Britain, [1977?]. — [35]p,plate : ill ; 30cm.
Cover title.
Pbk : £10.00
(B77-33921)

668.1 — SURFACE ACTIVE AGENTS
668'.1'0941 — Surface-active agents. *Great Britain. Lists*
Hollis, Gordon L. Surfactants UK : a catalogue of surface active agents available in the United Kingdom / compiled and edited by Gordon L. Hollis. — Darlington (34 Edinburgh Drive, Darlington, Co. Durham, DL3 8AT) : Tergo-Data, 1976. — 188p : ill ; 30cm.
Index.
Pbk : £7.50
(B77-01640)

668.3 — ADHESIVES AND RELATED PRODUCTS
668'.3 — Adhesives & sealants
Industrial adhesives and sealants / edited by B.S. Jackson. — London : Hutchinson, 1976. — 303p,[24]p of plates : ill ; 23cm.
Index.
ISBN 0-09-126900-8 : £5.75
(B77-11299)

668'.3 — Adhesives. Testing. *Standards*
British Standards Institution. British Standard methods of test for adhesives = Méthodes d'essai des adhésifs = Prüfmethoden für Klebstoffe / British Standards Institution. — London : B.S.I.
Part D4 = Partie D4 = Teil D4 : Determination of staining potential = Détermination de la capacité de tacher = Bestimmung des Fleckenpotentials. — 1976. — 4p ; 30cm. — (BS5350 : Part D4 : 1976)
Pierced for binder.
ISBN 0-580-09397-2 Sd : £1.15
(B77-02440)

British Standards Institution. British Standard methods of test for adhesives = Méthodes d'essai des adhesifs = Prüfmethoden für Klebstoffe / British Standards Institution. — London : B.S.I.
Part E1 = Partie E1 = Teil E1 : Guide to statistical analysis = Guide pour l'analyse statistique = Hinweise zur statistischen Analyse. — 1976. — Folder(4p) ; 30cm. — (BS5350 : Part E1 : 1976)
Pierced for binder.
ISBN 0-580-09335-2 : £1.20
(B77-11300)

668'.3 — Bonding. Adhesives. Testing
Anderson, Garron P. Analysis and testing of adhesive bonds / [by] Garron P. Anderson, S. John Bennett, K. Lawrence DeVries. — New York [etc.] ; London : Academic Press, 1977. — xviii,255p : ill ; 24cm.
Index.
ISBN 0-12-056550-1 : £14.90
(B77-32018)

668'.3'012 — Adhesives. *Classification schedules*
British Standards Institution. Classification of adhesives = Classification des adhésifs = Klassifikation von Klebstoffen / British Standards Institution. — London : B.S.I., 1976. — [2],12,[2]p ; 30cm. — (BS5407 : 1976)
Pierced for binder.
ISBN 0-580-09417-0 Sd : £3.10
(B77-09131)

668.4 — PLASTICS
Handbook of plastics and elastomers / Charles A. Harper editor-in-chief. — New York ; London [etc.] : McGraw-Hill, [1976]. — 1024p in various pagings : ill, facsims, form ; 24cm.
Published in the United States: 1975. — Bibl.: p.480-481. — Index.
ISBN 0-07-026681-6 : £23.30
Also classified at 678
(B77-03121)

Society of the Plastics Industry. Plastics engineering handbook of the Society of the Plastics Industry, Inc. — 4th ed. / edited by Joel Frados. — New York ; London [etc.] : Van Nostrand Reinhold, 1976. — xvii,909p : ill ; 26cm.
Previous ed.: New York : Reinhold ; London : Chapman and Hall, 1960. — Index.
ISBN 0-442-22469-9 : £32.25
(B77-01641)

668.4 — Flame-retardant polymers
Flame-retardant polymeric materials / edited by Menachem Lewin, S.M. Atlas and Eli M. Pearce. — New York ; London : Plenum Press, [1976]. — xii,457p : ill ; 24cm.
Published in the United States: 1975. — Index.
ISBN 0-306-30840-1 : £28.35
(B77-03658)

668.4 — Plastics. Design
Millett, Robert. Design & technology, plastics / by R. Millett. — Oxford [etc.] : Pergamon, 1977. — 102p : ill(some col) ; 23x25cm.
Index.
ISBN 0-08-020553-4 Pbk : £1.80
(B77-26405)

668.4'02'75 — Plastics industries. Trade names. *Great Britain. Lists*
New trade names in the rubber and plastics industries / RAPRA. — Shrewsbury (Shawbury, Shrewsbury SY4 4NR) : Rubber and Plastics Research Association.
1975. — [1977]. — 180p in various pagings ; 30cm.
ISBN 0-902348-09-4 Sd : £10.00
Also classified at 678'.2'0275
(B77-13127)

668.4'03 — Polymers. *Encyclopaedias*
Encyclopedia of polymer science and technology : plastics, resins, rubbers, fibers / editorial board Herman F. Mark, Norman G. Gaylord, Norbert M. Bikales. — New York ; London [etc.] : Interscience.
Supplement vol.1 : Acrylonitrile polymers, degradation to vinyl chloride / [editorial board Herman F. Mark, Norbert M. Bikales]. — 1976. — xix,674p : ill, port ; 28cm.
'This volume is dedicated to Professor Herman F. Mark on the happy occasion of his Eightieth Birthday' - p.v. — Index.
ISBN 0-471-56997-6 : £50.00
(B77-01642)

668.4'05 — Plastics. *Periodicals*
Plastics and rubber international. — London : Plastics and Rubber Institute.
Continues: Plastics and rubber.
Vol.2, no.1- ; Jan.-Feb. 1977-. — 1977-. — ill, ports ; 30cm.
Six issues a year. — 48p. in vol.2, no.1.
Sd : £3.00(£15.00 yearly)
ISSN 0309-4561
Also classified at 678'.2'05
(B77-08461)

Rubber and Plastics Research Association.
RAPRA news. — [Shrewsbury] ([Shawbury, Shrewsbury SY4 4NR]) : Rubber and Plastics Research Association.
Vol.1, no.1- ; May-June 1977-. — 1977-. — ill, ports ; 30cm.
Six issues a year. — 8p. in 1st issue.
Sd : Unpriced
ISSN 0140-041x
Also classified at 678'.2'05
(B77-20441)

668.4'12 — Hydro-plastic moulding
Bradbury, Farel. Hydro-plastic moulding : hpm / [by] Farel Bradbury. — Ross-on-Wye (P.O. Box 4, Ross-on-Wye, [Hereford and Worcester] HR9 6EB) : Hydatum, 1976. — 40p : ill ; 24cm.
ISBN 0-905682-00-9 Sd : £5.00
(B77-06200)

668.4'19 — Plastics materials. Inflammability. Investigation
British Plastics Federation. *Fire Committee.* A strategy for the investigation of plastics and fire / [prepared by the British Plastics Federation, Fire Committee]. — London : The Federation, 1976. — [3]leaves,9p ; 30cm. — (British Plastics Federation. Publications ; no.157/1)
ISBN 0-900213-44-2 Pbk : Unpriced
(B77-05527)

668'.419 — Plastics. Testing. *Standards*
British Standards Institution. British Standard methods of testing plastics = Méthodes d'essai des matières plastiques = Prüfverfahren für Kunststoffe / British Standards Institution. — London : B.S.I.
Part 1 = Partie 1 = Teil 1 : Thermal properties = Caractéristiques thermiques = Thermische Eigenschaften. Method 150B = Méthode 150B = Verfahren 150B : Determination of cold flex temperature of flexible polyvinyl compound = Détermination de la température de flexion à froid des composées polyvinyliques souples = Bestimmung der Kaltverformungstemperatur von biegbaren Polyvinyl-Verbindungen. — 1976. — 4p : 1 ill ; 30cm. — (BS2782 : Part 1 : Method 150B : 1976)
Pierced for binder.
ISBN 0-580-09287-9 Sd : £1.15
(B77-00848)

Part 1 = Partie 1 = Teil 1 : Thermal properties = Caractéristiques thermiques = Thermische Eigenschaften. Method 121A = Méthode 121A = Verfahren 121A : Determination of temperature of deflection under a bending stress of 1.8 MPa, of plastics and ebonite = Détermination de la température de fléchissement sous un effort de flexion de 1.8 MPa des matières plastiques et de l'ébonite = Bestimmung der Abbiegungstemperatur von Kunststoffen und Hartgummi bei einer Biegebeanspruchung von 1.8 MPa. Method 121B = Méthode 121B = Verfahren 121B : Determination of temperature of deflection under a bending stress of 0.45 MPa of plastics and ebonite ... Method 121C = Méthode 121C = Verfahren 121C : Determination of temperature of deflection under a bending stress, of rigid thermosetting resin bonded laminated sheet ... — London : B.S.I, 1976. — 4p : 1 ill ; 30cm. — (BS2782 : Part 1 : Methods 121A to 121C : 1976)
Pierced for binder.
ISBN 0-580-09267-4 Sd : £1.15
(B77-01643)

Part 1 = Partie 1 = Teil 1 : Thermal properties = Caractéristiques thermiques = Thermische Eigenschaften. Method 120A to 120E = Méthodes 120A à 120E = Verfahren 120A bis 120E : Determination of the Vicat softening temperature of thermoplastics = Détermination de la température de ramollissement Vicat des matières thermoplastiques = Bestimmung der Vicat-Erweichungstemperatur von Thermoplasten. — 1976. — 4p : 1 ill ; 30cm. — (BS2782 : Part 1 : Methods 120A to 120E : 1976)
Pierced for binder.
ISBN 0-580-09257-7 Sd : £1.15
(B77-00849)

Part 4 = Partie 4 = Teil 4 : Chemical properties = Caractéristiques chimiques = Chemische Eigenschaften. Method 432B = Méthode 432B = Verfahren 432B : Determination of the acid value of unsaturated polyester resins = Détermination de l'indice d'acide des résines de polyesters non saturés = Bestimmung des Säyrenwertes von ungesättingen Polyester-Harzen. — 1976. — 4p ; 30cm. — (BS2782 : Part 4 : Method 432B : 1976) (ISO 2114-1974)
Pierced for binder.
ISBN 0-580-09248-8 Sd : £1.15
(B77-00850)

British Standards Institution. British Standard methods of testing plastics = Méthodes d'essai des matières plastiques = Verfahren zur Prüfung von Kunststoffe / British Standards Institution. — London : B.S.I.
Part 3 = Partie 3 = Teil 3 : Mechanical properties = Caractéristiques mécaniques = Mechanische Eigenschaften. Methods 320A to 320F = Méthodes 320A à 320F = Verfahren 320A bis 320F : Tensile strength, elongation and elastic modulus = Résistance à la traction, allongement et module d'élasticité = Zugfestigkeit, Dehnung und Elastizitätsmodul. — 1976. — 10,[1]p : ill ; 30cm. — (BS2782 : Part 3 : Methods 320A to 320F : 1976)
Pierced for binder.
ISBN 0-580-09049-3 Sd : £2.00
(B77-07976)

668.4'19 — Resinography
Rochow, Theodore George. Resinography : an introduction to the definition, identification, and recognition of resins, polymers, plastics, and fibers / by Theodore George Rochow and Eugene George Rochow. — New York ; London : Plenum Press, [1977]. — xiv,193p : ill ; 24cm.
Published in the United States: 1976. — Bibl. — Index.
ISBN 0-306-30863-0 : £15.75
(B77-10861)

668.4'23 — Industrial chemicals: Emulsion polymers
Crystic Research Centre. Emulsion polymer handbook / Crystic Research Centre. — Wellingborough (Wollaston, Wellingborough, Northants. NN9 7RL) : [The Centre], 1974. — x,109p : ill ; 20cm. — (Crystic monograph ; no.3)
Bibl.: p.105. — Index.
Pbk : Unpriced
(B77-22002)

668.4'23 — Materials: Thermoplastics. Welding. *Manuals*
Engineering Equipment Users Association. Thermal and chemical welding of plastics materials / Engineering Equipment Users Association. — London (14 Belgrave Sq., SW1X 8PS) : E.E.U.A., 1976. — [6],82p : ill ; 30cm. — (Handbook ; no.35 : 1976)
Bibl.: p.77. — Index.
ISBN 0-85931-030-2 Sd : £4.50
(B77-10862)

668.4'235 — Nylon tubing. *Standards*
British Standards Institution. Specification for nylon tubing = Spécification des tubes en nylon = Spezifikation für Nylonrohre / British Standards Institution. — London : B.S.I.
Part 1 = Partie 1 = Teil 1 : Fully plasticized nylon tubing types 11 and 12 for use primarily in pneumatic installations = Tubes en nylon complètement plastifié, types 11 et 12, à utiliser surtout dans les installations pneumatiques = Vollplastizierte Nylonrohre, Typen 11 und 12, mit Haupverwendung in pneumatischen Anlagen. — 1976. — [2],6,[2]p : 1 ill ; 30cm. — (BS5409 : Part 1 : 1976)
Pierced for binder.
ISBN 0-580-09068-x Sd : £2.40
(B77-09132)

668.4'235 — Plastics: Nylon
Nelson, William Edgar. Nylon plastics technology / [by] W.E. Nelson. — London [etc.] : Newnes-Butterworths for the Plastics and Rubber Institute, 1976. — [8],230p : ill ; 23cm. — (Plastics and Rubber Institute. Monographs)
Index.
ISBN 0-408-00251-4 : £9.00
(B77-01649)

668.4'237 — Polyvinyl chloride. Manufacture
Open University. *ST294 Course Team.* Polyvinyl chloride, a case study / prepared by an Open University Course Team [the ST294 Course Team]. — Milton Keynes : Open University Press. — (Science and technology, a second level course : principles of chemical processes)
In 2 vols.
Part 1. — 1975. — 54p : ill(some col) ; 30cm. — (St294 ; CS1)
ISBN 0-335-04180-9 Pbk : £2.75
(B77-26406)

668.4'237 — Polyvinylidene chloride
Wessling, Ritchie A. Polyvinylidene chloride / [by] Ritchie A. Wessling. — New York ; London [etc.] : Gordon and Breach, 1977. — xii,199p : ill ; 23cm. — (Polymer monographs ; 5)
Index.
ISBN 0-677-01700-6 : £11.70
(B77-09817)

668.4'9 — Hospital equipment: Plastics containers. *Standards*
British Standards Institution. Specification for hospital hollow-ware made of plastics material = Spécification des ustensiles creux d'hôpital en matières plastiques = Spezifikation für Krankenhaus-Hohlkörper aus Kunststoffen / British Standards Institution. — London : B.S.I., 1977. — [2],8,[2]p : ill ; 30cm. — (BS5452 : 1977)
Pierced for binder.
ISBN 0-580-09571-1 Sd : £2.70
(B77-17631)

668.4'9 — Plastics laboratory equipment. *Standards*
British Standards Institution. Specification for plastics laboratory ware = Spécification des articles de laboratoire en matières plastiques = Spezifikation für Laboratoriumsartikel aus Kunststoff / British Standards Institution. — London : B.S.I.
Part 1 = Partie 1 = Teil 1 : Beakers = Bechers = Becher. — 1976. — [2],4,[2]p : ill ; 30cm. — (BS5404 : Part 1 : 1976)
Pierced for binder.
ISBN 0-580-09217-8 Sd : £1.50
(B77-03122)

668.4'9 — Plastics products. Design
Levy, Sidney. Plastics product design engineering handbook / [by] Sidney Levy, J. Harry DuBois. — New York ; London [etc.] : Van Nostrand Reinhold, 1977. — xv,332p : ill ; 24cm.
Index.
ISBN 0-442-24764-8 : £22.30
(B77-25063)

668.4'9 — Reinforced expanded plastics. *Conference proceedings*
Reinforced expanded plastics : one-day symposium organised by QMC Industrial Research Ltd, 26 March 1976. — [London] ([229 Mile End Rd, E1 4AA]) : [QMC Industrial Research Ltd], [1977]. — 108 leaves in various pagings : ill ; 30cm.
Sp : £10.00
(B77-26407)

668.4'94 — Glass fibre reinforced plastics
Crystic Research Centre. Polyester handbook / [Crystic Research Centre]. — [New ed.]. — Wellingborough (Wollaston, Wellingborough, Northants. NN9 7RL) : Crystic Research Centre, Scott Bader Co. Ltd, 1977. — x,116p : ill ; 20cm. — (Crystic monograph ; no.2)
Previous ed.: 1971. — Bibl.: p.108-109. — Index.
Pbk : Unpriced
(B77-30433)

668.4'94 — Reinforced plastics. *Conference proceedings*
Reinforced Plastics Congress, *Brighton, 1976.* Innovation : the basis of reinforced plastics : British Plastics Federation, Reinforced Plastics Group, Reinforced Plastics Congress 1976, Hotel Metropole, Brighton, England, 8-11 November 1976. — [London] : [British Plastics Federation, Reinforced Plastics Group], [1976]. — 259p : ill, maps, plans ; 30cm.
Cover title.
ISBN 0-900213-43-4 Pbk : £15.00
(B77-05528)

668.4'94 — Rubber toughened plastics
Bucknall, C B. Toughened plastics / [by] C.B. Bucknall. — London : Applied Science Publishers, 1977. — xvii,359p : ill ; 23cm.
Index.
ISBN 0-85334-695-x : £18.00
(B77-09133)

668.5 — PERFUMES AND COSMETICS
668'.55 — Cosmetics using herbs. *Recipes*
Beedell, Suzanne. Herbs for health and beauty / [by] Suzanne Beedell. — London : Sphere, 1977. — 174p : ill ; 18cm.
Originally published: 1972. — Bibl.: p.158-159. — Index.
ISBN 0-7221-1528-8 Pbk : £0.75
ISBN 0-7221-1531-8
Primary classification 615'.321
(B77-10379)

Huxley, Alyson. Natural beauty with herbs / [by] Alyson Huxley ; foreword by Muriel, Lady Dowding ; illustrated by Linda Diggins. — London : Darton, Longman and Todd, 1977. — 95p,[4]p of plates : ill(some col), col port ; 18cm. — (Herbwise ; 5)
ISBN 0-232-51388-0 Pbk : £0.99
(B77-30434)

668.6 — AGRICULTURAL CHEMICALS
668'.6'03 — Agricultural chemicals. *Dictionaries*
Marler, E E J. Pharmacological and chemical synonyms : a collection of names of drugs, pesticides and other compounds drawn from the medical literature of the world / compiled by E.E.J. Marler. — 6th ed. — Amsterdam ; Oxford : Excerpta Medica, 1976. — [8],472p ; 25cm.
Previous ed.: Amsterdam : Excerpta Medica, 1973.
£48.75
ISBN 90-219-0298-2 (Excerpta Medica)
Primary classification 615'.1'03
(B77-04840)

668'.62'5 — Fertilisers: Phosphates. Production. *Conference proceedings*
International Superphosphate Manufacturers' Association. *Technical Conference, The Hague, 1976.* New developments in phosphate fertilizer technology : proceedings of the 1976 Technical Conference of ISMA [International Superphosphate Manufacturers' Association] Ltd, the Hague, the Netherlands, 13-16 September 1976 / edited by L.J. Carpentier. — Amsterdam ; Oxford [etc.] : Elsevier, 1977. — viii,454p : ill ; 25cm.
ISBN 0-444-41535-1 : £30.00
(B77-21281)

669 — METALLURGY
669 — Extractive metallurgy. *Reviews of research*
Advances in extractive metallurgy, 1977 : an international symposium organized by the Institution of Mining and Metallurgy and held in London from 18 to 10 April, 1977 / edited by M.J. Jones. — London (44 Portland Place, W1N 4BR) : The Institution, [1977]. — vii, 244p : ill ; 30cm.
ISBN 0-900488-37-9 Pbk : £18.50
(B77-17632)

669 — Metals. Properties
British Steel Corporation. Which metals? / [British Steel Corporation and NCST Trent Polytechnic] ; material collected and arranged by Elizabeth Pedley and Cyril Gorham. — Sheffield (P.O. Box 64, The Mount, Sheffield S10 2PZ) : Market Promotion Department, British Steel Corporation, 1976. — 70p : ill ; 30cm.
Bibl.: p.69. — Index.
ISBN 0-9500451-3-6 Pbk : £1.50
(B77-16499)

669'.002'462 — Metals. *For engineering*
Nutt, Merle C. Metallurgy & plastics for engineers / [by] Merle C. Nutt. — Phoenix, Ariz. : Associated Lithographers ; Oxford [etc.] : Distributed by Pergamon, [1977]. — xv, 550p : ill ; 26cm.
Published in the United States: 1976. — Bibl. — Index.
ISBN 0-08-021684-6 : £12.50
(B77-10456)

669'.006'241 — Metallurgy. Organisations: Institution of Mining and Metallurgy. *Great Britain. Periodicals*
Institution of Mining and Metallurgy. IMM bulletin : bulletin of the Institution of Mining and Metallurgy. — London (44 Portland Place, W1N 4BR) : I.M.M.
No.830- ; Jan. 1976-. — 1976-. — 30cm.
Monthly. — 8p. in Jan. 1976 issue. — Continues: Institution of Mining and Metallurgy. Bulletin.
Sd : £6.00 yearly
ISSN 0308-9789
Primary classification 622'.06'241
(B77-04256)

669'.007'2 — Metals. Research. Techniques
Techniques involving extreme environment, nondestructive techniques, computer methods in metals research, and data analysis / editor R.F. Bunshah. — New York ; London [etc.] : Wiley. — (Techniques of metals research ; vol.7)
In 2 parts.
Part 2 ... / [by] S. Bhattacharya ... [et al.]. — 1976. — xii p,p529-943 : ill ; 24cm.
'A Wiley-Interscience publication'. — Bibl. — Index.
ISBN 0-471-12241-6 : £32.00
(B77-07489)

669'.009 — Metallurgy, to 1950
Tylecote, Ronald Frank. A history of metallurgy / [by] R.F. Tylecote. — London : Metals Society, 1976. — ix,182p : ill, maps ; 30cm.
Index.
ISBN 0-904357-06-6 Pbk : £10.00
(B77-06786)

669'.009'01 — Metallurgy, to 700. *Conference proceedings*
Aspects of early metallurgy : papers presented at a symposium on early metallurgy organised by the Historical Metallurgy Society and the British Museum Research Laboratory and held at the British Museum on 22nd and 23rd April 1977 / edited by W.A. Oddy. — [Sheffield] ([147 Whirlowdale Rd, Sheffield S7 2NG]) : [The Society], [1977]. — 177p : ill, maps ; 30cm.
Bibl.
Sp : Unpriced
(B77-25755)

669'.0282 — Ores. High temperature treatment
Alcock, Charles Benjamin. Principles of pyrometallurgy / [by] C.B. Alcock. — London [etc.] : Academic Press, 1976. — xiii,348p : ill ; 24cm.
Bibl. — Index.
ISBN 0-12-048950-3 : £8.80
(B77-05529)

669'.0284 — Metals. Production. Use of molten salts electrolysis. *Conference proceedings*
Molten salt electrolysis in metal production : an international symposium organized by the Institution of Mining and Metallurgy, with the cooperation of the Section sud-est de la Société française de métallurgie, and held in Grenoble, France, from 19 to 21 September, 1977. — London (44 Portland Place, W1N 4BR) : The Institution, 1977. — vii,73p : ill ; 30cm.
ISBN 0-900488-39-5 Pbk : £14.50
(B77-30435)

669.1 — METALLURGY OF FERROUS METALS
669'.1 — Iron & steel. Production. *Juvenile literature*
Saville, James Patrick. Iron and steel / [by] J.P. Saville. — Hove : Priory Press, 1976. — 89p : ill ; 20x23cm. — (World resources)
Map, ill. on lining papers. — Bibl.: p.87. — Index.
ISBN 0-85078-234-1 : £2.75
(B77-02441)

669.2/7 — METALLURGY OF NONFERROUS METALS
669'.22 — Gold. *Juvenile literature*
Law, Felicia. Gold / written by Felicia Law ; illustrated by Gary Rees. — London [etc.] : Collins, 1976. — 32p : col ill ; 22cm. — (Dandelions)
ISBN 0-00-651219-4 Sd : £0.50
(B77-02442)

669'.22'09 — Gold, to 1975
Mayhew, Vic. The 'Reader's digest' book of gold : a brief guide to the world's most alluring metal / compiled by Vic Mayhew. — London : Reader's Digest Association, 1976. — 48p : ill(chiefly col) ; 15cm.
Bibl.: p.48.
ISBN 0-276-00151-6 Sd : £0.30
(B77-04939)

669'.3 — Copper. Production
Biswas, Anil Kumar. Extractive metallurgy of copper / [by] A.K. Biswas and W.G. Davenport. — Oxford [etc.] : Pergamon, 1976. — xiii,438p,[5]p of plates : ill, maps ; 22cm. — (International series on materials science and technology ; vol.20) (Pergamon international library)
Bibl. — Index.
ISBN 0-08-019658-6 : £20.00
ISBN 0-08-019657-8 Pbk : £7.50
(B77-09818)

669'.4 — Lead. *Conference proceedings*
International Conference on Lead, *5th, Paris, 1974.* Lead 74 : edited proceedings [of the] Fifth International Conference on Lead, Paris, organized by European Lead Development Committee / [prepared by Barry Harris]. — London : Metal Bulletin, 1976. — 239p : ill, map ; 30cm.
'... held ... from 18-22 November 1974 ...' - Preface.
ISBN 0-900542-17-9 Pbk : £15.00
(B77-09819)

669'.5 — Zinc. Extraction
Open University. *ST294 Course Team.* Zinc, a case study / prepared by an Open University Course Team [the ST294 Course Team]. — Milton Keynes : Open University Press, 1975. — 35p : ill ; 30cm. — (ST294 ; CS3) (Science and technology, a second level course : principles of chemical processes)
Fold. sheet (leaf: col.ill.) as insert. — With SAW answers and comments.
ISBN 0-335-04189-2 Sd : £1.80
(B77-26408)

669.9 — PHYSICAL AND CHEMICAL METALLURGY
669'.9 — Metals. Structure & physical properties
Avner, Sidney Howard. Introduction to physical metallurgy / [by] Sidney H. Avner. — 2nd ed. — New York ; London [etc.] : McGraw-Hill, 1974. — viii,696p : ill ; 24cm.
Previous ed.: 1964. — Bibl. — Index.
ISBN 0-07-002499-5 : Unpriced
(B77-21282)

669'.94 — Alloys. Mechanical properties
Alloy and microstructural design / edited by John K. Tien, George S. Ansell. — New York [etc.] ; London : Academic Press, 1976 [i.e. 1977]. — xii,429p : ill ; 24cm. — (Materials science and technology)
Published in the United States: 1976. — Bibl. — Index.
ISBN 0-12-690850-8 : £28.05
(B77-13745)

669'.94 — Alloys. Shape memory effects. *Conference proceedings*
International Symposium on Shape Memory Effects and Applications, *Toronto, 1975.* Shape memory effects in alloys / edited by Jeff Perkins. — New York ; London : Plenum Press, 1975. — ix,583p : ill ; 26cm.
'A publication of the Metallurgical Society of AIME'. — 'Proceedings of the International Symposium on Shape Memory Effects and Applications held in Toronto, Ontario, Canada, May 19-22, 1975 ...' - title-page verso. — Index.
ISBN 0-306-30891-6 : £31.19
(B77-03659)

669'.94 — Metals. Reinforcement. Use of solid solutions. *Conference proceedings*
Physics of Solid-Solution Strengthening in Alloys *(Conference), Chicago, 1973.* Physics of solid solution strengthening / edited by E.W. Collings and H.L. Gegel. — New York ; London : Plenum Press, [1976]. — xii,306p : ill ; 26cm.
'... proceedings of a Symposium entitled "The Physics of Solid-Solution Strengthening in Alloys" which was held at McCormick Place, Chicago, on October 2, 1973 ...' - Preface. — 'A publication of The Metallurgical Society of AIME'. — Published in the United States: 1975. — Bibl. — Index.
ISBN 0-306-30890-8 : £17.33
(B77-05530)

669'.95 — Metallography
Rostoker, William. Interpretation of metallographic structures / [by] William Rostoker, James R. Dvorak. — 2nd ed. — New York [etc.] ; London : Academic Press, 1977. — xii,250p : ill ; 24cm.
Previous ed.: 1965. — Index.
ISBN 0-12-598260-7 : £17.40
(B77-25756)

669'.95 — Metals. Grain boundaries. Structure & physical properties. *Conference proceedings*
Institution of Metallurgists. *Spring Residential Conference, Jersey, 1976.* Grain boundaries : Spring Residential Conference, April 1976. — London (Northway House, Whetstone, N20 9LW) : The Institution, [1976]. — 225p in various pagings : ill ; 30cm. — (Series 3 ; no.5)
'papers ... presented at the Spring Residential Conference held at the Grouville Bay Hotel, Jersey from 9-12 April 1976 and organised by the Younger Metallurgists Committee of the Institution of Metallurgists' - title page verso.
ISBN 0-901462-03-9 Pbk : £11.00(£8.00 to members)
(B77-14826)

669'.95 — Metals. Mechanical properties. Effects of crystal defects. *Conference proceedings*
International School of Physics 'Enrico Fermi', *61st, Varenna, 1974.* Atomic structure and mechanical properties of metals : proceedings of the International School of Physics 'Enrico Fermi', course LXI, Varenna on Lake Como, Villa Monastero, 8th-20th July 1974 / edited by G. Caglioti. — Bologna : Società Italiana di fisica ; Amsterdam [etc.] ; Oxford : [Distributed by] North-Holland Publishing Co., 1976 [i.e. 1977]. — ii-xxiii,661p, plate : ill, ports ; 25cm.
At head of title: Italian Physical Society. — Second title page in Italian. — Cover title: Struttura atomica e proprietà meccaniche dei metalli. — Published in Italy : 1976.
ISBN 0-7204-0490-8 : £53.86
(B77-12565)

669'.96'722 — Aluminium & aluminium alloys. Chemical analysis. *Standards*
British Standards Institution. British Standard methods for the analysis of aluminium and aluminium alloys : Méthodes de l'analyse d'aluminium et des alliages d'aluminium = Verfahren zur Analyse von Aluminium und Aluminiumlegierungen / British Standards Institution. — London : B.S.I.
Part 24 = Partie 24 = Teil 24 : Nickel (atomic absorption method) = Nickel (méthode par absorption atomique) = Nickel (Atomabsorptionsverfahren). — 1976. — Folder (4p) ; 30cm. — (BS.1728 : Part 24 : 1976)
Pierced for binder.
ISBN 0-580-09308-5 : £1.15
(B77-01644)

Part 23 = Partie 23 = Teil 23 : Copper (atomic absorption method) = Cuivre (méthode par absorption atomique) = Kupfer (Atomabsorptionsverfahren). — 1976. — Folder (4p) ; 30cm. — (BS.1728 : Part 23 : 1976)
Pierced for binder.
ISBN 0-580-09298-4 : £1.15
(B77-01645)

670 — MANUFACTURES
670 — Gifts. *Buyers' guides*
Gifts annual buyer's guide. — London [etc.] : E. Benn.
1977. — 1977. — 140p : ill(some col) ; 30cm.
ISBN 0-510-49642-3 Pbk : £5.00
(B77-18889)

670 — Manufacture
Schey, John A. Introduction to manufacturing processes / [by] John A. Schey. — New York ; London [etc.] : McGraw-Hill, 1977. — xxi, 392p : ill ; 25cm.
With answers to selected problems. — Text on lining papers. — Bibl. — Index.
ISBN 0-07-055274-6 : £13.50
(B77-23572)

670'.21'6 — Kitemarked manufactured goods. *Buyers' guides*
British Standards Institution. The buyers guide / [British Standards Institution]. — Hemel Hempstead (Marylands Ave., Hemel Hempstead, Herts. HP2 4SQ) : B.S.I., Quality Assurance Dept.
1976. — [1976]. — [1],88p : ill(some col) ; 30cm.
Index.
Sd : Unpriced
(B77-02443)

670'.74'027642 — Museums. *Lancashire. Burnley. Towneley Hall Art Gallery and Museums. Museum of Local Crafts and Industries*
Towneley Hall Art Gallery and Museums. *Museum of Local Crafts and Industries.* Museum of Local Crafts & Industries. — [Burnley] ([Town Hall, Burnley, Lancs.]) : Burnley Borough Council, [1976]. — 24p : ill ; 16x22cm.
At head of title: Towneley Hall Art Gallery and Museums.
Sd : £0.15
(B77-07490)

670'.973 — Manufacture. *United States, ca 1800. Juvenile literature. Early works*
[The **book** of trades, or, Library of the useful arts. Part 1]. Little book of early American crafts and trades. — [1st American ed. reprinted] / edited, with a new introduction, by Peter Stockham. — New York : Dover Publications [etc.] ; London : Constable, 1976. — iii-xiv,140p,[14] leaves of plates,[8]p of plates : ill ; 16cm.
Facsimile reprint of: 1st American ed. part 1, originally published as 'Book of trades, or, Library of the useful arts'. White-Hall, N.Y. : Jacob Johnson, 1807.
ISBN 0-486-23336-7 Pbk : £1.40
(B77-15374)

671 — METAL MANUFACTURES
Amstead, Billy Howard. Manufacturing processes. — 7th ed. / [by] B.H. Amstead, Phillip F. Ostwald, Myron L. Begeman. — New York ; London [etc.] : Wiley, 1977. — xii, 739p : ill ; 24cm.
Text on lining papers. — Previous ed.: / by Myron L. Begeman and B.H. Amstead. 1969. — Bibl.: p.723-726. — Index.
ISBN 0-471-06245-6 : £15.40
(B77-11301)

671 — Metal products. Manufacture. *Manuals*
Tool and manufacturing engineers handbook : a reference work for manufacturing engineers. — 3rd ed. / revised under the supervision of the SME Publications Committee with the assistance of the SME technical divisions ; Daniel B. Dallas, editor-in-chief. — New York ; London [etc.] : McGraw-Hill [for the] Society of Manufacturing Engineers, 1976. — 2899p in various pagings : ill ; 24cm.
Previous ed.: published as 'Tool engineers handbook' / issued by the American Society of Tool and Manufacturing Engineers. New York : McGraw-Hill, 1959. — Bibl. — Index.
ISBN 0-07-059558-5 : £41.10
(B77-04940)

671 — Metals. Industrial processes
Rowe, Geoffrey Whaley. Principles of industrial metalworking processes / by Geoffrey W. Rowe. — [New] ed. — London : Edward Arnold, 1977. — xxii,407p : ill ; 25cm.
Previous ed.: published as 'An introduction to the principles of metalworking'. 1965. — Index.
ISBN 0-7131-3381-3 : £17.50
(B77-22004)

671.2 — Foundries. Molten metals & water. Explosions. *Reports, surveys*
Joint Standing Committee on Health, Safety and Welfare in Foundries. *Sub-committee on Continuous Casting and High Speed Melting.* A study of the causes of molten metal and water explosions : fourth report of the Sub-committee on Continuous Casting and High Speed Melting [of the] Joint Standing Committee on Health, Safety and Welfare in Foundries. — London : H.M.S.O., 1977. — 43p : ill ; 25cm.
Bibl.: p.42-43.
ISBN 0-11-883006-6 Sd : £1.75
(B77-16500)

671.2'5 — Die casting
The **diecasting** book / [edited] by Arthur Street. — Redhill (2 Queensway, Redhill, Surrey) : Portcullis Press, 1977. — [10],786p : ill, plans ; 25cm.
Bibl.: p.757-765. — Index.
ISBN 0-901994-98-7 : £28.00
(B77-32737)

671.3 — Metals. Forming
Blazynski, Tadeusz Zdzislaw. Metal forming : tool profiles and flow / [by] T.Z. Blazynski. — London [etc.] : Macmillan, 1976. — xii,379p : ill ; 24cm.
Index.
ISBN 0-333-19319-9 : £17.50
(B77-04941)

671.3'6 — Metals. Heat treatment. *Conference proceedings*
International Heat Treatment Conference, *16th, Stratford-upon-Avon, 1976.* Heat treatment '76 : proceedings of the 16th International Heat Treatment Conference organized jointly by Activity Group Committee VII of the Metals Society and the International Federation for the Heat Treatment of Materials, and held at Stratford-upon-Avon, 6-7 May 1976. — London : Metals Society, 1976. — vii,257p : ill ; 31cm.
Contains résumés in French, German and Russian. — Index.
ISBN 0-904357-05-8 : £22.50
(B77-06201)

671.5'2 — Castings. Welding. *Conference proceedings*
Welding of Castings *(Conference), Bradford, 1976.* Welding of Castings : an international conference arranged by the Welding Institute, the Steel Castings Research and Trade Association, and the BNF Metals Technology Centre, Bradford, 21-23 September 1976 : conference technical director D.N. Shackleton. — Cambridge : Welding Institute.
Vol.1 : Papers. — 1977. — [3],299p : ill ; 30cm.
ISBN 0-85300-108-1 Pbk : Unpriced
(B77-17633)

671.5'2 — Metals. Welding
Davies, Arthur Cyril. The science and practice of welding / [by] A.C. Davies. — 7th ed. — Cambridge [etc.] : Cambridge University Press, 1977. — xiii,713p : ill ; 21cm.
Previous ed.: 1972. — Index.
ISBN 0-521-21557-9 : £7.00
(B77-30436)

671.5'2 — Metals. Welding. *Conference proceedings*
Advances in welding processes : [proceedings of the] third international conference, Harrogate, 7-9 May 1974 : conference technical director J.C. Needham. — Cambridge : Welding Institute.
Vol.2 : Discussions. — 1975. — [3]p,p303-341 : ill ; 30cm.
Sd : Unpriced
(B77-20442)

671.5'2 — Metals. Welding. *Manuals*
Bainbridge, Cecil George. Welding / [by] C.G. Bainbridge. — 3rd ed. — Sevenoaks : Teach Yourself Books, 1977. — xii,181p : ill ; 18cm. — (Teach yourself books)
Previous ed.: 1973. — Index.
ISBN 0-340-21255-1 Pbk : £0.95
(B77-13746)

671.5'2 — Offshore structures. Underwater welding. *Conference proceedings*
Underwater welding for offshore installations. — Cambridge : Welding Institute, 1977. — [4], 129p : ill ; 30cm.
'[Papers presented at] an international seminar, sponsored by the Welding Institute, the UK Department of Energy, and the Society for Underwater Technology ... arranged in 1976 ...' - Foreword. — Bibl.: p.127-129.
ISBN 0-85300-106-5 Pbk : £10.50
(B77-09134)

671.5'2 — Welding
American Welding Society. Welding handbook / [American Welding Society]. — 7th ed. — Miami : American Welding Society ; London [etc.] : Distributed by Macmillan.
In 5 vols.
Vol.1 : Fundamentals of welding / Charlotte Weisman, editor. — 1976. — xv,373p : ill ; 24cm.
Previous ed.: New York : American Welding Society, 1968. — Bibl. — Index.
ISBN 0-87171-126-5 : £15.00
(B77-04942)

Lancaster, John Frederick. The metallurgy of welding, brazing and soldering / [by] J.F. Lancaster. — 2nd ed. — London : Allen and Unwin, 1974. — 3-303p : ill ; 23cm. — (Institution of Metallurgists. Modern metallurgical texts ; no.3)
This ed. originally published: 1970. — Bibl. — Index.
£5.50
ISBN 0-04-669004-2
Also classified at 671.5'6
(B77-03123)

671.5'212 — Arc welding
Griffin, Ivan H. Basic welding techniques : three books in one, arc, oxyacetylene, TIG & MIG / [by] Ivan H. Griffin, Edward M. Roden and Charles W. Briggs. — New York ; London [etc.] : Van Nostrand Reinhold, 1977. — 82,92, 114,[20]p : ill(some col) ; 27cm.
Certain portions originally published: in 'Basic arc welding' / by Ivan H. Griffin, Edward M. Roden. Albany, N.Y. : Delmar Publishers, 1971 - 'Basic oxyacetylene welding' / by Ivan H. Griffin, Edward M. Roden. Albany, N.Y. : Delmar Publishers, 1971 - 'Basic TIG & MIG welding' / by Ivan H. Griffin, Edward M. Roden. Albany, N.Y. : Delmar Publishers, 1971.
ISBN 0-442-22861-9 : £10.60
Also classified at 671.5'22
(B77-23573)

671.5'22 — Oxyacetylene welding
Griffin, Ivan H. Basic welding techniques : three books in one, arc, oxyacetylene, TIG & MIG / [by] Ivan H. Griffin, Edward M. Roden and Charles W. Briggs. — New York ; London [etc.] : Van Nostrand Reinhold, 1977. — 82,92, 114,[20]p : ill(some col) ; 27cm.
Certain portions originally published: in 'Basic arc welding' / by Ivan H. Griffin, Edward M. Roden. Albany, N.Y. : Delmar Publishers, 1971 - 'Basic oxyacetylene welding' / by Ivan H. Griffin, Edward M. Roden. Albany, N.Y. : Delmar Publishers, 1971 - 'Basic TIG & MIG welding' / by Ivan H. Griffin, Edward M. Roden. Albany, N.Y. : Delmar Publishers, 1971.
ISBN 0-442-22861-9 : £10.60
Primary classification 671.5'212
(B77-23573)

671.5'3 — Metals. Cutting
Trent, E M. Metal cutting / [by] E.M. Trent. — London [etc.] : Butterworth, 1977. — [11], 203p : ill ; 24cm.
Bibl.: p.197. — Index.
ISBN 0-408-10603-4 : £10.00
(B77-08462)

671.5'6 — Brazing & soldering
Lancaster, John Frederick. The metallurgy of welding, brazing and soldering / [by] J.F. Lancaster. — 2nd ed. — London : Allen and Unwin, 1974. — 3-303p : ill ; 23cm. — (Institution of Metallurgists. Modern metallurgical texts ; no.3)
This ed. originally published: 1970. — Bibl. — Index.
£5.50
ISBN 0-04-669004-2
Primary classification 671.5'2
(B77-03123)

671.5'6 — Soft solders. *Standards*
British Standards Institution. Specification for soft solders = Spécification des soudures tendres = Spezifikation für Weichlote / British Standards Institution. — 5th revision. — London : B.S.I., 1977. — [2],3,[2]p ; 30cm. — (BS219 : 1977)
Pierced for binder.
ISBN 0-580-09741-2 Sd : £1.60
(B77-15375)

671.7'35 — Ion plating. *Conference proceedings*
IPAT 77 *(Conference), Edinburgh, 1977.* IPAT 77 : proceedings [of a] conference [on] ion plating & allied techniques, Edinburgh, June, 1977. — [Edinburgh] ([14a Henderson Row, Edinburgh EH3 5DH]) : [CEP Consultants Ltd], [1977]. — [1],v,248p : ill ; 30cm.
ISBN 0-905941-00-4 Pbk : Unpriced
(B77-32738)

672 — FERROUS METALS MANUFACTURES
672'.2'5 — Steel. Continuous casting. *Conference proceedings*
Continuous casting of steel : proceedings of an international conference organized by the Metals Society, London and L'Institut de recherches [i.e. recherche] de la sidérurgie française (IRSID), and held in Biarritz, France on 31 May-2 June 1976 ... — London : Metals Society, 1977. — xi,324p : ill ; 31cm.
Index.
ISBN 0-904357-08-2 : £36.00
(B77-30437)

672'.5'2 — Steel. Fusion welding. *Standards*
National Coal Board. *Headquarters Inspection Service. Quality Control Branch.* Fusion welding of steel / [National Coal Board, Headquarters Inspection Service, Quality Control Branch]. — London : N.C.B., 1976. — [3],31p : ill, forms ; 22cm. — (Quality requirements ; 1)
ISBN 0-901429-94-5 Sd : Private circulation
(B77-01646)

672.8 — 1230-1420 MPa 2.5% nickel-chromium-molybdenum steel billets, bars, forgings & parts up to 150mm section. *Standards. For aerospace engineering*
British Standards Institution. Specification for 2.5% nickel-chromium-molybdenum (high carbon) steel billets, bars, forgings and parts = Spécification, billettes, barres, pièces forgées et éléments en acier (à haute teneur en carbone) à 2.5% nickel-chrome-molybdène = Spezifikation, Knüppel, Stäbe, Schmiedestücke und Stücke aus (kohlenstoffreichen) Stahl mit einem 2.5% Nickel-Chrom-Molybdän-Gehalt : (1230-1420 Mpa : limiting ruling section 150mm) = (1230-1420 Mpa : section limite de 150mm) = (1230-1420 Mpa : massgeblicher Grenzquerschnitt 150mm) / British Standards Institution. — London : B.S.I., 1976. — Folder (4p) ; 30cm. — (British Standard aerospace series = Série aérospatiale = Luftraumserie) (4S 99 : 1976)
Pierced for binder. — '(Superseding British Standard 3S 99)'.
ISBN 0-580-09488-x : £1.20
(B77-14315)

672.8 — 1760-1960 MPa 4% nickel-chromium-molybdenum vacuum arc remelted air-hardening steel billets, bars, forgings & parts up to 100mm section. *Standards. For aerospace engineering*
British Standards Institution. Specification for 4% nickel-chromium-molybdenum air-hardening steel (vacuum arc remelted) billets, bars, forgings and parts = Spécification, billettes, barres, pièces forgées et éléments en acier de trempe à l'air (réaffiné à arc sous vide) à 4% nickel-chrome-molybdène = Spezifikation, Knüppel, Stäbe, Schmiedestücke und Stücke aus (im Vakuumbogen wiedergeschmolzenem) Lufthärtestahl miteinem 4% Nickel-Chrom-Molybdän-Gehalt : (1760-1960 Mpa : limiting ruling section 100mm) = (1760-1960 Mpa = section limite de 100mm) = (1760-1960 Mpa : Massgeblicher Grenzquerschmitt 100mm) / British Standards Institution. — London : B.S.I., 1976. — Folder (4p) ; 30cm. — (British Standard aerospace series = Série aérospatiale = Luftraumserie) (25 146 : 1976)
Pierced for binder. — '(Superseding British Standard S146)'.
ISBN 0-580-09498-7 : £1.20
(B77-14827)

672'.8'23 — Cold-rolled steel sections. *Standards*
British Standards Institution. Specification for cold rolled steel sections = Spécification pour profilés en acier laminés à froid = Spezifikation für kaltgewalzte Stahlprofile / British Standards Institution. — 1st revision. — London : B.S.I., 1976. — [2],32,[2]p : ill ; 30cm. — (BS2994 : 1976)
Pierced for binder.
ISBN 0-580-09377-8 Sd : £5.80
(B77-10457)

672'.8'3 — Carbon steel forgings & manganese steel forgings. *Standards*
British Standards Institution. Specification for carbon steel forgings above 150mm ruling section = Spécification des pièces forgées en acier au carbone de section dominante supérieure à 150mm = Spezifikation für Schmiedestücke aus unlegiertem Stahl mit einem ausschlaggebenden Querschnitt über 150mm / British Standards Institution. — 4th revision. — London : B.S.I., 1976. — [2],8,[2] p : ill ; 30cm. — (BS29 : 1976)
Pierced for binder.
ISBN 0-580-09268-2 Sd : £2.40
(B77-10458)

673 — NONFERROUS METALS MANUFACTURES
673'.3'83 — Engineering components: Steel copper tube bending springs. *Standards*
British Standards Institution. Specification for bending springs for use with copper tubes for water, gas and sanitation = Spécification pour ressorts de flexion pour usages avec les tubes en cuivre pour le transport de l'eau, du gaz et pour les systèmes sanitaires = Spezifikation für Biegefedern zur Verwendung mit Kupferrohren für Wasser, Gas und Abwasserbeseitigung / British Standards Institution. — London : B.S.I., 1976. — [2],3,[2]p : ill ; 30cm. — (BS5431 : 1976)
Pierced for binder.
ISBN 0-580-09570-3 Sd : £1.60
(B77-11960)

673'.5 — Zinc die castings. Machining
Zinc Alloy Die Casters Association. Machining and forming zinc die castings / [Zinc Alloy Die Casters Association]. — Revised [ed.]. — London (34 Berkeley Sq., W1X 6AJ) : The Association, 1976. — 36p : ill ; 21cm.
Index.
ISBN 0-905219-01-5 Sd : Unpriced
(B77-11961)

673'.73'3 — Nickel bars & nickel alloy bars. *Standards*
British Standards Institution. Specification for nickel and nickel alloys, bar = Spécification du nickel et des alliages de nickel, barres = Spezifikation für Nickel und Nickellegierungen, Stähe / British Standards Institution. — 2nd revision. — London : B.S.I., 1976. — [2],13,[2] p ; 30cm. — (BS3076 : 1976)
Pierced for binder.
ISBN 0-580-09327-1 Sd : £4.00
(B77-03124)

673'.73'3 — Nickel wires & nickel alloy wires. *Standards*
British Standards Institution. Specification for nickel and nickel alloys, wire = Spécification du nickel et des alliages nickel fils = Spezifikation für Nickel und Nickellegierungen, Drähte / British Standards Institution. — 2nd revision. — London : B.S.I., 1976. — [2],7,[2] p ; 30cm. — (BS3075 : 1976)
Pierced for binder.
ISBN 0-580-09207-0 Sd : £2.40
(B77-03125)

673'.73'3 — Seamless nickel tubes & seamless nickel alloy tubes. *Standards*
British Standards Institution. Specification for nickel and nickel alloys, seamless tube = Spécification du nickel et des alliages de nickel, tubes sans soudure = Spezifikation für Nickel und Nickellegierungen, nahtlose Röhre / British Standards Institution. — 2nd revision. — London : B.S.I., 1977. — [2],12,[2]p ; 30cm. — (BS3074 : 1977)
Pierced for binder.
ISBN 0-580-09541-x Sd : £3.60
(B77-15376)

674 — TIMBER MANUFACTURES
674'.007'2042595 — Timber. Research organisations. *Buckinghamshire. Princes Risborough. Building Research Establishment. Princes Risborough Laboratory, to 1975*
Rendle, Bernard John. Fifty years of timber research : a short history of the Forest Products Research Laboratory, Princes Risborough / [by] B.J. Rendle. — London : H.M.S.O., 1976. — xii,117p,[12]p of plates : ill ; 25cm.
Bibl. — Index.
ISBN 0-11-670546-9 : £5.75
(B77-09820)

674'.142 — Sawn hardwood. Sizes. *Standards*
British Standards Institution. Specification for sizes of hardwoods and methods of measurement = Dimensions des bois durs et méthodes de mesure = Masse von Harthölzern und Messverfahren / British Standards Institution. — London : B.S.I., 1977. — [2],4, [2]p : ill ; 30cm. — (BS5450 : 1977)
Pierced for binder.
ISBN 0-580-09910-5 Sd : £1.60
(B77-15377)

674'.144 — Softwood
Building Research Establishment. A handbook of softwoods / [Building Research Establishment]. — 2nd ed. — London : H.M.S.O, 1977. — [5], 63p ; 30cm. — (Building Research Establishment. Reports)
Previous ed.: issued by the Forest Products Research Laboratory. 1957. — Index.
ISBN 0-11-470563-1 Sd : £3.75
(B77-27963)

674'.8 — Rural crafts connected with timber. *England, 1827-1930*
Sparkes, Ivan George. Woodland craftsmen / [by] Ivan G. Sparkes. — Aylesbury : Shire Publications, 1977. — 33p : ill, ports ; 21cm. — (Shire album ; 25)
Bibl.: p.32.
ISBN 0-85263-381-5 Sd : £0.50
(B77-32019)

674'.82'0941 — Coopering. *Great Britain*
Kilby, Kenneth. The village cooper / [by] K. Kilby. — Aylesbury : Shire Publications, 1977. — 32p : ill ; 21cm. — (Shire album ; 28)
Bibl.: p.32.
ISBN 0-85263-392-0 Sd : £0.50
(B77-30438)

675 — LEATHER AND FUR PROCESSING
675'.24 — Leather. Treatment. Use of sperm oil. *Great Britain. Reports, surveys*
British Leather Manufacturers' Research Association. Utilisation of sperm oil by the leather industry / British Leather Manufacturers' Research Association. — [London] : [Department of Industry], [1976]. — [6],48p ; 30cm.
ISBN 0-900209-00-3 Pbk : £2.75
(B77-03126)

676 — PULP AND PAPER TECHNOLOGY
676'.14 — Pulp & paper industries. Waste paper. Recycling. *Organisation for Economic Co-operation and Development countries. Reports, surveys*
Organisation for Economic Co-operation and Development. *Working Party on Pulp and Paper.* Prospects and policies for waste paper recycling in the pulp and paper industry / [Working Party on Pulp and Paper of the Industry Committee of the Organisation for Economic Co-operation and Development]. — Paris : O.E.C.D. ; [London] : [H.M.S.O.], 1976. — [2],ii,95p : ill ; 27cm.
'In 1975, the Industry Committee of the OECD instructed an ad hoc Working Party on Pulp and Paper to prepare a report on prospects and policies for waste paper recycling ...' - Preface.
Pbk : £3.00
ISBN 92-64-11521-8
(B77-01647)

676'.2 — Paper. *Juvenile literature*
Ellis, Rosemary. Paper-making / [by] Rosemary Ellis and Isabelle Symons. — London [etc.] : Bodley Head, 1976. — 48p : ill, facsims ; 26cm. — (Outlooks and insights series)
Index.
ISBN 0-370-01559-2 : £2.00
(B77-00879)

676.2 — Recycled paper. Use. *Great Britain. Friends of the Earth viewpoints*
Cohen, Colin. Ecological paper buying : why? how? where? / [by] Colin Cohen. — London (9 Poland St., W1V 3DG) : Friends of the Earth, 1976. — [1],24p : ill, samples ; 22cm.
Sd : Unpriced
(B77-30439)

676.2'06'241 — Paper & paperboard. Manufacture. Organisations. *Great Britain. British Paper and Board Industry Federation. Technical Division. Yearbooks*
British Paper and Board Industry Federation. *Technical Division.* Handbook and membership list / the British Paper and Board Industry Federation, Technical Division. — London : The Federation.
1975-1976. — [1977]. — vii,155p : ill ; 21cm.
Cover title. — Previously published: as 'Yearbook'.
Pbk : £3.50
ISSN 0140-2927
(B77-27964)

677 — TEXTILE MANUFACTURES
677'.022 — Woven fabrics. Design
Watson, William, *fl.1912.* Watson's advanced textile design : compound woven structures. — 4th ed. / [by] Z.J. Grosicki. — London [etc.] : Newnes-Butterworths, 1977. — [8],435p : ill ; 24cm.
Previous ed.: published as 'Advanced textile design'. London : Longman, 1947. — Index.
ISBN 0-408-00250-6 : £12.50
(B77-13128)

677'.02822 — Yarns. Open-end spinning. *Periodicals*
OE report : pilot issue. — Stockport : Textile Trade Press.
[Vol.1, no.1- ; Jan. 1977-]. — 1976-. — ill ; 30cm.
Six issues a year. — 12p. in 1st issue.
Sd : £25.00 yearly
ISSN 0309-2097
(B77-03660)

World oe bulletin. — Altrincham (Mayville House, Park Rd, Timperley, Altrincham, Cheshire WA15 6TQ) : Mayville Publishing (Bulletins) Ltd.
Issue 1-1- ; Oct. 1976-. — 1976-. — ill ; 30cm.
Monthly. — 12p. in 1st issue.
Sd : £45.00 for 10 issues
ISSN 0309-4820
(B77-09821)

677'.02824 — Weaving. *Great Britain. Periodicals*
The **weavers** journal. — [London] (c/o Federation of British Craft Societies, 80a Southampton Row, WC1B 4BA) : Association of the Guilds of Weavers, Spinners and Dyers.
No.97- ; Summer 1976-. — [1976]-. — ill ; 22cm.
Quarterly. 35p. in Summer 1976 issue. — Continues: Quarterly journal of the Guilds of Weavers, Spinners and Dyers.
Sd : £0.50(£1.80 yearly)
ISSN 0308-9207
(B77-01648)

677'.02825 — Yarns. Texturing. *Conference proceedings*
Developments in texturing : papers presented at a Shirley Institute conference on 20-21 October 1976. — Manchester : Shirley Institute, 1977. — [3],206p(2 fold) : ill ; 30cm. — (Shirley Institute. Publications ; S25 ISSN 0306-5154)
Pbk : £10.00(£7.50 to members of the Institute)
(B77-18274)

677'.02854 — Textile machinery: Warping machines. *Glossaries*
British Standards Institution. Glossary of terms relating to textile machinery and accessories, warping machinery and the preparation of warp for weaving = Lexique des termes relatifs au matériel pour l'industrie textile, matériel d'ourdissage, préparation de la chaîne pour le tissage = Lexikon von Begriffen mit Bezug auf Textilmaschinen und Zubehör, Kettvorbereitungsmaschinen, Kettvorbereitung für den Webvorgang / British Standards Institution. — London : B.S.I., 1976. — [2],22, [1]p : ill ; 30cm. — (BS5399 : 1976) (ISO 2544-1975)
Parallel text in English, French and Russian with an annex of German terms. — ISO title: Textile machinery and accessories - Warping machinery - Preparation of warp for weaving - Vocabulary. — Pierced for binder.
ISBN 0-580-09107-4 Sd : £4.00
(B77-03127)

677'.02862 — Yarns. *Conference proceedings*
Textile Institute. *Annual Conference, 60th, Harrogate, 1976.* The yarn revolution : new developments in the production of spun and textured yarns and their exploitation in fabric form : papers of the 60th Annual Conference of the Textile Institute, 1976, held at Harrogate. — Manchester : The Institute, 1976. — [4], 162p : ill ; 24cm.
Bibl.: p.23.
ISBN 0-900739-23-1 Pbk : £10.20
(B77-06787)

677'.02864'024746 — Fabrics. *For needlework*
Giles, Rosalie Phyllis. Fabrics for needlework / [by] Rosalie Giles. — 4th (metric) ed. — London [etc.] : Methuen, 1977. — ix,148p : ill, facsims, maps ; 22cm.
Previous ed.: 1970. — Index.
ISBN 0-423-89880-9 : £3.00
ISBN 0-423-89870-1 School ed. : £1.85
(B77-18890)

677'.0287 — Textiles. Testing
Lyle, Dorothy Siegert. Performance of textiles / [by] Dorothy Siegert Lyle. — New York ; London [etc.] : Wiley, 1977. — xvi,592p : ill ; 24cm.
Bibl.: p.567-579. — Index.
ISBN 0-471-01418-4 : £13.35
(B77-21283)

677'.0287 — Vertically oriented fabrics. Inflammability. Testing. *Standards*
British Standards Institution. Methods of test for flammability of vertically oriented textile fabrics and fabric assemblies subjected to a small igniting flame = Méthodes d'essai de la flammabilité des tissus textiles et des ensembles de tissus orientés dans le sens vertical et exposés à une petite flamme d'allumage = Methode zur Prüfung der Brennbarkeit von vertikal orientierten Flächengebilden und aus mehreren Lagen bestehenden Textilien mit dem Kleinbrenner / British Standards Institution. — London : B.S.I., 1976. — [2],15,[2]p : ill ; 30cm. — (BS5438 : 1976)
Pierced for binder.
ISBN 0-580-09299-2 Sd : £4.70
(B77-11302)

677'.21'0941 — Cotton fabrics. Manufacture. *Great Britain. Middle school texts*
Cox, Sarah. Textileworker / text by Sarah Cox ; photographs by Robert Golden. — Harmondsworth : Kestrel Books, 1976. — 32p : chiefly ill ; 27cm. — (People working)
ISBN 0-7226-5227-5 : £1.95
(B77-00309)

677'.21'52094276 — Cotton spinning machines. *Lancashire, 1738-1974*
Hills, Richard Leslie. Cotton spinning / by R.L. Hills. — [Manchester] ([97 Grosvenor St., Manchester M1 7HF]) : North Western Museum of Science and Industry, [1977]. — [1] ,22p : ill ; 21cm.
Bibl.: p.22.
Sd : £0.15
(B77-23574)

677'.31'0941 — Wool textiles. Manufacture. *Great Britain*
Brearley, Alan. The woollen industry : an outline of the woollen industry and its processes from fibre to fabric. — 2nd ed. / by Alan Brearley and John A. Iredale. — Leeds (Headingley La., Leeds LS6 1BW) : Wira, 1977. — viii,154p : ill ; 21cm.
Previous ed.: / by Alan Brearley. London : Pitman, 1965. — Bibl.: p.119-120. — Index.
ISBN 0-900820-10-1 Pbk : £3.00
(B77-22725)

677'.31'64 — Woven fabrics. *Wales. Welsh-English parallel texts*
Welsh Arts Council. Defnyddiau gwlân = Fabrics in wool : arddangosfa o ymgeisiadau dethol o'r gystadleuaeth agored a drefnwyd gan Gyngor Celfyddydau Cymru gyda chefnogaeth y Pwyllgor Crefftau Ymgynghorol = an exhibition of selected entries from the open competition organised by the Welsh Arts Council with the support of the Crafts Advisory Committee / [Welsh translation Siân Edwards]. — [Cardiff] : [The Council], [1977]. — [11]p : ill ; 30cm.
'Arddangosfa Deithiol Cyngor Celfyddydau Cymru = A Welsh Arts Council Touring Exhibition'. — Parallel Welsh and English text.
ISBN 0-905171-17-9 Sd : Unpriced
(B77-17634)

677'.473 — Beds. Mattresses. Covers. Polyurethane coated nylon fabrics. *Standards*
British Standards Institution. Specification for polyurethane coated nylon fabric for mattress covers = Spécification des tissu en nylon revêtu de polyuréthane par couvertures de matelas = Spezifikation für nylon tuch mit polyurethanbeschechtung für Matratzenüberzüge / British Standards Institution. — London : B.S.I., 1977. — [2],4, [2]p ; 30cm. — (BS5455 : 1977)
Pierced for binder.
ISBN 0-580-09621-1 Sd : £1.60
(B77-16987)

677'.4743 — Polyester textiles. *Conference proceedings*
Shirley International Seminar, *9th, Manchester?, 1977.* Polyester textiles : papers presented at the 9th Shirley International Seminar, 10-12 May, 1977. — Manchester : Shirley Institute, 1977. — [3],257p : ill ; 30cm. — (Shirley Institute. Publications ; S26 ISSN 0306-5154)
Sd : £15.00(£10.00 to members of the Shirley Institute)
(B77-33328)

677'.643'0941 — Carpets. *Great Britain. Consumers' guides*
Consumers' Association. *Advice Centre Servicing Unit.* Carpets : a consumer handbook / [Advice Centre Servicing Unit, Consumers' Association]. — London : The Association, 1976. — ix, 104p : ill(some col), col facsim ; 30cm.
Bibl.: p.75-76. — Index.
ISBN 0-85202-125-9 Pbk : £7.00
(B77-02444)

678 — ELASTOMERS AND ELASTOMER PRODUCTS
678 — Elastomeric threads. Testing. *Standards*
British Standards Institution. Methods of test for elastomeric threads = Méthodes d'essai des fils élastomeriques = Prüfverfahren für Elastomerdrähte / British Standards Institution. — London : B.S.I.
ISO title: Rubber threads.
Part 1 = Partie 1 = Teil 1 : Rubber threads = Fils élastiques = Gummidrähte. — 1976. — [2],10,[1]p : ill ; 30cm. — (BS5421 : Part 1 : 1976) (ISO 2321-1975)
Pierced for binder.
ISBN 0-580-09119-8 Sd : £3.10
(B77-10459)

678 — Elastomers & rubber
Handbook of plastics and elastomers / Charles A. Harper editor-in-chief. — New York ; London [etc.] : McGraw-Hill, [1976]. — 1024p in various pagings : ill, facsims, form ; 24cm.
Published in the United States: 1975. — Bibl.: p.480-481. — Index.
ISBN 0-07-026681-6 : £23.30
Primary classification 668.4
(B77-03121)

678.2/4 — RUBBER TECHNOLOGY

678'.2 — Rubber. *Juvenile literature*

Sowry, Jo. Rubber / [by] Jo Sowry. — Hove : Priory Press [etc.], 1977. — 90p : ill, map, plan, ports ; 20x22cm. — (World resources)
Ill. on lining paper. — Bibl.: p.87. — Index.
ISBN 0-85078-233-3 : £2.95
(B77-28742)

678'.2 — Rubber. Testing. Statistical methods. *Standards*

British Standards Institution. Guide to application of statistics to rubber testing = Guide pour l'application des statistiques aux essais des élastomères = Richtlinie für die Anwendung von Statistiken auf Gummiprüfung / British Standards Institution. — London : B.S.I., 1976. — [2],38p : ill ; 31cm. — (BS 5324 : 1976)
In binder.
ISBN 0-580-09450-2 Ls : £5.80
(B77-03128)

678'.2 — Test rubber mixes. Mixing & vulcanising. *Standards*

British Standards Institution. Specification for equipment and general procedure for mixing and vulcanizing rubber test mixes = Spécification pour l'appareillage et le mode opératoire général pour le mélangeage et la vulcanisation des mélanges d'essai à base d'élastomères = Spezifikation für Geräte und allegemeines Verfahren für die Mischung und Vulkanisierung von Elastomer-Prüfmischungen / British Standards Institution. — 2nd revision. — London : B.S.I., 1976. — [2],10,[2]p : ill ; 30cm. — (BS1674 : 1976)
Pierced for binder.
ISBN 0-580-09059-0 Sd : £3.10
(B77-09822)

678'.2'0275 — Rubber industries. Trade names. *Great Britain. Lists*

New trade names in the rubber and plastics industries / RAPRA. — Shrewsbury (Shawbury, Shrewsbury SY4 4NR) : Rubber and Plastics Research Association.
1975. — [1977]. — 180p in various pagings ; 30cm.
ISBN 0-902348-09-4 Sd : £10.00
Primary classification 668.4'02'75
(B77-13127)

678'.2'05 — Rubber. *Periodicals*

Plastics and rubber international. — London : Plastics and Rubber Institute.
Continues: Plastics and rubber.
Vol.2, no.1- ; Jan.-Feb. 1977-. — 1977-. — ill, ports ; 30cm.
Six issues a year. — 48p. in vol.2, no.1.
Sd : £3.00(£15.00 yearly)
ISSN 0309-4561
Primary classification 668.4'05
(B77-08461)

Rubber and Plastics Research Association. RAPRA news. — [Shrewsbury] ([Shawbury, Shrewsbury SY4 4NR]) : Rubber and Plastics Research Association.
Vol.1, no.1- ; May-June 1977-. — 1977-. — ill, ports ; 30cm.
Six issues a year. — 8p. in 1st issue.
Sd : Unpriced
ISSN 0140-041x
Primary classification 668.4'05
(B77-20441)

678'.22 — Rubber mixes. Mixing

Funt, John M. Mixing of rubbers / [by] John M. Funt. — Shrewsbury (Shawbury, Shrewsbury SY4 4NR) : Rubber and Plastics Research Association, 1977. — 276p in various pagings : ill ; 30cm.
Sp : Unpriced
(B77-26409)

678'.24 — Vulcanised rubber. Properties. Testing. *Standards*

British Standards Institution. Methods of testing vulcanized rubber = Méthodes d'essais des élastomères vulcanisés = Prüfverfahren für vulkanisierte Elastomere / British Standards Institution. — London : B.S.I.
ISO title: Vulcanized rubbers.
Part A10 = Partie A10 = Teil A10 : Determination of resistance to flex cracking (De Mattia-type machine) = Détermination de la résistance au craquelage par flexion (machine du type De Mattia) = Bestimmung des Widerstandes gegen Biegerissbildung (Maschine nach De Mattia). — 1st revision. — 1976. — [2],3,[1]p : ill ; 30cm. — (BS903 : Part A10 : 1976) (ISO132-1975)
Pierced for binder.
ISBN 0-580-09019-1 Sd : £1.50
(B77-09823)

Part A11 = Partie A11 = Teil A11 : Determination of resistance to cut growth (De Mattia-type machine) = Détermination de la résistance au developpement d'une craquelure (machine du type De Mattia) = Bestimmung des Widerstandes gegen Einschnitt-Weiterreiss (Maschine nach De Mattia). — 1st revision. — 1976. — [2],4,[1]p : ill ; 30cm. — (BS903 : Part A11 : 1976) (ISO133-1975)
Pierced for binder.
ISBN 0-580-09029-9 Sd : £1.50
(B77-09824)

678'.36 — Rubber high-pressure saturated steam hoses. *Standards*

British Standards Institution. Specification for rubber hose for high-pressure saturated steam = Spécification pour tuyaux en caoutchouc pour vapeur saturée à haute pression = Spezifikation für Gummischlaüche für Hochdrucksattdampf / British Standards Institution. — London : B.S.I., 1977. — [2],4,[2]p ; 30cm. — (BS5342 : 1977)
Pierced for binder.
ISBN 0-580-09342-5 Sd : £1.60
(B77-17635)

678'.36 — Smooth-bore water hoses. *Standards*

British Standards Institution. Specification for smooth-bore water suction and discharge hose with smooth or corrugated exterior = Spécification des tuyaux d'aspiration et d'évacuation d'eau à alésage lisse et à surface extérieure lisse ou ondulée = Spezifikation für glattkalibrige Wasseransavg- bwz. Ausflussschlaüche mit glatter oder wellenförmiger Aussenoberfläche / British Standards Institution. — 2nd revision. — London : B.S.I., 1977. — [2],3,[2]p ; 30cm. — (BS1102 : 1977)
Pierced for binder.
ISBN 0-580-09187-2 Sd : £1.60
(B77-17636)

678'.4 — Conductive rubber. *Conference proceedings*

Recent developments in conductive rubbers : proceedings of a RAPRA seminar held at Shawbury on Thursday 28th October 1976 / editor D.I. James. — Shrewsbury (Shawbury, Shrewsbury SY4 4NR) : Rubber and Plastics Research Association of Great Britain, 1977. — [5],50p : ill ; 30cm.
Sp : £5.00
(B77-32020)

678.7 — SYNTHETIC ELASTOMERS

678'.72 — Stereoregular elastomers

The **stereo** rubbers / edited by William M. Saltman. — New York ; London [etc.] : Wiley, 1977. — xi,897p : ill ; 24cm.
'A Wiley-Interscience publication'. — Index.
ISBN 0-471-74993-1 : £35.00
(B77-25066)

679.6 — MANUFACTURES. FIBRE AND BRISTLE PRODUCTS

679'.6 — Brushes & brooms. *Illustrations*

Klein, Louis Peace. Brushes and [brooms] / [by Lou Klein]. — London (61 North Wharf Rd, W2 1LA) : Pentagram Design, [1977]. — [40] p : of ill ; 21cm. — (Pentagram papers ; 3 ISSN 0309-2135)
Jacket title.
Pbk : £1.00
(B77-18275)

679.7 — MANUFACTURES. TOBACCO PRODUCTS

679'.7 — Tobacco & tobacco products. Measurement. Methods. *Standards*

British Standards Institution. Methods for determination of physical properties of tobacco and tobacco products = Méthodes pour la détermination des caractéristiques physiques du tabac et des produits du tabac = Verfahren zur Bestimmung der physikalischen Eigenschaften von Tabak und Tabakerzeugnissen / British Standards Institution. — London : B.S.I.
ISO title: Tobacco and tobacco products.
Part 1 = Partie 1 = Teil 1 : Loss of tobacco from the ends of cigarettes = Pertes de tabac par les extrémités des cigarettes = Tabakausfall von Zigarettenenden. — 1976. — [2],3,[1]p : 1 ill ; 30cm. — (BS5381 : Part 1 : 1976) (ISO3550-1975)
Pierced for binder.
ISBN 0-580-09540-1 Sd : £1.50
(B77-09825)

British Standards Institution. Methods for determination of physical properties of tobacco and tobacco products = Méthodes pour la détermination des caractéristiques physiques du tabac et des produits du tabac = Verfahren zur Bestimmung der physikalischen Eigenschaften von Tabak und Tabakerzeugnissen / British Standards Institution. — London : B.S.I.
ISO title: Tobacco and tobacco products.
Part 2 = Partie 2 = Teil 2 : Nominal diameter of cigarettes and filters = Diamètre nominal des cigarettes et filtres = Nenndurchmesser von Zigaretten und Filtern. — 1976. — [2],6,[1] p : ill ; 30cm. — (BS5381 : Part 2 : 1976) (ISO2971-1976)
Pierced for binder.
ISBN 0-580-09550-9 Sd : £2.40
(B77-09826)

680 — CRAFTS

680 — Crafts. *Cleveland. Directories*

Directory of artists and craftsmen in Cleveland. — Middlesbrough ([Gurney House, Gurney St., Middlesbrough, Cleveland TS1 1JL]) : Leisure and Amenities Dept., County of Cleveland.
1976. — [1976]. — [33]p : ill ; 21cm.
ISBN 0-904784-03-7 Sd : £0.25
ISSN 0308-9916
Primary classification 702'.5'4285
(B77-03136)

680 — Crafts. *England*

Gibbon, David. Crafts : today as yesterday : in colour / photography and text by David Gibbon ; produced by Ted Smart. — New Malden (80 Coombe Rd, New Malden, Surrey KT3 4QZ) : Colour Library International Ltd, 1976. — 63p : ill(chiefly col), col ports ; 29cm.
ISBN 0-904681-06-8 : £3.95
(B77-04943)

680 — Crafts. Organisations. *Great Britain. Federation of British Craft Societies*

Federation of British Craft Societies. Federation of British Craft Societies. — [London] ([80A Southampton Row, WC1B 4BA]) : [The Federation], [1976]. — 1v. : ill, 2 maps, ports ; 22cm.
Forty one sheets (81 sides) in cover.
£0.50
(B77-18891)

680 — Craftsmen. *Hampshire*

Norwood, John. Craftsmen at work / [by] John Norwood. — London : J. Baker, 1977. — 207p : ill ; 25cm.
Bibl.: p.199-200. — Index.
ISBN 0-212-97019-4 : £6.25 : CIP rev.
(B77-22726)

680 — Rural crafts. *Great Britain*

Arnold, James. The countryman's workshop / by James Arnold. — Wakefield : EP Publishing, 1977. — 164p : ill ; 20cm.
Originally published: London : Phoenix House, 1953.
ISBN 0-7158-1226-2 : £4.95 : CIP rev.
(B77-16988)

Rendell, Joan. Country crafts / [by] Joan Rendell. — London [etc.] : Routledge and Kegan Paul, 1977. — vii,63p : ill ; 23cm. — (The local search series)
Bibl.: p.62.
ISBN 0-7100-8604-0 : £2.95 : CIP rev.
(B77-14316)

680 — Rural crafts. *Manuals*

Pittaway, Andy. Country bazaar / by Andy Pittaway and Bernard Scofield. — [London] : Fontana, 1976. — 248p : ill, map ; 23cm.
Originally published: as '"Country bizarre's" country bazaar'. London : Architectural Press, 1974. — Bibl.
ISBN 0-00-634001-6 Pbk : £2.95
(B77-01650)

680 — Rural crafts. *Wales, to 1975*

John, Brian Stephen. Rural crafts of Wales / [by] Brian S. John. — Newport, Dyfed (Trefelin, Newport, Dyfed) : Greencroft Books, 1976. — [1],37p : ill, ports ; 21cm.
Bibl.: p.37.
ISBN 0-9504014-9-8 Sd : £0.65
(B77-03661)

681 — MANUFACTURES. PRECISION INSTRUMENTS

681 — Office machinery. Keyboards. Numeric keys. Layout. *Standards*

British Standards Institution. Specification for keyboard layouts for numeric applications on office machines and data processing equipment = Spécification des claviers pour des applications numériques sur les machines de bureau et les machines employées en traitement de l'information = Spezifikation für Tastaturanordnungen für numerische Anwendungen auf Büromaschinen und Datenverarbeitungsgeräten / British Standards Institution. — London : B.S.I., 1977. — [2],3,[1]p : ill ; 30cm. — (BS5448 : 1977) (ISO 3791-1976)
Pierced for binder.
ISBN 0-580-09930-x Sd : £1.60
Also classified at 681'.14
(B77-11962)

681.1 — MANUFACTURES. ANALOGUE AND DIGITAL INSTRUMENTS

681'.11 — Clocks & watches. Making. *Manuals. Early works*

Glasgow, David. Watch and clockmaking / by David Glasgow. — Wakefield : EP Publishing, 1977. — xii,341p : ill, music ; 20cm.
Facsimile reprint of: 1st ed. London : Cassell, 1885. — Index.
ISBN 0-7158-1215-7 : £4.95
(B77-17637)

681'.11'09 — Clocks & watches, to 1976

Jagger, Cedric. The world's great clocks & watches / [by] Cedric Jagger. — London [etc.] : Hamlyn, 1977. — 256p : ill(some col), facsims, ports ; 31cm.
Col. ill. on lining papers. — Bibl.: p.254. — Index.
ISBN 0-600-34027-9 : £4.95
(B77-32021)

681'.11'0922 — Clocks & watches. Manufacture. Pinchbeck family. *London, 1670-1783*

Shenton, Rita Kathleen. Christopher Pinchbeck and his family / by Rita Shenton. — Ashford, Kent (P.O. Box 22, Ashford, Kent [TN23 1DN]) : Brant Wright Associates Ltd, 1976. — 3-71p : ill, facsims, geneal table, ports ; 22cm.
Bibl.: p.71.
ISBN 0-903512-06-8 : £6.75
(B77-07977)

681'.11'0924 — Horology. Harrison, John, b.1693

Laycock, W S. The lost science of John 'Longitude' Harrison / by W.S. Laycock. — Ashford, Kent (P.O. Box 22, Ashford, Kent) : Brant Wright Associates Ltd, 1976. — 159p : ill, facsim, port ; 26cm.
Bibl.: p.153. — Index.
ISBN 0-903512-07-6 : £18.75
(B77-05531)

681'.112 — 30 hour long case clocks. Automatic winding mechanisms. Making. *Manuals*

Wilding, John, *b.1924.* Automatic winding for a 30 hour longcase clock / by John Wilding. — Ashford, Kent (PO Box 22, Ashford, Kent) : Brant Wright Associates Ltd, 1975. — [2],12p : ill ; 26cm.
Fold. sheet in pocket.
ISBN 0-903512-03-3 : £4.75
(B77-04312)

681'.113 — 30 hour weight driven alarm clocks. Making. *Manuals*

Wilding, John, *b.1924.* A 30-hour weight driven alarm clock / by John Wilding. — Ashford, Kent (P.O. Box 22, Ashford, Kent) : Brant Wright Associates Ltd, [1976]. — [4],71p : ill ; 26cm.
Jacket title: How to make a replica of an 18th century 30 hour weight driven alarm clock.
ISBN 0-903512-04-1 : £8.25
(B77-04313)

681'.113 — Clocks. Maintenance & repair. *Manuals*

Smith, Eric, *b.1940.* Clocks : their working and maintenance / [by] Eric Smith. — Newton Abbot [etc.] : David and Charles, 1977. — 224p : ill ; 23cm.
Bibl.: p.216-218. — Index.
ISBN 0-7153-7424-9 : £4.95
(B77-28743)

681'.113 — Congreve clocks. Making. *Manuals*

Wilding, John, *b.1924.* How to make a Congreve rolling ball clock / by John Wilding. — Ashford, Kent (P.O. Box 22, Ashford, Kent) : Brant Wright Associates Ltd, 1976. — [4],iii, 76p : ill, plans ; 25cm.
Spine title: A Congreve clock.
ISBN 0-903512-05-x : £9.75
(B77-05532)

681'.113 — Long case clocks, to 1825

Bruton, Eric. The longcase clock / [by] Eric Bruton. — 2nd ed. — London [etc.] : Hart-Davis MacGibbon, 1976. — 246p : ill, facsims, ports ; 23cm.
Previous ed.: London : Arco, 1964. — Bibl.: p.238-239. — Index.
ISBN 0-246-10881-9 : £12.00
(B77-10460)

681'.113'0922 — Clockmakers. *Pennsylvania. Lancaster County, 1750-1850*

Wood, Stacy B C. Clockmakers of Lancaster County and their clocks, 1750-1850 / [by] Stacy B.C. Wood, Jr, Stephen E. Kramer, III ; with a study of Lancaster County clock cases by John J. Snyder, Jr. — New York ; London [etc.] : Van Nostrand Reinhold, 1977. — 224p : ill, facsims, maps, ports ; 29cm.
Index.
ISBN 0-442-29531-6 : £12.55
(B77-25067)

681'.113'0942714 — Museums. *Cheshire. Chester. Grosvenor Museum. Exhibits: Chester clocks. Catalogues*

Moore, Nicholas. Chester clocks and clockmakers / by Nicholas Moore. — Chester ([27 Grosvenor St., Chester CH11 2DD]) : Grosvenor Museum, [1977]. — [1],19[i.e. 21]p : ill ; 29cm.
Catalogue of an exhibition at the Grosvenor Museum. — Bibl.: p.16.
Sd : £0.40
(B77-16989)

681'.114'0275 — Watchmaking industries. Trade marks & trade names. *Great Britain. Lists*

'Watchmaker, jeweller & silversmith' directory of trade names & punch marks. — London : IPC Consumer Industries Press.
1977 : 41st ed. — [1977]. — 104p : ill ; 29cm.
Pbk : £3.00
(B77-17638)

681'.116 — Electric clocks. Making. *Manuals. Early works*

Electric clocks and chimes : a practical handbook ... / edited by Percival Marshall. — Kings Langley : Argus Books, 1976. — 159p : ill ; 19cm.
Facsimile reprint of: 1st ed. London : P. Marshall, 192-.
ISBN 0-85242-474-4 Pbk : £2.50
(B77-13129)

Way, Robert Barnard. How to make an electric clock / [by] R. Barnard Way. — Kings Langley : Model and Allied Publications, 1976. — vii,53p : ill, plans ; 19cm.
Originally published: London : P. Marshall, 1947.
ISBN 0-85242-473-6 Pbk : £1.50
(B77-13130)

681'.116'07402134 — Museums. *London. Kensington and Chelsea (London Borough). Science Museum. Exhibits: Electric clocks, to 1976. Catalogues*

Aked, Charles Kenneth. Electrifying time : [catalogue of] an exhibition at the Science Museum to commemorate the centenary of the death of Alexander Bain, 2nd January, 1877 : open 15th December 1976 to 11th April 1977 / compiled by Charles K. Aked. — Ticehurst (New House, High St., Ticehurst, Wadhurst, Sussex TN5 7AL) : Antiquarian Horological Society, 1976. — 106p : ill, plan, ports ; 25cm. — (Antiquarian Horological Society. Monographs ; no.10)
Bibl.
ISBN 0-901180-14-9 Pbk : Unpriced
(B77-25068)

681'.116'09034 — Electric clocks, 1800-1850. *Essays*

Aked, Charles Kenneth. A conspectus of electrical timekeeping / by Charles K. Aked. — [Wadhurst] ([New House, High St., Ticehurst, Wadhurst, Sussex]) : Antiquarian Horological Society, [1976]. — vii,80p : ill, facsims, ports ; 25cm. — (Antiquarian Horological Society. Monographs ; no.12)
Bibl.
Sd : £2.25
(B77-32739)

681'.14 — Data processing equipment. Keyboards. Numeric keys. Layout. *Standards*

British Standards Institution. Specification for keyboard layouts for numeric applications on office machines and data processing equipment = Spécification des claviers pour des applications numériques sur les machines de bureau et les machines employées en traitement de l'information = Spezifikation für Tastaturanordnungen für numerische Anwendungen auf Büromaschinen und Datenverarbeitungsgeräten / British Standards Institution. — London : B.S.I., 1977. — [2],3,[1]p : ill ; 30cm. — (BS5448 : 1977) (ISO 3791-1976)
Pierced for binder.
ISBN 0-580-09930-x Sd : £1.60
Primary classification 681
(B77-11962)

681.6/7 — MANUFACTURES. PRINTING, DUPLICATING, AND OTHER SPECIAL-PURPOSE MACHINERY

681'.6 — Microwriting machines: Peters microwriting machine. Performance

Stevens, Guy William Willis. The performance and significance of the Peters microwriting machine / by G.W.W. Stevens. — Guildford (8 High St., Guildford, Surrey GV2 5AJ) : Microfilm Association of Great Britain, 1976. — 15p : ill, facsim ; 21cm.
'Reprinted from "Microdoc" Vol.15, No.3, 1976' - title page verso.
ISBN 0-9500417-7-7 Sd : £1.30(£1.00 to members of the Association)
(B77-01651)

681'.62 — Offset printing equipment. *Great Britain. Buyers' guides*

Offset data index. — Tonbridge : Printing Trades Journal : [Distributed by] Benn Bros.
1977. — 1977. — 80p : ill ; 30cm.
ISBN 0-510-49409-9 Pbk : £4.00
ISSN 0308-4485
(B77-06202)

681'.7 — Electric industrial cleaning equipment. Safety measures. *Standards*

British Standards Institution. Specification for safety of electrical motor-operated industrial cleaning appliances = Spécification de la sécurité des appareils de nettoyage industriels à moteur électrique = Spezifikation für die Sicherheit von industriellen Reinigungsgeräten mit elektrischem Motor / British Standards Institution. — London : B.S.I.
Part 2 = Partie 2 = Teil 2 : Particular requirements = Exigences particulières = Besondere Anforderungen. Section 2.2 = Section 2.2 = Abschnitt 2.2 : Vacuum cleaners wet and/or dry = Aspirateurs fonctionnant à sec et/ou à l'eau = Staubsauger mit Trocken- oder Nassbetrieb. — 1976. — [2],6,[2]p : 1 ill ; 30cm. — (BS5415 : Part 2 : Section 2.2 : 1976)

Pierced for binder.
ISBN 0-580-09468-5 Sd : £2.70
(B77-16503)

Part 2 = Partie 2 = Teil 2 : Particular requirements = Exigences particulières = Besondere Anforderungen. Section 2.1 = Section 2.1 = Abschnitt 2.1 : Floor polishing, scrubbing and/or carpet cleaning machines = Machines à lustrer et à brosser les sols et/ou à nettoyer les tapis = Bohnermaschinen, Schevermaschinen und/oder Teppichreinigungsmaschinen. — 1976. — [2],4,[2]p : 1 ill ; 30cm. — (BS5415 : Part 2 : Section 2.1 : 1976)
Pierced for binder.
ISBN 0-580-09328-x Sd : £1.60
(B77-16501)

Part 1 = Partie 1 = Teil 1 : General requirements = Exigences générales = Allgemeine Anforderungen. — 1976. — [2],36,[2]p : ill ; 30cm. — (BS5415 : Part 1 : 1976)
Pierced for binder.
ISBN 0-580-09318-2 Sd : £6.60
(B77-16502)

681'.75 — Meteorological thermometers. *Standards*

British Standards Institution. Specification for meteorological thermometers = Thermomètres météorologiques = Meteorologische Thermometer / British Standards Institution. — 3rd revision. — London : B.S.I., 1976. — [2],8,[2]p : ill ; 30cm. — (BS692 : 1976)
Pierced for binder.
ISBN 0-580-09350-6 Sd : £2.70
(B77-11963)

681'.753 — English barometers, 1680-1860
Goodison, Nicholas. English barometers, 1680-1860 : a history of domestic barometers and their makers and retailers / [by] Nicholas Goodison. — Revised and enlarged ed. — Woodbridge : Antique Collectors' Club, 1977. — 3-388p,plate : ill(some col), facsims ; 28cm. Ill. on lining papers. — Previous ed.: London : Cassell, 1969. — Bibl.: p.375-377. — Index.
ISBN 0-902028-52-9 : £15.00
(B77-33329)

681'.753 — English barometers, ca 1690-ca 1920
Banfield, Edwin. Antique barometers : an illustrated survey / [by] Edwin Banfield. — Bristol (11 Folleigh Drive, Long Ashton, Bristol [BS18 9JD]) : Wayland Publications, [1977]. — ix,119p : ill ; 23cm.
Bibl.: p.117. — Index.
ISBN 0-9505272-0-3 Sd : £2.00
(B77-09827)

681'.753 — Proton synchrotrons. *France. Air (Department). CERN 400 Ge V Super Proton Synchrotron. Design & construction*
Goldsmith, Maurice. Europe's giant accelerator : the story of the CERN 400 Ge V Proton Synchrotron / [by] Maurice Goldsmith and Edwin Shaw. — London : Taylor and Francis, 1977. — x,261p,xvi p of plates : ill(some col), facsim, maps, ports ; 27cm.
Index.
ISBN 0-85066-121-8 : £13.00
(B77-25069)

681'.753 — Secondary reference thermometers. *Standards*
British Standards Institution. Specification for secondary reference thermometers = Thermomètres - étalons secondaires = Sekundärbezugsthermometer / British Standards Institution. — 1st revision. — London : B.S.I., 1976. — [2],7,[1]p : ill ; 30cm. — (BS1900 : 1976)
Pierced for binder.
ISBN 0-580-09380-8 Sd : £2.70
(B77-11303)

681'.754 — Graduated pipettes. *Standards*
British Standards Institution. Specification for graduated pipettes (including blowout pipettes) = Spécification pour pipettes graduées (pipettes à soufflet inclues) = Spezifikation für kalibrierte Pipetten (einschliesslich Ausblaspipetten / British Standards Institution. — 3rd revision. — London : B.S.I., 1976. — [2],9,[1]p : ill ; 30cm. — (BS700 : 1976)
Pierced for binder.
ISBN 0-580-09098-1 Sd : £2.70
(B77-11304)

681'.76 — Medical equipment: Gas cylinders. *Standards*
British Standards Institution. Specification for medical gas cylinders, valves and yoke connections = Spécification des bouteilles à gaz, robinets et raccords à chape pour usage médical = Spezifikation für Gaszylinder, Ventile und Jochanschlüsse für Medizinische Zwecke / British Standards Institution. — 2nd revision. — London : B.S.I., 1976. — [2],16,[2] p : ill(some col) ; 30cm. — (BS1319 : 1976)
Pierced for binder.
ISBN 0-580-09197-x Sd : £4.00
(B77-09828)

681'.763 — Agricultural equipment. *Buyers' guides. For developing countries*
Boyd, John, *b.1946.* Tools for agriculture : a buyer's guide to low cost agricultural implements / compiled by John Boyd ; [for the Intermediate Technology Development Group]. — 2nd ed. — London (9 King St., WC2E 8HN) : Intermediate Technology Publications Ltd, 1976. — 173p : ill ; 30cm.
Previous ed.: 1973.
ISBN 0-903031-22-1 Pbk : £4.00
(B77-09135)

681'.766 — Pressure vessels. *Standards*
British Standards Institution. Specification for pressure containers for paint and other substances = Spécification pour récipients sous pression pour peintures et autres matières = Spezifikation für Druckbehälter für Anstrichfarben und andere Stoffe / British Standards Institution. — 2nd revision. — London : B.S.I., 1977. — [2],8,[2]p : ill ; 30cm. — (BS1101 : 1977)
Pierced for binder.
ISBN 0-580-09399-9 Sd : £2.70
(B77-15378)

Chuse, Robert. Pressure vessels : the ASME Code simplified / [by] Robert Chuse. — 5th ed. — New York ; London [etc.] : McGraw-Hill, 1977. — vi,233p : ill, forms, map ; 24cm.
Previous ed.: published as 'Unfired pressure vessels'. New York : F.W. Dodge Corp., 1960. — Bibl.: p.228. — Index.
ISBN 0-07-010872-2 : £13.90
(B77-25757)

681'.766 — Pressure vessels. Components. *Standards*
British Standards Institution. Specification for pressure vessel details (dimensions) = Spécification des détails des récipients à pression (dimensions) = Spezifikation für die Einzelheiten von Druckbehältern (Masse) / British Standards Institution. — London : B.S.I.
Part 4 = Partie 4 = Teil 4 : Standardized pressure vessels = Récipients à pression normalisés = Genormte Druckbehälter. — 1977. — [2],8,[2]p : ill ; 30cm. — (BS5276 : Part 4 : 1977)
Pierced for binder.
ISBN 0-580-09795-1 Sd : £2.70
(B77-33922)

681'.766 — Pressure vessels. Components. Creep. *Conference proceedings*
Failure of components operating in the creep range : conference sponsored [i.e. organized] by the Pressure Vessels Section of the Applied Mechanics Group of the Institution of Mechanical Engineers, London, 27 April 1976. — London [etc.] : Mechanical Engineering Publications for the Institution, 1977. — [5], 58p : ill ; 30cm. — (Institution of Mechanical Engineers. Conference publications ; 1976-4)
ISBN 0-85298-359-x Pbk : £10.00
(B77-32740)

681'.766 — Pressure vessels. Components. Inspection. *Conference proceedings*
Third conference on periodic inspection of pressurized components - sponsored [i.e. organised] by the Pressure Vessels Section of the Applied Mechanics Group of the Institution of Mechanical Engineers [held] London, 20-22 September 1976. — London [etc.] : Mechanical Engineering Publications for the Institution, 1977. — [5],189p : ill ; 31cm. — (Institution of Mechanical Engineers. Conference publications ; 1976-10)
Spine title: Periodic inspection of pressurized components.
ISBN 0-85298-349-2 : £19.00
(B77-32741)

681'.766 — Pressure vessels. Stress analysis
Developments in stress analysis for pressurised components / edited by R.W. Nichols. — London : Applied Science Publishers, 1977. — x,210p : ill ; 23cm. — (Developments series)
Index.
ISBN 0-85334-724-7 : £14.00
(B77-15962)

681'.7677 — Textile machinery. Yarn winding equipment. Cones. Dimensions. *Standards*
British Standards Institution. British Standard specification for basic dimensions of cones and tubes for winding textile yarns / British Standards Institution. — London : B.S.I.
Part 1 : Cones for yarn winding (cross wound), half angle of the cone 3° 30'. — 3rd revision. — 1976. — Folder (4p) : ill ; 30cm. — (BS 2547 : Part 1 : 1976) (ISO 112-1975)
Pierced for binder. — ISO title: Textile machinery and accessories - Cones for yarn winding (cross wound) - Half angle of the cone 3° 30'.
ISBN 0-580-09117-1 : £1.15
(B77-03129)

682 — BLACKSMITHING
682'.0942 — Blacksmithing. *England, to 1976*
Bailey, Jocelyn. The village blacksmith / [by] Jocelyn Bailey. — Aylesbury : Shire Publications, 1977. — 33p : ill, coat of arms, ports ; 21cm. — (Shire album ; 24)
Bibl.: p.33.
ISBN 0-85263-380-7 Sd : £0.50
(B77-32742)

682'.1'0941 — Farriery. *Great Britain*
Hickman, John. Farriery : a complete illustrated guide / [by] John Hickman ; [line drawings by John Christiansen]. — London [etc.] : J.A. Allen, 1977. — 240p : ill ; 26cm.
Bibl.: p.233-234. — Index.
ISBN 0-85131-228-4 : £8.50 : CIP rev.
(B77-11964)

683.3 — LOCKS
683'.32'075 — Locks & keys. Collecting. *Periodicals*
The **lock** collectors newsletter. — Bournemouth (38 Calvin Rd, Winton, Bournemouth BH9 1LN) : 'Lock collectors newsletter'.
Vol.1, no.1- ; Apr. 1975-. — [1975]-. — ill ; 30cm.
Six issues a year. — 6p. in 1st issue. — Bibl.
Sd : £2.00
ISSN 0309-4480
(B77-13747)

683.4 — FIREARMS
683'.4'009 — Firearms, to 1976
Wilkinson, Frederick. The world's great guns / [by] Frederick Wilkinson. — London [etc.] : Hamlyn, 1977. — 256p : ill(chiefly col), facsims, ports(some col) ; 30cm.
Col. ill. on lining papers. — Bibl.: p.254. — Index.
ISBN 0-600-39364-x : £4.95
(B77-28744)

683'.4'00904 — Firearms, 1900-1974
Cadiou, Yves. Modern firearms / [by] Yves Cadiou, Alphonse Richard ; translated from the French by Simon Pleasance. — London [etc.] : Routledge and Kegan Paul, 1977. — 224p : ill(some col), port ; 30cm.
Translation of: 'Les armes à feu modernes'. Paris : Denoël, 1975. — Bibl.: p.219. — Index.
ISBN 0-7100-8424-2 : £12.00
(B77-06788)

683'.4'00904 — Firearms, 1939-1973
Smith, Walter Harold Bingham-Black. Small arms of the world : a basic manual of small-arms : the classic / by W.H.B. Smith. — 10 ed. / completely revised by Joseph E. Smith. — [London] ([2 Hampstead High St., NW3 1PR]) : A and W Visual Library, [1976]. — 768p : ill, port ; 28cm.
This ed. originally published: Harrisburg, Pa : Stackpole ; London : Arms and Armour Press, 1973. — Index.
ISBN 0-89104-021-8 Pbk : £6.95
(B77-06789)

683'.42 — Spring operated air rifles. Internal ballistics
Cardew, G V. The air gun from trigger to muzzle / by G.V. Cardew, G.M. Cardew and E.R. Elsom. — [Great Britain] : [The authors], 1976. — 2-96p : ill ; 21cm.
Index.
Pbk : £2.95
ISBN 0-9505108-0-7
(B77-00310)

683'.43 — Luger pistols, 1875-1976
Walter, John. Luger : an illustrated history of the handguns of Hugo Borchardt and Georg Luger, 1875 to the present day / [by] John Walter. — London : Arms and Armour Press [etc.], 1977. — 256p : ill, facsims, ports ; 30cm.
Bibl.: p.250-254. — Index.
ISBN 0-85368-131-7 : £12.95
(B77-30440)

683'.43 — Pistols
Jane's pocket book of pistols and sub-machine guns / edited by Denis Archer. — London : Macdonald and Jane's, 1976. — 237p : ill ; 13x19cm. — ([Jane's pocket book ; 16])
Index.
ISBN 0-354-01012-3 : £3.75
ISBN 0-354-01013-1 Pbk : £2.75
Also classified at 623.4'424
(B77-08463)

683.8 — MANUFACTURES. HOUSEHOLD EQUIPMENT
683'.8 — English household equipment, 1682-ca 1900
Fearn, Jacqueline. Domestic bygones / [by] Jacqueline Fearn. — Aylesbury : Shire Publications, 1977. — 33p : ill ; 21cm. — (Shire album ; 20)
Bibl.: p.33.
ISBN 0-85263-349-1 Sd : £0.50
(B77-32022)

683'.8 — English household kitchen equipment, to ca 1930. *Collectors' guides*
Curtis, Tony, *b.1939.* Kitchen equipment / compiled by Tony Curtis. — Galashiels : Lyle Publications, 1977. — 3-126p : chiefly ill ; 16cm. — (Antiques and their values)
Index.
ISBN 0-902921-41-x : £1.50
(B77-33923)

683'.8'09034 — Household appliances. Inventions, 1860-1930
De Haan, David. Antique household gadgets and appliances, c.1860 to 1930 / [by] David de Haan. — Poole : Blandford Press, 1977. — ix, 165p : ill(chiefly col) ; 20cm.
Index.
ISBN 0-7137-0791-7 : £3.25
(B77-13748)

683'.82 — Aluminium foil catering containers. *Standards*
British Standards Institution. Specification for aluminium foil catering containers = Spécification des récipients d'approvisionnement en lame d'aluminium = Spezifikation für Lebensmittelbehälter aus Alufolie / British Standards Institution. — London : B.S.I., 1977. — [2],4,[2]p : ill ; 30cm. — (BS5439 : 1977)
Pierced for binder.
ISBN 0-580-09670-x Sd : £1.60
(B77-12566)

683'.82 — Cast aluminium frying pans & cast aluminium saucepans. *Standards*
British Standards Institution. Specification for cast aluminium saucepans and frying pans = Specification des casseroles et des poêles en aluminium moulé = Spezifikation für Kochtöpfe und Bratpfannen aus Gussaluminium / British Standards Institution. — 1st revision. — London : B.S.I., 1976. — [2],4,[2]p : ill ; 30cm. — (BS1859 : 1976)
Pierced for binder.
ISBN 0-580-09158-9 Sd : £1.50
(B77-09136)

683'.82 — Cooking utensils
The **cooks'** catalogue : a critical selection of the best, the necessary and the special in kitchen equipment and utensils : over 4000 items including 200 extraordinary recipes plus cooking folklore and 1700 illustrations produced with the assistance of the world's leading food authorities / introduction by James Beard ; edited by James Beard ... [et al.]. — New York [etc.] ; London : Harper and Row, [1976]. — x,566p : ill, facsims, port ; 29cm.
Published in the United States: 1975. — Bibl.: p.530-536. — Index.
ISBN 0-06-011563-7 : £11.95
Also classified at 641.5
(B77-07491)

683'.83 — Household electric equipment. Maintenance & repair. *Manuals*
Heiserman, David L. Handbook of major appliance troubleshooting and repair / [by] David L. Heiserman. — Englewood Cliffs ; London [etc.] : Prentice-Hall, 1977. — xiii, 333p : ill ; 24cm.
With answers. — Index.
ISBN 0-13-380295-7 : £12.80
(B77-11305)

Small appliance servicing guide : motor-driven and resistance-heated appliances / edited by Robert Scharff. — New York ; London [etc.] : McGraw-Hill, 1976. — ix,259p : ill ; 29cm.
Index.
ISBN 0-07-055142-1 : £8.50
(B77-01652)

683'.83 — Household electric equipment. Safety. *Standards*
British Standards Institution. Specification for safety of household electrical appliances = Spécification relative à la sécurité des appareils électriques domestiques = Spezifikation bezüglich der Sicherheit von elektrischen Haushaltsgeräten / British Standards Institution. — London : B.S.I.
Part 2 = Partie 2 = Teil 2 : Particular requirements = Exigences spécifiques = Spezifische Anforderungen. Section 2.34 = Section 2.34 = Abschnitt 2.34 : Room air conditioners = Appareils pour la climatisation des locaux = Zimmerklimaanlager. — 1976. — [2],8,[2]p : ill ; 30cm. — (BS3456 : Part 2 : Section 2.34 : 1976)
Pierced for binder.
ISBN 0-580-09334-4 Sd : £2.40
(B77-00851)

British Standards Institution. Specification for safety of household electrical appliances = Spécification relative à la sécurité des appareils électrodomestiques = Spezifikation bezüglich der Sichenheit von elektrischen Haushaltsgeräten / British Standards Institution. — London : B.S.I.
Part 2 = Partie 2 = Teil 2. Particular requirements = Exigences spécifiques = Besondere Anforderungen. Section 2.42 = Section 2.42 = Abschnitt 2.42 : Battery-operated lawnmowers = Tondeuses à batteries = Rasenmäher mit Batteriebetrieb. — 1977. — [2],6,[2]p : ill ; 30cm. — (BS3456 : Part 2 : Section 2.42 : 1977)
Pierced for binder.
ISBN 0-580-08829-4 Sd : £2.70
(B77-13131)

British Standards Institution. Specification for safety of household electrical appliances = Spécification relative à la sécurité des appareils électrodomestiques = Spezifikation bezüglich der Sicherheit von elektrischen Haushaltsgeräten / British Standards Institution. — London : B.S.I.
Part 2 = Partie 2 = Teil 2 : Particular requirements = Exigences spécifiques = Besondere Anforderungen. Section 2.41 = Section 2.41 = Abschnitt 2.41 : Room heating and similar appliances for use in children's nurseries and similar situations = Appareils de chauffage des locaux et appareils similaires pour usage dans les crèches, les jardins d'enfants, les chambres des enfants et locaux similaires = Raumbeheizungs- und ähnliche Geräte zur Verwendung in Kinderhorten, -gärten, -zimmern und ähnlichen Orten. — 1977. — [2],7,[1]p ; 30cm. — (BS3456 : Part 2 : Section 2.41 : 1977)
Pierced for binder.
ISBN 0-580-09770-6 Sd : £2.70
(B77-10461)

683'.83 — Vacuum cleaners. Armatures. Rewinding. *Amateurs' manuals*
Banner, E C. Rewinding armatures and repairing vac cleaners and power tools / by E.C. Banner. — Manchester ([c/o Magnum Associates, Brinksway Trading Estate, Brinksway, Stockport, Cheshire]) : Magnum Publications, [1976]. — [3],129p : ill ; 26cm.
ISBN 0-900144-03-3 Sp : £4.00
Primary classification 621.9'52
(B77-15333)

683'.88 — Gas-fired catering equipment. *Standards*
British Standards Institution. Specification for gas heated catering appliances = Spécification pour les appareils de grande cuisine utilisant les combustibles gazeux = Spezifikation für gasbeheizte Grossküchengeräte / British Standards Institution. — London : B.S.I.
Part 4 = Partie 4 = Teil 4 : Fryers = Friteuses = Friteusen. — 1976. — [2],13,[2]p : ill ; 30cm. — (BS5314 : Part 4 : 1976)
Pierced for binder.
ISBN 0-580-09457-x Sd : £4.00
(B77-11965)

684 — WOODWORKING, METALWORKING, FURNITURE MAKING, FURNISHINGS

684'.0021'2 — Furnishings. *Technical data. Serials*
Fabrics, wallcoverings & furniture. — Edenbridge (25 High St., Edenbridge, Kent) : A4 Publications Ltd. — (Architects' and specifiers' guide series)
1975-6. — 1975. — 184p : ill ; 30cm.
ISBN 0-510-07007-8 Pbk : £3.50
Also classified at 690'.1'2
(B77-25070)

684'.00941 — Furnishings. *Great Britain. Buyers' guides*
Design Centre, *London.* The Design Centre furnishing buyers' guide. — London : [Design Council].
1977. — [1977]. — 20,[2]p : chiefly col ill ; 30cm.
Sd : Unpriced
ISSN 0140-0045
(B77-23576)

684'.08 — Wood turning. *Amateurs' manuals*
Nish, Dale L. Creative woodturning / [by] Dale L. Nish. — London (67 Worship St., EC2A 2EL) : Stobart and Son Ltd, 1976. — vii,248p : ill(some col), ports ; 29cm.
Originally published: Provo, Utah : Brigham Young University Press, 1975. — Index.
ISBN 0-85442-006-1 : £7.50
(B77-13132)

684'.08 — Woodworking
Groneman, Chris Harold. General woodworking / [by] Chris H. Groneman. — 5th ed. — New York ; London [etc.] : McGraw-Hill, 1976. — xii,404p,[16]p of plates : ill(chiefly col), map ; 25cm. — (McGraw-Hill publications in industrial education)
Form on lining paper. — Previous ed.: 1971. — Index.
ISBN 0-07-024985-7 : £8.10
(B77-04314)

684'.08 — Woodworking. *Amateurs' manuals*
Basic carpentry. — London [etc.] : Marshall Cavendish, 1977. — 64p : ill(chiefly col) ; 30cm.
'This material was first published by Marshall Cavendish Ltd. in the publication 'Encyclopedia of crafts"' - title page verso.
ISBN 0-85685-244-9 : £1.99
(B77-30441)

Martenson, Alf. Woodwork in easy steps / [by] Alf Martenson ; [photographs by Peter Kibbles]. — London : Studio Vista, 1976. — 64p : col ill ; 29cm.
Bibl.: p.64.
ISBN 0-289-70740-4 : £1.95
(B77-07492)

684'.08 — Woodworking. *Amateurs' manuals. Juvenile literature*
Simmons, John, *b.1925.* Carpentry is easy : when you know how / [author John Simmons]. — London : Marshall Cavendish, 1974. — 48p : ill(chiefly col) ; 32cm. — (A 'Golden hands' book)
ISBN 0-85685-075-6 : £0.99
(B77-19509)

684'.08 — Woodworking. *For Irish students. Secondary school texts*
Lingane, J. Basic woodwork / [by] J. Lingane. — Tallaght : Folens, [1977]. — 93p : ill, 2 maps ; 25cm. — (Intermediate and Group Certificate)
Index.
Pbk : Unpriced
(B77-32743)

684'.08 — Woodworking. *Manuals*
Groneman, Chris Harold. Technical woodworking / [by] Chris H. Groneman, Everett R. Glazener. — 2nd ed. — New York ; London [etc.] : McGraw-Hill, 1976. — xiv, 434p,[8]p of plates : ill(some col), forms, map ; 25cm.
Form on lining paper. — Previous ed.: New York : McGraw-Hill, 1966. — Index.
ISBN 0-07-024964-4 : £10.70
(B77-04945)

684'.08 — Woodworking. *Secondary school texts*
Brazier, Geoffrey William. Woodwork / [by] G.W. Brazier, N.A. Harris. — 3rd ed., metric. — St Albans : Hart-Davis Educational, 1976. — xi,365p : ill ; 20cm.
This ed. originally published: London : Chatto and Windus, 1971. — Index.
ISBN 0-247-12762-0 Pbk : £1.25(non-net)
ISBN 0-7010-0555-6 (Chatto and Windus Educational) : £1.95
(B77-05533)

Hay, John, *b.1910 (Apr.).* Woodwork / [by] J. Hay. — Amended ed. — London : Blackie, 1976. — [8],213p : ill ; 26cm.
Previous ed.: i.e. Metric ed., published as 'Woodwork for schools'. Aylesbury : Intertext, 1973.
ISBN 0-216-90249-5 : £3.45
ISBN 0-216-90187-1 Pbk : £2.45 (non-net)
(B77-00311)

684'.08'06241 — Woodworking. Organisations. *Great Britain. Institute of Carpenters. Periodicals*
Institute of Carpenters. The journal of the Institute of Carpenters. — Richmond, Surrey (24 Ormond Rd, Richmond, Surrey) : The Institute.
Continues: Incorporated British Institute of Certified Carpenters. Journal.
Issue no.243- ; Jan. 1977-. — [1977]-. — ill, ports ; 24cm.
Quarterly. — [2],20p. in 1st issue.
Sd : £0.50
ISSN 0140-2501
(B77-32023)

684'.08'076 — Woodworking. *Exercises, worked examples. For Irish students. Secondary school texts. Irish-English parallel texts*
Ó Luasaigh, Donnchadh. Cleachtaí adhmadóireachta = Woodwork exercises / [le] Donnchadh Ó Luasaigh. — Baile Átha Cliath [i.e. Dublin] : Helicon, [1976]. — [4],61p : chiefly ill ; 21x30cm.
Parallel Irish text and English translation.
ISBN 0-904916-58-8 Sd : £1.10
(B77-03662)

684'.09 — Metalworking. *Secondary school texts*
Reen, Michael. Intermediate metalwork / [by] Michael Reen. — Dublin : Helicon, 1977. — [3],108p : ill ; 21cm. — (Study assessment series)
Fill-in book.
Sd : £1.65
(B77-27240)

Strefford, John. Metalwork technology for schools and colleges / [by] John Strefford, Guy McMurdo ; illustrated by David Leek. — Huddersfield : Schofield and Sims, 1976. — 93p : ill(some col) ; 22cm.
Index.
ISBN 0-7217-4007-3 Pbk : £0.95
(B77-09829)

684'.09'071242 — Secondary schools. Curriculum subjects: Metalwork. Design. *England. For teaching*
Davies, M G. Mode 3 Design in metalwork / [by] M.G. Davies, J.V. Robbins. — London : Mills and Boon, 1974. — 85p : ill ; 21x30cm.
ISBN 0-263-05700-3 Sp : £0.95
(B77-11966)

684'.09'076 — Metalworking. *Questions & answers. Secondary school texts*
Objective and completion tests in C.S.E. metalwork theory / general editor Ernest Clarke. — London : J. Murray, 1977. — [6], 85p : ill ; 22cm.
With answers.
ISBN 0-7195-3369-4 Sd : £0.95
(B77-27241)

684.1 — Furniture. Components: Threaded inserts. *Technical data*
Langston, Christopher. Furniture hardware, group 'B' : threaded inserts / by C. Langston. — Stevenage (Maxwell Rd, Stevenage, Herts. SG1 2EW) : Furniture Industry Research Association, 1976. — [4],66p : ill ; 21cm. — (Furniture Industry Research Association. Manuals)
Sp : £5.00(£2.00 to members)
(B77-12567)

684.1 — Hospital equipment: Angular trolleys, dressings trolleys & instrument trolleys. *Standards*
British Standards Institution. Specification for hospital trolleys for instruments, dressings and for anaesthetists' use including angular trolleys = Spécification des chariots d'hôpital pour les instruments, les pansements et pour l'usage des anesthésistes, y compris les chariots angulaires = Spezifikation für Krankenhauswagen für Instrumente, Verbände sowie auch zur Verwendung durch Anästhesiste einschliesslich eckiger Wagen / British Standards Institution. — 1st revision. — London : B.S.I., 1977. — [2] ,4,[2]p : ill ; 30cm. — (BS4068 : 1977)
Pierced for binder.
ISBN 0-580-09610-6 Sd : £1.60
(B77-11967)

684.1'04 — Cabinet-making. *Manuals*
Hayward, Charles Harold. Cabinet making for beginners / [by] Charles H. Hayward. — Revised and enlarged [ed.]. — London : Evans Bros, 1975. — vi,209p : ill ; 23cm.
This ed. originally published: 1960. — Index.
ISBN 0-237-44339-2 : £3.95
(B77-32744)

684.1'04'0924 — Cabinet-making. *Personal observations*
Krenov, James. A cabinetmaker's notebook / [by] James Krenov ; [photographs by Bengt Carlèn]. — London : Studio Vista, 1976. — 132p : ill(some col) ; 29cm.
Also published: New York : Van Nostrand Reinhold, 1976. — Index.
ISBN 0-289-70754-4 : £6.50
(B77-09830)

684.1'042 — Wooden furniture for young persons. Making. *Manuals*
Brooks, Brian. Furniture for children / [by] Brian Brooks. — London : Evans Bros, 1977. — 103p : ill ; 26cm.
ISBN 0-237-44793-2 : £5.25
(B77-05534)

684.1'042 — Wooden furniture. Making. *Manuals*
Dal Fabbro, Mario. How to build modern furniture / [by] Mario Dal Fabbro. — 3rd ed. — New York ; London [etc.] : McGraw-Hill, [1977]. — viii,216p : ill ; 25cm.
This ed. published in the United States: 1976. — Previous ed.: New York : F.W. Dodge Corporation, 1957. — Index.
ISBN 0-07-015185-7 : £8.00
(B77-10462)

Stamberg, Peter S. Instant furniture : low-cost, well-designed, easy-to-assemble tables, chairs, couches, beds, desks, and storage systems / [by] Peter S. Stamberg ; with designs by Gerrit J. Rietveld ... [et al.] ; photography by the Globus Brothers. — New York ; London [etc.] : Van Nostrand Reinhold, 1976. — 160p : ill ; 28cm.
Index.
ISBN 0-442-27935-3 Pbk : £9.70
ISBN 0-442-27934-5 Pbk : £5.95
(B77-14828)

Taylor, Victor John. Modern furniture construction / [by] Victor J. Taylor. — London : Evans Bros, 1977. — 144p : ill ; 22cm.
Index.
ISBN 0-237-44829-7 : £5.25
(B77-20443)

684.1'042'0942 — English wooden furniture. Designs. *Catalogues*
Council for Small Industries in Rural Areas. Furniture designs / Council for Small Industries in Rural Areas. — London : CoSIRA, [1977]. — [43]leaves : of ill ; 15x21cm.
Cover title.
Pbk : Unpriced
(B77-13133)

684.1'044 — Antique furniture. Restoration. *Manuals*
Hook, Albert G. The work of restoration of antique furniture / by Albert G. Hook. — [Hove] ([2a Somerhill Ave., Hove, Sussex]) : [Lockholt and Co. Ltd], [1977]. — [1],iv,94p : ill ; 21cm.
Cover title: The wonderful world of period furniture.
Pbk : Unpriced
(B77-24364)

684.1'044 — Wooden furniture. Renovation. *Amateurs' manuals*
Basic furniture renovation / [edited by Gabrielle Weaver]. — London [etc.] : Marshall Cavendish, 1977. — [4],64p : ill(chiefly col) ; 28cm.
'This material has previously appeared in the publication "The Encyclopedia of Crafts"' - title page verso.
ISBN 0-85685-295-3 : £1.75
(B77-26410)

Gaston, Desmond. Care and repair of furniture / [by] Desmond Gaston ; [drawings by Malcolm Ward]. — Glasgow [etc.] : Collins, 1977. — 176p : ill ; 25cm.
Index.
ISBN 0-00-435485-0 : £3.95
(B77-22727)

684.1'2 — Furniture. Upholstery. Ignition by lighted cigarettes & lighted matches. *Research reports*
Marchant, Roger Philip. The ignitability of upholstery by smokers' materials / by R.P. Marchant. — Stevenage : Furniture Industry Research Association, 1977. — [3],43p : ill ; 30cm.
Sp : £3.00(free to members of FIRA)
(B77-32024)

684.1'6 — Hospital equipment: Bedside lockers. *Standards*
British Standards Institution. Specification for hospital bedside lockers = Spécification des armoires d'hôpital destinées à être placées à côté des lits = Spezifikation für Schränke zur Stellung neben Krankenhausbetten / British Standards Institution. — London : B.S.I.
Part 2 = Partie 2 = Teil 2 : General purpose lockers of wooden construction with facilities for hanging day clothes = Armoires en bois d'usage général permettant l'accrochage des vêtements de jour = Allgemeingebräuchliche Holzschränke mit Möglichkeiten zur Aufhängung von Tageskleidern. — 1976. — [2], 4,[2]p ; 30cm. — (BS1765 : Part 2 : 1976)
Pierced for binder.
ISBN 0-580-09247-x Sd : £1.50
(B77-00852)

684.3 — Hospitals. Bedding. *Standards*
British Standards Institution. Specification for hospital bedding = Spécification de la literie pour usage dans les hôpitaux = Spezifikation für Beltzeug zur Verwendung in Krankenhäusern / British Standards Institution. — London : B.S.I.
Part 3 = Partie 3 = Teil 3 : Flexible polyurethane pillows = Oreillers souples en polyuréthane = Flexibel Kopfkissen aus Polyurethan. — 1976. — [8]p ; 30cm. — (BS5223 : Part 3 : 1976)
Pierced for binder.
ISBN 0-580-09129-5 Sd : £1.60
(B77-10463)

686 — PRINTING AND RELATED ACTIVITIES

686 — Books. Production. *Juvenile literature*
Leach, Alison. Books / by Alison Leach ; illustrated by Sally Holmes. — London [etc.] : F. Watts, 1977. — 56p : ill(chiefly col), facsims(some col), port ; 22cm. — (A first look book)
Index.
ISBN 0-85166-643-4 : £1.95
(B77-28745)

686'.03 — Books. Production & marketing. *Encyclopaedias*
Jacob, Henry. A pocket dictionary of publishing terms : including explanations and definitions of words and phrases commonly used in the production and distribution of books / [by] Henry Jacob ; [edited by Antony Kamm]. — London : Macdonald and Jane's, 1976. — [10], 70p : ill ; 18cm.
Bibl.: p.70.
ISBN 0-354-04016-2 Sd : £0.85
(B77-00312)

686.2 — PRINTING

686.2 — Periodicals. Printing
British Printing Industries Federation. Printing and finishing / [prepared by the British Printing Industries Federation, Periodical Publishers Association, British Paper and Board Industry Federation]. — London (11 Bedford Row, WC1R 4DX) : B.P.I.F. : P.P.A. : B.P.B.I.F., 1975. — 20p : ill, facsims ; 21cm.
ISBN 0-85168-091-7 Sd : £0.75
(B77-08464)

686.2 — Printed ephemera printed by Rampant Lions Press, 1973. *Collections*
Rampant Lions Press. Portfolio two / [compiled by Will & Sebastian Carter at the Rampant Lions Press]. — [Cambridge] ([12 Chesterton Rd, Cambridge CB4 3AB]) : [Rampant Lions Press], [1974]. — Portfolio : ill, port ; 29cm.
Twenty-five items. — Limited ed. of 500 copies.
Unpriced
(B77-05535)

686.2 — Printing. *Conference proceedings*
International Conference of Printing Research Institutes, *13th, Wildhaus, 1975.* Advances in printing science and technology : proceedings of the 13th International Conference of Printing Research Institutes, Wildhaus, Switzerland, May 1975 / edited by W.H. Banks ; for the International Association of Research Institutes for the Graphic Arts Industry. — London [etc.] (Estover Rd, Plymouth PL6 7PZ) : Pentech Press Ltd, 1977. — x,412p : ill, forms ; 23cm.
ISBN 0-7273-0102-0 : £15.00
(B77-14317)

686.2 — Printing by private presses. *Periodicals*
Albion : a journal of printing and typography. — Hitchin (26 West Hill, Hitchin, Herts.) : Dodman Press.
Vol.1, no.1- ; Apr. 1977-. — [1977]-. — ill(some col), facsims ; 26cm.
Three issues a year. — [17]p.,[3]p. of plates in 1st issue.
Sd : £1.00 yearly
ISSN 0140-2781
(B77-33925)

686.2'03 — Printing. *Dictionaries*
Dictionary of printing terms : a comprehensive guide to the terms most commonly used in printing, paper, typesetting, origination, finishing, point of sale, premiums and promotions, etc. / edited by Ian Foster. — Revised ed. — London (58 Parker St., WC2B 5QB) : 'Print Buyer' Magazine Ltd, 1976. — 112p : ill ; 19cm.
Previous ed.: 1975.
ISBN 0-905768-00-0 Sd : £0.60
(B77-07978)

686.2'09 — Printing, to 1976. *Juvenile literature*
Rees, Gary. The story of books / illustrated by Gary Rees ; written by Vivienne Driscoll. — London : Macdonald Educational, 1977. — [1], 44p : ill(chiefly col), facsims, col ports ; 25cm. — (Toppers history)
Index.
ISBN 0-356-05443-8 : £1.50
(B77-13134)

686.2'092'4 — Printing. Caxton, William. *England. Biographies*
Knight, Charles. [William Caxton, the first English printer]. William Caxton and Charles Knight / [by Charles Knight]. — [1st ed. reprinted] ; with an introduction by Kenneth Day. — London : Wynkyn de Worde Society : Distributed by Lund Humphries, 1976. — 264p in various pagings : ill, ports ; 16cm.
Includes original pagings. — Facsimile reprint. — 'William Caxton, the first English printer' originally published: London : C. Knight, 1844.
ISBN 0-85331-391-1 Pbk : £2.95
(B77-08465)

Pearman, Naomi. The Lincoln Caxton / [by] Naomi Pearman. — [Lincoln] ([Lincoln Minster Shop, Exchequergate, Lincoln]) : [Lincoln Cathedral Library], 1976. — 28p : ill ; 22cm. — (Lincoln Cathedral. Library. Publications ; no.1)
ISBN 0-9505083-0-6 Sd : £0.60
(B77-13135)

Sommerlad, Michael John. William Caxton : a quincentenary tribute / by Michael Sommerlad. — Colchester ([Sheepen Rd, Colchester]) : Faculty of Arts, Colchester Institute of Higher Education, [1976]. — 3-21p : ill, facsim ; 31cm.
Unpriced
(B77-27965)

686.2'092'4 — Printing. Ogilby, John. *England. Biographies*
Van Eerde, Katherine S. John Ogilby and the taste of his times / by Katherine S. Van Eerde. — Folkestone : Dawson, 1976. — 183p : ill, facsims, maps, port ; 28cm.
Ill. on lining papers. — Bibl.: p.173-179. — Index.
ISBN 0-7129-0690-8 : £12.00
(B77-07493)

686.2'092'4 — Printing. Worde, Wynkyn de. *Biographies*
Moran, James. Wynkyn de Worde : father of Fleet Street / [by] James Moran. — 2nd revised ed. — London : Wynkyn de Worde Society : Distributed by Lund Humphries, 1976. — 2-60p,fold plate : facsims, map ; 20cm.
Previous ed.: 1960. — Bibl.: p.55. — Index.
ISBN 0-85331-388-1 Pbk : £2.95
(B77-10464)

686.2'092'4 — Printing. Wright, John, fl.1720-1744. *Biographies*
McLaverty, J. Pope's printer, John Wright : a preliminary study / [by] J. McLaverty. — Oxford (Bodleian Library, Oxford OX1 3BG) : Oxford Bibliographical Society, 1976. — iv, 52p : ill ; 26cm. — (Oxford Bibliographical Society. Occasional publications ; no.11)
Bibl.: p.51-52. — Index. — Includes a list of books printed by John Wright.
ISBN 0-901420-32-8 Sd : Unpriced
(B77-25758)

686.2'0941 — Printing. *Great Britain, to 1967*
The **hero** as printer : essays to accompany an exhibition mounted by Aberdeen University Library in the Art Gallery, Aberdeen to commemorate the Caxton quincentenary / edited by C.A. McLaren. — Aberdeen ([King's College, Aberdeen AB9 2UB]) : Aberdeen University Library, 1976. — vii,62p,8p of plates : facsims ; 22cm.
Bibl.: p.61-62.
ISBN 0-9505322-0-7 Pbk : £1.00
(B77-11306)

686.2'0942 — Printing. *England, to 1976*
Hampson, Geoffrey. Five centuries of English printing / written by G. Hampson ... ; glossary and chronology compiled by Dan Chadwick ... — [Southampton] ([Civic Centre, Southampton SO9 4XF]) : Southampton Museums and Art Gallery, 1976. — [15]p : ill ; 21cm.
' ... published October 1976 in conjunction with the "Five centuries of English printing" exhibition held at Tudor Merchants Hall, Southampton, 15-31 October 1976'.
ISBN 0-901723-08-8 Sd : £0.25
(B77-04315)

686.2'09422'93 — Printing. *Berkshire. Reading, to ca 1975*
Reading Museum and Art Gallery. Printing : past, present and future : Reading celebrates Caxton's quincentenary / [Reading Museum and Art Gallery]. — [Reading] ([P.O. Box 17, Town Hall, Reading, RG1 1QN]) : Reading Museum and Art Gallery and Reading Libraries, 1976. — 23p,[8]p of plates : ill, facsims, ports ; 21x30cm.
Catalogue of an exhibition held at Reading Museum and Art Gallery, 1976. — Bibl.: p.22.
ISBN 0-9501247-6-1 Sd : £0.39
(B77-02446)

686.2'09429'98 — Printers. *Gwent. Chepstow, 1806-1976*
Waters, Ivor. Chepstow printers and newspapers / [by] Ivor Waters. — Revised [ed.]. — Chepstow ([c/o Hon. Sec. Mervyn Prothero, 1 Wyebank Close, Tutshill, Chepstow, Gwent NP6 7ET]) : The Chepstow Society, 1977. — iii,40p : ill, facsim, map, ports ; 21cm. — (Chepstow Society. Pamphlet series ; no.9)
Previous ed.: 1970.
ISBN 0-900278-38-2 Sd : Unpriced
Also classified at 072'.9'98
(B77-24365)

686.2'0945'31 — Printing. *Italy. Venice, 1400-1500*
Gerulaitis, Leonardas Vytautas. Printing and publishing in fifteenth century Venice / [by] Leonardas Vytautas Gerulaitis. — Chicago : American Library Association ; London : Mansell Information Publishing, 1976. — xiv, 190p ; 25cm.
Bibl.: p.164-179. — Index.
ISBN 0-7201-0628-1 : £10.00
(B77-09831)

686.2'17 — Latin alphabet. Display typefaces, 1837-1901. *Illustrations*
Victorian display alphabets : 100 complete fonts / selected and arranged by Dan X. Solo from the 'Solotype Typographers Catalog'. — New York : Dover Publications [etc.] ; London : Constable [etc.], 1976. — [3],100p : of ill ; 28cm. — (Dover pictorial archive series)
ISBN 0-486-23302-2 Pbk : £2.25
(B77-04946)

686.2'17 — Latin alphabet. Display typefaces. Art nouveau style. *Illustrations*
Art Nouveau display alphabets : 100 complete fonts / selected and arranged by Dan X. Solo from the 'Solotype Typographers Catalog'. — New York : Dover Publications [etc.] ; London : Constable, 1976. — [3],100p : of ill ; 28cm. — (Dover pictorial archive series)
ISBN 0-486-23386-3 Pbk : £2.15
(B77-23577)

686.2'2 — Typography. Design, ca 1920-1975
Plymouth College of Art and Design. *Department of Printing.* A mid-twentieth century typographical interlude / Department of Printing, Plymouth College of Art and Design. — [Plymouth] ([Plymouth, Devon]) : [The Department], [1976]. — 24,xx p : ill, facsims, ports ; 24cm.
On half-title page: Typographical interlude.
ISBN 0-905797-01-9 Sd : Unpriced
(B77-04947)

686.2'2'0924 — Books. Design. Morris, William, b.1834
Needham, Paul. William Morris and the art of the book / with essays on William Morris as book collector / by Paul Needham ; as calligrapher / by Joseph Dunlap ; and, as typographer / by John Dreyfus ; [edited by Paul Needham]. — New York : Pierpont Morgan Library ; London [etc.] : Oxford University Press, 1976. — 3-140,[1]p,cxiv[i.e. cxviii]p of plates : ill, facsims(some col), port ; 31cm.
Ill. on lining papers. — Includes a catalogue based on the Pierpont Morgan Library's exhibition "William Morris and the Art of the Book", September-November 1976.
ISBN 0-19-519910-3 : £30.00
Also classified at 020'.75
(B77-04948)

686.2'2'0924 — Typography. Burrett, Edward. *England, 1924-1975. Autobiographies*
Burrett, Edward. Full point : a typographer remembers / by Edward Burrett. — Esher (Full Point, New Rd, Esher, Surrey KT10 9PG) : Penmiel Press, 1976. — iii-xi,34,[1]p : ill(chiefly tipped in), ports(tipped in) ; 25cm.
Limited ed. of 125 numbered copies, of which 100 are for sale. — In slip case.
ISBN 0-905542-02-9 : £20.00
(B77-11307)

686.2'2'0942585 — Incunabula with St Albans imprints, 1480-1486. Typography. *Early works. Facsimiles*
Blades, William. Some account of the typography of St Alban's in the fifteenth century / by William Blades. — [1st ed. reprinted] ; with an introduction by Eric Vickers. — London : [Polytechnic of North London, School of Librarianship], 1976. — [14],16p,plate : 1 ill, port ; 22cm.
Limited ed. of 700 numbered copies. — Facsimile reprint of: 1st ed. s.l. : s.n., 1860.
ISBN 0-900639-10-5 Pbk : £2.75
(B77-07494)

686.2'24 — Printers' ornaments by George Bruce's Son and Company. *Specimen books*
George Bruce's Son and Company. [Specimens of printing types. *Selections].* Victorian frames, borders and cuts from the 1882 type catalog of George Bruce's Son and Co. — New York : Dover Publications [etc.] ; London : Constable, 1976. — [2],123p : chiefly ill ; 29cm. — (The Dover pictorial archive series)
'Specimens of printing types' originally published: New York : George Bruce's Son and Company, 1882.
ISBN 0-486-23320-0 Pbk : £2.40
(B77-13136)

686.2'24 — Words. Letters. Optical spacing
Kindersley, David. Optical letter spacing for new printing systems / [by] David Kindersley. — 2nd revised ed. — [s.l.] : Wynkyn de Worde Society ; London : Distributed by Lund Humphries, 1976. — 40p : ill ; 28x12cm.
Previous ed.: 1966. — Bibl.: p.39.
ISBN 0-85331-360-1 Pbk : £4.00
(B77-09832)

686.2'25 — Periodicals. Composition
British Printing Industries Federation. Composing / [prepared by the British Printing Industries Federation, Periodical Publishers Association, British Paper and Board Industry Federation]. — London (11 Bedford Row, WC1R 4DX) : B.P.I.F. ; London : P.P.A. : B.P.B.I.F., 1976. — 22p : form ; 21cm. — (Periodicals production)
ISBN 0-85168-090-9 Sd : £0.75
(B77-09137)

686.2'25 — Printing. Paste-up techniques. *Manuals*
Van Uchelen, Rod. Paste-up : production techniques and new applications / by Rod van Uchelen. — New York ; London [etc.] : Van Nostrand Reinhold, 1976. — 132p : ill(some col), facsims ; 24cm.
Index.
ISBN 0-442-29022-5 : £9.70
ISBN 0-442-29021-7 Pbk : £5.95
(B77-15963)

686.2'252 — British parliamentary papers: Hansard. Pages. Size. *Proposals*
Great Britain. *Parliament. House of Commons. Select Committee on House of Commons (Services).* Size of Hansard : fourth report from the Select Committee on House of Commons (Services), session 1976-77, together with part of the minutes of evidence taken before the Committee on 22 March and appendices. — London : H.M.S.O, [1977]. — xiii,20p ; 25cm. — ([1976-77 H.C.]298)
ISBN 0-10-229877-7 Sd : £0.70
(B77-13749)

686.2'315'0924 — Lithography. Griffits, Thomas Edgar. *Biographies*
Hawkes, Caroline. The pleasures of colour printing : a biography of Thomas Griffits, craftsman, 1883-1957 / by Caroline Hawkes. — [Stroud] ([Redcote, Bussage, Stroud, Glos. GL6 8AT]) : [The author], 1977. — [6],26[i.e.29]p : ill, ports ; 21cm.
Sd : Unpriced
(B77-29565)

United Kingdom food manufacturers / [Data Research Group]. — Amersham (Hill House, [Hill Ave.], Amersham, Bucks.) : The Group. [1977]. — 1977. — 128 leaves in various pagings ; 30cm.
ISBN 0-905570-84-7 Sp : £16.00
(B77-11665)

686.2'325 — Photolithography. Plates
British Printing Industries Federation. *Sheet-fed Offset Study Group.* Selecting the right litho plate / [prepared by the Sheet-fed Offset Study Group of the British Printing Industries Federation]. — London (11 Bedford Row, WC1R 4DX) : The Federation, 1976. — 39p : ill ; 21cm.
ISBN 0-85168-100-x Sd : £1.50
(B77-10465)

686.3 — BOOKBINDING
686.3'02 — Hand bookbinding. *Manuals*
Darley, Lionel Seabrook. Introduction to book binding / by Lionel S. Darley ; with sketches by the author. — London : Faber, 1976. — 120p,[4]p of plates : ill ; 21cm.
Originally published: 1965. — Bibl.: p.117. — Index.
ISBN 0-571-11105-x : £3.25
ISBN 0-571-11082-7 Pbk : £1.95
(B77-31324)

686.4 — PHOTOCOPYING
686.4'028 — Reprographic materials: Polymers
Warson, Henry. Polymers for carbon papers & the reprographic industries / by H. Warson. — Solihull (284 Warwick Rd, Solihull, W. Midlands B92 7AF) : Solihull Chemical Services, 1976. — ix p,187[i.e.190]leaves : ill ; 30cm.
ISBN 0-905827-00-7 Sp : £50.00
(B77-07495)

686.4'3 — COM. Processing & duplication. Techniques
Horder, Alan. Computer output microfilm : choice of processing and duplicating methods / [by] Alan Horder. — Hatfield (Hatfield Polytechnic, Endymion Rd Annexe, Hatfield, Herts. AL10 8AU) : National Reprographic Centre for documentation, 1976. — 33p ; 30cm. — (National Reprographic Centre for documentation. Publications ; no.6 ISSN 0307-9384)
ISBN 0-85267-103-2 Sp : £4.00(£3.00 to members)
ISBN 0-85267-104-0 Microfiche : £1.00(£0.70 to members)
(B77-02447)

687 — MANUFACTURES. CLOTHING
687'.021'2 — Fabrics for clothing. Metric measures. *Ready reckoners*
Morplan metric clothing trade reckoner : 1/2cm to 10cms every 1/2cm ... followed by useful conversion tables ... — London (230 Long La., SE1 4EQ) : Morrish and Company, 1975. — [202]p ; 16cm.
Pbk : £1.40
(B77-22005)

687'.16 — Industries. Personnel. Working clothing. *Standards*
British Standards Institution. Specification for workwear = Spécification des vêtements de travail = Spezifikation für Arbeitskleidung / British Standards Institution. — London : B.S.I., 1976. — [2],18p : ill ; 30cm. — (BS5426 : 1976)
Pierced for binder.
ISBN 0-580-09428-6 Sd : £4.00
(B77-02448)

688.4 — MANUFACTURES. SMOKERS' SUPPLIES
688'.4 — Clay tobacco pipes. *Cambridgeshire, to 1900*
Flood, Robert J. Clay tobacco pipes in Cambridgeshire / [by] Robert J. Flood. — Cambridge : Oleander Press, 1976. — 52p : ill ; 21cm.
Bibl.: p.50.
ISBN 0-902675-70-2 Sd : £1.20
(B77-10466)

688.6 — MANUFACTURES. CARRIAGES, WAGONS, CARTS, WHEELBARROWS
688.6 — Model horse-drawn vehicles. Making. *Manuals*
Thompson, John, *b.1937.* Making model horse-drawn vehicles / by John Thompson. — Fleet (1 Fieldway, Fleet, Hants.) : The author, 1976. — [86]p : ill, facsim ; 30cm.
Pbk : £3.10
(B77-16990)

688.7 — MANUFACTURES. RECREATIONAL EQUIPMENT
688.7 — Games. Equipment. Making. *Manuals. Juvenile literature*
Weiss, Harvey. Games & puzzles you can make yourself / [by] Harvey Weiss. — London : Hamilton, 1977. — [5],56p : ill(chiefly col) ; 24cm.
Originally published: New York : Crowell, 1976.
ISBN 0-241-89619-3 : £2.95
Primary classification 790
(B77-25119)

688.7'2 — Museums. *Norfolk. Norwich. Norwich Castle Museum. Exhibits: Educational toys, ca 1770-ca 1920. Catalogues*
Norfolk Museums Service. Teaching toys in the Norwich Museums collection / [Norfolk Museums Service] ; [text by] Rachel M.R. Young. — [Norwich] ([Castle Museum, Norwich NOR 6SB]) : The Service, 1975. — 24p,4p of plates : ill ; 22cm.
Originally published: Norwich : Castle Museum, 1966. — Bibl.: p.24.
ISBN 0-903101-21-1 Sd : £0.36
(B77-11968)

688.7'2'0222 — Toys. *Colouring books*
Toys colour copy book. — Maidenhead : Purnell, 1977. — [20]p : of ill(some col) ; 28cm.
Sd : £0.15
(B77-09138)

688.7'2'0740941 — Museums. Exhibits: Toys. *Great Britain. Directories*
Flick, Pauline. Discovering toys and toy museums / [by] Pauline Flick. — 2nd ed. — Princes Risborough : Shire Publications, 1977. — 70p : ill, facsims ; 18cm. — (Discovering series ; no.116)
Previous ed.: 1971. — Bibl.: p.68. — Index.
ISBN 0-85263-391-2 Pbk : £0.60
Primary classification 688.7'2'09
(B77-33926)

688.7'2'09 — Toys, to 1970
Flick, Pauline. Discovering toys and toy museums / [by] Pauline Flick. — 2nd ed. — Princes Risborough : Shire Publications, 1977. — 70p : ill, facsims ; 18cm. — (Discovering series ; no.116)
Previous ed.: 1971. — Bibl.: p.68. — Index.
ISBN 0-85263-391-2 Pbk : £0.60
Also classified at 688.7'2'0740941
(B77-33926)

688.7'2'09 — Toys, to 1975. *Juvenile literature*
Law, Felicia. Toys / written by Felicia Law ; illustrated by Christine Howes. — London [etc.] : Collins, 1975. — 32p : col ill ; 22cm. — (Dandelions)
ISBN 0-00-651188-0 Sd : £0.50
(B77-02449)

688.7'2'09 — Toys, to ca 1920. *Collectors' guides*
Cadbury, Betty. Playthings past / [by] Betty Cadbury. — Newton Abbot [etc.] : David and Charles, 1976. — 96p : ill ; 26cm.
Bibl.: p.94-95. — Index.
ISBN 0-7153-7191-6 : £4.95
(B77-05536)

688.7'2'09 — Toys, to ca 1958. *Collectors' guides*
Curtis, Tony, *b.1939.* Dolls & toys / compiled by Tony Curtis. — [Galashiels] : [Lyle Publications], [1977]. — 3-126p : chiefly ill ; 16cm. — (Antiques and their values)
Index.
ISBN 0-902921-45-2 : £1.50
(B77-33927)

688.7'2'09034 — Toys, ca 1800-ca 1920
Mackay, James. Nursery antiques / [by] James Mackay. — London : Ward Lock, 1976. — 136p : ill(some col), facsims ; 27cm.
Ill. on lining papers. — Index. — Includes chapters on children's clothing and nursery literature.
ISBN 0-7063-5019-7 : £3.95
(B77-04949)

688.7'2'0951 — Chinese toys, to 1976
Fawdry, Marguerite. Chinese childhood / [by] Marguerite Fawdry. — London (1 Scala St., W.1) : Pollocks Toy Theatres Ltd, 1977. — 192p : ill(some col), facsims, map, port ; 26cm.
Bibl.: p.187-188. — Index.
ISBN 0-9505588-0-x : £5.95
(B77-24366)

688.7'22 — Museums. *London. Tower Hamlets (London Borough). Bethnal Green Museum. Exhibits: Puppets, ca 1700-ca 1970. Illustrations*
Goodfellow, Caroline. Puppets / [by] Caroline Goodfellow ; [for the] Victoria & Albert Museum and [the] Bethnal Green Museum ; [photography Ken Jackson]. — London : H.M.S.O., 1976. — [12]p : chiefly col ill ; 16cm. — (Victoria and Albert Museum. Small colour books ; 15)
ISBN 0-11-290256-1 Sd : £0.40
(B77-09139)

688.7'22'09 — Dolls, to 1976
King, Constance Eileen. Dolls and dolls' houses / [by] Constance Eileen King. — London [etc.] : Hamlyn, 1977. — 256p : ill(some col) ; 31cm.
Col. ill. on lining papers. — Bibl.: p.254. — Index.
ISBN 0-600-32929-1 : £5.95
Also classified at 688.7'23'09
(B77-28747)

688.7'23 — Dolls' houses. *Stories, anecdotes*
ffolliott, Rosemary. De Bever Hall : the story of a stately dolls house / [by] Rosemary ffolliott ; photographs by Gordon Ledbetter. — London : Duckworth, 1976. — [4],75p : ill ; 28cm.
ISBN 0-7156-1018-x : £3.95
(B77-00869)

688.7'23'09 — Dolls' houses, to ca 1950
King, Constance Eileen. Dolls and dolls' houses / [by] Constance Eileen King. — London [etc.] : Hamlyn, 1977. — 256p : ill(some col) ; 31cm.
Col. ill. on lining papers. — Bibl.: p.254. — Index.
ISBN 0-600-32929-1 : £5.95
Primary classification 688.7'22'09
(B77-28747)

688.7'25 — Educational toys for mentally handicapped children. Design. *Research reports*
Sandhu, Jim Singh. Environmental design for handicapped children / [by] Jim Singh Sandhu, Horst Hendriks-Jansen. — Farnborough, Hants. : Saxon House, 1976. — xiii,222,[1]p : ill, plans ; 24cm.
Bibl.: p.219-222.
ISBN 0-566-00142-x : £9.75
Primary classification 725'.57
(B77-10873)

688.7'28 — Mechanical toys, to 1975
Hillier, Mary. Automata & mechanical toys : an illustrated history / by Mary Hillier. — London : Jupiter Books, 1976. — 200p : ill(some col), facsims, ports ; 26cm.
Ill. on lining papers. — Bibl.: p.196-197. — Index.
ISBN 0-904041-32-8 : £5.95
(B77-33330)

688.7'54'0222 — Pornographic translucent playing cards, ca 1850. *Illustrations*
Denning, Trevor. Transluscent [i.e. translucent] playing-cards / [by] Trevor Denning. — [Birmingham] ([91 Southam Rd, Birmingham B28 0AA]) : [The author], [1976]. — [1],51p : ill ; 21x31cm.
Limited ed. of 300 numbered copies, signed by the author.
ISBN 0-9505521-0-0 Pbk : £6.20
(B77-07496)

688.7'6'34 — Real tennis balls. Making. *Manuals*
Hamilton, *Sir* **Richard,** *bart.* How to make the real tennis ball from core to cover / [by] Richard Hamilton and Anthony Hobson. — London (The Queen's Club, West Kensington, W.14) : Tennis and Rackets Association, 1977. — [3],27p : ill ; 19cm.
Pbk : £1.00
(B77-24367)

688.7'9 — Fly fishing. Lures. Making. *Manuals*
Evanoff, Vlad. Make your own fishing lures / [by] Vlad Evanoff. — South Brunswick ; New York : Barnes ; London : Yoseloff, 1975. — 158p : ill ; 26cm.
Index.
ISBN 0-498-01617-x : £4.50
(B77-30442)

688.7'9 — Salmon. Fly fishing. Flies. Tying. *Manuals*
Pryce-Tannatt, T E. How to dress salmon flies : a handbook for amateurs / [by] T.E. Pryce-Tannatt. — [1st ed., reprinted] / with an appreciation by T. Donald Overfield ; additional material compiled by John Veniard and Freddie Riley ; drawings by Donald Downs. — London : A. & C. Black, 1977. — xxi,289p,xvi p of plates : ill(some col) ; 20cm.
Facsimile reprint of: 1st ed. 1914.
ISBN 0-7136-1618-0 : £4.75
(B77-13750)

690 — BUILDINGS. CONSTRUCTION
Boucher, Ronald Charles. Industrial studies for building craft students / [by] R.C. Boucher. — London [etc.] : Macmillan, 1976. — ix,96p : ill, form, map ; 25cm.
Bibl.: p.95.
ISBN 0-333-19589-2 Pbk : £2.95
(B77-02450)

Grundy, J T. Construction technology / [by] J.T. Grundy. — London : Edward Arnold.
Index.
Vol.1. — 1977. — viii,200p : ill, maps ; 22cm.
ISBN 0-7131-3387-2 Pbk : £2.95 : CIP rev.
(B77-29566)

690 — Buildings. Aerodynamics
Aynsley, R M. Architectural aerodynamics / by R.M. Aynsley, W. Melbourne and B.J. Vickery. — London : Applied Science Publishers, 1977. — xii,254p : ill, maps, plans ; 23cm. — (Architectural science series)
Index.
ISBN 0-85334-698-4 : £14.00
(B77-15964)

690 — Buildings. Construction. *Conference proceedings*
International Council for Building Research, Studies and Documentation. *Triennial Congress, 7th, Edinburgh, 1977.* Construction research international / edited by Keith Alsop. — Lancaster [etc.] : Construction Press.
In 2 vols. — Bibl.
[Vol.1]. — 1977. — [13],349p : ill, map ; 31cm.

'... contains the keynote papers that were specially commissioned for the technical sessions of the Seventh Triennial Congress of the International Council for [Building] Research, Studies and Documentation (CIB), held in Edinburgh in September 1977' - Preface. — Second title page in French, English and French preliminaries and summaries. — Includes 3 papers in French.
ISBN 0-904406-71-7 : Unpriced
(B77-28748)

690 — Buildings. Construction. *Manuals*
Handisyde, Cecil Charles. Everyday details / [by] Cecil C. Handisyde. — London : Architectural Press, 1976. — vii,109p : ill ; 30cm.
ISBN 0-85139-213-x Pbk : £3.75
(B77-09833)

Lingane, J. Basic building / [by] J. Lingane. — Tallaght : Folens, [1977]. — 178p : ill, plans ; 25cm. — (Leaving Certificate)
Pbk : £1.80
(B77-17639)

690 — Buildings. Construction. Sites. Electric equipment. *Great Britain. Manuals*
Great Britain. *Department of the Environment. Property Services Agency.* Electricity on building sites / Department of the Environment, Property Services Agency. — 3rd ed. — [London] : H.M.S.O., 1977. — Folder([5]p) : col ill ; 22cm. — (Advisory leaflet ; 59)
Previous ed.: 1971. — Bibl.: p.[5].
ISBN 0-11-670702-x : £0.15
(B77-14829)

690 — Buildings. Joints. Design & construction. *Manuals*
Martin, Bruce, *b.1917.* Joints in buildings / [by] Bruce Martin. — London : Godwin [etc.], 1977. — vii,226p : ill ; 31cm.
Bibl.: p.210-211. — Index.
ISBN 0-7114-4001-8 : £14.00
(B77-22728)

690'.021'2 — Buildings. Construction. *Technical data*
Smith, Sam, *b.1917.* Builder's detail sheets / by Sam Smith. — London (49 Hatton Garden, EC1N 8XS) : Northwood Publications Ltd, 1976. — [6],84 leaves : ill ; 30cm.
'These detail sheets were originally published in the "Building Trades Journal" over a period of two-and-a-half years' - Preface. — Originally published: 1973. — Previous control number ISBN 0-7198-2550-4.
Sp : £2.50
ISBN 0-7198-2550-4
(B77-03130)

690'.028 — Building equipment: Scaffolding. Safety measures. *Great Britain. Manuals*
Great Britain. *Health and Safety Executive.* Safety in construction work, scaffolding / Health and Safety Executive. — [2nd ed.]. — [London] : H.M.S.O., 1977. — [2],27p : ill ; 21cm. — (Health and safety at work ; 6D)
This ed.: issued by the Factory Inspectorate. 1968. — Bibl.: p.27.
ISBN 0-11-881452-4 Sd : £0.30
(B77-14830)

690'.028 — Building equipment: System scaffolding. Evaluation. *Reports, surveys*
Vickery, J E F. An evaluation of system scaffolding / by J.E.F. Vickery. — Ascot : Institute of Building, 1977. — [1],62p : ill ; 29cm. — (Institute of Building. Occasional papers ; no.13 ISSN 0306-6878)
ISBN 0-901822-45-0 Sd : Unpriced
(B77-18276)

690'.028 — Building machinery. Maintenance
Great Britain. *Department of the Environment. Property Services Agency.* Care of builders' machines / Department of the Environment, Property Services Agency. — 4th ed. — [London] : H.M.S.O., 1976. — Folder([5]p) : col ill ; 22cm. — (Advisory leaflet ; 33)
Previous ed.: 1953.
ISBN 0-11-670690-2 : £0.15
(B77-05537)

690'.03 — Buildings. Construction. *Dictionaries*
Dictionary of architecture and construction / edited by Cyril M. Harris. — New York ; London [etc.] : McGraw-Hill, [1976]. — xvii, 553p : ill, plans ; 25cm.
Published in the United States: 1975.
ISBN 0-07-026756-1 : £20.65
Primary classification 720'.3
(B77-01662)

690'.07'1141 — Colleges of further education. Curriculum subjects: Buildings. Construction. Teaching. Safety measures. *Great Britain. Manuals*
Southern Regional Council for Further Education. *Safety Working Party.* Safety recommendations to construction teachers / Southern Regional Council for Further Education, Safety Working Party ; [written by B. Lavender]. — [Reading] ([26 Bath Rd, Reading RG1 6NT]) : [The Council], [1976]. — [11]p ; 30cm. — (Safety booklet ; no.2)
ISBN 0-901271-28-4 Sd : £0.30
(B77-08466)

690'.07'20425892 — Buildings. Construction. Research organisations. *Hertfordshire. Garston. Building Research Establishment. Reports, surveys. Serials*
Building Research Establishment. Annual report / Building Research Establishment. — London : H.M.S.O.
1976. — 1977. — vi,69p,[8]p of plates : ill ; 30cm.
Bibl.: p.59-63. — Index.
ISBN 0-11-670549-3 Pbk : £3.00
ISSN 0071-7517
(B77-27966)

690'.0913 — Buildings. Construction. *Tropical regions*
Fullerton, Richard Lewis. Building construction in warm climates / [by] R.L. Fullerton. — Oxford [etc.] : Oxford University Press.
In 3 vols.
Vol.3. — 1977. — xiii,269,[2]p : ill, plans ; 20cm. — (Oxford tropical handbooks)
Index.
ISBN 0-19-859509-3 Pbk : £3.50 : CIP rev.
(B77-07498)

690'.1 — Buildings. Structural components. Performance. *Conference proceedings*
Performance of building structures : proceedings of the international conference held at Glasgow University from 31st March to 1st April 1976 / [edited by D.R. Green and I.A. MacLeod]. — Plymouth (Estover Rd, Plymouth PL6 7PZ) : Pentech Press, 1976. — [8],535p : ill, plans ; 25cm.
Bibl.: p.505-508.
ISBN 0-7273-1602-8 : £12.80
(B77-06203)

690'.1'2 — Buildings. External walls. *Technical data. Serials*
External walls. — Edenbridge (25 High St., Edenbridge, Kent) : A4 Publications Ltd. — (Architects' and specifiers' guide series)
[1976-7]. — 1976. — 224p : ill ; 30cm.
Index.
ISBN 0-510-07014-0 Pbk : £3.50
ISSN 0307-0107
(B77-25071)

[1977-8]. — 1977. — 204p : ill ; 30cm.
Index.
ISBN 0-510-07030-2 Pbk : £3.50
ISSN 0307-0107
(B77-25072)

690'.1'2 — Buildings. Internal partitions. *Technical data. Serials*
Ceilings & partitions. — Edenbridge (25 High St., Edenbridge, Kent) : A4 Publications Ltd. — (Architects' and specifiers' guide series)
1975-6. — 1975. — 320p : ill ; 30cm.
Bibl.: p.91.
ISBN 0-510-07011-6 Pbk : £3.50
Also classified at 690'.1'70212
(B77-25073)

[1976-7]. — 1976. — 280p : ill ; 30cm.
Bibl.: p.279. — Index.
ISBN 0-510-07025-6 Pbk : £3.50
Also classified at 690'.1'70212
(B77-25074)

690'.1'2 — Wall coverings. *Technical data. Serials*
Fabrics, wallcoverings & furniture. — Edenbridge (25 High St., Edenbridge, Kent) : A4 Publications Ltd. — (Architects' and specifiers' guide series)
1975-6. — 1975. — 184p : ill ; 30cm.
ISBN 0-510-07007-8 Pbk : £3.50
Primary classification 684'.0021'2
(B77-25070)

690'.1'2 — Wall lining materials. Choice. Criteria: Costs in use. *Great Britain*
Guide to the choice of wall and floor surfacing materials : a costs in use approach / based on a report by the National Building Agency ; edited by Harry Miller. — London : Hutchinson, 1976. — 71p : ill ; 31cm.
Bibl.: p.71.
ISBN 0-09-127650-0 : £6.50
Also classified at 698.9
(B77-00854)

690'.1'6 — Agricultural industries. Farms. Buildings. Floors. Construction. *Manuals*
Agricultural Development and Advisory Service. Floor construction and sheet roofing / Ministry of Agriculture, Fisheries and Food, ADAS. — London : H.M.S.O., 1977. — [1],30p : ill ; 25cm. — (Fixed equipment of the farm ; leaflet 38)
ISBN 0-11-240578-9 Sd : £0.60
Also classified at 695
(B77-16504)

690'.1'70212 — Ceilings. *Technical data. Serials*
Ceilings & partitions. — Edenbridge (25 High St., Edenbridge, Kent) : A4 Publications Ltd. — (Architects' and specifiers' guide series)
1975-6. — 1975. — 320p : ill ; 30cm.
Bibl.: p.91.
ISBN 0-510-07011-6 Pbk : £3.50
Primary classification 690'.1'2
(B77-25073)

[1976-7]. — 1976. — 280p : ill ; 30cm.
Bibl.: p.279. — Index.
ISBN 0-510-07025-6 Pbk : £3.50
Primary classification 690'.1'2
(B77-25074)

690'.1'8 — Buildings. Doors & windows. *Technical data. Serials*
Doors & windows. — Edenbridge (25 High St., Edenbridge, Kent) : A4 Publications Ltd. — (Architects' and specifiers' guide series)
[1977-8]. — 1977. — 240p : ill ; 30cm.
Bibl.: p.239. — Index.
ISBN 0-510-07029-9 Pbk : £3.50
(B77-25075)

690'.24 — Buildings. Maintenance. *Manuals*
Intermediate Technology Development Group. A manual on building maintenance / [Intermediate Technology Development Group]. — London (9 King St., WC2E 8HN) : Intermediate Technology Publications.
Vol.2 : Methods / by Derek Miles. — 1976. — iv,61p : ill ; 22cm.
Cover title.
ISBN 0-903031-40-x Pbk : £1.25
(B77-00314)

690'.24'0942534 — Buildings of historical importance. Maintenance & repair. *Lincolnshire. Lincoln*
Lincoln *(District). Department of Planning and Architecture.* Lincoln's older buildings : a guide to their repair and maintenance / [City of Lincoln Department of Planning and Architecture]. — Lincoln (City Hall, Beaumont Fee, Lincoln LN1 1DP) : [The Department], 1976. — [1],ii,20p : ill ; 30cm.
ISBN 0-902092-07-3 Sp : £1.50
(B77-02451)

690'.6'50942132 — Parish churches. *London. Westminster (London Borough). All Souls Church, Langham Place, London. Rebuilding, 1968-1976*
Endersbee, Mary. Hidden miracles at All Souls / [by] Mary Endersbee. — London : Lakeland, 1977. — 111p : ill, plan ; 18cm.
ISBN 0-551-00768-0 Pbk : £0.95
(B77-31325)

Inside story : the building project of All Souls Church, Langham Place / [editorial Lance Bidewell, Elrose Hunter]. — London ([Langham Place, W.1]) : [The Church], 1976. — 22p : ill, ports ; 30cm.
Sd : Unpriced
(B77-25076)

690'.8'3 — Houses. Construction. *Great Britain. Middle school texts*
Cox, Sarah. Buildingworker / text by Sarah Cox ; photographs by Robert Golden. — Harmondsworth : Kestrel Books, 1976. — 32p : chiefly ill ; 27cm. — (People working)
ISBN 0-7226-5228-3 : £1.95
(B77-00315)

690'.8'3 — Houses. Construction. *Juvenile literature*
Claxton, John. Bricks and mortar, sand and water / photographs John Claxton ; story Sally Doganis. — London : Hamilton, 1977. — [32] p : chiefly ill ; 26cm. — (All-in-a-day books)
ISBN 0-241-89371-2 : £2.50
(B77-31326)

Read, Brian. Wonder why book of building a house / [by] Brian Read ; illustrated by Toni Goffe. — London : Transworld, 1977. — [2], 20p : col ill ; 29cm.
Index. — Previous control number ISBN 0-552-57006-0.
ISBN 0-552-98040-4 : £1.35
ISBN 0-552-57006-0 Sd : £0.50
(B77-11308)

690'.8'6 — Vernacular houses. Maintenance & conversion. *Northern England*
Whittaker, Neville. The house and cottage handbook / [by] Neville Whittaker ; foreword by Sir John Summerson. — Durham (34 Saddler St., Durham) : Civic Trust for the North East, 1976. — 120p : ill(some col), plans ; 20x23cm.
Bibl.: p.114.
ISBN 0-905516-00-1 Pbk : £2.50
(B77-02452)

690'.8'6709417 — Farmhouses. Extension & improvement. *Ireland (Republic). Manuals*
O'Farrell, Fearghal. Farm-house conversions : a handbook on renovating the farm-home / [by] F. O'Farrell. — Dublin (19 Sandymount Ave., Dublin 4) : An Foras Talúntais, 1977. — [4], 95p : ill, plans ; 29cm. — (Agricultural Institute (Republic of Ireland). Handbook series ; no.11)
Bibl.: p.95.
ISBN 0-905442-15-6 Pbk : £2.50
(B77-27967)

691 — BUILDING MATERIALS

691 — Building components. Failure. *Readings*
Bickerdike, Allen, Rich and Partners. Design failures in buildings / prepared by Bickerdike, Allen, Rich & Partners in association with Turlogh O'Brien. — London : Godwin.
2nd series. — [1974]. — [1],29 leaves : ill ; 30cm.
In binder. — 'This material was first published in "Building" between 12 January and 28 December 1973' - leaf 1.
ISBN 0-7114-3407-7 Ls : £5.00
ISBN 0-7114-3406-9 Sp : £2.00
(B77-03663)

691 — Building components: Profiled weathering sheeting. *Standards*
British Standards Institution. Code of practice for performance and loading criteria for profiled sheeting in building / British Standards Institution. — London : B.S.I., 1976. — [2],46, [2]p : ill ; 30cm. — (BS5427 : 1976)
Pierced for binder.
ISBN 0-580-09387-5 Sd : £6.60
(B77-11309)

691 — Buildings. Hardware
Underwood, Grahame. AJ handbook of architectural ironmongery / [by] Grahame Underwood and John Planck. — London : Architectural Press, 1977. — viii,109p(4 fold) : ill, forms, plans ; 30cm.
Index.
ISBN 0-85139-310-1 Pbk : £3.75
(B77-17640)

691 — Parish churches. Building materials. *England, to 1913*
Cox, John Charles. The English parish church : an account of the chief building types & of their materials during nine centuries / by J. Charles Cox. — Wakefield : EP Publishing, 1976. — xx,338p,fold plate : ill, plans ; 20cm.
Facsimile reprint of: 1st ed. London : Batsford, 1914. — Index.
ISBN 0-7158-1174-6 : £4.95
Primary classification 726'.5'0942
(B77-05549)

691'.1 — Agricultural industries. Farms. Buildings. Materials: Timber. Preservation. *Great Britain. Manuals*
Agricultural Development and Advisory Service. Preservation of timber and metal / Ministry of Agriculture, Fisheries and Food, ADAS. — London : H.M.S.O., 1977. — [1],23,[1]p,[4]p of plates : ill ; 25cm. — (Fixed equipment of the farm ; leaflet 17)
Bibl.: p.19-21.
ISBN 0-11-241121-5 Sd : £0.70
Also classified at 691'.8
(B77-15965)

691'.1'05 — Construction materials: Timber. *Periodicals*
Concept in wood. — High Wycombe : Timber Research and Development Association.
[No.1]- ; Autumn 1976-. — 1976-. — col ill, plans ; 30cm.
Two issues a year. — 24p. in 1st issue.
Sd : £0.50
ISSN 0309-0868
(B77-04316)

691'.12 — Building components: Timber. Infestation. Detection & treatment. *For surveying*
Richardson, Stanley A. The surveyor's guide to timber decay diagnosis and treatment / by Stanley A. Richardson. — [Winchester] ([21 Hyde St., Winchester, Hants.]) : [Wykamol Limited], [1977]. — [1],36p : ill ; 19cm.
Originally published: Winchester : Richardson and Starling Ltd, 1971. — Bibl.: p.36. — Index.
Sd : £0.45
(B77-16991)

691'.12 — Timber. Damage by larvae of furniture beetles. Prevention. Preservatives. Effectiveness. Testing. *Standards*
British Standards Institution. Wood preservatives. Determination of the toxic values against Anobium punctatum (De Geer) by egg-laying and larval survival (laboratory method) = Produits de préservation des bois. Détermination du seuil d'efficacité contre Anobium punctatum (De Geer) par l'observation de la ponte et du taux de survie des larves (méthode de laboratoire) = Holzschutzmittel. Bestimmung der Grenze der Wirksamkeit gegenüber Anobium punctatum (De Geer) durch Beobachten der Eiablage und des Überlebens von Larven (Laboratoriumsverfahren) / British Standards Institution. — London : B.S.I., 1976. — [2],8, [2]p : 1 ill ; 30cm. — (BS5437 : 1977) (EN49)
Pierced for binder.
ISBN 0-580-09269-0 Sd : £2.70
(B77-11310)

691'.14 — Building materials: Timber. Damage by termites. Resistance. *Ghana. Research reports*
Williams, R M C. Evaluation of field and laboratory methods for testing termite resistance of timber and building materials in Ghana, with relevant biological studies / [by] R.M.C. Williams. — London : Centre for Overseas Pest Research, 1973. — 64p,[10]p of plates,leaf of plate : ill ; 30cm. — (Tropical pest bulletin ; 3)
English and French abstract. — Bibl.: p.62-63.
ISBN 0-85135-065-8 Sd : £1.85
Also classified at 691'.92
(B77-30443)

691'.8 — Agricultural industries. Farms. Buildings. Materials: Metals. Preservation. *Great Britain. Manuals*
Agricultural Development and Advisory Service. Preservation of timber and metal / Ministry of Agriculture, Fisheries and Food, ADAS. — London : H.M.S.O., 1977. — [1],23,[1]p,[4]p of plates : ill ; 25cm. — (Fixed equipment of the farm ; leaflet 17)
Bibl.: p.19-21.
ISBN 0-11-241121-5 Sd : £0.70
Primary classification 691'.1
(B77-15965)

691'.92 — Building materials: Plastics. Damage by termites. Resistance. *Ghana. Research reports*
Williams, R M C. Evaluation of field and laboratory methods for testing termite resistance of timber and building materials in Ghana, with relevant biological studies / [by] R.M.C. Williams. — London : Centre for Overseas Pest Research, 1973. — 64p,[10]p of plates,leaf of plate : ill ; 30cm. — (Tropical pest bulletin ; 3)
English and French abstract. — Bibl.: p.62-63.
ISBN 0-85135-065-8 Sd : £1.85
Primary classification 691'.14
(B77-30443)

691'.99 — Building materials. Bonding. Adhesives
Great Britain. *Department of the Environment. Property Services Agency.* Adhesives used in building / Department of the Environment, Property Services Agency. — 2nd ed. — [London] : H.M.S.O., 1976. — Folder ([5]p) : col ill ; 22cm. — (Advisory leaflet ; 77)
Previous ed.: / issued by the Ministry of Public Building and Works. 1969.
ISBN 0-11-670693-7 : £0.15
(B77-06204)

691'.99 — Buildings. Joints. Flexible sealants. Use. *Manuals*
Great Britain. *Department of the Environment. Property Services Agency.* Flexible sealing materials : where and how to use them / Department of the Environment, Property Services Agency. — 2nd ed. — [London] : H.M.S.O., 1976. — Folder ([5]p) : col ill ; 21cm. — (Advisory leaflet ; 70)
Previous ed.: / issued by the Ministry of Public Building and Works. 1968. — Bibl.: p.[5].
ISBN 0-11-670697-x : £0.15
(B77-11311)

692 — BUILDINGS. PLANS, SPECIFICATIONS, ESTIMATING, CONTRACTS

692 — Buildings. Dimensional coordination. *Conference proceedings*
Symposium on Dimensional Coordination, *Dublin, 1975.* Dimensional coordination in building : a review : proceedings of a symposium held in the Gresham Hotel, Dublin on August 26, 1975, under the auspices of An Foras Forbartha / [edited by Aodhagán Brioscú]. — Dublin : Foras Forbartha, 1976. — 81p : ill, plans ; 30cm.
'... the Symposium on Dimensional Coordination ...' - Introduction. — Cover title: Comhordú toiseach. san bhfoirgníocht = Dimensional coordination in building.
ISBN 0-900115-85-8 Sd : £1.50
(B77-03664)

692 — Buildings. Dimensional coordination. *Great Britain. Standards*
British Standards Institution. Draft for development guidance on dimensional co-ordination in building = Projet à développer guide pour la co-ordination dimensionnelle dans le bâtiment = Entwurf zur weiteren Ausarbeitung Hinweise für grössenmässige Koordination im Bauwesen / British Standards Institution. — London : B.S.I., 1977. — Portfolio : ill ; 31cm. — (DD51 : 1977)
Sheet ([2])p., 4 folders, 3 booklets. — Text on portfolio. — Pierced for binder.
£6.60
(B77-15379)

692'.2 — Buildings. External works. Architectural design. Detail drawings. *Illustrations*
National Building Agency. External works detail sheets / National Building Agency. — London : Architectural Press [etc.], 1977. — [6] p,142 leaves : ill, plan ; 31cm.
Bibl.
ISBN 0-85139-215-6 : Unpriced
ISBN 0-85139-214-8 Pbk : £4.95
(B77-26423)

692'.3'05 — Buildings. Construction. *Standards. Serials*
Specification : building methods and products. — London : Architectural Press.
1976-7 : 77th ed. / editor Dex Harrison. — [1976]. — 2v.(various pagings) : ill, maps, plans ; 30cm.
Bibl. — Index.
ISBN 0-85139-580-5 Pbk : £10.75
ISSN 0081-3567
(B77-03131)

692'.5 — Agricultural industries. Farms. Buildings. Construction. Standard costs. *Scotland. Lists. Serials*

Farm building cost guide. — Aberdeen (Craibstone, Bucksburn, Aberdeen AB2 9TR) : Scottish Farm Buildings Investigation Unit.
1977 / [by] H.J. Wight. — 1977. — vi,132p : ill, plans ; 15x22cm.
Index.
ISBN 0-902433-13-x Sd : £1.35
ISSN 0309-4146
(B77-14831)

692'.5 — Buildings. Construction. Contracts. Prices. Adjustment. Formulae. *Standards*

Great Britain. *Department of the Environment. Property Services Agency.* Price adjustment formulae for building contracts / [Property Services Agency]. — London : H.M.S.O.
Description of the indices. — Series 2 [ed.] / [revision by the National Consultative Council of the Building and Civil Engineering Industries, Standing Committee on Indices for Building Contracts]. — 1977. — [1],v,67p ; 30cm.
Previous ed.: / Building EDC, Steering Group on Building Price Adjustment Formulae. 1974.
ISBN 0-11-670791-7 Sd : £2.25
(B77-15380)

Guide to application and procedure. — Series 2 [ed.] / [revision by the National Consultative Council of the Building and Civil Engineering Industries, Standing Committee on Indices for Building Contracts]. — 1977. — iv,20p : form ; 30cm.
ISBN 0-11-670790-9 Sd : £2.25
(B77-15381)

692'.5 — Buildings. Construction. Estimating

Wainwright, Walter Howard. Practical builders' estimating / [by] W. Howard Wainwright & A.A.B. Wood. — 3rd ed. — London : Hutchinson, 1977. — 3-190p ; 24cm.
Previous ed.: London : Hutchinson Educational, 1970.
ISBN 0-09-129221-2 Pbk : £2.95
(B77-25760)

692'.5 — Buildings. Construction. Standard costs. *Great Britain. For estimating. Lists. Serials*

Griffiths' building price book : formerly 'The provincial and country builders' price book'. — Yeovil (Newton Rd, Yeovil, Somerset BA20 1NF) : Barton Publishers.
1977 : 23rd ed. / edited by Geoffrey Smith & Partners. — [1977]. — xviii,168,168p : ill, plans ; 30cm.
'Metric and imperial editions combined in one volume' - cover. — Index.
Pbk : Unpriced
(B77-26411)

Laxton's building price book. — Kingston upon Thames : Kelly's Directories.
1977 : 149th ed. / edited and revised throughout by N.R. Wheatley. — 1977. — xxiv,388p : ill ; 30cm.
Index.
ISBN 0-610-00489-1 Pbk : £7.00
ISSN 0305-6589
(B77-18277)

692'.5 — Local authority houses. Construction. Tendering. *England. Manuals. For local authorities*

Great Britain. *Department of the Environment.* Code of procedures for local authority housebuilding / Department of the Environment, Welsh Office. — [London] ([2 Marsham St., SW1P 3EB]) : [The Department], [1976]. — [28]p ; 30cm.
Pierced for binder.
Sd : Unpriced
Also classified at 692'.8
(B77-30444)

692'.8 — Local authority houses. Construction. Contractual arrangements. *England. Manuals. For local authorities*

Great Britain. *Department of the Environment.* Code of procedures for local authority housebuilding / Department of the Environment, Welsh Office. — [London] ([2 Marsham St., SW1P 3EB]) : [The Department], [1976]. — [28]p ; 30cm.
Pierced for binder.
Sd : Unpriced
Primary classification 692'.5
(B77-30444)

692'.8'0941 — Buildings. Construction. Small works. Contracts. Administration. *Great Britain. Manuals*

Bowyer, Jack. Small works contract documentation and how to administer it / [by] Jack Bowyer. — London : Architectural Press, 1976. — viii,95p : forms ; 31cm.
ISBN 0-85139-558-9 : £4.95
(B77-05538)

693 — BUILDINGS. CONSTRUCTION IN SPECIAL MATERIALS AND FOR SPECIAL PURPOSES

693.1 — Dry stone walls. Construction. *Manuals*

Rainsford-Hannay, Frederick. Dry stone walling / by F. Rainsford-Hannay. — 3rd ed. — Gatehouse of Fleet ([c/o Hon. Sec., Cally Estate Office, Gatehouse of Fleet, Kirkcudbrightshire DG7 2HX]) : Stewartry of Kirkcudbright, Drystane Dyking Committee, 1976. — [4],109p,[18]p of plates : ill(incl 1 col), facsim, port ; 22cm.
Previous ed.: 1972. — Index.
Pbk : Unpriced
(B77-29567)

693.1 — Stone masonry. *Amateurs' manuals*

Day, Roy. All about brickwork, stonework and concrete / [by] Roy Day. — London [etc.] : Hamlyn, 1976. — 112p : ill(some col) ; 29cm.
Index.
ISBN 0-600-30252-0 : £2.95
ISBN 0-600-30296-2 Pbk : £1.95
Primary classification 693.5
(B77-15382)

Working with bricks, concrete and stone. — London : Reader's Digest Association, 1976. — 48p : ill(some col) ; 27cm. — ('Reader's digest' basic guide)
'The text and illustrations in this book are taken from "The 'Reader's Digest' complete do-it-yourself manual" ...', 3rd ed., 2nd revise. London : Reader's Digest Association, 1975.
ISBN 0-276-00155-9 Sd : £0.75
Primary classification 693.2'1
(B77-19511)

693.1 — Stone masonry. *Standards*

British Standards Institution. Code of practice for stone masonry = Code de bonne pratique relatif à la maçonnerie en pierre = Richtlinien für Steinmallerwerk / British Standards Institution. — 1st revision. — London : B.S.I., 1976. — [2],39,[2]p : ill ; 30cm. — (BS5390 : 1976)
Pierced for binder. — '(Formerly CP121.201 and CP121.202)'.
ISBN 0-580-09426-x Sd : £5.80
(B77-02453)

693.2'1 — Brickwork. *Amateurs' manuals*

Day, Roy. All about brickwork, stonework and concrete / [by] Roy Day. — London [etc.] : Hamlyn, 1976. — 112p : ill(some col) ; 29cm.
Index.
ISBN 0-600-30252-0 : £2.95
ISBN 0-600-30296-2 Pbk : £1.95
Primary classification 693.5
(B77-15382)

Working with bricks, concrete and stone. — London : Reader's Digest Association, 1976. — 48p : ill(some col) ; 27cm. — ('Reader's digest' basic guide)
'The text and illustrations in this book are taken from "The 'Reader's Digest' complete do-it-yourself manual" ...', 3rd ed., 2nd revise. London : Reader's Digest Association, 1975.
ISBN 0-276-00155-9 Sd : £0.75
Also classified at 693.5; 693.1
(B77-19511)

693.2'1 — Brickwork. *Manuals*

Kreh, R T. Masonry skills / [by] R.T. Kreh, Sr. — New York ; London [etc.] : Van Nostrand Reinhold, 1976. — viii,325p : ill, plans ; 27cm.
Index.
ISBN 0-442-24548-3 : £7.60
(B77-00855)

693.2'1 — Brickwork. Bonding. *Exercises, worked examples*

Nash, William George. Brickwork bonding problems and solutions / [by] W.G. Nash. — London : Hutchinson, 1977. — 154p : chiefly ill ; 22cm.
ISBN 0-09-127871-6 Pbk : £1.85
(B77-25761)

693.2'1 — Buildings. Laterally loaded brick walls. Design. *Manuals*

Haseltine, Barry A. A simplified guide to the design of laterally loaded walls / by B.A. Haseltine and H.W.H. West. — Stoke-on-Trent (Queens Rd, Penkhull, Stoke-on-Trent ST4 7LQ) : British Ceramic Research Association, 1977. — 13,[1]p : ill ; 30cm. — (British Ceramic Research Association. Special publications ; no.90)
ISBN 0-900910-26-7 Sd : £4.00
(B77-10863)

693.3 — Buildings. Walls. Tiling. *Standards*

British Standards Institution. Code of practice for wall tiling = Code de bonne pratique pour carreaux muraux = Richtlinie für Wandfliesen / British Standards Institution. — London : B.S.I.
Part 1 = Partie 1 = Teil 1 : Internal ceramic wall tiling and mosaics in normal conditions = Carreaux et mosaïques céramiques pour revêtement des murs intérieurs dans les conditions normales = Keramische Fliesen und Mosaike für Innenwände unter normalen Bedingungen (formerly CP 212 : Part 1). — 1st revision. — 1976. — [2],30,[2]p : ill ; 30cm. — (BS5385 : Part 1 : 1976)
Pierced for binder.
ISBN 0-580-09286-0 Sd : £5.80
(B77-03132)

693.4 — Buildings. Concrete blockwork. *Standards*

Tovey, A K. Model specification for concrete blockwork / [by] A.K. Tovey. — Slough : Cement and Concrete Association, 1976. — [4], 12p ; 30cm.
Bibl.: p.12.
ISBN 0-7210-1053-9 Sd : £0.40
(B77-11312)

693.5 — Cattle housing. Concrete slats. Making. *Manuals*

Barnes, Maurice Malcolm. Concrete slats for cattle / [by] Maurice M. Barnes. — Slough : Cement and Concrete Association, 1977. — Folder([4]p) : ill ; 30cm. — (Farm note ; 4 ISSN 0307-0352)
ISBN 0-7210-1054-7 : £0.50
(B77-18278)

693.5 — Domestic concrete structures. *Amateurs' manuals*

Day, Roy. All about brickwork, stonework and concrete / [by] Roy Day. — London [etc.] : Hamlyn, 1976. — 112p : ill(some col) ; 29cm.
Index.
ISBN 0-600-30252-0 : £2.95
ISBN 0-600-30296-2 Pbk : £1.95
Also classified at 693.1; 693.2'1
(B77-15382)

Working with bricks, concrete and stone. — London : Reader's Digest Association, 1976. — 48p : ill(some col) ; 27cm. — ('Reader's digest' basic guide)
'The text and illustrations in this book are taken from "The 'Reader's Digest' complete do-it-yourself manual" ...', 3rd ed., 2nd revise. London : Reader's Digest Association, 1975.
ISBN 0-276-00155-9 Sd : £0.75
Primary classification 693.2'1
(B77-19511)

693.5 — Houses & flats. Building materials: Concrete. Handling on site. *Great Britain. Manuals*

Great Britain. *Department of the Environment. Property Services Agency.* Handling concrete on housing sites / Department of the Environment, Property Services Agency. — 4th ed. — [London] : H.M.S.O., 1977. — Folder([5]p) : col ill ; 21cm. — (Advisory leaflet ; 32)
Previous ed.: / issued by the Ministry of Public Building and Works. 1970. — Bibl.: p.[5].
ISBN 0-11-670703-8 : £0.20
(B77-18279)

693.5 — Houses. Improvement. Use of concrete. *Amateurs' manuals*

Beadle, David. Concrete round the house / by Dave Beadle. — 2nd ed. — London : Cement and Concrete Association, 1974. — [1],48p : ill ; 30cm.
Previous ed.: 1972.
ISBN 0-7210-0881-x Sd : £0.25
(B77-27242)

693.5'2 — Concrete floors. High-strength toppings. Construction. *Manuals*
Deacon, R Colin. High-strength concrete toppings for floors, including granolithic / [by] R. Colin Deacon. — Slough : Cement and Concrete Association, 1976. — [2],7p : ill ; 30cm. — (Cement and Concrete Association. Publications ; 48.040) (Cement and Concrete Association. Advisory notes)
ISBN 0-7210-1031-8 Sd : £0.65
(B77-03133)

693.5'2 — Recreation facilities. Playing surfaces. Construction. Use of concrete. *Manuals*
Enoch, M D. Concrete for sports and play areas / [by] M.D. Enoch. — Slough : Cement and Concrete Association, 1976. — [3],46p : ill, plans ; 30cm.
Bibl.: p.46.
ISBN 0-7210-1049-0 Sd : £2.50
(B77-20444)

693.5'4 — Reinforced concrete towers. Design
Pinfold, Geoffrey Markham. Reinforced concrete chimneys and towers / by Geoffrey M. Pinfold. — London : Cement and Concrete Association, 1975. — ix,233p : ill ; 24cm. — (Viewpoint publications)
ISBN 0-7210-0993-x : £5.00
Primary classification 697'.8
(B77-02454)

693.6 — Agricultural industries. Farms. Buildings. External walls. Rendering. *Manuals*
Barnes, Maurice Malcolm. Rendering for farm buildings / [by] Maurice M. Barnes. — Slough : Cement and Concrete Association, 1977. — Folder([6]p) : ill ; 30cm. — (Farm note ; 5 ISSN 0307-0352)
ISBN 0-7210-1055-5 : £0.50
(B77-18280)

693.6 — Plastering
Taylor, J.B. Plastering / [by] J.B. Taylor. — 2nd ed. — [London] : Godwin, 1977. — vii,229p,4p of plates : ill ; 25cm.
Previous ed.: 1970. — Bibl.: p.226-227. — Index.
ISBN 0-7114-4610-5 : £4.80
(B77-15383)

693.7'1 — Buildings. Steel structural components. Design. Use of specifications issued or endorsed by American Institute for Steel. *United States. Manuals*
Rice, Paul F. Structural design guide to AISC specifications for buildings / [by] Paul F. Rice, Edward S. Hoffman. — New York ; London [etc.] : Van Nostrand Reinhold, 1976. — viii, 360p : ill ; 27cm.
Index.
ISBN 0-442-26904-8 : £12.95
(B77-05539)

693.7'1 — Steel-framed buildings. Design. Structural analysis
Crawley, Stanley William. Steel buildings : analysis and design / [by] Stanley W. Crawley, Robert M. Dillon. — 2nd ed. / chapter 11 and appendixes D, E and F written in collaboration with the authors by Winfred O. Carter. — New York ; London [etc.] : Wiley, 1977. — xi,591p : ill, charts, plans ; 26cm.
With answers to problems. — Previous ed.: 1970. — Index.
ISBN 0-471-18552-3 : £15.25
(B77-23578)

693.8 — Buildings. Decay. Protection. *Manuals*
Richardson, Stanley A. Protecting buildings : how to combat dry rot, woodworm and damp / [by] Stanley A. Richardson. — Newton Abbot [etc.] : David and Charles, 1977. — 156p : ill ; 23cm.
Bibl.: p.151. — Index.
ISBN 0-7153-7321-8 : £4.95
(B77-21284)

693.8'2 — Buildings. Interiors. Ceiling lining materials & wall lining materials. Combustion. Surface spread of flames & heat release. Tests. Results. *Tables*
Fisher, Reynold Walter. Results of fire propagation tests on building products / [by] R.W. Fisher and Barbara F.W. Rogowski. — London : H.M.S.O. [for the] Department of the Environment and Fire Offices' Committee, Joint Fire Research Organisation, Fire Research Station, Building Research Establishment, 1976. — ix,21p : 1 ill ; 30cm. — (Building Research Establishment. Reports)
ISBN 0-11-670547-7 Sd : £1.50
(B77-29568)

693.8'2'0941 — Buildings. Fire resistance. Testing. *Great Britain. Reports, surveys*
Results of fire resistance tests on elements of building construction / compiled by R.W. Fisher and P.M.T. Smart. — London : H.M.S.O. [for the] Department of the Environment and Fire Offices' Committee, Joint Fire Research Organisation, Fire Research Station, Building Research Establishment. — (Building Research Establishment. Reports)
Vol.2. — 1977. — vii,27p : ill ; 30cm.
Index.
ISBN 0-11-670548-5 Sd : £1.15
(B77-27243)

693.8'32 — Buildings. Heat. Conservation
Electricity Council. Heat recovery / [Electricity Council]. — [London] ([30 Millbank, S.W.1]) : [The Council], [1977?]. — 16p : ill(chiefly col) ; 30cm.
Sd : Unpriced
(B77-32025)

693.8'32 — Residences. Thermal insulation. *Amateurs' manuals*
Colesby, John Allan. Keeping warm for half the cost / [by] J.A. Colesby & P.J. Townsend. — Dorchester (Stable Court, Chalmington, Dorchester, Dorset DT2 0HB) : Prism Press, 1975. — [4],90,[1]p : ill, map ; 22cm.
Also published: Mountsorrel : The author, 1975.
ISBN 0-904727-34-3 : Unpriced
ISBN 0-904727-35-1 Pbk : £1.50
(B77-27968)

693.8'32 — Residences. Thermal insulation. *Practical information*
Hudson, Mike. The great heat escape : a report on home insulation / by Mike Hudson. — Durham (Vane Tempest Hall, Durham) : Friends of the Earth, Durham, 1975. — [2],12,[2]p : ill ; 30cm.
ISBN 0-905605-00-4 Sd : £0.16
(B77-11969)

Northumbria Habitat. Wrap up warmer : a guide to cheap insulation & how to get it paid for / [Northumbria Habitat]. — [s.l.] : Northumbria Habitat ; Durham (Vane Tempest Hall, Gilesgate, Durham DH1 1QC) : Friends of the Earth (Durham), 1976. — [8]p : 1 ill ; 21cm.
ISBN 0-905605-02-0 Sd : £0.05
(B77-12568)

693.8'32 — Residences. Thermal insulation. *Practical information. Teaching kits*
Friends of the Earth, Durham. Home insulation project pack / [Friends of the Earth, Durham]. — Durham (Vane Tempest Hall, Gilesgate, Durham) : Friends of the Earth, Durham, [1976]. — 1v. : ill(some col), forms ; 22x36cm.
Twenty-one items in portfolio. — Bibl.
ISBN 0-905605-01-2 : £1.00
(B77-14318)

694 — CARPENTRY, JOINERY
694 — Buildings. Construction. Carpentry. *Manuals*
Ball, John E. Exterior and interior trim / [by] John E. Ball. — New York ; London [etc.] : Van Nostrand Reinhold, [1976]. — v,192p : ill ; 27cm.
Published in the United States: 1975. — Index.
ISBN 0-442-20543-0 : £4.75
(B77-03134)

694 — Construction materials: Timber. Use. *Standards*
British Standards Institution. Code of practice for the structural use of timber = Code de bonne pratique relatif à l'utilisation de bois de charpente = Richtlinien für Holz für Bauzwecke / British Standards Institution. — London : B.S.I.
Part 5 = Partie 5 = Teil 5 : Preservative treatments for constructional timber = Traitement de protection du bois de charpente = Schutzbehandlungen für Bauholz. — 2nd revision. — 1976. — [2],12,[2]p ; 30cm. — (BS5268 : Part 5 : 1977)
Pierced for binder. — '(Formerly CP 98)'.
ISBN 0-580-08897-9 Sd : £3.60
(B77-11313)

695 — ROOFING, AUXILIARY STRUCTURES
695 — Agricultural industries. Farms. Buildings. Roofing. *Manuals*
Agricultural Development and Advisory Service. Floor construction and sheet roofing / Ministry of Agriculture, Fisheries and Food, ADAS. — London : H.M.S.O., 1977. — [1],30p : ill ; 25cm. — (Fixed equipment of the farm ; leaflet 38)
ISBN 0-11-240578-9 Sd : £0.60
Primary classification 690'.1'6
(B77-16504)

695'.021'2 — Roof coverings. *Technical data. Serials*
Roofing. — Edenbridge (25 High St., Edenbridge, Kent) : A4 Publications Ltd. — (Architects' and specifiers' guide series)
1975-6. — 1975. — 348p : ill ; 30cm.
ISBN 0-510-07010-8 Pbk : £3.50
(B77-25077)

[1976-7]. — 1976. — 320p : ill ; 30cm.
Index.
ISBN 0-510-07018-3 Pbk : £3.50
(B77-25078)

[1977-8]. — 1977. — 288p : ill ; 30cm.
Index.
ISBN 0-510-07033-7 Pbk : £3.50
(B77-25079)

695'.3 — Concrete shell roofs. Design
Wilby, Charles Bryan. Concrete shell roofs / [by] C.B. Wilby and I. Khwaja. — London : Applied Science Publishers, 1977. — xiv,327p : ill ; 23cm.
Bibl.: p.143-147. — Index.
ISBN 0-85334-579-1 : £20.00
(B77-14832)

696 — PLUMBING, PIPE FITTING, HOT WATER SUPPLY
696 — Buildings. Engineering services
Andrews, Franklin Thomas. Building mechanical systems / [by] F.T. Andrews. — New York ; London [etc.] : McGraw-Hill, 1977. — ix, 401p : ill, forms, map ; 29cm.
Originally published: as 'The architect's guide to mechanical systems'. New York : Reinhold ; London : Chapman and Hall, 1966. — Bibl.: p.233. — Index.
ISBN 0-07-001847-2 : £18.40
(B77-25080)

McGuinness, William James. Building technology : mechanical & electrical systems / [by] William J. McGuinness, Benjamin Stein. — New York ; London [etc.] : Wiley, 1977. — xv, 596p : ill, forms, map, plans ; 29cm.
Bibl. — Index.
ISBN 0-471-58433-9 : £15.00
(B77-17641)

696'.1 — Residences. Plumbing. *Amateurs' manuals*
Day, Roy. All about plumbing and central heating / [by] Roy Day. — London [etc.] : Hamlyn, 1976. — 112p : ill(chiefly col) ; 29cm.
Index.
ISBN 0-600-30254-7 : £2.95
ISBN 0-600-30297-0 Pbk : £1.95
(B77-06205)

Hall, Ernest. Beginner's guide to domestic plumbing / [by] Ernest Hall. — Sevenoaks : Newnes Technical Books, 1977. — [7],200p : ill ; 19cm.
Index.
ISBN 0-408-00283-2 Pbk : £2.85
(B77-32026)

Hall, Ernest. Home plumbing / [by] Ernest Hall. — Sevenoaks : Newnes Technical Books, 1977. — [8],102p : ill(chiefly col) ; 25cm. — (Do it yourself)
Index.
ISBN 0-408-00246-8 Pbk : £2.90
(B77-16505)

696'.12 — Cold water. Water supply equipment: Plastics pipes. Use. *Manuals*
Great Britain. *Department of the Environment. Property Services Agency.* Plastic pipes for cold water supply / Department of the Environment, Property Services Agency. — 2nd ed. — [London] : H.M.S.O., 1977. — Folder ([5]p) : ill ; 21cm. — (Advisory leaflet ; 76)
Previous ed.: / issued by the Ministry of Public Building and Works. 1969. — Bibl.: p.[5].
ISBN 0-11-670701-1 : £0.15
(B77-11314)

696'.12 — Draw-off water taps. *Standards*
British Standards Institution. Specification for the performance of draw-off taps with metal bodies for water services = Spécification pour la performance des robinets d'alimentation à corps métallique pour les services d'eau = Spezifikation für die Leistung von Speisehähnen mit metallischem Körper für Wasserdienste ; [and], Specification for the performance of draw-off taps with plastics bodies for water services = Spécification pour la performance des robinets d'alimentation à corps en matières plastiques pour les services d'eau = Spezifikation für die Leistung von Speisehähnen mit Kunststoffkörper für Wasserdienste / British Standards Institution. — London : B.S.I.
Part 5 = Partie 5 = Teil 5 : Physio-chemical characteristics = Caractéristiques physio-chimiques = Physio-chemische Eigenschaften : materials, coatings = matériaux, revêtements = Materialüberzüge. — 1976. — [2],9,[1]p : ill ; 30cm. — (BS5412 : Part 5 : 1976) (BS5413 : Part 5 : 1976)
Pierced for binder.
ISBN 0-580-09058-2 Sd : £2.70
(B77-11971)

Part 4 = Partie 4 = Teil 4 : Mechanical and endurance characteristics = Caractéristiques mécaniques et d'endurance = Mechanische Eigenschaften und Daverhaftigkeit. — 1976. — [2],4,[2]p : 1 ill ; 30cm. — (BS5412 : Part 4 : 1976) (BS5413 : Part 4 : 1976)
Pierced for binder.
ISBN 0-580-09018-3 Sd : £1.60
(B77-11970)

Part 1 = Partie 1 = Teil 1 : Dimensional and design characteristics = Caractéristiques dimensionelles et de calcul = Abmessungs- und Berechnungseigenschaften. — 1976. — [2],12,[2]p : ill ; 30cm. — (BS5412 : Part 1 : 1976) (BS5413 : Part 1 : 1976)
Pierced for binder.
ISBN 0-580-09427-8 Sd : £3.60
(B77-11974)

Part 2 = Partie 2 = Teil 2 : Water tightness and pressure resistance characteristics = Caractéristiques d'étanchéité a l'eau et de résistance à pression = Wasserdichtigkeits- und Druckhaltungs-eigenschaften. — 1976. — [2],2,[2]p ; 30cm. — (BS5412 : Part 2 : 1976) (BS5413 : Part 2 : 1976)
Pierced for binder.
ISBN 0-580-09477-4 Sd : £1.60
(B77-11972)

Part 3 = Partie 1 [i.e. 3] = Teil 3 : Hydraulic characteristics = Caractéristiques hydrauliques = Hydraulische Eigenschaften. — 1976. — [2],5,[1]p : ill ; 30cm. — (BS5412 : Part 3 : 1976) (BS5413 : Part 3 : 1976)
Pierced for binder.
ISBN 0-580-09497-9 Sd : £2.70
(B77-11973)

696'.12 — Residences. Water supply systems. *For architecture*
Great Britain. *Department of the Environment. Housing Development Directorate.* Water services for housing / Housing Development Directorate, Department of the Environment. — [London] ([Room 1107, 1 Lambeth Palace Rd, SE1 7ER]) : [The Directorate].
Parts 1-4. — 1976. — [1],i,24p : ill ; 30cm. — (Housing development note ; 5)
Pierced for binder. — Bibl.
Sd : Unpriced
(B77-16992)

696'.12 — Underground copper alloy water stop valves. *Standards*
British Standards Institution. Specification for underground stopvalves for water services = Spécification des robinets d'arrêt souterrains pour les services d'eau = Spezifikation für unterirdische Abstellarmaturen für Wasserdienste / British Standards Institution. — London : B.S.I., 1976. — [2],14,[2]p : ill ; 30cm. — (BS5433 : 1976)
Pierced for binder.
ISBN 0-580-09630-0 Sd : £4.70
(B77-11975)

696'.13 — Buildings. Drainage systems. Flexible pipes. Installation. *Manuals*
Great Britain. *Department of the Environment. Property Services Agency.* Flexible drain and sewer pipes / Department of the Environment, Property Services Agency. — 3rd ed. — [London] : H.M.S.O., 1977. — Folder([5]p) : col ill ; 21cm. — (Advisory leaflet ; 66)
Previous ed.: 1971. — Bibl.: p.[5].
ISBN 0-11-670700-3 : £0.15
(B77-15966)

696'.182 — Lavatories. *Northumberland, to 1976*
Graham, Frank, *b.1913.* The Geordie netty : a short history and guide / by Frank Graham. — Newcastle upon Tyne : F. Graham, 1977. — 32p : ill ; 22cm. — (Northern history booklet ; no.1001 ISSN 0550-855x)
Sd : £0.50
(B77-29569)

696'.6 — Residences. Solar energy hot water supply systems. Installation. *Amateurs' manuals*
Kiely, Charles. Solar energy : a do-it-yourself manual / [by] Charles Kiely. — London [etc.] : Hamlyn, 1977. — 88p : ill, 2 charts, port ; 26cm.
Bibl.: p.85-86.
ISBN 0-600-38265-6 Pbk : £2.50
(B77-27244)

697 — HEATING, VENTILATING

697 — Buildings. Air conditioning, heating & ventilation equipment. Control systems
Haines, Roger William. Control systems for heating, ventilating and air conditioning / [by] Roger W. Haines. — 2nd ed. — New York ; London [etc.] : Van Nostrand Reinhold, 1977. — xvii,233p : ill ; 24cm. — (Van Nostrand Reinhold environmental engineering series)
Previous ed.: 1971. — Index.
ISBN 0-442-23031-1 : £11.75
(B77-23579)

697 — Buildings. Air conditioning, heating & ventilation equipment. Control systems. *Standards*
British Standards Institution. Guide to the selection and use of control systems for heating, ventilating and air conditioning installations = Guide pour le choix et l'utilisation des systèmes de contrôle des installations de chauffage, de ventilation et de climatisation = Hinweise zur Auswahl und Verwendung von Stevervorrichtungen für Heizungs- Belüftungs- und Klimaanlagen / British Standards Institution. — London : B.S.I., 1977. — [2],29,[2]p : ill ; 30cm. — (BS5384 : 1977)
Pierced for binder.
ISBN 0-580-09106-6 Sd : £6.60
(B77-11976)

697 — Buildings. Heating. Effects of meteorological conditions
Anapol'skaia, L E. Environmental factors in the heating of buildings / [by] L.E. Arapol'skaya and L.S. Gandin ; translated from Russian by H. Olaru ; translation edited by P. Greenberg. — New York [etc.] : Wiley ; Jerusalem ; London : Israel Program for Scientific Translations ; Chichester : Distributed by Wiley, [1977]. — ix,238p : ill, charts ; 25cm.
'A Halsted Press book'. — This translation published in the United States: 1975. — Translation of: 'Meteorologischeskie faktory teplovogo rezhima zdaniĭ'. Leningrad : Gidrometeoizdat, 1973. — Index.
ISBN 0-470-02557-3 : £16.40
(B77-11977)

697'.03 — Commercial buildings. Central heating systems. Efficiency. Determination. Use of degree days. *Great Britain*
Great Britain. *Department of Energy.* Degree days / Department of Energy. — London (Library, Thames House South, Millbank, SW1P 4QJ) : The Department, [1977]. — [1],12p : ill, map ; 21cm. — (Fuel efficiency booklet ; 7)
Bibl.: p.12.
ISBN 0-904552-16-0 Sd : Free
(B77-09140)

697'.03 — Residences. Central heating systems. *Consumers' guides*
Bowyer, John. Central heating : a complete guide / [by] John Bowyer. — Newton Abbot [etc.] : David and Charles, 1977. — 144p : ill ; 22cm.
Index.
ISBN 0-7153-7037-5 : £3.95
(B77-14833)

697'.03 — Residences. Central heating systems. *Standards*
British Standards Institution. Code of practice for central heating for domestic premises = Code de bonne pratique relatif au chauffage central pour les immeubles domestiques = Richtlinien Zentralheizung für Haushaltsgrundstücke / British Standards Institution. — London : B.S.I.
Part 1 = Partie 1 = Teil 1 : Forced circulation hot water systems = Systèmes à circulation d'eau chaude sous pression = Warmwasserraumversorgung mit Zwangsumlauf. — 1st revision. — 1977. — [2],14,[2]p : ill ; 30cm. — (BS5449 : Part 1 : 1977)
Pierced for binder. — 'formerly CP3006 : Part 1'.
ISBN 0-580-09511-8 Sd : £4.70
(B77-14834)

697'.042 — Household solid fuel heating appliances. Installation. *Manuals*
Great Britain. *Department of the Environment. Property Services Agency.* Installing solid fuel appliances / Department of the Environment, Property Services Agency. — [London] : H.M.S.O.
1 : Open fires and convectors. — 3rd ed. — 1977. — Folder([5]p) : ill ; 21cm. — (Advisory leaflet ; 30)
Previous ed.: / issued by the Ministry of Public Building and Works. 1969. — Bibl.: p.[5].
ISBN 0-11-670704-6 : £0.20
(B77-18281)

697'.042'0212 — Household solid fuel heating appliances. *Lists*
Approved domestic solid fuel appliances / issued jointly by the Solid Fuel Advisory Service [and the] Solid Smokeless Fuels Federation. — London (Hobart House, Grosvenor Place, SW1X 7AE) : Solid Fuel Advisory Service ; Wembley : Solid Smokeless Fuels Federation.
1976-7 : List no.33 (cancelling list number 32 dated 1975-6). — [1977]. — [2],28,[2]p ; 30cm. — (Cl/SfB(56))
'The official list of all appliances approved up to the 31st July, 1976 by the Domestic Solid Fuel Appliances Approval Scheme for the National Coal Board'. — Index.
Sd : Unpriced
(B77-12569)

697'.07 — Oil burning equipment. *Standards*
British Standards Institution. Code of practice for oil firing = Code de bonne pratique pour chauffe au mazout = Richtlinie für Ölfeuerung / British Standards Institution. — London : B.S.I.
Part 3 = Partie 3 = Teil 3 : Installations for furnaces, kilns, ovens and other industrial purposes = Installations pour fourneaux, fours, étuves et d'autres applications industrielle = Anlagen für Brennöfen, Schachtöfen, Backöfen und andere gewerbliche Zwecke. — 1976. — [2],34,[2]p : 1 ill ; 30cm. — (BS5410 : Part 3 : 1976)
Pierced for binder. — '(Formerly part of CP 3002 : Parts 1,2 and 3)'.
ISBN 0-580-09128-7 Sd : £5.80
(B77-09834)

697'.22'0222 — Stoves, 1750-1940. *Illustrations*
Reid, Jo. Stove book / [by] Jo Reid and John Peck. — London (51 Endell St., WC2H 9AJ) : Mathews Miller Dunbar Ltd, 1977. — [84]p : chiefly col ill ; 21cm.
ISBN 0-903811-22-7 Pbk : £2.95
(B77-33928)

697'.4 — Sealed hot water heating systems. Expansion vessels using internal diaphragms. *Standards*
British Standards Institution. Specification for expansion vessels using an internal diaphragm, for sealed hot water heating systems / British Standards Institution. — 1st revision. — London : B.S.I., 1976. — [2],6,[2]p : ill ; 30cm. — (BS4814 : 1976)
Pierced for binder.
ISBN 0-580-09177-5 Sd : £2.40
(B77-03665)

697'.54'05 — District heating. *Yearbooks*
District Heating Association. Annual handbook / District Heating Association. — Caterham (Bedford House, Stafford Rd, Caterham, Surrey CR3 6JA) : The Association.
1977 : 8th ed. — [1977]. — 68p : ill, plan, ports ; 30cm.
Index.
Pbk : £10.00
(B77-21285)

697'.78 — Buildings. Heating & air conditioning. Use of solar energy. *Manuals*
Kreider, Jan F. Solar heating and cooling : engineering, practical design and economics / [by] Jan F. Kreider, Frank Kreith. — Washington, D.C. : Scripta Book Company ; New York ; London [etc.] : McGraw-Hill, [1976]. — ix,342p : ill, maps, plans ; 24cm.
Published in the United States: 1975. — Bibl.: p.337-338. — Index.
ISBN 0-07-035473-1 : £18.70
(B77-03135)

697'.78 — Buildings. Solar energy heating systems. Testing. *Conference proceedings*
Testing of solar collectors and systems : [proceedings of] conference (C11) at the the [sic.] Royal Institution, April 1977. — London (c/o The Royal Institution, 21 Albemarle St., W1X 4BS) : International Solar Energy Society, UK Section, [1977]. — [1],82p : ill ; 30cm. — (International Solar Energy Society. UK Section. Conferences ; C11 ISSN 0306-7874)
Pbk : £4.50
(B77-20445)

697'.78 — Residences. Solar energy heating systems
Szokolay, Steven Vajk. Solar energy and building / [by] S.V. Szokolay. — 2nd ed. — London : Architectural Press [etc.], 1977. — [12],174p : ill, chart, plans ; 31cm.
Previous ed.: 1975. — Index.
ISBN 0-85139-570-8 : £6.95
(B77-32746)

697'.78 — Swimming pools. Heating. Use of solar energy. *Conference proceedings*
Solar energy for heating swimming pools : UK-ISES conference at the Polytechnic of the South Bank, London, January 1977. — London (c/o The Royal Institution, 21 Albemarle St., W.1) : UK Section of the International Solar Energy Society, [1977]. — [1],34p : ill ; 30cm. — (International Solar Energy Society. UK Section. Conferences ; C10 ISSN 0306-7874)
Cover title.
ISBN 0-904963-14-4 Pbk : £3.00(£1.00 to members)
(B77-13751)

697'.78'0973 — Buildings. Solar energy heating systems. *United States*
Anderson, Bruce. Solar energy : fundamentals in building design / [by] Bruce Anderson. — New York ; London [etc.] : McGraw-Hill, 1977. — ix,374p : ill, charts, plans ; 25cm.
Bibl.: p.359-370. — Index.
ISBN 0-07-001751-4 : £16.15
(B77-30445)

697'.78'0973 — Houses. Heating. Use of solar energy. *United States. Amateurs' manuals*
Daniels, George, *b.1914.* Solar homes and sun heating / [by] George Daniels. — New York [etc.] ; London : Harper and Row, 1976. — [9], 178p : ill, charts ; 22cm.
Index.
ISBN 0-06-010937-8 : £4.50
(B77-33331)

697'.8 — Gas appliances. Air vents & flues. *Standards*
British Standards Institution. Code of practice for flues and air supply for gas appliances of rated input not exceeding 60kW (1st and 2nd family gases) = Code de tonne pratique. Gaines d'évacuation et approvisionnement d'air pour les appareils à gaz de puissance nominale inférieure ou égale à 60kW (gaz des familles 1 et 2) = Richtlinie. Abfuhrrohre und Luftzufuhr für Gasgeräte mit einer Nennwärmebelastung bis 60kW (Gase der ersten und zweiten Familie) / British Standards Institution. — London : B.S.I.
Part 2 = Partie 2 = Teil 2 : Air supply = Approvisionnement d'air = Luftzufuhr. — 1976. — [2],7,[2]p : ill ; 30cm. — (BS5440 : Part 2 : 1976)
Pierced for binder.
ISBN 0-580-09800-1 Sd : £2.70
(B77-11978)

697'.8 — Heating systems. Multi-flue chimneys. Design
Great Britain. *Department of the Environment. Directorate of Civil Engineering Development.* Design of multi-flue chimneys / [Department of the Environment, Directorate of Civil Engineering Development]. — [London] : [The Directorate], [1977]. — vii,96p : ill ; 30cm.
Cover title: Multi flue chimneys : a design guide.
Sp : £5.00
Also classified at 628'.445
(B77-32027)

697'.8 — Reinforced concrete chimneys. Design
Pinfold, Geoffrey Markham. Reinforced concrete chimneys and towers / by Geoffrey M. Pinfold. — London : Cement and Concrete Association, 1975. — ix,233p : ill ; 24cm. — (Viewpoint publications)
ISBN 0-7210-0993-x : £5.00
Also classified at 693.5'4
(B77-02454)

697.9'2 — Buildings. Ventilation equipment. Noise. Control measures
Atkins Research and Development. The control of noise in ventilation systems : a designers' guide / Atkins Research and Development ; edited by M.A. Iqbal, T.K. Willson, R.J. Thomas. — London : Spon, 1977. — vii,107p : ill ; 31cm.
'Initially ... prepared as a guide for use within the Atkins Group ... it was decided to publish it as a guide for general use ...' - Preface. — Bibl.: p.103. — Index.
ISBN 0-419-11050-x : £9.00
(B77-11315)

697.9'3 — Air conditioning. Scientific aspects
Kimura, Ken-Ichi. Scientific basis of air conditioning / [by] Ken-Ichi Kimura. — London : Applied Science Publishers, 1977. — viii,269p : ill ; 23cm. — (Architectural science series)
Bibl.: p.259-263. — Index.
ISBN 0-85334-732-8 : £15.00
(B77-32747)

697.9'35'4 — Industrial buildings. Air conditioning equipment. Regulation. *Manuals*
Building Services Research and Information Association. Manual for regulating air conditioning installations / [Building Services Research and Information Association]. — Bracknell : B.S.R.I.A., 1975. — iv,48p : ill, form ; 30cm. — (Building Services Research and Information Association. Application guides ; 1/75)
Bibl.: p.48.
ISBN 0-86022-009-5 Sd : Unpriced
(B77-18892)

698 — BUILDINGS. DECORATING, GLAZING, ETC

698 — Buildings. Decorating
Tubb, Leslie Francis James. Painting and decorating / [by] L.F.J. Tubb. — 3rd ed. — London [etc.] : Macmillan, 1976. — ix,151p : ill ; 25cm. — (Basic building series)
Previous ed.: i.e. 2nd ed., revised. 1974. — Index.
ISBN 0-333-21159-6 Pbk : £2.25
(B77-13137)

698.9 — Contract carpeting. *Technical data. Serials*
Contract carpeting. — Edenbridge (25 High St., Edenbridge, Kent) : A4 Publications Ltd. — (Architects' and specifiers' guide series)
1975-6. — 1975. — 188p : ill ; 30cm.
ISBN 0-510-07012-4 Pbk : £3.50
(B77-25064)

[1976-7]. — 1976. — 160p : ill ; 30cm.
Index.
ISBN 0-510-07023-x Pbk : £3.50
(B77-27245)

698.9 — Floor coverings. Choice. Criteria: Costs in use. *Great Britain*
Guide to the choice of wall and floor surfacing materials : a costs in use approach / based on a report by the National Building Agency ; edited by Harry Miller. — London : Hutchinson, 1976. — 71p : ill ; 31cm.
Bibl.: p.71.
ISBN 0-09-127650-0 : £6.50
Primary classification 690'.1'2
(B77-00854)

698.9'05 — Floor coverings. *Serials*
Flooring. — Edenbridge (25 High St., Edenbridge, Kent) : A4 Publications Ltd. — (Architects' and specifiers' guide series)
[1976-7]. — 1976. — 224p : ill(some col) ; 30cm.
Index.
ISBN 0-510-07016-7 Pbk : £3.50
(B77-05540)

700 — ARTS
Barzun, Jacques. The use and abuse of art / by Jacques Barzun. — Princeton [N.J.] ; London : Princeton University Press, 1975. — [6],150p ; 22cm. — (Bollingen series ; 35) (A.W. Mellon lectures in the fine arts ; 22)
Originally published: 1974.
ISBN 0-691-01804-9 Pbk : Unpriced
(B77-18893)

700 — Arts. *Juvenile literature*
Currah, Ann. The creative arts / by Ann Currah ; foreword by James Burke. — Glasgow [etc.] : Collins, 1977. — 159p : ill(chiefly col) ; 25cm. — (This is our world)
Index.
ISBN 0-00-106127-5 : £3.95
(B77-25762)

700 — Arts. *League of Socialist Artists viewpoints*
League of Socialist Artists. Manifesto ; &, Theses on art. 3rd and enlarged ed. / the League of Socialist Artists. — London (18 Camberwell Church St., S.E.5) : The League, [1977]. — [1], 19p ; 33cm.
Previous ed. of 'Theses on art': 1973.
Sd : £0.40
(B77-33929)

700 — Arts. Censorship. *Great Britain. Periodicals*
Uncensored : journal of the Defence of Literature and the Arts Society. — London (18 Brewer St., W1R 4AS) : The Society.
No.1- ; Spring 1977-. — [1977]-. — ill ; 21cm.
Two issues a year. — [1],14p. in 1st issue.
Sd : £0.20
ISSN 0140-1351
(B77-28750)

700 — Arts, to 1976. Special themes: Swans
Lister, Raymond. For love of Leda / by Raymond Lister. — Linton (Linton, Cambs. [CB1 6NS]) : Windmill House Press, 1976. — [15]leaves : col ill tipped in ; 17cm.
Spine title: Leda. — Limited ed. of 14 signed copies. — In slip case.
Pbk : £50.00
(B77-18894)

700 — Visual arts
Preble, Duane. We create art creates us / [by] Duane Preble. — San Francisco : Canfield Press ; New York [etc.] ; London : Harper and Row, 1976. — [6],272p,[32]p of plates : ill(some col), plans, ports ; 31cm.
'Brief edition [i.e. abridgement] of: "Man creates art creates man"'. Berkeley : McCutchan Publishing, 1973. — Bibl.: p.260-263. — Index.
ISBN 0-06-386829-6 Pbk : Unpriced
(B77-01653)

700 — Visual arts. Related to dancing
Watts, Elizabeth. Towards dance and art : a study of relationships between two art forms / [by] Elizabeth Watts. — London : Lepus Books, 1977. — x,110p : ill ; 22cm.
Bibl.: p.104-106. — Index.
ISBN 0-86019-027-7 : £3.80
Also classified at 793.3
(B77-13752)

700 — Visual arts. Social aspects
Bell, Quentin. A demotic art / by Quentin Bell. — [Southampton] ([Highfield, Southampton SO9 5NH]) : University of Southampton, 1976. — 20p ; 21cm. — (Gwilym James memorial lecture ; 5th)
'... delivered at the University on Tuesday, 4 May, 1976'.
ISBN 0-85432-158-6 Sd : £0.40
(B77-03666)

700'.1 — Arts. Aesthetics
Chiari, Joseph. Art and knowledge / [by] Joseph Chiari. — London : Elek, 1977. — x,132p ; 23cm.
Bibl.: p.125-127. — Index.
ISBN 0-236-40017-7 : £5.25
(B77-13138)

Harbison, Robert. Eccentric spaces / [by] Robert Harbison. — London : Deutsch, 1977. — xii, 177p ; 24cm.
Index.
ISBN 0-233-96878-4 : £3.50
(B77-22006)

700'.1 — Arts. Semiotic aspects. *Readings*
Semiotics of art : Prague School contributions / edited by Ladislav Matejka and Irwin R. Titunik ; [translated from the French and Czech]. — Cambridge, Mass. ; London : M.I.T. Press, 1976. — xxi,298p ; 21cm.
Index.
ISBN 0-262-13117-x : £13.50
(B77-02455)

700'.5 — Arts. *Periodicals*
Artifact. — London (70 Warriner Gardens, SW11 4DX) : Rosedale Publications Ltd.
Issue 1- ; [June] 1976-. — [1976]-. — ill(some col), ports ; 30cm.
Quarterly. — 60p. in 1st issue. — Bibl.: p.8.
Sd : £0.75
ISSN 0309-202x
(B77-04950)

Ferment : a quarterly magazine of poetry, politics and the arts. — Edinburgh (2 Rochester Terrace, Edinburgh EH10) : Ferment Publications.
[No.1]- ; Sept. 1976-. — 1976-. — 21cm.
[2],30p. in 1st issue.
Sd : £0.45
(B77-19512)

Kipple. — London (4 Holmside Court, Nightingale La., Balham, SW12 5JW) : David Wingrove.
[No.] 1- ; Feb. 1977-. — 1977-. — 30cm.
45p. in 1st issue.
Sd : Unpriced
ISSN 0309-3301
(B77-16993)

700'.7'9 — Eisteddfodau. *Wales. Eisteddfod Genedlaethol Frenhinol Cymru, to 1976. Welsh texts*
Edwards, Hywel Teifi. Yr Eisteddfod : cyfrol ddathlu wythganmlwyddiant yr Eisteddfod, 1176-1976 / [gan] Hywel Teifi Edwards. — Llandysul : Gwasg Gomer [ar ran] Llys yr Eisteddfod Genedlaethol, 1976. — [11],85p : ill, facsims, ports ; 22cm.
Bibl.: p.85.
ISBN 0-85088-376-8 : £1.75
(B77-10467)

700'.8 — Arts. *League of Socialist Artists viewpoints. Readings*
League of Socialist Artists. Class war in the arts! : the League of Socialist Artists v. the 'art and culture' agencies of monopoly capital : a collection of documents in struggle against corporate reaction in art produced by the League of Socialist Artists since its foundation in May 1971. — [London] ([18 Camberwell Church St., S.E.5]) : [The League], [1976]. — [1],iv,52p : ill, facsims, port ; 30cm.
ISBN 0-9501540-7-5 Sd : £0.75
(B77-05541)

700'.92'2 — English arts. Bloomsbury Group
Shone, Richard. Bloomsbury portraits : Vanessa Bell, Duncan Grant, and their circle / [by] Richard Shone. — Oxford : Phaidon, 1976. — 272p,viii p of plates : ill(some col), facsims, ports(some col) ; 25cm.
Bibl.: p.266-269. — Index.
ISBN 0-7148-1628-0 : £8.95
(B77-16994)

700'.92'4 — Arts. Theories of Plato
Murdoch, Iris. The fire & the sun : why Plato banished the artists : based upon the Romanes Lecture 1976 / [by] Iris Murdoch. — Oxford : Clarendon Press, 1977. — [5],89p ; 23cm.
ISBN 0-19-824580-7 : £2.50 : CIP rev.
(B77-09835)

700'.92'4 — British experimental arts, 1972-1975. Projects designed by Willats, Stephen
Willats, Stephen. Art and social function : three projects / [by] Stephen Willats. — London : Latimer New Dimensions, 1976. — [4],51p,[68] p of plates : ill, facsims, forms, maps ; 24cm.
ISBN 0-901539-42-2 Pbk : £6.50
(B77-06792)

700'.92'4 — European arts, ca 1945-ca 1975. *Personal observations. Polish texts*
Laks, Szymon. Epiozody, epigramy, epistoly / Szymon Laks. — Londyn [i.e. London] : Oficyna Poetów i Malarzy, 1976. — 187p,[6]p of plates : ports ; 22cm.
Index.
ISBN 0-902571-89-3 Pbk : £3.50
(B77-06793)

700'.94 — European arts. Dadaism
Dada : monograph of a movement / edited by Willy Verkauf. — London : Academy Editions [etc.], 1975. — 109p : ill, facsims, ports ; 30cm.

Originally published: in English, German and French. Teufen : A. Niggli ; London : Tiranti, 1957. — Bibl.: p.98-105. — Index.
ISBN 0-85670-275-7 : £5.95
ISBN 0-85670-280-3 Pbk : £3.95
(B77-00316)

700'.941 — Popular arts. Social aspects. *Great Britain. Readings*
Arts in society / edited by Paul Barker. — [London] : Fontana, 1977. — 285p : ill ; 18cm. — (Fontana communications series)
'A "New Society" Collection'. — Index.
ISBN 0-00-633813-5 Pbk : £1.50
(B77-14835)

700'.9417 — Arts. *Ireland (Republic). Periodicals*
The **crane** bag. — [Dublin] ([Balnagowan, Palmerston Park, Dublin 6]) : ['The Crane Bag'].
Vol.1, no.1- ; Spring 1977-. — 1977-. — ill ; 25cm.
Two issues a year. — Cover title. — 93p., plate in 1st issue.
Pbk : £3.00 yearly
ISSN 0332-060x
(B77-25763)

700'.942 — English arts. Pre-Raphaelitism. *Critical studies*
Williamson, Audrey. Artists and writers in revolt : the Pre-Raphaelites / [by] Audrey Williamson. — Newton Abbot [etc.] : David and Charles, 1976. — 208p ; 23cm.
Bibl.: p.197-202. — Index.
ISBN 0-7153-7262-9 : £4.95
(B77-09141)

700'.9421 — Arts. *London, 1939-1945*
Hewison, Robert. Under siege : literary life in London, 1939-1945 / [by] Robert Hewison. — London : Weidenfeld and Nicolson, 1977. — x, 219p,[16]p of plates : ill, map, ports ; 23cm.
Bibl.: p.187-202. — Index.
ISBN 0-297-77326-7 : £6.00
(B77-22729)

700'.944'36 — Arts. *France. Paris, 1918-1939*
Monnier, Adrienne. The very rich hours of Adrienne Monnier / translated [from the French] with an introduction and commentaries by Richard McDougall. — London [etc.] : Millington, 1976. — viii,536p : ill, ports ; 24cm.

These translations also published: New York : Scribner, 1976. — 'Parts of this book were originally published in French in "Les Gazettes d'Adrienne Monnier, 1925-1945", René Julliard, 1953 ; "Dernières Gazettes et Ecrits divers", Mercure de France, 1961 ; "Rue de l'Odéon", Editions Albin Michel, 1960' - title page verso. — Index.
ISBN 0-86000-067-2 : £7.50
(B77-08467)

701 — VISUAL ARTS. PHILOSOPHY AND THEORY

701 — Visual arts. Political aspects
Triesman, Susan. Art and political action / prepared for the [Open University Art and Environment] Course Team by Susan Triesman and Janet Woollacott. — Milton Keynes : Open University Press, 1977. — 64p,[4]p of plates : ill(some col), facsim, ports ; 30cm. — ([Technology/arts/social sciences], a second level interdisciplinary course : art and environment ; unit 16) (TAD292 ; 16)
Bibl.: p.61-62.
ISBN 0-335-06215-6 Pbk : Unpriced
(B77-28751)

701'.15 — Artists. Development. Psychological aspects
Getzels, Jacob Warren. The creative vision : a longitudinal study of problem finding in art / [by] Jacob W. Getzels, Mihaly Csikszentmihalyi. — New York ; London [etc.] : Wiley, 1976. — x,293p : ill ; 24cm.
'A Wiley-Interscience publication'. — Bibl.: p.277-283. — Index.
ISBN 0-471-01486-9 : £14.30
(B77-04317)

701'.15 — Visual arts. Related to visual perception
Gombrich, Ernst Hans. Art and illusion : a study in the psychology of pictorial representation / by E.H. Gombrich. — 5th ed. — London : Phaidon, 1977. — xiv,386p,[4]p of plates : ill(some col), facsims, ports ; 26cm.
Previous ed.: 1972. — Bibl.: p.334. — Index.
ISBN 0-7148-1790-2 : £8.95
ISBN 0-7148-1756-2 Pbk : £5.50
(B77-28752)

701'.17 — Visual arts. Aesthetics
Schorr, Justin. Toward the transformation of art / [by] Justin Schorr. — Rutherford [etc.] : Fairleigh Dickinson University Press ; London (108 New Bond St., W1Y 0QX) : Associated University Press, 1974. — 118p ; 22cm.
Bibl.: p.114-116. — Index.
ISBN 0-8386-1382-9 : £2.75
(B77-25764)

701'.17 — Visual arts. Aesthetics. Theories of Ruskin, John
Williams, Catherine, *b.1943.* Ruskin's philosophy / by Catherine Williams. — Penzance (6 Morrab Place, Penzance, Cornwall TR18 4DG) : Triton Press, 1975. — [3],28p ; 20cm.
Unpriced
(B77-33930)

701'.8 — Visual arts. Linear perspective, ca 1400-ca 1450
Edgerton, Samuel Y. The Renaissance rediscovery of linear perspective / [by] Samuel Y. Edgerton, Jr. — New York [etc.] ; London : Harper and Row, 1976. — xvii,206p : ill, charts, maps ; 24cm.
Originally published: New York : Basic Books, 1975. — Index.
ISBN 0-06-430069-2 Pbk : £3.60
(B77-03667)

702 — VISUAL ARTS. MISCELLANY

702'.5'4285 — Visual arts. *Cleveland. Directories*
Directory of artists and craftsmen in Cleveland. — Middlesbrough ([Gurney House, Gurney St., Middlesbrough, Cleveland TS1 1JL]) : Leisure and Amenities Dept., County of Cleveland. 1976. — [1976]. — [33]p : ill ; 21cm.
ISBN 0-904784-03-7 Sd : £0.25
ISSN 0308-9916
Also classified at 680
(B77-03136)

702'.8 — Assemblages & collages. *Manuals*
McConnell, Gerald. Assemblage : three-dimensional picture making / [by] Gerald McConnell ; designed and edited by Howard Munce. — New York ; London [etc.] : Van Nostrand Reinhold, 1976. — 96p,[8]p of plates : ill(some col), ports ; 28cm.
ISBN 0-442-25264-1 : £8.20
ISBN 0-442-25263-3 Pbk : £5.20
(B77-09142)

702'.8 — Human figures. *Illustrations. For design*
Szabo, Marc. Drawing file for architects, illustrators and designers / [by] Marc Szabo. — New York ; London [etc.] : Van Nostrand Reinhold, 1976. — [257]p : of ill ; 31cm.
ISBN 0-442-27878-0 Pbk : £8.90
(B77-05542)

702'.8 — Visual arts. Techniques. *Manuals*
Hart, Tony. Fun with art / [by Tony Hart]. — London : Kaye and Ward [etc.], 1976. — 64p : ill ; 26cm. — ([Learning with fun])
ISBN 0-7182-0097-7 : £2.15
(B77-00317)

704 — VISUAL ARTS. SPECIAL ASPECTS

704'.054 — Visual arts by children. Theories
Kellogg, Rhoda. Analyzing children's art / [by] Rhoda Kellogg. — Palo Alto : Mayfield Publishing ; London : Muller, [1977]. — [4], 308p : ill ; 21cm.
Originally published: Palo Alto : National Press Books, 1969. — Bibl.: p.291-298. — Index.
£6.00
(B77-14836)

704.94'2'07402132 — Art galleries. *London. Westminster (London Borough). National Portrait Gallery. Exhibits, 1970-1976. Catalogues*
National Portrait Gallery. Concise catalogue, 1970-76 / National Portrait Gallery ; compiled by K.K. Yung. — London ([2 St Martin's Place] WC2H 0HE) : The Gallery, 1977. — [1], 56p ; 21cm.
Index.
ISBN 0-904017-19-2 Sd : £0.80
(B77-32028)

704.94'2'07402132 — Art galleries. *London. Westminster (London Borough). National Portrait Gallery. Reports, surveys. Serials*
National Portrait Gallery. Report of the Trustees / National Portrait Gallery. — London : H.M.S.O.
1975-76. — 1977. — 28p,[12]p of plates : ill, ports ; 25cm.
ISBN 0-11-290261-8 Sd : £1.25
(B77-10864)

704.94'32'091812 — Western visual arts, to 1900. Special subjects: Animals. *Critical studies*
Clark, Kenneth, *Baron Clark, b.1903.* Animals and men : their relationship as reflected in western art from prehistory to the present day / [by] Kenneth Clark. — London : Thames and Hudson, 1977. — 240p : ill(some col), col ports ; 28cm.
Ill. on lining papers. — Index.
ISBN 0-500-23257-1 : £10.50
(B77-26412)

704.94'4 — Arts centres. *London. Camden (London Borough). Camden Arts Centre. Exhibits: Visual arts. Special subjects: Doors. Catalogues*
Arkwright Arts Trust. Doors : [catalogue of an exhibition held] 14 December 1976-30 January 1977 [at] Camden Arts Centre ... [organised by the Arkwright Arts Trust]. — London (Camden Arts Centre, Arkwright Rd, NW3 6DG) : The Trust, [1976]. — 36p : ill ; 30cm.
ISBN 0-9505532-0-4 Sd : £1.00
(B77-09836)

704.94'7 — Aegean visual arts, to ca B.C.600. Special subjects: Gods. *Critical studies*
Coldstream, John Nicolas. Deities in Aegean art : before and after the Dark Age / by J.N. Coldstream. — London (Regent's Park, NW1 4NS) : Bedford College, 1977. — 19p : ill ; 25cm. — (Bedford College. Inaugural lectures)
'... delivered ... 27th October 1976'.
ISBN 0-900145-38-2 Sd : £0.65
(B77-28753)

704.948 — Religious visual arts
Burckhardt, Titus. Sacred art in East and West : its principles and methods / [by] Titus Burckhardt ; translated [from the French] by Lord Northbourne. — Bedfont : Perennial Books, 1976. — 160p,xvi p of plates : ill, facsims, plans ; 22cm.
This translation originally published: 1967. — Translation of: 'Principes et méthodes de l'art sacré'. Lyon : Derain, 1958.
ISBN 0-900588-11-x Pbk : £2.75
(B77-13139)

704.948'2 — Catacombs. Christian visual arts. Symbolism. *Italy. Rome*
Billon, B M. Early Christian art and symbolism / [by] B.M. Billon. — Ilfracombe : Stockwell, 1976. — 96p : ill, map, plan ; 19cm.
ISBN 0-7223-0935-x : £2.00
(B77-11979)

704.948'2'098 — Christian visual arts. *Latin America, 1520-1800*
Kelemen, Pál. Baroque and rococo in Latin America / by Pál Kelemen. — 2nd ed. — New York : Dover Publications [etc.] ; London : Constable, [1977]. — xix,313p,2-192p of plates : ill, map ; 28cm.
This ed. originally published: in 2 vols. 1967. — Bibl.: p.273-288. — Index.
ISBN 0-486-21698-5 Pbk : £7.10
(B77-30446)

704.948'4 — Western European visual arts, 1120-1886. Special subjects: Christ. Nativity. *Illustrations*
The **Christmas** story in masterpieces / introduced by David Kossoff. — London : Collins, 1977. — 72p : ill(some col), ports(some col) ; 29cm.
ISBN 0-00-216128-1 : £5.95
(B77-32029)

704.948'5 — Visual arts. Special subjects: Christ, to 1973. *Critical studies*
Bainton, Roland Herbert. Behold the Christ / [by] Roland H. Bainton assisted by Sumathi Devasahayam. — New York [etc.] ; London : Harper and Row, 1976. — 224p : ill ; 24cm.
'A Collins Associates book'. — Originally published: New York [etc.] ; London : Harper and Row, 1974. — Bibl.: p.223-224.
ISBN 0-06-060353-4 Pbk : £4.45
(B77-13753)

704.94'9'92972 — Visual arts, 1066-1976. Special subjects: Great Britain. Royal families
The **face** of monarchy : British royalty portrayed / [text by] Richard Ormond. — Oxford : Phaidon, 1977. — 207p : ill(some col), geneal table, chiefly ports(some col) ; 29cm.
Index.
ISBN 0-7148-1762-7 : £9.95
(B77-14837)

705 — VISUAL ARTS. PERIODICALS
705 — Visual arts. *Periodicals*
Seer / [School of Drawing and Painting, Duncan of Jordanstone College of Art]. — Dundee (Perth Rd, Dundee) : The College.
1- ; [1977]-. — [1977]-. — ill, music ; 30cm.
Published at irregular intervals. — [44]p. in 1st issue.
Sd : Unpriced
ISSN 0309-6262
(B77-16995)

705 — Visual arts. *Yearbooks*
Christie's review of the season. — London : Hutchinson [etc.].
1976 / edited by John Herbert. — 1976. — 516p : ill(some col), facsims(some col), ports(some col) ; 25cm.
Ill. on lining papers. — Index.
ISBN 0-09-128330-2 : £10.00
(B77-03137)

706 — VISUAL ARTS. ORGANISATIONS
706'.5 — Visual arts. Art dealing. Organisations. *London. Duveen Brothers (Firm), 1898-1931. Personal observations*
Fowles, Edward. Memories of Duveen Brothers / [by] Edward Fowles ; introduction by Sir Ellis Waterhouse. — London : Times Books, 1976. — [7],215p,[16]p of plates : ill, facsim, ports ; 24cm.
'Abridged by Michael Glover' - jacket. — Index.
ISBN 0-7230-0155-3 : £7.95
(B77-03138)

707 — VISUAL ARTS. STUDY AND TEACHING
707'.1'041 — Educational institutions. Curriculum subjects: Visual arts. *Great Britain. Reports, surveys*
Wayte, Nick. A study of aspects of art and design education / [by] Nick Wayte, David Cooper [and David Eyre]. — [Manchester] ([Hilton House, Hilton St., Manchester M1 2FE]) : Manchester Polytechnic, Institute of Advanced Studies.
[Part 1] / [by Nick Wayte, David Cooper]. — 1974. — [7],113,[8]p ; 30cm.
ISBN 0-905252-07-1 Sp : £3.00
(B77-06794)

Part 2 : The secondary sector / [by] David Eyre, David Cooper. — 1975. — [9],170,41p : ill, forms ; 30cm.
ISBN 0-905252-08-x Sp : £3.00
(B77-06795)

707'.1041 — Schools. Curriculum subjects: Visual arts. Teaching. *Great Britain*
Wooff, Terence. Developments in art teaching / [by] Terence Wooff. — London : Open Books, 1976. — xii,117p : ill, plans ; 21cm. — (The changing classroom)
Bibl.: p.112-113. — Index.
ISBN 0-7291-0039-1 : £3.90
ISBN 0-7291-0034-0 Pbk : £1.75
(B77-00856)

707'.11'41 — Artists. Professional education. Foundation courses. *Great Britain. Reports, surveys*
National Standing Conference for Foundation Education in Art and Design. *Working Party on Foundation Course Validation.* Report of the Working Party on Foundation Course Validation. — [London?] ([c/o P. Williams, Lincoln College of Art, Lincoln]) : National Standing Conference for Foundation Education in Art and Design, 1976. — [61]leaves : col map ; 30cm.
Cover title.
ISBN 0-9505536-0-3 Pbk : £1.00
(B77-06796)

707'.11'41 — Universities. *Great Britain. Open University. Curriculum subjects: Arts. Social aspects. Courses: Art and environment*
Open University. *Art and Environment Course Team.* Guide to the course / prepared for the [Open University, Art and Environment] Course Team by Christopher Crickmay. — [Milton Keynes] ([Walton Hall, Milton Keynes MK7 6AA]) : Open University, 1977. — 15p ; 30cm. — ([Technology/arts/social sciences], a second level interdisciplinary course : art and environment) (TAD292 ; G)
Sd : Unpriced
(B77-14319)

707'.11'42132 — Art schools. *London. Westminster (London Borough). Royal College of Art. Calendars*
Royal College of Art. Yearbook / Royal College of Art. — [London] ([Kensington Gore, SW7 2EU]) : [The College].
1976-1977. — [1976]. — 3-143p : ill, map, ports ; 23cm.
Previously published: in 2 vols as 'Calendar' and 'Royal College of Art, a pictorial'.
ISBN 0-902490-22-2 Pbk : Unpriced
ISSN 0309-1597
(B77-02456)

707'.11'42574 — Universities. *Oxfordshire. Oxford. University of Oxford. Curriculum subjects: Arts. Applications of digital computer systems. Reports, surveys*
Hockey, Susan M. Computing in the arts at Oxford University / [by] Susan M. Hockey. — Oxford (19 Banbury Rd, Oxford) : Oxford University Computing Service, 1976. — [1], 19p ; 21cm.
Sd : Unpriced
(B77-17642)

707'.12'429 — Secondary schools. Curriculum subjects: Visual arts. *Wales. Reports, surveys. Welsh-English parallel texts*
Great Britain. *Welsh Education Office. HM Inspectorate (Wales).* Art in the secondary schools of Wales = Celfyddyd yn ysgolion uwchradd Cymru : a progress report = adroddiad ar y sefyllfa bresennol / by H.M. Inspectors of Schools = gan Arolygwyr Ysgolion Ei Mawrhydi. — Cardiff [etc.] (31 Cathedral Rd, Cardiff) : Welsh Education Office, 1976. — 89,[1]p : ill, plan ; 30cm. — (Welsh education survey ; no.4)
Parallel English and Welsh texts.
Pbk : Unpriced
(B77-27246)

707'.4'094127 — Museums. *Scotland. Tayside Region. Dundee. Dundee City Museum and Art Gallery. Exhibits: Visual arts acquired with help of National Art-Collections Fund. Catalogues*
Deslandes, Gerald. The National Art-Collections Fund in Scotland : [an exhibition held] 5 March-2 April 1977 [organized by] Dundee Museums and Art Galleries / [catalogue by Gerald Deslandes, Joanna Mundy]. — [Dundee] ([Albert Sq., Dundee DD1 1DA]) : City of Dundee District Council, Museums and Art Galleries Department, 1977. — [12]p : ill, 2 ports ; 30cm.
ISBN 0-900344-39-3 Sd : £0.50
(B77-16506)

707'.5 — Art objects. Plunder by Hitler, Adolf. *Europe, 1938-1945*
Roxan, David. The jackdaw of Linz : the story of Hitler's art theft / [by] David Roxan and Ken Wanstall. — London [etc.] : White Lion Publishers, 1976. — xiv,197p,[32]p of plates : ill, plan, ports ; 23cm.
Originally published: London : Cassell, 1964. — Index.
ISBN 0-85617-266-9 : £4.75
(B77-03668)

708 — VISUAL ARTS. GALLERIES, MUSEUMS, PRIVATE COLLECTIONS
708'.22'56 — Museums. *East Sussex. Brighton. Royal Pavilion, Art Gallery and Museums, Brighton. Exhibits. Catalogues*
Royal Pavilion, Art Gallery and Museums, Brighton. Illustrated guide and introduction to the collections in the Art Gallery and Museum, Brighton / [photography by John Barrow]. — [Brighton] ([Royal Pavilion, Art Gallery and Museums, Brighton BN1 1UE]) : Brighton Borough Council Amenities Committee, 1975. — [24]p,[4]p of plates : ill(some col), ports(1 col) ; 24cm.
Sd : £0.50
Primary classification 914.22'56
(B77-06965)

708'.22'56 — Museums. *East Sussex. Brighton. Royal Pavilion, Art Gallery and Museums, Brighton. Exhibits. Catalogues. French texts*
Royal Pavilion, Art Gallery and Museums, Brighton. Le Pavillon Royal de Brighton / [Royal Pavilion, Art Gallery and Museums, Brighton] ; [photographies par Eric de Maré, Louis Klemantaski, John Barrow ; texte de David Higginbottom en collaboration avec le Directeur du Pavillon]. — [Brighton] ([The Royal Pavilion, Art Gallery and Museums, Brighton BN1 1UE]) : Brighton Borough Council Amenities Committee, [1976]. — [55] p : ill(chiefly col), facsims, ports ; 30cm.
Also available in English without catalogue pages.
ISBN 0-9502372-4-8 Sd : £0.45
Primary classification 914.22'56
(B77-01900)

708'.25'74 — Universities. *Oxfordshire. Oxford. University of Oxford. Stock: Visual arts*
Piper, David. The treasures of Oxford / [by] David Piper. — New York ; London : Paddington Press, 1977. — 144p,[12]p of plates(4 fold) : ill(some col), facsims, ports(some col) ; 29cm.
Ill. on lining papers. — Index.
ISBN 0-448-22836-x : £6.95
(B77-22007)

708'.941 — Art galleries. *Great Britain. Directories*
The **libraries,** museums and art galleries year book. — Cambridge : J. Clarke.
1976 / editors Adrian Brink & Derry Watkins. — 1976. — [2],254p ; 31cm.
Index.
ISBN 0-227-67824-9 : £15.00
Primary classification 021'.0025'41
(B77-00003)

708'.9'41 — Visual arts owned by British royal families, 973-1976. *Critical studies*
Plumb, John Harold. Royal heritage : the story of Britain's royal builders and collectors / by J.H. Plumb. — London : British Broadcasting Corporation, 1977. — 360p : ill(some col), facsims, ports(some col) ; 30cm.
'Published in association with the television series written by Huw Wheldon and J.H. Plumb'. — Ill. on lining papers. — Index.
ISBN 0-563-17082-4 : £10.00
Primary classification 941'.00992
(B77-19911)

708'.9413'4 — Art galleries. *Edinburgh. National Galleries of Scotland. Reports, surveys. Serials*
National Galleries of Scotland. Report of the Board of Trustees ... / the National Galleries of Scotland. — Edinburgh : H.M.S.O.
70th : 1976. — 1977. — 30p,[8]p of plates : ill, ports ; 25cm.
Bibl.: p.30.
ISBN 0-11-491489-3 Sd : £1.00
(B77-27969)

709 — VISUAL ARTS. HISTORICAL AND GEOGRAPHICAL TREATMENT

709 — Visual arts. Theories, 1400-1940. *Readings*
Artists on art : from the 14th to the 20th century / compiled and edited by Robert Goldwater and Marco Treves. — London : J. Murray, 1976. — xii,500p : ill, ports ; 21cm.
'... [The editors] have translated into English for the first time nearly one-half of the artists' writing quoted ...' - Foreword. — Originally published: New York : Pantheon Books, 1945. — Bibl.: p.480-488. — Index.
ISBN 0-7195-3312-0 Pbk : £3.50
(B77-13140)

709 — Visual arts, to 1975
Hartt, Frederick. Art : a history of painting, sculpture, architecture / [by] Frederick Hartt. — London : Thames and Hudson.
In 2 vols.
Vol.1 : Prehistory, ancient world, middle ages. — 1976. — 468p : ill(some col), facsims, maps, plans, ports(some col) ; 28cm.
Fold. cover. — Also published: Englewood Cliffs, N.J. : Prentice-Hall, 1976. — Bibl.: p.449-458. — Index.
ISBN 0-500-27082-1 Pbk : £6.95
(B77-20446)

Vol.2 : Renaissance, baroque, modern world. — 1977. — 527p : ill(some col), maps, ports(some col) ; 28cm.
Originally published: Englewood Cliffs, N.J. : Prentice-Hall, 1976. — Bibl.: p.505-515. — Index.
ISBN 0-500-27083-x Pbk : £6.95
(B77-14838)

709 — Visual arts, to 1975. *Essays*
Smith, Bernard, *b.1916.* The antipodean manifesto : essays in art and history / [by] Bernard Smith. — Melbourne ; London [etc.] : Oxford University Press, 1976. — ix,222p ; 23cm.
Index.
ISBN 0-19-550477-1 : £14.75
(B77-03139)

709 — Visual arts, to 1976. Occult aspects
Waldo-Schwartz, Paul. Art and the occult / [by] Paul Waldo-Schwartz. — London : Allen and Unwin, 1977. — vii,168p : ill, ports ; 26cm.
Originally published: New York : Braziller, 1975. — Bibl.: p.167-168.
ISBN 0-04-701008-8 : £6.95
ISBN 0-04-701009-6 Pbk : £3.50
(B77-24368)

709 — Western visual arts. Influence of Japanese visual arts, to 1975
Dialogue in art : Japan and the West / general editor Chisaburoh F. Yamada. — London : Zwemmer, 1976. — 334p : ill(some col), plans, ports(some col) ; 31cm.
Bibl.: p.321-328. — Index.
ISBN 0-87011-214-7 : £25.00
Primary classification 709'.52
(B77-13756)

709'.01'1 — Primitive visual arts, to 1965. *Critical studies*
Lommel, Andreas. Prehistoric and primitive man / [by] Andreas Lommel. — London [etc.] : Hamlyn, 1976. — 176p : ill(some col), maps ; 29cm. — (Landmarks of the world's art)
Originally published: New York : McGraw-Hill, 1966 ; London : Hamlyn, 1967. — Bibl.: p.171. — Index.
ISBN 0-600-37119-0 Pbk : £2.25
(B77-20447)

709'.01'109398 — Bulgarian visual arts, B.C.6000-B.C.1000. *Reports, surveys*
Raduncheva, Anna. Prehistoric art in Bulgaria from the fifth to the second millennium BC / [by] Anna Raduncheva ; translated from the Russian by Caroline M.A. Schuck. — Oxford : British Archaeological Reports, 1976. — [5], 54p,[59]p of plates : ill ; 30cm. — (British archaeological reports : supplementary series ; 13)
Translation of: 'Doistoricheskoe iskusstvo v Bolgarii'. Sofia : Sofia-Press, 1973. — Bibl.: p.43-47.
ISBN 0-904531-59-7 Pbk : £2.70
(B77-21286)

709'.01'1097 — Art galleries. *London. Lambeth (London Borough). Hayward Gallery. Exhibits: Visual arts of Indians of North America, to ca 1970. Catalogues*
Coe, Ralph T. Sacred circles : two thousand years of North American Indian art : exhibition organized by the Arts Council of Great Britain with the support of the British-American Associates, [held at the] Hayward Gallery, London, 7 October 1976-16 January 1977 : catalogue / by Ralph T. Coe. — [London] : Arts Council of Great Britain, 1976. — 236p : ill(some col), maps, ports ; 28cm.
Bibl.: p.29-31.
ISBN 0-7287-0095-6 : £5.00
ISBN 0-7287-0096-4 Pbk : £3.30
(B77-04951)

709'.01'1097 — Eskimo visual arts. *Critical studies*
Ritchie, Carson Irving Alexander. The Eskimo and his art / [by] Carson I.A. Ritchie. — London : Academy Editions [etc.], 1975. — 80p : ill, map ; 30cm.
ISBN 0-85670-014-2 : £4.95
Primary classification 970'.004'97
(B77-13450)

709'.01'109711 — Visual arts of Indians of North America. *British Columbia. Illustrations*
Steltzer, Ulli. Indian artists at work / [by] Ulli Steltzer. — Seattle ; London : University of Washington Press, 1977. — [9],163p : chiefly ill, ports ; 26cm.
ISBN 0-295-95536-8 : £11.25
(B77-32030)

709.01'1'0979 — Visual arts of Indians of North America. *United States. North-western states. Coastal regions, ca 1780-ca 1830. Transcripts of discussions*
Holm, Bill. Indian art of the Northwest coast : a dialogue on craftsmanship and aesthetics / [by] Bill Holm, Bill Reid. — [Houston] : Institute for the Arts, Rice University ; Seattle ; London : Distributed by the University of Washington Press, 1976. — 3-263p : ill(some col), ports ; 24cm.
Originally published in conjunction with an exhibition organized by the Institute for the Arts, Rice University, Houston: as 'A dialogue on form and freedom'. 1975.
ISBN 0-295-95531-7 : £16.00
(B77-07499)

709'.02 — Arts. Patronage. Organisations. *Great Britain. Arts Council of Great Britain. Exhibits: Visual arts, 1150-1600. Collections: Burrell Collection. Catalogues*
Arts Council of Great Britain. The Burrell Collection, medieval tapestries, sculpture, stained glass with paintings, alabasters, ivories and metalwork : [catalogue of an exhibition organised by the] Arts Council of Great Britain, 1977. — [London] : [Arts Council], 1977. — [38]p : ill ; 20x21cm.
ISBN 0-7287-0120-0 Sd : £0.80
(B77-13754)

709'.02 — European visual arts, 300-1300
Kitzinger, Ernst. The art of Byzantium and the medieval West : selected studies / by Ernst Kitzinger ; edited by W. Eugene Kleinbauer. — Bloomington ; London : Indiana University Press, [1977]. — xxi,419p : ill, facsims, plans ; 29cm.
Facsimile reprints. — This collection published in the United States: 1976. — Bibl.: p.397-400. — Index.
ISBN 0-253-31055-5 : £16.85
(B77-10468)

709'.02 — European visual arts, 500-1500. *Critical studies*
Lassus, Jean. The early Christian and Byzantine world / [by] Jean Lassus. — London [etc.] : Hamlyn, 1976. — 176p : ill(some col), facsims, map, plans, ports(some col) ; 29cm. — (Landmarks of the world's art)
Originally published: New York : McGraw-Hill ; London : Hamlyn, 1967. — Bibl.: p.171. — Index.
ISBN 0-600-33133-4 Pbk : £2.25
(B77-20448)

709'.02'3 — Western European visual arts, 1350-1500
Swaan, Wim. The late Middle Ages : art and architecture from 1350 to the advent of the Renaissance / [by] Wim Swaan ; with photographs by the author. — London : Elek, 1977. — 232p : ill(some col), facsim, map, plans, ports ; 32cm.
Bibl.: p.224-227. — Index.
ISBN 0-236-30911-0 : £18.00
(B77-33932)

709'.02'4 — European visual arts, 1400-1600
Dunbarton Art Panel. The Renaissance / Dunbarton Art Panel. — Glasgow [etc.] : Blackie, 1977. — 32p : ill ; 21x27cm. — (Topics in art history)
Bibl.: p.32. — List of filmstrips: p.32.
ISBN 0-216-90272-x Sd : £1.30
(B77-30447)

709'.03 — Anamorphic arts, to 1976. *Critical studies*
Baltrušaitis, Jurgis. Anamorphic art / by Jurgis Baltrušaitis ; translated [from the French] by W.J. Strachan. — Cambridge (21 Bateman St., Cambridge CB2 1NB) : Chadwyck-Healey Ltd, 1976. — viii,184p : ill, ports ; 29cm.
Ill. on lining papers. — Translation of: 'Anamorphoses ou Magie artificielle des effets merveilleux'. Nouv. éd.: Paris : Perrin, 1969. — Index.
ISBN 0-85964-029-9 : £10.00
(B77-22730)

709'.03'1 — European visual arts. Mannerism. *Critical studies*
Shearman, John, *b.1931.* Mannerism / [by] John Shearman. — Harmondsworth [etc.] : Penguin, 1977. — 216p : ill, facsim, plan, port ; 20cm. — (Style and civilisation) (A Pelican original)
Originally published: 1967. — Bibl.: p.207-208. — Index.
Pbk : £2.50
ISBN 0-14-020808-9
(B77-25765)

709'.03'2 — European visual arts, 1600-1800. *Critical studies*
Kitson, Michael. The age of baroque / [by] Michael Kitson. — London [etc.] : Hamlyn, 1976. — 176p : ill(some col), maps, plans, ports(chiefly col) ; 29cm. — (Landmarks of the world's art)
Originally published: New York : McGraw-Hill, 1966 ; London : Hamlyn, 1967. — Bibl.: p.172. — Index.
ISBN 0-600-30308-x Pbk : £2.25
(B77-20449)

709'.03'2 — European visual arts. Baroque style. *Critical studies*
Hubala, Erich. Baroque and Rococo art / [by] Erich Hubala ; [translated from the German]. — London : Weidenfeld and Nicolson, 1976. — 196p : ill(some col), plans, ports(some col) ; 23cm. — ([The universal history of art])
Translation of: 'Barock und Rokoko'. Stuttgart : C. Belser, 1971. — Bibl.: p.192-193. — Index.
ISBN 0-297-99444-1 : £4.25
Also classified at 709'.03'3
(B77-11316)

Martin, John Rupert. Baroque / [by] John Rupert Martin. — London : Allen Lane, 1977. — 367p : ill, plans, ports ; 25cm. — (Style and civilization)
Ill. on lining papers. — Bibl.: p.305-309. — Index.
ISBN 0-7139-0926-9 : £8.95
(B77-20450)

709'.03'3 — European visual arts. Rococo style. *Critical studies*
Hubala, Erich. Baroque and Rococo art / [by] Erich Hubala ; [translated from the German]. — London : Weidenfeld and Nicolson, 1976. — 196p : ill(some col), plans, ports(some col) ; 23cm. — ([The universal history of art])
Translation of: 'Barock und Rokoko'. Stuttgart : C. Belser, 1971. — Bibl.: p.192-193. — Index.
ISBN 0-297-99444-1 : £4.25
Primary classification 709'.03'2
(B77-11316)

709'.04 — Art galleries. *Edinburgh. Royal Scottish Academy. Exhibits: European visual arts, ca 1800-ca 1970. Catalogues*
Blackadder, Elizabeth. The Royal Scottish Academy 150th anniversary exhibition, 1826-1976 / [catalogue compiled by Elizabeth Blackadder et al.]. — [Edinburgh] : [Royal Scottish Academy], [1976]. — 3-96p : ill(some col), plans, ports(1 col) ; 22x25cm.
'Exhibition staged during the Edinburgh International Festival, [1976]' - Foreword. — Index.
ISBN 0-905783-00-x Pbk : £1.50
(B77-00857)

709'.04 — Arts centres. *London. Camden (London Borough). Camden Arts Centre. Exhibits: European visual arts, ca 1900-ca 1975 from Roland Collection. Catalogues*
The **Roland** Collection : [catalogue of an exhibition held] 15 September-10 October 1976, Camden Arts Centre, Arkwright Road, London NW3 ... organised by the Arkwright Arts Trust ... — [Woking] ([Tyle Court, Hockering Gardens, Woking, Surrey]) : [H.M. Roland], [1976]. — [48]p : ill ; 25cm.
ISBN 0-9504265-1-2 Sd : £0.50
(B77-03140)

709'.04 — Arts. Patronage. Organisations. *Wales. Welsh Arts Council. Exhibits: Visual arts purchased by the Contemporary Art Society for Wales, 1938-1977. Catalogues*
Contemporary Art Society for Wales. 40 mlynedd wedyn = 40 years on : arddangosfa o weithiau a bwrcaswyd er 1938 gan Gymdeithas Gelfyddyd Gyfoes Cymru = an exhibition of works purchased since 1938 by the Contemporary Art Society for Wales. — [Cardiff] : Welsh Arts Council, 1977. — [16]p : ill ; 22cm.
'A Welsh Arts Council touring exhibition'. — Parallel Welsh text and English translation.
ISBN 0-905171-16-0 Sd : Unpriced
(B77-30448)

709'.04 — European visual arts. Dadaism & surrealism
Scharf, Marina. Liberation through art : Dada and Surrealism / prepared by Marina Scharf ; for the [Open University] Course Team. — Milton Keynes : Open University Press, 1976. — 87p,[8]p of plates : ill(some col), facsims, ports ; 30cm. — (Arts, a third level course : modern art, 1848 to the present, styles and social implications ; units 13 and 14) (A351 ; 13 and 14)
Bibl.
ISBN 0-335-05155-3 Pbk : £2.60
(B77-03141)

709'.04 — Experimental visual arts. *Critical studies*
Auty, Giles. The art of self deception : an intelligible guide / [by] Giles Auty. — Bedford (Cranfield Book Service, Wharley End, Bedford) : Libertarian Books Ltd, 1977. — x, 172p : ill, facsim ; 23cm.
Index.
ISBN 0-905004-03-5 : £5.95
(B77-23581)

709'.04 — Visual arts, 1900-1976
Arnason, Hjorvardur Harvard. A history of modern art : painting, sculpture, architecture / [by] H.H. Arnason. — Revised and enlarged ed. — London : Thames and Hudson, 1977. — 740p : ill(some col), plans, ports(some col) ; 30cm.
Previous ed.: Englewood Cliffs, N.J. : Prentice-Hall, 1968 ; London : Thames and Hudson, 1969. — Bibl.: p.709-721. — Index.
ISBN 0-500-23261-x : £11.50
(B77-21287)

709'.04 — Visual arts, 1945-1976. *Glossaries*
Walker, John A. Glossary of art, architecture and design since 1945 : terms and labels describing movements, styles and groups derived from the vocabulary of artists and critics / [by] John A. Walker. — 2nd revised ed. — London : Bingley [etc.], 1977. — 352p ; 23cm.
Previous ed.: 1973. — Bibl.: p.309-312. — Index.
ISBN 0-85157-229-4 : £7.00
(B77-20451)

709'.04 — Visual arts, ca 1905-1975
Lucie-Smith, Edward. Art today : from abstract expressionism to superrealism / [by] Edward Lucie-Smith. — Oxford : Phaidon, 1977. — 504p : col ill ; 29cm.
Bibl.: p.501. — Index.
ISBN 0-7148-1806-2 : £11.95
(B77-29570)

709'.04 — Western avant garde arts, ca 1910-1968. *Critical studies*
Tomkins, Calvin. The bride and the bachelors : five masters of the avant-garde / by Calvin Tomkins. — [Expanded ed.]. — Harmondsworth [etc.] : Penguin, 1976. — [10], 306p,[16]p of plates : ill, facsim, ports ; 20cm.
Expanded ed. originally published: New York : Viking Press, 1968. — Index.
ISBN 0-14-004313-6 Pbk : Unpriced
(B77-00858)

709'.04 — Western avant-garde visual arts, 1900-1968. *Critical studies*
Parmelin, Hélène. Art anti-art : anartism explored / by Hélène Parmelin ; translated [from the French] by J.A. Underwood. — London : Boyars : Distributed by Calder and Boyars, 1977. — 76p ; 21cm. — (Signature series ; 24)
Translation of: 'L'art et les anartistes'. Paris : C. Bourgois, 1969.
ISBN 0-7145-2570-7 : £3.50
ISBN 0-7145-2571-5 Pbk : £1.50
(B77-12570)

709'.04 — Western visual arts, 1945-1974
Lucie-Smith, Edward. Movements in art since 1945 / [by] Edward Lucie-Smith. — Revised ed. — London : Thames and Hudson, 1975. — 288p : ill(some col), ports ; 22cm. — ([The world of art library])
Previous ed.: 1969. — Index.
ISBN 0-500-18153-5 : £4.50
(B77-10469)

709'.2'2 — Artists. *Great Britain, 1900-1950. Biographical dictionaries*
Waters, Grant M. Dictionary of British artists working 1900-1950 / by Grant M. Waters. — Eastbourne (47 South St., Eastbourne, E. Sussex) : Eastbourne Fine Art Publications. Vol.2. — [1976]. — [2],63p,[228]p of plates : ill(some col), ports ; 25cm.
Bibl.: p.57-58. — Index.
ISBN 0-902010-06-9 : Unpriced
(B77-27247)

709'.2'2 — Visual arts by women, ca 1900-1976. *Critical studies*
The **world** as we see it : graphics, paintings, sculpture ... / [by] Monica Sjöö ... [et al.] ; introduction Charlotte Yeldham. — London (16 Agincourt Rd, Hampstead N.W.3) : Arts Section, Camden Council for International Cooperation, 1977. — [1],15p : ill ; 21x30cm.
ISBN 0-906013-00-3 Sd : £0.30
(B77-16507)

709'.2'2 — Visual arts. Women artists, ca 400-1975
Petersen, Karen. Women artists : recognition and reappraisal, from the early Middle Ages to the twentieth century / [by] Karen Petersen & J.J. Wilson. — New York [etc.] ; London : Harper and Row, 1976. — [9],212p : ill, facsims, ports ; 24cm. — (Harper colophon books)
Bibl.: p.179-191. — Index.
ISBN 0-06-090387-2 Pbk : £4.45
(B77-03669)

709'.2'4 — American visual arts. Calder, Alexander. *Biographies*
Calder, Alexander. Calder's universe / [text] by Jean Lipman ; Ruth Wolfe, editorial director. — London : Thames and Hudson, 1977. — 352p : chiefly ill(some col), facsims(some col), ports ; 28cm.
Also published: New York : Viking Press, 1977. — Bibl.: p.341-345. — List of films : p.344-345. — Index.
ISBN 0-500-23234-2 : £12.50
(B77-04318)

709'.2'4 — Art galleries. *London. Kensington and Chelsea (London Borough). Taranman Limited. Exhibits: English visual arts. Clarke, Geoffrey, b.1924. Catalogues*
Taranman Limited. Geoffrey Clarke : early engraved work and iron sculpture ; [catalogue of an exhibition held at] Taranman ... 9 June-15 July, 1976. — London (236 Brompton Rd, S.W.3) : Taranman, [1976]. — [27]p : ill ; 24cm.
Also available in limited ed. of 300 copies. — Bibl.: p.[15].
Sd : £1.00
Limited ed. : £2.00
(B77-20452)

709'.2'4 — English visual arts. Long, Richard, b.1945. *Critical studies*
Compton, Michael. Some notes on the work of Richard Long / by Michael Compton. — [London] : [British Council], [1976]. — [22]p : ill, maps ; 30cm.
Published to accompany the installation in the British Pavilion XXXVII Venice Biennale 1976.
ISBN 0-900229-30-6 Sd : £1.00
(B77-07500)

709'.2'4 — Italian visual arts. Leonardo da Vinci. *Biographies. Juvenile literature*
Henrie, Jacqueline. Leonardo da Vinci : Italian artist, inventor and engineer / by Jacqueline Henrie ; illustrated by Louis Joos. — Edinburgh : W. and R. Chambers, 1977. — [28]p : ill(chiefly col), col ports ; 19x20cm. — (History makers)
ISBN 0-550-31931-x : £1.40
(B77-32748)

709'.2'4 — Museums. *Cardiff. National Museum of Wales. Exhibits: British visual arts. Evans, Merlyn. Catalogues*
Evans, Merlyn. Merlyn Evans, 1910-1973 : [catalogue of an exhibition held at] National Museum of Wales, Cardiff, 29 June-11 August 1974 [and at] Glasgow Museum and Art Gallery, 23 August-22nd September 1974. — [Cardiff] ([9 Museum Place, Cardiff CF1 3NX]) : Welsh Arts Council, 1974. — 40p : chiefly ill(incl 2 col) ; 21cm.
Pbk : £0.30
Also classified at 709'.2'4
(B77-03670)

709'.2'4 — Museums. *Scotland. Strathclyde Region. Glasgow. Glasgow Art Gallery and Museum. Exhibits: British visual arts. Evans, Merlyn. Catalogues*
Evans, Merlyn. Merlyn Evans, 1910-1973 : [catalogue of an exhibition held at] National Museum of Wales, Cardiff, 29 June-11 August 1974 [and at] Glasgow Museum and Art Gallery, 23 August-22nd September 1974. — [Cardiff] ([9 Museum Place, Cardiff CF1 3NX]) : Welsh Arts Council, 1974. — 40p : chiefly ill(incl 2 col) ; 21cm.
Pbk : £0.30
Primary classification 709'.2'4
(B77-03670)

709'.2'4 — Visual arts. Criticism. Clark, Kenneth, Baron Clark, b.1903, 1939-1974. *Autobiographies*
Clark, Kenneth, *Baron Clark, b.1903.* The other half : a self portrait / [by] Kenneth Clark. — London : J. Murray, 1977. — xii,261p,[16]p of plates : ill, ports ; 22cm.
Index.
ISBN 0-7195-3432-1 : £6.50
(B77-32031)

709'.2'4 — Visual arts. Criticism. Clark, Kenneth, Baron Clark, b.1903, to 1939. *Autobiographies*
Clark, Kenneth, *Baron Clark, b.1903.* Another part of the wood : a self-portrait / [by] Kenneth Clark. — London : Coronet, 1976. — 254p,[16]p of plates : ill, ports ; 18cm.
Originally published: London : J. Murray, 1974. — Index.
ISBN 0-340-20811-2 Pbk : £1.25
(B77-01654)

709'.38 — Classical visual arts, B.C.2000-A.D.400. *Critical studies*
Strong, Donald Emrys. The classical world / [by] Donald E. Strong. — London [etc.] : Hamlyn, 1976. — 176p : ill(some col), maps, plans, ports ; 29cm. — (Landmarks of the world's art)
Originally published: New York : McGraw-Hill, 1965 ; London : Hamlyn, 1967. — Bibl.: p.171. — Index.
ISBN 0-600-31917-2 Pbk : £2.25
(B77-20453)

709'.38 — Museums. *London. Camden (London Borough). British Museum. Department of Greek and Roman Antiquities. Exhibits: Ancient Greek & Ancient Roman visual arts*
British Museum. Greek and Roman art in the British Museum / [by] B.F. Cook. — London : British Museum Publications, 1976. — 194,[2] p : ill(incl 1 col), plans, ports ; 24cm.
Bibl.: p.193. — Index.
ISBN 0-7141-1249-6 : £4.95
ISBN 0-7141-1248-8 Pbk : £2.75
(B77-02457)

709'.39 — Ancient Middle Eastern visual arts, to ca B.C.500. *Critical studies*
Garbini, Giovanni. The ancient world / [by] Giovanni Garbini. — London [etc.] : Hamlyn, 1976. — 176p : ill(some col), maps, plans, ports ; 29cm. — (Landmarks of the world's art)

Originally published: New York : McGraw-Hill, 1966 ; London : Hamlyn, 1967. — Bibl.: p.171. — Index.
ISBN 0-600-30307-1 Pbk : £2.25
(B77-20454)

709'.4 — European visual arts. Chinoiserie, to 1920
Impey, Oliver. Chinoiserie : the impact of Oriental styles on Western art and decoration / [by] Oliver Impey. — London [etc.] : Oxford University Press, 1977. — 208p,[16]p of plates : ill(some col), facsims, maps, ports ; 25cm.
Bibl.: p.198-200. — Index.
ISBN 0-19-211444-1 : £7.95
(B77-10470)

709'.4 — European visual arts, to ca 1850. Images. *Essays*
Wittkower, Rudolf. Allegory and the migration of symbols / [by] Rudolf Wittkower. — London : Thames and Hudson, 1977. — 223p : ill, facsims, 2 maps, ports ; 26cm. — (The collected essays of Rudolf Wittkower ; 3)
Index.
ISBN 0-500-85004-6 : £12.50
(B77-11317)

709'.41 — Art galleries. *London. Lambeth (London Borough). Hayward Gallery. Exhibits: British visual arts, 1964-1977. Catalogues*
Hayward Gallery. 1977 Hayward annual : current British art selected by Michael Compton, Howard Hodgkin and William Turnbull : [catalogue of an exhibition held at the] Hayward Gallery, London, part one 25 May to 4 July, part two 20 July to 4 September. — [London] : Arts Council of Great Britain, 1977. — 140p : chiefly ill, ports ; 24cm.
ISBN 0-7287-0132-4 Pbk : £2.25
(B77-32749)

709'.41 — Art galleries. *London. Westminster (London Borough). Mall Galleries. Exhibits: British visual arts. Catalogues*
United Society of Artists. Fifty-sixth annual exhibition [of the] United Society of Artists [held] 27th August to 9th September 1976 at the Mall Galleries, The Mall, London, S.W.1. — [London] ([c/o The Secretary, 17 Carlton House Terrace, SW1Y 5BD]) : [The Society], [1976]. — [28]p,[9]p of plates : ill, forms ; 21cm.
ISBN 0-9505661-0-1 Sd : £0.50
(B77-13755)

709'.41 — Art galleries. *London. Westminster (London Borough). Royal Academy. Exhibits: British visual arts associated with celebrations of golden jubilee of Victoria, Queen of Great Britain, 1887. Catalogues*
Maas, Jeremy. "This brilliant year", Queen Victoria's Jubilee, 1887 / [by Jeremy Maas]. — London (Piccadilly, W1V 0DS) : Royal Academy of Arts, 1977. — 84p : ill(some col), facsim, ports(some col) ; 20x21cm.
Catalogue of an exhibition held at the Royal Academy, 19 March to 10 July 1977. — Index.

Pbk : £2.30
(B77-17643)

709'.41 — British visual arts. Vorticism
Cork, Richard. Vorticism and abstract art in the first machine age / [by] Richard Cork. — London : Gordon Fraser Gallery.
In 2 vols. — Col. ill. tipped in.
Vol.1 : Origins and development. — 1976. — xxiv,321p : ill(some col), facsims, ports ; 34cm.
Index.
ISBN 0-900406-24-0 : £29.00
(B77-23582)

Vol.2 : Synthesis and decline. — 1976. — xxiii p,p323-592 : ill(some col), facsims, ports ; 34cm.
Bibl.: p.567-578. — Index.
ISBN 0-900406-25-9 : £37.00
(B77-23583)

709'.41 — Visual arts. *Great Britain. Periodicals*
Artscribe. — London : ['Artscribe'] ; London (49 Endell St., W.C.2) : [Distributed by] Idea Books.
No.1- ; 1976-. — 1976-. — ill, facsims, ports ; 45cm.
Six issues a year. — 24p. in issue no.4.
Sd : £0.40
ISSN 0309-2151
(B77-05543)

709'.41 — Visual arts. *Great Britain. Yearbooks*
'Arts review' yearbook. — London (1 Whitehall Place, SW1A 2HE) : Eaton House Publishers Ltd.
1977 / editor John Gainsborough ; assistant editor Annabel Terry-Engell. — 1977. — 224p, [2]leaves of plates : ill, col map, ports ; 29cm.
ISBN 0-904831-04-3 Pbk : £3.25
ISSN 0309-3611
(B77-22008)

709'.411 — Art galleries. *Edinburgh. Fruit Market, Edinburgh. Exhibits: Scottish visual arts, 1968-1976. Catalogues*
Scottish Arts Council. Inscape : Ian Hamilton Finlay, Eileen Lawrence, Will Maclean, Glen Onwin, Fred Stiven, Ainslie Yule : [catalogue of] a Scottish Arts Council exhibition, selected by Paul Overy. — Edinburgh (19 Charlotte Sq., Edinburgh) : The Council, 1976. — 2-47p : ill ; 16cm.
ISBN 0-902989-34-0 Sd : £0.25
(B77-28754)

709'.42 — Art galleries. *London. Westminster (London Borough). Serpentine Gallery. Exhibits: English experimental visual arts. Catalogues*
Arts Council of Great Britain. 6 times : performances and installations exploring duration and change, 26 November-12 December [at the] Serpentine Gallery, Kensington Gardens, W.2 ... — [London] : Arts Council, [1976]. — Sheet ([2]p) : ill ; 42x59cm fold. to 21x20cm.
Unpriced
(B77-13142)

709'.42 — Art galleries. *London. Westminster (London Borough). Serpentine Gallery. Exhibits: English visual arts. Catalogues*
Serpentine Gallery. Summer show 4 ... : a mixed exhibition selected by Derek Boshier, Patrick Caulfield, and William Feaver : [catalogue of an exhibition held on the] 28 August-19 September 1976, Serpentine Gallery, Kensington Gardens, W.2. — [London] : Arts Council of Great Britain, [1976]. — 1v. ; 15x21cm.
Sixteen cards ([32] sides) in plastic envelope.
ISBN 0-7287-0123-5 : £0.50
(B77-04952)

709'.42 — English visual arts, ca 1890. *Readings from contemporary sources*
The **birth** of 'The Studio', 1893-1895. — [Woodbridge] : Antique Collectors' Club, [1976]. — [1],176,[1]p : ill, facsims, plans, ports ; 29cm.
Facsimile reprints of: 27 articles originally published between 1893 and 1895.
ISBN 0-902028-44-8 Pbk : £4.95
(B77-04319)

709'.426'5 — English arts: Visual arts by students of Cambridgeshire schools. *Illustrations*
Moving jewels : an anthology of writing and art / by Cambridgeshire schoolchildren ; [editor Christopher Martin]. — [Cambridge] ([c/o Cambridgeshire County Education Division, Shire Hall, Castle Hill, Cambridge CB3 9AP]) : EARO for the George Edwards Memorial Committee, [1977]. — 80p : ill(some col), port ; 21cm.
ISBN 0-904463-24-9 Pbk : £1.50
Also classified at 820'.8'09282
(B77-33933)

709'.43 — Art galleries. *London. Westminster (London Borough). Fischer Fine Art Limited. Exhibits: German visual arts, 1910-1939. Catalogues*
Fischer Fine Art Limited. Apocalypse and Utopia : a view of art in Germany, 1910-1939. — London (30 King St., S.W.1) : Fischer Fine Art Ltd, 1977. — 74p(2 fold) : ill(some col), facsims, ports ; 20cm.
Catalogue of an exhibition held at Fischer Fine Art Ltd, March to May 1977. — German abstract of introduction (sheet,[2]p.) as insert.
Pbk : £2.50
(B77-28755)

709'.43 — Art galleries. *London. Westminster (London Borough). National Gallery. Exhibits: German visual arts, 1390-1525. Catalogues*
Zehnder, Frank Günter. Late Gothic art from Cologne : [catalogue of] a loan exhibition [held] 5th April to 1st June 1977 [at] the National Gallery / [written by Frank Günter Zehnder, Alistair Smith et al. ; translation from the German by Heidi Grieve and Alistair Smith]. — London : The Gallery, 1977. — 164p,[8]p of plates : ill(some col), geneal table, map ; 21cm.
Index.
Pbk : £2.10
(B77-23584)

709'.437'1 — Bohemian visual arts, 1300-1500. *Critical studies*
Neumeister, Werner. Gothic art in Bohemia : architecture, sculpture and painting / [by] Ferdinand Seibt ... [et al.] ; edited by Erich Bachmann ; [photographs by Werner Neumeister ; translated from the German by Gerald Onn]. — Oxford : Phaidon, 1977. — 96p,[6]leaves,[160]p of plates(4 fold) : chiefly ill(some col), facsims(some col), map, plans ; 29cm.
Col. ill. chiefly tipped in. — These illustrations originally published: in 'Gotik in Böhmen'. / by Karl M. Swoboda. Munich : Prestel-Verlag, 1969. — Bibl.: p.90-92. — Index.
ISBN 0-7148-1413-x : £20.00
(B77-19514)

709'.45'31 — Visual arts. *Italy. Venice, to ca 1800. Guidebooks. Early works*
Ruskin, John. Ruskin's Venice / editor Arnold Whittick ; preface by Sir Ashley Clarke. — London : Godwin, 1976. — xv,325p : ill, maps, plans, port ; 24cm.
'Ruskin's Venetian index to "The stones of Venice" with amplifications from the body of the work as indicated by Ruskin' - note. — 'The stones of Venice', originally published: in 3 vols. London : Smith Elder, 1851-53. — Bibl.: p.307-312. — Index.
ISBN 0-7114-4802-7 : £7.50
(B77-03671)

709'.47 — Russian visual arts, 988-1917
Hamilton, George Heard. The art and architecture of Russia / [by] George Heard Hamilton. — 2nd ed. — Harmondsworth [etc.] : Penguin, 1975. — xxv,342p,leaf of plate,180p of plates : ill(incl 1 col), map, plans, ports ; 27cm. — (The pelican history of art)
In slip case. — Previous ed.: 1954. — Bibl.: p.317-322. — Index.
ISBN 0-14-056006-8 : £16.00
(B77-04320)

709'.47 — Soviet visual arts. Exhibitions. Destruction by government. *Soviet Union. Moscow. Readings from contemporary sources. Russian texts*
Iskusstvo pod bul'dozerom : siniaia kniga / sostavil Aleksandr Glezer. — London (40 Elsham Rd, W14 8HB) : Overseas Publications Interchange, [1977?]. — 163p : ill, facsim, port ; 18cm.
Second title page has English title 'Art under bulldozers'.
ISBN 0-903868-07-5 Pbk : £3.00
(B77-13143)

709'.492 — Art galleries. *London. Westminster (London Borough). National Gallery. Exhibits: Dutch visual arts, 1600-1700. Catalogues*
Brown, Christopher, *b.1948.* Art in seventeenth century Holland : the National Gallery, 30th September to 12th December 1976 : a loan exhibition / [catalogue compiled by Christopher Brown]. — London : National Gallery, 1976. — [2],144,[2]p(2 fold),[6]p of plates : ill(some col), col map, ports(some col) ; 25cm.
Pbk : Unpriced
(B77-01655)

709'.5 — Oriental visual arts. Aesthetics
Coomaraswamy, Ananda Kentish. On the traditional doctrine of art / [by] A.K. Coomaraswamy. — Ipswich (3 Cambridge Drive, Ipswich IP2 9EP) : Golgonooza Press, 1977. — 24p ; 23cm.
Sd : £0.90
(B77-33332)

709'.52 — Japanese visual arts. Influence of Western visual arts, to 1975
Dialogue in art : Japan and the West / general editor Chisaburoh F. Yamada. — London : Zwemmer, 1976. — 334p : ill(some col), plans, ports(some col) ; 31cm.
Bibl.: p.321-328. — Index.
ISBN 0-87011-214-7 : £25.00
Also classified at 709
(B77-13756)

709'.52 — Japanese visual arts, to ca 1935. *Critical studies*
Tsuda, Noritake. Handbook of Japanese art / by Noritake Tsuda. — Rutland, Vt [etc.] : Tuttle ; London : Distributed by Prentice Hall [etc.], 1976. — xxv,525p,[11] leaves of plates(1 fold) : ill, map, ports ; 19cm.
Originally published: Tokyo : Sanseido 1935 ; London : Allen and Unwin, 1937. — Bibl.: p.505-508. — Index.
ISBN 0-8048-1139-3 Pbk : £3.90
(B77-05544)

709'.54 — Museums. *London. Kensington and Chelsea (London Borough). Victoria and Albert Museum. Exhibits: Indian visual arts. Catalogues*
Indian art / [compiled by] Victoria and Albert Museum. — London : H.M.S.O., 1977. — vi, [70]p : chiefly ill, ports ; 25cm. — (Victoria and Albert Museum. Large picture books ; no.36)
Originally published: 1969.
Pbk : £3.25
ISBN 0-11-290006-2
(B77-33333)

709'.66 — West African visual arts
Price, Christine. Made in West Africa / by Christine Price. — London : Studio Vista, 1976. — x,150p : ill, map, ports ; 25cm.
Originally published: New York : Dutton, 1975. — Bibl.: p.147. — Index.
ISBN 0-289-70742-0 : £5.95
(B77-10471)

709'.67 — Sub-Saharan visual arts. Expounded by Sub-Saharan literatures
Duerden, Dennis. African art & literature : the invisible present / [by] Dennis Duerden. — London [etc.] : Heinemann Educational, 1977. — xiv,169p : ill ; 23cm.
Originally published: as 'The invisible present'. New York : Harper and Row, 1975. — Bibl.: p.155-160. — Index.
ISBN 0-435-91190-2 : £4.95
(B77-11980)

709'.7294 — Haitian visual arts, to 1972
Christensen, Eleanor Ingalls. The art of Haiti / [by] Eleanor Ingalls Christensen. — South Brunswick [etc.] : Barnes ; London : Yoseloff, 1975. — 77p,[48]p of plates : ill(some col), ports ; 32cm.
Bibl.: p.73-74. — Index.
ISBN 0-498-07926-0 : £6.00
(B77-28756)

709'.73 — Art galleries. *Merseyside (Metropolitan County). Liverpool. Walker Art Gallery. Exhibits: American visual arts, 1800-1900. Catalogues*
Morris, Edward. American artists in Europe, 1800-1900 : [catalogue of] an exhibition to celebrate the bicentenary of American independence [held at the] Walker Art Gallery, Liverpool, 14 November-2 January 1976-7 / [compiled by Edward Morris]. — [Liverpool] ([PO Box 95, Derby House, Exchange Flags, Liverpool L69 2JD]) : Merseyside County Council, [1976]. — 33p,[34]p of plates : ill, ports ; 30cm.
Index.
ISBN 0-901534-43-9 Sd : £2.25
(B77-04321)

709'.73 — Museums. *London. Kensington and Chelsea (London Borough). Victoria and Albert Museum. Exhibits: American visual arts, 1750-1800. Catalogues*
Victoria and Albert Museum. American art, 1750-1800 : towards independence : exhibition guide / Victoria and Albert Museum. — [London] : [The Museum], 1976. — 16p : ill, map, plan, ports ; 21cm.
'The Guide is divided into two sections : firstly an Introduction to American Art 1750-1800 ; secondly a room by room Guide ...' - title page verso.
Sd : £0.15
(B77-32750)

711 — ENVIRONMENT PLANNING
711 — Great Britain. Countryside. Policies of government. Great Britain. Parliament. House of Commons. Expenditure Committee. National parks and countryside. *Critical studies*
Great Britain. *Department of the Environment.* National Parks and the countryside, observations by the Secretaries of State for the Environment, for Scotland and for Wales on the sixth report of the Committee in session 1975-76 : first special report from the Expenditure Committee, session 1976-77. — London : H.M.S.O., [1977]. — 14p ; 25cm. — ([1976-77 H.C.]256)
ISBN 0-10-225677-2 Sd : £0.35
(B77-18282)

711'.05 — Environment planning. *Periodicals*
Face : University of Sheffield architectural studies. — [Sheffield] : [s.n.].
No.1- ; 1975-. — 1975-. — ill ; 30cm.
Monthly. — 12p. in no.5.
Sd : Unpriced
ISSN 0308-2229
Primary classification 720'.5
(B77-04324)

Martin Centre for Architectural and Urban Studies. Transactions of the Martin Centre for Architectural & Urban Studies, University of Cambridge. — Cambridge : Woodhead-Faulkner.
Vol.1- ; [1976]-. — 1976-. — ill, maps, plans ; 25cm.
Twice yearly. — [2],334p. in 1st issue. — Bibl.
Pbk : £14.50 yearly
ISSN 0309-2062
Also classified at 720'.5
(B77-07501)

711'.07'2041 — Great Britain. Environment planning. Research projects. *Lists. Serials*
Great Britain. *Department of the Environment. Library.* Research and surveys / [Department of the Environment, Headquarters Library]. — London (2 Marsham St., SW1P 3EB) : The Library. — (Great Britain. Department of the Environment. Library. Information series ; no.23)
1975. — 1976. — [2],v,197p ; 30cm.
Index.
ISBN 0-7184-0071-2 Pbk : Unpriced
(B77-15384)

711'.07'8 — Universities. *Tyne and Wear (Metropolitan County). Newcastle upon Tyne. University of Newcastle upon Tyne. Department of Town and Country Planning. Students. Individualised instruction. Role of audio-visual aids. Feasibility studies*
Stewart, James Henderson. The role of audio-visual self teaching packages : a pilot study of the acceptability of audio-visual self teaching packages in a Town and Country Planning School ... / [by] James H. Stewart. — Newcastle upon Tyne ([Newcastle upon Tyne NE1 7RU]) : [University of Newcastle upon Tyne, Department of Town and Country Planning], 1976. — [3],20,[8]leaves,plate : 1 ill ; 30cm.
Bibl.: p.20.
ISBN 0-905770-00-5 Sp : £1.00
(B77-01656)

711'.0941 — Great Britain. Environment planning. *Inquiry reports*
Great Britain. *Parliament. House of Commons. Expenditure Committee.* Planning procedures : eighth report from the Expenditure Committee, session 1976-77, together with the minutes of the evidence taken before the Environment Sub-committee in session 1975-76 and session 1976-77, appendices and index. — London : H.M.S.O.
Vol.1 : Report. — [1977]. — xlv p ; 25cm. — ([1976-77 H.C.]395-I) ([1975-76 H.C.]466) ([1976-77 H.C.]35)
ISBN 0-10-239577-2 Sd : £0.85
(B77-22009)

Vol.2 : Evidence. — [1977]. — xiv,706p : ill, form ; 25cm. — ([1976-77 H.C.]395-II) (1975-76 [H.C.]466) ([1976-77 H.C.]35)
ISBN 0-10-294477-6 Pbk : £13.80
(B77-28757)

Vol.3 : Appendices. — [1977]. — xiv p,p707-1224 : 1 ill ; 25cm. — ([1976-77 H.C.]395-III) (1975-76[H.C.]466) ([1976-77 H.C.]35)
ISBN 0-10-296577-3 Pbk : £7.10
(B77-28758)

711'.09411 — Scotland. Environment planning, 1971-1973. *Reports, surveys*
Planning Exchange. Changes in planning organisation and policy, 1971-73 / the Planning Exchange. — Glasgow (186 Bath St., Glasgow G2 4BG) : Planning Exchange, [1975]. — [3], 32p ; 30cm. — (Newsheet ; 2 ISSN 0307-1278)
Bibl.
ISBN 0-905011-12-0 Sd : £0.25
(B77-07979)

711'.12 — Environment planning. Structure plans. Plan making. Participation of public. Use of surveys. *Great Britain. Research reports*
Boaden, Noel. Sample surveys and public participation / [by] Noel Boaden and Raymond Walker. — Sheffield (c/o Ms I. Walkland, Department of Extramural Studies, University of Sheffield, 85 Wilkinson St., Sheffield S10 2GJ) : Linked Research Project into Public Participation in Structure Planning, 1976. — [1] ,ii,30,[2]p ; 30cm. — (Linked Research Project into Public Participation in Structure Planning. Interim research papers ; 10 ISSN 0307-5699)
ISBN 0-904856-08-9 Sd : £0.95
(B77-03142)

711'.12 — Great Britain. Environment planning. Structure plans. Plan making. Participation of public. Role of press. *Research reports*
Stringer, Peter. The press and publicity for public participation / [by] Peter Stringer. — Sheffield (c/o Ms I. Walkland, Department of Extramural Studies, University of Sheffield, 85 Wilkinson St., Sheffield S10 2GJ) : Linked Research Project into Public Participation in Structure Planning, 1977. — [1],iv,24,[2]p : 2 maps ; 30cm. — (Linked Research Project into Public Participation in Structure Planning. Interim research papers ; 12 ISSN 0307-5699)
Sd : £1.00
(B77-32032)

711'.3'094223 — Kent. Environment planning. Structure plans. Plan making. *Proposals*
Kent *(County). Planning Department.* Kent County structure plan / [Kent County Planning Department]. — Maidstone : Kent County Council.
Report of survey. — 1976. — [5],439p : ill, maps ; 21x30cm.
ISBN 0-905155-06-8 Pbk : £5.00
(B77-18896)

Written statement, consultative draft. — 1977. — [7],225p : 2 maps(1 col) ; 30cm.
Three fold. sheets (3 maps(2 col.)) in pocket.
ISBN 0-905155-08-4 Pbk : £2.00
(B77-18897)

711'.3'094225 — East Sussex. Environment planning. *Proposals*
East Sussex *(County). Planning Department.* County structure plan, 1977 review / East Sussex [County Planning Department]. — Lewes (Southover House, Southover Rd, Lewes, E. Sussex BN7 1YA) : The Department, 1977. — [5],64[i.e.70]p,fold plate : plan ; 30cm. — (Publication ; no.P/132)
Sd : £1.00
(B77-27970)

East Sussex *(County). Planning Department.* County structure plan, 1977 review, a consultative draft / East Sussex County Council [Planning Department]. — Lewes (Southover House, Southover Rd, Lewes, E. Sussex BN71 YA) : The Department, 1976. — [7],58[i.e.64]p, fold plate : map ; 30cm. — (Publication ; no.P/125)
ISBN 0-900348-50-x Sd : £1.00
(B77-09143)

711'.3'094225 — East Sussex. Environment planning. Structure plans. Plan making. *Proposals*
East Sussex *(County). Planning Department.* Submitted alterations and corrections to the county structure plan, 1975 / East Sussex County Council [Planning Department]. — Lewes : The Department, 1976. — [1],i,42p ; 30cm.
To be read in conjunction with the 'County structure plan, 1975'.
ISBN 0-900348-49-6 Sd : £1.00
(B77-04953)

711'.3'094225 — East Sussex. Environment planning. Structure plans. Plan making. *Reports, surveys*
East Sussex *(County). Planning Department.* County structure plan, 1977 review, report of survey, review of the submitted structure plan / East Sussex County Council [Planning Department]. — Lewes (Southover House, Southover Rd, Lewes, E. Sussex BN7 1YA) : [The Department], 1976. — [3],48p ; 30cm.
'This report provides the background to the Review of the submitted Structure Plan. Its contents will be assimilated into the County Structure Plan Report of Survey, when a further submission is made to the Secretary of State'.
Sd : £0.55
(B77-15385)

711'.3'0942291 — Environment planning. Structure plans. Plan making. Strategic choice methods. *Study regions: Berkshire. Newbury (District)*
Bather, Nicholas John. Strategic choice in practice : the West Berkshire Structure Plan experience / [by] N.J. Bather, C.M. Williams & A. Sutton. — Reading (Whiteknights, Reading RG6 2AB) : Department of Geography, University of Reading, 1976. — [3],ii,63p : ill, maps ; 21cm. — (Geographical papers ; no.50 ISSN 0305-5914)
Bibl.: p.63.
ISBN 0-7049-0460-8 Sd : £0.70
(B77-09144)

711'.3'0942336 — Dorset. Purbeck (District). Coastal regions. Environment planning. *Proposals*
Dorset *(County). Planning Department.* Purbeck Heritage Coast : report & proposals / Dorset County Council Planning Department. — [Dorchester] ([c/o County Librarian, County Library, Colliton Park, Dorchester DT1 1XJ]) : [The Council], 1977. — 66p in various pagings,10 leaves of plates(3 fold) : ill, maps(chiefly col) ; 30cm.
ISBN 0-85216-180-8 Pbk : £0.75
(B77-33334)

711'.3'094237 — Cornwall. Environment planning. Structure plans. Plan making. *Proposals*
Cornwall *(County). Planning Department.* Cornwall county structure plan, the policy choices / [Cornwall County Council, Planning Department]. — [Truro] ([County Hall, Truro, Cornwall TR1 3AY]) : [The Department], 1976. — [4],34p : form ; 30cm.
ISBN 0-902319-13-2 Sp : Unpriced
(B77-03672)

711'.3'094239 — Avon. Environment planning. Structure plans. Plan making. *Proposals*
Avon *(County). Planning Department.* Structure plan, options in outline / Avon County Council Planning Department. — Bristol (Avon House North, St James Barton, Bristol BS99 7NB) : [The Department], [1977]. — [72]p : ill, maps ; 30cm.
ISBN 0-86063-016-1 Sp : £0.80
(B77-21288)

711'.3'09424 — England. West Midlands. Environment planning. Monitoring. *Reports, surveys. Serials*
West Midlands Joint Monitoring Steering Group. Annual report of the [West Midlands] Joint Monitoring Steering Group. — Birmingham (102 New St., Birmingham B2 4HQ) : West Midland Regional Study ; Birmingham : Department of the Environment.
1st : 1975 : a developing strategy for the West Midlands. — 1975. — [5],38,[4]p,[5]leaves : plans ; 30cm.
ISBN 0-905940-00-8 Sp : £1.00
(B77-09837)

711'.3'094246 — Great Britain. Environment planning. Structure plans. Plan making. Participation of public. *Study regions: Staffordshire. Research reports*
Bridges, Lee. Structure plan examinations in public : a descriptive analysis / by Lee Bridges and Carol Vielba. — [Birmingham] ([P.O. Box 363, Birmingham B15 2TT]) : University of Birmingham, Institute of Judicial Administration, 1976. — x,87p ; 30cm.
ISBN 0-7044-0218-1 Sp : £1.25
Also classified at 711'.3'094254
(B77-12571)

711'.3'094246 — Members of public participating in structure planning. *Great Britain. Study regions: Staffordshire. Research reports*
Vielba, Carol A. A survey of those taking part in two structure plan examinations in public / by Carol A. Vielba. — [Birmingham] ([P.O. Box 363, Birmingham B15 2TT]) : University of Birmingham, Institute of Judicial Administration, 1976. — vi,72p : ill, forms ; 30cm.
ISBN 0-7044-0217-3 Sp : £1.25
Also classified at 711'.3'094254
(B77-12572)

711'.3'094253 — Lincolnshire. Environment planning. Structure plans. Plan making. Participation of public. *Reports, surveys*
Lincolnshire *(County). Planning Department.* Public participation and consultation : a background paper to the Lincolnshire structure plan / [Lincolnshire County Planning Department]. — [Lincoln] ([County Offices, Lincoln LN1 1Y]) : The Department, 1976. — 36p ; 30cm.
Cover title: Lincolnshire structure plan, background paper, public participation and consultation. — Summary (sheet;[2]p.) as insert. — 'Report of Survey : Part IV' - cover.
Sp : £0.35
(B77-22010)

711'.3'094254 — Great Britain. Environment planning. Structure plans. Plan making. Participation of public. *Study regions: Leicestershire. Research reports*
Bridges, Lee. Structure plan examinations in public : a descriptive analysis / by Lee Bridges and Carol Vielba. — [Birmingham] ([P.O. Box 363, Birmingham B15 2TT]) : University of Birmingham, Institute of Judicial Administration, 1976. — x,87p ; 30cm.
ISBN 0-7044-0218-1 Sp : £1.25
Primary classification 711'.3'094246
(B77-12571)

711'.3'094254 — Leicestershire. Environment planning. Structure plans. *Proposals*
Leicestershire *(County). Planning Department.* Leicestershire planning policies / [Leicestershire County Planning Department]. — [Leicester] ([County Hall, Glenfield, Leicester]) : Leicestershire County Council, 1976. — [2],40,[2]p : ill, col map ; 20x29cm.
ISBN 0-85022-011-4 Sd : £0.50
(B77-11981)

711'.3'094254 — Members of public participating in structure planning. *Great Britain. Study regions: Leicestershire. Research reports*
Vielba, Carol A. A survey of those taking part in two structure plan examinations in public / by Carol A. Vielba. — [Birmingham] ([P.O. Box 363, Birmingham B15 2TT]) : University of Birmingham, Institute of Judicial Administration, 1976. — vi,72p : ill, forms ; 30cm.
ISBN 0-7044-0217-3 Sp : £1.25
Primary classification 711'.3'094246
(B77-12572)

711'.3'0942545 — Leicestershire. Rutland (District). Environment planning. Structure plans. Plan making. *Proposals*
Leicestershire *(County). Planning Department.* Structure plan for Rutland : written statement / [Leicestershire County Planning Department]. — [Leicester] ([County Hall, Glenfield, Leicester]) : [Leicestershire County Council], 1977. — 94p in various pagings : maps ; 30cm.
Ls : Unpriced
(B77-17644)

Leicestershire *(County). Planning Department.* Structure plan for Rutland, written statement / Leicestershire County Council [Planning Department]. — Leicester (County Hall, Glenfield, Leicester [LE3 8RA]) : [The Department], 1977. — [5],64p,fold plate : maps, plans(1 col) ; 31cm.
Not the same as B77-17644. — Previous control number ISBN 0-85022-016-5.
Sp : £2.50
(B77-28759)

711'.3'0942545 — Leicestershire. Rutland (District). Environment planning. Structure plans. Plan making. Participation of public. *Reports, surveys*
Leicestershire *(County). Planning Department.* Structure plan for Rutland, report of publicity / [Leicestershire County Planning Department]. — Leicester (County Hall, Glenfield, Leicester [LE3 8RA]) : [The Department], 1977. — [3], 28p : ill, facsims ; 31cm.
ISBN 0-85022-014-9 Sd : £0.50
(B77-33934)

711'.3'094256 — Bedfordshire. Environment planning. Structure plans. Plan making. Participation of public. *Research reports*
Bedfordshire *(County). Council.* County structure plan, public participation, phase 2 report / [Bedfordshire County Council]. — [Bedford] ([County Hall, Bedford MK42 9AP]) : [The Council], 1976. — [225]p in various pagings : maps ; 30cm.
ISBN 0-901051-83-7 Sd : £1.50
(B77-11982)

Bedfordshire *(County). Council.* County structure plan, public participation, phase 2 : report / Bedfordshire [County Planning Department]. — [Bedford] ([County Hall, Bedford MK42 9AP]) : [The Department].
(Supplement). — 1977. — [5],9,[i.e.11]p ; 30cm.
Sd : £1.50
(B77-18283)

711'.3'094259 — Buckinghamshire. Environment planning. Structure plans. Plan making. *Proposals*
Buckinghamshire *(County). Council.* Buckinghamshire county structure plan 1976, written statement / [Buckinghamshire County Council]. — [Aylesbury] ([County Offices, Aylesbury, Bucks.]) : County Planning Department, [1976]. — [10],98p(4 fold),[6]leaves : ill, maps, 2 plans(1 col) ; 30cm.
'Form for objections or representations' ([3] leaves : sd) as insert. — Index.
ISBN 0-902805-75-4 Sp : £1.75
(B77-15968)

711'.3'094259 — Buckinghamshire. Environment planning. Structure plans. Plan making. Participation of public. *Reports, surveys*
Buckinghamshire *(County). Council.* Buckinghamshire county structure plan 1976, report on public participation / [Buckinghamshire County Council]. — [Aylesbury] ([County Hall, Aylesbury, Bucks.]) : [County Planning Department], [1976]. — [4],166p ; 30cm.
ISBN 0-902805-85-1 Sp : £1.00
(B77-16508)

711'.3'094264 — Suffolk. Environment planning. Structure plans. *Proposals*
Suffolk *(County). Planning Department.* Suffolk County structure plan, [written statement] / Suffolk County Planning Department. — Ipswich ([County Hall, Ipswich IP4 2JS]) : Suffolk County Council, 1977. — [4]leaves, 193[i.e.194]p,fold plate : ill, col maps ; 30cm.
ISBN 0-86055-011-7 Pbk : £1.75
(B77-18898)

711'.3'094264 — Suffolk. Environment planning. Structure plans. Plan making. *Proposals*
Suffolk *(County). Council.* Suffolk County structure plan, report of survey / Suffolk County Council. — [Ipswich] ([County Hall, Ipswich, Suffolk]) : [The Council].
[Appendix] 1 : Population. — 1977. — [5],42[i.e.44]p,[4]p of plates,[3] leaves of plates(1 fold) : ill, 2 maps(1 col) ; 30cm.
ISBN 0-86055-013-3 Sd : £0.75
(B77-21289)

[Appendix] 2 : Employment. — 1977. — [5], 74p,[3] leaves of plates(2 fold) : ill, 3 maps(2 col) ; 30cm.
ISBN 0-86055-014-1 Sd : £1.00
(B77-21290)

[Appendix] 3 : Housing. — 1977. — [5],40p : col map ; 30cm.
ISBN 0-86055-015-x Sd : £0.60
(B77-21291)

[Appendix] 4 : Shopping. — 1977. — [5],43p, plate : 2 maps(1 col) ; 30cm.
ISBN 0-86055-016-8 Sd : £0.60
(B77-21292)

[Appendix] 5 : Conservation and recreation. — 1977. — [5],42p,7 fold leaves of plates : maps(2 col) ; 30cm.
Bibl.: p.42.
ISBN 0-86055-017-6 Sd : £0.75
(B77-21293)

[Appendix] 6 : Communications. — 1977. — [5],31p,[5] leaves of plates(2 fold) : maps(some col) ; 30cm.
ISBN 0-86055-018-4 Sd : £0.75
(B77-21294)

[Appendix] 7 : Public sector services. — 1977. — [5],10p : col map ; 30cm.
ISBN 0-86055-026-5 Sd : Unpriced
(B77-21295)

[Appendix] 8 : Resources. — 1977. — [5],16p : col map ; 30cm.
ISBN 0-86055-019-2 Sd : £0.40
(B77-21296)

[Appendix] 9 : The county strategy. — 1977. — [5],20,xvii p : col map ; 30cm.
ISBN 0-86055-020-6 Sd : £0.60
(B77-21297)

[Appendix] 10 : Rural settlement. — 1977. — [5],39p : col map ; 30cm.
ISBN 0-86055-021-4 Sd : £0.60
(B77-21298)

[Appendix] 11 : Ipswich Sub-region. — 1977. — 104p in various pagings : ill, 2 forms, maps(1 col), col plan ; 30cm.
Includes: Ipswich and District transportation strategy, first public consultation report / Suffolk County Council, Ipswich Borough Council. Originally published: Ipswich : Suffolk County Council, 1974 - Ipswich transportation study, second public consultation report / Suffolk County Council, Borough of Ipswich. Originally published: Ipswich : Suffolk County Council, 1976.
ISBN 0-86055-022-2 Sd : £1.40
(B77-21299)

[Appendix] 12 : Western Suffolk Sub-region. — 1977. — [5],41p : maps(1 col) ; 30cm.
ISBN 0-86055-023-0 Sd : £0.60
(B77-21300)

[Appendix] 13 : Central Suffolk Sub-region. — 1977. — [5],13p : maps(1 col) ; 30cm.
ISBN 0-86055-024-9 Sd : £0.40
(B77-21301)

[Appendix] 14 : Lowestoft Sub-region. — 1977. — [5],29p : maps(2 col) ; 30cm.
ISBN 0-86055-025-7 Sd : £0.60
(B77-21302)

Suffolk *(County). Planning Department.* Suffolk County Structure Plan, report of survey : public consultation draft / [Suffolk County Planning Department]. — [1st ed., reprinted] ; [with addendum to the report of survey]. — [Ipswich] ([County Hall, Ipswich IP4 2JS]) : Suffolk County Council, 1977. — 58,[14]p,[10]fold leaves of plates : ill, maps ; 30cm.
Originally published: 1976.
ISBN 0-86055-012-5 Sd : £1.00
(B77-19515)

Suffolk *(County). Planning Department.* Suffolk County Structure Plan, report of survey : public consultation draft / [Suffolk County Planning Department]. — [Ipswich] ([County Hall, Ipswich IP4 2JS]) : Suffolk County Council, 1976. — 58,[12]p,[10]fold leaves of plates : ill, maps ; 30cm.
ISBN 0-86055-039-7 Sd : £1.00
(B77-19516)

711'.3'094264 — Suffolk. Environment planning. Structure plans. Publicity & representations. *Reports, surveys*

Suffolk *(County). Planning Department.* Suffolk County structure plan, report of publicity and representations / [Suffolk County Planning Department]. — Ipswich (County Hall, Ipswich [IP4 2JS]) : Suffolk County Council, [1977]. — 41p in various pagings : 1 ill, 2 facsims(1 col), col map ; 30cm.
Includes 'Suffolk, the next 15 years' as appendix.
ISBN 0-86055-028-1 Pbk : £0.50
(B77-18899)

711'.3'0942646 — Suffolk. Coastal regions. Environment planning. *Proposals*

Suffolk Coastal District. *Council.* Suffolk Heritage Coast : draft plan / Suffolk Coastal District Council, Suffolk County Council, Waveney District Council. — [Ipswich] ([County Hall, Ipswich IP4 2JS]) : Suffolk County Council, 1976. — 2 leaves,14[i.e.15],[3]p,7 leaves of plates : maps(chiefly col) ; 30cm.
ISBN 0-86055-003-6 Pbk : £0.80
(B77-06797)

711'.3'094265 — Cambridgeshire. Environment planning. Structure plans. *Proposals*

Cambridgeshire *(County). Planning Department.* Cambridgeshire structure plan, report on alternative strategies / [Cambridgeshire] County Planning Department. — Cambridge (Shire Hall, Cambridge) : Cambridgeshire County Council, 1976. — [5],14p : ill, maps(chiefly col) ; 30cm.
ISBN 0-902436-16-3 Sp : £0.75
(B77-11318)

711'.3'094267 — Essex. Environment planning. Structure plans. Plan making. *Proposals*

Essex *(County). Planning Department.* Alternatives : how the county could develop / Essex County Council [Planning Department]. — [Chelmsford] ([County Hall, Chelmsford CM1 1LF]) : [The Department], 1977. — [1],ii, 38p : col maps ; 30cm.
Cover title: Essex structure plan, alternatives.
Sp : £0.50
(B77-25766)

Essex *(County). Planning Department.* Essex structure plan, report on first consultation / Essex County Council [Planning Department]. — [Chelmsford] ([County Hall, Chelmsford CM1 1LF]) : [The Department], 1977. — [3], 20p ; 30cm.
Sd : £0.25
(B77-26413)

711'.3'094267 — North Essex & Central Essex. Environment planning. Structure plans. Plan making. *Proposals*

Essex *(County). Planning Department.* The alternatives in North & Central Essex / Essex County Council [Planning Department]. — [Chelmsford] ([County Hall, Chelmsford CM1 1LF]) : [The Department], 1977. — [53]p : 1 ill, col maps, col plans ; 30cm.
Cover title: Essex structure plan, the alternatives in North & Central Essex.
Sd : £0.60
(B77-25767)

711'.3'094267 — South Essex. Environment planning. Structure plans. *Proposals*

Essex *(County). Planning Department.* The alternatives in South Essex : the generation of alternative strategies / [Essex County Planning Department]. — [Chelmsford] ([County Hall, Chelmsford CM1 1LF]) : [The Department], 1977. — [5],61p : maps, plans(chiefly col) ; 30cm.
Cover title: Essex structure plan, the alternatives in South Essex.
Sd : £0.70
(B77-26414)

Essex *(County). Planning Department.* The alternatives in South Essex : the generation of alternative strategies / [Essex County Planning Department]. — [Chelmsford] ([County Hall, Chelmsford CM1 1LF]) : [The Department].
Appendices. — 1977. — [3],58p : map ; 30cm.
Cover title: Essex structure plan, the alternatives in South Essex. Appendices.
Sd : £0.70
(B77-26415)

711'.3'094267 — South Essex. Environment planning. Structure plans. Implications of national & regional planning. *Reports, surveys. For structure plan making*

Essex *(County). Planning Department.* South Essex, its regional context / Essex County Council [Planning Department]. — [Chelmsford] ([County Hall, Chelmsford CM1 1LF]) : [The Department], 1977. — [3],23p : 2 maps(1 col) ; 30cm.
Cover title: Essex structure plan, South Essex regional context.
Sd : £0.25
(B77-26416)

711'.3'09426715 — Essex. Braintree (District). Rural regions. Environment planning. *Proposals*

Braintree *(District). Council.* Rural planning, policy / Braintree District Council. — Braintree (Town Hall, Braintree, Essex) : The Council, 1977. — [95]p : maps ; 30cm.
Sd : £0.75
(B77-33335)

711'.3'09426752 — Essex. Chelmsford (District). Rural regions. Environment planning. *Reports, surveys*

Chelmsford *(District). Council.* Rural areas study, the rural environment / Chelmsford District Council. — Chelmsford (Planning Department, Burgess Well Rd, Chelmsford [CM1 1TR]) : [The Council], 1977. — [3],6[i.e. 8]p,[3] leaves of plates : maps ; 30cm. — (Subject report ; 8)
Sd : £0.20
(B77-17645)

711'.3'094282 — South Yorkshire (Metropolitan County). Environment planning. Structure plans. Plan making. *Proposals*

South Yorkshire *(Metropolitan County). Council.* South Yorkshire structure plan, report of survey / South Yorkshire County Council. — [Barnsley] ([Planning Department, County Hall, Barnsley, S. Yorkshire S70 2TN]) : The Council.
Vol.1 : The structure plan process. — 1977. — vi,16[i.e.24]p,3 leaves of plates(1 fold) : 2 ill, 2 col maps ; 21x30cm.
Page width varies.
ISBN 0-86046-003-7 Sp : £0.50
(B77-15969)

Vol.2 : Defining the key issues. — 1977. — xi, 137[i.e.229]p,[25]leaves,[42]p of plates : ill(incl 1 col), col maps ; 21x30cm.
Page width varies.
ISBN 0-86046-004-5 Sp : £2.00
(B77-15970)

Vol.3 : Developing strategic policies. — 1977. — xii,157[i.e.197]p,[6]leaves of plates(1 fold),[28]p of plates : ill, maps(chiefly col), col plans ; 21x30cm.
Page width varies.
ISBN 0-86046-005-3 Sp : £2.00
(B77-15971)

711'.3'094282 — South Yorkshire (Metropolitan County). Environment planning. Structure plans. Plan making. *Reports, surveys*

South Yorkshire *(Metropolitan County). Council.* South Yorkshire structure plan, draft written statement / South Yorkshire County Council. — [Barnsley] ([Planning Department, County Hall, Barnsley, S. Yorkshire S70 2TN]) : The Council, 1977. — ix,[4],142[i.e.162]p,[6] leaves of plates(3 fold) : ill, maps(1 col), col plans ; 21x30cm.
Plan on fold leaf in pocket. — Page width varies.
ISBN 0-86046-006-1 Sp : £2.00
(B77-16509)

711'.3'094283 — Humberside. Environment planning. Structure plans. Plan making. *Proposals*

Humberside *(County). Council.* Humberside structure plan : [background studies : consultation draft June 1976] / Humberside County Council. — [Beverley] ([c/o The Director of Planning, Manor Rd, Beverley, N. Humberside HU17 7BX]) : [The Council], [1977]. — 177p, 11 fold leaves of plates : ill, maps, plans ; 30cm.
Cover title.
Pbk : Unpriced
(B77-12573)

Humberside *(County). Council.* Humberside structure plan / Humberside County Council. — [Beverley] ([c/o The Director of Planning, Manor Rd, Beverley, N. Humberside HU17 7BX]) : [The Council].
[Background studies]. — 1976. — 181p,11 fold leaves of plates : maps ; 30cm.
Cover title.
ISBN 0-905972-01-5 Pbk : £4.25
(B77-15386)

[Participation]. — 1976. — 46p ; 30cm.
Cover title.
ISBN 0-905972-02-3 Pbk : £1.00
(B77-15387)

[Policies, submission draft]. — 1976. — 98p,6 fold leaves of plates : maps ; 30cm.
Cover title.
ISBN 0-905972-03-1 Pbk : £1.50
(B77-15388)

711'.3'094285 — Great Britain. Environment planning. Structure plans. Plan making. Participation of public. Role of consultants. *Study regions: Cleveland. Teesside. Reports, surveys*
Hampton, William. The role of consultants in the public participation process : the Teesside experience / [by] William Hampton and Raymond Walker. — Sheffield (c/o Mrs Iris Walkland, Department of Extramural Studies, University of Sheffield, 85 Wilkinson St., Sheffield S10 2GJ) : Linked Research Project into Public Participation in Structure Planning, 1975. — [4],14p : map ; 30cm. — (Linked Research Project into Public Participation in Structure Planning. Interim research papers ; 5)
ISBN 0-904856-05-4 Pbk : £0.60
(B77-02458)

711'.3'094293 — Clwyd. Environment planning. *Proposals*
Clwyd *(County). Planning Department.* Clwyd County structure plan, written statement (draft) / County of Clwyd [Planning Department]. — Mold (Shire Hall, Mold, Clwyd CH7 6NG) : [The Department], 1977. — [3],vii,189[i.e.209]p,[8]fold leaves of plates : maps(chiefly col), col plans ; 30cm.
Pbk : Unpriced
(B77-30449)

711'.4 — Organisation for Economic Co-operation and Development countries. Town planning. Related to choice by governments of passenger transport services. *Reports, surveys*
Round Table on Transport Economics, *33rd, Paris, 1976.* Report of the Thirty-third Round Table on Transport Economics held in Paris on 26th and 27th February, 1976 on the following topic, 'Impact of the structure and extent of urban development on the choice of modes of transport : the case of large conurbations' / [by P. Merlin]. — Paris : European Conference of Ministers of Transport, Economic Research Centre ; [London] : [H.M.S.O.], 1976. — 48p : ill, maps, plan ; 24cm. — (ECMT round table ; 33 ISSN 0531-9528)
Bibl.: p.36.
Pbk : £1.80
ISBN 92-821-1038-9
Primary classification 380.5'2
(B77-05998)

711'.4 — Town planning. Role of sociology. Theories
McDougall, G. Sociology in planning : a redefinition / [by] G. McDougall, J. Foulsham and J. Porter. — Hatfield (c/o Gabriel Newfield, School of Social Sciences, Hatfield Polytechnic, P.O. Box 109, Hatfield, Herts. AL10 9AB) : Organisation of Sociologists in Polytechnics and Cognate Institutions, 1977. — [2],27p ; 21cm. — (Organisation of Sociologists in Polytechnics and Cognate Institutions. SIP papers ; no.3)
ISBN 0-905509-02-1 Sd : £0.50(free to members)
(B77-14839)

711.4'01'9 — Town planning. Psychological aspects
Smith, Peter Frederick. The syntax of cities / [by] Peter F. Smith. — London : Hutchinson, 1977. — 271p : ill ; 24cm. — (The built environment)
Bibl.: p.264-266. — Index.
ISBN 0-09-127080-4 : £10.00
(B77-23585)

711'.4'06041 — Town planning. Organisations. *Great Britain. Directories*
Directory of official architecture & planning. — London : Godwin.
1977 : 21st ed. — 1977. — xiv,508p : ill, maps ; 23cm.
Index.
ISBN 0-7114-3410-7 : Unpriced
Primary classification 720'.6'041
(B77-13760)

711'.4'06241 — Town planning. Organisations. *Great Britain. Royal Town Planning Institute. Directories*
Royal Town Planning Institute. List of members / the Royal Town Planning Institute. — London : [R.T.P.I.].
1976, as at August. — [1977]. — [2],155p ; 21cm.
Cover title.
ISBN 0-901151-25-4 Pbk : £6.00(£0.90 to members)
(B77-06798)

711'.4'0942 — England. Urban regions. Environment planning. Political aspects. *Case studies*
Gladstone, Francis. The politics of planning / [by] Francis Gladstone. — London : Temple Smith, 1976. — 128p ; 23cm.
Index.
ISBN 0-85117-106-0 : £4.50
ISBN 0-85117-104-4 Pbk : £2.00
(B77-00318)

711'.4'0942 — Towns. Layout. *England, to 1975*
Aston, Michael. The landscape of towns / [by] Michael Aston and James Bond. — London : Dent, 1976. — 255p,[8]p of plates : ill, maps, plans ; 23cm. — (Archaeology in the field series)
Bibl.: p.221-238. — Index.
ISBN 0-460-04194-0 : £5.50
(B77-00319)

711'.4'09421 — Docks. Land. Redevelopment. *Port of London. Proposals*
Docklands Joint Committee. London docklands strategic plan / Docklands Joint Committee. — London (164 Westminster Bridge Rd, SE1 7RW) : Docklands Development Team, [1976]. — [1],115p : ill, maps, plans(some col) ; 30cm. — (Docks 150)
Previous control number B7702459.
ISBN 0-905065-11-5 Pbk : £1.50
(B77-02459)

Docklands Joint Committee. London docklands strategic plan, summary / Docklands Joint Committee. — [London] ([164 Westminster Bridge Rd, SE1 7RW]) : [Docklands Development Team], 1976. — Folder(4p) : col plan ; 30cm.
ISBN 0-905065-10-7 : Unpriced
(B77-02460)

711'.4'094212 — London (City). Areas destroyed by fires, 1666. Redevelopment
De Maré, Eric. Wren's London / by Eric de Maré. — London : [Joseph], 1975 [i.e. 1977]. — 128p : ill(some col), col coats of arms, facsims, maps(1 col), plans(1 col), ports(some col) ; 26cm.
Title page imprint: Folio Society. — Ill., maps on lining papers. — Originally published: London : Folio Society, 1975.
ISBN 0-7181-1586-4 : £5.00
Also classified at 720'.92'4
(B77-18284)

711'.4'0942132 — London. Westminster (London Borough). Covent Garden. Town planning. *Proposals*
Greater London Council. The Greater London Council (Covent Garden) GLC action area plan, written statement incorporating the proposals map. — [London] : G.L.C., 1976. — [5],153[i.e. 157],[1]p,[11] leaves of plates : plans(chiefly col) ; 30cm.
ISBN 0-7168-0855-2 Sd : £1.00
(B77-11983)

711'.4'0942165 — London. Lambeth (London Borough). Waterloo region. Environment planning. *Proposals*
Lambeth *(London Borough). Directorate of Development Services.* Waterloo district plan : written statement / London Borough of Lambeth [Directorate of Development Services]. — London ([138 Clapham Park Rd, SW4 7DD]) : The Directorate, 1976. — [5],24,23p ; 30cm.
Four fold sheets (col. maps) in pocket.
ISBN 0-902062-07-7 Sp : £1.25
(B77-09839)

Lambeth *(London Borough). Directorate of Development Services.* Waterloo district plan : written statement / London Borough of Lambeth [Directorate of Development Services]. — [New ed.]. — [London] ([138 Clapham Park Rd, SW4 7DD]) : [The Directorate], 1977. — [5],26,20p ; 30cm.
Five fold sheets (col. maps, col. plan) in pocket. — Previous ed.: 1976.
Sp : £1.25(£0.75 to residents of the borough)
(B77-18900)

711'.4'09422352 — Kent. Cranbrook. Town planning. *Proposals*
Kent *(County). Council.* Cranbrook, informal district plan including conservation study / Kent County Council. — [Maidstone] ([County Hall, Maidstone, Kent ME14 1XD]) : [The Council], 1976. — 89p in various pagings,[6]leaves of plates(4 fold) : ill, col maps, plans(some col) ; 30cm.
Pbk : £3.50
(B77-02461)

711'.4'09422372 — Kent. Snodland. Village planning. *Proposals*
Kent *(County). Planning Department.* Snodland informal district plan / [Kent County Planning Department]. — Maidstone (County Hall, Maidstone, Kent) : Kent County Council, 1976. — [7],25p,[2]fold leaves of plates : ill, col maps ; 30cm.
Sd : £1.35
(B77-01657)

711'.4'0942332 — Dorset. Blandford. Town planning. *Proposals*
Dorset *(County). Council.* Blandford draft district plan / Dorset County Council & North Dorset District Council. — [Blandford Forum] ([Chief Planning Officer, Nordon, Salisbury Rd, Blandford Forum DT11 7LL]) : [North Dorset District Council], 1976. — [4],17p,fold plate : map, col plan ; 30cm.
ISBN 0-85216-161-1 Sd : £0.20
(B77-04322)

711'.4'0942337 — Dorset. Poole. Town planning. *Proposals*
Dorset *(County). Council.* Poole district plan, modified draft / [Dorset County Council, Poole Borough Council]. — [Dorchester] ([County Hall, Dorchester, Dorset DT1 1XJ]) : Dorset County Council, [1976]. — [5],132[i.e. 142]p : ill, maps(chiefly col), plans(chiefly col) ; 30cm.
Cover title. — Two plans on 2 fold. leaves in pocket.
ISBN 0-85216-163-8 Pbk : £1.25
(B77-06799)

711'.4'09423592 — Devon. Ivybridge. Environment planning. Policies of Devon (County). Council, 1952-1976. *Reports, surveys*
Glyn-Jones, Anne. Village into town : a study of transition in South Devon / by Anne Glyn-Jones. — [Exeter] ([County Hall, Exeter]) : Devon County Council ; [Exeter] : University of Exeter, 1977. — [4],88p : 1 ill, maps ; 24cm.
ISBN 0-85989-057-0 Sd : Unpriced
(B77-24369)

711'.4'0942393 — Avon. Bristol. Environment planning. *Proposals*
University of Bristol. *Students' Union.* Just look at Bristol! : about planning & potential in cities / [University of Bristol Students' Union]. — Bristol (6 Buckingham Vale, Bristol 8) : Bristol Visual and Environmental Group, [1976?]. — [2],16,[2]p : ill, maps, plans ; 30cm.
ISBN 0-9504648-0-5 Sd : £0.60
(B77-30450)

711'.4'0942534 — Lincolnshire. Lincoln. Clasket Gate to Lower West Gate. Environment planning
Lincolnshire *(County). Planning Department.* Clasket Gate to Lower West Gate district plan, brief / [Lincolnshire County Planning Department and Lincoln City Department of Planning and Architecture]. — Lincoln (City Hall, Beaumont Fee, Lincoln LN1 1DF) : Lincoln City Department of Planning and Architecture ; Lincoln : Lincolnshire County Planning Department, 1977. — [1],6[i.e.7]p : map ; 30cm.
ISBN 0-902092-08-1 Sd : £0.12
(B77-13144)

711'.4'0942545 — Leicestershire. Lyddington. Village planning. *Reports, surveys*
Higgins, D C. Lyddington : an approach for the future / [by D.C. Higgins]. — [Lyddington] ([Lyddington, Leics.]) : The Lyddington Society, [1976]. — [3],28 leaves,fold plate : ill, plan ; 30cm.
Bibl.: leaf 8.
ISBN 0-9505553-0-4 Sp : Unpriced
(B77-07502)

711'.4'0942549 — Leicestershire. Groby. Village planning. Participation of public. *Reports, surveys*
Hinckley and Bosworth *(District). Council.*
Groby district plan / [Hinckley and Bosworth Borough Council]. — [Hinckley] ([Council Office, Argents Mead, Hinckley, Leics. LE10 1BZ]) : Department of Development and Amenity, The Council.
[Amendments]. — 1976. — [59]p,[2] fold leaves of plates : ill, map, plan ; 30cm.
Pierced for binder. — Three gummed labels in envelope as insert.
ISBN 0-905132-03-3 Sd : £1.75
(B77-03673)

Hinckley and Bosworth *(District). Council.*
Groby district plan, statement on publicity and consultations / [Hinckley and Bosworth Borough Council]. — [Hinckley] ([Council Offices, Argents Mead, Hinckley, Leics. LE10 1BZ]) : Department of Development and Amenity, [The Council], 1976. — [3],90p : ill, facsims, map, plans ; 30cm.
ISBN 0-905132-02-5 Sp : £0.50
(B77-03674)

711'.4'0942549 — Leicestershire. Ratby. Environment planning. Structure plans. *Proposals*
Hinckley and Bosworth *(District). Council.*
Ratby district plan : residents information booklet : your chance to comment on issues that affect you / Hinckley and Bosworth Borough Council. — Hinckley (Council Offices, Argents Mead, Hinckley, Leics.) : The Council, 1977. — 12p : ill, maps(1 col) ; 22cm.
Sd : Unpriced
(B77-17646)

711'.4'0942561 — Conservation areas. *Bedfordshire. Thurleigh. Thurleigh conservation area*
North Bedfordshire *(Borough). Department of Planning and Development.* Thurleigh and its conservation area / Department of Planning and Development, North Bedfordshire Borough Council. — [Bedford] ([Town Hall, Bedford MK40 1SJ]) : North Bedfordshire Borough Council, 1976. — [1],24,[2]p,fold plate : ill, 2 maps(1 col), 2 plans(1 col) ; 30cm.
Sd : £0.50
(B77-09145)

711'.4'0942574 — Urban regions. Environment planning. Participation of public. Political aspects. *Study regions: Oxfordshire. East Oxford*
Neighbourhood, Planning and Politics *(Conference), Oxford Polytechnic, 1975.*
Neighbourhood, planning and politics : a geography seminar series / John R. Gold, editor. — [Headington] ([Oxford OX3 0BP]) : Oxford Polytechnic, 1976. — [5],59p ; 30cm. — (Oxford Polytechnic. Discussion papers in geography ; no.1)
'The papers ... are the revised transcripts of a seminar series held at Oxford Polytechnic in the Summer of 1975 under the title of "Neighbourhood, planning, and politics"' - Editorial note.
Pbk : £0.50
Also classified at 711'.4'09713541
(B77-08468)

711'.4'0942597 — Buckinghamshire. Chesham. Environment planning. Plan making. *Proposals*
Chiltern *(District). Council.* Chesham town centre and waterside local plan : alternatives report / Chiltern District Council. — [Amersham] ([42 High St., Amersham, Bucks. HP7 0DL]) : [The Council], 1977. — [7],78,v p(4 fold) : ill, maps, plans ; 30cm.
ISBN 0-902805-76-2 Sd : £0.50
(B77-21303)

711'.4'0942656 — Cambridgeshire. Ely. Central areas. Environment planning. *Proposals*
East Cambridgeshire *(District). Planning Department.* Ely draft town centre plan / East Cambridgeshire District Council [Planning Department] ; report prepared by Bruce Lorimer, Jonathan Tucker ; graphics by Alan Stevens, Robert Powell. — Ely (The Grange, Nutholt La., Ely, Cambs.) : East Cambridgeshire District Council, 1976. — [4], 39,[1]p,[7]leaves : ill, col maps, plans(chiefly col) ; 30cm.
One leaf printed on both sides.
Sp : £0.50
(B77-11319)

711'.4'0942657 — Cambridgeshire. Bar Hill. Village planning. *Proposals*
South Cambridgeshire *(District). Planning Department.* Bar Hill draft local plan / South Cambridgeshire District Council [Planning Department]. — Cambridge (South Cambridgeshire Hall, Hills Rd, Cambridge [CB2 1PB]) : [The Department], 1975. — [1], 5p ; 30cm.
'Schedule of amendments to the "Bar Hill draft local plan"' (3p.) and fold. sheet (col. plan) as inserts.
Sd : £0.15
(B77-04954)

711'.4'0942657 — Cambridgeshire. Histon & Impington. Village planning. *Proposals*
South Cambridgeshire *(District). Planning Department.* Histon & Impington draft local plan / South Cambridgeshire District Council [Planning Department]. — Cambridge (South Cambridgeshire Hall, Hills Rd, Cambridge CB2 1PB) : [The Department], 1975. — [4],60p,8 leaves of plates(4 fold) : col maps, col plans ; 30cm.
'Schedule of amendments to the "Histon & Impington draft local plan"' (15[i.e.] 17p.) and 2 sheets (1 fold.) (col. plans) as insert.
Sd : £0.25
(B77-04955)

711'.4'0942657 — Cambridgeshire. Pampisford. Village planning. *Proposals*
South Cambridgeshire *(District). Planning Department.* Pampisford draft local plan / South Cambridgeshire District Council [Planning Department]. — Cambridge (South Cambridgeshire Hall, Hills Rd, Cambridge [CB2 1PB]) : [The Department], 1975. — Sheet : col plan ; 30x42cm.
'Pampisford interim local plan : amendments to the draft local plan' (sheet) as insert.
£0.10
(B77-04956)

711'.4'0942657 — Cambridgeshire. Sawston. Village planning. *Proposals*
South Cambridgeshire *(District). Planning Department.* Sawston draft local plan / South Cambridgeshire District Council [Planning Department]. — Cambridge (South Cambridgeshire Hall, Hills Rd, Cambridge CB2 1PB) : [The Department], 1975. — [3],32p,5 leaves of plates(2 fold) : col maps, 2 col plans ; 30cm.
'Schedule of amendments to the "Sawston draft local plan"' (6p.) and fold. sheet (col. plan) as inserts.
Sd : £0.25
(B77-04957)

711'.4'0942659 — Cambridgeshire. Cambridge. St Matthew's. Environment planning. *Proposals*
Cambridge *(District). Department of Architecture and Planning.* St Matthews district plan / City of Cambridge [Department of Architecture and Planning]. — [Cambridge] ([The Guildhall, Cambridge CB2 3QJ]) : [The Department], 1977. — [6],87[i.e.98]p,[12]leaves of plates(8 fold) : ill, maps, plans ; 30cm.
Sp : £2.50
(B77-27971)

Cambridge *(District). Department of Architecture and Planning.* St Matthew's draft local plan / [drawn up by the staff of the Cambridge City Architect and Planning Officer]. — [Cambridge] ([The Guildhall, Cambridge]) : The Department, 1976. — [7],50,[9]p,[14] leaves of plates : ill, maps, plans ; 29cm.
ISBN 0-902696-03-3 Sd : Unpriced
(B77-10866)

711'.4'0942659 — Cambridgeshire. Cambridge. Town planning. Rejected proposals, to 1966
Reeve, Frank Albert. The Cambridge that never was / [by] F.A. Reeve. — Cambridge : Oleander Press, 1976. — 40p : ill, maps, plans ; 21cm.
Bibl.: p.40.
ISBN 0-902675-72-9 Sd : £0.90
Also classified at 720'.9426'59
(B77-10472)

711'.4'09426712 — Essex. Stansted Mountfitchet. Village planning. *Proposals*
Uttlesford *(District). Planning Department.* Stansted village plan, 1976-1981 / Uttlesford District Council [Planning Department]. — [Dunmow] ([Council Office, Dunmow, Essex]) : [The Department], [1976]. — [2]leaves,32p,2 fold leaves of plates : 2 plans ; 30cm.
Sp : £0.75
(B77-13757)

711'.4'09426752 — Essex. South Woodham Ferrers. Environment planning
Essex *(County). Council.* South Woodham Ferrers : a new country town by the River Crouch / Essex County Council. — [Chelmsford] ([County Hall, Chelmsford, Essex]) : [The Council], [1977]. — [1],33p : ill, 2 maps, plans(some col) ; 21x31cm.
Sd : £1.00
(B77-19517)

711'.4'094436 — France. Paris. Town planning. *Secondary school texts*
Beswick, C. The new Paris / [by] C. Beswick ; [general editor P.J. Downes]. — Sevenoaks : Hodder and Stoughton, 1977. — 31p : ill(some col), 2 maps ; 19x25cm.
ISBN 0-340-21541-0 Sd : Unpriced
(B77-33935)

711'.4'09713541 — Urban regions. Environment planning. Participation of public. Political aspects. *Study regions: Ontario. Toronto*
Neighbourhood, Planning and Politics *(Conference), Oxford Polytechnic, 1975.*
Neighbourhood, planning and politics : a geography seminar series / John R. Gold, editor. — [Headington] ([Oxford OX3 0BP]) : Oxford Polytechnic, 1976. — [5],59p ; 30cm. — (Oxford Polytechnic. Discussion papers in geography ; no.1)
'The papers ... are the revised transcripts of a seminar series held at Oxford Polytechnic in the Summer of 1975 under the title of "Neighbourhood, planning, and politics"' - Editorial note.
Pbk : £0.50
Primary classification 711'.4'0942574
(B77-08468)

711'.4'09875 — Venezuela. Ciudad Guayana. Town planning
Appleyard, Donald. Planning a pluralist city : conflicting realities in Ciudad Guayana / [by] Donald Appleyard. — Cambridge, Mass. ; London : M.I.T. Press, 1976. — ix,310p : ill, maps, plans ; 27cm. — (Joint Center for Urban Studies. Publications)
Bibl.: p.300-305. — Index.
ISBN 0-262-01044-5 : £15.00
(B77-06800)

711'.4'09947 — Australian Capital Territory. Tuggeranong. Environment planning
McCoy, Kent. Landscape planning for a new Australian town / [by] Kent McCoy. — Amsterdam ; Oxford [etc.] : Elsevier, 1976. — xv,149p : ill, form, maps, plans ; 25cm. — (Developments in landscape management and urban planning ; 3)
'Reprinted from "Urban Ecology" Vol.1 No.2/3 pp.129-270'. — Condensed version of: 'The role of the landscape architect in Australian new town development'. Canberra : National Capital Development Commission, 1974. — Bibl.: p.145. — Index.
ISBN 0-444-41340-5 : £13.95
(B77-00320)

711'.5 — Utopian communities. Environment planning. Influence of ideologies. *United States, 1790-1960*
Hayden, Dolores. Seven American utopias : the architecture of communitarian socialism, 1790-1975 / [by] Dolores Hayden. — Cambridge, Mass. ; London : M.I.T. Press, 1976. — ix,401p : ill, facsims, maps, plans, port ; 26cm.
Bibl.: p.367-379. — Index.
ISBN 0-262-08082-6 : £12.75
(B77-01658)

711'.552 — Cities. Central business districts. Redevelopment. *United States*
Redstone, Louis Gordon. The new downtowns : rebuilding business districts / [by] Louis G. Redstone. — New York ; London [etc.] : McGraw-Hill, 1976. — xxi,330p : ill, maps, plans ; 29cm.
Index.
ISBN 0-07-051369-4 : £17.00
(B77-03143)

711'.558 — Outdoor recreation facilities. Planning
Jubenville, Alan. Outdoor recreation planning / [by] Alan Jubenville. — Philadelphia ; London [etc.] : Saunders, 1976. — xiv,399p : ill, forms, maps, plans ; 25cm.
Ill. on lining papers. — Bibl. — Index.
ISBN 0-7216-5228-x : £8.25
(B77-25768)

711'.558 — Outdoor recreation facilities. Sites. Choice. Criteria
Hockin, Richard. The site requirements and planning of outdoor recreation activities / [by] Richard Hockin, Brian Goodall, John Whittow. — Reading (Whiteknights, Reading RG6 2AB) : Department of Geography, University of Reading, 1977. — [2],ii,49p ; 21cm. — (Geographical papers ; no.54 ISSN 0305-5914)
Bibl.: p.48.
ISBN 0-7049-0464-0 Sd : £0.70
(B77-17647)

711'.558'0941 — Recreation facilities. Planning. Information systems. *Great Britain. Conference proceedings*
Information Systems for Recreation Planning *(Conference), University of Edinburgh, 1974.* CRRAG conference, 1974 : Information Systems for Recreation Planning, organised for the Countryside Recreation Research Advisory Group by the Tourism and Recreation Research Unit / edited by M.L. Owen, Brian S. Duffield and J.T. Coppock. — [Edinburgh] ([High School Yards, Edinburgh EH1 1NR]) : [Tourism and Recreation Research Unit], 1975. — xi,184p : ill, facsims, forms, maps ; 29cm. — (University of Edinburgh. Tourism and Recreation Research Unit. Research reports ; no.17 ISSN 0305-487x)
'... held at Edinburgh University on 23rd and 24th of September 1974 ; the theme was "Information Systems for Recreation Planning"' - Acknowledgements. — Bibl.: p.181.
ISBN 0-904828-05-0 Pbk : £4.00
(B77-04958)

711'.558'09422 — Recreation facilities. Planning. *Southern England. Periodicals*
Southern Council for Sport and Recreation. Newsletter / Southern Council for Sport and Recreation. — Reading (Watlington House, Watlington St., Reading RG1 4RJ) : [The Council].
No.1- ; Nov.1976-. — [1976]-. — 30cm.
Two issues a year. — [3],38p. in 1st issue.
Sd : Unpriced
ISSN 0309-2461
(B77-07503)

711'.558'09423 — Recreation facilities. Planning. *South-west England. Proposals*
South Western Sports Council. A regional strategy for sport and recreation in South West England / [South Western Sports Council]. — 2nd ed. — Crewkerne (Ashlands House, Ashlands, Crewkerne, Somerset TA18 7LQ) : The Council, 1976. — 192p : ill, maps ; 30cm. — (Sport for all)
Cover title. — Fold cover. — Previous ed.: 1975. — Bibl.: p.191-192.
ISBN 0-900979-49-6 Pbk : £4.00
(B77-10867)

711'.558'0942737 — Recreation land. *Greater Manchester (Metropolitan County). West Pennine Moors. Planning. Participation of public. Reports, surveys*
West Pennine Moors Plan (formerly Anglezarke Recreation Area Local Plan), public participation report. — Preston ([East Cliff County Offices, Preston PR1 3EX]) : Lancashire County Council, [Planning Department for] the Members' Steering Group, 1976. — [7],55p : map ; 21x30cm.
Prepared by a working party of officers from eight local authorities and the North West Water Authority, and approved by a steering group of members from these authorities.
ISBN 0-902228-26-9 Pbk : £0.25
Primary classification 711'.558'094276
(B77-10868)

711'.558'094276 — Recreation land. *Lancashire. West Pennine Moors. Planning. Participation of public. Reports, surveys*
West Pennine Moors Plan (formerly Anglezarke Recreation Area Local Plan), public participation report. — Preston ([East Cliff County Offices, Preston PR1 3EX]) : Lancashire County Council, [Planning Department for] the Members' Steering Group, 1976. — [7],55p : map ; 21x30cm.
Prepared by a working party of officers from eight local authorities and the North West Water Authority, and approved by a steering group of members from these authorities.
ISBN 0-902228-26-9 Pbk : £0.25
Also classified at 711'.558'0942737
(B77-10868)

711'.558'0971 — Outdoor recreation facilities. Planning. *Canada*
Hall, Robert, *b.1947.* Outdoor recreation provision in Canada / [by] Robert K. Hall. — [Headington] ([Headington, Oxford OX3 0PB]) : [Oxford Polytechnic], 1976. — [7],47p, [2]leaves,[4]leaves of plates : maps ; 30cm. — (Oxford Polytechnic. Discussion papers in geography ; no.2)
Pbk : Unpriced
(B77-12574)

711'.558'0973 — Recreation facilities. Planning. *United States*
Ezersky, Eugene M. Facilities in sports and physical education / [by] Eugene M. Ezersky, P. Richard Theibert. — Saint Louis : Mosby ; London : Distributed by Kimpton, 1976. — ix, 193p : ill, forms, plans ; 27cm.
Bibl.: p.161-162. — Index.
ISBN 0-8016-1534-8 : £8.55
(B77-04323)

711'.58 — Award winning housing schemes. *England*
Awards for good design in housing / [prepared by the Department of the Environment and the Central Office of Information]. — [London] : [Department of the Environment].
1975. — 1975. — [1],23,[1]p : ill, map, col plans ; 30cm.
Sd : Unpriced
(B77-32751)

1976. — 1976. — [1],33,[1]p : ill, maps, col plans ; 30cm.
Sd : Unpriced
(B77-32752)

711'.58 — Local authority housing estates: Cunningham Road Estate. Environment planning. Projects: Cunningham Road Improvement Scheme. *Cheshire. Widnes. Reports, surveys*
Spence, James. Community planning project : Cunningham Road Improvement Scheme : interim report / [by] James Spence & Alan Hedges. — London (16 Duncan Terrace, N1 8BZ) : Social and Community Planning Research ; [London] : Centre for Sample Surveys, 1976. — 149p in various pagings : ill, facsims, forms, maps, plans, ports ; 30cm.
ISBN 0-904607-08-9 Sp : £2.60
(B77-03144)

711'.58 — Multiple housing. Layout. Planning. *Manuals*
Untermann, Richard. Site planning for cluster housing / [by] Richard Untermann & Robert Small ; with assistance by Lynn Lewicki. — New York ; London [etc.] : Van Nostrand Reinhold, 1977. — ix,306p : ill, plans ; 22x28cm.
Index.
ISBN 0-442-28822-0 : £18.25
(B77-25082)

711'.58'0942254 — Residential areas. Planning. *East Sussex. Hove (District). Proposals*
Hove *(District). Planning Department.* Borough of Hove residential subject plan : policies and proposals as approved by the Hove Borough Council July 1976 / [Borough of Hove Planning Department]. — Hove (Town Hall Annexe, Third Ave., Hove, Sussex BN3 2PU) : [The Department], 1976. — [12]p : plans(1 col) ; 30cm.
Plan on fold. leaf in pocket.
ISBN 0-905301-01-3 Sd : £0.50
(B77-11320)

711'.58'0942534 — Residential areas. Planning. *Lincolnshire. Lincoln. Nettleham Glebe. Proposals*
Lincoln *(District). Department of Planning and Architecture.* Nettleham Glebe development design brief / [City of Lincoln Department of Planning and Architecture]. — Lincoln (City Hall, Beaumont Fee, Lincoln LN1 1DF) : [The Department], 1976. — 30p : 2 ill, maps, plans ; 30cm.
ISBN 0-902092-09-x Sp : £0.50
(B77-11321)

711'.59'0941 — Urban renewal. *Great Britain, 1965-1975. Reports, surveys*
Urban harvest : urban renewal in retrospect and prospect / edited by Stanley Millward. — Berkhamsted : Geographical Publications, 1977. — xviii,266p : ill, plans ; 24cm. — (Studies in land economy)
Bibl. — Index.
ISBN 0-900394-18-8 : £8.25 : CIP rev.
(B77-13758)

711'.59'0941 — Urban renewal. *Great Britain. Conference proceedings*
Urban renewal 1975 / edited by Stanley Millward. — [Salford] ([Salford, Lancs. M5 4WT]) : [University of Salford, Department of Civil Engineering], [1976]. — [14],129p : ill ; 31cm.
'Papers presented at a Symposium held in the Department of Civil Engineering, University of Salford 2 and 3 July 1975'. — '... tenth symposium in the Urban Renewal Series' - p.[13].
ISBN 0-901025-07-0 Sp : £2.00
(B77-01659)

711'.59'09421 — Inner London. Urban renewal. *Proposals*
Greater London Council. London we're staying here : rebirth of the inner city / [Greater London Council]. — London : G.L.C., 1977. — [1],16p : ill, port ; 21cm.
ISBN 0-7168-0868-4 Sd : Unpriced
(B77-27248)

711'.59'0942659 — General Improvement Areas. *Cambridgeshire. Cambridge. St Matthews General Improvement Area. Proposals*
Cambridge *(District). Environment Committee.* St Matthews general improvement area declaration report / [Cambridge City Council Environment Committee]. — [Cambridge] ([The Guildhall, Cambridge]) : [The Committee], 1976. — [2], 16[i.e. 24]p : ill, maps, plans ; 21x30cm.
ISBN 0-902696-05-x Sd : £0.30
(B77-11984)

711'.7'018 — Transport. Long-range planning. Methodology. *Great Britain. Urban regions*
Maltby, D. Urban transport planning and energy, techniques for long term appraisal / prepared for the Science Research Council by D. Maltby, I.G. Monteath [i.e. Monteith] and K.A. Lawler. — [Salford] ([Salford, M5 4WT]) : [University of Salford, Centre for Transport Studies], 1976. — [4],leaves,79[i.e.81]p,8 leaves of plates : ill ; 31cm. — (University of Salford. Centre for Transport Studies. Working papers ; 2 ISSN 0309-5738)
Bibl.: p.72-78.
Sp : Unpriced
(B77-18286)

711'.7'072042 — Transport. Planning by local authorities. Research. *England. Periodicals*
Royal Institute of Public Administration. *Local Government Operational Research Unit.* LGORU transportation news. — Reading (201 King's Rd, Reading RG1 4LH) : The Unit.
No.1- ; Spring 1975-. — [1975]-. — 30cm.
Published at irregular intervals. — Folder (4p.) as 1st issue.
Sd : Unpriced
ISSN 0309-5304
(B77-26417)

711'.7'091732 — Passenger transport. Planning. *Urban regions. Proposals*
Richards, Brian, *b.1928.* Moving in cities / [by] Brian Richards. — London [etc.] : Studio Vista, 1976. — 104p : ill, facsims, maps, plans ; 22cm.

Enlarged and revised ed. of: the author's 'New movement in cities'. 1966. — Bibl.: p.104.
ISBN 0-289-70583-5 : £4.50
(B77-10473)

711'.7'091732 — Traffic. Planning. *Metropolitan regions. Conference proceedings*
Symposium on the Future of Conurbation Transport, *10th, Holly Royde College, 1976.* Tenth symposium on the future of conurbation transport, October 19th-21st, 1976, Holly Royde College, Manchester. — Manchester (Manchester M13 9PL) : University of Manchester, Department of Extra-Mural Studies, [1977]. — [3],v,149p : ill ; 30cm.
Sd : £4.55
(B77-18287)

711'.7'091732 — Transport. Planning. *Urban regions*
Urban Transport Planning *(Conference), University of Leeds, 1976.* Urban transportation planning : current themes and future prospects / edited by Peter Bonsall, Quasim Dalvi, Peter J. Hills. — Tunbridge Wells : Abacus Press [etc.], 1977. — vi,386p : ill ; 23cm.
'The papers which form the major part of this book have been edited from material presented at a conference on Urban Transport Planning held at the University of Leeds in the spring of 1976' - Preface. — Bibl.
ISBN 0-85626-138-6 : £15.80 : CIP rev.
(B77-10869)

711'.7'0941 — Transport. Planning. *Great Britain, 1960-1975*
Starkie, David Nicholas Martin. Transportation planning, policy and analysis / by D.N.M. Starkie. — Oxford [etc.] : Pergamon, 1976. — xii,145p : ill ; 22cm. — (Urban and regional planning series ; vol.13 ISSN 0305-5582) (Pergamon international library)
Bibl.: p.119-122. — Index.
ISBN 0-08-020909-2 Pbk : £6.75
ISBN 0-08-020908-4 Pbk : £3.50
Primary classification 380.5'0941
(B77-07254)

711'.7'0942561 — Transport. Planning. *Bedfordshire. Bedford. Proposals*
Martin and Voorhees Associates. Bedford Urban Transportation Study : a transportation plan for 1991 / [Martin and Voorhees Associates and County Planning Department, Bedfordshire County Council]. — London : Martin and Voorhees Associates ; Bedford (County Hall, Bedford) : County Planning Department, Bedfordshire County Council, 1976. — [1],v[i.e. viii],87p,[23] leaves of plates(10 fold) : ill, maps(chiefly col), plan ; 30cm.
Sd : £5.00(the 2 vols)
(B77-32033)

Martin and Voorhees Associates. Bedford Urban Transportation Study : a transportation plan for 1991 / [Martin and Voorhees Associates and County Planning Department, Bedfordshire County Council]. — London : Martin and Voorhees Associates ; Bedford (County Hall, Bedford) : County Planning Department, Bedfordshire County Council.
(Appendices). — 1976. — [11]leaves,[39]leaves of plates(some fold) : maps ; 30cm.
Sd : Unpriced
(B77-32034)

711'.73 — Car parks. *Cambridgeshire. South Cambridgeshire (District). Standards*
South Cambridgeshire *(District). Planning Department.* Car parking : planning standards / South Cambridgeshire District Council Planning Department. — [Cambridge] ([South Cambridgeshire Hall, Hills Rd, Cambridge CB2 1PB]) : [The Department], [1974]. — [1],[2], 9p ; 30cm.
'Standards for car parking provision : amendment sheet' (sheet) as insert.
Sd : £0.10
(B77-04959)

711'.73 — Car parks. *Lancashire. Standards*
Lancashire *(County). Planning Department.* Car parking standards / [Lancashire County Planning Dept.]. — [Preston] ([East Cliff County Offices, Preston PR1 3EX]) : Lancashire County Council, 1976. — [2],20p ; 30cm.
ISBN 0-902228-24-2 Sd : £0.50
(B77-08469)

711'.73 — Car parks. Design. *Lancashire*
Lancashire *(County). Planning Department.* Design notes for car parks / [Lancashire County Planning Dept.]. — [Preston] ([East Cliff County Offices, Preston PR1 3EX]) : Lancashire County Council, 1976. — [2],12p : ill, plans ; 30cm.
ISBN 0-902228-25-0 Sd : £0.30
(B77-08470)

711'.73 — Residential areas. Roads. Planning. Environmental aspects. *Conference proceedings*
Streets for Living *(Conference), Dublin, 1976.* Streets for Living : proceedings of a conference on residential road design : organised by An Foras Forbartha at Jury's Hotel, Dublin, May 1976 / edited by Eoghan Brangan. — Dublin : Foras Forbartha, [1976]. — [3],93p : ill, map, plans ; 30cm.
'The conference [was] entitled "Streets for Living" ...' - Introduction.
ISBN 0-900115-88-2 Sd : £2.00
(B77-09840)

711'.73 — River crossings. Planning. *East London. Thames River. Proposals*
East London river crossing study : report of the Steering Group. — [London] : Greater London Council, 1975. — 32p,[11]fold leaves of plates : ill, maps, plans ; 30cm.
ISBN 0-7168-0741-6 Sp : Unpriced
(B77-11887)

711'.73'091732 — Traffic. Planning. *Urban regions*
Thomson, John Michael. Great cities and their traffic / [by] J. Michael Thomson. — London : Gollancz, 1977. — 344[i.e.346]p : ill, maps ; 21cm.
Bibl.: p.325-337. — Index.
ISBN 0-575-02146-2 : £8.95
(B77-25083)

711'.73'0942183 — Airports. *London. Hillingdon (London Borough). London Airport (Heathrow). Road traffic. Planning. Proposals*
British Airports Authority. Heathrow, keeping traffic moving, second consultative paper / British Airports Authority. — [London] ([2 Buckingham Gate, SW1E 6JL]) : [B.A.A.], 1976. — [1],19p,fold plate : ill(some col), col plans ; 30cm.
ISBN 0-903460-10-6 Sp : Unpriced
(B77-00321)

711'.73'0942313 — Road traffic. Planning. *Wiltshire. Swindon. Reports, surveys*
Wiltshire *(County). Department of Highways and Transportation.* The Swindon Transportation Study, final report / [Wiltshire County Council Department of Highways and Transportation, Freeman Fox and Associates]. — Trowbridge (County Hall, Trowbridge, Wilts.) : The Department ; London : Freeman Fox and Associates, 1976. — xii,168p : ill(some col), maps(chiefly col) ; 30cm.
ISBN 0-86080-004-0 Pbk : Unpriced
(B77-33936)

712 — LANDSCAPE DESIGN
712 — Garden features. Construction. *Amateurs' manuals*
Oldale, Adrienne. The outdoor handyman / [by] Adrienne and Peter Oldale. — London [etc.] : Collins, 1976. — 288p : ill ; 22cm.
Contents: Lawns, hedges and fences. Originally published: 1969 - Garden woodworking. Originally published: 1971 - Paths, walls and steps. Originally published: 1969.
ISBN 0-00-435487-7 : £3.50
(B77-09146)

712'.092'4 — Art galleries. *Lancashire. Lancaster. University of Lancaster. Scott Gallery. Exhibits: Items associated with Mawson, Thomas Hayton. Catalogues*
Beard, Geoffrey. Thomas H. Mawson, 1861-1933 : the life and work of a northern landscape architect / [by Geoffrey Beard and Joan Wardman]. — [Lancaster] ([Bailrigg, Lancaster]) : University of Lancaster, Visual Arts Centre, 1976. — 80p,[8]p of plates : ill, port ; 21cm.
'... catalogue ... to accompany an exhibition of Mawson's work held in the Scott Gallery, Visual Arts Centre, University of Lancaster, October-December 1976' - title page verso.
Sd : £0.70
(B77-11985)

712'.092'4 — Landscape design. Olmsted, Frederick Law. *United States. Biographies*
Roper, Laura Wood. F.L.O. : a biography of Frederick Law Olmsted / [by] Laura Wood Roper. — Baltimore ; London : Johns Hopkins University Press, 1973. — xix,555,[1]p : ill, map, plan, ports ; 25cm.
Index.
ISBN 0-8018-1508-8 : Unpriced
(B77-19518)

712'.092'4 — Landscape design. Olmsted, Frederick Law. *United States. Correspondence*
Olmsted, Frederick Law. The papers of Frederick Law Olmsted / Charles Capen McLaughlin, editor. — Baltimore ; London : Johns Hopkins University Press.
Vol.1 : The formative years, 1822 to 1852 / Charles E. Beveridge, associate editor. — 1977. — xx,423p : ill, geneal tables, maps, ports ; 25cm.
Index.
ISBN 0-8018-1798-6 : Unpriced
(B77-28760)

712'.0941 — Landscape design. *Great Britain. Manuals*
Marlowe, Olwen C. Outdoor design : a handbook for the architect and planner / [by] Olwen C. Marlowe. — London : Crosby Lockwood Staples, 1977. — xiii,301p : ill, map ; 25cm.
Bibl.: p.276-289. — Index.
ISBN 0-258-97017-0 : £17.50
(B77-07504)

712'.09415 — Landscape design. *Ireland, 1660-1845*
Malins, Edward. Lost demesnes : Irish landscape gardening, 1660-1845 / [by] Edward Malins & the Knight of Glin ; foreword by Desmond Guinness. — London : Barrie and Jenkins, 1976. — xvi,208p : ill, facsim, maps, plans, ports ; 31cm.
Ill. on lining papers. — Bibl.: p.198-200. — Index.
ISBN 0-214-20275-5 : £15.00
(B77-22011)

712'.6 — Gardens. Planning. *Amateurs' manuals*
Huxley, Anthony Julian. Garden planning and planting / by Eigel Kiaer with Hans Petersen ; [translated from the Danish by Gillian Hartz] ; English edition supervised and edited by Anthony Huxley ; illustrations by Verner Hancke. — Poole : Blandford Press, 1976. — 222p : col ill ; 19cm. — ([Blandford colour series])
Translation and adaptation of: 'Havens be planting i farver'. Copenhagen : Politikens, 1975.
ISBN 0-7137-0792-5 : £3.95
(B77-00859)

Midgley, Kenneth. Garden design / [by] Kenneth Midgley ; prepared in conjunction and collaboration with the Royal Horticultural Society. — London : Pelham, 1977. — 218,[5] p : ill, plans ; 21cm.
Originally published: Harmondsworth : Penguin, 1966. — Index.
ISBN 0-7207-0982-2 : £4.95
(B77-17648)

Whiten, Geoff. Growing pleasure : the reluctant gardener's handbook / [by] Geoff and Faith Whiten ; drawings by Frank Dickens. — London (27 Chancery La., WC2A 1NF) : Foxwood Publishing Ltd, 1977. — iv,59p : ill(some col), plans ; 23cm.
ISBN 0-904897-92-3 : £2.75
ISBN 0-904897-17-6 Pbk : £1.25
(B77-27249)

712'.6'0941 — Gardens. *Great Britain, to 1976*
Scott-James, Anne. The pleasure garden : an illustrated history of British gardening / [by] Anne Scott-James, Osbert Lancaster. — London : J. Murray, 1977. — 128p : ill ; 24cm.
Bibl.: p.123-125. — Index.
ISBN 0-7195-3438-0 : £3.50
(B77-31327)

712'.6'0942 — Landscape gardens. *England, 1700-1940*
Hadfield, Miles. The English landscape garden / [by] Miles Hadfield. — Aylesbury : Shire Publications, 1977. — 72p : ill, plans, port ; 21cm.
Index.
ISBN 0-85263-345-9 Pbk : £1.25
(B77-33937)

712'.6'09421 — Gardens. *London, to ca 1950*
Taylor, Gladys. Old London gardens / by Gladys Taylor. — Hornchurch : I. Henry, 1977. — 3-194p : ill, ports ; 21cm.
Originally published: London : Batsford, 1953. — Bibl.: p.187-188. — Index.
ISBN 0-86025-806-8 : £4.55
(B77-14320)

712'.6'0994 — Gardens. Design. *Australia*
Maloney, Betty. Designing Australian bush gardens / by Betty Maloney and Jean Walker ; edited by Barbara Mullins. — Sydney [etc.] ; London : A.H. and A.W. Reed, 1975. — 127p : ill ; 19cm.
Originally published: Sydney : Horowitz, 1966. — Index.
ISBN 0-589-07175-0 Pbk : £2.15
(B77-32753)

717 — Landscape design. Use of bricks
Handisyde, Cecil Charles. Hard landscape in brick / [by] Cecil C. Handisyde. — London : Architectural Press, 1976. — [4],74p : ill ; 30cm.
Bibl.: p.73. — Index.
ISBN 0-85139-283-0 Pbk : £3.25
(B77-11986)

719 — NATURAL LANDSCAPES
719 — Great Britain. Mountainous regions. Conservation. *Conference proceedings*
Conserving the Mountains *(Conference), Plas y Brenin National Mountaineering Centre, 1976.* Conference report : Conserving the Mountains, 26-28 November 1976. — [Manchester] ([Crawford House, Precinct Centre, Booth Street East, Manchester M13 9RZ]) : [British Mountaineering Council], [1977]. — [5],67p ; 21cm.
'National symposium, "Conserving the Mountains", Plas y Brenin National Mountaineering Centre, 26-28 November 1976' - note. — Bibl.
Sd : £1.00
(B77-20455)

719'.06'1411 — Scotland. Landscape conservation. Organisations: Countryside Commission for Scotland. *Accounts*
Countryside (Scotland) Act 1967, account : account of the Countryside Commission for Scotland ... for the year ended 31st March ... — London : H.M.S.O.
1975-76. — [1977]. — Folder (4p) ; 25cm. — ([1976-77 H.C.] 87)
ISBN 0-10-208777-6 : £0.15
(B77-07505)

719'.06'1411 — Scotland. Landscape conservation. Organisations: Countryside Commission for Scotland. *Reports, surveys. Serials*
Countryside Commission for Scotland. Report / Countryside Commission for Scotland. — [Perth] : The Commission ; [London] : Distributed by H.M.S.O.
9th : 1976. — 1977. — [8],40p,[4]p of plates : col ill, col map, col plan, col port ; 20cm.
ISBN 0-902226-39-8 Pbk : £1.65
(B77-18901)

719'.06'142 — England. Landscape conservation. Organisations: Countryside Commission. *Reports, surveys. Serials*
Countryside Commission. Report of the Countryside Commission for the year ended 30 September ... — London : H.M.S.O.
9th : 1976. — [1977]. — vi,86p,[6]p of plates(2 fold),fold leaf of plate : ill, maps(1 col), port ; 25cm. — ([1976-77 H.C.]242)
ISBN 0-10-224277-1 Sd : £2.65
ISSN 0308-6941
(B77-12575)

719'.06'2411 — Scotland. Landscape conservation. Organisations: National Trust for Scotland. *Yearbooks*
National Trust for Scotland. The National Trust for Scotland year book. — Edinburgh : The Trust.
1977. — [1977]. — 46p ; 21cm.
Sd : Unpriced
ISSN 0077-5916
Also classified at 720'.9411
(B77-19519)

719'.07'2041 — Great Britain. Landscape conservation. Research in British institutions. *Directories*
Countryside Commission. Research register / Countryside Commission. — Cheltenham (John Dower House, Crescent Place, Cheltenham, Glos. GL50 3RA) : The Commission.
No.8 : Autumn 1976 / compiled by A.J. Gerrard ... — [1976]. — 216,[51]p ; 30cm.
Index.
ISBN 0-902590-52-9 Sp : £5.00
ISSN 0307-532x
(B77-04960)

719'.0941 — Great Britain. Landscape conservation
Fairbrother, Nan. New lives, new landscapes / [by] Nan Fairbrother. — Harmondsworth [etc.] : Penguin, 1977. — 383p : ill, maps ; 20cm. — (Geography and environmental studies)
Originally published: London : Architectural Press, 1970. — Bibl.: p.371-374. — Index.
ISBN 0-14-021388-0 Pbk : £2.50
(B77-23587)

719'.0942 — Agricultural land. Landscape conservation. *England. Lowland regions. Proposals*
Countryside Commission. New agricultural landscapes, issues, objectives and action / Countryside Commission. — Cheltenham : [The Commission], 1977. — [3],12p ; 15x21cm. — (CCP102)
ISBN 0-902590-51-0 Sd : Free
(B77-09841)

719'.09427'8 — National parks. *Cumbria. Lake District. Lake District National Park. Agricultural land. Landscape conservation. Projects: Lake District Upland Management Experiment. Reports, surveys*
The **Lake** District Upland Management Experiment : a report sponsored by the Countryside Commission in conjunction with the Lake District Planning Board, 1969-76. — [Cheltenham] ([John Dower House, Crescent Place, Cheltenham, Glos. GL50 3RA]) : [The Countryside Commission], 1976. — [1],vi,41p : ill(chiefly col), col maps, port ; 30cm. — (CCP ; 93)
ISBN 0-902590-48-0 Sd : £1.60
(B77-03145)

719'.09427'83 — Agricultural land. Landscape conservation. Projects. *Cumbria. Great Langdale. Lake District Upland Management Experiment. Trails: Upland Management Trail, Great Langdale. Walkers' guides*
Countryside Commission. The Upland Management Trail, Great Langdale / Countryside Commission. — [Cheltenham] : [The Commission], [1976]. — [16]p(2 fold) : ill, col map ; 21cm.
Notebook format.
Sp : Unpriced
(B77-17649)

719'.32'0942353 — National parks. *Devon. Dartmoor. Dartmoor National Park. Environment planning. Proposals*
Dartmoor National Park Authority. Dartmoor National Park plan / [Dartmoor National Park Authority]. — [Exeter] ([County Hall, Exeter EX2 4QD]) : The Authority, 1977. — [7],57[i.e. 61]p,[14]p of plates : ill, facsim, maps ; 30cm.
ISBN 0-905981-00-6 Sd : Unpriced
(B77-27972)

719'.32'0942511 — National parks. *England. Peak District. Peak District National Park. Environment planning. Proposals*
Peak Park Joint Planning Board. Peak District National Park Structure Plan / [Peak Park Joint Planning Board]. — Bakewell (Aldern House, Bakewell, Derbyshire) : The Board, 1976. — 98p,fold plate : maps(1 col) ; 30cm.
ISBN 0-901428-32-9 Pbk : Unpriced
(B77-30451)

719'.32'0942511 — National parks. *England. Peak District. Peak District National Park. Reports, surveys*
Peak Park Joint Planning Board. Peak District National Park additional survey report / [Peak Park Joint Planning Board]. — Bakewell (National Park Office, Aldern House, Baslow Rd, Bakewell, Derbyshire) : The Board, 1977. — vi,143p : maps, plan ; 30cm.
'... supplements the Structure Plan : Report of Survey' - Preface.
ISBN 0-901428-37-x Pbk : £2.00
(B77-26418)

719'.32'094278 — National parks. *Cumbria. Lake District. Lake District National Park. Reports, surveys. Serials*
Lake District National Park : report / [Lake District Special Planning Board]. — [Kendal] ([County Offices, Kendal, Cumbria]) : [The Board].
24th : 1975-1976. — [1977]. — [1],37p,[4]p of plates : ill ; 21cm.
Sd : £0.10
(B77-10870)

Lake District National Park annual report / [Lake District Special Planning Board]. — [Kendal] ([County Offices, Kendal, Cumbria]) : [The Board].
25th : 1976-1977. — [1977]. — [1],39p,[4]p of plates : ill ; 21cm.
'... the Third Report of the Lake District Special Planning Board' - p.1. — Previously published as: 'Lake District National Park : report'.
Sd : £0.10
(B77-18288)

719'.32'0942956 — National parks. *South Wales. Brecon Beacons National Park. Environment planning. Proposals*
Brecon Beacons National Park Committee. National Park Plan / [Brecon Beacons National Park Committee]. — Brecon (Glamorgan St., Brecon, Powys) : The Committee, 1977. — 91, [5]p,6 fold leaves of plates : ill, col maps ; 30cm.
At head of title: Parc Cenedlaethol Bannau Brycheiniog = Brecon Beacons National Park. — Spine title: Brecon Beacons National Park Plan. — Index.
ISBN 0-905293-03-7 Pbk : £2.50
(B77-14840)

720 — ARCHITECTURE
720 — Architects. Overseas work. *Great Britain. Directories*
Overseas activities of British architects. — Frinton-on-Sea (Ashlyns House, Frinton-on-Sea, Essex) : British Data Service ; Farnham (2 The Mews, 6 West St., Farnham, Surrey) : Construction Marketing Services Ltd.
1976-77. — 1976. — [2],8,76 leaves ; 30cm.
ISBN 0-905923-04-9 Sp : £22.00
ISSN 0309-3174
(B77-09842)

720 — Architecture. *Conference proceedings*
Royal Institute of British Architects. *Annual Conference, University of Hull, 1976.* Architecture : opportunities, achievements : a report of the Annual Conference of the Royal Institute of British Architects held at the University of Hull, 14 to 17 July 1976 / edited by Barbara Goldstein. — London : RIBA Publications, 1977. — [1],120,[1]p : ill, plans, ports ; 30cm.
ISBN 0-900630-59-0 Pbk : £3.50
(B77-22731)

720 — Vernacular architecture
Rudofsky, Bernard. The prodigious builders : notes toward a natural history of architecture with special regard to those species that are traditionally neglected or downright ignored / [by] Bernard Rudofsky. — London : Secker and Warburg, 1977. — 383p : ill, plans ; 25cm.
Index.
ISBN 0-436-43730-9 : £8.75
(B77-31328)

720'.22'2 — Buildings. Architectural presentation drawings. *United States. Illustrations*
Presentation drawings by American architects / [compiled by] Alfred Kemper. — New York ; London [etc.] : Wiley, 1977. — [11],380p : chiefly ill, plans ; 29cm.
'A Wiley-Interscience publication'. — Index.
ISBN 0-471-01369-2 : £18.75
(B77-22732)

720'.22'2 — German architectural drawings. Jacoby, Helmut. *Illustrations*
Jacoby, Helmut. Helmut Jacoby, architectural drawings 1968-1976 / introduction by Derek Walker. — [London] : Thames and Hudson, 1977. — 112p : chiefly ill ; 29cm.
English and German text. — Also published: Stuttgart : Verlag Gerd Hatje, 1977.
ISBN 0-500-34074-9 : £12.00
(B77-30452)

720'.22'2 — Libraries. *London. Westminster (London Borough). Royal Institute of British Architects. Drawings Collection. Catalogues*
Royal Institute of British Architects. *Drawings Collection.* Catalogue of the Drawings Collection of the Royal Institute of British Architects. — Farnborough, Hants. : Gregg.
C.F.A. Voysey / [compiled] by Joanna Symonds. — 1976. — 95p,[56]p of plates : ill, plans ; 34cm.
Bibl.: p.10-12. — Index.
ISBN 0-576-15570-5 : £26.00
(B77-01660)

720'.22'2 — Scottish architectural drawings. Mackintosh, Charles Rennie. *Illustrations*

Mackintosh, Charles Rennie. Architectural sketches & flower drawings / by Charles Rennie Mackintosh ; [text by] Roger Billcliffe. — London : Academy Editions, 1977. — 96p : chiefly ill(some col) ; 30cm.
Bibl.: p.13.
ISBN 0-85670-315-x : £6.95
ISBN 0-85670-149-1 Pbk : £3.95
Also classified at 741.9'411
(B77-13759)

720'.23 — Architects. Registration. Organisations. *Great Britain. Architects Registration Council of the United Kingdom*

Architects Registration Council of the United Kingdom. Architects Registration Council of the United Kingdom. — [London] ([73 Hallam St., W1N 6EE]) : [The Council], 1976. — [1], 28p ; 21cm.
ISBN 0-901917-08-7 Sd : Unpriced
(B77-04961)

720'.25'41 — Architects. *Great Britain. Directories*

British Data Service. The BDS selective list of practising architects. — Frinton-on-Sea (Ashlyns House, Frinton-on-Sea, Essex) : British Data Service.
1976. — [1976]. — 353 leaves in various pagings ; 33cm.
Forty leaves printed on both sides. — Index.
ISBN 0-905923-03-0 Sp : Unpriced
ISSN 0309-3220
(B77-08471)

The **register** of architects / [Architects Registration Council of the United Kingdom]. — London (73 Hallam St., W1N 6EE) : The Council.
Vol.44 : 1977. — 1977. — xvii,731p ; 21cm.
Pbk : £2.00
ISSN 0306-6967
(B77-33938)

720'.28 — Architectural drawings. Techniques

Atkin, William Wilson. Architectural presentation techniques / [by] William Wilson Atkin. — New York ; London [etc.] : Van Nostrand Reinhold, 1976. — 196p : ill(some col), facsims, maps, plans ; 24cm.
Bibl.: p.194. — Index.
ISBN 0-442-20361-6 : £11.35
(B77-01661)

Dudley, Leavitt. Architectural illustration / [by] Leavitt Dudley. — Englewood Cliffs ; London [etc.] : Prentice-Hall, 1977. — xix,300p,[16]p of plates : ill(some col), maps, plans ; 29cm.
Bibl.: p.291. — Index.
ISBN 0-13-044610-6 : £20.00
(B77-17650)

720'.28 — Architectural drawings. Techniques. *Manuals*

McHugh, Robert C. Working drawing handbook : a guide for architects and builders / [by] Robert C. McHugh. — New York ; London [etc.] : Van Nostrand Reinhold, 1977. — ix,166p : ill, forms, plans ; 22x28cm.
Bibl.: p.163. — Index.
ISBN 0-442-25283-8 Pbk : Unpriced
ISBN 0-442-25284-6 Pbk : £5.30
(B77-27250)

Weidhaas, Ernest R. Architectural drafting and design / [by] Ernest R. Weidhaas. — 3rd ed. — Boston, Mass. ; London [etc.] : Allyn and Bacon, 1977. — [9],438p : ill(some col), plans(some col) ; 29cm.
'Portions of this book first appeared in "Architectural drafting and construction" ... [Boston, Mass. : Allyn and Bacon, 1974]' - title page verso. — Previous ed. of 'Architectural drafting and design': Boston, Mass. : Allyn and Bacon, 1972. — Bibl.: p.416-419. — Index.
ISBN 0-205-05624-5 : Unpriced
Also classified at 721
(B77-11322)

720'.28 — Architectural working drawings

Liebing, Ralph W. Architectural working drawings / [by] Ralph W. Liebing, Mimi Ford Paul. — New York ; London [etc.] : Wiley, 1977. — x,310p : ill, forms, maps, plans ; 29cm.

'A Wiley-Interscience Publication'. — Bibl.: p.305. — Index.
ISBN 0-471-53432-3 : £10.50
(B77-33336)

720'.3 — Architecture. *Dictionaries*

Dictionary of architecture and construction / edited by Cyril M. Harris. — New York ; London [etc.] : McGraw-Hill, [1976]. — xvii, 553p : ill, plans ; 25cm.
Published in the United States: 1975.
ISBN 0-07-026756-1 : £20.65
Also classified at 690'.03
(B77-01662)

720'.3 — Architecture. *Encyclopaedias*

Historic architecture sourcebook / edited by Cyril M. Harris. — New York ; London [etc.] : McGraw-Hill, 1977. — ix,581p : ill, maps, plans ; 25cm.
ISBN 0-07-026755-3 : £14.95
(B77-22733)

720'.5 — Architecture. *Periodicals*

Face : University of Sheffield architectural studies. — [Sheffield] : [s.n.].
No.1- ; 1975-. — 1975-. — ill ; 30cm.
Monthly. — 12p. in no.5.
Sd : Unpriced
ISSN 0308-2229
Also classified at 711'.05
(B77-04324)

Martin Centre for Architectural and Urban Studies. Transactions of the Martin Centre for Architectural & Urban Studies, University of Cambridge. — Cambridge : Woodhead-Faulkner.
Vol.1- ; [1976]-. — 1976-. — ill, maps, plans ; 25cm.
Twice yearly. — [2],334p. in 1st issue. — Bibl.
Pbk : £14.50 yearly
ISSN 0309-2062
Primary classification 711'.05
(B77-07501)

720'.6'041 — Architectural design. Organisations. *Great Britain. Directories*

Directory of official architecture & planning. — London : Godwin.
1977 : 21st ed. — 1977. — xiv,508p : ill, maps ; 23cm.
Index.
ISBN 0-7114-3410-7 : Unpriced
Also classified at 711'.4'06041
(B77-13760)

720'.6'1421 — Architectural design by Greater London Council. Department of Architecture and Civic Design. *London. Reports, surveys. Serials*

Greater London Council. *Department of Architecture and Civic Design.* Review / GLC architects [i.e. Department of Architecture and Civic Design]. — London : Academy Editions.
2. — 1977. — 96p : ill, plans ; 21cm.
ISBN 0-85670-308-7 : £5.50
ISBN 0-85670-307-9 Pbk : £3.95
(B77-17651)

720'.6'241 — Architectural design. Organisations. *Great Britain. Royal Institute of British Architects. Directories*

Royal Institute of British Architects. RIBA directory of practices. — London : R.I.B.A.
1977. — 1976. — 229p in various pagings : ill, form, 2 maps ; 30cm.
Index.
ISBN 0-900630-61-2 Pbk : £10.00
ISSN 0305-2435
(B77-10871)

720'.6'2411 — Architecture. Organisations. *Scotland. Royal Incorporation of Architects in Scotland. Yearbooks*

The **Scottish** architects directory : year book of the Royal Incorporation of Architects in Scotland. — [Edinburgh] ([Smith's Place House, Edinburgh]) : [Edinburgh Pictorial Ltd].

[1976]. — [1976]. — 204p : ill, plan, ports ; 30cm.
Cover title.
Pbk : £4.60
ISSN 0306-6584
(B77-11323)

720'.6'541 — Buildings designed by Owen Luder Partnership, to 1976. Architectural features

Wharton, Kate. Adventure in architecture : a profile of the Owen Luder Partnership / by Kate Wharton ; with a foreword by Lord Peddie. — London : Lund Humphries, 1977. — 143p : ill ; 20cm.
Index.
ISBN 0-85331-397-0 Pbk : £4.50
(B77-33939)

720'.7'22 — Architecture. Historiology. Historicism. Effects. *Western Europe*

Watkin, David. Morality and architecture : the development of a theme in architectural history and theory from the Gothic revival to the modern movement / by David Watkin. — Oxford : Clarendon Press, 1977. — x,126p ; 23cm.
Index.
ISBN 0-19-817350-4 : £2.95 : CIP rev.
(B77-22734)

720.9 — ARCHITECTURE. HISTORICAL AND GEOGRAPHICAL TREATMENT

720'.9 — Architecture, to 1976

Cowan, Henry Jacob. An historical outline of architectural science / by Henry J. Cowan. — 2nd ed. — London : Applied Science Publishers, 1977. — x,202p : ill, plans ; 22cm. — (Architectural science series)
Previous ed.: Amsterdam ; Barking : Elsevier, 1966. — Bibl.: p.169-188. — Index.
ISBN 0-85334-725-5 Pbk : Unpriced
(B77-24370)

720'.92'2 — Architects. *Western world, ca 1400-1976. Biographical dictionaries*

Who's who in architecture : from 1400 to the present day / edited by J.M. Richards. — London : Weidenfeld and Nicolson, 1977. — 368p : ill(some col), maps, plans ; 26cm.
Bibl.: p.360-361. — Index.
ISBN 0-297-77283-x : £8.75
(B77-23588)

720'.92'4 — Architectural design. Alberti, Leon Battista. *Italy. Critical studies*

Borsi, Franco. Leon Battista Alberti / [by] Franco Borsi ; [translated from the Italian by Rudolf G. Carpanini]. — Complete ed. — Oxford : Phaidon, 1977. — 397p : ill, facsims, plans(some col), ports ; 29cm.
Translation of: 'Leon Battista Alberti'. Milano : Electa editrice, 1975. — Bibl.: p.377-387. — Index.
ISBN 0-7148-1685-x : £29.50
(B77-30453)

720'.92'4 — Architectural design. Corbusier, Le. *Critical studies*

The **open** hand : essays on Le Corbusier / edited by Russell Walden. — Cambridge, Mass. ; London : M.I.T. Press, 1977. — xvi,484p : ill, facsims, maps, plans, ports ; 24cm.
Index.
ISBN 0-262-23074-7 : £17.50
(B77-25769)

720'.92'4 — Architectural design. Gaudí, Antonio

Mower, David. Gaudí / [by] David Mower. — London (30 Notting Hill Gate, W11 3HX) : Oresko Books Ltd, 1977. — 96p : ill(some col), plans, port ; 30cm.
Bibl.: p.95-96.
ISBN 0-905368-08-8 : £7.95
ISBN 0-905368-09-6 Pbk : £3.95
(B77-15972)

720'.92'4 — Architectural design. Gropius, Walter. *Biographies*

Gay, Peter, *b.1923.* Art and act : on causes in history : Manet, Gropius, Mondrian / [by] Peter Gay. — New York [etc.] ; London : Harper and Row, 1976. — xix,265p : ill, map, ports ; 24cm. — ('Critique' lectures ; 1974)
'... delivered at the Cooper Union [1974]'. — 'Icon editions'. — Bibl.: p.237-259. — Index.
ISBN 0-06-433248-9 : £9.75
Primary classification 759.4
(B77-02491)

720'.92'4 — Architectural design. Mackintosh, Charles Rennie. *Scotland*

Howarth, Thomas. Charles Rennie Mackintosh and the modern movement / [by] Thomas Howarth. — 2nd ed. — London [etc.] : Routledge and Kegan Paul, 1977. — li,335p, 96p of plates : ill, plans, ports ; 25cm.
Ill. on lining papers. — Previous ed.: 1952. — Bibl.: p.311-320. — Index.
ISBN 0-7100-8538-9 : £16.50 : CIP rev.
(B77-06206)

720'.92'4 — Architectural design. Mulholland, Roger. *Ireland. Biographies*

Brett, Charles Edward Bainbridge. Roger Mulholland : architect, of Belfast, 1740-1818 / by C.E.B. Brett. — [Belfast] ([30 College Garden, Belfast BT9 6BT]) : Ulster Architectural Heritage Society, 1976. — 20p : ill, map, plans, port ; 26cm.
ISBN 0-900457-20-1 Sd : £0.80
(B77-03146)

720'.92'4 — Architectural design. Palladio, Andrea. *Italy. Critical studies*
Ackerman, James Sloss. Palladio / by James S. Ackerman. — [2nd ed.]. — Harmondsworth [etc.] : Penguin, 1977. — 196p : ill, 2 maps, plans ; 20cm. — (The architect and society) (A Pelican original)
Previous ed.: 1966. — Bibl.: p.187-192. — Index.
ISBN 0-14-020845-3 Pbk : £1.50
(B77-18902)

720'.92'4 — Art galleries. *London. Tower Hamlets (London Borough). Whitechapel Art Gallery. Exhibits: Architectural design. Hawksmoor, Nicholas. Catalogues*
Downes, Kerry. Hawksmoor : an exhibition selected by Kerry Downes, [held at] Whitechapel Art Gallery, 23 March-1 May 1977 / [catalogue compiled by Kerry Downes]. — London : The Gallery, 1977. — 32p : ill ; 22cm.
Pbk : £1.15
(B77-18903)

720'.92'4 — Buildings designed by Kurokawa, Kisho, to 1976. Architectural features
Kurokawa, Kisho. Metabolism in architecture / [by] Kisho Kurokawa. — London : Studio Vista, 1977. — 208p : ill, plans, ports ; 26cm.
Bibl.: p.205-108.
ISBN 0-289-70733-1 : £10.50
(B77-25770)

720'.92'4 — Buildings designed by McCarthy, James Joseph. *Ireland*
Sheehy, Jeanne. J.J. McCarthy and the Gothic revival in Ireland / by Jeanne Sheehy. — [Belfast] ([4 Arthur Place, Belfast BT1 4HG]) : Ulster Architectural Heritage Society, 1977. — 71p : ill, plans ; 21cm.
Bibl.: p.70.
£3.00
(B77-24371)

720'.92'4 — Buildings designed by Wren, Sir Christopher. Architectural features. *London (City)*
De Maré, Eric. Wren's London / by Eric de Maré. — London : [Joseph], 1975 [i.e. 1977]. — 128p : ill(some col), col coats of arms, facsims, maps(1 col), plans(1 col), ports(some col) ; 26cm.
Title page imprint: Folio Society. — Ill., maps on lining papers. — Originally published: London : Folio Society, 1975.
ISBN 0-7181-1586-4 : £5.00
Primary classification 711'.4'094212
(B77-18284)

720'.92'4 — Museums. *Cheshire. Chester. Grosvenor Museum. Exhibits: Items associated with Harrison, Thomas. Catalogues*
Grosvenor Museum. The modest genius : [catalogue of] an exhibition of drawings and works of Thomas Harrison / [editor Margaret Gillison]. — [Chester] ([27 Grosvenor St., Chester CH1 2DD]) : [Grosvenor Museum], [1977]. — 26p : ill ; 21x30cm.
'The exhibition ... made possible through the joint co-operation of the Grosvenor Museum, the Cheshire County Museum Service and the North-West Museums and Art Gallery Service' - p.1.
Pbk : £0.40
(B77-17652)

720'.92'4 — Universities. *Edinburgh. University of Edinburgh. Department of Fine Art. Exhibits: Items associated with Bryce, David. Catalogues*
David Bryce, 1803-1876 : [catalogue of] an exhibition to mark the centenary of Scotland's great Victorian architect / [compiled by] Valerie Fiddes & Alistair Rowan. — Edinburgh ([Department of Fine Art, 19 George Sq., Edinburgh EH8 9JZ]) : University of Edinburgh, 1976. — 132p,leaf of plate,[40]p of plates : ill, plans, ports ; 24cm.
Catalogue of an exhibition mounted by the Department of Fine Art, the University of Edinburgh and held at Edinburgh, Dundee, Inverness, Aberdeen, Glasgow and London in turn from 11th December 1976 to 30th August 1977. — Cover title: Mr David Bryce.
ISBN 0-902511-19-x Pbk : £1.80
(B77-03147)

720'.941 — Architecture. *Great Britain, 1600-1850*
Three centuries of architectural craftsmanship / edited by Colin Amery. — London : Architectural Press [etc.], 1977. — xiv,3p,221p of plates : chiefly ill, plans ; 31cm.
Bibl.: p.1-3.
ISBN 0-85139-287-3 : £7.90
(B77-13145)

720'.941 — Architecture. *Great Britain, 1837-1901*
Seven Victorian architects : William Burn, Philip and Philip Charles Hardwick, Sydney Smirke, J.L. Pearson, G.F. Bodley, Alfred Waterhouse, Edwin Lutyens / edited by Jane Fawcett ; introduction by Nikolaus Pevsner. — London : Thames and Hudson, 1976. — 160p : ill, plans, ports ; 25cm. — (Victorian Society. Papers)
Index.
ISBN 0-500-34070-6 : £7.50
(B77-09147)

720'.941 — Architecture. *Great Britain, 1890-1914*
Service, Alastair. Edwardian architecture : a handbook to building design in Britain, 1890-1914 / [by] Alastair Service. — London : Thames and Hudson, 1977. — 216p : ill, plans ; 22cm. — ([The world of art library])
Bibl.: p.193-197. — Index.
ISBN 0-500-18158-6 : £5.50
(B77-33337)

720'.9411 — Architecture. *Scotland, ca 1960-1976*
Willis, Peter. New architecture in Scotland / [by] Peter Willis ; with drawings by Jon Ignatowicz. — London : Lund Humphries, [1977]. — 96p : ill, map, plans ; 20x21cm.
Index.
ISBN 0-85331-393-8 Pbk : £3.95
(B77-19520)

720'.9411 — Architecture. *Scotland, to 1967*
Hay, George, *b.1911.* Architecture of Scotland / by George Hay. — 2nd ed., revised and enlarged. — Stocksfield : Oriel Press, 1977. — 96p : ill, map, plans ; 22cm.
Previous ed.: 1969. — Index.
ISBN 0-85362-164-0 : £3.25
(B77-15389)

720'.9411 — Buildings of historical importance. Conservation. *Scotland. Reports, surveys. Serials*
Historic Buildings Council for Scotland. Report ... / Historic Buildings Council for Scotland. — Edinburgh : H.M.S.O.
1975-76. — [1977]. — [5],25p,[4]p of plates : ill ; 25cm. — ([1976-77 H.C.] 230)
ISBN 0-10-223077-3 Sd : £0.90
(B77-13146)

720'.9411 — Buildings of historical importance. Organisations: National Trust for Scotland. *Scotland. Yearbooks*
National Trust for Scotland. The National Trust for Scotland year book. — Edinburgh : The Trust.
1977. — [1977]. — 46p ; 21cm.
Sd : Unpriced
ISSN 0077-5916
Primary classification 719'.06'2411
(B77-19519)

720'.9414'43 — Architecture. *Scotland. Strathclyde Region. Glasgow, to 1975*
Glasgow at a glance : an architectural handbook / edited by A.M. Doak and Andrew McLaren Young ; with contributions from David Walker. — New and revised ed. ; foreword by Viscount Muirshiel. — London : Hale, 1977. — [128]p : chiefly ill, maps ; 20cm.

Previous ed.: i.e. 2nd ed. Glasgow : Collins, 1971. — Index.
ISBN 0-7091-5942-0 : £2.75
ISBN 0-7091-6088-7 Pbk : £1.35
(B77-15973)

720'.9418'35 — Architecture. *Dublin. Illustrations*
Martin, Liam Christopher. Dublin in decay : a book of memories / with pen & ink drawings by Liam C. Martin ; introduction by John Keating. — Dublin (32 St Alban's Rd, South Circular Rd, Dublin 8) : Cobblestone Press, 1976. — [9]p,42 leaves : of ill, port ; 21x30cm.
Limited ed. of 350 numbered copies signed by the artist.
ISBN 0-9503426-2-9 Pbk : £16.50
(B77-06207)

720'.942 — Architecture. *England, 950-1965*
Yarwood, Doreen. Outline of English architecture / [by] Doreen Yarwood. — New ed. — London : Batsford, 1977. — 48p,16p of plates : ill(some col), plans ; 31cm.
Previous ed.: 1965. — Bibl.: p.3. — Index.
ISBN 0-7134-0697-6 : £3.95
ISBN 0-7134-0698-4 Pbk : £2.25
(B77-18289)

720'.942 — Architecture. *England. Dictionaries*
Curl, James Stevens. English architecture : an illustrated glossary / [by] James Stevens Curl ; with a foreword by Lord Muirshiel ; and drawings by John J. Sambrook. — Newton Abbot [etc.] : David and Charles, [1977]. — 192p : ill, plans ; 26cm.
Bibl.: p.189-191.
ISBN 0-7153-7110-x : £9.50
(B77-27973)

720'.942 — Architecture. Queen Anne style. *England, 1860-1900*
Girouard, Mark. Sweetness and light : the 'Queen Anne' movement, 1860-1900 / [by] Mark Girouard. — Oxford : Clarendon Press, 1977. — xviii,250p,viii p of plates : ill(some col), facsims(some col), plans ; 29cm.
Index.
ISBN 0-19-817330-x : £15.00 : CIP rev.
(B77-14321)

720'.942 — Buildings of historical importance. Conservation. *England. Juvenile literature*
Young, Geoffrey. Conservation scene : how buildings are protected - and why / [by] Geoffrey Young ; illustrated with cartoons by Mel Calman and with photographs. — Harmondsworth [etc.] : Penguin, 1977. — 160p : ill, facsim, maps ; 20cm. — (Peacock books)
Index.
ISBN 0-14-047089-1 Pbk : £0.75
(B77-12576)

Young, Geoffrey. Conservation scene : how buildings are protected - and why / [by] Geoffrey Young ; illustrated with cartoons by Mel Calman and with photographs. — Harmondsworth : Kestrel Books, 1977. — 160p : ill, facsim, maps ; 21cm.
Index.
ISBN 0-7226-5239-9 : £2.75
(B77-12577)

720'.942 — Buildings of historical importance. Conservation. *England. Reports, surveys. Serials*
Historic Buildings Council for England. Report / Historic Buildings Council for England. — London : H.M.S.O.
22nd : for the period 1 April 1975 to 31 March 1976. — 1976. — xi,59p : ill ; 25cm. — ([1976-77 H.C.] 5)
ISBN 0-10-200577-x Sd : £1.50
(B77-05545)

720'.9421 — Architecture. *Inner London*
Greater London Council. Survey of London / Greater London Council ; general editor F.H.W. Sheppard. — London : Athlone Press.
Vol.39 : The Grosvenor Estate in Mayfair. Part 1 : General history. — 1977. — xvi,236,[1]p, leaf of plate,56p of plates : ill(incl 1 col), geneal table, maps, plans ; 30cm.
Two col. maps on 2 fold. leaves in pocket. — Index.
ISBN 0-485-48239-8 : £20.00
(B77-33338)

720'.9421 — Architecture. *London, 1837-1901*
Olsen, Donald James. The growth of Victorian London / [by] Donald J. Olsen. — London : Batsford, 1976. — 384p : ill, maps, plans ; 26cm.
Index.
ISBN 0-7134-3229-2 : £10.50
(B77-00860)

720'.9421 — Architecture. *London, 1870-1970*
Hobhouse, Hermione. Lost London : a century of demolition and decay / [by] Hermione Hobhouse. — London [etc.] : Macmillan, 1976. — vi,250p : ill, facsim, maps ; 28cm.
Ill. on lining papers. — Originally published: 1971. — Index.
ISBN 0-333-19826-3 Pbk : £3.95
(B77-03675)

720'.9421 — Buildings of historical importance: Buildings owned by Greater London Council. Architectural features. *London*
Greater London Council. Historic buildings in London : an inventory of historic buildings owned by the Greater London Council. — London : Academy Editions [for] the G.L.C., 1975. — 128p : ill, plans ; 30cm. — (London architectural monographs)
ISBN 0-85670-208-0 : £6.95
ISBN 0-85670-213-7 Pbk : £3.95
(B77-02462)

720'.9422'3 — Architecture. *Eastern Kent*
Newman, John. North East and East Kent / by John Newman. — 2nd ed. — Harmondsworth [etc.] : Penguin, 1976. — 548p,[64]p of plates : ill, map, plan ; 19cm. — (The buildings of England)
Previous ed.: 1969. — Index.
£5.00
ISBN 0-14-071039-6
(B77-16996)

720'.9422'3 — Architecture. *Western Kent*
Newman, John. West Kent and the Weald / by John Newman. — 2nd ed. — Harmondsworth [etc.] : Penguin, 1976. — 672p,[64]p of plates : ill, map, plan ; 19cm. — (The buildings of England)
Previous ed.: 1969. — Index.
£5.50
ISBN 0-14-071038-8
(B77-16997)

720'.9422'38 — Buildings of historical importance. Architectural features. *Kent. Tunbridge Wells*
Davis, Terence. Tunbridge Wells : the gentle aspect / [by] Terence Davis ; photographs by Charles Saumarez Smith. — London [etc.] : Phillimore, 1976. — xvi,72p : ill, map ; 26cm.
Ill. on lining papers. — Index.
ISBN 0-85033-250-8 : £4.95
(B77-30454)

720'.9422'93 — Architecture. *Berkshire. Reading, to 1974*
Reading, our architectural heritage / [by Eric Stanford et al.]. — [Reading] ([Blagrave St., Reading, Berks.]) : [Reading Museum and Art Gallery], [1975]. — [46]p(2 fold) : ill, map ; 21x30cm.
Published to accompany an exhibition held in 1975, organised by a working party under the chairmanship of Eric Stanford. — Bibl.: p.[44]-[46].
Sp : £0.95
(B77-20456)

720'.9423'35 — Buildings of historical importance. Architectural features. *Dorset. Weymouth. Walkers' guides*
Ricketts, Eric. The buildings of old Weymouth / written and sketched by Eric Ricketts. — [Weymouth] ([40a St Thomas St., Weymouth, Dorset]) : Longmans of Weymouth (Booksellers) Ltd.
Part 1 : From Wyke Regis to the south harbourside. — 1975. — [4],iv,117,[1]p : ill, maps, plans ; 21cm.
ISBN 0-905900-00-6 Pbk : £1.50
(B77-22012)
Part 2 : Melcombe Regis & Westham. — 1976. — [6],175[i.e.185]p : ill, maps ; 22cm.
Pbk : £2.00
(B77-22013)

720'.9423'595 — Architecture. *Devon. Torquay. Illustrations*
Meadfoot-Wellswood and Area Residents' Association. The charm of Torquay / Meadfoot-Wellswood and Area Residents' Association. — Torquay (Hon. Secretary, Rocklea, Parkhill Rd, Torquay [Devon]) : The Association, [1976]. — [24]p : chiefly ill, col map ; 21x26cm.
Previous control number ISBN 0-905854-01-2.
ISBN 0-905854-00-4 Sd : £0.65
(B77-04962)

720'.9423'93 — Buildings of historical importance. Architectural features. *Avon. Bristol, to 1976*
Brown, Dorothy, *b.1927.* Bristol and how it grew / [by] Dorothy Brown. — Bristol (6 Buckingham Vale, Bristol 8) : Bristol Visual and Environmental Group, [1975]. — [2],46p : ill, maps ; 30cm.
Bibl.: p.42.
Pbk : Unpriced
(B77-30455)

720'.9423'98 — Architecture. *Avon. Bath. Illustrations*
Coard, Peter. Vanishing Bath / [by] Peter Coard. — Bath : Kingsmead.
Part 3. — 1972. — [96]p : of ill ; 23cm.
ISBN 0-901571-61-x Pbk : £1.00
(B77-02463)

720'.9424'16 — Buildings of historical importance. Architectural features. *Gloucestershire. Cheltenham. Walkers' guides*
Cheltenham Art Gallery and Museum. Cheltenham historical walks / [Cheltenham Art Gallery and Museum]. — [Cheltenham] ([Clarence St., Cheltenham, Glos. GL50 3JT]) : Cheltenham Art Gallery and Museum.
No.1 : The Pittville Estate. — [1977]. — Folder([8]p.) : ill, map ; 21cm.
Unpriced
(B77-18904)

720'.9425'38 — Buildings of historical importance. Architectural features. *Lincolnshire. Stamford*
Royal Commission on Historical Monuments (England). The town of Stamford : an inventory of historical monuments / Royal Commission on Historical Monuments (England). — London : H.M.S.O., 1977. — xci,182,[1]p,leaf of plate,163p of plates : ill(some col), maps, plans ; 29cm.
Map (fold. sheet) in pocket. — Index.
ISBN 0-11-700712-9 : £25.00
ISBN 0-11-700715-3 Grey binding : £25.00
(B77-11987)

720'.9425'74 — Architecture. *Oxfordshire. Oxford*
Curl, James Stevens. The erosion of Oxford / [by] James Stevens Curl. — Oxford : Oxford Illustrated Press, 1977. — x,206p : ill ; 22cm.
ISBN 0-902280-40-6 Pbk : £2.95
(B77-17653)

Hinton, David Alban. Oxford buildings from medieval to modern / [written by] David A. Hinton ; [photographs by David Carpenter]. — [Revised ed.]. — Oxford : Ashmolean Museum, 1977. — [2],73p : ill ; 21x26cm.
Col. map on back cover verso. — Previous ed.: published as 'Oxford buildings from medieval to modern - exteriors'. Oxford : Oxford Archaeological Excavation Committee, 1972.
ISBN 0-900090-44-8 Pbk : Unpriced
(B77-23589)

720'.9425'8 — Architecture. *Hertfordshire*
Pevsner, *Sir* Nikolaus. Hertfordshire / by Nikolaus Pevsner. — 2nd ed. / revised by Bridget Cherry. — Harmondsworth [etc.] : Penguin, 1977. — 460p,[64]p of plates : ill, maps, plans ; 19cm. — (The buildings of England)
Previous ed.: London : Penguin Books, 1953. — Index.
ISBN 0-14-071007-8 : £4.75
(B77-18905)

720'.9426'46 — Buildings of historical importance. Conservation. *Suffolk. Woodbridge. Proposals*
Suffolk *(County)*. *Council.* Conservation in Woodbridge : an appraisal of its townscape and a policy for future change / Suffolk County Council. — Ipswich (County Hall, Ipswich, Suffolk) : Suffolk County Council, 1976. — [6], 55p,[6]leaves of plates(2 fold) : ill, maps(some col) ; 30cm.
ISBN 0-86055-009-5 Sd : £1.75
(B77-11988)

720'.9426'59 — Architecture. Rejected proposals. *Cambridgeshire. Cambridge, to 1966*
Reeve, Frank Albert. The Cambridge that never was / [by] F.A. Reeve. — Cambridge : Oleander Press, 1976. — 40p : ill, maps, plans ; 21cm.
Bibl.: p.40.
ISBN 0-902675-72-9 Sd : £0.90
Primary classification 711'.4'0942659
(B77-10472)

720'.9427'665 — Architecture. *Lancashire. Preston, ca 1960-ca 1975*
Brook, John. Preston's new buildings / by John Brook and Duncan Glen ; with photographs by Myra Jones and John Brook. — Preston (Graphics Division, Preston Polytechnic, Corporation St., Preston, Lancs.) : Harris Press, 1975. — [15]p : ill ; 27cm.
ISBN 0-905735-03-x Sd : Private circulation
(B77-01663)

720'.9428'8 — Buildings of historical importance. Architectural features. *Northumberland*
Allsopp, Bruce. Historic architecture of Northumberland and Newcastle upon Tyne / by Bruce Allsopp and Ursula Clark. — Stocksfield [etc.] : Oriel Press, 1977. — [4], 124p : chiefly ill, maps(on lining papers), plans ; 25cm.
ISBN 0-85362-170-5 : £5.00
(B77-31329)

720'.9429 — Architecture. *Wales, to 1939*
Hilling, John Bryan. The historic architecture of Wales : an introduction / [by] John B. Hilling ; [maps, plans and line drawings by John B. Hilling]. — Cardiff : University of Wales Press, 1976. — xiii,234p : ill, maps, plans ; 21cm.
Bibl.: p.218-222. — Index.
ISBN 0-7083-0626-8 : £5.50
(B77-06801)

720'.9429 — Buildings of historical importance. Conservation. *Wales. Reports, surveys. Serials*
Historic Buildings Council for Wales. Annual report / Historic Buildings Council for Wales = Cyngor Adeiladau Hanesyddol Cymru. — Cardiff : H.M.S.O.
23rd : 1975-76. — [1976]. — 14p,[2]p of plates : ill ; 25cm. — ([1975-76 H.C.] 634)
ISBN 0-10-263476-9 Sd : £0.35
(B77-04325)

720'.9437'12 — Architecture. *Czechoslovakia. Prague, ca 1650-ca 1800. Illustrations*
Uher, Vladimír. Dialogue of forms / introduction and commentary by Milan Pavlík ; photographs by Vladimír Uher ; [translated from the Czech by John Eisler]. — New York : St Martin's Press ; London : St James Press, 1976. — [180] p : chiefly ill ; 32cm.
Ill. on lining paper. — These illustrations originally published as: 'Dialog tvarů'. Prague : Odeon, 1974. — Bibl.: p.[175]-[178].
ISBN 0-900997-92-3 : £9.75
(B77-20457)

720'.945 — Architecture. *Italy, 1400-1600*
Lotz, Wolfgang. Studies in Italian Renaissance architecture / [by] Wolfgang Lotz ; editorial committee James S. Ackerman, W. Chandler Kirwin, Henry A. Millon ; translators [from the German and Italian] Margaret Breitenbach, Renate Franciscono, Paul Lunde. — Cambridge, Mass. ; London : M.I.T. Press, 1977. — xxv,220p : ill, plans ; 24cm.
Bibl.: p.209-211. — Index.
ISBN 0-262-12073-9 : £10.25
(B77-29572)

720'.946 — Architecture. *Spain, to 1976. Secondary school texts*
Tames, Richard. Buildings in Spain / [by] R. Tames. — London : Harrap, 1977. — 32p : ill ; 14x22cm. — (Discovering Spain)
ISBN 0-245-52818-0 Sd : £0.65
(B77-17654)

720'.9496'1 — Architecture. *Istanbul. Juvenile literature*
Leacroft, Helen. The buildings of Byzantium / [by] Helen and Richard Leacroft. — London : Hodder and Stoughton [etc.], 1977. — [1],41p : ill(some col), 2 maps ; 25cm.
Ill., ports on lining papers. — Index.
ISBN 0-340-16426-3 : £2.80
(B77-27974)

720'.9773'11 — Architecture. *Illinois. Chicago, to 1893*
Tallmadge, Thomas E. Architecture in old Chicago / [by] Thomas E. Tallmadge. — Chicago ; London : University of Chicago Press, 1975 [i.e. 1976]. — xv,218p,[5] leaves of plate,[24]p of plates : ill, plan ; 23cm.
Published in the United States: 1975. — Originally published: Chicago : University of Chicago Press, 1941. — Index.
ISBN 0-226-78947-0 Pbk : £3.00
(B77-02464)

720'.9794'94 — Architecture. *California. Los Angeles, to 1970*
Banham, Reyner. Los Angeles : the architecture of four ecologies / [by] Reyner Banham. — Harmondsworth [etc.] : Penguin, 1976. — 256p : ill, facsims, maps ; 20cm. — (Pelican books) (The architect and society)
Originally published: London : Allen Lane, 1971. — Bibl.: p.247-252. — Index.
Pbk : £1.75
ISBN 0-14-021178-0
(B77-04326)

721 — ARCHITECTURAL DESIGN
Broadbent, Geoffrey. Design in architecture : architecture and the human sciences / [by] Geoffrey Broadbent. — London [etc.] : Wiley, 1977. — xiv,504p : ill, forms, plans ; 23cm.
Originally published: 1973. — Bibl.: p.453-480. — Index.
ISBN 0-471-99527-4 Pbk : £4.95
(B77-23590)

721 — Architectural design. *Early works*
Palladio, Andrea. [I quattro libri dell'architettura. English]. The four books of architecture / [by] Andrea Palladio ; [translated from the Italian by Isaac Ware]. — [1738 ed. reprinted] ; with a new introduction by Adolf K. Placzek. — New York : Dover Publications [etc.] ; London : Constable, [1977]. — xx,110p,[4]leaves of plates,192p of plates in various pagings : ill, plans ; 31cm. — (Dover pictorial archive series)

This facsimile reprint published: New York : Dover Publications, 1965. — Facsimile reprint of: 1738 ed. London : I. Ware, 1738.
ISBN 0-486-21308-0 Pbk : £5.35
(B77-26419)

721 — Architectural design. *Manuals*
Planning. — 9th ed. / edited by Edward D. Mills. — London [etc.] : Newnes-Butterworths. In 5 vols. — Previous ed.: in 1 vol. / by S. Rowland Pierce, Patrick Cutbush, Anthony Williams. London : Iliffe, 1959.
Buildings for habitation, commerce and industry. — 1976. — 290p in various pagings : ill, plans ; 31cm.
Bibl. — Index.
ISBN 0-408-00226-3 : £12.00
(B77-06802)

Weidhaas, Ernest R. Architectural drafting and design / [by] Ernest R. Weidhaas. — 3rd ed. — Boston, Mass. ; London [etc.] : Allyn and Bacon, 1977. — [9],438p : ill(some col), plans(some col) ; 29cm.
'Portions of this book first appeared in "Architectural drafting and construction" ... [Boston, Mass. : Allyn and Bacon, 1974]' - title page verso. — Previous ed. of 'Architectural drafting and design': Boston, Mass. : Allyn and Bacon, 1972. — Bibl.: p.416-419. — Index.
ISBN 0-205-05624-5 : Unpriced
Primary classification 720'.28
(B77-11322)

721 — Architectural design. Behavioural aspects
Heimsath, Clovis. Behavioral architecture : towards an accountable design process / [by] Clovis Heimsath. — New York ; London [etc.] : McGraw-Hill, 1977. — xi,203p : ill, maps, plans ; 25cm. — ([An 'Architectural record' book])
Bibl.: p.189-192. — Index.
ISBN 0-07-027890-3 : £11.65
(B77-32035)

721 — Architectural design for handicapped persons. *Periodicals*
Design for special needs : the journal of the Centre on Environment for the Handicapped. — [London] ([126 Albert St., NW1 7NF]) : [C.E.H.].
No.10- ; May-Aug. 1976-. — [1976]-. — ill, ports ; 30cm.
Three issues a year. — [2],24p. in issue no.11. — Continues: Newsletter / Centre on Environment for the Handicapped. — Bibl.
Sd : £4.50 yearly
ISSN 0309-3042
Also classified at 362.4'028
(B77-10872)

721 — Architectural design for physically handicapped persons. *Great Britain*
Goldsmith, Selwyn. Designing for the disabled / [by] Selwyn Goldsmith. — 3rd ed., fully revised / diagrams by Louis Dezart. — London : RIBA Publications, 1976. — 525p : col ill, col plans ; 31cm.
Previous ed.: i.e. 2nd ed., 1967. — Bibl.: p.481-509. — Index.
ISBN 0-900630-50-7 : £20.00
(B77-00322)

721 — Architectural design. Social aspects
Crosby, Theo. The pessimist utopia / by Theo Crosby. — London (61 North Wharf Rd, W2 1LA) : Pentagram Design, [1976]. — 24p : ill ; 21cm. — (Pentagram papers ; 2 ISSN 0309-2135)
'The Lethaby lectures are delivered annually at the Royal College of Art ... In 1975 the lectures ... were delivered in two parts under the single title "The Pessimist Utopia"' - cover.
ISBN 0-905739-01-9 Sd : £1.00
(B77-04963)

721 — Architectural design. Social aspects. *Marxist viewpoints*
Tafuri, Manfredo. Architecture and utopia : design and capitalist development / [by] Manfredo Tafuri ; translated from the Italian by Barbara Luigia La Penta. — Cambridge, Mass. ; London : M.I.T. Press, 1976. — xi, 184p : ill, facsim, maps, plans ; 19cm.
Translation of: 'Progetto e utopia'. Roma-Bari : Laterza, 1973.
ISBN 0-262-20033-3 : £7.50
(B77-02465)

721 — Architectural design. Use of colour
Colour for architecture / [edited by] Tom Porter and Byron Mikellides. — London : Studio Vista, 1976. — 151p : ill(some col) ; 31cm.
Bibl.: p.145-146. — Index.
ISBN 0-289-70611-4 : £12.50
(B77-09843)

721 — Buildings. Renovation & remodelling. Design. *United States*
Recycling buildings : renovations, remodellings, restorations, and reuses / edited by Elisabeth Kendall Thompson. — New York ; London [etc.] : McGraw-Hill, 1977. — viii,213p : ill(some col), maps, plans ; 32cm. — ('Architectural record' books)
Index.
ISBN 0-07-002335-2 : £14.65
(B77-25771)

721 — Easily maintained buildings. Architectural design
Feldman, Edwin Barry. Building design for maintainability / [by] Edwin B. Feldman. — New York ; London [etc.] : McGraw-Hill, [1976]. — viii,232p : ill ; 21cm. — ('Architectural record' books)
Published in the United States : 1975. — Bibl.: p.195. — Index.
ISBN 0-07-020385-7 : £12.05
(B77-10474)

721 — Megastructures. Architectural design, ca 1930-ca 1970
Banham, Reyner. Megastructure : urban futures of the recent past / [by] Reyner Banham. — London : Thames and Hudson, 1976. — 224p : ill, plans ; 26cm.
Bibl.: p.221. — Index.
ISBN 0-500-34068-4 : £10.00
(B77-04964)

721'.01'8 — Architectural design. Methodology
Wade, John W. Architecture, problems and purposes : architectural design as a basic problem-solving process / by John W. Wade. — New York ; London [etc.] : Wiley, 1977. — xiii,350p,[2]fold p of plates,fold leaf of plate : ill ; 26cm.
Bibl. — Index.
ISBN 0-471-91305-7 : £15.00
(B77-21306)

721'.022'8 — Architectural models. Construction. *Manuals*
Hohauser, Sanford. Architectural and interior models : design and construction / [by] Sanford Hohauser. — New York ; London [etc.] : Van Nostrand Reinhold, [1977]. — [2],211p : ill ; 31cm.
Originally published: 1971. — Index.
ISBN 0-442-23479-1 Pbk : £6.80
(B77-29573)

721'.028'54 — Architectural design. Applications of computer systems
Cross, Nigel. The automated architect / [by] N. Cross. — London : Pion, 1977. — [11],178p : ill, plans ; 24cm. — (Research in planning and design ; 4)
Bibl.: p.155-171. — Index.
ISBN 0-85086-057-1 : £6.00
(B77-19521)

721'.042 — High-rise buildings. Analysis & design
Schueller, Wolfgang. High-rise building structures / [by] Wolfgang Schueller. — New York ; London [etc.] : Wiley, 1977. — xiii, 274p : ill, charts, plans ; 27cm.
'A Wiley-Interscience publication'. — Index.
ISBN 0-471-01530-x : £16.90
(B77-20458)

721'.0442 — Clay buildings. *Scotland. Grampian Region & Tayside Region*
Walker, Bruce. Clay buildings in north east Scotland / [by] Bruce Walker. — [Dundee etc.] ([c/o Mr A. Sprott, Hon. Secretary, 14 Villa Rd, South Queensferry, West Lothian]) : [Scottish Vernacular Buildings Working Group], [1977]. — 67p : ill, plans ; 21cm.
Sd : Unpriced
(B77-29574)

721'.044'4 — Concrete block buildings. Architectural design & construction
Gage, Michael. Design in blockwork / [by] Michael Gage, Tom Kirkbride. — 2nd ed. — London : Architectural Press, 1976. — 121p : ill, plans, 2 ports ; 30cm.
Previous ed.: London : Architectural Press for the Cement and Concrete Association, 1972. — Bibl.: p.120-121.
ISBN 0-85139-161-3 Pbk : £4.95
(B77-11989)

721'.08 — Architectural design. *Essays*
Rowe, Colin. The mathematics of the ideal villa, and other essays / [by] Colin Rowe. — Cambridge, Mass. ; London : M.I.T. Press, 1976. — vii,225p : ill, plans ; 26cm.
ISBN 0-262-18077-4 : £9.60
(B77-19522)

721'.09'04 — Universities. *Great Britain. Open University. Curriculum subjects: Visual arts. Courses: History of architecture and design, 1890-1939*
Project guide : and advanced recommended reading / [by Tim Benton et al.]. — Milton Keynes : Open University Press, 1976. — 39p : ill ; 30cm. — (A 305 ; PG) (Arts, a third level course : history of architecture and design, 1890-1939 ; project guide)
Bibl.
Sd : Unpriced
(B77-02466)

721'.09425'11 — National parks. *England. Peak District. Peak District National Park. Buildings. Architectural design. Standards*
Peak Park Joint Planning Board. Building design guide, Peak National Park / [Peak Park Joint Planning Board] ; [written and illustrated by Peter Knowles]. — Bakewell (Aldern House, Baslow Rd, Bakewell, Derbyshire) : The Board, 1976. — 123p in various pagings : ill(some col), form, col map, plans ; 31cm.
ISBN 0-901428-33-7 Sp : £2.30
(B77-05546)

721'.46 — Geodesic domes
Essential Structures Research Association. Sphere cells & surfaces / Essential Structures Research Association ; [written and researched by Graham Brand and Jim Bell]. — London (Architectural Association, School of Architecture, 34 Bedford Sq., WC1B 3ES) : E.S.R.A., [1976]. — [2],33p : ill ; 30cm.
Bibl.: p.33.
Sd : Unpriced
(B77-21307)

721'.5 — Anticlastic plastics roofs. Architectural design
Zerning, John. Design guide to anticlastic structures in plastic / [by] John Zerning. — [London] ([24 Park Steps, St George's Fields, W.2]) : The author, 1976. — 63p : ill, port ; 30cm.
Cover title. — Originally published: 1975.
Pbk : Unpriced
(B77-31330)

721'.5 — Tension roofs. *Conference proceedings*
International Conference on Tension Roof Structures, *London, 1974.* International Conference on Tension Roof Structures, London 1974 : conference manual. — London (35 Marylebone Rd, NW1 5LS) : The Short Course Unit, Polytechnic of Central London, [1977]. — 703p in various pagings : ill, plans ; 30cm.
Cover title. — '... International Conference on Tension Roof Structures, 8-10 April 1974, held at the Polytechnic of Central London' - inside front cover. — Bibl.
Pbk : £15.00
(B77-32745)

721'.8 — Windows. Design. *Manuals*
Pilkington Technical Advisory Service. Window glass design guide / [Pilkington Technical Advisory Service] ; edited by Denis Philip Turner. — London : Architectural Press [etc.], 1977. — viii,111p : ill, maps ; 30cm.
Index.
ISBN 0-85139-709-3 Pbk : £4.95
(B77-26420)

722 — ARCHITECTURE. ANCIENT AND ORIENTAL

722 — Architecture. Aeolic style. *Ancient world, B.C.1000-B.C.500*
Betancourt, Philip P. The Aeolic style in architecture : a survey of its development in Palestine, the Halikarnassos Peninsula and Greece, 1000-500 BC / by Philip P. Betancourt. — Princeton ; Guildford : Princeton University Press, 1977. — viii,169p,[24]p of plates : ill, maps, plans ; 29cm.
Bibl.: p.157-162. — Index.
ISBN 0-691-03922-4 : £18.80
(B77-30456)

722'.7 — Architecture. Mathematical aspects. *Ancient Rome, 527-565*
Warren, John, *b.1931.* Greek mathematics and the architects to Justinian / [by] John Warren. — [London] ([102 St Paul's Rd, N.1]) : [Coach Publishing], [1976]. — [4],14p : ill, plans ; 30cm. — (Art and archaeology research papers)
Bibl.: p.12.
ISBN 0-902608-02-9 Sd : £1.00
(B77-15390)

724 — ARCHITECTURE. MODERN PERIOD, 1400-
724.9 — Architectural design. *Europe, 1915-1930*
Benton, Tim. The new objectivity / prepared for the [Open University] course team by Tim Benton with contributions from ... [others]. — Milton Keynes : Open University Press, 1975. — 80p,[32]p of plates : ill, facsims, plans ; 30cm. — (Arts, a third level course : history of architecture and design, 1890-1939 ; units 11-12) (A305 ; 11 and 12)
Filmstrip (13fr. colour. 35mm.) in plastic envelope as insert. — Bibl.: p.5-7.
ISBN 0-335-00705-8 Pbk : £2.75
Also classified at 745.4'44
(B77-28761)

724.9 — Architectural design, 1890-1939. *Illustrations*
Radiovision booklet / [compiled by the Open University Course Team]. — Milton Keynes : Open University Press, 1975. — 112p : of ill, facsims, map, plans ; 30cm. — (Arts, a third level course : history of architecture and design, 1890-1939) (A305 ; RVB)
ISBN 0-335-00712-0 Pbk : £4.50
(B77-33940)

724.9 — Architectural design, ca 1900-1976
Jencks, Charles. The language of post-modern architecture / [by] Charles A. Jencks. — London : Academy Editions, 1977. — 104p : ill(some col), plans ; 30cm. — (An 'Architectural design' monograph)
Index.
ISBN 0-85670-320-6 : £7.95
ISBN 0-85670-325-7 Pbk : £4.95
(B77-22014)

724.9 — Architecture, 1900-1975
Brolin, Brent C. The failure of modern architecture / [by] Brent C. Brolin. — London : Studio Vista, 1976. — 128p : ill, plans ; 24cm.
Ill. on lining papers. — Bibl.: p.125-126. — Index.
ISBN 0-289-70753-6 : £6.00
(B77-09148)

725.1 — ARCHITECTURE. GOVERNMENT BUILDINGS
725'.15 — Magistrates' courts. Buildings. Architectural design. *Outer London. Reports, surveys*
Magistrates courthouses, design study, 1977. — [London] : Home Office : Greater London Council, [1977]. — [8],192p : ill, map, plans(some col) ; 30cm.
'This Study is based on a revision and amplification of the Greater London Council Design Study No.2 published in 1969 and results from a series of meetings by a Working Party set up jointly by the Greater London Council and the Home Office' - p.1.
ISBN 0-7168-0902-8 Pbk : £10.00
(B77-32036)

725.2 — ARCHITECTURE. COMMERCIAL BUILDINGS
725'.2'0941 — Commercial buildings. Architectural features. *Great Britain, 1927-1933. Illustrations*
Mackertich, Peter. Facade : a decade of British and American commercial architecture / [compiled] by Tony and Peter Mackertich ; photography by Peter Mackertich ; with an introduction by Bevis Hillier. — London (51 Endell St., WC2H 9AJ) : Mathews Miller Dunbar Ltd, 1976. — [83]p : chiefly col ill ; 21cm.
ISBN 0-903811-20-0 Pbk : £2.75
Also classified at 725'.2'0973
(B77-04965)

725'.2'0973 — Commercial buildings. Architectural features. *United States, 1927-1933. Illustrations*
Mackertich, Peter. Facade : a decade of British and American commercial architecture / [compiled] by Tony and Peter Mackertich ; photography by Peter Mackertich ; with an introduction by Bevis Hillier. — London (51 Endell St., WC2H 9AJ) : Mathews Miller Dunbar Ltd, 1976. — [83]p : chiefly col ill ; 21cm.
ISBN 0-903811-20-0 Pbk : £2.75
Primary classification 725'.2'0941
(B77-04965)

725'.23 — Offices. Buildings. Interiors. Architectural design. *Great Britain*
Planning office space / edited by Francis Duffy, Colin Cave, John Worthington. — London : Architectural Press [etc.], 1976. — vi,250p : ill, plans ; 31cm.
'... a heavily revised and updated version of a series first published in "The Architects' journal" ...' - jacket. — Bibl.: p.247. — Index.
ISBN 0-85139-505-8 : £16.00
(B77-05547)

725'.23'0973 — Offices. Buildings. Architectural design. *United States*
Office building design. — 2nd ed. / edited by Mildred F. Schmertz. — New York ; London [etc.] : McGraw-Hill, [1976]. — x,211p : ill, plans ; 32cm.
'An "Architectural record" book'. — This ed. published in the United States: 1975. — Previous ed.: published as 'Office buildings'. New York : F.W. Dodge, 1961. — Index.
ISBN 0-07-002320-4 : £19.50
(B77-05548)

725'.25 — Livery halls. *London (City). Fishmongers' Hall, London. Architectural features, 1444-1976*
Metcalf, Priscilla. The halls of the Fishmongers' Company : an architectural history of a riverside site / by Priscilla Metcalf. — London [etc.] : Phillimore, 1977. — xii,214p,leaf of plate,[28]p of plates : ill(incl 1 col), facsims, plans ; 26cm.
Bibl.: p.182-183. — Index.
ISBN 0-85033-243-5 : £12.00
(B77-30457)

725.3 — ARCHITECTURE. TRANSPORTATION AND STORAGE BUILDINGS
725'.3 — Railway services. *England. Great Western Railway. Buildings. Architectural features*
Vaughan, Adrian. A pictorial record of Great Western architecture / by A. Vaughan. — Oxford : Oxford Publishing, 1977. — vi,442p : ill, coats of arms, facsims, plans ; 28cm.
Ill. on lining papers. — Bibl.: p.vi. — Index.
ISBN 0-902888-22-6 : £11.50
(B77-24372)

725.4 — ARCHITECTURE. INDUSTRIAL BUILDINGS
725'.4 — Factories. Integration of engineering services. Architectural design aspects
The **integration** of building services engineering into the design and construction of process facilities : [proceedings of a] conference sponsored [i.e. organized] by the Process Engineering Group of the Institution of Mechanical Engineers and the Institution of Heating and Ventilating Engineers, London, 1-2 May 1974. — London [etc.] : Mechanical Engineering Publications for the Institution of Mechanical Engineers, 1975. — [8],72p : ill, plans ; 30cm. — (Institution of Mechanical Engineers. Conference publications ; CP15-1974)
ISBN 0-85298-306-9 : £9.50
(B77-12578)

725'.4'0941 — Industrial buildings. Architectural features. *Great Britain. Juvenile literature*
Allen, Eleanor. Industry / [by] Eleanor Allen. — London : A. and C. Black, 1977. — 32p : ill ; 26cm. — (Buildings as history)
Bibl.: p.31. — Index.
ISBN 0-7136-1758-6 : £1.75
(B77-31331)

725.5 — ARCHITECTURE. HEALTH AND WELFARE BUILDINGS
725'.51 — Hospitals. Laundries. Design. *England*
Great Britain. *Department of Health and Social Security.* Laundry. — Revised [ed.] / Department of Health and Social Security, Welsh Office. — [London] : H.M.S.O., 1977. — [2],38,[1]p : ill ; 30cm. — (Health building note ; 25)
Pierced for binder. — Previous ed.: / issued by Ministry of Health. 1964. (Hospital building note ; 25).
ISBN 0-11-320289-x Sd : £1.50
(B77-26421)

725'.52 — Hospitals. Psychiatric departments for long-stay patients. Extension & improvement. *Great Britain. Proposals*
Symons, Jean. Improving existing hospital buildings for long-stay residents / prepared for CEH by Jean Symons ; drawings by Peter Jones. — London (120 Albert St., NW1 7NE) : Centre on Environment for the Handicapped, [1977]. — 26p ; 30cm. — (Centre on Environment for the Handicapped. Design guides ; 1 ISSN 0301-7680)
Originally published: 1973.
Sd : £0.60
(B77-13761)

725'.57 — Residential institutions for mentally handicapped children. Architectural design. *Research reports*
Sandhu, Jim Singh. Environmental design for handicapped children / [by] Jim Singh Sandhu, Horst Hendriks-Jansen. — Farnborough, Hants. : Saxon House, 1976. — xiii,222,[1]p : ill, plans ; 24cm.
Bibl.: p.219-222.
ISBN 0-566-00142-x : £9.75
Also classified at 688.7'25
(B77-10873)

725.6 — ARCHITECTURE. PRISON AND REFORMATORY BUILDINGS
725'.6 — Community homes. Architectural design. *England. Manuals*
Great Britain. *Department of Health and Social Security.* Community homes design guidance : a small secure unit / Department of Health and Social Security. — [London] ([Alexander Fleming House, Elephant and Castle, SE1 6BY]) : [The Department], 1977. — 39p in various pagings : ill ; 30cm.
Sd : Unpriced
(B77-27251)

725.8 — ARCHITECTURE. RECREATION BUILDINGS
725'.8 — Outdoor sports facilities. Floodlighting. *Manuals*
Christy Electrical Contractors. Floodlighting of outdoor sports facilities : a brief guide on installation requirements, maintenance and costs / written for the National Playingfields Association by Christy Electrical Contractors Ltd. — 2nd ed. — London : The Association, 1976. — 52p : ill, plans ; 21cm.
Previous ed.: / by Christy Bros Ltd. 1970. — Bibl.: p.49. — Index.
ISBN 0-900858-63-x Sd : £1.25
(B77-09844)

725'.822'0942132 — National theatres. Buildings. *Great Britain. National Theatre. Architectural features*
The **National** Theatre : the 'Architectural review' guide / edited by Colin Amery. — London : Architectural Press, 1977. — [2],70p : ill(some col), facsim, map, ports ; 31cm.
Page width varies. — Originally published as a special issue of 'Architectural review'.
ISBN 0-85139-442-6 : £3.75
(B77-22016)

National Theatre. The complete guide to Britain's National Theatre / [contributors Richard Findlater ... et al.]. — Tadworth : Heinemann Educational, 1977. — 56p : ill, facsim, map, plans, ports ; 25cm.
ISBN 0-435-18656-6 Pbk : £1.50
(B77-26422)

725'.827 — Football stadiums and rugby stadiums. Design. Safety measures
Great Britain. *Home Office.* Guide to safety at sports grounds (football) / Home Office [and] Scottish Home and Health Department. — London : H.M.S.O., 1976. — iv,30p : 2 plans ; 21cm.
ISBN 0-11-340761-0 Sd : £0.75
(B77-07980)

725.9 — ARCHITECTURE. EXHIBITION BUILDINGS, MEMORIAL BUILDINGS, ETC.
725'.94 — Stoas. Architectural features. *Ancient Greece, to ca B.C.50*
Coulton, J J. The architectural development of the Greek stoa / by J.J. Coulton. — Oxford : Clarendon Press, 1976. — xviii,308p,leaf of plate,[8]p of plates : ill, plans ; 29cm. — (Oxford monographs on classical archaeology)
Bibl.: p.xiv-xviii. — Index.
ISBN 0-19-813215-8 : £15.00
(B77-22017)

726 — ARCHITECTURE. RELIGIOUS BUILDINGS

726'.1'45 — Hindu temples. Architectural features

Michell, George. The Hindu temple : an introduction to its meaning and forms / [by] George Michell. — London : Elek, 1977. — 192p : ill, map, plans ; 25cm.
Bibl.: p.185-186. — Index.
ISBN 0-236-40088-6 : £10.50
(B77-32754)

726'.5'0941 — Redundant churches. Conversion. *Great Britain. Case studies*

New life for old churches. — London : H.M.S.O. [for the] Department of the Environment, Scottish Development Department [and] Welsh Office, 1977. — [52]p : ill, maps, plans ; 25cm. — (Aspects of conservation ; 3)
Bibl.: p.[7].
ISBN 0-11-751065-3 Sd : £2.00
(B77-23591)

726'.5'09415 — Churches. Architectural features. *Ireland, to 1976. Secondary school texts*

Brioscú, Aodhagán. Irish churches / text Aodhagán Brioscú ; illustrations William Moore. — [Tallaght] : Folens, [1977]. — [1], 32p : col ill, plans ; 25cm. — (Irish environmental library series ; no.21)
Sd : £0.60
(B77-18906)

726'.5'0942 — Parish churches. Architectural features. *England, to 1913*

Cox, John Charles. The English parish church : an account of the chief building types & of their materials during nine centuries / by J. Charles Cox. — Wakefield : EP Publishing, 1976. — xx,338p,fold plate : ill, plans ; 20cm.
Facsimile reprint of: 1st ed. London : Batsford, 1914. — Index.
ISBN 0-7158-1174-6 : £4.95
Also classified at 691
(B77-05549)

726'.5'094212 — Churches. Architectural features. *London (City)*

Cobb, Gerald. London city churches / [by] Gerald Cobb. — New and revised ed. — London : Batsford, 1977. — 191p : ill, map, plans ; 26cm.
Previous ed.: i.e. 3rd ed. London : Corporation of London, 1971. — Bibl.: p.178-188. — Index.
ISBN 0-7134-3186-5 : £8.50
(B77-09149)

726'.5'09423 — Churches. Architectural features. *South-west England. Illustrations*

Churches of Wessex : an illustrated survey / [compiled] by Kenneth G. Ponting ; with a foreword by the Bishop of Bath & Wells. — Bradford-on-Avon : Moonraker Press, 1977. — 96p : ill(incl 1 col), map, ports ; 20x22cm.
Index.
ISBN 0-239-00163-x : £4.95
(B77-24373)

726'.5'094261 — Churches. Preservation. *Norfolk. Periodicals*

Norfolk Churches Trust. Newsletter / Norfolk Churches Trust Ltd. — Holt (The Old Rectory, Holt, [Norfolk]) : [The Trust].
[No.3]- ; Summer 1976-. — 1976-. — 21cm.
Annual. — Folder ([4]p.) as 3rd issue. — Continues: The Norfolk Society Committee for Country Churches.
Unpriced
(B77-04327)

726'.5'094264 — Churches. Architectural features. *Suffolk*

Suffolk churches : a pocket guide / edited by Jean Corke ... [et al.] ; with an introduction by Kenneth Clark. — Lavenham (Little Hall, Market Place, Lavenham, Sudbury, Suffolk) : Suffolk Historic Churches Trust, 1976. — [4], 76p : ill, facsim, map, plan ; 18cm.
Index.
ISBN 0-9505385-0-7 Pbk : £1.50
(B77-00323)

726'.5'094267 — Church of England. Redundant churches. Conservation & conversion. *Essex. Reports, surveys*

Couchman, Christine. Redundant churches in Essex / [prepared by Christine Couchman and John Hedges]. — Chelmsford ([c/o Planning Department, County Hall, Chelmsford, Essex CM1 1LF]) : [Essex County Planning Department], 1976. — [2],49p : ill, forms, map, plans ; 30cm.
Bibl.: p.46-47.
ISBN 0-901355-69-0 Sd : £1.00
(B77-02467)

726'.5'094531 — Churches. *Italy. Venice. Church of the Madonna dell'Orto. Restoration, 1968-1969*

Restoring Venice, the Church of the Madonna dell'Orto / edited by Ashley Clarke and Philip Rylands ; with contributions by ... [others]. — London : Elek, 1977. — 98p,[2]leaves of plates : ill(some col), plan ; 25cm.
Bibl.: p.93. — Index.
ISBN 0-236-40080-0 Pbk : £4.95
(B77-24374)

726'.5'094961 — Churches. Architectural features. *Turkey. Istanbul, ca 400-1975. Illustrations*

Mathews, Thomas Francis. The Byzantine churches of Istanbul : a photographic survey / [by] Thomas F. Mathews ; [plans and map prepared by Glenn Ruby and Robert Texter]. — University Park [Pa] ; London : Pennsylvania State University Press, 1976. — xx,405p : chiefly ill, facsim, map, plans ; 29cm.
Bibl. — Index.
ISBN 0-271-01210-2 : £37.50
(B77-11990)

726'.6'094 — Cathedrals. Architectural features. *Western Europe*

Grünenfelder, Josef. Cathedrals of Europe / text by Josef Grünenfelder ; photographs by Michael Wolgensinger ; translated [from the German] by David Lawrence Grambs. — Oxford : Elsevier-Phaidon, 1976. — [9],129p : col ill ; 30cm.
Translation of: 'Kathedralen'. Zürich : Silva, 1971.
ISBN 0-7290-0056-7 : £5.95
(B77-14841)

726'.6'0942 — Cathedrals. Architectural features. Date of building. *England*

Blakeney, H E. Pocket book of dates of the building of English medieval cathedrals / compiled by H.E. Blakeney. — [Canterbury] ([c/o Elvy & Gibbs Partnership, 11 Best La., Canterbury]) : [The author], [1977]. — 55p ; 17cm.
Cover title: Building dates of English medieval cathedrals. — Versos of most p. blank.
ISBN 0-9505618-0-0 Sd : £0.25
(B77-13147)

726'.6'0942656 — Cathedrals. *Cambridgeshire. Ely. Ely Cathedral. Architectural features. Juvenile literature*

Dowdy, Mac. Ely Cathedral task book / [text, graphics and artwork by Mac Dowdy]. — Ely (Back Hill, Ely, Cambridgeshire) : Ely Resource and Technology Centre, 1976. — [3],15p : ill, plans ; 30cm.
ISBN 0-904463-13-3 Sd : £0.20
(B77-14322)

726'.9 — Papal villas. *Vatican. Casino di Pio IV. Decorations*

Smith, Graham, *b.1942.* The Casino of Pius IV / [by] Graham Smith. — Princeton ; Guildford : Princeton University Press, 1977. — xvi,125p, [50]p of plates,leaf of plate : ill, facsims, plans ; 29cm.
Bibl.: p.113-117. — Index.
ISBN 0-691-03915-1 : £15.00
(B77-27975)

727 — ARCHITECTURE. EDUCATIONAL AND RESEARCH BUILDINGS

727'.1 — Educational institutions for pre-school children. Buildings. Architectural design. *Conference proceedings*

University of York. *Institute of Advanced Architectural Studies.* A right to be children : designing for the education of the under-fives : an account of two courses held at the Institute of Advanced Architectural Studies, University of York, April and July 1974 / [University of York, Institute of Advanced Architectural Studies] ; [prepared by Mary Medd]. — London : RIBA Publications, 1976. — 118p : ill, plans ; 30cm.
Bibl.: p.117.
ISBN 0-900630-58-2 Pbk : £3.00
(B77-04328)

727'.1'0942961 — Primary schools. Buildings. Design. *Wales. Rural regions. Study examples: Ysgol y Dderi. Reports, surveys*

Great Britain. *Welsh Education Office.* Ysgol y Dderi : an area school in Dyfed / Welsh Education Office. — Cardiff [etc.] (31 Cathedral Rd, Cardiff) : Welsh Education Office, 1976. — [1],69p : ill(some col), 2 maps(1 col), plans(some col) ; 30cm. — (Design study ; 2)
Pbk : Unpriced
(B77-16998)

727'.2 — Secondary schools. Music rooms. Architectural features. *England. Reports, surveys*

Music Accommodation Panel. Spaces for music / [prepared by the Music Accommodation Panel of the Music Advisers' National Association]. — Wembley (c/o Music Adviser, Brent Education Department, P.O. Box 1, 9 Park La., Wembley, Middx HA9 7RW) : The Association, [1977]. — [2],55p : plans ; 18x24cm.
Sd : £0.75
(B77-20459)

727'.3'0942574 — Universities. Buildings. Architectural features. *Oxfordshire. Oxford, 1957-1974*

Reed, David. New architecture in Oxford / [by] David Reed, Philip Opher ; foreword by Lord Bullock of Leafield. — Oxford (Oxford Polytechnic, Headington, Oxford [OX3 0BP]) : Urban Design, 1977. — [84]p : chiefly ill, map(on inside back cover), plans ; 20cm.
Pbk : Unpriced
(B77-32755)

727'.8 — Libraries. Buildings. Planning & architectural design

Thompson, Godfrey. Planning and design of library buildings / [by] Godfrey Thompson. — 2nd ed. — London : Architectural Press [etc.], 1977. — 189p : ill, plans ; 31cm.
Previous ed.: 1973. — Bibl.: p.180-185. — Index.
ISBN 0-85139-534-1 : £12.50
(B77-32037)

727'.8'0941 — Libraries. Buildings. Architectural design. *Great Britain. Serials*

New library buildings : architect-librarian assessments / [compiled by the Architect-Librarian Working Party]. — London : Library Association.
1976 issue : years 1973-1974 / edited by Herbert Ward. — 1976. — [10],269p : ill, col map, plans ; 30cm.
ISBN 0-85365-089-6 Pbk : £13.50(£10.80 to members of the Library Association)
ISSN 0307-9767
(B77-03676)

727.8'09429'61 — Universities. Colleges. Libraries. *Dyfed. Aberystwyth. Hugh Owen Library. Architectural features*

Percy Thomas Partnership. The Hugh Owen Library / [prepared by Percy Thomas Partnership, Swansea, and the staff of the College Library]. — Aberystwyth : University College of Wales, 1977. — [2],12[i.e.13]p : ill, plans ; 15x21cm.
ISBN 0-904222-04-7 Sd : Unpriced
(B77-28762)

728 — ARCHITECTURE. RESIDENCES

728'.0941 — Residences. Architectural features. *Great Britain. Serials*

Planahome. The Planahome book of house plans. — Salisbury (42 Chipper La., Salisbury, Wilts. SP1 1BP) : Planahome (House Designers) Ltd.
[1977] : 21st ed. — [1977]. — 271p : ill, maps(some col), plans ; 28cm.
Index.
ISBN 0-901820-06-7 Pbk : £4.50
(B77-09150)

728'.09426'4 — Residences. Architectural features. *Suffolk, ca 1375-1969*

Sandon, Eric. Suffolk houses : a study of domestic architecture / by Eric Sandon, with contributions by Stanley West & Elizabeth Owles ; drawings by John Western ; photographs by Helen Sandon, Liza Whipp & Baron Publishing. — Woodbridge (Church St., Woodbridge, Suffolk) : Baron Publishing, 1977. — 2-344p : ill(some col), coats of arms, facsims, maps, plans ; 31cm.
Ill. on lining papers. — Bibl.: p.341-344.
ISBN 0-902028-68-5 : £15.00
(B77-25773)

728'.097 — Residences constructed by amateurs. Architectural features. *North America. Illustrations*

Wampler, Jan. All their own : people and the places they build / by Jan Wampler. — Cambridge, Mass. : Schenkman ; New York ; London [etc.] : Wiley, 1977. — 203,[4]p : chiefly ill(some col), plans, ports(some col) ; 25cm.
Bibl.: p.[2].
ISBN 0-470-15152-8 : £11.80
(B77-13762)

728.3 — Converted structures: Houses. *Western world. Illustrations*
Fracchia, Charles A. Converted into houses / [text by] Charles A. Fracchia ; photographs by Jeremiah O. Bragstad. — London : Thames and Hudson, 1977. — 95p : chiefly col ill ; 25cm.
Originally published: New York : Viking Press, 1976.
ISBN 0-500-34069-2 : £7.50
(B77-09151)

728.3 — Houses. Architectural design. *Great Britain, 1919-1939*
Gould, Jeremy. Modern houses in Britain, 1919-1939 / by Jeremy Gould. — [London] ([c/o John Newman, Courtauld Institute of Art, 20 Portman Sq., W1H 0BE]) : Society of Architectural Historians of Great Britain, 1977. — 65,[23]p,[24]p of plates : ill, plans ; 24cm. — (Architectural history monographs ; no.1)
Index.
Pbk : £10.00
(B77-25774)

728.3 — Houses. Architectural design. *Great Britain. Serials*
House and bungalow plans. — London : Associated Newspapers Group. — (A 'Daily mail' publication)
[1976-77]. — [1976]. — 192p : ill(some col), plans ; 28cm.
Pbk : £0.90
(B77-09152)

728.3 — Houses. Architectural design. Plans. Making. *United States. Amateurs' manuals*
Curran, June. Drawing plans for your own home / [by] June Curran ; designs and illustrations by the author. — New York [etc.] ; London : McGraw-Hill, [1977]. — ix,180p : ill, plans ; 29cm.
Six plastic stencils in envelope attached to inside front cover. — Published in the United States: 1976. — Index.
ISBN 0-07-014925-9 : £20.70
ISBN 0-07-014922-4 Pbk : £14.95
(B77-13148)

728.3 — Houses. Exteriors. Architectural design. *Kent. Manuals*
Housing design guide / Kent Planning Officers. — [Maidstone] ([County Hall, Maidstone, Kent ME14 1XD]) : [Kent County Planning Department], 1976. — [1],59p : ill(some col), map, plans(some col) ; 30cm.
Bibl.: p.57. — Index.
ISBN 0-900947-99-3 Sd : £2.00
(B77-11324)

728.3 — Local authority houses & flats. Architectural features. *London, 1888-1975*
Greater London Council. *Department of Architecture and Civic Design.* Home sweet home : housing designed by the London County Council and Greater London Council architects, 1888-1975 / foreword by Kenneth Campbell ; [compiled by Judith Lever for the Information Office of the GLC's Department of Architecture and Civic Design]. — London : Academy Editions [for] the Greater London Council, 1976. — 111p : ill, map, plans ; 30cm. — (London architectural monographs)
'... based on the GLC's "Home Sweet Home" exhibition, held at the ICA Gallery at Nash House in 1973' - title page verso.
ISBN 0-85670-276-5 : £6.95
ISBN 0-85670-271-4 Pbk : £3.95
(B77-19523)

728.3 — Local authority houses. Architectural design. *England. Reports, surveys*
Great Britain. *Department of the Environment. Housing Development Directorate.* A survey of standards of design and specification in new local authority housing / Department of the Environment, Housing Development Directorate. — London (Room 1107, 1 Lambeth Palace Rd, SE1 7ER) : [The Directorate], 1976. — [2],33p : ill ; 30cm. — (Great Britain. Department of the Environment. Housing Development Directorate. Occasional paper ; 3/76)
ISBN 0-7184-0080-1 Sd : Unpriced
(B77-13150)

728.3 — Local authority housing. Design & construction. Organisations. *England. Directories*
Great Britain. *Department of the Environment. Housing Development Directorate.* Housing groups and consortia / Department of the Environment, Housing Development Directorate. — London (1 Lambeth Palace Rd, SE1 7ER) : The Directorate, 1977. — [1],46p ; 21x30cm.
Sp : Unpriced
(B77-20460)

728.3 — Residences for physically handicapped persons. *England. Reports, surveys*
Morton, Janis. Wheelchair housing : a survey of purpose-designed dwellings for disabled people / [by Janis Morton] ; [for the] Housing Development Directorate, Department of the Environment. — [London] ([2 Marsham St., SW1P 3EB]) : [The Directorate], [1977]. — [3], 44,39,[1]p : form ; 30cm.
Sp : Unpriced
(B77-21308)

728.3'1 — Flats. Architectural design. *Great Britain, to 1976*
Banham, Reyner. Mechanical services / prepared by Reyner Banham ; for the [Open University] Course Team. The modern flat / prepared by Stephen Bayley ; for the [Open University] Course Team. — Milton Keynes : Open University Press, 1975. — 80p,[32]p of plates : ill, plans, port ; 30cm. — (Arts, a third level course : history of architecture and design, 1890-1939 ; units 21-22) (A305 ; 21-22)
With answers. — Filmstrip (12 frames of col. ill.) in cellophane pocket. — Bibl.: p.4-5.
ISBN 0-335-00710-4 Pbk : £2.75
Primary classification 729
(B77-33941)

728.3'1 — Flats. Architectural design. *New York (City), 1869-1974*
Alpern, Andrew. Apartments for the affluent : a historical survey of buildings in New York / [by] Andrew Alpern ; with a foreword by Harmon H. Gladstone. — New York ; London [etc.] : McGraw-Hill, 1975. — x,66p : ill, plans ; 29cm.
Index.
ISBN 0-07-001372-1 : £14.75
(B77-02468)

728.3'1 — Town houses & flats. Architectural design. *United States*
Apartments, townhouses and condominiums / edited by Elisabeth Kendall Thompson. — [2nd ed.]. — New York ; London [etc.] : McGraw-Hill, [1976]. — viii,216p : ill, plans ; 31cm.
'An "Architectural record" book'. — This ed. published in the United States: 1975. — Previous ed.: published as 'Apartments and dormitories'. New York : F.W. Dodge, 1958. — Index.
ISBN 0-07-002321-2 : £16.55
(B77-04329)

728.3'1'09046 — Multiple family housing. Architectural design, 1961-1973. *German-English parallel texts*
Mackay, David, *b.1933.* Multiple family housing : from aggregation to integration / [by] David Mackay. — London : Thames and Hudson, 1977. — 160p : ill, maps, plans ; 27cm.
English and German text. — Also published: as 'Wohnungsbau vonder Addition zur Integration'. Stuttgart : Verlag Gerd Hatje, 1977. — Index.
ISBN 0-500-34071-4 : £15.00
(B77-27252)

728.6'4 — Bungalows. Architectural design. Plans
Architectural Services Planning Partnership. Architectural Services bungalow plans. — [Redhill] ([45 Station Rd, Redhill, Surrey]) : [The Partnership].
1976. — [1976]. — 202p : chiefly ill(some col), plans, ports ; 28cm.
Cover title. — Spine title: The Architectural Service book of bungalow plans. — Previously published as: 'Architectural Services book of bungalow plans'.
ISBN 0-903176-10-6 Pbk : £2.00
(B77-00861)

728.6'4 — Bungalows. Architectural features. *India (Republic). Bangalore, 1800-1920*
Pott, Janet. Old bungalows in Bangalore, South India / [by] Janet Pott ; in collaboration with Elizabeth Staley & Romola Chatterjee ; measured drawings by John Sambrook. — London (56 Addison Ave, W.11) : The author, 1977. — 72p : ill, map, plans ; 25cm.
ISBN 0-9505548-0-4 Pbk : £3.00
(B77-12579)

728.6'4 — Cottages. *Norfolk. Wiggenhall St Germans. Bank Cottage. Conversion. Personal observations*
Trewin, Ion. Norfolk cottage / [by] Ion Trewin. — London : Joseph, 1977. — 143p : ill, facsim, plan, ports ; 23cm.
ISBN 0-7181-1595-3 : £4.95
(B77-25775)

728.6'4 — Cottages. Architectural features. *Great Britain*
Reid, Richard. The Shell book of cottages / by Richard Reid. — London : Joseph, 1977. — 256p : ill, maps ; 22cm.
Bibl.: p.248-249. — Index.
ISBN 0-7181-1630-5 : £5.95
(B77-32038)

728.8'1'094121 — Castles. Architectural features. *Scotland. Grampian Region*
Scott, Schomberg. The castles of Mar / by Schomberg Scott. — Edinburgh : National Trust for Scotland, 1977. — [1],34p,[16]p of plates : ill(some col), map ; 21cm.
Sd : Unpriced
(B77-27976)

728.8'2'0945 — Architecture. Italy, 1400-1600. Expounded by Pythagorean geometry. *Study examples: Palaces*
Hersey, George Leonard. Pythagorean palaces : magic and architecture in the Italian Renaissance / [by] G.L. Hersey. — Ithaca ; London : Cornell University Press, 1976. — 218p : ill, facsims, ports, plans ; 26cm.
Bibl.: p.199-212. — Index.
ISBN 0-8014-0998-5 : £18.05
(B77-14323)

728.8'2'094528 — Palaces. *Italy. Mantua. Isola del Te. Palazzo del Te. Architectural features*
Verheyen, Egon. The Palazzo del Te in Mantua : images of love and politics / [by] Egon Verheyen ; with plans by Diane Finiello Zervas. — Baltimore ; London : Johns Hopkins University Press, 1977. — xvii,156,[1]p : ill, plans ; 29cm.
Bibl.: p.146-152. — Index. — Includes a catalogue raisonné of the decoration of the palace.
ISBN 0-8018-1809-5 : £20.00
(B77-30458)

728.8'3'09415 — Country houses. Architectural features. *Ireland, ca 1600-ca 1830. Illustrations*
Craig, Maurice James. Classic Irish houses of the middle size / by Maurice Craig. — London : Architectural Press [etc.], 1976. — vi,170p : ill, plans ; 31cm.
Bibl.: p.167. — Index.
ISBN 0-85139-114-1 : £11.95
(B77-03677)

728'.9 — Agricultural industries. Farms. Buildings. Architectural features. *Great Britain. Juvenile literature*
Allen, Eleanor. Farms / [by] Eleanor Allen. — London : A. and C. Black, 1977. — 32p : ill, map ; 26cm. — (Buildings as history)
Bibl.: p.2. — Index.
ISBN 0-7136-1757-8 : £1.75
(B77-31332)

728'.9 — Agricultural industries. Farms. Buildings. Design. *Scotland. Periodicals*
Farm buildings topics. — Edinburgh (6 South Oswald Rd, Edinburgh EH9 2HH) : East of Scotland College of Agriculture, Farm Buildings Advisory and Development Department.
No.1-. — [197-?]-. — ill, plans ; 30cm.
Published at irregular intervals. — 2 leaves as 2nd issue.
Sd : Unpriced
ISSN 0140-4423
(B77-30459)

729 — ARCHITECTURAL DETAIL AND DECORATION

729 — Buildings. Integration of engineering services. Architectural design aspects
Banham, Reyner. Mechanical services / prepared by Reyner Banham ; for the [Open University] Course Team. The modern flat / prepared by Stephen Bayley ; for the [Open University] Course Team. — Milton Keynes : Open University Press, 1975. — 80p,[32]p of plates : ill, plans, port ; 30cm. — (Arts, a third level course : history of architecture and design, 1890-1939 ; units 21-22) (A305 ; 21-22)
With answers. — Filmstrip (12 frames of col. ill.) in cellophane pocket. — Bibl.: p.4-5.
ISBN 0-335-00710-4 Pbk : £2.75
Also classified at 728.3'1
(B77-33941)

729'.0973 — Buildings. Interiors. Architectural features. *United States*
Interior spaces designed by architects / edited by Barclay F. Gordon. — New York ; London [etc.] : McGraw-Hill, [1976]. — x,230p : chiefly ill(some col), plans ; 31cm. — (An 'Architectural record' book)
Published in the United States: 1974. — '... photographs, drawing, specifications and descriptions as shown in "Architectural Record"' - jacket. — Index.
ISBN 0-07-002220-8 : £20.00
(B77-03678)

729'.25 — Buildings. Access by physically handicapped persons. *East Sussex. Hove. Technical data. For architectural design*
Hove *(District). Planning Department.* Access for the disabled : guidance notes for applicants / [Borough of Hove, Planning Department] ; [prepared by Rosalind Brown, Tim Cording]. — Hove (Town Hall Annexe, Third Ave., Hove, Sussex BN3 2PU) : Borough of Hove Planning Department, 1977. — [3],14p : ill, plans ; 30cm.
Sd : £0.25
(B77-30460)

729'.28 — Buildings. Interiors. Lighting. *Great Britain. Standards*
Illuminating Engineering Society. The IES code, interior lighting / the Illuminating Engineering Society. — [New ed.]. — London : The Society, 1977. — 128p : ill(some col) ; 30cm.
Previous ed.: 1973. — Bibl.: p.124-127. — Index.
ISBN 0-900957-24-7 Pbk : £5.50
(B77-15391)

729'.28 — Buildings. Lighting. Design
Lam, William M C. Perception and lighting as formgivers for architecture / [by] William M.C. Lam ; edited by Christopher Hugh Ripman. — New York ; London [etc.] : McGraw-Hill, 1977. — x,310p : chiefly ill(some col), plans ; 29cm.
Ill. on lining papers. — Bibl.: p.302-307. — Index.
ISBN 0-07-036094-4 : £24.40
(B77-21309)

729'.29 — Buildings. Interiors. Acoustics
Sound Research Laboratories. Practical building acoustics / Sound Research Laboratories Limited. — Sudbury : S.R.L. ; London : Distributed by Spon, 1976. — [5],226,[32]p : ill, form, plans ; 30cm.
Bibl. (4p.).
Pbk : £5.50
(B77-13763)

729'.7'09495 — Byzantine mosaics, to ca 1400
Demus, Otto. Byzantine mosaic decoration : aspects of monumental art in Byzantium / [by] Otto Demus. — London [etc.] : Routledge and Kegan Paul, 1976. — xiii,99,64p of plates : ill, plans ; 25cm.
Originally published: London : Kegan Paul, Trench, Trubner and Co., 1947. — Index.
ISBN 0-7100-1270-5 : £6.95
(B77-00324)

730 — SCULPTURES AND OTHER PLASTIC ARTS

730'.9 — Western sculptures, ca 500-1975. *Illustrations*
Hibbard, Howard. Masterpieces of Western sculpture : from medieval to modern / [by] Howard Hibbard. — London : Thames and Hudson, 1977. — 239p : ill(some col), ports(some col) ; 33cm.
Bibl.: p.239.
ISBN 0-500-23278-4 : £12.50
(B77-32039)

730'.92'2 — Sculptors, 1800-1900. *Biographical dictionaries*
Busse, Joachim. Internationales Handbuch aller Maler und Bildhauer des 19. Jahrhunderts : Busse-Verzeichnis / [von] Joachim Busse [zusammengestellt]. — Wiesbaden : Busse Kunst Dokumentation ; London : [Distributed by] Prior, 1977. — 72,[1],1403p,[70]p of plates,[5] leaves of plates : ill(chiefly col) ; 31cm.
Half title page verso: International directory of all XIXth century painters and sculptors ... — Spine title: Maler und Bildhauer des 19. Jahrhunderts. — Thumb indexed. — German, English, French, Italian and Spanish text.
£120.00
ISBN 3-9800062-0-4
Primary classification 759
(B77-23605)

730'.92'4 — Art galleries. *London. Kensington and Chelsea (London Borough). Taranman Limited. Exhibits: English sculptures. Brown, Ralph, b.1928. Catalogues*
Taranman Limited. Ralph Brown : a new sculpture & recent drawings : [catalogue of an exhibition held at] Taranman ... 14 October-15 November 1976. — [London] ([236 Brompton Rd, S.W.3]) : [Taranman Ltd], [1976]. — [19] p : ill ; 25cm.
Limited ed. of 300 copies. — Bibl.: p.[19].
Sd : £1.75
Primary classification 741.9'42
(B77-33944)

730'.92'4 — Art galleries. *London. Kensington & Chelsea (London Borough). Taranman Limited. Exhibits: English sculptures. Kneale, Bryan. Catalogues*
Taranman Limited. Bryan Kneale : small sculpture and maquettes : [catalogue of an exhibition held at] Taranman ... 1 June-12 July 1977. — [London] ([236 Brompton Rd, S.W.3]) : [Taranman Ltd], [1977]. — [23]p : ill ; 25cm.
Limited ed. of 300 copies.
Pbk : £2.00
(B77-33942)

730'.92'4 — Art galleries. *London. Westminster (London Borough). Serpentine Gallery. Exhibits: American sculptures. Lijn, Liliane. Catalogues*
Lijn, Liliane. Beyond light / [by] Liliane Lijn, Bill Culbert. — [London] : Arts Council of Great Britain, [1976]. — 1v. : chiefly ill(some col) ; 27cm.
'[Catalogue of an exhibition held at the] Serpentine Gallery, Kensington Gardens, London, 18 December 1976-16 January 1977, DLI Museum & Arts Centre, Durham, 2-20 February 1977' - note. — 'Liliane Lijn' ([16]p. : sd), 'Bill Culbert' ([16]p. : sd) in folder.
ISBN 0-7287-0118-9 : £1.50
Also classified at 730'.92'4
(B77-13764)

730'.92'4 — Art galleries. *London. Westminster (London Borough). Serpentine Gallery. Exhibits: English sculptures. Kenny, Michael, b.1941. Catalogues*
Kenny, Michael, *b.1941.* Michael Kenny, sculpture & drawings : [catalogue of an exhibition held at the] Serpentine Gallery, Kensington Gardens, W.2, 12 March-11 April 1977. — [London] : Arts Council of Great Britain, [1977]. — [1],16,[1]p : chiefly ill, port ; 30cm.
ISBN 0-7287-0129-4 Sd : £1.20
(B77-13765)

730'.92'4 — Art galleries. *London. Westminster (London Borough). Serpentine Gallery. Exhibits: New Zealand sculptures. Culbert, Bill. Catalogues*
Lijn, Liliane. Beyond light / [by] Liliane Lijn, Bill Culbert. — [London] : Arts Council of Great Britain, [1976]. — 1v. : chiefly ill(some col) ; 27cm.
'[Catalogue of an exhibition held at the] Serpentine Gallery, Kensington Gardens, London, 18 December 1976-16 January 1977, DLI Museum & Arts Centre, Durham, 2-20 February 1977' - note. — 'Liliane Lijn' ([16]p. : sd), 'Bill Culbert' ([16]p. : sd) in folder.
ISBN 0-7287-0118-9 : £1.50
Primary classification 730'.92'4
(B77-13764)

730'.92'4 — Art galleries. *London. Westminster (London Borough). Tate Gallery. Exhibits: American sculptures. Gabo, Naum. Catalogues*
Newman, Teresa. Naum Gabo, the constructive process / [by] Teresa Newman. — London : Tate Gallery Publications, 1976. — 63p : ill, ports ; 16cm.
Catalogue of an exhibition held at the Tate Gallery 13 November-12 December 1976. — Bibl.: p.63.
ISBN 0-905005-65-1 Pbk : £1.25
(B77-02469)

730'.92'4 — British culture. Dissemination. Organisations: British Council. Exhibits: English welded sculptures. Caro, Anthony. *Catalogues*
Caro, Anthony. Anthony Caro, table sculptures 1966-1977 : [catalogue of] a British Council exhibition. — London : British Council, [1977]. — [28]p : ill(some col), port ; 22x24cm.
Bibl.: p.[47].
ISBN 0-900229-31-4 Pbk : £1.75
(B77-13766)

730'.92'4 — English sculptures. Jonzen, Karin. *Illustrations*
Jonzen, Karin. Karin Jonzen, sculptor / foreword by Norman St John-Stevas ; introduction by Carel Weight. — London : Bachman and Turner, 1976. — 80p : chiefly ill, ports ; 26cm.
ISBN 0-85974-055-2 : £4.50
(B77-03679)

730'.92'4 — English sculptures. Milne, John, b.1931. *Critical studies*
Milne, John, *b.1931.* John Milne : sculptor / life and work by J.P. Hodin. — London : Latimer New Dimensions, 1977. — viii,96p : chiefly ill(some col), ports ; 25cm.
Col. ill. on lining papers. — Bibl.: p.96.
ISBN 0-901539-63-5 : £8.50
(B77-23592)

730'.92'4 — English sculptures. Moore, Henry, b.1898. *Illustrations*
Finn, David. Henry Moore / [photographs and text by David Finn ; foreword by Kenneth Clark ; commentaries by Henry Moore]. — London : Thames and Hudson, 1977. — 492p : chiefly ill(some col), ports ; 31cm.
Col. ill. on lining papers. — Col. ill. tipped in. — Originally published: as 'A Henry Moore odyssey'. New York : Abrams, 1976. — Index.
ISBN 0-500-23268-7 : £30.00
(B77-25776)

Moore, Henry, *b.1898.* Henry Moore : sculpture and drawings. — London : Lund Humphries : Zwemmer.
Vol.4 : Sculpture, 1964-73 / edited by Alan Bowness. — 1977. — 198p : chiefly ill ; 30cm.
Bibl.: p.26-30.
ISBN 0-85331-392-x : £12.00
(B77-23593)

730'.92'4 — English sculptures. Skeaping, John. *Autobiographies*
Skeaping, John. Drawn from life : an autobiography / [by] John Skeaping. — London : Collins, 1977. — 253p,[12]p of plates : ill, ports ; 23cm.
Index.
ISBN 0-00-216028-5 : £5.00
(B77-03148)

730'.92'4 — English sculptures. Tucker, William. *Illustrations*
Lynton, Norbert. William Tucker, sculptures / [text by Norbert Lynton]. — [London] : Arts Council of Great Britain, 1977. — [27]p : ill ; 20x21cm.
Catalogue of an Arts Council touring exhibition.
ISBN 0-7287-0133-2 Sd : £0.80
(B77-30461)

730'.92'4 — French sculptures. Degas, Edgar. *Critical studies*
Millard, Charles W. The sculpture of Edgar Degas / [by] Charles W. Millard. — Princeton ; Guildford : Princeton University Press, 1976. — xxiv,141p,leaf of plate,[80]p of plates : ill(incl 1 col) ; 27cm.
Bibl.: p.127-134. — Index.
ISBN 0-691-03898-8 : £15.80
(B77-15392)

730'.92'4 — Italian sculptures. Bernini, Giovanni Lorenzo. *Critical studies*
Hibbard, Howard. Bernini / [by] Howard Hibbard. — Harmondsworth [etc.] : Penguin, 1976. — 255p : ill, plans, ports ; 20cm. — (A pelican original)
Originally published: 1965. — Bibl.: p.231-232. — Index.
Pbk : £2.25
ISBN 0-14-020701-5
(B77-18290)

730'.92'4 — Italian sculptures. Rossellino, Bernardo. *Critical studies*
Schulz, Anne Markham. The sculpture of Bernardo Rossellino and his workshop / [by] Anne Markham Schulz. — Princeton ; Guildford : Princeton University Press, 1977. — xxiii,176p,[96]p of plates : ill ; 29cm.
Bibl.: p.133-166. — Index.
ISBN 0-691-03886-4 : £24.20
(B77-16511)

730'.94 — European sculptures, ca B.C.650-A.D.1970. *Lectures, speeches*
Wittkower, Rudolf. Sculpture : processes and principles / [by] Rudolf Wittkower. — London : Allen Lane, 1977. — 288p : ill ; 25cm.
Bibl.: p.277-280. — Index.
ISBN 0-7139-0878-5 : £8.50
(B77-22018)

730'.942 — Museums. *Lancashire. Burnley. Towneley Hall Art Gallery and Museums. Exhibits: English sculptures, 1900-1970. Catalogues*

Towneley Hall Art Gallery and Museums. 20th century British sculpture : from Northern public collections : [a catalogue of an exhibition held] April 10th-September 26th, 1976 [at] Towneley Hall Art Gallery & Museums. — Burnley ([Towneley Hall, Burnley, Lancs. BB11 3RQ]) : [The Gallery], [1976]. — [9]leaves ; 31cm.
Sheet ([2]p.) as insert.
Sd : £0.10
(B77-07506)

730'.944 — French sculptures, 1643-1715. *Critical studies*

Souchal, François. French sculptors of the 17th and 18th centuries : the reign of Louis XIV : illustrated catalogue / [by] François Souchal, with the collaboration of Françoise de la Moureyre, Henriette Dumuis ; [translated from the French by Elsie and George Hill]. — Oxford : Cassirer ; London : Distributed by Faber.
[Vol.1] : A-F. — 1977. — xvi,375p : ill, geneal tables(on lining papers), ports ; 30cm.
Bibl.: p.362-363. — Index.
ISBN 0-85181-062-4 : £50.00
(B77-30462)

730'.945'632 — Sculptures. *Italy. Rome, ca 1700-1750*

Enggass, Robert. Early eighteenth-century sculpture in Rome : an illustrated catalogue raisonné / [by] Robert Enggass. — University Park ; London : Pennsylvania State University Press, 1976. — 2v.(xv,243p,[162]p of plates) : ill, ports ; 30cm.
Bibl. — Index.
ISBN 0-271-01200-5 : £45.00
(B77-23594)

731 — SCULPTURES. MATERIALS, EQUIPMENT, TECHNIQUES, FORMS

731.4 — Clay sculptures & wax sculptures. Techniques. *Manuals*

DiValentin, Maria. Sculpture for beginners with clay & wax / by Maria and Louis DiValentin. — Combined ed. — New York : Sterling [etc.] ; London : Distributed by Ward Lock, 1976 [i.e. 1977]. — 208p,A-Hp of plates : ill(some col) ; 21cm. — (Arts & crafts books)
This ed. published in the United States: 1976. — Previous ed.: published in 2 vols as 'Sculpture for beginners', 1969 ; and as 'Sculpturing with wax', 1973. — Index.
£3.95
ISBN 0-7061-2016-7
(B77-13151)

731.4 — Sculptures. Techniques. *Manuals*

Stone, Anne. Sculpture : new ideas and techniques / [by] Anne Stone. — London : Bell, 1976. — 80p : chiefly ill ; 26cm.
Bibl.: p.79.
ISBN 0-7135-1943-6 : Unpriced
(B77-20461)

731.4'2 — Modelling in sand. *Manuals. Juvenile literature*

Reed, Bob. Sand creatures and castles : how to build them / [by] Bob and Pat Reed. — London : Hamilton, 1977. — 64p : ill, plans ; 24cm.
Originally published: New York : Holt, Rinehart and Winston, 1976.
ISBN 0-241-89618-5 : £2.75
(B77-24375)

731.4'2 — Modelling in self-hardening clay. *Manuals*

Tong, Gary. Modelling with self-hardening clay / [by] Gary Tong. — London : Pelham, 1977. — 96p : ill ; 26cm. — ([Pelham craft series])
Originally published: New York : Larousse, 1976.
ISBN 0-7207-0946-6 : £4.95
(B77-10475)

731.4'7 — Modelling in baker's clay. *Manuals*

Williamson, Ethie. Baker's clay : cutouts, sculptures, and projects with flour, salt, and water / [by] Ethie Williamson. — New York ; London [etc.] : Van Nostrand Reinhold, 1976 [i.e. 1977]. — 96p,[8]p of plates : ill(some col) ; 28cm.
Published in the United States: 1976. — Index.
ISBN 0-442-29487-5 : £8.20
ISBN 0-442-29486-7 Pbk : £5.20
(B77-09845)

731.4'7 — Pottery sculptures. Techniques

Bitters, Stan. Environmental ceramics / [by] Stan Bitters ; Micha Langer, photographer. — New York [etc.] ; London : Van Nostrand Reinhold, [1977]. — 144p : ill(some col) ; 29cm.
Published in the United States: 1976. — Bibl.: p.141. — Index.
ISBN 0-442-20781-6 : £12.35
(B77-11991)

731'.549'094111 — Stone monumental sculptures. *Scotland. Highlands & Islands, ca 1300-ca 1600*

Steer, K A. Late medieval monumental sculpture in the west Highlands / by K.A. Steer and J.W.M. Bannerman, with a contribution by G.H. Collins. — [Edinburgh] : Royal Commission on the Ancient and Historical Monuments of Scotland : [Distributed by H.M.S.O.], 1977. — xxvi,230p,[2]leaves of plates,43p of plates : ill, maps(1 col), ports ; 29cm.
Bibl.: p.xxi-xxvi. — Index.
ISBN 0-11-491383-8 : £14.50
(B77-15974)

731'.75 — Masks. *Cut-out books*

Make and know masks / [main drawings by Anthony Colbert]. — [London] ([Wheatsheaf House, Carmelite St., E.C.4]) : GeminiScan Ltd, 1974. — [2],24,[1]p : ill(chiefly col), col map ; 33cm.
Six leaves, with versos blank, are perforated for making press-out models.
ISBN 0-85691-007-4 Sd : Unpriced
(B77-20462)

731'.76 — Churchyards. Gravestones. *Scotland. Tayside Region. Angus (District), 1600-1707*

Davidson, Flora. An inventory of the seventeenth century tombstones of Angus / by Flora Davidson assisted by John Davidson. — Arbroath ([17 Inchcape Rd, Arbroath, Angus]) : [The authors], 1977. — [4],xxvii[i.e. xxviii],92[i.e.93]leaves,[25]leaves of plates : ill, coats of arms, maps ; 32cm.
In binder. — Bibl.: p.xxvi.
Ls : £15.00
(B77-30463)

731'.76'0942 — Churches. Monuments. *England, 1780-1840*

Penny, Nicholas. Church monuments in romantic England / [by] Nicholas Penny. — New Haven ; London : Yale University Press for the Paul Mellon Centre for Studies in British Art, 1977. — xi,236p : ill ; 26cm.
Bibl.: p.225-226. — Index.
ISBN 0-300-02075-9 : £10.00
(B77-25085)

731'.76'097471 — New York Harbour. Statue of Liberty, to ca 1970

Trachtenberg, Marvin. The Statue of Liberty / [by] Marvin Trachtenberg. — Harmondsworth [etc.] : Penguin, 1977. — 3-224p : ill, maps, plan, ports ; 23cm.
Originally published: London : Allen Lane, 1976. — Index.
ISBN 0-14-004513-9 Pbk : Unpriced
(B77-28763)

731'.82 — Sculptures. Special subjects: Human figures. Techniques. *Manuals*

Mills, John William. Head and figure modelling / [by] John W. Mills. — London : Batsford, 1977. — 137p : ill, ports ; 26cm.
Ill. on lining papers. — Index.
ISBN 0-7134-3258-6 : £4.95
(B77-25086)

731'.82 — Ships. Figureheads, to ca 1950

Norton, Peter, *b.1913.* Ships' figureheads / [by] Peter Norton. — Newton Abbot [etc.] : David and Charles, 1976. — 144p : ill, ports ; 24cm.
Bibl.: p.136-138. — Index.
ISBN 0-7153-7253-x : £4.95
(B77-00862)

731'.82'0941 — Art galleries. *London. Westminster (London Borough). Mall Galleries. Exhibits: British portrait busts. Society of Portrait Sculptors. Catalogues*

Society of Portrait Sculptors. Twenty third annual exhibition of the Society of Portrait Sculptors : [catalogue of the exhibition] at the Mall Galleries, The Mall, London S.W.1, 3rd to 16th December 1976. — [London] ([17 Carlton House Terrace, SW1Y 5BD]) : [The Society], [1976]. — [27]p : ports ; 21cm.
ISBN 0-901035-03-3 Sd : £0.50
(B77-11992)

731'.82'0942383 — Cathedrals. *Somerset. Wells. Wells Cathedral. West front. Sculptures. Guidebooks*

Colchester, Linzee Sparrow. The west front of Wells Cathedral / [text by L.S. Colchester ; illustrations from photographs by Arthur Gardner]. — 5th ed. revised. — [Wells] ([c/o 22 Vicars' Close, Wells, Somerset BA5 2UJ]) : Friends of Wells Cathedral, 1976. — [2],13p(1 fold),[8]p of plates : ill ; 22cm.
Previous ed.: 1974.
ISBN 0-902321-18-8 Sd : £0.25
(B77-01664)

731'.82'094281 — English alabaster tomb sculptures. Special subjects: Human figures. *Yorkshire, ca 1380-ca 1550*

Routh, Pauline E. Medieval effigial alabaster tombs in Yorkshire / [by] Pauline E. Routh. — Ipswich : Boydell Press, 1976. — 155p : ill ; 23cm.
Bibl.: p.10-11. — Index.
ISBN 0-85115-073-x : £7.50
(B77-09153)

731'.89'794109 — Chessmen, to 1936. *Collectors' guides*

Liddell, Donald M. Chessmen / by Donald M. Liddell with the collaboration of Gustavus A. Pfeiffer and J. Maunoury. — London [etc.] : White Lion Publishers, 1976. — xii,171p,[96]p of plates : ill ; 29cm.
Originally published: New York : Harcourt, Brace, 1937. — Bibl.: p.164-167. — Index.
ISBN 0-7274-0251-x : £8.50
(B77-23595)

732 — PRIMITIVE, ANCIENT, ORIENTAL SCULPTURE

732'.2'09361423 — Prehistoric rock carvings. *Scotland. Strathclyde Region. Argyll and Bute (District)*

Morris, Ronald W B. The prehistoric rock art of Argyll / [by] Ronald W.B. Morris. — Poole : Dolphin Press, 1977. — 128p : ill, maps ; 24cm.
Bibl.: p.125-128.
ISBN 0-85642-043-3 : £3.75
ISBN 0-85642-059-x Pbk : £1.50
(B77-16999)

732'.2'09364 — Palaeolithic rock carvings. *France. Aventignan. Grotte de Gargas. Reports, surveys. French-English parallel texts*

Barrière, Cl. L'art pariétal de la Grotte de Gargas = Palaeolithic art in the Grotte de Gargas / [par] Cl. Barrière ; avec la collaboration du Ali Sahly et des élèves de l'Institut d'art préhistorique de Toulouse ; translated [from the French] by W.A. Drapkin. — Oxford : British Archaeological Reports, 1976. — 2v.([25],409p(18 fold),fold plate) : ill, map, plans ; 30cm. — (British archaeological reports : supplementary series ; 14)
Spine title: Grotte de Gargas. — French text with English translations. — With 5 leaves of overlays. — Bibl.: p.[17]-[20].
ISBN 0-904531-47-3 Pbk : £8.50
(B77-22020)

732'.2'09669 — Universities. Colleges. *Cardiff. University College, Cardiff. Exhibits: Nigerian sculptures. Catalogues*

Cardiff University Art Group. Nigerian traditional sculpture : [catalogue of an exhibition held at] Central Hall, University College, Cardiff, 23 April to 17 May 1974 presented by Cardiff University Art Group. — Cardiff ([Cathays Park, Cardiff]) : University College, Cardiff, 1974. — [48]p : ill ; 26cm.
Bibl.: p.[9].
ISBN 0-901426-12-1 Sd : Unpriced
(B77-18907)

732'.2'09669 — Yoruba sculptures

Thompson, Robert Farris. Black gods and kings : Yoruba art at UCLA / by Robert Farris Thompson. — Bloomington ; London : Indiana University Press, 1976 [i.e. 1977]. — 230p in various pagings,[10]p of plates : ill(some col), maps, plan ; 29cm.
Originally published: Los Angeles : University of California, Museum and Laboratories of Ethnic Arts and Technology, 1971. — Bibl.(3p.).
ISBN 0-253-31204-3 : £14.00
(B77-10874)

732'.4 — Temples. Erotic sculptures. *India, ca 500-ca 1400. Critical studies*

Lannoy, Richard. The eye of love in the temple sculpture of India / [by] Richard Lannoy ; with drawings by Harry Baines. — London [etc.] : Rider, 1976 [i.e. 1977]. — 160p : ill ; 24cm.
Bibl.: p.159-160.
ISBN 0-09-127760-4 : Unpriced
ISBN 0-09-127761-2 Pbk : £2.95
(B77-13152)

732'.5 — Assyrian palaces. *Iraq. Mosul. North Palace of Ashurbanipal, Nineveh. Sculptures. Illustrations*
Barnett, Richard David. Sculptures from the north palace of Ashurbanipal at Nineveh (668-627 BC) / by R.D. Barnett. — London : British Museum Publications Ltd for the Trustees of the British Museum, 1976. — xv, 75p,[166]leaves of plates(6 fold) : ill, facsims, maps, plans(some col), ports ; 52cm.
Bibl.: p.69-70.
ISBN 0-7141-1046-9 : £60.00
(B77-18291)

732'.8 — Museums. *London. Camden (London Borough). Petrie Museum. Exhibits: Ancient Egyptian relief sculptures & stelae. Collections: Petrie Collection. Catalogues*
Petrie Museum. Egyptian stelae, reliefs and paintings from the Petrie Collection / [catalogue by] H.M. Stewart. — Warminster : Aris and Phillips. — ([The modern Egyptology series])
Part 1 : The New Kingdom. — 1976. — x,72p, 53p of plates : ill ; 30cm.
Bibl. — Index.
ISBN 0-85668-026-5 : £10.00
(B77-03149)

732'.8'07402142 — Museums. *London. Camden (London Borough). Petrie Museum. Exhibits: Ancient Egyptian sculptures, to ca B.C.650. Collections: Petrie Collection. Catalogues*
Petrie Museum. Egyptian sculpture : archaic to Saite, from the Petrie Collection / [catalogue by] Anthea Page ; with an introduction and translations by H.S. Smith. — Warminster : Aris and Phillips, 1976. — xviii,[2],124p : ill ; 30cm. — ([The modern Egyptology series])
Bibl. — Index.
ISBN 0-85668-025-7 : £12.00
(B77-03150)

733 — CLASSICAL SCULPTURE
733 — Classical portrait sculptures. *Critical studies*
Hinks, Roger Packman. Greek and Roman portrait sculpture / [by] R.P. Hinks. — [2nd ed.]. — London : British Museum Publications for the Trustees of the British Museum, 1976. — 93p : ports ; 24cm.
Previous ed.: London : British Museum, Department of Greek and Roman Antiquities, 1935.
ISBN 0-7141-1252-6 : £3.75
ISBN 0-7141-1253-4 Pbk : £1.95
(B77-27253)

733'.5 — Ancient Roman portrait reliefs, ca B.C.170-ca A.D.200. *Critical studies*
Bonanno, Anthony. Portraits and other heads on Roman historical relief up to the age of Septimius Severus / [by] Anthony Bonanno. — Oxford : British Archaeological Reports, 1976. — [21],227p,[76]p of plates : ill ; 30cm. — (British archaeological reports : supplementary series ; 6 ISSN 0306-1205)
Bibl.: p.215-227.
ISBN 0-904531-38-4 Pbk : £5.90
(B77-01665)

735 — SCULPTURE. MODERN PERIOD, 1400-
735'.22'094 — European sculptures, 1800-1900
Rheims, Maurice. 19th century sculpture / [by] Maurice Rheims ; translated [from the French] by Robert E. Wolf. — London : Thames and Hudson, 1977. — 430,[3]p : ill(some col), ports(1 col) ; 31cm.
Col. ill. tipped in. — Translation of: 'La sculpture au XIXe siècle'. Paris : Arts et métiers graphiques, 1972. — Bibl.: p.417-418. — Index.
ISBN 0-500-23265-2 : £18.00
(B77-27254)

736 — CARVING AND CARVINGS
736'.2 — Museums. *London. Kensington and Chelsea (London Borough). Victoria and Albert Museum. Exhibits: Gemstone figurines. Fabergé, Peter Carl. Catalogues*
Snowman, Abraham Kenneth. Fabergé / [catalogue compiled and written by Kenneth Snowman]. — [Kingston upon Thames] ([Neville House, Eden St., Kingston upon Thames, Surrey KT1 1BY]) : Debrett's Peerage, 1977. — [16]p : ill, port ; 21cm.
'[Catalogue of an] exhibition at the Victoria and Albert Museum, June-September 1977' - title page verso.
ISBN 0-905209-07-9 Sd : £0.15
(B77-21310)

736'.2028 — Lapidary. *Manuals*
Creative crafts from rocks & gemstones / [edited by Isabel Moore]. — London [etc.] : Marshall Cavendish, 1976. — 73p : ill(chiefly col) ; 30cm. — ([Golden Hands])
Ill. on lining papers. — 'Parts of this material were first published ... in the partwork "Crafts"' - title page verso. — Index.
ISBN 0-85685-175-2 : £1.99
(B77-11993)

736'.223'0937 — Universities. Colleges. *Cambridgeshire. Cambridge. Corpus Christi College, Cambridge. Exhibits: Ancient Roman intaglios, 1-200. Collections: Lewis Collection. Catalogues*
Corpus Christi College, *Cambridge.* The Lewis collection of engraved gemstones in Corpus Christi College, Cambridge / [compiled by] Martin Henig. — Oxford : British Archaeological Reports, 1975. — [6],94p,[58]p of plates, leaf of plate : ill ; 30cm. — (British archaeological reports : supplementary series ; 1)
Catalogue of the collection. — Bibl.: p.10-12.
ISBN 0-904531-33-3 : £2.90
Primary classification 736'.223'0938
(B77-03151)

736'.223'0938 — Universities. Colleges. *Cambridgeshire. Cambridge. Corpus Christi College, Cambridge. Exhibits: Ancient Greek intaglios, 1-200. Collections: Lewis Collection. Catalogues*
Corpus Christi College, *Cambridge.* The Lewis collection of engraved gemstones in Corpus Christi College, Cambridge / [compiled by] Martin Henig. — Oxford : British Archaeological Reports, 1975. — [6],94p,[58]p of plates, leaf of plate : ill ; 30cm. — (British archaeological reports : supplementary series ; 1)
Catalogue of the collection. — Bibl.: p.10-12.
ISBN 0-904531-33-3 : £2.90
Also classified at 736'.223'0937
(B77-03151)

736.4'09669'4 — Igala wood carvings & Igbo wood carvings: Ikenga
Boston, John. Ikenga figures among the north-west Igbo and the Igala / [by] John Boston. — London (14 West Central St., WC1A 1JH) : Ethnographica [etc.], 1977. — [7],120p : ill(some col), maps ; 31cm.
ISBN 0-905788-01-x : Unpriced
(B77-23596)

736'.4'09931 — Maori wood carvings
Phillipps, William John. Maori carving illustrated / by W.J. Phillipps. — 2nd ed. — Wellington [N.Z.] [etc.] ; London : A.H. and A.W. Reed, 1976. — 48p : ill, ports ; 25cm.
This ed. originally published: 1972.
ISBN 0-589-00201-5 Sd : £1.05
(B77-20463)

736'.5 — Castles. *London. Tower Hamlets (London Borough). Tower of London. Inscriptions*
Barter, Sarah. Inscriptions / [text by Sarah Barter]. — [London] : H.M.S.O. for the Department of the Environment, 1976. — [1], 36,[2]p : ill, ports ; 20cm. — (Treasures of the Tower)
ISBN 0-11-670448-9 Sd : £0.45
(B77-09846)

736'.5'0924 — Stone carving. *Cork (County). Cork. Personal observations*
Murphy, Seamus. Stone mad / [by] Seamus Murphy ; with illustrations by William Harrington and initial letters by the author. — [New and revised ed.]. — London [etc.] : Routledge and Kegan Paul, 1977 [i.e.1976]. — x,229p : ill, port ; 22cm.
This ed. originally published: 1966.
ISBN 0-7100-8542-7 Pbk : £2.25
(B77-02470)

736'.6'09 — Shell carvings, to 1974
Ritchie, Carson Irving Alexander. Shell carving : history and techniques / [by] Carson I.A. Ritchie. — South Brunswick ; New York : Barnes ; London : Yoseloff, 1974. — 208p : ill ; 29cm.
Index.
ISBN 0-498-07928-7 : £4.00
(B77-29575)

736'.9 — Cloth sculptures. Techniques. *Manuals*
Franklin, Sheila. Cloth sculpture / [text and models by Sheila Franklin ; photographs by Jeet Jain]. — London : Search Press, 1975. — 32p : ill(some col) ; 17cm. — (Leisure crafts ; 52)
Sd : £0.50
(B77-10476)

736'.94 — Ice & snow sculptures. *Manuals*
Haskins, Jim. Snow sculpture and ice carving / by Jim Haskins. — New York : Macmillan ; London : Collier Macmillan, 1974 [i.e. 1976]. — 91p : ill ; 29cm.
Published in the United States: 1974. — Index.
ISBN 0-02-548880-5 : £4.50
ISBN 0-02-000600-4 Pbk : £3.50
(B77-04966)

736'.98 — Origami. *Manuals*
Harbin, Robert. Origami : the art of paper folding / [by] Robert Harbin. — London : Coronet.
4. — 1977. — vi,186p : chiefly ill ; 18cm.
Bibl.: p.185-186.
ISBN 0-340-21822-3 Pbk : £0.75
(B77-22735)

Have fun with origami / [compiled by] Robert Harbin ; illustrated by Keith Jones. — London : Severn House : [Distributed by Hutchinson], 1977. — 128p : chiefly ill ; 21cm. — (Look-in)
Originally published: London : Independent Television Books Ltd, 1975.
ISBN 0-7278-0225-9 : £2.50
(B77-14324)

736'.98 — Paper. Cutting & folding. *School texts*
Ely Resource and Technology Centre. Green book / [prepared by Mary Cullen ... et al., for the Ely Resource and Technology Centre]. — London [etc.] : Hutchinson for Leapfrogs, 1976. — [1],15 leaves : of ill ; 21x30cm. — (Network : with few words)
ISBN 0-09-127741-8 Sd : £0.35(non-net)
(B77-02471)

Folds / [by Ray Hemmings ... et al.]. — London [etc.] : Hutchinson for Leapfrogs, 1976. — [1], 16,[1]p : of ill ; 21cm. — (Network : action books)
ISBN 0-09-127031-6 Sd : £0.35(non-net)
(B77-02472)

736'.98'028 — Paper sculptures. Techniques. *Manuals*
Fabri, Ralph. Sculpture in paper / by Ralph Fabri. — New York : Watson-Guptill ; London : Pitman, 1976. — 165p : ill(some col) ; 26cm.
Originally published: New York : Watson-Guptill, 1966. — Index.
ISBN 0-273-00978-8 Pbk : £4.95 : CIP rev.
(B77-07981)

737 — NUMISMATICS
737'.03 — Numismatics. *Dictionaries*
Chamberlain, Christopher Churchill. The world of coins : a dictionary of numismatics / [by] C.C. Chamberlain. — 3rd ed. / revised by Arthur Blair. — London : Teach Yourself Books, 1976. — 203p,[8]p of plates : ill ; 18cm. — (Teach yourself books)
Previous ed.: published as 'Numismatics'. London : Teach Yourself Books, 1969?. — Bibl. : p.199-203.
ISBN 0-340-21022-2 Pbk : £1.50
(B77-14842)

737'.2 — Honours: Decorations & orders, to 1974. *Collectors' guides*
Měřička, Václav. The book of orders and decorations / text by Václav Měřička ; [translated from the Czech by Ruth Shepherd and Eliška Říhová] ; photographs by Jindřich Marco ; [edited by Alec A. Purves]. — London [etc.] : Hamlyn, [1976]. — 248p : ill(some col), ports ; 29cm.
Ports on lining papers. — Bibl.: p.239-241.
ISBN 0-600-36731-2 : £4.50
(B77-01666)

737'.2 — Military forces. Decorations. *Collectors' guides*
Arden, Yves. Military medals and decorations : a price guide for collectors / [by] Yves Arden. — Newton Abbot [etc.] : David and Charles, 1976. — 224p,[8]p of plates : ill ; 23cm.
Bibl.: p.220-224.
ISBN 0-7153-7274-2 : £4.95
(B77-02473)

737'.2 — Peace medals presented to Indians of North America. *United States, 1789-1905*
Prucha, Francis Paul. Indian peace medals in American history / [by] Francis Paul Prucha. — Lincoln [Neb.] ; London : University of Nebraska Press, [1976]. — xiv,186p : ill, coat of arms, facsims, ports ; 27cm.
Originally published: Madison : State Historical Society of Wisconsin, 1971. — Bibl.: p.165-172. — Index.
ISBN 0-8032-0890-1 : £12.00
(B77-05550)

737'.3'094279 — Manx tokens, to 1977
Mackay, James. The Pobjoy encyclopaedia of Isle of Man coins and tokens / by James A. Mackay. — Sutton (Mint House, Oldfields Rd, Sutton, Surrey) : Pobjoy Mint Ltd, 1977. — [3], 73p : ill(some col) ; 23cm.
Spine title: Isle of Man coins and tokens. — Bibl.: p.72-73.
£3.50
Primary classification 737.4'9'4279
(B77-20464)

737.4 — Coins. Hoards. *Catalogues*
Coin hoards. — London ([c/o The Department of Coins and Medals, British Museum, WC1B 3DG]) : Royal Numismatic Society.
Vol.1. — 1975. — [4],124p : ill ; 24cm.
Index.
ISBN 0-901405-08-6 : £4.50
(B77-09154)

737.4'021'6 — Coins, to 1975. *Catalogues*
Reinfeld, Fred. Catalogue of the world's most popular coins. — 9th ed. / by Fred Reinfeld and Burton Hobson. — New York : Sterling [etc.] ; London : Distributed by Ward Lock, 1976. — 480p : chiefly ill ; 27cm.
Previous ed.: New York : President Coin Corporation ; London : Oak Tree Press, 1971. — Index.
ISBN 0-7061-2205-4 : £10.00
(B77-12580)

737.4'075 — Coins. Collecting. *Manuals*
Paramount International Coin Ltd. Collecting currency : a guide to numismatics and notaphily / [Paramount International Coin Ltd]. — London (238 Grand Buildings, Trafalgar Sq., WC2N 5EZ) : Paramount International Coin Ltd, 1975. — 23p : ill, facsims, port ; 18x25cm.
Sd : Unpriced
Also classified at 769'.55'075
(B77-31333)

737.4'9'37 — Ancient Roman bronze coins. *Spain. Gerona*
Villaronga, Leandre. The aes coinage of Emporion / [by] Leandre Villaronga ; translated from the Spanish by Elisabeth Weeks. — Oxford : British Archaeological Reports, 1977. — [8],84p,xv leaves of plates : ill ; 30cm. — (British archaeological reports : supplementary series ; 23)
Bibl.: p.[8].
ISBN 0-904531-70-8 Pbk : £2.20
(B77-24376)

737.4'9'37 — Ancient Roman coins
Reece, Richard. Introduction to Roman coins / [by] Richard Reece. — Cirencester ([Park St., Cirencester, Glos.]) : Corinium Museum, [1975]. — [8]p : ill, map ; 16x21cm. — (Corinium Museum. Brief guides)
Sd : £0.15
(B77-17655)

737.4'9'37 — Museums. *London. Camden (London Borough). British Museum. Stock: Ancient Roman coins. Catalogues*
British Museum. Coins of the Roman Empire in the British Museum. — 2nd ed. / prepared by R.A.G. Carson. — London : British Museum Publications Ltd.
Vol.2 : Vespasian to Domitian / [prepared] by Harold Mattingly. — 1976. — cvii,485p,83 leaves of plates : ill ; 25cm.
Half-title: A catalogue of the Roman coins in the British Museum. — Previous ed.: 1930. — Bibl.: p.xcviii-ci. — Index.
ISBN 0-7141-0832-4 : £25.00
(B77-00863)

British Museum. Coins of the Roman Empire in the British Museum. — London : British Museum Publications Ltd.
Vol.6 : Severus Alexander to Balbinus and Pupienus / [prepared] by R.A.G. Carson. — 1976. — ix,313p,47 leaves of plates : ill ; 25cm.
Half-title: A catalogue of the Roman coins in the British Museum. — Originally published: 1962. — Bibl.: p.105-108. — Index.
ISBN 0-7141-0809-x : £25.00
(B77-27255)

737.4'9'37 — Museums. *Scotland. Strathclyde Region. Glasgow. Hunterian Museum, University of Glasgow. Stock: Ancient Roman coins. Collections: Hunter Coin Cabinet. Catalogues*
Hunter Coin Cabinet. Roman imperial coins in the Hunter Coin Cabinet, University of Glasgow / by Anne S. Robertson. — London [etc.] : Oxford University Press.
3 : Pertinax to Aemilian. — 1977. — cxiv,327p, 88 leaves of plates : ill ; 26cm.
Bibl.: p.xxvii-xxxvi. — Index.
ISBN 0-19-713306-1 : £33.00
(B77-25087)

737.4'9'38 — Ancient Greek coins, to ca 500
Kraay, Colin Mackennal. Archaic and classical Greek coins / [by] Colin M. Kraay. — London : Methuen, 1976. — xxvi,390p,64p of plates : ill, maps ; 26cm.
Bibl.: p.335-344. — Index.
ISBN 0-416-12310-4 : £30.00
(B77-01667)

737.4'9'38 — Human settlements. *Turkey. Geyre. Aphrodisias. Ancient Greek & Ancient Roman coins, to 305. Lists*
MacDonald, David J. Greek and Roman coins from Aphrodisias / [by] David J. MacDonald. — Oxford : British Archaeological Reports, 1976. — [10],50p,iii leaves of plates : ill, map ; 30cm. — (British archaeological reports : supplementary series ; 9)
Spine title: Coins from Aphrodisias. — Bibl.: p.[9]-[10].
ISBN 0-904531-41-4 Sd : £1.25
(B77-02474)

737.4'9'396 — Ancient Central Asian coins, B.C.330-A.D.226
Mitchener, Michael. Indo-Greek and Indo-Scythian coinage / by Michael Mitchener. — Sanderstead : Hawkins Publications ; London : Distributed by Seaby.
In 9 vols.
Vol.5 : Establishment of the Scythians in Afghanistan and Pakistan : the Parthians, the dynasties of Otannes and Vonones, the conquests of Maues, circa 130 to 40 BC. — 1976. — [2],xxi p,p391-480 : ill, maps ; 31cm.
Bibl.: p.vii-xv.
ISBN 0-904173-10-0 Pbk : Unpriced
(B77-26424)

Mitchiner, Michael. Indo-Greek and Indo-Scythian coinage / by Michael Mitchiner. — Sanderstead : Hawkins Publications ; London : Distributed by Seaby.
In 9 vols.
Vol.6 : The dynasty of Azes : circa 60 to 1 BC. — 1976. — [2]p,p481-579,xvii p : ill, maps ; 31cm.
Bibl.: p.vii-xv.
ISBN 0-904173-11-9 Pbk : £18.00
(B77-21311)

Vol.7 : The decline of the Indo-Scythians : the satraps Zeionises, Kharahostes, Rujuvula etc. Contemporaries of the Indo-Scythians : the Yaudheyas, Arjunayanas, various Janapadas etc. — 1976. — [2]p,p581-673,xix p : ill, maps ; 31cm.
Bibl.: p.vii-xv.
ISBN 0-904173-12-7 Pbk : £18.00
(B77-21312)

Vol.8 : The Indo-Parthians : their Kushan neighbours. — 1976. — [2]p,p675-783,xix p : ill, maps ; 31cm.
Bibl.: p.vii-xv.
ISBN 0-904173-13-5 Pbk : £18.00
(B77-21313)

Vol.9 : Greeks, Sakas and their contemporaries in Central and Southern India : Indo-Parthian, Western Satraps, Chutus, Abhiràs, Satavahanas. — 1976. — [2]p,p785-924,xx p : ill, maps ; 31cm.
Bibl.: p.v-xi.
ISBN 0-904173-14-3 Pbk : £18.00
(B77-21314)

737.4'9'398 — Thracian coins, to ca 40
IUrkova, Iordanka. Coins of the ancient Thracians / [by] Yordanka Youroukova ; translated from the Bulgarian by V. Athanassov. — Oxford : British Archaeological Reports, 1976. — [5],129p,xxviii p of plates : ill ; 30cm. — (British archaeological reports : supplementary series ; 4)
Spine title: Thracian coins. — Bibl.: p.105-111. — Index.
ISBN 0-904531-36-8 : £2.80
(B77-00325)

737.4'9'41 — British coins. *Catalogues*
British Academy. Sylloge of coins of the British Isles / [British Academy]. — London : Oxford University Press : Spink.
24 : Ancient British, Anglo-Saxon and Norman coins in West Country museums / by A.J.H. Gunstone. — 1977. — xxxvi,99p : ill ; 26cm.
Bibl.: p.xxxiv-xxxv. — Index.
ISBN 0-19-725972-3 : £10.50
(B77-27256)

737.4'9'41 — British coins, 1066-1977
Linecar, Howard Walter Arthur. British coin designs & designers / [by] H.W.A. Linecar. — London : Bell, 1977. — xiii,146p : ill, geneal tables ; 25cm.
Bibl.: p.141. — Index.
ISBN 0-7135-1931-2 : £10.50
(B77-33340)

737.4'9'415 — Irish coins, 995-. *Collectors' guides*
Collectors' coins - Ireland. — [Torquay] : [Rotographic Publications].
1977 : 2nd ed. — [1976]. — [2],50p : ill ; 16cm.
ISBN 0-901170-99-2 Sd : £0.40
(B77-06803)

737.4'9'42 — English coins, 1760-. *Collectors' guides*
Collectors' coins - England. — [Torquay] : [Rotographic Publications].
1977 : 4th ed. — [1976]. — [2],82p : ill ; 16cm.
ISBN 0-901170-17-8 Sd : £0.50
(B77-06208)

737.4'9'42 — English coins, to ca 1950
Brooke, George Cyril. English coins from the seventh century to the present day / by George C. Brooke. — 3rd ed., revised. — London : Spink, 1976. — xii,300p,lxxii p of plates : ill ; 23cm.
This ed. originally published: London : Methuen, 1950. — Bibl. — Index.
ISBN 0-900696-72-9 : £5.50
(B77-01668)

737.4'9'42 — English obsidional coins, 1642-1649
Nelson, Philip. The obsidional money of the Great Rebellion, 1642-1649 / by Philip Nelson. — London (61 St John St., E.C.1) : Andrew Publishing Co., 1976. — [3],71p,plate : ill, maps ; 21cm.
Facsimile reprint of: 1st ed. Liverpool : W.M. Murphy, 1907. — Index.
ISBN 0-903681-06-4 Pbk : £3.00
(B77-14325)

737.4'9'42 — Museums. *Cardiff. National Museum of Wales. Stock: Anglo-Saxon coins. Catalogues*
Dykes, D W. Anglo-Saxon coins in the National Museum of Wales / [by] D.W. Dykes. — [Cardiff] : [National Museum of Wales], [1977]. — [1],31p : ill, maps ; 25cm.
'an expanded reprint from "Amgueddfa, Bulletin of the National Museum of Wales" 24 Winter 1976' - p.1. — Bibl.: p.26.
Sd : Unpriced
(B77-27257)

737.4'9'4279 — Manx coins, to 1977
Mackay, James. The Pobjoy encyclopaedia of Isle of Man coins and tokens / by James A. Mackay. — Sutton (Mint House, Oldfields Rd, Sutton, Surrey) : Pobjoy Mint Ltd, 1977. — [3], 73p : ill(some col) ; 23cm.
Spine title: Isle of Man coins and tokens. — Bibl.: p.72-73.
£3.50
Also classified at 737'.3'094279
(B77-20464)

737.4'9'51 — Universities. Numismatic cabinets. *Norway. Oslo. Universitet i Oslo. Myntkabinett. Stock: Chinese coins, B.C.1122-A.D.1864. Collections: Schjöth Collection. Catalogues*
Universitetet i Oslo. *Myntkabinett.* Chinese currency : the currency of the Far East : the Schjöth Collection at the Numismatic Cabinet of the University of Oslo, Norway / by F. Schjöth. — London (61 St John St., E.C.1) : Andrew Publishing Co., 1976. — [5],88p,132p of plates : ill ; 34cm.
Facsimile reprint of: 1st ed., published as: 'The currency of the Far East'. Oslo : Aschehoug ; London : Luzac, 1929.
ISBN 0-903681-05-6 : £16.00
(B77-13153)

737'.6'0951 — Chinese seals, ca B.C.300-ca 1950
Lai, T'ien-ch'ang. Chinese seals / [by] T.C. Lai ; introduction by Jui-fong L. Chang. — Seattle ; London : University of Washington Press, 1976. — xx,[4],200p : ill, facsims ; 23cm.
ISBN 0-295-95517-1 : £8.00
(B77-03680)

738 — CERAMICS

738'.02'78 — European pottery & porcelain. Potters' marks, ca 1500- ca 1900. *Identification manuals*

Macdonald-Taylor, Margaret. A dictionary of marks : metalwork, furniture, ceramics / compiled and edited by Margaret Macdonald-Taylor. — Revised ed. ; with an introduction by Bevis Hillier. — London : 'Connoisseur', 1976. — 319p,plate : ill(incl 1 col) ; 22cm.
Previous ed.: i.e. Revised ed. / introduction by L.G.G. Ramsey. 1973. — Bibl.: p.311-312. — Index.
ISBN 0-900305-11-8 : £3.95
Primary classification 739'.02'78
(B77-06210)

738'.074'02132 — Museums. *London. Westminster (London Borough). Wallace Collection. Exhibits: Ceramics. Catalogues*

Wallace Collection. Catalogue of ceramics / Wallace Collection. — London (Manchester Sq., W1M 6BN) : Trustees of the Wallace Collection.
Bibl.: p.386-406. — Index.
1 : Pottery, maiolica, faience, stoneware / by A.V.B. Norman. — 1976. — vi,443p : ill(some col) ; 24cm.
ISBN 0-900785-06-3 Pbk : £4.00
(B77-04967)

738'.074'02753 — Universities. Art galleries. *Merseyside (Metropolitan County). Liverpool. University of Liverpool. Art Gallery. Exhibits: Pottery & porcelain. Catalogues*

University of Liverpool. The University of Liverpool art collections : a selection of paintings, watercolours, woodcuts and ceramics, displayed in number 3, Abercromby Square / [catalogue by Andrew W. Moore]. — [Liverpool] ([c/o The University Archivist, Senate House, Abercromby Sq., P.O. Box 147, Liverpool L69 3BX]) : [University of Liverpool], 1977. — [3],v,60p : ill ; 21x30cm.
'University art collections - a recent acquisition' ([4]p.: ill; Sd) as insert. — Bibl.: p.59-60.
Sd : Unpriced
Primary classification 759.2
(B77-30492)

738'.0942 — Mason porcelain & ironstone ware, 1796-1853

Haggar, Reginald George. Mason porcelain and ironstone, 1796-1853 : Miles Mason and the Mason Manufactories / by Reginald Haggar and Elizabeth Adams. — London : Faber, 1977. — 2-135p,A-H,[80]p of plates : ill(some col), facsim, plan ; 26cm. — (Faber monographs on pottery and porcelain)
Bibl.: p.125-126. — Index.
ISBN 0-571-10945-4 : £15.00
(B77-14843)

738'.0942 — Museums. *East Sussex. Brighton. Royal Pavilion, Art Gallery and Museums, Brighton. Exhibits: English ceramics, ca 1785-ca 1955. Special subjects: Landscape. Catalogues*

Royal Pavilion, Art Gallery and Museums, Brighton. China postcards : [catalogue of] an exhibition of landscape views on ceramics from the Ian Henderson collection, [held] July 13th-August 22nd, 1976 [at the] Royal Pavilion, Art Gallery and Museums, Brighton. — [Brighton] ([North Gate House, Church St., Brighton BN1 1VE]) : [Royal Pavilion Art Gallery and Museums], [1976]. — [5],52p,[4]p of plates : ill ; 21cm.
Bibl.: p.52.
ISBN 0-9502372-5-6 Sd : £0.50
(B77-08475)

738'.09424'5 — Museums. *Salop. Shrewsbury. Clive House Museum. Exhibits: Salop pottery & porcelain, ca 1630-ca 1950. Catalogues*

Clive House Museum. Shropshire pottery and porcelain : a brief guide to the collection displayed in Clive House Museum. — Revised ed. / by Michael Messenger. — [Shrewsbury] ([College Hill, Shrewsbury, Salop.]) : Shrewsbury Museums, 1974. — [1],22p : ill ; 22cm.
Previous ed.: 1969. — Bibl.: p.21.
Sd : Unpriced
(B77-04968)

738'.095 — Art galleries & museums. Exhibits: Oriental pottery & porcelain, to 1900. *Illustrations*

Oriental ceramics : the world's great collections / honorary supervisors Fujio Koyama, John A. Pope. — Tokyo : Kodansha ; Warminster : [Distributed by] Aris and Phillips.
In 12 vols. — Limited ed. of 300 numbered copies. — Col. plates tipped in. — Each vol. individually boxed.
Vol.1 : Tokyo National Museum / [introduction and selections, Seizo Hayashiya, Gakuji Hasebe ; notes, Seizo Hayashiya et al.]. — 1976. — [4],343p : ill(some col) ; 38cm.
Japanese and English introductions, captions and notes.
£100.00
(B77-09155)

Vol.2 : National Museum of Korea / [selection and notes, Sunu Choi]. — 1976. — [4],323p : ill(some col) ; 38cm.
Japanese and English introductions, captions and notes.
£100.00
(B77-09156)

Vol.5 : The British Museum / [selection and notes, Ralph Pinder-Wilson et al.]. — 1976. — [4],294p : ill(some col) ; 38cm.
Japanese and English introductions, captions and notes.
£100.00
(B77-09157)

Vol.6 : Victoria & Albert Museum / [selection and notes, John G. Ayers]. — 1976. — [4],294, [1]p : ill(some col) ; 38cm.
Japanese and English introductions, captions and notes.
£100.00
(B77-09158)

Vol.7 : Percival David Foundation of Chinese Art / [selection and notes, Margaret Medley]. — 1976. — [4],319p : ill(some col) ; 38cm.
Japanese and English introductions, captions and notes.
£100.00
(B77-09159)

Vol.8 : Musée Guimet. — 1976. — [4],327,[1] p : ill(some col) ; 38cm.
Japanese and French introductions, captions and notes, English preliminaries.
£100.00
(B77-09160)

Vol.9 : Museum of Far Eastern Antiquities, Stockholm / [selection and notes, Bo Gyllensvärd]. — 1976. — [4],310p : ill(some col) ; 38cm.
Japanese and English introductions, captions and notes.
£100.00
(B77-09161)

Vol.10 : The Freer Gallery of Art / [selection and notes, Josephine H. Knapp, Esin Atil]. — 1976. — [4],319p : ill(some col) ; 38cm.
Japanese and English introductions, captions and notes.
£100.00
(B77-09162)

738'.095 — Asian ceramic products, 618-907. *Conference proceedings*

Pottery and metalwork in T'ang China : their chronology & external relations : a colloquy held 29 June to 2 July 1970 / edited by William Watson. — 2nd ed. — [London] ([c/o School of Oriental and African Studies, University of London, W.C.1]) : Percival David Foundation of Chinese Art, 1976. — [5],87p : ill ; 26cm. — (Colloquies on art and archaeology in Asia ; no.1)
Cover title. — Previous ed.: 1971. — Bibl.: p.75-77.
ISBN 0-7286-0027-7 Pbk : £3.00
Also classified at 739'.095
(B77-00864)

738'.095 — Oriental ceramic ware. *History. Serials*

Oriental Ceramic Society. Transactions of the Oriental Ceramic Society. — [London] ([31B Torrington Sq., W.C.1]) : The Society.
1973-1974, 1974-1975. — [1976]. — xxi,32, 152p,[4] leaves of plates,28,[108]p of plates : ill(some col), 2 ports ; 29cm.
Includes: Chinese jade throughout the ages : catalogue of an exhibition organised by the Arts Council of Great Britain and the Oriental Ceramic Society, 1st May-22nd June 1975 at the Victoria and Albert Museum / by Jessica Rawson, John Ayers.
ISBN 0-903421-14-3 : £15.00
ISSN 0306-0926
(B77-16513)

738'.0959 — South-east Asian ceramics. Dating & identification

Brown, Roxanna M. The ceramics of South-east Asia : their dating and identification / [by] Roxanna M. Brown. — Kuala Lumpur ; London [etc.] : Oxford University Press, 1977. — xiv,82p,[43],43p of plates : ill(some col), maps, plan ; 29cm. — (Oxford in Asia studies in ceramics)
Bibl.: p.71-76. — Index.
ISBN 0-19-580315-9 : £26.00
(B77-25778)

738.1 — POTTERY MAKING

738.1 — Pottery. Making. *Amateurs' manuals*

Dickerson, John. Pottery in easy steps / [by] John Dickson ; [photographs by Alain Le Garsmeur]. — London : Studio Vista, 1976. — 64p : col ill ; 29cm.
Bibl.: p.64.
ISBN 0-289-70721-8 : £1.95
(B77-07507)

738.1 — Pottery. Making. *Manuals*

Beck, Charles, *b.1904.* Throwing pottery : 72 projects with illustrations of 170 pots : new approaches and developments based on throwing / by Charles Beck. — Burnley (P.O. Box 61, Burnley BB12 8LH) : Isles House Publications, 1977. — 52p : ill ; 22cm. — (Pottery series ; no.2)
Sd : Unpriced
(B77-27977)

Birks, Tony. The potter's companion / [by] Tony Birks. — 2nd ed. — London : Batsford, 1977. — 208p : ill(some col), plan ; 22cm.
Previous ed.: London : Collins, 1974. — Index.
ISBN 0-7134-0944-4 : £3.95
ISBN 0-7134-0945-2 Pbk : £2.50
(B77-33341)

Casson, Michael. The craft of the potter / by Michael Casson ; edited by Anna Jackson. — London : British Broadcasting Corporation, 1977. — 128p : ill(some col), ports ; 30cm.
'Published to accompany a series of programmes prepared in consultation with the BBC Further Education Advisory Council' - title page verso. — Bibl.: p.128. — Includes 2 chapters by Lynne Reeve.
ISBN 0-563-16127-2 Pbk : £2.75
(B77-30464)

Gale, John, *b.1942.* Pottery / [by] John Gale. — Sevenoaks : Teach Yourself Books, 1977. — 240p : ill ; 20cm. — (Teach yourself books)
Bibl.: p.233. — Index.
ISBN 0-340-21518-6 Pbk : £2.25
(B77-19524)

738.1 — Salt-glazed pottery. Making

Starkey, Peter. Saltglaze / [by] Peter Starkey. — London : Pitman, 1977. — viii,88p : ill ; 21cm. — (Ceramic skillbooks)
Bibl.: p.86. — Index.
ISBN 0-273-01081-6 : £2.95 : CIP rev.
ISBN 0-273-00998-2 Pbk : £1.95
(B77-12581)

Troy, Jack. Salt-glazed ceramics / by Jack Troy. — New York : Watson-Guptill ; London : Pitman, 1977. — 160p : ill(some col) ; 29cm.
Bibl.: p.156-157. — Index.
ISBN 0-273-01053-0 : £11.50 : CIP rev.
(B77-22022)

738.1'03 — Pottery. Making. *Encyclopaedias*

Fournier, Robert. Illustrated dictionary of practical pottery / [by] Robert Fournier ; photographs by John Anderson ; diagrams by Sheila Fournier. — Revised ed. — New York ; London [etc.] : Van Nostrand Reinhold, 1977. — 256p : ill(some col) ; 26cm.
Previous ed.: 1973. — Bibl.: p.254. — List of films: p.255.
ISBN 0-442-22447-8 : £7.00
(B77-17656)

738.1'2 — Pottery. Making. Clay

Hamer, Frank. Clays / [by] Frank and Janet Hamer. — London : Pitman [etc.], 1977. — [5], 90p : ill ; 21cm. — (Ceramic skillbooks)
Bibl.: p.80-81. — Index.
ISBN 0-273-01085-9 : £2.95 : CIP rev.
ISBN 0-273-01000-x Pbk : £1.95
(B77-13154)

738.1'3 — Pottery. Making. Pottery kilns. Construction. *Manuals*

Gregory, Ian. Kiln building / [by] Ian Gregory. — London : Pitman [etc.], 1977. — viii,88p : ill, plans ; 21x21cm. — (Ceramic skillbooks)
Bibl.: p.86. — Index.
ISBN 0-273-01086-7 : £2.95 : CIP rev.
ISBN 0-273-01001-8 Pbk : £1.95
(B77-13155)

738.1'4 — Pottery & porcelain. Restoration. *Manuals*

André, Jean Michel. The restorer's handbook of ceramics and glass / [by] Jean-Michel André ; [translated from the French by J.A. Underwood]. — New York ; London [etc.] : Van Nostrand Reinhold, 1976. — 129,[1]p : ill(some col) ; 22cm.
Translation of: 'Restauration de la céramique et du verre'. Fribourg : Office du livre, 1976. — Bibl.: p.127. — Index.
ISBN 0-442-20363-2 : Unpriced
(B77-24377)

738.1'4 — Pottery & porcelain. Special subjects: Animals & human figures. Techniques. *Manuals*

Ruscoe, William. Sculpture for the potter / [by] William Ruscoe. — London : Academy Editions [etc.], 1975. — 80p,[16]p of plates : ill ; 23cm. — (A Scopas handbook)
Bibl.: p.74.
ISBN 0-85670-212-9 : £3.95
ISBN 0-85670-217-x Pbk : £1.95
(B77-00865)

738.1'5 — Porcelain. Painting. *Manuals*

Taylor, Doris Wark. China painting, step by step / [by] Doris W. Taylor, Anne Button Hart ; photographs by Darlene Bekkhedal. — New York ; London [etc.] : Van Nostrand Reinhold, [1977]. — x,234p,[16] leaves of plates : ill(some col) ; 24cm.
Some leaves printed on both sides. — Originally published: Princeton, N.J. ; London : Van Nostrand, 1962. — Index.
ISBN 0-442-28441-1 Pbk : £7.10
(B77-17657)

738.2 — PORCELAIN

738.2'094 — European porcelain, 1700-1800

Ducret, Siegfried. The colour treasury of eighteenth century porcelain / text by Siegfried Ducret ; photographs by Michael Wolgensinger ; translated [from the German] by Christine Friedlander. — Oxford : Elsevier-Phaidon, 1976. — [6],138p : col ill, facsims ; 30cm.
This translation also published: New York : Crowell, 1976. — Translation of: 'Porzellan des 18. Jahrhunderts'. Zürich : Silva, 1971. — Index.
ISBN 0-7290-0051-6 : £5.95
(B77-14844)

738.2'0942 — English porcelain, 1745-1850. *Collectors' guides*

Honey, William Bowyer. Old English porcelain : a handbook for collectors / by W.B. Honey. — 3rd ed. revised, expanded and reset / revised by Franklin A. Barrett. — London : Faber, 1977. — iii-xxxiv,440p,[4]p of plates : ill(some col) ; 23cm.
Previous ed.: 1948. — Bibl.: p.414-423. — Index.
ISBN 0-571-04902-8 : £13.00 : CIP rev.
(B77-13156)

738.2'0951 — Chinese export porcelain, to ca 1800

Chinese export porcelain : an historical survey / edited by Elinor Gordon. — New York : Main Street/Universe Books ; London : [Distributed] by Bell, 1977. — 175p,[8]p of plates : ill(some col), facsim, ports ; 29cm. — ('Antiques' magazine library ; 3)
Articles reprinted from 'Antiques' magazine. — Originally published: New York : Main Street/Universe Books, 1975. — Index.
£8.50
(B77-21315)

738.2'0951 — Museums. *London. Kensington and Chelsea (London Borough). Victoria and Albert Museum. Exhibits: Chinese porcelain, 1368-1644. Illustrations*

Victoria and Albert Museum. Ming porcelains / Victoria & Albert Museum ; [text by] John Ayers. — London : H.M.S.O., 1977. — [12] : chiefly col ill ; 16cm. — (Victoria and Albert Museum. Small colour books ; 17)
ISBN 0-11-290260-x Sd : £0.40
(B77-17000)

738.2'7 — Art galleries. *Greater Manchester (Metropolitan County). Manchester. Manchester City Art Gallery. Exhibits: Worcester transfer printed porcelain. Collections: Dykes Collection. Catalogues*

Manchester City Art Gallery. Transfer-printed Worcester porcelain at Manchester City Art Gallery : a catalogue / by Emmeline Leary and Peter Walton. — [Manchester] ([Central Library, St Peter's Sq., Manchester M2 4PD]) : City of Manchester Cultural Services, [1976]. — 52p : ill, port ; 20x21cm.
Bibl.: p.50-51. — Index.
ISBN 0-901673-08-0 Sd : £1.50
(B77-06209)

738.2'7 — Chinese blue & white porcelain, to 1976

Macintosh, Duncan. Chinese blue & white porcelain / [by] Duncan Macintosh. — Newton Abbot [etc.] : David and Charles, 1977. — 152p : ill(some col), map ; 29cm.
Bibl.: p.146-147. — Index.
ISBN 0-7153-7434-6 : £8.50
(B77-25088)

738.2'7 — Museums. *London. Westminster (London Borough). Wallace Collection. Exhibits: Sèvres porcelain, 1755-1781. Catalogues*

Wallace Collection. Sèvres porcelain / Wallace Collection ; [text] by R.A. Cecil. — London (Manchester Sq., W1M 6BN) : Trustees of the Wallace Collection, 1976. — [4]p,11p of plates(2 fold) : ill(chiefly col) ; 18cm.
ISBN 0-900785-08-x Sd : £0.45
(B77-05551)

738.2'7 — Wedgwood Fairyland lustreware porcelain, 1912-1929

Des Fontaines, Una. Wedgwood fairyland lustre : the work of Daisy Makeig-Jones / [by] Una des Fontaines. — New York : Born-Hawes ; London (36 Dover St., W1X 3RB) : Sotheby Parke Bernet Publications Ltd, 1975. — xiv, 298p : ill(some col), facsims, geneal table, ports ; 31cm.
Ill. on lining papers. — Bibl.: p.291-292. — Index.
ISBN 0-85667-022-7 : £30.00
(B77-18908)

738.2'8 — Porcelain tableware, ca 1750-1900

Cushion, John Patrick. Pottery & porcelain tablewares / [by] John P. Cushion. — London : Studio Vista, 1976. — 240p : ill(some col) ; 27cm.
Ill. on lining papers. — Bibl.: p.140. — Index.
ISBN 0-289-70729-3 : £8.95
Also classified at 738.3'8
(B77-09847)

738.3 — EARTHENWARE AND STONEWARE

738.3'092'4 — English pottery. Cardew, Michael. *Critical studies*

Michael Cardew : a collection of essays / with an introduction by Bernard Leach ; and contributions by Michael Cardew ... [et al.]. — London (12 Waterloo Place, SW1Y 4AU) : Crafts Advisory Committee, 1976. — 80p : ill, facsims, ports ; 20cm.
Bibl.: p.77-79. — Index.
ISBN 0-903798-07-7 : £3.00
ISBN 0-903798-03-4 Pbk : £1.75
(B77-32756)

738.3'092'4 — Museums. *London. Kensington and Chelsea (London Borough). Victoria and Albert Museum. Exhibits: English pottery. Leach, Bernard. Catalogues*

Victoria and Albert Museum. The art of Bernard Leach : [catalogue of] a loan retrospective exhibition, March to May 1977 / Victoria and Albert Museum. — London : [The Museum], 1977. — 29p : ill ; 21cm.
Bibl.: p.28. — Index.
Sd : £0.25
(B77-16514)

738.3'092'4 — Museums. *Staffordshire. Longton. Gladstone Pottery Museum. Exhibits: English pottery. Smith, Sampson. Catalogues*

Woolliscroft, Kathleen. Sampson Smith, manufacturer of all kinds of figures in great variety : a celebration : [catalogue of an exhibition held] 9th November to 5th December 1976 [at] Gladstone Pottery Museum, Longton, Stoke on Trent / [written by Kathleen Woolliscroft] ; [for Gladstone Pottery Museum]. — [Stoke-on-Trent] ([52 Wallis Way, Milton, Stoke-on-Trent, Staffs.]) : [The author], 1976. — 106p : ill, plan ; 15x21cm.
Cover title: Sampy. — Bibl.: p.105-106.
Sd : £0.90
(B77-03681)

738.3'0933 — Universities. *Norway. Oslo. Universitetet i Oslo. Stock: Ancient Palestinian pottery. Collections: Ustinov Collection*

Skupinska-Lovset, Ilona. The Ustinov Collection / [by] Ilona Skupinska-Lovset. — Oslo [etc.] : Universitetsforlaget ; Henley on Thames (37 Queen St., Henley on Thames, Oxon. R69 1AJ) : Global Book Resources Ltd. The Palestinian pottery. — 1976. — 177,[1]p,xl p of plates : ill, map ; 25cm.
Bibl.: p.7-11.
ISBN 0-200-01564-8 Pbk : £9.90
(B77-04969)

738.3'09361 — Romano-British coarse pottery

Romano-British coarse pottery : a student's guide / edited by Graham Webster. — 3rd ed. — London (7 Marylebone Rd, NW1 5HA) : Council for British Archaeology, 1976. — 37p : ill ; 21cm. — (Council for British Archaeology. Research reports ; 6)
Previous ed.: 1969. — Bibl.: p.21-30.
ISBN 0-900312-38-6 Sd : £1.25
(B77-03682)

738.3'0937 — Ancient Roman pottery. *Northumberland. Chesterholm, ca 70-ca 115. Lists*

Hird, Louise. A report on the pottery found in the Pre-Hadrianic levels at Vindolanda during the excavations of 1972-1975 / by Louise Hird. — Hexham (Bardon Mill, Hexham, [Northd]) : Vindolanda Trust, 1977. — 59p : ill ; 30cm. — (Vindolanda ; 5)
Cover title: The Pre-Hadrianic pottery.
ISBN 0-9505636-0-9 Sd : Unpriced
(B77-11994)

738.3'0941 — British pottery, 1870-1940

Coysh, Arthur Wilfred. British art pottery, 1870-1940 / [by] A.W. Coysh. — Newton Abbot [etc.] : David and Charles, 1976. — 96p : ill ; 24cm.
Bibl.: p.93. — Index.
ISBN 0-7153-7252-1 : £4.95
(B77-05552)

738.3'0941 — Museums. *London. Tower Hamlets (London Borough). Bethnal Green Museum. Exhibits: British royal commemorative pottery, 1660-1935. Collections: James Blewitt Collection. Catalogues*

May, John, *b.1926.* Jubilation : royal commemorative pottery from the collection of James Blewitt : [catalogue of an] exhibition [held] May to September 1977 [at the] Bethnal Green Museum of Childhood / [compiled by John May]. — London ([Museum House, Cambridge Heath Rd, E.2]) : [The Museum], 1977. — 26p,[32]p of plates : ill ; 15x21cm.
ISBN 0-905209-04-4 Sd : £1.50
(B77-17001)

738.3'0942 — Country houses. *West Yorkshire (Metropolitan County). Leeds. Temple Newsam House. Exhibits: English pottery, ca 1650-ca 1750. Collections: Leeds Collection. Catalogues*

Temple Newsam House. Creamware and other English pottery at Temple Newsam House, Leeds : a catalogue of the Leeds Collection / [compiled] by Peter Walton. — Bradford [etc.] ([The Country Press, Bradford, W. Yorkshire BD8 8DH]) : Manningham Press : [Distributed by Lund Humphries], 1976. — xi,293p : ill(some col), facsims, port ; 30cm.
'The collection is housed in ... Temple Newsam House, Lotherton Hall, and the City Art Gallery' - Preface. — Col. ill. tipped in. — Bibl.: p.281-284. — Index.
ISBN 0-905564-00-6 : £35.00
(B77-03683)

738.3'09424'6 — Staffordshire pottery. Special themes: England. Social life, 1700-1897

Sekers, David. Popular Staffordshire pottery / [by] David Sekers. — London : Joseph, 1977. — 48p : ill(some col) ; 19cm. — (Folio miniatures)
Ill. on lining papers. — Bibl.: p.32.
ISBN 0-7181-1590-2 : £1.95
(B77-29576)

738.3'09424'6 — Staffordshire pottery, to 1905

Rhead, G Woolliscroft. Staffordshire pots & potters / by G. Woolliscroft Rhead and Frederick Alfred Rhead ; with 120 illustrations in half tone, and 90 drawings in pen line by the authors. — Wakefield : EP Publishing, 1977. — [1],xvi,384p,[68] leaves of plates : ill ; 23cm.
Facsimile reprint of: 1st ed. London : Hutchinson, 1906. — Index.
ISBN 0-7158-1235-1 : £8.95 : CIP rev.
(B77-18909)

738.3'09426'4 — Pottery. Remains. *Suffolk, to ca 1700. Identification manuals*

Suffolk Archaeological Unit. Introductory guide to pottery & worked flints in Suffolk / compiled by the Suffolk Archaeological Unit. — Ipswich (County Hall, Ipswich [IP4 2JS]) : Suffolk County Council, [1976]. — [3],56,[1]p : ill ; 22cm.
Bibl.
ISBN 0-86055-008-7 Sd : £0.75
(B77-08476)

738.3'0985'2 — Ica Valley pottery. Style. *Southern Peru, 1350-1570*
Menzel, Dorothy. Pottery style and society in ancient Peru : art as a mirror of history in the Ica Valley, 1350-1570 / [by] Dorothy Menzel. — Berkeley [etc.] ; London : University of California Press, [1977]. — xiii,279p,64p of plates : ill ; 29cm.
Published in the United States: 1976. — Bibl.: p.257-260. — Index.
ISBN 0-520-02970-4 : £20.00
(B77-13767)

738.3'7 — Houses. *London. Kensington and Chelsea (London Borough). Kensington Church Street. No.141 Kensington Church Street. Exhibits: Royal Doulton stoneware, 1870-1925. Catalogues*
Dennis, Richard, *b.1937.* Catalogue of an exhibition of Doulton stoneware and terracotta, 1870-1925, part 1 : 28th September to 9th October, 1971 at 141 Kensington Church Street, London, W.8 / [compiled by Richard Dennis]. — London (144 Kensington Church St., W.8) : The author, 1971. — [265]p : ill(incl 2 col), facsims ; 25cm.
Cover title: Doulton stoneware pottery. — Bibl. : p.[256].
ISBN 0-903685-00-0 Pbk : Unpriced
(B77-04330)

738.3'7 — Museums. *Oxfordshire. Oxford. Ashmolean Museum. Exhibits: Chinese greenware, B.C.400-A.D.1100. Catalogues*
Ashmolean Museum. Catalogue of Chinese greenware / by Mary Tregear. — Oxford : Clarendon Press, 1976 [i.e. 1977]. — xii,84p,leaf of plate,[70]p of plates : ill(incl 1 col), maps ; 29cm.
Catalogue of the collection in the Ashmolean Museum, Oxford.
ISBN 0-19-813167-4 : £25.00
(B77-13768)

738.3'8 — Cream pots, 1866-ca 1920. *Collectors' guides*
Hunt, Chris. Collecting cream pots / by Chris Hunt ; [photographs by Paul Rhodes]. — Bradford : John England ; Bradford (23 Grove House Cres., Bradford, W. Yorkshire) : Distributed by the author, 1977. — 3-50p : ill, facsims ; 22cm.
Sd : £1.00
(B77-25779)

738.3'8 — Pots. Monochrome lids, ca 1840-1918. *Collectors' guides*
Heath, June. Identifying and valuing black and white pot lids / by June Heath ; editing and indexing E.S. Thompson ; photographs M.J. Coffin. — Southampton (7 Maple Rd, Bitterne, Southampton, Hants.) : Southern Collectors Publications, [1977]. — [126]p : chiefly ill ; 21cm.
Bibl.: p.[12]. — Index.
ISBN 0-905438-03-5 Pbk : £2.25
(B77-22736)

738.3'8 — Pots. Monochrome lids, ca 1860-ca 1920. *Collectors' guides*
Dale, Ronald. The price guide to black and white pot-lids / [by] Ronald Dale. — Woodbridge : Antique Collectors' Club, 1977. — 3-471p : ill ; 21cm. — (Antique Collectors' Club. Price guides)
Index.
ISBN 0-902028-53-7 : £7.95
(B77-33342)

738.3'8 — Pottery tableware, ca 1750-1900
Cushion, John Patrick. Pottery & porcelain tablewares / [by] John P. Cushion. — London : Studio Vista, 1976. — 240p : ill(some col) ; 27cm.
Ill. on lining papers. — Bibl.: p.140. — Index.
ISBN 0-289-70729-3 : £8.95
Primary classification 738.2'8
(B77-09847)

738.3'8 — Toothpaste pots. Lids. *Collectors' guides*
The tooth paste pot lid booklet / compiled by Ben Swanson. — Black Notley (Greenacres, Church Rd, Black Notley, Essex) : Bottles and Relics Publications, [1977?]. — [6],147[i.e. 149]p : ill, chiefly facsims ; 21cm.
Pbk : Unpriced
(B77-32040)

738.3'82'09377 — Apulian pottery: Red figure vases. Paintings. Symbolism, 300-400. Expounded by Ancient Greek religious doctrine of future life
Smith, H R W. Funerary symbolism in Apulian vase-painting / by H.R.W. Smith ; edited by J.K. Anderson. — Berkeley [etc.] ; London : University of California Press, 1976. — x,303p, [50]p of plates : ill ; 26cm. — (University of California. Publications : classical studies ; vol.12)
Bibl.: p.285-289. — Index.
ISBN 0-520-09469-7 Pbk : Unpriced
(B77-11325)

738.4 — ENAMELS

738.4 — Enamelling. *Amateurs' manuals*
Fairfield, Del. Enamelling / [by] Del Fairfield ; photographs by Peter Haines ; drawings by Helen Fairfield. — Sevenoaks : Teach Yourself Books, 1977. — 164p : ill ; 18cm. — (Teach yourself books)
ISBN 0-340-21550-x Pbk : £1.75
(B77-19525)

Untracht, Oppi. Enameling on metal / [by] Oppi Untracht ; photographs by the author ... [and others]. — London : Pitman, 1977. — 191p : ill, ports ; 26cm.
Originally published: New York : Greenberg, 1957 ; London : Pitman, 1958. — Bibl.: p.182. — Index.
ISBN 0-273-01092-1 Pbk : £4.95
(B77-25089)

Winter, Edward. Enamel painting techniques : glass fused on metals : jewellery, tiles, free forms, plaques and murals / [by] Edward Winter. — London : Applied Science Publishers, [1977]. — xiii,86p,leaf of plate,118p of plates : chiefly ill(some col) ; 25cm.
Originally published: Amsterdam ; Barking : Elsevier, 1970. — Bibl.: p.78-82. — Index.
ISBN 0-85334-717-4 Pbk : £5.00
(B77-17658)

739 — ART METALWORK

739 — Containers: Anglo-Saxon metal hanging bowls
Longley, David. Hanging-bowls, penannular brooches and the Anglo-Saxon connection / [by] David Longley. — Oxford : British Archaeological Reports, 1975. — [8],49p : ill, maps ; 30cm. — (British archaeological reports ; 22 ISSN 0306-1205)
Cover title: The Anglo-Saxon connection. — Bibl.: p.44-49.
ISBN 0-904531-25-2 Pbk : £0.95
Also classified at 739.27'8
(B77-03152)

739'.02'78 — British art metalwork. Hallmarks & makers' marks, ca 1500-ca 1900. *Identification manuals*
Macdonald-Taylor, Margaret. A dictionary of marks : metalwork, furniture, ceramics / compiled and edited by Margaret Macdonald-Taylor. — Revised ed. ; with an introduction by Bevis Hillier. — London : 'Connoisseur', 1976. — 319p,plate : ill(incl 1 col) ; 22cm.
Previous ed.: i.e. Revised ed. / introduction by L.G.G. Ramsey. 1973. — Bibl.: p.311-312. — Index.
ISBN 0-900305-11-8 : £3.95
Also classified at 738'.02'78
(B77-06210)

739'.092'4 — British art metalwork. Designs by Knox, Archibald: Designs for Liberty and Company, 1897-1909. *Illustrations*
Knox, Archibald. The designs of Archibald Knox for Liberty & Co. / by A.J. Tilbrook, jointly edited with Gordon House. — London (109 Highbury New Park, N5 2HG) : Ornament Press Ltd, 1976. — 283p : chiefly ill, facsims, ports ; 22cm.
Bibl.: p.279-280. — Index.
ISBN 0-905464-00-1 : Unpriced
(B77-22737)

739'.095 — Asian metalware, 618-907. *Conference proceedings*
Pottery and metalwork in T'ang China : their chronology & external relations : a colloquy held 29 June to 2 July 1970 / edited by William Watson. — 2nd ed. — [London] ([c/o School of Oriental and African Studies, University of London, W.C.1]) : Percival David Foundation of Chinese Art, 1976. — [5],87p : ill ; 26cm. — (Colloquies on art and archaeology in Asia ; no.1)
Cover title. — Previous ed.: 1971. — Bibl.: p.75-77.
ISBN 0-7286-0027-7 Pbk : £3.00
Primary classification 738'.095
(B77-00864)

739.2 — WORK IN PRECIOUS METALS

739.2'0937 — Museums. *London. Camden (London Borough). British Museum. Exhibits: Ancient Roman gold & silver products. Catalogues*
British Museum. Wealth of the Roman world, AD 300-700 / edited by J.P.C. Kent and K.S. Painter. — London : British Museum Publications Ltd for the Trustees, 1977. — 190p : ill(some col), maps ; 26cm.
Catalogue of an exhibition held at the British Museum, 1st April-1st October, 1977. — Bibl.: p.189-190.
ISBN 0-7141-0062-5 : £5.00
ISBN 0-7141-0061-7 Pbk : £1.95
(B77-27258)

739.2'094 — European goldware & silverware, 1540-1620
Hayward, John Forrest. Virtuoso goldsmiths and the triumph of mannerism, 1540-1620 / [by] J.F. Hayward. — London (34 New Bond St., W1A 2AA) : Sotheby Park Bernet Publications Ltd, 1976. — 751p : ill(some col), ports ; 34cm.
Bibl.: p.729-731. — Index.
ISBN 0-85667-005-7 : £48.00
(B77-13157)

739.2'0942 — English goldware & silverware, to 1900
Cripps, Wilfred Joseph. Old English plate : ecclesiastical, decorative, and domestic, its makers and marks / by Wilfred Joseph Cripps. — Library ed. — Wakefield : EP Publishing, 1977. — xx,519p,13 leaves of plates : ill ; 23cm.
Facsimile reprint of: Library ed. London : J. Murray, 1901. — Index.
ISBN 0-7158-1236-x : £8.95 : CIP rev.
(B77-18910)

739.2'274 — Museums. *London. Westminster (London Borough). Wallace Collection. Exhibits: Western European gold snuff boxes, 1730-1809. Catalogues*
Wallace Collection. Gold boxes / Wallace Collection ; [text] by A.V.B. Norman. — London (Manchester Sq., W1M 6BN) : Trustees of the Wallace Collection, 1975. — [16]p : col ill ; 18cm.
ISBN 0-900785-07-1 Sd : £0.45
(B77-05553)

739.2'2744'36 — Museums. *London. Kensington and Chelsea (London Borough). Victoria and Albert Museum. Exhibits: Parisian gold snuff boxes, 1700-1800. Illustrations*
Victoria and Albert Museum. French gold boxes / Victoria & Albert Museum ; [text by] Charles Truman. — London : H.M.S.O., 1977. — [12]p : chiefly col ill ; 16cm. — (Victoria and Albert Museum. Small colour books ; 16)
ISBN 0-11-290259-6 Sd : £0.40
(B77-16515)

739.2'3'0278 — Dutch metal products. Forged silver hallmarks, 1600-1803. *Lists. Dutch texts*
Citroen, Karel Adolf. Valse źilvermerken in Nederland / [door] K.A. Citroen. — Amsterdam [etc.] ; Oxford : North-Holland Publishing Co., 1977. — viii,73p : ill ; 23x11cm.
ISBN 0-7204-0522-x : £8.33
(B77-29577)

739.2'3'737 — Ancient Roman antiquities: Christian silver products. *Cambridgeshire. Water Newton*
Painter, K S. The Water Newton early Christian silver / [by] K.S. Painter. — London : British Museum Publications Ltd for the Trustees, 1977. — 48p : ill, maps ; 24cm.
ISBN 0-7141-1364-6 Pbk : £1.50
(B77-27978)

739.2'3'737 — Museums. *London. Camden (London Borough). British Museum. Department of Greek and Roman Antiquities. Exhibits: Ancient Roman silver products: Mildenhall treasure*
Painter, K S. The Mildenhall treasure : Roman silver from East Anglia / [by] K.S. Painter. — London : British Museum Publications Ltd, 1977. — 79p : ill, maps ; 25cm.
Bibl.: p.48.
ISBN 0-7141-1365-4 Pbk : £1.50 : CIP rev.
(B77-07508)

739.2'3'741 — English silver products, 1800-1900
Culme, John. Nineteenth-century silver / [by] John Culme. — London [etc.] : Hamlyn for Country Life Books, 1977. — 232p : ill(some col), facsims, plan, ports ; 31cm.
Bibl.: p.225-226. — Index.
ISBN 0-600-39134-5 : £17.50
(B77-23597)

739.2'3'7415 — Irish silverware, to 1973
Bennett, Douglas. Irish silver / [by] Douglas Bennett. — Norwich : Jarrold and Sons, 1976. — [28]p(2 fold) : ill(some col) ; 25cm. — (The Irish heritage series ; 7)
Sd : £0.10
(B77-02475)

739.2'3'742 — English silverware: Tea making equipment, 1670-1900
De Castres, Elizabeth. A collector's guide to tea silver, 1670-1900 / [by] Elizabeth de Castres. — London : Muller, 1977. — 136p,[32]p of plates : ill ; 26cm.
Bibl.: p.129. — Index.
ISBN 0-584-10289-5 : £7.50 : CIP rev.
(B77-17002)

739.27 — JEWELLERY
Blakemore, Kenneth. The retail jeweller's guide / [by] Kenneth Blakemore ; technical adviser G.F. Andrews. — 3rd ed. — London [etc.] : Newnes-Butterworths, 1976. — [7],323p : ill ; 23cm.
Previous ed.: London : Iliffe, 1973. — Index.
ISBN 0-408-00266-2 : £9.00
(B77-02476)

739.27 — Jewellery. Making. *Manuals*
Bowie, Hamish. Jewellery making / [by] Hamish Bowie ; colour photography by Christopher Walton ; and line illustrations by V.J. Taylor and the author. — Newton Abbot [etc.] : David and Charles, 1976. — 166p : ill(some col) ; 26cm. — ([Step-by-step series])
Bibl.: p.163. — Index.
ISBN 0-7153-7044-8 : £4.95
(B77-04970)

Edwards, Rod. The techniques of jewellery / [by] Rod Edwards. — London : Batsford, 1977. — 5-240p,[10]p of plates : ill(some col), plan ; 26cm.
Bibl.: p.230-232. — Index.
ISBN 0-7134-0197-4 : £5.95
(B77-33343)

Fairfield, Del. Jewellery making / [by] Del Fairfield ; photographs by Peter Haines ; drawings by Helen Fairfield. — London : Teach Yourself Books, 1976. — 170p : ill ; 18cm. — (Teach yourself books)
ISBN 0-340-20386-2 Pbk : £1.50
(B77-00326)

739.27 — Jewellery. Repair. *Amateurs' manuals*
Hardy, Richard Allen. The jewelry repair manual. — 2nd ed. / [by] R. Allen Hardy ; with illustrations by the author. — New York ; London [etc.] : Van Nostrand Reinhold, [1977]. — ix,253p : ill ; 24cm.
This ed. originally published: Princeton ; London : Van Nostrand, 1967. — 'Some of the material in this revised edition appeared originally in "The American Horologist & Jeweler" ...' - title page verso. — Index.
ISBN 0-442-03130-0 : £6.05
(B77-22023)

739.27'09 — Jewellery, to ca 1950. *Collectors' guides*
Poynder, Michael. The price guide to jewellery, 3000 B.C.-1950 A.D. / by Michael Poynder. — [Woodbridge] : Antique Collectors' Club, 1976. — 385p : ill(some col) ; 28cm. — (Antique Collectors' Club. Price guides)
Bibl.: p.385. — Index.
ISBN 0-902028-50-2 : £15.00
(B77-05554)

739.27'09'034 — Jewellery, 1837-1901
Armstrong, Nancy. Victorian jewelry / [by] Nancy Armstrong. — London [etc.] : Studio Vista, 1976. — 158,[2]p : ill(some col), ports ; 29cm.
Bibl.: p.157-158. — Index.
ISBN 0-289-70672-6 : £8.00
(B77-09848)

739.27'094 — Art galleries. Exhibits: European jewellery. *Great Britain, 1965-1975. Catalogues*
Scottish Arts Council. Jewellery in Europe : an exhibition of progressive work / selected by Ralph Turner. — Edinburgh (19 Charlotte Sq., Edinburgh EH2 4DF) : The Council, 1975. — 55,[1]p : ill, facsims, ports ; 23cm.
'A touring exhibition organised by the Scottish Arts Council and the Crafts Advisory Committee to be held at : The Scottish Arts Council Gallery ... Edinburgh ... 20 December 1975-18 January 1976 ... [and elsewhere]'. — Bibl.
Sp : Unpriced
(B77-20465)

739.27'094 — Country houses. *London. Camden (London Borough). Kenwood House. Exhibits: European jewellery, 1720-1880. Collections: Hull Grundy Collection*
Iveagh Bequest. Jewellery from the Hull Grundy Collection : an illustrated account of the collection of 18th and 19th century jewellery presented to Kenwood by Mrs John Hull Grundy, 1975-6 / the Iveagh Bequest, Kenwood ... ; [text prepared by Lindsay Stainton]. — London : Greater London Council, 1976. — [20]p : ill ; 20x21cm.
ISBN 0-7168-0850-1 Sd : £0.35
(B77-15975)

739.27'0941 — Art galleries. Exhibits: British jewellery. *Australia & West Germany. 1971-1976. Catalogues*
Crafts Advisory Committee. On tour = Auf Tournee : 10 British jewellers in Germany and Australia = Zehn britische Goldschmiede in Deutschland und Australien / [Crafts Advisory Committee]. — [London] ([12 Waterloo Place, SW1Y 4AU]) : [The Committee], [1976]. — 52p : ill(some col), ports ; 20x21cm.
English and German text. — '[Catalogue of] an exhibition organised by the Crafts Advisory Committee in conjunction with the British Council, London, 1965-76'.
ISBN 0-903798-16-6 Pbk : Unpriced
(B77-03684)

739.27'5 — Jewellery. Engraving. *Manuals*
Hardy, Richard Allen. The jewelry engravers manual. — Revised ed. / [by] R. Allen Hardy and John J. Bowman ; illustrations by R. Allen Hardy. — New York ; London [etc.] : Van Nostrand Reinhold, 1976. — v,143p : ill ; 23cm.
Previous ed.: / by John J. Bowman. New York : Van Nostrand Reinhold, 1954 ; London : Macmillan, 1955. — Index.
ISBN 0-442-20965-7 Pbk : £3.45
(B77-19526)

739.27'8 — Anglo-Saxon penannular brooches
Longley, David. Hanging-bowls, penannular brooches and the Anglo-Saxon connection / [by] David Longley. — Oxford : British Archaeological Reports, 1975. — [8],49p : ill, maps ; 30cm. — (British archaeological reports ; 22 ISSN 0306-1205)
Cover title: The Anglo-Saxon connection. — Bibl.: p.44-49.
ISBN 0-904531-25-2 Pbk : £0.95
Primary classification 739
(B77-03152)

739.4 — IRONWORK
739'.47 — Decorative cast ironwork, to 1976
Robertson, Edward Graeme. Cast iron decoration : a world survey / [by] E. Graeme Robertson and Joan Robertson. — London : Thames and Hudson, 1977. — 336p : ill ; 29cm.
Bibl.: p.324-331. — Index.
ISBN 0-500-23254-7 : £14.00
(B77-11995)

739'.4741 — British decorative cast ironwork,1800-1900
Owen, Michael, *b.1938.* Antique cast iron / [by] Michael Owen. — Poole : Blandford Press, 1977. — x,127p : ill ; 23cm.
Index.
ISBN 0-7137-0833-6 : £3.75
(B77-21316)

739.5 — WORK IN COPPER, BRASS, TIN ETC.
739'.512'0945 — Museums. *London. Kensington and Chelsea (London Borough). Victoria and Albert Museum. Exhibits: Italian bronze sculptures, ca 1490-ca 1590. Illustrations*
Radcliffe, Anthony. Italian Renaissance bronzes / [by] Anthony Radcliffe. — London : H.M.S.O., 1976. — [12]p : chiefly col ill ; 16cm. — (Victoria and Albert Museum. Small colour books ; 14)
ISBN 0-11-290243-x Sd : £0.40
(B77-09163)

739'.52'0941 — Monumental brasses. *Great Britain*
Norris, Malcolm. Brass rubbing / [by] Malcolm Norris. — London [etc.] : Pan Books, 1977. — 112p : ill, facsims, ports ; 25cm. — (Pan craft books)
Originally published: London : Studio Vista, 1965. — Bibl.: p.103-106. — Index.
ISBN 0-330-25095-7 Pbk : £1.50
Primary classification 760
(B77-19548)

739'.52'094261 — Churches. Monumental brasses. *Norfolk*
Greenwood, Roger. The brasses of Norfolk churches / by Roger Greenwood and Malcolm Norris. — Holt (The Old Rectory, Holt [Norfolk]) : Norfolk Churches Trust, 1976. — [1],52,[1]p : ill ; 30cm.
Index.
ISBN 0-9502838-3-5 Sd : £1.50
(B77-13158)

739'.52'094264 — Monumental brasses. Special subjects: Knights. *Suffolk, ca 1325-1623*
Felgate, T M. Knights on Suffolk brasses / by T.M. Felgate. — Ipswich (6 Great Colman St., Ipswich, Suffolk) : East Anglican Magazine Ltd, 1976. — 136p : ill, coats of arms ; 21cm.
ISBN 0-900227-22-2 Pbk : £2.95
(B77-07983)

739'.533 — Pewterware. *Collectors' guides*
Massé, Henri Jean Louis Joseph. Chats on old pewter / by H.J.L.J. Massé. — Revised ed. / edited and revised by Ronald F. Michaelis. — Wakefield : EP Publishing, 1977. — 240p,leaf of plate,[36]p of plates : ill ; 19cm.
This ed. originally published: London : E. Benn, 1949. — Index.
ISBN 0-7158-1224-6 : £5.50 : CIP rev.
(B77-18911)

739'.533'0278 — British pewterware. Hallmarks, ca 1400-ca 1850
Peal, Christopher Arthur. More pewter marks / [compiled by] Christopher A. Peal ; [for the Pewter Society]. — Norwich (12 Stratford Cres., Cringleford, Norwich NR4 7SF) : The compiler, 1976. — 117p : ill ; 22x31cm.
ISBN 0-9505288-0-3 : £15.00
(B77-03153)

739'.533'0278 — Pewterware. Hallmarks, to 1940
Stará, D. Pewter marks of the world / [by] D. Stará ; [translated from the Czech MS by Joy Moss-Kohoutová]. — London [etc.] : Hamlyn, 1977. — 260p : ill ; 20cm.
Index.
ISBN 0-600-37090-9 : £1.75
(B77-27259)

739'.54 — Lead objects. Casting. *Amateurs' manuals*
Horton, Gordon Tom. Lead casting for pleasure and profit : including casting methods, mould making and materials / by Gordon T. Horton ; illustrations A. Payne, photographs M.J. Coffin. — Southampton (7 Maple Rd, Bitterne, Southampton) : Southern Collectors Publications, [1976]. — [1],24p : ill ; 21cm.
ISBN 0-905438-02-7 Sd : £0.65
(B77-01669)

739.7 — ARMS AND ARMOUR
739.7'074'0215 — Museums. *London. Tower Hamlets (London Borough). Tower of London. Armouries. Exhibits. Catalogues*
Tower of London. *Armouries.* The Armouries of the Tower of London / [by] H.L. Blackmore. — London : H.M.S.O.
1 : Ordnance. — 1976. — ix,425p,[2]leaves of plates(1 fold),80p of plates : ill(incl 1 col), coats of arms, facsims, map, ports ; 29cm.
At head of title: Department of the Environment. — Bibl.: p.213-214. — Index.
ISBN 0-11-670251-6 : £30.00
(B77-16516)

739.7'2'09 — Edged weapons, to 1975. *Collectors' guides*
Stephens, Frederick John. Edged weapons : a collector's guide / [by] Frederick J. Stephens. — Bourne End : Spurbooks, 1976. — 160p : ill, port ; 25cm. — ([Spurbooks illustrated history series])
Bibl.: p.157. — Index.
ISBN 0-904978-18-4 : £6.00
(B77-06211)

739.7'4'43 — Flintlock pistols, 1600-1850. *Collectors' guides*
Wilkinson, Frederick. Flintlock pistols : an illustrated reference guide to flintlock pistols from the 17th to the 19th century / by F. Wilkinson. — London : Arms and Armour Press [etc.], 1976. — 75p : ill, facsims, port ; 22cm.
Originally published: 1968. — Bibl.: p.71-73.
ISBN 0-85368-251-8 Pbk : £1.25
(B77-09849)

741 — DRAWING
741 — Colouring books. *Texts*
Bock, Valerie. The umbrella girl : a painting book from Thailand / [text by Valerie Bock ; drawings by Jeanette Taylor]. — London : Leprosy Mission, 1976. — [16]p : ill ; 22cm.
Sd : £0.20
Primary classification 823'.9'1J
(B77-03778)

Bond, Michael. Paddington carpenter / [by] Michael Bond. — [London] : Collins, 1977. — [19]p : chiefly ill(some col) ; 28cm. — (Bond, Michael. Paddington's colouring books)
ISBN 0-00-143179-x Sd : £0.30
Primary classification 823'.9'1J
(B77-34213)

Bond, Michael. Paddington conjurer / [by] Michael Bond. — [London] : Collins, 1977. — [19]p : ill(some col) ; 28cm. — (Bond, Michael. Paddington's colouring books)
ISBN 0-00-143176-5 Sd : £0.30
Primary classification 823'.9'1J
(B77-33455)

Bond, Michael. Paddington cook / [by] Michael Bond. — [London] : Collins, 1977. — [19]p : chiefly ill(some col) ; 28cm. — (Bond, Michael. Paddington's colouring books)
ISBN 0-00-143178-1 Sd : £0.25
Primary classification 823'.9'1J
(B77-33456)

Bond, Michael. Paddington golfer / [by] Michael Bond. — [London] : Collins, 1977. — [19]p : ill(some col) ; 28cm. — (Bond, Michael. Paddington's colouring books)
ISBN 0-00-143177-3 Sd : £0.30
Primary classification 823'.9'1J
(B77-33457)

Jemima Puddle-Duck's painting book / from the original designs by Beatrix Potter. — London [etc.] : F. Warne, [1976]. — [16]p : ill ; 22cm. — ([Potter painting books])
ISBN 0-7232-1995-8 Sd : £0.40
Primary classification 823'.9'1J
(B77-04438)

Jeremy Fisher's painting book / from the original designs by Beatrix Potter. — London [etc.] : F. Warne, [1976]. — [16]p : ill ; 22cm. — ([Potter painting books])
ISBN 0-7232-1994-x Sd : £0.40
Primary classification 823'.9'1J
(B77-04439)

My super fun colouring book. — Maidenhead : Purnell, 1977. — 4v. : of ill ; 28cm.
ISBN 0-361-03789-9 Sd : £0.40
(B77-07984)

Peter Rabbit's painting book / from the original designs by Beatrix Potter. — London [etc.] : F. Warne, [1976]. — [16]p : ill ; 22cm. — ([Potter painting books])
ISBN 0-7232-1993-1 Sd : £0.40
Primary classification 823'.9'1J
(B77-04442)

Spano, Ann. Alice in Wonderland : based on Walt Disney Productions' cartoon feature film / this adaptation by Ann Spano. — London : New English Library, 1977. — 128p : ill(some col) ; 20cm. — (A read and colour book)
ISBN 0-450-03278-7 Pbk : £0.80
Primary classification 823'.9'1J
(B77-09996)

Tom Kitten's painting book / from the original designs by Beatrix Potter. — London [etc.] : F. Warne, [1976]. — [16]p : ill ; 22cm. — ([Potter painting books])
ISBN 0-7232-1996-6 Sd : £0.40
Primary classification 823'.9'1J
(B77-04445)

741 — Fill-in books. *Texts*
Noddy play pad. — Maidenhead : Purnell, 1977. — [128]p : ill ; 14x21cm.
Notebook format. — With answers.
Pbk : £0.20
(B77-07985)

Sooty play pad. — Maidenhead : Purnell, 1977. — [128]p : ill ; 14x21cm.
Notebook format. — With answers.
Pbk : £0.20
(B77-07986)

Walt Disney play pad. — Maidenhead : Purnell, 1977. — 2v.([128]p;[128]p) : chiefly ill ; 21x14cm.
Notebook format. — With answers.
ISBN 0-361-03798-8 Pbk : £0.40
(B77-09850)

741'.092'2 — Illustrations. Special subjects: Wars, 1853-1905. Illustrators
Hodgson, Pat. The war illustrators / compiled and written by Pat Hodgson. — London : Osprey Publishing, 1977. — 191p : ill, facsims, ports ; 26cm.
Bibl.: p.31-32. — Index.
ISBN 0-85045-079-9 : £5.95
(B77-24378)

741'.092'4 — English drawings. Peake, Mervyn. *Periodicals*
Mervyn Peake review. — Ipswich (c/o Administrative Secretary, Central Library, Northgate St., Ipswich, Suffolk) : Mervyn Peake Society.
Continues: The Mervyn Peake Society newsletter.
No.3- ; Autumn 1976-. — 1976-. — ill, facsims ; 21cm.
Two issues a year. — 36p. in 3rd issue.
Sd : Free to members
ISSN 0309-1309
Also classified at 823'.9'12
(B77-05555)

741'.092'4 — English drawings. Wain, Louis. Special subjects: Pets: Cats. *Critical studies*
Wain, Louis. Catland / illustrated by Louis Wain ; introduced [i.e. text written] by Rodney Dale. — London : Duckworth, 1977. — [32]p : col ill ; 29cm.
ISBN 0-7156-1164-x : £4.95
(B77-33943)

741'.092'4 — English illustrations. Caldecott, Randolph. *Correspondence*
Caldecott, Randolph. Yours pictorially : illustrated letters of Randolph Caldecott / edited by Michael Hutchins. — London [etc.] : F. Warne, 1976. — x,284p,[8]p of plates : ill, facsims(some col), port ; 24cm.
Index.
ISBN 0-7232-1981-8 : £7.95
(B77-02477)

741'.092'4 — English illustrations. Dulac, Edmund. *Biographies*
White, Colin, *b.1927.* Edmund Dulac / [by] Colin White. — London : Studio Vista, 1976. — 208p : ill(some col), facsims, map, music, plan, ports ; 29cm.
Index.
ISBN 0-289-70751-x : £10.50
(B77-09164)

741'.092'4 — English illustrations. Robinson, William Heath. *Biographies*
Day, Langston. The life and art of W. Heath Robinson / by Langston Day. — Wakefield : EP Publishing, 1976. — 270p,[10] leaves of plates,[10]p of plates : ill, port ; 23cm.
Originally published: London : H. Joseph, 1947.
ISBN 0-7158-1180-0 : £4.95
(B77-15976)

741'.092'4 — French drawings. Moreau, Gustave. *Critical studies*
Mathieu, Pierre Louis. Gustave Moreau : complete edition of the finished paintings, watercolours and drawings / [by] Pierre-Louis Mathieu ; [translated from the French by James Emmons]. — Oxford : Phaidon, 1977. — 400p : ill(some col), ports ; 29cm.
Translation of: 'Gustave Moreau'. Fribourg : Office du livre SA, 1977?. — Bibl.: p.382-388. — Index.
ISBN 0-7148-1733-3 : £35.00(£29.95 before publication)
Primary classification 759.4
(B77-14330)

741.2 — DRAWINGS. MATERIALS, EQUIPMENT, TECHNIQUES
741.2 — Drawings. Point & line. Techniques. *Manuals. For primary school teaching*
Röttger, Ernst. Creative drawing : point and line / [by] Ernst Röttger and Dieter Klante ; [translated from the German]. — London : Batsford, 1976. — 143p : chiefly facsim ; 20cm. — (Creative play series ; 4)
This translation originally published: 1964. — Translation of: 'Punkt und Linie'. 3 Aufl. Ravensburg : O. Maier, 1963.
ISBN 0-7134-2353-6 Pbk : £2.50
(B77-03154)

741.2 — Drawings. Techniques
Goldstein, Nathan. The art of responsive drawing / [by] Nathan Goldstein. — 2nd ed. — Englewood Cliffs ; London [etc.] : Prentice-Hall, 1977. — xii,355p : ill, ports ; 29cm.
Previous ed.: 1973. — Bibl.: p.348. — Index.
ISBN 0-13-048629-9 : £12.75
(B77-23598)

741.2 — Drawings. Techniques. *Manuals*
Harnest, Sepp. Sketching and drawing / [by] Sepp Harnest ; [translated from the German by Christopher McIntosh]. — Yeovil : Haynes, 1976. — 96p : ill ; 17cm. — (Foulis spectrum books)
Translation of: 'Zeichnen und skizzieren'. Bern : Hallwag, 197-?.
ISBN 0-85429-540-2 Pbk : £0.85
(B77-03155)

Mendelowitz, Daniel Marcus. A guide to drawing / [by] David M. Mendelowitz. — Revised and expanded ed. — New York ; London [etc.] : Holt, Rinehart and Winston, 1976. — viii,296p : ill(some col) ; 28cm.
Previous ed.: published as 'Drawing, a study guide'. 1967. — Index.
ISBN 0-03-089937-0 : £13.90
ISBN 0-03-086565-4 Pbk : £7.75
(B77-03685)

Taubes, Frederic. The quickest way to draw well / by Frederic Taubes. — Harmondsworth [etc.] : Penguin, 1977. — 94p : ill ; 23cm. — (Penguin handbooks)
Originally published: New York : Studio, 1958 ; London : Pitman, 1961.
ISBN 0-14-046275-9 Pbk : £1.50
(B77-26425)

741.5 — CARTOONS, CARICATURES
741.5'942 — English comics. *Texts. Juvenile literature*
Basil Brush holiday special. — London (382 Edgware Rd, W2 1EP) : Polystyle Publications Ltd, 1977. — 47p : of ill(some col) ; 28cm.
Sd : £0.30
(B77-25091)

Cheeky weekly. — London : IPC Magazines.
No.1- ; 22 Oct. 1977-. — 1977-. — chiefly ill(some col) ; 29cm.
Thirty-two p. in 1st issue.
Sd : £0.08
ISSN 0140-7139
(B77-33344)

Fury. — Sevenoaks (Fourth Floor, Tubs Hill House, London Rd, Sevenoaks, Kent) : 'Fury'.
No.1 - ; Mar. 16th 1977-. — 1977-. — chiefly ill ; 29cm.
Weekly. — 32p. in 1st issue.
Sd : £0.09
(B77-14845)

'Mighty TV comic's' Popeye holiday special. — London (382 Edgware Rd, W2 1EP) : Polystyle Publications Ltd, 1977. — 47p : of ill(some col) ; 28cm.
Sd : £0.30
(B77-25092)

Pink panther holiday special, and the Inspector. — London (382 Edgware Rd, W2 1EP) : Polystyle Publications Ltd, 1977. — 47p : of ill ; 28cm.
Sd : £0.30
(B77-25093)

Sooty's holiday special. — London (382 Edgware Rd, W2 1EP) : Polystyle Publications Ltd, 1977. — 47p : chiefly ill(some col) ; 28cm.
Sd : £0.30
(B77-25094)

Tarzan weekly. — London (30 Langham St., W1N 5LB) : Byblos Productions Ltd.
[No.1]- ; 11th June 1977-. — 1977-. — chiefly ill(some col) ; 28cm.
[32]p. in 24th Sept. 1977 issue.
Sd : £0.12
ISSN 0140-4652
(B77-28765)

Tom and Jerry holiday special : plus Barney Bear and Droopy. — London (382 Edgware Rd, W2 1EP) : Polystyle Publications Ltd, 1977. — 47p : of ill(some col) ; 28cm.
Sd : £0.30
(B77-25095)

741.5'09'04 — Humorous cartoons, 1900-1976. *Critical studies*
Hewison, William. The cartoon connection : the art of pictorial humour / as seen by William Hewison. — London : Elm Tree Books, 1977. — 144p : chiefly ill ; 27cm.
Index.
ISBN 0-241-89483-2 : £5.50
(B77-27979)

741.5'941 — British comics, 1950-1962. *Extracts, selections*
The **best** of 'Eagle' / edited by Marcus Morris. — London : Joseph : Ebury Press, 1977. — 194p : ill(some col), maps(1 col), ports ; 31cm.
Text, ill. on lining papers. — Facsimile reprints. — Index.
ISBN 0-7181-1566-x : £5.95
(B77-26426)

741.5'9411 — Scottish humorous strip cartoons. *Collections from individual artists. Serials*
The **Broons** : selected from the 'Sunday post' and earlier Broons books. — Glasgow [etc.] : D.C. Thomson.
[1977]. — 1977. — [98]p : of ill ; 28cm.
Pbk : £0.75
(B77-32041)

741.5'942 — Art galleries. *London. Westminster (London Borough). National Portrait Gallery. Exhibits: English cartoons: Cartoons for "Vanity Fair". Catalogues*
National Portrait Gallery. Catalogue of original 'Vanity fair' cartoons in the National Portrait Gallery / by Richard Ormond. — London : The Gallery, 1976. — 20p ; 21cm.
Cover title: Original 'Vanity fair' cartoons in the National Portrait Gallery'. — '... to coincide with the "Vanity Fair" exhibition, held at the National Portrait Gallery, July to August 1976' - Introduction. — Index.
ISBN 0-904017-09-5 Sd : £0.10
(B77-13160)

741.5'942 — English caricatures. Cruikshank, George. *Illustrations*
Cruikshank, George. The caricatures of George Cruikshank / [text by] John Wardroper. — London : Gordon Fraser Gallery, 1977. — 144p : chiefly ill(some col), facsim, port ; 24x25cm.
Bibl.: p.142. — Index.
ISBN 0-900406-85-2 : £15.00
(B77-30467)

741.5'942 — English caricatures. Gillray, James. *Illustrations*
Gillray, James. The satirical etchings of James Gillray / edited by Draper Hill. — New York : Dover Publications [etc.] ; London : Constable, 1976. — ii-xxxii,142p,viii p of plates : chiefly ill(some col) ; 31cm.
ISBN 0-486-23340-5 Pbk : £3.60
(B77-22738)

741.5'942 — English comics. *Texts*
Positive feedback. — Henley-on-Thames (21 Nicholas Rd, Henley-on-Thames, Oxon. RG9 1RB) : Positive Feedback Comics.
No.1- ; [1977]-. — 1977-. — chiefly ill ; 31cm.
19p. in 1st issue.
Sd : £0.30
(B77-30468)

741.5'942 — English humorous cartoons. *Collections*
The **Armada** book of cartoons / selected by Mary Danby. — London : Armada, 1977. — [126]p : of ill ; 19cm.
Originally published: 1972.
ISBN 0-00-691300-8 Pbk : £0.40
(B77-15977)

The **second** Armada book of cartoons / selected by Mary Danby. — London : Armada, 1977. — [126]p : of ill ; 18cm.
This collection originally published: 1973.
ISBN 0-00-691301-6 Pbk : £0.40
(B77-15978)

The **third** Armada book of cartoons / selected by Mary Danby. — London : Armada, 1977. — [126]p : of ill ; 18cm.
ISBN 0-00-691149-8 Pbk : £0.40
(B77-15979)

741.5'942 — English humorous cartoons. *Collections from individual artists*
Heath, Michael. The 'Punch' cartoons of Heath / introduced by Alan Coren. — London : Harrap, 1976. — [64]p : of ill ; 20cm.
ISBN 0-245-53026-6 Pbk : £1.00
(B77-00327)

Lancaster, *Sir* **Osbert.** The social contract : new pocket cartoons / by Osbert Lancaster. — London : J. Murray, 1977. — 71p : of ill ; 19cm.
ISBN 0-7195-3439-9 : £1.25
(B77-30469)

Robinson, William Heath. Devices / contrived by Heath Robinson ; with a foreword by K.R.G. Browne. — London : Duckworth, 1977. — 116p : of ill ; 23cm.
Originally published: as 'Let's laugh'. London : Hutchinson, 1940.
ISBN 0-7156-1268-9 : £3.50
(B77-30470)

Trog. The world of Trog / introduced by James Cameron. — London : Robson, 1977. — 96p : of ill ; 26cm.
ISBN 0-86051-020-4 : £3.25
(B77-29578)

741.5'942 — English humorous cartoons. *Juvenile literature. Collections*
The **Piccolo** book of cartoons / compiled by Deborah and Roy Manley ; cover illustration by David Bull. — London [etc.] : Pan Books, 1977. — [93]p : of ill ; 18cm. — (Piccolo original)
ISBN 0-330-25128-7 Pbk : £0.45
(B77-27980)

741.5'942 — English humorous cartoons. Special subjects: Children. *Collections from individual artists*
Thelwell. Thelwell's brat race. — London : Eyre Methuen, 1977. — 128p : of ill ; 22cm.
ISBN 0-413-45390-1 : £2.50
(B77-28766)

741.5'942 — English humorous cartoons. Special subjects: France. Paris. *Collections from individual artists*
Shaw, Irwin. Paris! Paris! / [text] by Irwin Shaw and [illustrations by] Ronald Searle. — London : Weidenfeld and Nicolson, 1977. — [11],211p : ill ; 24cm.
ISBN 0-297-77275-9 : £4.95
Primary classification 914.4'36'0483
(B77-19103)

741.5'942 — English humorous cartoons. Special subjects: Golf. *Collections from individual artists*
Bateman, Henry Mayo. H.M. Bateman on golf. — Weybridge (The Oil Mills, Weybridge, Surrey) : Whittet Books, 1977. — 5-78p : of ill ; 14x18cm.
ISBN 0-905483-03-0 : £1.75
(B77-29579)

741.5'942 — English humorous cartoons. Special subjects: Livestock: Dogs. *Collections from individual artists*
Steadman, Ralph. Dog bodies / [by] Ralph Steadman. — New York ; London : Paddington Press, 1977. — [32]p : of ill ; 23cm.
Originally published: London : Abelard-Schuman, 1970.
ISBN 0-448-22975-7 Sd : £0.75
(B77-16517)

741.5'942 — English humorous cartoons. Special subjects: Music. *Collections from individual artists*
Bateman, Henry Mayo. H.M. Bateman on music. — Weybridge (The Oil Mills, Weybridge, Surrey) : Whittet Books, 1977. — 3-61p : of ill ; 14x18cm.
ISBN 0-905483-02-2 : £1.50
(B77-29580)

741.5'942 — English humorous cartoons. Special subjects: Pets: Cats. *Collections from individual artists*
Angrave, Bruce. Cat-alogue / [by] Bruce Angrave. — Glasgow [etc.] : Collins, 1976. — [64]p : of ill ; 16cm.
ISBN 0-00-410325-4 : £0.75
(B77-07987)

Angrave, Bruce. Magnifi-cat / [by] Bruce Angrave. — Glasgow [etc.] : Collins, 1977. — [63]p : of ill ; 16cm.
ISBN 0-00-410327-0 : £0.95
(B77-33345)

741.5'942 — English humorous cartoons. Special subjects: Railway services, to 1975. *Collections*
The **railway** cartoon book / [compiled by] Ken and Kate Baynes. — Newton Abbot [etc.] : David and Charles, 1976. — 96p : of ill, facsims, port ; 25cm.
ISBN 0-7153-7354-4 : £2.95
(B77-04331)

741.5'942 — English humorous cartoons. Special subjects: Recorder playing. *Collections from individual artists*
King, Ronald, *b.1906.* Recorder humour : cartoons / by Ronald King. — London (48 Great Marlborough St., W1V 2BN) : Schott & Co., 1976. — 37p : of ill ; 17cm.
ISBN 0-901938-57-2 Sd : £0.60
(B77-04332)

741.5'942 — English humorous cartoons. Special subjects: Robots. *Collections from individual artists*
Heath, Michael. Michael Heath's automata. — London : A.P. Rushton ; London (219 Eversleigh Rd, S.W.11) : Distributed by Big O Publishing Ltd, 1976. — [20]leaves : of ill ; 30cm.
Sd : £1.50
(B77-29581)

741.5'942 — English humorous cartoons. Special subjects: Roman Catholic Church. *Collections from individual artists*
Ryan, John, *b.1921.* Rolling in the aisles : cartoons on an ecclesiastical theme / by John Ryan. — Great Wakering : Mayhew-McCrimmon, 1975. — [62]p : of ill ; 11x15cm.
ISBN 0-85597-088-x Sd : £0.35
(B77-19527)

Van Zeller, Hubert. Cracks in the clouds / by Hubert van Zeller (erstwhile Brother Choleric). — Chulmleigh : Augustine, 1976. — 64p : of ill ; 29cm.
ISBN 0-85172-750-6 Pbk : £2.50
(B77-14326)

741.5'942 — English humorous cartoons. Special subjects: Sailing. *Collections from individual artists*
Peyton, Mike. Come sailing again / [by] Mike Peyton. — Lymington : Nautical Publishing Co., 1976. — 96p : chiefly ill, port ; 22cm.
ISBN 0-245-52991-8 : £1.95
(B77-13161)

Peyton, Mike. Hurricane Zoë and other sailing / [by] Mike Peyton. — Lymington : Nautical Publishing Co., 1977. — 96p : of ill ; 22cm.
ISBN 0-245-53132-7 : £2.25
(B77-22739)

741.5'942 — English humorous cartoons. Special subjects: Signs of the zodiac. *Collections from individual artists*
McKie, Roy. Roy McKie's zodiac book. — Glasgow [etc.] : Collins, 1977. — [64]p : chiefly col ill ; 21cm.
ISBN 0-00-410717-9 Pbk : £0.95
(B77-31335)

741.5'942 — English humorous cartoons. Special subjects: Transport. *Collections from individual artists*
Emett, Rowland. Alarms and excursions, and other transports transfixed / by Emett. — London : J. Murray, 1977. — [96]p : of ill ; 29cm.
Does not include any railway cartoons.
ISBN 0-7195-3428-3 : £3.95
(B77-28767)

741.5'942 — English humorous cartoons, to 1976. Special subjects: Christianity. *Collections*
Bring me laughter : a collection of cartoons / compiled and introduced by Eric Morecambe and Ernie Wise. — London : Mowbrays, 1977. — 3-62p : chiefly ill ; 21cm.
Index.
ISBN 0-264-66422-1 Pbk : £0.95
(B77-28768)

741.5'942 — English humorous strip cartoons. *Collections from individual artists*
Browne, Chris. Captain Kremmen and the Krells / [original concept by Kenny Everett ; written by Chris Browne ; designed and drawn by Roger Wade Walker ; lettering by Chris Welch]. — London : Corgi, 1977. — [64]p : col ill ; 28cm.
ISBN 0-552-98033-1 Pbk : £1.50
(B77-32042)

Graham. Fred Basset, the hound that's almost human, no.24 / by Graham. — London : Associated Newspaper Group, [1977]. — [80]p : of ill ; 14x22cm.
Sd : £0.40
(B77-18912)

741.5'942 — English humorous strip cartoons. *Collections from individual artists. Juvenile literature*
Thompson, Graham. Alan Parker's Bugsy Malone / illustrated by Graham Thompson. — London : Armada, 1976. — [64]p : of col ill ; 30cm.
ISBN 0-00-691247-8 Pbk : £0.95
(B77-13159)

741.5'942 — English humorous strip cartoons. *Collections from individual artists. Serials*
Tidy, Bill. Fosdyke saga / by Bill Tidy. — London : Mirror Group Books.
6 : a new volume from the famous 'Daily mirror' strip. — 1977. — [160]p : of ill ; 13x22cm.
ISBN 0-85939-098-5 Pbk : £0.95
(B77-31336)

741.5'942 — English humorous strip cartoons, to 1977. *Collections. Periodicals*
Ally Sloper. — London (94 Leonard St., EC2A 4RH) : Alan Class ; London : Denis Gifford.
No.1-4. — 1976-1977. — chiefly ill, ports ; 28cm.
Published at irregular intervals. — [36]p. in 1st issue.
Sd : £0.30
(B77-18292)

741.5'9429 — Welsh humorous cartoons. Special subjects: Welsh persons. *Collections from individual artists*
Gren. More of my Wales / by Gren. — Llandybie : C. Davies, 1973. — [128]p : of ill, port ; 19x23cm.
ISBN 0-7154-0099-1 Pbk : £0.50
(B77-19528)

741.5'944 — French humorous strip cartoons. *Collections from individual artists*
Loup, Jean Jacques. The architect / [by] Loup. — London : Cape, 1977. — [33]p : of col ill ; 26cm.
Also published: Milan : Emme, 1977.
ISBN 0-224-01398-x : £2.50
(B77-30471)

741.5'944 — French humorous strip cartoons. *Collections from individual artists. English texts*
Goscinny. Asterix and Caesar's gift / text by Goscinny ; drawings by Uderzo ; translated [from the French] by Anthea Bell and Derek Hockridge. — London [etc.] : Hodder and Stoughton, 1977. — 48p : of col ill ; 30cm.
Translation of: 'Le cadeau de César'. Paris : Dargaud, 1974.
ISBN 0-340-21588-7 : £1.80
(B77-21318)

Goscinny. Asterix and the chieftain's shield / text by Goscinny ; drawings by Uderzo ; translated [from the French] by Anthea Bell and Derek Hockridge. — London [etc.] : Hodder and Stoughton, 1977. — 48p : of col ill ; 30cm.
Translation of: 'Le bouclier arverne'. Paris : Dargaud, 1968.
ISBN 0-340-21394-9 : £1.80
(B77-04971)

Goscinny. Asterix and the Goths / text by Goscinny ; drawings by Uderzo ; translated [from the French] by Anthea Bell and Derek Hockridge. — Leicester : Knight Books, 1977. — 47p : of col ill, col map ; 21cm. — (Colour knights)
This translation originally published: Leicester : Brockhampton Press, 1974. — Translation of: 'Astérix et les Goths'. Paris : Dargaud, 1963.
ISBN 0-340-22171-2 Pbk : £0.60
(B77-26427)

Goscinny. Asterix and the great crossing / text by Goscinny ; drawings by Uderzo ; translated [from the French] by Anthea Bell and Derek Hockridge. — London [etc.] : Hodder and Stoughton, 1977. — 48p : of col ill, col map ; 29cm.
This translation originally published: 1976. — Translation of: 'La grande traversée'. Neuilly : Dargaud, 1975.
ISBN 0-340-21589-5 Pbk : £0.95
(B77-21319)

Goscinny. Asterix and the soothsayer / text by Goscinny ; drawings by Uderzo ; translated [from the French] by Anthea Bell and Derek Hockridge. — London [etc.] : Hodder and Stoughton, 1976. — 48p : of col ill ; 29cm.
This translation originally published: Leicester : Brockhampton Press, 1975. — Translation of: 'Le devin'. Paris : Dargaud, 1972.
ISBN 0-340-20697-7 Pbk : £0.80
(B77-00866)

Goscinny. The Mansions of the Gods / text by Goscinny ; drawings by Uderzo ; translated [from the French] by Anthea Bell and Derek Hockridge. — Leicester : Knight Books, 1977. — 47p : col ill ; 21cm. — (An Asterix adventure) (Colour knight)
This translation originally published: Leicester : Brockhampton Press, 1973. — Translation of: 'Les Maisons des dieux'. Paris : Dargaud, 1971.
ISBN 0-340-21538-0 Pbk : £0.60
(B77-06804)

Hergé. Tintin and the Picaros / [by] Hergé ; [translated from the French by Leslie Lonsdale-Cooper and Michael Turner]. — London : Methuen, 1977. — [2],62p : chiefly col ill ; 30cm. — (Hergé. Adventures of Tintin)
This translation originally published: 1976. — Translation of: 'Tintin et les Picaros'. Paris : Casterman, 1976.
ISBN 0-416-57990-6 Pbk : £0.85
(B77-27981)

741.5'944 — French humorous strip cartoons. *Collections from individual artists. Latin texts*
Goscinny. Asterix apud Gothos / composuit Goscinny ; pinxit Uderzo ; in Latinum convertit Rubricastellanus. — Stuttgardiae [i.e. Stuttgart] : Sumptibus Deltae ; Leicester : Brockhampton Press, 1976. — 47p : chiefly col ill, col map ; 30cm.
Ill. on lining papers. — Translation of: 'Astérix et les Goths'. Paris : Dargaud, 1963.
Unpriced
(B77-32757)

741.5'944 — French humorous strip cartoons. *Collections from individual artists. Welsh texts*
Goscinny. Asterix a Cleopatra / testun gan Goscinny ; lluniau gan Uderzo ; troswyd o'r Ffrangeg gan Alun Jones. — Caerdydd [i.e. Cardiff] : Gwasg y Dref Wen, 1976. — 48p : col ill, col map ; 30cm.
Translation of: 'Astérix et Cléopâtre'. Paris : Dargaud, 1965.
ISBN 0-904910-26-1 : £1.85
(B77-04333)

Goscinny. Asterix y Galiad / testun gan Goscinny ; lluniau gan Uderzo ; troswyd o'r Ffrangeg gan Alun Jones. — Caerdydd [i.e. Cardiff] : Gwasg y Dref Wen, 1976. — 48p : col ill, col map ; 30cm.
Translation of: 'Astérix le Gaulois'. Paris : Dargaud, 1961.
ISBN 0-904910-25-3 : £1.85
(B77-04334)

Goscinny. Asterix ym Mhrydain / testun gan Goscinny ; lluniau gan Uderzo ; troswyd o'r Ffrangeg gan Alun Jones. — Caerdydd [i.e. Cardiff] : Gwasg y Dref Wen, 1976. — 48p : col ill, col map ; 30cm.
Translation of: 'Astérix chez les Bretons'. Paris : Dargaud, 1966.
ISBN 0-904910-27-x : £1.85
(B77-04335)

741.5'973 — American comics. *Encyclopaedias*
Fleisher, Michael L. The encyclopedia of comic book heroes / [by] Michael L. Fleisher, assisted by Janet E. Lincoln. — New York : Collier Books ; London : Collier Macmillan.
Vol.1 : Batman. — 1976. — ii-xxi,387p : ill, facsims ; 28cm.
ISBN 0-02-080090-8 Pbk : £6.75
(B77-11996)

Vol.2 : Wonder Woman. — 1976. — ii-xxiii, 253p : ill, facsims ; 28cm.
ISBN 0-02-080080-0 Pbk : £6.00
(B77-11997)

741.5'973 — American humorous cartoons. *Collections from individual artists*
Arno, Peter. Peter Arno's sizzling platter. — London : Duckworth, 1977. — [7],118p : of ill, port ; 29cm.
Spine title: Sizzling platter. — Originally published: New York : Simon and Schuster, 1949 ; London : Hale, 1952.
ISBN 0-7156-1269-7 : £3.95
(B77-27982)

Hamilton, William, *b.1939.* Introducing William Hamilton. — London : Wildwood House, 1977. — [96]p : of ill ; 18x20cm.
'Of the 90 drawings in this book 37 appeared originally in "The New Yorker" ... the remainder were syndicated internationally under the title "The New Society" by Chronicle Features' - title page verso.
ISBN 0-7045-0306-9 Pbk : £2.50
(B77-33346)

Hamilton, William, *b.1939.* William Hamilton's anti-social register. — Harmondsworth [etc.] : Penguin, 1977. — [191]p : of ill ; 18x21cm.
Originally published: San Francisco : Chronicle Books, 1974.
ISBN 0-14-004384-5 Pbk : £1.95
(B77-22025)

Hart, Johnny. BC it's a funny world / [by] Johnny Hart. — London : Coronet, 1976. — [127]p : of ill ; 18cm.
Originally published: New York : Fawcett Publications, 1974.
ISBN 0-340-20762-0 Pbk : £0.50
(B77-03686)

Thurber, James. Men, women and dogs / [by] James Thurber. — [1st ed. reprinted] ; with a new introduction by Wilfrid Sheed. — London : W.H. Allen, 1977. — 224p : of ill ; 24cm.
This ed. originally published: New York : Dodd, Mead, 1975.
ISBN 0-491-01958-0 : £4.50
(B77-17660)

741.5'973 — American humorous cartoons. *Collections. Periodicals*
Cracked. — London (30 Langham St., W1N 5LB) : Byblos Productions Ltd.
No.1- ; [1976?]-. — [1976?]-. — chiefly ill ; 28cm.
Monthly. — 38p. in 1st issue.
Sd : £0.25
(B77-30472)

741.5'973 — American humorous cartoons. Special subjects: Children. Christian life. Prayer. *Collections from individual artists*
Ketcham, Hank. Well God I goofed again / by Hank Ketcham. — London : Collins, 1976. — [65]p : chiefly col ill ; 19cm.
Ill. on lining papers. — Originally published: San Francisco : Determined Productions, 1975.
ISBN 0-00-184921-2 : £1.00
(B77-03687)

741.5'973 — American humorous strip cartoons. *Collections from individual artists*
Hart, Johnny. BC, life is a 50p paperback / [by] Johnny Hart. — London : Coronet, 1977. — [127]p : of ill ; 18cm.
Originally published: as 'BC truckin' on down'. New York : Fawcett Publications, 1975.
ISBN 0-340-21784-7 Pbk : £0.50
(B77-18913)

Parker, Brant. The wizard of Id frammin at the jim jam frippin in the krotz / [by] Brant Parker and Johnny Hart. — London : Coronet, 1977. — [127]p : of ill ; 18cm.
This collection originally published: New York : Fawcett, 1974.
ISBN 0-340-21817-7 Pbk : £0.50
(B77-32043)

Schulz, Charles Monroe. Watch out, Charlie Brown : selected cartoons from 'You're out of sight, Charlie Brown'. Vol.2 / [by] Charles M. Schulz. — London : Coronet, 1977. — [127]p : of ill ; 18cm.
Originally published: New York : Fawcett Publishing, 1975. — 'You're out of sight, Charlie Brown' originally published: New York : Holt, Rinehart and Winston, 1970.
ISBN 0-340-21797-9 Pbk : £0.50
(B77-28769)

741.5'973 — American humorous strip cartoons. *Collections from individual artists. Juvenile literature*
Emberley, Ed. W.O.O., the Wizard of Op / by Ed Emberley. — London : Dent, 1977. — [32] p : chiefly ill ; 23cm.
Originally published: as 'The Wizard of Op'. Boston, Mass. : Little, Brown, 1975.
ISBN 0-460-06794-x : £1.95 : CIP rev.
(B77-07509)

741.5'994 — Australian humorous cartoons. *Collections from individual artists*
Kim, *b.1941.* Love is : cartoons from the 'Daily mail' / [by Kim]. — [London] : [Associated Newspapers].
No.11. — [1977]. — [80]p : of ill ; 13cm.
Cover title. — 'Copyright 1971 Los Angeles Times Syndicate' - note.
Pbk : £0.30
(B77-22026)

741.6 — COMMERCIAL ART

741.6'01'48 — Graphic design. Symbols. *Dictionaries*

A dictionary of graphic clichés / compiled by Philip Thompson & Peter Davenport. — London (61 North Wharf Rd, W2 1LA) : Pentagram Design.
[ABC]. — [1976]. — [24]p : ill, facsims ; 21cm. — (Pentagram papers ; 1)
Fold. covers.
ISBN 0-905739-00-0 Sd : £1.00
(B77-00853)

741.6'05 — Graphic design. *Serials*

Graphic lines. — Preston (c/o Preston Polytechnic, Corporation St., Preston, Lancs.) : Harris Press.
1975 / edited by Duncan Glen. — 1975. — 56p : ill(incl 1 col) ; 23cm.
ISBN 0-905735-00-5 Pbk : Unpriced
(B77-00313)

741.6'0941 — Commercial arts. *Great Britain. Illustrations. Serials*

Association of Illustrators. The Association of Illustrators annual. — London : Studio Vista.
1. — 1976. — [164]p : of ill(some col) ; 29cm.
'A permanent record of an Exhibition of Illustration held at Thumb Gallery, 20/21 D'Arblay Street, London W.1., from 11th to 30th October 1976'. — Index.
ISBN 0-289-70757-9 : £9.95
(B77-10477)

741.64'0942 — English illustrations. Illustrations for books, 1790-1914. Illustrations. *Lists*

Ray, Gordon Norton. The illustrator and the book in England from 1790 to 1914 / [by] Gordon N. Ray ; [formal bibliographical descriptions by Thomas V. Lange ; photography by Charles V. Passela]. — New York : Pierpont Morgan Library ; London [etc.] : Oxford University Press, 1976. — iii-xxxiii,336p,leaf of plate : ill(some col), facsims, ports ; 31cm.
'The present volume depends almost entirely on the collection of ... [the author]' - Preface. — Ill. on lining papers. — Bibl.: p.317-325. — Index.
ISBN 0-19-519883-2 : £33.00
(B77-03156)

741.64'2'09034 — Illustrated children's books. Illustrations, 1794-1950. *Illustrations*

When we were young : two centuries of children's book illustration / [compiled by] William Feaver. — London : Thames and Hudson, 1977. — 96p : chiefly ill(some col) ; 28cm.
ISBN 0-500-27075-9 Pbk : £2.95
(B77-13162)

741.65 — American illustrated magazines & British illustrated magazines. Special subjects: Science fiction. Illustrations, ca 1920-ca 1975. *Illustrations*

Science fiction art / compiled & introduced by Brian Aldiss. — London : New English Library, 1975. — 128p : chiefly ill(some col) ; 38cm.
Index.
ISBN 0-450-02772-4 Pbk : £2.95
(B77-18293)

741.65 — British illustrated magazines. Special subjects: Science fiction: Science fiction monthly. Illustrations, 1970-1975. *Illustrations*

Visions of the future / [compiled by Janet Sacks]. — [London] : New English Library, 1976. — 128p : chiefly col ill ; 35cm.
'Compiled ... from ... "Science Fiction Monthly" ...' - title page verso.
ISBN 0-450-02835-6 : £5.95
(B77-05556)

741.65 — Illustrated magazines in English. Special subjects: Horror. Illustrations, 1800-1974. *Illustrations*

Terror! : a history of horror illustrations from the pulp magazines / [compiled by] Peter Haining ; designed by Christopher Scott. — London : Souvenir Press, 1976. — 176p : chiefly ill, facsims(some col) ; 28cm.
ISBN 0-285-62257-9 : £4.95
(B77-01670)

741.67'2 — Men's clothing. Fashion design. Drawings. Techniques. *Manuals*

Ireland, Patrick John. Drawing and designing menswear / [by] Patrick John Ireland. — London : Batsford, 1976. — 96p : chiefly ill ; 25cm.
ISBN 0-7134-3227-6 : £3.95
ISBN 0-7134-3228-4 Pbk : £2.95
(B77-02478)

741.9 — DRAWINGS. COLLECTIONS

741.9'411 — Arts. Patronage. Organisations. *Scotland. Scottish Arts Council. Exhibits: Scottish drawings. Dingwall, Kenneth. Catalogues*

Dingwall, Kenneth. Kenneth Dingwall : paintings, drawings and constructions : [catalogue of an exhibition held at] the Scottish Arts Council Gallery, 19 Charlotte Square, Edinburgh, 10 June to 3 July 1977. — Edinburgh (19 Charlotte Sq., Edinburgh) : Scottish Arts Council, 1977. — 3-71p : chiefly ill(some col), port ; 22x23cm.
Fold. cover.
ISBN 0-902989-41-3 Pbk : Unpriced
Primary classification 759.9411
(B77-25794)

741.9'411 — Scottish drawings. Mackintosh, Charles Rennie. Special subjects: Flowering plants. *Illustrations*

Mackintosh, Charles Rennie. Architectural sketches & flower drawings / by Charles Rennie Mackintosh ; [text by] Roger Billcliffe. — London : Academy Editions, 1977. — 96p : chiefly ill(some col) ; 30cm.
Bibl.: p.13.
ISBN 0-85670-315-x : £6.95
ISBN 0-85670-149-1 Pbk : £3.95
Primary classification 720'.22'2
(B77-13759)

741.9'42 — Art galleries. *London. Camden (London Borough). Courtauld Institute of Art. Gallery. Exhibits: English landscape drawings, 1700-1900. Catalogues*

Courtauld Institute of Art. English landscape drawings and watercolours from the collections of the Courtauld Institute of Art : [catalogue of an exhibition held at the] Courtauld Institute Galleries, Woburn Square, London WC1, May-June 1977. — London (Woburn Sq., W.C.1) : The Institute, 1977. — iv,14p ; 22cm.
Sd : Unpriced
Primary classification 758'.1'0942
(B77-32763)

741.9'42 — Art galleries. *London. Greenwich (London Borough). Woodlands Art Gallery. Exhibits: English drawings. Cooke, Jean & Cummings, Diana. Catalogues*

Woodlands Art Gallery. Jean Cooke and Diana Cumming : paintings and drawings : [catalogue of an exhibition held] 5 to 27 June 1976 [at] Woodlands Art Gallery. — London ([c/o Woodlands Art Gallery], 90 Mycenae Rd, SE3 7SE) : London Borough of Greenwich, [1976]. — [11]p : ill ; 21cm.
ISBN 0-9504033-9-3 Sd : Unpriced
Primary classification 759.2
(B77-11337)

741.9'42 — Art galleries. *London. Kensington and Chelsea (London Borough). Taranman Limited. Exhibits: English drawings. Brown, Ralph, b.1928. Catalogues*

Taranman Limited. Ralph Brown : a new sculpture & recent drawings : [catalogue of an exhibition held at] Taranman ... 14 October-15 November 1976. — [London] ([236 Brompton Rd, S.W.3]) : [Taranman Ltd], [1976]. — [19] p : ill ; 25cm.
Limited ed. of 300 copies. — Bibl.: p.[19].
Sd : £1.75
Also classified at 730'.92'4
(B77-33944)

741.9'42 — Art galleries. *London. Kensington and Chelsea (London Borough). Taranman Limited. Exhibits: English drawings. Meadows, Bernard. Catalogues*

Taranman Limited. Bernard Meadows : drawings for sculpture : [catalogue of an exhibition held at] Taranman ... 12 November-31 December 1975. — [London] ([236 Brompton Rd, S.W.3]) : [Taranman Ltd], [1975]. — [14]p,8 leaves of plates : ill ; 24cm.
Limited ed. of 400 copies. — Bibl.: p.[14].
Pbk : £2.50
(B77-33945)

741.9'42 — Art galleries. *London. Westminster (London Borough). Fischer Fine Art Limited. Exhibits: English abstract drawings. Stephenson, Cecil. Catalogues*

Stephenson, Cecil. Cecil Stephenson, 1889-1965 : paintings, gouaches and drawings, 1932-1957 : [catalogue of an exhibition held at Fischer Fine Art Ltd] October-November 1976. — London (30 King St., St James's, S.W.1) : Fischer Fine Art Ltd, [1976]. — [14]p : ill(some col), port ; 18cm.
ISBN 0-904867-09-9 Sd : £0.80
Primary classification 759.2
(B77-01686)

741.9'42 — Art galleries. Exhibits: English drawings. Donagh, Rita. *Great Britain. Catalogues*

Donagh, Rita. Rita Donagh, paintings and drawings : [catalogue of an exhibition held at the] Whitworth Art Gallery, University of Manchester, Whitworth Park, Manchester M15 6ER, 26 February-9 April 1977 ... [and elsewhere]. — [Manchester] : Whitworth Art Gallery ; [London] : Arts Council of Great Britain, 1977. — [48]p : chiefly ill(some col), facsim, maps, port ; 20x22cm.
ISBN 0-7287-0127-8 Sd : £1.20
Primary classification 759.2
(B77-13782)

741.9'42 — Art galleries. Exhibits: English drawings. Farington, Joseph. *England. Catalogues*

Farington, Joseph. Joseph Farington, watercolours and drawings : [catalogue of an exhibition held at] Bolton Museum and Art Gallery 16 July to 13 August 1977, Hastings Museum and Art Gallery 27 August to 9 October 1977, [and at] Ashmolean Museum, Oxford 5 November to 3 December 1977. — [Bolton] : Bolton Metropolitan Borough Arts Department, [1977]. — 3-116p : ill, port ; 20x21cm.
Pbk : £1.00
(B77-26428)

741.9'42 — English drawings. Adler, Jeremy. *Illustrations*

Adler, Jeremy. The Amsterdam quartet / [by] Jeremy Adler. — London (47 Wetherby Mansions, SW5 9BH) : Alphabox Press, 1976. — 1v. : of ill ; 18cm.
Five sheets ([5]p.) in polythene bag. — Limited ed. of 250 copies of which 50 are numbered and signed by the author.
ISBN 0-904504-07-7 : £0.25
ISBN 0-904504-08-5 Signed ed. : £1.50
(B77-11998)

741.9'42 — English drawings. Baskin, Leonard. *Illustrations*

Hughes, Ted. Cave birds / poems by Ted Hughes ; drawings by Leonard Baskin. — London : Scolar Press, 1975. — 1v. ; 74cm.
Limited ed. of 100 signed, numbered copies. — Folder ([11]fold leaves) and [1],10 sheets : of ill. all in portfolio. — '... each poem is accompanied by a facsimile of a draft selected from the poet's working papers' - colophon.
£125.00
Primary classification 821'.9'14
(B77-10530)

741.9'42 — English drawings. Constable, John, b.1776. Special subjects: Suffolk. East Bergholt region, 1796-1832. *Illustrations*

Kenyon, Lionel Frederick Robert. As John Constable saw it / [by L.F.R. Kenyon]. — Dedham (Duchy Barn, Dedham, Essex) : Council for the Protection of Rural England, Countryside Centre, [1976]. — [11]p : ill ; 30cm.
ISBN 0-9505348-0-3 Sd : £0.25
Primary classification 914.26'48
(B77-00507)

741.9'42 — English drawings. Lowry, Laurence Stephen. *Illustrations*

Lowry, Laurence Stephen. The drawings of L.S. Lowry : public and private / with an introduction and notes by Mervyn Levy. — London : Jupiter Books, 1976. — 31p,[21],282p of plates : ill(some col), facsim, ports ; 30cm.
Bibl.: p.31.
ISBN 0-904041-69-7 : £12.50
(B77-27983)

741.9'42 — English drawings. Pre-Raphaelitism. Special subjects: England. Social conditions, ca 1850-ca 1860. *Critical studies*

Grieve, Alastair Ian. The art of Dante Gabriel Rossetti - 1. 'Found' ; [and], 2. The Pre-Raphaelite modern-life subject / [by] A.I. Grieve. — Norwich (65 Newmarket Rd, Norwich) : Real World Publications, 1976. — [3],58p : ill, facsim ; 30cm.
Bibl.: p.[3].
Pbk : £2.50
Primary classification 756
(B77-14851)

741.9'42 — English drawings. Rider, Bevan. Special subjects: Great Britain. Harness horses. *Illustrations*

Rider, Bevan. Horses in harness today / [by] Bevan Rider. — London : Kaye and Ward, 1977. — 128p,plate : ill(incl 1 col) ; 23cm.
ISBN 0-7182-1148-0 : £3.50
Primary classification 636.1'4
(B77-28695)

741.9'42 — English drawings. Vicari, Andrew. *Illustrations*
Algosaibi, Ghazi A. From the Orient and the desert : poems / by Ghazi A. Algosaibi ; drawings by Andrew Vicari. — Stocksfield [etc.] : Oriel Press, 1977. — vi,25,[1]p : ill ; 22cm.
Limited ed. of 1000 numbered copies. — Ill. on lining papers.
ISBN 0-85362-165-9 : £5.00
Primary classification 821
(B77-18339)

741.9'42 — English illustrations. Caldecott, Randolph. Illustrations for books. *Illustrations*
Caldecott, Randolph. Randolph Caldecott : 'lord of the nursery' / [text by] Rodney K. Engen. — London (30 Notting Hill Gate, W.11) : Oresko Books Ltd, 1976. — 104p : ill(some col), facsims, port ; 30cm.
Bibl.: p.104.
ISBN 0-905368-02-9 : £7.95
ISBN 0-905368-03-7 Pbk : £3.95
(B77-15980)

Caldecott, Randolph. The Randolph Caldecott picture book. — London [etc.] : F. Warne, 1976. — 128p in various pagings : ill(some col) ; 24cm.
Contents: The diverting history of John Gilpin - The house that Jack built - The queen of hearts - The farmer's boy.
ISBN 0-7232-1997-4 : £2.50
(B77-02479)

Caldecott, Randolph. Randolph Caldecott's John Gilpin and other stories. — London [etc.] : F. Warne, 1977. — 80p : chiefly ill(some col) ; 31cm.
Contents: The diverting history of John Gilpin. — The house that Jack built - The frog he would a-wooing go - The milkmaid.
ISBN 0-7232-2062-x : £4.50
(B77-33946)

741.9'42 — English illustrations. Greenaway, Kate. Illustrations for children's books. *Illustrations*
Greenaway, Kate. Kate Greenaway / [text by] Rodney K. Engen. — London : Academy Editions [etc.], 1976. — 68p : chiefly ill(some col), port ; 30cm.
Bibl.: p.61-68.
ISBN 0-85670-246-3 : £5.95
ISBN 0-85670-241-2 Pbk : £2.95
(B77-04336)

Greenaway, Kate. Kate Greenaway. — London : Academy Editions, 1977. — [4],50 leaves : chiefly col ill, port ; 24cm.
Leaves printed on both sides.
ISBN 0-85670-358-3 Pbk : £2.95
(B77-33947)

Greenaway, Kate. The Kate Greenaway book / [compiled by] Bryan Holme. — [London] : F. Warne, 1976. — 144p : ill(some col), facsims, music ; 24cm.
Originally published: New York : Viking Press, 1976. — Bibl.: p.140-142. — Index.
ISBN 0-7232-1987-7 : £4.95
Also classified at 820'.8'09282
(B77-04337)

741.9'42 — English illustrations. Rackham, Arthur. Illustrations for Ring des Nibelungen by Wagner, Richard. *Illustrations*
Wagner, Richard. [Der Ring des Nibelungen. English]. The ring of the Niblung / [by] Richard Wagner ; with illustrations by Arthur Rackham ; translated by Margaret Armour. — London : Heinemann.
Ill. on lining papers. — Facsimile reprint of: 1st ed. of this translation. 1910-11.
Siegfried ; &, Twilight of the gods. — 1976. — vi,182p,[29]leaves of plates : ill(chiefly col) ; 25cm.
ISBN 0-434-61980-9 : £9.00
Primary classification 782.1'2
(B77-04347)

The Rhinegold ; &, The Valkyrie. — 1976. — vi,160p,[33]leaves of plates : ill(chiefly col) ; 25cm.
ISBN 0-434-61981-7 : £9.00
Primary classification 782.1'2
(B77-04348)

741.9'42 — English illustrations. Robinson, Charles. Illustrations for children's books. *Illustrations*
Robinson, Charles. Charles Robinson / [text] by Leo de Freitas. — London : Academy Editions [etc.], 1976. — 88p : chiefly ill(some col) ; 30cm.
Bibl.: p.83-87.
ISBN 0-85670-277-3 : £6.95
ISBN 0-85670-282-x Pbk : £3.95
(B77-18914)

741.9'42 — Museums. *Cambridgeshire. Cambridge. Fitzwilliam Museum. Exhibits: English drawings. Constable, John, b.1776. Catalogues*
Fitzwilliam Museum. John Constable R.A., 1776-1837 : a catalogue of drawings and watercolours, with a selection of mezzotints by David Lucas after Constable for 'English landscape scenery', in the Fitzwilliam Museum, Cambridge / [text by] Reg Gadney. — [London] : Arts Council of Great Britain, 1976. — 151p : ill(some col), facsims, ports ; 24cm.
Index.
ISBN 0-7287-0099-9 Pbk : Unpriced
Primary classification 759.2
(B77-03691)

741.9'42 — Museums. *Cardiff. National Museum of Wales. Exhibits: English drawings. John, Gwen. Catalogues*
John, Gwen. Gwen John at the National Museum of Wales / written by A.D. Fraser Jenkins. — Cardiff : The Museum, 1976. — [40]p : chiefly ill(some col), facsim, ports ; 16x23cm.
'All the works reproduced are in the collection of the Museum'.
ISBN 0-7200-0097-1 Sd : £0.85
Primary classification 759.2
(B77-23607)

741.9'42 — Museums. *Oxford. Oxfordshire. Ashmolean Museum. Exhibits: English drawings. Tolkien, John Ronald Reuel. Catalogues*
Ashmolean Museum. Catalogue of an exhibition of drawings by J.R.R. Tolkien at the Ashmolean Museum, Oxford, 14th December-27th February, 1976-1977 and at the National Book League, 7 Albemarle Street, London W1, 2nd March-7th April, 1977 / [selected and compiled by the Countess of Caithness and Ian Lowe]. — Oxford : Ashmolean Museum ; London : N.B.L., 1976. — [37]p : ill, port ; 24cm.
Cover title: Drawings by Tolkien. — Bibl.: p.[36]-[37].
ISBN 0-900090-42-1 Sd : Unpriced
ISBN 0-85353-251-6 (NBL) : Unpriced
(B77-07510)

741.9'42 — Museums. *Oxfordshire. Oxford. Ashmolean Museum. Exhibits: Drawings by teachers at Ruskin Drawing School, 1912-1930. Catalogues*
Ashmolean Museum. The Ruskin Drawing School under Sydney Carline (Master 1922-1929) and his staff : [catalogue of an exhibition held at the] Ashmolean Museum, Oxford, 9 July-28 August 1977. — Oxford : The Museum, 1977. — x,12p : 2 ill ; 21cm.
ISBN 0-900090-46-4 Sd : £0.75
(B77-27984)

741.9'429 — Art galleries. *London. Greenwich (London Borough). Woodlands Art Gallery. Exhibits: Welsh drawings. Llwyd Roberts, John Richard. Catalogues*
Woodlands Art Gallery. Llwyd Roberts : watercolours and drawings of places in the Borough of Greenwich : [catalogue of an exhibition held] 18 December 1976 to 18 January 1977 [at] Woodlands Art Gallery. — London ([c/o Woodlands Art Gallery], 90 Mycenae Rd, SE3 7SE) : London Borough of Greenwich, [1976]. — [15]p : ill ; 21cm.
Cover title: Llwyd Roberts, 1875-1940.
ISBN 0-9504033-6-9 Sd : Unpriced
Primary classification 759.29
(B77-11338)

741.9'43 — Art galleries. *London. Kensington and Chelsea (London Borough). Taranman Limited. Exhibits: German pastel drawings. Hartmann, Gerd. Catalogues*
Taranman Limited. Gerd Hartmann : die Welt als Wille und Verstellung : [catalogue of an exhibition held at] Taranman ... 20 April-21 May 1977. — [London] ([236 Brompton Rd, S.W.3]) : [Taranman Ltd], [1977]. — [19]p : ill ; 25cm.
English and German text. — Limited ed. of 300 copies.
Sd : £1.75
(B77-33948)

741.9'44 — French drawings. Degas, Edgar. *Catalogues*
Reff, Theodore. The notebooks of Edgar Degas : a catalogue of the thirty-eight notebooks in the Bibliothèque nationale and other collections / [by] Theodore Reff. — Oxford : Clarendon Press, 1976 [i.e. 1977]. — 2v.(xii,167p,[27]p of plates,[2] leaves of plates;[4]p, [272]p of plates : ill(some col), facsims ; 34cm.
'More than twelve hundred of the pages are reproduced ...' - book jacket. — Bibl.: p.153-154. — Index.
ISBN 0-19-817333-4 : £45.00
(B77-14327)

741.9'45 — Art galleries. *London. Camden (London Borough). Courtauld Institute of Art. Gallery. Exhibits: Italian drawings, 1590-1770. Catalogues*
Courtauld Institute of Art. Drawings by Guercino and other baroque masters : [catalogue of an exhibition held] February-March 1977 [at the] Courtauld Institute Galleries, Woburn Square, London WC1. — [London] ([20 Portman Sq., W.1]) : [The Institute], [1977]. — [2],25p ; 22cm.
Sd : Unpriced
(B77-17661)

741.9'45 — Art galleries. *New Jersey. Princeton. Princeton University. Art Museum. Exhibits: Italian drawings, 1395-1840. Catalogues*
Princeton University. *Art Museum.* Catalogue of Italian drawings in the Art Museum, Princeton University / by Felton Gibbons. — Princeton ; Guildford : Princeton University Press, 1977. — 2v.(xviii,272p;xxi p,[433]p of plates) : ill, ports ; 29cm.
Index.
ISBN 0-691-03888-0 : £48.50
(B77-28770)

741.9'45 — Italian drawings. Botticelli, Sandro. Illustrations for Divina commedia. *Illustrations*
Botticelli, Sandro. The drawings by Sandro Botticelli for Dante's 'Divine Comedy' : after the originals in the Berlin museums and the Vatican / [introductory text by] Kenneth Clark ; [commentaries compiled and written by George Robinson]. — London : Thames and Hudson, 1976. — 218p : ill(some col), facsim(on lining papers) ; 37cm.
'Extracts from Dante's "Divine Comedy" "The Inferno" "The Purgatorio" "The Paradiso" translated by John Ciardi' - title page verso.
ISBN 0-500-23256-3 : £35.00
Also classified at 851'.1
(B77-04972)

741.9'45 — Museums. *Oxfordshire. Oxford. Ashmolean Museum. Exhibits: Italian drawings, ca 1430-ca 1780. Catalogues*
Ashmolean Museum. Italian drawings in Oxford : from the collections of the Ashmolean Museum and Christ Church / text and commentary by Terisio Pignatti ; [translated from the Italian by Barbara Luigia la Penta]. — Oxford : Phaidon, 1977. — 256p : ill(chiefly col), ports(some col) ; 32cm.
In slip case. — Translation of: 'I grandi disegni italiani nelle collezioni di Oxford'. Milan : Silvana Editoriale d'Arte, 1976. — Bibl.: p.83-86. — Index.
ISBN 0-7148-1764-3 : £30.00
Also classified at 741.9'45
(B77-30473)

741.9'45 — Universities. Colleges. *Oxfordshire. Oxford. Christ Church, University of Oxford. Exhibits: Italian drawings, ca 1470-ca 1655. Catalogues*
Ashmolean Museum. Italian drawings in Oxford : from the collections of the Ashmolean Museum and Christ Church / text and commentary by Terisio Pignatti ; [translated from the Italian by Barbara Luigia la Penta]. — Oxford : Phaidon, 1977. — 256p : ill(chiefly col), ports(some col) ; 32cm.
In slip case. — Translation of: 'I grandi disegni italiani nelle collezioni di Oxford'. Milan : Silvana Editoriale d'Arte, 1976. — Bibl.: p.83-86. — Index.
ISBN 0-7148-1764-3 : £30.00
Primary classification 741.9'45
(B77-30473)

741.9'46 — Spanish drawings, 1400-1800. *Illustrations*
Angulo, Diego. A corpus of Spanish drawings / by Diego Angulo & Alfonso E. Pérez Sánchez. — London : Harvey Miller.
[Vol.2] : Madrid, 1600-1650. — 1977. — 199p : ill ; 34cm.
Bibl.: p.9-11. — Index.
ISBN 0-905203-06-2 : £35.00
(B77-30474)

741.9'489 — Danish illustrations. Nielsen, Kay. Illustrations for books. *Illustrations*
Nielsen, Kay. The unknown paintings of Kay Nielsen / edited by David Larkin ; with an elegy by Hildegarde Flanner. — London [etc.] : Pan Books, 1977. — [19]p,42 leaves of plates : chiefly ill(chiefly col) ; 29cm.
Also published: Bearsville, N.Y. : Peacock Press, 1977.
ISBN 0-330-25235-6 Pbk : £2.95
(B77-31337)

741.9'492 — Art galleries. *Greater Manchester (Metropolitan County). Manchester. Whitworth Art Gallery. Exhibits: Dutch landscape drawings from Musées Royaux des Beaux-Arts de Belgique, 1600-1700. Catalogues*
Musées Royaux des Beaux-Arts de Belgique. Landscape in Flemish and Dutch drawings of the 17th century from the collections of the Musée Royaux des Beaux-Arts de Belgique, Brussels : [catalogue of an exhibition held] 14th October to 15th December, 1976, Whitworth Art Gallery, University of Manchester / [selection and catalogue by Eliane de Wilde]. — Manchester (Whitworth Park, Manchester M15 6ER) : [Whitworth Art Gallery, University of Manchester], [1976]. — 94p : ill ; 26cm.
Bibl.: p.52. — Index.
ISBN 0-903261-06-5 Pbk : £1.50
Also classified at 741.9'493
(B77-07511)

741.9'492 — Art galleries. *London. Camden (London Borough). Courtauld Institute of Art. Gallery. Exhibits: Dutch drawings. Collections: Witt Collection. Catalogues*
Courtauld Institute of Art. Dutch drawings from the Witt Collection. — [London] ([Woburn Sq., WC1H 0AA]) : Courtauld Institute of Art.
The Witt Collection is part of the Institute's collection of drawings.
Pt 1 : Landscape. — [1972]. — [4],13p ; 22cm.
Catalogue of an exhibition held at the Institute Galleries, January to March 1972.
Sd : Unpriced
(B77-12582)

Pt 2 : Other than landscape. — [1977]. — [2], 22p : ill ; 22cm.
Catalogue of an exhibition held at the Institute Galleries, November 1976-February 1977.
Sd : Unpriced
(B77-12583)

741.9'492 — Dutch illustrations. Bruna, Dick. Illustrations for children's books. *Critical studies*
Kohnstamm, Dolf. The extra in the ordinary : children's books by Dick Bruna / [by] Dolf Kohnstamm ; [illustrations, Dick Bruna ; translated from the Dutch by Patricia Crampton]. — [London] ([4A Hereford Rd, W2 4AA]) : Mercis Ltd, 1976. — 29p : ill(chiefly col), facsims(chiefly col) ; 30cm.
Folder ([3]p.: col. facsims) as insert. — Originally published: in Dutch. s.l. : s.n., 1974?.
Pbk : £2.50
(B77-28771)

741.9'493 — Art galleries. *Greater Manchester (Metropolitan County). Manchester. Whitworth Art Gallery. Exhibits: Flemish landscape drawings from Musées Royaux des Beaux-Arts de Belgique, 1600-1700. Catalogues*
Musées Royaux des Beaux-Arts de Belgique. Landscape in Flemish and Dutch drawings of the 17th century from the collections of the Musée Royaux des Beaux-Arts de Belgique, Brussels : [catalogue of an exhibition held] 14th October to 15th December, 1976, Whitworth Art Gallery, University of Manchester / [selection and catalogue by Eliane de Wilde]. — Manchester (Whitworth Park, Manchester M15 6ER) : [Whitworth Art Gallery, University of Manchester], [1976]. — 94p : ill ; 26cm.
Bibl.: p.52. — Index.
ISBN 0-903261-06-5 Pbk : £1.50
Primary classification 741.9'492
(B77-07511)

741.9'493 — Museums. *London. Camden (London Borough). British Museum. Exhibits: Flemish drawings. Rubens, Sir Peter Paul. Catalogues*
Rubens, *Sir* Peter Paul. Rubens, drawings and sketches : catalogue of an exhibition at the Department of Prints and Drawings in the British Museum, 1977 / by John Rowlands. — London : British Museum Publications Ltd for the Trustees of the British Museum, 1977. — 173p : ill(some col), ports(some col) ; 29cm.
ISBN 0-7141-0753-0 : £6.95 : CIP rev.
ISBN 0-7141-0754-9 Pbk : £3.00
(B77-15393)

741.9'497 — Yugoslav naive drawings, 1930-1976. *Illustrations*
Naive art : paintings from Yugoslavia : 120 illustrations / selected and introduced by Boris Kelemen. — Oxford : Phaidon, 1977. — [16]p, 96p of plates : chiefly ill(chiefly col), ports(some col) ; 42cm. — (Giant art paperbacks)
Originally published: with text in Serbo-Croat as 'Naivno slikarstvo u Jugoslaviji'. Zagreb : Spektar, 1977. — Bibl.: p.[16].
ISBN 0-7148-1795-3 Pbk : £4.50
Primary classification 759.9497
(B77-31348)

741.9'71 — Arts. Patronage. Organisations. *Great Britain. Arts Council of Great Britain. Exhibits: Canadian drawings. Martin, Agnes. Catalogues*
Arts Council of Great Britain. Agnes Martin, paintings and drawings, 1957-1975. — [London] : Arts Council, 1977. — 47p : col ill ; 21cm.
Catalogue of an exhibition organised by the Arts Council at the Hayward Gallery. — Bibl.: p.41-43. — Includes facsimile of manuscript of 'We are in the midst of reality responding with joy', the text of a lecture given by Agnes Martin at Yale University, New Haven, Connecticut, on 5 April 1976.
ISBN 0-7287-0128-6 Pbk : £1.35
Primary classification 759.11
(B77-13781)

741.9'73 — American drawings, to 1973. *Critical studies*
Stebbins, Theodore E. American master drawings and watercolors : a history of works on paper from colonial times to the present / [by] Theodore E. Stebbins, Jr, with the assistance of John Caldwell and Carol Troyen. — New York [etc.] ; London : Harper and Row [for] the Drawing Society, 1976. — xv,464p : ill(some col), facsims, ports(some col) ; 29cm.
Bibl.: p.437-453. — Index.
ISBN 0-06-014068-2 : £37.50
ISBN 0-06-014069-0 Pbk : £11.95
Primary classification 759.13
(B77-30490)

741.9'73 — American illustrations. Kent, Rockwell. *Illustrations*
Kent, Rockwell. The illustrations of Rockwell Kent : 231 examples from books, magazines and advertising art / selected by Fridolf Johnson with the collaboration of John F.H. Gorton ; with an introduction by Fridolf Johnson. — New York : Dover Publications [etc.] ; London : Constable, [1977]. — ii-xiv, 130p : chiefly ill, facsims ; 29cm.
Published in the United States: 1976. — Bibl.: p.129-130.
ISBN 0-486-23305-7 Pbk : £2.80
(B77-11999)

741.9'73 — Art galleries. *Dublin. National Gallery of Ireland. Exhibits: American drawings, ca 1760-ca 1920 from John Davis Hatch Collection. Catalogues*
Burger, Gary. 100 American drawings : [catalogue of a] loan exhibition from the collection of John Davis Hatch ... [held at the] National Gallery of Ireland, Dublin, 7th September-8th October 1976 ... [and elsewhere] / [by Gary Burger]. — Dublin (Merrion Sq., Dublin 2) : The Gallery, 1976. — [174]p : ill, ports ; 25cm. — (Heim Gallery. Heim exhibition catalogues ; no.26)
Bibl.: p.[72].
ISBN 0-903162-03-2 Pbk : Unpriced
(B77-04973)

741.9'73 — Art galleries. *Edinburgh. Fruit Market, Edinburgh. Exhibits: American drawings. Conde, Miguel. Catalogues*
Conde, Miguel. Miguel Conde, paintings and drawings : [catalogue of an exhibition held at] the Fruit Market ..., Edinburgh, Scotland, 10 July-7 August 1976. — Edinburgh : Scottish Arts Council, 1976. — [17]p : chiefly ill(some col), port ; 15x21cm.
ISBN 0-902989-32-4 Sd : £0.40
Primary classification 759.13
(B77-02490)

741.9'86'1 — Colombian drawings. Botero, Fernando. *Illustrations*
Botero, Fernando. Fernando Botero / [text by] Klaus Gallwitz ; [translated from the German by John Gabriel]. — London : Thames and Hudson, 1976. — 88p : chiefly ill(some col), ports ; 21x23cm. — (Art now)
Originally published: in German. Stuttgart : Gerd Hatje, 1976. — Bibl.: p.86-88.
ISBN 0-500-09117-x : £5.00
Primary classification 759.986'1
(B77-07524)

741.9'931 — New Zealand drawings. McIntyre, Peter. Special subjects: New Zealand. Wellington, 1948-1974. *Illustrations*
McIntyre, Peter. Peter McIntyre's Wellington. — Wellington [N.Z.] [etc.] ; London : A.H. and A.W. Reed, 1975. — [76]p : chiefly ill(some col), ports ; 28cm.
Col. ill. tipped in. — Ill. on lining papers.
ISBN 0-589-00936-2 : £12.60
Primary classification 993.12'7
(B77-01956)

743 — DRAWINGS. SPECIAL SUBJECTS

743'.4 — Drawings. Special subjects: Human figures. Techniques. *Manuals*
Mugnaini, Joseph. The hidden elements of drawing / [by] Joseph Mugnaini. — New York [etc.] ; London : Van Nostrand Reinhold, 1974. — 211p : ill ; 28cm.
ISBN 0-442-25722-8 Pbk : £5.95
(B77-18294)

743'.4 — Man. Anatomy. *For visual arts*
Kramer, Jack, *b.1923.* Human anatomy & figure drawing : the integration of structure and form / [by] Jack Kramer. — New York ; London [etc.] : Van Nostrand Reinhold, 1972. — 143p : ill(some col) ; 29cm.
Bibl.: p.139. — Index.
ISBN 0-442-24516-5 : Unpriced
(B77-21320)

743'.43 — Drawings. Special subjects: Men: Nudes. Techniques. *Manuals*
Sheppard, Joseph. Drawing the male figure / by Joseph Sheppard. — New York : Watson-Guptill ; London : Pitman, 1976. — 159p : chiefly ill ; 29cm.
Bibl.: p.159.
ISBN 0-273-00974-5 : £8.50
(B77-09851)

743'.44 — Women. *Illustrations. For drawings*
Jennings, Thomas. The female figure in movement / [by] Thomas Jennings. — New York : Watson-Guptill ; London : Pitman, [1977]. — 175p : of ill ; 31cm.
Originally published: New York : Watson-Guptill, 1971.
ISBN 0-273-00976-1 Pbk : £4.95 : CIP rev.
(B77-07988)

743'.49 — Drawings. Special subjects: Man. Face. *Manuals. Juvenile literature*
Emberley, Ed. Ed Emberley's drawing book of faces. — London [etc.] : Dent, 1977. — 32p : of col ill ; 20x25cm.
Originally published: Boston, Mass. : Little, Brown, 1975. — Index.
ISBN 0-460-06808-3 : £2.50 : CIP rev.
(B77-23599)

743'.49 — Drawings. Special subjects: Man. Hands. Techniques. *Manuals*
Hogarth, Burne. Drawing dynamic hands / by Burne Hogarth. — New York : Watson-Guptill ; London : Pitman, 1977. — 144p : chiefly ill ; 29cm.
Bibl.: p.142. — Index.
ISBN 0-273-01049-2 : £7.95 : CIP rev.
(B77-21321)

743'.49 — Drawings. Special subjects: Man. Head. Techniques. *Manuals*
Gordon, Louise. Drawing the human head : including techniques and the anatomy of the head and neck / [by] Louise Gordon. — London : Batsford, 1977. — 120p : ill, 2 ports ; 26cm.
Index.
ISBN 0-7134-0236-9 : £4.50
ISBN 0-7134-0237-7 Pbk : £2.50
(B77-19529)

743'.6 — Drawings. Special subjects: Animals. *Manuals. Juvenile literature*
Emberley, Ed. Ed Emberley's drawing book of animals. — London [etc.] : Dent, 1977. — [32] p : of col ill, port ; 20x25cm.
Originally published: Boston, Mass. : Little, Brown, 1970.
ISBN 0-460-06809-1 : £2.50 : CIP rev.
(B77-23600)

743'.6 — Drawings. Special subjects: Animals. Techniques. *Manuals*
Davy, Don. Drawing animals and birds / [by] Don Davy. — Poole : Blandford Press, 1977. — 96p : chiefly ill ; 25cm.
ISBN 0-7137-0839-5 Pbk : £2.50
(B77-30475)

743'.6'09 — Books on zoology. Illustrations, 1480-1910. Special subjects: Animals. *Critical studies*
Knight, David, *b.1936.* Zoological illustration : an essay towards a history of printed zoological pictures / [by] David Knight. — Folkestone : Dawson [etc.], 1977. — xii,204p : ill, facsims ; 23cm.
Ill. on lining papers. — Bibl. — Index.
ISBN 0-7129-0786-6 : £10.00 : CIP rev.
(B77-20466)

743'.8'36 — Landscape drawings. Techniques. *Manuals*
Cozens, Alexander. [A new method of assisting the invention in drawing original compositions of landscape]. A new method of landscape / [by] Alexander Cozens. — [1st ed. reprinted] ; with a new introduction by Michael Marqusee. — [London] : Paddington Press, 1977. — xi,[3], 35,[28]p : ill ; 28cm. — (Masterpieces of the illustrated book)
Facsimile reprint of: 1st ed., originally published as 'A new method of assisting the invention in drawing original compositions of landscape'. London : The author, 1785.
ISBN 0-448-22120-9 Pbk : £2.50
(B77-15394)

Johnston, Frederick Charles. Sketching & painting : a step by step introduction / [by] F.C. Johnston. — London [etc.] : Macmillan, 1976. — 5-157p : ill(some col) ; 26cm.
Index.
ISBN 0-333-19143-9 : £3.95
Primary classification 751.4
(B77-00875)

743'.9'210904 — Drawings. Special subjects: Nudes, 1900-1975. *Illustrations*
From naked to nude : life drawing in the twentieth century / [compiled by] Georg Eisler. — London : Thames and Hudson, 1977. — 104p : chiefly ill(some col) ; 28cm.
Bibl.: p.104.
ISBN 0-500-27087-2 Pbk : £2.95
(B77-13769)

745 — DECORATIVE AND MINOR ARTS
745'.03 — Decorative arts. *Encyclopaedias*
Fleming, John, *b.1919.* The Penguin dictionary of decorative arts / [by] John Fleming and Hugh Honour. — London : Allen Lane, 1977. — 896p : ill ; 22cm.
ISBN 0-7139-0941-2 : £9.50
(B77-27985)

745'.092'2 — Decorative arts. Artists, 1875-1930. Monograms, signatures & symbols. *Dictionaries*
Haslam, Malcolm. Marks and monograms of the modern movement, 1875-1930 : a guide to the marks of artists, designers, retailers and manufacturers from the period of the aesthetic movement to art deco and style moderne / [by] Malcolm Haslam. — Guildford [etc.] : Lutterworth Press, 1977. — 192p ; 26cm.
Index.
ISBN 0-7188-2291-9 : £7.50
(B77-33949)

745'.092'4 — French decorative arts. Gallé, Emile. *Illustrations*
Garner, Philippe. Emile Gallé / [by] Philippe Garner. — London : Academy Editions, 1976. — 167p : ill(some col), ports(1 col) ; 32cm.
Bibl.: p.163. — Index.
ISBN 0-85670-129-7 : £17.50
(B77-26429)

745'.0941 — British folk art, 1600-1900
Ayres, James. British folk art / [by] James Ayres. — London : Barrie and Jenkins, 1977. — 144p,[24]p of plates : ill(some col), coat of arms, facsims, plans ; 26cm.
Bibl.: p.138. — Index.
ISBN 0-214-20269-0 : £8.50
(B77-32758)

745'.0944 — Museums. *Avon. Bristol. City of Bristol Museum and Art Gallery. Exhibits: French decorative arts. Art nouveau style. Catalogues*
Witt, Cleo. French Art Nouveau from English collections : [catalogue of an exhibition held at the] City of Bristol Museum and Art Gallery April 15th-May 28th 1977, Brighton Museum and Art Gallery June 14th-July 24th 1977 / by Cleo Witt. — [Bristol] ([Queen's Rd, Bristol BS8 1RL]) : City of Bristol Museum and Art Gallery, [1977]. — [1],29p : ill, 2 ports ; 20x21cm.
Index.
ISBN 0-900199-08-3 Sd : Unpriced
Also classified at 745'.0944
(B77-22740)

745'.0944 — Museums. *East Sussex. Brighton. Brighton Museum and Art Gallery. Exhibits: French decorative arts. Art nouveau style. Catalogues*
Witt, Cleo. French Art Nouveau from English collections : [catalogue of an exhibition held at the] City of Bristol Museum and Art Gallery April 15th-May 28th 1977, Brighton Museum and Art Gallery June 14th-July 24th 1977 / by Cleo Witt. — [Bristol] ([Queen's Rd, Bristol BS8 1RL]) : City of Bristol Museum and Art Gallery, [1977]. — [1],29p : ill, 2 ports ; 20x21cm.
Index.
ISBN 0-900199-08-3 Sd : Unpriced
Primary classification 745'.0944
(B77-22740)

745'.0947 — Russian decorative arts, 1682-1894
In the Russian style / edited by Jacqueline Onassis ; with the co-operation of the Metropolitan Museum of Art ; introduction by Audrey Kennett ; designed by Bryan Holme. — London : Thames and Hudson, 1977. — 184p : ill(some col), facsim, ports ; 29cm.
Originally published: New York : Viking Penguin, 1976. — Bibl.: p.183.
ISBN 0-500-23266-0 : £10.00
Primary classification 391'.00947
(B77-21069)

745'.0947 — Russian folk art
Pronin, Alexander. Russian folk arts / [by] Alexander and Barbara Pronin. — South Brunswick [etc.] : Barnes ; London : Yoseloff, 1975. — 192p,[12]p of plates : ill(some col) ; 32cm.
Bibl.: p.184. — Index.
ISBN 0-498-01276-x : £8.00
(B77-28772)

745'.0952 — Japanese decorative arts, 900-1900. *Conference proceedings*
Artistic personality and decorative style in Japanese art : [proceedings of] a colloquy held 21-23 June 1976 / edited by William Watson. — [London] : University of London School of Oriental and African Studies, [1977]. — [7], 187p : ill, facsims ; 26cm. — (Colloquies on art & archaeology in Asia ; no.6)
ISBN 0-7286-0042-0 Pbk : £4.00
(B77-22027)

745'.09748 — Pennsylvania Dutch decorative arts. Motifs
Lichten, Frances. Folk art motifs of Pennsylvania / [by] Frances Lichten. — New York : Dover Publications [etc.] ; London : Constable, 1976. — viii,71p,[16]p of plates : ill(some col) ; 29cm. — (Dover pictorial archive series)
Originally published: New York : Hastings House, 1954.
ISBN 0-486-23303-0 Pbk : £2.40
(B77-12000)

745.1 — Antiques. *Collectors' guides*
Coysh, Arthur Wilfred. Don't throw it away / [by] A.W. Coysh. — Newton Abbot [etc.] : David and Charles, 1977. — 104p,8p of plates : ill, facsims ; 22cm.
Index.
ISBN 0-7153-7429-x : £3.50
(B77-33950)

Hughes, Therle. Introduction to antiques / [by] Therle Hughes. — [Feltham] : Country Life Books ; London [etc.] : Distributed by Hamlyn, 1977. — 144p : ill ; 23cm.
'... developed from material originally published by "Homes and Gardens" in 1971' - title page verso. — Index.
ISBN 0-600-30346-2 : £3.00
(B77-33951)

Mackay, James. Yesterday's junk, tomorrow's antiques / [by] John Bedford ; revised and updated by James Mackay. — London : Macdonald and Jane's, 1977. — vi,168p : ill, facsims ; 25cm.
Adaptations of: 'Looking in junkshops'. London : Parrish, 1961 ; 'More looking in junkshops'. London : Parrish, 1962 ; 'Still looking for junk'. London : Macdonald and Co., 1969. — Bibl.: p.163-167.
ISBN 0-356-08429-9 : £4.95
(B77-25780)

745.1 — Boxes, to ca 1930. *Collectors' guides*
Curtis, Tony, *b.1939.* Caddies & boxes / compiled by Tony Curtis. — [Galashiels] : [Lyle Publications], [1977]. — 3-126p : chiefly ill ; 16cm. — (Antiques and their values)
Index.
ISBN 0-902921-42-8 : £1.50
(B77-33952)

745.1 — Potential antiques. *Collectors' guides*
Bamford, Joan. Collecting antiques for the future / [by] Joan Bamford. — Guildford : Lutterworth Press : Richard Smart Publishing, 1976. — 184p : ill, facsims, map, ports ; 23cm.
Bibl.: p.173. — Index.
ISBN 0-7188-7008-5 : £4.50
(B77-05557)

745.1 — Small antiques
Van de Gohm, Richard. Collecting small antiques and bygones / [by] Richard van de Gohm. — London : Gifford, 1975. — 304p,[16]p of plates : ill(some col) ; 26cm.
Ill., text on lining papers. — Index.
ISBN 0-7071-0345-2 : £4.95
(B77-15981)

745.1 — Tableware: Collectors' plates. *Catalogues*
The **Bradford** book of collector's plates : the official guide to all editions traded on the world's largest exchange / the Bradford Exchange. — New York ; London [etc.] : McGraw-Hill.
1976 / edited under the direction of Nadja K. Bartels, John G. McKinven. — [1977]. — I12, [127],A18p : ill, ports ; 29cm.
Published in the United States: 1976. — Index.
ISBN 0-07-007057-1 : £8.25
(B77-14328)

745.1'028 — Antiques. Restoration. *Encyclopaedias*
Savage, George. The art and antique restorers' handbook : a dictionary of materials and processes used in the restoration & preservation of all kinds of works of art / by George Savage. — Revised ed. — London : Barrie and Jenkins, 1976. — [6],142p ; 23cm.
This ed. originally published: London : Barrie and Rockliff, 1967. — Bibl.: p.133. — Index.
ISBN 0-214-20268-2 : £2.50
Primary classification 069'.53
(B77-01135)

745.1'095 — Oriental antiques, to ca 1900
Moorhouse, Judith. Collecting Oriental antiques / [by] Judith Moorhouse ; with a chapter on ceramics by Dries Blitz. — London [etc.] : Hamlyn, 1976. — 128p : ill(some col) ; 29cm.
Ill. on lining papers. — Bibl.: p.125. — Index.
ISBN 0-600-36720-7 : £2.95
(B77-06805)

745.2 — INDUSTRIAL DESIGN
Walker, David. Design : the man-made object / prepared for the [Open University] Technology Foundation Course Team by David Walker with Nigel Cross. — Milton Keynes : Open University Press, 1976. — 100p : ill, plans ; 30cm. — (The man-made world, a foundation course ; units 33-34) (T100 ; 33-4)
With answers to warming-up exercises. — 'This unit, together with unit 32(1976), replaces units 32-4 first published in 1971' - title page verso.
ISBN 0-335-02547-1 Pbk : Unpriced
(B77-04974)

745.2 — Industrial design. *Conference proceedings*
Design for Need *(Conference), Royal College of Art, 1976.* Design for need : the social contribution of design : an anthology of papers presented to the Symposium at the Royal College of Art, London, April 1976 / edited by Julian Bicknell, Liz McQuiston. — Oxford [etc.] : Pergamon for ICSID, 1977. — [5],154p : ill ; 26cm.
'The idea for Design for Need ... came from many sources' - Foreword.
ISBN 0-08-021500-9 : £9.50
(B77-25096)

745.2'06'2417 — Industrial design. Organisations. *Ireland (Republic). Design Ireland*
Irish Export Board. Design Ireland : to promote and assist improvement in the standard of industrial design in Ireland / [Irish Export Board]. — Dublin (Merrion Hall, Strand Rd, Sandymount, Dublin 4) : The Board, [1977]. — [13]p : ill(some col), port ; 30cm.
Fold. cover.
Sd : Unpriced
(B77-32759)

745.2'07'1141 — Higher education institutions. Curriculum subjects: Industrial design. Courses. *Great Britain. Directories*
Design courses in Britain / Design Council. — London : The Council.
1977-78 ed. — 1977. — 40p ; 21cm.
ISBN 0-85072-057-5 Sd : £1.00
ISSN 0309-4499
(B77-11326)

745.4 — DESIGN AND DECORATION

745.4 — Design. Figure-ground relationships. *Manuals*

Bothwell, Dorr. Notan : the dark-light principle of design / [by] Dorr Bothwell and Marlys Frey. — New York ; London [etc.] : Van Nostrand Reinhold, [1977]. — 79p : ill ; 21cm.
Originally published: 1968.
ISBN 0-442-20732-8 Pbk : £2.80
(B77-10478)

745.4 — Design. Patterns. *Illustrations*

Proctor, Richard M. The principles of pattern : for craftsmen and designers / [by] Richard M. Proctor. — New York ; London [etc.] : Van Nostrand Reinhold, [1977]. — 135p,[4]leaves of plates : chiefly ill ; 21cm.
Originally published: 1969. — Bibl.: p.134-135.
ISBN 0-442-26639-1 Pbk : £3.75
(B77-09165)

745.4 — Form. *For design*

Kranz, Stewart. Understanding visual forms : fundamentals of two and three dimensional design / [by] Stewart Kranz and Robert Fisher ; [photography by Douglas Abbott and Robert Fisher]. — New York ; London [etc.] : Van Nostrand Reinhold, 1976 [i.e. 1977]. — 127p : ill ; 16x23cm.
'Based on the design continuum concept'. — Notebook format. — Published in the United States: 1976.
ISBN 0-442-24542-4 Pbk : £4.25
(B77-10875)

745.4 — Graphics. Background patterns. *Illustrations*

Hornung, Clarence Pearson. Background patterns, textures and tints : 92 full-page plates for artists and designers / [by] Clarence P. Hornung. — New York : Dover Publications ; London : Constable, 1976. — [95]p : of ill ; 28cm. — (Dover pictorial archive series)
ISBN 0-486-23260-3 Pbk : £2.10
(B77-00328)

745.4 — Moiré patterns. *Illustrations*

Grafton, Carol Belanger. Optical designs in motion with moiré overlays / [by] Carol Belanger Grafton. — New York : Dover Publications [etc.] ; London : Constable, 1976. — [31]p : of ill ; 31cm.
Plastic ill. sheet in pocket.
ISBN 0-486-23284-0 Sd : £2.25
(B77-05558)

745.4 — Three-dimensional designs

Wong, Wucius. Principles of three-dimensional design / [by] Wucius Wong. — New York ; London [etc.] : Van Nostrand Reinhold, 1977. — 112p : chiefly ill ; 20cm.
ISBN 0-442-29561-8 Pbk : £3.45
(B77-22028)

745.4'07'1041 — Schools. Curriculum subjects: Design. *Great Britain*

Eggleston, John. Developments in design education / [by] John Eggleston. — London : Open Books, 1976. — x,138p : ill, plans ; 21cm. — (The changing classroom)
Bibl.: p.133-136. — Index.
ISBN 0-7291-0097-9 : £3.90
ISBN 0-7291-0092-8 Pbk : £1.75
(B77-01671)

745.4'4 — Decorative arts. Designs, to 1880. *Illustrations*

Leighton, John. Suggestions in design : three thousand years of ornaments, styles, motifs : more than 1000 original drawings / by John Leighton ; with a new introduction by Edward Lucie-Smith. — New York ; London : Paddington Press, 1977. — 9,101,[17]p : of ill ; 28cm.
These illustrations originally published: London : Blackie, 1880.
ISBN 0-448-22615-4 Pbk : £2.95
(B77-14846)

745.4'4 — Design. Patterns, to 1976

Justema, William. Pattern : a historical panorama / [by] William Justema. — London : Elek, 1976. — vi,202p : chiefly ill ; 29cm.
Bibl.: p.198-199. — Index.
ISBN 0-236-40072-x : £10.00
(B77-16518)

745.4'44 — Design, 1900-1975. *Conference proceedings*

Conference on Twentieth Century Design History, *2nd, Middlesex Polytechnic, 1976.* Leisure in the twentieth century : history of design : fourteen papers given at the Second Conference on Twentieth Century Design History, 1976. — London : Design Council Publications : Distributed by Heinemann Educational, 1977. — 99p : ill, facsims, plans ; 30cm.
'... held at Middlesex Polytechnic in April 1976' - Introduction.
ISBN 0-435-86500-5 Pbk : £10.00
(B77-20467)

745.4'44 — European design, 1915-1930

Benton, Tim. The new objectivity / prepared for the [Open University] course team by Tim Benton with contributions from ... [others]. — Milton Keynes : Open University Press, 1975. — 80p,[32]p of plates : ill, facsims, plans ; 30cm. — (Arts, a third level course : history of architecture and design, 1890-1939 ; units 11-12) (A305 ; 11 and 12)
Filmstrip (13fr. colour. 35mm.) in plastic envelope as insert. — Bibl.: p.5-7.
ISBN 0-335-00705-8 Pbk : £2.75
Primary classification 724.9
(B77-28761)

745.4'49'24 — American designs. Rowe, William, b.1941. Special subjects: Organisms. *Illustrations*

Rowe, William, *b.1941.* Flora and fauna design fantasies / by William Rowe. — New York : Dover Publications [etc.] ; London : Constable, 1976. — [3],72p : chiefly ill ; 29cm.
ISBN 0-486-23289-1 Pbk : £2.10
(B77-00329)

745.4'49'51 — Chinese decorative arts. Motifs, to 1900. *Illustrations*

Style, motif and design in Chinese art / [compiled by] Michael Ridley. — Poole : Blandford Press, 1977. — 144p : of ill ; 23cm.
ISBN 0-7137-2502-8 : £3.25
(B77-16519)

745.5 — HANDICRAFTS

745.5 — Handicrafts. *Manuals*

Abeles, Kim Victoria. Crafts, cookery, and country living / [by] Kim Victoria Abeles. — New York ; London [etc.] : Van Nostrand Reinhold, 1976. — [9],165p : ill ; 28cm.
Bibl.: p.160-161. — Index.
ISBN 0-442-20236-9 Pbk : £5.65
Also classified at 641.5
(B77-01672)

Home handicrafts : an exciting new range of designs for the home and family / edited by Mary Harding. — [London] : Octopus Books, [1977]. — 3-254p : ill(chiefly col) ; 29cm.
Col. ill. on lining papers. — 'This book is adapted from "Magic Touch"' - p.7.
ISBN 0-7064-0610-9 : £4.95
(B77-32044)

Stokes, Peter. Working with materials / [by] Peter Stokes. — Sunbury-on-Thames [etc.] : Nelson, 1976. — 63p : ill(some col) ; 18x26cm. — (Nelson integrated craft ; 2)
ISBN 0-17-431061-7 Pbk : £0.95
(B77-04975)

745.5 — Handicrafts. *Manuals. Juvenile literature*

Bassingthwaighte, Inger. Presents for the family / [by] Inger Bassingthwaighte. — London : Studio Vista, 1977. — 44p : ill ; 26cm. — (Something to do)
Index.
ISBN 0-289-70693-9 : £2.25
(B77-18295)

Berry, Roland. Berry's book of cunning contraptions. — London : A. and C. Black, 1977. — 64p : ill ; 23cm.
Index.
ISBN 0-7136-1700-4 : £1.75
(B77-25097)

Brown, Rosalie. Goodchild's handicrafts for all seasons / devised and drawn by Rosalie Brown. — Wendover (70 Carrington Cres., Wendover, Bucks.) : John Goodchild [for] the Girl Guides Association.
Book no.3. — 1976. — 47p : ill ; 17cm.
Book no.3 has title: 'Handcrafts for all seasons'.
ISBN 0-903445-21-2 Sd : £0.30
(B77-11327)

Book no.4. — 1976. — 47p : ill ; 17cm.
Book no.4 has title: 'Handcrafts for all seasons'.
ISBN 0-903445-22-0 Sd : £0.30
(B77-11328)

Deacon, Eileen. 'Magpie' make and do / [by] Eileen Deacon ; illustrated by Laura Potter. — London : Independent Television Books Ltd : Arrow Books, 1977. — 96p : ill ; 20cm. — (Look-in books)
'In association with Thames Television'.
ISBN 0-09-915430-7 Pbk : £0.65
(B77-31338)

Evans, Hazel, *b.1928.* Breaktime / [by] Hazel Evans ; illustrated by Rowan Barnes Murphy. — London : Independent Television Books Ltd : Arrow Books, 1977. — 95p : ill ; 20cm. — (Look-in books)
ISBN 0-09-915500-1 Pbk : £0.65
(B77-30476)

Nossek, Patricia. What shall we make? / [by] Patricia Nossek ; illustrations by Philip Nossek. — Tadworth : World's Work, 1977. — 96p : ill ; 24cm.
ISBN 0-437-62713-6 : £3.50
(B77-22741)

Pountney, Kate. Creative crafts for children / [by] Kate Pountney. — London : Faber, 1977. — 3-64p : ill ; 26cm.
ISBN 0-571-10948-9 : £2.95 : CIP rev.
(B77-10479)

Scott, Nancy. Making presents / [by] Nancy Scott ; illustrations by Moira McGregor. — London : Pan Books, 1977. — 89p : ill ; 20cm. — (Piccolo craft books)
ISBN 0-330-25187-2 Pbk : £0.50
(B77-33347)

Young crafts / edited by Sue Walker. — South Melbourne ; London [etc.] : Macmillan, [1977]. — 72p : ill(some col) ; 25cm.
Published in Australia: 1976. — Bibl.: p.72.
ISBN 0-333-21070-0 : £2.95
(B77-09166)

745.5 — Handicrafts. *Primary school texts & middle school texts*

Hobbyhorse : a lucky dip of things to make / [editor-in-chief Miguel Azada ; translated from the Spanish]. — London : Studio Vista.
In 6 vols.
1 / [drawings by Javier Pereda ; photographs by Lea Levi]. — 1976. — 64p : chiefly col ill ; 28cm.
Translation of: 'Carrusel.1'. Madrid : Ediciones Altea, 1974. — Index.
ISBN 0-289-70744-7 : £1.50
(B77-13770)

Hobbyhorse : a lucky dip of things to make / [editor-in-chief Miguel Azada ; translated from the Spanish]. — London : Studio Vista.
In 6 vols.
2 / [drawings by Pilar Ruiz ; photographs by Lea Levi]. — 1976. — 64p : chiefly col ill ; 28cm.
Translation of: 'Carrusel.2'. Madrid : Ediciones Altea, 1974. — Index.
ISBN 0-289-70745-5 : £1.50
(B77-13771)

Hobbyhorse : a lucky dip of things to make / [editor-in-chief Miguel Azada ; translated from the Spanish]. — London : Studio Vista.
In 6 vols.
3 / [drawings by Javier Pereda ; photographs by Lea Levi]. — 1976. — 64p : chiefly ill(chiefly col) ; 28cm.
Translation of: 'Carrusel.3'. Madrid : Ediciones Altea, 1974. — Index.
ISBN 0-289-70746-3 : £1.50
(B77-13772)

Hobbyhorse : a lucky dip of things to make / [editor-in-chief Miguel Azada ; translated from the Spanish]. — London : Studio Vista.
In 6 vols.
4 / [drawings by Pilar Ruiz ; photographs by Lea Levi]. — 1976. — 64p : chiefly ill(chiefly col) ; 28cm.
Translation of: 'Carrusel.4'. Madrid : Ediciones Altea, 1974. — Index.
ISBN 0-289-70747-1 : £1.50
(B77-13773)

Hobbyhorse : a lucky dip of things to make / [editor-in-chief Miguel Azada ; translated from the Spanish]. — London : Studio Vista.
In 6 vols.
5 / [drawings by Javier Pereda ; photographs by Lea Levi]. — 1976. — 64p : chiefly ill(some col) ; 28cm.
Translation of: 'Carrusel.5'. Madrid : Ediciones Altea, 1975. — Index.
ISBN 0-289-70748-x : £1.50
(B77-13774)

Hobbyhorse : a lucky dip of things to make / [editor-in-chief Miguel Azada ; translated from the Spanish]. — London : Studio Vista.
In 6 vols.
6 / [drawings by Pilar Ruiz ; photographs by Lea Levi]. — 1976. — 64p : chiefly ill(some col) ; 28cm.
Translation of: 'Carrusel.6'. Madrid : Ediciones Altea, 1975. — Index.
ISBN 0-289-70749-8 : £1.50
(B77-13775)

745.5 — Handicrafts. *Primary school texts. Cards*
Akers, John. Squeezebox : craft activity pack / [by] John Akers and Marilyn Andreetti ; illustrations by Pam Warner. — Sunbury-on-Thames [etc.] : Nelson, 1976. — 1v. : ill(chiefly col) ; 28cm.
Fold. sheet ([1]p.) : 1 col. ill., folder ([4]p.), 10 cards ([20] sides) : col. ill. ; 25x75cm. fold. to 25x19cm. in polythene bag.
ISBN 0-17-412311-6 : Unpriced
(B77-12001)

745.5 — Handicrafts. Decoration. *Manuals*
Seguin, Robert. Ideas for decoration / [by] Robert Seguin and Marthe Seguin-Fontes ; translated [from the French] by Marion Hunter ; illustrations by the authors with the help of Jean-Philippe Seguin ; photographs by Boris Teplitzky. — London : Evans Bros, 1977. — 3-187p : ill(some col) ; 25cm.
Translation of: '757 idées pour tout décorer'. Paris : Editions Fleurus, 1977.
ISBN 0-237-44873-4 : £4.50
(B77-24379)

745.5 — Handicrafts. Special subjects: Fish. *Manuals. Juvenile literature*
Janvier, Jeannine. Fantastic fish you can make / by Jeannine Janvier ; photographs by Boris Téplitzky ; [translated from the French by Maxine Hobson]. — New York : Sterling [etc.] ; London : Distributed by Ward Lock, 1976. — 32p : ill(chiefly col) ; 22cm. — (Easy craft series)
Translation of: 'Merveilleux poissons'. Paris : Editions Fleurus, 1975. — Index.
ISBN 0-7061-2527-4 : £2.50
(B77-21323)

745.5 — Handicrafts. Special themes: Bible. *Manuals. Juvenile literature*
Stuart, Monica. Come, hear and see : creative activities for use with Bible stories / [by] Monica Stuart and Gill Soper ; with drawings by Juliet Renny. — London : Faber, 1976. — 96p : ill ; 19x25cm.
ISBN 0-571-10935-7 : £3.50
ISBN 0-571-11099-1 Pbk : £2.50
(B77-00867)

745.5 — Handicrafts using bottles & handicrafts using cans. *Manuals. Juvenile literature*
McPhee Gribble Publishers. Bottles & cans : using them again / written and produced by McPhee Gribble Publishers ; illustrated by David Lancashire. — Harmondsworth [etc.] : Puffin Books, 1977. — [34]p : chiefly ill(chiefly col) ; 20cm. — (Practical puffins)
Originally published: Harmondsworth : Kestrel Books, 1976.
ISBN 0-14-049140-6 Sd : £0.50
(B77-25781)

745.5 — Handicrafts using fruit & vegetables. *Manuals. Juvenile literature*
Smithson, Sheila. Playing with fruit and vegetables / [by] Sheila Smithson. — London : Studio Vista, 1976. — 44p : ill ; 26cm. — (Something to do)
Index.
ISBN 0-289-70692-0 : £2.25
Also classified at 641.6'4; 641.6'5
(B77-19530)

745.5 — Handicrafts using nuts & handicrafts using seeds. *Manuals*
Nassiet, Claude. What to make with nuts & grains / by Claude Nassiet ; photographs by Pierre Roche ; drawings by Jeannine Janvier ; [translated from the French by Maxine Hobson]. — New York : Sterling [etc.] ; London : Distributed by Ward Lock, 1976. — 32p : col ill ; 22cm. — (Easy craft series)
Translation of: 'Coques et grains'. Paris : Editions Fleurus, 1975. — Index.
ISBN 0-7061-2529-0 : £2.50
(B77-15395)

745.5 — Handicrafts using pine cones. *Manuals*
Ploquin, Geneviève. What to make with pine cones / by Geneviève Ploquin ; photographs by Boris Téplitzky ; [translated from the French by Maxine Hobson]. — New York : Sterling [etc.] ; London : Distributed by Ward Lock, 1976. — 32p : ill(chiefly col) ; 22cm. — (Easy craft series)
Translation of: 'Avec des pommes de pin'. Paris : Editions Fleuris, 1975. — Index.
ISBN 0-7061-2530-4 : £2.50
(B77-16520)

745.5 — Handicrafts using scrap materials. *Manuals*
Alkema, Chester Jay. Alkema's scrap magic : how to turn your trash can into a treasure chest / by Chester Jay Alkema ; photographs by the author. — New York : Sterling [etc.] ; London : Distributed by Ward Lock, 1976. — 120p : ill(chiefly col), port ; 25cm.
Index.
ISBN 0-7061-2504-5 : £7.95
(B77-25782)

745.5 — Handicrafts using scrap materials. *Manuals. Juvenile literature*
Law, Felicia. Junk / by Felicia Law ; pictures by Janet Ahlberg. — Glasgow [etc.] : Collins, 1977. — [64]p : col ill ; 24cm.
Cover title: Things to make from junk. — Originally published: 1974.
ISBN 0-00-103358-1 Pbk : £0.95
(B77-23601)

745.5 — Handicrafts using seashore materials. *United States. Manuals. Juvenile literature*
Kohn, Bernice. The beachcomber's book / by Bernice Kohn ; illustrated by Arabelle Wheatley. — Harmondsworth [etc.] : Puffin Books, 1976. — 96p : ill ; 20x23cm. — (Picture puffin)
Originally published: New York : Viking Press, 1970. — Bibl.: p.94. — Index.
ISBN 0-14-049158-9 Pbk : Unpriced
(B77-04338)

745.5'02'4054 — Handicrafts for children. *For parents & for teaching*
Arnold, Arnold. The world book of arts and crafts for children / [by] Arnold Arnold. — London : Pan Books, 1977. — 286p : ill ; 18cm. — (Child development series)
Originally published: New York : Crowell, 1975 ; London : Macmillan, 1976. — Index.
ISBN 0-330-25180-5 Pbk : £0.90
(B77-33348)

Arnold, Arnold. The world book of arts & crafts for children / [by] Arnold Arnold. — London [etc.] : Macmillan, 1976. — 286p : ill ; 23cm.
Spine title: Arts & crafts for children. — Originally published: New York : Crowell, 1975. — Index.
ISBN 0-333-21295-9 : £4.95
(B77-00868)

745.5'02'40543 — Handicrafts for children, 3-8 years. *For parents & for teaching*
Winer, Yvonne. Busy hands : craft activities for the very young / by Yvonne Winer ; photography by Ivan Fox. — London [etc.] : Angus and Robertson, 1977. — 48p : ill ; 22cm.
ISBN 0-207-13052-3 : £2.50
(B77-32046)

745.5'028 — Handicraft equipment. Making. *Manuals*
Abrams, A Jay. Building craft equipment : an illustrated manual / [by] A. Jay Abrams and Carol W. Abrams. — London [etc.] : Pitman, 1977. — 208p : ill ; 29cm.
Originally published: New York : Praeger, 1976.
ISBN 0-273-00065-9 : £6.50
(B77-06806)

745.5'0941 — Handicrafts. *Great Britain, ca 1880*
Wiseman, E J. Victorian do-it-yourself : handicrafts and pastimes of the 1880s / [by] E.J. Wiseman. — Newton Abbot [etc.] : David and Charles, 1976. — 168p : ill, plans ; 26cm.
'... selection of practical advice and technical drawings from "Amateur work"' - jacket.
ISBN 0-7153-7307-2 : £5.00
(B77-07989)

745.5'0951 — Handicrafts. *China*
Carter, Michael. Crafts of China / [by] Michael Carter. — London : Aldus Books, 1977. — 144p : ill(chiefly col), col map ; 27cm. — (Crafts of the world)
ISBN 0-490-00402-4 : £4.25
(B77-33349)

745.5'0972 — Handicrafts. *Mexico*
Sayer, Chloë. Crafts of Mexico / [by] Chloë Sayer ; photographed by Marcos Ortiz. — London : Aldus Books, 1977. — 144p : ill(chiefly col), col map ; 27cm. — (Crafts of the world)
Ill. on lining papers. — Bibl.: p.144.
ISBN 0-490-00400-8 : £4.25
(B77-18915)

745.51 — Handicrafts using toothpicks & handicrafts using ice-cream sticks. *Manuals*
Bowman, Bruce. Toothpick sculpture & ice-cream stick art / by Bruce Bowman. — New York : Sterling [etc.] ; London : Distributed by Ward Lock, 1976. — 64p,A-H p of plates : ill(some col) ; 21cm.
Index.
ISBN 0-7061-2523-1 : £3.95
(B77-15396)

745.53'1 — Handicrafts using leather. *Manuals*
Dorné, David. Easy-to-do leathercraft projects : with full-size templates / [by] David Dorné. — New York : Dover Publications [etc.] ; London : Constable, 1976. — 32p,[16]leaves of plates : ill ; 28cm.
ISBN 0-486-23319-7 Sd : £1.55
(B77-12002)

745.54 — Handicrafts using card. *Manuals. Juvenile literature*
Law, Felicia. Card / by Felicia Law ; pictures by Janet Ahlberg. — Glasgow [etc.] : Collins, 1977. — [64]p : col ill ; 24cm.
Cover title: Things to make from card. — Originally published: 1974.
ISBN 0-00-103357-3 Pbk : £0.95
(B77-24380)

745'.54 — Handicrafts using newspaper. *Manuals*
Eisner, Vivienne. Crafting with newspapers / by Vivienne Eisner & William Shisler ; drawings by Guy Brison-Stack. — New York : Sterling [etc.] ; London : Distributed by Ward Lock, 1976. — 48p : ill(some col) ; 20cm. — (Little craft book series)
Index.
ISBN 0-7061-2505-3 : £2.25
(B77-25783)

Eisner, Vivienne. The newspaper everything book : how to make 150 useful objects from old newspapers / [by] Vivienne Eisner and Adelle Weiss. — London : Kaye and Ward, 1977. — 127p : ill ; 28cm.
Originally published: New York : Dutton, 1975. — Index.
ISBN 0-7182-1154-5 : £3.50
ISBN 0-7182-1168-5 Pbk : £2.50
(B77-25098)

745.54 — Handicrafts using papier-mâché. *Manuals*
Capon, Robin. Papier mâché / [by] Robin Capon. — London : Batsford, 1977. — 96p : ill ; 21cm.
Bibl.: p.91. — Index.
ISBN 0-7134-3235-7 : £3.50
(B77-07990)

745.59 — Mosaics. Making. *Manuals*
Hutton, Helen. Mosaic making techniques / [by] Helen Hutton. — New ed. — London : Batsford, 1977. — 138p,[4]p of plates : ill(some col) ; 26cm.
Ill. on lining papers. — Previous ed.: published as 'Mosaic making', 1966. — Bibl.: p.133. — Index.
ISBN 0-7134-0258-x : £4.50
(B77-17003)

745.59'2 — Braided string animals. Making. *Manuals*
Morin, Claude. Braided cord animals you can make / by Claude Morin ; drawings by Wiegeist, photographs by Jean-Pierre Tesson ; [translated from the French by Maxine Hobson]. — New York : Sterling [etc.] ; London : Distributed by Ward Lock, 1976. — 32p : ill(some col) ; 22cm. — (Easy craft series)
Translation of: 'La ficelle trissée'. Paris : Editions Fleurus, 1974. — Index.
ISBN 0-7061-2524-x : £2.50
(B77-26430)

745.59'2 — Handicrafts. Special subjects: Birds. Making. *Manuals*
Janvier, Jeannine. Fabulous birds you can make / by Jeannine Janvier ; photographs by Jean-Pierre Tesson ; [translated from the French by Maxine Hobson]. — New York : Sterling [etc.] ; London : Distributed by Ward Lock, 1976. — 32p : ill(chiefly col) ; 22cm. — (Easy craft series)
Translation of: 'Merveilleux oiseaux'. Paris : Editions Fleurus, 1974. — Index.
ISBN 0-7061-2526-6 : £2.50
(B77-26431)

745.59'2 — Moving toys. Making. *Manuals*
McLaughlin, Terence. Working toys and models / [by] Terence McLaughlin. — London : Pelham, 1977. — 95p : ill ; 26cm. — (Pelham craft series)
ISBN 0-7207-0971-7 : £4.50
(B77-25099)

745.59'2 — Toy prehistoric animals. Making. *Manuals. Juvenile literature*
Dean, Audrey Vincente. Make a prehistoric monster / [by] Audrey Vincente Dean. — London : Faber, 1977. — 76p : ill ; 26cm.
ISBN 0-571-10802-4 : £3.95 : CIP rev.
ISBN 0-571-11140-8 Pbk : £2.25
(B77-13776)

745.59'2 — Toys made from corks. Making. *Manuals*
Ploquin, Genevieve. Cork toys you can make / by Genevieve Ploquin ; photographs by Jean-Pierre Tesson ; [translated from the French by Maxine Hobson]. — New York : Sterling [etc.] ; London : Distributed by Ward Lock, 1976. — 32p : ill(chiefly col) ; 22cm. — (Easy craft series)
Translation of: 'Bouchons dociles'. Paris : Editions Fleurus, 1974. — Index.
ISBN 0-7061-2525-8 : £2.50
(B77-22742)

745.59'2 — Toys of items associated with Indians of North America. Making. *Manuals*
Gogniat, Maurice. Indian toys you can make / by Maurice Gogniat ; photographs by Jean-Pierre Tesson ; [translated from the French by Maxine Hobson]. — New York : Sterling [etc.] ; London : Distributed by Ward Lock, 1976. — 32p : ill(chiefly col) ; 22cm. — (Easy craft series)
Translation of: 'Jeux d'Indiens'. Paris : Editions Fleurus, 1974. — Index.
ISBN 0-7061-2528-2 : £2.50
(B77-25100)

745.59'2 — Toys of items associated with Western states, United States, ca 1855-ca 1875. Making. *Manuals*
Gogniat, Maurice. Wild West toys you can make / by Maurice Gogniat ; photographs by Jean-Pierre Tesson ; [translated from the French by Maxine Hobson]. — New York : Sterling [etc.] ; London : Distributed by Ward Lock, 1976. — 32p : ill(chiefly col) ; 22cm. — (Easy craft series)
Translation of: 'Jeux du Far-West'. Paris : Editions Fleurus, 1975. — Index.
ISBN 0-7061-2531-2 : £2.50
(B77-18296)

745.59'2 — Wooden toys. Making. *Manuals*
Toys from wood : original designs / by Brian Brooks, Albert Lain and John Money ; edited by Peter Scaife. — London : Evans Bros, 1976. — 104p : ill, plans ; 26cm.
ISBN 0-237-44806-8 : £4.00
(B77-01673)

745.59'22 — Paper costume dolls. *Cut-out books*
Lowndes, Rosemary. Make your own history of costume / written and designed by Rosemary Lowndes and Claude Kaïler. — London : Macdonald and Jane's, 1977. — [95]p : chiefly col ill ; 30cm.
ISBN 0-356-08418-3 Pbk : £3.50
Also classified at 391'.009
(B77-25784)

745.59'22 — Paper dolls. *Cut-out books*
Amanda doll dressing book. — Maidenhead : Purnell, 1977. — [20]p : ill(some col) ; 26cm.
Sd : £0.15
ISBN 0-361-03794-5
Primary classification 823'.9'1J
(B77-12151)

Joanna doll dressing book. — Maidenhead : Purnell, 1977. — [20]p : ill(some col) ; 26cm.
Sd : £0.15
ISBN 0-361-03794-5
Primary classification 823'.9'1J
(B77-12156)

Katy doll dressing book. — Maidenhead : Purnell, 1977. — [20]p : ill(some col) ; 26cm.
Sd : £0.15
ISBN 0-361-03794-5
Primary classification 823'.9'1J
(B77-12157)

Tracy doll dressing book. — Maidenhead : Purnell, 1977. — [20]p : ill(some col) ; 26cm.
Sd : £0.15
ISBN 0-361-03794-5
Primary classification 823'.9'1J
(B77-12163)

Walt Disney's Cinderella doll dressing book. — Maidenhead : Purnell, 1977. — [20]p : ill(some col) ; 26cm.
Sd : £0.30
ISBN 0-361-03804-6
Primary classification 823'.9'1J
(B77-12164)

Walt Disney's Snow White doll dressing book. — Maidenhead : Purnell, 1977. — [20]p : ill(some col) ; 26cm.
Sd : £0.30
ISBN 0-361-03804-6
Primary classification 823'.9'1J
(B77-12165)

745.59'22 — Puppets. Making. *Manuals. Juvenile literature*
Evans, Delphine. The piccolo puppet book / [by] Delphine Evans ; cover and text illustrations by Juliet Stanwell-Smith. — London : Pan Books, 1977. — 95p : ill ; 20cm. — (Piccolo original)
ISBN 0-330-25040-x Pbk : £0.55
(B77-25785)

745.59'23 — Dolls' houses. Furniture. Making. *Manuals*
Duda, Margaret B. Dollhouse accessories : how to design and make them / by Margaret B. Duda ; photography by Jon Sheckler. — South Brunswick ; New York : Barnes ; London : Yoseloff, 1976. — 3-129p,[8]p of plates : ill(some col), port ; 27cm.
Originally published: 1975. — Bibl.: p.129.
ISBN 0-498-01557-2 : £4.00
(B77-30477)

745.59'23 — Dolls' houses. Making. *Manuals*
Fairlie, Barbara L. All about doll houses / by Barbara L. Fairlie with Charlotte L. Clarke ; photographs by Otto Maya ; drawings by Jaime Iribarren. — London : Hale, 1978. — 240p,[11] p of plates : ill(some col) ; 29cm.
Originally published: Indianapolis : Bobbs-Merrill, 1975. — Index.
ISBN 0-7091-6526-9 : £6.50
(B77-30478)

745.59'23'0973 — American dolls' houses, ca 1750. Making. *Manuals*
Woodruff, Marie. Early America in miniatures, the 18th century / by Marie Woodruff ; photography by Charles E. Woodruff. — New York : Sterling [etc.] ; London : Distributed by Ward Lock, 1976. — 176p,[8]p of plates : ill(some col) ; 26cm.
Index.
ISBN 0-7061-2510-x : £5.95
(B77-22743)

745.59'23'0973 — Museums. *New York (City). Museum of the City of New York. Stock: Dolls' houses: Stettheimer Dollhouse*
Noble, John, *b.1923.* A fabulous dollhouse of the twenties : the famous Stettheimer Dollhouse at the Museum of the City of New York / [by] John Noble. — New York : Dover Publications [etc.] ; London : Constable, 1976. — 2-48p : ill, port ; 28cm.
ISBN 0-486-23375-8 Sd : £1.25
(B77-19531)

745.59'24 — Felt ornaments. *Patterns*
Deems, Betty. Easy-to-make felt ornaments for Christmas and other occasions with full-size templates / by Betty Deems. — New York : Dover Publications [etc.] ; London : Constable, 1976. — 32p,16 leaves of plates : ill ; 28cm. — (Dover needlework series)
'... a new collection of ornaments from "Heirloom ornaments", published by Betty Deems in 1974 and "Heirloom ornaments II", published by Betty Deems in 1975' - title page verso.
ISBN 0-486-23389-8 Sd : £1.65
(B77-11329)

745.59'24 — Miniature soft toys. Making. *Manuals*
Greenhowe, Jean. Making miniature toys and dolls / [by] Jean Greenhowe. — London : Batsford, 1977. — 118p,[4]p of plates : ill(some col) ; 26cm.
ISBN 0-7134-3271-3 : £3.95
ISBN 0-7134-0799-9 Pbk : Unpriced
(B77-24381)

745.59'24 — Soft toy dinosaurs & soft toy dragons. Making. *Manuals*
Peake, Pamela. Pamela Peake's how to make dinosaurs and dragons. — Glasgow [etc.] : Collins, 1976. — 112p,[12]p of plates : ill(some col) ; 29cm.
Index.
ISBN 0-00-411837-5 : £4.95
ISBN 0-00-411839-1 Pbk : £1.95
(B77-10480)

745.59'24 — Soft toys. Making. *Manuals*
Bradshaw-Smith, Gillian. Soft toys with flair / [by] Gillian Bradshaw-Smith ; illustrated with drawings by the author and with photographs by Bob Hanson. — Newton Abbot [etc.] : David and Charles, 1976. — 128p,[8]p of plates : ill(some col) ; 25cm.
Originally published: as 'Adventures in toymaking'. New York : Taplinger, 1976.
ISBN 0-7153-7245-9 : £3.95
(B77-00870)

Gifts to make for children / [edited by Sarah Parr]. — London [etc.] : Marshall Cavendish, 1976. — 73p : ill(chiefly col) ; 30cm. — ([Golden Hands])
Ill. on lining papers. — 'This material was first published in "Golden Hands Monthly" and "Fashion Maker"' - title page verso.
ISBN 0-85685-188-4 : £1.99
(B77-12003)

Gray, Ilse. Soft toys, dolls and puppets in easy steps / [by] Ilse Gray. — London : Studio Vista, 1977. — 64p : col ill ; 29cm.
Bibl.: p.64.
ISBN 0-289-70758-7 : £2.25
(B77-25101)

745.59'28 — Balsa models. Making
Solarbo book of balsa models. — Kings Langley : Argus Books, 1976. — 99p : ill ; 26cm. — (MAP technical publication)
Previous ed.: Hemel Hempstead : Model and Allied Publications, 1968. — Index.
ISBN 0-85242-462-0 Pbk : £2.50
(B77-12584)

745.59'28 — Model villages. Making. *Manuals*
Williams, Guy Richard. Making a miniature village / [by] Guy R. Williams. — Harmondsworth [etc.] : Puffin Books, 1977. — 87,[1]p,[4]p of plates : ill, plan ; 20cm. — (Puffin books)
Originally published: London : Faber, 1970.
ISBN 0-14-030908-x Pbk : £0.75
(B77-17662)

745.59'28 — Plastics models. Airbrushing. *Manuals*
Goldman, Richard M. Airbrushing for modellers / by Richard M. Goldman and Murray Rubenstein. — 2nd ed. — London : Almark Publishing, 1977. — 48p : ill(some col) ; 20x21cm.
Previous ed.: 1974.
Pbk : £1.75
ISBN 0-85524-177-2
(B77-18916)

745.59'28 — Scale models. Decoration. *Manuals*
Huntley, Ian D. Painting and lining scale models / [by] Ian D. Huntley. — Kings Langley : Model and Allied Publications, 1976. — 94p : ill, plan ; 22cm. — (MAP technical publication)
ISBN 0-85242-479-5 : £3.50
ISBN 0-85242-454-x Pbk : £1.95
(B77-10481)

745.59'28 — Wooden model American buildings & wooden model American furniture. Making. *Manuals*
Maginley, C J. America in miniatures : how to make models of early American houses, furniture, and vehicles / [by] C.J. Maginley ; illustrated by Elizabeth D. McKee and James MacDonald ; photographs by Joseph Moffa. — New York ; London : Harcourt Brace Jovanovich, 1976. — x,99p : ill ; 24x27cm.
'Compiled from the author's "Models of America's past" and "Historic models of early America"' - Library of Congress Cataloguing in Publication data.
ISBN 0-15-105587-4 : £7.10
(B77-22029)

745.59'282 — Military models. Making. *Manuals*
Cassin-Scott, Jack. Making model soldiers of the world / [by] Jack Cassin-Scott. — Edinburgh [etc.] : J. Bartholomew, 1977. — 5-156p : ill(some col) ; 24cm.
Originally published: London : Stephen Hope Books, 1973. — Bibl.: p.148-149. — Index.
ISBN 0-7028-1016-9 Pbk : £1.95
(B77-22744)

Featherstone, Donald. Better military modelling / [by] Donald Featherstone. — London : Kaye and Ward, 1977. — 96p : ill ; 23cm.
Bibl.: p.95-96.
ISBN 0-7182-1447-1 : £2.25
(B77-12004)

745.59'282 — Military models. Painting & detailing. *Manuals*
Dilley, Roy. Painting & detailing military miniatures / by Roy Dilley & Bryan Fosten. — London : Almark Publishing, 1977. — 36p : ill(some col) ; 20x21cm. — (Focus on modelling techniques ; no.1)
ISBN 0-85524-281-7 Pbk : £1.50
(B77-30479)

745.59'282 — Model castles & forts. Construction. *Manuals. Juvenile literature*
Warner, Philip. Making model forts and castles / [by] Philip Warner. — London : Bell, 1976. — 64p : ill, plans ; 20cm.
ISBN 0-7135-1892-8 Pbk : £1.85
(B77-09852)

745.59'282 — Model soldiers. Making. *Manuals*
Windrow, Martin Clive. Model soldiers / [by] Martin Windrow and Gerry Embleton. — Cambridge : Stephens [for] Airfix Products Ltd, 1976. — 64p : ill ; 23cm. — ('Airfix magazine' guide ; 19)
ISBN 0-85059-234-8 : £1.40
(B77-00871)

745.59'3 — Art galleries. *Nebraska. Lincoln. Sheldon Memorial Art Gallery. Exhibits: American carved wooden decoy ducks. Catalogues*
Sheldon Memorial Art Gallery. The bird decoy : an American art form : a catalog of carvings exhibited at the Sheldon Memorial Art Gallery, Lincoln, Nebraska / edited by Paul A. Johnsgard. — Lincoln [Neb.] ; London : University of Nebraska Press, [1977]. — xii, 191p,[4]p of plates : ill(some col) ; 26cm.
Published in the United States: 1976. — Bibl.: p.185. — Index.
ISBN 0-8032-0887-1 : £14.40
(B77-13163)

745.59'32 — Lampshades. Making. *Manuals*
Lampshades to make / [edited by Linda Doeser]. — London [etc.] : Marshall Cavendish, 1976. — 88p : ill(chiefly col) ; 30cm. — (['Golden hands'])
'This material first appeared in other Marshall Cavendish publications' - title page verso. — Index.
ISBN 0-85685-193-0 : £2.95
(B77-27260)

745.59'33 — Decorative candles. Making. *Manuals*
Jameson, Norma. Tie-dye, batik and candlemaking in easy steps / [by] Norma Jameson and Ann Hirst-Smith. — London : Studio Vista, 1976. — 64p : ill(chiefly col) ; 28cm.
Bibl.: p.64.
ISBN 0-289-70723-4 : £1.95
Primary classification 746.6
(B77-08481)

745.59'41 — Handicrafts. Special themes: Christmas. *Manuals*
Innes, Jocasta. Christmas do-it-yourself / [by] Jocasta Innes. — London : Sphere, 1975. — 128p : ill ; 20cm.
ISBN 0-7221-4921-2 Pbk : £0.70
(B77-19532)

745.59'41 — Handicrafts using paper. Special themes: Christmas. *Juvenile literature. Cards*
Instruction cards for handicrafts. — Leicester : Dryad Press, 1976. — Portfolio : chiefly col ill ; 17x25cm.
Title supplied by cataloguer. — 8 cards ([16] sides).
ISBN 0-85219-117-0 : Unpriced
(B77-02480)

745.59'42 — Jewellery. Making. *Amateurs' manuals*
Clarke, Patti. Jewelry in easy steps / [by] Patti Clarke [et al.] ; [photographs by Peter Kibbles]. — London : Studio Vista, 1977. — 64p : col ill ; 29cm.
Bibl.: p.64.
ISBN 0-289-70720-x : £2.25
(B77-21324)

745.59'43 — Paper flowers. Making. *Manuals*
Janitch, Valerie. Paper flowers / [by] Valerie Janitch. — London : Ward Lock, 1976. — 96p : ill(some col) ; 27cm.
Index.
ISBN 0-7063-5047-2 : £3.50
(B77-12585)

745.59'43 — Ribbon flowers. Making. *Manuals*
Ounsworth, Magda. Ribbon flowermaking / by Magda Ounsworth and Anne Hamilton. — Helensburgh (24 Bain Cres., Helensburgh, Dunbartonshire) : The authors, 1976. — 63p : ill(some col) ; 26cm.
£2.20
(B77-30480)

745.6 — LETTERING, ILLUMINATION, HERALDIC DESIGN

745.6 — Calligraphy & manuscript illumination. *Manuals*
Johnston, Edward. Writing & illuminating, & lettering / by Edward Johnston ; with diagrams and illustrations by the author and Noel Rooke. — London : Pitman [etc.], 1977. — xxx,439p : ill, facsims ; 19cm.
Originally published: London : John Hogg, 1906.
ISBN 0-273-01064-6 Pbk : £4.95 : CIP rev.
(B77-07513)

745.6'1 — Lettering. *Manuals*
Hewitt, Graily. Lettering for students & craftsmen / by Graily Hewitt. — London : Seeley, 1976. — 3-336p : ill, facsims ; 20cm.
Facsimile reprint of: 1st ed., 1930. — Index.
ISBN 0-85422-135-2 : £6.95
(B77-21325)

Switkin, Abraham. Hand lettering today / [by] Abraham Switkin. — New York [etc.] ; London : Harper and Row, 1976. — xi,212p : ill ; 29cm.
ISBN 0-06-014204-9 : £7.95
(B77-33953)

745.6'1 — Lettering. Design
Biggs, John Reginald. Letter-forms & lettering : towards an understanding of the shapes of letters / [by] John R. Biggs. — Poole : Blandford Press, 1977. — 128p : ill, facsims, map ; 26cm.
Bibl.: p.128.
ISBN 0-7137-0795-x : £3.25
(B77-10876)

745.6'1 — Ornamental alphabets. *Illustrations*
Earnshaw, Anthony. Seven secret alphabets / [by] Anthony Earnshaw. — London : Cape, [1977]. — 64p : of ill ; 25cm.
Originally published: 1972.
ISBN 0-224-01383-1 Pbk : £2.50 : CIP rev.
(B77-05559)

Koch, Rudolf. The little ABC book of Rudolf Koch / [designed by Rudolf Koch and Berthold Wolpe ; cut in wood and metal by Fritz Kredel and Gustav Eichenauer]. — [1st ed. reprinted] ; with a memoir by Fritz Kredel and a preface by Warren Chappell. — Boston, Mass. : David R. Godine ; London ([16 Groveway, SW9 0AR]) : The Merrion Press [etc.], 1976. — [20]p,[29] leaves ; 15x23cm.
Folder ([4]p.) : 1 ill. as insert. — Facsimile reprint of: 1st ed., published as 'Das ABC Büchlein'. Leipzig : Insel-verlag, 1934.
ISBN 0-87923-196-3 : £6.00
(B77-02481)

Larcher, Jean. Fantastic alphabets / by Jean Larcher. — New York : Dover Publications ; London : Constable, 1976. — 3-72p : port ; 29cm. — (Dover pictorial archive series)
English and French foreword.
ISBN 0-486-23412-6 Pbk : £2.15
(B77-31339)

745.6'197 — Humanistic writing, ca 1410-1603
Bodleian Library. Humanistic script of the fifteenth and sixteenth centuries / [Bodleian Library]. — Oxford ([Broad St., Oxford]) : The Library, 1976[i.e.1977]. — 8p,[24]p of plates : facsims ; 22cm. — (Bodleian Library. Picture books)
Originally published: 1960.
ISBN 0-900177-39-x Sd : £0.60
(B77-14847)

745.6'197 — Italic writing. *Manuals*
Thomson, George Lawrie. The new better handwriting / [by] George L. Thomson. — Edinburgh : Canongate Publishing [etc.], 1977. — [2],45p : ill, geneal table, map ; 19x23cm.
Bibl.: p.44-45.
ISBN 0-903937-47-6 : £3.50
ISBN 0-903937-48-4 Pbk : Unpriced
(B77-30481)

745.6'197 — Latin alphabet. Calligraphy
Fairbank, Alfred. A book of scripts / by Alfred Fairbank. — [New ed.]. — London : Faber, 1977. — 47p,80p of plates : ill, facsims ; 21cm.
Previous ed.: Harmondsworth : Penguin, 1968. — Bibl.: p.39-42.
ISBN 0-571-10876-8 : £3.50
ISBN 0-571-11080-0 Pbk : £1.95
(B77-22745)

745.6'199'27 — Islamic calligraphy, to 1975. *Critical studies*
Khatibi, Abdelkebir. The splendour of Islamic calligraphy / [by] Abdelkebir Khatibi, Mohammed Sijelmassi ; [translated from the French by James Hughes]. — London : Thames and Hudson, 1976. — 254p : ill(some col), facsims(some col) ; 31cm.
Translation of: 'L'art calligraphique arabe'. Paris : Editions Du Chêne, 1976. — Bibl.: p.250-251.
ISBN 0-500-23252-0 : £18.00
(B77-03688)

745.6'7 — Illuminated manuscripts. Illuminations, to 700. *Critical studies*
Weitzmann, Kurt. Late Antique and Early Christian book illumination / [by] Kurt Weitzmann. — London : Chatto and Windus, 1977. — 127p : ill(chiefly col) ; 28cm.
Also published: as 'Late Antique-Early Christian painting'. New York : Braziller, 1977. — Bibl.: p.25-27.
ISBN 0-7011-2243-9 Pbk : £4.95 : CIP rev.
(B77-09853)

745.6'7'094 — Carolingian illuminated manuscripts. Illuminations. *Illustrations*
Carolingian painting / introduction by Florentine Mütherich ; provenances and commentaries by Joachim E. Gaehde. — London : Chatto and Windus, 1977. — 127p : ill(chiefly col) ; 28cm.
Bibl.: p.23.
ISBN 0-7011-2241-2 Pbk : £4.95 : CIP rev.
(B77-09167)

745.6'7'094 — Celtic illuminated manuscripts, ca 600-ca 800. Illuminations. *Critical studies*
Nordenfalk, Carl. Celtic and Anglo-Saxon painting : book illumination in the British Isles, 600-800 / [by] Carl Nordenfalk. — London : Chatto and Windus, 1977. — 127p : ill(chiefly col), facsims(chiefly col) ; 28cm.
Bibl.: p.27-28.
ISBN 0-7011-2242-0 Pbk : £4.95 : CIP rev.
Also classified at 745.6'7'0941
(B77-09854)

745.6'7'0941 — Anglo-Saxon illuminated manuscripts, ca 600-ca 800. Illuminations. *Critical studies*
Nordenfalk, Carl. Celtic and Anglo-Saxon painting : book illumination in the British Isles, 600-800 / [by] Carl Nordenfalk. — London : Chatto and Windus, 1977. — 127p : ill(chiefly col), facsims(chiefly col) ; 28cm.
Bibl.: p.27-28.
ISBN 0-7011-2242-0 Pbk : £4.95 : CIP rev.
Primary classification 745.6'7'094
(B77-09854)

745.7 — DECORATIVE COLOURING

745.7 — Handicrafts. Use of colour. *Manuals*
Colourcraft. — London : Search Press, 1976. — 124p : ill(chiefly col) ; 26cm.
'Some of the photographs, drawing and in a few cases texts in this volume appeared originally in books published in the Leisure Crafts series ...' - p.124.
ISBN 0-85532-363-9 : £4.25
(B77-08477)

745.7'3'0942 — English decorative arts, 1837-1901. Stencils. *Collections*
Day, Joanne Christene. Art nouveau : cut & use stencils : 66 full-size stencils printed on durable stencil paper / [by] Joanne C. Day. — New York : Dover Publications [etc.] ; London : Constable, 1977. — [32]leaves : of ill ; 28cm.
Cover title.
ISBN 0-486-23443-6 Pbk : £1.95
(B77-30482)

Grafton, Carol Belanger. Victorian cut & use stencils / [by] Carol Belanger Grafton. — New York : Dover Publications ; London : Constable [etc.], 1976. — [32]leaves : of ill ; 28cm.
Cover title. — '55 full-size stencils printed on durable stencil paper' - cover.
ISBN 0-486-23385-5 Pbk : £2.00
(B77-12586)

745.7'3'0973 — American decorative arts. Stencils, 1924-1934. Patterns. *Illustrations*
A treasury of stencil designs for artists and craftsmen / edited and with an introduction by Martin J. Isaacson and Dorothy A. Rennie. — New York : Dover Publications [etc.] ; London : Constable, 1976. — [3],60p : of ill ; 28cm. — (Dover pictorial archive series)
'... designs ... from the collection of Edward H. Bowers ... Most of them are taken from the notebook in which he recorded the stencil designs he used. The others are reproduced from actual stencils which were not recorded in his notebook, though they had been in his possession' - Introduction.
ISBN 0-486-23307-3 Pbk : £1.40
(B77-00330)

745.92 — FLOWER ARRANGEMENT
745.92 — Flower arrangement. *Manuals*
Fields, Nora. Flower arranging for parties / [by] Nora Fields. — South Brunswick [etc.] : Barnes ; London : Yoseloff, 1975. — 169p,[8]p of plates : ill(some col) ; 29cm.
Index.
ISBN 0-498-01316-2 : £6.25
(B77-27986)

Hicks, David, *b.1929.* The David Hicks book of flower arranging / as told to Maureen Gregson ; introduction by Julia Clements. — London [etc.] : Marshall Cavendish, 1976. — 88p : ill(chiefly col) ; 30cm.
Index.
ISBN 0-85685-171-x : £2.95
(B77-12005)

Massingham, Betty. 'Homes and gardens' book of flower arrangement / [by] Betty Massingham ; photographs by John Miller. — London [etc.] : Hamlyn, 1976. — 160p : col ill ; 33cm.
Index.
ISBN 0-600-34494-0 : £4.95
(B77-13164)

Smith, George, *b.1934.* Flower arranging in house and garden / [by] George Smith ; drawings by Charles Stitt. — London : Pelham, 1977. — 96p,[16]p of plates : ill(some col) ; 26cm.
Bibl.: p.90. — Index.
ISBN 0-7207-0958-x : £5.95
(B77-32047)

Stevenson, Violet. Flower arranging & house-plants / [by] Violet Stevenson. — London : Sphere, 1975. — 160p : ill(chiefly col) ; 22cm. — ('Good housekeeping' family library)
Originally published: London : Ebury Press, 1973. — Index.
ISBN 0-7221-3949-7 Pbk : £0.95
Also classified at 635.9'65
(B77-19533)

745.92 — Flowering plants. Preservation. *Manuals*
Bugbee, Audrey Steiner. How to dry flowers the easy way / [by] Audrey Steiner Bugbee ; with photographs by John Murphy and Timothy Cross. — Large print [ed.]. — London : Prior [etc.], 1977. — xiii,126p : ill ; 25cm.
Originally published: Boston, Mass. : Houghton Mifflin, 1975.
ISBN 0-86043-045-6 : £4.50
(B77-12006)

Everlasting flowers / edited by Moyna McWilliam and Dorothy Shipman. — London [etc.] : Marshall Cavendish, 1976. — 88,[1]p : ill(chiefly col) ; 30cm. — ([Golden Hands])
Col. ill. on lining papers.
ISBN 0-85685-170-1 : £2.50
(B77-12007)

Smith, Margaret. Pressed flowers / [text and models by Margaret Smith ; drawings by John M. Smith]. — London : Search Press, 1976. — 32p : ill(some col) ; 17cm. — (Leisure crafts ; 55)
Previous control number B7709855.
ISBN 0-85532-498-8 Sd : £0.50
(B77-09855)

745.92 — Handicrafts using cloth flowers. *Manuals*
Woods, Pamela. Flowers from fabrics / [by] Pamela Woods. — Newton Abbot [etc.] : David and Charles, 1976. — 120p : ill(some col) ; 27cm. — ([Step by step series])
Index.
ISBN 0-7153-7254-8 : £4.50
(B77-01674)

745.92 — Handicrafts using preserved plants. *Manuals*
Foster, Maureen. Flower preserving for beginners / by Maureen Foster ; drawings by Bryan Foster ; photographs by Ron Brockland. — London : Pelham, 1977. — 48p,[8]p of plates : ill(some col) ; 22cm. — (Craft and design)
Bibl.: p.48.
ISBN 0-7207-0955-5 : £3.50
(B77-33350)

745.92'252 — Ikebana. *Manuals*
Davidson, Georgie. Ikebana : the art of Japanese flower arrangement / by Georgie Davidson in collaboration with Beata Bishop ; [photography Ronald A. Chapman ; Sumie painting Mary Millar]. — London : Barrie and Jenkins, 1976. — 143,[1]p,[8]p of plates : ill(some col), facsim ; 29cm.
Originally published: London : W.H. Allen, 1967.
ISBN 0-214-20360-3 : £6.50
(B77-00331)

745.92'5 — Handicrafts using herbs. *Manuals*
Walker, Elizabeth, *b.1922.* Herbs for fun / [by] Elizabeth Walker ; illustrated by Linda Diggins. — London : Darton, Longman and Todd, 1977. — 96p,[4]p of plates : ill(some col) ; 18cm. — (Herbwise ; 4)
Bibl.: p.88-89. — Index. — Contains chapters on the use of herbs in perfumes & cookery.
ISBN 0-232-51368-6 Pbk : £0.95
(B77-33351)

745.92'6 — Abbeys & cathedrals. Flower arrangement. *England, 1966-1976*
Clements, Julia. Flowers in praise : church festivals and decorations / [by] Julia Clements. — London : Batsford, 1977. — 96p,[8]p of plates : chiefly ill(some col) ; 26cm.
ISBN 0-7134-3260-8 : £5.95
(B77-26432)

746 — TEXTILE HANDICRAFTS
746 — Needlework. *Manuals*
The **complete** book of knitting, crochet & embroidery. — London [etc.] : Marshall Cavendish, 1976. — [8],488p : ill(chiefly col) ; 28cm.
Spine title: Knitting, crochet & embroidery. — 'This material was first published ... in the publications "Golden hands monthly", "Encyclopedia of crafts" and "Fashion maker"' - title page verso. — Index.
ISBN 0-85685-198-1 : £4.95
(B77-25786)

Lowcock, Eileen. Needlework for pleasure / [by] Eileen Lowcock. — London : Sphere, 1975. — 160p : ill(some col) ; 22cm. — ('Good housekeeping' family library)
Originally published: London : Ebury Press, 1973. — Index.
ISBN 0-7221-3950-0 Pbk : £0.95
(B77-19534)

746 — Needlework. *Manuals. Juvenile literature*
Wigg, Dora. Let's sew / [by] Dora Wigg and Catherine Topham. — London : Evans Bros, 1977. — 32,[2]p : ill(chiefly col) ; 21cm. — (Starting points)
ISBN 0-237-44741-x Sd : £0.65
(B77-13777)

746 — Needlework. Designs
Zimiles, Martha Rogers. A treasury of needlework designs / [by] Martha Rogers Zimiles. — New York ; London [etc.] : Van Nostrand Reinhold, 1976. — 208p : chiefly ill ; 36cm.
Pierced for binder. — Index.
ISBN 0-442-29584-7 Pbk : £5.80
(B77-13165)

746 — Needlework. Special themes: American colonial artefacts. *Patterns*
Grow, Judith. Classic needlework : contemporary designs inspired by the American past / [by] Judith Grow ; with photographs by Kenneth Kaplowitz. — New York ; London [etc.] : Van Nostrand Reinhold, 1976. — 112p : ill(some col) ; 24cm.
Index.
ISBN 0-442-22881-3 : £10.50
(B77-14848)

746 — Needlework. Special themes: Bible. *Patterns. Juvenile literature*
Meyer, Carolyn. The needlework book of Bible stories / by Carolyn Meyer ; illustrated by Janet McCaffery. — New York ; London : Harcourt Brace Jovanovich, 1975 [i.e. 1976]. — [7],87p : ill ; 24cm.
Published in the United States: 1975.
ISBN 0-15-256793-3 : £1.85
(B77-07515)

746 — Textiles. Conservation. *Manuals*
Finch, Karen. Caring for textiles / [by] Karen Finch and Greta Putnam ; line drawings by Danielle Bosworth ; foreword by Donald King. — London : Barrie and Jenkins, 1977. — 104p : ill ; 26cm.
Bibl.: p.98. — Index.
ISBN 0-214-20396-4 : £3.95
(B77-26433)

746'.03 — Needlework. *Encyclopaedias*
Clabburn, Pamela. The needleworker's dictionary / [by] Pamela Clabburn ; American contributing editor Helene von Rosenstiel. — London [etc.] : Macmillan, 1976. — 296p : ill(some col), ports ; 29cm.
Text on lining papers. — Bibl.: p.288-292.
ISBN 0-333-18756-3 : £9.95
(B77-02482)

746'.04'63 — Handicrafts using felts. *Manuals. Juvenile literature*
Douet, Kathleen. All about felt / by Kathleen Douet and Valerie Jackson. — London : Pelham, 1977. — 48p,[8]p of plates : ill(some col) ; 22cm. — (Craft and design)
ISBN 0-7207-0936-9 : £3.50
(B77-33352)

746'.074 — Museums. Stock: Textiles. Collections. *Directories*
Textile collections of the world / editor Cecil Lubell. — London [etc.] : Studio Vista.
Vol.1 : United States & Canada : an illustrated guide to textile collections in United States and Canadian museums / with essays on the traditions of North American textile design by Andrew Hunter Whiteford, Robert Riley, Dorothy K. Burnham. — 1976. — 336p : ill(some col) ; 29cm.
Also published: New York : Van Nostrand Reinhold, 1976. — Index.
ISBN 0-289-70755-2 : £12.00
(B77-10482)

Vol.2 : United Kingdom, Ireland : an illustrated guide to textile collections in the United Kingdom and Ireland. — 1976. — 240p : ill(some col), map ; 29cm.
Originally published: New York : Van Nostrand Reinhold, 1975. — Index.
ISBN 0-289-70756-0 : £10.00
(B77-10483)

746'.076 — Needlework. *Questions & answers. Secondary school texts*
Hartley, K M. Topics and questions in needlework / [by] K.M. Hartley and J.M. Roe. — London : Heinemann Educational, 1977. — [5],74p : ill ; 25cm.
ISBN 0-435-42835-7 Pbk : £1.00
(B77-28773)

Hartley, K M. Topics and questions in needlework / [by] K.M. Hartley and J.M. Roe. — London : Heinemann Educational, 1977. — [5],116p : ill ; 25cm.
With answers. — Ill. on inside covers.
ISBN 0-435-42836-5 Pbk : £1.80
(B77-32760)

746'.0941 — Needlework. *Great Britain, 1837-1910*
Warren, Geoffrey. A stitch in time : Victorian and Edwardian needlecraft / [by] Geoffrey Warren. — Newton Abbot [etc.] : David and Charles, 1976. — 144p : ill, port ; 24cm.
Bibl.: p.137-139. — Index.
ISBN 0-7153-7218-1 : £4.95
(B77-01675)

746'.0947 — Needlework. Russian folk motifs. *Patterns*
[Russkiĭ narodnyĭ ornament. Vyp.1. *English. Selections].* Russian peasant design motifs for needleworkers and craftsmen / [selected by] V. Stasov. — New York : Dover Publications [etc.] ; London : Constable, 1976. — 32p : of ill ; 28cm. — (Dover pictorial archive series)
'... a new selection of 30 plates from "Russkiĭ narodnyĭ ornament. Vyp.1" [St Petersburg, Obshchestvo Pooshchreniia Khudozhnikov, 1872]' - title page verso.
ISBN 0-486-23235-2 Sd : £1.15
(B77-12008)

746'.0958'4 — Turkestan textiles
Leix, Alfred. Turkestan and its textile crafts / [by] Alfred Leix. — Basingstoke (Wheathold Green, Ramsdell, Basingstoke, Hants. RG26 5SA) : Crosby Press, 1974. — 54p : ill, map ; 18x24cm.
'This work was originally published as issue number forty of "CIBA Review" ; it was issued from Basle, Switzerland in August 1941' - title page verso.
ISBN 0-903580-10-1 : Unpriced
(B77-19535)

746.1 — HANDICRAFTS. SPINNING AND WEAVING
746.1'2 — Wool. Combing & spinning. *Amateurs' manuals*
Teal, Peter. Hand woolcombing and spinning : a guide to worsteds from the spinning-wheel / [by] Peter Teal. — Poole : Blandford Press, 1976. — 184p,[8]p of plates : ill(some col), facsim, port ; 23cm.
Ill. on lining papers. — Index.
ISBN 0-7137-0814-x : £4.75
(B77-02483)

746.1'4 — Handicrafts: Card weaving & board weaving. *Manuals*
Gordon, Linda. Weaving with card and board looms / [by] Linda Gordon. — Leicester : Dryad Press, 1976. — 16p : ill(chiefly col) ; 15x21cm. — (Dryad leaflet ; 510)
ISBN 0-85219-115-4 Sd : Unpriced
(B77-12009)

746.1'4 — Handicrafts: Off-loom weaving. *Manuals*
Rainey, Sarita R. Weaving without a loom / [by] Sarita R. Rainey. — Revised ed. — Englewood Cliffs ; London [etc.] : Prentice-Hall, 1977. — xix,136p,[8]p of plates : ill(some col) ; 24cm. — (The creative handicrafts series)
'A spectrum book'. — Previous ed.: Worcester, Mass. : Davis Publications, 1966. — Bibl.: p.135-136.
ISBN 0-13-947796-9 Pbk : £6.35
(B77-33954)

746.1'4 — Handicrafts: Weaving. *Manuals*
Chetwynd, Hilary. Weaving in easy steps / [by] Hilary Chetwynd ; [photographs by Peter Kibbles]. — London : Studio Vista, 1977. — 64p : col ill ; 29cm.
Bibl.: p.64.
ISBN 0-289-70759-5 : £2.25
(B77-22030)

Straub, Marianne. Hand weaving and cloth design / [by] Marianne Straub. — London : Pelham, 1977. — 152p : ill(some col), form ; 25cm.
Bibl.: p.148. — Index.
ISBN 0-7207-0968-7 : £5.75
(B77-08478)

Tod, Osma Gallinger. The joy of handweaving / by Osma Gallinger Tod. — [2nd revised ed.]. — New York : Dover Publications [etc.] ; London : Constable, 1977. — [1],xv,326p : ill, port ; 26cm.
This ed. originally published: Princeton ; London : Van Nostrand, 1964. — Bibl.: p.320-322. — Index.
ISBN 0-486-23458-4 Pbk : £3.20
(B77-24382)

746.1'4 — Handicrafts: Weaving using frame looms. *Manuals*
Redman, Jane. Frame-loom weaving / [by] Jane Redman. — New York [etc.] ; London : Van Nostrand Reinhold, 1976. — 144p : ill(some col) ; 24cm.
Bibl.: p.136-137. — Index.
ISBN 0-442-26860-2 : £9.60
(B77-00872)

746.2 — LACE MAKING AND RELATED HANDICRAFTS
746.2'09 — Lace, to 1901
Palliser, *Mrs* Bury. History of lace / by Mrs Bury Palliser. — [New and revised ed.] / entirely revised, re-written, and enlarged under the editorship of M. Jourdain and Alice Dryden. — Wakefield : EP Publishing, 1976. — xvi,536p,[150]leaves of plates(1 fold) : ill, ports ; 26cm.
Facsimile reprint of: 1902 ed. London : Sampson Low, 1902. — Index.
ISBN 0-7158-1183-5 : £15.00
(B77-26434)

746.2'2 — Bobbin lace. Making. *Manuals*
Dawson, Amy. Bobbin lacemaking for beginners / [by] Amy Dawson. — Poole : Blandford Press, 1977. — 88p : ill ; 23cm.
Bibl.: p.83. — Index.
ISBN 0-7137-0817-4 : £1.75
(B77-20468)

Nottingham, Pamela. The technique of bobbin lace / [by] Pamela Nottingham. — London : Batsford, 1976. — 222p : ill(some col) ; 26cm.
Index.
ISBN 0-7134-3230-6 : £5.95
(B77-00332)

746.2'2 — English Maltese bobbin lace. Making. *Manuals*
Hamer, Margaret. Pillow lace / [by Margaret Hamer and Kathleen Waller]. — [Bedford] ([13 Abbey Rd, Bedford]) : [M. Hamer].
[Book 1] / by Margaret Hamer. — [1975]. — [1],15p : ill ; 22cm.
ISBN 0-9505738-0-9 Sd : £0.40
(B77-15397)

Book 2 : English Maltese type lace edging with corners / by Margaret Hamer. — [1977]. — [1] ,15p : ill ; 22cm.
Fold. plate as insert.
ISBN 0-9505738-1-7 Sd : £0.50
(B77-15398)

746.3 — TAPESTRIES
746.3 — Tapestries. Weaving. *Amateurs' manuals*
Tapestry & canvaswork / [edited by Gabrielle Weaver]. — London [etc.] : Marshall Cavendish, [1977]. — 88p : ill(some col) ; 30cm.
Col. ill. on lining papers. — Cover title: 'Golden hands' tapestry & canvaswork. — 'This material has previously appeared in the publications "Golden hands", "Golden hands monthly", "Creative canvaswork" and "Encyclopedia of crafts"' - title page verso.
ISBN 0-85685-187-6 : £2.50
Also classified at 746.4'4
(B77-13166)

746.3'941 — Arts. Patronage. Organisations. *Scotland. Scottish Arts Council. Exhibits: Scottish small tapestries, 1976. Catalogues*
Scottish Arts Council. Small tapestries : a Scottish Arts Council exhibition / selected by Maureen Hodge and Fiona Mathison. — Edinburgh (19 Charlotte Sq., Edinburgh EH2 4DF) : The Council, 1976. — 36,[1]p : ill, port ; 16cm.
Exhibition held at Aberdeen Art Gallery and Museum, Aberdeen, 18th December 1976 to 9th January 1977.
ISBN 0-902989-37-5 Sd : Unpriced
(B77-29582)

746.3'942 — Art galleries. *London. Greenwich (London Borough). Woodlands Art Gallery. Exhibits: English woven tapestries, 1971-1976. Catalogues*
Woodlands Art Gallery. Mary Rhodes, her embroiderers and tapestry-weavers : [catalogue of an exhibition held] 6 May to 1 June 1976 [at the] Woodlands Art Gallery. — London (c/o Woodlands Art Gallery, 90 Mycenae Rd, SE3 7SE) : London Borough of Greenwich, [1976]. — [12]p : ill ; 21cm.
ISBN 0-9504033-8-5 Sd : Unpriced
Also classified at 746.4'4'0942
(B77-11330)

746.4 — BASKETRY, KNITTING, EMBROIDERY, ETC.
746.4 — Curve stitching. *Manuals*
String art encyclopedia. — New York : Sterling [etc.] ; London : Distributed by Ward Lock, 1976. — 128p,[24]p of plates : ill(some col) ; 26cm.
Index.
ISBN 0-7061-2174-0 : £4.50
(B77-00333)

746.4 — Handicrafts using string. *Manuals. Juvenile literature*
Fletcher, Helen Jill. String projects / [by] Helen Jill Fletcher ; illustrated by Françoise Webb. — Tadworth : World's Work, 1976. — 62p : ill(chiefly col) ; 22cm. — (Crafts for children)
Originally published: New York : Doubleday, 1974.
ISBN 0-437-40130-8 : £2.90
(B77-13167)

746.4 — Macramé. *Manuals*
Barnes, Charles. Creative macrame projects : with step-by-step instructions for 64 useful and attractive articles / [by] Charles Barnes and David P. Blake ; in collaboration with William Baker. — New York : Dover Publications [etc.] ; London : Constable, 1976. — 3-256p : ill ; 21cm.
Originally published: as 'Macrame fashions and furnishings'. Great Neck, N.Y. : Hearthside Press, 1972. — Index.
ISBN 0-486-23370-7 Pbk : £1.95
(B77-13778)

746.4 — Three-dimensional curve stitching. *Manuals*
Eales, Patricia. Stringcraft in 3D / [text and models by Patricia and Brian Eales ; photographs by John Morphett]. — London : Search Press, 1976. — 32p : ill(some col), plans ; 17cm. — (Leisure crafts ; 54)
Sd : £0.50
(B77-10484)

746.4'1 — American baskets, 1970-1975. *Critical studies*
Rossbach, Ed. The new basketry / [by] Ed Rossbach. — New York ; London [etc.] : Van Nostrand Reinhold, 1976. — 128p : chiefly ill, ports ; 29cm.
Bibl.: p.126. — Index.
ISBN 0-442-27055-0 : £10.65
(B77-03157)

746.4'1 — Appalachian basketry. *Manuals*
Stephenson, Sue H. Basketry of the Appalachian mountains / [by] Sue H. Stephenson. — New York ; London [etc.] : Van Nostrand Reinhold, 1977. — 112p : ill ; 28cm.
Bibl.: p.110-111. — Index.
ISBN 0-442-27972-8 Pbk : £6.05
(B77-25102)

746.4'1 — Basketry. *Manuals*
Wright, Dorothy, *b.1910.* The complete book of baskets and basketry / [by] Dorothy Wright ; illustrations by David Button, Susan Smith, Malcolm Couch. — Newton Abbot [etc.] : David and Charles, 1977. — 192p : ill(some col) ; 26cm.
Bibl.: p.183-184. — Index.
ISBN 0-7153-7449-4 : £5.95
(B77-33955)

746.4'1 — Handicrafts: Rushworking. *Manuals*
Brotherton, Germaine. Rush and leafcraft / [by] Germaine Brotherton. — London : Batsford, 1977. — 80p : ill(some col) ; 26cm.
Bibl.: p.78.
ISBN 0-7134-0383-7 : £3.95
ISBN 0-7134-0384-5 Pbk : £2.35
(B77-25103)

746.4'1 — Maori basketry. *Manuals*
Pendergrast, Mick. Maori basketry for beginners, te mahi kete : a practical guide for craftworkers, setting out the preparation of materials, and weaving techniques for Maori baskets / [by] Mick Pendergrast. — Wellington [N.Z.] [etc.] ; London : A.H. and A.W. Reed, 1975. — 64p : ill, port ; 26cm.
Bibl.: p.64.
ISBN 0-589-00764-5 : £3.00
(B77-19536)

746.4'32 — Knitting. *Manuals*
Dawson, Pam. A complete guide to knitting / [by] Pam Dawson. — London [etc.] : Marshall Cavendish, [1976]. — [4],160p : ill(chiefly col) ; 28cm.
'This material was first published by Marshall Cavendish Limited in the publication "Fashion Maker"' - note.
ISBN 0-85685-189-2 : £2.95
ISBN 0-85685-047-0 Pbk : £1.99
(B77-08479)

De Negri, Eve. Knitting and crochet in easy steps / [by] Eve de Negri ; [photographs by Alain le Garsmeur and Peter Kibbles]. — London : Studio Vista, 1977. — 64p : col ill ; 29cm.
Bibl.: p.64.
ISBN 0-289-70760-9 : £2.25
Also classified at 746.4'34
(B77-21326)

746.4'32 — Knitting. *Manuals. Juvenile literature*
Compton, Rae. Knitting things / [by] Rae Compton and Michael Harvey ; text illustrations by Moira Buj. — London : Severn House : [Distributed by Hutchinson], 1976. — 112p : ill ; 21cm.
Originally published: London : Pan Books, 1976.
ISBN 0-7278-0299-2 : £2.95
(B77-27261)

746.4'32 — Knitting. *Patterns*
Dawson, Pam. Knitting fashion / by Pam Dawson ; edited by Jenny Rogers. — London : British Broadcasting Corporation, 1976. — 176p : ill(some col), facsim ; 30cm.
'... Ten 25 minute programmes first transmitted between October 11 and December 13th, 1976, BBC-2 at 7.05 p.m' '... prepared in consultation with the BBC Further Education Advisory Council' - title page verso. — Index.
ISBN 0-563-16059-4 Pbk : £2.20
Also classified at 746.4'34
(B77-02484)

Mariano, Linda. The encyclopedia of knitting and crochet stitch patterns / by Linda Mariano. — New York [etc.] ; London : Van Nostrand Reinhold, 1977. — 319p : ill(some col) ; 29cm.
ISBN 0-442-25117-3 : £9.85
Also classified at 746.4'34
(B77-27262)

Roberts, Patricia. Knitting patterns : exclusive knitwear designs for all the family / [by] Patricia Roberts ; [photography by John Carter ; illustrations by Michael Wells]. — London : Macdonald and Jane's, 1977. — [143] p : ill(chiefly col) ; 31cm.
ISBN 0-354-08508-5 : £5.95
(B77-30483)

746.4'32 — Machine knitting. *Amateurs' manuals*
Anthony, Jane. Machine knitting : a practical guide / [by] Jane Anthony. — London : Macdonald and Jane's, 1977. — [5],138p : ill ; 25cm.
Index.
ISBN 0-354-04137-1 : £4.50
(B77-22746)

746.4'34 — Crocheting. *Manuals*
A **complete** guide to crochet / edited by Pam Dawson. — London [etc.] : Marshall Cavendish, [1976]. — [4],160p : ill(chiefly col) ; 28cm.
'This material was first published by Marshall Cavendish Limited in the publication "Fashion Maker"' - note.
ISBN 0-85685-190-6 : £2.95
ISBN 0-85685-057-8 Pbk : £1.99
(B77-08480)

Crochet stitches & edgings : with instructions for left-handed workers. — Glasgow : Coats Sewing Group, 1976. — 112p : ill ; 15cm. — (Coats Sewing Group. Books ; no.1246)
Cover title.
ISBN 0-85196-106-1 Pbk : Unpriced
Primary classification 746.4'34
(B77-12587)

De Negri, Eve. Knitting and crochet in easy steps / [by] Eve de Negri ; [photographs by Alain le Garsmeur and Peter Kibbles]. — London : Studio Vista, 1977. — 64p : col ill ; 29cm.
Bibl.: p.64.
ISBN 0-289-70760-9 : £2.25
Primary classification 746.4'32
(B77-21326)

Stalling, Mary. Crochet / [by] Mary Stalling. — London : Octopus Books, 1977. — 4-93p : ill(chiefly col) ; 28cm.
ISBN 0-7064-0641-9 : £1.99
(B77-15982)

746.4'34 — Crocheting. *Manuals. Juvenile literature*
Broughton, Wynne. Crochet / by Wynne Broughton ; with illustrations by Eric Winter. — Loughborough : Ladybird Books, 1977. — 51p : ill(chiefly col) ; 18cm. — (Learnabout) (A ladybird book : series 634)
Text on lining papers. — Originally published: as 'Learning to crochet'. 1975.
£0.24
ISBN 0-7214-0406-5
(B77-32048)

746.4'34 — Crocheting. *Patterns*
Dawson, Pam. Knitting fashion / by Pam Dawson ; edited by Jenny Rogers. — London : British Broadcasting Corporation, 1976. — 176p : ill(some col), facsim ; 30cm.
'... Ten 25 minute programmes first transmitted between October 11 and December 13th, 1976, BBC-2 at 7.05 p.m' '... prepared in consultation with the BBC Further Education Advisory Council' - title page verso. — Index.
ISBN 0-563-16059-4 Pbk : £2.20
Primary classification 746.4'32
(B77-02484)

746.4'34 — Crocheting. Motifs. *Patterns*
Mariano, Linda. The encyclopedia of knitting and crochet stitch patterns / by Linda Mariano. — New York [etc.] ; London : Van Nostrand Reinhold, 1977. — 319p : ill(some col) ; 29cm.
ISBN 0-442-25117-3 : £9.85
Primary classification 746.4'32
(B77-27262)

746.4'34 — Decorative edgings. Crocheting. *Patterns*
Crochet stitches & edgings : with instructions for left-handed workers. — Glasgow : Coats Sewing Group, 1976. — 112p : ill ; 15cm. — (Coats Sewing Group. Books ; no.1246)
Cover title.
ISBN 0-85196-106-1 Pbk : Unpriced
Also classified at 746.4'34
(B77-12587)

746.4'4 — Appliqué: Mola. *Manuals*
Auld, Rhoda Landsman. Molas : what they are : how to make them : ideas they suggest for creative appliqué / [by] Rhoda Landsman Auld ; photographs by Lawrence Auld. — New York ; London [etc.] : Van Nostrand Reinhold, 1977. — 112p,[8]p of plates : ill(some col), 2 maps ; 29cm.
Bibl.: p.109-110. — Index.
ISBN 0-442-20379-9 : £10.25
(B77-21327)

746.4'4 — Canvas embroidery. *Manuals*
Christensen, Jo Ippolito. The needlepoint book : 303 stitches with patterns and projects / [by] Jo Ippolito Christensen ; drawings by Lynn Lucas Jones ; photographs by James T. Long. — Englewood Cliffs ; London [etc.] : Prentice-Hall, 1976. — xvi,384p,[16]p of plates : ill(some col) ; 25cm.
'A spectrum book'. — Bibl.: p.371-374. — Index.
ISBN 0-13-610980-2 : £13.10
ISBN 0-13-610972-1 Pbk : £7.25
(B77-01677)

Sidney, Sylvia. Question and answer book on needlepoint / [by] Sylvia Sidney. — New York ; London [etc.] : Van Nostrand Reinhold, [1977]. — 128p : ill(some col), port ; 29cm.
Published in the United States: 1974. — Bibl.: p.126. — Index.
ISBN 0-442-27882-9 : £10.65
(B77-07518)

Tapestry & canvaswork / [edited by Gabrielle Weaver]. — London [etc.] : Marshall Cavendish, [1977]. — 88p : ill(some col) ; 30cm.
Col. ill. on lining papers. — Cover title: 'Golden hands' tapestry & canvaswork. — 'This material has previously appeared in the publications "Golden hands", "Golden hands monthly", "Creative canvaswork" and "Encyclopedia of crafts"' - title page verso.
ISBN 0-85685-187-6 : £2.50
Primary classification 746.3
(B77-13166)

746.4'4 — Canvas embroidery. *Patterns*
Jones, Diana. Patterns for canvas embroidery / [by] Diana Jones. — London : Batsford, 1977. — 94p,[4]p of plates : ill(some col) ; 26cm.
Index.
ISBN 0-7134-3285-3 : £3.95
(B77-17663)

746.4'4 — Canvas embroidery. Designs based on American patchwork quilts. *Patterns*
Fontana, Frank. Patchwork quilt designs for needlepoint : charted for easy use / [by] Frank Fontana. — New York : Dover Publications [etc.] ; London : Constable, 1976. — [1],v,41,[1] p : of ill(some col) ; 28cm. — (Dover needlework series)
ISBN 0-486-23300-6 Sd : £1.15
(B77-03689)

746.4'4 — Canvas embroidery. Designs. Charting. *Manuals*
Weiss, Rita. Design and chart your own needlepoint / [by] Rita Weiss. — New York : Dover Publications [etc.] ; London : Constable, 1976. — [2],13,[64]p : ill(some col) ; 28cm. — (Dover needlework series)
Sixty-four p. of translucent charting paper.
ISBN 0-486-23301-4 Sd : £1.50
(B77-11331)

746.4'4 — Canvas embroidery. Pennsylvania Dutch designs. *Patterns*
Loeb, Marcia. Pennsylvania Dutch needlepoint designs, charted for easy use / [by] Marcia Loeb. — New York : Dover Publications [etc.] ; London : Constable, 1976. — vii,37p : chiefly ill(some col) ; 28cm. — (Dover needlework series)
ISBN 0-486-23299-9 Sd : £1.15
(B77-11332)

746.4'4 — Central European embroidery. Cross-stitch. *Patterns*
Gierl, Irmgard. Cross stitch patterns / [by] Irmgard Gierl ; [translated from the German]. — London : Batsford, 1977. — [4],88,[3]p : chiefly ill ; 23cm.
Translation of: 'Stickereien in Bauernstuben'. Rosenheim : Rosenheimer, 1973.
ISBN 0-7134-0287-3 Pbk : £1.75
(B77-24383)

746.4'4 — Crewel embroidery. *Manuals*
Young, Eleanor R. Crewel embroidery / by Eleanor R. Young. — New York ; London : F. Watts, 1976. — [7],63,[1]p : ill ; 25cm. — (A concise guide)
Index.
ISBN 0-531-00341-8 : £1.95
(B77-20469)

746.4'4 — Crewel embroidery. Designs
Anderson, Fay. Crewel embroidery / [by] Fay Anderson. — London : Octopus Books, 1977. — 5-93p : ill(some col) ; 27cm.
Jacket title: The colour book of crewel embroidery.
ISBN 0-7064-0638-9 : £1.99
(B77-22031)

746.4'4 — Danish embroidery. Cross-stitch. Motifs based on American state flowers. *Patterns*
Bengtsson, Gerda. US state flowers in counted cross stitch / [by] Gerda Bengtsson and the Danish Handcraft Guild with Ginnie Thompson ; diagrams prepared by Judie Schall. — New York ; London [etc.] : Van Nostrand Reinhold, 1977. — 96p : chiefly ill(chiefly col) ; 28cm.
Index.
ISBN 0-442-20683-6 Pbk : £7.55
(B77-31341)

746.4'4 — Embroidery. *Manuals*
Brittain, Judy. 'Vogue' book of fashion embroidery / [written and edited by Judy Brittain]. — Glasgow [etc.] : Collins, 1976. — 96p : ill(some col) ; 29cm.
Spine title: Vogue fashion embroidery. — Index.
ISBN 0-00-435046-4 : £2.95
(B77-19537)

A **complete** guide to embroidery / introduction by Pam Dawson. — London [etc.] : Marshall Cavendish, [1976]. — [4],160p : ill(chiefly col) ; 28cm.
'... first published by Marshall Cavendish Limited in the publications Fashion Maker, Golden Hands Monthly and the Encyclopedia of Crafts' - p.[4].
ISBN 0-85685-191-4 : £2.95
ISBN 0-85685-141-8 Pbk : £1.99
(B77-15399)

De Denne, Lynette. Embroidery / [by] Lynette de Denne. — Sevenoaks [etc.] : Teach Yourself Books, 1977. — ix,178p,16p of plates : ill ; 18cm. — (Teach yourself books)
Bibl.: p.164-166. — Index.
ISBN 0-340-22395-2 Pbk : £1.590
(B77-27987)

Embroidery in easy steps / edited by Christine Risley ; [photographs by Peter Kibbles]. — London : Studio Vista, 1976. — 64p : ill(chiefly col) ; 29cm.
Bibl.: p.64.
ISBN 0-289-70722-6 : £1.95
(B77-07516)

Holz, Loretta. Teach yourself embroidery / [by] Loretta Holz ; illustrated with photographs and drawings by the author. — Tadworth : World's Work, 1977. — [1],154p : ill ; 24cm.
Originally published: as 'Teach yourself stitchery'. New York : Lothrop, Lee and Shepard, 1974. — Index.
ISBN 0-437-47341-4 : £3.50
(B77-21328)

John, Edith. Experimental embroidery / [by] Edith John. — London [etc.] : Batsford, 1976. — 120p,[4]p of plates : ill(some col) ; 25cm.
Originally published: 1975. — Bibl.: p.114. — Index.
ISBN 0-7134-1014-0 Pbk : £3.75
(B77-23602)

Simpson, Jane. Embroidery / [by] Jane Simpson. — [New] ed. — London : Octopus Books, 1977. — 4-92p : ill(chiefly col) ; 28cm.
Previous ed.: published as 'The basic book of embroidery'. 1973.
ISBN 0-7064-0639-7 : £1.99
(B77-15983)

746.4'4 — Embroidery. *School texts*
Nicholson, Joan Mary. Embroidery for schools / [by] Joan Nicholson. — London : Batsford, 1977. — 96p : ill ; 23cm.
Bibl.: p.96.
ISBN 0-7134-0134-6 : £2.95
(B77-21329)

746.4'4 — Embroidery. Blackwork. *Manuals*
Gostelow, Mary. Blackwork / [by] Mary Gostelow. — London : Batsford, 1976. — 160p, 4p of plates : ill(some col), map, ports(some col) ; 26cm.
Bibl.: p.151. — Index.
ISBN 0-7134-3259-4 : £4.95
(B77-01676)

746.4'4 — Embroidery. Colour. Techniques. *Manuals*
Howard, Constance. Embroidery and colour / [by] Constance Howard. — London : Batsford, 1976. — 216p : ill(some col) ; 26cm.
Bibl.: p.6. — Index.
ISBN 0-7134-3125-3 : £5.50
(B77-07517)

746.4'4 — Embroidery. Stitches. *Manuals*
50 free style embroidery stitches. — Glasgow : Coats Sewing Group, 1976. — 132p : ill(some col) ; 15cm. — (Coats Sewing Group. Books ; no.1243)
Index.
ISBN 0-85196-105-3 Pbk : £0.50
(B77-07519)

Petersen, Grete. Handbook of stitches : 200 embroidery stitches, old and new, with descriptions, diagrams and samplers / by Grete Petersen and Elsie Svennas ; [translated from the Danish by Anne Wilkins] ; foreword by Jacqueline Enthoven. — New York ; London [etc.] : Van Nostrand Reinhold, [1977]. — 64, [3]p,[10]p of plates,leaf of plate : chiefly ill ; 16x23cm.
This translation originally published: London : Batsford, 1970. — Translation of 'Sting og somme'. Kobenhavn : Host and Sons, 1959, with the addition of material from 'Märkbok'. Kobenhavn : Host and Sons, 1966?. — Index.
ISBN 0-442-26533-6 Pbk : £3.00
(B77-25787)

746.4'4 — Embroidery. Use of printing
Newland, Mary. Printing and embroidery / [by] Mary Newland, Carol Walklin ; photography by Colin Walklin. — London : Batsford, 1977. — 89p,[4]p of plates : ill(some col) ; 26cm.
Bibl.: p.85. — Index.
ISBN 0-7134-0136-2 : £4.95
(B77-33956)

746.4'4 — Machine embroidery. *Manuals*
Foss, Mildred B. Creative embroidery with your sewing machine / [by] Mildred B. Foss. — Englewood Cliffs ; London [etc.] : Prentice-Hall, 1976. — x,118p : ill ; 25cm. — (The creative handicraft series)
Index.
ISBN 0-13-189365-3 : £8.00
ISBN 0-13-189357-2 Pbk : £2.90
(B77-00873)

746.4'4 — Museums. *London. Kensington and Chelsea (London Borough). Victoria and Albert Museum. Exhibits: English embroidery. Flower motifs, ca 1100-1900. Catalogues*
Victoria and Albert Museum. Flowers in English embroidery / Victoria & Albert Museum. — 2nd ed. — London : H.M.S.O, 1976. — [6],26p of plates : ill ; 18cm. — (Victoria and Albert Museum. Small picture books ; no.2)
This ed. originally published: 1963.
ISBN 0-11-290241-3 Sd : £0.65
(B77-01678)

746.4'4 — Parish churches. *Suffolk. Great Bealings. St Mary's Church, Great Bealings. Hassocks. Making*
Brown, Cynthia. Hassocks for your church : how we made them at Great Bealings / [by] Cynthia Brown. — [Great Bealings] ([Great Bealings, Woodbridge, Suffolk]) : [St Mary's Church], [1976]. — 36p : ill ; 12x19cm.
ISBN 0-9505054-0-4 Pbk : £0.95
(B77-06212)

746.4'4 — Textured embroidery. *Manuals*
Harding, Valerie. Textures in embroidery / [by] Valerie Harding. — London : Batsford, 1977. — 84p,[4]p of plates : ill(some col) ; 26cm.
Index.
ISBN 0-7134-0027-7 : £3.95
(B77-24384)

746.4'4 — Turkish embroidery. *Manuals*
Ramazanoğlu, Gülseren. Turkish embroidery / [by] Gülseren Ramazanoğlu. — New York ; London [etc.] : Van Nostrand Reinhold, 1976. — 104p : ill(some col) ; 24cm.
Index.
ISBN 0-442-26799-1 : £7.17
(B77-02485)

746.4'4'0942 — Art galleries. *London. Greenwich (London Borough). Woodlands Art Gallery. Exhibits: English embroidery, 1971-1976. Catalogues*
Woodlands Art Gallery. Mary Rhodes, her embroiderers and tapestry-weavers : [catalogue of an exhibition held] 6 May to 1 June 1976 [at the] Woodlands Art Gallery. — London (c/o Woodlands Art Gallery, 90 Mycenae Rd, SE3 7SE) : London Borough of Greenwich, [1976]. — [12]p : ill ; 21cm.
ISBN 0-9504033-8-5 Sd : Unpriced
Primary classification 746.3'942
(B77-11330)

746.4'4'094972 — Croatian embroidery, to 1914
Etnografski Muzej, *Zagreb.* Yugoslavia-Croatian folk embroidery : designs and techniques / foreword by Jelka Radauš Ribarić ; description of techniques by Blažena Szenczi ; photographs by Mitja Koman ; [translated from the Serbo-Croat by Janko Paravić ; edited by Viktor Kipcić]. — New York ; London [etc.] : Van Nostrand Reinhold, 1976 [i.e. 1977]. — 76p : chiefly col ill ; 24cm.
'The selection for this book has been made from the ... collection of the Ethnographic Museum in Zagreb' - Foreword. — This translation published in the United States: 1976. — 'Originally published as a dual-language edition under the Yugoslavian title "Vezak vezla" and the English title "Croatian folk embroidery". [Zagreb] : Grafički zavod Hrvatske, 1973' - title page verso.
ISBN 0-442-26905-6 : £6.25
(B77-14329)

746.4'6 — Patchwork. *Manuals*
Hellegers, Louisa. Pictures in patchwork / [by] Marie-Janine Solvitt ; photographs from 'Elle' ; [drawings by the author ; translated from the French by Walter A. Simpson ; adapted by Louisa B. Hellegers]. — New York : Sterling [etc.] ; London : Distributed by Ward Lock, 1977. — 112p : ill(some col) ; 24cm.
Adaptation of: 'Le patchwork'. Paris : Dessain et Tolra, 1976. — Index.
ISBN 0-7061-2552-5 : £5.95
(B77-31342)

746.4'6 — Patchwork & quilting. *Manuals*
Gutcheon, Beth. The perfect patchwork primer / [by] Beth Gutcheon ; illustrated by Barbara Stockwell and Jeffrey Gutcheon ; photographs by Bevan Davies. — Harmondsworth [etc.] : Penguin, 1976. — 267p : ill ; 26cm. — (Penguin handbooks)
Originally published: New York : D. McKay, 1973 ; Harmondsworth : Penguin, 1974. — Bibl.: p.256. — Index.
ISBN 0-14-046212-0 Pbk : £1.75
(B77-02486)

746.6 — TEXTILE HANDICRAFTS. PRINTING AND DYEING
746.6 — Fabrics. Batik. *Amateurs' manuals*
Martin, Beryl, *b.1925.* Batik for beginners / by Beryl Martin. — Revised ed. — London [etc.] : Angus and Robertson, 1977. — [5],42p : ill(some col) ; 22cm.
Previous ed.: 1971.
ISBN 0-207-95759-2 : £2.80
(B77-30484)

Samuel, Evelyn. Introducing batik / [by] Evelyn Samuel. — London : Batsford, 1977. — 80p,[8] p of plates : ill(some col) ; 20cm.
Originally published: 1968. — Bibl.: p.80.
ISBN 0-7134-2445-1 Pbk : £2.95
(B77-27988)

746.6 — Fabrics. Batik & tie-dyeing. *Amateurs' manuals*
Anderson, Fay. Tie dyeing & batik / [by] Fay Anderson. — [New] ed. — London : Octopus Books, 1977. — 4-93p : ill(chiefly col) ; 28cm.
Previous ed.: published as 'Tie-dyeing and batik' / by Mary Frame, Helen Anstey. 1974.
ISBN 0-7064-0640-0 : £1.99
(B77-16521)

Jameson, Norma. Tie-dye, batik and candlemaking in easy steps / [by] Norma Jameson and Ann Hirst-Smith. — London : Studio Vista, 1976. — 64p : ill(chiefly col) ; 28cm.
Bibl.: p.64.
ISBN 0-289-70723-4 : £1.95
Also classified at 745.59'33
(B77-08481)

746.6 — Fabrics. Dyeing & printing. *Amateurs' manuals*
Johnston, Meda Parker. Design on fabrics / [by] Meda Parker Johnston, Glen Kaufman. — New York ; London [etc.] : Van Nostrand Reinhold, [1977]. — 156p : ill(some col) ; 28cm.
Originally published: 1967. — Bibl.: p.153. — Index.
ISBN 0-442-24170-4 Pbk : £5.95
(B77-13779)

746.6'095 — Textiles. Dyeing. Asian techniques, to 1976. Artistic aspects
Larsen, Jack Lenor. The dyer's art : ikat, batik, plangi / [by] Jack Lenor Larsen with ... [others] ; photographs by Bob Hanson. — New York [etc.] ; London : Van Nostrand Reinhold, 1976. — 272p : chiefly ill(chiefly col), map ; 36cm.
Bibl.: p.247-257. — Index.
ISBN 0-442-24685-4 : £23.00
(B77-24385)

746.7 — TEXTILE HANDICRAFTS. RUGS AND CARPETS
746.7 — Rugs. Making. *Manuals*
Creative rug making / [edited by Sue Simmons]. — London [etc.] : Marshall Cavendish, 1976. — 88p : chiefly ill(chiefly col) ; 29cm. — ([A 'Golden hands' crafts book])
Col. ill. on lining papers. — 'This material has previously appeared in other publications of Marshall Cavendish Limited' - title page verso.
ISBN 0-85685-161-2 : £2.50
(B77-13168)

746.7'2 — Art galleries. *London. Tower Hamlets (London Borough). Whitechapel Art Gallery. Exhibits: Kilims. Catalogues*
Whitechapel Art Gallery. Kilims : plain-weave tapestries from Persia, Turkey and the Caucasus : [catalogue of an exhibition held at] Whitechapel Art Gallery, 23 March to 1 May 1977. — London : The Gallery, [1977]. — [10] p ; 17cm.
'Exhibition compiled by David Black and Clive Loveless' - title page verso.
Sd : £0.25
(B77-22032)

746.7'5 — Oriental carpets
Harris, Nathaniel. Rugs and carpets of the Orient / [by] Nathaniel Harris. — London [etc.] : Hamlyn, 1977. — 96p : ill(chiefly col), map ; 33cm.
Col. ill. on lining papers.
ISBN 0-600-31928-8 : £2.95
(B77-20470)

746.7'5 — Oriental carpets, to ca 1913
Erdmann, Kurt. Oriental carpets : an account of their history / [by] Kurt Erdmann ; translated [from the German] by Charles Grant Ellis. — Fishguard ([PO Box 100, Fishguard, Dyfed]) : Crosby Press, 1976. — 80p,[132]p of plates,viii leaves of plates : ill(some col) ; 28cm.
This translation originally published: London : Zwemmer, 1961. — Translation of: 'Der orientalische Knüpfteppich'. Tübingen : Ernst Warmuth, 1955. — Bibl.: p.59-69.
ISBN 0-903580-35-7 : £16.50
(B77-19538)

746.7'5 — Oriental rugs & carpets
Izmidlian, Georges. Oriental rugs and carpets today : how to choose and enjoy them / [by] Georges Izmidlian. — Newton Abbot [etc.] : David and Charles, 1977. — 128p : ill(some col), 2 maps ; 26cm.
Bibl.: p.128.
ISBN 0-7153-7416-8 : £4.95
(B77-29583)

746.7'5 — Oriental rugs, to ca 1920. *Collectors' guides*
Oriental rugs / compiled by Tony Curtis. — [Galashiels] : [Lyle Publications], [1977]. — 3-125p : chiefly ill ; 16cm. — (Antiques and their values)
Index.
ISBN 0-902921-51-7 : £1.50
(B77-33957)

746.7'55 — Persian rugs, 1800-1925. *Illustrations*
Benardout, Raymond. Nomadic Persian and Turkoman weaving / [by] Raymond Benardout. — London (5 William St., SW1X 9HL) : Raymond Benardout, 1977. — [36]p : ill(some col) ; 24cm.
Catalogue of an exhibition held at Raymond Benardout (Gallery).
£7.50
Also classified at 746.7'58'4
(B77-21330)

Benardout, Raymond. Tribal and nomadic rugs / by Raymond Benardout. — London (5 William St., Knightsbridge, SW1X 9HL) : Raymond Benardout, 1976. — [22]p : col ill ; 29cm.
ISBN 0-9503968-1-8 Sd : Unpriced
Also classified at 746.7'58'4
(B77-13169)

746.7'561 — Antique dealers. *London. Kensington and Chelsea (London Borough). Raymond Bernardout (Firm). Exhibits: Turkish rugs. Catalogues*

Benardout, Raymond. Turkish rugs. — London (5 William St., SW1X 9HL) : Raymond Benardout, 1975. — [14]p,32p of plates : ill(some col) ; 18cm.
Author: Raymond Benardout. — Catalogue of an exhibition held at Raymond Benardout (Gallery) from 9 to 29 November 1975. — Bibl. : p.[8].
ISBN 0-9503968-2-6 : £4.75
ISBN 0-9503968-3-4 Pbk : £3.50
(B77-13170)

746.7'561 — Turkish carpets, to 1700

Erdmann, Kurt. The history of the early Turkish carpet / by Kurt Erdmann ; translated [from the German] by Robert Pinner ; and bibliography of Kurt Erdmann on carpets compiled by Hanna Erdmann. — London : P.O. Box 127, NW8 8NT : Oguz Press, 1977. — xvi,101p,viii leaves of plates : ill(some col), port ; 25cm.
Translation of: 'Der türkische Teppich des 15. Jahrhunderts'. Istanbul : Maarif Basimevi, 1957. — Bibl.: p.81-101.
ISBN 0-905820-02-9 : Unpriced
(B77-21331)

746.7'58 — Central Asian carpets, 1800-1900

Blikslager, Bert. Central Asian carpets : 8 October 1976 / [by Bert Blikslager] ; [with a contribution by Jon Thompson]. — London : Lefevre and Partners ; Fishguard ([PO Box 100, Fishguard, Dyfed]) : Distributed by the Crosby Press, 1976. — [75]p : ill(chiefly col) ; 29cm.
Produced to coincide with a sale of Oriental carpets.
ISBN 0-903580-40-3 : £12.00
(B77-18917)

746.7'58'1 — Turkoman carpets. Motifs. Ethnographic aspects

Azadi, Siawosch. Turkoman carpets, and the ethnographic significance of their ornaments / [by] Siawosch Azadi ; translated [from the German] by Robert Pinner. — [New ed.]. — Fishguard ([PO Box 100, Fishguard, Dyfed]) : Crosby Press, 1975. — [5],48,[77]p : ill(chiefly col), col map ; 31cm.
Translation and revision of: 'Turkmenische Teppiche ...'. Hamburg : Museum für Volkerkunde, 1970. — Bibl.: p.44-46.
ISBN 0-903580-30-6 : £24.75
(B77-18918)

746.7'58'4 — Turkestan rugs, 1800-1925. *Illustrations*

Benardout, Raymond. Nomadic Persian and Turkoman weaving / [by] Raymond Benardout. — London (5 William St., SW1X 9HL) : Raymond Benardout, 1977. — [36]p : ill(some col) ; 24cm.
Catalogue of an exhibition held at Raymond Benardout (Gallery).
£7.50
Primary classification 746.7'55
(B77-21330)

Benardout, Raymond. Tribal and nomadic rugs / by Raymond Benardout. — London (5 William St., Knightsbridge, SW1X 9HL) : Raymond Benardout, 1976. — [22]p : col ill ; 29cm.
ISBN 0-9503968-1-8 Sd : Unpriced
Primary classification 746.7'55
(B77-13169)

746.9 — TEXTILE HANDICRAFTS. COSTUME, FURNISHINGS, ETC

746.9'2 — Tee-shirts. Transfers. *Collections. For hand colouring*

Sibbett, Ed. Iron-on t-shirt transfers for hand coloring / [by] Ed Sibbett, Jr. — New York : Dover Publications [etc.] ; London : Constable, 1976. — [50]p ; 28cm.
Twenty-four designs, with instructions on inside covers.
ISBN 0-486-23395-2 Sd : £1.20
(B77-11333)

746.9'2 — Women's clothing. Crocheting & knitting. *Patterns. Periodicals*

'Weekend' patterns for sewing, knitting and crochet. — [London] : [Associated Newspapers Group].
[No.1]-. — [197-?]-. — ill(some col) ; 30cm.
64p. in 1977 spring and summer edition.
Sd : £0.40
ISBN 0-85144-146-7
Primary classification 646.4'04'05
(B77-14811)

746.9'2 — Women's clothing. Decoration by hand. *Manuals*

Boutique attire / by the editors of Time-Life Books. — [London] ([42 Conduit St., W.1]) : Time Life Books [etc.], 1976. — 184p : chiefly col ill ; 30cm. — (The art of sewing)
Originally published: New York : Time Inc., 1975. — Index.
ISBN 0-7054-0363-7 : £5.95
Primary classification 646.4'04
(B77-15942)

746.9'2 — Women's clothing. Design. *Secondary school texts*

Nelms, Ivy. Fashion and clothing technology / [by] Ivy Nelms. — Amersham : Hulton, 1976. — [4],159p : ill(some col) ; 25cm.
ISBN 0-7175-0682-7 Pbk : £2.80
Primary classification 646.4'04
(B77-09798)

746.9'2 — Women's clothing. Fashion design. *Western Europe, 1901-1939*

Robinson, Julian. The golden age of style / [by] Julian Robinson. — London : Orbis Books, 1976. — 128p : ill(chiefly col), ports(1 col) ; 30cm.
Bibl.: p.126. — Index.
ISBN 0-85613-243-8 : £5.95
ISBN 0-85613-262-4 Pbk : £3.95
(B77-15984)

746.9'2 — Women's clothing. Fashion design. *Western Europe, 1920-1960. Illustrations*

Peacock, John. Fashion sketchbook, 1920-1960 / [by] John Peacock ; with a foreword by Mary Quant. — London : Thames and Hudson, 1977. — 128p : chiefly col ill ; 28cm.
ISBN 0-500-27090-2 Pbk : £2.50
(B77-23603)

746.9'2'0904 — Haute couture, 1900-1976

Carter, Ernestine. The changing world of fashion : 1900 to the present / [by] Ernestine Carter ; introduction by Diana Vreeland. — London : Weidenfeld and Nicolson, 1977. — 256p : ill(some col), facsims, ports ; 29cm.
Bibl.: p.241-243. — Index.
ISBN 0-297-77349-6 : £8.50
(B77-28774)

746.9'2'09044 — Haute couture, 1940-1950

Robinson, Julian. Fashion in the forties / [by] Julian Robinson. — London [etc.] : Academy Editions [etc.], 1976. — 103p : ill(some col) ; 30cm.
Pbk : £3.95
(B77-30485)

746.9'2'0922 — Women's clothing. Fashion. Women, 1918-1976. *Biographies*

Keenan, Brigid. The women we wanted to look like / [by] Brigid Keenan. — London : Macmillan, 1977. — 224p : ill(some col), ports(some col) ; 31cm.
Bibl.: p.221. — Index.
ISBN 0-333-21345-9 : £7.95 : CIP rev.
(B77-22033)

746.9'2'0941 — British haute couture. *Illustrations. Periodicals*

Collections London. — London (Market Place, Oxford Circus, W1N 8EJ) : R.D. Franks Publications.
No.1- ; Spring-Summer 1977-. — [1977]-. — ill(some col) ; 31cm.
Two issues a year. — Cover title. — [64]p. in 1st issue.
Pbk : £3.00
ISSN 0309-4391
(B77-12010)

747 — INTERIOR DESIGN

747'.05 — Interior design. *Serials*

Decorative art and modern interiors. — London : Studio Vista ; New York ; London [etc.] : Van Nostrand Reinhold.
1977 : Vol.66 / edited by Maria Schofield. — 1977. — xvi,184p : ill(some col) ; 29cm.
English captions, English, German, Spanish, French and Japanese introduction.
ISBN 0-289-70726-9 : £12.50
(B77-13171)

747.2'147'1 — Buildings. Interior design. *New York (City), 1893-1916. Illustrations*

Byron, Joseph. New York interiors at the turn of the century : in 131 photographs by Joseph Byron from the Byron Collection of the Museum of the City of New York / text by Clay Lancaster. — New York : Dover Publications [for] the Museum ; London : Constable, 1976. — xviii,154p : ill, ports ; 28cm.
ISBN 0-486-23359-6 Pbk : £3.60
(B77-25104)

747'.7 — Bed-sitters. Interior design

Rowlands, Sue. One room living / [by] Sue Rowlands. — London : Design Council, 1977. — 71p : ill(some col) ; 21x22cm. — (Design Centre, London. Books)
ISBN 0-85072-053-2 : £3.95
ISBN 0-85072-052-4 Pbk : £1.95
(B77-19539)

747'.75 — Residences. Living rooms. Interior design

Dyson, Katie. Letts do up the living room / [by] Katie Dyson. — London [etc.] : Letts, 1975. — 95p : ill(some col) ; 21cm.
ISBN 0-85097-139-x Pbk : £1.40
(B77-15985)

747'.77 — Residences. Bedrooms. Interior design

Dyson, Katie. Letts do up the bedroom / [by] Katie Dyson. — London [etc.] : Letts, 1975. — 95p : ill(some col) ; 21cm.
ISBN 0-85097-140-3 Pbk : £1.40
(B77-16522)

747'.78 — Bathrooms. Interior design

Kira, Alexander. The bathroom / [by] Alexander Kira. — New and expanded ed. — Toronto [etc.] ; London : Bantam, 1977. — xviii,493,[1] p : ill ; 18cm.
This ed. originally published: New York : Viking Press ; Harmondsworth : Penguin, 1976. — Index.
ISBN 0-552-62676-7 Pbk : £1.25
(B77-30486)

747'.78 — Residences. Bathrooms. Interior design

Dyson, Katie. Letts do up the bathroom / [by] Katie Dyson. — London [etc.] : Letts, 1975. — 95p : ill(some col) ; 21cm.
ISBN 0-85097-138-1 Pbk : £1.40
(B77-15986)

747'.791 — Residences. Rooms for leisure activities. Interior design

Barty, Euan. Rooms for recreation / [by] Euan Barty. — London : Design Council, 1977. — 69p : ill(some col) ; 21x22cm. — (Design Centre, London. Books)
ISBN 0-85072-055-9 : £3.95
ISBN 0-85072-054-0 Pbk : £1.95
(B77-18919)

747'.797 — Residences. Kitchens. Interior design

Dyson, Katie. Letts do up the kitchen / [by] Katie Dyson. — London [etc.] : Letts, 1975. — 95p : ill(some col) ; 21cm.
ISBN 0-85097-137-3 Pbk : £1.40
(B77-15987)

747'.8'8 — Residences. Interior design. *Amateurs' manuals*

Gilliatt, Mary. How to decorate without a decorator : a realistic guide to interior design / by Mary Gilliatt ; book design by Janet Odgis ; photos by Michael Dunne with Michael Nicholson and others. — London : Thames and Hudson, 1977. — 271,[1]p : ill(some col), plans ; 29cm.
Index.
ISBN 0-500-01189-3 : £12.50
(B77-31343)

Green, Shirley. Doing up your home / [by] Shirley Green. — London : Sphere, 1975. — 160p : ill(chiefly col) ; 22cm. — ('Good housekeeping' family library)
Originally published: London : Ebury Press, 1973. — Index.
ISBN 0-7221-3952-7 Pbk : £0.95
(B77-19540)

The **guide** to home design and decorating / edited by Barbara Chandler. — London (59 Grosvenor St., W.1) : Sundial Books Ltd, 1977. — 4-157p : ill(chiefly col) ; 29cm.
Spine title: The St Michael guide to home design and decorating. — Index.
ISBN 0-904230-33-3 : £2.99
(B77-33353)

Liman, Ellen. Everything in its place : a practical guide to room improvement / [by] Ellen Liman ; drawings by Nancy Stahl. — Newton Abbot [etc.] : David and Charles, 1977. — 120p : ill, plans ; 23x29cm.
ISBN 0-7153-7442-7 : £3.95
(B77-32049)

747'.8'80941 — Residences. Interior design. *Great Britain, ca 1890-ca 1910. Illustrations*
Lemere, H Bedford. The opulent eye : late Victorian and Edwardian taste in interior design / [text] by Nicholas Cooper ; with photographic plates by H. Bedford Lemere. — London : Architectural Press, 1976. — [5], 258p : chiefly ill ; 31cm.
Index.
ISBN 0-85139-004-8 : £8.95
(B77-04976)

747'.8'80942 — Residences. Interior design. *England, 1650-1820*
Strange, Thomas Arthur. A guide to collectors : 3500 illustrations, English furniture, decoration, woodwork and allied arts during the last half of the seventeenth century, the whole of the eighteenth century & the early part of the nineteenth / by Thomas Arthur Strange. — [New ed.]. — Wakefield : EP Publishing, 1977. — [9],368p : ill ; 29cm.
Cover title: English furniture, decoration, woodwork and allied arts. — New ed. originally published: London : Simpkin, Marshall, Hamilton, Kent, 1903.
ISBN 0-7158-1210-6 : £10.00
(B77-18920)

748 — HANDICRAFTS. GLASS
748.2'904 — Glassware, 1870-1975
Beard, Geoffrey William. International modern glass / [by] Geoffrey Beard. — London : Barrie and Jenkins, 1976. — 264p,[8]p of plates : ill(some col), ports ; 31cm.
Bibl.: p.254-256. — Index.
ISBN 0-214-20081-7 : £16.50
(B77-13780)

748.2'92 — English glassware, to 1900
Cheltenham Art Gallery and Museum. English glass / [Cheltenham Art Gallery and Museum]. — [Cheltenham] ([Clarence St., Cheltenham, Glos. GL50 3JT]) : The Art Gallery and Museum, [1977]. — Folder([8]p) : ill ; 21cm.
£0.15
(B77-17004)

748.2'92 — Museums. *Oxfordshire. Oxford. Ashmolean Museum. Exhibits: English drinking glasses, 1700-1800. Illustrations*
Ashmolean Museum. English drinking glasses in the Ashmolean Museum, Oxford. — [Oxford] ([University of Oxford, Oxford OX1 2PH]) : [The Museum], 1977. — [2],32,[1]p : chiefly ill ; 19cm.
ISBN 0-900090-45-6 Sd : £0.65
(B77-32050)

748.2'99'3 — Museums. *Avon. Bristol. City of Bristol Museum and Art Gallery. Exhibits: Ancient Mediterranean glassware. Collections: Bomford Collection. Catalogues*
Thomas, Nicholas, *b.1928.* Ancient glass : the Bomford collection of pre-Roman & Roman glass on loan to the City of Bristol Museum & Art Gallery / [catalogue compiled by Nicholas Thomas ; photographs by Derek Balmer]. — [Bristol] ([Queen's Rd, Bristol BS8 1RL]) : The Museum and Art Gallery, 1976. — [2],47p : ill(chiefly col) ; 30cm.
Bibl.: p.45-47.
ISBN 0-900199-06-7 Sd : £2.00
(B77-19541)

748.2'99'41 — British glassware, 1837-1901
Wills, Geoffrey. Victorian glass / [by] Geoffrey Wills. — London : Bell, 1976. — xi,96p,[24]p of plates : ill, port ; 25cm.
Bibl.: p.85-86. — Index.
ISBN 0-7135-1949-5 : £6.50
(B77-04977)

748.2'99'411 — Scottish glassware, to 1937
Fleming, Arnold. Scottish and Jacobite glass / by Arnold Fleming ; with a foreword by Alexander O. Curle. — Wakefield : EP Publishing, 1977. — xv,196p,[1],lvi leaves of plates : ill, facsim, port ; 26cm.
Facsimile reprint of: 1st ed., Glasgow : Jackson, 1938. — Index.
ISBN 0-7158-1207-6 : £8.50
(B77-14849)

748.2'99'415 — Irish glassware, to 1975
Boydell, Mary. Irish glass / [by] Mary Boydell. — Norwich : Jarrold and Sons, 1976. — [28] p(2 fold) : ill(some col), facsim, port ; 25cm. — (The Irish heritage series ; 5)
Bibl.: p.[27].
ISBN 0-900346-09-4 Sd : £0.70
(B77-01679)

748.5 — Handicrafts using stained glass. *Manuals*
Wood, Paul Winthrop. Artistry in stained glass / by Paul W. Wood. — New York : Sterling [etc.] ; London : Distributed by Ward Lock, 1976. — 96p,[8]p of plates : ill(some col) ; 26cm.
Index.
ISBN 0-7061-2104-x : £3.95
(B77-02487)

748.5 — Stained glass
Lee, Lawrence, *b.1909.* The appreciation of stained glass / [by] Lawrence Lee. — London [etc.] : Oxford University Press, 1977. — x, 118p : ill(some col) ; 21cm. — (The appreciation of the arts ; 9)
Index.
ISBN 0-19-211913-3 : £5.50
(B77-10877)

748.5 — Stained glass panels. *Patterns*
Sibbett, Ed. Stained glass pattern book : 88 designs for workable projects / [by] Ed Sibbett, Jr. — New York : Dover Publications [etc.] ; London : Constable, 1976. — [2],62p : of ill ; 28cm. — (Dover pictorial archive series)
ISBN 0-486-23360-x Pbk : £1.50
(B77-11334)

748.5'9 — Stained glass windows, to 1975
Lee, Lawrence, *b.1909.* Stained glass / [by] Lawrence Lee, George Seddon, Francis Stephens ; with photographs by Sonia Halliday and Laura Lushington. — London : Mitchell Beazley, 1976. — 207p : ill(chiefly col), col coats of arms, col map, plans(chiefly col), ports(chiefly col) ; 38cm.
In slip case. — Bibl.: p.207. — Index.
ISBN 0-85533-069-4 : £25.00
(B77-00334)

748.5'925'85 — Cathedrals. *Hertfordshire. St Albans. St Albans Cathedral. Stained glass windows*
Skeat, Francis W. Stained glass windows of St Albans Cathedral / by Francis W. Skeat. — Chesham : Barracuda Books ; Luton : White Crescent Press, 1977. — xiii,130p,24p of plates : ill(some col), col coats of arms, facsims, plan(on lining papers) ; 31cm.
Also available in a limited ed. of 500 numbered copies. — Bibl.: p.120-122. — Index.
ISBN 0-86023-044-9 : £12.00
(B77-23604)

748.6 — Art galleries. *West Midlands (Metropolitan County). Dudley (District). Dudley Museum and Art Gallery. Exhibits: English rock crystal glass, 1878-1925. Catalogues*
Wolfenden, Ian. English 'rock crystal' glass, 1878-1925 : [catalogue of an exhibition held at] Dudley Art Gallery, 14th August-18th September 1976 / [by Ian Wolfenden]. — [Dudley] ([3 St James's Rd, Dudley, W. Midlands]) : Dudley Metropolitan District, Leisure and Recreation Department, [1976]. — [59]p : ill(incl 1 col) ; 21cm.
ISBN 0-900911-14-x Sd : £1.00
(B77-00874)

748.8 — Bottles. *Collectors' guides*
Fletcher, Edward. Antique bottles in colour / [by] Edward Fletcher ; photography Jeremy McCabe, Nico Mavroyenis, Frank Welch. — Poole : Blandford Press, 1976. — 166p : ill(chiefly col) ; 20cm.
Bibl.: p.166.
ISBN 0-7137-0793-3 : £2.95
(B77-02488)

748.8 — British bottles. *Collectors' guides*
Fletcher, Edward. The best of British bottles / [by] Edward Fletcher. — Braintree (Greenacres, Church Rd., Black Notley, Braintree, Essex) : Bottles and Relics Publications. — (Bottle collectors' library series ; no.3)
Book 1 : Glass. — 1975. — 100p : ill, facsims ; 21cm.
Index.
Pbk : £0.90
(B77-27263)

748.8 — East & West Sussex bottles. *Collectors' guides*
Askey, Derek. Sussex bottle collectors guide / [by] Derek Askey. — Brighton ([20 Surrenden Rd, Brighton BN1 6PP]) : [The author], [1977]. — 2-120p : ill, facsim ; 21cm.
Bibl.: p.118-119. — Index.
Pbk : £0.95
(B77-31344)

748.8 — European sealed bottles, 1630-1930. *Collectors' guides*
Morgan, Roy. Sealed bottles : their history and evolution (1630-1930) / by Roy Morgan ; researched by Roy Morgan & Gordon Litherland. — Burton-on-Trent (458C Stanton Rd, Burton-on-Trent, Staffs. DE15 9RS) : Midlands Antique Bottle Publishing, [1977]. — 120p : ill, 2 ports ; 22cm.
Bibl.: p.114. — Index.
ISBN 0-905447-01-8 : £4.50
(B77-25789)

748.8 — Ink bottles. *Collectors' guides*
Tansley, June. The collector's book of ink bottles / by June Tansley. — Bembridge ([21 Brook Furlong, Bembridge, Isle of Wight]) : The author.
3 : another 160+ 'inks', drawn full size & text & price-guide. — [1977]. — 84p : ill ; 21cm.
ISBN 0-905591-03-8 Sd : £1.35
(B77-10485)

749 — FURNITURE AND ACCESSORIES
749.2 — Antique furniture. *Collectors' guides*
Johnson, Peter, *b.1930 (Feb.).* Collecting antique furniture / [by] Peter Johnson. — London [etc.] : Hamlyn, 1976. — 128p : ill(some col) ; 30cm.
Ill. on lining papers. — Index.
ISBN 0-600-39136-1 : £2.95
(B77-01680)

749.2 — Furniture, to 1975
The **history** of furniture / introduction by Sir Francis Watson ; [editor Anne Charlish]. — London : Orbis Books, 1976. — 344p : ill(chiefly col), 3 facsims(1 col), ports(chiefly col) ; 32cm.
Ill. on lining papers. — In slip case. — Bibl.: p.332-335. — Index.
ISBN 0-85613-202-0 : £12.50
(B77-15988)

749.2'03 — Furniture, ca 1550-ca 1900
Synge, Lanto. Furniture in colour / [by] Lanto Synge ; photography Bob Loosemore. — Poole : Blandford Press, 1977. — 144p : ill(chiefly col) ; 20cm.
Bibl.: p.134. — Index.
ISBN 0-7137-0794-1 : £3.25
(B77-27264)

749.2'1'3 — American vernacular furniture, 1600-1900. *Encyclopaedias*
Filbee, Marjorie. Dictionary of country furniture / [by] Marjorie Filbee. — London : 'Connoisseur', 1977. — 200p : ill ; 26cm.
Bibl.: p.194-195. — Index.
ISBN 0-900305-17-7 : £6.00
Primary classification 749.2'2
(B77-32051)

749.2'2 — English furniture, 1500-1910. *Collectors' guides*
Bly, John. Discovering English furniture / [by] John Bly. — Combined and revised ed. — Aylesbury : Shire Publications, 1976. — 200p : ill, facsims ; 18cm. — (Discovering series ; no.223)
Index. — Contents: Discovering English furniture, 1500-1720. Originally published: Tring : Shire Publications, 1971 - Discovering English furniture, 1720-1830. Originally published: Tring : Shire Publications, 1971 - Discovering Victorian and Edwardian furniture. Originally published: 1973.
ISBN 0-85263-359-9 Pbk : £1.25
(B77-10878)

749.2'2 — English vernacular furniture, 1600-1900. *Encyclopaedias*
Filbee, Marjorie. Dictionary of country furniture / [by] Marjorie Filbee. — London : 'Connoisseur', 1977. — 200p : ill ; 26cm.
Bibl.: p.194-195. — Index.
ISBN 0-900305-17-7 : £6.00
Also classified at 749.2'1'3
(B77-32051)

749.2'2 — Museums. *Gloucestershire. Cheltenham. Cheltenham Art Gallery and Museum. Exhibits: English furniture. Barnsley, Ernest & Barnsley, Sidney. Catalogues*
Cheltenham Art Gallery and Museum. Good citizen's furniture : the work of Ernest and Sidney Barnsley : [catalogue of an exhibition held at Cheltenham Art Gallery & Museum 5th November 1976-15th January 1977]. — [Cheltenham] ([Clarence St., Cheltenham GL50 3JT]) : [The Art Gallery and Museum], [1976]. — [49]p : ill, ports ; 15x21cm.
Cover title.
ISBN 0-905157-01-x Sd : 75p
(B77-07520)

749.2'2 — Museums. *Lancashire. Burnley. Towneley Hall Art Gallery and Museums. Exhibits: English children's furniture. Catalogues*
Towneley Hall Art Gallery and Museums. Children's furniture, 1600-1900. — [Burnley] ([Towneley Hall, Burnley, Lancs. BB11 3RQ]) : [The Gallery], [1977]. — 39p : ill ; 22cm.
Catalogue of an exhibition held at Towneley Hall Art Gallery and Museums, 2nd April-2nd October, 1977.
Sd : £0.30
(B77-20471)

749.2'94 — Wooden furniture, ca 1170-1565. *Sources of data: European visual arts*
Wright, Arthur, *b.1947.* Medieval furniture / written and illustrated by A.C. Wright. — [Southend-on-Sea] ([Central Library, Victoria Ave., Southend SS2 6EX]) : Museums Service, Borough of Southend-on-Sea, 1976. — [40] leaves : ill ; 21x31cm. — (Southend-on-Sea (District). Libraries, Art Gallery and Museum Service. Museum publications ; no.19)
ISBN 0-900690-14-3 Pbk : £0.50
(B77-03158)

749'.3 — Chairs & couches, to ca 1900. *Collectors' guides*
Curtis, Tony. Chairs & couches / compiled by Tony Curtis. — Galashiels : Lyle Publications, 1977. — 3-125p : chiefly ill ; 16cm. — (Antiques and their values)
Index.
ISBN 0-902921-47-9 : £1.50
(B77-33958)

750 — PAINTINGS
750'.74'02132 — Art galleries. *London. Westminster (London Borough). Tate Gallery. Reports, surveys. Serials*
Tate Gallery. The Tate Gallery. — London : Tate Gallery Publications.
1974-6 : illustrated biennial report and catalogue of acquisitions. — 1976. — 3-103p : ill(some col), col port ; 25cm.
ISBN 0-905005-70-8 Pbk : £1.50
(B77-06807)

750'.74'02556 — Country houses. *Northamptonshire. Daventry (District). Althorp House. Stock: Paintings. Catalogues*
Garlick, Kenneth. A catalogue of pictures at Althorp / compiled by K.J. Garlick. — [London] ([Hon. Secretary, Paul Mellon Centre for Studies in British Art (London), 20 Bloomsbury Sq., WC1A 2NP]) : Walpole Society, 1976. — xv,128p,leaf of plate,32p of plates : ill, ports ; 29cm. — (Walpole Society. Publications ; vol.45)
Index.
ISBN 0-9502374-1-8 : Unpriced(subscribers only)
(B77-04339)

750'.74'02659 — Museums. *Cambridgeshire. Cambridge. Fitzwilliam Museum. Exhibits: Paintings. Catalogues*
Fitzwilliam Museum. Catalogue of paintings / Fitzwilliam Museum Cambridge. — Cambridge [etc.] : Cambridge University Press for the Fitzwilliam Museum.
In 3 vols.
Vol.3 : British school / by J.W. Goodison. — 1977. — x,311p,64p of plates : ill, ports ; 23cm.

Index.
ISBN 0-521-21620-6 : £15.00
ISBN 0-521-21639-5 Set of 3 vols : £27.00
(B77-32761)

751 — PAINTINGS. MATERIALS, EQUIPMENT, TECHNIQUES, FORMS
751 — Paintings. Materials & techniques. *Amateurs' manuals*
Mills, John FitzMaurice. Painting for pleasure / [by] John FitzMaurice Mills. — London [etc.] : Hamlyn, 1977. — 144p : ill(some col), ports(2 col) ; 29cm.
Index.
ISBN 0-600-00230-6 : £2.95
(B77-22034)

751.4 — Landscape paintings. Naturalism. Techniques. *Manuals*
De Reyna, Rudy. Magic realist landscape painting / by Rudy de Reyna. — New York : Watson-Guptill ; London : Pitman, 1976. — 168p : ill(some col) ; 29cm.
Bibl.: p.165. — Index.
ISBN 0-273-00121-3 : £7.95
(B77-26435)

751.4 — Landscape paintings. Techniques. *Manuals*
Johnston, Frederick Charles. Sketching & painting : a step by step introduction / [by] F.C. Johnston. — London [etc.] : Macmillan, 1976. — 5-157p : ill(some col) ; 26cm.
Index.
ISBN 0-333-19143-9 : £3.95
Also classified at 743'.8'36
(B77-00875)

751.4 — Paintings. Composition. Techniques. *Manuals*
Poore, Henry Rankin. Composition in art / [by] Henry Rankin Poore. — Revised and enlarged ed. — New York : Dover Publications ; London : Constable, 1976. — 96p,[8]p of plates : ill(some col), ports ; 28cm.
This ed. originally published: New York : Sterling Publishing Co., 1967. — Index.
ISBN 0-486-23358-8 Pbk : £2.15
(B77-25790)

751.4 — Paintings. Special subjects: Women: Nudes. Techniques. *Manuals*
Serra, Francesc. Painting the nude / [by] Francesc Serra, J.M. Parramon ; [translated from the Spanish]. — Kings Langley : Fountain Press, 1976. — 112p : chiefly ill(some col), ports ; 26cm. — (Improve your painting and drawing ; no.14) (Fountain art series)
Translation of: 'El desnudo al óleo'. Spain : s.n., 1976.
ISBN 0-85242-449-3 Pbk : Unpriced
(B77-02489)

751.4 — Paintings. Techniques. *Manuals*
Garbo, Norman. Pull up an easel / [by] Norman Garbo. — Revised ed. — South Brunswick ; New York : Barnes ; London : Yoseloff, 1976. — x,261p : ill ; 26cm. — (Barnes large type editions)
Previous ed.: New York : Barnes, 1955 ; London : Yoseloff, 1968.
ISBN 0-498-01854-7 : £4.25
(B77-29584)

Lobley, Robert. Your book of painting / [by] Robert Lobley. — London : Faber, 1977. — 68p : ill ; 16x22cm. — (The your book series)
Index.
ISBN 0-571-10776-1 : £2.50 : CIP rev.
(B77-24386)

751.4'22 — Watercolour paintings. Techniques. *Manuals*
Dorf, Barbara. Guide to water colour painting / [by] Barbara Dorf. — London : Sphere, 1977. — 201p : ill ; 18cm.
Originally published: as 'Beginner's guide to water colour painting'. London : Pelham, 1972. — Index.
ISBN 0-7221-3027-9 Pbk : £0.75
(B77-28775)

751.4'22'0922 — American watercolour paintings, ca 1970. Techniques. *Personal observations. Collections*
40 watercolorists and how they work : from the pages of 'American artist' / [edited] by Susan E. Meyer. — New York : Watson-Guptill ; London : Pitman, 1976 [i.e. 1977]. — 176p : chiefly ill(some col), ports ; 31cm.
Index.
ISBN 0-273-00971-0 : £9.50 : CIP rev.
(B77-07991)

751.4'26 — Acrylic portrait paintings. Techniques. *Manuals*
Van Wyk, Helen. Acrylic portrait painting / by Helen Van Wyk. — New York : Watson-Guptill ; London : Pitman, 1976 [i.e. 1977]. — 174p : chiefly ill(some col), ports(some col) ; 28cm. — (Art instruction paperbacks)
Originally published: New York : Watson Guptill, 1970. — Index.
ISBN 0-273-00975-3 Pbk : £4.95 : CIP rev.
(B77-07992)

751.4'5 — Oil landscape paintings. Colour. Techniques. *Amateurs' manuals*
Curtis, Roger William. Color in outdoor painting / by Roger W. Curtis ; edited by Charles Movalli. — New York : Watson-Guptill ; London : Pitman, 1977. — 152p : ill(some col) ; 29cm.
Bibl.: p.149. — Index.
ISBN 0-273-01048-4 : £9.95 : CIP rev.
(B77-21332)

751.4'5 — Oil paintings. Brushwork. Techniques. *Manuals*
Gruppé, Emile Albert. Brushwork : a guide to expressive brushwork for oil painting / by Emile A. Gruppé ; edited by Charles Movalli. — New York : Watson-Guptill ; London : Pitman, 1977. — 151p : ill(some col), port ; 29cm.
Bibl.: p.149. — Index.
ISBN 0-273-01047-6 : £10.75 : CIP rev.
(B77-22035)

751.4'5 — Oil paintings. Techniques. *Amateurs' manuals*
Dorf, Barbara. A guide to painting in oils / [by] Barbara Dorf. — London : Sphere, 1977. — 202p : ill ; 18cm.
Originally published: as 'Beginner's guide to painting in oils'. London : Pelham, 1971. — Bibl. — Index.
ISBN 0-7221-3026-0 Pbk : £0.75
(B77-31345)

751.4'5 — Oil paintings. Techniques. *Manuals*
Kominsky, Nancy. The third book of paint along with Nancy Kominsky : oil painting made easy. — Glasgow [etc.] : Collins, 1976. — 72p : ill(some col) ; 27cm.
'The third book of the HTV series' - cover.
ISBN 0-00-411841-3 Pbk : £1.75
(B77-28776)

751.4'5 — Oil portrait paintings. Techniques. *Manuals*
Finck, Furman J. Complete guide to portrait painting / by Furman J. Finck. — New York : Watson-Guptill ; London : Pitman, 1977. — 207p : ill(some col), ports(some col) ; 28cm. — (Art instruction paperbacks)
Originally published: New York : Watson-Guptill, 1970 ; London : Pitman, 1974. — Index.
ISBN 0-273-01089-1 Pbk : £5.50 : CIP rev.
(B77-22036)

751.4'5 — Oil seascape paintings. Techniques. *Manuals*
Robinson, Earl John. The seascape painter's problem book / by E. John Robinson. — New York : Watson-Guptill ; London : Pitman, 1976. — 167p : ill(some col) ; 29cm.
Bibl.: p.163. — Index.
ISBN 0-273-00972-9 : £7.95
(B77-03159)

751.6 — Paintings. Analysis. Scientific techniques. *For conservation*
Hours, Madeleine. Conservation and scientific analysis of painting / [by] Madeleine Hours ; [translated from the French by Anne G. Ward]. — New York ; London [etc.] : Van Nostrand Reinhold, 1976. — 128p : ill(some col), ports(1 col) ; 22cm.
Translation of: 'L'analyse scientifique et conservation des peintures'. Fribourg : Office du livre, 1976. — Bibl.: p.121-124. — Index.
ISBN 0-442-23549-6 : £15.20
(B77-30487)

751.6 — Paintings. Conservation & restoration. *Conference proceedings*
Congress on Conservation of Paintings and the Graphic Arts, *Lisbon, 1972.* Conservation and restoration of pictorial art / edited by Norman Brommelle and Perry Smith. — London [etc.] : Butterworth, 1976. — xv,270p,leaf of plate,[4]p of plates : ill(some col), facsims ; 31cm.
'... papers presented at a Congress in Lisbon of the International Institute for Conservation of Historic and Artistic Works in October 1972 on Conservation of Paintings and the Graphic Arts' - Preface. — Bibl.: p.198-201. — Index.
ISBN 0-408-70712-7 : £18.00
(B77-04340)

751.7'7'09545 — Museums. *Pakistan. Lahore. Lahore Museum. Exhibits: Pahari miniature paintings, ca 1660-ca 1850. Catalogues*
Lahore Museum. Pahari paintings and Sikh portraits in the Lahore Museum / by F.S. Aijazuddin ; foreword by W.G. Archer. — London [etc.] (Russell Chambers, Covent Garden, W.C.2) : Sotheby Parke Bernet Publications [etc.], 1977. — iii-xxviii,[2],101p, leaf,xvi,111p of plates : ill(some col), ports(some col) ; 30cm.
Bibl.: p.92-93. — Index.
ISBN 0-85667-029-4 : £25.00
(B77-24387)

753/758 — PAINTING. SPECIAL SUBJECTS
753 — European paintings, 1500-1973. Special subjects: Fantasy. *Illustrations*
Fantastic painters / [compiled and with text by] Simon Watney. — London : Thames and Hudson, 1977. — [88]p : chiefly col ill ; 28cm.
ISBN 0-500-53010-6 Pbk : £2.50
(B77-25105)

753'.5'0973 — American paintings. Abstract expressionism, to 1970. *Critical studies*
Sandler, Irving. The triumph of American painting : a history of abstract expressionism / [by] Irving Sandler. — New York[[etc.] ; London : Harper and Row, [1977]. — xv,301p : ill, ports ; 26cm.
'Icon Editions'. — Originally published: New York : Praeger, 1970. — Bibl.: p.281-298. — Index.
ISBN 0-06-430075-7 Pbk : £5.15
(B77-15989)

755'.2 — Monasteries. *Israel. Sinai. Monastery of Saint Catherine. Byzantine painted icons. Catalogues*
Monastery of Saint Catherine. The Monastery of Saint Catherine at Mount Sinai, the icons. — Princeton ; Guildford : Princeton University Press.
Catalogue of the icons.
Vol.1 : From the sixth to the tenth century / [by] Kurt Weitzmann ; with photographs by John Galey. — 1976. — xvii,107p,[16],cxxii p of plates,leaf of plate : ill(some col), ports(some col) ; 36cm.
Bibl. — Index.
ISBN 0-691-03543-1 : £63.30
(B77-14850)

755'.2 — Russian painted icons, to ca 1700. *Critical studies*
Russian icons / [compiled by] Konrad Onasch ; [translated from the German by I. Grafe]. — Oxford : Phaidon, 1977. — 19p,48p of plates : col ill ; 31cm. — ([Phaidon colour plate series])

Translation of: 'Altrussische Ikonen'. Berlin : Union Verlag, 1977.
ISBN 0-7148-1792-9 : £3.95
(B77-32052)

755'.9'43 — Tibetan tangkas. *Illustrations*
Victoria and Albert Museum. Tibetan tangkas / Victoria & Albert Museum ; [text by] John Lowry. — London : H.M.S.O., 1977. — [4],9p : chiefly col ill ; 16cm. — (Victoria and Albert Museum. Small colour books ; 18)
ISBN 0-11-290264-2 Sd : £0.40
(B77-20472)

756 — British paintings. Special subjects: Great Britain. Social life, 1837-1901
Wood, Christopher, *b.1941.* Victorian panorama : paintings of Victorian life / [by] Christopher Wood. — London : Faber, 1976. — 260p,[8] leaves of plates : ill(some col), ports ; 26cm.
Bibl.: p.248-251. — Index.
ISBN 0-571-10780-x : £12.50
Also classified at 941.081
(B77-01681)

756 — English paintings. Pre-Raphaelitism. Special subjects: England. Social conditions, ca 1850-ca 1860. *Critical studies*
Grieve, Alastair Ian. The art of Dante Gabriel Rossetti - 1. 'Found' ; [and], 2. The Pre-Raphaelite modern-life subject / [by] A.I. Grieve. — Norwich (65 Newmarket Rd, Norwich) : Real World Publications, 1976. — [3],58p : ill, facsim ; 30cm.
Bibl.: p.[3].
Pbk : £2.50
Also classified at 741.9'42; 759.2
(B77-14851)

756 — Paintings, 1525-1977. Special subjects: United States. Western states. Frontier life, 1525-1850. *Illustrations*
The **pioneers** : images of the frontier / selected and introduced by Joseph Czestochowski. — Oxford : Phaidon, 1977. — [16]p,96p of plates : chiefly ill(chiefly col), col map, ports(some col) ; 41cm. — (Giant art paperbacks)
ISBN 0-7148-1775-9 Pbk : £4.50
(B77-32762)

757 — European paintings. Special subjects: Working classes. Social life, 1870-1914
Work and struggle : the painter as witness, 1870-1914 / [text by] Edward Lucie-Smith and [compiled by] Celestine Dars. — New York ; London : Paddington Press, 1977. — 248p : chiefly ill(some col) ; 29cm.
ISBN 0-448-22616-2 : £8.95
(B77-16523)

757'.0941 — Art galleries. *London. Lambeth (London Borough). Hayward Gallery. Exhibits: British paintings, ca 1950-1975. Special subjects: Human figures. Catalogues*
Arts Council of Great Britain. The human clay : an exhibition / selected by R.B. Kitaj [for the] Arts Council of Great Britain. — [London] : Arts Council of Great Britain, 1976. — [64]p ; chiefly ill ; 22cm.
ISBN 0-7287-0101-4 Pbk : £1.20
(B77-01682)

757'.0942 — English portrait paintings, 1558-1603. *Critical studies*
Strong, Roy. The cult of Elizabeth : Elizabethan portraiture and pageantry / [by] Roy Strong. — [London] : Thames and Hudson, 1977. — 227p : ill(incl 1 col), facsim, geneal table, ports(3 col) ; 26cm.
Index.
ISBN 0-500-23263-6 : £11.50
Also classified at 394'.5'0942
(B77-27265)

757'.4 — Art galleries. *London. Westminster (London Borough). National Portrait Gallery. Exhibits: Portrait paintings of Helena Rubinstein held in stock of Helena Rubinstein Foundation. Catalogues*
Helena Rubinstein Foundation. Portraits of Helena Rubinstein. — London : National Portrait Gallery, 1977. — [31]p : ports(some col) ; 25cm.
Catalogue of an exhibition held at the National Portrait Gallery, 6 May-19 June 1977. — With one exception, all the exhibits are in the collection of the Helena Rubinstein Foundation, New York. — Originally published: New York : Helena Rubinstein Foundation, 1976.
ISBN 0-904017-17-6 Pbk : £1.00
(B77-25791)

757'.4 — English portrait paintings. Special subjects: Great Britain. Charlotte, Queen, consort of George III, King of Great Britain. *Critical studies*
Levey, Michael. A royal subject : portraits of Queen Charlotte / [by] Michael Levey. — London : National Gallery, 1977. — [1],24p : ports ; 28cm.
Sd : £0.75
(B77-32053)

757'.8'0954 — Indian erotic paintings, ca 1600-ca 1900. *Critical studies*
Erotic art of India / [text by] Philip Rawson. — London : Thames and Hudson, 1977. — [88]p : col ill ; 28cm.
ISBN 0-500-53009-2 Pbk : £2.50
(B77-27266)

758'.1'09 — Landscape paintings, to 1970. *Critical studies. Juvenile literature*
Hollmann, Eckhard. Looking at landscapes / [by] Eckhard Hollmann and Hellmar Penndorf ; [translated from the German by Neil Jones]. — London : Robson Books, 1976. — 59p : ill(some col) ; 25cm. — (Through artists' eyes)
Translation of: 'Wie Maler die Landschaft sehen'. Leipzig : Edition Leipzig, 1973.
ISBN 0-903895-42-0 : £1.60
(B77-01684)

758'.1'0942 — Art galleries. *London. Camden (London Borough). Courtauld Institute of Art. Gallery. Exhibits: English watercolour landscape paintings, 1700-1900. Catalogues*
Courtauld Institute of Art. English landscape drawings and watercolours from the collections of the Courtauld Institute of Art : [catalogue of an exhibition held at the] Courtauld Institute Galleries, Woburn Square, London WC1, May-June 1977. — London (Woburn Sq., W.C.1) : The Institute, 1977. — iv,14p ; 22cm.
Sd : Unpriced
Also classified at 741.9'42
(B77-32763)

758'.2'0942 — Guildhalls. *London (City). Guildhall, London. Exhibits: English marine paintings. Royal Society of Marine Artists. Catalogues*
Royal Society of Marine Artists. Catalogue of the thirty-first annual exhibition [of] the Royal Society of Marine Artists, 8th October to 5th November 1976, held at Guildhall, London E.C.2. — [London] ([17 Carlton House Terrace, SW1Y 5BD]) : [The Society], [1976]. — 26p : ill ; 14x21cm.
Index.
ISBN 0-9505660-0-4 Sd : £0.50
(B77-11336)

758'.3 — Museums. *France. Paris. Muséum Nationale d'Histoire Naturelle. Exhibits: French watercolour paintings, 1800-1911. Special subjects: Vertebrates. Illustrations*
Grassé, P P. Larousse animal portraits / [by] P.P. Grassé ; consultant editor Maurice Burton ; [translated from the French by John Bailie]. — London [etc.] : Hamlyn, 1977. — 174p : col ill ; 29cm.
Translation of: 'Le plus beau bestiaire du monde'. Paris : Librairie Larousse, 1970.
ISBN 0-600-35507-1 : £6.95
Also classified at 596'.0022'2
(B77-25792)

759 — PAINTING. HISTORICAL AND GEOGRAPHICAL TREATMENT
759 — European paintings. Paintings imitated by Keating, Tom. *Catalogues*
Keating, Tom. The Tom Keating catalogue : illustrations to 'The fake's progress' / edited and with an introduction by Geraldine Norman. — London : Hutchinson, 1977. — 104p : ill, facsim, ports ; 24cm.
Includes drawings by Keating and drawings imitated by Keating.
ISBN 0-09-129610-2 : £9.50
Primary classification 759.2
(B77-21336)

759 — Painters, 1800-1900. *Biographical dictionaries*
Busse, Joachim. Internationales Handbuch aller Maler und Bildhauer des 19. Jahrhunderts : Busse-Verzeichnis / [von] Joachim Busse [zusammengestellt]. — Wiesbaden : Busse Kunst Dokumentation ; London : [Distributed by] Prior, 1977. — 72,[1],1403p,[70]p of plates,[5] leaves of plates : ill(chiefly col) ; 31cm.
Half title page verso: International directory of all XIXth century painters and sculptors ... — Spine title: Maler und Bildhauer des 19. Jahrhunderts. — Thumb indexed. — German, English, French, Italian and Spanish text.
£120.00
ISBN 3-9800062-0-4
Also classified at 730'.92'2
(B77-23605)

Norman, Geraldine. Nineteenth-century painters and painting : a dictionary / [by] Geraldine Norman. — [London] : Thames and Hudson, 1977. — 240p : ill(some col), ports(some col) ; 28cm.
Bibl.: p.223-229.
ISBN 0-500-23249-0 : £20.00
(B77-32054)

759 — Paintings. Painters, 1837-1901. Monograms, signatures & symbols. *Dictionaries*
Nahum, Peter. Victorian painters' monograms : a practical means of identification to almost 2000 signatures / [by] Peter Nahum. — Slough [etc.] : Foulsham, 1977. — 221p : facsims ; 18cm. — (A pocket identification guide)
'... developed out of the original work, "Monograms of Victorian and Edwardian artists"...' - title page verso. — Index.
ISBN 0-572-00973-9 Pbk : £2.25
(B77-30488)

759.03 — European paintings, 1400-1500. *Critical studies*
Meiss, Millard. The painter's choice : problems in the interpretation of renaissance art / [by] Millard Meiss. — New York [etc.] ; London : Harper and Row, 1976. — x,374p : ill, facsims, plan, ports ; 24cm.
'Icon Editions'. — Index.
ISBN 0-06-435657-4 : £14.60
ISBN 0-06-430068-4 Pbk : £6.45
(B77-15990)

759.05 — European paintings, 1800-1900. Orientalism. *Critical studies*
Jullian, Philippe. The orientalists : European painters of Eastern scenes / by Philippe Jullian ; [translated from the French by Helga and Dinah Harrison]. — Oxford : Phaidon, 1977. — 210p : ill(some col), ports ; 26x29cm.
Translation of: 'Les orientalistes'. Fribourg : Office du livre, 1977. — Bibl.: p.198-202. — Index.
ISBN 0-7148-1780-5 : £29.95
(B77-30489)

759.05 — European paintings, 1860-1913. Influence of Japanese prints
Whitford, Frank. Japanese prints and Western painters / [by] Frank Whitford. — London : Studio Vista, 1977. — 264p : ill(some col), ports(some col) ; 29cm.
Ill. on lining papers. — Bibl.: p.257-261. — Index.
ISBN 0-289-70752-8 : £12.50
(B77-20473)

759'.05 — European paintings. Classicism, ca 1750-ca 1850. Compared with romanticism, ca 1750- ca 1850
Clark, Kenneth, *Baron Clark, b.1903.* The Romantic rebellion : Romantic versus classic art / [by] Kenneth Clark. — London : Omega, 1976. — 366p,[24]p of plates : ill(some col), ports(some col) ; 25cm.
Based on the television series. — Originally published: London : J. Murray ; London : Sotheby Parke Bernet Publications Ltd, 1973. — Index.
ISBN 0-86007-718-7 Pbk : £2.95
(B77-09856)

759.05 — Western paintings, to ca 1910. Impressionism. Techniques
Dunstan, Bernard. Painting methods of the Impressionists / by Bernard Dunstan. — New York : Watson-Guptill ; London : Pitman, 1976. — 184p : ill(some col), facsims, ports(some col) ; 29cm.
Bibl.: p.180. — Index.
ISBN 0-273-00970-2 : Unpriced : CIP rev.
(B77-07993)

759.06 — Art galleries. *London. Westminster (London Borough). Thomas Gibson Fine Art Ltd. Exhibits: Western paintings, 1949-1968. Catalogues*
Ossorio, Alfonso. Fourteen paintings : De Kooning, Dubuffet, Ossorio, Pollock, Still / [catalogue notes written by Alfonso Ossorio ; colour photographs by Bruce C. Jones]. — London (9a New Bond St., W1Y 9PE) : Thomas Gibson Fine Art Ltd, 1976. — [44]p(2 fold) : col ill tipped in, ports ; 31cm.
ISBN 0-905536-01-0 : Unpriced
(B77-03690)

759.06 — European avant garde paintings, 1900-1925. *Political aspects*
Shapiro, Theda. Painters and politics : the European avant-garde and society, 1900-1925 / [by] Theda Shapiro. — New York ; Oxford [etc.] : Elsevier, 1976. — xx,341p : ill, facsims, ports ; 25cm.
Bibl.: p.296-322. — Index.
ISBN 0-444-99012-7 : £9.37
(B77-15991)

759.06 — Paintings, 1920-1975. *Critical studies*
Wolfe, Tom. The painted word / [by] Tom Wolfe. — Toronto [etc.] ; London : Bantam, 1976[i.e.1977]. — [4],120,[1]p : ill, ports ; 18cm.
Originally published: New York : Farrar, Straus and Giroux, 1975.
ISBN 0-553-02502-3 Pbk : £0.65
(B77-10486)

759'.074'0941 — Great Britain. Royal families. Private collections: Paintings
Millar, Oliver. The Queen's pictures / [by] Oliver Millar. — London : Weidenfeld and Nicolson : British Broadcasting Corporation, 1977. — 240p,[48]p of plates : ill(some col), ports(some col) ; 30cm.
Bibl.: p.225. — Index.
ISBN 0-297-77267-8 : £15.00
ISBN 0-563-17211-8 (B.B.C.) : £15.00
(B77-21333)

759.11 — Art galleries. *London. Greenwich (London Borough). Woodlands Art Gallery. Exhibits: Canadian paintings. McGugan, Ian. Catalogues*
Woodlands Art Gallery. Ian McGugan and Ed Perera : paintings : [catalogue of an exhibition held] 9 October to 9 November 1976 [at] Woodlands Art Gallery. — London ([c/o Woodlands Art Gallery], 90 Mycenae Rd, SE3 7SE) : London Borough of Greenwich, [1976]. — [11]p : ill ; 21cm.
Sheet (1 side) as insert.
ISBN 0-9504033-5-0 Sd : Unpriced
Also classified at 759.9549'3
(B77-12011)

759.11 — Arts. Patronage. Organisations. *Great Britain. Arts Council of Great Britain. Exhibits: Canadian paintings. Martin, Agnes. Catalogues*
Arts Council of Great Britain. Agnes Martin, paintings and drawings, 1957-1975. — [London] : Arts Council, 1977. — 47p : col ill ; 21cm.
Catalogue of an exhibition organised by the Arts Council at the Hayward Gallery. — Bibl.: p.41-43. — Includes facsimile of manuscript of 'We are in the midst of reality responding with joy', the text of a lecture given by Agnes Martin at Yale University, New Haven, Connecticut, on 5 April 1976.
ISBN 0-7287-0128-6 Pbk : £1.35
Also classified at 741.9'71
(B77-13781)

759.13 — American marine paintings. Homer, Winslow. *Critical studies*
Beam, Philip C. Winslow Homer / [by] Philip C. Beam. — New York ; London [etc.] : McGraw-Hill, [1976]. — 48p : ill, port ; 28cm. — (Color slide program of the great masters ; no.16)
Twenty col. slides (film) (2x2 in.) in pockets. — Published in the United States: 1975. — Bibl.: p.48.
ISBN 0-07-004215-2 : £8.90
(B77-05560)

759.13 — American paintings. Meneeley, Ed. *Critical studies*
Kenedy, Robert Christopher. Ed Meneeley / [by R.C. Kenedy]. — [London] ([c/o Victoria and Albert Museum, South Kensington, SW7 2RL]) : [The author], 1976. — Folder([6]p) ; 26cm.
Accompanies an exhibition held at the Oliver Dowling Gallery in Dublin 15 November-4 December 1976. — Bibl.: p.[6].
Unpriced
(B77-32764)

759.13 — American paintings. New realism, ca 1960-ca 1970. *Illustrations*
Hyperrealism / [text] by Linda Chase ; introduction by Salvador Dali. — London : Academy Editions, 1975. — 76p : chiefly ill(some col), facsim, ports ; 31cm.
These illustrations originally published: with French text. Paris : Filipacchi, 1973.
ISBN 0-85670-243-9 Pbk : £3.95
(B77-07521)

759.13 — American paintings. Ramos, Mel. *Illustrations*
Ramos, Mel. Mel Ramos / with a text by Elizabeth Claridge. — London : Mathews Miller Dunbar : Distributed by Idea Books, 1975. — 158p : chiefly ill(some col) ; 30cm.
Bibl.: p.152-153. — Index.
Pbk : Unpriced
(B77-29585)

759.13 — American watercolour paintings, to 1973. *Critical studies*
Stebbins, Theodore E. American master drawings and watercolors : a history of works on paper from colonial times to the present / [by] Theodore E. Stebbins, Jr, with the assistance of John Caldwell and Carol Troyen. — New York [etc.] ; London : Harper and Row [for] the Drawing Society, 1976. — xv,464p : ill(some col), facsims, ports(some col) ; 29cm.
Bibl.: p.437-453. — Index.
ISBN 0-06-014068-2 : £37.50
ISBN 0-06-014069-0 Pbk : £11.95
Also classified at 741.9'73
(B77-30490)

759.13 — Art galleries. *Edinburgh. Fruit Market, Edinburgh. Exhibits: American paintings. Conde, Miguel. Catalogues*
Conde, Miguel. Miguel Conde, paintings and drawings : [catalogue of an exhibition held at] the Fruit Market ..., Edinburgh, Scotland, 10 July-7 August 1976. — Edinburgh : Scottish Arts Council, 1976. — [17]p : chiefly ill(some col), port ; 15x21cm.
ISBN 0-902989-32-4 Sd : £0.40
Also classified at 741.9'73
(B77-02490)

759.2 — Art galleries. *Edinburgh. Scottish National Gallery of Modern Art. Exhibits: English paintings. Clough, Prunella. Catalogues*
Clough, Prunella. Recent paintings by Prunella Clough : [catalogue of an exhibition held at the] Scottish National Gallery of Modern Art, Royal Botanic Garden, Edinburgh, 18 September-17 October 1976 [and at the] Serpentine Gallery, Kensington Gardens, London W2, 23 October-21 November 1976. — [London] : Arts Council of Great Britain, [1976]. — [17]p : chiefly ill ; 25cm.
ISBN 0-7287-0106-5 Sd : £0.80
(B77-04341)

759.2 — Art galleries. *London. Greenwich (London Borough). Woodlands Art Gallery. Exhibits: English paintings. Cooke, Jean & Cumming, Diana. Catalogues*
Woodlands Art Gallery. Jean Cooke and Diana Cumming : paintings and drawings : [catalogue of an exhibition held] 5 to 27 June 1976 [at] Woodlands Art Gallery. — London ([c/o Woodlands Art Gallery], 90 Mycenae Rd, SE3 7SE) : London Borough of Greenwich, [1976]. — [11]p : ill ; 21cm.
ISBN 0-9504033-9-3 Sd : Unpriced
Also classified at 741.9'42
(B77-11337)

759.2 — Art galleries. *London. Greenwich (London Borough). Woodlands Art Gallery. Exhibits: English paintings. Palmer, Frederick. Catalogues*
Woodlands Art Gallery. Frederick Palmer and Max Middleton : paintings, drawings and prints : [catalogue of an exhibition held] 13 November to 14 December 1976 [at] Woodlands Art Gallery. — London ([c/o Woodlands Art Gallery], 90 Mycenae Rd, SE3 7SE) : London Borough of Greenwich, [1976]. — [11]p : ill ; 21cm.
ISBN 0-905950-00-3 Sd : Unpriced
Primary classification 760'.092'4
(B77-11340)

759.2 — Art galleries. *London. Lambeth (London Borough). Hayward Gallery. Exhibits: English paintings. Wynter, Bryan. Catalogues*
Wynter, Bryan. Bryan Wynter, 1915-1975 : paintings, kinetics and works on paper : [catalogue of an exhibition held at the] Hayward Gallery, London, 5 to 30 August 1976. — [London] : Arts Council of Great Britain, 1976. — [28]p : chiefly ill(some col), port ; 30cm.
Bibl.: p.[21].
ISBN 0-7287-0100-6 Sd : £1.50
(B77-01685)

759.2 — Art galleries. *London. Westminster (London Borough). Fischer Fine Art Limited. Exhibits: English abstract paintings. Stephenson, Cecil. Catalogues*
Stephenson, Cecil. Cecil Stephenson, 1889-1965 : paintings, gouaches and drawings, 1932-1957 : [catalogue of an exhibition held at Fischer Fine Art Ltd] October-November 1976. — London (30 King St., St James's, S.W.1) : Fischer Fine Art Ltd, [1976]. — [14]p : ill(some col), port ; 18cm.
ISBN 0-904867-09-9 Sd : £0.80
Also classified at 741.9'42
(B77-01686)

759.2 — Art galleries. *London. Westminster (London Borough). Michael Parkin Fine Art Limited. Exhibits: English paintings. Luard, Lowes Dalbiac. Catalogues*
Michael Parkin Fine Art Limited. Lowes Dalbiac Luard, 1872-1944 : [catalogue of an exhibition held] 17 February-19 March 1977, [at the Parkin Gallery]. — London (11 Motcomb St., SW1X 8LB) : Michael Parkin Fine Art Ltd, [1977]. — [25]p : ill, ports ; 20x21cm.
Sd : £1.00
(B77-19542)

759.2 — Art galleries. *London. Westminster (London Borough). National Portrait Gallery. Exhibits: English portrait paintings. Zoffany, John. Catalogues*
Webster, Mary. Johan Zoffany, 1733-1810 / [by] Mary Webster. — London ([2 St Martin's Place, WC2H 0HE]) : National Portrait Gallery, 1976. — 96p : ill, ports ; 25cm.
Catalogue of an exhibition held at the National Portrait Gallery from 14 January to 27 March 1977. — Index.
ISBN 0-904017-11-7 Pbk : £1.75
(B77-18298)

759.2 — Art galleries. *London. Westminster (London Borough). Royal Academy. Exhibits: English paintings. Monnington, Sir Thomas. Catalogues*
Egerton, Judy. Drawings and paintings by Sir Thomas Monnington, 1902-1976 / [catalogue by Judy Egerton]. — [London] ([Piccadilly, W1V 0DS]) : Royal Academy of Arts, 1977. — 33p : ill, ports ; 30cm.
Catalogue of an exhibition held at the Royal Academy of Arts, 8 October to 13 November 1977.
Sd : £3.00
(B77-33354)

759.2 — Art galleries. *London. Westminster (London Borough). Serpentine Gallery. Exhibits: English collages. Thubron, Harry. Catalogues*
Thubron, Harry. Harry Thubron : [catalogue of an exhibition held at the] Serpentine Gallery, Kensington Gardens, London W2, 23 October-21 November 1976 / [introduction by Martin Shuttleworth]. — [London] : Arts Council of Great Britain, [1976]. — [20]p : chiefly ill(some col) ; 25cm.
ISBN 0-7287-0105-7 Sd : £1.35
(B77-04342)

759.2 — Art galleries. *London. Westminster (London Borough). Spink and Son Limited. Exhibits: English watercolour paintings. Catalogues*
Spink and Son Limited. English watercolour drawings : annual exhibition, 1977 [held] 18 April-13 May ... [at Spink and Son Limited]. — London [etc.] : Spink, [1977]. — 44p : ill, ports ; 23cm.
Sd : Unpriced
(B77-21334)

759.2 — Art galleries. Exhibits: English paintings. Donagh, Rita. *Great Britain. Catalogues*
Donagh, Rita. Rita Donagh, paintings and drawings : [catalogue of an exhibition held at the] Whitworth Art Gallery, University of Manchester, Whitworth Park, Manchester M15 6ER, 26 February-9 April 1977 ... [and elsewhere]. — [Manchester] : Whitworth Art Gallery ; [London] : Arts Council of Great Britain, 1977. — [48]p : chiefly ill(some col), facsim, maps, port ; 20x22cm.
ISBN 0-7287-0127-8 Sd : £1.20
Also classified at 741.9'42
(B77-13782)

759.2 — Art galleries. Exhibits: English paintings. Frost, Terry. *Great Britain. Catalogues*
Frost, Terry. Terry Frost, paintings, drawings and collages : [catalogue of an exhibition organised by the] Arts Council [and] South West Arts, 1976-77. — [London] : Arts Council of Great Britain, 1976. — 48p : chiefly ill(some col) ; 18cm.
Bibl.: p.22.
ISBN 0-7287-0117-0 Pbk : £1.50
(B77-13783)

759.2 — Arts. Patronage. Organisations. *Great Britain. Arts Council of Great Britain. Exhibits: English paintings. Stephenson, Ian. Catalogues*
Stephenson, Ian. Ian Stephenson, paintings 1955-66 and 1966-77 : [catalogue of an exhibition held at the] Hayward Gallery, London, 2 March-24 April 1977, Arnolfini Gallery, Bristol, 7 May-25 June 1977, Turnpike Gallery, Leigh, 6 August-4 September 1977. — [London] : Arts Council of Great Britain, 1977. — 55p : chiefly ill(some col), ports ; 20x21cm.
Bibl.: p.54-55.
ISBN 0-7287-0121-9 Pbk : £3.00
(B77-13784)

759.2 — Arts. Patronage. Organisations. *Great Britain. Arts Council of Great Britain. Exhibits: English paintings. Tunnard, John. Catalogues*
Glazebrook, Mark. John Tunnard, 1900-1971 : [catalogue of an exhibition held at the] Royal Academy of Arts, 5 March-11 April 1977 ... [and elsewhere] / [by Mark Glazebrook]. — [London] : [Arts Council of Great Britain], 1977. — 54p : ill(incl 1 col), ports ; 25cm.
One col. ill. tipped in. — Bibl.: p.46.
ISBN 0-7287-0122-7 Pbk : £2.25
(B77-13785)

759.2 — English marine paintings. Wilcox, Leslie Arthur. *Lists*
Wilcox, Leslie Arthur. Leslie A. Wilcox, R.I., R.S.M.A. / [text] by Frank G.G. Carr. — Leigh-on-Sea : F. Lewis, 1977. — 47p,[38] leaves of plates : ill(incl 2 col) ; 30cm.
Catalogue of the artist's work. — Limited ed. of 600 copies. — Col. ill. tipped in.
ISBN 0-85317-049-5 : £15.50
(B77-25106)

759.2 — English miniature portrait paintings. Hilliard, Nicholas. Portrait of a young man. Sitter. Identity: Shakespeare, William
Hotson, Leslie. Shakespeare by Hilliard / [by] Leslie Hotson. — London : Chatto and Windus, 1977. — 3-210p,[2]leaves of plates,[2]p of plates : ill, ports(chiefly col) ; 23cm.
Index.
ISBN 0-7011-2226-9 : £6.50
(B77-27267)

759.2 — English paintings, 1837-1901. *Critical studies*
Bell, Quentin. Victorian artists / [by] Quentin Bell. — [1st ed. reprinted] ; completely redesigned with additional colour plates. — London : Academy Editions, 1975. — [6],130p, [8]p of plates : ill(some col), ports ; 30cm.
Originally published: London : Routledge and Kegan Paul, 1967. — Bibl.: p.123-127. — Index.
ISBN 0-85670-151-3 Pbk : £3.95
(B77-20474)

759.2 — English paintings, 1900-ca 1970. *Critical studies*
Rothenstein, *Sir* John. Modern English painters / by John Rothenstein. — London : Macdonald and Jane's.
In 3 vols.
[Vol.1] : Sickert to Smith. — Revised ed. ; with new preface and biographies. — 1976. — [4], 268p,32p of plates : ill, ports ; 23cm.
Previous ed.: i.e. 1st ed., London : Eyre and Spottiswoode, 1952. — Index.
ISBN 0-356-08120-6 : £5.25
(B77-00876)

[Vol.2] : Lewis to Moore. — Revised ed. ; with new preface and biographies. — 1976. — [5], 349p,32p of plates : ill, ports ; 23cm.
Previous ed.: i.e. 1st ed., London : Eyre and Spottiswoode, 1956. — Index.
ISBN 0-356-08213-x : £5.25
(B77-00877)

Rothenstein, *Sir* John. Modern English painters / by John Rothenstein. — London : Macdonald and Jane's.
In 3 vols.
[Vol.3] : Wood to Hockney. — 1974[i.e.1976]. — 262p,[24]p of plates : ill, ports ; 23cm.
Originally published: London : Macdonald, 1974. — Index.
£5.25
ISBN 0-356-04608-7
(B77-00878)

759.2 — English paintings. Arkle, William. *Illustrations*
Arkle, William. The paintings of William Arkle concerning The Great Gift. — Sudbury : Spearman, 1977. — [3],92p : col ill ; 25cm.
Spine title: The Great Gift.
ISBN 0-85435-204-x Pbk : £2.95
(B77-27989)

759.2 — English paintings. Blake, William. *Illustrations*
Blake, William. William Blake / [text by] William Vaughan. — London : Thames and Hudson, 1977. — [8]p,40 leaves of plates : chiefly col ill, col facsims, col port ; 28cm.
Leaves printed on both sides.
ISBN 0-500-53013-0 Pbk : £2.50
Also classified at 769'.92'4
(B77-33959)

759.2 — English paintings. Cuneo, Terence. *Autobiographies*
Cuneo, Terence. The mouse & his master : the life and work of Terence Cuneo. — London ([65 Marylebone High St., W.1]) : New Cavendish Books, 1977. — 244p : chiefly ill(some col), facsims, ports(some col) ; 28x34cm.
Also available in a limited ed. signed by the author. — Ill. on lining papers. — Index.
ISBN 0-904568-08-3 : £25.00
ISBN 0-904568-09-1 Signed ed. : Unpriced
(B77-32055)

759.2 — English paintings. Frith, William Powell, 1858-1865. *Critical studies*
Maas, Jeremy. The Prince of Wales's wedding : the story of a picture / [by] Jeremy Maas. — London : Cameron and Tayleur ; Newton Abbot : Distributed by David and Charles, 1977. — 100p : ill, facsims, plan, ports(some col) ; 26cm.
Index.
ISBN 0-7153-7419-2 : £5.95
Also classified at 941.081'092'2
(B77-20475)

759.2 — English paintings. Gainsborough, Thomas. *Biographies*
Worman, Isabelle. Thomas Gainsborough : a biography, 1727-1788 / by Isabelle Worman. — Lavenham : Dalton, 1976. — 148p : ill, ports(some col) ; 24cm.
Bibl.: p.145. — Index.
ISBN 0-900963-69-7 : £4.80
(B77-04978)

759.2 — English paintings. Hockney, David. *Autobiographies*
Hockney, David. David Hockney / by David Hockney ; edited by Nikos Stangos ; introductory essay hy Henry Geldzahler. — London : Thames and Hudson, 1977. — 312p : ill(some col), ports(some col) ; 28cm.
Originally published: 1976. — Index.
ISBN 0-500-09108-0 : £10.00
(B77-18299)

759.2 — English paintings. Lowry, Laurence Stephen. *Illustrations*
Lowry, Laurence Stephen. Selected paintings of L.S. Lowry : oils and watercolours / with an introduction and notes by Mervyn Levy. — London : Jupiter Books, 1976. — 3-31p,[95]p of plates : ill(chiefly col), ports(chiefly col) ; 29cm.

Bibl.: p.31.
ISBN 0-904041-62-x Pbk : £4.75
(B77-27990)

759.2 — English paintings. Pre-Raphaelitism. *Critical studies*
The **Pre-Raphaelites** / [text by] James Harding. — London : Academy Editions, 1977. — 96p : chiefly ill(some col), ports ; 30cm.
Index.
ISBN 0-85670-336-2 : £6.95
ISBN 95670-335-4 Pbk : £3.95
(B77-27991)

759.2 — English paintings. Pre-Raphaelitism. *Illustrations*
The **Pre-Raphaelites** / [compiled by] Andrea Rose. — Oxford : Phaidon, 1977. — 16p,48p of plates : col ill ; 31cm. — ([Phaidon colour plate series])
ISBN 0-7148-1791-0 : £3.95
(B77-27992)

759.2 — English paintings. Rossetti, Dante Gabriel. *Biographies*
Dobbs, Brian. Dante Gabriel Rossetti : an alien Victorian / [by] Brian and Judy Dobbs. — London : Macdonald and Jane's, 1977. — ix, 257p,[16]p of plates : ill, ports ; 24cm.
Index.
ISBN 0-354-04032-4 : £7.95
(B77-30491)

759.2 — English paintings. Rossetti, Dante Gabriel. 'Found'. *Critical studies*
Grieve, Alastair Ian. The art of Dante Gabriel Rossetti - 1. 'Found' ; [and], 2. The Pre-Raphaelite modern-life subject / [by] A.I. Grieve. — Norwich (65 Newmarket Rd, Norwich) : Real World Publications, 1976. — [3],58p : ill, facsim ; 30cm.
Bibl.: p.[3].
Pbk : £2.50
Primary classification 756
(B77-14851)

759.2 — English paintings. Stubbs, George. *Illustrations*
Stubbs, George. Stubbs / [text by] William Gaunt. — Oxford : Phaidon, 1977. — 16p,48p of plates : chiefly col ill ; 32cm. — ([Phaidon colour plate series])
Bibl.: p.14.
ISBN 0-7148-1808-9 : £3.95
(B77-27993)

759.2 — English paintings. Tuesday Group of Art. *Illustrations*
Tuesdays / [editor Kay Stout]. — London (11 Belsize Sq., N.W.3) : The Tuesday Group [of Art], [1976]. — [47]p : of ill ; 21cm.
ISBN 0-904936-06-6 Sd : £1.50
(B77-01687)

759.2 — English portrait paintings. Sutherland, Graham. *Illustrations*
Sutherland, Graham. Portraits by Graham Sutherland / [text by] John Hayes. — London ([2 St Martin's Place], London WC2H 0HE) : National Portrait Gallery, 1977. — 96p : chiefly ports(some col), ill ; 27cm.
'Published for the exhibition held at the National Portrait Gallery from 24 June to 16 Oct 1977' - title page verso. — Bibl.: p.7.
ISBN 0-904017-18-4 Pbk : Unpriced
(B77-23606)

759.2 — English watercolour landscape paintings. Goodwin, Albert. *Critical studies*
Smith, Hammond. Albert Goodwin, RWS, 1845-1932 / by Hammond Smith. — Leigh-on-Sea : F. Lewis, 1977. — 64p,44 leaves of plates : ill, geneal table, ports ; 30cm.
Limited ed. of 500 copies.
ISBN 0-85317-047-9 : £15.50
(B77-12588)

759.2 — English watercolour paintings. Jones, Henry, b.1838. Special subjects: Birds. *Illustrations*
Jones, Henry, *b.1838.* The bird paintings of Henry Jones / [text by] Bruce Campbell ; foreword by the Duke of Edinburgh ; preface by Lord Zuckermann. — [London] ([202 Great Suffolk St., SE1 1PR]) : Folio Fine Editions [for] the Zoological Society of London, 1976. — [105]p : col ill ; 40x47cm.
Limited ed. of 500 numbered copies. — Half leather. — In slip case.
£300.00
(B77-26436)

759.2 — English watercolour paintings. Thorburn, Archibald. Special subjects: Great Britain. Animals. *Illustrations*
Thorburn, Archibald. Thorburn's naturalist's sketchbook. — [New ed.] ; with an introduction by Robert Dougall. — London : Joseph, 1977. — 136p : ill(some col) ; 27cm.
Previous ed.: published as 'A naturalist's sketchbook'. London : Longmans, 1919. — Index.
ISBN 0-7181-1567-8 : £6.50
Primary classification 591.9'41
(B77-15291)

759.2 — European paintings. English fakes. Keating, Tom. *Autobiographies*
Keating, Tom. The fake's progress : being the cautionary history of the master painter & simulator Tom Keating as recounted with the utmost candour & without fear or favour to Frank Norman ; together with a dissertation upon the traffic in works of art by Geraldine Norman [entitled Art trading and art faking]. — London : Hutchinson, 1977. — 272p,leaf of plate,[12]p of plates : ill, facsim, ports ; 24cm.
ISBN 0-09-129420-7 : £5.50
(B77-21335)

759.2 — European paintings. English fakes. Keating, Tom. *Catalogues*
Keating, Tom. The Tom Keating catalogue : illustrations to 'The fake's progress' / edited and with an introduction by Geraldine Norman. — London : Hutchinson, 1977. — 104p : ill, facsim, ports ; 24cm.
Includes drawings by Keating and drawings imitated by Keating.
ISBN 0-09-129610-2 : £9.50
Also classified at 759
(B77-21336)

759.2 — Museums. *Cambridgeshire. Cambridge. Fitzwilliam Museum. Exhibits: English watercolour paintings. Constable, John, b.1776. Catalogues*
Fitzwilliam Museum. John Constable R.A., 1776-1837 : a catalogue of drawings and watercolours, with a selection of mezzotints by David Lucas after Constable for 'English landscape scenery', in the Fitzwilliam Museum, Cambridge / [text by] Reg Gadney. — [London] : Arts Council of Great Britain, 1976. — 151p : ill(some col), facsims, ports ; 24cm.
Index.
ISBN 0-7287-0099-9 Pbk : Unpriced
Also classified at 741.9'42
(B77-03691)

759.2 — Museums. *Cardiff. National Museum of Wales. Exhibits: English paintings. John, Gwen. Catalogues*
John, Gwen. Gwen John at the National Museum of Wales / written by A.D. Fraser Jenkins. — Cardiff : The Museum, 1976. — [40]p : chiefly ill(some col), facsim, ports ; 16x23cm.
'All the works reproduced are in the collection of the Museum'.
ISBN 0-7200-0097-1 Sd : £0.85
Also classified at 741.9'42
(B77-23607)

759.2 — Museums. *Cumbria. Brampton. LYC Museum and Gallery. Exhibits: English paintings. Blacker, Thetis. Special subjects: Fabulous beasts. Catalogues*
LYC Museum and Gallery. Mantic paintings & mythographs : works from 'A bestiary of mythical creatures' and 'Notes from the magic flute' by Thetis Blacker : [catalogue of an exhibition held from 1st to 30th April 1977 at the LYC Museum and Art Gallery]. — Banks Brampton (Cumbria CA8 2JH) : LYC Museum, [1977]. — [32]p : ill, port ; 14cm.
Sd : Unpriced
Also classified at 769'.9'24
(B77-23608)

759.2 — Museums. *Cumbria. Brampton. LYC Museum and Gallery. Exhibits: English paintings. Palmer, Tony, b.1945. Catalogues*
Palmer, Tony, *b.1945.* Artist in fantasy land : 'over the hills and far away' : paintings and drawings by Tony Palmer : [catalogue of an] exhibition [held] 1st to 31st May 1977 ... [at the] LYC Museum ... — Brampton, Cumbria (Banks, Brampton, Cumbria CA8 2JH) : LYC Museum, [1977]. — [15]p : ill, port ; 14cm.
'37'.
Pbk : £0.15
(B77-18921)

759.2 — Museums. *Oxfordshire. Oxford. Ashmolean Museum. Exhibits: English oil paintings. Philpot, Glyn. Catalogues*
Ashmolean Museum. Glyn Philpot, R.A., 1884-1937 : [catalogue of] a commemorative exhibition [held at the] Ashmolean Museum Oxford 15th September-28th November 1976. — Oxford ([University of Oxford, Oxford OX1 2PH]) : The Museum, 1976. — ix,12p : ill, ports ; 21cm.
ISBN 0-900090-41-3 Sd : £0.75
(B77-07522)

759.2 — Universities. Art galleries. *Merseyside (Metropolitan County). Liverpool. University of Liverpool. Art Gallery. Exhibits: English paintings. Catalogues*
University of Liverpool. The University of Liverpool art collections : a selection of paintings, watercolours, woodcuts and ceramics, displayed in number 3, Abercromby Square / [catalogue by Andrew W. Moore]. — [Liverpool] ([c/o The University Archivist, Senate House, Abercromby Sq., P.O. Box 147, Liverpool L69 3BX]) : [University of Liverpool], 1977. — [3],v,60p : ill ; 21x30cm.
'University art collections - a recent acquisition' ([4]p.: ill; Sd) as insert. — Bibl.: p.59-60.
Sd : Unpriced
Also classified at 738'.074'02753
(B77-30492)

759.28'47 — Watercolour paintings. Painters. *North Yorkshire. Scarborough & Whitby. Biographies*
Bullamore, Colin P. Scarborough and Whitby watercolourists / by Colin P. Bullamore. — [Whitby] ([Carr Hill Farm, Sleights, Whitby, N. Yorkshire YO21 1RS]) : The author, 1975. — 47p,[8]p of plates : ill, ports ; 22cm.
Bibl.: p.46-47.
ISBN 0-9504109-1-8 Sd : Unpriced
(B77-12012)

759.29 — Art galleries. *London. Greenwich (London Borough). Woodlands Art Gallery. Exhibits: Welsh watercolour paintings. Llwyd Roberts, John Richard. Catalogues*
Woodlands Art Gallery. Llwyd Roberts : watercolours and drawings of places in the Borough of Greenwich : [catalogue of an exhibition held] 18 December 1976 to 18 January 1977 [at] Woodlands Art Gallery. — London ([c/o Woodlands Art Gallery], 90 Mycenae Rd, SE3 7SE) : London Borough of Greenwich, [1976]. — [15]p : ill ; 21cm.
Cover title: Llwyd Roberts, 1875-1940.
ISBN 0-9504033-6-9 Sd : Unpriced
Also classified at 741.9'429
(B77-11338)

759.3 — Art galleries. Exhibits: German paintings. Bissier, Julius. Paintings from Kunstsammlung Nordrhein-Westfalen. *Great Britain. Catalogues*
Bissier, Julius. Julius Bissier, 1893-1965 : [catalogue of] an exhibition from the Kunstsammlung Nordrhein-Westfalen, Düsseldorf [held at] the National Gallery of Ireland, Dublin, 5 March to 3 April [1977], City Museum and Art Gallery, Birmingham, 16 April to 15 May [1977], Graves Art Gallery, Sheffield, 21 May to 19 June [1977]. — [London] : Arts Council, 1977. — 60p : ill(some col), port ; 22x23cm.
Bibl.: p.59-60.
ISBN 0-7287-0125-1 : £3.30
ISBN 0-7287-0124-3 Pbk : £2.25
(B77-13786)

759.3 — German paintings, 1907-1918. *Illustrations*
The **Blue** Rider / [text by] Peter Vergo. — Oxford : Phaidon [etc.], 1977. — 16p,48p of plates : chiefly col ill ; 31cm. — ([Phaidon colour plates series])
Bibl.: p.14.
ISBN 0-7148-1749-x : £3.95
(B77-22037)

759.3 — German paintings. Ehret, Georg Dionysius. *Biographies*
Calmann, Gerta. Ehret : flower painter extraordinary : an illustrated biography / [by] Gerta Calmann. — Oxford : Phaidon, 1977. — 3-160p : ill(some col), ports ; 35cm.
Bibl.: p.150-155. — Index.
ISBN 0-7148-1776-7 : £16.00
(B77-26437)

759.3 — German paintings. Elsheimer, Adam. *Critical studies*
Elsheimer, Adam. Adam Elsheimer : paintings, drawings, prints / [text by] Keith Andrews. — Oxford : Phaidon, 1977. — 178p,[2] leaves of plates,[2]p of plates : chiefly ill(some col), ports ; 29cm.
Bibl.: p.171. — Index. — Includes a catalogue raisonné.
ISBN 0-7148-1770-8 : £25.00
(B77-28777)

759.36 — Austrian paintings. Klimt, Gustav. *Illustrations*
Klimt, Gustav. Gustav Klimt. — London : Academy Editions, 1976. — 47p : of col ill, ports(chiefly col) ; 39cm.
Cover title: Gustav Klimt, a poster book. — Versos of most leaves blank.
ISBN 0-85670-301-x Pbk : £4.95
(B77-16524)

759.38 — Polish paintings. Topolski, Feliks. Buckingham Palace panoramas. *Illustrations*
Topolski, Feliks. Feliks Topolski's Buckingham Palace panoramas / with a foreword by Prince Philip, Duke of Edinburgh ; appreciation, Bernard Denvir ; collage, Feliks Topolski with Peter Ford ; photography, Marcus Harrison. — London [etc.] : Quartet Books, 1977. — [4], 112p(4 fold) : ill(chiefly col), facsims, port ; 30cm.
ISBN 0-7043-2142-4 : £11.50
(B77-27268)

759.4 — Art galleries. *London. Kensington and Chelsea (London Borough). Taranman Limited. Exhibits: French tempera paintings. Marq, Charles. Catalogues*
Taranman Limited. Charles Marq : drawings in tempera : [catalogue of an exhibition held at] Taranman ... 24 November-31 December 1976. — [London] ([236 Brompton Rd, S.W.3]) : [Taranman Ltd], [1976]. — [20]p,8 leaves of plates : ill ; 24cm.
Limited ed. of 300 copies.
Pbk : £3.00
(B77-33960)

759.4 — Arts. Patronage. Organisations. *Great Britain. Arts Council of Great Britain. Exhibits: French paintings, 1800-1900. Collections: Burrell Collection. Catalogues*
Wells, William. The Burrell Collection, 19th century French paintings : [catalogue of an exhibition organised by the] Arts Council of Great Britain, 1977-78 / [by William Wells]. — [London] : [Arts Council], 1977. — [30]p : ill, port ; 20x21cm.
ISBN 0-7287-0119-7 Sd : £0.70
(B77-13787)

759.4 — French paintings. Cézanne, Paul. *Biographies*
McLeave, Hugh. A man and his mountain : the life of Cézanne / [by] Hugh McLeave. — London : W.H. Allen, 1977. — xii,324p ; 23cm.
ISBN 0-491-02071-6 : £5.95
(B77-27269)

759.4 — French paintings. Cézanne, Paul. *Correspondence*
Cézanne, Paul. Letters [of] Paul Cézanne / edited by John Rewald ; [translated from the French by Marguerite Kay]. — 4th ed. (revised and enlarged). — Oxford : Cassirer ; [London] : [Distributed by Faber], 1976. — 374p ; 22cm.
'This new edition not only presents ... a completely revised translation, but contains many more letters and documents than the first English edition of 1941' - Preface. — Includes poems in French. — Previous ed. of this translated collection: 1946. — Translation of: 'Paul Cézanne, correspondance'. Paris : Grasset, 1937. — Index.
ISBN 0-85181-061-6 : £6.50
(B77-09168)

759.4 — French paintings. Courbet, Gustave. *Critical studies*
Courbet in perspective / edited by Petra ten-Doesschate Chu. — Englewood Cliffs ; London [etc.] : Prentice-Hall, 1977. — xi,161p, [12]p of plates : ill, ports ; 24cm. — (The artists in perspective series)
Bibl.: p.145-149. — Index.
ISBN 0-13-184432-6 : Unpriced
ISBN 0-13-184424-5 Pbk : £3.20
(B77-17006)

759.4 — French paintings. Degas, Edgar. *Critical studies*
Reff, Theodore. Degas, the artist's mind / [by] Theodore Reff. — London : Thames and Hudson, 1976. — 352p : ill(some col), facsims, ports ; 26cm.
Index.
ISBN 0-500-09120-x : £15.00
(B77-00335)

759.4 — French paintings. Fragonard, Jean Honoré. *Illustrations*
Fragonard, Jean Honoré. Fragonard / [text by] David Wakefield. — London (30 Notting Hill Gate, W11) : Oresko Books, 1976. — 88p : chiefly ill(some col), ports ; 30cm.
Bibl.: p.88.
ISBN 0-905368-01-0 : £7.95
ISBN 0-905368-05-3 Pbk : £3.95
(B77-15992)

759.4 — French paintings. Icart, Louis. *Critical studies*
Schnessel, S Michael. Icart / by S. Michael Schnessel ; introduction by Katharine M. McClinton. — London : Studio Vista, 1976. — xiv,178p : ill(some col), ports ; 32cm.
Also published: New York : Potter, 1976. — Bibl.: p.174-175. — Index.
ISBN 0-289-70761-7 : £10.50
Primary classification 769'.92'4
(B77-15404)

759.4 — French paintings. Impressionism
Impressionism / [compiled] by the editors of 'Réalités' ; preface by René Huyghe ; [translated from the French]. — London : Octopus Books, 1977. — 320p : chiefly ill(chiefly col), facsim, ports(some col) ; 32cm.
Translation of: 'L'Impressionisme'. Paris : Hachette, 1973. — Bibl.: p.318. — Index.
ISBN 0-7064-0690-7 : £10;95
(B77-30493)

759.4 — French paintings. Impressionism. *Dictionaries*
A **dictionary** of Impressionism / [biographies by Raymond Cogniat, Frank Elgar, Jean Selz] ; [with an introduction by Jean Selz]. — London : Eyre Methuen, 1977. — 168p : ill(some col) ; 19cm.
This translation originally published: 1973. — Translation of: 'Dictionnaire de l'impressionisme'. Paris : Hazan, 1972. — Bibl.: p.166-168.
ISBN 0-413-38280-x Pbk : £2.50
(B77-31346)

759.4 — French paintings. Impressionism. *Illustrations*
Muller, Joseph Emile. Impressionism / text by Joseph-Emile Muller. — Bourne End, Bucks. : Spurbooks, [1976]. — 31p,[79]p of plates : col ill, col ports ; 18cm.
ISBN 0-902875-71-x : £2.50
(B77-03692)

759.4 — French paintings. Ingres, Jean Auguste Dominique. *Critical studies*
Ingres, Jean Auguste Dominique. Ingres / [text by] Jon Whiteley. — London (30 Notting Hill Gate, W.11) : Oresko Books Ltd, 1977. — 88p : ill(some col), ports(some col) ; 30cm.
Bibl.: p.16.
ISBN 0-905368-10-x : £7.95
ISBN 0-905368-11-8 Pbk : £3.95
(B77-16525)

759.4 — French paintings. La Tour, Georges de. *Critical studies*
La Tour, Georges de. Georges de La Tour / [text by] Christopher Wright. — Oxford : Phaidon, 1977. — 16p,48p of plates : chiefly col ill ; 32cm. — ([Phaidon colour plate series])
Bibl.: p.14.
ISBN 0-7148-1807-0 : £3.95
(B77-28778)

759.4 — French paintings. Manet, Edouard. *Biographies*
Gay, Peter, *b.1923.* Art and act : on causes in history : Manet, Gropius, Mondrian / [by] Peter Gay. — New York [etc.] ; London : Harper and Row, 1976. — xix,265p : ill, map, ports ; 24cm. — ('Critique' lectures ; 1974)
'... delivered at the Cooper Union [1974]'. — 'Icon editions'. — Bibl.: p.237-259. — Index.
ISBN 0-06-433248-9 : £9.75
Also classified at 759.9492; 720'.92'4
(B77-02491)

759.4 — French paintings. Manet, Edouard. *Critical studies*
Hanson, Anne Coffin. Manet and the modern tradition / [by] Anne Coffin Hanson. — New Haven ; London : Yale University Press, 1977. — xvii,222p,[80]p of plates : ill(some col), facsims, ports(1 col) ; 26cm.
Bibl.: p.210-216. — Index.
ISBN 0-300-01954-8 : £14.50
(B77-32765)

759.4 — French paintings. Manet, Edouard. *Illustrations*
Manet, Edouard. Manet / [text by] John Richardson. — 3rd ed. — Oxford : Phaidon, 1976. — 16,48p of plates : chiefly col ill, col ports ; 32cm. — ([Phaidon colour plate series])
Previous ed.: 1972.
ISBN 0-7148-1743-0 : £3.95
(B77-17007)

759.4 — French paintings. Millet, Jean François. *Critical studies*
Millet, Jean François. Millet / [text by] Griselda Pollock. — London (30 Notting Hill Gate, W.11) : Oresko Books Ltd, 1977. — 96p : chiefly ill(some col), ports ; 30cm.
Bibl.: p.95-96.
ISBN 0-905368-12-6 : £7.95
ISBN 0-905368-13-4 Pbk : £3.95
(B77-33355)

759.4 — French paintings. Monet, Claude Oscar. *Illustrations*
Monet, Claude Oscar. Monet / [text by] John House. — Oxford : Phaidon, 1977. — 16p,48p of plates : chiefly col ill ; 31cm. — ([Phaidon colour plate series])
Bibl.: p.14.
ISBN 0-7148-1809-7 : £3.95
(B77-30494)

759.4 — French paintings. Moreau, Gustave. *Critical studies*
Mathieu, Pierre Louis. Gustave Moreau : complete edition of the finished paintings, watercolours and drawings / [by] Pierre-Louis Mathieu ; [translated from the French by James Emmons]. — Oxford : Phaidon, 1977. — 400p : ill(some col), ports ; 29cm.
Translation of: 'Gustave Moreau'. Fribourg : Office du livre SA, 1977?. — Bibl.: p.382-388. — Index.
ISBN 0-7148-1733-3 : £35.00(£29.95 before publication)
Also classified at 741'.092'4
(B77-14330)

759.4 — French paintings. Post-impressionism. *Illustrations*
The **post-impressionists** / [text by] Frank Elgar. — Oxford : Phaidon, 1977. — 16p,48p of plates : chiefly col ill, col ports ; 31cm. — ([Phaidon colour plate series])
ISBN 0-7148-1810-0 : £3.95
(B77-29586)

759.4 — French paintings. Redouté, Pierre Joseph. *Biographies*
Ridge, Antonia. The man who painted roses : the story of Pierre-Joseph Redouté / [by] Antonia Ridge. — Large print ed. — Leicester : Ulverscroft, 1976. — [5],487p ; 23cm. — (Ulverscroft large print series : [non-fiction])
Originally published: London : Faber, 1974.
ISBN 0-85456-496-9 : £2.65
(B77-00880)

759.4 — French paintings. Rousseau, Henri. *Critical studies*
Rousseau, Henri. Henri Rousseau : 'le douanier' / [text by] Carolyn Keay. — London : Academy Editions, 1976. — 192p : ill(some col), facsims, ports ; 32cm.
Spine title: Rousseau. — Bibl.: p.185-191. — List of films : p.190. — Index. — Includes parallel French text and English translation of a poem by Guillaume Apollinaire.
ISBN 0-85670-168-8 : £15.75
(B77-17664)

759.4 — French paintings. Rousseau, Henri. Local associations: France. Paris. Rue Perrel
Grey, Roch. A visit to the Rue Perrel : from Roch Grey's 'Henri Rousseau' / illustrated by Peter Lord. — Wantage ([28 Bosley's Orchard, Grove, Wantage, Oxon.]) : The Black Swan Press, 1976. — [3],6p : ill ; 20cm.
Limited ed. of 310 copies. — 'Henri Rousseau' originally published: Rome : Valori Plastici, 1924.
ISBN 0-905475-03-8 Sd : £1.05
(B77-11339)

759.4 — French paintings. Toulouse-Lautrec, Henri de. *Illustrations*
Toulouse-Lautrec, Henri de. Toulouse-Lautrec / [text by] Richard Shone. — London : Thames and Hudson, 1977. — [88]p : col ill, col ports ; 28cm.
ISBN 0-500-53012-2 Pbk : £2.50
(B77-27270)

Toulouse-Lautrec, Henri de. Toulouse-Lautrec / [text by] Edward Lucie-Smith. — Oxford : Phaidon, 1977. — 16p,48p of plates : chiefly col ill, col ports ; 31cm. — ([Phaidon colour plate series])
Bibl.: p.14.
ISBN 0-7148-1802-x : £3.95
(B77-28779)

759.4 — Museums. *Cardiff. National Museum of Wales. Exhibits: French paintings. Debré, Olivier. Catalogues. French-Welsh-English parallel texts*
Debré, Olivier. O. Debré / [translation, French-English Jane McGovern, English-Welsh Siân Edwards]. — [Cardiff] : Welsh Arts Council, 1977. — [18]p : chiefly ill ; 25cm.
Catalogue of an exhibition held at the National Museum of Wales, 1977. — Booklet ([10]p.: ports: Sd), [3]cards ([6] sides: col. ill.) in pocket. — Parallel English, French and Welsh text.
Sd : £0.75
(B77-17665)

759.5 — Italian paintings, 1401-1612
Hale, John Rigby. Italian Renaissance painting : from Masaccio to Titian / [by] John Hale. — Oxford : Phaidon, 1977. — 271p : ill(some col), ports(some col) ; 29cm.
Bibl.: p.263. — Index.
ISBN 0-7148-1599-3 : £13.95
(B77-23609)

759.5 — Italian paintings. Botticelli, Sandro. *Critical studies*
Ettlinger, L D. Botticelli / [by] L.D. and Helen S. Ettlinger. — London : Thames and Hudson, 1976. — 216p : ill(some col) ; 22cm. — ([The world of art library])
Bibl.: p.208. — Index.
ISBN 0-500-18156-x : £4.50
(B77-04343)

759.5 — Italian paintings. Botticelli, Sandro. Adoration of the Magi. *Critical studies*
Hatfield, Rab. Botticelli's Uffizi 'Adoration' : a study in pictorial content / [by] Rab Hatfield. — Princeton ; Guildford : Princeton University Press, 1976. — xv,151p,[50]p of plates(2 fold) : ill(incl 1 col), ports ; 25cm. — (Princeton essays on the arts ; 2)
Bibl.: p.133-139. — Index.
ISBN 0-691-03912-7 : £10.10
ISBN 0-691-00310-6 Pbk : £4.15
(B77-06808)

759.5 — Italian paintings. Canaletto, b.1697. *Critical studies*
Constable, William George. Canaletto, Giovanni Antonio Canal, 1697-1768 / by W.G. Constable. — 2nd ed. / revised by J.G. Links. — Oxford : Clarendon Press, 1976. — 2v.(xvi, 723,xivp,leaf of plate,232p of plates) : ill, facsims, geneal table, port ; 26cm.
Previous ed.: 1962. — Bibl.: p.180-186. — Index.
ISBN 0-19-817324-5 : £40.00
(B77-12013)

Links, Joseph Gluckstein. Canaletto and his patrons / [by] J.G. Links. — London : Elek, 1977. — xvi,112p,[72]p of plates : ill(some col), facsim, map(on lining papers), ports ; 26cm.
Bibl.: p.105-109. — Index.
ISBN 0-236-40061-4 : £9.75
(B77-19543)

759.5 — Italian paintings. Correggio. *Critical studies*
Gould, Cecil. The paintings of Correggio / [by] Cecil Gould. — London : Faber, 1976. — 3-307p,[2] leaves of plates,[204]p of plates : ill(some col) ; 29cm.
Bibl.: p.290-295. — Index.
ISBN 0-571-10580-7 : £50.00
(B77-08483)

759.5 — Italian paintings. Gaddi, Agnolo. *Critical studies*
Cole, Bruce. Agnolo Gaddi / [by] Bruce Cole. — Oxford : Clarendon Press, 1977. — xiv,101p, [52]p of plates : ill ; 30cm. — (Oxford studies in the history of art and architecture)
Bibl.: p.91-95. — Index.
ISBN 0-19-817339-3 : £12.50
(B77-27271)

759.5 — Italian paintings. Giotto. *Critical studies*
Cole, Bruce. Giotto and Florentine painting, 1280-1375 / [by] Bruce Cole. — New York [etc.] ; London : Harper and Row, 1976. — x, [1],209p : ill ; 22cm.
Bibl.: p.195-197. — Index.
ISBN 0-06-430900-2 : £8.15
ISBN 0-06-430071-4 Pbk : £3.95
(B77-08484)

759.5 — Italian paintings. Piero della Francesca. Legend of the true cross. *Critical studies*
Podro, Michael. Piero della Francesca's 'Legend of the true cross' / by Michael I. Podro. — [Newcastle upon Tyne] (The Registrar, The University of Newcastle upon Tyne, [Newcastle upon Tyne] NE1 7RU) : University of Newcastle upon Tyne, 1974. — 20,[1]p : ill ; 25cm. — (Charlton lectures on art ; 55th)
'... delivered in the University of Newcastle upon Tyne [on 12th November 1973]'.
ISBN 0-900565-91-8 Sd : £1.00
(B77-19544)

759.5 — Italian portrait paintings. Annigoni, Pietro. *Autobiographies*
Annigoni, Pietro. An artist's life / [by] Pietro Annigoni ; as told to Robert Wraight. — London : W.H. Allen, 1977. — 224p,[32]p of plates : ill, ports ; 24cm.
Index.
ISBN 0-491-01948-3 : £6.95
(B77-19545)

759.5 — Museums. *Oxfordshire. Oxford. Ashmolean Museum. Department of Western Art. Exhibits: Italian paintings. 1300-1600. Catalogues*
Ashmolean Museum. A catalogue of the earlier Italian paintings in the Ashmolean Museum / compiled by Christopher Lloyd. — Oxford : Clarendon Press, 1977. — xxvii,223p,leaf of plate,[82]p of plates : ill, facsims, ports ; 24cm.
Index.
ISBN 0-19-817342-3 : £15.00
(B77-15993)

759.5 — Palaces. *Italy. Florence. Palazzo Pitti. Sala della Stufa & Sala Planetario. Italian frescoes. Pietro da Cortona. Critical studies*
Campbell, Malcolm. Pietro da Cortona at the Pitti Palace : a study of the Planetary Rooms and related projects / [by] Malcolm Campbell. — Princeton ; Guildford : Princeton University Press, 1977. — xviii,307p,iv,[96]p of plates : ill(some col) ; 29cm. — (Princeton monographs in art and archaeology ; 41)
Bibl.: p.289-293. — Index.
ISBN 0-691-03891-0 : £33.80
(B77-27272)

759.5'31 — Art galleries. Exhibits: Venetian paintings from National Gallery. *England, 1700-1800. Catalogues*
National Gallery. The National Gallery lends : pictures from eighteenth-century Venice. — [London] : Arts Council, 1976. — [26]p : ill, 2 ports ; 21cm.
'Places of showing: Bristol City Museum & Art Gallery 23rd October-5th December 1976, Norwich, Castle Museum 11th December-23rd January 1977, Wolverhampton, Central Art Gallery 31st January-13th March 1977' - title page verso.
ISBN 0-7287-0111-1 Sd : £0.75
(B77-04979)

759.6 — Spanish paintings. El Greco. *Illustrations*
El Greco. El Greco / [text by] David Davies. — Oxford : Phaidon, 1976. — 16p,48p of plates : col ill, col ports ; 31cm. — ([Phaidon colour plate series])
ISBN 0-7148-1740-6 : £3.95
(B77-22747)

759.6 — Spanish paintings. Goya y Lucientes, Francisco José de. *Illustrations*
Goya y Lucientes, Francisco José de. Goya / [text by] Sarah Symmons. — London (30 Notting Hill Gate, W.11) : Oresko Books Ltd, 1977. — 104p : chiefly ill(some col), ports(some col) ; 31cm.
Bibl.: p.22-24.
ISBN 0-905368-14-2 : £8.95
ISBN 0-905368-15-0 Pbk : £4.95
(B77-29587)

759.6 — Spanish paintings. Goya y Lucientes, Francisco José de. Criticism, 1771-1975
Glendinning, Nigel. Goya and his critics / [by] Nigel Glendinning. — New Haven ; London : Yale University Press, 1977. — xii,340p : ill, facsim, ports ; 26cm.
Bibl.: p.255-285. — Index.
ISBN 0-300-02011-2 : £15.50
(B77-25107)

759.6 — Spanish paintings. Picasso, Pablo. *Critical studies*
Malraux, André. Picasso's mask / [by] André Malraux ; translated and annotated by June Guicharnaud with Jacques Guicharnaud. — London : Macdonald and Jane's, 1976. — xi, 273p : ill ; 22cm.
Translation of 'La tête d'obsidienne'. Paris : Gallimard, 1974.
ISBN 0-354-04015-4 : £6.50
(B77-03160)

Picasso in perspective / edited by Gert Schiff. — Englewood Cliffs ; London [etc.] : Prentice-Hall, 1976. — viii,184p,[16]p of plates : ill, port ; 24cm. — (The artists in perspective series)
Bibl.: p.179-182.
ISBN 0-13-675801-0 : Unpriced
ISBN 0-13-675793-6 Pbk : £3.15
(B77-16526)

759.6 — Spanish paintings. Picasso, Pablo. Studios, 1973. *Illustrations*
Duncan, David Douglas. The silent studio / [by] David Douglas Duncan. — London : Collins, 1976. — 112p : chiefly ill, ports ; 28cm.
Ill. on lining papers.
ISBN 0-00-216768-9 : £5.50
(B77-00336)

759.6 — Spanish paintings. Velazquez, Diego Rodriguez de Silva y. *Critical studies*
Kahr, Madlyn Millner. Velázquez : the art of painting / [by] Madlyn Millner Kahr. — New York [etc.] ; London : Harper and Row, 1976. — xii,233p : ill, facsims, ports ; 24cm. — (Icon editions)
Bibl.: p.221-225. — Index.
ISBN 0-06-433575-5 : £9.75
ISBN 0-06-430079-x Pbk : £4.50
(B77-22038)

759.81 — Norwegian paintings. Munch, Edvard. *Illustrations*
Munch, Edvard. Edvard Munch / [edited by] Ian Dunlop. — London : Thames and Hudson, 1977. — [88]p : col ill, col ports ; 28cm.
ISBN 0-500-53011-4 Pbk : £2.50
(B77-27273)

Munch, Edvard. Munch / [text by] John Boulton Smith. — Oxford : Phaidon, 1977. — 16p,48p of plates : chiefly col ill ; 32cm. — ([Phaidon colour plate series])
Bibl.: p.14.
ISBN 0-7148-1799-6 : £3.95
(B77-29588)

759.89 — Danish paintings. Jorn, Asger, 1954-1964. *Critical studies*
Atkins, Guy. Asger Jorn, the crucial years, 1954-1964 : a study of Asger Jorn's artistic development from 1954 to 1964 and a catalogue of his oil paintings from that period / [by] Guy Atkins ; with the help of Troels Andersen. — London : Lund Humphries, 1977. — 396p : ill(some col), facsims, ports ; 30cm.
Col. ill. tipped in. — Bibl.: p.231-307. — Index.
ISBN 0-85331-398-9 : £37.50
(B77-18300)

759.938 — Ancient Greek paintings. Colour & shading. *Techniques*
Bruno, Vincent J. Form and colour in Greek painting / [by] Vincent J. Bruno. — London : Thames and Hudson, 1977. — 123p,16p of plates : ill(chiefly col) ; 26cm.
Also published: New York : Norton, 1977. — Bibl.: p.115-117. — Index.
ISBN 0-500-23267-9 : £10.00
(B77-23610)

759.94 — Art galleries. *London. Westminster (London Borough). National Gallery. Exhibits. Catalogues*
National Gallery. The National Gallery, London / [by] Homan Potterton ; with a preface by Michael Levey. — London : Thames and Hudson, 1977. — 216p : ill(some col), plan, ports(some col) ; 21cm. — (The world of art library)
Bibl.: p.24. — Includes a complete catalogue of the paintings.
ISBN 0-500-20161-7 Pbk : £2.50
(B77-30495)

759.94 — Art galleries. *London. Westminster (London Borough). National Gallery. Exhibits. Illustrations*
National Gallery. The National Gallery, London / [text by] Michael Wilson. — London : Orbis Books, 1977. — 136p : chiefly ill(chiefly col), plan, ports(chiefly col) ; 30cm.
Ill. on lining papers.
ISBN 0-85613-314-0 : £6.25
(B77-29589)

759.94 — Art galleries. *Ohio. Toledo. Toledo Museum of Art. Exhibits: European paintings. Catalogues*
Toledo Museum of Art. European paintings / Toledo Museum of Art. — Toledo, Ohio : The Museum ; University Park, Pa. ; London : Distributed by Pennsylvania State University Press, 1976. — 396p : ill(some col), ports(1 col) ; 26cm.
ISBN 0-271-01249-8 : £16.85
ISBN 0-271-02148-x Pbk : £9.35
(B77-26438)

759.94 — European paintings, ca 1400-ca 1950. *Critical studies*
Gaunt, William. The W.H. Smith treasury of painting through five centuries / by William Gaunt. — [Oxford] : Phaidon for W.H. Smith and Son Ltd, 1976. — 3-66p,iii,76p of plates : ill(chiefly col), ports(chiefly col) ; 29cm.
ISBN 0-7148-1778-3 : £4.95
(B77-03693)

759.94 — European wall paintings, to 1909
Gombrich, Ernst Hans. Means and ends : reflections on the history of fresco painting / [by] E.H. Gombrich. — London : Thames and Hudson, 1976. — 72p : ill ; 22cm. — (Walter Neurath memorial lectures ; 8)
8 ... the eight of the Walter Neurath memorial lectures ... given annually each spring ... ' - half title page verso.
ISBN 0-500-55008-5 : £3.50
(B77-10487)

759.94 — Museums. *Kent. Maidstone. Maidstone Museum and Art Gallery. Exhibits: European paintings, ca 1400-ca 1870. Catalogues*
Maidstone Museum and Art Gallery. Foreign paintings catalogue [of the] Maidstone Museum and Art Gallery / [compiled by] Susan Legouix. — Maidstone (St Faith's St., Maidstone, Kent) : Maidstone Borough Council for the Maidstone Museum and Art Gallery, 1976. — 52p : ill, ports ; 20x22cm.
Index.
ISBN 0-905567-00-5 Sd : £0.80
(B77-04980)

759.94 — Museums. *London. Westminster (London Borough). Wallace Collection. Exhibits: European paintings, 1480-1890. Catalogues*
Wallace Collection. Forty paintings / Wallace Collection. — London (Manchester Sq., W1M 6BN) : Trustees of the Wallace Collection, 1977. — [7],40p : chiefly col ill, col ports ; 18cm.
Pbk : £1.25
(B77-25793)

759.94 — Museums. Stock: European paintings. Collections: Kress Collection. *United States, 1400-1900. Catalogues*
Eisler, Colin Tobias. Paintings from the Samuel H. Kress collection : European schools, excluding Italian / by Colin Eisler. — Oxford : Phaidon Press for the Samuel H. Kress Foundation, 1977. — xii,639p,[64]p of plates : ill(some col), coat of arms, ports(some col) ; 31cm.
Bibl.: p.xi-xii. — Index.
ISBN 0-7148-1453-9 : £18.00
(B77-12014)

759.941 — Art galleries. *London. Westminster (London Borough). Royal Academy. Exhibits: British paintings, 1952-1977. Catalogues*
Royal Academy. British painting 1952-1977. — London (Piccadilly, W1V 0DS) : Royal Academy of Arts, 1977. — 129p : of ill, ports ; 20x21cm.
Catalogue of an exhibition held at and organized by the Royal Academy, 24 Sept.-20 Nov. 1977. — Index.
Pbk : £2.95
(B77-32056)

759.941 — British naïve paintings, 1900-1976. *Critical studies*
Twentieth century British naïve and primitive artists / [compiled by] Eric Lister and Sheldon Williams. — London : Astragal Books, 1977. — viii,100p,[16]p of plates : chiefly ill(some col) ; 26cm.
Bibl.: p.96-100.
ISBN 0-85139-083-8 : £8.95
(B77-33356)

759.941 — British paintings, 1880-1940. *Biographical dictionaries*
Johnson, Jane. The dictionary of British artists, 1880-1940 : an Antique Collectors' Club research project, listing 41,000 artists / compiled by J. Johnson and A. Greutzner. — Woodbridge : Antique Collectors' Club, 1976. — [3],567p ; 29cm.
ISBN 0-902028-36-7 : £17.50
(B77-07523)

759.941 — British paintings, 1900-1976. *Critical studies*
The **century** of change : British painting since 1900 / [compiled by] Richard Shone. — Oxford : Phaidon, 1977. — 240p : chiefly ill(some col), ports ; 29cm.
Bibl.: p.46. — Index.
ISBN 0-7148-1782-1 : £12.95
(B77-32057)

759.941 — British watercolour paintings, 1750-1850. *Critical studies*
British watercolours, 1750 to 1850 / [text by] Andrew Wilton. — Oxford : Phaidon, 1977. — 3-208p : ill(some col), col port ; 29cm.
Bibl.: p.59-61. — Index.
ISBN 0-7148-1713-9 : £12.95
(B77-29590)

759.941 — British watercolour paintings, to 1920. *Biographical dictionaries*
Mallalieu, H L. The dictionary of British watercolour artists up to 1920 / [compiled by] H.L. Mallalieu. — [Woodbridge] : Antique Collectors' Club, 1976. — 299p : ill, geneal tables ; 29cm.
Jacket spine title: British watercolour artists up to 1920.
ISBN 0-902028-48-0 : £15.00
(B77-08485)

759.941 — Museums. *London. Kensington and Chelsea (London Borough). Victoria and Albert Museum. Exhibits: British watercolour paintings, 1740-ca 1880. Catalogues*
Victoria and Albert Museum. Forty two British watercolours from the Victoria and Albert Museum / [by] John Murdoch. — London : [The Museum], 1977. — [3]p,42 leaves of plates : ill, port ; 20x21cm.
Catalogue of an exhibition held at Phoenix Art Museum and five other American and Canadian art galleries. — Leaves printed on both sides.
ISBN 0-901486-99-x Pbk : £1.30
(B77-12015)

759.9411 — Arts. Patronage. Organisations. *Scotland. Scottish Arts Council. Exhibits: Scottish paintings. Dingwall, Kenneth. Catalogues*
Dingwall, Kenneth. Kenneth Dingwall : paintings, drawings and constructions : [catalogue of an exhibition held at] the Scottish Arts Council Gallery, 19 Charlotte Square, Edinburgh, 10 June to 3 July 1977. — Edinburgh (19 Charlotte Sq., Edinburgh) : Scottish Arts Council, 1977. — 3-71p : chiefly ill(some col), port ; 22x23cm.
Fold. cover.
ISBN 0-902989-41-3 Pbk : Unpriced
Also classified at 741.9'411
(B77-25794)

759.9411 — Museums. *Oxfordshire. Oxford. Ashmolean Museum. Department of Western Art. Exhibits: Scottish paintings, 1940-1976. Catalogues*
Hall, Douglas, *b.1926.* Four contemporary Scottish painters : Eardley, Haig, Philipson, Pulsford : [catalogue of an exhibition held at the] Ashmolean Museum, Oxford, 15 September-30 October 1977 / [by Douglas Hall]. — Oxford ([University of Oxford, Oxford OX1 2PH]) : The Museum, 1977. — 15,[1]p : ill ; 18x21cm.
ISBN 0-900090-48-0 Sd : Unpriced
(B77-30496)

759.9411 — Scottish paintings, 1837-1939. *Critical studies*
Hardie, William R. Scottish painting, 1837-1939 / [by] William Hardie. — London : Studio Vista, 1976. — 112p,[96]p of plates : ill(some col), ports ; 29cm.
Ill. on lining papers. — Bibl.: p.105-109. — Index.
ISBN 0-289-70482-0 : £12.00
(B77-09857)

759.9411 — Scottish paintings. Cadell, Francis Campbell Boileau; Hunter, Leslie, b.1879 & Peploe, Samuel John. *Biographies*
Honeyman, Tom John. Three Scottish colourists : S.J. Peploe, F.C.B. Cadell, Leslie Hunter / [by] T.J. Honeyman. — Edinburgh : P. Harris, 1977. — xi,122p,[24]p of plates : ill, ports ; 16cm.
Originally published: London : Nelson, 1950. — Index.
ISBN 0-904505-25-1 : £2.00
(B77-17008)

759.9411 — Scottish paintings. Eardley, Joan. *Critical studies*
Buchanan, William. Joan Eardley / by William Buchanan. — Edinburgh : Edinburgh University Press, 1976. — [4],91p : ill(some col), ports ; 16x22cm. — (Modern Scottish painters ; no.5)
Bibl.: p.88.
ISBN 0-85224-301-4 : £2.50
(B77-18301)

759.9411 — Scottish paintings. McEwen, Rory. Special subjects: Tulips. *Illustrations*
Blunt, Wilfrid. Tulips & tulipomania / by Wilfrid Blunt. — Fully revised ed. / with sixteen plates from paintings by Rory McEwen. — London ([32 Englands La., N.W.3]) : Basilisk Press, 1977. — 100p : ill(some col), facsim, port ; 30cm.
Limited ed. of 515 signed copies, of which 500 are for sale and numbered, the remainder being lettered. — Quarter leather. — Col. ill. tipped in. — Accompanied by 8 sheets (col. ill.;59x52cm) all in box (62cm). — Previous ed.: published as 'Tulipomania'. Harmondsworth : Penguin, 1950. — Bibl.: p.95-96. — Index.
£314.60
Primary classification 635.9'34'324
(B77-25018)

759.9411 — Scottish paintings. Maxwell, John. *Critical studies*
McClure, David. John Maxwell / by David McClure. — Edinburgh : Edinburgh University Press, 1976. — [4],69p : ill(some col), ports ; 16x22cm. — (Modern Scottish painters ; no.4)
Bibl.: p.66.
ISBN 0-85224-300-6 : £2.25
(B77-18302)

759.9411 — Scottish paintings. Nasmyth family. *Critical studies*
Johnson, Peter, *b.1930 (Feb.).* The Nasmyth family of painters ... / by Peter Johnson & Ernlé Money. — Leigh-on-Sea : F. Lewis, 1977. — 64p,[35]leaves of plates : ill, ports ; 30cm.
Limited ed. of 500 copies. — Bibl.: p.64.
ISBN 0-85317-045-2 : £15.50
(B77-18303)

759.9411 — Scottish paintings. Painters, 1586-1976. *Biographical dictionaries*
Investing in Scottish pictures / edited by Paul Harris. — Edinburgh : P. Harris ; London [etc.] : Sotheby's Belgravia, 1977. — 96p,[8]p of plates : ill ; 16cm.
Bibl.: p.93-94.
ISBN 0-904505-18-9 : £2.00
(B77-15994)

759.9411 — Scottish paintings. Philipson, Robin. *Critical studies*
Lindsay, Maurice. Robin Philipson / by Maurice Lindsay. — Edinburgh : Edinburgh University Press, 1976. — [4],79p : ill(some col), ports ; 16x22cm. — (Modern Scottish painters ; no.6)
Bibl.: p.75.
ISBN 0-85224-302-2 : £2.25
(B77-33357)

759.9415 — Art galleries. *Texas. Dallas. Dallas Museum of Fine Arts. Exhibits: Irish watercolour paintings from National Gallery of Ireland, 1675-1925. Catalogues*
National Gallery of Ireland. Irish watercolours, 1675-1925 : from the National Gallery of Ireland : [catalogue of] a loan exhibition at the Dallas Museum of Fine Arts [held] October-November 1976. — Dublin (Dublin 2) : National Gallery of Ireland, 1976. — 23p, [30]p of plates, leaf of plate : ill, ports ; 23cm.
Bibl.: p.6.
ISBN 0-903162-04-0 Pbk : Unpriced
(B77-04344)

759.9492 — Art galleries. *London. Westminster (London Borough). Alan Jacobs Gallery. Exhibits: Dutch landscape paintings. Goyen, Jan van. Catalogues*
Alan Jacobs Gallery. Jan van Goyen, 1596-1656, poet of the Dutch landscape : paintings from museums and private collections in Great Britain. — London : Alan Jacobs Gallery ; Bradford [etc.] : Distributed by Lund Humphries, 1977. — 112p : ill(some col), port ; 25cm.
'Published to coincide with the exhibition "Jan van Goyen, poet of the Dutch landscape", 20 April-25 May 1977, at the Alan Jacobs Gallery ...' - title page verso. — Bibl.: p.38-39. — Index.
ISBN 0-9503121-2-6 : Unpriced
ISBN 0-9503121-3-4 Pbk : Unpriced
(B77-19546)

759.9492 — Dutch paintings, 1600-1700. *Collectors' guides*
Jacobs, Alan. 17th century Dutch and Flemish painters : a collectors' guide / compiled by Alan Jacobs. — London [etc.] : McGraw-Hill, 1976. — 297p : ill(some col), ports ; 22x28cm.
Revision of: 'A classified synopsis of the principal painters of the Dutch and Flemish schools, their scholars, imitators and analogists' / by George Stanley. London : H.G. Bohn, 1855. — Bibl.: p.277. — Index.
ISBN 0-07-084477-1 : £25.00
Also classified at 759.9493
(B77-06213)

759.9492 — Dutch paintings, 1600-1700. *Lists. Facsimiles*
Groot, C Hofstede de. A catalogue raisonné of the works of the most eminent Dutch painters of the seventeenth century / based on the work of John Smith ; by C. Hofstede de Groot ; [translated from the German by Edward G. Hawke]. — Teaneck : Somerset House ; Cambridge (21 Bateman St., Cambridge CB2 1NB) : Chadwyck-Healey, 1976. — 2v. ; 23cm.
Four facsimile pages printed on each page. — Facsimile reprint of: 1st ed. of this translation. London : Macmillan, 1907-1927. — Index.
ISBN 0-85964-027-2 : £72.00
(B77-03694)

759.9492 — Dutch paintings, 1600-ca 1700. *Illustrations*
Dutch & Flemish painting : 110 illustrations / selected & introduced by Christopher Brown. — Oxford : Phaidon, 1977. — [16]p,96p of plates : chiefly ill(chiefly col), ports(chiefly col) ; 42cm.
ISBN 0-7148-1772-4 Pbk : £4.50
Also classified at 759.9493
(B77-25108)

759.9492 — Dutch paintings, ca 1450-ca 1700. *Critical studies*
Leymarie, Jean. Dutch painting / by Jean Leymarie ; [translated from the French by Stuart Gilbert]. — Geneva : Editions d'Art Albert Skira ; London : Macmillan, 1977. — 214p : col ill(tipped in) ; 35cm.
Translation of: 'Peinture hollandaise'. Geneva : Editions d'Art Albert Skira, 1974. — Bibl.: p.201-204. — Index.
ISBN 0-333-21540-0 : £25.00
(B77-10879)

759.9492 — Dutch paintings, ca 1600- ca 1710. *Illustrations*
Wiesner, Herbert. Master painters of Holland : Dutch painting in the seventeenth century / [by] Herbert Wiesner. — Oxford : Phaidon Press, 1976. — 31p,[80]p of plates : ill(some col), ports ; 29cm.
ISBN 0-7148-1779-1 : £5.95
(B77-01688)

759.9492 — Dutch paintings. Hals, Frans. *Illustrations*
Hals, Frans. Frans Hals / [text by] Christopher Wright. — Oxford : Phaidon, 1977. — 15p,48p of plates : col ill, col ports ; 31cm. — ([Phaidon colour plate series])
Also published: New York : Dutton, 1977. — Bibl.: p.15.
ISBN 0-7148-1750-3 : £3.95
(B77-23611)

759.9492 — Dutch paintings. Mondrian, Piet. *Biographies*
Gay, Peter, *b.1923.* Art and act : on causes in history : Manet, Gropius, Mondrian / [by] Peter Gay. — New York [etc.] ; London : Harper and Row, 1976. — xix,265p : ill, map, ports ; 24cm. — ('Critique' lectures ; 1974)
'... delivered at the Cooper Union [1974]'. — 'Icon editions'. — Bibl.: p.237-259. — Index.
ISBN 0-06-433248-9 : £9.75
Primary classification 759.4
(B77-02491)

759.9492 — Dutch paintings. Steen, Jan. Special subjects: Biblical themes & classical antiquity. *Critical studies*
Kirschenbaum, Baruch D. The religious and historical paintings of Jan Steen / [by] Baruch D. Kirschenbaum. — Oxford : Phaidon, 1977. — 261p : ill(incl 1 col tipped in), ports ; 29cm.
Also published: New York : Allenheld and Schram, 1977. — Bibl.: p.251-255. — Index.
ISBN 0-7148-1777-5 : £20.00
(B77-19547)

759.9492 — Dutch paintings. Van Gogh, Vincent. *Illustrations*
Van Gogh, Vincent. Vincent van Gogh / [text by] Richard Shone. — London : Thames and Hudson, 1977. — [8]p,40 leaves of plates : chiefly col ill, col ports ; 28cm.
Leaves printed on both sides.
ISBN 0-500-53016-5 Pbk : £2.50
(B77-31347)

759.9492 — Dutch paintings. Vermeer, Jan. *Illustrations*
Vermeer, Jan. Vermeer / [text by] Christopher Wright. — London (30 Notting Hill Gate, W11 3HX) : Oresko Books Ltd, 1976. — 87p : ill(some col), port ; 30cm.
Bibl.: p.82-85. — Index.
ISBN 0-905368-00-2 : £7.95
ISBN 0-905368-04-5 Pbk : £3.95
(B77-16527)

759.9493 — Flemish paintings, 1420-1640. *Illustrations*
Flemish painting / [text by] Anthea Peppin and William Vaughan. — Oxford : Phaidon, 1977. — 16p,48p of plates : chiefly col ill, col ports ; 31cm. — ([Phaidon colour plates series])
ISBN 0-7148-1747-3 : £3.95
(B77-22039)

759.9493 — Flemish paintings, 1600-1700. *Collectors' guides*
Jacobs, Alan. 17th century Dutch and Flemish painters : a collectors' guide / compiled by Alan Jacobs. — London [etc.] : McGraw-Hill, 1976. — 297p : ill(some col), ports ; 22x28cm.
Revision of: 'A classified synopsis of the principal painters of the Dutch and Flemish schools, their scholars, imitators and analogists' / by George Stanley. London : H.G. Bohn, 1855. — Bibl.: p.277. — Index.
ISBN 0-07-084477-1 : £25.00
Primary classification 759.9492
(B77-06213)

759.9493 — Flemish paintings, 1600-ca 1700. *Illustrations*
Dutch & Flemish painting : 110 illustrations / selected & introduced by Christopher Brown. — Oxford : Phaidon, 1977. — [16]p,96p of plates : chiefly ill(chiefly col), ports(chiefly col) ; 42cm.
ISBN 0-7148-1772-4 Pbk : £4.50
Primary classification 759.9492
(B77-25108)

759.9493 — Flemish paintings. Bruegel, Pieter
Gibson, Walter S. Bruegel / [by] Walter S. Gibson. — London : Thames and Hudson, 1977. — 216p : ill(some col), map ; 22cm. — ([The world of art library])
Bibl.: p.207-209. — Index.
ISBN 0-500-18159-4 : £4.50
(B77-21337)

759.9493 — Flemish paintings. Rubens, Sir Peter Paul. *Illustrations*
Rubens, *Sir* **Peter Paul.** Rubens : 108 reproductions / compiled and with an introduction by Keith Roberts. — Oxford : Phaidon, 1977. — [16]p,96p of plates : chiefly ill(chiefly col), ports(chiefly col) ; 42cm.
ISBN 0-7148-1796-1 Pbk : £4.50
(B77-26439)

759.9493 — Flemish paintings. Rubens, Sir Peter Paul. Influence of Italy
Jaffé, Michael. Rubens and Italy / [by] Michael Jaffé. — Oxford : Phaidon, 1977. — 128p,[207] p of plates : ill(some col), ports(some col) ; 29cm.
Bibl.: p.121-123. — Index.
ISBN 0-7148-1575-6 : £35.00
(B77-23612)

759.9495 — Greek gouache paintings. Vassos, John. Illustrations for books. *Illustrations*
Vassos, John. 'Contempo', 'Phobia' and other graphic interpretations / [by] John Vassos ; with a foreword by P.K. Thomajan. — New York : Dover Publications [etc.] ; London : Constable, 1976. — ii-xi,115p : of ill, ports ; 31cm.
ISBN 0-486-23338-3 Pbk : £3.60
(B77-13172)

759.9497 — Yugoslav naive paintings, 1930-1976. *Illustrations*
Naive art : paintings from Yugoslavia : 120 illustrations / selected and introduced by Boris Kelemen. — Oxford : Phaidon, 1977. — [16]p, 96p of plates : chiefly ill(chiefly col), ports(some col) ; 42cm. — (Giant art paperbacks)
Originally published: with text in Serbo-Croat as 'Naivno slikarstvo u Jugoslaviji'. Zagreb : Spektar, 1977. — Bibl.: p.[16].
ISBN 0-7148-1795-3 Pbk : £4.50
Also classified at 741.9'497
(B77-31348)

759.951 — Arts. Patronage. Organisations. *Great Britain. Arts Council of Great Britain. Exhibits: Chinese folk paintings, ca 1965-1974. Catalogues*
Brett, Guy. Peasant paintings from Hu county, Shensi province, China = Chung-Kuo Hu-hsien nung-min hua / [by Guy Brett]. — [London] : Arts Council of Great Britain, 1976. — 68p : chiefly ill(some col) ; 20x21cm.
Transliterated Chinese parallel title. — Catalogue of an Arts Council exhibition held at the Warehouse Gallery, Covent Garden, from 18 November to 23 December 1976'. — Includes two poems by Mao Tse-tùng in Chinese with parallel English translation.
ISBN 0-7287-0103-0 Pbk : £1.50
(B77-04981)

759.954'12 — Mithila paintings. *Illustrations*
Véquaud, Yves. The art of Mithila : ceremonial paintings from an ancient kingdom / [by] Yves Véquaud ; [translated from the French by George Robinson]. — London : Thames and Hudson, 1977. — 112p : ill(some col) ; 28cm.
Translation of: 'L'art du Mithila'. Paris : Les presses de la connaissance, 1976.
ISBN 0-500-27093-7 Pbk : £3.50
(B77-32058)

759.9549'3 — Art galleries. *London. Greenwich (London Borough). Woodlands Art Gallery. Exhibits: Sri Lanka paintings. Perera, Ed. Catalogues*
Woodlands Art Gallery. Ian McGugan and Ed Perera : paintings : [catalogue of an exhibition held] 9 October to 9 November 1976 [at] Woodlands Art Gallery. — London ([c/o Woodlands Art Gallery], 90 Mycenae Rd, SE3 7SE) : London Borough of Greenwich, [1976]. — [11]p : ill ; 21cm.
Sheet (1 side) as insert.
ISBN 0-9504033-5-0 Sd : Unpriced
Primary classification 759.11
(B77-12011)

759.955 — Persian oil paintings, ca 1725-ca 1900. *Illustrations*
Robinson, Basil William. Persian oil paintings / [by] B.W. Robinson. — London : H.M.S.O., 1977. — [12]p : col ill ; 16cm. — (Victoria and Albert Museum. Small colour books ; 20)
ISBN 0-11-290268-5 Sd : £0.40
(B77-25795)

759.955 — Royal courts. Iranian paintings. *Iran, ca 1570-1600*
Welch, Anthony. Artists for the Shah : late sixteenth-century painting at the Imperial Court of Iran / [by] Anthony Welch. — New Haven ; London : Yale University Press, 1976. — xvii, 233p,16p of plates : ill(some col), facsims(some col) ; 24cm.
Bibl.: p.221-223. — Index.
ISBN 0-300-01915-7 : £16.50
(B77-09169)

759.986'1 — Colombian paintings. Botero, Fernando. *Illustrations*
Botero, Fernando. Fernando Botero / [text by] Klaus Gallwitz ; [translated from the German by John Gabriel]. — London : Thames and Hudson, 1976. — 88p : chiefly ill(some col), ports ; 21x23cm. — (Art now)
Originally published: in German. Stuttgart : Gerd Hatje, 1976. — Bibl.: p.86-88.
ISBN 0-500-09117-x : £5.00
Also classified at 741.9'86'1
(B77-07524)

759.9931 — New Zealand paintings. Conly, Maurice. Special subjects: Antarctic. Ross Sea region. *Illustrations*
Conly, Maurice. Ice on my palette / [paintings and sketches by] Maurice Conly ; text by Neville Peat. — Christchurch, N.Z. [etc.] ; London : Whitcoulls, 1977. — 64p : ill(chiefly col), 2 col maps ; 27x35cm.
ISBN 0-7233-0500-5 : £11.45
Also classified at 919.8'9
(B77-23613)

759.9931 — New Zealand paintings. McIntyre, Peter. Special subjects: New Zealand. Wellington, 1948-1974. *Illustrations*
McIntyre, Peter. Peter McIntyre's Wellington. — Wellington [N.Z.] [etc.] ; London : A.H. and A.W. Reed, 1975. — [76]p : chiefly ill(some col), ports ; 28cm.
Col. ill. tipped in. — Ill. on lining papers.
ISBN 0-589-00936-2 : £12.60
Primary classification 993.12'7
(B77-01956)

759.994 — Art galleries. *London. Westminster (London Borough). Fischer Fine Art Limited. Exhibits: Australian paintings. Boyd, Arthur. Catalogues*
Boyd, Arthur. Arthur Boyd : recent paintings, 1977. — London (30 King St., S.W.1) : Fischer Fine Art Ltd, [1977]. — [28]p : chiefly ill(chiefly col) ; 18cm.
Bibl.: p.[24].
ISBN 0-904867-10-2 Pbk : £1.50
(B77-14331)

760 — GRAPHIC ARTS

760 — Brass rubbings. Techniques
Norris, Malcolm. Brass rubbing / [by] Malcolm Norris. — London [etc.] : Pan Books, 1977. — 112p : ill, facsims, ports ; 25cm. — (Pan craft books)
Originally published: London : Studio Vista, 1965. — Bibl.: p.103-106. — Index.
ISBN 0-330-25095-7 Pbk : £1.50
Also classified at 739'.52'0941
(B77-19548)

760 — Graphic arts, 1450-1972. Special subjects: War. *Illustrations*
Battle art : images of war : 106 reproductions / selected & introduced by Denis Thomas. — Oxford : Phaidon, 1977. — [15]p,96p of plates : chiefly ill(chiefly col), col ports ; 42cm. — (Giant art paperbacks)
ISBN 0-7148-1773-2 Pbk : £4.50
(B77-32766)

760 — Graphic arts. Special subjects: Cats, ca 1600-1975. *Illustrations*
The illustrated cat / compiled by Jean-Claude Saurès ; designed by Seymour Chwast ; edited by William E. Maloney. — London : Omnibus Press, 1976. — 72p : chiefly ill(some col), facsims(some col) ; 33cm.
'A Push Pin Press/Omnibus Press book'.
ISBN 0-86001-295-6 Pbk : £2.95
(B77-17666)

760 — Museums. *Oxfordshire. Oxford. Ashmolean Museum. Exhibits: Brass rubbings*
Ashmolean Museum. Rare brass rubbings from the Ashmolean collection / [by] Jerome Bertram. — Oxford ([University of Oxford, Oxford OX1 2PH]) : The Museum, 1977. — [40]p : ill, ports ; 22cm.
Bibl.: p.[5].
ISBN 0-900090-34-0 Sd : £0.75
(B77-22748)

760 — Rubbings. Techniques. *Manuals. Juvenile literature*
Openshaw, Patricia. Fun with making rubbings / [by] Patricia Openshaw. — London : Kaye and Ward [etc.], 1977. — 64p : ill ; 26cm. — ([Learning with fun])
With answers.
ISBN 0-7182-0099-3 : £2.15
(B77-17667)

760'.074'02789 — Museums. *Cumbria. Brampton. LYC Museum and Gallery. Arts Room. Exhibits: Graphic arts by visitors. Serials*
LYC arts. — Brampton (Banks, Brampton, Cumbria CA8 2JH) : LYC Press, 1976. — [32] p : chiefly ill, facsims ; 14cm.
ISBN 0-9504537-2-2 Sd : £0.15
(B77-05561)

760'.092'2 — Graphic arts. Artists, to 1975. Monograms, signatures & symbols. *Dictionaries*
Caplan, Hillier Harris. The classified directory of artists signatures, symbols & monograms / [compiled by] H.H. Caplan. — London : Prior, 1976. — [5],viii,738[i.e.744]p : chiefly facsims ; 31cm.
English text, English, French, German, Spanish and Italian introduction.
ISBN 0-86043-004-9 : £29.50
(B77-00337)

760'.092'4 — Art galleries. *London. Greenwich (London Borough). Woodlands Art Gallery. Exhibits: English graphic arts. Middleton, Max. Catalogues*
Woodlands Art Gallery. Frederick Palmer and Max Middleton : paintings, drawings and prints : [catalogue of an exhibition held] 13 November to 14 December 1976 [at] Woodlands Art Gallery. — London ([c/o Woodlands Art Gallery], 90 Mycenae Rd, SE3 7SE) : London Borough of Greenwich, [1976]. — [11]p : ill ; 21cm.
ISBN 0-905950-00-3 Sd : Unpriced
Also classified at 759.2
(B77-11340)

760'.092'4 — Art galleries. *Nottinghamshire. Nottingham. Nottingham University Art Gallery. Exhibits: New Zealand graphic arts. Boswell, James, b.1906. Catalogues*
Nottingham University Art Gallery. James Boswell, 1906-71, drawings, illustrations and paintings / [Nottingham University Art Gallery]. — [Nottingham] (Department of Fine Art, Portland Building, [University of Nottingham, University Park, Nottingham NG7 2RD]) : The Gallery, 1976. — 32p : ill, port ; 25cm.
Catalogue of an exhibition held 22 November-16 December 1976. — 'Handlist' / by Ronald Pickvance (folder ([4]p.)) as insert. — Bibl.: p.32.
ISBN 0-9504622-1-7 Sd : £0.50
(B77-06809)

760'.092'4 — Australian graphic arts. Lindsay, Norman. *Biographies*
Hetherington, John, *b.1907.* Norman Lindsay : the embattled Olympian / [by] John Hetherington. — Melbourne ; London [etc.] : Oxford University Press, 1976. — xv,272p,leaf of plate,[20]p of plates : ill(incl 1 col), ports ; 24cm.
Ill. on lining papers. — Originally published: 1973. — Bibl.: p.259-262. — Index.
£6.50
(B77-27274)

760'.092'4 — English graphic arts. Hogarth, William. *Biographies*
Lindsay, Jack. Hogarth : his art and his world / [by] Jack Lindsay. — London : Hart-Davis MacGibbon, 1977. — x,277p,[32]p of plates : ill, ports ; 24cm.
Bibl.: p.260-268. — Index.
ISBN 0-246-10837-1 : £10.00
(B77-19549)

760'.092'4 — English graphic arts. Lear, Edward. *Biographies*
Lehmann, John. Edward Lear and his world / [by] John Lehmann. — [London] : Thames and Hudson, 1977. — 128p : ill, facsims, ports ; 24cm.
Bibl.: p.118-119. — Index.
ISBN 0-500-13061-2 : £3.95
(B77-28780)

760'.092'4 — English graphic arts. Woodroffe, Patrick. *Illustrations*
Woodroffe, Patrick. 'Mythopoeikon' : fantasies, monsters, nightmares, daydreams : the paintings, book-jacket illustrations and record-sleeve designs of Patrick Woodroffe ; with a commentary by the artist. — [Limpsfield] ([The Bower, High St., Limpsfield, Surrey RH8 0DY]) : [Dragon's World Ltd], [1976]. — 156p : chiefly ill(chiefly col), col facsims, col ports ; 31cm.
ISBN 0-905071-09-3 : £6.95
IBSBN 0-905071-08-5 Pbk : £3.95
(B77-27275)

760'.092'4 — French graphic arts. Redon, Odilon. *Critical studies*
Hobbs, Richard. Odilon Redon / [by] Richard Hobbs. — London : Studio Vista, 1977. — 192p : ill(some col), ports(some col) ; 29cm.
Bibl.: p.173-178. — Index.
ISBN 0-289-70615-7 : £10.50
(B77-14332)

760'.092'4 — Great Britain. Army. Royal Army Medical Corps. Colleges: Royal Army Medical College. Exhibits: English graphic arts. Grundy, John Hull. Catalogues
Burgess, N R H. Exhibition of works by John Hull Grundy : [catalogue of an exhibition held] 6th December 1976 to 28 January 1977, 10am to 4pm, in the Study Centre of the Royal Army Medical College ... / [compiled by N.R.H. Burgess]. — [London] ([Millbank, S.W.1]) : [Royal Army Medical College], [1976]. — [11] p : ill ; 25cm.
ISBN 0-9505525-0-x Sd : Unpriced
(B77-09858)

760'.092'4 — Museums. *Cumbria. Brampton. LYC Museum and Gallery. Exhibits: Scottish graphic arts. Stansfield, Elsa. Catalogues*
Stansfield, Elsa. The time machine, 'everything is round' : a sequence by Elsa Stansfield : [catalogue of an] exhibition [held] 1st to 31st May 1977 ... [at the] LYC Museum ... — Brampton, Cumbria (Banks, Brampton, Cumbria CA8 2JH) : LYC Museum, [1977]. — [19]p : ill, port ; 14cm.
'36'. — Bibl.: p.[10].
Pbk : £0.15
(B77-18922)

760'.092'4 — Scottish graphic arts. McBey, James, 1883-1911. *Autobiographies*
McBey, James. The early life of James McBey : an autobiography, 1883-1911 / edited by Nicolas Barker. — Oxford [etc.] : Oxford University Press, 1977. — ix,131p,leaf of plate,16p of plates : ill, ports ; 24cm.
ISBN 0-19-211738-6 : £5.50 : CIP rev.
(B77-07525)

760'.094 — European graphic arts. Art nouveau style, 1890-1910. *Illustrations*
Art nouveau posters & graphics / [compiled by] Roger Sainton. — London : Academy Editions, 1977. — 95p : chiefly ill(some col), facsims(some col) ; 30cm.
Index. — Previous control number ISBN 0-85670-324-9.
ISBN 0-85670-322-2 : £6.95
ISBN 0-85670-323-0 Pbk : £3.95
(B77-18923)

760'.094 — European graphic arts. Symbolist movement, ca 1880-ca 1910
Jullian, Philippe. The Symbolists / [by] Philippe Jullian ; [translated from the French by Mary Anne Stevens]. — 2nd ed. [i.e. 1st ed reprinted]. — Oxford : Phaidon, 1977. — 240p : chiefly ill(some col), ports(some col) ; 24cm.
This translation originally published: London : Phaidon, 1973. — Translation of: 'Les Symbolistes'. Neuchatel : Ides et Calendes, 1972. — Index.
ISBN 0-7148-1739-2 Pbk : £4.95
(B77-33358)

760'.0947 — Russian graphic arts, 1920-1976. *Illustrations*
Unofficial art from the Soviet Union / [text] by Igor Golomshtok and Alexander Glezer ; introduction by Sir Roland Penrose ; edited by Michael Scammell. — London : Secker and Warburg, 1977. — xvi,172p : chiefly ill(some col), ports(some col) ; 26cm.
Bibl.: p.165-172.
ISBN 0-436-47700-9 : £7.95
(B77-15400)

760'.28 — Monoprints. Techniques. *Manuals. Juvenile literature*
Baulig, Elisabeth. Let's make monoprints / [by] Elisabeth and Pierre Baulig. — London : Evans Bros, 1977. — 32,[1]p : ill(chiefly col) ; 21cm. — (Starting points)
ISBN 0-237-44862-9 Sd : £0.65
(B77-15401)

760'.28 — Prints. Making. *Manuals. Juvenile literature*
Rockwell, Harlow. Printmaking / by Harlow Rockwell. — Tadworth : World's Work, 1977. — [4],59p : ill(chiefly col) ; 22cm.
Ill. on lining papers. — Originally published: Garden City, N.Y. : Doubleday, 1974.
ISBN 0-437-71651-1 : £2.50
(B77-33359)

760'.28 — Prints. Making. *Manuals. School texts*
Prints / [by Ray Hemmings ... et al.]. — Ely : Leapfrogs Limited, 1976. — [1],17,[1]p : ill ; 21cm. — (Network : action books)
ISBN 0-905531-00-0 Sd : £0.30(non-net)
ISBN 0-09-128341-8 (Hutchinson) : £0.30 non-net
(B77-02492)

761 — RELIEF PRINTS
761'.2 — Woodcuts. Techniques. *Manuals*
Banister, Manly. Wood block cutting & printing / by Manly Banister ; photos, drawings, and prints by the author. — New York : Sterling [etc.] ; London : Distributed by Ward Lock, 1976. — 72p : ill(some col) ; 22cm.

Index.
ISBN 0-7061-2500-2 : £3.95
(B77-12589)

763 — LITHOGRAPHY
763'.028 — Lithographs. Techniques. *Manuals*
Vicary, Richard. The Thames and Hudson manual of advanced lithography / [by] Richard Vicary. — London : Thames and Hudson, 1977. — 192p : ill(some col), facsims(3 col), ports ; 25cm. — (The Thames and Hudson manuals)
Bibl.: p.186-189. — Index.
ISBN 0-500-67010-2 : £6.00
(B77-22040)

769 — PRINTS
769'.4'2074094134 — Art galleries. *Edinburgh. Scottish National Portrait Gallery. Exhibits: Portrait engravings, 1500-1900. Catalogues*
Stevenson, Sara. A face for any occasion : some aspects of portrait engraving / [by] Sara Stevenson. — [Edinburgh] ([Portrait Gallery Buildings, Queen St., Edinburgh 2]) : Trustees of the National Galleries of Scotland [for the] Scottish National Portrait Gallery, 1976. — viii, 127p : ill, facsims, ports ; 25cm.
Bibl.: p.126.
Pbk : Unpriced
(B77-23614)

769'.4'28 — French erotic picture postcards, 1900-1920. *Critical studies*
Hammond, Paul. French undressing : naughty postcards from 1900 to 1920 / by Paul Hammond. — London : Jupiter Books, 1976. — 136p : ill(some col) ; 31cm.
Bibl.: p.136.
ISBN 0-904041-40-9 : £4.95
(B77-15402)

769'.4'2809041 — Erotic picture postcards, c1900-c1930. *Illustrations*
Erotic postcards / [compiled by] Barbara Jones and William Ouellette. — London : Macdonald and Jane's, 1977. — 127p : chiefly ill(some col), ports ; 27cm.
ISBN 0-354-04139-8 : £4.95
(B77-27276)

769'.4'34 — Dutch engravings, 1612. Special subjects: Flowering plants. *Illustrations*
Sweerts, Emanuel. [Florilegium Emanuelis Sweerti. English]. Early floral engravings : all 110 plates from the 1612 'Florilegium' / by Emanuel Sweerts ; edited by E.F. Bleiler. — New York : Dover Publications [etc.] ; London : Constable, 1976. — xv p,67,43 leaves of plates : ill, ports ; 31cm. — (The Dover pictorial archive series)
'[Includes] translations of the original advertisement, preface and planting instructions ; identifying captions that incorporate material from the original text ...' - title page verso. — Leaves of plates printed on both sides. — 'Florilegium Emanuelis Sweerti' originally published: Frankfurt am Main : Sweerts, 1612. — Index.
ISBN 0-486-23038-4 Pbk : £4.80
(B77-14333)

769'.4'37 — British picture postcards, 1890-1923. Special subjects: Seaside resorts. *Illustrations*
Beside the seaside : a picture postcard album / [compiled by] Harriet Bridgeman & Elizabeth Drury. — London : Elm Tree Books, 1977. — 144p : chiefly ill, facsims, 2 maps ; 24cm.
Bibl.: p.14.
ISBN 0-241-89596-0 : £5.95
(B77-23615)

769'.4'37 — English picture postcards, 1900- . Special subjects: Sailing vessels. *Illustrations*
Old postcard views : from the Walter Dowsett collection / compiled by Alan Cordell, Peter Ferguson, Alan Pearsall. — Twickenham (17 Court Way, Twickenham, Middx) : Nautical Pictorial.
No.1 : River Thames. — 1976. — 40p : chiefly ill, maps, port ; 30cm.
Sd : £1.50
(B77-13788)

769'.4'938522 — Advertising posters, to 1945. Special subjects: Rail travel
The **golden** age of the railway poster / [compiled by] J.T. Shackleton. — London : New English Library, 1976. — 128p : ill, chiefly facsims(chiefly col) ; 35cm.
Ill. on lining papers.
ISBN 0-450-02875-5 : £5.95
(B77-23616)

769'.4'9629130941469 — Postcards. Special subjects: Lanark aviation meetings, 1910
Malcolm, Donald. The Scottish international aviation meeting, Lanark, 6-13 August 1910 : a philatelic monograph / by Donald Malcolm. — [Paisley] ([42 Garry Drive, Paisley, Renfrewshire]) : The author, 1975. — 23p : ill, facsims, ports ; 24cm.
Limited ed. of 600 numbered copies.
ISBN 0-9505654-0-7 Sd : £2.00
(B77-14852)

769'.4'97821 — French advertising posters, 1868-1930. Special subjects: Opera. *Illustrations*
French opera posters, 1868-1930 / [compiled by] Lucy Broido. — New York : Dover Publications [etc.] ; London : Constable, 1976. — xxv p,52p of plates : chiefly ill(chiefly col) ; 32cm.
Bibl.: p.vii. — Index.
ISBN 0-486-23306-5 Pbk : £2.85
(B77-27277)

769'.4'97911 — Advertising posters. Special subjects: Buffalo Bill's Wild West, 1885-1905. *Illustrations*
100 posters of Buffalo Bill's Wild West / [compiled] by Jack Rennert. — London : Hart-Davis MacGibbon, 1976. — 112p,2p of plates(2 fold) : chiefly ill(chiefly col), facsims, ports(chiefly col) ; 41cm. — (The poster art library)
ISBN 0-246-10959-9 Pbk : £5.00
(B77-30497)

769'.4'979143090915 — Advertising posters. Special subjects: Cinema films: Science fiction films, 1933-1973. *Illustrations*
Science-fiction and horror movie posters in full color / edited by Alan Adler. — New York : Dover Publications [etc.] ; London : Constable, 1977. — viii,40p : chiefly col ill ; 37cm.
Col. ill. on inside covers.
ISBN 0-486-23452-5 Pbk : £4.25
Also classified at 769'.4'979143090916
(B77-33961)

769'.4'979143090916 — Advertising posters. Special subjects: Cinema films: Horror films, 1933-1973. *Illustrations*
Science-fiction and horror movie posters in full color / edited by Alan Adler. — New York : Dover Publications [etc.] ; London : Constable, 1977. — viii,40p : chiefly col ill ; 37cm.
Col. ill. on inside covers.
ISBN 0-486-23452-5 Pbk : £4.25
Primary classification 769'.4'979143090915
(B77-33961)

769'.4'9791430941 — Arts. Patronage. Organisations. *Wales. Welsh Arts Council. Exhibits: British advertising posters. Special subjects: Cinema films, to 1976. Catalogues*
Welsh Arts Council. Selling dreams : posteri ffilm o Brydain ac America 1890-1976 = British and American film posters 1890-1976 / [photography Colin Molyneux ; Welsh translation from the English by Siân Edwards]. — [Cardiff] : Welsh Arts Council, [1977]. — [1],84p(6 fold) : chiefly ill(some col), facsims ; 30cm.
Catalogue of a Welsh Arts Council touring exhibition. — Cover title. — Parallel English and Welsh text.
ISBN 0-905171-20-9 Pbk : Unpriced
Also classified at 769'.4'9791430973
(B77-18924)

769'.4'9791430973 — Arts. Patronage. Organisations. *Wales. Welsh Arts Council. Exhibits: American advertising posters. Special subjects: Cinema films, to 1976. Catalogues*
Welsh Arts Council. Selling dreams : posteri ffilm o Brydain ac America 1890-1976 = British and American film posters 1890-1976 / [photography Colin Molyneux ; Welsh translation from the English by Siân Edwards]. — [Cardiff] : Welsh Arts Council, [1977]. — [1],84p(6 fold) : chiefly ill(some col), facsims ; 30cm.
Catalogue of a Welsh Arts Council touring exhibition. — Cover title. — Parallel English and Welsh text.
ISBN 0-905171-20-9 Pbk : Unpriced
Primary classification 769'.4'9791430941
(B77-18924)

769'.4'99410820922 — British picture postcards. Special subjects: Great Britain. Royal families, 1923-1973. *Illustrations*
One hundred and forty-four picture postcards of Her Majesty Queen Elizabeth II and her family / compiled by Mary Dunkin. — London [etc.] : Omnibus Press, 1977. — [50]p : of ill(some col), chiefly ports(some col) ; 28cm.
ISBN 0-86001-310-3 Pbk : £3.95
(B77-27278)

769'.5 — Art galleries. *London. Greenwich (London Borough). Woodlands Art Gallery. Exhibits: Valentines, 1700-1950. Catalogues*
Woodlands Art Gallery. Valentines : [catalogue of an exhibition held] 14 February to 14 March 1976 [at the] Woodlands Art Gallery. — London (c/o Woodlands Art Gallery, 90 Mycenae Rd, SE3 7SE) : London Borough of Greenwich, [1976]. — [12]p : ill ; 21cm.
ISBN 0-9504033-4-2 Sd : Unpriced
(B77-10488)

769'.5 — Beer mats. *Great Britain. Lists*
Brittain, Dennis G. United Kingdom brewery mat catalogue : current breweries / compiled by Dennis G. Brittain. — [Northwich] ([c/o M.J. Powell, 10 Pinetree Close, Barnton, Northwich, Cheshire]) : British Beermat Collectors' Society.
Section 1. — 1976 [i.e. 1977]. — 46p ; 21cm.
' ... the mats listed herin being from breweries "A-B" ... ' - Foreword.
ISBN 0-9505645-0-8 Sd : Private circulation
(B77-12590)

769'.5 — Books. Organisations. *Great Britain. National Book League. Exhibits: British engraved bookplates, 1925-1975. Catalogues*
Bookplate Society. Bookplate designers, 1925-1975 : catalogue of the Bookplate Society's Third Biennial Exhibition, held at the National Book League, 7 Albemarle Street, London W.1, Saturday 16th to Thursday 28th October 1976. — [London] ([c/o Secretary, 32 Barrowgate Rd, W4 4QY]) : [Bookplate Society] ; [London] : [Private Libraries' Association], 1976. — [50]p,[4]p of plates : ill ; 26cm.
Index.
ISBN 0-900002-43-3 Sd : £0.65
(B77-03695)

769'.5 — British bawdy comic picture postcards. *Illustrations*
The **2nd** Bamforth's saucy postcard annual. — London [etc.] : Pan Books, 1977. — [64]p : of col ill ; 18cm.
ISBN 0-330-25305-0 Pbk : £0.75
(B77-29591)

Bamforth's saucy postcard annual. — London [etc.] : Pan Books, 1976. — [96]p : of col ill ; 18cm.
ISBN 0-330-24810-3 Pbk : £0.70
(B77-02493)

769'.5 — British cigarette cards, 1888-. *Lists*
Bagnall, Charles Lane. British cigarette card issues / compiled 1950 by C.L. Bagnall. — London (34 Wellesley Rd, Chiswick, W4 4BP) : London Cigarette Card Co. Ltd.
Part 1 : 1888-1919. Catalogue. — 3rd revised ed. / by Ian A. Laker and F.C. Doggett. — 1977. — [1],ix,54p : ill ; 21cm.
'... for use with "Handbook part 1"'. — Previous ed.: / by Dorothy Bagnall and Ian A. Laker. 1975. — Index.
Sd : £1.50
(B77-32767)

769'.5 — British postcards, 1894-1939. *Catalogues*
Picton's priced catalogue of British pictorial postcards and postmarks, 1894-1939 / [compiled by] M.R. Hewlett. — Chippenham (Citadel Works, Bath Rd, Chippenham, Wilts. SN15 2AA) : B.P.H. Publications Ltd, 1976. — [3],104p,[12]p of plates : ill, facsims ; 21cm.
Cover title: Picton's postcard catalogue. — Previous ed.: 1973. — Bibl.: p.71-75. — Index.
ISBN 0-902633-39-2 Sd : £2.00
(B77-10489)

769'.5 — Disc records. Sleeves. Illustrations. *Illustrations*
Album cover album / edited by Storm Thorgerson (Hipgnosis) & Roger Dean ; introduced by Dominy Hamilton ... — Limpsfield (Limpsfield, Surrey RH8 0DY) : Dragon's World Ltd, 1977. — 2-160p : chiefly col facsims ; 31cm.
Index.
ISBN 0-905895-00-2 : £9.50
ISBN 0-905895-01-0 Pbk : £4.95
(B77-25109)

769'.5 — Ephemera. Collecting. *Periodicals*
The **ephemerist** : journal of the Ephemera Society. — London (10 Fitzroy Sq., W1P 5AH) : The Society.
Vol.1, no.1- ; Nov. 1975-. — 1975-. — facsims, ports ; 30cm.
Six issues a year. — Folder (4p.) as 1st issue.
£0.50
ISSN 0309-4383
(B77-11341)

769'.5 — New York (City). Historiology. Organisations: New-York Historical Society. Collections: Bella C. Landauer Collection. Exhibits: American advertising posters, ca 1842-1897. *Illustrations*
New-York Historical Society. American advertising posters of the nineteenth century : from the Bella C. Landauer Collection of the New-York Historical Society / [compiled by] Mary Black. — New York : Dover Publications [etc.] ; London : Constable, 1976. — viii,119p : chiefly ill(some col), facsims ; 36cm.
Col. ill. on inside covers. — Index.
ISBN 0-486-23356-1 Pbk : £5.00
(B77-30498)

769'.5 — Picture postcards, 1900-1929
Fantasy postcards / [compiled by] William Ouellette ; with an introduction by Barbara Jones. — London : Sphere, 1976. — 96p : chiefly ill(some col) ; 24x30cm.
Originally published: Garden City, N.Y. : Doubleday, 1975.
ISBN 0-7221-6569-2 Pbk : £1.95
(B77-09170)

769'.5 — United States. Levy, Lester S. Private collections: American sheet music. Illustrations: Lithographs, 1800-1900. *Critical studies*
Levy, Lester S. Picture the songs : lithographs from the sheet music of nineteenth-century America / [by] Lester S. Levy. — Baltimore ; London : Johns Hopkins University Press, [1977]. — x,214p : facsims(some col), ports(some col) ; 29cm.
Published in the United States: 1976. — Bibl.: p.206-211. — Index.
ISBN 0-8018-1814-1 : £15.95
(B77-13173)

769'.55'075 — Paper money. Collecting. *Manuals*
Beresiner, Yasha. A collector's guide to paper money / [by] Yasha Beresiner. — London : Deutsch, 1977. — 255p,[8]p of plates : ill, facsim(some col), forms, 2 ports ; 26cm.
Bibl.: p.244-246. — Index.
ISBN 0-233-96594-7 : £6.95 : CIP rev.
(B77-21338)

Paramount International Coin Ltd. Collecting currency : a guide to numismatics and notaphily / [Paramount International Coin Ltd]. — London (238 Grand Buildings, Trafalgar Sq., WC2N 5EZ) : Paramount International Coin Ltd, 1975. — 23p : ill, facsims, port ; 18x25cm.
Sd : Unpriced
Primary classification 737.4'075
(B77-31333)

769'.55942 — English banknotes, to 1976. *Collectors' guides*
Stanley Gibbons Limited. Collect British banknotes : a Stanley Gibbons priced catalogue of British Treasury and Bank of England notes. — 2nd ed. — London : Gibbons, 1977. — vi, 58p : ill ; 19cm.
'This edition is a condensation of Vincent Duggleby's "English Paper Money" prepared by James Negus' - title page verso. — Previous ed.: 1970.
ISBN 0-85259-960-9 Sd : £0.75
(B77-29592)

769'.56 — Postal services. Mail. Civil censorship devices. *West Indies, 1939-1945*
Roses Caribbean Philatelic Society. West Indian censorship devices / [Roses Caribbean Philatelic Society] ; [general editor G.G. Ritchie]. — Harrogate (16 Stray Walk, Harrogate, [N. Yorkshire] HG2 8HU) : The editor, 1977. — [1],102p : ill, facsims ; 30cm. — (Roses Caribbean philatelic handbook ; no.2)
Limited ed. of 250 numbered copies.
Sd : Unpriced
(B77-32768)

769'.56'0216 — Postage stamps. *Catalogues*
Stanley Gibbons Limited. Stanley Gibbons foreign stamp catalogue, overseas. — London : Gibbons.
[Vol.] 2 : D-J. — 2nd ed. — 1976. — xxii, B826p : ill, facsims ; 22cm.
Previous ed.: 1974. — Index to 'Overseas', vols 1-4 and 'Europe', vols 1-3.
ISBN 0-85259-825-4 Pbk : £6.50
ISSN 0305-8093
(B77-06214)

[Vol.] 3 : K-O. — 1977. — xxii,C694p : ill ; 22cm.
Index.
ISBN 0-85259-890-4 Pbk : £6.50
ISSN 0305-8093
(B77-27279)

Stanley Gibbons Limited. Stanley Gibbons stamps of the world : an illustrated and priced guide to the postage stamps of the whole world, excluding changes of paper, perforation, shade and watermark. — London : Gibbons.
1978 : 43rd ed. — 1977. — xii,1588p : ill, facsims ; 29cm.
Cover title: Stamps of the world. — Index.
ISBN 0-85259-940-4 : £8.95
ISSN 0081-4210
(B77-32059)

769'.56'075 — Postage stamps. Specialised collections. Collecting. *Manuals*
Wise, Ernest Harold. Forming a specialised stamp collection / [by] Ernest H. Wise. — London : Gibbons, 1976. — 30p : ill, facsims ; 20cm. — (Stanley Gibbons Limited. Guides)
ISBN 0-85259-840-8 Sd : £0.75
(B77-05562)

769'.562'0922 — Postage stamps. Forgers, ca 1860-ca 1940
Tyler, Varro Eugene. Philatelic forgers, their lives and works / by Varro E. Tyler. — London : Lowe, 1976. — iv,60p : facsims, ports ; 25cm.
Index.
£4.00
(B77-01689)

769'.569 — United Nations postage stamps, to 1966
Goodey, Ramon. A study of the first United Nations regular and airmail postage stamps, 1951-1966 / by Ramon Goodey. — [Chelmsford] ([403 Main Rd, Broomfield, Chelmsford, Essex CM1 5EJ]) : [The author], 1976. — [9],120p,leaf of plate,[26]p of plates : ill, ports ; 23cm.
Cover title: United Nations regular and airmail postage stamps, 1951-1966. — In binder.
Ls : £5.00
(B77-11342)

769'.569171'241 — Commonwealth postage stamps. *Catalogues. Serials*
Stanley Gibbons Limited. Stanley Gibbons British Commonwealth stamp catalogue : including post-independence issues of Ireland, Pakistan, Rhodesia and South Africa. — London : Gibbons.
1978 : Eightieth ed. — 1977. — xxvi,989p : ill ; 24cm.
ISBN 0-85259-935-8 : £6.95
ISSN 0068-1903
(B77-32769)

769'.569171'241 — Commonwealth postage stamps, 1952-. *Catalogues. Serials*
The **Commonwealth** Queen Elizabeth II stamp catalogue. — Bristol (7 Richmond Hill Ave., Bristol BS8 1BQ) : Urch, Harris and Co. Ltd.
1978 ed. : (including Ireland and South Africa) / edited by Brian Purcell. — [1977]. — 635,xxi p : ill, facsims ; 24cm.
Index.
Pbk : £8.00
(B77-31349)

769'.5694 — European postage stamps. *Catalogues*
Stanley Gibbons Limited. Stanley Gibbons foreign stamp catalogue, Europe. — London : Gibbons.
[Vol.]1 : A-F. — 3rd ed. — 1977. — xxii,566p : ill, facsims ; 22cm.
Previous ed.: 1974. — Index to 'Europe', vols 1-3 and 'Overseas', vols 1-4.
ISBN 0-85259-870-x Pbk : £6.00
ISSN 0305-8085
(B77-19550)

[Vol.]2 : G-P. — 3rd ed. — 1977. — xxii, 694p : ill ; 22cm.
Previous ed.: 1974.
ISBN 0-85259-885-8 Pbk : £6.50
ISSN 0305-8085
(B77-32770)

769'.56941 — British postage stamps. *Catalogues*
Stanley Gibbons Limited. Stanley Gibbons Great Britain specialised stamp catalogue. — London : Gibbons.
Vol.4 : Queen Elizabeth II decimal issues. — 1976. — xiv,238p : ill ; 23cm.
Index.
ISBN 0-85259-770-3 : £5.00
ISSN 0072-7229
(B77-17009)

769'.56941 — British postage stamps, 1840-. *Catalogues. Serials*
Collect British stamps : a Stanley Gibbons checklist of the stamps of Great Britain / originally devised and compiled by Eric Allen. — London : Gibbons.
19th ed. — 1976. — 53p : ill(chiefly col) ; 20cm.
ISBN 0-85259-835-1 Sd : £0.85
ISSN 0069-5262
(B77-06810)

Stanley Gibbons Limited. Collect British stamps : a Stanley Gibbons checklist of the stamps of Great Britain / originally devised and compiled by Eric Allen. — London : Gibbons.
20th ed. — 1977. — 55p : ill(chiefly col) ; 20cm.
ISBN 0-85259-880-7 Sd : £0.90
ISSN 0069-5262
(B77-22041)

769'.56941 — British postage stamps. Collecting. *Periodicals*
The **philatelic** review. — Bristol (40 Whiteladies Rd, Bristol BS8 2LG) : Candlish McCleery Ltd.
Vol.1, no.1- ; Jan. 1977-. — 1977-. — ill, facsims ; 16x21cm.
Quarterly. — [1],24,viii p. in 1st issue.
Sd : £0.50
ISSN 0309-9350
(B77-29593)

769'.569423'4 — Channel Islands postage stamps, to 1977. *Catalogues*
Collect Channel Islands stamps : a Stanley Gibbons checklist of the stamps and postal history of the Channel Islands. — London : Gibbons.
6th ed. — 1977. — 50p : ill(chiefly col), facsims(1 col) ; 20cm.
ISBN 0-85259-855-6 Sd : £0.85
ISSN 0306-5103
(B77-18304)

769'.569427'9 — Isle of Man postage stamps, to 1977. *Catalogues*
Collect Isle of Man stamps : a Stanley Gibbons checklist of the stamps and postal history of the Isle of Man. — London : Gibbons.
2nd ed. — 1977. — 31p : ill(chiefly col), facsims, map ; 20cm.
ISBN 0-85259-865-3 Sd : £0.85
ISSN 0307-7098
(B77-18305)

769'.569428'1 — Yorkshire temporary handstamps, 1840-1974. *Catalogues*
Ward, Ronald. The temporary handstamps of Yorkshire and administrative areas / by Ronald Ward and William A. Sedgwick. — Sheffield (c/o Ronald Ward, 48 Banner Cross Rd, Ecclesall, Sheffield S11 9HR) : Yorkshire Postal History Society, 1977. — [1],28,[4]p,19 leaves of plates : facsims ; 26cm. — (Yorkshire Postal History Society. Special series ; no.2)
Bibl.(1p.).
ISBN 0-9500053-9-8 Pbk : £1.50
(B77-16528)

769'.569689'4 — Zambian postage stamps, 1963-1965
Drysdall, Alan R. The stamps and postal history of Northern Rhodesia and Zambia, 1963-1965 / by Alan R. Drysdall. — London : Lowe, 1976. — [2],ii,38p : facsims, map, ports ; 25cm.
ISBN 0-85397-053-x Sd : £2.75
(B77-06811)

769'.56994 — Australian postage stamps, 1913-1976. *Catalogues*
The **colour** catalogue of Australian stamps. — Southsea [etc.] (P.O. Box 7, Southsea PO4 0RA) : David Mortimer, 1976. — [1],30p : chiefly col ill ; 23cm.
ISBN 0-905556-00-3 Sd : £1.25
(B77-15403)

769'.5699423'12 — Wiltshire postmarks: Chippenham postmarks, to 1974
Williamson, W T. Chip.nham postal markings and some postal history / by W.T. Williamson. — Chippenham (35 Wood La., Chippenham, Wilts. SN15 3DW) : The author, 1977. — [2], 31p : facsims ; 22cm.
Sd : £1.00
(B77-26440)

769'.56994'8 — Norfolk Island postmarks, to 1974
Pacific Islands Study Circle of Great Britain. Norfolk Island cancellations and postal markings : study / by the Pacific Islands' Study Circle of Great Britain ; compiled by D.A.R. Murray Brown. — [Cheltenham] ([c/o The editor, 'Pacifica', 108 Leckhampton Rd, Cheltenham, Glos. GL53 0BX]) : [The Study Circle], [1974?]. — [1],i,35p : facsims, 2 maps ; 30cm.
Bibl.: p.33-34.
Sd : £1.50
(B77-17668)

769'.9 — Prints, to 1962
Cleaver, James. A history of graphic art / [by] James Cleaver. — Wakefield : EP Publishing, 1977. — 282p,[64]p of plates : ill, facsims ; 23cm.
Originally published: London : Owen, 1963. — Bibl.: p.261-267. — Index.
ISBN 0-7158-1209-2 : £6.50
(B77-25110)

769'.9 — Prints, to 1975
Eichenberg, Fritz. The art of the print : masterpieces, history, techniques / [by] Fritz Eichenberg. — London : Thames and Hudson, 1976. — 611p : ill(some col), facsims(some col), ports(some col) ; 30cm.
Bibl.: p.590-595. — Index. — Includes contributions by other writers.
ISBN 0-500-23253-9 : £21.00
(B77-00338)

769'.92'2 — Art galleries. *Greater Manchester (Metropolitan County). Manchester. Whitworth Art Gallery. Exhibits: English prints. Orobiej, Bill & Whitehead, Alan. Catalogues*
Orobiej, Bill. Prints by Bill Orobiej and Alan Whitehead : [catalogue of an exhibition held] 15 January-12 February 1977 ... [at the] Whitworth Art Gallery, University of Manchester, Whitworth Park, Manchester M15 6ER / [compiled by Christopher Allan]. — [Manchester] ([University of Manchester, Whitworth Park, Manchester M15 6ER]) : [Whitworth Art Gallery], [1977]. — [20]p : chiefly ill, 2 ports ; 21x21cm.
Sd : £0.50
(B77-27994)

769'.92'4 — American posters. Glaser, Milton. *Illustrations*
Glaser, Milton. The Milton Glaser poster book. — London : Academy Editions, 1977. — 47p : chiefly col ill ; 39cm.
Pages printed on one side only. — Also published: New York : Harmony Books, 1977. — Index.
Pbk : Unpriced
(B77-33962)

769'.92'4 — American printed labels. Sibbett, Ed. Special subjects: Christmas. *Collections*
Sibbett, Ed. Christmas labels, gummed and perforated : 96 colorful labels / designed by Ed Sibbett, Jr. — New York : Dover Publications [etc.] ; London : Constable, 1976. — [13] leaves : of col ill ; 28cm.
ISBN 0-486-23351-0 Sd : £1.65
(B77-02494)

769'.92'4 — Art galleries. *Essex. Maldon. Haagensen Gallery. Exhibits: English etchings. Haagensen, Frederick Hans. Catalogues*
Haagensen, Frederick Hans. Catalogue, Frederick Hans Haagensen, 1877-1943 ... — [Maldon, Essex] ([Haagensen Gallery, 2 High St., Maldon, Essex]) : Audrey M. Haagensen, 1976. — 87p : ill, ports ; 18x23cm.
ISBN 0-9505398-0-5 Pbk : £1.50
(B77-03696)

769'.92'4 — Art galleries. *Nottinghamshire. Nottingham. Nottingham University Art Gallery. Exhibits: Hungarian etchings. Vasarhelyi, Vera. Catalogues*
Vasarhelyi, Vera. Vera Vasarhelyi : pictures, graphics and collaborations / [catalogue compiled by Joanne Frew]. — [Nottingham] (Portland Building, University Park [Nottingham]) : University of Nottingham Art Gallery, 1977. — [19]p : ill ; 24cm.
Catalogue of an exhibition held 22 February-12 March 1977.
ISBN 0-9504622-2-5 Sd : £0.15
(B77-16529)

769'.92'4 — Art galleries. *Oxfordshire. Oxford. Studio One Gallery. Exhibits: English wood engravings. Gill, Eric. Catalogues*
Studio One Gallery. A tribute to Eric Gill / Studio One Gallery, Betty Clark. — [Oxford] (214 Banbury Rd, Oxford OX2 7BY) : Studio One Gallery, 1976. — [10]p : port ; 22cm.
Catalogue of an exhibition held at Studio One Gallery, 22-30 November 1976.
ISBN 0-9505455-0-3 Sd : £0.20
(B77-03697)

769'.92'4 — Arts. Patronage. Organisations. *Great Britain. Arts Council of Great Britain. Exhibits: Belgian etchings. Rops, Félicien. Catalogues*
Arts Council of Great Britain. Félicien Rops : [catalogue of] an Arts Council touring exhibition, 1976-77. — [London] : [Arts Council], [1976]. — 32p : ill, port ; 26cm.
ISBN 0-7287-0116-2 Sd : £1.00
(B77-13789)

769'.92'4 — English engravings. Blake, William: Illustrations for Night thoughts, or, The complaint and the consolation by Young, Edward, b.1683. *Illustrations*
Young, Edward, *b.1683.* Night thoughts, or, The complaint and the consolation / illustrated by William Blake ; text by Edward Young ; edited, with an introduction and commentary, by Robert Essick, Jenijoy La Belle. — New York : Dover Publications [etc.] ; London : Constable, [1976]. — 127p in various pagings : ill ; 31cm.
Includes original pagings. — Facsimile reprint of: 1797 ed. originally published as 'The complaint and the consolation, or, Night thoughts'. London : Richard Edwards, 1797. — Bibl.: p.xix-xxi.
ISBN 0-486-20219-4 Pbk : £2.80
Primary classification 821'.5
(B77-02550)

769'.92'4 — English linocuts. Weissenborn, Hellmuth. *Illustrations*
Weissenborn, Hellmuth. Ruins : a picture anthology of human genius, aggression, neglect & folly / [by] Hellmuth Weissenborn. — London ([7 Harley Gardens, SW10 9SW]) : Acorn Press, 1977. — [49]p : col ill ; 27x39cm.
Includes extracts in German and Latin. — Limited ed. of 60 numbered and signed copies. — In slip case.
Pbd : £60.00
(B77-32771)

769'.92'4 — English prints. Blake, William. *Illustrations*
Blake, William. William Blake / [text by] William Vaughan. — London : Thames and Hudson, 1977. — [8]p,40 leaves of plates : chiefly col ill, col facsims, col port ; 28cm.
Leaves printed on both sides.
ISBN 0-500-53013-0 Pbk : £2.50
Primary classification 759.2
(B77-33959)

769'.92'4 — English prints. Crane, Walter. Special subjects: Socialism, 1886-1896. *Illustrations*
Crane, Walter. Cartoons for the cause : designs and verses for the Socialist and Labour movement, 1886-1896 / by Walter Crane. — [1st ed. reprinted] ; with a foreword by John Betjeman. — London ([97 Ferme Park Rd, N8 9SA]) : Journeyman Press ; [London] : Marx Memorial Library, 1976. — [20] leaves : chiefly ill ; 43cm.
Limited ed. of 600 copies of which 100 have been signed by John Betjeman. — Some leaves printed on both sides. — Facsimile reprint of: 1st ed.: London : Twentieth Century Press, 1896.
ISBN 0-904526-13-5 Sd : £3.95
ISBN 0-904526-14-3 Signed ed. : £12.00
Also classified at 821'.8
(B77-13174)

769'.92'4 — English prints. Lubbock, Joseph Guy. *Illustrations*
Lubbock, Joseph Guy. Perceptions of the earth / original prints and text by J.G. Lubbock. — London (30 Long Acre, WC2E 9LT) : Bertram Rota (Publishing) Ltd, 1977. — [43]p : col ill ; 34cm.
Full leather. — In slip case.
Unpriced
Primary classification 828'.9'1408
(B77-31580)

769'.92'4 — French etchings. Icart, Louis. *Critical studies*
Schnessel, S Michael. Icart / by S. Michael Schnessel ; introduction by Katharine M. McClinton. — London : Studio Vista, 1976. — xiv,178p : ill(some col), ports ; 32cm.
Also published: New York : Potter, 1976. — Bibl.: p.174-175. — Index.
ISBN 0-289-70761-7 : £10.50
Also classified at 759.4
(B77-15404)

769'.92'4 — French lithographs. Delacroix, Eugène. Illustrations for 'Faust'. *Illustrations*
Goethe, Johann Wolfgang von. [Faust. Part 1. English]. Faust / [by] Johann Wolfgang von Goethe ; with eighteen lithographs by Eugène Delacroix ; with a new introduction by Michael Marqusee. — [London] : Paddington Press, 1977. — 174p : ill, port ; 28cm. — (Masterpieces of the illustrated book)
These illustrations originally published: with French translation. Paris : C. Motte, 1828.
ISBN 0-448-22184-5 Pbk : £2.95
Primary classification 832'.6
(B77-16634)

769'.92'4 — French lithographs. Redon, Odilon. *Illustrations*
Redon, Odilon. Odilon Redon / edited by Carolyn Keay ; introduction by Thomas Walters. — London : Academy Editions, 1977. — 80p : chiefly ill(some col) ; 30cm.
ISBN 0-85670-240-4 : £5.95
ISBN 0-85670-245-5 Pbk : £2.95
(B77-18925)

769'.92'4 — German advertising posters. Hohlwein, Ludwig. *Illustrations*
Hohlwein, Ludwig. Hohlwein posters in full color. — New York : Dover Publications [etc.] ; London : Constable, 1976. — 48p : of col ill ; 36cm.
ISBN 0-486-23408-8 Pbk : £4.25
(B77-33963)

769'.92'4 — Italian etchings. Piranesi, Giovanni Battista. Special subjects: Italy. Rome. Ancient Roman antiquities. *Illustrations*
Piranesi, Giovanni Battista. Views of Rome, then and now / 41 etchings by Giovanni Battista Piranesi ; corresponding photographs and text by Herschel Levit. — New York : Dover Publications [etc.] ; London : Constable, 1976. — iii-xxvii p,41,41p of plates : chiefly ill ; 38cm.
Opposite pages of plates numbered in duplicate. — Bibl.: p.viii.
ISBN 0-486-23339-1 Pbk : £4.25
Also classified at 779'.4'0924
(B77-25111)

769'.92'4 — Museums. *Cumbria. Brampton. LYC Museum and Gallery. Exhibits: Dutch screen prints. Hooykaas, Else Madelon. Catalogues*
Hooykaas, Else Madelon. The time-machine, a dialogue with time and space : 10 silkscreen prints by Else Madelon Hooykaas : [catalogue of an] exhibition [held] 1st to 31st May 1977 ... [at the] LYC Museum ... — Brampton, Cumbria (Banks, Brampton, Cumbria CA8 7JH) : LYC Museum, [1977]. — [19]p : ill, port ; 14cm.
'35'. — Bibl.: p.[8].
Pbk : £0.15
(B77-18926)

769'.9'24 — Museums. *Cumbria. Brampton. LYC Museum and Gallery. Exhibits: English prints. Blacker, Thetis. Special subjects: Mozart, Wolfgang Amadeus. Zauberflöte, Die. Catalogues*
LYC Museum and Gallery. Mantic paintings & mythographs : works from 'A bestiary of mythical creatures' and 'Notes from the magic flute' by Thetis Blacker : [catalogue of an exhibition held from 1st to 30th April 1977 at the LYC Museum and Art Gallery]. — Banks Brampton (Cumbria CA8 2JH) : LYC Museum, [1977]. — [32]p : ill, port ; 14cm.
Sd : Unpriced
Primary classification 759.2
(B77-23608)

769'.92'4 — Museums. *Oxfordshire. Oxford. Ashmolean Museum. Department of Western Art. Exhibits: Czechoslovakian engravings. Hollar, Václav. Catalogues*
Parry, Graham. Wenceslaus Hollar in England : [catalogue of] a tercentenary exhibition [held at the] Ashmolean Museum, 1 October-27 November 1977 / [text by Graham Parry]. — [Oxford] ([University of Oxford, Oxford OX1 2PH]) : [The Museum], 1977. — [1],19p : port ; 26cm.
ISBN 0-900090-47-2 Sd : £0.65
(B77-32060)

769'.942 — Art galleries. *London. Westminster (London Borough). Tate Gallery. Exhibits: English lithographs: Lithographs by artists associated with Curwen Press. Catalogues*
Gilmour, Pat. Artists at Curwen : a celebration of the gift of artists' prints from the Curwen Studio / [by] Pat Gilmour. — London : Tate Gallery Publications, 1977. — 167p,32p of plates,leaf of plate : ill(chiefly col) ; 26cm.
Published to accompany an exhibition held at the Tate Gallery, 23 February-11 April 1977. — Index. — Includes the catalogue of the exhibition.
ISBN 0-905005-80-5 : £8.00
ISBN 0-905005-75-9 Pbk : £4.75
(B77-12016)

769'.942 — English prints, 1837-1901. *Illustrations*
Victorian engravings / [compiled by] Rodney K. Engen ; edited by Hilary Beck. — London : Academy Editions [etc.], 1975. — 96p : chiefly ill, ports ; 30cm.
Bibl.: p.96.
ISBN 0-85670-225-0 : Unpriced
ISBN 0-85670-220-x Pbk : Unpriced
(B77-19551)

769'.952 — Japanese prints, 1660-1894. *Illustrations*
Japanese prints / [text by] Cecilia Whitford. — London : Thames and Hudson, 1977. — [8]p,40 leaves of plates : chiefly ill(chiefly col), facsim, col ports ; 28cm.
Leaves printed on both sides.
ISBN 0-500-53014-9 Pbk : £2.50
(B77-33964)

769'.952 — Japanese prints. Ukiyo-e style. *Illustrations*
Japanese graphic art / [compiled by] Lubor Hájek ; [translated from the Czech by Helena Krejčová ; revised by Věra Gissing]. — London : Octopus Books, 1976. — 39p,[96]p of plates : chiefly ill(chiefly col), ports(chiefly col) ; 30cm.
ISBN 0-7064-0521-8 : £4.95
(B77-13175)

769'.973 — Art galleries. *West Yorkshire (Metropolitan County). Leeds. Leeds City Art Galleries. Exhibits: American prints, 1913-1963. Catalogues*
Museum of Modern Art, New York. *International Council.* American prints, 1913-1963 : [catalogue of] an exhibition circulated under the auspices of the International Council of the Museum of Modern Art, New York, [held at] Leeds City Art Gallery, 16 July-22 August 1976. — [London] : Arts Council of Great Britain, 1976. — 36p : ill ; 21cm.
Bibl. — Index.
ISBN 0-7287-0097-2 Pbk : £0.90
(B77-01690)

770 — PHOTOGRAPHY
Langford, Michael John. Basic photography : a primer for professionals / [by] Michael J. Langford. — 4th ed. — London [etc.] : Focal Press, 1977. — [2],397p,[52]p of plates : ill ; 24cm.
Previous ed.: 1973. — Bibl.: p.371-373. — Index.
ISBN 0-240-50954-4 : £6.95
ISBN 0-240-50955-2 Pbk : £4.95
(B77-31350)

Worlds within worlds : a journey into the unknown / [by] Michael Marten ... [et al.]. — London : Secker and Warburg, 1977. — 208p : ill(some col), col charts, maps(chiefly col) ; 28cm.
ISBN 0-436-27340-3 : £7.95
ISBN 0-436-27341-1 Pbk : £3.95
(B77-33965)

770 — Photography. *Transcripts of interviews*
Danziger, James. Interviews with master photographers / [by] James Danziger and Barnaby Conrad III. — New York ; London : Paddington Press, 1977. — 5-175p,[24]p of plates : ill, ports ; 25cm.
ISBN 0-448-22183-7 : £5.95
(B77-18927)

770 — Photo-sensitive imaging systems
Jacobson, Kurt I. Imaging systems / [by] Kurt I. Jacobson and Ralph E. Jacobson. — London [etc.] : Focal Press, 1976. — 319p : ill ; 25cm.
Index.
ISBN 0-240-50790-8 : £11.95
(B77-04345)

770'.28 — Photography. *Amateurs' manuals*
Greenhill, Richard. Photography / [by] Richard Greenhill, Margaret Murray, Jo Spence. — London : Macdonald Educational, 1977. — 96p : ill(some col), facsims ; 21cm. — (Macdonald guidelines)
Bibl.: p.91. — Index.
ISBN 0-356-06010-1 Pbk : £1.00
(B77-13176)

770'.28 — Photography. *Manuals*
Hedgecoe, John. The photographer's handbook / [photographs by] John Hedgecoe ; [text by Leonard Ford]. — London : Ebury Press, 1977. — 352p : chiefly ill(some col) ; 25cm.
Index.
ISBN 0-85223-123-7 : £8.95
(B77-29594)

Kodak. Kodak handbook for the professional photographer. — [Revised ed.]. — [London] : Kodak.
Vol.1 : Films and papers - their behaviour, handling, processing and use. — 1975. — 107p in various pagings : ill(chiefly col) ; 30cm.
Pierced for binder. — Previous ed.: Ruislip : Kodak, 1974. — Bibl. — Index.
ISBN 0-901023-12-4 Sd : £3.00
(B77-01691)

770'.28 — Photography. *Manuals. Juvenile literature*
Wright, Christopher, *b.1937.* Pocket money photography / [by] Christopher Wright ; cover illustration by Michael Jackson ; text illustrations by John Kilday ; photographs by the author. — London : Severn House : [Distributed by Hutchinson], 1976. — 93p,[8]p of plates : ill ; 20cm.
Originally published: London : Pan Books, 1975.
ISBN 0-7278-0164-3 : £2.50
(B77-10880)

770'.28 — View cameras. *Manuals*
Stroebel, Leslie. View camera technique / [by] Leslie Stroebel. — 3rd ed. revised. — London [etc.] : Focal Press, 1976. — 311p : ill ; 25cm.
Previous ed.: 1972. — Index.
ISBN 0-240-50901-3 : £7.00
(B77-01692)

770'.282 — 35mm cameras. *Manuals*
Foothorap, Robert. Independent photography : a biased guide to 35mm technique and equipment / by Robert Foothorap, with Vickie Golden ; illustrated by Gretchen Shields. — European ed. / edited by Roger Perry. — New York ; London [etc.] : Omnibus Press, 1976. — [8],227p : ill ; 23cm.
Previous ed.: San Francisco : Straight Arrow Books, 1975. — Bibl.: p.221-222. — Index.
ISBN 0-86001-294-8 Pbk : £2.95
(B77-17010)

770'.282 — 35mm single lens reflex cameras. *Amateurs' manuals*
Mason, Reg Herbert. Photography using a 35mm camera / [by] R.H. Mason, M. Decron ; drawings by P. Dupuis. — [London] : Chancerel : Barrie and Jenkins, 1977. — 2-91p : ill, 2 ports ; 21cm. — (Action books)
Ill. on lining papers.
ISBN 0-905703-01-4 : £1.75
(B77-22749)

Watkins, Derek. SLR photography : a handbook of the single lens reflex / [by] Derek Watkins. — Newton Abbot [etc.] : David and Charles, 1976. — 128p : ill ; 26cm.
Bibl.: p.124. — Index.
ISBN 0-7153-7301-3 : £4.95
(B77-18928)

770'.282 — Cameras. *Amateurs' manuals*
Reynolds, Clyde. The photoguide to cameras / [by] Clyde Reynolds. — London [etc.] : Focal Press, 1976. — 233p : ill(some col) ; 19cm. — (The Focal photoguides)
Index.
ISBN 0-240-50963-3 Pbk : £2.25
(B77-09171)

770'.5 — Photography. *Annuals*
Photography year book. — [Watford] : Fountain Press.
1977 / edited by John Sanders. — [1977]. — [266]p : chiefly ill(some col), ports(some col) ; 29cm.
Ill. on lining papers. — English, German and Spanish text.
ISBN 0-85242-466-3 : £7.50
ISSN 0079-1865
(B77-09859)

770'.6'241 — Photography as a profession. Organisations. *Great Britain. Institute of Incorporated Photographers. Directories*
Institute of Incorporated Photographers. IIP register. — Ware (Amwell End, Ware, Herts. SG12 9HN) : I.I.P.
1975-6. — 1975. — 200p : ill ; 22cm.
Previously published: as 'Register of incorporated photographers'. — Bibl.: p.193. — Index.
Pbk : Unpriced
ISSN 0140-3982
(B77-27995)

1976-7. — 1976. — 180p : ill ; 22cm.
Index.
Pbk : Unpriced
ISSN 0140-3982
(B77-29595)

770'.9 — Photography. *History. Periodicals*
History of photography : an international quarterly. — London : Taylor and Francis.
Vol.1, no.1 - ; Jan. 1977-. — 1977-. — ill, facsims, plans, ports ; 30cm.
92p. in 1st issue.
Pbk : £3.25(£12.00 yearly)
ISSN 0308-7298
(B77-12017)

770'.9'034 — Photography, 1800-1900
Thomas, Alan. The expanding eye : photography and the nineteenth-century mind / [by] Alan Thomas. — London : Croom Helm, 1978 [i.e. 1977]. — 171p : ill, ports ; 29cm.
Bibl.: p.165-166. — Index.
ISBN 0-85664-161-8 : £8.95 : CIP rev.
(B77-18929)

770'.9'034 — Photography, 1800-1910
Coe, Brian. The birth of photography : the story of the formative years, 1800-1900 / by Brian Coe. — London (120B Pentonville Rd, N1 9JB) : Ash and Grant, 1976. — 144p : ill, facsims, ports ; 29cm.
Bibl.: p.140. — Index.
ISBN 0-904069-06-0 : £4.95
ISBN 0-904069-07-9 Pbk : £2.95
(B77-06812)

770'.92'4 — Photography. Jacobs, Sylvester. *Autobiographies*
Jacobs, Sylvester. Born black / by Sylvester Jacobs with Linette Martin. — London [etc.] : Hodder and Stoughton, 1977. — 128p ; 18cm. — (Hodder Christian paperbacks)
ISBN 0-340-22178-x Pbk : £0.80
(B77-32061)

770'.92'4 — Photography. Warren, Allan. *Autobiographies*
Warren, Allan. The confessions of a society photographer / [by] Allan Warren. — London : Jupiter Books, 1976. — xi,214p : ill, ports ; 24cm.
ISBN 0-904041-68-9 : £3.95
(B77-17011)

770'.92'4 — Portrait photography. Nadar, Félix
Nadar, Félix. Nadar / [text by] Nigel Gosling. — London : Secker and Warburg, 1976. — [6], 298p : ill, facsim, chiefly ports ; 31cm.
Index.
ISBN 0-436-18610-1 : £9.75
(B77-04982)

771 — PHOTOGRAPHY. EQUIPMENT AND MATERIALS
771 — Photographic equipment. *United States. Buyers' guides*
The **photography** catalog / edited by Norman Snyder, with Carole Kismaric and Don Myrus. — New York [etc.] ; London : Harper and Row, 1976. — 255p : ill, facsims, form, ports ; 31cm.
Bibl. — Index.
ISBN 0-06-013979-x Pbk : £4.95
(B77-25796)

771.3 — Cameras. *Juvenile literature*
Hewitt, James. What makes a camera work? / [by] James Hewitt ; pictures by David Armitage. — London : Muller, 1977. — 47p : ill ; 22cm. — (How does it work)
Index.
ISBN 0-584-64305-5 : £2.50 : CIP rev.
(B77-07526)

771.3 — Unusual cameras, to 1975
Glassman, Carl. Hocus focus : the world's weirdest cameras / by Carl Glassman. — New York ; London : F. Watts, 1976. — [7],87,[1]p : ill, facsims, 2 ports ; 26cm.
Bibl.: p.84. — Index.
ISBN 0-531-00350-7 : £2.95
(B77-18306)

771.3'1 — Fed 4L cameras & Zorki 4 & 4K cameras. *Manuals*
Gaunt, Leonard. The Zorki and Fed book for Zorki 4K, Zorki 4 and Fed 4L camera users / [by] Leonard Gaunt. — London [etc.] : Focal Press, 1976. — 120p : ill(some col) ; 22cm. — (Focal camera books)
Index.
ISBN 0-240-50940-4 Pbk : £2.50
(B77-04983)

771.3'1 — Nikon cameras & Nikkormat cameras. *Manuals*
Keppler, Herbert. The Nikon and Nikkormat way / [by] Herbert Keppler. — London [etc.] : Focal Press, 1977. — 473p : ill(some col), port ; 22cm.
Index.
ISBN 0-240-50943-9 : Unpriced
(B77-20476)

771.3'1 — Nikon F cameras. *Manuals*
Reynolds, Clyde. The Nikon book : for F2 and F users / [by] Clyde Reynolds. — London [etc.] : Focal Press, 1977. — 136p : ill(some col) ; 22cm. — (Focal camera books)
Index.
ISBN 0-240-50905-6 Pbk : £2.50
(B77-21339)

771.3'1 — Olympus OM-1 & OM-2 cameras. *Manuals*
Gaunt, Leonard. The Olympus book : for OM1 and OM2 users / [by] Leonard Gaunt. — London [etc.] : Focal Press, 1977. — 136p : ill(some col) ; 22cm. — (Focal camera books)
ISBN 0-240-50942-0 Pbk : £2.50
(B77-31351)

771.3'1 — Pentax K series cameras. *Manuals*
Reynolds, Clyde. The Asahi Pentax book for K2, KX, KM and K1000 users / [by] Clyde Reynolds. — London [etc.] : Focal Press, 1976. — 136p : ill(some col) ; 22cm. — (Focal camera books)
ISBN 0-240-50935-8 Pbk : £2.50
(B77-06813)

771.3'52 — Cameras. Lenses. *Manuals*
Gaunt, Leonard. The focalguide to lenses / [by] Leonard Gaunt. — London [etc.] : Focal Press, 1977. — 206p : ill(some col) ; 19cm.
Index.
ISBN 0-240-50959-5 Pbk : £2.25 : CIP rev.
(B77-11343)

Ray, Sidney F. The lens in action / [by] Sidney F. Ray. — London [etc.] : Focal Press, 1976. — 201p : ill(chiefly col) ; 22cm. — (Media manuals)
Bibl.: p.194-196.
ISBN 0-240-50879-3 Pbk : £2.95
(B77-02495)

772 — PHOTOGRAPHY. METALLIC SALTS PROCESSES
772'.12'0973 — American daguerreotypes, 1840-1850. *Critical studies*
Newhall, Beaumont. The daguerreotype in America / by Beaumont Newhall. — 3rd revised ed. — New York : Dover Publications [etc.] ; London : Constable, 1976. — 2-175p, [96]p of plates : ill, ports ; 29cm.
Previous ed.: New York : Duell Sloan and Pearce, 1961. — Bibl.: p.169-170. — Index.
ISBN 0-486-23322-7 Pbk : £4.25
(B77-25797)

774 — HOLOGRAPHY
Collier, Robert J. Optical holography / [by] Robert J. Collier, Christoph B. Burckhardt, Lawrence H. Lin. — New York [etc.] ; London : Academic Press, 1971 [i.e. 1977]. — xvii,605p,[4]p of plates : ill(some col) ; 23cm.
Originally published: 1971. — Bibl.: p.xvi-xvii. — Index.
ISBN 0-12-181052-6 Pbk : £11.70
(B77-30499)

Françon, Maurice. Holography / [by] M. Françon. — United Kingdom ed. / expanded and revised from the French edition ; translated [from the French] by Grace Marmor Spruch. — New York ; London : Academic Press, 1974. — xi,143p : ill ; 24cm.
Previous ed.: published as 'Holographie'. Paris : Masson, 1969. — Bibl.: p.121-139. — Index.
ISBN 0-12-265750-0 : Unpriced
(B77-19552)

774 — Holography. Applications
Kock, Winston Edward. Engineering applications of lasers and holography / [by] Winston E. Kock. — New York ; London : Plenum Press, [1976]. — xv,400p : ill, ports ; 24cm. — (Optical physics and engineering)
Published in the United States: 1975. — Bibl.: p.389-390. — Index.
ISBN 0-306-30849-5 : £15.75
Primary classification 621.36'6
(B77-05475)

778.3 — PHOTOGRAPHY. SCIENTIFIC AND TECHNOLOGICAL APPLICATIONS
778.3'1 — Photomicrographs. *Illustrations. Juvenile literature*
Wolberg, Barbara J. Zooming in : photographic discoveries under the microscope / text by Barbara J. Wolberg ; photographs by Lewis R. Wolberg. — New York ; London : Harcourt Brace Jovanovich, 1974. — 64p : ill ; 29cm.
Bibl.: p.64.
ISBN 0-15-299970-1 : £3.25
(B77-15995)

778.3'5 — Aerial photography. Applications
The **uses** of air photography / edited by J.K.S. St Joseph. — New ed. / with contributions by D.E. Coombe ... [et al.]. — London : J. Baker, 1977. — 196p : ill, maps ; 26x32cm.
Previous ed.: / edited by J.K.S. St Joseph with contributions by Lord Esher and others. 1966. — Bibl. — Index.
ISBN 0-212-97016-x : £9.50
(B77-18930)

778.4 — STEREOSCOPIC PHOTOGRAPHY AND PROJECTION
778.4 — Three-dimensional photographic images. Techniques
Okoshi, Takanori. Three-dimensional imaging techniques / [by] Takanori Okoshi ; [translated from the Japanese]. — New York [etc.] ; London : Academic Press, 1976 [i.e. 1977]. — xi,403p : ill ; 24cm.
This translation published in the United States: 1976. — Translation and revision of: 'Sanjigen gazo kogaku'. Tokyo : Sangyo Tosho, 1972. — Index.
ISBN 0-12-525250-1 : £10.65
(B77-13177)

778.4'09'03 — Stereoscopic photography, to ca 1920
Jones, John, *b.1926.* Wonders of the stereoscope / [by] John Jones. — London : Cape, 1976. — 2v. : ill(some col), facsims, ports(some col) ; 27cm.
126p. in one vol. and 48 cards(ill.(some col)) with viewer in case, all in slip case. — Bibl.: p.125.
ISBN 0-224-01344-0 : £12.50
(B77-03161)

778.5 — CINEMATOGRAPHY
778.5'028'54044 — Cinematography. Applications of digital computer systems
Levitan, Eli L. Electronic imaging techniques : a handbook of conventional and computer-controlled animation, optical, and editing processes / [by] Eli L. Levitan. — New York ; London [etc.] : Van Nostrand Reinhold, 1977. — 195p : ill(some col), form ; 24cm.
Index.
ISBN 0-442-24771-0 : £13.65
(B77-26442)

778.5'3 — Cinematographic equipment: Cameras
Raimondo Souto, Hector Mario. The technique of the motion picture camera / by H. Mario Raimondo Souto. — 3rd revised and enlarged ed. — London [etc.] : Focal Press, 1977. — 381p : ill, form ; 23cm. — (The library of communication techniques)
Previous ed.: 1969. — Index.
ISBN 0-240-50917-x : £7.25
(B77-14853)

778.5'3 — Cinematography. *Manuals*
Adams, William B. Handbook of motion picture production / [by] William B. Adams ; line illustrations by Len Keennon. — New York ; London [etc.] : Wiley, 1977. — xi,352p : ill, forms ; 29cm.
'A Wiley-Interscience publication'. — Bibl.: p.343-344. — Index.
ISBN 0-471-00459-6 : £13.45
(B77-21340)

778.5'3'028 — Cinematography equipment: Cameras & lighting equipment
Samuelson, David W. Motion picture camera and lighting equipment : choice and technique / [by] David W. Samuelson. — London [etc.] : Focal Press, 1977. — 220p : ill ; 22cm. — (Media manuals)
Bibl.: p.220.
ISBN 0-240-50948-x Pbk : £2.95
(B77-22750)

778.5'342 — Colour cinematography. Processing, 1900-1975
Ryan, Roderick T. A history of motion picture color technology / [by] Roderick T. Ryan. — London [etc.] : Focal Press, 1977. — 278p : ill, facsims ; 25cm.
Include facsimile reprints of early instructions for cameramen. — Bibl.: p.234-235. — Index.
ISBN 0-240-50953-6 : £15.50
(B77-29596)

778.5'347 — Cinematography. Animation. Mechanics. *School texts*
Animations / [by Ray Hemmings ... et al.]. — London [etc.] : Hutchinson for Leapfrogs, 1975. — [1],16,[1]p : ill ; 21cm. — (Network : action books)
ISBN 0-09-124901-5 Sd : £0.30
(B77-02496)

778.5'347 — Cinematography. Animation. Techniques. *Manuals*
Salt, Brian George Daniel. Basic animation stand techniques / by Brian G.D. Salt. — Oxford [etc.] : Pergamon, 1977. — 239p : ill, forms ; 26cm.
Index.
ISBN 0-08-021368-5 : £6.25
(B77-22042)

778.5'347'0904 — Animated films. Production, to 1975. *Readings*
Experimental animation : an illustrated anthology / [compiled by] Robert Russett and Cecile Starr. — New York ; London [etc.] : Van Nostrand Reinhold, 1976. — 224p : ill, ports ; 24cm.
Bibl.: p.213-214. — List of films: p.214-215. — Index.
ISBN 0-442-27194-8 : £11.20
ISBN 0-442-27195-6 Pbk : £6.70
(B77-16530)

778.5'349 — Cinematography. *Amateurs' manuals*
Dean, Peter. Home movies : make and project your own films / by Peter Dean ; drawings by G. Pestarque. — London : Chancerel : Barrie and Jenkins, 1977. — 2-91p : ill, port ; 21cm. — (Action books)
Ill. on lining papers.
ISBN 0-905703-08-1 : £1.75
(B77-27996)

778.5'3491 — Super 8mm cinematography. *Amateurs' manuals*
Watkins, Derek. Cine photography made easy / [by] Derek Watkins. — Newton Abbot [etc.] : David and Charles, 1977. — 126p : ill ; 22cm. — (David & Charles leisure & travel series)
Bibl.: p.124. — Index.
ISBN 0-7153-7437-0 : £1.95
(B77-24389)

778.59 — Television programmes. Cinematography. *Manuals*
Englander, Adolphe Arthur. Filming for television / [by] A. Arthur Englander, Paul Petzold ; preface by Kenneth Clark. — London [etc.] : Focal Press, 1976. — 266p : ill, facsims, plans, ports ; 24cm.
Index.
ISBN 0-240-50961-7 : £6.95
(B77-01693)

778.7 — PHOTOGRAPHY UNDER SPECIAL CONDITIONS
778.7'2 — Photography. Use of lighting. *Amateurs' manuals*
Petzold, Paul. The photoguide to lighting / [by] Paul Petzold. — London [etc.] : Focal Press, 1977. — 261p : ill(some col) ; 19cm. — (The Focal photoguides)
Index.
ISBN 0-240-50962-5 Pbk : £2.25
(B77-13790)

778.7'3 — Underwater photography. *Manuals*
Glover, T. A manual of underwater photography / [by[T. Glover, G.E. Harwood, J.N. Lythgoe. — London [etc.] : Academic Press, 1977. — xiii,219p : ill ; 24cm.
Bibl.: p.202-203. — Index.
ISBN 0-12-286750-5 : £9.60
(B77-22043)

778.8 — TRICK PHOTOGRAPHY
778.8 — Photomontage. *Manuals*
Croy, Otto Roman. Croy's camera trickery / [translated from the German by W.D. Emanuel]. — London [etc.] : Focal Press, 1977. — 136p : ill, facsims ; 25cm.
Translation of: 'Fotomontage und Verfremdung'. Vollständig überarb. und erw. Neufassung. Düsseldorf : Wilhelm Knapp, 1974. — Index.
ISBN 0-240-50958-7 : £4.50
(B77-11344)

778.9 — PHOTOGRAPHY OF SPECIAL SUBJECTS
778.9'2 — Portrait photography. *Amateurs' manuals*
Mason, Reg Herbert. Portraiture at home / [by] R.H. Mason. — [Watford] : Fountain Press, 1977. — 157p,[8]p of plates : chiefly ill(some col) ; 24cm.
Bibl.: p.157.
ISBN 0-85242-488-4 : £4.95
(B77-23617)

778.9'24 — Glamour photography. Modelling
Wells, Stanley, *b.1924.* Pin-up model : a course in modelling / by Stanley Wells ; photography by Henry Dobkin. — London : Hale, 1977. — 142p,[16]p of plates : ill ; 21cm.
ISBN 0-7091-6456-4 : £3.50
(B77-31352)

778.9'32 — Photography. Special subjects: Animals. *Manuals*
Hosking, Eric. Wildlife photography : a field guide / [by] Eric Hosking and John Gooders. — London : Arrow Books, 1976. — 181p,[32]p of plates : ill(some col) ; 20cm.
Originally published: London : Hutchinson, 1973. — Bibl.: p.171-172. — Index.
ISBN 0-09-913740-2 Pbk : £1.95
(B77-00339)

778.9'32 — Photography, to ca 1940. Special subjects: Birds & mammals. *Critical studies*
Guggisberg, Charles Albert Walter. Early wildlife photographers / by C.A.W. Guggisberg ; foreword by Eric Hosking. — Newton Abbot [etc.] : David and Charles, 1977. — 128p : ill, facsim, ports ; 24cm.
Bibl.: p.120-127. — Index.
ISBN 0-7153-7328-5 : £4.95
(B77-21341)

778.9'34 — Photography. Special subjects: Flowering plants. *Manuals*
Angel, Heather. Flowers / [by] Heather Angel. — Kings Langley : Fountain Press, 1975. — 96p : ill(some col) ; 18cm. — (Photographing nature)
Bibl.: p.95. — Index.
ISBN 0-85242-424-8 Pbk : £1.75
(B77-06215)

778.9'36 — Photography. Special subjects: Mountains. *Manuals*

Milner, Cyril Douglas. The photoguide to mountains : for the backpacker and climber / [by] Douglas Milner. — London [etc.] : Focal Press, 1977. — 184p : ill(some col) ; 19cm. — (Focal photoguides)
Bibl.: p.180-181. — Index.
ISBN 0-240-50969-2 Pbk : £2.25 : CIP rev.
(B77-16531)

778.9'9'92972 — Photography, 1850-1976. Special subjects: Great Britain. Royal families

Happy and glorious : six reigns of royal photography / with contributions by Cecil Beaton ... [et al.] ; edited by Colin Ford. — London [etc.] : Angus and Robertson, 1977. — 136p : ill(some col), facsims, geneal table, ports(some col) ; 25cm.
'... most [of the illustrations] have been specially chosen from the exhibition ... which the [National Portrait] Gallery has mounted to celebrate Her Majesty's Silver Jubilee' - Foreword. — List of films: p.126-131. — Index.
ISBN 0-207-95744-4 : £4.80
(B77-14854)

Happy and glorious : 130 years of royal photographs / with contributions by Cecil Beaton ... [et al.] ; edited by Colin Ford. — London ([2 St Martin's Place] WC2H 0HE) : National Portrait Gallery, 1977. — 136p : ill, facsims, ports(some col) ; 24cm.
Index.
ISBN 0-904017-14-1 Pbk : £1.50
(B77-16532)

779 — PHOTOGRAPHY. COLLECTIONS

779'.092'4 — American photography, 1850-1900. *Collections from individual artists*

Stieglitz, Alfred. Alfred Stieglitz / [text by Dorothy Norman]. — London : Gordon Fraser Gallery, 1976. — 95p : chiefly ill, ports ; 21cm. — (The history of photography series ; 3)
Also published: New York : Aperture, 1976. — Bibl.: p.94-95.
ISBN 0-900406-79-8 : £3.95
(B77-27997)

779'.092'4 — American photography, 1900-1950. *Collections from individual artists*

Callahan, Henry. Callahan / edited with an introduction by John Szarkowski. — Millerton, N.Y. : Aperture [for] the Museum of Modern Art ; London : Gordon Fraser Gallery, 1976. — 203p : of ill ; 32cm.
'... published ... on the occasion of a major exhibition of the photographs of Harry Callahan held at the Museum of Modern Art from December 2, 1976 to February 8, 1977' - title page verso. — Bibl.: p.197-199.
ISBN 0-900406-83-6 : £19.95
(B77-11345)

Strand, Paul. Paul Strand : sixty years of photographs / profile by Calvin Tomkins. — London : Gordon Fraser Gallery, 1976. — 183p : chiefly ill, ports ; 30cm.
'[With] excerpts from correspondence, interviews and other documents'. — 'The introductory text of this work appeared originally in "The New Yorker", [1974] in a slightly different form' - title page verso. — Bibl.: p.178-181.
ISBN 0-900406-81-x : £15.00
(B77-10881)

779'.092'4 — American photography, 1950-. *Collections from individual artists*

Bullock, Wynn. Wynn Bullock / [text by David Fuess]. — London : Gordon Fraser Gallery, 1976. — 95p : chiefly ill ; 21cm. — (The history of photography series ; 4)
Versos of leaves 13-87 blank. — Also published: Millerton : Aperture, 1976. — Bibl.: p.92-93. — List of films: p.93.
ISBN 0-900406-80-1 : £3.95
(B77-27998)

Eggleston, William. William Eggleston's guide / essay by John Szarkowski. — New York : Museum of Modern Art ; Cambridge, Mass. ; London : Distributed by M.I.T. Press, 1976. — 112p : chiefly col ill, port ; 24cm.
ISBN 0-87070-317-x : £9.35
(B77-01694)

McCartney, Linda. Linda's pictures : a collection of photographs / photographs and words by Linda McCartney ; reviewed by Paul McCartney. — London : Cape, 1976. — xv,[5] p,148p of plates : chiefly ill(some col), chiefly ports(some col) ; 33cm.
ISBN 0-224-01370-x : £7.50
(B77-01695)

779'.092'4 — Art galleries. *London. Lambeth (London Borough) Hayward Gallery. Exhibits: American photography. Weston, Edward, b.1886. Catalogues*

Haworth-Booth, Mark. Edward Weston / [by Mark Haworth-Booth]. — [London] : Arts Council, 1977. — [18]p : ill ; 21cm.
'Published ... on the occasion of the Edward Weston exhibition at the Hayward Gallery, London, 2 March to 24 April 1977' - title page verso. — Bibl.: p.[18].
ISBN 0-7287-0126-x Sd : £0.60
(B77-13791)

779'.092'4 — Art galleries. *London. Westminster (London Borough). National Portrait Gallery. Exhibits: English photography. Stone, Sir Benjamin. Catalogues*

Stone, *Sir* Benjamin. Sir Benjamin Stone, 1838-1914, & the National Photographic Record Association, 1897-1910 / [text by Colin Ford]. — [London] ([2 St Martin's Place, WC2H 0HE]) : National Portrait Gallery, 1974. — 32p : chiefly ill, facsim, ports ; 24cm.
Catalogue of an exhibition held at the National Portrait Gallery 1974.
ISBN 0-904017-13-3 Sd : £0.50
(B77-03162)

779'.092'4 — Art galleries. *Oxfordshire. Oxford. Museum of Modern Art, Oxford. Exhibits: American photography. Evans, Walker. Catalogues*

Museum of Modern Art, *New York.* Walker Evans : photographs : [catalogue of] an exhibition circulated under the auspices of the International Council of the Museum of Modern Art, New York [held at the] Museum of Modern Art, Oxford, 18 September-31 October 1976. — [London] : Arts Council of Great Britain, 1976. — [16]p : ill, 2 ports ; 21cm.
ISBN 0-7287-0110-3 Pbk : £0.65
(B77-04984)

779'.092'4 — Art galleries. *Oxfordshire. Oxford. Museum of Modern Art, Oxford. Exhibits: German photography. Rinke, Klaus. Catalogues*

Rinke, Klaus. Klaus Rinke : [catalogue of an exhibition held at the] Museum of Modern Art, Oxford, January 11th-February 15th 1976 / [translation from the German by Barbara Flynn]. — [Oxford] ([30 Pembroke St., Oxford OX1 1BP]) : [The Museum], [1976]. — [176]p : of ill ; 26cm.
Pbk : £3.00
(B77-00340)

779'.092'4 — Arts. Patronage. Organisations. *Wales. Welsh Arts Council. Exhibits: Dutch photography. Dibbets, Jan. Catalogues*

Scottish Art Council. Jan Dibbets / [with an essay by Marcel Vos]. — Edinburgh (19 Charlotte Sq., Edinburgh) : Scottish Arts Council ; Cardiff : Welsh Arts Council, [1977]. — [16]p,[18]p of plates,[2] leaves of plates : ill(some col) ; 19x26cm.
Cover title. — Text on inside front cover. — 'A Scottish Arts Council and Welsh Arts Council Exhibition organised with the assistance of Arnolfini Gallery, Bristol' - cover . — Plate width varies. — Bibl.: p.[15].
Pbk : Unpriced
(B77-29597)

779'.092'4 — English photography, 1950-. *Collections from individual artists*

Bailey, David. Mixed moments / [by] David Bailey. — London (2 Honduras St., WC1Y 0TX) : The author : Olympus Optical Co. (UK) Ltd, 1976. — 142p : chiefly ill(some col), ports(chiefly col) ; 31cm.
ISBN 0-9505268-0-0 : £6.95
(B77-32062)

Hamilton, David, *b.1933.* The best of David Hamilton / text by Denise Couttès. — London : Collins, 1977. — 3-143p : chiefly ill(chiefly col) ; 30cm.
'... the best photographs from David Hamilton's fist three books, "Dreams of a young girl", "Sisters", and "La Danse" ...' - jacket.
ISBN 0-00-216078-1 : £8.00
(B77-09172)

Hopkins, Thurston. Thurston Hopkins / [text by] Robert Muller. — London : Gordon Fraser Gallery [for] the Arts Council of Great Britain, 1977. — 14p,73p of plates : chiefly ill, ports ; 29cm. — (Gordon Fraser photographic monographs ; 6)
ISBN 0-900406-67-4 Pbk : Unpriced
(B77-18307)

Slinger, Penelope. An exorcism / [by] Penny Slinger. — London : Villiers Publications for Empty-Eye ; Sudbury : Distributed by Spearman, 1977. — [149]p : chiefly ill(some col) ; 23x29cm.
English, French, German and Italian introductory material and captions.
ISBN 0-85435-274-0 : £17.50
(B77-27999)

779'.092'4 — French photography, 1900-1950. *Collections from individual artists*

Cartier-Bresson, Henri. Henri Cartier-Bresson. — London : Gordon Fraser Gallery, 1976. — 95p : chiefly ill, ports ; 21cm. — (The history of photography series ; book 1)
Versos of leaves 9-85 blank. — Also published: Millerton : Aperture, 1976. — Bibl.: p.93-94.
ISBN 0-900406-76-3 : £3.95
(B77-28781)

779'.092'4 — German photomontages, 1900-1950. *Collections from individual artists*

Heartfield, John. Photomontages of the Nazi period / [by] John Heartfield. — London [etc.] : Gordon Fraser Gallery [for] Universe Books, 1977. — 143p : chiefly ill, ports ; 26cm.
Accompanying text translated from the German. — Bibl.: p.142.
ISBN 0-900406-20-8 : £7.00
ISBN 0-900406-23-2 Pbk : £3.95
(B77-25798)

779'.092'4 — Swiss photography, 1950-. Special subjects: Items resembling faces. *Collections from individual artists*

Robert, Jean Ed. Face to face / concept and photography Jean-Ed. Robert. — [London] ([61 North Wharf Rd, W2 1LA]) : [Pentagram Design], [1977]. — [42]p : of ill ; 21cm. — ([Pentagram papers ; 4 ISSN 0309-2135])
Pbk : £1.00
(B77-22751)

779'.0973 — Art galleries. *Washington (State). Seattle. Seattle Art Museum. Exhibits: American photography, to 1975. Collections: Monsen Collection of American Photography. Catalogues*

Seattle Art Museum. American photography : past into present : prints from the Monsen Collection of American Photography [in the] Seattle Art Museum / selected and with an introduction by Anita Ventura Mozley. — [Seattle] : Seattle Art Museum ; Seattle ; London : Distributed by the University of Washington Press, 1976. — 156p : chiefly ill, ports ; 29cm.
Exhibition catalogue. — Bibl.: p.155.
ISBN 0-295-95508-2 : £16.00
ISBN 0-295-95509-0 Pbk : £8.00
(B77-06216)

779'.2'0924 — American portrait photography, 1900-1950. Special subjects: Celebrities. *Collections from individual artists*

Eisenstaedt, Alfred. Eisenstaedt's album : fifty years of friends and acquaintances / with an introduction by Philip B. Kunhardt, Jr. — London : Thames and Hudson, 1976. — [224] p : of ill, chiefly ports, facsims ; 30cm.
ISBN 0-500-54041-1 : £9.50
(B77-09860)

779'.2'0924 — American portrait photography, 1950-. *Collections from individual artists*

Avedon, Richard. Portraits / [by Richard Avedon] ; [with an essay by Harold Rosenberg]. — London : Thames and Hudson, [1976]. — [141]p(incl [6]fold) : chiefly ports ; 31cm.
Also published: New York : Farrar, Straus and Giroux, 1976.
ISBN 0-500-54042-x : £10.50
(B77-05563)

779'.2'0924 — Art galleries. *London. Westminster (London Borough). National Portrait Gallery. Exhibits: Portrait photography. Man, Felix H. Catalogues*

Man, Felix H. Felix H. Man : reportage portraits, 1929-76 : [catalogue of an exhibition held at the] National Portrait Gallery [1 October 1976 to 2 January 1977]. — London (London WC2H 0HE) : The Gallery, 1976. — [19]p : chiefly ports ; 24cm.
Bibl.: p.[8].
ISBN 0-904017-10-9 Sd : £0.30
(B77-01696)

779'.2'0924 — Australian photography, 1950-. Special subjects: Transsexuals & transvestites. *Collections from individual artists*
Kay, Barry. The other women / by Barry Kay. — London (51 Endell St., WC2H 9AJ) : Mathews Miller Dunbar Ltd, 1976. — [117]p : of ports ; 30cm.
ISBN 0-903811-17-0 Pbk : £3.95
(B77-27280)

779'.2'0924 — English portrait photography, 1850-1900. *Collections from individual artists*
Cameron, Julia Margaret. The Herschel album : an album of photographs / by Julia Margaret Cameron ; presented to Sir John Herschel. — London ([2 St Martin's Place, WC2H 0HE]) : National Portrait Gallery, 1975. — [6]p,26p of plates : ill, ports ; 26cm.
'... published in connection with the first exhibition of the Album, 14 November 1975 to 29 February 1976' - Preface.
ISBN 0-904017-03-6 Sd : £0.60
(B77-07994)

779'.2'0924 — English portrait photography, 1900-1950. Special subjects: Artists & intellectuals. *Collections from individual artists*
Morrell, *Lady* **Ottoline.** Lady Ottoline's album : snapshops and portraits of her famous contemporaries (and of herself) / photograhed for the most part by Lady Ottoline Morrell ; from the collection of her daughter, Julian Vinogradoff ; with an introduction by Lord David Cecil ; edited by Carolyn G. Heilbrun. — London : Joseph, 1976. — vii,118p : chiefly ports ; 24cm.
Originally published: New York : Knopf, 1976. — Index.
ISBN 0-7181-1483-3 : £7.50
(B77-09861)

779'.2'0973 — American portrait photography, 1900-1950. Special subjects: Cinema films. Acting. Stars, 1926-1949. *Collections*
Hollywood glamor portraits : 145 photos of stars, 1926-1949 / edited by John Kobal. — New York : Dover Publications [etc.] ; London : Constable, 1976. — xiv,144p : of ill, ports ; 29cm.
Index.
ISBN 0-486-23352-9 Pbk : £4.00
(B77-09173)

779'.24'0924 — American photography, 1950- . Special subjects: Women. *Collections from individual artists*
Arnold, Eve. The unretouched woman / [by] Eve Arnold. — London : Cape, 1976. — 199p : chiefly ill(some col), ports(some col) ; 29cm.
ISBN 0-224-01315-7 : £7.95
(B77-18931)

779'.24'0924 — French anamorphic photography, 1900-1950. Special subjects: Women: Nudes. *Collections from individual artists*
Kertész, André. Distortions / [by] André Kertész ; edited by Nicolas Ducrot ; with an introduction by Hilton Kramer. — London : Thames and Hudson, 1977. — [7]p,[80]leaves of plates,[14]p of plates : chiefly ill ; 29cm.
Originally published: New York : Knopf, 1976.
ISBN 0-500-54046-2 : £12.50
(B77-22752)

779'.24'0924 — German photography, 1900-1950. Special subjects: Women. *Collections from individual artists*
Newton, Helmut. White women / [by] Helmut Newton ; designed by Bea Feitler. — London : Quartet Books, 1976. — xiv,107,[2]p : of ill(some col), ports(some col) ; 32cm.
Also published: New York : Stonehill, 1976.
ISBN 0-7043-2140-8 : £9.95
(B77-05564)

779'.25 — Photography, 1950- . Special subjects: Children. *Collections*
The **family** of children / [editor, Jerry Mason]. — London : Cape, 1977. — 192p : of ill ; 29cm.
'A Ridge Press Book'. — Also published: New York : Grosset and Dunlap, 1977.
ISBN 0-224-01569-9 : £5.95 : CIP rev.
(B77-24391)

779'.3'0924 — American photography, 1950- . Special subjects: Natural objects. *Collections from individual artists*
Feininger, Andreas. The mountains of the mind : a fantastic journey into reality / [by] Andreas Feininger. — London : Thames and Hudson, 1977. — 160p : chiefly ill(some col) ; 29cm.
ISBN 0-500-54047-0 : £12.50
(B77-32063)

779'.37'07402162 — Museums. *London. Greenwich (London Borough). National Maritime Museum. Exhibits: Marine photography. Catalogues*
National Maritime Museum. General catalogue of historic photographs / National Maritime Museum. — [London] ([Greenwich, SE10 9NF]) : The Museum.
Vol.2 : Merchant sailing ships. — 1976. — xii, 193,[20]p,[4]p of plates : ill ; 28cm.
Index.
ISBN 0-905555-00-7 Pbk : £2.00
(B77-12018)

779'.4'0924 — American photography, 1950-. Special subjects: Italy. Rome. Ancient Roman antiquities. *Collections from individual artists*
Piranesi, Giovanni Battista. Views of Rome, then and now / 41 etchings by Giovanni Battista Piranesi ; corresponding photographs and text by Herschel Levit. — New York : Dover Publications [etc.] ; London : Constable, 1976. — iii-xxvii p,41,41p of plates : chiefly ill ; 38cm.
Opposite pages of plates numbered in duplicate. — Bibl.: p.viii.
ISBN 0-486-23339-1 Pbk : £4.25
Primary classification 769'.92'4
(B77-25111)

779'.4'0924 — German photography, 1950-. Special subjects: Buildings. Walls. *Collections from individual artists*
Schaewen, Deidi von. Walls / by Deidi von Schaewen. — London : Thames and Hudson, 1977. — xvi,142[i.e.136]p(8 fold) : of ill(some col) ; 28cm.
Also published: New York : Pantheon Books, 1977. — Index.
ISBN 0-500-27102-x Pbk : £4.95
(B77-33967)

779'.9'9414430810924 — Scottish photography, 1850-1900. Special subjects: Scotland. Strathclyde Region. Glasgow. Streets, 1868-1877. *Collections from individual artists*
Annan, Thomas. Photographs of the old closes and streets of Glasgow, 1868-1877 : with a supplement of 15 related views / [by] Thomas Annan ; with a new introduction by Anita Ventura Mozley. — New York : Dover Publications [etc.] ; London : Constable, 1977. — xvii p,55p of plates : chiefly ill ; 31cm.
Contents: 'Photographs of old closes, streets & etc. taken 1868-1877'. Originally published: Glasgow : Glasgow City Improvement Trust, 1878-79 - 15 photographs from the 1900 edition 'Old closes & streets, a series of photogravures, 1868-1899'. Originally published: Glasgow : James Maclehose & Sons, 1900.
ISBN 0-486-23442-8 Pbk : £3.60
(B77-24392)

779'.9'942081 — Art galleries. *London. Greenwich (London Borough). Woodlands Art Gallery. Exhibits: English photography. Special subjects: England. Social life, 1837-1901*
Woodlands Art Gallery. Victorian street scenes : Mr Coulthurst's Salford, 1889-1894, Mr Spurgeon's Greenwich, 1884-1887 (a magic lantern lecture) : an exhibition of photographs 10 January-10 February 1976 [at] Woodlands Art Gallery. — London ([c/o Woodlands Art Gallery], 90 Mycenae Rd, SE3 [7SE]) : [London Borough of Greenwich], [1976]. — Folder ([4]p) : ill ; 21cm.
ISBN 0-9504033-7-7 : Unpriced
(B77-12019)

779'.9'9420830924 — English photography, 1900-1950. Special subjects: England. Social life, 1930-1940. *Collections from individual artists*
Brandt, Bill. Bill Brandt, early photographs, 1930-1942. — [London] : Arts Council of Great Britain, [1975?]. — [18]p : chiefly ill ; 25cm.
Issued in conjunction with a touring exhibition. — Bibl.: p.[18].
ISBN 0-7287-0056-5 Sd : Unpriced
(B77-18932)

780 — MUSIC
The **book** of music / [editor Gill Rowley]. — London : Macdonald Educational, 1977. — 192p : ill(some col), facsims, maps(chiefly col), music, plans(some col), ports ; 31cm.
Index.
ISBN 0-356-05579-5 : £8.50
(B77-33362)

The **comprehensive** study of music / [by] William Brandt ... [et al.]. — New York [etc.] ; London : Harper and Row.
Anthology of music from Debussy through Stockhausen. — 1976. — viii,286p : of music ; 28cm.
ISBN 0-06-161420-3 7PGP : £5.20
(B77-15996)

The **music** forum. — New York ; Guildford : Columbia University Press.
Vol.4 / Felix Salzer, editor, Carl Schachter, associate editor, Hedi Siegel, editorial assistant. — 1976. — xi,403p : facsims, music ; 26cm.
Index.
ISBN 0-231-03934-4 : £14.35
(B77-15405)

The **musical** companion / edited by A.L. Bacharach & J.R. Pearce. — Revised ed. — London : Gollancz, 1977. — 800p,plate : facsim, music ; 21cm.
Previous ed.: published as 'The new musical companion' / edited by A.L. Bacharach. 1957. — Index.
ISBN 0-575-02263-9 : £6.50
(B77-33968)

780 — Music. *Juvenile literature*
Doniach, Shula. Every child's book of music and musicians / [by] Shula Doniach. — 2nd revised ed. — London [etc.] : Burke, 1974. — 128p : ill, facsims, music, ports ; 26cm.
Previous ed.: 1961. — Index.
ISBN 0-222-00178-x : £2.50
(B77-19553)

780 — Music. *Secondary school texts*
Brace, Geoffrey. Listen! music and you / [by] Geoffrey Brace and Ian Burton. — Cambridge [etc.] : Cambridge University Press, 1977. — vi, 66p : ill, music, ports ; 21x22cm.
Bibl.: p.66.
ISBN 0-521-21240-5 Pbk : £1.75
(B77-28000)

780'.01 — Musicology. *Reviews of research*
Current thought in musicology / edited by John W. Grubbs, with the assistance of ... [others]. — Austin ; London : University of Texas Press, 1976. — xv,313p : ill, facsims, music ; 26cm. — (Symposia in the arts and the humanities ; no.4)
'... the result of a symposium held at the University of Texas at Austin in 1971' - jacket. — Index.
ISBN 0-292-71017-8 : £9.80
(B77-03163)

780'.07 — Music. *Sociological perspectives*
Whose music? : a sociology of musical languages / [by] John Shepherd ... [et al.] ; foreword by Howard S. Becker. — London : Latimer Press, 1977. — xiv,300p : ill, music ; 23cm.
Bibl.: p.259-266. — Index.
ISBN 0-901539-51-1 : £12.00
ISBN 0-901539-62-7 Pbk : £5.95
(B77-28001)

780'.07 — Society. Influence of music
Small, Christopher, *b.1927.* Music, society, education : a radical examination of the prophetic function of music in Western, Eastern and African cultures with its impact on society and its use in education / by Christopher Small. — London : J. Calder : [Distributed by Calder and Boyars], 1977. — [6],234p ; 23cm. — (Platform books)
Index.
ISBN 0-7145-3530-3 : £6.95
ISBN 0-7145-3614-8 Pbk : Unpriced
(B77-23618)

780'.1 — Music. *Phenomenological viewpoints*
In search of musical method / edited by F.J. Smith. — London [etc.] : Gordon and Breach, 1976. — [7],149,[1]p : music ; 24cm.
'The articles in this book are also ... published in the journal "Music and Man", Vol.2, Nos 1/2 (1976)' - title page verso. — Bibl.
ISBN 0-677-12640-9 : £7.10
(B77-01697)

780'.15 — Music. *For music appreciation*
Kamien, Roger. Music : an appreciation / [by] Roger Kamien. — New York ; London [etc.] : McGraw-Hill, 1976. — xxvi,579p : ill, music, ports ; 25cm.
Bibl.: p.546-552. — List of sound discs : p.552-554. — Index.
ISBN 0-07-033266-5 : £10.40
(B77-03698)

Ratner, Leonard Gilbert. Music : the listener's art / [by] Leonard G. Ratner. — 3rd ed. — New York ; London [etc.] : McGraw-Hill, 1977. — xiii,306p : ill, facsims, music ; 25cm.
Previous ed.: New York : McGraw-Hill, 1966. — Bibl.: p.289-291. — Index.
ISBN 0-07-051221-3 : £9.70
(B77-20477)

780'.15 — Music. Appreciation. *Juvenile literature*
Cardus, *Sir* Neville. What is music? / [by] Sir Neville Cardus ; edited by Margaret Hughes ; illustrated by Richard Hook ; record list by Peter Gammond. — London [etc.] : White Lion Publishers, 1977. — 144p : ill ; 23cm. — (The White Lion music library)
List of sound discs: p.129-142.
ISBN 0-7285-0017-5 : £4.50
ISBN 0-7285-0009-9 Pbk : £1.95
(B77-22044)

780'.23 — Music. *Great Britain. Career guides. For graduates*
Fortescue, Margaret. Careers with music for graduates / [written by Margaret Fortescue and Geoffrey Perrin]. — 2nd ed. — Norwich (Careers Centre, University of East Anglia, University Plain, Norwich NR4 7TJ) : University of East Anglia, 1976. — [2],27p ; 21cm. — (University of East Anglia. Careers information sheets)
Previous ed.: published as 'Careers with music ...' 1975. — Bibl.: p.21-22.
Sd : £0.35
(B77-26443)

780'.3 — Music. *Encyclopaedias*
Westrup, *Sir* Jack Allan. Collins encyclopedia of music / [by] Sir Jack Westrup and F.Ll. Harrison. — Completely revised [ed.] / revised by Conrad Wilson. — London [etc.] : Collins, 1976. — 608p : ill, facsims, music, ports ; 26cm.
Previous ed.: published as 'Collins music encyclopedia', 1959. — Bibl.
ISBN 0-00-434331-x : £7.95
(B77-20478)

780'.3 — Music. *Polyglot glossaries*
Leach, Robert, *b.1949*. Musical thesaurus : a dictionary of musical language / compiled by Robert Leach. — Oxford (36 Great Clarendon St., Oxford) : Hannon, 1976. — [2],ii,47p : ill ; 21cm.
English, Italian and German text, English, Italian, French and German general terms.
Sd : £1.00
(B77-13792)

780'.42 — Pop music
Bygrave, Mike. Rock / author Mike Bygrave ; art director Linda Nash ; special consultant Paul Murray. — London : Hamilton, 1977. — 4-61p : chiefly ill(some col), ports(some col) ; 30cm.
Ill. on lining papers.
ISBN 0-241-89643-6 : £2.75
(B77-21342)

780'.42 — Rock music. *Chronologies*
Marchbank, Pearce. The illustrated rock almanac / compiled, written and edited by Pearce Marchbank and Miles. — New York ; London : Paddington Press, 1977. — 191p : ill, facsims, ports ; 28cm.
ISBN 0-448-22675-8 Pbk : £2.95
(B77-22753)

780'.42 — Rock music. *Encyclopaedias*
Logan, Nick. The illustrated 'New musical express' encyclopedia of rock / [compiled and written by Nick Logan and Bob Woffinden]. — London [etc.] : Hamlyn, 1977. — 256p : ill(chiefly col), ports(chiefly col) ; 31cm. — (A Salamander book)
Col. ill. on lining papers. — Originally published: 1976. — Index.
ISBN 0-600-33147-4 : £4.95
(B77-20479)

The **'New** musical express' book of rock / edited by Nick Logan ; updated by Rob Finnis. — London : Star Books, 1975. — 429p,[12]p of plates : ports ; 19cm.
Cover title: 'The NME book of rock'. — 'Parts of this book have already appeared in separate issues of ... the 'New musical express' ...' - p.1.
ISBN 0-352-30074-4 Pbk : £0.75
(B77-19554)

780'.42 — Rock music, 1955-1975
Yorke, Ritchie. The history of rock 'n' roll / [by] Ritchie Yorke ; prepared in association with CHUM Ltd. — London : Eyre Methuen, 1976. — 174p : ill(some col), facsims, ports(some col) ; 28cm.
Also published: Toronto : Methuen, 1976.
ISBN 0-413-37640-0 Pbk : £2.50
(B77-14855)

780'.42'02573 — Popular music. *United States. Directories*
Wootton, Richard. Honky tonkin' : a guide to music USA / [by] Richard Wootton and Charlie McKissack. — [London] ([21 Melbourne Court, Anersley Rd, S.E.20]) : [The authors], [1977]. — 27p : ill ; 22cm.
Sd : £0.50
(B77-29598)

780'.42'05 — Pop music. *Periodicals*
Hot press. — [Dublin] : [Steady Rolling Publishing Ltd] ; [London] ([4 Monmouth Place, W.2]) : [Distributed by Paper Chain]. Vol.1, no.1- ; 9th June 1977-. — [1977]-. — ill, ports ; 45cm.
Fortnightly. — 32p. in 7th issue.
Sd : £0.20
ISSN 0332-0847
(B77-30500)

National rockstar. — London : IPC Magazines. [1]- ; Oct. 23, 1976-. — 1976-. — ill, ports ; 42cm.
Weekly. — 40p. in 1st issue.
Sd : £0.12
(B77-04346)

780'.42'0904 — Pop music, to 1977. *Juvenile literature*
Dufour, Barry. The world of pop and rock / written and devised by Barry Dufour ; special consultant Dave Laing. — London : Macdonald Educational, 1977. — 4-61p : ill(some col), facsims, ports(some col) ; 29cm.
Bibl.: p.60. — Index.
ISBN 0-356-05591-4 : £2.50
ISBN 0-356-05763-1 Pbk : £1.95
(B77-32064)

780'.42'0904 — Popular music, ca 1900-1975
Palmer, Tony, *b.1941*. All you need is love : the story of popular music / [by] Tony Palmer ; edited by Paul Medlicott. — London : Weidenfeld and Nicolson : Chappell, 1976. — xii,323p : ill, facsims(some col), ports ; 29cm.
Based on a sixteen part television series. — Index.
ISBN 0-297-77251-1 : £6.50
(B77-05565)

780'.42'0922 — American country music. *Biographical dictionaries*
Shestack, Melvin. The country music encyclopaedia / by Melvin Shestack. — London [etc.] : Omnibus Press, 1977. — xv,378p : ill, ports ; 27cm.
Originally published: New York : Crowell, 1974. — List of sound discs: p.325-375.
ISBN 0-86001-308-1 : £5.95
(B77-33363)

780'.42'0922 — Pop music. Negro stars, 1950-1976
Pascall, Jeremy. The stars & superstars of black music / [produced by Jeremy Pascall and Rob Burt]. — London : Phoebus, 1977. — 128p : col facsim, ports(some col) ; 31cm.
Ill. on lining papers. — 'This material first appeared in "The story of pop"' - title page verso.
ISBN 0-7026-0065-2 : £2.95
(B77-11346)

780'.42'0924 — Rock music. *Great Britain, 1967-1975. Personal observations*
Rock on the road / edited and photographed by Mick Gold. — [London] : Futura Publications, [1976]. — 160p : ill, ports ; 25cm.
ISBN 0-86007-323-8 Pbk : £1.95
(B77-10490)

780'.42'0973 — American country music. *Great Britain. Serials*
British Country Music Association. Yearbook / British Country Music Association. — Newton Abbot (PO Box 2, Newton Abbot, Devon) : The Association.
1977. — [1977]. — 80p : ill, ports ; 21cm.
Cover title.
Pbk : £1.25
ISSN 0308-4698
(B77-19555)

780'.42'0979 — West Coast American rock music, ca 1960-1976
West Coast story / [edited by Rob Burt & Patsy North]. — London [etc.] : Hamlyn ; London : Phoebus, 1977. — 96p : ill(some col), ports(some col) ; 31cm.
Ill. on lining papers. — 'This material first appeared in "The story of pop" 1973, 74, 75' - title page verso.
ISBN 0-600-39393-3 : £2.95
(B77-32774)

780'.5 — Music. *Yearbooks*
International music guide. — London : Tantivy Press [etc.].
1977 / edited by Derek Elley. — [1976]. — 288p : ill, ports ; 21cm.
ISBN 0-904208-12-5 Pbk : £2.50
ISSN 0140-7147
(B77-33364)

780'.6'241 — Music. Organisations. *Great Britain. Incorporated Society of Musicians. Directories*
Incorporated Society of Musicians. Handbook and register of members / the Incorporated Society of Musicians. — [London] ([10 Stratford Place, W1N 9AE]) : [The Society]. 1977. — 1976. — 232,72,66p : ill, map ; 21cm.
Cover title.
Pbk : £6.00
(B77-16533)

780'.7 — Education. Curriculum subjects: Music. *Serials*
International Society for Music Education. ISME yearbook. — Mainz ; London [etc.] ([48 Great Marlborough St., W1V 2BN]) : B. Schott's Söhne.
Vol.3 : 1975-76 : Music as a dimension of lifelong education : papers and recommendations of the 12th International Conference, Montreux, Switzerland, 1976. — 1976. — [1],134p ; 22cm.
At head of title: International music education.
Pbk : £8.00
(B77-12591)

780'.7 — Private music teachers. *Great Britain. Directories*
Professional register of private teachers of music / the Incorporated Society of Musicians. — London (10 Stratford Place, W1N 9AE) : The Society.
1977. — [1976]. — [2],66p : map ; 21cm.
ISBN 0-902900-10-2 Sd : £1.00
(B77-07527)

780'.72 — Schools. Curriculum subjects: Music. Teaching. *Manuals*
Gelineau, R Phyllis. Experiences in music / [by] R. Phyllis Gelineau. — 2nd ed. — New York ; London [etc.] : McGraw-Hill, 1976. — xii,440p, [14] leaves of plates : ill, music ; 24cm.
Previous ed.: New York : McGraw-Hill, 1970. — Bibl. — Lists of music. — Lists of sound discs. — Lists of films. — Index.
ISBN 0-07-023092-7 Sp : £9.90
(B77-05566)

780'.72 — Schools. Curriculum subjects: Music. Teaching methods, ca 1840-1975
Some great music educators : a collection of essays / general editor Kenneth Simpson. — Borough Green : Novello, 1976. — 128p,[2] leaves of plates,[12]p of plates : ill, music, ports ; 22cm.
Bibl. — Index.
ISBN 0-85360-065-1 Pbk : £1.70
(B77-02497)

780'.72 — Schools. Curriculum subjects: Music. Teaching. Research. *United States*
Research in music behavior : modifying music behavior in the classroom / edited by Clifford K. Madsen, R. Douglas Greer and Charles H. Madsen, Jr. — New York ; London : Teachers College Press, 1975. — vii,277p : ill, forms ; 24cm.
Bibl.
ISBN 0-8077-2436-x : Unpriced
(B77-19556)

780'.79'41 — Music festivals. Organisations. *Great Britain. British Federation of Music Festivals. Yearbooks*
British Federation of Music Festivals. Year book / the British Federation of Music Festivals incorporating the Music Teachers' Association. — London (106 Gloucester Place, W1H 3DB) : The Federation.
1977. — [1977]. — [6],112p : ill, ports ; 21cm.
ISBN 0-901532-07-x Sd : £1.00
ISSN 0309-8044
(B77-14856)

780'.8 — Music. *Essays*
Bruxner, Mervyn. The value of music : essays / by Mervyn Bruxner. — London : Bedford Square Press, 1977. — [4],iv,51p : port ; 21cm.
ISBN 0-7199-0911-2 Sd : £1.00
(B77-18308)

Debussy, Claude. Debussy on music : the critical writings of the great French composer Claude Debussy / collected and introduced by François Lesure ; translated [from the French] and edited by Richard Langham Smith. — London : Secker and Warburg, 1977. — xxv, 353,[2]p ; 22cm.
Translation of: 'Monsieur Croche et autres écrits'. Paris : Gallimard, 1971. — Index.
ISBN 0-436-12559-5 : £6.90
(B77-25112)

780.9 — MUSIC. HISTORICAL AND GEOGRAPHICAL TREATMENT

780'.9 — Music, to 1880. *Essays. Early works*
Wagner, Richard. Wagner on music and drama : a selection from Richard Wagner's prose works / arranged, & with an introduction by Albert Goldman & Evert Sprinchorn ; translated [from the German] by H. Ashton Ellis. — London : Gollancz, 1977. — 447p ; 23cm.
These translations originally published: New York : Dutton, 1964 ; London : Gollancz, 1970.
£6.50
ISBN 0-575-00443-6
(B77-23619)

780'.9 — Music, to 1975
Dearling, Robert. The Guinness book of music facts and feats / [by] Robert and Celia Dearling with Brian Rust. — Enfield : Guinness Superlatives, 1976. — 288p : ill(some col), facsims, music, col plan, ports(some col) ; 25cm.
Text on lining papers. — Bibl.: p.279. — Index.
ISBN 0-900424-63-x : £6.50
(B77-13178)

780'.9 — Music, to ca 1920
The **pelican** history of music / edited by Alec Robertson and Denis Stevens. — Harmondsworth [etc.] : Penguin. — (A pelican original)
Bibl.: p.241-242. — Index.
3 : Classical and Romantic. — 1976. — [1], 251p : ill, music ; 18cm.
Originally published: 1968.
ISBN 0-14-020494-6 Pbk : £0.75
(B77-15997)

780'.9 — Western music, to 1973
Headington, Christopher. A history of Western music / [by] Christopher Headington. — St Albans : Triad, 1977. — 399p : music ; 20cm.
Originally published: as 'The Bodley Head history of Western music'. London : Bodley Head, 1974. — Bibl.: p.386-387. — Index.
ISBN 0-586-08357-x Pbk : £1.95
(B77-08486)

780'.9 — Western music, to ca 1970. *Case studies. Secondary school texts*
Bennett, F. Roy. Enjoying music / [by] Roy Bennett. — London : Longman.
Book 1. — 1977. — [1],64p : ill, facsims, music, ports ; 19x25cm.
ISBN 0-582-22179-x Sd : £0.95
(B77-30501)

780'.902 — Early music. *Periodicals*
Early music news. — London (27 Lanhill Rd, W9 2BS) : 'Early music news'.
No.1- ; Aug. 1977-. — 1977-. — 30cm.
Monthly. — Folder ([4]p.) as 1st issue.
£1.00 yearly
ISSN 0140-1696
(B77-33365)

780'.904 — Music, 1918-1976
Whittall, Arnold. Music since the First World War / [by] Arnold Whittall. — London : Dent, 1977. — ix,277p : music ; 25cm.
Bibl.: p.271-272. — Index.
ISBN 0-460-04255-6 : £7.95
(B77-33969)

780'.92'2 — Music. *Biographical dictionaries*
International who's who in music and musicians' directory. — Cambridge (International Biographical Centre, Cambridge CB2 3QP) : International Who's Who in Music.
8th ed. : [1977] / edited by Adrian Gaster. — 1977. — xv,1178p ; 26cm.
ISBN 0-900332-44-1 : Unpriced
ISSN 0307-2894
(B77-22754)

780'.92'2 — Music. Composers, ca 1760-ca 1900. *Biographies. Humorous texts*
Borge, Victor. My favourite intervals / by Victor Borge and Robert Sherman ; drawings by Thomas Winding. — London : Sphere, 1977. — 187p : ill ; 18cm.
Originally published: as 'My favorite intermissions', Garden City, N.Y. : Doubleday, 1971 ; and as 'My favourite intervals', London : Woburn Press, 1974.
ISBN 0-7221-1780-9 Pbk : £0.85
(B77-31353)

780'.92'2 — Polish music. Composers, 1930-1975. *Critical studies*
Maciejewski, B M. Twelve Polish composers / [by] B.M. Maciejewski ; with a foreword by the Earl of Harewood. — London (10 Blenheim Cres., South Croydon CR2 6BN) : Allegro Press, 1976. — 3-229p,[2] leaves of plates,[76]p of plates : ill, facsims, music, ports ; 23cm.
Lists of works.: p.207-212. — Index.
ISBN 0-9505619-0-8 : £3.75
(B77-11347)

780'.92'4 — American music. Hermann, Bernard. *Biographies*
Johnson, Edward. Bernard Herrmann, Hollywood's music-dramatist : a biographical sketch with a filmography, catalogue of works, discography and bibliography / by Edward Johnson ; foreword by Miklós Rózsa. — Rickmansworth (22 Pheasants Way, Rickmansworth, Herts.) : Triad Press, 1977. — 60p : facsims, music, ports ; 30cm. — (Triad Press bibliographical series ; no.6)
List of films: p.33-37. — List of music: p.39-41. — List of sound discs: p.43-56. — Bibl.: p.57-59.
Pbk : £3.50
(B77-25799)

780'.92'4 — American music. Ives, Charles. *Critical studies*
Hitchcock, Hugh Wiley. Ives / [by] H. Wiley Hitchcock. — London [etc.] : Oxford University Press, 1977. — 95p : music ; 22cm. — (Oxford studies of composers ; 14)
Bibl.: p.95.
ISBN 0-19-315439-0 Pbk : £3.25 : CIP rev.
(B77-10491)

780'.92'4 — American music. Stravinsky, Igor. *Biographies*
Tierney, Neil. The unknown country : a life of Igor Stravinsky / [by] Neil Tierney. — London : Hale, 1977. — 272p,[16]p of plates : ill, music, ports ; 24cm.
Bibl.: p.264-265. — Index.
ISBN 0-7091-6092-5 : £6.95
(B77-21343)

780'.92'4 — American music. Stravinsky, Igor. *Critical studies*
Routh, Francis. Stravinsky / by Francis Routh. — London : Dent, 1975 [i.e. 1977]. — ix,202p, [8]p of plates : music, ports ; 19cm. — (The master musicians series) (An Aldine paperback)
Originally published: 1975. — Bibl.: p.188-191. — Index.
ISBN 0-460-02172-9 Pbk : £2.95
(B77-32065)

780'.92'4 — Art galleries. *London. Southwark (London Borough). South London Art Gallery. Exhibits: Items associated with Lambert, Constant. Catalogues*
South London Art Gallery. Constant Lambert, 1905-1951 : a souvenir of the exhibition at the South London Art Gallery, Peckham Road, London SE5 8UH, 17 September-7 October 1976 ... — [London] ([20 Lordship La., SE22 8HN]) : [London Borough of Southwark Council], [1976]. — 40p : ill, facsims, music, ports ; 30cm.
Catalogue ([10]p.) as insert.
ISBN 0-9500243-9-2 Sd : £0.50
(B77-02498)

780'.92'4 — Art galleries. *London. Westminster (London Borough). Covent Garden Gallery. Exhibits: Items associated with Tippett, Sir Michael. Catalogues*
A man of our time, Michael Tippett. — London : Schott, 1977. — [12],126p : chiefly ill(some col), facsims, ports(some col) ; 23x25cm.
Catalogue of an exhibition held at Covent Garden Gallery, July 1977. — List of works: p.15-20. — List of sound discs: p.115-119.
ISBN 0-901938-64-5 Pbk : Unpriced
(B77-24393)

780'.92'4 — Austrian music. Bruckner, Anton. *Critical studies*
Watson, Derek. Bruckner / by Derek Watson. — London : Dent, [1977]. — ix,174p,[8]p of plates : ill, facsims, music, ports ; 20cm. — (The master musicians series)
Originally published: 1975. — Bibl.: p.167-169. — Index. — Previous control number ISBN 0-460-02171-0.
£2.95
ISBN 0-460-02171-0 Pbk (Aldine paperbacks) : £2.25
ISBN 0-460-03144-9
(B77-17669)

780'.92'4 — Austrian music. Haydn, Joseph. *Biographies*
Butterworth, Neil. Haydn : his life and times / [by] Neil Butterworth. — Tunbridge Wells : Midas Books, 1977. — 144p : ill, facsims, music, ports ; 26cm.
Bibl.: p.7. — Index.
ISBN 0-85936-070-9 : £5.95
(B77-14857)

780'.92'4 — Austrian music. Haydn, Joseph. *Critical studies*
Landon, Howard Chandler Robbins. Haydn, chronicle and works / [by H.C. Robbins Landon]. — [London] : [Thames and Hudson]. In 5 vols.
[Vol.5] : Haydn, the late years, 1801-1809. — [1977]. — 495p,[20]p of plates : ill(some col), facsims, music, ports(some col) ; 27cm.
Bibl.: p.433-469. — Index.
ISBN 0-500-01167-2 : £25.00
(B77-30503)

Landon, Howard Chandler Robbins. Haydn : chronicle and works / [by H.C. Robbins Landon]. — [London] : [Thames and Hudson]. In 5 vols.
Haydn in England, 1791-1795. — [1976]. — 640p,[20]p of plates : ill(incl 1 col), facsims, music, ports(some col) ; 26cm.
Bibl.: p.17-18. — Index.
ISBN 0-500-01164-8 : £25.00
(B77-03164)

Landon, Howard Chandler Robbins. Haydn : chronicle and works / [by H.C. Robbins Landon]. — London : Thames and Hudson. In 5 vols.
Haydn, the years of 'The creation', 1796-1800. — 1977. — 656p,[20]p of plates : ill(some col), facsims, music, ports(some col) ; 27cm.
Bibl.: p.16-18. — Index.
ISBN 0-500-01166-4 : £25.00
(B77-21344)

780'.92'4 — Austrian music. Mahler, Gustav. *Biographies*
Kennedy, Michael, *b.1926.* Mahler / by Michael Kennedy. — London : Dent, 1977. — xii,196p, [8]p of plates : ill, facsim, music, ports ; 19cm. — (The master musicians series) (An Aldine paperback)
Originally published: 1974. — Bibl.: p.187-189. — List of works: p.172-180. — Index.
ISBN 0-460-02161-3 Pbk : £2.50
(B77-31354)

780'.92'4 — Austrian music. Mahler, Gustav. *Documents*
Mahler, a documentary study / compiled and edited by Kurt Blaukopf ; with contributions by Zoltan Roman ; [translated from the German by Paul Baker et al.]. — London : Thames and Hudson, 1976. — 280p : ill(some col), facsims(some col), col map, plans, ports(some col) ; 32cm.
Translation of: 'Mahler : sein Leben, sein Werk und seine Welt im zeitgenössischen Bildern und Texten'. Vienna : Universal Edition, 1976. — Index.
ISBN 0-500-01170-2 : £12.50
(B77-00881)

780'.92'4 — Austrian music. Mahler, Gustav, 1897-1907
Gustav Mahler in Vienna / contributors Pierre Boulez ... [et al.] ; edited by Sigrid Wiesmann ; [translated from the German by Anne Shelley]. — London : Thames and Hudson, 1977. — 165,[1]p : chiefly ill(some col), facsims, music, ports(1 col) ; 28x30cm.
Translation of: 'Gustav Mahler und Wien'. Stuttgart : Belser, 1976.
ISBN 0-500-01179-6 : £15.00
(B77-15406)

780'.92'4 — Austrian music. Mozart, Wolfgang Amadeus. *Biographies*
Woodford, Peggy. Mozart : his life and times / [by] Peggy Woodford. — Tunbridge Wells : Midas Books, 1977. — 144p : ill, facsims, map, music, ports ; 26cm.
Bibl.: p.7. — Index.
ISBN 0-85936-063-6 : £5.95
(B77-14858)

780'.92'4 — Austrian music. Mozart, Wolfgang Amadeus. Influence of freemasonry
Thomson, Katharine. The Masonic thread in Mozart / by Katharine Thomson. — London : Lawrence and Wishart, 1977. — 207p : music ; 23cm.
Bibl.: p.195-197. — List of sound discs: p.198-199. — Index.
ISBN 0-85315-381-7 : £5.00
(B77-27281)

780'.92'4 — Austrian music. Schoenberg, Arnold. *Biographies*
Stuckenschmidt, Hans Heinz. Schoenberg : his life, world and work / [by] H.H. Stuckenschmidt ; translated from the German by Humphrey Searle. — London : J. Calder : [Distributed by Calder and Boyars], 1977. — 581p : ill, facsims, music, ports ; 23cm.
Translation of: 'Schönberg : Leben, Umwelt, Werk'. Zürich : Atlantis-Verlag, 1974. — Bibl.: p.562-564. — List of works: p.558-561. — Index.
ISBN 0-7145-3532-x : £12.50
(B77-29599)

780'.92'4 — Austrian music. Schubert, Franz. *Biographies*
Wechsberg, Joseph. Schubert : his life, his work, his time / [by] Joseph Wechsberg. — London : Weidenfeld and Nicolson, 1977. — 224p : ill(some col), facsims, music, ports(some col) ; 26cm.
Music on lining papers. — Bibl.: p.220. — Index.
ISBN 0-297-77371-2 : £6.95
(B77-29600)

780'.92'4 — Austrian music. Schubert, Franz. *Critical studies*
Hutchings, Arthur. Schubert / by Arthur Hutchings. — Revised ed. — London : Dent, 1973 [i.e. 1976]. — vi,233p,[8]p of plates : ill, 2 facsims, music, ports ; 19cm. — (Aldine paperbacks) (The master musicians series)
This ed. originally published: 1973. — Bibl.: p.216-218. — Index.
ISBN 0-460-02111-7 Pbk : £1.95
(B77-01698)

780'.92'4 — Concentration camps. *Poland. Oświęcim. Auschwitz concentration camp. Women prisoners: Musicians, 1944-1945. Personal observations*
Fénelon, Fania. The musicians of Auschwitz / [by] Fania Fénelon with Marcelle Routier ; translated from the French by Judith Landry. — London : Joseph, 1977. — ix,262p ; 23cm.
Translation of: 'Sursis pour l'orchestre'. Paris : Stock, 1976.
ISBN 0-7181-1609-7 : £5.50
(B77-33970)

780'.92'4 — English music. Elgar, Sir Edward, bart. *Periodicals*
Elgar Society. The Elgar Society newsletter. — [New Barnet] ([104 Crescent Rd, New Barnet, Herts.]) : ['Elgar Society Newsletter'].
Continued by: Elgar Society newsletter, new series.
[Issue no.1-10 ; Sept.1973-Sept.1976]. — [1973-1976]. — 10v. ; 26cm.
Three issues a year.
Sd : Unpriced
ISSN 0309-4405
(B77-15407)

Elgar Society. Elgar Society newsletter, new series. — New Barnet (104 Crescent Rd, New Barnet, Herts.) : 'Elgar Society newsletter'.
No.1- ; Jan. 1977-. — 1977-. — port ; 21cm.
Three issues a year. — 32p. in issue no.1. — Continues: Elgar Society newsletter.
Sd : Free to members of the Society
ISSN 0309-4405
(B77-10882)

780'.92'4 — English music. Pearsall, Robert Lucas de. *Biographies*
Hunt, Edgar. Robert Lucas Pearsall : the 'compleat gentleman' and his music (1795-1856) / by Edgar Hunt ; based on the researches of the late Hubert Hunt. — Amersham (Rose Cottage, Bois La., Chesham Bois, Amersham, Bucks. HP6 6BP) : The author, 1977. — viii,140p,leaf of plate,[12]p of plates : ill, coats of arms, facsims, geneal table, map, music, ports ; 23cm.
Bibl.: p.134. — Index.
ISBN 0-9505831-0-3 Pbk : £5.00
(B77-25113)

780'.92'4 — French music. Berlioz, Hector. *Autobiographies*
Berlioz, Hector. [Mémoires de Hector Berlioz. English]. The memoirs of Hector Berlioz, member of the French Institute : including his travels in Italy, Germany, Russia and England, 1803-1865 / translated [from the French] and edited by David Cairns. — 2nd ed. — London : Gollancz, 1977. — 636p,[24]p of plates : ill, facsims, geneal table, maps, music, ports ; 24cm.
This ed. originally published: New York : Norton, 1975. — Translation of: 'Mémoires de Hector Berlioz'. Paris : M. Lévy, 1870. — Bibl.: p.615-616. — Index.
ISBN 0-575-02396-1 : £8.50
(B77-32775)

780'.92'4 — French music. Berlioz, Hector. *Critical studies*
Dickinson, Alan Edgar Frederic. The music of Berlioz / [by] A.E.F. Dickinson. — London : Faber, [1977]. — 3-280p,leaf of plate,[8]p of plates : ill, facsim, music, ports ; 25cm.
Originally published: 1972. — Bibl.: p.263-273. — List of works: p.259-261. — Index.
ISBN 0-571-10017-1 Pbk : £2.75
(B77-08487)

780'.92'4 — French music. Bizet, Georges. *Critical studies*
Dean, Winton. Bizet / by Winton Dean. — [3rd ed.]. — London : Dent, 1975 [i.e. 1977]. — x, 306p,[8]p of plates : ill, facsims, music, ports ; 19cm. — (The master musicians series) (An Aldine paperback)
This ed. originally published: 1975. — Bibl.: p.280-282. — Index.
ISBN 0-460-02170-2 Pbk : £2.95
(B77-17670)

780'.92'4 — French music. Boulez, Pierre. *Biographies*
Peyser, Joan. Boulez : composer, conductor, enigma / [by] Joan Peyser. — London : Cassell, 1977. — [7],303p,[16]p of plates : ill, facsims, music, ports ; 24cm.
Contains poems by René Char, Henri Michaux and Mallarmé in French with English translation. — Originally published: New York : Schirmer, 1976. — Index.
ISBN 0-304-29901-4 : £7.50
(B77-28002)

780'.92'4 — French music. Debussy, Claude. Influence of poetry in French, 1848-1900
Wenk, Arthur B. Claude Debussy and the poets / [by] Arthur B. Wenk. — Berkeley [etc.] ; London : University of California Press, 1976. — x,345p : music ; 25cm.
Bibl.: p.319-340. — Index.
ISBN 0-520-02827-9 : £14.65
(B77-03699)

780'.92'4 — French music. Debussy, Claude. Influence of symbolism in French poetry, ca 1885-ca 1910. Compared with influence of impressionism in French paintings, ca 1850-ca 1890
Jarocinski, Stefan. Debussy : impressionism and symbolism / [by] Stefan Jarocinski ; translated from the French by Rollo Myers. — London (48 Great Marlborough St., W1V 2BN) : Eulenberg Books, 1976. — xv,175p : music ; 23cm.
Translation of: 'Debussy'. Paris : Editions du Seuil, 1971. — Originally published: in Polish. Kraków ; Polskie Wydawn. 1966.
ISBN 0-903873-20-6 : Unpriced
ISBN 0-903873-09-5 Pbk : £2.50
(B77-04985)

780'.92'4 — French music. Ravel, Maurice. *Critical studies*
Nichols, Roger. Ravel / by Roger Nichols. — London : Dent, 1977. — xi,199p,[8]p of plates : ill, facsims, music, ports ; 20cm. — (The master musicians series)
Bibl.: p.186-189. — List of works: p.172-177. — Index.
ISBN 0-460-03146-5 : £3.95 : CIP rev.
ISBN 0-460-02189-3 Pbk
(B77-06217)

Orenstein, Arbie. Ravel : man and musician / by Arbie Orenstein. — New York ; London : Columbia University Press, 1975 [i.e. 1977]. — xix,291p,32p of plates : ill, facsims, music, ports ; 24cm.
Published in the United States: 1975. — Bibl.: p.271-276. — List of works: p.219-245. — List of sound discs: p.247-270. — Index.
ISBN 0-231-03902-6 : £6.85
(B77-10883)

780'.92'4 — German music. Bach, Johann Sebastian. *Biographies*
Robertson, Alec. Bach : a biography, with a survey of books, editions and recordings / by Alec Robertson. — London : Bingley [etc.], 1977. — 140p ; 23cm. — (The concertgoer's companions)
Bibl.: p.53-71. — List of music : p.72-106. — List of sound discs p.107-129. — Index.
ISBN 0-85157-138-7 : £2.25
(B77-17671)

780'.92'4 — German music. Brahms, Johannes. *Biographies*
Chissell, Joan. Brahms / [by] Joan Chissell. — London : Faber, 1977. — 104p : ill, facsims, music, ports ; 23cm. — (The great composers)
Bibl.: p.98. — List of music: p.99-100. — Index.
ISBN 0-571-10791-5 : £3.25
(B77-20480)

780'.92'4 — German music. Brahms, Johannes. *Critical studies*
Jacobson, Bernard. The music of Johannes Brahms / [by] Bernard Jacobson. — London : Tantivy Press [etc.], 1977. — 222p,[8]p of plates : ill, music, ports ; 24cm.
Spine title: Brahms. — Bibl.: p.177-178. — List of music: p.179-180. — List of sound discs: p.180-207. — Index.
ISBN 0-904208-26-5 : £6.50
(B77-32776)

780'.92'4 — German music. Mendelssohn, Felix. *Critical studies*
Radcliffe, Philip. Mendelssohn / by Philip Radcliffe. — Revised [ed.]. — London : Dent, 1976. — x,214p,[8]p of plates : ill, facsim, music, ports ; 20cm. — (The master musicians series)
Previous ed.: 1967. — Bibl.: p.204-206. — List of works: p.183-198. — Index. — Contains a catalogue of the composer's works.
ISBN 0-460-03123-6 : £3.95
ISBN 0-460-02180-x Pbk : £2.95
(B77-17672)

780'.92'4 — German music. Schumann, Robert. *Critical studies*
Robert Schumann : the man and his music / edited by Alan Walker ; [contributors] Frank Cooper ... [et al.]. — London : Barrie and Jenkins, 1976. — xii,489p,leaf of plate,[12]p of plates : ill, facsims, geneal table, music, ports ; 23cm.
Originally published: 1972. — Bibl.: p.442-445. — List of works: p.447-479. — Index.
Pbk : £4.95
ISBN 0-214-66805-3
(B77-06815)

780'.92'4 — German music. Weber, Carl Maria von. *Biographies*
Warrack, John. Carl Maria von Weber / [by] John Warrack. — 2nd ed. — Cambridge [etc.] : Cambridge University Press, 1976. — 411p : ill, facsim, geneal table, map, music, ports ; 24cm.
Previous ed.: London : Hamilton, 1968. — List of works.: p.379-390. — Bibl.: p.391-395. — Index.
ISBN 0-521-21354-1 : £12.50
ISBN 0-521-29121-6 Pbk : £3.95
(B77-01699)

780'.92'4 — Hungarian music. Liszt, Franz. *Critical studies*
Franz Liszt : the man and his music / edited by Alan Walker ; [contributors] Sacheverell Sitwell ... [et al.]. — London : Barrie and Jenkins, 1976. — xv,472p,leaf of plate,[24]p of plates : ill, facsims, music, ports ; 23cm.
Originally published: 1970. — Bibl.: p.387-389. — List of works: p.390-463. — Index.
ISBN 0-214-20345-x Pbk : £4.95
(B77-06816)

780'.92'4 — Music. *Personal observations*
Heath, Edward. Music, a joy for life / [by] Edward Heath. — London : Sidgwick and Jackson, 1976. — 208p : ill(some col), facsims, music, plan, ports(some col) ; 26cm.
Index.
ISBN 0-283-98349-3 : £5.95
(B77-01700)

780'.92'4 — Norwegian music. Grieg, Edvard. *Critical studies*
Horton, John. Grieg / by John Horton. — London : Dent, 1975 [i.e. 1976]. — xv,255p,[8] p of plates : ill, facsims, music, ports ; 19cm. — (The master musicians series) (An Aldine paperback)
Originally published: 1974. — List of works: p.212-233. — Bibl.: p.240-244. — Index.
ISBN 0-460-02169-9 Pbk : £1.95
(B77-00882)

780'.92'4 — Russian music. Mussorgsky, Modest. *Critical studies*
Calvocoressi, Michael Dimitri. Mussorgsky / by M.D. Calvocoressi ; completed by Gerald Abraham. — Revised ed. / revised [by Gerald Abraham]. — London : Dent, 1974[i.e.1977]. — viii,216p,[8]p of plates : ill, facsims, music, ports ; 19cm. — (The master musicians series) (An Aldine paperback)
This ed. originally published: 1974. — Bibl.: p.209-210. — List of works: p.201-204. — Index.
ISBN 0-460-02141-9 Pbk : £2.50
(B77-17673)

780'.92'4 — Russian music. Tchaikovsky, Peter. *Biographies*
Garden, Edward. Tchaikovsky / by Edward Garden. — London : Dent, 1976. — viii,194p, [8]p of plates : ill, facsims, music, ports ; 20cm. — (The master musicians series)
Originally published: 1973. — Bibl.: p.185-188. — List of works: p.169-178. — Index.
ISBN 0-460-03142-2 : £3.25
ISBN 0-460-02187-7 Pbk : £1.95
(B77-17013)

780'.92'4 — Spanish music. Falla, Manuel de. *Critical studies*
Crichton, Ronald. Manuel de Falla : descriptive catalogue of his works / by Ronald Crichton. — London : J. and W. Chester, 1976. — [5], 80p,plate : ill, facsims, maps ; 26cm.
Index.
ISBN 0-9502767-5-8 : Unpriced
(B77-29601)

780'.9423'98 — Music. *Avon. Bath, 1700-1800*
Turner, Anthony John. Science and music in eighteenth century Bath : [catalogue of] an exhibition in the Holburne of Menstrie Museum, Bath, 22 September 1977-29 December 1977 / catalogue by A.J. Turner, with the assistance of I.D. Woodfield and contributions by H.S. Torrens. — Bath (Claverton Down, Bath, Avon BA2 7AY) : University of Bath, 1977. — viii,131p : ill, facsims, music, ports ; 21cm.
Bibl.: p.117-123.
ISBN 0-900843-83-7 Sd : Unpriced
Primary classification 520'.92'4
(B77-33778)

780'.9424'6 — Music. *North Staffordshire, 1850-1918*
Nettel, Reginald. North Staffordshire music : a social experiment / [by] Reginald Nettel. — Rickmansworth (22 Pheasants Way, Rickmansworth, Herts.) : Triad Press, 1977. — 64p : ill, facsims, ports ; 25cm.
Ill. on lining papers. — Limited ed. of 300 numbered copies. — Bibl.: p.62. — Index.
ISBN 0-902070-19-3 : £4.50 : CIP rev.
(B77-06814)

781 — MUSIC. PRINCIPLES AND TECHNIQUES

781'.07'1141 — Universities. *Great Britain. Open University. Curriculum subjects: Music. Elements. Courses: 'Elements of music'*
Open University. Course guide / [prepared by the Open University Course Team]. — [Milton Keynes] ([Walton Hall, Milton Keynes, MK7 6AA]) : Open University, 1977. — 12p ; 21x30cm. — (Arts, a second level course : elements of music) (A241 ; CG)
Bibl.
Sd : Unpriced
(B77-32778)

781'.1 — Music. Neuropsychological aspects
Music and the brain : studies in the neurology of music / edited by Macdonald Critchley and R.A. Henson ; with a foreword by Sir Michael Tippett. — London : Heinemann Medical, 1977. — xiv,459p : ill, facsim, music, port ; 24cm.
Bibl. — Index.
ISBN 0-433-06703-9 : £11.50
(B77-08488)

781'.2 — Music. Rudiments
Barsham, Dinah. Rudiments of music / prepared for the [Open University] Course Team by Dinah Barsham ; recorder tuition by Ian Graham-Jones. — Milton Keynes : Open University Press.
In 3 vols.
1. — 1977. — 40p : ill, facsim, music ; 21x30cm. — (Arts, a second level course : elements of music ; unit 1) (A241 ; 1)
With answers.
ISBN 0-335-05330-0 Sd : Unpriced
(B77-32066)

2. — 1977. — 29p : ill, music ; 21x30cm. — (A241 ; 2) (Arts, a second level course : elements of music ; unit 2)
ISBN 0-335-05331-9 Sd : Unpriced
(B77-12020)

3. — 1977. — 27p : ill, music ; 21x30cm. — (Arts, a second level course : elements of music ; unit 3) (A241 ; 3)
With answers.
ISBN 0-335-05332-7 Sd : Unpriced
(B77-32067)

781'.22 — European music. Tonality, 1900-1920
Samson, Jim. Music in transition : a study of tonal expansion and atonality, 1900-1920 / [by] Jim Samson. — London : Dent, 1977. — [11], 242p : music ; 25cm.
Bibl.: p.235. — Index.
ISBN 0-460-04245-9 : £7.50
(B77-30504)

781'.22 — Music. Tonality
George, Graham. Tonality and musical structure / [by] Graham George. — London : Faber, [1977]. — 3-231p : ill, music ; 22cm.
Originally published: 1970. — Bibl.: p.217-225. — Index.
ISBN 0-571-10016-3 Pbk : £2.25
(B77-15408)

781'.22 — South Indian ragas
Kaufmann, Walter, *b.1907.* The r¯agas of South India : a catalogue of scalar material / by Walter Kaufmann. — Bloomington ; London : Indiana University Press, [1977]. — xxxiv, 723p : chiefly music ; 24cm.
Published in the United States: 1976. — Index.
ISBN 0-253-39508-9 : £18.75
(B77-10884)

781'.23'0207 — Music. Terminology. *Humorous texts*
Hopkins, Antony. Downbeat music guide / [by] Antony Hopkins ; illustrated by Marc. — London [etc.] : Oxford University Press, 1977. — 96p : ill, music ; 19cm.
ISBN 0-19-311322-8 : £1.95
(B77-32068)

781.3 — MUSIC. HARMONY

Barsham, Dinah. Harmony / prepared for the [Open University] Course Team by Dinah Barsham ; recorder tuition by Ian Graham-Jones. — Milton Keynes : Open University Press.
In 7 vols.
2. — 1977. — 27p : ill, facsim, music ; 21x30cm. — (Arts, a second level course : elements of music ; unit 5) (A241 ; 5)
With answers.
ISBN 0-335-05334-3 Sd : Unpriced
(B77-32069)

3. — 1977. — 28p : ill, music ; 21x30cm. — (Arts, a second level course : elements of music ; unit 6) (A241 ; 6)
With answers.
ISBN 0-335-05335-1 Sd : Unpriced
(B77-32070)

4. — 1977. — 23p : ill, music ; 21x30cm. — (Arts, a second level course : elements of music ; unit 7) (A241 ; 7)
With answers.
ISBN 0-335-05336-x Sd : Unpriced
(B77-32071)

5. — 1977. — 26p : ill, facsim, music ; 21x30cm. — (Arts, a second level course : elements of music ; unit 8) (A241 ; 8)
With answers.
ISBN 0-335-05337-8 Sd : Unpriced
(B77-32072)

Steinitz, Paul. Harmony in context : a new approach to understanding harmony without conventional exercises / by Paul Steinitz and Stella Sterman. — Croydon (250 Purley Way, Croydon, CR9 4QD) : Belwin-Mills Music Ltd.

Workbook. — 1976. — [3],i,100p : music ; 26cm.
ISBN 0-9503671-4-1 Pbk : £2.95
(B77-02499)

781.3'6 — Music. Modulation. *Manuals*
Siebert, Edrich. A practical guide to modulation / by Edrich Siebert. — London ([89 Vicarage Rd, NW10 2UA]) : Studio Music Co., [1976]. — [1],24p : music ; 24cm.
ISBN 0-905925-02-5 Sd : £0.50
(B77-08489)

781.5 — MUSICAL FORMS

781.5'7 — Jazz. Elements
Dankworth, Avril. Jazz : an introduction to its musical basis / [by] Avril Dankworth. — London [etc.] : Oxford University Press, 1975. — xi,91p : ill, music ; 20cm.
Originally published: 1968. — Bibl.: p.86. — Index.
ISBN 0-19-316501-5 Pbk : £1.10
(B77-05567)

781.5'73'0973 — Blues. *United States, to 1975*
Oakley, Giles. The devil's music : a history of the blues / [by] Giles Oakley. — London : British Broadcasting Corporation, 1976. — 287p : ill, facsims, map, ports ; 24cm.
Bibl.: p.271-275. — Index.
ISBN 0-563-16012-8 Pbk : £3.00
(B77-03700)

781.6 — MUSIC. COMPOSITION AND PERFORMANCE

781.6'1 — Music. Composition. *Middle school texts*
Davies, John Stephen. Beginning to compose / [by] John Stephen Davies. — London : Oxford University Press Music Department.
Book 1 : Writing melodies. — 1976. — [3], 28p : of ill ; 18x25cm.
ISBN 0-19-321063-0 Sd : £0.65
(B77-03165)

Book 2 : Writing in two parts. — 1976. — [3], 24p : of ill, music ; 18x25cm.
ISBN 0-19-321064-9 Sd : £0.65
(B77-03166)

Information and instructions for books 1 and 2. — 1976. — [3],19p : ill, music ; 26cm.
ISBN 0-19-321062-2 Sd : £1.00
(B77-03167)

781.6'35 — Music. Conducting. *Manuals*
Miles, Maurice. Are you beating two or four? : some hints to help you make up your mind / [by] Maurice Miles. — Sevenoaks : Novello, 1977. — 54p : ill, music ; 22cm.
Pbk : £1.25
(B77-17674)

781.7 — MUSIC OF ETHNIC AND NATIONAL ORIENTATION

781.7'092'2 — American folk music. *Biographical dictionaries*
Baggelaar, Kristin. The folk music encyclopaedia / by Kristin Baggelaar & Donald Milton. — London [etc.] : Omnibus Press, 1977. — xi,419p : facsims, ports ; 27cm.
Originally published: as 'Folk music, more than a song'. New York : Crowell, 1976.
ISBN 0-86001-309-x : £5.95
(B77-33971)

781.7'2'924 — Jewish music. *Encyclopaedias*
Nulman, Macy. Concise encyclopedia of Jewish music / [by] Macy Nulman. — New York ; London [etc.] : McGraw-Hill, [1976]. — xii, 276p : ill, facsims, music, ports ; 24cm.
Published in the United States: 1975.
ISBN 0-07-047546-6 : £12.40
(B77-01701)

781.7'41 — Folk music. *Great Britain. Directories*
The **folk** directory / [English Folk Dance and Song Society]. — London : The Society.
1977 / edited by Bonnie Shaljean. — 1977. — 176p : ill, map ; 22cm.
ISBN 0-85418-116-4 Pbk : £1.50(£0.75 to members)
(B77-32073)

781.7'42 — English folk music, to 1976
Pegg, Bob. Folk : a portrait of English traditional music, musicians and customs / [by] Bob Pegg. — London : Wildwood House, 1976. — 128p : ill, music ; 30cm.
Bibl.: p.121-122. — List of sound discs and tapes: p.123-128.
ISBN 0-7045-0195-3 Pbk : £3.25
(B77-03168)

781.7'497 — Bulgarian music & Yugoslav music, to 1974. *German texts*
Cvetko, Dragotin. Musikgeschichte der Südslawen / [von] Dragotin Cvetko. — Kassel [etc.] ; London ([32 Great Titchfield St., W1P 7AD]) : Bärenreiter, 1975. — 272p : music ; 24cm.
Bibl.: p.237-251. — Index.
£10.08
(B77-07995)

781.7'5 — Asian music. *Serials*
Musica Asiatica. — London : Oxford University Press, Music Department.
1 / edited by Laurence Picken. — 1977. — viii, 165p : ill, music ; 24cm.
ISBN 0-19-323234-0 Pbk : £9.00
ISSN 0140-6078
(B77-31356)

781.7'54 — Indian music
Massey, Reginald. The music of India / by Reginald & Jamila Massey ; foreword by Ravi Shankar. — London : Kahn and Averill, 1976. — 189p : ill, music, ports ; 23cm.
Bibl.: p.177-178. — List of sound discs: p.179-180. — Index.
ISBN 0-900707-40-2 : £4.80
(B77-09174)

781.7'597 — Vietnamese music, to 1966
Pham-Duy. Musics of Vietnam / by Pham Duy ; edited by Dale R. Whiteside. — Carbondale [etc.] : Southern Illinois University Press ; London [etc.] : Feffer and Simons, 1975. — xx, 161p,fold leaf ; 23cm. — (Southern Illinois University. Centennial publications)
Bibl.: p.153-155. — Index.
ISBN 0-8093-0644-1 : £7.94
(B77-22756)

781.91 — MUSICAL INSTRUMENTS
781.9'1 — Musical instruments using scrap materials. Making. *Manuals*
Jardine, Maggie. Bang! rattle!! shake!!! : a simple guide to making musical instruments from scrap materials / by Maggie Jardine ; illustrations by Wilma Harper. — Nuneaton : National Association of Youth Clubs, [1977]. — [16]p : ill ; 22cm.
ISBN 0-901528-78-1 Sd : £0.35
(B77-29602)

781.9'1 — Orchestras. Musical instruments. *Juvenile literature*
Hosier, John. Instruments of the orchestra / [by] John Hosier ; with a preface by Yehudi Menuhin. — 2nd ed. — London : Oxford University Press, Music Department, 1977. — 72p : ill, music ; 18cm.
'... prepared in conjunction with gramophone records originally issued by EMI Records Limited' - Introduction. — Previous ed.: 1961.
ISBN 0-19-321351-6 Sd : £0.95
(B77-09862)

781.9'1'09 — Musical instruments, to 1976
Diagram Group. Musical instruments of the world : an illustrated encyclopaedia / by the Diagram Group. — [London] : Paddington Press [etc.], 1976. — 320p : ill(some col), map, music, ports ; 29cm.
Ill. on lining papers. — Bibl.: p.314-315. — Index.
ISBN 0-8467-0134-0 : £8.95
(B77-30505)

781.9'1'09 — Musical instruments, to ca 1930. *Collectors' guides*
Curtis, Tony, *b.1939.* Musical instruments / compiled by Tony Curtis. — [Galashiels] : [Lyle Publications], [1977]. — 3-126p : chiefly ill ; 16cm. — (Antiques and their values)
Index.
ISBN 0-902921-50-9 : £1.50
(B77-33972)

781.9'1'0932 — Ancient Egyptian royal tombs. *Egypt. Valley of the Kings. Tomb of Tutankhamun, Pharaoh of Egypt. Grave goods: Musical instruments*
Manniche, Lise. Musical instruments from the tomb of Tut'ankhamun / by Lise Manniche. — Oxford ([Ashmolean Museum, Beaumont St., Oxford]) : Griffith Institute, 1976. — [6],15p, 12p of plates : ill ; 29cm. — (Tut'ankhamun's tomb series ; 6)
ISBN 0-900416-05-x : £4.00
(B77-03169)

781.9'1'094 — European musical instruments, ca 800-ca 1600
Montagu, Jeremy. The world of medieval & Renaissance musical instruments / [by] Jeremy Montagu. — Newton Abbot [etc.] : David and Charles, 1976. — 136p : ill(some col), facsims(some col), plans ; 26cm.
Ill. on lining papers. — Bibl.: p.132-133. — Index.
ISBN 0-7153-7280-7 : £7.50
(B77-00883)

782.1 — OPERA
782.1'03 — Opera. *Encyclopaedias*
Forbes, Elizabeth. Opera from A to Z / [by] Elizabeth Forbes. — London : Kaye and Ward [etc.], 1977. — 153p : ill ; 23cm.
ISBN 0-7182-1139-1 : £3.50
(B77-17014)

782.1'06'242188 — Amateur operatic societies. *London. Haringey (London Borough). Hornsey. Hornsey Operatic and Dramatic Society, to 1976*
Young, John. The Hornsey Operatic & Dramatic Society : an illustrated souvenir of 50 years of HODS / written by John Young ; illustrations arranged by John Saxon-Jones. — [London] : [The Society], 1976. — 36p : ill, ports ; 30cm.
'[Issued] to celebrate the fiftieth anniversary of the first performance by the Society on Thursday 21 October 1926'.
ISBN 0-9505652-0-2 Sd : £1.50
(B77-13793)

782.1'09 — Opera, to 1975
Jefferson, Alan. The glory of opera / [by] Alan Jefferson. — Newton Abbot [etc.] : David and Charles, 1976. — 192p : ill(some col), facsims, ports ; 30cm.
Ill. on lining papers. — Bibl.: p.190. — Index.
ISBN 0-7153-7265-3 : £6.50
(B77-00884)

782.1'09 — Opera, to 1976
May, Robin. Opera / [by] Robin May. — Sevenoaks : Teach Yourself Books, 1977. — 216p,16p of plates : ill, facsim ; 18cm. — (Teach yourself books)
Bibl.: p.206-207. — List of music: p.201-205. — Index.
ISBN 0-340-21847-9 Pbk : £1.50
(B77-24394)

782.1'09'034 — Opera, ca 1800-ca 1840
Dent, Edward Joseph. The rise of romantic opera / [by] Edward J. Dent ; edited by Winton Dean. — Cambridge [etc.] : Cambridge University Press, 1976. — x,198p ; 23cm.
'Lectures originally delivered at Cornell University, 1937-8' - Library of Congress Cataloging in Publication data. — Index.
ISBN 0-521-21337-1 : £6.50
(B77-00341)

782.1'0924 — Opera. Directing. Gatti-Casazza, Giulio. *Autobiographies*
Gatti-Casazza, Giulio. Memories of the opera / [by] Giulio Gatti-Casazza. — [1st ed. reprinted] ; [with new preface]. — London : J. Calder : [Distributed by Calder and Boyars], 1977. — xxix,326p,[14]p of plates : ill, ports ; 23cm. — ([Opera library])
Originally published: New York : Scribner, 1941. — Index.
ISBN 0-7145-3518-4 : £9.50
(B77-22757)

782.1'092'4 — Opera in German. Wagner, Richard. *Biographies*
Newman, Ernest. The life of Richard Wagner / [by] Ernest Newman. — London : Cassell, 1976. — 4v. : music ; 24cm.
In slip case. — Originally published: New York : Knopf, 1933-46 ; London : Cassell, 1933-47. — Bibl. — Indexes.
ISBN 0-304-29763-1 : £34.00
(B77-08490)

Osborne, Charles, *b.1927.* Wagner and his world / [by] Charles Osborne. — London : Thames and Hudson, 1977. — 128p : ill, facsims, music, ports ; 24cm.
Bibl.: p.121. — Index.
ISBN 0-500-13060-4 : £3.95
(B77-15998)

782.1'092'4 — Opera in German. Wagner, Richard. *Critical studies*
Mander, Raymond. The Wagner companion / [by] Raymond Mander and Joe Mitchenson ; with a musical appreciation and an essay on the Bayreuth Festival centenary celebrations by Barry Millington. — London : W.H. Allen, 1977. — x,246,[16]p of plates : ill, facsim ; 25cm.
Bibl.: p.228-229. — Index.
ISBN 0-491-01856-8 : £7.50
(B77-32779)

Newman, Ernest. Wagner nights / [by] Ernest Newman. — London : Pan Books, 1977. — vii, 771p : ill, music ; 20cm. — (Picador)
Originally published: London : Putnam, 1949. — Index.
ISBN 0-330-25070-1 Pbk : £2.50
(B77-09863)

Wagner 1976 : a celebration of the Bayreuth festival / [edited by Stewart Spencer]. — London ([c/o 25 Balcombe St., NW1 6HE]) : The Wagner Society, 1976. — 287p,leaf of plate,[24]p of plates : ill, facsims, music, ports ; 22cm.
English text, parallel German text and English translation. — Index.
ISBN 0-905800-00-1 Pbk : £3.75
(B77-00342)

782.1'092'4 — Opera in German. Wagner, Richard. Ring des Nibelungen. Composition
Westernhagen, Curt von. The forging of the 'Ring' : Richard Wagner's composition sketches for 'Der Ring des Nibelungen' / [by] Curt von Westernhagen ; translated [from the German] by Arnold and Mary Whittall. — Cambridge [etc.] : Cambridge University Press, 1976. — ix, 248p : facsims, music ; 24cm.
Translation of: 'Die Entstehung des "Ring"'. Zürich : Atlantis, 1973. — Bibl.: p.244-246. — Index.
ISBN 0-521-21293-6 : £7.50
(B77-00343)

782.1'092'4 — Opera in Italian. Mozart, Wolfgang Amadeus. *Critical studies*
Mann, William Somervell. The operas of Mozart / [by] William Mann. — London : Cassell, 1977. — ix,656p : music ; 24cm.
Bibl.: p.641-644. — Index.
ISBN 0-304-29381-4 : £15.00
(B77-19557)

782.1'09'24 — Opera in Italian. Verdi, Giuseppe. *Documents*
Verdi : a documentary study / compiled, edited and translated [from the Italian] by William Weaver. — [London] : Thames and Hudson, [1977]. — 256p : ill(some col), facsims(some col), col map, music, ports(some col) ; 31cm.
Index. — Includes selections from Verdi's correspondence.
ISBN 0-500-01184-2 : £20.00
(B77-28783)

782.1'092'4 — Opera. Singing. Te Wiata, Inia. *Biographies*
Te Wiata, Beryl. Most happy fella : a biography of Inia Te Wiata / [by] Beryl Te Wiata. — Wellington, N.Z. [etc.] ; London : A.H. and A.W. Reed, 1976. — xi,307p,[16]p of plates : ill, ports ; 23cm.
Ill. on lining papers. — Index.
ISBN 0-589-00954-0 : Unpriced
(B77-33973)

782.1'2 — Opera in German. Einem, Gottfried von. *Librettos*
Blacher, Boris. Kabale und Liebe : Oper in 2 Teilen (9 Bildern) nach Friedrich von Schiller / Libretto von Boris Blacher und Lotte Ingrisch ; Musik von Gottfried von Einem. — London : Boosey and Hawkes, 1976. — 83p ; 19cm.
ISBN 0-85162-027-2 Pbk : £1.50
(B77-02500)

782.1'2 — Opera in German. Wagner, Richard. *Librettos. English texts*
Wagner, Richard. [Der Ring des Nibelungen. English]. The ring of the Niblung / [by] Richard Wagner ; with illustrations by Arthur Rackham ; translated by Margaret Armour. — London : Heinemann.
Ill. on lining papers. — Facsimile reprint of: 1st ed. of this translation. 1910-11.
Siegfried ; &, Twilight of the gods. — 1976. — vi,182p,[29]leaves of plates : ill(chiefly col) ; 25cm.
ISBN 0-434-61980-9 : £9.00
Also classified at 741.9'42
(B77-04347)

The Rhinegold ; &, The Valkyrie. — 1976. — vi,160p,[33]leaves of plates : ill(chiefly col) ; 25cm.
ISBN 0-434-61981-7 : £9.00
Also classified at 741.9'42
(B77-04348)

782.1'2 — Opera in German. Wagner, Richard. *Librettos. German-English parallel texts*
Wagner, Richard. [Der Ring des Nibelungen. English & German]. The ring of the Nibelung / [by] Richard Wagner ; German text with English translation by Andrew Porter. — London : Faber, 1977. — xx,329p ; 24cm.
Parallel German text and English translation, English preliminaries. — This translation originally published: as 'The ring'. Folkestone : Dawson, 1976.
ISBN 0-571-10020-1 Pbk : £4.80
(B77-26444)

782.1'2 — Opera in Italian. Monteverdi, Claudio. *Librettos. Italian-English parallel texts*
Busenello, G F. L'incoronazione di Poppea = The coronation of Poppaea : opera in a prologue and three acts, first performed in Venice, 1642 : Italian and English libretto / [music by] Claudio Monteverdi ; original text by G.F. Busenello ; English singing version by Arthur Jacobs. — Sevenoaks : Novello, 1976. — v[i.e.vii],2-111p ; 21cm.
Parallel Italian text and English translation.
Pbk : £2.55
(B77-18310)

782.8 — THEATRE MUSIC

782.8'1'0922 — Musical shows in English. Hart, Larry & Rodgers, Richard. *Biographies*

Marx, Samuel. Rodgers & Hart : bewitched, bothered, and bedevilled / by Samuel Marx and Jan Clayton. — London : W.H. Allen, 1977. — 287p,[16]p of plates : ill, facsims, ports ; 24cm.
Originally published: New York : Putnam, 1976. — Index.
ISBN 0-491-02060-0 : £4.95
(B77-22758)

782.8'1'0922 — Operettas in English. Gilbert, Sir William Schwenck & Sullivan, Sir Arthur, 1890-1900. *Critical studies*

Wolfson, John. Final curtain : the last Gilbert and Sullivan operas / [by] John Wolfson. — London [etc.] : Chappell : Deutsch, 1976. — xiv,293p : ill(incl 2 col), facsims, music, plans, ports ; 26cm.
Bibl.: p.285-286. — Index. — Includes facsimile reprints of the printed rehearsal librettos of 'Utopia (Limited)' and 'The Grand Duke', and twenty unpublished Gilbert lyrics.
ISBN 0-903443-12-0 : £7.95
(B77-08492)

782.8'1'0924 — Ballad opera in English. Gay, John, b.1685. Beggar's opera. *Critical studies*

Lewis, Peter Elfed. John Gay, 'The beggar's opera' / by Peter Elfed Lewis. — London : Edward Arnold, 1976. — 64p ; 20cm. — (Studies in English literature ; no.61)
Bibl.: p.62-63. — Index.
ISBN 0-7131-5895-6 : £2.95
ISBN 0-7131-5896-4 Pbk : £1.65
(B77-06218)

782.8'1'0924 — Musical shows in English. Words. Hart, Larry. *Biographies*

Thou swell, thou witty : the life and lyrics of Lorenz Hart / edited and with a memoir by Dorothy Hart. — New York [etc.] ; London : Harper and Row, 1976. — 192p : ill, facsims, music, ports ; 31cm.
List of plays and films: p.186-191.
ISBN 0-06-011776-1 : Unpriced
(B77-30506)

782.8'1'0973 — American musical shows, 1903-1975. *Illustrations. Questions & answers*

Green, Stanley, *b.1923.* The Broadway musical : a picture quiz book / [by] Stanley Green. — New York : Dover Publications [etc.] ; London : Constable, 1977. — [128]p : ill ; 24cm.
With answers. — Index.
ISBN 0-486-23403-7 Pbk : £2.50
(B77-32074)

782.8'1'2 — Children's musical plays in English. Hamel-Cooke, Chris. *Librettos*

Goss, Bernard. The fantastic fairground / by Bernard Goss ; music by Chris Hamel-Cooke ; lyrics by Denis Bond. — London [etc.] : French, 1976. — [6],50p ; 22cm.
Six men, 2 women. — Music available separately.
ISBN 0-573-05036-8 Pbk : £1.00
(B77-01702)

782.8'1'2 — Children's musical plays in English. O'Gorman, Denis. *Librettos*

O'Gorman, Denis. The rebels' inn : a short musical play for junior and middle schools / text and songs Denis O'Gorman ; accompaniment Jim Brand. — Pinner : Grail Publications, 1976. — 47p : music, port ; 25cm.

ISBN 0-901829-34-x Sd : £0.85
(B77-03701)

782.8'1'2 — Children's musical plays in English. Parker, Jim. *Librettos*

Daly, Wally K. Follow the star / book and lyrics by Wally K. Daly ; music by Jim Parker. — [London] : [Chappell], [1976]. — v,57p ; 26cm.
Music available separately.
Pbk : £1.50
(B77-02501)

782.8'1'2 — Children's musical plays in English. Wood, David, b.1944. *Librettos*

Wood, David, *b.1944.* The gingerbread man : a musical play / [by] David Wood. — London [etc.] : French, 1977. — [6],55p : 1 ill ; 22cm.
Four men, 2 women.
ISBN 0-573-05042-2 Pbk : £1.10 : CIP rev
(B77-12626)

Wood, David, *b.1944.* Old Mother Hubbard : a family musical / by David Wood. — London [etc.] : French, 1976. — [6],73p : plans ; 22cm.
Nine men, 4 women, supers.
ISBN 0-573-06449-0 Pbk : £0.90
(B77-10492)

Wood, David, *b.1944.* The papertown paperchase : a musical play / [book, lyrics and music] by David Wood. — London [etc.] : French, 1976. — [6],67p : plans ; 22cm.
Twelve characters, supers.
ISBN 0-573-05032-5 Pbk : £1.00
(B77-04349)

782.8'1'2 — Musical plays in English. Braden, John. *Librettos*

Foster, Paul. Marcus Brutus / [by] Paul Foster. Silver Queen Saloon / [text by Paul Foster ; lyrics Paul Foster and John Braden ; music John Braden]. — London : J. Calder : [Distributed by Calder and Boyars], 1977. — 159p : music ; 21cm. — (Playscript ; 77)
'Silver Queen Saloon' originally published: New York : French, 1976.
ISBN 0-7145-3564-8 : £5.50
Primary classification 812'.5'2
(B77-17047)

782.8'1'2 — Musical plays in English. Edwards, Sherman. *Librettos*

Edwards, Sherman. 1776 : a musical play (based on a conception of Sherman Edwards) / book by Peter Stone ; music and lyrics by Sherman Edwards. — Harmondsworth [etc.] : Penguin, 1976. — xv,176p,[8]p of plates : ill, facsim, ports ; 18cm. — (Penguin plays)
Twenty-five men, 2 women. — Originally published: New York : Viking Press, 1970. — Bibl.: p.174-176.
ISBN 0-14-048139-7 Pbk : Unpriced
(B77-04350)

782.8'1'2 — Musical plays in English. McDonald, James; Vos, David & Gerlach, Robert. *Librettos*

McDonald, James. Something's afoot : a new murder mystery musical / book, music and lyrics by James McDonald, David Vos & Robert Gerlach ; additional music by Ed Linderman. — New York ; London [etc.] : French, 1975. — 69p : plan ; 21cm. — (French's musical library)
Six men, 4 women.
ISBN 0-573-68072-8 Sd : £1.65
(B77-14859)

782.8'1'2 — Musical plays in English. Marvin, Mel. *Librettos*

Tesich, Steve. Gorky : a play with music / by Steve Tesich ; lyrics by Steve Tesich ; music by Mel Marvin. — New York ; London [etc.] : French, 1976. — 58p : plan ; 22cm. — (French's musical library)
ISBN 0-573-68077-9 Sd : £1.65
(B77-07529)

782.8'1'2 — Musical plays in English. Parr, Andrew. *Librettos*

Gardiner, John. The Dracula spectacula : a spooky musical / book and lyrics by John Gardiner ; music by Andrew Parr. — [London] : [Evans Bros], [1976]. — [8],80p : plan ; 21cm.

Music available separately.
ISBN 0-237-75012-0 Pbk : £0.75
(B77-11348)

782.8'1'2 — Musical plays in English. Previn, André. *Librettos*

Mercer, Johnny. J.B. Priestley's 'The Good Companions' / music by André Previn ; lyrics by Johnny Mercer ; book by Ronald Harwood. — London : Chappell, [1976]. — vi,78p ; 26cm.

Cover title: Good Companions : the musical of the novel by J.B. Priestley. — Music available separately.
Pbk : £1.50
(B77-02502)

782.8'1'2 — Musical plays in English. Reiser, Dave & Sharkey, Jack. *Librettos*

Sharkey, Jack. Hope for the best : a musical comedy in three acts / book, music and lyrics by Jack Sharkey and Dave Reiser. — New York ; London [etc.] : French, 1977. — 81p : plan ; 19cm. — (French's acting edition)
Three men, 3 women. — Music available separately.
ISBN 0-573-61044-4 Sd : £1.65
(B77-25114)

782.8'1'2 — Musical plays in English. Wann, Jim & Simpson, Bland. *Librettos*

Wann, Jim. Diamond studs : the life of Jesse James / book by Jim Wann ; music and lyrics by Bland Simpson and Jim Wann. — New York [etc.] ; London : French, 1976. — 59p : plan ; 21cm. — (French's musical library)
Twelve men, 8 women.
ISBN 0-573-68076-0 Sd : £1.60
(B77-00344)

782.8'1'2 — Musical shows in English. Grant, Micki. *Librettos*

Grant, Micki. Don't bother me, I can't cope : a musical entertainment / by Micki Grant ; conceived by Vinnette Carroll. — New York ; London [etc.] : French, 1972. — 66p : 1 ill ; 22cm. — (French's musical library)
ISBN 0-573-68080-9 Sd : £1.65
(B77-26445)

782.8'1'2 — Musical shows in English. Songs. Words. *Texts*

Gershwin, Ira. Lyrics on several occasions : a selection of stage & screen lyrics written for sundry situations, and now arranged in arbitrary categories. To which have been added many informative annotations & disquisitions on their why & wherefore, their whom-for, their how, and matters associative / by Ira Gershwin. — London : Elm Tree Books, 1977. — xvi,362,ix p ; 23cm.
Originally published: New York : Knopf, 1959. — Index.
ISBN 0-241-89634-7 : £4.95
(B77-12021)

782.8'1'2 — Operettas in English. Sullivan, Sir Arthur. *Librettos*

Gilbert, *Sir* **William Schwenck.** The first night Gilbert and Sullivan : containing complete librettos of the fourteen operas, exactly as presented at their première performances / [by W.S. Gilbert] ; edited with a prologue and copious descriptive particulars by Reginald Allen ; and a foreword by Bridget D'Oyly Carte. — Revised centennial ed. — London : Chappell, [1976]. — xxi,465p : ill, facsims, music, ports ; 30cm.
This ed. originally published: Avon, Conn. : Cardavon Press, 1975. — Bibl.: p.462-465.
ISBN 0-903443-10-4 : £10.95
(B77-08493)

783 — RELIGIOUS MUSIC

783'.026 — English church music. *Essays. Serials*

English church music : a collection of essays. — Croydon (Addington Palace, Croydon CR9 5AD) : Royal School of Church Music.
1977. — [1977]. — 3-55p,plate : music, port ; 22cm.
Bibl.: p.30.
ISBN 0-85402-067-5 Pbk : £1.56
(B77-32780)

783'.026 — English church music, ca 1100-1975

Routley, Erik. A short history of English church music / [by] Erik Routley. — London [etc.] : Mowbrays, 1977. — vi,122p : music ; 22cm.
Index.
ISBN 0-264-66125-7 Pbk : £2.95
(B77-21347)

783'.026'3 — Church of England. Parish churches. Music. *Manuals*

Dakers, Lionel. A handbook of parish music : a working guide for clergy and organists / by Lionel Dakers. — London [etc.] : Mowbrays, 1976. — xv,133p : music ; 19cm.
Bibl.: p.122-127. — Index.
ISBN 0-264-66261-x Pbk : £1.95
(B77-00345)

783'.029'6 — Ashkenazic religious songs, to 1914

Werner, Eric. A voice still heard : the sacred songs of the Ashkenazic Jews / [by] Eric Werner. — University Park [Penn.] ; London : Pennsylvania State University Press, 1976. — xiii,350p : 1 col ill tipped in, music ; 26cm. — (Leo Baeck Institute. Series)
Index.
ISBN 0-271-01167-x : £14.00
(B77-33366)

783'.06'21 — Church music. Organisations: Royal School of Church Music. *Periodicals*

Church music quarterly. — Croydon (Addington Palace, Croydon CR9 5AD) : Royal School of Church Music.
Continues: Promoting church music.
Vol.9, no.57- ; Jan. 1977-. — 1977-. — ill, ports ; 25cm.
Thirty two p. in vol.9, no.57.
Sd : £0.40(£1.70 yearly)
ISSN 0307-6334
(B77-09864)

783'.06'21 — Church music. Organisations: Royal School of Church Music, to 1977

Royal School of Church Music. The Royal School of Church Music. — [Croydon] ([Addington Palace, Croydon CR9 5AD]) : [R.S.C.M.], [1977]. — [35]p : ill, coat of arms, music, ports ; 30cm.
ISBN 0-85402-065-9 Sd : £0.75
(B77-12022)

783′.092′4 — English church music. Gray, Jonathan
Temperley, Nicholas. Jonathan Gray and church music in York, 1740-1840 / by Nicholas Temperley. — [York] : [St Anthony's Press], 1977. — [3],30p,plate : 1 ill ; 21cm. — (Borthwick papers ; no.51 ISSN 0524-0913)
Sd : £0.60
(B77-22759)

783′.092′4 — English church music. Wesley, Samuel Sebastian. *Biographies*
Chappell, Paul. Dr S.S. Wesley, 1810-1876 : portrait of a Victorian musician / [by] Paul Chappell ; with a foreword by Lionel Dakers. — Great Wakering : Mayhew-McCrimmon, 1977. — x,210p : ill, music, ports ; 21cm.
Bibl.: p.185-186. — List of compositions, musical scores and printed editions: p.171-184. — Index.
ISBN 0-85597-198-3 Pbk : £5.00
(B77-24395)

783′.092′4 — English church music. Wesley, Samuel Sebastian. *Periodicals*
Wesley Society of Great Britain. Gazette / the Wesley Society of Great Britain. — Bideford [etc.] ([c/o D.M. Baker, 52 Redwood Ave., Melton Mowbray, Leics. LE13 1TZ]) : The Society.
Vol.1, no.1- ; Apr. 19th, 1976-. — 1976-. — 21cm.
Three issues a year. — [16]p. in 1st issue.
Sd : Unpriced
ISSN 0309-0442
(B77-03702)

783.2′1 — Cathedral. *Hampshire. Winchester. Winchester Cathedral. Church music: Tropes, ca 1000-1100. Critical studies*
Planchart, Alejandro Enrique. The repertory of tropes at Winchester / [by] Alejandro Enrique Planchart. — Princeton ; Guildford : Princeton University Press, 1977. — 2v.(xiii,392p;xi,395p) : music ; 25cm.
Bibl.: vol.2, p.343-360. — Index.
ISBN 0-691-09121-8 : £16.90
(B77-29603)

783.2′3 — West Frankish church music: Sequences, ca 800-ca 900. *Critical studies*
Crocker, Richard L. The early medieval sequence / [by] Richard L. Crocker. — Berkeley [etc.] ; London : University of California Press, 1977. — x,470p : facsims, music ; 29cm.
Bibl.: p.449-452. — Index.
ISBN 0-520-02847-3 : £22.50
(B77-25800)

783.2′9 — Idoma funeral chants. *English texts*
Iles, Norman. The great ceremony : the songs, chants, and poems of a pagan funeral / [reconstructed by Norman Iles]. — Morecambe (381 Marine Rd, Morecambe, Lancs.) : The author, 1977. — [1],84p : ill ; 30cm.
Cover title: A pagan funeral. — 'The source of this re-creation ... is a booklet in album no.AHM 4221, "Music of the Idoma of Nigeria", Asch Records, 701 Seventh Ave., NYC, USA' - Introduction.
ISBN 0-9500776-5-8 Sd : £2.00
(B77-15409)

783.6′2′0942 — Carols in English, to 1550. Words. *Anthologies*
The **early** English carols / edited by Richard Leighton Greene. — 2nd ed., revised and enlarged. — Oxford : Clarendon Press, 1977. — clxxiii,517p,plate : facsim ; 24cm.
Previous ed.: 1935. — Bibl.: p.297-341. — Index.
ISBN 0-19-812715-4 : £25.00
(B77-13794)

783.9′092′2 — Hymns. Music. British composers, to 1975. *lists*
Hayden, Andrew J. British hymn writers and composers : a check-list giving their dates & places of birth & death / by Andrew J. Hayden and Robert F. Newton. — Croydon (c/o Addington Palace, Croydon CR9 5AD) : Hymn Society of Great Britain and Ireland, 1977. — [94]p ; 21cm.
Bibl.: p.[4].
ISBN 0-9505589-0-7 Pbk : £2.40
Also classified at 245′.092′2
(B77-08494)

783.9′092′4 — Hymns. Music. Ieuan Gwyllt. *Biographies. Welsh texts*
Davies, Thomas James. Ieuan Gwyllt (Y Parchedig John Roberts) / gan T.J. Davies. — Llandysul : Gwasg Gomer, 1977. — 111p : facsims, music ; 19cm.
ISBN 0-85088-476-4 Pbk : £0.90
(B77-32075)

784 — VOCAL MUSIC

784′.092′2 — American rock music. Grateful Dead, to 1972
Harrison, Hank. The Grateful Dead / [by] Hank Harrison. — London : Star Books, 1975. — 175p,[8]p of plates : ill, ports ; 18cm.
Originally published: as 'The Dead book : a social history of the Grateful Dead'. New York : Links, 1973.
ISBN 0-352-30093-0 Pbk : £0.70
(B77-19558)

784′.092′2 — British rock music. Small Faces (Group) & Stewart, Rod, to 1976
Pidgeon, John. Rod Stewart and the changing Faces / [by] John Pidgeon. — St Albans : Panther, 1976. — 144p,[8]p of plates : ill, facsims, geneal table, ports ; 18cm.
List of records: p.135-142.
ISBN 0-586-04650-x Pbk : £0.60
(B77-03170)

784′.092′2 — Pop music. Arrows (Group). *Biographies*
Harry, Bill. Arrows : the official story / [by] Bill Harry. — London : Everest, 1976. — 141p,[8]p of plates : ill, ports ; 18cm.
ISBN 0-903925-61-3 Pbk : £0.50
(B77-07996)

784′.092′2 — Pop music. Beatles, to 1964
Braun, Michael. Love me do : the Beatles' progress / [by] Michael Braun. — Harmondsworth [etc.] : Penguin, 1977. — 143p : ill, ports ; 18cm.
Originally published: 1964.
Pbk : Unpriced
(B77-32781)

784′.092′2 — Pop music. Beatles, to 1971
McCabe, Peter. Apple to the core : the unmaking of the Beatles / [by] Peter McCabe & Robert D. Schonfeld. — London : Martin Brian and O'Keeffe, 1977. — 3-209p ; 18cm.
Originally published: New York : Pocket Books ; London : Martin Brian and O'Keeffe, 1972.
Pbk : Unpriced
ISBN 0-85616-090-3
(B77-31357)

784′.092′2 — Pop music. Groups. *Study examples: Wings (Group)*
Gelly, David. The facts about a pop group, featuring Wings / by David Gelly ; photographed by Homer Sykes ; introduction by Paul McCartney. — London : G. Whizzard Publications Ltd : Deutsch, 1976. — [4],54p : ill(some col), facsim, music, ports(some col) ; 29cm. — (Fact books)
Ill. on lining papers.
ISBN 0-233-96771-0 : £1.95
(B77-08495)

784′.092′2 — Pop music. Queen, to 1975
Pryce, Larry. Queen / [by] Larry Pryce. — London : Star Books, 1976. — 124p,[8]p of plates : ports ; 18cm.
List of sound discs : p.123-124.
ISBN 0-352-39746-2 Pbk : £0.50
(B77-11349)

784′.092′2 — Pop music. Rolling Stones, to 1974
The **Rolling** Stones / edited by David Dalton. — [New ed.]. — London : Star Books, 1975. — 186p,12p of plates : ill, ports ; 18cm.
Previous ed.: New York : Amsco Music Publishing ; London : Music Sales Ltd, 1972. — List of sound discs : p.180-186.
ISBN 0-352-30092-2 Pbk : £0.50
(B77-19559)

784′.092′2 — Pop music. Rolling Stones, to 1976
Pascall, Jeremy. The Rolling Stones / [written and edited by Jeremy Pascall]. — London [etc.] : Hamlyn, 1977. — 96p : ill(some col), ports(some col) ; 31cm.
Ill. on lining papers. — List of sound discs: p.94-96.
ISBN 0-600-37596-x : £1.99
(B77-19560)

784′.092′2 — Pop music. Singing. Osmonds, The. *Serials*
Osmonds' world : the official year book of the Osmonds. — London : IPC Magazines.
1978. — [1977]. — 3-70p : ill(some col), ports(some col) ; 27cm. — (A Fleetway annual)
Cover title. — Spine title: Osmonds' yearbook. — Ill., ports on lining papers.
ISBN 0-85037-378-6 : £1.35
(B77-33367)

784′.092′2 — Pop music. Slik. *Biographies*
Tremlett, George. Slik / [by] George Tremlett. — London : Futura Publications, 1976. — 144p, [16]p of plates : facsims, ports ; 18cm.
ISBN 0-86007-197-9 Pbk : £0.60
(B77-13795)

784′.092′2 — Pop music. Wings (Group), to 1976
Jasper, Tony. Paul McCartney and Wings / [by] Tony Jasper. — London : Octopus Books, 1977. — 3-93p : ill(some col), ports(chiefly col) ; 30cm.
Col. ill. on lining papers. — List of sound discs: p.93.
ISBN 0-7064-0663-x : £2.50
(B77-30507)

784′.092′4 — Blues. Singing. Joplin, Janis. *United States. Biographies*
Friedman, Myra. Buried alive : a biography of Janis Joplin / [by] Myra Friedman. — London : Star Books, 1975. — 284p,[8]p of plates : ports ; 18cm.
Originally published: New York : Morrow, 1973 ; London : W.H. Allen, 1974.
ISBN 0-352-30077-9 Pbk : £0.75
(B77-19561)

784′.092′4 — British rock music. Singing. Stewart, Rod. *Biographies*
Jasper, Tony. Rod Stewart / [by] Tony Jasper. — London : Octopus Books, 1977. — 3-94p : chiefly ill(some col), ports(chiefly col) ; 31cm.
Col. port. on lining papers. — List of sound discs : p.75-85.
ISBN 0-7064-0666-4 : £2.50
(B77-28004)

Tremlett, George. The Rod Stewart story / [by] George Tremlett. — London : Futura Publications, 1976. — 143p,[16]p of plates : ill, ports ; 18cm.
ISBN 0-86007-351-3 Pbk : £0.60
(B77-10493)

784′.092′4 — Flemish vocal music. Josquin des Prés. *Conference proceedings*
International Josquin Festival-Conference, *Julliard School, 1971.* Josquin des Prez : proceedings of the International Josquin Festival-Conference held at the Julliard School at Lincoln Center in New York City, 21-25 June 1971 : sponsored by the American Musicological Society in cooperation with the International Musicological Society and the Renaissance Society of America / edited by Edward E. Lowinsky, in collaboration with Bonnie J. Blackburn. — London [etc.] : Oxford University Press, 1976 [i.e. 1977]. — xix,787p, [2]leaves of plates(1 fold),44p of plates : ill, coat of arms, facsims(1 col), music ; 27cm & 3 sound discs(6s.; 7in. 33 1/3rpm).
In slip case. — Index.
ISBN 0-19-315229-0 : £25.00
(B77-17675)

784′.092′4 — German vocal music. Bach, Johann Sebastian, 1723-1750. *Chronologies*
Dürr, Alfred. Zur Chronologie der Leipziger Vokalwerke J.S. Bachs / [von] Alfred Dürr. — 2.Aufl. ; mit Anmerkungen und Nachträgen versehener Nachdruck aus Bach-Jahrbuch 1957. — Kassel [etc.] ; London ([32 Great Titchfield St., W1P 7AD]) : Bärenreiter, 1976. — 175p ; 23cm. — (Gesellschaft für Musikforschung. Musikwissenschaftliche Arbeiter ; Nr.26)
Previous ed.: Berlin : Evangelische Verlagsanstalt, 1958.
Pbk : £6.72
ISBN 3-7618-0544-6
(B77-25115)

784′.092′4 — Jamaican pop music. Marley, Bob
Dalrymple, Henderson. Bob Marley : music, myth & the Rastas / [by] Henderson Dalrymple. — Sudbury (37 Priory Ave., Sudbury, Middx) : Carib-Arawak Publishers, 1976. — 77,[1]p : ill, ports ; 21cm.
ISBN 0-9505688-0-5 Sd : £1.00
Also classified at 289.9
(B77-16534)

784′.092′4 — Jazz. Singing. Holiday, Billie. *Biographies*
Chilton, John. Billie's blues : a survey of Billie Holiday's career, 1933-1959 / [by] John Chilton ; foreword by Buck Clayton. — London [etc.] : Quartet Books, 1977. — [7],259, [4]p : facsims, ports ; 22cm.
Originally published: 1975. — Bibl.: p.239-259. — Index.
ISBN 0-7043-3114-4 Pbk : £1.95
(B77-28005)

784′.092′4 — Jazz. Singing. Melly, George. *Autobiographies*
Melly, George. Owning-up / [by] George Melly ; illustrated by Trog. — Harmondsworth [etc.] : Penguin, 1977. — 251p : ill ; 18cm.
Originally published: London : Weidenfeld and Nicolson, 1965.
Pbk : £0.75
ISBN 0-14-002936-2
(B77-30508)

784′.092′4 — Jazz. Singing. Melly, George, 1944-1947. *Autobiographies*
Melly, George. Rum, bum and concertina / [by] George Melly. — London : Weidenfeld and Nicolson, 1977. — [5],183p ; 23cm.
ISBN 0-297-77341-0 : £4.95
(B77-25801)

784′.092′4 — Music hall. Singing. Lauder, Sir Harry, b.1870. *Great Britain. Autobiographies*
Lauder, *Sir* Harry, *b.1870.* Roamin' in the gloamin' / by Sir Harry Lauder. — Wakefield : EP Publishing, 1976. — [5],11-287p ; 20cm.
Facsimile reprint of: 1st ed., London : Hutchinson, 1928. — Index.
ISBN 0-7158-1176-2 : £4.00
(B77-17676)

784′.092′4 — Pop music. Lennon, John. *Biographies*
Fawcett, Anthony. John Lennon, one day at a time : a personal biography of the seventies / by Anthony Fawcett. — London : New English Library, 1977. — 192p : ill, facsims, ports ; 26cm.
Originally published: New York : Grove Press, 1976. — Bibl.: p.191. — List of sound discs: p.188-190.
ISBN 0-450-03073-3 Pbk : £3.95
(B77-09865)

784′.092′4 — Pop music. Previn, Dory. *Autobiographies*
Previn, Dory. Midnight baby : an autobiography / [by] Dory Previn. — London : Elm Tree Books, 1977. — x,246p ; 23cm.
Originally published: New York : Macmillan, 1976.
ISBN 0-241-89650-9 : £3.95
(B77-11350)

784′.092′4 — Pop music. Singing. John, Elton. *Biographies*
Newman, Gerald. Elton John / by Gerald Newman with Joe Bivona ; introduction by Henry Edwards. — London : New English Library, 1976. — 159p ; 18cm.
List of sound discs: p.156-159. — Also published: Bergenfield, N.J. : Signet Books, 1976.
ISBN 0-450-03235-3 Pbk : £0.60
(B77-03171)

784′.092′4 — Pop music. Singing. John, Elton. *Transcripts of interviews*
Gambaccini, Paul. A conversation with Elton John and Bernie Taupin / by Paul Gambaccini. — New York ; London : Flash Books ; London (78 Newman St., W.1) : Distributed by Book Sales Ltd, [1976]. — 112p : ill, ports ; 26cm.
Published in the United States: 1975. — List of gramophone records: p.110-111.
ISBN 0-8256-3063-0 Pbk : £1.95
Also classified at 784′.092′4
(B77-02503)

Gambaccini, Paul. Elton John and Bernie Taupin / [by Paul Gambaccini]. — London : Star Books, 1975. — 117p,[16]p of plates : ports ; 18cm.
Originally published: as 'A conversation with Elton John and Bernie Taupin'. New York : Flash Books, 1975 ; London : Distributed by Book Sales Ltd, 1976. — List of sound discs : p.115-117.
ISBN 0-352-30058-2 Pbk : £0.50
Also classified at 784′.092′4
(B77-19562)

784′.092′4 — Pop music. Singing. Presley, Elvis. *Biographies*
Elvis : a tribute to the king of rock'n'roll : remembering you. — London : IPC Magazines, 1977. — 62p : ill(some col), ports(some col) ; 30cm.
List of films: p.62. — List of sound discs: p.62.
Sd : £0.65
(B77-28784)

Harbinson, William Allen. The life and death of Elvis Presley / by W.A. Harbinson ; designed by Stephen Ridgeway. — Revised ed. — London : Joseph, 1977. — 160p : chiefly ill, ports ; 28cm.
Previous ed.: published as 'Elvis Presley'. London : Joseph, 1975.
ISBN 0-7181-1681-x Pbk : £3.50
(B77-33974)

Mann, May. Elvis and the Colonel / [by] May Mann. — New York ; London : Drake, 1975. — [6],273p,[6]p of plates : ports ; 24cm.
ISBN 0-8473-1004-3 : Unpriced
(B77-15999)

784′.092′4 — Pop music. Singing. Richard, Cliff. *Autobiographies*
Richard, Cliff. Which one's Cliff? / [by] Cliff Richard ; [with Bill Latham]. — London [etc.] : Hodder and Stoughton, 1977. — 156p, [16]p of plates : ill, ports ; 21cm.
ISBN 0-340-22074-0 : £2.95
(B77-33368)

784′.092′4 — Pop music. Singing. Stardust, Alvin. *Biographies*
Tremlett, George. The Alvin Stardust story / [by] George Tremlett. — London : Futura Publications, 1976. — 144p,[16]p of plates : ports ; 18cm.
ISBN 0-86007-301-7 Pbk : £0.60
(B77-09866)

784′.092′4 — Pop music. Tours by John, Elton, 1976. *Illustrations*
Taupin, Bernie. Elton : it's a little bit funny / text by Bernie Taupin ; pictures by David Nutter ; dedication by Elton John. — Harmondsworth [etc.] : Penguin, 1977. — 144p : ill(some col), chiefly ports(some col) ; 28cm.
Also published: New York : Viking Press, 1977.
ISBN 0-14-004680-1 Pbk : £2.50
(B77-31358)

784′.092′4 — Pop songs in English. Words. Taupin, Bernie. *Transcripts of interviews*
Gambaccini, Paul. A conversation with Elton John and Bernie Taupin / by Paul Gambaccini. — New York ; London : Flash Books ; London (78 Newman St., W.1) : Distributed by Book Sales Ltd, [1976]. — 112p : ill, ports ; 26cm.
Published in the United States: 1975. — List of gramophone records: p.110-111.
ISBN 0-8256-3063-0 Pbk : £1.95
Primary classification 784′.092′4
(B77-02503)

Gambaccini, Paul. Elton John and Bernie Taupin / [by Paul Gambaccini]. — London : Star Books, 1975. — 117p,[16]p of plates : ports ; 18cm.
Originally published: as 'A conversation with Elton John and Bernie Taupin'. New York : Flash Books, 1975 ; London : Distributed by Book Sales Ltd, 1976. — List of sound discs : p.115-117.
ISBN 0-352-30058-2 Pbk : £0.50
Primary classification 784′.092′4
(B77-19562)

784′.092′4 — Popular music. Singing. Jolson, Al. *Biographies*
Freedland, Michael. Al Jolson / [by] Michael Freedland. — London : Abacus, 1975. — 268p, [16]p of plates : ill, ports ; 20cm.
Originally published: London : W.H. Allen, 1972. — Index.
ISBN 0-349-11333-5 Pbk : £1.45
(B77-19563)

784′.092′4 — Popular music. Singing. Sinatra, Frank. *Biographies*
Scaduto, Anthony. Frank Sinatra / [by] Tony Scaduto. — London : Sphere, 1977. — 159p,[8] p of plates : ill, ports ; 18cm.
Originally published: London : Joseph, 1976.
ISBN 0-7221-7656-2 Pbk : £0.85
(B77-21348)

784′.092′4 — Popular music. Singing. Sinatra, Frank. Performances, to 1976. *Lists*
Ridgway, John, *b.1943.* The Sinatrafile / by John Ridgway. — Birmingham (Miramar, Rowney Green La., Alvechurch, Birmingham B48 7QF) : John Ridgway Books.
Part 1 : [Non commercial]. — 1977. — x,310p : facsims, ports ; 25cm.
Limited ed. of 1,000 copies. — Bibl.: p.287. — List of sound discs: p.243-271.
ISBN 0-905808-00-2 : £13.00
ISBN 0-905808-01-0 Pbk : £11.00
(B77-14860)

784′.092′4 — Rock music. Hendrix, Jimi. *Biographies*
Knight, Curtis. Jimi : an intimate biography of Jimi Hendrix / [by] Curtis Knight. — London : Star Books, 1975. — 223p,[8]p of plates : ports ; 18cm.
Originally published: London : W.H. Allen, 1974. — List of sound discs : p.209-218. — Index.
ISBN 0-352-30047-7 Pbk : £0.60
(B77-19564)

784′.092′4 — Singing. Biermann, Wolf. Political aspects. *Trotskyist viewpoints*
Posadas, J. The singer Biermann, the function of criticism and the construction of socialism / [by] J. Posadas. — London (24 Cranbourn St., W.C.2) : Revolutionary Workers Party (Trotskyist), [1977]. — [1],6,[1]p ; 22cm. — (A 'European Marxist review' publication)
At head of title: Workers of the world, unite!.
Sd : £0.05
(B77-30509)

784′.092′4 — Singing. McCormack, John, Count. *Biographies*
Ledbetter, Gordon T. The great Irish tenor / [by] Gordon T. Ledbetter. — London : Duckworth, 1977. — 160p : ill, facsims, ports ; 25cm.
Bibl.: p.157. — Index.
ISBN 0-7156-1172-0 : £5.95
(B77-20481)

784′.092′4 — Singing. Piaf, Edith. *Biographies*
Edith Piaf / text ... by Simone Berteaut ; [translated from the French by Ghislaine Boulanger] ; edited by Michael Leitch ; ... music compilation by Peter Foss. — London (78 Newman St., W1P 3LA) : Wise Publications, 1976. — 117p : chiefly music, ports ; 31cm.
Cover title: Piaf. — Text from: 'Piaf' / by Simone Berteaut ; translated from the French by Ghislaine Boulanger. London : W.H. Allen, 1970. — Includes 20 songs.
ISBN 0-86001-112-7 Pbk : £3.95
(B77-17677)

784′.092′4 — Singing. Trapp, Maria Augusta. *Autobiographies*
Trapp, Maria Augusta. The sound of music : the story of the Trapp family singers / [by] Maria Augusta Trapp. — London [etc.] : White Lion Publishers, 1976. — 287p,[8]leaves of plates : ill, ports ; 23cm.
Originally published: as 'The story of the Trapp family singers', Philadelphia : Lippincott, 1949 ; and as 'The Trapp family singers', London : Bles, 1953.
ISBN 0-7274-0193-9 : £3.95
(B77-01703)

784′.092′4 — Songs in French. Poulenc, Francis. *Critical studies*
Bernac, Pierre. Francis Poulenc : the man and his songs / by Pierre Bernac ; translated [from the French MS.] by Winifred Radford ; with a foreword by Sir Lennox Berkeley. — London : Gollancz, 1977. — 233p,leaf of plate,[6]p of plates : ports ; 23cm.
Bibl.: p.225. — Index.
ISBN 0-575-02328-7 : £8.50
(B77-31359)

784′.0942 — Bawdy songs in English, 1830-1840. Words. *Anthologies. Facsimiles*
Bawdy songs of the early music hall / selected, with an introduction, by George Speaight. — London [etc.] : Pan Books, 1977. — 96p : ill, music ; 25cm.
This collection originally published: Newton Abbot : David and Charles, 1975. — Facsimile reprints of selections from various song-books originally published by William West of London.
ISBN 0-330-25195-3 Pbk : £1.25
(B77-32076)

784′.0942 — Songs in English. Origins
Harrowven, Jean. The origins of rhymes, songs and sayings / [by] Jean Harrowven. — London : Kaye and Ward, 1977. — xii,356p : ill, ports ; 23cm.
Bibl.: p.333-334. — Index.
ISBN 0-7182-1123-5 : £5.25
Primary classification 398.8
(B77-28555)

784′.0942 — Songs in English. Words. *Texts*
Boyce, Max. Max Boyce, his songs and poems / introduction by Barry John ; cartoons by Gren. — St Albans : Panther, 1976. — 63p : ill ; 18cm.
Includes two songs in Welsh.
ISBN 0-586-04621-6 Pbk : £0.50
(B77-05568)

784′.09429 — Popular songs in Welsh. Words. *Anthologies. For non-Welsh speaking students*
50 o ganeuon i'r dysgwyr / casgliad gan Alun Ifans. — Aberaeron ([Aberaeron, Dyfed]) : Gwasg Aeron, 1977. — [2],48p : ill ; 22cm.
Sd : £0.65
(B77-33369)

784'.0944 — Songs in French. Performance. Interpretation
Bernac, Pierre. The interpretation of French song / by Pierre Bernac ; translations of song texts by Winifred Radford. — London : Gollancz, 1976. — xvi,327p : music ; 21cm.
Originally published: London : Cassell, 1970. — Index.
ISBN 0-575-02207-8 : £7.50
(B77-00346)

784'.3'00924 — Lieder. Schubert, Franz. *Critical studies. German texts*
Fischer-Dieskau, Dietrich. Auf den Spuren der Schubert-Lieder : Werden, Wesen, Wirkung / [von] Dietrich Fischer-Dieskau. — Kassel [etc.] ; London ([32 Great Titchfield St., W1P 7AD]) : Bärenreiter [etc.], 1976. — 371p : ill, facsims, music, ports ; 18cm.
Originally published: Wiesbaden : Brockhaus, 1971. — Bibl.: p.356-357. — Index.
Pbk : £2.18
(B77-08496)

784.3'00943 — Lieder. Words. *Anthologies. English texts*
The **Penguin** book of lieder / edited and translated by S.S. Prawer. — Harmondsworth [etc.] : Penguin, 1977. — 201p : music ; 20cm.
Parallel German text and English translation. — Originally published: 1964. — Bibl.: p.191-193. — Index.
ISBN 0-14-070844-8 Pbk : £1.00
(B77-17015)

784.4'94114 — Folk songs in Gaelic: Western Isles folk songs : South Uist folk songs. *Gaelic-English parallel texts. Collections*
Shaw, Margaret Fay. Folksongs and folklore of South Uist / by Margaret Fay Shaw. — 2nd ed. — Oxford [etc.] : Oxford University Press, 1977. — xiv,306p,[2]leaves of plates,32p of plates : ill, map, music, ports ; 25cm.
Songs and proverbs in Gaelic with English translations. — Previous ed.: London : Routledge and Kegan Paul, 1955. — Bibl.: p.293-297. — Index.
ISBN 0-19-920085-8 : £12.50
(B77-30510)

784.4'9415 — Irish folk songs, to 1976
O Boyle, Seán. The Irish song tradition / [by] Seán O Boyle. — Dublin : G. Dalton ; Dublin (11 Clare St., Dublin 1) : Distributed by the O Brien Press, 1976. — 93p : music ; 22cm.
Includes songs in English and Irish.
ISBN 0-9505173-0-5 : £4.50
ISBN 0-9505173-1-3 Pbk : £1.50
(B77-05569)

784.4'9422'5 — Folk songs in English: East Sussex folk songs. *Collections*
Copper, Bob. Early to rise : a Sussex boyhood / [by] Bob Copper. — London : Heinemann, 1976. — [9],267p,[12]p of plates : ill, music, port ; 23cm.
Ill. on lining papers.
ISBN 0-434-14457-6 : £4.90
Primary classification 942.2'56
(B77-01932)

784.4'9423 — Folk songs in English. Pagan symbolism. *Sources of data: South-west English folk songs*
Stewart, Bob. Where is Saint George? : pagan imagery in English folksong / [by] Bob Stewart. — Bradford-on-Avon : Moonraker Press, 1977. — [5],138p : ill, music ; 22cm.
Bibl.: p.133-134. — Index.
ISBN 0-239-00169-9 : £3.95
(B77-23621)

784.6'24 — Children's action songs. *Collections*
Nelson, Esther L. Musical games for children of all ages / by Esther L. Nelson ; illustrations by Shizu Matsuda. — New York : Sterling [etc.] ; London : Distributed by Ward Lock, 1977. — 72p : ill, music ; 23x26cm.
Published in the United States: 1976. — Index.
ISBN 0-7061-2520-7 : £3.50
Also classified at 796.1'3
(B77-25116)

784.6'24'00942 — Children's songs in English. *Texts*
Zemach, Margot. Hush, little baby / [by] Margot Zemach. — Harmondsworth : Kestrel Books, 1976. — [32]p : col ill, music ; 22x25cm.
Also published: New York : Dutton, 1976.
ISBN 0-7226-5024-8 : £2.75
(B77-02504)

784.7'6'91497 — Folk songs in English: Gypsy songs. *Collections*
Travellers' songs from England and Scotland / [compiled by] Ewan MacColl and Peggy Seeger. — London [etc.] : Routledge and Kegan Paul, 1977. — xii,387p : music ; 24cm.
Bibl.: p.368-384. — Index.
ISBN 0-7100-8436-6 : £11.95 : CIP rev.
(B77-19565)

785 — MUSIC. INSTRUMENTAL ENSEMBLES
785 — Instrumental music. *Critical studies*
Hopkins, Antony. Talking about music : symphonies, concertos and sonatas / [by] Antony Hopkins ; illustrated by John Barkwith. — London [etc.] : Pan Books, 1977. — [13], 462p : ill, music ; 20cm.
Index. — Contents: Talking about symphonies. Originally published: London : Heinemann Educational, 1961 - Talking about concertos. Originally published: London : Heinemann Educational, 1964 - Talking about sonatas. London : Heinemann Educational, 1971.
ISBN 0-330-24824-3 Pbk : £1.50
Also classified at 785.1'1; 785.6; 786.4'1
(B77-27282)

785 — Orchestral music
Howes, Frank. Full orchestra : a guide to orchestral music / [by] Frank Howes. — Revised and extended ed. — London [etc.] : White Lion Publishers, 1976. — 233p : ill, music ; 21cm.
Previous ed.: published as 'Fontana guide to orchestral music'. London : Fontana, 1958. — Bibl.: p.224-226. — Index.
ISBN 0-85617-998-1 : £3.25
(B77-01704)

785'.0284 — Music for young players. Orchestration. *Manuals*
Oboussier, Philippe. Arranging music for young players : a handbook on basic orchestration / [by] Philippe Oboussier. — London : Oxford University Press, 1977. — [8],175p : music ; 26cm.
Bibl.: p.166. — Index.
ISBN 0-19-321495-4 Pbk : Unpriced
(B77-25117)

785'.06'24167 — Youth orchestras. *Belfast. Belfast Youth Orchestra, to 1975*
McNeilly, Norman. The music makers / [by] Norman McNeilly. — Belfast ([Linfield Industrial Estate, Linfield Rd, Belfast]) : Academy Organization [for] the Friends of the Belfast Youth Orchestra, 1976. — [8],84p : ill, facsims, music, ports ; 30cm.
Bibl.: p.83.
ISBN 0-905784-00-6 Pbk : Unpriced
(B77-01705)

785'.06'2421 — Symphony orchestras. *London. Philharmonia Orchestra, 1947-1975. Personal observations*
Beavan, Peter. Philharmonia days : a few brief memories of my early days with the Philharmonia Orchestra / [by] Peter Beavan. — London (15 Dungarvan Ave., S.W.15) : The Cock Robin Press, 1976. — [15]p ; 20cm.
Limited ed. of 200 copies.
ISBN 0-9500594-7-1 Sd : Private circulation
(B77-07997)

785'.06'2421 — Symphony orchestras. *Study examples: London Symphony Orchestra*
Amis, John. The facts about a symphony orchestra : featuring the London Symphony Orchestra / by John Amis ; photographed by Philip Sayer ; introduction by André Previn. — London : G. Whizzard Publications Ltd : [Distributed by] Deutsch, 1977. — [7],43p : ill(some col), music, ports(some col) ; 29cm. — (Fact book)
Ill. on lining papers.
ISBN 0-233-96770-2 : £2.25
(B77-31360)

785'.06'66 — Popular music. Big bands, 1912-1976
Jackson, Arthur. The world of big bands : the sweet and swinging years / [by] Arthur Jackson ; foreword by Edmund Anderson. — Newton Abbot [etc.] : David and Charles, 1977. — 3-130p : ill, ports ; 27cm.
Bibl.: p.124. — Index.
ISBN 0-7153-7359-5 : £4.95
(B77-20482)

785'.06'660924 — Popular music. Dance bands, 1919-1955. *Personal observations*
Colin, Sid. And the bands played on / [by] Sid Colin. — London : Elm Tree Books, 1977. — 136p : ill, facsims, ports ; 24cm.
Ports on lining papers. — List of sound discs: p.136.
ISBN 0-241-89589-8 : £5.50
(B77-18933)

785'.06'660924 — Popular music. Dance bands. Cotton, Billy. *Great Britain. Biographies*
Maxwell, John. The greatest Billy Cotton Band Show / by John Maxwell. — London : Jupiter Books, 1976. — xii,155p : ill, facsims, ports ; 26cm.
Sound disc in pocket. — Index.
ISBN 0-904041-31-x : £3.95
(B77-17678)

785'.06'720976335 — Jazz. Brass bands. *Louisiana. New Orleans, to 1976*
Schafer, William J. Brass bands and New Orleans jazz / [by] William J. Schafer ; with assistance from Richard B. Allen. — Baton Rouge ; London ([c/o American University Publishers Group, 70 Great Russell St., WC1B 3BY]) : Louisiana State University Press, 1977. — ix,134p : ill, music, ports ; 20x23cm.
Bibl.: p.100-102. — List of sound discs: p.102-105. — Index.
ISBN 0-8071-0280-6 : £9.35
ISBN 0-8071-0282-2 Pbk : £5.25
(B77-32077)

785'.092'4 — American popular music. Big bands. Miller, Glenn. *Critical studies*
Snow, George. Glenn Miller & the age of swing / conceived, designed and produced by George Snow ; written by Jonathan Green ... — London (8 Berwick St., W.1) : Dempsey and Squires, 1976. — 128p : ill, facsims, music, ports ; 27cm.
Cover title: George Snow presents Glenn Miller & the age of swing. — List of sound discs: p.127. — Index.
ISBN 0-86044-007-9 Pbk : £3.50
(B77-22760)

785'.092'4 — Music. Conducting. Beecham, Sir Thomas, bart. *Essays*
Beecham remembered / [compiled and edited by] Humphrey Procter-Gregg. — New ed. — London : Duckworth, 1976. — ix,212p,leaf of plate,[8]p of plates : ill, music, ports ; 23cm.
Previous ed.: published as 'Sir Thomas Beecham, conductor and impresario, as remembered by his friends and colleagues'. Windermere : The author, 1973. — List of sound discs : p.196-199. — Bibl.: p.204-205. — Index.
ISBN 0-7156-1117-8 : £5.95
(B77-01706)

785'.092'4 — Popular music. Big bands. Last, James. *Biographies*
Willox, Bob. James Last / [by] Bob Willox. — London : Everest, 1976. — 207p,[16]p of plates : ill, ports ; 23cm.
List of sound discs : p.5-6.
ISBN 0-905018-12-5 : £3.95
(B77-05570)

785.1'1 — Symphonies. *Critical studies*
Hopkins, Antony. Talking about music : symphonies, concertos and sonatas / [by] Antony Hopkins ; illustrated by John Barkwith. — London [etc.] : Pan Books, 1977. — [13], 462p : ill, music ; 20cm.
Index. — Contents: Talking about symphonies. Originally published: London : Heinemann Educational, 1961 - Talking about concertos. Originally published: London : Heinemann Educational, 1964 - Talking about sonatas. London : Heinemann Educational, 1971.
ISBN 0-330-24824-3 Pbk : £1.50
Primary classification 785
(B77-27282)

785.1'1'0924 — Austrian symphonies. Haydn, Joseph. *Critical studies*
Hodgson, Antony. The music of Joseph Haydn, the symphonies / [by] Antony Hodgson. — London : Tantivy Press [etc.], 1976. — 208p, [12]p of plates : ill(some col), music, plans, ports(1 col) ; 24cm.
Bibl.: p.159-161. — List of sound discs: p.162-201. — Index.
ISBN 0-904208-21-4 : £6.50
(B77-33370)

785.1'2 — Brass band music. Instrumentation. *Manuals*
Siebert, Edrich. A practical guide to instrumentation for the brass band / by Edrich Siebert. — London (89 Vicarage Rd, NW10 2UA) : Studio Music Co., 1976. — 16p : music ; 24cm.
ISBN 0-905925-01-7 Sd : £0.50
(B77-08498)

785.4'1 — Latin American ballroom dance music. Rhythm. *For percussion instrument playing*
Hanmer, Ronald. Learn to play - the Latin-American way! : a guide for the rhythm section / by Ronald Hanmer. — London (89 Vicarage Rd, NW10 2YA) : Studio Music Co., 1976. — 24p : ill, music, port ; 25cm.
ISBN 0-905925-00-9 Sd : £0.50
(B77-09175)

785.4'2 — Jazz
Harrison, Max. A jazz retrospect / [by] Max Harrison. — Newton Abbot [etc.] : David and Charles [etc.], 1976. — 223p ; 23cm.
Index.
ISBN 0-7153-7279-3 : £5.95
(B77-06817)

785.4'2'05 — Jazz. *Periodicals*
Jazz journal international. — London (7 Carnaby St., W1V 1PG) : Billboard Ltd.
Continues: Jazz journal.
Vol.30, no.5- ; May 1977-. — 1977-. — ill, ports ; 28cm.
Monthly. — 52p. in Vol.30, no.8.
Sd : £0.45(£6.50 yearly)
ISSN 0140-2285
(B77-32078)

785.4'2'0904 — Jazz, to 1958
Jazz / edited by Nat Hentoff and Albert J. McCarthy ; introduction by Graham Collier. — London [etc.] : Quartet Books, 1977. — x, 342p : music ; 22cm.
Originally published: New York : Rinehart, 1959.
ISBN 0-7043-3151-9 Pbk : £2.95
(B77-30511)

785.4'2'0922 — Jazz. Musicians. *United States. Transcripts of interviews*
Wilmer, Valerie. Jazz people / [by] Valerie Wilmer ; photographs by the author. — New ed. [i.e. 2nd ed. reprinted]. — London [etc.] : Quartet Books, 1977. — 167p : ports ; 22cm.
This ed. originally published: London : Allison and Busby, 1971. — Index.
ISBN 0-7043-3163-2 Pbk : £2.25
(B77-30512)

785.4'2'0924 — Jazz. *Great Britain, 1941-1975. Personal observations*
Godbolt, Jim. All this and 10% / [by] Jim Godbolt. — London : Hale, 1976. — 208p,[12] p of plates : ports ; 23cm.
Index.
ISBN 0-7091-5841-6 : £4.95
(B77-00347)

785.4'2'0924 — Jazz. Ellington, Duke. *Autobiographies*
Ellington, Duke. Music is my mistress / by Edward Kennedy Ellington. — London : Quartet Books, 1977. — iii-xv,523p : ill, facsims, music, ports ; 21cm.
Originally published: Garden City, N.Y. : Doubleday, 1973 ; London : W.H. Allen, 1974. — Bibl.: p.523. — List of sound discs: p.491-492. — List of works: p.493-522.
ISBN 0-7043-3090-3 Pbk : £3.95
(B77-15410)

785.4'2'0924 — Jazz. Ellington, Duke. *Biographies*
Jewell, Derek. Duke : a portrait of Duke Ellington / [by] Derek Jewell. — London : Elm Tree Books, 1977. — 192p,[16]p of plates : ports ; 24cm.
Ports on lining papers. — Bibl.: p.184-186. — Index.
ISBN 0-241-89579-0 : £5.50
(B77-15411)

785.6 — Concertos. *Critical studies*
Hopkins, Antony. Talking about music : symphonies, concertos and sonatas / [by] Antony Hopkins ; illustrated by John Barkwith. — London [etc.] : Pan Books, 1977. — [13], 462p : ill, music ; 20cm.
Index. — Contents: Talking about symphonies. Originally published: London : Heinemann Educational, 1961 - Talking about concertos. Originally published: London : Heinemann Educational, 1964 - Talking about sonatas. London : Heinemann Educational, 1971.
ISBN 0-330-24824-3 Pbk : £1.50
Primary classification 785
(B77-27282)

785.7'04'710924 — German string quartets. Beethoven, Ludwig van. *Critical studies*
Kerman, Joseph. The Beethoven quartets / [by] Joseph Kerman. — London [etc.] : Oxford University Press, 1975. — [11],386,viii,[3]p : music ; 25cm.
Originally published: New York : Knopf ; London : Oxford University Press, 1967. — Bibl.: p.383-386. List of works: p.i-iv. — Index.
ISBN 0-19-315135-9 : £6.00
(B77-00348)

786 — MUSIC. KEYBOARD INSTRUMENTS

786'.092'4 — German keyboard music. Bach, Johann Sebastian. Wohltemperierte Klavier. Performance. Interpretation
Keller, Hermann. 'The well-tempered clavier' by Johann Sebastian Bach / [by] Hermann Keller ; translated [from the German] by Leigh Gerdine. — London : Allen and Unwin, 1976. — 3-207p : facsim, music ; 23cm.
Translation of: '"Das wohltemperierte Klavier" von Johann Sebastian Bach'. Kassel : Bärenreiter, 1965. — Bibl.: p.204-205.
ISBN 0-04-786005-7 : £7.50
(B77-02505)

786.1'09'03 — Keyboard string instruments, 1500-1800
Keyboard instruments : studies in keyboard organology, 1500-1800 / edited by Edwin M. Ripin. — New York : Dover Publications [etc.] ; London : Constable, 1977. — ix,86p,[54] p of plates,[3]leaves of plates : ill, facsims, ports ; 21cm.
Originally published: Edinburgh : Edinburgh University Press, 1971.
ISBN 0-486-23363-4 Pbk : £2.10
(B77-20483)

786.1'092'2 — Piano playing. Lhevinne, Josef & Lhevinne, Rosina. *Biographies*
Wallace, Robert K. A century of music-making : the lives of Josef & Rosina Lhevinne / [by] Robert K. Wallace. — Bloomington ; London : Indiana University Press, [1977]. — xiii,350p, [18]p of plates : ill, facsim, ports ; 24cm.
Published in the United States: 1976. — Bibl.: p.333-335. — List of sound discs: p.337-340. — Index.
ISBN 0-253-31330-9 : £14.05
(B77-13179)

786.1'092'4 — Italian piano music. Clementi, Muzio
Plantinga, Leon. Clementi : his life and music / [by] Leon Plantinga. — London [etc.] : Oxford University Press, 1977. — xiii,346p,leaf of plate,8p of plates : 1 ill, facsims, music, ports ; 25cm.
Bibl.: p.328-335. — Index.
ISBN 0-19-315227-4 : £15.00
(B77-20484)

786.1'092'4 — Piano playing. Hess, Dame Myra. *Biographies*
McKenna, Marian Cecilia. Myra Hess : a portrait / [by] Marian C. McKenna. — London : Hamilton, 1976. — xii,319p,16p of plates : ill, facsim, music, ports ; 24cm.
Music on lining papers. — List of sound discs : p.281-290. — Index.
ISBN 0-241-89522-7 : £6.95
(B77-02506)

786.1'092'4 — Piano playing. Liberace
Liberace. The things I love / [by] Liberace ; edited by Tony Palmer. — New York : Grosset and Dunlap ; [Leicester] ([Euston St., Freemen's Common, Aylestone Rd, Leicester LE2 7SS]) : Distributed by WHS Distributors, 1976. — 224p : ill(some col), facsims, ports(some col) ; 28cm.
ISBN 0-448-12718-0 : £4.50
ISBN 0-448-12719-9 Pbk : £1.95
(B77-23622)

786.1'092'4 — Polish piano music. Chopin, Frédéric. *Biographies*
Melville, Derek. Chopin : a biography, with a survey of books, editions and recordings / by Derek Melville. — London : Bingley [etc.], 1977. — 108p ; 23cm. — (The concertgoer's companions)
Bibl.: p.62-78. — List of music: p.79-91. — List of sound discs: p.93-99. — Index.
ISBN 0-85157-230-8 : £2.25
(B77-17016)

786.2'1 — Pianos. *Juvenile literature*
Crow, David. The piano / by David Crow ; illustrated by Virginia Smith ; general editor J.P. Rutland. — London [etc.] : F. Watts, 1977. — 48p : ill(some col), music, ports(some col) ; 18x23cm.
Bibl.: p.46. — Index.
ISBN 0-85166-596-9 : £1.75
(B77-16000)

786.2'1'09 — Pianos, to 1975
Grover, David S. The piano : its story from zither to grand / [by] David S. Grover. — London : Hale, 1976. — 223p,[32]p of plates : ill, facsim, music, port ; 23cm.
Bibl.: p.211-212. — Index.
ISBN 0-7091-5673-1 : £5.00
(B77-00885)

Harrison, Sidney. Grand piano / [by] Sidney Harrison. — London : Faber, 1976. — 272p,[8] p of plates : ill, music ; 23cm.
Index.
ISBN 0-571-10386-3 : £6.95
(B77-07998)

786.2'1'09042 — Pianos, ca 1926. *Early works*
Nalder, Lawrence M. The modern piano / by Lawrence M. Nalder. — [1st ed. reprinted] ; [with an introduction by Robert Morgan]. — Old Woking (The Gresham Press, Old Woking, Surrey GU22 9LH) : Unwin Brothers Ltd, 1977. — xii,192p : ill, music ; 24cm.
Facsimile reprint of: 1st ed. London : 'Musical opinion', 1927.
ISBN 0-905418-10-7 : £10.00
ISBN 0-905418-11-5 Pbk : £7.00
(B77-29604)

786.2'2'0222 — Museums. *London. Kensington and Chelsea (London Borough). Victoria and Albert Museum. Exhibits: Early keyboard string instruments. Illustrations*
Victoria and Albert Museum. Early keyboard instruments / Victoria and Albert Museum ; [written] by Raymond Russell. — London : H.M.S.O., 1976. — [32]p : chiefly ill ; 18cm. — (Victoria and Albert Museum. Small colour books ; 48)
Originally published: 1959.
ISBN 0-11-290240-5 Pbk : £0.65
(B77-00886)

786.2'21'07402 — England. Thomas, Michael. Private collections: Harpsichords. *Catalogues*
The **keyboard** instruments of Michael Thomas. — [Chesham Bois] ([Rose Cottage, Bois La., Chesham Bois, Bucks.]) : [English Harpsichord Magazine], 1976. — [16]p : ill ; 25cm.
ISBN 0-9505395-0-3 Sd : £0.50
Also classified at 786.2'22'07402
(B77-10885)

786.2'22'07402 — England. Thomas, Michael. Private collections: Clavichords. *Catalogues*
The **keyboard** instruments of Michael Thomas. — [Chesham Bois] ([Rose Cottage, Bois La., Chesham Bois, Bucks.]) : [English Harpsichord Magazine], 1976. — [16]p : ill ; 25cm.
ISBN 0-9505395-0-3 Sd : £0.50
Primary classification 786.2'21'07402
(B77-10885)

786.2'3 — Pianos. Manufacture. *Manuals*
Wolfenden, Samuel. A treatise on the art of pianoforte construction / by Samuel Wolfenden. — Revised ed., [i.e. 1st ed. reprinted]. — Old Woking (The Gresham Press, Old Woking, Surrey) : Unwin Bros Ltd, 1977. — [15],274, [10]p,[4]p of plates : ill, port ; 24cm.
Facsimile reprint of: 1st ed., London : Unwin Bros, 1916. — Index. — Includes supplement first published 1927.
ISBN 0-905418-09-3 Pbk : Unpriced
(B77-33975)

786.3'04'1 — Piano playing. Techniques. *Manuals*
Hofmann, Josef. Piano playing ; with, Piano questions answered / [by] Josef Hofmann. — [New ed. reprinted] ; with a new introduction by Gregor Benko. — New York : Dover Publications [etc.] ; London : Constable [etc.], 1976. — iii-xxi,89,xvi,3-183p,[3]leaves of plates,[6]p of plates : ill, music, ports ; 21cm.
Facsimile reprint of: New ed. Philadelphia : Theodore Presser, 1920. — Index.
ISBN 0-486-23362-6 Pbk : £2.65
(B77-15412)

786.3'04'1 — Songs. Accompaniment: Piano playing. *Manuals*
Foster, Anthony. Sing it, play it! : basic piano accompanying for the adult beginner / by Anthony Foster. — Brighton (55 North St., Brighton [BN1 1RH]) : Downs Music, 1976. — 47p : ill, music ; 21cm.
ISBN 0-9505394-0-6 Sd : £1.50
(B77-03172)

786.3'04'10924 — Piano playing. Teaching. Ashburnham, George. *Autobiographies*
Ashburnham, George. The story of unique piano tuition / by George Ashburnham. — 4th ed. — Sutton (22 Effingham Close, Sutton, Surrey SM2 6AG) : Ashburnham School of Music, 1977. — [1],iii,119p,plate : facsims, music, port ; 22cm.
Previous ed.: 1976.
Unpriced
(B77-25802)

786.4'1 — Piano sonatas. *Critical studies*
Hopkins, Antony. Talking about music : symphonies, concertos and sonatas / [by] Antony Hopkins ; illustrated by John Barkwith. — London [etc.] : Pan Books, 1977. — [13], 462p : ill, music ; 20cm.
Index. — Contents: Talking about symphonies. Originally published: London : Heinemann Educational, 1961 - Talking about concertos. Originally published: London : Heinemann Educational, 1964 - Talking about sonatas. London : Heinemann Educational, 1971.
ISBN 0-330-24824-3 Pbk : £1.50
Primary classification 785
(B77-27282)

786.6'22'4 — German organ music. Bach, Johann Sebastian. *Critical studies*
Sitwell, *Sir* Sacheverell, *bart.* Fugue : a study of J.S. Bach's organ preludes and fugues / [by] Sacheverell Sitwell. — [Daventry] (['Pennywick', Badby, Daventry, Northants.]) : [The author], [1976]. — [1],28p ; 22cm.
ISBN 0-903591-29-4 Sd : Unpriced
(B77-10886)

786.6'241 — Musical instruments: British pipe organs. Preservation. *Great Britain. Periodicals*
British Institute of Organ Studies. BIOS reporter. — Mansfield (c/o Hon. Secretary, 1 Oak Bank Close, Mansfield, Notts. NG19 7BW) : British Institute of Organ Studies. Vol.1, no.1- ; (Jan. 1977)-. — 1977-. — 21cm.
Quarterly. — 10p. in 1st issue.
Sd : Free to members
ISSN 0309-8052
(B77-29605)

786.6'241 — Musical instruments: British pipe organs, to ca 1960
Clutton, Cecil. The British organ / [by] Cecil Clutton and Austin Niland. — Wakefield : EP Publishing, 1976. — 320p : ill ; 23cm.
Originally published: London : Batsford, 1963. — Bibl.: p.305. — Index.
ISBN 0-7158-1159-2 : £8.00
(B77-26446)

786.6'2421'32 — Chapels of ease. *London. Westminster (London Borough). St Peter's Church, Vere Street, London. Musical instruments: Pipe organs, to 1976*
All Souls Church, *Langham Place, London.* The organs of All Souls Church, Langham Place, London and St Peter's Church, Vere Street, London / by Colin Goulden. — London ([All Souls Vestry, 2 All Souls Place, W1N 3DB]) : All Souls Church, 1976. — [4],15p : ill ; 21x18cm.
Sd : £0.40
Primary classification 786.6'2421'32
(B77-03173)

786.6'2421'32 — Parish churches. *London. Westminster (London Borough). All Souls Church, Langham Place, London. Musical instruments: Pipe organs, to 1976*
All Souls Church, *Langham Place, London.* The organs of All Souls Church, Langham Place, London and St Peter's Church, Vere Street, London / by Colin Goulden. — London ([All Souls Vestry, 2 All Souls Place, W1N 3DB]) : All Souls Church, 1976. — [4],15p : ill ; 21x18cm.
Sd : £0.40
Also classified at 786.6'2421'32
(B77-03173)

786.6'2423'12 — Parish churches. *Wiltshire. Chippenham. St Andrew's Parish Church, Chippenham. Musical instruments: Pipe organs, to 1975*
Kent, Christopher, *b.1949.* The organ of St Andrew's Parish Church, Chippenham : a historical monograph / by Christopher Kent. — [West Harrow] ([c/o The author, Drury Rd, West Harrow, Middx HA1 4B2]) : The Vicar and Churchwardens, 1976. — 30p : ill, facsim ; 19cm.
ISBN 0-9505581-0-9 Sd : £0.40
(B77-09867)

786.7 — Churches. Pipe organ playing. *Amateurs' manuals*
Cooper, Janette. The reluctant organist / by Janette Cooper. — Croydon (Addington Palace, Croydon CR9 5AD) : Royal School of Church Music, 1976. — 31p : music ; 22cm. — (Royal School of Church Music. Handbooks ; 1)
List of music: p.31.
ISBN 0-85402-066-7 Sd : £0.50
(B77-24396)

786.7 — Electronic organ playing. *Amateurs' manuals*
Ashburnham, George. The pocket organ tutor / by George Ashburnham. — Sutton (22 Effingham Close, Sutton, Surrey SM2 6AG) : Ashburnham School of Music, [1977]. — [1], 129p : ill, music ; 22cm.
Index.
£8.95
(B77-31361)

786.9'7 — Two row chromatic button accordion playing. *Manuals*
McDowell, John, *b.1943.* Button keyed accordeon / by John McDowell. — [Gosport] ([25 Broadsands Drive, Gosport, Hants. PO12 2SB]) : Metrorange Publications, [1977]. — [3], 26p : music ; 21cm.
Sd : £0.20
(B77-27283)

786.9'7'0924 — Accordion playing. Shand, Jimmy. *Biographies*
Phillips, David, *b.1914.* Jimmy Shand / by David Phillips. — Dundee (15 Shore Terrace, Dundee) : D. Winter and Son Ltd, 1976. — 166p,[32]p of plates : ill, ports ; 22cm.
List of sound discs: p.132-143.
ISBN 0-902804-05-7 : £3.50
(B77-07530)

787 — MUSIC. STRING INSTRUMENTS

787'.1 — Violins. *Juvenile literature*
Robinson, Marjorie. The violin and viola / by Marjorie Robinson ; illustrated by Virginia Smith ; general editor J.P. Rutland. — London [etc.] : F. Watts, 1976. — 48p : ill(some col), col map, music, ports ; 18x22cm.
Bibl.: p.46. — Index.
ISBN 0-85166-595-0 : £1.75
Also classified at 787'.2
(B77-00349)

787'.10714 — Violin music. Baroque style. Performance. Interpretation
Donington, Robert. String playing in baroque music / [by] Robert Donington ; with recorded illustrations by Yehudi Menuhin, George Malcolm, Robert Donington. — London : Faber, 1977. — 126p : music ; 26cm & sound disc(2s.;12 in. 33 1/3 rpm).
Bibl.: p.121. — Index.
ISBN 0-571-10014-7 : £8.80
(B77-21349)

787'.1'0924 — Violin playing. Menuhin, Yehudi. *Autobiographies*
Menuhin, Yehudi. Unfinished journey / [by] Yehudi Menuhin. — London : Macdonald and Jane's, 1977. — xvii,393p,[48]p of plates : music, ports ; 24cm.
Index.
ISBN 0-354-04146-0 : £5.95
(B77-15413)

787'.12 — Violins. Manufacture. Techniques. *Early works. Facsimiles*
Heron-Allen, Edward. Violin-making as it was and is : being a historical, theoretical and practical treatise on the science and art of violin-making for the use of violin makers and players, amateur and professional / by Ed Heron-Allen ; with upwards of 200 illustrations by the author ; preceded by an essay on the violin and its position as a musical instrument. — 2nd ed. — London : Ward Lock, 1977. — xxii,366p,[6]leaves of plates(3 fold) : ill, port ; 23cm.
Facsimile reprint of: 2nd ed., 1885. — Bibl.: p.329-343. — Index.
£7.50
ISBN 0-7063-1045-4
(B77-27284)

787'.2 — Violas. *Juvenile literature*
Robinson, Marjorie. The violin and viola / by Marjorie Robinson ; illustrated by Virginia Smith ; general editor J.P. Rutland. — London [etc.] : F. Watts, 1976. — 48p : ill(some col), col map, music, ports ; 18x22cm.
Bibl.: p.46. — Index.
ISBN 0-85166-595-0 : £1.75
Primary classification 787'.1
(B77-00349)

787'.6 — Martin fretted string instruments, to 1973
Longworth, Mike. Martin guitars : a history / by Mike Longworth. — London [etc.] : Omnibus Press ; London (78 Newman St., W1P 3LA) : Distributed by Music Sales Ltd, [1976]. — [10], 118,[48]p : ill, facsims, ports ; 26cm.
Originally published: Cedar Knolls, N.J. : Colonial Press, 1975.
ISBN 0-86001-231-x Pbk : £2.95
(B77-05571)

787'.61 — Fender electric guitars, to 1976
Achard, Ken. The Fender guitar / [by] Ken Achard. — London (20 Denmark St., WC2H 8NE) : Musical New Services Ltd, 1977. — iv, 68p : ill, port ; 26cm.
'A "Guitar" magazine project'.
Pbk : £2.95
(B77-29606)

787'.61 — Gibson electric guitars, to 1976
Bishop, Ian Courtney. The Gibson guitar from 1950 / [by] Ian Courtney Bishop. — London (20 Denmark St., WC2H 8NE) : Musical New Services Ltd, 1977. — iv,95p : ill, ports ; 26cm.
'A "Guitar" magazine project'.
Pbk : £2.95
(B77-29607)

787'.61'0712 — Guitar playing. Folk techniques. *Manuals*
Pearse, John. Hold down a chord : folk guitar for beginners / [by] John Pearse. — London : British Broadcasting Corporation, 1977. — 32, [1]p : ill ; 28cm.
'... written to accompany ten BBC television broadcasts ... originally televised in 1967'. — Originally published: 1967.
ISBN 0-563-07132-x Sd : £0.75
(B77-33372)

787'.61'0924 — British rock music. Guitar playing. Clapton, Eric. *Transcripts of interviews*
Turner, Steve. Conversations with Eric Clapton / [by] Steve Turner. — London : Abacus, 1976. — 116p,[24]p of plates : ports ; 20cm.
List of sound discs: p.112-116.
ISBN 0-349-13402-2 Pbk : £1.25
(B77-07999)

787'.61'0924 — Guitar playing. Segovia, Andrés, to 1920. *Autobiographies*
Segovia, Andrés. Andrés Segovia : an autobiography of the years 1893-1920 / translated [from the Spanish MS.] by W.F. O'Brien. — London : Boyars : Distributed by Calder and Boyars, 1977. — xi,207p : ill, ports ; 23cm.
Spine title: Segovia : an autobiography 1893-1920. — This translation originally published: New York : Macmillan, 1976. — Index.
ISBN 0-7145-2635-5 : £6.95
(B77-30513)

787'.61'0924 — Spanish guitar music. Sor, Fernando. *Biographies*
Jeffery, Brian. Fernando Sor : composer and guitarist / [by] Brian Jeffery. — London : Preachers' Court, Charterhouse, EC1M 6AS : Tecla Editions, 1977. — 3-197p : ill, facsims, geneal table, music, ports ; 29cm.
Includes facsimile reprint of the article 'Sor' from 'Encyclopédie pittoresque de la musique' of A. Ledhuy and H. Bertini. Paris, 1835. — List of music: p.146-185. — Index.
ISBN 0-9502241-4-6 : £7.75
ISBN 0-9502241-5-4 Pbk : £5.60
(B77-21350)

787'.61'2 — Guitars. Acoustics
Strassenburg, Arnold Adolph. The guitar : a module on wave motion and sound / [by] A.A. Strassenburg, Bill G. Aldridge, Gary S. Waldman. — New York [etc.] ; London : McGraw-Hill, [1976]. — [4],81p : ill ; 28cm. — (Physics of technology)
Published in the United States: 1975.
ISBN 0-07-001716-6 Sd : £2.30
(B77-10494)

787'.61'52 — Spanish guitar music. *Collections. Facsimiles*
Guerau, Francisco. Poema harmónico / [por] Francisco Guerau. — Complete facsimile ed. / with an introduction and English translation by Brian Jeffery. — London (Preachers' Court, Charterhouse, EC1M 6AS) : Tecla Editions, 1977. — 3-87p : chiefly music ; 22x28cm.
Facsimile reprint of: 1st ed. Madrid : En la Imprenta de Manuel Ruiz de Murga, 1694.
ISBN 0-8494-0045-7 Pbk : Unpriced
(B77-30514)

787'.9 — Japanese koto music: Tegotomono
Wade, Bonnie C. Tegotomono : music for the Japanese koto / [by] Bonnie C. Wade. — Westport, Conn. ; London : Greenwood Press, 17976. — xxv,379,[1]p : ill, map, music ; 26cm. — (Contributions in intercultural and comparative studies ; no.2)
Bibl.: p.359-363. — List of sound discs : p.364. — Index.
ISBN 0-8371-8908-x : £15.95
(B77-18311)

788 — MUSIC. WIND INSTRUMENTS
788'.01'09 — Musical instruments: Brass instruments, to 1975
Baines, Anthony. Brass instruments : their history and development / [by] Anthony Baines. — London : Faber, 1976. — 3-298p,xvi p of plates : ill, music, ports ; 23cm.
Bibl.: p.267-278. — Index.
ISBN 0-571-10600-5 : £12.50
(B77-00350)

788'.41'0924 — French horn playing. Brain, Dennis. *Biographies*
Pettitt, Stephen. Dennis Brain : a biography / by Stephen Pettitt ; with an appreciation by Benjamin Britten. — London : Hale, 1976. — 192p,[8]p of plates : ill, music, ports ; 23cm.
List of sound discs: p.175-184. — Index.
ISBN 0-7091-5772-x : £5.00
(B77-01707)

788'.51'0712 — Flute playing. *Manuals. Early works*
Quantz, Johann Joachim. [Versuch einer Anweisung die Flöte traversiere zu spielen. English]. On playing the flute / [by] Johann Joachim Quantz ; a complete translation [from the German] with an introduction and notes by Edward R. Reilly. — London : Faber, 1976. — xxxix,368p : ill, facsim, music ; 24cm.
This translation originally published: 1966. — 'Versuch einer Anweisung die Flöte traversiere zu spielen' originally published : Berlin : Voss, 1752. — Bibl.: p.345-353. — Index.
ISBN 0-571-06698-4 : £8.50
ISBN 0-571-11033-9 Pbk : £4.95
(B77-09176)

788'.51'0712 — Flute playing. Avant garde techniques. *Manuals*
Dick, Robert, *b.1950.* The other flute : a performance manual of contemporary techniques / [by] Robert Dick. — London [etc.] : Oxford University Press, Music Department, 1975. — v,154p : ill, music ; 28cm.
Folder ([5]p. : of music) and sound disc (2s. ; 7in. 33 1/3 rpm.) in pocket.
ISBN 0-19-322125-x Sp : £6.75
(B77-10887)

788'.53'0712 — Recorder playing. *Manuals. Secondary school texts*
Dolmetsch, Carl. Advanced recorder technique / [by] Carl Dolmetsch. — Revised ed. — Leeds : E.J. Arnold, 1977. — 51p : ill, music, port ; 25cm.
Previous ed.: published as 'The school recorder book. 3'. E.J. Arnold, 1974.
ISBN 0-560-02040-6 Sd : £1.00
(B77-32079)

788'.53'09 — Recorders & recorder music, to 1976
Hunt, Edgar. The recorder and its music / [by] Edgar Hunt. — Revised and enlarged ed. — London (48 Great Marlborough St., W1V 2BN) : Eulenberg Books, 1977. — xvi,184p,[16] p of plates : ill, music, ports ; 23cm.
Previous ed.: London : Jenkins, 1962. — Bibl.: p.168-177. — Index.
ISBN 0-903873-31-1 : £4.50
ISBN 0-903873-05-2 Pbk : £3.00
(B77-29608)

788'.6'06241 — Clarinet & saxophone playing. Organisations. *Great Britain. Clarinet and Saxophone Society of Great Britain. Periodicals*
Clarinet and Saxophone Society of Great Britain. CASS News. — Norwich (c/o A. Milne, 100 Long John Hill, Norwich) : [C.A.S.S.].
Issue no.1- ; [1976]-. — [1976]-. — 30cm.
Published at irregular intervals. — 5 leaves in 1st issue.
Sd : Unpriced
ISSN 0308-9053
(B77-01708)

788'.66'0924 — Jazz. Performance. Saxophone playing. Coltrane, John. *Biographies*
Cole, Bill. John Coltrane / by Bill Cole. — New York : Schirmer Books ; London : Collier Macmillan, 1976. — viii,264p : ill, music, ports ; 24cm.
Bibl.: p.241-250. — Index.
ISBN 0-02-870660-9 : £9.00
(B77-18934)

788'.7'0712 — Oboe playing
Goossens, Léon. Oboe / [by] Léon Goossens and Edwin Roxburgh. — London : Macdonald and Jane's, 1977. — xv,236p,16p of plates : ill, facsim, music, port ; 22cm. — (Yehudi Menuhin music guides)
Bibl.: p.216-219. — List of sound discs: p.221-229. — Index.
ISBN 0-356-08416-7 : £5.95
ISBN 0-356-08417-5 Pbk : £3.25
Primary classification 788'.7'09
(B77-20485)

788'.7'0712 — Oboe playing. *Manuals*
Rothwell, Evelyn. The oboist's companion / [by] Evelyn Rothwell. — [Oxford] : Oxford University Press.
In 3 vols.
Vol.3. — 1977. — iv,60p : ill ; 31cm.
Index.
ISBN 0-19-322337-6 Pbk : Unpriced
(B77-25803)

788'.7'09 — Oboes & oboe music, to 1976
Goossens, Léon. Oboe / [by] Léon Goossens and Edwin Roxburgh. — London : Macdonald and Jane's, 1977. — xv,236p,16p of plates : ill, facsim, music, port ; 22cm. — (Yehudi Menuhin music guides)
Bibl.: p.216-219. — List of sound discs: p.221-229. — Index.
ISBN 0-356-08416-7 : £5.95
ISBN 0-356-08417-5 Pbk : £3.25
Also classified at 788'.7'0712
(B77-20485)

788'.9 — Scottish Highland bagpipes, to 1900. *Early works*
Manson, W L. The Highland bagpipe : its history, literature and music, with some account of the traditions, superstitions and anecdotes relating to the instrument and its tunes / by W.L. Manson. — Wakefield : EP Publishing, 1977. — xv,9-420p,[8] leaves of plates : ill, ports ; 19cm.
Facsimile reprint of: 1st ed. Paisley : A. Gardner, 1901. — Bibl.: p.383-387. — Index.
ISBN 0-7158-1213-0 : £6.50
(B77-16535)

789.01 — MUSIC. PERCUSSION INSTRUMENTS
789'.01'0924 — Percussion instrument playing. Blades, James. *Autobiographies*
Blades, James. Drum roll : a professional adventure from the circus to the concert hall / [by] James Blades. — London : Faber, 1977. — xvi,275p,[16]p of plates : ill, facsim, music, ports ; 23cm.
Index.
ISBN 0-571-10107-0 : £6.50 : CIP rev.
(B77-07531)

789'.5 — Bells. *Juvenile literature*
Law, Felicia. Bells / written by Felicia Law ; illustrated by Michael Brownlow. — London [etc.] : Collins, 1977. — 32p : col ill, music ; 22cm. — (Dandelions)
ISBN 0-00-651261-5 Sd : £0.50
(B77-32080)

789'.5 — Bells. Partial tones. *Early works*
Simpson, Arthur Barwick. Why bells sound out of tune / [by] A.B. Simpson. — Oxford ([36 Great Clarendon St., Oxford]) : J. Hannon and Co., [1976]. — [1],25p : 1 ill ; 20cm.
Originally published: as 'Why bells sound out of tune and how to cure them'. London : Skeffington, 1897.
ISBN 0-904233-06-5 : £2.25
(B77-06219)

789'.5'0941 — Churches. Bells. *Great Britain. Lists*
Dove, Ronald Hammerton. A bellringer's guide to the church bells of Britain and ringing peals of the world / compiled by Ronald H. Dove. — 5th ed. — Aldershot (28 Ayling La., Aldershot, [Hants. GU11 3LZ]) : Viggers, 1976. — ii-viii,198p ; 19cm.
Spine title: Church bells of Britain. — Previous ed.: 1968.
ISBN 0-9505557-0-3 : £2.25
(B77-08000)

789'.5'0942 — Churches. Bells. *England*
Walters, Henry Beauchamp. Church bells of England / by H.B. Walters ; illustrated by 170 photographs and drawings. — Wakefield : EP Publishing, 1977. — xx,400p,plate : ill, coat of arms, facsim ; 22cm.
Facsimile reprint of: 1st ed. London : Henry Frowde, 1912. — Bibl.: p.ix-xx. — Index.
ISBN 0-7158-1225-4 : £10.50 : CIP rev.
(B77-12593)

789'.5'0942446 — Cathedrals. *Hereford and Worcester. Hereford. Hereford Cathedral. Bells*
Eisel, John C. The bells of Hereford Cathedral / by John C. Eisel. — [Hereford] ([The Cathedral, Hereford HR1 2NG]) : Friends of Hereford Cathedral Publications Committee, 1977. — 20p : ill, facsims ; 22cm. — (Hereford Cathedral. Publications)
Sd : £0.30
(B77-28785)

789'.5'0942544 — Parish churches. *Leicestershire. Kings Norton. St John the Baptist, Kings Norton. Bells. Restoration*
St John the Baptist, *Kings Norton.* Bell restoration fund / St John the Baptist, Kings Norton, Leicester. — [Kings Norton] ([Kings Norton, Leics.]) : [St John the Baptist], [1977]. — [1],24p : ill, ports ; 24cm.
ISBN 0-9505633-0-7 Sd : £0.25
(B77-12023)

789.7 — MUSIC. MECHANICAL INSTRUMENTS
789.7'09 — Mechanical musical instruments, to 1974
Crowley, Terence Eldon. Discovering mechanical music / [by] T.E. Crowley. — [2nd ed.]. — Aylesbury : Shire Publications, 1977. — 48p : ill, facsims ; 18cm. — (Discovering series ; 200)

Previous ed.: 1975. — Bibl.: p.45-46. — Index.
ISBN 0-85263-371-8 Pbk : £0.50
(B77-32782)

789.8 — MUSICAL BOXES
789.8'06'241 — Musical boxes. Collecting. Organisations: Musical Box Society of Great Britain. *Directories*
Musical Box Society of Great Britain. Directory of members / the Musical Box Society of Great Britain. — Edenbridge (Bylands, Crockham Hill, Edenbridge, Kent) : The Society.
[1976]. — 1976. — 32p : ill ; 30cm.
ISBN 0-9505657-0-9 Sd : £1.15
(B77-14334)

789.9 — ELECTRONIC MUSICAL INSTRUMENTS, MUSIC RECORDING
789.9 — Aleatoric electronic music. Projects
Orton, Richard. Electronic sound / prepared for the [Open University, Art and Environment] Course Team by Richard Orton. — Milton Keynes : Open University Press, 1976. — 22,[1] p : ill, form ; 30cm. — ([Technology/arts/social sciences], a second level interdisciplinary course : art and environment ; unit 11) (TAD 292 ; unit 11)
Bibl.: p.20. — List of sound discs: p.20.
ISBN 0-335-06210-5 Sd : Unpriced
(B77-14861)

789.9 — Electronic music. Technical aspects
Sear, Walter. A guide to electronic music and synthesizers / by Walter Sear. — London (78 Newman St., W1P 3LA) : Omnibus Press, [1977]. — 90p : ill ; 23cm.
Originally published: as 'The new world of electronic music'. New York : Alfred Publishing Co., 1972.
ISBN 0-86001-210-7 Pbk : Unpriced
(B77-11351)

789.9 — Electronic music, to 1976
Ernst, David. The evolution of electronic music / [by] David Ernst. — New York : Schirmer ; London : Collier Macmillan, 1977. — xl,274p : ill, music ; 24cm.
Bibl.: p.249-256. — Lists of sound discs. — List of music: p.256-8. — Index.
ISBN 0-02-870880-6 Pbk : £6.75
(B77-27285)

789.9 — Electronic musical instruments. Technical aspects
Towers, Thomas Dundas. Master electronics in music / [by] T.D. Towers. — Sevenoaks : Newnes Technical Books [etc.], 1976. — [7], 120p : ill(chiefly col) ; 22cm.
Index.
ISBN 0-408-00262-x Pbk : £2.50
(B77-04986)

789.9 — Music. Use of electronic equipment
Jenkins, John, *b.1936.* Electric music : a practical manual / [by] John Jenkins and Jon Smith. — Bloomington ; London : Indiana University Press, 1976 [i.e. 1977]. — [8],168p : ill ; 22cm.
Originally published: Newton Abbot : David and Charles, 1975. — Index.
ISBN 0-253-31944-7 : £6.75
ISBN 0-253-20195-0 Pbk : £2.25
(B77-10888)

789.9'12 — Music. Disc records available in Great Britain. *Consumers' guides*
'**Records** and recording' classical guide. — Tunbridge Wells : Midas Books.
77 / edited by Ateş Orga. — 1977. — [7], 360p ; 21cm.
Index.
ISBN 0-85936-086-5 Pbk : £2.95
ISSN 0309-8508
(B77-33976)

789.9'136'210924 — Opera. Singing. Callas, Maria. Recordings. *Critical studies*
Ardoin, John. The Callas legacy / [by] John Ardoin. — London : Duckworth, 1977. — xiii, 224p,plate : port ; 23cm.
Bibl.: p.212-213. — Index.
ISBN 0-7156-0975-0 : £5.95
(B77-10495)

790 — RECREATIONS
790 — Games. *Manuals. Juvenile literature*
Weiss, Harvey. Games & puzzles you can make yourself / [by] Harvey Weiss. — London : Hamilton, 1977. — [5],56p : ill(chiefly col) ; 24cm.
Originally published: New York : Crowell, 1976.
ISBN 0-241-89619-3 : £2.95
Also classified at 688.7
(B77-25119)

790 — Recreations. Projects. *For recreation leadership*
Vannier, Maryhelen. Recreation leadership / [by] Maryhelen Vannier. — 3rd ed. — Philadelphia : Lea and Febiger ; London : Kimpton, 1977. — ix,387p : ill, forms ; 25cm.
Previous ed.: published as 'Methods and materials in recreation leadership'. Belmont, Calif. : Wadsworth Publishing Co., 1966. — Bibl. — Index.
ISBN 0-8121-0548-6 : £9.35
(B77-19566)

790'.025'41 — Vacation facilities for families. *Great Britain. Directories*
Britain, children on holiday / [British Tourist Authority]. — London : B.T.A.
[1977]. — 1977. — [2],64p : map ; 22cm. — (British Tourist Authority. Information sheets ; no.341/77/14)
English text, French, German, Spanish, Dutch, Italian and English introduction.
ISBN 0-85630-383-6 Sd : £0.30
(B77-33373)

790'.025'42 — Vacation activities. *England. Directories*
Special interest & hobby holidays in England / English Tourist Board. — [London] : The Board.
'77 / [edited by Denise Carter]. — [1977]. — [2],31,[1]p : ill ; 21cm.
Index.
ISBN 0-903265-66-4 Sd : £0.30
(B77-09177)

790'.025'42 — Vacation activities. *England. Directories. For families*
Titchmarsh, Peter. The family guide to where to go : over 800 places of interest for family fun / [compiled by Peter and Helen Titchmarsh]. — [New ed.]. — [Norwich] : [Jarrold and Sons], [1977]. — 125p : ill, maps ; 21cm. — (The Jarrold 'White Horse' series)
Cover title. — Previous ed.: 1972. — Index.
ISBN 0-85306-709-0 Pbk : £0.99
(B77-15414)

790'.025'42498 — Leisure facilities. *West Midlands (Metropolitan County). Coventry. Directories*
City of Coventry leisure handbook. — Carshalton : Home Publishing Co., [1977]. — 40,[1]p : ill ; 21cm.
Sd : Unpriced
(B77-25120)

790'.025'42574 — Leisure facilities & recreation facilities. *Oxfordshire. Oxford. Directories*
Oxford recreation and leisure handbook : a booklet for citizens and visitors. — London : Burrow, 1977. — 20,[2]p(2 fold) : ill, map ; 19cm.
Cover title: Recreation for you.
Sd : Unpriced
(B77-32081)

790'.0941 — Great Britain. Elizabeth II, Queen of Great Britain. Silver jubilee celebrations, 1977. *Calendars*
Britain, 1952-1977 : the Queen's Silver Jubilee celebrations, 1977. — 2nd ed. — London : British Tourist Authority : London Tourist Board, 1977. — [2],72p : map ; 21cm.
Previous ed.: 1977.
Sd : Unpriced
(B77-32082)

Britain, 1952-1977 : the Queen's Silver Jubilee celebrations, 1977. — London : British Tourist Authority : London Tourist Board, 1977. — , 32p : map ; 21cm.
Sd : Unpriced
(B77-05572)

790'.09411 — Public events. *Scotland. Calendars*
Events in Scotland / Scottish Tourist Board. — Edinburgh : The Board. — (Scottish Tourist Board. Information booklets)
January-December 1977. — [1976]. — 32p : 1 ill ; 21x10cm.
Sd : Unpriced
(B77-23623)

790'.0942 — Public events. *England. Calendars*
Events in England / English Tourist Board. — [London] : [The Board].
1977. — [1977]. — 141p : ill ; 21cm.
Cover title.
ISBN 0-903265-70-2 Pbk : Free
(B77-09178)

May 1977-April 1978. — [1977]. — 204p : ill ; 21cm.
Cover title.
Pbk : Unpriced
(B77-20486)

790'.09421 — Public events. *London. Calendars. Periodicals*
London week / British Tourist Authority. — [London] : B.T.A.
[No.1]- ; 1976-. — [1976]-. — ill ; 21cm.
Weekly. — 8p. in 29 Oct.-5 Nov. 1976 issue.
Sd : Unpriced
ISSN 0308-9150
(B77-03174)

790'.09426'57 — Leisure facilities & recreation facilities. *Cambridgeshire. South Cambridgeshire (District). Reports, surveys. For structure plan making*
South Cambridgeshire *(District). Planning Department.* Recreation / South Cambridgeshire District Council [Planning Department]. — Cambridge (South Cambridgeshire Hall, Hills Rd, Cambridge CB2 1PB) : [The Department], 1976. — [4],68p,7 leaves of plates : map, plans ; 30cm.
Sd : £0.25
(B77-04987)

790'.0973 — Community recreation facilities. *United States*
Butler, George Daniel. Introduction to community recreation / prepared for the National Recreation and Park Association ; [by] George D. Butler. — 5th ed. — New York ; London [etc.] : McGraw-Hill, 1976. — xiv, 538p : ill ; 24cm.
Previous ed.: New York : McGraw-Hill, 1967. — Bibl.: p.515-526. — Index.
ISBN 0-07-009361-x : £10.75
(B77-06220)

790.1 — Activities. Projects
Nicholson, Simon. Interactive art and play / prepared for the [Open University Art and Environment] Course Team by Simon Nicholson. — Milton Keynes : Open University Press, 1976. — 64p,[12]p of plates : ill(some col), facsim, form, map ; 30cm. — ([Technology/arts/social sciences], a second level interdisciplinary course : art and environment ; unit 10) (TAD292 ; unit 10)
ISBN 0-335-06209-1 Pbk : £1.20
(B77-04988)

790.1 — Leisure activities. *Manuals. Juvenile literature*
Free time news / [edited] by Eva Wilson. — London : Fontana, 1977. — [2],92p : ill ; 19cm. — (Lions original)
Index.
ISBN 0-00-671204-5 Pbk : £0.50
(B77-28006)

790.1 — Seaside activities. *Colouring books*
At the seaside. — Maidenhead : Purnell, 1977. — [48]p : ill ; 28cm. — (Colour and learn)
Fill-in book.
Pbk : £0.15
(B77-09179)

790.13 — Games for one person. *Manuals. Juvenile literature*
Pick, John Barclay. 100 more games for one player / [by] J.B. Pick ; illustrated by Anna Barnard. — [London] : Armada, 1976. — 3-121p : ill ; 20cm.
Selection, with revisions, of games from: '180 games for one player'. London : Phoenix House, 1954.
ISBN 0-00-690956-6 Pbk : £0.40
(B77-04351)

790.13'2'05 — Collecting. *Periodicals*
Collecting today : (incorporating Amateur collector). — Trowbridge : R.J. Culverhouse ; London (10 North Tenter St., E.1) : Distributed by Concorde Distribution.
Vol.1, no.1- ; Mar. 1977-. — 1977-. — ill, facsims, ports ; 30cm.
Monthly. — 36p. in 1st issue.
Sd : £0.25
ISSN 0309-7277
(B77-22761)

790.13'2'05 — Collecting. *Serials*
Collectors year book. — Burton upon Trent (458C Stanton Rd, Burton upon Trent) : MAB Publishing.
'77 / compiled by Gordon Litherland and Ian Waterfield. — [1977]. — 200p : ill, coats of arms, facsims, maps, ports ; 21cm.
ISBN 0-905447-02-6 Pbk : £2.50
(B77-09869)

790.13'2'08 — Collecting. *Essays*
Hillier, Bevis. The new antiques / [by] Bevis Hillier. — London : Times Books, 1977. — 216p : ill ; 26cm.
ISBN 0-7230-0152-9 : £5.95
(B77-33977)

790.19'22 — Activities connected with grouping: Activities for pre-school children. *Cut-out books*
Grender, Iris. Sorting & matching / by Iris Grender ; designed and illustrated by Geoffrey Butcher. — [Kenley] : Three Four Five, [1976]. — [4],p,12 leaves : chiefly ill(chiefly col) ; 20x22cm. — (Pre-school activity books)
Leaves perforated at inside edge, some divided into sections. — Col. ill. on verso of 3 leaves.
ISBN 0-903016-41-9 Pbk : £0.60
(B77-13180)

790.19'22 — Activities connected with numeration: Activities for pre-school children. *Cut-out books*
Grender, Iris. Counting games / by Iris Grender ; designed and illustrated by Geoffrey Butcher. — [Kenley] : Three Four Five, [1976]. — [4]p,12 leaves : chiefly ill(chiefly col) ; 20x22cm. — (Pre-school activity books)
Leaves perforated at inside edge, some divided into sections. — Col. ill. on verso of 2 leaves.
ISBN 0-903016-42-7 Pbk : £0.60
(B77-13181)

790.19'22 — Activities for children. *Juvenile literature*
Bond, Michael. Fun and games with Paddington / [by] Michael Bond ; pictures by Ivor Wood. — Glasgow [etc.] : Collins, 1977. — 4-61p : ill(chiefly col), col map ; 27cm.
ISBN 0-00-138045-1 : £1.75
(B77-28786)

Brandreth, Gyles. Fun & games for every day of the year / [by] Giles [i.e. Gyles] Brandreth ; illustrated by David Farris. — Leicester : Knight Books, 1976. — 128p : ill ; 18cm.
With answers.
ISBN 0-340-20225-4 Pbk : £0.45
(B77-00887)

Brandreth, Gyles. Knight book of fun and games for a rainy day / [by] Gyles Brandreth ; illustrated by David Farris. — Leicester : Knight Books, 1976. — 126p : ill ; 18cm.
With answers.
ISBN 0-340-19781-1 Pbk : £0.45
(B77-06818)

Chetwood, Doreen. What's in a game? / [by] Doreen Chetwood ; designed and illustrated by John Gough. — Edinburgh : Oliver and Boyd, 1976. — 32p : ill(chiefly col), facsim ; 25cm. — (You at home)
Bibl.: p.32.
ISBN 0-05-003006-x Sd : £0.70
(B77-06819)

Home and away : a holiday book / compiled by Eva Wilson ; with illustrations by Brian Robins. — London : Collins, 1975. — 125p : ill ; 20cm. — (Lions)
ISBN 0-00-670994-x Pbk : £0.35
(B77-04989)

The **Know** How make & do encyclopedia / written and devised by Heather Amery ... [et al.] ; compiled by Christopher Rawson ; designed by John Jamieson ... [et al.] ; illustrated by Colin King ... [et al.]. — London : Usborne, 1976. — 4-157p : col ill ; 29cm.
Bibl.: p.157. — Index.
ISBN 0-86020-035-3 : £2.50
(B77-09870)

Miller, Russell. The Chivers Jelly book of 101 things to do, make & play / [text Russell Miller] ; [editor Yvonne Deutch ; illustrator Robin Arkell]. — [London] : [Marshall Cavendish], [1976]. — [64]p : ill(chiefly col) ; 21cm.
'Some of this material was first published in a Marshall Cavendish special' - colophon.
ISBN 0-85685-173-6 Pbk : Unpriced
(B77-22046)

790.19'22 — Activities for children. *Juvenile literature. Welsh texts*
Williams, Cen. Ffau'r Llewod! : cannoedd o bethau i blant / gan Cen Williams. — Talybont, Ceredigion (Talybont, Ceredigion SY24 5ER) : Y Lolfa, 1977. — 95p : ill ; 19cm. — (Pocedlyfrau'r Lolfa)
With answers.
ISBN 0-904864-43-x Pbk : £0.75
(B77-25804)

790.19'22 — Games for children. *Collections*
Kay, George. The Beaver book of games for indoors and outdoors / [by] George and Cornelia Kay ; illustrated by Robin Anderson. — London [etc.] : Beaver Books, 1977. — 125p : ill ; 20cm.
ISBN 0-600-34033-3 Pbk : £0.55
(B77-13182)

790.19'22 — Seaside activities for children. *Juvenile literature*
Law, Felicia. Beside the seaside / [by] Felicia Law ; illustrated by Annie Bennett. — London : Collins, 1976. — 96p : ill ; 20cm. — (Lions)
ISBN 0-00-671120-0 Pbk : £0.45
(B77-09180)

790.19'22 — Winter activities for children. *Juvenile literature*
Gundrey, Elizabeth. The winter book / [by] Elizabeth Gundrey ; illustrated by Zena Flax and Jim Hodgson. — London : Methuen, 1977. — 128p : ill, charts ; 26cm.
ISBN 0-416-84800-1 : £2.95
(B77-28787)

790.19'22'02542 — Vacation activities for unaccompanied children. *England. Directories*
'**Breakaway**' holidays for unaccompanied children / English Tourist Board. — [London] : The Board.
'77 / [edited by Denise Carter]. — [1977]. — [2],36p : ill, port ; 21cm.
Index.
ISBN 0-903265-67-2 Sd : £0.35
(B77-09181)

790.19'6 — Physical activities for handicapped persons
Vannier, Maryhelen. Physical activities for the handicapped / [by] Maryhelen Vannier. — Englewood Cliffs ; London [etc.] : Prentice-Hall, 1977. — xiv,338p : ill, facsims, forms ; 24cm.
Bibl. — List of films.: p.327. — Index.
ISBN 0-13-665638-2 : £10.85
(B77-12594)

790.2'092'2 — Entertainers. *Annuals*
'**Fab** 208'. — London : IPC Magazines.
1978. — [1977]. — 71p : ill, ports(some col) ; 27cm. — (A Fleetway annual)
Cover title.
ISBN 0-85037-379-4 : £1.35
(B77-32783)

791 — PUBLIC ENTERTAINMENT
791 — Beauty contests: Miss World Contest, to 1975
Short, Don. Miss World : the naked truth / [by] Don Short. — London : Everest, 1976. — 153p,[24]p of plates : ports ; 18cm.
ISBN 0-905018-23-0 Pbk : £0.75
(B77-22762)

791 — Public performances based on Sherlock Holmes stories by Doyle, Sir Arthur Conan, to 1975
Pointer, Michael. The Sherlock Holmes file / [by] Michael Pointer. — Newton Abbot [etc.] : David and Charles, 1976. — 168p : ill, facsims, ports ; 26cm.
List of films: p.160-163. — Index.
ISBN 0-7153-7033-2 : £4.50
(B77-02507)

791'.029'4 — Entertainments. Ustinov, Peter. *Autobiographies*
Ustinov, Peter. Dear me / [by] Peter Ustinov. — London : Heinemann, 1977. — viii,280p,24p of plates : ill, ports ; 25cm.
Index.
ISBN 0-434-81711-2 : £5.90
(B77-27286)

791'.09 — Entertainments, to 1976. *Juvenile literature*
Harvey, Jack, *b.1942.* History of entertainment / [by] Jack Harvey. — London : Macdonald Educational, 1977. — 2-46p : ill(some col), plan, ports(some col) ; 25cm. — (Macdonald new reference library)
Bibl.: p.44. — Index.
ISBN 0-356-05800-x : £1.50
(B77-33374)

791'.092'2 — Comedians associated with Goon Show. *Biographies*
Draper, Alfred. The story of the Goons / [by] Alfred Draper with John Austin and Harry Edgington. — London : Severn House : [Distributed by Hutchinson], 1977. — 191p,[16] p of plates : ill, ports ; 21cm.
Originally published: London : Everest, 1976.
ISBN 0-7278-0248-8 : £3.95
(B77-33978)

791'.092'4 — Comedy. Askey, Arthur. *Autobiographies*
Askey, Arthur. Before your very eyes / [by] Arthur Askey. — Sevenoaks : Coronet, 1977. — 191p,[8]p of plates : ill, facsims, ports ; 18cm.
Originally published: London : Woburn Press, 1975.
ISBN 0-340-21985-8 Pbk : £0.95
(B77-31362)

791'.092'4 — Comedy. Benny, Jack. *Biographies*
Fein, Irving Ashley. Jack Benny : an intimate biography / [by] Irving A. Fein ; introduction by George Burns. — Large print [ed.]. — London : Prior [etc.], 1977. — 2v.(xvii,642p) ; 24cm.
Originally published: in 1 vol. New York : Putnam ; London : W.H. Allen, 1976.
ISBN 0-86043-024-3 : £7.50
(B77-23624)

791'.092'4 — Comedy. Burns, George. *Autobiographies*
Burns, George. Living it up, or, They still love me in Altoona! / by George Burns. — London : W.H. Allen, 1977. — 251p,[16]p of plates : ports ; 23cm.
Originally published: New York : Putnam, 1976.
ISBN 0-491-01828-2 : £4.95
(B77-17017)

791'.092'4 — Comedy. Miller, Max. *Biographies*
East, John Marlborough. Max Miller, the Cheeky Chappie / [by] John M. East. — London : W.H. Allen, 1977. — 196p,[8]p of plates : ports ; 23cm.
List of sound discs: p.186-189. — Index.
ISBN 0-491-02260-3 : £4.95
(B77-25805)

791'.092'4 — Comedy. Sahl, Mort. *Autobiographies*
Sahl, Mort. Heartland / [by] Mort Sahl. — New York ; London : Harcourt Brace Jovanovich, [1977]. — [4],158p ; 22cm.
Published in the United States: 1976.
ISBN 0-15-139820-8 : £4.60
(B77-10496)

791'.092'4 — Comedy. Yarwood, Mike. *Autobiographies*
Yarwood, Mike. And this is me! / [by] Mike Yarwood. — London : Star Books, 1975. — 126p,[8]p of plates : ports ; 18cm.
Originally published: London : Jupiter Books, 1974.
ISBN 0-352-39830-2 Pbk : £0.50
(B77-10889)

791'.092'4 — Entertainments. Milton, Billy. *Autobiographies*
Milton, Billy. Milton's paradise mislaid. — London : Jupiter Books, 1976. — ix,218p : ill, facsims, ports ; 24cm.
Index.
ISBN 0-904041-67-0 : £3.75
(B77-17679)

791'.092'4 — Entertainments. Murray, Pete. *Great Britain. Autobiographies*
Murray, Pete. One day I'll forget my trousers / [by] Pete Murray. — London : Everest, 1976. — [6],289p,[16]p of plates : ill, ports ; 18cm.
Joint author: Jeremy Hornsby. — Originally published: 1975.
ISBN 0-905018-18-4 Pbk : £0.75
(B77-23625)

791'.0946 — Entertainments. *Spain. Secondary school texts*
Escribano, J G. Entertainment in Spain / by J.G. Escribano and S. Escribano. — London : Harrap, 1977. — 32p : ill, facsims, map ; 14x22cm. — (Discovering Spain)
ISBN 0-245-52817-2 Sd : £0.65
(B77-18312)

791.1 — PUBLIC ENTERTAINMENT. TRAVELLING SHOWS
791.1 — Entertainments: Fairs. *Norfolk. Barsham. Barsham Faire. Organisation*
Build another Barsham : a guide to Faire making. — [Beccles] ([c/o Colour Artisans, Beccles, Suffolk]) : Sandra Bell, 1976. — [28]p : ill, facsims, map, plan ; 30cm.
Pbk : Unpriced
(B77-17680)

791.1 — Fairground equipment, to 1975
Braithwaite, David. Fairground architecture / by David Braithwaite. — 2nd ed. revised. — London (9 Fitzroy Sq., W1P 5AH) : Hugh Evelyn, 1976. — 195[i.e. 199]p : ill(some col), facsims, map, plans ; 25cm. — (Excursions into architecture)
Previous ed.: i.e. 1st ed. 1968. — Bibl.: p.183-184. — Index.
ISBN 0-238-78997-7 : £8.50
(B77-00351)

791.1'2'0973 — Minstrel shows. *United States, 1800-1900*
Toll, Robert C. Blacking up : the minstrel show in nineteenth century America / [by] Robert C. Toll. — London [etc.] : Oxford University Press, 1977. — x,310p : ill, facsims, ports ; 21cm. — (A galaxy book)
Originally published: New York : Oxford University Press, 1974. — Bibl.: p.285-302. — Index.
ISBN 0-19-502172-x Pbk : £2.75
(B77-19567)

791.3 — CIRCUSES
791.3'09 — Circuses, to 1976
Bentley, Nicolas. The history of the circus / [by] Nicolas Bentley. — London : Joseph, 1977. — 48p : ill(some col), facsims(chiefly col), ports(some col) ; 19cm. — (Folio miniatures)
Ill. on lining papers.
ISBN 0-7181-1589-9 : £1.95
(B77-29609)

791.3'092'4 — Circuses. Chipperfield, Jimmy. *Autobiographies*
Chipperfield, Jimmy. My wild life / [by] Jimmy Chipperfield. — London : Pan Books, 1976. — 256p,[16]p of plates : ill, facsim, ports ; 18cm.
Originally published: London : Macmillan, 1975. — Index.
ISBN 0-330-24819-7 Pbk : £0.75
(B77-00888)

791.3'0941 — Circuses. *Great Britain. Secondary school texts*
Fairs & circuses / [compiled by] John Foster & Rod Hunt. — Basingstoke [etc.] : Macmillan, 1977. — [1],32p : ill, facsim ; 20x21cm. — (Investigations)
Bibl.
ISBN 0-333-16839-9 Sd : £0.55
Primary classification 394'.6'0941
(B77-27798)

791.3'3'0942 — Museums. *Nottinghamshire. Nottingham. Nottingham Castle Museum. Exhibits: Items associated with clowns in England, to 1976*
Rattenbury, Arnold. Clowning : June 11 to September 4 1977 : an exhibition / designed and catalogued for Nottingham Festival 1977 by Arnold Rattenbury. — [Nottingham] ([Nottingham NG1 6EL]) : Nottingham Castle Museum, 1977. — [96]p : ill, facsims, port ; 21cm.
Cover title: The story of English clowning.
Pbk : Unpriced
(B77-25121)

791.43 — CINEMA
Bresson, Robert. Notes on cinematography / [by] Robert Bresson ; translated [from the French] by Jonathan Griffin. — New York : Urizen Books ; London : [Distributed by] Pluto Press, 1977. — [7],72p ; 23cm.
Translation of: 'Notes sur le cinématographe'. Paris : Gallimard, 1975.
ISBN 0-916354-28-8 : £4.00
(B77-32083)

791.43 — Cinema films based on plays of Shakespeare, William
Jorgens, Jack J. Shakespeare on film / [by] Jack J. Jorgens. — Bloomington ; London : Indiana University Press, 1977. — xiii,337p : ill ; 24cm.
Index.
ISBN 0-253-35196-0 : £11.25
(B77-28788)

791.43 — Cinema films produced by Ealing Studios, to 1959
Barr, Charles. Ealing Studios / [by] Charles Barr. — London : Cameron and Tayleur ; Newton Abbot : Distributed by David and Charles, 1977. — 198p : ill ; 26cm.
Index.
ISBN 0-7153-7420-6 : £6.95
(B77-20487)

791.43 — Cinema films: Remakes, to 1974
Druxman, Michael B. Make it again, Sam : a survey of movie remakes / [by] Michael B. Druxman. — South Brunswick ; New York : Barnes ; London : Yoseloff, 1975. — 285p : ill ; 29cm.
List of films: p.215-285.
ISBN 0-498-01470-3 : £6.25
(B77-03703)

791.43 — Oscar winning cinema films, to 1976
Pickard, Roy. The Oscar movies from A-Z / [by] Roy Pickard. — London : Muller, 1977. — [7], 247p,[48]p of plates : ill, ports ; 24cm.
Index.
ISBN 0-584-10288-7 : £6.95 : CIP rev.
(B77-25806)

791.43'01 — Cinema films. Aesthetics. *Essays*
Giannetti, Louis Daniel. Godard and others : essays on film form / [by] Louis D. Giannetti. — Rutherford [etc.] : Fairleigh Dickinson University Press ; London : Tantivy Press, [1976]. — 184p : ill ; 26cm.
Published in the United States: 1975. — Index.
ISBN 0-8386-1291-1 : £4.50
(B77-03704)

791.43'0233 — Motion picture films. Continuity. *Manuals*
Rowlands, Avril. Script continuity and the production secretary in film and TV / [by] Avril Rowlands. — London [etc.] : Focal Press, 1977. — 160p : ill, forms, plan ; 22cm. — (Media manuals)
Bibl.: p.156.
ISBN 0-240-50949-8 Pbk : £2.75
Also classified at 791.45'0233
(B77-28789)

791.43'0233'0922 — American cinema films, 1917-1975. Directors. *Critical studies. Juvenile literature*
Lloyd, Ronald. American film directors : the world as they see it / [by] Ronald Lloyd. — New York ; London : F. Watts, 1976. — 143p : ill ; 24cm.
Index.
ISBN 0-531-01110-0 : £2.95
(B77-16001)

791.43'0233'0922 — American cinema films. Directing. *Personal observations. Collections*
The **men** who made the movies : interviews with Frank Capra, George Cukor, Howard Hawks, Alfred Hitchcock, Vincente Minnelli, King Vidor, Raoul Walsh, and William A. Wellman / by Richard Schickel. — London : Elm Tree Books, 1977. — xi,308p : ill, ports ; 24cm.
'... evolved from a ... television series first shown in the United States ... and since screened in England on BBC2' - jacket. — Originally published: New York : Atheneum, 1975. — Index.
ISBN 0-241-89583-9 : £5.95
(B77-09182)

791.43'0233'0922 — Canadian cinema films. Directors, ca 1968-1974
Hofsess, John. Inner views : ten Canadian film-makers / [by] John Hofsess. — Toronto [etc.] ; London : McGraw-Hill, [1976]. — 171p : ill, ports ; 23cm.
Originally published: Toronto ; New York : McGraw-Hill Ryerson, 1975.
ISBN 0-07-082190-9 : Unpriced
ISBN 0-07-082199-2 Pbk : Unpriced
(B77-05573)

791.43'0233'0924 — American cinema films. Directing. Capra, Frank
Poague, Leland A. The cinema of Frank Capra : an approach to film comedy / [by] Leland A. Poague. — South Brunswick ; New York : Barnes ; London : Tantivy Press, 1975. — 252p : ill, ports ; 29cm.
Bibl.: p.248-250. — List of films: p.235-247. — Index.
ISBN 0-498-01506-8 : £6.50
(B77-32084)

791.43'0233'0924 — American cinema films. Directing. Cukor, George
Clarens, Carlos. George Cukor / [by] Carlos Clarens. — London : Secker and Warburg [for] the British Film Institute, 1976. — 192p : ill, ports ; 20cm. — (Cinema one ; 28)
List of films: p.127-191.
ISBN 0-436-09942-x : £4.90
ISBN 0-436-09943-8 Pbk : £2.90
(B77-01709)

791.43'0233'0924 — British documentary films. Directing. Wilcox, Pamela. *Autobiographies*
Wilcox, Pamela. Between hell and Charing Cross / [by] Pamela Wilcox. — London : Allen and Unwin, 1977. — 3-168p ; 23cm.
ISBN 0-04-920051-8 : £3.50
(B77-30515)

791.43'0233'0924 — Cinema films directed by Fellini, Federico. *Critical studies*
Murray, Edward. Fellini the artist / [by] Edward Murray. — Bembridge (Hapgood House, Station Rd, Bembridge, Isle of Wight) : BCW Publishing Limited, 1977. — xiii,256p : ill, port ; 22cm.
Originally published: New York : Ungar, 1976. — Bibl.: p.243-244. — List of films: p.239-242. — Index.
ISBN 0-904159-49-3 : £6.50
(B77-28790)

791.43'0233'0924 — Cinema films directed by Forde, Walter
Walter Forde / edited by Geoff Brown. — London : British Film Institute, 1977. — [3], 52p ; 21cm.
Sd : £0.55
(B77-25122)

791.43'0233'0924 — Cinema films directed by Hitchcock, Alfred
Spoto, Donald. The art of Alfred Hitchcock : fifty years of his motion pictures / [by] Donald Spoto. — London : W.H. Allen, 1977. — xv, 525p : ill, ports ; 24cm.
Originally published: New York : Hopkinson and Blake, 1976. — List of films: p.501-515. — Bibl.: p.516. — Index.
£7.50
(B77-27287)

791.43'0233'0924 — Cinema films directed by Lang, Fritz
Eisner, Lotte Henriette. Fritz Lang / by Lotte H. Eisner ; [translated from the German MS. by Gertrud Mander and edited by David Robinson]. — London : Secker and Warburg, 1976. — 416p : ill, facsim, ports ; 25cm.
Bibl.: p.405-406. — List of films: p.407-413.
ISBN 0-436-14232-5 : £9.75
(B77-02508)

791.43'0233'0924 — Cinema films directed by Renoir, Jean
Braudy, Leo Beal. Jean Renoir : the world of his films / [by] Leo Braudy. — London : Robson, 1977. — 288p,[56]p of plates : ill, plan, ports ; 23cm.
Bibl.: p.274-278. — List of films: p.221-273. — Index.
ISBN 0-86051-005-0 : £5.95
(B77-18313)

791.43'0233'0924 — Danish cinema films. Directing. Dreyer, Carl Theodor. *Critical studies*
Nash, Mark. Dreyer / by Mark Nash. — London : British Film Institute, 1977. — [3], 81p ; 21cm.
Bibl.: p.81.
ISBN 0-85170-068-3 Pbk : £0.75
(B77-33979)

791.43'0233'0924 — French cinema films. Directing. Renoir, Jean
Gilliatt, Penelope. Jean Renoir : essays, conversations, reviews / by Penelope Gilliatt. — New York ; London [etc.] : McGraw-Hill, 1975 [i.e. 1976]. — [7],136p,[16]p of plates : ill ; 21cm.
Published in the United States: 1975. — List of films: p.87-131. — Index. — Previous control number ISBN 0-07-023224-5.
ISBN 0-07-023225-3 : £4.95
ISBN 0-07-023224-5 Pbk : £1.60
(B77-02509)

791.43'0233'0924 — French cinema films. Directing. Rivette, Jacques. *Transcripts of interviews*
Rivette, Jacques. Rivette : texts and interviews / edited and introduced by Jonathan Rosenbaum ; translated [from the French] by Amy Gateff and Tom Milne. — London : British Film Institute, 1977. — [3],101p ; 21cm.
Bibl.: p.99-101. — List of films: p.91-98.
ISBN 0-85170-064-0 Pbk : £0.75
(B77-25123)

791.43'0233'0924 — French cinema films. Directing. Vadim, Roger. *Autobiographies*
Vadim, Roger. Memoirs of the devil / [by] Roger Vadim ; translated [from the French] by Peter Beglan. — London : Hutchinson, 1976. — 192p,[16]p of plates : ports ; 23cm.
Translation of: 'Mémoires du diable'. Paris : Stock, 1975. — Index.
ISBN 0-09-127670-5 : £3.95
(B77-03705)

791.43'0233'0924 — Italian cinema films. Directing. Fellini, Federico. *Critical studies*
Rosenthal, Stuart. The cinema of Federico Fellini / [by] Stuart Rosenthal. — South Brunswick ; New York : Barnes ; London : Tantivy Press, 1976. — 190p : ill, ports ; 26cm.
Bibl.: p.185-187. — List of films: p.175-184. — Index.
ISBN 0-904208-90-7 : £4.75
(B77-30516)

791.43'025 — Cinema films. Special effects, to 1973
Brosnan, John. Movie magic : the story of special effects in the cinema / [by] John Brosnan. — Revised ed. — London : Abacus, 1977. — 207p,[32]p of plates : ill, ports ; 20cm.
Previous ed.: London : Macdonald and Jane's, 1974. — Bibl.: p.196. — Index.
ISBN 0-349-10368-2 Pbk : £2.50
(B77-13183)

791.43'026 — Art galleries. *Greater Manchester (Metropolitan County). Manchester. Whitworth Art Gallery. Exhibits: Women's costumes used in cinema films made in Hollywood, to 1976*
Regan, Michael. Hollywood film costume : [catalogue of an exhibition held at the] Whitworth Art Gallery, University of Manchester, Whitworth Park, Manchester M15 6ER, 2nd June-23rd July 1977 / [by Michael Regan]. — [Manchester] ([University of Manchester, Whitworth Park, Manchester M15 6ER]) : [The Gallery], 1977. — 48p : ill, ports ; 20x21cm.
Bibl.: p.46-47.
ISBN 0-903261-07-3 Sd : £1.00
(B77-24397)

791.43'026 — Cinema films. Women's costumes. Design. *California. Los Angeles. Hollywood, to 1975*
Chierichetti, David. Hollywood costume design / [by] David Chierichetti. — London [etc.] : Studio Vista, 1976. — 192p : ill(some col), ports ; 28cm.
Originally published: New York : Harmony Books, 1976. — Lists of films.: p.169-188. — Index.
ISBN 0-289-70730-7 : £7.95
(B77-09183)

791.43'026 — Cinema films. Women's costumes. Design, to 1975
Leese, Elizabeth. Costume design in the movies / [by] Elizabeth Leese. — Bembridge (Hapgood House, Station Rd, Bembridge, Isle of Wight) : BCW Publishing Ltd, 1976. — 166,[2]p : ill(some col), ports ; 31cm.
Ill., port. on lining papers. — Index.
ISBN 0-904159-32-9 : £8.50
(B77-00352)

791.43'027 — Cinema films. Make-up. Techniques. *Manuals*
Westmore, Michael G. The art of theatrical makeup for stage and screen / [by] Michael G. Westmore ; illustrated by Al Mayton. — New York ; London [etc.] : McGraw-Hill, 1973. — 11,155p : ill, forms ; 28cm.
Index.
ISBN 0-07-069485-0 Pbk : £6.25
Primary classification 792'.027
(B77-03177)

791.43'028'0922 — American cinema films. Acting. Abbott, Bud & Costello, Lou. *Biographies*
Thomas, Bob. Bud & Lou : the Abbott & Costello story / by Bob Thomas. — London : W.H. Allen, 1977. — 224p : ill, ports ; 24cm.
Also published: Philadelphia : Lippincott, 1977. — List of films: p.203-209. — Index.
ISBN 0-491-02212-3 : £5.50
(B77-33980)

791.43'028'0922 — American cinema films. Acting. Fonda family, 1905-1973. *Biographies*
Brough, James, *b.1918.* The fabulous Fondas / [by] James Brough. — London : Star Books, 1975. — [9],243p,[8]p of plates : ill, ports ; 18cm.
Originally published: New York : David McKay ; London : W.H. Allen, 1973.
ISBN 0-352-30056-6 Pbk : £0.65
(B77-19568)

791.43'028'0922 — American cinema films. Acting. Gable, Clark & Lombard, Carole. *Biographies*
Harris, Warren Gene. Gable and Lombard / [by] Warren G. Harris. — London : Corgi, 1977. — 207p : ill, chiefly ports ; 18cm.
Originally published: New York : Simon and Schuster, 1974 ; London : Cassell, 1976. — Index.
ISBN 0-552-10436-1 Pbk : £0.85
(B77-17681)

791.43'028'0922 — American cinema films: Comedies. Actors & actresses, 1920-1930
Manchel, Frank. The talking clowns : from Laurel and Hardy to the Marx brothers / by Frank Manchel. — New York ; London : F. Watts, 1976. — [10],129p : ill, ports ; 24cm.
Bibl.: p.119-121. — Index.
ISBN 0-531-01153-4 : £2.95
(B77-17682)

791.43'028'0922 — American cinema films: Westerns, 1920-1976. Actors
Horwitz, James. They went thataway / [by] James Horwitz. — London : W.H. Allen, 1977. — v,281p : ill ; 23cm.
Originally published: New York : Dutton, 1976.
ISBN 0-491-01818-5 : £5.95
(B77-16536)

791.43'028'0922 — American silent cinema films. Acting. Stars. *Biographies*
Slide, Anthony. The idols of silence / [by] Anthony Slide. — South Brunswick ; New York : Barnes ; London : Yoseloff, 1976. — 208p : ill, ports ; 29cm.
Bibl.: p.119-207.
ISBN 0-498-01611-0 : £6.50
(B77-30517)

791.43'028'0922 — Cinema films. Acting. Burton, Richard, b.1925. Interpersonal relationships with Taylor, Elizabeth, b.1932
David, Lester. Richard & Elizabeth / by Lester David & Jhan Robbins. — London : A. Barker, 1977. — [11],242p : ill, ports ; 23cm.
Also published: New York : Funk and Wagnalls, 1977. — Index.
ISBN 0-213-16660-7 : £4.95
(B77-30518)

791.43'028'0922 — Cinema films. Acting. Supporting actresses. *California. Los Angeles. Hollywood, 1930-1973*
Barris, Alex. Hollywood's other women / [by] Alex Barris. — South Brunswick ; New York : Barnes ; London : Yoseloff, 1975. — 212p : ill, ports ; 29cm.
Index.
ISBN 0-498-01488-6 : £6.00
(B77-33375)

791.43'028'0922 — Cinema films featuring Eddy, Nelson & MacDonald, Jeanette
Knowles, Eleanor. The films of Jeanette MacDonald and Nelson Eddy / [by] Eleanor Knowles ; with film credits by John Robert Cocchi ; music credits and discography by J. Peter Bergman. — South Brunswick ; New York : Barnes ; London : Tantivy Press, 1975. — 469p : ill, facsims, ports ; 32cm.
List of sound discs: p.396-443. — Index.
ISBN 0-498-01218-2 : £10.00
(B77-31363)

791.43'028'0922 — Cinema films: Horror films. Actors. *Biographies*
Beck, Calvin Thomas. Heroes of the horrors / by Calvin Thomas Beck. — New York : Collier Books ; London : Collier Macmillan, 1975. — xiv,353p : ill, facsims, ports ; 27cm.
List of films: p.339-353.
ISBN 0-02-508190-x Pbk : £4.75
(B77-06221)

791.43'028'0922 — Cinema films produced by Selznick, David O., 1936-1957. Actors & actresses. *Biographies*
Bowers, Ronald L. The Selznick players / [by] Ronald Bowers ; editorial assistant, C. Leigh Hibbard Church. — South Brunswick ; New York : Barnes ; London : Yoseloff, 1976. — 255p : ill, ports ; 29cm.
Bibl.: p.246. — Index.
ISBN 0-498-01375-8 : £6.25
(B77-30519)

791.43'028'0924 — American cinema films. Acting, 1937-1972. *Personal observations*
Hope, Bob, *b.1904.* The road to Hollywood : my love affair with the movies / by Bob Hope and Bob Thomas. — London : W.H. Allen, 1977. — 2-271p : ill, facsims ; 29cm.
Also published: Garden City, N.Y. : Doubleday, 1977.
ISBN 0-491-02150-x : £6.50
(B77-33981)

791.43'028'0924 — American cinema films. Acting. Baxter, Anne. *Autobiographies*
Baxter, Anne. Intermission : a true tale / [by] Anne Baxter. — London : W.H. Allen, 1977. — 384p ; 23cm.
Originally published: New York : Putnam, 1976.
ISBN 0-491-02480-0 : £4.95
(B77-23626)

791.43'028'0924 — American cinema films. Acting. Cagney, James. *Critical studies*
McGilligan, Patrick. Cagney : the actor as auteur / [by] Patrick McGilligan. — South Brunswick ; New York : Barnes ; London : Tantivy Press, 1975. — 240p : ill, ports ; 26cm.
Bibl.: p.236-238. — List of films: p.214-234. — Index.
ISBN 0-904208-45-1 : £5.00
(B77-30520)

791.43'028'0924 — American cinema films. Acting. Chaplin, Sir Charles, b.1889. *Biographies*
Hoyt, Edwin Palmer. Sir Charlie / [by] Edwin P. Hoyt. — London : Hale, 1977. — 206p,[16]p of plates : ill, ports ; 23cm.
Bibl.: p.197-198. — Index.
ISBN 0-7091-6192-1 : £4.50
(B77-29610)

791.43'028'0924 — American cinema films. Acting. Clift, Montgomery. *Biographies*
LaGuardia, Robert. Montgomery Clift : a biography / by Robert LaGuardia. — London : W.H. Allen, 1977. — xi,304p : ill, ports ; 24cm.
Also published: New York : Arbor House, 1977. — List of films: p.285-287. — Index.
ISBN 0-491-02320-0 : £5.95
(B77-25124)

791.43'028'0924 — American cinema films. Acting. Cooper, Gary. *Biographies*
Carpozi, George. The Gary Cooper story / [by] George Carpozi, Jr. — London : Star Books, 1975. — 221p,[8]p of plates : ill, ports ; 18cm.
Originally published: New Rochelle : Arlington House, 1970 ; London : W.H. Allen, 1971. — List of films: p.201-221.
ISBN 0-352-30086-8 Pbk : £0.75
(B77-19569)

791.43'028'0924 — American cinema films. Acting. Eastwood, Clint. *Biographies*
Agan, Patrick. Clint Eastwood, the man behind the myth / [by] Patrick Agan. — London : Hale, 1977. — 189p,[12]p of plates : ill ; 23cm.
Originally published: New York : Pyramid Books, 1975. — List of films: p.171-189.
ISBN 0-7091-6159-x : £3.95
(B77-32784)

Douglas, Peter. Clint Eastwood : movin' on / [by] Peter Douglas. — London : Star Books, 1975. — viii,147p,12p of plates : ill, ports ; 18cm.
Originally published: Chicago : Regnery, 1974. — List of films: p.127-142. — Index.
ISBN 0-352-30083-3 Pbk : £0.60
(B77-18935)

791.43'028'0924 — American cinema films. Acting. Flynn, Errol. *Biographies*
Godfrey, Lionel. The life and crimes of Errol Flynn / [by] Lionel Godfrey. — London : Hale [etc.], 1977. — 176p,[24]p of plates : ill, ports ; 23cm.
Bibl.: p.159-160. — List of films: p.161-165. — List of sound discs: p.166-168. — Index.
ISBN 0-7091-6091-7 : £4.50
(B77-31364)

791.43'028'0924 — American cinema films. Acting. Garbo, Greta. *Biographies*
Payne, Robert, *b.1911.* The great Garbo / [by] Robert Payne. — London : W.H. Allen, 1976. — [7],198p,[24]p of plates : ill, facsim, ports ; 23cm.
Bibl.: p.191-192. — Index.
ISBN 0-491-01538-0 : £4.95
(B77-00889)

791.43'028'0924 — American cinema films. Acting. Garbo, Greta. *Illustrations*
Garbo / [compiled by] Ture Sjolander ; [translated from the Swedish]. — New York [etc.] ; London : Harper and Row, 1971. — 139p : ill, facsims, geneal table, chiefly ports ; 31cm.
These illustrations originally published: as 'Garbo' / text av Oscar Hedlund. Stockholm : Askild och Karnekull, 1971.
ISBN 0-06-013926-9 : Unpriced
(B77-20488)

791.43'028'0924 — American cinema films. Acting. Garland, Judy. *Critical studies*
Juneau, James. Judy Garland / by James Juneau. — London : Star Books, 1976. — 159p : ill, ports ; 20cm. — (The Star illustrated history of the movies)
Originally published: New York : Pyramid Publications, 1974. — Bibl.: p.145-146. — List of films: p.147-151. — Index.
ISBN 0-352-39841-8 Pbk : £0.80
(B77-19570)

791.43'028'0924 — American cinema films. Acting. Garland, Judy, to 1935. *Biographies*
Dahl, David. Young Judy / [by] David Dahl and Barry Kehoe. — St Albans : Mayflower, 1977. — 238p,[8]p of plates : ill, ports ; 18cm.
Originally published: New York : Mason/Charter, 1975 ; London : Hart-Davis MacGibbon, 1976. — Bibl.: p.235-238.
ISBN 0-583-12592-1 Pbk : £0.95
(B77-22047)

791.43'028'0924 — American cinema films. Acting. Hayworth, Rita. *Biographies*
Kobal, John. Rita Hayworth : the time, the place and the woman / by John Kobal. — London : W.H. Allen, 1977. — 416p : ill, coat of arms, ports ; 24cm.
List of films: p.340-407. — Index.
ISBN 0-491-02330-8 : £6.95
(B77-25125)

791.43'028'0924 — American cinema films. Acting. Lemmon, Jack. *Biographies*
Widener, Don. Lemmon : a biography / by Don Widener. — London : W.H. Allen, 1977. — vii, 247p,[32]p of plates : ill, ports ; 24cm.
Originally published: New York : Macmillan, 1975. — Index.
ISBN 0-491-01578-x : £4.95
(B77-08499)

791.43'028'0924 — American cinema films. Acting. Love, Bessie. *Autobiographies*
Love, Bessie. From Hollywood with love / [by] Bessie Love. — London : Elm Tree Books, 1977. — 160p : ill, ports ; 24cm.
List of films: p.148-156. — Index.
ISBN 0-241-89342-9 : £5.95
(B77-29611)

791.43'028'0924 — American cinema films. Acting. MacLaine, Shirley, 1970-1974. *Autobiographies*
MacLaine, Shirley. You can get there from here / [by] Shirley MacLaine. — London : Corgi, 1977. — [5],218p ; 18cm.
Originally published: London : Bodley Head, 1975.
ISBN 0-552-10411-6 Pbk : £0.70
(B77-13184)

791.43'028'0924 — American cinema films. Acting. Marx, Groucho. *Correspondence*
Marx, Groucho. The Groucho letters / [by] Groucho Marx. — London : Sphere, 1976. — 252p ; 18cm.
Originally published: New York : Simon and Schuster ; London : Joseph, 1967.
ISBN 0-7221-5858-0 Pbk : £0.75
(B77-31365)

791.43'028'0924 — American cinema films. Acting. Presley, Elvis, to 1972
Lichter, Paul. Elvis in Hollywood / [by] Paul Lichter. — London : Hale, 1977. — 188p : ill, col facsims, ports(1 col) ; 28cm.
Originally published: New York : Simon and Schuster, 1975. — List of sound discs: p.183-185.
ISBN 0-7091-5733-9 Pbk : £2.50
(B77-13185)

791.43'028'0924 — American cinema films. Acting. Valentino, Rudolph. *Biographies*
Botham, Noel. Valentino : the love god / [by] Noel Botham and Peter Donnelly. — London : Everest, 1976. — 248p,[32]p of plates : ill, facsim, ports ; 19cm.
List of films : p.245-248.
ISBN 0-903925-49-4 : £4.25
ISBN 0-903925-99-0 Pbk : £0.75
(B77-04990)

Walker, Alexander. Rudolph Valentino / [by] Alexander Walker. — London : Sphere, 1977. — 92p,[32]p of plates : ill, ports ; 18cm.
Originally published: New York : Stein and Day ; London : Elm Tree Books, 1976. — Bibl. : p.88. — List of films: p.83-87. — Index.
ISBN 0-7221-8868-4 Pbk : £0.95
(B77-28791)

791.43'028'0924 — American silent cinema films. Acting. Pickford, Mary, b.1893. *Biographies*
Windeler, Robert. Mary Pickford : sweetheart of the world / [by] Robert Windeler. — London : Star Books, 1975. — xii,226p,[8]p of plates : ill, ports ; 18cm.
Originally published: as 'Sweetheart : the story of Mary Pickford'. London : W.H. Allen, 1973. — Bibl.: p.219. — List of films: p.204-218. — Index.
ISBN 0-352-30046-9 Pbk : £0.75
(B77-19571)

791.43'028'0924 — Cinema films. Acting. Baker, Sir Stanley, b.1928. *Biographies*
Storey, Anthony. Stanley Baker : portrait of an actor / [by] Anthony Storey. — London : W.H. Allen, 1977. — 160p,[16]p of plates : ill, ports ; 23cm.
List of films: p.139-160.
ISBN 0-491-02230-1 : £3.95
(B77-25126)

791.43'028'0924 — Cinema films. Acting. Bogarde, Dirk, to ca 1960. *Autobiographies*
Bogarde, Dirk. A postillion struck by lightning / [by] Dirk Bogarde. — London : Chatto and Windus, 1977. — [12],268p,leaf of plate,10p of plates : ill, ports ; 23cm.
Ill. on lining papers. — Index.
ISBN 0-7011-2207-2 : £4.95 : CIP rev.
(B77-05574)

791.43'028'0924 — Cinema films. Acting. Brando, Marlon. *Critical studies*
Jordan, René. Marlon Brando / by René Jordan. — London : Star Books, 1975. — 157,[1]p : ill ; 20cm. — ([Star] illustrated history of the movies)
Originally published: New York : Pyramid Publications, 1973. — Bibl.: p.149. — List of films: p.150-153. — Index.
ISBN 0-352-30062-0 Pbk : £0.70
(B77-19572)

791.43'028'0924 — Cinema films. Acting. Fonda, Jane. *Biographies*
Kiernan, Thomas. Jane Fonda / [by] Thomas Kiernan. — St Albans : Mayflower, 1976. — xviii,430p ; 18cm.
Originally published: as 'Jane : an intimate biography of Jane Fonda', New York : Putnam, 1973 ; and as 'Jane Fonda', London : Talmy Franklin, 1973.
ISBN 0-583-12717-7 Pbk : £1.25
(B77-04352)

791.43'028'0924 — Cinema films. Acting. Gable, Clark. *Biographies*
Tornabene, Lyn. Long live the king : a biography of Clark Gable / by Lyn Tornabene. — London : W.H. Allen, 1977. — 396p,[32]p of plates : ill, facsims, ports ; 24cm.
Originally published: New York : Putnam, 1976. — Index.
ISBN 0-491-02470-3 : £5.95
(B77-27288)

791.43'028'0924 — Cinema films. Acting. Lee, Christopher, b.1922. *Autobiographies*
Lee, Christopher, *b.1922.* Tall, dark and gruesome : an autobiography / [by] Christopher Lee. — London : W.H. Allen, 1977. — 284p, leaf of plate,[32]p of plates : ill, coat of arms, ports ; 23cm.
Index.
ISBN 0-491-01968-8 : £4.95
(B77-27289)

791.43'028'0924 — Cinema films. Acting. Rathbone, Basil. *Biographies*
Druxman, Michael B. Basil Rathbone : his life and his films / [by] Michael B. Druxman. — South Brunswick [etc.] : Barnes ; London : Yoseloff, 1976. — 359p : ill, ports ; 26cm.
Originally published: 1975.
ISBN 0-498-01471-1 : £4.25
(B77-28792)

791.43'028'0924 — Cinema films featuring Bogart, Humphrey
Pettigrew, Terence. The Bogart file / [by] Terence Pettigrew. — London [etc.] : Golden Eagle Press, 1977. — 213p,[32]p of plates : ill, ports ; 23cm.
List of films: p.183-206. — Index.
ISBN 0-901482-25-0 : £4.50
(B77-20489)

791.43'028'0924 — Cinema films featuring Brando, Marlon
Braithwaite, Bruce. The films of Marlon Brando / [by] Bruce Braithwaite. — 2nd ed. — Bembridge (Hapgood House, Station Rd, Bembridge, Isle of Wight) : BCW Publishing, 1977. — 47p : ill, ports ; 21cm.
Previous ed.: 1974. — List of films: p.35-45.
ISBN 0-904159-39-6 Sd : £0.95
(B77-28007)

791.43'028'0924 — Cinema films featuring Caine, Michael
Andrews, Emma. The films of Michael Caine / [by] Emma Andrews. — 2nd ed. — Bembridge (Hapgood House, Station Rd, Bembridge, Isle of Wight) : BCW Publishing, 1977. — 47p : ill, ports ; 21cm.
Previous ed.: 1974. — List of films: p.37-46.
ISBN 0-904159-41-8 Sd : £0.95
(B77-28793)

791.43'028'0924 — Cinema films featuring Connery, Sean
Andrews, Emma. The films of Sean Connery / [by] Emma Andrews. — 2nd ed. — Bembridge (Hapgood House, Station Rd, Bembridge, Isle of Wight) : BCW Publishing, 1977. — 47p : ill, ports ; 21cm.
Previous ed.: 1974. — List of films: p.36-45.
ISBN 0-904159-44-2 Sd : £0.95
(B77-28794)

791.43'028'0924 — Cinema films featuring Dean, James
Whitman, Mark. The films of James Dean / by Mark Whitman. — 3rd ed. — Bembridge (Hapgood House, Station Rd, Bembridge, Isle of Wight) : BCW Publishing, 1977. — 47p : ill, ports ; 21cm.
Previous ed.: 1975. — Bibl.: p.45. — List of films: p.43-45.
ISBN 0-904159-43-4 Sd : £0.95
(B77-28795)

791.43'028'0924 — Cinema films featuring Eastwood, Clint
Whitman, Mark. The films of Clint Eastwood / [by] Mark Whitman. — 3rd ed. — Bembridge (Hapgood House, Station Rd, Bembridge, Isle of Wight) : BCW Publishing, 1977. — 47p : ill, ports ; 21cm.
Previous ed.: 1975. — List of films: p.35-45.
ISBN 0-904159-36-1 Sd : £0.95
(B77-29612)

791.43'028'0924 — Cinema films featuring Garland, Judy
Baxter, Brian, *b.1938.* The films of Judy Garland / [by] Brian Baxter. — 2nd ed. — Bembridge (Hapgood House, Station Rd, Bembridge, Isle of Wight) : BCW Publishing, 1977. — 47p : ill, ports ; 21cm.
Previous ed.: 1974. — Bibl.: p.44. — List of films: p.36-43. — List of sound discs: p.44.
ISBN 0-904159-46-9 Sd : £0.95
(B77-28796)

791.43'028'0924 — Cinema films featuring Heston, Charlton
Williams, John, *b.1944.* The films of Charlton Heston / by John Williams. — 2nd ed. — Bembridge (Hapgood House, Station Rd, Bembridge, Isle of Wight) : BCW Publishing, 1977. — 47p : ill, ports ; 21cm.
Previous ed.: 1974. — List of films: p.34-45.
ISBN 0-904159-42-6 Sd : £0.95
(B77-28797)

791.43'028'0924 — Cinema films featuring Keaton, Buster. *Illustrations*
The **best** of Buster : the classic comedy scenes direct from the films of Buster Keaton / edited by Richard J. Anobile. — London : Elm Tree Books, 1976. — 256p : of ill, facsims ; 28cm.
ISBN 0-241-89518-9 : £5.95
ISBN 0-241-89519-7 Pbk : £3.50
(B77-01710)

791.43'028'0924 — Cinema films featuring McQueen, Steve
Campbell, Joanna. The films of Steve McQueen / [by] Joanna Campbell. — 2nd ed. — Bembridge (Hapgood House, Station Rd, Bembridge, Isle of Wight) : BCW Publishing, 1977. — 47p : ill, ports ; 21cm.
Previous ed.: 1973. — List of films: p.38-45.
ISBN 0-904159-27-2 Sd : £0.95
(B77-28798)

791.43'028'0924 — Cinema films featuring Minnelli, Liza
D'Arcy, Susan. The films of Liza Minnelli / [by] Susan d'Arcy. — 2nd ed. — Bembridge (Hapgood House, Station Rd, Bembridge, Isle of Wight) : BCW Publishing, 1977. — 47p : ill, ports ; 21cm.
Previous ed.: 1973. — List of films: p.41-45.
ISBN 0-904159-35-3 Sd : £0.95
(B77-28799)

791.43'028'0924 — Cinema films featuring Moore, Roger
Williams, John, *b.1944.* The films of Roger Moore / [by] John Williams. — 2nd ed. — Bembridge (Hapgood House, Station Rd, Bembridge, Isle of Wight) : BCW Publishing, 1977. — 47p : ill, ports ; 21cm.
Previous ed.: 1974. — List of films: p.39-45.
ISBN 0-904159-45-0 Sd : £0.95
(B77-29613)

791.43'028'0924 — Cinema films featuring Newman, Paul, b.1925
Thompson, Kenneth. The films of Paul Newman / [by] Kenneth Thompson. — 3rd ed. — Bembridge (Hapgood House, Station Rd, Bembridge, Isle of Wight) : BCW Publishing, 1977. — 47p : ill, ports ; 21cm.
Previous ed.: 1975. — List of films: p.35-45.
ISBN 0-904159-26-4 Sd : £0.95
(B77-28800)

791.43'028'0924 — Cinema films featuring Nicholson, Jack
Braithwaite, Bruce. The films of Jack Nicholson / [by] Bruce Braithwaite. — Bembridge (Hapgood House, Station Rd, Bembridge, Isle of Wight) : BCW Publishing, 1977. — 47p : ill, ports ; 21cm.
List of films: p.36-45.
ISBN 0-904159-47-7 Sd : £0.95
(B77-28801)

791.43'028'0924 — Cinema films featuring Price, Vincent
McAsh, Iain F. The films of Vincent Price / [by] Iain F. McAsh. — 2nd ed. — Bembridge (Hapgood House, Station Rd, Bembridge, Isle of Wight) : BCW Publishing, 1977. — 47p : ill, ports ; 21cm.
Previous ed.: 1974. — List of films: p.36-45.
ISBN 0-904159-40-x Sd : £0.95
(B77-28802)

791.43'028'0924 — Cinema films featuring Redford, Robert
Castell, David. The films of Robert Redford / by David Castell. — 3rd ed. — Bembridge (Hapgood House, Station Rd, Bembridge, Isle of Wight) : BCW Publishing, 1977. — 47p : ill, ports ; 21cm.
Previous ed.: 1975. — List of films: p.37-45.
ISBN 0-904159-37-x Sd : £0.95
(B77-29614)

791.43'028'0924 — Cinema films featuring Shearer, Norma
Jacobs, Jack. The films of Norma Shearer / [by] Jack Jacobs and Myron Braum. — South Brunswick ; New York : Barnes ; London : Yoseloff, 1976. — 250p : ill, ports ; 29cm.
ISBN 0-498-01552-1 : £7.00
(B77-30521)

791.43'028'0924 — Cinema films featuring Streisand, Barbra

Castell, David. The films of Barbra Streisand / by David Castell. — 3rd ed. — Bembridge (Hapgood House, Station Rd, Bembridge, Isle of Wight) : BCW Publishing, 1977. — 47p : ill, ports ; 21cm.
Previous ed.: 1975. — List of films: p.43-45.
ISBN 0-904159-34-5 Sd : £0.95
(B77-28803)

791.43'028'0924 — Cinema films featuring Taylor, Elizabeth, b.1932

D'Arcy, Susan. The films of Elizabeth Taylor / [by] Susan d'Arcy. — 3rd ed. — Bembridge (Hapgood House, Station Rd, Bembridge, Isle of Wight) : BCW Publishing, 1977. — 47p : ill, ports ; 21cm.
Previous ed.: 1974. — List of films: p.35-45.
ISBN 0-904159-38-8 Sd : £0.95
(B77-28804)

791.43'028'0924 — Cinema films featuring Wayne, John, b.1907

Eyles, Allen. John Wayne and the movies / [by] Allen Eyles. — South Brunswick ; New York : Barnes ; London : Tantivy Press, 1976. — 320p : ill, ports ; 29cm.
Index.
ISBN 0-498-01449-5 : £6.00
(B77-31366)

791.43'028'0924 — Silent cinema films featuring Keaton, Buster

Moews, Daniel. Keaton : the silent features close up / [by] Daniel Moews. — Berkeley [etc.] ; London : University of California Press, 1977. — x,337p : 1 ill ; 22cm.
Index.
ISBN 0-520-03126-1 : £8.95
ISBN 0-520-03155-5 Pbk : £2.95
(B77-21351)

791.43'03 — Cinema films. *Encyclopaedias*

Halliwell, Leslie. Halliwell's film guide : a survey of 8000 English-language movies. — London [etc.] : Hart-Davis MacGibbon, 1977. — xii, 897p : ill, facsims, ports ; 26cm.
Index.
ISBN 0-246-10982-3 : £12.50
(B77-31367)

Halliwell, Leslie. Halliwell's filmgoer's companion / [by] Leslie Halliwell. — 6th ed. — London [etc.] : Granada, 1977. — xvii, 825p : ill, facsims, ports ; 26cm.
Previous ed.: published as 'The filmgoer's companion'. St Albans : Paladin, 1976. — Bibl.: p.819-821. — List of films: p.797-804.
ISBN 0-246-10981-5 : £10.00
(B77-28008)

791.43'05 — Cinema films. *Annuals*

Cinema. — London (181 Queen Victoria St., EC4V 4DD) : Independent Magazines (Publishing) Ltd.
'77 / [edited by David Castell]. — 1976. — 3-159p : ill(some col), ports(some col) ; 30cm.
Index.
ISBN 0-904894-01-0 Pbk : £3.95
ISSN 0307-6016
(B77-13796)

791.43'05 — Cinema films. *Reports, surveys. Serials*

Film review. — London : W.H. Allen.
1977-78 / edited by F. Maurice Speed. — 1977. — 192p : ill, facsims, ports ; 21x23cm.
Bibl.: p.154-167. — List of films: p.124-153. — Index.
ISBN 0-491-02211-5 : £5.95
(B77-33982)

791.43'05 — Cinema films. *Serials*

The films of -. — Bembridge (Hapgood House, Bembridge, Isle of Wight PO35 5NN) : BCW Publishing Ltd.
Originally published: in 6 issues a year.
1975 / [by] John Williams. — 1976. — 2-94,[1] p : ill, ports ; 22cm.
Index.
ISBN 0-904159-31-0 Sd : £1.50
ISSN 0305-2184
(B77-05575)

791.43'06'241 — Cinema films: Feature films. Organisations. *Great Britain. British Film Institute. Production Board*

BFI Production Board / edited by Alan Lovell. — London : British Film Institute, 1976. — iii, 68p ; 21cm.
Cover title: Production Board. — List of films: p.62-66.
ISBN 0-85170-059-4 Sd : £0.70
(B77-14339)

791.43'08 — Cinema films. *Readings*

Movies and methods : an anthology / edited by Bill Nichols. — Berkeley [etc.] ; London : University of California Press, 1976. — xi, 640p : ill ; 24cm.
Bibl. — Index.
ISBN 0-520-02890-2 : £16.00
ISBN 0-520-03151-2 Pbk : £5.50
(B77-13186)

791.43'09'04 — Cinema films, 1956-1976. *Reviews*

Walker, Alexander. Double takes : notes and afterthoughts on the movies, 1956-76 / [by] Alexander Walker. — London : Elm Tree Books, 1977. — xi,260p ; 23cm.
Index.
ISBN 0-241-89395-x : £5.95
(B77-16002)

791.43'09'047 — Cinema films, 1972-1975. *Reviews*

Kael, Pauline. Reeling / [by] Pauline Kael. — London : Boyars : Distributed by Calder and Boyars, 1977. — xiv,497p ; 24cm.
This collection originally published: Boston, Mass. : Little, Brown, 1976. — Index.
ISBN 0-7145-2581-2 : £9.95
ISBN 0-7145-2582-0 Pbk : £4.95
(B77-15415)

791.43'0909'15 — Cinema films: Science fiction films, to 1975

Manchel, Frank. An album of great science fiction films / by Frank Manchel. — New York ; London : F. Watts, 1976. — 96p : ill ; 29cm.
Bibl.: p.94. — Index.
ISBN 0-531-00345-0 : £2.95
(B77-15416)

791.43'0909'16 — Cinema films: Horror films, to 1976

Frank, Alan. Horror films / [by] Alan Frank. — London [etc.] : Hamlyn, 1977. — 5-189p : ill(some col), ports ; 33cm.
Ill. (incl. 1 col.) on lining papers. — Bibl.: p.183. — Index.
ISBN 0-600-37068-2 : £3.95
(B77-31368)

791.43'0909'32 — American cinema films: Westerns, ca 1950-1976

French, Philip. Westerns : aspects of a movie genre / [by] Philip French. — Revised ed. — London : Secker and Warburg [for] the British Film Institute, 1977. — 208p : ill ; 20cm. — (Cinema one ; 25)
Previous ed.: 1973. — Bibl.: p.206-208. — List of films: p.200-205.
ISBN 0-436-09944-6 : £3.50
ISBN 0-436-09945-4 Pbk : £1.90
(B77-33983)

791.43'0909'32 — American cinema films: Westerns, to 1972. *Questions & answers*

Cocchi, John. The Westerns : a picture quiz book / [by] John Cocchi. — New York : Dover Publications [etc.] ; London : Constable, 1976. — [130]p : of ill ; 24cm.
With answers. — Index.
ISBN 0-486-23288-3 Pbk : £2.25
(B77-04353)

791.43'0909'32 — Cinema films: Westerns, to 1972

Calder, Jenni. There must be a Lone Ranger : the myth and reality of the American Wild West / [by] Jenni Calder. — London : Abacus, 1976. — xiii,241p,[8]p of plates : ill, facsim, ports ; 19cm.
Originally published: London : Hamilton, 1974. — Bibl.: p.231-234. — List of films : p.228-230. — Index.
ISBN 0-349-10479-4 Pbk : £0.95
Also classified at 823'.0874
(B77-07532)

Fenin, George N. The Western from silents to the seventies / [by] George N. Fenin and William K. Everson. — Revised ed. — Harmondsworth [etc.] : Penguin, 1977. — xix, 396p : ill, facsim, ports ; 22cm.
This ed. originally published: New York : Grossman, 1973. — Previous ed.: published as 'The Western from silents to cinerama'. New York : Orion Press, 1962. — Index.
ISBN 0-14-004416-7 Pbk : £2.95
(B77-21352)

791.43'0909'351 — Cinema films: Horror films, 1910-1975. Special subjects: Frankenstein

The **Frankenstein** file / [edited by] Peter Haining. — London : New English Library, 1977. — 128p : ill, facsims, ports ; 27cm.
List of films: p.125-126.
ISBN 0-450-03305-8 Pbk : £3.50
Also classified at 823'.9'1209351
(B77-29615)

791.43'0909'352 — American cinema films, 1931-1974. Characters: Reporters

Barris, Alex. Stop the presses! : the newspaperman in American films / [by] Alex Barris. — South Brunswick ; New York : Barnes ; London : Yoseloff, 1976. — 211p : ill, ports ; 29cm.
Index.
ISBN 0-498-01603-x : £8.50
(B77-30522)

791.43'0909'352 — American cinema films, to 1976. Characters: Women. *Juvenile literature*

Manchel, Frank. Women on the Hollywood screen / by Frank Manchel. — New York ; London : F. Watts, 1977. — [6],122p : ill, ports ; 27cm.
Bibl.: p.118-120. — Index.
ISBN 0-531-00389-2 : £2.95
(B77-30523)

791.43'0909'353 — Cinema films. Special themes: Homosexuality

Gays and film / edited by Richard Dyer. — London : British Film Institute, 1977. — iv, 73p ; 21cm.
'[Published] in conjunction with a National Film Theatre season'. — Bibl.: p.72-73. — List of films: p.58-71.
ISBN 0-85170-065-9 Pbk : £0.75
(B77-25807)

791.43'0909'375 — Cinema films: Horror films. Special subjects: Monsters

Gifford, Denis. Monsters of the movies / [by] Denis Gifford. — London : Carousel Books, 1977. — 95p : ill ; 20cm. — (Carousel books)
ISBN 0-552-54118-4 Pbk : £0.45
(B77-29616)

791.43'0909'375 — Cinema films: Horror films, to 1974. Special themes: Vampires

Pirie, David. The vampire cinema / [by] David Pirie. — London [etc.] : Hamlyn, 1977. — 176p : ill(some col), facsims(some col), map, 4 ports ; 31cm. — (A Quarto book)
Ill. on lining papers. — Bibl.: p.176. — Index.
ISBN 0-600-39157-4 : £3.95
(B77-22048)

Ursini, James. The vampire film / [by] James Ursini and Alain Silver. — South Brunswick ; New York : Barnes ; London : Tantivy Press, [1976]. — 238p : ill ; 26cm.
Originally published: South Brunswick ; New York : Barnes, 1975. — Bibl.: p.231-235. — List of films: p.145-230. — Index.
ISBN 0-904208-40-0 : £4.25
(B77-04991)

791.43'0909'38 — Surrealist cinema films, to 1975

Gould, Michael. Surrealism and the cinema : (open-eyed screening) / by Michael Gould. — South Brunswick [etc.] : Barnes ; London : Tantivy Press, 1976. — [1],171p : ill ; 26cm.
Bibl.: p.165-166. — Index.
ISBN 0-904208-55-9 : £4.00
(B77-17018)

791.43'092'2 — Cinema films. *Biographical dictionaries*

Thomson, David, *b.1941.* A biographical dictionary of the cinema / [by] David Thomson. — London : Secker and Warburg, 1975 [i.e. 1976]. — ix,629p ; 24cm.
Originally published: 1975.
ISBN 0-436-52011-7 Pbk : £3.90
(B77-03175)

791.43'092'2 — Cinema films. *California. Los Angeles. Hollywood. Personal observations. Collections*

Marchak, Alice. The super secs / [by] Alice Marchak and Linda Hunter. — London : Corgi, 1976. — [5],280,[1]p ; 18cm.
Originally published: New York : Bantam, 1975.
ISBN 0-552-10282-2 Pbk : £0.70
(B77-04992)

791.43'092'4 — Cinema films. *California. Los Angeles. Hollywood, 1935-1960. Personal observations*

Niven, David. Bring on the empty horses / [by] David Niven. — Sevenoaks : Coronet, 1976. — 352p,[24]p of plates : ill, ports ; 18cm.
Originally published: London : Hamilton, 1975. — Index.
ISBN 0-340-20915-1 Pbk : £0.95
(B77-13187)

791.4'3'0942 — Cinema films. *England, to 1896*
Barnes, John, *b.1920.* The beginnings of the cinema in England / [by] John Barnes. — Newton Abbot [etc.] : David and Charles, 1976. — 240p : ill, facsims, ports ; 26cm.
List of films: p.201-219. — Index.
ISBN 0-7153-7089-8 : £7.50
(B77-00890)

791.43'09471 — Finnish cinema films, to 1975. *Critical studies*
Cowie, Peter. Finnish cinema / by Peter Cowie. — London : Tantivy Press [etc.], 1976. — 128p : ill, ports ; 17cm.
Bibl.: p.126-127. — Index.
ISBN 0-904208-56-7 : £3.25
(B77-32085)

791.43'0973 — American cinema films, to 1974
Kuhns, William. Movies in America / [by] William Kuhns. — South Brunswick [etc.] : Barnes ; London : Tantivy Press, 1975. — [8], 248p : ill, ports ; 22x29cm.
Bibl.: p.244-245. — Index.
ISBN 0-498-01640-4 : £5.00
(B77-28009)

791.43'0983 — Chilean cinema films. Political aspects. *Transcripts of interviews*
Chilean cinema / edited and introduced by Michael Chanan. — London : British Film Institute, 1976. — [7],102p ; 21cm.
Bibl.: p.100-120. — List of films: p.97-99.
ISBN 0-85170-058-6 Pbk : £0.75
(B77-12595)

791.43'3 — Animated feature films, to 1974
Edera, Bruno. Full length animated feature films / by Bruno Edera ; edited by John Halas. — London [etc.] : Focal Press, 1977. — 198p : ill(some col), ports ; 29cm. — (The library of animation technology)
Bibl.: p.193-194. — Index.
ISBN 0-240-50818-1 : £13.50
(B77-15417)

791.43'3 — Animated films, to 1975
The **great** movie cartoon parade / introduction by John Halas ; notes by David Rider. — London ([101 Ladbroke Grove, W11 1PG]) : Triune Books, 1976. — 120p : chiefly ill(some col), music, port ; 38cm.
Index.
ISBN 0-85674-076-4 Pbk : £3.50
(B77-06222)

791.43'52 — Cinema films, 1915-1973. Special themes: Swashbuckling. *Critical studies*
Richards, Jeffrey. Swordsmen of the screen, from Douglas Fairbanks to Michael York / by Jeffrey Richards. — London [etc.] : Routledge and Kegan Paul, 1977. — [15],296p : ill ; 25cm. — (Cinema and society)
Bibl.: p.284-286. — Index.
ISBN 0-7100-8478-1 : £8.95
(B77-21353)

791.43'52 — Cinema films: Detective films, to 1976. Characters: Sherlock Holmes. *Critical studies*
Davies, David Stuart. Holmes of the movies : the screen career of Sherlock Holmes / [by] David Stuart Davies ; foreword by Peter Cushing. — London : New English Library, 1976. — 175p : ill, port ; 26cm.
List of films: p.163-174.
ISBN 0-450-03065-2 : £6.95
(B77-21354)

791.43'53 — Ethnographic motion picture films
Heider, Karl Gustav. Ethnographic film / by Karl G. Heider. — Austin ; London : University of Texas Press, 1976. — xiv,166p : ill, form ; 24cm.
Bibl.: p.153-157. — List of films : p.135-152. — Index.
ISBN 0-292-72020-3 : £7.50
(B77-19573)

791.43'7 — American cinema films: King Kong, 1976. Production, 1975-1976
Bahrenburg, Bruce. The creation of Dino de Laurentiis' 'King Kong' / by Bruce Bahrenburg. — London : Star Books, 1976. — xi,273p : ill, ports ; 18cm.
ISBN 0-352-30006-x Pbk : £0.60
(B77-25127)

791.43'7 — American cinema films: 'Othello'. Production, 1949-1950. *Diaries*
Mac Liammóir, Micheál. Put money in thy purse : the filming of Orson Welles' 'Othello' / [by] Micheál Mac Liammóir ; with a preface by Orson Welles. — 2nd, revised ed. — London : Eyre Methuen, 1976. — xii,258p,[8]p of plates : ill, ports ; 20cm.
Previous ed.: London : Methuen, 1952.
ISBN 0-413-31890-7 : £4.50
ISBN 0-413-36740-1 Pbk : £2.25
(B77-02510)

791.43'7 — British cinema films. *Scripts*
Monty Python's second film : a first draft / by Graham Chapman ... [et al.]. — London : Eyre Methuen, 1977. — 284p in various pagings : ill(some col), facsims(some col) ; 25cm.
Cover title: Monty Python and the Holy Grail (Book). — Spine title: Monti Python ik den Holie Gräilen (Bok).
ISBN 0-413-38520-5 Pbk : £3.50
(B77-31369)

791.43'7 — British cinema films: Legend of the werewolf. Production, 1974-1975
Buscombe, Edward. Making 'Legend of the Werewolf' / by Edward Buscombe. — London (81 Dean St., W1V 6AA) : British Film Institute, Educational Advisory Service, 1976. — 2-121,[1]p : ill, facsims, plan, ports ; 21cm.
ISBN 0-85170-057-8 Pbk : £0.95
(B77-12596)

791.43'7 — British cinema films: Tales of Beatrix Potter. Production
Godden, Rumer. The tale of the tales : the Beatrix Potter ballet / [by] Rumer Godden ; including illustrations by Beatrix Potter designs by Christine Edzard and photographs from the E.M.I. film production 'Tales of Beatrix Potter'. — London [etc.] : F. Warne, 1976. — 208p : ill(chiefly col), facsims, music, ports ; 30cm.
Originally published: 1971.
£7.95
ISBN 0-7232-1421-2
(B77-04993)

791.43'7 — Cinema films directed by Thorsen, Sven: Cinema films on Christ. Proposals. *Church of England viewpoints*
Leonard, Graham. A speech by the Rt Revd Graham Leonard, Bishop of Truro, chairman of the Board of Social Responsibility to the General Synod of the Church of England, on the Thorsen film. — London : Church Literature Association, 1976. — [8]p ; 21cm.
'[Delivered] 8 November 1976'.
ISBN 0-85191-097-1 Sd : £0.10
(B77-10497)

791.43'7 — French cinema films. *Scripts. French texts*
Cocteau, Jean. Orphée : the play and the film / [by] Jean Cocteau ; edited with an introduction and selection of film-stills by E. Freeman. — Oxford : Blackwell, 1976. — xliii,129p,16p of plates : ill, plan, ports ; 19cm. — (Blackwell's French texts)
French texts, English introduction and notes. — Bibl.: p.xliii. — Contents: Orphée. Originally published: Paris : s.n., 1927 - Orphée, film. Originally published: Paris : Editions de la Parade, 1951.
ISBN 0-631-00720-2 Pbk : £3.25
Primary classification 842'.9'12
(B77-05742)

791.43'7 — French documentary cinema films on occupation of France by German military forces. *Scripts*
Ophuls, Marcel. The sorrow and the pity : chronicle of a French city under the German occupation, a film / by Marcel Ophuls ; introduction by Stanley Hoffman ; filmscript translated [from the French MS.] by Mireille Johnston ; biographical and appendix material by Mireille Johnston. — St Albans : Paladin, 1975. — xxxix,194p : ill, facsims, map, ports ; 20cm.
Originally published: New York : Outerbridge and Lazard, 1972.
ISBN 0-586-08177-1 Pbk : £1.00
(B77-21355)

791.43'7 — Polish cinema films: Shadow line. Production, 1973-1976. *Personal observations*
Sulik, Boleslaw. A change of tack : making 'The shadow line' / [by] Boleslaw Sulik. — London : British Film Institute, Educational Advisory Service, 1976. — 113p : ill, ports ; 21cm.
Pbk : £1.25
(B77-31370)

791.43'7 — Russian cinema films: King Lear. Production. *Personal observations*
Kozintsev, Grigoriĭ M. 'King Lear', the space of tragedy : the diary of a film director / [by] Grigori Kozintsev ; translated [from the Russian] by Mary Mackintosh ; with a foreword by Peter Brook. — London : Heinemann Educational, 1977. — xii,260p,[8]p of plates : ill ; 24cm.
Translation of: 'Prostranstvo tragedii'. Leningrad : Iskusstvo, 1973. — Index.
ISBN 0-435-18519-5 : £8.50
(B77-13188)

791.44 — RADIO

791.44'028'0924 — Radio & television programmes. Broadcasting. Dimbleby, Richard. *Great Britain. Biographies*
Dimbleby, Jonathan. Richard Dimbleby / [by] Jonathan Dimbleby. — Sevenoaks : Coronet, 1977. — 409p,[8]p of plates : ill, facsim, map, ports ; 18cm.
Originally published: London : Hodder and Stoughton, 1975. — Bibl.: p.396-397. — Index.
ISBN 0-340-21308-6 Pbk : £1.00
(B77-17683)

791.44'028'0924 — Radio programmes. Broadcasting. Weir, Molly. *Great Britain. Autobiographies*
Weir, Molly. Stepping into the spotlight / [by] Molly Weir. — London : Arrow Books, 1976. — 190p ; 18cm.
Originally published: London : Hutchinson, 1975.
ISBN 0-09-914170-1 Pbk : £0.60
(B77-13797)

Weir, Molly. Walking into the Lyons' den / [by] Molly Weir. — London : Hutchinson, 1977. — 192p ; 23cm.
ISBN 0-09-129030-9 : £3.50
(B77-28010)

791.44'0941 — Broadcasting services. *Great Britain. British Broadcasting Corporation. Radio programmes, 1975-1976. Reports, surveys*
British Broadcasting Corporation. What's Auntie been up to? / BBC. — London : B.B.C., 1976. — [68]p : ill(chiefly col), col map, ports(chiefly col) ; 21cm.
'... based mainly on the [BBC's] Annual Report and Accounts for 1975-6 ...' - p.3.
ISBN 0-563-17257-6 Sd : £0.30
Primary classification 791.45'0941
(B77-08500)

791.44'3 — Disc jockeys. *Great Britain. Biographical dictionaries*
The **music** spinners : Britain's radio DJs / edited by Nik Oakley & Dave Gotz. — London (77 New Bond St., W.1) : MRP Books, 1976. — [4] ,127p : ill, ports ; 20cm.
ISBN 0-905590-01-5 Pbk : £1.99
(B77-26447)

791.44'3 — Disc jockeys. Techniques. *Manuals*
Emperor Rosko. Emperor Rosko's DJ book / ideas by Rosko ; translated into English and written down by Johnny Beerling. — London : Everest, 1976. — 224p,[24]p of plates : ill, facsim, ports ; 21cm.
Index.
ISBN 0-903925-92-3 : £3.50
ISBN 0-903925-91-5 Pbk : £0.95
(B77-08001)

791.44'5 — Broadcasting services. *Great Britain. British Broadcasting Corporation. Medical radio programmes. Reports, surveys*
The **BBC's** medical programmes & their effects on lay audiences : a study for the BBC General Advisory Council. — London : British Broadcasting Corporation, 1976. — [1],63,[1]p ; 26cm.
ISBN 0-563-17262-2 Sd : Unpriced
Also classified at 791.45'5
(B77-09184)

791.44'5 — Broadcasting services. *Scotland. British Broadcasting Corporation. Scottish Region. Religious radio programmes*
Falconer, Ronald Hugh Wilson. Message, media, mission / [by] Ronald Falconer. — Edinburgh : St Andrew Press, 1977. — x,138p ; 21cm. — (The Baird lectures ; 1975)
ISBN 0-7152-0349-5 : Unpriced
ISBN 0-7152-0358-4 Pbk : £2.00
Also classified at 791.45'5
(B77-30524)

791.44'5 — Radio programmes: News programmes. *United States, 1935-1941*
Culbert, David Holbrook. News for everyman : radio and foreign affairs in thirties America / [by] David Holbrook Culbert. — Westport, Conn. ; London : Greenwood Press, 1976. — xvi,239p ; 22cm.
Bibl.: p.211-229. — Index.
ISBN 0-8371-8260-3 : Unpriced
(B77-20490)

791.44'7 — Radio programmes. Comedies: Goon Show. *Great Britain. Scripts*
Milligan, Spike. The Goon Show scripts / written and selected by Spike Milligan ; with drawings by Peter Sellers, Harry Secombe, Spike Milligan. — London : Sphere, 1976. — [191]p : ill, facsims, ports ; 21cm.
Originally published: London : Woburn Press, 1972.
ISBN 0-7221-6074-7 Pbk : £0.95
(B77-16003)

791.44'7 — Radio programmes. Comedies: Goon Show. *Great Britain, to 1975*
Wilmut, Roger. The Goon Show companion : a history and goonography / written and compiled by Roger Wilmut ; with a personal memoir by Jimmy Grafton. — London : Sphere, 1977. — 191p,[4]p of plates : ill, ports ; 24cm.
Originally published: London : Robson, 1976. — Bibl.: p.185. — List of sound recordings: p.155-179. — List of films: p.180-184. — Index.
ISBN 0-7221-9182-0 Pbk : £0.95
(B77-29617)

791.45 — TELEVISION
791.45 — Video art, to 1975. *Critical studies*
Video art : an anthology / compiled and edited by Ira Schneider and Beryl Korot ... — New York ; London : Harcourt Brace Jovanovich, [1977]. — 286p : ill, facsims, plan, ports ; 24cm.
Published in the United States: 1976. — Bibl.: p.187.
ISBN 0-15-193632-3 : £12.20
ISBN 0-15-193634-x Pbk : £6.10
(B77-09185)

791.45'0232 — Television programmes. Production. *Manuals*
Millerson, Gerald. Effective TV production / [by] Gerald Millerson. — London [etc.] : Focal Press, 1976. — 192p : ill(chiefly col), plan ; 22cm. — (Media manuals)
Bibl.: p.186.
ISBN 0-240-50950-1 Pbk : £2.95
(B77-01711)

791.45'0233 — Television programmes. Continuity. *Manuals*
Rowlands, Avril. Script continuity and the production secretary in film and TV / [by] Avril Rowlands. — London [etc.] : Focal Press, 1977. — 160p : ill, forms, plan ; 22cm. — (Media manuals)
Bibl.: p.156.
ISBN 0-240-50949-8 Pbk : £2.75
Primary classification 791.43'0233
(B77-28789)

791.45'028'0924 — Broadcasting services. *Great Britain. British Broadcasting Corporation. Television programmes: News programmes. Broadcasting. Dougall, Robert. Autobiographies*
Dougall, Robert. In and out of the box : an autobiography / [by] Robert Dougall. — [London] : Fontana, 1975. — 319p,[8]p of plates : ports ; 18cm.
Originally published: London : Collins ; Harvill Press, 1973.
ISBN 0-00-613669-9 Pbk : £0.75
(B77-00353)

791.45'028'0924 — Television programmes. Drama: Coronation Street. Acting. Phoenix, Pat. *Autobiographies*
Phoenix, Pat. All my burning bridges / [by] Pat Phoenix. — London : Star Books, 1976. — 188p,[8]p of plates : ill, ports ; 19cm.
Originally published: London : Arlington Books, 1974.
ISBN 0-352-39839-6 Pbk : £0.60
(B77-10890)

791.45'0941 — Broadcasting services. *Great Britain. British Broadcasting Corporation. Television programmes, 1975-1976. Reports, surveys*
British Broadcasting Corporation. What's Auntie been up to? / BBC. — London : B.B.C., 1976. — [68]p : ill(chiefly col), col map, ports(chiefly col) ; 21cm.
'... based mainly on the [BBC's] Annual Report and Accounts for 1975-6 ...' - p.3.
ISBN 0-563-17257-6 Sd : £0.30
Also classified at 791.44'0941
(B77-08500)

791.45'0941 — Commercial television services. *Great Britain. Independent Television Authority. Television programmes, to 1976*
Eye on TV : the first 21 years of Independent Television. — London (247 Tottenham Court Rd., W1P 0AU) : Independent Television Publications, 1976. — 348p : ill(some col), col maps, ports(some col) ; 28cm. — ('TV times' book)
ISBN 0-900727-61-6 : £10.00
(B77-27290)

791.45'0941 — Television programmes. *Great Britain, 1972-1976. Reviews*
James, Clive. Visions before midnight : television criticism from 'the Observer', 1972-1976 / [by] Clive James. — London : Cape, 1977. — 176p ; 23cm.
ISBN 0-224-01386-6 : £3.95 : CIP rev.
(B77-07533)

791.45'5 — Broadcasting services. *Great Britain. British Broadcasting Corporation. Medical television programmes. Reports, surveys*
The **BBC**'s medical programmes & their effects on lay audiences : a study for the BBC General Advisory Council. — London : British Broadcasting Corporation, 1976. — [1],63,[1]p ; 26cm.
ISBN 0-563-17262-2 Sd : Unpriced
Primary classification 791.44'5
(B77-09184)

791.45'5 — Broadcasting services. *Scotland. British Broadcasting Corporation. Scottish Region. Religious television programmes*
Falconer, Ronald Hugh Wilson. Message, media, mission / [by] Ronald Falconer. — Edinburgh : St Andrew Press, 1977. — x,138p ; 21cm. — (The Baird lectures ; 1975)
ISBN 0-7152-0349-5 : Unpriced
ISBN 0-7152-0358-4 Pbk : £2.00
Primary classification 791.44'5
(B77-30524)

791.45'5 — Children's television programmes. *United States*
Barcus, F Earle. Children's television : an analysis of programming and advertising / [by] F. Earle Barcus, with Rachel Wolkin. — New York ; London : Praeger, 1977. — xxix,219p ; 25cm. — (Praeger special studies in US economic, social and political issues)
ISBN 0-275-23210-7 : £12.40
(B77-22049)

791.45'5 — Children's television programmes. Production. Implications of visual literacy. *United States*
Amey, L J. Visual literacy : implications for the production of children's television programs / [by] L.J. Amey. — London (21 Gwendolen Ave., [SW15 6ET]) : Vine Press, 1976. — iii,55,[1]leaves ; 28cm. — (Dalhousie University. Dalhousie University Libraries and Dalhousie University School of Library Service occasional papers ; no.11)
Bibl.: leaves: 52-55.
ISBN 0-905305-02-7 Sd : £2.50
(B77-11352)

791.45'5 — Television programmes: Documentary films. *Great Britain*
Vaughan, Dai. Television documentary usage / [by] Dai Vaughan ... ; [for] the British Film Institute, Educational Advisory Service. — London : B.F.I., 1976. — iv,39p ; 21cm. — (British Film Institute. Television monographs ; 6 ISSN 0306-2929)
List of films: p.37-39.
ISBN 0-85170-060-8 Sd : £0.55
(B77-12024)

791.45'5 — Television programmes: News programmes. Bias. *United States*
Altheide, David L. Creating reality : how TV news distorts events / [by] David L. Altheide ; introduction by Arthur J. Vidich. — Beverly Hills ; London : Sage Publications, [1977]. — [5],221p ; 23cm. — (Sage library of social research ; vol.33)
Published in the United States: 1976. — Bibl.: p.217-220.
ISBN 0-8039-0671-4 : £8.65
ISBN 0-8039-0672-2 Pbk : £4.55
(B77-12025)

791.45'5 — Television programmes. Special subjects: Great Britain. Politics. *Great Britain*
Tracey, Michael. The production of political television / [by] Michael Tracey. — London [etc.] : Routledge and Kegan Paul, 1978. — xiii,283p ; 24cm.
Bible.: p.263-277. — Index.
ISBN 0-7100-8689-x Pbk : £4.95 : CIP rev.
(B77-25128)

791.45'7 — Television programmes. Comedies: Two Ronnies. *Scripts*
Barker, Ronnie. It's goodnight from him : the best of 'The two Ronnies' / [by] Ronnie Barker ; illustrated by John Painter ; designed by David Cox. — London [etc.] : Hodder and Stoughton, 1976. — 95p : ill(chiefly col) ; 29cm.
ISBN 0-340-20525-3 : £2.95
(B77-03706)

Nice to be with you again! / [compiled by] Peter Vincent. — London : Star Books, 1977. — [4], 139p : ill ; 18cm.
Cover title: More of the two Ronnies.
ISBN 0-352-30108-2 Pbk : £0.60
(B77-23627)

791.45'7 — Television programmes: Documentary films on General Strike, Great Britain, 1926. *Scripts*
Kee, Robert. General strike report ... / by Robert Kee. — Leeds (The Television Centre, Leeds LS3 1JS) : Yorkshire Television Ltd, 1976. — 56p ; 21cm.
'This publication is a reproduction of the television scripts which were written by Robert Kee'.
Pbk : Unpriced
(B77-21356)

791.45'7 — Television programmes. Drama: Onedin Line
McLeay, Alison. The world of the Onedin Line / [by] Alison McLeay. — Newton Abbot [etc.] : David and Charles, 1977. — 143p : ill(some col), facsim, ports ; 25cm.
Bibl.: p.141. — Index.
ISBN 0-7153-7398-6 : £4.95
(B77-24398)

791.45'7 — Television programmes. Sports programmes: 'Superstars'
Vine, David. The Superstars / [by] David Vine. — Henley-on-Thames : A. Ellis, 1977. — 128p : ill, ports ; 21cm.
ISBN 0-85628-057-7 Pbk : £1.95 : CIP rev.
(B77-13798)

791.45'7 — Television programmes: Star Trek. *Questions & answers*
Razzi, James. Star trek puzzle manual : puzzles, mazes and trivia to baffle, enlighten and amuse Star trek fans everywhere / based on the television series created by Gene Roddenberry ; [written by] James Razzi ; [assisted by] Sondra Marshak and Myrna Culbreath. — Toronto [etc.] ; London : Bantam, 1976. — 128p : ill ; 28cm.
With answers.
ISBN 0-552-99001-9 Pbk : £1.50
Primary classification 793.7'3
(B77-08003)

791.5 — MINIATURE, TOY, SHADOW THEATRES
791.5 — Black box theatres. *Manuals. Juvenile literature*
Kodicek, Susan. Black theatre for children / [by] Susan Kodicek ; illustrated by Peter Lang. — London : Pelham, 1977. — 71p : ill ; 22cm.
ISBN 0-7207-0977-6 : £3.25
(B77-22050)

791.8 — ANIMAL PERFORMANCES

791.8 — Cockfighting, to ca 1930

Atkinson, Herbert. Cock-fighting and game fowl : from the note-books of Herbert Atkinson of Ewelme ; together with, The life and letters of John Harris, the Cornish cocker / [by H.A.] ; ten plates in colour and twelve in black and white from paintings and drawings by the author ; edited and with an introductory memoir by Game Cock. — Liss : Spur Publications, 1977. — viii,253p,[21]leaves of plates : ill(some col), col port ; 26cm.
Facsimile reprint of: 1st ed. Bath : Bayntun, 1938. — Index.
ISBN 0-904558-23-1 : £9.00
(B77-12597)

791.8 — Rodeos. *United States*

Porter, Willard H. Roping and riding : fast horses and short ropes / [by] Willard H. Porter. — South Brunswick ; New York : Barnes ; London : Yoseloff, 1975. — 232p : ill, ports ; 26cm.
Index.
ISBN 0-498-01549-1 : £4.00
(B77-26448)

791.8'2'09 — Bull-fighting, to 1975

Hay, Doddy. The bullfight / [by] Doddy Hay. — London : New English Library, 1976. — 128p, [8]p of plates : ill(some col), plan, ports ; 31cm.
Bibl.: p.126. — Index.
ISBN 0-450-03066-0 : £5.95
(B77-10891)

792 — THEATRE

Triesman, Susan. Body, mind, stage and street / prepared for the [Open University Art and Environment] Course Team by Susan Triesman. — Milton Keynes : Open University Press, 1976. — 58,[1]p,[2]p of plates : ill(some col), facsim ; 30cm. — (A second level interdisciplinary course : art and environment ; unit 12) (TAD292 ; 12)
Bibl.: p.55-56.
ISBN 0-335-06211-3 Pbk : £1.20
(B77-02511)

Wilson, Edwin. The theater experience / [by] Edwin Wilson. — New York ; London [etc.] : McGraw-Hill, 1976. — xii,371p : ill ; 24cm.
Bibl.: p.353-354. — Index.
ISBN 0-07-070661-1 : Unpriced
ISBN 0-07-070662-x Pbk : £7.45
(B77-03707)

792 — Theatre. Censorship. *England, 1737-1824*

Conolly, L W. The censorship of English drama, 1737-1824 / by L.W. Conolly. — San Marino [Calif.] : Huntington Library ; Folkestone : [Distributed by] Dawson, 1976. — xii,223p : 1 ill, facsims, port ; 24cm.
Index.
ISBN 0-87328-068-7 : £9.00
(B77-32785)

792'.02 — Stagecraft. *Manuals. Juvenile literature*

McCallum, Andrew. Fun with stagecraft / [by] Andrew McCallum ; line drawings by E.J. O'Toole. — London : Kaye and Ward [etc.], 1977. — 60p : ill, plans, port ; 26cm. — ([Learning with fun])
ISBN 0-7182-0098-5 : £2.15
(B77-13189)

792'.0226 — Theatre in education

O'Toole, John. Theatre in education : new objectives for theatre, new techniques in education / [by] John O'Toole. — London [etc.] : Hodder and Stoughton, 1976. — ix, 165p : ill ; 17x20cm.
Bibl.: p.162. — Index.
ISBN 0-340-20617-9 : £4.95
ISBN 0-340-20618-7 Pbk : £2.40
(B77-10498)

792'.0233'0924 — Theatre. Directing. Clurman, Harold. *United States. Autobiographies*

Clurman, Harold. All people are famous : (instead of an autobiography) / [by Harold Clurman]. — New York ; London : Harcourt Brace Jovanovich, [1976]. — xiv,327p ; 22cm.
Published in the United States: 1974. — Index.
ISBN 0-15-104775-8 : £5.10
(B77-06820)

792'.0233'0924 — Theatre. Directing. Guthrie, Sir Tyrone. *Great Britain. Biographies*

Forsyth, James, *b.1913.* Tyrone Guthrie : a biography / [by] James Forsyth. — London : Hamilton, 1976. — xi,372p,[12]p of plates : ill, ports ; 23cm.
List of theatrical productions : p.349-353. — List of works : p.355. — Index.
ISBN 0-241-89471-9 : £7.95
(B77-00891)

792'.0233'0924 — Theatre. Directing. Logan, Joshua. *United States. Autobiographies*

Logan, Joshua. Josh : my up and down, in and out life / by Joshua Logan. — London : W.H. Allen, 1977. — [7],408p : ill, ports ; 24cm.
Originally published: New York : Delacorte Press, 1976. — Index.
ISBN 0-491-02040-6 : £5.95
(B77-25129)

792'.025 — Theatre. Stage lighting. *Manuals*

Bentham, Frederick. The art of stage lighting / [by] Frederick Bentham. — 2nd ed. — London [etc.] : Pitman, 1976. — xiii,361p : ill ; 26cm.
Previous ed.: 1968. — Index.
ISBN 0-273-00210-4 : £7.50
(B77-00892)

792'.025'0228 — Stage design. Models. Making. *Manuals*

Payne, Darwin Reid. Materials and craft of the scenic model / [by] Darwin Reid Payne. — Carbondale [etc.] : Southern Illinois University Press ; London [etc.] : Feffer and Simons, 1976. — xix,116p : ill ; 19x27cm.
Bibl.: p.107-110. — Index.
ISBN 0-8093-0778-2 : £18.00
ISBN 0-8093-0783-9 Pbk : £3.90
(B77-03176)

792'.027 — Theatre. Make-up. Techniques. *Manuals*

Westmore, Michael G. The art of theatrical makeup for stage and screen / [by] Michael G. Westmore ; illustrated by Al Mayton. — New York ; London [etc.] : McGraw-Hill, 1973. — 11,155p : ill, forms ; 28cm.
Index.
ISBN 0-07-069485-0 Pbk : £6.25
Also classified at 791.43'027
(B77-03177)

792'.027 — Theatre. Make-up. Techniques. *Manuals. Juvenile literature*

Bruun-Rasmussen, Ole. Make-up, costumes and masks : for the stage / by Ole Bruun-Rasmussen and Grete Petersen ; [translated from the Danish by Kathleen Margaret Brondal]. — New York : Sterling [etc.] ; London : Distributed by Ward Lock, [1977]. — 96p : ill ; 21cm.
Published in the United States: 1976. — Translation of: 'Sjove masker af papir'. Copenhagen : Host, 1972 ; and 'Sminkning og maskering'. Copenhagen : Host, 1975. — Index.
ISBN 0-7061-2519-3 : £3.50
Also classified at 646.4'7
(B77-13190)

792'.028 — Acting. *Manuals*

Glenn, Stanley L. The complete actor / [by] Stanley L. Glenn. — Boston, Mass. ; London : Allyn and Bacon, 1977. — xii,339p : ill, ports ; 24cm.
Bibl. — Index.
ISBN 0-205-05580-x : Unpriced
(B77-17020)

Ting : Theatre of Mistakes. Elements of performance art / [compiled] by Anthony Howell and Fiona Templeton. — Revised ed. — London (11 Ascham St., N.W.5) : The Ting, Theatre of Mistakes, 1977. — 83p : ill, plan ; 21cm.
'Derived from exercises contributed to workshops by performers with The Ting : Theatre of Mistakes, 1974-76'. — Limited ed. of 800 copies. — Previous ed.: 1976.
Sp : Unpriced
(B77-25808)

792'.028'07 — Actors. Training. Theories of Stanislavskiĭ, Konstantin Sergeevich

Moore, Sonia. The Stanislavski system : the professional training of an actor : digested from the teachings of Konstantin S. Stanislavski / by Sonia Moore. — New revised ed. — Harmondsworth [etc.] : Penguin, 1976. — xxi, 106p ; 18cm. — (Penguin handbooks)
This ed. originally published: New York : Viking Press, 1965 ; London : Gollancz, 1966. — Index.
ISBN 0-14-046259-7 Pbk : Unpriced
(B77-14862)

792'.028'07 — Actors. Training. *Manuals*

Barker, Clive. Theatre games : a new approach to drama training / [by] Clive Barker. — London : Eyre Methuen, 1977. — xi,226p : ill, plan ; 21cm.
Bibl.: p.225-226.
ISBN 0-413-45370-7 : £4.95
ISBN 0-413-45380-4 Pbk : £2.95
(B77-30525)

792'.028'0922 — Actors. *Great Britain. Directories*

Spotlight. Actors. — London (42 Cranbourn St., WC2H 7AP) : 'The Spotlight'.
1977-78 ed. — [1977]. — 2v.(xxxii,2016p) : of ports ; 26cm.
Thumb indexed. — Indexes. — Includes 'Agents & production A-Z'.
Pbk : Unpriced
ISSN 0309-0183
(B77-18936)

792'.028'0922 — Actresses. *Great Britain. Directories*

Spotlight. Actresses. — London (42 Cranbourn St., WC2H 7AP) : 'The Spotlight'.
1977-78. A-K. — [1977]. — xii,805p : of ports ; 26cm.
Thumb indexed. — Index.
Pbk : £6.30
ISSN 0308-9827
(B77-32786)

1977-78. L-Z. — [1977]. — p xv-xxv,807-1763 : of ports ; 26cm.
Thumb indexed. — Index. — Includes children A-Z.
Pbk : £6.30
ISSN 0308-9827
(B77-32787)

792'.028'0924 — Acting. Evans, Dame Edith. *Great Britain, 1946-1971. Biographies*

Batters, Jean. Edith Evans : a personal memoir / by Jean Batters. — London : Hart-Davis MacGibbon, 1977. — 159p,[8]p of plates : ill, ports ; 22cm.
Index.
ISBN 0-246-10994-7 : £4.50
(B77-27291)

792'.028'0924 — Acting. Evans, Dame Edith. *Great Britain. Biographies*

Forbes, Bryan. Ned's girl : the authorised biography of Dame Edith Evans / [by] Bryan Forbes. — London : Elm Tree Books, 1977. — xvii,297p,[24]p of plates : facsim, ports ; 24cm.
Index.
ISBN 0-241-89600-2 : £5.95
(B77-27292)

792'.028'0924 — Acting. Leigh, Vivien. *Great Britain. Biographies*

Edwards, Anne. Vivien Leigh : a biography / by Anne Edwards. — London : W.H. Allen, 1977. — 318p,[32]p of plates : ill, facsim, ports ; 24cm.
Also published: New York : Simon and Schuster, 1977. — Index.
ISBN 0-491-02140-2 : £6.95
(B77-25130)

792'.028'0924 — Acting. Martin, Mary, b.1913. *Autobiographies*

Martin, Mary, *b.1913.* My heart belongs / by Mary Martin. — London : W.H. Allen, 1977. — 320p : ports ; 24cm.
Originally published: New York : Morrow, 1976. — Index.
ISBN 0-491-01668-9 : £5.00
(B77-12026)

792'.028'0924 — Acting. Massey, Raymond, to 1921. *Autobiographies*

Massey, Raymond. When I was young / by Raymond Massey. — London : Robson, 1977. — 271p : ill, ports ; 24cm.
Originally published: Toronto : McClelland and Stewart, 1976.
ISBN 0-903895-85-4 : £4.95
(B77-21357)

792'.028'0924 — Acting. Twiggy. *Autobiographies*

Twiggy. Twiggy : an autobiography. — St Albans : Mayflower, 1976. — 160p,[16]p of plates : ill, ports ; 18cm.
Originally published: London : Hart-Davis MacGibbon, 1975.
ISBN 0-583-12564-6 Pbk : £0.60
(B77-00893)

792'.028'0924 — Acting. Ullman, Liv. *Autobiographies*

Ullmann, Liv. Changing / by Liv Ullmann ; [translated from the Norwegian by the author in collaboration with Gerry Bothmer and Erik Friis]. — London : Weidenfeld and Nicolson, 1977. — [7],244p ; 23cm.
Translation of: 'Forandringen'. Oslo? : Helge Ericsen, 1976.
ISBN 0-297-77285-6 : £4.95
(B77-13799)

792'.028'0924 — Theatre. Acting. Bernhardt, Sarah. *France. Autobiographies*
Bernhardt, Sarah. My double life : the memoirs of Sarah Bernhardt / [translated from the French]. — London : Owen, 1977. — vi,453p, [8]p of plates : ports ; 22cm.
Facsimile reprint of: 1st ed. of this translation. London : Heinemann, 1907. — Translation of: 'Ma double vie'. Paris : Charpentier et Fasquelle, 1907. — Index.
ISBN 0-7206-0502-4 : £6.95
(B77-14340)

792'.028'0924 — Theatre. Acting. Bernhardt, Sarah. *France. Biographies*
Richardson, Joanna. Sarah Bernhardt and her world / [by] Joanna Richardson. — London : Weidenfeld and Nicolson, 1977. — 232p : ill(some col), facsims, ports(some col) ; 26cm.
Bibl.: p.225. — Index.
ISBN 0-297-77253-8 : £6.00
(B77-11353)

792'.028'0924 — Theatre. Acting. Cibber, Susannah Maria. *Great Britain. Biographies*
Nash, Mary. The provoked wife : the life and times of Susannah Cibber / [by] Mary Nash. — London : Hutchinson, 1977. — xii,369p : ill, facsims, ports ; 25cm.
Also published: Boston, Mass. : Little, Brown, 1977. — Bibl.: p.353-358. — Index.
ISBN 0-09-129380-4 : £6.95
(B77-28805)

792'.028'0924 — Theatre. Acting. Du Maurier, Sir Gerald. *Great Britain. Biographies*
Du Maurier, *Dame* **Daphne.** Gerald : a portrait / [by] Daphne Du Maurier. — Harmondsworth [etc.] : Penguin, 1977. — 252p ; 19cm.
Originally published: London : Gollancz, 1934.
Pbk : £0.75
ISBN 0-14-003048-4
(B77-09186)

792'.028'0924 — Theatre. Acting. Kemble, Fanny. *Great Britain. Biographies*
Marshall, Dorothy. Fanny Kemble / [by] Dorothy Marshall. — London : Weidenfeld and Nicolson, 1977. — vii,280p,[8]p of plates : ill, ports ; 23cm.
Bibl.: p.4-5. — Index.
ISBN 0-297-77282-1 : £6.50
(B77-20491)

792'.028'0924 — Theatre. Acting. Terry, Ellen. *Great Britain. Biographies*
Prideaux, Tom. Love or nothing : the life and times of Ellen Terry / [by] Tom Prideaux. — London [etc.] : Millington, 1976. — xi,288p,[16] p of plates : ill, facsim, ports ; 23cm.
Ill. on lining papers. — Originally published: New York : Scribner, 1975. — Bibl.: p.273-277. — Index.
ISBN 0-86000-074-5 : £5.50
(B77-26449)

792'.028'0924 — Theatre. Acting. Thorndike, Dame Sybil. *Great Britain. Biographies*
Morley, Sheridan. Sybil Thorndike : a life in the theatre / [by] Sheridan Morley ; preface by Sir John Gielgud. — London : Weidenfeld and Nicolson, 1977. — 183p : facsims, ports ; 26cm.
Index.
ISBN 0-297-77388-7 : £5.95
(B77-30526)

792'.028'0924 — Theatre. Olivier, Laurence, Baron Olivier. *Great Britain. Biographies*
Cottrell, John. Laurence Olivier / [by] John Cottrell. — [London] : Coronet, 1977. — 478p, [8]p of plates : ill, ports ; 18cm.
Originally published: London : Weidenfeld and Nicolson, 1975. — Bibl.: p.447-452. — Index.
ISBN 0-340-21804-5 Pbk : £1.50
(B77-27293)

792'.03 — Theatre. *Encyclopaedias*
Illustrated encyclopaedia of world theatre / [translated from the German by Estella Schmid] ; introduction [and revision] by Martin Esslin. — London : Thames and Hudson, 1977. — 320p : ill, facsims, ports ; 30cm.
Translation and revision of: 'Friedrichs Theaterlexikon' / by Karl Gröning and Werner Kliess. Velber bei Hannover : Friedrich Verlag, 1969. — Index.
ISBN 0-500-01174-5 : £12.50
(B77-30527)

792'.07'10411 — Educational institutions. Curriculum subjects: Drama. *Scotland. Periodicals*
ID : information for drama. — Edinburgh (Drama Department, Moray House College of Education, Holyrood Rd, Edinburgh EH8 8AQ) : Moray House College of Education. [No.1]- ; [June 1974]-. — [1974]-. — ill, facsims ; 21cm.
Three issues a year. — 54 [i.e. 55]p. in 1st issue.
Sd : £1.00
ISSN 0309-6319
(B77-27294)

792'.07'10411 — Schools. Curriculum subjects: Drama. *Scotland. Reports, surveys*
Working Party on Drama. Drama in Scottish schools : a discussion document : report of the Working Party on Drama appointed by the Secretary of State for Scotland on the recommendation of the Consultative Committee on the Curriculum. — Edinburgh : H.M.S.O., 1977. — ix,33p ; 22cm.
ISBN 0-11-491503-2 Sd : £0.90
(B77-28806)

792'.07'1042 — Schools. Activities: Drama. *England. Reports, surveys*
Slade, Peter. New trends / [by] Peter Slade. — [Birmingham] : Educational Drama Association, [1976?]. — 14p ; 22cm.
'Based on his opening address at the Conference of the Welsh Education Office, 7th July 1972'.
Pbk : Unpriced
(B77-04354)

792'.07'1042 — Schools. Activities: Drama. Role of professional actors. *England. Reports, surveys*
Great Britain. *Department of Education and Science.* Actors in schools / Department of Education and Science. — London : H.M.S.O., 1976. — vi,73p ; 21cm. — (Education survey ; 22)
ISBN 0-11-270382-8 Sd : £1.00
(B77-15418)

792'.07'12 — Middle schools. Activities: Drama
Slade, Peter. Drama and the middle school : report as from the Educational Drama Association for the Middle Years of Schooling Research Project, University of Lancaster / [by] Peter Slade. — 2nd ed. — [Birmingham] : Educational Drama Association, [1976?]. — 17p : plans ; 21cm.
Previous ed.: Bromley : Educational Drama Association, 1971.
Sd : Unpriced
(B77-06223)

792'.07'12 — Middle schools. Activities: Drama. *Middle school texts. Cards*
Norris, Jay. Drama resource cards / [by] Jay Norris, Mike Evans. — London : Longman, 1977. — Portfolio : ill ; 25cm.
Booklet ([2],13p.), 80 cards ([72] sides).
ISBN 0-582-36204-0 : £5.75
(B77-30528)

792'.07'12 — Secondary schools. Activities: Drama. *Exercises, worked examples. Secondary school texts*
Ideas in action / [edited by B.A. Phythian]. — London : Hodder and Stoughton.
3 / [by] P.W. Thomson & C. Goodhead. — 1976. — iv,92p : ill, form, map, plan ; 22cm.
ISBN 0-340-17725-x Pbk : £0.95
(B77-05576)

792'.07'12 — Secondary schools. Curriculum subjects: Drama. *For teaching*
Seely, John. Dramakit / [by] John Seely. — Oxford [etc.] : Oxford University Press, 1977. — vi,193p : ill, maps, music, plans ; 31cm.
In binder.
ISBN 0-19-913238-0 Ls : £5.95
(B77-22763)

792'.07'1241 — Secondary schools. Curriculum subjects: Drama. Projects: Schools Council Drama Teaching Project (10-16). *Great Britain. Reports, surveys*
Schools Council Drama Teaching Project, 10-16. Learning through drama : report of the Schools Council Drama Teaching Project (10-16), Goldsmiths' College, University of London / [prepared by] Lynn McGregor, Maggie Tate, Ken Robinson. — London [etc.] : Heinemann Educational for the Schools Council, 1977. — [5],224p : 1 ill ; 23cm.
Bibl.: p.217-218.
ISBN 0-435-18564-0 : £5.25
ISBN 0-435-18565-9 Pbk : £2.50
(B77-20492)

792'.07'1241 — Secondary schools. Curriculum subjects: Drama. Teaching. *Great Britain*
Drama guidelines / [by] Cecily O'Neill ... [et al.]. — London : Heinemann Educational, 1977. — 75p ; 30cm.
Originally published: London : 'London drama', 1976. — Index.
ISBN 0-435-18670-1 Sd : £1.25
(B77-23628)

792'.074'022392 — Museums. *Kent. Tenterden. Ellen Terry Memorial Museum. Guidebooks*
National Trust. Ellen Terry's house, Smallhythe, Tenterden, Kent / [National Trust] ; [written by Audrey Lucas]. — [London] : The Trust, 1977. — 9p,[4]p of plates : ill, ports ; 22cm.
Sd : £0.15
(B77-33984)

792'.08 — Theatre. *Essays*
Arden, John. To present the pretence : essays on the theatre and its public ... / [by] John Arden ; selected, with commentaries by the author. — London : Eyre Methuen, 1977. — 216p ; 21cm.
'(Including two essays written in collaboration with Margaretta D'Arcy)'.
ISBN 0-413-38150-1 : £5.50
ISBN 0-413-38160-9 Pbk : £3.25
(B77-28011)

792.09 — THEATRE. HISTORICAL AND GEOGRAPHICAL TREATMENT

792'.09'034 — Theatre, 1835-1967. *Readings from contemporary sources*
The **theory** of the modern stage : an introduction to modern theatre and drama / edited by Eric Bentley. — [1st ed.] reprinted with revisions. — Harmondsworth [etc.] : Penguin, 1976. — 493p ; 18cm. — (A pelican original)
This ed. originally published: 1968. — Bibl.: p.485. — Index.
ISBN 0-14-020947-6 Pbk : £1.25
(B77-04355)

792'.09181'2 — Popular theatre. *Western world, to 1976. Conference proceedings*
Western Popular Theatre *(Conference), University of Manchester, 1974.* Western popular theatre : the proceedings of a symposium sponsored by the Manchester University Department of Drama / edited by David Mayer and Kenneth Richards. — London : Methuen, 1977. — x,277p : ill, facsims ; 23cm.
'... papers ... delivered at the third University of Manchester International Theatre Symposium, held at Langdale Hall in April, 1974. The theme ... was "Western Popular Theatre"' - Preface. — Bibl.: p.228.
ISBN 0-416-82220-7 : £6.20
(B77-16537)

792'.092'2 — Theatre. *Great Britain & United States. Biographical dictionaries*
Who's who in the theatre : a biographical record of the contemporary stage. — 16th ed. / edited by Ian Herbert with Christine Baxter, London, Robert E. Finley, New York. — London : Pitman [etc.], 1977. — xxvi,1389p ; 21cm.
Previous ed.: 1972. — Index.
ISBN 0-273-00163-9 : £15.00
(B77-16538)

792'.092'4 — Experimental theatre. Performances by companies of International Centre of Theatre Research. *West Africa. Personal observations*
Heilpern, John. Conference of the birds : the story of Peter Brook in Africa / by John Heilpern. — London : Faber, 1977. — 3-317p : map ; 23cm.
ISBN 0-571-10372-3 : £5.95 : CIP rev.
(B77-17021)

792'.092'4 — Theatre. Hayward, Brooke. *United States. Autobiographies*
Hayward, Brooke. Haywire / [by] Brooke Hayward. — London : Cape, 1977. — [9], 325p : ill, ports ; 24cm.
Also published: New York : Knopf, 1977.
ISBN 0-224-01426-9 : £4.95 : CIP rev.
(B77-22051)

792'.092'4 — Theatre. Payne, Ben Iden. *United States. Autobiographies*
Payne, Ben Iden. A life in a wooden O : memoirs of the theatre / [by] Ben Iden Payne. — New Haven ; London : Yale University Press, 1977. — xvii,204,[1]p : ill, plan, ports ; 26cm.
Bibl.: p.197-199. — Index.
ISBN 0-300-02064-3 : £7.50
(B77-25131)

792'.0941 — Theatre. Influence of Christian rituals. *Great Britain, 1066-1485*
Edwards, Francis, *b.1908.* Ritual and drama : the mediaeval theatre / [by] Francis Edwards ; with line drawings by George Tuckwell. — Guildford [etc.] : Lutterworth Press, 1976. — 127p,8p of plates : ill ; 22cm.
Bibl.: p.116-118. — Index.
ISBN 0-7188-2180-7 Pbk : £2.95
(B77-05577)

792'.0942 — Theatre. *England, 1590-1625. Correspondence & diaries. Manuscripts. Facsimiles*
Henslowe, Philip. The Henslowe papers / edited, with an introduction by R.A. Foakes. — London : Scolar Press, 1977. — 2v.([536]p;[749]p(6 fold)) ; 36cm.
Four fold. sheets ([8]p.) in pocket (Vol.1) and 7 fold. sheets ([14]p.) in pocket (Vol.2). — Facsimile reproduction of manuscripts at Dulwich College, consisting of letters and papers relating to Henslowe, Alleyn and the Fortune Theatre and including Henslowe's diary. — Bibl.: p.[8]-[9] (Vol.1).
ISBN 0-85967-355-3 : £95.00
(B77-26450)

792'.0942 — Theatre. *England, to ca 1975*
The **Revels** history of drama in English / [general editors Clifford Leech and T.W. Craik]. — London : Methuen.
Vol.5 : 1660-1750 / [by] John Loftis ... [et al.]. — 1976. — xxxi,331p,[32]p of plates : ill, facsim, plan, ports ; 25cm.
Ill. on lining papers. — Bibl.: p.297-319. — Index.
ISBN 0-416-13060-7 : £13.00
ISBN 0-416-81370-4 Pbk : £6.95
Primary classification 822'.009
(B77-05621)

792'.0942 — Theatre. England, ca 1550-1644. Related to drama in English, 1558-1625
Bradbrook, Muriel Clara. The living monument : Shakespeare and the theatre of his time / [by] M.C. Bradbrook. — Cambridge [etc.] : Cambridge University Press, 1976. — xv,287p, 4p of plates : ill, map ; 23cm.
Index.
ISBN 0-521-21255-3 : £8.50
Primary classification 822.3'3
(B77-01775)

792'.09421 — Theatre. *London*
Hurren, Kenneth. Theatre inside out / [by] Kenneth Hurren. — London : W.H. Allen, 1977. — [7],213p ; 23cm.
Index.
ISBN 0-491-02170-4 : £4.95
(B77-28012)

792'.09421 — Theatres. *London, to 1969*
Mander, Raymond. Lost theatres of London / [by] Raymond Mander and Joe Mitchenson. — New and revised ed. — London : New English Library, 1976. — 240p : ill, facsims, maps, ports ; 28cm.
Previous ed.: London : Hart-Davis, 1968.
ISBN 0-450-02838-0 : £14.95
(B77-07535)

792'.09421 — Theatres. *London, to 1976*
Roose-Evans, James. London theatre : from the Globe to the National / [by] James Roose-Evans. — Oxford : Phaidon, 1977. — 160p : ill, ports ; 24cm.
Ill. on lining papers. — Bibl.: p.154-156. — Index.
ISBN 0-7148-1766-x : £6.95
(B77-28807)

792'.09421'44 — Theatres. *London. Hackney (London Borough). Curtain (Theatre), 1577-1626*
Linnell, Rosemary. The Curtain Playhouse / by Rosemary Linnell ... — [London] ([26 Commercial St., E1 6LP]) : Curtain Theatre, 1977. — 64p : ill, facsim, maps, plans ; 21cm.
Bibl.: p.64.
Pbk : £1.50
(B77-31371)

792'.09421'65 — Theatres. *London. Lambeth (London Borough). Old Vic, to 1976*
Roberts, Peter. The Old Vic story : a nation's theatre, 1818-1976 / [by] Peter Roberts. — London : W.H. Allen, 1976. — x,203p,[24]p of plates : ill, facsims, ports ; 25cm.
Bibl.: p.193. — Index.
ISBN 0-491-01747-2 : £5.95
(B77-03178)

792'.09424'89 — Amateur theatre. Companies. *Warwickshire. Studley. Cygnet Players, to 1976*
The **Cygnet** Players : a short history, 1958-1976. — Studley (13 Gunners La., Studley, Warwickshire) : K.A.F. Brewin for the Society, 1976. — 32p : ill, ports ; 21cm.
ISBN 0-9505570-0-5 Sd : £0.45
(B77-10499)

792'.09425'57 — Theatres. *Northamptonshire. Northampton. Northampton Repertory Theatre, to 1975*
Reynolds, Ernest. Northampton Repertory Theatre / by Ernest Reynolds. — [Northampton] ([Guildhall Rd, Northants. NN1 1EA]) : [The Theatre], 1976. — 20p : ill(incl 1 col), ports ; 22cm.
'... commissioned to commemorate the Golden Jubilee of the Northampton Repertory Players 1927-1977' - p.4.
ISBN 0-9505442-0-5 Sd : £0.50
(B77-03179)

792'.0943 — Volksbühne. *Germany, 1890-1976*
Davies, Cecil William. Theatre for the people : the story of the Volksbühne / [by] Cecil W. Davies. — Manchester : Manchester University Press, 1977. — ix,181p : 1 ill, map ; 23cm.
Bibl.: p.145-148. — Index.
ISBN 0-7190-0666-x : £4.95
(B77-30529)

792'.0944 — Theatre. *France, 1594-1673*
Arnott, Peter Douglas. An introduction to the French theatre / [by] Peter D. Arnott. — London [etc.] : Macmillan, 1977. — xii,164p ; 23cm.
Bibl.: p.159-160. — Index.
ISBN 0-333-17647-2 : £8.95
(B77-23629)

792'.0947 — Theatre. *Soviet Union, ca 1875-1925. Russian texts*
Red'ko, A E. Teatr i evoliutsiia teatral'nykh form = The theatre and the evolution of theatrical forms / A.E. Red'ko. — Letchworth : Prideaux Press, 1977. — [2],132p ; 21cm. — (Russian titles for the specialist ; no.106 ISSN 0305-3741)
Russian title transliterated. — Russian text. — Second title page in Russian. — Facsimile reprint of: 1st ed. Leningrad? : Izdanie M. i S. Sabashnikovykh, 1926.
Pbk : £1.80
(B77-27295)

792.1 — TRAGEDY AND SERIOUS DRAMA
792.1 — Religious drama in European languages. Performance, ca 1100-ca 1500
Nagler, Alois Maria. The medieval religious stage : shapes and phantoms / [by] A.M. Nagler ; [translated from the German by George C. Schoolfield]. — New Haven ; London : Yale University Press, 1976. — xii, 108p : ill, facsims, plans ; 26cm.
Index.
ISBN 0-300-01986-6 : £8.25
(B77-09187)

792.2 — COMEDY AND MELODRAMA
792.2 — Commedia dell'arte. *Critical studies*
Nicoll, Allardyce. The world of Harlequin : a critical study of the Commedia dell'Arte / by Allardyce Nicoll. — Cambridge [etc.] : Cambridge University Press, 1976. — xvi,243p : ill, coat of arms, facsims ; 29cm.
Originally published: 1963. — Index.
ISBN 0-521-05834-1 : £12.50
ISBN 0-521-29132-1 Pbk : £5.00
(B77-03180)

792.7 — MUSIC HALL, REVUE, NIGHT CLUBS, ETC
792.7 — Striptease. Bruce, Honey. *United States. Autobiographies*
Bruce, Honey. Honey : the life and loves of Lenny's shady lady / [by] Honey Bruce ; with Dana Benenson. — London [etc.] : Mayflower, 1977. — 288p ; 18cm.
Originally published: Chicago : Playboy Press, 1976.
ISBN 0-583-13031-3 Pbk : £0.80
(B77-33985)

792.7'028'0922 — Music hall. Entertainers. *Great Britain, 1850-1975. Biographical dictionaries*
Busby, Roy. British music hall : an illustrated who's who from 1850 to the present day / [by] Roy Busby. — London [etc.] : Elek, 1976. — 191p : ill, facsims, ports ; 25cm.
ISBN 0-236-40053-3 : £12.50
(B77-01712)

792.7'0941 — Music hall. *Great Britain, to 1914. Illustrations*
Music hall / [compiled by] Roy Hudd. — London : Methuen, 1976. — [128]p : chiefly ill, facsims, ports ; 24cm. — (Picturefile)
ISBN 0-413-33430-9 Pbk : £1.95
(B77-01713)

792.7'0941 — Music hall. *Great Britain, to 1920*
Scott, Harold. The early doors : origins of the music hall / [by] Harold Scott. — Wakefield : EP Publishing, 1977. — [4],3-259p,leaf of plate,[12]p of plates : ill, facsims ; 22cm.
Originally published: London : Nicholson and Watson, 1946. — Bibl.: p.255-259. — Index.
ISBN 0-7158-1219-x : £5.95 : CIP rev.
(B77-09188)

792.8 — BALLET
Woodward, Ian. Ballet / [by] Ian Woodward. — Sevenoaks : Teach Yourself Books, 1977. — ix, 430p : ill, facsims, music, plan, ports ; 20cm. — (Teach yourself books)
Bibl.: p.411-414. — Index.
ISBN 0-340-21517-8 Pbk : £2.95
(B77-19574)

792.8'026'0222 — Ballet. Companies. *Soviet Union. Ballets Russes. Costumes. Design. Bakst, Leon. Illustrations*
Bakst, Léon. Bakst. — London : Academy Editions, 1977. — [7]p,48 leaves of plates : ill(chiefly col) ; 24cm.
Leaves printed on both sides.
ISBN 0-85670-311-7 Pbk : £2.95
(B77-13800)

792.8'028'0922 — Ballet. Companies. *Soviet Union. Bolshoi Ballet. Ballet dancers*
Bolshoi's young dancers : Vladimir Vassiliev ... [et al.] / [compiled by Noi Avaliani and Leonid Zhdanov ; translated from the Russian by Natalie Ward ; photographs by Leonid Zhdanov]. — Moscow : Progress Publishers ; London (37 Grays Inn Rd, WC1X 8PS) : [Distributed by] Central Books Ltd, 1975. — 309p : chiefly ill, facsims, music, ports ; 27cm.
Ill. on lining papers. — Translation of: 'Molodye artisty Bol'shogo Baleta'. USSR : s.n., [197-].
ISBN 0-7147-0859-3 : £3.00
(B77-13191)

792.8'03 — Ballet. *Encyclopaedias*
The **encyclopedia** of dance & ballet / edited by Mary Clarke & David Vaughan. — London [etc.] : Pitman, 1977. — 376p : ill(some col), ports ; 26cm.
Bibl.: p.373-374.
ISBN 0-273-01088-3 : £13.50
(B77-32086)

Koegler, Horst. The concise Oxford dictionary of ballet / [by] Horst Koegler. — English ed. — London [etc.] : Oxford University Press, 1977. — viii,583p ; 21cm.
Previous ed.: published as 'Friedrichs Ballettlexikon'. Velber bei Hanover : Friedrich, 1972. — Bibl.: p.vii.
ISBN 0-19-311314-7 : £4.95
(B77-13192)

792.8'09'03 — Ballet, to 1976
Bland, Alexander. A history of ballet and dance in the western world / [by] Alexander Bland. — London : Barrie and Jenkins, 1976. — 192p : ill(some col), facsim, music, ports(some col) ; 31 cm.
Index.
ISBN 0-214-20305-0 : £7.95
Also classified at 793.3'09
(B77-01714)

Crisp, Clement. The colourful world of ballet / [by] Clement Crisp and Edward Thorpe. — London (59 Grosvenor St., W.1) : Sundial Books Ltd, 1977. — 96p : ill(chiefly col), ports(chiefly col) ; 33cm.
Col. ill. on lining papers. — Index.
ISBN 0-904230-39-2 : £1.99
(B77-29618)

792.8'092'2 — Ballet dancers, ca 1920-1975. *Transcripts of interviews*
Gruen, John. The private world of ballet / [by] John Gruen. — Harmondsworth [etc.] : Penguin, 1976. — xv,464p : ports ; 20cm.
Originally published: New York : Viking Press, 1975. — Index.
ISBN 0-14-004343-8 Pbk : Unpriced
(B77-02512)

792.8'092'2 — Ballet. Dancing. Sibley, Antoinette & Dowell, Anthony. *Transcripts of interviews*
Spatt, Leslie E. Sibley & Dowell / photographs by Leslie Spatt ; text by Nicholas Dromgoole ; [with transcriptions of conversations between Antoinette Sibley and Anthony Dowell]. — London : Collins, 1976. — 223p : chiefly ill, ports ; 29cm.
Ports on lining papers.
ISBN 0-00-211047-4 : £9.50
(B77-04356)

792.8'092'4 — Art galleries. *London.* *Westminster (London Borough). Tate Gallery. Exhibits: Items associated with Baccelli, Giovanna. Catalogues*
Einberg, Elizabeth. Gainsborough's 'Giovanna Baccelli' / [by] Elizabeth Einberg. — London : Tate Gallery Publications, 1976. — 40p : ports ; 16x17cm.
Catalogue of an exhibition held 3 November-12 December 1976 at the Tate Gallery. — Bibl.: p.40. — Includes an essay on Giovanna Baccelli.
ISBN 0-905005-60-0 Pbk : £0.90
(B77-02513)

792.8'092'4 — Ballet. Choreography. Ashton, Sir Frederick
Vaughan, David, *b.1924.* Frederick Ashton and his ballets / [by] David Vaughan. — London : A. and C. Black, 1977. — xxi,522p : ill, ports ; 26cm.
Ill. on lining papers. — Bibl.: p.503-509. — Index.
ISBN 0-7136-1689-x : £12.00 : CIP rev.
(B77-06224)

792.8'092'4 — Ballet. Dancing, Baryshnikov, Mikhail
Baryshnikov, Mikhail. Baryshnikov at work : Mikhail Baryshnikov discusses his roles / photographs by Martha Swope ; text edited and introduced by Charles Engell France. — London : A. and C. Black, 1977. — 252p : ill, ports ; 30cm.
Originally published: New York : Knopf, 1976.
ISBN 0-7136-1750-0 : £15.00
(B77-17022)

792.8'092'4 — Ballet. Dancing. Grey, Beryl. *Biographies*
Gillard, David. Beryl Grey : a biography / [by] David Gillard. — London : W.H. Allen, 1977. — ix,214p,[24]p of plates : ill, ports ; 24cm.
Bibl.: p.202-203. — Index.
ISBN 0-491-02221-2 : £5.95
(B77-28808)

792.8'092'4 — Ballet. Dancing. Nureyev, Rudolf
Bland, Alexander. The Nureyev image / [by] Alexander Bland. — London [etc.] : Studio Vista, 1976. — 288p : ill, facsim, ports ; 31cm.
ISBN 0-289-70362-x : £8.95
(B77-08002)

Nureyev. — London : Dance Books [for] Victor Hochhauser Ltd, 1976. — [64]p : ill, ports ; 29cm.
ISBN 0-903102-23-4 : £3.00
ISBN 0-903102-24-2 Pbk : £1.50
(B77-13193)

792.8'092'4 — Ballet. Dancing. Zucchi, Virginia. *Biographies*
Guest, Ivor. The divine Virginia : a biography of Virginia Zucchi / [by] Ivor Guest. — New York [etc.] : Dekker ; [London] : [Distributed by Dance Books], 1977. — [2],xv,187,[1]p,[18]p of plates : ill, ports ; 24cm.
Bibl.: p.177-180. — Index.
ISBN 0-8247-6492-7 : £9.50
(B77-19575)

792.8'0942 — Ballet. Companies. *England. Ballet Rambert, to 1976*
Ballet Rambert. 50 years of Ballet Rambert, 1926-1976 / edited by Clement Crisp, Anya Sainsbury, Peter Williams. — [London] ([Mercury Theatre Trust, 94 Chiswick High Rd, W4 1SH]) : [Ballet Rambert], 1976. — [1], 64,[1]p : ill, facsim, ports ; 32cm.
ISBN 0-9505478-0-8 Pbk : £1.00
(B77-04994)

792.8'0942 — Ballet. Companies. *England. Royal Ballet, to 1973. Essays*
De Valois, *Dame* **Ninette.** Step by step : the formation of an establishment / [by] Ninette de Valois. — London : W.H. Allen, 1977. — [10], 204p,[32]p of plates : ill, ports ; 23cm.
Index.
ISBN 0-491-01598-4 : £4.50
(B77-08501)

792.8'2 — Ballet. Techniques. *Manuals*
Kirstein, Lincoln. The classic ballet : basic technique and terminology / historical development by Lincoln Kirstein ; descriptive text by Muriel Stuart ; illustrations by Carlus Dyer ; with a preface by George Balanchine. — London : A. and C. Black, 1977. — xii,243p : ill ; 22x27cm.
Originally published: New York : Knopf, 1952 ; London : Longmans, 1953. — Index.
ISBN 0-7136-1751-9 : £7.50
(B77-19576)

Lawson, Joan, *b.1906.* Beginning ballet : a concentrated primer for ballet students of all ages / [by] Joan Lawson ; with original introduction by Kay Ambrose. — London : A. and C. Black, 1977. — [6],113p : ill ; 22cm.
Index. — '... comprises "Beginners, please!" by the late Kay Ambrose and "Dressing for the ballet" by the late Peter Revitt and Joan Lawson, who has reworked some of the material from both books' - title page verso.
ISBN 0-7136-1649-0 : £3.75 : CIP rev.
(B77-07536)

Messerer, Asaf. Classes in classical ballet / [by] Asaf Messerer ; translated [from the Russian] by Oleg Briansky. — London : Dance Books [etc.], 1976. — 494p : ill, ports ; 24cm.
This translation originally published: Garden City : Doubleday, 1975. — Translation of: 'Uroki klassicheskogo tantsa'. Moscow : Iskusstvo, 1967.
ISBN 0-903102-25-0 : £7.50
(B77-17023)

792.8'2 — Ballet. Techniques: Cecchetti method. *Manuals*
Beaumont, Cyril William. A manual of the theory and practice of classical theatrical dancing (classical ballet) (Cecchetti method) / by Cyril W. Beaumont and Stanislas Idzikowski ; with a preface by Enrico Cecchetti. — Revised ed. — London (70 Gloucester Place, W1H 4AJ) : Imperial Society of Teachers of Dancing, 1977. — 272p : ill ; 22cm.
Previous ed.: i.e. New and revised ed. / illustrations by Randolph Schwabe ; revised by Cyril W. Beaumont. London : The author, 1932. — Index.
Pbk : £5.00
(B77-32788)

792.8'4 — Ballet. Bruce, Christopher. Black angels. Production
Austin, Richard. Birth of a ballet / by Richard Austin ; line drawings by Judy Ling Wong ; photographs by Alan Cunliffe ; with a foreword by Christopher Bruce. — London : Vision Press, 1976. — 151p,[8]p of plates : ill, ports ; 23cm.
ISBN 0-85478-044-0 : £4.20
(B77-02514)

792.9 — THEATRE. SPECIFIC PRODUCTIONS
792.9 — Drama in English. Shakespeare, William. *Promptbooks. Facsimiles*
Shaw, Glen Byam. 'Macbeth' onstage : an annotated facsimile of Glen Byam Shaw's 1955 promptbook / edited by Michael Mullin. — Columbia ; London : University of Missouri Press, 1976 [i.e. 1977]. — 256p : ill, plans, port ; 29x32cm.
Ill. on lining paper. — Published in the United States: 1976. — Includes the text of the play.
ISBN 0-8262-0212-8 : £20.80
(B77-13801)

792.9 — Drama in English. Shakespeare, William. Directing. *Transcripts of interviews*
Berry, Ralph. On directing Shakespeare : interviews with contemporary directors / [by] Ralph Berry. — London : Croom Helm [etc.], 1977. — 135p,[16]p of plates : ill, ports ; 23cm.
Index.
ISBN 0-85664-329-7 : £5.95
(B77-04995)

792.9 — Drama in English. Shakespeare, William. Performance, 1800-1976
Styan, John Louis. The Shakespeare revolution : criticism and performance in the twentieth century / [by] J.L. Styan. — Cambridge [etc.] : Cambridge University Press, 1977. — ix,292p : ill ; 22cm.
Bibl.: p.264-274. — Index.
ISBN 0-521-21193-x : £6.50
Also classified at 822.3'3
(B77-27296)

792.9 — Drama in English. Shakespeare, William. Production by Royal Shakespeare Theatre Company at Stratford-upon-Avon, 1959-1974. *Critical studies*
Wells, Stanley, *b.1930.* Royal Shakespeare : four major productions at Stratford-upon-Avon ... / [by] Stanley Wells. — Manchester : Manchester University Press, 1977. — 81p : ill ; 22cm.
'... delivered as lectures at Furman University, South Carolina, U.S.A. in 1976'. — '... reprinted ... from the sesquicentennial issue of "Furman Studies", N.S. Volume 23' - cover.
ISBN 0-7190-0547-7 Pbk : £1.50 : CIP rev.
(B77-16004)

793 — INDOOR GAMES AND AMUSEMENTS
793 — Games using toy shops. *Collections. Juvenile literature*
Evans, Hilary. Playing shops / [by] Hilary Evans. — London : Studio Vista, 1977. — 44p : ill ; 26cm. — (Something to do)
Index.
ISBN 0-289-70691-2 : £2.25
(B77-19577)

793 — Indoor activities. *Manuals*
Foulsham's bumper fun book : a great guide to home amusement. — London : Foulsham, 1976. — 255p : ill, music ; 20cm.
Spine title: Bumper fun book.
ISBN 0-572-00957-7 Pbk : £0.75
(B77-02515)

793 — Indoor games. *Manuals*
Ainslie, Tom. Ainslie's complete Hoyle / illustrations by Jill Schwartz. — London : New English Library, 1977. — xvii,526p : ill ; 24cm.
Originally published: New York : Simon and Schuster, 1975. — Index.
ISBN 0-450-03201-9 : £7.50
(B77-16005)

The **book** of games / edited by Richard Sharp and John Piggott. — London (11 St John's Hill, S.W.11) : Artus Publishing Co. Ltd, 1977. — 3-186p : col ill ; 30cm.
Col. ill. on lining papers. — Index.
£2.99
(B77-32789)

Diagram Group. The way to play : the illustrated encyclopedia of the games of the world / by the Diagram Group. — Toronto [etc.] ; London : Bantam, 1977. — 320p : ill(chiefly col) ; 28cm.
Originally published: New York : London : Paddington Press, 1975. — Index.
ISBN 0-552-98016-1 Pbk : £2.95
(B77-28013)

793 — Indoor games. *Manuals. Juvenile literature*
Yeatman, Linda. The best book of indoor games / [by] Linda Yeatman ; illustrated by Richard Fowler. — [London] : Hodder Causton for Rowntree Mackintosh Ltd, 1975. — 63p : col ill ; 32cm.
ISBN 0-340-18922-3 Pbk : £1.60
(B77-01715)

793.3 — Dancing
Dance studies. — St Peter (Les Bois, St Peter, Jersey, C.I.) : Centre for Dance Studies.
Vol.1 / edited by Roderyk Lange. — 1976. — ix,87p,[32] leaves of plates : ill, music, port ; 21cm.
ISBN 0-9505503-0-2 Pbk : £3.00
(B77-06821)

793.3 — Dancing. Related to visual arts
Watts, Elizabeth. Towards dance and art : a study of relationships between two art forms / [by] Elizabeth Watts. — London : Lepus Books, 1977. — x,110p : ill ; 22cm.
Bibl.: p.104-106. — Index.
ISBN 0-86019-027-7 : £3.80
Primary classification 700
(B77-13752)

793.3'09 — Dancing, to ca 1500
Bland, Alexander. A history of ballet and dance in the western world / [by] Alexander Bland. — London : Barrie and Jenkins, 1976. — 192p : ill(some col), facsim, music, ports(some col) ; 31 cm.
Index.
ISBN 0-214-20305-0 : £7.95
Primary classification 792.8'09'03
(B77-01714)

793.3'19411 — Scottish country dancing. *Manuals*
Johnstone, Jackie. The Loreburn dances ... / devised by Jackie Johnstone. — Dumfries : [The author].
Book 2. — 1976. — [18]p ; 21cm.
ISBN 0-9505469-0-9 Sd : Unpriced
(B77-03181)

Scottish country dancing. — Wakefield : EP Publishing, 1977. — 36,[1]p : ill ; 15x22cm. — (Know the game)
'Produced in collaboration with the Royal Scottish Country Dance Society'.
ISBN 0-7158-0535-5 : Unpriced
ISBN 0-7158-0534-7 Sd : £0.50
(B77-30530)

793.3'19411 — Scottish country dancing for children. *Collections*
Gradon, Sheila Anne. The St Columban book of Scottish country dances for children / [by Sheila Gradon]. — Liverpool (50 Wicks Cres., Formby, Liverpool L37 1PW) : Hugh Foss (Formby), [1976]. — [3],15p : ill ; 21cm.
ISBN 0-904102-16-5 Sd : £0.30
(B77-01716)

793.3'1942 — English country dancing. *Manuals*
Set and honour : 18 English country dances / collected by Cecil Sharp ; edited by Margaret Grant. — Borough Green : Novello, 1976. — [4],24p : music ; 25cm.
'The notation of these dances taken from Playford's "English Dancing Master" is based on Cecil Sharp's original transcription and the practical experience and teaching of Mrs Margaret Grant. The instructions are not given in full detail but are intended as an "aide memoire". The dances included ... are taken from "The Country Dance Book, Part II, published by Novello and Company Limited"' - Preface.
Sd : £0.65
(B77-06225)

793.3'2 — Body movements. Analysis. Notation
Benesh, Rudolf. Reading dance : the birth of choreology / by Rudolf and Joan Benesh. — London : Souvenir Press, 1977. — xvi,139p : ill, music, ports ; 25cm. — (A condor book)
ISBN 0-285-62291-9 : £4.50 : CIP rev.
(B77-15419)

793.3'2 — Body movements: Medau movements
Braithwaite, Molly. Medau rhythmic movement / by Molly Braithwaite. — [3rd ed.]. — Wallington (c/o The Secretary, 58 Montagu Gardens, Wallington, Surrey SM6 0NF) : Medau Society of Great Britain & Northern Ireland, [1976]. — 80p : ill, ports ; 26cm.
Previous ed.: 1955. — Bibl.: p.79. — Index.
ISBN 0-9505535-0-6 Pbk : £1.75
(B77-09871)

793.3'2 — Improvised dancing. *Manuals*
Slade, Peter. Natural dance : developmental movement and guided action / [by] Peter Slade. — London [etc.] : Hodder and Stoughton, 1977. — [8],280p : ill ; 24cm.
Index.
ISBN 0-340-20933-x : £6.95
ISBN 0-340-20934-8 Pbk : £3.95
(B77-29619)

793.3'2 — Jazz dance. *Manuals*
Cayou, Dolores Kirton. Modern jazz dance / [by] Dolores Kirton Cayou. — London : Dance Books, 1976. — ii-xii,148p : ill, ports ; 22cm.
Originally published: Palo Alto : National Press Books, 1971.
ISBN 0-903102-15-3 : £4.00
ISBN 0-903102-16-1 Pbk : £2.00
(B77-17024)

793.3'2 — Modern dance
Salter, Alan. The curving air / [by] Alan Salter with Stina Grist ; and five line drawings by Brian Smithies. — London (20 Dartmouth Hill, SE10 8AJ) : Human Factors Associates, 1977. — 164p : ill ; 21cm.
ISBN 0-9505899-0-x Pbk : £2.00
(B77-30531)

793.3'2 — Theatrical dance. Production
Dance : the art of production / edited by Joan Schlaich, Betty DuPont. — Saint Louis : Mosby ; London : Distributed by Kimpton, 1977. — xiii,161p : ill, forms, plan ; 23cm.
Index.
ISBN 0-8016-4346-5 Pbk : £5.30
(B77-19578)

793.3'2'07 — Dancing. Teaching. Organisations. *Great Britain. Laban Art of Movement Guild. Directories*
Laban Art of Movement Guild. List of members / Laban Art of Movement Guild. — [Addlestone] ([Laban Art of Movement Centre, Woburn Hill, Addlestone, Surrey KT15 2QD]) : [The Guild].
1976 : compiled 1st April, 1976. — [1976]. — [1],20p ; 21cm.
Sd : Unpriced
(B77-17684)

793.3'2'08 — Theatrical dance. *Critical studies. Readings*
Jowitt, Deborah. Dance beat : selected views and reviews, 1967-1976 / [by] Deborah Jowitt. — New York [etc.] : Marcel Dekker ; London : Distributed by Dance Books, 1977. — xi,211p ; 23cm.
Index.
ISBN 0-8247-6506-0 Pbk : £6.00
(B77-18314)

793.3'2'0924 — Educational institutions. Curriculum subjects: Dancing. Teaching. Influence of Laban, Rudolf. *England*
Foster, John, *b.1929.* The influences of Rudolph [i.e. Rudolf] Laban / [by] John Foster. — London : Lepus Books, 1977. — 184p ; 23cm.
Bibl.: p.171-180. — Index.
ISBN 0-86019-015-3 : £5.00
(B77-14341)

793.3'2'0924 — Modern dance. Choreography. Horton, Lester. *United States. Biographies*
Warren, Larry. Lester Horton : modern dance pioneer / [by] Larry Warren. — New York [etc.] : Dekker ; [London] : [Distributed by Dance Books], 1977. — [2],xvii,267p,[1]p : ill, facsims, ports ; 24cm.
Index.
ISBN 0-8247-6503-6 : £7.50
(B77-19579)

793.3'2'0973 — Modern dance. *United States, to 1976*
Mazo, Joseph H. Prime movers : the makers of modern dance in America / [by] Joseph H. Mazo. — London : A. and C. Black, 1977. — 3-322p : ill, facsims, ports ; 24cm.
Also published: New York : Morrow, 1977. — Bibl.: p.302-311. — Index.
ISBN 0-7136-1737-3 : £6.75 : CIP rev.
(B77-22052)

793.3'3 — Latin American ballroom dancing. *Manuals*
Imperial Society of Teachers of Dancing. *Latin-American Dance Branch Committee.* Popular variations in Latin-American dancing / [edited by Elizabeth Romain on behalf of the Latin-American Dance Branch Committee], Imperial Society of Teachers of Dancing. — London (70 Gloucester Place, W1H 4AJ) : The Society, [1976]. — [4],46p ; 21cm.
Incorporates 'Latin, popular variations'. 1972.
Sd : £1.50
(B77-33377)

793.3'5 — North-eastern English sword dancing. *Manuals*
Sharp, Cecil James. The sword-dances of Northern England / [by] Cecil J. Sharp. — Wakefield : EP Publishing, 1977. — [4],112p, 43p,115p,[17]leaves of plates : ill, facsim, music ; 20cm.
Facsimile reprint of: 1st ed., originally published in 3 vols. London : Novello, 1911-3. — Part III is reprinted from 2nd ed., 1952.
ISBN 0-7158-1211-4 : £4.25
(B77-17685)

793.7'3 — General knowledge. *Questions & answers*
Ask the family : questions and answers from the BBC TV quiz game. — London : British Broadcasting Corporation.
3 / illustrated by Graham Bingham. — 1976. — 96p : ill ; 18cm.
With answers.
ISBN 0-563-17187-1 Pbk : £0.45
(B77-01717)

Brandreth, Gyles. Pears all the year round quiz book / [by] Gyles Brandreth. — London : Pelham, 1977. — 222p : ill ; 21cm.
With answers.
ISBN 0-7207-1018-9 : £3.50
ISBN 0-7207-1019-7 Pbk : £2.25
(B77-33378)

Dr Seuss. The cat's quizzer / by Dr Seuss. — London : Collins, 1977. — [1],64p : chiefly col ill ; 29cm. — (Beginner books) (I can read it all by myself)
With answers. — Originally published: New York : Random House, 1976.
ISBN 0-00-171167-9 : £1.95
(B77-17025)

Fletcher, Cyril. The generation quiz book / with Cyril Fletcher representing the 1920s, 1930s and 1940s and Gyles Brandreth representing the 1950s, 1960s and 1970s. — [London] : Fontana, 1976. — 126p ; 18cm.
With answers. — Originally published: London : Luscombe, 1975.
ISBN 0-00-634148-9 Pbk : £0.60
(B77-15420)

Robinson, Tom. Third piccolo quiz book / [by] Tom Robinson. — London [etc.] : Pan Books, 1977. — [143]p : ill ; 18cm. — (Piccolo original)
With answers.
ISBN 0-330-25115-5 Pbk : £0.45
(B77-31372)

'University Challenge' quiz book / compiled by Jean Sedley. — London (247 Tottenham Court Rd, W1P 0AU) : Independent Television Books ; London : Arrow Books, 1977. — 112p ; 18cm.
With answers.
ISBN 0-09-915520-6 Pbk : £0.65
(B77-32087)

793.7'3 — General knowledge. *Questions & answers. Juvenile literature*
May, Robin. Runaround quiz book / compiled by Robin May ; illustrated by Tony Morris. — London : Independent Television Books Ltd : Arrow Books, 1977. — 95p : ill, ports ; 20cm. — (Look-in books)
'From the Southern Television series' - cover. — With answers.
ISBN 0-09-915450-1 Pbk : £0.65
(B77-32088)

Thaw, George. The George Thaw quiz book. — London : Muller, 1977. — 63p : ill, ports ; 26cm.
With answers.
ISBN 0-584-10318-2 : £1.95 : CIP rev.
(B77-22764)

A third book of 'How' : a general knowledge question and answer book / compiled by Robin May ; text illustrations by David Jefferis. — London [etc.] : Pan Books, 1975. — [2],87p : ill, maps ; 20cm. — (A piccolo-'TV times' original)
Based on the Southern Television network series.
ISBN 0-330-24568-6 Pbk : £0.35
(B77-08502)

793.7'3 — Logical puzzles. *Collections*
Emmet, Eric Revell. 101 brain puzzlers / [by] E.R. Emmet. — New York [etc.] ; London : Harper and Row, [1977]. — x,254p : ill ; 18cm.
With answers. — Originally published: as '101 brain-puzzlers for the young of all ages'. London : Macmillan, 1967.
ISBN 0-06-465070-7 Pbk : £1.30
(B77-14863)

793.7'3 — Mudcrack. *Fill-in books*
Schensted, Craige. Mudcrack pad : the game of strategy all the family can enjoy / edited by Craige Schensted and Charles Titus. — [London] : Longman, 1976. — [66]p : of ill(some col) ; 21x24cm.
Cover title. — Notebook format. — Originally published: New York : Neo Press, 1970.
ISBN 0-582-18635-8 Pbk : £0.85
(B77-03708)

793.7'3 — Pictorial puzzles. *Collections. Juvenile literature*
Webb, Leslie Walter. Fifth piccolo picture puzzle book / devised and drawn by Leslie W. Webb. — London [etc.] : Pan Books, 1977. — [95]p : chiefly ill ; 20cm. — (Piccolo original)
With answers.
ISBN 0-330-25117-1 Pbk : £0.40
(B77-30532)

793.7'3 — Puzzles. *Collections*
Booth-Jones, Charles. The Beaver book of brain ticklers / [by] Charles Booth-Jones ; illustrated by Michael Jackson and Lesley Smith. — London [etc.] : Beaver Books, 1977. — 109p : ill ; 20cm.
With answers.
ISBN 0-600-31396-4 Pbk : £0.50
(B77-26451)

Fixx, James F. Games for the superintelligent / by James F. Fixx. — London : Muller, 1977. — ix,86p : ill ; 22cm.
With answers. — Originally published: Garden City, N.Y. : Doubleday, 1972.
ISBN 0-584-10162-7 Pbk : £0.95
(B77-20493)

Fixx, James F. More games for the superintelligent / by James F. Fixx. — London : Muller, 1977. — ix,101p : ill ; 22cm.
With answers. — Originally published: New York : Doubleday, 1976.
ISBN 0-584-10258-5 Pbk : £0.95
(B77-20494)

Razzi, James. Star trek puzzle manual : puzzles, mazes and trivia to baffle, enlighten and amuse Star trek fans everywhere / based on the television series created by Gene Roddenberry ; [written by] James Razzi ; [assisted by] Sondra Marshak and Myrna Culbreath. — Toronto [etc.] ; London : Bantam, 1976. — 128p : ill ; 28cm.
With answers.
ISBN 0-552-99001-9 Pbk : £1.50
Also classified at 791.45'7
(B77-08003)

793.7'3 — Puzzles. *Collections. Juvenile literature*
Brandreth, Gyles. 101 brain teasers and mind benders / [by] Gyles Brandreth ; illustrated by Ann Axworthy. — [London] : Carousel Books, 1977. — 121p : ill ; 20cm. — (Carousel books)
ISBN 0-552-54116-8 Pbk : £0.45
(B77-17686)

Holt, Michael. The second big book of puzzles / by Michael Holt and Ronald Ridout ; illustrated by Peter Edwards. — Harmondsworth [etc.] : Puffin Books, 1976. — 170p : ill ; 18cm. — (Puffin books)
Originally published: Harmondsworth : Longman Young Books, 1973.
ISBN 0-14-030826-1 Pbk : £0.40
(B77-02516)

Mottahedin, Yasmin. The Armada round the world quiz book / written and illustrated by Yasmin Mottahedin. — London : Armada, 1976. — 123p : ill, maps ; 18cm.
With answers.
ISBN 0-00-691029-7 Pbk : £0.40
(B77-01718)

Shepherd, Walter. Picture puzzles / [by] Walter Shepherd. — London [etc.] : Beaver Books, 1976. — 92p : ill ; 20cm.
With answers.
ISBN 0-600-37117-4 Pbk : £0.50
(B77-13194)

What's the answer?. — London [etc.] : Beaver Books, 1976. — 111p : ill ; 20cm.
With answers.
ISBN 0-600-33607-7 Pbk : £0.50
(B77-13802)

793.7'3 — Puzzles: Mazes. *Collections*
Phillips, Dave. Graphic and op-art mazes / [by] David Phillips. — New York : Dover [etc.] ; London : Constable, 1976. — [56]p : of ill(some col) ; 28cm.
ISBN 0-486-23373-1 Pbk : £1.05
(B77-28014)

793.7'3 — Puzzles: Mazes. *Collections. Juvenile literature*
Brandreth, Gyles. Knight book of mazes / [by] Gyles Brandreth and David Farris. — Leicester : Knight Books, 1975. — 127p : of ill ; 18cm.
With answers.
ISBN 0-340-19784-6 Pbk : £0.40
(B77-08503)

Koziakin, Vladimir. Mazes for fun / [by] Vladimir Koziakin. — London : Pan Books. — (Piccolo)
No.4. — 1977. — [64]p : of ill ; 20cm.
With solutions. — Originally published: New York : Grosset & Dunlap, 1974.
ISBN 0-330-25074-4 Pbk : £0.35
(B77-12598)

Lear, Edward. Edward Lear's book of mazes. — London : Carousel, 1977. — 109p : ill ; 20cm.
With answers. — Contents: Nonsense songs and limericks / by Edward Lear - Amazing mazes / by Gyles Brandreth and David Farris.
ISBN 0-552-52077-2 Pbk : £0.45
Also classified at 821'.8
(B77-28809)

793.7'3 — Puzzles. Special subjects: Animals. *Collections. Juvenile literature*
Morris, Johnny. Animal quiz / [by] Johnny Morris. — London [etc.] : Beaver Books, 1976. — 110p : ill ; 20cm.
With answers.
ISBN 0-600-30314-4 Pbk : £0.50
(B77-13803)

793.7'3 — Puzzles. Special subjects: Earth. *Collections. Juvenile literature*
Stein, Nora. Our earth / [written and planned by Nora Stein]. — London : Macdonald Educational, 1977. — [1],25p : col ill, col map ; 20cm. — (Macdonald quiz books)
With answers.
ISBN 0-356-05534-5 Sd : £0.35
(B77-14342)

793.7'3 — Puzzles. Special subjects: Pets. *Collections. Juvenile literature*
Stein, Nora. Pets / [written and planned by Nora Stein]. — London : Macdonald Educational, 1977. — [1],25p : col ill ; 20cm. — (Macdonald quiz books)
With answers.
ISBN 0-356-05535-3 Sd : £0.35
(B77-13804)

793.7'3 — Puzzles. Special subjects: Plants. *Collections. Juvenile literature*
Stein, Nora. Plants and flowers / [written and planned by Nora Stein]. — London : Macdonald Educational, 1977. — [1],25p : col ill ; 20cm. — (Macdonald quiz books)
With answers.
ISBN 0-356-05536-1 Sd : £0.35
(B77-14343)

793.7'3 — Puzzles. Special subjects: Seashore. *Collections. Juvenile literature*
Stein, Nora. Seaside / [written and planned by Nora Stein]. — London : Macdonald Educational, 1977. — [1],25p : col ill ; 20cm. — (Macdonald quiz books)
With answers.
ISBN 0-356-05537-x Sd : £0.35
(B77-14344)

793.7'3 — Puzzles. Special subjects: Sports & games. *Collections. Juvenile literature*
Stein, Nora. Sports and games / [written and planned by Nora Stein]. — London : Macdonald Educational, 1977. — [1],25p : col ill ; 20cm. — (Macdonald quiz books)
With answers.
ISBN 0-356-05538-8 Sd : £0.35
(B77-14345)

793.7'3 — Scrabble. *Manuals*
Hinch, Derryn. The Scrabble book / [by] Derryn Hinch. — Revised British ed. — London [etc.] : Macmillan, 1977. — [8],184p : ill ; 23cm.
Previous ed.: New York : Mason, Charter, 1976. — Index.
ISBN 0-333-23073-6 : £3.95 : CIP rev.
(B77-22765)

793.7'3 — Tangram. *Manuals*
Elffers, Joost. Tangram : the ancient Chinese shapes game / [by] Joost Elffers ; translated by R.J. Hollingdale. — Harmondsworth [etc.] : Penguin, 1976. — 264p in various pagings : chiefly ill, facsims ; 19cm.
Seven puzzle pieces in plastic envelope. — Translation of: 'Tangram'. 2.Aufl. Köln : M. DuMont Schauberg, 1974. — Bibl.: p.29-31.
ISBN 0-14-004181-8 Pbk : £1.95
(B77-03182)

793.7'3 — Word games. *Collections*
Robson, Ann. Word games for all the family / [by] Ann & John Robson. — Leicester : Knight Books, 1977. — 94p ; 18cm.
Originally published: Toronto : Paperjacks, 1974.
ISBN 0-340-20484-2 Pbk : £0.50
(B77-24399)

793.7'3'05 — Puzzles. *Collections. Juvenile literature. Serials*
The '**Jack** and Jill' book of games and puzzles. — London : IPC Magazines.
1978. — 1977. — 96p : chiefly ill ; 27cm. — (A Fleetway annual)
ISBN 0-85037-332-8 Pbk : £0.85
(B77-33986)

793.7'3'05 — Puzzles. *Collections. Periodicals*
One across. — Horsham : Micron Publications Ltd ; Horsham (Faygate, Horsham, W. Sussex) : Distributed by Wells Gardner, Darton and Co. Ltd.
Vol.1, no.1- ; Jan. 1974?-. — 1974?-. — ill, ports ; 25cm.
Monthly. — 36p. in July 1977 issue. — With answers.
Sd : £0.30
ISSN 0305-912x
(B77-32089)

793.73'2 — Crossword puzzles. *Collections*
The **30th** Pan book of crosswords / edited by L.W. Burgess. — London [etc.] : Pan Books, 1976. — [128]p ; 18cm.
Cover title: The Pan book of crosswords. 30. — With answers.
ISBN 0-330-24841-3 Pbk : £0.40
(B77-04357)

The **31st** Pan book of crosswords / edited by L.W. Burgess. — London [etc.] : Pan Books, 1977. — [128]p ; 18cm.
With answers.
ISBN 0-330-25136-8 Pbk : £0.45
(B77-28810)

Coltman, David. The fifth Arrow book of crosswords / compiled by David Coltman. — London [etc.] : Arrow Books, 1977. — [95]p ; 18cm.
With answers.
ISBN 0-09-914600-2 Pbk : £0.50
(B77-17026)

'**Daily** mail' book of crossword puzzles no.8 : 72 quick puzzles, 72 cryptic puzzles. — London : Associated Newspapers Group, [1977?]. — [128]p ; 19cm.
With answers.
Pbk : £0.40
(B77-33987)

'**Daily** mirror' crossword book 46. — London : Mirror Group Books, 1977. — [128]p : ill ; 18cm.
With answers.
ISBN 0-85939-079-9 Pbk : £0.35
(B77-13195)

'**Daily** mirror' crossword book 48. — London : Mirror Group Books, 1977. — [126]p ; 19cm.
With answers.
ISBN 0-85939-087-x Pbk : £0.35
(B77-27297)

'**Daily** mirror' quizword book 6 / compiled by L.C. Browne. — London : Mirror Group Books, 1977. — [128]p ; 19cm.
With answers.
ISBN 0-85939-082-9 Pbk : £0.35
(B77-18938)

The '**Daily** telegraph' 50th anniversary crossword book. — Harmondsworth [etc.] : Penguin, 1975. — 142p ; 19cm. — (Penguin crossword puzzles)
ISBN 0-14-003988-0 Pbk : £0.50
(B77-09189)

'**Evening** news' book of crossword puzzles. — London : Associated Newspapers Group.
No.30. — [1977]. — 127p ; 18cm.
With solutions.
ISBN 0-85144-141-6 Pbk : £0.35
(B77-09872)

The **fourth** Penguin book of 'Sunday telegraph' crosswords. — Harmondsworth [etc.] : Penguin, 1977. — 187p ; 18cm. — (Penguin crossword puzzles)
With answers.
ISBN 0-14-004344-6 Pbk : £0.65
(B77-25809)

Harding, Frederick. The fifteenth Fontana book of crosswords / [by] Frederick Harding. — [London] : Fontana, 1976. — 192p ; 18cm.
With answers.
ISBN 0-00-614265-6 Pbk : £0.45
(B77-09190)

Harding, Frederick. The sixteenth Fontana book of crosswords / [by] Frederick Harding. — [London] : Fontana, 1977. — 191p ; 18cm.
With answers.
ISBN 0-00-614549-3 Pbk : £0.50
(B77-17027)

Jones, Christopher. Structural crossword puzzles / [by] Christopher Jones ; illustrated by Dan Pearce. — London : Longman.
Stage 6. — 1977. — [4],59p : ill ; 20cm.
With answers.
ISBN 0-582-55068-8 Sd : £0.42
(B77-11354)

Julius, Edward. Bantam one a day crosswords / by Edward Julius. — Toronto [etc.] ; London : Bantam.
2. — 1975. — 142,[1]p ; 18cm.
With answers.
ISBN 0-552-66455-3 Pbk : £0.40
(B77-18939)

McKay, Tim. Crosswords galore number nine / [by Tim McKay]. — [London] : [Beaverbrook Newspapers], [1977]. — [128]p : ill, ports ; 19cm.
Cover title. — With answers. — 'A "Daily Express" publication'.
ISBN 0-85079-082-4 Pbk : £0.35
(B77-15421)

Parsons, Colin. 76 new crossword puzzles / by Colin Parsons. — [Sutton] ([15 Temple Way, Sutton, Surrey]) : Spartan Books, 1976. — 173p ; 18cm.
With answers.
ISBN 0-905532-00-7 Pbk : £0.40
(B77-10500)

Patterson, Christopher. The eleventh Fontana book of crosswords / [by] Christopher Patterson. — [London] : Fontana, 1977. — 192p ; 18cm.
With answers. — Originally published: 1973.
ISBN 0-00-614527-2 Pbk : £0.45
(B77-17028)

Patterson, Christopher. The tenth Fontana book of crosswords / [by] Christopher Patterson. — [London] : Fontana, 1977. — 192p ; 18cm.
With answers. — Originally published: 1973.
ISBN 0-00-615063-2 Pbk : £0.50
(B77-27298)

Patterson, Christopher. The thirteenth Fontana book of crosswords / [by] Christopher Patterson. — [London] : Fontana, 1977. — 190p ; 18cm.
With answers. — Originally published: 1974.
ISBN 0-00-614652-x Pbk : £0.45
(B77-17029)

The **Penguin** book of 'Sunday times' crosswords. — Harmondsworth [etc.] : Penguin. — (Penguin crossword puzzles)
2nd / compiled by Elizabeth and Derek Jewell with Solver's Guide by the authors. — 1976. — 223p ; 18cm.
With answers.
ISBN 0-14-004160-5 Pbk : £0.60
(B77-01719)

The **second** Penguin book of 'Sun' crosswords. — Harmondsworth [etc.] : Penguin, 1975. — 187p ; 18cm. — (Penguin crossword puzzles)
With answers.
ISBN 0-14-004050-1 Pbk : £0.50
(B77-19580)

Stokes, Leslie. The first Fontana book of crosswords / [by] Leslie Stokes. — [London] : Fontana, 1977. — 192p ; 18cm.
With answers. — Originally published: 1967.
ISBN 0-00-614416-0 Pbk : £0.45
(B77-17030)

The '**Sunday** express' book of skeleton crosswords. — Harmondsworth [etc.] : Penguin, 1977. — 181p ; 20cm. — (Penguin crossword puzzles)
With answers.
ISBN 0-14-004424-8 Pbk : £0.60
(B77-32090)

The **third** Penguin book of 'Sun' crosswords. — Harmondsworth [etc.] : Penguin, 1977. — 187p ; 18cm. — (Penguin crossword puzzles)
With answers.
ISBN 0-14-004226-1 Pbk : £0.50
(B77-13196)

Woolley, Reg. The fourth Arrow book of crosswords / compiled by Reg Woolley. — London : Arrow Books, 1977. — [5],68,[19]p ; 18cm.
With answers.
ISBN 0-09-914150-7 Pbk : £0.50
(B77-09873)

793.73'2 — Crossword puzzles. *Collections. Juvenile literature*

Armada book of picture crosswords. — London : Armada Books.
2nd / [by] Douglas and Christina Power. — 1976. — [96]p : chiefly ill ; 20cm.
With answers.
ISBN 0-00-691062-9 Pbk : £0.40
(B77-01720)

Cavendish, Mavis. The young puffin book of crosswords / by Mavis Cavendish ; illustrated by Stuart Kettle. — Harmondsworth [etc.] : Puffin Books, 1977. — 95p : ill ; 20cm. — (A young puffin original)
With answers to numbered puzzles.
ISBN 0-14-030885-7 Pbk : £0.40
(B77-16006)

'**Daily** mirror' junior crossword book 25. — London : Mirror Group Books, 1976. — [128] p : ill ; 18cm.
With answers.
ISBN 0-85939-068-3 Pbk : £0.30
(B77-02517)

'**Daily** mirror' junior crossword book 26. — London : Mirror Group Books, 1977. — [128] p ; 19cm.
With answers.
ISBN 0-85939-080-2 Pbk : £0.35
(B77-13197)

'**Daily** mirror' junior crossword book 27. — London : Mirror Group Books, 1977. — [128] p ; 18cm.
With answers.
ISBN 0-85939-086-1 Pbk : £0.35
(B77-28811)

Fourth Knight book of crosswords / compiled by Roy S. Philpott. — Leicester : Knight Books, 1977. — [96]p ; 18cm.
With answers.
ISBN 0-340-19618-1 Pbk : £0.45
(B77-14864)

Newton, Robert, *b.1915.* The twelfth Armada crossword book / compiled by Robert Newton. — London : Armada Paperbacks, 1977. — [7], 100,[19]p : ill ; 18cm.
Cover title: 12th Armada crossword book. — With answers.
ISBN 0-00-690822-5 Pbk : £0.40
(B77-05578)

The **Starfish** third junior crosswords. — Cobham : Starfish Books, [1976]. — 144p : ill ; 18cm.
With answers.
ISBN 0-900708-99-9 Pbk : £0.40
(B77-06226)

793.73'2 — Crossword puzzles. *Collections. Welsh texts*

Ab Ifor, Gwynfor. Gwirion bôs! : croeseiriau a phosau / gan Gwynfor ab Ifor, Alice Williams a Dafydd Meirion. — Y Groeslon ([Bryn Mair, Dolydd, y Groeslon, Caernarfon, Gwynedd]) : Cyhoeddiadau Mei, 1977. — 47p ; 13x19cm.
ISBN 0-905775-01-5 Sd : £0.45
(B77-33379)

793.73'2 — Crossword puzzles. Special subjects: Yorkshire. *Collections*

Knox, Philip. Yorkshire crosswords : 50 crosswords and answers / compiled by Philip Knox. — Clapham, N. Yorkshire : Dalesman, 1976. — [63]p ; 21cm.
ISBN 0-85206-369-5 Pbk : £0.60
(B77-15422)

793.7'4 — Games for children: Number games. *Collections*

Hurwitz, Abraham Benjamin. Number games for children / [by] Abraham B. Hurwitz, Arthur Goddard, David T. Epstein. — English ed. / abridged and adapted ... by J.A. Gillham. — London : Teach Yourself Books, 1976. — 153p : ill ; 18cm. — (Teach yourself books)
Previous ed.: published as 'Number games to improve your child's arithmetic'. New York : Funk and Wagnalls, 1975. — Index.
ISBN 0-340-20769-8 Pbk : £0.95
(B77-23630)

793.7'4 — Games using pocket electronic calculators. *Collections*

Olney, Ross. Pocket calculator fun & games / by Ross and Pat Olney ; illustrated by Gretchen Lopez. — New York ; London : F. Watts, 1977. — [8],86,[1]p : ill ; 22cm.
Index.
ISBN 0-531-00387-6 : £2.25
(B77-28812)

Vine, James. Fun and games with your electronic calculator / by James Vine. — London : Babani Press, 1977. — 63p ; 18cm.
Originally published: as 'Boggle'. Los Angeles : Price, Stern, Sloan Publishers, 1975.
ISBN 0-85934-041-4 Pbk : £0.75
(B77-23631)

793.7'4 — Mathematical puzzles. *Collections*

Gardner, Martin. Further mathematical diversions / [by] Martin Gardner. — Harmondsworth [etc.] : Penguin, 1977. — 255p : ill ; 20cm. — (Pelican books)
Originally published: as 'The unexpected hanging, and other mathematical diversions', New York : Simon and Schuster, 1969 ; and as 'Further mathematical diversions', London : Allen and Unwin, 1970. — Bibl.: p.245-255.
ISBN 0-14-021996-x Pbk : £0.80
(B77-33988)

Gardner, Martin. Mathematical carnival : from penny puzzles, card shuffles, and tricks of lightning calculators to roller coaster rides into the fourth dimension ... / [by] Martin Gardner. — London : Allen and Unwin, 1976. — xii, 274p : ill ; 22cm.
'A new round-up of tantalizers from "Scientific American"'. — Originally published: New York : Knopf, 1975. — Bibl.: p.267-274.
ISBN 0-04-793025-x : £6.50
(B77-02518)

Hunter, James Alston Hope. Mathematical brain-teasers / [by] J.A.H. Hunter. — Corrected and enlarged [ed.]. — New York : Dover Publications [etc.] ; London : Constable, 1976. — iii-ix,111p : ill ; 22cm.
With answers. — Previous ed.: published as 'Hunter's math brain teasers'. New York : Bantam, 1965.
ISBN 0-486-23347-2 Pbk : £1.40
(B77-12027)

793.7'4 — Mathematical puzzles. *Collections. Juvenile literature*

Emmet, Eric Revell. The puffin book of brainteasers / [by] Eric Emmet. — Harmondsworth [etc.] : Puffin Books, 1976. — 317p : ill ; 18cm. — (Puffin books)
With answers.
ISBN 0-14-030886-5 Pbk : £0.65
(B77-04358)

793.8 — Conjuring. *Amateurs' manuals*

Baron, Harry. Close-up magic / [by] Harry Baron ; photographs by Eric Braithwaite ; drawings by Wayne Boughen Design. — London : Sphere, 1977. — 160p : ill ; 18cm.
Originally published: as 'Close-up magic for beginners'. London : Kaye and Ward, 1972. — Index.
ISBN 0-7221-1469-9 Pbk : £0.85
(B77-31373)

Delvin, Jack. Magic of the masters / [by] Jack Delvin ; with special artwork by the Hayward Art Group. — London [etc.] : Hamlyn, 1977. — 240p : ill(some col) ; 20cm.
Bibl.: p.234.
ISBN 0-600-36238-8 : £2.50
(B77-13198)

Fisher, John, *b.1945.* John Fisher's magical hoaxes / illustrated by Ann Fisher. — Leicester : Knight Books, 1977. — 128p : ill ; 18cm.
Originally published: as 'John Fisher's magic book'. London : Muller, 1968.
ISBN 0-340-20585-7 Pbk : £0.70
(B77-26452)

Lorayne, Harry. The magic book : the complete beginner's guide to anytime, anywhere, sleight-of-hand magic / [by] Harry Lorayne ; illustrations by Richard Kaufman. — London : W.H. Allen, 1977. — 306p : ill ; 24cm.
Also published: New York : Putnam, 1977.
ISBN 0-491-02411-8 : £5.00
(B77-32091)

Reed, Graham, *b.1937.* Magical miracles you can do / [by] Graham Reed ; illustrated by Dennis Patten. — London : Kaye and Ward, 1977. — [9],84p : ill, facsims ; 23cm.
Bibl.: p.80.
ISBN 0-7182-1153-7 : £2.95
(B77-22766)

Sharps, Les. Sharp sorcery / by Les Sharps. — Bideford (64 High St., Bideford, Devon) : Supreme Magic Company Ltd, 1977. — 76p : ill ; 25cm.
Unpriced
(B77-28813)

793.8 — Conjuring. *Amateurs' manuals. Juvenile literature*

Amery, Heather. The KnowHow book of jokes and tricks / [by] Heather Amery and Ian Adair ; illustrated by Colin King ; designed by John Jamieson. — London : Usborne, 1977. — 32p : col ill ; 28cm. — (Know how books)
ISBN 0-86020-033-7 : £1.95
ISBN 0-86020-034-5 Pbk : £0.90
(B77-28814)

Carrick, Malcolm. Making magic / [by] Malcolm Carrick ; illustrated by the author. — Ealing : Carousel Books, 1976. — [63]p : chiefly ill ; 20cm. — (Carousel books)
ISBN 0-552-54114-1 Pbk : £0.40
(B77-04359)

Eldin, Peter. The trickster's handbook / [by] Peter Eldin ; with drawings by Roger Smith. — London : Armada Books, 1976. — 126p : ill ; 19cm.
ISBN 0-00-691084-x Pbk : £0.40
(B77-03183)

Gibson, Walter Brown. Junior magic : easy-to-learn tricks or magic made simple / [by] Walter B. Gibson. — New York : Sterling [etc.] ; London : Distributed by Ward Lock, 1977. — 287p : ill ; 20cm.
'Adapted from "Magic made simple" [Garden City, N.Y. : Made Simple Books, 1963]' - title page verso. — Index.
ISBN 0-7061-2549-5 : £3.50
(B77-26453)

Nixon, David. David Nixon's magic box / [by] David Nixon ; text illustrations by David Jefferis and Hardy [and] Escasany. — London : Severn House : [Distributed by Hutchinson], 1977. — 93p : ill ; 21cm.
Based on the Thames Television series. — Originally published: London : Pan Books, 1973.
ISBN 0-7278-0174-0 : £2.75
(B77-20495)

Severn, Bill. Magic from your pocket / [by] Bill Severn ; illustrated by Juliet Stanwell-Smith. — Revised ed. — London : Armada Books, 1976. — 125p : ill ; 18cm.
Previous ed.: London : Faber, 1965. — Index.
ISBN 0-00-691010-6 Pbk : £0.40
(B77-05579)

793.8 — Conjuring. *Early works*
Magic : stage illusions, special effects and trick photography / compiled and edited by Albert A. Hopkins ; with an introduction by Henry Ridgely Evans. — New York : Dover Publications [etc.] ; London : Constable, 1976. — ii-xii,556p : ill, plans, port ; 22cm.
Facsimile reprint of : 'Magic : stage illusions and scientific diversions, including trick photography'. New York : Munn and Co., 1901. — Bibl.: p.539-550. — Index.
ISBN 0-486-23344-8 Pbk : £3.60
(B77-13199)

793.8 — Conjuring. *Manuals*
Booth, John, *b.1912.* The John Booth classics / by John Booth. — Bideford (64 High St., Bideford, Devon) : The Supreme Magic Co., [1975]. — 354p in various pagings : ill, facsims, ports ; 23cm.
Originally published: Philadelphia : Kanter's Magic Shop, 1941. — Originally published: Philadelphia : Kanter's Magic Shop, 1941. — Contents: A conjurer's reminiscences - Forging ahead in magic. Originally published: Philadelphia : Kanter's Magic Shop, 1941 - Marvels of mystery. Originally published : Kanter's Magic Shop, 1941.
Unpriced
(B77-16007)

Cameron, Charles W. Devil's diary / by Charles W. Cameron ; illustrations by the author. — Bideford (64 High St., Bideford, Devon) : Supreme Magic Co., 1976. — 52p : ill ; 25cm.
ISBN 0-901127-13-2 Sd : £2.00
(B77-03184)

Kaye, Marvin. The complete magician / [by] Marvin Kaye ; edited by John Salisse. — London [etc.] : Pan Books, 1976. — 278p : ill ; 20cm.
Originally published: as 'The Stein and Day handbook of magic', New York : Stein and Day, 1973 ; and as 'The complete magician', London : Macmillan, 1974. — Bibl.: p.277-278. — Index.
ISBN 0-330-24828-6 Pbk : £1.00
(B77-00354)

Page, Patrick. The big book of magic / [by] Patrick Page ; illustrated by Eric Mason. — London : Sphere, 1977. — 304p : ill ; 20cm.
Originally published: London : Wolfe, 1976.
ISBN 0-7221-6664-8 Pbk : £1.25
(B77-33989)

793.8 — Conjuring. Hypnotism. *Manuals*
Miller, Hugh. Hypnotism / by Hugh Miller. — Bideford (64 High St., Bideford, Devon) : Supreme Magic Company Ltd, 1976. — 56p : ill ; 24cm.
Four cards ([4] sides) as insert. — Originally published: 1971.
ISBN 0-901127-18-3 Sd : £4.50
(B77-03709)

793.8 — Conjuring. Mental tricks. *Amateurs' manuals*
Carlisle, Stanton. Mentalism de luxe / by Stanton Carlisle ; edited by Ken de Courcy (who also illustrated the book). — [Bideford] ([64 High St., Bideford, Devon]) : [Supreme Magic Company], [1976?]. — 36p : ill, port ; 25cm.
'A Supreme Magic publication'.
ISBN 0-901127-11-6 Sd : £2.50
(B77-03710)

793.8 — Conjuring. Mental tricks. *Manuals*
Carlisle, Stanton. Master-mentality / by Stanton Carlisle ; with a pertinent foreword and impertinent drawings by Ken de Courcy. — Bideford (64 High St., Bideford, Devon) : Supreme Magic Co., [1976]. — 87p : ill, ports ; 26cm.
Bibl.: p.86.
ISBN 0-901127-14-0 : £5.00
(B77-05580)

Setterington, Arthur. The power of perception / by Arthur Setterington. — Bideford (64 High St., Bideford, Devon) : Supreme Magic Co. Ltd, 1976. — 35p : ill ; 25cm.
ISBN 0-901127-19-1 Sd : £2.50
(B77-05581)

793.8 — Conjuring. Performance. *Manuals*
De Courcy, Ken. Deceiver's discourse / by Ken de Courcy. — Bideford (64 High St., Bideford, Devon) : Supreme Magic Co., [1976]. — 24p : ill, ports ; 25cm.
ISBN 0-901127-17-5 : £1.50
(B77-04360)

793.8 — Conjuring. Techniques, 1895-1925
Gibson, Walter Brown. Houdini's magic : prepared from Houdini's private notebooks and memoranda with the assistance of Beatrice Houdini, widow of Houdini, and Bernard M.L. Ernst president of the parent assembly of the Society of American Magicians / by Walter B. Gibson. — [1st ed. reprinted] ; introduction by Milbourne Christopher. — Toronto [etc.] ; London : Bantam, 1976. — xiv,207,[1]p : ill ; 18cm.
Originally published: New York : Harcourt, Brace, 1932.
ISBN 0-552-60397-x Pbk : £0.65
(B77-18315)

793.8 — Escapology. Techniques, 1895-1925
Gibson, Walter Brown. Houdini's escapes : prepared from Houdini's private notebooks and memoranda with the assistance of Beatrice Houdini, widow of Houdini, and Bernard M.L. Ernst, president of the parent assembly of the Society of American Magicians / by Walter B. Gibson. — [1st ed. reprinted] ; introduction by Milbourne Christopher. — Toronto [etc.] ; London : Bantam, 1976. — xv,208p : ill ; 18cm.

Originally published: New York : Harcourt, Brace and Co., 1930.
ISBN 0-552-60398-8 Pbk : £0.65
(B77-18316)

793.8 — Tricks using doves. *Manuals*
Adair, Ian. Adair's encyclopaedia of dove magic. — Bideford (64 High St., Bideford, Devon) : Supreme Magic Company.
In 4 vols.
Vol.4 / illustrated by the author (plus guest illustrators), photographs by A.C. Littlejohns and Ian Adair and guest photographers. — [1975]. — 438p : ill, ports ; 26cm.
Index.
ISBN 0-901127-15-9 : Unpriced
(B77-04361)

793.8 — Tricks using glove puppets. *Manuals*
Carlisle, Stanton. Puppetrix / by Stanton Carlisle. — [Bideford] ([64 High St., Bideford, Devon]) : [Supreme Magic Co.], [1976]. — 16p : ill ; 25cm.
Cover title: Puppetrix supreme.
ISBN 0-901127-12-4 Sd : £1.50
(B77-04362)

793.8'09 — Conjuring, to 1975
Gibson, Walter. Secrets of the great magicians / by Walter Gibson ; illustrated by Kyuzo Tsugami. — Glasgow [etc.] : Collins, 1976. — 143p : ill ; 25cm.
Originally published as: 'Secrets of magic, ancient and modern'. New York : Grosset and Dunlap, 1967.
ISBN 0-00-103329-8 Pbk : £1.25
(B77-19581)

793.8'092'2 — Conjurors, to 1975. *Juvenile literature*
Butler, William Vivian. The greatest magicians on earth : the workers of some of history's most incredible wonders - with an account of their feats, tricks, illusions, miracles and spells / [by] William Vivian Butler ; cover illustrations by George Underwood ; text illustrations by Mary French. — London : Pan Books, 1976. — 122p : ill ; 18cm. — (Piccolo)
Bibl.: p.121-122. — Includes chapters on Merlin, Nostradamus and Mesmer.
ISBN 0-330-24762-x Pbk : £0.40
(B77-00894)

793.8'092'4 — Escapology. Houdini, Harry. *Biographies*
Shavelson, Melville. The great Houdinis : a vaudeville / [by] Mel Shavelson. — London : Star Books, 1977. — 175p : port on inside front cover ; 19cm.
Also published: London : W.H. Allen, 1977.
ISBN 0-352-39557-5 Pbk : £0.60
(B77-26454)

Shavelson, Melville. The great Houdinis : a vaudeville / [by] Melville Shavelson. — London : W.H. Allen, 1977. — 175p,[16]p of plates : ill, facsims, ports ; 23cm.
ISBN 0-491-01798-7 : £3.95
(B77-16539)

793'.9 — Proprietary board war games. *Manuals*
Palmer, Nicholas. The comprehensive guide to board wargaming / [by] Nicholas Palmer. — London : A. Barker, 1977. — 224p : ill(some col), facsims ; 25cm.
With answers. — 2 fold. sheets ([4]p.), perforated card in pocket.
ISBN 0-213-16646-1 : £6.50
(B77-25810)

793'.9 — War games based on American Civil War. *Manuals*
Wise, Terence. American Civil War wargaming / [by] Terence Wise. — Cambridge : Stephens [for] Airfix Products Ltd, 1977. — 64p : ill, map, plans ; 23cm. — ('Airfix magazine' guide ; 24)
Bibl.: p.56.
ISBN 0-85059-258-5 : £1.60
(B77-28015)

793'.9 — War games based on army operations involving tanks. *Manuals*
Tank battles in miniature. — Cambridge : Stephens.
4 : A wargamers' guide to the Mediterranean Campaigns, 1943-1945 / [by] Donald Featherstone. — 1977. — 152p : ill, maps ; 23cm.
Bibl.: p.148-150. — Index.
ISBN 0-85059-275-5 : £3.95 : CIP rev.
(B77-18317)

793'.9 — War games based on battles, B.C.3000-A.D.1945
Featherstone, Donald. War games through the ages / [by] Donald F. Featherstone. — London : Paul.
Vol.4 : 1861 to 1945. — 1976. — 240p,[8]p of plates : ill ; 23cm.
Bibl.: p.223-234. — Index.
ISBN 0-09-126520-7 : £5.50
(B77-06227)

793'.9 — War games based on European battles, 1512-1658
Featherstone, Donald. Wargaming, pike-and-shot / [by] Donald Featherstone. — Newton Abbot [etc.] : David and Charles [etc.], 1977. — 160p : maps, plans ; 23cm.
Bibl.: p.155-157. — Index.
ISBN 0-7153-7251-3 : £4.50
(B77-12028)

793'.9 — War games based on events involving imaginary Saxon characters. *Rules*
Knowles, Eric. The quest of Thane Tostig : fantasy war game rules / by Eric & William Knowles. — Barnet (48 East View, Barnet, Herts. EN5 5TN) : Navwar Productions Limited, 1977. — [2],12,[1]p : ill, plan ; 21cm.
Sd : £0.65
(B77-30533)

793'.9 — War games based on Napoleonic Wars. *Manuals*
Quarrie, Bruce. Napoleon's campaigns in miniature : a wargamers' guide to the Napoleonic Wars, 1796-1815 / [by] Bruce Quarrie ; foreword by David G. Chandler. — Cambridge : Stephens, 1977. — 192p : ill, maps, plans ; 25cm.
Bibl.: p.191-192.
ISBN 0-85059-283-6 : £4.95 : CIP rev.
(B77-22053)

793'.9 — War games based on naval battles, 1756-1815. *Rules*
Birnie, S. Action undersail, 1756-1815 / by S. Birnie. — Bolton (72 Philips Ave., Farnworth, Bolton BL4 9BJ) : Georgiann Press, 1976. — [1],40 leaves : ill ; 30cm.
Card ([2]p.) as insert. — Bibl.: leaf 38-39.
ISBN 0-9505480-0-6 Sp : £1.30
(B77-04363)

794 — INDOOR GAMES OF SKILL
794 — Darts. *Manuals*
Scott, Graham. Dart games people play now / by G. Scott. — [Sheffield] ([65 Dalewood Rd, Sheffield 8]) : [The author], [1976]. — [18]p ; 14cm.
ISBN 0-9505484-0-5 Sd : £0.50
(B77-04364)

794 — Darts. *Periodicals*
Darts world. — Croydon (15 Katharine St., Croydon, Surrey) : C.N.A. Publications.
No.1- ; Nov.-Dec. 1972-. — [1972]-. — ill, ports ; 30cm.
Monthly. — 35p. in 1st issue.
Sd : £0.30
ISSN 0140-6000
(B77-32790)

794 — Monopoly. *Manuals*
Monopoly. — Wakefield : EP Publishing, 1977. — 27,[1]p : ill ; 14x21cm. — (Know the game)
'Produced in collaboration with John Waddington Ltd'.
ISBN 0-7158-0532-0 Sd : £0.50
(B77-31374)

794.1 — CHESS
Abrahams, Gerald. Brilliance in chess / [by] Gerald Abrahams. — London [etc.] : Pitman, 1977. — vii,143p : ill ; 24cm.
Descriptive notation. — Index.
ISBN 0-273-00034-9 : £4.95 : CIP rev.
(B77-07537)

Bell, Robert Charles. Discovering chess / by R.C. Bell. — Aylesbury : Shire Publications, 1976. — 56p : ill ; 18cm. — (Discovering series ; no.221)
Bibl.: p.55. — Index.
ISBN 0-85263-357-2 Pbk : £0.50
(B77-09191)

794.1'092'4 — Chess. Staunton, Howard. *Biographies*
Levy, David Neil Laurence. Howard Staunton / [by] D.N.L. Levy. — Nottingham (12 Burton Ave., Carlton, Nottingham NG4 1PT) : The Chess Player, 1975. — 3-142p,[5]p of plates : ill, facsims, ports ; 21cm.
Descriptive notation.
ISBN 0-900928-44-1 Pbk : £1.80
(B77-03185)

794.1'2 — Chess. *Manuals*
Abramov, Lev IAkovlevich. Chess, move by move / written by L. Abramov ; translated [from the Russian] and edited by B. Cafferty. — Nottingham (12 Burton Ave., Carlton, Nottingham NG4 1PT) : The Chess Player, 1976. — 111p : ill, ports ; 21cm.
Descriptive notation. — Originally published in Russian: s.l. : s.n., 1971.
ISBN 0-900928-67-0 Pbk : £1.50
(B77-00895)

Barden, Leonard. Chess : master the moves / [by] Leonard Barden ; drawings by G. Domenech. — London : Chancerel : Barrie and Jenkins, 1977. — 2-91p : ill, ports ; 21cm. — (Action books)
Ill. on lining papers.
ISBN 0-905703-12-x : £1.75
(B77-28016)

Bott, Raymond. Discovering chess / [by] Raymond Bott and Stanley Morrison. — Revised ed. — London : Sphere, 1977. — 5-148p : ill ; 18cm.
Algebraic notation. — This ed. originally published: London : Faber, 1973. — Index.
ISBN 0-7221-1788-4 Pbk : £0.75
(B77-25811)

Brady, Frank Robert. Chess : how to improve your technique / by Frank Brady. — New York ; London : F. Watts, 1974. — [5],64,[1]p : ill ; 25cm. — (A concise guide)
Bibl.: p.59-60. — Index.
ISBN 0-531-02730-9 : £2.50
(B77-20496)

Finkelstein, Milton. Self-taught chess for beginners and intermediates / [by] Milton Finkelstein. — London [etc.] : White Lion Publishers, 1976. — ix,270p : ill ; 21cm.
Descriptive notation. — With answers. — Originally published as: 'Chess for beginners and intermediates', Bronxville, N.Y. : Self Taught Publications, 1962 ; and as 'Self-taught chess for beginners and intermediates', Garden City, N.Y. : Doubleday, 1975.
ISBN 0-7274-0286-2 : £4.25
(B77-04996)

Gillam, A J. Play chess / [by] A.J. Gillam. — Nottingham (12 Burton Ave., Carlton, Nottingham NG4 1PT) : Chess Player Ltd, 1977. — 127p : ill ; 21cm. — (Discovering chess series ; book 1)
Algebraic notation.
ISBN 0-900928-87-5 Pbk : £0.95
(B77-30534)

Wicker, Kevin. How to play chess / [by] Kevin Wicker ; with a foreword by David Pritchard ; illustrated by Karel Feuerstein. — London [etc.] : Hamlyn, 1977. — 3-60p : ill(chiefly col) ; 25cm.
Algebraic notation. — Bibl.: p.58. — Index.
ISBN 0-600-31918-0 : £1.50
(B77-32092)

794.1'2 — Chess. *Manuals. Facsimiles*
Cessolis, Jacobus de. The game of chess / [by] Jacobus de Cessolis ; translated [from the French] and printed by William Caxton, c.1483. — Reproduced in facsimile from the copy at Trinity College, Cambridge ; with an introduction by N.F. Blake. — London : Scolar Press, 1976. — [175]p : ill ; 29cm.
Limited ed. of 500 copies. — Facsimile reprint of: 2nd ed. Westminster : Explicit per Caxton, 1483? - Written originally in Latin under the title of 'Liber de ludo scaccorum' which was based on 'De regimine principum' by AEgidius Romanus. This translation was based on a French version which was itself based on two separate French translations made by Jean de Vignay and Jean Farron or Ferron.
ISBN 0-85967-306-5 : £12.50
(B77-03711)

794.1'2 — Chess. *Manuals. Juvenile literature*
Leeming, Joseph. The first book of chess / by Joseph Leeming. — Revised ed. / revised by Robert S. Fenton. — New York ; London : F. Watts, 1977. — [7],64p : ill ; 23cm.
Descriptive notation. — Previous ed.: New York : F. Watts, 1953 ; London : F. Watts, 1971. — Index.
ISBN 0-85166-677-9 : £2.25
(B77-33380)

794.1'2 — Chess. Checkmates. *Manuals*
Hooper, David. Play for mate / [by] David Hooper, Bernard Cafferty. — London : Bell, 1977. — vii,244p : ill ; 23cm.
Descriptive notation.
ISBN 0-7135-1872-3 : Unpriced
(B77-21358)

794.1'2 — Chess. Sacrifices. *Manuals*
Shamkovich, Leonid A. Chess sacrifices / [by] Leonid Shamkovich ; [translated from the Russian by A. Kalnajs]. — Nottingham : Chess Player, 1976. — 184p : ill ; 21cm.
Descriptive notation. — Translation of: 'Zhertva v shakhmatakh'. Moskva : Fizkul'tura i sport, 1971.
ISBN 0-900928-99-9 Pbk : £2.95
(B77-33990)

794.1'2 — Chess. Strategy. *Manuals*
Lisitsyn, G M. First book of chess strategy / [by] G.M. Lisitsyn, B. Cafferty. — Nottingham ([12 Newstead Grove, Nottingham]) : 'The chess player', 1976. — 96p : ill ; 21cm.
Descriptive notation.
ISBN 0-900928-69-7 Pbk : £1.20
(B77-01721)

Lisitsyn, G M. Second book of chess strategy / [by] G.M. Lisitsyn, B. Cafferty. — Nottingham (12 Burton Ave., Carlton, Nottingham NG4 1PT) : 'The chess player', 1976. — 71p : ill ; 21cm.
Descriptive notation.
Pbk : £1.70
(B77-04997)

794.1'2 — Chess. Strategy. *Manuals. Juvenile literature*
Walker, John Norman. Attacking the king / [by] J.N. Walker. — Oxford [etc.] : Oxford University Press, 1976. — xv,173,[1]p : ill ; 21cm.
Algebraic notation. — Index.
ISBN 0-19-217556-4 : £2.95
ISBN 0-19-217557-2 Pbk : £1.50
(B77-02519)

794.1'22 — Chess. Opening: Sicilian Defence. Rossolimo Variation. *Manuals*
Pickett, Leonard M. Rossolimo variation : 1 P-K4 P-QB4 2 N-KB3 N-QB4 3 B-N5 / [by] L.M. Pickett. — Nottingham ([12 Burton Ave., Carlton, Nottingham NG4 1PT]) : 'The chess player', [1977]. — 71p : ill ; 21cm. — (Sicilian defence ; 9)
Descriptive notation.
ISBN 0-900928-91-3 Pbk : £1.75
(B77-18318)

794.1'22 — Chess. Openings. *Manuals*
Levy, David Neil Laurence. An opening repertoire for the attacking club player / [by] David Levy, Raymond Keene. — London : Batsford, 1976. — ix,157p : ill ; 22cm. — (The Batsford club player's library) (Batsford chess books)
Descriptive notation.
ISBN 0-7134-3137-7 Pbk : £2.50
(B77-25812)

Pickett, Leonard M. Enterprising strategy in the opening / [by] Leonard M. Pickett. — Nottingham (12 Burton Ave., Carlton, Nottingham NG4 1PT) : 'The Chess Player', 1975. — 62p : ill ; 19cm.
ISBN 0-900928-48-4 Pbk : £1.00
(B77-00896)

Schwob, Pierre R. The chess tutor, opening moves / [by] Pierre R. Schwob and George F. Kane. — London : Barrie and Jenkins, 1976. — iii-xxix,268p : chiefly ill ; 23cm. — (The chess tutor series)
Descriptive notation. — Also published: New York : Mason/Charter, 1976. — Bibl.: p.263-264. — Index.
ISBN 0-214-20328-x : £5.95
(B77-11355)

794.1'22 — Chess. Openings: Bird's Opening. *Manuals*
Pickett, Leonard M. A modern approach to Bird's opening / [by] L.M. Picket [i.e. Pickett]. — Nottingham (12 Burton Ave., Carlton, Nottingham NG4 1PT) : 'Chess player', 1975. — 28p : ill ; 20cm. — (No.182)
Sd : £0.60
(B77-01722)

794.1'22 — Chess. Openings: Centre Game. *Manuals*
Pickett, Leonard M. Centre game and Danish gambit / [by] L.M.Pickett. — Nottingham ([12 Newstead Grove, Nottingham]) : 'The chess player', 1976. — 54p : ill ; 19cm.
ISBN 0-900928-49-2 Pbk : £1.00
(B77-01723)

794.1'22 — Chess. Openings: English Opening. *Manuals*
Cafferty, Bernard. English opening / [by] Bernard Cafferty. — 2nd ed. — Nottingham (12 Burton Ave., Carlton, Nottingham NG4 1PT) : The Chess Player, 1977. — 152p : ill ; 21cm.
Descriptive notation. — Previous ed.: 1973. — 'Based on a book by B. Shatskes originally published in Russian' - title page verso.
ISBN 0-900928-92-1 Pbk : £2.95
(B77-16540)

794.1'22 — Chess. Openings: Four Knights. *Manuals*
Pickett, Leonard M. Four knights and Belgrade gambit / [by] L.M. Pickett. — Nottingham ([12 Newstead Grove, Nottingham]) : 'The chess player', 1976. — 80p : ill ; 19cm.
ISBN 0-900928-51-4 Pbk : £1.20
(B77-01724)

794.1'22 — Chess. Openings: Giuoco Piano. *Manuals*
Harding, Timothy David. The Italian Game : 1 P-K4 P-K4 2 N-KB3 N-QB3 3 B-B4 Giuoco Piano, Evans Gambit, Two Knights Defence, Hungarian Defence / [by] T.D. Harding, G.S. Botterill. — London : Batsford, 1977. — viii, 136p : ill ; 23cm. — (Contemporary chess openings) (Batsford chess books)
Descriptive notation. — Bibl.: p.vi. — Index.
ISBN 0-7134-3261-6 : £4.10
(B77-09192)

794.1'22 — Chess. Openings: King's Indian Defence. *Manuals*
Pickett, Leonard M. Enterprising strategy in the King's Indian defence / [by] L.M. Pickett. — Nottingham (12 Burton Ave., Carlton, Nottingham NG4 1PT) : 'The chess player', 1975. — 56p : ill ; 21cm.
Contributions to the text by Norman R. Oliver et al.
ISBN 0-900928-54-9 Sd : £1.00
(B77-01725)

794.1'22 — Chess. Openings: King's Indian Defence. Sämisch Variation. *Manuals*
Keene, Raymond Dennis. How to play the king's Indian, Saemisch variation / [by] R.D. Keene. — Nottingham (12 Burton Ave., Carlton, Nottingham NG4 1PT) : 'Chess player', 1976. — 80p : ill ; 21cm.
Descriptive notation.
ISBN 0-900928-84-0 Pbk : £1.70
(B77-06822)

794.1'22 — Chess. Openings: Queen's Gambit Declined. Exchange Variation. *Manuals*
Wicker, Kevin. How to play the queen's gambit exchange variation / [by] K. Wicker. — Nottingham (12 Burton Ave., Carlton, Nottingham NG4 1PT) : 'Chess player', 1976. — 96p : ill ; 21cm.
ISBN 0-900928-70-0 Pbk : £1.50
(B77-01726)

794.1'22 — Chess. Openings: Ruy Lopez. Delayed Exchange Ruy Lopez Deferred. *Manuals*
Pickett, Leonard M. The DERLD (Delayed Exchange Ruy Lopez Deferred) / [by] Leonard Pickett. — Nottingham (12 Burton Ave., Carlton, Nottingham NG4 1PT) : The Chess Player Ltd, 1975. — 71p : ill ; 21cm.
Descriptive notation.
ISBN 0-900928-52-2 Sd : £1.50
(B77-03712)

794.1'22 — Chess. Openings: Scotch Game. *Manuals*
Botterill, George Steven. The Scotch : 1 P-K4 P-K4 2 N-KB3 N-QB3 3 P-Q4 PXP Scotch Game, Scotch Four Knights, Scotch Gambit, Goring Gambit / [by] G.S. Botterill, T.D. Harding. — London : Batsford, 1977. — xviii, 140p : ill ; 23cm. — (Contemporary chess openings) (Batsford chessbooks)
Descriptive notation. — Bibl.: p.134. — Index.
ISBN 0-7134-0224-5 : £4.25
(B77-24401)

Swift, A K. Scotch game / compiled by A.K. Swift ; editted [i.e. edited] by L.M. Pickett. — Nottingham ([15 Newstead Grove, Nottingham]) : 'The chess player', 1976. — 71p : ill ; 18cm. — (Scotch opening ; 1)
Descriptive notation.
ISBN 0-900928-47-6 Pbk : £1.00
(B77-03713)

794.1'22 — Chess. Openings: Scotch Game. Goring Gambit. *Manuals*
Swift, A K. Goring gambit / compiled by A.K. Swift ; edited by L.M. Pickett. — Nottingham ([15 Newstead Grove, Nottingham]) : 'The chess player', 1976. — 63p : ill ; 18cm. — (Scotch opening ; 3)
Descriptive notation.
ISBN 0-900928-45-x Pbk : £1.00
(B77-03714)

794.1'22 — Chess. Openings: Scotch Game. Scotch Gambit. *Manuals*
Swift, A K. Scotch gambit / compiled by A.K. Swift ; edited by L.M. Pickett. — Nottingham ([15 Newstead Grove, Nottingham]) : 'The chess player', 1976. — 101p : ill ; 18cm. — (Scotch opening ; 2)
Descriptive notation.
ISBN 0-900928-46-8 Pbk : £1.40
(B77-03715)

794.1'22 — Chess. Openings: Sicilian Defence. Closed System. *Manuals*
Pickett, Leonard M. Closed variation / [by] L.M. Pickett, A.K. Swift. — Nottingham ([15 Newstead Grove, Nottingham]) : 'The chess player', 1976. — 72p : ill ; 21cm. — (Sicilian defence ; 6)
Descriptive notation.
ISBN 0-900928-64-6 Pbk : £1.40
(B77-03716)

794.1'22 — Chess. Openings: Sicilian Defence. Four Knights' Variation. *Manuals*
Pickett, Leonard M. Four knights variation / [by] L.M. Pickett, A.K. Swift. — Nottingham ([12 Newstead Grove, Nottingham]) : 'The chess player', 1976. — 95p : ill ; 18cm. — (Sicilian defence ; 5)
Descriptive notation. — Index. — Also includes a survey of the Najdorf, Richter-Rauzer and Sozin Variations.
ISBN 0-900928-63-8 Pbk : £1.50
(B77-03717)

794.1'22 — Chess. Openings: Sicilian Defence. Maróczy Bind. *Manuals*
Pickett, Leonard M. Gurgenidze system, accelerated fianchetto / [by] L.M. Pickett. — Nottingham ([12 Newstead Grove, Nottingham]) : 'The chess player', 1976. — 63p : ill ; 19cm. — (Sicilian defence ; 4)
Descriptive notation.
Pbk : £1.00
(B77-03718)

794.1'22 — Chess. Openings: Sicilian Defence. Moscow Variation. *Manuals*
Pickett, Leonard M. Moscow variation : 1 P-K4 P-QB4 2 N-KB3 p-Q3 3 B-N5+ / [by] L.M. Pickett. — Nottingham (12 Burton Ave., Carlton, Nottingham NG4 1PT) : The Chess Player, 1976. — 78p : ill ; 21cm. — (Sicilian defence ; 8)
Descriptive notation.
ISBN 0-900928-85-9 Pbk : £1.70
(B77-12599)

794.1'22 — Chess. Openings: Sicilian Defence. Najdorf Variation. *Manuals*
Adams, Jimmy. Main line Najdorf / [by] Jimmy Adams. — Nottingham (12 Burton Ave., Carlton, Nottingham NG4 1PT) : The Chess Player, 1977. — 104p : ill ; 22cm. — (Sicilian defence ; 10)
Descriptive notation.
ISBN 0-900928-90-5 Pbk : £2.30
(B77-12600)

Stean, Michael. Sicilian, Najdorf / [by] Michael Stean. — London : Batsford, 1976. — xiv, 127p : ill ; 22cm. — (Specialist chess openings) (Batsford chess books)
Algebraic notation. — Index.
ISBN 0-7134-0098-6 : £3.95
ISBN 0-7134-0099-4 Pbk : £2.50
(B77-28017)

794.1'22 — Chess. Openings: Sicilian Defence. P-KB4 variations. *Manuals*
Pickett, Leonard M. Lines with P-KB4 / [by] L.M. Pickett, A.K. Swift. — Nottingham ([15 Newstead Grove, Nottingham]) : 'The chess player', 1976. — 63p : ill ; 21cm. — (Sicilian defence ; 7)
Descriptive notation. — Index.
ISBN 0-900928-65-4 Pbk : £1.00
(B77-03719)

794.1'22 — Chess. Openings: Sicilian Defence. Scheveningen Variation. *Manuals*
Pritchett, Craig. The Sicilian Scheveningen / [by] Craig Pritchett. — London : Batsford, 1977. — x,206p : ill ; 23cm. — (Contemporary chess openings) (Batsford chess books)
Descriptive notation. — Index.
ISBN 0-7134-0087-0 : £5.75
(B77-22768)

794.1'22 — Chess. Openings: Vienna Opening. *Manuals*
Harding, Timothy David. Vienna opening / [by] T.D. Harding. — Nottingham (12 Burton Ave., Carlton, Nottingham NG4 1PT) : 'Chess player', 1976. — 104p : ill ; 21cm.
Bibl.: p.8. — Index.
ISBN 0-900928-68-9 Pbk : £1.95
(B77-01727)

794.1'22'03 — Chess. Openings. *Encyclopaedias*
Enciklopedija šahovskih otvaranja ... = Encyclopedia of chess openings / [editor-in-chief Aleksandar Matanović for 'Šahovski informator']. — Beograd [i.e. Belgrade] : 'Šahovski informator' ['Chess informant'] ; London : Batsford. — ([A Batsford chess book])
In 5 vols. — Serbo-Croatian, Russian, English, German, French, Spanish, Italian and Swedish text. — Algebraic notation.
[Vol.] D : 1. d4 d5, 1. d4 sf6 2. c4 g6 [with] d7-d5. — 1977. — 404p : ill ; 25cm.
ISBN 0-7134-3210-1 : £12.00
(B77-09874)

794.1'24 — Chess. End games using bishops. *Manuals*
Averbakh, IUriĭ L'vovich. Bishop endings / [by] Yuri Averbakh ; translated [from the Russian] by Mary Lasher. — London : Batsford, 1977. — viii,167p : ill ; 23cm. — (Contemporary chess endings) ([Batsford chess books])
Descriptive notation. — Translation and revision of: selections from vol.2 of 'Shakhmatnye okonchaniia', originally published in 3 vols. Moskva : Fizkul'tura i sport, 1956-62. — Index.
ISBN 0-7134-0096-x : £4.95
(B77-33991)

794.1'24 — Chess. Endgames. *Manuals*
Euwe, Max. A guide to chess endings / [by] Max Euwe and David Hooper. — New York : Dover Publications [etc.] ; London : Constable, 1976. — iii-viii,248p : ill ; 22cm.
Descriptive notation. — Originally published: London : Routledge and Kegan Paul, 1959. — Index.
ISBN 0-486-23332-4 Pbk : £2.50
(B77-12601)

Griffiths, P C. The endings : in modern theory and practice / [by] P.C. Griffiths. — London : Bell, 1976. — viii,176p : ill ; 23cm.
ISBN 0-7135-1953-3 : £4.75
(B77-06823)

794.1'24 — Chess. Endgames. Problems. *Collections*
Pick of the best chess problems / compiled by B.P. Barnes. — Kingswood : Elliot Right Way Books, 1976. — 157p : ill ; 18cm. — (Paperfronts)
Algebraic notation. — Index.
ISBN 0-7160-0627-8 Pbk : £0.40
(B77-01728)

794.1'42 — Chess. Play with pawns. *Manuals*
Sokol'skiĭ, Alekseĭ Pavlovich. Pawns in action / [by] A.P. Sokolsky ; translated [from the Russian] by Bernard Cafferty. — Nottingham (12 Burton Ave., Carlton, Nottingham NG4 1PT) : 'The chess player', 1976. — 85p : ill ; 19cm.
Descriptive notation. — Translation of: 'Peshki v dvizhenii'. Moskva : Fizkul'tura i sport, 1962.
ISBN 0-900928-66-2 Pbk : £1.20
(B77-01729)

794.1'5 — Chess. Combinations, to 1976. *Collections*
Keene, Raymond Dennis. The chess combination from Philidor to Karpov / by Raymond Keene. — Oxford [etc.] : Pergamon, 1977. — xiii, 162p ; 22cm. — (Pergamon international library) (Pergamon chess series)
Descriptive notation.
ISBN 0-08-019758-2 : £4.25
(B77-30535)

794.1'5 — Chess. Games played by junior Soviet players, 1960-1975. *Collections*
Soltis, Andrew. The younger school of Soviet chess / [by] Andrew Soltis. — London : Bell, 1976. — xxv,253p : ill ; 23cm. — ([Bell chess books])
Descriptive notation. — Index.
ISBN 0-7135-1956-8 : £6.25
(B77-25132)

794.1'52 — Chess. Grandmaster matches. Games, 1770-1938. *Collections*
Tartakover, Saveliĭ Grigor'evich. 500 master games of chess / by S. Tartakower and J. du Mont. — New York : Dover Publications ; London : Constable, 1975. — xxvii,665p,iv p : ill ; 22cm.
Originally published: in 2 vols. London : Bell, 1952. — Index.
ISBN 0-486-23208-5 Pbk : £4.20
(B77-02520)

794.1'52 — Chess. Master matches. Games, 1912-1939. *Collections*
Euwe, Max. Meet the masters : eight great chess players and their most characteristic games / by Max Euwe ; translated from the Dutch by L. Prins and B.H. Wood. — 2nd ed. — New York : Dover Publications [etc.] ; London : Constable, 1975 [i.e. 1976]. — ii-viii,279p : ill, port ; 21cm.
Descriptive notation. — This ed. originally published: as 'Meet the masters : the modern chess champions and their most characteristic games'. London : Pitman, 1946.
ISBN 0-486-23207-7 Pbk : £2.30
(B77-02521)

794.1'52 — Chess. Master matches. Games, 1920-1974. *Collections*
Cafferty, Bernard. Chess with the masters / [by] B. Cafferty, A.J. Gillam. — Nottingham (12 Burton Ave., Carlton, Nottingham NG4 1DP) : The Chess Player Ltd, 1977. — 80p : ill ; 21cm.
Descriptive notation.
ISBN 0-900928-95-6 Pbk : £1.25
(B77-33381)

794.1'52 — Chess. Master matches. Games, 1941-1944. *Collections*
Fine, Reuben. Fifty chess masterpieces, 1941-1944 / by Reuben Fine. — New York : Dover Publications [etc.] ; London : Constable, 1977. — v,218p : ill ; 22cm.
Descriptive notation. — Originally published: as 'Chess marches on!'. New York : Chess review, 1945. — Index.
ISBN 0-486-23450-9 Pbk : £2.50
(B77-33992)

794.1'57 — Chess. Chess Olympiad, Haifa, 1976
Keene, Raymond Dennis. Haifa Chess Olympiad 1976 / [by] R.D. Keene & D.N.L. Levy. — Nottingham (12 Burton Ave., Carlton, Nottingham) : The Chess Player Ltd, 1977. — xvi,128p : ill, ports ; 21cm.
Algebraic notation.
ISBN 0-906042-02-x Pbk : £3.50
(B77-32791)

794.1'57 — Chess. US Open Chess Championship. 72nd, Ventura, 1971. Games. *Collections*
US Open Chess Championship, *72nd, Ventura, 1971.* 72nd annual US Open Chess Championship, Ventura, California, 8-20 August 1971 / edited by Jack L. Spence. — Nottingham (15 Newstead Grove, Nottingham) : The Chess Player, [1976]. — xxii,130p : ill, ports ; 19cm.
Index.
Pbk : £2.70
(B77-01730)

794.1'57 — Chess. US Open Chess Championship, 73rd, Atlantic City, 1972. Games. *Collections*
US Open Chess Championship, *73rd, Atlantic City, 1972.* 73rd annual US Open Chess Championship, August 13-25, 1972, Atlantic City, New Jersey / compiled by Jack L. Spence. — [Nottingham] ([15 Newstead Grove, Nottingham]) : The Chess Player, [1976]. — 116p : ill ; 19cm.
Pbk : £2.50
(B77-01731)

794.1'57 — Chess. World Championship Candidates' matches, 1974. *Collections*
Byrne, Robert, *b.1928.* Anatoly Karpor : the road to the world chess championship / by Robert Byrne. — Toronto [etc.] ; London : Bantam, 1976. — [9],177,[1]p : ill ; 18cm.
Descriptive notation.
ISBN 0-553-02876-6 Pbk : £0.75
(B77-08004)

794.1'59 — Chess. Games played by Fischer, Bobby. Compared with games played by earlier world champions. *Collections*
Euwe, Max. Bobby Fischer and his predecessors in the World Chess Championship / [by] Max Euwe. — London : Bell, 1976. — xiv,200p : ill ; 22cm.
Descriptive notation.
ISBN 0-7135-1955-x : Unpriced
(B77-23632)

794.1'59 — Chess. Games played by Lasker, Emanuel. *Collections*
Lasker, Emanuel. Emanuel Lasker. — Nottingham (12 Burton Ave., Carlton, Nottingham NG4 1PT) : The Chess Player Ltd.

Vol.3 / edited by K. Whyld. — 1976. — 104p ; 25cm.
Descriptive notation. — Index.
ISBN 0-900928-89-1 Pbk : £2.95
(B77-12029)

794.1'7 — Chess. Playing. Applications of digital computer systems. *Conference proceedings*
Advances in computer chess. — Edinburgh : Edinburgh University Press.
1 / M.R.B. Clarke, editor. — 1977. — v,118p : ill ; 26cm.
'... a symposium was held at Oxford in March 1975 ... organised jointly by the Atlas Computer Laboratory of the Science Research Council and the Artificial Intelligence & Simulation of Behaviour group ...' - jacket. — Algebraic and descriptive notation. — Bibl.
ISBN 0-85224-292-1 : £3.50
(B77-18319)

794.1'8 — Fairy chess. Problems. *Collections*
Fairy Chess Correspondence Circle. An album of fairy chess / by members of the Fairy Chess Correspondence Circle ; edited by A.S.M. Dickins. — 2nd ed. — Kew Gardens (6a Royal Parade, Kew Gardens, Surrey TW9 3QD) : The Q Press, [1976]. — 28,[1]p : ill ; 21cm.
Algebraic notation. — Limited ed. of 50 numbered copies. — Previous ed.: 1970. — Index.
ISBN 0-901911-13-5 Sd : £2.10
(B77-01732)

794.2 — DRAUGHTS AND SIMILAR GAMES
794.2 — Go. *Manuals*
Fairbairn, John. Invitation to go / [by] John Fairbairn. — Oxford [etc.] : Oxford University Press, 1977. — [7],85p : ill, ports ; 21cm.
Index.
ISBN 0-19-217547-5 : £2.60
ISBN 0-19-217546-7 Pbk : £1.30
(B77-23633)

794.2 — Mastermind. *Manuals*
Ault, Leslie H. The official 'Mastermind' handbook / [by] Leslie H. Ault. — London : New English Library, 1976. — [7],136p : ill, form ; 19cm.
Originally published: New York : Signet, 1976.
ISBN 0-450-03245-0 Pbk : £0.60
(B77-03186)

794.6 — TENPIN BOWLING
794.6 — Tenpin bowling. *Manuals*
Schunk, Carol. Bowling / [by] Carol Schunk ; illustrated by James Bonner. — 2nd ed. — Philadelphia ; London [etc.] : Saunders, 1976. — ii-viii,106p : ill, forms ; 23cm. — (Saunders physical activity series)
Previous ed.: 1970. — Bibl.: p.105-106.
ISBN 0-7216-8026-7 Pbk : £2.25
(B77-01733)

794.73 — SNOOKER
Pot black / compiled by Reg Perrin. — New revised ed. — London : British Broadcasting Corporation, 1977. — 96p : ill, ports ; 20cm.
Previous ed.: 1975.
ISBN 0-563-17271-1 Pbk : £0.70
(B77-13200)

794.7'3 — Snooker. *Manuals*
Charlton, Eddie. Winning snooker / with Eddie Charlton. — London [etc.] : Macmillan, 1976. — 113p : col ill, col ports ; 25cm.
Includes the text of the Billiards and Snooker Control Council's 'Rules of snooker' and 'General rules'.
ISBN 0-333-21063-8 : £2.95
(B77-03720)

Davis, Fred, *b.1913.* Snooker / [by] Fred Davis. — London : A. and C. Black, 1977. — 95p : ill, ports ; 22cm. — (Black's picture sports)
Bibl.: p.90-91.
ISBN 0-7136-1740-3 : £1.95 : CIP rev.
(B77-16541)

Davis, Joe. How I play snooker / [by] Joe Davis. — [2nd, i.e. revised ed.]. — London : Star Books, 1975. — 174p : ill, port ; 22cm.
Revised ed. originally published: London : Country Life, 1956.
ISBN 0-352-30057-4 Pbk : £0.80
(B77-06825)

795 — GAMES OF CHANCE
795 — Betting. *Manuals*
Tunbridge, Frederick Charles. The guaranteed betting systems / by F.C. Tunbridge. — Larkhall ([76 Church St.], Larkhall, Lanarkshire ML9 1HE) : TV Technic Publications, 1977. — 2-43p ; 26cm.
ISBN 0-905059-14-x Sd : Unpriced
(B77-14865)

795 — Casinos. Gambling. *Manuals*
Graham, Virginia L. A book on casino gambling / written by a mathematician and a computer expert, Virginia L. Graham, C. Ionescu Tulcea. — New York ; London [etc.] : Van Nostrand Reinhold, 1976. — xii,122p : ill ; 21cm.
Spine title: Casino gambling. — Bibl.: p.108. — Index.
ISBN 0-442-23632-8 Pbk : Unpriced
(B77-02522)

Hughes, Barrie. The educated gambler : a guide to casino games / [by] Barrie Hughes. — London : Paul, 1976. — 222p : ill ; 24cm.
Bibl.: p.217-218. — Index.
ISBN 0-09-127700-0 : £4.95
Also classified at 301.5'7
(B77-02523)

795 — Gambling. *Manuals*
Figgis, Eric Lenox. Gamblers handbook / [by] E. Lenox Figgis. — London [etc.] : Hamlyn, 1976. — 240p : ill(some col), facsims ; 20cm.
Index.
ISBN 0-600-34011-2 : £2.50
(B77-28815)

795 — Games of chance. Cheating. *Manuals*
Fisher, John, *b.1945.* Never give a sucker an even break : a guide for the interested reader to knavery and sharp practice / by John Fisher. — London : Elm Tree Books, 1976. — 128p : ill ; 25cm.
ISBN 0-241-89439-5 : £4.50
(B77-02524)

795 — Pinball machines. *Periodicals*
Replay : the monthly newsletter of the Pinball Owner's Association. — Mitcham (c/o The editor, 2 Love La., Mitcham, Surrey CR4 3AG) : [The Association].
Supersedes: News bulletin / Pinball Owners' Association.
Vol.1, no.1- ; Jan. 1977-. — 1977-. — ill, ports ; 30cm.
Monthly. — [10]p. in vol.1, no.2.
Sd : Unpriced
ISSN 0140-5438
(B77-32792)

795 — Pinball machines, to 1975
McKeown, Harry. Pinball portfolio / [by] Harry McKeown. — London : New English Library, 1976. — 160p : ill(some col), facsims(some col), ports ; 35cm.
Index.
ISBN 0-450-02848-8 : £5.95
(B77-07538)

795 — Pinball machines, to 1976
Pinball : an illustrated history / [compiled by] Michael Colmer ; design by Alex Vining. — London ([17 Oakley Rd, N1 3LL]) : Pierrot Publishing Ltd, 1976. — 120p : chiefly ill(some col), facsim, ports ; 26cm.
Index.
ISBN 0-905310-04-7 Pbk : £2.95
(B77-04365)

795'.01 — Betting. Applications of precognition. *Manuals*
Briggs, Harold William. The psychology of psychic gambling / by Harold W. Briggs. — Reading (118 Dee Rd, Tilehurst, Reading RG3 4BL) : The author, 1976. — [2],17p ; 29cm.
Sd : Unpriced
(B77-22054)

795'.1 — Backgammon. *Manuals*
Clay, R A. Backgammon / [by] R.A. Clay. — Sevenoaks : Teach Yourself Books, 1977. — x, 164p : ill ; 18cm. — (Teach yourself books)
ISBN 0-340-22233-6 Pbk : £1.75
(B77-32093)

Jacoby, Oswald. The backgammon book / [by] Oswald Jacoby, John R. Crawford. — Harmondsworth [etc.] : Penguin, 1976. — 224p : ill(some col), facsims, ports ; 26cm. — (Penguin handbooks)
Originally published: New York : Viking Press ; London : Macmillan, 1970.
ISBN 0-14-046260-0 Pbk : Unpriced
(B77-02525)

Martyn, Phillip. Phillip Martyn on backgammon / written with the assistance of Stuart Wheeler. — London : Paul, 1976. — 188p : ill ; 24cm.
ISBN 0-09-127970-4 : £3.95
(B77-03721)

Ratip, Arman. How to play backgammon / [by] Arman Ratip ; illustrated by Karel Feuerstein. — London [etc.] : Hamlyn, 1977. — 3-61p : ill(chiefly col) ; 25cm.
Bibl.: p.60. — Index.
ISBN 0-600-31394-8 : £1.50
(B77-32094)

795'.1 — Dice games. *Manuals*
Frey, Skip. Complete book of dice games / [by] Skip Frey. — London : Hale, 1977. — 192p : ill ; 19cm.
Originally published: New York : Hart Publishing Co., 1975.
ISBN 0-7091-6007-0 : £2.50
(B77-11356)

795'.2 — Casinos. *France. Nice. Casino Municipale. Roulette, 1966. Personal observations*
Leigh, Norman. Thirteen against the bank / [by] Norman Leigh. — Harmondsworth [etc.] : Penguin, 1977. — 203p ; 18cm.
Originally published: London : Weidenfeld and Nicolson, 1976.
ISBN 0-14-004445-0 Pbk : £0.75
(B77-28018)

795'.3 — Domino games. *Collections*
Berndt, Fredrick. The domino book : games, solitaire, puzzles / [by] Fredrick Berndt. — Toronto [etc.] ; London : Bantam, 1975. — xii, 195p : ill ; 18cm. — (Bantam game books)
Originally published: Nashville : Nelson, 1974.
ISBN 0-552-66491-x Pbk : £0.65
(B77-32793)

795'.3 — Mah-jongg. *Manuals*
Bell, Robert Charles. Discovering mah-jong / [by] R.C. Bell. — Aylesbury : Shire Publications, 1976. — 48p : ill ; 18cm. — (Discovering series ; no.222)
Bibl.: p.45-46. — Index.
ISBN 0-85263-358-0 Pbk : £0.50
(B77-10501)

Millington, A D. The complete book of mah-jongg / [by] A.D. Millington ; foreword by David Pritchard. — London : Barker, 1977. — viii,200p : ill ; 23cm.
Bibl.: p.199-200.
ISBN 0-213-16622-4 : £4.25
(B77-10502)

Whitney, Eleanor Noss. A mah jong handbook : how to play, score, and win the modern game / [by] Eleanor Noss Whitney. — London [etc.] : Pan Books, 1977. — 237p : ill ; 18cm.
Originally published: Rutland, Vt. : Tuttle ; London : Prentice-Hall, 1964.
ISBN 0-330-25229-1 Pbk : £1.00
(B77-32794)

795.4 — CARD GAMES
795.4 — Card games. *Manuals*
Hervey, George Frangopulo. Card games for all the family / [by] George F. Hervey. — Sevenoaks : Teach Yourself Books, 1977. — xii, 100p ; 18cm. — (Teach yourself books)
Index.
ISBN 0-340-22234-4 Pbk : £0.95
(B77-31375)

795.4 — Card games for four players. *Manuals*
Parlett, David. Card games for four / [by] David Parlett. — Sevenoaks : Teach Yourself Books, 1977. — xi,215p : ill ; 18cm. — (Teach yourself books)
ISBN 0-340-22232-8 Pbk : £1.95
(B77-33382)

795.4 — Card games for three players. *Manuals*
Parlett, David. Card games for three / [by] David Parlett. — Sevenoaks : Teach Yourself Books, 1977. — vi,264p : ill ; 18cm. — (Teach yourself books)
ISBN 0-340-21519-4 Pbk : £1.50
(B77-14866)

795.4 — Cribbage
Anderson, Douglas. All about cribbage / [by] Douglas Anderson. — Large print ed. — London : Prior [etc.], 1977. — [8],135p ; 25cm.
Originally published: New York : Winchester Press, 1971 ; Folkestone : Bailey and Swinfen, 1974.
ISBN 0-86043-101-0 : £4.50
(B77-27299)

795.4'12 — Poker. *Manuals*
Spanier, David. Total poker / [by] David Spanier. — London : Secker and Warburg, 1977. — 255p : ill, port ; 23cm.
Index.
ISBN 0-436-47886-2 : £3.90
(B77-18940)

795.4'13 — Russian whist. *Manuals. Facsimiles*
Collinson, John. Biritch, or, Russian whist / [by] John Collinson. — Richmond-upon-Thames (P.O. Box 7, Hounslow TW3 2LA) : Bibliagora, 1977. — [15]p : ports(1 col) tipped in ; 22cm.
Limited ed. of 250 copies. — Full leather. — Facsimile reprint of: 1st ed. London, 1886?.
ISBN 0-906031-00-1 : £27.50
(B77-32795)

795.4'15 — Contract bridge. *Manuals*
Cohen, Ben. The ABC of contract bridge : being a complete outline of the Acol bidding system and the card play of contract bridge especially prepared for beginners / by Ben Cohen and Rhoda Lederer. — 3rd ed. / revised by Rhoda Lederer. — London [etc.] : Allen and Unwin, 1977. — 287p : ill ; 20cm.
With answers. — Previous ed.: 1972.
ISBN 0-04-793028-4 Pbk : £3.50
(B77-24403)

Ewen, Robert B. Contract bridge : how to improve your technique / by Robert B. Ewen ; edited by Albert Dormer. — Revised ed. — London : Hale, 1977. — 124p : ill ; 21cm.
Previous ed.: New York : Watts, 1975. — Bibl.: p.119-120. — Index.
ISBN 0-7091-6033-x : £2.95
(B77-16542)

Flint, Jeremy. How to play bridge / [by] Jeremy Flint ; illustrated by Hana Feuerstein. — London [etc.] : Hamlyn, 1977. — 3-62p : ill(chiefly col) ; 25cm.
Bibl.: p.61. — Index.
ISBN 0-600-31397-2 : £1.50
(B77-32095)

Goren, Charles Henry. Goren's bridge complete : completely updated and revised edition of the standard work for all bridge players. — New ed. — London : Barrie and Jenkins, 1977. — xiv,690p ; 24cm.
This ed. originally published: New York : Doubleday, 1973. — Previous ed.: published as 'Bridge complete'. London : Barrie and Rockliff, 1964. — Index.
ISBN 0-214-20385-9 : £7.95
(B77-11357)

Markus, Rixi. Bid boldly, play safe / [by] Rixi Markus. — [New ed.]. — London [etc.] : Bodley Head, 1977. — 285p ; 21cm.
Previous ed.: London : Blond, 1966.
ISBN 0-370-30060-2 : £4.50
(B77-33383)

Milnes, Eric Charles. Learn to play bridge / [by] Eric C. Milnes and Paul Lukacs. — London : Kaye and Ward, 1977. — 153p ; 23cm.
With answers.
ISBN 0-7182-1145-6 : £2.95
(B77-10892)

Mollo, Victor. Bridge course complete : a new method of bridge tuition with over 200 quizzes / [by] Victor Mollo. — London : Faber, 1977. — 237p ; 21cm.
ISBN 0-571-11122-x : £5.50 : CIP rev
(B77-23634)

Squire, Norman, *b.1907.* A guide to bridge / [by] Norman Squire. — London : Sphere, 1977. — 151p ; 18cm.
Originally published: as 'Beginner's guide to bridge'. London : Pelham, 1971. — Index.
ISBN 0-7221-8091-8 Pbk : £0.75
(B77-31376)

795.4'15 — Contract bridge. Conventions
Kearse, Amalya. Bridge conventions complete / [by] Amalya Kearse. — Revised and expanded [ed.]. — London : A. and C. Black, 1977. — 656p ; 23cm.
Previous ed.: New York : Hart, 1975. — Index.
ISBN 0-7136-1744-6 : £6.50 : CIP rev.
(B77-07539)

795.4'15 — Contract bridge. Problems. *Collections*
Truscott, Alan. Master bridge by question and answer / [by] Alan Truscott. — British ed. / conversion to British bidding by Tony & Rhoda Lederer. — London : Allen and Unwin, [1977]. — 3-260p : ill ; 22cm.
This ed. originally published: 1973.
ISBN 0-04-793026-8 Pbk : £1.95
(B77-13805)

795.4'15'0924 — Contract bridge. Reese, Terence. *Autobiographies*
Reese, Terence. Bridge at the top / [by] Terence Reese ; with an introduction by Victor Mollo. — London : Faber, 1977. — ii-xiii,143p ; 21cm.
Index.
ISBN 0-571-11123-8 : £4.25 : CIP rev.
(B77-12602)

795.4'153 — Contract bridge. Card play. *Manuals*
Reese, Terence. The play of the cards / [by] Terence Reese and Albert Dormer. — New ed. — London : Hale, 1977. — 224p ; 23cm. — (Hale bridge books)
Previous ed.: Harmondsworth : Penguin, 1967.
ISBN 0-7091-5873-4 : £4.50
(B77-17687)

795.4'153 — Contract bridge. Deceptive play. *Manuals*
Reese, Terence. Snares and swindles in bridge / [by] Terence Reese and Roger Trézel. — London : Ward Lock, 1977. — 64p ; 20cm. — (Master bridge series) (A Hyperion book)
ISBN 0-7063-5310-2 Pbk : £1.50
(B77-20497)

795.4'153 — Contract bridge. Elimination play. *Manuals*
Reese, Terence. Elimination play in bridge / [by] Terence Reese and Roger Trézel. — London : Ward Lock, 1977. — 77p ; 20cm. — (Master bridge series) (A Hyperion book)
ISBN 0-7063-5323-4 Pbk : Unpriced
(B77-20498)

795.4'153 — Duplicate bridge. Card play. Problems. *Collections*
Kelsey, Hugh Walter. Test your match play / [by] H.W. Kelsey. — London : Faber, 1977. — 3-190p ; 23cm.
ISBN 0-571-11005-3 : £4.50
(B77-08005)

795.4'158 — Contract bridge. Card play. Games. *Collections*
Karpin, Fred Leon. Winning play in tournament and duplicate bridge : how the experts triumph / [by] Fred L. Karpin ; with a foreword by Alfred Sheinwold. — New York : Dover Publications [etc.] ; London : Constable, 1976. — iii-xiii,241,[1]p ; 22cm.
Originally published: New York : New American Library, 1968.
ISBN 0-486-23333-2 Pbk : £2.15
(B77-13201)

795.4'158 — Contract bridge. Games. *Collections*
Cotter, Edmond Patrick Charles. The 'Financial times' book of bridge / [by] E.P.C. Cotter ; edited by Derek Rimmington. — London : Hale, 1977. — 176p ; 23cm. — (Hale bridge books)
ISBN 0-7091-6271-5 : £4.25
(B77-28019)

795.4'3 — Card games: Patience. *Manuals*
Collie, Margaret. Games of patience : thirty-three ways to play / [by] Margaret Collie. — Havant : K. Mason, 1977. — [1],64p : ill ; 15cm.
ISBN 0-85937-062-3 Sd : £0.50
(B77-18320)

Hervey, George Frangopulo. The illustrated book of card games for one : over 120 games of patience / [by] George F. Hervey ; illustrated by Karel Feuerstein. — London [etc.] : Hamlyn, 1977. — 159p : col ill ; 27cm.
ISBN 0-600-34037-6 : £2.95
(B77-24404)

Parlett, David. Patience games / by David Parlett. — Wakefield : EP Publishing, 1976. — 48,[1]p : ill ; 14x21cm. — (Know the game)
'Published in collaboration with "Games & puzzles" magazine'. — Bibl.: p.48.
ISBN 0-7158-0501-0 Sd : £0.45
(B77-33993)

795.4'3 — Card games: Patience. *Manuals. Juvenile literature*
Belton, John. Card games for one / authors John Belton, Joella Cramblit. — London [etc.] : Foulsham, 1976. — 47p : col ill ; 24cm.
Originally published: as 'Solitaire games'. Milwaukee : Raintree Editions, 1975.
ISBN 0-572-00947-x Pbk : £1.95
(B77-00897)

795.4'38 — Card tricks. *Manuals*
Baron, Harry. Card tricks / [by] Harry Baron ; photographs by Reg Salmon ; drawings by Harry Baron ; additional drawings by Wayne Boughen. — London : Sphere, 1977. — [136]p : ill, ports ; 18cm.
Originally published: as 'How to do card tricks and entertain people'. London : Kaye, 1960.
ISBN 0-7221-1468-0 Pbk : £0.85
(B77-32096)

Fulves, Karl. Self-working card tricks : 72 foolproof card miracles for the amateur magician / [by] Karl Fulves ; with 42 illustrations by Joseph K. Schmidt. — New York : Dover Publications [etc.] ; London : Constable, 1976. — ix,113p : ill ; 22cm.
ISBN 0-486-23334-0 Pbk : £1.05
(B77-12603)

795.4'38 — Card tricks using giant card fans. *Manuals*
Ganson, Lewis. Lewis Ganson's fan finale : a routine with giant card fans. — Bideford (64 High St., Bideford, Devon) : Supreme Magic Company Ltd, 1976. — [15]p : ill, port ; 25cm.
ISBN 0-901127-16-7 Sd : £2.00
(B77-04998)

796 — SPORTS AND GAMES
796 — Sports & games. *Juvenile literature*
Goffe, Toni. Wonder why book of the XYZ of sport / written and illustrated by Toni Goffe. — London : Transworld, 1977. — [2],32p : col ill ; 29cm.
Index. — Previous control number ISBN 0-552-57008-7.
ISBN 0-552-98042-0 : £1.35
ISBN 0-552-57008-7 Sd : £0.50
(B77-12604)

796 — Sports. Systems analysis
Optimal strategies in sports / edited by Shaul P. Ladany and Robert E. Machol. — Amsterdam [etc.] ; Oxford : North-Holland Publishing Co., 1977. — xx,231p : ill ; 23cm. — (Studies in management science and systems ; vol.5)
Bibl.: p.207-224. — Index.
ISBN 0-7204-0528-9 : £18.67
(B77-25813)

796'.01 — Sports. Aesthetic aspects
Lowe, Benjamin. The beauty of sport : a cross-disciplinary inquiry / [by] Benjamin Lowe. — Englewood Cliffs ; London [etc.] : Prentice-Hall, 1977. — xix,327p : ill ; 24cm.
Bibl.: p.304-320. — Index.
ISBN 0-13-066589-4 : £9.55
(B77-18321)

796'.01 — Sports. Psychological aspects
Butt, Dorcas Susan. Psychology of sport : the behavior, motivation, personality, and performance of athletes / [by] Dorcas Susan Butt ; sketches by Jay. — New York ; London [etc.] : Van Nostrand Reinhold, [1977]. — xii, 196p : ill, ports ; 24cm.
Published in the United States: 1976. — Bibl.: p.175-183. — Index.
ISBN 0-442-21226-7 : £9.85
ISBN 0-442-21227-5 Pbk : £5.30
(B77-10503)

Singer, Robert N. Myths and truths in sports psychology / [by] Robert N. Singer. — New York [etc.] ; London : Harper and Row, [1976]. — ix,133p : ill ; 21cm. — (Issues in contemporary physical education)
Published in the United States: 1975. — Bibl. — Index.
ISBN 0-06-046225-6 Pbk : £3.40
(B77-04366)

796'.02'07 — Sports & games. *Humorous texts*
Rushton, William. Pigsticking, a joy for life : a gentleman's guide to sporting pastimes / by William Rushton ; illustrated by William Rushton. — London : Macdonald and Jane's, 1977. — 176 : ill, facsims, ports ; 25cm.
Index.
ISBN 0-354-08500-x : £4.95
(B77-28020)

796'.022'2 — Sports & games. *Illustrations. Juvenile literature*
Blanco, Josette. Sport / by Josette Blanco ; illustrated by Claude d'Ham. — Purton (Restrop Manor, Purton, Wilts.) : Child's Play (International) Ltd, [1977]. — [20]p : chiefly col ill ; 22cm. — (Child's Play moments ; book 1)
Page width varies.
ISBN 0-85953-039-6 : £0.90
ISBN 0-85953-035-3 Pbk : £0.45
(B77-13202)

796'.025 — Outdoor vacation activities for students. *Directories*
Sport and adventure holidays / the Central Bureau for Educational Visits & Exchanges. — London [etc.] (43 Dorset St., W1H 3FN) : The Bureau.
[1976] / edited by Hilary Sewell. — 1976. — 106p : ill ; 20cm.
Previously published: as 'Sport and adventure holidays at home & abroad'.
ISBN 0-900087-30-7 Pbk : £0.85
(B77-04999)

796'.025'42 — Outdoor vacation activities. *England. Directories*
Outdoor activity & sports holidays in England / English Tourist Board. — [London] : The Board.
'77 / [edited by Denise Carter]. — [1977]. — [2],52p : ill ; 21cm.
ISBN 0-903265-63-x Sd : £0.45
(B77-09193)

796'.025'426 — Outdoor recreation facilities. *East Anglia. Directories*
Eastern Sports Council. Countryside recreation projects / Eastern Sports Council. — [2nd ed.]. — Bedford (26 Bromham Rd, Bedford MK40 2QP) : The Council, 1976. — [5],38p ; 22cm.
Previous ed.: 1972.
Sd : £0.50
(B77-09194)

796'.03 — Sports & games. *Encyclopaedias*
The **Oxford** companion to sports and games / edited by John Arlott ; line drawings by Carl James. — St Albans : Paladin, 1977. — viii, 1010p : ill, plans ; 20cm.
Originally published: London : Oxford University Press, 1975.
ISBN 0-586-08313-8 : £3.25
(B77-25134)

796'.05 — Sports & games. *Juvenile literature. Serials*
'**Tiger**' book of sport. — London : IPC Magazines.
[1978]. — 1977. — 2-95p : ill(some col), map, ports(some col) ; 28cm. — (A Fleetway annual)
ISBN 0-85037-374-3 : £1.25
ISSN 0140-7120
(B77-33384)

796'.06'241 — Sports. Organisations. *Great Britain. Directories*
Sport : a guide to governing bodies / compiled by the Information Centre of the Sports Council. — London : Sports Council.
1977. — 1977. — [3],142p ; 30cm.
Index.
ISBN 0-900979-45-3 Pbk : £3.50
(B77-16543)

796'.06'2421 — Psychiatric hospitals. Personnel. Sports. Organisations. *London. London Mental Hospitals Sports Association. Yearbooks*
London Mental Hospitals Sports Association. Journal and yearbook / London Mental Hospitals Sports Association. — London (86 Edgware Rd, W2 2EA) : Waltham Publications.
[1977] / editor A.M. Puzey, asst editor L.G. Atkins. — [1977]. — 207p : ill, ports ; 22cm.
Cover title: London mental hospitals yearbook. 1977. — Supersedes: London mental hospitals journal.
ISBN 0-902570-20-x Sd : Unpriced
ISSN 0309-7358
(B77-16544)

796'.06'2422 — Sports. Organisations. *Central Southern England. Southern Council for Sport and Recreation. Reports, surveys*
Southern Council for Sport and Recreation. The Southern Council for Sport and Recreation. — Reading (Watlington House, Watlington St., Reading RG1 4RJ) : [The Council], 1977. — 15p : map ; 21cm.
ISBN 0-900979-55-0 Sd : Unpriced
(B77-16545)

796'.068 — Sports grounds. Playing areas. Hard porous surfaces. *Reports, surveys*
National Playing Fields Association. Hard porous (waterbound) surfaces for recreation / [National Playing Fields Association]. — London : N.P.F.A., 1976. — [1],31p ; 22cm.
Bibl.: p.28. — Index.
ISBN 0-900858-62-1 Sd : £0.75
(B77-09875)

796'.07 — Education. Role of sports. *France & Great Britain. Conference proceedings*
The **place** of sport in education : report of an Anglo-French Symposium held at the Crystal Palace National Sports Centre, September 6th-10th 1976 in conjunction with the French State Department for Youth and Sport. — London (10 Nottingham Place, W1M 4AX) : Physical Education Association of Great Britain and Northern Ireland, 1976. — [2],182p : forms ; 30cm.
'Comparative studies in physical education : France'. — Bibl.
ISBN 0-900985-13-5 Sp : £3.00
Also classified at 613.7'07
(B77-14867)

796'.076 — Sports & games. *Questions & answers*
Sportsquiz. — London (360 South Lambeth Rd, S.W.8) : Allen Sporting Publications Ltd ; London : Sportsvision Ltd.
No.1- ; Oct. 1977-. — [1977]-. — ill(some col), ports(some col) ; 28cm.
Monthly. — 'A "World of Sport" publication'. — 54p. in 1st issue.
Sd : £0.30
ISSN 0140-5349
(B77-30536)

796'.077 — Sports & games. Coaching schemes. *England. East Midlands*
East Midlands Sports Council. Directory of coaching awards / East Midlands Sports Council. — [Nottingham] ([26 Muster Rd, West Bridgford, Nottingham NG2 7PL]) : [The Council], [1977]. — [128]p : 1 ill ; 30cm.
Cover title.
ISBN 0-905163-07-9 Pbk : £1.00
(B77-13203)

796'.08 — Sports & games. *Essays*
Houlihan, Con. Come all you loyal heroes / by Con Houlihan. — Dublin (21 Great Denmark St., Dublin 1) : Olympic Press Ltd, 1977. — 91p ; 19cm.
Pbk : £1.00
(B77-33994)

796'.09 — Sports & games, to 1976
Jewell, Brian. Sports and games : history and origins / [by] Brian Jewell. — Tunbridge Wells : Midas Books, 1977. — 148p : ill, ports ; 26cm. — ([Heritage of the past])
Ill. on lining papers. — Bibl.: p.141-142. — Index.
ISBN 0-85936-075-x : £5.95
(B77-22055)

796'.0941 — Sports. *Great Britain. Secondary school texts*
McIver, Nick. Sport / by Nick McIver. — [Harlow] : Longman, 1977. — 12p : ill, ports ; 30cm. — (Young Britain)
ISBN 0-582-74066-5 Sd : £0.33
(B77-28816)

796'.09411 — Sports & games. *Scotland*
Directory of Scottish sport. — Edinburgh (1 St Colme St., Edinburgh EH3 6AA) : Scottish Sports Council.
1977. — [1977]. — 255p in various pagings ; 21cm.
Bibl.
Sd : £1.50
ISSN 0140-279x
(B77-32097)

796'.0942 — Sports facilities. Joint provision & multiple use. *England. Reports, surveys*
Eastern Sports Council. Joint provision of sport facilities / Eastern Sports Council. — Bedford (26 Bromham Rd, Bedford MK40 2QP) : The Council, 1976. — [2],40p ; 22cm.
Bibl.: p.37-39.
ISBN 0-905101-03-0 Sd : £0.50
(B77-05000)

796'.09424 — Schools. Sports facilities. Multiple use. *England. West Midlands. Inquiry reports*
West Midlands Sports Council. Dual use of education facilities / the West Midlands Sports Council. — [Birmingham] (7 Highfield Rd, Birmingham B15 3EG]) : [The Council], 1976. — [1],64p ; 30cm. — (Providing for sport ; 3)
Addendum (2,3p. : Sd) as insert. — Bibl.: p.62-64.
ISBN 0-904465-02-0 Sd : £1.25
(B77-11359)

796'.0944 — Sports. *France. Secondary school texts*
Sykes, Ben. Sport in France / [by] Ben Sykes. — London : Harrap, 1977. — [1],16,[1]p : ill, ports ; 14x22cm. — ([Destination France] : life French style)
ISBN 0-245-53055-x Sd : £0.35
(B77-15423)

796'.0947 — Sports. *Soviet Union, 1861-1976*
Riordan, James. Sport in Soviet Society : development of sport and physical education in Russia and the USSR / [by] James Riordan. — Cambridge [etc.] : Cambridge University Press, 1977. — ix,435p : ill ; 23cm. — (Soviet and East European studies)
Bibl.: p.420-429. — Index.
ISBN 0-521-21284-7 : £10.00
(B77-18941)

796'.0947 — Sports. *Soviet Union. Reports, surveys*
Speak, Michael Arthur. Physical education, recreation and sport in the USSR / by M.A. Speak and V.H. Ambler. — Lancaster (Bailrigg, Lancaster LA1 4YW) : Centre for Physical Education, University of Lancaster, 1976. — [3],92,xxi,[1]p : ill, form ; 21cm.
Bibl.: p.xiii-xviii.
ISBN 0-901699-37-3 Pbk : £1.50
Primary classification 613.7
(B77-02336)

796'.0968 — Sports. International competitions. Effects of apartheid, 1959-1970
Lapchick, Richard Edward. The politics of race and international sport : the case of South Africa / [by] Richard Edward Lapchick. — Westport, Conn. ; London : Greenwood Press, 1975. — xxx,268p ; 22cm. — (University of Denver. Center on International Race Relations. Studies in human rights ; no.1)
Bibl.: p.253-256. — Index.
ISBN 0-8371-7691-3 : £11.50
(B77-18942)

796'.0973 — Intramural sports & intramural games. Organisation & administration. *United States*
Hyatt, Ronald W. Intramural sports : organization and administration / [by] Ronald W. Hyatt. — Saint Louis : Mosby ; London : Distributed by Kimpton, 1977. — ix,299p : ill, forms ; 26cm.
Bibl. — Index.
ISBN 0-8016-2320-0 Pbk : £7.25
(B77-22769)

796'.0973 — Sports & games. *United States*
Michener, James Albert. Michener on sport. — London : Corgi, 1977. — 635p : ill ; 18cm.
Originally published: as 'Sports in America', New York : Random House ; and as 'Michener on sport', London : Secker and Warburg, 1976. — Index.
ISBN 0-552-10554-6 Pbk : £1.50
(B77-22056)

796.1'3 — Dancing games for children
Nelson, Esther L. Musical games for children of all ages / by Esther L. Nelson ; illustrations by Shizu Matsuda. — New York : Sterling [etc.] ; London : Distributed by Ward Lock, 1977. — 72p : ill, music ; 23x26cm.
Published in the United States: 1976. — Index.
ISBN 0-7061-2520-7 : £3.50
Primary classification 784.6'24
(B77-25116)

796.323 — BASKETBALL
796.32'32 — Basketball. *Manuals*
Coleman, Brian Edward. Basketball / [by] Brian Coleman, Peter Ray. — Wakefield : EP Publishing, 1976. — 119p : ill ; 21cm. — (EP sport series)
ISBN 0-7158-0587-8 : £3.00
(B77-15424)

796.33 — FOOTBALL

796.33 — Gaelic football. Teams. *Kerry (County). Kerry County Gaelic Football Team, 1903-1976*

Barry, John. Years of glory : the story of Kerry's All-Ireland Senior victories (23 football, 1 hurling) / authors John Barry and Eamon Horan ; with a message from Tom Moriarty ; and a foreword by Gerald McKenna. — Tralee (The Kerryman Ltd, Clash Industrial Estate, Tralee) : The authors, 1977. — 238p : ill, ports ; 21cm.
Col. ports on back cover.
Pbk : £2.00
(B77-29620)

796.332 — AMERICAN FOOTBALL

796.33'2'0922 — American football, 1972. *Personal observations. Collections*

Plimpton, George. Mad ducks and bears / [by] George Plimpton. — London : Deutsch, 1974 [i.e. 1977]. — ii-xi,423p : 2 ill ; 22cm.
Originally published: New York : Random House, 1973.
ISBN 0-233-96536-x : £3.95
(B77-10504)

796.333 — RUGBY FOOTBALL

796.33'3'05 — Rugby Union football. *Yearbooks*

Rothmans rugby yearbook : (incorporating Playfair rugby annual). — London : Queen Anne Press.
1977-78 / editor Vivian Jenkins. — 1977. — 368p : ill, ports ; 22cm.
ISBN 0-354-09019-4 : Unpriced
ISSN 0306-9605
(B77-28817)

796.33'3'09034 — Rugby Union football, to 1976

Rea, Chris. Rugby : a history of rugby union football / [by] Chris Rea. — London [etc.] : Hamlyn, 1977. — 216p : ill(some col), facsims, ports ; 26cm.
Index.
ISBN 0-600-37591-9 : £4.95
(B77-25135)

796.33'3'0924 — Rugby Union football. McCormick, William Fergus. *New Zealand. Biographies*

Veysey, Alex. Fergie / [by] Alex Veysey. — London : Pelham, 1977. — 192p,[16]p of plates : ill, ports ; 23cm.
Originally published: Christchurch, N.Z. ; London : Whitcoulls, 1976.
ISBN 0-7207-0995-4 : £4.50
(B77-17688)

796.33'3'0924 — Rugby Union football. Thomas, Watcyn. *Wales. Autobiographies*

Thomas, Watcyn. Rugby-playing man / [by] Watcyn Thomas ; foreword by Vivian Jenkins. — London : Pelham, 1977. — 102p,[8]p of plates : ill, ports ; 23cm.
Index.
ISBN 0-7207-0952-0 : £3.75
(B77-10505)

796.33'3'09931 — Rugby Union football. *New Zealand, 1875-1965. Illustrations*

Focus on rugby / [compiled by] Gordon Slatter. — Christchurch, N.Z. [etc.] ; London : Whitcoulls, 1976 [i.e. 1977]. — 136p,[2]leaves of plates : of ill, ports ; 27cm.
Published in New Zealand : 1976. — Index.
ISBN 0-7233-0457-2 Pbk : Unpriced
(B77-11360)

796.33'32 — Rugby Union football. *Manuals*

Craven, D H. Rugby handbook / [by] D.H. Craven. — [New ed.]. — Wakefield : EP Publishing, 1977. — [9],250p ; 23cm.
This ed. originally published: Wellington, N.Z. : A.H. and A.W. Reed, 1975.
ISBN 0-7158-0616-5 : £3.50 : CIP rev.
(B77-16546)

Craven, Danie. Rugby handbook / [by] D.H. Craven. — Wellington [N.Z.] [etc.] ; London : A.H. and A.W. Reed, [1976]. — [9],250p : ill ; 25cm.
Spine title: Craven rugby handbook. — Originally published: Cape Town : Tafelberg, 1974.
ISBN 0-589-00915-x : £7.75
(B77-08006)

Wallace, Jim. The rugby game : a manual for coaches and players / [by] Jim Wallace. — Wellington [etc.] ; London : A.H. and A.W. Reed, 1976. — ix,176,[1]p,[16]p of plates : ill, ports ; 26cm.
Also published: London : Kaye and Ward, 1976.
ISBN 0-589-00960-5 : £7.75
(B77-20499)

Williams, Ray, *b.1927.* Skilful rugby / [by] Ray Williams. — London : Souvenir Press, 1976. — 239p : ill ; 25cm.
Bibl.: p.219.
ISBN 0-285-62233-1 : £4.00
(B77-01734)

796.333'3'0924 — Rugby Union football. Davies, Mervyn. *Wales. Autobiographies*

Davies, Mervyn. Number 8 / [by] Mervyn Davies ; with David Parry-Jones ; foreword by John Dawes. — London : Pelham, 1977. — 208p,[16]p of plates : ill, ports ; 23cm.
ISBN 0-7207-0980-6 : £4.25
(B77-21359)

796.33'362'0941 — Rugby Union football. Clubs: Barbarians. *Great Britain, to 1976*

Starmer-Smith, Nigel. The Barbarians : the official history of the Barbarian Football Club / [by] Nigel Starmer-Smith. — London : Macdonald and Jane's, 1977. — 240p : ill, facsims, ports ; 23cm.
ISBN 0-354-08501-8 : £5.95
(B77-17031)

796.33'362'0942987 — Rugby Union football. Clubs. *Cardiff. Cardiff Rugby Club, 1876-1975*

Davies, Danny Ellis. Cardiff Rugby Club : history and statistics, 1876-1975 / [by] D.E. Davies. — 2nd ed. — Risca : Starling Press, 1976. — 435p,[32]p of plates : ill, facsim, map, ports ; 23cm.
Previous ed.: Cardiff : Cardiff Athletic Club, 1975.
ISBN 0-903434-24-5 : £4.50
(B77-05582)

796.33'362'0942995 — Rugby Union football. Clubs. *Gwent. Blaina. Blaina Rugby Football Club, 1875-1976*

Evans, Barbara M. Blaina Rugby Football Club, 1875-1976 : memories of Mutton Tump / [by] Barbara M. Evans. — Risca : Starling Press, 1976. — 137p,leaf of plate,[50]p of plates : ill, facsims, ports ; 22cm.
Ports on lining papers.
ISBN 0-903434-22-9 : £3.00
(B77-05583)

796.33'374 — Rugby Union football. Tours by All Blacks. *South Africa, 1976*

McLean, Terry. Goodbye to glory : the 1976 All Black tour of South Africa / [by] Terry McLean. — London : Pelham, 1977. — vii, 176p,[16]p of plates : ill, ports ; 23cm.
Originally published: Wellington, N.Z. : Reed, 1976.
ISBN 0-7207-0997-0 : £4.95
(B77-28021)

796.33'374 — Rugby Union football. Tours by British Lions. *New Zealand, 1977*

John, Barry. The long lost tour : Lions '77 / [by] Barry John, Graham Thorne. — Swansea : C. Davies, 1977. — 135p : ill, ports ; 20cm.
ISBN 0-7154-0432-6 Pbk : £1.50
(B77-32796)

796.33'375 — Rugby Union football. International matches played by English teams, to 1976

Bowker, Barry Morrison. England rugby : a history of the national side, 1871-1976 / [by] Barry Bowker ; with a foreword by M.R. Steele-Bodger. — London : Cassell, 1976. — xiv,199p,[16]p of plates : ill, ports ; 22cm.
Index.
ISBN 0-304-29546-9 : £4.25
(B77-09195)

796.334 — ASSOCIATION FOOTBALL

The **Hamlyn** international book of soccer / contributors Michael Archer ... [et al.]. — London [etc.] : Hamlyn, 1977. — 208p : ill(some col), facsim, ports(some col) ; 27cm.
Ill. on lining papers. — Index.
ISBN 0-600-38247-8 : £2.95
(B77-33995)

Macdonald, Malcolm. Win! / [by] Malcolm Macdonald. — London : Pelham, 1977. — 157, [8]p of plates : ill, ports ; 23cm.
ISBN 0-7207-1014-6 : £3.95
(B77-30537)

796.33'4 — Association football. *Juvenile literature*

Peacock, Frank. Let's go to the soccer match / [by] Frank Peacock ; editor Henry Pluckrose. — London [etc.] : F. Watts, 1977. — 32p : col ill ; 22cm. — (Let's go series)
ISBN 0-85166-639-6 : £1.95
(B77-28022)

Tagholm, John. Football : how much do you really know? / [by] John Tagholm ; illustrated by Robin Anderson. — London : Severn House : [Distributed by Hutchinson], 1976. — 128p : ill, ports ; 21cm. — (Look-in books)
Originally published: London : Independent Television Books Ltd, 1975. — Bibl.: p.126. — Index.
ISBN 0-7278-0182-1 : £2.50
(B77-00898)

796.33'4'02022 — Association football. *Rules*

Referees' chart and players' guide to the laws of Association football. — London [etc.] : Pan Books [for the Football Association].
1977-1978 : revised ed. / authorised by the International Football Association Board. — 1977. — 63p : ill ; 20cm.
ISBN 0-330-25302-6 Pbk : £0.40
(B77-33996)

796.33'4'027 — Association football. Clubs. Colours

Tyler, Martin. Soccer club colours / [by] Martin Tyler. — London [etc.] : Hamlyn, 1976. — 5-60p : col ill ; 23cm.
Ill. on lining paper.
ISBN 0-600-38206-0 : £1.00
(B77-01735)

796.33'4'05 — Association football. *Annuals*

International football book. — London : Souvenir Press.
No.18 / edited by Eric Batty ; with contributions by Terry Yorath ... [et al.]. — 1976. — 142p : ports ; 24cm.
ISBN 0-285-62230-7 : £2.50
(B77-04367)

No.19 / edited by Eric Batty ; with contributions by John Toshack ... [et al.]. — 1977. — 144p : ports ; 24cm.
ISBN 0-285-62292-7 : £3.00
(B77-25814)

'The **topical** times' football book. — London [etc.] : D.C. Thomson.
1978. — [1977]. — 4-125p : chiefly ill(some col), facsims, ports(some col) ; 28cm.
Ill. on lining papers. — Index.
£1.05
(B77-31377)

796.33'4'05 — Association football. *Annuals. Juvenile literature*

'Shoot!' annual. — London : IPC Magazines.
1978. — 1977. — 2-127p : ill(some col), ports(some col) ; 28cm. — (A Fleetway annual)
ISBN 0-85037-354-9 : £1.25
(B77-32797)

796.33'4'05 — Association football. *Yearbooks*

Rothmans football yearbook. — London : Queen Anne Press.
1976-77 / compiled by Leslie Vernon and Jack Rollin ; [edited by Peter Dunk]. — [1976]. — 875p,[8]p of plates : ill, ports ; 21cm.
ISBN 0-362-00259-2 Pbk : £2.50
ISSN 0080-4088
(B77-06826)

796.33'4'076 — Association football. *Questions & answers. Juvenile literature*

Jeffery, Gordon. The Armada football quiz book no.2 / [by] Gordon Jeffery. — London : Armada, 1975. — 126p : ill, facsims, 2 maps ; 18cm.
With answers. — Originally published: 1973.
ISBN 0-00-691038-6 Pbk : £0.30
(B77-32798)

796.33'4'076 — Association football. *Questions & answers. Juvenile literature. Serials*

Jeffery, Gordon. Football quiz / by Gordon Jeffery. — London : Armada.
1976. — 1976. — [96]p,[8]p of plates : ill, ports ; 18cm.
With answers.
ISBN 0-00-690951-5 Pbk : £0.40
(B77-13806)

796.33'4'076 — Association football. *Questions & answers. Serials*

'Shoot' soccer quiz book. — London : IPC Magazines.
1977. — 1976. — 2-79p : ill(some col), ports(some col) ; 28cm. — (A Fleetway annual)
With answers.
ISBN 0-85037-303-4 : £1.30
(B77-01736)

1978. — 1977. — 3-79p : ill(some col), ports(some col) ; 28cm. — (A Fleetway annual)
With answers.
ISBN 0-85037-355-7 : £1.35
(B77-32799)

796.33'4'077 — Association football. Coaching. *Manuals*
Yonker, Donald Y. Soccer : coaching to win / [by] Donald Y. Yonker and Alexander Weide. — South Brunswick ; New York : Barnes ; London : Yoseloff, 1976. — 171p : ill ; 26cm.
ISBN 0-498-01663-3 : £4.25
(B77-30538)

796.33'4'0904 — Association football, to 1976
Macdonald, Roger. Soccer : a pictorial history / by Roger Macdonald ; with a foreword by Bobby Moore. — Glasgow [etc.] : Collins, 1977. — 192p : chiefly ill(some col), facsims, ports(some col) ; 26cm.
Ports on lining papers. — Index.
ISBN 0-00-434554-1 : £4.95
(B77-29621)

796.33'4'0924 — Association football. Channon, Mike. *Great Britain. Autobiographies*
Channon, Mike. Home and away : an autobiography / [by] Mike Channon ; with Neil Ewart. — London : Paul, 1977. — 123p,[12]p of plates : ill, ports ; 23cm.
ISBN 0-09-131290-6 : £3.95
(B77-33997)

796.33'4'0924 — Association football. Clubs. *England. Manchester City Football Club, 1965-1976. Personal observations*
Doyle, Mike, *b.1946.* Manchester City, my team / [by] Mike Doyle. — London : Souvenir Press, 1977. — 173p,[16]p of plates : ill, ports ; 23cm.
ISBN 0-285-62306-0 : £3.95 : CIP rev.
(B77-22057)

796.33'4'0924 — Association football. Dean, Dixie. *Great Britain. Biographies*
Walsh, Nick. Dixie Dean : the life story of a goal scoring legend / [by] Nick Walsh. — London : Macdonald and Jane's, 1977. — [2],221p,[8]p of plates : ill, ports ; 23cm.
ISBN 0-354-08515-8 : £4.95
(B77-33385)

796.33'4'0924 — Association football. Macari, Lou. *Autobiographies*
Macari, Lou. United we shall not be moved / [by] Lou Macari. — London : Souvenir Press, 1976. — 187p,[8]p of plates : ports ; 23cm.
Contains a chapter by Tommy Docherty.
ISBN 0-285-62260-9 : £3.50
(B77-01737)

796.33'4'0924 — Association football. Pelé. *Brazil. Autobiographies*
Pelé. Pelé : my life and the beautiful game : the autobiography of Pelé / by Pelé and Robert L. Fish. — London : New English Library, 1977. — 255,[1]p : ill, ports ; 26cm.
Also published: Garden City, N.Y. : Doubleday, 1977.
ISBN 0-450-03230-2 : £3.95
(B77-29622)

796.33'4'0924 — Association football. Shankly, Bill. *Great Britain. Autobiographies*
Shankly, Bill. Shankly. — St Albans : Mayflower, 1977. — 187p,[8]p of plates : ill, ports ; 18cm.
Originally published: London : A. Barker, 1976.
ISBN 0-583-12788-6 Pbk : £0.75
(B77-25136)

796.33'4'0924 — Association football. Toshack, John. *Great Britain*
The **Tosh** annual / [by John Toshack et al.]. — London : Duckworth, 1977. — 2-62p : chiefly ill, ports ; 29cm.
Ports. on lining papers.
ISBN 0-7156-1259-x : £1.35
(B77-33998)

796.33'4'0941 — Association football. *Great Britain. Annuals*
Football champions. — Maidenhead : Purnell.
[1976] / edited by Ken Johns. — 1976. — 3-62p : ill(some col), ports(some col) ; 28cm.
Ill., ports on lining papers.
ISBN 0-361-03504-7 : £0.85
(B77-01738)

796.33'4'0941 — Association football. *Great Britain. Yearbooks*
Football Association. The Football Association year book. — London [etc.] : Clowes.
1977-1978. — [1977]. — 142p : ill, ports ; 20cm.
ISBN 0-85194-056-0 Pbk : £1.20
ISSN 0071-724x
(B77-30539)

'**News** of the world' football annual. — London (Bouverie St., E.C.4) : 'News of the World' Ltd.

1976-77 : 90th year of publication / [edited by Frank Butler and Patrick Collins]. — [1977]. — 384p,[16]p of plates : ill, ports ; 15cm.
Pbk : £0.50
ISSN 0305-4780
(B77-30540)

796.33'4'09411 — Association football. *Scotland. Annuals*
The **Scottish** football book. — London : Paul.
No.22 / edited by Hugh Taylor. — 1976. — 128p : ill, ports ; 25cm.
ISBN 0-09-127460-5 : £1.95
(B77-17689)

796.33'42 — Association football. *Manuals*
Diagram Group. Enjoying soccer / by the Diagram Group. — New York ; London : Paddington Press, 1977. — 159p : ill, 2 ports ; 24cm.
Index.
ISBN 0-448-22182-9 Pbk : £1.95
(B77-20500)

Sexton, Dave. Tackle soccer / [by] Dave Sexton. — London : Paul, 1977. — 172p : ill, ports ; 20cm.
ISBN 0-09-129900-4 : £3.25
ISBN 0-09-129901-2 Pbk : £1.75
(B77-32800)

796.33'42 — Association football. *Manuals. Juvenile literature*
Leslie, Stephen. Action football / [by] Stephen Leslie ; illustrated by Robert Bond. — London : Transworld, 1977. — [88]p : chiefly ill ; 13x20cm. — (A tracker action book)
ISBN 0-552-56008-1 Pbk : £0.45
(B77-29623)

796.33'42'0222 — Association football. *Manuals. Illustrations*
Blanchflower, Danny. Football / by Danny Blanchflower ; script Iain Reid ; drawings by Horak. — Paris : Chancerel ; Leicester (Euston St., Freeman's Common, Aylestone Rd, Leicester LE2 7SS) : [Distributed by] WHS Distributors, 1975. — 96p : chiefly ill, ports ; 17x23cm. — (Learn through strips)
'From the Sunday Express' - cover.
Pbk : £0.95
ISBN 2-85429-010-0
(B77-20501)

796.33'426 — Association football. Goalkeeping. *Manuals*
Clemence, Ray. Clemence on goalkeeping / [by] Ray Clemence ; with John Keith ; photographs by Harry Ormesher. — Guildford : Lutterworth Press ; [Great Britain] : Richard Smart Publishing, 1977. — 156p : ill, ports ; 23cm.
Index.
ISBN 0-7188-7016-6 : £4.95
(B77-32098)

796.33'462'0942185 — Association football. Clubs. *Great Britain. Study examples: Queen's Park Rangers Football Club*
Road, Alan. The facts about a football club, featuring Queens Park Rangers / by Alan Road ; photographed by Bryn Campbell ; introduction by Bobby Charlton. — London : G. Whizzard Publications Ltd : Deutsch, 1976. — [5],53p : ill(some col), ports(some col) ; 29cm. — (Factbooks)
Ill. on lining papers.
ISBN 0-233-96772-9 : £1.95
(B77-08007)

796.33'462'0942674 — Association football. Clubs. *England. Old Foresters Football Club, to 1976*
Adams, P C. From little acorns : a centennial review of the Old Foresters Football Club and its place in the history of the game / by P.C. Adams. — Windsor (Adams, Middleton and Partners Ltd, 27 High St., Windsor, Berks. SL4 1LH) : The author, [1976]. — [4],82p : ill, facsims, ports ; 30cm.
ISBN 0-9505531-0-7 Pbk : £3.00
(B77-08504)

796.33'463'0941 — Association football. League tables. *Great Britain, 1899-1977. Collections*
Football league tables : 1889 to the present / [editor Jim Mallory ; assistant editor Jeanette Tannock]. — Glasgow [etc.] : Collins, 1977. — 153p ; 20cm.
ISBN 0-00-435009-x Pbk : £0.65
(B77-27300)

796.33'463'0941443 — Association football. Clubs. *Scotland. Glasgow Celtic Football Club. Annuals*
Playing for Celtic. — London : Paul.
No.8 / edited by Rodger Baillie. — 1976. — 128p : ill, ports ; 24cm.
ISBN 0-09-127470-2 : £2.25
(B77-05584)

796.33'463'0941443 — Association football. Clubs. *Scotland. Glasgow Rangers Football Club. Annuals*
Playing for Rangers. — London : Paul.
No.9 / edited by Ken Gallacher. — 1977. — 96p,[8]p of plates : ill(some col), ports(some col) ; 24cm.
ISBN 0-09-131231-0 Pbk : £2.50
(B77-33386)

796.33'463'0941443 — Association football. Clubs. *Scotland. Partick Thistle Football Club, to 1976*
Archer, Ian. The Jags : the centenary history of Partick Thistle Football Club / by Ian Archer. — Glasgow : Molendinar Press, 1976. — 95p : ill, plan, ports ; 20cm.
ISBN 0-904002-19-5 : £1.25
(B77-02526)

796.33'463'0941835 — Association football. Clubs. *Ireland (Republic). Bohemians Football Club, to 1976*
Reid, Tony. Bohemian AFC : official club history, 1890-1976 / compiled and edited [i.e. written] by Tony Reid. — Dublin (3 Lower Abbey St., Dublin 1) : Tara Publishing Company Ltd for Bohemian Association Football Club, [1977]. — [1],64p : ill, ports ; 25cm.
Sd : £0.75
(B77-32099)

796.33'463'0942491 — Association football. Clubs. *England. Wolverhampton Wanderers Football Club, to 1975*
Young, Percy Marshall. Centenary Wolves / by Percy M. Young. — [Wolverhampton] ([Molineux Grounds, Wolverhampton, W. Midlands]) : Wolverhampton Wanderers F.C. (1923) Ltd, 1976. — [12],209p,[48]p of plates : ill, facsims, ports ; 22cm.
Index.
ISBN 0-9505245-0-6 : £3.75
(B77-15425)

796.33'463'0942494 — Association football. Clubs. *England. West Bromwich Albion Football Club, 1939-1946. Statistics*
Matthews, Tony, *b.1943 (April).* Albion through the war : a statistical history of West Bromwich Albion's fortunes during the Second World War / by Tony Matthews. — [West Bromwich] ([The Hawthorns, Halfords La., West Bromwich, W. Midlands]) : West Bromwich Albion Football Club, 1976. — [2],29p : ports ; 21cm.
ISBN 0-9505585-0-8 Sd : £0.40
(B77-10506)

796.33'463'0942733 — Association football. Clubs. *England. Manchester United Football Club. Serials*
The **Manchester** United football book. — London : Paul.
No.12 / edited by David Meek. — 1977. — 128p : ill, ports ; 24cm.
ISBN 0-09-131250-7 : £2.50
ISSN 0308-8405
(B77-28818)

796.33'463'0942733 — Association football. Clubs. *England. Manchester United Football Club, to 1977*
Hodgson, Derek. The Manchester United story / [by] Derek Hodgson. — London : A. Barker, 1977. — 149p : ill, ports ; 26cm.
Ill. on lining papers.
ISBN 0-213-16631-3 : £3.50
(B77-24406)

796.33'466 — Association football. European Cup. Role of Liverpool Football Club. *Europe, 1964-1977*
Keith, John. Liverpool, champions of Europe : the players' official story / [by] John Keith ; foreword by Ian Callaghan ; colour photography by Harry Ormesher. — London : Duckworth ; Liverpool : Elmwood, 1977. — 3-62p,[8]p of plates : ill(some col), map, ports(some col) ; 29cm.
Ill. on lining papers. — Includes contributions by others.
ISBN 0-7156-1270-0 : £2.95
(B77-31378)

796.34 — RACKET GAMES
796.34'09 — Racket games, to 1974. *Juvenile literature*
Barrett, John, *b.1931 (Apr.).* Tennis and racket games / by John Barrett. — London : Macdonald Educational, 1975. — 3-62p : ill(chiefly col), col maps, ports(some col) ; 29cm. — (Macdonald library of sport)
Col. ill. on lining papers. — Index.
ISBN 0-356-05093-9 : £1.75
(B77-03187)

796.342 — TENNIS
796.34'2'05 — Lawn tennis. *Periodicals*
Tennis today. — London : Allen Sporting Publications Ltd : [Distributed by] Seymour Press.
Issue no.1- ; July 1976-. — 1976-. — ill, ports(some col) ; 28cm.
Monthly. — 58[i.e.59]p. in 1st issue.
Sd : £0.35
ISSN 0140-5497
(B77-30541)

796.34'2'05 — Lawn tennis. *Reports, surveys. Serials*
World of tennis : a BP yearbook. — London : Macdonald and Jane's.
1977 / edited by John Barrett ; compiled by Lance Tingay ; biographies by Steve Flink. — 1977. — 384p : ill, ports ; 22cm.
Index.
ISBN 0-354-09011-9 Pbk : £3.25
ISSN 0305-6325
(B77-25815)

796.34'2'06241 — Lawn tennis. Organisations. *Great Britain. Lawn Tennis Association. Yearbooks*
Lawn Tennis Association. The Lawn Tennis Association handbook. — London (Baron's Court, W14 9EG) : The Association.
1977. — 1977. — xx,374p : ill, forms ; 17cm.
Pbk : £2.25
(B77-32801)

796.34'2'09 — Lawn tennis, to 1976
Tingay, Lance. Tennis, a pictorial history / by Lance Tingay. — New and revised ed. ; foreword by Jack Kramer. — Glasgow : Collins, 1977. — 168p : ill(some col), facsim, ports(some col) ; 26cm.
Previous ed.: published as 'History of lawn tennis in pictures'. London : T. Stacey, 1973. — Index.
ISBN 0-00-434553-3 : £4.95
(B77-32100)

796.34'2'0924 — Lawn tennis. Rosewall, Ken. *Biographies*
Rowley, Peter. Twenty years at the top / by Peter Rowley ; with Ken Rosewall. — London : Cassell, 1976. — [11],239p,[8]p of plates : ill, ports ; 23cm.
Spine title: Rosewall, twenty years at the top. — Index.
ISBN 0-304-29735-6 : £4.50
(B77-09196)

796.34'2'0924 — Lawn tennis. Tilden, William Tatem. *Biographies*
Deford, Frank. Big Bill Tilden : the triumphs and the tragedy / by Frank Deford. — London : Gollancz, 1977. — 286p,[16]p of plates : ports ; 23cm.
'This work is an outgrowth of a two-part magazine series written by Mr Deford for "Sports illustrated" (January 13, January 20, 1975)' - title page verso. — Originally published: New York : Simon and Schuster, 1976. — Index.
ISBN 0-575-02305-8 : £5.25
(B77-25137)

796.34'2'0942193 — Lawn tennis. Competitions. *London. Merton (London Borough). Lawn Tennis Championships, to 1977*
Medlycott, James. 100 years of the Wimbledon Tennis Championships / [by] James Medlycott. — London [etc.] : Hamlyn, 1977. — 4-93p : ill, ports ; 29cm.
Ill. on lining papers.
ISBN 0-600-38768-2 : £2.50
(B77-30542)

Robertson, Max. Wimbledon, 1877-1977 / [by] Max Robertson. — London : A. Barker, 1977. — xii,180p : ill, facsim, ports ; 26cm.
ISBN 0-213-16643-7 : £4.50
(B77-25138)

Tingay, Lance. 100 years of Wimbledon / [by] Lance Tingay. — Enfield : Guinness Superlatives, 1977. — 256p : ill(some col), facsims, ports(some col) ; 31cm.
Index.
ISBN 0-900424-71-0 : £8.50
(B77-21360)

796.34'22 — Lawn tennis. *Manuals*
Brown, Jim. Tennis without lessons / [by] Jim Brown. — Englewood Cliffs ; London [etc.] : Prentice-Hall, 1977. — ix,159p : ill ; 24cm.
Bibl.: p.153-154. — Index.
ISBN 0-13-903252-5 : £7.20
(B77-14346)

Deflassieux, A. Tennis : basic techniques and tactics / [by] A. Deflassieux ; adapted [i.e. translated from the French] by Barbara Wancke ; drawings by R. Garel. — [London] : Chancerel Publishers Ltd : Barrie and Jenkins, 1977. — 2-91p : ill, ports ; 21cm. — (Action books)
Ill. on lining papers. — Translation of: 'Le tennis'. Paris : Chancerel, 1976.
ISBN 0-905703-02-2 : £1.75
(B77-25139)

Ravensdale, Tom. Tennis / [by] Tom Ravensdale ; with photographs bythe author. — Leicester : Knight Books, 1977. — 96p : ill(some col) ; 21cm. — (Illustrated teach yourself)
Index.
ISBN 0-340-20584-9 Pbk : £1.80
(B77-23635)

Tennis strokes and strategies. — London [etc.] : Hodder and Stoughton, 1976. — 215p : ill(some col), ports ; 29cm. — (The classic instruction series)
'"Tennis strokes and strategies" ... represents the best of the "Tennis" instructional portfolios, along with the best of the instruction that has appeared in other sections of the magazine' - Introduction. — Originally published: New York : Simon and Schuster, 1975.
ISBN 0-340-20722-1 : £4.95
(B77-13204)

796.34'22 — Lawn tennis. Strokes. *Manuals*
Mastering your tennis strokes / [by] Charlie Pasarell ... [et al.] ; edited by Larry Sheehan. — London : Cassell, 1977. — [5],201p : ill, ports ; 27cm.
Originally published: New York : Atheneum, 1976.
ISBN 0-304-29917-0 Pbk : £4.50
(B77-30543)

796.343 — SQUASH RACKETS
796.34'3 — Squash rackets. *Manuals*
Barrington, Jonah, *b.1941.* Tackle squash / [by] Jonah Barrington with John Hopkins. — London : Paul, 1976. — 104p : ill, ports ; 20cm.
ISBN 0-09-127880-5 : £2.95
ISBN 0-09-127881-3 Pbk : £1.75
(B77-20502)

Beddington, John. Play better squash / [by] John Beddington. — 2nd ed. — London : Macdonald and Jane's, 1977. — 128p : ill, plans ; 22cm.
Previous ed.: London : Queen Anne Press, 1974. — Includes the rules of squash.
ISBN 0-354-08506-9 : £3.95
ISBN 0-354-08507-7 Pbk : £2.25
(B77-32101)

Hawkey, Richard Bladworth. A guide to squash / [by] Richard Hawkey. — London : Sphere, 1977. — 157p,[16]p of plates : ill ; 18cm.
Originally published: as 'Beginners guide to squash'. London : Pelham, 1973. — Index.
ISBN 0-7221-4415-6 Pbk : £0.85
(B77-28819)

Hunt, Geoff. Geoff Hunt on squash / edited by Alan Trengove. — 2nd revised ed. — London : Cassell, 1977. — 160p : ill, ports ; 23cm.
Previous ed. i.e. 1st ed.: 1974.
ISBN 0-304-29925-1 Pbk : £2.50
(B77-27301)

796.34'3'05 — Squash rackets. *Yearbooks*
Squash Rackets Association. Annual handbook / Squash Rackets Association. — London (70 Brompton Rd, SW3 1DX) : [The Association]. 1976-77. — [1976]. — 432p : ill, plans, ports(some col) ; 19cm.
Pbk : £2.50
(B77-01739)

796.345 — BADMINTON
796.34'5 — Badminton. *Manuals*
Hashman, Judy Devlin. Starting badminton / [by] Judy Hashman and C.M. Jones. — London : Ward Lock, 1977. — 96p : ill ; 21cm. — (A Hyperion book)
ISBN 0-7063-5126-6 : £2.95 : CIP rev.
(B77-17032)

796.346 — TABLE TENNIS
796.34'6 — Table tennis. *Manuals*
Barnes, Chester. Advanced table tennis techniques : how the world's top players win / by Chester Barnes ; with line drawings by Sylvia Gainsford. — London [etc.] : Angus and Robertson, 1977. — 112p : ill, ports ; 22cm.
ISBN 0-207-95721-5 : £3.60
ISBN 0-207-95745-2 Pbk : £1.95
(B77-13205)

Myers, Harold. Table tennis / [by] Harold Myers. — London : Faber, 1977. — 121p : ill ; 20cm.
Index.
ISBN 0-571-11001-0 Pbk : £1.50 : CIP rev.
(B77-05001)

796.352 — GOLF
Humphreys, Eric. The Dunlop golfer's companion / by Eric Humphreys. — Lavenham : Eastland Press, 1977. — 128p : ill, ports ; 24cm.
Index.
ISBN 0-903214-09-1 : £4.20
(B77-30544)

796.352 — Golf. *Mystic viewpoints. Stories, anecdotes*
Murphy, Michael. Golf in the Kingdom / [by] Michael Murphy. — London : Abacus, 1976. — 175p ; 20cm.
Originally published: New York : Viking Press, 1972 ; London : Latimer New Dimensions, 1974. — Bibl.: p.175.
ISBN 0-349-12464-7 Pbk : £0.95
(B77-06827)

796.352'05 — Golf. *Yearbooks*
Golfer's handbook. — Glasgow (113 St Vincent St., Glasgow G2 5HU) : The Golfer's Handbook.
1977 : seventy-fourth year of publication / editor Eileen Gibb ... — 1977. — xxxii,681p : ill, ports ; 22cm.
Index.
ISBN 0-900403-12-8 : £7.00
ISSN 0072-498x
(B77-12030)

World of golf. — London : Macdonald and Jane's.
1977 / edited by George Simms. — 1977. — 224p : ill, ports ; 22cm.
ISBN 0-354-09001-1 Pbk : £3.95
ISSN 0309-8257
(B77-23636)

796.352'06 — Golf. Clubs. *Great Britain. Directories*
United Kingdom golf clubs / [Data Research Group]. — Amersham (Hill House, [Hill Ave.], Amersham, Bucks.) : The Group.
[1975]. — 1975. — 132 leaves in various pagings ; 30cm.
ISBN 0-905570-69-3 Sp : £12.00
(B77-06228)

796.352'068 — Golf courses
The **world** atlas of golf / contributing editor Pat Ward-Thomas. — London : Mitchell Beazley, 1976. — 280p : ill(chiefly col), col maps, plans(chiefly col), ports(some col) ; 30cm.
Index.
ISBN 0-85533-088-0 : £12.95
(B77-00355)

796.352'068'094 — Golf courses. *Europe. Directories*
Eurogolf : your second golf club. — [Members ed.]. — London (409 Hendon Way, NW4 3LH) : Eurogolf Ltd.
1975/6 / consultants Henry Longhurst ... [et al.]. — [1975]. — [2],269p : ill(some col), col maps, ports ; 22cm.
Index.
Unpriced(free to members)
(B77-33999)

Golf in the sun : a recommendation of some of the best places to play and stay throughout Europe, the Mediterranean, Bermuda, the Caribbean, West Indies, South Africa and Thailand. — London (Sherborne House, Hadley Highstone, Barnet, Herts.) : Fairgreen Publications Ltd.
1977 / [edited] by Michael Gedye ; with contributions from Peter Alliss, Peter Dobereiner and Gary Player. — [1976]. — 160, [7]p : ill(some col), maps(some col), ports(1 col) ; 18cm.
ISBN 0-902863-04-5 Pbk : £1.25
(B77-06828)

796.352'068'0941 — Golf courses. *Great Britain. Directories*
Steel, Donald. The golf course guide / by Donald Steel. — 4th revised ed. — Glasgow [etc.] : Collins [for] the 'Daily telegraph', 1977. — 176p : maps ; 27cm.
Previous ed.: i.e. Completely revised ed. 1974. — Index.
ISBN 0-00-412083-3 Pbk : £1.95
(B77-17690)

796.352'068'09411 — Golf courses. *Scotland. Directories*
Scotland, home of golf / Scottish Tourist Board. — [Edinburgh] : Scottish Tourist Board. 1977. — [1977]. — 48p : ill, 2 maps, port ; 30cm.
ISBN 0-85419-116-x Sd : £0.50
(B77-15426)

796.352'068'0941292 — Golf courses. *Scotland. Fife Region. St Andrews. Old Course, to 1976*
Taylor, Dawson. St Andrews, cradle of golf / [by] Dawson Taylor. — South Brunswick ; New York : Barnes ; London : Yoseloff, 1976. — 207p,[8]p of plates : ill(some col), facsims, plans, ports(some col) ; 29cm.
Bibl.: p.202-203. — Index.
ISBN 0-498-01442-8 : £6.25
(B77-33387)

796.352'09417 — Golf. *Ireland (Republic). Serials*
Golf. — Blackrock : Sports Enterprises Ltd ; Blackrock (40 Sydney Ave., Blackrock, Co. Dublin) : Distributed by Quality Publications Ltd.
77 / editor Pat Ruddy. — 1977. — 77p : ill(some col), ports(some col) ; 30cm.
Pbk : £0.90
(B77-09876)

796.352'3 — Golf. *Manuals*
Alliss, Peter. Easier golf / [by] Peter Alliss and Paul Trevillion. — London : Paul, 1977. — 142p : ill ; 22cm.
Originally published: 1969.
ISBN 0-09-095941-8 Pbk : £2.25
(B77-30545)

Grout, Jack. Let me teach you golf as I taught Jack Nicklaus / by Jack Grout with Dick Aultman ; illustrated by Jim McQueen. — London : Cassell, 1977. — ix,164p : ill ; 27cm.
Originally published: New York : Atheneum, 1975.
ISBN 0-304-29787-9 : £4.95
(B77-13206)

Miller, Johnny. Pure golf / by Johnny Miller ; with Dale Shankland ; foreword by John Geertsen ; illustrations by Jim McQueen. — London [etc.] : Hodder and Stoughton, 1977. — 192p,leaf of plate,[14]p of plates : ill(some col), port ; 26cm.
Originally published: Garden City, N.Y. : Doubleday, 1976.
ISBN 0-340-20979-8 : £4.95
(B77-22770)

Nicklaus, Jack. Total golf techniques / by Jack Nicklaus ; with Ken Bowden ; illustrated by Jim McQueen. — London : Heinemann, 1977. — 157p : col ill ; 29cm.
'Published originally as the Jack Nicklaus "Lesson Tee" series in Golf Digest Magazine, U.S.A.' - title page verso.
ISBN 0-434-51351-2 : £4.50
(B77-23637)

Redford, Ken. Success in golf / [by] Ken Redford and Nick Tremayne. — London : J. Murray, 1977. — 86p : ill, ports ; 23cm. — (Success sportsbooks)
ISBN 0-7195-2862-3 : £2.50
(B77-18322)

Townsend, Peter, *b.1946.* Golf : 100 ways to improve your game / [by] Peter Townsend ; script Iain Reid ; drawings by Richard Hughes. — [London] : Chancerel : Barrie and Jenkins, 1977. — 2-90p : ill, ports ; 21cm. — (Action books)
Ill. on lining papers.
ISBN 0-905703-00-6 : £1.75
(B77-22058)

796.352'64'05 — Professional golf. *Yearbooks*
McCormack, Mark Hume. The world of professional golf : Mark H. McCormack's golf annual. — London : Collins.
1977. — 1977. — [7],563p,[32]p of plates : ill, ports ; 24cm.
ISBN 0-00-216879-0 : £7.25
(B77-25816)

796.352'74'0941 — Professional golf. *Great Britain, to 1977*
Cousins, Geoffrey. Lords of the links : the story of professional golf / [by] Geoffrey Cousins. — London : Hutchinson, 1977. — 176,[12]p of plates : ill, ports ; 23cm.
Index.
ISBN 0-09-131560-3 : £4.95
(B77-31379)

796.352'74'09415 — Professional golf. Matches. *Ireland. Serials*
Golf circuit : a review of the past 12 months / [Professional Golfers' Association, Irish Section]. — [Dublin] ([3 Lower Abbey St., Dublin 1]) : [Tara Publishing Co. Ltd].
[1977] / compiled and edited by Seamus Smith. — [1977]. — [1],68p : ill, ports ; 24cm.
Sd : £0.75
(B77-22059)

796.355 — HOCKEY
796.35'5 — Women's hockey. *Manuals*
Read, Brenda. Better hockey for girls / by Brenda Read ; on behalf of the All England Women's Hockey Association Coaching Sub-Committee. — Revised ed. — London : Kaye and Ward [etc.], 1976. — 95p : ill, plans, ports ; 23cm.
Previous ed.: 1971.
ISBN 0-7182-1445-5 : £2.05
(B77-24407)

796.35'5'019 — Women's hockey. Psychological aspects
Weir, Marie. Hockey coaching : a psychological approach to the women's game / [by] Marie Weir. — London : Kaye and Ward, 1977. — 187p,[8]p of plates : ill ; 23cm.
ISBN 0-7182-1113-8 : £4.25
(B77-18323)

796.35'5'0202 — Women's hockey. *Rules*
Cook, P E G. Hockey rules simplified : a short guide for players and umpires / compiled by ... P.E.G. Cook and M.E. Bawden ; edited by Joyce Whitehead. — Lechlade (Kencot, Lechlade [Glos.]) : Marjorie Pollard Publications Ltd, [1977]. — Folder ([4]p) : plan ; 23cm.
ISBN 0-902596-13-6 : £0.20
(B77-13207)

796.35'5'062424 — Men's hockey. Organisations. *England. Midlands. Midland Counties Hockey Association. Yearbooks*
Midland Counties Hockey Association. Handbook / The Midland Counties Hockey Association. — [Solihull] ([The Secretary, 564 Warwick Rd, Solihull, W. Midlands B91 1AD]) : [The Association].
1976-77. — [1977]. — 140p : 1 ill ; 16cm.
ISBN 0-9505656-0-1 Sd : £0.50
(B77-13807)

796.358 — CRICKET
796.358'02'07 — Cricket. *Humorous texts*
Parkinson, Michael, *b.1935.* Bats in the pavilion : a follow-on from 'Cricket mad' / [by] Michael Parkinson ; drawings by Derek Adler. — London : Paul, 1977. — [6],114p : ill ; 21cm.
ISBN 0-09-131750-9 : £3.25
(B77-32802)

796.358'03 — Cricket. *Encyclopaedias*
Golesworthy, Maurice. Encyclopaedia of cricket / compiled by Maurice Golesworthy. — 6th ed. — London : Hale, 1977. — 222p,[16]p of plates : ill, ports ; 23cm.
Previous ed.: 1974. — Bibl.: p.12. — Index.
ISBN 0-7091-6020-8 : £4.95
ISBN 0-7091-6034-8 Pbk : £1.95
(B77-25140)

796.358'05 — Cricket. *Annuals*
Cricket. — London (Lord's Ground, N.W.8) : Test and County Cricket Board.
'76 / editor R.J. Roe. — [1976]. — 36p : ill(some col), ports(chiefly col) ; 30cm.
Sd : £0.40
(B77-20503)

'77 / editor R.J. Roe. — [1977]. — 36p : ill(chiefly col), ports(chiefly col) ; 30cm.
Sd : £0.50
(B77-20504)

Playfair cricket annual. — London : Queen Anne Press.
1975 : 28th ed. / edited by Gordon Ross ; statistics by Michael Fordham and Barry McCaully. — [1975]. — 224p : ill ; 14cm.
ISBN 0-362-00226-6 Pbk : £0.50
ISSN 0079-2314
(B77-18943)

1976 : 29th ed. / edited by Gordon Ross ; statistics by Michael Fordham and Geoffrey Saulez. — [1976]. — 224p : ill ; 14cm.
ISBN 0-362-00270-3 Pbk : £0.50
ISSN 0079-2314
(B77-18944)

796.358'05 — Cricket. *Yearbooks*
Playfair cricket annual. — London : Queen Anne Press.
1977 : 30th ed. / edited by Gordon Ross ; statistics by Michael Fordham and Geoffrey Saulez. — [1977]. — 224p : ill ; 14cm.
ISBN 0-354-09015-1 Pbk : £0.60
ISSN 0079-2314
(B77-17033)

World of cricket. — London : Queen Anne Press.

1977 / edited by Trevor Bailey ; compiled by Bill Frindall. — 1977. — 222p : ill, ports ; 22cm.
ISBN 0-354-09007-0 Pbk : £3.95
ISSN 0309-8206
(B77-21361)

796.358'08 — Cricket. *Anthologies*
The **cricket** addict's archive / edited by Benny Green. — London : Elm Tree Books, 1977. — xiii,241p : ill ; 23cm.
ISBN 0-241-89610-x : £5.50
(B77-21362)

796.358'08 — Cricket. *Essays*
Cardus, *Sir* **Neville.** Cardus on cricket : a selection from the cricket writings of Sir Neville Cardus / chosen and introduced by Sir Rupert Hart-Davis. — [New ed.]. — London : Souvenir Press, 1977. — 256p : ill ; 23cm.
Previous ed.: published as 'The essential Neville Cardus' London : Cape, 1949.
ISBN 0-285-62284-6 : £5.50 : CIP rev.
(B77-17691)

796.358'09 — Cricket, to 1976
Arlott, John. Arlott and Trueman on cricket / edited by Gilbert Phelps. — London : British Broadcasting Corporation, 1977. — 280p : ill(some col), facsims, ports(some col) ; 24cm.
'... accompanies the BBC Further Education Television programmes, "Arlott and Trueman on Cricket", first shown on BBC2 ... starting on 11 April 1977 ... Published to accompany a series of programmes prepared in consultation with the BBC Further Education Advisory Council' - title page verso. — Includes an anthology of cricket literature.
ISBN 0-563-16115-9 : £4.75
(B77-20505)

796.358'092'4 — Cricket. *Gloucestershire, 1946-1976. Personal observations*
Craven, Nico. Suddenly it was summer / [by] Nico Craven ; foreword by Frank Keating. — [Seascale] ([The Coach House, Ponsonby, Seascale, Cumbria CA20 1BX]) : [The author], [1977]. — 97p,plate : 1 col ill ; 21cm.
£2.50
(B77-25141)

796.358'092'4 — Cricket. Chappell, Ian. *Autobiographies*
Chappell, Ian. Cricket in our blood : an autobiography / [by] Ian Chappell. — London : Paul, 1976 [i.e. 1977]. — 206p,[32]p of plates : ill, ports ; 22cm.
Originally published: as 'Chappelli : Ian Chappell's life story'. Richmond, Vic. : Hutchinson of Australia, 1976.
ISBN 0-09-128650-6 : £3.95
(B77-21363)

796.358'092'4 — Cricket. Cowdrey, Colin. *Autobiographies*
Cowdrey, Colin. M.C.C. : the autobiography of a cricketer / [by] Colin Cowdrey. — Sevenoaks : Coronet, 1977. — 253p,[12]p of plates : facsim, ports ; 18cm.
Originally published: London : Hodder and Stoughton, 1976. — Index.
ISBN 0-340-21570-4 Pbk : £0.85
(B77-19582)

796.358'092'4 — Cricket. Denness, Mike. *Autobiographies*
Denness, Mike. I declare / [by] Mike Denness. — London : A. Barker, 1977. — 162p,[12]p of plates : ill, ports ; 23cm.
ISBN 0-213-16657-7 : £4.50
(B77-22060)

796.358'092'4 — Cricket. Dodds, Thomas Carter. *Autobiographies*
Dodds, Thomas Carter. Hit hard and enjoy it / by T.C. 'Dickie' Dodds ; with a preface by Sir Neville Cardus. — Tunbridge Wells (Beech Hanger, Ashurst, Tunbridge Wells, Kent) : The Cricketer Ltd, 1976. — 120p,[8]p of plates : ill, chiefly ports ; 22cm.
ISBN 0-902211-04-8 : £4.00
ISBN 0-902211-05-6 Pbk : £1.95
(B77-07540)

796.358'092'4 — Cricket. Peebles, Ian. *Autobiographies*
Peebles, Ian. Spinner's yarn / [by] Ian Peebles ; foreword by Lord Cobham. — London : Collins, 1977. — 222p,[8]p of plates : ill, ports ; 22cm.
Index.
ISBN 0-00-216516-3 : £4.95
(B77-21364)

796.358'092'4 — Cricket. Sobers, Sir Gary. *Biographies*
Bailey, Trevor, *b.1923.* Sir Gary : a biography / [by] Trevor Bailey ; with a foreword by Richie Benaud. — [London] : Fontana, 1977. — 190p, [4]p of plates : ill, ports ; 18cm.
Originally published: London : Collins, 1976. — Index.
ISBN 0-00-634850-5 Pbk : £0.95
(B77-32102)

796.358'092'4 — Cricket. Steele, David. *Autobiographies*
Steele, David. Come in number 3 / [by] David Steele ; with John Morris. — London : Pelham, 1977. — 192p,[16]p of plates : ill, ports ; 23cm.
ISBN 0-7207-0966-0 : £4.50
(B77-20506)

796.358'092'4 — Cricket. Trueman, Fred. *Autobiographies*
Trueman, Fred. Ball of fire : an autobiography / [by] Fred Trueman. — St Albans : Mayflower, 1977. — 173p,[8]p of plates : ill, ports ; 18cm.
Originally published: London : Dent, 1976. — Index.
ISBN 0-583-12755-x Pbk : £0.60
(B77-20507)

796.358'2 — Cricket. *Manuals*
Bradman, *Sir* Donald. Cricket / [by] Sir Donald Bradman. — Revised and updated [ed.] / photographs by Patrick Eagar ; drawings by Reg Cartwright. — Leicester : Knight Books, 1977. — 96p : ill(some col), facsim, plan, ports(some col) ; 21cm. — (Illustrated teach yourself)
Previous ed.: published as 'How to play cricket'. London : Hodder and Stoughton, 1953. — Index.
ISBN 0-340-21498-8 Pbk : £1.80
(B77-05002)

796.358'2 — Cricket. *Manuals. Juvenile literature*
Boycott, Geoff. Geoff Boycott's book for young cricketers. — London : Paul, 1976. — 64p : chiefly ill, ports ; 25cm.
ISBN 0-09-126930-x : £2.95
ISBN 0-09-126931-8 Pbk : £1.75
(B77-01740)

796.358'2'024372 — Cricket. *Manuals. For teaching*
Tyson, Frank. Complete cricket coaching illustrated / [by] Frank Tyson. — London : Pelham, 1977. — viii,152p : ill ; 25cm.
Originally published: West Melbourne : Nelson, 1976. — Index.
ISBN 0-7207-1002-2 : £4.00
ISBN 0-7207-1012-x Pbk : £2.50
(B77-21365)

796.358'22'0922 — Cricket. Fast bowlers, ca 1820-1974
Frith, David, *b.1937.* The fast men : a 200-year cavalcade of speed bowlers / [by] David Frith ; preface by John Arlott. — Revised and up-dated ed. — London : Corgi, 1977. — 221p, [16]p of plates : ill, facsim, ports ; 18cm.
Previous ed.: Wokingham : Van Nostrand Reinhold, 1975. — Bibl.: p.209-210. — Index.
ISBN 0-552-10435-3 Pbk : £0.75
(B77-20508)

796.358'24 — Cricket. Wicket-keeping. *Manuals*
Knott, Alan. Alan Knott on wicket-keeping. — London : Paul, 1977. — 64p : ill, ports ; 25cm.
ISBN 0-09-129470-3 : £3.25
ISBN 0-09-129471-1 Pbk : £1.95
(B77-20509)

796.358'62'0924 — Club cricket. *England, ca 1960-1976. Personal observations*
Redbourn, Dick. The domestic cricketer : memoirs / by Dick Redbourn. — Tunbridge Wells : Midas Books, 1977. — 128p : ill, ports ; 21cm.
ISBN 0-85936-093-8 Pbk : £1.65
(B77-22061)

796.358'62'0942842 — Cricket. Clubs. *North Yorkshire. Harrogate. Harrogate Cricket Club, to 1976*
Greaves, George L. Over the summers again : a history of Harrogate Cricket Club / by George L. Greaves. — Harrogate (County Ground, St George's Rd, Harrogate [N. Yorkshire]) : Harrogate Cricket Club, 1976. — 171p,[16]p of plates : ill, ports ; 25cm.
Bibl.: p.168.
ISBN 0-9505493-0-4 : £4.50
(B77-05003)

796.358'63'094297 — Cricket. Clubs. *Glamorgan. Glamorgan County Cricket Club, to 1976. Records of achievement*
Thomas, Wayne. Glamorgan CCC book of cricket records (1921-1976) / by Wayne Thomas. — Woking (Knaphill, Woking, Surrey) : Davies and Sons (Publishers) Ltd, [1977]. — [4],87p : ill, ports ; 22cm.
'... published to commemorate the Club's fiftieth first-class season in 1976'.
ISBN 0-9505750-0-3 Sd : £1.00
(B77-16547)

796.358'65 — Cricket. Test matches, to 1977
Greig, Tony. Test match cricket : a personal view / [by] Tony Greig. — London [etc.] : Hamlyn, 1977. — 176p : ill(some col), ports(some col) ; 27cm.
Index.
ISBN 0-600-31971-7 : £3.95
(B77-24408)

796.358'65 — Cricket. Tours by Marylebone Cricket Club team. *India, 1976-1977. Personal observations*
Martin-Jenkins, Christopher. MCC in India, 1976-77 / [by] Christopher Martin-Jenkins. — London : Macdonald and Jane's, 1977. — 190p, [16]p of plates : ports ; 23cm.
ISBN 0-354-04151-7 : £4.95
(B77-31380)

796.358'65 — Cricket. Tours by Marylebone Cricket Club team. Test matches. *Australia, 1946-1975. Personal observations*
Swanton, Ernest William. Swanton in Australia with MCC, 1946-75 / with foreword by Sir Robert Menzies ; and introduction by Sir Donald Bradman. — [London] : Fontana, 1977. — 224p,[8]p of plates : ill, ports ; 18cm.
Originally published: London : Collins, 1975. — Index.
Pbk : £0.95
(B77-32803)

796.358'65 — Cricket. Tours by West Indian cricket team. Test matches. *England. Scores, 1976. Statistics*
Frindall, Bill. Frindall's score book, England versus West Indies, 1976 / [photographs by Patrick Eagar]. — [Birmingham] ([CJ House, Wrentham St., Birmingham B5 6QT]) : [Lonsdale Press], [1976]. — 111p : of facsims, ill, ports ; 22x30cm.
ISBN 0-905051-02-5 : £4.35
(B77-27302)

796.4 — ATHLETICS
796.4'01'531 — Athletics. Mechanics
Dyson, Geoffrey Harry George. The mechanics of athletics / [by] Geoffrey H.G. Dyson. — 7th ed. — London [etc.] : Hodder and Stoughton, 1977. — 267p : ill ; 23cm.
Previous ed.: London : University of London Press, 1973. — Bibl.: p.257-259. — Index.
ISBN 0-340-20034-0 : £6.50
(B77-27303)

796.4'03 — Athletics. *Encyclopaedias*
Watman, Melvyn. Encyclopaedia of athletics / compiled by Mel Watman ; foreword by Harold Abrahams. — 4th ed. — London : Hale, 1977. — 240p,[16]p of plates : ports ; 23cm.
Previous ed.: 1973.
ISBN 0-7091-5443-7 : £4.95
(B77-25817)

796.4'06'241 — Athletics. Organisations. *Great Britain. Amateur Athletic Association. Yearbooks*
Amateur Athletic Association. Handbook / Amateur Athletic Association. — London : [A.A.A.].
1977-78. — [1977]. — 156p : ill, plans ; 18cm.
Pbk : £1.00
(B77-32804)

796.4'07'1042 — Schools. Activities: Athletics. *England. Yearbooks*
English Schools Athletic Association. Handbook of the Association / the English Schools Athletic Association. — Houghton-le-Spring ([c/o Hon. Secretary, 'Dunelm', Houghton Rd, Newbottle, Houghton-le-Spring, Tyne and Wear DH4 4EF]) : [The Association].
1976. — [1976]. — [2],52p ; 19cm.
ISBN 0-9504669-1-3 Sd : £0.20
(B77-00356)

796.4'07'1073 — Educational institutions. Activities: Athletics. Fund raising. *United States*
Bronzan, Robert T. Public relations, promotions, and fund-raising for athletic and physical education programs / [by] Robert T. Bronzan. — New York ; London [etc.] : Wiley, 1977. — xiv,268p : ill, facsims, ports ; 24cm.
Bibl.: p.259-262. — Index.
ISBN 0-471-01540-7 : £10.00
Primary classification 659.2'9'7694071073
(B77-11946)

796.4'0938 — Ancient Greek athletics. *Secondary school texts*
Buchanan, David. Greek athletics / [by] David Buchanan. — London : Longman, 1976. — [1], 48,[1]p : ill, maps ; 16x22cm. — (Aspects of Greek life)
Bibl.
ISBN 0-582-20059-8 Sd : £0.65
(B77-09197)

796.4'0941 — Athletics. *Great Britain. Records of achievement. Yearbooks*
UK athletics annual / compiled by the National Union of Track Statisticians. — Hungerford (12 Bridge St., Hungerford, Berks.) : Goss Grant Ltd for NUTS.
1977. — 1977. — 6 leaves,7-188p : port ; 21cm.
Index.
ISBN 0-904612-04-x Pbk : £1.50
(B77-25818)

796.4'09415 — Women's athletics. *Ireland, to 1976*
Pozzoli, Peter R. Irish women's athletics / [by] Peter R. Pozzoli. — London (155 Ordnance Rd, Enfield [Middx]) : Women's Track and Field World, 1977. — 302p : ill, col coats of arms, facsims, ports ; 29cm.
Pbk : £5.00
(B77-32805)

796.4'1 — Gymnastics. *Manuals*
Kaneko, Akitomo. Olympic gymnastics / by Akitomo Kaneko ; [translated from the Japanese by Tomoko and Jeffrey Cousminer]. — New York : Sterling [etc.] ; London : Distributed by Ward Lock, 1976. — 256p : ill, ports ; 26cm.
Originally published: in Japanese. Tokyo : Kodansha, 1971. — Index.
ISBN 0-7061-2202-x : £8.95
(B77-13208)

Prestidge, Pauline. Better gymnastics / [by] Pauline Prestidge ; photographs by Jim Prestidge. — London : Kaye and Ward [etc.], 1977. — 91p : ill, ports ; 22cm.
ISBN 0-7182-1450-1 : £2.50
(B77-24409)

796.4'1 — Gymnastics. *Manuals. For girls*
Ryan, Frank. Gymnastics for girls / [by] Frank Ryan. — Harmondsworth [etc.] : Penguin, 1977. — xiii,433p : ill ; 28cm. — (Penguin handbooks)
Originally published: New York : Viking Press, 1976.
ISBN 0-14-046271-6 Pbk : £3.50
(B77-33388)

796.4'1 — Gymnastics. *Manuals. For women*
Coulton, Jill. Women's gymnastics / [by] Jill Coulton. — Wakefield : EP Publishing, 1977. — 116p : ill ; 21cm. — (EP sport series)
ISBN 0-7158-0592-4 : £3.50
(B77-23638)

Temple, Cliff. Gymnastics for girls / [by] Cliff Temple and Peter Tatlow. — London : Pelham, 1977. — 64p : ill, ports ; 26cm. — (Pelham pictorial sports instruction series)
ISBN 0-7207-1013-8 : £3.50
(B77-28023)

796.4'1 — Schools. Curriculum subjects: Gymnastics. Exercises. Teaching
Mauldon, Elizabeth. Teaching gymnastics / [by] E. Mauldon, J. Layson. — London : Macdonald and Evans, 1975. — xiv,192p,[14]p of plates : ill ; 22cm.
Originally published: 1965. — Index.
ISBN 0-7121-2001-7 Pbk : £2.75
(B77-16548)

796.4'1 — Schools. Students: Girls. Curriculum subjects: Gymnastics. Teaching
Fidler, Janet. Olympic gymnastics for girls / [by] Janet Fidler, Brian Steele. — Altrincham : Sherratt, 1976. — 128p : ill ; 21cm.
ISBN 0-85427-050-7 Pbk : £2.50
(B77-17034)

796.4'1 — Weight training. *Manuals*
Lear, John. Weight training / by John Lear. — Wakefield : EP Publishing, 1977. — 45p : ill ; 14x21cm. — (Know the game)
'Published in collaboration with the British Amateur Weight Lifters' Association'. — Bibl.: p.45.
ISBN 0-7158-0494-4 Sd : £0.45
(B77-16008)

796.4'2 — Athletics. Track & field events. *Manuals*
Johnson, Carl Thomas. Success in athletics / [by] Carl Johnson. — London : J. Murray, 1977. — 96p : ill, ports ; 23cm. — (Success sportsbooks)
ISBN 0-7195-3375-9 : £2.50
(B77-18324)

796.4'2 — Orienteering
Martin, Toy. Map & compass fundamentals orienteering / [by] Toy Martin, Dave Lotty. — Sydney [etc.] ; London : A.H. and A.W. Reed, 1976. — 79p : ill, forms, maps ; 25cm.
With answers. — Index.
ISBN 0-589-07192-0 Pbk : £3.90
(B77-17692)

Rand, Jim. This is orienteering / [by] Jim Rand and Tony Walker. — London : Pelham [for] the British Orienteering Federation, 1976. — 144p : ill, maps ; 26cm.
Bibl.: p.133. — List of films: p.133-134. — Index.
ISBN 0-7207-0928-8 : £5.50
(B77-00357)

796.4'2'05 — Athletics. Track & field events. *Yearbooks*
Athletics. — London : Queen Anne Press.
1977 / editor Ron Pickering ; compiler Mel Watman. — 1977. — 223p : ill, ports ; 22cm.
ISBN 0-354-09009-7 Pbk : £3.95
ISSN 0305-6171
(B77-25819)

796.4'2'071042 — Schools. Curriculum subjects: Athletics. Track & field events. Teaching. *England. Manuals*
Watts, Denis Claude Vernon. Athletics for schools / [by] Denis Watts and Bill Marlow. — London : Pelham, 1976. — 96p,[16]p of plates : ill ; 23cm.
ISBN 0-7207-0742-0 : £3.95
(B77-01741)

796.4'26 — Athletics. Marathon running, to 1976
Campbell, Gail. Marathon : the world of the long-distance athlete / [by] Gail Campbell. — New York : Sterling [etc.] ; London : Distributed by Ward Lock, 1977. — 176p : ill, maps, ports ; 27cm.
Index.
ISBN 0-7061-2551-7 : £4.95
Primary classification 797.2'1
(B77-31384)

796.4'26 — Athletics. Track events. *Manuals*
Whitehead, Nick. Track athletics / [by] Nick Whitehead. — Wakefield : EP Publishing, 1976. — 108p : ill, 2 ports ; 21cm. — (EP sport series)
Bibl.: p.108.
ISBN 0-7158-0586-x : £3.50
(B77-27304)

796.4'3 — Athletics. Field events. Judging. *Manuals*
Sinfield, Cyril. How to judge field events / [by] Cyril Sinfield. — [New ed.]. — London : Amateur Athletic Association, 1976. — 45p : ill, port ; 21cm. — (Amateur Athletic Association. Instructional booklets)
Previous ed.: published as 'The technique of judging track events' / by Victor Charles Sealy. 1968.
ISBN 0-85134-053-9 Sd : £1.00
(B77-08505)

796.4'3 — Athletics. Triple jump. *Manuals*
McNab, Tom. Triple jump / by Tom McNab. — [New ed.]. — London (70 Brompton Rd, SW3 1EE) : British Amateur Athletic Board, [1977]. — 56p : ill, ports ; 21cm. — (British Amateur Athletic Board. Instructional books)
Previous ed.: London : Amateur Athletic Association, 1968.
Sd : £1.25
(B77-32103)

796.4'7 — Acrobatics. *Manuals*
Gedney, Judith M. Tumbling and balancing : basic skills and variations / [by] Judith M. Gedney. — Englewood Cliffs ; London [etc.] : Prentice-Hall, 1977. — xvii,172p : ill ; 25cm.
Index.
ISBN 0-13-932798-3 : £8.75
(B77-25142)

796.4'7 — Trampolining. *Manuals*
Horne, Dennis Edward. Trampolining : a complete handbook / [by] Dennis E. Horne. — New ed. — London [etc.] : Faber, 1978. — 3-176p,[16]p of plates : ill, ports ; 23cm.
Previous ed.: 1968. — Index.
ISBN 0-571-04868-4 : £4.95 : CIP rev.
ISBN 0-571-04945-1 Pbk : £2.75
(B77-19583)

796.4'8'09 — Olympic Games, to 1972. *Records of achievement*
Benagh, Jim. Incredible Olympic feats / [by] Jim Benagh. — New York ; London [etc.] : McGraw-Hill, 1976. — xii,178p : ill ; 21cm.
ISBN 0-07-004426-0 Pbk : £3.30
(B77-07541)

796.4'8'09047 — Olympic Games. Sporting events, 1976. *Records of achievement*
Olympic report '76 / editor James Coote. — London : Kemp, 1976. — x,222p,[20]p of plates : ill, ports ; 23cm.
ISBN 0-905255-03-8 : £3.50
(B77-16009)

796.5 — OUTDOOR LIFE

796.5'1'0941 — Recreations: Walking. *Great Britain. Manuals*
Greenbank, Anthony. Walking, hiking and backpacking / [by] Anthony Greenbank. — London : Constable, 1977. — 256p : ill, form, maps ; 18cm.
Bibl.: p.234-241. — Index.
ISBN 0-09-460280-8 : £3.50
(B77-18325)

796.5'1'09411 — Recreations: Walking. *Scotland. Guidebooks*
Moir, Donald Grant. Scottish hill tracks : old highways and drove roads / [by] D.G. Moir. — Revised ed. — Edinburgh : Bartholomew.
In 2 vols.
1 : Southern Scotland. — 1975. — 80p : maps ; 19cm.
Previous ed.: 1947. — Index.
ISBN 0-85152-721-3 Sd : £0.50
(B77-02527)

796.5'1'0941434 — Recreations: Walking. *Scotland. Strathclyde Region. Milngavie. Guidebooks*
Walk this way : favourite walks round Milngavie ... / [edited by Edward Davidson ; assisted by Stella Lardner]. — Milngavie (163 Mugdock Rd, Milngavie, Dunbartonshire) : Heatherbank Press, 1976. — [41]p : ill, 2 facsims ; 18cm.
ISBN 0-905192-03-6 Sd : £0.40
(B77-09877)

796.5'1'09421 — Recreations: Walking. *London. Thames River region. Guidebooks*
Chesterton, Gervaise J. Riverside walks for Londoners / by Gervaise J. Chesterton and Martin Worth. — Deal (6 Liverpool Rd, Deal, Kent) : The Towers Press, 1976. — 48p : ill, maps ; 22cm.
ISBN 0-905588-00-2 Pbk : £0.95
(B77-08506)

796.5'1'09422 — Long-distance footpaths. *Southern England. Ridgeway. Recreations: Walking. Guidebooks*
Cull, Elizabeth. Walks along the Ridgeway / [by] Elizabeth Cull. — 2nd (revised) ed. — Bourne End, Bucks. : Spurbooks, 1977. — 56p,[8]p of plates : ill, maps ; 19cm. — (A Spurbook footpath guide)
Previous ed.: 1975. — Bibl.: p.56.
ISBN 0-904978-86-9 Pbk : £0.75
(B77-24410)

Westacott, Hugh Douglas. A practical guide to walking the Ridgeway Path / [by] H.D. Westacott. — 3rd ed. — Buckingham (Adstock Cottage, Adstock, Buckingham MK18 2HZ) : Footpath Publications, 1977. — [2],24p : ill, maps ; 21cm.
Previous ed.: 1976.
ISBN 0-9503696-9-1 Sd : £0.60
(B77-18326)

796.5'1'094221 — Recreations: Walking. *Surrey. Guidebooks*
Bagley, William Alfred. London countryside walks for motorists, south western area / by Wm A. Bagley ; illustrated with sketch maps and photographs by the author. — Harrow : Gerrard, 1976. — 104p,[8]p of plates : ill, maps ; 21cm. — (Walks for motorists series)
ISBN 0-900397-38-1 Pbk : £1.00
(B77-23639)

796.5'1'094223 — Recreations: Walking. *North Kent. Guidebooks*
Bagley, William Alfred. London countryside walks for motorists, South Eastern area / by Wm A. Bagley ; illustrated with sketch maps and photographs by the author. — Harrow : Gerrard, 1976. — 103p,[6]p of plates : ill, maps ; 21cm. — (Walks for motorists series)
Pbk : £1.00
(B77-25143)

796.5'1'09423 — Recreations: Walking. *South-west England. Guidebooks*
Severnside : a guide to family walks / edited by Stephen Taylor. — London : Croom Helm, 1977. — 154p : ill, maps ; 23cm.
ISBN 0-85664-385-8 : £5.50 : CIP rev.
ISBN 0-85664-390-4 Pbk : £2.95
(B77-09878)

796.5'1'094233 — Long-distance footpaths. *Dorset. Coastal regions. Dorset Coast Path. Recreations: Walking. Guidebooks*
Westacott, Hugh Douglas. A practical guide to walking the Dorset Coast Path, Lyme Regis to Bournemouth / [by] H.D. Westacott. — Buckingham (Adstock Cottage, Adstock, Buckingham MK18 2HZ) : Footpath Publications, 1977. — [2],24p : ill, maps ; 21cm.
ISBN 0-9503696-6-7 Sd : £0.60
(B77-20510)

796.5'1'094235 — Long-distance footpaths. *Devon. Coastal regions. Devon South Coast Path. Recreations: Walking. Guidebooks*
Westacott, Hugh Douglas. A practical guide to walking the Devon South Coast Path, Plymouth to Lyme Regis / [by] H.D. Westacott. — [2nd ed.]. — [Buckingham] ([Adstock Cottage, Adstock, Buckingham MK18 2HZ]) : [Footpath Publications], [1977]. — [3],29p : ill, maps ; 21cm.
Previous ed.: 1976.
ISBN 0-905904-00-1 Sd : £0.60
(B77-20511)

796.5'1'09424 — Long-distance footpaths. *Welsh Marches. Offa's Dyke Path. Recreations: Walking. Guidebooks*
Kay, Ernest, *b.1931.* Walks along Offa's Dyke / compiled by Ernest & Katherine Kay ; on behalf of the Offa's Dyke Association. — Bourne End, Bucks. : Spurbooks, 1977. — 64p : maps ; 19cm. — (A Spurbooks footpath guide)
Bibl.: p.62.
ISBN 0-904978-24-9 Pbk : £0.75
(B77-25820)

796.5'1'0942416 — Recreations: Walking. *Gloucestershire. Cheltenham region. Guidebooks*
Kershaw, Ronald. Hill walks around Cheltenham / [by] R. Kershaw. — Gloucester (Shire Hall, Gloucester) : Gloucestershire County Council, 1976. — 83p : ill, maps ; 21cm.
Originally published: in serial form in the 'Gloucestershire echo' 'Pathways for pleasure' series. 1974. — Bibl.: p.83.
ISBN 0-904950-02-6 Sd : £0.70
(B77-09198)

796.5'1'0942417 — Recreations: Walking. *England. Cotswolds. Guidebooks*
Price, Peter Antony. Cotswolds walks for motorists, southern area : 30 circular walks / [by] Peter A. Price ; 30 sketch maps by the author ; 8 photographs [by W.R. Bawden]. — Harrow : Gerrard, 1976. — 104p,[4]p of plates : ill, maps ; 21cm. — (Walks for motorists [series])
ISBN 0-900397-40-3 Pbk : £0.90
(B77-03722)

796.5'1'094257 — Recreations: Walking. *Oxfordshire. Guidebooks*
Hammond, Nigel. Walks in Oxfordshire / [by] Nigel Hammond. — Bourne End : Spurbooks, 1977. — 64p : maps ; 19cm. — (A Spurbooks footpath guide)
ISBN 0-904978-25-7 Pbk : £0.75
(B77-23640)

796.5'1'0942586 — Recreations: Walking. *Hertfordshire. Welwyn Region. Guidebooks*
Mid-Herts. Footpaths Society. More footpath walks in mid Herts. for motorists / [Mid-Herts. Footpaths Society]. — [Welwyn Garden City] ([c/o The Secretary, 1 Templewood, Welwyn Garden City, Herts. AL8 7HT]) : [The Society], [1976]. — 32p : ill, maps ; 21cm.
Sd : £0.50
(B77-33389)

796.5'1'0942846 — Recreations: Walking. *North Yorkshire. North York Moors. White Rose Walk. Guidebooks*
White, Geoffrey. The White Rose Walk / by Geoffrey White. — 2nd ed. — Clapham, N. Yorkshire : Dalesman, 1976. — [1],32p : ill, maps ; 19cm. — (A Dalesman mini-book)
Previous ed.: 1973.
ISBN 0-85206-324-5 Sd : £0.30
(B77-00358)

796.5'1'094288 — Recreations: Walking. *Great Britain. Cheviot Hills. Guidebooks*
Ramblers' Association. *Northern Area.* Ramblers' Cheviot : twelve walks in the Cheviot Hills / Ramblers' Association, Northern Area. — Revised [ed.]. — Newcastle-upon-Tyne : H. Hill, 1976. — 84p : ill, maps ; 22cm.
Previous ed.: 1969.
ISBN 0-900463-07-4 Sd : £1.00
(B77-12031)

796.5'1'094288 — Recreations: Walking. *Northumberland. Guidebooks*
Ramblers' Association. *Northern Area.* Ramblers' 'Through Northumberland'... / Ramblers' Association, Northern Area ; [illustrated by Betty Fletcher]. — Newcastle upon Tyne : F. Graham, 1977. — 78p : ill, maps ; 22cm.
ISBN 0-85983-094-2 Sd : £0.80
(B77-34000)

796.5'1'0942956 — Recreations: Walking. *Powys. Brecon Beacons. Guidebooks*
Brecon Beacons National Park Committee. Walking in the Beacons / [Brecon Beacons National Park Committee]. — [Brecon] ([Glamorgan St., Brecon, Powys]) : The Committee, 1977. — Folder([8]p) : map ; 21cm. — (Information sheet ; no.25)
£0.03
(B77-18327)

796.5'1'0942956 — Recreations: Walking. *Powys. Brecon. Guidebooks*
Brecon Beacons National Park Committee. Some short walks around Brecon / [Brecon Beacons National Park Committee]. — [Brecon] ([Glamorgan St., Brecon, Powys]) : The Committee, 1977. — Folder([6]p) ; 21cm. — (Information sheet ; no.24)
£0.03
(B77-18328)

796.5'22 — Hill walking. *Galway (County). Connemara. Twelve Bens. Guidebooks*
Twelve Bens : hill walkers and rock climbers guide / edited by Joss Lynam ; illustrated by Sean Rothery. — Dublin : Federation of Mountaineering Clubs of Ireland ; Leicester (249 Knighton Church Rd, Leicester) : [Distributed by] Cordee Publishing, 1971. — [2],29p : 1 ill, map ; 16cm. — (Federation of Mountaineering Clubs of Ireland. Guides)
' ... revised and updated from: 'Selected climbs on Ben Corr". 1967 ; and "The twelve Bens". 1953' - title page verso. — Bibl.: p.29.
ISBN 0-902940-03-1 Sd : £0.60
Primary classification 796.5'22
(B77-14351)

796.5'22 — Hill walking. *Great Britain. Manuals*
Lumley, Peter. The Spur book of hill trekking / by Peter Lumley. — Bourne End, Bucks. : Spurbooks, 1977. — 64p : ill, maps ; 19cm. — (A Spurbook venture guide)
ISBN 0-904978-67-2 Pbk : £0.90
(B77-17035)

796.5'22 — Hill walking. *Scotland. Highlands. Manuals*
Gilbert, Richard Frank. Hillwalking in Scotland / by Richard F. Gilbert. — Gloucester : Thornhill Press, 1976. — 31p : ill, map ; 20cm. — (A Thornhill guide ; 5)
ISBN 0-904110-40-0 Sd : £0.40
(B77-12032)

796.5'22 — Hill walking. *Scotland. Highlands. Mountains: Munros. Personal observations*
Gilbert, Richard Frank. Memorable Munros : an account of the ascent of the 3,000 ft peaks in Scotland / by Richard Gilbert. — [York?] : [The author] ; Leicester (249 Knighton Church Rd, Leicester) : Distributed by Cordee, 1976. — [2],100p : ill ; 23cm.
Index.
ISBN 0-904405-01-x Pbk : £1.95
(B77-32104)

796.5'22 — Hill walking & rock climbing. *Great Britain. Manuals. Juvenile literature*
Unsworth, Walter. Walking and climbing / [by] Walt Unsworth. — London [etc.] : Routledge and Kegan Paul, 1977. — vii,71p : ill ; 24cm. — (The local search series)
Bibl.: p.68-70.
ISBN 0-7100-8596-6 : £2.95 : CIP rev.
(B77-13808)

796.5'22 — Mountaineering
Mountaineers. *Climbing Committee.* Mountaineering : the freedom of the hills / The Climbing Committee of the Mountaineers. — 3rd ed. / editor Peggy Ferber ; Textbook Revision Committee Sam Fry ... [et al.] ; illustrations Robert Cram and Ramona Hammerly. — Seattle : The Mountaineers ; Leicester (249 Knighton Church Rd, Leicester) : [Distributed by] Cordee Publishing, 1975. — xv,478p : ill, charts, maps ; 24cm.
This ed. originally published: Seattle : The Mountaineers, 1974. — Bibl. — Index.
ISBN 0-916890-01-5 : £6.95
(B77-25144)

796.5'22 — Mountaineering. *Essays. Welsh texts*
Rees, Ioan Bowen. Mynyddoedd : ysgrifau a cherddi / gan Ioan Bowen Rees ; ynghyd â darluniau gan John Wright. — Llandysul : Gwasg Gomer, 1975. — [9],102p : ill, maps ; 21cm.
Bibl.: p.101-102.
ISBN 0-85088-338-5 Pbk : £1.50
(B77-02528)

796.5'22 — Mountaineering. *Europe. Alps. Mont Blanc range. Manuals*
Collomb, Robin Gabriel. Mont Blanc range. — [New ed.] / compiled and edited by Robin G. Collomb, W.H. O'Connor. — London : Alpine Club ; Reading : [Distributed] by West Col Productions. — (Alpine Club guide books)
In 3 vols. — Previous ed.: published in 2 vols. as 'Selected climbs in the Mont Blanc range' / by Robin G. Collomb & Peter Crew. 1967.
Vol.1 : Trélatête, Mont Blanc, Maudit, Tacul, Brenva. — 1976. — 221p : ill ; 17cm.
Bibl.: p.9-11. — Index.
ISBN 0-900523-20-4 : £4.50
(B77-06829)

796.5'22 — Mountaineering. *Ireland. Manuals*
Wall, C W. Mountaineering in Ireland / by C.W. Wall ; with an introduction by R. Lloyd Praeger. — [Revised ed.] / revised by Joss Lynam ; and including a list of the mountains of Ireland attaining an altitude of 2000ft or over. — Dublin : Federation of Mountaineering Clubs of Ireland ; Leicester (249 Knighton Church Rd, Leicester) : [Distributed by] Cordee Publishing, 1976. — 111p : map ; 16cm. — (Federation of Mountaineering Clubs of Ireland. Guides)
Previous ed.: i.e. 2nd ed. Dublin : Irish Tourist Association, 1944. — Bibl.: p.83-84.
ISBN 0-902940-01-5 Sd : £1.00
(B77-14347)

796.5'22 — Mountaineering. *Manuals*
Banks, Mike. Mountaineering for beginners / [by] Mike Banks ; with drawings by Toby Buchan. — London : Seeley Service, 1977. — 92p : ill ; 23cm.
ISBN 0-85422-125-5 : £3.50
(B77-10508)

Roscoe, Donald Thomas. Mountaineering : a manual for teachers & instructors / [by] D.T. Roscoe. — London : Faber, 1976. — iii-xi, 181p,[8]p of plates : ill ; 23cm.
Bibl.: p.177-178. — Index.
ISBN 0-571-09456-2 : £5.95
(B77-00359)

796.5'22 — Mountaineering. *North America, to 1975*
Jones, Chris, *b.1939.* Climbing in North America / [by] Chris Jones. — Berkeley [etc.] ; London : University of California Press for the American Alpine Club, 1976. — xi,392p : ill, facsims, ports ; 23cm.
Bibl. — Index.
ISBN 0-520-02976-3 : £10.50
(B77-14348)

796.5'22 — Mountaineering. *Switzerland. Alps. Eiger. North Face, 1935-1973*
Harrer, Heinrich. The White Spider : the story of the north face of the Eiger / [by] Heinrich Harrer ; with additional chapters by Heinrich Harrer and Kurt Maix ; translated from the German by Hugh Merrick. — 2nd revised ed. — London : Hart-Davis MacGibbon, 1976. — 312p,fold leaf of plate,[40]p of plates : ill(some col), ports ; 24cm.
Previous ed. of this translation: 1965. — Translation and revision of: 'Die weisse Spinne'. Wien : Ullstein, 1958. — Index.
ISBN 0-246-64109-6 : £6.00
(B77-30546)

796.5'22 — Mountaineering & rock climbing. *Manuals*
Law, Donald. Starting mountaineering and rock climbing / [by] Donald Law ; photographs by John Clements. — Newton Abbot [etc.] : David and Charles, 1977. — 143p : ill ; 23cm.
Bibl.: p.141-143.
ISBN 0-7153-7322-6 : £3.50
(B77-22772)

796.5'22 — Mountaineering, to 1975
Clark, Ronald William. Men, myths and mountains / [by] Ronald W. Clark. — London : Weidenfeld and Nicolson, 1976. — viii,292p : ill, facsim, maps, ports ; 26cm.
Bibl.: p.279-284. — Index.
ISBN 0-297-77264-3 : £9.95
(B77-14349)

796.5'22 — Mountaineering, to 1976
Newby, Eric. Great ascents : a narrative history of mountaineering / [by] Eric Newby. — Newton Abbot [etc.] : David and Charles, 1977. — 208p : ill(some col), facsim, maps, ports(1 col) ; 26cm.
Bibl.: p.205-206. — Index.
ISBN 0-7153-7408-7 : £6.50
(B77-29624)

796.5'22 — Mountains. *For climbing*
Bueler, William M. Mountains of the world : a handbook for climbers & hikers / by William M. Bueler. — Seattle : The Mountaineers ; Leicester (249 Knighton Church Rd, Leicester) : Distributed by Cordee, 1977. — 279p : maps ; 18cm.
Originally published: Rutland, Vt. : Tuttle ; London : Prentice-Hall, 1970. — Index.
ISBN 0-916890-49-x Pbk : £3.25
(B77-31381)

796.5'22 — National parks. *Washington (State). North Cascades National Park. Mountaineering, 1937-1976. Personal observations*
Beckey, Fred. Challenge of the North Cascades / by Fred Beckey ; maps by Dee Molenaar. — Seattle : The Mountaineers ; [Leicester] ([249 Knighton Church Rd, Leicester]) : [Distributed by Cordee], 1977. — v-xvi,280p : ill, maps, ports ; 21cm.
Originally published: Seattle : The Mountaineers, 1969.
ISBN 0-916890-21-x Pbk : £3.25
(B77-32807)

796.5'22 — Rock climbing. *Antrim (County). Coastal regions. Manuals*
Antrim coast rockclimbs : interim guide / edited by Mick Curran. — [New ed.] / additional information by Calvin Torrans. — [Dublin] : Federation of Mountaineering Clubs of Ireland ; Leicester (249 Knighton Church Rd, Leicester) : [Distributed by] Cordee Publishing, 1975[i.e.1976]. — 33,4p : maps ; 16cm. — (Federation of Mountaineering Clubs of Ireland. Guides)
Previous ed.: 1975.
ISBN 0-902940-02-3 : £0.60
(B77-14868)

796.5'22 — Rock climbing. *Cumbria. Pillar Rock. Manuals*
Cram, Alan Geoffrey. Pillar group / by A.G. Cram ; illustrated by W. Heaton Cooper. — [New ed.]. — Todmorden] (['Owlers', Todmorden, Lancs.]) : Fell and Rock Climbing Club of the English Lake District, 1977. — [12],160p,plate : ill(1 col), map ; 16cm. — (Fell and Rock Climbing Club of the English Lake District. Guides) (Climbing guides to the English Lake District)
Map on inside front cover. — Previous ed.: 1968. — Index.
ISBN 0-85028-015-x Pbk : £2.50
(B77-26455)

796.5'22 — Rock climbing. *Derbyshire. Chew Valley region. Manuals*
Chew Valley. — [New ed.] / editor Bob Whittaker. — [Dunblane] : Peak [District] Committee of the British Mountaineering Council ; Leicester (249 Knighton Church Rd, Leicester LE2 3JQ) : [Distributed by] Cordee, 1976. — iv,154p : ill, maps ; 17cm. — (Rock climbs in the Peak : new series ; vol.2)
Previous ed.: published as 'Rock climbs in the Peak' / edited by Eric Byne. Vol.2 : The Saddleworth - Chew Valley area'. London : Cade, 1965. — Bibl.: p.153.
ISBN 0-903908-30-1 Pbk : £2.40
(B77-08507)

796.5'22 — Rock climbing. *Derbyshire. Stanage region. Manuals*
Stanage area. — [New ed.] / editors B. Griffiths and A. Wright. — [Dunblane] : Peak [District] Committee of the British Mountaineering Council ; Leicester (249 Knighton Church Rd, Leicester LE2 3JQ) : [Distributed by] Cordee, 1976. — vi,199p : ill, maps ; 18cm. — (Rock climbs in the Peak : new series ; vol.1)
Previous ed.: published as 'Rock climbs in the Peak' / edited by Eric Byne. Vol.1 : The Sheffield Stanage area'. London : Cade, 1964. — Bibl.: p.196.
ISBN 0-903908-25-5 Pbk : £2.40
(B77-08508)

796.5'22 — Rock climbing. *Devon. Dartmoor. Manuals*
Moulam, Anthony John James. Dartmoor / [by] Tony Moulam. — Reading : West Col Productions, 1976. — 68p : ill, map ; 17cm. — (West Col regional and coastal climbing guides)
Spine title: Dartmoor climbers' guide.
ISBN 0-901516-86-4 : £2.50
(B77-08008)

796.5'22 — Rock climbing. *Dorset. Manuals*
Dorset. — Completely revised ed. / edited by R.J. Crewe. — [Swanage] : The editor ; Leicester (249 Knighton Church Rd, Leicester) : [Distributed by] Cordee Publishing, 1977. — xxii,232p : ill, maps ; 16cm.
Previous ed.: / edited by R.C. White. London : Climbers' Club, 1969. — Contents: Lulworth/Portland / by R.L.M. Shepton - Swanage / by R.J. Crewe.
ISBN 0-904405-04-4 Pbk : £3.50
(B77-22773)

796.5'22 — Rock climbing. *Down (County). Mourne Mountains. Manuals*
Mourne rock-climbs / edited by John Forsythe. — [Ireland] : Federation of Mountaineering Clubs of Ireland ; [Leicester] ([249 Knighton Church Rd, Leicester]) : [Distributed by Cordee Publishing], 1973. — 88p : ill ; 15cm. — (Federation of Mountaineering Clubs of Ireland. Guides)
ISBN 0-902940-05-8 Sd : £0.80
(B77-14350)

796.5'22 — Rock climbing. *Galway (County). Connemara. Twelve Bens. Manuals*
Twelve Bens : hill walkers and rock climbers guide / edited by Joss Lynam ; illustrated by Sean Rothery. — Dublin : Federation of Mountaineering Clubs of Ireland ; Leicester (249 Knighton Church Rd, Leicester) : [Distributed by] Cordee Publishing, 1971. — [2],29p : 1 ill, map ; 16cm. — (Federation of Mountaineering Clubs of Ireland. Guides)
' ... revised and updated from: 'Selected climbs on Ben Corr". 1967 ; and "The twelve Bens". 1953' - title page verso. — Bibl.: p.29.
ISBN 0-902940-03-1 Sd : £0.60
Also classified at 796.5'22
(B77-14351)

796.5'22 — Rock climbing. *Great Britain. Manuals*
Disley, John. Tackle climbing / [by] John Disley. — Revised ed. — London : Paul, 1977. — 144p : ill, chart, maps, port ; 20cm.
Previous ed.: published as 'Tackle climbing this way'. 1959. — Bibl.: p.135-136.
ISBN 0-09-129270-0 : £3.50
ISBN 0-09-129271-9 Pbk : £1.45
(B77-20512)

796.5'22 — Rock climbing. *Gwynedd. Clogwyn du'r Arddu. Manuals*
Sharp, Alec. Clogwyn du'r Arddu. — 3rd ed. / by Alec Sharp ; diagrams by R.B. Evans and map by Ken Wilson. — [Dunblane] : Climbers' Club ; [Leicester] ([249 Knighton Church Rd, Leicester]) : [Distributed by Cordee Publishing], 1976. — [5],99p : ill, maps(on lining papers) ; 17cm. — (Climbers' Club. Guides to Wales ; 4)
Previous ed.: / by H.I. Banner and P. Clew. 1967.
ISBN 0-901601-30-6 : £2.40
(B77-12605)

796.5'22 — Rock climbing. *Gwynedd. Eastern Snowdonia. Manuals*
Moulam, Anthony John James. Snowdon east / by A.J.J. Moulam ; natural history notes by R. Goodier ; diagrams by Steve Knott and L. Barker. — [Dunblane] : Climbers' Club ; [Leicester] ([249 Knighton Church Rd, Leicester]) : [Distributed by Cordee Publishing], 1970. — [8],vii,191p : ill, maps(on lining papers) ; 16cm. — (Climbers' Club. Guides to Wales ; 9)
Pbk : £2.25
(B77-14352)

796.5'22 — Rock climbing. *Gwynedd. Glyder Fach & Tryfan. Manuals*
Moulam, Anthony John James. Tryfan and Glyder Fach / by A.J.J. Moulam. — 4th ed. / with diagrams by R.B. Evans. — [Dunblane] : The Climbers' Club ; Leicester (249 Knighton Church Rd, Leicester) : [Distributed by] Cordee Publishing, 1973. — [2],159p : ill, maps(on lining papers) ; 16cm. — (Climbers' Club. Guides to Wales)
Previous ed.: London : Climbers' Club, 1966. — Index.
ISBN 0-901601-20-9 Pbk : Unpriced
(B77-14353)

796.5'22 — Rock climbing. *Gwynedd. Llanberis Pass. Cwm Glas. Manuals*
Crew, Peter. Cwm Glas. — 2nd ed. / by P. Crew and I. Roper, with a geological note by N.J. Soper, a natural history note by Evan Roberts ; diagrams by R.B. Evans and photographs by K.J. Wilson and L.R. Holliwell. — [Dunblane] : Climbers' Club ; [Leicester] ([249 Knighton Church Rd, Leicester]) : [Distributed by Cordee Publishing], 1971. — [8],ii,157p : ill, maps(on lining papers) ; 16cm. — (Climbers' Club. Guides to Wales ; 5)
Previous ed.: published as 'Llanberis south' / by Peter Crew. London : Camtors, Jackson and Warr, 1966.
ISBN 0-901601-31-4 Pbk : £2.25
(B77-14354)

796.5'22 — Rock climbing. *Gwynedd. Lliwedd. Manuals*
Drasdo, Harold. Lliwedd. — 3rd ed. / by H. Drasdo ; with geological notes by Dave Thomas, natural history notes by Rawdon Goodier, and illustrations by Steve Knott. — [Dunblane] : Climbers' Club ; Leicester (249 Knighton Church Rd, Leicester) : [Distributed by] Cordee Publishing, 1972. — [8],ii,161p : ill, maps(on lining papers) ; 16cm. — (Climbers' Club. Guides to Wales ; 7)
Previous ed.: i.e. New and revised ed. / by C.W.F. Noyce and J.M. Edwards. London : s.n., 1939.
Pbk : £1.80
(B77-14355)

796.5'22 — Rock climbing. *Wicklow (County). Wicklow Mountains. Manuals*
Wicklow rock-climbs : (Glendalough and Luggala) / edited by Pat Redmond. — [Dublin] : Federation of Mountaineering Clubs of Ireland ; Leicester (249 Knighton Church Rd, Leicester) : [Distributed by] Cordee Publishing, 1973. — 86p : ill ; 16cm. — (Federation of Mountaineering Clubs of Ireland. Guides)
Sd : £0.80
(B77-14356)

796.5'22'024055 — Climbing. Techniques. *For adolescents. Manuals*
Greenbank, Anthony. Climbing for young people / by Anthony Greenbank. — London : Harrap, 1977. — 128p : ill ; 23cm.
Index.
ISBN 0-245-53112-2 : £2.75
(B77-21366)

Greenbank, Anthony. Climbing for young people / [by] Anthony Greenbank ; cover photograph by Pete Smith. — London : Pan Books, 1977. — 128p : ill ; 20cm. — (Piccolo)
Also published: London : Harrap, 1977. — Index.
ISBN 0-330-25139-2 Pbk : £0.60
(B77-27305)

796.5'22'03 — Mountaineering. *Encyclopaedias*
Unsworth, Walter. Encyclopedia of mountaineering / [compiled by] Walt Unsworth. — [Revised ed.]. — Harmondsworth [etc.] : Penguin, 1977. — 398p,16p of plates : ill, maps, ports ; 20cm. — (Penguin reference books)
Previous ed.: London : Hale, 1975. — Bibl. — Index.
ISBN 0-14-051075-3 Pbk : £1.50
(B77-22062)

796.5'22'0924 — Mountaineering. Hillary, Sir Edmund. *Autobiographies*
Hillary, *Sir* Edmund. Nothing venture, nothing win / [by] Edmund Hillary. — [Sevenoaks] : Coronet, 1977. — 381p,[24]p of plates : ill(some col), maps, ports(some col) ; 18cm.
Originally published: London : Hodder and Stoughton, 1975. — Index.
ISBN 0-340-21296-9 Pbk : £1.25
(B77-08509)

796.5'22'0924 — Mountaineering. Shipton, Eric. *Autobiographies*
Shipton, Eric. That untravelled world : an autobiography / by Eric Shipton ; line illustrations by Biro. — London : Hodder and Stoughton, 1977. — 286p,[16]p of plates : ill, maps, ports ; 23cm.
Maps on lining papers. — Originally published: 1969. — Index.
ISBN 0-340-21609-3 : £4.95
(B77-22774)

796.5'22'0924 — Mountaineering. Tenzing Norgay. *Himalayas. Everest, 1953-1976. Autobiographies*
Tenzing Norgay. After Everest : an autobiography / by Tenzing Norgay Sherpa ; as told to Malcolm Barnes. — London : Allen and Unwin, 1977. — 3-184p,[24]p of plates : ill(some col), 2 maps, ports(some col) ; 23cm.
ISBN 0-04-920050-x : £4.95
(B77-22063)

796.5'25'0941 — Great Britain. Caves. Exploration
Mason, Edmund John. Caves and caving in Britain / [by] Edmund J. Mason. — London : Hale, 1977. — 208p,[24]p of plates : ill, maps ; 23cm.
Bibl.: p.197-200. — Index.
ISBN 0-7091-6195-6 : £4.50
(B77-22775)

796.54 — Backpacking. *Manuals*
Adshead, Robin. The Spur book of back packing / by Robin Adshead. — Bourne End, Bucks. : Spurbooks, 1976. — 64p : ill, map ; 19cm. — (Spur venture guide series)
ISBN 0-904978-69-9 Pbk : £0.90
(B77-12033)

796.54 — Backpacking. *Nepal. Manuals*
Armington, Stan. Exploring Nepal / [by] Stan Armington. — Glendale, Calif. : La Siesta Press ; Leicester (249 Knighton Church Rd, Leicester) : Cordee Publishing, 1975. — 72p, fold plate : ill, maps ; 22cm.
Index.
ISBN 0-910856-62-1 Pbk : £2.20
(B77-12606)

796.54 — Backpacking. *Wales. Personal observations*
Styles, Showell. Backpacking in Wales / [by] Showell Styles. — London : Hale, 1977. — 3-158p,[12]p of plates : ill, maps ; 21cm.
ISBN 0-7091-5958-7 : £3.95
(B77-13809)

796.54 — Camping. *Juvenile literature*
Harwood, David. Camping / by David Harwood ; illustrations by Eric Winter ; cartoons by Martin Aitchison. — Loughborough : Ladybird Books, 1977. — 52p : col ill ; 18cm. — (Learnabout)
Text, col. ill. on lining papers.
ISBN 0-7214-0455-3 : £0.24
(B77-25821)

796.54 — Camping. *Manuals*
Lumley, Peter. How to go camping / by Peter Lumley. — [London] ([50a Sheen La., SW14 8LP]) : Continental Leisure Publications Ltd, [1977]. — 96p : ill, map, plan ; 21cm.
ISBN 0-905136-07-1 Pbk : £0.95
(B77-20513)

Nicholls, Peter. Camping for beginners / [by] Peter Nicholls. — Sydney [etc.] ; London : A.H. and A.W. Reed, 1976. — 111p : ill, form, maps ; 22cm.
Bibl.: p.111.
ISBN 0-589-07193-9 Pbk : £3.00
(B77-17693)

796.54 — Camping. *Teaching kits*
Brand, Ron. Camping / by Ron Brand ; illustrated by Therese Carmona ... [et al.]. — London : Jackdaw [for] Thames Television, 1977. — Portfolio : ill(some col), col map ; 23x26cm. — (Magpies)
Twelve sheets (9 fold) ([24] sides). — Bibl.(1p.).
ISBN 0-305-62134-3 : £0.99
(B77-25822)

796.6 — CYCLING
796.6 — Bicycles. Racing. Tour de France. *France, 1976*
Nicholson, Geoffrey. The great bike race / by Geoffrey Nicholson. — London [etc.] : Hodder and Stoughton, 1977. — 192p : 1 ill, maps ; 23cm.
Ill. on lining papers. — Index.
ISBN 0-340-21719-7 : £4.95
(B77-25145)

796.6 — Long-distance cycling, to 1976
Campbell, Gail. Marathon : the world of the long-distance athlete / [by] Gail Campbell. — New York : Sterling [etc.] ; London : Distributed by Ward Lock, 1977. — 176p : ill, maps, ports ; 27cm.
Index.
ISBN 0-7061-2551-7 : £4.95
Primary classification 797.2'1
(B77-31384)

796.6'02'436 — Cycling. *Manuals. For cub scouting*
Cyclist / [by A.A.R.]. — 2nd revision. — Glasgow : Brown and Ferguson, 1976. — 32p : ill ; 16cm. — (Cub Scout badge series ; no.1)
Previous ed.: i.e. 1st revision. 1970.
ISBN 0-85174-031-6 Sd : £0.25
(B77-04368)

796.6'09 — Cycling, to 1975
Durry, J. The Guinness guide to bicycling / written by J. Durry ; [translated from the French by Vivienne Menkes] ; edited by J.B. Wadley. — Enfield : Guinness Superlatives, 1977. — 2-221p : ill(some col), facsims, col map, ports(some col) ; 30cm.
Translation of: 'Le vélo'. Paris : Denoël, 1976.
ISBN 0-900424-62-1 : £8.50
(B77-24411)

796.6'0941 — Cycling. *Great Britain. Serials*
Cyclists Touring Club. Handbook / Cyclists Touring Club. — Godalming (69 Meadrow, Godalming, Surrey GU7 3HS) : Cyclists Touring Club.
1977. — 1977. — 120p : ill, map ; 16cm.
ISBN 0-902237-09-8 Pbk : Unpriced
(B77-14357)

796.6'09421 — Cycling. *London. Manuals*
Kensington and Chelsea Friends of the Earth. On your bike! : a guide to cycling in London / [Kensington and Chelsea Friends of the Earth]. — London (93 Lexham Gardens, W.8) : Kensington and Chelsea FOE, 1977. — [2], 24p : 1 ill, maps ; 22cm.
Bibl.: p.18.
Sd : £0.20
(B77-34001)

796.7 — MOTORING
796.7 — Motorcycle touring
Craven, Ken. Ride it! : the complete book of motorcycle touring / [by] Ken Craven. — Yeovil : Haynes, 1977. — 3-134p : ill, forms, ports ; 28cm. — (A Foulis motorcycling book)
ISBN 0-85429-223-3 : £3.95
(B77-21367)

796.7 — Motorcycling
Forsdyke, Graham. The love of motorcycling / [by] Graham Forsdyke. — [London] : Octopus Books, [1977]. — 96p : ill(chiefly col), col ports ; 33cm.
Col. ill. on lining papers. — Index.
ISBN 0-7064-0601-x : £2.95
(B77-25146)

796.7 — Motorcycling. *Periodicals*
On two wheels. — London : Orbis.
Vol.1, Part 1- ; 1976-. — 1976-. — ill(chiefly col), facsims(1 col), ports(some col) ; 30cm.
Weekly. — [1],20p. in 1st issue.
Sd : £0.38
ISSN 0309-5584
(B77-14358)

796.7'09'04 — Motoring. *Records of achievement*
Car facts and feats : a record of everyday motoring and automotive achievement / edited by Anthony Harding ; with contributions by Anthony Bird ... [et al.]. — 2nd ed. revised. — Enfield : Guinness Superlatives, 1976. — 256p : ill(some col), facsims, ports(some col) ; 24cm.
Spine title: Guinness book of car facts & feats. — Previous ed.: 1971. — Index.
ISBN 0-900424-64-8 : £4.95
(B77-01742)

796.7'09'041 — Motoring, to ca 1914
Montagu, Edward Douglas-Scott-Montagu, *Baron.* Behind the wheel : the magic and manners of early motoring / [by] Lord Montagu of Beaulieu & F. Wilson McComb. — New York ; London : Paddington Press, 1977. — 224p : ill, facsims, map, ports ; 26cm.
Ill. on lining papers. — Bibl.: p.221-222. — Index.
ISBN 0-448-22676-6 : £8.50
(B77-22776)

796.7'092'4 — Motoring, 1947-1975. *Personal observations*
Sedgwick, Stanley. Motoring my way / [by] Stanley Sedgwick. — London : Batsford, 1976. — 192p : ill, maps, ports ; 26cm.
Index.
ISBN 0-7134-3262-4 : £6.95
(B77-02529)

796.72 — MOTOR RACING
796.7'2 — Cars. Rallying
Brittan, Nick. All about motor sport / [by] Nick Brittan. — London [etc.] : W.H. Allen, 1977. — 160p : ill, ports ; 23cm.
Index.
ISBN 0-491-02450-9 : £3.25
Primary classification 796.7'2
(B77-20514)

796.7'2 — Cars. Rallying. *Great Britain. Periodicals*
Rally sport. — London (360 South Lambeth Rd, S.W.8) : Allen Sporting Publications Ltd.
Supersedes: Welsh rally sport.
Issue no.1- ; 1974-. — [1974]-. — ill(some col), maps, ports ; 29cm.
Monthly. — 40p.,[4]p. of plates in 27th issue.
Sd : £0.35
ISSN 0140-542x
(B77-33390)

796.7'2 — Cars. Rallying. *Manuals*
Sclater, Chris. Rallying : a practical guide to successful competition / [by] Chris Sclater & Martin Holmes. — London : Faber, 1977. — 127p : ill, maps, ports ; 20cm.
ISBN 0-571-11000-2 Pbk : £1.95 : CIP rev.
(B77-06229)

796.7'2 — Ford Escort cars sponsored by Ford Motor Company. Competitions Department. Rallying, 1968-1976
Robson, Graham. The works Escorts / [by] Graham Robson. — Yeovil : Haynes, 1977. — 255p : ill, ports ; 24cm.
Index.
ISBN 0-85429-179-2 : £5.95
(B77-25823)

796.7'2 — Formula 1 racing cars. Racing, 1966-1975
Sheldon, Paul. Milestones behind the marques / [by] Paul Sheldon. — Newton Abbot [etc.] : David and Charles, 1976. — 128p : ill ; 18x24cm.
Index.
ISBN 0-7153-7267-x : £4.95
(B77-05004)

796.7'2 — Production car sports
Hudson-Evans, Richard. Competing with production cars / [by] Richard Hudson-Evans. — London : Batsford, 1977. — 155p,[24]p of plates : ill, ports ; 23cm.
Index.
ISBN 0-7134-0132-x : £4.50
(B77-25147)

796.7'2 — Racing cars. Racing
Brittan, Nick. All about motor sport / [by] Nick Brittan. — London [etc.] : W.H. Allen, 1977. — 160p : ill, ports ; 23cm.
Index.
ISBN 0-491-02450-9 : £3.25
Also classified at 796.7'2
(B77-20514)

796.7'2 — Racing cars. Racing. *For slow learning adolescents*
Royston, Robert. Racing cars and bikes / [text by Robert Royston] ; [planned and edited by Angela Wilkinson]. — London : Macdonald Educational, 1977. — 3-46p : ill(chiefly col), col maps, ports(chiefly col) ; 25cm. — (Action world)
Index.
ISBN 0-356-05567-1 : £1.50
Also classified at 796.7'5
(B77-28024)

796.7'2 — Racing cars. Racing. *Hereford and Worcester. Shelsley Walsh. Shelsley Walsh hill-climb, to 1976*
Seventy years of Shelsley Walsh : the story of the oldest motoring speed event in the world with a continuous history (war years apart) over the same course / edited by Harold C. Hastings. — Droitwich (31 St Andrews St., Droitwich WR9 8DY) : Midland Automobile Club, 1976. — 112p : ill, facsim, map, ports ; 22cm.
Ill., map on lining papers.
ISBN 0-9505631-0-2 : £3.95
(B77-12034)

796.7'2 — Racing cars. Racing. Grands Prix. *Great Britain, 1926-1976*
Nye, Doug. The British Grand Prix, 1926-1976 / [by] Doug Nye. — London : Batsford, 1977. — 144p : ill, maps, ports ; 26cm.
Index.
ISBN 0-7134-3283-7 : £4.95
(B77-21368)

796.7'2 — Racing cars. Road racing, to 1973
Jones, Chris, *b.1947.* Road race / [by] Chris Jones. — London : Allen and Unwin, 1977. — 3-240p : ill, maps, ports ; 26cm.
Bibl.: p.230-232. — Index.
ISBN 0-04-796045-0 : £5.50
(B77-31382)

796.7'2'05 — Racing cars. Racing. *French-English parallel texts. Serials*
Fédération internationale de l'automobile. FIA annuaire du sport automobile = Year book of automobile sport / Fédération internationale de l'automobile. — Cambridge : Stephens.
1977. — [1977]. — 763p in various pagings : ill, maps, ports ; 15cm.
French and English text, French, English, German and Italian section headings, some captions and keys.
ISBN 0-85059-248-8 Pbk : £5.95
(B77-09879)

796.7'2'05 — Racing cars. Racing. *Yearbooks*
Autocourse. — Richmond (1 Church Terrace, Richmond, Surrey TW10 6SE) : Hazleton Securities Ltd.
[1976-77] / editor Mike Kettlewell ; ... chief photographer Nigel Snowdon ; ... lap charts Angela Poulter ... — 1976. — 256p : ill(some col), plans, ports(some col) ; 33cm.
ISBN 0-905138-01-5 : £8.95
(B77-04369)

International motor racing. — London : Queen Anne Press. — (A Marlboro yearbook)
1977 / edited by Barrie Gill. — 1977. — 218p : ill, ports ; 22cm.
ISBN 0-354-09003-8 Pbk : £3.95
ISSN 0309-6750
(B77-17036)

John Player motor sport yearbook. — London : Queen Anne Press.
1976 / edited by Barrie Gill. — 1976. — 336p : ill, ports ; 21cm.
Index.
ISBN 0-362-00254-1 Pbk : £2.95
ISSN 0305-6228
(B77-06831)

796.7'2'0904 — Racing cars. Racing, to 1975
Nye, Doug. Great moments in sport, motor racing / [by] Doug Nye. — London : Pelham, 1976. — 176p,[16]p of plates : ill, ports ; 23cm.
Index.
ISBN 0-7207-0763-3 : £2.25
(B77-00899)

796.7'2'0922 — Racing cars. Racing. Hunt, James, b.1947 & Lauda, Niki
Benson, David. Hunt v Lauda : Grand Prix season, 1976 / by David Benson. — London : Beaverbrook Newspapers, 1976. — 143p : ill, ports ; 19cm.
At head ot title: Daily express.
ISBN 0-85079-080-8 Pbk : £0.80
(B77-05586)

796.7'2'0924 — Cars. Rallying. Clark, Roger, b.1939. *Autobiographies*
Clark, Roger, *b.1939.* Sideways - to victory! / [by] Roger Clark ; in collaboration with Graham Robson. — Croydon : Motor Racing Publications, 1976. — 256p : ill, ports ; 23cm.
ISBN 0-900549-29-7 : £4.50
(B77-00900)

796.7'2'0924 — Formula 1 racing cars. Racing, 1970-1976. *Personal observations*
Lauda, Niki. Formula 1 : the art and technicalities of Grand Prix driving / [by] Niki Lauda ; [translated from the German by David Irving]. — London : Kimber, 1977. — 245p : ill(some col), ports(some col), plans ; 25cm.
This translation also includes a transcription of an interview with Harry Carpenter for BBC's 'Sportsnight' 13th October, 1976. — Translation of 'Formel 1'. Wien : Orac, 1975.
ISBN 0-7183-0145-5 : £8.95
(B77-27306)

796.7'2'0924 — Racing cars. Racing, 1927-1974. *Personal observations*
Bruce, *Mrs* Victor. Nine lives plus : record-breaking on land, sea and in the air : an autobiographical account / [by] Mrs Victor Bruce. — London : Pelham, 1977. — 192p : ill, facsims, map, ports ; 22cm.
Index.
ISBN 0-7207-0974-1 : £4.50
(B77-18945)

796.7'2'0924 — Racing cars. Racing. Eyston, G.E.T.. *Autobiographies*
Eyston, G E T. Safety last / [by] G.E.T. Eyston. — [London] : Vincent Publishing Company ; Spalding (41 High St., Spalding, Lincs.) : Distributed by the Turnpike Bookshop, 1975. — 159p : ill, facsims, ports ; 20cm.
ISBN 0-9504186-6-8 : £3.95
(B77-02530)

796.7'2'0924 — Racing cars. Racing. Hill, Graham. *Autobiographies*
Hill, Graham. Graham / [by] Graham Hill ; with Neil Ewart. — London [etc.] : Hutchinson, 1976. — 175p,[24]p of plates : ill, ports(some col) ; 23cm.
ISBN 0-09-127930-5 : £3.95
(B77-10509)

Hill, Graham. Graham / [by] Graham Hill ; with Neil Ewart. — London [etc.] : Arrow Books, 1977. — 175p,[16]p of plates : ill, ports ; 18cm.
Originally published: London : Hutchinson, 1976.
ISBN 0-09-915250-9 Pbk : £0.70
(B77-28820)

796.7'2'0924 — Racing cars. Racing. Hunt, James, b.1947. *Biographies*
Williams, Peter, *b.1946 (Dec.).* The story of James Hunt / by Peter Williams. — Brentwood (Sovereign House, High St., Brentwood, Essex CM14 4SE) : NPC, 1976. — 3-86p : ill(incl 1 col), ports ; 28cm.
Sd : £0.80
(B77-01743)

796.7'2'0924 — Racing cars. Racing. Hunt, James, b.1947, 1976. *Autobiographies*
Hunt, James, *b.1947.* James Hunt against all odds / [by] Eoin Young ; with James Hunt ; edited by David Hodges. — London [etc.] : Hamlyn, [1977]. — 176p : ill(some col), ports(some col) ; 25cm.
Ill. on lining papers. — Index.
ISBN 0-600-35250-1 : £3.95
(B77-22777)

796.7'2'0941 — Racing cars. Hill-climbing & sprinting. *Great Britain*
Boucher, Robin. Drive it! : the complete book of hillclimbing and sprinting / [by] Robin Boucher ; [illustration Terry Davey]. — Yeovil : Haynes, 1977. — 3-124p : ill, maps, ports ; 28cm.
'A Foulis motoring book' - half title page verso.
ISBN 0-85429-226-8 : £3.95
(B77-25824)

796.7'2'0941 — Racing cars. Racing. *Great Britain. Yearbooks*
Motor sport year book including fixture list. — London (31 Belgrave Sq., [SW1X 8QH]) : Royal Automobile Club, Motor Sport Division.
1977. — [1977]. — 163p : ill, maps ; 19cm.
Spine title: RAC motor sport year book & fixture list.
Pbk : £2.00
(B77-32105)

796.7'2'0973 — Racing cars. Racing. *United States, to 1973*
Bochroch, Albert R. American automobile racing : an illustrated history / [by] Albert R. Bochroch. — [1st ed. reprinted] ; [with a new preface by the author]. — Harmondsworth [etc.] : Penguin, 1977. — 260p : ill(some col), ports(some col) ; 28cm.
Originally published: New York : Viking Press ; Cambridge : Stephens, 1974. — Bibl.: p.253-254. — Index.
ISBN 0-14-004417-5 Pbk : Unpriced
(B77-26456)

796.75 — MOTORCYCLE RACING
796.7'5 — Motorcycling. Display teams. *Great Britain. Great Britain. Army. Royal Signals Motorcycle Display Team, to 1977*
Ladd, James David. The White Helmets : the Royal Signals Motor Cycle Display Team / [by] James Ladd. — Yeovil : Haynes, 1977. — 3-165p : ill, port ; 24cm.
'A Foulis motorcycling book' - title page verso. — Index.
ISBN 0-85429-218-7 : £4.95
(B77-22778)

796.7'5 — Racetracks. *Leicestershire. Kirkby Mallory. Mallory Park. Racing motorcycles, 1931-1951. Racing, 1976. Illustrations*
Main-Smith, Bruce. The first post-vintage racing scene (1931-1951) / [photographs by Bruce Main-Smith and Brian Holder]. — Leatherhead (P.O. Box 20, Leatherhead, Surrey) : Bruce Main-Smith and Co. Ltd, 1977. — 64p : of ill, ports ; 21cm.
Sd : £1.50
(B77-25825)

796.7'5 — Racetracks. *Leicestershire. Kirkby Mallory. Mallory Park. Racing motorcycles, to 1931. Racing, 1976. Illustrations*
Main-Smith, Bruce. The first vintage racing scene (pre-1931) / [photographs by Bruce Main-Smith and Brian Holder]. — Leatherhead (P.O. Box 20, Leatherhead, Surrey) : Bruce Main-Smith and Co. Ltd, 1977. — 64p : of ill, ports ; 21cm.
Sd : £1.50
(B77-25826)

796.7'5 — Racing motorcycles. Junior moto-cross. *Manuals*
Hooper, Royston. The Topliner book of moto-cross / [by] Royston Hooper. — Basingstoke [etc.] : Macmillan, 1977. — 112p, [8]p of plates : ill ; 18cm. — (Topliners)
Cover title: Moto-cross.
ISBN 0-333-21853-1 Pbk : £0.45 : CIP rev.
(B77-05005)

796.7'5 — Racing motorcycles. Off-road racing
Forsdyke, Graham. Off road motor cycle sport / [by] Graham Forsdyke. — London [etc.] : Hamlyn, 1976. — 5-156p : ill(some col), ports ; 26cm.
Ill. on lining papers. — Index.
ISBN 0-600-36735-5 : £2.50
(B77-09199)

796.7'5 — Racing motorcycles. Racing. *For slow learning adolescents*
Royston, Robert. Racing cars and bikes / [text by Robert Royston] ; [planned and edited by Angela Wilkinson]. — London : Macdonald Educational, 1977. — 3-46p : ill(chiefly col), col maps, ports(chiefly col) ; 25cm. — (Action world)
Index.
ISBN 0-356-05567-1 : £1.50
Primary classification 796.7'2
(B77-28024)

796.7'5 — Racing motorcycles. Speedway racing. Teams. Records. *Fill-in books*
Speedway record book. — Hove (Waterloo St., Hove, Sussex BN3 1AH) : Denbee Publications Ltd.
1977. — 1977. — 117p : ill ; 26cm.
Unpriced
ISBN 0-905128-00-3
(B77-17037)

796.7'5 — Trail motorcycles. Trail riding. *Manuals*
Melling, Frank. Ride it! : the complete book of trail bike riding / [by] Frank Melling. — Yeovil : Haynes, 1976. — 3-135p : ill, facsims, ports ; 28cm.
'A Foulis motorcycling book' - half title page verso.
ISBN 0-85429-221-7 : £3.95
ISBN 0-85696-180-9 Pbk : £2.50
(B77-05587)

796.7'5 — Trials motorcycles. Racing. *Manuals*
Beesley, Tom. The Mick Andrews book of trials / [written and photographed by Tom Beesley ; in conjunction with Mick Andrews]. — Cambridge : Stephens, [1976]. — 3-222p, plate : chiefly ill, ports ; 21cm.
Also published: Irvine, Calif. : Trippe, Cox Associates, 1976.
ISBN 0-85059-271-2 Pbk : £3.95
(B77-03723)

796.7'5'03 — Racing motorcycles. Racing, to 1976. *Encyclopaedias*
Carrick, Peter. Encyclopaedia of motor-cycle sport / compiled by Peter Carrick. — London : Hale [etc.], 1977. — 224p,[16]p of plates : ill, ports ; 24cm.
Index.
ISBN 0-7091-5784-3 : £5.25
(B77-13209)

796.7'5'05 — Racing motorcycles. Racing. *Annuals*
Motocourse : the motorcycle road racing annual. — Richmond, Surrey (1 Church Terrace, Richmond, Surrey TW10 6SE) : Hazleton Securities Ltd.
[1976-77] / editor Chris Carter. — 1976. — 200p : ill(some col), maps, ports ; 33cm.
ISBN 0-905138-02-3 : £7.95
ISSN 0309-4642
(B77-09880)

'Motor cycle news' yearbook. — Peterborough (117 Park Rd, Peterborough) : EMAP National Publications Ltd [etc.].
1976-77 / edited by Frank Ward. — 1977. — 128p : ill(some col), ports ; 24cm.
Previously published: as 'Motor cycle news' annual.
ISBN 0-85059-244-5 Pbk : £1.95
(B77-09200)

796.7'5'05 — Racing motorcycles. Speedway racing. *Serials*
Speedway yearbook. — Ipswich (37 Lower Brook St., Ipswich IP1 1AQ) : Studio Publications.
1977 / edited by Peter Oakes. — 1977. — 232p : ill, ports ; 24cm.
Index.
ISBN 0-904584-29-1 Pbk : £2.95
ISSN 0309-8915
(B77-26457)

796.7'5'0904 — Racing motorcycles. Racing, to 1976
Carrick, Peter. Great moments in sport, motor cycle racing / [by] Peter Carrick. — London : Pelham, 1977. — 142p,[15]p of plates : ill, ports ; 23cm.
Index.
ISBN 0-7207-0972-5 : £4.50
(B77-15427)

796.7'5'0924 — Racing motorcycles. Racing. Read, Phil. *Autobiographies*
Read, Phil. Phil Read : the real story / Phil Read ; in association with Graeme Wright. — London : Macdonald and Jane's, 1977. — 192p, [8]p of plates : ill, ports ; 23cm.
ISBN 0-354-04024-3 : £4.25
(B77-14359)

796.7'5'0924 — Racing motorcycles. Racing. Sheene, Barry. *Autobiographies*
Sheene, Barry. Barry Sheene : the story so far - / [edited by Ian Beacham]. — Ipswich (7 King St., Ipswich, Suffolk) : Studio Publications, 1976. — 160p : ill(some col), ports(some col) ; 25cm.
ISBN 0-904584-21-6 : £4.00
(B77-23641)

796.7'5'0924 — Racing motorcycles. Speedway racing. Collins, Peter, b.1954. *Autobiographies*
Collins, Peter, *b.1954.* The Peter Collins speedway book / edited [with contributions] by Richard Bott. — London : Paul, 1977. — 112p, [4]p of plates : ill(some col), ports(some col) ; 25cm.
ISBN 0-09-129400-2 : £2.95
(B77-25148)

796.76 — KARTING
796.7'6 — Karts. Racing
Burgess, Alan Thomas. Starting karting / by Alan T. Burgess. — 5th ed. — Chislehurst : Lodgemark Press, [1976?]. — 40p : ill, maps ; 19cm.
Previous ed.: 1972.
ISBN 0-85077-051-3 Pbk : £0.70
(B77-05006)

796.79 — CARAVANNING
796.7'9 — Caravanning. *Manuals*
Leonard, Frank, *b.1927.* How to choose and use a caravan / [by] Frank Leonard. — Yeovil : Haynes, [1977]. — 3-173p : ill, facsim, forms, maps, plans ; 24cm.
Index.
ISBN 0-85429-227-6 Pbk : £3.95
(B77-24412)

796.812 — WRESTLING
796.8'12 — Wrestling. *Manuals*
Carson, Ray Fritziof. Systematic championship wrestling / [by] Ray F. Carson, Jr. — South Brunswick [etc.] : Barnes ; London : Yoseloff, 1973. — 328p : ill, facsim ; 26cm.
Bibl.: p.324-325. — Index.
ISBN 0-498-01140-2 : £3.75
(B77-19584)

Clayton, Thompson. Wrestling for fun / [by] Thompson Clayton. — South Brunswick ; New York : Barnes ; London : Yoseloff, 1973. — 87p : ill ; 27cm.
Bibl.: p.79-84. — Index.
ISBN 0-498-01170-4 : £2.75
(B77-19585)

796.815 — JUJITSUS
796.8'15'06241 — Jujitsus. Organisations. *Great Britain. Directories*
Milom (J.) Ltd. Associations & societies ; and, List of clubs / J. Milom Ltd. — Manchester (68 Great Ducie St., Manchester M3 1ND) : [J. Milom Ltd], 1976. — 12,4,102p : map ; 33cm.
Sd : Unpriced
(B77-17038)

796.8'15'07 — Jujitsus. Instructors. *Great Britain. Directories*
Milom (J.) Ltd. List of instructors and associates & societies / J. Milom Ltd. — Manchester (68 Great Ducie St., Manchester M3 1ND) : [J. Milom Ltd], 1976. — [2],12,26p : map ; 33cm.
Sd : Unpriced
(B77-17039)

796.8'152 — Judo. *Manuals*
Glass, George. Competitive judo : throwing techniques and weight control / [by] George Glass. — London : Faber, 1977. — 93p : ill ; 20cm.
Bibl.: p.91. — Index.
ISBN 0-571-10915-2 Pbk : £1.75 : CIP rev.
(B77-13810)

White, David, *b.1942.* Judo : the practical way / [by] David White ; drawings by Max Lenvers. — [London] : Chancerel : Barrie and Jenkins, 1977. — 2-91p : ill, ports ; 21cm. — (Action books)
Ill. on lining papers. — Bibl.: p.88.
ISBN 0-905703-04-9 : £1.75
(B77-22065)

796.8'153 — Karate. *Manuals*
Donovan, Ticky. Special competition karate / [by] Ticky Donovan, Dominique Valera. — [London?] ([c/o Panda Printing Ltd, 376 High St. North, London E.12]) : Donovan and Valera Ltd, [1977]. — [1],94p : chiefly ill, ports ; 21cm.
ISBN 0-9505627-0-x Sd : Unpriced
(B77-10893)

Nagamine, Shoshin. The essence of Okinawan karate-do (Shorin-ryu) / by Shoshin Nagamine. — Rutland, Vt [etc.] : Tuttle ; London : Prentice-Hall, 1976. — 278p : ill ; 24cm.
Ill. on lining papers. — Index.
ISBN 0-8048-1163-6 : Unpriced
(B77-06230)

Nakayama, Masatoshi. Dynamic karate : instruction by the master / by Masatoshi Nakayama ; translated [from the Japanese] by Herman Kauz. — London : Ward Lock, 1976. — 308p : ill(incl 1 col) ; 27cm.
Translated from the 9th Japanese ed., Tokyo : Kodansha International, 1976.
£8.50
ISBN 0-7063-1714-9
(B77-09881)

796.8'153'024042 — Karate. *Manuals. For women*
Sugano, Jun. Karate and self-defense for women / [by] Jun Sugano. — London : Ward Lock, [1976]. — 119p : chiefly ill(some col) ; 25cm.
ISBN 0-7063-5220-3 : £4.95
(B77-05007)

796.8'159 — Kung fu. *Manuals*
Dennis, Felix. The beginner's guide to kung-fu / [by] Felix Dennis, Paul Simmons. — [London] : Sphere, 1976. — [154]p : ill ; 20cm.
Originally published: London : Wildwood House, 1974. — Bibl.: p.[154].
ISBN 0-7221-2903-3 Pbk : £0.65
(B77-15428)

796.8'159 — Kung fu. Praying Mantis techniques. *Manuals*
Un, Ho Bun. Praying mantis Kung fu / by H.B. Un. — London (683 Fulham Rd, S.W.6) : Paul H. Crompton Ltd, 1975. — [7],83p : chiefly ill, ports ; 20cm.
Originally published: 1974.
Unpriced
(B77-01744)

796.8'159 — T'ai chi ch'üan. *Manuals*
Soo, Chee. The Chinese art of T'ai Chi Ch'uan / [by] Chee Soo. — London : Gordon and Cremonesi, 1976. — 116p : ill ; 20cm.
Index.
ISBN 0-86033-037-0 : £4.50
(B77-08510)

796.83 — BOXING
796.8'3'0922 — Prizefighting. Sayers, Tom. Matches with Heenan, John Carmel, b.1835. *England*
Lloyd, Alan. The great prize fight / [by] Alan Lloyd. — London : Cassell, 1977. — xii,188p, [8]p of plates : ill, ports ; 22cm.
Bibl.: p.181-184. — Index.
ISBN 0-304-29780-1 : £4.50
(B77-15429)

796.8'3'0924 — Boxing. *London. Croydon (London Borough), 1922-1976. Personal observations*
Fisher, Tom. Boxing was my sport : the story of Croydon boxers from 1920 in words and pictures / [by] Tom Fisher ; written [i.e. edited] by Gilbert M. Allnutt. — West Wickham : Belvedere Printing Co. Ltd ; Beckenham (6 South Eden Park Rd, Beckenham, Kent) : [Distributed by the editor], 1976. — [4],61[i.e. 64]p,[20]p of plates : ill, ports ; 21cm.
Index.
ISBN 0-9505417-0-2 Pbk : £2.00
(B77-01745)

796.8'3'0924 — Boxing. Marciano, Rocky. *Biographies*
Skehan, Everett M. Rocky Marciano / by Everett M. Skehan ; with family assistance by Peter, Louis and Mary Anne Marciano. — London : Robson, 1977. — [12],369p,[8]p of plates : ill, ports ; 24cm.
Also published: Boston, Mass. : Houghton Mifflin, 1977.
ISBN 0-86051-021-2 : £5.75 : CIP rev
(B77-23642)

796.8'3'0924 — Boxing. Mills, Freddie. *Biographies*
Birtley, Jack. Freddie Mills : his life and death / [by] Jack Birtley. — London : New English Library, 1977. — 206p,[8]p of plates : 1 ill, ports ; 22cm.
ISBN 0-450-03210-8 : £4.95
(B77-31383)

796.8'3'0924 — Boxing. Muhammad Ali. *Autobiographies*
Muhammad Ali. The greatest : my own story / [by] Muhammad Ali ; with Richard Durham. — St Albans : Mayflower, 1976. — 510p ; 18cm.
Originally published: New York : Random House, 1975 ; London : Hart-Davis MacGibbon, 1976.
ISBN 0-583-12613-8 Pbk : £0.75
(B77-13210)

796.8'3'0924 — Prizefighting. Donnelly, Dan. *Biographies*
Myler, Patrick. Regency rogue : Dan Donnelly, his life and legends / [by] Patrick Myler. — Dublin (11 Clare St., Dublin 2) : The O'Brien Press, 1976. — 168p : ill, facsims, music, ports ; 22cm.
Bibl.: p.160-161. — Index.
ISBN 0-905140-06-0 : £4.50
(B77-03724)

796.9 — WINTER SPORTS
796.9'09 — Winter sports, to 1976
Flower, Raymond. The story of ski-ing and other winter sports / by Raymond Flower ; with a foreword by Jean-Claude Killy. — London [etc.] : Angus and Robertson, 1976. — 240p : ill(some col), facsims, ports ; 26cm.
Index.
ISBN 0-207-95704-5 : £6.00
(B77-01746)

796.91 — ICE SKATING
796.9'1 — Ice skating. *Manuals*
Hügin, Otto. The technique of skating / [by] Otto Hügin & Jack Gerschwiler ; translated [from the German] by A.D. Simons. — London : Cassell and Collier Macmillan, 1977. — 183p : ill, ports ; 23cm.
Originally published: in German. Thun : Ott, 1973.
ISBN 0-304-29541-8 : £4.00
(B77-13811)

796.9'1 — Ice skating: Figure skating. *Juvenile literature*
Wolter, Carlo. Figure skating / by Carlo Wolter. — New York ; London : F. Watts, 1977. — [7],64p : ill, ports ; 23cm. — (A first book)
Index.
ISBN 0-531-00396-5 : £1.95
(B77-30547)

796.93 — SKIING
'Ski' magazine's encyclopedia of skiing / edited by Robert Scharff. — Updated [ed.]. — New York [etc.] ; London : Harper and Row, [1976]. — xi,427p : ill, ports ; 26cm.
This ed. published in the United States: 1974. — Previous ed.: New York : Harper and Row, 1970.
ISBN 0-06-013918-8 : £12.70
ISBN 0-06-013919-6 Pbk : £4.45
(B77-01747)

796.9'3 — Alpine skiing. *Manuals*
Brown, Terence Henry Charles. The Spur book of parallel ski-ing / by Terry Brown and Rob Hunter. — Bourne End, Bucks. : Spurbooks, 1977. — 64p : ill ; 19cm. — (A Spur book venture guide)
ISBN 0-904978-82-6 Pbk : £0.90
(B77-33391)

796.9'3 — Cross-country skiing. *Manuals*
Brown, Terence Henry Charles. The Spur book of cross country ski-ing / by Terry Brown and Rob Hunter. — Bourne End, Bucks. : Spurbooks, 1977. — 64p : ill ; 19cm. — (A Spur book venture guide)
ISBN 0-904978-85-0 Pbk : £0.90
(B77-33392)

796.9'3 — Skiing. *Manuals*
Brown, Terence Henry Charles. The Spur book of ski-ing / by Terry Brown and Rob Hunter. — Bourne End, Bucks. : Spurbooks, 1976. — 62p : ill ; 19cm. — (A Spurbook venture guide)
ISBN 0-904978-77-x Pbk : £0.90
(B77-09882)

Kent, Bill. Better skiing / [by] Bill Kent and Peter Roberts. — London : Kaye and Ward [etc.], 1976. — 96p : ill, port ; 23cm.
Bibl.: p.96.
ISBN 0-7182-1448-x : £2.15
(B77-01748)

796.9'3'094 — Skiing. *Western Europe. Practical information. Serials*
'Daily mail' skier's holiday guide. — London (4 Douro Place, W8 5PH) : Ski Specialists Ltd ; Glasgow : Wm Teacher and Sons Ltd.
1976-77 / [editor David G. Ross]. — [1976]. — 384p : ill(some col), form, col maps, ports ; 22cm.
Previously published: as 'Skier's holiday guide'.
ISBN 0-904126-02-1 Pbk : £2.85
ISSN 0309-5134
(B77-14360)

796.9'3'09411 — Skiing. *Scotland. Practical information. Serials*
Winter sports in Scotland / Scottish Tourist Board. — Edinburgh : The Board. — (Scottish Tourist Board. Information booklets)
1976-1977. — [1976]. — 38,[28]p : 1 ill ; 21x10cm.
Sd : Unpriced
(B77-22066)

796.95 — TOBOGGANING AND COASTING
796.9'5'0624947 — Tobogganing. Organisations. *Switzerland. St Moritz. St Moritz Tobogganing Club, to 1976*
Seth-Smith, Michael. The Cresta Run : history of the St Moritz Tobogganing Club / [by] Michael Seth-Smith ; foreword by H.R.H. The Prince Philip, Duke of Edinburgh. — London [etc.] : Foulsham, 1976. — 272p,leaf of plate,[32]p of plates : ill(some col), facsims, plan, ports(some col) ; 26cm.
Index.
ISBN 0-572-00949-6 : £7.50
Primary classification 796.9'5'094947
(B77-08511)

796.9'5'094947 — Tobogganing courses: Cresta Run. *Switzerland. St Moritz, to 1976*

Seth-Smith, Michael. The Cresta Run : history of the St Moritz Tobogganing Club / [by] Michael Seth-Smith ; foreword by H.R.H. The Prince Philip, Duke of Edinburgh. — London [etc.] : Foulsham, 1976. — 272p,leaf of plate,[32]p of plates : ill(some col), facsims, plan, ports(some col) ; 26cm.
Index.
ISBN 0-572-00949-6 : £7.50
Also classified at 796.9'5'0624947
(B77-08511)

797.1 — BOATING

797.1 — Boating. *Manuals*

Beavis, Bill. The A-Z of cheaper boating : a practical guide / [by] Bill Beavis ; illustrated by Alan Roy. — London : Paul, 1977. — 127p : ill, plans ; 23cm.
ISBN 0-09-129060-0 : £3.75
ISBN 0-09-129061-9 Pbk : £2.25
(B77-25149)

797.1 — Inland waterways. Cruising. *Great Britain. Manuals*

Davenport, Sheila. Canal and river cruising / [by Sheila Davenport]. — Wakefield : EP Publishing, 1977. — 40,[1]p : ill, 2 maps, plan ; 14x21cm. — (Know the game)
'Produced in collaboration with the Inland Waterways Association'.
ISBN 0-7158-0498-7 Sd : £0.45
(B77-20515)

Liley, John. Inland cruising companion / [by] John Liley. — London : Stanford Maritime, 1977. — 159p : ill ; 22cm.
Index.
ISBN 0-540-07167-6 Pbk : £2.50
(B77-24413)

797.1 — Inland waterways. Cruising. *Great Britain. Serials*

The **Belmont** beginners guide to inland waterways activities. — [Harrow] ([29 Tenby Ave., Harrow, Middx HA3 8RU]) : [Belmont Press].
[1976] : 1st ed. / [editor John S. Lawes]. — [1976]. — [1],31p : ill, 2 maps ; 21cm. — (Belmont waterways series)
ISBN 0-905366-04-2 Sd : £0.15
(B77-08512)

The **Belmont** guide to inland waterways activities : the guide to all your leisure activities on the waterways. — [Harrow] ([29 Tenby Ave., Harrow, Middx HA3 8RU]) : [Belmont Press].
1977 / [editor John S. Lawes]. — [1976]. — [1],48p : ill, maps, plans ; 21cm.
ISBN 0-905366-03-4 Sd : £0.35
(B77-09201)

A **lazy** man's guide to holidays afloat. — Oxford (7 Walton Well Rd, Oxford OX2 6ED) : Boat Enquiries Ltd.
1976 : 10th annual ed. / edited by Roger Frankland ; assisted by the staff of Boat Enquiries Ltd. — 1976. — 64,65p : ill, forms, maps(some col), plans ; 21cm.
ISBN 0-901156-09-4 Pbk : £0.30
(B77-11361)

797.1'02'47991 — Boating. *Manuals. For angling*

McCristal, Vic. The fisherman's boat / [by] Vic McCristal. — Sydney [etc.] ; London : A.H. and A.W. Reed, 1976. — 120p : ill, ports ; 25cm.
ISBN 0-589-07182-3 Pbk : Unpriced
(B77-25150)

797.1'0941 — Inland waterways. Boating. *Great Britain. Manuals*

Colborne, C L. Practical boat handling on rivers and canals / [by] C.L. Colborne. — Newton Abbot [etc.] : David and Charles, 1977. — 134p : ill, map ; 23cm.
Index.
ISBN 0-7153-7061-8 : £2.95
(B77-12607)

797.1'09417 — Boating. *Ireland (Republic). Periodicals*

Irish boats & yachting. — Dublin (4 Portobello Place, Dublin 8) ; London : 'Irish Boats and Yachting'.
Mar.-Apr. 1977-. — 1977-. — ill, map, plans, ports ; 29cm.
Six issues a year. — 3-70p. in 1st issue.
Sd : £0.30
(B77-26458)

797.1'09429'56 — National parks. *South Wales. Brecon Beacons National Park. Boating. Practical information*

Brecon Beacons National Park Committee. Boating and sailing / [Brecon Beacons National Park Committee]. — [Brecon] ([Glamorgan St., Brecon, Powys]) : The Committee, 1977. — Folder([6]p) ; 22cm. — (Information sheet ; no.8)
£0.03
(B77-18329)

797.1'22 — Canoeing. *Manuals*

Brailsford, John. Canoeing / [by] John Brailsford and Stephen Baker. — Oxford : Oxford Illustrated Press, 1977. — [7],82p : ill, ports ; 26cm.
ISBN 0-902280-41-4 : £3.25
(B77-26459)

Williams, Peter. Canoeing / [by] Peter Williams. — London : Pelham, 1977. — 88p : ill ; 26cm. — (Pelham pictorial sports instruction series)
ISBN 0-7207-0983-0 : £3.95
(B77-34002)

797.1'22 — Wildwater canoeing. *Manuals*

Steidle, R. Wildwater canoeing / [by] R. Steidle ; [translated from the German by Wendy Gill]. — Wakefield : EP Publishing, 1977. — 140p : ill, port ; 21cm. — (EP sport series)
Translation of: 'Wildwasserfahren-technik, training, taktik'. Munich : BLV Verlagsgesellschaft, 1976.
ISBN 0-7158-0562-2 : £3.95
(B77-30548)

797.1'23 — Rowing. *Manuals*

Chant, Christopher. Rowing for everyone / [by] Christopher Chant. — Newton Abbot [etc.] : David and Charles, 1977. — 125p : ill ; 22cm. — (David and Charles leisure and travel series)
Bibl.: p.124. — Index.
ISBN 0-7153-7363-3 : £1.95
(B77-20516)

Howard, Ronnie. Knowing rowing : an illustrated introduction to rowing and sculling / [by] Ronnie Howard with Nigel Hunt. — London : Allen and Unwin, 1977. — 96p : ill ; 26cm.
Bibl.: p.96.
ISBN 0-04-797002-2 : £4.95
(B77-20517)

797.1'24 — Sailing. *Manuals*

The **complete** book of sailing / edited by Peter Cook and Barbara Webb. — London : Ward Lock, 1977. — 304p : ill(some col), chart, plans ; 26cm.
Index.
ISBN 0-7063-5125-8 : £5.95
(B77-28025)

Dawson, Christopher, *b.1927.* Tackle sailing / [by] Christopher Dawson. — 3rd ed. — London : Paul, 1977. — 152p,[8]p of plates : ill ; 20cm.
Previous ed.: published as 'Tackle sailing this way'. 1968. — Bibl.: p.139-142.
ISBN 0-09-128640-9 : £2.95
ISBN 0-09-128641-7 Pbk : £1.45
(B77-21369)

Mellor, John, *b.1945.* Sailing can be simple / [by] John Mellor. — London : Souvenir Press, 1977. — 311p : ill, charts, facsims, map ; 23cm.
Bibl.: p.296-299.
ISBN 0-285-62276-5 : £5.50 : CIP rev.
(B77-13812)

Toghill, Jeff. Sailing for beginners / [by] Jeff Toghill. — Sydney [etc.] ; London : A.H. and A.W. Reed, 1974. — 111p : ill ; 22cm.
ISBN 0-589-07129-7 Pbk : £2.55
(B77-17696)

797.1'24 — Sailing boats. Sailing. *Manuals*

Knox-Johnston, Robin. Sailing / [by] Robin Knox-Johnston. — London [etc.] : Collins [etc.], 1977. — 128p : ill(chiefly col), maps(1 col), ports(some col) ; 26cm. — (International library)
Col. ill. on lining papers. — Bibl.: p.126. — Index.
ISBN 0-00-100178-7 : £3.50
ISBN 0-00-103332-8 Pbk : 1.95
(B77-22779)

797.1'24 — Sailing dinghies. Cruising. *Great Britain. Manuals*

Dye, Margaret. The Spur book of dinghy cruising / by Margaret Dye ; with illustrations by Terry Brown. — Bourne End : Spurbooks, 1977. — 64p : ill, maps ; 19cm. — (A Spurbook venture guide)
ISBN 0-904978-68-0 Pbk : £0.90
(B77-22780)

797.1'24 — Sailing dinghies. Sailing. *Manuals*

Andrews, James Sydney. Simple sailing / [by] Jim Andrews. — Tadworth : World's Work, 1975. — 93p : ill ; 20cm.
Index.
ISBN 0-437-23200-x : £2.90
ISBN 0-437-23201-8 Pbk : £1.50
(B77-00360)

797.1'24 — Wind surfing. *Manuals*

Mares, Uwe. Windsurfing / by Uwe Mares, Reinhart Winkler ; translated into English [from the German] by Barbara Webb with technical assistance by David Pelly. — Lymington : Nautical Publishing Co., 1976. — 92p : ill ; 22cm.
Translation of: 'Windsurfing'. Bielefeld : Delius Klasing, 1976?. — Index.
ISBN 0-245-53011-8 : £2.75
(B77-01749)

797.1'24'03 — Yachting. *Polyglot dictionaries*

Webb, Barbara, *b.1929.* Yachtsman's 8 language dictionary : English, French, German, Dutch, Danish, Italian, Spanish, Portuguese / [by] Barbara Webb. — 2nd ed. — London : Coles, 1977. — 160p : ill, maps ; 13x20cm.
Previous ed.: published as 'Ready about!', 1965.
ISBN 0-229-11575-6 : £3.95
(B77-14361)

797.1'24'06242847 — Yachting. Organisations. *North Yorkshire. Scarborough. Scarborough Yacht Club, to 1976*

James, W H. Scarborough Sailing Club, Scarborough Yacht Club : a history / [by] W.H. James ; with contributions and sketches by Norman W.L. Sanderson. — [Beverley] (['Maes-y-Coed', Molescroft, Beverley, N. Humberside HU17 7EP]) : [The author], 1976. — [1],106p : ill(1 col), map, ports ; 16x22cm.
ISBN 0-9505431-0-1 : £4.00
(B77-03725)

797.1'25 — Motor cruisers. Cruising. *Great Britain. Manuals*

Kinsey, Terry Leander. Start motor cruising / [by] T.L. Kinsey. — Wakefield : EP Publishing, 1977. — 116p : ill, map ; 21cm. — (EP sport series)
Bibl.: p.115-116.
ISBN 0-7158-0564-9 : Unpriced
(B77-28821)

797.1'25'0222 — Motorboating. *Manuals. Illustrations*

Searl, Crab. Plain sailing, power boat / by Crab Searl ; drawings by Gary Keane. — Paris : Chancerel ; Leicester (Euston St., Freeman's Common, Aylestone Rd, Leicester LE2 7SS) : [Distributed by] WHS Distributors, 1975. — 96p : chiefly ill, charts, ports ; 17x23cm. — (Learn through strips)
'These strips were first published in the London Evening News' - note.
Pbk : £0.95
ISBN 2-85429-012-7
(B77-20518)

797.1'4 — J class yachts. Racing, ca 1930-1937

Dear, Ian. Enterprise to Endeavour : the J-class yachts / [by] Ian Dear. — London : I. Allan, 1977. — 160p : ill, facsims, ports, plans ; 30cm.
Ill. on lining papers. — Bibl.: p.159. — Index.
ISBN 0-7110-0804-3 : £6.95
(B77-27307)

797.1'4 — Racing motorboats. Speed records, to 1973

Villa, Leo. The world water speed record / by Leo Villa and Kevin Desmond ; with a foreword by Sir Thomas Sopwith. — London : Batsford, 1976. — x,206p,[16]p of plates : ill, ports ; 23cm.
Bibl.: p.200. — Index.
ISBN 0-7134-3065-6 : £4.75
(B77-00361)

797.1'4 — Racing sailing boats. Racing

Creagh-Osborne, Richard. This is racing : tactics and strategy in action / [by] Richard Creagh-Osborne. — Lymington : Nautical Publishing Co., 1977. — xii,179p : ill(chiefly col), charts(some col), facsims, port ; 21cm.
Bibl.: p.179.
ISBN 0-245-53070-3 : £5.50
(B77-13813)

797.1'4 — Sailing dinghies. Racing. *Periodicals*
International dinghy racing. — London (34 Buckingham Palace Rd, SW1W 0RE) : Ocean Publications Ltd.
Vol.1, no.1- ; 1977-. — 1977-. — ill(some col), ports ; 28cm.
Quarterly. — 3-42p. in 1st issue.
Sd : £0.40
ISSN 0309-5479
(B77-20519)

797.1'4 — Sailing ships. Sailing. Operation Sail, 1976
The **tall** ships : a sailing celebration / text by Hyla M. Clark ; introductions by Frank O. Braynard and Tony Cribbs. — New York : Tree Communications ; Cambridge : Stephens, 1976. — 128p : chiefly ill(chiefly col), col maps, ports ; 28cm.
'Published in association with Operation Sail 1976'. — 'A Tree Communications/Alexis Gregory Book'.
ISBN 0-85059-273-9 Pbk : £3.95
(B77-07542)

797.1'4 — Yachts. Offshore racing. *Manuals*
Offshore manual international / edited by Peter Johnson with Robert Humphreys (Europe), Roger Marshall (USA) ; illustrated by Peter Milne. — Lymington : Nautical Publishing Co., 1977. — 172p : ill(chiefly col), facsim, forms, col map ; 22cm.
Bibl.: p.168-169. — Index.
ISBN 0-245-53039-8 : £4.85
(B77-17040)

797.1'4 — Yachts. Racing. Competitions. America's Cup, 1958-1974
Hoyt, Norris Dresser. The twelve metre challenges for the America's Cup / text by Norris D. Hoyt ; paintings and drawings by Joseph W. Golinkin. — London [etc.] : Angus and Robertson, 1977. — 252p : ill(some col) ; 23x26cm.
ISBN 0-207-95779-7 : £10.95
(B77-27308)

797.1'4 — Yachts. Racing. Financial Times Clipper Race, 1975-1976
Beilby, Alec. To beat the clippers : the 'Financial Times' Clipper Race, 1975-6 / [by] Alec Beilby. — London : Allen Lane, 1976. — xix,212p,[8]p of plates : ill(some col), map, ports ; 24cm.
Maps on lining papers.
ISBN 0-7139-0967-6 : £6.95
(B77-03726)

797.1'4 — Yachts. Racing. Rules: International Yacht Racing Union. Yacht racing rules, 1977-1980. *Texts with commentaries*
Twiname, Eric. The rules book : the 1977-80 Yacht Racing Rules explained / [by] Eric Twiname. — London [etc.] : Coles, 1977. — [6] ,122p : ill ; 19cm.
Includes the text of the rules, Parts I, IV, V, VI and appendices 2, 3 and 6.
ISBN 0-229-11577-2 Pbk : £2.50
(B77-30550)

797.1'4 — Yachts. Racing. Schooners: Westward (Ship), to 1947
Hamilton-Adams, C P. The racing schooner 'Westward' / [by] C.P. Hamilton-Adams. — London : Stanford Maritime, 1976. — 109p : ill, plans, ports ; 21x27cm.
ISBN 0-540-07155-2 : £4.95
(B77-14362)

797.1'4'0924 — Yachts. Racing. Royal Western/Observer Singlehanded Transatlantic Race, 1976. *Personal observations*
Francis, Clare. Come hell or high water / [by] Clare Francis. — London : Pelham, 1977. — 198p,[16]p of plates : ill, 2 maps, ports ; 22cm.
ISBN 0-7207-0985-7 : £4.25
(B77-08009)

Francis, Clare. Come hell or high water / [by] Clare Francis. — London : Sphere, 1977. — 199p,[8]p of plates : ill, maps, ports ; 18cm.
Originally published: London : Pelham, 1977.
ISBN 0-7221-3641-2 Pbk : £0.95
(B77-22781)

Woods, Stuart. Blue water, green skipper / [by] Stuart Woods. — London : Stanford Maritime, 1977. — 190p : ill, map, plans, ports ; 24cm.
ISBN 0-540-07168-4 : £4.95
(B77-22067)

797.1'4'0924 — Yachts. Racing. Royal Western/Observer Singlehanded Transatlantic Race, 1976. Trimarans: FT (ship). *Personal observations*
Palmer, David. The Atlantic challenge : the story of trimaran FT / [by] David Palmer. — London [etc.] : Hollis and Carter, 1977. — 187p,[12]p of plates : ill, charts, plans, ports ; 23cm.
Charts on lining papers.
ISBN 0-370-30031-9 : £4.95
(B77-34003)

797.1'73 — Water skiing. *Manuals*
Water skiing. — Wakefield : EP Publishing, 1977. — 35,[1]p : ill, ports ; 14x21cm. — (Know the game)
'Produced in collaboration with the British Water Ski Federation' - cover. — Bibl.: p.35.
ISBN 0-7158-0496-0 Sd : £0.50
(B77-30551)

797.2 — SWIMMING AND DIVING
797.2'1 — Competitive swimming. *Manuals*
Haller, David. Swimming / [by] David Haller. — London : Pelham, 1977. — 61p : ill, ports ; 26cm. — (Pelham pictorial sports instruction series)
ISBN 0-7207-0954-7 : £2.95
(B77-14363)

797.2'1 — Long-distance swimming, to 1976
Campbell, Gail. Marathon : the world of the long-distance athlete / [by] Gail Campbell. — New York : Sterling [etc.] ; London : Distributed by Ward Lock, 1977. — 176p : ill, maps, ports ; 27cm.
Index.
ISBN 0-7061-2551-7 : £4.95
Also classified at 796.4'26; 796.6
(B77-31384)

797.2'1 — Swimming
Gallagher, Harry. Harry Gallagher on swimming. — Revised ed. — London : Pelham, 1976. — 231p,fold leaf,[4]p of plates : ill ; 23cm.
Previous ed.: 1970. — Index.
£4.25
ISBN 0-7207-0335-2
(B77-25827)

797.2'1 — Swimming. *Manuals*
Hogg, John Mervyn. Success in swimming / [by] John Hogg. — London : J. Murray, 1977. — 96p : ill ; 23cm. — (Success sportsbooks)
ISBN 0-7195-3376-7 : £2.50
(B77-18946)

Spitz, Mark. The Mark Spitz complete book of swimming / [by] Mark Spitz and Alan LeMond ; photographs by Neil Leifer. — London : Pelham, 1977. — [8],182p : ill, ports ; 26cm.
Originally published: New York : Crowell, 1976. — Index.
ISBN 0-7207-0969-5 : £5.75
(B77-19586)

Wilkie, David, *b.1954.* Winning with Wilkie : a guide to better swimming / [by] David Wilkie ; with Athole Still. — London : Paul, 1977. — 95p : ill, ports ; 25cm.
'Based on the Scottish Television series'.
ISBN 0-09-129550-5 : £3.25
(B77-17697)

Wilson, Charlie. Swimming : learning, training, competing / [by] Charlie Wilson ; drawings by J. Arbeau. — London : Chancerel : Barrie and Jenkins, 1977. — 2-91p : chiefly ill, ports ; 21cm. — (Action books)
Ill. on lining papers.
ISBN 0-905703-06-5 : £1.75
(B77-23643)

797.21 — Swimming. *Manuals. For parents*
Hoyle, Julie. Swimming for the family / [by] Julie Hoyle. — Guildford : Lutterworth Press : Richard Smart Publishing, 1977. — 72p : ill, ports ; 21cm. — (Leisure series)
ISBN 0-7188-7010-7 Pbk : £1.95
(B77-29625)

797.2'1 — Swimming. Crawl sprinting
Gallagher, Harry. Sprint the crawl / [by] Harry Gallagher ; with a special chapter on US sprint performances by Buck Dawson. — London : Pelham, 1976. — 158p : ill, ports ; 23cm.
Index.
ISBN 0-7207-0905-9 : £4.95
(B77-01750)

797.2'1'07 — Babies. Swimming. Teaching. *For parents*
Timmermans, Claire. How to teach your baby to swim / [by] Claire Timmermans. — London : Heinemann, 1977. — 159p : ill, ports ; 23cm.
Originally published: New York : Stein and Day, 1975.
ISBN 0-434-78000-6 Pbk : £2.50
(B77-32808)

797.2'1'0924 — Swimming. Wilkie, David, b.1954. *Great Britain. Autobiographies*
Wilkie, David, *b.1954.* David Wilkie / with Pat Besford, Tommy Long. — London : Kemps, 1976. — 180p,[32]p of plates : ill, ports ; 23cm.
Spine title: Wilkie.
ISBN 0-905255-22-4 : £3.50
(B77-08513)

797.2'3 — Recreations: Underwater diving. *Manuals*
British Sub-Aqua Club. The British Sub Aqua Club diving manual : a comprehensive guide to the techniques of underwater swimming. — 9th ed. / edited by Leo Zanelli. — [London] ([Club Administrative Agent, 25 Orchard Rd, Kingston-upon-Thames, Surrey]) : The Club, 1976. — 506p : ill, charts, forms, map ; 22cm.
Previous ed.: 1975. — Bibl.: p.478-482. — Index. — Previous control number ISBN 0-902988-14-x.
£3.75
ISBN 0-902988-14-x
(B77-03727)

797.2'3 — Recreations: Underwater diving. *Manuals. For instructors*
Hazzard, Jeremy. Diving officers' handbook. — 5th ed. / compiled by Jeremy Hazzard ; and based on the earlier works of George F. Brookes and George T. Skuse ; foreword by Mike Todd. — London (70 Brompton Rd, SW3 1HA) : British Sub-Aqua Club, 1976. — 84p in various pagings : ill, forms ; 30cm.
Previous ed.: / by George F. Brookes ; revised by George T. Skuse. 1973. — Index. — Previous control number B7707543.
ISBN 0-902988-14-x Pbk : Unpriced
(B77-07543)

797.2'3 — Skin diving & snorkelling. *Manuals*
Dobbs, Horace. Snorkelling and skindiving : an introduction / [by] Horace E. Dobbs. — Oxford : Oxford Illustrated Press, 1976. — 96p : ill, ports ; 26cm.
ISBN 0-902280-37-6 : £2.95
(B77-14364)

797.2'3 — Underwater swimming & diving. *Manuals*
Brookes, George Frederick. Underwater swimming / by George F. Brookes and Robert B. Matkin ; in collaboration with the British Sub-Aqua Club. — Revised ed. — Wakefield : EP Publishing, 1976. — 41,[1]p : ill(some col) ; 14x21cm. — (Know the game)
Previous ed.: i.e. New ed., 1974.
Sd : £0.45
ISBN 0-7158-0204-6
(B77-28822)

Marcante, Duilio. This is sport - diving technique : a handbook for beginners / [by] Duilio Marcante ; [translated from the Italian by Ann Levi]. — Lymington : Nautical Publishing Co., 1977. — ii-viii,144p : ill(chiefly col) ; 21cm.
Index.
ISBN 0-245-52862-8 : £5.85
(B77-28026)

797.2'3'09711 — Recreations: Underwater diving. Sites. *British Columbia. Coastal waters. Practical information*
Pratt-Johnson, Betty. 141 dives in the protected waters of Washington and British Columbia / [by] Betty Pratt-Johnson. — Vancouver ; London (42 New Broad St., EC2M 1QY) : Gordon Soules Economic and Marketing Research [etc.], 1976. — 394p : ill, charts, maps, port ; 22cm.
Index.
ISBN 0-919574-10-6 Pbk : £5.95
Also classified at 797.2'3'09797
(B77-31385)

797.2'3'09797 — Recreations: Underwater diving. Sites. *Washington (State). Coastal waters. Practical information*
Pratt-Johnson, Betty. 141 dives in the protected waters of Washington and British Columbia / [by] Betty Pratt-Johnson. — Vancouver ; London (42 New Broad St., EC2M 1QY) : Gordon Soules Economic and Marketing Research [etc.], 1976. — 394p : ill, charts, maps, port ; 22cm.
Index.
ISBN 0-919574-10-6 Pbk : £5.95
Primary classification 797.2'3'09711
(B77-31385)

797.5 — AIR SPORTS
797.5'5 — Recreations: Gliding. *Manuals*
Scull, Bill. Gliding and soaring / [by] Bill Scull. — London : Pelham, 1977. — 64p : ill ; 26cm. — (Pelham pictorial sports instruction series)
Bibl.: p.64.
ISBN 0-7207-0934-2 : £3.20
(B77-16549)

797.5'5 — Recreations: Hang gliding. *Great Britain. Conference proceedings*
Hang Gliding Seminar, *Queen Elizabeth Country Park, 1976.* Hang gliding : some problems and possible solutions : a report of a seminar held in October 1976. — [Reading] ([Watlington House, Watlington St., Reading RG1 4RJ]) : Sports Council, Southern Region, [1976]. — [4], 38p ; 30cm.
'Hang Gliding Seminar - Queen Elizabeth Country Park, Hampshire, October 16th 1976' - p.[4].
ISBN 0-900979-51-8 Sd : £1.00
(B77-13814)

797.5'5 — Recreations: Hang gliding. *Manuals*
Mackay, Bob. Hang gliding / by Bob Mackay. — 2nd ed. — Gloucester : Thornhill Press, 1976. — 32p : ill ; 19cm. — (A Thornhill guide ; 6)
'Official rules of the British Hang Gliding Association', folder ([4]p) as insert. — Previous ed.: 1976.
ISBN 0-904110-41-9 Sd : £0.50
(B77-07544)

Welch, Ann. Hang glider pilot / [by] Ann Welch & Gerry Breen. — London : J. Murray, 1977. — 128p : ill, chart ; 19cm.
Index.
ISBN 0-7195-3377-5 Pbk : £2.75
(B77-20520)

797.5'5 — Recreations: Tow launched hang gliding. *Manuals*
Poynter, Dan. Manned kiting : the basic handbook of tow launched hang gliding / by Dan Poynter. — Santa Barbara : The author ; Leicester (249 Knighton Church Rd, Leicester) : [Distributed by] Cordee Publishing, 1975. — 101p : ill, facsims, plans ; 23cm.
Originally published: 1974.
ISBN 0-915516-04-7 Pbk : £3.00
(B77-13815)

798 — EQUESTRIAN SPORTS AND ANIMAL RACING
798'.05 — Equestrian sports. *Annuals. Juvenile literature*
Pony Club. The Pony Club annual. — Maidenhead : Purnell.
1978 / edited by Genevieve Murphy. — 1977. — 3-94p : ill, ports ; 29cm.
With answers. — Ill. on lining papers.
ISBN 0-361-03904-2 : £1.75
(B77-32106)

'Pony' magazine annual. — Maidenhead : Purnell.
1978 / edited by Michael Williams. — 1977. — 3-78p : ill, ports ; 27cm.
Ill. on lining papers.
ISBN 0-361-03899-2 : £1.50
ISSN 0305-1234
(B77-32809)

798'.09'04 — Equestrian sports, ca 1900-1975
Churchill, Peter, *b.1933.* The sporting horse / [by] Peter Churchill. — London [etc.] : Marshall Cavendish, 1976. — 120p : ill(some col), col plan, ports(some col) ; 29cm.
Ill. on lining paper. — Index.
ISBN 0-85685-139-6 : £2.50
(B77-13816)

798.2 — HORSEMANSHIP
798'.2 — Horsemanship. *Manuals. Juvenile literature*
Bowes-Lyon, Sarah. Horsemanship as it is today / by Sarah Bowes-Lyon. — London : Dent, 1977. — [16],94p,[5]leaves of plates : ill(chiefly col) ; 25cm.
Facsimile reprint of: 1st ed. 1933.
ISBN 0-460-06826-1 : £5.50
(B77-28027)

798'.2'06241 — Livestock: Ponies. Horsemanship. Organisations. *Great Britain. Pony Club, to 1975*
Webber, Toni. The Pony Club : past and present / by Toni Webber. — London : Luscombe, 1976. — 168p,[20]p of plates : ill, ports ; 25cm.
Index.
ISBN 0-86002-049-5 : £4.95
(B77-01751)

798'.2'0924 — Horsemanship. *Personal observations*
Dickens, Monica. Talking horses / [by] Monica Dickens ; text illustrations by Margery Gill. — London : Pan Books, 1977. — 140p : ill ; 20cm. — (Piccolo)
Originally published: London : Heinemann, 1973.
ISBN 0-330-25114-7 Pbk : £0.50
(B77-21370)

798'.2'094 — Horsemanship. *Western Europe*
Kidd, Jane. Horsemanship in Europe / [by] Jane Kidd ; foreword by Sir Mike Ansell. — London : J.A. Allen, 1977. — 224p,[16]p of plates : ill, ports ; 23cm.
Index.
ISBN 0-85131-243-8 : £4.95 : CIP rev.
(B77-13817)

798'.23 — Horsemanship: Dressage. *Manuals*
De Kunffy, Charles. Creative horsemanship / [by] Charles de Kunffy. — South Brunswick ; New York : Barnes ; London : Yoseloff, 1975. — 224p : ill, ports ; 26cm.
Bibl.: p.8-12. — Index.
ISBN 0-498-01386-3 : £4.00
(B77-29626)

798'.23 — Livestock: Horses. Riding. *Manuals*
Blixen-Finecke, Hans von, *baron.* The art of riding / [by] Hans von Blixen-Finecke. — London : J.A. Allen, 1977. — 120p : ill ; 21cm.
ISBN 0-85131-253-5 Pbk : £1.75
(B77-16550)

Pullein-Thompson, Josephine. Ride better and better / [by] Josephine Pullein-Thompson ; illustrated by Priscilla Goodfield. — Leicester : Knight Books, 1977. — [6],122p : ill ; 18cm.
Originally published: Glasgow : Blackie, 1974.
ISBN 0-340-20078-2 Pbk : £0.60
(B77-32107)

798'.23 — Livestock: Horses. Riding. *Manuals. Juvenile literature*
Owen, Robert, *b.1918.* Riding and schooling / [by] Robert Owen and John Bullock ; illustrated by James Val and Peter Kesteven. — London [etc.] : Beaver Books, 1977. — 77p,[8]p of plates : ill ; 20cm. — (Young riders guides)
ISBN 0-600-37582-x Pbk : £0.55
(B77-31387)

Owen, Robert, *b.1918.* The young rider / [by] Robert Owen & John Bullock. — Feltham : Country Life Books, 1977. — 144p : ill(some col) ; 26cm.
ISBN 0-600-39527-8 : £2.95
(B77-28823)

Pullein-Thompson, Christine. Good riding / [by] Christine Pullein-Thompson ; illustrated by Christine Bousfield. — London : Severn House : [Distributed by Hutchinson], 1977. — 126p : ill ; 21cm.
Originally published: London : Armada Books, 1975.
ISBN 0-7278-0259-3 : £2.75
(B77-13211)

798'.23 — National parks. *South Wales. Brecon Beacons National Park. Pony trekking. Practical information*
Brecon Beacons National Park Committee. Pony trekking / [Brecon Beacons National Park Committee]. — [Brecon] ([Glamorgan St., Brecon, Powys]) : The Committee, 1977. — Folder([6]p) ; 21cm. — (Information sheet ; no.10)
£0.03
(B77-18330)

798'.23'0222 — Livestock: Horses. Riding. *Manuals. Illustrations*
Herbert, Ivor. Come riding / by Ivor Herbert ; drawings by George Stokes. — Paris : Chancerel ; Leicester (Euston St., Freeman's Common, Aylestone Rd, Leicester LE2 7SS) : [Distributed by] WHS Distributors, 1975. — 96p : chiefly ill, ports ; 17x23cm. — (Learn through strips)
'These strips were first published in the London Evening News' - note.
Pbk : £0.95
ISBN 2-85429-014-3
(B77-20521)

798'.23'05 — Livestock: Horses. Riding. *Yearbooks*
Embassy horse and rider yearbook. — London : Macdonald and Jane's.
1977 / edited by Pamela Macgregor-Morris & Alan Smith. — 1977. — 288p : ill, map, ports ; 21cm.
Spine title: Horse and rider yearbook 1977. — Previously published: as 'W.D. & H.O. Wills horse and rider yearbook'.
ISBN 0-354-09005-4 Pbk : £3.25
ISSN 0305-621x
(B77-16551)

798'.23'07 — Livestock: Horses. Riding by children. Teaching. *Manuals*
Roberts, Pamela. Teaching the child rider : some practical notes for parents and trainee instructors / by Pamela Roberts. — London : J.A. Allen, 1976. — 102p,leaf of plate,[16]p of plates : ill ; 21cm.
Originally published: 1968.
Pbk : £1.30
ISBN 0-85131-195-4
(B77-03728)

798'.24 — Eventing
Beale, Jeremy J. Eventing in focus / text and commentary by Jeremy J. Beale ; photographs by Alix Coleman. — London [etc.] : Angus and Robertson, 1976. — 160p,[8]p of plates : ill(some col), ports(some col) ; 29cm.
Ill. on lining papers. — Also published: Philadelphia : Lippincott, 1976.
ISBN 0-207-95727-4 : £6.80
(B77-01752)

Campbell, Judith. Eventing / [by] Judith Campbell ; photographs by Srdja Djukanovic. — London : Barker, 1976. — xi,116p,[24]p of plates : ill, ports ; 26cm.
ISBN 0-213-16613-5 : £3.95
(B77-00362)

798'.24 — Horse shows. *Manuals*
Baker, Jennifer. The horse show / by Jennifer Baker ; with photographs by Leslie Lane. — London [etc.] : Allen and Unwin, 1977. — 3-111p : ill ; 21cm.
Index.
ISBN 0-04-798001-x : £2.95
(B77-30552)

Spooner, Glenda. The handbook of showing : basic conformation, defects, unsoundness, breeds, types, horse and pony societies, breeding, showing in hand and under saddle, judges and judging, and a complete guide to show organization / [by] Glenda Spooner. — Revised [ed.]. — London : J.A. Allen, 1977. — 264p,[24]p of plates : ill, forms ; 22cm.
Previous ed.: London : Museum Press, 1968. — Bibl.: p.260. — Index.
ISBN 0-85131-240-3 Pbk : Unpriced
(B77-18947)

798'.24 — Riding exhibitions: Dressage. *Manuals*
Green, Carol. Dressage explained : a horseman's handbook / [by] Carol Green. — London : Ward Lock, 1977. — 96p : ill(some col), ports ; 20cm. — (Concorde books)
Originally published: Tunbridge Wells : Midas Books, 1974.
ISBN 0-7063-5393-5 Pbk : £1.50
(B77-21230)

Podhajsky, Alois. The art of dressage : basic principles of riding and judging / [by] Alois Podhajsky ; translated [from the German] by Eva Podhajsky ; with 28 photographs of the medalists at the Olympic Games dressage tests 1912 to 1972 by Werner Menzendorf and others. — London : Harrap, 1976. — [7],184p, [16]p of plates : forms, ports ; 23cm.
This translation also published: Garden City, N.Y. : Doubleday, 1976. — Translation of: 'Reiten und Richten im Enfahrungen und Vorschläge'. München : Nymphenburger, 1974. — Index.
ISBN 0-245-53027-4 : £4.25
(B77-00818)

798'.24 — Three-day eventing
Silver, Caroline. Eventing : the book of the three-day event / text by Caroline Silver ; photographs by Akhtar Hussein ; adviser Lucinda Prior-Palmer. — London : Collins, 1976. — 176p : ill(some col), map, ports(some col) ; 30cm.
Index.
ISBN 0-00-216780-8 : £6.95
(B77-00363)

798'.24'0942185 — Horse shows: Horse of the Year Show. *London. Brent (London Borough), to 1975*
Williams, Dorian. Horse of the Year : the story of a unique horse show / [by] Dorian Williams. — Newton Abbot [etc.] : David and Charles, 1976. — 168p : ill(some col), ports(some col) ; 24cm.
Index.
ISBN 0-7153-7258-0 : £3.95
(B77-03729)

798'.25 — Show jumping. *Manuals*
Dawes, Alison. Showjumping for horses & riders / [by] Alison Dawes ; foreword by Sir Michael Ansell. — Maidenhead : Sampson Low, 1977. — 152p : ill(some col), ports(some col) ; 29cm.
Index.
ISBN 0-562-00036-4 : £4.95
(B77-14365)

798'.25'0924 — Show jumping. Smith, Harvey. *Autobiographies*
Smith, Harvey. Harvey / [by] Harvey Smith ; with Victor Green. — London [etc.] : White Lion Publishers, 1977. — 160p,[8]p of plates : ill, ports ; 21cm.
Originally published: London : Arrow Books, 1976. — Index.
ISBN 0-7274-0305-2 : £3.75
(B77-20522)

798'.25'0924 — Showjumping. Schockemöhle, Alwin. *Autobiographies*
Schockemöhle, Alwin. Alwin Schockemöhle / [by] Alwin Schockemöhle ; with Ulrich Kaiser ; translated [from the German] by Stella and Vernon Humphries ; foreword by David Broome. — London [etc.] : Angus and Robertson, 1977. — 176p : ill(some col), ports ; 25cm.
Originally published: in German. Munich : Copress-Verlag, 1976.
ISBN 0-207-95774-6 : £4.95
(B77-28029)

798.4 — HORSE RACING
798'.4'00941 — Racehorses. Racing. *Great Britain*
Campbell, Barry. Horse racing in Britain / [by] Barry Campbell. — London : Joseph, 1977. — 348p,[12]p of plates : ill, maps, plan, ports ; 23cm.
Bibl.: p.339-340. — Index.
ISBN 0-7181-1427-2 : £7.50
(B77-08010)

798'.4'00941 — Racehorses. Racing. *Great Britain. Yearbooks*
Directory of the turf. — London ([59 High St., Ascot, Berks. SL5 7HP]) : Stud and Stable Ltd.

1973 / edited by Peter Towers-Clark and Michael Ross. — [1973]. — [3],viii,727,[20]p : ill, maps ; 26cm.
Index.
£5.50
(B77-19587)

1976 / edited by Peter Towers-Clark and Michael Ross. — [1976]. — [3],viii,694,[20]p : ill, maps ; 26cm.
Index.
£11.00
(B77-19588)

Horse racing. — London : Macdonald and Jane's [for the William Hill Organization].
1977 / edited by Tom Cosgrove. — 1977. — 224p : ill, ports ; 22cm.
Continues: William Hill racing year book.
ISBN 0-354-09016-x Pbk : £3.95
ISSN 0309-6769
(B77-17698)

Ruff's guide to the turf and the 'Sporting life' annual. — London : 'Sporting life'.
1977 / edited by Julian Simcocks. — [1977]. — iii-xxii,500p : ill, ports ; 21cm.
£8.50
(B77-17041)

798'.401 — Racehorses. Racing. Bookmaking
Sidney, Charles. The art of legging / [by] Charles Sidney. — London (c/o Hazell Watson and Viney Ltd, Aylesbury, Bucks) : Maxline International, 1976. — xi,227p,[12]p of plates : ill, ports ; 23cm.
Bibl.: p.220-221. — Index.
ISBN 0-905861-00-0 : £7.00
(B77-05008)

798'.401 — Racehorses. Racing. Totalisator betting. Organisations. *Great Britain. Horserace Totalisator Board. Inquiry reports*
Great Britain. *Parliament. House of Commons. Select Committee on Nationalised Industries.* The Horserace Totalisator Board : second report from the Select Committee on Nationalised Industries, session 1976-77, report, together with minutes of proceedings of the Committee, minutes of evidence and appendices. — London : H.M.S.O., [1977]. — lx,166p ; 25cm. — ([1976-77 H.C.]344)
ISBN 0-10-234477-9 Pbk : £4.60
(B77-23644)

798'.43 — Flat racing racehorses: Bustino & Grundy. *Great Britain*
Hawkins, Christopher. The race of the century : Grundy and Bustino at Ascot / [by] Christopher Hawkins. — London : Allen and Unwin, 1976. — 159p,[12]p of plates : ill, facsim, ports ; 23cm.
ISBN 0-04-796046-9 : £3.95
(B77-00364)

798'.43'0924 — Flat racing. Jockeys: Longden, Johnny. *Biographies*
Beckwith, Brainerd Kellogg. The Longden legend / [by] B.K. Beckwith. — South Brunswick [etc.] : A.S. Barnes ; London : Yoseloff, 1973. — 235p : ill, ports ; 27cm.
Index.
ISBN 0-498-01242-5 : £4.00
(B77-18948)

798'.43'0941 — Flat racing racehorses. *Great Britain. Performance records. Serials*
Racehorses. — Halifax : Portway Press.
1976 / [compiled and produced under the direction of Phil Bull and Reg Griffin by members of the Timeform Organization]. — 1977. — [1],989p : ill ; 19cm. — (A 'Timeform' publication)
ISBN 0-900599-22-7 : £15.00
(B77-32108)

798'.45 — Point-to-point horses. *Great Britain. Lists. Serials*
'Horse and hound' hunter chasers and point-to-pointers. — London : IPC Magazines.
1977 / edited and compiled by Geoffrey Sale and Iain Mackenzie. — 1977. — 494p : ill ; 18cm.
Previously published: as 'Hunter chasers and point-to-pointers'.
ISBN 0-85037-320-4 : £4.95
(B77-04370)

The **'Pointer'** point-to-point handbook. — Lymm (Cinema Buildings, Lymm, Cheshire WA13 0QQ) : 'The Pointer'.
1977 / compiled by David Coulton. — 1977. — 3-288p ; 15cm.
Folder ([6]p.) as insert. — Index.
ISBN 0-901188-06-9 Pbk : £2.80
(B77-09202)

798'.45 — Steeplechasing horses: Red Rum
Herbert, Ivor. Red Rum / [by] Ivor Herbert. — [New ed.]. — London : Arrow Books, 1977. — 334p,[16]p of plates : ill, ports ; 18cm.
Previous ed.: London : Luscombe : Mitchell Beazley, 1974.
ISBN 0-09-914760-2 Pbk : £0.95
(B77-16552)

798'.45'0924 — National Hunt racing. Jockeys: Fletcher, Brian. *Great Britain. Autobiographies*
Fletcher, Brian. My rum life / [by] Brian Fletcher ; edited by Michael Litchfield. — Kettering (72 St Peter's Ave., Kettering, Northants NN16 0HB) : Viking Books, 1977. — 158p ; 18cm.
Index.
ISBN 0-905862-00-7 Pbk : £0.85
(B77-23645)

798'.45'0941 — National Hunt racehorses. *Great Britain. Performance records. Serials*
Chasers & hurdlers. — Halifax : Portway Press. — (Timeform. Publications)
1975-76 / [compiled and produced by D.P. Adams et al.]. — 1976. — 676p : ill ; 19cm.
Text, ill. on lining papers.
ISBN 0-900599-23-5 : £12.50
(B77-03188)

798.6 — DRIVING AND COACHING
798'.6 — Livestock: Horses. Driving. *Manuals*
Walrond, Sallie. A guide to driving horses / [by] Sallie Walrond. — London : Pelham, 1977. — [7],136p,[12]p of plates : ill, ports ; 21cm. — (Pelham horsemaster series)
Originally published: London : Nelson, 1971. — Index.
ISBN 0-7207-1009-x : £4.25
(B77-23646)

798.8 — RACING ANIMALS OTHER THAN HORSES
798'.8 — Racing pigeons. Racing. *Yearbooks*
'Homing world' stud book. — Cheltenham (The Reddings, Cheltenham, Glos. GL51 6RN) : Royal Pigeon Racing Association.
1977 : 15th olympiad ed. — [1977]. — 416p : ill, forms, ports ; 20cm.
ISBN 0-900204-08-7 Pbk : £1.40
Primary classification 636.5'96
(B77-10427)

799 — FIELD SPORTS
799'.06'241 — Field sports. Organisations. *Great Britain. British Field Sports Society. Periodicals*
British Field Sports Society. BFSS news bulletin. — London (26 Caxton St., SW1H 0RG) : The Society.
[No.1]- ; 1974-. — [1974]-. — 30cm.
Published at irregular intervals. — Folder ([4]p.) as issue for Jan. 1976.
Unpriced
(B77-16011)

799'.0941 — Blood sports. *Great Britain*
Page, Robin. The hunter and the hunted : a countryman's view of blood sports / [by] Robin Page. — London : Davis-Poynter, 1977. — 243p,[8]p of plates : ill ; 23cm.
Bibl.: p.241-243.
ISBN 0-7067-0203-4 : £5.00
(B77-10510)

799.1 — RECREATIONS. FISHING
799.1'092'4 — Angling. *Australia. Personal observations*
McCristal, Vic. The rivers & the sea / by Vic McCristal. — Sydney [etc.] ; London : A.H. and A.W. Reed, 1974. — 175p,[8]p of plates : ill(some col), ports(1 col) ; 25cm.
ISBN 0-589-07124-6 : £6.90
(B77-19589)

799.1'09415 — Recreations: Fishing. *Ireland. Periodicals*
Fishing Ireland. — Dublin (Reprographis Ltd, Greenhills Industrial Estate, Walkinstown, Dublin 12) : Repro Publications.
July 1977-. — 1977-. — ill, maps, ports ; 30cm.

Monthly. — 32p. in 1st issue.
Sd : £0.40
ISSN 0332-074x
(B77-32109)

799.1'1'09427 — Freshwater angling. *Northern England. Practical information*
Northern anglers' handbook. — 14th ed. / [compiled by Edward Hinchliffe]. — Clapham, N. Yorkshire : Dalesman, 1976. — 152p : ill ; 14cm.
Previous ed.: / compiled by Bill Peyton. 1974. — Index.
ISBN 0-85206-329-6 Pbk : £0.60
(B77-03189)

799.1'1'09429 — Natural resources: Water. Reservoirs. Angling. *Wales. Practical information*
Welsh National Water Development Authority. Reservoir fishing in Wales / [Welsh National Water Development Authority]. — Brecon (Cambrian Way, Brecon, Powys) : The Authority, [1977]. — Fold sheet : 1 ill, maps ; 42x60cm fold to 21x10cm.
ISBN 0-86097-014-0 : £0.15
(B77-16553)

799.1'1'094292 — Freshwater angling. *Gwynedd. Practical information*
Welsh National Water Development Authority. *Gwynedd River Division.* A guide to fishing in the Welsh National Water Development Authority, Gwynedd River Division / [Welsh National Water Development Authority, Gwynedd River Division]. — Caernarfon (Highfield, Caernarfon, Gwynedd LL55 1HR) : The Division, 1976. — 19p in various pagings ; 30cm.
Sd : Unpriced
(B77-21372)

799.1'1'094293 — Freshwater angling. *Clwyd. Practical information*
Welsh National Water Development Authority. *Dee and Clwyd River Division.* A guide to angling facilities in the area / Welsh National Water Development Authority, Dee & Clwyd River Division. — Chester (2 Vicar's La., Chester) : The Division, 1976. — [1],54p : ill, maps ; 22cm.
ISBN 0-86097-006-x Sd : Unpriced
(B77-10894)

799.1'2 — Angling. Knots & rigs. *Manuals*
Lewers, Dick. Fishing knots & rigs / [by] Dick Lewers ; with line illustrations by the author. — Revised and enlarged [ed.]. — Sydney [etc.] ; London : A.H. and A.W. Reed, 1976. — 70p : ill ; 19cm.
This ed. originally published: 1972.
ISBN 0-589-07127-0 Pbk : £1.65
(B77-25828)

799.1'2 — Big game fish. Angling. *Africa & Europe. Coastal regions. Manuals*
Goddard, John. Big fish from salt water : a guide to tackle, techniques and species in British, European and African waters / [by] John Goddard, with contributions by Leslie Moncrieff and Mike Millman. — London [etc.] : E. Benn, 1977. — xi,244p : ill, ports ; 25cm.
Bibl.: p.238. — Index.
ISBN 0-510-22504-7 : £9.50
(B77-22068)

799.1'2 — Coarse fish. Angling. *Manuals*
Bartles, Bill. Coarse fishing / [by] Bill Bartles. — London : A. and C. Black, 1977. — 96p : ill, facsim ; 22cm. — (Black's picture sports)
Bibl.: p.90.
ISBN 0-7136-1741-1 : £1.95 : CIP rev.
(B77-17699)

Graham, Colin, *b.1929.* Coarse fishing for beginners / [by] Colin Graham. — Revised ed. — London : Macdonald and Jane's, 1977. — [9],139p,[8]p of plates : ill, ports ; 23cm.
Previous ed.: London : Queen Anne Press, 1974. — Bibl.: p.138-139.
ISBN 0-354-08503-4 : £3.95
(B77-15430)

Successful angling : coarse fishing tackle and methods / [by] Richard Walker ... [et al.]. — London : Paul, 1977. — 152p : ill, ports ; 23cm.
Bibl.: p.145-146. — Index.
ISBN 0-09-129280-8 : £3.95
ISBN 0-09-129281-6 Pbk : £2.25
(B77-28031)

799.1'2 — Coarse fish. Angling. Baits. *Encyclopaedias*
Graham, Colin, *b.1929.* The new encyclopaedia of coarse fishing baits / [by] Colin Graham. — New ed. — London : Macdonald and Jane's, 1977. — [5],151p,[8]p of plates : ill, 2 ports ; 23cm.
Previous ed.: London : Queen Anne Press, 1974.
ISBN 0-354-08502-6 : £3.95
(B77-16012)

799.1'2 — Coarse fish. Angling. Matches. *England. Manuals*
Ashurst, Kevin. World class match fishing / [by] Kevin Ashurst. — London : Cassell, 1977. — viii,152p : ill ; 21cm. — ([Modern angling series])
Index.
ISBN 0-304-29729-1 : £3.50
(B77-19590)

799.1'2 — Float fishing
Lane, Billy. Float fishing : tackle and techniques for still and running water / [by] Billy Lane ; foreword by Colin Graham. — London : Cassell, 1976. — [6],117p : ill, port ; 21cm. — ([Modern angling series])
Index.
ISBN 0-304-29466-7 : £3.25
(B77-09883)

799.1'2 — Fly fishing. *Manuals*
The **complete** fly-fisher / edited by C.F. Walker. — 2nd ed. — London : Barrie and Jenkins, 1976. — 304p,[36]p of plates : ill(some col), maps ; 24cm. — ([The angler's library])
This ed. originally published: London : Jenkins, 1969. — Index.
£5.50
ISBN 0-257-65718-4
(B77-29628)

The **essence** of fly fishing / [by] Donald Downs ... [et al.]. — Winchester : Shurlock, 1976. — 128p,[4]p of plates : ill(some col) ; 19cm.
Index.
ISBN 0-903330-25-3 Pbk : £1.50
(B77-08011)

799.1'2 — Fly-fishing. Flies. Scotcher, George. Fly fisher's legacy. *Critical studies*
Heddon, Jack. Scotcher notes : bibliographical, biographical and historical notes to George Scotcher's 'Fly fisher's legacy - ', circa 1810, with comments on the fly-dressings / [by] Jack Heddon ; [illustrated by John Simpson]. — London (4 Cawdor Cres., W7 2DD) : Honey Dun Press, 1975. — [6],30p,vi leaves of plates : col ill ; 23cm.
Limited ed. of 165 numbered copies, signed by the author and artist, of which 150 copies are for sale. — Quarter leather. — In box. — Scotcher's black gnat tipped in. — Bibl.: p.7-8.
ISBN 0-904104-02-8 : £25.00
(B77-12035)

799.1'2 — Freshwater angling. *Great Britain. Manuals*
Forbes, David Carl. Rough river and small stream fishing / [by] David Carl Forbes ; with illustrations by the author ; foreword by Donald Downs. — London : Cassell, 1977. — x,150p : ill, ports ; 21cm. — ([Modern angling series])
Index.
ISBN 0-304-29731-3 : £3.50
(B77-20523)

799.1'2 — Freshwater angling. *Manuals. Illustrations*
Mitchell, John, *b.1928.* Fresh water angling / by John Mitchell ; drawings by George Stokes. — Paris : Chancerel ; Leicester (Euston St., Freeman's Common, Aylestone Rd, Leicester LE2 7SS) : [Distributed by] WHS Distributors, 1975. — 96p : chiefly ill, ports ; 17x23cm. — (Learn through strips)
'These strips were first published in the London Evening News' - note.
Pbk : £0.95
ISBN 2-85429-009-7
(B77-20524)

799.1'2 — Marine fish. Angling. *Scotland. Coastal waters. Practical information*
Scotland for sea angling. — Edinburgh : Scottish Tourist Board [for] the Scottish Federation of Sea Anglers.
[1976]. — [1976]. — 77p : maps ; 21cm.
'... the official guide of the Scottish Federation of Sea Anglers ... The material gathered ... is checked by the Scottish Tourist Board' - note.
ISBN 0-85419-110-0 Sd : £0.40
(B77-00365)

799.1'2 — Sea angling. *Great Britain*
Stoker, Hugh. The modern sea angler / by Hugh Stoker ; illustrated with half-tones and line drawings by the author. — 5th ed. — London : Hale, 1977. — 222p,8p of plates : ill, port ; 23cm.
Previous ed.: 1971. — Index.
ISBN 0-7091-6019-4 : £2.95
(B77-26460)

799.1'2 — Sea angling. *Great Britain. Manuals*
Housby, Trevor Raymond. Sea angling around Britain / by Trevor Housby. — London : Barrie and Jenkins, 1977. — 158p : ill, maps ; 19cm. — (The angler's library)
Index.
ISBN 0-214-20259-3 : £2.95
(B77-18331)

Sea angling with the specimen hunters : big-fish tactics of the experts / edited by Hugh Stoker. — London [etc.] : E. Benn, 1977. — 216p : ill, map, ports ; 23cm.
Index.
ISBN 0-510-22899-2 : £4.95
ISBN 0-510-22900-x Pbk : £2.95
(B77-13212)

Wiggin, Maurice. Sea fishing for beginners / [by] Maurice Wiggin ; drawings by W.J. Pezare. — New ed. — London : A. and C. Black, 1977. — 136p : ill ; 20cm.
Previous ed.: London : J. Baker, 1970.
ISBN 0-7136-1734-9 : £2.25
(B77-14366)

799.1'2 — Swing tipping. *Manuals*
Foster, Fred. Fred Foster's swing tipping and other modern techniques / foreword by Colin Graham. — London : Cassell, 1976. — vii, 113p : ill, ports ; 21cm. — ([Modern angling series])
Index.
ISBN 0-304-29467-5 : £3.25
(B77-10511)

799.1'2'05 — Angling. *Serials*
'Angler's mail' annual. — London : IPC Magazines.
1977. — 1976. — 95p : ill(some col), ports ; 28cm. — (A Fleetway annual)
Cover title.
ISBN 0-85037-287-9 : £1.30
(B77-01753)

1978. — 1977. — 95p : ill(some col), ports(some col) ; 18cm. — (A Fleetway annual)
Cover title.
ISBN 0-85037-322-0 : £1.45
(B77-32811)

799.1'2'0941 — Angling. *Great Britain*
Encyclopedia of fishing in the British Isles / edited by Michael Prichard. — Glasgow [etc.] : Collins, 1976. — 256p : ill(chiefly col), col maps, col ports ; 31cm.
Col. ill. on lining papers. — Index.
ISBN 0-00-435017-0 : £4.95
(B77-16013)

799.1'6 — Wreck fishing. *Manuals*
Gammon, Clive. Wreck fishing / [by] Clive Gammon ; colour plates by Keith Linsell. — Reading : Osprey Publishing, 1975. — 48p : ill(some col), ports ; 24cm. — (The Osprey anglers)
ISBN 0-85045-219-8 Pbk : £1.50
(B77-10512)

799.1'6'0941 — Sea fishing. *Great Britain. Amateurs' manuals*
Wrangles, Alan. Sea fishing for fun / [by] Alan Wrangles and Jack P. Tupper. — Newton Abbot [etc.] : David and Charles, 1977. — 127p : ill ; 22cm. — (David & Charles leisure & travel series)
Bibl.: p.125. — Index.
ISBN 0-7153-7362-5 : £1.95
(B77-21373)

799.1'7'31 — Tope. Angling. *Manuals*
Gammon, Clive. Tope / [by] Clive Gammon ; colour plates by Keith Linsell. — Reading : Osprey Publishing, 1975. — 48p : ill(some col), ports ; 24cm. — (The Osprey anglers)
ISBN 0-85045-216-3 Pbk : £1.50
(B77-09884)

799.1'7'52 — Barbel. Angling. *Manuals*
Howcroft, Ian R. Barbel / [by] Ian R. Howcroft ; colour plates by Keith Linsell. — Reading : Osprey Publishing, 1975. — 48p : ill(some col), map, ports ; 24cm. — (The Osprey anglers)
ISBN 0-85045-218-x Pbk : £1.50
(B77-08514)

799.1'7'52 — Chub. Angling. *Manuals*
Seaman, Kenneth. The complete chub angler / by Kenneth Seaman. — Newton Abbot [etc.] : David and Charles, 1976. — 131p : ill ; 23cm.
Bibl.: p.127. — Index.
ISBN 0-7153-7310-2 : £4.50
(B77-10895)

799.1'7'52 — Tench. Angling. *Manuals*
Rickards, Barrie. Fishing for big tench / [by] Barrie Rickards and Ray Webb. — London (323 Upper St., N.1) : Rod and Gun Publishing Ltd, 1976. — 176p : ill, ports ; 22cm.
Bibl.: p.175-176.
ISBN 0-903643-03-0 : £4.50
(B77-03730)

799.1'7'55 — Natural resources: Water. Reservoirs. Trout. Fly fishing
Church, Bob. Reservoir trout fishing / [by] Bob Church. — London : Cassell, 1977. — vi,136p : ill, ports ; 21cm. — ([Modern angling series])
Index.
ISBN 0-304-29698-8 : £3.50
(B77-22070)

799.1'7'55 — Salmon. Angling. *Anthologies*
A portrait of salmon fishing / written and compiled by Geoffrey Nickson. — Rugby (124A Hillmorton Rd, Rugby, Warwickshire CV22 5AN) : Antony Atha, 1976. — 112p : col ill ; 26x31cm.
In slip case. — Quarter leather.
ISBN 0-904475-16-6 : £40.00
(B77-04371)

799.1'7'55 — Trout. Fly fishing
Venables, Bernard. Fishing for trout with Mr Cherry and Jim / by Bernard Venables. — London : E. Benn, 1972. — 32,[1]p : ill ; 18x22cm. — (An 'Angling times' book)
Originally published: Peterborough, Northants. : 'Angling times', 1962.
ISBN 0-510-23241-8 Sd : £0.45
(B77-19591)

799.1'7'55 — Trout. Fly fishing. *Australia*
Massy, Carl. Fly fishing for trout / [by] Carl Massy. — Sydney [etc.] ; London : A.H. and A.W. Reed, 1976. — 174p : ill, col maps on lining papers, ports ; 22cm.
ISBN 0-589-07183-1 : £6.90
(B77-18332)

Northen, R I. Shopping centres : a developer's guide to planning and design / [by] R.I. Northen, M. Haskoll. — Reading : Centre for Advanced Land Use Studies, College of Estate Management, 1977. — [8],89p : ill(some col), maps, plans ; 30cm. — (Planning for people)
ISBN 0-902132-33-4 Pbk : £5.50
(B77-16510)

799.1'7'55 — Trout. Fly fishing. Flies. *New Zealand*
Draper, Keith. Trout flies in New Zealand / by Keith Draper. — Wellington [etc.] ; London : A.H. and A.W. Reed, 1975. — 182,[1]p : ill(some col) ; 22cm.
Originally published: 1971. — Bibl.: p.178.
ISBN 0-589-00655-x : £3.90
(B77-00366)

799.2 — HUNTING
799.2'13 — Game animals. Rough shooting. *Manuals. Humorous texts*
Tickner, John. Tickner's rough shooting / written and illustrated by John Tickner ; with a foreword by John Anderton. — Revised ed. ; including new chapter on training gundogs. — Saul (Saul, Glos.) : The Standfast Press, 1976. — 93p : ill ; 23cm.
Previous ed.: i.e. 1st ed. London : Putnam, 1964.
ISBN 0-904602-02-8 : £2.50
(B77-16554)

799.2'13'0941 — Game animals. Shooting. *Great Britain. Amateurs' manuals*
Smith, Guy Newman. Gamekeeping and shooting for amateurs / by Guy N. Smith. — Liss (Hill Brow, Liss, Hants. GU33 7PU) : The Spur Publications Co., 1976. — viii,166p : ill ; 23cm. — (Field sports library)
ISBN 0-904558-17-7 : £3.90
Also classified at 639'.95'0941
(B77-05588)

799.2'3 — Ferreting. *Manuals*
Plummer, David Brian. Modern ferreting / [by] David Brian Plummer. — Ipswich : Boydell Press, 1977. — 128p : ill ; 23cm.
ISBN 0-85115-083-7 : £4.50
(B77-29629)

799.2'32 — Falconry. *Manuals*
Woodford, Michael. A manual of falconry / by Michael Woodford ; with chapters on rook hawking and game hawking by J.G. Mavrogordato and S.E. Allen ; and a foreword by Lord Portal of Hungerford. — 3rd ed. — London : A. and C. Black, 1977. — xvi,194p, [8]leaves of plates : ill, port ; 23cm.
Previous ed.: 1966. — Index.
ISBN 0-7136-1746-2 : £4.25 : CIP rev.
(B77-13213)

799.2'34 — Hunting with hounds. Hunts. *Directories*
Baily's hunting directory. — London : J.A. Allen.
1976-77 : No.70 : containing details of hunts, including their countries, histories and former Masters of Foxhounds, Harriers, Staghounds, Draghounds, Beagles, Basset Hounds, Otterhounds and Bloodhounds in the United Kingdom and Ireland ; hunts of America, the Commonwealth and Europe ; results of hound shows ; three maps showing boundaries of foxhounds and one of distribution of hare hunts. — 1976. — xxx,416p,[3]fold leaves of plates : ill, maps(chiefly col) ; 23cm.
ISBN 0-85131-251-9 : £6.50
(B77-02531)

799.2'4'0924 — Game birds. Shooting. *Great Britain. Personal observations*
Rawlins, J E F. Bridle & gun : essays of an undistinguished sportsman / by J.E.F. Rawlins. — Old Buckenham (Old Buckenham, Norfolk) : Wildfowl Publications, 1973. — 130p : ill, port ; 23cm.
ISBN 0-903731-01-0 : £2.90
(B77-19592)

799.2'44'028 — Wildfowl. Shooting. Use of decoys
Becker, Adolph Carl. Decoying waterfowl / [by] A.C. Becker, Jr. — South Brunswick [etc.] : Barnes ; London : Yoseloff, 1973. — 247p : ill, ports ; 26cm.
Bibl.: p.242-243. — Index.
ISBN 0-498-01070-8 : £4.50
(B77-20525)

799.2'44'0941 — Wildfowling. *Great Britain*
Marchington, John. The practical wildfowler / [by] John Marchington ; photographs by the author ; drawings by Tom Banks ; with a foreword by Arthur Cadman. — London : A. and C. Black, 1977. — 143p,[4]p of plates : ill ; 25cm.
Bibl.: p.135. — Index.
ISBN 0-7136-1739-x : £5.95 : CIP rev.
(B77-16555)

799.2'5'09415 — Mammals. Hunting. *Ireland. Early works*
Stringer, Arthur. The experienced huntsman / by Arthur Stringer. — [1st ed. reprinted] / edited by James Fairley ; illustrated by Raymond Piper. — Belfast : Blackstaff Press, 1977. — vii, 177p : ill, facsim, map ; 23cm.
Originally published: Belfast : James Blow, 1714. — Bibl.: p.168. — Index.
ISBN 0-85640-103-x : £5.50
(B77-31388)

799.2'59'322 — Hares. Coursing
Coursing : the pursuit of game with gazehounds / [general editor Richard Grant-Rennick]. — Saul (Saul, Glos.) : Standfast Press, [1976]. — [14],303p : ill(some col), ports ; 30cm. — (Standfast sporting library)
Bibl.: p.263-269.
ISBN 0-9502148-9-2 : £15.00
(B77-03190)

799.2'59'322 — Rabbits. Ferreting. *Manuals*
Samuel, Ernest, *b.1890.* Rabbiting and ferreting / by E. Samuel and J. Ivester Lloyd ; photographs by K.H. Purkiss and Oliver Pike. — 7th ed. — London (26 Caxton St., SW1H 0RG) : British Fields Sports Society, 1976. — 67p : ill ; 22cm. — (British Field Sports Society. Booklets)
Previous ed.: 1974.
ISBN 0-903549-09-3 Sd : £0.30
Primary classification 636'.97'4447
(B77-04917)

799.2'59'74442 — Foxes. Hunting. Hunts. *East Anglia. Puckeridge and Newmarket and Thurlow Combined Hunts, to 1976*
Brander, Michael. Portrait of a hunt : the history of the Puckeridge and Newmarket and Thurlow Combined Hunts / [by] Michael Brander. — London : Hutchinson, 1976. — xvi,192p,leaf of plate,[36]p of plates : ill(some col), facsims, ports ; 25cm.
Bibl.: p.186-187. — Index.
ISBN 0-09-127800-7 : £7.50
(B77-28032)

799.2'59'74442 — Foxes. Hunting. Peel, John, b.1776. *Cumbria*
John Peel : the man, the myth and the song : a book to celebrate his bi-centenary / with an introduction by Melvyn Bragg. — Carlisle (12 Lonsdale St., Carlisle, [Cumbria]) : 'Cumbria weekly digest', [1976]. — [2],88p : ill, facsim, geneal tables, music, ports ; 22cm.
ISBN 0-905390-01-6 Sd : £0.60
(B77-04373)

799.2'6'0924 — Big game. Hunting. *New Zealand. South Westland. Personal observations*
Harker, Peter. Hunting with Harker / [by] Peter Harker and Keith Eunson. — Wellington [etc.] ; London : A.H. and A.W. Reed, 1976. — xiii,137p : ill, map, ports ; 26cm.
ISBN 0-589-00950-8 : £5.65
(B77-31389)

799.2'6'0924 — Big game. Hunting. Finch Hatton, Denys. *East Africa. Biographies*
Trzebinski, Errol. Silence will speak : a study of the life of Denys Finch Hatton and his relationship with Karen Blixen / by Errol Trzebinski. — London : Heinemann, 1977. — xx,348p,[16]p of plates : ill, map, ports ; 24cm.
Index.
ISBN 0-434-79500-3 : £7.50
(B77-29630)

799.32 — ARCHERY
799.3'2 — Archery. *Manuals*
Pszczola, Lorraine. Archery / [by] Lorraine Pszczola ; illustrated by James Bonner. — 2nd ed. — Philadelphia ; London [etc.] : Saunders, 1976. — ii-viii,105p : ill, forms ; 23cm. — (Saunders physical activities series)
Previous ed.: 1971. — Bibl.: p.105.
ISBN 0-7216-7389-9 Pbk : £2.50
(B77-14367)

799.3'2'062411 — Archery. Organisations. *Scotland. Royal Company of Archers, 1951-1976*
Blair, *Sir* **Alastair.** The history of the Royal Company of Archers, 1951-1976 / by Sir Alastair Blair. — [Edinburgh] ([c/o William Blackwood & Sons, Ltd, 32 Thistle St., Edinburgh]) : [Royal Company of Archers], 1977. — ix,169p ; 22cm.
Index.
Pbk : £7.00
(B77-33393)

800 — LITERATURE
801 — Literature. Semiotic aspects. *French texts*
Mounin, G. Sémiologies des textes littéraires / [par] G. Mounin 1. — London : Athlone Press, 1977. — 24p ; 22cm. — (The Cassal Bequest lecture ; 1976)
Bibl.: p.22-24.
ISBN 0-485-16107-9 Sd : £1.00
(B77-14869)

801 — Literature. Semiotics. Lotman, Jüri. *Critical studies*
Shukman, Ann. Literature and semiotics : a study of the writings of Yu. M. Lotman / [by] Ann Shukman. — Amsterdam [etc.] ; Oxford : North-Holland Publishing Co., 1977. — xii, 239p : 1 ill, port ; 23cm. — (Meaning and art ; vol.1)
Bibl.: p.205-231. — Index.
ISBN 0-7204-0413-4 : £21.08
(B77-16014)

801 — Literature. Theories of Marxists, to 1975
Williams, Raymond. Marxism and literature / [by] Raymond Williams. — Oxford [etc.] : Oxford University Press, 1977. — v,218p ; 21cm. — (Marxist introductions)
Bibl.: p.213-217. — Index.
ISBN 0-19-876056-6 : £3.75 : CIP rev.
ISBN 0-19-876061-2 Pbk : £1.75
(B77-06231)

801'.95 — Literature. Criticism. Applications of psychoanalysis
Literary criticism and psychology / edited by Joseph P. Strelka. — University Park ; London : Pennsylvania State University Press, [1977]. — xii,306[i.e.308]p : 1 ill ; 24cm. — (Yearbook of comparative criticism ; vol.7)
Published in the United States: 1976. — Bibl. — Index.
ISBN 0-271-01218-8 : £11.05
(B77-14870)

801'.95 — Literature. Criticism. Use of paraphrases
Carey, John. Wording and rewording : paraphrase in literary criticism / by John Carey. — Oxford : Clarendon Press, 1977. — 21p ; 22cm. — (University of Oxford. Inaugural lectures)
'... delivered ... on 4 June 1976'.
ISBN 0-19-951510-7 Sd : £0.90 : CIP rev.
(B77-05009)

801'.95 — Literature, to 1975. Historical criticism, 1800-1975. *Readings*
Weimann, Robert. Structure and society in literary history : studies in the history and theory of historical criticism / [by] Robert Weimann. — London : Lawrence and Wishart, 1977. — xi,273p ; 23cm.
Originally published: Charlottesville : University Press of Virginia, 1976. — Index.
ISBN 0-85315-397-3 : £5.00
(B77-23647)

801'.95'02854044 — Literature. Criticism. Applications of digital computer systems. *Conference proceedings*
International Symposium on the Use of the Computer in Linguistic and Literary Research, *3rd, Cardiff, 1974.* The computer in literary and linguistic studies : (proceedings of the Third International Symposium) / edited by Alan Jones and R.F. Churchhouse. — Cardiff : University of Wales Press, 1976. — viii,362p : ill, facsims ; 23cm.
'The Third International Symposium on the Use of the Computer in Linguistic and Literary Research ... held at Cardiff in April 1974' - Introduction. — Bibl. — Index.
ISBN 0-7083-0590-3 : £10.00
Primary classification 410'.028'54044
(B77-02227)

801'.95'08 — Literature. Criticism. *Essays*
Richards, Ivor Armstrong. Complementarities : uncollected essays [of] I.A. Richards / edited by John Paul Russo. — Manchester : Carcanet New Press, 1977. — xxiv,293p : ill ; 23cm.
This collection originally published: Cambridge, Mass. : Harvard University Press, 1976. — Index.
ISBN 0-85635-156-3 : £6.00
Primary classification 809
(B77-13216)

801'.951'0942 — Poetry. English criticism, 1837-1900
Starzyk, Lawrence J. The imprisoned splendor : a study of Victorian critical theory / [by] Lawrence J. Starzyk. — Port Washington, N.Y. ; London : Kennikat Press, 1977. — xii, 200p ; 23cm. — (Kennikat Press national university publications : literary criticism series)
Bibl.: p.2. — Index.
ISBN 0-8046-9169-x : £8.90
(B77-30553)

803 — Literature. *Dictionaries*
Cuddon, John Anthony. A dictionary of literary terms / [by] J.A. Cuddon. — London : Deutsch, 1977. — [12],745p ; 23cm. — (The language library)
ISBN 0-233-96716-8 : £11.50
(B77-14368)

807'.6 — Literature. *Questions & answers*
Booker, Christopher. The Booker quiz / [compiled by] Christopher Booker. — London : British Broadcasting Corporation ; London [etc.] : Routledge and Kegan Paul, 1976. — 96p : ill, facsims, ports ; 24cm.
'Six hundred and sixty questions on the world of books, based on the BBC 1 "Read all about it" quiz' - cover. — With answers.
ISBN 0-563-17183-9 Pbk : £1.50
ISBN 0-7100-8504-4 (Routledge and Kegan Paul) : £1.50
(B77-06833)

807'.9 — Literature. Prizes. *Lists*
Literary and library prizes. — 9th ed. / revised and edited by Olga S. Weber. — New York ; London : Bowker, 1976. — viii,544p ; 24cm.
Previous ed.: 1973. — Index.
ISBN 0-8352-0897-4 : £18.00
(B77-05010)

808 — Literature. Language. *Case studies*
Barthes, Roland. Sade, Fourier, Loyola / [by] Roland Barthes ; translated [from the French] by Richard Miller. — London : Cape, 1977. — viii,184p : ill ; 23cm.
This translation originally published: New York : Hill and Wang, 1976. — Translation of: 'Sade, Fourier, Loyola'. Paris : Éditions du Seuil, 1971.
ISBN 0-224-01308-4 : £5.95 : CIP rev.
(B77-22071)

808 — Swahili language. Style
Maw, Joan. Swahili style : a study / [by] Joan Maw. — London : University of London, School of Oriental and African Studies, 1974. — vii,77p ; 26cm.
ISBN 0-7286-0000-5 Pbk : Unpriced
Also classified at 896'.392'09
(B77-19593)

808 — Writers in English. Pseudonyms, 1900-1974. *Dictionaries*
Atkinson, Frank, *b.1922.* Dictionary of literary pseudonyms : a selection of popular modern writers in English / [by] Frank Atkinson. — 2nd ed. — London : Bingley [etc.], 1977. — viii,248p ; 23cm.
Previous ed.: published as 'Dictionary of pseudonyms and pen-names'. London : Bingley, 1975.
ISBN 0-85157-239-1 : £4.75
(B77-32110)

808'.009'024 — European literatures, 1350-1600. Rhetoric
Lanham, Richard Alan. The motives of eloquence : literary rhetoric in the Renaissance / [by] Richard A. Lanham. — New Haven ; London : Yale University Press, 1976. — xiii,234p ; 22cm.
Bibl.: p.229-230. — Index.
ISBN 0-300-02002-3 : £8.25
(B77-09885)

808'.02 — Microforms. Copy. Preparation. *Standards*
British Standards Institution. Recommendations for preparation of copy for microcopying = Recommandations pour la préparation du manuscrit en vue de faire des microcopies = Empfehlungen für die Vorbereitung von Manuskript zur Mikroverfilmung / British Standards Institution. — London : B.S.I., 1977. — [2],4,[2]p : ill ; 30cm. — (BS5444 : 1977)
Pierced for binder.
ISBN 0-580-09369-7 Sd : £1.60
(B77-15431)

808'.02 — Theses. Preparation. *United States. Manuals*
Turabian, Kate Larimore. Student's guide for writing college papers / [by] Kate L. Turabian. — 3rd ed. — Chicago ; London : University of Chicago Press, 1976. — ix,256p ; 21cm.
Previous ed.: 1969. — Bibl.: p.183-244. — Index.
ISBN 0-226-81622-2 : £4.50
ISBN 0-226-81623-0 Pbk : £2.35
(B77-31390)

808'.02'025 — Authorship. *Directories*
Writers' & artists' yearbook. — London : A. and C. Black.
1977 : 70th annual edition. — 1977. — xii, 462p ; 20cm.
Index.
ISBN 0-7136-1709-8 Pbk : £1.75
ISSN 0084-2664
(B77-08012)

808'.042 — English language. American usage. Composition
Corbett, Edward P J. The little English handbook : choices and conventions / [by] Edward P.J. Corbett. — 2nd ed. — New York ; London [etc.] : Wiley, 1977. — xx, 224p : ill, facsims ; 18cm.
Previous ed.: 1973. — Index.
ISBN 0-471-17229-4 Pbk : £2.65
(B77-17700)

Corbett, Edward P J. The little rhetoric / [by] Edward P.J. Corbett. — New York ; London [etc.] : Wiley, 1977. — xv,357p : ill, facsims ; 18cm.
Index.
ISBN 0-471-17231-6 Pbk : £3.35
(B77-17042)

Corbett, Edward P J. The little rhetoric and handbook / [by] Edward P.J. Corbett. — [Combined ed.]. — New York ; London [etc.] : Wiley, 1977. — xix,523,[1]p : ill, facsims ; 19cm.
Text on lining papers. — '... combined edition of two separately published books - "The little rhetoric" and the second edition of "The little English handbook : choices and conventions"' - Preface. — Index.
ISBN 0-471-17232-4 : £4.65
(B77-17701)

Irmscher, William F. The Holt guide to English : a contemporary handbook of rhetoric, language and literature / [by] William F. Irmscher. — 2nd ed. — New York ; London [etc.] : Holt, Rinehart and Winston, 1976. — xx,539p,[2]p of plates : 3 col ill, facsims, 3 col maps ; 25cm.
Text on lining papers. — Previous ed.: New York : Holt, Rinehart and Winston, 1972. — Bibl. — Index.
ISBN 0-03-089842-0 : £6.75
(B77-03731)

808'.042 — English language. Composition. *For undergraduates*
Brown, Harry M. The contemporary college writer : patterns in prose / [by] Harry M. Brown. — New York ; London [etc.] : Van Nostrand, 1977. — xii,244p : ill ; 21cm.
Index.
ISBN 0-442-21110-4 Pbk : £4.00
(B77-27309)

808'.042 — Verbal communication. *Manuals*
Dineen, Jacqueline. Talking your way to success : the persuasive power of words / by Jacqueline Dineen. — Wellingborough : Thorsons, 1977. — 95p ; 23cm. — ([Business success series])
Bibl.: p.77-78.
ISBN 0-7225-0376-8 : £2.50
(B77-30555)

Fellows, Hugh P. The art and skill of talking with people : a new guide to personal and business success / by Hugh P. Fellows ; illustrations by Charles Miller. — [London] : Heron Books, [1977]. — 224p : ill ; 24cm.
Originally published: Englewood Cliffs : Prentice-Hall, 1964. — Index.
ISBN 0-900948-84-1 : Unpriced
(B77-09886)

808.042 — Writing. Techniques. *Manuals*
Clark, Leonard, *b.1905.* Writing for the public / by Leonard Clark. — Gloucester : Thornhill Press, 1976. — 31p ; 20cm. — (A Thornhill guide ; 3)
ISBN 0-904110-38-9 Sd : £0.40
(B77-11362)

Lambuth, David. The golden book on writing / by David Lambuth and others. — [New ed.] ; foreword by Budd Schulberg. — Harmondsworth [etc.] : Penguin, 1976. — xiv, 81p ; 18cm. — (Penguin handbooks)
This ed. originally published: United States: s.n., 1963.
ISBN 0-14-046263-5 Pbk : Unpriced
(B77-06232)

808'.042'071 — Schools. Curriculum subjects: English language. Composition. Teaching
Kohl, Herbert Ralph. Writing, maths & games in the open classroom / [by] Herbert R. Kohl. — London : Methuen, 1977. — xi,200p : ill ; 21cm.
Originally published: as 'Math, writing & games in the open classroom'. New York : New York Review, 1974.
ISBN 0-416-83930-4 : £4.00
ISBN 0-416-83940-1 Pbk : £2.35
Primary classification 510'.7'8
(B77-12420)

808'.042'071041 — Schools. Curriculum subjects: Writing. Projects. *Great Britain. Case studies. For teaching*
Hoffman, Mary. Reading, writing and relevance / [by] Mary Hoffman. — London : Hodder and Stoughton [for] the United Kingdom Reading Association, 1976. — 109p ; 22cm. — (Open University. Set books) (Teaching of reading monographs)
Index.
ISBN 0-340-21025-7 Pbk : £1.35
Primary classification 428'.4'071041
(B77-06632)

808'.042'076 — English language. Composition. *Exercises, worked examples. For Nigerian students. Secondary school texts*
Kanelli, Sheelagh. Advanced English composition / [by] Sheelagh Kanelli. — London [etc.] : Evans Bros, 1977. — iv,72p ; 22cm.
ISBN 0-237-28970-9 Sd : £1.30
(B77-08515)

808'.042'076 — English language. Composition. *Exercises, worked examples. Secondary school texts*
Coleby, Allan Alfred. English for communication / [by] A.A. Coleby. — 2nd ed. — London : J. Murray, 1977. — vii,39p : ill(some col), 2 maps(1 col), col plans ; 22cm.
Previous ed.: 1970.
ISBN 0-7195-3448-8 Sd : £0.65
(B77-32111)

Lamb, Geoffrey Frederick. Exercises in composition and comprehension (CSE standard) / by G.F. Lamb. — London : Harrap, 1976. — 159p : ill, map ; 20cm.
Originally published: 1968.
ISBN 0-245-53038-x Pbk : £1.70
Primary classification 428'.2
(B77-10788)

808'.04275 — English language. Composition. *Samplers*
Detail & pattern : essays for composition / [compiled by] Robert Baylor. — 3rd ed. — New York ; London [etc.] : McGraw-Hill, 1976. — xiv,208p : ill ; 23cm.
Previous ed.: 1972.
ISBN 0-07-004145-8 Pbk : £5.75
(B77-05011)

808'.043'1076 — German language. Composition. *Exercises, worked examples. Secondary school texts*
Richardson, Geoffrey. Schreib' bald! / by G. Richardson and Anne Meinhold ; illustrated by Jane Michaelis. — London : Edward Arnold, 1977. — 64p : ill ; 25cm.
German text, English preface. — Previous control number ISBN 0-7131-0086-9.
ISBN 0-7131-0056-7 Sd : £1.25
(B77-13818)

808'.066'0016425 — Computer systems. Software. Documents on software. Preparation
Lomax, Jeffrey David. Documentation of software products : recommendations for producers and users / by J.D. Lomax. — Manchester : NCC Publications, 1977. — xi, 60p : 1 ill, facsims, form ; 21cm.
Bibl. — Index.
ISBN 0-85012-166-3 Pbk : £4.50 : CIP rev.
(B77-06233)

808'.066'3 — Authorship by social scientists. *United States. Manuals*
Mullins, Carolyn Johns. A guide to writing and publishing in the social and behavioral sciences / [by] Carolyn J. Mullins. — New York ; London [etc.] : Wiley, 1977. — xvi, 431p : forms ; 22cm.
'A Wiley-Interscience publication'. — Bibl.: p.411-417. — Index.
ISBN 0-471-62420-9 : Unpriced
ISBN 0-471-02708-1 Pbk : Unpriced
(B77-23648)

808'.066'34602 — Contracts. Drafting. *Common law countries. For businessmen*
Wincor, Richard. Contracts in plain English / [by] Richard Wincor. — New York ; London [etc.] : McGraw-Hill, 1976. — xv,143p : forms ; 24cm.
Index. — Includes English, French and German texts of the European Convention Relating to the Formalities Required for Patent Applications and English translation of the Japanese text of the Treaty of Commerce and Negotiation between Japan and Great Britain in 1894.
ISBN 0-07-070966-1 : £9.55
(B77-08516)

808'.066'5 — Periodical articles on science. Writing. *Manuals*
Booth, Vernon. Writing a scientific paper / [by] Vernon Booth. — 4th ed. — London (Biochemical Society Book Depot, P.O. Box 32, Colchester CO2 8HP) : Biochemical Society, 1977. — 28p ; 25cm.
Third edition (1975) published in "Biochemical Society Transactions" 3, 1-26 ...' - p.2.
Sd : £1.00
(B77-27310)

808'.066'574 — Research reports in biology. Writing. *Manuals*
Dudley, Hugh Arnold Freeman. The presentation of original work in medicine and biology / [by] Hugh Dudley. — Edinburgh [etc.] : Churchill Livingstone, 1977. — vii,99p : ill ; 22cm.
Bibl. — Index.
ISBN 0-443-01583-x Pbk : £2.50
Also classified at 808'.066'61
(B77-20526)

808'.066'6 — Technical reports. Writing. *Manuals*
Souther, James W. Technical report writing. — 2nd ed. / [by] James W. Souther and Myron L. White. — New York ; London [etc.] : Wiley, 1977. — ix,93p : ill, map ; 29cm.
'A Wiley-Interscience Publication'. — Previous ed.: / by James W. Souther. New York : Wiley ; London : Chapman and Hall, 1957. — Bibl.: p.87-89. — Index.
ISBN 0-471-81412-1 : £7.25
(B77-25152)

808'.066'6 — Technical writing. *Manuals. For Irish students*
Reen, Michael. Ten aids to technical writing for intermediate, Leaving Certificate pupils and craft apprentices / [by] Michael Reen. — Dublin : Helicon : Distributed by Educational Company of Ireland, 1977. — 23p : ill ; 21cm.
Sd : £0.28
(B77-28033)

808'.066'61 — Periodical articles on medicine. Writing. *Manuals*
Thorne, Charles. Thorne's better medical writing. — 2nd ed. / [by] Stephen Lock. — Tunbridge Wells : Pitman Medical, 1977. — x,118p : ill ; 23cm.
Previous ed.: published as 'Better medical writing' / by Charles Thorne (i.e. Stephen Lock and Tony Smith). London : Pitman Medical, 1970. — Bibl.: p.114-115. — Index.
ISBN 0-272-79413-9 : £3.50
(B77-14871)

808'.066'61 — Research reports on medicine. Writing. *Manuals*
Dudley, Hugh Arnold Freeman. The presentation of original work in medicine and biology / [by] Hugh Dudley. — Edinburgh [etc.] : Churchill Livingstone, 1977. — vii,99p : ill ; 22cm.
Bibl. — Index.
ISBN 0-443-01583-x Pbk : £2.50
Primary classification 808'.066'574
(B77-20526)

808'.066'791 — Broadcasting services. *Great Britain. British Broadcasting Corporation. Radio & television programmes. Scripts. Writing. Manuals*
British Broadcasting Corporation. Writing for the BBC : a guide for professional and part-time freelance writers on possible markets for their work within the British Broadcasting Corporation / [British Broadcasting Corporation]. — 5th ed. — London : B.B.C., 1977. — [3],75p ; 21cm.
'The material on which this book is based was compiled and edited by Norman Longmate ...' - title page verso. — Previous ed.: 1974.
ISBN 0-563-17278-9 Sd : £0.75
(B77-23649)

808'.066'791 — Cinema films & television programmes. Scripts. Writing. *Secondary school texts*
Bennett, Rodney. The writer's approach to the TV-film script / by Rodney Bennett. — London : Harrap, 1976. — 49p : ill, facsims, plan, ports ; 25cm.
ISBN 0-245-52412-6 Sd : £0.95
(B77-06834)

808'.066'9142 — Parish churches. Guidebooks. Writing. *England. Manuals*
Dymond, David. Writing a church guide / by David Dymond ; bibliography prepared by David M. Williams. — London : CIO Publishing for the Council for Places of Worship and the Standing Conference for Local History, [1977]. — [3],20p,iv p of plates : ill, facsim, plan ; 21cm.
Bibl.: p.17-20.
ISBN 0-7151-7530-0 Sd : £0.75
(B77-28034)

808.1 — Poetry. Composition
Jacob, Max. Advice to a young poet / by Max Jacob ; translated from the French and introduced by John Adlard ; with a preface by Edmond Jabès, and an afterword by Jacques Evrard ; both translated [from the French] by John Adlard. — London : Menard Press, 1976. — 40p : facsims ; 22cm.
Afterword in French with English translation. — Translation of: 'Conseils à un jeune poète'. 2.éd. Paris : Gallimard, 1945.
ISBN 0-903400-17-0 Sd : £0.75
(B77-13819)

808.1 — Poetry in English. Composition. *Primary school texts*
Lane, Sheila Mary. Poems for writing / [by] Sheila M. Lane, Marion Kemp. — Glasgow [etc.] : Blackie.
In 2 vols.
1. — 1976. — 47p : ill ; 24cm.
ISBN 0-216-90171-5 Sd : £0.98
(B77-12036)

2. — 1976. — 47p : ill ; 24cm.
ISBN 0-216-90172-3 Sd : £0.98
(B77-12037)

808.1 — Poetry in English. Composition. *Serials*
The **poet's** yearbook. — London (1 Herbert Rd, N11 2QN) : Poet's Yearbook Ltd.
1977 / compiled and edited by S.T. Gardiner. — 1977. — 204p ; 21cm.
Index.
ISBN 0-905106-01-6 Pbk : £2.45
(B77-14872)

808.1'08 — Poetry. *Lectures, speeches*
Wain, John. Professing poetry / [by] John Wain. — London [etc.] : Macmillan, 1977. — x,396p : music ; 23cm.
Index.
ISBN 0-333-22641-0 : £6.95 : CIP rev.
(B77-22072)

808.2 — Drama. Composition. *Secondary school texts*
Howarth, Tony. The writer's approach to the play / [by] Tony Howarth. — London : Harrap, 1976. — 48p : ill, facsims, plan, ports ; 25cm.
ISBN 0-245-52416-9 Sd : £0.95
(B77-02532)

808.2 — Drama. Reading. *Manuals*
Hayman, Ronald. How to read a play / [by] Ronald Hayman. — London : Eyre Methuen, 1977. — 96p ; 21cm.
ISBN 0-413-33300-0 : £3.50
ISBN 0-413-33310-8 Pbk : £1.50
(B77-25153)

808.2'076 — Drama. *Exercises, worked examples. Secondary school texts*
Farquhar-Smith, Ann. More plays to finish / [by] Ann Farquhar-Smith. — Amersham : Hulton, 1976. — 124p ; 20cm.
ISBN 0-7175-0762-9 Pbk : £0.90
(B77-09203)

808.2'3 — Animated films. Scripts. Writing. *Manuals*
Hayward, Stan. Scriptwriting for animation / [by] Stan Hayward. — London [etc.] : Focal Press, 1977. — 160p : ill, forms, music ; 22cm. — (Media manuals)
Text on inside from cover. — Bibl.: p.157.
ISBN 0-240-50967-6 Pbk : £2.50 : CIP rev.
(B77-16556)

808.3'3 — Fiction. Forms: Novels. Composition. *Secondary school texts*
Blishen, Edward. The writer's approach to the novel / by Edward Blishen. — London : Harrap, 1976. — 59p : ill, facsims, ports ; 25cm.
ISBN 0-245-52415-0 Sd : £1.15
(B77-02533)

808.3'876 — Science fiction. Social aspects
Science fiction at large : a collection of essays by various hands about the interface between science fiction and reality / edited by Peter Nicholls. — London : Gollancz, 1976. — 224p : ill ; 23cm.
'... a series of lectures delivered at the Institute of Contemporary Arts in London, from January to March 1975' - Introduction.
ISBN 0-575-02178-0 : £5.95
(B77-00901)

808.3'876'05 — Science fiction. *Periodicals*
Science fiction forum : the journal of the Nottingham Science Fiction Group. — Nottingham (233 Cinderhill Rd, Bulwell, Nottingham) : The Group.
Vol.1, no.1- ; [Nov. 1976]-. — [1976]-. — ill ; 26cm.
Three issues a year. — [2],26p. in 1st issue.
Sd : £0.20
(B77-13820)

808.3'876'05 — Science fiction in English. Composition. *Periodicals*
Cyclotron : a quarterly SF writers' bulletin. — Cheltenham (c/o Graham R. Poole, 23 Russet Rd, Cheltenham, Glos. GL51 7LN) : Grapevine Publications.
[No.1]- ; July 1976-. — 1976-. — ill ; 30cm.
[Eight] p. with insert (4p.) in 1st issue.
Sd : £0.25
(B77-13214)

808.5 — Oral communication. *Manuals*
Asante, Molefi K. Contemporary public communication : applications / [by] Molefi K. Asante, Jerry K. Frye. — New York [etc.] ; London : Harper and Row, 1977. — xii,240p : ill ; 24cm.
Bibl. — Index.
ISBN 0-06-046321-x : £8.20
(B77-17043)

Bormann, Ernest Gordon. Speech communication : a comprehensive approach / [by] Ernest G. Bormann & Nancy C. Bormann. — 2nd ed. — New York [etc.] ; London : Harper and Row, 1977. — xii,436p : ill ; 24cm.

Previous ed.: New York : Harper and Row, 1972. — Bibl. — Index.
ISBN 0-06-040859-6 Pbk : £6.70
(B77-17044)

Reid, Loren. Speaking well / [by] Loren Reid. — 3rd ed. — New York ; London [etc.] : McGraw-Hill, 1977. — xi,420p : ill ; 24cm. — (McGraw-Hill series in speech)
Previous ed.: New York : McGraw-Hill, 1972. — Bibl. — Index.
ISBN 0-07-051783-5 Pbk : £6.25
(B77-22782)

Speech communication in society / [by] Charles R. Gruner ... [et al.]. — 2nd ed. — Boston [Mass.] ; London [etc.] : Allyn and Bacon, 1977. — ix,2-292p : ill, 2 forms ; 24cm.
Previous ed.: Boston, Mass. : Allyn and Bacon, 1972. — Index.
ISBN 0-205-05732-2 Pbk : Unpriced
(B77-17045)

808.5 — Voice production. *Manuals*
Morrison, Malcolm. Clear speech : practical speech correction and voice improvement / [by] Malcolm Morrison. — London [etc.] : Pitman, 1977. — iv,76p : ill ; 23cm.
Bibl.: p.75-76.
ISBN 0-273-01016-6 Pbk : £1.50 : CIP rev.
(B77-08013)

Turner, James Clifford. Voice and speech in the theatre / [by] J. Clifford Turner. — 3rd ed. / revised by Malcolm Morrison. — London : Pitman, 1977. — xi,146p : ill, music ; 22cm. — (Theatre and stage series)
Previous ed.: 1956. — Index.
ISBN 0-273-00219-8 Pbk : £2.50
(B77-13215)

808.5'1 — Public speaking. *Manuals*
Barrett, Harold. Practical uses of speech communication / [by] Harold Barrett. — 4th ed. — New York ; London [etc.] : Holt, Rinehart and Winston, 1977. — viii,303p : ill, facsims ; 24cm.
Previous ed.: published as 'Practical methods in speech'. 1973. — Index.
ISBN 0-03-089967-2 Pbk : £6.50
(B77-20527)

Hasling, John. The audience, the message, the speaker / [by] John Hasling. — 2nd ed. — New York ; London [etc.] : McGraw-Hill, 1976. — xi,125p : 1 ill ; 23cm. — (McGraw-Hill series in speech)
Previous ed.: published as 'The message, the speaker, the audience'. New York : McGraw-Hill, 1971. — Index.
ISBN 0-07-026990-4 Pbk : £4.10
(B77-04374)

Perkins, Margaret. Confident speaking / by Margaret Perkins. — Revised ed. — Wellinborough [i.e. Wellingborough] : A. Thomas, 1977. — 62p ; 18cm. — (A practical psychology handbook)
Previous ed.: published as 'Speech mastery in 15 lessons'. London : Thorsons, 1971.
ISBN 0-85454-047-4 Pbk : £0.60
(B77-30556)

808.53 — Broadcasting services. Interviews. *For interviewees*
Brand, John. Hello, good evening and welcome- : a guide to being interviewed on television and radio / by John Brand. — London : Shaw and Sons, 1977. — 31p : ill, maps ; 19cm.
'A Shaway publication'.
ISBN 0-7219-0760-1 Sd : £0.55
(B77-28035)

808.56 — Conversation. *Manuals*
Russell, Elliot. Hold your own in conversation, with the joy of feeling at ease / by Elliot Russell. — Revised, rewritten ed. — Kingswood : Elliot Right Way Books, 1977. — 124p ; 18cm. — (Paperfronts)
Previous ed.: i.e. 2nd ed. published as 'The conversation secret'. 1965.
ISBN 0-7160-0631-6 Pbk : £0.50
(B77-18333)

808.6 — Correspondence. *Manuals. Secondary school texts*
Summers, Vivian. Letter writing for schools and colleges / [by] Vivian Summers. — 2nd ed. — Exeter : Wheaton, 1977. — 48p : ill ; 27cm.
ISBN 0-08-021901-2 Pbk : £0.70
ISBN 0-08-021776-1 Pbk non-net : Unpriced
(B77-30557)

808.8 — LITERATURE. GENERAL ANTHOLOGIES
808.8'003 — Literature, ca 1560-1954. *Anthologies. English texts*
A **book** of delights : an anthology of words and pictures / chosen and arranged by John Hadfield. — London : Hamilton, 1977. — 224p : col ill, music, col ports ; 22cm.
Ill. on lining papers. — Previous ed.: London : Hulton Press, 1954. — Index.
ISBN 0-241-89727-0 : £4.95
(B77-27311)

808.8'036 — Literature, to 1976. Special subjects: Pets: Cats. *Anthologies. English texts*
Nine lives : an anthology of poetry and prose concerning cats / compiled by Kenneth Lillington ; illustrated by Maurice Wilson. — London : Deutsch, 1977. — 154p : ill ; 23cm.
ISBN 0-233-96927-6 : £3.50
(B77-30558)

808.81 — Poetry. African writers, to 1975. *Anthologies. Secondary school texts. English texts*
A **selection** of African poetry / introduced and annotated by K.E. Senanu and T. Vincent. — [Harlow] : Longman, 1976. — [6],224p ; 22cm.
ISBN 0-582-60141-x Pbk : £1.20
(B77-02534)

808.81 — Poetry in European languages, to 1976. *Anthologies. English texts*
Watkins, Vernon. Selected verse translations : with an essay on the translation of poetry / [by] Vernon Watkins ; introduction by Michael Hamburger ; textual editor Ruth Pryor. — London : Enitharmon Press, 1977. — 79p ; 22cm.
ISBN 0-901111-75-9 : £3.45
ISBN 0-901111-76-7 Pbk : £1.95
(B77-20528)

808.81'5 — Religious poetry, ca 600-1965. *Anthologies. English texts*
The **mystic** in love : a treasury of world mystical poetry / edited by Shelley Gross. — Toronto [etc.] ; London : Bantam, 1976. — xxvii,194,[1] p ; 18cm.
This collection originally published: New York : Citadel Press, 1966. — Bibl.: p.179-181. — Index.
ISBN 0-552-68263-2 Pbk : £0.65
(B77-01754)

808.81'9'355 — Poetry, 1558-1976. Special subjects: Transport. *Anthologies. Juvenile literature*
Moving along : poems of travel and transport / collected by Barbara Ireson ; illustrated by John Glover. — London : Evans Bros, 1977. — 128p : ill ; 22cm.
Index.
ISBN 0-237-44853-x : £3.75
(B77-25154)

808.82'04 — Drama in European languages, 1900-. *Anthologies. English texts*
14 great plays. — [London] : [Heinemann] : [Octopus Books], [1977]. — 3-859p ; 25cm.
ISBN 0-905712-20-x : £4.95
(B77-26461)

808.83'1 — Short stories in European languages, 1800- : Horror stories. *English texts. Anthologies. Serials*
Uncanny tales / selected by Dennis Wheatley. — London : Sphere.
3. — 1975. — 235p ; 18cm. — (The Dennis Wheatley library of the occult ; vol.37)
ISBN 0-7221-9039-5 Pbk : £0.60
(B77-08014)

808.83'1 — Short stories in European languages, 1840-1976. *Anthologies. English texts*
The **realm** of fiction : 74 short stories. — 3rd ed. / [edited by] James B. Hall, Elizabeth C. Hall. — New York ; London [etc.] : McGraw-Hill, 1977. — xviii,634p,[2]p of plates : 1 ill, ports ; 23cm.
Previous ed.: / edited by James B. Hall. New York : McGraw-Hill, 1970.
ISBN 0-07-025594-6 Pbk : £5.95
(B77-24416)

808.83'1 — Short stories in European languages, ca 1850-. *Anthologies. Welsh texts*
Storïau tramor. — Llandysul : Gwasg Gomer.
2 / golygydd Bobi Jones. — 1975. — 161p ; 23cm.
ISBN 0-85088-321-0 : £2.25
(B77-01755)

3 / golygydd Bobi Jones. — 1976. — 148p ; 22cm.
ISBN 0-85088-450-0 : £2.25
(B77-05012)

4 : Storïau Tschechoff / golygydd W. Gareth Jones ; [cyfieithiwyd o'r Rwsieg]. — 1977. — 225p ; 22cm.
ISBN 0-85088-413-6 : £3.50
(B77-29631)

808.83'1 — Short stories in European languages, to 1975. *Anthologies. English texts*
The **short** story : an introduction / [edited by] Wilfred Stone, Nancy Huddleston Packer, Robert Hoopes. — New York ; London [etc.] : McGraw-Hill, 1976. — x,598p ; 24cm.
Bibl.: p.591-592. — Index.
ISBN 0-07-061689-2 Pbk : £6.60
(B77-05013)

808.86'9'354 — Love letters, ca 200-1945. *Anthologies. English texts*
Love letters : an anthology / chosen by Antonia Fraser ; illustrations by James Hutcheson. — Harmondsworth [etc.] : Penguin, 1977. — xxi, 247p : ill ; 18cm.
This collection originally published: London : Weidenfeld and Nicolson, 1976.
ISBN 0-14-004203-2 Pbk : £0.80
(B77-28036)

808.88'2 — Humorous quotations, ca 1550-ca 1970. *Anthologies. English texts*
I wish I'd said that! : an anthology of witty replies / collected by Kenneth Edwards ; introduced by Frank Muir. — London : Abelard-Schuman, 1976. — 78p ; 21cm.
ISBN 0-200-72467-3 : £1.95
ISBN 0-200-72474-6 Pbk : £0.95
(B77-00367)

I wish I'd said that too! : an anthology of witty replies / collected by Kenneth Edwards. — London : Abelard, 1977. — 64p ; 21cm.
ISBN 0-200-72529-7 : £1.75
ISBN 0-200-72528-9 Pbk : £0.80
(B77-32813)

808.88'2 — Quotations. *Anthologies. For public speaking*
Prochnow, Herbert Victor, *b.1897.* The public speaker's treasure chest : a compendium of source material to make your speech sparkle / by Herbert V. Prochnow [and Herbert V. Prochnow, Jr]. — 2nd ed. (revised and enlarged). — Wellingborough : A. Thomas, 1977. — ix,516p ; 22cm.
This ed. originally published: New York : Harper and Row, 1964 ; Preston : A. Thomas, 1965. — Index.
ISBN 0-85454-031-8 Pbk : £3.00
(B77-17702)

808.88'2 — Quotations, to ca 1970. *Anthologies. English texts*
Bartlett, John. Familiar quotations : a collection of passages, phrases and proverbs traced to their sources in ancient and modern literature / by John Bartlett. — 14th ed., revised and enlarged / Emily Morison Beck editor. — London [etc.] : Macmillan, 1977. — xix,1750p ; 24cm.
Cover title: Bartlett's familiar quotations. — This ed. originally published: Boston, Mass. : Little, Brown, 1968. — Index.
ISBN 0-333-21845-0 : £7.95
(B77-25155)

These have been my inspiration / compiled by Gladys Tinker. — Revised ed. — [Huddersfield] : [Advertiser Press], [1976]. — 40p ; 20cm.
Previous ed.: Holmfirth : Charlesworths, 1971.
ISBN 0-900028-23-8 : £1.50
(B77-00902)

808.88'2 — Quotations, to ca 1975. Special subjects: Science. *Anthologies. English texts*
The **harvest** of a quiet eye : a selection of scientific quotations / by Alan L. Mackay ; edited by Maurice Ebison ; with a foreword by Sir Peter Medawar. — Bristol [etc.] : Institute of Physics, 1977. — xii,192p : ill, ports ; 24cm.
Index.
ISBN 0-85498-031-8 : £5.20
(B77-01756)

809 — LITERATURE. HISTORY AND CRITICAL STUDIES
809 — Literature. *Critical studies*
Muir, Kenneth. The singularity of Shakespeare, and other essays / [by] Kenneth Muir. — Liverpool : Liverpool University Press, 1977. — vii,235p ; 23cm. — (Liverpool English texts and studies)
Index.
ISBN 0-85323-433-7 : £9.75
Primary classification 822.3'3
(B77-32830)

809 — Literature. *Critical studies. Essays*
Lewis, Wyndham, *b.1884.* Enemy salvoes : selected literary criticism / by Wyndham Lewis ; edited with sectional introductions and notes by C.J. Fox ; general introduction by C.H. Sisson. — London : Vision Press, 1975. — 272p ; 23cm.
Index.
ISBN 0-85478-323-7 : £4.95
(B77-08015)

Richards, Ivor Armstrong. Complementarities : uncollected essays [of] I.A. Richards / edited by John Paul Russo. — Manchester : Carcanet New Press, 1977. — xxiv,293p : ill ; 23cm.
This collection originally published: Cambridge, Mass. : Harvard University Press, 1976. — Index.
ISBN 0-85635-156-3 : £6.00
Also classified at 801'.95'08
(B77-13216)

Wilson, Edmund. Letters on literature and politics, 1912-1972 / [by] Edmund Wilson ; edited by Elena Wilson ; introduction by Daniel Aaron ; foreword by Leon Edel. — London [etc.] : Routledge and Kegan Paul, 1977. — xxxvii,768p : ill, facsims, ports ; 24cm.
Also published: New York : Farrar, Straus and Giroux, 1977. — Index.
ISBN 0-7100-8761-6 : £12.50 : CIP rev.
Also classified at 909.82'08
(B77-25156)

809 — Literature. *Critical studies. Periodicals*
Essays in poetics : the journal of the British Neo-formalist Circle. — Keele ([Department of Russian Studies, University of Keele, Keele, Staffs. ST5 5BG]) : ['Essays in poetics'].
Vol.1, no.1- ; Apr. 1976-. — 1976-. — 21cm.
Two issues a year. — [2],iii,98p. in 1st issue. — Bibl.
Pbk : £1.25
ISSN 0308-888x
(B77-03732)

809 — Literature in European languages, 1625-1920. *Essays*
Woolf, Virginia. Books and portraits : some further selections from the literary and biographical writings of Virginia Woolf / edited by Mary Lyon. — London : Hogarth Press, 1977. — x,221p ; 23cm.
ISBN 0-7012-0405-2 : £5.50 : CIP rev.
(B77-10514)

809 — Literature in European languages, to 1970. *Critical studies. Essays*
Todoroc, Tzvetan. The poetics of prose / [by] Tzvetan Todorov ; translated from the French by Richard Howard ; with a new foreword by Jonathan Culler. — Oxford : Blackwell, 1977. — 272p ; 22cm.
Translation of: 'La poétique de la prose'. Paris : Editions du Seuil, 1971. — Index.
ISBN 0-631-18230-6 : £8.75
(B77-28824)

809 — Literature. Mythopoeic aspects. Related to historiography. *Conference proceedings*
English Institute, *Columbia University.* The literature of fact : selected papers from the English Institute / edited with a foreword by Angus Fletcher. — New York ; Guildford : Columbia University Press, 1976. — xxvii, 172p ; 21cm.
'The "Literature of fact" occupied the attention of the English Institute during two sessions of its meetings, in 1974 and 1975' - Foreword.
ISBN 0-231-04144-6 : £5.90
Also classified at 907'.2
(B77-06234)

809 — Western literatures. Attitudes of Russians, 1954-1964
Friedberg, Maurice. A decade of euphoria : Western literature in post-Stalin Russia, 1954-64 / [by] Maurice Friedberg. — Bloomington ; London : Indiana University Press, 1977. — xi,371p ; 24cm.
List of films: p.349. — Index.
ISBN 0-253-31675-8 : £13.15
(B77-25157)

809'.034 — European literatures, 1809-1967. *Critical studies*
Miller, Ronald Duncan. Beyond anarchy : studies in modern literature / by R.D. Miller. — Harrogate (8 Lancaster Rd, Harrogate, [N. Yorkshire]) : Duchy Press, 1976. — [5],265p ; 26cm.
Bibl.: p.263-265.
ISBN 0-9500617-6-x Pbk : £5.00
(B77-00368)

809'.034 — Literature, ca 1850-ca 1960. *Critical studies*
Wilson, Colin. The strength to dream : literature and the imagination / [by] Colin Wilson. — London : Abacus, 1976. — 254p ; 20cm.
Originally published: London : Gollancz, 1962. — Index.
ISBN 0-349-13735-8 Pbk : £1.50
(B77-06235)

809'.04 — Literature, 1900-1975. Criticism. *Exercises, worked examples*
Elkins, William R. Literary reflections / [by] William R. Elkins, Jack L. Kendall, John R. Willingham. — 3rd ed. — New York ; London [etc.] : McGraw-Hill, 1976. — xxii,501,[1]p : ill ; 24cm.
Previous ed.: New York : McGraw-Hill, 1971. — Index.
ISBN 0-07-019182-4 Pbk : £7.45
(B77-05014)

809'.04 — Literature in European languages, ca 1900-1972. *Critical studies*
Josipovici, Gabriel. The lessons of modernism, and other essays / [by] Gabriel Josipovici. — London [etc.] : Macmillan, 1977. — xiv,208p ; 23cm.
Index.
ISBN 0-333-21440-4 : £8.95
(B77-25830)

809'.04 — Literature in European languages, ca 1900-ca 1970. *Critical studies*
Jennings, Elizabeth. Seven men of vision : an appreciation / by Elizabeth Jennings. — London : Vision Press, 1976. — 249p ; 23cm.
Bibl.: p.249.
ISBN 0-85478-253-2 : £5.40
(B77-04375)

809.1 — Orally transmitted poetry. Related to epic poetry of Homer. *Essays*
Kirk, Geoffrey Stephen. Homer and the oral tradition / [by] G.S. Kirk. — Cambridge [etc.] : Cambridge University Press, 1976. — viii,223p ; 23cm.
Index.
ISBN 0-521-21309-6 : £7.50
Primary classification 883'.01
(B77-05749)

809.1 — Poetry in European languages. Translations into English language. Shelley, Percy Bysshe. *Critical studies*
Webb, Timothy. The violet in the crucible : Shelley and translation / [by] Timothy Webb. — Oxford : Clarendon Press, 1976. — xiii, 364p ; 23cm.
Bibl.: p.337-349. — Index.
ISBN 0-19-812059-1 : £12.00
Also classified at 809.2
(B77-12608)

809.1'008 — Poetry. *Critical studies. Essays*
Snodgrass, William DeWitt. In radical pursuit : critical essays and lectures / [by] W.D. Snodgrass. — New York [etc.] ; London : Harper and Row, 1977. — xiii,364p ; 21cm. — (Harper colophon books)
This collection originally published: New York : Harper and Row, 1975.
ISBN 0-06-090575-1 Pbk : £2.25
(B77-34006)

809.1'01 — Poetry in European languages. Role of analogy, to ca 1350
Damon, Phillip. Modes of analogy in ancient and medieval verse / by Phillip Damon. — Berkeley [etc.] ; London : University of California Press, 1973. — [5]p,p261-334 ; 24cm. — (California library reprint series)
Originally published: Berkeley : University of California Press, 1961.
ISBN 0-520-02366-8 : Unpriced
(B77-19594)

809.1'03 — Poetry in European languages, 1690-1965. *Critical studies. Essays*
Paz, Octavio. The siren & the seashell, and other essays on poets and poetry / [by] Octavio Paz ; translated [from the Spanish] by Lysander Kemp and Margaret Sayers Peden ; illustrated by Barry Moser. — Austin ; London : University of Texas Press, 1976. — viii,188p : ports ; 22cm. — (The Texas pan American series)
'The essays ... are [selected and translated] from "Cuadrivio" ... Mexico City : Editorial Joaquín Mortiz, 1965 ; ... "Las peras del olmo" ... Mexico City : Universidad Nacional Autónoma de México, 1957 ; ... "Puertas al campo" ... Mexico City : Universidad Nacional Autónoma de México, 1966' - Editor's note. — Index.
ISBN 0-292-77521-0 : £8.00
(B77-06835)

809.1'9'353 — Poetry. Special themes: Self-discovery. Study examples: Poetry in European languages, ca 1300-ca 1930
Raine, Kathleen. The inner journey of the poet / [by] Kathleen Raine. — Ipswich (3 Cambridge Drive, Ipswich IP2 9EP) : Golgonooza Press, 1976. — 24p ; 24cm.
Limited ed. of 500 numbered copies of which nos.1-100 are signed by the author and have a signed autolithograph by Cecil Collins. — '... first written as a lecture delivered at the College of Psychic Studies' conference at Winchester, in 1975, and published in the College journal, "Light" ... rewritten and given in the form of a public lecture ... in March 1976, and published in the [Analytical Psychology] Club's magazine, "Harvest" ... further revised for the present publication'.
ISBN 0-903880-13-x Sd : £1.00
ISBN 0-903880-12-1 Signed ed.: £5.00
(B77-05589)

809.1'9'38 — Poetry in European languages, 1797-1933. Special themes: Soul. *Critical studies*
Nalbantian, Suzanne. The symbol of the soul from Hölderlin to Yeats : a study in metonymy / [by] Suzanne Nalbantian. — London [etc.] : Macmillan, 1977. — vii,151p ; 23cm.
Bibl.: p.144-148. — Index.
ISBN 0-333-21399-8 : £7.95
(B77-12038)

809.2 — Drama in European languages, to 1972. *Critical studies*
Stone, Brian. Sophocles to Fugard / [by] Brian Stone and Pat Scorer. — London : British Broadcasting Corporation, 1977. — 127p : ill ; 20cm.
'... an illustrated introduction to the sixteen fifty-minute drama programmes which are being shown on BBC television as part of the Open University's course A 307 : Drama' - cover.
ISBN 0-563-17267-3 Pbk : £1.50
(B77-18949)

809.2 — Drama in European languages. Translations into English language. Shelley, Percy Bysshe. *Critical studies*
Webb, Timothy. The violet in the crucible : Shelley and translation / [by] Timothy Webb. — Oxford : Clarendon Press, 1976. — xiii, 364p ; 23cm.
Bibl.: p.337-349. — Index.
ISBN 0-19-812059-1 : £12.00
Primary classification 809.1
(B77-12608)

809.2'034 — Drama in European languages, 1850-1960. *Critical studies*
Williams, Raymond. Drama from Ibsen to Brecht / [by] Raymond Williams. — 2nd revised ed. — Harmondsworth [etc.] : Penguin, 1976. — xi,408p ; 18cm. — (Pelican books)
Second revised ed. originally published: London : Chatto and Windus, 1968. — Previous ed.: published as 'Drama from Ibsen to Eliot'. Harmondsworth : Penguin, 1964. — Index.
Pbk : £1.10
(B77-03191)

809.3'034 — Fiction in European languages, 1800-1900. Use of free indirect speech
Pascal, Roy. The dual voice : free indirect speech and its functioning in the nineteenth-century European novel / [by] Roy Pascal. — Manchester : Manchester University Press [etc.], 1977. — ix,150p ; 23cm.
ISBN 0-7190-0654-6 : £5.50
(B77-09204)

809.3'04 — Fiction in European languages, 1900-1975. *Critical studies*
Lindsay, Jack. Decay and renewal : critical essays on twentieth century writing / [by] Jack Lindsay. — Sydney : Wild and Woolley ; London : Lawrence and Wishart, 1976. — 447p ; 22cm.
Includes 'The elephant and the lotus'. Originally published: Bombay : Kutub Popular, 1965.
ISBN 0-85315-379-5 : £7.50
(B77-20529)

809.3'04 — Fiction in European languages, 1900-1976. Related to psychological theories, 1900-1976
May, Keith M. Out of the maelstrom : psychology and the novel in the twentieth century / [by] Keith M. May. — London : Elek, 1977. — xvi,135p ; 23cm.
Bibl.: p.127-132. — Index.
ISBN 0-236-40095-9 : £5.50
Also classified at 150'.9'04
(B77-23650)

809.3'876 — Science fiction, to 1975. *Critical studies. Readings*
Science fiction : a collection of critical essays / edited by Mark Rose. — Englewood Cliffs ; London [etc.] : Prentice-Hall, 1976. — xi,174p ; 22cm. — (Twentieth century views)
Bibl.: p.173-174.
ISBN 0-13-794966-9 : £6.20
ISBN 0-13-794958-8 Pbk : £2.30
(B77-06836)

809.3'9'17 — Fiction in European languages. Picaresque novels, to 1965. *Critical studies*
Sieber, Harry. The picaresque / [by] Harry Sieber. — London : Methuen, 1977. — viii, 85p ; 20cm. — (The critical idiom ; 33)
Bibl.: p.75-79. — Index.
ISBN 0-416-82710-1 : £2.35
ISBN 0-416-82720-9 Pbk : £1.20
(B77-10897)

809.3'9'3 — Fiction in European languages, 1605-ca 1920. Special themes: Desire. *Critical studies*
Girard, René. Deceit, desire, and the novel : self and other in literary structure / by René Girard ; translated [from the French] by Yvonne Freccero. — Baltimore ; London : Johns Hopkins University Press, 1976. — [9], 318p ; 22cm.
This translation originally published: Baltimore : Johns Hopkins University Press, 1965. — Translation of: 'Mensonge romantique et vérité romanesque'. Paris : Grasset, 1961. — Index.
ISBN 0-8018-1830-3 Pbk : £3.40
(B77-15432)

809.3'9'3 — Fiction in European languages, 1900-1945. Special subjects: World War 1. *Critical studies*
The **First** World War in fiction : a collection of critical essays / edited by Holger Klein. — London [etc.] : Macmillan, 1976. — x,246p ; 23cm.
Bibl.: p.233-235. — Index.
ISBN 0-333-18823-3 : £8.95
(B77-07545)

809.3'9'352 — Fiction in European languages, 1945-1974. Special themes: Jews. Persecution, 1939-1945. *Critical studies*
Langer, Lawrence L. The holocaust and the literary imagination / [by] Lawrence L. Langer. — New Haven ; London : Yale University Press, 1977. — xiii,300p ; 24cm.
Index.
ISBN 0-300-02121-6 Pbk : £3.75
(B77-33395)

809.3'9'353 — Fiction in European languages, 1837-1901. Special subjects: Adultery. *Critical studies*
Armstrong, Judith. The novel of adultery / [by] Judith Armstrong. — London [etc.] : Macmillan, 1976. — viii,182p ; 23cm.
Bibl.: p.175-178. — Index.
ISBN 0-333-19680-5 : £5.95
(B77-09887)

809.3'9'37 — Fiction in European languages, 1800-1976. Special themes: Magic. *Critical studies*
Ziolkowski, Theodore. Disenchanted images : a literary iconology / [by] Theodore Ziolkowski. — Princeton ; Guildford : Princeton University Press, 1977. — xi,273p ; 23cm.
Index.
ISBN 0-691-06334-6 : £9.40
(B77-34007)

809'.894 — European literatures. *Reviews of research*
The **year's** work in modern language studies. — London (c/o The Hon. Treasurer, King's College, Strand, WC2R 2LS) : Modern Humanities Research Association.
1975 : Vol.37 / edited by Glanville Price and David A. Wells. — 1976. — xi,1006p ; 23cm.
Index.
ISBN 0-900547-44-8 : £16.00
Primary classification 400
(B77-14680)

809'.91'5 — Western European literatures, 1400-1976. Typology. *Conference proceedings*
Literary uses of typology : from the late Middle Ages to the present / Earl Miner, editor. — Princeton ; Guildford : Princeton University Press, 1977. — xxi,403,[3]p ; 23cm.
Revised versions of the papers presented to a seminar sponsored by the Department of English, Princeton University, in April 1974. — Index.
ISBN 0-691-06327-3 : £18.80
(B77-24417)

809'.92'3 — Orally transmitted narrative literature in European languages. *Critical studies*
Wilson, Anne. Traditional romance and tale : how stories mean / [by] Anne Wilson. — Ipswich : Brewer [etc.], 1976. — xii,116p ; 23cm.
Bibl.: p.111-115. — Index.
ISBN 0-85991-021-0 : £5.00
(B77-14369)

809'.933'2 — Literature in European languages, 1900-1945. Special themes: Egypt. Alexandria. *Critical studies*
Pinchin, Jane Lagoudis. Alexandria still : Forster, Durrell and Cavafy / [by] Jane Lagoudis Pinchin. — Princeton ; Guildford : Princeton University Press, 1977. — xiii,245p : map ; 23cm. — (Princeton essays in literature)
Bibl.: p.227-237. — Index.
ISBN 0-691-06283-8 : £10.20
(B77-23651)

809'.933'2 — Literature, to 1975. Special subjects: India
Bissoondoyal, Basdeo. India in world literature / by B. Bissoondoyal. — London : Luzac, 1976. — viii,103p ; 22cm.
Index.
ISBN 0-7189-0245-9 : £3.00
(B77-05015)

809'.933'52 — European literatures, ca 1810-1976. Characters: Heroes
Calder, Jenni. Heroes : from Byron to Guevara / [by] Jenni Calder. — London : Hamilton, 1977. — xii,211p,8p of plates : ill, ports ; 23cm.
Index.
ISBN 0-241-89536-7 : £6.95
Also classified at 920'.009'034
(B77-12609)

809'.933'52 — European literatures, ca 600-ca 1650. Characters: Heroes. *Conference proceedings*
Concepts of the hero in the Middle Ages and the Renaissance / edited by Norman T. Burns and Christopher Reagan. — London [etc.] : Hodder and Stoughton, 1976. — xiii,293p,[32]p of plates : ill ; 24cm.
'... contains papers of the Fourth and Fifth Annual Conferences of the Center for Medieval and Early Renaissance Studies, State University of New York at Binghamton, 2-3 May 1970, 1-2 May 1971' - title page verso. — Originally published: Albany : State University of New York Press, 1975. — Bibl.
ISBN 0-340-19660-2 : £10.50
(B77-08517)

809'.933'53 — European literatures, to 1975. Special themes: Boredom. *Critical studies*
Kuhn, Reinhard Clifford. The demon of noontide : ennui in Western literature / [by] Reinhard Kuhn. — Princeton ; Guildford : Princeton University Press, [1977]. — xvi, 395p : ill ; 25cm.
Published in the United States: 1976. — Bibl.: p.379-386. — Index.
ISBN 0-691-06311-7 : £17.40
(B77-09888)

810.9 — AMERICAN LITERATURE. HISTORY AND CRITICAL STUDIES

810'.9 — English literature. American writers, 1800-1915. *Critical studies*
Brooks, Van Wyck. Our literary heritage : a pictorial history of the writer in America / [by] Van Wyck Brooks & Otto Bettmann. — New York ; London : Paddington Press, [1977]. — ix,246p : ill, facsims, ports ; 28cm.
Originally published: as 'Our literary heritage', New York : Dutton, 1956 ; and as 'A pictorial history of American literature', London : Dent, 1957. — Index.
ISBN 0-448-22061-x Pbk : £3.95
(B77-16557)

810'.9'001 — English literature. American writers, 1607-1830. *Critical studies*
American literature, 1764-1789 : the revolutionary years / Everett Emerson, editor. — Madison ; London : University of Wisconsin Press, 1977. — xvi,301,[1]p ; 24cm.
Bibl. — Index.
ISBN 0-299-07270-3 : £11.25
(B77-25158)

810'.9'0052 — English literature. American writers, 1900-1945. *Biographies*
Cowley, Malcolm. Exile's return : a literary odyssey of the 1920s / by Malcolm Cowley. — [New ed.]. — Harmondsworth [etc.] : Penguin, 1976. — vi,322p ; 20cm.
This ed. originally published: New York : Viking Press, 1951. — Index.
ISBN 0-14-004392-6 Pbk : Unpriced
(B77-11363)

810'.9'0052 — English literature. American writers, 1900-1975. *Critical studies. Essays*
Coxe, Louis Osborne. Enabling acts : selected essays in criticism / by Louis Coxe. — Columbia [Miss.] ; London : University of Missouri Press ; [London] : [Distributed by American University Publishers], 1976. — [9], 164p : ports ; 23cm.
ISBN 0-8262-0200-4 : £7.65
(B77-06236)

Farrell, James Thomas. Literary essays, 1954-1974 / [by] James T. Farrell ; collected and edited by Jack Alan Robbins. — Port Washington ; London : Kennikat Press, 1976. — ix,147p ; 23cm. — (Kennikat Press national university publications : literary criticism series)
ISBN 0-8046-9125-8 : £8.45
(B77-21374)

810'.9'0052 — English literature. American writers. Southern states writers, 1900-1976. *Critical studies*
Gray, Richard. The literature of memory : modern writers of the American South / by Richard Gray. — London : Edward Arnold, 1977. — xi,377p ; 24cm.
Bibl.: p.325-369. — Index.
ISBN 0-7131-5861-1 : £12.50
(B77-22783)

810'.9'32 — English literature. American negro writers, to 1976. Special themes: Africa. *Critical studies*
Berghahn, Marion. Images of Africa in Black American literature / [by] Marion Berghahn. — London [etc.] : Macmillan, 1977. — x,230p ; 23cm.
Bibl.: p.224-228. — Index.
ISBN 0-333-22326-8 : £8.95
(B77-34008)

810'.9'356 — English literature. American writers, 1900-1975. Special themes: Cars. *Critical studies*
Dettelbach, Cynthia Golomb. In the driver's seat : the automobile in American literature and popular culture / [by] Cynthia Golomb Dettelbach. — Westport, Conn. ; London : Greenwood Press, 1976. — xii,139p : ill, ports ; 22cm. — (Contributions in American studies ; no.25)
Bibl.: p.129-132. — Index.
ISBN 0-8371-8593-9 : £8.95
(B77-17703)

810'.9'38 — English literature. American writers. Special subjects: Self. Political aspects, to 1973. *Critical studies*
Warren, Robert Penn. Democracy and poetry / [by] Robert Penn Warren. — Cambridge, Mass. ; London : Harvard University Press, 1976. — xvi,102p ; 22cm. — (Jefferson lecture in the humanities ; 1974)
Originally published: 1975.
£4.50
ISBN 0-674-19625-2
Also classified at 321.8'0973
(B77-04376)

810'.9'896 — English literature. American negro writers, 1900-1945. *Critical studies*
Perry, Margaret, *b.1933.* Silence to the drums : a survey of the literature of the Harlem renaissance / [by] Margaret Perry. — Westport, Conn. ; London : Greenwood Press, 1976. — xv,3-193,[1]p ; 22cm. — (Contributions in Afro-American and African studies ; no.18)
Bibl.: p.175-187. — Index.
ISBN 0-8371-7847-9 : £10.25
(B77-17704)

810'.9'971 — English literature. Canadian writers, to 1972. *Critical studies*
Waterston, Elizabeth. Survey : a short history of Canadian literature / by Elizabeth Waterston. — Toronto ; London [etc.] : Methuen, 1973. — [8],215p : ill ; 18cm. — (Methuen Canadian literature series)
Bibl. — Index.
ISBN 0-458-90950-5 : Unpriced
ISBN 0-458-90930-0 Pbk : £2.75
(B77-21375)

810'.9'9729 — English literature. West Indian writers, 1900-. *Critical studies*
Ramchand, Kenneth. An introduction to the study of West Indian literature / [by] Kenneth Ramchand. — Sunbury-on-Thames [etc.] : Nelson Caribbean, 1976. — ix,183p ; 22cm.
Bibl.: p.180-183.
ISBN 0-17-566058-1 Pbk : £2.50
(B77-05029)

811 — AMERICAN POETRY

811 — Poetry in English. Bahamian writers, 1945-. *Texts*
Turner, Telcine. Song of the surreys / by Telcine Turner ; illustrations by James O. Rolle. — London [etc.] : Macmillan, 1977. — [4],59p : ill ; 14x22cm.
ISBN 0-333-21279-7 Sd : £0.60
(B77-13823)

811 — Poetry in English. Barbadian writers, 1945-. *Texts*
Brathwaite, Edward. Mother poem / [by] Edward Kamau Brathwaite. — Oxford [etc.] : Oxford University Press, 1977. — x,122p ; 22cm.
ISBN 0-19-211859-5 Pbk : £2.95 : CIP rev.
(B77-17046)

Kizerman, Rudolph. I'm here : poems of soul / by Rudolph Kizerman ; with an introduction by Andrew Salkey and a final rap from Ted Joans. — London (23 Bedford Row, WC1R 5BH) : Blackbird Books Ltd, 1975. — [12], 98p : ill ; 20cm.
ISBN 0-901813-01-x Pbk : Unpriced
(B77-03195)

Suttle, Charles Richard William. Awakened from the dreadful grips of slumber / by C.W.R. [i.e. C.R.W.] Suttle. — Chesterfield (26 Southdown Ave., Loudsley Green, Chesterfield, Derbyshire [S40 4QL]) : The author, [1976]. — [16]p : ports ; 21cm.
ISBN 0-9502017-2-3 Sd : £0.60
(B77-07554)

811'.008 — Poetry in English. American writers, to 1976. *Anthologies*

The **Penguin** book of American verse / edited with an introduction by Geoffrey Moore. — Harmondsworth [etc.] : Penguin, 1977. — 656p ; 19cm.
Bibl.: p.604-638. — Index.
ISBN 0-14-042198-x Pbk : £1.75
(B77-13217)

811'.009 — Poetry in English. American writers, 1668-1892. *Critical studies*

Gelpi, Albert Joseph. The tenth muse : the psyche of the American poet / [by] Albert Gelpi. — Cambridge, Mass. ; London : Harvard University Press, 1975. — xxi,327p ; 25cm.
Index.
ISBN 0-674-87441-2 : £11.25
(B77-19595)

811'.009 — Poetry in English. American writers, to 1960. *Critical studies*

Pearce, Roy Harvey. The continuity of American poetry / by Roy Harvey Pearce. — Princeton ; Guildford : Princeton University Press, 1977. — xv,442p ; 24cm.
Originally published: Princeton : Princeton University Press, 1961. — Index.
ISBN 0-691-01254-7 Pbk : £4.10
(B77-24418)

811.2 — AMERICAN POETRY, 1776-1830
811'.2 — Poetry in English. American writers, 1776-1830. *Texts*

Moore, Clement Clarke. [A visit from St Nicholas]. The night before Christmas / [by] Clement Clarke Moore ; illustrated by Elisa Trimby. — London [etc.] : E. Benn, 1977. — [24]p : chiefly col ill ; 22cm.
ISBN 0-510-09806-1 : £2.50
(B77-22073)

811.3 — AMERICAN POETRY, 1830-1861
811'.3 — Poetry in English. American writers, 1830-1861. *Texts*

Longfellow, Henry Wadsworth. Hiawatha / [by Henry Longfellow]. — Kettering (27 Mill Dale Rd, Kettering, [Northants.]) : J.L. Carr Publisher, [1977]. — [19]p ; 13cm.
ISBN 0-900847-76-x Sd : £0.20
(B77-07546)

Longfellow, Henry Wadsworth. The song of Hiawatha / by H.W. Longfellow ; line drawings by Kiddell-Monroe. — London : Dent [etc.], 1972. — viii,214p : ill(chiefly col) ; 22cm. — ([Children's illustrated classics ; no.46])
Originally published: with these illustrations, 1960.
ISBN 0-460-05046-x : £2.50
(B77-10898)

Whitman, Walt. The portable Walt Whitman / selected and with notes by Mark Van Doren. — Revised ed. / revised by Malcolm Cowley ; with a chronology and a bibliographical check list by Gay Wilson Allen. — Harmondsworth [etc.] : Penguin, 1977. — xxxvii,648p ; 19cm. — (The Viking portable library)
This ed. of this collection originally published: as 'Walt Whitman'. New York : Viking Press, 1974. — Bibl.: p.641-648. — Contents include: Democratic vistas. Originally published: Washington, D.C. : Redfield, 1871 - Specimen days. Originally published: as 'Specimen days and collect'. Philadelphia : West, 1882-1883.
ISBN 0-14-015078-1 Pbk : £1.95
(B77-34009)

811'.3 — Poetry in English. American writers. Whitman, Walt. Leaves of grass. *Critical studies*

Marki, Ivan. The trial of the poet : an interpretation of the first edition of 'Leaves of grass' / by Ivan Marki. — New York ; Guildford : Columbia University Press, [1977]. — xvii,301p ; 24cm.
Published in the United States: 1976. — Bibl.: p.285-295. — Index.
ISBN 0-231-03984-0 : £12.14
(B77-09205)

811.52 — AMERICAN POETRY, 1900-1945
811'.5'2 — Poetry in English. American writers, 1900-1945. *Texts*

Aiken, Conrad. A little who's zoo of mild animals / [by] Conrad Aiken ; illustrated by John Vernon Lord. — London : Cape, 1977. — [32]p : ill(chiefly col) ; 28cm.
ISBN 0-224-01351-3 : £2.95 : CIP rev.
(B77-06237)

Armour, Richard. Sea full of whales / [by] Richard Armour ; Paul Galdone drew the pictures. — Tadworth : World's Work, 1976. — [37]p : chiefly ill(some col) ; 26cm.
Originally published: New York : McGraw-Hill, 1974.
ISBN 0-437-24006-1 : £2.40
(B77-00903)

Cather, Willa. April twilights (1903) : poems / by Willa Cather ; edited with an introduction by Bernice Slote. — Revised ed. — Lincoln, [Neb.] ; London : University of Nebraska Press, 1976. — xlviii,88p,leaf of plate,[2]p of plates : 2 facsims, port ; 21cm.
'A Bison book'. — This ed. originally published: Lincoln, Neb. : University of Nebraska Press, 1968. — Bibl.: p.75-88.
ISBN 0-8032-5851-8 Pbk : £1.80
(B77-05590)

Dewey, John. The poems of John Dewey / edited with an introduction by Jo Ann Boydston. — Carbondale [etc.] ; Southern Illinois University Press ; London [etc.] : Feffer and Simons, 1977. — lxviii,153p ; 24cm.
Index.
ISBN 0-8093-0800-2 : £11.20
(B77-34010)

Fisher, Aileen. In the woods, in the meadow, in the sky / by Aileen Fisher ; illustrated by Margot Tomes. — Tadworth : World's Work, 1977. — 64p : ill ; 24cm.
Originally published: New York : Scribner, 1965 ; Tadworth : World's Work, 1967. — Index.
ISBN 0-437-40100-6 : £2.10
(B77-31391)

Johnson, James Weldon. God's trombones : seven negro sermons in verse / by James Weldon Johnson ; drawings by Aaron Douglas ; lettering by C.B. Falls. — Harmondsworth [etc.] : Penguin, 1976. — [8],56p,[16]p of plates : ill ; 18cm. — (The Penguin poets)
Originally published: New York : Viking Press, 1927.
ISBN 0-14-042217-x Pbk : Unpriced
(B77-09206)

Pound, Ezra. Collected early poems of Ezra Pound / edited by Michael John King ; with an introduction by Louis L. Martz. — London : Faber, 1977. — xxii,330p : facsims, port ; 24cm.
This collection originally published: New York : New Directions, 1976. — Index.
ISBN 0-571-10930-6 : £12.00
(B77-13218)

Sandeen, Ernest. Like any road anywhere : new poems / [by] Ernest Sandeen. — Notre Dame [Ind.] ; London : University of Notre Dame Press, 1976. — lx,100p ; 23cm.
ISBN 0-268-01255-5 Pbk : £4.00
(B77-03192)

Warren, Robert Penn. Selected poems, 1923-1975 / [by] Robert Penn Warren. — London : Secker and Warburg, 1976. — iii-xvii, 325,[1]p ; 25cm.
Also published: New York : Random House, 1976.
ISBN 0-436-56316-9 : £7.95
(B77-10515)

811'.5'2 — Poetry in English. American writers. Crosby, Harry. *Biographies*

Wolff, Geoffrey. Black Sun : the brief transit and violent eclipse of Harry Crosby / [by] Geoffrey Wolff. — London : Hamilton, 1977. — ii-xv, 367,[1]p,[16]p of plates : ill, ports ; 25cm.
Originally published: New York : Random House, 1976. — Bibl.: p.351-359. — Index.
ISBN 0-241-89529-4 : £4.95
(B77-08016)

811'.5'2 — Poetry in English. American writers. Hughes, Langston. *Critical studies*

Jemie, Onwuchekwa. Langston Hughes : an introduction to the poetry / [by] Onwuchekwa Jemie. — New York ; Guildford : Columbia University Press, 1976. — xxxiii,234p ; 20cm. — (Columbia introductions to twentieth-century American poetry)
Bibl.: p.215-224. — Index.
ISBN 0-231-03780-5 : £6.30
(B77-13821)

811'.5'2 — Poetry in English. American writers. Lowell, Robert. *Critical studies*

Chambers, Barry. Robert Lowell / prepared by Barry Chambers ; for the [Open University] Course Team. — Milton Keynes : Open University Press, 1976. — 48p : ill, port ; 30cm. — (Arts, a third level course : twentieth century poetry ; unit 27) (A306 ; 27)
Bibl.: p.47.
ISBN 0-335-05118-9 Pbk : £0.95
(B77-02535)

811'.5'2 — Poetry in English. American writers. Pound, Ezra. *Critical studies*

Davie, Donald. Ezra Pound / [by] Donald Davie. — Harmondsworth [etc.] : Penguin, 1976. — x, 134p ; 19cm. — (Penguin modern masters)
Originally published: as 'Pound'. London : Fontana, 1975. — Bibl.: p.121-125. — Index.
ISBN 0-14-004318-7 Pbk : Unpriced
(B77-02536)

811'.5'2 — Poetry in English. American writers. Pound, Ezra. Cantos, The. I-XVI. *Critical studies*

Bush, Ronald. The genesis of Ezra Pound's 'Cantos' / [by] Ronald Bush. — Princeton ; Guildford : Princeton University Press, [1977]. — xv,327,[1]p : ill ; 23cm.
Published in the United States: 1976. — Index.
ISBN 0-691-06308-7 : £11.50
(B77-08518)

811'.5'2 — Poetry in English. American writers. Stevens, Wallace. *Critical studies*

Bloom, Harold. Wallace Stevens, the poems of our climate / by Harold Bloom. — Ithaca ; London : Cornell University Press, 1977. — xi, 413p ; 24cm.
Index.
ISBN 0-8014-0840-7 : £12.00
(B77-34011)

Weston, Susan B. Wallace Stevens : an introduction to the poetry / [by] Susan B. Weston. — New York ; Guildford : Columbia University Press, 1977. — xxii,151p : 21cm. — (Columbia introductions to twentieth-century American poetry)
Bibl.: p.147-148. — Index.
ISBN 0-231-03990-5 : £7.80
(B77-27312)

811'.5'2 — Poetry in English. American writers. Stevens, Wallace. Romanticism. *Critical studies*

Bornstein, George. Transformations of romanticism in Yeats, Eliot, and Stevens / [by] George Bornstein. — Chicago ; London : University of Chicago Press, 1976[i.e.1977]. — xiii,263,[1]p ; 24cm.
Published in the United States: 1976. — Index.
ISBN 0-226-06643-6 : £11.25
Primary classification 821'.8'0914
(B77-14879)

811'.5'205 — Poetry in English. American writers, 1900-1945. Periodicals with American imprints: 'Poetry', 1912-1922

Williams, Ellen. Harriet Monroe and the poetry renaissance : the first ten years of 'Poetry', 1912-22 / [by] Ellen Williams. — Urbana [etc.] ; London : University of Illinois Press, 1977. — xiv,312p ; 24cm.
Bibl.: p.297-300. — Index.
ISBN 0-252-00478-7 : £6.70
(B77-25159)

811'.5'208 — Poetry in English. American writers, 1900-1945. *Anthologies*

The **American** long poem : an annotated selection / [by] Stephen Fender. — London : Edward Arnold, 1977. — ix,254p ; 23cm.
Bibl.: p.237-240.
ISBN 0-7131-5922-7 Pbk : £3.95
(B77-30559)

811.54 — AMERICAN POETRY, 1945-
811'.5'4 — Poetry in English. American writers, 1945-. *Texts*

Aldrich, Jonathan. Croquet lover at the dinner table : poems / by Jonathan Aldrich. — Columbia ; London : University of Missouri Press, 1977. — 64p ; 23cm. — (A breakthrough book)
ISBN 0-8262-0205-5 : £4.60
(B77-25831)

Ashbery, John. Self-portrait in a convex mirror : poems / by John Ashbery. — Manchester : Carcanet New Press, 1977. — [11],83p ; 23cm.
Originally published: New York : Viking Press, 1975.
ISBN 0-85635-209-8 : £2.25
(B77-19596)

Asimov, Isaac. Lecherous limericks / [by] Isaac Asimov ; boldly illustrated by Arthur Robins. — London : Corgi, 1977. — 205p : ill ; 18cm.
Cover title: Asimov's lecherous limericks. — This collection originally published: New York : Walker, 1975.
ISBN 0-552-10553-8 Pbk : £0.75
(B77-28825)

Bail, Grace Shattuck. Shadow fingers : poems / by Grace Shattuck Bail. — London : Mitre Press, 1976. — 72p ; 19cm.
ISBN 0-7051-0237-8 : £1.60
(B77-05591)

Berry, Wendell. Clearing / [by] Wendell Berry. — New York ; London : Harcourt Brace Jovanovich, 1977. — [9],52p ; 21cm.
ISBN 0-15-118150-0 : £4.50
ISBN 0-15-618051-0 Pbk : £1.90
(B77-31392)

Berry, Wendell. The country of marriage / [by] Wendell Berry. — New York ; London : Harcourt Brace Jovanovich, [1976]. — [8],53p ; 21cm. — (A harvest book)
Published in the United States: 1975.
ISBN 0-15-622697-9 Pbk : £1.55
(B77-06238)

Bishop, Elizabeth. Geography III / [by] Elizabeth Bishop. — London : Chatto and Windus, 1977. — [10],50p ; 22cm.
This collection originally published: New York : Farrar, Straus and Giroux, 1976.
ISBN 0-7011-2238-2 Pbk : £2.50 : CIP rev
(B77-16558)

Bowers, Edgar. Living together : new and selected poems / [by] Edgar Bowers. — Manchester : Carcanet New Press, 1977. — 84p ; 23cm.
ISBN 0-85635-221-7 : £2.90
(B77-30560)

Breier, Morton A. Aleph zero / [by] Morton A. Breier. — Staines (44 Penton Rd, Staines, Middx TW18 2LD) : Alex Scott Publications, 1976. — [94]p : ill ; 26cm.
ISBN 0-9505526-0-7 : £4.25
(B77-05592)

Broumas, Olga. Beginning with O / [by] Olga Broumas ; foreword by Stanley Kunitz. — New Haven ; London : Yale University Press, 1977. — xiii,74p ; 21cm. — (Yale series of younger poets ; vol.72)
ISBN 0-300-02106-2 : £5.00
ISBN 0-300-02111-9 Pbk : £2.15
(B77-25160)

Cole, William, *b.1919.* A boy named Mary Jane, and other silly verse / by William Cole ; illustrated by George MacClain. — New York ; London : F. Watts, 1977. — 64p : ill ; 22cm.
ISBN 0-531-01144-5 : £1.95
(B77-29632)

Connellan, Leo. First selected poems [of] Leo Connellan. — [Pittsburgh] : University of Pittsburgh Press ; London : Feffer and Simons : [Distributed by Transatlantic Book Service], 1976. — [7],70p ; 21cm. — (Pitt poetry series)
ISBN 0-8229-5268-8 Pbk : £2.20
(B77-05593)

Creeley, Robert. Myself / [by] Robert Creeley. — Knotting : Sceptre Press, 1977. — [10]p ; 21cm.
Limited ed. of 250 numbered copies of which nos.1-50 are signed by the poet.
Sd : £1.00
Signed ed.: £7.00
(B77-15433)

Deesen, Herbert C. Precious moments / by Herbert C. Deesen. — London [etc.] : Regency Press, 1976. — 94p ; 22cm.
ISBN 0-7212-0481-3 Pbk : £0.60
(B77-10516)

Dressel, Jon. Hard love and a country : poems / by Jon Dressel. — Swansea : C. Davies, 1977. — 46p ; 22cm. — (The Triskel poets ; 20)
Pbk : £0.90
(B77-23652)

Dylan, Bob. Writings and drawings / [by] Bob Dylan. — St Albans : Panther, 1974. — 479p : ill ; 20cm.
Originally published: New York : Knopf, 1972 ; London : Cape, 1973. — Index.
ISBN 0-586-04088-9 Pbk : £1.50
(B77-20531)

Engels, John. Blood mountain / [by] John Engels. — Pittsburgh : University of Pittsburgh Press ; London : Feffer and Simons, 1977. — [9],54,[1]p ; 22cm. — (Pitt poetry series)
Limited ed. of 550 hardbound copies, 50 of which are specially bound and numbered and signed by the author.
ISBN 0-8229-3338-1 : £5.21
ISBN 0-8229-5277-7 Pbk : £2.22
ISBN 0-8229-3289-x Signed ed. : £22.50
(B77-32113)

Froman, Robert. Seeing things / written and designed by Robert Froman. — London : Abelard, 1977. — 64p ; 21cm. — (A grasshopper book)
Originally published: New York : Crowell, 1974.
ISBN 0-200-72435-5 : £1.75
ISBN 0-200-72436-3 Pbk : £0.50
(B77-22074)

Green, Rose Basile. Primo vino / [by] Rose Basile Green. — South Brunswick [etc.] : Barnes ; London : Yoseloff, 1974. — 83p ; 22cm.
ISBN 0-498-01660-9 : £2.25
(B77-23653)

Halperin, Mark. Backroads / [by] Mark Halperin. — [Pittsburgh] : University of Pittsburgh Press ; London : Feffer and Simons : [Distributed by Transatlantic Book Service], 1976. — [7],68p ; 21cm. — (Pitt poetry series)
ISBN 0-8229-3311-x : Unpriced
ISBN 0-8229-5266-1 Pbk : £2.20
(B77-05594)

Hanzlicek, C G. Stars : poems / by C.G. Hanzlicek. — Columbia ; London : University of Missouri Press, 1977. — [8],69,[1]p ; 23cm. — (A breakthrough book)
ISBN 0-8262-0226-8 : £4.50
(B77-34012)

Hardison, Osborne Bennett. Pro musica antiqua : poems / by O.B. Hardison, Jr. — Baton Rouge ; London : Louisiana State University Press ; [London] : [Distributed by Transatlantic Book Service], 1977. — [7],55p ; 22cm.
ISBN 0-8071-0295-4 Pbk : £6.00
ISBN 0-8071-0296-2 Pbk : £3.00
(B77-33396)

Hoffman, Daniel Gerard. Able was I ere I saw Elba : selected poems, 1954-74 / [by] Daniel Hoffman. — London : Hutchinson, 1977. — 114p ; 22cm.
ISBN 0-09-128241-1 Pbk : £2.95
(B77-09889)

Hunter, Paul. Pullman : a songbook from aboard the train / by Paul Hunter. — Seattle ; London : University of Washington Press, 1976. — [11],67p : ill(on lining papers) ; 25cm.
ISBN 0-295-95427-2 : £4.80
(B77-05016)

Jong, Erica. Loveroot / [by] Erica Jong. — London : Secker and Warburg, 1977. — [9], 114,[1]p ; 23cm.
Originally published: New York : Holt, Rinehart and Winston, 1975.
ISBN 0-436-22446-1 : £3.90
(B77-15434)

Liddy, James. Corca Bascinn / [by] James Liddy. — Dublin : Dolmen Press, 1977. — 64p ; 22cm.
ISBN 0-85105-314-9 Pbk : £2.50
(B77-32114)

Lindsey, Jim. In lieu of Mecca / [by] Jim Lindsey. — [Pittsburgh] : University of Pittsburgh Press ; London : Feffer and Simons : [Distributed by Transatlantic Book Service], 1976. — [9],66p ; 21cm. — (Pitt poetry series)
ISBN 0-8229-5267-x Pbk : £2.20
(B77-06239)

McElroy, Colleen J. Music from home : selected poems / by Colleen J. McElroy ; with preface by John Gardner and an introduction by Knute Skinner. — Carbondale [etc.] : Southern Illinois University Press ; London [etc.] : Feffer and Simons, 1976. — xvii,100p ; 23cm. — (Sagittarius poetry series)
Index.
ISBN 0-8093-0774-x : Unpriced
(B77-14370)

McKuen, Rod. Coming close to the earth / [by] Rod McKuen. — London : Elm Tree Books, 1977. — 160p : ill ; 22cm.
ISBN 0-241-89717-3 : £3.50
ISBN 0-241-89762-9 Limited ed. : £7.50
(B77-30561)

Mahoney, John Joseph. The wine of the muses : forty poems / by John J. Mahoney. — London : Mitre Press, 1976. — 58p ; 22cm.
ISBN 0-7051-0247-5 : £1.90
(B77-05595)

Merrill, James. Divine comedies : poems / by James Merrill. — Oxford [etc.] : Oxford University Press, 1977. — [5],138p ; 23cm.
ISBN 0-19-211867-6 Pbk : £2.95
(B77-32115)

Miller, Calvin. The singer / [by] Calvin Miller. — London : Falcon Books, 1976. — 151p : ill ; 22cm.
Originally published: Downers Grove : Inter Varsity Press, 1975.
ISBN 0-85491-537-0 Pbk : £1.50
(B77-02537)

Miller, Calvin. The song / [by] Calvin Miller. — London : Falcon Books, 1977. — 168p : ill ; 22cm.
Also published: Downers Grove : Inter-Varsity Press, 1977.
ISBN 0-85491-544-3 Pbk : £1.75
(B77-28037)

Morgan, Frederick. Poems of the two worlds / [by] Frederick Morgan. — Urbana [etc.] ; London : University of Illinois Press, 1977. — [9],131p ; 21cm.
ISBN 0-252-00604-6 : £6.00
ISBN 0-252-00605-4 Pbk : £3.00
(B77-28038)

Richardson, James, *b.1950.* Reservations : poems / by James Richardson. — Princeton ; Guildford : Princeton University Press, 1977. — [8],75,[1]p ; 23cm. — (Princeton series of contemporary poets)
ISBN 0-691-06329-x : £5.65
ISBN 0-691-01334-9 Pbk : £2.25
(B77-34013)

Rivers, Henry. A canticle for winds : poems / by Henry Rivers. — Oxford : Alden Press, 1976. — vii,97p ; 23cm.
ISBN 0-900040-20-3 : £3.00
(B77-05017)

Schulman, Grace. Burn down the icons : poems / by Grace Schulman. — Princeton ; Guildford : Princeton University Press, 1976. — [10],65p ; 23cm. — (Princeton series of contemporary poets)
ISBN 0-691-06317-6 : £6.05
ISBN 0-691-01330-6 Pbk : £3.20
(B77-06240)

Sexton, Anne. 45 Mercy Street / [by] Anne Sexton ; edited by Linda Gray Sexton. — London : Secker and Warburg, 1977. — xi, 114p ; 23cm.
Originally published: Boston, Mass. : Houghton Mifflin, 1976.
ISBN 0-436-44750-9 : £3.90
(B77-15435)

Sexton, Anne. The awful rowing toward God / by Anne Sexton. — London : Chatto and Windus, 1977. — 64p ; 22cm.
ISBN 0-7011-2201-3 Pbk : £2.50
(B77-07547)

Smith, Dave. Cumberland Station : poems / by Dave Smith. — Urbana [etc.] ; London : University of Illinois Press, 1976. — [11],94p ; 21cm.
ISBN 0-252-00581-3 : £6.00
ISBN 0-252-00582-1 Pbk : £2.60
(B77-14873)

Soto, Gary. The elements of San Joaquin / [by] Gary Soto. — Pittsburgh : University of Pittsburgh Press ; London : Feffer and Simons, 1977. — [8],56p ; 21cm. — (Pitt poetry series)
ISBN 0-8229-3335-7 : £5.21
ISBN 0-8229-5279-3 Pbk : £2.20
(B77-32116)

Stokesbury, Leon. Often in different landscapes / by Leon Stokesbury ; photographs by Frank Armstrong. — Austin ; London : University of Texas Press, 1976. — viii,69p : ill ; 20cm. — (The University of Texas Press poetry series ; no.1)
ISBN 0-292-76004-3 : £7.20
ISBN 0-292-76005-1 Pbk : £3.20
(B77-05596)

Stone, Ruth. Cheap : new poems and ballads / [by] Ruth Stone. — New York ; London : Harcourt Brace Jovanovich, [1976]. — [9], 101p ; 21cm. — (A harvest book)
Published in the United States: 1975.
ISBN 0-15-117034-7 : £5.65
ISBN 0-15-616798-0 Pbk : £2.70
(B77-06241)

Terris, Virginia R. Tracking : poems / by Virginia R. Terris. — Urbana [etc.] ; London : University of Illinois Press, 1976. — [7],70p ; 21cm.
ISBN 0-252-00602-x : £6.00
ISBN 0-252-00603-8 Pbk : £2.60
(B77-14874)

Thurman, Judith. Flashlight, and other poems / by Judith Thurman ; illustrated by Reina Rubel. — Harmondsworth : Kestrel Books, 1977. — [8],35p : ill ; 22cm.
Originally published: New York : Atheneum, 1976.
ISBN 0-7226-5411-1 : £1.95
(B77-26462)

Wagoner, David. Collected poems, 1956-1976 / [by] David Wagoner. — Bloomington ; London : Indiana University Press, 1976. — xvii,301p ; 25cm.
ISBN 0-253-11245-1 : £9.45
(B77-01757)

Wier, Dara. Blood, hook & eye / by Dara Wier. — Austin ; London : University of Texas Press, 1977. — ix,70p ; 24cm. — (University of Texas Press poetry series ; no.2)
ISBN 0-292-70720-7 : £6.00
ISBN 0-292-70721-5 Pbk : £3.00
(B77-23654)

Wilbur, Richard. The mind-reader : new poems / by Richard Wilbur. — London : Faber, 1977. — 3-80p ; 20cm.
This collection originally published: New York : Harcourt Brace Jovanovich, 1976.
ISBN 0-571-11070-3 Pbk : £2.50 : CIP rev.
(B77-07548)

Woods, John. Striking the earth / [by] John Woods. — Bloomington ; London : Indiana University Press, 1976. — 2-93p ; 22cm.
ISBN 0-253-18550-5 : £5.60
(B77-03193)

811'.5'4 — Poetry in English. American writers. Bevington, Helen, 1960-1969. *Autobiographies*

Bevington, Helen. Along came the witch : a journal in the 1960's / [by] Helen Bevington. — New York ; London : Harcourt Brace Jovanovich, 1976. — [9],223p ; 22cm.
ISBN 0-15-105080-5 : £6.05
(B77-06837)

811'.5'4 — Poetry in English. American writers. McKuen, Rod. *Autobiographies*

McKuen, Rod. Finding my father : one man's search for identity / [by] Rod McKuen. — London : Elm Tree Books, 1977. — 255p : ill, facsim, ports ; 23cm.
Originally published: Los Angeles : Coward, McCann and Geoghegan, 1976. — Bibl.: p.245-247. — Index.
ISBN 0-241-89625-8 : £4.95
(B77-14875)

811'.5'4 — Poetry in English. American writers. Plath, Sylvia. Images & themes. Psychological aspects

Holbrook, David. Sylvia Plath : poetry and existence / by David Holbrook. — London : Athlone Press, 1976. — [9],308p ; 23cm.
Bibl.: p.298-302. — Index.
ISBN 0-485-11143-8 : £7.00
(B77-06242)

811'.5'4 — Poetry in English. American writers. Roethke, Theodore. *Critical studies*

La Belle, Jenijoy. The echoing wood of Theodore Roethke / [by] Jenijoy La Belle. — Princeton ; Guildford : Princeton University Press, 1976. — xi,174p ; 23cm. — (Princeton essays in literature)
Index.
ISBN 0-691-06312-5 : £8.00
(B77-07549)

811'.5'4 — Poetry in English. Canadian writers, 1945-. *Texts*

Lochhead, Douglas. The full furnace : collected poems / [by] Douglas Lochhead. — Toronto [etc.] : McGraw-Hill Ryerson ; New York ; London [etc.] : [McGraw-Hill], [1976]. — [13], 168p ; 23cm.
This collection published in Canada : 1975. — Index.
ISBN 0-07-082239-5 : Unpriced
ISBN 0-07-082238-7 Pbk : Unpriced
(B77-05018)

Rowe, Terry. To you with love / [by] Terry Rowe. — 2nd ed. — London : Souvenir Press, 1977. — [6],103p ; 23cm.
This ed. originally published: Toronto : Lester and Orpen, 1973.
ISBN 0-285-62271-4 : £2.25
(B77-09207)

811'.5'4 — Poetry in English. Puerto Rican writers, 1945-. *Texts*

Arrillaga, Maria. New York in the sixties / by Maria Arrillaga. — Bakewell (Youlgrave, Bakewell, Derbyshire) : Hub Publications Ltd, 1976. — [3],20p : port ; 21cm.
ISBN 0-905049-11-x Sd : £0.90
(B77-05019)

812.52 — AMERICAN DRAMA, 1900-1945
812'.5'2 — Drama in English. American writers, 1900-1945. *Texts*

Foster, Paul. Marcus Brutus / [by] Paul Foster. Silver Queen Saloon / [text by Paul Foster ; lyrics Paul Foster and John Braden ; music John Braden]. — London : J. Calder : [Distributed by Calder and Boyars], 1977. — 159p : music ; 21cm. — (Playscript ; 77)
'Silver Queen Saloon' originally published: New York : French, 1976.
ISBN 0-7145-3564-8 : £5.50
Also classified at 782.8'1'2
(B77-17047)

Miller, Arthur. The crucible / [by] Arthur Miller ; text and criticism edited by Gerald Weales. — Harmondsworth [etc.] : Penguin, 1977. — xxi,484p ; 20cm. — (Viking critical library)
This edition originally published: New York : Viking Press, 1971. — Bibl.: p.477-484.
ISBN 0-14-015507-4 Pbk : £1.95
(B77-27313)

Miller, Arthur. The portable Arthur Miller / edited, with an introduction, by Harold Clurman. — Harmondsworth [etc.] : Penguin, 1977. — xxv,566p ; 18cm. — (The Viking portable library)
This collection originally published: New York : Viking Press, 1971. — Bibl.: p.563-566. — Includes: Death of a salesman - The crucible - Incident at Vichy - The price - The misfits.
ISBN 0-14-015071-4 Pbk : Unpriced
(B77-09890)

Miller, Arthur. A view from the bridge : a play in two acts / by Arthur Miller. — [Revised ed.] ; with a new introduction [by the author]. — Harmondsworth [etc.] : Penguin, 1977. — x, 86p ; 20cm. — (Penguin plays)
This ed. originally published: New York : Viking Press, 1960.
ISBN 0-14-048135-4 Pbk : Unpriced
(B77-32117)

Patrick, John, *b.1905.* Love nest for three / by John Patrick. — New York ; London [etc.] : French, 1974. — 71p : plan ; 19cm.
Six men, 3 women, super.
ISBN 0-573-61612-4 Sd : £1.65
(B77-24419)

812'.5'2 — Drama in English. American writers. Hellman, Lillian. *Autobiographies*

Hellman, Lillian. Pentimento : a book of portraits / by Lillian Hellman. — London : Quartet Books, 1976. — [5],297p ; 20cm.
Originally published: Boston, Mass. : Little, Brown, 1973 ; London : Macmillan, 1974.
ISBN 0-7043-3105-5 Pbk : £1.50
(B77-03194)

812'.5'2 — Drama in English. American writers. Hellman, Lillian, ca 1935-ca 1960. *Autobiographies*

Hellman, Lillian. Scoundrel time / by Lillian Hellman ; introduction by James Cameron ; commentary by Garry Wills. — London [etc.] : Macmillan, 1976. — 172p,[12]p of plates : ill, ports ; 23cm.
Originally published: Boston, Mass. : Little, Brown, 1976.
ISBN 0-333-21101-4 : £4.95
(B77-01758)

812'.5'2 — Drama in English. American writers. Miller, Arthur. Death of a salesman. *Study outlines*

Altena, I. Notes on Arthur Miller's 'Death of a salesman' / compiled by I. Altena and A.M. Aylwin. — London [etc.] : Methuen, 1976. — [5],42p ; 22cm. — (Study-aid series)
Bibl.: p.42.
ISBN 0-413-36990-0 Sd : £0.60
(B77-13219)

812.54 — AMERICAN DRAMA, 1945-
812'.5'4 — Drama in English. American writers, 1945-. *Texts*

Allison, John, *b.1939.* Stand by your beds, boys : a comedy in three acts / by John Allison and Ray Scantlin. — New York ; London [etc.] : French, 1977. — 83p : plan ; 19cm.
Four men, 2 women, 1 boy.
ISBN 0-573-61610-8 Sd : £1.55
(B77-26463)

Calandra, Anthony C. Life in excellence : a drama in one act / by Anthony C. Calandra. — New York ; London [etc.] : French, 1977. — 48p : plan ; 19cm.
Five men, 3 women.
ISBN 0-573-62287-6 Sd : Unpriced
(B77-10899)

Carmichael, Fred. Foiled by an innocent maid, or, The curse of the iron horse : an old fashioned meller-drammer in one act / by Fred Carmichael. — New York ; London [etc.] : French, 1977. — 41p ; 19cm.
Two men, 4 women.
ISBN 0-573-62169-1 Sd : £0.75
(B77-22784)

Carmichael, Fred. Whatever happened to Mrs Kong? : a comedy in two acts / by Fred Carmichael. — New York ; London [etc.] : French, 1977. — 96p : plans ; 19cm.
Four men, 4 women.
ISBN 0-573-61816-x Sd : £1.65
(B77-23655)

Carter, Steve. Eden : a drama in three acts / by Steve Carter. — New York ; London [etc.] : French, 1976. — 99p : plan ; 19cm.
Four men, 4 women.
ISBN 0-573-60873-3 Sd : £1.65
(B77-21376)

Christopher, Jay. Not with my daughter! : a comedy in three acts / by Jay Christopher. — New York ; London [etc.] : French, 1976. — 69p : plan ; 19cm.
Three men, 3 women.
ISBN 0-573-61321-4 Sd : £1.55
(B77-06243)

Clinton, Edward. The lady who cried fox : a comedy in two acts / by Edward Clinton. — New York ; London [etc.] : French, [1976]. — 60p : plan ; 19cm.
Published in the United States: 1975.
ISBN 0-573-61190-4 Sd : £1.55
(B77-05020)

Cole, Tom. Medal of honor rag : a full length play in one act / by Tom Cole. — New York ; London [etc.] : French, 1977. — 50p : plan ; 19cm.
Three men.
ISBN 0-573-64018-1 Sd : £1.55
(B77-26464)

Crittenden, Jordan. Unexpected guests : a comedy in two acts / by Jordan Crittenden. — New York ; London [etc.] : French, 1977. — 72p : plan ; 19cm.
Five men, 3 women, supers.
ISBN 0-573-61744-9 Sd : £1.65
(B77-28826)

Dee, Peter. A sea of white horses : a play in two acts / by Peter Dee. — New York ; London [etc.] : French, 1976. — 69p : plan ; 19cm.
Two men, 2 women.
ISBN 0-573-61511-x Sd : £1.55
(B77-05021)

Dvoracek, D K. The maturing of Jonathan Pruneberg : a comedy in two acts / by D.K. Dvoracek. — New York ; London [etc.] : French, 1977. — 96,[1]p : plan ; 19cm.
Three men, 3 women.
ISBN 0-573-61285-4 Pbk : £1.65
(B77-28827)

Elliott, Paul C. Perspective : a drama in one act / by Paul C. Elliott. — New York ; London [etc.] : French, 1977. — 22p : plan ; 19cm.
Two men, 5 women.
ISBN 0-573-62424-0 Sd : £0.75
(B77-25832)

Feiffer, Jules. Knock knock : a comedy in three acts / by Jules Feiffer. — New York ; London [etc.] : French, [1977]. — 78p : plans ; 19cm.
Four men, 1 woman. — Originally published: New York : Hill and Wang, 1976.
ISBN 0-573-61127-0 Sd : £1.55
(B77-11364)

Flynn, Louis. Madness on Madrona Drive : a comedy in three acts / by Louis Flynn. — New York ; London [etc.] : French, 1977. — 90p : plan ; 19cm.
Seven men, 5 women.
ISBN 0-573-61207-2 Sd : £1.65
(B77-24420)

Galvin, W Randolph. The baby sitter : a comedy in two acts / by W. Randolph Galvin. — New York ; London [etc.] : French, 1977. — 65p ; 19cm.
One man, 4 women.
ISBN 0-573-60650-1 Sd : £1.65
(B77-28828)

Gardner, Herb. Thieves : a comedy in two acts / by Herb Gardner. — New York ; London [etc.] : French, 1977. — 83p ; 19cm.
Eleven men, 4 women.
ISBN 0-573-61712-0 Sd : £1.65
(B77-32118)

Hall, Nick. Going ape : a farce in two acts / by Nick Hall. — New York [etc.] ; London : French, [1976]. — 83p : plan ; 19cm.
Three men, 2 women. — Published in the United States: 1975.
ISBN 0-573-60974-8 Sd : £1.60
(B77-00904)

Hauptman, William. Comanche Cafe ; and, Domino Courts / by William Hauptman. — [London] : French, [1977]. — [1],63p : 2 plans ; 19cm. — (French's acting edition)
ISBN 0-573-62131-4 Sd : £1.55
(B77-15436)

Hayes, Joseph. Impolite comedy : a comedy in three acts / by Joseph Hayes. — New York ; London [etc.] : French, 1977. — 93p ; 19cm.
Three men, 3 women.
ISBN 0-573-61084-3 Sd : £1.55
(B77-11365)

Heifner, Jack. Vanities : a comedy in three scenes / by Jack Heifner. — New York ; London [etc.] : French, 1976. — 67p ; 19cm.
Three women.
ISBN 0-573-63014-3 Sd : £1.55
(B77-25833)

Kidd, Virginia. Happily ever once upon : a fairy tale parody in three acts / by Virginia Kidd. — New York ; London [etc.] : French, 1977. — 57p : plans ; 19cm.
Three men, 4 women, supers.
ISBN 0-573-61043-6 Sd : £1.55
(B77-11366)

Kvares, Donald. Smoking pistols : a tragicomedy in one act / by Donald Kvares. — New York ; London [etc.] : French, [1977]. — 29p : plan ; 19cm.
One man, 1 woman. — Published in the United States: 1976.
ISBN 0-573-62512-3 Sd : £0.75
(B77-11367)

Lee, Robert E. Sounding brass : a new play about the 13th apostle / by Robert E. Lee. — New York ; London [etc.] : French, 1976. — 61p : plan ; 19cm.
Eight men, 3 women, supers.
ISBN 0-573-61609-4 Sd : £1.55
(B77-06244)

Lim, Paul Stephen. Conpersonas : a recreation in two acts / by Paul Stephen Lim. — New York ; London etc. : French, 1977. — 77p ; 19cm.
Three men, 2 women.
ISBN 0-573-60748-6 Sd : £1.55
(B77-22785)

Lowe, Frank. James Thurber's 'The 13 clocks' / adapted for the stage by Frank Lowe. — New York ; London [etc.] : French, 1976. — 59p : plans ; 19cm.
Thirteen men, 2 women.
ISBN 0-573-65122-1 Sd : £1.55
(B77-06245)

Mamet, David. American buffalo : a drama in two acts / by David Mamet. — New York ; London [etc.] : French, 1977. — 87p : plan ; 19cm.
Three men.
ISBN 0-573-64021-1 Sd : £1.65
(B77-32119)

Marowitz, Charles. Artaud at Rodez / [by] Charles Marowitz. — London : Boyars : Distributed by Calder and Boyars, 1977. — 112p ; 21cm.
ISBN 0-7145-2631-2 : £4.95
ISBN 0-7145-2632-0 Pbk : £1.95
(B77-28039)

Montley, Patricia. Bible herstory : a one-act comedy in six scenes for an all-female cast / by Patricia Montley. — New York ; London [etc.] : French, 1975. — 48p : ill ; 19cm.
Five to 18 women.
ISBN 0-573-63211-1 Sd : £1.55
(B77-15437)

Murray, John. The monkey walk : a comedy in two acts / by John Murray. — Revised and rewritten [ed.]. — New York ; London [etc.] : French, 1977. — 90p : ill, music, plan ; 19cm.
One man, 1 woman. — This ed. originally published: 1975.
ISBN 0-573-61284-6 Sd : £1.65
(B77-23656)

O'Brien, John. The bottled-up man : a play in one act / by John O'Brien. — New York ; London [etc.] : French, 1977. — 15p : plan ; 19cm.
One man, 1 woman.
ISBN 0-573-62063-6 Sd : £0.30
(B77-28829)

Patrick, John, *b.1907.* Sex on the sixth floor : three one act plays / by John Patrick. — New York ; London [etc.] : French, 1974. — 79p : plan ; 19cm.
ISBN 0-573-61611-6 Sd : £1.65
(B77-23657)

Patrick, Robert. The golden circle : a fantastic farce : a two act play / by Robert Patrick. — New York ; London [etc.] : French, [1977]. — 63p : plans ; 19cm.
Eight men, 4 women. — Published in the United States: 1970?.
ISBN 0-573-62202-7 Sd : Unpriced
(B77-11368)

Patrick, Robert. Play-by-play : (a spectacle of ourselves) : a verse farce in two acts / by Robert Patrick. — New York ; London [etc.] : French, 1975. — 56p ; 19cm.
Four men, two women.
ISBN 0-573-61441-5 Sd : £1.55
(B77-12039)

Perry, Jack. The indoor sport : a comedy in three acts / by Jack Perry. — New York ; London [etc.] : French, 1976. — 107p : plan ; 19cm.
Three men, 3 women.
ISBN 0-573-61085-1 Sd : £1.55
(B77-25161)

Poston, Dick. Burlesque humor revisited : a history-like comedy run-down from the world of burlesque condensed into twelve classic sketches / [by] Dick Poston. — New York ; London [etc.] : French, 1977. — 117p ; 19cm.
Two men, 1 woman.
ISBN 0-573-62062-8 Sd : £1.80
(B77-28830)

Rabe, David William. Streamers : a drama in two acts / by David Rabe. — Revised and rewritten [ed.]. — New York ; London [etc.] : French, 1977. — 105p : plan ; 19cm.
Ten men. — This ed. originally published: 1975.
ISBN 0-573-64019-x Sd : £1.55
(B77-15438)

Sharkey, Jack. The creature creeps! : a comedy in three acts / by Jack Sharkey. — New York ; London [etc.] : French, 1977. — 109p : music, plan ; 19cm.
Four men, 8 women.
ISBN 0-573-60750-8 Sd : £1.65
(B77-21377)

Sharkey, Jack. Dream lover : a romantic comedy in three acts / by Jack Sharkey. — New York ; London [etc.] : French, 1977. — 118p : plan ; 19cm.
Three men, 2 women.
ISBN 0-573-60766-4 Sd : £1.65
(B77-24421)

Sharkey, Jack. Rich is better : a comedy in three acts / by Jack Sharkey. — New York ; London [etc.] : French, 1977. — 109p : plan ; 19cm.
Two men, 2 women.
ISBN 0-573-61459-8 Sd : £1.65
(B77-33397)

Sharkey, Jack. Take a number, darling : a comedy in three acts / by Jack Sharkey. — New York ; London [etc.] : French, 1976. — 111p : music, plans ; 19cm.
Three men, 3 women.
ISBN 0-573-61714-7 Sd : £1.55
(B77-15439)

Swift, Allen. Checking out : a comedy in two acts / by Allen Swift. — New York ; London [etc.] : French, 1975. — 72p : plan ; 19cm.
Seven men, 1 woman.
ISBN 0-573-60749-4 Sd : £1.55
(B77-22786)

Thornber, Geoffrey. Quest for a golden key : a magical adventure in two acts / by Geoffrey Thornber. — Macclesfield (35 Sandringham Rd, Macclesfield, Cheshire SK10 1QB) : New Playwrights' Network, [1977]. — 97p ; 18cm.
Six men, 7 women, 1 child.
Pbk : £1.25
(B77-18950)

Williams, Tennessee. The rose tattoo ; [and], Camino real ; [and], Orpheus descending / [by] Tennessee Williams. — Harmondsworth [etc.] : Penguin, 1976. — 347p ; 18cm. — (Penguin plays)
'The rose tattoo' originally published: New York : New Directions, 1951 ; London : Secker and Warburg, 1954. — 'Camino real' originally published: Norfolk, Conn. : New Directions, 1953 ; London : Secker and Warburg, 1956. — 'Orpheus descending' originally published: New York : New Directions, 1958 ; London : Secker and Warburg, 1958.
ISBN 0-14-048131-1 Pbk : £1.50
(B77-01759)

812'.5'4 — Drama in English. American writers. Williams, Tennessee. ***Autobiographies***

Williams, Tennessee. Memoirs [of] Tennessee Williams. — London : Star Books, 1977. — xv, 268p,[8]p of plates : ill, ports ; 19cm.
Originally published: Garden City, N.Y. : Doubleday, 1975 ; London : W.H. Allen, 1976. — Index.
ISBN 0-352-39558-3 Pbk : £0.85
(B77-23658)

812'.5'4 — Drama in English. Canadian writers, 1945-. ***Texts***

French, David. Of the fields, lately : a drama / by David French. — New York ; London [etc.] : French, 1975. — [9],101p : plan ; 22cm.
Three men, 1 woman.
ISBN 0-573-61356-7 Sd : £1.65
(B77-33398)

813 — AMERICAN FICTION

813'.009 — Fiction in English. American negro writers, to 1974. ***Critical studies***

Rosenblatt, Roger. Black fiction / [by] Roger Rosenblatt. — Cambridge, Mass. ; London : Harvard University Press, 1976. — [11],211p ; 22cm.
Also available in a series of audiocassettes. — Originally published: Cambridge, Mass. : Harvard University Press, 1974. — Bibl.: p.201-203. — Index. — Previous control number ISBN 0-674-07620-6.
£6.40
ISBN 0-674-07622-2 Pbk : £3.00
ISBN 0-674-07620-6
(B77-05025)

813'.009 — Fiction in English. American writers, 1789-1900. ***Critical studies***

Spengemann, William C. The adventurous muse : the poetics of American fiction, 1789-1900 / [by] William C. Spengemann. — New Haven ; London : Yale University Press, 1977. — ix, 290p ; 24cm.
Bibl.: p.277-284. — Index.
ISBN 0-300-02042-2 : £11.25
(B77-25162)

813'.009'32 — Fiction in English. American writers, to 1860. Special themes: Cities

Stout, Janis P. Sodoms in Eden : the city in American fiction before 1860 / [by] Janis P. Stout. — Westport, Conn. ; London : Greenwood Press, 1976. — 163p ; 22cm. — (Contributions in American studies ; no.19)
Bibl.: p.143-155. — Index.
ISBN 0-8371-8585-8 : £10.25
(B77-17048)

813'.009'352 — Fiction in English. American writers, 1790-1890. Special themes: Indians of North America

Barnett, Louise K. The ignoble savage : American literary racism, 1790-1890 / [by] Louise K. Barnett. — Westport, Conn. ; London : Greenwood Press, 1975. — xii,220p : 1 ill ; 22cm. — (Contributions in American studies ; no.18)
Bibl.: p.205-213. — Index.
ISBN 0-8371-8281-6 : £11.50
(B77-18334)

813'.0876 — Science fiction in English. American writers, 1900-1970. Social aspects

Bainbridge, William Sims. The spaceflight revolution : a sociological study / [by] William Sims Bainbridge. — New York ; London [etc.] : Wiley, [1977]. — x,294p : ill ; 24cm. — (Science, culture and society)
'A Wiley-Interscience publication'. — Published in the United States: 1976. — Bibl.: p.282-289. — Index.
ISBN 0-471-04306-0 : £12.55
Primary classification 301.5
(B77-12311)

813.2 — AMERICAN FICTION, 1776-1830
813'.2 — Fiction in English. American writers. Cooper, James Fenimore. *Critical studies*

Peck, H Daniel. A world by itself : the pastoral moment in Cooper's fiction / [by] H. Daniel Peck. — New Haven ; London : Yale University Press, 1977. — xiv,213p ; 22cm.
Bibl.: p.191-199. — Index.
ISBN 0-300-02027-9 : £9.00
(B77-25163)

813.3 — AMERICAN FICTION, 1830-1861
813'.3 — Fiction in English. American writers, 1830-1861. *Texts*

Melville, Herman. The portable Melville / edited and with an introduction by Jay Leyda. — Harmondsworth [etc.] : Penguin, 1976. — xxii, 746p ; 18cm. — (The Viking portable library)
This collection originally published: New York : Viking Press, 1952. — Includes: Typee - Billy Budd.
ISBN 0-14-015058-7 Pbk : £1.95
(B77-09208)

813'.3 — Fiction in English. American writers. Hawthorne, Nathaniel. *Critical studies*

Dauber, Kenneth. Rediscovering Hawthorne / [by] Kenneth Dauber. — Princeton ; Guildford : Princeton University Press, 1977. — xii,235p : 1 ill ; 23cm.
Index.
ISBN 0-691-06323-0 : £10.10
(B77-34014)

Dryden, Edgar A. Nathaniel Hawthorne : the poetics of enchantment / [by] Edgar A. Dryden. — Ithaca ; London : Cornell University Press, 1977. — 182,[2]p ; 23cm.
Bibl.: p.173-176. — Index.
ISBN 0-8014-1028-2 : £8.00
(B77-20532)

813'.3 — Fiction in English. American writers. Melville, Herman. Moby-Dick. *Critical studies. Readings*

Twentieth century interpretations of 'Moby-Dick' : a collection of critical essays / edited by Michael T. Gilmore. — Englewood Cliffs ; London [etc.] : Prentice-Hall, 1977. — iv,123p ; 21cm.
'A Spectrum book'. — Bibl.: p.121-123.
ISBN 0-13-586057-1 : £6.35
ISBN 0-13-586032-6 Pbk : £2.00
(B77-23659)

813'.3 — Short stories in English. American writers, 1830-1861. *Texts*

Poe, Edgar Allan. The illustrated Edgar Allan Poe : a selection of the tales together with a poem / edited and with an introduction by Roy Gasson. — London : Jupiter Books, 1976. — xix,236,[2]p,viii,48p of plates : ill(some col), 2 ports ; 26cm.
Bibl.: p.233-236. — List of films: p.229-232.
ISBN 0-904041-57-3 : £5.50
(B77-16015)

813.4 — AMERICAN FICTION, 1861-1900
813'.4 — Fiction in English, 1861-1900. American writers. *Texts. Facsimiles*

James, Henry. The American : the version of 1877 revised in autograph and typescript for the New York edition of 1907 / [by] Henry James ; reproduced in facsimile from the original in the Houghton Library, Harvard University ; with an introduction by Rodney G. Dennis. — Ilkley [etc.] : Scolar Press, 1976. — [5],478p ; 29cm.
'In the preparation of his working sheets Henry James used pages of two (or more) copies of the two-volume edition published in 1883, in London by Macmillan as volumes 6 and 7 of the Collective Edition ... [however] the text of the New York Edition as issued contains many variants from the version here presented' - Introduction.
ISBN 0-85967-224-7 : £25.00
(B77-05022)

813'.4 — Fiction in English. American writers, 1861-1900. *Texts*

Alcott, Louisa May. Little women / [by] Louisa M. Alcott. — Abridged [ed.]. — Maidenhead : Purnell, 1977. — 194p : 1 ill ; 21cm. — (A Purnell classic)
ISBN 0-361-03554-3 : £0.50
(B77-12040)

Coolidge, Susan. What Katy did at school / [by] Susan Coolidge. — Abridged [ed.]. — Maidenhead : Purnell, 1976. — 111p : 1 ill ; 21cm. — (A Purnell classic)
ISBN 0-361-03550-0 : £0.50
(B77-10517)

Coolidge, Susan. What Katy did next / [by] Susan Coolidge. — Abridged [ed.]. — Maidenhead : Purnell, 1976. — 121p : 1 ill ; 21cm. — (A Purnell classic)
ISBN 0-361-03547-0 : £0.50
(B77-10518)

James, Henry. The portable Henry James / edited and with an introduction by Morton Dauwen Zabel. — Revised ed. / revised ... by Lyall H.P. Powers. — Harmondsworth [etc.] : Penguin, 1977. — viii,696p ; 18cm. — (The Viking portable library)
Revised ed. originally published: 1968. — Bibl.: p.682-696.
ISBN 0-14-015055-2 Pbk : £1.95
(B77-34015)

James, Henry. The Princess Casamassima / [by] Henry James ; with the author's preface. — Harmondsworth [etc.] : Penguin, 1977. — 537p ; 19cm. — (Penguin modern classics)
ISBN 0-14-004102-8 Pbk : £1.25
(B77-18335)

Twain, Mark. [Selections]. The portable Mark Twain / edited by Bernard Devoto. — Harmondsworth [etc.] : Penguin, 1977. — viii, 790p ; 18cm. — (The Viking portable library)
This collection originally published: New York : Viking Press, 1946. — Bibl.: p.787-790. — Includes: Huckleberry Finn - The mysterious stranger.
ISBN 0-14-015020-x Pbk : £1.95
(B77-27314)

Twain, Mark. Huckleberry Finn / [by] Mark Twain. — Abridged [ed.]. — Maidenhead : Purnell, 1976. — 143p : 1 ill ; 21cm. — (A Purnell classic)
ISBN 0-361-03540-3 : £0.40
(B77-00905)

Twain, Mark. The prince and the pauper : a tale for young people of all ages / by Mark Twain ; illustrated by Robert Hodgson. — London : Dent, 1976. — [11],248p,[6]p of plates : ill, facsim ; 18cm. — (A Dent dolphin)
Originally published: 1968.
ISBN 0-460-02706-9 Pbk : £0.60
(B77-07550)

Twain, Mark. [Tom Sawyer]. The adventures of Tom Sawyer / [by] Mark Twain. — Abridged [ed.]. — Maidenhead : Purnell, 1977. — 148p : 1 ill ; 21cm. — (A Purnell classic)
This ed. originally published: London : Bancroft, 1966.
ISBN 0-361-03561-6 : £0.50
(B77-22787)

Wallace, Lew. Ben-Hur / [by] Lew Wallace. — Abridged [ed.]. — Maidenhead : Purnell, 1976. — 176p : 1 ill ; 21cm. — (A Purnell classic)
ISBN 0-361-03539-x : £0.40
(B77-00369)

813'.4 — Fiction in English. American writers. Howells, William Dean. *Plot outlines*

Carrington, George C. Plots and characters in the fiction of William Dean Howells / [by] George C. Carrington, Jr and Ildikó de Papp Carrington ; with a foreword by George Arms. — Hamden, Conn. : Archon Books ; Folkestone : Distributed by Dawson, 1976. — xxiii,306p ; 23cm. — (The plots and characters series)
List of works: p.xix-xxiii.
ISBN 0-7129-0779-3 : £13.75
Also classified at 813'.4
(B77-31393)

813'.4 — Fiction in English. American writers. Howells, William Dean. Characters. *Dictionaries*

Carrington, George C. Plots and characters in the fiction of William Dean Howells / [by] George C. Carrington, Jr and Ildikó de Papp Carrington ; with a foreword by George Arms. — Hamden, Conn. : Archon Books ; Folkestone : Distributed by Dawson, 1976. — xxiii,306p ; 23cm. — (The plots and characters series)
List of works: p.xix-xxiii.
ISBN 0-7129-0779-3 : £13.75
Primary classification 813'.4
(B77-31393)

813'.4 — Fiction in English. American writers. James, Henry. Ambassadors, The; Golden bowl & Wings of the dove. Style

Yeazell, Ruth Bernard. Language and knowledge in the late novels of Henry James / [by] Ruth Bernard Yeazell. — Chicago ; London : University of Chicago Press, 1976. — viii,143p ; 23cm.
Index.
ISBN 0-226-95094-8 : £6.80
(B77-02538)

813'.4 — Fiction in English. American writers. Twain, Mark. Huckleberry Finn. *Critical studies*

Egan, Michael. Mark Twain's 'Huckleberry Finn' : race, class and society / [by] Michael Egan. — London : Chatto and Windus for Sussex University Press, 1977. — 135p ; 20cm. — (Text and context)
Bibl.: p.135.
ISBN 0-85621-060-9 : £3.50
ISBN 0-85621-061-7 Pbk : £1.75
(B77-05023)

813'.4 — Short stories in English. American writers, 1861-1900. *Texts*

Harris, Joel Chandler. Brer Rabbit / [by] Joel Chandler Harris ; selected and edited by Marcus Crouch ; illustrated by William Stobbs. — London : Pelham, 1977. — 112p : ill ; 23cm.
ISBN 0-7207-0986-5 : £3.50
(B77-29633)

813.52 — AMERICAN FICTION, 1900-1945
813'.5'2 — Fiction in English. American witers. McCullers, Carson. *Biographies*

Carr, Virginia Spencer. The lonely hunter : a biography of Carson McCullers / by Virginia Spencer Carr. — London : Owen, 1977. — xxi, 598p,[16]p of plates : ill, geneal tables, ports ; 23cm.
Originally published: Garden City, N.Y. : Doubleday, 1975. — List of works: p.581. — Index.
ISBN 0-7206-0506-7 : £8.50
(B77-16560)

813'.5'2 — Fiction in English. American writers. Burroughs, Edgar Rice. *Biographies*

Porges, Irwin. Edgar Rice Burroughs : the man who created Tarzan / [by] Irwin Porges ; Hulbert Burroughs, pictorial editor ; introduction by Ray Bradbury. — London : New English Library [etc.], 1976. — xx,820p, [8]p of plates : ill(some col), facsims, form, maps, plan, ports ; 29cm.
Originally published: Provo : Brigham Young University Press, 1975. — Bibl.: p.787-799. — Index.
ISBN 0-450-03048-2 : £19.50
(B77-04377)

813'.5'2 — Fiction in English. American writers. Burroughs, Edgar Rice. *Periodicals*

The **fantastic** worlds of Edgar Rice Burroughs. — Stevenage (113 Chertsey Rise, Stevenage, Herts.) : British Edgar Rice Burroughs Society. 1st issue- ; Summer 1976-. — [1976]-. — ill, maps ; 30cm.
Quarterly. — 28p. in 1st issue.
Sd : Unpriced
ISSN 0140-3427
(B77-32120)

813'.5'2 — Fiction in English. American writers. Cather, Willa. *Biographies*
Lewis, Edith. Willa Cather living : a personal record / by Edith Lewis. — Lincoln [Neb.] ; London : University of Nebraska Press, 1976. — xviii,197p ; 21cm.
'A Bison book'. — Originally published: New York : Knopf, 1953.
ISBN 0-8032-5849-6 Pbk : £2.40
(B77-06246)

813'.5'2 — Fiction in English. American writers. Chandler, Raymond. *Critical studies*
The **world** of Raymond Chandler / edited by Miriam Gross ; introduction by Patricia Highsmith. — London : Weidenfeld and Nicolson, 1977. — ix,190p,[24]p of plates : ill, ports ; 24cm.
Bibl.: p.185-186.
ISBN 0-297-77362-3 : £5.95
(B77-32121)

813'.5'2 — Fiction in English. American writers. Chandler, Raymond. *Notebooks*
Chandler, Raymond. The notebooks of Raymond Chandler ; and, English summer : a gothic romance / by Raymond Chandler ; illustrated by Edward Gorey ; edited by Frank MacShane. — London : Weidenfeld and Nicolson, 1977. — [7],113p : ill, facsims, ports ; 24cm.
This collection originally published: New York : Ecco Press, 1976.
ISBN 0-297-77430-1 : £4.50
Also classified at 823'.9'1F
(B77-32122)

813'.5'2 — Fiction in English. American writers. Dreiser, Theodore. *Plot outlines*
Gerber, Philip L. Plots and characters in the fiction of Theodore Dreiser / [by] Philip L. Gerber. — Hamden, Conn. : Archon Books ; Folkestone : Dawson, 1977. — xxi,153p ; 23cm. — (The plots and characters series)
ISBN 0-7129-0758-0 : £9.00
Also classified at 813'.5'2
(B77-31394)

813'.5'2 — Fiction in English. American writers. Dreiser, Theodore. Characters. *Dictionaries*
Gerber, Philip L. Plots and characters in the fiction of Theodore Dreiser / [by] Philip L. Gerber. — Hamden, Conn. : Archon Books ; Folkestone : Dawson, 1977. — xxi,153p ; 23cm. — (The plots and characters series)
ISBN 0-7129-0758-0 : £9.00
Primary classification 813'.5'2
(B77-31394)

813'.5'2 — Fiction in English. American writers. Faulkner, William. Sound and the fury. *Critical studies*
Bleikasten, André. The most splendid failure : Faulkner's 'The sound and the fury' / [by] André Bleikasten. — Bloomington ; London : Indiana University Press, 1976. — xi,275p : facsims ; 22cm.
Bibl.: p.243-268. — Index.
ISBN 0-253-33877-8 : £10.00
(B77-05024)

813'.5'2 — Fiction in English. American writers. Fitzgerald, Francis Scott. Great Gatsby. *Critical studies*
Whitley, John Stuart. F. Scott Fitzgerald, 'The great Gatsby' / by John S. Whitley. — London : Edward Arnold, 1976. — 64p ; 20cm. — (Studies in English literature ; no.60)
Bibl.: p.62. — Index.
ISBN 0-7131-5872-7 : £2.95
ISBN 0-7131-5873-5 Pbk : £1.50
(B77-01760)

813'.5'2 — Fiction in English. American writers. Fitzgerald, Francis Scott. Great Gatsby. *Study outlines*
Altena, I. Notes on F. Scott Fitzgerald's 'The great Gatsby' / compiled by I. Altena. — London [etc.] : Methuen, 1976. — [5],41p : ill ; 22cm. — (Study-aid series)
Bibl.: p.41.
ISBN 0-413-37020-8 Sd : £0.60
(B77-13220)

813'.5'2 — Fiction in English. American writers. Fitzgerald, Francis Scott. Last tycoon. *Critical studies*
Bruccoli, Matthew Joseph. 'The last of the novelists' : F. Scott Fitzgerald and 'The last tycoon' / [by] Matthew J. Bruccoli. — Carbondale [etc.] : Southern Illinois University Press ; London [etc.] : Feffer and Simons, 1977. — [9],163p : facsims ; 24cm.
ISBN 0-8093-0820-7 : Unpriced
(B77-29634)

813'.5'2 — Fiction in English. American writers. Hemingway, Ernest, 1921-1926. *Autobiographies*
Hemingway, Ernest. A moveable feast / [by] Ernest Hemingway. — St Albans : Triad, 1977. — 140p ; 18cm.
Originally published: New York : Scribner ; London : Cape, 1964.
ISBN 0-586-04464-7 Pbk : £0.75
(B77-29635)

813'.5'2 — Fiction in English. American writers. Hemingway, Ernest, 1949-1961. *Biographies*
Hemingway, Mary Welsh. How it was / [by] Mary Welsh Hemingway. — London : Weidenfeld and Nicolson, 1977. — vi,537,xi p,[24]p of plates : ill, facsims, ports ; 24cm.
Ill. on lining papers. — Originally published: New York : Knopf, 1976. — Index.
ISBN 0-297-77265-1 : £6.95
Also classified at 070'.92'4
(B77-12041)

813'.5'2 — Fiction in English. American writers. Hemingway, Ernest. Old man and the sea. *Study outlines*
Bonynge, Fiona. Brodie's notes on Ernest Hemingway's 'The old man and the sea' / [by] Fiona Bonynge. — London [etc.] : Pan Books, 1977. — [3],41p ; 20cm. — (Pan revision aids)
Bibl.: p.7.
ISBN 0-330-50073-2 Pbk : £0.60
(B77-34016)

813'.5'2 — Fiction in English. American writers. London, Jack. *Biographies*
Barltrop, Robert. Jack London : the man, the writer, the rebel / [by] Robert Barltrop. — London : Pluto Press, 1976. — xiv,206p : ill, facsim, ports ; 23cm.
Bibl.: p.196-199. — Index.
ISBN 0-904383-18-0 : £4.50
(B77-10519)

813'.5'2 — Fiction in English. American writers. Morris, Wright. *Critical studies*
Conversations with Wright Morris : critical views and responses / edited with an introduction by Robert E. Knoll. — Lincoln, Neb. ; London : University of Nebraska Press, 1977. — xiv, 211p : ill ; 21cm.
Bibl.: p.169-206. — Index.
ISBN 0-8032-0904-5 : £7.50
ISBN 0-8032-5854-2 Pbk : £3.00
(B77-21378)

813'.5'2 — Fiction in English. American writers. Steinbeck, John. Grapes of wrath. *Study outlines*
Handley, Graham. Brodie's notes on John Steinbeck's 'The grapes of wrath' / [by] Graham Handley. — London [etc.] : Pan Books, 1977. — 82p ; 20cm. — (Pan study aids)
Bibl.: p.9-10.
ISBN 0-330-50067-8 Pbk : £0.60
(B77-34017)

813'.5'2 — Fiction in English. American writers. Steinbeck, John. Of mice and man & Pearl, The. *Study outlines*
Handley, Graham. Brodie's notes on John Steinbeck's 'Of mice and men' and 'The pearl' / [by] Graham Handley. — London [etc.] : Pan Books, 1977. — [3],68p ; 20cm. — (Pan study aids)
Bibl.: p.5.
ISBN 0-330-50066-x Pbk : £0.60
(B77-34018)

813'.5'2 — Fiction in English. American writers. Steinbeck, John. Of mice and men. *Study outlines*
Burton, Harry McGuire. Notes on John Steinbeck's 'Of mice and men' / compiled by H.M. Burton. — London [etc.] : Methuen, 1976. — [3],28p ; 22cm. — (Study-aid series)
Bibl.: p.28.
ISBN 0-413-34840-7 Sd : £0.60
(B77-13221)

813'.5'208032 — Fiction in English. American writers, 1900-1972. Special subjects: United States, to 1970. *Extracts, selections*
Understanding American history through fiction / [compiled by] Warren A. Beck, Myles L. Clowers. — New York ; London [etc.] : McGraw-Hill.
In 2 vols. — Published in the United States: 1974.
Vol.1. — [1976]. — xi,200p ; 23cm.
ISBN 0-07-004217-9 Pbk : £4.55
(B77-08017)

Vol.2. — [1976]. — xi,210p ; 23cm.
ISBN 0-07-004218-7 Pbk : £4.55
(B77-08018)

813'.5'209 — Fiction in English. American negro writers, 1900-1945. *Critical studies*
Singh, Amritjit. The novels of the Harlem renaissance : twelve black writers, 1923-1933 / [by] Amritjit Singh. — University Park ; London : Pennsylvania State University Press, 1976. — [8],175p ; 24cm.
Bibl.: p.153-164. — Index.
ISBN 0-271-01208-0 : £9.00
(B77-05026)

813.54 — AMERICAN FICTION, 1945-

813'.5'4 — Fiction in English. American writers. Asimov, Isaac. *Critical studies*
Isaac Asimov / edited by Joseph D. Olander and Martin Harry Greenberg ; afterword by Isaac Asimov. — Edinburgh : P. Harris, 1977. — 247p ; 22cm. — (Writers of the 21st century)
Also published: New York : Taplinger, 1977. — Bibl.: p.217-233. — Index.
ISBN 0-904505-40-5 : £6.00
(B77-29636)

Patrouch, Joseph F. The science fiction of Isaac Asimov / [by] Joseph F. Patrouch, Jr. — St Albans : Panther, 1976. — 325p ; 18cm.
Originally published: Garden City, N.Y. : Doubleday, 1974. — Bibl.: p.313-317.
ISBN 0-586-04393-4 Pbk : £0.75
(B77-00906)

813'.5'4 — Fiction in English. American writers. Barth, John. *Critical studies*
Morrell, David. John Barth : an introduction / [by] David Morrell. — University Park [Pa] ; London : Pennsylvania State University Press, [1977]. — xviii,194p : ill, facsims, map ; 24cm.
Published in the United States: 1976. — Bibl.: p.176-189. — Index.
ISBN 0-271-01220-x : £7.50
(B77-10520)

813'.5'4 — Fiction in English. American writers. Burroughs, William, b.1914. *Critical studies*
Mottram, Eric. William Burroughs : the algebra of need / [by] Eric Mottram. — London : Boyars : Distributed by Calder and Boyars, 1977. — 282p ; 23cm. — ([Critical appraisals series])
Bibl.: p.273-282.
ISBN 0-7145-2562-6 : £5.95
(B77-22788)

813'.5'4 — Fiction in English. American writers. Humphrey, William, to 1937. *Autobiographies*
Humphrey, William. Farther off from heaven / [by] William Humphrey. — London : Chatto and Windus, 1977. — [9],242p ; 21cm.
Also published: New York : Knopf, 1977.
ISBN 0-7011-2249-8 : £5.25 : CIP rev.
(B77-14876)

813'.5'4 — Fiction in English. American writers. Kerouac, Jack, ca 1965. *Autobiographies*
Kerouac, Jack. Satori in Paris / [by] Jack Kerouac. — London [etc.] : Quartet Books, 1977. — [5],116p ; 18cm.
Originally published: New York : Grove Press, 1966 ; London : Deutsch, 1967.
ISBN 0-7043-3144-6 Pbk : £0.95
(B77-22789)

813'.5'4 — Fiction in English. American writers. Mailer, Norman. Interpersonal relationships with Baldwin, James
Weatherby, William John. Squaring off : Mailer v. Baldwin / [by] W.J. Weatherby. — London : Robson, 1977. — [5],217p ; 25cm.
Originally published: New York : Mason/Charter, 1977. — Bibl.: p.216-217.
ISBN 0-903895-89-7 : £4.50
Also classified at 818'.5'409
(B77-18336)

813'.5'4 — Fiction in English. American writers. Nabokov, Vladimir. *Biographies*
Field, Andrew. Nabokov : his life in part / [by] Andrew Field. — London : Hamilton, 1977. — [13],285p,[8]p of plates : coat of arms, ports ; 25cm.
ISBN 0-241-02479-x : £8.50
(B77-25834)

813'.5'4 — Fiction in English. American writers. Nabokov, Vladimir. Works originally written in Russian. Compared with originals
Grayson, Jane. Nabokov translated : a comparison of Nabokov's Russian and English prose / by Jane Grayson. — Oxford [etc.] : Oxford University Press, 1977. — xi,257p ; 23cm. — (Oxford modern languages and literature monographs)
Bibl.: p.232-251. — Index.
ISBN 0-19-815527-1 : £9.50
Primary classification 891.7'3'42
(B77-12182)

813'.5'4 — Fiction in English. American writers. O'Connor, Flannery. *Critical studies*
May, John Richard. The pruning word : the parables of Flannery O'Connor / [by] John R. May. — Notre Dame, Ind. ; London : University of Notre Dame Press, 1976. — xxv, 178p ; 21cm.
Bibl.: p.170-174. — Index.
ISBN 0-268-01518-x : £8.80
(B77-06247)

813'.5'4 — Fiction in English. American writers. Vonnegut, Kurt. *Critical studies*
Giannone, Richard. Vonnegut : a preface to his novels / [by] Richard Giannone. — Port Washington ; London : Kennikat Press, 1977. — [7],136p ; 23cm. — (Kennikat Press national university publications : literary criticism series)
Bibl.: p.132-134. — Index.
ISBN 0-8046-9167-3 : £7.60
(B77-29637)

813'.5'4 — Fiction in English. American writers. West, Jessamyn. *Autobiographies*
West, Jessamyn. Encounters with death and life : memoirs / [by] Jessamyn West. — London : Gollancz, 1977. — [9],180p ; 21cm.
Originally published: as 'The woman said yes'. New York : Harcourt, Brace, Jovanovich, 1976.
ISBN 0-575-02292-2 : £4.50
(B77-17049)

813'.5'409 — Fiction in English. American writers, 1945-. *Critical studies*
McConnell, Frank DeMay. Four postwar American novelists : Bellow, Mailer, Barth and Pynchon / [by] Frank D. McConnell. — Chicago ; London : University of Chicago Press, 1977. — xxix,206p ; 23cm.
Index.
ISBN 0-226-55684-0 : £10.50
(B77-28040)

813'.5'4093 — Fiction in English. American writers, 1945- . Special subjects: War. *Critical studies*
Jones, Peter G. War and the novelist : appraising the American war novel / [by] Peter G. Jones ; with a foreword by M.L. Rosenthal. — Columbia ; London : University of Missouri Press, 1976. — xiv,260,[1]p : ill ; 23cm.
Ill. on lining papers. — Bibl.: p.239-256. — Index.
ISBN 0-8262-0211-x : £9.35
(B77-15440)

814.52 — AMERICAN ESSAYS, 1900-1945
814'.5'2 — Essays in English. American writers, 1900-1945. *Texts*
O'Hara, John. 'An artist is his own fault' : John O'Hara on writers and writing / edited, with an introduction, by Matthew J. Bruccoli. — Carbondale [etc.] : Southern Illinois University Press ; London [etc.] : Feffer and Simons, 1977. — xv,226p ; 21cm.
ISBN 0-8093-0796-0 : £6.72
(B77-09209)

814.54 — AMERICAN ESSAYS, 1945-
814'.5'4 — Essays in English. American writers, 1945-. *Texts*
Vidal, Gore. Matters of fact and fiction : essays, 1973-1976 / [by] Gore Vidal. — London : Heinemann, 1977. — ix,285p ; 23cm.
This collection also published: New York : Random House, 1977.
ISBN 0-434-82964-1 : £6.00
(B77-22790)

Vidal, Gore. On our own now / [by] Gore Vidal. — St Albans : Panther, 1976. — 423p ; 18cm.
Originally published: as 'Homage to Daniel Shays : collected essays, 1952-1972'. New York : Vintage Books, 1973 ; and as 'Collected essays, 1952-1972'. London : Heinemann, 1974.
ISBN 0-586-04282-2 Pbk : £1.50
(B77-08019)

817 — AMERICAN SATIRE AND HUMOUR
817'.008'03 — Humour in English. American writers, 1775-1975. Special subjects: United States. Politics. *Anthologies*
Pardon us, Mr President! : American humor on politics / edited and introduced by Arthur Power Dudden. — [New ed.]. — South Brunswick ; New York : Barnes ; London : Yoseloff, 1975. — 3-613p : ill ; 22cm.
Previous ed.: published as 'The assault of laughter'. New York : Yoseloff, 1962.
ISBN 0-498-01566-1 : £4.25
(B77-30562)

817.52 — AMERICAN SATIRE AND HUMOUR, 1900-1945
817'.5'2 — Humour in English. American writers, 1900-1945. *Texts*
Thurber, James. Fables for our time, and famous poems illustrated / by James Thurber. — New York [etc.] ; London : Harper and Row, 1974. — [6],154p : ill ; 18cm. — (Perennial library)
Originally published: New York ; London : Harper, 1940.
ISBN 0-06-080319-3 Pbk : £0.85
(B77-28831)

Thurber, James. The owl in the attic, and other perplexities / [by] James Thurber. — New York [etc.] ; London : Harper and Row, [1977]. — [10],113,[1]p : ill ; 19cm. — (Perennial library)
Originally published: New York ; London : Harper, 1931.
ISBN 0-06-080351-7 Pbk : £0.70
(B77-28832)

818 — AMERICAN MISCELLANY
818'.08 — Autobiographical prose in English. American negro writers, to 1973. *Critical studies*
Smith, Sidonie. Where I'm bound : patterns of slavery and freedom in Black American autobiography / [by] Sidonie Smith. — Westport, Conn. ; London : Greenwood Press, 1974. — xi,194p ; 22cm. — (Contributions in American studies ; no.16)
Bibl.: p.181-186. — Index.
ISBN 0-8371-7337-x : £9.75
(B77-19597)

818.2 — AMERICAN MISCELLANY, 1776-1830
818'.2'09 — English literature. American writers. Irving, Washington. *Critical studies*
Roth, Martin. Comedy and America : the lost world of Washington Irving / [by] Martin Roth. — Port Washington ; London : Kennikat Press, 1976. — xiv,205p ; 23cm. — (Kennikat Press national university publications : literary criticism series)
Index.
ISBN 0-8046-9132-0 : £10.60
(B77-18337)

818.3 — AMERICAN MISCELLANY, 1830-1861
818'.3'09 — English literature. American writers, 1830-1861. *Texts*
Poe, Edgar Allan. Edgar Allan Poe / selected and edited with an introduction and notes by Philip Van Doren Stern. — Harmondsworth [etc.] : Penguin, 1977. — xxgviii,666p ; 19cm. — (The Viking portable library)
Cover title: The portable Poe. — This collection originally published: New York : Viking Press, 1945. — Bibl.: p.665-666.
ISBN 0-14-015012-9 Pbk : £1.95
(B77-26465)

Thoreau, Henry David. The portable Thoreau / edited, and with an introduction, by Carl Bode. — Revised ed. — Harmondsworth [etc.] : Penguin, 1977. — vi,698p ; 18cm. — (The Viking portable library)
This ed. originally published: New York : Viking Press, 1964. — Bibl.: p.697-698. — Includes: Walden.
ISBN 0-14-015031-5 Pbk : £1.95
(B77-14371)

818'.3'09 — English literature. American writers. Poe, Edgar Allan. *Readings*
The **Edgar** Allan Poe scrapbook : articles, essays, letters, anecdotes, illustrations, photographs and memorabilia about the legendary American genius / edited by Peter Haining ; foreword by Robert Bloch. — London : New English Library, 1977. — 144p : ill, facsims, ports ; 31cm.
ISBN 0-450-03208-6 : £6.50
(B77-25165)

818.4 — AMERICAN MISCELLANY, 1861-1900
818'.4'09 — English literature. American writers. Twain, Mark. *Plot outlines*
Gale, Robert Lee. Plots and characters in the works of Mark Twain / [by] Robert L. Gale ; with a foreword by Frederick Anderson. — Hamden, Conn. : Archon Books ; Folkestone : [Distributed by] Dawson, 1973. — 2v.(l,1300p) ; 23cm.
Bibl.: p.xlix-l.
ISBN 0-7129-0782-3 : £21.00
Also classified at 818'.4'09
(B77-30563)

818'.4'09 — English literature. American writers. Twain, Mark. Characters. *Dictionaries*
Gale, Robert Lee. Plots and characters in the works of Mark Twain / [by] Robert L. Gale ; with a foreword by Frederick Anderson. — Hamden, Conn. : Archon Books ; Folkestone : [Distributed by] Dawson, 1973. — 2v.(l,1300p) ; 23cm.
Bibl.: p.xlix-l.
ISBN 0-7129-0782-3 : £21.00
Primary classification 818'.4'09
(B77-30563)

818.52 — AMERICAN MISCELLANY, 1900-1945
818'.5'203 — Diaries in English. American writers, 1900-1945. *Texts*
Nin, Anaïs. The journals of Anaïs Nin. — London : Owen.
[Vol.6] : 1955-1966 / edited and with a preface by Gunther Stuhlmann. — 1977. — xvii,414p, [16]p of plates : ill, ports ; 22cm.
Originally published: New York : Harcourt, Brace, Jovanovich, 1976. — Index.
ISBN 0-7206-0444-3 : £7.50
(B77-15441)

818'.5'208 — Humorous prose in English. American writers, 1900-1945. *Texts*
Thurber, James. Let your mind alone! and other more or less inspirational pieces / by James Thurber ; with drawings by the author. — New York [etc.] ; London : Harper and Row, 1976. — x,245p : ill ; 18cm. — (Perennial library)
This collection originally published: New York : London : Harper and Brothers, 1937.
ISBN 0-06-080375-4 Pbk : £1.10
(B77-07551)

818'.5'208 — Prose in English. American writers, 1900-1945. *Texts*
Rexroth, Kenneth. An autobiographical novel / [by] Kenneth Rexroth. — Weybridge (The Oil Mills, Weybridge, Surrey) : Whittet Books Ltd, 1977. — xiii,367p ; 23cm.
Originally published: Garden City, N.Y. : Doubleday, 1966.
ISBN 0-905483-00-6 : £6.50
ISBN 0-905483-01-4 Pbk : £2.95
(B77-12042)

Sandoz, Mari. Hostiles and friendlies : selected short writings of Mari Sandoz. — Landmark ed. — Lincoln, Neb. ; London : University of Nebraska Press, 1976[i.e.1977]. — iii-xxi,250p, [4]p of plates : ill, map, ports ; 24cm.
This collection originally published: Lincoln, Neb. : University of Nebraska Press, 1959. — Bibl.: p.241-244.
ISBN 0-8032-0161-3 : £10.80
(B77-11369)

818'.5'209 — English literature. American writers, 1900-1945. *Texts*
Parker, Dorothy, *b.1893.* The portable Dorothy Parker. — Revised and enlarged ed. ; with a new introduction by Brendan Gill. — New York ; Harmondsworth [etc.] : Penguin, 1976[i.e.1977]. — xxviii,610p ; 18cm. — (Viking portable library)
This ed. originally published: as 'The portable Dorothy Parker', New York : Viking Press, 1973 ; and as 'The collected Dorothy Parker', London : Duckworth, 1973. — Index.
ISBN 0-14-015074-9 Pbk : £1.95
(B77-10521)

818'.5'209 — English literature. American writers. McAlmon, Robert. *Autobiographies*
McAlmon, Robert. McAlmon and the lost generation : a self-portrait / edited with a commentary by Robert E. Knoll. — Landmark ed. — Lincoln, Neb. ; London : University of Nebraska Press, 1976. — viii,397p,[16]p of plates : ill, ports ; 24cm.
Originally published: 1962. — Bibl.: p.367-386. — Index.
ISBN 0-8032-0225-3 : £15.00
(B77-11370)

818'.5'209 — English literature. American writers. Stein, Gertrude, 1903-1932. *Autobiographies*
Stein, Gertrude. The autobiography of Alice B. Toklas / [by] Gertrude Stein. — Harmondsworth [etc.] : Penguin, 1977. — 272p ; 18cm.
Originally published: London : J. Lane, 1933.
ISBN 0-14-002531-6 Pbk : £0.75
(B77-28833)

818'.5'209 — English literature. American writers. Taber, Gladys. *Autobiographies*
Taber, Gladys. Harvest of yesterdays / [by] Gladys Taber ; drawings by Pamela Johnson. — Large print [ed.]. — London : Prior [etc.], 1976. — xiii,357p : ill ; 24cm.
Also published: Philadelphia : Lippincott, 1976.

ISBN 0-86043-020-0 : £4.95
(B77-09210)

818'.5'209 — English literature. American writers. White, William Allen. *Biographies*
McKee, John DeWitt. William Allen White : maverick on Main Street / [by] John DeWitt McKee. — Westport, Conn. ; London : Greenwood Press, 1975. — iii-x,264p ; 22cm. — (Contributions in American studies ; no.17)
Bibl.: p.239-254. — Index.
ISBN 0-8371-7533-x : £11.50
(B77-17705)

818.54 — AMERICAN MISCELLANY, 1945-
818'.5'407 — Documentary novels in English. American writers, 1945-1976. *Critical studies*
Zavarzadeh, Mas'ud. The mythopoeic reality : the postwar American nonfiction novel / [by] Mas'ud Zavarzadeh. — Urbana [etc.] ; London : University of Illinois Press, 1976. — ix,262p ; 24cm.
Bibl.: p.229-258. — Index.
ISBN 0-252-00523-6 : £7.50
(B77-31395)

818'.5'408 — Humorous prose in English. American writers, 1945-. *Texts*
Donleavy, James Patrick. The unexpurgated code : a complete manual of survival & manners / [by] J.P. Donleavy ; with drawings by the author. — Harmondsworth [etc.] : Penguin, 1976. — 3-321p : ill ; 19cm.
Originally published: New York : Delacorte Press/S. Lawrence ; London : Wildwood House, 1975.
ISBN 0-14-004282-2 Pbk : £0.95
(B77-02539)

Rosenbloom, Joseph. Doctor Knock-Knock's official knock-knock dictionary / by Joseph Rosenbloom ; illustrated by Joyce Behr. — New York : Sterling [etc.] ; London : Distributed by Ward Lock, 1977. — 128p : ill ; 22cm.
Originally published: 1976. — Index.
ISBN 0-7061-2509-6 : £2.50
(B77-22791)

818'.5'408 — Prose in English. American writers, 1945- . Special subjects: Pets: Cats. *Texts*
Rampa, Mama San Ra-ab. Pussy willow / [by] Mama San Ra-ab Rampa. — London : Corgi, 1976. — 3-159p : ill ; 18cm.
Cover title: Pussywillow.
ISBN 0-552-10261-x Pbk : £0.50
(B77-01761)

818'.5'408 — Prose in English. American writers, 1945-. *Texts*
Plath, Sylvia. Johnny Panic and the bible of dreams, and other prose writings / [by] Sylvia Plath. — London : Faber, 1977. — 3-250p ; 21cm.
ISBN 0-571-11120-3 : £4.95 : CIP rev.
(B77-23660)

Vonnegut, Kurt. Wampeters, foma & granfalloons / [by] Kurt Vonnegut, Jr. — St Albans : Panther, 1976. — 255,[1]p ; 18cm.
This collection originally published: as 'Wampeters, foma and granfalloons (opinions)'. New York : Delacorte Press, 1974 ; London : Cape, 1975.
ISBN 0-586-04256-3 Pbk : £0.75
(B77-00907)

818'.5'409 — English literature. American writers. Baldwin, James. Interpersonal relationships with Mailer, Norman
Weatherby, William John. Squaring off : Mailer v. Baldwin / [by] W.J. Weatherby. — London : Robson, 1977. — [5],217p ; 25cm.
Originally published: New York : Mason/Charter, 1977. — Bibl.: p.216-217.
ISBN 0-903895-89-7 : £4.50
Primary classification 813'.5'4
(B77-18336)

818'.5'409 — English literature. American writers. Baraka, Imamu Amiri. *Critical studies*
Benston, Kimberly W. Baraka : the renegade and the mask / [by] Kimberly W. Benston. — New Haven ; London : Yale University Press, 1976. — xxi,290p ; 22cm.
Bibl.: p.278-283. — Index.
ISBN 0-300-01958-0 : £9.00
(B77-08520)

820 — ENGLISH LITERATURE
820'.3 — English literature. Writers, to 1976. *Encyclopaedias*
Eagle, Dorothy. The Oxford literary guide to the British Isles / compiled and edited by Dorothy Eagle, Hilary Carnell. — Oxford : Clarendon Press, 1977. — xiii,415,[31]p : maps ; 21cm.
Bibl.: p.415. — Index.
ISBN 0-19-869123-8 : £3.95
Primary classification 941'.003
(B77-18475)

820'.6'241 — English literature. Organisations. *Great Britain. Directories*
English Association. The English Association handbook of societies and collections / edited by Alicia C. Percival. — London : Library Association for the English Association, 1977. — [1],xii,139p ; 21cm.
Index.
ISBN 0-85365-449-2 Pbk : £2.50(£2.00 to members of the associations) : CIP rev.
Primary classification 420'.6'241
(B77-23338)

820'.7'1141 — Universities. English literature teachers. *Great Britain. Directories*
Mruck, Martin L. Handbook of university teachers of English language and literature, linguistics and Celtic studies in Great Britain and Ireland / [compiled and] edited by Martin L. Mruck. — London (11 Arlington St., S.W.1) : Deutscher Akademischer Austauschdienst, 1975. — vii,235p ; 24cm.
Index.
Pbk : Unpriced
Primary classification 420'.7'1141
(B77-22523)

820'.8 — English literature. *Anthologies*
The **essential** self : an introduction to literature / [edited by] Paul Berry. — New York ; London [etc.] : McGraw-Hill, 1976. — xvi,439p ; 24cm.

Published in the United States: 1975.
ISBN 0-07-005048-1 Pbk : £6.25
(B77-05027)

820'.8 — English literature. *Anthologies. Juvenile literature*
Pleasure trove / [edited by] Jennifer Curry ; illustrated by William Geldart. — London [etc.] : Beaver Books, 1976. — 126p : ill ; 20cm.
ISBN 0-600-37127-1 Pbk : £0.55
(B77-14372)

820'.8 — English literature. *Anthologies. Secondary school texts*
Interplay / [compiled by] John Watts. — London : Longman.
Book 2. — 1976. — vii,216p : ill ; 24cm.
ISBN 0-582-21670-2 Pbk : £1.65
(B77-09211)

820'.8'001 — English literature, 1066-1400. *Anthologies*
Fourteenth century verse & prose / edited by Kenneth Sisam. — [1st ed. reprinted] ; with corrections. — Oxford : Clarendon Press, 1975. — xlvii,460p : map ; 20cm.
Middle English text and glossary, English introduction and notes. — Originally published in 2 vols. : 1921-22. — Bibl.: p.xlvi-xlvii. — Index. — Includes: A middle English vocabulary / by J.R.R. Tolkien. Originally published: 1922.
ISBN 0-19-811391-9 : £5.50
ISBN 0-19-871093-3 Pbk : £2.75
(B77-00908)

820'.8'002 — English literature, 1400-1625. *Anthologies*
Sixteenth-century English poetry and prose : a selective anthology / [edited by] Paul Delany, Jeffrey Ford, Robert W. Hanning with the collaboration of Joyce F. Leana. — New York ; London [etc.] : Holt, Rinehart and Winston, 1976. — xii,563p : geneal table ; 24cm.
Bibl.: p.555-557. — List of sound discs: p.553-554. — Index.
ISBN 0-03-085102-5 Pbk : £8.75
(B77-02540)

820'.8'003 — English literature, 1558-1625. *Anthologies*
Passages of early modern English / selected by Charles Barber. — [Leeds] ([Leeds LS2 9JT]) : School of English, University of Leeds, 1976. — [3],31p ; 30cm. — (Leeds studies in English)
ISBN 0-902296-18-3 Sp : Unpriced
(B77-02541)

820'.8'008 — English literature, 1837-1900. *Anthologies. Manuscripts. Facsimiles*
The '**Rectory** magazine' / edited by Lewis Carroll. — Austin ; London : University of Texas Press, [1976]. — [26],117p : ill ; 21cm.
Published in the United States: 1975. — 'facsimile of the original manuscript, which is located in the Humanities Research Center of the University of Texas at Austin' - jacket.
ISBN 0-292-77010-3 : £6.00
(B77-05597)

820'.8'00912 — English literature, 1900-. *Anthologies*
New writing and writers. — London : J. Calder : [Distributed by Calder and Boyars].
13 / by Samuel Beckett ... [et al.]. — 1976. — 224p : ports ; 21cm.
Previously published: as 'New writers'.
ISBN 0-7145-3552-4 : £4.95
ISBN 0-7145-3541-9 Pbk : £2.25
(B77-03775)

820'.8'00914 — English literature, 1945-. *Anthologies*
The **string** and feather review / [edited by Richard Hemmings]. — [Northampton] ([c/o R. Hemmings, 19 Celeborn Place, Overstone Lodge, Northampton NN3 4SA]) : Portsmouth Polytechnic, [1976]. — [1],20p ; 26cm.
ISBN 0-900234-02-4 Sd : £0.10
(B77-04378)

820'.8'00914 — English literature, 1945-. *Anthologies. Periodicals*
Forever : poetry and prose. — Didsbury (c/o M. O'Neill, Flat 1, 43 Moorland Rd, Didsbury, Manchester 20) : Forever Publications.
Issue no.1- ; [1976]-. — 1976-. — 21cm.
Published at irregular intervals. — [34]p. in 1st issue.
Sd : £0.30
ISSN 0140-3141
(B77-31396)

Oasis magazine. — Glasgow (John MacIntyre Building, The University, Glasgow 12) : [Glasgow University, Students Representative Council].
Vol.1, no.1- ; 1975-. — 1975-. — ill ; 22cm.
Quarterly. — [2],29p.(1 fold) in Vol.2, no.6.
Sd : £0.20
ISSN 0309-9091
(B77-28041)

820'.8'00914 — English literature, 1945-. *Anthologies. Serials*
The E and B annual. — Corby : Excello and Bollard.
1976 : Tea bags. — 1976. — [20]p ; 30cm.
ISBN 0-904339-40-8 Sd : Unpriced
(B77-04379)

820'.8'015 — Fantasy literature in English. *Periodicals*
Vortex : a monthly journal of fantasy, science and speculative fiction. — [Great Britain] : Cerberus Publishing Limited ; Faygate (Faygate, W. Sussex) : Distributed by Wells, Gardner and Darton and Co. Limited.
Vol.1, no.1- ; Jan. 1977-. — 1977-. — ill(some col), ports ; 28cm.
Forty-eight p. in 4th issue.
Sd : £0.45
(B77-33399)

820'.8'033 — English literature, to 1976. Special subjects: Autumn. *Anthologies*
The **autumn** book : a collection of prose and poetry / chosen and arranged by James Reeves ; illustrated by Colin McNaughton. — London : Heinemann, 1977. — 192p : ill ; 24cm.
ISBN 0-434-95896-4 : £4.50
(B77-31397)

820'.8'0352 — English literature, to 1975. Special subjects: Women. *Anthologies*
Who am I this time? : female portraits in British and American literature / [edited by] Carol Pearson, Katherine Pope. — New York ; London [etc.] : McGraw-Hill, 1976. — xiii, 305p : ill, ports ; 24cm.
Bibl.: p.299-303.
ISBN 0-07-049032-5 Pbk : £5.40
(B77-06838)

820'.8'0353 — English literature, to 1976. Special themes: Courage & joy. *Anthologies*
Now for the good news / [compiled by] Robert Dougall. — London [etc.] : Mowbrays, 1976. — xiv,146p ; 23cm.
ISBN 0-264-66379-9 : £4.25
(B77-02542)

820'.8'0355 — English literature, 1900-1976. Special subjects: Cinema films. *Anthologies*
The **film** addict's archive / edited by Philip Oakes. — London : Elm Tree Books, 1977. — xii,212p : 1 ill ; 23cm. — ([Addict's archive series])
ISBN 0-241-89384-4 : £5.95
(B77-17706)

820'.8'0355 — English literature. Scottish writers, 1945- . Special subjects: Alcoholic drinks. Consumption. *Anthologies*
The **rhythm** of the glass : Scots writers look at drinking in prose and poetry / edited by Paul Harris. — Edinburgh : P. Harris, 1977. — 87p : ill ; 22cm.
ISBN 0-904505-14-6 Pbk : Unpriced
(B77-31398)

820'.8'036 — English literature, to 1975. Special subjects: Animals. *Anthologies. Secondary school texts*
Anchor books. — Edinburgh : W. and R. Chambers.
Men and animals / [compiled by] Esmor Jones. — 1976. — 93p : ill ; 21cm.
ISBN 0-550-72032-4 Pbk : £1.00
(B77-24423)

820'.8'036 — English literature, to 1975. Special subjects: Oceans. *Anthologies. Secondary school texts*
Anchor books. — Edinburgh : W. and R. Chambers.
The sea / [compiled by] Anthony Adams. — 1976. — 96p : ill ; 21cm.
ISBN 0-550-72031-6 Pbk : £1.00
(B77-25166)

820'.8'09282 — Children's literature in English, 1300-1900. *Anthologies*
Greenaway, Kate. The Kate Greenaway book / [compiled by] Bryan Holme. — [London] : F. Warne, 1976. — 144p : ill(some col), facsims, music ; 24cm.
Originally published: New York : Viking Press, 1976. — Bibl.: p.140-142. — Index.
ISBN 0-7232-1987-7 : £4.95
Primary classification 741.9'42
(B77-04337)

820'.8'09282 — English literature. Compositions by children, 1945-. *Anthologies. Serials*
Children as writers. — London : Heinemann Educational.
3 : award-winning entries from the 17th 'Daily mirror' Children's Literary Competition. — 1976. — xvi,152p ; 23cm.
ISBN 0-435-13404-3 : £3.50
ISBN 0-435-13405-1 Pbk : £1.50
(B77-00909)

Children as writers. — London : Heinemann.
4 : award-winning entries from the 18th Daily Mirror Children's Literary Competition / foreword by Michael Baldwin. — 1977. — xv, 125p ; 23cm.
ISBN 0-435-13406-x : £3.80
ISBN 0-435-13405-1 Pbk : £1.50
(B77-26466)

820'.8'09282 — English literature: Literature by students of Cambridgeshire schools, 1945-1976. *Anthologies*
Moving jewels : an anthology of writing and art / by Cambridgeshire schoolchildren ; [editor Christopher Martin]. — [Cambridge] ([c/o Cambridgeshire County Education Division, Shire Hall, Castle Hill, Cambridge CB3 9AP]) : EARO for the George Edwards Memorial Committee, [1977]. — 80p : ill(some col), port ; 21cm.
ISBN 0-904463-24-9 Pbk : £1.50
Primary classification 709'.426'5
(B77-33933)

820'.8'09282 — English literature: Literature by students of Lerwick Primary School, 1945-. *Anthologies*
Lerwick Primary School. Young dawn : the Shetland scene through the eyes of the rising generation / [Lerwick Primary School] ; photos by Dennis Coutts. — [Lerwick] : [Lerwick Primary School] ; Lerwick ([77 Commercial St., Lerwick, Shetland ZE1 0AJ]) : [Distributed by] Shetland Times Ltd, 1976. — [4],107p : ill, music ; 22cm.
Sd : Unpriced
(B77-06839)

820'.8'09283 — English literature. Australian writers. Compositions by adolescents, 1975-1976. *Anthologies*
Youth writes : a collection of original writings by young people of secondary school age in Australia and the South Pacific / ... [compiled] by the Youth Writes Fellowship Incorporated. — Sydney [etc.] ; London : A.H. and A.W. Reed.
1975 & 1976 / editor Marcia Kirsten, assistant editor Marjorie Aldred. — 1975. — 95p : 2 ports ; 24cm.
ISBN 0-589-09168-9 Pbk : £1.45
(B77-32814)

820'.8'09411 — English literature. Scottish writers, 1945-. *Periodicals*
Association of Scottish Literary Studies. ASLS newsletter. — [Aberdeen] ([c/o University of Aberdeen, Aberdeen AB9 1FX]) : [A.S.L.S.].
Supersedes: Scottish literary news.
[No.1]- ; Dec. 1976-. — [1976]-. — 21cm.
Published at irregular intervals. — 9p. in 1st issue.
Sd : Unpriced
ISSN 0140-1629
(B77-25835)

820'.8'094129 — English literature. Fife writers, 1945-. *Anthologies. Periodicals*
Words. — Markinch (Arts Administration Centre, Bowling Green Rd, Markinch, Fife) : 'Words'.
Autumn 1976-. — 1976-. — ports ; 30cm.
[1],58p. in Autumn 1976 issue.
Sd : £0.60
(B77-16016)

820'.8'09426 — English literature. East Anglian writers, 1945-1976. *Anthologies*
Writers of East Anglia / selected and edited by Angus Wilson ; poetry adviser John Holloway. — London : Secker and Warburg, 1977. — xiii, 238p ; 23cm.
ISBN 0-436-57517-5 : £4.50
(B77-28834)

820.9 — ENGLISH LITERATURE. HISTORY AND CRITICAL STUDIES

820'.9 — English literature. *Critical studies, 1853-1871. Essays*
Simpson, Richard. Richard Simpson as critic / edited by David Carroll. — London [etc.] : Routledge and Kegan Paul, 1977. — x,355p ; 23cm. — (The Routledge critics series)
Index. — Includes essays on Dante and Hugo.
ISBN 0-7100-8514-1 : £9.50 : CIP rev.
(B77-17707)

820'.9 — English literature. *Critical studies. Serials*
Essays and studies. — London : J. Murray.
1977 : being volume thirty of the new series of essays and studies / collected for the English Association by W. Moelwyn Merchant. — 1977. — [7],109p ; 23cm.
ISBN 0-7195-3370-8 : £5.00
(B77-32815)

Literary monographs. — Madison, Wis. ; London : University of Wisconsin Press for the Department of English.
Vol.8 : Mid-nineteenth century writers : Eliot, De Quincey, Emerson / edited by Eric Rothstein and Joseph Anthony Wittreich, Jr. — 1976. — [7],216p ; 25cm.
ISBN 0-299-06950-8 : £10.00
(B77-05598)

The **yearbook** of English studies. — London (c/o Hon. Treasurer, MHRA, King's College, Strand, WC2R 2LS) : Modern Humanities Research Association.
Vol.7 : 1977 / edited by G.K. Hunter and C.J. Rawson ; assistant editor Jenny Mezciems. — 1977. — x,340p,iv p of plates : ill ; 25cm.
ISBN 0-900547-45-6 : £10.00
ISSN 0306-2473
(B77-11371)

The **year's** work in English studies. — London : J. Murray for the English Association.
Vol.55 : 1974 / edited by James Redmond and ... [others]. — 1976. — 610p ; 23cm.
Index.
ISBN 0-7195-3329-5 : £10.00
(B77-05028)

820'.9 — English literature, 1558-1975. Influence of Shakespeare, William
Shakespeare, aspects of influence / edited by G.B. Evans. — Cambridge, Mass. ; London : Harvard University Press, 1976. — [11],212p ; 22cm. — (Harvard English studies ; 7)
ISBN 0-674-80330-2 : £9.40
ISBN 0-674-80331-0 Pbk : £3.00
(B77-08521)

820'.9 — English literature, 1702-1900. *Critical studies*
Southall, Raymond. Literature, the individual and society : critical essays on the eighteenth and nineteenth centuries / by Raymond Southall. — London : Lawrence and Wishart, 1977. — 184p ; 22cm.
'... based upon lectures delivered ... at the Universities of Sheffield and Wollongong' - Prologue. — Index.
ISBN 0-85315-380-9 Pbk : £2.95
(B77-15442)

820'.9 — English literature, ca 1590-ca 1975. *Critical studies. Essays*
Wilbur, Richard. Responses : prose pieces, 1953-1976 / [by] Richard Wilbur. — New York ; London : Harcourt Brace Jovanovich, 1976. — xii,238p ; 22cm.
ISBN 0-15-176930-3 : £7.10
ISBN 0-15-676550-0 Pbk : £2.80
(B77-22792)

820'.9 — English literature. Criticism, 1750-1900
Parrinder, Patrick. Authors and authority : a study of English literary criticism and its relation to culture, 1750-1900 / [by] Patrick Parrinder. — London [etc.] : Routledge and Kegan Paul, 1977. — viii,199p ; 24cm.
'Routledge direct editions'. — Bibl.: p.185-194. — Index.
ISBN 0-7100-8686-5 Pbk : £3.75
(B77-27315)

820'.9 — English literature. Criticism. Stephen, Sir Leslie. *Autobiographies*
Stephen, *Sir* Leslie. Sir Leslie Stephen's mausoleum book / with an introduction by Alan Bell. — Oxford : Clarendon Press, 1977. — xxxiii,118p,leaf of plate,[4]p of plates : ports ; 23cm.
Spine title: Mausoleum book. — Index.
ISBN 0-19-812084-2 : £4.25 : CIP rev.
(B77-19598)

820'.9 — English literature. Style
Brett, Raymond Laurence. An introduction to English studies / [by] R.L. Brett. — 2nd ed. — London : Edward Arnold, 1976. — [5],88p ; 20cm.
Previous ed.: 1965. — Bibl. — Index.
ISBN 0-7131-5884-0 Pbk : £1.65
(B77-02543)

820'.9 — English literature, to 1900. *Festschriften*
An **English** miscellany : presented to W.S. Mackie / edited by Brian S. Lee. — Cape Town ; London [etc.] : Oxford University Press, 1977. — 218p,[3] leaves of plates : facsim, ports ; 22cm.
ISBN 0-19-570101-1 : £6.50
(B77-24424)

820'.9 — English literature, to 1939. *Critical studies*
Legouis, Emile. A short history of English literature / by Émile Legouis ; translated [from the French MS.] by V.F. Boyson and J. Coulson. — Oxford : Clarendon Press, 1971. — xvi,404p,[12] leaves of plates,[28]p of plates : ill, facsims, ports ; 20cm.
Originally published: 1934. — Index.
ISBN 0-19-811561-x : £4.00
(B77-17708)

820'.9 — English literature, to 1960. *Critical studies*
Coombes, Henry. English literature made simple / [by] H. Coombes. — London : W.H. Allen, 1977. — x,294p ; 22cm. — (Made simple books ISSN 0464-2902)
Bibl.: p.287-288. — Index.
ISBN 0-491-02001-5 : Unpriced
ISBN 0-491-02011-2 Pbk : £1.75
(B77-28835)

820'.9 — English literature, to 1976. *Critical studies*
Contemporary approaches to English studies / edited by Hilda Schiff. — London : Heinemann Educational for the English Association [etc.], 1977. — [5],105p ; 23cm.
Bibl.
ISBN 0-435-18806-2 : £3.80
ISBN 0-435-18807-0 Pbk : £1.50
(B77-06248)

820'.9 — English literature, to ca 1970. Role of spoken English language. Rhythm
Harding, Denys Wyatt. Words in rhythm : English speech rhythm in verse and prose / [by] D.W. Harding. — Cambridge [etc.] : Cambridge University Press, 1976. — vii,166p ; 23cm. — (The Clark lectures ; 1971-1972)
Bibl.: p.159-161. — Index.
ISBN 0-521-21267-7 : £5.95
(B77-02544)

820'.9 — English literature. Writers, 1066-1702. Handwriting. *Facsimiles*
Petti, Anthony Gretano. English literary hands from Chaucer to Dryden / [by] Anthony G. Petti. — London : Edward Arnold, 1977. — ix, 133p : ill, facsims ; 29cm.
Bibl.: p.126-128. — Index.
ISBN 0-7131-5871-9 : £14.50
(B77-26467)

820'.9 — English literature. Writers. Local associations: East Sussex. Hastings, ca 1600-1960
Brodribb, Gerald. Hastings and men of letters / by Gerald Brodribb. — Revised ed. — [Hastings] ([39b High St., Hastings, Sussex]) : Old Hastings Preservation Society, 1971. — 51p,[4]p of plates : ill ; 19cm.
Previous ed.: Hastings : Hastings Public Library, 1954. — Bibl.: p.45-48. — Index.
ISBN 0-9505279-1-2 Sd : £0.30
(B77-00910)

820'.9 — English popular literature, 1540-1897. *Critical studies*
Neuburg, Victor Edward. Popular literature : a history and guide : from the beginning of printing to the year 1897 / [by] Victor E. Neuburg. — Harmondsworth [etc.] : Penguin, 1977. — 302p : ill, facsims ; 18cm. — (A pelican original)
Bibl.: p.265-297. — Index.
ISBN 0-14-021837-8 Pbk : £1.25
(B77-22076)

820'.9'001 — English literature, 1066-1400. Style. Linguistic aspects
Blake, Norman Francis. The English language in medieval literature / [by] Norman Blake. — London [etc.] : Dent [etc.], 1977. — 190p ; 23cm. — (Everyman's university library)
Bibl.: p.183-184. — Index.
ISBN 0-460-10273-7 : £7.95 : CIP rev.
(B77-12610)

820'.9'001 — English literature. Influence of Bible, to 1400
Fowler, David C. The Bible in early English literature / by David C. Fowler. — London : Sheldon Press, 1977. — x,263p : facsim(on lining papers) ; 24cm.
Originally published: Seattle : University of Washington Press, 1976. — Bibl.: p.247-254. — Index.
ISBN 0-85969-117-9 : £11.50
(B77-22793)

820'.9'001 — English literature. Influence of Islamic countries, 1066-1400
Metlitzki, Dorothee. The matter of Araby in medieval England / [by] Dorothee Metlitzki. — New Haven ; London : Yale University Press, 1977. — xiii,320p,[8]p of plates : ill, facsims, maps, port ; 24cm.
Index.
ISBN 0-300-02003-1 : £11.25
(B77-27316)

820'.9'003 — English literature, 1558-1625. *Critical studies*
Helgerson, Richard. The Elizabethan prodigals / [by] Richard Helgerson. — Berkeley [etc.] ; London : University of California Press, 1976. — x,178p ; 23cm.
Index.
ISBN 0-520-03264-0 : £6.70
(B77-24425)

820'.9'003 — English literature, 1558-1702. *Critical studies*
Kermode, Frank. English Renaissance literature : introductory lectures / [by] Frank Kermode, Stephen Fender, Kenneth Palmer. — London : Gray-Mills Publishing, 1974. — [6],145p ; 23cm.
ISBN 0-85641-022-5 : £6.50
ISBN 0-85641-023-3 Pbk : Unpriced
(B77-27317)

820'.9'005 — English literature, 1702-1800. *Critical studies*
Carnochan, W B. Confinement and flight : an essay on English literature of the eighteenth century / [by] W.B. Carnochan. — Berkeley [etc.] ; London : University of California Press, 1977. — xi,201p : ill ; 21cm.
Bibl.: p.193-196. — Index.
ISBN 0-520-03188-1 : £8.25
(B77-24426)

820'.9'007 — English literature, 1800-1900. Compared with French literature, 1815-1900
Sabin, Margery. English Romanticism and the French tradition / [by] Margery Sabin. — Cambridge, Mass. ; London : Harvard University Press, 1976. — xv,294p ; 24cm.
Index.
ISBN 0-674-25686-7 : £11.25
Also classified at 840'.9'007
(B77-05599)

820'.9'008 — English literature, 1837-1900. Influence of Sand, George
Thomson, Patricia. George Sand and the Victorians : her influence and reputation in nineteenth-century England / [by] Patricia Thomson. — London [etc.] : Macmillan, 1977. — ix,283p ; 23cm.
Bibl.: p.271-275. — Index.
ISBN 0-333-19819-0 : £6.95
(B77-22795)

820'.9'008 — English literature, 1837-1945. *Critical studies. Essays*
Ellmann, Richard. Golden codgers : biographical speculations / [by] Richard Ellmann. — New York ; London : Oxford University Press, 1976. — xiii,193p ; 21cm. — (A galaxy book)
Originally published: London : Oxford University Press, 1973. — Index.
ISBN 0-19-519845-x Pbk : £2.00
(B77-02545)

820'.9'008 — English literature, 1837-1975. Political aspects. *Essays*
Watson, George, *b.1927.* Politics and literature in modern Britain / [by] George Watson. — London [etc.] : Macmillan, 1977. — 190p ; 23cm.
Index.
ISBN 0-333-21741-1 : £5.95
ISBN 0-333-21743-8 Pbk : £2.50
(B77-31399)

820'.9'00912 — English literature, 1900-. *Transcripts of interviews*
Writers at work : the 'Paris review' interviews. — London : Secker and Warburg.
4th series / edited by George Plimpton ; introduced by Wilfrid Sheed. — 1976. — xvii, 459p : facsims, ports ; 22cm.
Includes interviews with Borges and Seferis.
ISBN 0-436-37610-5 : £6.50
(B77-09212)

820'.9'00912 — English literature, 1900-1945. *Critical studies*
Pritchard, William Harrison. Seeing through everything : English writers 1918-1940 / [by] William H. Pritchard. — London : Faber, 1977. — 234p ; 23cm.
Index.
ISBN 0-571-10167-4 : £5.95 : CIP rev.
(B77-07552)

820'.9'00912 — English literature, 1900-1945. *Critical studies. Readings*
Towards standards of criticism : selections from 'The calendar of modern letters', 1925-7 / chosen and with introductions by F.R. Leavis. — London : Lawrence and Wishart, 1976. — xxiii,200p ; 21cm.
This collection originally published: 1933. — Index.
ISBN 0-85315-388-4 Pbk : £2.75
(B77-07553)

820'.9'00912 — English literature, 1900-1945. Modernism. *Critical studies*
Faulkner, Peter. Modernism / [by] Peter Faulkner. — London : Methuen, 1977. — x, 86p ; 20cm. — (The critical idiom ; 35)
Bibl.: p.76-81. — Index.
ISBN 0-416-83700-x : £2.35
ISBN 0-416-83710-7 Pbk : £1.20
(B77-12043)

820'.9'00912 — English literature, 1900-1945. Political aspects
Morris, John Anthony. Writers and politics in modern Britain (1880-1950) / [by] J.A. Morris. — London [etc.] : Hodder and Stoughton, 1977. — vii,109p ; 22cm.
Bibl.: p.vi-vii.
ISBN 0-340-18440-x Pbk : £1.75
(B77-16561)

820'.9'00912 — English literature, 1900-1957. Writers. *Personal observations*
Stanford, Derek. Inside the forties : literary memoirs, 1937-1957 / [by] Derek Stanford. — London : Sidgwick and Jackson, 1977. — viii, 242p,[16]p of plates : ill, ports ; 23cm.
Index.
ISBN 0-283-98215-2 : £6.95
(B77-17050)

820'.9'00912 — English literature, 1900-1972. Influence of Golden bough by Frazer, Sir James George
Vickery, John B. The literary impact of 'The golden bough' / by John B. Vickery. — Princeton ; Guildford : Princeton University Press, 1976 [i.e. 1977]. — ix,435p ; 24cm.
Originally published: Princeton : Princeton University Press, 1973. — Index.
ISBN 0-691-01331-4 Pbk : £4.70
(B77-09213)

820'.9'00912 — English literature, 1900-1976. *Critical studies*
Lodge, David. Modernism, antimodernism and postmodernism / [by] David Lodge. — [Birmingham] : University of Birmingham, 1977. — [2],13p ; 21cm. — (University of Birmingham. Inaugural lectures)
'... delivered in the University of Birmingham on 2 December 1976' - title page verso.
ISBN 0-7044-0247-5 Sd : Unpriced
(B77-17709)

820'.9'00912 — English literature, 1900-1976. Comprehension. *Exercises, worked examples. For West African students. Secondary school texts*
Prose and poetry unseens for certificate literature in English / [compiled by] Rosina Umelo. — London [etc.] : Macmillan.
[Pupils' ed.]. — 1976. — vi,90p ; 22cm.
ISBN 0-333-19824-7 Pbk : £1.25
(B77-17710)

Teachers' ed. — 1976. — vi,138p ; 22cm.
ISBN 0-333-19825-5 Pbk : £3.15
(B77-17711)

820'.9'3 — English literature, 1837-1900. Special themes: Great Britain. Social conditions, 1832-1867. *Critical studies*
Brantlinger, Patrick. The spirit of reform : British literature and politics, 1832-1867 / [by] Patrick Brantlinger. — Cambridge, Mass. ; London : Harvard University Press, 1977. — x, 293p : ill, ports ; 24cm.
Index.
ISBN 0-674-83315-5 : £9.80
(B77-23662)

820'.9'353 — English literature, 1066-1558. Special themes: Curiosity & Christian pilgrimages. *Critical studies*
Zacher, Christian. Curiosity and pilgrimage : the literature of discovery in fourteenth-century England / [by] Christian K. Zacher. — Baltimore ; London : Johns Hopkins University Press, 1976. — x,196,[2]p ; 24cm.
Index.
ISBN 0-8018-1778-1 : £7.65
(B77-00370)

820'.9'9282 — Children's literature in English, 1800-1900. *Critical studies. Readings from contemporary sources*
A peculiar gift : nineteenth century writings on books for children / selected and edited by Lance Salway. — Harmondsworth : Kestrel Books, 1976. — 573p : ill ; 23cm.
Bibl.: p.537-556. — Index.
ISBN 0-7226-5140-6 : £8.95
(B77-02546)

820'.9'9282 — Children's literature in English, 1945-1976. *Critical studies. Readings*
Good writers for young readers : critical essays / edited by Dennis Butts. — St Albans : Hart-Davis Educational, 1977. — 144p ; 22cm.
Bibl.: p.142-144.
ISBN 0-247-12798-1 Pbk : £2.00
(B77-25836)

820'.9'9411 — English literature. Scottish writers, 1400-1558. *Conference proceedings*
International Conference on Scottish Language and Literature, Medieval and Renaissance, *1st, Edinburgh, 1975.* Bards and makars : Scottish language and literature : medieval and Renaissance / edited by Adam J. Aitken, Matthew P. McDiarmid, Derick S. Thomson. — [Glasgow] : University of Glasgow Press, 1977. — viii,250p ; 22cm.
'... a selection of the papers read at the First International Conference on Scottish Language and Literature, Medieval and Renaissance, held in Edinburgh from September 10-16, 1975' - title page verso. — Bibl.: p.213.
ISBN 0-85261-132-3 : £15.00
(B77-24427)

820'.9'9411 — English literature. Scottish writers, to 1976. *Critical studies*
Lindsay, Maurice. History of Scottish literature / [by] Maurice Lindsay. — London : Hale, 1977. — 496p ; 24cm.
Bibl.: p.449-462. — Index.
ISBN 0-7091-5642-1 : £8.95
(B77-13822)

820'.9'9415 — English literature. Irish writers, 1837-1945. *Critical studies*
Henn, Thomas Rice. Last essays / [by] Thomas Rice Henn. — Gerrards Cross : Smythe, 1976. — 253p ; 23cm.
Spine title: T.R. Henn's last essays.
ISBN 0-901072-03-6 : £5.50
(B77-00371)

820'.9'94174 — English literature. Galway (County) writers. *Biographical dictionaries*
Maher, Helen. Galway authors : a contribution towards a biographical and bibliographical index, with an essay on the history and literature in Galway / by Helen Maher. — Galway ([County Library Headquarters, Courthouse, Galway]) : Galway County Libraries, 1976. — [8],vi,116p ; 22cm.
Index.
ISBN 0-9505595-0-4 : £3.75
Also classified at 891.6'2'0994174
(B77-17051)

820'.9'968 — English literature. South African writers. *Conference proceedings*
Aspects of South African literature / edited by Christopher Heywood. — London [etc.] : Heinemann [etc.], 1976. — xv,192p ; 23cm. — ([Studies in African literature])
'... papers ... from contributions to two conferences which were held in March and April 1975, at the University of Texas at Austin, and in England at the University of York' - Acknowledgements. — Index.
ISBN 0-435-91340-9 : £6.00
ISBN 0-435-91341-7 Pbk : £2.60
(B77-02547)

821 — ENGLISH POETRY
821 — Poetry in English. Australian writers, 1890-1945. *Texts*
Dennis, Clarence James. C.J. Dennis' book for kids : a full colour edition of C.J. Dennis' rollicking rhymes / illustrated by Lee Whitmore. — London [etc.] : Angus and Robertson, 1976. — [86]p : col ill ; 30cm.
Originally published: as 'A book for kids'. Australia? : s.n., 1921.
ISBN 0-207-13359-x : £3.20
(B77-13222)

821 — Poetry in English. Australian writers, 1945-. *Texts*
James, Clive. Fan-mail : seven verse letters / [by] Clive James. — London : Faber, 1977. — 3-61p ; 20cm.
ISBN 0-571-11058-4 Pbk : £1.95 : CIP rev.
(B77-09891)

821 — Poetry in English. Finnish writers, 1945-. *Texts*
Lindroos, Rubio Tapani. Memories of discreet rooms / [by] Rubio Tapani Lindroos. — Banstead (109 High St., Banstead, Surrey) : Ibis Books, 1977. — [7],43p ; 21cm.
ISBN 0-9501960-5-3 Pbk : £1.75
(B77-18338)

821 — Poetry in English. Greek writers, 1945-. *Texts*
Goumas, Yannis. Signing on, and other poems, 1974-1977 / [by] Yannis Goumas. — Knotting : Sceptre Press, 1977. — 48p ; 21cm.
Pbk : £1.00
(B77-27318)

821 — Poetry in English. Indian writers, 1947-. *Texts*
Daruwalla, Keki N. Crossing of rivers / [by] Keki N. Daruwalla. — Delhi ; London [etc.] : Oxford University Press, 1976. — 58p ; 22cm. — (New poetry in India) (Three crowns books)
ISBN 0-19-560691-4 Pbk : £1.25
(B77-29638)

Kumar, Shiv Kumar. Subterfuges / [by] Shiv K. Kumar. — Delhi ; London [etc.] : Oxford University Press, 1976. — 48p ; 22cm. — (New poetry in India) (Three crowns books)
ISBN 0-19-560688-4 Pbk : £1.25
(B77-29639)

Ramanujan, Attipat Krishnaswami. Selected poems [of] A.K. Ramanujan. — Delhi ; London [etc.] : Oxford University Press, 1976. — [8],56p ; 22cm. — (New poetry in India) (Three crowns books)
ISBN 0-19-560689-2 Pbk : £1.25
(B77-29640)

821 — Poetry in English. Libyan writers, 1945-. *Texts*
Fekini, Hazami. Summer idylls / by Hazami Gadara-Fekini. — London [etc.] : Regency Press, 1977. — 77p,[11]leaves of plates : col ill ; 23cm.
£2.40
(B77-33400)

821 — Poetry in English. Maltese writers, 1945-. *Texts*
Fenech, Victor. London pictures, and other poems / [by] Victor Fenech ; with drawings by Rigby Graham. — Leicester (396 Aylestone Rd, Leicester) : Cog Private Press ; Wymondham : Brewhouse Private Press, 1976. — [24]p : ill ; 25cm.
Limited ed. of 120 numbered copies.
£6.00
(B77-20533)

821 — Poetry in English. New Zealand writers, 1900-1975. *Anthologies*
An **anthology** of twentieth century New Zealand poetry / selected by Vincent O'Sullivan. — 2nd ed. — Wellington [N.Z.] ; London [etc.] : Oxford University Press, 1976. — xxix,439p ; 21cm.
Previous ed.: London : Oxford University Press, 1970. — Bibl. — Index.
ISBN 0-19-558002-8 : Unpriced
ISBN 0-19-558003-6 Pbk : £3.50
(B77-14373)

821 — Poetry in English. New Zealand writers, 1907-. *Texts*
Baxter, James Keir. The bone chanter : unpublished poems, 1945-72 / [by] James K. Baxter ; chosen and introduced by J.E. Weir. — Oxford [etc.] : Oxford University Press, 1976. — 107p ; 22cm.
ISBN 0-19-558019-2 Pbk : £3.50
(B77-32123)

Baxter, James Keir. The holy life and death of Concrete Grady : various uncollected and unpublished poems / [by] James K. Baxter ; chosen and introduced by J.E. Weir. — Oxford [etc.] : Oxford University Press, 1976. — 99p ; 22cm.
ISBN 0-19-558021-4 Pbk : £3.50
(B77-31400)

821 — Poetry in English. New Zealand writers. Baxter, James Keir. *Critical studies*
O'Sullivan, Vincent, *b.1937.* James K. Baxter / by Vincent O'Sullivan. — Wellington [N.Z.] ; London [etc.] : Oxford University Press, [1977]. — 64p ; 22cm. — (New Zealand writers and their work)
Published in New Zealand: 1976. — Bibl.: p.62-64.
ISBN 0-19-558010-9 Pbk : £2.75
(B77-13824)

821 — Poetry in English. New Zealand writers. Brasch, Charles. *Critical studies*
Bertram, James. Charles Brasch / by James Bertram. — Wellington [N.Z.] ; London [etc.] : Oxford University Press, [1977]. — 60p ; 22cm. — (New Zealand writers and their work)
Published in New Zealand: 1976. — Bibl.: p.59-60.
ISBN 0-19-558015-x Pbk : £3.50
(B77-13825)

821 — Poetry in English. New Zealand writers. Compositions by secondary school students, 1945-. *Anthologies*
Dandelion daughter : an anthology of recent poems by New Zealand secondary school pupils (fifth series) / selected and edited by Helen M. Hogan. — Christchurch, N.Z. [etc.] ; London : Whitcoulls, 1977. — 80p ; 21cm.
Index.
ISBN 0-7233-0525-0 Sd : £2.10
(B77-27319)

821 — Poetry in English. Nigerian writers, 1945-. *Texts*
Okogie, M O, *Prince.* The God indwelling : gem poems of Nigeria / [by] Prince M.O. Okogie. — Ilfracombe : Stockwell, 1977. — 128p : port ; 19cm.
ISBN 0-7223-0984-8 : £2.50
(B77-21379)

Soyinka, 'Wole. Ogun Abibimañ / [by] Wole Soyinka. — London [etc.] : Collings, 1976. — [8],24p ; 20cm.
ISBN 0-86036-031-8 Pbk : £1.50
(B77-08522)

Williams, Lari. Drumcall : an anthology of poetry / by Lari Williams. — London (c/o Gadd and Pen, The Africa Centre, [38 King St., W.C.2]) : Barbican Books [etc.], [1976]. — 56p : ill, port ; 20cm.
ISBN 0-905507-00-2 Pbk : £0.75
(B77-06840)

821 — Poetry in English. Pakistani writers, 1947-. *Anthologies*
Rafat, Taufiq. Wordfall : three Pakistani poets : Taufiq Rafat, Maki Kureishi, Kaleem Omar ; edited by Kaleem Omar. — Karachi ; London [etc.] : Oxford University Press, 1975 [i.e. 1977]. — vii,78p ; 21cm. — (A three crowns book)
Published in Pakistan: 1975.
ISBN 0-19-577217-2 Pbk : £3.50
(B77-10522)

821 — Poetry in English. Polish writers, 1945-. *Texts*
Strzalkowski, Wieslaw. Awakening : poems / by Wieslaw Strzalkowski. — Breakish : Aquila, 1977. — 23p ; 21cm.
Also available in a limited ed. of 26 copies, signed and lettered by the author.
ISBN 0-7275-0148-8 Sd : £0.30
ISBN 0-7275-0149-6 Signed ed. : £1.50
(B77-16017)

821 — Poetry in English. Saudi Arabian writers, 1945-. *Texts*
Algosaibi, Ghazi A. From the Orient and the desert : poems / by Ghazi A. Algosaibi ; drawings by Andrew Vicari. — Stocksfield [etc.] : Oriel Press, 1977. — vi,25,[1]p : ill ; 22cm.
Limited ed. of 1000 numbered copies. — Ill. on lining papers.
ISBN 0-85362-165-9 : £5.00
Also classified at 741.9'42
(B77-18339)

821 — Poetry in English. South African writers, 1909-1961. *Texts*
Wright, David, *b.1920.* To the gods the shades : new & collected poems / [by] David Wright. — Manchester : Carcanet New Press, 1976. — 152p ; 23cm.
ISBN 0-85635-181-4 : £3.90
(B77-00911)

821 — Poetry in English. South African writers, 1961-. *Texts*
Sepamla, Sydney Sipho. The Soweto I love / [by] Sipho Sepamla. — London : Collings [etc.], 1977. — [7],53p ; 20cm.
ISBN 0-86036-065-2 Pbk : £1.50
(B77-21380)

821 — Poetry in English. Swedish writers, 1945-. *Texts*
Sprenger, Madeleine. One single day / [by] Madeleine Sprenger. — London : Senate Books, 1976. — 32p ; 21cm.
ISBN 0-900656-03-4 Sd : £2.00
(B77-05030)

821'.008 — Children's poetry in English, 1558-1975. *Anthologies*
Eight and a half : poems / compiled by Geoffrey Palmer and Noel Lloyd ; with illustrations by Denis Wrigley. — London [etc.] : Warne, 1976. — 32p : col ill ; 25cm.
Cover title.
ISBN 0-7232-1895-1 Pbk : £0.60
(B77-13826)

Nine and a half : poems / compiled by Geoffrey Palmer and Noel Lloyd ; with illustrations by Denis Wrigley. — London [etc.] : Warne, 1976. — p.33-64 : ill(chiefly col) ; 25cm.
Cover title.
ISBN 0-7232-1896-x Pbk : £0.60
(B77-13827)

Ten and a half : poems / compiled by Geoffrey Palmer and Noel Lloyd ; with illustrations by Denis Wrigley. — London [etc.] : Warne, 1976. — p.65-96 : col ill ; 25cm.
Cover title.
ISBN 0-7232-1897-8 Pbk : £0.60
(B77-13828)

821'.008 — Children's poetry in English, to 1976. *Anthologies*
The **rhyming** rainbow : poems / selected and illustrated by Cicely Mary Barker. — Glasgow [etc.] : Blackie [etc.], 1977. — [31]p : ill(some col) ; 18cm.
ISBN 0-216-90387-4 : £1.10
ISBN 0-216-90388-2 Pbk : £0.50
(B77-27320)

821'.008 — Poetry in English. *Anthologies. Serials*
The **fireside** book : a picture and a poem for every mood / chosen by David Hope. — London : D.C. Thomson.
[1978]. — 1977. — [102]p : col ill ; 19cm.
Col. ill. on lining papers.
£0.70
(B77-32124)

821'.008 — Poetry in English, 1250-1918. *Anthologies*
The **Oxford** book of English verse, 1250-1918 / chosen and edited by Sir Arthur Quiller-Couch. — New ed. — Oxford : Clarendon Press, 1974. — xxxii,1166p ; 19cm.
This ed. originally published: 1939. — Index.
ISBN 0-19-812107-5 : £4.50
(B77-06249)

821'.008 — Poetry in English, 1558-. *Anthologies. For Caribbean students. Secondary school texts*
Out for stars : an anthology of poetry for Caribbean secondary schools. — London [etc.] : Macmillan.
2 / selected by Neville and Undine Giuseppi. — 1976. — 109p ; 22cm.
ISBN 0-333-19899-9 Pbk : £0.60
(B77-16562)

821'.008 — Poetry in English, 1800-1976. *Anthologies. Juvenile literature*
Ichikawa, Satomi. From morn to midnight / [illustrated by] Satomi Ichikawa ; children's verses chosen by Elaine Moss. — London : Heinemann, 1977. — [32]p : chiefly col ill ; 23x25cm.
ISBN 0-434-94363-0 : £2.90
(B77-25837)

821'.008 — Poetry in English, ca 1500- ca 1970. *Anthologies*
Poetry for pleasure : a choice of poetry & verse on a variety of themes / made by Ian Parsons and illustrated by John Ward. — London : Chatto and Windus, 1977. — 352p : ill ; 21cm.
Index.
ISBN 0-7011-2279-x : £4.50 : CIP rev.
(B77-20534)

821'.008 — Poetry in English, to 1945. *Anthologies*
Poets of the English language / [edited by W.H. Auden and Norman Holmes Pearson]. — Harmondsworth [etc.] : Penguin. — (The Viking portable library)
In 5 vols.
[Vol.3] : Restoration and Augustan poets : Milton to Goldsmith. — 1977. — xliv,622p ; 19cm.
This collection originally published: New York : Viking Press, 1950 ; London : Eyre and Spottiswoode, 1952. — Index.
ISBN 0-14-015051-x Pbk : £1.95
(B77-28043)

821'.008 — Poetry in English, to ca 1950. *Anthologies*
The **London** book of English verse / selected by Herbert Read and Bonamy Dobrée. — 2nd revised ed. — London : Eyre Methuen, 1977. — xxxv,891p ; 19cm.
This ed. originally published: London : Eyre and Spottiswoode, 1952. — Index.
ISBN 0-413-21710-8 : £4.95
ISBN 0-413-37830-6 Pbk : £1.95
(B77-24428)

821'.008 — Poetry in English, to ca 1970. *Anthologies*
A **book** of faith / [compiled by] Elizabeth Goudge. — London [etc.] : Hodder and Stoughton, 1976. — 352p ; 23cm.
Index.
ISBN 0-340-19400-6 : £4.50
(B77-09214)

821'.008 — Poetry in English, to ca 1970. *Anthologies. Juvenile literature*
This world : an anthology of poetry for young people / [compiled by] M.M. Flynn and J. Groom ; illustrated by R. Wenban. — Rushcutters Bay ; Oxford [etc.] : Pergamon, 1976. — [8],208p : ill ; 25cm.
This anthology originally published: 1970. — Index.
ISBN 0-08-017482-5 : Unpriced
ISBN 0-08-017485-x Pbk : Unpriced
(B77-23663)

821'.008 — Poetry in English, to ca 1976. *Anthologies. Juvenile literature*
The **new** dragon book of verse / edited by Michael Harrison and Christopher Stuart-Clark. — Oxford [etc.] : Oxford University Press, 1977. — [5],267p : ill ; 20cm.
Index.
Unpriced
ISBN 0-19-831240-4
ISBN 0-19-831241-5 Pbk : £1.95
(B77-22796)

821'.008 — Poetry in English. Welsh writers, 1623-1976. *Anthologies*
The **Oxford** book of Welsh verse in English / chosen by Gwyn Jones. — Oxford [etc.] : Oxford University Press, 1977. — xxxvii,313p ; 19cm.
Includes some poems translated from the Welsh. — Index.
ISBN 0-19-211858-7 : £3.95
Primary classification 891.6'6'1008
(B77-13947)

821'.008'032 — Poetry in English, to 1975. Special subjects: England. *Anthologies*
Poet's England. — London (137 Fowler's Walk, W.5) : Brentham Press.
1 : Buckinghamshire, Berkshire, Oxfordshire / compiled by Margaret Tims ; line drawings by Gillian Durrant. — 1976. — 66p : ill, map ; 23cm.
ISBN 0-9503459-8-9 Pbk : £1.50
(B77-10900)

821'.008'033 — Poetry in English, to 1976. Special themes: Special occasions. *Anthologies. Juvenile literature*
Time's delights : poems for all seasons / chosen by Raymond Wilson ; illustrated by Meg Rutherford. — London [etc.] : Beaver Books, 1977. — 173p : ill ; 20cm.
Index.
ISBN 0-600-37128-x Pbk : £0.60
(B77-14877)

821'.008'033 — Poetry in English, to ca 1970. Special subjects: Christmas. *Anthologies. Juvenile literature*
A **single** star : an anthology of Christmas poetry / compiled and arranged by David Davis ; illustrated by Margery Gill. — Harmondsworth [etc.] : Puffin Books, 1976. — 96p : ill ; 19cm. — (Puffin books)
This collection originally published: London : Bodley Head, 1973. — Index.
ISBN 0-14-030876-8 Pbk : £0.45
(B77-02548)

821'.008'035 — Children's poetry in English. Special subjects: Man. *Anthologies*
People / poems selected by Dennis Saunders ; photographs by Vincent Oliver. — London : Evans Bros, 1977. — 32,[1]p : col ill ; 21cm. — (Poems and pictures)
ISBN 0-237-44848-3 Sd : £0.70
(B77-19599)

821'.008'0355 — Children's poetry in English. Special subjects: Social life. *Anthologies*
Town and country / poems selected by Dennis Saunders ; photographs by Vincent Oliver. — London : Evans Bros, 1977. — 32,[1]p : col ill ; 21cm. — (Poems and pictures)
ISBN 0-237-44849-1 Sd : £0.70
(B77-19600)

821'.008'0355 — Poetry in English, 1250-1916. Special subjects: Great Britain. Social life, 1250-1916. *Anthologies*
The **Penguin** book of everyday verse : social and documentary poetry, 1250-1916 / edited with an introduction by David Wright. — London : Allen Lane, 1976. — 542p ; 21cm.
Index.
ISBN 0-7139-1002-x : £6.95
(B77-02549)

821'.008'036 — Children's poetry in English. Special subjects: Nature. *Anthologies*
Miracles / poems selected by Dennis Saunders ; photographs by Vincent Oliver. — London : Evans Bros, 1977. — 32,[1]p : col ill ; 21cm. — (Poems and pictures)
ISBN 0-237-44847-5 Sd : £0.70
(B77-19601)

821'.008'036 — Children's poetry in English. Special subjects: Vertebrates. *Anthologies*
Creatures large / poems selected by Dennis Saunders ; photographs by Vincent Oliver. — London : Evans Bros, 1977. — 32,[1]p : col ill ; 21cm. — (Poems and pictures)
ISBN 0-237-44850-5 Sd : £0.70
(B77-19602)

821'.008'037 — Children's poetry in English. Special themes: Occultism. *Anthologies*
Hist whist : poems of magic and mystery, witches and ghosts / collected by Dennis Saunders ; cover illustration by Alan Lee ; text illustrations by Kathy Wyatt. — London : Pan Books, 1977. — 95p : ill ; 20cm. — (Piccolo)
This collection originally published: London : Evans Bros, 1975. — Index.
ISBN 0-330-25205-4 Pbk : £0.50
(B77-30564)

821'.009 — Poetry. Analysis. *Study examples: Poetry in English, 1637-ca 1890. Essays*
Hill, Archibald A. Constituent and pattern in poetry / by Archibald A. Hill. — Austin ; London : University of Texas Press, 1976. — xiv,157p ; 24cm.
Index.
ISBN 0-292-72010-6 : £9.00
(B77-04380)

821'.009 — Poetry in English, 1800-1975. *Critical studies*
Pinsky, Robert. The situation of poetry : contemporary poetry and its traditions / by Robert Pinsky. — Princeton ; Guildford : Princeton University Press, [1977]. — xi,188p ; 23cm. — (Princeton essays in literature)
Published in the United States: 1976. — Index.
ISBN 0-691-06314-1 : £9.70
(B77-12044)

821'.009 — Poetry in English, ca 1350-1975. *Transcripts of discussions*
English poetry / [edited by Alan Sinfield]. — London (85 Linden Gardens, W2 4EU) : Sussex Books, 1976. — 3-239[i.e.238]p ; 21cm. — (Questions in literature)
Bibl.
ISBN 0-905272-00-5 : Unpriced
ISBN 0-905272-01-3 Pbk : Unpriced
(B77-08523)

821'.009 — Poetry in English. Criticism. Eliot, Thomas Stearns. *Critical studies*
The **literary** criticism of T.S. Eliot : new essays / collected and edited by David Newton-de Molina. — London : Athlone Press, 1977. — vii,216p ; 23cm.
Index. — Includes comments on his criticism of other literary forms.
ISBN 0-485-11167-5 : £6.50
(B77-22797)

821'.009 — Poetry. Role of insight. *Study examples: Poetry in English, 1620-1920*
Holloway, John. The proud knowledge : poetry, insight and the self, 1620-1920 / [by] John Holloway. — London [etc.] : Routledge and Kegan Paul, 1977. — viii,264p ; 23cm.
Bibl.: p.259-261. — Index.
ISBN 0-7100-8541-9 : £6.75
(B77-19603)

821'.009'3 — Poetry in English, 1390-1960. Special subjects: War. *Anthologies*
War poetry : an anthology / edited with introduction & commentaries [by] D.L. Jones. — Oxford [etc.] : Pergamon, [1976]. — xi, 142p ; 20cm. — (Commonwealth and international library : Pergamon Oxford English series)
This collection originally published: 1968. — Index.
ISBN 0-08-012622-7 Pbk : £0.90
(B77-00912)

821'.04 — Ballads in English. Words. *Critical studies. Readings*
Ballad studies / edited by E.B. Lyle. — Cambridge [etc.] : Brewer [etc.] for the Folklore Society, 1976. — [11],212p : music ; 23cm. — (Mistletoe series)
Contains material on the music of the ballads.
ISBN 0-85991-020-2 : £3.50
(B77-03733)

821'.04 — Broadside ballads in English, 1702-1837. Words. *Facsimiles. Anthologies*
Broadside ballads of the 18th and early 19th centuries : reproductions from the original 32 / selected by J. Stevens Cox. — St Peter Port : Toucan Press, 1976. — [20]p : ill, of facsims ; 30cm.
ISBN 0-85694-091-7 Sd : £1.50
(B77-05600)

821'.04 — Elegiac poetry in English, 1637-1866. *Critical studies*
Smith, Eric, *b.1940.* By mourning tongues : studies in English elegy / [by] Eric Smith. — Ipswich : Boydell Press [etc.], 1977. — [9], 149p ; 23cm.
Index.
ISBN 0-85115-075-6 : £5.00
(B77-31401)

821'.04 — Lyric poetry in English, 1600-1970. *Critical studies. Essays*
Hardy, Barbara. The advantage of lyric : essays on feeling in poetry / [by] Barbara Hardy. — London : Athlone Press, 1977. — [9],142p ; 23cm.
Index.
ISBN 0-485-11162-4 : £5.50
(B77-14878)

821'.04 — Poetry in English. Sonnets, 1558-1625. *Anthologies*
Elizabethan sonnets / edited by Maurice Evans. — London [etc.] : Dent [etc.], 1977. — xxxi, 238p ; 19cm.
Index.
ISBN 0-460-10554-x Pbk : Unpriced : CIP rev.
ISBN 0-460-11554-5 Pbk : £2.95
(B77-17052)

821'.07 — Limericks in English, to 1975. *Critical studies*
Harrowven, Jean. The limerick makers / [by] Jean Harrowven. — London : Research Publishing Co., 1976. — 128,[4]p of plates : ill, facsims, port ; 23cm.
Bibl.: p.124-125. — Index.
ISBN 0-7050-0040-0 : £3.00
(B77-00372)

821.1 — ENGLISH POETRY, 1066-1400
821'.1 — Poetry in English, 1066-1400. *Texts*
Chaucer, Geoffrey. [Canterbury tales. English]. The Canterbury tales / [by] Geoffrey Chaucer ; an illustrated selection rendered into modern English by Nevill Coghill. — London : Allen Lane, 1977. — 374p,[32]p of plates : ill(some col), facsims ; 25cm.
These translations originally published: Harmondsworth : Penguin, 1951.
ISBN 0-7139-0262-0 : £7.95
(B77-13223)

Chaucer, Geoffrey. [Canterbury tales. Knight's tale]. The knight's tale / [by] Chaucer ; edited by J.A.W. Bennett. — 2nd ed. revised. — London : Harrap, 1976. — 208p : ill ; 18cm. — (Harrap's English classics)
Middle English text, English introduction and notes. — This ed. originally published: 1958. — Bibl.: p.208.
ISBN 0-245-53013-4 Pbk : £1.35
(B77-10901)

Chaucer, Geoffrey. [Canterbury tales. Pardoner's tale]. The pardoner's tale / [by] Chaucer ; edited by Nevill Coghill and Christopher Tolkien. — London : Harrap, 1976. — 172p, plate : 1 ill ; 18cm. — (Harrap's English classics)
Middle English text, English introduction and notes. — Originally published: 1958. — Bibl.: p.60.
ISBN 0-245-53016-9 Pbk : £1.00
(B77-10902)

Cleanness / edited by J.J. Anderson. — Manchester : Manchester University Press [etc.], 1977. — ix,177p : 1 ill ; 23cm. — (Old and Middle English texts)
Middle English text, modern English introduction, notes and glossary. — '... transcribed from the facsimile of MS Cotton Nero A.x. published by the Early English Text Society, and checked against the manuscript in the British Library' - Preface. — Bibl.: p.8-10. — Index.
ISBN 0-7190-0665-1 : £8.50
(B77-19604)

821'.1 — Poetry in English. Chaucer, Geoffrey. *Biographies*
Chute, Marchette. Geoffrey Chaucer of England / written and decorated by Marchette Chute. — London : Souvenir Press, 1977. — 347p ; 22cm. — (A condor book)
Originally published: New York : Dutton, 1946 ; London : Hale, 1951. — Bibl.: p.323-332. — Index.
ISBN 0-285-64832-2 : £3.95
ISBN 0-285-64833-0 Pbk : £2.50
(B77-12045)

Gardner, John, *b.1933.* The life and times of Chaucer / by John Gardner ; ornaments by J. Wolf. — London : Cape, 1977. — [1],ix,328,x p : ill ; 25cm.
Originally published: New York : Knopf, 1976. — Index.
ISBN 0-224-01387-4 : £7.50 : CIP rev.
(B77-24429)

821'.1 — Poetry in English. Chaucer, Geoffrey. *Critical studies*
Burlin, Robert Bradford. Chaucerian fiction / [by] Robert B. Burlin. — Princeton ; Guildford : Princeton University Press, 1977. — x,292p ; 23cm.
Index.
ISBN 0-691-06322-2 : £10.90
(B77-31402)

David, Alfred. The strumpet muse : art and morals in Chaucer's poetry / [by] Alfred David. — Bloomington ; London : Indiana University Press, 1976. — vii,280p,plate : ill ; 25cm.
Index.
ISBN 0-253-35517-6 : £11.25
(B77-20535)

Evans, Gillian. Chaucer / [by] Gillian Evans. — Glasgow [etc.] : Blackie, 1977. — [7],150p : ill, facsims, maps ; 22cm. — (Authors in their age)
Bibl.: p.143-145. — Index.
ISBN 0-216-90192-8 : £3.50
ISBN 0-216-90184-7 Pbk : £2.20
(B77-31403)

Gardner, John, *b.1933.* The poetry of Chaucer / [by] John Gardner. — Carbondale [etc.] : Southern Illinois University Press ; London [etc.] : Feffer and Simons, 1977. — xxvii,408p ; 25cm.
Index.
ISBN 0-8093-0772-3 : £11.25
(B77-12046)

Geoffrey Chaucer : a collection of original articles / edited by George D. Economou. — New York ; London [etc.] : McGraw-Hill, [1977]. — ii-xi,148p ; 21cm. — (Contemporary studies in literature)
Published in the United States: 1975. — Bibl.
ISBN 0-07-018968-4 Pbk : £2.05
(B77-10523)

821'.1 — Poetry in English. Chaucer, Geoffrey. Canterbury tales. Knight's tale. *Study outlines*
Notes on Chaucer's 'The knight's tale'. — London [etc.] : Methuen, 1976. — [5],40p ; 22cm. — (Study-aid series)
Bibl.: p.40. — Contains a modern English prose version of the tale.
ISBN 0-413-36980-3 Sd : £0.60
(B77-13224)

821'.1 — Poetry in English. Chaucer, Geoffrey. Canterbury tales. Nun's priest's tale. *Study outlines*
Notes on Chaucer's 'The nonne preestes tale'. — London [etc.] : Methuen, 1976. — [3],28p ; 22cm. — (Study-aid series)
Bibl.: p.28. — Contains a modern English version of the tale.
ISBN 0-413-36970-6 Sd : £0.60
(B77-13829)

821'.1 — Poetry in English. Chaucer, Geoffrey. Troilus and Criseyde. *Critical studies*
Rowe, Donald Wallace. O love, O charite! : contraries harmonized in Chaucer's 'Troilus' / [by] Donald W. Rowe. — Carbondale [etc.] : Southern Illinois University Press ; London [etc.] : Feffer and Simons, 1976. — ix,201p ; 22cm.
Index.
ISBN 0-8093-0697-2 : Unpriced
(B77-00373)

821'.1 — Poetry in English. Langland, William. Piers Plowman. Compared with Faerie Queene
Anderson, Judith H. The growth of a personal voice : 'Piers Plowman' and 'The faerie queene' / [by] Judith H. Anderson. — New Haven ; London : Yale University Press, 1976. — ix,240p ; 24cm.
Index.
ISBN 0-300-02000-7 : £9.90
Also classified at 821'.3
(B77-08524)

821'.1'08 — Poetry in English, 1066-1400. *Anthologies*
The owl and the nightingale ; [and], Cleanness ; [and], St Erkenwald / translated [from the Middle English] and introduced by Brian Stone. — Harmondsworth [etc.] : Penguin, 1977. — 264p ; 19cm. — (Penguin classics)
These translations originally published: 1971. — Bibl.: p.253-256. — Index.
Pbk : £0.80
ISBN 0-14-044245-6
(B77-29641)

821'.1'08 — Poetry in English, 1066-1400. *Anthologies. Facsimiles*
The Thornton manuscript (Lincoln Cathedral MS. 91) / introductions by D.S. Brewer & A.E.B. Owen. — [Facsimile ed.] reprinted with introductions revised. — London : Scolar Press, 1977. — xxii,[642]p ; 36cm.
'[A facsimile reprint of] the Lincoln manuscript, now Lincoln Cathedral MS. 91 (formerly A.S.2.) ... [probably written c.1430-50]' - Introduction. — Facsimile ed. originally published: 1975. — Bibl.: p.xxi-xxii.
ISBN 0-85967-352-9 : £50.00
Primary classification 091
(B77-28345)

821'.1'08 — Poetry in English, 1066-1558. *Anthologies*
English verse, 1300-1500 / edited by John Burrow. — London [etc.] : Longman, 1977. — xxvii,397p ; 22cm. — (Longman annotated anthologies of English verse ; vol.1)
Middle English texts, modern English introduction and notes. — Bibl.: p.391-394. — Index.
ISBN 0-582-48367-0 : £9.95
ISBN 0-582-48368-9 Pbk : £4.50
(B77-21381)

821'.1'08 — Poetry in English, 1066-1558. *Anthologies. Manuscripts. Facsimiles*
The Findern manuscript : Cambridge University Library MS.Ff.I.6 / introduction [and description] by Richard Beadle & A.E.B. Owen. — London : Scolar Press, 1977. — xxxiii,[332] p : ill ; 28cm.
Middle English text, English introduction and description. — Facsimile reproduction. — Bibl.: p.xxxi-xxxiii.
ISBN 0-85967-351-0 : £30.00
(B77-26468)

821'.1'09 — Alliterative poetry in English, 1066-1400. *Critical studies*
Turville-Petre, Thorlac. The alliterative revival / [by] Thorlac Turville-Petre. — Cambridge : Brewer [etc.], 1977. — viii,152p ; 25cm.
Bibl.: p.146-147. — Index.
ISBN 0-85991-019-9 : £7.50
(B77-23664)

821'.1'09 — Poetry in English, to 1558. *Critical studies*
Pearsall, Derek Albert. Old English and Middle English poetry / [by] Derek Pearsall. — London [etc.] : Routledge and Kegan Paul, 1977. — xiv,352p ; 24cm. — (The Routledge history of English poetry ; vol.1)
Index.
ISBN 0-7100-8396-3 : £8.75
(B77-09892)

821'.1'09353 — Poetry in English, 1066-1558. Special themes: Dreams & visions. *Critical studies*
Spearing, Anthony Colin. Medieval dream-poetry / [by] A.C. Spearing. — Cambridge [etc.] : Cambridge University Press, 1976. — vii,236p ; 23cm.
Bibl.: p.229-231. — Index.
ISBN 0-521-21194-8 : £8.50
ISBN 0-521-29069-4 Pbk : £3.00
(B77-04381)

821.2 — ENGLISH POETRY, 1400-1558
821'.2'08 — Poetry in English. 1400-1558. *Anthologies*
Three early Tudor poets : a selection from Skelton, Wyatt and Surrey / edited with an introduction and notes by Nicholas Bielby. — Exeter : Wheaton, 1976. — 231p ; 17cm. — (Wheaton studies in literature)
Bibl.: p.227-228. — Index.
ISBN 0-08-020385-x Pbk : £1.40
(B77-03734)

821.3 — ENGLISH POETRY, 1558-1625
821'.3 — Poetry in English, 1558-1625. *Texts*
Donne, John. The flea / [by] John Donne ; design in relief by Willow Legge. — Guildford ([22 Sydney Rd, Guildford GU1 3LL]) : Circle Press, 1977. — [8]p : ill ; 31cm.
Limited ed. of 75 copies, signed by the artist.
Sd : £5.00
(B77-29642)

Drayton, Michael. Selected poems [of] Michael Drayton / edited by Vivien Thomas. — Manchester : Carcanet New Press, 1977. — 96p ; 19cm. — (Fyfield books)
ISBN 0-85635-225-x : £2.50
ISBN 0-85635-226-8 Pbk : £0.95
(B77-28837)

Shakespeare, William. [Sonnets]. Shakespeare's sonnets. — Wantage (Grove, Wantage, Oxon.) : Black Swan Press, 1974. — [85]p ; 29cm.
Limited ed. of 190 numbered copies. — Quarter leather.
£27.00
(B77-26469)

Shakespeare, William. [Sonnets]. Sonnets [of] William Shakespeare. — London [etc.] : Spring Books, 1977. — [80]p ; 21cm.
ISBN 0-600-38266-4 : £1.25
(B77-22798)

Spenser, Edmund. [The faerie queen. *Selections]*.
The faerie queene : a selection / [by] Edmund Spenser ; introduction by Douglas Brooks-Davies. — London : Dent [etc.], 1976. — xxii,526p ; 19cm. — (Everyman's library)
Bibl.: p.xxi-xxii.
ISBN 0-460-00443-3 : £1.70
ISBN 0-460-01443-9 Pbk : £1.50
(B77-01762)

821'.3 — Poetry in English. Herbert, George, b.1593. *Concordances*
Di Cesare, Mario Anthony. A concordance to the complete writings of George Herbert / edited [i.e. compiled] by Mario A. Di Cesare and Rigo Mignani. — Ithaca ; London : Cornell University Press, 1977. — xv,1319p ; 25cm. — (The Cornell concordances)
ISBN 0-8014-1106-8 : Unpriced
(B77-28838)

821'.3 — Poetry in English. Shakespeare, William. Sonnets. 122. *Critical studies*
Marrian, Francis John Morton. Shakespeare's sonnet friend as pioneer of the New World / by F.J.M. Marrian. — London (1 Coulson St., S.W.3) : The author, 1977. — 22p ; 22cm.
Sd : £1.00
(B77-28839)

821'.3 — Poetry in English. Sidney, Sir Philip. *Critical studies*
Hamilton, A C. Sir Philip Sidney : a study of his life and works / by A.C. Hamilton. — Cambridge [etc.] : Cambridge University Press, 1977. — viii,216p ; 23cm.
Bibl.: p.209-211. — Index.
ISBN 0-521-21423-8 : £6.50
(B77-26470)

821'.3 — Poetry in English. Spenser, Edmund. Faerie Queene. *Critical studies*
Nohrnberg, James. The analogy of 'The faerie queene' / [by] James Nohrnberg. — Princeton ; Guildford : Princeton University Press, [1977]. — xxi,870p ; 25cm.
Published in the United States: 1976. — Index.
ISBN 0-691-06307-9 : £32.20
(B77-10903)

821'.3 — Poetry in English. Spenser, Edmund. Faerie Queene. *Critical studies, 1715-1975. Readings*
Spenser, 'The Faerie Queene' : a casebook / edited by Peter Bayley. — London [etc.] : Macmillan, 1977. — 253p ; 21cm. — (Casebook series)
Bibl.: p.247-248. — Index.
ISBN 0-333-19394-6 : £4.95
ISBN 0-333-19395-4 Pbk : £2.25
(B77-12047)

821'.3 — Poetry in English. Spenser, Edmund. Faerie Queene. Book 1 & 2. *Critical studies*
Brooks-Davies, Douglas. Spenser's 'Faerie queene' : a critical commentary on Books I and II / [by] Douglas Brooks-Davies. — Manchester : Manchester University Press [etc.], 1977. — x,198p : ill, facsims ; 20cm.
Bibl.
ISBN 0-7190-0683-x : £5.75
ISBN 0-7190-0698-8 Pbk : Unpriced
(B77-30565)

821'.3 — Poetry in English. Spenser, Edmund. Faerie Queene. Compared with Piers Plowman
Anderson, Judith H. The growth of a personal voice : 'Piers Plowman' and 'The faerie queene' / [by] Judith H. Anderson. — New Haven ; London : Yale University Press, 1976. — ix,240p ; 24cm.
Index.
ISBN 0-300-02000-7 : £9.90
Primary classification 821'.1
(B77-08524)

821'.3'08 — Poetry in English. Scottish writers, 1558-1702. *Anthologies. Facsimiles*
[A **choice** collection of comic and serious Scots poems both ancient and modern]. James Watson's choice collection of comic and serious Scots poems. — [1st ed. reprinted] / edited by Harriet Harvey Wood. — Edinburgh ([27 George Sq., Edinburgh EH8 9LD]) : Scottish Text Society.
In 2 vols. — Facsimile reprint of: 1869 reprint of 1st ed., originally published in 3 vols. Edinburgh : Watson, 1706-11.
Vol.1. — 1977. — 428p in various pagings ; 23cm. — (Scottish Text Society. Publications : 4th series ; 10)
Index.
£6.50(£5.00 to members of the Society)
(B77-29643)

821.4 — ENGLISH POETRY, 1625-1702
821'.4 — English literature. Puritan writers, 1625-1702. *Study examples: Poetry in English. Milton, John. Paradise lost*
Berry, Boyd McCulloch. Process of speech : Puritan religious writing & 'Paradise lost' / [by] Boyd M. Berry. — Baltimore ; London : Johns Hopkins University Press, 1976. — xiii,305p : 1 ill ; 24cm.
Index.
ISBN 0-8018-1779-x : £9.45
(B77-00374)

821'.4 — Poetry in English, 1625-1702. *Texts*
Marvell, Andrew. The complete poems [of] Andrew Marvell / edited by Elizabeth Story Donno. — Harmondsworth [etc.] : Penguin, 1976. — 314p ; 19cm. — (Penguin English poets)
This collection originally published: 1972. — Bibl.: p.17-20. — Index. — Includes poems in Latin and one in Greek with English translations.
ISBN 0-14-042213-7 Pbk : £0.90
(B77-01763)

Milton, John. 'Lycidas' of John Milton. — Dublin (Hewitt & Hewitt, 69 Fitzwilliam Sq., Dublin 2) : Laurel House Press (Minor Publications), 1977. — [12]p : 3 ill ; 23cm.
Cover title: John Milton's 'Lycidas'.
Sd : Unpriced
(B77-28044)

Milton, John. Samson Agonistes, sonnets, &c. / [by] John Milton ; edited by John Broadbent and Robert Hodge ; with translations of selected Latin and Italian poetry by Robert Hodge. — Cambridge [etc.] : Cambridge University Press, 1977. — xiv,235p ; 21cm. — (The Cambridge Milton for schools and colleges)
Includes 5 poems in Italian and 4 in Latin, with parallel English translations. — Bibl.
ISBN 0-521-21474-2 Pbk : Unpriced
(B77-18952)

821'.4 — Poetry in English. Dryden, John. *Critical studies*
Wykes, David. A preface to Dryden / [by] David Wykes. — London [etc.] : Longman, 1977. — xix,236p : ill, coat of arms, facsims, geneal table, map, ports ; 22cm. — (Preface books)
Bibl.: p.225-226. — Index.
ISBN 0-582-35101-4 : £4.00
ISBN 0-582-35102-2 Pbk : £2.25
(B77-18953)

821'.4 — Poetry in English. Dryden, John. Annus mirabilis. Political aspects
McKeon, Michael. Politics and poetry in Restoration England : the case of Dryden's 'Annus mirabilis' / [by] Michael McKeon. — Cambridge, Mass. ; London : Harvard University Press, 1975 [i.e. 1976]. — xiv,336p : ill, facsims, ports ; 24cm.
Published in the United States: 1975. — Bibl.: p.285-326. — Index.
ISBN 0-674-68755-8 : £11.25
(B77-05031)

821'.4 — Poetry in English. Marvell, Andrew. *Critical studies*
King, Bruce, *b.1933.* Marvell's allegorical poetry / [by] Bruce King. — New York ; Cambridge : Oleander Press, 1977. — 208p : port ; 23cm.
Index.
ISBN 0-902675-60-5 : £3.75 : CIP rev.
(B77-06841)

821'.4 — Poetry in English. Milton, John. *Biographies*
Hill, Christopher, *b.1912.* Milton and the English revolution / by Christopher Hill. — London : Faber, 1977. — iii-xviii,541p ; 24cm.
Bibl.: p.496-517. — Index.
ISBN 0-571-10198-4 : £12.50 : CIP rev.
ISBN 0-571-11170-x Pbk : Unpriced
(B77-17053)

Rowse, Alfred Leslie. Milton the Puritan : portrait of a mind / [by] A.L. Rowse. — London [etc.] : Macmillan, 1977. — 297p ; 23cm.
Index.
ISBN 0-333-21850-7 : £5.95
(B77-30566)

821'.4 — Poetry in English. Milton, John. *Critical studies*
Jones, Esmor. Milton / [by] Esmor Jones. — Glasgow [etc.] : Blackie, 1977. — [6],122p : ill, facsims, maps, ports ; 22cm. — (Authors in their age)
Bibl.: p.116-117. — Index.
ISBN 0-216-90370-x : £3.50
ISBN 0-216-90353-x Pbk : £1.95
(B77-28045)

Milton / [translated from the Italian]. — Maidenhead : Sampson Low, 1977. — 136p : ill(some col), col coat of arms, facsims, ports(chiefly col) ; 22cm. — (Giants of literature)
Originally published: in Italian. Milan : Arnoldo Mondadori Editore, 1968?. — Bibl.: p.131.
ISBN 0-562-00049-6 : £2.75
(B77-10904)

821'.4 — Poetry in English. Milton, John. Paradise lost. *Critical studies*
Stein, Arnold. The art of presence : the poet and 'Paradise lost' / by Arnold Stein. — Berkeley [etc.] ; London : University of California Press, 1977. — ix,190p ; 24cm.
Index.
ISBN 0-520-02956-9 : £8.25
(B77-21383)

821'.4 — Poetry in English. Milton, John. Paradise lost. Structure
Steadman, John Marcellus. Epic and tragic structure in 'Paradise lost' / [by] John M. Steadman. — Chicago ; London : University of Chicago Press, [1977]. — xi,189p ; 23cm.
Published in the United States: 1976. — Bibl.: p.143-150. — Index.
ISBN 0-226-77134-2 : £11.25
(B77-11372)

821'.4'09355 — Poetry in English, 1625-1702. Special subjects: Country houses. *Critical studies*
McClung, William A. The country house in English renaissance poetry / [by] William A. McClung. — Berkeley [etc.] ; London : University of California Press, 1977. — [10], 192p : ill, map, plans ; 23cm.
Index.
ISBN 0-520-03137-7 : £7.50
(B77-22799)

821.5 — ENGLISH POETRY, 1702-1745
821'.5 — Poetry in English, 1702-1745. *Texts*
Cameron, Archibald. Archibald Cameron's lament / edited, & with an introduction by G. Ross Roy. — London : Quarto Press, 1977. — [1],18p ; 21cm. — (Scottish poetry reprints ; no.3)
Limited ed. of 325 numbered copies.
Sd : Unpriced
(B77-28840)

Morning MDCCXLV. — Dublin ([c/o The Old Library, Trinity College], Dublin [2]) : Trinity Closet Press, 1977. — Folder([4]p) ; 26cm.
ISBN 0-9505512-0-1 : £0.20
(B77-05032)

Pope, Alexander. [Poems]. Collected poems [of] Alexander Pope / edited, with an introduction, by Bonamy Dobrée. — London : Dent [etc.], 1975. — xvii,408p ; 19cm. — (Everyman's library)
This collection originally published: London : Dent, 1924. — Bibl.: p.x-xii. — Index.
ISBN 0-460-00760-2 : £2.30
ISBN 0-460-01760-8 Pbk : £1.20
(B77-06842)

Swift, Jonathan. Selected poems [of] Jonathan Swift / edited by C.H. Sisson. — Manchester : Carcanet New Press, 1977. — 91p ; 19cm. — (Fyfield books)
ISBN 0-85635-134-2 : £2.50
ISBN 0-85635-135-0 Pbk : £0.95
(B77-24431)

Thomas Gray and William Collins : poetical works / edited by Roger Lonsdale. — Oxford [etc.] : Oxford University Press, 1977. — xxiii, 232p : 3 facsims ; 21cm. — (Oxford standard authors)
Bibl.: p.223-227. — Index.
ISBN 0-19-254170-6 : £5.50 : CIP rev.
ISBN 0-19-281169-x Pbk : £2.25
Primary classification 821'.6
(B77-07555)

Young, Edward, *b.1683.* Night thoughts, or, The complaint and the consolation / illustrated by William Blake ; text by Edward Young ; edited, with an introduction and commentary, by Robert Essick, Jenijoy La Belle. — New York : Dover Publications [etc.] ; London : Constable, [1976]. — 127p in various pagings : ill ; 31cm.
Includes original pagings. — Facsimile reprint of: 1797 ed. originally published as 'The complaint and the consolation, or, Night thoughts'. London : Richard Edwards, 1797. — Bibl.: p.xix-xxi.
ISBN 0-486-20219-4 Pbk : £2.80
Also classified at 769'.92'4
(B77-02550)

821'.5 — Poetry in English. Pope, Alexander. Special themes: Morals
Leranbaum, Miriam. Alexander Pope's 'Opus magnum', 1729-1744 / [by] Miriam Leranbaum. — Oxford : Clarendon Press, 1977. — xv,187p, plate : facsim ; 23cm.
Bibl.: p.xv. — Index.
ISBN 0-19-812051-6 : £8.50 : CIP rev.
(B77-08525)

821'.5'09 — Poetry in English, 1702-1800. Influence of landscape gardening
Hunt, John Dixon. The figure in the landscape : poetry, painting, and gardening during the eighteenth century / [by] John Dixon Hunt. — Baltimore ; London : Johns Hopkins University Press, 1976. — xv,271,[1]p : ill, plans, ports ; 25cm.
Index.
ISBN 0-8018-1795-1 : £11.20
(B77-22800)

821.6 — ENGLISH POETRY, 1745-1800
821'.6 — Poetry in English, 1745-1800. *Texts*
Burns, Robert. [Poems. Selected poems]. Poems and songs of Robert Burns : a completely new edition, including over 60 poems appearing for the first time in a collected edition, of which some have never before been published / edited and introduced by James Barke. — London [etc.] : Collins, 1976. — 736[i.e.738]p,[30]p of plates : ill, facsims, ports ; 19cm. — (Collins classics)
This collection originally published: 1955. — Index.
ISBN 0-00-420224-4 : £3.50
(B77-11373)

Fergusson, Robert. Fergusson : a bi-centenary handsel : seventeen poems / selected by Robert Garioch. A vision of angels : a one-act play / by Anne Smith. — Edinburgh : Reprographia, 1974. — 72p : 1 ill ; 22cm.
Four men, 2 women.
Sd : £1.30
Also classified at 822'.9'14
(B77-19605)

Goldsmith, Oliver. [Selected works]. Poems and plays / [by] Oliver Goldsmith. — New ed., completely revised / edited by Tom Davis. — London : Dent [etc.], 1975 [i.e. 1977]. — xxx, 258p : facsims ; 19cm.
This ed. originally published: 1975. — Bibl.: p.xxvii.
Pbk : £2.95
ISBN 0-460-10415-2
Primary classification 822'.6
(B77-31426)

Thomas Gray and William Collins : poetical works / edited by Roger Lonsdale. — Oxford [etc.] : Oxford University Press, 1977. — xxiii, 232p : 3 facsims ; 21cm. — (Oxford standard authors)
Bibl.: p.223-227. — Index.
ISBN 0-19-254170-6 : £5.50 : CIP rev.
ISBN 0-19-281169-x Pbk : £2.25
Also classified at 821'.5
(B77-07555)

821'.6 — Poetry in English, 1745-1800. *Texts. Manuscripts. Facsimiles*
Burns, Robert. [Poems. Selected poems]. A holograph of lines from 'The bonny banks of Ayr' and a version of 'Tibby, I hae see the day' / [by] Robert Burns ; introduction and notes by Gerald Campbell. — Richmond, Surrey : Keepsake Press, 1976. — [10]p : facsims ; 31cm.
Limited ed. of 150 copies.
ISBN 0-901924-41-5 Sd : Unpriced
(B77-05033)

821'.6 — Poetry in English. Burns, Robert. *Biographies*
Douglas, Hugh. Robert Burns : a life / [by] Hugh Douglas. — London : Hale, 1976. — 240p,[12]p of plates : ill, ports ; 23cm.
Bibl.: p.231-233. — Index.
ISBN 0-7091-5798-3 : £5.50
(B77-01764)

821'.6 — Poetry in English. Burns, Robert. Local associations: South-west Scotland. *Guidebooks*
Fergus, Andrew. Discovering the Burns country / [by] Andrew Fergus. — Aylesbury : Shire Publications, 1976. — 54p : ill, maps ; 18cm. — (Discovering series ; no.220)
Index.
ISBN 0-85263-354-8 Sd : £0.50
(B77-09215)

821'.6 — Poetry in English. Percy, Thomas. *Correspondence*
Percy, Thomas. The Percy letters / Cleanth Brooks & A.F. Falconer, general editors. — New Haven ; London : Yale University Press. [Vol.7] : The correspondence of Thomas Percy & William Shenstone / edited by Cleanth Brooks. — 1977. — xxxiv,324,[1]p ; 24cm.
Index.
ISBN 0-300-01924-6 : £13.40
(B77-16563)

821'.6'0914 — Poetry in English, 1745-1837. Romanticism. *Critical studies*
Cooke, Michael G. The Romantic will / [by] Michael G. Cooke. — New Haven ; London : Yale University Press, 1976. — xviii,279p ; 22cm.
Bibl.: p.253-270. — Index.
ISBN 0-300-01961-0 : £10.80
(B77-09216)

821.7 — ENGLISH POETRY, 1800-1837
821'.7 — Poetry in English, 1800-1837. *Texts*
Blake, William. The complete poems [of] William Blake / edited by Alicia Ostriker. — Harmondsworth [etc.] : Penguin, 1977. — 1071p ; 19cm. — (Penguin English poets)
Bibl.: p.15-18. — Index.
ISBN 0-14-042215-3 Pbk : £2.95
(B77-34019)

Byron, George Gordon, *Baron Byron.* Don Juan / [by] Lord Byron ; edited by T.G. Steffan, E. Steffan and W.W. Pratt ; with revisions by T.G. Steffan. — Harmondsworth [etc.] : Penguin, 1977. — 756p ; 18cm. — (Penguin English poets)
Bibl.: p.27-31.
ISBN 0-14-042216-1 Pbk : £1.95
(B77-25838)

Coleridge, Samuel Taylor. [Selections]. The portable Coleridge / edited and with an introduction by I.A. Richards. — Harmondsworth [etc.] : Penguin, 1977. — x, 630p ; 18cm. — (The Viking portable library)
This collection originally published: New York : Viking Press, 1950. — Index.
ISBN 0-14-015048-x Pbk : £1.95
(B77-34020)

Crabbe, George. Peter Grimes / [by] George Crabbe. — Kettering (27 Mill Dale Rd, Kettering) : J.L. Carr, [1977]. — [19]p : 1 ill ; 13cm.
Sd : £0.20
(B77-17712)

Keats, John. [Poems]. John Keats, the complete poems / edited by John Barnard. — 2nd ed. — Harmondsworth [etc.] : Penguin, 1976. — 3-731p ; 18cm. — (Penguin English poets)
Previous ed.: 1973. — Index.
ISBN 0-14-042210-2 Pbk : £1.75
(B77-08020)

Shelley, Percy Bysshe. [Poems. Selected poems]. Selected poems [of] Percy Bysshe Shelley / edited, with an introduction and notes by Timothy Webb. — London : Dent [etc.], 1977. — xl,232p ; 20cm. — ([Everyman's university library])
Index.
ISBN 0-460-10186-2 : £4.95 : CIP rev.
ISBN 0-460-11186-8 Pbk : £2.95
(B77-17054)

Wordsworth, William. Poems / [by] William Wordsworth ; edited by John O. Hayden. — Harmondsworth [etc.] : Penguin. — (Penguin English poets)
Vol.1. — 1977. — 1066p ; 18cm.
Index.
ISBN 0-14-042211-0 Pbk : £3.75
(B77-07556)

Vol.2. — 1977. — 1104p ; 18cm.
Index.
ISBN 0-14-042212-9 Pbk : £3.75
(B77-07557)

Wordsworth, William. The prelude, 1798-1799 / by William Wordsworth ; edited by Stephen Parrish. — Ithaca : Cornell University Press ; Hassocks : Harvester Press, 1977. — xi,313p : facsims ; 24cm. — (The Cornell Wordsworth)
' ... this book presents the earliest version of Wordsworth's ... poem ... ' - jacket. — Bibl.: p.xi.
ISBN 0-85527-169-8 : £12.50
(B77-06250)

821'.7 — Poetry in English. Blake, William. *Biographies*
Davis, Michael, *b.1925.* William Blake : a new kind of man / [by] Michael Davis. — London : Elek, 1977. — 181p,[40]p of plates : ill(some col), facsims(some col), ports ; 24cm.
Bibl.: p.165-170. — Index.
ISBN 0-236-40054-1 : £6.75
(B77-12048)

821'.7 — Poetry in English. Blake, William. *Critical studies*
Mellor, Anne Kostelanetz. Blake's human form divine / [by] Anne Kostelanetz Mellor. — Berkeley [etc.] ; London : University of California Press, 1974. — xxiii,354p : ill, facsims ; 24cm.
Index.
ISBN 0-520-02065-0 : Unpriced
(B77-18954)

821'.7 — Poetry in English. Blake, William. Influence of philosophy of Berkeley, George
Raine, Kathleen. Berkeley, Blake and the New Age / [by] Kathleen Raine. — Ipswich (3 Cambridge Drive, Ipswich IP2 9EP) : Golgonooza Press, 1977. — 24p ; 23cm. — (Berkeley lecture ; 1975)
Sd : £0.90
Signed ed. : Unpriced
(B77-34021)

821'.7 — Poetry in English. Byron, George Gordon, Baron Byron. *Biographies*
Marchand, Leslie Alexis. Byron : a portrait / [by] Leslie A. Marchand. — London : Futura Publications, 1976. — xvii,518,xxxiv,[1]p,[8]p of plates : geneal tables, 2 maps, ports ; 20cm. — (An Omega book)
Originally published: New York : Knopf, 1970 ; London : J. Murray, 1971. — Bibl.: p.514-518. — Index.
ISBN 0-86007-738-1 Pbk : £1.75
(B77-12049)

821'.7 — Poetry in English. Byron, George Gordon, Baron Byron. *Correspondence & diaries*
Byron, George Gordon, *Baron Byron.* Byron's letters and journals : the complete and unexpurgated text of all the letters available in manuscript and the full printed version of all others / edited by Leslie A. Marchand. — London : J. Murray.
Vol.7 : 1820 : Between two worlds. — 1977. — [5],282p,plate : ports ; 23cm.
Includes original text and English translations of those letters written in Italian. — Bibl.: p.271. — Index.
ISBN 0-7195-3345-7 : £6.50
(B77-22801)

821'.7 — Poetry in English. Byron, George Gordon, Baron Byron. *Critical studies*
Bell, Arnold Craig. Byron : his achievement and significance / [by] A. Craig Bell. — Darley (Darley, Harrogate, N. Yorkshire) : Grian-aig Press, 1976. — xiv,120p ; 23cm.
Bibl.: p.113. — Index.
ISBN 0-9500714-6-3 Pbk : £2.20
(B77-04382)

821'.7 — Poetry in English. Byron, George Gordon, Baron Byron. Relations with Shelley, Percy Bysshe
Robinson, Charles Edward. Shelley and Byron : the snake and eagle wreathed in fight / [by] Charles E. Robinson. — Baltimore ; London : Johns Hopkins University Press, 1976. — xi, 292p ; 24cm.
Index.
ISBN 0-8018-1707-2 : £10.05
(B77-05034)

821'.7 — Poetry in English. Coleridge, Samuel Taylor. *Critical studies*
Beer, John Bernard. Coleridge's poetic intelligence / [by] John Beer. — London : Macmillan, 1977. — xviii,318p ; 23cm.
Index.
ISBN 0-333-21312-2 : £8.95
(B77-07558)

821'.7 — Poetry in English. Crabbe, George. *Critical studies*
Bareham, Terence. George Crabbe / [by] Terence Bareham. — London : Vision Press, 1977. — 245p ; 23cm. — (Vision critical studies)
Index.
ISBN 0-85478-084-x : £5.95
(B77-30567)

821'.7 — Poetry in English. Keats, John. *Critical studies*
Allott, Miriam. John Keats / by Miriam Allott ; edited by Ian Scott-Kilvert. — Harlow : Longman for the British Council, 1976. — 62p, plate : port ; 22cm. — (Writers and their work ; 253)
Bibl.: p.55-62.
ISBN 0-582-01257-0 Sd : £0.40
(B77-29644)

Ende, Stuart A. Keats and the sublime / [by] Stuart A. Ende. — New Haven ; London : Yale University Press, 1976. — xviii,201p : facsim ; 22cm.
Index.
ISBN 0-300-02010-4 : £9.00
(B77-26471)

821'.7 — Poetry in English. Keats, John. Religious beliefs
Ryan, Robert M. Keats : the religious sense / by Robert M. Ryan. — Princeton ; Guildford : Princeton University Press, 1976. — [7],236p ; 23cm.
Bibl.: p.219-229. — Index.
ISBN 0-691-06316-8 : £10.10
(B77-05601)

821'.7 — Poetry in English. Moore, Thomas, b.1779. *Biographies*
White, Terence de Vere. Tom Moore : the Irish poet / [by] Terence de Vere White. — London : Hamilton, 1977. — xiv,281p,[8]p of plates : ports ; 23cm.
Bibl.: p.271-273. — Index.
ISBN 0-241-89622-3 : £7.50
(B77-21384)

821'.7 — Poetry in English. Shelley, Percy Bysshe. *Biographies*
Holmes, Richard, *b.1945.* Shelley : the pursuit / [by] Richard Holmes. — London : Quartet Books, 1976. — xv,829p,[16]p of plates : ill, facsim, ports ; 22cm.
Originally published: London : Weidenfeld and Nicolson, 1974. — Bibl.: p.736-738. — Index.
ISBN 0-7043-3111-x Pbk : £2.95
(B77-03196)

821'.7 — Poetry in English. Shelley, Percy Bysshe. *Critical studies*
Curran, Stuart. Shelley's 'Annus mirabilis' : the maturing of an epic vision / by Stuart Curran. — San Marino, Calif. : Huntington Library ; Folkestone : [Distributed by] Dawson, 1975. — xxii,255p : ill, facsims ; 24cm.
Bibl.: p.xxii. — Index.
ISBN 0-87328-064-4 : £10.25
(B77-30568)

821'.7 — Poetry in English. Shelley, Percy Bysshe. Gothic aspects
Murphy, John V. The dark angel : Gothic elements in Shelley's works / [by] John V. Murphy. — Lewisburg : Bucknell University Press ; London (108 New Bond St., W1Y 0QX) : Associated University Press, 1975. — 199p ; 22cm.
Bibl.: p.186-193. — Index.
ISBN 0-8387-1407-2 : £4.50
(B77-01765)

821'.7 — Poetry in English. Symbolism. Study examples: Coleridge, Samuel Taylor
Barth, John Robert. The symbolic imagination : Coleridge and the Romantic tradition / [by] J. Robert Barth. — Princeton ; Guildford : Princeton University Press, 1977. — xi,155p ; 23cm. — (Princeton essays in literature)
Bibl.: p.145-150. — Index. — Includes a chapter on William Wordsworth.
ISBN 0-691-06320-6 : £8.10
(B77-16564)

821'.7 — Poetry in English. Wordsworth, William. Lyrical ballads. *Critical studies*
Jordan, John Emory. Why the 'Lyrical ballads'? : the background, writing, and character of Wordsworth's 1798 'Lyrical ballads' / by John E. Jordan. — Berkeley [etc.] ; London : University of California Press, 1976. — xii, 212p ; 23cm.
Bibl.: p.187-189. — Index.
ISBN 0-520-03124-5 : £7.80
(B77-13225)

821'.7 — Poetry in English. Wordsworth, William. Special themes: Mysticism
Wlecke, Albert O. Wordsworth and the sublime / [by] Albert O. Wlecke. — Berkeley [etc.] ; London : University of California Press, 1973. — xii,163p ; 23cm. — (Perspectives in criticism ; 23)
Index.
ISBN 0-520-02233-5 : Unpriced
(B77-19606)

821'.7'09 — Poetry in English, 1800-1837. *Reviews, to 1824. Anthologies*
Romantic bards and British reviewers : a selected edition of the contemporary reviews of the works of Wordsworth, Coleridge, Byron, Keats and Shelley / edited by John O. Hayden. — Lincoln, Neb. ; London : University of Nebraska Press, 1976. — xix,433p ; 24cm.
Originally published: Lincoln, Neb. : University of Nebraska Press ; London : Routledge and Kegan Paul, 1971. — Bibl.: p.429-433.
ISBN 0-8032-0773-5 : £18.00
(B77-06251)

821'.7'0914 — Poetry in English, 1800-1837. Romanticism. *Critical studies, to 1969. Readings*
The **romantic** imagination : a casebook / edited by John Spencer Hill. — London [etc.] : Macmillan, 1977. — 241p ; 23cm. — (Casebook series)
Bibl.: p.228-233. — Index.
ISBN 0-333-21234-7 : £5.95 : CIP rev.
ISBN 0-333-21235-5 Pbk : £2.50
(B77-21385)

821.8 — ENGLISH POETRY, 1837-1900
821'.8 — Poetry in English, 1837-1900. *Texts*
Belloc, Hilaire. Matilda who told lies and was burned to death / [by] Hilaire Belloc ; pictures by Steven Kellogg. — London : F. Warne, 1977. — [32]p : ill ; 25cm.
Originally published: New York : Dial Press, 1970.
ISBN 0-7232-2053-0 : £2.50
(B77-33401)

Browning, Robert, *b.1812.* The Pied Piper of Hamelin / [by] Robert Browning ; illustrated by Harold Jones. — London [etc.] : Angus and Robertson, 1976. — [48]p : col ill ; 25cm.
Originally published: London : Oxford University Press, 1962.
ISBN 0-207-95673-1 : £2.80
(B77-06843)

Carr, H.D. Rosa coeli ; [and], Rosa mundi ; [and], Rosa inferni / by H.D. Carr (Aleister Crowley) ; with original compositions by Auguste Rodin. — London (49a Museum St., W.C.1) : Neptune Press, 1976. — [2],47p : ill ; 31cm.
Limited ed. of 500 numbered copies. — Facsimile reprints. — 'Rosa coeli' originally published: London : Chiswick Press, 1907. — 'Rosa mundi' originally published: Paris : Ph. Renouard, 1905. — 'Rosa inferni' originally published: London : Chiswick Press, 1907.
ISBN 0-9505001-2-7 Sd : £7.50
(B77-10905)

Carroll, Lewis. The hunting of the Snark : an agony in eight fits / by Lewis Carroll ; illustrated by John Minnion. — London (302 Wood Green High Rd, N.22) : John Minnion, 1976. — [1],39p : ill ; 30cm.
ISBN 0-9504847-1-7 Pbk : £1.50
(B77-11374)

Carroll, Lewis. Jabberwocky / [by Lewis Carroll] ; drawings by John Minnion. — London (302 High Rd, N.22) : Aloes Books, 1973. — [16]p : chiefly ill ; 30cm.
Limited ed. of 1000 copies.
Sd : Unpriced
(B77-11375)

Carroll, Lewis. Jabberwocky : Lewis Carroll's poem / illustrated by John Minnion. — London (302 Wood Green High Rd, N.22) : The artist, 1975. — [14]p : ill ; 30cm.
Originally published: s.l. : John Minnion and Aloes Books, 1973.
ISBN 0-9504847-0-9 Sd : £0.90
(B77-10906)

Carroll, Lewis. Lewis Carroll's 'Jabberwocky' / illustrations by Jane Breskin Zalben ; with annotations by Humpty Dumpty. — New York ; London : F. Warne, 1977. — [32]p : col ill ; 21x23cm.
ISBN 0-7232-6145-8 : £3.95
(B77-34022)

Crane, Walter. Cartoons for the cause : designs and verses for the Socialist and Labour movement, 1886-1896 / by Walter Crane. — [1st ed. reprinted] ; with a foreword by John Betjeman. — London ([97 Ferme Park Rd, N8 9SA]) : Journeyman Press ; [London] : Marx Memorial Library, 1976. — [20] leaves : chiefly ill ; 43cm.
Limited ed. of 600 copies of which 100 have been signed by John Betjeman. — Some leaves printed on both sides. — Facsimile reprint of: 1st ed.: London : Twentieth Century Press, 1896.
ISBN 0-904526-13-5 Sd : £3.95
ISBN 0-904526-14-3 Signed ed. : £12.00
Primary classification 769'.92'4
(B77-13174)

Hardy, Thomas, *b.1840.* Poems of Thomas Hardy : a new selection / selected, with an introduction and notes, by T.R.M. Creighton. — Revised ed. — London [etc.] : Macmillan, 1977. — xvi,368p ; 23cm.
Previous ed.: 1974. — Index.
ISBN 0-333-22679-8 : £5.95
ISBN 0-333-22680-1 Pbk : £1.95
(B77-26472)

Hogan, Michael. Drunken Thady and the Bishop's lady : a legend of Thomond Bridge / by Michael Hogan, the Bard of Thomond ; edited, with an introduction and notes, by Críostóir Ó Floinn. — [Dun Laoghaire] ([47 Pairc Arnold, Dun Laoghaire, Co. Baile Atha Cliath]) : [The editor], [1977?]. — 68p : ill, map(on cover) ; 19cm.
Pbk : £1.00
(B77-34023)

Kipling, Rudyard. Kipling : a selection / by James Cochrane. — Harmondsworth [etc.] : Penguin, 1977. — 313p ; 18cm. — (The Penguin poets)
Spine title: Selected verse. — Index.
ISBN 0-14-042206-4 Pbk : £1.25
(B77-18340)

Lear, Edward. Edward Lear's book of mazes. — London : Carousel, 1977. — 109p : ill ; 20cm.
With answers. — Contents: Nonsense songs and limericks / by Edward Lear - Amazing mazes / by Gyles Brandreth and David Farris.
ISBN 0-552-52077-2 Pbk : £0.45
Primary classification 793.7'3
(B77-28809)

Shorter, Dora Sigerson. The tricolour : poems of the Irish revolution / by Dora Sigerson Shorter. — [Enlarged ed.] / [edited by Dan Barry]. — Cork (San Toye, Ballyvolane Rd, Cork) : CFN, 1976. — 48p : 2 ill, ports ; 22cm.
Previous ed.: Dublin : Maunsel and Roberts, 1922.
Sd : £0.50
(B77-18341)

821'.8 — Poetry in English. Blunt, Wilfred Scawen. Interpersonal relationships with Wyndham, George
Egremont, Max. The cousins : the friendship, opinions and activities of Wilfrid Scawen Blunt and George Wyndham / [by] Max Egremont. — London : Collins, 1977. — 320p,[8]p of plates : ill, geneal table(on lining papers), ports ; 23cm.
Bibl.: p.305-309. — Index.
ISBN 0-00-216134-6 : £6.50
Also classified at 941'.081'0924
(B77-07559)

821'.8 — Poetry in English. Browning, Robert, b.1812. Correspondence with Carlyle, Thomas. *Critical studies*
Sanders, Charles Richard. The Carlyle-Browning correspondence and relationship / by Charles Richard Sanders. — Manchester (Manchester M3 3EH) : John Rylands University Library of Manchester, 1975. — [1],67p ; 25cm.
'Reprinted from the "Bulletin of the John Rylands University Library of Manchester", Vol.57, No.1, Autumn, 1974 and Vol.57, No.2, Spring, 1975'.
ISBN 0-905578-02-3 Sd : £1.50
Primary classification 828'.8'08
(B77-04448)

821'.8 — Poetry in English. Browning, Robert, b.1812, to 1835. *Biographies*
Maynard, John. Browning's youth / [by] John Maynard. — Cambridge, Mass. ; London : Harvard University Press, 1977. — xx,490p : ill, facsims, geneal tables, map, ports ; 24cm.
Index.
ISBN 0-674-08441-1 : £13.65
(B77-30569)

821'.8 — Poetry in English. Field, Michael. *Biographies*
Ricketts, Charles. Michael Field / by Charles Ricketts ; edited by Paul Delaney. — Edinburgh ([137 Warrender Park Rd, Edinburgh EH9 1DS]) : Tragara Press, 1976. — vii,12p,[2]leaves of plates : ports ; 24cm.
Limited ed. of 125 numbered copies.
ISBN 0-902616-32-3 Sd : £6.00
(B77-09893)

821'.8 — Poetry in English. Fitzgerald, Edward, b.1809. *Biographies*
Jewett, Iran B Hassani. Edward FitzGerald / [by] Iran B. Hassani Jewett. — London : Prior [etc.], 1977. — 173p : port ; 21cm. — (Twayne's English authors series ; TEAS 205)
Bibl.: p.165-170. — Index.
ISBN 0-86043-091-x : £4.95
(B77-28046)

821'.8 — Poetry in English. Hardy, Thomas, b.1840. *Critical studies*
Pinion, Francis Bertram. A commentary on the poems of Thomas Hardy / [by] F.B. Pinion. — London [etc.] : Macmillan, 1976. — xviii,293p, 8p of plates : ill, facsims, maps, ports ; 23cm.
Index.
ISBN 0-333-17918-8 : £10.00
(B77-02551)

821'.8 — Poetry in English. Hopkins, Gerard Manley. *Biographies*
Bergonzi, Bernard. Gerard Manley Hopkins / by Bernard Bergonzi. — London [etc.] : Macmillan, 1977. — xvii,202p ; 23cm. — (Masters of world literature series)
Bibl.: p.193-194. — Index.
ISBN 0-333-21522-2 : £7.95
(B77-20536)

821'.8 — Poetry in English. Hopkins, Gerard Manley. Language
Milroy, James. The language of Gerard Manley Hopkins / [by] James Milroy. — London : Deutsch, 1977. — xiv,264p ; 23cm. — (The language library)
Bibl.: p.262-264.
ISBN 0-233-96916-0 : £7.95 : CIP rev.
(B77-24432)

821'.8 — Poetry in English. Seaman, Sir Owen, bart. *Biographies*
Adlard, John. Owen Seaman : his life and work / by John Adlard. — London (3 Kemplay Rd, Hampstead NW3 1TA) : The Eighteen Nineties Society, 1977. — viii,139p,leaf of plate,p2-6 of plates : facsim, ports ; 22cm. — (Makers of the nineties)
Limited ed. of 750 numbered copies. — Index.
ISBN 0-905744-00-4 : £10.50
ISBN 0-9504108-3-7 Pbk : £4.65
(B77-15444)

821'.8 — Poetry in English. Tennyson, Alfred, Baron Tennyson. Style. *Critical studies*
Shaw, William David. Tennyson's style / by W. David Shaw. — Ithaca ; London : Cornell University Press, 1976. — 347p,[2]p ; 23cm.
Bibl.: p.307-331. — Index.
ISBN 0-8014-1021-5 : £9.75
(B77-13226)

821'.8 — Poetry in English. Yeats, William Butler. *Biographies*
O'Connor, Frank. A gambler's throw : memories of W.B. Yeats / by Frank O'Connor. — Edinburgh ([137 Warrender Park Rd, Edinburgh EH9 1DS]) : Tragara Press, 1975. — [16]p : port ; 23cm.
'... the text of a radio talk ... on 13th February 1966' - note. — Limited ed. of 95 numbered copies.
ISBN 0-902616-21-8 Sd : Unpriced
(B77-19607)

821'.8 — Poetry in English. Yeats, William Butler. *Critical studies, 1884-1939. Readings*
W.B. Yeats, the critical heritage / edited by A. Norman Jeffares. — London [etc.] : Routledge and Kegan Paul, 1977. — xvi,483p ; 23cm. — (The critical heritage series)
Bibl.: p.437-439. — Index.
ISBN 0-7100-8480-3 : £8.25 : CIP rev.
(B77-21387)

821'.8 — Poetry in English. Yeats, William Butler. *Transcripts of interviews*
W.B. Yeats : interviews and recollections / edited by E.H. Mikhail. — London [etc.] : Macmillan.

In 2 vols.
Vol.1 / with a foreword by A. Norman Jeffares. — 1977. — xviii,197p ; 23cm.
ISBN 0-333-19711-9 : £7.95
(B77-17713)

Vol.2. — 1977. — xi p,p199-426 ; 23cm.
Bibl.: p.416-417. — Index.
ISBN 0-333-19712-7 : £7.95
(B77-17714)

821'.8 — Poetry in English. Yeats, William Butler. Local associations: Galway (County). Gort. Castles: Ballylee Castle
Hanley, Mary. Thoor Ballylee : home of William Butler Yeats / [by] Mary Hanley & Liam Miller ; with a foreword by T.R. Henn. — 2nd ed., revised. — Dublin : Dolmen Press, 1977. — 32p : ill, facsim, map, plans, ports ; 25cm.
'... a development of a lecture delivered by Mary Hanley to the Kiltartan Society at Coole Park on 19 June 1961, rearranged with additional matter by Liam Miller' - title page verso. — Previous ed.: 1965.
ISBN 0-85105-300-9 Sd : £1.50
(B77-23665)

821'.8 — Poetry in English. Yeats, William Butler. Local associations: Sligo (County). Sligo region
Kirby, Sheelah. The Yeats country : a guide to the Sligo district and other places in the West of Ireland associated with the life and work of W.B. Yeats / [by] Sheelah Kirby ; with drawings by Ruth Brandt. — New ed. — Dublin : Dolmen Press, 1977. — 93p : ill, map ; 19cm.
This ed. originally published: 1969. — Bibl.: p.85-86. — Index.
ISBN 0-85105-333-5 Pbk : £1.60
(B77-22802)

821'.8 — Poetry in English. Yeats, William Butler. Romanticism. *Critical studies*
Bornstein, George. Transformations of romanticism in Yeats, Eliot, and Stevens / [by] George Bornstein. — Chicago ; London : University of Chicago Press, 1976[i.e.1977]. — xiii,263,[1]p ; 24cm.
Published in the United States: 1976. — Index.
ISBN 0-226-06643-6 : £11.25
Primary classification 821'.8'0914
(B77-14879)

821'.8'09 — Poetry in English, 1837-1945. *Critical studies*
Perkins, David. A history of modern poetry / [by] David Perkins. — Cambridge, Mass. ; London : Belknap Press of Harvard University Press.
In 2 vols.
From the 1890s to the high modernist mode. — 1976. — xv,623p ; 23cm.
Index.
ISBN 0-674-39941-2 : £13.15
(B77-04383)

821'.8'0914 — Poetry in English, 1837-1945. Romanticism. *Critical studies*
Bornstein, George. Transformations of romanticism in Yeats, Eliot, and Stevens / [by] George Bornstein. — Chicago ; London : University of Chicago Press, 1976[i.e.1977]. — xiii,263,[1]p ; 24cm.
Published in the United States: 1976. — Index.
ISBN 0-226-06643-6 : £11.25
Also classified at 821'.8; 821'.9'12; 811'.5'2
(B77-14879)

821.912 — ENGLISH POETRY, 1900-1945
821'.9'12 — Poetry in English, 1900-1945. *Texts*
Auden, Wystan Hugh. Sue / [by] W.H. Auden. — Oxford (4 Benson Place, Oxford) : Sycamore Press, 1977. — Folder([5]p) ; 21cm. — (Sycamore broadsheet ; 23)
ISBN 0-9500635-9-2 : Unpriced
(B77-10524)

Beckett, Samuel. Collected poems in English and French / [by] Samuel Beckett. — London : J. Calder : [Distributed by Calder and Boyars], 1977. — xi,147p ; 21cm.
ISBN 0-7145-3608-3 : £4.50
ISBN 0-7145-3613-x Pbk : Unpriced
Also classified at 841'.9'14
(B77-16566)

Betjeman, *Sir* John. Continual dew : a little book of bourgeois verse / by John Betjeman. — London : J. Murray, 1977. — [9],45,[6]p : ill ; 22cm.
Facsimile reprint: of 1st ed. 1937.
ISBN 0-7195-3395-3 : £2.95
(B77-25839)

Betjeman, *Sir* John. Summoned by bells / [by] John Betjeman. — [New ed.]. — London : J. Murray, 1976. — [11],115p : ill, facsim, ports ; 24cm.
Previous ed.: 1960.
ISBN 0-7195-3349-x : £3.00
ISBN 0-7195-3350-3 Pbk : £1.75
(B77-02552)

Bishop, Mary, *b.1905.* Prairie summer, and other poems / by Mary (Davidson) Bishop. — [New enlarged ed.]. — [Minety] ([Minety, Wilts. SN16 9QU]) : [Taylor and Sons], [1977]. — xiii,25p,plate : 2 ports ; 21cm.
Previous ed. of this collection: published as 'In heaven's view'. Hounslow : Cedar Press, 1958.
Pbk : Unpriced
(B77-32125)

Cameron, Clare. Memories of Eden / [by] Clare Cameron. — London : Mitre Press, 1976. — 64p ; 19cm.
ISBN 0-7051-0249-1 Pbk : £1.20
(B77-05602)

Colum, Pádraic. Irish elegies : memorabilia of Roger Casement, Thomas MacDonagh, Kuno Meyer, John Butler Yeats, Arthur Griffith, Michael Collins, Thomas Hughes Kelly, Dudley Digges, James Joyce, William Butler Yeats, Monsignor Padraig de Brun, Seumas O'Sullivan, Allen, Larkin & O'Brien / by Padraic Colum. — 4th ed. ; with three additional poems ; introduction by Liam Miller. — Dublin : Dolmen Press, 1976. — 32p ; 22cm.
Previous ed.: 1963.
ISBN 0-85105-315-7 : £4.50
(B77-05035)

Day Lewis, Cecil. Poems of C. Day Lewis, 1925-1972 / chosen and with an introduction by Ian Parsons. — London : Cape : Hogarth Press, 1977. — xviii,345p ; 21cm.
Index.
ISBN 0-224-01294-0 : £6.50
ISBN 0-7012-0427-3 (Hogarth Press) : £6.50
(B77-06844)

Durrell, Lawrence. Selected poems of Lawrence Durrell / selected and with an introduction by Alan Ross. — London : Faber, 1977. — 3-96p ; 21cm.
Index.
ISBN 0-571-04943-5 : £2.95 : CIP rev.
ISBN 0-571-04944-3 Pbk : £1.50
(B77-16567)

Fuller, Roy, *b.1912.* Poor Roy / [by] Roy Fuller ; Nicolas Bentley drew the pictures. — London : Deutsch, 1977. — 64p : ill ; 21cm.
ISBN 0-233-96802-4 : £1.95
(B77-09894)

Garton, Charles. Strays : selected poems / by Charles Garton. — [Bodmin] ([Trehil Court, Bodmin, Cornwall]) : [The author], 1976. — [14]p : port ; 15cm.
ISBN 0-9505768-0-8 Sd : £0.45
(B77-16568)

Geoffrey, Wallace. Monday, Thursday, Sunday : poems / by Wallace Geoffrey ; illustrated by Pavla Davey. — Andoversford (Manor Farm, Andoversford, Glos.) : The Whittington Press, 1976. — viii,55p : ill, port ; 26cm.
Limited ed. of 100 numbered copies.
ISBN 0-904845-05-2 : £2.50
(B77-00913)

Graham, William Sydney. Implements in their places / [by] W.S. Graham. — London : Faber, 1977. — 3-85p ; 20cm.
ISBN 0-571-10955-1 Pbk : £1.95
(B77-24433)

Hauser, Jacob. Green & golden rhyme : sonnets / by Jacob Hauser ; with a preface by John Cowper Powys. — [Bakewell] : Hub Publications, 1977. — [5],26p ; 21cm.
'Athenaeum books series'.
ISBN 0-905049-28-4 Sd : £0.60
(B77-22803)

Hopkins, Kenneth. By invitation only : poems / by Kenneth Hopkins. — North Walsham (12 New Rd, North Walsham, Norfolk NR28 9DF) : Warren House Press, 1977. — 16p ; 21cm.
ISBN 0-902107-13-5 Sd : £1.05
(B77-16018)

Lawrence, David Herbert. [Poems]. The complete poems of D.H. Lawrence / collected and edited with an introduction and notes by Vivian de Sola Pinto and Warren Roberts. — Harmondsworth [etc.] : Penguin, 1977. — vii, 1079p ; 20cm. — (The Penguin poets)
This collection originally published: in 2 vols. London : Heinemann, 1964. — Index.
ISBN 0-14-042220-x Pbk : £3.00
(B77-12611)

MacCaig, Norman. Tree for strings / by Norman MacCaig. — London : Hogarth Press, 1977. — 64p ; 22cm. — (The Phoenix living poets)
ISBN 0-7011-2220-x Pbk : £2.25 : CIP rev.
(B77-12612)

MacDiarmid, Hugh, *b.1892.* Selected poems [of] Hugh MacDiarmid / selected and edited by David Craig and John Manson. — Harmondsworth [etc.] : Penguin, 1976. — 124p ; 18cm. — (The Penguin poets)
This collection originally published: 1970.
Pbk : £1.00
ISBN 0-14-042123-8
(B77-01766)

Norris, Leslie. Ravenna Bridge / [by] Leslie Norris. — Knotting : Sceptre Press, [1977]. — [7]p ; 21cm.
Limited ed. of 150 numbered copies of which nos 1-50 are signed by the poet.
Sd : Unpriced
(B77-31405)

Raine, Kathleen. The oval portrait, and other poems / by Kathleen Raine. — London : Enitharmon Press : Hamilton, 1977. — 67p ; 23cm.
ISBN 0-901111-96-1 : £3.00
ISBN 0-241-89516-2 (Hamilton) : £3.00
(B77-20538)

Reid, Forrest. The suppressed dedication and envoy of 'The garden god' / [by] Forrest Reid ; with an introduction by Brian Taylor now for the first time printed. — London (30 Baker St., W.1) : D'Arch Smith, [1976]. — [6]p : ill, port ; 21cm.
Limited ed. of 105 numbered copies.
ISBN 0-903394-05-7 Sd : £3.00
(B77-06845)

Scaife, Christopher Henry Oldham. Tones & overtones : selected poems, 1926-1976 / by C.H.O. Scaife. — London ([83 North Rd, Hythe, Kent]) : [The author], 1976. — 122p, leaf of plate,[2]p of plates : ill, ports ; 23cm.
Limited ed. of 400 numbered copies.
ISBN 0-9505677-0-1 : £2.50
(B77-11376)

Sitwell, ***Sir*** **Sacheverell,** *bart.* Credo, or an affirmation / [by] Sacheverell Sitwell. — [Daventry] (['Pennywick', Badby, Daventry, Northants.]) : [The author], [1977]. — [1],23p ; 22cm.
Sd : £0.50
(B77-09895)

Sitwell, ***Sir*** **Sacheverell,** *bart.* Placebo / [by] Sacheverell Sitwell. — [Daventry] (['Pennywick', Badby, Daventry, Northants.]) : [The author], [1977]. — [1],24p ; 22cm.
ISBN 0-903591-31-6 Sd : £0.50
(B77-09896)

Sitwell, ***Sir*** **Sacheverell,** *bart.* Serenade to a sister : (full version) / [by] Sacheverell Sitwell. — [Daventry] (['Pennywick', Badby, Daventry, Northants.]) : [The author], [1977]. — [10]p ; 22cm.
ISBN 0-903591-28-6 Sd : £0.50
(B77-09897)

Sitwell, ***Sir*** **Sacheverell,** *bart.* To Henry Woodward, the harlequin / [by] Sacheverell Sitwell. — [Daventry] (['Pennywick' Badby, Daventry, Northants.]) : [The author], [1977]. — [13]p ; 22cm.
This collection originally published: as 'To Henry Woodward'. London : Covent Garden Press, 1972.
ISBN 0-903591-30-8 Sd : £0.50
(B77-09898)

Sitwell, ***Sir*** **Sacheverell,** *bart.* Two themes, taken one at a time / [by] Sacheverell Sitwell. — [Daventry] (['Pennywick', Badby, Daventry, Northants.]) : [The author], [1977]. — [12]p ; 22cm.
ISBN 0-903591-27-8 Sd : £0.50
(B77-09899)

Strong, Patience. Golden hours / [by] Patience Strong. — [1st ed. reprinted] ; with new illustrations. — London : Muller, 1977. — [5], 58p : ill(some col) ; 22cm.
Originally published: 1952.
ISBN 0-584-10746-3 : £2.25
(B77-22079)

Strong, Patience. Out into the sunshine / [by] Patience Strong. — London : Muller, 1977. — [33]p : chiefly col ill ; 17cm.
ISBN 0-584-10693-9 Sd : £0.45
(B77-27321)

Welch, Denton. Dumb instrument : poems and fragments / [by] Denton Welch ; edited with an introduction and notes by Jean-Louis Chevalier ; decorations by Denton Welch. — London : Enitharmon Press, 1976. — 58,[1]p : ill ; 23cm.
Limited ed. of 660 copies, of which 60 have been printed on blue paper and specially bound.

ISBN 0-901111-70-8 : £3.75
ISBN 0-901111-74-0 Pbk : £2.25
(B77-11377)

821'.9'12 — Poetry in English. Eliot, Thomas Stearns. *Critical studies*
Spender, Stephen. T.S. Eliot / [by] Stephen Spender. — Harmondsworth [etc.] : Penguin, 1976. — xv,269p ; 19cm. — (Penguin modern masters)
Originally published: as 'Eliot'. London : Fontana, 1975. — Bibl.: p.255-258. — Index.
ISBN 0-14-004321-7 Pbk : £0.95
(B77-05036)

821'.9'12 — Poetry in English. Eliot, Thomas Stearns. Romanticism. *Critical studies*
Bornstein, George. Transformations of romanticism in Yeats, Eliot, and Stevens / [by] George Bornstein. — Chicago ; London : University of Chicago Press, 1976[i.e.1977]. — xiii,263,[1]p ; 24cm.
Published in the United States: 1976. — Index.
ISBN 0-226-06643-6 : £11.25
Primary classification 821'.8'0914
(B77-14879)

821'.9'12 — Poetry in English. Eliot, Thomas Stearns, to 1928. *Biographies*
Gordon, Lyndall. Eliot's early years / [by] Lyndall Gordon. — Oxford [etc.] : Oxford University Press, 1977. — xiii,174p,16p of plates : ill, ports ; 22cm.
Index.
ISBN 0-19-812078-8 : £4.95
(B77-24434)

821'.9'12 — Poetry in English. Eliot, Thomas Stearns. Waste land. *Critical studies*
Miller, James Edwin. T.S. Eliot's personal waste land : exorcism of the demons / [by] James E. Miller, Jr. — University Park ; London : Pennsylvania State University Press, 1977. — xiii,176p ; 24cm.
Index.
ISBN 0-271-01237-4 : £9.75
(B77-20539)

821'.9'12 — Poetry in English. Hopkin, William Edward. *Biographies*
Kader, Noel M. William Edward Hopkin / [by] Noel M. Kader. — [Eastwood] ([165 Nottingham Rd, Eastwood, Notts.]) : [The author], [1977]. — [2],20p : ill, facsim, ports ; 21cm.
Sd : £0.75
(B77-18342)

821'.9'12 — Poetry in English. Jones, David, b.1895. *Critical studies*
David Jones Weekend School, *Aberystwyth, 1975.* David Jones : eight essays on his work as writer and artist : being the first transactions of Yr Academi Gymreig (English Section) / edited by Roland Mathias. — Llandysul : Gomer Press, 1976. — 144p,[4]leaves of plates : col ill, col facsim, port ; 22cm.
'... substantially the papers that the respective contributors gave to the David Jones Weekend School at Aberystwyth early in September 1975 ... held under the auspices of the English Section of Yr Academi Gymreig ...' - Preface. — Bibl.: p.139-144.
ISBN 0-85088-372-5 : £3.25
(B77-09217)

821'.9'12 — Poetry in English. Jones, David, b.1895 & MacDiarmid, Hugh, b.1892. *Critical studies*
Pacey, Philip. Hugh MacDiarmid and David Jones, Celtic wonder-voyagers / by Philip Pacey. — Preston : Akros Publications, 1977. — 19p ; 26cm.
Sd : £0.65
(B77-25840)

821'.9'12 — Poetry in English. MacDiarmid, Hugh, b.1892. *Critical studies*
Glen, Duncan. Hugh MacDiarmid : an essay for 11th August 1977 / by Duncan Glen. — Preston : Akros Publications, 1977. — 12,[1]p ; 21cm.
Limited ed. of 300 numbered copies signed by the author.
ISBN 0-900036-88-5 Sd : £1.25
(B77-14374)

Morgan, Edwin. Hugh MacDiarmid / by Edwin Morgan ; edited by Ian Scott-Kilvert. — Harlow : Longman for the British Council, 1976. — 39p,plate : port ; 22cm. — (Writers and their work)
Bibl.: p.34-39.
ISBN 0-582-01258-9 Sd : £0.40
(B77-14880)

821'.9'12 — Poetry in English. Owen, Wilfred. *Biographies*
Stallworthy, Jon. Wilfred Owen / [by] Jon Stallworthy. — Oxford [etc.] : Oxford University Press, 1977. — xiv,333p,[2] leaves of plates : ill, facsims, geneal tables, map, plans, ports ; 21cm.
Originally published: London : Oxford University Press, 1974. — Bibl.: p.305-324. — Index.
ISBN 0-19-281215-7 Pbk : £2.50 : CIP rev.
(B77-05037)

821'.9'12 — Poetry in English. Raine, Kathleen, 1946-1976. *Autobiographies*
Raine, Kathleen. The lion's mouth : concluding chapters of autobiography / [by] Kathleen Raine. — London : Hamilton, 1977. — [4], 163p ; 23cm.
ISBN 0-241-89756-4 : £4.95
(B77-29645)

821'.9'12 — Poetry in English. Spender, Stephen. *Autobiographies*
Spender, Stephen. World within world : the autobiography of Stephen Spender. — London : Faber, 1977. — ix,349p ; 20cm.
Originally published: London : Hamilton, 1951. — Index.
ISBN 0-571-10212-3 Pbk : £2.95
(B77-25170)

821'.9'12 — Poetry in English. Spender, Stephen. *Critical studies*
Weatherhead, Andrew Kingsley. Stephen Spender and the thirties / [by] A. Kingsley Weatherhead. — Lewisburg : Bucknell University Press ; London (108 New Bond St., W1Y 0QX) : Associated University Presses, 1975. — 3-241p ; 22cm.
Bibl.: p.222-235. — Index.
£5.25
(B77-28841)

821'.9'12 — Poetry in English. Thomas, Dylan. *Biographies*
Ferris, Paul. Dylan Thomas / by Paul Ferris. — London [etc.] : Hodder and Stoughton, 1977. — 399p,[16]p of plates : ill, facsims, ports ; 24cm.
Bibl.: p.373-375. — Index.
ISBN 0-340-19564-9 : £7.50
(B77-19608)

FitzGibbon, Constantine. The life of Dylan Thomas / [by] Constantine FitzGibbon. — London : Dent, 1975. — ix,422p,[8]p of plates : facsims, ports ; 22cm.
Originally published: 1965. — List of broadcasts: p.395-399. — List of film scripts: p.400-402. — List of lectures and readings from America: p.403-410. — Index.
ISBN 0-460-03494-4 : £3.00
ISBN 0-460-02174-5 Pbk : £2.25
(B77-07560)

821'.9'12 — Poetry in English. Thomas, Dylan. *Personal observations*
Jones, Daniel. My friend Dylan Thomas / [by] Daniel Jones. — London [etc.] : Dent, 1977. — xi,116p,[4]p of plates : ports ; 23cm.
ISBN 0-460-04314-5 : £3.95 : CIP rev.
(B77-07561)

821'.9'12 — Poetry in English. Thomas, Dylan. Local associations: Dyfed & West Glamorgan
Perkins, Derek Cyril. The world of Dylan Thomas / by D.C. Perkins. — Swansea : Celtic Educational, [1975]. — 79p : ill(some col), facsim, maps ; 16x22cm.
Bibl.: p.77.
ISBN 0-86005-102-1 : £0.95
ISBN 0-86005-101-3 Pbk : Unpriced
(B77-09218)

821'.9'1208 — Poetry in English, 1900-. *Anthologies. Secondary school texts*
Double take : a book of verse comparison / edited by A.F. Bolt. — London : Harrap, 1976. — [7],55p ; 22cm.
ISBN 0-245-52874-1 Sd : £0.80
(B77-00914)

821'.9'1208 — Poetry in English, 1900-. *Primary school texts. For Caribbean students. Anthologies*

Parang : a poetry anthology for Caribbean primary schools. — [Kingston, Jamaica] : Nelson Caribbean ; Sunbury-on-Thames [etc.] : Nelson.
Book 2 / edited by Cecil Gray. — 1977. — viii, 103p : ill ; 22cm.
Index.
ISBN 0-17-566080-8 Pbk : £0.90
(B77-30570)

821'.9'1208 — Poetry in English, 1900-1975. *Anthologies. Juvenile literature*

My world : poems from 'Living language' / edited by Joan Griffiths. — London : British Broadcasting Corporation, 1976. — 144p : ill ; 24cm.
Index.
ISBN 0-563-17071-9 : £2.75
(B77-05038)

821'.9'1208 — Poetry in English, 1900-1976. *Anthologies. Juvenile literature*

Bulls eyes : poems / chosen by Brian Thompson ; illustrated by Janet Archer ... [et al.]. — London : Longman, 1977. — [1],65p : ill(some col) ; 24cm.
ISBN 0-582-19034-7 Sd : Unpriced
(B77-15448)

Bulls eyes : poems / chosen by Brian Thompson ; illustrated by Janet Archer ... [et al.]. — Harmondsworth : Kestrel Books, 1977. — [2],64p : ill(some col) ; 25cm.
ISBN 0-7226-5231-3 : £2.94
(B77-15449)

Rhyme time : poems / collected by Barbara Ireson ; illustrated by Lesley Smith. — London [etc.] : Beaver Books, 1977. — 188p : ill ; 20cm.
Index.
ISBN 0-600-37584-6 Pbk : £0.60
(B77-14375)

821'.9'1208 — Poetry in English. Cambridgeshire writers, 1900-. *Anthologies*

Cambridge town & gown : poetry from the provinces / edited ... by C.W. Osborne. — Cambridge (7 Enniskillen Rd, Chesterton, Cambridge CB4 1SQ) : The editor, 1976. — 44p : 1 ill ; 21cm. — (Cambridge poetry series ; no.3)
Limited ed. of 500 copies. — Index.
ISBN 0-9504649-2-9 Sd : £0.54
(B77-04384)

821'.9'1208 — Poetry in English. Scottish writers, 1900-. *Anthologies*

Twelve modern Scottish poets / edited by Charles King. — London [etc.] (138 Park La., W1Y 3DD) : Lion Library, 1976. — 205p ; 25cm.
Originally published: London : University of London Press, 1971. — Bibl.: p.195-199. — Index.
£3.95
ISBN 0-7082-0025-7
(B77-00915)

821'.9'1208 — Poetry in English. Welsh writers, 1900-. *Anthologies. Secondary school texts*

Dragon's hoard : an anthology of modern poetry for Welsh secondary schools / edited by Sam Adams and Gwilym Rees Hughes. — Llandysul : Gwasg Gomer, 1976. — 133p ; 22cm.
Poems in Welsh and English. — 'The poems in the Welsh language are accompanied by translations' - Foreword. — Index.
ISBN 0-85088-322-9 Pbk : £1.50
Also classified at 891.6'6'1208
(B77-03197)

Wales today : a collection of poems and pictures for children / edited by Don Dale-Jones and W. Randal Jenkins. — Llandysul : Gomer Press, 1976. — 3-144p : ill ; 21cm.
Index.
ISBN 0-85088-377-6 Pbk : £1.25
(B77-06252)

821'.9'120803 — Poetry in English, 1900-1945. Special subjects: World War 1. *Anthologies*

Men who march away : poems of the First World War / [edited with an introduction by] I.M. Parsons. — London : Chatto and Windus, 1978. — 192p ; 22cm.
This collection originally published: 1965. — Index.
ISBN 0-7011-2276-5 Pbk : I.50 : CIP rev.
(B77-31406)

821'.9'1209 — Poetry in English, 1900-. *Critical studies*

Holbrook, David. Lost bearings in English poetry / [by] David Holbrook. — London : Vision Press, 1977. — 255p ; 23cm. — (Vision critical studies)
' ... incorporates the substance of the Sir D. Owen Evans Memorial Lectures delivered at the University College of Wales, Aberystwyth ... 1975-76' - title page verso. — Bibl.: p.245-247. — Index.
ISBN 0-85478-493-4 : £5.80
(B77-14376)

821'.9'1209 — Poetry in English, 1900-1945. *Critical studies, 1911-1959. Readings*

Georgian poetry, 1911-1922, the critical heritage / edited by Timothy Rogers. — London [etc.] : Routledge and Kegan Paul, 1977. — xvi,435p ; 23cm. — (The critical heritage series)
Bibl.: p.418-420. — Index.
ISBN 0-7100-8278-9 : £7.50
(B77-12613)

821'.9'1209 — Poetry in English, 1900-1945. Influence of classical myths

Feder, Lillian. Ancient myth in modern poetry / [by] Lillian Feder. — Princeton ; Guildford : Princeton University Press, 1977. — xiv,432p ; 25cm.
Originally published: Princeton : Princeton University Press, 1972. — Index.
ISBN 0-691-06207-2 : £11.30
ISBN 0-691-01336-5 Pbk : £3.80
(B77-25171)

821'.9'1209 — Poetry in English, 1900-1966. *Critical studies, 1938-1966. Readings*

Modern poets on modern poetry / edited by James Scully. — [London] : Fontana, 1977. — 285p ; 18cm.
Originally published: as 'Modern poetics'. New York : McGraw Hill, 1965.
ISBN 0-00-634864-5 Pbk : £1.25
(B77-16569)

821'.9'1209 — Poetry in English, 1900-1976. *Critical studies. Essays*

Fraser, George Sutherland. Essays on twentieth-century poets / [by] George Fraser. — [Leicester] : Leicester University Press, 1977. — 255p ; 24cm.
ISBN 0-7185-1156-5 Pbk : £3.95 : CIP rev.
(B77-16570)

821'.9'12093 — Poetry in English, 1900-1945. Special subjects: World War 1. *Critical studies*

Gregson, James Michael. Poetry of the First World War / by J.M. Gregson. — London : Edward Arnold, 1976. — 72p ; 19cm. — (Studies in English literature ; no.64)
Bibl.: p.70-71. — Index.
ISBN 0-7131-5930-8 : £3.30
ISBN 0-7131-5931-6 Pbk : £1.60
(B77-09900)

821.914 — ENGLISH POETRY, 1945-

821'.9'14 — Poetry in English, 1945-. *Texts*

Abrahams, John. The abandoned maze / by John Abrahams. — Walton-on-Thames : Outposts Publications, 1977. — 28p ; 21cm.
ISBN 0-7205-0511-9 Sd : £0.60
(B77-13830)

Abse, Dannie. Collected poems, 1948-1976 / [by] Dannie Abse. — London : Hutchinson, 1977. — xi,204p ; 23cm.
ISBN 0-09-128470-8 : £4.95
ISBN 0-09-128471-6 Pbk : £2.50
(B77-18955)

Adams, Fred, *b.1917.* Jungle of the mind / by Fred Adams. — Walton-on-Thames : Outposts Publications, 1977. — 20p ; 21cm.
ISBN 0-7205-0503-8 Sd : £0.40
(B77-05603)

Adams, Richard, *b.1920.* The adventures & brave deeds of the ship's cat on the Spanish Maine : together with the most lamentable losse of the 'Alcestis' & triumphant firing of the port of Chagres / truthfully narrated in verses by Richard Adams and in divers cunning and fantastical pictures by Alan Aldridge with Harry Willock. — London : Cape, 1977. — [32]p : col ill ; 29cm.
Cover title: The ship's cat.
ISBN 0-224-01441-2 : £2.95 : CIP rev.
(B77-18343)

Aitken, Michael. The school : poems / by Michael Aitken. — Breakish : Aquila, 1976. — [23]p ; 21cm.
Also available in a limited ed. of 26 copies, signed and lettered by the author.
ISBN 0-7275-0129-1 Sd : £0.30
ISBN 0-7275-0130-5 Signed ed. : £1.50
(B77-15450)

Anderson, Lilian. Solo voyager : poems / by Lilian Anderson ; cover design Mark Williams. — Bridgend (83 Pyle Inn Way, Pyle, Bridgend, M. Glam.) : Speed Limit Publications, 1977. — [16]p ; 26cm. — (Speed Limit booklet ; 2)
ISBN 0-9505634-0-4 Sd : £0.20
(B77-09901)

Angus-Butterworth, Lionel Milner. Poems of life and death / [by] L.M. Angus-Butterworth. — [Ashton-on-Mersey] ([Ashton New Hall, Ashton-on-Mersey, Cheshire]) : [The author], 1977. — 24p : port ; 21cm.
ISBN 0-9501956-3-4 Sd : £0.75
(B77-11378)

Ank, Elbo. Woman, nail & screw : Zen at the workbed / by Elbo Ank. — Corby (10 Minden Close, Danesholme, Corby, Northants. NN18 9EW) : Excello and Bollard, 1976. — [2],28,[1] p ; 15cm.
ISBN 0-904339-41-6 Sd : £0.25
(B77-11379)

Appleby, Lynne. Animal poems for youngsters / by Lynne Appleby. — [Redcar] ([56 West Dyke Rd, Redcar, Cleveland TS10 LHQ]) : [The author], [1977]. — [1],23p ; 19cm.
ISBN 0-9505717-2-5 Sd : £0.45
(B77-14377)

Appleby, Lynne. Little poems for little people / by Lynne Appleby. — [Redcar] ([56 West Dyke Rd, Redcar, Cleveland TS10 LHQ]) : [The author], [1977]. — [1],22p ; 19cm.
ISBN 0-9505717-0-9 Sd : £0.45
(B77-14378)

Appleby, Lynne. People you meet : (poems for the young) / [by] Lynne Appleby. — [Redcar] ([56 West Dyke Rd, Redcar, Cleveland TS10 LHQ]) : [The author], [1977]. — [1],24p ; 19cm.
ISBN 0-9505717-1-7 Sd : £0.45
(B77-14379)

Appleyard, Eileen. Please read on / by Eileen Appleyard. — London [etc.] : Regency Press, 1976. — 32p ; 22cm.
'This publication is the prize awarded by Regency Press for the "Spring Poets 1976 Competition"'.
ISBN 0-9505448-0-9 Sd : £0.50
(B77-01767)

Archer, Francis. Certain things / by Francis Archer. — [London] ([30 Carmichael Court, Barnes, SW13 0HA]) : [The author], 1976. — [2],154p ; 21cm.
Pbk : £1.00
(B77-30571)

Archer, Francis. Far more : love poems / by Francis Archer. — [S.l.] ([c/o Spotlight Publications, The Broadway, Crowborough, E. Sussex]) : [The author], 1976. — [3],30p ; 21cm.
ISBN 0-9503330-4-2 Sd : £0.50
(B77-01768)

Armstrong, C M. Two weather poems / [by] C.M. Armstrong. — Knotting : Sceptre Press, [1977]. — [4]leaves ; 21cm.
Limited ed. of 150 numbered copies of which nos 1-50 are signed by the poet.
Sd : Unpriced
(B77-31407)

Armstrong, James. Letter to a friend, and other poems / by James Armstrong. — Walton-on-Thames : Outposts Publications, 1977. — 12p ; 21cm.
ISBN 0-7205-0507-0 Sd : £0.30
(B77-12050)

Arnold, Jeannette. Willow seeds and wild roses : prose and poetry / by Jeannette Arnold. — London : Mitre Press, 1977. — 62p,plate : 1 ill ; 20cm.
ISBN 0-7051-0256-4 : £1.60
Also classified at 828'.9'1408
(B77-20540)

Arrowsmith, Pat. Breakout : poems & drawings from prison / by Pat Arrowsmith. — [Edinburgh] ([1 Buccleuch Place, Edinburgh EH8 9LW]) : Edinburgh University Student Publications Board, 1975. — 23p : ill ; 21cm.
ISBN 0-9501890-8-1 Sd : £0.30
(B77-18956)

Austin, Josephine. Knee deep in short buttercups / [by] Josephine Austin. — London : Mitre Press, 1977. — 59p ; 20cm.
ISBN 0-7051-0260-2 : £1.60
(B77-34024)

AWood, Anthony. The poetry of Anthony AWood : 'Tiger's flower songs'. — London (Flat 145, Brooke Rd, N16 7RP) : The author. [Vol.2]. — 1976. — [22]p ; 15cm.
Limited ed. of 106 copies.
ISBN 0-9505126-1-3 Sd : £8.40
(B77-06846)

Ayres, Pam. Some more of me poetry / [by] Pam Ayres ; introduced and illustrated by Roy Garnham Elmore. — London (223 Regent St., W1R 8TD) : Galaxy Records, 1976. — 48p : ill, music ; 21cm.
ISBN 0-9504774-1-9 Pbk : £1.00
(B77-00375)

Baird, Maisie. Simple poems / by Maisje Baird. — [Renfrew] ([28 Beechwood Drive, Renfrew PA4 0PN]) : [The author], [1977]. — [1],24p ; 21cm.
ISBN 0-9505824-0-9 Sd : £0.40
(B77-27322)

Baldwin, Joan. Tranquillity / by Joan Baldwin ; illustrations by Pat Catlin. — London [etc.] : Regency Press, 1977. — 32p : ill ; 19cm.
Sd : £0.60
(B77-34025)

Barber, Barbara. Pastiche / by Barbara Barber. — London [etc.] : Regency Press, 1977. — 32p ; 22cm.
ISBN 0-7212-0495-3 Sd : Unpriced
(B77-15451)

Barker, Reginald John. Creation, and other poems / [by] R.J. Barker. — Ludlow (Bridge House, Leinthall Starkes, Ludlow, Shropshire SY8 2HP) : [The author], [1976]. — 84p ; 20cm.
ISBN 0-9505490-0-2 : £1.50
(B77-05039)

Barker, Thomas. Blessings more abundant : monologues / by Thomas Barker. — Ilkeston : Moorley's Bible and Bookshop, [1977]. — [1], 31,[1]p ; 22cm.
ISBN 0-901495-97-2 Sd : £0.30
(B77-21388)

Barlow, Thelma. Doubts / by Thelma Barlow. — [Colchester] ([135 Hazelton Rd, Colchester, Essex]) : [The author], 1976. — [32]p ; 21cm.
ISBN 0-9505518-0-5 Sd : £0.60
(B77-05604)

Barnes, Keith. Devolution, evolution and revolution / [by] Keith Barnes. — Ilfracombe : Stockwell, 1976. — 48p ; 15cm.
ISBN 0-7223-0958-9 : £1.65
(B77-10907)

Barnett, Anthony. Fear and misadventure ; [and], Mud settles / [by] Anthony Barnett. — London : Ferry Press, 1977. — 3-94p ; 20cm.
Limited ed. of 350 copies.
Pbk : £1.80
(B77-27323)

Barycz, Richard Ignatius. Poems upon several occasions and to several persons / [by R.I. Barycz]. — London ([16 Musgrove Rd, SE14 5PW]) : The author, 1976. — [20]p ; 15cm.
Sd : Free for self addressed envelope or in exchange for similar publication
(B77-30572)

Beake, Fred. Legends from Mammon : poems and translations, 1974-76 / by Fred Beake. — Bath (12 Dartmouth Ave., Bath BA2 1AT) : The author, 1976. — 36p ; 21cm.
ISBN 0-9505391-0-4 Pbk : £0.50
(B77-00916)

Beeching, R C. Wings / [by] R.C. Beeching. — Stanford-Le-Hope (53 Prospect Ave., Stanford-Le-Hope, Essex) : Bream Press, [1977]. — [41]p ; 21cm.
Sd : £0.20
(B77-14380)

Beer, Doris. Med i' 'Alifax : 44 poems in dialect / by Doris Beer. — Driffield : Ridings Publishing Co., 1977. — 48p ; 18cm.
Sd : £0.60
(B77-22805)

Bell, Andrew. See you at the beautiful feast / by Andrew Bell ; illustrations by Mick Sparksman and Meg Amsden ; calligraphy Ruth Sparksman. — Lowestoft (13 Wollaston Rd, Lowestoft, Suffolk) : Tamlyn Books, 1976. — [31]p : ill, port ; 21cm.
ISBN 0-9505744-0-6 Pbk : Unpriced
(B77-15452)

Bell, D M. Moods and moments / [by] D.M. Bell. — Ilfracombe : Stockwell, 1976. — 16p : ill ; 18cm.
ISBN 0-7223-0983-x Pbk : £0.30
(B77-10908)

Bellerby, Frances. Frances Bellerby. — London : Enitharmon Press, 1975. — [7]p,plate(tipped in) : port ; 19cm.
Two poems.
Sd : Unpriced
(B77-16019)

Benenson, Michael. The blood is warm / by Michael Benenson. — Walton-on-Thames : Outposts Publications, 1977. — 20p ; 21cm.
Sd : £0.40
(B77-22806)

Benveniste, Asa. Loose use / [by] Asa Benveniste. — Newcastle upon Tyne (24 Coquet Terrace, Heaton, Newcastle upon Tyne 6) : Pig Press, [1977]. — [12]p ; 21cm.
'This edition of approx. 100 copies is produced to coincide with a reading by Asa Benveniste at the Colpitts Hotel, Durham on Jan. 21st 1977 at 8.00 p.m.' - Note.
ISBN 0-903997-24-x Sd : £0.20
(B77-09902)

Berry, Eileen. The strange truth / by Eileen Berry. — Walton-on-Thames : Outposts Publications, 1977. — 12p ; 21cm.
Sd : £0.30
(B77-26473)

Berry, Paul, *b.1953.* After silence / [by] Paul Berry. — [New] ed. — King's Lynn (King's Lynn, Norfolk) : Scree Publications, 1976. — [17]p ; 21cm.
Previous ed.: London : Good Elf/Coarsecrash Press, 1973.
Sd : £0.30
(B77-34026)

Bevan, Gwen. See it in colour / by Gwen Bevan. — Walton-on-Thames : Outposts Publications, 1977. — 16p ; 21cm.
ISBN 0-7205-0513-5 Sd : £0.35
(B77-16020)

Birna, Inga. Poems / [by] Inga Birna. — Ilfracombe : Stockwell, 1977. — 16p ; 15cm.
ISBN 0-7223-1055-2 Pbk : £0.30
(B77-34027)

Blackburn, Thomas. Post mortem / [by] Thomas Blackburn. — Liverpool (123 The Albany, Old Hall St., Liverpool L3 9EG) : Rondo Publications, 1977. — 39p ; 22cm.
ISBN 0-85619-014-4 Pbk : £1.95
(B77-28842)

Boadella, David. Broken waters / by David Boadella. — Weymouth (186 Newstead Rd, Weymouth, [Dorset] DT4 0DY) : Word and Action (Dorset), 1976. — [2],18p ; 21cm. — (Poets in Dorset ; 2)
Sd : £0.50
(B77-18344)

Bodecker, Niels Mogens. Let's marry said the cherry, and other nonsense poems / written and illustrated by N.M. Bodecker. — London : Faber, 1977. — 79p : ill ; 21cm.
Originally published: New York : Atheneum, 1974.
ISBN 0-571-11093-2 : £2.50 : CIP rev.
(B77-17715)

Bonner, Roger. Driftwood : poems and translations / by Roger Bonner. — Bakewell : Hub Publications, 1977. — [4],28p ; 21cm.
ISBN 0-905049-19-5 Sd : £0.90
(B77-27324)

Bosley, Keith. Dark summer : a sequence of poems / [by] Keith Bosley. — London (23 Fitzwarren Gardens, N19 3TR) : Menard Press, 1976. — 32p ; 22cm.
ISBN 0-903400-16-2 Sd : £0.45
(B77-12051)

Bowker, Ed. Hercules in Hove / by Ed Bowker ; drawings by Sean MacTomas. — London ([10 Uphill Grove, Mill Hill] NW7 4NJ) : Scrinium Press, 1977. — 26,[1]p : ill ; 23cm.
Limited ed. of 100 copies.
Pbk : £1.75
(B77-34028)

Boyle, Charles. Affinities / [by] Charles Boyle. — Manchester : Carcanet New Press, 1977. — 56p ; 23cm.
ISBN 0-85635-222-5 : £2.00
(B77-26474)

Brandon, Alfred J. Poems [of] Alfred J. Brandon. — Ilfracombe : Stockwell, 1977. — 24p ; 19cm.

ISBN 0-7223-1025-0 Pbk : £0.30
(B77-21389)

Bresslaw, Bernard. Ode to the Dead Sea Scrolls / [by] Bernard Bresslaw. — [Leicester] ([78 Cambridge St., Leicester LE3 0JP]) : New Broom Private Press, 1977. — [8]p : ill ; 13cm.
Limited ed. of 60 copies signed by the printer.
ISBN 0-901870-28-5 Sd : £0.75
(B77-24435)

Briar, Bridget. The collected works of Bridget Briar. — London [etc.] : Regency Press, 1977. — 32p ; 19cm.
Sd : £0.60
(B77-34029)

Brinn, Lesley. Tenderness / [by] Lesley Brinn. — Ilfracombe : Stockwell, 1977. — 16p ; 15cm.
ISBN 0-7223-1084-6 Pbk : £0.30
(B77-34030)

Britter, Michael. 410 light years out from the Pleiades / by Michael Britter. — Walton-on-Thames : Outposts Publications, 1977. — 12p ; 21cm.
Sd : £0.30
(B77-22807)

Britter, Michael. Acceleration through a universe / by Michael Britter. — Walton-on-Thames : Outposts Publications, 1977. — 12p ; 21cm.
ISBN 0-7205-0500-3 Sd : £0.35
(B77-05040)

Britter, Michael. A tendency to magic / by Michael Britter. — Walton-on-Thames : Outposts Publications, 1977. — 12p ; 21cm.
ISBN 0-7205-0508-9 Sd : £0.30
(B77-12052)

Brock, Edwin. Song of the battery hen : selected poems, 1959-1975 / [by] Edwin Brock. — London : Secker and Warburg, 1977. — 105p ; 23cm.
Index.
ISBN 0-436-06884-2 : £3.50
(B77-10525)

Brown, George MacKay. Selected poems / by George MacKay Brown. — London : Hogarth Press, 1977. — 95p ; 23cm.
ISBN 0-7012-0429-x : £3.50 : CIP rev.
(B77-09219)

Brown, Stewart. Room service / poems by Stewart Brown ; images by Barry Hesson. — Falmouth (Woodlane, Falmouth, Cornwall) : Falmouth School of Art, 1977. — [20]p ; 26cm.

Fold. covers.
ISBN 0-9505680-0-7 Sd : £0.75
(B77-33402)

Buck, Paul, *b.1946.* Sentence. And would be superfluous / [by] Paul Buck. — Hebden Bridge (12 Foster Clough, Hebden Bridge, W. Yorkshire HX7 5QZ) : Pressed Curtains, [1977]. — [18]p : chiefly ill ; 11x15cm. — (Pressed Curtains performance series)
Also available in a limited ed. of 28 copies signed by the author, 26 being lettered and offered for sale.
ISBN 0-9504368-3-6 Pbk : £0.45
Signed ed. : £2.00
(B77-09220)

Buck, Paul, *b.1946.* Within the process of change / [by] Paul Buck. — Newcastle upon Tyne (24 Coquet Terrace, Heaton, Newcastle upon Tyne 6) : Pig Press, 1976. — [8]p : ill ; 21cm.
Limited ed. of approximately 50 copies. — '... produced to coincide with a reading by Allen Fisher & Paul Buck at the Colpitts Hotel, Durham on Nov. 19th 1976 at 7.30 p.m.' - p.[8].
ISBN 0-903997-16-9 Sd : £0.20
(B77-00376)

Bura, Paul. The coming of the giants : poems / by Paul Bura. — London : Mitre Press, 1977. — 64p ; 19cm.
ISBN 0-7051-0251-3 : £1.60
(B77-13831)

Burcher, Joseph James. The poems of Joseph James Burcher (a grandson of Arundel, Sussex, England) Bancroft, Ontario, Canada. — Arundel ([c/o Castle Press, 12c High St., Arundel, Sussex BN18 9AB]) : The author, 1976. — 28p ; 18cm.
ISBN 0-9505647-0-2 Sd : £3.00
(B77-11380)

Burford, Ted. Cranefly incident : poems / by Ted Burford. — London (15 Woodfield Rd, Ealing, W.5) : Ealing Press, 1976. — 35p ; 21cm.
ISBN 0-904397-01-7 Sd : £0.75
(B77-10526)

Burgess, Anthony. Moses : a narrative / [by] Anthony Burgess. — London (8 Berwick St., W.1) : Dempsey and Squires, 1976. — 190,[2] p : music ; 22cm.
Also published: New York : Stonehill Publishing, 1976.
ISBN 0-86044-000-1 : £4.50
(B77-19610)

Burgess, Desmond. All that is left / by Desmond Burgess. — Hailsham (4 Garfield Rd, Hailsham, E. Sussex BN27 2BB) : 'Rhyme and Reason', 1977. — 28p ; 21cm.
ISBN 0-905855-04-3 Sd : £0.50
(B77-12053)

Burgess, Desmond. Battling for Britain / by Desmond Burgess. — Hailsham (4 Garfield Rd, Hailsham, Sussex BN27 2BB) : Rhyme and Reason, 1976. — [1],28p ; 21cm.
ISBN 0-905855-00-0 Sd : £0.50
(B77-03735)

Burgess, Desmond. Believing in Britain / [by Desmond Burgess]. — Hailsham (4 Garfield Rd, Hailsham, E. Sussex BN27 2BB) : 'Rhyme and Reason', 1977. — 28,[1]p ; 22cm.
Sd : £0.50
(B77-31408)

Burgess, Desmond. First the kingdom / by Desmond Burgess. — Hailsham (4 Garfield Rd, Hailsham, E. Sussex BN27 2BB) : Rhyme and Reason, 1977. — 28p ; 21cm.
Sd : £0.50
(B77-25841)

Burgess, Desmond. The shining light / by Desmond Burgess. — Hailsham (4 Garfield Rd, Hailsham, E. Sussex BN27 2BB) : 'Rhyme and Reason', 1976. — [1],28p ; 21cm.
ISBN 0-905855-01-9 Sd : £0.50
(B77-02553)

Burgess, Desmond. A Silver Jubilee trilogy / [by] Desmond Burgess. — Hailsham (4 Garfield Rd, Hailsham, E. Sussex BN27 2BB) : Rhyme & Reason, 1977. — Folder([3]p.) ; 21cm.
Unpriced
(B77-32816)

Burgess, Desmond. Think on these things / [by] Desmond Burgess. — 2nd ed. — Hailsham (4 Garfield Rd, Hailsham, E. Sussex) : Rhyme & Reason, 1976. — 32p ; 21cm.
Previous ed.: i.e. Limited ed. 1975.
ISBN 0-905855-02-7 Sd : £0.50
(B77-04385)

Burgess, Desmond. Weep no more for freedom / [by] Desmond Burgess. — [Hailsham] ([4 Garfield Rd, Hailsham, E. Sussex BN27 2BB]) : [The author], 1976. — 28p ; 21cm.
ISBN 0-905855-03-5 Sd : £0.60
(B77-04386)

Burnett, Alfred David. The heart's undesign / [by] David Burnett ; with two wood engravings by Joan Hassall. — Edinburgh ([137 Warrender Park Rd, Edinburgh EH9 1DS]) : Tragara Press, 1977. — 2-55p : ill ; 20cm.
Limited ed. of 200 copies of which 10 have been bound in boards and signed by the author.
ISBN 0-902616-37-4 Pbk : £1.50
(B77-28843)

Burnett, Anne. Reflections on life / [by] Anne Burnett. — Ilfracombe : Stockwell, 1977. — 64p ; 15cm.
ISBN 0-7223-1038-2 : £1.50
(B77-23666)

Burns, Jim, *b.1936.* Playing it cool / [by] Jim Burns. — Swansea (104 Bryn Rd, Swansea, W. Glam. SA2 0AU) : Galloping Dog Press, 1976. — 24p ; 21cm.
Limited ed. of 300 copies of which 10 are numbered and signed by the author.
ISBN 0-904837-00-9 Sd : £0.40
Signed ed. : £2.00
(B77-00377)

Burns, Richard, *b.1943.* Inhabitable space / [by] Richard Burns. — Groningen : John Morann ; Cambridge (20 Tenison Ave., Cambridge) : Distributed by Bragora Press, 1976. — [8]p ; 21cm.
Sd : £0.20
(B77-05605)

Butler, Gwendoline June. The white daisies, and other poems / [by] Gwendoline June Butler. — Ilfracombe : Stockwell, 1977. — 40p ; 15cm.
ISBN 0-7223-1010-2 : £1.35
(B77-23667)

Caccia, David. Poems and aphorisms / [by] David Caccia. — [London] ([Studio 4, 59 South Edwards Sq., W.8]) : [The author], [1977]. — 114 leaves in various pagings ; 21cm.
Cover title.
Pbk : £1.00
(B77-13832)

Caccia, David. Sonnets / [by] David Caccia. — [London] ([Studio 4, 59 South Edwards Sq., W.8]) : [The author], [1977]. — 64 leaves ; 21cm.
Cover title.
Pbk : £1.00
(B77-13833)

Cadaxa, Armindo Bonanco Menol. Elegies from the lesser Sierras / [by] A.B.M. Cadaxa. — London : Mitre Press, 1976. — 35p ; 19cm.
ISBN 0-7051-0244-0 : £1.60
(B77-05606)

Caddick, Arthur. The ballad of Michael Joseph, the Captain of Cornwall (1947) / by Arthur Caddick. — Penzance (Nancledra, Penzance, Cornwall) : The author, 1977. — [8]p ; 17cm.
Sd : £0.50
(B77-25842)

Calder, Dave. Leaf of mouth : poems / by Dave Calder. — Liverpool (14 Harringay Ave., Liverpool L18 1JE) : Toulouse Press, 1976. — [24]p ; 20cm.
Sheet([2]p.) as insert.
Sd : £0.35
(B77-17716)

Cameron, John Cullen. Poetical works / by John Cullen Cameron. — [3rd ed. i.e. 1st ed. reprinted]. — Ilfracombe : Stockwell, [1977]. — 44p ; 19cm.
Originally published: 1969.
ISBN 0-7223-0024-7 Pbk : Unpriced
(B77-16571)

Carey, Jack. Woods and mirrors : poems / by Jack Carey. — London (3 Cadogan Sq., SW1X 0HT) : Salamander Imprint, 1976. — 78p ; 24cm.
Also available in a limited ed. of 50 copies, numbered and signed by the author.
ISBN 0-904632-04-0 : £3.95
ISBN 0-904632-05-9 Pbk : £2.25
Signed ed. : Unpriced
(B77-13834)

Carpenter, Andrew. The confounded eye / [by] Andrew Carpenter ; [with and original drawing by Jim Stewart]. — Dublin (6 Richmond Hill, Monkstown, Dublin) : The Cadenus Press, 1976. — [22]p : 1 ill ; 23cm.
Limited ed. of 100 numbered copies signed by the poet and artist.
ISBN 0-904375-03-x Sd : £7.50
(B77-08021)

Carpenter, Joyce Frances. Attitude / by Joyce Frances Carpenter. — Bordage (Tudor House, Bordage, Guernsey) : Etcetera Press, 1976. — 2-26,[1]p ; 21cm.
ISBN 0-905119-01-0 Sd : £0.45
(B77-08526)

Carradice, Phil John. Fading islands : a concern with aspects of growing up / by Phil J. Carradice. — Corby (10 Minden Close, Danesholme, Corby, Northants. NN18 9EW) : Excello and Bollard, [1977]. — [13]p ; 30cm.
ISBN 0-904339-43-2 Sd : £0.25
(B77-11381)

Carradice, Phil John. Slit here / by Phil Carradice. — Corby : Excello and Bollard, 1977. — [20]p ; 26cm.
ISBN 0-904339-56-4 Sd : Unpriced
(B77-26475)

Carroll, Anthony. My poems I leave to you / [by] Anthony Carroll. — Fermoy ; Youghal ([Saint Anne's, Kilcoran Rd, Youghal, Co. Cork]) : [The author], [1977]. — [1],24p ; 22cm.
Sd : £0.50
(B77-28844)

Carte, Michael. Full circle / by Michael Carte. — Walton-on-Thames : Outposts Publications, 1977. — 12p ; 21cm.
Sd : £0.30
(B77-22808)

Carter, Gerda. Bouquet of thorns and other poems / written and illustrated by Gerda Carter. — [London] ([24 The Boltons, S.W.10]) : The authoress, 1977. — 95p : ill ; 21cm.
Sd : £1.20
(B77-34031)

Carter, Martin, *b.1927.* Poems of succession / [by] Martin Carter. — London [etc.] : New Beacon Books, 1977. — 117p ; 23cm.
ISBN 0-901241-20-2 : £4.00
ISBN 0-901241-21-0 Pbk : £1.95
(B77-22809)

Cathie, Diarmid. In transit : an entertainment / [by] Diarmid Cathie. — London (21 Gloucester Cres., N.W.1) : John Gill, 1976. — Sheet ; 61x45cm fold to 21x15cm.
Limited ed. of 125 numbered copies of which nos. 1-25 are signed by the poet.
£1.00
(B77-00917)

Catling, Brian. Pleiades in nine / [by] B. Catling. — London (28 Albion Drive, E8 4ET) : Albion Village Press, 1976. — [48]p : ill ; 21cm.
Limited ed. of 200 copies, with 15 further copies casebound, numbered and signed, and containing additional holograph material.
ISBN 0-903924-17-x Pbk : £0.90
ISBN 0-903924-16-1 Signed ed. : £5.00
(B77-05041)

Caulton, J Stewart. Christmas rhymes and woodcuts for children & others / by J. Stewart Caulton. — London : Church Literature Association, 1977. — 5-32p : ill ; 18cm.
Facsimile reprint of: 1st ed. London : Society of SS. Peter and Paul, 1923.
Sd : £0.40
(B77-34032)

Cavaliero, Glen. Paradise stairway / [by] Glen Cavaliero. — Manchester : Carcanet New Press, 1977. — 54p ; 23cm.
ISBN 0-85635-223-3 : £2.00
(B77-29646)

Cavanagh, Sybil. Some aspects of life / as observed or fancied by Sybil Cavanagh. — [London] ([12 Grange Court, Holly St., E.8]) : Timothy L. Wood, 1977. — [28]p ; 21cm.
Signed by the author.
Sd : Unpriced
(B77-27325)

Chafer-Ford, L J. An anthology of original prose and poetry / written by Chafer-Ford. — Nottingham (c/o 17 Chalfont Drive, Aspley, Nottingham NG8 3LS) : The author, 1976. — [5],55p : ill, ports ; 22cm.
ISBN 0-9505575-0-1 Sd : Unpriced
(B77-08527)

Chambers, Nancy. Stickleback, stickleback / by Nancy Chambers ; with pictures by Charles Front. — Harmondsworth : Kestrel Books, 1977. — 25p : col ill ; 21cm. — (A Minnow book)
ISBN 0-7226-5259-3 : £1.30
(B77-22810)

Channell, Eric. On the city wall, and other Chester poems / by Eric Channell. — Chester (c/o Chester Arts and Recreation Trust, The Centre, Market Sq., Chester, [Cheshire]) : Cestrian Press, 1975. — v,61p ; 21cm.
ISBN 0-904448-04-5 Pbk : £0.90
(B77-00918)

Chapman, Muriel. Comes in the light : a selection of poems / by Muriel Chapman. — Bakewell : Hub Publications, 1976. — [2],18p ; 21cm.
ISBN 0-905049-12-8 Sd : £0.45
(B77-14381)

Chillingworth, Sidney. A bright light - and a taper / by Sidney Chillingworth. — Walton-on-Thames : Outposts Publications, 1977. — [5],36p ; 21cm.
Pbk : £1.50
(B77-18345)

Christopher, Ellen. Candles in the dark / [by Ellen Christopher]. — London (13 Blithfield St., W.8) : Hilary Press, [1977]. — 2-29p ; 22cm.
Sd : £0.15
(B77-18957)

Chub, A. Bunions onions / by A. Chub. — [Aberdeen] ([Skean Dhu Hotel, Dyce, Aberdeen]) : [The author], [1976]. — [2],33p ; 22cm.
ISBN 0-9505452-0-1 Sd : £0.40
(B77-03198)

Clay, Frank R. Lust into dust / [by] Frank R. Clay. — Ilfracombe : Stockwell, 1976. — 40p ; 18cm.
ISBN 0-7223-0982-1 Pbk : £0.45
(B77-10909)

Cokeley, Francis P. The collected poetry of Francis P. Cokeley. — London : Regency Press, 1976. — 32p ; 19cm.
ISBN 0-7212-0485-6 Sd : £0.60
(B77-09903)

Cole, David, *b.1928.* Meeting places, and other poems / by David Cole. — Oxford : Mowbrays, 1977. — viii,52p ; 23cm.
ISBN 0-264-66436-1 : £2.00
(B77-13227)

Conway, Paul. Poems / by Paul Conway. — Bray (149 Ardmore Park, Bray, Co. Wicklow) : Cicero Publications, 1977. — [1],48p : ill ; 23cm.
Sd : Unpriced
(B77-25843)

Cook, Alan F. A selection of the poems of Alan F. Cook (born 1949). — Nuneaton (Griff Lodge South, Griff La., Nuneaton, Warwickshire) : Griff Small Press, 1977. — 7 leaves ; 30cm.
Sd : Unpriced
(B77-32817)

Cook, Anne. Selected poems / by Anne Cook. — [London] ([183A Clapham Manor St., SW4 6DB]) : Crossed Keys Publication, 1976. — 12p ; 21cm.
ISBN 0-9501069-3-3 Sd : Unpriced
(B77-16572)

Cook, Michael James. Of faith and fortune / by Michael J. Cook. — Walton-on-Thames : Outposts Publications, 1977. — 48p ; 21cm.
Sd : £1.00
(B77-21390)

Cooney, Anthony. Rosary : a cycle of fifteen poems / [by] Anthony Cooney. — Liverpool (17 Hadassah Grove, Liverpool L17 8XH) : 'Liverpool newsletter', [1976]. — [19]p ; 22cm.
ISBN 0-9505383-0-2 Sd : £0.20
(B77-00919)

Cooper, Dorothy, *b.1924.* Sunshine and shadow / [by] Dorothy Cooper ; illustrated by Stuart J.C. Avery. — Ilfracombe : Stockwell, 1977. — 32p : ill ; 19cm.
ISBN 0-7223-1018-8 Pbk : £0.50
(B77-23668)

Corbluth, Elsa. Brown harvest / by Elsa Corbluth. — Weymouth (186 Newstead Rd, Weymouth, Dorset DT4 0DY) : Word and Action (Dorset), 1976. — [2],18p ; 21cm. — (Poets in Dorset ; 1)
Sd : £0.50
(B77-18346)

Covey, C R. Reflections in a sullen eye / [by] C.R. Covey. — Ilfracombe : Stockwell, 1977. — 20p ; 15cm.
ISBN 0-7223-1059-5 Pbk : £0.30
(B77-34033)

Cox, Charles Anderson. The aporetic / by Charles Anderson Cox. — Walton-on-Thames : Outposts Publications, 1977. — 52p ; 21cm.
Sd : £1.10
(B77-18347)

Cox, Morris. Intimidations of mortality : poems on Victorian themes with psychological implications / [by] Morris Cox. — London : Gogmagog Private Press ; London (30 Long Acre, WC2E 9LT) : Distributed by Bertram Rota Ltd, 1977. — [7],11[i.e.22]p : ill(chiefly col) ; 24cm.
Limited ed. of 90 copies, signed and numbered by the author.
£12.00
(B77-34034)

Crabtree, Richard. Wild oats / by Richard Crabtree. — 2nd ed. — Sheffield (c/o Parker Press Ltd, Vicar La., Sheffield S1 2EX) : The Sheffield Poetry Workshop, 1977. — [22]p ; 21cm.
Previous ed.: 1976.
Sd : £0.50
ISBN 0-9505641-0-9
(B77-24436)

Crabtree, Richard. Wild oats / by Richard Crabtree. — Sheffield (c/o Parker Press, Vicar La., Sheffield S1 2EX) : Sheffield Poetry Workshop, 1976. — [22]p ; 21cm.
ISBN 0-9505641-0-9 Sd : £0.50
(B77-14881)

Croome, Pam. Still in the wild lands / by Pam Croome. — Bakewell : Hub Publications, 1977. — [2],14p ; 21cm.
ISBN 0-905049-17-9 Sd : £0.60
(B77-22811)

Crossley-Holland, Kevin. The dream-house : poems / by Kevin Crossley-Holland. — London : Deutsch, 1976. — 63p ; 23cm.
ISBN 0-233-96805-9 : £1.95
(B77-00378)

Cumberlege, Marcus. The poetry millionaire / by Marcus Cumberlege. — Swanage (4 Alexandra Terrace, Swanage, Dorset) : Dollar of Soul Press, 1977. — [24]p : ill ; 20cm.
Limited ed. of 200 numbered copies of which the first 25 are signed.
ISBN 0-9504504-3-x Sd : £0.45
Signed ed. : £1.00
(B77-25844)

Cunningham, A W. Into the westering sun : poems in peace and war / [by] A.W. Cunningham. — Ilfracombe : Stockwell, 1976. — 103p ; 19cm.
ISBN 0-7223-0973-2 : £1.95
(B77-22080)

Cutlack, Madeline Joyce. My scrapbook of poems / [by] Madeline J. Cutlack. — [New ed.]. — Ilfracombe : Stockwell, 1977. — 79p ; 15cm.
Previous ed.: 1976. — Previous control number ISBN 0-7223-0879-5.
£1.25
ISBN 0-7223-0879-5
(B77-23669)

Cutler, Ivor. A flat man / [by] Ivor Cutler ; with drawings by Phyllis April King. — London : Trigram Press, 1977. — 71p ; 21cm.
Limited ed. of 1000 copies, of which 250 are cased and the remainder paperback. 26 copies of the cased ed. are signed and lettered by the author and artist.
ISBN 0-85465-054-7 : £3.25
ISBN 0-85465-053-9 Pbk : £1.75
ISBN 0-85465-055-5 Signed ed.: £6.30
(B77-23670)

Dagley, Bertha L. Knobs and chairs and pump handles / by Bertha L. Dagley. — Walton-on-Thames : Outposts Publications, 1976. — 16p ; 21cm.
ISBN 0-7205-0501-1 Sd : £0.30
(B77-05607)

Dale, Peter, *b.1938.* Cross channel / [by] Peter Dale. — Sutton (26 Cedar Rd, Sutton, Surrey) : Hippopotamus Press, 1977. — 33p ; 21cm.
Also available in limited ed. of 25 copies numbered and signed by the author.
Pbk : £1.50
ISBN 0-904179-14-1
ISBN 0-904179-15-x Signed ed. : £5.00
(B77-25845)

Dale, Peter, *b.1938.* Mortal fire / [by] Peter Dale. — Expanded [ed.]. — London (5 Cranbourne Court, Albert Bridge Rd, SW11 4PE) : Agenda Editions, 1976. — ix,181p ; 24cm.
Previous ed.: London : Macmillan, 1970.
ISBN 0-902400-16-9 : £3.75
ISBN 0-902400-17-7 Pbk : £2.40
(B77-05608)

Danielli, Mary. The amaranth / [by] Mary Danielli. — London : Mitre Press, 1977. — 145p : ill ; 19cm.
ISBN 0-7051-0241-6 : £2.00
(B77-24438)

Das, Deep Kumar. Highs and lows / [by] Deep K. Das. — Ilfracombe : Stockwell, 1976. — 31p ; 15cm.
ISBN 0-7223-0966-x : £1.10
(B77-10910)

Davie, Donald. In the stopping train & other poems / [by] Donald Davie. — Manchester : Carcanet New Press, 1977. — 55p ; 23cm.
£2.00
(B77-26476)

Davis, Geoff. The man in the white suit / by Geoff Davis. — Walton-on-Thames : Outposts Publications, 1977. — 20p ; 21cm.
ISBN 0-7205-0512-7 Sd : £0.40
(B77-16021)

Davis, Owen. Ace of fools / [by] Owen Davis. — Swanage (4 Alexander Terrace, Swanage, Dorset) : Dollar of Soul Press, [1977]. — [33] p : ill ; 21cm.
Limited ed. of 200 numbered copies, of which 25 copies are also signed by the author and illustrator.
ISBN 0-9504504-2-1 Sd : £0.45
Signed ed. : £1.00
(B77-14382)

Davis, Owen. It rains it rains shepherdess / by Owen Davis. — Sheffield (5 Ashgate Close, Sheffield SI0 3DL) : Rivelin Press, 1977. — [2], 18p ; 26cm.
Limited ed. of 200 copies.
ISBN 0-904524-17-5 Sd : £0.40
(B77-18348)

De Bijl, Jordana. To the dunes / [by] Jordana de Bijl. — [Oxford] ([60 Hurst St., Oxford]) : [Ziprint Parchment], 1977. — 76p ; 21cm.
Pbk : £1.50
(B77-33403)

De Lima, Arthur. Bits and pieces / [by] Arthur De Lima ; illustrated by J.B. Simon. — Ilfracombe : Stockwell, 1976. — 96p : ill ; 15cm.
ISBN 0-7223-0956-2 : £1.75
(B77-10911)

De Picarda, Guy. Zongs vrom a Zummerzet wine-zellar / by Guy de Picarda. — Wells (Newton House, Cross, Somerset) : The author, 1976. — 7p ; 21cm.
Limited ed. of 200 copies.
ISBN 0-9505404-0-4 Sd : Unpriced
(B77-00920)

Deane, Seamus. Rumours / [by] Seamus Deane. — Dublin : Dolmen Press, 1977. — 54,[1]p ; 22cm.
ISBN 0-85105-320-3 Pbk : £2.50
(B77-28047)

Dearn, Keith N. Hunter / [by] Keith N. Dearn. — [Huddersfield] (4 Nowell Place, Almondbury, [Huddersfield] HD5 8PB) : Hilltop Press, [1976]. — [6]p ; 21cm.
ISBN 0-905262-02-6 Sd : £0.15
(B77-06253)

Dick, J P. Silence and empty mirrors / [by] J.P. Dick. — [Kingston upon Thames] ([1 Rayleigh Court, Kingston upon Thames KT1 3NF]) : [Court Poetry Press], [1977]. — 32p ; 21cm.
ISBN 0-906010-04-7 Sd : £0.35
(B77-30573)

Dickinson, Barbara. Gaze an eagle blind / by Barbara Dickinson ; cover design by John Churchill ... — Guildford (10 Ashcroft, Shalford, Guildford, Surrey) : Guildford Poets Press, 1977. — 24p ; 21cm.
ISBN 0-904673-06-5 Sd : Unpriced
(B77-30574)

Dinnicombe, Olive. Walking with Jesus : children's recitations / [by] Olive Dinnicombe. — Ilkeston : Moorley's Bible and Bookshop, [1977]. — [1],48p ; 21cm.
Index.
ISBN 0-901495-91-3 Sd : £0.38
(B77-17717)

Donaghey, Betty. Autumn green, and other poems / [by] Betty Donaghey. — Walton-on-Thames : Outposts Publications, 1977. — 32p ; 21cm.
Sd : £0.80
(B77-28048)

Donnachie, James. Humorous rhymes and words without music / [by] James Donnachie ; illustrated by Peter Butler. — Ilfracombe : Stockwell, 1977. — 59p : ill ; 19cm.
Spine title: Humorous rhymes -.
ISBN 0-7223-0868-x : £1.75
(B77-23671)

Donovan, Jo. A white light from the sea / by Jo Donovan. — Walton-on-Thames : Outposts Publications, 1977. — 20p ; 21cm.
Sd : Unpriced
(B77-22812)

Downie, Freda. A stranger here / [by] Freda Downie. — London : Secker and Warburg, 1977. — 55p ; 23cm.
ISBN 0-436-13250-8 : £2.90
(B77-10527)

Dowthwaite, G. The collected poetry of G. Dowthwaite. — London [etc.] : Regency Press, 1977. — 32p ; 19cm.
Sd : £0.60
(B77-27326)

Drake, D M. The collected poetry of D.M. Drake. — London : Regency Press, 1977. — 32p ; 19cm.
Sd : Unpriced
(B77-24439)

Duckworth, Jean. Where footsteps tread : Christian poetry / by Jean Duckworth. — Ilkeston : Moorley's Bible and Bookshop, [1976]. — [1],40p ; 21cm.
Index.
ISBN 0-901495-90-5 Sd : £0.35
(B77-05609)

Duffy, Maureen. Evesong / [by] Maureen Duffy ; illustrations by Celia Berridge. — London (39 Wardour St., W1V 3HA) : Sappho Publications, 1975. — 62,[1]p : ill ; 21cm.
ISBN 0-905834-00-3 Pbk : £1.10
(B77-01769)

Duncan, Ronald. For the few / by Ronald Duncan. — [Bideford] ([Welcombe, Bideford, Devon]) : Rebel Press, 1977. — 63p ; 23cm.
Unpriced
(B77-32818)

Dundrow, Michael. West of Tamar / by Michael Dundrow. — Walton-on-Thames : Outposts Publications, 1977. — 20p ; 21cm.
ISBN 0-7205-0510-0 Sd : £0.40
(B77-13835)

Dunstan, Ruth Tomlin. Dawn till dusk : lyrical verses / by Ruth (Tomlin) Dunstan. — [Solihull] ([102 Redlands Rd, Solihull, Warwickshire]) : [The author], 1976. — [2], 25p ; 20cm.
ISBN 0-902315-03-x Sd : £0.60
(B77-00921)

Earley, Tom. The sad mountain / by Tom Earley. — London : Chatto and Windus : Hogarth Press, 1971. — 40p ; 23cm. — (The phoenix living poets)
Originally published: 1970. — Previous control number ISBN 0-7011-1613-7.
£1.05
ISBN 0-7011-1613-7
(B77-23672)

Earley, Tom. The sad mountain / by Tom Earley. — London : Chatto and Windus : Hogarth Press, 1971. — 40p ; 23cm. — (The phoenix living poets)
Originally published: 1970.
£1.05
ISBN 0-7011-1613-7
(B77-19611)

Earnshaw, Joan. Mr Gander, Mrs Goose and family, and other poems / [by] Joan Earnshaw ; illustrated by the author. — Ilfracombe : Stockwell, 1977. — 63p : ill ; 19cm.
ISBN 0-7223-0998-8 : £1.50
(B77-23673)

Eden, Edward. Inverse strands / by Edward Eden. — Walton-on-Thames : Outposts Publications, 1976. — 20p ; 21cm.
ISBN 0-7205-0498-8 Sd : £0.40
(B77-01770)

Eggleston, Jessie. The turning year / by Jessie Eggleston. — Bakewell : Hub Publications, 1977. — [2],23p : 1 ill ; 21cm.
ISBN 0-905049-24-1 Sd : £0.75
(B77-28845)

Eglinton, Edna. Pisgah / by Edna Eglinton. — Walton-on-Thames : Outposts Publications, 1977. — 20p ; 21cm.
ISBN 0-7205-0506-2 Sd : £0.40
(B77-12054)

Ellis, Gwen. Jubilee year / by Gwen Ellis. — [West Lavington] ([Hollycot, 99 Littleton Panell, West Lavington, Wilts.]) : [The author], [1977]. — Folder([3]p) ; 19cm.
Unpriced
(B77-24440)

Ellis, Gwen, *b.1918.* Moonshine : poems featuring the Wiltshire dialect, including some poems of local historical interest / by Gwen Ellis ; illustrated by Rosalind Hooper. — [West Lavington] ([99 Littleton Panell, West Lavington, Devizes, Wilts.]) : [The author], [1976]. — 54p : ill ; 19cm.
ISBN 0-9505663-0-6 Sd : £0.95
(B77-14383)

Elsted, Crispin. 14 changes on a s̆ao of Huang Bau-xi / [by] Crispin Elsted. — [Boughton Monchelsea] ([13 Church St., Boughton Monchelsea, Kent]) : Barbarian Press, 1977. — [67]p ; 29cm.
Limited ed. of 100 signed, numbered copies of which 15 are bound in leather and also signed by Huang Bau-xi.
£8.00
(B77-32126)

Emerson, Giles. The mark of the fool / by Giles Emerson. — Walton-on-Thames : Outposts Publications, 1977. — 12p ; 21cm.
Sd : £0.35
(B77-28049)

Enters, Ian. Outside this communion / by Ian Enters. — Walton-on-Thames : Outposts Publications, 1977. — 20p ; 21cm.
Sd : £0.40
(B77-29647)

Erimus. Tom Boyes, Deealsman : a selection of poems / by Erimus. — [Whitby] ([Castle Houses, Danby, Whitby, N. Yorkshire YO21 2NP]) : [William E. Fall], [1977]. — [11],34p : ill, port ; 21cm.
ISBN 0-9504829-1-9 Sd : Unpriced
(B77-14384)

Ewart, Gavin. The first eleven : a collection of poems / by Gavin Ewart. — Hatch End (30 Grimsdyke Rd, Hatch End, Middx) : Poet and Printer, 1977. — 20p ; 22cm.
Sd : £0.60
(B77-22081)

Fainlight, Ruth. Two fire poems / [by] Ruth Fainlight. — Knotting (Knotting, Beds.) : Sceptre Press, [1977]. — [4]leaves ; 21cm.
Limited ed. of 150 numbered copies of which the first 50 are signed.
Sd : £0.95
Signed ed. : Unpriced
(B77-32127)

Fassnidge, Chris. Gathering : poems, 1972-1976 / by Chris Fassnidge. — Weymouth (186 Newstead Rd, Weymouth, Dorset DT4 0DY) : Word and Action (Dorset), 1976. — [2],18p ; 21cm. — (Poets in Dorset ; 3)
Sd : £0.50
(B77-18349)

Fawcett, Dorothy. Judas, and other selected poems / [by] Dorothy Fawcett. — Ilfracombe : Stockwell, 1976. — 16p ; 15cm.
ISBN 0-7223-0974-0 Pbk : £0.30
(B77-10912)

Feakes, Kenneth. Spaces between / by Kenneth Feakes. — Walton-on-Thames : Outposts Publications, 1977. — 28p ; 21cm.
Sd : £0.70
(B77-28050)

Fearn, Susan. Marking time / [by] Susan Fearn. — Breakish : Aquila/The Phaethon Press, 1976. — [23]p ; 20cm.
Also available in a limited ed. of 26 copies signed and lettered by the author.
ISBN 0-7275-0180-1 Sd : £0.40
ISBN 0-7275-0181-x Signed ed.: £1.50
(B77-09221)

Ffinch, Michael. The beckwalker, and other poems / [by] Michael Ffinch. — London : Latimer New Dimensions, 1977. — viii,53p ; 23cm.
Includes 'The undertaker poet' originally published: London : Latimer Press, 1968.
ISBN 0-901539-60-0 : £2.95
(B77-22813)

Fiacc, Padraic. Nights in the bad place / [by] Padraic Fiacc ; images by Deborah Brown. — Belfast : Blackstaff Press, 1977. — 48p : ill ; 21cm.
ISBN 0-85640-111-0 Pbk : £1.75
(B77-28051)

Finch, Vivienne. The owl master : a poem sequence / by Vivienne Finch ; with illustrations by Peter Barnfield. — Bristol (15 Ladman Rd, Bristol BS14 8QH) : Xenia Press, 1977. — [32]p : ill ; 21cm.
ISBN 0-9502843-7-8 Sd : £1.00
(B77-22814)

Fisher, Allen. Gripping the rail : pit stop 13 to 20 with part of a coda / [by] Allen Fisher. — Newcastle upon Tyne (24 Coquet Terrace, Heaton, Newcastle upon Tyne 6) : Pig Press, 1976. — [16]p : ill ; 21cm.
Limited ed. of approximately 100 copies. — '... produced to coincide with a reading by Allen Fisher & Paul Buck at the Colpitts Hotel, Durham on Nov. 19th 1976 at 7.30 p.m.' - p.[16].
ISBN 0-903997-15-0 Sd : £0.20
(B77-00379)

Fisher, Allen. Paxton's beacon / [by Allen Fisher]. — Todmorden : Arc Publications, 1976. — [15]leaves : ill ; 21x30cm.
Limited ed. of 250 copies of which 15 are numbered and signed by the author.
ISBN 0-902771-57-4 Sd : £0.60(£1.50 signed ed.)
ISBN 0-902771-58-2 Signed ed. : £1.50
(B77-00922)

Fisher, Roy. Four poems / [by] Roy Fisher. — Newcastle upon Tyne (24 Coquet Terrace, Heaton, Newcastle upon Tyne 6) : Pig Press, 1976. — [8]p : 2 ill ; 21cm.
Limited ed. of ca 75 copies.
ISBN 0-903997-22-3 Sd : £0.20
(B77-03199)

Fleischner, Lewis. Nightspaces : poems / by Lewis Fleischner. — London (310 Westbourne Park Rd, W.11) : Cash and Co., 1976. — 38,[1] p ; 21cm.
Limited ed. of 500 numbered copies, signed by the author.
ISBN 0-900656-05-0 Sd : Unpriced
(B77-10528)

Fletcher, Colin. Windows : poems / by Colin Fletcher ; drawings by Trevor Skempton ; photographs by Sean Sprague. — Nottingham (24 Lea Rd, Ravenshead, Nottingham) : The author, [1977]. — [3],37p : ill ; 21cm.
Pbk : £1.20
(B77-28846)

Fletcher, Cyril. Odd odes & oddities / [by] Cyril Fletcher ; illustrated by Roy Garnham Elmore. — London (223 Regent St., W1R 8TD) : Galaxy Records, 1977. — 44p : ill ; 21cm.
ISBN 0-9504774-2-7 Pbk : £1.00
(B77-07562)

Flynn, Frank. Songs Frankenstein sang / [by] Frank Flynn. — Lower Bebington (55 Townfield La., Lower Bebington, Wirral, Cheshire) : Our Publications, 1977. — 47p ; 21cm.
Sd : £1.00
(B77-26477)

Fooks, Alfred. Head and heart / [by] Alfred Fooks. — Ilfracombe : Stockwell, 1976. — 40p ; 19cm.
ISBN 0-7223-0964-3 : £1.35
(B77-10913)

Forbes, Sarah. I thought we were friends / by Sarah Forbes. — London : G. Whizzard Publications Ltd : [Distributed by] Deutsch, 1977. — [7],40p : ill ; 25cm.
ISBN 0-233-96931-4 Pbk : £1.75
(B77-29648)

Ford, Hilda Minnie. Riding in the spray / by Hilda Ford. — Walton-on-Thames : Outposts Publications, 1977. — 12p ; 21cm.
ISBN 0-7205-0504-6 Sd : £0.30
(B77-05610)

Francis, Mabel Aylena. The collected poetry of Mabel Aylena Francis. — London [etc.] : Regency Press, 1977. — 32p ; 19cm.
ISBN 0-7212-0491-0 Sd : Unpriced
(B77-15453)

Francis, Morgan. The sun lights and the sun shades : poems / by Morgan Francis. — [Cardiff] ([37 Oakfield St., Roath, Cardiff CF2 3RE]) : [The author], 1976. — [12],17p : port ; 23cm.
ISBN 0-9505601-0-3 Pbk : £1.00
(B77-09904)

Fraser, Douglas, *b.1910.* Where the dark branches part : a sequence of love poems / [by] Douglas Fraser. — Loanhead (Edgefield Rd, Loanhead, Midlothian EH20 9SY) : Macdonald Publishers, 1977. — 36p ; 22cm.
ISBN 0-904265-17-x Sd : £1.50
(B77-34035)

Freegard, Stella. Carried forward / by Stella Freegard. — London [etc.] : Regency Press, 1977. — 32p ; 22cm.
ISBN 0-7212-0496-1 Sd : Unpriced
(B77-15454)

Frost, Hardy. In Dorset of course : poems / by Hardy Frost. — Sherborne : Abbey Press, L. Coldwell (Printing), 1976. — 43p ; 19cm.
ISBN 0-9505382-0-5 Sd : £0.85
(B77-00923)

Fulker, Tina. Winter / by Tina Fulker. — Bridgend (83 Pyle Inn Way, Pyle, Bridgend, M. Glam.) : Speed Limit Publications, 1977. — [10]p ; 26cm. — (Speed Limit booklet ; 3)
Sd : £0.15
(B77-28847)

Fuller, John, *b.1937.* Bel and the dragon / [by] John Fuller. — Oxford (4 Benson Place, Oxford) : Sycamore Press, 1977. — [12]p ; 21cm.
'The 1977 Oxford Prize Poem on a Sacred Subject'. — Limited ed. of 160 copies numbered and signed by the author.
Sd : £1.50
(B77-33404)

Fulton, Robin, *b.1937.* Between flights : eighteen poems / by Robin Fulton. — Egham (4 Northcroft Villas, Northcroft Rd, Englefield Green, Egham, Surrey TW20 0DZ) : Interim Press, 1976. — 22,[1]p ; 22cm.
Limited ed. of 200 copies, of which 20 are numbered and signed by the author.
ISBN 0-904675-06-8 Sd : £0.40
ISBN 0-904675-07-6 Signed ed. : Unpriced
(B77-08022)

Furnival, Christine. Prince of sapphires / by Christine Furnival. — Breakish : Aquila, 1976. — 23p ; 21cm.
Also available in a limited ed. of 26 copies, signed and lettered by the author.
ISBN 0-7275-0135-6 Sd : £0.30
ISBN 0-7275-0136-4 Signed ed. : £1.50
(B77-15455)

Gaddum, Richard H. My world passport / by Richard H. Gaddum. — Nottingham (c/o National Westminster Bank Ltd, 1 Beech Ave., Nottingham NG7 7LJ) : Roundabout Books, 1977. — [1],16 leaves : col ill ; 21cm.
Leaves printed on both sides.
ISBN 0-9505897-0-5 Sd : Unpriced
(B77-28848)

Gardner, Lily. The dance of progress / by Lily Gardner. — Walton-on-Thames : Outposts Publications, 1977. — 20p ; 21cm.
Sd : £0.40
(B77-22815)

Garioch, Robert. Collected poems [of] Robert Garioch. — Loanhead (Edgefield Rd, Loanhead, Midlothian EH20 9SY) : Macdonald Publishers, 1977. — xiv,208p ; 23cm.
ISBN 0-904265-14-5 : £6.95
(B77-21391)

Garlick, Raymond. Incense : poems 1972-1975 / [by] Raymond Garlick. — Llandysul : Gwasg Gomer, 1976. — 64p ; 23cm.
ISBN 0-85088-339-3 : £1.00
(B77-06254)

Garrett, Florence Rome. On the hill / by Florence Rome Garrett. — Bakewell : Hub Publications, 1977. — [2],21p ; 21cm.
ISBN 0-905049-26-8 Sd : £0.90
(B77-27327)

Garrison, Philip. Lime tree notes / [by] Philip Garrison. — [Pensnett] ([10 Consort Cres., Commonside, Pensnett, Staffs.]) : Grosseteste Press, 1976. — 14,[1]p ; 22cm.
Limited ed. of 300 numbered copies of which the first 30 are signed. — 'This book is also issued as "Grosseteste Review", Volume 9 no.4' - title page verso.
ISBN 0-901597-52-x Sd : £0.40
ISBN 0-901597-53-8 Signed ed. : £1.50
(B77-12055)

Gaul, A. Poems of Ryedale / [by] A. Gaul. — Ilfracombe : Stockwell, 1977. — 24p ; 15cm.
ISBN 0-7223-0992-9 Pbk : £0.30
(B77-10914)

George, Glenda. Slit here / [by] Glenda George. — Hebden Bridge (12 Foster Clough, Hebden Bridge, W. Yorkshire HX7 5QZ) : Pressed Curtains, 1976. — [25]leaves : ill ; 26cm.
Also available in a limited ed. of 15 numbered and signed copies.
Sd : £0.60
Signed ed. : £2.00
(B77-26478)

Gibbs, Jean. My way / by Jean Gibbs. — London [etc.] : Regency Press, 1977. — 32p ; 22cm.
ISBN 0-7212-0497-x Sd : Unpriced
(B77-15456)

Gilbertson, Richard. Cornish aerie, and other poems / by Richard Gilbertson ; drawings by Rigby Graham. — [Leicester] ([78 Cambridge St., Leicester LE3 0JP]) : New Broom Private Press, 1977. — [20]p : ill ; 19cm.
Limited ed. of 175 numbered and signed copies of which nos 1-50 include a handwritten poem.
ISBN 0-901870-27-7 Sd : Unpriced
(B77-25846)

Gilchrist, Marjory. The London tree / by Marjory Gilchrist. — Walton-on-Thames : Outposts Publications, 1977. — 40p ; 21cm.
Sd : £0.80
(B77-02554)

Gilmore, Charlie. The leggings & the bandoliers : a poem / by Charlie Gilmore. — Dublin (30 Gardiner Place, Dublin 1) : Repsol Publications, 1976. — [1],8,[1]p ; 19cm.
ISBN 0-86064-003-5 Sd : £0.20
(B77-17718)

Gittings, Christine. Dreamer's canvas : poems / by Christine Gittings. — London : Mitre Press, [1977]. — 53p ; 19cm.
ISBN 0-7051-0250-5 : £1.60
(B77-08023)

Glen, Duncan. Gaitherings : poems in Scots / by Duncan Glen. — Preston : Akros Publications, 1977. — 91p ; 21cm.
'Twenty-five copies are numbered and signed by the author' - title page verso. — Word leet/glossary ([12]p.) as insert.
ISBN 0-900036-87-7 Pbk : £1.25
(B77-08024)

Glen, Duncan. Of philosophers and tinks : a sequence of poems / by Duncan Glen. — Preston : Akros Publications, 1977. — 34p ; 23cm.
'... a sequence from "Realities : poems of sequences"' - title page verso. — Limited ed. of 300 copies of which the first 25 are numbered and signed by the author.
Sd : £0.85
Signed ed.: £1.25
(B77-26479)

Gohorry, John. Five poems / [by] John Gohorry. — King's Langley : Kit-Cat Press, 1977. — [12]p ; 21cm.
Sd : £0.75
(B77-29649)

Gonzalez, John. Fuss / by John Gonzalez. — Corby (10 Minden Close, Danesholme, Corby, Northants. NN18 9EW) : Excello & Bollard, [1977]. — [24]p ; 15cm.
ISBN 0-904339-44-0 Sd : £0.10
(B77-12056)

Gordon, Janette R. Left by the tide : poems / by Janette R. Gordon. — Aberdeen : Alex P. Reid, 1977. — 131p ; 21cm.
Pbk : £1.50
(B77-24441)

Graham, Paula. Escape in thoughts / by Paula Graham ; illustrations by Michel Stin. — Crowborough ('Kiambu', Luxford Rd, Crowborough, Sussex TN6 2PL) : Major-Minor Books, [1976]. — [3],26p : ill ; 22cm.
ISBN 0-9505481-0-3 Sd : £0.60
(B77-03736)

Graham-Mitchell, Gwendoline. No root of bitterness / by Gwendoline Graham-Mitchell. — London : Regency Press, 1977. — 32p ; 19cm.
Sd : Unpriced
(B77-24442)

Grant, James Russell. The excitement of being Sam : earth-poetry in English / by James Russell Grant. — Walton-on-Thames : Outposts Publications, 1977. — 24p ; 21cm.
Sd : £0.60
(B77-28052)

Grant, Michael, *b.1940.* Orders of exchange / by Michael Grant. — Todmorden : Arc Publications, 1977. — [17]p ; 21cm.
Limited ed. of 250 copies of which 15 are numbered and signed by the author.
ISBN 0-902771-61-2 Sd : £0.36
ISBN 0-902771-62-0 Signed and numbered ed. : Unpriced
(B77-25847)

Gray, Barbara, *b.1934.* A thousand dreams, and other poems / by Barbara Gray. — London : Regency Press, 1977. — 32p ; 22cm.
Sd : £0.60
(B77-25848)

Green, J C R. A beaten image : poems for several places, 1968-1976 / by J.C.R. Green. — Breakish : Aquila, 1977. — [24]p ; 18cm.
Limited ed. of 125 copies, of which 25 have been signed and numbered by the author.
ISBN 0-7275-0186-0 Sd : £0.30
ISBN 0-7275-0187-9 Signed ed. : £1.50
(B77-15457)

Green, Stanley Roger. A suburb of Belsen : the poetry of Stanley Roger Green / with drawings by Geoffrey Roper. — Edinburgh : P. Harris, 1977. — 88p : ill ; 23cm.
ISBN 0-904505-21-9 : £6.00
ISBN 0-904050-22-7 Pbk : £1.95
(B77-14882)

Gregory, Raymond George. But then : other poems / by R.G. Gregory. — Weymouth (186 Newstead Rd, Weymouth, Dorset DT4 0DY) : Word and Action (Dorset), 1976. — [2],18p ; 21cm. — (Poets in Dorset ; 5)
Sd : £0.50
(B77-18350)

Gregory, Robin. Sea-bird in the western sunrise / by Robin Gregory. — Bakewell : Hub Publications, 1977. — [3],32p ; 21cm.
ISBN 0-905049-22-5 Sd : £0.66
(B77-14385)

Griffiths, Bill. Six walks around Tenby / [by] Bill Griffiths. — [London] ([21 Earls Court Sq., S.W.5]) : Earthgrip Press, 1976. — [8] leaves ; 21cm.
Includes one poem in French.
ISBN 0-905194-03-9 Sd : Unpriced
(B77-09905)

Grinter, June. A handful of thoughts : children's recitations / by June Grinter. — Ilkeston : Moorley's Bible and Bookshop, [1977]. — 25p ; 21cm.
Index.
ISBN 0-901495-93-x Sd : £0.25
(B77-13228)

Ground, Hannah. New poems and true short stories / by Hannah Ground. — [Alfreton] ([172 Mansfield Rd, Alfreton, Derbyshire DE5 7JQ]) : [The author], [1977]. — [3],35p : ill, ports ; 19cm.
Sd : £1.25
Also classified at 942.5'1'0810924
(B77-27328)

Grubb, David Herbert Watkins. Last days of the eagle, and other poems / by David H.W. Grubb. — London (16 Haslemere Rd, N.8) : Oxus Press, 1976. — [2],38p ; 22cm.
ISBN 0-905501-02-0 : £2.60
ISBN 0-905501-01-2 Pbk : £1.20
(B77-17719)

Guest, Harry. Two poems / [by] Harry Guest. — Knotting : Sceptre Press, 1977. — [8]p ; 21cm.
Limited ed. of 150 numbered copies, of which nos 1-50 are signed by the poet.
ISBN 0-7068-0340-x Sd : £0.95
ISBN 0-7068-0341-8 Signed ed : £5.00
(B77-09222)

Gunson, Douglas. Shadow show / by Douglas Gunson. — Norwich (18A Cricket Ground Rd, Norwich) : The author, 1977. — [8]p ; 21cm.
Sd : Unpriced
(B77-26480)

Haddow, Hilda May. Pictures in the sky / [by] Hilda May Haddow ; illustrated by J.B. Simon. — Ilfracombe : Stockwell, 1977. — 32p : ill ; 18cm.
ISBN 0-7223-1004-8 Pbk : £0.50
(B77-25172)

Hagan-Smith, Pamela. Children's poems / by Pamela Hagan-Smith. — [Falmouth] ([5 Park Cres., Falmouth, Cornwall TR11 2DL]) : [The author].
[Book 1] / illustrated by Gaye Lush. — 1977. — [27]p : ill ; 22cm.
'A Lanarca publication' - p.[3].
Sd : Unpriced
(B77-26481)

Hamburger, Michael. Palinode : a poet's progress / [by] Michael Hamburger. — Knotting : Sceptre Press, [1977]. — [3]leaves ; 21cm.
Limited ed. of 150 numbered copies, of which nos 1-50 are signed by the poet.
Sd : Unpriced
Signed ed. : Unpriced
(B77-32819)

Hamburger, Michael. Real estate / [by] Michael Hamburger. — Manchester : Carcanet New Press, 1977. — 96p ; 23cm.
ISBN 0-85635-216-0 : £2.50
ISBN 0-85635-234-9 Pbk : £1.95
(B77-18958)

Hammond, Clifford. Reflections / by Clifford Hammond. — Walton-on-Thames : Outposts Publications, 1977. — 24p ; 21cm.
Sd : £0.50
(B77-29650)

Hampden-Jackson, Mary. Lyrical and meditative poems / [by] Mary Hampden-Jackson. — London [etc.] : Regency Press, 1975. — 100p ; 22cm.
ISBN 0-7212-0420-1 Pbk : £0.60
(B77-10529)

Harbinson, Robert. Songs out of oriel / [by] Robert Harbinson. — London (BCM-Productions, WC1V 6XX) : G.H. and R. Hart, 1974. — 3-142p : ill ; 23cm.
ISBN 0-9503516-0-1 Pbk : £1.50
(B77-19612)

Harding, Cory. Jeanee with the light brown hair / [by] Cory Harding. — London (176 Peckham Rye, S.E.22) : Editions Grand Hotel des Palmes a Palerme, 1977. — [7]leaves ; 30cm.
Sd : £0.20
(B77-17056)

Harris, S M. Poems of reality / [by] S.M. Harris. — Ilfracombe : Stockwell, 1977. — 32p ; 15cm.
ISBN 0-7223-1050-1 Pbk : £0.45
(B77-23674)

Harrison, Roy. Hieronymus Bosch at the zoo, and other poems / [by] Roy Harrison. — London (19 South Hill Park, NW3 2ST) : Red Candle Press, 1977. — [2],30p ; 21cm.
Pbk : £0.60
(B77-18959)

Harsent, David. Dreams of the dead / [by] David Harsent. — Oxford [etc.] : Oxford University Press, 1977. — [7],55p ; 22cm.
ISBN 0-19-211875-7 Pbk : £2.50 : CIP rev.
(B77-20541)

Hartnett, Michael. Poems in English / [by] Michael Hartnett. — Dublin : Dolmen Press, 1977. — 80p,plate : port ; 23cm.
ISBN 0-85105-313-0 : £6.00
(B77-28053)

Harvey, Andrew. Winter scarecrow : poems / by Andrew Harvey ; with an introduction by John Wain. — Ilkley (Festival Office, Ilkley, W. Yorkshire LS29 8HF) : Proem Pamphlets, 1977. — [19]p ; 19cm.
ISBN 0-905125-01-0 Sd : £0.35
(B77-13836)

Henderson, Pamela M. The vale / by Pamela M. Henderson. — Walton-on-Thames : Outposts Publications, 1977. — 16p ; 21cm.
Sd : £0.35
(B77-22082)

Henderson Smith, Stephen Lane. Filterings / by S.L. Henderson Smith. — Walton-on-Thames : Outposts Publications, 1977. — 52p ; 21cm.
Sd : £1.00
(B77-22816)

Henri, Adrian. City hedges : poems, 1970-76 / [by] Adrian Henri. — London : Cape, 1977. — 64p ; 22cm. — (Cape poetry paperbacks)
ISBN 0-224-01423-4 Pbk : £1.25 : CIP rev.
(B77-22083)

Herbert, Allan. When the nights were sub-titled : poems, 1975 / [by] Allan Herbert. — Pyle (83 Pyle Inn Way, Pyle, Bridgend, M. Glam.) : Speed Limit Publications, 1977. — [16]p ; 21cm. — (Speed Limit booklet ; 10)
Sd : £0.15
(B77-32128)

Hesketh, Phoebe. Preparing to leave : poems / by Phoebe Hesketh. — London : Enitharmon Press, 1977. — 36p ; 22cm.
ISBN 0-901111-99-6 : £2.40
ISBN 0-905289-00-5 Pbk : Unpriced
(B77-29651)

Hewitt, John, *b.1907.* Time enough : poems new and revised / by John Hewitt. — Belfast : Blackstaff Press, 1976. — [5],37p ; 22cm.
ISBN 0-85640-097-1 Pbk : £1.50
(B77-05611)

Hilton, Jeremy. Short stout ghosts : a selection of poems from community studies / by Jeremy Hilton. — Sheffield (5 Ashgate Close, Sheffield S10 3DL) : Rivelin Press, 1977. — [2],16p ; 26cm.
Limited ed. of 200 copies.
ISBN 0-904524-16-7 Sd : £0.40
(B77-18960)

Hochheiser, Marilyn. A view through the thicket / by Marilyn Hochheiser. — Walton-on-Thames : Outposts Publications, 1977. — 36p ; 21cm.
Sd : £0.90
(B77-21392)

Hoddes, Sidney. Poems about - / by Sidney Hoddes ; cover photograph, Susan Sterne. — Liverpool (14 Harringay Ave., Liverpool L18 1JE) : Toulouse Press, 1976. — [2],38p ; 22cm.
Sd : £0.50
(B77-18351)

Holloway, John. Planet of winds : poems / by John Holloway. — London [etc.] : Routledge and Kegan Paul, 1977. — vii,76p ; 23cm.
ISBN 0-7100-8515-x : £2.95
(B77-17720)

Holmes, Philip. A place to stand : poems 1969-76 / [by] Philip Holmes ; with drawings by Peter Coleman. — London : Anvil Press Poetry : Distributed by Collings, 1977. — 95p : ill ; 22cm.
ISBN 0-85646-034-6 Pbk : £2.25
(B77-34036)

Horsbrugh, Wilma. The bold bad bus, and other rhyming stories / [by] Wilma Horsbrugh ; illustrated by Gerald Rose. — New ed. — London : British Broadcasting Corporation, 1977. — 72p : ill ; 24cm.
'BBC Play Away' - cover. — 'All of these verses have been broadcast in BBC children's programmes' - note. — Previous ed.: 1973.
ISBN 0-563-17256-8 Pbk : £0.70
(B77-12614)

Howell, Anthony. The Mekon / [by] Anthony Howell. — [London] ([40 Walford Rd, N16 8ED]) : The Many Press, 1976. — [15]p ; 21cm.
Sd : £0.30
(B77-17057)

Howell, Jim. Survivals / [by] Jim Howell. — Stockport (8 Cavendish Rd, Heaton Mersey, Stockport, Cheshire SK4 3DN) : Harry Chambers Peterloo Poets, 1976. — 56p : 1 ill, port ; 23cm.
ISBN 0-905291-00-x Pbk : £1.35
(B77-34037)

Hubbard, Frank. Wings for victory / by Frank Hubbard. — [Canterbury] ([3 Kings Rd, Dylesham, Canterbury, Kent CT3 3HD]) : [The author], [1977]. — [58]p : ports ; 21cm.
Sd : £0.50
(B77-28054)

Hughes, Bill. The smashed rainbow : more poems / by Bill Hughes. — Ilkeston : Moorley's Bible and Bookshop, [1977]. — 29p ; 21cm.
ISBN 0-86071-008-4 Sd : £0.33
(B77-29652)

Hughes, R A. Bits and pieces / by R.A. Hughes. — London : Regency Press, 1976. — 32p ; 20cm.
Sd : £0.60
(B77-00924)

Hughes, Rex. The wedding presents : a Jubilee poem / by Rex Hughes. — North Walsham (12 New Rd, North Walsham, Norfolk NR28 9DF) : Warren House Press, 1977. — [5],7p ; 21cm.
Sd : Unpriced
(B77-32129)

Hughes, Ted. Cave birds / poems by Ted Hughes ; drawings by Leonard Baskin. — London : Scolar Press, 1975. — 1v. ; 74cm.
Limited ed. of 100 signed, numbered copies. — Folder ([11]fold leaves) and [1],10 sheets : of ill. all in portfolio. — '... each poem is accompanied by a facsimile of a draft selected from the poet's working papers' - colophon.
£125.00
Also classified at 741.9'42
(B77-10530)

Hughes, Ted. Gaudete / by Ted Hughes. — London : Faber, 1977. — 200p ; 23cm.
ISBN 0-571-11076-2 : £4.50 : CIP rev.
(B77-07563)

Hughes, Ted. Meet my folks! / [by] Ted Hughes ; illustrated by George Adamson. — Harmondsworth [etc.] : Puffin Books, 1977. — 62p : ill ; 19cm. — (Puffin books)
Originally published: London : Faber, 1961.
ISBN 0-14-030865-2 Pbk : £0.30
(B77-24443)

Hughes, Ted. Sunstruck / [by] Ted Hughes. — Knotting : Sceptre Press, [1977]. — [7]p ; 16cm.
Limited ed. of 300 numbered copies of which nos 1-100 are signed by the poet.
Sd : Unpriced
(B77-31409)

Hyatt, Mark. A different mercy / [by] Mark Hyatt. — Cambridge (c/o David Trotter, Magdalene College, Cambridge) : Infernal Methods, 1976. — 67p ; 21cm.
Limited ed. of 250 copies.
ISBN 0-905795-02-4 Sd : £1.50
(B77-10915)

Ingham, Charles. The Alexander Graham Bell poems / by Charles Ingham. — London ([40 Walford Rd, N16 8ED]) : Many Press, 1977. — [15]p ; 15cm.
Limited ed. of 100 numbered copies of which 15 are signed.
Sd : £0.40
(B77-23675)

Jacobs, A C. The proper blessing : poems / by A.C. Jacobs. — London (23 Fitzwarren Gardens, N.19) : The Menard Press, 1976. — 39p ; 22cm.
ISBN 0-903400-24-3 Pbk : £1.20
(B77-11382)

James, Martin. From the ears of the stars / [by] Martin James. — London : Workshop Press, 1976. — 40p ; 21cm.
ISBN 0-902705-36-9 : £2.50
ISBN 0-902705-37-9 Pbk : £1.00
(B77-09906)

James, Trevor. It's like feeding the pigs on alderman's fare : poems and drawings / by Trevor James. — London (Devon House, South Rd, Forest Hill, SE23 2UF) : Caligula Books, 1976. — [2],14p : ill ; 21cm.
ISBN 0-9504214-1-3 Pbk : £0.65
(B77-11383)

James, Vin. The song of fading day / [by] Vin James. — Ilfracombe : Stockwell, 1977. — 37p ; 15cm.
ISBN 0-7223-1052-8 : £1.50
(B77-31410)

Jarman, Archie. The ballad of Brighton beach / [by] Archie Jarman. — [London] ([13 Blithfield St., W.8]) : [Hilary Press], [1977]. — [1],28p ; 24cm.
Sd : £0.10
(B77-18961)

Jay, Peter. Lifelines : poems / by Peter Jay. — Edinburgh (14 Greenhill Place, Edinburgh 10) : Malcolm Rutherford for SATIS, 1977. — [2], 22p ; 21cm.
Limited ed. of 300 numbered copies.
Sd : £0.40
(B77-34038)

Jennings, Elizabeth. Consequently I rejoice / [by] Elizabeth Jennings. — Manchester : Carcanet Press, 1977. — 70p ; 23cm.
ISBN 0-85635-218-7 : £3.00
ISBN 0-85635-219-5 Pbk : £2.00
(B77-32820)

Johnson, Andy. Thought tracks out / [by] Andy Johnson. — [Kingston upon Thames] ([1 Rayleigh Court, Kingston upon Thames KT1 3NF]) : [Court Poetry Press], [1977]. — 15p ; 21cm.
ISBN 0-906010-05-5 Sd : £0.25
(B77-30575)

Johnstone, Robert. Our lives are Swiss / by Robert Johnstone. — Belfast (70 Eglantine Ave., Belfast BT9 6DY) : Ulsterman Publications, 1977. — 20p ; 22cm.
Sd : £0.20
(B77-17058)

Jones, Bramwell. Cadence notes : poems / by Bramwell Jones. — Swansea : C. Davies, 1977. — 24p ; 22cm. — (The Triskel poets ; 19)
Pbk : £0.60
(B77-23676)

Jones, Peter, *b.1929 (Apr.).* The garden end : new & selected poems / [by] Peter Jones. — Manchester : Carcanet New Press, 1977. — 116p ; 23cm.
ISBN 0-85635-170-9 : £2.90
(B77-29653)

Jones, Richard. Us / by Richard Jones. — Corby (10 Minden Close, Danesholme, Corby, Northants. NN18 9EW) : Excello & Bollard, [1977]. — [17]p ; 15cm.
ISBN 0-904339-46-7 Sd : £0.10
(B77-12057)

Jones, Richard, *b.1951.* Love suite : a poem / by Richard Jones. — Breakish : Aquila, 1976. — [16]p ; 21cm.
Also available in a limited ed. of 26 copies, signed and lettered by the author.
ISBN 0-7275-0156-9 Sd : £0.25
ISBN 0-7275-0157-7 Signed ed.: £1.25
(B77-15458)

Jones, Sally Roberts. Strangers and brothers : a radio poem / by Sally Roberts Jones. — Port Talbot (3 Crown St., Port Talbot, [W. Glam.]) : Alun Books, [1976]. — 18p ; 18cm.
Limited ed. of 500 numbered copies. — 'This poem was commissioned by BBC Wales, and was broadcast on April 4th, 1975' - p.3.
ISBN 0-9505643-0-3 Sd : £0.50
(B77-10916)

Jones, Thomas Henry. The collected poems of T. Harri Jones / edited and with an introduction by Julian Croft and Don Dale-Jones. — Llandysul : Gomer Press, 1977. — xix,267p ; 19cm.
Index. — Includes: The enemy in the heart - Songs of a mad prince - The beast at the door - The colour of cockcrowing.
ISBN 0-85088-412-8 : £3.50
(B77-21393)

Jowett, Sue. The Gnookaroos / [by] Sue Jowett ; illustrated by B.J. Blackmore and Sue Jowett. — Ilfracombe : Stockwell, 1976. — [8]p : col ill ; 19cm.
ISBN 0-7223-0977-5 Sd : £0.30
(B77-23677)

Kader, Noel M. Potpourri / [by] Noel M. Kader. — [Eastwood] ([165 Nottingham Rd, Eastwood, Notts. NG16 3GJ]) : [The author], [1977?]. — [3],18p : port ; 21cm.
Limited ed. of 150 numbered copies.
Sd : Unpriced
(B77-27329)

Kazantzis, Judith. Minefield / [by] Judith Kazantzis. — London : Sidgwick and Jackson, 1977. — [4],43p ; 23cm.
ISBN 0-283-98386-8 : £3.00
ISBN 0-283-98406-6 Pbk : £1.00
(B77-22084)

Kempson, David. Brain-bleed / by David Kempson. — Walton-on-Thames : Outposts Publications, 1977. — 20p ; 21cm.
Sd : £0.40
(B77-21394)

Kenedy, Robert Christopher. Six love poems / by R.C. Kenedy. — London ([16 Brookfield Rd, Bedford Park, W4 1DQ]) : Lugano Review for Dalmas and Ricour, 1977. — [10]p ; 30cm.
ISBN 0-9502642-1-0 Sd : £3.00
(B77-12058)

Kerr, J. A fern-clad comely kay / by J. Kerr. — London : Regency Press, 1977. — 32p ; 22cm.
Sd : Unpriced
(B77-27330)

King, Patrick. Still running / by Patrick King. — Belfast (70 Eglantine Ave., Belfast BT9 6DY) : Ulsterman Publications, 1977. — 23p ; 22cm.
Sd : £0.20
(B77-17059)

King, Peter John. A secret tear / [by] Peter J. King. — London (c/o Consortium of London Presses, National Poetry Centre, 21 Earls Court Sq., S.W.5) : Tapocketa Press, 1976. — 47p ; 21cm.
ISBN 0-905687-00-0 Pbk : £0.40
(B77-03737)

Knight, John, *b.1906.* Adam's Eve : poems / by John Knight ; illustrations by Jill Lewin. — St Ives, Cornwall (Goonhilly, St Ives, Cornwall) : Michael Snow, [1976]. — [16]p : ill ; 30cm.
Limited ed. of 200 numbered copies. — Three sheets ([3]leaves : ill.) in pocket.
ISBN 0-9505600-0-6 Sd : £2.00
(B77-09223)

Knopp, Ben. Evolution, strong delusion : a poem / by Ben Knopp. — Eastbourne (Fingella, 1 Hillside, East Dean, Eastbourne, E. Sussex BN20 0HE) : The author, 1977. — [1], 6p ; 21cm.
Sd : Unpriced
(B77-33405)

Krapf, Norbert. Song of the music stand / [by] Norbert Krapf. — Knotting : Sceptre Press, [1977]. — [7]p ; 21cm.
Limited ed. of 150 numbered copies, of which nos 1-50 are signed by the poet.
Sd : Unpriced
Signed ed. : Unpriced
(B77-32821)

Kuhner, Herbert. Broadsides & pratfalls / by Herbert Kuhner. — London (23 Fitzwarren Gardens, N19 3TR) : Menard Press, [1977]. — 48p ; 22cm.
ISBN 0-903400-15-4 Pbk : £0.75
(B77-11384)

Laing, Ronald David. Do you love me? : an entertainment in conversation and verse / [by] R.D. Laing. — Harmondsworth [etc.] : Penguin, 1977. — [4],60p ; 19cm.
Also published: London : Allen Lane, 1977. — Originally published: New York : Pantheon Books, 1976.
ISBN 0-14-004087-0 Pbk : £0.50
(B77-22085)

Laing, Ronald David. Do you love me? : an entertainment in conversation and verse / [by] R.D. Laing. — London : Allen Lane, 1977. — [4],60p ; 23cm.
Originally published: New York : Pantheon Books, 1976.
ISBN 0-7139-0995-1 : £2.50
(B77-21395)

Lark, Catherine. Fervour and fun / [by] Catherine Lark. — Ilfracombe : Stockwell, 1977. — 72p ; 15cm.
ISBN 0-7223-1069-2 : £1.35
(B77-34039)

Law, T S. A pryle o aces / [by] T.S. Law. — Larkhall (Blackwood Cottage, The Marlage, By Larkhall, Strathclyde, Scotland) : Fingerpost Publications, 1977. — [5],33p ; 21cm.
Sd : £1.00
(B77-25173)

Lawson, Ada East. The stars were bright / by Ada Lawson. — Walton-on-Thames : Outposts Publications, 1977. — 12p ; 21cm.
Sd : £0.30
(B77-21396)

Lee, Robin. The view from John Keats / by Robin Lee. — Walton-on-Thames : Outposts Publications, 1977. — 44p ; 21cm.
Sd : £1.00
(B77-22086)

Lehmann, Pauline M. The collected poetry of Pauline M. Lehmann. — London : Regency Press, 1976. — 32p ; 19cm.
ISBN 0-7212-0483-x Sd : Unpriced
(B77-09907)

Leisk, Ronald. Poems of a practical mystic / [by] Ronald Leisk. — Ilfracombe : Stockwell, 1977. — 40p ; 15cm.
ISBN 0-7223-1026-9 : £1.35
(B77-23678)

Lester, Paul. A funny brand of freedom / [by] Paul Lester. — Birmingham (Tower St., Birmingham B19 3UY) : Arts Lab Press, 1975. — [12]p ; 22cm.
Sd : £0.30
(B77-32130)

Lewis-Smith, Anne. Dinas Head, and other places / [by] Anne Lewis-Smith. — London : Mitre Press, 1977. — 64p ; 20cm.
ISBN 0-7051-0261-0 : £1.60
(B77-23679)

Lindley, John. Pacific envelope / [by] John Lindley. — Stockport (19 All Saints Rd, Heaton Norris, Stockport [Cheshire]) : The author, 1976. — [41]p ; 22cm.
ISBN 0-9505534-0-9 Sd : £0.35
(B77-07564)

Lindop, Grevel. Fools' paradise / [by] Grevel Lindop. — Manchester : Carcanet New Press, 1977. — 64p ; 23cm.
ISBN 0-85635-215-2 : £2.00
(B77-20542)

Lindsay, Maurice. Walking without an overcoat : poems, 1972-6 / [by] Maurice Lindsay. — London : Hale, 1977. — 48p ; 19cm.
ISBN 0-7091-6160-3 : £2.50
(B77-20543)

Livingstone, Felicity. From pocket to pavement / by Felicity Livingstone. — Walton-on-Thames : Outposts Publications, 1977. — 48p ; 21cm.
Sd : £1.00
(B77-22817)

Lloyd, Theodora. Song of the iron hoop (and other poems) / by Theodora Lloyd. — Llandysul : Gomer Press, 1976. — 77p ; 22cm.
ISBN 0-85088-400-4 Pbk : £1.00
(B77-05612)

Lloyd-Bedford, Patrick. Sebastian Melmoth, and other poems / [by] Patrick Lloyd-Bedford. — London : Mitre Press, 1977. — 64p ; 20cm.
ISBN 0-7051-0259-9 : £1.60
(B77-34040)

Lobban, Mabel. The sleeping beauty in verse / [by] Mabel Lobban ; illustrated by Cora E.M. Paterson. — Ilfracombe : Stockwell, 1977. — 16p : ill ; 19cm.
ISBN 0-7223-1047-1 Sd : £0.35
(B77-31411)

Logan, Chris. The day moves / [by] Chris Logan. — Horsham : Causeway Press, 1977. — 26p ; 20cm.
Limited ed. of 75 numbered copies.
Sd : £0.50
(B77-21397)

Logue, Christopher. Abecedary / verse by Christopher Logue ; pictures by Bert Kitchen. — London : Cape, 1977. — [40]p : ill, ports ; 26cm.
ISBN 0-224-01562-1 : £2.50 : CIP rev.
(B77-24444)

Longville, Tim. Between the river and the sea / [by] Tim Longville. — [Lincoln] : Grosseteste Press, 1976. — 14,[1]p ; 22cm.
Limited ed. of 300 copies of which the first 30 were signed by the author. — '... also issued as "Grosseteste Review", Vol.9, no.5' - colophon.
ISBN 0-901597-50-3 Sd : £0.30
(B77-12059)

Longville, Tim. To intimate distance / [by] Tim Longville. — [Pensnett] : Grosseteste Press, 1976. — 38,[1]p ; 22cm.
Limited ed. of 300 copies of which the first 30 were signed by the author. — '... also issued as a part of "Grosseteste Review", Vol.9, no.2' - colophon.
ISBN 0-901597-49-x Sd : £0.40
(B77-00380)

Longwill, James. A man's jacket / [by James Longwill]. — Newcastle upon Tyne : Pig Press, 1977. — [16]p ; 21cm.
Limited ed. of 200 numbered copies.
ISBN 0-903997-29-0 Sd : Unpriced
(B77-28055)

Love is helpless / by a non-poet. — Exeter (105 Fore St., Exeter, Devon) : Exeter Publishing, 1976. — [52]p ; 22cm.
ISBN 0-905780-01-9 Sd : £0.60
(B77-05042)

Loveday, John, *b.1926.* Particularities / [by] John Loveday. — Berkhamsted ([37 Lombardy Drive, Berkhamsted, Herts.]) : Priapus Press, 1977. — [11]p ; 21cm.
Limited ed. of 160 copies of which 40 are signed and numbered by the author.
Sd : £0.25
Signed ed.: £0.70
(B77-18962)

Lund, Harry. Light 'n shade / [by] Harry Lund. — Ilfracombe : Stockwell, 1977. — 24p ; 19cm.
ISBN 0-7223-1044-7 : £1.25
(B77-33406)

McCarthy, Ulli. Intra Venus songs / [by] Ulli McCarthy. — Todmorden : Arc Publications, 1976. — [23]p ; 19cm.
Limited ed. of 200 copies of which 15 are signed and numbered by the author.
ISBN 0-902771-59-0 Sd : £0.30
ISBN 0-902771-60-4 Signed ed. : £1.00
(B77-00381)

McCarthy, Ulli. Triptych / [by] Ulli McCarthy. — Newcastle upon Tyne : Pig Press, 1977. — [18]leaves ; 29cm.
Limited ed. of 200 copies.
ISBN 0-903997-26-6 Sd : Unpriced
(B77-28056)

McCorkindale, William Ferguson. Poems / by Bill McCorkindale ; in aid of Oxfam. — Aberdeen (171 Victoria Rd, Aberdeen) : Rainbow Books, 1976. — Folder([6])p ; 21cm.
'No.3'.
ISBN 0-9503025-6-2 : £0.10
(B77-05613)

McFadden, Roy. Verifications / [by] Roy McFadden. — Belfast : Blackstaff Press, 1977. — [6],40,[1]p ; 22cm.
ISBN 0-85640-112-9 Pbk : £1.75
(B77-25174)

McGee, Shelagh. Smile please ; [and, Witches] / by Shelagh McGee. — London : Robson Books, 1976. — [56]p : ill(chiefly col) ; 20cm.
Bound tête-bêche. — Ill., col. ill. on lining papers.
ISBN 0-903895-82-x : £1.50
(B77-00925)

MacGregor, Bryan. The stillness in the heart / by Bryan MacGregor. — Breakish : Aquila, 1976. — [2],21p ; 21cm.
Also available in a limited ed. of 26 copies, signed and lettered by the author.
ISBN 0-7275-0182-8 Sd : £0.40
ISBN 0-7275-0183-6 Signed ed.: £1.50
(B77-15459)

Machin, Norman. Watching and waiting / by Norman Machin. — Walton-on-Thames : Outposts Publications, 1977. — 16p ; 21cm.
Sd : £0.35
(B77-21398)

McKay, C G. The algebraist, and other poems / by C.G. McKay. — Edinburgh ([137 Warrender Park Rd, Edinburgh EH9 1DS]) : Tragara Press, 1977. — 15p ; 21cm.
Limited ed. of 100 numbered copies, of which nos 1-25 have been printed on Barcham Green Canterbury hand-made paper.
ISBN 0-902616-35-8 Sd : £1.50
(B77-24445)

McKinley, Hugh. Star-music : (heard in Párnassus and Pindus Mountains, August 1973) / by Hugh McKinley. — Bakewell : Hub Publications, 1976. — [3],23p ; 21cm.
ISBN 0-905049-25-x Sd : £0.60
(B77-14386)

McKinley, Hugh. The transformation of Faust, and other poems / [by] Hugh McKinley. — Ipswich (3 Cambridge Drive, Ipswich IP2 9EP) : Golgonooza Press, 1977. — 28p,plate : 1 ill ; 23cm.
ISBN 0-903880-15-6 Sd : £0.90
(B77-14387)

Maclean, Alasdair. Waking the dead / by Alasdair Maclean. — London : Gollancz, 1976. — 80p ; 22cm. — (Gollancz poets)
ISBN 0-575-02203-5 Pbk : £2.95
(B77-00382)

McLeod, Edward. Magnolia / by Edward McLeod. — Corby : Excello and Bollard, 1977. — [19]p ; 27cm.
ISBN 0-904339-59-9 Sd : Unpriced
(B77-23680)

MacMiàdhachain, Pádraig. The secret door : poems / by Pádraig MacMiàdhachain. — Swanage (4 Arcade Terrace, Swanage, Dorset) : Macintyre Saul Publications, 1977. — 54,[3]p ; 18cm.
ISBN 0-9505888-0-6 Sd : £1.25
(B77-25849)

Magee, Wes. Creature of the bay : set of poems / by Wes Magee. — Kingston upon Thames ([1 Rayleigh Court, Kingston upon Thames, Surrey KT1 3NF]) : Court Poetry Press, 1977. — 12p ; 21cm.
Limited ed. of 100 copies of which 26 have been lettered A-Z, signed and dated.
ISBN 0-906010-01-2 Sd : £0.25
Signed ed. : Unpriced
(B77-33407)

Magee, Wes. Reptile rhymes / [written by Wes Magee ; illustrated by Peter Barnfield]. — Bristol (15 Ladman Rd, Bristol [BS14 8QH]) : Xenia Press, 1977. — Folder([4]p) : col ill ; 28cm.
ISBN 0-9502843-6-x : £0.20
(B77-13837)

Mahon, Derek. Light music / by Derek Mahon. — Belfast (70 Eglantine Ave., Belfast BT9 6DY) : Ulsterman Publications, 1977. — 23p ; 22cm.
Sd : £0.20
(B77-16573)

Maillard, Phil. A North American journal / [by] Phil Maillard. — Cardiff (20 Newfoundland Ave., Cardiff CF4 3LA) : Blackweir Press, 1976. — [2],14,[1]leaves : ill ; 30cm.
Limited ed. of 300 copies.
ISBN 0-905686-00-4 Sd : £0.50
(B77-01771)

Mallin, Rupert. Audrey ribbons : poems / by Rupert Mallin. — Pyle (83 Pyle Inn Way, Pyle Bridgend, M. Glam.) : Speed Limit Publications, 1977. — [13]p ; 26cm. — (Speed Limit booklet ; 14)
Sd : £0.15
(B77-30576)

Mann, Hilda. The collected poetry of Hilda Mann. — London : Regency Press, [1976]. — 32p ; 20cm.
Sd : £0.60
(B77-00926)

Manning, Elfrida. Growing tall / [by] Elfrida Manning. — Southampton (48 Alma Rd, Southampton) : Advent Books, 1977. — 3-23p ; 22cm. — (Advent poem ; no.11)
Limited ed. of 100 copies.
Sd : £1.20
(B77-28057)

Manning, Hugo. Dylan Thomas : a poem / by Hugo Manning ; with linocuts by Paul Peter Piech. — London : Enitharmon Press, 1977. — 37p : col ill ; 23cm.
Limited ed. of 550 copies of which 50 are signed by the author and artist.
ISBN 0-901111-93-7 : £3.50
(B77-26482)

Marks-Smith, Harrison. If you have a standpoint / by Harrison M. Smith. — Walton-on-Thames : Outposts Publications, 1977. — 18p ; 21cm.
Sd : £0.50
(B77-28849)

Marriage, Alwyn. Beautiful man / by Alwyn Marriage. — Walton-on-Thames : Outposts Publications, 1977. — 36p ; 21cm.
Sd : £0.90
(B77-30577)

Marshall Douglas. Upstair neighbours / by Douglas Marshall. — Belfast (70 Eglantine Ave., Belfast BT9 6DY) : Ulsterman Publications, 1977. — 16p ; 22cm.
'"Office of Solitude" is a version of "Offici de Solitud" by the Catalan poet, Francesc Parcerisas' - p.16.
Sd : £0.20
(B77-17060)

Martin, Tony, *b.1933.* A week is too long / by Tony Martin. — Bridgend (83 Pyle Inn Way, Pyle, Bridgend, M. Glam.) : Speed Limit Publications, 1977. — [16]p ; 21cm. — (Speed Limit booklet ; no.8)
Sd : £0.15
(B77-26483)

Mary Agnes, *Sister.* A world of stillness / [by] Sister Mary Agnes. — Gloucester : Thornhill Press, 1976. — [35]p ; 20cm.
ISBN 0-904110-50-8 Sd : £0.60
(B77-14388)

Massey, Ephraim. Poems / by Ephraim Massey ; illustrated by Abraham Bazak. — Edinburgh ([137 Warrender Park Rd, Edinburgh EH9 1DS]) : Tragara Press, 1977. — 43p,plate : ill ; 21cm.
Limited ed. of 200 copies of which 26 are on Barcham Green hand-made paper, lettered A-Z and signed by the author and artist. The remainder are numbered 27-200.
ISBN 0-902616-34-x Pbk : Unpriced
(B77-24446)

Mathews, Aidan Carl. Windfalls / [by] Aidan Carl Mathews. — Dublin : Dolmen Press, 1977. — 42,[1]p ; 22cm.
ISBN 0-85105-325-4 Pbk : £2.50
(B77-31412)

Matthews, Paul. Blank walls / [by] Paul Matthews. — London (18 Hayes Court, New Park Rd, SW2 4EX) : Aloes Books, 1973. — [35]p : 2 ill ; 21cm.
Limited ed. of 220 copies. — Ill. tipped in.
ISBN 0-85652-011-x Sd : £0.50
(B77-00927)

Matthias, John. Two poems / [by] John Matthias. — Knotting : Sceptre Press, [1977]. — [7]p ; 21cm.
Limited ed. of 150 numbered copies of which the first 50 are signed.
Sd : £0.95
Signed ed. : £4.95
(B77-16022)

Mays, John Barron. Nicer than humans / [by] John Barron Mays ; cover by Angela Mays. — London (14 Barlby Rd, W10 6AR) : Autolycus Publications, 1977. — 19p ; 21cm.
ISBN 0-903413-17-5 Sd : £0.75
(B77-14883)

Mengham, Rod. Beds of scrapings : prose / by Rod Mengham. — Horsham : Causeway Press, 1977. — [21]p ; 20cm.
Limited ed. of 250 numbered copies.
Sd : £0.60
(B77-21399)

Merchant, William Moelwyn. Breaking the code / [by] Moelwyn Merchant. — [Llandyssul] : Gomer Press, 1975. — 3-58p,[4]p of plates : ill ; 25cm.
ISBN 0-85088-327-x Pbk : £1.00
(B77-00928)

Metz, Barbara Treadwell. Wishes and dreams / [by] Barbara Treadwell Metz. — Ilfracombe : Stockwell, 1977. — 16p ; 15cm.
ISBN 0-7223-1053-6 Pbk : £0.30
(B77-31413)

Middleton, Christopher. Eight elementary inventions / [by] Christopher Middleton. — Knotting : Sceptre Press, 1977. — [7]p ; 21cm.
Limited ed. of 150 numbered copies of which nos 1-50 are signed by the poet.
ISBN 0-7068-0338-8 Sd : £0.95
ISBN 0-7068-0339-6 Signed ed. : £5.25
(B77-09224)

Miller, David, *b.1950.* The preparation : consisting of The preparation / by David Miller. And, Upon unruled wrapper / by Allen Fisher. — London ([12 Kings Court, King St., W.6]) : X Press, 1977. — [13]leaves ; 30cm.
Sd : £0.40
(B77-19613)

Miller, Lanette Bradford. Mid-day / by Lanette Bradford Miller. — Walton-on-Thames : Outposts Publications, 1977. — [3],52p ; 22cm.
Pbk : £1.50
(B77-32822)

Milligan, Spike. Poems [of] Spike Milligan / drawings [by] Dante Gabriel Rossetti. — Leicester (78 Cambridge St., Leicester) : New Broom Private Press, 1977. — [21]p : ill ; 20cm.
Limited ed. of 140 numbered copies.
ISBN 0-901870-29-3 Sd : £3.50
(B77-26484)

Milne, Ewart. Cantata under Orion / [by] Ewart Milne. — Breakish : Aquila, 1976. — 54p ; 22cm. — (Aquila poetry)
Also available in limited ed. of 25 copies, signed and numbered by the author.
ISBN 0-7275-0141-0 : £2.50
ISBN 0-7275-0143-7 Pbk : £1.25
ISBN 0-7275-0142-9 Signed ed. : £4.20
(B77-08528)

Milne, John Clark. Poems / [by] John C. Milne. — Aberdeen : Aberdeen University Press, 1976. — 168p ; 22cm.
This collection originally published: 1963.
ISBN 0-900015-35-7 Pbk : £2.00
(B77-11385)

Mitchell, Adrian. The annotated 'Out loud' / by Adrian Mitchell. — 1st annotated ed. — London (14 Talacre Rd, NW5 3PE) : Writers and Readers Publishing Cooperative, 1976. — [79]p : ill, facsims ; 22cm.
Previous ed. published: as 'Out loud'. London : Cape Goliard, 1969.
ISBN 0-904613-33-x Pbk : £1.00
(B77-09908)

Mole, John. The mortal room / [by] John Mole. — Berkhamsted ([37 Lombardy Drive, Berkhamsted, Herts.]) : Priapus Press, 1977. — [7]p ; 21cm. — (Priapus poets)
Limited ed. of 160 copies, of which 40 are numbered and signed by the poet.
ISBN 0-905448-06-5 Sd : £0.25
ISBN 0-905448-07-3 Signed ed. : £0.60
(B77-09909)

Mole, John. Our ship / [by] John Mole. — London : Secker and Warburg, 1977. — 62p ; 23cm.
ISBN 0-436-28450-2 : £2.90
(B77-10531)

Montague, John. Poisoned lands / [by] John Montague. — New ed. — Dublin : Dolmen Press ; London : Oxford University Press, 1977. — 63p ; 21cm.
Previous ed.: published as 'Poisoned lands and other poems'. London : MacGibbon and Kee, 1961.
ISBN 0-85105-319-x Pbk : £2.25
ISBN 0-19-211869-2 (Oxford University Press) : £2.25
(B77-17061)

Montgomery, Stuart. From 'Calypso' / [by] Stuart Montgomery. — Hasty ed. — Newcastle upon Tyne (24 Coquet Terrace, Heaton, Newcastle upon Tyne 6) : Pig Press, 1976. — [8]p : 2 ill ; 21cm.
Limited ed. of approximately 75 copies.
ISBN 0-903997-23-1 Sd : £0.20
(B77-03200)

Mooney, Maire. Golden Sundays / by Maire Mooney. — Walton-on-Thames : Outposts Publications, 1977. — 16p ; 21cm.
Sd : £0.35
(B77-29654)

Moore, George Albert. Collected sandwiches / [by] George A. Moore. — Pyle (83 Pyle Inn Way, Pyle, Bridgend, M. Glam.) : Speed Limit Publications, 1977. — [16]p ; 26cm. — (Speed Limit booklet ; 11)
'All the poems in this collection originally appeared in "Sandwiches", 1975-1977' - note.
Sd : £0.15
(B77-30578)

Morgan, Edwin. The new divan / [by] Edwin Morgan. — Manchester : Carcanet New Press, 1977. — 118p ; 23cm.
ISBN 0-85635-211-x : £3.00
ISBN 0-85635-212-8 Pbk : £2.00
(B77-16574)

Morgan, Robert. Voices in the dark : a verse play / by Robert Morgan. — Todmorden : Arc Publications, 1976. — [1],39p ; 23cm.
Limited ed. of 400 copies of which 175 are cloth bound and 15 are numbered and signed by the author. — Originally published: in 'Anglo-Welsh review'. Vol.17 (40).
ISBN 0-902771-56-6 : £2.00
ISBN 0-902771-55-8 Pbk : £0.60
(B77-22818)

Morland, Harold. Flowering reeds, and other poems / [by] Harold Morland. — Ambleside (Hill Top, Hawkshead Hill, Ambleside, Cumbria LA22 0PN) : The author, 1977. — 3-52p : ill ; 20cm.
Cover title: Flowering reeds.
ISBN 0-904803-04-x Sd : £0.40
(B77-07565)

Morland, Harold. With music ceasing / [by] Harold Morland. — Penzance (11 Parade St., Penzance, Cornwall) : Ark Press, 1975. — 55, [1]p : ill ; 25cm.
Limited ed. of 250 copies.
ISBN 0-904356-02-7 : Unpriced
(B77-19614)

Morris, Brian, *b.1930.* Tide race : poems / by Brian Morris. — Llandysul : Gomer Press, 1976. — 50p ; 22cm.
ISBN 0-85088-420-9 : £1.50
(B77-05614)

Morris, Tina. 850 / by Tina Morris. — Corby : Excello and Bollard, [1977]. — [16]p ; 16cm. — (E & B minibook ; no.9)
ISBN 0-904339-52-1 Sd : Unpriced
(B77-34042)

Morriss, Fred. My reflections / [by] Fred Morriss. — Ilfracombe : Stockwell, 1976. — 127p ; 19cm.
ISBN 0-7223-0963-5 : £1.95
(B77-25175)

Morwenna. A late harvest, and other poems / by Morwenna ; illustrated by Donald R. Rawe. — Padstow ([14 Market St.], Padstow, Cornwall) : Lodenek Press, 1976. — 48p : ill ; 21cm.
Index.
ISBN 0-902899-45-7 Sd : £0.35
(B77-13229)

Motion, Andrew. The pleasure steamers / [by] Andrew Motion. — Oxford (4 Benson Place, Oxford) : Sycamore Press, 1977. — Folder ([5]p) ; 21cm. — (Sycamore broadsheet ; 24)
ISBN 0-906003-00-8 : Unpriced
(B77-14389)

Mottram, Eric. Tunis / by Eric Mottram. — Sheffield (5 Ashgate Close, Sheffield S10 3DL) : Rivelin Press, 1977. — [1],15,[1]p ; 26cm.
Limited ed. of 200 copies, signed by the author and artist.
ISBN 0-904524-15-9 Sd : £0.40
(B77-18352)

Moxon, Robert. Spiegel / by Robert Moxon. — London [etc.] : Regency Press, 1977. — 32p ; 22cm.
Sd : £0.60
(B77-27331)

Muldoon, Paul. Mules / [by] Paul Muldoon. — London : Faber, 1977. — 3-59p ; 20cm.
ISBN 0-571-11077-0 Pbk : £1.95 : CIP rev.
(B77-10532)

Murray, Eleanor. The pulsing earth / by Eleanor Murray. — Walton-on-Thames : Outposts Publications, 1977. — 24p ; 21cm.
ISBN 0-7205-0509-7 Sd : £0.50
(B77-12060)

Musgrave, Susan. For Charlie Beaulieu in Yellowknife who told me go back to the South and write another poem about Indians / [by] Susan Musgrave. — Knotting : Sceptre Press, [1977]. — [4]leaves ; 21cm.
Limited ed. of 150 numbered copies of which the first 50 are signed by the author.
Sd : £0.95
Signed ed. : £5.00
(B77-15460)

Musgrave, Susan. Two poems for the blue moon / [by] Susan Musgrave. — Knotting : Sceptre Press, [1977]. — [4]leaves ; 21cm.
Limited ed. of 150 numbered copies, of which nos 1-50 are signed by the poet.
Sd : Unpriced
Signed ed. : Unpriced
(B77-32823)

Naphray, A R. Pyromania. — Wednesbury (2 Engine La., Wednesbury, West Midlands [WS10 8SA]) : 'Bavie' Publications.
Author: A.R. Naphray.
[No.1]. — 1976. — [24]leaves,[4]leaves of plates : ports ; 30cm.
ISBN 0-9505560-0-9 Pbk : £1.25
(B77-07566)

[No.2]. — 1976. — [17]leaves,[3]leaves of plates : ports ; 30cm.
ISBN 0-9505560-1-7 Pbk : £1.25
(B77-07567)

[No.3]. — 1976. — [17]leaves,[3]leaves of plates : ports ; 30cm.
ISBN 0-9505560-2-5 Pbk : £1.25
(B77-07568)

Neville, Frank. Mushrooms in the high grass / [by] Frank Neville. — Roscrea ([Roscrea, Co. Tipperary]) : Parkmore Press, 1977. — 36p ; 21cm.
Limited ed. of 200 signed and numbered copies.

Sd : Unpriced
(B77-28058)

Nicholson, Norman. Cloud on Black Combe / [by] Norman Nicholson. — Newcastle upon Tyne (24 Coquet Terrace, Heaton, Newcastle upon Tyne 6) : Pig Press, 1976. — [8]p : ill ; 21cm.
Limited ed. of approximately 75 copies. — '... produced to coincide with a reading by Norman Nicholson at the Colpitts Hotel, Durham on Thursday Oct. 14th 1976 at 7.30 p.m.' - p.[8]. — Originally published: Hitchin : Cellar Press, 1975.
ISBN 0-903997-17-7 Sd : £0.20
(B77-00383)

Nickl, Peter. The crocodile / [by] Peter Nickl, Binette Schroeder ; English verse by Christopher Logue. — London : Cape, 1976. — [26]p : chiefly col ill ; 27cm.
These illustrations originally published with German text. Hamburg : Nord-Sud Verlag, 1975.
ISBN 0-224-01330-0 : £3.50
(B77-01772)

Noiprox, Max. Maxims / by Max Noiprox. — Corby : Excello and Bollard, 1977. — 23p ; 16cm.
ISBN 0-904339-60-2 Sd : Unpriced
(B77-32824)

Nuttall, Jeff. Objects / [by] Jeff Nuttall. — London : Trigram Press, 1976. — [64]p ; 22cm.

Also available in limited cloth bound ed. of 200 copies of which 26 have been lettered and signed by the author.
ISBN 0-85465-045-8 Pbk : £1.50
ISBN 0-85465-047-4 Cased ed. : £2.75
ISBN 0-85465-046-6 Lettered and signed ed. : Unpriced
(B77-00384)

Ó Hehir, Diana. Summoned : poems / by Diana Ó Hehir. — Columbia ; London : University of Missouri Press, 1976. — 63p ; 21cm. — (A breakthrough book)
ISBN 0-8262-0204-7 : £4.50
(B77-14884)

O'Brien, Joy. The joyful stranger / by Joy O'Brien. — Bakewell : Hub Publications, 1977. — [3],12p ; 21cm.
ISBN 0-905049-36-5 Sd : £0.90
(B77-32825)

O'Connor, John, *b.1926.* From the edge of spring / [by] John O'Connor. — Dublin (Ballyboden, Dublin 14) : Good Counsel Press, [1977?]. — [2],iv,115p ; 21cm.
Pbk : £2.00
(B77-25850)

Officer, Sharon Diane. A quiet moment / [by] Sharon Diane Officer. — London [etc.] : Regency Press, 1977. — 32p ; 19cm.
Sd : £0.60
(B77-33408)

Oldham, Mary. My loves / [by] Mary Oldham. — Ilfracombe : Stockwell, 1977. — 24p ; 15cm.

Includes 1 poem in French.
ISBN 0-7223-1057-9 Sd : £0.30
(B77-25851)

Oliver, Colin. In the open : poems / [by] Colin Oliver ; drawings [by] Alex Rolfe. — Ipswich (Nacton, Ipswich) : Shollond Publications, [1977]. — 30p : ill ; 25cm.
Sd : Unpriced
(B77-17062)

O'Neill, Michael. The ever birds of space / by Michael O'Neill. — Corby : Excello and Bollard, 1977. — [24]p ; 16cm.
ISBN 0-904339-58-0 Sd : Unpriced
(B77-23681)

Oram, Neil. Beauty's shit / [by] Neil Oram. — [London] ([3 Lancaster Grove, N.W.3]) : Zum Zum Books, [1976]. — 85,[3]p ; 21cm.
ISBN 0-905194-02-0 Sd : £0.50
(B77-10533)

Orchard, William. Voices in the wind : an epic of Cornwall / by William Orchard ; with Vignettes by Ilene. — London [etc.] : Regency Press, 1977. — 72p : ill ; 23cm.
£2.00
(B77-28059)

Ormsby, Frank. A store of candles / [by] Frank Ormsby. — Oxford [etc.] : Oxford University Press, 1977. — viii,54p ; 22cm.
'Poetry Book Society choice' - cover.
ISBN 0-19-211870-6 Pbk : £1.95 : CIP rev.
(B77-28850)

Osbourn, H J L. Selected poems / by H.J.L. Osbourn. — Beckenham (84 High St., Beckenham, Kent BR3 1ED) : Welmont Publishing, 1977. — 92p : ill ; 21cm. — (The Welmont poets)
ISBN 0-905530-00-4 Pbk : £1.50
(B77-00385)

Osers, Ewald. Wish you were here : a sequence of holiday postcards / by Ewald Osers. — Bakewell (Youlgrave, Bakewell, Derbyshire) : Hub Publications Ltd, 1976. — [4],18,[1]p ; 21cm.
ISBN 0-905049-14-4 Sd : £0.75
(B77-03738)

Owen, Gari. Strawberry dust / by Gari Owen. — Bridgend (83 Pyle Inn Way, Pyle, Bridgend, Mid Glamorgan) : Speed Limit Publications, 1977. — [12]p ; 21cm. — (Speed Limit booklet ; 6)
Sd : £0.15
(B77-26485)

Owens, Philip, *b.1947.* To hymn the miracle / by Philip Owens. — Walton-on-Thames : Outposts Publications, 1977. — 24p ; 21cm.
Sd : £0.50
(B77-22087)

Oxley, William. Eve free / [by] William Oxley. — Knotting : Sceptre Press, 1974. — Fold sheet ([4]p) ; 11x15cm.
Limited ed. of 150 numbered copies, of which nos. 1-50 are signed by the poet.
Unpriced
Signed ed.: Unpriced
(B77-02555)

Oxley, William. Superficies / by William Oxley. — Breakish : Aquila, 1976. — 15p ; 21cm.
Also available in a limited ed. of 26 copies, signed and lettered by the author.
ISBN 0-7275-0158-5 Sd : £0.20
ISBN 0-7275-0159-3 Signed ed.: £1.25
(B77-15461)

Pain, Margaret. No dark legend / by Margaret Pain. — Bakewell : Hub Publications, 1977. — [2],21p ; 21cm.
ISBN 0-905049-16-0 Sd : £0.60
(B77-14390)

Parr, Stephen. Equinox : poems for a new year / by Stephen Parr ; illustrations by Heather Jackson. — Purley (3 Plough La., Purley, Surrey) : Aryatara Publications, 1976. — 39p : ill ; 25cm.
Limited ed. of 300 copies.
ISBN 0-9505644-0-0 Pbk : Unpriced
(B77-10917)

Parrett, Ray. Love's joys and sorrows / by Ray Parrett. — London ([12c Grange Court, Holly St., Queensbridge Rd, E8 3JD]) : Typographic Press, 1977. — [8]leaves ; 18cm.
Limited ed. of 40 copies.
Sd : Unpriced
(B77-26486)

Parry, Stephen. Twenty short poems / [by] Stephen Parry. — [London] (28 Shrewsbury Ave., S.W.14) : Polyptoton, 1977. — [5],18p ; 18cm.
Sd : £0.75
(B77-22088)

Patchett, John. Springtime in the High Street / by John Patchett. — Walton-on-Thames : Outposts Publications, 1977. — 16p ; 21cm.
Sd : £0.35
(B77-22089)

Paterson, Andrew Barton. The man from Snowy river / poem by A.B. Paterson ; illustrated by Annette Macarthur-Onslow. — Sydney ; London : Collins, 1977. — [32]p ; col ill ; 22x27cm.
ISBN 0-00-185025-3 : £2.95
(B77-25176)

Patten, Brian. The sly cormorant and the fishes : new adaptations into poetry of the Aesop fables / [by] Brian Patten ; illustrated by Errol Le Cain. — Harmondsworth : Kestrel Books, 1977. — 64p : ill(some col) ; 24cm.
ISBN 0-7226-5360-3 : £2.75
(B77-30579)

Patterson, Cyril. Thistledown 2 / [by] Cyril Patterson. — [Whitley Bay] : [Elpar Poem Productions] ; Consett (114 Greenways, Delves Lane, Consett, Co. Durham) : [Distributed by] the author, [1977]. — 40p ; 21cm.
ISBN 0-9505628-0-7 Sd : £0.50
(B77-10918)

Patterson, Cyril. Trust / [by] Cyril Patterson. — Corby (10 Minden Close, Danesholme, Corby, Northants. NN18 9EW) : Excello and Bollard, [1977]. — [17]p ; 15cm.
ISBN 0-904339-45-9 Sd : £0.10
(B77-12061)

Paulin, Tom. A state of justice / by Tom Paulin. — London : Faber, 1977. — 47p ; 20cm.
ISBN 0-571-10982-9 Pbk : £1.95
(B77-12062)

Penn, Prudence. Verses for children / [by] Prudence Penn ; illustrated by Cora E.M. Paterson. — Ilfracombe : Stockwell, 1977. — 32p : ill ; 18cm.
ISBN 0-7223-0979-1 Pbk : £0.45
(B77-10919)

Peskett, William. A killing in the grove / by William Peskett. — Belfast (70 Eglantine Ave., Belfast BT9 6DY) : Ulsterman Publications, 1977. — 16,[1]p ; 22cm.
Sd : £0.20
(B77-16575)

Phillips, Pam. This and that / by Pam Phillips. — [London] : T.L. Wood, 1977. — [20]p ; 26cm.
Sd : Unpriced
(B77-28851)

Pick, John Barclay. A small occasion for rejoicing / [by] J.B. Pick, Peter Pick ; cover Gene Pick. — Billesdon ([Billesdon, Leicester]) : Bay Tree, 1977. — [46]p ; 15cm.
Sd : Unpriced
(B77-28852)

Pilcher, Barry Edgar. Poem to Hagia Sophia / by Barry Edgar Pilcher ; [edited by David Miller]. — Neath Abbey (16 Rhydhir, Longford, Neath Abbey [W. Glam.]) : Cwm Nedd Press, 1977. — [10]p ; 22cm.
Sd : £0.25
(B77-30580)

Pitt, E M. Pathos and whimsey / [by] E.M. Pitt. — Ilfracombe : Stockwell, 1976. — 24p ; 15cm.
ISBN 0-7223-0976-7 Pbk : £0.30
(B77-10920)

Please, Keith. Black hole off Crete / [by] Keith Please. — Guildford ([22 Sydney Rd, Guildford GU1 3LL]) : Circle Press, 1977. — [3]p(3fold) : 1 col ill ; 30cm.
Limited ed. of 300 copies, of which nos 1-100 are signed.
Sd : £5.00
(B77-29655)

Pluckwell, George. Just life poems / by George Pluckwell. — Rowhedge (13 Head St., Rowhedge, Colchester, Essex) : Modern Poets, 1977. — [12]p ; 22cm.
ISBN 0-9504538-1-1 Sd : £0.25
(B77-12063)

Potts, Patricia. Seasons of life / [by] Patricia Potts. — Ilfracombe : Stockwell, 1977. — 24p ; 15cm.
ISBN 0-7223-1037-4 Pbk : £0.30
(B77-21400)

Powell, Neil, *b.1948.* At the edge / [by] Neil Powell. — Manchester : Carcanet New Press, 1977. — 61p ; 23cm.
ISBN 0-85635-214-4 : £2.00
(B77-18963)

Preston, Stanley. I dreamed I died / by Stanley Preston. — Manchester (35 Chatcombe Rd, Manchester M22 6RQ) : The author, 1977. — [1],32p ; 21cm.
Sd : £0.40
(B77-34043)

Price, David Watkin. And that was / [by] David Watkin Price. — Kingston upon Thames ([1 Rayleigh Court, Kingston upon Thames, Surrey KT1 3NF]) : Court Poetry Press, [1977]. — 23, [1]p ; 21cm.
ISBN 0-906010-02-0 Sd : £0.35
(B77-31414)

Pudney, John. Living in a one-sided house : poems / by John Pudney ; [illustrations by Toni Goffe]. — London : Shepheard-Walwyn, 1976. — 48p : ill ; 25cm.
ISBN 0-85683-032-1 : £2.75
(B77-04387)

Pugh, Sheenagh. Crowded by shadows : poems / by Sheenagh Pugh. — Swansea : C. Davies, 1977. — 32p ; 22cm. — (The Triskel poets ; 21)
Pbk : £0.75
(B77-23682)

Pulsford, Doris. Inner persuasions / [by] Doris Pulsford. — Hunton Bridge : Kit-Cat Press, 1977. — [24]p ; 22cm.
Limited ed. of 120 numbered copies.
Sd : £1.50
(B77-17063)

Purser, John. The counting stick / [by] John Purser. — Breakish : Aquila, 1976. — 46p ; 22cm. — (Aquila poetry)
Also available in a cloth bound ed. of 25 copies numbered and signed by the author.
ISBN 0-7275-0163-1 : £2.50
ISBN 0-7275-0162-3 Signed ed. : £4.20
ISBN 0-7275-0164-x Pbk : £1.25
(B77-09225)

Pyper, Betty. Visions : Christian poetry / [by] Betty Pyper. — Ilkeston : Moorley's Bible and Bookshop, [1977]. — 45p ; 21cm.
Index.
ISBN 0-86071-010-6 Sd : £0.45
(B77-34044)

Quenby, David C. Yesterday's prisoner / [by] David C. Quenby. — Ilfracombe : Stockwell, 1973. — 46p ; 15cm.
ISBN 0-7223-0399-8 : £1.65
(B77-31415)

Ramage, David. Anadyomene / by David Ramage. — Durham [etc.] (35 South St., Durham) : [The author], 1976. — Folder([3]p) ; 19cm.
Unpriced
(B77-26487)

Rathkey, William Arthur. Twenty five poems / by W.A. Rathkey. — London (15 Dungarvan Ave., S.W. 15) : Cock Robin Press, 1976. — [7] ,17,[1]p ; 20cm.
Limited ed. of 100 copies.
ISBN 0-9500594-6-3 Sd : Unpriced
(B77-00929)

Rawsterne, Mick. Bust / by Mick Rawsterne. — Corby (10 Minden Close, Danesholme, Corby, Northants. NN18 9EW) : Excello & Bollard, [1977]. — [21]p ; 15cm.
ISBN 0-904339-47-5 Sd : £0.10
(B77-12064)

Rawsterne, Mick. Luminous void / by Mick Rawsterne. — Corby : Excello and Bollard, 1977. — [18]p ; 31cm.
ISBN 0-904339-61-0 Sd : Unpriced
(B77-33409)

Rawsterne, Mick. Trade letter / by Mick Rawsterne and Zack Samuel. — Corby : Excello and Bollard, [1977]. — [16]p ; 22cm.
ISBN 0-904339-48-3 Sd : Unpriced
(B77-12615)

Read, David. More meditations of a common Catholic / by David Read. — [London] ([48 Howitt Rd, N.W.3]) : [The author], 1977. — [2],38p ; 21cm.
Sd : £0.60
(B77-31416)

Read, David. Rhymed reflections of a common Catholic / by David Read. — [London] ([48 Howitt Rd, Belsize Park, N.W.3]) : The author, 1976. — [2],42p ; 21cm.
ISBN 0-9505454-0-6 Sd : £0.50
(B77-03201)

Reading, Peter. Nothing for anyone / [by] Peter Reading. — London : Secker and Warburg, 1977. — 54p ; 23cm.
ISBN 0-436-40981-x : £2.90
(B77-28060)

Redgrove, Peter. The fortifiers, the vitrifiers and the witches / [by] Peter Redgrove. — Knotting : Sceptre Press, [1977]. — [7]p ; 21cm.
Limited ed. of 150 numbered copies, of which nos 1-50 are signed by the poet.
Sd : Unpriced
Signed ed. : Unpriced
(B77-32826)

Redgrove, Peter. From every chink of the ark, and other new poems / by Peter Redgrove. — London [etc.] : Routledge and Kegan Paul, 1977. — viii,268p ; 23cm.
ISBN 0-7100-8531-1 : £4.95 : CIP rev.
(B77-08025)

Redgrove, Peter. Skull event / [by] Peter Redgrove. — Knotting : Sceptre Press, 1977. — [3]leaves ; 21cm.
Limited ed. of 150 numbered copies, of which nos 1-50 are signed by the poet.
ISBN 0-7068-0342-6 Sd : £0.95
ISBN 0-7068-0343-4 Signed ed. : £4.95
(B77-09226)

Reed, Frances. Poems of the Highlands and Islands / [by] Frances Reed. — London : The author ; Ilfracombe : [Distributed by] Stockwell, 1977. — 46p ; 15cm.
ISBN 0-7223-1021-8 Pbk : Unpriced
(B77-23683)

Reed, Irene. Whinmoor breezes : poems / by Irene Reed. — Newcastle-on-Tyne (6 Whinmoor Place, Cowgate, Newcastle-on-Tyne NE5 3BA) : The author, 1976. — [2],16,[1]p ; 16cm.
Limited ed. of 210 copies.
ISBN 0-9505474-0-9 Sd : Unpriced
(B77-03202)

Reed, Jeremy. Count Bluebeard / by Jeremy Reed. — Breakish : Aquila, 1976. — 23p ; 21cm.
Also available in limited ed. of 26 copies, signed and lettered by the author.
ISBN 0-7275-0160-7 Sd : £0.30
ISBN 0-7275-0161-5 Signed ed. : £1.50
(B77-15462)

Reed, Jeremy. The isthmus of Samuel Greenberg / [by] Jeremy Reed. — London : Trigram Press, 1976. — [48]p : port ; 22cm. — (A botulus book)
Limited ed. of 256 copies of which 26 lettered copies are signed by the author.
ISBN 0-85465-043-1 Pbk : £1.25
ISBN 0-85465-044-x Signed ed. : £3.50
(B77-00930)

Robbins, Jon. The way it goes / [by] Jon Robbins. — Weymouth (186 Newstead Rd, Weymouth, Dorset DT4 0DY) : Word and Action (Dorset), 1977. — [2],17,[1]p ; 21cm. — (Poets in Dorset ; 4)
Sd : £0.50
(B77-18353)

Roberts, George. Whispering hopes of self expression / by George Roberts. — [Tunstall] ([7 Queen's Ave., The Boulevard, Tunstall, Staffs.]) : [The author], 1977. — [7],88[i.e.99]p : 1 ill ; 21cm.
Sd : £0.88
(B77-31417)

Robinett, Jane. First letter to Fairbanks, Alaska / [by] Jane Robinett. — Knotting : Sceptre Press, [1977]. — [7]p ; 21cm.
Limited ed. of 150 numbered copies of which the first 50 are signed.
Sd : £0.95
Signed ed.: £4.95
(B77-16023)

Rose, Charles. Pomes dad did / by Charles Rose ; illustrations by Leon Olin and Sylvia Gainsford. — Canterbury ([79 Northgate, Canterbury, Kent]) : Hawthorn Publications, [1977?]. — [53]p : ill(some col) ; 21cm.
Pbk : £0.70
(B77-18354)

Rosen, Michael. Wouldn't you like to know / words by Michael Rosen ; pictures by Quentin Blake. — London : Deutsch, 1977. — 3-95p : ill ; 22cm.
ISBN 0-233-96902-0 : £2.50
(B77-19615)

Ross, Andrew Christie Gordon. A mixed bag of golfing verse / by A.C. Gordon Ross. — Glasgow : Brown and Ferguson, 1977. — 83p ; 19cm.
ISBN 0-85174-291-2 Pbk : £1.35
(B77-28853)

Rothwell, Elizabeth. Brown smoke and dark amber / [by] Elizabeth Rothwell. — [Lincoln] : Grosseteste Press, 1976. — 23,[1]p ; 23cm.
Limited ed. of 300 copies of which the first 30 were signed by the poet and contained an additional hand-written poem by her. — '... also issued as "Grosseteste Review", vol.9, no.3' - title page verso.
ISBN 0-901597-51-1 Sd : £0.40
(B77-12065)

Rowe, Albert. St Ives boy's summer : poems / by Albert Rowe. — Breakish : Aquila, 1977. — 23p ; 21cm.
Also available in limited ed. of 26 copies, signed and lettered by the author.
ISBN 0-7275-0184-4 Sd : £0.30
ISBN 0-7275-0185-2 Signed ed. : £1.50
(B77-15463)

Rowe, Tony. Nor time reality : twenty seven poems / by Tony Rowe. — London : Mitre Press, 1977. — 32p ; 19cm.
ISBN 0-7051-0265-3 : £1.60
(B77-33410)

Sarat. Sisera's child / by Sarat ; illustrations by R. Burrows. — London (43 New Oxford St., W.C.1.) : The Caduceus Press, 1976. — 71p : ill ; 19cm.
ISBN 0-7212-0475-9 Pbk : £1.00
(B77-03203)

Schmidt, Michael. My brother Gloucester : new poems / [by] Michael Schmidt. — Cheadle : Carcanet Press, 1976. — 64p ; 22cm.
Also published: Chester Springs, Pa : Dufour Editions, 1976.
ISBN 0-85635-189-x Pbk : £1.90
(B77-03739)

Scott, Eddie. Freezing in the heat / by Eddie Scott. — [Ipswich] ([11 Ashcroft Rd, Ipswich, Suffolk]) : [The author], 1976. — [5],51p ; 19cm.
ISBN 0-9505539-0-5 : £1.95
(B77-05615)

Scupham, Peter. The hinterland / [by] Peter Scupham. — Oxford [etc.] : Oxford University Press, 1977. — vi,58p ; 22cm.
ISBN 0-19-211871-4 Pbk : £1.95
(B77-28854)

Seabrooke, Alan. Random choice / [by] Alan Seabrooke. — Ipswich (3 Friars St., Ipswich) : The Calver Press, 1977. — [2],65p ; 18cm.
Sd : £0.95
(B77-21401)

Seaton, Meg. The far side of Eden / by Meg Seaton. — London (Agincourt Rd, N.W.3) : Fleet Community Education Centre, [1977]. — 24p ; 21cm.
ISBN 0-9505895-0-0 Sd : £0.40
(B77-29656)

Seed, John. Spaces in / [by] John Seed. — Newcastle upon Tyne : Pig Press, 1977. — 20p : 1 ill ; 21cm.
Limited ed. of 200 numbered copies.
ISBN 0-903997-28-2 Sd : Unpriced
(B77-34045)

Sethi, Zaid Sarwar. Solitude : poems on life and love / by Zaid Sarwar Sethi. — [London] ([85 Emmanuel Rd, S.W.12]) : [The author], 1977. — [1],39p ; 21cm.
Sd : £1.00
(B77-26488)

Shaw, John, *b.1916.* The collected poetry of John Shaw. — London [etc.] : Regency Press, 1977. — 32p ; 19cm.
ISBN 0-7212-0492-9 Sd : Unpriced
(B77-15464)

Shepherd, Bill. The Antonine poems / [by] Bill Shepherd. — [London] (40 Walford Rd, N.16) : The Many Press, [1976]. — [22]p ; 21cm.
Limited ed. of 100 copies.
Sd : £0.30
(B77-16576)

Sherman, Bill. Mermaids / [by] Bill Sherman. — Hove (6 Davigdor Rd, Hove, Sussex) : X Press, 1977. — [16]leaves ; 30cm.
Pbk : £0.30
(B77-32827)

Shore, Henry. Room 98 / by Henry Shore. — Walton-on-Thames : Outposts Publications, 1977. — 56p ; 21cm.
Pbk : £1.00
(B77-23684)

Sillitoe, Alan. Day-dream communiqué / [by] Alan Sillitoe. — Knotting : Sceptre Press, [1977]. — [7]p ; 21cm.
Limited ed. of 150 numbered copies of which nos 1-50 are signed by the poet.
Sd : Unpriced
(B77-31418)

Sills-Docherty, Jonathan. From bottoms to tops and back again : too late roles for erogenous and other zones ... / by Jonathan Sills-Docherty. — Manchester (43 Cornbrook Park Rd, Old Trafford, Manchester M15 4EH) : The author, 1977. — [6]p34p ; 21cm.
Sd : Unpriced
(B77-34046)

Sills-Docherty, Jonathan. Words on paper / by Jonathan Sills-Docherty. — Manchester (43 Cornbrook Park Rd, Old Trafford, Manchester M15 4EH) : The author, 1977. — 20p ; 21cm.
Sd : Unpriced
(B77-27332)

Simmons, James. Judy Garland and the cold war / [by] James Simmons. — Belfast : Blackstaff Press, 1976. — [4],59p ; 22cm.
ISBN 0-85640-106-4 Pbk : £1.75
(B77-06255)

Simms, Colin. Voices / [by] Colin Simms. — London ([40 Walford Rd, N.16]) : Many Press, 1977. — [24]p ; 21cm.
'The cover is a silkscreen print by Steve Herne' - note. — Limited ed. of 200 numbered copies of which nos 1-15 have been signed by the poet and artist.
Sd : £0.75
(B77-24447)

Simpson, John Gregory. Colours of springtime : poems / [by] John G. Simpson. — [Ilkeston] : [Moorley's Bible and Bookshop], [1977]. — 16p ; 21cm.
Index.
Sd : Unpriced
(B77-22090)

Simpson, John Gregory. Ilkeston at yuletime : poems of local scenes and recollections / by John G. Simpson. — [Ilkeston] ([366 Nottingham Rd, Ilkeston, Derbyshire DE7 5BN]) : [The author], [1976]. — [1],11p ; 21cm.
ISBN 0-9504658-2-8 Sd : £0.20
(B77-05043)

Sinclair, Iain. The penances / [by] Iain Sinclair. — London (40 Walford Rd, N16 8ED) : The Many Press, 1977. — [20]p : ill ; 21cm.
Limited ed. of 200 copies.
Sd : £0.60
(B77-26489)

Singer, Burns. Selected poems [of] Burns Singer / edited by Anne Cluysenaar. — Manchester : Carcanet New Press, 1977. — xxiii,122p ; 23cm.
ISBN 0-85635-177-6 : £2.90
(B77-26490)

Skelton, Robin. Three poems / [by] Robin Skelton. — Knotting : Sceptre Press, [1977]. — [7]p ; 21cm.
Limited ed. of 150 numbered copies of which the first 50 are signed.
Sd : £0.95
Signed ed. : £5.25
(B77-16024)

Smallshaw, Judith. Copper farthings / by Judith Smallshaw. — Walton-on-Thames : Outposts Publications, 1977. — 32p ; 21cm.
Sd : £0.70
(B77-22819)

Smart, Elizabeth. A bonus / [by] Elizabeth Smart. — London (21 Formosa St., W.9) : Polytantric Press, 1977. — 55p ; 21cm.
ISBN 0-905150-01-5 Pbk : £1.95
(B77-11386)

Smith, Iain Crichton. In the middle / [by] Iain Crichton Smith. — London : Gollancz, 1977. — 64p ; 22cm. — (Gollancz poets)
ISBN 0-575-02227-2 Pbk : £2.95
(B77-24448)

Smith, Tom. A countryman's view / [by] Tom Smith. — Ilfracombe : Stockwell, 1976. — 24p ; 15cm.
ISBN 0-7223-0993-7 Pbk : £0.30
(B77-10921)

Sneyd, Steve. Two humps not one : poems / by Steve Sneyd. — Pyle (83 Pyle Inn Way, Pyle, Bridgend, M. Glam. CF33 6LP) : Speed Limit Publications, 1977. — [12]p ; 26cm. — (Speed Limit booklet ; 7)
Sd : £0.15
(B77-24449)

Spain, Mary. A quickening joy / [by] Mary Spain. — London : Broomsleigh Press, 1976. — 40p ; 19cm.
Index.
ISBN 0-904646-17-3 : £1.60
(B77-05616)

Stallybrass, Donald. Perseus : poems / by Donald Stallybrass. — Bakewell : Hub Publications, 1977. — [2],17p ; 21cm.
ISBN 0-905049-20-9 Sd : £0.60
(B77-14391)

Stanton, Harry. Intimate thoughts / [by] Harry Stanton. — Nottingham (42 Redland Grove, Carlton, Nottingham) : Carlton House Press, 1977. — vi,74p ; 18cm.
ISBN 0-906103-00-2 Pbk : Unpriced
(B77-28061)

Stapleton, Wilson. Trophies of empire : poems / by Wilson Stapleton. — Huddersfield (4 Nowell Place, Almondbury, Huddersfield HD5 8PS) : Hilltop Press, 1977. — [8],[1]leaves ; 31cm.
Sd : £0.25
(B77-26491)

Stathatos, John. Maps and tracings / [by] John Stathatos. — London (16 Haslemere Rd, N.8) : Oxus Press, 1976. — 15p ; 21cm.
Includes: Bombers. Originally published: Knotting : Sceptre Press, 1976 - December light, Cape Lizard. Originally published: Hitchin : Mandeville Press, 197-?.
ISBN 0-905501-00-4 Sd : £0.60
(B77-17721)

Steadman, Diane. Today my hands are ten years older / by Diane Steadman. — Bakewell : Hub Publications, 1977. — [2],17p ; 21cm.
ISBN 0-905049-27-6 Sd : £0.60
(B77-32828)

Stevens, Frank. Pony tales in verse / [words by] Frank Stevens & [illustrations by] Maureen Paul. — London [etc.] : White Lion Publishers, 1976. — 29p : col ill ; 25cm.
ISBN 0-85686-227-4 : £3.25
(B77-06256)

Stevens, Patrick. Declaration of independence / by Patrick Stevens ; edited by John Emuss. — Guildford (10 Ashcroft, Shalford, Guildford, Surrey) : Guildford Poets Press, 1976. — 32p ; 21cm.
ISBN 0-904673-04-9 Sd : £0.50
(B77-07569)

Stevenson, Anne. Cliff walk : a poem / by Anne Stevenson ; with a drawing by Anne Newnham. — Richmond, Surrey : Keepsake Press, 1977. — [4] leaves : 1 ill ; 24cm. — (Keepsake poem ; 30)
Limited ed. of 180 copies of which 12 are signed by the author and the artist.
Sd : Unpriced
Signed ed.: Unpriced
(B77-32131)

Stevenson, Anne. Enough of green / [by] Anne Stevenson. — Oxford [etc.] : Oxford University Press, 1977. — ix,44p ; 22cm.
ISBN 0-19-211874-9 Pbk : £2.25 : CIP rev.
(B77-20544)

Stinton, Judith. Owl house / by Judith Stinton ; illustrated by Philip Lord and the author. — Wantage (28 Bosley's Orchard, Grove, Wantage, Oxon.) : The Black Swan Press, 1976. — [3],18p : ill ; 19cm.
ISBN 0-905475-04-6 Sd : £1.05
(B77-09910)

Stiven, Tessa. Poetry of persons / [by] Tessa Stiven. — Feltham : Quarto Press, 1976. — [32]p ; 22cm.
Limited ed. of 375 copies.
ISBN 0-901105-15-5 Sd : £0.50
(B77-00386)

Stiven, Tessa. While it is yet day / [by] Tessa Stiven. — London : Quarto Press, 1977. — [40] p ; 21cm.
Limited ed. of 425 copies.
Sd : £0.50
(B77-27333)

Stiven, Tessa. While it is yet day / [by] Tessa Stiven. — London : Quarto Press, 1977. — [40] p ; 22cm.
Limited ed. of 425 numbered copies.
Sd : £0.50
(B77-28855)

Stock, Queenie F. Down memory lane / by Queenie F. Stock. — London [etc.] : Regency Press, 1977. — 32p ; 22cm.
ISBN 0-7212-0494-5 Sd : £0.60
(B77-15465)

Stockdale, Louise, *Lady.* The blossoming tree : poems and illustrations / by Louise Stockdale ; with a foreword by the Countess of Longford. — [Basingstoke] ([Hoddington House, Upton Grey, Basingstoke, Hants.]) : [The author], 1977. — 92p : ill(some col) ; 28cm.
£2.75
(B77-29657)

Stokes, Daniel P. Buying a sweater : a poem / by Daniel P. Stokes ; with a linocut by Daphne Lord. — Richmond, Surrey : Keepsake Press, 1977. — [4] leaves : 1 col ill ; 24cm. — (Keepsake poem ; 31)
Limited ed. of 180 copies of which 12 are signed by the author and the artist.
Sd : Unpriced
Signed ed. : Unpriced
(B77-32132)

Stroud, Elizabeth. The collected poetry of Elizabeth Stroud. — London [etc.] : Regency Press, 1976. — 32p ; 19cm.
ISBN 0-7212-0493-7 Sd : Unpriced
(B77-15466)

Sutherland-Smith, James. Death of a Nixen / [by James Sutherland-Smith]. — London (40 Walford Rd, N16 8ED) : Many Press, 1977. — Folder([4]p) ; 21cm. — (Many Press broadsheet ; no.2)
Limited ed. of 100 copies, of which ten have been signed by the poet.
£0.20
(B77-28062)

Sykes, Graham. Owls & swimmers / by Graham Sykes, Andy Darlington. — Corby : Excello and Bollard, [1977]. — [12]p ; 21cm.
ISBN 0-904339-50-5 Sd : Unpriced
(B77-16025)

Sylvester, Debonnaire. Rhyming roads to Rome / [by] Debonnaire Sylvester. — London : Mitre Press, 1977. — 80p ; 19cm.
ISBN 0-7051-0253-x : £1.60
(B77-20545)

Symes, Gordon. After Rowlandson : a poem / by Gordon Symes ; with a drawing by Thomas Rowlandson. — Richmond, Surrey : Keepsake Press, 1977. — [4] leaves : 1 ill ; 24cm. — (Keepsake poem ; 32)
Limited ed. of 180 copies of which 12 are signed by the author.
Sd : Unpriced
Signed ed. : Unpriced
(B77-32133)

Thom, Martin. The bloodshed, the shaking house / [by] Martin Thom. — [Hove] ([6 Davigdor Rd, Hove, E. Sussex]) : X Press, 1977. — [49] leaves ; 31cm.
ISBN 0-905758-01-3 Sd : Unpriced
(B77-13230)

Thomas, Donald Michael. Orpheus in Hell / [by] D.M. Thomas. — Knotting : Sceptre Press, 1977. — [4]leaves ; 21cm.
Limited ed. of 150 numbered copies, of which nos 1-50 are signed by the poet.
ISBN 0-7068-0346-9 Sd : £0.95
ISBN 0-7068-0347-7 Signed ed : £5.00
(B77-09227)

Thomas, Edward Boaden. Anne Clifford : a woman for all seasons : a biographical poem / by Edward Boaden Thomas. — [Bakewell] : [Hub Publications], [1977]. — [7],112p ; 21cm.
ISBN 0-905049-43-8 Pbk : £3.00
(B77-34047)

Thomas, Richard, *b.1926.* Rapture of the depths / by Richard Thomas.— Walton-on-Thames : Outposts Publications, 1977. — 40p ; 21cm.
ISBN 0-7205-0505-4 Sd : £0.80
(B77-09228)

Thomas, Ronald Stuart. Laboratories of the spirit / [by] R.S. Thomas. — Gregynog : Gwasg Gregynog ; [Cardiff] : University of Wales Press, 1976. — [8],73p ; 30cm.
Limited ed. of 190 numbered copies, of which 175 are bound in quarter leather and 15 are numbered I to XV, bound in full leather and are signed by the poet. — Originally published: London : Macmillan, 1975.
£60.00
Signed ed.: £230.00
(B77-10534)

Thompson, Robert, *b.1933.* Nomadic cycle / by Robert Thompson. — Walton-on-Thames : Outposts Publications, 1977. — 16p ; 21cm.
Sd : £0.40
(B77-28856)

Thwaite, Anthony. A portion for foxes / [by] Anthony Thwaite. — Oxford [etc.] : Oxford University Press, 1977. — viii,48p ; 22cm.
ISBN 0-19-211872-2 Pbk : £2.25
(B77-22820)

Tipp, James Edward. A rainbow of thoughts / by James Tipp. — [Orpington] ([St Pauls Cray, Orpington, Kent]) : [Rev. J.E. Tipp], [1977]. — [1],iv,52p ; 21cm.
Sd : Unpriced
(B77-28857)

Tompkins, John. Portraits of Bath / by John Tompkins ; drawings by Grace D. Bratton. — Bath : Kingsmead, 1976. — 48p : ill ; 26cm.
ISBN 0-901571-78-4 : £1.75
ISBN 0-901571-80-6 Pbk : £0.95
Also classified at 914.23'98'048570222
(B77-03204)

Torrance, Chris. The magic door : a cycle / by Chris Torrance. — London : Albion Village Press.
Book 2 : Citrinas. — 1977. — [48]p : ill ; 25x11cm.
Limited ed. of 300 copies of which 15 are casebound and contain additional holograph material. — Spine title: Citrinas.
Pbk : £0.90
(B77-28858)

Toshack, John. Gosh it's Tosh / [by] John Toshack ; foreword by Kevin Keegan ; preface by John Keith ; photography by Harry Ormesher. — London : Duckworth [etc.], 1976. — 95p : ill, facsim, ports ; 19x25cm.
ISBN 0-7156-1197-6 : £4.95
ISBN 0-7156-1198-4 Pbk : £2.25
(B77-06257)

Tower, Christopher. A distant fluting : poems and sonnets / by Christopher Tower ; illustrations by Roland Pym. — London : Weidenfeld and Nicolson, 1977. — [4],800p,[16] leaves of plates : ill(some col) ; 25cm.
ISBN 0-297-77300-3 : £6.50
(B77-30581)

Triggs, Tony D. Janus / [by] Tony D. Triggs. — Breakish : Aquila, 1976. — 15p ; 21cm.
Also available in a limited ed. of 26 copies, signed and lettered by the author.
ISBN 0-7275-0133-x Sd : £0.20
ISBN 0-7275-0134-8 Signed ed.: £1.25
(B77-15467)

Tucker, Alan. The crystal carol, and other poems / [by] Alan Tucker ; drawings by Steve Wallhead. — Wymondham : Brewhouse Private Press, 1976. — [12]p : ill ; 21cm.
Limited ed. of 80 copies.
ISBN 0-900190-41-8 : £6.00
(B77-05044)

Twite, Irene. Always the horizon / by Irene Twite. — Kingston upon Thames ([1 Rayleigh Court, Kingston upon Thames, Surrey KT1 3NF]) : Court Poetry Press, 1977. — 24p ; 21cm.
ISBN 0-906010-00-4 Sd : £0.35
(B77-28859)

Ursic, Vlasta. Stolen pictures / by Vlasta Ursic ; preface by Sir Herbert Read. — Burslem (Burslem, Stoke-on-Trent, Staffs) : Warwick Savage, 1977. — [7],39p : 1 port ; 21cm.
'Limited edition'.
ISBN 0-9505712-0-2 Sd : Unpriced
(B77-27335)

Vatsa, Mamman Jiya. ABC rhymes / by Mamman J. Vatsa. — Walton-on-Thames : Outposts Publications, 1977. — 12p ; 21cm.
Sd : £0.30
(B77-21402)

Vatsa, Mamman Jiya. Reflections on Warminster / by Mamman J. Vatsa. — Walton-on-Thames : Outposts Publications, 1977. — 12p ; 21cm.
Originally published: 1975.
Sd : £0.30
(B77-21403)

Vessey, David. Poems from Florida and elsewhere / by David Vessey. — London (10 Uphill Grove, Mill Hill, NW7 4NJ) : Scrinium Press, 1977. — 36p ; 23cm.
Limited ed. of 120 copies.
Pbk : Unpriced
(B77-33411)

Violetta. A variety of verse / [by] Violetta. — Ilfracombe : Stockwell, 1977. — 19p ; 15cm.
ISBN 0-7223-1035-8 Pbk : £0.30
(B77-33412)

Voneld, Ruth. Nursery poems of creatures great and small / [by] Ruth Voneld ; illustrated by Cora E.M. Paterson. — Ilfracombe : Stockwell, 1977. — 40p : ill ; 19cm.
ISBN 0-7223-1039-0 Pbk : £0.45
(B77-31419)

Walkin, Jimmy. A selection of poems / by Jimmy Walkin. — Bradford (806 Leeds Rd, Bradford [W. Yorkshire] BD3 9TY) : James John Hopkinson, Printers, [1977]. — [1],29,[1] p ; 22cm.
Sd : £1.00
(B77-22821)

Walwin, Peggy Christison. Vacation in Oxford / [by] Peggy C. Walwin ; illustrations by Michael Seacome. — Gloucester (c/o John Jennings (Gloucester) Ltd, [Brunswick Rd, Gloucester GL1 1HN]) : The author, 1977. — 44p : ill ; 19cm.
ISBN 0-9505409-1-9 : Unpriced
(B77-22822)

Ward, Dave. Angel veins / [by] Dave Ward. — Bridgend (83 Pyle Inn Way, Pyle, Bridgend, M. Glam.) : Speed Limit Publications, 1977. — [24]p ; 21cm. — (Speed Limit booklet ; 5)
Sd : £0.15
(B77-30582)

Ward, Dave. Ceremonies/rituals / by Dave Ward. — Corby : Excello and Bollard, 1977. — [14]p ; 15cm.
ISBN 0-904339-62-9 Sd : Unpriced
(B77-33413)

Ward, Dave. Tuff stuff : poems / by Dave Ward ; cover design Mark Williams. — Bridgend (83 Pyle Inn Way, Pyle, Bridgend, M. Glam.) : Speed Limit Publications, 1977. — [12]p ; 26cm. — (Speed Limit booklet ; 1)
ISBN 0-9505634-1-2 Sd : £0.15
(B77-09911)

Ward, Dave. Yesterdays loving / [by] Dave Ward. — Breakish : Aquila, 1976. — [14]p ; 21cm.
Also available in a limited ed. of 26 copies, signed and lettered by the author.
ISBN 0-7275-0154-2 Sd : £0.25
ISBN 0-7275-0155-0 Signed ed. : £1.25
(B77-15468)

Ward, Geoffrey. Tales from the snowline / by Geoffrey Ward. — Horsham (47 Cambridge Rd, Horsham, W. Sussex) : Causeway Press, 1977. — [19]p ; 21cm.
Limited ed. of 250 copies of which 20 are numbered and signed by the author.
ISBN 0-903955-01-6 Sd : £0.60
ISBN 0-903955-02-4 Signed ed. : Unpriced
(B77-16026)

Ward, Philip. impostors and their imitators : poems / [by] Philip Ward. — Cambridge : Oleander Press, [1977]. — iv,44p ; 21cm. — (Oleander modern poets ; 7)
ISBN 0-900891-22-x Pbk : £1.35 : CIP rev.
(B77-17722)

Waterman, Andrew. From the other country / [by] Andrew Waterman. — Manchester : Carcanet New Press, 1977. — 63p ; 23cm.
Includes: 'Last fruit'. Hitchin : Mandeville Press, 1974.
ISBN 0-85635-213-6 : £2.00
(B77-16027)

Waters, Ivor. Collected verse [of] Ivor Waters. — Chepstow (41 Hardwick Ave., Chepstow, Gwent NP6 5DS) : The author, 1977. — x, 112p ; 23cm.
Limited ed. of 100 copies.
ISBN 0-9500079-9-4 : £3.00
(B77-16577)

Watson, Owen V. Strong i'th'arm : the rhymes of a Marlpool miner / [by] Owen V. Watson. — [Marlpool] ([161 Roper Ave., Marlpool, Langley Mill, Nottingham]) : [The author], 1975. — [1],25p : ill ; 21cm.
ISBN 0-9505340-0-5 Sd : Unpriced
(B77-03740)

Watson, Roderick. True history on the walls / [by] Roderick Watson. — Loanhead (Edgefield Rd, Loanhead, Midlothian) : M. Macdonald, 1976. — 64p ; 22cm.
'Lines Review editions - 6' - title page verso.
ISBN 0-904265-15-3 Pbk : £2.00
(B77-08026)

Webb, Harri. Rampage and revel / [by] Harri Webb. — Llandysul : Gomer Press, 1977. — 63p ; 19cm.
Includes 2 poems in Welsh.
ISBN 0-85088-443-8 : £0.75
(B77-28860)

Wedlake, George Eardley Chester. Rum rhymes : very light verse / by Eardley Wedlake. — Bridgwater (42 Wembdon Rise, Bridgwater [Somerset]) : The author, 1977. — 24p ; 22cm.
Sd : £0.40
(B77-23685)

Weissbort, Daniel. Soundings / [by] Daniel Weissbort. — Manchester : Carcanet New Press, 1977. — 64p ; 23cm.
ISBN 0-85635-217-9 : £2.25
(B77-31420)

Welch, John, *b.1942.* Estuary / [by] John Welch. — London (40 Walford Rd, N.16) : Many Press, [1977]. — Folder ([4]p) ; 15cm. — (Many Press broadsheet ; no.1)
£0.10
(B77-17723)

Wells, Robert, *b.1947.* The winter's task : poems / [by] Robert Wells. — Manchester : Carcanet New Press, 1977. — 63p ; 23cm.
ISBN 0-85635-210-1 : £2.00
(B77-11387)

Wheeler, David J C. The Hangman's an inkpot : a selection of verse by a North Devon poet / by David J.C. Wheeler. — Ilfracombe (74 Channel View, Ilfracombe) : The author, [1977]. — [23]p ; 21cm.
ISBN 0-9505678-0-9 Sd : £0.30
(B77-12066)

Whistler, Laurence. A bridge on the Usk / [by] Laurence Whistler. — [Birmingham] ([9 Crosbie Rd, Harborne, Birmingham B17 9BG]) : [F.E. Pardoe], 1976. — [11]p ; 20cm.
Limited ed. of 120 numbered copies.
ISBN 0-9500523-3-7 Sd : £3.00
(B77-12067)

Whitaker, James. A touch of green, and other poems / [by James Whitaker]. — Stanford-Le-Hope (53 Prospect Ave., Stanford-Le-Hope, Essex) : The Bream Press, 1976. — 12p ; 21cm.
ISBN 0-9502259-6-7 Sd : £0.20
(B77-04388)

White, B C. Poems from the West Country / [by] B.C. White. — Ilfracombe : Stockwell, 1976. — 103p : port ; 15cm.
ISBN 0-7223-0953-8 : £1.50
(B77-10922)

White, Celia, *b.1906.* After the sermon : poems / by Celia White ; cover drawings by Ann Holehouse. — London (14 Barlby Rd, W10 6AR) : Autolycus Publications, 1977. — 28p ; 21cm.
ISBN 0-903413-21-3 Sd : £1.20
(B77-34048)

White, Eric Walter. Beginnings / [by] Eric Walter White. — Hatch End (30 Grimsdyke Rd, Hatch End, Middx [HA5 4PW]) : Poet and Printer, 1976. — 30p ; 21cm.
ISBN 0-900597-15-1 : £1.80
ISBN 0-900597-16-x Pbk : £0.75
(B77-05617)

White, Ivan. Removal of an exhibition / [by] Ivan White ; [designer-photographer Robert Golden ; editor Richard Appignanesi]. — London (14 Talacre Rd, NW5 3PE) : Writers and Readers Publishing Cooperative, 1976. — 64p : ill ; 20cm. — (Poetry in progress)
Bibl.: p.63-64.
ISBN 0-904613-23-2 Pbk : £0.60
(B77-09912)

White, Kenneth, *b.1936.* A walk along the shore / by Kenneth White ; with nine screen-prints by John Christie. — Guildford (22 Sydney Rd, Guildford, Surrey GU1 3LL) : Circle Press Publications, 1977. — [62]p,[9] leaves of plates : col ill ; 34cm.
Limited ed. of 95 copies.
£75.00
(B77-29658)

Whitehill, Kate. Poems of love and life / [by] Kate Whitehill. — Ilfracombe : Stockwell, 1977. — 56p ; 15cm.
ISBN 0-7223-1046-3 : £1.50
(B77-23686)

Whitehouse, A K. Confident / by A.K. Whitehouse. — Corby : Excello and Bollard, [1977]. — [16]p ; 15cm.
'An Excello & Bollard Minibook'.
ISBN 0-904339-53-x Sd : Unpriced
(B77-26492)

Whiteing, Eileen. Cross currents : poems by a Sussex housewife / [by] Eileen Whiteing. — Bakewell : Hub Publications, 1977. — [2],10p ; 21cm.
ISBN 0-905049-18-7 Sd : £0.75
(B77-22823)

Wilkins, Maurice. Poems of love & human freedom / [by] Maurice Wilkins. — Dublin ([c/o The Dolmen Press, North Richmond Industrial Estate, North Richmond St., Dublin 1]) : The Five Lamps Press, 1977. — 44p ; 22cm.
Sd : Unpriced
(B77-22824)

Wilkinson, John Lawton. The Central Line : a novel / [by] John Lawton Wilkinson. — Cambridge (c/o David Trotter, Magdalene College, Cambridge) : Infernal Methods, 1976. — [54]p ; 21cm.
Limited ed. of 300 copies, of which 20 numbered and signed copies contain additional holograph material.
ISBN 0-905795-00-8 Sd : £1.20
ISBN 0-905795-01-6 Numbered ed. : £3.00
(B77-00387)

Williams, Mark. Habits and other poems / by Mark Williams. — Corby : Excello and Bollard, 1977. — [23]p ; 15cm.
ISBN 0-904339-64-5 Sd : Unpriced
(B77-33414)

Williams, Mark. Lungs : poems / by Mark Williams. — Bridgend (83 Pyle Inn Way, Pyle, Bridgend, M. Glam.) : Speed Limit Publications, 1977. — [38]p ; 26cm. — (Speed Limit booklet ; 4)
Sd : £0.30
(B77-29659)

Williams, Thomas Beverly. The collected poetry of Thomas Beverly Williams. — London : Regency Press, [1976]. — 32p ; 20cm.
ISBN 0-9505456-0-0 Sd : £0.60
(B77-03205)

Williamson, Peter. The gift of life : poems / by Peter Williamson. — London (137 Fowler's Walk, W.5) : Brentham Press, 1976. — 16p ; 21cm.
ISBN 0-9503459-9-7 Sd : £0.60
(B77-09229)

Wills, M. Hues and colours / [by] M. Wills. — Ilfracombe : Stockwell, 1977. — 23p ; 18cm.
ISBN 0-7223-1012-9 Pbk : £0.30
(B77-25852)

Wilmer, Clive. The dwelling-place / [by] Clive Wilmer. — Manchester : Carcanet New Press, 1977. — 59p ; 23cm.
ISBN 0-85635-232-2 : £2.00
(B77-29660)

Wilson, Esmé. Shared thoughts / [by] Esmé Wilson. — [Weymouth] ([9 Grafton Ave., Radipole, Weymouth, Dorset DT4 9RZ]) : [The author], 1976. — 48p : ill ; 22cm.
ISBN 0-9505408-0-3 Sd : £0.75
(B77-00931)

Wilson, Leigh. Loving is lonely / [by] Leigh Wilson. — Ilfracombe : Stockwell, 1977. — 22p ; 15cm.
ISBN 0-7223-1002-1 Pbk : £0.30
(B77-10923)

Wilyman, Geoffrey Steven S. Togetherness / [by] G.S.S. Wilyman ; illustrated by Julian Moore ; with a foreword by Roy Castle. — Ilfracombe : Stockwell, 1977. — 16p : ill ; 15cm.
ISBN 0-7223-1013-7 Sd : £0.30
(B77-21404)

Wong, Alan L. The hermit : poems and drawings / by Alan L. Wong. — London : Mitre Press, 1977. — 66p : ill ; 20cm.
ISBN 0-7051-0246-7 : £1.80
(B77-20546)

Woolley, Marta Johanna. Forgotten path : poems / by Marta Johanna Woolley ; with two original coloured drawings by the author. — Saltburn-by-the-Sea (The Moorings, Mount Pleasant, Staithes, Saltburn-by-the-Sea, Cleveland TS13 5DG) : Anchor Publications, 1977. — [1],iv[i.e.x],76,[2]leaves,[2]leaves of plates : col ill ; 31cm.
Limited ed., numbered and signed by the author.
ISBN 0-9504157-4-x : £2.80
(B77-28063)

Woolsey, Gamel. Twenty eight sonnets / by Gamel Woolsey. — North Walsham (12 New Rd, North Walsham, Norfolk NR28 9DF) : Warren House Press, 1977. — 34p ; 22cm.
Pbk : £2.25
(B77-27336)

Wray, Michael. Stereotypes / by Michael Wray. — [Bristol] ([Wick Court, Wick, Bristol]) : The author, 1977. — [28]p ; 21cm.
Sd : Unpriced
(B77-31421)

Wright, David, *b.1920.* A view of the north : poems / by David Wright. — Ashington : MidNAG ; Manchester : Carcanet Press, 1976. — 48p ; 22cm.
ISBN 0-85635-202-0 Pbk : £1.75
(B77-10535)

Wrintmore, Frederick Henry. Goodness and mercy : selected poems / by F.H. Wrintmore. — Overstrand (24 Harbord Rd, Overstrand, Cromer, Norfolk NR27 0PN) : The author, [1977]. — 63p,plate : port ; 19cm.
Pbk : £0.60
(B77-25853)

Wroe, Malcolm. Sparks and embers / by Malcolm Wroe. — Walton-on-Thames : Outposts Publications, 1977. — 16p ; 21cm.
ISBN 0-7205-0502-x Sd : £0.35
(B77-05618)

Wyatt, Bill. Spring dreams & autumn wine / by Bill Wyatt. — Pyle (83 Pyle Inn Way, Pyle, Bridgend, M. Glam.) : Speed Limit Publications, 1977. — [23]p ; 21cm. — (Speed Limit booklet ; 13)
Sd : £0.15
(B77-32134)

Young, Kate Bush. The Christmas garland / [by] Kate Bush Young. — Ilfracombe : Stockwell, 1976. — 16p ; 18cm.
ISBN 0-7223-0988-0 Pbk : £0.25
(B77-10924)

821'.9'14 — Poetry in English. Brock, Edwin. *Autobiographies*

Brock, Edwin. Here, now, always / [by] Edwin Brock. — London : Secker and Warburg, 1977. — 153p ; 23cm.
ISBN 0-436-06883-4 : £3.90
(B77-06847)

821'.9'14 — Poetry in English. Montague, John. *Critical studies*

Kernowski, Frank. John Montague / [by] Frank Kernowski. — Lewisburg : Bucknell University Press ; London (108 New Bond St., W1Y 0QX) : Associated University Press, 1975. — 73p ; 21cm. — (The Irish writers series)
Bibl.: p.73.
ISBN 0-8387-7807-0 : £2.50
ISBN 0-8387-7983-2 Pbk : Unpriced
(B77-26493)

821'.9'14 — Poetry in English. Morgan, Edwin. *Transcripts of interviews*

Walker, Marshall. Edwin Morgan : an interview / by Marshall Walker. — Preston : Akros Publications, 1977. — 23p7 ; 23cm.
'... reprinted from "Akros"' - title page verso.
ISBN 0-900036-89-3 Sd : £0.65
(B77-16028)

821'.9'14 — Poetry in English. Scannell, Vernon, 1975-1976. *Autobiographies*

Scannell, Vernon. A proper gentleman / [by] Vernon Scannell. — London : Robson, 1977. — 160p ; 23cm.
ISBN 0-903895-86-2 : £3.95 : CIP rev.
(B77-23687)

821'.9'14 — Poetry in English. Warner, Francis. *Critical studies. Festschriften*

Francis Warner : poet and dramatist / edited by Tim Prentki. — Knotting : Sceptre Press, 1977. — viii,156p,plate : 2 ill, port ; 22cm.
Essays published in honour of the fortieth birthday of Francis Warner. — Bibl.: p.vi.
ISBN 0-7068-0378-7 : £3.75
Also classified at 822'.9'14
(B77-32135)

821'.9'1408 — Poetry in English, 1945-. *Anthologies*

Autumn anthology : a biographical anthology of one hundred poets / edited by S.T. Gardiner. — London (1 Herbert Rd, N11 2QN) : Poet's Yearbook Publications, 1977. — 82p ; 21cm.
ISBN 0-905106-03-2 Sd : £1.25
(B77-13231)

Bourner, Brian. In two minds : poems / by Brian Bourner and John Pole ; illustrated by Gordon Robertson. — London (26 Somerset Rd, W.13) : The authors, 1975. — 34p : ill ; 21cm.
Sd : £0.40
(B77-13838)

Child, Mark. Vestiges / [by] Mark Child, Alan Roe. — [Swindon] ([40 Ashbury Ave., Nythe, Swindon SN3 3LY]) : [M. Child], [1977]. — 38p : ill ; 21cm.
Sd : £0.40
(B77-22091)

Flights : poetry from Sheffield (and elsewhere) / editor Gerard Langley. — Sheffield (Western Bank, Sheffield S10) : Union of Students, Sheffield University, [1977]. — [2],34p ; 21cm.
'An Arrows production'.
Sd : £0.10
(B77-26494)

Fraser, Steve. Move still, still so / [by] Steve Fraser, Simon Fraser. — Sherborne, Dorset (35 Kings Rd, Sherborne, Dorset) : Zeds Magazine, [1977]. — 20p : ill ; 15x21cm.
Sd : £0.75
(B77-34049)

Just something to buy / [edited by John Woodward]. — Nottingham (18 Durham Cres., Bulwell, Nottingham [NG6 9AN]) : B.K. Poems, 1976. — [24]p : 1 ill ; 22cm.
ISBN 0-9504763-1-5 Sd : £0.25
(B77-05619)

Milne, E M. Readable rhymes / [by] E.M. Milne and E.A. Bright. — London : Mitre Press, 1976. — 64p ; 19cm.
ISBN 0-7051-0245-9 : £1.60
(B77-08027)

A **poetry** quintet : poems / by Angus Nicolson ... [et al.]. — London : Gollancz, 1976. — 96p ; 22cm. — (Gollancz poets)
ISBN 0-575-02156-x Pbk : £3.20
(B77-00388)

Richmond poets / Richmond Poetry Group. — Twickenham (c/o 72 Heathfield South, Twickenham, Middx TW2 7SS) : The Group.
1977 / edited by Brian Louis Pearce. — 1977. — [24]p ; 21cm.
ISBN 0-9505637-0-6 Sd : £0.40
(B77-14885)

Songs without music / by Rod Argent ... [et al.]. — London (8 Cleveland Sq., W.2) : Bongi Books, 1976. — 47,[1]p ; 21cm.
Cover title.
ISBN 0-905602-00-5 Pbk : £1.00
(B77-08028)

Spring collection / [by] Richard Carlile ... [et al.]. — Hitchin (2 Taylor's Hill, Hitchin, Herts.) : Mandeville Press, 1977. — [24]p ; 23cm.
ISBN 0-904533-28-x Sd : £0.60
(B77-22092)

Steam Press portfolio. — [London] ([Turret Bookshop, 285 Russell Court, Woburn Place, WC1H 0NF]) : [Steam Press].
No.3 / by Fleur Adcock ... [et al.] ; [illustrations by] Ralph Steadman. — [1977]. — Portfolio : col ill ; 46x30cm.
Limited ed. of 50 numbered sets, signed by the authors and artist. — 9 sheets (9 sides).
ISBN 0-904382-01-x : £42.00
(B77-13232)

Symes, Gordon. Gordon Symes, Janet Harrison, Philip Crick. — London : Chatto and Windus, 1977. — 64p ; 22cm. — (Treble poets ; 3)
ISBN 0-7011-2212-9 Pbk : £2.50 : CIP rev.
(B77-06848)

Szirtes, George. A Mandeville troika / [by] George Szirtes, Neil Powell, Peter Scupham. — Hitchin (2 Taylor's Hill, Hitchin, Herts.) : Mandeville Press, 1977. — [11]p : ill ; 23cm.
Limited ed. of 150 numbered copies of which the first 50 are signed.
ISBN 0-904533-26-3 Sd : Unpriced
(B77-12616)

Thursday evening anthology / edited by Farida Majid ; drawings by Feliks Topolski. — London (3 Cadogan Sq., SW1X 0HT) : Salamander Imprint, 1977. — 72p : ill ; 25cm.
Also available in a signed and numbered ed. of 200 copies.
ISBN 0-904632-06-7 Pbk : £3.50
ISBN 0-904632-07-5 Signed ed. : £20.00
(B77-34050)

A **treasury** of modern poets : an anthology of contemporary verse. — London [etc.] : Regency Press.
[1977]. — [1977]. — 280p ; 23cm.
£4.00
(B77-34051)

821'.9'1408 — Poetry in English, 1945-. *Anthologies. Periodicals*

Counterpoint. — Kingston upon Thames (c/o The editor, 1 Rayleigh Court, Kingston upon Thames, Surrey KT1 3NF) : 'Counterpoint'.
Issue no.1- ; Spring 1977-. — [1977]-. — 21cm.

Quarterly. — 48p. in 1st issue.
Sd : £0.40
ISSN 0309-3328
(B77-33415)

821'.9'1408 — Poetry in English, 1945-. *Anthologies. Serials*

20th century poets : an anthology of contemporary verse. — London [etc.] : Regency Press.
[1976]. — [1977]. — 310p : 1 ill ; 23cm.
ISBN 0-7212-0489-9 : £4.00
(B77-20547)

Autumn anthology : an anthology of contemporary verse. — London [etc.] : Regency Press.
[1976]. — [1976]. — 279p : 1 ill ; 23cm.
ISBN 0-7212-0478-3 : £4.00
(B77-10536)

Collected poems. — Ilfracombe : Stockwell.
1976. Vol.2. — 1976. — 112p ; 15cm.
Index.
ISBN 0-7223-1007-2 : £1.85
(B77-10537)

Editor's choice : an anthology of selected contemporary verse. — London [etc.] : Regency Press.
'77. — [1977]. — 464p ; 23cm.
ISBN 0-7212-0476-7 : £4.00
(B77-09913)

Kaleidoscope of verse : an anthology of contemporary verse. — London [etc.] : Regency Press.
'76. — [1976]. — 275p ; 23cm.
ISBN 0-7212-0467-8 : £3.20
(B77-00389)

Living poets : an anthology of contemporary verse. — London [etc.] : Regency Press.
'77. — [1977]. — 304p : ill ; 23cm.
£4.00
(B77-24450)

New poems : a PEN anthology of contemporary poetry. — London : Hutchinson.
1977-78 / edited by Gavin Ewart. — 1977. — 192p ; 21cm.
ISBN 0-09-131790-8 : £4.95
(B77-32136)

New poetry : an anthology. — London : Arts Council of Great Britain.
2 / edited by Patricia Beer & Kevin Crossley-Holland. — 1976. — 3-284p ; 22cm.
ISBN 0-7287-0108-1 : £3.80
ISBN 0-7287-0109-x Pbk : £2.00
(B77-02556)

New poets : an anthology of contemporary verse. — London [etc.] : Regency Press.
77. — [1977]. — 324p ; 23cm.
£4.00
(B77-24451)

Poems. — Llandysul : Gomer Press.
'76 : an anthology of poems by Welsh writers selected from work which has appeared during the last two years / editor Glyn Jones. — 1976. — 89p ; 21cm.
ISBN 0-85088-460-8 Pbk : £1.25
(B77-05620)

Poetry dimension annual : the best of the poetry year. — London : Robson Books.
4 / edited by Dannie Abse. — 1976. — 176p ; 21cm.
ISBN 0-903895-71-4 : £3.95
ISBN 0-903895-72-2 Pbk : £1.75
(B77-00390)

Poetry international : an anthology of contemporary verse. — London [etc.] : Regency Press.
1976. — [1976]. — 322p ; 23cm.
ISBN 0-7212-0482-1 : £4.00
(B77-09914)

821'.9'1408 — Poetry in English. Chesham writers, 1945-. *Anthologies*

Chesham Poetry Society. With Chesham in mind / the Chesham Poetry Society. — Chesham (170 White Hill, Chesham, Bucks.) : The Society, 1976. — 46p ; 21cm.
ISBN 0-9505467-0-4 Sd : £0.75
(B77-04389)

821'.9'1408 — Poetry in English. Civil service writers, 1945-. *Anthologies. Serials*

Focus / [Poetry Workshop, Society of Civil Service Authors]. — Stockport (42 Seal Rd, Bramhall, Stockport, Cheshire SK7 2JS) : The Workshop.
1977 / edited by John Ward. — [1977]. — [2], 18p ; 20cm.
Previously published: as 'Broadsheet'.
Sd : Unpriced
ISSN 0140-0878
(B77-32137)

821'.9'1408 — Poetry in English. Dorset writers, 1945-. *Anthologies*

Seventy Dorset poets : a Word and Action (Dorset) anthology, 1976-1977. — Weymouth (186 Newstead Rd, Weymouth, Dorset DT4 0DY) : Word and Action (Dorset), 1977. — [2] ,58p ; 21cm.
Cover title: 70 Dorset poets. — Index.
Sd : £0.80
(B77-18355)

Under Dorset skies : second anthology of the works of members of the Dorset Poets (1972) Society / edited by Malcolm Payne ; cover by Ann Jackson. — Blandford Forum (14 Bryanston St., Blandford Forum, Dorset DT11 7AZ) : The Society, 1976. — 72p : 1 ill ; 21cm.

ISBN 0-9504518-1-9 Pbk : £0.85
(B77-00391)

821'.9'1408 — Poetry in English. East Anglian writers, 1945-1976. *Anthologies*
A **selection** of poems from new East Anglian poets / compiled by S.P. Dutchyn. — Haddenham (13 The Green, Haddenham, Cambs. CB6 3TA) : The compiler, 1977. — [3], 24p ; 21cm.
Sd : Unpriced
(B77-20548)

821'.9'1408 — Poetry in English. Feminist writers, 1945-. *Anthologies*
Cutlasses & earrings / [edited by Michelene Wandor and Michele Roberts]. — London (71 Belsize La., N.W.3) : Playbooks, 1977. — 58p ; 21cm.
ISBN 0-904732-01-0 Sd : £0.50
(B77-15469)

821'.9'1408 — Poetry in English. Merchant seaman writers, 1945-. *Anthologies*
Voices from the sea : poems by merchant seamen / selected by Ronald Hope. — London : Harrap [for] the Marine Society, 1977. — 91p ; 23cm.
ISBN 0-245-53113-0 : £2.60
(B77-21405)

821'.9'1408 — Poetry in English. North-eastern Surrey writers, 1945-. *Anthologies. Periodicals*
Poetry in North East Surrey *(Group).* Pines / Poetry in North East Surrey. — Caterham (45 Manor Ave., Caterham [Surrey]) : Pines Poets. No.1- ; [1977]-. — 1977-. — ill ; 21cm.
Published at irregular intervals. — [28]p. in 1st issue.
Sd : £0.25
ISSN 0140-0444
(B77-19616)

821'.9'1408 — Poetry in English. Preston Polytechnic writers, 1945-. *Anthologies*
Preston Polytechnic poets : Duncan Glen, Ian Harrow, Philip Pacey, Hugh Probyn / edited by Duncan Glen ; with illustrations by John Hodkinson. — Preston (Preston Polytechnic, Preston, Lancs.) : Harris Press, 1977. — 53p : ill ; 21cm.
ISBN 0-905735-04-8 Pbk : Unpriced
(B77-15470)

821'.9'1408 — Poetry in English. Scottish writers, 1945-. *Anthologies*
A **sense** of belonging : six Scottish poets of the seventies / compiled by Brian Murray and Sydney Smyth. — Glasgow [etc.] : Blackie, 1977. — vi,58p ; 21cm.
ISBN 0-216-90369-6 : £2.00
ISBN 0-216-90264-9 Educational ed. : £1.50
(B77-22825)

821'.9'1408 — Poetry in English. Walthamstow Poetry Group writers, 1945-. *Anthologies*
Poet tree centaur : a Walthamstow Group anthology / [compiled by Gerda Mayer]. — London (c/o Gerda Mayer, 12 Margaret Ave., E.4) : Oddments, [1973?]. — [15]p ; 26cm.
Sd : Unpriced
(B77-18964)

821'.9'14080351 — Poetry in English, 1945-. *Special subjects: Printing. Savage, Toni. Anthologies*
Poems for Toni Savage / [by Spike Milligan et al. ; illustrations by Rigby Graham]. — [Ilkley] (37 The Grove, Ilkley, W. Yorkshire) : The Janus Studio, 1976. — [15]p : 1 ill ; 21cm.
Limited ed. of 100 numbered copies.
ISBN 0-9505317-0-7 Sd : £1.25
(B77-00932)

821'.9'1408038 — Poetry in English, 1945-. Special subjects: Christianity. *Anthologies. Periodicals*
Symphony : a magazine of Christian poetry. — Reading (c/o Keith Barrett, Esq., 202 Fairwater Drive, Woodley, Reading RG5 3JF) : 'Symphony'.
No.1- ; Spring 1976-. — 1976-. — 21cm.
Two issues a year. — 23p. in issue no.2.
Sd : £0.54 yearly
ISSN 0308-4566
(B77-03206)

821'.9'1409 — Poetry in English, 1945-. *Critical studies*
Homberger, Eric. The art of the real : poetry in England and America since 1939 / [by] Eric Homberger. — London [etc.] : Dent [etc.], 1977. — x,246p ; 23cm. — ([Everyman's university library])
Bibl.: p.231-239. — Index.
ISBN 0-460-10084-x : £5.95
ISBN 0-460-11084-5 Pbk : £2.95
(B77-28064)

821'.9'1409 — Poetry in English, 1945-. Influence of public performances
Morgan, Edwin. East European poets / prepared for the [Open University] Course Team by Edwin Morgan. Poetry in public / prepared for the [Open University] Course Team by Alasdair Clayre. — Milton Keynes : Open University Press, 1976. — 54p : ports ; 30cm. — (Arts, a third level course : twentieth century poetry ; unit 32) (A306 ; 32)
Bibl.
ISBN 0-335-05123-5 Pbk : £0.95
Primary classification 891.8
(B77-04461)

821'.9'1409 — Poetry in English. Campbell, Donald, b.1940 & Glen, Duncan. *Critical studies*
Mason, Leonard. Two younger poets : Duncan Glen and Donald Campbell : a study of their Scots poetry / [by] Leonard Mason. — Preston : Akros Publications, 1976. — 75p ; 24cm.
Bibl.
ISBN 0-900036-86-9 Pbk : £0.75
(B77-09230)

821'.9'1409 — Poetry in English. Gunn, Thom & Hughes, Ted. *Critical studies*
Bold, Alan. Thom Gunn and Ted Hughes / [by] Alan Bold. — Edinburgh : Oliver and Boyd, 1976. — [7],136p ; 19cm. — (Modern writers series)
Bibl.: p.133-136.
ISBN 0-05-002855-3 : £2.80
ISBN 0-05-002854-5 Pbk : £1.40
(B77-00392)

821'.9'14093 — Poetry in English, 1945- . Special themes: Violence. *Critical studies*
Ries, Lawrence R. Wolf masks : violence in contemporary poetry / [by] Lawrence R. Ries. — Port Washington ; London : Kennikat Press, 1977. — [6],162p ; 23cm. — (Kennikat Press national university publications : literary criticism series)
Bibl.: p.156-159. — Index.
ISBN 0-8046-9168-1 : £8.90
(B77-27337)

822 — ENGLISH DRAMA
822 — Drama in English. Australian writers, 1945-. *Texts*
Williamson, David, *b.1942.* David Williamson's 'The removalists' / with notes on authority & violence, past & present by Ian Turner, Frank Galbally and Kerry Milte ; further comment by Bruce Petty ; director's notes by John Bell ; edited by Sylvia Lawson. — Sydney : Currency Press ; London : Eyre Methuen, 1975. — 128p : ill, facsims ; 19cm. — (Currency Methuen plays)
Originally published: Sydney : Currency Press, 1972.
ISBN 0-86937-035-9 Pbk : Unpriced
ISBN 0-86937-017-0 Pbk : £1.50
(B77-25854)

822 — Drama in English. Kenyan writers, 1945-. *Texts*
Ngugi wa Thiong'o. The trial of Dedan Kimathi / [by] Ngugi wa Thiong'o and Micere Githae Mugo. — London [etc.] : Heinemann Educational, 1977. — [10],85p ; 19cm. — (African writers series ; 191)
Originally published: Nairobi : Heinemann Educational Books (East Africa) Ltd, 1976.
ISBN 0-435-90191-5 Pbk : £0.85
(B77-32829)

822 — Drama in English. New Zealand writers. Mason, Bruce. *Critical studies*
McNaughton, Howard. Bruce Mason / by Howard McNaughton. — Wellington [N.Z.] ; London [etc.] : Oxford University Press, [1977]. — 53p ; 22cm. — (New Zealand writers and their work)
Published in New Zealand: 1976. — Bibl.: p.50-53.
ISBN 0-19-558016-8 Pbk : £2.75
(B77-13839)

822 — Drama in English. South African writers, 1961-. *Texts*
Fugard, Athol. Dimetos ; and, Two early plays / [by] Athol Fugard. — Oxford [etc.] : Oxford University Press, 1977. — [5],164p ; 21cm.
Contents: Dimetos - Nongogo - No-good Friday.
ISBN 0-19-211390-9 : £4.25 : CIP rev.
ISBN 0-19-281210-6 Pbk : £1.95
(B77-07570)

822 — Drama in English. Ugandan writers, 1945-. *Texts*
Rugyendo, Mukotani. The barbed wire, & other plays / [by] Mukotani Rugyendo. — London [etc.] : Heinemann Educational, 1977. — [5], 112p ; 19cm. — (African writers series ; 187)
ISBN 0-435-90187-7 Pbk : £1.30
(B77-22093)

822'.009 — Drama in English, to ca 1950. *Festschriften*
English drama : forms and development : essays in honour of Muriel Clara Bradbrook / edited by Marie Axton and Raymond Williams ; with an introduction by Raymond Williams. — Cambridge [etc.] : Cambridge University Press, 1977. — x,263p ; 24cm.
Bibl.: 241.247. — Index.
ISBN 0-521-21588-9 : £7.50
(B77-29661)

822'.009 — Drama in English, to ca 1975. *Critical studies*
The **Revels** history of drama in English / [general editors Clifford Leech and T.W. Craik]. — London : Methuen.
Vol.5 : 1660-1750 / [by] John Loftis ... [et al.]. — 1976. — xxxi,331p,[32]p of plates : ill, facsim, plan, ports ; 25cm.
Ill. on lining papers. — Bibl.: p.297-319. — Index.
ISBN 0-416-13060-7 : £13.00
ISBN 0-416-81370-4 Pbk : £6.95
Also classified at 792'.0942
(B77-05621)

822'.02 — Drama in English, 1945- . Television plays. *Anthologies. Secondary school texts*
The **pressures** of life : four television plays / by Richard Harris ... [et al.] ; selected and edited by Michael Marland ; with questions for discussion and writing by Chris Buckton. — London : Longman, 1977. — vii,174p : ill, facsims ; 20cm. — (Longman imprint books)
Contents: Reasonable suspicion / by Richard Harris - A right dream of delight / by Michael O'Neill and Jeremy Seabrook - Speech day / by Barry Hines - The piano / by Julia Jones.
ISBN 0-582-23329-1 Pbk : £1.05
(B77-14886)

822'.041 — Drama in English, 1945- . One-act plays. *Anthologies. Secondary school texts*
Second playbill / edited by Alan Durband. — New ed. — London : Hutchinson. — (Hutchinson playbill series)
Previous ed.: 1973. — Contents: Terraces / by Willy Russell - The jolly good fellow / by John Kershaw - The man without a name / by David Shellan - Who is Bobby Valentine? / by Ken Taylor - The New Model Army / by Phillips and Girling.
1. — 1977. — 170p ; 19cm.
ISBN 0-09-131201-9 Pbk : £0.95
(B77-34052)

The **windmill** book of one-act plays. — London : Heinemann Educational.
9th : Six plays / by Margaret Wood ; with introduction and notes. — 1977. — vi,160p ; 19cm.
Contents: Home is the sailor - Top table - Covenant with death - Withington warrior - A kind of justice - 'Peace hath her victories ...'.
ISBN 0-435-23959-7 Pbk : £1.00
(B77-07571)

822'.041 — Drama in English, 1945-. One-act plays. *Anthologies*
Contemporary one-act plays / selected and introduced by James Redmond and Hallam Tennyson. — London [etc.] : Heinemann Educational for the English Association, 1976. — xiv,170p ; 19cm.
Contents include: 'If you're Glad, I'll be Frank' / by Tom Stoppard. Originally published: London : Faber, 1976.
ISBN 0-435-23723-3 Pbk : £1.50
(B77-04390)

Counterpoint : a fine selection of one act plays. — Macclesfield (35 Sandringham Rd, Macclesfield, Cheshire SK10 1QB) : New Playwrights' Network, [1977]. — [1],35,20,28p : 2 plans ; 18cm. — (Triad ; 15)
Contents: Death and Nellie Miller / by Jack Boswell - Ruins : a drama for women / by Doris M. Day - The face of the angel / by Taylor Lovering.
Pbk : £1.40
(B77-34053)

Extremities : a fine selection of one act plays. — Macclesfield (35 Sandringham Rd, Macclesfield, Cheshire SK10 1QB) : New Playwrights' Network, [1977]. — [1],31,17,27p : plan ; 18cm. — (Triad ; 14)
Contents: The seven cream jugs / by David Coe, freely adapted from a short story by Hector Munro - The night is far spent / by Cecil Davies - Wilfred slept here / by Don Carroll.
Pbk : £1.40
(B77-31422)

Spelling trouble : a fine selection of one act plays. — Macclesfield (35 Sandringham Rd, Macclesfield, Cheshire SK10 1QB) : New Playwrights' Network, [1977]. — [1],23,30,26p : plans ; 18cm. — (Triad ; 12)
Contents: Shock tactics / by Mary Lee - Men of letters / adapted by Fred Partridge from 'La Grammaire' by Eugene Labiche - Ducks and Mr Drake / by Derek Hoddinott.
ISBN 0-903653-32-x Pbk : £1.25
(B77-10925)

822'.051 — Drama in English. Tragedies, 1625-1702. *Anthologies*
Restoration tragedies / edited with an introduction by James Sutherland. — London [etc.] : Oxford University Press, 1977. — xii, 441p : facsims ; 20cm.
Bibl.: p.439-441. — Contents: All for love / by John Dryden - Lucius Junius Brutus / by Nathaniel Lee - The unhappy favourite / by John Banks - Venice preserved / by Thomas Otway - Oroonoko / by Thomas Southerne.
ISBN 0-19-281176-2 Pbk : £2.95
(B77-12617)

822'.051 — Drama in English. Tragedy. Theories of Dennis, John, b.1657, Dryden, John & Rymer, Thomas. *Critical studies*
Grace, Joan Carroll. Tragic theory in the critical works of Thomas Rymer, John Dennis, and John Dryden / [by] Joan C. Grace. — Rutherford [etc.] : Fairleigh Dickinson University Press ; London (108 New Bond St., W1Y 0QX) : Associated University Presses, 1975. — 143p ; 22cm.
Bibl.: p.130-136. — Index.
ISBN 0-8386-1312-8 : £3.75
(B77-01773)

822'.051 — Miracle plays in English, 1400-1558. *Anthologies. Manuscripts. Facsimiles*
[Towneley plays]. The Towneley cycle : a facsimile of Huntington MS. HM 1 / with an introduction by A.C. Cawley and Martin Stevens. — [Leeds] : University of Leeds, School of English, 1976. — xix p,132 leaves,plate : ill(incl 1 col) ; 33cm. — (Leeds texts and monographs : medieval drama facsimiles ; 2)
'Issued jointly by the Huntington Library [and Art Gallery], San Marino, California and by "Leeds studies in English", University of Leeds' - title page verso. — Facsimile reprint of: 1st ed., 1480?.
ISBN 0-902296-16-7 Pbk : £14.00
(B77-00393)

822'.051 — Miracle plays in English. York plays. *Anthologies*
[York plays. *Selections].* The Passion : selected from the 15th century cycle of York mystery plays / in a version by the [National Theatre] Company with Tony Harrison. — London : Collings, 1977. — 64p : plan ; 26cm.
ISBN 0-86036-071-7 Sd : £1.95
(B77-32138)

822'.051 — Morality plays in English, 1420-1500. *Critical studies*
Miyajima, Sumiko. The theatre of man : dramatic technique and stagecraft in the English medieval moral plays / by Sumiko Miyajima. — Clevedon (Six Ways, Clevedon, Avon) : Clevedon Printing Co. Ltd, 1977. — vi, 193p ; 23cm.
Bibl.: p.173-188. — Index.
ISBN 0-9505919-0-4 : £6.00
(B77-31423)

822.3 — ENGLISH DRAMA, 1558-1625
822'.3 — Drama in English, 1558-1625. *Texts*
Beaumont, Francis. The faithful friends / [by Francis Beaumont and John Fletcher ; text prepared by G.M. Pinciss]. — [London] ([c/o Dr E. Brennan, Westfield College, Kidderpore Ave., NW3 7ST]) : Malone Society, 1975. — ii-xx,107p,[6]p of plates : facsims ; 22cm. — (Malone Society. Reprints)
'... the unique manuscript in the Dyce collection at the Victoria and Albert Museum ...' - title page verso.
Unpriced
(B77-08529)

Fletcher, John, *b.1579.* The two noble kinsmen / [by] William Shakespeare and John Fletcher ; edited by N.W. Bawcutt. — Harmondsworth [etc.] : Penguin, 1977. — 249p ; 19cm. — (New Penguin Shakespeare)
Bibl.: p.47-50.
ISBN 0-14-070730-1 Pbk : £1.25
(B77-27338)

Jonson, Ben. [Bartholomew Fair]. Bartholmew Fair / [by] Ben Jonson ; edited by G.R. Hibbard. — London : E. Benn [etc.], 1977. — xxxvi,180p ; 20cm. — (The new mermaids)
Bibl.: p.xxxvi.
ISBN 0-510-33710-4 Pbk : £1.95
(B77-18965)

Middleton, Thomas. A fair quarrel / [by] Thomas Middleton and William Rowley ; edited by George R. Price. — London : Edward Arnold, 1977. — xxvi,138p ; 21cm. — (Regents Renaissance drama series)
This ed. originally published: Lincoln, Neb. : University of Nebraska Press, 1976.
ISBN 0-7131-5959-6 : £8.00
ISBN 0-7131-5960-x Pbk : £3.95
(B77-18356)

The **wasp**, or, Subject's precedent / [text prepared by J.W. Lever]. — London ([c/o Dr E. Brennan, Westfield College, Kidderpore Ave., NW3 7ST]) : Malone Society, 1976. — ii-xxi,100p,[7]p of plates : facsims ; 22cm. — (Malone Society. Reprints)
'... a unique manuscript in the Duke of Northumberland's library at Alnwick Castle (MS.507) ...' - p.5.
Unpriced
(B77-08530)

822'.3 — Drama in English. Jonson, Ben. *Critical studies*
Parfitt, George. Ben Jonson : public poet and private man / [by] George Parfitt. — London : Dent, 1976. — ix,181p ; 23cm.
Bibl.: p.175-177. — Index.
ISBN 0-460-10429-2 : £5.95
(B77-01774)

822'.3 — Drama in English. Marlowe, Christopher. *Biographies*
Hilton, Della. Who was Kit Marlowe? : the story of the poet and playwright / [by] Della Hilton. — London : Weidenfeld and Nicolson, 1977. — xi,163p,[8]p of plates : ill, facsims, ports ; 23cm.
Bibl.: p.159-160. — Index.
ISBN 0-297-77247-3 : £5.00
(B77-07572)

822'.3 — Drama in English. Marlowe, Christopher. *Critical studies*
Weil, Judith. Christopher Marlowe : Merlin's prophet / [by] Judith Weil. — Cambridge [etc.] : Cambridge University Press, 1977. — vii,219p ; 23cm.
Bibl.: p.207-213. — Index.
ISBN 0-521-21554-4 : £7.50
(B77-28065)

822'.3 — Drama in English. Tourneur, Cyril. Revenger's tragedy. *Critical studies*
Ayres, Philip J. Tourneur, 'The Revenger's tragedy' / by Philip J. Ayres. — London : Edward Arnold, 1977. — 64p ; 20cm. — (Studies in English literature ; no.68)
Bibl.: p.63. — Index.
ISBN 0-7131-5937-5 : £3.50
ISBN 0-7131-5938-3 Pbk : £1.90
(B77-14392)

822'.3'09 — Drama in English, 1558-1625. *Critical studies. Festschriften*
English Renaissance drama : essays in honor of Madeleine Doran & Mark Eccles / edited by Standish Henning, Robert Kimbrough, Richard Knowles. — Carbondale [etc.] : Southern Illinois University Press ; London [etc.] : Feffer and Simons, 1976. — xi,186p ; 24cm.
Bibl.: p.179-182. — Index.
ISBN 0-8093-0777-4 : £7.50
(B77-34054)

822'.3'09 — Drama in English, 1558-1625. Related to English theatre, ca 1550-1644
Bradbrook, Muriel Clara. The living monument : Shakespeare and the theatre of his time / [by] M.C. Bradbrook. — Cambridge [etc.] : Cambridge University Press, 1976. — xv,287p, 4p of plates : ill, map ; 23cm.
Index.
ISBN 0-521-21255-3 : £8.50
Primary classification 822.3'3
(B77-01775)

822.3'3 — Drama in English. Shakespeare, William. *Biographies*
Chute, Marchette. Shakespeare of London / by Marchette Chute. — London : Souvenir Press, 1977. — xiii,397p,[2] leaves of plates : map ; 22cm.
Originally published: New York : Dutton, 1949 ; London : New English Library, 1962. — Bibl.: p.363-372. — Index.
ISBN 0-285-64841-1 : £4.95
ISBN 0-285-64840-3 Pbk : £3.50
(B77-32139)

Rowse, Alfred Leslie. Shakespeare the Elizabethan / [by] A.L. Rowse. — London : Weidenfeld and Nicolson, 1977. — 128p : ill(some col), coat of arms, facsims, 3 maps(1 col), ports(some col) ; 29cm.
Ill. on lining papers. — Index.
ISBN 0-297-77254-6 : £4.95
(B77-20549)

Schoenbaum, Samuel. William Shakespeare : a compact documentary life / [by] S. Schoenbaum. — [New ed.]. — Oxford : Clarendon Press, 1977. — xix,376p : ill, coat of arms, facsims, ports ; 22cm.
Ill. on lining papers. — Previous ed.: published as 'William Shakespeare : a documentary life'. 1975. — Index.
ISBN 0-19-812575-5 : £6.75
(B77-23689)

822.3'3 — Drama in English. Shakespeare, William. *Biographies. Secondary school texts*
Birch, Beverley. Shakespeare, man of the theatre / [written and planned by Beverley Birch] ; illustrated by Gordon King. — London : Macdonald Educational, 1977. — 2-47p : col ill, ports ; 29cm. — (Macdonald famous people)
Index.
ISBN 0-356-05167-6 : £1.60
(B77-10538)

822.3'3 — Drama in English. Shakespeare, William. *Critical studies*
Brownlow, F W. Two Shakespearean sequences : Henry VI to Richard II and Pericles to Timon of Athens / [by] F.W. Brownlow. — London [etc.] : Macmillan, 1977. — ix,245p ; 23cm.
Index.
ISBN 0-333-21679-2 : £7.95
(B77-22094)

Muir, Kenneth. The singularity of Shakespeare, and other essays / [by] Kenneth Muir. — Liverpool : Liverpool University Press, 1977. — vii,235p ; 23cm. — (Liverpool English texts and studies)
Index.
ISBN 0-85323-433-7 : £9.75
Also classified at 809
(B77-32830)

Schwartz, Elias. The mortal worm : Shakespeare's master theme / [by] Elias Schwartz. — Port Washington ; London : Kennikat Press, 1977. — viii,119,[1]p ; 23cm. — (Kennikat Press national university publications : literary criticism series)
Index.
ISBN 0-8046-9137-1 : £7.60
(B77-25178)

Shakespeare / [translated from the Italian]. — Maidenhead : Sampson Low, 1977. — 135p : ill(chiefly col), facsims, ports(chiefly col) ; 22cm. — (Giants of literature)
Originally published: in Italian. Milan : Arnoldo Mondadori, 1968?.
ISBN 0-562-00047-x : £2.75
(B77-10926)

Speaight, Robert. Shakespeare : the man and his achievement / [by] Robert Speaight. — London : Dent, 1977. — vii,384p,[16]p of plates : ill, facsims, geneal table, map, ports ; 24cm.
Bibl.: p.375-377. — Index.
ISBN 0-460-04268-8 : £6.50
(B77-06258)

822.3'3 — Drama in English. Shakespeare, William. *Critical studies. Serials*

Shakespeare survey : an annual survey of Shakespearian study and production. — Cambridge [etc.] : Cambridge University Press. 30 : ['Henry IV' to 'Hamlet'] / edited by Kenneth Muir. — 1977. — viii,214p,viii p of plates : ill, plans, port ; 26cm.
Index.
ISBN 0-521-21636-2 : £10.50
ISSN 0080-9152
(B77-31424)

822.3'3 — Drama in English. Shakespeare, William. *Encyclopaedias*

Halliday, Frank Ernest. A Shakespeare companion / [by] F.E. Halliday. — Revised ed. — London : Duckworth [etc.], [1977]. — 571p, leaf of plate,32p of plates : ill, facsims, geneal tables, maps(on lining papers), ports ; 23cm.
Revised ed. originally published: 1964. — Bibl.: p.545-566.
ISBN 0-7156-0309-4 : £12.50
(B77-22826)

822.3'3 — Drama in English. Shakespeare, William. *Esperanto texts*

Shakespeare, William. [Twelfth night. Esperanto]. Epifanio, aŭ, Kiel vi volas / Ŝekspiro ; el la angla tradukis William Auld. — Glasgow (16 Woodlands Drive, Coatbridge ML5 1LE) : Eldonejo Kardo, 1977. — [5],71p ; 21cm.
ISBN 0-905149-02-5 Pbk : £1.80
(B77-13840)

822.3'3 — Drama in English. Shakespeare, William. *Secondary school texts*

Presenting Shakespeare / written [i.e. edited] and arranged by R.C. Peat. — London : Harrap, 1976. — 247p ; 18cm.
This collection originally published: 1947.
ISBN 0-245-53047-9 Pbk : £1.80
(B77-12618)

822.3'3 — Drama in English. Shakespeare, William. *Texts*

Shakespeare, William. Antony and Cleopatra / [by] William Shakespeare ; edited by Emrys Jones. — Harmondsworth [etc.] : Penguin, 1977. — 299p ; 18cm. — (New Penguin Shakespeare)
Bibl.: p.49-53.
ISBN 0-14-070731-x Pbk : £0.75
(B77-27339)

Shakespeare, William. As you like it / [by William Shakespeare] ; edited by Isabel J. Bisson. — Oxford : Clarendon Press, 1975. — 190p : ill ; 17cm. — (The new Clarendon Shakespeare)
Originally published: 1941.
ISBN 0-19-831925-8 Pbk : £0.60
(B77-07573)

Shakespeare, William. [King Henry IV. Part 2]. The second part of King Henry the Fourth / [by] William Shakespeare ; edited by P.H. Davison. — Harmondsworth [etc.] : Penguin, 1977. — 313p : music ; 19cm. — (New Penguin Shakespeare)
Cover title: Henry IV, part 2. — Bibl.: p.41-45.
ISBN 0-14-070728-x Pbk : £0.75
(B77-27340)

Shakespeare, William. [King Richard II]. The tragedy of King Richard II / [by William Shakespeare] ; edited by J.H. Walter. — London : Heinemann Educational, 1977. — [5], 246p : ill ; 20cm. — (Players' Shakespeare)
Text on lining papers.
ISBN 0-435-19013-x : £1.25
(B77-24452)

Shakespeare, William. [A midsummer night's dream]. A midsummer-night's dream / [by William Shakespeare] ; edited by F.C. Horwood. — Oxford : Clarendon Press, [1977]. — 192p,[4]p of plates : ill, facsim ; 17cm. — (The new Clarendon Shakespeare)
Originally published: 1939.
ISBN 0-19-831926-6 Pbk : £0.60
(B77-07574)

Shakespeare, William. [A midsummer night's dream]. A midsummer-night's dream / by William Shakespeare ; with illustrations by Arthur Rackham. — London : Heinemann, 1977. — [7],134p,[40]p of plates : ill(chiefly col) ; 26cm.
Facsimile reprint of: 1st ed. 1908.
ISBN 0-434-61982-5 : £7.50
(B77-23690)

822.3'3 — Drama in English. Shakespeare, William. Antony and Cleopatra. *Critical studies. Readings*

Twentieth century interpretations of 'Antony and Cleopatra' : a collection of critical essays / edited by Mark Rose. — Englewood Cliffs ; London [etc.] : Prentice-Hall, 1977. — vi,138p ; 21cm.
'A Spectrum book'. — Bibl.: p.137-138.
ISBN 0-13-038612-x : £5.55
ISBN 0-13-038604-9 Pbk : £2.00
(B77-23691)

822.3'3 — Drama in English. Shakespeare, William, ca 1600-ca 1615. *Critical studies*

Bradbrook, Muriel Clara. The living monument : Shakespeare and the theatre of his time / [by] M.C. Bradbrook. — Cambridge [etc.] : Cambridge University Press, 1976. — xv,287p, 4p of plates : ill, map ; 23cm.
Index.
ISBN 0-521-21255-3 : £8.50
Also classified at 822'.3'09; 792'.0942
(B77-01775)

822.3'3 — Drama in English. Shakespeare, William. Characters. *Critical studies*

Fiedler, Leslie Aaron. The stranger in Shakespeare / [by] Leslie A. Fiedler. — St Albans : Paladin, 1974. — 222p ; 20cm.
Originally published: New York : Stein and Day, 1972 ; London : Croom Helm, 1973. — Index.
ISBN 0-586-08142-9 Pbk : £0.90
(B77-20550)

822.3'3 — Drama in English. Shakespeare, William. Compared with Virgil

Knight, George Wilson. Vergil and Shakespeare / by G. Wilson Knight. — Exeter : University of Exeter, 1977. — [1],26,[1]p ; 21cm. — (Jackson Knight memorial lecture ; 9th)
'Delivered at the University of Exeter 27th February 1976'.
ISBN 0-85989-037-6 Sd : £0.50
Also classified at 871'.01
(B77-15472)

822.3'3 — Drama in English. Shakespeare, William. Coriolanus. *Critical studies, 1765-1971. Readings*

Shakespeare, 'Coriolanus' : a casebook / edited by B.A. Brockman. — London [etc.] : Macmillan, 1977. — 236p ; 22cm. — (Casebook series)
Bibl.: p.225-227. — Index.
ISBN 0-333-19574-4 : £5.95
ISBN 0-333-19575-2 Pbk : Unpriced
(B77-22827)

822.3'3 — Drama in English. Shakespeare, William. Criticism, 1800-1976

Styan, John Louis. The Shakespeare revolution : criticism and performance in the twentieth century / [by] J.L. Styan. — Cambridge [etc.] : Cambridge University Press, 1977. — ix,292p : ill ; 22cm.
Bibl.: p.264-274. — Index.
ISBN 0-521-21193-x : £6.50
Primary classification 792.9
(B77-27296)

822.3'3 — Drama in English. Shakespeare, William. Hamlet. Psychological aspects

Lidz, Theodore. Hamlet's enemy : madness and myth in 'Hamlet' / [by] Theodore Lidz. — London : Vision Press, 1976. — xiii,258p : 1 ill ; 24cm.
Originally published: New York : Basic Books, 1975. — Bibl.: p.243-246. — Index.
ISBN 0-85478-433-0 : £4.95
(B77-09231)

822.3'3 — Drama in English. Shakespeare, William. Historical plays. Related to historical events

Saccio, Peter. Shakespeare's English kings : history, chronicle, and drama / [by] Peter Saccio. — London [etc.] : Oxford University Press, 1977. — viii,268p : geneal tables, maps, ports ; 20cm.
Bibl.: p.247-257. — Index.
ISBN 0-19-281224-6 Pbk : £1.75
(B77-24453)

822.3'3 — Drama in English. Shakespeare, William. Julius Caesar. *Critical studies*

Daiches, David. Shakespeare, 'Julius Caesar' / by David Daiches. — London : Edward Arnold, 1976. — 63p ; 19cm. — (Studies in English literature ; no.65)
Bibl.: p.62. — Index.
ISBN 0-7131-5927-8 : £3.30
ISBN 0-7131-5928-6 Pbk : £1.60
(B77-10539)

822.3'3 — Drama in English. Shakespeare, William. King Lear. *Critical studies*

Reibetanz, John. The Lear world : a study of 'King Lear' in its dramatic context / [by] John Reibetanz. — London : Heinemann, 1977. — xi,142p ; 26cm.
Also published: Toronto : University of Toronto Press, 1977. — Index.
ISBN 0-435-18770-8 : £6.80
(B77-31425)

822.3'3 — Drama in English. Shakespeare, William. Linguistic aspects

Hulme, Hilda Mary. Explorations in Shakespeare's language : some problems of word meaning in the dramatic text / [by] Hilda M. Hulme. — London : Longman, 1977. — xii, 351p ; 22cm.
Originally published: London : Longmans, 1962. — Bibl.: p.340-341. — Index.
ISBN 0-582-48726-9 Pbk : £3.95
(B77-33416)

822.3'3 — Drama in English. Shakespeare, William. Love's labour's lost. *Critical studies*

Carroll, William C. The great feast of language in 'Love's labour's lost' / by William C. Carroll. — Princeton ; Guildford : Princeton University Press, 1976. — xii,279,[1]p ; 23cm.
Bibl.: p.243-254. — Index.
ISBN 0-691-06309-5 : £10.50
(B77-06849)

822.3'3 — Drama in English. Shakespeare, William. Macbeth. *Critical studies*

Twentieth century interpretations of 'Macbeth' : a collection of critical essays / edited by Terence Hawkes. — Englewood Cliffs ; London [etc.] : Prentice-Hall, 1977. — iv,140p ; 21cm.
Bibl.: p.139-140.
ISBN 0-13-541458-x : £5.55
ISBN 0-13-541441-5 Pbk : £1.95
(B77-17064)

822.3'3 — Drama in English. Shakespeare, William. Macbeth. *Critical studies. Readings*

Aspects of 'Macbeth' : articles reprinted from 'Shakespeare survey' / edited by Kenneth Muir and Philip Edwards. — Cambridge [etc.] : Cambridge University Press, 1977. — ix,86p,xvi p of plates : ill ; 26cm.
ISBN 0-521-21500-5 : £6.50
ISBN 0-521-29176-3 Pbk : £2.95
(B77-22828)

822.3'3 — Drama in English. Shakespeare, William. Macbeth. *Study outlines. For Irish students. Secondary school texts*

Britton, Tony. 'Macbeth' / [by] Tony Britton. — Dublin : Helicon, 1977. — [3],58p ; 21cm. — (Helicon student guides)
Bibl.: p.58.
Sd : £0.66
(B77-33417)

822.3'3 — Drama in English. Shakespeare, William. Othello. *Critical studies. Readings*

Aspects of 'Othello' : articles reprinted from 'Shakespeare survey' / edited by Kenneth Muir and Philip Edwards. — Cambridge [etc.] : Cambridge University Press, 1977. — x,110p, xvi p of plates : ill ; 26cm.
ISBN 0-521-21499-8 : £6.50
ISBN 0-521-29175-5 Pbk : £2.95
(B77-22829)

822.3'3 — Drama in English. Shakespeare, William. Religious aspects

Bennell, Margaret. Shakespeare's flowering of the spirit / by Margaret Bennell ; edited and completed by Isabel Wyatt. — East Grinstead (Peredur, East Grinstead, Sussex) : Lanthorn Press, 1971. — [11],253p : ill(on lining papers), port ; 22cm.
£2.80
(B77-29663)

822.3'3 — Drama in English. Shakespeare, William. Satire

Birney, Alice Lotvin. Satiric catharsis in Shakespeare : a theory of dramatic structure / [by] Alice Lotvin Birney. — Berkeley [etc.] ; London : University of California Press, 1973. — xi,158p ; 21cm.
Bibl.: p.149-155. — Index.
ISBN 0-520-02214-9 : Unpriced
(B77-20551)

822.3'3 — Drama in English. Shakespeare, William. Sources & analogues. *Critical studies*

Jones, Emrys, *b.1931.* The origins of Shakespeare / [by] Emrys Jones. — Oxford : Clarendon Press, 1977. — vii,290p ; 22cm.
Index.
ISBN 0-19-812080-x : £10.00
(B77-09915)

822.3'3 — Drama in English. Shakespeare, William. Special subjects: Dreams & visions
Arthos, John. Shakespeare's use of dream and vision / [by] John Arthos. — London : Bowes and Bowes, 1977. — 208p ; 23cm.
Index.
ISBN 0-370-30007-6 : £5.00
(B77-12619)

822.3'3 — Drama in English. Shakespeare, William. Tragedies. Characters: Heroes. *Critical studies*
Knight, George Wilson. Shakespeare's dramatic challenge : on the rise of Shakespeare's tragic heroes / [by] G. Wilson Knight. — London : Croom Helm [etc.], 1977. — 181p : port ; 23cm.
Index.
ISBN 0-85664-309-2 : £5.95
(B77-09232)

822.3'3 — Drama in English. Shakespeare, William. Troilus and Cressida. *Critical studies, 1679-1975. Readings*
Shakespeare, 'Troilus and Cressida' : a casebook / edited by Priscilla Martin. — London [etc.] : Macmillan, 1976. — 253p ; 21cm. — (Casebook series)
Bibl.: p.239-240. — Index.
ISBN 0-333-18641-9 : £4.95
(B77-05622)

822.4 — ENGLISH DRAMA, 1625-1702
822'.4 — Drama in English, 1625-1702. *Texts*
Buckingham, George Villiers, *2nd Duke of.* The rehearsal / [by] George Villiers, Duke of Buckingham ; [edited, with a commentary by] D.E.L. Crane. — Durham : University of Durham, 1976. — xvii,107p ; 23cm. — (University of Durham. Publications)
Bibl.: p.101-103.
ISBN 0-900926-26-0 : £3.50
(B77-17065)

Dryden, John. The works of John Dryden / [general editor H.T. Swedenberg, Jr, et al.]. — Berkeley [etc.] ; London : University of California Press.
Vol.15 : Plays : 'Albion and Albanius', 'Don Sebastian', 'Amphitryon' / [editor Earl Miner, textual editor George R. Guffey, associate editor Franklin B. Zimmerman]. — 1976. — xv,568p,[4]leaves of plates : ill, facsims, music, port ; 24cm.
Bibl.: p.321. — Index.
ISBN 0-520-02129-0 : £26.00
(B77-12620)

Farquhar, George. The recruiting officer / [by] George Farquhar ; edited by John Ross. — London : E. Benn [etc.], 1977. — xli,141p : facsims, map, music, port ; 20cm. — (The new mermaids)
Bibl.: p.xli.
ISBN 0-510-33731-7 Pbk : £1.95
(B77-25855)

Otway, Thomas. The orphan / [by] Thomas Otway ; edited by Aline Mackenzie Taylor. — London : Edward Arnold, 1977. — xxx,118p ; 21cm. — (Regents Restoration drama series)
This ed. originally published: Lincoln, Neb. : University of Nebraska Press, 1976.
ISBN 0-7131-5947-2 : £8.00
ISBN 0-7131-5948-0 Pbk : £3.95
(B77-24454)

Polwhele, Elizabeth. The frolicks, or, The lawyer cheated (1671) / [by] Elizabeth Polwhele ; edited from the manuscript in the Cornell University Libraries by Judith Milhous and Robert D. Hume. — Ithaca ; London : Cornell University Press, 1977. — 154,[3]p : ill, facsims ; 23cm.
'Edition of Cornell Mss. Bd. Rare P P77' - Preface.
ISBN 0-8014-1030-4 : Unpriced
(B77-34055)

Southerne, Thomas. Oroonoko / [by] Thomas Southerne ; edited by Maximillian E. Novak and David Stuart Rodes. — London : Edward Arnold, 1977. — xlii,143p ; 21cm. — (Regents Restoration drama series)
This ed. originally published: Lincoln, Neb. : University of Nebraska Press, 1976.
ISBN 0-7131-5950-2 : £8.00
ISBN 0-7131-5951-0 Pbk : £3.95
(B77-24455)

822'.4 — Drama in English. Behn, Aphra. *Biographies*
Duffy, Maureen. The passionate shepherders : Aphra Behn, 1640-89 / [by] Maureen Duffy. — London : Cape, 1977. — 324p,[8]p of plates : ill, facsims, geneal table, map, ports ; 23cm.
Facsim. on lining papers. — Bibl.: p.305-307. — Index.
ISBN 0-224-01349-1 : £7.50 : CIP rev.
(B77-08531)

822'.4 — Drama in English. Farquhar, George. Beaux' stratagem & Recruiting officer. *Critical studies, 1706-1973. Readings*
Farquhar, 'The recruiting officer' and 'The beaux' stratagem' : a casebook / edited by Raymond A. Anselment. — London [etc.] : Macmillan, 1977. — 230p ; 23cm. — (Casebook series)
Spine title: 'The recruiting officer' and 'The beaux' stratagem'. — Bibl.: p.221. — Index.
ISBN 0-333-21145-6 : £5.95
ISBN 0-333-21146-4 Pbk : £2.50
(B77-24456)

822'.4 — Drama in English. Vanbrugh, Sir John. *Biographies*
Anthony, John, *b.1928.* Vanbrugh : an illustrated life of Sir John Vanbrugh, 1664-1726 / [by] John Anthony. — Aylesbury : Shire Publications, 1977. — 48p : ill, facsim, ports ; 21cm. — (Lifelines ; 42)
Bibl.: p.47. — Index.
ISBN 0-85263-339-4 Pbk : £0.60
(B77-29664)

822.6 — ENGLISH DRAMA, 1745-1800
822'.6 — Drama in English, 1745-1800. *Texts*
Goldsmith, Oliver. [Selected works]. Poems and plays / [by] Oliver Goldsmith. — New ed., completely revised / edited by Tom Davis. — London : Dent [etc.], 1975 [i.e. 1977]. — xxx, 258p : facsims ; 19cm.
This ed. originally published: 1975. — Bibl.: p.xxvii.
Pbk : £2.95
ISBN 0-460-10415-2
Also classified at 821'.6
(B77-31426)

O'Keeffe, John. Wild oats, or, The strolling gentlemen : a comedy in five acts / by John O'Keeffe ; the text as prepared and directed by Clifford Williams for the Royal Shakespeare Company ; with an introduction and editorial material by the director. — London : Heinemann Educational, 1977. — xvi,88p ; 19cm. — (The Hereford plays)
ISBN 0-435-23722-5 Pbk : £1.50
(B77-13233)

822'.6 — Drama in English. Sheridan, Richard Brinsley. *Critical studies*
Loftis, John. Sheridan and the drama of Georgian England / [by] John Loftis. — Oxford : Blackwell, 1976. — xi,174p ; 23cm. — (Plays and playwrights)
Bibl.: p.161-164. — Index.
ISBN 0-631-14880-9 : £5.00
(B77-07575)

822'.6 — Folk plays in English, 1745-1800. *Texts. Manuscripts. Facsimiles*
[The **Revesby** sword play]. Morrice dancers at Revesby : reproduced from the manuscript in the British Library / with an introduction by M.J. Preston, M.G. Smith and P.S. Smith. — Sheffield (Sheffield S10 2TN) : Centre for English Cultural Tradition and Language, University of Sheffield, 1976. — [2],36p ; 30cm. — (University of Sheffield. Centre for English Cultural Tradition and Language. CECTAL facsimiles ; no.1 ISSN 0309-4154)
Facsimile reprint of the script of a performance of the Revesby sword play as performed on October 20th, 1779.
Sd : £0.75
(B77-13841)

822.8 — ENGLISH DRAMA, 1837-1900
822'.8 — Drama in English, 1837-1900. *Texts*
Barrie, *Sir* **James Matthew,** *bart.* Peter Pan : a fantasy in five acts / by J.M. Barrie. — London [etc.] : French, 1977. — [4],83p ; 19cm.
Originally published in: 'The plays of J.M. Barrie'. London : Hodder and Stoughton, 1928.

ISBN 0-573-05041-4 Pbk : £0.80 : CIP rev.
(B77-12621)

Barrie, *Sir* **James Matthew,** *bart.* Quality Street / [by] J.M. Barrie. — London [etc.] : Hodder and Stoughton, 1977. — 120p : ill ; 19cm. — (Pilot books)
Five men, 8 women. — Originally published: 1913.
ISBN 0-340-22206-9 Pbk : £0.85
(B77-25179)

822'.8 — Drama in English. Barrie, Sir James Matthew, bart. *Critical studies*
Wright, Allen. J.M. Barrie : glamour of twilight / [by] Allen Wright. — Edinburgh (36 North Castle St., Edinburgh EH2 3BN) : Ramsay Head Press, 1976. — 96p ; 19cm. — (New assessments)
Bibl.: p.96.
ISBN 0-902859-37-4 : £2.50
(B77-07576)

822'.8 — Drama in English. Gregory, Isabella Augusta, Lady. *Biographies. Readings*
Lady Gregory : interviews and recollections / edited by E.H. Mikhail. — London [etc.] : Macmillan, 1977. — xii,113p ; 23cm.
Index.
ISBN 0-333-22327-6 : £7.95 : CIP rev.
(B77-15473)

822'.8 — Drama in English. Pinero, Sir Arthur Wing. *Correspondence*
Pinero, *Sir* **Arthur Wing.** The collected letters of Sir Arthur Pinero / edited by J.P. Wearing. — Minneapolis : University of Minnesota Press ; London [etc.] : Oxford University Press, [1976]. — xi,302p ; 24cm.
Spine title: Pinero letters. — Published in the United States: 1974. — Index.
ISBN 0-8166-0717-6 : Unpriced
(B77-03207)

822'.8 — Drama in English. Wilde, Oscar. *Critical studies*
Bird, Alan. The plays of Oscar Wilde / [by] Alan Bird. — London : Vision Press, 1977. — 220p ; 23cm. — (Vision critical studies)
Bibl.: p.213-214. — Index.
ISBN 0-85478-064-5 : £5.40
(B77-29665)

822'.8 — Drama in English. Yeats, William Butler. *Critical studies*
Miller, Liam. The noble drama of W.B. Yeats / [by] Liam Miller. — Dublin : Dolmen Press [etc.], 1977. — xv,365p,[16]p of plates : ill, facsims, music, plans, ports ; 26cm. — (New Yeats papers ; 13)
Bibl.: p.337-341. — Index.
ISBN 0-85105-301-7 : £20.00
(B77-25856)

822'.8 — Drama in English. Yeats, William Butler. Cuchulain cycle. *Critical studies*
Friedman, Barton R. Adventures in the deeps of the mind : the 'Cuchulain cycle' of W.B. Yeats / [by] Barton R. Friedman. — Princeton ; Guildford : Princeton University Press, 1977. — xiii,151,[1]p ; 23cm. — (Princeton essays in literature)
Index.
ISBN 0-691-06325-7 : £7.80
(B77-28861)

822'.8'08 — Drama in English, 1837-1900. Parodies of Shakespeare, William. *Anthologies*
Nineteenth-century Shakespeare burlesques / [selected by Stanley Wells]. — London : Diploma Press.
In 5 vols.
Vol.1 : John Poole and his imitators / with an introduction by Stanley Wells. — 1977. — xxvii,235p ; 22cm.
Cover title: Shakespeare burlesques. — Contents: Hamlet travestie / by John Poole - Romeo and Juliet travesty / by R. Gurney - Richard III travestie / by William By - King Richard III travestie.
ISBN 0-86015-015-1 : £12.50
(B77-22830)

822.912 — ENGLISH DRAMA, 1900-1945
822'.9'12 — Drama in English, 1900-1945. *Texts*
Beckett, Samuel. Ends and odds : plays and sketches / by Samuel Beckett. — London : Faber, 1977. — 104p : plans ; 21cm.
ISBN 0-571-10978-0 : £2.75 : CIP rev.
(B77-07577)

Durbridge, Francis. Murder with love : a thriller / [by] Francis Durbridge. — London [etc.] : French, 1977. — [3],68p : plan ; 22cm.
Six men, 3 women.
ISBN 0-573-11302-5 Pbk : £1.10
(B77-27341)

Galsworthy, John. Escape : an episodic play / [by] John Galsworthy. — [1st ed. reprinted] / with school and acting notes by John Hampden. — London : Duckworth, 1977. — [4],76p ; 23cm.
Nineteen men, 6 women, 1 girl, supers. — This ed. originally published: 1964.
ISBN 0-7156-1219-0 : £4.95
ISBN 0-7156-1220-4 Pbk : £1.50
(B77-19617)

Galsworthy, John. Justice : a tragedy in four acts / [by] John Galsworthy. — [1st ed. reprinted] / with school and acting notes by John Hampden. — London : Duckworth, 1977. — iv-vii,3-94p ; 23cm.
Seventeen men, 1 woman, supers. — This ed. originally published: 1964.
ISBN 0-7156-1221-2 : £4.95
ISBN 0-7156-1222-0 Pbk : £1.50
(B77-19618)

Galsworthy, John. Loyalties : a drama in three acts / [by] John Galsworthy. — [1st ed. reprinted] / with school and acting notes by John Hampden. — London : Duckworth, 1977. — viii,3-86p ; 23cm.
Seventeen men, 3 women. — This ed. originally published: 1963.
ISBN 0-7156-1223-9 : £4.95
ISBN 0-7156-1224-7 Pbk : £1.50
(B77-19619)

Galsworthy, John. The silver box : a comedy in three acts / [by] John Galsworthy. — [1st ed. reprinted] / with school and acting notes by John Hampden. — London : Duckworth, 1977. — ii-vii,3-76p ; 23cm.
Eleven men, 7 women, supers. — This ed. originally published: 1964.
ISBN 0-7156-1227-1 : £4.95
ISBN 0-7156-1228-x Pbk : £1.50
(B77-32140)

Galsworthy, John. Strife : a drama in three acts / [by] John Galsworthy ; with school and acting notes by John Hampden. — London : Duckworth, 1977. — [5],90p ; 23cm.
Twenty-two men, 2 women. — Originally published: 1964.
ISBN 0-7156-1225-5 : £4.95
ISBN 0-7156-1226-3 Pbk : £1.50
(B77-32141)

Granville-Barker, Harley. The Madras house : a comedy in four acts / [by] Harley Granville Barker ; with an introduction and notes by Margery Morgan. — London : Eyre Methuen, 1977. — xxxii,160p ; 20cm. — (Methuen's theatre classics)
Eight men, 17 women. — Originally published: London : Sidgwick and Jackson, 1911.
ISBN 0-413-38440-3 : £4.50
ISBN 0-413-38430-6 Pbk : £2.25
(B77-28066)

Johnston, Denis. The dramatic works of Denis Johnston. — Gerrards Cross : Smythe.
In 2 vols.
Vol.1. — 1977. — [4],395p ; 23cm.
Contents: The old lady says 'No!' - The scythe and the sunset - Storm song - The dreaming dust - 'Strange occurrence on Ireland's Eye'.
ISBN 0-901072-52-4 : £9.75
ISBN 0-901072-71-0 Limited signed ed. : £40.00
(B77-18966)

Maugham, William Somerset. Selected plays [of] W. Somerset Maugham. — London : Pan Books, 1976. — 448p ; 18cm.
Contents: Sheppey - The sacred flame - The circle - The constant wife - Our betters.
ISBN 0-330-24238-5 Pbk : £1.25
(B77-02557)

Watkins, Vernon. The influences / [by] Vernon Watkins. — Hayes, Middx (91 Wimborne Ave., Hayes, Middx) : Bran's Head Books Ltd, 1976. — [40]p ; 24cm.
Limited ed. of 350 copies.
ISBN 0-905220-08-0 : £8.00
(B77-08532)

822'.9'12 — Drama in English. Eliot, Thomas Stearns. Murder in the cathedral. *Study outlines*

Gallagher, Michael Paul. T.S. Eliot, 'Murder in the cathedral' / [by] Michael Paul Gallagher. — Dublin : Gill and Macmillan, 1977. — 39p ; 21cm. — (Study-guide series)
Bibl.: p.39.
ISBN 0-7171-0825-2 Sd : £0.60
(B77-17066)

822'.9'12 — Drama in English. Sherriff, Robert Cedric. Journey's end. *Study outlines*

Altena, I. Notes on R.C. Sherriff's 'Journey's end' / compiled by I. Altena. — London [etc.] : Methuen, 1976. — [3],28p ; 22cm. — (Study-aid series)
Bibl.: p.28.
ISBN 0-413-37000-3 Sd : £0.60
(B77-13234)

822'.9'12 — Drama in English. Synge, John Millington. *Transcripts of interviews*

J.M. Synge : interviews and recollections / edited by E.H. Mikhail ; foreword by Robin Skelton. — London [etc.] : Macmillan, 1977. — xiv, 138p ; 23cm.
Index.
ISBN 0-333-19770-4 : £6.95
(B77-17724)

822'.9'1209 — Verse drama in English, 1900-1975. *Critical studies*

Hinchcliffe, Arnold P. Modern verse drama / [by] Arnold P. Hinchcliffe. — London : Methuen, 1977. — xiii,80p ; 20cm. — (The critical idiom ; 32)
Bibl.: p.77-78. — Index.
ISBN 0-416-83250-4 : £2.35
ISBN 0-416-83260-1 Pbk : £1.20
(B77-12622)

822.914 — ENGLISH DRAMA, 1945-

822'.9'14 — Drama in English, 1945-. *Texts*

Astell, Betty. Aladdin : a pantomime / by Betty Astell. — [London] : Evans Bros, [1977]. — [10],60,[1]p ; 23cm.
Seven men, 3 women, supers.
ISBN 0-237-75013-9 Sd : Unpriced
(B77-32142)

Ayckbourn, Alan. Confusions : five interlinked one-act plays / [by] Alan Ayckbourn. — London [etc.] : French, 1977. — [4],68p : plans ; 22cm.
Three men, 2 women.
ISBN 0-573-11073-5 Pbk : £1.00
(B77-11388)

Ayckbourn, Alan. Ernie's incredible illucinations : a play / by Alan Ayckbourn. — London [etc.] : French, 1976. — [3],20,[2]p : plan ; 19cm.
Fifteen men, 7 women, supers. — Originally published: in 'Playbill. 1' / edited by Alan Durband. London : Hutchinson Educational, 1970.
ISBN 0-573-12063-3 Sd : £0.50
(B77-00933)

Ayckbourn, Alan. Three plays / [by] Alan Ayckbourn. — London : Chatto and Windus, 1977. — 229p ; 20cm.
Contents: Absurd person singular. Originally published: London : French, 1974 - Absent friends. Originally published: London : French, 1975 - Bedroom farce.
ISBN 0-7011-2203-x : £4.95 : CIP rev.
(B77-05623)

Barker, Howard. Stripwell ; [and], Claw / [by] Howard Barker. — London : J. Calder : [Distributed by Calder and Boyars], 1977. — 230p ; 21cm. — (Playscript ; 79)
ISBN 0-7145-3566-4 : £6.50
(B77-25857)

Barnes, Peter, *b.1931.* The frontiers of farce / adaptations by Peter Barnes of George[s] Feydeau's 'The purging' ; [and], Frank Wedekind's 'The singer'. — London : Heinemann Educational, 1977. — viii,64p ; 19cm.
'The purging': 4 men, 3 women. — 'The singer': 5 men, 3 women.
ISBN 0-435-23063-8 Pbk : £1.30
(B77-08533)

Barstow, Stan. Joby : a television play / by Stan Barstow ; dramatized from his own novel ; edited by Marilyn Davies. — London [etc.] : Blackie, 1977. — [10],86p;[4]p of plates : ill ; 21cm. — (Student drama series)
'... a Yorkshire Television colour production ... first transmitted in two episodes on 12 and 19 January, 1975'. — note. — Adaptation of: 'Joby'. London : Joseph, 1964. — Bibl.: p.85.
ISBN 0-216-90180-4 Pbk : £1.60
(B77-26495)

Bate, Sam. Decline and fall : a play / [by] Sam Bate. — London [etc.] : French, 1977. — [5], 24p ; 19cm.
Three men, 5 women.
ISBN 0-573-02349-2 Sd : £0.35 : CIP rev.
(B77-12623)

Bate, Sam. Murder at eight : a thriller / [by] Sam Bate. — London [etc.] : French, 1977. — [4],28p : plan ; 19cm.
Six women.
ISBN 0-573-03371-4 Sd : £0.35
(B77-16578)

Beech, Marjorie. Young Mr Dickens / by Marjorie Beech. — Macclesfield (35 Sandringham Rd, Macclesfield, Cheshire SK10 1QB) : New Playwrights' Network, [1977]. — 72p ; 18cm.
Seven men, 11 women.
Pbk : £1.40
(B77-22831)

Berkoff, Steven. East ; [and], Agamemnon ; [and], The fall of the house of Usher / [by] Steven Berkoff. — London : J. Calder : [Distributed by Calder and Boyars], 1977. — 139p : ill ; 21cm. — (Playscript ; 78)
ISBN 0-7145-3610-5 : £4.95
(B77-17725)

Bingham, Jack. To father with love / by Jack Bingham. — Macclesfield (35 Sandringham Rd, Macclesfield, Cheshire SK10 1QB) : New Playwrights' Network, 1976. — 83,[3]p : plan ; 18cm.
Four men, 3 women.
ISBN 0-903653-27-3 Pbk : £1.25
(B77-03741)

Bond, Edward. Plays [of] Edward Bond. — London : Eyre Methuen. — (The master playwrights series)
1 : Saved ; [and], Early morning. [New ed.] [and], The Pope's wedding / with an author's note, 'On violence'. — 1977. — 312p ; 18cm.
'Saved' originally published: London : Methuen, 1966. — Previous ed. of: 'Early morning'. London : Calder and Boyars, 1968. — 'The Pope's wedding' originally published: London : Methuen, 1971.
ISBN 0-413-45410-x Pbk : £1.25
(B77-28067)

Booth, Anthony. Deadline dawn : a play / [by] Anthony Booth. — London [etc.] : French, 1977. — vii,30,[2]p : plan ; 19cm.
Two men, 2 women.
ISBN 0-573-02347-6 Pbk : £0.35
(B77-13235)

Bowen, John. Florence Nightingale : a play / by John Bowen. — London [etc.] : French, 1976. — [6],62p : plan ; 22cm.
'... a flexible cast of at least seven men and six or more women' - cover.
ISBN 0-573-01131-1 Pbk : £1.00
(B77-00934)

Brenton, Howard. Weapons of happiness / [by] Howard Brenton. — London : Eyre Methuen, 1976. — 78p ; 20cm. — (Methuen modern plays)
ISBN 0-413-36660-x : £3.25
ISBN 0-413-36650-2 Pbk : £1.25
(B77-00935)

Brown, Alan, *b.1951.* Wheelchair Willie ; [and], Brown ale with Gertie ; [and], O'Connor / [by] Alan Brown. — London : J. Calder, 1977. — 221p : ill ; 21cm. — (Playscript ; 80)
ISBN 0-7145-3652-0 : £5.95
(B77-30584)

Browne, Felicity. The family dance : a play / by Felicity Browne. — London [etc.] : French, 1976. — [3],60p : plan ; 22cm.
Four men, 3 women.
ISBN 0-573-11124-3 Pbk : £1.00
(B77-05624)

Bryden, Bill. Old movies : a play / by Bill Bryden. — London : Heinemann [for] the National Theatre, 1977. — [6],65p ; 19cm. — (National Theatre. Plays)
Seven men, 2 women.
ISBN 0-435-23141-3 Pbk : £1.75
(B77-23692)

Campton, David. The do-it-yourself Frankenstein outfit / by David Campton. — [Leicester] ([35 Liberty Rd, Glenfield, Leicester LE3 8JF]) : The author, [1977]. — 20p ; 21cm.
Eight children.
ISBN 0-901615-29-3 Sd : Unpriced
(B77-18357)

Campton, David. Us and them : a play / [by] David Campton. — London [etc.] : French, 1977. — [4],15p ; 19cm.
Three players and supers.
ISBN 0-573-02346-8 Sd : £0.35
(B77-10540)

Carpenter, Joyce Frances. Away in a manger : a one act modern nativity play / by Joyce Frances Carpenter. — Bakewell : Hub Publications, 1977. — 28p ; 21cm.
Three men, 4 women, supers.
ISBN 0-905049-39-x Sd : £0.60
(B77-31427)

Carter, Beatrix. Afternoon theatre : a play in one act for five women / by Beatrix Carter. — London : Kenyon-Deane, 1977. — [2],13p ; 21cm.
ISBN 0-7155-0222-0 Sd : £0.40
(B77-10927)

Cooney, Ray. Move over, Mrs Markham : a comedy in two acts / by Ray Cooney and John Chapman. — New York ; London [etc.] : French, [1977]. — [5],107p : plan ; 19cm.
Four men, 5 women. — Originally published: London : English Theatre Guild, 1972.
ISBN 0-573-61282-x Sd : £1.55
(B77-12068)

Coppel, Alec. Cadenza : a play in two acts / by Alec Coppel. — Hornchurch : I. Henry, 1977. — 71p ; 20cm. — (Chameleons' dramascripts)
Three men, 2 women.
ISBN 0-86025-809-2 Pbk : £1.40
(B77-09916)

Cox, Constance. Lady Audley's secret : a melodrama / [by] Constance Cox. — London [etc.] : French, 1976. — [3],24p : plan ; 24cm.
Four men, 8 women.
ISBN 0-573-02345-x Sd : £0.35
(B77-06259)

Cox, Constance. Mansfield Park : a comedy in three acts / adapted from the novel by Jane Austen by Constance Cox. — Bakewell : Hub Publications, 1977. — [1],72p : plan ; 21cm.
Five men, 6 woman.
ISBN 0-905049-15-2 Sd : £0.90
(B77-26496)

Cregan, David. Poor Tom ; &, Tina : two plays / by David Cregan. — London : Eyre Methuen, 1976. — 64p ; 21cm. — (Methuen's new theatrescripts ; no.5)
ISBN 0-413-37470-x Sd : £1.00
(B77-04391)

Croot, Arnold. The miraculous beam : a play in three acts / by Arnold Croot. — [Christchurch] ([Abbotswood, Stour Way, Christchurch, Dorset]) : [The author], [1977]. — [1],62p ; 21cm.
Cover title: Mortgage on the house redeemed by the miraculous beam. — 12 men, male supers.
Sd : £1.00
(B77-32831)

Dale, Adrian. Murder behind the mask / [by] Adrian Dale. — London [etc.] : French, 1977. — [5],23p ; 19cm.
Eight women.
ISBN 0-573-03373-0 Sd : £0.35 : CIP rev.
(B77-30585)

Darbon, Leslie. Double edge : a play / by Leslie Darbon and Peter Whelan. — London [etc.] : French, 1976. — [3],56p ; 22cm.
Three men, 1 woman.
ISBN 0-573-11103-0 Pbk : £1.00
(B77-00394)

Davenport, David Victor. SS and WI sketches and plays / by David V. Davenport. — Melksham : Venton : White Horse Library, 1977. — 55p : ill ; 21cm. — (White Horse library)
ISBN 0-85475-138-6 : £2.50
ISBN 0-85966-048-6 Pbk : Unpriced
(B77-18358)

Day, Doris Maria. Ever been had? : a comedy / [by] Doris M. Day. — London [etc.] : French, 1977. — [3],22p ; 19cm.
Five women.
ISBN 0-573-03370-6 Sd : £0.35
(B77-17067)

Deary, Terence. Teaching through theatre : six practical projects / [by] Terence Deary. — London [etc.] : French, 1977. — ix,49,[1]p : ill, form ; 22cm.
ISBN 0-573-09040-8 Pbk : £1.50
(B77-24457)

Dougall, Edwin. Tatties and herring : a farce / by Edwin Dougall. — Glasgow : Brown and Ferguson, 1977. — 29p ; 18cm. — (Scottish plays ; no.32)
Six men, 5 women.
ISBN 0-85174-283-1 Sd : £0.40
(B77-18359)

Drane, David. Toe nailed to the floor / by David Drane. — Lowestoft (12 The Street, Rushmere, Lowestoft, Suffolk) : Dark Lantern Press, [1976]. — [26]p : ill ; 26cm.
ISBN 0-9504647-0-8 : £1.25
ISBN 0-9504647-1-6 Pbk : Unpriced
(B77-00395)

Edgar, David. Wreckers / [by] David Edgar ; [with music by the 7:84 Band]. — London : Eyre Methuen, 1977. — [6],46,[11]p : music ; 21cm. — (Methuen's new theatrescripts ; no.6)
Twelve men, 8 women, extras.
ISBN 0-413-38510-8 Sd : £1.20
(B77-31428)

Evans, Charles, *b.1937.* A fool among foes : a play in three acts / by Charles Evans. — Macclesfield (35 Sandringham Rd, Macclesfield, Cheshire SK10 1QB) : New Playwrights Network, [1977?]. — 71p : 1 ill, music, plan ; 18cm.
Seven men, 3 women. — '... loosely based on incidents recalled by Corporal William Todd in his "Contemporary journal of the Seven Years War"'.
Pbk : £1.25
(B77-26497)

Featherstone, Anne. Yesterday's tomorrow : a Christian play / by Anne Featherstone. — Ilkeston : Moorley's Bible and Bookshop, [1977]. — 26p ; 21cm.
Three men, 2 women.
ISBN 0-86071-000-9 Sd : £0.24
(B77-34056)

Fergusson, Robert. Fergusson : a bi-centenary handsel : seventeen poems / selected by Robert Garioch. A vision of angels : a one-act play / by Anne Smith. — Edinburgh : Reprographia, 1974. — 72p : 1 ill ; 22cm.
Four men, 2 women.
Sd : £1.30
Primary classification 821'.6
(B77-19605)

Fight for Shelton Bar : a documentary from the Victoria Theatre, Stoke-on-Trent / with introduction and notes by the director, Peter Cheeseman. — London : Eyre Methuen, 1977. — [7],63p,[8]p of plates : ill, ports ; 21cm. — (Methuen's new theatrescripts ; no.10)
ISBN 0-413-38040-8 Sd : £1.20
(B77-28068)

Frayn, Michael. Alphabetical order ; and, Donkeys' years / [by] Michael Frayn. — London : Eyre Methuen, 1977. — [4],165p ; 20cm. — ([A Methuen modern play])
'Alphabetical order' 4 men, 3 women ; 'Donkeys' years' 8 men, 1 woman. — 'Alphabetical order' originally published: London : French, 1976.
ISBN 0-413-37980-9 : £3.95
ISBN 0-413-37990-6 Pbk : £1.75
(B77-27342)

Frayn, Michael. Clouds / [by] Michael Frayn. — London : Eyre Methuen, 1977. — [4],84p ; 20cm. — ([A Methuen modern play])
Four men, 1 woman. — Also published: London : French, 1977.
ISBN 0-413-38000-9 : £3.50
ISBN 0-413-38010-6 Pbk : £1.50
(B77-27343)

Frayn, Michael. Clouds / by Michael Frayn. — London [etc.] : French, 1977. — [3],84p ; 19cm. — (French's acting edition)
Four men, 1 woman.
ISBN 0-573-11083-2 Pbk : £1.00
(B77-15475)

Frayn, Michael. Donkeys' years : a play / by Michael Frayn. — London [etc.] : French, 1977. — [3],92p : plans ; 19cm.
Eight men, 1 woman.
ISBN 0-573-11097-2 Pbk : £1.00 : CIP rev.
(B77-06850)

Freeman, Dave. A bedfull of foreigners : a comedy / by Dave Freeman. — London [etc.] : French, 1976. — [3],86p : plan ; 22cm.
Four men, 3 women.
ISBN 0-573-11043-3 Pbk : £1.00
(B77-10541)

Graham-Jones, Susanna. Il campiello : a Venetian comedy / by Carlo Goldoni ; English version by Susanna Graham-Jones & Bill Bryden. — London : Heinemann Educational [for] the National Theatre, 1976. — vii,64p ; 19cm. — (National Theatre. Plays)
ISBN 0-435-23359-9 Pbk : £1.25
(B77-00936)

Gray, Nicholas Stuart. The other Cinderella : a three act play for children / by Nicholas Stuart Gray. — New York ; London [etc.] : French, [1977]. — 117p : ill ; 19cm.
Five men, 5 women. — Originally published: London : Oxford University Press, 1958.
ISBN 0-573-65090-x Sd : £1.65
(B77-11389)

Gray, Simon. Dog days / [by] Simon Gray. — London : Eyre Methuen, 1976. — 96p ; 20cm. — ([Methuen's modern plays])
ISBN 0-413-37260-x : Unpriced
ISBN 0-413-37270-7 Pbk : £1.50
(B77-00396)

Gregory, Raymond George. Robin Goodfellow in summer / [by] R.G. Gregory. — Weymouth (186 Newstead Rd, Weymouth Dorset DT4 0DY) : Word and Action (Dorset).
1. — 1976. — [2],18p ; 21cm.
'... the first play in a sequence of five [seasonal] plays concerning Robin Goodfellow and Kate Brick'. — 2 men, 1 woman.
Sd : £0.50
(B77-18360)

Gribble, Dorothy Rose. Edgar Allan Poe's 'The cask of Amontillado' / adapted for the stage by Dorothy Rose Gribble. — Newbury (Westridge, Highclere, Newbury, Berks.) : Plantagenet Productions, 1977. — [2],8p ; 21cm.
Two men.
ISBN 0-9505213-6-1 Sd : £0.40
(B77-16029)

Gribble, Dorothy Rose. My servant must not fail : a story of black magic in Renaissance times / written by Dorothy Rose Gribble. — Newbury (Westridge, Highclere, Newbury, Berks.) : Plantagenet Productions, 1977. — [3], 14p ; 21cm.
ISBN 0-9505213-4-5 Sd : £0.50
(B77-09917)

Gribble, Dorothy Rose. The pretty chickens : an ill-natured comedy / written by Dorothy Rose Gribble. — Newbury (Westridge, Highclere, Newbury, Berks.) : Plantagenet Productions, 1977. — [2],10p ; 21cm.
One man, 1 woman.
ISBN 0-9505213-5-3 Sd : £0.45
(B77-16030)

Gribble, Dorothy Rose. Seed of glory : a confession / written by Dorothy Rose Gribble. — Newbury (Westridge, Highclere, Newbury, Berks.) : Plantagenet Productions, 1977. — [2], 5p ; 21cm.
ISBN 0-9505213-3-7 Sd : £0.35
(B77-09918)

Gribble, Dorothy Rose. The taming of the shrew as related by Petruchio and Katherine : scenes from Shakespeare's comedy / with linking dialogue [i.e. adapted] by Dorothy Rose Gribble. — Newbury (Westridge, Highclere, Newbury, Berks.) : Plantagenet Productions, 1976. — [2],16p ; 21cm.
One man, 1 woman.
ISBN 0-9505213-2-9 Sd : £0.55
(B77-09233)

Gribble, Dorothy Rose. Twelfth night as remembered by Feste and Maria : scenes from Shakespeare's comedy / with linking dialogue [i.e. adapted] by Dorothy Rose Gribble. — Newbury (Westridge, Highclere, Newbury, Berks.) : Plantagenet Productions, 1976. — [2], 25p : music ; 21cm.
One man, 1 woman.
ISBN 0-9505213-1-0 Sd : £0.75
(B77-09234)

Gribble, Dorothy Rose. Will you forgo all food? : the legend of a haunting / written by Dorothy Rose Gribble. — Newbury (Westridge, Highclere, Newbury, Berks.) : Plantagenet Productions, 1977. — [2],8p ; 21cm.
One man, 1 woman.
Sd : £0.40
(B77-16031)

Griffiths, Trevor. All good men ; and, Absolute beginners : two plays for television / by Trevor Griffiths. — London : Faber, 1977. — 110p ; 20cm.
ISBN 0-571-10815-6 Pbk : £1.95 : CIP rev.
(B77-09235)

Griffiths, Trevor. Through the night ; and, Such impossibilities : two plays for television / by Trevor Griffiths. — London : Faber, 1977. — 3-128p ; 20cm.
ISBN 0-571-11158-0 Pbk : £1.95 : CIP rev.
(B77-09236)

Groves, Paul. Action stations : seven plays to read or record / [by] Paul Groves, Nigel Grimshaw. — London : Edward Arnold, 1977. — 64p ; 22cm.
ISBN 0-7131-0106-7 Sd : £0.75
(B77-14887)

Hall, Willis. Christmas crackers : a play for children / [by] Willis Hall. — London : French : Heinemann Educational, 1976. — 54p ; 19cm.
Six men, 2 women, 1 boy.
ISBN 0-573-05040-6 Pbk : £0.85
ISBN 0-435-23369-6 (Heinemann Educational) : £0.85
(B77-05625)

Hampton, Christopher. Treats : a play / by Christopher Hampton. — London [etc.] : French, 1976. — [4],42,[2]p : plan ; 22cm.
Two men, 1 woman.
ISBN 0-573-11458-7 Sd : £0.80
(B77-03742)

Hampton, Christopher, *b.1946.* Savages : a play in two acts / by Christopher Hampton. — Revised and rewritten [ed.]. — New York [etc.] ; London : French, 1976. — 94p : plan ; 19cm.
Eight men, 1 woman, supers. — Previous ed.: London : Faber, 1974.
ISBN 0-573-61512-8 Sd : £1.55
(B77-00937)

Harding, Huntly. The licentious fly : a comedy / [by] Huntley Harding. — London [etc.] : French, 1977. — [3],68p : plan ; 22cm.
Six men, 3 women.
ISBN 0-573-11235-5 Pbk : £1.10 : CIP rev.
(B77-16032)

Hardy, Joan, *b.1952.* Just the beginning : a Christmas play / by Joan Hardy. — Ilkeston : Moorley's Bible and Bookshop, [1976]. — 16p ; 21cm.
Nine men, 1 woman, supers.
ISBN 0-901495-85-9 Sd : £0.16
(B77-00397)

Hardy, Joan, *b.1952.* A man called Jesus / [by] Joan Hardy. — Ilkeston : Moorley's Bible and Bookshop, [1977]. — 20p ; 21cm.
ISBN 0-86071-001-7 Sd : £0.18
(B77-12069)

Hare, David. Fanshen : a play / by David Hare ; based on the book by William Hinton. — London [etc.] : French, 1976. — 69p ; 19cm. — (French's theatre scripts)
Seven men, 2 women. — Also published: London : Faber, 1976.
ISBN 0-573-01703-4 Pbk : £1.00
(B77-25180)

Harrison, Tony. Bow down / [by] Tony Harrison. — London : Collings, 1977. — 25p ; 26cm.
ISBN 0-86036-067-9 Sd : £1.95
(B77-32144)

Hastings, Charlotte. The restless evil : a play / [by] Charlotte Hastings. — London [etc.] : French, 1977. — [4],66p : music, plan ; 22cm.
Three men, 7 women.
ISBN 0-573-11370-x Pbk : £1.00
(B77-11390)

Hillman, Barry Leslie. Six for the Charleston : a Twenties skit / by Barry L. Hillman. — Macclesfield (35 Sandringham Rd, Macclesfield, Cheshire SK10 1QB) : New Playwrights' Network, [1976]. — 83,[2]p : plan ; 18cm.
Four men, 6 women.
ISBN 0-903653-28-1 Pbk : £1.25
(B77-03743)

Home, William Douglas. Betzi : a play / by William Douglas Home. — London [etc.] : French, 1977. — [3],74p : plans ; 22cm.
Eleven men, 5 women.
ISBN 0-573-11033-6 Pbk : £1.10 : CIP rev.
(B77-09237)

Hoxton Hall Community Theatre and Education Project. Who killed William Corder? : a new play / [Hoxton Hall Community Theatre and Education Project]. — [London] ([128A Hoxton St., N.1]) : The Project, [1977]. — [33]leaves ; 30cm.
Cover title. — ' ... the result of a series of improvisations based on the story of Maria Marten ... The script is the end point of these improvisations' - leaf [3].
ISBN 0-9503952-2-6 Pbk : Unpriced
(B77-09238)

Hurley, Kathy. The alchemist's book : one of the adventurous encounters of Q. Dapperwhiskers Spats and his friend Churchy : a play to be presented by adults for children / book by Kathy Hurley ; music by Jerry Markoe. — New York ; London [etc.] : French, 1976. — 47p : music, plan ; 19cm.
Seven men, 3 women, supers.
ISBN 0-573-65216-3 Sd : £1.15
(B77-00938)

Hutchence, Keith. Out on a limb : a comedy in another vein (a one act play) / by Keith Hutchence & Anthony Cree. — Oxford (36 Great Clarendon St., Oxford) : J. Hannon & Co. (Publishers), 1976. — [2],15p ; 21cm.
ISBN 0-904233-07-3 Sd : £0.50
(B77-12070)

Jarvis, Martin. Bright boy / by Martin Jarvis. — London [etc.] : French, 1977. — [6],26p : plan ; 19cm.
Four men.
ISBN 0-573-04202-0 Sd : £0.35 : CIP rev.
(B77-27345)

Jones, Dedwydd. Bard : a play on the life and times of Twm O'r Nant / by Dedwydd Jones. — Cambridge (1 Jesus Terrace, New Sq., Cambridge) : The Land of Cokaygne Limited, 1974. — 3-91p ; 18cm.
ISBN 0-904063-06-2 Pbk : £0.65
(B77-20552)

Jones, Elwyn, *b.1923.* Softly, softly : five scripts from the BBC Television series / [by] Elwyn Jones ; with an introduction by the author ; selected by Michael Marland. — London : Longman, 1976. — 170p : ill, port ; 19cm. — (Longman imprint books)
Contents: Private mischief - Power of the press - In the public gaze - Priorities - On the third day.
ISBN 0-582-23341-0 Pbk : £0.95
(B77-00939)

Keefe, Barrie. A mad world, my masters / [by] Barrie Keefe. — London : Eyre Methuen, 1977. — 54p ; 21cm. — (Methuen's new theatrescripts ; no.9)
ISBN 0-413-38590-6 Sd : £1.20
(B77-28069)

Langley, Lee. Baggage : a comedy / by Lee Langley. — London [etc.] : French, 1977. — [3],64p : plan ; 22cm.
Three men, 4 women.
ISBN 0-573-11036-0 Pbk : £1.00
(B77-15476)

Lee, Irene M. The deepest need : a harvest play / [by] Irene M. Lee. — Ilkeston : Moorley's Bible and Bookshop, [1977?]. — 8,[1] p ; 21cm.
Two boys, 4 girls.
ISBN 0-86071-004-1 Sd : £0.14
(B77-27346)

Lee, Irene M. The staff of life : a Bible play for harvest / [by] Irene M. Lee. — Ilkeston : Moorley's Bible and Bookshop, [1977]. — 12, [1]p ; 22cm.
Five boys, 2 girls.
ISBN 0-86071-005-x Sd : £0.14
(B77-25858)

Lee, Maureen. The visitor : a thriller / by Maureen Lee. — London [etc.] : French, 1977. — [3],22p : plan ; 19cm.
Four women.
ISBN 0-573-03372-2 Sd : £0.35 : CIP rev.
(B77-12624)

Leyin, John. Last in - first out : a comedy in three acts / by John Leyin. — Macclesfield (35 Sandringham Rd, Macclesfield, Cheshire SK10 1QB) : New Playwrights Network, 1976. — 75, [6]p : plans ; 18cm.
Eight men, 3 women, supers.
ISBN 0-903653-30-3 Pbk : £1.25
(B77-08029)

Livings, Henry. Pongo plays 1-6 : six short plays / by Henry Livings ; with music by Alex Glasgow. — Revised ed. — London : Methuen, 1976. — 64p : music ; 20cm. — (Methuen young drama)
Previous ed.: 1971.
ISBN 0-413-36730-4 Pbk : £1.00
(B77-09919)

Lucas, Victor. Strangers in the house : a comedy / by Victor Lucas. — [Revised ed.]. — London ([Montague House, Russell Sq., W.C.1]) : Evans Plays, [1977]. — 91p : plan ; 22cm.
Three men, 6 women. — Previous ed. : 1970.
ISBN 0-237-49127-3 Pbk : Unpriced
(B77-10928)

McGrath, John. Fish in the sea / [by] John McGrath. — London : Pluto Press, 1977. — [8],82p ; 22cm. — (Pluto plays)
Ten men, 4 women.
ISBN 0-904383-26-1 Pbk : £1.50
(B77-27347)

McGrath, John. Little Red Hen / [by] John McGrath. — London : Pluto Press, 1977. — [10],51p ; 22cm. — (Pluto plays)
ISBN 0-904383-31-8 Pbk : £1.50
(B77-27348)

McLaren, C A. The meretricious muse of C.A. McLaren and W.J.S. Kirton. — [Aberdeen] ([c/o Waverley Press, Aberdeen]) : [The authors], [1976]. — [27]p ; 21cm.
ISBN 0-9505109-0-4 Sd : Unpriced
(B77-00398)

Mankowitz, Wolf. The Hebrew lesson : a play / by Wolf Mankowitz. — [London] : [Evans Bros], 1976. — [4],16p ; 21cm. — (Evans one act plays)
Includes passages in Yiddish, Gaelic and Hebrew.
ISBN 0-237-75027-9 Sd : £0.50
(B77-29667)

Manktelow, Bettine. They call it murder : a play / [by] Bettine Manktelow. — London [etc.] : French, 1977. — [5],65p : plan ; 22cm.
Three men, 4 women.
ISBN 0-573-11449-8 Pbk : £1.00 : CIP rev.
(B77-12625)

Marcus, Frank. Blind date : an anecdote / by Frank Marcus. — London [etc.] : French, 1977. — 18p ; 19cm. — (French's theatre scripts)
One man, 1 woman.
ISBN 0-573-02505-3 Sd : £0.40 : CIP rev.
(B77-32145)

Maskell, Valerie. Just a song at twilight : a play / [by] Valerie Maskell. — London [etc.] : French, 1977. — [3],13,[3]p : music ; 19cm.
Two men, 4 women.
ISBN 0-573-02348-4 Sd : £0.35
(B77-15477)

Meadowcroft, Ernest. Cradle and shrine : historical play / by Ernest Meadowcroft. — Brentwood : Emma, 1977. — 44p ; 19cm.
ISBN 0-901044-31-8 Sd : £1.25
(B77-22833)

Mercer, David, *b.1928.* Huggy Bear, and other plays / [by] David Mercer. — London : Eyre Methuen, 1977. — 142p ; 20cm. — ([A Methuen modern play])
Contents: Huggy Bear - The Arcata promise - A superstition.
ISBN 0-413-38310-5 : £4.95
ISBN 0-413-38320-2 Pbk : £2.90
(B77-28070)

Moran, Jane. Parable plays / [by] Jane Moran. — London : Edward Arnold, 1977. — 78p ; 22cm.
ISBN 0-7131-0112-1 Sd : £0.98
(B77-19620)

Murphy, Thomas. The sanctuary lamp / [by] Thomas Murphy. — Dublin (Knocksedan House, Swords, Co. Dublin) : Poolbeg Press, 1976. — 78p ; 19cm.
Five men, 2 women.
ISBN 0-905169-02-6 Pbk : £0.90
(B77-25859)

Nichols, Peter, *b.1927.* Privates on parade : a play with songs in two acts / by Peter Nichols. — London : Faber, 1977. — 109p ; 20cm.
Ten men, 1 woman.
ISBN 0-571-11142-4 Pbk : £1.95 : CIP rev.
(B77-07578)

Odd sequence : a fine selection of one act plays. — Macclesfield (35 Sandringham Rd, Macclesfield, Cheshire SK10 1QB) : New Playwrights' Network, [1976]. — [1],29,21,27p : plans ; 18cm. — (Triad ; 10)
Contents: Cat / by John Reason - The mute / by Eleanor Worsley - Shame the devil / by Alison McMaster.
ISBN 0-903653-29-x Pbk : £1.25
(B77-03744)

Poliakoff, Stephen. City sugar : a play / by Stephen Poliakoff. — London [etc.] : French, 1976. — [4],68p : music, plans ; 22cm.
Four men, 3 women.
ISBN 0-573-11072-7 Pbk : £1.00
(B77-00940)

Poliakoff, Stephen. Hitting town : a play / by Stephen Poliakoff. — London [etc.] : French, 1976. — [3],44p ; 19cm.
One man, 2 women.
ISBN 0-573-11179-0 Sd : £0.40
(B77-11391)

Poliakoff, Stephen. Hitting town ; &, City sugar : two plays / by Stephen Poliakoff. — London : Eyre Methuen, 1976. — 76p,[2]leaves of plates : music ; 21cm. — (Methuen's new theatrescripts)
'City sugar' also published: London : French, 1976.
ISBN 0-413-34940-3 Sd : £1.00
(B77-05045)

Poliakoff, Stephen. Strawberry fields / [by] Stephen Poliakoff. — London : Eyre Methuen, 1977. — 53p ; 21cm. — (A Methuen new theatrescript ; no.8)
Four men, 3 women.
ISBN 0-413-38470-5 Sd : £1.20
(B77-25860)

Rayburn, Joyce. Out on a limb : a play / by Joyce Rayburn. — London [etc.] : French, 1977. — [3],57p : plan ; 22cm.
Three men, 3 women.
ISBN 0-573-11323-8 Pbk : £1.00 : CIP rev.
(B77-19621)

Redgrove, Peter. Miss Carstairs dressed for blooding, and other plays / by Peter Redgrove. — London : Boyars : [Distributed by Calder and Boyars], 1977. — 103p ; 21cm. — (Signature series ; 25)
Contents: Miss Carstairs dressed for blooding - In the country of the skin - Three pieces for voices. Originally published: Woodford Green : Poet and Printer, 1972.
ISBN 0-7145-2556-1 : £3.50
(B77-23693)

Richards, Alun. Plays for players / by Alun Richards. — [Llandysul] : [J.D. Lewis], 1975. — 367p ; 22cm.
Contents: The big breaker - The victuallers' ball - The snowdropper - The horizontal life.
ISBN 0-85088-290-7 : £3.75
(B77-13236)

Richardson, Alan, *b.1949.* Brodie the broadsword : a border comedy / by Alan Richardson. — Glasgow : Brown and Ferguson, 1977. — 78p ; 18cm. — (Scottish plays)
Four men, 5 women.
ISBN 0-85174-308-0 Pbk : £0.75
(B77-28071)

Richardson, Alan, *b.1949.* Farewell ploy : a Border comedy / by Alan Richardson. — Glasgow : Brown and Ferguson, 1977. — 42p ; 18cm. — (Scottish plays ; no.64)
Four men, 4 women.
ISBN 0-85174-290-4 Sd : £0.40
(B77-34057)

Robbins, Norman. Wedding of the year : a comedy / [by] Norman Robbins. — London [etc.] : French, 1977. — [5],81p : plan ; 22cm.
Four men, 6 women.
ISBN 0-573-11473-0 Pbk : £0.80
(B77-11392)

Robertson, Jane. Fast - and lose : a one-act play for six women / by Jane Robertson. — London : Kenyon-Deane, 1977. — [2],21p ; 21cm.
ISBN 0-7155-0221-2 Sd : £0.40
(B77-09920)

Ross, Stella. Vin extraordinaire : a play / by Stella Ross. — London [etc.] : French, 1977. — [3],20p : plan ; 19cm.
Four men, 3 women.
ISBN 0-573-12290-3 Sd : £0.35 : CIP rev.
(B77-29668)

Rudkin, David. Ashes / by David Rudkin. — London [etc.] : French, [1977]. — 53p : music ; 19cm. — (French's theatre scripts)
Two men, 2 women.
ISBN 0-573-01707-7 Pbk : £1.00
(B77-13237)

Shaffer, Peter. Equus : a play in two acts / by Peter Shaffer. — New York ; London [etc.] : French, [1976]. — 106p : plan ; 19cm.
Five men, 4 women, supers. — Originally published: London : Deutsch, 1973.
ISBN 0-573-60872-5 Sd : £1.55
(B77-06260)

Shaffer, Peter. White liars / by Peter Shaffer. — Revised [ed.]. — London [etc.] : French, 1976. — [3],35p : plan ; 19cm.
'A revised version presented at the Shaw Theatre, 1976' - 2 men, 1 woman. — Previous ed.: 1968.
ISBN 0-573-12302-0 Sd : £0.35
(B77-17726)

Sharkey, Jack. The murder room : a mystery farce in three acts / by Jack Sharkey. — New York ; London [etc.] : French, 1977. — 107,[1] p : plan ; 19cm.
Three men, 3 women.
ISBN 0-573-61283-8 Sd : £1.55
(B77-16579)

Shirley, Rae. Scarlet ribbon : a play / by Rae Shirley. — London [etc.] : French, 1977. — [3], 59p : plan ; 22cm.
Two men, 6 women.
ISBN 0-573-11406-4 Pbk : £1.00
(B77-15478)

Stoppard, Tom. A separate peace : a play in one act / by Tom Stoppard. — New York ; London [etc.] : French, [1977]. — 30p ; 19cm.
Two men, 4 women.
ISBN 0-573-62513-1 Sd : £0.75
(B77-23694)

Storey, David. The changing room / [by] David Storey ; with an introduction by E.R. Wood. — London : Heinemann Educational, 1977. — xxvii,9-91p ; 20cm. — (The Hereford plays)
Originally published: London : Cape, 1972.
ISBN 0-435-22836-6 : £1.00
(B77-13238)

Stott, Mike. Funny peculiar : a farce / by Mike Stott. — Hornchurch : I. Henry, 1977. — 63, [1]p ; 20cm. — (Chameleons' dramascripts)
Seven men, 3 women.
ISBN 0-86025-811-4 Pbk : £1.40
(B77-13842)

Tasca, Jules. Five one act plays by Mark Twain / adapted from his short stories by Jules Tasca. — New York ; London [etc.] : French, [1977]. — 73p ; 19cm.
This collection originally published: as 'Twain's damned human race'. s.l. : s.n., 1976.
ISBN 0-573-60040-6 Sd : £1.65
(B77-23695)

Taylor, Don. The roses of Eyam : a play / [by] Don Taylor. — London [etc.] : French, 1976. — [5],89p ; 22cm.
Thirty-five men, 22 women.
ISBN 0-573-11386-6 Pbk : £1.00
(B77-07579)

Taylor, George, *b.1906.* Taylor made : a fine selection of one act plays / by George Taylor. — Macclesfield (35 Sandringham Rd, Macclesfield, Cheshire SK10 1QB) : New Playwrights' Network, [1977]. — [1],27,28,20p : plans ; 18cm. — (Triad ; 11)
Contents: The old fiddle - Happy the bride - Second time of asking.
ISBN 0-903653-31-1 Pbk : £1.25
(B77-08534)

Taylor, Ian, *b.1932.* Tarantara! Tarantara! : a musical play / [by] Ian Taylor. — London [etc.] : French, 1976. — [4],68p : plan ; 22cm.
Five men, 3 women, supers. — Includes lyrics by W.S. Gilbert.
ISBN 0-573-08043-7 Pbk : £1.00
(B77-00941)

Von Linden, Cia. The schizophrenic : a play in four acts / [by] Cia von Linden. — Ilfracombe : Stockwell, 1976. — 96p ; 18cm.
ISBN 0-7223-0960-0 Pbk : £1.50
(B77-10929)

Walker, David, *b.1947.* Next stage : thirteen plays for written or improvised extension / [by] David Walker. — London : Edward Arnold, 1977. — 64p ; 22cm.
ISBN 0-7131-0147-4 Sd : £0.75
(B77-21406)

Waterhouse, Keith. Saturday, Sunday, Monday : a play in three acts / by Eduardo de Filippo ; English adaptation by Keith Waterhouse & Willis Hall. — New York [etc.] ; London : French, 1974. — 112,[1]p : geneal table ; 19cm.

Eleven men, 6 women. — This adaptation also published: London : Heinemann Educational, 1974.
ISBN 0-573-61513-6 Sd : £1.60
(B77-00942)

Wesker, Arnold. Three plays / [by] Arnold Wesker. — Harmondsworth [etc.] : Penguin, 1976. — 206p ; 19cm. — (Penguin plays)
Contents: The kitchen. New ed. Originally published, London : Cape, 1961 - The four seasons. Originally published, London: Cape, 1966 - Their very own and golden city. Originally published, London: Cape, 1966.
ISBN 0-14-048133-8 Pbk : £0.95
(B77-01776)

Whitehead, Ted. Mecca / [by] Ted Whitehead. — London : Faber, 1977. — 3-88p ; 20cm.
Three women, 5 men.
ISBN 0-571-10981-0 Pbk : £1.95
(B77-13239)

Whitemore, Hugh. Stevie : a play from the life and work of Stevie Smith / [by] Hugh Whitemore. — London [etc.] : French, 1977. — [3],47p : plan ; 22cm.
One man, 2 women.
ISBN 0-573-11418-8 : £1.10 : CIP rev.
(B77-28073)

Williams, Heathcote. Hancock's last half hour / [by] Heathcote Williams. — London (21 Formosa St., W.9) : Polytantric Press, 1977. — 40p : port ; 20cm.
ISBN 0-905150-04-x : £1.00
ISBN 0-905150-05-8 Pbk : Unpriced
(B77-32832)

Wilson, Pat. 3 sheep, 2 1/2 kangaroos / by Pat Wilson. — Bakewell : Hub Publications, 1977. — [3],27p ; 21cm.
Three men, 3 women.
ISBN 0-905049-21-7 Sd : £0.60
(B77-25861)

Wood, Margaret, *b.1910.* A moving story : a play / [by] Margaret Wood. — London [etc.] : French, 1977. — [3],25p : plan ; 19cm.
Two men, 4 women.
ISBN 0-573-12168-0 Sd : £0.35 : CIP rev.
(B77-28074)

Wood, Margaret, *b.1910.* Parochial problems : a play / [by] Margaret Wood. — London [etc.] : French, 1977. — [3],25p : plan ; 19cm.
Five men, 3 women.
ISBN 0-573-12199-0 Sd : £0.35 : CIP rev.
(B77-29669)

Wood, Margaret, *b.1910.* A person of no consequence : a play / by Margaret Wood. — London [etc.] : French, 1976. — [3],20,[3]p ; 19cm.
Eight women.
ISBN 0-573-03369-2 Sd : £0.35
(B77-00943)

Yeldham, Peter. Fringe benefits : a comedy / [by] Peter Yeldham and Donald Churchill. — London [etc.] : French, 1977. — [3],72p : plan ; 22cm.
Three men, 4 women.
ISBN 0-573-11146-4 Pbk : £1.10 : CIP rev.
(B77-14888)

822'.9'14 — Drama in English. Arden, John. Serjeant Musgrave's dance. *Study outlines*

Aylwin, Anthony Maxwell. Notes on John Arden's 'Serjeant Musgrave's dance' / compiled by A.M. Aylwin. — London [etc.] : Methuen, 1976. — [7],38p ; 22cm. — (Study-aid series)
Bibl.: p.37-38.
ISBN 0-413-34850-4 Sd : £0.60
(B77-14889)

822'.9'14 — Drama in English. Behan, Brendan. *Critical studies*

Kearney, Colbert. The writings of Brendan Behan / [by] Colbert Kearney. — Dublin : Gill and Macmillan, 1977. — xi,155p ; 23cm.
Bibl.: p.151-152. — Index.
ISBN 0-7171-0817-1 : £7.50
(B77-25862)

822'.9'14 — Drama in English. Pinter, Harold. *Critical studies*

Dukore, Bernard Frank. Where laughter stops : Pinter's tragicomedy / [by] Bernard F. Dukore. — Columbia, Miss. ; London : University of Missouri Press ; [London] : [Distributed by American University Publishers], [1977]. — [5], 74p ; 21cm.
'A literary frontiers edition'. — Published in the United States: 1976. — Bibl.: p.74.
ISBN 0-8262-0208-x Pbk : £4.40
(B77-10542)

Esslin, Martin. Pinter : a study of his plays / by Martin Esslin. — 3rd expanded ed. — London : Eyre Methuen, 1977. — [1],273p,8p of plates : ill ; 19cm. — (Modern theatre profiles)
Previous ed.: 1973. — Bibl.: p.253-261. — Index.
Pbk : £2.75
ISBN 0-413-29740-3
(B77-19622)

822'.9'14 — Drama in English. Pinter, Harold. Caretaker, The. *Study outlines*
Aylwin, Anthony Maxwell. Notes on Harold Pinter's 'The caretaker' / compiled by A.M. Aylwin. — London [etc.] : Methuen, 1976. — [2],29p ; 22cm. — (Study-aid series)
Bibl.: p.28-29.
ISBN 0-413-34830-x Sd : £0.60
(B77-13240)

822'.9'14 — Drama in English. Warner, Francis. *Critical studies. Festschriften*
Francis Warner : poet and dramatist / edited by Tim Prentki. — Knotting : Sceptre Press, 1977. — viii,156p,plate : 2 ill, port ; 22cm.
Essays published in honour of the fortieth birthday of Francis Warner. — Bibl.: p.vi.
ISBN 0-7068-0378-7 : £3.75
Primary classification 821'.9'14
(B77-32135)

822'.9'1402541 — Dramatists. *Great Britain. Directories*
New playwrights directory. — London [etc.] (44 Earlham St., W.C.2) : TQ Publications Ltd. 1976 / compiled and edited by Catherine Itzin. — 1976. — 62p ; 21cm. — ('Theatrefacts' supplements : directory series ; no.2)
Index.
ISBN 0-904844-05-6 Sd : £1.50
(B77-06851)

822'.9'1408 — Children's plays in English, 1945-. *Anthologies*
Assinder, Peter. Playtime plays : a volume of action scripts for younger children / by Peter Assinder, Michael Kilgarriff & Shelagh Hodson. — London : Kenyon-Deane, 1977. — 40 leaves in various pagings ; 21x26cm.
Ls : £0.80
(B77-30587)

822'.9'1408 — Drama in English, 1945-. *Anthologies*
Dennis, Richard, *b.1940.* Music hall miscellany / by Richard Dennis, Michael Kilgarriff and Malcolm Sircom ; introduced and edited by Michael Kilgarriff. — London [etc.] : French, 1977. — xix,73p : music, plan ; 19cm.
Contents: The molecatcher / realized by Malcolm Sircom - Who will man the lifeboat? / devised by Michael Kilgarriff - The tram-track tragedy / by Richard Dennis and Michael Kilgarriff - The master and the maid / by Michael Kilgarriff.
ISBN 0-573-00013-1 Pbk : £0.80
(B77-11393)

Mixed doubles : an entertainment on marriage / by Alan Ayckbourn ... [et al.]. — London : French, 1977. — 90p ; 19cm.
Originally published: London : Methuen, 1970.
ISBN 0-573-01584-8 Pbk : Unpriced
(B77-13241)

Play ten / ten short plays ; by James Saunders ... [et al.] ; edited by Robin Rook. — London : Edward Arnold, 1977. — [3],91p ; 22cm.
ISBN 0-7131-0156-3 Pbk : £1.50 : CIP rev.
(B77-16033)

822'.9'1409 — Drama in English, 1945-. *Biographical dictionaries*
Contemporary dramatists. — 2nd ed. / editor James Vinson ; associate editor D.L. Kirkpatrick ; with a preface by Ruby Cohn. — London : St James Press [etc.], 1977. — xiv, 1088p ; 24cm. — (Contemporary writers of the English language ; vol.3)
Previous ed.: 1973. — Bibl. — Index.
ISBN 0-900997-86-9 : £15.00
(B77-32833)

822'.9'1409 — Drama in English, 1945-1976. *Critical studies*
Taylor, John Russell. Anger and after : a guide to the new British drama / [by] John Russell Taylor. — 2nd ed., revised. — London : Eyre Methuen, 1977. — 391p,leaf of plate,[14]p of plates : ill, ports ; 20cm. — (An Eyre Methuen dramabook)
This ed. originally published: London : Methuen, 1969. — Index.
ISBN 0-413-34930-6 Pbk : £3.00
(B77-23696)

823 — ENGLISH FICTION
823 — Fiction in English. African writers, 1945-. *Critical studies*
Gakwandi, Shatto Arthur. The novel and contemporary experience in Africa / [by] Shatto Arthur Gakwandi. — London [etc.] : Heinemann Educational, 1977. — [6],136p ; 23cm.
Bibl.: p.131-132. — Index.
ISBN 0-435-91320-4 : £5.00
ISBN 0-435-91321-2 Pbk : £1.90
Also classified at 843
(B77-34058)

823 — Fiction in English. Australian writers. White, Patrick. Voss. *Critical studies*
Walsh, William. Patrick White, 'Voss' / by William Walsh. — London : Edward Arnold, 1976. — 53p ; 20cm. — (Studies in English literature ; no.62)
Bibl.: p.50-51. — Index.
ISBN 0-7131-5897-2 : £2.95
ISBN 0-7131-5898-0 Pbk : £1.60
(B77-04392)

823 — Fiction in English. New Zealand writers. Mansfield, Katherine. *Correspondence & diaries*
Mansfield, Katherine. The letters and journals of Katherine Mansfield : a selection / edited by C.K. Stead. — Harmondsworth [etc.] : Penguin, 1977. — 285p ; 19cm. — (Penguin modern classics)
ISBN 0-14-004201-6 Pbk : £0.95
(B77-28862)

Mansfield, Katherine. The letters and journals of Katherine Mansfield : a selection / edited by C.K. Stead. — London : Allen Lane, 1977. — 285p ; 23cm.
ISBN 0-7139-1069-0 : £5.75
(B77-28863)

823 — Fiction in English. Nigerian writers. Achebe, Chinua. *Critical studies*
Killam, Gordon Douglas. The writings of Chinua Achebe / [by] G.D. Killam. — Revised ed. — London [etc.] : Heinemann Educational, 1977. — viii,132p ; 22cm. — (Studies in African literature)
Previous ed.: published as 'The novels of Chinua Achebe'. 1969.
ISBN 0-435-91665-3 Pbk : £1.50
(B77-26498)

823 — Fiction in English. Nigerian writers. Achebe, Chinua. Things fall apart. *Critical studies*
Turkington Kate. Chinua Achebe, 'Things fall apart' / by Kate Turkington. — London : Edward Arnold, 1977. — 63,[1]p ; 20cm. — (Studies in English literature ; no.66)
Bibl.: p.63. — Index.
ISBN 0-7131-5932-4 : £3.50
ISBN 0-7131-5933-2 Pbk : £1.95
(B77-14890)

823 — Short stories in English. New Zealand writers. Sargeson, Frank. *Critical studies*
Copland, R A. Frank Sargeson / by R.A. Copland. — Wellington [N.Z.] ; London [etc.] : Oxford University Press, [1977]. — 47p ; 22cm. — (New Zealand writers and their work)
Published in New Zealand: 1976. — Bibl.: p.46-47.
ISBN 0-19-558004-4 Pbk : £2.75
(B77-13843)

823'.009 — Fiction in English, 1702-1900. *Critical studies*
Skilton, David. The English novel : Defoe to the Victorians / [by] David Skilton. — Newton Abbot [etc.] : David and Charles [etc.], 1977. — 200p ; 23cm. — (Comparative literature)
Bibl.: p.192-193. — Index.
ISBN 0-7153-7392-7 : £6.50
(B77-22095)

823'.009'16 — Fiction in English, to ca 1960: Ghost stories. *Critical studies*
Briggs, Julia. Night visitors : the rise and fall of the English ghost story / [by] Julia Briggs. — London : Faber, 1977. — 238p ; 23cm.
Bibl.: p.213-225. — Index.
ISBN 0-571-11113-0 : £6.95 : CIP rev.
(B77-09239)

823'.009'352 — Fiction in English. Women writers, 1745-1975. Special themes: Role of women in society
Zeman, Anthea. Presumptuous girls : women and their world in the serious woman's novel / [by] Anthea Zeman. — London : Weidenfeld and Nicolson, 1977. — [7],185p ; 23cm.
Index.
ISBN 0-297-77256-2 : £5.25
(B77-12071)

823'.009'354 — Fiction in English, 1745-1945. Special subjects: Love. *Critical studies*
Cockshut, Anthony Oliver John. Man and woman : a study of love and the novel, 1740-1940 / [by] A.O.J. Cockshut. — London : Collins, 1977. — 221p ; 22cm.
Index.
ISBN 0-00-216503-1 : £4.50
(B77-24458)

823'.01 — Children's short stories in English, 1837-1960. Special subjects: Witches. *Anthologies*
Witches, witches, witches / selected by Helen Hoke ; pictures by W.R. Lohse. — New enlarged ed. — New York ; London : F. Watts, 1977. — [9],230p : ill ; 24cm.
Previous ed.: New York : F. Watts, 1958 ; London : Chatto and Windus, 1960.
ISBN 0-531-01823-7 : £3.50
(B77-24459)

823'.01 — Fantasy stories in English, 1837-1945. *Anthologies*
England invaded : a collection of fantasy fiction / edited and introduced by Michael Moorcock. — London : W.H. Allen, 1977. — vii,245p ; 23cm.

'The stories ... come from the popular magazines of the Victorian and Edwardian era : "Pearson's", "The Strand", "Harmsworth's" and "Cassell's"' - jacket.
ISBN 0-491-02191-7 : £4.95
(B77-32147)

823'.01 — Short stories in English, 1800-1976: Horror stories. *Anthologies*
Tales of a monster hunter / selected by Peter Cushing. — London : Barker, 1977. — ix,208p, [8]p of plates : ill, ports ; 22cm.
ISBN 0-213-16628-3 : £4.25
(B77-12072)

823'.01 — Short stories in English, 1837-1900: Horror stories. *Anthologies*
Terror by gaslight / edited by Hugh Lamb. — Sevenoaks : Coronet, 1977. — 222p ; 18cm.
This collection originally published: London : W.H. Allen, 1975.
ISBN 0-340-21303-5 Pbk : £0.70
(B77-09240)

Victorian tales of terror / edited by Hugh Lamb. — London : Coronet, 1976. — 287p ; 18cm.
This collection originally published: London : W.H. Allen, 1974.
ISBN 0-340-20817-1 Pbk : £0.80
(B77-03208)

823'.01 — Short stories in English, 1837-1901: Horror stories. *Anthologies*
Reign of terror / edited by Michel Parry. — London : Severn House : [Distributed by Hutchinson], 1977. — 187p ; 21cm. — (Great Victorian horror stories)
This collection originally published: London : Corgi, 1976.
ISBN 0-7278-0340-9 : £3.50 : CIP rev.
(B77-25863)

Reign of terror, the 1st Corgi book of great Victorian horror stories / edited by Michel Parry. — London : Corgi, 1976. — 187p ; 18cm.
ISBN 0-552-10335-7 Pbk : £0.65
(B77-06852)

Reign of terror, the 2nd Corgi book of great Victorian horror stories / edited by Michel Parry. — London : Corgi, 1977. — 190p ; 18cm.
ISBN 0-552-10390-x Pbk : £0.70
(B77-13242)

Victorian nightmares / edited by Hugh Lamb. — London : W.H. Allen, 1977. — 224p ; 23cm.
ISBN 0-491-02030-9 : £3.95
(B77-17727)

823'.01 — Short stories in English, 1837-1925: Horror stories. *Anthologies*
Vincent Price presents the price of fear / edited by Richard Davis. — London : Severn House : [Distributed by Hutchinson], 1977. — 189p ; 21cm.
Also published: London : Everest, 1977.
ISBN 0-7278-0272-0 : £3.25
(B77-29670)

823'.01 — Short stories in English, 1837-1945: Ghost stories. *Anthologies*
The **best** ghost stories / introduction by Charles Fowkes. — London [etc.] : Hamlyn, 1977. — 750p ; 21cm.
ISBN 0-600-38242-7 : £2.95
(B77-24460)

Thirteen famous ghost stories / edited and selected by Peter Underwood. — London [etc.] : Dent [etc.], 1977. — 203p ; 18cm.
ISBN 0-460-01749-7 Pbk : £0.75 : CIP rev.
(B77-23697)

823'.01 — Short stories in English, 1837-1945: Horror stories. *Anthologies*
The **supernatural** omnibus : being a collection of stories of apparitions, witchcraft, werewolves, diabolism, necromancy, satanism, divination, sorcery, goety, voodoo, possession, occult, doom and destiny / edited, with an introduction, by Montague Summers. — Harmondsworth [etc.] : Penguin.
In 2 vols. — This collection originally published: in 1 vol. London : Gollancz, 1931.
Vol.1 : Hauntings and horror. — 1976. — 429p ; 18cm.
ISBN 0-14-004184-2 Pbk : £0.95
(B77-04393)

823'.01 — Short stories in English, 1837-1975. Special subjects: Oceans. *Anthologies*
Waves of terror : weird stories about the sea / edited by Michel Parry. — London : Gollancz, 1976. — 208p ; 21cm. — ([Gollancz fantasy & macabre])
ISBN 0-575-02184-5 : £3.95
(B77-02559)

823'.01 — Short stories in English, 1860-1976: Horror stories. Special subjects: Vampires. *Anthologies*
The **rivals** of Dracula : a century of vampire fiction / edited by Michel Parry. — London : Corgi, 1977. — 190p ; 18cm.
Bibl.: p.178. — List of films : p.179-190.
ISBN 0-552-10410-8 Pbk : £0.65
(B77-17068)

823'.01 — Short stories in English, 1867-1976: Horror stories. *Anthologies*
Gaslight tales of terror / edited by R. Chetwynd-Hayes. — [London] : Fontana, 1976. — 191p ; 18cm.
ISBN 0-00-614149-8 Pbk : £0.50
(B77-12073)

823'.01 — Short stories in English, 1869-1951: Horror stories. Special subjects: Werewolves. *Anthologies*
Book of the werewolf / edited by Brian J. Frost. — London : Sphere, 1976. — 325p ; 18cm.
Originally published: 1973.
ISBN 0-7221-3687-0 Pbk : £0.60
(B77-07580)

823'.01 — Short stories in English, ca 1820-1974: Horror stories. *Anthologies*
More of Christopher Lee's new chamber of horrors / edited by Peter Haining. — St Albans : Mayflower, 1976. — 159p ; 18cm.
This collection originally published: in 'Christopher Lee's new chamber of horrors'. London : Souvenir Press, 1974.
ISBN 0-583-12636-7 Pbk : £0.60
(B77-05046)

823'.01 — Short stories in English, ca 1840-1976: Horror stories. Special subjects: Graves. *Anthologies*
Return from the grave / edited by Hugh Lamb. — London : W.H. Allen, 1976. — [2],199p ; 23cm.
ISBN 0-491-01937-8 : £3.50
(B77-00399)

823'.0872 — Detective fiction in English, 1794-1917. *Critical studies*
Ousby, Ian. Bloodhounds of heaven : the detective in English fiction from Godwin to Doyle / [by] Ian Ousby. — Cambridge, Mass. ; London : Harvard University Press, 1976. — xiii,194p : ill ; 24cm.
Index.
ISBN 0-674-07657-5 : £7.50
(B77-04395)

823'.0872 — Detective fiction in English, 1837-1945. Special subjects: Women detectives. *Anthologies*
Crime on her mind : fifteen stories of female sleuths from the Victorian era to the forties / edited and with introductions by Michele B. Slung. — Harmondsworth [etc.] : Penguin, 1977. — 378p ; 19cm. — (Penguin crime fiction)
This collection originally published: New York : Pantheon Books, 1975 ; London : Joseph, 1976. — Bibl.: p.377-378.
ISBN 0-14-004331-4 Pbk : £0.95
(B77-25182)

823'.0872 — Detective fiction in English, to 1939. *Critical studies*
Mystery! : an illustrated history of crime and detective fiction / [compiled by] Peter Haining ; designed by Christopher Scott. — London : Souvenir Press, 1977. — 176p : chiefly ill(some col), facsims, maps ; 28cm.
ISBN 0-285-62218-8 : £5.50
(B77-34060)

823'.0872 — Detective fiction in English, to 1974. *Special subjects: Detectives*
Pate, Janet. The book of sleuths / [by] Janet Pate. — London : New English Library, 1977. — 5-124p : ill, coat of arms, facsims, plan ; 31cm.
'A Webb & Bower book' - title page verso. — Ill. on lining papers. — Bibl. — Lists of films.
ISBN 0-450-03083-0 : £4.95
(B77-14891)

823'.0872 — Detective stories in English, 1837-1945. *Anthologies*
Great tales of detection : nineteen stories / chosen by Dorothy L. Sayers. — London : Dent, 1976. — iii-xvi,382p ; 19cm. — (Everyman's library)
This collection originally published: as 'Tales of detection'. 1936.
ISBN 0-460-00928-1 : Unpriced
ISBN 0-460-01928-7 Pbk : £0.95
(B77-03209)

823'.0872 — Spy fiction in English, 1900- . Writers. *Biographical dictionaries*
McCormick, Donald, *b.1911.* Who's who in spy fiction / [compiled by] Donald McCormick. — London : Elm Tree Books, 1977. — [5],216p ; 23cm.
Bibl.: p.215-216.
ISBN 0-241-89447-6 : £4.95
(B77-20554)

823'.0874 — Fiction in English. Westerns, to 1972. *Critical studies*
Calder, Jenni. There must be a Lone Ranger : the myth and reality of the American Wild West / [by] Jenni Calder. — London : Abacus, 1976. — xiii,241p,[8]p of plates : ill, facsim, ports ; 19cm.
Originally published: London : Hamilton, 1974. — Bibl.: p.231-234. — List of films : p.228-230. — Index.
ISBN 0-349-10479-4 Pbk : £0.95
Primary classification 791.43'0909'32
(B77-07532)

823'.0876 — Science fiction in English, 1726-1960. *Anthologies*
Ten science fiction stories / edited by R.A. Banks. — London [etc.] : Hodder and Stoughton, 1977. — 156p ; 22cm.
ISBN 0-340-21371-x Pbk : £1.20
(B77-14892)

823'.0876 — Science fiction in English: Paperback books with British imprints. *Reviews. Periodicals*
Paperback parlour : a bimonthly review of British paperback SF. — Oxford (c/o 1 Lewell Ave., Old Marston, Oxford OX3 0RL) : P. Stephenson-Payne.
Vol.1, no.1- ; [1977?]-. — [1977?]-. — 30cm.
Six issues a year. — 8p. in 1st issue.
Sd : £0.10(free to UK members of the British Science Fiction Association)
(B77-14893)

823'.0876 — Science fiction in English. Special themes: Man. Biology
Isaacs, Leonard. Darwin to double helix : the biological theme in science fiction / [by] Leonard Isaacs ; [for] Science in a Social Context. — London [etc.] : Butterworth, 1977. — 64p ; 22cm.
Bibl.
ISBN 0-408-71302-x Pbk : £1.00
(B77-17069)

823.2 — ENGLISH FICTION, 1400-1558

823'.2 — Fiction in English, 1400-1558. *Texts*
Malory, *Sir* Thomas. Le morte d'Arthur / [by] Sir Thomas Malory. — London : Dent [etc.]. — (Everyman's library)
In 2 vols.
Vol.1 / introduction by Sir John Rhys. — 1976. — xxxviii,401p ; 19cm.
Facsimile reprint. — Originally published: 1906.

ISBN 0-460-00045-4 : £2.95
ISBN 0-460-01045-x Pbk : £1.20
(B77-13844)

Vol.2. — 1976. — xvi,411p ; 19cm.
Facsimile reprint. — Originally published: 1906.

ISBN 0-460-00046-2 : £1.60
ISBN 0-460-01046-8 Pbk : £1.20
(B77-13845)

Malory, *Sir* Thomas. Works [of] Malory / edited by Eugène Vinaver. — 2nd ed. [reprinted with some omissions and revisions]. — Oxford [etc.] : Oxford University Press, 1977. — xv, 811p ; 21cm.
This revision of Vinaver's 2nd ed. originally published: London : Oxford University Press, 1971.
ISBN 0-19-281217-3 Pbk : £3.50 : CIP rev.
(B77-09921)

823'.2 — Fiction in English, 1400-1558. *Texts. Facsimiles*
Malory, *Sir* Thomas. Le morte d'Arthur / [by] Sir Thomas Malory. — London : Scolar Press, 1976. — [895]p : ill ; 30cm.
Limited ed. of 500 numbered copies. — 'Reproduced in facsimile from the copy in the Pierpont Morgan Library, New York, with an introduction by Paul Needham'.
ISBN 0-85967-302-2 : £75.00
(B77-03210)

823.3 — ENGLISH FICTION, 1558-1625

823'.3 — Fiction in English, 1558-1625. *Texts*
Sidney, *Sir* Philip. [Arcadia]. The Countess of Pembroke's Arcadia / [by] Sir Philip Sidney ; edited with an introduction and notes by Maurice Evans. — Harmondsworth [etc.] : Penguin, 1977. — 870p ; 18cm. — (Penguin English library)
ISBN 0-14-043111-x Pbk : £2.00
(B77-28866)

823.4 — ENGLISH FICTION, 1625-1702

823'.4 — Fiction in English, 1625-1702. *Texts. Facsimiles*
Garfield, John, *fl.1660-1663.* The wandring whore, numbers 1-5, 1660-1661 / by John Garfield. — [Exeter] ([Amory Buildings, Rennes Drive, Exeter EX4 4RJ]) : 'The Rota', 1977. — 81p in various pagings ; 21cm.
'Issue no.1 ... is reproduced ... from a copy in the Guildhall Library, London ... Issues 2-4 are reproduced from copies in the Thomason collection ... of the British Library ... Issue no.5 is reproduced ... [from the copy in] the Huntington Library, San Marino, California' - Prefatory note. — Facsimile reprints.
ISBN 0-904617-07-6 Sd : Unpriced
(B77-28867)

823.5 — ENGLISH FICTION, 1702-1745

823'.5 — Fiction in English, 1702-1745. *Texts*
Defoe, Daniel. [Moll Flanders]. The fortunes and misfortunes of the famous Moll Flanders, &c. ... / [by] Daniel Defoe ; edited with an introduction by G.A. Starr. — London [etc.] : Oxford University Press, 1976. — xxxiv,408p ; 21cm.
This ed. originally published: 1971. — Bibl.: p.xxxi-xxxii.
ISBN 0-19-281194-0 Pbk : £1.50
(B77-03211)

Defoe, Daniel. Robinson Crusoe / [by] Daniel Defoe. — Abridged [ed.]. — Maidenhead : Purnell, 1976. — 188p : 1 ill ; 21cm. — (A Purnell classic)
ISBN 0-361-03544-6 : £0.50
(B77-05626)

Defoe, Daniel. [Robinson Crusoe]. The life and strange surprizing adventures of Robinson Crusoe, of York, mariner ... / [by] Daniel Defoe ; edited with an introduction by J. Donald Crowley. — London [etc.] : Oxford University Press, 1976. — xxx,316p,[2]leaves of plates : map ; 21cm.
This ed. originally published: 1972. — Bibl.: p.xxvii-xxviii.
ISBN 0-19-281195-9 Pbk : £1.50
(B77-03745)

Swift, Jonathan. Gulliver's travels / [by] Jonathan Swift ; introduction and notes by A.L. Rowse. — London [etc.] : Pan Books, 1977. — 299p : 1 ill, facsim, maps ; 18cm. — (Pan classics)
Bibl.: p.299.
ISBN 0-330-25190-2 Pbk : £0.70
(B77-26499)

Swift, Jonathan. Gulliver's travels / [by] Jonathan Swift. — Abridged [ed.]. — Maidenhead : Purnell, 1976. — 126p : 1 ill ; 21cm. — (A Purnell classic)
ISBN 0-361-03543-8 : £0.50
(B77-05627)

823'.5'0924 — Fiction in English, 1702-1800. *Plot outlines*

Johnson, Clifford R. Plots and characters in the fiction of eighteenth-century English authors / [by] Clifford R. Johnson. — Hamden, Conn. : Archon Books ; Folkestone : Dawson. — (The plots and characters series)
In 2 vols.
Vol.1 : Jonathan Swift, Daniel Defoe, and Samuel Richardson. — 1977. — xx,270p ; 23cm.
ISBN 0-7129-0762-9 : £10.00
Also classified at 823'.5'0927
(B77-32834)

823'.5'0927 — Fiction in English, 1702-1800. Characters. *Dictionaries*

Johnson, Clifford R. Plots and characters in the fiction of eighteenth-century English authors / [by] Clifford R. Johnson. — Hamden, Conn. : Archon Books ; Folkestone : Dawson. — (The plots and characters series)
In 2 vols.
Vol.1 : Jonathan Swift, Daniel Defoe, and Samuel Richardson. — 1977. — xx,270p ; 23cm.
ISBN 0-7129-0762-9 : £10.00
Primary classification 823'.5'0924
(B77-32834)

823.6 — ENGLISH FICTION, 1745-1800

823'.6 — Fiction in English, 1745-1800. *Texts*

Johnson, Samuel. [Rasselas]. The history of Rasselas, Prince of Abissinia / [by] Samuel Johnson ; edited with an introduction by D.J. Enright. — Harmondsworth [etc.] : Penguin, 1976. — 157p ; 19cm. — (Penguin English library)
Bibl.: p.36.
ISBN 0-14-043108-x Pbk : £0.60
(B77-01777)

Johnson, Samuel. [Rasselas]. The history of Rasselas, Prince of Abissinia / [by] Samuel Johnson ; edited with an introduction by Geoffrey Tillotson and Brian Jenkins. — Oxford [etc.] : Oxford University Press, 1977. — xxx,145p ; 21cm.
This ed. originally published: London : Oxford University Press, 1971.
ISBN 0-19-281197-5 Pbk : £1.50 : CIP rev.
(B77-05047)

Walpole, Horace, *Earl of Orford.* The castle of Otranto : a Gothic story / by Horace Walpole ; introduction by Devendra P. Varma ; lithographs by Charles Keeping. — London : Folio Society, 1976. — 142p,[6]leaves of plates : col ill ; 23cm.
In slip case. — 'The text follows the collected edition of 1798 ...' - title page verso.
ISBN 0-85067-103-5 : £4.50(to members only)
(B77-02560)

Wollstonecraft, Mary. Mary, a fiction ; and, The wrongs of woman / [by] Mary Wollstonecraft ; edited with an introduction by Gary Kelly. — London [etc.] : Oxford University Press, 1976. — xxxi,231p ; 21cm. — (Oxford English novels)
Bibl.: p.xxiv-xxv.
ISBN 0-19-255367-4 : £5.75
(B77-00944)

823'.6 — Fiction in English. Smollett, Tobias. *Critical studies*

Grant, Damian. Tobias Smollett : a study in style / [by] Damian Grant. — Manchester : Manchester University Press [etc.], 1977. — xii, 232p ; 23cm.
Bibl.: p.223-226. — Index.
ISBN 0-7190-0607-4 : £8.95
(B77-06261)

823'.6'09 — Autobiographical fiction in English, 1745-1800. Compared with autobiographical prose in English, 1745-1800

Spacks, Patricia Meyer. Imagining a self : autobiography and novel in eighteenth-century England / [by] Patricia Meyer Spacks. — Cambridge, Mass. ; London : Harvard University Press, 1976. — [9],342p ; 25cm.
Index.
ISBN 0-674-44005-6 : £11.25
Also classified at 828'.6'0809
(B77-09241)

823'.6'09 — Fiction in English, 1745-1837. *Critical studies*

Kelly, Gary. The English Jacobin novel, 1780-1805 / [by] Gary Kelly. — Oxford : Clarendon Press, 1976. — xi,291p ; 23cm.
Bibl.: p.270-282. — Index.
ISBN 0-19-812062-1 : £10.00
(B77-03746)

823.7 — ENGLISH FICTION, 1800-1837

823'.7 — Fiction in English, 1800-1837. *Texts*

Austen, Jane. Pride and prejudice / [by] Jane Austen ; illustrations by Jenny Thorne. — Maidenhead : Purnell, 1977. — 364p,[8]leaves of plates : ill(some col) ; 21cm. — (A Purnell de luxe classic)
ISBN 0-361-03871-2 : £1.50
(B77-19623)

Austen, Jane. Sanditon / [by] Jane Austen and another lady. — London : Corgi, 1976. — 318p ; 18cm.
Originally published: Boston, Mass. : Houghton Mifflin ; London : P. Davies, 1975.
ISBN 0-552-10297-0 Pbk : £0.75
(B77-03212)

Austen, Jane. The Watsons / [by] Jane Austen and another. — London : P. Davies, 1977. — [4],235p ; 23cm.
ISBN 0-432-00751-2 : £3.90
(B77-11394)

Marryat, Frederick. The children of the New Forest / [by] Captain Marryat ; illustrations by Derick Bown. — Maidenhead : Purnell, 1977. — 356p,[8]leaves of plates : ill(some col) ; 21cm. — (A Purnell de luxe classic)
ISBN 0-361-03869-0 : £1.50
(B77-23698)

Maturin, Charles Robert. Melmoth the Wanderer : a tale / [by] Charles Robert Maturin ; edited with an introduction by Althea Hayter. — Harmondsworth [etc.] : Penguin, 1977. — 3-720p ; 18cm. — (Penguin English library)
Bibl.: p.31.
ISBN 0-14-043110-1 Pbk : £1.95
(B77-15479)

Scott, *Sir* **Walter,** *bart.* The supernatural short stories of Sir Walter Scott / edited with an introduction by Michael Hayes. — London : J. Calder : [Distributed by Calder and Boyars], 1977. — 217p ; 21cm. — (The Scottish library)

Contents: The tapestried chamber - My Aunt Margaret's mirror - Wandering Willie's tale - The two drovers - The Highland widow.
ISBN 0-7145-3616-4 : £5.25
(B77-20555)

823'.7 — Fiction in English. Austen, Jane. *Biographies*

Llewelyn, Margaret. Jane Austen : a character study / by Margaret Llewelyn. — London : Kimber, 1977. — 189p : geneal table ; 23cm.
Bibl.: p.182-185. — Index.
ISBN 0-7183-0345-8 : £3.95
(B77-29671)

Vipont, Elfrida. A little bit of ivory : a life of Jane Austen / [by] Elfrida Vipont. — London : Hamilton, 1977. — [7],148p : geneal table ; 23cm.
Bibl.: p.148.
ISBN 0-241-89534-0 : £3.25
(B77-19624)

823'.7 — Fiction in English. Austen, Jane. *Conference proceedings*

Jane Austen Bicentennial Conference, *University of Alberta, 1975.* Jane Austen's achievement : papers delivered at the Jane Austen Bicentennial Conference at the University of Alberta / edited by Juliet McMaster. — London [etc.] : Macmillan, 1976. — xvii,139p ; 23cm.
Index.
ISBN 0-333-21127-8 : £6.95
(B77-03747)

823'.7 — Fiction in English. Austen, Jane. *Critical studies*

Moler, Kenneth L. Jane Austen's art of allusion / [by] Kenneth L. Moler. — Lincoln [Neb.] ; London : University of Nebraska Press, 1977. — vii,233p ; 22cm.
Originally published: Lincoln, Neb. : University of Nebraska Press, 1968. — Index.
ISBN 0-8032-0124-9 : £9.50
(B77-33418)

823'.7 — Fiction in English. Austen, Jane. Emma. *Critical studies*

Jefferson, Douglas William. Jane Austen's 'Emma' : a landmark in English fiction / [by] Douglas Jefferson. — London : Chatto and Windus for Sussex University Press, 1977. — 89p ; 20cm. — (Text and context)
Bibl.: p.88-89.
ISBN 0-85621-058-7 : £3.00
ISBN 0-85621-059-5 Pbk : £1.50
(B77-05628)

823'.7 — Fiction in English. Austen, Jane. Local associations: Hampshire. Chawton. Chawton Manor

Carpenter, T Edward. The story of Jane Austen's Chawton home / by T. Edward Carpenter. — [Chawton] ([c/o Chawton Manor, Chawton, Alton, Hants.]) : Jane Austen Memorial Trust, [1976]. — [1],7p ; 22cm.
Sd : Unpriced
(B77-16580)

823'.7 — Fiction in English. Austen, Jane. Northanger Abbey & Persuasion. *Critical studies, 1818-1975. Readings*

Jane Austen, 'Northanger Abbey' and 'Persuasion' : a casebook / edited by B.C. Southam. — London [etc.] : Macmillan, 1976. — 250p ; 21cm. — (Casebook series)
Bibl.: p.243. — Index.
ISBN 0-333-19207-9 : £4.95
(B77-05629)

823'.7 — Fiction in English. Peacock, Thomas Love. *Critical studies, 1818-1970. Readings*

Peacock, the satirical novels : a casebook / edited by Lorna Sage. — London [etc.] : Macmillan, 1976. — 253p ; 21cm. — (Casebook series)
Bibl.: p.247-248. — Index.
ISBN 0-333-18410-6 : £4.95
(B77-05630)

823'.7 — Fiction in English. Scott, Sir Walter, bart. Siege of Malta. *Critical studies*

Sultana, Donald. 'The siege of Malta' rediscovered : an account of Sir Walter Scott's Mediterranean journey and his last novel / [by] Donald E. Sultana. — Edinburgh : Scottish Academic Press, 1977. — xii,215p,leaf of plate,[8]p of plates : ill, facsims(on lining paper), maps, ports ; 24cm.
Ill. on lining paper. — Bibl.: p.196-199. — Index.
ISBN 0-7073-0131-9 : £7.50
Primary classification 828'.7'09
(B77-29777)

823'.7 — Fiction in English. Shelley, Mary Wollstonecraft. *Biographies*

Florescu, Radu. In search of Frankenstein / [by] Radu Florescu ; with contributions by Alan Barbour & Matei Cazacu. — London : New English Library, 1977. — xii,244p : ill, coat of arms, facsims, geneal tables, maps, ports ; 25cm.
Originally published: Boston, Mass. : New York Graphic Society, 1975. — Bibl.: p.243-244. — List of films: p.239-242.
ISBN 0-450-03434-8 Pbk : £5.95
Also classified at 823'.7
(B77-29672)

823'.7 — Fiction in English. Shelley, Mary Wollstonecraft. Frankenstein. *Critical studies*

Florescu, Radu. In search of Frankenstein / [by] Radu Florescu ; with contributions by Alan Barbour & Matei Cazacu. — London : New English Library, 1977. — xii,244p : ill, coat of arms, facsims, geneal tables, maps, ports ; 25cm.
Originally published: Boston, Mass. : New York Graphic Society, 1975. — Bibl.: p.243-244. — List of films: p.239-242.
ISBN 0-450-03434-8 Pbk : £5.95
Primary classification 823'.7
(B77-29672)

823'.7'09 — Fiction in English, 1800-1900. *Critical studies*

Doubleday, Neal Frank. Variety of attempt : British and American fiction in the early nineteenth century / [by] Neal Frank Doubleday. — Lincoln [Neb.] ; London : University of Nebraska Press, 1976. — [9], 218p ; 23cm.
Index.
ISBN 0-8032-0876-6 : £10.40
(B77-05048)

823'.7'0924 — Fiction in English. Women writers, 1800-1900. *Plot outlines*

Halperin, John. Plots and characters in the fiction of Jane Austen, the Brontës, and George Eliot / [by] John Halperin and Janet Kunert. — Hamden, Conn. : Archon Books ; Folkestone : Dawson, 1976. — xii,282p ; 23cm. — (The plots and characters series)
ISBN 0-7129-0757-2 : £10.00
Also classified at 823'.7'0927
(B77-33419)

823'.7'0927 — Fiction in English. Women writers, 1800-1900. Characters. *Dictionaries*

Halperin, John. Plots and characters in the fiction of Jane Austen, the Brontës, and George Eliot / [by] John Halperin and Janet Kunert. — Hamden, Conn. : Archon Books ; Folkestone : Dawson, 1976. — xii,282p ; 23cm. — (The plots and characters series)
ISBN 0-7129-0757-2 : £10.00
Primary classification 823'.7'0924
(B77-33419)

823.8 — ENGLISH FICTION, 1837-1900

823'.8 — Fiction in English, 1837-1900. *Texts*

Ainsworth, William Harrison. Beau Nash, or, Bath in the eighteenth century / [by] William Harrison Ainsworth. — Bath : Chivers, 1977. — [5],314p ; 19cm.
Based on the life of Beau Nash.
ISBN 0-85997-273-9 : £5.20(£3.90 to members of the Library Association)
(B77-29673)

Ballantyne, Robert Michael. The coral island / [by] R.M. Ballantyne ; illustrations by Derick Brown. — Maidenhead : Purnell, 1977. — 290p,[8]leaves of plates : ill(some col) ; 21cm. — (A Purnell de luxe classic)
ISBN 0-361-03868-2 : £1.50
(B77-25183)

Ballantyne, Robert Michael. The coral island / [by] R.M. Ballantyne. — Abridged [ed.]. — Maidenhead : Purnell, 1976. — 184p : 1 ill ; 21cm. — (A Purnell classic)
ISBN 0-361-03545-4 : £0.50
(B77-05631)

Blackmore, Richard Doddridge. Lorna Doone / [by] R.D. Blackmore. — Abridged [ed.]. — Maidenhead : Purnell, 1977. — 184p : 1 ill ; 21cm. — (A Purnell classic)
ISBN 0-361-03564-0 : £0.50
(B77-28075)

Boothby, Guy. Doctor Nikola / [by] Guy Boothby. — Large print ed. — Bath : Lythway Press, 1977. — xvii,394p ; 23cm. — (Lythway classics of crime and detection)
ISBN 0-85046-741-1 : £4.95
(B77-29674)

Brontë, Charlotte. Jane Eyre / [by] Charlotte Brontë ; edited, with an introduction, by Margaret Smith. — London [etc.] : Oxford University Press, 1976. — xxxviii,479p : music ; 21cm.
Originally published: 1973. — Bibl.: p.xxxiii-xxxvi.
ISBN 0-19-281198-3 Pbk : £1.50
(B77-08030)

Brontë, Charlotte. Jane Eyre / [by] Charlotte Brontë. — Abridged [ed.]. — Maidenhead : Purnell, 1977. — 174p : 1 ill ; 21cm. — (A Purnell classic)
ISBN 0-361-03551-9 : £0.50
(B77-10930)

Brontë, Emily. Wuthering Heights / [by] Emily Brontë. — Abridged [ed.]. — Maidenhead : Purnell, 1977. — 159p : 1 ill ; 21cm. — (A Purnell classic)
This ed. originally published: London : Bancroft, 1967.
ISBN 0-361-03562-4 : £0.50
(B77-22834)

Carroll, Lewis. Alice in Wonderland / [by] Lewis Carroll. — Maidenhead : Purnell, 1977. — 112p : ill ; 21cm. — (A Purnell classic)
ISBN 0-361-03556-x : £0.50
(B77-14894)

Carroll, Lewis. [Alice in Wonderland]. Alice's adventures in Wonderland ; and, Through the looking-glass / by Lewis Carroll ; with the original engravings by John Tenniel of which 8 have been redrawn in colour by Diana Stanley. — London : Dent [etc.], 1977. — x,246p,8 leaves of plates : ill(some col) ; 22cm. — (Children's illustrated classics)
Originally published: 1954.
ISBN 0-460-02754-9 Pbk : £1.75
(B77-25184)

Carroll, Lewis. Through the looking glass / [by] Lewis Carroll. — Maidenhead : Purnell, 1977. — 112p : ill ; 21cm. — (A Purnell classic)
ISBN 0-361-03552-7 : £0.50
(B77-10931)

Carroll, Lewis. [Through the looking-glass]. Alice through the looking-glass / [by] Lewis Carroll ; with fifty illustrations by John Tenniel. — Giant illustrated ed. — London : Academy Editions [etc.], 1977. — 96p : ill ; 28cm.
ISBN 0-85670-216-1 Pbk : £1.95
(B77-26500)

Carroll, Lewis. The wasp in a wig : a 'suppressed' episode of 'Through the looking-glass, and what Alice found there' / [by] Lewis Carroll ; with a preface, introduction and notes by Martin Gardner. — London [etc.] : Macmillan, 1977. — 37,[3]p : ill, facsims ; 23cm.
Also published: New York : Lewis Carroll Society of North America, 1977.
ISBN 0-333-23727-7 : £1.95
(B77-34061)

Collins, Wilkie. Armadale / by Wilkie Collins. — New York : Dover Publications [etc.] ; London : Constable, 1977. — [2],597p : ill ; 22cm.
Facsimile reprint. — '... republication of the work as originally published serially in "The Cornhill Magazine", November 1864 to June 1866 (Volumes X-XIII)' - title page verso.
ISBN 0-486-23429-0 Pbk : £3.60
(B77-25185)

Collins, Wilkie. Armadale / [by] Wilkie Collins. — London (40 William IV St., WC2N 4DF) : Zodiac Press, 1975. — [4],559p ; 21cm.
ISBN 0-7011-1375-8 : £3.50
(B77-24461)

Dickens, Charles. [Selected works]. Three novels / [by] Charles Dickens. — London [etc.] : Spring Books, 1977. — 1088p : ill ; 21cm.
Contents: Oliver Twist - A tale of two cities - Great expectations.
ISBN 0-600-32930-5 : £2.75
(B77-30588)

Dickens, Charles. Hard times / [by] Charles Dickens ; introduction and notes by George Levine. — London [etc.] : Pan Books, 1977. — 297p ; 18cm. — (Pan classics)
Bibl.: p.295-297.
ISBN 0-330-25191-0 Pbk : £0.70
(B77-27350)

Dickens, Charles. Hard times : for these times / [by] Charles Dickens ; with a foreword by Asa Briggs. — St Albans : Panther, 1977. — xiv, 7-303p ; 18cm.
ISBN 0-586-04371-3 Pbk : £0.75
(B77-24462)

Dickens, Charles. Oliver Twist / [by] Charles Dickens. — Abridged [ed.]. — Maidenhead : Purnell, 1976. — 194p : 1 ill ; 21cm. — (A Purnell classic)
ISBN 0-361-03549-7 : £0.50
(B77-10932)

Falkner, John Meade. A midsummer night's marriage / by John Meade Falkner ; illustrations by Jonathan Clarke. — Edinburgh ([137 Warrender Park Rd, Edinburgh EH9 1DS]) : Tragara Press, 1977. — 2-35p : ill ; 23cm.
Limited ed. of 160 numbered copies, of which nos 1-10 are printed on Barcham Green hand-made paper.
ISBN 0-902616-36-6 : £6.50
(B77-24463)

Gaskell, Elizabeth Cleghorn. Cranford / [by] Elizabeth Gaskell ; edited with an introduction by Elizabeth Porges Watson. — Oxford [etc.] : Oxford University Press, 1977. — xix,200p ; 21cm.
This ed. originally published: in the 'Oxford English novels' series. 1972. — Bibl.: p.xv-xvi.
ISBN 0-19-281207-6 Pbk : £1.50 : CIP rev.
(B77-05632)

Gaskell, Elizabeth Cleghorn. North and south / [by] Elizabeth Gaskell ; edited with an introduction by Angus Easson. — Oxford [etc.] : Oxford University Press, 1977. — xxv, 447p ; 21cm.
This ed. originally published: in the 'Oxford English novels' series. 1973. — Bibl.: p.xxi-xxii.
ISBN 0-19-281196-7 Pbk : £1.75 : CIP rev.
(B77-04396)

Gaskell, Elizabeth Cleghorn. North and south / [by] Elizabeth Cleghorn Gaskell ; introduction by Esther Alice Chadwick. — London : Dent [etc.], 1975. — iii-xx,424p ; 19cm. — (Everyman's library)
Everyman ed. originally published: 1914. — Bibl.: p.xv.
ISBN 0-460-00680-0 : £1.40
ISBN 0-460-01680-6 Pbk : £0.95
(B77-07581)

Gissing, George. In the year of Jubilee / [by] George Gissing ; with a new introduction by Gillian Tindall ; and textual notes by P.F. Kropholler. — Hassocks : Harvester Press, 1976 [i.e. 1977]. — xxiv,457p ; 19cm. — (Society and the Victorians ; no.27)
Facsimile reprint of: New ed. London : Lawrence and Bullen, 1895. — Originally published: in 3 vols. London : Lawrence and Bullen, 1894. — Bibl.: p.455-457.
ISBN 0-85527-064-0 : £5.95 : CIP rev.
(B77-05049)

Gissing, George. Our friend the charlatan / [by] George Gissing ; edited with a new introduction and notes by Pierre Coustillas. — Hassocks : Harvester Press, 1976 [i.e. 1977]. — xxxiii,453p, [5]leaves of plates : ill ; 19cm. — (Society and the Victorians ; no.28)
Facsimile reprint of: 1st ed. London : Chapman and Hall, 1901. — Bibl.: p.451-453.
ISBN 0-85527-199-x : £5.95 : CIP rev.
(B77-05050)

Gissing, George. The whirlpool / [by] George Gissing. — [1st ed. reprinted] / edited and with a new introduction and notes by Patrick Parrinder. — Hassocks : Harvester Press, 1977. — xxvi,467p ; 19cm.
Facsimile reprint of: 1st ed. London : Lawrence and Bullen, 1897. — Bibl.: p.465-467.
ISBN 0-85527-789-0 : £6.50 : CIP rev.
(B77-23700)

Grahame, Kenneth. Bertie's escapade / by Kenneth Grahame ; illustrated by Ernest H. Shepard. — London : Methuen, 1977. — [4], 28p : ill ; 20cm.
Originally published: 1949.
ISBN 0-416-57950-7 : £1.95
(B77-28076)

Grahame, Kenneth. The reluctant dragon / [by] Kenneth Grahame ; illustrated by Peggy Fortnum. — [London] : Fontana, 1977. — 74p : ill ; 20cm. — (Lions)
Originally published: London : Bodley Head, 1959. — '... an extract from "Dream Day[s]" first published by the Bodley Head in 1898' - title page verso.
ISBN 0-00-670544-8 Pbk : £0.45
(B77-16034)

Hardy, Thomas, *b.1840.* An indiscretion in the life of an heiress / [by] Thomas Hardy. — [1st ed. reprinted] / edited with an introduction by Terry Coleman. — London : Hutchinson, 1976. — 125p ; 23cm.
First ed. originally published: in a limited ed. of 100 numbered copies. London : Privately printed, 1934.
ISBN 0-09-126010-8 : £2.95
(B77-06262)

Henty, George Alfred. In the heart of the Rockies : a story of adventure in Colorado / by G.A. Henty. — Abridged [ed.]. — London [etc.] : Foulsham, 1977. — 223p ; 23cm. — (The Foulsham Henty library)
Previous ed.: 1953.
ISBN 0-572-00965-8 : £1.95
(B77-23701)

Henty, George Alfred. The treasure of the Incas : a story of adventure in Peru / by G.A. Henty. — Abridged [ed.]. — London [etc.] : Foulsham, 1977. — 223p ; 23cm. — (The Foulsham Henty library)
Previous ed.: London : Latimer House, 1953.
ISBN 0-572-00963-1 : £1.95
(B77-23702)

Hope, Anthony. The prisoner of Zenda / [by] Anthony Hope ; introduction by Roger Lancelyn Green. — London [etc.] : Dent [etc.], 1977. — xv,140p ; 19cm. — (Everyman's library ; no.637)
Bibl.: p.xiii.
ISBN 0-460-00637-1 Pbk : £2.40
ISBN 0-460-01637-7 Pbk : £0.65
(B77-25186)

Hughes, Thomas, *b.1822.* Tom Brown's schooldays / [by] Thomas Hughes. — Abridged [ed.]. — Maidenhead : Purnell, 1977. — 220p : 1 ill ; 21cm. — (A Purnell classic)
ISBN 0-361-03558-6 : £0.50
(B77-16035)

Jerome, Jerome Klapka. Three men in a boat ; also, Diary of a pilgrimage ; [and], Three men on the bummel / [by] Jerome K. Jerome ; original illustrations by A. Frederics, G.G. Fraser, L. Raven Hill. — London [etc.] : Spring Books, 1977. — 828p in various pagings : ill, port ; 21cm.
Facsimile reprints.
ISBN 0-600-38767-4 : £2.50
(B77-20556)

Le Fanu, Sheridan. Uncle Silas : a tale of Bartram-Haugh / by J.S. Le Fanu. — Bath : Chivers, 1977. — 19-480p ; 21cm.
ISBN 0-85997-246-1 : £6.00(£4.50 to members of the Library Association)
(B77-23703)

Moore, George. Esther Waters / [by] George Moore ; introduction by Walter Allen. — London : Dent [etc.], 1976. — x,362p ; 19cm. — (Everyman's library)
This ed. originally published: 1936. — Bibl.: p.x.
ISBN 0-460-01933-3 Pbk : £1.00
(B77-16036)

Morrison, Arthur. Cunning Murrell / [by] Arthur Morrison. — Ipswich : Boydell Press, 1977. — viii,310p ; 18cm. — (The Essex library)
Facsimile reprint of: 1st ed. London : Methuen, 1900.
ISBN 0-85115-085-3 : £3.50
(B77-34062)

Nesbit, Edith. The princess & the cat / [by] E. Nesbit ; illustrated by Michael Pollard. — London : Abelard-Schuman : Sadler, 1977. — 63p : ill ; 21cm. — (A grasshopper book)
ISBN 0-200-72424-x : £1.75
ISBN 0-200-72425-8 Pbk : £0.50
(B77-17072)

Nesbit, Edith. The railway children / by E. Nesbit ; illustrated by Charles Mozley. — London : Dent, 1977. — 234p,[6]leaves of plates : ill(some col) ; 22cm. — (A children's illustrated classics paperback)
Originally published: with these illustrations. 1975.
ISBN 0-460-02751-4 Pbk : £1.75
(B77-25864)

Sewell, Anna. Black Beauty / by Anna Sewell ; illustrated by Joy Hawken ; foreword by Olive Jones. — London [etc.] : Collins, 1976. — 192p : ill(some col) ; 23cm. — (Classics for today)
ISBN 0-00-184042-8 : £3.50
(B77-00400)

Sewell, Anna. Black beauty / [by] Anna Sewell. — Abridged [ed.]. — Maidenhead : Purnell, 1977. — 128p : 1 ill ; 21cm. — (A Purnell classic)
ISBN 0-361-03555-1 : £0.50
(B77-16037)

Somerville, Edith OEnone. The real Charlotte / by E. OE. Somerville and Martin Ross. — London : Quartet Books, 1977. — [7],344p ; 20cm.
ISBN 0-7043-3099-7 Pbk : £1.75
(B77-12074)

Stevenson, Robert Louis. Kidnapped / [by] Robert Louis Stevenson ; edited with an introduction by M.R. Ridley. — London [etc.] : Dent, 1977. — xv,160p ; 18cm. — (Everyman's library)
Originally published: with 'Catriona'. 1962.
ISBN 0-460-01762-4 Pbk : £0.60
(B77-28077)

Stevenson, Robert Louis. Kidnapped / [by] Robert Louis Stevenson. — Abridged [ed.]. — Maidenhead : Purnell, 1977. — 136p : 1 ill ; 21cm. — (A Purnell classic)
This ed. originally published: London : Bancroft, 1966.
ISBN 0-361-03560-8 : £0.50
(B77-22835)

Stevenson, Robert Louis. Treasure Island / [by] Robert Louis Stevenson. — Abridged ed. — [London] : Armada Books, 1977. — 192p : map ; 18cm.
This ed. originally published: London : Collins, 1964.
ISBN 0-00-691334-2 Pbk : £0.40
(B77-27351)

Stevenson, Robert Louis. Treasure Island / [by] Robert Louis Stevenson. — Abridged [ed.]. — Maidenhead : Purnell, 1977. — 152p : 1 ill ; 21cm. — (A Purnell classic)
ISBN 0-361-03553-5 : £0.50
(B77-12075)

Trollope, Anthony. Barchester towers / [by] Anthony Trollope ; introduction by Julian Symons ; drawings by Peter Reddick. — London : Folio Society, 1977. — 462p : ill, maps(on lining papers) ; 23cm.
ISBN 0-85067-105-1 : £6.95(to members only)
(B77-07582)

Whitechurch, Victor Lorenzo. Stories of the railway / by V.L. Whitechurch. — [1st ed. reprinted] ; foreword by Bryan Morgan. — London [etc.] : Routledge and Kegan Paul, 1977. — [13],248,[7]p : ill, facsims, plans, port ; 21cm.
Facimile reprint of: 1st ed., originally published as 'Thrilling stories of the railway'. London : C. Arthur Pearson, 1912.
ISBN 0-7100-8635-0 : £3.75
(B77-25865)

Wilde, Oscar. [Fairy stories. Selected fairy stories]. The happy prince, and other tales / [by] Oscar Wilde ; illustrated in colour and black and white by Charles Robinson. — London : Pan Books, 1977. — [1],134,[2]p,[8]p of plates : ill(some col) ; 23cm. — (Piccolo gift book series)
Facsimile reprint of: illustrated ed. London : Duckworth, 1913.
ISBN 0-330-24857-x Pbk : £1.25
(B77-13243)

Wilde, Oscar. The happy prince / [by] Oscar Wilde ; illustrated by Kaj Beckman. — London : Kaye and Ward, 1977. — [29]p : col ill ; 22x27cm.
ISBN 0-7182-1164-2 : £2.25
(B77-30589)

Zangwill, Israel. Children of the ghetto : a study of a peculiar people / [by] Israel Zangwill ; with an introduction by V.D. Lipman. — [Leicester] : Leicester University Press, 1977. — 27,ii-viii,410p : map ; 20cm. — (The Victorian library)
Facsimile reprint of: 3rd ed. London : Heinemann, 1893.
ISBN 0-7185-5028-5 : £6.00
(B77-05051)

823'.8 — Fiction in English. Brontë, Charlotte. *Critical studies*
Blom, Margaret Howard. Charlotte Brontë / by Margaret Howard Blom. — London : Prior [etc.], 1977. — 176p : port ; 21cm. — (Twayne's English authors series ; TEAS 203)
Bibl.: p.169-174. — Index.
ISBN 0-86043-090-1 : £4.95
(B77-28078)

823'.8 — Fiction in English. Brontë, Charlotte, 1849-1855. *Biographies*
Banks, Lynne Reid. Path to the silent country : Charlotte Brontë's years of fame / [by] Lynne Reid Banks. — London : Weidenfeld and Nicolson, 1977. — xv,208p ; 23cm.
ISBN 0-297-77319-4 : £4.25
(B77-27352)

823'.8 — Fiction in English. Carroll, Lewis. Through the looking-glass. Special subjects: Chess. *Critical studies*
Dickins, Anthony Stewart Mackay. Alice in Fairyland : a lecture to the Lewis Carroll Society on the 14th November 1975 at County Hall, London / by A.S.M. Dickins. — Kew Gardens (6a Royal Parade, Kew Gardens, Surrey TW9 3QD) : The author, 1976. — 24, [1]p : ill ; 21cm.
Limited ed. of 250 copies, of which the first 100 are signed by the author. — 'Reprinted from the Society's magazine "Jabberwocky" Winter 1976'.
ISBN 0-901911-11-9 Sd : £1.00
(B77-01778)

823'.8 — Fiction in English. Dickens, Charles. *Critical studies*
Dickens / [translated from the Italian]. — Maidenhead : Sampson Low, 1977. — 136p : ill(chiefly col), facsims, ports(chiefly col) ; 22cm. — (Giants of literature)
Originally published: in Italian. Milan : Arnoldo Mondadori, 1968?. — Bibl.: p.131.
ISBN 0-562-00048-8 : £2.75
(B77-11395)

823'.8 — Fiction in English. Dickens, Charles. David Copperfield. *Critical studies*
Collins, Philip. Charles Dickens, 'David Copperfield' / by Philip Collins. — London : Edward Arnold, 1977. — 64p ; 20cm. — (Studies in English literature ; no.67)
Bibl.: p.62-63. — Index.
ISBN 0-7131-5935-9 : £3.30
ISBN 0-7131-5936-7 Pbk : £1.70
(B77-13846)

823'.8 — Fiction in English. Dickens, Charles. Hard times. *Study outlines. For Irish students. Secondary school texts*
Jennings, John. 'Hard times' / [by] John Jennings. — Dublin : Helicon, 1977. — 56p ; 21cm. — (Helicon student guides)
Bibl.: p.56.
Sd : £0.58
(B77-34063)

823'.8 — Fiction in English. Dickens, Charles. Local associations: England
Hardwick, Michael. Dickens's England / by Michael & Mollie Hardwick ; photography by Michael Hardwick. — London : Dent, 1976. — xi,172p,[32]p of plates : ill, facsims ; 22cm.
Originally published: 1970. — Bibl.: p.162-163. — Index.
£3.95
ISBN 0-460-03925-3
(B77-00401)

823'.8 — Fiction in English. Dickens, Charles. Nicholas Nickleby. *Study outlines*
Arkin, Marcus. Notes on Charles Dickens' 'Nicholas Nickleby' / compiled by Marcus Arkin. — London [etc.] : Methuen, 1976. — [7] ,67p ; 22cm. — (Study-aid series)
Bibl.: p.67.
ISBN 0-413-36960-9 Sd : £0.60
(B77-13244)

823'.8 — Fiction in English. Eliot, George. *Biographies*
Adams, Kathleen. George Eliot : a brief biography / by Kathleen Adams ; illustrated by William J. Adams. — 3rd ed. — [Warwick] ([Shire Hall, Warwick CV34 4RR]) : Warwickshire County Council, 1976. — 28p : ill ; 23cm.
Previous ed.: Nuneaton : Nuneaton Borough Council, 1972. — Bibl.: p.27-28.
ISBN 0-904937-02-x Sd : £0.25
(B77-12076)

823'.8 — Fiction in English. Eliot, George. *Critical studies*
Liddell, Robert. The novels of George Eliot / [by] Robert Liddell. — London : Duckworth, 1977. — 193p ; 23cm.
Index.
ISBN 0-7156-0992-0 : £7.95
(B77-34064)

823'.8 — Fiction in English. Eliot, George. Characters. *Dictionaries*
Hartnoll, Phyllis. Who's who in George Eliot / [by] Phyllis Hartnoll. — London : Elm Tree Books, 1977. — viii,183p ; 21cm.
ISBN 0-241-89428-x : £3.95
(B77-08031)

823'.8 — Fiction in English. Eliot, George. Daniel Deronda. *Critical studies. Conference proceedings*
Daniel Deronda : a centenary symposium / edited by Alice Shalvi ; [for] the Institute of Languages and Literature, the Hebrew University of Jerusalem. — Jerusalem : Jerusalem Academic Press ; Stanmore (103 Stanmore Hill, Stanmore, Middx) : Distributed by Michael Katanka (Books) Ltd, 1976 [i.e. 1977]. — [1],156p ; 22cm.
'... held in Spring 1976 ... The papers ... are here presented in lightly edited form ...' - note. — Published in Israel: 1976.
ISBN 0-902291-74-2 Pbk : £3.50
(B77-12077)

823'.8 — Fiction in English. Gaskell, Elizabeth Cleghorn. *Biographies. Juvenile literature*
Brill, Barbara. Elizabeth Gaskell / by Barbara Brill ; with illustrations by Roger Hall. — Loughborough : Ladybird Books, 1977. — 52p : col ill, facsim, col ports ; 18cm. — (Ladybird history series ; 45)
Col. ill., text on lining papers. — Index.
ISBN 0-7214-0454-5 : £0.24
(B77-18365)

823'.8 — Fiction in English. Gissing, George. *Biographies*
Collie, Michael. George Gissing, a biography / [by] Michael Collie. — Folkestone : Dawson, 1977. — 189p ; 23cm.
Bibl.: p.182-186. — Index.
ISBN 0-7129-0770-x : £7.00 : CIP rev.
ISBN 0-208-01700-3 (Archon)
(B77-10543)

823'.8 — Fiction in English. Hardy, Thomas, b.1840. *Critical studies*
Page, Norman. Thomas Hardy / by Norman Page. — London [etc.] : Routledge and Kegan Paul, 1977. — xiii,195p ; 23cm.
Bibl.: p.187-190. — Index.
ISBN 0-7100-8614-8 : £5.50
(B77-26501)

Pinion, Francis Bertram. Thomas Hardy : art and thought / [by] F.B. Pinion. — London [etc.] : Macmillan, 1977. — x,214p ; 23cm.
Index.
ISBN 0-333-19730-5 : £7.95
(B77-25187)

Thomas Hardy after fifty years / edited by Lance St John Butler. — London [etc.] : Macmillan, 1977. — xiv,153p ; 23cm.
Index.
ISBN 0-333-21487-0 : £7.95 : CIP rev.
(B77-19625)

823'.8 — Fiction in English. Hardy, Thomas, b.1840. *Critical studies. Conference proceedings*
Thomas Hardy Society. *Summer School, 2nd, Weymouth College of Education, 1975.* Budmouth essays on Thomas Hardy : papers presented at the 1975 Summer School [of the Thomas Hardy Society] / edited by F.B. Pinion. — Dorchester ([c/o] Hon. Secretary, The Vicarage, Haselbury Plucknett, Crewkerne, Somerset TA18 7PB) : The Society, 1976. — 228p ; 22cm.
'... held ... at the College of Education, Weymouth ...' - Preface. — Index.
ISBN 0-904398-15-3 Pbk : £3.60
(B77-34065)

823'.8 — Fiction in English. Hardy, Thomas, b.1840. Jude the obscure. *Study outlines*
Baker, Isadore Lewis. Brodie's notes on Thomas Hardy's 'Jude the obscure' / [by] I.L. Baker. — London [etc.] : Pan Books, 1977. — [3],124p ; 20cm. — (Pan revision aids)
Bibl.: p.1-2.
ISBN 0-330-50062-7 Pbk : £0.60
(B77-34066)

823'.8 — Fiction in English. Hardy, Thomas, b.1840. Return of the native. *Study outlines*
Arkin, Marcus. Notes on Thomas Hardy's 'The return of the native' / compiled by Marcus Arkin. — London [etc.] : Methuen, 1976. — [5],38p ; 22cm. — (Study-aid series)
Bibl.: p.38.
ISBN 0-413-37010-0 Sd : £0.60
(B77-13245)

823'.8 — Fiction in English. Kingsley, Charles. *Critical studies*
Hartley, Allan John. The novels of Charles Kingsley : a Christian social interpretation / [by] Allan John Hartley. — Folkestone ([Warner House, Bowles Well Gardens, Folkestone, Kent CT19 6PH]) : The Hour-Glass Press, 1977. — xii,188p,[2] leaves of plates : 2 ports ; 28cm.
Index.
ISBN 0-561-01000-5 : £6.00
(B77-05633)

823'.8 — Fiction in English. Meredith, George, b.1828. *Biographies*
Williams, David, *b.1909.* George Meredith : his life and lost love / [by] David Williams. — London : Hamilton, 1977. — xii,227p,[8]p in plates : ill, ports ; 23cm.
Bibl.: p.219-220. — Index.
ISBN 0-241-89630-4 : £7.95
(B77-21407)

823'.8 — Fiction in English. Moore, George. *Autobiographies*
Moore, George. Hail and farewell : ave, salve, vale / [by] George Moore. — [2nd ed. reprinted with new introduction and notes] / edited by Richard Cave. — Gerrards Cross : Smythe, 1976. — 774p,[16]p of plates : ill, ports ; 24cm.
This ed. originally published: in 2 vols. London : Heinemann, 1925. — Bibl.: p.755-756. — Index.
ISBN 0-900675-64-0 : £17.50
(B77-05634)

823'.8 — Fiction in English. Rolfe, Fr. *Biographies*
Benkovitz, Miriam Jeannette. Frederick Rolfe, Baron Corvo : a biography / [by] Miriam J. Benkovitz. — London : Hamilton, 1977. — xv,332p,xii p of plates : ill, facsims, ports ; 23cm.
Also published: New York : Putnam, 1977. — Index.
ISBN 0-241-89512-x : £6.50
(B77-08536)

823'.8 — Fiction in English. Rolfe, Fr. *Correspondence to Bainbridge, Harry*
Rolfe, Fr. Letters to Harry Bainbridge / [by] Frederick William Rolfe, Baron Corvo ; edited with an introduction by Miriam J. Benkovitz. — London : Enitharmon Press, 1977. — 47p ; 22cm.
Limited ed. of 395 copies, of which 45 copies are specially bound and numbered I to XLV. — Index.
ISBN 0-901111-95-3 : Unpriced
Special ed.: Unpriced
(B77-27353)

823'.8 — Fiction in English. Thackeray, William Makepeace. *Critical studies*
Carey, John. Thackeray : prodigal genius / [by] John Carey. — London : Faber, 1977. — 3-208p ; 23cm.
Index.
ISBN 0-571-11126-2 : £6.95 : CIP rev.
(B77-22836)

823'.8 — Fiction in English. Trollope, Anthony. *Critical studies*
Kincaid, James Russell. The novels of Anthony Trollope / [by] James R. Kincaid. — Oxford : Clarendon Press, 1977. — xiii,302p ; 23cm.
Bibl.: p.261-284. — Index.
ISBN 0-19-812077-x : £9.75
(B77-20557)

Terry, R C. Anthony Trollope : the artist in hiding / [by] R.C. Terry. — London [etc.] : Macmillan, 1977. — xiii,286p,8p of plates : ill, port ; 23cm.
Bibl.: p.250-260. — Index.
ISBN 0-333-21923-6 : £8.95 : CIP rev.
(B77-24464)

823'.8 — Fiction in English. Trollope, Anthony. Special subjects: England. Politics, 1860-1880. *Critical studies*
Halperin, John. Trollope and politics : a study of the Pallisers and others / [by] John Halperin. — London [etc.] : Macmillan, 1977. — x,318p : port ; 23cm.
Bibl.: p.305-307. — Index.
ISBN 0-333-21694-6 : £8.95
(B77-20558)

823'.8 — Short stories in English, 1837-1900. *Texts*
Hardy, Thomas, *b.1840.* The stories of Thomas Hardy / [edited by F.B. Pinion]. — New Wessex ed. — [London] : [Macmillan].
In 3 vols.
Vol.3 : Old Mrs Chundle, and other stories. — [1977]. — 240p : 3 ill ; 23cm.
ISBN 0-333-19983-9 : £5.50
(B77-20559)

Vol.1. — [1977]. — 384p : map, port ; 23cm.
Contents: Wessex tales - A group of noble dames.
ISBN 0-333-19982-0 : £5.50
(B77-20560)

Vol.2. — [1977]. — 504p : map, port ; 23cm.
Contents: Life's little ironies - A changed man, The waiting supper, and other tales.
ISBN 0-333-19984-7 : £5.50
(B77-20561)

Hornung, Ernest William. [The amateur cracksman]. Raffles, the amateur cracksman / by Ernest William Hornung ; illustrated by F.C. Yohn. — [1st ed. reprinted]. — Lincoln [Neb.] ; London : University of Nebraska Press, 1976. — [2],xvii,244p,[2] leaves of plates : ill ; 21cm.
'A Bison book'. — Facsimile reprint. — 'The amateur cracksman' originally published: London : Methuen, 1899.
ISBN 0-8032-5836-4 Pbk : £1.50
(B77-16581)

Kipling, Rudyard. [Selections]. The man who would be king, and other stories / [by] Rudyard Kipling. — London : Pan Books, 1976. — 188p ; 18cm.
This collection originally published: 1975.
ISBN 0-330-24662-3 Pbk : £0.50
(B77-08032)

Morrison, Arthur. Martin Hewitt, investigator / [by] Arthur Morrison. — Large print ed. — Bath : Lythway Press, 1977. — xi,270p ; 23cm. — (Lythway classics of crime and detection)
ISBN 0-85046-729-2 : £4.50
(B77-23704)

Nesbit, Edith. Fairy stories / [by] E. Nesbit ; illustrated by Brian Robb ; edited by Naomi Lewis. — London [etc.] : E. Benn, 1977. — xx,171p : ill ; 22cm.
ISBN 0-510-16000-x : £2.95
(B77-20562)

O'Brien, Fitz-James. The fantastic tales of Fitz-James O'Brien / edited with an introduction by Michael Hayes. — London : J. Calder : [Distributed by Calder and Boyars], 1977. — 149p ; 23cm.
ISBN 0-7145-3617-2 : £4.95
(B77-29675)

Riddell, *Mrs* **Joseph H.** The collected ghost stories of Mrs J.H. Riddell / selected and introduced by E.F. Bleiler. — New York : Dover Publications [etc.] ; London : Constable, 1977. — [1],xxvi,[1],345p,[5]p of plates : ill, facsims, port ; 22cm.
Bibl.: p.341-344.
ISBN 0-486-23430-4 Pbk : £3.60
(B77-32148)

823'.8'0803 — Fiction in English, 1837-1900. Special subjects: Science. *Anthologies*
Beyond the gaslight : science in popular fiction, 1895-1905 / [edited by] Hilary & Dik Evans ; with illustrations from the Mary Evans Picture Library. — London : Muller, 1976. — 160p : ill, facsims ; 26cm.
Ill. on lining papers.
ISBN 0-584-31017-x : £4.95
(B77-03213)

823'.8'09 — Fiction in English, 1837-1975. *Critical studies. Transcripts of discussions*
The **English** novel / [edited by C.T. Watts]. — London (Sussex Publications Ltd, 85 Linden Gardens, W2 4EU) : Sussex Books, 1976. — 200p ; 21cm. — (Questions in literature)
Bibl.: p.195-200.
ISBN 0-905272-02-1 : £3.60(library ed)
ISBN 0-905272-03-x Pbk : £1.85
(B77-08537)

823'.8'09 — Fiction in English. Brontë family. *Biographies*
James, Donna. Brontë life / [by] Donna James. — Manchester (40 Leominster Drive, Manchester 22) : Peter Riley, 1977. — [4],26p : ill, ports ; 21cm.
Bibl.: p.26.
Sd : £0.50
(B77-22096)

823'.8'09 — Fiction in English. Brontë family. Local associations: West Yorkshire (Metropolitan County). Haworth
Bentley, Phyllis. Haworth of the Brontës / by Phyllis Bentley and John Ogden. — Lavenham : Dalton, 1977. — 103p : ill, facsims, map(on lining paper), plan(on lining paper), ports ; 23cm.
Index.
ISBN 0-900963-75-1 : £3.80
(B77-23705)

823'.8'09 — Fiction in English. Brontë sisters. *Critical studies*
Winnifrith, Tom. The Brontës / by Tom Winnifrith. — London [etc.] : Macmillan, 1977. — viii,181p ; 23cm. — (Masters of world literature series)
Bibl.: p.171-178. — Index.
ISBN 0-333-21610-5 : £5.95
(B77-22097)

823'.8'09 — Fiction in English. Gaskell, Elizabeth Cleghorn; Hardy, Thomas, b.1840 & Rutherford, Mark. *Critical studies*
Lucas, John, *b.1937.* The literature of change : studies in the nineteenth-century provincial novel / [by] John Lucas. — Hassocks : Harvester Press [etc.], 1977. — xii,217p ; 23cm.
Index.
ISBN 0-85527-079-9 : £7.50 : CIP rev.
(B77-07583)

823'.8'09 — Fiction in English. Women writers, 1837-1975. *Critical studies*
Showalter, Elaine. A literature of their own : British women novelists from Brontë to Lessing / [by] Elaine Showalter. — Princeton ; Guildford : Princeton University Press, 1977. — viii,378,[1]p ; 23cm.
Bibl.:. p.351-365. — Index.
ISBN 0-691-06318-4 : £14.20
(B77-14895)

823'.8'0915 — Fantasy fiction in English, 1837-1957. *Critical studies*
Irwin, W R. The game of the impossible : a rhetoric of fantasy / [by] W.R. Irwin. — Urbana [etc.] ; London : University of Illinois Press, [1977]. — xii,215p ; 24cm.
Published in the United States: 1976. — Bibl.: p.199-205. — Index.
ISBN 0-252-00587-2 : £8.00
(B77-14393)

823'.8'0932 — Fiction in English, 1837-1945. Special subjects: Developing countries. *Critical studies*
Goonetilleke, D C R A. Developing countries in British fiction / [by] D.C.R.A. Goonetilleke. — London [etc.] : Macmillan, 1977. — ix,282p ; 23cm.
Bibl.: p.271-276. — Index.
ISBN 0-333-19767-4 : £8.95
(B77-15480)

823'.8'0936 — Fiction in English, 1837-1945. Special subjects: Nature. *Critical studies*

Alcorn, John. The nature novel from Hardy to Lawrence / [by] John Alcorn. — London [etc.] : Macmillan, 1977. — x,139p ; 23cm.
Bibl.: p.129-135. — Index.
ISBN 0-333-21195-2 : £7.95
(B77-10933)

823'.8'0938 — Fiction in English, 1837-1900. Special subjects: Christian church. *Critical studies*

Wolff, Robert Lee. Gains and losses : novels of faith and doubt in Victorian England / by Robert Lee Wolff. — London : J. Murray, 1977. — xiv,537p,16 p of plates : ill, ports ; 24cm.
Also published: New York : Garland, 1977. — Bibl.: p.507-516. — Index.
ISBN 0-7195-3388-0 : £10.50
(B77-21408)

823.91F — ENGLISH FICTION, 1900-. NOVELS

Aalben, Patrick. The grab / by Patrick Aalben. — London : Hale, 1977. — 192p ; 20cm.
ISBN 0-7091-6319-3 : £3.25
(B77-28079)

Abbey, Ruth. Dream of terror / [by] Ruth Abbey. — London : Hale, 1976. — 158p ; 21cm.
ISBN 0-7091-5679-0 : £3.25
(B77-01779)

Ableman, Paul. Tornado Pratt : a novel / by Paul Ableman. — London : Gollancz, 1977. — 223p ; 20cm.
ISBN 0-575-02387-2 : £4.95
(B77-30590)

Adam, Nicolas. The triplehip cracksman / [by] Nicolas Adam. — London : Cape, 1977. — 223p ; 21cm.
ISBN 0-224-01376-9 : £3.50 : CIP rev.
(B77-09922)

Adams, Clifton. Hogan's way / [by] Clifton Adams. — [London] : Fontana, 1976. — 160p ; 18cm.
Originally published: London : Collins, 1964.
ISBN 0-00-614406-3 Pbk : £0.50
(B77-12627)

Adams, Norman. Blood Dirk / by Norman Adams. — London : Hale, 1977. — 176p ; 21cm.
ISBN 0-7091-6067-4 : £3.50
(B77-19626)

Adams, Philippa. Nine months / [by] Philippa Adams. — Basingstoke [etc.] : Macmillan, 1977. — 112p ; 18cm. — (Topliners)
For adolescents.
ISBN 0-333-21754-3 Pbk : £0.45 : CIP rev.
(B77-05052)

Adams, Richard, *b.1920.* The plague dogs / [by] Richard Adams ; with illustrations and diagrams by A. Wainwright. — London : Allen Lane : Collings, 1977. — xiii,461p : ill, maps ; 23cm.
ISBN 0-7139-1055-0 : £4.50
(B77-25866)

Adler, Renata. Speedboat / [by] Renata Adler. — London : Hamilton, 1977. — [9],178p ; 21cm.
Originally published: New York : Random House, 1976.
ISBN 0-241-89708-4 : £3.95
(B77-23706)

Adler, Warren. Trans-Siberian Express / [by] Warren Adler. — London [etc.] : Macmillan, 1977. — 368p ; 23cm.
Also published: New York : Putnam, 1977.
ISBN 0-333-22306-3 : £4.95
(B77-22098)

Agamon, David. The stone captain / by David Agamon. — London : Hale, 1977. — 3-173p ; 21cm.
ISBN 0-7091-6220-0 : £3.50
(B77-28080)

Agnew, Spiro T. The Canfield decision / [by] Spiro T. Agnew. — London : W.H. Allen, 1977. — [5],344p ; 24cm.
Originally published: Chicago : Playboy Press, 1976.
ISBN 0-491-01998-x : £4.95
(B77-17728)

Aidoo, Christina Ama Ata. Our sister Killjoy, or, Reflections from a black-eyed squint / [by] Ama Ata Aidoo. — London : Longman, 1977. — [6],134p ; 20cm. — (African creative writing series)
ISBN 0-582-64134-9 Pbk : £0.95
(B77-26502)

Aiken, Joan. Died on a rainy Sunday / [by] Joan Aiken. — London : Sphere, 1976. — 143p ; 18cm.
Originally published: London : Gollancz, 1972.
ISBN 0-7221-1052-9 Pbk : £0.55
(B77-06263)

Aiken, Joan. The five-minute marriage / [by] Joan Aiken. — London : Gollancz, 1977. — 3-264p ; 21cm.
ISBN 0-575-02331-7 : £3.95
(B77-29676)

Aiken, Joan. Last movement / by Joan Aiken. — London : Gollancz, 1977. — 251p ; 21cm. — ([Gollancz thriller])
ISBN 0-575-02257-4 : £3.95
(B77-16582)

Aird, Catherine. Parting breath / [by] Catherine Aird. — London : Collins [for] the Crime Club, 1977. — 224p ; 21cm.
ISBN 0-00-231616-1 : £3.25
(B77-31429)

Albrand, Martha. A day in Monte Carlo / [by] Martha Albrand. — London [etc.] : White Lion Publishers, 1977. — 158p ; 21cm.
Originally published: New York : Random House ; London : Hodder and Stoughton, 1959.
ISBN 0-7274-0219-6 : £3.25
(B77-06264)

Albrand, Martha. The mask of Alexander / [by] Martha Albrand. — London [etc.] : White Lion Publishers, 1977. — 191p ; 21cm.
Originally published: New York : Random House, 1955 ; London : Hodder and Stoughton, 1956.
ISBN 0-7274-0321-4 : £3.75
(B77-19627)

Albrand, Martha. No surrender / by Martha Albrand. — London : Severn House : [Distributed by Hutchinson], 1976. — 174p ; 21cm.
Originally published: London : Chatto and Windus, 1943.
ISBN 0-7278-0156-2 : £2.95
(B77-06265)

Albrand, Martha. A taste of terror / by Martha Albrand. — London [etc.] : Hodder and Stoughton, 1976. — 192p ; 21cm.
ISBN 0-340-20540-7 : £3.50
(B77-00945)

Alding, Peter. Murder is suspected / [by] Peter Alding. — London : Long, 1977. — 184p ; 20cm.
ISBN 0-09-131520-4 : £3.50
(B77-27354)

Aldiss, Brian Wilson. Cryptozoic / [by] Brian Aldiss. — London : Sphere, 1977. — 187p ; 18cm. — (Sphere science fiction)
Originally published: as 'An age', London : Faber, 1967 ; and as 'Cryptozoic', Garden City, N.Y. : Doubleday, 1968 ; London : Sphere, 1973.
ISBN 0-7221-1104-5 Pbk : £0.75
(B77-22837)

Aldiss, Brian Wilson. Hothouse / [by] Brian Aldiss. — London : Sphere, 1977. — 206p ; 18cm. — (Sphere science fiction)
Originally published: London : Faber, 1962.
ISBN 0-7221-1103-7 Pbk : £0.75
(B77-22838)

Aldiss, Brian Wilson. Non-stop / [by] Brian W. Aldiss. — London [etc.] : Pan Books, 1977. — 204p ; 18cm. — (Pan science fiction)
Originally published: London : Faber, 1958.
Pbk : £0.60
ISBN 0-330-24638-0
(B77-25867)

Aldridge, James. One last glimpse / by James Aldridge. — London : Joseph, 1977. — v, 182p ; 21cm.
ISBN 0-7181-1564-3 : £4.25
(B77-12628)

Alexander, Dair. Olivia / by Dair Alexander. — London : Hale, 1977. — 160p ; 20cm.
ISBN 0-7091-5919-6 : £3.10
(B77-09923)

Algren, Nelson. A walk on the wild side / [by] Nelson Algren. — Harmondsworth [etc.] : Penguin, 1977. — [5],346p ; 19cm.
Originally published: New York : Farrar, Straus and Cudahy, 1956 ; London : Spearman, 1957.
ISBN 0-14-003565-6 Pbk : £1.10
(B77-32836)

Allardyce, Paula. The gentle sex / [by] Paula Allardyce. — St Albans : Mayflower, 1977. — 190p ; 18cm.
Originally published: London : Hodder and Stoughton, 1974.
ISBN 0-583-12518-2 Pbk : £0.60
(B77-08538)

Allardyce, Paula. Miss Philadelphia Smith / [by] Paula Allardyce. — London [etc.] : Hodder and Stoughton, 1977. — 224p ; 21cm.
ISBN 0-340-21456-2 : £3.75
(B77-20563)

Allardyce, Paula. The respectable Miss Parkington-Smith / [by] Paula Allardyce. — St Albans : Mayflower, 1977. — 190p ; 18cm.
Originally published: London : Hodder and Stoughton, 1964.
ISBN 0-583-12745-2 Pbk : £0.60
(B77-14896)

Allbeury, Ted. The man with the president's mind / [by] Ted Allbeury. — London : P. Davies, 1977. — [6],218p ; 23cm.
ISBN 0-432-00426-2 : £3.95
(B77-18967)

Allbeury, Ted. Palomino blonde / [by] Ted Allbeury. — St Albans : Mayflower, 1976. — 158p ; 18cm.
Originally published: London : P. Davies, 1975.
ISBN 0-583-12700-2 Pbk : £0.50
(B77-03748)

Alldritt, Keith. The lover next door / [by] Keith Alldritt. — London : Deutsch, 1977. — 208p ; 21cm.
ISBN 0-233-96880-6 : £3.50
(B77-22099)

Allen, Jay Presson. Just tell me what you want / [by] Jay Presson Allen. — London : Corgi, 1977. — [6],344p ; 18cm.
Originally published: New York : Dutton ; London : Heinemann, 1975.
ISBN 0-552-10399-3 Pbk : £0.85
(B77-23707)

Allen, Judy. Song for solo and persistent chorus / [by] Judy Allen. — London : Hamilton, 1977. — [5],118p ; 23cm.
For adolescents.
ISBN 0-241-89698-3 : £2.95
(B77-32837)

Allen, Michael. Spence in Petal Park / [by] Michael Allen. — London : Constable, 1977. — 173p ; 21cm. — (Constable crime)
ISBN 0-09-461890-9 : £3.95
(B77-23708)

Allen, Paul, *b.1948.* Apeland / by Paul Allen. — Toronto [etc.] ; London : Bantam, 1977. — [7], 183,[1]p ; 18cm.
Originally published: New York : Viking Press, 1976.
ISBN 0-552-60385-6 Pbk : £0.65
(B77-31430)

Allerton, Jay. Vote for a silk gown / [by] Jay Allerton ; edited by Lesley Saxby. — London (110 Warner Rd, S.E.5) : Troubadour, 1976. — [4],176p ; 18cm.
Originally published: London : Macdonald and Jane's, 1974.
ISBN 0-86007-326-2 Pbk : £0.50
(B77-08539)

Allgood, Marcus. D-Day Dawson / [by] Marcus Allgood. — London : New English Library, 1977. — 128p : ill ; 18cm.
ISBN 0-450-03324-4 Pbk : £0.60
(B77-28081)

Alther, Lisa. Kinflicks / [by] Lisa Alther. — Harmondsworth [etc.] : Penguin, 1977. — 570p ; 18cm.
Originally published: New York : Knopf ; London : Chatto and Windus, 1976.
ISBN 0-14-004410-8 Pbk : £0.95
(B77-33420)

Alther, Lisa. Kinflicks / [by] Lisa Alther. — London : Chatto and Windus, 1976. — [4], 505p ; 23cm.
Also published: New York : Knopf, 1976.
ISBN 0-7011-2191-2 : £4.95
(B77-09924)

Alvarez, Alfred. Hers / [by] A. Alvarez. — Harmondsworth [etc.] : Penguin, 1977. — 218p ; 19cm.
Originally published: London : Weidenfeld and Nicolson, 1974.
ISBN 0-14-004267-9 Pbk : £0.80
(B77-24465)

Ambler, Eric. The dark frontier / [by] Eric Ambler. — Large print ed. — Leicester : Ulverscroft, 1977. — [4],411p ; 23cm. — (Ulverscroft large print series : [adventure])
Originally published: London : Hodder and Stoughton, 1936.
ISBN 0-7089-0030-5 : Unpriced
(B77-34067)

Ambler, Eric. Doctor Frigo / [by] Eric Ambler. — [London] : Fontana, 1976. — [6],245p ; 18cm.
Originally published: London : Weidenfeld and Nicolson, 1974.
ISBN 0-00-613996-5 Pbk : £0.70
(B77-12629)

Ambler, Eric. The Schirmer inheritance / [by] Eric Ambler. — [London] : Fontana, 1977. — 189p ; 19cm.
Originally published: London : Heinemann, 1953.
ISBN 0-00-614658-9 Pbk : £0.70
(B77-22839)

Ambler, Eric. Send no more roses / [by] Eric Ambler. — London : Weidenfeld and Nicolson, 1977. — 269p ; 23cm.
ISBN 0-297-77277-5 : £3.95
(B77-21409)

Ambler, Eric. Uncommon danger / [by] Eric Ambler. — [London] : Fontana, 1977. — 220p ; 18cm.
Originally published: London : Hodder and Stoughton, 1937.
ISBN 0-00-615011-x Pbk : £0.70
(B77-22100)

Ames, Francis. Callahan goes south / [by] Francis H. Ames. — Large print [ed.]. — London : Prior [etc.], 1977. — [3],329p ; 25cm.
Originally published: Garden City, N.Y. : Doubleday, 1976.
ISBN 0-86043-079-0 : £4.95
(B77-34068)

Ames, Jennifer. Nurse's story / by Jennifer Ames. — London : Hale, 1977. — 159p ; 20cm.
Originally published: London : Collins, 1965.
ISBN 0-7091-6242-1 : £3.20
(B77-28082)

Ames, Jennifer. This sinister island / [by] Jennifer Ames. — Revised ed. — Bath : Lythway Press, 1976. — [4],284p ; 23cm.
Large print ed. — This ed., i.e. Revised ed. originally published: London : Collins, 1968.
ISBN 0-85046-667-9 : £4.15
(B77-00402)

Amis, Kingsley. Lucky Jim / [by] Kingsley Amis. — Harmondsworth [etc.] : Penguin, 1976. — 251p ; 18cm.
Originally published: London : Gollancz, 1954.
ISBN 0-14-001648-1 Pbk : £0.60
(B77-03749)

Amis, Martin. Dark secrets / [by] Martin Amis. — St Albans : Triad, 1977. — 224p ; 18cm.
Originally published: as 'Dead babies'. London : Cape, 1975.
ISBN 0-586-04482-5 Pbk : £0.60
(B77-14897)

Anderson, Garrett. Brennan's book : a novel / by Garrett Anderson. — Edinburgh : P. Harris, 1977. — 318p ; 23cm.
ISBN 0-905882-02-4 : £4.95
(B77-28083)

Anderson, James, *b.1936.* Appearance of evil / [by] James Anderson. — London : Constable, 1977. — 218p ; 21cm. — (Constable crime)
ISBN 0-09-461470-9 : £3.50
(B77-07584)

Anderson, John Richard Lane. Death in the Caribbean / by J.R.L. Anderson. — London : Gollancz, 1977. — 159p ; 21cm. — ([Gollancz thriller])
ISBN 0-575-02321-x : £3.50
(B77-31431)

Anderson, John Richard Lane. Death in the city / by J.R.L. Anderson. — London : Gollancz, 1977. — 192p ; 21cm. — ([Gollancz thriller])
ISBN 0-575-02272-8 : £3.95
(B77-20564)

Anderson, Poul. Brain wave / [by] Poul Anderson. — [1st ed. reprinted] ; introduction by Brian W. Aldiss. — London : New English Library, 1976. — 192p ; 22cm. — (SF master series)
Originally published: New York : Ballantine Books, 1954 ; London : Heinemann, 1955.
ISBN 0-450-02981-6 : £4.95
(B77-01780)

Anderson, Poul. Brain wave / [by] Poul Anderson. — [1st ed. reprinted] ; introduction by Brian W. Aldiss. — London : New English Library, 1977. — 192p ; 18cm. — (SF master series)
This ed. originally published: 1976.
ISBN 0-450-03004-0 Pbk : £0.80
(B77-24466)

Anderson, Poul. The dancer from Atlantis / [by] Poul Anderson. — London : Sphere, 1977. — 171p ; 18cm. — ([Sphere science fiction])
Originally published: Garden City, N.Y. : Doubleday, 1971.
ISBN 0-7221-1163-0 Pbk : £0.75
(B77-31432)

Anderson, Poul. Ensign Flandry / [by] Poul Anderson. — London : Severn House : [Distributed by Hutchinson], 1977. — 217p ; 21cm.
Originally published: Philadelphia : Chilton Books, 1966 ; London : Coronet, 1976.
ISBN 0-7278-0338-7 : £3.50
(B77-31433)

Anderson, Poul. Fire time / [by] Poul Anderson. — St Albans : Panther, 1977. — 255p ; 18cm. — (Panther science fiction)
Originally published: Garden City, N.Y. : Doubleday, 1974.
ISBN 0-586-04392-6 Pbk : £0.75
(B77-08540)

Anderson, Poul. A midsummer tempest / [by] Poul Anderson. — London : Severn House ([Distributed by Hutchinson]), 1976. — [3], 228p ; 21cm.
Originally published: Garden City, N.Y. : Doubleday, 1974 ; London : Futura Publications, 1975. — Previous control number ISBN 0-442-25061-4.
ISBN 0-7278-0311-5 : £3.25
(B77-00403)

Anderson, Sylvia. As the twig is bent / [by] Sylvia Anderson. — St Ives, Cornwall : United Writers Publications, 1976. — 252p ; 22cm.
ISBN 0-901976-19-9 : £3.95
(B77-02561)

Anderson, Verily. Daughters of divinity / [by] Verily Anderson. — Large print ed. — Bath : Chivers, 1977. — [7],360p ; 22cm.
Originally published: London : Hart-Davis, 1960.
ISBN 0-85997-248-8 : £5.40(£4.05 to members of the Library Association)
(B77-21410)

Andrew, Prudence. The hooded falcon / [by] Prudence Andrew. — Large print ed. — Bath : Chivers, 1977. — [5],385p ; 22cm.
Originally published: London : New Authors, 1960.
ISBN 0-85997-231-3 : £5.60(£4.20 to members of the Library Association)
(B77-22840)

Andrew, Prudence. Where are you going to, my pretty maid? / [by] Prudence Andrew. — London : Heinemann, 1977. — 92p ; 21cm. — (Pyramid books)
ISBN 0-434-95820-4 : £2.20
(B77-34069)

Andrews, A.A. Buffalo township / by A.A. Andrews. — London : Hale, 1977. — 157p ; 20cm.
ISBN 0-7091-6142-5 : £3.10
(B77-20565)

Andrews, A.A. Four Aces / by A.A. Andrews. — London : Hale, 1977. — 157p ; 20cm.
ISBN 0-7091-5953-6 : £2.80
(B77-09925)

Andrews, Jane. File on St Peters / by Jane Andrews. — London : Hale, 1976. — 160p ; 20cm.
ISBN 0-7091-5852-1 : £2.95
(B77-00404)

Andrews, Jane. Focus on St Peter's / by Jane Andrews. — London : Hale, 1977. — 152p ; 20cm.
ISBN 0-7091-6343-6 : £3.40
(B77-30591)

Andrews, Lucilla. In storm and in calm / [by] Lucilla Andrews. — Large print ed. — Leicester : Ulverscroft, 1977. — [7],383p ; 23cm. — (Ulverscroft large print series : [romance])
Originally published: London : Harrap, 1975.
ISBN 0-85456-509-4 : £2.65
(B77-08033)

Andrews, Lynda M. Elizabeth, the witch's daughter / by Lynda M. Andrews. — London : Hale, 1977. — 175p ; 21cm.
Bibl.: p.175. — Based on the early life of Elizabeth I.
ISBN 0-7091-6072-0 : £3.70
(B77-19628)

Andrews, Lynda M. The Tudor heritage / [by] Lynda M. Andrews. — London : Hale, 1977. — 173p ; 21cm.
ISBN 0-7091-6210-3 : £3.50
(B77-28084)

Angoff, Charles. Mid-century / [by] Charles Angoff. — South Brunswick ; New York : Barnes ; London : Yoseloff, 1974. — 349p ; 22cm.
ISBN 0-498-01339-1 : £3.00
(B77-29677)

Anne, David. Rabid / [by] David Anne. — London : W.H. Allen, 1977. — [6],249p ; 23cm.
ISBN 0-491-01748-0 : £3.95
(B77-06266)

Anthony, David. Stud game / [by] David Anthony. — London : Collins [for] the Crime Club, 1977. — 249p ; 21cm.
ISBN 0-00-231790-7 : £2.95
(B77-18968)

Anthony, Evelyn. Clandara / [by] Evelyn Anthony. — London : Sphere, 1976. — 293p ; 18cm.
Originally published: Garden City, N.Y. : Doubleday ; London : Hurst and Blackett, 1963.
ISBN 0-7221-1191-6 Pbk : £0.60
(B77-14898)

Anthony, Evelyn. Curse not the King / [by] Evelyn Anthony. — London : Hutchinson, 1977. — 256p ; 21cm.
Originally published: London : Museum Press, 1954. — Based on the life of Paul the First of Russia.
ISBN 0-09-128550-x : £3.95
(B77-09926)

Anthony, Evelyn. Elizabeth / [by] Evelyn Anthony. — London : Hutchinson, 1976. — 286p ; 21cm.
Originally published: London : Museum Press, 1960. — Based on the life of Elizabeth I.
ISBN 0-09-125950-9 : £3.95
(B77-12630)

Anthony, Evelyn. Far fly the eagles / [by] Evelyn Anthony. — London : Hutchinson, 1977. — 222p ; 21cm.
Originally published: London : Museum Press, 1955. — Based on the life of Alexander I, Tsar of Russia.
ISBN 0-09-128560-7 : £3.95
(B77-09242)

Anthony, Evelyn. The French bride / [by] Evelyn Anthony. — London : Sphere, 1976. — 255p ; 18cm.
Originally published: Garden City, N.Y. : Doubleday, 1964 ; London : Arrow Books, 1966.
ISBN 0-7221-1193-2 Pbk : £0.75
(B77-06267)

Anthony, Evelyn. The legend / [by] Evelyn Anthony. — London : Sphere, 1976. — 219p ; 18cm.
Originally published: London : Hutchinson, 1969.
ISBN 0-7221-1195-9 Pbk : £0.65
(B77-00405)

Anthony, Evelyn. The legend / [by] Evelyn Anthony. — London : Sphere, 1977. — 219p ; 18cm.
Originally published: London : Hutchinson, 1969.
ISBN 0-7221-1210-6 Pbk : £0.85
(B77-31434)

Anthony, Evelyn. The Persian ransom / [by] Evelyn Anthony. — London : Corgi, 1977. — 237p ; 18cm.
Originally published: London : Hutchinson, 1975.
ISBN 0-552-10421-3 Pbk : £0.80
(B77-20566)

Anthony, Evelyn. The Poellenberg inheritance / [by] Evelyn Anthony. — Large print ed. — Leicester : Ulverscroft, 1976. — [5],414p ; 23cm. — (Ulverscroft large print series : [fiction])
Originally published: London : Hutchinson, 1972.
ISBN 0-85456-504-3 : £2.65
(B77-08541)

Anthony, Evelyn. The rendezvous / [by] Evelyn Anthony. — London : Sphere, 1977. — 186p ; 18cm.
Originally published: London : Hutchinson, 1967.
ISBN 0-7221-1211-4 Pbk : £0.85
(B77-31435)

Anthony, Michael, *b.1932.* The games were coming / [by] Michael Anthony ; introduction by Kenneth Ramchand, study questions by Jean D'Costa. — London [etc.] : Heinemann, 1977. — xviii,108p ; 19cm. — (Caribbean writers series ; 17)
Originally published: London : Deutsch, 1963. — Bibl.: p.xviii.
ISBN 0-435-98033-5 Pbk : £0.85
(B77-23709)

Anthony, Piers. Omnivore / [by] Piers Anthony. — London : Corgi, 1977. — 173p ; 18cm.
Originally published: London : Faber, 1969.
ISBN 0-552-10528-7 Pbk : £0.70
(B77-25868)

Anthony, Piers. Orn / [by] Piers Anthony. — London : Corgi, 1977. — 235p ; 18cm. — (Corgi science fiction)
ISBN 0-552-10506-6 Pbk : £0.75
(B77-26503)

Anthony, Piers. Rings of ice / [by] Piers Anthony. — [London] : Fontana, 1977. — 159p ; 18cm. — (Fontana science fiction)
Originally published: New York : Avon, 1974 ; London : Millington, 1975.
ISBN 0-00-614615-5 Pbk : £0.65
(B77-32149)

Apter, T E. Adonis' garden / [by] T.E. Apter. — London : Heinemann, 1977. — [4],211p ; 23cm.
ISBN 0-434-02305-1 : £3.90
(B77-09927)

Arbor, Jane. A girl named Smith / by Jane Arbor. — London : Mills and Boon, 1977. — 187p ; 17cm.
Originally published: 1960.
ISBN 0-263-72348-8 Pbk : £0.35
(B77-06853)

Arbor, Jane. Tree of paradise / by Jane Arbor. — London : Mills and Boon, 1976. — 186p ; 17cm.
ISBN 0-263-72313-5 Pbk : £0.30
(B77-00406)

Archer, Jeffrey. Shall we tell the President? / [by] Jeffrey Archer. — London : Cape, 1977. — 220p ; 23cm.
ISBN 0-224-01563-x : £3.95 : CIP rev.
(B77-20567)

Areo, Agbo. Director! / [by] Agbo Areo. — London [etc.] : Macmillan, 1977. — [4],121p ; 18cm. — (Pacesetters)
For adolescents.
ISBN 0-333-23055-8 Pbk : £0.59
(B77-31436)

Armour, Jill. Miranda / by Jill Armour. — London : Hale, 1977. — 185p ; 20cm.
ISBN 0-7091-5969-2 : £3.10
(B77-12078)

Armstrong, Evelyn Stewart. Valdoro's mistress / [by] Evelyn Stewart Armstrong. — London : Macdonald and Jane's, 1976. — [4],220p ; 21cm. — (A troubadour)
ISBN 0-354-04050-2 : £3.75
(B77-00407)

Armstrong, Richard. Sea change / [by] Richard Armstrong ; illustrated by Michel Leszczynoki. — London [etc.] : White Lion Publishers, 1977. — [7],212p : ill ; 21cm.
Originally published: London : Dent, 1948. — For adolescents.
ISBN 0-85686-222-3 : £2.75
(B77-18969)

Armstrong, Thomas. The Crowthers of Bankdam / by Thomas Armstrong. — London : Collins, 1976. — 640p ; 21cm.
Originally published: 1940.
ISBN 0-00-221102-5 : £3.75
(B77-01781)

Arnim, Mary Annette, *Gräfin von.* Mr Skeffington / [by] Elizabeth [i.e. Mary Annette] von Arnim. — Large print ed. — Bath : Chivers, 1976. — [5],452p ; 23cm.
Originally published: London : Heinemann, 1940.
ISBN 0-85997-195-3 : £5.60(£4.20 to members of the Library Association)
(B77-02562)

Arnold, Alan. Sarah / [by] Alan Arnold. — [London] : Fontana, 1976. — 189p ; 18cm.
'Based on the screenplay for the Reader's Digest film, "The Incredible Sarah" ...'. — Cover title : The incredible Sarah.
ISBN 0-00-614442-x Pbk : £0.65
(B77-01782)

Arnold, Alan. Sarah / [by] Alan Arnold. — London : Severn House : [Distributed by Hutchinson], 1977. — 189p ; 21cm.
Spine title: The incredible Sarah. — 'Based on the screenplay for the Reader's Digest film, "The incredible Sarah" ...'. — Originally published: London : Fontana, 1976.
ISBN 0-7278-0228-3 : £3.25
(B77-08542)

Arnold, Edwin Lester. Lieut Gulliver Jones : his vacation / [by] Edwin Lester Arnold ; introduction by Roger Lancelyn Green. — London : New English Library, 1977. — 206p ; 18cm. — (SF master series)
Originally published: United States : s.n. ; London : Brown, Langham and Co., 1905.
ISBN 0-450-03365-1 Pbk : £0.90
(B77-30592)

Arrighi, Mel. Conscience of a killer / by Mel Arrighi. — London : Hale, 1977. — [4],180p ; 20cm.
Originally published: as 'Navona 1000'. United States: s.n., 1976.
ISBN 0-7091-5893-9 : £3.15
(B77-13246)

Arthur, Ruth Mabel. An old magic / by Ruth Arthur ; illustrated by Margery Gill. — London : Gollancz, 1977. — [9],175p : ill ; 20cm.
For adolescents.
ISBN 0-575-02356-2 : £3.40
(B77-31437)

Arvay, Harry. Blow the four winds / [by] Harry Arvay. — London : Corgi, 1977. — 172p ; 18cm.
ISBN 0-552-10448-5 Pbk : £0.70
(B77-26504)

Arvay, Harry. The Swiss deal / [by] Harry Arvay. — London : Corgi, 1976. — 126p ; 18cm.
ISBN 0-552-10319-5 Pbk : £0.50
(B77-04397)

Ashe, Gordon. A blast of trumpets / [by] John Creasey as Gordon Ashe. — Large print [ed.]. — London : Prior [etc.], 1976. — [3],289p ; 24cm.
Originally published: London : Long, 1975.
ISBN 0-86043-034-0 : £4.95
(B77-07585)

Ashe, Rosalind. Moths / [by] Rosalind Ashe. — London : Hutchinson, 1976. — 240p ; 21cm.
ISBN 0-09-126490-1 : £3.75
(B77-05053)

Ashe, Rosalind. Moths / [by] Rosalind Ashe. — Harmondsworth [etc.] : Penguin, 1977. — 211p ; 18cm.
Originally published: London : Hutchinson, 1976.
ISBN 0-14-004506-6 Pbk : £0.80
(B77-27355)

Ashford, Jeffrey. Hostage to death / [by] Jeffrey Ashford. — London : Long, 1977. — 183p ; 20cm.
ISBN 0-09-129290-5 : £3.50
(B77-30593)

Ashton, Elizabeth. Mountain heritage / by Elizabeth Ashton. — London : Mills and Boon, 1977. — 187p ; 17cm.
Originally published: 1976.
ISBN 0-263-72337-2 Pbk : £0.35
(B77-06854)

Ashton, Elizabeth. Sanctuary in the desert / by Elizabeth Ashton. — London : Mills and Boon, 1976. — 186p ; 17cm.
ISBN 0-263-72299-6 Pbk : £0.30
(B77-00408)

Ashton, Helen. Family cruise : a marine comedy / [by] Helen Ashton. — Large print ed. — Bath : Chivers, 1977. — [7],373p ; 22cm.
Originally published: London : Gollancz, 1934.
ISBN 0-85997-266-6 : £5.80(£4.35 to members of the Library Association)
(B77-34070)

Ashton, Helen. The half-crown house / [by] Helen Ashton. — Large print ed. — Bath : Chivers, 1977. — [7],386p : geneal table ; 22cm.
Originally published: London : Collins, 1956.
ISBN 0-85997-232-1 : £5.60(£4.20 to members of the Library Association)
(B77-20568)

Ashton, Helen. Letty Landon / [by] Helen Ashton. — Large print ed. — Bath : Chivers, 1977. — [7],487p ; 22cm.
Originally published: New York : Dodd, Mead ; London : Collins, 1951. — Bibl.: p.483-485. — Based on the life of Letty Landon.
ISBN 0-85997-203-8 : £5.60(£4.20 to members of the Library Association)
(B77-09928)

Ashton, Helen. The swan of Usk / [by] Helen Ashton. — Large print ed. — Bath : Chivers, 1976. — xiii,487p ; 22cm.
Originally published: London : Collins, 1940. — Based on the life of Henry Vaughan.
ISBN 0-85997-196-1 : £5.60(£4.20 to members of the Library Association)
(B77-02563)

Ashton, Joe. Grass roots / [by] Joe Ashton. — London [etc.] : Quartet Books, 1977. — [4], 236p ; 23cm.
ISBN 0-7043-2118-1 : £4.50
(B77-30594)

Asimov, Isaac. Authorised murder / [by] Isaac Asimov. — St Albans : Panther, 1977. — 240p ; 18cm.
Originally published: as 'Murder at the ABA', Garden City, N.Y. : Doubleday ; and as 'Authorised murder', London : Gollancz, 1976.
ISBN 0-586-04641-0 Pbk : £0.80
(B77-24467)

Asimov, Isaac. A whiff of death / [by] Isaac Asimov. — London : Sphere, 1977. — 157p ; 18cm.
Originally published: as 'The death dealers', New York : Avon, 1958 ; and as 'A whiff of death', London : Gollancz, 1968.
ISBN 0-7221-1260-2 Pbk : £0.85
(B77-28869)

Astley, Juliet. The fall of Midas / [by] Juliet Astley. — London : Corgi, 1977. — 221p ; 18cm.
Originally published: London : Joseph, 1976.
ISBN 0-552-10572-4 Pbk : £0.75
(B77-31438)

Athar, Ikbal. The years of their lives / [by] Ikbal Athar. — London : Macdonald and Jane's, 1976. — [7],439p ; 23cm.
ISBN 0-356-04703-2 : £4.50
(B77-01783)

Atkins, Meg Elizabeth. Samain / [by] Meg Elizabeth Atkins. — London : Cassell, 1977. — [9],226p ; 21cm.
ISBN 0-304-29847-6 : £3.95
(B77-28870)

Atkinson, Hugh. Crack-up / [by] Hugh Atkinson. — St Albans : Mayflower, 1977. — [5],137p ; 18cm.
Originally published: London : Hart-Davis, MacGibbon, 1974.
ISBN 0-583-12466-6 Pbk : £0.50
(B77-13247)

Atwood, Margaret. Lady Oracle / [by] Margaret Atwood. — London : Deutsch, 1977. — 345p ; 21cm.
Originally published: Toronto : McClelland and Stewart, 1976.
ISBN 0-233-96884-9 : £4.95
(B77-26505)

Auchincloss, Louis. The dark lady / [by] Louis Auchincloss. — London : Weidenfeld and Nicolson, 1977. — [9],246p ; 23cm.
Also published: Boston, Mass. : Houghton Mifflin, 1977.
ISBN 0-297-77350-x : £4.95
(B77-30595)

Audemars, Pierre. The healing hands of death / [by] Pierre Audemars. — London : Long, 1977. — 184p ; 20cm.
ISBN 0-09-128780-4 : £3.25
(B77-16583)

Audsley, Catherine. The golden island : an adventure story of 1920 / written by Catherine Audsley, at the age of 11. — Ilfracombe : Stockwell, 1977. — 63p : facsims ; 19cm.
ISBN 0-7223-1093-5 : £2.25
(B77-32150)

Avallone, Michael. The big stiffs / by Michael Avallone. — London : Hale, 1977. — 173p ; 20cm.
ISBN 0-7091-6184-0 : £3.25
(B77-26506)

Avery, Richard. The death worms of Kratos / [by] Edmund Cooper writing as Richard Avery. — London : Severn House : [Distributed by Hutchinson], 1977. — 142p ; 21cm. — (Avery, Richard. Expendables ; vol.1)
Originally published: London : Coronet, 1975.
ISBN 0-7278-0267-4 : £3.15
(B77-24468)

Axton, David. Prison of ice / [by] David Axton. — London : W.H. Allen, 1976. — 219p ; 22cm.
ISBN 0-491-01638-7 : £3.95
(B77-06268)

Ayres, Ruby Mildred. All over again / [by] Ruby M. Ayres. — Large print ed. — Bath : Lythway Press, 1977. — [4],348p ; 23cm.
Originally published: New York : Doubleday, 1934 ; London : Hodder and Stoughton, 1935.
ISBN 0-85046-722-5 : £4.70
(B77-34071)

Ayres, Ruby Mildred. Living apart / [by] Ruby M. Ayres. — Large print ed. — Bath : Lythway Press, 1977. — [5],279p ; 23cm.
Originally published: London : Hodder and Stoughton, 1938.
ISBN 0-85046-747-0 : £4.50
(B77-33421)

Ayres, Ruby Mildred. Young shoulders / [by] Ruby M. Ayres. — London : Severn House : [Distributed by Hutchinson], 1976. — 192p ; 21cm.
Originally published: London : Hodder and Stoughton, 1947.
ISBN 0-7278-0216-x : £3.15
(B77-03750)

Babson, Marian. The lord mayor of death / [by] Marian Babson. — London [etc.] : Collins [for] the Crime Club, 1977. — 193p ; 21cm.
ISBN 0-00-231474-6 : £2.95
(B77-09929)

Babson, Marian. Murder sails at midnight / [by] Marian Babson. — Large print ed. — Leicester : Ulverscroft, 1977. — [4],301p ; 23cm. — (Ulverscroft large print series : [mystery])
Originally published: London : Collins for the Crime Club, 1975.
ISBN 0-7089-0041-0 : £2.95
(B77-28085)

Bach, Richard. Illusions / [by] Richard Bach. — London : Heinemann, 1977. — 144p ; 23cm.
Also published: New York : Delacorte Press, 1977.
ISBN 0-434-04101-7 : £2.90
(B77-21411)

Bagley, Desmond. The enemy / [by] Desmond Bagley. — London : Collins, 1977. — 322p ; 22cm.
ISBN 0-00-221583-7 : £4.25
(B77-20569)

Bagley, Desmond. High citadel / [by] Desmond Bagley. — Large print ed. — Leicester : Ulverscroft, 1977. — [5],544p ; 23cm. — (Ulverscroft large print series : [adventure, suspense])
Originally published: London : Collins, 1965.
ISBN 0-85456-522-1 : £2.65
(B77-13847)

Bagley, Desmond. The spoilers / [by] Desmond Bagley. — London : Collins, 1977. — 317p ; 21cm.
Originally published: 1969.
£3.00
ISBN 0-00-221742-2
(B77-19629)

Bailey, Paul, *b.1937 (Feb.).* Peter Smart's confessions / [by] Paul Bailey. — London : Cape, 1977. — 191p ; 21cm.
ISBN 0-224-01358-0 : £3.95 : CIP rev.
(B77-07586)

Bainbridge, Beryl. Harriet said - / [by] Beryl Bainbridge. — [London] : Fontana, 1977. — 158p ; 18cm.
Originally published: London : Duckworth, 1972.
ISBN 0-00-614650-3 Pbk : £0.65
(B77-14899)

Bainbridge, Beryl. Injury time / [by] Beryl Bainbridge. — London : Duckworth, 1977. — 158p ; 21cm.
ISBN 0-7156-1246-8 : £3.95
(B77-28086)

Bainbridge, Beryl. A quiet life / [by] Beryl Bainbridge. — [London] : Fontana, 1977. — 156p ; 18cm.
Originally published: London : Duckworth, 1976.
ISBN 0-00-614801-8 Pbk : £0.75
(B77-27356)

Baker, Donna. Moon over the mountains / by Donna Baker. — London : Hale, 1977. — 156p ; 20cm.
ISBN 0-7091-6332-0 : £3.40
(B77-32151)

Baker, Ivon. Death and variations / by Ivon Baker. — New York ; St Martin's ; London : Hale, 1977. — 175p ; 20cm.
ISBN 0-7091-6295-2 : £3.25
(B77-28087)

Balchin, Nigel. Mine own executioner / by Nigel Balchin. — London : Collins, 1976. — [2], 256p ; 21cm.
Originally published: 1945.
£3.00
ISBN 0-00-221511-x
(B77-16584)

Baldwin, Faith. Thursday's child / [by] Faith Baldwin. — London : Hale, 1977. — [5],218p ; 20cm.
ISBN 0-7091-5897-1 : £3.10
(B77-12631)

Baldwin, Faith. Thursday's child / [by] Faith Baldwin. — Large print [ed.]. — London : Prior [etc.], 1977. — [7],358p ; 24cm.
Originally published: New York : Holt, Rinehart and Winston, 1976.
ISBN 0-86043-014-6 : £4.95
(B77-12079)

Baldwin, James. Another country / [by] James Baldwin. — London : Corgi, 1976. — [7],338p ; 18cm.
Originally published: New York : Dial Press, 1962 ; London : Joseph, 1963.
ISBN 0-552-10324-1 Pbk : £0.85
(B77-04398)

Baldwin, James. Giovanni's room / [by] James Baldwin. — London : Corgi, 1977. — 127p ; 18cm.
Originally published: New York : Dial Press, 1956 ; London : Joseph, 1957.
ISBN 0-552-10378-0 Pbk : £0.50
(B77-16038)

Baldwin, James. Go tell it on the mountain / [by] James Baldwin. — London : Corgi, 1976. — 254p ; 18cm.
Originally published: New York : Knopf, 1953 ; London : Joseph, 1954.
ISBN 0-552-10291-1 Pbk : £0.75
(B77-00409)

Baldwin, James. If Beale Street could talk / [by] James Baldwin. — London : Corgi, 1976. — 173p ; 18cm.
Originally published: New York : Dial Press ; London : Joseph, 1974.
ISBN 0-552-10290-3 Pbk : £0.65
(B77-00410)

Balham, Joe. Regan and the human pipe line / [by] Joe Balham. — London : A. Barker, 1977. — 157p ; 23cm.
'Based on the TV series "The Sweeney"' - jacket.
ISBN 0-213-16650-x : £3.75
(B77-32152)

Balham, Joe. Regan and the Lebanese shipment / [by] Joe Balham. — London : A. Barker, 1977. — 157p ; 23cm.
'Based on the T.V. series "The Sweeney"' - jacket.
ISBN 0-213-16633-x : £3.75
(B77-22841)

Ball, David, *b.1942.* The contortionist : a concentrate fiction in prose / [by] David Ball. — Colchester (44 Queens Rd, Wivenhoe, Colchester, Essex) : Paperbag Book Club. Part 1. — 1976. — [1],41p : ill ; 30cm.
Pierced for binder.
ISBN 0-905336-01-1 Ls : £1.00
(B77-06855)

Ballantyne, David. The Cunninghams / [by] David Ballantyne. — Christchurch [N.Z.] [etc.] ; London : Whitcoulls, 1976. — 239p ; 21cm.
Originally published: London : Hale, 1963.
ISBN 0-7233-0478-5 : Unpriced
ISBN 0-7233-0461-0 Pbk : £3.45
(B77-05054)

Ballard, James Graham. High-rise / [by] J.G. Ballard. — St Albans : Triad, 1977. — 173p ; 18cm.
Originally published: London : Cape, 1975.
ISBN 0-586-04456-6 Pbk : £0.60
(B77-23710)

Ballard, Todhunter. Home to Texas / by Todhunter Ballard. — London : Hale, 1977. — [5],159p ; 20cm.
Originally published: Garden City, N.Y. : Doubleday, 1974.
ISBN 0-7091-6031-3 : £2.95
(B77-14900)

Ballinger, Bill Sanborn. The ultimate warrior / [by] Bill S. Ballinger ; based on a screenplay of the same title by Robert Clouse. — London : Star Books, 1976. — 140p ; 19cm.
Also published: New York : Warner, 1976.
ISBN 0-352-39805-1 Pbk : £0.50
(B77-06269)

Ballinger, W.A. The voyagers / [by] W.A. Ballinger. — London : New English Library. Part 2 : There and back again. — 1977. — 206p ; 21cm.
ISBN 0-450-03441-0 : £4.95
(B77-32838)

Banks, Barbara. Dragonseeds / [by] Barbara Banks. — New York : St Martin's Press ; London : Hale, 1977. — 3-190p ; 21cm.
ISBN 0-7091-6098-4 : £3.70
(B77-19630)

Banks, Lynne Reid. The L-shaped room / [by] Lynne Reid Banks ; with a specially written introduction by the author ; and a sequence of photographs by Lance Browne ; editor Chris Buckton. — London : Longman, 1976. — ix, 309p : ill ; 19cm. — (Longman imprint books)
'The L-shaped room' originally published: London : Chatto and Windus, 1960.
ISBN 0-582-23358-5 Pbk : £1.10
(B77-05055)

Banks, Lynne Reid. My darling villain / [by] Lynne Reid Banks. — London [etc.] : Bodley Head, 1977. — 238p ; 23cm. — (A book for new adults)
For adolescents.
ISBN 0-370-11034-x : £3.25
(B77-06856)

Bannatyne, Jack. Torpedo squadron / [by] Jack Bannatyne. — London : New English Library, 1977. — 159p ; 18cm.
Originally published: London : Hale, 1975.
ISBN 0-450-03468-2 Pbk : £0.70
(B77-22101)

Banning, John. Goodbye to Istanbul / [by] John Banning. — London : New English Library, 1977. — 140p ; 18cm.
ISBN 0-450-03114-4 Pbk : £0.65
(B77-12080)

Barak, Michael. The secret list of Heinrich Roehm / [by] Michael Barak. — Large print ed. — London : Prior [etc.], 1976. — [6],415p ; 24cm.
Originally published: London : Weidenfeld and Nicolson, 1976.
ISBN 0-86043-018-9 : £5.50
(B77-07587)

Barlas, Chris. Man about the house / adapted by Chris Barlas ; based on the television series of the same name by Johnnie Mortimer and Brian Cooke. — London : Severn House, 1976. — 191p ; 21cm.
ISBN 0-7278-0193-7 : £3.25
(B77-05635)

Barnard, Christiaan Neethling. The unwanted / [by] Christiaan Barnard & Siegfried Stander. — London : Arrow Books, 1977. — [5],390p ; 18cm.
Originally published: Cape Town : Tafelberg, 1974 ; London : Hutchinson, 1976.
ISBN 0-09-914220-1 Pbk : £0.80
(B77-22102)

Barnard, Eveline. The Brothers are walking / [by] Eveline Barnard. — London : Dobson, 1976. — 136p ; 21cm.
For adolescents.
ISBN 0-234-77577-7 : £2.50
(B77-00946)

Barnard, Robert. Blood brotherhood / [by] Robert Barnard. — London : Collins [for] the Crime Club, 1977. — 196p ; 21cm.
ISBN 0-00-231048-1 : £3.25
(B77-24469)

Barnard, Robert. Death on the high C's / [by] Robert Barnard. — London : Collins [for] the Crime Club, 1977. — 195p ; 21cm.
ISBN 0-00-231217-4 : £2.95
(B77-00947)

Barnes, Lilian. Captive love / by Lilian Barnes. — London : Hale, 1977. — 189p ; 20cm.
ISBN 0-7091-6311-8 : £3.20
(B77-28871)

Barnes, Margaret Campbell. Brief gaudy hour / [by] Margaret Campbell Barnes. — London : Sphere, [1976]. — 390p ; 18cm.
Originally published: London : Macdonald and Co., 1949. — Based on the life of Anne Boleyn.
ISBN 0-7221-2209-8 Pbk : £0.95
(B77-02565)

Barnes, Margaret Campbell. Isabel the Fair / [by] Margaret Campbell Barnes. — London : Sphere, 1977. — 287p ; 18cm.
Originally published: London : Macdonald, 1957. — Based on the life of Isabel, wife of Edward II.
ISBN 0-7221-2224-1 Pbk : £0.95
(B77-20570)

Barnes, Margaret Campbell. The king's bed / [by] Margaret Campbell Barnes. — London : Macdonald and Jane's, 1976. — 251p ; 21cm.
Originally published: London : Macdonald and Co., 1961.
£3.95
ISBN 0-356-01756-7
(B77-00411)

Barnes, Margaret Campbell. The king's bed / [by] Margaret Campbell Barnes. — London : Sphere, 1977. — 251p ; 18cm.
Originally published: London : Macdonald and Co., 1961.
ISBN 0-7221-2226-8 Pbk : £0.95
(B77-18970)

Barnes, Margaret Campbell. The king's fool / [by] Margaret Campbell Barnes. — London : Sphere, 1977. — 300p ; 18cm.
Originally published: London : Macdonald and Co., 1959.
ISBN 0-7221-2210-1 Pbk : £0.95
(B77-18971)

Barnes, Margaret Campbell. Lady on the coin / [by] Margaret Campbell Barnes and Hebe Elsna. — London : Sphere, [1977]. — 255p ; 18cm.
Originally published: London : Macdonald, 1963. — Based on the lives of Charles II and Frances Stuart.
ISBN 0-7221-2221-7 Pbk : £0.95
(B77-12632)

Barnes, Margaret Campbell. Mary of Carisbrooke / [by] Margaret Campbell Barnes. — London : Sphere, 1977. — 365p ; 18cm.
Originally published: London : Macdonald, 1956. — Bibl.: p.365.
ISBN 0-7221-2219-5 Pbk : £0.95
(B77-12633)

Barnes, Margaret Campbell. My lady of Cleves / [by] Margaret Campbell Barnes. — London : Macdonald and Jane's, 1976. — 316p ; 21cm.
Originally published: London : Macdonald and Co., 1946.
ISBN 0-356-01750-8 : £3.95
(B77-00948)

Barnes, Margaret Campbell. My lady of Cleves / [by] Margaret Campbell Barnes. — London : Sphere, [1976]. — 366p ; 18cm.
Originally published: London : Macdonald and Co., 1946. — Based on the life of Anne of Cleves.
ISBN 0-7221-2207-1 Pbk : £0.95
(B77-02566)

Barnes, Margaret Campbell. The passionate brood / [by] Margaret Campbell Barnes. — London : Sphere, 1972 [i.e. 1977]. — 296p ; 18cm.
Originally published: as 'Like us they lived'. London : Macdonald, 1944.
ISBN 0-7221-2220-9 Pbk : £0.95
(B77-12634)

Barnes, Margaret Campbell. The Tudor Rose / [by] Margaret Campbell Barnes. — London : Sphere, 1977. — 349p : geneal table ; 18cm.
Originally published: London : Macdonald and Co., 1953. — Based on the life of Elizabeth of York, wife of King Henry VII.
ISBN 0-7221-2222-5 Pbk : £0.95
(B77-18972)

Barnes, Margaret Campbell. With all my heart / [by] Margaret Campbell Barnes. — London : Sphere, 1972[i.e.1976]. — 288p : geneal table ; 18cm.
Originally published: London : Macdonald and Co., 1951. — Based on the lives of Catherine of Braganza and Charles II.
ISBN 0-7221-2206-3 Pbk : £0.95
(B77-02567)

Barnes, Margaret Campbell. Within the hollow crown / [by] Margaret Campbell Barnes. — London : Sphere, 1977. — 366p ; 18cm.
Originally published: Philadelphia : Macrae Smith, 1947 ; London : Macdonald and Co., 1948. — Based on the life of Richard II.
ISBN 0-7221-2223-3 Pbk : £0.95
(B77-21412)

Barnes, Margaret Campbell. Within the hollow crown / [by] Margaret Campbell Barnes. — Revised ed. — London : Macdonald and Jane's, 1976. — 316p : geneal table ; 21cm.
Revised ed. originally published: London : Macdonald and Co., 1958. — Based on the life of Richard II.
£3.95
ISBN 0-356-01753-2
(B77-00949)

Baron, Alexander. The lowlife / by Alexander Baron. — Hornchurch : I. Henry, 1977. — 191p ; 21cm.
Originally published: London : Collins, 1963.
ISBN 0-86025-096-2 : £3.10
(B77-10544)

Barr, Donald. Space relations : a slightly gothic interplanetary tale / [by] Donald Barr. — London : Futura Publications, 1975. — [5], 249p ; 18cm. — (An orbit book)
Originally published: New York : Charterhouse Books, 1973 ; London : Millington, 1974.
ISBN 0-86007-841-8 Pbk : £0.65
(B77-08543)

Barr, Elisabeth. Castle heritage / [by] Elisabeth Barr. — London : Hale, 1977. — 192p ; 21cm.
ISBN 0-7091-6008-9 : £3.50
(B77-17729)

Barr, Elisabeth. The storm witch / [by] Elisabeth Barr. — London : Hale, 1976. — 190p ; 21cm.
ISBN 0-7091-5580-8 : £3.25
(B77-01784)

Barrett, Geoffrey John. The halls of the Evolvulus / [by] G.J. Barrett. — London : Hale, 1977. — 189p ; 21cm. — (Hale SF)
ISBN 0-7091-4948-4 : £3.25
(B77-05636)

Barrett, Geoffrey John. The other side of red / [by] G.J. Barrett. — London : Hale, 1977. — 172p ; 21cm. — (Hale SF)
ISBN 0-7091-5380-5 : £3.25
(B77-17730)

Barrett, Geoffrey John. Robotia / [by] G.J. Barrett. — London : Hale, 1977. — 172p ; 21cm. — (Hale SF)
ISBN 0-7091-5487-9 : £3.60
(B77-26507)

Barrett, Max. The house across the park / by Max Barrett. — London : Hale, 1977. — 221p ; 21cm.
ISBN 0-7091-6151-4 : £3.80
(B77-23711)

Barris, Chuck. You and me, babe / [by] Chuck Barris. — London : Coronet, 1976. — 189p ; 18cm.
Originally published: New York : Harper's Magazine Press ; London : Hodder and Stoughton, 1974.
ISBN 0-340-21017-6 Pbk : £0.60
(B77-03214)

Barstow, Stan. A kind of loving / [by] Stan Barstow. — London : Corgi, 1977. — 272p ; 18cm.
Originally published: London : Joseph, 1960.
ISBN 0-552-10445-0 Pbk : £0.75
(B77-19631)

Barstow, Stan. The watchers on the shore / [by] Stan Barstow. — London : Corgi, 1977. — [2], 206p ; 18cm.
Originally published: London : Joseph, 1966.
ISBN 0-552-10446-9 Pbk : £0.75
(B77-20571)

Barth, John. Chimera / [by] John Barth. — London [etc.] : Quartet Books, 1977. — [7], 308p ; 20cm.
Originally published: New York : Random House, 1972 ; London : Deutsch, 1974.
ISBN 0-7043-3113-6 Pbk : £1.50
(B77-18973)

Barthelme, Donald. The dead father / [by] Donald Barthelme. — London [etc.] : Routledge and Kegan Paul, 1977. — [5],177p ; 23cm.
Originally published: New York : Farrar, Straus & Giroux, 1975.
ISBN 0-7100-8639-3 : £3.95 : CIP rev.
(B77-09243)

Bartlett, Eric George. Smoking flax : a novel / by E.G. Bartlett. — London : Mitre Press, 1977. — 164p ; 22cm.
ISBN 0-7051-0262-9 : £2.60
(B77-34072)

Barton, Jon. Forest of death / [by] Jon Barton. — London : Corgi, 1977. — 128p ; 18cm. — (Barton, Jon. Deathshop ; 2)
ISBN 0-552-10351-9 Pbk : £0.50
(B77-08544)

Barton, Jon. Lightning strikes / [by] Jon Barton. — London : Corgi, 1977. — 126p ; 18cm. — (Barton, Jon. Deathshop ; 3)
ISBN 0-552-10401-9 Pbk : £0.60
(B77-16039)

Basile, Gloria Vitanza. The godson / [by] Gloria Vitanza Basile. — London : Corgi, 1976. — [6], 634p ; 18cm.
ISBN 0-552-10320-9 Pbk : £0.95
(B77-04399)

Basnett, Fred. Gropers, or, A splendid view of St Pancras / by Fred Basnett. — London : Gollancz, 1977. — 384p ; 21cm.
ISBN 0-575-02213-2 : £4.95
(B77-10934)

Bates, Herbert Ernest. A crown of wild myrtle / [by] H.E. Bates. — Large print ed. — Bath : Chivers, 1977. — [5],191p ; 22cm.
Originally published: London : Joseph, 1962.
ISBN 0-85997-233-x : £5.60(£4.20 to members of the Library Association)
(B77-21413)

Baum, Vicki. Berlin hotel / [by] Vicki Baum. — Large print ed. — Bath : Chivers, 1977. — [5], 410p ; 22cm.
Originally published: as 'Hotel Berlin '43'. New York : Doubleday, Doran ; London : Joseph, 1944.
ISBN 0-85997-205-4 : £5.60(£4.20 to members of the Library Association)
(B77-09930)

Baum, Vicki. Grand hotel / [by] Vicki Baum ; [translated from the German by Basil Creighton]. — London [etc.] : Pan Books, 1977. — 271p ; 18cm.
This translation originally published: London : Bles, 1930. — Translation of 'Menschen im Hotel'. Berlin : Ullstein, 1929.
ISBN 0-330-02895-2 Pbk : £0.75
(B77-25869)

Bawden, Nina. George beneath a paper moon / [by] Nina Bawden. — Harmondsworth [etc.] : Penguin, 1977. — 192p ; 18cm.
Originally published: London : Allen Lane, 1974.
ISBN 0-14-003813-2 Pbk : £0.70
(B77-27357)

Bawden, Nina. The Odd Flamingo / [by] Nina Bawden. — Large print ed. — Bath : Chivers, 1977. — [5],312p ; 22cm.
Originally published: London : Collins, 1954.
ISBN 0-85997-249-6 : £4.80(£3.60 to members of the Library Association)
(B77-22842)

Bawden, Nina. Tortoise by candlelight / [by] Nina Bawden. — Harmondsworth [etc.] : Penguin, 1977. — 234p ; 19cm.
Originally published: London : Longmans, 1963.
ISBN 0-14-004223-7 Pbk : £0.80
(B77-28088)

Bax, Martin. The hospital ship / [by] Martin Bax. — London : Pan Books, 1977. — 204p ; 20cm. — (Picador)
Originally published: London : Cape, 1976. — Bibl.: p.202-204.
ISBN 0-330-25251-8 Pbk : £0.95
(B77-34073)

Baxter, Alida. Don't hang up, Sophie - it's God / [by] Alida Baxter. — London : W.H. Allen, 1977. — 144p ; 23cm.
ISBN 0-491-02061-9 : £3.50
(B77-26508)

Bayley, Barrington John. Collision with Chronos : a novel / [by] Barrington J. Bayley. — London : Allison and Busby, 1977. — 169p ; 23cm.
Originally published: as 'Collision course'. New York : Daw Books, 1973.
ISBN 0-85031-222-1 : £3.95
(B77-28089)

Beaton, Janet. An affair of hearts / by Janet Beaton. — London : Hale, 1977. — 175p ; 20cm.
ISBN 0-7091-6201-4 : £3.20
(B77-32839)

Beattie, Tasman. The Zambesi break / [by] Tasman Beattie. — London : Eyre Methuen, 1977. — [5],169p ; 21cm.
ISBN 0-413-37400-9 : £3.50
(B77-27358)

Beaty, David. Electric train / [by] David Beaty. — London : Coronet, 1977. — 236p ; 18cm.
Originally published: London : Secker and Warburg, 1975.
ISBN 0-340-21820-7 Pbk : £0.85
(B77-22103)

Beaty, David. Excellency / [by] David Beaty. — London : Secker and Warburg, 1977. — [5], 231p ; 23cm.
ISBN 0-436-03914-1 : £4.10
(B77-21414)

Beaty, David. Excellency / [by] David Beaty. Chase the wind / [by] E.V. Thompson. The badgers of Summercombe / [by] Ewan Clarkson. Overboard / [by] Hank Searls. — Collector's library ed. — London : Reader's Digest Association [etc.], 1977. — 510,[1]p : ill(chiefly col), ports ; 21cm. — ('Reader's digest' condensed books)
ISBN 0-340-22366-9 : £3.97
(B77-32153)

Beck, Harry. Casadora / by Harry Beck. — London : Hale, 1977. — 5-156p ; 19cm.
ISBN 0-7091-5729-0 : £3.25
(B77-30596)

Beck, Harry. The lawbreaker / by Harry Beck. — London : Hale, 1977. — 152p ; 20cm.
ISBN 0-7091-5652-9 : £3.10
(B77-20572)

Beck, Harry. Sawgrass Range / [by] Harry Beck. — London : Hale, 1976. — 157p ; 20cm.
ISBN 0-7091-5488-7 : £2.70
(B77-00412)

Beck, Harry. Utah summer / by Harry Beck. — London : Hale, 1977. — 152p ; 20cm.
ISBN 0-7091-5497-6 : £2.95
(B77-14394)

Becker, Stephen. The Chinese bandit / [by] Stephen Becker. — St Albans : Triad, 1977. — 300p : map ; 18cm.
Originally published: New York : Random House, 1975 ; London : Chatto and Windus, 1976.
ISBN 0-586-04457-4 Pbk : £0.75
(B77-27359)

Beilby, Richard. Gunner : a novel of the retreat from Crete / [by] Richard Beilby. — London [etc.] : Angus and Robertson, 1977. — [6], 313p ; 23cm.
ISBN 0-207-95742-8 : £4.80
(B77-22843)

Bell, Josephine. Such a nice client / by Josephine Bell. — London [etc.] : Hodder and Stoughton, 1977. — 191p ; 20cm.
ISBN 0-340-21851-7 : £3.75
(B77-28090)

Bell, Josephine. The trouble in Hunter ward / by Josephine Bell. — London [etc.] : Hodder and Stoughton, 1976. — 191p ; 20cm.
ISBN 0-340-20973-9 : £3.15
(B77-00950)

Bell, Thomas, *b.1903.* Out of this furnace / by Thomas Bell. — [1st ed. reprinted] ; with an afterword by David P. Demarest Jr. — [Pittsburg] : University of Pittsburg Press ; London : Feffer and Simons, 1976. — [7],424p ; 21cm.
Originally published: Boston, Mass. : Little, Brown, 1941.
ISBN 0-8229-3321-7 : £5.96
ISBN 0-8229-5273-4 Pbk : £2.63
(B77-32154)

Bellamann, Henry. Kings Row / [by] Henry Bellamann. — Bath : Chivers, 1977. — 3-562p ; 21cm.
Originally published: New York : Simon and Schuster, 1940 ; London : Cape, 1941.
ISBN 0-85997-245-3 : £6.00(£4.50 to members of the Library Association)
(B77-18974)

Bellamy, Guy. The secret lemonade drinker / [by] Guy Bellamy. — London : Secker and Warburg, 1977. — [5],153p ; 23cm.
ISBN 0-436-03940-0 : £3.50
(B77-05637)

Bellow, Saul. The adventures of Augie March / [by] Saul Bellow. — Harmondsworth [etc.] : Penguin, 1977. — 617p ; 18cm.
Originally published: New York : Viking Press, 1953 ; London : Weidenfeld and Nicolson, 1954.
ISBN 0-14-002494-8 Pbk : £1.25
(B77-12081)

Bellow, Saul. Dangling man / [by] Saul Bellow. — Harmondsworth [etc.] : Penguin, 1977. — 159p ; 19cm.
Originally published: New York : Vanguard Press, 1944 ; London : Lehmann, 1946.
ISBN 0-14-001862-x Pbk : £0.50
(B77-12082)

Bellow, Saul. Henderson the Rain King : a novel / [by] Saul Bellow. — Harmondsworth [etc.] : Penguin, 1977. — [6],341p ; 20cm.
Originally published: New York : Viking Press ; London : Weidenfeld and Nicolson, 1959.
ISBN 0-14-004229-6 Pbk : £0.95
(B77-22844)

Bellow, Saul. Humboldt's gift / [by] Saul Bellow. — Harmondsworth [etc.] : Penguin, 1977. — 475p ; 19cm.
Originally published: New York : Viking Press ; London : Secker and Warburg, 1975.
ISBN 0-14-004162-1 Pbk : £0.95
(B77-15481)

Bellow, Saul. Mr Sammler's planet / [by] Saul Bellow. — Harmondsworth [etc.] : Penguin, 1977. — 3-286p ; 18cm.
Originally published: New York : Viking Press ; London : Weidenfeld and Nicolson, 1970.
ISBN 0-14-004419-1 Pbk : £0.90
(B77-32840)

Bellow, Saul. Seize the day / [by] Saul Bellow. — Harmondsworth [etc.] : Penguin, 1977. — 126p ; 19cm.
Originally published: New York : Viking Press, 1956 ; London : Weidenfeld and Nicolson, 1957.
ISBN 0-14-002495-6 Pbk : £0.55
(B77-12083)

Bellow, Saul. The victim / [by] Saul Bellow. — Harmondsworth [etc.] : Penguin, 1977. — 238p ; 18cm.
Originally published: New York : Vanguard Press, 1947 ; London : Lehmann, 1948.
ISBN 0-14-002493-x Pbk : £0.60
(B77-12635)

Benchley, Peter. The deep / [by] Peter Benchley. — London [etc.] : Pan Books, 1977. — 251,[1] p ; 18cm.
Originally published: Garden City, N.Y. : Doubleday ; London : Deutsch, 1976.
ISBN 0-330-25044-2 Pbk : £0.75
(B77-20573)

Benedictus, David. The fourth of June / [by] David Benedictus. — London : Sphere, 1977. — 176p ; 18cm.
Originally published: London : Blond, 1962.
ISBN 0-7221-1588-1 Pbk : £0.85
(B77-30597)

Benedictus, David. The rabbi's wife / [by] David Benedictus. — London : Sphere, 1977. — 189p ; 18cm.
Originally published: London : Blond and Briggs, 1976.
ISBN 0-7221-1579-2 Pbk : £0.85
(B77-30598)

Bennett, Dorothea. The jigsaw man / [by] Dorothea Bennett. — London [etc.] : Bodley Head, 1977. — 256p ; 21cm.
Originally published: New York : Coward, McCann and Geoghegan, 1976.
ISBN 0-370-10618-0 : £3.50
(B77-14395)

Bennett, Margot. The man who didn't fly / [by] Margot Bennett. — London : Remploy, 1977. — 191p ; 19cm.
Originally published: London : Eyre and Spottiswoode, 1955.
ISBN 0-7066-0718-x : £3.00
(B77-34074)

Bennetts, Pamela. The house in Candle Square / [by] Pamela Bennetts. — London : Hale, 1977. — 188p ; 21cm.
ISBN 0-7091-5876-9 : £3.50
(B77-22104)

Bennetts, Pamela. Stephen and the sleeping saints / [by] Pamela Bennetts. — New York : St Martin's Press ; London : Hale, 1977. — 190p ; 21cm.
ISBN 0-7091-5629-4 : £3.50
(B77-08034)

Benson, Barbara. The underlings / [by] Barbara Benson. — London : Constable, 1977. — 189p ; 23cm.
ISBN 0-09-461760-0 : £4.50
(B77-22845)

Bentley, Edmund Clerihew. Trent's last case / [by] E.C. Bentley. — Large print ed. — Bath : Lythway Press, 1976. — x,342p ; 22cm. — (Lythway classics of crime and detection)
Originally published: London : Nelson, 1913.
ISBN 0-85046-687-3 : £4.45
(B77-02568)

Bentley, Nicolas. Inside information / [by] Nicolas Bentley. — Harmondsworth [etc.] : Penguin, 1977. — 138p ; 19cm. — (Penguin crime fiction)
Originally published: London : Deutsch, 1974.
ISBN 0-14-004277-6 Pbk : £0.60
(B77-14901)

Bentley, Peter. Destined to survive / by Peter Bentley. — London : Hale, 1977. — 155p ; 21cm. — (Hale SF)
ISBN 0-7091-6316-9 : £3.60
(B77-28091)

Bentley, Phyllis. The house of Moreys / [by] Phyllis Bentley. — Large print ed. — Bath : Chivers, 1976. — [7],530p ; 22cm.
Originally published: London : Gollancz, 1953.
ISBN 0-85997-198-8 : 5.60(£4.20 to members of the Library Association)
(B77-03215)

Bentley, Phyllis. The partnership / [by] Phyllis Bentley. — Large print ed. — Bath : Chivers, 1977. — [9],291p ; 22cm.
Originally published: London : E. Benn, 1928.
ISBN 0-85997-267-4 : £5.00(£3.75 to members of the Library Association)
(B77-34075)

Benton, Kenneth. Craig and the Midas touch / [by] Kenneth Benton. — London : Sphere, 1977. — 216p ; 18cm.
Originally published: London : Macmillan ; 1975.
ISBN 0-7221-1619-5 Pbk : £0.65
(B77-09931)

Benton, Kenneth. Death on the Appian Way / [by] Kenneth Benton. — London : New English Library, 1977. — 205p : maps ; 18cm.
Originally published: London : Chatto and Windus, 1974.
ISBN 0-450-02733-3 Pbk : £1.10
(B77-34076)

Benton, Kenneth. The red hen conspiracy / [by] Kenneth Benton. — London [etc.] : Macmillan, 1977. — 192p ; 21cm.
ISBN 0-333-21940-6 : £3.50
(B77-26509)

Benton, Will. Cayuse country / by Will Benton. — London : Hale, 1977. — 160p ; 20cm.
ISBN 0-7091-6457-2 : £3.25
(B77-32841)

Benton, Will. Indian summer / by Will Benton. — London : Hale, 1977. — 159p ; 20cm.
ISBN 0-7091-5976-5 : £2.95
(B77-13248)

Berg, Rilla. Legacy of thorns / by Rilla Berg. — London : Hale, 1977. — 189p : geneal table ; 20cm.
ISBN 0-7091-6188-3 : £3.20
(B77-23712)

Berger, Thomas. Who is Teddy Villanova? / [by] Thomas Berger. — London : Eyre Methuen, 1977. — [7],247p ; 21cm.
Also published: New York : Delacorte Press, 1977.
ISBN 0-413-38410-1 : £3.95
(B77-27360)

Bergman, Andrew. Hollywood and LeVine / [by] Andrew Bergman. — London [etc.] : Arrow Books, 1977. — [7],216p ; 18cm.
Originally published: New York : Holt, Rinehart and Winston, 1975.
ISBN 0-09-914090-x Pbk : £0.65
(B77-17073)

Bermant, Chaim. The second Mrs Whitberg / [by] Chaim Bermant. — Large print ed. — London : Prior [etc.], 1977. — [3],354p ; 25cm.
Originally published: London : Allen and Unwin, 1976.
ISBN 0-86043-081-2 : £4.95
(B77-34078)

Bermant, Chaim. The squire of Bor Shachor : a novel / by Chaim Bermant. — London : Allen and Unwin, 1977. — 3-191p ; 23cm.
ISBN 0-04-823138-x : £4.50
(B77-19632)

Berry, Francis. I tell of Greenland : an edited translation of the Sau ...[thorn]arkrokur manuscripts / [by] Francis Berry. — London [etc.] : Routledge and Kegan Paul, 1977. — xxi,205p : 2 maps ; 25cm.
ISBN 0-7100-8591-5 : £4.95 : CIP rev.
(B77-12084)

Berry, Wendell. The memory of Old Jack / [by] Wendell Berry. — New York ; London : Harcourt Brace Jovanovich, [1976]. — [7], 223p ; 19cm.
Published in the United States: 1974.
ISBN 0-15-658670-3 Pbk : £1.55
(B77-06270)

Berry-Hart, Alice. Ching-a-ring-a-ring-ching, or, Three Victorian sisters in Shanghai / [by] Alice Berry-Hart. — London : Collings, 1977. — [4], 484p : map(on lining papers) ; 22cm.
ISBN 0-86036-043-1 : £6.00
(B77-29678)

Betteridge, Anne. A place for everyone / [by] Anne Betteridge. — London : Hurst and Blackett, 1977. — 183p ; 20cm.
ISBN 0-09-129310-3 : £3.50
(B77-28092)

Bevan, Gloria. Bachelor territory / by Gloria Bevan. — London : Mills and Boon, 1977. — 187p ; 17cm.
ISBN 0-263-72384-4 Pbk : £0.35
(B77-21415)

Beyea, Basil. The golden mistress / [by] Basil Beyea. — London : Pan Books, 1977. — 3-381, [1]p ; 18cm.
Originally published: New York : Simon and Schuster, 1975 ; London : Heinemann, 1976.
ISBN 0-330-25149-x Pbk : £0.80
(B77-28872)

Beynon, John, *b.1903.* The secret people / [by] John Wyndham writing as John Beynon. — [London] : Coronet, 1977. — 192p ; 18cm.
Cover has author statement: / John Wyndham. — Originally published: London : Newnes, 1935. — Previous control number ISBN 0-340-15834-4.
Pbk : £0.60
ISBN 0-340-15834-4
(B77-27361)

Beynon, John, *b.1903.* Stowaway to Mars / [by] John Wyndham writing as John Beynon. — [London] : Coronet, 1977. — 189p ; 18cm.
Cover has author statement: / John Wyndham. — Originally published: as 'Planet plane'. London : Newnes, 1936 ; and as 'Stowaway to Mars'. London : Coronet, 1972. — Previous control number ISBN 0-340-15835-2.
Pbk : £0.60
ISBN 0-340-15835-2
(B77-27362)

Bickers, Richard Townshend. Summer of no surrender / [by] Richard Townshend Bickers. — London : Corgi, 1977. — 189p ; 18cm.
Originally published: London : Hale, 1976.
ISBN 0-552-10498-1 Pbk : £0.70
(B77-21416)

Bickham, Jack Miles. Twister / [by] Jack M. Bickham. — London [etc.] : Macmillan, 1977. — [9],397p ; 21cm.
Originally published: Garden City, N.Y. : Doubleday, 1976.
ISBN 0-333-21779-9 : £4.95
(B77-22105)

Billington, Rachel. Beautiful : a modern romance / [by] Rachel Billington. — Harmondsworth [etc.] : Penguin, 1977. — 171p ; 18cm.
Originally published: London : Heinemann, 1974.
ISBN 0-14-004165-6 Pbk : £0.70
(B77-20574)

Bingham, John, *Baron Clanmorris.* The double agent / by John Bingham. — London : Gollancz, 1977. — 192p ; 21cm. — ([Gollancz vintage thriller])
Originally published: 1966.
ISBN 0-575-00860-1 : £3.50
(B77-22846)

Bingham, John, *Baron Clanmorris.* The marriage bureau murders / [by] John Bingham. — London [etc.] : Macmillan, 1977. — 190p ; 21cm.
ISBN 0-333-21753-5 : £3.25
(B77-19633)

Binner, Ina. Ravine Edge / [by] Ina Binner. — London : Hale, 1977. — 184p ; 21cm.
ISBN 0-7091-5961-7 : £3.50
(B77-22106)

Bird, Kenneth. Himself beats the Bill / [by] Kenneth Bird ; illustrated by Adrian Bird. — London : Macdonald and Jane's, 1977. — [4], 102p : ill ; 23cm.
ISBN 0-354-08010-5 : £2.75
(B77-09244)

Bishop, Michael. Stolen faces / [by] Michael Bishop. — London : Gollancz, 1977. — [9], 176p ; 21cm. — ([Gollancz SF])
ISBN 0-575-02285-x : £3.75
(B77-19634)

Black, Betty, *b.1927.* The sisterhood / [by] Betty Black and Casey Bishop. — London : W.H. Allen, 1977. — 160p ; 23cm.
ISBN 0-491-02390-1 : £3.50
(B77-23713)

Black, Gavin. The bitter tea / [by] Gavin Black. — London : Fontana, 1975. — 189p ; 18cm.
Originally published: New York : Harper and Row, 1972 ; London : Collins, 1973.
ISBN 0-00-613988-4 Pbk : £0.50
(B77-07588)

Black, Gavin. Dead man calling / [by] Gavin Black. — [London] : Fontana, 1977. — 192p ; 18cm.
Originally published: London : Collins, 1962.
ISBN 0-00-614785-2 Pbk : £0.70
(B77-31439)

Black, Gavin. Killer moon / [by] Gavin Black. — [London] : Fontana, 1977. — 190p ; 18cm.
Originally published: as 'A moon for killers'. London : Collins for the Crime Club, 1976.
ISBN 0-00-614779-8 Pbk : £0.70
(B77-25870)

Black, Gavin. Suddenly, at Singapore / [by] Gavin Black. — [London] : Fontana, 1977. — 192p ; 18cm.
Originally published: London : Collins, 1961.
ISBN 0-00-614784-4 Pbk : £0.70
(B77-30599)

Black, Hermina. Cinderella in sunlight / [by] Hermina Black. — London : Sphere, 1977. — 189p ; 18cm.
Originally published: London : Hodder and Stoughton, 1958.
ISBN 0-7221-1686-1 Pbk : £0.65
(B77-16040)

Black, Hermina. Enchanted oasis / [by] Hermina Black. — London : Sphere, 1977. — 206p ; 18cm.
Originally published: London : Hale, 1947.
ISBN 0-7221-1691-8 Pbk : £0.65
(B77-16041)

Black, Hermina. The girl from Van Leydens / [by] Hermina Black. — London : Sphere, 1977. — 175p ; 18cm.
Originally published: London : Hodder and Stoughton, 1959.
ISBN 0-7221-1688-8 Pbk : £0.65
(B77-16042)

Black, Hermina. In pursuit of Perilla / [by] Hermina Black. — London : Sphere, 1977. — 174p ; 18cm.
Originally published: London : Hodder and Stoughton, 1958.
ISBN 0-7221-1689-6 Pbk : £0.65
(B77-16043)

Black, Hermina. In the time of lilacs / [by] Hermina Black. — Sevenoaks : Coronet, 1977. — 192p ; 18cm.
Originally published: London : Hodder and Stoughton, 1975.
ISBN 0-340-21254-3 Pbk : £0.60
(B77-18975)

Black, Hermina. The lost years / by Hermina Black. — London [etc.] : Hodder and Stoughton, 1976. — 192p ; 20cm.
ISBN 0-340-20022-7 : £3.25
(B77-00951)

Black, Hermina. Love's cross-roads / [by] Hermina Black. — London : Hale, 1977. — 176p ; 20cm.
Originally published: 1953.
ISBN 0-7091-6120-4 : £3.10
(B77-17731)

Black, Hermina. When the desert blooms / [by] Hermina Black. — London [etc.] : White Lion Publishers, 1976. — 248p ; 20cm.
Originally published: London : Hale, 1941.
ISBN 0-7274-0217-x : £3.50
(B77-05056)

Black, Jett. Whipcrack at Caraway / [by] Jett Black. — London : Hale, 1977. — 160p ; 20cm.
ISBN 0-7091-6284-7 : £3.25
(B77-32842)

Black, Laura. Glendraco / [by] Laura Black. — London : Hamilton, 1977. — [4],364p ; 23cm.
ISBN 0-241-89658-4 : £4.50
(B77-19635)

Black, Lionel. Outbreak / by Lionel Black. — Hornchurch : I. Henry, 1977. — 176p ; 21cm.
Originally published: London : Cassell, 1968.
ISBN 0-86025-099-7 : £2.85
(B77-09932)

Blackburn, John. The Cyclops goblet / [by] John Blackburn. — London : Cape, 1977. — 184p ; 20cm.
ISBN 0-224-01377-7 : £3.50 : CIP rev.
(B77-06271)

Blackmore, Jane. Dance on a hornet's nest / [by] Jane Blackmore. — Large print ed. — Bath : Lythway Press, 1977. — [4],267p ; 22cm.
Originally published: London : Collins, 1970.
ISBN 0-85046-691-1 : £4.30
(B77-10935)

Blackmore, Jane. Silver unicorn / [by] Jane Blackmore. — London : Collins, 1977. — 159p ; 19cm.
ISBN 0-00-233789-4 : £2.75
(B77-09933)

Blackstock, Charity. I met murder on the way / by Charity Blackstock. — London [etc.] : Hodder and Stoughton, 1977. — 224p ; 21cm.
ISBN 0-340-21746-4 : £3.95
(B77-28873)

Blackwood, Caroline. Great granny Webster / [by] Caroline Blackwood. — London : Duckworth, 1977. — 135p ; 23cm.
ISBN 0-7156-1190-9 : £3.95
(B77-28093)

Blagowidow, George. The last train from Berlin / [by] George Blagowidow. — London : Hamilton, 1977. — [9],206p ; 21cm.
Also published: Garden City, N.Y. : Doubleday, 1977.
ISBN 0-241-89797-1 : £3.95
(B77-28094)

Blair, Iain. Bone / [by] Iain Blair. — London : Sphere, 1977. — 189p ; 18cm.
ISBN 0-7221-1709-4 Pbk : £0.75
(B77-28095)

Blair, Iain. Duff / [by] Iain Blair. — London : Sphere, 1977. — 174p ; 18cm.
ISBN 0-7221-1708-6 Pbk : £0.75
(B77-19636)

Blair, Iain. True / [by] Iain Blair. — London : Sphere, 1977. — 192p ; 18cm.
ISBN 0-7221-1707-8 Pbk : £0.65
(B77-15482)

Blair, Kathryn. The fair invader / [by] Kathryn Blair. — London [etc.] : Mills and Boon, 1976. — 185p ; 18cm. — (Mills and Boon classics)
Originally published: 1952.
ISBN 0-263-72229-5 : £0.35
(B77-14902)

Blair, Kathryn. The tulip tree / [by] Kathryn Blair. — London [etc.] : Mills and Boon, 1976. — 186p ; 18cm. — (Mills and Boon classics)
Originally published: 1958.
ISBN 0-263-72219-8 Pbk : £0.35
(B77-11396)

Blake, George, *b.1893.* The innocence within / [by] George Blake. — London : Remploy, 1976. — 253p ; 20cm.
Originally published: London : Collins, 1955.
ISBN 0-7066-0678-7 : £2.75
(B77-03751)

Blake, Margaret. Walk softly and beware / by Margaret Blake. — London : Hale, 1977. — 191p ; 20cm.
ISBN 0-7091-5936-6 : £3.10
(B77-09934)

Blake, Monica. The dark horseman / by Monica Blake. — London : Hale, 1977. — 159p ; 21cm.
ISBN 0-7091-6249-9 : £3.50
(B77-28874)

Blake, Monica. Pelham's Folly / [by] Monica Blake. — London : Hale, 1977. — 157p ; 21cm.
ISBN 0-7091-6136-0 : £3.50
(B77-34079)

Blake, Nicholas. The beast must die / [by] Nicholas Blake. — Large print ed. — Bath : Lythway Press, 1977. — [4],347p ; 23cm. — (Lythway classics of crime and detection)
Originally published: London : Collins, 1938.
ISBN 0-85046-715-2 : £4.65
(B77-30600)

Blake, Nicholas. The deadly joker / [by] Nicholas Blake. — London : Collins [for] the Crime Club, 1977. — 256p ; 21cm.
Originally published: London : Collins, 1963.
ISBN 0-00-231096-1 : £3.25
(B77-27363)

Blake, Nicholas. The dreadful hollow / [by] Nicholas Blake. — Large print ed. — Bath : Chivers, 1977. — [7],397p ; 22cm.
Originally published: London : Collins, 1953.
ISBN 0-85997-256-9 : £6.00(£4.50 to members of the Library Association)
(B77-34080)

Blake, Nicholas. A question of proof / [by] Nicholas Blake. — Large print ed. — Bath : Lythway Press, 1977. — xi,338p ; 22cm. — (Lythway classics of crime & detection)
Originally published: London : Collins, 1935. — Bibl.: p.ix-x.
ISBN 0-85046-740-3 : £4.75
(B77-30601)

Blake, Nicholas. The whisper in the gloom / [by] Nicholas Blake. — Large print ed. — Bath : Chivers, 1977. — [6],410p ; 22cm.
Originally published: London : Collins, 1954.
ISBN 0-85997-250-x : £5.80(£4.35 to members of the Library Association)
(B77-21417)

Blake, Nicholas. The widow's cruise / by Nicholas Blake. — London : Collins for the Crime Club, 1976. — 192p ; 21cm.
Originally published: London : Collins, 1959.
ISBN 0-00-231917-9 : £2.75
(B77-17732)

Blankenship, William Douglas. Tiger Ten / [by] William D. Blankenship. — St Albans : Mayflower, 1977. — 232p ; 18cm.
Originally published: New York : Putnam, 1976.
ISBN 0-583-12752-5 Pbk : £0.75
(B77-23714)

Blanshard, Audrey. The Chelbeck charger / by Audrey Blanshard. — London : Hale, 1977. — 176p ; 21cm.
ISBN 0-7091-5962-5 : £3.50
(B77-21418)

Blanshard, Audrey. Granborough's filly / [by] Audrey Blanshard. — London : Hale, 1976. — 176p ; 21cm.
ISBN 0-7091-5472-0 : £3.25
(B77-01785)

Blanshard, Audrey. The shy young Denbury / by Audrey Blanshard. — London : Hale, 1977. — 191p ; 21cm.
ISBN 0-7091-5828-9 : £3.50
(B77-17074)

Blatty, William Peter. The exorcist / [by] William Peter Blatty. — London : Corgi, 1977. — 320p ; 18cm.
Originally published: New York : Harper and Row ; London : Blond and Briggs, 1971.
ISBN 0-552-10535-x Pbk : £0.75
(B77-32843)

Bleasdale, Alan. Scully / [by] Alan Bleasdale. — London : Arrow Books, 1977. — 215p ; 18cm.
Originally published: London : Hutchinson, 1975.
ISBN 0-09-913920-0 Pbk : £0.60
(B77-28096)

Bleasdale, Alan. Who's been sleeping in my bed? / [by] Alan Bleasdale. — London : Hutchinson, 1977. — 220p ; 21cm.
ISBN 0-09-128610-7 : £3.50
(B77-13848)

Blish, James. Fallen star / [by] James Blish. — London : Arrow Books, 1977. — 224p ; 18cm. — (Arrow science fiction)
Originally published: London : Faber, 1957.
ISBN 0-09-914180-9 Pbk : £0.60
(B77-05057)

Blishen, Edward. Roaring boys : a schoolmaster's agony / [by] Edward Blishen. — Large print ed. — Bath : Chivers, 1977. — xiv,385p ; 22cm.
Originally published: London : Thames and Hudson, 1955.
ISBN 0-85997-257-7 : £5.80(£4.35 to members of the Library Association)
(B77-34081)

Bloch, Robert. Firebug / [by] Robert Bloch. — London : Corgi, 1977. — 156p ; 18cm.
Originally published: Evanston, Ill. : Regency Books, 1961.
ISBN 0-552-10403-5 Pbk : £0.60
(B77-16044)

Bloch, Robert. Psycho / [by] Robert Bloch. — London : Corgi, 1977. — 126p ; 18cm.
Originally published: New York : Simon and Schuster, 1959 ; London : Hale, 1960.
ISBN 0-552-10402-7 Pbk : £0.60
(B77-16045)

Bloom, Ursula. The dragonfly / [by] Ursula Bloom. — Large print ed. — Bath : Lythway Press, 1977. — [4],299p ; 22cm.
Originally published: London : Hutchinson, 1968.
ISBN 0-85046-699-7 : £4.60
(B77-17733)

Bloom, Ursula. Gipsy flower / [by] Ursula Bloom. — Large print ed. — Bath : Lythway Press, 1977. — [5],222p ; 23cm.
Originally published: London : Hale, 1949.
ISBN 0-85046-731-4 Pbk : £2.35
(B77-32844)

Bloom, Ursula. Now Barabbas was a robber : the story of the man who lived that Christ might die / [by] Ursula Bloom. — London : Severn House : [Distributed by Hutchinson], 1977. — 254p ; 21cm.
Originally published: under the name Deborah Mann. London : Corgi, 1968.
ISBN 0-7278-0328-x : £3.75
(B77-34082)

Bloom, Ursula. To-morrow for apricots / [by] Ursula Bloom. — Large print ed. — Bath : Lythway Press, 1977. — [7],309p ; 22cm.
Originally published: London : Hutchinson, 1929.
ISBN 0-85046-692-x : £4.45
(B77-11397)

Blyth, Robert. Festival : a novel / [by] Robert Blyth. — Edinburgh : Canongate Publishing, 1977. — vi,156p ; 23cm.
ISBN 0-903937-32-8 : £3.95
ISBN 0-903937-33-6 Pbk : Unpriced
(B77-25871)

Boast, Philip. The assassinators / [by] Philip Boast. — London [etc.] : Millington, 1976. — [4],248p ; 23cm.
ISBN 0-86000-058-3 : £3.50
(B77-16046)

Boateng, Yaw M. The return / [by] Yaw M. Boateng. — London [etc.] : Heinemann Educational, 1977. — [8],120p : map ; 19cm. — (African writers series ; 186)
ISBN 0-435-90186-9 Pbk : £1.00
(B77-25189)

Bocca, Geoffrey. Nadine / [by] Geoffrey Bocca. — St Albans : Mayflower, 1977. — 285p ; 18cm.
Originally published: New York : Putnam, 1974 ; London : Hart-Davis MacGibbon, 1976.
ISBN 0-583-12550-6 Pbk : £0.75
(B77-27364)

Bogner, Norman. Seventh Avenue / [by] Norman Bogner. — London : Corgi, 1977. — 413p ; 18cm.
Originally published: as 'Divorce'. London : Deutsch, 1966.
ISBN 0-552-10667-4 Pbk : £0.95
(B77-27365)

Boland, John. Holocaust / [by] John Boland. — London [etc.] : White Lion Publishers, 1977. — 192p ; 21cm.
Originally published: London : Futura Publications, 1974.
ISBN 0-7274-0253-6 : £3.75
(B77-17734)

Bova, Ben. The duelling machine / [by] Ben Bova. — Harmondsworth [etc.] : Puffin Books, 1977. — 204p ; 19cm. — (Puffin books)
Originally published: as 'The dueling machine', New York : Holt, Rinehart and Winston, 1969 ; and as 'The duelling machine', London : Faber, 1971.
ISBN 0-14-030909-8 Pbk : £0.55
(B77-15483)

Bova, Ben. Millennium : a novel about people and politics in the year 1999 / by Ben Bova. — London : Macdonald and Jane's, 1976. — [5], 277,[1]p ; 21cm.
Also published: New York : Random House, 1976.
ISBN 0-354-04158-4 : £4.25
(B77-18976)

Bova, Ben. The multiple man : a novel of suspense / by Ben Bova. — London : Gollancz, 1977. — [5],210p ; 21cm. — ([Gollancz thriller])
Originally published: Indianapolis : Bobbs-Merrill, 1976.
ISBN 0-575-02293-0 : £3.75
(B77-25872)

Bova, Ben. Star watchman / [by] Ben Bova. — London : Sphere, 1977. — 187p ; 18cm. — (Sphere science fiction)
Originally published: New York : Holt, Rinehart and Winston, 1964 ; London : Dobson, 1972.
ISBN 0-7221-1793-0 Pbk : £0.75
(B77-22847)

Bowden, Jim. Incident at Bison Creek / by Jim Bowden. — London : Hale, 1977. — 155p ; 20cm.
ISBN 0-7091-6424-6 : £3.25
(B77-32845)

Bowdler, Roger. The bawd's footman / [by] Roger Bowdler. — London : Sphere, 1977. — 224p ; 18cm.
Originally published: London : W.H. Allen, 1973.
ISBN 0-7221-1801-5 Pbk : £0.75
(B77-18977)

Bowdler, Roger. George and Mildred / [by Roger Bowdler] ; [adapted from the series by] Johnnie Mortimer and Brian Cooke. — London [etc.] : Arrow Books, 1977. — 207p ; 18cm.
ISBN 0-09-916060-9 Pbk : £0.70
(B77-29679)

Bowdler, Roger. George and Mildred / by Roger Bowdler ; based on a Thames Television series by Johnnie Mortimer and Brian Cooke ... — London : Severn House : [Distributed by Hutchinson], 1977. — 207p ; 20cm.
ISBN 0-7278-0274-7 : £3.25
(B77-29680)

Bowdler, Roger. Robin's nest / based on the Thames Television series by Johnnie Mortimer & Brian Cooke ; this novelization by Roger Bowdler. — London : Severn House : [Distributed by Hutchinson], 1977. — 206p ; 21cm.
ISBN 0-7278-0290-9 : £3.50
(B77-28875)

Bowdler, Roger. This year, next year / [created by] John Finch ; novelisation by Roger Bowdler. — London : Severn House : [Distributed by Hutchinson], 1977. — 272p ; 21cm.
'... based upon the Granada Television series of the same name' - p.1.
ISBN 0-7278-0264-x : £3.50
(B77-30602)

Bowdler, Roger. The voyage of the 'Snapdragon' / [by] Roger Bowdler. — London (73 Langford Court, Langford Place, N.W.8) : Parnassus Press, 1976. — [5],245p ; 23cm.
ISBN 0-9503795-1-4 : £4.00
(B77-06272)

Box, Sydney. Alibi in the rough / by Sydney Box. — London : Hale, 1977. — 176p ; 20cm.
ISBN 0-7091-6235-9 : £3.25
(B77-22107)

Boyar, Jane. World class / [by] Jane and Burt Boyar. — Sevenoaks : Coronet, 1977. — 446p ; 18cm.
Originally published: New York : Random House, 1975 ; London : Hodder and Stoughton, 1976.
ISBN 0-340-21787-1 Pbk : £1.00
(B77-26510)

Boyd, Shylah. American made / [by] Shylah Boyd. — London : Corgi, 1977. — 416p ; 18cm.
Originally published: New York : Farrar, Straus and Giroux, 1975 ; London : Macdonald and Jane's, 1976.
ISBN 0-552-10376-4 Pbk : £0.95
(B77-34083)

Boyer, Richard L. The giant rat of Sumatra / [by] Richard L. Boyer. — London : W.H. Allen, 1977. — vii,216p ; 23cm.
Originally published: New York : Warner Books, 1976.
ISBN 0-491-02310-3 : £3.95
(B77-19637)

Boyers, Barbara. Search for Susan / [by] Barbara Boyers. — London : Dobson, 1976. — 136p ; 21cm.
For adolescents.
ISBN 0-234-77710-9 : £2.50
(B77-00952)

Brackett, Leigh. The ginger star / [by] Leigh Brackett. — London : Sphere, 1976. — [5], 186p : map ; 18cm. — (Sphere science fiction)
Originally published: New York : Ballantine, 1974.
ISBN 0-7221-1834-1 Pbk : £0.60
(B77-06273)

Bradbury, Malcolm. The history man / [by] Malcolm Bradbury. — London : Arrow Books, 1977. — [6],230p ; 18cm.
Originally published: London : Secker and Warburg, 1975.
ISBN 0-09-914910-9 Pbk : £0.80
(B77-30603)

Bradbury, Ray. Dandelion wine / [by] Ray Bradbury. — St Albans : Panther, 1977. — 192p ; 18cm.
Originally published: Garden City, N.Y. : Doubleday ; London : Hart-Davis, 1957.
ISBN 0-586-04360-8 Pbk : £0.65
(B77-12636)

Bradbury, Ray. The silver locusts / [by] Ray Bradbury. — St Albans : Panther, 1977. — 221p ; 18cm.
Originally published: London : Hart-Davis, 1951.
ISBN 0-586-04362-4 Pbk : £0.75
(B77-08545)

Bradbury, Ray. Something wicked this way comes / [by] Ray Bradbury. — St Albans : Panther, 1977. — 220p ; 18cm.
Originally published: New York : Simon and Schuster, 1962 ; London : Hart-Davis, 1963.
ISBN 0-586-04357-8 Pbk : £0.75
(B77-22848)

Braddon, Russell. The finalists / [by] Russell Braddon. — London : Joseph, 1977. — 224p : plan ; 23cm.
ISBN 0-7181-1596-1 : £4.25
(B77-28876)

Bradford, Will. Lightning strike / by Will Bradford. — London : Hale, 1977. — 151p ; 20cm.
ISBN 0-7091-5781-9 : £2.95
(B77-05638)

Bradford, Will. Outlaw town / by Will Bradford. — London : Hale, 1977. — 155p ; 20cm.
ISBN 0-7091-6455-6 : £3.10
(B77-28877)

Bradley, Concho. The juniper shadow / by Concho Bradley. — London : Hale, 1977. — 155p ; 20cm.
ISBN 0-7091-6454-8 : £3.25
(B77-32846)

Brady, Ryder. Instar / by Ryder Brady. — London : New English Library, 1977. — [5], 233p ; 21cm.
Originally published: Garden City, N.Y. : Doubleday, 1976.
ISBN 0-450-03196-9 : £4.50
(B77-13249)

Brady, Terence. Victoria / [by] Terence Brady & Charlotte Bingham. — London : Star Books, 1975. — 188p ; 18cm.
Originally published: London : W.H. Allen, 1972.
ISBN 0-352-30090-6 Pbk : £0.50
(B77-19638)

Brady, Terence. Yes - honestly / [by] Terence Brady and Charlotte Bingham. — London : Sphere, 1977. — 175p ; 18cm.
'Based on the London Weekend Television series' - cover.
ISBN 0-7221-1846-5 Pbk : £0.65
(B77-06274)

Brady, Terence. Yes - honestly / [by] Terence Brady and Charlotte Bingham. — London : Severn House : [Distributed by Hutchinson], 1977. — 175p ; 21cm.
'From the London Weekend Television series ...' title page verso. — Originally published: London : Sphere, 1977.
ISBN 0-7278-0257-7 : £3.25
(B77-19639)

Bragg, Melvyn. The hired man / [by] Melvyn Bragg. — Sevenoaks : Coronet, 1977. — 208p ; 18cm.
Originally published: London : Secker and Warburg, 1969.
ISBN 0-340-21807-x Pbk : £0.85
(B77-26511)

Brain, Robert. Kolonialagent : a novel with an appendix / [by] Robert Brain. — London : Faber, 1977. — [4],188p ; 21cm.
ISBN 0-571-10992-6 : £3.95
(B77-16585)

Braine, John. Finger of fire / [by] John Braine. — London : Eyre Methuen, 1977. — 231p ; 21cm.
ISBN 0-413-36590-5 : Unpriced
(B77-19640)

Braine, John. The jealous God / [by] John Braine. — London (11 New Fetter La., EC4P 4EE) : Magnum Books, 1977. — 3-287p ; 18cm.
Originally published: London : Eyre and Spottiswoode, 1964.
ISBN 0-413-36630-8 Pbk : £0.70
(B77-14396)

Braly, Malcolm. On the yard / [by] Malcolm Braly. — Harmondsworth [etc.] : Penguin, 1977. — 286p ; 18cm.
Originally published: Boston, Mass. : Little, Brown, 1967 ; London : Hutchinson, 1968.
ISBN 0-14-004455-8 Pbk : £1.00
(B77-34084)

Bramble, Forbes. Regent Square / [by] Forbes Bramble. — London : Hamilton, 1977. — [7], 407p : 2 maps ; 23cm.
ISBN 0-241-89660-6 : £4.95
(B77-19641)

Brand, Christianna. Death in high heels / by Christianna Brand. — Hornchurch : I. Henry, 1976. — 224p ; 21cm.
Originally published: London : John Lane, 1941.
ISBN 0-86025-076-8 : £3.10
(B77-05639)

Brand, Christianna. Green for danger / [by] Christianna Brand. — Large print ed. — Bath : Lythway Press, 1977. — viii,351p ; 22cm. — (Lythway classics of crime and detection)
Originally published: London : Bodley Head, 1943.
ISBN 0-85046-727-6 : £4.80
(B77-22108)

Brand, Christianna. Tour de force / by Christianna Brand. — Hornchurch : I. Henry, 1977. — 191p : 1 ill ; 21cm.
Originally published: London : Joseph, 1955.
ISBN 0-86025-114-4 : £3.50
(B77-31440)

Brand, Max. Dr Kildare's trial / [by] Max Brand. — London [etc.] : White Lion Publishers, 1977. — 144p ; 21cm.
Originally published: New York : Dodd, Mead, 1942 ; London : Hodder and Stoughton, 1944.
ISBN 0-7274-0315-x : £3.25
(B77-21419)

Brand, Max. Golden lightning / [by] Max Brand. — London [etc.] : White Lion Publishers, 1977. — [4],251p ; 21cm.
Originally published: New York : Dodd, Mead, 1964 ; London : Hodder and Stoughton, 1965.
ISBN 0-7274-0238-2 : £3.50
(B77-12637)

Brand, Max. The King Bird rides / [by] Max Brand. — Large print ed. — Leicester : Ulverscroft, 1977. — [4],430p ; 23cm. — (Ulverscroft large print series : [Western])
Originally published: New York : Dodd, Mead ; London : Hodder and Stoughton, 1936.
ISBN 0-85456-524-8 : £2.65
(B77-13849)

Brand, Max. Larramee's ranch / [by] Max Brand. — London [etc.] : White Lion Publishers, 1976. — [7],207p ; 20cm.
Originally published: New York : Dodd, Mead, 1966 ; London : Hodder and Stoughton, 1967.
ISBN 0-85617-109-3 : £3.50
(B77-03752)

Brand, Max. The last showdown / [by] Max Brand. — London [etc.] : Hodder and Stoughton, 1976. — [4],251p ; 20cm.
Originally published: United States : Street and Smith, 1929.
ISBN 0-340-20950-x : £3.15
(B77-02569)

Brand, Max. Rawhide justice / by Max Brand. — London : Hale, 1977. — [4],248p ; 20cm.
Originally published: United States : Street and Smith, 1933.
ISBN 0-7091-6037-2 : £3.10
(B77-17075)

Brand, Max. The seven of diamonds / [by] Max Brand. — London : Remploy, 1976. — 190p ; 19cm.
Originally published: New York : Dodd, Mead ; London : Hodder and Stoughton, 1935.
ISBN 0-7066-0693-0 : £3.00
(B77-14903)

Brand, Max. Young Dr Kildare / by Max Brand. — Hornchurch : I. Henry, 1977. — 158p ; 21cm.
Originally published: New York : Dodd, Mead, 1941 ; London : Hodder and Stoughton, 1966.
ISBN 0-86025-129-2 : £3.25
(B77-30604)

Brant, Lewis. Bullets at sunset / by Lewis Brant. — London : Hale, 1977. — 160p ; 20cm.
ISBN 0-7091-5977-3 : £2.95
(B77-12638)

Brason, John. Secret army / [by] John Brason. — London : British Broadcasting Corporation, 1977. — 256p ; 22cm.
Based on the BBC Television series of the same name and narrates the events leading up to the first episode of the series.
ISBN 0-563-17401-3 : £3.75
(B77-34085)

Brautigan, Richard. The abortion : a historical romance, 1966 / [by] Richard Brautigan. — London : Pan Books, 1977. — 171p ; 20cm. — (Picador)
Originally published: Simon and Schuster, 1971 ; London : Cape, 1973.
Pbk : £0.80
ISBN 0-330-24189-3
(B77-34086)

Brautigan, Richard. A Confederate general from Big Sur / [by] Richard Brautigan. — London : Pan books, 1977. — xii,116p : port(on inside front cover) ; 20cm. — (Picador)
Originally published: New York : Grove Press, 1964 ; London : Cape, 1970.
Pbk : £0.75
ISBN 0-330-23565-6
(B77-34087)

Brautigan, Richard. Sombrero fallout : a Japanese novel / [by] Richard Brautigan. — London : Cape, 1977. — 3-187p ; 23cm.
Originally published: New York : Simon and Schuster, 1976.
ISBN 0-224-01371-8 : £3.50 : CIP rev.
(B77-06275)

Brautigan, Richard. Willard and his bowling trophies : a perverse mystery / [by] Richard Brautigan. — London : Pan Books, 1977. — 123p ; 20cm. — (Picador)
Originally published: New York : Simon and Schuster, 1975 ; London : Cape, 1976.
ISBN 0-330-25250-x Pbk : £0.80
(B77-34088)

Brawley, Ernest. The rap / [by] Ernest Brawley. — London : New English Library, 1976. — 540p ; 18cm.
Originally published: New York : Atheneum, 1974 ; London : Secker and Warburg, 1975.
ISBN 0-450-02913-1 Pbk : £1.50
(B77-01786)

Bremner, Marjorie. Murder amid proofs / by Marjorie Bremner. — London : Remploy, 1976. — 191p ; 19cm.
Originally published: London : Hodder and Stoughton, 1955.
ISBN 0-7066-0687-6 : £2.75
(B77-10545)

Brennan, Will. The border pawn / by Will Brennan. — London : Hale, 1977. — 156p ; 20cm.
ISBN 0-7091-6326-6 : £3.10
(B77-28878)

Brennan, Will. The ghost rider / by Will Brennan. — London : Hale, 1977. — 156p ; 20cm.
ISBN 0-7091-6173-5 : £3.10
(B77-31441)

Brent, Madeleine. Kirkby's changeling / [by] Madeleine Brent. — London [etc.] : Pan Books, 1977. — 318p ; 18cm.
Originally published: London : Souvenir Press, 1975.
ISBN 0-330-25144-9 Pbk : £0.80
(B77-26512)

Brent, Madeleine. Merlin's Keep / [by] Madeleine Brent. — London : Souvenir Press, 1977. — 368p ; 21cm.
ISBN 0-285-62296-x : £3.95 : CIP rev.
(B77-20576)

Breton-Smith, Clare. A soft pillow / by Clare Breton-Smith. — London : Hale, 1977. — 160p ; 20cm.
ISBN 0-7091-5984-6 : £3.10
(B77-14397)

Brett, Rosalind. Tangle in sunshine / [by] Rosalind Brett. — Large print ed. — Leicester : Ulverscroft, 1976. — [5],359p ; 23cm. — (Ulverscroft large print series : [romance])
Originally published: London : Mills and Boon, 1957.
ISBN 0-85456-502-7 : £2.65
(B77-08546)

Brett, Simon. Star trap : a crime novel / by Simon Brett. — London : Gollancz, 1977. — 191p ; 21cm. — ([Gollancz detection])
ISBN 0-575-02299-x : £3.95
(B77-25873)

Brewis, Henry. The road to Clartiehole / written and illustrated by Henry Brewis. — [Whitehaven] ([Catherine St., Whitehaven, Cumbria]) : [West Cumberland Farmers], [1976]. — 51p : ill(some col) ; 21cm.
ISBN 0-9504367-2-0 Sd : £0.60
(B77-05640)

Bridge, Susan Rosemary. Escape without pardon / [by] S.R. Bridge. — London : Hale, 1976. — 160p ; 21cm.
ISBN 0-7091-5462-3 : £2.95
(B77-11398)

Bridge, Susan Rosemary. For love or duty / [by] S.R. Bridge. — London : Hale, 1977. — 191p ; 21cm.
ISBN 0-7091-6304-5 : £3.85
(B77-29681)

Briggs, Jean. The flame of the Borgias / [by] Jean Briggs. — London (110 Warner Rd, S.E.5) : Troubadour, 1976. — 336p ; 18cm.
Originally published: London : Collins, 1974. — Based on the lives of Pietro Bembo and Lucrezia Borgia.
ISBN 0-86007-329-7 Pbk : £0.75
(B77-08547)

Briggs, Victor. The sacred ground / [by] Victor Briggs. — London : New English Library, 1977. — 352p ; 19cm. — (Briggs, Victor. Way ahead ; part 1)
Originally published: 1975.
ISBN 0-450-03338-4 Pbk : £1.50
(B77-28097)

Briggs, Victor. Such were the joys / [by] Victor Briggs. — London : New English Library, 1977. — 302p ; 21cm.
ISBN 0-450-03231-0 : £4.95
(B77-27366)

Briggs, Victor. Yours is the earth / [by] Victor Briggs. — London : New English Library, 1977. — 288p ; 21cm. — (Briggs, Victor. Way ahead ; part 3)
ISBN 0-450-03080-6 : £4.50
(B77-21420)

Bristow, Gwen. Celia Garth / [by] Gwen Bristow. — Bath : Chivers, 1977. — 407p ; 21cm.
Originally published: New York : Crowell, 1959 ; London : Eyre and Spottiswoode, 1960.
£5.40(£4.05 to members of the Library Association)
ISBN 0-85594-889-2
(B77-19642)

Britt, Katrina. If today be sweet / by Katrina Britt. — London : Mills and Boon, 1976. — 188p ; 17cm.
ISBN 0-263-72326-7 Pbk : £0.30
(B77-05641)

Britton, Anna. Fike's point / [by] Anna Britton. — London [etc.] : Angus and Robertson, 1977. — [4],148p ; 23cm.
ISBN 0-207-95764-9 : £3.95
(B77-27367)

Broat, Isidore. The junketeers / [by] I.G. Broat. — St Albans : Panther, 1977. — 288p ; 18cm.
Originally published: London : Barrie and Jenkins, 1976.
ISBN 0-586-04636-4 Pbk : £0.75
(B77-22849)

Brock, Rose. Longleaf / [by] Rose Brock. — London : Arrow Books, 1977. — [4],290p ; 18cm.
Originally published: New York : Harper ; London : Harrap, 1974.
ISBN 0-09-914100-0 Pbk : £0.70
(B77-12639)

Broderick, John. The pride of summer / [by] John Broderick. — London [etc.] : Pan Books, 1977. — 252p ; 18cm.
Originally published: London : Harrap, 1976.
ISBN 0-330-25026-4 Pbk : £0.75
(B77-12640)

Brome, Vincent. The embassy / [by] Vincent Brome. — London [etc.] : White Lion Publishers, 1977. — [4],252p ; 21cm.
Originally published: London : Cassell, 1972.
ISBN 0-7274-0287-0 : £4.25
(B77-33422)

Brome, Vincent. The surgeon / [by] Vincent Brome. — London [etc.] : White Lion Publishers, 1977. — [4],281p ; 21cm.
Originally published: London : Cassell, 1967.
ISBN 0-7274-0282-x : £3.95
(B77-15484)

Bromige, Iris. The bend in the river / [by] Iris Bromige. — London : Coronet, 1976. — 190p ; 18cm.
Originally published: London : Hodder and Stoughton, 1975.
ISBN 0-340-21000-1 Pbk : £0.50
(B77-00953)

Bromige, Iris. The broken bough / [by] Iris Bromige. — Large print ed. — Leicester : Ulverscroft, 1977. — [9],317p ; 23cm. — (Ulverscroft large print series : [romance])
Originally published: London : Hodder and Stoughton, 1973.
ISBN 0-7089-0044-5 : £2.95
(B77-28098)

Bromige, Iris. A distant song / by Iris Bromige. — London [etc.] : Hodder and Stoughton, 1977. — 191p ; 20cm.
ISBN 0-340-21574-7 : £3.50
(B77-25874)

Bromige, Iris. Family group / [by] Iris Bromige. — London [etc.] : White Lion Publishers, 1977. — 220p ; 21cm.
Originally published: London : Hodder and Stoughton, 1958.
ISBN 0-85617-967-1 : £3.50
(B77-12085)

Bromige, Iris. The gay intruder / [by] Iris Bromige. — London [etc.] : White Lion Publishers, 1976. — 190p ; 21cm.
Originally published: London : Hodder and Stoughton, 1954.
ISBN 0-85617-927-2 : £3.25
(B77-00954)

Bromige, Iris. Golden summer / [by] Iris Bromige. — London : Coronet, 1977. — 191p ; 18cm.
Originally published: London : Hodder and Stoughton, 1972.
ISBN 0-340-16857-9 Pbk : £0.65
(B77-24470)

Bromige, Iris. A haunted landscape / by Iris Bromige. — London [etc.] : Hodder and Stoughton, 1976. — 191p ; 20cm.
ISBN 0-340-20587-3 : £2.95
(B77-13850)

Bromige, Iris. Laurian Vale / [by] Iris Bromige. — London : Corgi, 1977. — [4],188p ; 18cm. — (A Corgi romance)
Originally published: London : Hodder and Stoughton, 1952.
ISBN 0-552-10405-1 Pbk : £0.50
(B77-16047)

Bromige, Iris. Rough weather / [by] Iris Bromige. — Large print ed. — Leicester : Ulverscroft, 1977. — [7],330p ; 23cm. — (Ulverscroft large print series : [romance])
Originally published: London : Hodder and Stoughton, 1972.
ISBN 0-85456-529-9 : £2.65
(B77-13851)

Bromige, Iris. Shall love be lost? / [by] Iris Bromige. — London : Corgi, 1976. — [5], 184p ; 18cm. — (A Corgi romance)
Originally published: as 'The house of conflict'. London : Hodder and Stoughton, 1953.
ISBN 0-552-10330-6 Pbk : £0.50
(B77-04400)

Bromige, Iris. Stay but till tomorrow / [by] Iris Bromige. — London : Corgi, 1976. — [4], 188p ; 18cm.
Originally published: London : Hodder and Stoughton, 1975.
ISBN 0-552-10356-x Pbk : £0.50
(B77-09245)

Bromige, Iris. The wind in the reeds / [by] Iris Bromige. — London : Corgi, 1977. — 189p ; 18cm. — (A Corgi romance)
Originally published: London : Herbert Jenkins, 1953.
ISBN 0-552-10460-4 Pbk : £0.50
(B77-23715)

Bromley, Gordon. A midsummer night's crime / by Gordon Bromley. — London : Hale, 1977. — 173p : ill ; 20cm.
ISBN 0-7091-5916-1 : £3.15
(B77-08035)

Brookes, Ewart. Wind along the waste / [by] Ewart Brookes. — London [etc.] : White Lion Publishers, 1976. — 240p ; 20cm.
Originally published: London : Jarrolds, 1962.
ISBN 0-7274-0189-0 : £3.50
(B77-05058)

Brophy, John. Immortal sergeant / [by] John Brophy. — London : Corgi, 1977. — 220p ; 18cm.
Originally published: London : Collins, 1942.
ISBN 0-552-10352-7 Pbk : £0.75
(B77-09246)

Brophy, John. Man, woman and child / [by] John Brophy. — London : Remploy, 1976. — 319p ; 20cm.
Originally published: London : Collins, 1938.
ISBN 0-7066-0683-3 : £2.75
(B77-03216)

The **Brothers**. — London [etc.] : White Lion Publishers.
Book 3 / [by] Lee Mackenzie. — 1977. — 208p ; 21cm.
Based on the BBC TV series. — Originally published: London : Sphere, 1974.
ISBN 0-7274-0298-6 : £3.50
(B77-12641)

The **brothers**. — London [etc.] : White Lion Publishers.
Book 4 / [by] Lee Mackenzie. — 1977. — 202p ; 21cm.
Based on the BBC TV series. — Originally published: London : Sphere, 1975.
ISBN 0-7274-0204-8 : £3.75
(B77-18366)

Brown, George Mackay. Greenvoe / [by] George Mackay Brown. — [1st ed., reprinted] / with commentary and notes by D.M. Budge. — London : Longman, 1977. — xv,272p : map ; 19cm. — (The heritage of literature series)
Originally published: London : Hogarth Press, 1972.
ISBN 0-582-34872-2 Pbk : £0.95
(B77-13250)

Brown, George Mackay. Magnus / [by] George Mackay Brown. — London : Quartet Books, 1977. — 206p ; 20cm.
Originally published: London : Hogarth Press, 1973.
ISBN 0-7043-3148-9 Pbk : £1.50
(B77-20577)

Brown, Jamieson. Destroyers will rendezvous / [by] Jamieson Brown. — London [etc.] : White Lion Publishers, 1977. — 288p ; 21cm.
Originally published: London : Jarrolds, 1959.
ISBN 0-7274-0194-7 : £3.50
(B77-12642)

Brown, Mandy. The lilac quest / [by] Mandy Brown. — London : Hale, 1976. — 181p ; 20cm.
ISBN 0-7091-5504-2 : £2.95
(B77-03217)

Brown, Roy, *b.1921.* The cage / [by] Roy Brown. — London : Abelard-Schuman, 1977. — 151p ; 23cm.
ISBN 0-200-72459-2 : £3.50
(B77-03753)

Browne, Gerald Austin. Slide / [by] Gerald A. Browne. — London : Hart-Davis MacGibbon, 1977. — 237p ; 23cm.
Originally published: New York : Arbor House, 1976.
ISBN 0-246-10973-4 : £3.95
(B77-17076)

Browne, Tom, *b.1943.* One of Barney's girls / [by] Tom Browne. — Basingstoke [etc.] : Macmillan, 1977. — [6],119p ; 18cm. — (Topliners)
ISBN 0-333-22747-6 Pbk : £0.45 : CIP rev.
(B77-19643)

Browne, Tom, *b.1943.* The Santa Claus plot. — Basingstoke : : Macmillan, Jan. 1978. — 1v. — (Topliner tridents)
Previous control number ISBN 0-333-23553-3. — For adolescents.
ISBN 0-333-23633-5 : CIP entry
(B77-32847)

Browning, William. Grimm Grange / [by] William Browning. — London : Gollancz, 1977. — 158p ; 21cm.
ISBN 0-575-02363-5 : £3.50
(B77-27368)

Bruce, Leo. Death in Albert Park / [by] Leo Bruce. — London [etc.] : White Lion Publishers, 1977. — 239p ; 21cm.
Originally published: London : W.H. Allen, 1964.
ISBN 0-7274-0116-5 : £3.75
(B77-20578)

Brunner, John, *b.1934.* The squares of the city / [by] John Brunner. — [London] : Fontana, 1977. — [1],311p ; 18cm. — (Fontana science fiction)
Originally published: New York : Ballantine Books, 1965 ; Harmondsworth : Penguin, 1969.
ISBN 0-00-614610-4 Pbk : £0.80
(B77-31442)

Brunner, John, *b.1934.* Total eclipse / [by] John Brunner. — London : Futura Publications, 1976. — [4],187p ; 18cm. — (An orbit book)
Originally published: London : Weidenfeld and Nicolson, 1975.
ISBN 0-86007-883-3 Pbk : £0.60
(B77-08548)

Brunner, John, *b.1934.* Web of everywhere / [by] John Brunner. — London : New English Library, 1977. — 143p ; 18cm.
Originally published: New York : Bantam, 1974.
ISBN 0-450-03094-6 Pbk : £0.60
(B77-13852)

Buchan, John, *1st Baron Tweedsmuir.* The dancing floor / [by] John Buchan. — Large print ed. — Bath : Chivers, 1977. — [9],386p : map ; 23cm.
Originally published: London : Hodder and Stoughton, 1926.
ISBN 0-85997-258-5 : £5.80(£4.35 to members of the Library Association)
(B77-33423)

Buchan, John, *1st Baron Tweedsmuir.* Salute to adventurers / [by] John Buchan. — London : Hutchinson, 1976. — 366p ; 20cm.
Facsimile reprint of: 1st ed. London : Nelson, 1915.
ISBN 0-09-127750-7 : £3.95
(B77-03754)

Buchan, Sinclair. Singleton's mill / [by] Sinclair Buchan. — Sydney ; London [etc.] : Hodder and Stoughton, 1975[i.e.1977]. — 173p ; 22cm.
Published in Australia: 1975.
ISBN 0-340-19758-7 : £3.25
(B77-09247)

Buchanan, Peter. Under the doctor / [by] Peter Buchanan. — London : Sphere, 1977. — 141p ; 18cm.
ISBN 0-7221-2035-4 Pbk : £0.65
(B77-06857)

Buck, Pearl Sydenstricker. All under heaven / [by] Pearl S. Buck. — London [etc.] : Pan Books, 1977. — 156p ; 18cm.
Originally published: New York : Day ; London : Eyre Methuen, 1973.
Pbk : £0.50
ISBN 0-330-24553-8
(B77-34089)

Buck, Pearl Sydenstricker. The goddess abides / [by] Pearl S. Buck. — London [etc.] : Pan Books, 1977. — 172p ; 18cm.
Originally published: New York : Day ; London : Eyre Methuen, 1972.
Pbk : £0.50
ISBN 0-330-24208-3
(B77-34090)

Buck, Pearl Sydenstricker. God's men / [by] Pearl S. Buck. — London [etc.] : White Lion Publishers, 1976. — [4],450p ; 21cm.
Originally published: London : Methuen, 1951.
ISBN 0-7274-0216-1 : £4.25
(B77-05059)

Buck, Pearl Sydenstricker. Imperial woman / [by Pearl S. Buck. — London [etc.] : White Lion Publishers, 1977. — 432p ; 21cm.
Originally published: New York : Day ; London : Methuen, 1956. — Based on the life of Tz'u-hsî, Empress Dowager of China.
ISBN 0-7274-0211-0 : £4.75
(B77-12643)

Buck, Pearl Sydenstricker. Voices in the house / [by] Pearl S. Buck. — London [etc.] : White Lion Publishers, 1977. — [4],220p ; 21cm.
Originally published: New York : Day, 1953 ; London : Methuen, 1954.
ISBN 0-7274-0239-0 : £3.75
(B77-19644)

Buck, William. Ramayana / [retold] by William Buck ; with an introduction by B.A. van Nooten ; illustrated by Shirley Triest. — Berkeley [etc.] ; London : University of California Press, 1976. — xxxi,432p : ill, map ; 22cm.
Ill. on lining papers.
ISBN 0-520-02016-2 : £11.95
(B77-13251)

Buckingham, Nancy. The jade dragon / [by] Nancy Buckingham. — London (11 New Fetter La., EC4P 4EE) : Magnum Books, 1977. — 3-206p ; 18cm.
Originally published: London : Hale, 1976.
ISBN 0-413-37240-5 Pbk : £0.65
(B77-15485)

Buckingham, Nancy. Shroud of silence / [by] Nancy Buckingham. — London (11 New Fetter La., EC4P 4EE) : Magnum Books, 1977. — 191p ; 18cm.
Originally published: London : Hale, 1970.
ISBN 0-413-37230-8 Pbk : £0.65
(B77-16048)

Buckley, Eunice. Prisoners of hate / [by] Eunice Buckley. — London : Hale, 1977. — 172p ; 21cm.
ISBN 0-7091-5861-0 : £3.25
(B77-13252)

Buckley, Eunice. You've got to have gold / [by] Eunice Buckley. — Large print ed. — Leicester : Ulverscroft, 1977. — [4],516p ; 22cm. — (Ulverscroft large print series : [romance])
Originally published: London : Hale, 1972.
ISBN 0-85456-527-2 : £2.65
(B77-13853)

Buckley, William Frank. Saving the Queen / [by] William F. Buckley, Jr. — Large print [ed.]. — London : Prior [etc.], 1976. — [11],528p ; 24cm.
Originally published: Garden City, N.Y. : Doubleday ; London : W.H. Allen, 1976.
ISBN 0-86043-010-3 : £6.75
(B77-07589)

Budrys, Algis. Michaelmas / by Algis Budrys. — London : Gollancz, 1977. — 3-253p ; 21cm. — ([Gollancz SF])
Also published: New York : Berkley, 1977.
ISBN 0-575-02375-9 : £3.95
(B77-29682)

Bullock, Michael. Randolph Cranstone and the glass thimble : a parabolic fiction / [by] Michael Bullock. — London : Boyars : Distributed by Calder and Boyars, 1977. — 120p : ill ; 23cm.
Originally published: as 'Randolph Cranstone and the pursuing river'. Vancouver : Rainbow Press, 1975.
ISBN 0-7145-2506-5 : £4.95
(B77-10936)

Burchell, Mary. Elusive harmony / by Mary Burchell. — London : Mills and Boon, 1976. — 188p ; 17cm.
ISBN 0-263-72314-3 Pbk : £0.30
(B77-00955)

Burchell, Mary. Love him or leave him / by Mary Burchell. — London : Mills and Boon, 1976. — 187p ; 17cm.
Originally published: 1950.
ISBN 0-263-72346-1 Pbk : £0.30
(B77-05642)

Burgess, Anthony. Abba Abba / [by] Anthony Burgess. — London : Faber, 1977. — 127p ; 21cm.
Contains poems by Giuseppe Gioacchino Belli translated into English.
ISBN 0-571-11125-4 : £3.95 : CIP rev
Also classified at 851'.7
(B77-07590)

Burgess, Anthony. Beard's Roman women : a novel / [by] Anthony Burgess ; photographs by David Robinson. — London : Hutchinson, 1977. — [1],155,[1],[16]p of plates : ill(some col) ; 24cm.
Originally published: New York : McGraw-Hill, 1976.
ISBN 0-09-128400-7 : £4.25
(B77-09248)

Burgess, Anthony. The doctor is sick / [by] Anthony Burgess. — London : Heinemann, 1977. — [5],261p ; 20cm.
Originally published: 1960.
ISBN 0-434-09810-8 : £3.50
(B77-21421)

Burgess, Anthony. The wanting seed / [by] Anthony Burgess. — London : Heinemann, 1977. — [6],285p ; 20cm.
Originally published: 1962.
£3.50
ISBN 0-434-09806-x
(B77-20579)

Burgess, Eric, *b.1912.* The mants of Myrmedon / [by] Eric Burgess and Arthur Friggens. — London : Hale, 1977. — 189p ; 21cm. — (Hale SF)
ISBN 0-7091-5880-7 : £3.25
(B77-05643)

Burke, Jackson Frederick. Location shots / [by] J.F. Burke. — London (11 New Fetter La., London EC4P 4EE) : Magnum Books, 1977. — [4],140p ; 18cm.
Originally published: New York : Harper and Row ; London : Constable, 1974.
ISBN 0-413-37090-9 Pbk : £0.60
(B77-09935)

Burke, John, *b.1922.* The black charade : a Dr Caspian story / [by] John Burke. — London : Weidenfeld and Nicolson, 1977. — [5],186p ; 23cm.
ISBN 0-297-77328-3 : £3.95
(B77-19645)

Burke, John, *b.1922.* A hard day's night / [by] John Burke. — London : Pan Books, 1977. — 121p,[8]p of plates : ill, ports ; 18cm.
'Based on the original screenplay by Alun Owen' - cover. — Originally published: 1964.
Pbk : Unpriced
(B77-29683)

Burke, John, *b.1922.* Luke's kingdom / [by] John Burke. — London : Severn House : [Distributed by Hutchinson], 1977. — 192p ; 21cm.
'Based on the popular television series' - jacket. — Originally published: London : Fontana, 1976.
ISBN 0-7278-0242-9 : £3.25
(B77-18978)

Burke, Lee John. The Cairo counterplot / by Lee John Burke. — London : Hale, 1977. — 189p ; 20cm.
ISBN 0-7091-6462-9 : £3.25
(B77-28099)

Burley, William John. The schoolmaster : a novel / by W.J. Burley. — London : Gollancz, 1977. — 160p ; 21cm. — ([Gollancz detection])
ISBN 0-575-02252-3 : £3.75
(B77-13253)

Burmeister, Jon. The darkling plain / [by] Jon Burmeister. — London : Sphere, 1977. — 373p : plan ; 18cm.
Originally published: London : Joseph, 1970.
ISBN 0-7221-2078-8 Pbk : £0.85
(B77-19646)

Burmeister, Jon. The edge of the coast / [by] Jon Burmeister. — London : Sphere, 1977. — 189p ; 18cm.
Originally published: London : Joseph, 1968.
ISBN 0-7221-2082-6 Pbk : £0.75
(B77-20580)

Burmeister, Jon. A hot and copper sky / [by] Jon Burmeister. — London : Sphere, 1977. — 3-304p ; 18cm.
Originally published: London : Joseph, 1969.
ISBN 0-7221-2076-1 Pbk : £0.85
(B77-19647)

Burmeister, Jon. The protector conclusion / [by] Jon Burmeister. — London : Joseph, 1977. — 191p ; 23cm.
ISBN 0-7181-1576-7 : £4.20
(B77-15486)

Burmeister, Jon. Running scared / [by] Jon Burmeister. — London : Sphere, 1977. — 303p ; 18cm.
Originally published: London : Joseph, 1972.
ISBN 0-7221-2083-4 Pbk : £0.95
(B77-19648)

Burnley, Judith. The wife / [by] Judith Burnley. — London : Heinemann, 1977. — [6],132p ; 23cm.
ISBN 0-434-09855-8 : £2.90
(B77-06276)

Burroughs, Edgar Rice. The cave girl / [by] Edgar Rice Burroughs. — London : Tandem, 1977. — 220p ; 19cm.
Originally published: Chicago : McClurg, 1925.
ISBN 0-426-18323-1 Pbk : £0.60
(B77-22850)

Burroughs, Edgar Rice. The lost continent / [by] Edgar Rice Burroughs. — London : Tandem, 1977. — 126p ; 18cm.
Originally published: as 'Beyond thirty'. South Ozone Park, N.Y. : Science Fiction & Fantasy Publications, 1957.
ISBN 0-426-18331-2 Pbk : £0.60
(B77-24471)

Burroughs, William, *b.1914.* Junky / [by] William S. Burroughs. — Complete and unexpurgated ed. ; with an introduction by Allen Ginsberg. — Harmondsworth [etc.] : Penguin, 1977. — xvii,158p ; 18cm.
Previous ed.: published as 'Junk' / under the name William Lee, New York : Ace Books, 1953 ; and as 'Junkie', New York : Ace Books, 1964 ; London : New English Library, 1966.
ISBN 0-14-004351-9 Pbk : £0.60
(B77-25875)

Burroway, Janet. Raw silk / [by] Janet Burroway. — London : Gollancz, 1977. — [6], 314p ; 21cm.
Originally published: Boston, Mass. : Little, Brown, 1976.
ISBN 0-575-02308-2 : £4.95
(B77-19649)

Burton, Anthony. The master idol / [by] Anthony Burton. — London : Futura Publications, 1976. — [5],298p ; 18cm.
Originally published: London : Macdonald and Jane's, 1975.
ISBN 0-86007-373-4 Pbk : £0.75
(B77-12086)

Burton, Anthony. A place to stand / [by] Anthony Burton. — London : Macdonald and Jane's, 1977. — [5],245p ; 23cm. — (A troubadour)
ISBN 0-354-04100-2 : £4.50
(B77-10937)

Burton, Hester. To Ravensrigg / [by] Hester Burton ; illustration by Victor G. Ambrus. — London : Oxford University Press, 1976. — ix, 148p : 1 ill ; 23cm.
For adolescents.
ISBN 0-19-271393-0 : £2.95
(B77-00956)

Burton, Miles. Look alive / by Miles Burton. — Hornchurch : I. Henry, 1977. — 192p ; 21cm.
Originally published: London : Collins, 1949.
ISBN 0-86025-119-5 : £3.35
(B77-22109)

Bush, Christopher. The case of the dead man gone / [by] Christopher Bush. — London [etc.] : White Lion Publishers, [1977]. — 191p ; 21cm.
Originally published: London : Macdonald and Co., 1961.
ISBN 0-85617-406-8 : £3.50
(B77-15487)

Butler, David, *b.1927.* Edward the Seventh / [by] David Butler. — London : Futura Publications.
In 2 vols.
Book 1 : Prince of hearts. — 1974. — 327p ; 18cm.
' ... based on the ... research ... for his [David Butler's] television series on the life of Edward VII ... ' - half title page. — Also published: London : Weidenfeld and Nicolson, 1974.
ISBN 0-86007-129-4 Pbk : £0.60
(B77-09249)

Butler, Gwendoline. The brides of Friedberg / [by] Gwendoline Butler. — London [etc.] : Macmillan, 1977. — 192p : geneal table(on lining papers) ; 21cm.
ISBN 0-333-21814-0 : £3.75
(B77-19650)

Butler, Margaret. This turbulent priest / [by] Margaret Butler. — London [etc.] : Macmillan, 1977. — 334p : geneal table ; 21cm.
Bibl.: p.333-334. — Based on the last years of the quarrel between King Henry II and Archbishop Thomas Becket.
ISBN 0-333-21539-7 : £3.95
(B77-15488)

Butler, Richard, *b.1925.* The men that God forgot / [by] Richard Butler. — London : Corgi, 1977. — 223p ; 18cm.
Originally published: London : Hutchinson, 1975. — Bibl.: p.222-223.
ISBN 0-552-10469-8 Pbk : £0.75
(B77-30605)

Butterworth, Michael. The man in the Sopwith Camel / [by] Michael Butterworth. — [London] : Fontana, 1977. — 192p ; 18cm.
Originally published: London : Collins, 1974.
ISBN 0-00-614780-1 Pbk : £0.70
(B77-22110)

Butterworth, Michael. Queens of Deliria / [by] Michael Butterworth. — London : Star Books, 1977. — 191p ; 19cm.
ISBN 0-352-39602-4 Pbk : £0.80
(B77-20581)

Bygraves, Max. The milkman's on his way / [by] Max Bygraves. — London : W.H. Allen, 1977. — 189p ; 23cm.
ISBN 0-491-02290-5 : £3.50
(B77-19651)

Byrd, Elizabeth. Rest without peace / [by] Elizabeth Byrd. — Large print ed. — Bath : Firecrest, 1977. — [4],363p ; 23cm.
Originally published: London : Macmillan, 1974. — Based on the lives of Burke and Hare.
ISBN 0-85119-014-6 : £4.80
(B77-33424)

Cadell, Elizabeth. The fledgling / [by] Elizabeth Cadell. — London : Coronet, 1977. — 188p ; 18cm.
Originally published: London : Hodder and Stoughton, 1975.
ISBN 0-340-21234-9 Pbk : £0.60
(B77-09250)

Cadell, Elizabeth. Game in diamonds / [by] Elizabeth Cadell. — Sevenoaks : Coronet, 1977. — 188p ; 18cm.
Originally published: London : Hodder and Stoughton, 1976.
ISBN 0-340-21981-5 Pbk : £0.80
(B77-34091)

Cadell, Elizabeth. Game in diamonds / [by] Elizabeth Cadell. — Large print [ed.]. — London : Prior [etc.], 1977. — [5],365p ; 25cm.
Originally published: London : Hodder and Stoughton, 1976.
ISBN 0-86043-063-4 : £4.95
(B77-33425)

Cadell, Elizabeth. Parson's House / [by] Elizabeth Cadell. — London [etc.] : Hodder and Stoughton, 1977. — 189p ; 21cm.
ISBN 0-340-21616-6 : £3.50
(B77-17077)

Caidin, Martin. Cyborg IV / by Martin Caidin. — London : W.H. Allen, 1977. — 3-205p ; 23cm.
Originally published: New York : Arbor House, 1975.
ISBN 0-491-01878-9 : £3.95
(B77-14398)

Caidin, Martin. Whip / [by] Martin Caidin. — London : Corgi, 1977. — [9],242,[1]p ; 18cm.
Originally published: Boston, Mass. : Houghton Mifflin, 1976.
ISBN 0-552-10379-9 Pbk : £0.85
(B77-16586)

Cain, James Mallahan. Rainbow's end / [by] James M. Cain. — London : Magnum Books, 1977. — 191p ; 18cm.
Originally published: New York : Mason, Charter ; London : W.H. Allen, 1975.
ISBN 0-417-02020-1 Pbk : £0.70
(B77-24472)

Caine, Jeffrey. The cold room / [by] Jeffrey Caine. — London : W.H. Allen, 1976. — 189p ; 23cm.
ISBN 0-491-01628-x : £3.50
(B77-06277)

Caine, Jeffrey. Heathcliff : a novel / [by] Jeffrey Caine. — London : W.H. Allen, 1977. — [5], 216p ; 23cm.
ISBN 0-491-02201-8 : £4.50
(B77-28100)

Caine, Rebecca. Child of Tahiti / by Rebecca Caine. — London : Mills and Boon, 1977. — 188p ; 18cm.
Originally published: 1976.
ISBN 0-263-72331-3 Pbk : £0.35
(B77-06858)

Cairncross, George. A friend of the people : being one man's saga of the sixties and dedicated to all those who were there / by George Cairncross. — Filey (31 Belle Vue St., Filey, N. Yorkshire YO14 9HU) : Fiasco Publications, [1977]. — [1],72p ; 26cm.
ISBN 0-903711-29-x Sd : £0.35
(B77-12087)

Calde, Mark A. Shadowboxer / by Mark A. Calde. — London : Hale, 1977. — 192p ; 20cm.
Originally published: New York : Putnam, 1976.
ISBN 0-7091-6318-5 : £3.25
(B77-28879)

Caldecott, Moyra. The tall stones / [by] Moyra Caldecott. — London : Collings, 1977. — [6], 234p ; 23cm.
ISBN 0-86036-032-6 : £4.95
(B77-13854)

Caldecott, Moyra. The temple of the sun / [by] Moyra Caldecott. — London : Collings, 1977. — [7],232p ; 23cm.
ISBN 0-86036-048-2 : £4.95
(B77-28880)

Calder, Robert. The dogs : a novel / by Robert Calder. — London [etc.] : Hodder and Stoughton, 1976. — [7],228p ; 21cm.
Also published: New York : Delacorte Press, 1976.
ISBN 0-340-21269-1 : £3.75
(B77-00957)

Caldwell, Taylor. Captains and the kings / [by] Taylor Caldwell. — [London] : Fontana, 1977. — 442p ; 18cm.
Originally published: Garden City, N.Y. : Doubleday, 1972 ; London : Collins, 1973. — Bibl.: p.441-442.
ISBN 0-00-614869-7 Pbk : £1.25
(B77-32155)

Caldwell, Taylor. Ceremony of the innocent / [by] Taylor Caldwell. — Abridged [ed.]. — London : Collins, 1977. — 350p ; 22cm.
Full ed.: Garden City, N.Y. : Doubleday, 1976.
ISBN 0-00-222113-6 : £3.95
(B77-15489)

Caldwell, Taylor. Dynasty of death / [by] Taylor Caldwell. — [London] : Fontana, 1977. — 668p ; 18cm.
Originally published: New York : Scribner, 1938 ; London : Collins, 1939.
ISBN 0-00-615015-2 Pbk : £1.50
(B77-22111)

Caldwell, Taylor. The eagles gather / [by] Taylor Caldwell. — [London] : Fontana, 1977. — 478p ; 18cm.
Originally published: London : Collins, 1940.
ISBN 0-00-615016-0 Pbk : £1.25
(B77-22112)

Caldwell, Taylor. The final hour / [by] Taylor Caldwell. — [London] : Fontana, 1977. — 608p ; 18cm.
Originally published: New York : Scribner, 1944 ; London : Collins, 1945.
ISBN 0-00-615017-9 Pbk : £1.25
(B77-22113)

Caldwell, Taylor. Glory and the lightning / [by] Taylor Caldwell. — [London] : Fontana, 1977. — 380p ; 18cm.
Originally published: Garden City, N.Y. : Doubleday, 1974 ; London : Collins, 1975.
ISBN 0-00-615026-8 Pbk : £1.00
(B77-27369)

Caldwell, Taylor. Great lion of God : a novel based on the life of Saint Paul / [by] Taylor Caldwell ; a condensation by the editors of Reader's Digest Condensed Books. — Large print ed. — Leicester : Ulverscroft, 1976. — [4] ,394,[2]p ; 23cm. — (Ulverscroft large print series : [fiction])
This condensation originally published: Pleasantville, N.Y. ; London : Reader's Digest Association, 197-?. — Based on the life of St Paul.
ISBN 0-85456-553-1 : £2.65
(B77-08036)

Caldwell, Taylor. A prologue to love / [by] Taylor Caldwell. — [London] : Fontana, 1977. — 733p ; 18cm.
Originally published: London : Collins, 1962.
ISBN 0-00-615018-7 Pbk : £1.50
(B77-30606)

Caldwell, Taylor. The romance of Atlantis / [by] Taylor Caldwell with Jess Stearn. — [London] : Fontana, 1976. — 286p ; 18cm.
Originally published: New York : Morrow, 1975.
ISBN 0-00-614447-0 Pbk : £0.75
(B77-01787)

Caldwell, Taylor. The romance of Atlantis / [by] Taylor Caldwell with Jess Stearn. — London : Severn House : [Distributed by Hutchinson], 1977. — 3-286p ; 21cm.
Originally published: New York : Morrow, 1975 ; London : Fontana, 1976.
ISBN 0-7278-0252-6 : £3.75
(B77-17078)

Caldwell, Taylor. Tender victory / [by] Taylor Caldwell. — Bath : Chivers, 1976. — 512p ; 21cm.
Originally published: London : Collins, 1956.
£5.40(£4.05 to members of the Library Association)
ISBN 0-85594-638-5
(B77-05644)

Caldwell, Taylor. This side of innocence / [by] Taylor Caldwell. — [London] : Fontana, 1977. — 510p ; 18cm.
Originally published: London : Collins, 1947.
ISBN 0-00-615020-9 Pbk : £1.25
(B77-30607)

Calin, Harold. Panzer! / [by] Harold Calin. — London : New English Library, 1977. — 144p ; 18cm.
Originally published: as 'Return to the Ardennes'. United States : s.n., 1968.
ISBN 0-450-03403-8 Pbk : £0.70
(B77-23716)

Callison, Brian. A frenzy of merchantmen / [by] Brian Callison. — London : Collins, 1977. — 206p ; 22cm.
ISBN 0-00-222239-6 : £3.50
(B77-10546)

Callison, Brian. A ship is dying / [by] Brian Callison. — [London] : Fontana, 1977. — 191p ; 18cm.
Originally published: London : Collins, 1976.
ISBN 0-00-614495-0 Pbk : £0.70
(B77-28101)

Callison, Brian. A web of salvage / [by] Brian Callison. — [London] : Fontana, 1977. — 191p ; 18cm.
Originally published: London : Collins, 1973.
ISBN 0-00-614842-5 Pbk : £0.70
(B77-27370)

Callow, Philip. Janine : a novel / by Philip Callow. — London [etc.] : Bodley Head, 1977. — 148p ; 21cm.
ISBN 0-370-30033-5 : £3.50
(B77-23717)

Campbell, James, *b.1920.* Bomber stream broken / [by] James Campbell. — Henley-on-Thames (Kestrel House, Peppard Common, Henley-on-Thames, [Oxon]) : Cressrelles Publishing Company, 1976. — 238p ; 21cm.
ISBN 0-85956-024-4 : £3.50
(B77-02570)

Campbell, Karen. Thunder on Sunday / [by] Karen Campbell. — [London] : Fontana, 1976. — 191p ; 18cm.
Originally published: London : Collins, 1972.
ISBN 0-00-614334-2 Pbk : £0.60
(B77-09251)

Campsie, Alistair Keith. By law protected : a novel / by Alistair Campsie. — Edinburgh : Canongate Publishing, 1976. — [6],201p ; 23cm.
ISBN 0-903937-27-1 : £3.50
(B77-14904)

Canning, Victor. The circle of the gods / [by] Victor Canning. — London : Heinemann, 1977. — [9],178p ; 23cm.
ISBN 0-434-10791-3 : £3.90
(B77-28102)

Canning, Victor. Doubled in diamonds / [by] Victor Canning. — London : Pan Books, 1977. — 205p ; 18cm.
Originally published: London : Heinemann, 1966.
Pbk : £0.70
ISBN 0-330-02125-7
(B77-24473)

Canning, Victor. The Kingsford mark / [by] Victor Canning. — London : Pan Books, 1977. — 204p ; 18cm.
Originally published: London : Heinemann, 1975.
ISBN 0-330-25176-7 Pbk : £0.70
(B77-32156)

Canning, Victor. The melting man / [by] Victor Canning. — London : Pan Books, 1977. — 237p ; 18cm.
Originally published: London : Heinemann, 1968.
Pbk : £0.70
ISBN 0-330-02538-4
(B77-27371)

Cannon, Elliott. The big chip / [by] Elliott Cannon. — London : Hale, 1976. — 184p ; 20cm.
ISBN 0-7091-5560-3 : £2.95
(B77-03755)

Cannon, Elliott. A nice guy like me / by Elliott Cannon. — London : Hale, 1977. — 192p ; 20cm.
ISBN 0-7091-6074-7 : £3.15
(B77-22851)

Cannon, Elliott. The treachery trade / by Elliott Cannon. — London : Hale, 1977. — 192p ; 20cm.
ISBN 0-7091-6292-8 : £3.25
(B77-26513)

Cardew, Christopher. Pellafino / [by] Christopher Cardew. — Ilfracombe : Stockwell, 1976. — 132p ; 19cm.
ISBN 0-7223-0954-6 : £2.50
(B77-10938)

Carmichael, Harry. A grave for two / [by] Harry Carmichael. — London : Collins [for] the Crime Club, 1977. — 192p ; 21cm.
ISBN 0-00-231263-8 : £2.95
(B77-18979)

Carnegie, Sacha. The banners of revolt / [by] Sacha Carnegie. — London : P. Davies, 1977. — 279p ; 23cm. — (Carnegie, Sacha. Destiny of eagles ; [5])
ISBN 0-432-02076-4 : £4.90
(B77-28103)

Carney, Daniel. The wild geese / [by] Daniel Carney. — London : Heinemann, 1977. — [5], 237p ; 23cm.
ISBN 0-434-10860-x : £3.90
(B77-14905)

Carpentier, Charles. Flight one / [by] Charles Carpentier. — London : Sphere, 1977. — 272p ; 18cm.
Originally published: New York : Simon and Schuster, 1972 ; London : Eyre Methuen, 1973.
ISBN 0-7221-2202-0 Pbk : £0.85
(B77-22114)

Carpentier, Charles. Flight one / [by] Charles Carpentier. — London : Sphere, 1975. — 272p ; 18cm.
Originally published: New York : Simon and Schuster, 1972 ; London : Eyre Methuen, 1973.
ISBN 0-7221-2204-7 Pbk : £0.60
(B77-09252)

Carr, John Dickson. The Blind Barber / [by] John Dickson Carr. — Large print ed. — Bath : Lythway Press, 1976. — ix,3-407p ; 22cm. — (Lythway classics of crime and detection)
Originally published: New York : London : Harper, 1934.
ISBN 0-85046-688-1 : £4.70
(B77-02571)

Carr, John Dickson. The case of the constant suicides / by John Dickson Carr. — London : Hamilton, 1977. — 166p ; 21cm. — (A fingerprint book)
Originally published: London : Hamilton, 1941.
ISBN 0-241-89719-x : £3.95
(B77-27372)

Carr, John Dickson. He who whispers / [by] John Dickson Carr. — Large print ed. — Bath : Lythway Press, 1977. — [5],358p ; 23cm.
Originally published: London : Hamilton, 1946.
ISBN 0-85046-709-8 : £4.80
(B77-21422)

Carr, John Dickson. The hollow man / by John Dickson Carr. — London : Remploy, 1977. — 304p : 1 ill, plan ; 19cm. — ([Deerstalker series])
Facsimile reprint of: 1st ed. London : Hamilton, 1935.
ISBN 0-7066-0698-1 : £3.00
(B77-34092)

Carr, John Dickson. The man who could not shudder / by John Dickson Carr. — London : Severn House : [Distributed by Hutchinson], 1977. — [5],150p ; 21cm.
Originally published: New York ; London : Harper, 1940.
ISBN 0-7278-0277-1 : £3.25
(B77-22852)

Carr, John Dickson. The problem of the wire cage / [by] John Dickson Carr. — London : Severn House : [Distributed by Hutchinson], 1977. — [4],168p ; 21cm.
Originally published: London : Hamilton, 1940.
ISBN 0-7278-0249-6 : £3.25
(B77-17079)

Carr, John Dickson. Till death do us part / by John Dickson Carr. — London : Hamilton, 1977. — 224p ; 21cm. — (A fingerprint book)
Originally published: New York : Harper and Row ; London : Hamilton, 1944.
ISBN 0-241-89639-8 : £3.75
(B77-18980)

Carr, Margaret. Twin tragedy / by Margaret Carr. — London : Hale, 1977. — 185p ; 20cm.
ISBN 0-7091-6087-9 : £3.15
(B77-17080)

Carr, Philippa. Lament for a lost lover / [by] Philippa Carr. — London : Collins, 1977. — 347p : geneal table ; 22cm.
ISBN 0-00-222417-8 : £4.25
(B77-22115)

Carr, Philippa. The lion triumphant / [by] Philippa Carr. — [London] : Fontana, 1977. — 351p ; 18cm.
Originally published: London : Collins, 1974.
ISBN 0-00-614649-x Pbk : £0.80
(B77-13855)

Carr, Philippa. The miracle at St Bruno's / [by] Philippa Carr. — [London] : Fontana, 1977. — 352p ; 18cm.
Originally published: London : Collins, 1972.
ISBN 0-00-614335-0 Pbk : £0.80
(B77-13856)

Carr, Philippa. Saraband for two sisters / [by] Philippa Carr. — [London] : Fontana, 1977. — 351p : geneal table ; 18cm.
Originally published: London : Collins, 1976.
ISBN 0-00-614488-8 Pbk : £0.80
(B77-13254)

Carr, Philippa. The witch from the sea / [by] Philippa Carr. — [London] : Fontana, 1977. — 319p ; 18cm.
Originally published: London : Collins, 1975.
ISBN 0-00-615007-1 Pbk : £0.75
(B77-22116)

Carrington, Leonora. The hearing trumpet / [by] Leonora Carrington ; illustrations by Pablo Weisz-Carrington. — London [etc.] : Routledge and Kegan Paul, 1977. — [2],158p : ill ; 23cm.
Originally published: translated from English into French as 'Le cornet acoustique'. Paris : Flammarion, 1974.
ISBN 0-7100-8637-7 : £3.50 : CIP rev.
(B77-07591)

Carroll, James. Madonna red / [by] James Carroll. — London [etc.] : Hodder and Stoughton, 1977. — 282p ; 21cm.
Originally published: Boston, Mass. : Little, Brown, 1976.
ISBN 0-340-21596-8 : £3.95
(B77-17735)

Carstens, Netta. While the gentlemen go by / [by] Netta Carstens. — London : Hale, 1977. — 174p ; 21cm.
ISBN 0-7091-6276-6 : £3.50
(B77-28104)

Carter, Angela. The passion of new Eve / by Angela Carter. — London : Gollancz, 1977. — 191p ; 21cm. — ([Gollancz fantasy & macabre])
ISBN 0-575-02247-7 : £3.95
(B77-13255)

Carter, Forrest. Gone to Texas / [by] Forrest Carter. — London : Futura Publications, 1976. — viii,206p : ill ; 18cm.
Originally published: as 'The rebel outlaw : Josey Wales'. Gantt : Whipporwill, 1973 ; London : Weidenfeld and Nicolson, 1975.
ISBN 0-86007-331-9 Pbk : £0.60
(B77-08549)

Carter, John. The diamond mercenaries / [by] John Carter. — London : Futura Publications, 1976. — 219p ; 18cm.
'Based on the screenplay by Michael Winder, Val Guest and Gerald Sansord' - title page verso.
ISBN 0-86007-342-4 Pbk : £0.60
(B77-08550)

Carter, John. The eagle's nest / [by] John Carter. — London : Barker, 1977. — [2],190p ; 23cm. — (The new avengers)
ISBN 0-213-16635-6 : £3.75
(B77-12644)

Carter, Lin. Black legion of Callisto / [by] Lin Carter. — London : Futura Publications, 1975. — 3-203p : 1 ill ; 18cm. — (An orbit book)
Originally published: New York : Dell, 1972.
ISBN 0-86007-825-6 Pbk : £0.45
(B77-09253)

Carter, Nevada. The lost trail / by Nevada Carter. — London : Hale, 1977. — 160p ; 20cm.
ISBN 0-7091-6016-x : £2.95
(B77-14906)

Carter, Peter, *b.1929.* Under Goliath / [by] Peter Carter. — Oxford [etc.] : Oxford University Press, 1977. — [5],169p : 1 ill ; 23cm.
For adolescents.
ISBN 0-19-271405-8 : £2.95 : CIP rev.
(B77-07592)

Cartland, Barbara. The adventurer / [by] Barbara Cartland. — London : Arrow Books, 1977. — 208p ; 18cm.
Originally published: as 'But never free'. London : Hutchinson, 1937.
ISBN 0-09-916050-1 Pbk : £0.50
(B77-29684)

Cartland, Barbara. Again this rapture / [by] Barbara Cartland. — London : Arrow Books, 1977. — 192p ; 18cm.
Originally published: London : Hutchinson, 1947.
ISBN 0-09-914460-3 Pbk : £0.50
(B77-12088)

Cartland, Barbara. Bewitched / [by] Barbara Cartland. — London : Hurst and Blackett, 1977. — 174p ; 20cm.
Originally published: London : Corgi, 1975.
ISBN 0-09-128280-2 : £3.25
(B77-19652)

Cartland, Barbara. Conquered by love / [by] Barbara Cartland. — London [etc.] : Pan Books, 1977. — 154p ; 18cm.
ISBN 0-330-24854-5 Pbk : £0.50
(B77-06859)

Cartland, Barbara. The curse of the clan / [by] Barbara Cartland. — London [etc.] : Pan Books, 1977. — 3-160p ; 18cm.
ISBN 0-330-25261-5 Pbk : £0.50
(B77-31443)

Cartland, Barbara. Dance on my heart / [by] Barbara Cartland. — London : Arrow Books, 1977. — 191p ; 18cm.
ISBN 0-09-914530-8 Pbk : £0.50
(B77-17081)

Cartland, Barbara. The disgraceful duke / [by] Barbara Cartland. — London : Corgi, 1976. — 188p ; 18cm.
ISBN 0-552-10305-5 Pbk : £0.50
(B77-02572)

Cartland, Barbara. The dragon and the pearl / [by] Barbara Cartland. — London : Hutchinson, 1977. — 160p ; 20cm.
ISBN 0-09-131810-6 : £3.75
(B77-31444)

Cartland, Barbara. The dream and the glory / [by] Barbara Cartland. — London [etc.] : Pan Books, 1977. — 153p ; 18cm.
ISBN 0-330-24853-7 Pbk : £0.50
(B77-06860)

Cartland, Barbara. The dream within / [by] Barbara Cartland. — Revised ed. — London : Arrow Books, 1977. — 256p ; 18cm.
This ed. originally published: 1972.
Pbk : £0.50
ISBN 0-09-906350-6
(B77-05060)

Cartland, Barbara. A duel with destiny / [by] Barbara Cartland. — London : Corgi, 1977. — 160p ; 18cm.
ISBN 0-552-10549-x Pbk : £0.50
(B77-28105)

Cartland, Barbara. The golden gondola / [by] Barbara Cartland. — London : Arrow Books, 1977. — 256p ; 18cm.
Originally published: London : Hutchinson, 1958.
ISBN 0-09-914450-6 Pbk : £0.50
(B77-05061)

Cartland, Barbara. The impetuous duchess / [by] Barbara Cartland. — London : Hurst and Blackett, 1977. — 174p ; 20cm.
Originally published: London : Corgi, 1975.
ISBN 0-09-128290-x : £3.25
(B77-19653)

Cartland, Barbara. The karma of love / [by] Barbara Cartland. — London : Hurst and Blackett, 1977. — 185p ; 20cm.
Originally published: London : Corgi, 1974.
ISBN 0-09-129000-7 : £3.25
(B77-19654)

Cartland, Barbara. Kiss the moonlight / [by] Barbara Cartland. — London [etc.] : Pan Books, 1977. — 157p ; 18cm.
ISBN 0-330-25088-4 Pbk : £0.50
(B77-20582)

Cartland, Barbara. Look, listen and love / [by] Barbara Cartland. — London [etc.] : Pan Books, 1977. — 156p ; 18cm.
ISBN 0-330-25171-6 Pbk : £0.50
(B77-28881)

Cartland, Barbara. Love at forty / [by] Barbara Cartland. — London : Arrow Books, 1977. — 204p ; 18cm.
ISBN 0-09-914940-0 Pbk : £0.50
(B77-31445)

Cartland, Barbara. Love in pity / [by] Barbara Cartland. — London : Arrow Books, 1977. — 208p ; 18cm.
ISBN 0-09-913350-4 Pbk : £0.50
(B77-10547)

Cartland, Barbara. Love is innocent / [by] Barbara Cartland. — London : Arrow Books, 1977. — 188p ; 18cm.
Originally published: London : Hutchinson, 1975.
ISBN 0-09-915140-5 Pbk : £0.50
(B77-20583)

Cartland, Barbara. Love locked in / [by] Barbara Cartland. — London [etc.] : Pan Books, 1977. — 157p ; 18cm.
ISBN 0-330-25089-2 Pbk : £0.50
(B77-20584)

Cartland, Barbara. Love on the run / [by] Barbara Cartland. — London : Arrow Books, 1977. — 192p ; 18cm.
Originally published: under the name Barbara McCorquodale. London : Ward Lock, 1965.
ISBN 0-09-915210-x Pbk : £0.50
(B77-21423)

Cartland, Barbara. The magic of love / [by] Barbara Cartland. — London [etc.] : Pan Books, 1977. — 155p ; 18cm.
ISBN 0-330-25045-0 Pbk : £0.50
(B77-12089)

Cartland, Barbara. The magnificent marriage / [by] Barbara Cartland. — London [etc.] : Hurst and Blackett, 1977. — 191p ; 20cm.
Originally published: London : Corgi, 1974.
ISBN 0-09-131180-2 : £3.50
(B77-27373)

Cartland, Barbara. The marquis who hated women / [by] Barbara Cartland. — London [etc.] : Pan Books, 1977. — 157p ; 18cm.
ISBN 0-330-25168-6 Pbk : £0.50
(B77-25876)

Cartland, Barbara. The mysterious maid-servant / [by] Barbara Cartland. — London : Hutchinson, 1977. — 175p ; 20cm.
ISBN 0-09-128230-6 : £3.50
(B77-06278)

Cartland, Barbara. The outrageous lady / [by] Barbara Cartland. — London [etc.] : Pan Books, 1977. — 155p ; 18cm.
ISBN 0-330-25260-7 Pbk : £0.50
(B77-31446)

Cartland, Barbara. The passionate pilgrim / [by] Barbara Cartland. — London : Arrow Books, 1977. — 256p ; 18cm.
Originally published: London : Rich and Cowan, 1952.
ISBN 0-09-915330-0 Pbk : £0.50
(B77-34093)

Cartland, Barbara. The reluctant bride / [by] Barbara Cartland. — London : Arrow Books, 1977. — 223p ; 18cm.
Originally published: London : Hutchinson, 1970.
ISBN 0-09-908590-9 Pbk : £0.50
(B77-31447)

Cartland, Barbara. The reluctant bride / [by] Barbara Cartland. — London : Arrow Books, 1977. — 223p ; 18cm.
Originally published: London : Hutchinson, 1970.
Pbk : £0.50
ISBN 0-09-908590-9
(B77-32848)

Cartland, Barbara. A rhapsody of love / [by] Barbara Cartland. — London [etc.] : Pan Books, 1977. — 157p ; 18cm.
ISBN 0-330-25169-4 Pbk : £0.50
(B77-26514)

Cartland, Barbara. The shadow of sin / [by] Barbara Cartland. — London : Hurst and Blackett, 1977. — 184p ; 20cm.
Originally published: London : Corgi, 1975.
ISBN 0-09-128970-x : £3.25
(B77-19655)

Cartland, Barbara. A sword to the heart / [by] Barbara Cartland. — London [etc.] : Hurst and Blackett, 1977. — 191p ; 20cm.
Originally published: London : Corgi, 1975.
ISBN 0-09-131170-5 : £3.50
(B77-27374)

Cartland, Barbara. The taming of Lady Lorinda / [by] Barbara Cartland. — London [etc.] : Pan Books, 1977. — 155p ; 18cm.
ISBN 0-330-25028-0 Pbk : £0.50
(B77-12090)

Cartland, Barbara. This time it's love / [by] Barbara Cartland. — London : Arrow Books, 1977. — 190p ; 18cm.
ISBN 0-09-915870-1 Pbk : £0.50
(B77-29685)

Cartland, Barbara. The unpredictable bride / [by] Barbara Cartland. — London [etc.] : Arrow Books, 1976. — 192p ; 18cm.
Originally published: London : Hutchinson, 1964.
Pbk : £0.50
ISBN 0-09-908110-5
(B77-03756)

Cartland, Barbara. Vote for love / [by] Barbara Cartland. — London : Corgi, 1977. — 142p ; 18cm.
ISBN 0-552-10404-3 Pbk : £0.50
(B77-16049)

Cartland, Barbara. The wild, unwilling wife / [by] Barbara Cartland. — London [etc.] : Pan Books, 1977. — 156p ; 18cm.
ISBN 0-330-25172-4 Pbk : £0.50
(B77-28882)

Cartwright, Justin. Fighting men / [by] Justin Cartwright ; based on an original script by Brian Clemens. — London : A. Barker, 1977. — 159p ; 23cm. — (The new avengers)
ISBN 0-213-16642-9 : £3.75
(B77-20585)

Carvic, Heron. Odds on Miss Seeton / [by] Heron Carvic. — Large print ed. — London : Prior [etc.], 1976. — [7],303p ; 24cm.
Originally published: New York : Harper and Row, 1975 ; London : P. Davies, 1976.
ISBN 0-86043-012-x : £4.95
(B77-07593)

Casey, Kevin. Dreams of revenge / [by] Kevin Casey. — London : Faber, 1977. — [6],135p ; 21cm.
ISBN 0-571-11049-5 : £3.25
(B77-08037)

Cassady, Claude. The hideout / by Claude Cassady. — London : Hale, 1977. — 158p ; 20cm.
ISBN 0-7091-6442-4 : £3.10
(B77-28883)

Castle, Brenda. Interlude in Sardinia / by Brenda Castle. — London : Hale, 1977. — 157p ; 20cm.
ISBN 0-7091-6367-3 : £3.40
(B77-30608)

Castle, Brenda. The man from Amsterdam / by Brenda Castle. — London : Hale, 1976. — 155p ; 20cm.
ISBN 0-7091-5820-3 : £2.95
(B77-00413)

Castle, Brenda. Tarnished hero / by Brenda Castle. — London : Hale, 1977. — 176p ; 20cm.
ISBN 0-7091-6154-9 : £3.20
(B77-22117)

Castle, Frank. Dakota boomtown / [by] Frank Castle. — Large print ed. — Leicester : Ulverscroft, 1977. — [5],352p ; 23cm. — (Ulverscroft large print series : [Western])
Originally published: New York : Fawcett, 1958 ; London : White Lion Publishers, 1974.
ISBN 0-85456-544-2 : £2.95
(B77-21424)

Catherall, Arthur. Death of an oil rig / [by] Arthur Catherall ; illustrated by Geoffrey Whittam. — London [etc.] : White Lion Publishers, 1976. — 172p : ill ; 21cm.
Originally published: London : Dent, 1967.
ISBN 0-85686-211-8 : £2.75
(B77-00414)

Cato, Nancy. Brown sugar / [by] Nancy Cato. — London : Pan Books, 1977. — 256p : geneal table ; 18cm.
Originally published: London : Heinemann, 1974.
ISBN 0-330-25003-5 Pbk : £0.70
(B77-06861)

Catto, Max. The empty tiger / [by] Max Catto. — London : Joseph, 1977. — 224p ; 21cm.
ISBN 0-7181-1618-6 : £4.25
(B77-27375)

Catto, Max. I have friends in heaven / [by] Max Catto. — London [etc.] : White Lion Publishers, 1977. — [4],201p ; 21cm.
Originally published: London : Heinemann, 1965.
ISBN 0-7274-0262-5 : £4.25
(B77-33426)

Catto, Max. King oil / [by] Max Catto. — London [etc.] : White Lion Publishers, 1977. — £3.50.
Originally published: New York : Simon and Schuster ; London : Heinemann, 1970.
ISBN 0-7274-0257-9
(B77-05645)

Cave, Emma. Little Angie / [by] Emma Cave. — London : Deutsch, 1977. — 205p ; 21cm.
ISBN 0-233-96910-1 : £3.50
(B77-20586)

Cave, Peter. The crime commandos / [by] Peter Cave. — London : Everest, 1976. — 173p ; 18cm.
ISBN 0-903925-98-2 Pbk : £0.50
(B77-05646)

Cave, Peter. House of cards / [by] Peter Cave. — London : Barker, 1977. — 160p ; 23cm. — (The new avengers)
ISBN 0-213-16636-4 : £3.75
(B77-12645)

Cavendish, Clare. Doctor in charge / by Clare Cavendish. — London : Hale, 1977. — 192p ; 20cm.
ISBN 0-7091-6241-3 : £3.20
(B77-19656)

Cecil, Henry, *b.1902.* Friends at court / [by] Henry Cecil. — Large print ed. — Bath : Chivers, 1977. — [5],314p ; 22cm.
Originally published: London : Joseph, 1956.
ISBN 0-85997-234-8 : £5.60(£4.20 to members of the Library Association)
(B77-21425)

Cecil, Henry, *b.1902.* Hunt the slipper / [by] Henry Cecil. — London : Joseph, 1977. — 151p ; 21cm.
ISBN 0-7181-1578-3 : £3.75
(B77-08551)

Cecil, Henry, *b.1902.* Independent witness / by Henry Cecil. — Hornchurch : I. Henry, 1977. — 172p ; 21cm.
Originally published: London : Joseph, 1963.
ISBN 0-86025-116-0 : £3.25
(B77-34094)

Chace, Isobel. A canopy of rose leaves / by Isobel Chace. — London : Mills and Boon, 1976. — 188p ; 19cm.
ISBN 0-263-09040-x : £1.95
(B77-12646)

Chace, Isobel. The clouded veil / by Isobel Chace. — London : Mills and Boon, 1976. — 186p ; 19cm.
ISBN 0-263-09016-7 : £1.95
(B77-10548)

Chace, Isobel. The flamboyant tree / by Isobel Chace. — London : Mills and Boon, 1976. — 192p ; 18cm.
Originally published: 1972.
ISBN 0-263-72333-x Pbk : £0.30
(B77-00958)

Chance, John Newton. The frightened fisherman / by John Newton Chance. — London : Hale, 1977. — 176p ; 20cm.
ISBN 0-7091-5760-6 : £3.25
(B77-21426)

Chance, John Newton. The house of the dead ones / by John Newton Chance. — London : Hale, 1977. — 175p ; 20cm.
ISBN 0-7091-5624-3 : £3.15
(B77-13857)

Chance, John Newton. The mists of treason / [by] John Newton Chance. — Large print ed. — Bath : Lythway Press, 1977. — 202p ; 22cm.
Originally published: London : Hale, 1970.
ISBN 0-85046-732-2 Pbk : £2.20
(B77-32157)

Chandler, Arthur Bertram. Star courier / [by] A. Bertram Chandler. — London : Hale, 1977. — 159p ; 21cm. — (Hale SF)
ISBN 0-7091-6073-9 : £3.60
(B77-28884)

Chandler, Raymond. The big sleep ; [and], The high window ; [and], The lady in the lake ; [and], The long goodbye ; [and], Playback ; [and], Farewell my lovely / [by] Raymond Chandler. — London : Heinemann : Secker and Warburg : Octopus Books, 1977. — 3-862p ; 25cm.
ISBN 0-905712-14-5 : £4.95
(B77-29686)

Chandler, Raymond. The notebooks of Raymond Chandler ; and, English summer : a gothic romance / by Raymond Chandler ; illustrated by Edward Gorey ; edited by Frank MacShane. — London : Weidenfeld and Nicolson, 1977. — [7],113p : ill, facsims, ports ; 24cm.
This collection originally published: New York : Ecco Press, 1976.
ISBN 0-297-77430-1 : £4.50
Primary classification 813'.5'2
(B77-32122)

Chaney, Jill. The buttercup field / [by] Jill Chaney. — London : Dobson, 1976. — 152p ; 21cm.
For adolescents.
ISBN 0-234-77654-4 : £2.50
(B77-00959)

Chant, Joy. The grey mane of morning / by Joy Chant. — London : Allen and Unwin, 1977. — 3-262p ; 23cm.
ISBN 0-04-823137-1 : £3.95
(B77-24474)

Chapdelaine, Perry Anthony. The laughing terran / [by] Perry A. Chapdelaine. — London : Hale, 1977. — 176p ; 21cm. — (Hale SF)
ISBN 0-7091-5892-0 : £3.25
(B77-09936)

Chapdelaine, Perry Anthony. Swampworld west / [by] Perry A. Chapdelaine. — London : Coronet, 1976. — 191p ; 18cm.
Originally published: Morley : Elmfield Press, 1974.
ISBN 0-340-20814-7 Pbk : £0.70
(B77-00960)

Chaplin, Patrice. By Flower and Dean Street ; &, The love apple / [by] Patrice Chaplin. — London : Duckworth, 1976. — [4],159p ; 23cm.

ISBN 0-7156-1113-5 : £3.25
(B77-00415)

Chaplin, Patrice. Having it away / [by] Patrice Chaplin. — London : Duckworth, 1977. — 126p ; 23cm.
ISBN 0-7156-1274-3 : £3.95
(B77-30609)

Chappell, Mollie. Country air / [by] Mollie Chappell. — London : Collins, 1977. — 160p ; 20cm.
ISBN 0-00-233118-7 : £2.75
(B77-17082)

Chappell, Mollie. The loving heart / [by] Mollie Chappell. — London : Collins, 1977. — 260p ; 19cm.
ISBN 0-00-233477-1 : £2.95
(B77-26515)

Chappell, Mollie. Seton's wife / [by] Mollie Chappell. — London : Collins, 1975. — 159p ; 19cm.
ISBN 0-00-233755-x : £1.25
(B77-06279)

Chard, Brigid. Ferret summer / [by] Brigid Chard. — London : Collings, 1975. — [5], 135p ; 21cm.
ISBN 0-901720-70-4 : £2.50
(B77-19657)

Chard, Judy. The other side of sorrow / by Judy Chard. — London : Hale, 1977. — 154p ; 20cm.
ISBN 0-7091-6104-2 : £3.20
(B77-20587)

Charles, Robert. The prey of the falcon : a counter-terror dossier / [by] Robert Charles. — London : Hale, 1977. — 185p ; 21cm.
ISBN 0-7091-5537-9 : £3.50
(B77-13256)

Charles, Robert. The snarl of the lynx / by Robert Charles. — London : Hale, 1977. — 190p ; 21cm.
ISBN 0-7091-6169-7 : £3.70
(B77-28106)

Charles, Robert. The venom of The Cobra / [by] Robert Charles. — London : Hale, 1977. — 192p ; 21cm.
ISBN 0-7091-5720-7 : £3.70
(B77-34095)

Charles, Theresa. Crisis at St Chad's / by Theresa Charles. — London : Hale, 1977. — 160p ; 20cm.
ISBN 0-7091-6185-9 : £3.20
(B77-22853)

Charles, Theresa. Fairer than she / [by] Theresa Charles. — Large print ed. — Bath : Lythway Press, 1977. — [5],430p ; 23cm.
Originally published: London : Cassell, 1953.
ISBN 0-85046-710-1 : £4.85
(B77-20588)

Charles, Theresa. Rainbow after rain / by Theresa Charles. — London : Hale, 1977. — 160p ; 20cm.
ISBN 0-7091-5970-6 : £3.10
(B77-14907)

Charteris, Leslie. The Saint in Miami / [by] Leslie Charteris. — London [etc.] : White Lion Publishers, 1976. — 190p ; 21cm.
Originally published: Garden City, N.Y. : Doubleday, 1940 ; London : Hodder and Stoughton, 1941.
ISBN 0-7274-0134-3 : £3.25
(B77-00416)

Chase, James Hadley. But a short time to live / [by] James Hadley Chase. — London : Corgi, 1977. — 190p ; 18cm.
Originally published: under the name Raymond Marshall. London : Jarrolds, 1951.
ISBN 0-552-10477-9 Pbk : £0.65
(B77-26516)

Chase, James Hadley. Do me a favour, drop dead / [by] James Hadley Chase. — London : Corgi, 1977. — 173p ; 18cm.
Originally published: London : Hale, 1976.
ISBN 0-552-10574-0 Pbk : £0.65
(B77-30610)

Chase, James Hadley. I hold the four aces / [by] James Hadley Chase. — London : Hale, 1977. — 189p ; 21cm.
ISBN 0-7091-5634-0 : £3.25
(B77-14399)

Chase, James Hadley. In a vain shadow / [by] James Hadley Chase. — London : Hale, 1977. — 190p ; 21cm.
Originally published: under the name Raymond Marshall. London : Jarrolds, 1951.
ISBN 0-7091-6346-0 : £3.25
(B77-28885)

Chase, James Hadley. The joker in the pack / [by] James Hadley Chase. — London : Corgi, 1977. — 175p ; 18cm.
Originally published: London : Hale, 1975.
ISBN 0-552-10426-4 Pbk : £0.60
(B77-18981)

Chase, James Hadley. Lady here's your wreath / [by] James Hadley Chase. — London : Corgi, 1977. — 160p ; 18cm.
Originally published: under the name Raymond Marshall. London : Jarrolds, 1940.
ISBN 0-552-10328-4 Pbk : £0.60
(B77-13257)

Chase, James Hadley. Meet Mark Girland / [by] James Hadley Chase. — London : Hale, 1977. — 569p in various pagings ; 21cm.
Contents: This is for real. Originally published: 1965 - You have yourself a deal. Originally published: 1966 - Have this one on me. Originally published: 1967.
ISBN 0-7091-5818-1 : £4.95
(B77-21427)

Chase, James Hadley. Miss Shumway waves a wand / [by] James Hadley Chase. — London : Corgi, 1977. — 221p ; 18cm.
Originally published: London : Jarrolds, 1944.
ISBN 0-552-10381-0 Pbk : £0.65
(B77-18982)

Chase, James Hadley. Mission to Venice / [by] James Hadley Chase. — London : Hale, 1977. — 192p ; 21cm.
Originally published: under the name Raymond Marshall. 1954.
ISBN 0-7091-6390-8 : £3.50
(B77-30611)

Chase, James Hadley. My laugh comes last / [by] James Hadley Chase. — London : Hale, 1977. — 190p ; 21cm.
ISBN 0-7091-6119-0 : £3.70
(B77-28107)

Chase, James Hadley. No orchids for Miss Blandish / [by] James Hadley Chase. — London : Corgi, 1977. — 189p ; 18cm.
Originally published: London : Jarrolds, 1939.
ISBN 0-552-10522-8 Pbk : £0.60
(B77-26517)

Chase, James Hadley. The sucker punch / [by] James Hadley Chase. — London : Corgi, 1977. — 204p ; 18cm.
Originally published: under the name Raymond Marshall. London : Jarrolds, 1954.
ISBN 0-552-10575-9 Pbk : £0.65
(B77-30612)

Chase, James Hadley. There's always a price tag / [by] James Hadley Chase. — London : Hale, 1977. — 254p ; 21cm.
Originally published: 1956.
ISBN 0-7091-6389-4 : £3.50
(B77-30613)

Chase, James Hadley. Trusted like the fox / [by] James Hadley Chase. — London : Hale, 1977. — 192p ; 21cm.
Originally published: under the name Raymond Marshall. London : Jarrolds, 1948.
ISBN 0-7091-6349-5 : £3.25
(B77-28108)

Chase, James Hadley. You never know with women / [by] James Hadley Chase. — London : Corgi, 1976. — 190p ; 18cm.
Originally published: London : Jarrolds, 1949.
ISBN 0-552-10276-8 Pbk : £0.60
(B77-04401)

Chastain, Thomas. The Christmas bomber : a novel / by Thomas Chastain. — London [etc.] : Cassell, 1976. — [5],227p : ill ; 23cm.
Originally published: as '911'. New York : Mason-Charter, 1976.
ISBN 0-304-29759-3 : £3.95
(B77-07594)

Cheever, John. Falconer / [by] John Cheever. — London : Cape, 1977. — [5],211p ; 21cm.
Also published: New York : Knopf, 1977.
ISBN 0-224-01401-3 : £3.95 : CIP rev.
(B77-12091)

Chester, Charlie. Overture to anthem / [by] Charlie Chester. — London : New English Library, 1977. — 218p ; 21cm.
ISBN 0-450-03444-5 : £4.95
(B77-32158)

Chester, Roy. The Damocles factor / [by] Roy Chester. — London : Long, 1977. — 183p ; 19cm.
ISBN 0-09-131840-8 : £3.50
(B77-30614)

Childers, Erskine. The riddle of the sands : a record of secret service / by Erskine Childers. — [1st ed. reprinted] ; foreword by Erskine Hamilton Childers ; introduction by the Earl of Longford. — London : Sidgwick and Jackson, 1977. — 287p : map ; 18cm.
Originally published: London : Smith, Elder, 1903.
ISBN 0-283-98420-1 Pbk : £0.95
(B77-34096)

Chilson, Robert. The shores of Kansas / by Robert Chilson. — London : Hale, 1977. — 220p ; 21cm. — (Hale SF)
Originally published: United States: s.n., 1976.
ISBN 0-7091-6417-3 : £3.60
(B77-28109)

Chisholm, Mary Mackellar. The clown in the windmill / [by] Mary Mackellar Chisholm. — London : Corgi, 1977. — 156p ; 18cm.
ISBN 0-552-10504-x Pbk : £0.50
(B77-21428)

Chisholm, Matt. Kill McAllister / [by] Matt Chisholm. — St Albans : Mayflower, 1977. — 142p ; 18cm.
Originally published: London : Panther, 1969.
ISBN 0-583-12683-9 Pbk : £0.50
(B77-27376)

Chisholm, Matt. McAllister / [by] Matt Chisholm. — St Albans : Mayflower, 1977. — 123p ; 18cm.
Originally published: 1963.
ISBN 0-583-12679-0 Pbk : £0.40
(B77-08038)

Chisholm, Matt. McAllister strikes / [by] Matt Chisholm. — St Albans : Mayflower, 1977. — 127p ; 18cm.
Originally published: as 'The last gun'. London : Panther Books, 1966.
ISBN 0-583-12680-4 Pbk : £0.40
(B77-12647)

Chisholm, Matt. Tough to kill / [by] Matt Chisholm. — St Albans : Mayflower, 1977. — 140p ; 18cm.
Originally published: London : Panther, 1968.
ISBN 0-583-12682-0 Pbk : £0.50
(B77-25190)

Christie, *Dame* Agatha. Appointment with death / [by] Agatha Christie. — [London] : Fontana, 1977. — 160p ; 18cm.
Originally published: New York : Dodd, Mead, 1938 ; London : Collins for the Crime Club, 1939.
ISBN 0-00-614045-9 : £0.65
(B77-30615)

Christie, *Dame* Agatha. At Bertram's Hotel / [by] Agatha Christie. — The Greenway ed. — London : Collins for the Crime Club, 1977. — 3-253p ; 21cm.
Originally published: 1965.
ISBN 0-00-231001-5 : £2.95
(B77-24475)

Christie, *Dame* Agatha. Curtain : Poirot's last case / [by] Agatha Christie. — [London] : Fontana, 1977. — 188p ; 18cm.
Originally published: London : Collins, 1975.
ISBN 0-00-614277-x Pbk : £0.70
(B77-30616)

Christie, *Dame* Agatha. Curtain : Poirot's last case / [by] Agatha Christie. — Large print ed. — Leicester : Ulverscroft, 1976. — [4],325p ; 23cm. — (Ulverscroft large print series : [mystery])
Originally published: London : Collins, 1975.
ISBN 0-85456-498-5 : £2.65
(B77-08552)

Christie, *Dame* Agatha. Destination unknown / [by] Agatha Christie. — Greenway ed. — London : Collins for the Crime Club, 1977. — 192p ; 21cm.
Originally published: 1954.
ISBN 0-00-231089-9 : £3.00
(B77-33427)

Christie, *Dame* Agatha. Evil under the sun / [by] Agatha Christie. — [London] : Fontana, 1977. — 189p : map ; 18cm.
Originally published: London : Collins, 1941.
ISBN 0-00-613982-5 Pbk : £0.65
(B77-15490)

Christie, *Dame* Agatha. The hollow / [by] Agatha Christie. — London [etc.] : Pan Books, 1975. — 219p ; 18cm.
Originally published: London : Collins, 1946.
ISBN 0-330-24431-0 Pbk : £0.60
(B77-07595)

Christie, *Dame* Agatha. Murder is easy / [by] Agatha Christie. — [London] : Fontana, 1977. — 190p ; 18cm.
Originally published: London : Collins, 1939.
ISBN 0-00-614657-0 Pbk : £0.65
(B77-21429)

Christie, *Dame* Agatha. The murder of Roger Ackroyd / [by] Agatha Christie. — Greenway ed. — London : Collins for the Crime Club, 1976. — 288p ; 21cm.
This ed. orginally published: 1967.
ISBN 0-00-231509-2 : £3.00
(B77-17083)

Christie, *Dame* Agatha. The murder on the links / [by] Agatha Christie. — Large print ed. — Leicester : Ulverscroft, 1977. — [4],349p ; 23cm. — (Ulverscroft large print series : [mystery])
Originally published: London : Lane, 1923.
ISBN 0-85456-516-7 : £2.65
(B77-13858)

Christie, *Dame* Agatha. The mysterious Mr Quin / [by] Agatha Christie. — Large print ed. — Leicester : Ulverscroft, 1977. — [10],457p ; 23cm. — (Ulverscroft large print series : [mystery])
Originally published: New York : Dodd, Mead ; London : Collins, 1930.
ISBN 0-85456-546-9 : £2.95
(B77-29687)

Christie, *Dame* Agatha. Ordeal by innocence / [by] Agatha Christie. — [London] : Fontana, 1977. — 192p ; 18cm.
Originally published: London : Collins, 1958.
ISBN 0-00-614629-5 Pbk : £0.65
(B77-22118)

Christie, *Dame* Agatha. Postern of fate / [by] Agatha Christie. — Glasgow : Collins, 1976. — 221p ; 18cm.
Originally published: 1973.
ISBN 0-00-614255-9 Pbk : £0.60
(B77-07596)

Christie, *Dame* Agatha. Sparkling cyanide / [by] Agatha Christie. — London : Pan Books, 1977. — 189p ; 18cm.
Originally published: London : Collins, 1945.
ISBN 0-330-25236-4 Pbk : £0.60
(B77-22119)

Christie, *Dame* Agatha. Ten little niggers / [by] Agatha Christie. — Greenway ed. — London : Collins for the Crime Club, 1977. — 252p ; 21cm.
Originally published: 1939.
ISBN 0-00-231835-0 : £3.50
(B77-34097)

Christie, *Dame* Agatha. They came to Baghdad / [by] Agatha Christie. — [London[: Fontana, 1977. — 192p ; 18cm.
Originally published: London : Collins, 1951.
ISBN 0-00-615034-9 Pbk : £0.70
(B77-30617)

Christie, *Dame* Agatha. Third girl / [by] Agatha Christie. — [London] : Fontana, 1977. — 190p ; 18cm.
Originally published: London : Collins, 1966.
ISBN 0-00-615119-1 Pbk : £0.70
(B77-30618)

Christie, *Dame* Agatha. Towards zero / [by] Agatha Christie. — Harmondsworth [etc.] : Penguin, [1977]. — 192p : map ; 18cm. — (Penguin crime fiction)
Originally published: London : Collins, 1944.
ISBN 0-14-004213-x Pbk : £0.60
(B77-07597)

Christopher, John, *b.1922.* Empty world / [by] John Christopher. — London : Hamilton, 1977. — [5],134p ; 23cm.
ISBN 0-241-89751-3 : £3.25
(B77-28110)

Christopher, Kate. A nest of serpents / by Kate Christopher. — London : Gollancz, 1977. — 352p ; 21cm.
Based on the life of Sir Thomas Overbury.
ISBN 0-575-02330-9 : £4.95
(B77-28886)

Church, Richard. The porch / [by] Richard Church. — Bath : Chivers, 1976. — 355p ; 19cm.
Originally published: London : Dent, 1937.
ISBN 0-85997-227-5 : £5.80(£4.35 to members of the Library Association)
(B77-06280)

Church, Richard. The room within / [by] Richard Church. — Bath : Chivers, 1977. — 399p ; 19cm.
Originally published: London : Dent, 1940.
ISBN 0-85997-239-9 : £5.80(£4.35 to members of the Library Association)
(B77-16050)

Church, Richard. The stronghold / [by] Richard Church. — Bath : Chivers, 1976. — [8],360p ; 19cm.
Originally published: London : Dent, 1939.
ISBN 0-85997-228-3 : £5.80(£4.35 to members of the Library Association)
(B77-06281)

Churchill, Rosemary. Conflict for a crown : the story of King Edward VI's reign / by Rosemary Churchill. — London : Hale, 1977. — 206p ; 21cm.
ISBN 0-7091-5829-7 : £3.25
(B77-09937)

Churchward, John. The rainbow deaths : a novel / by John Churchward. — London : New English Library, 1977. — 192p ; 21cm.
ISBN 0-450-03082-2 : £4.50
ISBN 0-450-03371-6 Pbk : £0.75
(B77-13258)

Churchward, John. What beck'ning ghost? / [by] John Churchward. — London : New English Library, 1977. — [6],199p ; 18cm.
Originally published: 1975.
ISBN 0-450-02972-7 Pbk : £0.85
(B77-13859)

Clare, Elizabeth. Down by the willows / by Elizabeth Clare. — London : Hale, 1977. — 159p ; 20cm.
ISBN 0-7091-5971-4 : £3.10
(B77-17084)

Clark, Badger. Cow-country killer / by Badger Clark. — London : Hale, 1976. — 151p ; 20cm.
ISBN 0-7091-5591-3 : £2.70
(B77-01788)

Clark, Badger. Secret Mesa / by Badger Clark. — London : Hale, 1977. — 158p ; 20cm.
ISBN 0-7091-6243-x : £3.10
(B77-22854)

Clark, Douglas. The gimmel flask / by Douglas Clark. — London : Gollancz, 1977. — 175p ; 21cm. — ([Gollancz detection])
ISBN 0-575-02332-5 : £3.75
(B77-27377)

Clark, Douglas. Table d'hote / by Douglas Clark. — London : Gollancz, 1977. — 189p ; 21cm. — ([Gollancz detection])
ISBN 0-575-02238-8 : £3.80
(B77-07598)

Clarke, Anna. The lady in black / [by] Anna Clarke. — London : Collins for the Crime Club, 1977. — 193p ; 21cm.
Bibl.: p.192-193. — Based on the lives of George Meredith and Frederic Chapman.
ISBN 0-00-231449-5 : £2.95
(B77-09938)

Clarke, Anna. Letter from the dead / [by] Anna Clarke. — London : Collins [for] the Crime Club, 1977. — 180p ; 21cm.
ISBN 0-00-231476-2 : £3.25
(B77-28111)

Clarke, Arthur Charles. Childhood's end / [by] Arthur C. Clarke. — London [etc.] : Pan Books, 1977. — 189p ; 18cm. — (Pan science fiction)
Originally published: New York : Ballantine Books, 1953 ; London : Sidgwick and Jackson, 1954.
ISBN 0-330-10573-6 Pbk : £0.60
(B77-25877)

Clarke, Arthur Charles. The deep range / [by] Arthur C. Clarke. — London [etc.] : Pan Books, 1976. — 204p ; 18cm. — (Pan science fiction)
Originally published: New York : Harcourt, Brace ; London : Muller, 1957.
Pbk : £0.70
ISBN 0-330-02570-8
(B77-34098)

Clarke, Arthur Charles. Imperial earth : a fantasy of love and discord / [by] Arthur C. Clarke. — London [etc.] : Pan Books, 1977. — 287p : 1 ill ; 18cm.
Originally published: London : Gollancz, 1975.
ISBN 0-330-25004-3 Pbk : £0.75
(B77-20589)

Clarke, Roy. Last of the summer wine / [by] Roy Clarke. — London : Severn House : [Distributed by Hutchinson], 1977. — 160p ; 21cm.
Originally published: London : Coronet, 1974.
ISBN 0-7278-0291-7 : £3.25
(B77-25878)

Clarke, Thomas Ernest Bennett. The man who seduced a bank / [by] T.E.B. Clarke. — London : Joseph, 1977. — 224p ; 21cm.
ISBN 0-7181-1621-6 : £4.25
(B77-20590)

Clavell, James. Sh¯ogun / [by] James Clavell. — Sevenoaks : Coronet, 1976. — 1243,[2]p ; 18cm.
Originally published: London : Hodder and Stoughton, 1975.
ISBN 0-340-20917-8 Pbk : £1.93
(B77-00961)

Cleary, Beverly. Fifteen / by Beverly Cleary. — Harmondsworth [etc.] : Puffin Books, 1977. — 175p ; 18cm. — (Puffin books)
Originally published: New York : Morrow, 1956 ; Harmondsworth : Penguin : 1962. — For adolescents.
ISBN 0-14-030948-9 Pbk : £0.50
(B77-14908)

Cleary, Jon. The fall of an eagle / [by] Jon Cleary. — Large print ed. — Bath : Chivers, 1977. — [7],399p ; 23cm.
Originally published: New York : Morrow, 1964 ; London : Collins, 1965.
ISBN 0-85997-235-6 : £5.60(£4.20 to members of the Library Association)
(B77-22855)

Cleary, Jon. A flight of chariots / [by] Jon Cleary. — London : Fontana, 1977. — 348p ; 18cm.
Originally published: London : Collins, 1964.
ISBN 0-00-614587-6 Pbk : £0.80
(B77-30619)

Cleary, Jon. High road to China : a novel / by Jon Cleary. — London : Collins, 1977. — 276p ; 22cm.
ISBN 0-00-222002-4 : £3.50
(B77-07599)

Cleary, Jon. Peter's pence / [by] Jon Cleary. — [London] : Fontana, 1977. — 253p ; 18cm.
Originally published: London : Collins, 1974.
ISBN 0-00-614428-4 Pbk : £0.75
(B77-30620)

Cleeve, Brian Talbot. Kate / [by] Brian Cleeve. — London : Cassell, 1977. — [2],345p ; 21cm.
ISBN 0-304-29753-4 : £3.95
(B77-22856)

Cleeve, Brian Talbot. Sara / [by] Brian Cleeve. — Sevenoaks : Coronet, 1977. — 320p ; 18cm.
Originally published: London : Cassell, 1976.
ISBN 0-340-22494-0 Pbk : £1.25
(B77-34099)

Clegg, Michael. Porpoise song / [by] Michael Clegg ; illustrated by Susan O'Carroll. — London : Macdonald and Jane's, 1977. — [5], 119p : ill ; 23cm.
ISBN 0-354-08021-0 : £3.25
(B77-13259)

Clewes, Dorothy. Merry-go-round / [by] Dorothy Clewes. — London [etc.] : White Lion Publishers, 1977. — 190p ; 21cm.
Originally published: London : Hodder and Stoughton, 1954.
ISBN 0-7274-0241-2 : £3.50
(B77-12092)

Clews, Roy. Young Jethro / [by] Roy Clews. — London : Corgi, 1977. — 270p ; 18cm.
Originally published: London : Heinemann, 1975.
ISBN 0-552-10363-2 Pbk : £0.75
(B77-09254)

Clifford, Francis. Drummer in the dark / [by] Francis Clifford. — London : Coronet, 1977. — 175p ; 18cm.
Originally published: London : Hodder and Stoughton, 1976.
ISBN 0-340-21818-5 Pbk : £0.70
(B77-25191)

Clifford, Francis. The green fields of Eden / [by] Francis Clifford. — London [etc.] : Hodder and Stoughton, 1977. — 207p ; 21cm.
Originally published: 1963.
ISBN 0-340-21597-6 : £3.95
(B77-19658)

Clifford, Francis. Overdue / [by] Francis Clifford. — London [etc.] : Hodder and Stoughton, 1977. — 221p ; 21cm.
Originally published: London : Hamilton, 1957.
ISBN 0-340-21598-4 : £3.95
(B77-19659)

Climie, David. Backs to the land / [by] David Climie. — London : Pan Books, 1977. — 192p ; 18cm.
'Based on the new Anglia Television series'.
ISBN 0-330-25241-0 Pbk : £0.60
(B77-20591)

Clive, William. Fighting Mac : the climb to disaster of Sir Hector Macdonald, KCB, DSO, 1853-1903 / [by] William Clive. — London [etc.] : Macmillan, 1977. — 3-305p ; 21cm.
Bibl.: p.303-305.
ISBN 0-333-21148-0 : £3.95
(B77-07600)

Clive, William. The tune that they play / [by] William Clive. — London : Sphere, 1977. — 188p ; 18cm.
Originally published: London : Macmillan, 1973. — Bibl.: p.187.
ISBN 0-7221-2428-7 Pbk : £0.65
(B77-09939)

Cloete, Stuart. The abductors / [by] Stuart Cloete. — London : Fontana, 1977. — 479p : ill ; 18cm.
Originally published: New York : Simon & Schuster, 1966 ; London : Collins, 1970. — Bibl.: p.475-479.
ISBN 0-00-614769-0 Pbk : £0.95
(B77-18367)

Clute, John. The disinheriting party : a novel / by John Clute. — London : Allison and Busby, 1977. — 144p ; 23cm.
ISBN 0-85031-134-9 : £4.50
ISBN 0-85031-195-0 Pbk : £1.95
(B77-31448)

Clydesdale, Abby. Sign of the witch / [by] Abby Clydesdale. — London : Hale, 1977. — 205p ; 21cm.
ISBN 0-7091-6101-8 : £3.70
(B77-26518)

Coburn, L J. The first shot / [by] L.J. Coburn. — London : Sphere, 1977. — 142p ; 18cm. — (Coburn, L J. Caleb Thorn ; 1)
ISBN 0-7221-2462-7 Pbk : £0.65
(B77-21430)

Coburn, L J. The raiders / [by] L.J. Coburn. — London : Sphere, 1977. — 141p ; 18cm. — (Coburn, L J. Caleb Thorn ; 2)
ISBN 0-7221-2463-5 Pbk : £0.65
(B77-32159)

Cochrane, Ian. A streak of madness / [by] Ian Cochrane. — Harmondsworth [etc.] : Penguin, 1977. — 170p ; 18cm.
Originally published: London : Allen Lane, 1973.
ISBN 0-14-004295-4 Pbk : £0.70
(B77-25192)

Cockain, Frank. The inside out man / [by] Frank Cockain. — London : Futura Publications, 1975. — 252p ; 18cm.
ISBN 0-86007-208-8 Pbk : £0.65
(B77-08039)

Coetzee, J M. In the heart of the country / [by] J.M. Coetzee. — London : Secker and Warburg, 1977. — [4],139p ; 23cm.
'Sections 85-94 have appeared in South Africa in the magazine "Standpunte 124", August 1976' - title page verso.
ISBN 0-436-25670-3 : £3.50
(B77-23718)

Cogswell, Theodore R. Spock Messiah / by Theodore R. Cogswell and Charles A. Spano, Jr ; based on the television series created by Gene Roddenberry. — London : Corgi, 1977. — [5],182p ; 18cm.
Cover title: Startrek, Spock Messiah. — Originally published: New York : Bantam, 1976.
ISBN 0-552-10281-4 Pbk : £0.60
(B77-08040)

Cohn, Nik. King Death / [by] Nik Cohn. — London : Pan Books, 1977. — 125p ; 20cm. — (Picador)
Originally published: New York : Harcourt Brace Jovanovich, 1975.
ISBN 0-330-25113-9 Pbk : £0.75
(B77-19660)

Coker, Elizabeth Boatwright. Daughter of strangers / [by] Elizabeth Boatwright Coker. — Toronto [etc.] ; London : Bantam, 1977. — [5], 408,[1]p ; 18cm.
Originally published: New York : Dutton, 1950 ; London : Heinemann, 1952.
ISBN 0-553-10508-6 Pbk : £0.85
(B77-28112)

Cole, Adrian. The coming of the Voidal / by Adrian Cole ; illustrated by Jim Pitts. — Burton-on-Trent (37 Hawkins La., Burton-on-Trent, Staffs. DE14 1PT) : Spectre Press, 1977. — 24p : ill ; 22cm.
ISBN 0-905416-01-5 Sd : £1.00
(B77-25193)

Cole, Adrian. Paths in darkness / by Adrian Cole. — London : Hale, 1977. — 190p ; 21cm. — (Hale SF)
ISBN 0-7091-6051-8 : £3.25
(B77-19661)

Coles, Janis. Lucy Grey / by Janis Coles. — London : Hale, 1977. — 157p ; 21cm.
ISBN 0-7091-6204-9 : £3.50
(B77-22120)

Collins, Jackie. Lovers & gamblers / [by] Jackie Collins. — London : W.H. Allen, 1977. — [5], 657p ; 22cm.
ISBN 0-491-02052-x : £5.95
(B77-32160)

Collins, Jackie. Sunday Simmons and Charlie Brick / [by] Jackie Collins. — London : Sphere, 1977. — 283p ; 18cm.
Originally published: London : W.H. Allen, 1971.
ISBN 0-7221-2467-8 Pbk : £0.75
(B77-18983)

Collins, Max. Blood money / [by] Max Collins. — London : New English Library, 1977. — 175p ; 18cm.
Originally published: New York : Curtis Books, 1973.
ISBN 0-450-02975-1 Pbk : £0.75
(B77-05647)

Collins, Michael, *b.1924.* The blood-red dream / [by] Michael Collins. — London : Hale, 1977. — [5],186p ; 20cm.
Originally published: New York : Dodd, Mead, 1976.
ISBN 0-7091-6234-0 : £3.25
(B77-22857)

Compton-Burnett, *Dame* **Ivy.** Elders and betters / by I. Compton-Burnett. — London : Gollancz, 1977. — 304p ; 21cm.
Originally published: 1944.
ISBN 0-575-02371-6 : £4.50
(B77-28113)

Compton-Burnett, *Dame* **Ivy.** Mother and son / by I. Compton-Burnett. — London : Gollancz, 1977. — 208p ; 21cm.
Originally published: 1955.
ISBN 0-575-02353-8 : £3.95
(B77-27378)

Comyns, Barbara. Our spoons came from Woolworths / [by] Barbara Comyns. — Large print ed. — Bath : Chivers, 1977. — [7],261p ; 22cm.
Originally published: London : Eyre and Spottiswoode, 1950.
ISBN 0-85997-259-3 : £4.80(£3.60 to members of the Library Association)
(B77-26519)

Concannon, Thomas Patrick. Sunset at Chalgrove / [by] T.P. Concannon. — London : Hale, 1977. — 192p ; 21cm.
ISBN 0-7091-6351-7 : £3.85
(B77-32849)

Condon, Richard. Bandicoot / [by] Richard Condon. — London : Hutchinson, 1978. — 208p ; 23cm.
ISBN 0-09-131780-0 : £4.50
(B77-34100)

Coney, Michael Greatrey. Brontomek! / [by] Michael Coney. — London [etc.] : Pan Books, 1977. — 223p ; 18cm. — (Pan science fiction)
Originally published: London : Gollancz, 1976.
ISBN 0-330-25334-4 Pbk : £0.70
(B77-31449)

Coney, Michael Greatrey. Charisma / [by] Michael Coney. — London [etc.] : Pan Books, 1977. — 220p ; 18cm. — (Pan science fiction)
Originally published: London : Gollancz, 1975.
ISBN 0-330-25090-6 Pbk : £0.60
(B77-20592)

Coney, Michael Greatrey. Winter's children / [by] Michael Coney. — London : Sphere, [1977]. — 174p ; 18cm.
Originally published: London : Gollancz, 1974.
ISBN 0-7221-2461-9 Pbk : £0.60
(B77-06282)

Conlon, Kathleen. A twisted skein / [by] Kathleen Conlon. — [London] : Fontana, 1977. — 251p ; 18cm.
Originally published: London : Collins, 1975.
ISBN 0-00-614664-3 Pbk : £0.70
(B77-22121)

Connolly, Ray. Trick or treat? / [by] Ray Connolly. — St Albans : Panther, 1977. — 170p ; 18cm.
Originally published: London : W.H. Allen, 1975.
ISBN 0-586-04416-7 Pbk : £0.60
(B77-13260)

Conrad, Joseph. The portable Conrad / edited, and with an introduction and notes, by Morton Dauwen Zabel. — Revised ed. / revised by Frederick R. Karl. — Harmondsworth [etc.] : Penguin, 1976. — vi,762p ; 18cm. — (Viking portable library)
This ed. originally published: New York : Viking Press, 1969. — Bibl.: p.758-762.
ISBN 0-14-015033-1 Pbk : £1.95
(B77-09255)

Conrad, Joseph. Selected tales from Conrad / edited with an introduction and commentary by Nigel Stewart. — London : Faber, 1977. — 224p ; 19cm.
Bibl. — Contents: An outpost of progress - Karain : a memory - The secret sharer - The planter of Malata.
ISBN 0-571-10763-x Pbk : £2.25
(B77-19662)

Conroy, Pat. The great Santini / [by] Pat Conroy. — London : Collins, 1977. — [7], 536p ; 22cm.
Originally published: Boston, Mass. : Houghton Mifflin, 1976.
ISBN 0-00-222262-0 : £4.95
(B77-18368)

Conway, Celine. Full tide / [by] Celine Conway. — London [etc.] : Mills and Boon, 1976. — 186p ; 18cm. — (Mills and Boon classics)
Originally published: 1954.
ISBN 0-263-72220-1 Pbk : £0.35
(B77-11399)

Conway, Laura. I bequeath / [by] Laura Conway. — Revised ed. — London : Collins, 1976. — 160p ; 20cm.
Previous ed.: / published under the name Hebe Elsna. London : Hale, 1955.
ISBN 0-00-233336-8 : £2.75
(B77-00962)

Conway, Laura. Safety for my love / [by] Laura Conway. — Large print ed. — Bath : Lythway Press, 1976. — [5],297p ; 22cm.
Originally published: London : Collins, 1963.
ISBN 0-85046-683-0 : £4.30
(B77-06862)

Conway, Laura. A way through the maze / [by] Laura Conway. — Large print ed. — Bath : Lythway Press, 1977. — [4],299p ; 23cm.
Originally published: London : Collins, 1963.
ISBN 0-85046-700-4 : £4.60
(B77-17085)

Conway, Peter. Cradle snatch / by Peter Conway. — London : Hale, 1976. — 188p ; 20cm.
ISBN 0-7091-5881-5 : £2.95
(B77-01789)

Conway, Peter, *b.1929.* A word in her ear / by Peter Conway. — London : Hale, 1977. — 157p ; 20cm.
ISBN 0-7091-6419-x : £3.25
(B77-34101)

Cook, Kenneth, *b.1929.* Bloodhouse / [by] Kenneth Cook. — London : Pan Books, 1977. — 126p ; 18cm.
Originally published: London : Heinemann, 1974.
ISBN 0-330-25193-7 Pbk : £0.70
(B77-28887)

Cook, Robin, *b.1940.* Coma : a novel / by Robin Cook. — London [etc.] : Macmillan, 1977. — [5],306p ; 23cm.
Also published: Boston, Mass. : Little, Brown, 1977.
ISBN 0-333-22314-4 : £4.95
(B77-26520)

Cooke, Phyl. The shadow beast / [by] Phyl Cooke. — London : Collins, 1977. — 159p ; 20cm.
ISBN 0-00-233790-8 : £2.95
(B77-30621)

Cookson, Catherine. Fanny McBride / [by] Catherine Cookson. — London : Corgi, 1977. — 222p ; 18cm.
Originally published: London : Macdonald, 1959.
ISBN 0-552-10394-2 Pbk : £0.75
(B77-13261)

Cookson, Catherine. The gambling man / [by] Catherine Cookson. — London : Corgi, 1977. — 316p ; 18cm.
Originally published: London : Heinemann, 1975.
ISBN 0-552-10450-7 Pbk : £0.85
(B77-30622)

Cookson, Catherine. The girl : a novel / by Catherine Cookson. — London : Heinemann, 1977. — [7],307p ; 23cm.
ISBN 0-434-14266-2 : £4.10
(B77-28888)

Cookson, Catherine. Life and Mary Ann / [by] Catherine Cookson. — Large print ed. — Leicester : Ulverscroft, 1977. — [4],354p ; 23cm. — (Ulverscroft large print series : [general fiction])
Originally published: London : Macdonald and Co., 1962.
ISBN 0-7089-0049-6 : £2.95
(B77-28114)

Cookson, Catherine. Maggie Rowan / [by] Catherine Cookson. — Large print ed. — Leicester : Ulverscroft, 1977. — [6],568p ; 23cm. — (Ulverscroft large print series : [general fiction])
Originally published: London : Macdonald and Co., 1954.
ISBN 0-7089-0005-4 : £2.95
(B77-32850)

Cookson, Catherine. Our John Willie / [by] Catherine Cookson. — Large print [ed.]. — London : Prior [etc.], 1977. — [2],306p ; 25cm.
Originally published: London : Macdonald and Co., 1974.
ISBN 0-86043-039-1 : £4.95
(B77-21431)

Cookson, Catherine. Slinky Jane / [by] Catherine Cookson. — Large print ed. — Leicester : Ulverscroft, 1977. — [4],414p ; 23cm. — (Ulverscroft large print series : [general fiction])
Originally published: London : Macdonald and Co., 1959.
ISBN 0-85456-530-2 : £2.65
(B77-13860)

Cooper, Dominic. Sunrise / by Dominic Cooper. — London : Chatto and Windus, 1977. — 224p ; 21cm.
ISBN 0-7011-2218-8 : £3.95 : CIP rev.
(B77-07601)

Cooper, Edmund, *b.1926.* All Fools' Day / [by] Edmund Cooper. — Sevenoaks : Coronet, 1977. — 192p ; 18cm.
Originally published: London : Hodder and Stoughton, 1966.
Pbk : £0.75
ISBN 0-340-02860-2
(B77-29688)

Cooper, Edmund, *b.1926.* Prisoner of fire / [by] Edmund Cooper. — Sevenoaks : Coronet, 1977. — 191p ; 18cm.
Originally published: London : Hodder and Stoughton, 1974.
ISBN 0-340-21242-x Pbk : £0.60
(B77-13262)

Cooper, Edmund, *b.1926.* Who needs men? / [by] Edmund Cooper. — Sevenoaks : Coronet, 1977. — 192p ; 18cm.
Originally published: London : Hodder and Stoughton, 1972. — Previous control number ISBN 0-340-18614-3.
Pbk : £0.75
ISBN 0-340-18614-3
(B77-29689)

Cooper, Jilly. Bella / [by] Jilly Cooper. — London : Corgi, 1977. — 171p ; 18cm.
Originally published: London : Arlington Books, 1976.
ISBN 0-552-10427-2 Pbk : £0.50
(B77-16587)

Cooper, Jilly. Emily / [by] Jilly Cooper. — London : Arlington Books, 1975. — [6],186p ; 21cm.
ISBN 0-85140-244-5 : £2.25
(B77-00963)

Cooper, Jilly. Harriet / [by] Jilly Cooper. — London : Corgi, 1977. — 190p ; 18cm.
Originally published: London : Arlington Books, 1976.
ISBN 0-552-10576-7 Pbk : £0.50
(B77-31450)

Cooper, Jilly. Harriet / [by] Jilly Cooper. — London : Arlington Books, 1976. — 232p ; 21cm.
ISBN 0-85140-241-0 : £2.95
(B77-00964)

Cooper, Jilly. Octavia / [by] Jilly Cooper. — London : Arlington Books, 1977. — [6],210p ; 21cm.
ISBN 0-85140-260-7 : £3.25
(B77-19663)

Cooper, Louise. In memory of Sarah Bailey / [by] Louise Cooper. — London : New English Library, 1977. — 143p ; 19cm.
ISBN 0-450-03101-2 Pbk : £0.60
(B77-08553)

Cooper, Morton. Rich people / [by] Morton Cooper. — London : W.H. Allen, 1977. — [5], 360p ; 23cm.
Also published: New York : H. Evans, 1977.
ISBN 0-491-02121-6 : £4.95
(B77-33428)

Cooper, Parley J. Dark desires / [by] Parley J. Cooper. — London : Sphere, 1977. — 320p ; 18cm.
Originally published: New York : Pocket Books, 1976.
ISBN 0-7221-2493-7 Pbk : £0.85
(B77-18984)

Cooper, Roderick. Blood on blue denim / [by] Roderick Cooper. — London : Hale, 1977. — 158p ; 20cm.
ISBN 0-7091-6436-x : £3.25
(B77-28889)

Cooper, Simon. Exhibition / [by] Simon Cooper. — London : Magnum Books, 1977. — 320p ; 18cm.
Originally published: London : Souvenir Press, 1975.
ISBN 0-413-37450-5 Pbk : £0.80
(B77-16051)

Copper, Basil. Death squad / [by] Basil Copper. — London : Hale, 1977. — 3-172p ; 20cm. — (Copper, Basil. .38 specials ; 25)
ISBN 0-7091-5965-x : £3.15
(B77-21433)

Copper, Basil. The year of the dragon / [by] Basil Copper. — London : Hale, 1977. — 157p ; 20cm. — (Copper, Basil. .38 specials)
ISBN 0-7091-5749-5 : £3.15
(B77-05648)

Cordell, Alexander. The bright Cantonese / [by] Alexander Cordell. — Large print ed. — Leicester : Ulverscroft, 1977. — [7],342p ; 23cm. — (Ulverscroft large print series : [adventure, suspense])
Originally published: London : Gollancz, 1967.
ISBN 0-7089-0058-5 : £2.95
(B77-32161)

Cordell, Alexander. The sinews of love / [by] Alexander Cordell. — Bath : Chivers, 1977. — 256p ; 21cm.
Originally published: London : Gollancz, 1965.
ISBN 0-85997-240-2 : £5.60(£4.20 to members of the Library Association)
(B77-15491)

Cordell, Alexander. This sweet and bitter earth / [by] Alexander Cordell. — London [etc.] : Hodder and Stoughton, 1977. — 447p ; 23cm.
ISBN 0-340-21743-x : £4.95
(B77-21434)

Corder, Eric. Hellbottom / [by] Eric Corder. — London : Star Books, 1975. — [6],310p ; 18cm.
Originally published in the United States: s.n., 1972 ; London : W.H. Allen, 1974.
ISBN 0-352-30067-1 Pbk : £0.75
(B77-05649)

Corlett, William. The gate of Eden / [by] William Corlett. — Basingstoke [etc.] : Macmillan, 1977. — 142p ; 18cm. — (Topliner redstars)
Originally published: London : Hamilton, 1974. — For adolescents.
ISBN 0-333-21392-0 Pbk : £0.50 : CIP rev.
(B77-05083)

Corlett, William. Return to the gate / [by] William Corlett. — Basingstoke [etc.] : Macmillan, 1977. — 143p ; 18cm. — (Topliner redstars)
Originally published: London : Hamilton, 1975. — For adolescents.
ISBN 0-333-21393-9 Pbk : £0.50 : CIP rev.
(B77-05084)

Corley, Edwin. Sargasso / [by] Edwin Corley. — London : Joseph, 1977. — [4],259p ; 23cm.
Also published: Garden City, N.Y : Doubleday, 1977.
ISBN 0-7181-1627-5 : £4.50
(B77-22122)

Cormier, Robert. I am the cheese : a novel / by Robert Cormier. — London : Gollancz, 1977. — [5],234p ; 21cm.
Also published: New York : Pantheon Books, 1977. — For adolescents.
ISBN 0-575-02372-4 : £3.20
(B77-28890)

Corrie, Jane. The Bahamian pirate / by Jane Corrie. — London : Mills and Boon, 1976. — 174p ; 19cm.
ISBN 0-263-09059-0 : £1.95
(B77-14400)

Corrie, Jane. Green paddocks / by Jane Corrie. — London : Mills and Boon, 1976. — 188p ; 19cm.
ISBN 0-263-09038-8 : £1.95
(B77-12648)

Corrie, Jane. The impossible boss / by Jane Corrie. — London : Mills and Boon, 1977. — 192p ; 17cm.
Originally published: 1975.
ISBN 0-263-72407-7 Pbk : £0.35
(B77-20593)

Cory, Desmond. Bennett / [by] Desmond Cory. — London [etc.] : Macmillan, 1977. — 191p ; 21cm.
ISBN 0-333-21757-8 : £3.50
(B77-22858)

Cosgrave, Patrick. Cheyney's law / [by] Patrick Cosgrave. — London [etc.] : Macmillan, 1977. — 159p ; 21cm.
ISBN 0-333-21635-0 : £3.25
(B77-19664)

Couldrey, Vivienne. Bird with one wing / by Vivienne Couldrey. — London : Hale, 1977. — 191p ; 20cm.
ISBN 0-7091-5948-x : £3.10
(B77-17086)

Coulter, Stephen. The Château / [by] Stephen Coulter. — London : Pan Books, 1977. — 447p ; 18cm.
Originally published: London : Heinemann, 1974.
ISBN 0-330-25001-9 Pbk : £0.80
(B77-12093)

Couper, Elspeth. Danger in scarlet / by Elspeth Couper. — London : Hale, 1977. — 160p ; 20cm.
ISBN 0-7091-6298-7 : £3.40
(B77-32851)

Couper, Elspeth. The fairest valley / by Elspeth Couper. — London : Hale, 1977. — 152p ; 20cm.
ISBN 0-7091-6082-8 : £3.20
(B77-30623)

Courtis, Gerald. The big noise / [by] Gerald Courtis. — London : Hale, 1977. — 185p ; 20cm.
ISBN 0-7091-6045-3 : £3.15
(B77-13861)

Cowan, Evelyn. Portrait of Alice : a novel / by Evelyn Cowan. — Edinburgh : Canongate Publishing, 1976. — [6],170p ; 23cm.
ISBN 0-903937-26-3 : £3.30
(B77-14401)

Cowen, Frances. The lost one / by Frances Cowen. — London : Hale, 1977. — 173p ; 20cm.
ISBN 0-7091-5935-8 : £3.15
(B77-13862)

Cowen, Frances. The silent pool / [by] Frances Cowen. — London : Hale, 1977. — 168p ; 20cm. — ([Hale crime])
ISBN 0-7091-6111-5 : £3.25
(B77-19665)

Cox, Richard. SAM 7 / [by] Richard Cox. — London : Hutchinson, 1977. — 367p : map ; 23cm.
ISBN 0-09-128820-7 : £4.50
(B77-17087)

Cox, William Robert. Bigger than Texas / [by] William R. Cox. — Large print ed. — Leicester : Ulverscroft, 1977. — [5],290p ; 23cm. — (Ulverscroft large print series : [Western])
Originally published: New York : Fawcett, 1963 ; London : Gold Lion Books, 1974.
ISBN 0-7089-0007-0 : £2.95
(B77-32162)

Coxe, George Harmon. The hidden key / [by] George Harmon Coxe. — London [etc.] : White Lion Publishers, 1976. — 187,[1]p ; 21cm.
Originally published: New York : Knopf, 1963 ; London : Hammond, 1964.
ISBN 0-7274-0070-3 : £3.25
(B77-00965)

Coxe, George Harmon. The inside man / [by] George Harmon Coxe. — Large print ed. — Leicester : Ulverscroft, 1977. — [5],376p ; 23cm. — (Ulverscroft large print series : [mystery])
Originally published: New York : Knopf, 1974 ; London : Hale, 1975.
ISBN 0-85456-517-5 : £2.65
(B77-13863)

Coxe, George Harmon. No place for murder / [by] George Harmon Coxe. — Large print ed. — London : Prior [etc.], 1977. — [7],369p ; 24cm.
Originally published: New York : Knopf, 1975 ; London : Hale, 1976.
ISBN 0-86043-028-6 : £4.95
(B77-12649)

Coxhead, Elizabeth. One green bottle / [by] Elizabeth Coxhead. — Large print ed. — Bath : Chivers, 1976. — [6],393p ; 22cm.
Originally published: London : Faber, 1951.
ISBN 0-85997-199-6 : £5.60(£4.20 to members of the Library Association)
(B77-02573)

Coxhead, Elizabeth. A wind in the west / [by] Elizabeth Coxhead. — Bath : Chivers, 1977. — 3-290p ; 19cm.
Originally published: London : Faber, 1949.
ISBN 0-85997-274-7 : £5.40(£4.05 to members of the Library Association)
(B77-29690)

Cradock, Fanny. War comes to Castle Rising / [by] Fanny Cradock. — London : W.H. Allen, 1977. — xiv,337p : geneal table ; 23cm.
ISBN 0-491-02092-9 : £4.95
(B77-32163)

Craven, Sara. Strange adventure / by Sara Craven. — London : Mills and Boon, 1977. — 188p ; 17cm.
ISBN 0-263-72390-9 Pbk : £0.35
(B77-20594)

Cravens, Gwyneth. The Black Death / by Gwyneth Cravens and John S. Marr. — London : Weidenfeld and Nicolson, 1977. — [13],302p ; 23cm.
Also published: New York : Dutton, 1977.
ISBN 0-297-77297-x : £4.50
(B77-18985)

Crawford, Sheila. The foundling / [by] Sheila Crawford ; illustrated by Katinka Crampton. — Oxford [etc.] : Oxford University Press, 1977. — [6],147p : ill ; 23cm.
For adolescents.
ISBN 0-19-271408-2 : £2.95 : CIP rev.
(B77-17088)

Creasey, John, *b.1908.* Death to my killer / [by] John Creasey. — London [etc.] : White Lion Publishers, 1977. — 190p ; 21cm.
Originally published: under the name Jeremy York. London : Andrew Melrose, 1950.
ISBN 0-7274-0254-4 : £3.75
(B77-16588)

Creasey, John, *b.1908.* Find Inspector West / [by] John Creasey. — Large print ed. — Bath : Lythway Press, 1976. — [11],302p ; 22cm.
Originally published: London : Hodder and Stoughton, 1957.
ISBN 0-85046-681-4 : £4.35
(B77-06863)

Creasey, John, *b.1908.* The flood / [by] John Creasey. — Large print ed. — Leicester : Ulverscroft, 1977. — [7],383p ; 23cm. — (Ulverscroft large print series : [mystery])
Originally published: London : Hodder and Stoughton, 1956.
ISBN 0-85456-508-6 : £2.65
(B77-08554)

Creasey, John, *b.1908.* The mark of the crescent : a Department Z adventure / [by] John Creasey. — Revised ed. — Leicester : Ulverscroft, 1977. — [4],365p ; 23cm. — (Ulverscroft large print series : [mystery])
Revised ed. originally published: London : Long, 1970.
ISBN 0-7089-0042-9 : £2.95
(B77-28115)

Creasey, John, *b.1908.* The thunder-maker : a new Dr Palfrey adventure / by John Creasey. — London [etc.] : Hodder and Stoughton, 1976. — 189p ; 20cm.
ISBN 0-340-18380-2 : £2.95
(B77-09256)

Creasey, John, *b.1908.* The Toff and the crooked copper / by John Creasey. — London [etc.] : Hodder and Stoughton, 1977. — 160p ; 20cm.
'The 57th book of the Toff'.
ISBN 0-340-21654-9 : £3.40
(B77-17089)

Creasey, John, *b.1908.* The touch of death / [by] John Creasey. — Large print ed. — Leicester : Ulverscroft, 1977. — [5],376p ; 23cm. — (Ulverscroft large print series : [mystery])
Originally published: London : Hodder and Stoughton, 1954.
ISBN 0-85456-536-1 : Unpriced
(B77-19666)

Cresswell, Jasmine. Forgotten marriage / by Jasmine Cresswell. — London : Hale, 1977. — 189p ; 20cm.
ISBN 0-7091-6265-0 : £3.20
(B77-28891)

Crews, Harry. A feast of snakes / [by] Harry Crews. — London : Secker and Warburg, 1977. — [7],177p ; 23cm.
Originally published: New York : Atheneum, 1976.
ISBN 0-436-11441-0 : £3.50
(B77-02574)

Crisp, N J. The odd job man / [by] N.J. Crisp. — London : Raven Books, 1977. — [5],215p ; 23cm.
ISBN 0-354-04114-2 : £3.95
(B77-20595)

Crisp, Quentin. Love made easy / [by] Quentin Crisp. — London : Duckworth, 1977. — 154p ; 23cm.
ISBN 0-7156-1188-7 : £3.95
(B77-09257)

Crispin, Edmund. The glimpses of the moon : a novel / by Edmund Crispin. — London : Gollancz, 1977. — 287p ; 21cm. — ([Gollancz detection])
ISBN 0-575-02259-0 : £4.25
(B77-17736)

Crispin, Edmund. The moving toyshop : a detective story / by Edmund Crispin. — London : Gollancz, 1977. — 224p : map ; 21cm. — ([Gollancz vintage detection])
Originally published: 1946.
£3.75
ISBN 0-575-00250-6
(B77-25879)

Crispin, Edmund. The moving toyshop / [by] Edmund Crispin. — Harmondsworth [etc.] : Penguin, 1977. — 205p : map ; 19cm. — (Penguin crime fiction)
Originally published: London : Gollancz, 1946.
Pbk : £0.70
ISBN 0-14-001315-6
(B77-29691)

Croft-Cooke, Rupert. Nine days with Edward / [by] Rupert Croft-Cooke. — London [etc.] : White Lion Publishers, 1977. — vii,279p ; 21cm.
Originally published: London : Macmillan, 1952.
ISBN 0-85617-178-6 : £3.95
(B77-18986)

Crofts, Freeman Wills. The cask / by Freeman Wills Crofts. — London : Remploy, 1977. — viii,357p : 1 ill ; 19cm. — ([Deerstalker series])
Facsimile reprint of: 1st ed. London : Collins, 1920.
ISBN 0-7066-0714-7 : £3.35
(B77-34102)

Crofts, Freeman Wills. Inspector French's greatest case / [by] Freeman Wills Crofts. — Large print ed. — Bath : Lythway Press, 1977. — [3],396p ; 23cm. — (Lythway classics of crime and detection)
Originally published: London : Collins, 1925.
ISBN 0-85046-716-0 : £4.85
(B77-30624)

Cronin, Archibald Joseph. Lady with carnations / [by] A.J. Cronin. — Large print ed. — Bath : Firecrest, 1977. — [5],289p ; 23cm.
Originally published: London : Gollancz, 1976.
ISBN 0-85119-011-1 : £4.40
(B77-18987)

Cronin, Archibald Joseph. The minstrel boy / [by] A.J. Cronin. — London : New English Library, 1977. — 287p ; 18cm.
Originally published: London : Gollancz, 1975.
ISBN 0-450-03279-5 Pbk : £0.95
(B77-13864)

Cronin, Archibald Joseph. Shannon's way / [by] A.J. Cronin. — London : New English Library, 1977. — 288p ; 18cm.
Originally published: London : Gollancz, 1948.
ISBN 0-450-03313-9 Pbk : £0.80
(B77-18988)

Cronin, Archibald Joseph. A song of sixpence / [by] A.J. Cronin. — London : New English Library, 1977. — 255p ; 18cm.
Originally published: London : Heinemann, 1964.
ISBN 0-450-03312-0 Pbk : £0.75
(B77-18989)

Cronin, Michael, *b.1907.* The Macamba project / [by] Michael Cronin. — London : Hale, 1977. — 192p ; 21cm.
ISBN 0-7091-5995-1 : £3.50
(B77-19667)

Cronin, Michael, *b.1907.* A pair of knaves / [by] Michael Cronin. — London : Hale, 1977. — 176p ; 21cm.
ISBN 0-7091-5676-6 : £3.25
(B77-05650)

Cronin, Michael, *b.1907.* Unfinished business / [by] Michael Cronin. — London : Hale, 1977. — 191p ; 21cm.
ISBN 0-7091-6278-2 : £3.70
(B77-29692)

Crosby, John, *b.1912.* The company of friends / [by] John Crosby. — London : Cape, 1977. — 228p ; 23cm.
ISBN 0-224-01399-8 : £3.95 : CIP rev.
(B77-16589)

Crosby, John, *b.1912.* Snake : a novel / [by] John Crosby. — London : Cape, 1977. — 240p ; 23cm.
Originally published: as 'Nightfall'. New York : Stein and Day, 1976.
ISBN 0-224-01310-6 : £3.95
(B77-06864)

Crosby, John, *b.1912.* The white telephone / [by] John Crosby. — [London] : Coronet, 1976. — 219p ; 18cm.
Originally published: London : Joseph, 1974.
ISBN 0-340-21013-3 Pbk : £0.80
(B77-00966)

Cross, Amanda. The question of Max / [by] Amanda Cross. — Large print ed. — London : Prior [etc.], 1977. — [3],323p ; 25cm.
Originally published: New York : Knopf ; London : Gollancz, 1976.
ISBN 0-86043-068-5 : £4.95
(B77-34103)

Crowley, John. The deep / [by] John Crowley. — London : New English Library, 1977. — [9], 180p ; 19cm.
Originally published: Garden City, N.Y. : Doubleday, 1975.
ISBN 0-450-03069-5 : £2.95
ISBN 0-450-03353-8 Pbk : £0.85
(B77-09258)

Crowther, Bruce. Dead man's cocktail / by Bruce Crowther. — London : Hale, 1976. — 184p ; 20cm.
ISBN 0-7091-5707-x : £2.95
(B77-01790)

Crowther, Bruce. Underkill / [by] Bruce Crowther. — London : Hale, 1976. — 206p ; 20cm.
ISBN 0-7091-5664-2 : £2.95
(B77-11400)

Curtis, Marjorie. Palm-thatched hospital / [by] Marjorie Curtis. — London : Hale, 1977. — 160p ; 20cm.
ISBN 0-7091-6331-2 : £3.40
(B77-30625)

Curtis, Marjorie. A time to remember / by Marjorie Curtis. — London : Hale, 1977. — 159p ; 20cm.
ISBN 0-7091-6042-9 : £3.20
(B77-34104)

Curtis, Marjorie. Wife for a rancher / by Marjorie Curtis. — London : Hale, 1977. — 158p ; 20cm.
ISBN 0-7091-5821-1 : £3.10
(B77-13263)

Curtis, Sydney Albert. The evil that men do / by Sydney Albert Curtis. — London : Hale, 1977. — 192p ; 20cm.
ISBN 0-7091-6009-7 : £3.25
(B77-12094)

Curtis, Tony, *b.1925.* Kid Andrew Cody & Julie Sparrow : a novel / by Tony Curtis. — London : W.H. Allen, 1977. — 307p ; 23cm.
Also published: Garden City, N.Y. : Doubleday, 1977.
ISBN 0-491-02032-5 : £4.50
(B77-34105)

Curtiss, Ursula. Dig a little deeper / [by] Ursula Curtiss. — London [etc.] : Macmillan, 1976. — [5],184p ; 21cm.
Originally published: as 'The birthday gift'. New York : Dodd, Mead, 1976.
ISBN 0-333-19761-5 : £2.95
(B77-00967)

Cussler, Clive. Iceberg / [by] Clive Cussler. — London : Sphere, 1977. — 252p ; 18cm.
Originally published: New York : Dodd, Mead, 1975 ; London : Sphere, 1976.
Pbk : £0.75
ISBN 0-7221-2737-5
(B77-23719)

Cussler, Clive. Mayday! / [by] Clive Cussler. — London : Sphere, 1977. — 237p ; 18cm.
ISBN 0-7221-2739-1 Pbk : £0.85
(B77-22859)

Cussler, Clive. Raise the Titanic! / [by] Clive Cussler. — London : Joseph, 1977. — [5], 314p : map ; 23cm.
Originally published: New York : Viking Press, 1976.
ISBN 0-7181-1579-1 : £4.25
(B77-15492)

Dailey, Janet. Fiesta San Antonio / by Janet Dailey. — London : Mills and Boon, 1977. — 188p ; 17cm.
ISBN 0-263-72382-8 Pbk : £0.35
(B77-21435)

Dailey, Janet. The night of the Cotillion / by Janet Dailey. — London : Mills and Boon, 1976. — 188p ; 18cm.
Previous control number ISBN 0-263-72316-x.
ISBN 0-263-09032-9 : £1.95
ISBN 0-263-72316-x Pbk : £0.30
(B77-00417)

Daish, Elizabeth. The Breton slippers / by Elizabeth Daish. — London : Hale, 1977. — 184p ; 20cm.
ISBN 0-7091-6322-3 : £3.40
(B77-30626)

Daish, Elizabeth. A touch of silk embroidery / by Elizabeth Daish. — London : Hale, 1977. — 192p ; 20cm.
ISBN 0-7091-6172-7 : £3.20
(B77-34106)

Dalgleish, James. The duke's right hand / by James Dalgleish. — London : Hale, 1977. — 3-190p ; 21cm.
ISBN 0-7091-6162-x : £3.70
(B77-23720)

Danbury, Iris. The scented island / by Iris Danbury. — London : Mills and Boon, 1976. — 189p ; 19cm.
ISBN 0-263-09054-x : £1.95
(B77-14402)

Dancer, J.B. Evil breed / [by] J.B. Dancer. — Sevenoaks : Coronet, 1977. — 128p ; 18cm. — (Dancer, J.B. The lawmen ; book 2)
ISBN 0-340-21828-2 Pbk : £0.65
(B77-22123)

Dane, Eva. A lion by the mane / [by] Eva Dane. — London : Macdonald and Jane's, 1977. — [4],184p ; 21cm. — (A troubadour)
ISBN 0-354-04118-5 : £3.50
(B77-19668)

Daniel, Elaine. A wilder kind of music / by Elaine Daniel. — London : Hale, 1977. — 157p ; 20cm.
ISBN 0-7091-6190-5 : £3.20
(B77-26521)

Daniels, Jeffery Robert. Firegold / [by] J.R. Daniels. — London : Corgi, 1977. — 188p ; 18cm.
Originally published: London : Macmillan, 1975.
ISBN 0-552-10422-1 Pbk : £0.65
(B77-19669)

Darby, Catherine. The falcon and the moon / [by] Catherine Darby. — London : Hale, 1977. — 221p : geneal table ; 21cm.
ISBN 0-7091-5550-6 : £3.95
(B77-29693)

Darby, Catherine. The Falcon tree / [by] Catherine Darby. — London : Hale, 1977. — 190p : geneal table ; 21cm.
ISBN 0-7091-5444-5 : £3.70
(B77-19670)

Darby, Catherine. A pride of falcons / [by] Catherine Darby. — London : Hale, 1977. — 191p : geneal table ; 21cm.
ISBN 0-7091-5296-5 : £3.50
(B77-13264)

Darby, Catherine. Season of the falcon / [by] Catherine Darby. — London : Hale, 1976. — 206p ; 21cm.
ISBN 0-7091-5295-7 : £3.25
(B77-00418)

Darcy, Clare. Elyza / by Clare Darcy. — London : Raven Books : Macdonald and Jane's, 1977. — [5],240p ; 23cm.
Originally published: New York : Walker, 1976.
ISBN 0-354-04102-9 : £3.50
(B77-13265)

Darcy, Clare. Lady Pamela / by Clare Darcy. — London : Wingate, 1977. — [5],280p ; 23cm.
Originally published: New York : Walker, 1975.
ISBN 0-85523-261-7 : £3.95
(B77-17090)

Darcy, Clare. Regina / [by] Clare Darcy. — London : Raven Books, 1977. — [4],217p ; 23cm.
Originally published: New York : Walker, 1976.
ISBN 0-354-04168-1 : £3.95
(B77-29694)

Darke, Marjorie. The first of Midnight / [by] Marjorie Darke ; with illustrations by Anthony Morris. — Harmondsworth : Kestrel Books, 1977. — 191p : ill ; 23cm.
ISBN 0-7226-5304-2 : £3.50
(B77-13865)

Date, John H. Escape route M6 / by John H. Date. — London : Hale, 1977. — 187p ; 20cm.
ISBN 0-7091-6215-4 : £3.25
(B77-26522)

Davenport, Marcia. East side, West side / [by] Marcia Davenport. — Bath : Chivers, 1976. — 384p ; 19cm.
Originally published: London : Collins, 1948.
ISBN 0-85594-153-7 : £4.60(£3.45 to members of the Library Association)
(B77-05651)

Davenport, Marcia. The valley of decision / [by] Marcia Davenport. — [London] : Fontana, 1977. — 795p ; 18cm.
Originally published: New York : Scribner, 1942 ; London : Collins, 1944.
ISBN 0-00-614762-3 Pbk : £1.25
(B77-25880)

Davie-Martin, Hugh. The pearl of Oyster Island / by Hugh Davie-Martin. — London : Hale, 1977. — 189p ; 20cm.
ISBN 0-7091-6228-6 : £3.25
(B77-19671)

Davies, Iris. Return to Tip Row / by Iris Davies. — London : Hale, 1977. — 192p ; 21cm.
ISBN 0-7091-6123-9 : £3.70
(B77-34107)

Davies, Jack. Le hold-up / [by] Jack Davies. — London : W.H. Allen, 1977. — 190p ; 23cm.
ISBN 0-491-02020-1 : £3.50
(B77-17737)

Davies, Jack. Paper tiger / [by] Jack Davies. — London : Star Books, 1975. — [5],212p ; 18cm.
Originally published: London : W.H. Allen, 1974.
ISBN 0-352-30053-1 Pbk : £0.50
(B77-05652)

Davies, Rhys. The red hills / [by] Rhys Davies. — Large print ed. — Bath : Chivers, 1977. — [4],299p ; 22cm.
Originally published: London : Putnam, 1932.
ISBN 0-85997-268-2 : £5.00(£3.75 to members of the Library Association)
(B77-34108)

Davies, Robertson. World of wonders / [by] Robertson Davies. — London : W.H. Allen, 1977. — [7],358p ; 23cm.
Originally published: New York : Viking Press, 1976.
ISBN 0-491-02200-x : £4.50
(B77-22860)

Davis, John Gordon. Cape of storms / [by] John Gordon Davis. — London : Corgi, 1977. — 381p ; 18cm.
Originally published: London : Joseph, 1970.
ISBN 0-552-10447-7 Pbk : £0.85
(B77-24476)

Davis, John Gordon. Leviathan / [by] John Gordon Davis. — London : Joseph, 1977. — [8],306p ; 23cm.
Originally published: New York : Dutton, 1976.
ISBN 0-7181-1506-6 : £4.50
(B77-10939)

Davis, Maggie. The sheik / [by] Maggie Davis. — London [etc.] : Hart-Davis MacGibbon, 1978. — 365p ; 23cm.
Originally published: New York : Morrow, 1977.
ISBN 0-246-11027-9 : £4.95
(B77-32164)

Davis, Margaret Thomson. Roots of bondage / [by] Margaret Thomson Davis. — London : Allison and Busby, 1977. — 272p ; 23cm.
ISBN 0-85031-196-9 : £4.25
(B77-28116)

Dawson, Janis. Changing scenes / by Janis Dawson. — London : Hale, 1977. — 156p ; 20cm.
ISBN 0-7091-6026-7 : £3.10
(B77-21436)

Day, Robert, *b.1941.* The last cattle drive / [by] Robert Day. — London : Secker and Warburg, 1977. — 223p ; 22cm.
Also published: New York : Putnam, 1977.
ISBN 0-436-12555-2 : £4.10
(B77-28117)

De Felitta, Frank. Audrey Rose / [by] Frank De Felitta. — London : Pan Books, 1977. — 380p ; 18cm.
Originally published: New York : Putnam, 1975 ; London : Collins, 1976.
ISBN 0-330-25023-x Pbk : £0.75
(B77-12650)

De Klerk, Willem Abraham. The thirstland / [by] W.A. de Klerk. — London : Collings, 1977. — [6],463p ; 24cm.
Text, map on lining papers.
ISBN 0-86036-045-8 : £8.50
(B77-30627)

De Polnay, Peter. Driftsand / [by] Peter de Polnay. — London : W.H. Allen, 1977. — 217p ; 21cm.
ISBN 0-491-02380-4 : £4.50
(B77-23721)

Deal, Borden. Bluegrass / [by] Borden Deal. — London : New English Library, 1977. — xii, 468p ; 22cm.
Originally published: Garden City, N.Y. : Doubleday, 1976.
ISBN 0-450-03443-7 : £5.50
(B77-32165)

Deane, Sonia. Doctor's mistress / [by] Sonia Deane. — London : Hurst and Blackett, 1977. — 171p ; 20cm.
ISBN 0-09-128990-4 : £3.25
(B77-30628)

Deeping, Warwick. Paradise Place / [by] Warwick Deeping. — Large print ed. — Bath : Chivers, 1977. — [5],407p ; 22cm.
Originally published: London : Cassell, 1949.
ISBN 0-85997-219-4 : £5.60(£4.20 to members of the Library Association)
(B77-13866)

Deighton, Len. Only when I larf / [by] Len Deighton. — London : Sphere, 1977. — 251p ; 18cm.
Originally published: London : Joseph, 1968.
ISBN 0-7221-2906-8 Pbk : £0.85
(B77-10549)

Deighton, Len. Yesterday's spy / [by] Len Deighton. — St Albans : Panther, 1977. — 224p ; 18cm.
Originally published: London : Cape, 1975.
ISBN 0-586-04347-0 Pbk : £0.60
(B77-08555)

Delaney, John. Blood brand : a James Gunn novel / by John Delaney. — London [etc.] : Mews Books ; London : Distributed by New English Library, 1977. — 127p ; 19cm. — (Delaney, John. James Gunn ; 4)
ISBN 0-452-00062-9 Pbk : £0.50
(B77-05653)

Delany, Samuel R. The jewels of Aptor / [by] Samuel R. Delany. — London : Sphere, 1977. — 159p ; 18cm. — (Sphere science fiction)
Originally published: New York : Ace Books, 1962 ; London : Gollancz, 1968.
Pbk : £0.75
ISBN 0-7221-2192-2
(B77-23722)

Delany, Samuel R. Triton / [by] Samuel R. Delaney. — London : Corgi, 1977. — [11], 369p ; 18cm.
Originally published: New York : Bantam Books, 1976.
ISBN 0-552-10579-1 Pbk : £0.85
(B77-31451)

Dell, Ethel May. The hundredth chance / by Ethel M. Dell ; condensed by Barbara Cartland. — London : Corgi, 1977. — [7],306p ; 18cm. — (Barbara Cartland's library of love ; 5)
Full ed. originally published: London : Hutchinson, 1917.
ISBN 0-552-10543-0 Pbk : £0.60
(B77-27379)

Dell, Ethel May. The knave of diamonds / by Ethel M. Dell ; condensed by Barbara Cartland. — London : Corgi, 1977. — [5],280p ; 18cm. — (Barbara Cartland's library of love)
Originally published: London : T. Fisher Unwin, 1913.
ISBN 0-552-10441-8 Pbk : £0.50
(B77-26523)

Dell, Ethel May. The way of an eagle / by Ethel M. Dell ; condensed by Barbara Cartland. — London : Corgi, 1977. — [7],193,[1]p ; 18cm. — (Barbara Cartland's library of love ; 7)
Full ed. originally published: London : T. Fisher Unwin, 1912.
ISBN 0-552-10588-0 Pbk : £0.60
(B77-32166)

Delman, David. The Nice murderers / [by] David Delman. — London : Collins [for] the Crime Club, 1977. — 220p ; 20cm.
ISBN 0-00-231582-3 : £3.25
(B77-31452)

Delroy, Margaret. The starry heights / by Margaret Delroy. — London : Hale, 1977. — 191p ; 20cm.
ISBN 0-7091-5898-x : £3.10
(B77-08041)

Dene, Bryony. Hermit Island / by Bryony Dene. — London : Hale, 1977. — 157p ; 20cm.
ISBN 0-7091-5899-8 : £3.10
(B77-08042)

Denker, Henry. The experiment : a novel / by Henry Denker. — London : W.H. Allen, 1977. — 256p ; 23cm.
Originally published: New York : Simon and Schuster, 1976.
ISBN 0-491-02010-4 : £3.95
(B77-17091)

Denker, Henry. The starmaker / [by] Henry Denker. — London : W.H. Allen, 1977. — 384p ; 23cm.
Also published: New York : Simon and Schuster, 1977.
ISBN 0-491-02161-5 : £4.95
(B77-28118)

Dennison, Diana. Bitter rain / by Diana Dennison. — London : Hale, 1977. — 187p ; 20cm.
ISBN 0-7091-6012-7 : £3.10
(B77-20596)

Denver, Lee. Cheyenne Jones, maverick marshall / by Lee Denver. — London : Hale, 1977. — 156p ; 20cm.
ISBN 0-7091-6084-4 : £2.95
(B77-13266)

Desai, Anita. Fire on the mountain / [by] Anita Desai. — London : Heinemann, 1977. — [9], 146p : 1 ill ; 23cm.
ISBN 0-434-18631-7 : £3.50
(B77-24478)

Devon, Sarah. Doctor's housekeeper / [by] Sarah Devon. — Large print ed. — Bath : Lythway Press, 1977. — [5],178p ; 22cm.
Originally published: London : Gresham, 1967.
ISBN 0-85046-733-0 Pbk : £2.20
(B77-34109)

Devon, Sarah. Noakes end / by Sarah Devon. — London : Hale, 1977. — 160p ; 20cm.
ISBN 0-7091-6128-x : £3.20
(B77-20597)

DeWeese, Gene. The doll with opal eyes / by Jean DeWeese. — London : Hale, 1977. — [7], 182p ; 20cm.
Originally published: Garden City, N.Y. : Doubleday, 1976.
ISBN 0-7091-5894-7 : £3.15
(B77-05654)

Dewhurst, Eileen. Curtain fall / [by] Eileen Dewhurst. — London [etc.] : Macmillan, 1977. — 219p ; 21cm.
ISBN 0-333-21310-6 : £3.50
(B77-17092)

Dexter, Colin. Last bus to Woodstock / [by] Colin Dexter. — London : Pan Books, 1977. — 205p ; 18cm.
Originally published: London : Macmillan, 1975.
ISBN 0-330-24896-0 Pbk : £0.60
(B77-09259)

Dexter, Colin. Last seen wearing / [by] Colin Dexter. — London : Pan Books, 1977. — 222p ; 18cm.
Originally published: London : Macmillan, 1976.
ISBN 0-330-25148-1 Pbk : £0.70
(B77-21437)

Dexter, Colin. The silent world of Nicholas Quinn / [by] Colin Dexter. — London [etc.] : Macmillan, 1977. — 254p : plan ; 21cm.
ISBN 0-333-21626-1 : £3.50
(B77-19672)

Dexter, Ross. The black duke / by Ross Dexter. — London : Hale, 1977. — 159p ; 20cm.
ISBN 0-7091-6302-9 : £3.10
(B77-28119)

Dexter, Ted. Testkill / [by] Ted Dexter and Clifford Makins. — Harmondsworth [etc.] : Penguin, 1977. — 189p : facsim ; 18cm. — (Penguin crime fiction)
Originally published: London : Allen and Unwin, 1976.
ISBN 0-14-004466-3 Pbk : £0.60
(B77-25194)

Di Giovanni, Norman Thomas. 1900 / [by] Norman Thomas Di Giovanni. — [London] : Fontana, 1977. — 283p ; 18cm.
ISBN 0-00-614476-4 Pbk : £0.75
(B77-34110)

Dick, Kay. They : a sequence of unease / [by] Kay Dick. — Harmondsworth [etc.] : Penguin, 1977. — 94p ; 19cm.
ISBN 0-14-004469-8 Pbk : £0.70
(B77-29695)

Dick, Kay. They : a sequence of unease / [by] Kay Dick. — London : Allen Lane, 1977. — 94p ; 21cm.
ISBN 0-7139-1056-9 : £2.95
(B77-29696)

Dick, Philip Kindred. Counter clock world / [by] Philip K. Dick. — London [etc.] : White Lion Publishers, 1977. — 160p ; 21cm.
Originally published: New York : Berkley, 1967.
ISBN 0-85617-199-9 : £3.25
(B77-14909)

Dick, Philip Kindred. Counter-clock world / [by] Philip K. Dick. — Sevenoaks : Coronet, 1977. — 158p ; 18cm.
Originally published: New York : Berkeley, 1967 ; London : White Lion Publishers, 1977.
ISBN 0-340-21830-4 Pbk : £0.70
(B77-22124)

Dick, Philip Kindred. The crack in space / [by] Philip K. Dick. — London : Eyre Methuen, 1977. — 188p ; 18cm.
ISBN 0-413-36530-1 Pbk : £0.70
(B77-10550)

Dick, Philip Kindred. Deus Irae / [by] Philip K. Dick & Roger Zelazny. — London : Gollancz, 1977. — [7],182p ; 21cm. — ([Gollancz SF])
Originally published: Garden City, N.Y. : Doubleday, 1976.
ISBN 0-575-02307-4 : £3.75
(B77-31453)

Dick, Philip Kindred. The Game-players of Titan / [by] Philip K. Dick. — London : Sphere, 1977. — 157p ; 18cm. — (Sphere science fiction)
Originally published: New York : Ace Books, 1963 ; London : Sphere, 1969.
ISBN 0-7221-2961-0 Pbk : £0.65
(B77-20598)

Dick, Philip Kindred. A scanner darkly / [by] Philip K. Dick. — London : Gollancz, 1977. — [4],220p ; 21cm.
Also published: Garden City, N.Y. : Doubleday, 1977.
ISBN 0-575-02381-3 : £3.50
(B77-31454)

Dick, Philip Kindred. The simulacra / [by] Philip K. Dick. — London : Eyre Methuen, 1977. — 220p ; 19cm.
Originally published: New York : Ace Books, 1964.
ISBN 0-413-37750-4 : £2.95
(B77-28892)

Dick, Philip Kindred. We can build you / [by] Philip K. Dick. — [London] : Fontana, 1977. — 208p ; 18cm.
Originally published: New York : Daw Books, 1972.
ISBN 0-00-614616-3 Pbk : £0.70
(B77-29697)

Dick, Philip Kindred. The world Jones made : science fiction / by Philip K. Dick. — London : Sidgwick and Jackson [etc.], 1976. — 160p ; 18cm.
Originally published: New York : Ace Books, 1956 ; London : Sidgwick and Jackson, 1968.
ISBN 0-283-98364-7 Pbk : £0.60
(B77-01791)

Dickens, Monica. Flowers on the grass / [by] Monica Dickens. — Harmondsworth [etc.] : Penguin, 1977. — 255p ; 19cm.
Originally published: London : Joseph, 1949.
ISBN 0-14-001808-5 Pbk : £0.65
(B77-08043)

Dickens, Monica. The happy prisoner / [by] Monica Dickens. — Harmondsworth [etc.] : Penguin, 1976. — 311p ; 18cm.
Originally published: London : Joseph, 1946.
ISBN 0-14-001271-0 Pbk : £0.70
(B77-08044)

Dickens, Monica. Last year when I was young / [by] Monica Dickens. — Large print ed. — Bath : Firecrest, 1977. — [4],364p ; 23cm.
Originally published: London : Heinemann, 1974.
ISBN 0-85119-012-x : £4.75
(B77-18990)

Dickens, Monica. My turn to make the tea / [by] Monica Dickens. — Harmondsworth [etc.] : Penguin, 1977. — 222p ; 19cm.
Originally published: London : Joseph, 1951.
ISBN 0-14-001751-8 Pbk : £0.60
(B77-07602)

Dickinson, Margaret. Pride of the Courtneys / [by] Margaret Dickinson. — London [etc.] : White Lion Publishers, 1977. — 175p ; 21cm.
Originally published: London : Hale, 1968.
ISBN 0-7274-0215-3 : £3.25
(B77-34111)

Dickinson, Peter. The blue hawk / [by] Peter Dickinson ; illustrated by David Smee. — Harmondsworth [etc.] : Puffin Books, 1977. — 237p ; 18cm. — (Puffin books)
Originally published: London : Gollancz, 1976.
ISBN 0-14-030929-2 Pbk : £0.60
(B77-30629)

Dickinson, Peter. King and joker / [by] Peter Dickinson. — Large print [ed.]. — London : Prior [etc.], 1977. — [5],423p : geneal table ; 24cm.
Originally published: London : Hodder and Stoughton, 1976.
ISBN 0-86043-057-x : £4.95
(B77-22125)

Dickson, Gordon Rupert. Dorsai! / [by] Gordon R. Dickson. — London : Sphere, 1976. — 176p ; 18cm.
Originally published: as 'The genetic general'. New York : Ace Books, 1960.
ISBN 0-7221-2951-3 Pbk : £0.50
(B77-08045)

Dickson, Gordon Rupert. The outposter / [by] Gordon R. Dickson. — London : Sphere, 1975. — 187p ; 18cm.
'A slightly different version of this work was first published in "Analog, science fiction-science fact"' - title page verso. — Originally published: Philadelphia : Lippincott, 1972 ; London : Hale, 1973.
ISBN 0-7221-2955-6 Pbk : £0.60
(B77-13267)

Dickson, Gordon Rupert. Soldier, ask not / [by] Gordon R. Dickson. — London : Sphere, 1975. — 216p ; 18cm. — (Sphere science fiction)
Originally published: New York : Dell, 1967.
ISBN 0-7221-2952-1 Pbk : £0.60
(B77-08046)

Dickson, Gordon Rupert. Tactics of mistake / [by] Gordon R. Dickson. — London : Sphere, 1976. — 238p ; 18cm.
Originally published: Garden City, N.Y. : Doubleday, 1971 ; London : Sphere, 1975.
ISBN 0-7221-2954-8 Pbk : £0.60
(B77-07603)

Didion, Joan. A book of common prayer / [by] Joan Didion. — London : Weidenfeld and Nicolson, 1977. — 3-272p ; 23cm.
ISBN 0-297-77269-4 : £4.25
(B77-19673)

Dillon, Catherine. Constantine Cay / [by] Catherine Dillon. — London (11 New Fetter La., EC4P 4EE) : Magnum Books, 1977. — 254p ; 18cm.
Originally published: London : Hodder and Stoughton, 1975.
ISBN 0-413-36940-4 Pbk : £0.70
(B77-14403)

Dillon, Catherine. Rockfire / by Catherine Dillon. — London [etc.] : Hodder and Stoughton, 1977. — 253p ; 21cm.
ISBN 0-340-21264-0 : £3.75
(B77-13867)

Dines, Michael. Abrams and Jones, homicide / by Michael Dines. — London : Hale, 1977. — 188p ; 20cm.
ISBN 0-7091-6078-x : £3.15
(B77-17093)

Dingwell, Joyce. Inland paradise / by Joyce Dingwell. — London : Mills and Boon, 1976. — 188p ; 19cm.
ISBN 0-263-09042-6 : £1.95
(B77-12651)

DiPego, Gerald. With a vengeance / [by] Gerald DiPego. — London [etc.] : Macmillan, 1977. — [5],262p ; 21cm.
ISBN 0-333-22341-1 : £4.50
(B77-28893)

Dixon, Roger. Christ on trial / [by] Roger Dixon ; based on the original story by Basil Bova and Roger Dixon. — [London] : Fontana, 1976. — 255p ; 18cm.
Originally published: New York : Pinnacle Books, 1973 ; London : Collins, 1974.
ISBN 0-00-624191-3 Pbk : £0.65
(B77-10940)

Dixon, Roger. Going to Jerusalem / [by] Roger Dixon. — London : Collins, 1977. — 224p ; 22cm.
ISBN 0-00-221420-2 : £3.95
(B77-13868)

Dixon, Roger. The Messiah / [by] Roger Dixon. — [London] : Fontana, 1976. — 288p ; 18cm.
Originally published: London : Collins, 1975.
ISBN 0-00-624440-8 Pbk : £0.75
(B77-10941)

Dixon, Rosie. Confessions of a babysitter / [by] Rosie Dixon. — London : Futura Publications, 1976. — 160p ; 18cm.
ISBN 0-86007-335-1 Pbk : £0.50
(B77-08556)

Dixon, Rosie. Confessions of a personal secretary / [by] Rosie Dixon. — London : Futura Publications, 1976. — 157p ; 18cm.
ISBN 0-86007-388-2 Pbk : £0.50
(B77-12652)

Doctorow, E L. Ragtime / [by] E.L. Doctorow. — London : Pan Books, 1977. — 236p ; 18cm.
Originally published: New York : Random House ; London : Macmillan, 1975.
ISBN 0-330-24648-8 Pbk : £0.75
(B77-09940)

Doctorow, E L. Ragtime / [by] E.L. Doctorow. — Large print [ed.]. — London : Prior [etc.], 1976. — [9],467p ; 24cm.
Originally published: New York : Random House ; London : Macmillan, 1975.
ISBN 0-86043-011-1 : £5.95
(B77-07604)

Doctorow, E L. Welcome to hard times / [by] E.L. Doctorow. — London [etc.] : Pan Books, 1977. — 155p ; 18cm.
Originally published: as 'Welcome to hard times', New York : Simon and Schuster, 1960 ; and as 'Bad man from Bodie', London : Deutsch, 1961.
ISBN 0-330-25085-x Pbk : £0.60
(B77-25195)

Donaldson, William. Both the ladies and the gentlemen / [by] William Donaldson. — London : Futura Publications, 1977. — 199p ; 18cm.
Originally published: London : Talmy Franklin, 1975.
ISBN 0-86007-278-9 Pbk : £0.75
(B77-08557)

Donnelly, Jane. The silver cage / by Jane Donnelly. — London : Mills and Boon, 1976. — 188p ; 19cm.
Previous control number ISBN 0-263-72298-8.
ISBN 0-263-09011-6 : £1.95
ISBN 0-263-72298-8 Pbk : £0.30
(B77-00419)

Douglas, Colin, *b.1945.* The greatest breakthrough since lunchtime / [by] Colin Douglas. — Edinburgh : Canongate Publishing, 1977. — [4],176p ; 23cm.
ISBN 0-903937-38-7 : £3.95
(B77-25881)

Douglas, Colin, *b.1945.* The houseman's tale / [by] Colin Douglas. — [London] : Fontana, 1977. — 222p ; 18cm.
Originally published: Edinburgh : Canongate, 1975.
ISBN 0-00-614473-x Pbk : £0.75
(B77-16052)

Douglas, Felicity. Within these walls / [by] Felicity Douglas. — London : Futura Publications, 1975. — 187p ; 18cm.
'... based on the scripts by David Butler and Felicity Douglas for the London Weekend Television series "Within these walls"' - title page verso.
ISBN 0-86007-162-6 Pbk : £0.40
(B77-08558)

Douglas, George, *b.1902.* End of the line / by George Douglas. — London : Hale, 1977. — 189p ; 20cm.
ISBN 0-7091-6306-1 : £3.25
(B77-26524)

Douglas, John, *b.1931.* A walk down Summer Lane / [by] John Douglas ; with a foreword by Archie Hill. — Kineton : Roundwood Press, 1977. — xi,137p ; 23cm.
ISBN 0-900093-66-8 : £3.75
(B77-32852)

Douglas, Lloyd Cassel. The big fisherman / [by] Lloyd C. Douglas. — London : Corgi, 1977. — 501p ; 18cm.
Originally published: London : Peter Davies, 1949.
ISBN 0-552-10451-5 Pbk : £1.25
(B77-30630)

Douglas, Richard. The rig / [by] Richard Douglas. — London [etc.] : White Lion Publishers, 1977. — 251p ; 21cm.
Originally published: London : Futura Publications, 1975.
ISBN 0-7274-0258-7 : £3.50
(B77-12653)

Douglas, Thorne. Killraine / [by] Thorne Douglas. — Sevenoaks : Coronet, 1977. — 190p ; 18cm.
Originally published: New York : Fawcett Publications, 1975.
ISBN 0-340-21752-9 Pbk : £0.65
(B77-28894)

Doyle, *Sir* **Arthur Conan.** The lost world : being an account of the recent amazing adventures of Professor E. Challenger, Lord John Roxton, Professor Summerlee, and Mr E.D. Malone of the 'Daily gazette' / [by] Arthur Conan Doyle. — London : Folio Society, 1977. — 195p,[11] leaves of plates : ill, map ; 23cm.
In slip case. — Originally published: London : Hodder and Stoughton, 1912.
£4.95(to members only)
(B77-31455)

Doyle, *Sir* **Arthur Conan.** The lost world : being an account of the recent amazing adventures of Professor E. Challenger, Lord John Roxton, Professor Summerlee and Mr Ed Malone of the 'Daily Gazette'. — London [etc.] : Pan Books, 1977. — [7],214p : 1 ill, 2 maps ; 18cm.
Originally published: London : Hodder and Stoughton, 1912.
ISBN 0-330-25107-4 Pbk : £0.70
(B77-20599)

Doyle, *Sir* **Arthur Conan.** The Maracot Deep / [by] Sir Arthur Conan Doyle. — London [etc.] : Pan Books, 1977. — 128p ; 18cm.
Originally published: in 'The Maracot Deep, and other stories'. London : J. Murray, 1929.
ISBN 0-330-25108-2 Pbk : £0.60
(B77-20600)

Dozois, Gardner. Nightmare blue / [by] Gardner Dozois and George Alec Effinger. — [London] : Fontana, 1977. — 190p ; 18cm. — (Fontana science fiction)
Originally published: United States : Berkeley Medallion Books, 1975.
ISBN 0-00-614617-1 Pbk : £0.70
(B77-31456)

Drabble, John Frederick. Scawsby / [by] John Drabble. — London : Weidenfeld and Nicolson, 1977. — [5],247p ; 23cm.
ISBN 0-297-77280-5 : £4.50
(B77-13268)

Drabble, Margaret. The ice age : a novel / by Margaret Drabble. — London : Weidenfeld and Nicolson, 1977. — 297p ; 23cm.
ISBN 0-297-77368-2 : £4.25
(B77-25882)

Drabble, Margaret. The millstone / [by] Margaret Drabble. — Harmondsworth [etc.] : Penguin, 1977. — 172p ; 18cm. — (Peacock books)
Originally published: London : Weidenfeld and Nicolson, 1965.
ISBN 0-14-047097-2 Pbk : £0.50
(B77-12095)

Drabble, Margaret. The realms of gold / [by] Margaret Drabble. — Harmondsworth [etc.] : Penguin, 1977. — 358p ; 19cm.
Originally published: London : Weidenfeld and Nicolson, 1975.
ISBN 0-14-004360-8 Pbk : £0.95
(B77-14910)

Drake, Francis. Double identity / by Francis Drake. — London : Hale, 1977. — 159p ; 20cm.
ISBN 0-7091-6291-x : £3.25
(B77-26525)

Drew, Eleanor. Burn all your bridges / [by] Eleanor Drew. — London : Macdonald and Jane's, 1977. — [4],156p ; 21cm. — (A Troubador)
ISBN 0-354-04119-3 : £3.95
(B77-24479)

Drew, John. Seven nights in Japan / [by] John Drew. — London : Futura Publications, 1976. — 159p ; 18cm.
ISBN 0-86007-334-3 Pbk : £0.50
(B77-08559)

Drewe, Robert. The savage crows / [by] Robert Drewe. — Sydney ; London : Collins, 1976. — 264p ; 22cm.
ISBN 0-00-221589-6 : £4.50
(B77-22126)

Driscoll, Peter. The Barboza credentials : a novel / by Peter Driscoll. — London : Macdonald and Jane's, 1976. — 334p ; 22cm.
ISBN 0-354-04028-6 : £3.95
(B77-01792)

Driscoll, Peter. In connection with Kilshaw / [by] Peter Driscoll. — London : Sphere, 1975. — 251p ; 18cm.
Originally published: London : Macdonald and Jane's, 1974.
ISBN 0-7221-3061-9 Pbk : £0.75
(B77-01793)

Driscoll, Peter. The Wilby conspiracy / [by] Peter Driscoll. — London : Sphere, 1975. — 3-269p ; 18cm.
Originally published: London : Macdonald and Co., 1973.
ISBN 0-7221-3062-7 Pbk : £0.75
(B77-01794)

Drummond, Ivor. The necklace of skulls / [by] Ivor Drummond. — London : Joseph, 1977. — [4],185p ; 21cm.
ISBN 0-7181-1552-x : £3.95
(B77-10942)

Drury, Allen. Return to Thebes / [by] Allen Drury. — London : Joseph, 1977. — xvi,272p : geneal table ; 25cm.
Also published: Garden City, N.Y. : Doubleday, 1977.
ISBN 0-7181-1583-x : £5.50
(B77-24480)

Dryland, Gordon. Curious conscience / [by] Gordon Dryland. — Palmerston North : Dunmore Press ; London : Hale, 1977. — 190p ; 21cm.
ISBN 0-7091-6205-7 : £3.70
(B77-22127)

Du Maurier, *Dame* Daphne. The loving spirit / [by] Daphne du Maurier. — London : Pan Books, 1976. — 351p : geneal table ; 18cm.
Originally published: London : Heinemann, 1931.
ISBN 0-330-24244-x Pbk : £0.75
(B77-08047)

Du Maurier, *Dame* Daphne. Mary Anne : a novel / by Daphne du Maurier. — London [etc.] : Pan Books, 1976. — 381p ; 18cm.
Originally published: London : Gollancz, 1954. — Based on the life of Mary Anne Clarke.
ISBN 0-330-24839-1 Pbk : £0.75
(B77-02575)

Du Vall, Stephen. The song of Hero : a legend / by Stephen Du Vall. — Perth, W. Australia : The author ; Ilfracombe : Distributed by Stockwell, 1977. — 56p ; 18cm.
ISBN 0-7223-1015-3 Pbk : Unpriced
(B77-31457)

Dudley, Ernest. The blind beak : a novel about the fabulous Sir John Fielding, blind magistrate and detective, his renowned Bow Street Runners and his secret agent, Nick Rathburn, gamester and rakehell / by Ernest Dudley. — London : Remploy, 1976. — 222p ; 20cm.
Originally published: London : Hale, 1954. — Based on the life of Sir John Fielding.
ISBN 0-7066-0688-4 : £2.75
(B77-10551)

Dulack, Tom. The stigmata of Dr Constantine / [by] Tom Dulack. — Toronto [etc.] ; London : Bantam, 1976 [i.e. 1977]. — [9],340,[1]p ; 18cm.
Originally published: New York : Harpers Magazine Press, 1974.
ISBN 0-553-02195-8 Pbk : £0.75
(B77-09260)

Dunbar, Jean. An heir for Maryvale / by Jean Dunbar. — London : Mills and Boon, 1976. — 188p ; 19cm.
ISBN 0-263-09023-x : £1.95
(B77-10552)

Duncan, Alex. The best of vets / [by] Alex Duncan ; [condensed by Jo Deitch]. — London : W.H. Allen, 1977. — [5],233p ; 23cm.
'... condensed ... from "It's a vet's life" ... "The vet has nine lives" ... "Vets in the belfry" ... by Alex Duncan - title page verso.
ISBN 0-491-02051-1 : £3.95
(B77-34112)

Duncan, Jane. My friends George and Tom / [by] Jane Duncan. — Large print ed. — London : Prior [etc.], 1977. — [3],455p ; 25cm.
Originally published: London [etc.] : Macmillan, 1976.
ISBN 0-86043-064-2 : £5.50
(B77-33429)

Duncan, Robert Lipscomb. Dragons at the gate / [by] Robert L. Duncan. — London : Sphere, 1977. — 255p ; 18cm.
Originally published: New York : Morrow, 1975 ; London : Joseph, 1976.
ISBN 0-7221-0414-6 Pbk : £0.75
(B77-18991)

Duncan, William Murdoch. Murder of a cop / [by] W. Murdoch Duncan. — London : Long, 1976. — 187p ; 20cm.
ISBN 0-09-127190-8 : £3.25
(B77-12654)

Dunmore, Spencer. Collision / [by] Spencer Dunmore. — London [etc.] : Pan Books, 1977. — 254p ; 18cm.
Originally published: London : P. Davies, 1974. — Bibl.: p.254.
Pbk : £0.75
ISBN 0-330-24606-2
(B77-31458)

Dunmore, Spencer. Final approach / [by] Spencer Dunmore. — London [etc.] : Pan Books, 1977. — 284p ; 18cm.
Originally published: London : P. Davies, 1976.
ISBN 0-330-25206-2 Pbk : £0.80
(B77-31459)

Dunne, Lee. The virgin cabbies / [by] Lee Dunne. — London : Futura Publications, 1976. — 188p ; 18cm.
ISBN 0-86007-317-3 Pbk : £0.60
(B77-09261)

Dunnett, Dorothy. Pawn in frankincense / [by] Dorothy Dunnett. — London : Sphere, 1976. — 576p : map ; 18cm.
Originally published: London : Cassell, 1969.
ISBN 0-7221-3141-0 Pbk : £0.95
(B77-15493)

Dunsany, Edward Plunkett, *Baron*. The curse of the wise woman / [by] Lord Dunsany. — London : Sphere, 1976. — 173p ; 18cm. — (The Dennis Wheatley library of the occult ; vol.40)
Originally published: London : Heinemann, 1933.
ISBN 0-7221-3135-6 Pbk : £0.60
(B77-15494)

Durbridge, Francis. A game of murder / [by] Francis Durbridge. — London : Coronet, 1977. — 160p ; 18cm.
Originally published: London : Hodder and Stoughton, 1975.
ISBN 0-340-21302-7 Pbk : £0.60
(B77-09262)

Durbridge, Francis. The other man / [by] Francis Durbridge. — Large print ed. — Leicester : Ulverscroft, 1977. — [5],311p ; 23cm. — (Ulverscroft large print series : [mystery])
Originally published: London : Hodder and Stoughton, 1958.
ISBN 0-85456-547-7 : £2.75
(B77-28895)

Durham, John, *b.1916*. Nightrider's moon / by John Durham. — London : Hale, 1977. — 152p ; 20cm.
ISBN 0-7091-6114-x : £3.10
(B77-27380)

Durham, John, *b.1916*. Signal rock range / by John Durham. — London : Hale, 1977. — 152p ; 20cm.
ISBN 0-7091-5836-x : £2.95
(B77-08048)

Durham, John, *b.1916*. Tomahawk Meadow / by John Durham. — London : Hale, 1977. — 158p ; 20cm.
ISBN 0-7091-6085-2 : £2.95
(B77-20601)

Durman, Hilda. Call for Greenacres / [by] Hilda Durman. — London : Hale, 1977. — 160p ; 20cm.
ISBN 0-7091-6035-6 : £3.20
(B77-19674)

Durman, Hilda. Meadow's End / by Hilda Durman. — London : Hale, 1977. — 159p ; 20cm.
ISBN 0-7091-6155-7 : £3.20
(B77-28120)

Durrell, Lawrence. The black book : a novel / by Lawrence Durrell. — London : Faber, 1977. — 3-244p ; 20cm.
Originally published: Paris : Obelisk, 1938 ; London : Faber, 1973.
ISBN 0-571-11075-4 Pbk : £1.95
(B77-08049)

Dwyer, K.R. Dragonfly / [by] K.R. Dwyer. — London : P. Davies, 1977. — [5],244p ; 23cm.
Originally published: New York : Random House, 1975.
ISBN 0-432-03550-8 : £3.50
(B77-08050)

Dwyer-Joyce, Alice. The banshee tide / [by] Alice Dwyer-Joyce. — London : Hale, 1977. — 189p ; 21cm.
ISBN 0-7091-5549-2 : £3.50
(B77-19675)

Dwyer-Joyce, Alice. The diamond cage / [by] Alice Dwyer-Joyce. — Large print ed. — Leicester : Ulverscroft, 1977. — [5],288p ; 23cm. — (Ulverscroft large print series : [romance])
Originally published: New York : St Martin's Press ; London : Hale, 1976.
ISBN 0-7089-0011-9 : £2.95
(B77-22128)

Dwyer-Joyce, Alice. The gingerbread house / [by] Alice Dwyer-Joyce. — New York : St Martin's Press ; London : Hale, 1977. — 224p ; 21cm.
ISBN 0-7091-5785-1 : £3.60
(B77-12655)

Dwyer-Joyce, Alice. The storm of wrath / [by] Alice Dwyer-Joyce. — New York : St Martins Press ; London : Hale, 1977. — [2],205p ; 20cm.
ISBN 0-7091-6309-6 : £3.70
(B77-28896)

Dyke, Carol Hamilton. The Demarel inheritance / by Carol Hamilton Dyke. — London : Hale, 1976. — 184p ; 20cm.
ISBN 0-7091-5685-5 : £2.95
(B77-01795)

Dyke, Carol Hamilton. Dragon's bane / by Carol Hamilton Dyke. — London : Hale, 1977. — 176p ; 20cm.
ISBN 0-7091-6013-5 : £3.20
(B77-22129)

Dyke, Carol Hamilton. Summer folly / by Carol Hamilton Dyke. — London : Hale, 1977. — 190p ; 20cm.
ISBN 0-7091-5822-x : £3.10
(B77-16590)

Dymoke, Juliet. Shadows on a throne / [by] Juliet Dymoke. — London : Wingate, 1976. — 187p ; 23cm.
ISBN 0-85523-074-6 : £3.50
(B77-00968)

Early, Richard Elliott. Apprentice : a historical novel / by Richard E. Early. — London [etc.] : Routledge and Kegan Paul, 1977. — [8],179p ; 23cm.
Based on the life of Thomas Early.
ISBN 0-7100-8692-x : £4.50 : CIP rev.
(B77-18992)

Eastwood, Helen. The ghostly melody / by Helen Eastwood. — London : Hale, 1977. — 175p ; 21cm.
ISBN 0-7091-6275-8 : £3.50
(B77-28897)

Eaton, Evelyn. The king is a witch / [by] Evelyn Eaton. — London : Sphere, 1976. — 219p ; 18cm. — (Dennis Wheatley library of the occult ; vol.38)
Originally published: London : Cassell and Collier Macmillan, 1965.
ISBN 0-7221-3192-5 Pbk : £0.60
(B77-14911)

Ebel, Suzanne. The double rainbow / [by] Suzanne Ebel. — London : Collins, 1977. — 157p ; 19cm.
ISBN 0-00-233181-0 : £2.75
(B77-08560)

Eberhart, Mignon Good. Call after midnight / [by] M.G. Eberhart. — London [etc.] : White Lion Publishers, 1977. — 256p ; 21cm.
Originally published: New York : Random House, 1964 ; London : Collins, 1965.
ISBN 0-7274-0294-3 : £3.75
(B77-19676)

Eberhart, Mignon Good. Five passengers from Lisbon / by Mignon G. Eberhart. — Hornchurch : I. Henry, 1977. — 159p ; 21cm.
Originally published: New York : Random House ; London : Collins, 1946.
ISBN 0-86025-117-9 : £3.25
(B77-19677)

Eberhart, Mignon Good. RSVP murder / by Mignon G. Eberhart. — Hornchurch : I. Henry, 1976. — 224p ; 21cm.
Originally published: New York : Random House, 1965 ; London : Collins, 1966.
ISBN 0-86025-102-0 : £3.10
(B77-01796)

Eberhart, Mignon Good. Speak no evil / by Mignon G. Eberhart. — London : Remploy, 1976. — 252p ; 19cm.
Originally published: London : Collins, 1941.
ISBN 0-7066-0681-7 : £2.75
(B77-04403)

Eberhart, Mignon Good. Witness at large / [by] M.G. Eberhart. — London [etc.] : White Lion Publishers, 1977. — 192p ; 21cm.
Originally published: New York : Random House, 1966 ; London : Collins, 1967.
ISBN 0-7274-0289-7 : £3.75
(B77-16053)

Eckert, Allan Wesley. The HAB theory / [by] Allan W. Eckert. — London : Sphere, 1977. — 717p ; 18cm.
Originally published: Boston, Mass. : Little, Brown, 1976.
ISBN 0-7221-3204-2 Pbk : £1.50
(B77-30631)

Eden, Dorothy. Afternoon for lizards / [by] Dorothy Eden. — Large print ed. — Leicester : Ulverscroft, 1977. — [9],318p ; 23cm. — (Ulverscroft large print series : [romance])
Originally published: London : Hodder and Stoughton, 1962.
ISBN 0-7089-0056-9 : £2.95
(B77-32167)

Eden, Dorothy. The house on Hay Hill / [by] Dorothy Eden. — London : Coronet, 1976. — 224p ; 18cm.
This collection also published: New York : Fawcett Publications, 1976.
ISBN 0-340-21479-1 Pbk : £0.60
(B77-02576)

Eden, Dorothy. Listen to danger / [by] Dorothy Eden. — Large print ed. — Leicester : Ulverscroft, 1977. — [7],375p ; 23cm. — (Ulverscroft large print series : [romantic suspense])
Originally published: London : Macdonald and Co., 1958.
ISBN 0-7089-0035-6 : Unpriced
(B77-34113)

Eden, Dorothy. The Salamanca drum / [by] Dorothy Eden. — London [etc.] : Hodder and Stoughton, 1977. — 3-284p ; 23cm.
ISBN 0-340-21747-2 : £3.95
(B77-25883)

Eden, Dorothy. The time of the dragon / [by] Dorothy Eden. — Large print ed. — Leicester : Ulverscroft, 1977. — [4],475p ; 23cm. — (Ulverscroft large print series : [romantic suspense])
Originally published: London : Hodder and Stoughton, 1975.
ISBN 0-7089-0048-8 : Unpriced
(B77-28121)

Eden, Dorothy. The voice of the dolls / [by] Dorothy Eden. — Large print ed. — Leicester : Ulverscroft, 1977. — [7],371p ; 23cm. — (Ulverscroft large print series : [romantic suspense])
Originally published: London : Macdonald and Co., 1950.
ISBN 0-85456-539-6 : £2.95
(B77-19678)

Eden, Dorothy. Whistle for the crows / [by] Dorothy Eden. — Large print ed. — Leicester : Ulverscroft, 1977. — [7],355p ; 23cm. — (Ulverscroft large print series : [romantic suspense])
Originally published: London : Hodder and Stoughton, 1962.
ISBN 0-7089-0023-2 : £2.95
(B77-20602)

Edgar, Josephine. The Lady of Wildersley / [by] Josephine Edgar ; edited by Lesley Saxby. — London (110 Warner Rd, S.E.5) : Troubadour, 1976. — [4],178p ; 18cm.
Originally published: London : Macdonald and Jane's, 1975.
ISBN 0-86007-354-8 Pbk : £0.50
(B77-08561)

Edson, John Thomas. The bull whip breed / by J.T. Edson. — London : Hale, 1977. — 159p ; 20cm.
Originally published: London : Corgi, 1968.
ISBN 0-7091-3222-0 : £3.25
(B77-32168)

Edson, John Thomas. 'Cap' Fog, Texas Ranger, meet Mr J.G. Reeder / [by] J.T. Edson. — London : Corgi, 1977. — 205p ; 18cm.
ISBN 0-552-10578-3 Pbk : £0.60
(B77-32169)

Edson, John Thomas. Doc Leroy, MD / [by] J.T. Edson. — London : Corgi, 1977. — 191p ; 18cm.
ISBN 0-552-10406-x Pbk : £0.50
(B77-16591)

Edson, John Thomas. Gun wizard / by J.T. Edson. — London : Hale, 1977. — 160p ; 20cm.
Originally published: London : Corgi, 1969.
ISBN 0-7091-3223-9 : £2.95
(B77-09941)

Edson, John Thomas. The hard riders / [by] J.T. Edson. — Large print ed. — Leicester : Ulverscroft, 1977. — [5],318p ; 23cm. — (Ulverscroft large print series : [Western])
Originally published: London : Brown, Watson, 1962.
ISBN 0-7089-0040-2 : Unpriced
(B77-34114)

Edson, John Thomas. Ole Devil and the Caplocks / by J.T. Edson. — London : Corgi, 1976. — 203p ; 18cm.
ISBN 0-552-10158-3 Pbk : £0.50
(B77-05655)

Edson, John Thomas. Ole Devil and the mule train / [by] J.T. Edson. — London : Corgi, 1976. — 159p ; 18cm.
ISBN 0-552-10332-2 Pbk : £0.50
(B77-04404)

Edson, John Thomas. Sagebrush sleuth / by J.T. Edson. — London : Hale, 1977. — 157p ; 20cm.
Originally published: London : Corgi, 1968.
ISBN 0-7091-3221-2 : £2.95
(B77-18369)

Edson, John Thomas. A town called Yellowdog / [by] J.T. Edson. — Large print ed. — Leicester : Ulverscroft, 1977. — [4],309p ; 23cm. — (Ulverscroft large print series : [Western])
Originally published: London : Brown, Watson, 1966.
ISBN 0-7089-0062-3 : £2.95
(B77-32170)

Edwards, Alexander. The black bird : a novel / by Alexander Edwards ; based on the screenplay written and directed by David Giler ; story by Don M. Mankiewicz and Gordon Cotler. — London : Star Books, 1976. — 128p ; 18cm.
Originally published: New York : Warner Paperback Library, 1975.
ISBN 0-352-39817-5 Pbk : £0.45
(B77-06283)

Edwards, Ernie. It all started / author Ernie Edwards. — Plymouth (Mount House, Shaugh Prior, Plymouth PL7 5HA) : John Edwards, [1977]. — [34]p : port ; 21cm.
ISBN 0-9505573-2-3 Sd : Unpriced
(B77-13269)

Edwards, Ernie. The lucky prisoner / author Ernie Edwards. — Plymouth (Mount House, Shaugh Prior, Plymouth PL7 5HA) : John Edwards, [1977]. — [22]p : port ; 21cm.
ISBN 0-9505573-1-5 Sd : Unpriced
(B77-13270)

Edwards, John Ernest. From Glastonbury to Dartmoor : a story / written by J.E. Edwards. — [Plymouth] ([c/o Mount Clogg, Shaugh Prior, Plymouth PL7 5HA]) : [The author], [1977]. — [3],29p ; 21cm.
ISBN 0-9505573-0-7 Sd : £0.47
(B77-07605)

Edwards, John Ernest. How a convict became a farmer / by J.E. Edwards. — Plymouth ([c/o Mount Clogg], Shaugh Prior, Plymouth [PL7 5HA]) : The author, [1977]. — [1],16p ; 21cm.
ISBN 0-9505573-3-1 Sd : Unpriced
(B77-13271)

Edwards, Rachelle. A spy for Napoleon / by Rachelle Edwards. — London : Hale, 1977. — 3-172p ; 21cm.
ISBN 0-7091-5699-5 : £3.50
(B77-05063)

Edwards, Samuel. The exploiters / [by] Samuel Edwards. — London : Pan Books, 1977. — 320p ; 18cm.
Originally published: New York : Praeger, 1974 ; London : Heinemann, 1975.
ISBN 0-330-25106-6 Pbk : £0.80
(B77-26526)

Edwards, Samuel. Neptune / [by] Samuel Edwards. — London : Heinemann, 1977. — [5],185p ; 23cm.
Originally published: / under the name Noel Bertram Gerson. New York : Dodd, Mead, 1976.
ISBN 0-434-28820-9 : £3.50
(B77-06865)

Egan, Lesley. The blind search / [by] Lesley Egan. — London : Gollancz, 1977. — [7],175p ; 21cm.
ISBN 0-575-02341-4 : £3.95
(B77-22861)

Egleton, Clive. State visit / [by] Clive Egleton. — London [etc.] : Hodder and Stoughton, 1976. — 221p ; 23cm.
ISBN 0-340-21270-5 : £3.95
(B77-00969)

Elder, Michael. Oil-seeker / [by] Michael Elder. — London : Hale, 1977. — 189p ; 21cm. — (Hale SF)
ISBN 0-7091-5933-1 : £3.25
(B77-09942)

Eldridge, Roger. The shadow of the gloom-world / [by] Roger Eldridge. — London : Gollancz, 1977. — 191p ; 21cm.
ISBN 0-575-02277-9 : £3.60
(B77-19679)

Elgin, Elizabeth. The Manchester affair / by Elizabeth Elgin. — London : Hale, 1977. — 184p ; 20cm.
ISBN 0-7091-6105-0 : £3.20
(B77-26527)

Elkin, Stanley. Alex and the gypsy : three short novels / [by] Stanley Elkin. — Harmondsworth [etc.] : Penguin, 1977. — 315p ; 18cm.
Originally published: as 'Searches and seizures', New York : Random House, 1973 ; and as 'Eligible men', London : Gollancz, 1974. — Contents: Alex and the gypsy - The making of Ashenden - The condominium.
ISBN 0-14-004562-7 Pbk : £0.95
(B77-27381)

Ellin, Stanley. Stronghold / [by] Stanley Ellin. — Harmondsworth [etc.] : Penguin, 1977. — 294p ; 18cm. — (Penguin crime fiction)
Originally published: New York : Random House, 1974 ; London : Cape, 1975.
ISBN 0-14-004336-5 Pbk : £0.80
(B77-15495)

Elliot, John, *b.1918.* Blood upon the snow : a novel / by John Elliot. — London : Souvenir Press, 1977. — 334p ; 23cm.
ISBN 0-285-62247-1 : £4.00
(B77-18370)

Elliott, Janice. A loving eye / [by] Janice Elliott. — London [etc.] : Hodder and Stoughton, 1977. — 256p ; 23cm.
ISBN 0-340-21848-7 : £4.25
(B77-28122)

Elliston, Valerie. The tides of spring / [by] Valerie Elliston. — [London] : Fontana, 1977. — 315p ; 18cm.
Originally published: London : Collins, 1975.
ISBN 0-00-614489-6 Pbk : £0.80
(B77-13272)

Elsna, Hebe. Beyond reasonable doubt / [by] Hebe Elsna. — London : Collins, 1977. — 159p ; 19cm.
Originally published: London : Hale, 1962.
ISBN 0-00-233052-0 : £2.75
(B77-09943)

Elsna, Hebe. The love match / [by] Hebe Elsna. — Large print ed. — Bath : Lythway Press, 1976. — [5],355p ; 23cm.
Originally published: London : Hale, 1956.
ISBN 0-85046-684-9 : £4.55
(B77-06866)

Elvin, Harold. The gentle Russian / [by] Harold Elvin. — [London etc.] (Crooks Cottage, Gilsland, Cumbria) : Pacific Press Ltd, [1975 i.e. 1976]. — 5-204p ; 23cm.
ISBN 0-905472-00-4 : £3.50
(B77-08051)

Emecheta, Buchi. The slave girl : a novel / [by] Buchi Emecheta. — London : Allison and Busby, 1977. — 179p ; 23cm.
ISBN 0-85031-221-3 : £3.95
(B77-25884)

Enefer, Douglas. Ice in the sun / by Douglas Enefer. — London : Hale, 1977. — 190p ; 19cm.
ISBN 0-7091-5927-7 : £3.15
(B77-09944)

Engel, Marian. Bear : a novel / by Marian Engel. — London [etc.] : Routledge and Kegan Paul, 1977. — 141p ; 23cm.
Originally published: New York : Atheneum, 1976.
ISBN 0-7100-8603-2 : £3.50
(B77-13869)

Erdman, Paul. The crash of '79 / [by] Paul E. Erdman. — London : Secker and Warburg, 1977. — 350p : 1 ill, col maps(on lining papers) ; 23cm.
Originally published: New York : Simon and Schuster, 1976.
ISBN 0-436-14830-7 : £3.90
(B77-04405)

Erskine, Rosalind. The Passion-Flower Hotel / by Rosalind Erskine. — Hornchurch : I. Henry, 1977. — 156p ; 21cm.
Originally published: London : Cape, 1962.
ISBN 0-86025-111-x : £2.95
(B77-12656)

Escott, Jonathan. Shadow of Katie / by Jonathan Escott. — London : Hale, 1977. — 207p ; 21cm.
ISBN 0-7091-6198-0 : £3.70
(B77-26528)

Esler, Anthony. The blade of Castlemayne / [by] Anthony Esler. — London (110 Warner Rd, S.E.5) : Troubadour, 1976. — 288p ; 18cm.
Originally published: New York : Morrow, 1974 ; London : Weidenfeld and Nicolson, 1975.
ISBN 0-86007-344-0 Pbk : £0.75
(B77-08562)

Esmond, Harriet. The eye stones / [by] Harriet Esmond. — [London] : Coronet, 1976. — 223p ; 18cm.
Originally published: London : Collins, 1975.
ISBN 0-340-21005-2 Pbk : £0.80
(B77-00970)

Esmond, Harriet. The Florian signet / [by] Harriet Esmond. — London : Collins, 1977. — 252p ; 22cm.
ISBN 0-00-222248-5 : £3.95
(B77-08052)

Essex, Mary. I love my love / by Mary Essex. — London : Hale, 1977. — 157p ; 20cm.
ISBN 0-7091-6141-7 : £3.20
(B77-20603)

Evans, Ian. Star maidens : a novel / [by] Ian Evans. — London : Corgi, 1977. — 175p ; 18cm.
'... based on the television series created by Eric Paice' - cover.
ISBN 0-552-10418-3 Pbk : £0.60
(B77-16592)

Evans, Jean. A brittle glory / [by] Jean Evans. — London : Hale, 1977. — 192p ; 21cm.
Based on the life of King Edward II.
ISBN 0-7091-6179-4 : £3.50
(B77-28124)

Evans, Jean. The king's own / by Jean Evans. — London : Hale, 1977. — 173p ; 21cm.
Based on the life of Charles II.
ISBN 0-7091-5865-3 : £3.25
(B77-14912)

Evans, Stuart. The caves of alienation / [by] Stuart Evans. — London : Hutchinson, 1977. — 412p ; 23cm.
ISBN 0-09-128590-9 : £4.95
(B77-13273)

Evans, Stuart. The gardens of the Casino / [by] Stuart Evans. — London : Hutchinson, 1976. — 288p ; 21cm.
ISBN 0-09-124630-x : £4.25
(B77-05064)

Eyers, John. Survivors, genesis of a hero / [by] John Eyers. — London : Weidenfeld and Nicolson, 1977. — 189p ; 23cm.
'Based on the format and characters created by Terry Nation' - title page verso.
ISBN 0-297-77336-4 : £3.95
(B77-23723)

Faid, Mary. The daughter at home / by Mary Faid. — London : Hale, 1977. — 191p ; 20cm.
ISBN 0-7091-5949-8 : £3.10
(B77-09263)

Faid, Mary. The Marshalls of Croma / by Mary Faid. — London : Hale, 1977. — 156p ; 20cm.
ISBN 0-7091-6423-8 : £3.20
(B77-28898)

Fair, A.A. Some women won't wait / by Erle Stanley Gardner writing under the name of A.A. Fair. — Large print ed. — Leicester : Ulverscroft, 1977. — [4],396p ; 23cm. — (Ulverscroft large print series : [mystery])
Jacket has author statement: / Erle Stanley Gardner. — Originally published: New York : Morrow, 1953 ; London : Heinemann, 1958.
ISBN 0-7089-0021-6 : £2.95
(B77-22862)

Falkirk, Richard. Blackstone and the Scourge of Europe / [by] Richard Falkirk. — London : Eyre Methuen, 1976. — 192p ; 18cm.
Originally published: 1974.
ISBN 0-413-34600-5 Pbk : £0.60
(B77-03757)

Falkirk, Richard. Blackstone on Broadway / [by] Richard Falkirk. — London : Eyre Methuen, 1977. — 189p ; 21cm.
ISBN 0-413-33590-9 : £3.75
(B77-27382)

Farmer, Penelope. Year king / by Penelope Farmer. — London : Chatto and Windus, 1977. — 232p ; 21cm.
For adolescents.
ISBN 0-7011-2231-5 : £3.50 : CIP rev.
(B77-16082)

Farmer, Philip José. A feast unknown : volume IX of 'The memoirs of Lord Grandrith', edited by Philip José Farmer / [by] Philip José Farmer. — London : Quartet Books, 1975. — 2-286p ; 18cm.
Originally published: North Hollywood : Essex House, 1969.
ISBN 0-7043-1211-5 Pbk : £0.95
(B77-01797)

Farmer, Philip José. Hadon of ancient Opar / [by] Philip José Farmer. — London : Magnum Books, 1977. — 222p : maps ; 18cm.
Originally published: New York : Daw Books, 1974.
ISBN 0-417-01800-2 Pbk : £0.75
(B77-25885)

Farmer, Philip José. The stone god awakens / [by] Philip José Farmer. — St Albans : Panther, 1976. — 205p ; 18cm. — (Panther science fiction)
Originally published: United States : s.n. : 1970.
ISBN 0-586-04226-1 Pbk : £0.60
(B77-03218)

Farrar, Kate. Rebel's ride / by Kate Farrar. — London : Hale, 1977. — 158p ; 21cm.
ISBN 0-7091-6279-0 : £3.50
(B77-32171)

Farrar, Stewart. The serpent of Lilith / [by] Stewart Farrar. — London : Arrow Books, 1976. — 3-254p ; 18cm.
ISBN 0-09-913510-8 Pbk : £0.70
(B77-12096)

Farrar, Stewart. The sword of Orley / [by] Stewart Farrar. — London : Joseph, 1977. — 235p ; 21cm.
ISBN 0-7181-1587-2 : £3.95
(B77-17094)

Farren, Mick. The neural atrocity / [by] Mick Farren. — St Albans : Mayflower, 1977. — 191p ; 18cm. — (Mayflower science fantasy)
ISBN 0-583-12603-0 Pbk : £0.60
(B77-08563)

Farrington, Robert. Tudor agent / [by] Robert Farrington. — St Albans : Mayflower, 1977. — 302p : geneal table, maps ; 18cm.
Originally published: London : Chatto and Windus, 1974.
ISBN 0-583-12658-8 Pbk : £0.75
(B77-07606)

Farris, John. The fury / [by] John Farris. — London : Macdonald and Jane's, 1977. — [7], 341p ; 23cm.
Originally published: Chicago : Playboy Press, 1976.
ISBN 0-354-04125-8 : £4.50
(B77-06867)

Farris, John. Sharp practice / [by] John Farris. — London : Futura Publications, 1976. — [7], 277p ; 18cm.
Originally published: New York : Simon and Schuster, 1974 ; London : Weidenfeld and Nicolson, 1975.
ISBN 0-86007-314-9 Pbk : £0.65
(B77-08564)

Faulkner, William. As I lay dying / [by] William Faulkner. — Large print ed. — Bath : Lythway Press, 1977. — [5],290p ; 23cm.
Originally published: New York : J. Cape, H. Smith, 1930 ; London : Chatto and Windus, 1935.
ISBN 0-85046-719-5 : £4.50
(B77-26529)

Faulkner, William. The reivers : a reminiscence / [by] William Faulkner. — Harmondsworth [etc.] : Penguin, 1976. — 254p ; 19cm. — (Penguin modern classics)
Originally published: New York : Random House ; London : Chatto and Windus, 1962.
Pbk : £0.60
ISBN 0-14-002993-1
(B77-01798)

Faulkner, William. Soldiers' pay / [by] William Faulkner. — Harmondsworth [etc.] : Penguin, 1976. — 266p ; 18cm. — (Penguin modern classics)
Originally published: New York : Boni and Liveright, 1926 ; London : Chatto and Windus, 1930.
ISBN 0-14-000123-9 Pbk : £0.75
(B77-07607)

Feinstein, Elaine. Children of the rose / [by] Elaine Feinstein. — Harmondsworth [etc.] : Penguin, 1976. — 171p ; 18cm.
Originally published: London : Hutchinson, 1975.
ISBN 0-14-004189-3 Pbk : £0.70
(B77-01799)

Feinstein, Elaine. The crystal garden / [by] Elaine Feinstein. — Harmondsworth [etc.] : Penguin, 1976. — 139p ; 18cm.
Originally published: as 'The glass alembic'. London : Hutchinson, 1973.
ISBN 0-14-004190-7 Pbk : £0.70
(B77-02577)

Fellows, Catherine. The Heywood inheritance / [by] Catherine Fellows. — London : Coronet, 1976. — 191p : geneal table ; 18cm.
Originally published: London : Hodder and Stoughton, 1975.
ISBN 0-340-21019-2 Pbk : £0.70
(B77-03219)

Fen, Elisaveta. All thy waves : a novel / by Elisaveta Fen. — London : Hamilton, 1977. — [4],284p ; 21cm.
ISBN 0-241-89725-4 : £4.25
(B77-19680)

Ferrand, Georgina. Call back yesterday / by Georgina Ferrand. — London : Hale, 1977. — 159p ; 20cm.
ISBN 0-7091-6310-x : £3.20
(B77-28899)

Ferrand, Georgina. House of glass / by Georgina Ferrand. — London : Hale, 1977. — [5],199p ; 21cm.
Originally published: New York : Ballantine, 1975.
ISBN 0-7091-6002-x : £3.70
(B77-30632)

Ferrand, Georgina. Shadows of the past / by Georgina Ferrand. — London : Hale, 1977. — 171p ; 20cm.
ISBN 0-7091-5991-9 : £3.10
(B77-17738)

Ferrand, Georgina. The thickening light / [by] Georgina Ferrand. — London : Hale, 1977. — [7],184p ; 21cm.
ISBN 0-7091-5650-2 : £3.50
(B77-08053)

Ferrars, Elizabeth. Blood flies upwards / [by] Elizabeth Ferrars. — London : Collins [for] the Crime Club, 1976. — 192p ; 21cm.
ISBN 0-00-231060-0 : £2.95
(B77-03220)

Ferrars, Elizabeth. The cup and the lip / [by] Elizabeth Ferrars. — [London] : Fontana, 1977. — [4],186p ; 18cm.
Originally published: London : Collins, 1975.
ISBN 0-00-614642-2 Pbk : £0.60
(B77-09264)

Ferrars, Elizabeth. Drowned rat / [by] Elizabeth Ferrars. — Large print ed. — Leicester : Ulverscroft, 1977. — [4],295p ; 23cm. — (Ulverscroft large print series : [mystery])
Originally published: London : Collins for the Crime Club, 1975.
ISBN 0-7089-0053-4 : £2.95
(B77-32172)

Ferrars, Elizabeth. Hanged man's house / [by] Elizabeth Ferrars. — Harmondsworth [etc.] : Penguin, 1977. — 171p ; 18cm. — (Penguin crime fiction)
Originally published: London : Collins for the Crime Club, 1974.
ISBN 0-14-004299-7 Pbk : £0.60
(B77-18993)

Ferrars, Elizabeth. Murders anonymous / [by] Elizabeth Ferrars. — London : Collins [for] the Crime Club, 1977. — 195p ; 20cm.
ISBN 0-00-231578-5 : £3.25
(B77-31460)

Ferrars, Elizabeth. The pretty pink shroud / [by] Elizabeth Ferrars. — London [etc.] : Collins [for] the Crime Club, 1977. — 196p ; 21cm.
ISBN 0-00-231641-2 : £2.95
(B77-13274)

Field, Penelope. Someone is watching / [by] Penelope Field. — Large print [ed.]. — London : Prior [etc.], 1977. — [4],376p ; 25cm.

Originally published: Boston, Mass. : Little, Brown, 1976.
ISBN 0-86043-061-8 : £4.95
(B77-21439)

Field, Rachel. And now to-morrow / [by] Rachel Field. — Bath : Chivers, 1977. — 287p ; 21cm.

Originally published: London : Collins, 1943.
ISBN 0-85997-242-9 : £5.60(£4.20 to members of the Library Association)
(B77-16593)

Fielding, Joy. The transformation : a novel / by Joy Fielding. — London : W.H. Allen, 1977. — 286p ; 23cm.
Originally published: Chicago : Playboy Press, 1976.
ISBN 0-491-02111-9 : £4.95
(B77-28900)

Figes, Eva. Nelly's version / [by] Eva Figes. — London : Secker and Warburg, 1977. — 218p ; 23cm.
ISBN 0-436-15601-6 : £3.90
(B77-31461)

Finley, Glenna. Journey to love / [by] Glenna Finley. — London : New English Library, 1977. — 159p ; 18cm.
Originally published: New York : New American Library, 1970.
ISBN 0-450-03308-2 Pbk : £0.60
(B77-19681)

Firbank, Ronald. Concerning the eccentricities of Cardinal Pirelli / [by] Ronald Firbank. — London : Duckworth, 1977. — [2],74p ; 23cm.
Originally published: London : Grant Richards, 1926.
ISBN 0-7156-1095-3 : £4.95
ISBN 0-7156-1099-6 Pbk : £1.50
(B77-19682)

Firbank, Ronald. Prancing nigger / [by] Ronald Firbank. — London : Duckworth, 1977. — 3-77p ; 22cm.
Originally published: as 'Prancing nigger', New York : Brentano's, 1924 ; and as 'Sorrow in sunlight', London : Brentano's, 1924.
ISBN 0-7156-1094-5 : Unpriced
ISBN 0-7156-1098-8 Pbk : £1.50
(B77-20604)

Firbank, Ronald. Valmouth / [by] Ronald Firbank. — London : Duckworth, 1977. — 3-127p ; 23cm.
Originally published: London : Grant Richards, 1919.
ISBN 0-7156-1093-7 : £4.95
ISBN 0-7156-1097-x Pbk : £1.50
(B77-20605)

Fischer, David E. The last flying tiger : a novel / by David E. Fischer. — London : W.H. Allen, 1977. — [7],279p ; 23cm.
Originally published: New York : Scribner, 1976.
ISBN 0-491-02062-7 : £4.95
(B77-32173)

Fisher, Clay. Black Apache / by Clay Fisher. — Toronto [etc.] ; London : Bantam, 1976. — xiii, 209p ; 18cm.
ISBN 0-552-62825-5 Pbk : £0.50
(B77-17739)

Fisher, George. Operation VIP / by George Fisher. — London : Hale, 1977. — 172p ; 20cm.
ISBN 0-7091-5779-7 : £3.15
(B77-09265)

Fisher, Graham. Villain of the piece : a Mike King adventure / [by] Graham Fisher. — London : Macdonald and Jane's, 1977. — [5], 214p ; 21cm.
ISBN 0-354-04209-2 : £3.95
(B77-28125)

Fitzgerald, Francis Scott. The great Gatsby / [by] F. Scott Fitzgerald. — Large print ed. — Bath : Lythway Press, 1977. — [6],257p ; 22cm.
Originally published: New York : C. Scribner's Sons, 1925 ; London : Chatto and Windus, 1926.
ISBN 0-85046-734-9 Pbk : £2.35
(B77-32853)

Fitzgerald, Penelope. The golden child / [by] Penelope Fitzgerald. — London : Duckworth, 1977. — 159p : ill ; 23cm.
ISBN 0-7156-1263-8 : £4.95
(B77-28126)

Fleetwood, Frances. Concordia : the story of Francesca da Rimini, told by her daughter / [by] Frances Fleetwood. — London : Sphere, 1975. — 275p ; 18cm.
Originally published: London : W.H. Allen, 1971.
ISBN 0-7221-3542-4 Pbk : £0.95
(B77-16594)

Fleetwood, Frances. Concordia errant : the story of Francesca da Rimini's daughter / [by] Frances Fleetwood. — London : Sphere, 1975. — 304p : geneal tables ; 18cm.
Originally published: London : W.H. Allen, 1973. — Based on the life of Concordia Malatesta.
ISBN 0-7221-3543-2 Pbk : £0.95
(B77-16595)

Fleetwood, Hugh. An artist and a magician / [by] Hugh Fleetwood. — London : Hamilton, 1977. — 189p ; 21cm.
ISBN 0-241-89729-7 : £4.25
(B77-28127)

Fleetwood, Hugh. The girl who passed for normal / [by] Hugh Fleetwood. — London [etc.] : Pan Books, 1977. — 156p ; 18cm.
Originally published: London : Hamilton, 1973.

ISBN 0-330-24370-5 Pbk : £0.60
(B77-19683)

Fleischer, Leonore. The Lords of Flatbush / [by] Leonore Fleischer. — Toronto [etc.] ; London : Bantam, 1977. — vi,134p ; 18cm.
'Based on a screenplay by Stephen F. Verona, Gayle Gleckler and Martin Davidson' - cover.
ISBN 0-552-61138-7 Pbk : £0.65
(B77-34115)

Fleming, Joan. Every inch a lady : a murder of the fifties / [by] Joan Fleming. — London : Collins [for] the Crime Club, 1977. — 193p ; 21cm.
ISBN 0-00-231216-6 : £3.25
(B77-22130)

Fleming, Joan. Maiden's prayer / by Joan Fleming. — London : Severn House : [Distributed by Hutchinson], 1977. — 192p ; 21cm.
Originally published: London : Collins, 1957.
ISBN 0-7278-0221-6 : £3.15
(B77-09266)

Fleming, Joan. The man who looked back / by Joan Fleming. — London : Hamilton, 1977. — 224p ; 21cm. — (A fingerprint book)
Originally published: London : Hutchinson, 1951.
ISBN 0-241-89721-1 : £3.95
(B77-27383)

Fleming, Joan. Polly put the kettle on / by Joan Fleming. — London : Hamilton, 1977. — 208p : plan ; 21cm. — (A fingerprint book)
Originally published: London : Hutchinson, 1952.
ISBN 0-241-89662-2 : £3.75
(B77-18994)

Fleming, Joan. When I grow rich / by Joan Fleming. — London : Severn House : [Distributed by Hutchinson], 1977. — 256p ; 21cm.
Originally published: New York : Washburn ; London : Collins for the Crime Club, 1962.
ISBN 0-7278-0226-7 : £3.25
(B77-19684)

Fletcher, David, *b.1940.* Only children / [by] David Fletcher. — London [etc.] : Macmillan, 1977. — 192p ; 21cm.
ISBN 0-333-21632-6 : £3.50
(B77-21440)

Fletcher, Inglis. Men of Albemarle / [by] Inglis Fletcher. — Toronto [etc.] ; London : Bantam, [1977]. — xii,500p ; 18cm.
Originally published: Indianapolis : Bobbs-Merrill, 1942.
ISBN 0-552-62565-5 Pbk : £0.65
(B77-12657)

Fletcher, Inglis. Raleigh's Eden / by Inglis Fletcher. — Toronto [etc.] ; London : Bantam, [1977]. — x,598p ; 18cm. — (Fletcher, Inglis. Carolina series)
Originally published: Indianapolis : Bobbs-Merrill, 1940.
ISBN 0-552-62786-0 Pbk : £0.60
(B77-21441)

Fletcher, Inglis. Roanoke hundred / [by] Inglis Fletcher. — Toronto [etc.] ; London : Bantam, [1976]. — [10],501,[1]p ; 18cm.
Originally published: Indianapolis : Bobbs-Merrill, 1948. — Based on the life of Sir Richard Grenville.
ISBN 0-552-62683-x Pbk : £0.65
(B77-02578)

Fletcher, Inglis. Toil of the brave / [by] Inglis Fletcher. — Toronto [etc.] ; London : Bantam, 1971. — xii,548p ; 18cm.
Originally published: Indianapolis : Bobbs-Merrill, 1946.
ISBN 0-552-68072-9 Pbk : £0.80
(B77-26530)

Fletcher, Inglis. The wind in the forest / by Inglis Fletcher. — Toronto [etc.] ; London : Bantam, 1975 [i.e. 1977]. — xii,416,[1]p ; 18cm.

Originally published: Indianapolis : Bobbs-Merrill, 1957 ; London : Hutchinson, 1958.
ISBN 0-552-68085-0 Pbk : £0.60
(B77-09945)

Fletcher, Lucille. Eighty dollars to Stamford / [by] Lucille Fletcher. — London : Hale, 1977. — [4],151p ; 20cm. — ([Hale crime])
Originally published: New York : Random House, 1975.
ISBN 0-7091-6138-7 : £3.15
(B77-17740)

Fletcher, Margaret. The tempestuous affair / by Margaret Fletcher. — London : Hale, 1977. — 185p ; 20cm.
ISBN 0-7091-6240-5 : £3.20
(B77-20606)

Foley, Lorette. Bury by night / by Lorette Foley. — London : Hale, 1977. — 3-189p ; 20cm.
ISBN 0-7091-6213-8 : £3.25
(B77-19685)

Foley, Rae. The Barclay place / [by] Rae Foley. — London : Hale, 1976. — [4],215p ; 20cm.
Originally published: New York : Dodd Mead, 1975.
ISBN 0-7091-5752-5 : £3.15
(B77-01800)

Foley, Rae. Where Helen lies / [by] Rae Foley. — London : Hale, 1977. — [9],214p ; 20cm.
Originally published: New York : Dodd, Mead, 1976.
ISBN 0-7091-6233-2 : £3.25
(B77-22863)

Follett, James. Crown court / [by] James Follett. — London : A. Barker, 1977. — 174p ; 23cm.
ISBN 0-213-16651-8 : £3.75
(B77-31462)

Follett, Ken. The shakeout / [by] Ken Follett. — London : Coronet, 1976. — 157p ; 18cm.
Originally published: Lewes : Harwood Smart Publishing Co., 1975.
ISBN 0-340-21018-4 Pbk : £0.60
(B77-02579)

Foord, William Spencer. Cupid's copse / by W.S. Foord. — London : Hale, 1977. — 156p ; 20cm.
ISBN 0-7091-5998-6 : £3.10
(B77-16596)

Foord, William Spencer. Kiss the summer goodbye / by W.S. Foord. — London : Hale, 1977. — 191p ; 20cm.
ISBN 0-7091-6134-4 : £3.20
(B77-25886)

Forbes, Colin. Avalanche Express / [by] Colin Forbes. — London : Collins, 1977. — 276p ; 22cm.
ISBN 0-00-222006-7 : £3.95
(B77-14913)

Forbes, Colin, *b.1923.* The stone leopard / [by] Colin Forbes. — London : Pan Books, 1977. — 254p ; 18cm.
Originally published: London : Collins, 1975.
ISBN 0-330-24817-0 Pbk : £0.75
(B77-13870)

Ford, Elizabeth. The amber cat / [by] Elizabeth Ford. — London : Hurst and Blackett, 1976. — 185p ; 20cm.
ISBN 0-09-126570-3 : £3.25
(B77-05656)

Ford, Elizabeth. Open day at the manor / [by] Elizabeth Ford. — London [etc.] : Hurst and Blackett, 1977. — 185p ; 20cm.
ISBN 0-09-129540-8 : £3.50
(B77-28128)

Ford, Hilary. Castle Malindine / [by] Hilary Ford. — London [etc.] : Pan Books, 1977. — 239p ; 18cm.
Originally published: London : Hamilton, 1975.
ISBN 0-330-24859-6 Pbk : £0.70
(B77-06868)

Forde, Nicholas. Engaged in murder / by Nicholas Forde. — London : Hale, 1977. — 169p ; 20cm.
ISBN 0-7091-6139-5 : £3.15
(B77-17741)

Forde, Nicholas. Urgent wedding / by Nicholas Forde. — London : Hale, 1977. — 191p ; 20cm.
ISBN 0-7091-5917-x : £3.15
(B77-07608)

Foreman, Russell. The ringway virus / [by] Russell Foreman. — London : New English Library, 1977. — 288p ; 18cm.
Originally published: London : Millington, 1976.
ISBN 0-450-03272-8 Pbk : £0.90
(B77-22864)

Foreman, Russell. The ringway virus / by Russell Foreman. — London [etc.] : Millington, 1976. — [6],294p ; 23cm.
ISBN 0-86000-046-x : £3.50
(B77-15496)

Forester, Cecil Scott. Brown on Resolution / [by] C.S. Forester. — St Albans : Triad : Mayflower, 1977. — 155p ; 18cm.
Originally published: London : John Lane, 1929.
ISBN 0-583-12818-1 Pbk : £0.60
(B77-21442)

Forester, Cecil Scott. Death to the French / [by] C.S. Forester. — St Albans : Triad, 1977. — 155p : map ; 18cm.
Originally published: London : Lane, 1932.
ISBN 0-583-12820-3 Pbk : £0.60
(B77-25196)

Forester, Cecil Scott. Payment deferred / [by] C.S. Forester. — Large print ed. — Bath : Lythway Press, 1977. — ix,286p ; 23cm. — (Lythway classics of crime and detection)
Originally published: London : Lane, 1926.
ISBN 0-85046-717-9 : £4.55
(B77-28901)

Forester, Cecil Scott. The ship ; [and], Mr Midshipman Hornblower ; [and], The earthly paradise ; [and], The general ; [and], The captain from Connecticut ; [and], The 'African Queen' / [by] C.S. Forester. — London : Heinemann : Secker and Warburg : Octopus Books, [1977]. — 3-861p : ill ; 25cm.
ISBN 0-905712-02-1 : £3.95
(B77-13275)

Forster, Edward Morgan. The Lucy novels : early sketches for 'A room with a view' / [by] E.M. Forster. — Abinger ed. — London : Edward Arnold, 1977. — xii,132p : ill(on lining papers) ; 23cm.
Limited ed. of 1000 numbered copies.
ISBN 0-7131-5954-5 : £12.50
(B77-22131)

Forster, Edward Morgan. A room with a view / [by] E.M. Forster. — Abinger ed. — London : Edward Arnold, 1977. — xix,237p : ill(on lining papers) ; 23cm.
'A room with a view' originally published: 1908.
ISBN 0-7131-5946-4 : £7.95
(B77-22132)

Foster, Alan Dean. Icerigger / [by] Alan Dean Foster. — London : New English Library, 1976. — 319p ; 18cm.
Originally published: New York : Ballantine, 1974 ; London : New English Library, 1976.
ISBN 0-450-03042-3 Pbk : £0.95
(B77-01801)

Foster, Alan Dean. Midworld / [by] Alan Dean Foster. — London : Macdonald and Jane's, 1977. — [7],213p ; 21cm.
Originally published: United States : Science Fiction Book Club, 1975.
ISBN 0-354-04154-1 : £3.95
(B77-22133)

Foster, John, *b.1944.* King Cinder / [by] John Foster. — London : British Broadcasting Corporation, 1977. — 139p ; 24cm.
'... based on the successful BBC 1 series [first shown in autumn 1977]' - jacket.
ISBN 0-563-17296-7 : £3.25
(B77-34116)

Fowles, John. Daniel Martin / [by] John Fowler. — London : Cape, 1977. — 704p ; 21cm.
ISBN 0-224-01490-0 : £4.95 : CIP rev.
(B77-22134)

Fowles, John. The magus / [by] John Fowles. — Revised ed. ; with a foreword by the author. — London : Cape, 1977. — 656p ; 21cm.
Ill. on lining papers. — Previous ed.: 1966.
ISBN 0-224-01392-0 : £4.95 : CIP rev.
(B77-09267)

Foxall, Peter Augustus. A dishonest way to die / by P.A. Foxall. — London : Hale, 1977. — 183p ; 20cm.
ISBN 0-7091-6320-7 : £3.50
(B77-32174)

Foxall, Peter Augustus. Inspector Derben and the widow maker / by P.A. Foxall. — London : Hale, 1977. — 156p ; 20cm.
ISBN 0-7091-6055-0 : £3.25
(B77-22135)

Foxall, Peter Augustus. Inspector Derben's war / by P.A. Foxall. — London : Hale, 1976. — 156p ; 20cm.
ISBN 0-7091-5882-3 : £2.95
(B77-01802)

Foxall, Peter Augustus. No life for a loser / by P.A. Foxall. — London : Hale, 1977. — 156p ; 20cm.
ISBN 0-7091-6054-2 : £3.15
(B77-14914)

Francis, Dick. High stakes / [by] Dick Francis. — London [etc.] : Pan Books, 1977. — 190p ; 18cm.
Originally published: London : Joseph, 1975.
ISBN 0-330-24836-7 Pbk : £0.70
(B77-12097)

Francis, Dick. In the frame / [by] Dick Francis. — Large print ed. — Leicester : Ulverscroft, 1977. — [7],382p ; 23cm. — (Ulverscroft large print series : [adventure, suspense])
Originally published: London : Joseph, 1976.
ISBN 0-7089-0060-7 : £2.95
(B77-32175)

Francis, Dick. In the frame / [by] Dick Francis. Baker's hawk / [by] Jack Bickham. Bring on the empty horses / [by] David Niven. Lord of the far island / [by] Victoria Holt. The Hessian / [by] Howard Fast. — Collector's library ed. — London : Reader's Digest Association [etc.], 1976. — 510,[2]p : ill(chiefly col), ports ; 21cm. — ('Reader's digest' condensed books ; [vol. 90])
ISBN 0-340-21665-4 : £2.95
(B77-01810)

Francis, Dick. Risk / [by] Dick Francis. — London : Joseph, 1977. — 252p ; 21cm.
ISBN 0-7181-1636-4 : £3.95
(B77-28129)

Frankau, Pamela. The offshore light / [by] Pamela Frankau. — London [etc.] : White Lion Publishers, 1977. — [7],283p : map ; 21cm.
Originally published: London : Heinemann, 1952.
ISBN 0-7274-0371-0 : £3.95
(B77-25887)

Frankau, Pamela. Slaves of the lamp / [by] Pamela Frankau. — London [etc.] : White Lion Publishers, 1977. — [6],422p ; 21cm.
Originally published: London : Heinemann, 1965.
ISBN 0-7274-0259-5 : £4.95
(B77-15497)

Franklin, Max. Starsky & Hutch / created and written by William Blinn ; adapted by Max Franklin. — London : Barker, 1977. — [4], 186p ; 22cm.
'Based upon the BBC television series ...'. — Originally published: New York : Ballantine Books, 1976.
ISBN 0-213-16640-2 : £3.75
(B77-13276)

Franklin, Max. Starsky & Hutch, death ride / created by William Blinn ; based upon the television play by Ed Laska ; adapted by Max Franklin. — London : Barker, 1977. — [4], 153p ; 23cm.
'Based upon the BBC Television Series ...' - title page. — Originally published: New York : Ballantine Books, 1976.
ISBN 0-213-16656-9 : £3.75
(B77-28130)

Franklin, Max. Starsky & Hutch, kill Huggy Bear / created by William Blinn ; based upon the television play by Fred Freiberger ; adapted by Max Franklin. — London : Barker, 1977. — [4],153p ; 23cm.
'Based upon the BBC television series ... '. — Originally published: New York : Ballantine Books, 1976.
ISBN 0-213-16641-0 : £3.75
(B77-13277)

Fraser, Anthea. Home through the dark / [by] Anthea Fraser. — Large print [ed.]. — London : Prior [etc.], 1977. — [5],332p ; 25cm.
Originally published: Aylesbury : Milton House Books, 1974.
ISBN 0-86043-046-4 : £4.95
(B77-21443)

Fraser, Anthea. Whistler's Lane / [by] Anthea Fraser. — Large print [ed.]. — London : Prior [etc.], 1977. — [5],358p ; 24cm.
Originally published: Aylesbury : Milton House, 1975.
ISBN 0-86043-019-7 : £4.95
(B77-11401)

Fraser, James, *b.1924 (Feb.).* Hearts ease in death : a Detective Superintendent Aveyard novel / [by] James Fraser. — London : Barrie and Jenkins, 1977. — 192p ; 21cm.
ISBN 0-214-20311-5 : £3.95
(B77-16597)

Fraser, *Lady* **Antonia.** Quiet as a nun / [by] Antonia Fraser. — London : Weidenfeld and Nicolson, 1977. — [7],176p ; 23cm.
ISBN 0-297-77292-9 : £3.95
(B77-19686)

Frayn, Michael. The tin men / [by] Michael Frayn. — [London] : Fontana, 1977. — 158p ; 18cm.
Originally published: London : Collins, 1965.
ISBN 0-00-615066-7 Pbk : £0.75
(B77-34117)

Frayn, Michael. Towards the end of the morning / [by] Michael Frayn. — [London] : Fontana, 1977. — 223p ; 18cm.
Originally published: London : Collins, 1967.
ISBN 0-00-615067-5 Pbk : £0.85
(B77-34118)

Freeborn, Brian. Ten days, Mister Cain? / [by] Brian Freeborn. — London : Secker and Warburg, 1977. — [5],185p ; 23cm.
ISBN 0-436-16469-8 : £3.50
(B77-15498)

Freed, Donald. The killing of RFK / [by] Donald Freed. — London : Sphere, 1977. — 192p ; 18cm.
Originally published: New York : Dell, 1975.
ISBN 0-7221-3655-2 Pbk : £0.85
(B77-28902)

Freedman, Nancy. Joshua, son of none / [by] Nancy Freedman. — London [etc.] : Panther, 1977. — 235p ; 18cm.
Originally published: New York : Delacorte Press, 1973 ; London : Hart-Davis MacGibbon, 1974.
ISBN 0-586-04251-2 Pbk : £0.75
(B77-28131)

Freeling, Nicolas. Gadget / [by] Nicolas Freeling. — London : Heinemann, 1977. — [12],244p ; 23cm.
ISBN 0-434-27182-9 : £4.50
(B77-28132)

Freeman, Cynthia. A world full of strangers / by Cynthia Freeman. — Toronto [etc.] ; London : Bantam, 1976. — [7],631,[1]p ; 18cm.
Originally published: New York : Arbor House, 1975.
ISBN 0-552-10285-7 Pbk : £0.85
(B77-02580)

Freeman, Mary. An Edwardian childhood : 'rosemary and rue' / by Mary Freeman. — Sherborne : Abbey Press. L. Coldwell (Printing), 1976. — 12p ; 21cm.
ISBN 0-900011-04-1 Sd : £0.30
(B77-00420)

Freemantle, Brian. Charlie Muffin / [by] Brian Freemantle. — London : Cape, 1977. — 192p ; 21cm.
ISBN 0-224-01312-2 : £3.50 : CIP rev
(B77-05657)

Fremlin, Celia. The spider-orchid / by Celia Fremlin. — London : Gollancz, 1977. — 174p ; 21cm. — ([Gollancz suspense])
ISBN 0-575-02326-0 : £3.75
(B77-21444)

Fresson, Iris Muriel. No greater love / by I.M. Fresson. — London : Hale, 1977. — 190p ; 20cm.
ISBN 0-7091-5900-5 : £3.10
(B77-09946)

Friedman, Rosemary. The life situation / [by] Rosemary Friedman. — London : Barrie and Jenkins, 1977. — [5],276p ; 23cm.
ISBN 0-214-20382-4 : £3.95
(B77-21445)

Frith, Nigel. The spear of mistletoe : an epic / [by] Nigel Frith. — London [etc.] : Routledge and Kegan Paul, 1977. — [5],293p : ill(on lining papers) ; 24cm.
ISBN 0-7100-8569-9 : £4.95 : CIP rev.
(B77-08054)

Fullerton, Alexander. The blooding of the guns / [by] Alexander Fullerton. — London [etc.] : Pan Books, 1977. — 256p ; 18cm.
Originally published: London : Joseph, 1976.
ISBN 0-330-25052-3 Pbk : £0.75
(B77-13871)

Fullerton, Alexander. Sixty minutes for St George / [by] Alexander Fullerton. — London : Joseph, 1977. — 224p ; 23cm.
ISBN 0-7181-1575-9 : £4.20
(B77-17095)

Fullerton, Alexander. The yellow Ford / [by] Alexander Fullerton. — St Albans : Mayflower, 1977. — 237p ; 18cm.
Originally published: London : P. Davies, 1959.

ISBN 0-583-12463-1 Pbk : £0.65
(B77-09268)

Fullerton, Charles. If chance a stranger / [by] Charles Fullerton. — Large print ed. — Leicester : Ulverscroft, 1977. — [7],431p ; 23cm. — (Ulverscroft large print series : [general fiction])
Originally published: London : Harvill Press, 1958.
ISBN 0-7089-0025-9 : £2.95
(B77-22136)

Fulton, Len. The grassman / [by] Len Fulton. — Harmondsworth [etc.] : Penguin, 1977. — 368p ; 18cm.
Originally published: Berkeley : Thorp Spring Press, 1974.
ISBN 0-14-004163-x Pbk : £0.95
(B77-12098)

Gadney, Reg. The champagne Marxist / [by] Reg Gadney. — London : Hutchinson, 1977. — 182p ; 23cm.
ISBN 0-09-131150-0 : £3.95
(B77-29698)

Gage, Nicholas. The Bourlotas fortune / [by] Nicholas Gage. — London : Corgi, 1977. — [6],503,[1]p : geneal table, map ; 18cm.
Originally published: New York : Holt, Rinehart and Winston, 1975 ; London : Weidenfeld and Nicolson, 1976.
ISBN 0-552-10473-6 Pbk : £0.95
(B77-25888)

Gaines, Diana. Nantucket woman / [by] Diana Gaines. — London [etc.] : Hutchinson, 1977. — 351p : ill ; 23cm.
Originally published: New York : Dutton, 1976.

ISBN 0-09-128540-2 : £3.95
(B77-09269)

Gainham, Sarah. The cold dark night / [by] Sarah Gainham. — London : Severn House : [Distributed by Hutchinson], 1977. — 238p ; 21cm.
Originally published: London : Barker, 1957.
ISBN 0-7278-0217-8 : £3.25
(B77-13278)

Gainham, Sarah. Mythmaker / [by] Sarah Gainham. — London : Severn House : [Distributed by Hutchinson], 1976. — 254p ; 20cm.
Originally published: London : Barker, 1957.
ISBN 0-7278-0305-0 : £3.25
(B77-06284)

Gall, Grant. The long ride home / [by] Grant Gall. — Colchester ([Hewitt Photo-Lith Ltd, Whitewell Rd, Colchester, Essex CO2 7DE]) : Shield Press, 1977. — 196p ; 19cm.
ISBN 0-9505068-0-x : £3.95
(B77-30633)

Gall, Sandy. Gold scoop / [by] Sandy Gall. — London : Collins, 1977. — 3-209p ; 22cm.
ISBN 0-00-221355-9 : £3.95
(B77-28133)

Gallagher, Patricia. The sons and the daughters / by Patricia Gallagher. — London : Corgi, 1976. — [5],345p ; 18cm.
Originally published: London : Muller, 1961.
ISBN 0-552-10269-5 Pbk : £0.85
(B77-00421)

Gallico, Paul. Scruffy / [by] Paul Gallico. — Harmondsworth [etc.] : Penguin, 1977. — 288p ; 18cm.
Originally published: London : Joseph, 1962.
ISBN 0-14-002628-2 Pbk : £0.80
(B77-07609)

Gallico, Paul. The zoo gang / [by] Paul Gallico. — London : Pan Books, 1977. — 236p ; 18cm.
Originally published: London : Heinemann, 1971.
Pbk : £0.75
ISBN 0-330-23603-2
(B77-19687)

Gann, Ernest Kellogg. Of good and evil / [by] Ernest K. Gann. — Large print ed. — Bath : Chivers, 1977. — vii,504p ; 23cm.
Originally published: New York : Simon and Schuster ; London : Hodder and Stoughton, 1963.
ISBN 0-85997-251-8 : £6.60(£4.95 to members of the Library Association)
(B77-22137)

Gardam, Jane. The summer after the funeral / [by] Jane Gardam. — Harmondsworth [etc.] : Penguin, 1977. — 155,[1]p ; 18cm. — (Peacock books)
Originally published: London : Hamilton, 1973. — For adolescents.
ISBN 0-14-047084-0 Pbk : £0.55
(B77-12099)

Gardner, Erle Stanley. The case of the careless cupid / [by] Erle Stanley Gardner. — Large print [ed.]. — London : Prior [etc.], 1977. — ix,330p ; 25cm.
Originally published: New York : Morrow, 1968 ; London : Heinemann, 1973.
ISBN 0-86043-054-5 : £4.95
(B77-22865)

Gardner, Erle Stanley. The case of the empty tin / [by] Erle Stanley Gardner. — London : Severn House : [Distributed by Hutchinson], 1977. — [5],276p ; 21cm.
Spine title: Perry Mason, the case of the empty tin. — Originally published: New York : Morrow, 1941 ; London : Cassell, 1943.
ISBN 0-7278-0254-2 : £3.50
(B77-14404)

Gardner, Erle Stanley. The case of the fabulous fake / [by] Erle Stanley Gardner. — London (11 New Fetter La., EC4P 4EE) : Magnum Books, 1977. — 222p ; 18cm.
Originally published: New York : Morrow, 1969 ; London : Heinemann, 1974.
ISBN 0-413-37420-3 Pbk : £0.65
(B77-13872)

Gardner, Erle Stanley. The case of the gilded lily ... / [by] Erle Stanley Gardner. — London : Heinemann : Octopus Books, 1976. — 976p ; 25cm.
Jacket title: Perry Mason in 8 famous cases.
ISBN 0-7064-0575-7 : £3.95
(B77-00422)

Gardner, Erle Stanley. The case of the half-wakened wife / [by] Erle Stanley Gardner. — Large print ed. — Leicester : Ulverscroft, 1977. — [7],440p ; 23cm. — (Ulverscroft large print series : [mystery])
Originally published: New York : M.S. Mill, 1945 ; London : Cassell, 1949.
ISBN 0-85456-545-0 : £2.95
(B77-28903)

Gardner, Erle Stanley. The case of the hesitant hostess / [by] Erle Stanley Gardner. — London : Magnum Books, 1977. — 206p ; 18cm.
Originally published: New York : Morrow, 1953 ; London : Heinemann, 1959.
ISBN 0-413-37690-7 Pbk : £0.65
(B77-25889)

Gardner, Erle Stanley. The case of the musical cow / [by] Erle Stanley Gardner. — London (11 New Fetter La., EC4P 4EE) : Magnum Books, 1977. — [6],250p ; 18cm.
Originally published: New York : Morrow, 1950 ; London : Heinemann, 1957.
ISBN 0-413-37430-0 Pbk : £0.65
(B77-13873)

Gardner, Erle Stanley. The case of the postponed murder / [by] Erle Stanley Gardner. — London : Heinemann, 1977. — 220p ; 20cm.
Originally published: New York : Morrow, 1973.
ISBN 0-434-28233-2 : £3.50
(B77-22138)

Gardner, Erle Stanley. The case of the worried waitress / [by] Erle Stanley Gardner. — London : Magnum Books, 1977. — vii,212p ; 18cm.
'A Perry Mason mystery' - cover. — Originally published: New York : Morrow, 1966 ; London : Heinemann, 1972.
ISBN 0-413-37700-8 Pbk : £0.65
(B77-25197)

Gardner, Jerome. Two-bit town / by Jerome Gardner. — London : Hale, 1977. — 159p ; 19cm.
ISBN 0-7091-6443-2 : £3.10
(B77-28904)

Gardner, Jerome. The underhand mail / [by] Jerome Gardner. — London : Hale, 1976. — 156p ; 20cm.
ISBN 0-7091-5884-x : £2.70
(B77-01803)

Gardner, John, *b.1926.* The revenge of Moriarty / [by] John Gardner. — London [etc.] : Pan Books, 1977. — 303p ; 18cm.
Originally published: London : Weidenfeld and Nicolson, 1975.
ISBN 0-330-25231-3 Pbk : £0.80
(B77-28905)

Gardner, John, *b.1926.* The Werewolf trace / [by] John Gardner. — London [etc.] : Hodder and Stoughton, 1977. — 219p ; 23cm.
ISBN 0-340-21271-3 : £3.95
(B77-10553)

Gardner, John, *b.1933.* October light / [by] John Gardner. — London : Cape, 1977. — [10],401p ; 23cm.
Originally published: New York : Knopf, 1976.
ISBN 0-224-01388-2 : £4.95 : CIP rev.
(B77-08565)

Garfield, Brian. Death sentence / [by] Brian Garfield. — London : Pan Books, 1977. — 157p ; 18cm.
Originally published: New York : Evans, 1975 ; London : Macmillan, 1976.
ISBN 0-330-25118-x Pbk : £0.70
(B77-19688)

Garfield, Brian. Hopscotch / [by] Brian Garfield. — London : Pan Books, 1976. — 208p ; 18cm.
Originally published: New York : M. Evans ; London : Macmillan, 1975.
ISBN 0-330-24848-0 Pbk : £0.70
(B77-02581)

Garfield, Brian. Kolchak's gold / [by] Brian Garfield. — London : Pan Books, 1977. — 331p : 3 maps ; 18cm.
Originally published: New York : McKay ; London : Heinemann, 1974.
ISBN 0-330-24594-5 Pbk : £0.75
(B77-08055)

Garfield, Brian. Recoil / by Brian Garfield. — London [etc.] : Macmillan, 1977. — 335p ; 23cm.
ISBN 0-333-21406-4 : £3.95
(B77-12658)

Garfield, Brian. The Romanov succession / [by] Brian Garfield. — London : Pan Books, 1977. — 303p ; 18cm.
Originally published: New York : McKay ; London : Macmillan, 1974.
ISBN 0-330-24838-3 Pbk : £0.75
(B77-34119)

Garnett, Bill. Down bound train / [by] Bill Garnett. — St Albans : Mayflower, 1977. — 173p ; 18cm.
Originally published: London : Hale, 1973.
ISBN 0-583-12525-5 Pbk : £0.60
(B77-08056)

Garnett, David. Up she rises / [by] David Garnett. — London [etc.] : Macmillan, 1977. — 272p ; 21cm.
ISBN 0-333-21492-7 : £3.95
(B77-15499)

Garrett, Charles C. The massacre trail / [by] Charles C. Garrett. — London : Sphere, 1977. — 143p ; 18cm. — (Garrett, Charles C. Gunslinger ; [1])
Bibl.: p.5-6.
ISBN 0-7221-5009-1 Pbk : £0.65
(B77-32176)

Garrison, Jim. The star spangled contract / by Jim Garrison. — London : W.H. Allen, 1977. — [5],372p ; 24cm.
Originally published: New York : McGraw-Hill, 1976.
ISBN 0-491-01928-9 : £4.50
(B77-17096)

Garve, Andrew. The file on Lester / [by] Andrew Garve. — Large print ed. — Bath : Lythway Press, 1977. — [4],268p ; 22cm.
Originally published: London : Collins, 1974.
ISBN 0-85046-721-7 : £4.45
(B77-26531)

Garve, Andrew. Murderer's fen / [by] Andrew Garve. — Large print ed. — Bath : Chivers, 1977. — [5],274p ; 22cm.
Originally published: London : Collins, 1966.
ISBN 0-85997-269-0 : £4.80(£3.60 to members of the Library Association)
(B77-34120)

Gash, Jonathan. The Judas pair / [by] Jonathan Gash. — London : Collins [for] the Crime Club, 1977. — 210p ; 21cm.
ISBN 0-00-231383-9 : £3.25
(B77-23724)

Gaskell, Jane. Atlan / [by] Jane Gaskell. — London [etc.] : White Lion Publishers, 1977. — 286p ; 21cm.
Originally published: London : Hodder and Stoughton, 1965.
ISBN 0-7274-0330-3 : £3.95
(B77-12659)

Gaskin, Catherine. Corporation wife / [by] Catherine Gaskin. — London : Collins, 1977. — 384p ; 21cm.
Originally published: Garden City, N.Y. : Doubleday ; London : Collins, 1960.
£3.95
ISBN 0-00-221132-7
(B77-20607)

Gaskin, Catherine. I know my love / [by] Catherin Gaskin. — London : Collins, 1976. — 384p ; 21cm.
Originally published: 1962.
ISBN 0-00-221346-x : £3.25
(B77-10554)

Gaskin, Catherine. The property of a gentleman / [by] Catherine Gaskin ; a condensation by the editors of Reader's Digest Condensed Books. — Large print ed. — Leicester : Ulverscroft, 1976. — [4],352p ; 23cm. — (Ulverscroft large print series : [fiction])
This condensation originally published: Pleasantville, N.Y. ; London : Reader's Digest Association, 1975?.
ISBN 0-85456-552-3 : £2.65
(B77-08566)

Gast, Kelly P. Murphy's trail / [by] Kelly P. Gast. — London : Hale, 1977. — [5],185p ; 20cm.
Originally published: Garden City, N.Y. : Doubleday, 1976.
ISBN 0-7091-6143-3 : £3.10
(B77-31463)

Gaston, Bill. Winter of the Wildcat / [by] Bill Gaston. — London : Hale, 1977. — 3-190p ; 21cm.
ISBN 0-7091-5815-7 : £3.50
(B77-13279)

Gavin, Bernard. Ring of fire / [by] Bernard Gavin. — London : W.H. Allen, 1977. — [5], 281p ; 23cm.
ISBN 0-491-02190-9 : £4.95
(B77-25890)

Gawaine, John. The diamond seeker / [by] John Gawaine. — Johannesburg ; London [etc.] : Macmillan, 1976. — 184p,plate : maps(on lining papers), port ; 22cm.
Based on the life of John Thoburn Williamson.
ISBN 0-86954-029-7 : £3.95
(B77-09947)

Gaye, Carol. A summer to decide / [by] Carol Gaye. — Large print ed. — Bath : Lythway Press, 1977. — [5],306p ; 21cm.
Originally published: London : Collins, 1959.
ISBN 0-85046-693-8 : £4.45
(B77-10943)

Gaye, Carol. There'll be another spring / [by] Carol Gaye. — London : Hale, 1977. — 192p ; 20cm.
Originally published: London : Collins, 1963.
ISBN 0-7091-5808-4 : £3.20
(B77-34121)

Geddes, Paul. Hangman / [by] Paul Geddes. — London : Faber, 1977. — 176p ; 21cm.
ISBN 0-571-11098-3 : £3.95 : CIP rev.
(B77-19689)

Gentry, Peter. Rafe / [by] Peter Gentry. — London : Coronet, 1977. — 304p ; 18cm.
Originally published: New York : Fawcett, 1976.
ISBN 0-340-21796-0 Pbk : £0.85
(B77-31464)

Gibbons, Floyd. The Red Napoleon / by Floyd Gibbons. — [1st ed. reprinted] ; with an afterword by John Gardner. — Carbondale [etc.] : Southern Illinois University Press ; London [etc.] : Feffer and Simons, 1976. — [5], 486,[1]p : ill, maps, plans ; 20cm. — (Lost American fiction)
Facsimile reprint of: 1st ed. New York : J. Cape and H. Smith, 1929.
ISBN 0-8093-0764-2 : Unpriced
(B77-00423)

Gibbons, Stella. Cold Comfort Farm / [by] Stella Gibbons. — Harmondsworth [etc.] : Penguin, 1977. — 233p ; 18cm.
Originally published: London : Longman, 1932.
ISBN 0-14-000140-9 Pbk : £0.70
(B77-12100)

Gibbons, Stella. Cold Comfort Farm / [by] Stella Gibbons ; with water-colour drawings by Quentin Blake. — London : Folio Society, 1977. — 203p,[9]leaves of plates : col ill ; 23cm.
Originally published: London : Longmans, 1932.
ISBN 0-85067-108-6 : £5.95(to members only)
(B77-13280)

Gibbons, Stella. The shadow of a sorcerer / [by] Stella Gibbons. — London : Remploy, 1976. — 285p ; 19cm.
Originally published: Sevenoaks : Hodder and Stoughton, 1955.
ISBN 0-7066-0699-x : £3.00
(B77-14915)

Gibbs, Mary Ann. The moon in a bucket / [by] Mary Ann Gibbs. — Sevenoaks : Coronet, 1977. — [5],182p ; 18cm.
Originally published: London : Hurst and Blackett, 1972.
ISBN 0-340-21241-1 Pbk : £0.65
(B77-12660)

Gibbs, Mary Ann. A most romantic city / [by] Mary Ann Gibbs. — Sevenoaks : Coronet, 1977. — 157p ; 18cm.
Originally published: London : Hurst and Blackett, 1976.
ISBN 0-340-21988-2 Pbk : £0.75
(B77-29699)

Gibbs, Mary Ann. A wife for the admiral / [by] Mary Ann Gibbs. — Sevenoaks : Coronet, 1977. — 208p ; 18cm.
Originally published: London : Hurst and Blackett, 1974.
ISBN 0-340-21240-3 Pbk : £0.60
(B77-12661)

Gibson, George. Captain Incognito / [by] George Gibson. — Lymington : Nautical Publishing Co. ; London : [Distributed by] Harrap, 1977. — 207p ; 21cm.
ISBN 0-245-53040-1 : £3.95
(B77-32177)

Gifford, Thomas. The Cavanaugh quest / by Thomas Gifford. — London : Hamilton, 1977. — 375p ; 21cm.
Originally published: New York : Putnam, 1976.
ISBN 0-241-89533-2 : £3.95
(B77-06285)

Gilbert, Anna. A family likeness / [by] Anna Gilbert. — London [etc.] : Hodder and Stoughton, 1977. — 223p ; 21cm.
ISBN 0-340-21335-3 : £3.75
(B77-17097)

Gilbert, Anna. The look of innocence / [by] Anna Gilbert. — Sevenoaks : Coronet, 1977. — 223p ; 18cm.
Originally published: London : Hodder and Stoughton, 1975.
ISBN 0-340-21795-2 Pbk : £0.70
(B77-28906)

Gilbert, Anthony. And death came too / by Anthony Gilbert. — London : Hamilton, 1977. — [5],170p ; 21cm. — (A fingerprint book)
Originally published: London : Collins, 1956.
ISBN 0-241-89511-1 : £3.75
(B77-12662)

Gilbert, Anthony. He came by night / [by] Anthony Gilbert. — London [etc.] : White Lion Publishers, 1977. — [4],215p ; 21cm.
Originally published: London : Collins for the Crime Club, 1944.
ISBN 0-7274-0225-0 : £3.50
(B77-14916)

Gilbert, Anthony. A nice little killing / [by] Anthony Gilbert. — Large print ed. — Bath : Lythway Press, 1977. — [5],374p ; 22cm.
Originally published: London : Collins for the Crime Club, 1974.
ISBN 0-85046-746-2 : £4.90
(B77-32855)

Gilbert, Harriet. Tide race : a novel / by Harriet Gilbert. — London : Constable, 1977. — [4], 231p ; 21cm.
ISBN 0-09-461570-5 : £3.95
(B77-13281)

Gilchrist, Rupert. Dragonard / [by] Rupert Gilchrist. — London : Corgi, 1976. — 240p ; 18cm. — (Gilchrist, Rupert. Dragonard trilogy ; 1)
Originally published: London : Souvenir Press, 1975.
ISBN 0-552-10149-4 Pbk : £0.75
(B77-05658)

Gilchrist, Rupert. Dragonard blood / [by] Rupert Gilchrist. — London : Souvenir Press, 1977. — 311p : geneal table ; 21cm. — (Gilchrist, Rupert. Dragonard trilogy ; [3])
ISBN 0-285-62283-8 : £3.95
(B77-18371)

Gilchrist, Rupert. The master of Dragonard Hill / [by] Rupert Gilchrist. — London : Corgi, 1977. — [7],305,[1]p ; 18cm. — (Gilchrist, Rupert. Dragonard trilogy ; 2)
Originally published: London : Souvenir Press, 1976.
ISBN 0-552-10420-5 Pbk : £0.85
(B77-16598)

Gill, B M. Target Westminster / by B.M. Gill. — London : Hale, 1977. — 190p ; 20cm.
ISBN 0-7091-6076-3 : £3.15
(B77-16599)

Gill, Judy. Catherine's image / [by] Judy Gill. — London : Hale, 1977. — 183p ; 20cm.
ISBN 0-7091-6057-7 : £3.20
(B77-19690)

Gill, Judy. A harvest of jewels / by Judy Gill. — London : Hale, 1977. — 191p ; 20cm.
ISBN 0-7091-6217-0 : £3.20
(B77-26532)

Gillott, Jacky. Crying out loud : a novel / [by] Jacky Gillott. — London [etc.] : Hodder and Stoughton, 1976. — 256p ; 23cm.
ISBN 0-340-21127-x : £4.25
(B77-00971)

Gilman, Dorothy. The clairvoyant countess / [by] Dorothy Gilman. — Large print ed. — London : Prior [etc.], 1976. — [7],329p ; 24cm.
Originally published: under the name Dorothy Gilman Butters. Garden City, N.Y. : Doubleday, 1975.
ISBN 0-86043-025-1 : £4.95
(B77-07610)

Gilman, Dorothy. Mrs Pollifax on safari / [by] Dorothy Gilman. — London : Hale, 1977. — [9],182p ; 20cm.
Also published: Garden City, N.Y. : Doubleday, 1977.
ISBN 0-7091-6293-6 : £3.25
(B77-26533)

Gilman, George G. Bloody border / [by] George G. Gilman. — London : New English Library, 1977. — 126p ; 18cm. — (Adam Steele ; no.13)
ISBN 0-450-03179-9 Pbk : £0.55
(B77-19691)

Gilman, George G. The day democracy died / [by] George G. Gilman. — London : New English Library, 1977. — 125p ; 18cm. — (Gilman, George G. Edge ; 24)
ISBN 0-450-03176-4 Pbk : £0.60
(B77-28907)

Gilman, George G. Death trail / [by] George G. Gilman. — London : New English Library, 1977. — 126p ; 18cm. — (Adam Steele ; 12)
ISBN 0-450-03095-4 Pbk : £0.50
(B77-12101)

Gilman, George G. Delta duel / [by] George G. Gilman. — London : New English Library, 1977. — 125p ; 18cm. — (Adam Steel ; no.14)
ISBN 0-450-03180-2 Pbk : £0.55
(B77-29700)

Gilman, George G. Echoes of war / [by] George G. Gilman. — London : New English Library, 1977. — 125p ; 18cm. — (Gilman, George G. Edge ; no.23)
ISBN 0-450-03175-6 Pbk : £0.55
(B77-25891)

Gilman, George G. Rhapsody in red / [by] George G. Gilman. — London : New English Library, 1976. — 125p ; 19cm. — (Gilman, George G. Edge ; no.21)
ISBN 0-450-02938-7 Pbk : £0.50
(B77-05659)

Gilman, George G. River of death / [by] George G. Gilman. — London : New English Library, 1977. — 127p ; 18cm. — (Adam Steele ; 15)
ISBN 0-450-03181-0 Pbk : £0.60
(B77-30634)

Gilman, J.D. KG 200 : the force with no face / by J.D. Gilman and John Clive. — London : Souvenir Press, 1977. — 3-363p ; 21cm.
ISBN 0-285-62274-9 : £3.95
(B77-18372)

Gissing, Frances. Gold cord and pot-pourri / [by] Frances Gissing. — Ilfracombe : Stockwell, 1976. — 195p ; 23cm.
ISBN 0-7223-0896-5 : £3.00
(B77-10555)

Glasser, Ronald Joel. Ward 402 / [by] Ronald J. Glasser. — Sevenoaks : Coronet, 1976. — 158p ; 18cm.
Originally published: New York : Braziller, 1973 ; London : Garnstone Press, 1974.
ISBN 0-340-20004-9 Pbk : £0.60
(B77-00972)

Glassford, Wilfred. Alpha-Omega / [by] Wilfred Glassford. — London : New English Library, 1977. — 127p ; 18cm.
ISBN 0-450-02889-5 Pbk : £0.60
(B77-25892)

Glazebrook, Philip. The Burr Wood / by Philip Glazebrook. — London : Gollancz, 1977. — 252p ; 21cm.
ISBN 0-575-02264-7 : £4.75
(B77-22139)

Glemser, Bernard. Grand opening : a novel / by Bernard Glemser. — London : Eyre Methuen, 1977. — [4],268p ; 19cm.
Originally published: Boston, Mass. : Little, Brown, 1976.
ISBN 0-413-38420-9 : £2.95
(B77-28908)

Glendenning, Donn. High ridge country / by Donn Glendenning. — London : Hale, 1977. — 160p ; 20cm.
ISBN 0-7091-5941-2 : £2.95
(B77-08057)

Glendenning, Donn. The hunter of Faro Canyon / by Donn Glendenning. — London : Hale, 1977. — 160p ; 20cm.
ISBN 0-7091-6244-8 : £3.10
(B77-22866)

Glenn, James. Stedman's law / by James Glenn. — London : Hale, 1977. — 157p ; 20cm.
ISBN 0-7091-6083-6 : £2.95
(B77-20608)

Glenn, James. The tumbleweed stage / by James Glenn. — London : Hale, 1977. — 160p ; 20cm.
ISBN 0-7091-6166-2 : £3.10
(B77-26534)

Gloag, John. Artorius rex / [by] John Gloag. — London : Cassell, 1977. — ix,197p : map ; 21cm.
ISBN 0-304-29827-1 : £3.95
(B77-20609)

Glut, Donald Frank. Bones of Frankenstein / [by] Donald F. Glut. — London : New English Library, 1977. — 109p ; 18cm. — (Glut, Donald Frank. New adventures of Frankenstein ; 3)
ISBN 0-450-03407-0 Pbk : £0.60
(B77-28909)

Glut, Donald Frank. Frankenstein lives again / [by Donald F. Glut]. — London [etc.] : Mews Books ; London : Distributed by New English Library, 1977. — 110p ; 18cm. — (Glut, Donald Frank. New adventures of Frankenstein ; 1)
ISBN 0-452-00060-2 Pbk : £0.55
(B77-05660)

Glut, Donald Frank. Terror of Frankenstein / [by Donald F. Glut]. — [London] : [Mews Books] : [Distributed by New English Library], 1977. — 128p ; 18cm. — (Glut, Donald Frank. New adventures of Frankenstein ; 2)
ISBN 0-452-00066-1 Pbk : £0.55
(B77-09270)

Glyn, Elinor. The reason why / by Elinor Glyn ; condensed by Barbara Cartland. — London : Corgi, 1977. — [7],246,[1]p ; 18cm. — (Barbara Cartland's library of love ; 6)
Full ed. originally published: London : Duckworth, 1911.
ISBN 0-552-10560-0 Pbk : £0.60
(B77-28910)

Godden, Jon. Ahmed and the old lady / [by] Jon Godden. — Large print [ed.]. — London : Prior [etc.], 1977. — ix,380p ; 25cm.
Originally published: as 'Ahmed's lady'. London : Chatto and Windus, 1975.
ISBN 0-86043-088-x : £4.95
(B77-34122)

Godden, Rumer. Black narcissus / [by] Rumer Godden. — Large print ed. — Bath : Chivers, 1977. — [5],361p ; 22cm.
Originally published: London : Davies, 1939.
ISBN 0-85997-220-8 : £5.60(£4.20 to members of the Library Association)
(B77-13874)

Godden, Rumer. The peacock spring / [by] Rumer Godden. — Harmondsworth [etc.] : Penguin, 1977. — 286p ; 19cm. — (Peacock books)
Originally published: London : Macmillan, 1975.
ISBN 0-14-047099-9 Pbk : £0.80
(B77-20610)

Godey, John. The talisman / by John Godey. — London : W.H. Allen, 1977. — 383p ; 23cm.
Originally published: New York : Putnam, 1976.
ISBN 0-491-02012-0 : £5.95
(B77-31465)

Goff, Oliver. The eye of the peacock / [by] Oliver Goff. — London : Magnum Books, 1977. — [5],218p ; 18cm.
Originally published: London : Eyre Methuen, 1975.
ISBN 0-413-36560-3 Pbk : £0.70
(B77-16054)

Golding, William. Lord of the flies / [by] William Golding. — Large print ed. — Bath : Lythway Press, 1977. — [5],322p ; 23cm.
Originally published: London : Faber, 1954.
ISBN 0-85046-707-1 : £4.65
(B77-21446)

Goldman, William, *b.1931.* The princess bride : S. Morgenstern's classic tale of true love and high adventure : the 'good parts' version / abridged by [i.e. by] William Goldman. — London : Pan Books, 1976. — [2],283p ; 18cm.
Originally published: New York : Harcourt, Brace, Jovanovich, 1973 ; London : Macmillan, 1975.
ISBN 0-330-24790-5 Pbk : £0.80
(B77-02582)

Goldstein, Arthur D. A person shouldn't die like that / [by] Arthur D. Goldstein. — Large print [ed.]. — London : Prior [etc.], 1977. — [5], 360p ; 24cm.
Originally published: New York : Random House, 1972.
ISBN 0-86043-031-6 : £4.95
(B77-12102)

Goodfield, June. Courier to Peking / [by] June Goodfield. — London : Arrow Books, 1977. — 255p ; 18cm.
Originally published: London : Hart-Davis, MacGibbon, 1973.
ISBN 0-09-914040-3 Pbk : £0.70
(B77-05065)

Goolden, Barbara. Unborn tomorrow / [by] Barbara Goolden. — London : Heinemann, 1977. — 186p ; 21cm.
ISBN 0-434-30211-2 : £3.90
(B77-32178)

Gordon, Giles. Enemies : a novel about friendship / [by] Giles Gordon. — Hassocks : Harvester Press, 1977. — 224p ; 21cm.
ISBN 0-85527-660-6 : £4.50 : CIP rev.
(B77-07611)

Gordon, John, *b.1925.* The ghost on the hill / by John Gordon. — Harmondsworth [etc.] : Penguin, 1977. — 171p ; 18cm. — (Peacock books)
Originally published: Harmondsworth : Kestrel Books, 1976.
ISBN 0-14-047094-8 Pbk : £0.50
(B77-12663)

Gordon, Rex. No man Friday / [by] Rex Gordon. — [1st ed. reprinted] ; introduction by Alan Brien. — London : New English Library, 1977. — 207p ; 22cm. — (SF master series)
Originally published: London : Heinemann, 1956.
ISBN 0-450-03204-3 : £5.95
(B77-21447)

Gordon, Richard. The invisible victory / [by] Richard Gordon. — London : Heinemann, 1977. — [5],310p ; 23cm.
ISBN 0-434-30244-9 : £3.90
(B77-10556)

Gordon, Richard. The sleep of life / [by] Richard Gordon. — Harmondsworth [etc.] : Penguin, 1976. — [5],305p ; 19cm.
Originally published: London : Heinemann, 1975.
ISBN 0-14-004324-1 Pbk : £0.85
(B77-18373)

Gordon, Stuart. Three-eyes / [by] Stuart Gordon. — St Albans : Panther, 1976. — 316p : maps ; 18cm. — (Panther science fiction)
Originally published: New York : Daw Books, 1975 ; London : Sidgwick and Jackson, 1976.
ISBN 0-586-04710-7 Pbk : £0.95
(B77-21448)

Gordon, Yvonne. Holiday heartache / by Yvonne Gordon. — London : Hale, 1977. — 158p ; 20cm.
ISBN 0-7091-5901-3 : £3.10
(B77-05661)

Gordon, Yvonne. Moment of magic / by Yvonne Gordon. — London : Hale, 1977. — 183p ; 20cm.
ISBN 0-7091-6221-9 : £3.20
(B77-34123)

Goulart, Ron. Crackpot / [by] Ron Goulart. — London : Hale, 1977. — [7],150p ; 21cm. — (Hale SF)
ISBN 0-7091-6342-8 : £3.75
(B77-30635)

Goulart, Ron. Gadget man / [by] Ron Goulart. — London : New English Library, 1977. — 111p ; 18cm.
Originally published: Garden City, N.Y. : Doubleday, 1971.
ISBN 0-450-03405-4 Pbk : £0.60
(B77-20611)

Goulart, Ron. The hellhound project / [by] Ron Goulart. — London : Hale, 1976. — [4],156p ; 21cm. — (Hale SF)
Originally published: Garden City, N.Y. : Doubleday, 1975.
ISBN 0-7091-5619-7 : £3.25
(B77-08058)

Goulart, Ron. Vampirella / [by] Ron Goulart. — London : Sphere.
1 : Bloodstalk. — 1976. — 139p ; 18cm.
Originally published: New York : Warner Books, 1975.
ISBN 0-7221-3979-9 Pbk : £0.65
(B77-02583)

2 : On alien wings. — 1977. — 143p ; 18cm.
Originally published: New York : Warner Books, 1975.
ISBN 0-7221-3980-2 Pbk : £0.65
(B77-06869)

3 : Deadwalk. — 1977. — 144p ; 18cm.
Originally published: New York : Warner, 1976.
ISBN 0-7221-3981-0 Pbk : £0.65
(B77-15500)

Gould, Lois. A sea-change / by Lois Gould. — London : W.H. Allen, 1977. — 5-163p ; 22cm.
Originally published: New York : Simon and Schuster, 1976.
ISBN 0-491-02151-8 : £3.95
(B77-25893)

Graham, Carroll. Queer people / by Carroll and Garrett Graham. — [1st ed. reprinted] ; afterword by Budd Schulberg. — Carbondale [etc.] : Southern Illinois University Press ; London [etc.] : Feffer and Simons, 1976. — [2], 284p ; 20cm. — (Lost American fiction)
Facsimile reprint of: 1st ed. New York : Vanguard Press, 1930.
ISBN 0-8093-0784-7 : Unpriced
(B77-10944)

Graham, Neill. Motive for murder : a Solo Malcolm thriller / [by] Neill Graham. — London [etc.] : Long, 1977. — 184p ; 20cm.
ISBN 0-09-128790-1 : £3.25
(B77-17098)

Graham, Robert. Attar's revenge : an Attar the merman novel / by Robert Graham. — London [etc.] : Mews Books ; London : Distributed by New English Library, 1977. — 127p ; 18cm. — (Graham, Robert. Attar the merman ; 1)
Originally published: New York : Pocket Books, 1975.
ISBN 0-452-00077-7 Pbk : £0.55
(B77-12103)

Graham, Winston. The black moon : a novel of Cornwall, 1794-5 / [by] Winston Graham. — [London] : Fontana, 1977. — 384p : geneal tables ; 18cm. — (Graham, Winston. Poldark novels ; 5)
Originally published: London : Collins, 1973.
ISBN 0-00-615085-3 Pbk : £0.95
(B77-27384)

Graham, Winston. The four swans : a novel of Cornwall, 1795-7 / [by] Winston Graham. — London [etc.] : Collins, 1976. — [6],409p : geneal table(on lining papers) ; 22cm.
ISBN 0-00-222246-9 : £3.95
(B77-02584)

Graham, Winston. The four swans : a novel of Cornwall, 1795-7 / [by] Winston Graham. — [London] : Fontana, 1977. — 443p : geneal tables ; 18cm. — (Graham, Winston. Poldark novels ; 6)
Originally published: London : Collins, 1976.
ISBN 0-00-615086-1 Pbk : £1.00
(B77-27385)

Graham, Winston. Night without stars / [by] Winston Graham. — [London] : Fontana, 1976. — 223p ; 18cm.
Originally published: London : Hodder and Stoughton, 1950.
ISBN 0-00-614245-1 Pbk : £0.60
(B77-08567)

Graham, Winston. Woman in the mirror / [by] Winston Graham. — [London] : Fontana, 1977. — 192p ; 18cm.
'Some of this book is based on an earlier novel by the author, "The giant's chair", published in 1938 [by Ward Lock, London]' - note. — Originally published: London : Bodley Head, 1975.
ISBN 0-00-614270-2 Pbk : £0.70
(B77-30636)

Grant, Catherine. To Matthew, a father / by Catherine Grant. — London : Hale, 1977. — 160p ; 20cm.
ISBN 0-7091-6113-1 : £3.20
(B77-21449)

Grant, James. Island of gold / [by] James Grant. — London : Muller, 1977. — [4],148p ; 23cm.
ISBN 0-584-31051-x : £3.95
(B77-19692)

Grant, James. The rose medallion / [by] James Grant. — London : Muller, 1977. — [4],186p ; 23cm.
ISBN 0-584-31112-5 : £3.95 : CIP rev.
(B77-17099)

Grant, Maxwell. Hands in the dark : from the Shadow's private annals / as told to Maxwell Grant. — London : New English Library, 1977. — 156p ; 18cm. — (Grant, Maxwell. Shadow ; no.4)
Originally published: New York : Pyramid Publications, 1975.
ISBN 0-450-02884-4 Pbk : £0.65
(B77-09271)

Grant, Roderick. The clutch of caution / [by] Roderick Grant. — London : New English Library, 1977. — 126p ; 18cm.
Originally published: 1975.
ISBN 0-450-03535-2 Pbk : £0.75
(B77-34124)

Grau, Shirley Ann. Evidence of love / [by] Shirley Ann Grau. — London : Hamilton, 1977. — [7],227p ; 21cm.
Also published: New York : Knopf, 1977.
ISBN 0-241-89739-4 : £3.95
(B77-28134)

Graves, Richard Latshaw. The black gold of Malaverde / [by] Richard L. Graves. — St Albans : Mayflower, 1977. — 3-273p : map ; 18cm.
Originally published: New York : Stein and Day, 1973 ; London : Hart-Davis MacGibbon, 1974.
ISBN 0-583-12532-8 Pbk : £0.65
(B77-13282)

Graves, Robert. I, Claudius : from the autobiography of Tiberius Claudius, Emperor of the Romans, born BC 10, murdered and deified AD 54 / [by] Robert Graves. — London : Eyre Methuen, 1976. — vi,281p,fold leaf : geneal table ; 23cm.
Originally published: London : Barker, 1934.
ISBN 0-413-37070-4 : £3.95
(B77-00424)

Gray, Dulcie. The Devil wore scarlet / by Dulcie Gray. — Hornchurch : I. Henry, 1976. — 190p ; 21cm.
Originally published: London : Macdonald and Co., 1964.
ISBN 0-86025-100-4 : £2.95
(B77-05066)

Gray, Dulcie. The murder of love / by Dulcie Gray. — Hornchurch : I. Henry, 1977. — 173p ; 21cm.
Originally published: London : Macdonald and Co., 1967.
ISBN 0-86025-115-2 : £2.95
(B77-13283)

Gray, Edwyn. Tokyo Torpedo / [by] Edwyn Gray. — London : Futura Publications, 1976. — 192p ; 18cm. — (Gray, Edwyn. U-Boat ; 3)
ISBN 0-86007-281-9 Pbk : £0.60
(B77-09272)

Gray, Francine du Plessix. Lovers and tyrants / [by] Francine du Plessix Gray. — London : Deutsch, 1977. — 3-316p ; 21cm.
Originally published: New York : Simon and Schuster, 1976.
ISBN 0-233-96846-6 : £4.95
(B77-22867)

Gray, Juliet. Bouquet of white roses / by Juliet Gray. — London : Hale, 1977. — 169p ; 20cm.
ISBN 0-7091-6254-5 : £3.20
(B77-26535)

Gray, Juliet. A touch of tenderness / by Juliet Gray. — London : Hale, 1977. — 156p ; 20cm.
ISBN 0-7091-5972-2 : £3.10
(B77-14917)

Gray, Nicholas Stuart. Killer's cookbook / by Nicholas Stuart Gray. — London : Dobson, 1976. — [6],184p ; 21cm.
ISBN 0-234-77668-4 : £3.95
(B77-23725)

Gray, Stephen. Visible people / [by] Stephen Gray. — London : Collings [etc.], 1977. — [4], 195p ; 23cm.
ISBN 0-86036-046-6 : £5.00
(B77-19693)

Grayson, Laura. House of clay / [by] Laura Grayson. — London : Hale, 1977. — 176p ; 21cm.
ISBN 0-7091-6110-7 : £3.70
(B77-25894)

Greathead, Joan. The hiding hole : a tale of the penal days in the time of Elizabeth I / [by] Joan Greathead. — Ilfracombe : Stockwell, 1977. — 23p ; 18cm.
ISBN 0-7223-1065-x Pbk : £0.85
(B77-31466)

Green, Christina. Mistress of Moorhill / by Christina Green. — London : Hale, 1977. — 192p ; 20cm.
ISBN 0-7091-6264-2 : £3.40
(B77-30637)

Green, Cliff. Break of day / [by] Cliff Green. — Sevenoaks : Coronet, 1977. — 160p ; 18cm.
Originally published: Hornsby, N.S.W. : Hodder and Stoughton, 1976.
ISBN 0-340-22034-1 Pbk : £0.60
(B77-26536)

Green, Henry. Blindness : a novel / by Henry Green. — London : Hogarth Press, 1977. — [7] ,254p ; 21cm.
Facsimile reprint of: 1st ed. London : Dent, 1926.
ISBN 0-7012-0434-6 : £3.95 : CIP rev.
(B77-09273)

Greenberg, Dave. The super cops : play it to a bust / [by] Dave Greenberg. — London : Futura Publications, 1977. — viii,247p ; 18cm.
Originally published: as 'Play it to a bust : the super cops'. New York : Hawthorn Books, 1975.
ISBN 0-86007-285-1 Pbk : £0.65
(B77-08568)

Greene, Constance C. I know you, Al / [by] Constance C. Greene. — Harmondsworth : Kestrel Books, 1977. — 109,[1]p ; 23cm.
Originally published: New York : Viking Press, 1975. — For adolescents.
ISBN 0-7226-5361-1 : £2.50
(B77-23726)

Greene, Gael. Blue skies, no candy / [by] Gael Greene. — London : Raven Books, 1977. — 288p ; 23cm.
Originally published: New York : Morrow, 1976.
ISBN 0-354-04228-9 : £4.95
(B77-23727)

Greene, Graham. The heart of the matter ; [and], Stamboul train ; [and], A burnt-out case ; [and], The third man ; [and], The quiet American ; [and], Loser takes all ; [and], The power and the glory / [by] Graham Greene. — London : Heinemann : Octopus Books, 1977. — 3-856p ; 25cm.
ISBN 0-905712-01-3 : £3.95
(B77-14918)

Greene, Graham. Stamboul train : an entertainment / [by] Graham Greene. — Harmondsworth [etc.] : Penguin, 1977. — 216p ; 18cm. — (Peacock books)
Originally published: London : Heinemann, 1932.
ISBN 0-14-047108-1 Pbk : £0.70
(B77-33430)

Greene, Graham. The third man ; and, The fallen idol / [by] Graham Greene. — Large print ed. — Bath : Lythway Press, 1977. — xi,209p ; 22cm.
Originally published: London : Heinemann, 1950.
ISBN 0-85046-697-0 : £4.20
(B77-11402)

Greene, Harris. FSO-1 / [by] Harris Greene. — London : New English Library, 1977. — [5], 186p ; 21cm.
Also published: Garden City, N.Y. : Doubleday, 1977.
ISBN 0-450-03589-1 : £4.95
(B77-32179)

Greenhough, Terry. Thoughtworld / [by] Terry Greenhough. — London : New English Library, 1977. — 144p ; 21cm.
ISBN 0-450-03197-7 : £3.95
(B77-15501)

Greer, Ben. Slammer / [by] Ben Greer. — London : Hale, 1977. — [7],268,[1]p ; 21cm.
Originally published: New York : Atheneum, 1975.
ISBN 0-7091-5744-4 : £3.95
(B77-08059)

Gregson, Maureen. 1990 / based on a series created by Wilfred Greatorex ; novelization by Maureen Gregson ; novelization based on scripts by Wilfred Greatorex, Edmund Ward and Arden Winch. — London : Sphere, 1977. — 199p ; 18cm.
ISBN 0-7221-4009-6 Pbk : £0.85
(B77-31467)

Greig, Maysie. I loved her yesterday / [by] Maysie Greig. — Large print ed. — Bath : Lythway Press, 1976. — [6],351p ; 22cm.
Originally published: London : Collins, 1945.
ISBN 0-85046-685-7 : £4.55
(B77-06870)

Grex, Leo. Death throws no shadow / by Leo Grex. — London : Hale, 1976. — 192p ; 20cm.
ISBN 0-7091-5875-0 : £2.95
(B77-00425)

Grey, Francesca. The dancing place / by Francesca Grey. — London : Hale, 1977. — 185p ; 20cm.
ISBN 0-7091-6330-4 : £3.40
(B77-32180)

Grey, Naidra. Foxglove summer / [by] Naidra Grey. — London : P. Davies, 1977. — ix,210p ; 23cm.
ISBN 0-432-06365-x : £3.50
(B77-00973)

Grey, Zane. The call of the canyon / [by] Zane Grey. — London [etc.] : White Lion Publishers, 1977. — 157p ; 21cm.
Originally published: New York : Harper; London : Hodder and Stoughton, 1924.
ISBN 0-7274-0295-1 : £3.50
(B77-06286)

Grey, Zane. Fighting caravans / [by] Zane Grey. — London [etc.] : White Lion Publishers, 1977. — 255p ; 21cm.
Originally published: New York ; London : Harper, 1929.
ISBN 0-7274-0285-4 : £3.75
(B77-15502)

Grey, Zane. West of the Pecos / [by] Zane Grey. — London : Sphere, [1977]. — 208p ; 18cm.
Originally published: New York : Harper ; London : Hodder and Stoughton, 1937.
ISBN 0-7221-4068-1 Pbk : £0.60
(B77-13284)

Grey, Zane. Western Union / [by] Zane Grey. — London : Sphere, 1975. — 220p ; 18cm.
Originally published: New York ; London : Harper ; London : Hodder and Stoughton, 1939.
ISBN 0-7221-4070-3 Pbk : £0.65
(B77-09274)

Grey, Zane. Wilderness trek / [by] Zane Grey. — London [etc.] : White Lion Publishers, 1976. — [4],263p ; 21cm.
Originally published: New York : Harper, 1944 ; London : Hodder and Stoughton, 1945.
ISBN 0-7274-0290-0 : £3.75
(B77-05067)

Grey, Zane. Wyoming / by Zane Grey. — Hornchurch : I. Henry, 1977. — 223p ; 21cm.
Originally published: New York : Harper, 1953 ; London : Hodder and Stoughton, 1954.
ISBN 0-86025-110-1 : £3.65
(B77-20612)

Gribble, Leonard. Crime on her hands / by Leonard Gribble. — London : Hale, 1977. — 183p ; 20cm.
ISBN 0-7091-6317-7 : £3.25
(B77-28911)

Grice, Frederick. Nine days' wonder / [by] Frederick Grice ; illustrated by Paul Ritchie. — London : Oxford University Press, 1976. — [6], 121p : ill ; 23cm.
For adolescents.
ISBN 0-19-271394-9 : £2.95
(B77-02585)

Griffin, Gwyn. Shipmaster / [by] Gwyn Griffin. — London [etc.] : White Lion Publishers, 1976. — 384p ; 21cm.
Originally published: London : Collins, 1961.
ISBN 0-7274-0164-5 : £4.50
(B77-03221)

Griffin, John. Anarchists' moon / [by] John Griffin. — London : Hale, 1977. — 208p : map ; 20cm.
ISBN 0-7091-6290-1 : £3.25
(B77-28135)

Griffin, John. Seeds of destruction / by John Griffin. — London : Hale, 1977. — 192p : map ; 20cm.
ISBN 0-7091-5833-5 : £3.15
(B77-09948)

Griffin, John, *b.1935.* Skulker Wheat, and other stories / [by] John Griffin. — London : Heinemann, 1977. — [5],86p ; 21cm. — (Pyramid books)
For adolescents.
ISBN 0-434-95818-2 : £2.10
(B77-13385)

Griffiths, Peter, *b.1944.* Final approach / [by] Peter Griffiths. — London : Hale, 1977. — 188p ; 21cm.
ISBN 0-7091-6338-x : £3.85
(B77-32181)

Grimwood, Ken. Breakthrough / [by] Ken Grimwood. — London : W.H. Allen, 1977. — [5],234p ; 23cm.
Originally published: Garden City, N.Y. : Doubleday, 1976.
ISBN 0-491-01698-0 : £3.95
(B77-10557)

Grogan, Emmett. Final score / [by] Emmett Grogan. — London : Heinemann, 1977. — [7], 292p ; 23cm.
Originally published: New York : Holt, Rinehart and Winston, 1976.
ISBN 0-434-30650-9 : £3.90
(B77-02586)

Grubb, Davis. The night of the hunter / [by] Davis Grubb. — Harmondsworth [etc.] : Penguin, 1977. — 220p ; 18cm.
Originally published: New York : Harper, 1953 ; London : Hamilton, 1954.
ISBN 0-14-004426-4 Pbk : £0.75
(B77-31468)

Guest, Judith. Ordinary people / [by] Judith Guest. — London : Collins, 1977. — 252p ; 21cm.
Originally published: New York : Viking Press, 1976.
ISBN 0-00-221613-2 : £3.50
(B77-06287)

Guild, Nicholas. The lost and found man / by Nicholas Guild. — London : Hale, 1977. — [7], 213p ; 20cm.
Originally published: New York : Harpers Mag. Press, 1975.
ISBN 0-7091-6420-3 : £3.25
(B77-28136)

Gulliver, Sam. The Vulcan bulletins / [by] Sam Gulliver. — London : Sphere, 1976. — 160p ; 18cm.
Originally published: London : Hodder and Stoughton, 1974.
ISBN 0-7221-4144-0 Pbk : £0.60
(B77-06288)

Gunn, James. The joy makers / [by] James Gunn. — St Albans : Panther, 1976. — 204p ; 18cm. — (Panther science fiction)
Originally published: New York : Bantam Books, 1961 ; London : Gollancz, 1963.
ISBN 0-586-04266-0 Pbk : £0.60
(B77-13875)

Gunn, James. Kampus : a novel / by James E. Gunn. — Toronto [etc.] ; London : Bantam, 1977. — [5],308,[1]p ; 18cm.
ISBN 0-552-62693-7 Pbk : £0.75
(B77-28912)

Gunn, James. This fortress world / [by] James Gunn. — London : Sphere, 1977. — 192p ; 18cm. — (Sphere science fiction)
Originally published: New York : Gnome Press, 1955.
ISBN 0-7221-4145-9 Pbk : £0.65
(B77-10558)

Gunn, Neil Miller. Butcher's broom / by Neil M. Gunn. — London : Souvenir Press, 1977. — 429p ; 20cm.
Originally published: Edinburgh : Porpoise Press, 1934.
ISBN 0-285-62278-1 : £3.95
ISBN 0-285-62288-9 Pbk : £2.00
(B77-19694)

Gunn, Victor. Death comes laughing / [by] Victor Gunn. — Large print ed. — Bath : Lythway Press, 1977. — [5],319p ; 22cm.
Originally published: London : Collins, 1952.
ISBN 0-85046-696-2 : £4.55
(B77-11403)

Gunn, Victor. The treble chance murder / [by] Victor Gunn. — Large print ed. — Leicester : Ulverscroft, 1977. — [4],364p ; 23cm. — (Ulverscroft large print series : [mystery])
Originally published: London : Collins, 1958.
ISBN 0-7089-0008-9 : £2.95
(B77-22140)

Haas, Ben. The house of Christina / [by] Ben Haas. — London : P. Davies, 1977. — 411,[1] p ; 23cm.
ISBN 0-432-06534-2 : £4.50
(B77-18995)

Hackforth-Jones, Gilbert. All stations to Malta / [by] Gilbert Hackforth-Jones. — London : White Lion Publishers, 1977. — 222p ; 21cm.
Originally published: London : Hodder and Stoughton, 1971.
ISBN 0-7274-0325-7 : £3.95
(B77-18996)

Hackforth-Jones, Gilbert. Crack of doom / by Gilbert Hackforth-Jones. — London : Remploy, 1976. — 223p ; 19cm.
Originally published: London : Hodder and Stoughton, 1961.
ISBN 0-7066-0701-5 : £3.00
(B77-15503)

Haddad, C A. The Moroccan / [by] C.A. Haddad. — London : W.H. Allen, 1977. — 253p ; 23cm.
Originally published: New York : Harper and Row, 1975.
ISBN 0-491-01618-2 : £3.95
(B77-07612)

Haddon, Celia. Venus reveal'd : the amorous adventures of Francis Lysaght / edited [i.e. written] by Celia Haddon. — London : Davis-Poynter, 1977. — x,165p ; 23cm.
ISBN 0-7067-0221-2 : £5.00
(B77-30638)

Hailey, Arthur. Hotel / [by] Arthur Hailey ; a condensation by the editors of Reader's Digest Condensed Books. — Large print ed. — Leicester : Ulverscroft, 1977. — [5],287p ; 23cm. — (Ulverscroft large print series : [fiction])
This condensation originally published: Pleasantville, N.Y. : Reader's Digest Association, 197-?.
ISBN 0-85456-557-4 : £2.65
(B77-15504)

Hailey, Arthur. The moneychangers / [by] Arthur Hailey. — London [etc.] : Pan Books, 1976. — 476p ; 18cm.
Originally published: London : Joseph : Souvenir Press, 1975.
ISBN 0-330-24603-8 Pbk : £0.95
(B77-03222)

Haldeman, Joe. Mindbridge / by Joe Haldeman. — London : Macdonald and Jane's, 1977. — [6],186p ; 21cm.
Originally published: New York : St Martin's Press, 1976.
ISBN 0-354-04144-4 : £3.95
(B77-13285)

Hale, Arlene. One more bridge to cross / [by] Arlene Hale. — Large print [ed.]. — London : Prior [etc.], 1976. — [9],455p ; 24cm.
Originally published: Boston, Mass. : Little, Brown, 1975.
ISBN 0-86043-013-8 : £5.95
(B77-07613)

Hale, Arlene. The other side of the world / [by] Arlene Hale. — Large print [ed.]. — London : Prior [etc.], 1977. — [7],406p ; 24cm.
Originally published: Boston, Mass. : Little, Brown, 1976.
ISBN 0-86043-037-5 : £4.95
(B77-12104)

Hales, Edward Elton Young. Chariot of fire / [by] E.E.Y. Hales. — London [etc.] : Hodder and Stoughton, 1977. — 191p ; 21cm.
ISBN 0-340-22153-4 : £3.95
(B77-28913)

Haley, Alex. Roots / [by] Alex Haley. — London : Hutchinson, 1977. — ix,688p ; 23cm.
Originally published: Garden City, N.Y. : Doubleday, 1976.
ISBN 0-09-129680-3 : £5.95
(B77-19695)

Halil, Lola. I remember Cyprus - : a novel / by Lola Halil. — London (P.O. Box 159, NW1 7HZ) : The author, 1977. — [5],192p ; 20cm.
ISBN 0-905506-01-4 : £2.50
(B77-10559)

Hall, Adam. The Kobra manifesto / [by] Adam Hall. — Large print [ed.]. — London : Prior [etc.], 1977. — [7],480p ; 25cm.
Originally published: London : Collins, 1976.
ISBN 0-86043-058-8 : £5.95
(B77-21450)

Hall, Adam. The Mandarin cypher / [by] Adam Hall. — [London] : Fontana, 1977. — 224p ; 18cm.
Originally published: London : Collins, 1975.
ISBN 0-00-614828-x Pbk : £0.70
(B77-13286)

Hall, Adam. The Quiller memorandum / [by] Adam Hall. — [London] : Fontana, 1977. — 192p ; 18cm.
Originally published: as 'The Berlin memorandum', London : Collins, 1965 ; and as 'The Quiller memorandum', New York : Simon and Schuster, 1965 ; London : Fontana, 1967.
ISBN 0-00-614493-4 Pbk : £0.70
(B77-18997)

Hall, Robert Lee. Exit Sherlock Holmes : the great detective's final days / [by] Robert Lee Hall. — London : J. Murray, 1977. — iii-xi, 238p ; 22cm.
Also published: New York : Scribner, 1977.
ISBN 0-7195-3440-2 : £3.95
(B77-32182)

Hall, S G. The rape of the catalog / [by] S.G. Hall. — Brighton : Noyce, 1977. — [1],10p ; 30cm.
Sd : Unpriced
(B77-20613)

Hall, Willis. The Fuzz / [by] Willis Hall. — Sevenoaks : Coronet, 1977. — 174p ; 18cm.
'Based on the Thames Television series "The Fuzz" created and written by Willis Hall'.
ISBN 0-340-22703-6 Pbk : £0.75
(B77-29701)

Hallahan, William H. The Ross forgery / [by] William H. Hallahan. — London : Gollancz, 1977. — [4],204p ; 21cm. — ([Gollancz thriller])
Originally published: Indianapolis : Bobbs-Merrill, 1973.
ISBN 0-575-02367-8 : £3.75
(B77-28137)

Hamill, W D. Dreaming time / [by] W.D. Hamill. — Ilfracombe : Stockwell, 1977. — 86p ; 19cm.
ISBN 0-7223-0985-6 : £2.50
(B77-21451)

Hamilton, Jessica. Baxter : a novel of inhuman evil / [by] Jessica Hamilton. — London : Harrap, 1977. — 142p ; 23cm.
ISBN 0-245-53178-5 : £2.95
(B77-29702)

Hamilton, Julia. The changeling queen / by Julia Hamilton. — London : Hale, 1977. — 176p ; 21cm.
ISBN 0-7091-6202-2 : £3.70
(B77-34126)

Hamilton, Virginia. Arilla sun down / [by] Virginia Hamilton. — London : Hamilton, 1977. — [5],248p ; 23cm.
Originally published: as 'Arilla'. New York : Greenwillow Books, 1976.
ISBN 0-241-89548-0 : £3.60
(B77-09949)

Hamilton, Virginia. M.C. Higgins, the great / [by] Virginia Hamilton. — London : Collins, 1976. — 220p ; 18cm. — (Lions)
Originally published: New York : Macmillan, 1974 ; London : Hamilton, 1975. — For adolescents.
ISBN 0-00-671172-3 Pbk : £0.60
(B77-01804)

Hammand, Norman Bentley. De Monterey and the losing side / [by] N.B. Hammand. — London : Hale, 1977. — 223p ; 21cm.
ISBN 0-7091-5745-2 : £3.60
(B77-12664)

Hammett, Dashiell. The Maltese falcon / [by] Dashiell Hammett. — Large print ed. — Bath : Lythway Press, 1977. — [5],344p ; 22cm.
Originally published: New York : London : Knopf, 1930.
ISBN 0-85046-698-9 : £4.60
(B77-10945)

Hammond, Jane. Gunpowder treason / [by] Jane Hammond. — London : Hale, 1976. — 189p ; 21cm.
ISBN 0-7091-5371-6 : £3.25
(B77-01805)

Hammond, Jane. The queen's assassin / [by] Jane Hammond. — London : Hale, 1977. — 3-171p ; 21cm.
ISBN 0-7091-5611-1 : £3.50
(B77-21452)

Hammond, Jane. The red queen / [by] Jane Hammond. — London : Hale, 1976. — 191p ; 21cm.
ISBN 0-7091-5297-3 : £3.10
(B77-11404)

Hammond, Jane. The silver madonna / by Jane Hammond. — London : Hale, 1977. — 160p ; 21cm.
ISBN 0-7091-5528-x : £3.25
(B77-14405)

Hammond, Jane. Witch of the White House / [by] Jane Hammond. — London : New English Library, 1977. — 141p ; 18cm.
Originally published: London : Hale, 1976.
ISBN 0-450-03406-2 Pbk : £0.70
(B77-23728)

Hampson, Anne. Fire meets fire / by Anne Hampson. — London : Mills and Boon, 1977. — 188p ; 17cm.
Originally published: 1976.
ISBN 0-263-72340-2 Pbk : £0.35
(B77-06871)

Hampson, Anne. Harbour of love / by Anne Hampson. — London : Mills and Boon, 1977. — 186p ; 17cm.
ISBN 0-263-72389-5 Pbk : £0.35
(B77-20614)

Hampson, Anne. Satan and the nymph / by Anne Hampson. — London : Mills and Boon, 1976. — 188p ; 18cm.
ISBN 0-263-72297-x Pbk : £0.30
(B77-00974)

Hanley, Clifford. The taste of too much / [by] Clifford Hanley. — London [etc.] : White Lion Publishers, 1977. — 198p ; 21cm.
Originally published: London : Hutchinson, 1960.
ISBN 0-7274-0203-x : £3.50
(B77-08060)

Hanley, James. Sailor's song / [by] James Hanley. — London : Kimber, 1977. — 224p ; 21cm.
Originally published: London : Nicholson and Watson, 1943.
ISBN 0-7183-0115-3 : £3.25
(B77-19696)

Hanrahan, Barbara. The albatross muff : a novel / by Barbara Hanrahan. — London : Chatto and Windus, 1977. — 206p ; 21cm.
ISBN 0-7011-2197-1 : £4.50
(B77-18998)

Harbinson, William Allen. Instruments of death / [by] W.A. Harbinson. — London : Corgi, 1977. — 413p ; 18cm.
Originally published: 1973.
ISBN 0-552-10252-0 Pbk : £0.95
(B77-16600)

Harbinson, William Allen. The MacKinnons / [by] W.A. Harbinson and Lindsay Galloway. — London : Severn House, 1977. — 173p ; 21cm.
'Based on the ... BBC TV series ...' - p.1.
ISBN 0-7278-0244-5 : £3.25
(B77-32183)

Harding, Duncan. Flotilla attack / [by] Duncan Harding. — London : Futura Publications, 1976. — 190p ; 18cm. — (Destroyer ; 1)
ISBN 0-86007-300-9 Pbk : £0.60
(B77-08569)

Harding, Duncan. Torpedo boat / [by] Duncan Harding. — London [etc.] : White Lion Publishers, 1977. — 192p ; 21cm.
Originally published: London : Futura Publications, 1976.
ISBN 0-7274-0279-x : £3.75
(B77-16601)

Harding, Duncan. Torpedo boat / [by] Duncan Harding. — London : Futura Publications, 1976. — 192p ; 18cm.
ISBN 0-86007-376-9 Pbk : £0.60
(B77-12105)

Harding, Duncan. Tug of war : (December 22nd-December 31st 1941) / [by] Duncan Harding. — London : Seeley Service, 1976. — 190p ; 21cm. — ([Seeley Service war fiction])
Originally published: London : Futura Publications, 1975.
ISBN 0-85422-123-9 : £3.95
(B77-00426)

Hardwick, Michael. The cedar tree, autumn of an age : a novel / by Michael Hardwick. — London : Corgi, 1977. — 175p ; 18cm.
'The second novel based on the ... ATV series created by Alfred Shaughnessy' - note.
ISBN 0-552-10438-8 Pbk : £0.65
(B77-25895)

Hardwick, Michael. The cedar tree, autumn of an age : a novel / by Michael Hardwick. — London : Severn House : [Distributed by Hutchinson], 1977. — 175p ; 21cm.
'Based on the television series created by Alfred Shaughnessy'.
ISBN 0-7278-0304-2 : £3.25
(B77-28138)

Hardwick, Michael. The four musketeers : the revenge of Milady / by Michael Hardwick ; based on Alexander Salkind's film of 'The four musketeers' with screenplay by George MacDonald Fraser ; based on the novels of Alexander Dumas. — Hornchurch : I. Henry, 1977. — [4],122,[1]p ; 21cm.
Originally published: London : Corgi, 1975.
ISBN 0-86025-125-x : £3.10
(B77-27386)

Hardwick, Mollie. Beauty's daughter : the story of Lady Hamilton's 'lost' child / [by] Mollie Hardwick. — London : Sphere, 1977. — 368p ; 18cm.
Originally published: London : Eyre Methuen, 1976.
ISBN 0-7221-4297-8 Pbk : £0.95
(B77-31469)

Hardwick, Mollie. Charlie is my darling : a novel / by Mollie Hardwick. — London : Eyre Methuen, 1977. — 317p ; 23cm.
ISBN 0-413-34230-1 : £4.95
(B77-22868)

Hardwick, Mollie. The Duchess of Duke Street / [by] Mollie Hardwick. — Large print ed. — Leicester : Ulverscroft.
[Book 1] : The way up. — 1977. — [5],365p ; 23cm. — (Ulverscroft large print series : [historical romance])
'... based on the first five episodes of the [BBC] television series' - note. — Originally published: London : Hamilton, 1976.
ISBN 0-7089-0059-3 : £2.95
(B77-32184)

Hardwick, Mollie. The Duchess of Duke Street / [by] Mollie Hardwick. — Large print ed. — Bath : Firecrest.
Book 1 : The way up. — 1977. — [5],330p ; 22cm.
'... based on the first five episodes of the BBC Television series ...' - Acknowledgement. — Originally published: London : Hamilton : Futura, 1976.
ISBN 0-85119-016-2 : £4.65
(B77-28139)

Book 2 : The golden years. — 1977. — [7], 271p ; 22cm.
'... based on episodes in the B.B.C. Television serial ...' - Acknowledgement. — Originally published: London : Hamilton, 1976.
ISBN 0-85119-015-4 : £4.65
(B77-28140)

Hardwick, Mollie. The Duchess of Duke Street / [by] Mollie Hardwick. — London : Futura Publications.
[Book 1] : The way up. — 1976. — 190p ; 18cm.
'... based on the first five episodes of the [BBC] television series ...' - title page verso. — Also published: London : Hamilton, 1976.
ISBN 0-86007-409-9 Pbk : £0.60
(B77-13287)

Hardwick, Mollie. The Duchess of Duke Street / [by] Mollie Hardwick. — London : Hamilton.
Book 2 : The golden years. — 1976. — 189p ; 21cm.
'... based on episodes in the BBC television serial ...' - Acknowledgement.
ISBN 0-241-89494-8 : £3.50
(B77-01806)

Book 3 : The world keeps turning. — 1977. — 240p ; 21cm.
Based on the BBC television serial.
ISBN 0-241-89632-0 : £3.95
(B77-27387)

Hardwick, Mollie. Mrs Bridges' story / [by] Mollie Hardwick. — London : Sphere, 1976. — 123p ; 18cm.
Originally published: 1975.
ISBN 0-7221-4293-5 Pbk : £0.50
(B77-08061)

Hardy, Adam. Close quarters / [by] Adam Hardy. — London : New English Library, 1977. — 128p ; 18cm. — (Hardy, Adam. Fox ; no.14)
ISBN 0-450-02892-5 Pbk : £0.50
(B77-12665)

Hargrave, Leonie. Clara Reeve / [by] Leonie Hargrave. — London : Arrow Books, 1977. — [6],442p : geneal table ; 18cm.
Originally published: London : Hutchinson, 1975.
ISBN 0-09-914920-6 Pbk : £0.95
(B77-31470)

Harmon, Sandra. A girl like me / [by] Sandra Harmon. — London : Corgi, 1977. — [7], 213p ; 18cm.
Originally published: New York : Dutton, 1975.
ISBN 0-552-10350-0 Pbk : £0.75
(B77-13288)

Harper, David. The hanged men / [by] David Harper. — London : Hamilton, 1977. — [5], 218p ; 21cm.
Originally published: New York : Dodd, Mead, 1976.
ISBN 0-241-89605-3 : £3.75
(B77-19697)

Harper, Stephen. Live till tomorrow / [by] Stephen Harper. — London : Collins, 1977. — 195p ; 22cm.
ISBN 0-00-222405-4 : £2.95
(B77-00975)

Harris, Alfred. Baroni / [by] Alfred Harris. — London : Hale, 1977. — 256p ; 23cm.
Originally published: New York : Putnam, 1975.
ISBN 0-7091-6200-6 : £3.95
(B77-30639)

Harris, Evelyn. Against the flame / by Evelyn Harris. — London : Hale, 1977. — 185p ; 20cm.
ISBN 0-7091-6011-9 : £3.15
(B77-13289)

Harris, Hyde. Kyd for hire : a crime novel / by Hyde Harris. — London : Gollancz, 1977. — 176p ; 21cm. — ([Gollancz thriller])
ISBN 0-575-02365-1 : £4.25
(B77-29703)

Harris, John, *b.1916.* Army of shadows : a novel of the Resistance / [by] John Harris. — London : Hutchinson, 1977. — 287p : maps(on lining papers) ; 23cm.
ISBN 0-09-128450-3 : £3.95
(B77-13876)

Harris, John, *b.1916.* The claws of mercy / [by] John Harris. — Large print ed. — Leicester : Ulverscroft, 1977. — [5],507p ; 23cm. — (Ulverscroft large print series : [adventure, suspense])
Originally published: London : Hurst and Blackett, 1955.
ISBN 0-7089-0004-6 : £2.95
(B77-28914)

Harris, John, *b.1916.* The interceptors : a Martin Falconer story / [by] John Harris ; illustrated by Oliver Elmes. — London : Hutchinson, 1977. — 192p : ill, map ; 21cm.
ISBN 0-09-128630-1 : £3.25
(B77-21453)

Harris, John, *b.1916.* The professionals / [by] John Harris ; illustrated by Oliver Elmes. — Harmondsworth [etc.] : Puffin Books, 1977. — 188,[1]p : ill ; 19cm. — (Puffin books)
Originally published: London : Hutchinson, 1973.
ISBN 0-14-030918-7 Pbk : £0.50
(B77-18374)

Harris, John, *b.1916.* Road to the coast / [by] John Harris. — Large print ed. — Leicester : Ulverscroft, 1977. — [4],466p ; 23cm. — (Ulverscroft large print series : [adventure, suspense])
Originally published: London : Hutchinson, 1959.
ISBN 0-85456-531-0 : £2.65
(B77-13877)

Harris, John, *b.1916.* The sea shall not have them / [by] John Harris. — London [etc.] : Arrow Books, 1977. — 256p ; 18cm.
Originally published: London : Hurst and Blackett, 1953.
Pbk : £0.70
ISBN 0-09-910330-3
(B77-17100)

Harris, John, *b.1916.* Take or destroy! / [by] John Harris. — London : Arrow Books, 1977. — 286p ; 18cm.
Originally published: London : Hutchinson, 1976.
ISBN 0-09-914210-4 Pbk : £0.75
(B77-30640)

Harris, Leonard, *b.1929.* The Masada plan : a novel / by Leonard Harris. — London : Joseph, 1977. — [5],314p ; 23cm.
Originally published: New York : Crown, 1976.
ISBN 0-7181-1600-3 : £4.50
(B77-18999)

Harris, MacDonald. The balloonist : a novel / by MacDonald Harris. — London : Gollancz, 1977. — [5],273p : ill ; 21cm.
ISBN 0-575-02254-x : £4.75
(B77-18375)

Harris, Ralph, *b.1920.* Spring call / [by] Ralph Harris. — London : P. Davies, 1977. — [5], 216p ; 23cm.
ISBN 0-432-06500-8 : £3.90
(B77-19000)

Harris, Thomas. Black Sunday / [by] Thomas Harris. — Sevenoaks : Coronet, 1977. — 318p ; 18cm.
Originally published: New York : Putnam ; London : Hodder and Stoughton, 1975.
ISBN 0-340-20530-x Pbk : £0.85
(B77-09275)

Harris, Walter, *b.1925.* To catch a rat / [by] Walter Harris. — London : A. Barker, 1977. — 160p ; 23cm. — (The new avengers)
ISBN 0-213-16637-2 : £3.75
(B77-25198)

Harris, Wilson, *b.1921.* Da Silva da Silva's cultivated wilderness ; and, Genesis of the clowns / by Wilson Harris. — London : Faber, 1977. — [4],148p : 2 ill ; 21cm.
ISBN 0-571-10819-9 : £3.95
(B77-13290)

Harrison, Elizabeth. Ambulance call / [by] Elizabeth Harrison. — London : Corgi, 1977. — 142p ; 18cm. — (Harrison, Elizabeth. Central Hospital romance series ; no.9)
Originally published: London : Hurst and Blackett, 1972.
ISBN 0-552-10355-1 Pbk : £0.50
(B77-09276)

Harrison, Elizabeth. Corridors of healing / [by] Elizabeth Harrison. — London : Corgi, 1976. — 174p ; 18cm. — (Harrison, Elizabeth. Central Hospital romance series ; no.8)
Originally published: London : Ward Lock, 1968.
ISBN 0-552-10329-2 Pbk : £0.50
(B77-04406)

Harrison, Elizabeth. The Ravelston affair / [by] Elizabeth Harrison. — London : Corgi, 1976. — 173p ; 18cm. — (Harrison, Elizabeth. Central Hospital romance series ; no.7)
Originally published: London : Ward Lock, 1967.
ISBN 0-552-10304-7 Pbk : £0.45
(B77-02587)

Harrison, Elizabeth. To mend a heart / [by] Elizabeth Harrison. — London : Hurst and Blackett, 1977. — 184p ; 19cm.
ISBN 0-09-129890-3 : £3.50
(B77-30641)

Harrison, Harry. Deathworld / [by] Harry Harrison. — London : Sphere. — (Sphere science fiction)
In 3 vols.
1. — 1977. — 157p ; 18cm.
Originally published: New York : Bantam Books, 1960 ; Harmondsworth : Penguin, 1963.
ISBN 0-7221-4416-4 Pbk : £0.65
(B77-12666)

2. — 1977. — 160p ; 18cm.
Originally published: as 'The ethical engineer'. London : Gollancz, 1964.
ISBN 0-7221-4417-2 Pbk : £0.65
(B77-12667)

3. — 1977. — 157p ; 18cm.
Originally published: London : Faber, 1969.
ISBN 0-7221-4418-0 Pbk : £0.65
(B77-12668)

Harrison, Harry. Planet of the damned / [by] Harry Harrison. — London : Futura Publications, 1976. — [5],169p ; 18cm.
Originally published: as 'Planet of the damned', s.l. : s.n., 1962 ; and as 'Sense of obligation', London : Dobson, 1967.
ISBN 0-86007-855-8 Pbk : £0.50
(B77-09277)

Harrison, Harry. Queen Victoria's revenge / [by] Harry Harrison. — London : Severn House : [Distributed by Hutchinson], 1977. — [5],161p ; 21cm.
Originally published: Garden City, N.Y. : Doubleday, 1974.
ISBN 0-7278-0229-1 : £3.25
(B77-08570)

Harrison, Harry. Skyfall / [by] Harry Harrison. — London : Corgi, 1977. — 270p ; 18cm.
Originally published: London : Faber, 1976.
ISBN 0-552-10542-2 Pbk : £0.85
(B77-28141)

Harrison, Harry. Star smashers of the Galaxy Rangers / [by] Harry Harrison. — London : Futura Publications, 1976. — 190p ; 18cm. — (An orbit book)
Originally published: New York : Putnam, 1973 ; London : Faber, 1974.
ISBN 0-86007-850-7 Pbk : £0.60
(B77-08571)

Harrison, Harry. The technicolor time machine / [by] Harry Harrison. — London : Futura Publications, 1976. — 174p ; 18cm. — (An orbit book)
Originally published: New York : Doubleday, 1967 ; London : Faber, 1968.
ISBN 0-86007-887-6 Pbk : £0.60
(B77-08572)

Harrison, William, *b.1933.* Africana / [by] William Harrison. — London : Hamilton, 1977. — 252p : maps ; 21cm.
Originally published: New York : Morrow, 1977.
ISBN 0-241-89724-6 : £3.95
(B77-22869)

Hart, George. The Punch and Judy murders / [by] George Hart. — London : Golden Eagle Press, 1977. — 194p ; 23cm.
ISBN 0-901482-26-9 : £3.50
(B77-19698)

Hart, Jon. The mercenaries, black blood / [by] Jon Hart. — St Albans : Mayflower, 1977. — 128p ; 18cm.
ISBN 0-583-12589-1 Pbk : £0.50
(B77-13291)

Hart, Jon. The mercenaries, triangle of death / [by] Jon Hart. — St Albans : Mayflower, 1977. — 128p ; 18cm.
ISBN 0-583-12591-3 Pbk : £0.50
(B77-25199)

Hart, Ted. Ted Willis' 'Hunters Walk' : a novel / by Ted Hart. — London : Severn House : [Distributed by Hutchinson], 1976. — 192p ; 21cm.
'Based on the original television format by Ted Willis'.
ISBN 0-7278-0307-7 : £3.15
(B77-00427)

Hart, Tom. They call it murder / [by] Tom Hart. — London [etc.] : Quartet Books, 1977. — [7], 120p ; 23cm.
ISBN 0-7043-2153-x : £3.95
(B77-32185)

Hartshorne. The Mexican assassin / [by] Hartshorne. — London : Hale, 1977. — 350p ; 21cm.
ISBN 0-7091-5862-9 : £3.95
(B77-15505)

Harvey, John, *b.1938.* Scott Mitchell, junkyard angel / [by] John Harvey. — London : Sphere, 1977. — 143p ; 18cm.
Cover title: Junkyard angel.
ISBN 0-7221-4407-5 Pbk : £0.65
(B77-13292)

Hastings, Michael. The trader of Skull Island / [by] Michael Hastings. — London : Macdonald and Jane's, 1977. — 190p ; 23cm.
ISBN 0-354-04101-0 : £3.75
(B77-13293)

Hastings, Phyllis. The death-scented flower / by Phyllis Hastings. — London : Hale, 1977. — 192p ; 21cm.
ISBN 0-7091-5877-7 : £3.50
(B77-14919)

Hastings, Phyllis. House of the twelve Caesars / [by] Phyllis Hastings. — London : Corgi, 1976. — 186p ; 18cm.
Originally published: London : Hale, 1975.
ISBN 0-552-10152-4 Pbk : £0.60
(B77-05662)

Hawke, Elton. Keep it up downstairs / [by] Elton Hawke. — London : Everest, 1976. — [2],156p,[8]p of plates : ill ; 18cm.
'... based on the film of the same name ...' - note.
ISBN 0-905018-07-9 Pbk : £0.60
(B77-06289)

Hay, Ian. A safety match / by Ian Hay ; condensed by Barbara Cartland. — London : Corgi, 1977. — [5],181,[1]p ; 18cm. — (Barbara Cartland's library of love ; 4)
Full ed. originally published: Edinburgh : Blackwood, 1911.
ISBN 0-552-10489-2 Pbk : £0.50
(B77-20615)

Haycox, Ernest. No law and order / [by] Ernest Haycox. — Large print ed. — Leicester : Ulverscroft, 1977. — [5],466p ; 23cm. — (Ulverscroft large print series : [Western])
Originally published: as 'Alder Gulch', Boston, Mass. : Little, Brown ; and as 'No law and order', London : Hodder and Stoughton, 1942.
ISBN 0-7089-0018-6 : £2.95
(B77-22141)

Hayden, Jay. Wanderer of the open range / by Jay Hayden. — London : Hale, 1977. — 157p ; 20cm.
ISBN 0-7091-5837-8 : £2.95
(B77-09950)

Hayden, Sterling. Voyage : a novel of 1896 / [by] Sterling Hayden. — London : Raven Books, 1977. — 700p ; 23cm.
Originally published: New York : Putnam, 1976.
ISBN 0-354-04182-7 : £6.95
(B77-30642)

Hayes, Joseph. The long dark night / [by] Joseph Hayes. — London [etc.] : Pan Books, 1977. — 416p ; 18cm.
Originally published: New York : Putnam ; London : Deutsch, 1974.
ISBN 0-330-25079-5 Pbk : £0.80
(B77-23729)

Haysom, Derrick. Ice trap / by Derrick Haysom. — London : Hale, 1977. — 190p ; 20cm.
ISBN 0-7091-6171-9 : £3.25
(B77-19699)

Heald, Tim. John Steed : an authorized biography / [by] Tim Heald. — London : Weidenfeld and Nicolson.
Vol.1 : Jealous in honour. — 1977. — [7], 197p ; 23cm.
ISBN 0-297-77434-4 : £4.95
(B77-30643)

Healey, Ben. Captain Havoc / [by] Ben Healey. — London : Hale, 1977. — [5],217p ; 21cm.
ISBN 0-7091-6381-9 : £3.95
(B77-32187)

Heath-Miller, Mavis. The sound of winter / [by] Mavis Heath-Miller. — London : Collins, 1976. — 159p ; 20cm.
ISBN 0-00-233788-6 : £2.75
(B77-00428)

Heath-Miller, Mavis. The stubble field / [by] Mavis Heath-Miller. — London : Collins, 1977. — 158p ; 20cm.
ISBN 0-00-233743-6 : £2.95
(B77-29704)

Heath-Miller, Mavis. A time for silence / [by] Mavis Heath-Miller. — London : Collins, 1977. — 158p ; 20cm.
ISBN 0-00-233825-4 : £2.75
(B77-19700)

Heaven, Constance. The Astrov inheritance / [by] Constance Heaven. — London : Pan Books, 1977. — 235p ; 18cm.
Originally published: London : Heinemann, 1973.
Pbk : £0.60
ISBN 0-330-23848-5
(B77-23730)

Heaven, Constance. Castle of Eagles / [by] Constance Heaven. — London : Pan Books, 1977. — 206p ; 18cm.
Originally published: London : Heinemann, 1974.
ISBN 0-330-24665-8 Pbk : £0.60
(B77-19701)

Heaven, Constance. The fires of Glenlochy / [by] Constance Heaven. — London : Pan Books, 1977. — 238p ; 18cm.
Originally published: London : Heinemann, 1976.
ISBN 0-330-25061-2 Pbk : £0.60
(B77-19702)

Heaven, Constance. The house of Kuragin / [by] Constance Heaven. — London : Pan Books, 1977. — 206p ; 18cm.
Originally published: London : Heinemann, 1972.
Pbk : £0.60
ISBN 0-330-23724-1
(B77-21454)

Heaven, Constance. The night of the wolf / [by] Constance Heaven. — London [etc.] : Pan Books, 1977. — 285p ; 18cm.
Originally published: under the name Constance Fecher. London : Hale, 1972.
ISBN 0-330-25062-0 Pbk : £0.60
(B77-19703)

Heaven, Constance. The place of stones / [by] Constance Heaven. — London : Pan Books, 1977. — 219p ; 18cm.
Originally published: London : Heinemann, 1975.
ISBN 0-330-24780-8 Pbk : £0.60
(B77-19704)

Hebden, Mark. The league of eighty-nine / [by] Mark Hebden. — London : Hamilton, 1977. — [4],219p ; 21cm.
ISBN 0-241-89604-5 : £3.95
(B77-10560)

Hedges, Joseph. The Revenger, angel of destruction / [by] Joseph Hedges. — London : Sphere, 1977. — 141p ; 18cm.
ISBN 0-7221-4465-2 Pbk : £0.60
(B77-09951)

Hedges, Joseph. The Revenger, Mexican mourning / [by] Joseph Hedges. — London : Sphere, 1975. — 188p ; 18cm.
ISBN 0-7221-4459-8 Pbk : £0.50
(B77-08062)

Hedges, Joseph. The Revenger, the chauffeur-driven pyre / [by] Joseph Hedges. — London : Sphere, 1976. — 160p ; 18cm.
ISBN 0-7221-4456-3 Pbk : £0.50
(B77-08063)

Hedges, Joseph. The Revenger, the gates of death / [by] Joseph Hedges. — London : Sphere, 1976. — 143p ; 18cm.
ISBN 0-7221-4454-7 Pbk : £0.60
(B77-13294)

Hedges, Joseph. The Revenger, the stainless steel wreath / [by] Joseph Hedges. — London : Sphere, 1975. — 190p ; 18cm.
ISBN 0-7221-4460-1 Pbk : £0.60
(B77-13295)

Heinlein, Robert Anson. The door into summer / [by] Robert Heinlein. — London [etc.] : Pan Books, 1977. — 190p ; 18cm. — (Pan science fiction)
Originally published: Garden City, N.Y. : Doubleday, 1957 ; London : Gollancz, 1967.
Pbk : £0.60
ISBN 0-330-02516-3
(B77-28142)

Heinlein, Robert Anson. The green hills of earth / [by] Robert Heinlein. — London [etc.] : Pan Books, 1977. — 189p ; 18cm. — (Pan science fiction)
Originally published: London : Sidgwick and Jackson, 1954.
ISBN 0-330-10679-1 Pbk : £0.60
(B77-26538)

Heinlein, Robert Anson. Podkayne of Mars / [by] Robert A. Heinlein. — London : New English Library, 1977. — 157p ; 21cm.
Originally published: as 'Podkayne of Mars, her life and times', New York : Putnam, 1963 ; and as 'Podkayne of Mars', London : New English Library, 1969.
ISBN 0-450-03431-3 : £3.95
(B77-24482)

Heinlein, Robert Anson. Rocketship Galileo / [by] Robert A. Heinlein. — London : New English Library, 1977. — 159p ; 21cm.
Originally published: New York : Scribner, 1947 ; London : New English Library, 1971.
ISBN 0-450-03212-4 : £3.75
(B77-32188)

Heley, Veronica. Fear for Frances / by Veronica Heley. — London : Hale, 1977. — 190p ; 21cm.
ISBN 0-7091-6050-x : £3.70
(B77-19705)

Hemingway, Ernest. Across the river and into the trees / [by] Ernest Hemingway. — London [etc.] : Triad, 1977. — 221p ; 18cm.
Originally published: New York : Scribner ; London : Cape, 1950.
ISBN 0-586-04466-3 Pbk : £0.75
(B77-32189)

Hemingway, Ernest. The essential Hemingway. — St Albans : Triad, 1977. — 461p ; 18cm.
This collection originally published: London : Cape, 1947. — 'Containing one complete novel ['Fiesta'], extracts from three others, twenty-five short stories and a chapter from "Death in the afternoon"'. — 'Fiesta' originally published: as 'The sun also rises', New York : C. Scribner's Sons, 1926 ; and as 'Fiesta', London : Cape, 1927'.
ISBN 0-586-04473-6 Pbk : £1.25
(B77-15506)

Hemingway, Ernest. A farewell to arms / [by] Ernest Hemingway. — St Albans : Triad, 1977. — 236p ; 18cm.
Originally published: New York : Scribner ; London : Cape, 1929.
ISBN 0-586-04471-x Pbk : £0.75
(B77-08064)

Hemingway, Ernest. For whom the bell tolls / [by] Ernest Hemingway. — St Albans : Triad, 1976. — 413p ; 18cm.
Originally published: New York : C. Scribner's Sons, 1940 ; London : Cape, 1941.
ISBN 0-586-04469-8 Pbk : £0.90
(B77-03758)

Hemingway, Ernest. For whom the bell tolls ; [and], The snows of Kilimanjaro ; [and], Fiesta ; [and], The short happy life of Francis Macomber ; [and], Across the river and into the trees ; [and], The old man and the sea / [by] Ernest Hemingway. — London : Heinemann : Secker and Warburg : Octopus Books, 1977. — 2-862p ; 25cm.
ISBN 0-905712-03-x : £3.95
(B77-13296)

Hemingway, Ernest. Islands in the stream / [by] Ernest Hemingway. — Harmondsworth [etc.] : Penguin, 1977. — [9],405p : 2 maps ; 19cm.
Originally published: New York : Scribner ; London : Collins, 1970.
Pbk : £0.90
ISBN 0-14-003479-x
(B77-24483)

Hemingway, Ernest. To have and have not / [by] Ernest Hemingway. — St Albans : Triad, 1977. — 191p ; 18cm.
Originally published: London : Cape, 1937.
ISBN 0-586-04470-1 Pbk : £0.75
(B77-20616)

Hemingway, Ernest. The torrents of spring : a romantic novel in honour of the passing of a great race / [by] Ernest Hemingway. — [1st ed. reprinted] ; [with a new] introduction by David Garnett. — St Albans : Triad, 1977. — 108p ; 18cm.
Originally published: New York : Scribners, 1926 ; London : Cape, 1933.
ISBN 0-586-04463-9 Pbk : £0.75
(B77-27388)

Hemstock, Patricia. Rosalie / by Patricia Hemstock. — London : Hale, 1977. — 3-204p ; 21cm.
ISBN 0-7091-6203-0 : £3.70
(B77-26539)

Henegan, J M. Pulse / [by] J.M. Henegan. — London : J. Calder : [Distributed by Calder and Boyars], 1977. — 224p ; 21cm.
ISBN 0-7145-3618-0 : £5.95
(B77-20617)

Hennessy, Max. The lion at sea / [by] Max Hennessy. — London : Hamilton, 1977. — [4], 314p ; 23cm.
ISBN 0-241-89745-9 : £4.95
(B77-30644)

Henriques, Veronica. Tom's sister / [by] Veronica Henriques. — London : Secker and Warburg, 1977. — 253p ; 23cm.
ISBN 0-436-19305-1 : £3.90
(B77-20618)

Henry, Will. From where the sun now stands / [by] Will Henry. — Toronto [etc.] ; London : Bantam, 1976. — [7],245,[3]p : map ; 18cm.
Originally published: New York : Random House, 1960 ; London : Hammond, 1962. — Bibl.
ISBN 0-552-62581-7 Pbk : £0.50
(B77-02588)

Hentoff, Nat. This school is driving me crazy / [by] Nat Hentoff. — London [etc.] : Angus and Robertson, 1977. — [5],151p ; 23cm.
Originally published: New York : Delacorte Press, 1976. — For adolescents.
ISBN 0-207-95763-0 : £3.80
(B77-30645)

Heppenstall, Rayner. Two moons : a novel / [by] Rayner Heppenstall. — London : Allison and Busby, 1977. — 194p ; 23cm.
ISBN 0-85031-198-5 : £4.50
ISBN 0-85031-199-3 Pbk : £1.95
(B77-28916)

Hepple, Anne. Janet Forsythe / [by] Anne Hepple. — Large print ed. — Leicester : Ulverscroft, 1976. — [5],339p ; 23cm. — (Ulverscroft large print series : [romance])
Originally published: London : Hutchinson, 1956.
ISBN 0-85456-501-9 : £2.65
(B77-08573)

Herbert, Ivor. The filly / [by] Ivor Herbert. — London : Heinemann, 1977. — [5],211p ; 23cm.
ISBN 0-434-32761-1 : £3.90
(B77-21455)

Herbert, James. The fog / [by] James Herbert. — London : New English Library, 1976. — 267p ; 18cm.
Originally published: 1975.
ISBN 0-450-03045-8 Pbk : £0.75
(B77-06872)

Herbert, James. The survivor / [by] James Herbert. — London : New English Library, 1976. — 206p ; 22cm.
ISBN 0-450-03067-9 : £4.50
(B77-01807)

Herbert, Nan. The late awakening / by Nan Herbert. — London : Hale, 1977. — 190p ; 20cm.
ISBN 0-7091-5950-1 : £3.10
(B77-12669)

Herbert, *Sir* Alan Patrick. The secret battle / [by] A.P. Herbert ; with an introduction by Winston S. Churchill. — London : Hutchinson, 1976. — viii,216p ; 20cm.
Facsimile reprint of: 1st ed. London : Methuen, 1919.
ISBN 0-09-126600-9 : £3.50
(B77-03759)

Herbert, *Sir* Alan Patrick. The water gipsies / [by] A.P. Herbert. — London : Hutchinson, 1976. — 383p ; 20cm.
Originally published: London : Methuen, 1930.
ISBN 0-09-126590-8 : £3.95
(B77-03223)

Herbert, Xavier. Poor fellow my country / [by] Xavier Herbert. — London [etc.] : Pan Books, 1977. — 1466p ; 22cm.
Originally published: Sydney : Collins, 1975.
ISBN 0-330-25233-x : £6.95
(B77-33431)

Herlihy, James Leo. Midnight cowboy / [by] James Leo Herlihy. — St Albans : Triad, 1977. — 191p ; 18cm.
Originally published: New York : Simon and Schuster, 1965 ; London : Cape, 1966.
ISBN 0-586-02590-1 Pbk : £0.75
(B77-24484)

Herron, Shaun. The bird in last year's nest / [by] Shaun Herron. — [Sevenoaks] : Coronet, 1977. — 303p ; 18cm.
Originally published: New York : M. Evans ; London : Cape, 1974.
ISBN 0-340-21312-4 Pbk : £0.85
(B77-15507)

Hersey, John. White Lotus / [by] John Hersey. — Toronto [etc.] ; London : Bantam, 1976. — [11],691,[1]p ; 18cm.
Originally published: New York : Knopf ; London : Hamilton, 1965.
ISBN 0-552-62267-2 Pbk : £0.85
(B77-02589)

Hershan, Stella K. The naked angel / [by] Stella K. Hershan. — London : Sphere, 1977. — 267p ; 18cm.
Originally published: in the United States, 1971 ; London : Hale, 1973.
ISBN 0-7221-4530-6 Pbk : £0.85
(B77-30646)

Herzog, Arthur. Earth sound / [by] Arthur Herzog. — London : Pan Books, 1977. — 205p ; 18cm.
Originally published: New York : Simon and Schuster ; London : Heinemann, 1975.
ISBN 0-330-25059-0 Pbk : £0.70
(B77-19706)

Herzog, Arthur. Heat / [by] Arthur Herzog. — London : Heinemann, 1978 [i.e. 1977]. — 251p ; 23cm.
Also published: New York : Simon and Schuster, 1977.
ISBN 0-434-32767-0 : £4.50
(B77-30647)

Herzog, Arthur. Orca / [by] Arthur Herzog. — London [etc.] : Pan Books, 1977. — 191p ; 18cm.
Originally published: New York : Pocket Books, 1977.
ISBN 0-330-25348-4 Pbk : £0.70
(B77-23731)

Hewitt, Jenny. Sally makes a change / [by] Jenny Hewitt. — London [etc.] : Macmillan, 1977. — [4],121p ; 18cm. — (Topliners)
For adolescents.
ISBN 0-333-22638-0 Pbk : £0.45
(B77-34127)

Hewlett, Jennifer. The Denninghams / [by] Jennifer Hewlett. — London : Hale, 1977. — 184p : geneal table ; 21cm.
ISBN 0-7091-6164-6 : £3.70
(B77-21456)

Heyer, Georgette. The Black Moth / [by] Georgette Heyer. — Large print ed. — Leicester : Ulverscroft, 1977. — [10],546p ; 23cm. — (Ulverscroft large print series : [historical romance])
Originally published: London : Constable, 1921.
ISBN 0-7089-0015-1 : £2.95
(B77-22143)

Heyer, Georgette. Friday's child / [by] Georgette Heyer. — Large print ed. — Leicester : Ulverscroft, 1977. — [4],701p ; 22cm. — (Ulverscroft large print series : [historical romance])
Originally published: London : Heinemann, 1944.
ISBN 0-7089-0036-4 : Unpriced
(B77-34128)

Heyer, Georgette. Lady of quality / [by] Georgette Heyer. — Large print ed. — Leicester : Ulverscroft, 1977. — [4],507p ; 23cm. — (Ulverscroft large print series : [fiction])
Originally published: London : Bodley Head, 1972.
ISBN 0-85456-512-4 : £2.65
(B77-08065)

Heyer, Georgette. My lord John / [by] Georgette Heyer. — London [etc.] : Pan Books, 1977. — 384p : geneal table ; 18cm.
Originally published: London : Bodley Head, 1975. — Based on the life of John of Lancaster, Duke of Bedford.
ISBN 0-330-25014-0 Pbk : £0.80
(B77-25896)

Heyer, Georgette. Sylvester, or, The wicked uncle / [by] Georgette Heyer. — Large print ed. — Leicester : Ulverscroft, 1976. — [4], 639p ; 23cm. — (Ulverscroft large print series : [fiction])
Originally published: London : Heinemann, 1957.
ISBN 0-85456-494-2 : £2.65
(B77-00429)

Heyer, Georgette. These old shades / [by] Georgette Heyer. — Large print ed. — Leicester : Ulverscroft, 1977. — [4],612p ; 23cm. — (Ulverscroft large print series : [historical romance])
Originally published: London : Heinemann, 1926.
ISBN 0-85456-542-6 : Unpriced
(B77-19707)

Heyer, Georgette. These old shades ; [and], Sprig muslin ; [and], Sylvester ; [and], The Corinthian ; [and], The convenient marriage / [by] Georgette Heyer. — London : Heinemann : Octopus Books, 1977. — 3-862p : ill ; 25cm.
ISBN 0-905712-19-6 : £4.95
(B77-21457)

Heym, Stefan. The King David report : a novel / by Stefan Heym. — London : Quartet Book, 1977. — 255p ; 20cm.
Originally published: in German translation as 'Die König David Bericht', München (Munich) : Kindler Verlag, 1972 ; and in English as 'The King David report', London : Hodder and Stoughton, 1973.
ISBN 0-7043-3159-4 Pbk : £1.95
(B77-32190)

Hickman, Hal. The bachelor party / by Hal Hickman. — London : Hamilton, 1977. — [4], 187p ; 21cm.
ISBN 0-241-89592-8 : £3.75
(B77-12670)

Hicks, Margery. The happy year / [by] Margery Hicks. — St Ives, Cornwall : United Writers Publications, 1977. — 188p ; 21cm.
ISBN 0-901976-39-3 Pbk : £1.95
(B77-20619)

Higgins, George Vincent. A city on a hill / [by] George V. Higgins. — Sevenoaks : Coronet, 1977. — 205p ; 18cm.
Originally published: New York : Knopf ; London : Secker and Warburg, 1975.
ISBN 0-340-21786-3 Pbk : £0.80
(B77-28917)

Higgins, George Vincent. Dreamland / [by] George V. Higgins. — London : Secker and Warburg, 1977. — [5],181p ; 23cm.
Also published: Boston, Mass. : Little, Brown, 1977.
ISBN 0-436-19585-2 : £3.90
(B77-28918)

Higgins, Jack. A fine night for dying / [by] Jack Higgins. — London : Arrow Books, 1977. — 184p ; 18cm.
Originally published: under the name Martin Fallon. London : Long, 1969.
ISBN 0-09-915900-7 Pbk : £0.65
(B77-23732)

Higgins, Jack. Hell is always today / [by] Jack Higgins. — London : Arrow Books, 1977. — 183p ; 18cm.
Originally published: / under the name Harry Patterson. London : Lang, 1968.
ISBN 0-09-913990-1 Pbk : £0.60
(B77-05068)

Higgins, Jack. The last place God made / [by] Jack Higgins. — London : Pan Books, 1977. — 191p ; 18cm.
Originally published: London : Collins, 1971.
ISBN 0-330-25329-8 Pbk : £0.70
(B77-28919)

Higgins, Jack. The savage day / [by] Jack Higgins. — London : Pan Books, 1977. — 220p ; 18cm.
Originally published: London : Collins, 1972.
ISBN 0-330-25328-x Pbk : £0.70
(B77-28920)

Higgins, Jack. Storm warning / [by] Jack Higgins. — London : Pan Books, 1977. — 237p : map ; 18cm.
Originally published: London : Collins, 1976.
ISBN 0-330-25035-3 Pbk : £0.80
(B77-25897)

Higgins, Jack. Storm warning / [by] Jack Higgins. — Large print [ed.]. — London : Prior [etc.], 1977. — [8],482p : map ; 25cm.
Originally published: London : Collins, 1976.
ISBN 0-86043-047-2 : £5.50
(B77-21458)

Higgins, Jack. Toll for the brave / [by] Jack Higgins. — London : Arrow Books, 1977. — 184p ; 18cm.
Originally published: under the name Harry Patterson. London : Long, 1971.
ISBN 0-09-914000-4 Pbk : £0.60
(B77-05069)

Highsmith, Patricia. Edith's diary / [by] Patricia Highsmith. — London : Heinemann, 1977. — [5],312p ; 23cm.
ISBN 0-434-33516-9 : £4.50
(B77-19001)

Hildick, Edmund Wallace. Vandals / [by] Wallace Hildick. — London : Hamilton, 1977. — [5],248p ; 21cm.
ISBN 0-241-89517-0 : £3.95
(B77-06873)

Hildick, Wallace. The loop / [by] Wallace Hildick. — London : Hamilton, 1977. — [4], 218p ; 21cm.
ISBN 0-241-89582-0 : £3.95
(B77-27389)

Hill, Deborah. This is the house / [by] Deborah Hill. — London : P. Davies, 1977. — 413p ; 23cm.
Originally published: New York : Coward, McCann and Geoghegan, 1976.
ISBN 0-432-06733-7 : £3.95
(B77-02590)

Hill, Pamela. The green salamander : a historical novel / [by] Pamela Hill. — London [etc.] : Hodder and Stoughton, 1977. — 288p : coat of arms(on lining papers), geneal table(on lining papers) ; 23cm.
Based on the life of Margaret Douglas, Countess of Lennox.
ISBN 0-340-20992-5 : £3.95
(B77-10561)

Hill, Pamela. Maddalena / [by] Pamela Hill. — London : Severn House : [Distributed by Hutchinson], 1977. — [4],271p ; 21cm.
Originally published: London : Cassell, 1963.
ISBN 0-7278-0316-6 : £3.75
(B77-28143)

Hill, Pamela. Whitton's folly / [by] Pamela Hill. — Sevenoaks : Coronet, 1977. — 286p ; 18cm.
Originally published: London : Hodder and Stoughton, 1975.
ISBN 0-340-21524-0 Pbk : £0.80
(B77-14920)

Hill, Peter. The fanatics / [by] Peter Hill. — London : P. Davies, 1977. — [4],150p ; 23cm.
ISBN 0-432-06734-5 : £3.90
(B77-30648)

Hill, Peter. The hunters / [by] Peter Hill. — Sevenoaks : Coronet, 1977. — [5],185p ; 18cm.
Originally published: London : P. Davies, 1976.
ISBN 0-340-21976-9 Pbk : £0.80
(B77-29705)

Hill, R Lance. King of White Lady / [by] R. Lance Hill. — London [etc.] : Pan Books, 1977. — 256p ; 18cm.
Originally published: Toronto : Lester and Orpen, 1975 ; London : Souvenir Press, 1976.
ISBN 0-330-25224-0 Pbk : £0.75
(B77-32191)

Hill, R Lance. Nails / [by] R. Lance Hill. — London [etc.] : Pan Books, 1977. — 287p ; 18cm.
Originally published: Toronto : Lester and Orpen, 1974 ; London : Souvenir Press, 1975.
ISBN 0-330-25055-8 Pbk : £0.75
(B77-13878)

Hill, Reginald. Another death in Venice / [by] Reginald Hill. — London : Collins [for] the Crime Club, 1976. — 192p ; 21cm.
ISBN 0-00-231015-5 : £2.95
(B77-02591)

Hill, Susan. In the springtime of the year / [by] Susan Hill. — Harmondsworth [etc.] : Penguin, 1977. — 170p ; 18cm.
Originally published: London : Hamilton, 1974.
ISBN 0-14-004110-9 Pbk : £0.60
(B77-12106)

Hilliar, Michael. Come dance with me / [by] Michael Hilliar. — Belfast : Blackstaff Press, 1977. — [4],146,[1]p ; 22cm.
ISBN 0-85640-100-5 : £4.50
(B77-19708)

Hilliard, Nerina. Sister to Meryl / by Nerina Hilliard. — London : Mills and Boon, 1976. — 186p ; 18cm.
ISBN 0-263-72315-1 Pbk : £0.30
(B77-00976)

Hilton, Margery. Young Ellis / [by] Margery Hilton. — London [etc.] : Mills and Boon, 1976. — 185p ; 18cm. — (Mills and Boon classics)
Originally published: 1966.
ISBN 0-263-72230-9 Pbk : £0.35
(B77-14921)

Hinde, Thomas. For the good of the company / [by] Thomas Hinde. — London : Remploy, 1976. — 254p ; 19cm.
Originally published: London : Hutchinson, 1961.
ISBN 0-7066-0692-2 : £2.75
(B77-10562)

Hinde, Thomas. Our father / [by] Thomas Hinde. — [London] : Coronet, 1977. — 351p ; 18cm.
Originally published: London : Hodder and Stoughton, 1975.
ISBN 0-340-21318-3 Pbk : £0.85
(B77-19709)

Hines, Barry. The blinder / [by] Barry Hines. — Harmondsworth [etc.] : Penguin, 1977. — 240p ; 18cm. — (Peacock books)
Originally published: London : Joseph, 1966. — For adolescents.
ISBN 0-14-047096-4 Pbk : £0.60
(B77-12107)

Hinton, Nigel. Collision course / [by] Nigel Hinton. — London : Oxford University Press, 1976. — [5],144p ; 23cm.
For adolescents.
ISBN 0-19-271387-6 : £2.95
(B77-00977)

Hinton, S.E. That was then, this is now / [by] S.E. Hinton. — [London] : Fontana, 1977. — 126p ; 18cm. — (Lions)
Originally published: New York : Viking Press ; London : Gollancz, 1971.
ISBN 0-00-671399-8 Pbk : £0.60
(B77-34129)

Hintze, Naomi A. Listen, please listen / [by] Naomi A. Hintze. — Toronto [etc.] ; London : Bantam, [1977]. — [7],182p ; 18cm.
Originally published: New York : Random House, 1973 ; London : Hale, 1975.
ISBN 0-552-66877-x Pbk : £0.50
(B77-12671)

Hinxman, Margaret. One-way cemetery / [by] Margaret Hinxman. — London : Collins [for] the Crime Club, 1977. — 196p ; 21cm.
ISBN 0-00-231611-0 : £3.25
(B77-20620)

Hirschfeld, Burt. Acapulco / [by] Burt Hirschfeld. — London : Sphere, 1977. — 350p ; 18cm.
Originally published: New York : Arbor House, 1971 ; London : W.H. Allen, 1972.
ISBN 0-7221-4584-5 Pbk : £0.95
(B77-22144)

Hirschfeld, Burt. Aspen / [by] Burt Hirschfeld. — London : Corgi, 1976. — [5],374,[1]p ; 18cm.
Originally published: United States : s.n., 1975 ; London : W.H. Allen, 1976.
ISBN 0-552-10296-2 Pbk : £0.85
(B77-02592)

Hirschfeld, Burt. Father Pig / [by] Burt Hirschfeld. — London : W.H. Allen, 1977. — 173p ; 23cm.
Originally published: New York : Arbor House, 1972.
ISBN 0-491-02072-4 : £3.75
(B77-32192)

Hirschfeld, Burt. Fire island / [by] Burt Hirschfeld. — London : Sphere, 1976. — [4], 440p ; 18cm.
Originally published: New York : Lancer Books, 1970 ; London : W.H. Allen, 1971.
ISBN 0-7221-4581-0 Pbk : £0.95
(B77-25898)

Hirschfeld, Burt. Generation of victors / [by] Burt Hirschfeld. — London : Sphere, 1975. — 413p ; 18cm.
Originally published: New York : Arbor House, 1973 ; London : W.H. Allen, 1974.
ISBN 0-7221-4565-9 Pbk : £0.75
(B77-07614)

Hirschfeld, Burt. Generation of victors / [by] Burt Hirschfeld. — London : Sphere, 1977. — 413p ; 18cm.
Originally published: New York : Arbor House, 1973 ; London : W.H. Allen, 1974.
ISBN 0-7221-4586-1 Pbk : £0.95
(B77-22145)

Hirschfeld, Burt. Moment of power / [by] Burt Hirschfeld. — London : W.H. Allen, 1977. — 447p ; 23cm.
Originally published: New York : Pocket Books, 1971.
ISBN 0-491-02400-2 : £4.95
(B77-24485)

Hirst, George. Back to the Golden Mile / [by] George Hirst. — London : Sphere, 1975. — 154p ; 18cm.
ISBN 0-7221-4561-6 Pbk : £0.50
(B77-09278)

Hirst, William. Robbers' roost / by William Hirst. — London : Hale, 1977. — 158p ; 20cm.
ISBN 0-7091-6345-2 : £3.25
(B77-32193)

Hoban, Russell. Turtle diary / [by] Russell Hoban. — London : Pan Books, 1977. — 191p ; 20cm. — (Picador)
Originally published: London : Cape, 1975.
ISBN 0-330-25050-7 Pbk : £0.80
(B77-12108)

Hodder-Williams, Christopher. The silent voice : a novel / by Christopher Hodder-Williams. — London : Weidenfeld and Nicolson, 1977. — 240p ; 23cm.
ISBN 0-297-77382-8 : £4.50
(B77-29706)

Hodge, Jane Aiken. One way to Venice / [by] Jane Aiken Hodge. — Sevenoaks : Coronet, 1977. — 224p ; 18cm.
Originally published: London etc. : Hodder and Stoughton, 1974.
ISBN 0-340-21250-0 Pbk : £0.70
(B77-19002)

Hodge, Jane Aiken. Runaway bride / [by] Jane Aiken Hodge. — London [etc.] : Hodder and Stoughton, 1977. — [4],202p ; 23cm.
Originally published: New York : Fawcett, 1975 ; London : Coronet, 1976.
ISBN 0-340-20969-0 : £3.95
(B77-19710)

Hodgman, Helen. Blue skies / [by] Helen Hodgman. — London : Duckworth, 1976. — 104p ; 23cm.
ISBN 0-7156-1177-1 : £2.95
(B77-05663)

Hoffman, Louise. Edge of betrayal / by Louise Hoffman. — London : Hale, 1977. — 184p ; 20cm.
ISBN 0-7091-5902-1 : £3.10
(B77-12672)

Hogan, Ray. The hasty hangman : a novel / by Ray Hogan. — London [etc.] : Mews Books ; London : Distributed by New English Library, 1977. — 112p ; 18cm.
Originally published: New York : Ace, 1960.
ISBN 0-452-00069-6 Pbk : £0.55
(B77-08574)

Holden, Ursula. Turnstiles / [by] Ursula Holden. — London : London Magazine Editions, 1977. — 144p ; 23cm.
ISBN 0-904388-20-4 : £4.50
(B77-08575)

Holdstock, Robert. Earthwind / [by] Robert Holdstock. — London : Faber, 1977. — [6], 245p ; 21cm.
ISBN 0-571-11119-x : £4.25 : CIP rev.
(B77-19711)

Holdstock, Robert. Eye among the blind / [by] Robert Holdstock. — London [etc.] : Pan Books, 1976. — 219p ; 18cm.
Also published: London : Faber, 1976.
ISBN 0-330-25178-3 Pbk : £0.70
(B77-26540)

Holdsworth, Jean. The stooping falcon : a novel of the life of Alexander Pope / [by] Jean Holdsworth. — London : Constable, 1977. — 240p ; 23cm.
ISBN 0-09-461690-6 : £4.50
(B77-22870)

Holland, Cecelia. Two ravens / [by] Cecelia Holland. — London : Gollancz, 1977. — [5], 199p ; 21cm.
Also published: New York : Knopf, 1977.
ISBN 0-575-02370-8 : £3.95
(B77-27390)

Holland, Isabelle. Darcourt / [by] Isabelle Holland. — London : Collins, 1977. — [6], 377p ; 22cm.
Originally published: New York : Weybright and Talley, 1976.
ISBN 0-00-222154-3 : £3.95
(B77-22146)

Holland, Isabelle. Kilgaren / [by] Isabelle Holland. — [London] : Fontana, 1977. — 190p ; 18cm.
Originally published: New York : Weybright and Talley, 1974 ; London : Collins, 1975.
ISBN 0-00-614663-5 Pbk : £0.70
(B77-29707)

Holland, Sheila. The caring kind / by Sheila Holland. — London : Hale, 1976. — 184p ; 20cm.
ISBN 0-7091-5587-5 : £2.95
(B77-11405)

Holland, Sheila. The devil and Miss Hay / [by] Sheila Holland. — London : Hale, 1977. — 157p ; 21cm.
ISBN 0-7091-5786-x : £3.25
(B77-09952)

Holmes, Clare Frances. Season of innocence / [by] Clare Frances Holmes. — London : Hale, 1976. — 3-172p ; 21cm.
ISBN 0-7091-5719-3 : £3.25
(B77-01808)

Holmes, Clare Frances. Shadows of the lamp / by Clare Frances Holmes. — London : Hale, 1977. — 189p ; 21cm.
ISBN 0-7091-6048-8 : £3.50
(B77-20621)

Holroyd, Sam. Tibb's house / [by] Sam Holroyd. — London : New English Library, 1977. — 112p ; 18cm.
ISBN 0-450-02873-9 Pbk : £0.50
(B77-05664)

Holt, Victoria. Bride of Pendorric / [by] Victoria Holt. — London : Collins, 1977. — 320p ; 21cm.
Originally published: 1963.
ISBN 0-00-221057-6 : £3.25
(B77-19712)

Holt, Victoria. Bride of Pendorric / [by] Victoria Holt. — [London] : Fontana, 1977. — 284p ; 18cm.
Originally published: London : Collins, 1963.
ISBN 0-00-614867-0 Pbk : £0.70
(B77-13879)

Holt, Victoria. The devil on horseback / [by] Victoria Holt. — London : Collins, 1977. — 334p ; 22cm.
ISBN 0-00-222422-4 : £4.25
(B77-23733)

Holt, Victoria. The House of a Thousand Lanterns / [by] Victoria Holt. — [London] : Fontana, 1976. — 320p ; 18cm.
Originally published: London : Collins, 1974.
ISBN 0-00-614349-0 Pbk : £0.75
(B77-09279)

Holt, Victoria. The king of the castle / [by] Victoria Holt. — London : Collins, 1976. — 319p ; 21cm.
Originally published: 1967.
ISBN 0-00-221408-3 : £3.25
(B77-14922)

Holt, Victoria. Kirkland revels / by Victoria Holt. — London : Collins, 1976. — 320p ; 21cm.
Originally published: 1962.
ISBN 0-00-221403-2 : £3.00
(B77-14923)

Holt, Victoria. The legend of the seventh virgin / [by] Victoria Holt. — London : Collins, 1977. — 3-318p ; 21cm.
Originally published: 1965.
ISBN 0-00-221456-3 : £3.95
(B77-34130)

Holt, Victoria. Lord of the Far Island / [by] Victoria Holt. — [London] : Fontana, 1977. — 254p ; 18cm.
Originally published: London : Collins, 1975.
ISBN 0-00-614999-5 Pbk : £0.80
(B77-21459)

Holt, Victoria. The pride of the peacock / [by] Victoria Holt. — Large print [ed.]. — London : Prior [etc.], 1977. — [5],651p ; 25cm.
Originally published: London : Collins, 1976.
ISBN 0-86043-059-6 : £6.50
(B77-22147)

Holt, Victoria. The secret woman / [by] Victoria Holt. — [London] : Fontana, 1977. — 320p ; 18cm.
Originally published: London : Collins, 1970.
ISBN 0-00-614783-6 Pbk : £0.75
(B77-13880)

Holt, Victoria. The shadow of the lynx / [by] Victoria Holt. — London [etc.] : Collins, 1976. — 319p ; 22cm.
Originally published: 1971.
£3.00
ISBN 0-00-221735-x
(B77-15508)

Holtby, Winifred. Mandoa, Mandoa! : a comedy of irrelevance / [by] Winifred Holtby. — Bath : Chivers, 1977. — [1],382[i.e.383]p ; 21cm.
Facsimile reprint of: 1st ed. London : Collins, 1933.
£5.60(£4.20 to members of the Library Association)
ISBN 0-85594-614-8
(B77-16055)

Hone, Joseph. The Paris trap / [by] Joseph Hone. — London : Secker and Warburg, 1977. — [7],254p ; 23cm.
ISBN 0-436-20086-4 : £4.50
(B77-28921)

Hone, Joseph. The sixth directorate / [by] Joseph Hone. — Sevenoaks : Coronet, 1977. — [7], 337p ; 18cm.
Originally published: London : Secker and Warburg, 1975.
ISBN 0-340-19982-2 Pbk : £1.25
(B77-29708)

Honeyman, Brenda. At the king's court / [by] Brenda Honeyman. — London : Hale, 1977. — 189p ; 21cm.
Based on the life of Richard II.
ISBN 0-7091-5746-0 : £3.50
(B77-13297)

Honeyman, Brenda. The King's tale / by Brenda Honeyman. — London : Hale, 1977. — 175p ; 21cm.
ISBN 0-7091-6041-0 : £3.50
(B77-19713)

Honeyman, Brenda. Macbeth, King of Scots / [by] Brenda Honeyman. — London : Hale, 1977. — 5-188p ; 20cm.
ISBN 0-7091-6303-7 : £3.85
(B77-32856)

Hooker, Richard. MASH goes to Hollywood / [by] Richard Hooker and William E. Butterworth. — London : Sphere, 1977. — 190p ; 18cm.
Originally published: New York : Pocket Books, 1976.
ISBN 0-7221-4647-7 Pbk : £0.65
(B77-16602)

Hooker, Richard. MASH goes to Las Vegas / [by] Richard Hooker and William E. Butterworth. — London : Sphere, 1977. — 240p ; 18cm.
Originally published: New York : Pocket Books, 1976.
ISBN 0-7221-4649-3 Pbk : £0.65
(B77-06874)

Hooker, Richard. MASH goes to Miami / [by] Richard Hooker and William E. Butterworth. — London : Sphere, 1977. — 236p ; 18cm.
Originally published: United States : s.n., 1976.
ISBN 0-7221-4646-9 Pbk : £0.75
(B77-31471)

Hooker, Richard. MASH goes to Morocco / [by] Richard Hooker and William E. Butterworth. — London : Sphere, 1977. — 221p ; 18cm.
Originally published: New York : Pocket Books, 1975.
ISBN 0-7221-4648-5 Pbk : £0.65
(B77-10563)

Hooker, Richard. MASH goes to New Orleans / [by] Richard Hooker and William E. Butterworth. — London : Sphere, 1976. — 187p ; 18cm.
Originally published: New York : Pocket Books, 1975.
ISBN 0-7221-4650-7 Pbk : £0.65
(B77-02593)

Hoover, H M. Children of Morrow / [by] H.M. Hoover. — London [etc.] : Beaver Books, 1977. — 157p ; 20cm.
Originally published: New York : Four Winds Press, 1973 ; London : Methuen, 1975. — For adolescents.
ISBN 0-600-31952-0 Pbk : £0.60
(B77-30649)

Hoover, Ralph. Jabberwocky / [by] Ralph Hoover. — London [etc.] : Pan Books, 1977. — 159p ; 18cm.
Based on the screenplay of the film 'Jabberwocky' by Terry Gilliam and Charles Alverson inspired by Lewis Carroll's poem.
ISBN 0-330-25012-4 Pbk : £0.60
(B77-12673)

Hope, Amanda. The Pengelly face / [by] Amanda Hope. — London : Hale, 1977. — 188p ; 21cm.
ISBN 0-7091-5866-1 : £3.50
(B77-13298)

Hopkins, Tim. On target / [by] Tim Hopkins. — London : Macdonald and Jane's, 1977. — [4], 109p ; 21cm.
For adolescents.
ISBN 0-354-08012-1 : £2.95
(B77-09280)

Horbury, James. Embassy / [by] James Horbury. — London : W.H. Allen, 1977. — [4],204p ; 23cm.
ISBN 0-491-02210-7 : £4.50
(B77-25899)

Horner, Lance. Six-fingered stud / [by] Lance Horner. — London [etc.] : Pan Books, 1977. — 350p ; 18cm.
Originally published: London : W.H. Allen, 1975.
ISBN 0-330-25022-1 Pbk : £0.80
(B77-12109)

Horsley, David. Sunset showdown / [by] David Horsley. — London : Hale, 1977. — 159p ; 20cm.
ISBN 0-7091-6129-8 : £2.95
(B77-17742)

Hoult, Norah. Two girls in the big smoke / [by] Norah Hoult. — London : Hale, 1977. — 175p ; 21cm.
ISBN 0-7091-6140-9 : £3.50
(B77-22871)

Household, Geoffrey. Dance of the dwarfs / by Geoffrey Household. — Hornchurch : I. Henry, 1977. — 159p ; 21cm.
Originally published: London : Joseph, 1968.
ISBN 0-86025-120-9 : £3.25
(B77-31472)

Household, Geoffrey. Hostage, London : the diary of Julian Despard / [by] Geoffrey Household. — London : Joseph, 1977. — 190p ; 21cm.
ISBN 0-7181-1573-2 : £3.95
(B77-19003)

Household, Geoffrey. A time to kill / by Geoffrey Household. — Hornchurch : I. Henry, 1977. — 124p ; 21cm.
Originally published: London : Joseph, 1952.
ISBN 0-86025-122-5 : £2.90
(B77-19714)

Houston, James. Ghost Fox / [by] James Houston. — London : Collins, 1977. — [12], 303p : ill, map ; 22cm.
Also published: New York : Harcourt Brace Jovanovich, 1977.
ISBN 0-00-222276-0 : £4.50
(B77-21460)

Houston, Will. Colorado trail / by Will Houston. — London : Hale, 1977. — 160p ; 20cm.
ISBN 0-7091-5955-2 : £2.80
(B77-09953)

Houston, Will. Gila Pass / by Will Houston. — London : Hale, 1977. — 158p ; 20cm.
ISBN 0-7091-6004-6 : £3.10
(B77-22872)

Houston, Will. Howe / by Will Houston. — London : Hale, 1977. — 160p ; 20cm.
ISBN 0-7091-6174-3 : £3.10
(B77-28144)

Howard, Clark. The killings / [by] Clark Howard. — London [etc.] : Pan Books, 1977. — 239p ; 18cm.
Originally published: New York : Dial Press, 1973 ; London : Souvenir Press, 1974.
ISBN 0-330-24804-9 Pbk : £0.75
(B77-09954)

Howard, Hartley. Fall guy / [by] Hartley Howard. — Large print ed. — Bath : Lythway Press, 1976. — [6],346p ; 22cm.
Originally published: London : Collins, 1960.
ISBN 0-85046-682-2 : £4.50
(B77-06875)

Howard, Lesley. Invitation to paradise / [by] Lesley Howard. — London : New English Library, 1977. — 143p ; 18cm.
Originally published: London : Cassell, 1974.
ISBN 0-450-03409-7 Pbk : £0.70
(B77-24486)

Howard, Mary. The Spanish summer / [by] Mary Howard. — London : Collins, 1977. — 277p ; 21cm.
'First published in an abridged version 1976' - title page verso.
ISBN 0-00-222470-4 : £3.95
(B77-20622)

Howard, Mary. Two loves have I : a romance / [by] Mary Howard. — London : Severn House : [Distributed by Hutchinson], 1977. — 192p ; 21cm.
Originally published: London : Collins, 1951.
ISBN 0-7278-0215-1 : £3.25
(B77-08576)

Howard, Robert Ervin. Almuric / [by] Robert E. Howard. — London : Sphere, 1977. — 155p ; 18cm.
Originally published: New York : Ace Books, 1964 ; London : New English Library, 1971.
ISBN 0-7221-4717-1 Pbk : £0.65
(B77-06876)

Howatch, Susan. Call in the night / [by] Susan Howatch. — Large print ed. — Leicester : Ulverscroft, 1977. — [4],298p ; 22cm. — (Ulverscroft large print series : [romantic suspense])
Originally published: New York : Ace Books, 1967 ; London : Hamilton, 1972.
ISBN 0-7089-0014-3 : £2.95
(B77-22148)

Howatch, Susan. The rich are different / [by] Susan Howatch. — London : Hamilton, 1977. — 704p ; 23cm.
ISBN 0-241-89653-3 : £4.95
(B77-19715)

Howatch, Susan. The waiting sands / [by] Susan Howatch. — Large print ed. — Leicester : Ulverscroft, 1977. — [5],311p ; 23cm. — (Ulverscroft large print series : [romantic suspense])
Originally published: New York : Ace Books, 1966 ; London : Hamilton, 1972.
ISBN 0-85456-541-8 : Unpriced
(B77-19716)

Howlett, John, *b.1940.* Tango November / [by John Howlett]. — London : Arrow Books, 1977. — 269p ; 18cm.
Originally published: London : Hutchinson, 1976.
ISBN 0-09-914850-1 Pbk : £0.75
(B77-30650)

Hoyle, Jill. Rings on my finger / by Jill Hoyle. — London : Hale, 1977. — 183p ; 20cm.
ISBN 0-7091-6156-5 : £3.20
(B77-22149)

Hoyle, *Sir* **Fred.** The incandescent ones / [by] Fred Hoyle and Geoffrey Hoyle ; edited by Barbara Hoyle. — London : Heinemann, 1977. — [7],183p ; 23cm.
ISBN 0-434-34928-3 : £3.50
(B77-21461)

Hoyle, Trevor. Q, seeking the mythical future / [by] Trevor Hoyle. — St Albans : Panther, 1977. — 189p ; 18cm. — (Panther science fiction)
Bibl.: p.189.
ISBN 0-586-04366-7 Pbk : £0.60
(B77-25900)

Hoyle, Trevor. The sexless spy / [by] Trevor Hoyle. — London : Sphere, 1977. — 160p ; 18cm.
ISBN 0-7221-4759-7 Pbk : £0.65
(B77-12674)

Hubank, Roger. North wall / [by] Roger Hubank. — London : Hutchinson, 1977. — [4], 191p : map ; 21cm.
ISBN 0-09-129840-7 : £3.95
(B77-28145)

Huddy, Delia. My kind of cake. — Basingstoke : Macmillan, Jan. 1978. — 1v. — (Topliner tridents)
For adolescents. — Previous control number ISBN 0-333-23556-8.
ISBN 0-333-23632-7 : CIP entry
(B77-32857)

Huffaker, Clair. Seven Ways from Sundown / [by] Clair Huffaker. — London [etc.] : White Lion Publishers, 1976. — 124p ; 21cm.
Originally published: New York : Fawcett, 1960 ; London : Futura Publications, 1974.
ISBN 0-7274-0157-2 : £2.95
(B77-03760)

Hughes, John Lewis. Before the crying ends / [by] John L. Hughes. — London [etc.] : Bodley Head, 1977. — 154p ; 21cm.
ISBN 0-370-10612-1 : £3.50
(B77-05070)

Hughes, Lynn. Hawkmoor : adventures of Twm Sion Cati / [by] Lynn Hughes. — Harmondsworth [etc.] : Penguin, 1977. — 205p ; 19cm.
Bibl.: p.203-204.
ISBN 0-14-004501-5 Pbk : £0.75
(B77-29709)

Hughes, Richard, *b.1900.* A high wind in Jamaica / [by] Richard Hughes. — Large print ed. — Bath : Lythway Press, 1976. — [5], 296p ; 23cm.
Originally published: London : Chatto and Windus, 1929.
ISBN 0-85046-679-2 : £4.25
(B77-06877)

Hughes, Richard, *b.1900.* In hazard / [by] Richard Hughes. — St Albans : Triad, 1977. — 155p ; 18cm.
Originally published: London : Chatto and Windus, 1938.
ISBN 0-586-04486-8 Pbk : £0.60
(B77-25901)

Hughes, Richard, *b.1900.* In hazard : a sea story / [by] Richard Hughes. — Large print ed. — Bath : Lythway Press, 1977. — [5],263p ; 22cm.
Originally published: London : Chatto and Windus, 1938.
ISBN 0-85046-735-7 Pbk : £2.20
(B77-34132)

Hughes, William. Aces high / [by] William Hughes. — London : Futura Publications, 1976. — 191p ; 18cm.
'Based on a screenplay by Howard Barker' - cover.
ISBN 0-86007-363-7 Pbk : £0.60
(B77-09281)

Hulke, Malcolm. Crossroads, a new beginning / [by] Malcolm Hulke. — London : Everest, 1975. — 187p ; 18cm.
'Based on stories from the television serial originally devised by Hazel Adair and Peter Ling'. — Originally published: 1974.
ISBN 0-903925-12-5 Pbk : £0.40
(B77-05665)

Hulke, Malcolm. Crossroads, a time for living / [by] Malcolm Hulke. — London : Everest, 1976. — 190p ; 18cm.
'Based on stories from the television serial originally devised by Hazel Adair and Peter Ling'.
ISBN 0-905018-04-4 Pbk : £0.55
(B77-05666)

Hulke, Malcolm. Crossroads, something old, something new / [by] Malcolm Hulke. — London : Everest, 1976. — 191p ; 18cm.
'Based on story themes by Hazel Adair, Don Houghton, and Peter Ling for the television serial originally devised by Hazel Adair and Peter Ling'. — Also published: London : White Lion Publishers, 1976.
ISBN 0-903925-96-6 Pbk : £0.50
(B77-05667)

Humana, Charles. Youth is the enemy / [by] Charles Humana. — London : Allison and Busby, 1977. — 212p ; 23cm.
ISBN 0-85031-216-7 : £3.95
(B77-28146)

Hunt, John, *b.1916.* Law along the border / by John Hunt. — London : Hale, 1977. — 152p ; 20cm.
ISBN 0-7091-5357-0 : £2.95
(B77-15509)

Hunt, John, *b.1916.* The Skyline Trail / by John Hunt. — London : Hale, 1977. — 152p ; 20cm.
ISBN 0-7091-5590-5 : £3.10
(B77-23734)

Hunter, Alan. Gently where the birds are / [by] Alan Hunter. — London : Cassell, 1976. — 173p ; 21cm.
ISBN 0-304-29752-6 : £3.25
(B77-08066)

Hunter, Christine. The day will dawn / by Christine Hunter. — London : Hale, 1977. — 189p ; 20cm.
ISBN 0-7091-6058-5 : £3.20
(B77-30651)

Hunter, Elizabeth, *b.1934.* The realms of gold / by Elizabeth Hunter. — London : Mills and Boon, 1977. — 188p ; 17cm.
Originally published: 1976.
ISBN 0-263-72341-0 Pbk : £0.35
(B77-07615)

Hunter, Evan. The Chisholms / [by] Evan Hunter. — London : Corgi, 1977. — 238p ; 18cm.
Originally published: London : Hamilton, 1976.
ISBN 0-552-10518-x Pbk : £0.75
(B77-26541)

Hunter, Evan. Me and Mr Stenner / [by] Evan Hunter. — London : Hamilton, 1977. — 157, [1]p ; 22cm.
Originally published: Philadelphia : Lippincott, 1976. — 'Portions of this novel appeared previously in the "Ladies' Home Journal"' - title page verso. — For adolescents.
ISBN 0-241-89555-3 : £2.50
(B77-10564)

Hunter, Evan. Mothers and daughters / [by] Evan Hunter. — London : Corgi, 1977. — 543p ; 18cm.
Originally published: New York : Simon and Schuster ; London : Constable, 1961.
ISBN 0-552-10364-0 Pbk : £0.95
(B77-10946)

Hunter, Evan. Strangers when we meet / [by] Evan Hunter. — London : Corgi, 1977. — 317p ; 18cm.
Originally published: New York : Simon and Schuster ; London : Constable, 1958.
Pbk : £0.85
ISBN 0-552-10365-9
(B77-10947)

Hunter, Evan. Streets of gold / [by] Evan Hunter. — London : Pan Books, 1977. — [7], 471p ; 18cm.
Originally published: New York : Harper and Row, 1974 ; London : Macmillan, 1975.
ISBN 0-330-25122-8 Pbk : £0.95
(B77-25902)

Hunter, Jack Dayton. The Blue Max / [by] Jack D. Hunter. — London : Corgi, 1977. — [7], 280p ; 18cm.
Originally published: London : Muller, 1965.
ISBN 0-552-10393-4 Pbk : £0.75
(B77-12675)

Hunter, Joan. Cavalier / [by] Joan Hunter. — London : Hale, 1977. — 206p ; 21cm.
Bibl.: p.205-206.
ISBN 0-7091-5700-2 : £3.60
(B77-15510)

Hunter, Joan. Rupert the devil / [by] Joan Hunter. — London : Hale, 1976. — 206p ; 21cm.
Bibl.: p.205-206. — Based on the life of Rupert, of the Rhine.
ISBN 0-7091-5581-6 : £3.25
(B77-01809)

Hunter, Joe. Vampire mission / [by] Joe Hunter. — London : New English Library, 1977. — 159p ; 18cm. — (Hunter, Joe. Attack force ; no.4)
ISBN 0-450-02906-9 Pbk : £0.70
(B77-12676)

Hunter, John, *b.1903.* This range is mine / [by] John Hunter. — London : Hale, 1977. — [4], 153p ; 20cm.
Originally published: s.l. : s.n., 1975.
ISBN 0-7091-5908-0 : £2.95
(B77-08067)

Hunter, Mollie. The ghosts of Glencoe / [by] Mollie Hunter. — London : Hamilton, 1976. — 160p : maps ; 23cm.
Originally published: London : Evans Bros, 1966.
ISBN 0-241-89478-6 : £2.75
(B77-00430)

Hutchinson, Ray Coryton. A child possessed / [by] R.C. Hutchinson. — London : Joseph, 1977. — 351p ; 21cm.
Originally published: London : Bles, 1964.
ISBN 0-7181-1644-5 : £5.00
(B77-20623)

Huth, Angela. South of the lights / [by] Angela Huth. — London : Collins, 1977. — 277p ; 21cm.
ISBN 0-00-222473-9 : £4.25
(B77-22150)

Huth, Angela. Sun child / [by] Angela Huth. — [London] : Fontana, 1977. — 224p ; 18cm.
Originally published: London : Collins, 1975.
ISBN 0-00-614840-9 Pbk : £0.75
(B77-30652)

Hutton, Ann. Edge of the deep / by Ann Hutton. — London : Hale, 1977. — 189p ; 20cm.
ISBN 0-7091-5937-4 : £3.10
(B77-08068)

Huxley, Aldous. Antic hay / [by] Aldous Huxley. — St Albans : Triad, 1977. — 250p ; 18cm.
Originally published: London : Chatto and Windus, 1923.
ISBN 0-586-04433-7 Pbk : £0.95
(B77-24487)

Huxley, Aldous. Brave new world / [by] Aldous Huxley. — St Albans : Triad, 1977. — 206p ; 18cm.
Originally published: London : Chatto and Windus, 1932.
ISBN 0-586-04434-5 Pbk : £0.75
(B77-22873)

Huxley, Aldous. Crome yellow / [by] Aldous Huxley. — St Albans : Triad, 1977. — 174p ; 18cm.
Originally published: London : Chatto and Windus, 1921.
ISBN 0-586-04436-1 Pbk : £0.65
(B77-13299)

Hyde, Eleanor. Tudor mausoleum / by Eleanor Hyde. — London : Hale, 1977. — 3-157p ; 21cm.
ISBN 0-7091-6274-x : £3.70
(B77-32194)

Hyde, Eleanor. Tudor murder / by Eleanor Hyde. — London : Hale, 1977. — 191p ; 21cm.
ISBN 0-7091-5630-8 : £3.50
(B77-08069)

Hynd, Noel. Revenge / [by] Noel Hynd. — London : New English Library, 1977. — 285p ; 19cm.
Originally published: London : W.H. Allen, 1976.
ISBN 0-450-03255-8 Pbk : £0.95
(B77-30653)

Idle, Eric. Hello sailor / [by] Eric Idle. — London : Futura Publications, 1975. — [6], 169p ; 18cm. — (A contact book)
Also published: London : Weidenfeld and Nicolson, 1975.
ISBN 0-86007-235-5 Pbk : £0.50
(B77-08577)

Ike, Vincent Chukwuemeka. Sunset at dawn : a novel about Biafra / [by] Chukwuemeka Ike. — London : Collins : Harvill Press, 1976. — 255p : map ; 21cm.
ISBN 0-00-261807-9 : £3.50
(B77-00431)

Ingate, Mary. This water laps gently / [by] Mary Ingate. — London [etc.] : Macmillan, 1977. — 190p ; 21cm.
ISBN 0-333-21209-6 : £3.25
(B77-10565)

Innes, Hammond. The angry mountains / [by] Hammond Innes. — [London] : Fontana, 1977. — 255p ; 18cm.
Originally published: London : Collins, 1950.
ISBN 0-00-614858-1 Pbk : £0.70
(B77-18376)

Innes, Hammond. The big footprints / [by] Hammond Innes. — London : Collins, 1977. — 349p : maps ; 22cm.
ISBN 0-00-221422-9 : £3.95
(B77-08070)

Innes, Hammond. Golden soak / [by] Hammond Innes. — [London] : Fontana, 1977. — 286p : maps ; 18cm.
Originally published: London : Collins, 1973.
ISBN 0-00-615064-0 Pbk : £0.75
(B77-31473)

Innes, Hammond. Killer mine / [by] Hammond Innes. — Collected ed. — London : Collins, 1976. — 223p ; 21cm.
Originally published: 1947.
£2.75
ISBN 0-00-221416-4
(B77-16603)

Innes, Hammond. North Star / [by] Hammond Innes. — [London] : Fontana, 1977. — 256p : maps ; 18cm.
Originally published: London : Collins, 1974.
ISBN 0-00-614592-2 Pbk : £0.75
(B77-09282)

Innes, Hammond. 'North Star' / [by] Hammond Innes. — Large print ed. — Leicester : Ulverscroft, 1977. — [9],543p ; 23cm. — (Ulverscroft large print series : [adventure, suspense])
Originally published: London : Collins, 1974.
ISBN 0-7089-0027-5 : £2.95
(B77-19717)

Innes, Michael. Appleby at Allington / by Michael Innes. — London : Gollancz, 1977. — 189p ; 20cm. — ([Gollancz vintage detection])
Originally published: 1968.
£3.30
ISBN 0-575-00078-3
(B77-29710)

Innes, Michael. The bloody wood / by Michael Innes. — London : Gollancz, 1977. — 192p ; 20cm. — ([Gollancz vintage detection])
Originally published: 1966.
ISBN 0-575-01020-7 : £3.20
(B77-10566)

Innes, Michael. A change of heir / by Michael Innes. — London : Gollancz, 1977. — 192p ; 20cm. — ([Gollancz vintage detection])
Originally published: 1966.
ISBN 0-575-02359-7 : £3.30
(B77-29711)

Innes, Michael. A connoisseur's case / by Michael Innes. — London : Gollancz, 1977. — 192p ; 20cm. — ([Gollancz vintage detection])
Originally published: 1962.
ISBN 0-575-01021-5 : £3.20
(B77-10567)

Innes, Michael. Honeybath's haven / by Michael Innes. — London : Gollancz, 1977. — 191p ; 21cm. — ([Gollancz detection])
ISBN 0-575-02364-3 : £3.95
(B77-28922)

Innes, Michael. The long farewell / [by] Michael Innes. — Large print ed. — Bath : Lythway Press, 1977. — viii,295p ; 22cm. — (Lythway classics of crime and detection)
Originally published: London : Gollancz, 1958.
ISBN 0-85046-728-4 : £4.60
(B77-21462)

Innes, Michael. The mysterious commission / by Michael Innes. — Harmondsworth [etc.] : Penguin, 1977. — 192p ; 18cm. — (Penguin crime fiction)
Originally published: London : Gollancz, 1974.
ISBN 0-14-004437-x Pbk : £0.65
(B77-27391)

Innes, Michael. What happened at Hazelwood / [by] Michael Innes. — Harmondsworth [etc.] : Penguin, 1976. — 238p ; 18cm. — (Penguin crime fiction)
Originally published: London : Gollancz, 1946.
ISBN 0-14-002650-9 Pbk : £0.65
(B77-01811)

Iroh, Eddie. Forty-eight guns for the general / [by] Eddie Iroh. — London [etc.] : Heinemann Educational, 1976. — [6],218p ; 19cm. — (African writers series ; 189)
ISBN 0-435-90189-3 Pbk : £1.70
(B77-23735)

Irwin, Frances. Fire across the march / by Frances Irwin. — London : Hale, 1977. — 152p ; 21cm.
ISBN 0-7091-5734-7 : £3.50
(B77-05668)

Irwin, Frances. The winter killing / [by] Frances Irwin. — London : Hale, 1977. — 175p ; 21cm.
ISBN 0-7091-6360-6 : £3.70
(B77-32195)

Isaacson, Knight. The store / [by] Knight Isaacson. — London : Star Books, 1977. — 220p ; 19cm.
Originally published: New York : Walker, 1974 ; London : W.H. Allen, 1975.
ISBN 0-352-39840-x Pbk : £0.60
(B77-10568)

Israel, Peter. The French kiss : a novel / by Peter Israel. — London [etc.] : Hodder and Stoughton, 1977. — [5],233p ; 21cm.
Originally published: New York : Crowell, 1976.
ISBN 0-340-21336-1 : £3.50
(B77-11406)

Jacks, Oliver. Autumn heroes / by Oliver Jacks. — London [etc.] : Hodder and Stoughton, 1977. — 256p : map(on lining papers) ; 21cm.
ISBN 0-340-21739-1 : £4.25
(B77-34133)

Jacks, Oliver. Man on a short leash / [by] Oliver Jacks. — Sevenoaks : Coronet, 1977. — 192p ; 18cm.
Originally published: London : Hodder and Stoughton, 1974.
ISBN 0-340-21306-x Pbk : £0.60
(B77-12677)

Jackson, Basil. Flameout / [by] Basil Jackson. — London : Hale, 1977. — 287p : 2 ill ; 23cm.
Originally published: New York : Norton, 1976.
ISBN 0-7091-6175-1 : £4.25
(B77-19718)

Jackson, Basil. Rage under the Arctic / [by] Basil Jackson. — London : Hale, 1977. — 220p : map ; 21cm.
Originally published: New York : Norton, 1974.
ISBN 0-7091-5415-1 : £3.60
(B77-13300)

Jackson, Basil. Supersonic / [by] Basil Jackson. — London : Sphere, 1977. — 190p ; 18cm.
Originally published: New York : Norton, 1975 ; London : Hale, 1976.
ISBN 0-7221-4951-4 Pbk : £0.85
(B77-28923)

Jackson, Shirley. The haunting of Hill House / [by] Shirley Jackson. — London : Corgi, 1977. — 189p ; 18cm.
Originally published: New York : Viking Press, 1959 ; London : Joseph, 1960.
ISBN 0-552-10389-6 Pbk : £0.65
(B77-13301)

Jacob, Naomi. 'Honour come back' / [by] Naomi Jacob. — London : Hurst and Blackett, 1976. — 352p ; 20cm.
Originally published: London : Hutchinson, 1935.
ISBN 0-09-125050-1 : £3.50
(B77-17101)

Jacob, Naomi. Jacob Ussher / [by] Naomi Jacob. — Large print ed. — Bath : Chivers, 1977. — [6],432p ; 22cm.
Originally published: London : Eyre and Spottiswoode, 1925. — Adaptation of: 'Birds of a feather' / by Henry V. Esmond.
ISBN 0-85997-221-6 : £5.60(£4.20 to members of the Library Association)
(B77-13881)

Jacob, Naomi. Sally Scarth / [by] Naomi Jacob. — London : Hutchinson, 1976. — 320p ; 20cm.
Originally published: 1940.
ISBN 0-09-127590-3 : £3.50
(B77-00978)

Jacob, Naomi. Search for a background / [by] Naomi Jacob. — London : Hurst and Blackett, 1976. — 287p ; 20cm.
Originally published: London : Hutchinson, 1960.
ISBN 0-09-125060-9 : £3.50
(B77-17102)

Jacobson, Dan. The confessions of Josef Baisz : a novel / by Dan Jacobson. — London : Secker and Warburg, 1977. — [4],204p ; 23cm.
ISBN 0-436-22045-8 : £3.90
(B77-28147)

Jacobson, Dan. The wonder-worker / [by] Dan Jacobson. — Harmondsworth [etc.] : Penguin, 1977. — 139p ; 19cm.
Originally published: London : Weidenfeld and Nicolson, 1973.
ISBN 0-14-004077-3 Pbk : £0.70
(B77-07616)

Jaffe, Rona. Family secrets / [by] Rona Jaffe. — London : New English Library.
In 2 vols. — Originally published: in 1 vol. New York : Simon and Schuster, 1974 ; London : Hodder and Stoughton, 1975.
Vol.1. — 1977. — 253p ; 18cm.
ISBN 0-450-02899-2 Pbk : £0.80
(B77-05669)

Vol.2. — 1977. — 255p ; 18cm.
ISBN 0-450-03096-2 Pbk : £0.80
(B77-05670)

Jahn, Mike. The six million dollar man, wine, women and war : a novel / by Michael Jahn ; from the teleplay by Glen A. Larson ; based on a character created by Martin Caidin. — London : Wingate, 1976. — 155p ; 21cm.
ISBN 0-85523-111-4 : £2.95
(B77-00979)

James, David. Croc / [by] David James. — London : New English Library, 1977. — 157p ; 18cm.
Originally published: New York : Belmont-Tower Books, 1976.
ISBN 0-450-03347-3 Pbk : £0.60
(B77-25200)

James, Donald. A spy at evening / [by] Donald James. — London : Collins, 1977. — 220p ; 22cm.
ISBN 0-00-222466-6 : £3.95
(B77-17103)

James, Phyllis Dorothy. The black tower / [by] P.D. James. — London : Sphere, 1977. — 288p ; 18cm.
Originally published: London : Faber, 1975.
ISBN 0-7221-4972-7 Pbk : £0.75
(B77-09283)

James, Phyllis Dorothy. Cover her face / [by] P.D. James. — London : Sphere, 1977. — 207p ; 18cm.
Originally published: London : Faber, 1962.
ISBN 0-7221-4956-5 Pbk : £0.75
(B77-09284)

James, Phyllis Dorothy. Death of an expert witness / [by] P.D. James. — London : Faber, 1977. — [6],265p ; 21cm.
ISBN 0-571-11107-6 : £3.95 : CIP rev.
(B77-23736)

James, Phyllis Dorothy. A mind to murder / [by] P.D. James. — Harmondsworth [etc.] : Penguin, 1977. — 221p ; 18cm. — (Penguin crime fiction)
Originally published: London : Faber, 1963.
Pbk : £0.55
ISBN 0-14-003850-7
(B77-29712)

James, Phyllis Dorothy. Shroud for a nightingale / [by] P.D. James. — London : Sphere, 1977. — 300p ; 18cm.
Originally published : London : Faber, 1971.
ISBN 0-7221-4955-7 Pbk : £0.75
(B77-09285)

James, Phyllis Dorothy. Unnatural causes / [by] P.D. James. — London : Sphere, 1977. — 218p ; 18cm.
Originally published: London : Faber, 1967.
ISBN 0-7221-4957-3 Pbk : £0.75
(B77-09286)

James, Phyllis Dorothy. An unsuitable job for a woman / [by] P.D. James. — London : Sphere, 1977. — 205p ; 18cm.
Originally published: London : Faber, 1972.
ISBN 0-7221-4953-0 Pbk : £0.75
(B77-09287)

James, Rebecca. The house is dark / [by] Rebecca James. — London : New English Library, 1977. — [9],227p ; 22cm.
Originally published: Garden City, N.Y. : Doubleday, 1976.
ISBN 0-450-03211-6 : £4.95
(B77-30654)

James, Sally. Miranda of the island / by Sally James. — London : Hale, 1977. — 176p ; 21cm.
ISBN 0-7091-6163-8 : £3.50
(B77-22151)

James, William M. Apache, duel to the death / [by] William M. James. — London : Sphere, 1975. — 125p ; 18cm.
ISBN 0-7221-4990-5 Pbk : £0.45
(B77-09288)

James, William M. Apache, knife in the night / [by] William M. James. — London : Sphere, 1975. — 125p ; 18cm.
ISBN 0-7221-4989-1 Pbk : £0.40
(B77-08071)

Jameson, Storm. The intruder / [by] Storm Jameson. — London [etc.] : White Lion Publishers, 1977. — [4],236p ; 21cm.
Originally published: London : Macmillan, 1956.
ISBN 0-85617-067-4 : £3.75
(B77-16056)

Jancath, Matthew. Seatag / [by] Matthew Jancath. — Swansea : C. Davies, 1977. — 271p ; 22cm.
ISBN 0-7154-0405-9 : £3.95
(B77-17743)

Janes, Kathleen. The testing time / [by] Kathleen Janes. — London : Corgi, 1977. — 128p ; 18cm. — (A Corgi romance)
ISBN 0-552-10502-3 Pbk : £0.50
(B77-22152)

Jeans, Angela. To cherish a dream / [by] Angela Jeans. — London : New English Library, 1976. — 174p ; 18cm.
ISBN 0-450-02897-6 Pbk : £0.60
(B77-06878)

Jefferis, Barbara. Half angel / [by] Barbara Jefferis ; with illustrations by Sarah van Niekerk. — Large print ed. — Bath : Chivers, 1977. — [6],195p : ill ; 22cm.
Originally published: London : Dent, 1960.
ISBN 0-85997-222-4 : £5.60(£4.20 to members of the Library Association)
(B77-13882)

Jeffries, Roderic. Troubled deaths / [by] Roderic Jeffries. — London : Collins [for] the Crime Club, 1977. — 208p ; 21cm.
ISBN 0-00-231840-7 : £3.25
(B77-27392)

Jenkins, Geoffrey. A bridge of magpies / [by] Geoffrey Jenkins. — [London] : Fontana, 1977. — 222p : map ; 18cm.
Originally published: London : Collins, 1974.
ISBN 0-00-614680-5 Pbk : £0.75
(B77-21463)

Jenkins, Thelma H. John Bunyan's 'The Holy War' / [retold] by Thelma H. Jenkins ; [illustrations by Lewis F. Lupton] ; foreword by D. Martyn Lloyd-Jones. — Welwyn [etc.] : Evangelical Press, 1976. — xii,171p : ill ; 22cm.
ISBN 0-85234-074-5 Pbk : £1.50
(B77-06879)

Jennings, Paul. And now for something exactly the same : a novel / by Paul Jennings. — London : Gollancz, 1977. — 190p ; 21cm.
ISBN 0-575-02258-2 : £4.20
(B77-20624)

Jenson, Martin. The echo on the stairs / [by] Martin Jenson. — London : New English Library, 1977. — 125p ; 18cm.
ISBN 0-450-03122-5 Pbk : £0.55
(B77-12110)

Jesmer, Elaine. Number one with a bullet / [by] Elaine Jesmer. — London : Futura Publications, 1976. — [7],424p ; 18cm. — (A contact book)
Originally published: New York : Farrar, Straus and Giroux ; London : Weidenfeld and Nicolson, 1974.
ISBN 0-86007-297-5 Pbk : £0.90
(B77-08578)

Jessup, Richard. The Cincinnati Kid / [by] Richard Jessup. — London [etc.] : Pan Books, 1977. — 156p ; 18cm.
Originally published: Boston, Mass. : Little, Brown, 1963 ; London : Gollancz, 1964.
ISBN 0-330-23441-2 Pbk : £0.60
(B77-21464)

Johnson, Barbara Ferry. Lionors / [by] Barbara Ferry Johnson. — London : Sphere, 1977. — 283p ; 18cm.
Originally published: New York : Avon Books, 1975.
ISBN 0-7221-5051-2 Pbk : £0.85
(B77-19004)

Johnson, Pamela Hansford. The holiday friend / [by] Pamela Hansford Johnson. — Harmondsworth [etc.] : Penguin, 1977. — 251p ; 19cm.
Originally published: London : Macmillan, 1972.
ISBN 0-14-004147-8 Pbk : £0.95
(B77-24488)

Johnson, Pamela Hansford. Too dear for my possessing / [by] Pamela Hansford Johnson. — Harmondsworth [etc.] : Penguin, 1976. — 304p ; 19cm.
Originally published: London : Collins, 1940.
ISBN 0-14-004148-6 Pbk : £0.95
(B77-24489)

Johnston, Jennifer. Shadows on our skin / [by] Jennifer Johnston. — London : Hamilton, 1977. — 191p ; 21cm.
ISBN 0-241-89661-4 : £3.50
(B77-15511)

Johnston, Velda. Deveron Hall / [by] Velda Johnston. — Large print [ed.]. — London : Prior [etc.], 1977. — [5],299p ; 25cm.
Originally published: New York : Dodd, Mead, 1976.
ISBN 0-86043-055-3 : £4.95
(B77-22153)

Johnston, Velda. The Frenchman / [by] Velda Johnston. — Large print [ed.]. — London : Prior [etc.], 1976. — [5],295p ; 24cm.
Also published: New York : Dodd, Mead, 1976.
ISBN 0-86043-022-7 : £4.75
(B77-07617)

Jones, Annabel. The radiant dove / [by] Annabel Jones. — London : Sphere, 1976. — 158p ; 18cm.
Originally published: London : Joseph, 1974.
ISBN 0-7221-5073-3 Pbk : £0.55
(B77-06290)

Jones, Diana Wynne. Drowned Ammet / [by] Diana Wynne Jones. — London [etc.] : Macmillan, 1977. — [7],255p ; 21cm.
ISBN 0-333-22620-8 : £3.95
(B77-34134)

Jones, Douglas C. The court-martial of George Armstrong Custer / [by] Douglas C. Jones. — London : W.H. Allen, 1977. — [7],291p : chart, ports ; 24cm.
Originally published: New York : Scribner, 1976.
ISBN 0-491-02490-8 : £4.50
(B77-17744)

Jones, Elwyn, *b.1923.* Barlow comes to judgement / [by] Elwyn Jones. — London : Corgi, 1977. — 125p ; 18cm.
Based on the BBC television series. — Originally published: London : Barker, 1974.
ISBN 0-552-10338-1 Pbk : £0.60
(B77-09289)

Jones, Elwyn, *b.1923.* Barlow exposed / [by] Elwyn Jones. — London : Corgi, 1977. — 144p ; 18cm.
Originally published: London : Weidenfeld and Nicolson, 1976.
ISBN 0-552-10547-3 Pbk : £0.60
(B77-28148)

Jones, James. A touch of danger / [by] James Jones. — [London] : Fontana, 1977. — 349p ; 18cm.
Originally published: London : Collins, 1973.
ISBN 0-00-614777-1 Pbk : £0.95
(B77-27393)

Jones, Mervyn. Nobody's fault / [by] Mervyn Jones. — London : Quartet Books, 1977. — [7], 198p ; 23cm.
ISBN 0-7043-2135-1 : £4.25
(B77-13302)

Jong, Erica. How to save your own life : a novel / by Erica Jong. — London : Secker and Warburg, 1977. — [7],310p ; 23cm.
Also published: New York : Holt, Rinehart and Winston, 1977.
ISBN 0-436-22445-3 : £3.90
(B77-13303)

Jordan, Humfrey. Spoiling for mischief / by Humfrey Jordan. — London : Remploy, 1976. — 223p ; 19cm.
Originally published: London : Hodder and Stoughton, 1958.
ISBN 0-7066-0704-x : £3.00
(B77-15512)

Jordan, Matt. Brigham's way / [by] Matt Jordan. — London : Jenkins, 1976. — 159p ; 21cm.
ISBN 0-214-20209-7 : £2.95
(B77-08579)

Jordan, Matt. Jacob's road / [by] Matt Jordan. — London : Jenkins, 1976. — 164p ; 21cm.
ISBN 0-214-20254-2 : £2.95
(B77-08580)

Joseph, Michael Kennedy. A soldier's tale / [by] M.K. Joseph. — [London] : Fontana, 1977. — 152p ; 18cm.
Originally published: Auckland ; London : Collins, 1976.
ISBN 0-00-614491-8 Pbk : £0.70
(B77-13304)

Josipovici, Gabriel. Migrations / [by] Gabriel Josipovici. — Hassocks : Harvester Press, 1977. — 232p ; 21cm.
ISBN 0-85527-799-8 : £4.50 : CIP rev.
(B77-06880)

Joyce, Cyril. A crime to fit the punishment / by Cyril Joyce. — London : Hale, 1977. — 175p ; 20cm.
ISBN 0-7091-5996-x : £3.15
(B77-14406)

Joyce, Cyril. Twice a victim / by Cyril Joyce. — London : Hale, 1977. — 187p ; 20cm.
ISBN 0-7091-6232-4 : £3.25
(B77-22874)

Joyce, James, *b.1882.* The essential James Joyce / [edited] with an introduction and notes by Harry Levin. — St Albans : Triad, 1977. — 528p ; 18cm.
This collection originally published: London : Cape, 1948. — Contents: Dubliners - A portrait of the artist as a young man - Exiles - Collected poems - Extracts from 'Ulysses' and 'Finnegans Wake'.
ISBN 0-586-04474-4 Pbk : £1.50
(B77-28149)

Joyce, James, *b.1882.* A portrait of the artist as a young man / [by] James Joyce. — [1st ed., reprinted] / with six drawings by Robin Jacques. — St Albans : Triad, 1977. — 228p ; 18cm.
Originally published: London : 'The egoist', 1916.
ISBN 0-586-04475-2 Pbk : £0.75
(B77-14924)

Joyce, James, *b.1882.* Stephen Hero : part of the first draft of 'A portrait of the artist as a young man' / [by] James Joyce ; edited with an introduction by Theodore Spencer. — Revised ed. / with additional material and a foreword by John J. Slocum and Herbert Cahoon. — St Albans : Triad, 1977. — 220p ; 18cm.
Previous ed.: London : Cape, 1944.
ISBN 0-586-04477-9 Pbk : £1.25
(B77-27394)

Joyce, James, *b.1882.* Ulysses : a facsimile of the manuscript / [by] James Joyce ; with a critical introduction by Harry Levin and a bibliographical preface by Clive Driver. — London : Faber [for] the Philip H. & A.S.W. Rosenbach Foundation, 1975. — 3v.([3],45, [415]p;[470]p;[2],4,[184]p) : col facsims ; 30cm.
In slip case. — 3rd vol. has subtitle: 'The manuscript and first printings compared' / annotated by Clive Driver.
ISBN 0-571-10701-x : £60.00
(B77-05671)

Judd, Denis. The adventures of Long John Silver / [by] Denis Judd. — London : Joseph, 1977. — 219p ; 23cm.
ISBN 0-7181-1504-x : £3.95
(B77-08072)

Kamm, Josephine. The starting point / [by] Josephine Kamm. — London : Heinemann Educational, 1976. — 136p ; 20cm. — (The new windmill series)
Originally published: Leicester : Brockhampton Press, 1975. — For adolescents.
ISBN 0-435-12210-x : £0.85
(B77-03224)

Kanin, Garson. A thousand summers / [by] Garson Kanin. — St Albans : Panther, 1976. — 207p ; 18cm.
Originally published: Garden City, N.Y. : Doubleday, 1973 ; St Albans : Hart-Davis MacGibbon, 1974.
ISBN 0-586-04250-4 Pbk : £0.60
(B77-03761)

Kapp, Colin. Manalone / [by] Colin Kapp. — St Albans : Panther, 1977. — 197p ; 18cm. — (Panther science fiction)
ISBN 0-586-04234-2 Pbk : £0.75
(B77-25903)

Kastle, Herbert. Cross-country / [by] Herbert Kastle. — St Albans : Mayflower, 1977. — 319p ; 18cm.
Originally published: New York : Delacorte Press ; London : W.H. Allen, 1975.
ISBN 0-583-12581-6 Pbk : £0.75
(B77-07618)

Kastle, Herbert David. The gang / [by] Herbert Kastle. — London : W.H. Allen, 1977. — 316p ; 23cm.
Originally published: New York : Dell, 1976.
ISBN 0-491-02171-2 : £4.95
(B77-28150)

Kata, Elizabeth. A patch of blue / [by] Elizabeth Kata. — Harmondsworth [etc.] : Penguin, 1977. — 172p ; 18cm. — (Peacock books)
Originally published: as 'Be ready with bells and drums'. New York : St Martins Press ; London : Joseph, 1961. — For adolescents.
ISBN 0-14-047113-8 Pbk : £0.55
(B77-27395)

Katz, Robert, *b.1933.* The Cassandra Crossing / a novelization by Robert Katz ; based on the screenplay by Tom Mankiewicz, Robert Katz and George Pan Cosmatos. — London [etc.] : Pan Books, 1977. — 153p : 2 ill ; 18cm.
ISBN 0-330-24397-7 Pbk : £0.60
(B77-13883)

Katz, Shelley. Alligator / [by] Shelley Katz. — London : Sphere, 1977. — 269p ; 18cm.
Also published: New York : Dell, 1977.
ISBN 0-7221-5148-9 Pbk : £0.95
(B77-31475)

Kaufman, Margaret. Summer song / by Margaret Kaufman. — London : Hale, 1977. — 185p ; 20cm.
ISBN 0-7091-5903-x : £3.10
(B77-12111)

Kay, Mara. Storm warning / [by] Mara Kay. — London [etc.] : Beaver Books, 1977. — 190p ; 18cm.
Originally published: London : Macmillan, 1976. — For adolescents.
ISBN 0-600-38240-0 Pbk : £0.55
(B77-30655)

Kazan, Elia. The arrangement / [by] Elia Kazan. — [London] : Fontana, 1977. — 526p ; 18cm.
Originally published: London : Collins, 1967.
ISBN 0-00-614411-x Pbk : £1.25
(B77-15513)

Keating, Henry Raymond Fitzwalter. Bats fly up for Inspector Ghote / [by] H.R.F. Keating. — Harmondsworth [etc.] : Penguin, 1977. — 191p ; 19cm. — (Penguin crime fiction)
Originally published: London : Collins for the Crime Club, 1974.
ISBN 0-14-004161-3 Pbk : £0.65
(B77-17745)

Kebbell, Janet. Morgan's folly / by Janet Kebbell. — London : Hale, 1977. — 190p ; 20cm.
ISBN 0-7091-5985-4 : £3.10
(B77-14925)

Keegan, William. A real killing : a novel / by William Keegan. — London : Weidenfeld and Nicolson, 1977. — [5],184p ; 23cm.
ISBN 0-297-77260-0 : £3.95
(B77-13305)

Keene, Carolyn. The whispering statue / [by] Carolyn Keene. — London : Armada, 1977. — 160p : 1 ill ; 19cm. — (Keene, Carolyn. Nancy Drew mystery stories ; no.14)
Originally published: New York : Grosset and Dunlap, 1937 ; London : Collins, 1972.
ISBN 0-00-691304-0 Pbk : £0.45
(B77-18377)

Keenleyside, David. Where the mountain falls / by David Keenleyside. — Toronto : Nelson, Foster and Scott ; London : Hale, 1977. — 192p ; 23cm.
ISBN 0-7091-6131-x : £3.70
(B77-20625)

Kelley, Edith Summers. Weeds / [by] Edith Summers Kelley. — [1st ed. reprinted] ; with an afterword [and textual note] by Matthew J. Bruccoli. — Carbondale [Ill.] : Southern Illinois University Press ; London [etc.] : Feffer and Simons, 1974. — [4],345p ; 21cm. — (Lost American fiction)
Originally published: New York : Harcourt, Brace, 1923 ; London : Cape, 1924.
ISBN 0-8093-0587-9 : Unpriced
(B77-10569)

Kelley, Ray. Blue grass range / by Ray Kelley. — London : Hale, 1977. — 154p ; 20cm.
ISBN 0-7091-5802-5 : £3.10
(B77-22875)

Kelley, Ray. Justice in New Mexico / by Ray Kelley. — London : Hale, 1976. — 151p ; 20cm.
ISBN 0-7091-5498-4 : £2.70
(B77-01812)

Kelley, Ray. Sixgun assassin / by Ray Kelley. — London : Hale, 1977. — 157p ; 20cm.
ISBN 0-7091-5599-9 : £2.95
(B77-17104)

Kelly, Gwen. The middle-aged maidens / [by] Gwen Kelly. — London : Hamilton, [1977]. — [6],224p ; 22cm.
Originally published: Melbourne : Nelson, 1976.

ISBN 0-241-89792-0 : £3.50
(B77-28151)

Kemelman, Harry. Tuesday the rabbi saw red / [by] Harry Kemelman. — Harmondsworth [etc.] : Penguin, 1977. — 267p ; 18cm. — (Penguin crime fiction)
Originally published: New York : A. Fields Books ; London : Hutchinson, 1974.
ISBN 0-14-004249-0 Pbk : £0.80
(B77-07619)

Kemelman, Harry. Wednesday the Rabbi got wet / [by] Harry Kemelman. — Large print ed. — London : Prior [etc.], 1977. — [5],497p ; 25cm.
Originally published: London : Hutchinson, 1976.
ISBN 0-86043-113-4 : £5.95
(B77-34135)

Keneally, Thomas. Blood red, sister rose / [by] Thomas Keneally. — [London] : Fontana, 1976. — 352p : geneal table, maps ; 18cm.
Originally published: London : Collins, 1974. — Based on the life of Joan of Arc.
ISBN 0-00-614403-9 Pbk : £0.85
(B77-12112)

Keneally, Thomas. Season in purgatory / [by] Thomas Keneally. — [London] : Fontana, 1977. — 190p ; 18cm.
Originally published: London : Collins, 1976.
ISBN 0-00-615025-x Pbk : £0.75
(B77-30656)

Keneally, Thomas. A victim of the aurora / [by] Thomas Keneally. — London [etc.] : Collins, 1977. — 222p : 2 maps ; 22cm.
ISBN 0-00-222493-3 : £4.50
(B77-25904)

Kennaway, James. Silence / by James Kennaway. — Harmondsworth [etc.] : Penguin, 1977. — 93p ; 18cm.
Originally published: London : Cape, 1972.
ISBN 0-14-004076-5 Pbk : £0.50
(B77-07620)

Kenrick, Tony. The Chicago girl / by Tony Kenrick. — London : Joseph, 1977. — 223p ; 21cm.
Originally published: New York : Putnam, 1976.
ISBN 0-7181-1568-6 : £4.25
(B77-12678)

Kenrick, Tony. The kidnap kid / [by] Tony Kenrick. — London : Sphere, 1976. — 224p ; 18cm.
Originally published: as 'Stealing Lillian'. New York : McKay, 1975 ; London : Joseph, 1975.
ISBN 0-7221-5161-6 Pbk : £0.75
(B77-02594)

Kent, Alexander. In gallant company / [by] Alexander Kent. — London : Hutchinson, 1977. — 287p : maps(on lining papers) ; 23cm.
ISBN 0-09-128830-4 : £3.95
(B77-22876)

Kent, Simon. The lions at the kill / [by] Simon Kent. — London : Remploy, 1976. — 224p ; 19cm.
Originally published: London : Hutchinson, 1959.
ISBN 0-7066-0682-5 : £2.75
(B77-04407)

Kenyon, Michael. Mr Big / [by] Michael Kenyon. — London : Fontana, 1977. — 224p ; 18cm.
Originally published: London : Collins, 1975.
ISBN 0-00-614583-3 Pbk : £0.70
(B77-05672)

Kenyon, Michael. The rapist / [by] Michael Kenyon. — London [etc.] : Collins [for] the Crime Club, 1977. — 196p ; 21cm.
ISBN 0-00-231713-3 : £2.95
(B77-17105)

Keppel, Charlotte. When I say goodbye, I'm Clary Brown / [by] Charlotte Keppel. — London [etc.] : Hodder and Stoughton, 1977. — [5],246p ; 21cm.
Originally published: as 'My name is Clary Brown'. New York : Random House, 1976.
ISBN 0-340-20704-3 : £3.75
(B77-13884)

Kern, Seymour. Fifty / [by] Seymour Kern. — London : New English Library, 1977. — 271p ; 18cm.
Originally published: 1975.
ISBN 0-450-02898-4 Pbk : £0.95
(B77-28925)

Kerouac, Jack. Maggie Cassidy / [by] Jack Kerouac. — London [etc.] : Quartet Books, 1977. — 155p : 1 ill ; 18cm.
Originally published: New York : Avon Book Division, Hearst Corporation, 1959 ; London : Hamilton, 1960.
ISBN 0-7043-3141-1 Pbk : £0.95
(B77-20626)

Kerouac, Jack. Pic / [by] Jack Kerouac. — London [etc.] : Quartet Books, 1977. — [7], 83p ; 18cm.
Originally published: New York : Grove Press, 1971 ; and, together with 'The subterraneans', London : Deutsch, 1971.
ISBN 0-7043-3142-x Pbk : £0.75
(B77-21465)

Kerouac, Jack. Vanity of Duluoz : an adventurous education, 1935-46 / [by] Jack Kerouac. — London [etc.] : Quartet Books, 1977. — [5],214p ; 18cm.
Originally published: New York : Coward-McCann, 1968 ; London : Deutsch, 1969.
ISBN 0-7043-3145-4 Pbk : £0.95
(B77-20627)

Kerr, Carole. Love all start / by Carole Kerr. — London : Hale, 1977. — 154p ; 20cm.
ISBN 0-7091-6308-8 : £3.20
(B77-26542)

Kerr, M.E. The son of someone famous / [by] M.E. Kerr. — Harmondsworth [etc.] : Penguin, 1977. — 175p ; 18cm. — (Peacock books)
Originally published: New York : Harper and Row, 1974 ; London : Gollancz, 1975. — For adolescents.
ISBN 0-14-047110-3 Pbk : £0.70
(B77-32858)

Kershaw, H V. Coronation Street, early days / [by] H.V. Kershaw. — London [etc.] : White Lion Publishers, 1977. — 208p ; 21cm.
Originally published: St Albans : Mayflower, 1976.
ISBN 0-7274-0268-4 : £3.50
(B77-14926)

Kershaw, H V. Coronation Street, trouble at the Rovers / [by] H.V. Kershaw. — London [etc.] : White Lion Publishers, 1977. — 156p ; 21cm.
'... based on the Granada TV series' - jacket. — Originally published: St Albans : Mayflower, 1976.
ISBN 0-7274-0390-7 : £3.75
(B77-34136)

Kesey, Ken. Sometimes a great notion : a novel / by Ken Kesey. — Harmondsworth [etc.] : Penguin, 1977. — [7],628p ; 20cm.
Originally published: New York : Viking Press, 1964 ; London : Methuen, 1966.
ISBN 0-14-004529-5 Pbk : £1.75
(B77-26543)

Kessler, Leo. The Black Cossacks / [by] Leo Kessler. — London : Severn House : [Distributed by Hutchinson], [1977]. — 192p : map ; 21cm.
Originally published: London : Futura Publications, 1975.
ISBN 0-7278-0320-4 : £3.50 : CIP rev.
(B77-22154)

Kessler, Leo. Forced march / [by] Leo Kessler. — London [etc.] : White Lion Publishers, 1977. — 188p : plan ; 21cm.
Originally published: London : Futura Publications, 1976.
ISBN 0-7274-0316-8 : £3.75
(B77-25201)

Kessler, Leo. Forced march / [by] Leo Kessler. — London : Futura Publications, 1976. — 188p : plan ; 18cm.
ISBN 0-86007-358-0 Pbk : £0.60
(B77-12113)

Kessler, Leo. Sabres of the Reich / [by] Leo Kessler. — London : Futura Publications, 1976. — 191p ; 18cm. — (Kessler, Leo. Black Cossacks ; 2)
ISBN 0-86007-387-4 Pbk : £0.60
(B77-13306)

Ketchum, Cliff. The border men / by Cliff Ketchum. — London : Hale, 1977. — 156p ; 20cm.
ISBN 0-7091-6145-x : £3.10
(B77-34137)

Keyes, Daniel. The contaminated man / [by] Daniel Keyes. — St Albans : Mayflower, 1977. — 3-208p ; 18cm.
Originally published: as 'The touch'. New York : Harcourt, Brace and World, 1968 ; London : Hale, 1971.
ISBN 0-583-12434-8 Pbk : £0.65
(B77-14927)

Keyes, Frances Parkinson. Dinner at Antoine's / [by] Frances Parkinson Keyes. — Bath : Chivers, 1977. — 416p : ill ; 23cm.
Originally published: New York : Messner, 1948 ; London : Eyre and Spottiswoode, 1949.
ISBN 0-85997-247-x : £6.00(£4.50 to members of the Library Association)
(B77-19719)

Keyes, Frances Parkinson. Queen Anne's lace / [by] Frances Parkinson Keyes. — Large print ed. — Bath : Chivers, 1977. — [9],397p ; 22cm.
Originally published: New York : Liveright, 1930 ; London : Eyre and Spottiswoode, 1940.
ISBN 0-85997-223-2 : £5.60(£4.20 to members of the Library Association)
(B77-13885)

Keyes, Frances Parkinson. The royal box / [by] Frances Parkinson Keyes. — Bath : Chivers, 1977. — 5-317p ; 23cm.
Originally published: New York : Messner ; London : Eyre and Spottiswoode, 1954.
ISBN 0-85997-275-5 : £5.80(£4.35 to members of the Library Association)
(B77-29713)

Kidd, Flora. The bargain bride / by Flora Kidd. — London : Mills and Boon, 1976. — 187p ; 17cm.
ISBN 0-263-72324-0 Pbk : £0.30
(B77-05673)

Kidd, Flora. Strange as a dream / [by] Flora Kidd. — Large print ed. — Leicester : Ulverscroft, 1977. — [4],330p ; 23cm. — (Ulverscroft large print series : [romance])
Originally published: London : Mills and Boon, 1968.
ISBN 0-7089-0034-8 : Unpriced
(B77-34138)

Kidd, Flora. Visit to Rowanbank / [by] Flora Kidd. — London [etc.] : Mills and Boon, 1976. — 186p ; 18cm. — (Mills and Boon classics)
Originally published: 1966.
ISBN 0-263-72223-6 Pbk : £0.35
(B77-11407)

Kiely, Benedict. Proxopera : a novel / by Benedict Kiely. — London : Gollancz, 1977. — 93p ; 21cm.
ISBN 0-575-02322-8 : £2.95
(B77-19005)

Killick, Brian. The Camelot Club / [by] Brian Killick. — London : Hamilton, 1977. — [4], 216p ; 21cm.
ISBN 0-241-89607-x : £3.95
(B77-10570)

Kilworth, Garry. In solitary / [by] Garry Kilworth. — London : Faber, 1977. — [6], 131p ; 21cm.
ISBN 0-571-11096-7 : £3.95 : CIP rev.
(B77-17106)

Kimbrough, Emily. Better than oceans / [by] Emily Kimbrough. — Large print [ed.]. — London : Prior [etc.], 1977. — [5],365p ; 24cm.
Originally published: New York : Harper and Row, 1976.
ISBN 0-86043-103-7 : £4.95
(B77-26544)

King, Betty. Emma Hamilton / [by] Betty King. — London : Hale, 1976. — 204p ; 21cm.
Bibl.: p.7.
ISBN 0-7091-5612-x : £3.25
(B77-01813)

King, Betty. Mountains divide us / [by] Betty King. — London : Hale, 1977. — 224p ; 21cm.
ISBN 0-7091-5867-x : £3.60
(B77-16604)

King, Betty. Owen Tudor / [by] Betty King. — London : Hale, 1977. — 191p ; 21cm.
Bibl.: p.6. — Based on the life of Owen Tudor.
ISBN 0-7091-6280-4 : £3.85
(B77-32196)

King, Francis, *b.1923.* Danny Hill : memoirs of a prominent gentleman / edited [i.e. written] with an introduction by Francis King. — London : Hutchinson, 1977. — 188p ; 21cm.
ISBN 0-09-131540-9 : £3.95
(B77-30657)

King, Harold, *b.1945.* Four days / [by] Harold King. — London : Sphere, 1977. — 317p ; 18cm.
Originally published: Indianapolis : Bobbs Merrill, 1976.
ISBN 0-7221-5263-9 : £0.95
(B77-31476)

King, Stephen, *b.1947.* Carrie / [by] Stephen King. — London : New English Library, 1977. — 189p ; 18cm.
Originally published: Garden City, N.Y. : Doubleday ; London : New English Library, 1974.
ISBN 0-450-03034-2 Pbk : £0.75
(B77-08581)

King, Stephen, *b.1947.* 'Salem's Lot / [by] Stephen King. — London : New English Library, 1977. — [7],439p ; 18cm.
Originally published: Garden City, N.Y. : Doubleday, 1975 ; London : New English Library, 1976.
ISBN 0-450-03106-3 Pbk : £1.25
(B77-08582)

King, Stephen, *b.1947.* The shining / [by] Stephen King. — London : New English Library, 1977. — [7],447p ; 22cm.
Also published: Garden City, N.Y. : Doubleday, 1977.
ISBN 0-450-03220-5 : £4.95
(B77-25202)

King, Vincent. Time snake and superclown / [by] Vincent King. — London : Futura Publications, 1976. — 191p ; 18cm. — (An orbit book)
ISBN 0-86007-890-6 Pbk : £0.60
(B77-08583)

Kingsley, Bettina. The house on the drive : a novel / by Bettina Kingsley. — London [etc.] : Mews Books ; London : Distributed by New English Library, 1977. — 143p ; 18cm. — (A Mews mystery romance)
Originally published: New York : Dell, 1975.
ISBN 0-452-00071-8 Pbk : £0.55
(B77-08584)

Kitchen, Paddy. The marriage ring / [by] Paddy Kitchen and Dulan Barber ; based on the TV series 'Couples', developed by Tony Parker ; foreword by Anna Raeburn ; introduction by Tony Parker. — London : Star Books, 1976. — 172p ; 18cm.
ISBN 0-352-39895-7 Pbk : £0.60
(B77-06291)

Kitchen, Paddy. The marriage ring / [by] Paddy Kitchen and Dulan Barber ; based on the TV series 'Couples', developed by Tony Parker ; foreword by Anna Raeburn ; introduction by Tony Parker. — London : W.H. Allen, 1977. — 172p ; 23cm.
Originally published: London : Star Books, 1976.
ISBN 0-491-01888-6 : £3.50
(B77-14407)

Knebel, Fletcher. Seven days in May / [by] Fletcher Knebel and Charles W. Bailey, II ; a condensation by the editors of Reader's Digest Condensed Books. — Large print ed. — Leicester : Ulverscroft, 1977. — [4],350p,[2]p ; 23cm. — (Ulverscroft large print series : [fiction])
This condensation originally published: Pleasantville, N.Y. ; London : Reader's Digest Association, 196-?.
ISBN 0-85456-555-8 : £2.65
(B77-08585)

Knight, Alanna. A drink for the bridge / [by] Alanna Knight. — London : Corgi, 1977. — 190p ; 18cm.
Originally published: London : Macmillan, 1976.
ISBN 0-552-10496-5 Pbk : £0.70
(B77-25905)

Knight, Bernard. Madoc, Prince of America / [by] Bernard Knight. — London : Hale [etc.], 1977. — 3-189p ; 21cm.
Based on the legend of Madoc, bastard son of the King of North Wales.
ISBN 0-7091-5868-8 : £3.50
(B77-17107)

Knight, Leonard Alfred. The pawn / [by] Leonard A. Knight. — Large print ed. — Bath : Chivers, 1977. — [9],396p ; 22cm.
Originally published: London : Sampson Low, 1931.
ISBN 0-85997-252-6 : £5.80(£4.35 to members of the Library Association)
(B77-22155)

Knox, Alexander. The kidnapped surgeon / [by] Alexander Knox. — London [etc.] : Macmillan, 1977. — 214p : 2 maps ; 21cm.
ISBN 0-333-21304-1 : £3.95
(B77-10948)

Knox, Bill. Death department : a Thane and Moss case / [by] Bill Knox. — Large print ed. — Leicester : Ulverscroft, 1977. — [4],348p ; 23cm. — (Ulverscroft large print series : [mystery])
Originally published: London : Long, 1959.
ISBN 0-7089-0043-7 : Unpriced
(B77-28152)

Knox, Bill. Hellspout : a Webb Carrick story / [by] Bill Knox. — Large print ed. — Leicester : Ulverscroft, 1977. — [7],289p ; 23cm. — (Ulverscroft large print series : [mystery])
Originally published: London : Long, 1976.
ISBN 0-7089-0019-4 : £2.95
(B77-22156)

Knox, Bill. Pilot error : a Thane and Moss case / [by] Bill Knox. — London : Long, 1977. — 185p ; 20cm.
ISBN 0-09-128310-8 : £3.25
(B77-09290)

Knox, Bill. The Tallyman / [by] Bill Knox. — London : Arrow Books, 1977. — 183p ; 18cm.
Originally published: London : Long, 1969.
ISBN 0-09-915310-6 Pbk : £0.70
(B77-30658)

Knox, Bill. Witchrock / [by] Bill Knox. — London : Long, 1977. — 184p ; 19cm.
ISBN 0-09-131850-5 : £3.50
(B77-30659)

Knox, Oliver. Asylum / [by] Oliver Knox. — London : Collins, 1977. — 168p ; 22cm.
ISBN 0-00-222418-6 : £4.25
(B77-28926)

Konigsburg, Elaine Lobl. Father's arcane daughter / by E.L. Konigsburg. — London [etc.] : Macmillan, 1977. — [4],118p ; 21cm.
Originally published: New York : Atheneum, 1976.
ISBN 0-333-21427-7 : £2.95
(B77-11408)

Koning, Hans. Death of a schoolboy / [by] Hans Koning. — London : Quartet Books, 1977. — [4],187p ; 23cm.
ISBN 0-7043-2095-9 : £3.95
(B77-06881)

Koontz, Dean R. Demon seed / [by] Dean R. Koontz. — London : Corgi, 1977. — [7],182p ; 18cm.
Originally published: Toronto ; New York : Bantam, 1973.
ISBN 0-552-10567-8 Pbk : £0.70
(B77-29714)

Koontz, Dean R. Night chills / [by] Dean R. Koontz. — London : W.H. Allen, 1977. — xiii, 334p ; 22cm.
Originally published: New York : Atheneum, 1976. — Bibl.: p.333-334.
ISBN 0-491-02491-6 : £4.95
(B77-31477)

Koontz, Dean R. Time thieves / [by] Dean R. Koontz. — London : Dobson, 1977. — 109p ; 21cm.
Originally published: New York : Ace Books, 1972.
ISBN 0-234-77368-5 : £3.95
(B77-28927)

Kops, Bernard. Partners / [by] Bernard Kops. — London : New English Library, 1977. — 252p ; 18cm.
Originally published: London : Secker and Warburg, 1975.
ISBN 0-450-03090-3 Pbk : £0.90
(B77-05674)

Kops, Bernard. The passionate past of Gloria Gaye / [by] Bernard Kops. — London : New English Library, 1977. — 156p ; 18cm.
Originally published: London : Secker and Warburg, 1971.
ISBN 0-450-03297-3 Pbk : £0.75
(B77-30660)

Kops, Bernard. Settle down Simon Katz / [by] Bernard Kops. — London : New English Library, 1977. — 160p ; 18cm.
Originally published: London : Secker and Warburg, 1973.
ISBN 0-450-02869-0 Pbk : £0.70
(B77-19720)

Kosinski, Jerzy. Cockpit / [by] Jerzy Kosinski. — London : Corgi, 1976. — [11],273,[2]p ; 18cm.
Originally published: Boston, Mass. : Houghton Mifflin ; London : Hutchinson, 1975.
ISBN 0-552-10322-5 Pbk : £0.75
(B77-04408)

Kosinski, Jerzy. The painted bird / [by] Jerzy Kosinski. — London : Corgi, 1976. — 222p ; 18cm.
Originally published: Boston, Mass. : Houghton Mifflin, 1965 ; London : W.H. Allen, 1966.
ISBN 0-552-10323-3 Pbk : £0.65
(B77-04409)

Koster, R M. The dissertation : a novel / by R.M. Koster. — Toronto [etc.] ; London : Bantam, 1976. — xviii,556,[1]p : geneal table ; 18cm.
Originally published: New York : Harper's Magazine Press, 1975.
ISBN 0-553-02682-8 Pbk : £0.95
(B77-19006)

Kotzwinkle, William. The fan man / [by] William Kotzwinkle. — Harmondsworth [etc.] : Penguin, 1977. — 141p ; 19cm.
Originally published: New York : Avon ; Henley-on-Thames : Ellis, 1974.
ISBN 0-14-004191-5 Pbk : £0.60
(B77-15514)

Kotzwinkle, William. Fata Morgana / [by] William Kotzwinkle. — London : Hutchinson, 1977. — [8],209p : ill ; 21cm.
Also published: New York : Knopf, 1977.
ISBN 0-09-131630-8 : £3.95
(B77-29715)

Kotzwinkle, William. Swimmer in the secret sea : a novel / by William Kotzwinkle. — Henley-on-Thames : A. Ellis, 1976. — [5],89p ; 18cm.
'This work appeared in slightly different form in "Redbook magazine" and appears in "Prize stories 1975 : the O. Henry awards" published by Doubleday and Company, Inc' - title page verso.
ISBN 0-85628-036-4 : £2.95
(B77-03225)

Kroll, Burt. Trail to Boot Hill / by Burt Kroll. — London : Hale, 1977. — 156p ; 20cm.
ISBN 0-7091-5922-6 : £2.95
(B77-05675)

Kurelek, William. Lumberjack / paintings and story by William Kurelek. — London : Collins, 1977. — [48]p : col ill ; 23x29cm.
Originally published: Montreal : Tundra Books, 1974.
ISBN 0-00-183725-7 : £3.50
(B77-21466)

Kyle, Duncan. Terror's cradle / [by] Duncan Kyle. — [London] : Fontana, 1976. — 222p ; 18cm.
Originally published: London : Collins, 1975.
ISBN 0-00-614675-9 Pbk : £0.70
(B77-01814)

Kyle, Elisabeth. The burning hill / [by] Elisabeth Kyle. — London : P. Davies, 1977. — 202p ; 21cm.
ISBN 0-432-08493-2 : £3.90
(B77-28928)

Kyle, Elisabeth. The captain's house / [by] Elisabeth Kyle ; illustrated by Cheslie D'Andrea. — London [etc.] : White Lion Publishers, 1977. — [6],246p : ill ; 21cm.
Originally published: London : P. Davies, 1952.
ISBN 0-85686-277-0 : £3.25
(B77-14928)

La Bern, Arthur. Nightmare / [by] Arthur La Bern. — London [etc.] : Pan Books, 1977. — 158p ; 18cm.
Originally published: London : W.H. Allen, 1975.
ISBN 0-330-25056-6 Pbk : £0.60
(B77-13886)

Laffeaty, Christina. The blue scarab / by Christina Laffeaty. — London : Hale, 1977. — 192p ; 20cm.
ISBN 0-7091-5928-5 : £3.10
(B77-17746)

Laffeaty, Christina. Lamorna / by Christina Laffeaty. — London : Hale, 1977. — 186p ; 20cm.
ISBN 0-7091-5790-8 : £3.10
(B77-08073)

Laffeaty, Christina. The rage of heaven / by Christina Laffeaty. — London : Hale, 1977. — 192p ; 20cm.
ISBN 0-7091-6216-2 : £3.20
(B77-31478)

Lafferty, R A. Arrive at Easterwine : the autobiography of a ktistec machine, as conveyed to R.A. Lafferty. — London : Dobson, 1977. — [7],216p ; 23cm. — (Dobson science fiction)
Originally published: New York : Scribner, 1971.
ISBN 0-234-72013-1 : £3.95
(B77-34139)

Lake, Nara. The grass tree / by Nara Lake. — London : Hale, 1977. — 5-188p ; 21cm.
ISBN 0-7091-5830-0 : £3.50
(B77-05676)

Lake, Nara. The smiling stranger / by Nara Lake. — London : Hale, 1977. — 188p ; 21cm.
ISBN 0-7091-5831-9 : £3.50
(B77-17108)

Lake, Peter A. Leffert's disease : a novel / by Peter A. Lake. — London : W.H. Allen, 1977. — [7],214p ; 23cm.
Originally published: Indianapolis : Bobbs-Merrill, 1976.
ISBN 0-491-02481-9 : £3.95
(B77-28153)

Laker, Rosalind. The smuggler's bride / [by] Rosalind Laker. — London : Corgi, 1977. — 190,[1]p ; 18cm. — (Corgi Georgian romance series)
Originally published: Garden City, N.Y. : Doubleday, 1975 ; London : Hale, 1976.
ISBN 0-552-10524-4 Pbk : £0.60
(B77-26545)

Lamb, Charlotte. Star-crossed / by Charlotte Lamb. — London : Mills and Boon, 1976. — 189p ; 19cm.
ISBN 0-263-09017-5 : £1.95
(B77-09955)

Lambert, Derek. The great land / [by] Derek Lambert. — London : Arlington Books, 1977. — 463p ; 23cm.
ISBN 0-85140-253-4 : £4.95
(B77-32859)

Lambert, Derek. Touch the lion's paw / [by] Derek Lambert. — London : Corgi, 1977. — [4],252p ; 18cm.
Originally published: London : Arlington Books, 1975.
ISBN 0-552-10345-4 Pbk : £0.75
(B77-09291)

Lambert, Eric. Watermen / [by] Eric Lambert. — London [etc.] : White Lion Publishers, 1976. — 192p ; 21cm.
Originally published: London : Muller, 1956.
ISBN 0-7274-0067-3 : £3.25
(B77-01815)

Lamont, Marianne. Nine moons wasted / [by] Marianne Lamont. — London : Constable, 1977. — 349p ; 23cm.
ISBN 0-09-461630-2 : £4.50
(B77-19721)

L'Amour, Louis. The broken gun / by Louis L'Amour. — London : Hale, 1977. — 160p ; 20cm.
Originally published: New York : Bantam, 1965 ; London : Transworld, 1966.
ISBN 0-7091-4296-x : £3.10
(B77-32197)

L'Amour, Louis. Chancy / [by] Louis L'Amour. — Large print ed. — Leicester : Ulverscroft, 1977. — [5],281,[3]p ; 23cm. — (Ulverscroft large print series : [Western])
Originally published: New York : Bantam ; London : Corgi, 1968.
ISBN 0-7089-0029-1 : £2.95
(B77-20628)

L'Amour, Louis. The high graders / by Louis L'Amour. — London : Hale, 1977. — 157p ; 20cm.
Originally published: New York : Bantam ; London : Transworld, 1965.
ISBN 0-7091-4294-3 : £2.95
(B77-14408)

L'Amour, Louis. Kiowa trail / by Louis L'Amour. — London : Hale, 1976. — 148p ; 20cm.
Originally published: London : Transworld, 1964.
ISBN 0-7091-4293-5 : £2.70
(B77-01816)

L'Amour, Louis. Mustang man / [by] Louis L'Amour. — Large print ed. — Leicester : Ulverscroft, 1977. — [4],274p ; 23cm. — (Ulverscroft large print series : [western])
Originally published: London : Transworld, 1966.
ISBN 0-7089-0051-8 : £2.95
(B77-28154)

L'Amour, Louis. Over on the dry side / [by] Louis L'Amour. — Large print ed. — London : Prior [etc.], 1977. — [5],309p ; 24cm.
Originally published: New York : Saturday Review Press, 1975 ; London : Corgi, 1976.
ISBN 0-86043-042-1 : Unpriced
(B77-22877)

L'Amour, Louis. The quick and the dead / [by] Louis L'Amour. — Large print ed. — London : Prior [etc.], 1977. — [5],264p ; 25cm.
Originally published: London : Corgi, 1974.
ISBN 0-904000-95-8 : £4.75
(B77-12679)

L'Amour, Louis. Rivers west / [by] Louis L'Amour. — Large print [ed.]. — London : Prior [etc.], 1976. — [5],280p ; 24cm.
Originally published: New York : Saturday Review Press ; London : Corgi, 1975.
ISBN 0-904000-96-6 : £4.75
(B77-07621)

L'Amour, Louis. The Sackett brand / by Louis L'Amour. — London : Hale, 1977. — 156p ; 20cm.
Originally published: London : Transworld, 1965.
ISBN 0-7091-4295-1 : £3.10
(B77-28929)

L'Amour, Louis. Showdown at Yellow Butte / [by] Louis L'Amour. — Large print ed. — Leicester : Ulverscroft, 1977. — [7],277p ; 23cm. — (Ulverscroft large print series : [Western])
Originally published: / under the name Jim Mayo, New York : Ace Books, 1953 ; and / under the name Louis L'Amour, London : Tandem, 1972.
ISBN 0-85456-533-7 : £2.65
(B77-13887)

L'Amour, Louis. To tame a land / [by] Louis L'Amour. — Large print ed. — Leicester : Ulverscroft, 1976. — [5],269,[3]p ; 23cm. — (Ulverscroft large print series : [Western])
Originally published: London : Fawcett, 1956.
ISBN 0-85456-506-x : £2.65
(B77-08586)

L'Amour, Louis. To the far blue mountains / [by] Louis L'Amour. — London : Corgi, 1977. — 288p ; 18cm.
Originally published: New York : Saturday Review Press, 1976.
ISBN 0-552-10550-3 Pbk : £0.65
(B77-28155)

L'Amour, Louis. To the far blue mountains / [by] Louis L'Amour. — Large print [ed.]. — London : Prior [etc.], 1977. — [5],540p ; 25cm.
Originally published: New York : Saturday Review Press, 1976 ; London : Corgi, 1977.
ISBN 0-86043-114-2 : £5.95
(B77-34140)

L'Amour, Louis. Where the long grass blows / [by] Louis L'Amour. — London : Corgi, 1977. — [4],185p ; 18cm.
ISBN 0-552-10357-8 Pbk : £0.50
(B77-08074)

Lance, Leslie. Cousins by courtesy / by Leslie Lance. — London : Hale, 1977. — 172p ; 20cm.
ISBN 0-7091-5904-8 : £3.10
(B77-17109)

Landsborough, Gordon. Benghazi breakout / [by] Gordon Landsborough. — London : Wingate, 1977. — 238p ; 23cm. — (Landsborough, Gordon. Glasshouse gang series)
ISBN 0-85523-331-1 : £3.95
(B77-17110)

Landsborough, Gordon. The dead commando / [by] Gordon Landsborough. — London : Wingate, 1977. — 208p ; 23cm. — (Landsborough, Gordon. Glasshouse gang series ; 4)
ISBN 0-85523-321-4 : £3.95
(B77-22157)

Lane, Jane. A secret chronicle / [by] Jane Lane. — London : P. Davies, 1977. — [5],153p ; 23cm.
ISBN 0-432-08578-5 : £3.90
(B77-32198)

Lane, Roumelia. Himalayan moonlight / by Roumelia Lane. — London : Mills and Boon, 1977. — 186p ; 17cm.
ISBN 0-263-72385-2 Pbk : £0.35
(B77-21467)

Lang, Frances. The prince's pleasure / [by] Frances Lang. — London : Hale, 1977. — 176p ; 21cm.
ISBN 0-7091-6340-1 : £3.70
(B77-29716)

Langley, Robert. Death stalk / [by] Bob Langley. — London : Joseph, 1977. — 192p ; 21cm.
ISBN 0-7181-1572-4 : £3.95
(B77-14409)

Lant, Harvey. The Sarbo gang / by Harvey Lant. — London : Hale, 1976. — 155p ; 20cm.
ISBN 0-7091-5856-4 : £2.70
(B77-01817)

Larkin, Polly. Diary of an usherette / [by] Polly Larkin. — London : New English Library, 1977. — 128p ; 18cm.
ISBN 0-450-02940-9 Pbk : £0.50
(B77-13888)

Lathen, Emma. Banking on death / by Emma Lathen. — London : Gollancz, 1977. — [7], 166p ; 21cm.
Originally published: New York : Macmillan, 1961 ; London : Gollancz, 1962.
ISBN 0-575-02283-3 : £3.50
(B77-13889)

Lauben, Philip. Shall we send flowers? / by Philip Lauben. — London : Hale, 1976. — 192p ; 20cm.
ISBN 0-7091-5796-7 : £2.95
(B77-00432)

Lauder, Stuart. The standing stone : a novel / by Stuart Lauder. — London : Gollancz, 1977. — 199p ; 21cm.
ISBN 0-575-02323-6 : £4.75
(B77-20629)

Lauder, William. The uncanny / [by] William Lauder. — London [etc.] : Arrow Books, 1977. — 140p ; 18cm.
ISBN 0-09-916010-2 Pbk : £0.65
(B77-29717)

Laumer, Keith. A plague of demons / [by] Keith Laumer. — Sevenoaks : Coronet, 1977. — 159p ; 18cm.
Originally published: New York : Berkeley Publishing Corporation, 1965 ; Harmondsworth : Penguin, 1967.
ISBN 0-340-21793-6 Pbk : £0.60
(B77-29718)

Laumer, Keith. Planet run / [by] Keith Laumer and Gordon R. Dickson. — London : Hale, 1977. — 167p ; 21cm. — (Hale SF)
Originally published: Garden City, N.Y. : Doubleday, 1967.
ISBN 0-7091-6000-3 : £3.25
(B77-17748)

Laumer, Keith. The shape changer / by Keith Laumer. — London : Hale, 1977. — 189p ; 21cm. — (Hale SF)
Originally published: New York : Putnam, 1972.
ISBN 0-7091-5980-3 : £3.25
(B77-14929)

Laurence, Margaret, *b.1926.* A jest of God / [by] Margaret Laurence. — Toronto [etc.] ; London : Bantam, 1977. — [5],246,[1]p ; 18cm.
Originally published: Toronto : McClelland and Stewart ; London : Macmillan, 1966.
ISBN 0-552-60400-3 Pbk : £0.75
(B77-24490)

Lauria, Frank. Communion / by Frank Lauria. — Toronto [etc.] ; London : Bantam, 1977. — [7],179p ; 18cm.
'Based on an original story by Rose Mary Ritvo and Alfred Sole'. — cover.
ISBN 0-553-11241-4 Pbk : £0.75
(B77-27396)

Lawrence, David Herbert. The portable D.H. Lawrence / edited and with an introduction by Diana Trilling. — Harmondsworth [etc.] : Penguin, 1977. — viii,692p ; 18cm. — (The Viking portable library)
This collection originally published: New York : Viking Press, 1947.
ISBN 0-14-015028-5 Pbk : £1.95
(B77-34141)

Lawrence, Louise. The power of stars / [by] Louise Lawrence. — London : Collins, 1976. — 159p ; 18cm. — (Lions)
Originally published: London : Collins, 1972. — For adolescents.
ISBN 0-00-671006-9 Pbk : £0.50
(B77-30661)

Le Carré, John. The honourable schoolboy / [by] John le Carré. — London [etc.] : Hodder and Stoughton, 1977. — 32p : col maps(on lining papers) ; 23cm.
ISBN 0-340-22042-2 : £4.95
(B77-29719)

Le Carré, John. The naive and sentimental lover / [by] John le Carré. — London [etc.] : Pan Books, 1977. — 431p ; 18cm.
Originally published: London : Hodder and Stoughton, 1971.
Pbk : £1.00
ISBN 0-330-23293-2
(B77-19722)

Le Guin, Ursula Kroeber. The word for world is forest / by Ursula K. Le Guin. — London : Gollancz, 1977. — 128p ; 21cm. — (Gollancz SF)
Originally published: New York : Berkley Publishing Corporation, 1976.
ISBN 0-575-02302-3 : £3.25
(B77-30662)

Lea, Alec. Beth Varden at sunset / [by] Alec Lea. — London : Dobson, 1977. — 160p : map ; 21cm.
ISBN 0-234-72026-3 : £2.95
(B77-28156)

Lea, Alec. Deep down and high up / [by] Alec Lea. — London : Dobson, 1976. — 128p : map ; 21cm.
For adolescents.
ISBN 0-234-77602-1 : £2.50
(B77-00980)

Lea, Timothy. Confessions from a luxury liner / [by] Timothy Lea. — London : Futura Publications, 1976. — 156p ; 18cm.
ISBN 0-86007-298-3 Pbk : £0.50
(B77-08587)

Lea, Timothy. Confessions from a nudist colony / [by] Timothy Lea. — London : Futura Publications, 1976. — 159p ; 18cm.
ISBN 0-86007-359-9 Pbk : £0.50
(B77-12115)

Lea, Timothy. Confessions of a film extra / [by] Timothy Lea. — London : Sphere, 1975. — 159p ; 18cm.
Originally published: 1973.
ISBN 0-7221-9351-3 Pbk : £0.50
(B77-13307)

Lea, Timothy. Confessions of a travelling salesman / [by] Timothy Lea. — London : Sphere, 1976. — 155p ; 18cm.
Originally published: 1973.
ISBN 0-7221-9303-3 Pbk : £0.50
(B77-13308)

Leach, Christopher, *b.1925.* The lies of Boyo Butler. — Basingstoke : : Macmillan, Jan. 1978. — 1v. — (Topliner tridents)
For adolescents. — Previous control number ISBN 0-333-23554-1.
ISBN 0-333-23634-3 : CIP entry
(B77-32199)

Leader, Charles. A wreath for Miss Wong / [by] Charles Leader. — London : Hale, 1977. — 185p ; 21cm.
ISBN 0-7091-5647-2 : £3.25
(B77-05677)

Leader, Charles. A wreath of cherry blossom / [by] Charles Leader. — London : Hale, 1977. — 188p ; 21cm.
ISBN 0-7091-5895-5 : £3.50
(B77-17749)

Leasor, James. The Chinese widow / [by] James Leasor. — London : Corgi, 1977. — 318p ; 18cm.
Originally published: London : Heinemann, 1975.
ISBN 0-552-10512-0 Pbk : £0.85
(B77-22158)

Leasor, James. Passport in suspense / [by] James Leasor. — London : Corgi, 1977. — 251p ; 18cm.
Originally published: London : Heinemann, 1967.
ISBN 0-552-10587-2 Pbk : £0.80
(B77-32200)

Leasor, James. Passport to peril / [by] James Leasor. — London : Corgi, 1977. — 239p ; 18cm.
Originally published: London : Heinemann, 1966.
ISBN 0-552-10586-4 Pbk : £0.80
(B77-32201)

Lee, Fleming. The Saint returns / [adapted by Fleming Lee] ; [edited by] Leslie Charteris. — London [etc.] : White Lion Publishers, 1977. — 190p ; 21cm.
This collection originally published: Garden City, N.Y. : Doubleday for the Crime Club, 1968 ; London : Hodder and Stoughton, 1969. — Contents: The dizzy daughter / original story by D.R. Mottram ; teleplay by Leigh Vance - The gadget lovers / original teleplay by John Kruse.
ISBN 0-7274-0224-2 : £3.50
(B77-06292)

Lee, John, *b.1931.* The ninth man / [by] John Lee. — London : Corgi, 1977. — 319p ; 18cm.
Originally published: Garden City, N.Y. : Doubleday ; London : Cassell, 1976.
ISBN 0-552-10396-9 Pbk : £0.85
(B77-13309)

Lee, Ranger. Winding River range / [by] Ranger Lee. — [London] : Fontana, 1976. — 160p ; 18cm. — (A Fontana Western)
Originally published: London : Collins, 1948.
ISBN 0-00-614390-3 Pbk : £0.45
(B77-06293)

Lees, Marguerite. The secret song / by Marguerite Lees. — London : Mills and Boon, 1976. — 187p ; 19cm.
ISBN 0-263-09058-2 : £1.95
(B77-14410)

Lees, Marguerite. Still waters / [by] Marguerite Lees. — Large print ed. — Leicester : Ulverscroft, 1977. — [5],362p ; 23cm. — ([Ulverscroft large print series : romance])
Originally published: London : Mills and Boon, 1968.
ISBN 0-7089-0045-3 : £2.95
(B77-28157)

Leeson, Robert. The white horse / [by] Robert Leeson. — London : Collins, 1977. — 266p : map ; 22cm.
ISBN 0-00-184925-5 : £3.50
(B77-12680)

Lehman, Ernest. The French Atlantic affair / [by] Ernest Lehman. — London [etc.] : Macmillan, 1977. — [5],468,[1]p ; 23cm.
Also published: New York : Atheneum, 1977.
ISBN 0-333-22315-2 : £4.95
(B77-34142)

Leiber, Fritz. The big time / [by] Fritz Leiber. — London : Severn House : [Distributed by Hutchinson], 1976. — 171p ; 21cm.
Originally published: New York : Ace Books, 1961 ; London : New English Library, 1965.
ISBN 0-7278-0218-6 : £3.15
(B77-03762)

Leiber, Fritz. The green millennium / [by] Fritz Leiber. — London : Severn House : [Distributed by Hutchinson], 1977. — [4],220p ; 21cm.
Originally published: New York : Abelard Press, 1953 ; London : Abelard-Schuman, 1960.
ISBN 0-7278-0233-x : £3.15
(B77-17111)

Leigh, Roberta. Man without a heart / by Roberta Leigh. — London : Mills and Boon, 1977. — 186p ; 17cm.
Originally published: 1976.
ISBN 0-263-72334-8 Pbk : £0.35
(B77-06882)

Leigh, Roberta. Pretence / [by] Roberta Leigh. — Large print ed. — Bath : Lythway Press, 1977. — [4],308p ; 22cm.
Originally published: London : Hutchinson, 1956.
ISBN 0-85046-748-9 : £4.70
(B77-34143)

Leighton, Edward. A light from tomorrow / by Edward Leighton. — London : Hale, 1977. — 191p ; 21cm.
ISBN 0-7091-6075-5 : £3.25
(B77-17750)

Leighton, Edward. Lord of the lightning / by Edward Leighton. — London : Hale, 1977. — 176p ; 21cm. — (Hale SF)
ISBN 0-7091-6183-2 : £3.60
(B77-22878)

Leighton, Edward. Out of earth's deep / [by] Edward Leighton. — London : Hale, 1977. — 5-180p ; 21cm. — (Hale SF)
ISBN 0-7091-5994-3 : £3.25
(B77-17112)

Leitch, Maurice. Stamping ground / [by] Maurice Leitch. — London [etc.] : Quartet Books, 1977. — [11],209p ; 19cm.
Originally published: London : Secker and Warburg, 1975.
ISBN 0-7043-3167-5 Pbk : £1.25
(B77-28930)

Lemarchand, Elizabeth. Cyanide with compliments / [by] Elizabeth Lemarchand. — Large print ed. — Leicester : Ulverscroft, 1977. — [5],339p ; 23cm. — (Ulverscroft large print series : [mystery])
Originally published: London : MacGibbon and Kee, 1972.
ISBN 0-85456-507-8 : £2.65
(B77-08588)

Lemarchand, Elizabeth. Unhappy returns / [by] Elizabeth Lemarchand. — London : Hart-Davis MacGibbon, 1977. — 175p : map ; 21cm.
ISBN 0-246-10969-6 : £3.50
(B77-15515)

Leonard, Elmore. Fifty-two pickup / [by] Elmore Leonard. — London [etc.] : Pan Books, 1977. — 190p ; 18cm.
Cover title: 52 pick-up. — Originally published: New York : Delacorte Press ; London : Secker and Warburg, 1974.
ISBN 0-330-25024-8 Pbk : £0.60
(B77-12681)

Leonard, Elmore. Unknown man no.89 : a novel / by Elmore Leonard. — London : Secker and Warburg, 1977. — [7],264p ; 23cm.
ISBN 0-436-24435-7 : £3.90
(B77-21468)

Leslie, Colin. Feud royal / by Colin Leslie. — London : Hale, 1977. — 191p ; 21cm.
ISBN 0-7091-5923-4 : £3.50
(B77-14411)

Leslie, David Stuart. Two-way mirror - : a novel / by David Stuart Leslie. — London : Macdonald and Jane's, 1977. — [9],198p ; 23cm.
ISBN 0-354-04208-4 : £4.50
(B77-28931)

Leslie, Doris. The warrior king : the reign of Richard the Lion Heart / [by] Doris Leslie. — London : Heinemann, 1977. — [6],275p ; 21cm.
ISBN 0-434-41828-5 : £4.50
(B77-31479)

Lester, Jane. The reluctant heart / by Jane Lester. — London : Hale, 1977. — 157p ; 20cm.
ISBN 0-7091-6044-5 : £3.20
(B77-28158)

Lester, Julius. Basketball game / [by] Julius Lester. — Harmondsworth [etc.] : Penguin, 1977. — 92p ; 18cm. — (Peacock books)
Originally published: in 'Two love stories'. New York : Dial Press, 1972 ; Harmondsworth : Kestrel, 1974. — For adolescents.
ISBN 0-14-047106-5 Pbk : £0.50
(B77-27397)

Levin, Ira. The boys from Brazil / [by] Ira Levin. — London [etc.] : Pan Books, 1977. — 238p ; 18cm.
Originally published: New York : Random House ; London : Joseph, 1976.
ISBN 0-330-25015-9 Pbk : £0.80
(B77-21469)

Levin, Ira. The boys from Brazil / [by] Ira Levin. — Large print [ed.]. — London : Prior [etc.], 1977. — [5],456p ; 24cm.
Originally published: London : Joseph, 1976.
ISBN 0-86043-023-5 : £5.75
(B77-12116)

Levin, Ira. A kiss before dying / [by] Ira Levin. — Large print ed. — Bath : Lythway Press, 1976. — viii,424p ; 23cm. — (Lythway classics of crime and detection)
Originally published: New York : Simon and Schuster, 1953 ; London : Joseph, 1954.
ISBN 0-85046-690-3 : £4.75
(B77-03226)

Lewis, Clive Staples. The pilgrim's regress : an allegorical apology for Christianity, reason and romanticism / [by] C.S. Lewis. — [New and revised ed.]. — [London] ([14 St James's Place, S.W.1]) : Fount Paperbacks, 1977. — 250p : map ; 18cm.
This ed. originally published: London : Geoffrey Bles, 1943.
ISBN 0-00-623859-9 Pbk : £0.95
(B77-18378)

Lewis, Hilda, *b.1896.* Rose of England / [by] Hilda Lewis. — London : Hutchinson, 1977. — 192p ; 23cm.
Based on the life of Mary, Queen, consort of Louis XII, King of France.
ISBN 0-09-129090-2 : £3.95
(B77-28159)

Lewis, James. The shadows of death / by James Lewis. — Harrow (16 College Rd, Harrow, Middx) : J.M.C. Publications, 1976. — 253p ; 19cm.
ISBN 0-9504362-1-6 Pbk : £0.75
(B77-12682)

Lewis, Janet, *b.1899.* The wife of Martin Guerre / [by] Janet Lewis. — Harmondsworth [etc.] : Penguin, 1977. — 95p ; 19cm.
Originally published: San Francisco : Colt Press, 1941 ; London : Rapp and Carroll, 1967.
ISBN 0-14-004193-1 Pbk : £0.50
(B77-18379)

Lewis, Maynah. The other side of paradise / [by] Maynah Lewis. — London : Corgi, 1977. — 159p ; 18cm.
Originally published: London : Collins, 1975.
ISBN 0-552-10348-9 Pbk : £0.60
(B77-17113)

Lewis, Maynah. These my children / [by] Maynah Lewis. — London : Collins, 1977. — 158p ; 20cm.
ISBN 0-00-233853-x : £2.75
(B77-14930)

Lewis, Roy, *b.1933.* Nothing but foxes / [by] Roy Lewis. — London : Collins [for] the Crime Club, 1977. — 193p : geneal table ; 21cm.
ISBN 0-00-231583-1 : £2.95
(B77-19723)

Lewis, Stephen, *b.1947.* The bestsellers / [by] Stephen Lewis. — London : Coronet, 1977. — 319p ; 18cm.
Originally published: New York : Fawcett, 1976.
ISBN 0-340-21967-x Pbk : £1.00
(B77-22159)

Lewis, Ted. Jack Carter and the Mafia pigeon / [by] Ted Lewis. — London : Joseph, 1977. — 219p ; 21cm.
ISBN 0-7181-1372-1 : £4.25
(B77-19724)

Lewis, Ted. Jack Carter's law / [by] Ted Lewis. — London : Sphere, 1976. — 212p ; 18cm.
Originally published: London : Joseph, 1974.
ISBN 0-7221-5523-9 Pbk : £0.60
(B77-06294)

Lewty, Marjorie. To catch a butterfly / by Marjorie Lewty. — London : Mills and Boon, 1977. — 189p ; 17cm.
ISBN 0-263-72381-x Pbk : £0.35
(B77-21470)

Ley, Alice Chetwynd. At dark of the moon / [by] Alice Chetwynd Ley. — London : Hale, 1977. — 192p ; 21cm.
ISBN 0-7091-5698-7 : £3.50
(B77-05071)

Ley, Alice Chetwynd. The Georgian rake / [by] Alice Chetwynd Ley. — London : Corgi, 1977. — [5],218p ; 18cm. — (Corgi Georgian romance series)
Originally published: London : Hale, 1960.
ISBN 0-552-10482-5 Pbk : £0.50
(B77-26546)

Ley, Alice Chetwynd. The jewelled snuffbox / [by] Alice Chetwynd Ley. — London : Corgi, 1977. — [9],178p ; 18cm. — (Corgi Georgian romance series)
Originally published: London : Hale, 1959.
ISBN 0-552-10481-7 Pbk : £0.50
(B77-26547)

Lieberman, Herbert. City of the dead / [by] Herbert Lieberman. — London : Hutchinson, 1976. — 368p ; 23cm.
Also published: New York : Simon and Schuster, 1976.
ISBN 0-09-127120-7 : £3.95
(B77-13310)

Lillis, Molly. Where crickets sing / by Molly Lillis. — London : Hale, 1977. — 172p ; 20cm.
ISBN 0-7091-5951-x : £3.10
(B77-13311)

Lindall, Edward. A lively form of death / [by] Edward Lindall. — Sevenoaks : Coronet, 1977. — 184p ; 18cm.
Originally published: London : Constable, 1972.
ISBN 0-340-21809-6 Pbk : £0.60
(B77-26548)

Lindley, Erica. The Brackenroyd inheritance / by Erica Lindley. — London : Millington, 1976. — [3],247,[1]p ; 23cm.
ISBN 0-86000-072-9 : £3.50
(B77-15516)

Lindop, Audrey Erskine. Nicola / [by] Audrey Erskine Lindop. — London [etc.] : White Lion Publishers, 1977. — 319p ; 21cm.
Originally published: New York : Doubleday, 1959 ; London : Collins, 1964.
ISBN 0-85617-327-4 : £3.75
(B77-17751)

Lindop, Audrey Erskine. The tall headlines / [by] Audrey Erskine Lindop. — Large print ed. — Bath : Chivers, 1977. — [6],463p ; 23cm.
Originally published: London : Heinemann, 1950.
ISBN 0-85997-207-0 : £5.60(£4.20 to members of the Library Association)
(B77-09956)

Lindsay, Philip. The gentle knight / [by] Philip Lindsay. — Large print ed. — Bath : Chivers, 1977. — xiii,433p ; 22cm.
Originally published: London : Hutchinson, 1942.
ISBN 0-85997-208-9 : £5.60(£4.20 to members of the Library Association)
(B77-09957)

Lindsay, Philip. The merry mistress / [by] Philip Lindsay. — London : Hutchinson, 1976. — 304p ; 20cm.
Originally published: 1952. — Based on the life of Jane Shore.
ISBN 0-09-123360-7 : £3.95
(B77-12683)

Lindsay, Philip. A piece for candlelight / [by] Philip Lindsay. — London : Hutchinson, 1976. — 304p ; 20cm.
Originally published: 1953. — Based on the life of Mary 'Perdita' Robinson.
ISBN 0-09-123280-5 : £3.95
(B77-12684)

Lindsay, Philip. Through midnight streets / [by] Philip Lindsay. — Large print ed. — Bath : Chivers, 1976. — xv,512p ; 23cm.
Originally published: London : Hutchinson, 1957.
ISBN 0-85997-200-3 : £5.60(£4.20 to members of the Library Association)
(B77-02595)

Lindsay, Rachel. Alien corn / [by] Rachel Lindsay. — London [etc.] : Mills and Boon, 1976. — 188p ; 18cm. — (Mills and Boon classics)
Originally published: London : Hutchinson, 1954.
ISBN 0-263-72218-x Pbk : £0.35
(B77-11409)

Lindsay, Rachel. A man to tame / by Rachel Lindsay. — London : Mills and Boon, 1977. — 187p ; 17cm.
Originally published: 1976.
ISBN 0-263-72342-9 Pbk : £0.35
(B77-06883)

Lindsay, Rachel. Roman affair / by Rachel Lindsay. — London : Mills and Boon, 1976. — 187p ; 17cm.
ISBN 0-263-72312-7 Pbk : £0.30
(B77-00433)

Lindsay, Rachel. Tinsel star / by Rachel Lindsay. — London : Mills and Boon, 1976. — 187p ; 17cm.
ISBN 0-263-72323-2 Pbk : £0.30
(B77-05678)

Lingard, Joan. The reunion / [by] Joan Lingard. — London : Hamilton, 1977. — [5],135p ; 23cm.
ISBN 0-241-89753-x : £3.25
(B77-29720)

Linton, Cathy. The silver rose bowl / [by] Cathy Linton. — London : Corgi, 1977. — 127p ; 18cm. — (Linton, Cathy. St Lawrence's romances ; no.6)
ISBN 0-552-10548-1 Pbk : £0.50
(B77-28160)

Littell, Robert, *b.1935.* Sweet reason / [by] Robert Littell. — Sevenoaks : Coronet, 1977. — 192p ; 18cm.
Originally published: London : Hodder and Stoughton, 1974.
ISBN 0-340-21313-2 Pbk : £0.75
(B77-15517)

Lively, Penelope. The road to Lichfield / [by] Penelope Lively. — London : Heinemann, 1977. — [5],216p ; 23cm.
ISBN 0-434-42735-7 : £3.90
(B77-21471)

Livingston, Margaret. The Agnew inheritance / [by] Margaret Livingston. — London : Hale, 1977. — 204p ; 21cm.
ISBN 0-7091-6208-1 : £3.60
(B77-26549)

Llewellyn, Richard. At sunrise, the rough music / [by] Richard Llewellyn. — London : New English Library, 1977. — 286p ; 18cm.
Originally published: London : Joseph, 1976.
ISBN 0-450-03270-1 Pbk : £0.90
(B77-23737)

Llewellyn, Richard. Green, green my valley now / [by] Richard Llewellyn. — London : New English Library, 1977. — 221p : maps ; 18cm.
Originally published: London : Joseph, 1975.
ISBN 0-450-03087-3 Pbk : £0.75
(B77-12117)

Llewellyn, Richard. Mr Hamish Gleave / [by] Richard Llewellyn. — Large print ed. — Bath : Chivers, 1977. — [4],507p ; 22cm.
Originally published: London : Joseph, 1956.
ISBN 0-85997-224-0 : £5.60(£4.20 to members of the Library Association)
(B77-13890)

Llewellyn, Richard. Tell me now, and again / [by] Richard Llewellyn. — London : Joseph, 1977. — 284p ; 21cm.
ISBN 0-7181-1598-8 : £4.95
(B77-28161)

Llewellyn, Sam. Gurney's revenge / [by] Sam Llewellyn. — London : Arlington Books, 1977. — 235p ; 23cm.
ISBN 0-85140-271-2 : £3.50
(B77-27398)

Lockley, Ronald Mathias. Seal woman / [by] Ronald Lockley ; illustrations by Robert Gillmor. — [London] : Methuen [etc.], 1976. — [4],154p ; 18cm.
Originally published: London : Rex Collings, 1974.
ISBN 0-454-00049-9 Pbk : £0.70
(B77-03763)

Lockridge, Ross. Raintree County / [by] Ross Lockridge, Jr. — Abridged ed. / abridged by Edmund Fuller. — London [etc.] : Pan Books, 1977. — [6],442p : map ; 18cm.
This ed. originally published: New York : Dell, 1957 ; London : Pan Books, 1958.
ISBN 0-330-25240-2 Pbk : £0.95
(B77-31480)

Lofts, Norah. Blossom like the rose / by Norah Lofts. — London [etc.] : Hodder and Stoughton, 1977. — 286p ; 21cm.
Originally published: London : Gollancz, 1939.
ISBN 0-340-20122-3 : £3.95
(B77-22160)

Lofts, Norah. Charlotte / [by] Norah Lofts. — Large print ed. — Leicester : Ulverscroft, 1976. — [8],525p ; 23cm. — (Ulverscroft large print series : [fiction])
Originally published: London : Hodder and Stoughton, 1972.
ISBN 0-85456-503-5 : £2.65
(B77-08075)

Lofts, Norah. Gad's Hall / [by] Norah Lofts. — London [etc.] : Hodder and Stoughton, 1977. — 254p ; 22cm.
ISBN 0-340-21595-x : £3.95
(B77-30664)

Lofts, Norah. The homecoming / [by] Norah Lofts. — Sevenoaks : Coronet, 1977. — 285p ; 18cm.
Originally published: London : Hodder and Stoughton, 1975.
ISBN 0-340-21803-7 Pbk : £0.75
(B77-20630)

Lofts, Norah. I met a gypsy / [by] Norah Lofts. — Large print ed. — Leicester : Ulverscroft, 1977. — [5],287p ; 23cm. — (Ulverscroft large print series : [historical romance])
Originally published: London : Methuen, 1935.
ISBN 0-85456-519-1 : £2.65
(B77-13891)

Lofts, Norah. The lonely furrow / [by] Norah Lofts. — London [etc.] : Hodder and Stoughton, 1976. — 317p : geneal table ; 23cm.
ISBN 0-340-20667-5 : £3.95
(B77-13892)

Lofts, Norah. The road to revelation / [by] Norah Lofts. — Large print ed. — Leicester : Ulverscroft, 1977. — [7],525p ; 23cm. — (Ulverscroft large print series : [historical romance])
Originally published: London : P. Davies, 1941.
ISBN 0-85456-540-x : Unpriced
(B77-20631)

Logan, Jake. Slocum and the widow Kate / [by] Jake Logan. — London : New English Library, 1977. — 140p ; 18cm. — (Logan, Jake. Slocum ; no.3)
Originally published: Chicago : Playboy Press, 1975.
ISBN 0-450-03257-4 Pbk : £0.60
(B77-29721)

London, Jack. The call of the wild / by Jack London ; with two colour plates and line drawings in the text by Charles Pickard. — London : Dent [etc.], 1977. — [7],113p,[4]leaves of plates : ill(2 col) ; 22cm. — (Children's illustrated classics)
Originally published: New York : Macmillan, 1903.
ISBN 0-460-02752-2 Pbk : £1.75
(B77-25906)

London, Jack. White Fang / [by] Jack London ; illustrated by John Glover. — London [etc.] : Beaver Books, 1976. — 206p : ill ; 20cm.
Originally published: New York : Macmillan, 1905 ; London : Methuen, 1907.
ISBN 0-600-39378-x Pbk : £0.60
(B77-12685)

Long, Freda Margaret. For the love of Albert / by Freda M. Long. — London : Hale, 1977. — 3-207p ; 21cm.
Based on the life of Queen Victoria.
ISBN 0-7091-5792-4 : £3.60
(B77-14412)

Long, Freda Margaret. The master of Frinton Park / by Freda M. Long. — London : Hale, 1977. — 208p ; 21cm.
ISBN 0-7091-6066-6 : £3.70
(B77-22879)

Longstreet, Stephen. The bank : a novel / by Stephen Longstreet. — London : W.H. Allen, 1977. — 378p ; 23cm.
Originally published: New York : Putnam, 1976.
ISBN 0-491-02220-4 : £4.95
(B77-24491)

Longstreet, Stephen. The Kingston fortune / [by] Stephen Longstreet. — London : W.H. Allen, 1977. — [7],405p ; 22cm.
Originally published: New York : Avon Books, 1975.
ISBN 0-491-01708-1 : £4.50
(B77-10949)

Loos, Mary. Belinda / [by] Mary Loos. — London : Corgi, 1977. — [6],537,[1]p ; 18cm.
Originally published: New York : Bantam, 1976.
ISBN 0-552-10347-0 Pbk : £0.95
(B77-16057)

Lorac, E.C.R. Murder by matchlight / by E.C.R. Lorac. — Hornchurch : I. Henry, 1977. — 160p ; 21cm.
Originally published: London : Collins, 1945.
ISBN 0-86025-097-0 : £2.95
(B77-12686)

Loraine, Philip. Ask the rattlesnake / [by] Philip Loraine. — [London] : Fontana, 1977. — 223p ; 18cm.
Originally published: London : Collins, 1975.
ISBN 0-00-614794-1 Pbk : £0.70
(B77-31481)

Lord, Graham. God and all his angels / [by] Graham Lord. — London : Hamilton, 1976. — [5],217p ; 21cm.
ISBN 0-241-89480-8 : £3.50
(B77-16605)

Lord, Graham. The spider and the fly / [by] Graham Lord. — London : Sphere, 1977. — 192p ; 18cm.
Originally published: London : Hamilton, 1974.
ISBN 0-7221-5632-4 Pbk : £0.75
(B77-13312)

Loring, Emilie. Love with honor / [by] Emilie Loring. — Large print [ed.]. — London : Prior [etc.], 1977. — [7],394p ; 24cm.
Originally published: Boston, Mass. : Little, Brown, 1969 ; London : Hale, 1970.
ISBN 0-86043-032-4 : £4.95
(B77-11410)

Loring, Emilie. No time for love / [by] Emilie Loring. — Large print ed. — Leicester : Ulverscroft, 1977. — [6],371p ; 23cm. — (Ulverscroft large print series : [romance])
Originally published: Boston, Mass. : Little, Brown, 1970 ; London : Hale, 1971.
ISBN 0-85456-538-8 : Unpriced
(B77-19725)

Loring, Emilie. There is always love / [by] Emilie Loring. — London : Hale, 1977. — [4], 187p ; 20cm.
Originally published: Boston, Mass. : Little, Brown, 1940 ; London : Foulsham, 1951.
ISBN 0-7091-5946-3 : £3.10
(B77-14413)

Lorrimer, Claire. A voice in the dark / [by] Claire Lorrimer. — London : Corgi, 1977. — 171p ; 18cm.
Originally published: London : Souvenir Press, 1967.
ISBN 0-552-10585-6 Pbk : £0.70
(B77-32202)

Lovelace, Delos W. King Kong / conceived by Edgar Wallace and Merian C. Cooper ; novelization by Delos W. Lovelace. — London : A. Barker, 1977. — 191p ; 23cm.
Originally published: New York : Grosset and Dunlap, 1976?.
ISBN 0-213-16649-6 : £3.95
(B77-33432)

Lovell, Marc. Dreamers in a haunted house / [by] Marc Lovell. — London : Hale, 1976. — [5],180p ; 20cm.
Originally published: Garden City, N.Y. : Doubleday, 1975.
ISBN 0-7091-5834-3 : £2.95
(B77-00434)

Lovell, Marc. Vampire in the shadows / [by] Marc Lovell. — Sevenoaks : Coronet, 1977. — 157p ; 18cm.
Originally published: as 'An enquiry into the existence of vampires', Garden City, N.Y. : Doubleday, 1974 ; and as 'Vampire in the shadows', London : Hale, 1976.
ISBN 0-340-21840-1 Pbk : £0.75
(B77-34144)

Lovesey, Peter. A case of spirits / [by] Peter Lovesey. — Harmondsworth [etc.] : Penguin, 1977. — 192p ; 19cm. — (Penguin crime fiction)
Originally published: London : Macmillan, 1975.
ISBN 0-14-004333-0 Pbk : £0.60
(B77-25203)

Lowden, Desmond. Bellman and true / [by] Desmond Lowden. — London [etc.] : Pan Books, 1977. — 159p ; 18cm.
Originally published: London : Eyre Methuen, 1975.
ISBN 0-330-25120-1 Pbk : £0.60
(B77-25907)

Lowell, J.R. Secrets / [by] J.R. Lowell. — London : New English Library, 1977. — 208p ; 18cm.
Originally published: 1976.
ISBN 0-450-03104-7 Pbk : £0.95
(B77-24492)

Lowry, Malcolm. Lunar caustic / [by] Malcolm Lowry ; edited by Earle Birney and Margerie Lowry ; with a foreword by Conrad Knickerbocker. — London : Cape, 1977. — 76p ; 21cm.
Originally published: 1968.
ISBN 0-224-01346-7 : £2.50
(B77-08076)

Luard, Nicholas. The Robespierre serial / [by] Nicholas Luard. — London : Sphere, 1976. — 191p ; 18cm.
Originally published: London : Weidenfeld and Nicolson, 1975.
ISBN 0-7221-5663-4 Pbk : £0.65
(B77-06295)

Lucas, George. Star wars : from the adventures of Luke Skywalker : a novel / by George Lucas. — London : Sphere, 1977. — 190p,[16]p of plates : col ill, col ports ; 18cm. — (Sphere science fiction)
ISBN 0-7221-5669-3 Pbk : £0.95
(B77-31482)

Lucie-Smith, Edward. The dark pageant : a novel about Gilles de Rais / by Edward Lucie-Smith. — London : Blond and Briggs, 1977. — 281p ; 23cm.
ISBN 0-85634-045-6 : £4.95
(B77-30665)

Ludlum, Robert. The Chancellor manuscript / [by] Robert Ludlum. — London [etc.] : Hart-Davis MacGibbon, 1977. — 464p ; 23cm.
ISBN 0-246-10985-8 : £4.50
(B77-19726)

Luke, Mary M. The Nonsuch lure / [by] Mary Luke. — London : Joseph, 1977. — 319p : map ; 23cm.
Originally published: New York : Coward, McCann and Geoghegan, 1976.
ISBN 0-7181-1585-6 : £4.50
(B77-14931)

Lurie, Alison. Love and friendship / [by] Alison Lurie. — Harmondsworth [etc.] : Penguin, 1977. — 351p ; 18cm.
Originally published: New York : Macmillan, 1962 ; London : Heinemann, 1963.
ISBN 0-14-004210-5 Pbk : £0.90
(B77-20632)

Lurie, Alison. The nowhere city / [by] Alison Lurie. — Harmondsworth [etc.] : Penguin, 1977. — 318p ; 18cm.
Originally published: London : Heinemann, 1965.
ISBN 0-14-004209-1 Pbk : £0.90
(B77-20633)

Lurie, Alison. The war between the Tates / [by] Alison Lurie. — Harmondsworth [etc.] : Penguin, 1977. — 380p ; 19cm.
Originally published: New York : Random House ; London : Heinemann, 1974.
ISBN 0-14-004208-3 Pbk : £0.95
(B77-20634)

Lutz, Giles Alfred. Stagecoach to hell / by Giles A. Lutz. — London : Hale, 1977. — [5],182p ; 20cm.
Originally published: Garden City, N.Y. : Doubleday, 1975.
ISBN 0-7091-6032-1 : £2.95
(B77-14932)

Lutz, Gunther. Panzer platoon, Blitzkrieg! / [by] Gunther Lutz. — London : Sphere, 1977. — 189p ; 18cm.
ISBN 0-7221-9149-9 Pbk : £0.75
(B77-22880)

Lutz, John. Buyer beware / by John Lutz. — London : Hale, 1977. — 188p ; 20cm.
Originally published: New York : Putnam, 1976.
ISBN 0-7091-6337-1 : £3.50
(B77-30666)

Lykiard, Alexis. The drive north : a novel / by Alexis Lykiard. — London : Allison and Busby, 1977. — 183p ; 23cm.
ISBN 0-85031-200-0 : £4.50
ISBN 0-85031-201-9 Pbk : £1.95
(B77-28162)

Lymington, John. The Laxham haunting / by John Lymington. — London [etc.] : Hodder and Stoughton, 1976. — 192p ; 20cm.
ISBN 0-340-21332-9 : £3.25
(B77-02596)

Lynch, Frances. The fine and handsome captain / [by] Frances Lynch. — Sevenoaks : Coronet, 1977. — 220p ; 18cm.
Originally published: London : Souvenir Press, 1975.
ISBN 0-340-21320-5 Pbk : £0.85
(B77-19727)

Lynch, Frances. Stranger at the wedding : a novel / by Frances Lynch. — London : Souvenir Press, 1977. — [5],249p ; 21cm.
ISBN 0-285-62246-3 : £3.50
(B77-09292)

Lynn, Jack. The turncoat / [by] Jack Lynn. — London : Sphere, 1977. — 351p ; 18cm.
Originally published: New York : Delacorte Press ; London : Robson Books, 1976.
ISBN 0-7221-5675-8 Pbk : £0.95
(B77-21472)

Lyons, Arthur. All God's children / [by] Arthur Lyons. — London : Robson, 1977. — 224p ; 23cm.
Originally published: New York : Mason/Charter, 1975.
ISBN 0-903895-99-4 : £3.50
(B77-13313)

Lyons, Arthur. The dead are discreet / [by] Arthur Lyons. — London : Robson, 1977. — [9],213p ; 23cm.
Originally published: New York : Mason and Lipscomb, 1974.
ISBN 0-903895-98-6 : £3.50
(B77-13314)

Mac Liammóir, Michéal. Enter a goldfish : memoirs of an Irish actor, young and old / by Michéal Mac Liammóir. — London : Thames and Hudson, 1977. — 192p : music ; 24cm.
ISBN 0-500-01181-8 : £3.95
(B77-25908)

MacArthur, Catherine. It was the lark / [by] Catherine MacArthur. — London : Macdonald and Jane's, 1977. — [5],217p ; 21cm. — (A troubadour)
ISBN 0-354-04116-9 : £3.50
(B77-11411)

Macaulay, *Dame* Rose. Orphan island / [by] Rose Macaulay. — Large print ed. — Bath : Chivers, 1977. — ix,431p ; 23cm.
Originally published: London : Collins, 1924.
ISBN 0-85997-260-7 : £6.20(£4.65 to members of the Library Association)
(B77-34145)

McBain, Ed. The con man / [by] Ed McBain. — Harmondsworth [etc.] : Penguin, 1977. — 166p : ill ; 18cm. — (Penguin crime fiction)
'An 87th Precinct mystery' - cover. — Originally published: New York : Permabooks, 1957 ; London : Boardman, 1960.
ISBN 0-14-001971-5 Pbk : £0.60
(B77-24493)

McBain, Ed. Cop hater / [by] Ed McBain. — Harmondsworth [etc.] : Penguin, 1977. — 171p : ill ; 18cm. — (Penguin crime fiction)
'An 87th Precinct mystery' - cover. — Originally published: New York : Permabooks, 1956 ; London : Boardman, 1958.
ISBN 0-14-001968-5 Pbk : £0.60
(B77-24494)

McBain, Ed. Give the boys a great big hand / [by] Ed McBain. — Harmondsworth [etc.] : Penguin, 1977. — 170p : 1 ill ; 18cm. — (Penguin crime fiction)
'An 87th Precinct mystery' - cover. — Originally published: New York : Simon and Schuster, 1960 ; London : Boardman, 1962.
ISBN 0-14-002310-0 Pbk : £0.60
(B77-25909)

McBain, Ed. Give the boys a great big hand : an 87th Precinct mystery / by Ed McBain. — London : Hamilton, 1977. — [7],179p ; 21cm. — (A fingerprint book)
Originally published: New York : Simon and Schuster, 1960 ; London : Boardman, 1962.
ISBN 0-241-89720-3 : £3.95
(B77-28163)

McBain, Ed. Guns : a novel / by Ed McBain. — London : Hamilton, 1977. — [5],213p ; 21cm.
Originally published: New York : Random House, 1976.
ISBN 0-241-89509-x : £3.50
(B77-04410)

McBain, Ed. The heckler / [by] Ed McBain. — Harmondsworth [etc.] : Penguin, 1977. — 174, [1]p : ill, plan ; 18cm. — (Penguin crime fiction)
'An 87th Precinct mystery' - cover. — Originally published: New York : Simon and Schuster, 1960 ; London : Boardman, 1962.
ISBN 0-14-002393-3 Pbk : £0.60
(B77-25910)

McBain, Ed. Killer's choice : an 87th precinct mystery / by Ed McBain. — London : Hamilton, 1977. — [6],177p : facsims ; 21cm. — (A fingerprint book)
Originally published: New York : Permabooks, 1958 ; London : Boardman, 1960.
ISBN 0-241-89510-3 : £3.75
(B77-12687)

McBain, Ed. Killer's choice / [by] Ed McBain. — Harmondsworth [etc.] : Penguin, 1977. — 155p : facsims ; 19cm. — (Penguin crime fiction)
Originally published: New York : Permabooks, 1958 ; London : Boardman, 1960.
Pbk : £0.60
ISBN 0-14-001972-3
(B77-25911)

McBain, Ed. Lady killer / [by] Ed McBain. — Harmondsworth [etc.] : Penguin, 1977. — 172p : ill ; 18cm. — (Penguin crime fiction)
'An 87th Precinct mystery' - cover. — Originally published: New York : Permabooks, 1958 ; London : Boardman, 1961.
ISBN 0-14-002019-5 Pbk : £0.60
(B77-25912)

McBain, Ed. Long time no see : an 87th Precinct mystery / by Ed McBain. — London : Hamilton, 1977. — [7],274p : facsims ; 21cm.
Also published: New York : Random House, 1977.
ISBN 0-241-89654-1 : £3.95
(B77-25204)

McBain, Ed. The mugger / [by] Ed McBain. — Harmondsworth [etc.] : Penguin, 1977. — 158p : ill, map ; 18cm. — (Penguin crime fiction)
'An 87th Precinct mystery' - cover. — Originally published: New York : Permabooks, 1956 ; London : Boardman, 1959.
ISBN 0-14-001969-3 Pbk : £0.60
(B77-24495)

McBain, Ed. The pusher / [by] Ed McBain. — Harmondsworth [etc.] : Penguin, 1977. — 158p ; 19cm. — (Penguin crime fiction)
'An 87th Precinct mystery' - cover. — Originally published: New York : Permabooks, 1956 ; London : Boardman, 1959.
ISBN 0-14-001970-7 Pbk : £0.60
(B77-24496)

McBain, Ed. The third 87th Precinct omnibus / [by] Ed McBain. — London : Hamilton, 1977. — [6],393p : ill ; 23cm.
Contents: Shotgun. Originally published: Garden City, N.Y. : Doubleday, 1968 ; London : Hamilton, 1969 - Jigsaw. Originally published: Garden City, N.Y. : Doubleday ; London : Hamilton, 1970 - Hail, hail, the gang's all here. Originally published: Garden City, N.Y. : Doubleday ; London : Hamilton, 1971.
ISBN 0-241-89691-6 : £4.95
(B77-28932)

MacBeth, George. The survivor / [by] George MacBeth. — London [etc.] : Quartet Books, 1977. — [7],136p ; 23cm.
ISBN 0-7043-2125-4 : £4.95
(B77-22881)

MacBeth, George. The transformation / [by] George MacBeth. — London [etc.] : Quartet Books, 1977. — 96p ; 20cm.
Originally published: London : Gollancz, 1975.
ISBN 0-7043-3152-7 Pbk : £1.50
(B77-22161)

McBratney, Sam. A dip of the antlers / [by] Sam McBratney. — London : Abelard-Schuman, 1977. — 94p ; 23cm.
For adolescents.
ISBN 0-200-72526-2 : £3.25
(B77-26550)

McCabe, Eugene. Victims : a tale from Fermanagh / by Eugene McCabe. — London : Gollancz, 1976. — 128p ; 21cm.
ISBN 0-575-02169-1 : £3.20
(B77-10571)

McCaffrey, Anne. Dragonquest : being the further adventures of the Dragonriders of Pern / [by] Anne McCaffrey. — London : Sphere, 1976. — 304p : map ; 18cm. — (Sphere science fiction)
Originally published: New York : Ballantine Books, 1971 ; London : Rapp and Whiting : Deutsch, 1973.
ISBN 0-7221-5906-4 Pbk : £0.70
(B77-13315)

McCaffrey, Anne. Dragonsinger : science fiction / by Anne McCaffrey. — London : Sidgwick and Jackson, 1977. — [8],264p : map ; 20cm.
Also published: New York : Atheneum, 1977.
ISBN 0-283-98401-5 : £3.95
(B77-22882)

McCaffrey, Anne. The Kilternan legacy / [by] Anne McCaffrey. — London [etc.] : Millington, 1976. — 269p ; 23cm.
ISBN 0-86000-068-0 : £3.50
(B77-17114)

McCaffrey, Anne. To ride Pegasus / [by] Anne McCaffrey. — London : Sphere, 1977. — 224p ; 18cm. — (Sphere science fiction)
Originally published: New York : Bantam, 1973 ; London : Dent, 1974.
ISBN 0-7221-5908-0 Pbk : £0.85
(B77-32203)

McCarry, Charles. The secret lovers / [by] Charles McCarry. — London : Hutchinson, 1977. — 285p ; 23cm.
Also published: New York : Dutton, 1977.
ISBN 0-09-129450-9 : £3.95
(B77-28933)

McCarthy, Shaun Lloyd. Lucky Ham / [by] Shaun McCarthy. — London [etc.] : Macmillan, 1977. — [5],217p ; 21cm.
ISBN 0-333-22367-5 : £4.95
(B77-19728)

McCloy, Helen. Cruel as the grave / by Helen McCloy. — London : Gollancz, 1977. — [9], 182p ; 21cm. — ([Gollancz thriller])
Originally published: New York : Dodd, Mead, 1976.
ISBN 0-575-02175-6 : £3.75
(B77-07622)

McClure, James. Snake / [by] James McClure. — Harmondsworth [etc.] : Penguin, 1977. — 192p ; 19cm. — (Penguin crime fiction)
Originally published: London : Gollancz, 1975.
ISBN 0-14-004472-8 Pbk : £0.80
(B77-34146)

McClure, James. The Sunday hangman / [by] James McClure. — London [etc.] : Macmillan, 1977. — 255p ; 21cm.
ISBN 0-333-19829-8 : £3.50
(B77-22883)

MacColla, Fionn. And the cock crew / [by] Fionn MacColla. — London : Souvenir Press, 1977. — 191p ; 20cm.
Originally published: Glasgow : MacLellan, 1945.
ISBN 0-285-62280-3 : £3.00
ISBN 0-285-62290-0 Pbk : £1.60
(B77-20635)

McCullers, Carson. Clock without hands / [by] Carson McCullers. — Harmondsworth [etc.] : Penguin, 1977. — 208p ; 19cm.
Originally published: Boston, Mass. : Houghton Mifflin ; London : Cresset Press, 1961.
ISBN 0-14-002317-8 Pbk : £0.70
(B77-33433)

McCullers, Carson. Reflections in a golden eye / [by] Carson McCullers. — Harmondsworth [etc.] : Penguin, 1977. — 125p ; 19cm.
Originally published: Boston, Mass. : Houghton Mifflin, 1941 ; London : Cresset Press, 1942.
ISBN 0-14-002692-4 Pbk : £0.55
(B77-33434)

McCullough, Colleen. The thorn birds / [by] Colleen McCullough. — London : Raven Books, 1977. — [9],533p ; 22cm.
Also published: New York : Harper and Row, 1977.
ISBN 0-354-04231-9 : £4.95
(B77-28934)

McCutchan, Philip. Beware the Bight of Benin / [by] Philip McCutchan. — London : Futura Publications, 1976. — 192p ; 18cm. — (A contact book)
Originally published: as 'Beware, beware the Bight of Benin'. London : Barker, 1974.
ISBN 0-86007-282-7 Pbk : £0.60
(B77-09293)

McCutchan, Philip. Call for Simon Shard / [by] Philip McCutchan. — Large print ed. — Leicester : Ulverscroft, 1976. — [4],326p ; 23cm. — (Ulverscroft large print series : [mystery])
Originally published: London : Harrap, 1974.
ISBN 0-85456-499-3 : £2.65
(B77-08077)

McCutchan, Philip. Coach north / by Philip McCutchan. — Large print ed. — Leicester : Ulverscroft, 1977. — [4],355p ; 23cm. — (Ulverscroft large print series : [mystery])
Originally published: London : Harrap, 1974.
ISBN 0-85456-535-3 : £2.95
(B77-20636)

McCutchan, Philip. The dead line / [by] Philip McCutchan. — London : Severn House : [Distributed by Hutchinson], 1977. — 176p ; 21cm.
Originally published: London : Harrap, 1966.
ISBN 0-7278-0276-3 : £3.25
(B77-19729)

McCutchan, Philip. The Eros affair : a 'Simon Shard' novel / by Philip McCutchan. — London [etc.] : Hodder and Stoughton, 1977. — 191p ; 21cm.
ISBN 0-340-21480-5 : £3.75
(B77-22884)

McCutchan, Philip. Halfhyde to the narrows / [by] Philip McCutchan. — London : Weidenfeld and Nicolson, 1977. — [4],180p ; 23cm.
ISBN 0-297-77321-6 : £3.95
(B77-19730)

McDonald, Eva. Cry treason thrice / [by] Eva McDonald. — London : Hale, 1977. — 204p ; 21cm.
ISBN 0-7091-5747-9 : £3.70
(B77-27399)

McDonald, Eva. The lady from Yorktown / [by] Eva McDonald. — Large print ed. — Leicester : Ulverscroft, 1977. — [7],303p ; 23cm. — (Ulverscroft large print series : [historical romance])
Originally published: London : Hale, 1972.
ISBN 0-7089-0002-x : £2.95
(B77-32205)

McDonald, Eva. Norman knight / [by] Eva McDonald. — London : Hale, 1977. — 156p ; 21cm.
ISBN 0-7091-5515-8 : £3.25
(B77-12118)

McDonald, Eva. The road to Glencoe / [by] Eva McDonald. — London : Hale, 1977. — 157p ; 21cm.
ISBN 0-7091-5322-8 : £3.50
(B77-20637)

Mcdonald, Gregory. Confess, Fletch : a novel / by Gregory Mcdonald. — London : Gollancz, 1977. — 192p ; 21cm. — ([Gollancz thriller])
Originally published: New York : Avon Books, 1976.
ISBN 0-575-02346-5 : £4.25
(B77-23738)

Mcdonald, Gregory. Fletch / [by] Gregory Mcdonald. — Large print [ed.]. — London : Prior [etc.], 1976. — [5],380p ; 24cm.
Originally published: Indianapolis : Bobbs-Merrill, 1974.
ISBN 0-86043-015-4 : £4.95
(B77-07623)

McDonald, Gregory. Running scared / by Gregory McDonald. — London : Gollancz, 1977. — [5],214p ; 21cm. — ([Gollancz thriller])
Originally published: New York : Obolensky, 1964.
ISBN 0-575-02204-3 : £3.80
(B77-08078)

MacDonald, John Christopher. Just keep dancin / [by] John Christopher MacDonald. — Ontario : Press Porcepic ; Ontario [etc.] ; London (1 Bedford Rd, N.2) : Distributed by Books Canada Ltd, 1975 [i.e. 1977]. — 173p : ill ; 22cm.
Published in Canada: 1975.
ISBN 0-88878-057-5 : £5.95
(B77-09294)

MacDonald, John Dann. Condominium : a novel / by John D. MacDonald. — London : Hale, 1977. — 447p ; 23cm.
Also published: Philadelphia : Lippincott, 1977.
ISBN 0-7091-6464-5 : £4.60
(B77-28164)

MacDonald, John Dann. The girl in the plain brown wrapper / [by] John D. MacDonald. — London [etc.] : Pan Books, 1977. — 219p ; 18cm.
'Travis McGee in "The girl in the plain brown wrapper"' - cover. — Originally published: Greenwich, Conn. : Fawcett, 1968 ; London : Hale, 1969.
Pbk : £0.60
ISBN 0-330-02888-x
(B77-26551)

MacDonald, John Dann. The long lavender look / [by] John D. MacDonald. — London [etc.] : Pan Books, 1977. — 223p ; 18cm.
'Travis McGee in "The long lavender look"' - cover. — Originally published: London : Fawcett, 1970.
Pbk : £0.60
ISBN 0-330-23623-7
(B77-26552)

MacDonald, John Dann. Murder for the bride / [by] John D. MacDonald. — London : Hale, 1977. — 174p ; 20cm.
Originally published: New York : Fawcett Publications, 1951 ; London : Muller, 1954.
ISBN 0-7091-4505-5 : £3.25
(B77-05680)

MacDonald, John Dann. Nightmare in pink / [by] John D. MacDonald. — Large print [ed.]. — London : Prior [etc.], 1976. — [7],310p ; 24cm.
Originally published: Philadelphia : Lippincott, 1964 ; London : Hale, 1966.
ISBN 0-86043-017-0 : £4.95
(B77-07624)

Macdonald, Malcolm, *b.1932.* The rich are with you always / [by] Malcolm Macdonald. — Sevenoaks : Hodder and Stoughton, 1977. — [6],483p : ill ; 22cm.
Originally published: New York : Knopf, 1976.
ISBN 0-340-20708-6 : £5.25
(B77-13893)

MacDonald, Philip. The rasp / [by] Philip MacDonald. — Large print ed. — Bath : Lythway Press, 1977. — xi,369p ; 23cm. — (Lythway classics of crime and detection)
Originally published: London : Collins, 1924.
ISBN 0-85046-718-7 : £4.85
(B77-31483)

Macdonald, Ross, *b.1915.* The blue hammer / [by] Ross Macdonald. — Large print [ed.]. — London : Prior [etc.], 1977. — [4],524p ; 24cm.
Originally published: New York : Knopf ; London : Collins, 1976.
ISBN 0-86043-044-8 : £5.95
(B77-22162)

Macdonald, Ross, *b.1915.* The far side of the dollar / [by] Ross Macdonald. — [London] : Fontana, 1977. — 256p ; 18cm.
Originally published: New York : Knopf ; London : Collins, 1965.
ISBN 0-00-614531-0 Pbk : £0.70
(B77-13316)

Macdonald, Ross, *b.1915.* The way some people die / [by] Ross Macdonald. — London : Severn House : [Distributed by Hutchinson], 1977. — 192p ; 21cm.
Originally published: New York : Knopf, 1951 ; London : Cassell, 1953.
ISBN 0-7278-0197-x : £3.25
(B77-04411)

Macdonald, Shelagh. No end to yesterday / [by] Shelagh Macdonald. — London : Deutsch, 1977. — 216p ; 21cm.
ISBN 0-233-96865-2 : £3.25
(B77-13894)

McDougall, Donald. Davie / [by] Donald McDougall. — London [etc.] : Macmillan, 1977. — 254p ; 23cm.
ISBN 0-333-22316-0 : £3.95
(B77-27400)

MacDougall, Ruth Doan. The cheerleader / [by] Ruth Doan MacDougall. — Toronto [etc.] ; London : Bantam, 1976. — [5],276,[1]p ; 18cm.
Originally published: New York : Putnam, 1973. — For adolescents.
ISBN 0-552-62633-3 Pbk : £0.60
(B77-02597)

McGahern, John. The barracks / [by] John McGahern. — London [etc.] : Quartet Books, 1977. — 191p ; 19cm.
Originally published: London : Faber, 1963.
ISBN 0-7043-3171-3 Pbk : £1.00
(B77-28935)

McGahern, John. The leavetaking / [by] John McGahern. — London : Quartet Books, 1977. — [1],195p ; 18cm.
Originally published: London : Faber, 1974.
ISBN 0-7043-3125-x Pbk : £0.95
(B77-12688)

MacGibbon, Jean. After the raft race / [by] Jean MacGibbon. — London : Heinemann, 1976. — 95p ; 21cm. — (Pyramid books)
For adolescents.
ISBN 0-434-95816-6 : £2.10
(B77-00981)

McGill, Gordon. Arthur / [by] Gordon McGill. — London : Sphere, 1976. — 189p ; 18cm.
Originally published: London : Joseph, 1974.
ISBN 0-7221-5918-8 Pbk : £0.60
(B77-15518)

McGill, Gordon. Superstud / [by] Gordon McGill. — London : Sphere, 1977. — 173p ; 18cm.
ISBN 0-7221-5942-0 Pbk : £0.65
(B77-21473)

McIlvanney, William. Laidlaw / by William McIlvanney. — London [etc.] : Hodder and Stoughton, 1977. — 224p ; 23cm.
ISBN 0-340-20727-2 : £3.95
(B77-20638)

MacInnes, Hamish. Death reel / [by] Hamish MacInnes. — London [etc.] : Hodder and Stoughton, 1976. — 192p ; 21cm.
ISBN 0-340-20725-6 : £3.40
(B77-13317)

MacInnes, Helen. Agent in place / [by] Helen MacInnes. — Large print [ed.]. — London : Prior [etc.], 1977. — 2v.([13],649p) ; 24cm.
Originally published: in 1 vol. London : Collins, 1976.
ISBN 0-86043-035-9 : £7.50
(B77-12119)

MacInnes, Helen. Assignment in Brittany / [by] Helen MacInnes. — [London] : Fontana, 1977. — 318p ; 18cm.
Originally published: Boston, Mass. : Little, Brown ; London : Harrap, 1942.
ISBN 0-00-614997-9 Pbk : £0.75
(B77-19007)

MacInnes, Helen. Decision at Delphi / [by] Helen MacInnes. — [London] : Fontana, 1977. — 444p : map ; 18cm.
Originally published: New York : Harcourt, Brace, 1960 ; London : Collins, 1961.
ISBN 0-00-614427-6 Pbk : £0.85
(B77-19008)

MacInnes, Helen. The double image / [by] Helen MacInnes. — [London] : Fontana, 1977. — 317p : map ; 18cm.
Originally published: New York : Harcourt, Brace and World ; London : Collins, 1966.
ISBN 0-00-614998-7 Pbk : £0.75
(B77-19009)

MacInnes, Helen. I and my true love / [by] Helen MacInnes. — [London] : Fontana, 1977. — 287p ; 18cm.
Originally published: New York : Harcourt, Brace ; London : Collins, 1953.
ISBN 0-00-614481-0 Pbk : £0.75
(B77-19010)

MacInnes, Helen. The snare of the hunter / [by] Helen MacInnes. — [London] : Fontana, 1976. — 252p : map ; 18cm.
Originally published: London : Collins, 1974.
ISBN 0-00-614414-4 Pbk : £0.70
(B77-12120)

MacInnes, Helen. The Venetian affair / [by] Helen MacInnes. — London : Collins, 1977. — 382p ; 21cm.
Originally published: New York : Harcourt, Brace and World, 1963 ; London : Collins, 1964.
ISBN 0-00-221876-3 : £3.25
(B77-23739)

McIntosh, J.T. Norman conquest 2066 / [by] J.T. McIntosh. — London : Corgi, 1977. — 156p ; 18cm.
ISBN 0-552-10484-1 Pbk : £0.70
(B77-26553)

McIntosh, J.T. This is the way the world begins / [by] J.T. McIntosh. — London : Corgi, 1977. — 205p ; 18cm.
ISBN 0-552-10432-9 Pbk : £0.70
(B77-19011)

McIntyre, Vonda N. The exile waiting / by Vonda N. McIntyre. — London : Gollancz, 1976. — 255p ; 21cm. — ([Gollancz SF])
Originally published: Garden City, N.Y. : Doubleday, 1975.
ISBN 0-575-02189-6 : £3.95
(B77-10572)

Macken, Walter. I am alone / [by] Walter Macken. — London : Pan Books, 1977. — 252p ; 18cm.
Originally published: London : Macmillan, 1949.
ISBN 0-330-25027-2 Pbk : £0.75
(B77-12689)

Mackenzie, Donald. Raven and the kamikaze / [by] Donald Mackenzie. — London [etc.] : Macmillan, 1977. — 192p ; 21cm.
ISBN 0-333-21974-0 : £3.50
(B77-27401)

MacKenzie, Donald. Raven and the Ratcatcher / [by] Donald MacKenzie. — London [etc.] : Macmillan, 1977. — 192p ; 21cm.
ISBN 0-333-21162-6 : £3.25
(B77-12121)

Mackenzie, Joan. No halo for Mimosa / by Joan Mackenzie. — London : Hale, 1977. — 157p ; 20cm.
ISBN 0-7091-5920-x : £3.10
(B77-14414)

Mackenzie, Lee. Emmerdale Farm : the legacy / [by] Lee Mackenzie. — London : Wingate, 1977. — 144p ; 21cm.
'Based on the successful Yorkshire Television series originated by Kevin Laffan'.
ISBN 0-85523-351-6 : £2.95
(B77-17115)

Mackenzie, *Sir* Compton. Hunting the fairies / [by] Compton Mackenzie. — Harmondsworth [etc.] : Penguin, 1977. — 313p ; 19cm.
Originally published: London : Chatto and Windus, 1949.
ISBN 0-14-001365-2 Pbk : £0.85
(B77-21474)

Mackenzie, *Sir* Compton. The Monarch of the Glen / [by] Compton Mackenzie. — Harmondsworth [etc.] : Penguin, 1977. — 315p ; 19cm.
Originally published: London : Chatto and Windus, 1941.
ISBN 0-14-001366-0 Pbk : £0.85
(B77-20639)

Mackenzie, *Sir* Compton. Thin ice / [by] Compton Mackenzie. — Harmondsworth [etc.] : Penguin, 1977. — 191p ; 19cm.
Originally published: London : Chatto and Windus, 1956.
ISBN 0-14-001369-5 Pbk : £0.70
(B77-20640)

Mackenzie, *Sir* Compton. Water on the brain / [by] Compton Mackenzie. — Harmondsworth [etc.] : Penguin, 1977. — 301p ; 19cm.
Originally published: London : Cassell, 1933.
ISBN 0-14-001368-7 Pbk : £0.85
(B77-20641)

Mackenzie, *Sir* Compton. Whisky galore / [by] Compton Mackenzie. — Harmondsworth [etc.] : Penguin, 1977. — 304p ; 18cm.
Originally published: London : Chatto and Windus, 1947.
ISBN 0-14-001220-6 Pbk : £0.75
(B77-20642)

Mackie, Charles. The wolf / [by] Charles Mackie. — London : Hale, 1977. — 175p : geneal table ; 21cm.
Based on the life of Sir Philip Hogeston.
ISBN 0-7091-5777-0 : £3.25
(B77-12690)

Mackie, Mary. Pamela / by Mary Mackie. — London : Hale, 1977. — 159p ; 20cm.
ISBN 0-7091-6079-8 : £3.40
(B77-30667)

Mackie, Mary. The unquiet summer / by Mary Mackie. — London : Hale, 1977. — 192p ; 20cm.
ISBN 0-7091-5789-4 : £3.10
(B77-13318)

Mackie, Mary. A voice in the fog / by Mary Mackie. — London : Hale, 1977. — 189p ; 20cm.
ISBN 0-7091-5938-2 : £3.20
(B77-20643)

McKie, Ronald. The crushing / [by] Ronald McKie. — Sydney ; London : Collins, 1977. — [4],252p ; 22cm.
ISBN 0-00-221591-8 : £3.95
(B77-10950)

Mackinlay, Leila. Strange involvement / [by] Leila Mackinlay. — Large print ed. — Bath : Lythway Press, 1977. — [5],241p ; 23cm.
Originally published: London : Hale, 1972.
ISBN 0-85046-749-7 : £4.40
(B77-33435)

MacKinnon, Charles. Farthingale's Folly : a novel / by Charles MacKinnon. — London : Muller, 1977. — [9],262p ; 23cm.
ISBN 0-584-31031-5 : £4.25
(B77-13319)

MacKinnon, Charles. The matriarch / [by] Charles MacKinnon. — London : Muller, 1976. — [9],362p ; 23cm.
Originally published: New York : Delacorte Press, 1975.
ISBN 0-584-31071-4 : £4.25
(B77-03764)

MacKintosh, Ian. HMS Hero / [by] Ian MacKintosh. — London : Futura Publications, 1976. — 158p ; 18cm. — (A contact book)
Spine title: Warship, HMS Hero. — Based on the BBC TV series 'Warship'. — Also published: London : Barker, 1976.
ISBN 0-86007-291-6 Pbk : £0.50
(B77-08589)

MacKintosh, Ian. Holt RN / [by] Ian MacKintosh. — London : Barker, 1977. — 142p ; 23cm.
'Based on the BBC TV series "Warship"'.
ISBN 0-213-16630-5 : £3.65
(B77-13320)

McKnight, Ivy. The Brady tree / by Ivy McKnight. — London : Hale, 1977. — 156p ; 20cm.
ISBN 0-7091-6238-3 : £3.20
(B77-30668)

McLachlan, Ian. The seventh hexagram : a novel / by Ian McLachlan. — London [etc.] : Hodder and Stoughton, 1977. — [9],278p ; 22cm.
Originally published: New York : Dial Press, 1976.
ISBN 0-340-21850-9 : £3.95
(B77-30669)

McLaglen, John J. The black widow / [by] John J. McLaglen. — London : Corgi, 1977. — 126p ; 18cm. — (McLaglen, John J. Herne the hunter ; 3)
ISBN 0-552-10385-3 Pbk : £0.50
(B77-10951)

McLaglen, John J. River of blood / [by] John J. McLaglen. — London : Corgi, 1976. — 141p ; 18cm. — (McLaglen, John J. Herne the hunter ; 2)
ISBN 0-552-10310-1 Pbk : £0.50
(B77-02598)

McLaglen, John J. Shadow of the vulture / [by] John J. McLaglen. — London : Corgi, 1977. — 126p ; 18cm. — (McLaglen, John J. Herne the hunter ; 4)
ISBN 0-552-10431-0 Pbk : £0.50
(B77-34147)

Maclaren, Deanna. The first of all pleasures / [by] Deanna Maclaren. — London : Sphere, 1977. — 191p ; 18cm.
Originally published: London : Gollancz, 1975.
ISBN 0-7221-5701-0 Pbk : £0.65
(B77-12691)

McLaughlin, Dean. Hawk among the sparrows : three science fiction novels / [by] Dean McLaughlin. — London : Hale, 1977. — [7], 198p ; 23cm. — (Hale SF)
'The stories in this book were first published in "Astounding science fiction" and/or its successor, "Analog science fiction - science fact"' - title page verso.
ISBN 0-7091-6263-4 : £3.80
(B77-34148)

McLaughlin, William Raffan Davidson. Antarctic raider / [by] W.R.D. McLaughlin. — St Albans : Mayflower, 1977. — 223p ; 18cm.
Originally published: London : Harrap, 1960.
ISBN 0-583-12640-5 Pbk : £0.65
(B77-13321)

McLaughlin, William Raffan Davidson. So thin is the line / [by] W.R.D. McLaughlin. — St Albans : Mayflower, 1977. — 156p ; 18cm.
Originally published: London : Harrap, 1963.
ISBN 0-583-12639-1 Pbk : £0.60
(B77-14933)

MacLean, Alistair. Circus / [by] Alistair MacLean. — [London] : Fontana, 1977. — 191p : plan ; 18cm.
Originally published: London : Collins, 1975.
ISBN 0-00-614889-1 Pbk : £0.70
(B77-15519)

MacLean, Alistair. The golden gate / [by] Alistair MacLean. — Large print ed. — Leicester : Ulverscroft, 1977. — [5],452p ; 23cm. — (Ulverscroft large print series : [adventure, suspense])
Originally published: London : Collins, 1976.
ISBN 0-7089-0003-8 : Unpriced
(B77-32206)

MacLean, Alistair. Goodbye California / [by] Alistair MacLean. — London : Collins, 1977. — 318p ; 22cm.
ISBN 0-00-222275-2 : £4.25
(B77-27402)

MacLean, Alistair. Ice Station Zebra / [by] Alistair MacLean. — [London] : Fontana, 1977. — 254p : plans ; 18cm.
Originally published: London : Collins, 1963.
ISBN 0-00-614421-7 Pbk : £0.70
(B77-15520)

MacLean, Alistair. Seawitch / [by] Alistair MacLean. — London : Collins, 1977. — 221p ; 22cm.
ISBN 0-00-222468-2 : £3.50
(B77-05072)

MacLean, Alistair. Where eagles dare / [by] Alistair MacLean. — London : Collins, 1976. — 256p ; 21cm.
Originally published: 1967.
ISBN 0-00-221924-7 : £2.50
(B77-14934)

Maclean, Charles. The pathetic phallus : a novel / by Charles Maclean. — London : London Magazine Editions, 1977. — 180p ; 23cm.
ISBN 0-904388-25-5 : £4.75
(B77-17116)

McLendon, James. Deathwork : a novel / by James McLendon. — London : Hamilton, 1978. — 5-327p ; 21cm.
Originally published: Philadelphia : Lippincott, 1977.
ISBN 0-241-89815-3 : £4.50 : CIP rev.
(B77-29722)

MacLeod, Robert, *b.1928.* A pay-off in Switzerland / [by] Robert MacLeod. — London : Long, 1977. — 183p ; 20cm.
ISBN 0-09-129300-6 : £3.50
(B77-28165)

MacLeod, Robert, *b.1928.* A witchdance in Bavaria / [by] Robert MacLeod. — Large print ed. — Leicester : Ulverscroft, 1977. — [7], 270p ; 23cm. — (Ulverscroft large print series : [mystery])
Originally published: London : Long, 1975.
ISBN 0-7089-0010-0 : £2.95
(B77-22885)

MacLeod, Sheila. Xanthe and the robots / [by] Sheila MacLeod. — London [etc.] : Bodley Head, 1977. — 248p ; 21cm.
ISBN 0-370-30014-9 : £4.95
(B77-17752)

McManus, Leslie. The Viking maiden : a Churchill's Vixens novel / by Leslie McManus. — London [etc.] : Mews Books ; London : Distributed by New English Library, 1977. — 112p ; 18cm. — (McManus, Leslie. Churchill's Vixens novels ; no.4)
ISBN 0-452-00039-4 Pbk : £0.55
(B77-12122)

McMaster, Mary. Star Island / by Mary McMaster. — London : Hale, 1976. — 184p ; 20cm.
ISBN 0-7091-5687-1 : £2.95
(B77-11412)

McMaster, Mary. To him who waits / by Mary McMaster. — London : Hale, 1977. — [4], 188p ; 20cm.
ISBN 0-7091-6027-5 : £3.20
(B77-19731)

McMenemy, Nickie. Zulu! / [by] Nickie McMenemy. — St Albans : Mayflower, 1977. — [5],216p ; 18cm.
Originally published: as 'Assegai!'. London : Macmillan, 1973.
Pbk : £0.75
ISBN 0-583-12386-4
(B77-28166)

McMullen, Mary. A country kind of death / [by] Mary McMullen. — London : Hale, 1976. — [7],178p ; 20cm.
Originally published: Garden City, N.Y. : Doubleday, 1975.
ISBN 0-7091-5681-2 : £2.95
(B77-01818)

McMullen, Mary. The Pimlico plot / [by] Mary McMullen. — London : Hale, 1977. — 3-192p ; 20cm.
Originally published: Garden City, N.Y. : Doubleday, 1975.
ISBN 0-7091-6096-8 : £3.15
(B77-15521)

McMurtry, Larry. Terms of endearment : a novel / by Larry McMurtry. — London : W.H. Allen, 1977. — 410p ; 23cm.
Originally published: New York : Simon and Schuster, 1975.
ISBN 0-491-01858-4 : £4.95
(B77-14415)

MacNaughton, David. Dido : a love story / by David MacNaughton. — London : Collins, 1977. — 222p : map ; 22cm.
ISBN 0-00-222158-6 : £3.95
(B77-25913)

McNear, Robert. Carpet of death / [by] Robert McNear. — London : Hale, 1976. — 189p ; 20cm.
ISBN 0-7091-5819-x : £2.95
(B77-00435)

MacNeil, Duncan. By command of the Viceroy : an 'Ogilvie' novel / [by] Duncan Macneil. — London : Corgi, 1977. — 207p ; 18cm.
Originally published: London : Hodder and Stoughton, 1975.
ISBN 0-552-10453-1 Pbk : £0.65
(B77-32207)

MacNeil, Duncan. Wolf in the fold / by Duncan MacNeil. — London [etc.] : Hodder and Stoughton, 1977. — 190p ; 20cm.
ISBN 0-340-21738-3 : £3.75
(B77-32860)

Maconochie, Kathleen. The little house / by Kathleen Maconochie. — London : Hale, 1977. — 190p ; 20cm.
ISBN 0-7091-5986-2 : £3.10
(B77-16606)

McVean, James. Bloodspoor / [by] James McVean. — London : Raven Books, 1977. — [5],279p ; 23cm. — (Raven books)
ISBN 0-354-04160-6 : £4.75
(B77-23740)

Madariaga, Salvador de. The heart of jade / [by] Salvador de Madariaga. — [London] : Fontana, 1977. — 511p ; 18cm.
Originally published: London : Collins, 1944.
ISBN 0-00-614676-7 Pbk : £0.95
(B77-05073)

Madison, Hank. Blood on the saddle / by Hank Madison. — London : Hale, 1976. — 154p ; 20cm.
ISBN 0-7091-5838-6 : £2.70
(B77-01819)

Magee, Bryan. Facing death : a novel / by Bryan Magee. — London : Kimber, 1977. — 447p ; 23cm.
ISBN 0-7183-0135-8 : £4.95
(B77-22163)

Magowan, Ronald. No flowers on my grave / by Ronald Magowan. — London : Hale, 1977. — 189p ; 20cm.
ISBN 0-7091-6053-4 : £3.15
(B77-13322)

Maguire, Conn. The reefs of Eden / [by] Conn Maguire. — London : New English Library, 1977. — 254p : map ; 19cm.
Originally published: New York : Pyramid, 1969 ; London : New English Library, 1970.
ISBN 0-450-03378-3 Pbk : £0.95
(B77-22886)

Maimane, Arthur. Victims : a novel / by Arthur Maimane. — London : Allison and Busby, 1976. — 231p ; 23cm.
ISBN 0-85031-162-4 : £3.95
(B77-01820)

Maine, Charles Eric. The mind of Mr Soames / [by] Charles Eric Maine. — [1st ed. reprinted] ; [with an] introduction by Harry Harrison. — London : New English Library, 1977. — 223p ; 18cm. — (SF master series)
Originally published: London : Hodder and Stoughton, 1961.
ISBN 0-450-03005-9 Pbk : £0.95
(B77-22887)

Maine, Charles Eric. Thirst! / [by] Charles Eric Maine. — Revised [ed.]. — London : Sphere, 1977. — 187p ; 18cm.
Previous ed.: published as 'The tide went out'. London : Hodder and Stoughton, 1958.
ISBN 0-7221-5720-7 Pbk : £0.65
(B77-13323)

Malcolm, Margaret. Flight to fantasy / by Margaret Malcolm. — London : Mills and Boon, 1976. — 186p ; 19cm.
ISBN 0-263-09033-7 : £1.95
(B77-09958)

Maling, Arthur. Ripoff / by Arthur Maling. — London : Hale, 1977. — 187p ; 20cm.
Originally published: New York : Harper and Row, 1976.
ISBN 0-7091-6353-3 : £3.50
(B77-30670)

Maling, Arthur. Ripoff / [by] Arthur Maling. — Large print [ed.]. — London : Prior [etc.], 1977. — [5],426p ; 25cm.
Originally published: New York : Harper and Row, 1976.
ISBN 0-86043-049-9 : £5.95
(B77-33436)

Maling, Arthur. Schroeder's game / by Arthur Maling. — London : Gollancz, 1977. — [4], 204p ; 21cm. — ([Gollancz thriller])
Also published: New York : Harper and Row, 1977.
ISBN 0-575-02316-3 : £3.95
(B77-21475)

Mallin, Tom. Lobe / [by] Tom Mallin. — London : Allison and Busby, 1977. — 272p ; 23cm.
ISBN 0-85031-202-7 : £4.50
ISBN 0-85031-203-5 Pbk : £1.95
(B77-31484)

Malloch, Peter. The big deal / [by] Peter Malloch. — London : Long, 1977. — 184p ; 20cm.
ISBN 0-09-128300-0 : £3.25
(B77-09959)

Mann, Deborah. Pilate's wife / [by] Deborah Mann. — London : Corgi, 1976. — 125p ; 18cm. — (A Corgi romance)
ISBN 0-552-10159-1 Pbk : £0.45
(B77-05681)

Manning, Frederic. The middle parts of fortune : Somme & Ancre, 1916 / [by] Frederic Manning ; introduction by Michael Howard. — London : P. Davies, 1977. — viii,247p ; 23cm.
Originally published: anonymously in a limited ed. London : Piazza Press, 1929.
ISBN 0-432-09081-9 : £4.50
(B77-22888)

Manning, Marsha. Day of roses / by Marsha Manning. — London : Mills and Boon, 1976. — 187p ; 19cm.
ISBN 0-263-09019-1 : £1.95
(B77-09960)

Manning, Olivia. The danger tree : a novel / by Olivia Manning. — London : Weidenfeld and Nicolson, 1977. — 196p ; 23cm.
ISBN 0-297-77296-1 : £4.25
(B77-22164)

Manning, Olivia. The rain forest / [by] Olivia Manning. — Harmondsworth [etc.] : Penguin, 1977. — 269p ; 18cm.
Originally published: London : Heinemann, 1974.
ISBN 0-14-004176-1 Pbk : £0.90
(B77-14935)

Manning, Val. Queen of the dragon ships / [by] Val Manning. — London : Hale, 1977. — 207p ; 21cm.
Bibl.: p.207.
ISBN 0-7091-6132-8 : £3.70
(B77-26555)

Mannion, Michael. Death cloud / [by] Michael Mannion. — London : New English Library, 1977. — 160p ; 18cm.
Originally published: New York : Belmont-Tower, 1976.
ISBN 0-450-03404-6 Pbk : £0.70
(B77-31485)

Manville, William Henry. Good-bye / [by] W.H. Manville. — London : Hamilton, 1977. — 316p : 2 facsims ; 21cm.
Also published: New York : Simon and Schuster, 1977.
ISBN 0-241-89741-6 : £3.95
(B77-27403)

Marchant, Catherine. The fen tiger / [by] Catherine Marchant, a pseudonym for Catherine Cookson. — Large print ed. — Bath : Chivers, 1977. — [5],313p ; 22cm.
Originally published: London : Macdonald & Co., 1963.
ISBN 0-85997-236-4 : £5.60(£4.20 to members of the Library Association)
(B77-21476)

Marchant, Catherine. Heritage of folly / [by] Catherine Marchant, a pseudonym for Catherine Cookson. — Large print ed. — Bath : Chivers, 1977. — [5],337p ; 22cm.
Originally published: London : Macdonald and Co., 1962.
ISBN 0-85997-225-9 : £5.60(£4.20 to members of the Library Association)
(B77-13895)

Marchant, Catherine. House of men / [by] Catherine Marchant, a pseudonym for Catherine Cookson. — Large print ed. — Bath : Chivers, 1977. — [5],326p ; 22cm.
Originally published: London : Macdonald, 1963.
ISBN 0-85997-206-2 : £5.60(£4.20 to members of the Library Association)
(B77-09961)

Marchant, Catherine. The iron façade / [by] Catherine Marchant. — London : Heinemann, 1976. — [4],183p ; 23cm.
Originally published: as 'Evil at Rogers Cross' United States : s.n., 1965.
ISBN 0-434-45032-4 : £3.50
(B77-09295)

Marchant, Catherine. Miss Mary Martha [i.e. Martha Mary] Crawford / [by] Catherine Marchant. — London : Corgi, 1976. — 319p ; 18cm.
Originally published: London : Heinemann, 1975.
ISBN 0-552-10321-7 Pbk : £0.75
(B77-05074)

Marchant, Catherine. The slow awakening / [by] Catherine Marchant. — London : Corgi, 1977. — 316p ; 18cm.
Originally published: London : Heinemann, 1976.
ISBN 0-552-10541-4 Pbk : £0.85
(B77-28168)

Mariner, David. The Beaufort dossier / [by] David Mariner. — London : Futura Publications, 1976. — 206p ; 18cm.
Originally published: London : Hale, 1973.
ISBN 0-86007-261-4 Pbk : £0.60
(B77-12123)

Mariner, David. Castle of the dead / [by] David Mariner. — London : Hale, 1977. — 224p ; 21cm.
ISBN 0-7091-5997-8 : £3.60
(B77-19732)

Mariner, David. The seventy minute fuse / [by] David Mariner. — London : Futura Publications, 1976. — 190p ; 18cm.
Originally published: as 'A white lie and no glory'. London : Hale, 1971.
ISBN 0-86007-356-4 Pbk : £0.60
(B77-12124)

Markandaya, Kamala. The golden honeycomb : a novel / by Kamala Markandaya. — London : Chatto and Windus, 1977. — x,469p ; 23cm.
ISBN 0-7011-2209-9 : £4.95 : CIP rev.
(B77-06296)

Markstein, George. Chance awakening / by George Markstein. — London : Souvenir Press, 1977. — 251p ; 21cm.
ISBN 0-285-62281-1 : £3.50
(B77-17753)

Markstein, George. The man from yesterday / [by] George Markstein. — London [etc.] : Pan Books, 1977. — 236p ; 18cm.
Originally published: London : Souvenir Press, 1976.
ISBN 0-330-25222-4 Pbk : £0.75
(B77-31486)

Marlowe, Derek. Do you remember England? / [by] Derek Marlowe. — Harmondsworth [etc.] : Penguin, 1977. — 187p ; 18cm.
Originally published: London : Cape, 1972.
ISBN 0-14-004443-4 Pbk : £0.75
(B77-27404)

Marlowe, Derek. Nightshade / [by] Derek Marlowe. — Harmondsworth [etc.] : Penguin, 1977. — 185p ; 18cm.
Originally published: London : Weidenfeld and Nicolson, 1975.
ISBN 0-14-004444-2 Pbk : £0.75
(B77-27405)

Marlowe, Derek. Somebody's sister / [by] Derek Marlowe. — Harmondsworth [etc.] : Penguin, 1977. — 154p ; 19cm.
Originally published: London : Cape, 1974.
ISBN 0-14-004442-6 Pbk : £0.70
(B77-27406)

Marlowe, Stephen. Too many chiefs / [by] Stephen Marlowe. — London : New English Library, 1977. — 284p ; 18cm.
Originally published: as 'The Cawthorn journals'. Englewood Cliffs : Prentice-Hall, 1975 ; London : W.H. Allen, 1976.
ISBN 0-450-03290-6 Pbk : £1.25
(B77-23741)

Marlowe, Stephen. Translation : a novel / by Stephen Marlowe. — London : W.H. Allen, 1977. — [6],246p ; 24cm.
Originally published: Englewood Cliffs ; London : Prentice-Hall, 1976.
ISBN 0-491-02370-7 : £4.95
(B77-24497)

Marquis, Max. The care takers / [by] Max Marquis. — London : Everest, 1976. — 286p ; 18cm. — (Marquis, Max. General hospital ; no.1)
'Based on the TV hit' - cover. — Originally published: as 'General hospital, the care takers'. London : Barker, 1975.
ISBN 0-905018-06-0 Pbk : £0.60
(B77-06297)

Marquis, Max. General hospital, a matter of life / [by] Max Marquis. — London : Barker, 1977. — 205p ; 23cm.
'Based on the TV hit' - jacket. — Also published: London : Everest, 1977.
ISBN 0-213-16618-6 : £3.65
(B77-06298)

Marric, J.J. Gideon's fog / [by] John Creasey writing as J.J. Marric. — Sevenoaks : Coronet, 1977. — 192p ; 18cm.
Originally published: London : Hodder and Stoughton, 1975.
ISBN 0-340-21233-0 Pbk : £0.60
(B77-09296)

Marric, J.J. Gideon's march / [by] John Creasey (J.J. Marric). — London : IPC Magazines, 1977. — 128p ; 18cm. — (Fleetway thriller library ; no.1)
Originally published: London : Hodder and Stoughton, 1962.
Pbk : £0.25
(B77-26556)

Marrington, Pauline. The October horse / [by] Pauline Marrington. — [Sevenoaks] : Coronet, 1977. — 249p ; 18cm.
Originally published: Sydney ; London : Hodder and Stoughton, 1975.
ISBN 0-340-21301-9 Pbk : £0.70
(B77-15522)

Marsh, *Dame* Ngaio. Clutch of constables / [by] Ngaio Marsh. — [London] : Fontana, 1977. — 222p : map ; 18cm.
Originally published: London : Collins for the Crime Club, 1968.
ISBN 0-00-614526-4 Pbk : £0.70
(B77-15523)

Marsh, *Dame* Ngaio. Death in a white tie / [by] Ngaio Marsh. — [London] : Fontana, 1977. — 256p : plan ; 18cm.
'A Roderick Alleyn mystery' - cover. — Originally published: London : Bles, 1938.
ISBN 0-00-614523-x Pbk : £0.70
(B77-15524)

Marsh, *Dame* Ngaio. The nursing home murder / [by] Ngaio Marsh. — London : Collins, 1976. — 190p ; 21cm.
Joint author: Henry Jellett. — Originally published: London : Bles, 1935.
ISBN 0-00-231590-4 : £2.75
(B77-18380)

Marsh, *Dame* **Ngaio.** The nursing home murder / by Ngaio Marsh and Henry Jellett. — [London] : Fontana, 1976. — 190p ; 18cm.
'A Roderick Alleyn mystery' - jacket. — Originally published: London : Bles, 1935.
ISBN 0-00-614404-7 Pbk : £0.65
(B77-01821)

Marsh, *Dame* **Ngaio.** Surfeit of lampreys / [by] Ngaio Marsh. — Harmondsworth [etc.] : Penguin, 1977. — 303p ; 19cm. — (Penguin crime fiction)
Originally published: London : Collins, 1941.
ISBN 0-14-001100-5 Pbk : £0.90
(B77-24498)

Marsh, *Dame* **Ngaio.** Vintage murder / [by] Ngaio Marsh. — [London] : Fontana, 1977. — 223p : plan ; 18cm.
Originally published: London : Collins, 1937.
ISBN 0-00-614525-6 Pbk : £0.75
(B77-27407)

Marshall, Bruce. The yellow streak / [by] Bruce Marshall. — London : Constable, 1977. — 224p ; 23cm.
ISBN 0-09-461650-7 : £4.50
(B77-24499)

Marshall, Joanne. Last act / [by] Joanne Marshall. — London : Collins, 1976. — 159p ; 19cm.
For adolescents.
ISBN 0-00-233471-2 : £2.75
(B77-02599)

Marshall, William. Thin air / [by] William Marshall. — London : Hamilton, 1977. — [6], 186p ; 21cm. — (Marshall, William. Yellowthread Street mysteries ; 4)
ISBN 0-241-89581-2 : £3.75
(B77-10573)

Marshall, William Leonard. The hatchet man : a Yellowthread Street mystery / [by] William Marshall. — London [etc.] : Pan Books, 1977. — 172p ; 18cm.
Originally published: London : Hamilton, 1976.
ISBN 0-330-25087-6 Pbk : £0.50
(B77-25914)

Marshall, William Leonard. Yellowthread Street / [by] William Marshall. — London [etc.] : Pan Books, 1977. — 128p ; 18cm. — (Marshall, William Leonard. Yellowthread Street mysteries)
Originally published: London : Hamilton, 1975.
ISBN 0-330-25086-8 Pbk : £0.50
(B77-25205)

Martin, David, *b.1937.* The ceremony of innocence / [by] David Martin. — London : Secker and Warburg, 1977. — [5],282p ; 23cm.
ISBN 0-436-27332-2 : £3.90
(B77-10574)

Martin, Gillian. The goat, the wolf, and the crab / [by] Gillian Martin. — London : Heinemann, 1977. — vi,186p ; 23cm.
ISBN 0-434-45140-1 : £3.50
(B77-28936)

Martin, Ian Kennedy. Regan and the deal of the century / [by] Ian Kennedy Martin. — London : Barker, 1977. — 157p ; 23cm.
Based on the TV series 'The Sweeney'.
ISBN 0-213-16611-9 : £3.75
(B77-06884)

Martin, Ian Kennedy. Regan and the Manhattan file / [by] Ian Kennedy Martin. — London : Futura Publications, 1976. — 160p ; 18cm. — (Martin, Ian Kennedy. Sweeney ; 2) (A contact book)
Originally published: London : Barker, 1975.
ISBN 0-86007-287-8 Pbk : £0.50
(B77-08590)

Martin, Ian Kennedy. Rekill / [by] Ian Kennedy Martin. — London : Heinemann, 1977. — 3-254p ; 23cm.
ISBN 0-434-45150-9 : £4.50
(B77-28937)

Martin, Jane. The harbinger / by Jane Martin. — London : Hale, 1977. — 186p ; 20cm.
ISBN 0-7091-5858-0 : £3.10
(B77-08079)

Martin, Peter, *b.1907.* The landsmen / by Peter Martin. — [1st ed. reprinted] ; [with an] afterword by Wallace Markfield. — Carbondale [etc.] : Southern Illinois University Press ; London [etc.] : Feffer and Simons, 1977. — [7], 379,[1]p ; 22cm. — (Lost American fiction)
Originally published: Boston, Mass. : Little, Brown, 1952.
ISBN 0-8093-0837-1 : £6.72
(B77-30671)

Martin, Philip. Gangsters : Kline / [by] Philip Martin. — London : Severn House : [Distributed by Hutchinson], 1977. — 160p ; 21cm.
Based on the BBC TV series, 'Kline'. — Originally published: London : Sphere, 1977.
ISBN 0-7278-0269-0 : £3.15
(B77-20644)

Martin, Philip. Gangsters / [by] Philip Martin. — London : Sphere.
[1]. — 1977. — 160p ; 18cm.
Based on the BBC television series.
ISBN 0-7221-5849-1 Pbk : £0.65
(B77-07625)

2. — 1977. — 176p ; 18cm.
Based on the BBC television series.
ISBN 0-7221-5848-3 Pbk : £0.85
(B77-32208)

Martin, Tom. Long Lance / by Tom Martin. — London : Hale, 1977. — 160p ; 20cm.
ISBN 0-7091-6460-2 : £3.25
(B77-32209)

Martin, Tom. The men from El Paso / by Tom Martin. — London : Hale, 1977. — 156p ; 20cm.
ISBN 0-7091-6144-1 : £3.10
(B77-20645)

Marton, George. Alarum / by George Marton. — London : W.H. Allen, 1977. — [4],220p ; 23cm.
ISBN 0-491-01848-7 : £3.95
(B77-14416)

Martyn, Lesley. Escape me never / by Lesley Martyn. — London : Hale, 1977. — 189p ; 20cm.
ISBN 0-7091-6422-x : £3.40
(B77-32210)

Mason, Chuck. Heller from Texas / by Chuck Mason. — London : Hale, 1977. — 159p ; 20cm.
ISBN 0-7091-5947-1 : £2.95
(B77-10575)

Mason, Francis van Wyck. Trumpets sound no more / [by] F. van Wyck Mason. — London : Hutchinson, 1976. — [11],297p : map(on lining papers) ; 24cm.
Originally published: Boston, Mass. : Little, Brown, 1975.
ISBN 0-09-126320-4 : £4.75
(B77-05682)

Mason, Richard. The world of Suzie Wong / [by] Richard Mason. — London : Collins, 1976. — 383p ; 21cm.
Originally published: 1957.
ISBN 0-00-221901-8 : £3.75
(B77-17754)

Massey, Charlotte. Polmarran Tower / [by] Charlotte Massey ; edited by Lesley Saxby. — London (110 Warner Rd, S.E.5) : Troubadour, 1976. — 273p ; 18cm.
Originally published: London : Macdonald and Jane's, 1975.
ISBN 0-86007-328-9 Pbk : £0.65
(B77-08591)

Massinger, Philip. Hardcore / [by] Philip Massinger. — London : Sphere, 1977. — 158p ; 18cm.
ISBN 0-7221-3564-5 Pbk : £0.65
(B77-10576)

Masters, John. Fandango Rock / [by] John Masters. — London : Sphere, 1976. — 330p ; 18cm.
Originally published: London : Joseph, 1959.
ISBN 0-7221-5977-3 Pbk : £0.65
(B77-05683)

Masters, John. The field-marshal's memoirs / [by] John Masters. — London : Sphere, 1976. — 303p ; 18cm.
Originally published: London : Joseph, 1975.
ISBN 0-7221-0408-1 Pbk : £0.65
(B77-05684)

Masters, Simon. Target, the men they once were / [by] Simon Masters. — London : British Broadcasting Corporation, 1977. — 204p ; 22cm.
Based on 'BBC-1 television series "Target"' - title-page verso.
ISBN 0-563-17402-1 : £3.25
(B77-34149)

Masterton, Graham. The manitou / by Graham Masterton. — London : Spearman, 1975. — 160p ; 23cm.
ISBN 0-85435-442-5 : £2.50
(B77-00982)

Mather, Anne. Devils mount / by Anne Mather. — London : Mills and Boon, 1976. — 188p ; 19cm.
ISBN 0-263-09025-6 : £1.95
(B77-10577)

Mather, Anne. The Medici lover / by Anne Mather. — London : Mills and Boon, 1977. — 189p ; 18cm.
ISBN 0-263-72383-6 Pbk : £0.35
(B77-20646)

Mather, Anne. The smouldering flame / by Anne Mather. — London : Mills and Boon, 1976. — 186p ; 17cm.
ISBN 0-263-72325-9 Pbk : £0.30
(B77-05685)

Mather, Anne. Storm in a rain barrel / [by] Anne Mather. — Large print ed. — Bath : Lythway Press, 1977. — [5],262p ; 23cm.
Originally published: London : Mills and Boon, 1971.
ISBN 0-85046-750-0 : £4.50
(B77-32861)

Mather, Anne. Wild enchantress / by Anne Mather. — London : Mills and Boon, 1977. — 187p ; 17cm.
Originally published: 1976.
ISBN 0-263-72332-1 Pbk : £0.35
(B77-06885)

Mather, Berkely. Genghis Khan / by Berkeley [i.e. Berkely] Mather. — Hornchurch : I. Henry, 1976. — 158p : 1 ill ; 21cm.
Originally published: London : Collins, 1965.
ISBN 0-86025-101-2 : £2.85
(B77-03227)

Mather, Berkely. The gold of Malabar / [by] Berkley [i.e. Berkely] Mather. — London [etc.] : White Lion Publishers, 1977. — 222p ; 21cm.
Originally published: London : Collins, 1967.
ISBN 0-7274-0266-8 : £3.75
(B77-15525)

Mather, Berkely. The memsahib / [by] Berkely Mather. — London : Collins, 1977. — 318p ; 22cm.
ISBN 0-00-221590-x : £4.50
(B77-20647)

Mather, Berkely. With extreme prejudice / [by] Berkely Mather. — [London] : Fontana, 1977. — 223p : maps ; 18cm.
Originally published: London : Collins, 1975.
ISBN 0-00-614477-2 Pbk : £0.70
(B77-05686)

Matheson, Richard. Bid time return / [by] Richard Matheson. — London : Sphere, 1977. — 255p ; 18cm.
Originally published: New York : Viking Press, 1975.
ISBN 0-7221-5894-7 Pbk : £0.85
(B77-09962)

Matheson, Richard. Hell house / [by] Richard Matheson. — Toronto [etc.] ; London : Bantam, [1977]. — [7],247,[1]p ; 18cm.
Originally published: New York : Viking Press, 1971 ; London : Corgi, 1973.
ISBN 0-552-66477-4 Pbk : £0.50
(B77-16607)

Matthews, Patricia. Love's avenging heart / [by] Patricia Matthews. — London : Corgi, 1977. — [5],501p ; 18cm.
Originally published: New York : Pinnacle Books, 1976.
ISBN 0-552-10494-9 Pbk : £1.00
(B77-25206)

Maugham, Robin. The barrier : a novel containing five sonnets by John Betjeman written in the style of the period / [by] Robin Maugham. — London [etc.] : Pan Books, 1977. — 182,[6]p ; 18cm.
Originally published: London : W.H. Allen, 1973.
ISBN 0-330-25166-x Pbk : £0.75
(B77-21477)

Maugham, William Somerset. Cakes and ale, or, The skeleton in the cupboard / [by] W. Somerset Maugham. — Harmondsworth [etc.] : Penguin, 1977. — 203p ; 19cm.
Originally published: London : Heinemann, 1930.
ISBN 0-14-000651-6 Pbk : £0.60
(B77-32211)

Maugham, William Somerset. Cakes and ale, or, The skeleton in the cupboard / [by] W. Somerset Maugham. — Large print ed. — Bath : Lythway Press, 1976. — xiii,322p ; 22cm.
Originally published: London : Heinemann, 1930.
ISBN 0-85046-680-6 : £4.40
(B77-06886)

Maugham, William Somerset. The moon and sixpence / [by] Somerset Maugham. — Harmondsworth [etc.] : Penguin, 1977. — 217p ; 18cm.
Originally published: London : Heinemann, 1919.
ISBN 0-14-000468-8 Pbk : £0.50
(B77-26557)

Maugham, William Somerset. The narrow corner / [by] W. Somerset Maugham. — Harmondsworth [etc.] : Penguin, 1977. — 218p ; 18cm.
Originally published: London : Heinemann, 1932.
ISBN 0-14-001859-x Pbk : £0.65
(B77-26558)

Maxtone-Graham, John. Dark brown in the river : a novel / by John Maxtone-Graham. — London : Hale, 1977. — xi,339p : map(on lining papers) ; 24cm.
Originally published: New York : Macmillan, 1976.
ISBN 0-7091-6247-2 : £4.50
(B77-26559)

Maxwell, John. HMS 'Bounty' / [by] John Maxwell. — London : Cape, 1977. — 287p ; 23cm.
Bibl.: p.287.
ISBN 0-224-01414-5 : £3.95 : CIP rev.
(B77-15526)

Maxwell, Vicky. The other side of summer / [by] Vicky Maxwell. — London : Collins, 1977. — 160p ; 19cm.
ISBN 0-00-233855-6 : £2.95
(B77-27408)

May, Jonathan, *b.1935.* Confessions from a sex clinic / [by] Jonathan May. — London : Sphere, 1976. — 139p ; 18cm.
ISBN 0-7221-5983-8 Pbk : £0.60
(B77-07626)

May, Jonathan, *b.1935.* Confessions of a games master / [by] Jonathan May. — London : Sphere, 1975. — 144p ; 18cm.
ISBN 0-7221-4986-7 Pbk : £0.40
(B77-13324)

May, Jonathan, *b.1935.* Confessions of a gasman / [by] Jonathan May. — London : Sphere, 1977. — 140p ; 18cm.
ISBN 0-7221-5000-8 Pbk : £0.65
(B77-32212)

May, Jonathan, *b.1935.* Confessions of a housewife / [by] Jonathan May. — London : Sphere, 1976. — 142p ; 18cm.
ISBN 0-7221-4999-9 Pbk : £0.50
(B77-06299)

May, Jonathan, *b.1935.* Confessions of a shop assistant / [by] Jonathan May. — London : Sphere, 1975. — 139p ; 18cm.
Originally published: 1974.
ISBN 0-7221-9350-5 Pbk : £0.40
(B77-13325)

May, Jonathan, *b.1935.* Confessions of a stuntman / [by] Jonathan May. — London : Sphere, 1977. — 141p ; 18cm.
ISBN 0-7221-4998-0 Pbk : £0.60
(B77-19733)

Maybury, Anne. Jessamy Court / [by] Anne Maybury. — [London] : Fontana, 1976. — 256p ; 18cm.
Originally published: New York : Random House, 1974 ; London : Collins, 1975.
ISBN 0-00-614201-x Pbk : £0.60
(B77-06887)

Maybury, Anne. The moonlit door / [by] Anne Maybury. — [London] : Fontana, 1977. — 188p ; 18cm.
Originally published: New York : Holt, Rinehart and Winston ; London : Collins, 1967.
ISBN 0-00-614474-8 Pbk : £0.65
(B77-30672)

Maybury, Anne. The terracotta palace / by Anne Maybury. — Toronto [etc.] ; London : Bantam, 1976. — [6],284p : 1 col ill ; 18cm.
Originally published: New York : Random House ; London : Hodder and Stoughton, 1970.
ISBN 0-553-02446-9 Pbk : £0.75
(B77-09297)

Mayhew, Margaret. The owlers / [by] Margaret Mayhew. — London : Hamilton, 1977. — [7], 207p ; 21cm.
ISBN 0-241-89591-x : £3.95
(B77-28169)

Maynard, Nan. If you can't catch, don't throw / [by] Nan Maynard. — London : Corgi, 1976. — [5],247p ; 18cm.
Originally published: London : Cassell, 1976.
ISBN 0-552-10349-7 Pbk : £0.75
(B77-09298)

Maynard, Nan. Losers weepers / by Nan Maynard. — London : Hale, 1977. — 175p ; 21cm.
ISBN 0-7091-6060-7 : £3.50
(B77-19734)

Mazzaro, Ed. One death in the red / [by] Ed Mazzaro. — London : New English Library, 1977. — 159p ; 18cm.
Originally published: 1976.
ISBN 0-450-02608-6 Pbk : £0.65
(B77-08592)

Meacock, Norma. The book of Muntu Dixon / [by] Norma Meacock. — Sudbury : Spearman, 1977. — 217p ; 20cm.
ISBN 0-85435-144-2 : £2.75
(B77-22889)

Meade, Richard. Gaylord's badge / [by] Richard Meade. — Large print [ed.]. — London : Prior [etc.], 1976. — [7],286p ; 24cm.
Originally published: under the name Ben Haas. New York : Doubleday, 1975.
ISBN 0-86043-021-9 : £4.50
(B77-07627)

Meadows, Rose. Castle Lucas / [by] Rose Meadows. — London : Hale, 1976. — 191p ; 21cm.
ISBN 0-7091-5236-1 : £3.25
(B77-01822)

Meadows, Rose. The Christmas rebellion / [by] Rose Meadows. — London : Hale, 1977. — 192p ; 21cm.
ISBN 0-7091-5692-8 : £3.50
(B77-14936)

Meadows, Rose. The crinoline Empress / [by] Rose Meadows. — London : Hale, 1976. — 191p ; 21cm.
Based on the life of the Empress Eugénie.
ISBN 0-7091-5166-7 : £3.10
(B77-11413)

Meadows, Rose. Slander most savage / [by] Rose Meadows. — London : Hale, 1977. — 192p ; 21cm.
Based on the life of Ernest, Duke of Cumberland, fifth son of George III.
ISBN 0-7091-6137-9 : £3.70
(B77-22165)

Megahy, Cooper. The hustlers / [by] Cooper Megahy. — London : Futura Publications, 1976. — 176p ; 18cm.
ISBN 0-86007-299-1 Pbk : £0.60
(B77-09299)

Meggs, Brown. The matter of paradise / [by] Brown Meggs. — [London] : Fontana, 1977. — 192p ; 18cm.
Originally published: New York : Random House, 1975 ; London : Collins, 1976.
ISBN 0-00-614662-7 Pbk : £0.70
(B77-30673)

Meggs, Brown. Saturday games / [by] Brown Meggs. — [London] : Fontana, 1976. — 191p ; 18cm.
Originally published: New York : Random House, 1974 ; London : Collins for the Crime Club, 1975.
ISBN 0-00-614388-1 Pbk : £0.60
(B77-10952)

Mehdevi, Anne Sinclair. Parveen / [by] Anne Mehdevi. — Harmondsworth [etc.] : Penguin, 1977. — 141p ; 18cm. — (Peacock books)
Originally published: New York : Knopf, 1969 ; London : Chatto and Windus, 1975. — For adolescents.
ISBN 0-14-047111-1 Pbk : £0.60
(B77-27409)

Melchior, Ib. The Haigerloch project / [by] Ib Melchior. — London : Souvenir Press, 1977. — [14],317p : map ; 23cm.
Originally published: New York : Harper and Row, 1977. — Bibl.: p.315-317.
ISBN 0-285-62295-1 : £3.95
(B77-30674)

Melly, Diana. The girl in the picture : a novel / by Diana Melly. — London : Duckworth, 1977. — 120p ; 23cm.
ISBN 0-7156-0964-5 : £3.25
(B77-13326)

Melville, Anne. The Lorimer line / [by] Anne Melville. — London : Heinemann, 1977. — [5], 377p ; 23cm.
ISBN 0-434-46270-5 : £4.90
(B77-31487)

Melville, Jennie. Dragon's Eye / [by] Jennie Melville. — London [etc.] : Macmillan, 1977. — 192p ; 21cm.
Originally published: New York : Simon and Schuster, 1976.
ISBN 0-333-19659-7 : £3.25
(B77-19735)

Menegas, Peter. The nature of the beast / [by] Peter Menegas. — London : Corgi, 1976. — [11],240p ; 18cm.
Originally published: New York : Bantam, 1975.
ISBN 0-552-10147-8 Pbk : £0.75
(B77-05687)

Messmann, Jon. The Moneta papers : a novel / by Jon Messmann. — London [etc.] : Mews Books ; London : Distributed by New English Library, 1977. — 158p ; 18cm. — (Messmann, Jon. Jefferson Boone, handyman ; 1)
Originally published: New York : Pyramid Books, 1973.
ISBN 0-452-00059-9 Pbk : £0.60
(B77-05688)

Mewshaw, Michael. Earthly bread / [by] Michael Mewshaw. — London : Secker and Warburg, 1977. — [7],212p ; 23cm.
Originally published: New York : Random House, 1976.
ISBN 0-436-27840-5 : £3.90
(B77-19012)

Meyer, Lawrence. A Capitol crime / [by] Lawrence Meyer. — London : Collins [for] the Crime Club, 1977. — 251p ; 21cm.
Originally published: New York : Viking Press, 1976.
ISBN 0-00-231079-1 : £3.25
(B77-27410)

Meyer, Nicholas. The seven per cent solution : being a reprint from the reminiscences of John H. Watson, MD / as edited [i.e. written] by Nicholas Meyer. — Large print ed. — Leicester : Ulverscroft, 1977. — [5],367p ; 23cm. — (Ulverscroft large print series : [mystery])
Originally published: New York : Dutton, 1974 ; London : Hodder and Stoughton, 1975.
ISBN 0-7089-0052-6 : £2.95
(B77-32213)

Meyer, Nicholas. Target practice / [by] Nicholas Meyer. — Sevenoaks : Coronet, 1977. — 143p ; 18cm.
Originally published: New York : Harcourt Brace Jovanovich, 1974 ; London : Hodder and Stoughton, 1975.
ISBN 0-340-21316-7 Pbk : £0.60
(B77-21478)

Meynell, Laurence. Folly to be wise / [by] Laurence Meynell. — London : Hale, 1977. — 218p ; 21cm.
ISBN 0-7091-6314-2 : £3.95
(B77-32214)

Meynell, Laurence. Hooky gets the wooden spoon : a Hooky Hefferman story / [by] Laurence Meynell. — London [etc.] : Macmillan, 1977. — 192p : map ; 21cm.
ISBN 0-333-22011-0 : £3.50
(B77-19736)

Meynell, Laurence. The little kingdom / [by] Laurence Meynell. — London : Hale, 1977. — 208p ; 21cm.
ISBN 0-7091-5931-5 : £3.60
(B77-30675)

Meynell, Laurence. The lost half hour / [by] Laurence Meynell. — London [etc.] : Macmillan, 1976. — 220p ; 21cm.
ISBN 0-333-19879-4 : £3.25
(B77-00436)

Meynell, Laurence. The vision splendid / [by] Laurence Meynell. — London : Hale, 1976. — 220p ; 21cm.
ISBN 0-7091-5535-2 : £3.50
(B77-01823)

Miall, Stuart. Curtains for Britain? / [by] Stuart Miall. — London : Bachman and Turner, 1976. — 3-234p ; 23cm. — (Debate)
ISBN 0-85974-053-6 : £4.50
(B77-05689)

Michaels, Barbara. House of many shadows / [by] Barbara Michaels. — London [etc.] : Pan Books, 1977. — 222p ; 18cm.
Originally published: New York : Dodd, Mead, 1974 ; London : Souvenir Press, 1975.
ISBN 0-330-25223-2 Pbk : £0.70
(B77-31488)

Michaels, Barbara. The sea king's daughter / [by] Barbara Michaels. — London : Souvenir Press, 1977. — [7],245p ; 22cm.
Originally published: New York : Dodd, Mead, 1975.
ISBN 0-285-62269-2 : £3.50
(B77-08593)

Michaels, Barbara. The sea king's daughter / [by] Barbara Michaels. — Large print [ed.]. — London : Prior [etc.], 1977. — [7],445p ; 25cm.
Originally published: New York : Dodd, Mead, 1975 ; London : Souvenir Press, 1977.
ISBN 0-86043-026-x : £5.50
(B77-22166)

Michaels, Barbara. Witch / [by] Barbara Michaels. — London [etc.] : Pan Books, 1977. — 206p ; 18cm.
Originally published: New York : Dodd, Mead, 1973 ; London : Souvenir Press, 1975.
ISBN 0-330-25078-7 Pbk : £0.60
(B77-20648)

Michel, Freda. Counter-parry / by Freda Michel. — London : Hale, 1977. — 187p ; 21cm.
ISBN 0-7091-5878-5 : £3.70
(B77-20649)

Michel, Freda. The Machiavellian marquess / by Freda Michel. — London : Hale, 1977. — 208p ; 21cm.
ISBN 0-7091-5787-8 : £3.25
(B77-09300)

Michel, Freda. Subterfuge / [by] Freda Michel. — London : Hale, 1977. — 192p ; 21cm.
ISBN 0-7091-6071-2 : £3.70
(B77-28170)

Michener, James Albert. Hawaii / [by] James A. Michener. — London : Secker and Warburg, 1976. — 5-1011p : geneal tables, maps(on lining papers) ; 23cm.
Originally published: New York : Random House, 1959 ; London : Secker and Warburg, 1960.
ISBN 0-436-27951-7 : £5.90
(B77-01824)

Middleton, Stanley. Ends and means / [by] Stanley Middleton. — London [etc.] : Hutchinson, 1977. — 255p ; 20cm.
ISBN 0-09-131110-1 : £4.50
(B77-30676)

Midgley, John, *b.1931.* Donovan / [by] John Midgley. — Sevenoaks : Coronet, 1977. — [5], 161p ; 18cm.
Originally published: Bath : Chivers, 1974.
ISBN 0-340-21322-1 Pbk : £0.65
(B77-19737)

Milburn, Constance. Christy / by Constance Milburn. — London : Hale, 1977. — 190p ; 20cm.
ISBN 0-7091-6186-7 : £3.20
(B77-21479)

Millar, Margaret. Ask for me tomorrow / [by] Margaret Millar. — London : Gollancz, 1977. — [7],179p ; 21cm. — ([Gollancz thriller])
Originally published: New York : Random House, 1976.
ISBN 0-575-02230-2 : £3.50
(B77-08080)

Miller, Hugh, *b.1937.* The saviour / [by] Hugh Miller. — London : New English Library, 1977. — 3-239p ; 22cm.
ISBN 0-450-03202-7 : £4.50
(B77-30677)

Miller, Hugh, *b.1937.* A soft breeze from hell / [by] Hugh Miller. — London : New English Library, 1976. — 142p ; 18cm.
ISBN 0-450-02937-9 Pbk : £0.60
(B77-00437)

Miller, Victor B. Marked for murder / [by] Victor B. Miller. — London : Star Books, 1976. — 156p ; 18cm.
'Based on the television series "Kojak" created by Abby Mann, adapted from the episode "Death is not a passing grade" written by Gene Kearney'. — Spine title: Kojak, marked for murder. — Originally published: s.l. : MCA Publishing, 1975.
ISBN 0-352-39744-6 Pbk : £0.50
(B77-10578)

Milligan, Spike. Puckoon / [by] Spike Milligan. — London : Joseph ; Walton-on-Thames : M. and J. Hobbs, 1977. — 164p : ill ; 21cm.
Originally published: London : Blond, 1963.
ISBN 0-7181-1271-7 : £3.95
(B77-20650)

Mills, James, *b.1932.* One just man / [by] James Mills. — London : Sphere, 1976. — 173p ; 18cm.
Originally published: New York : Simon and Schuster, 1974.
ISBN 0-7221-6085-2 Pbk : £0.65
(B77-02600)

Milne, Alan Alexander. The Red House mystery / [by] A.A. Milne. — Large print ed. — Bath : Lythway Press, 1977. — xv,312p ; 23cm.
Originally published: London : Methuen, 1922.
ISBN 0-85046-742-x : £4.75
(B77-29723)

Milne, Paula. Flights of angels / [by] Paula Milne. — London : Hale, 1976. — 191p ; 21cm.
'... from the BBC television series "Angels"' - p.2.
ISBN 0-7091-6039-9 : £3.25
(B77-00438)

Milne, Roseleen. Borrowed plumes / by Roseleen Milne. — London [etc.] : Hodder and Stoughton, 1977. — 189p ; 21cm.
ISBN 0-340-21741-3 : £3.75
(B77-30678)

Miss Read. Over the gate / [by] 'Miss Read' ; illustrated by J.S. Goodall. — Harmondsworth [etc.] : Penguin, 1977. — 202p : ill ; 19cm.
Originally published: London : Joseph, 1964.
ISBN 0-14-002900-1 Pbk : £0.65
(B77-17755)

Miss Read. Thrush Green / by 'Miss Read' ; illustrated by J.S. Goodall. — Harmondsworth [etc.] : Penguin, 1977. — 219p : ill ; 18cm.
Originally published: London : Joseph, 1959.
ISBN 0-14-001802-6 Pbk : £0.70
(B77-17756)

Miss Read. Village affairs / by Miss Read ; illustrations by J.S. Goodall. — London : Joseph, 1977. — 239p : ill ; 21cm.
ISBN 0-7181-1577-5 : £3.95
(B77-28171)

Mitchell, Gladys. The devil's elbow / [by] Gladys Mitchell. — London : Sheldon House : [Distributed by Hutchinson], 1975. — 223p ; 21cm.
Originally published: London : Joseph, 1951.
ISBN 0-7278-0093-0 : £2.75
(B77-07628)

Mitchell, Gladys. Fault in the structure / [by] Gladys Mitchell. — London : Joseph, 1977. — 191p ; 21cm.
ISBN 0-7181-1601-1 : £3.95
(B77-24500)

Mitchell, Gladys. Noonday and night / [by] Gladys Mitchell. — London : Joseph, 1977. — 191p ; 21cm.
ISBN 0-7181-1517-1 : £3.75
(B77-10579)

Mitchell, Ian. The old gold road / by Ian Mitchell. — London : Hale, 1977. — 189p ; 20cm. — ([Hale crime])
ISBN 0-7091-6214-6 : £3.25
(B77-34150)

Mitchell, James, *b.1926.* Death and bright water / [by] James Mitchell. — London : Corgi, 1976. — 253p ; 18cm.
Originally published: London : Hamilton, 1974.
ISBN 0-552-10157-5 Pbk : £0.75
(B77-05690)

Mitchell, James, *b.1926.* Smear job : a Callan novel / [by] James Mitchell. — London : Corgi, 1977. — 335p ; 18cm.
Originally published: London : Hamilton, 1975.
ISBN 0-552-10456-6 Pbk : £0.85
(B77-32215)

Mitchell, James, *b.1926.* When the boat comes in / [by] James Mitchell. — London : Corgi. 2 : The hungry years. — 1976. — 253p ; 18cm.
'Based on the BBC TV drama series' - cover.
ISBN 0-552-10344-6 Pbk : £0.75
(B77-00439)

Mitchell, James, *b.1926.* When the boat comes in / by James Mitchell. — London : Hamilton. Book 3 : Upwards and onwards. — 1977. — 222p ; 20cm.
ISBN 0-241-89779-3 : £4.25
(B77-31489)

Mitchell, Yvonne. But answer came there none : a novel / by Yvonne Mitchell. — London : Constable, 1977. — 158p : ill, music ; 20cm.
ISBN 0-09-461850-x : £3.75
(B77-30679)

Mitchison, Naomi. Memoirs of a spacewoman / [by] Naomi Mitchison ; introduction by Hilary Rubenstein. — London : New English Library, 1977. — 160p ; 18cm. — (SF master series)
Originally published: London : Gollancz, 1962.
ISBN 0-450-03000-8 Pbk : £0.70
(B77-13896)

Mitford, Nancy. The pursuit of love / [by] Nancy Mitford. — Large print ed. — Bath : Lythway Press, 1977. — [5],339p ; 23cm.
Originally published: London : Hamilton, 1945.
ISBN 0-85046-745-4 : £4.75
(B77-32862)

Mittelhölzer, Edgar. Children of Kaywana / [by] Edgar Mittelhölzer. — London : Secker and Warburg, 1976. — 302p : geneal table ; 19cm. — (Mittelhölzer, Edgar. Kaywana quartet)
Originally published: London : Nevill, 1952.
ISBN 0-436-28307-7 : £4.90
(B77-04412)

Mittelhölzer, Edgar. [Children of Kaywana. Part 2]. Kaywana heritage / [by] Edgar Mittelhölzer. — New ed. [i.e. 1st ed. reprinted]. — London : Secker and Warburg, 1976. — 254p : geneal table, map ; 19cm. — (Mittelhölzer, Edgar. Kaywana quartet)
Originally published: as the second part of 'Children of Kaywana'. London : Peter Nevill, 1952.
ISBN 0-436-28304-2 : £4.90
(B77-04413)

Mittelhölzer, Edgar. Kaywana blood / [by] Edgar Mittelhölzer. — London : Secker and Warburg, 1976. — 560p : geneal table, map ; 19cm. — (Mittelhölzer, Edgar. Kaywana quartet)
Originally published: 1958.
ISBN 0-436-28305-0 : £4.90
(B77-05691)

Mittelhölzer, Edgar. Kaywana stock / [by] Edgar Mittelhölzer. — London : Secker and Warburg, 1976. — 300p : geneal table ; 19cm. — (Mittelhölzer, Edgar. Kaywana quartet)
Originally published: as 'The harrowing of Hubertus', 1954.
ISBN 0-436-28306-9 : £4.90
(B77-04414)

Monsarrat, Nicholas. The nylon pirates / [by] Nicholas Monsarrat. — London [etc.] : Pan Books, 1977. — 349p ; 18cm.
Originally published: London : Cassell, 1960.
ISBN 0-330-10183-8 Pbk : £0.80
(B77-21480)

Monsarrat, Nicholas. The pillow fight / [by] Nicholas Monsarrat. — London [etc.] : Pan Books, 1977. — 333p ; 18cm.
Originally published: London : Cassell, 1965.
ISBN 0-330-20188-3 Pbk : £0.80
(B77-21481)

Monsarrat, Nicholas. The pillow fight / [by] Nicholas Monsarrat. — London [etc.] : White Lion Publishers, 1977. — [4],348p ; 21cm.
Originally published: London : Cassell, 1965.
ISBN 0-7274-0288-9 : £4.25
(B77-12125)

Montgomery, Lucy Maud. Emily of New Moon / [by] L.M. Montgomery. — [1st ed. reprinted] ; [with a] foreword by Lady Wilson. — London : Harrap, 1977. — xii,299p ; 23cm.
Originally published: New York : Stokes ; London : Hodder and Stoughton, 1923. — For adolescents.
ISBN 0-245-53179-3 : £3.95
(B77-30680)

Moody, Laurence. The greatest Tudor / [by] Laurence Moody. — London : Hale, 1977. — 159p ; 21cm.
Based on the life Elizabeth I.
ISBN 0-7091-5793-2 : £3.25
(B77-13327)

Moorcock, Michael. The condition of Muzak : a Jerry Cornelius novel / [by] Michael Moorcock ; illustrated by Richard Glyn Jones. — London : Allison and Busby, 1977. — 313p : ill ; 23cm. — (Moorcock, Michael. Jerry Cornelius tetralogy)
ISBN 0-85031-044-x : £4.50
(B77-28172)

Moorcock, Michael. The end of all songs / [by] Michael Moorcock. — St Albans : Mayflower, 1977. — xi,307p ; 18cm. — (Moorcock, Michael. Dancers at the end of time ; vol.3) (Mayflower science fantasy)
Originally published: St Albans : Hart-Davis MacGibbon, 1976.
ISBN 0-583-12105-5 Pbk : £0.95
(B77-24501)

Moorcock, Michael. The ice schooner / [by] Michael Moorcock. — London : Sphere, 1975. — 158p ; 18cm. — (Sphere science fiction)
Originally published: 1969.
ISBN 0-7221-6203-0 Pbk : £0.65
(B77-30681)

Moorcock, Michael. The transformation of Miss Mavis Ming : a romance of the end of time / by Michael Moorcock. — London : W.H. Allen, 1977. — 159p ; 23cm.
ISBN 0-491-01718-9 : £3.50
(B77-10580)

Moore, Brian. Catholics / [by] Brian Moore. — Harmondsworth [etc.] : Penguin, 1977. — 89p ; 19cm.
Originally published: London : Cape, 1972.
ISBN 0-14-004269-5 Pbk : £0.60
(B77-27411)

Moore, Brian. The doctor's wife / [by] Brian Moore. — London : Cape, 1976. — [5],277p ; 21cm.
ISBN 0-224-01322-x : £3.50
(B77-00440)

Moore, Brian. The emperor of ice-cream / [by] Brian Moore. — Harmondsworth [etc.] : Penguin, 1977. — [5],201p ; 18cm.
Originally published: New York : Viking Press, 1965.
ISBN 0-14-004449-3 Pbk : Unpriced
(B77-32863)

Moore, Brian. Fergus / [by] Brian Moore. — Harmondsworth [etc.] : Penguin, 1977. — 171p ; 18cm.
Originally published: New York : Holt, Rinehart and Winston, 1970 ; London : Cape, 1971.
ISBN 0-14-004270-9 Pbk : £0.60
(B77-27412)

Moore, Brian. The great Victorian collection / [by] Brian Moore. — Harmondsworth [etc.] : Penguin, 1977. — 172p ; 18cm.
Originally published: New York : Farrar, Straus ; London : Cape, 1975.
ISBN 0-14-004499-x Pbk : £0.70
(B77-27413)

Moore, Brian. I am Mary Dunne / [by] Brian Moore. — Harmondsworth [etc.] : Penguin, 1977. — 187p ; 18cm.
Originally published: New York : Viking Press ; London : Cape, 1968.
Pbk : £0.60
ISBN 0-14-003634-2
(B77-27414)

Moore, Brian. The luck of Ginger Coffey / [by] Brian Moore. — Harmondsworth [etc.] : Penguin, 1977. — 202p ; 18cm.
Originally published: Boston, Mass. : Little, Brown ; London : Deutsch, 1960.
ISBN 0-14-002115-9 Pbk : £0.60
(B77-27415)

Moore, John, *b.1907.* The blue field / [by] John Moore. — London [etc.] : Pan Books, 1976. — [8],215p ; 18cm. — (Moore, John, b.1907. Brensham trilogy)
Originally published: London : Collins, 1948.
Pbk : £0.70
ISBN 0-330-02870-7
(B77-02601)

Moore, John, *b.1907.* Brensham village / [by] John Moore. — London [etc.] : Pan Books, 1976. — [9],226p ; 18cm. — (Moore, John, b.1907. Brensham trilogy)
Originally published: London : Collins, 1946.
Pbk : £0.70
ISBN 0-330-02869-3
(B77-02602)

Moore, John, *b.1907.* Portrait of Elmbury / [by] John Moore. — London [etc.] : Pan Books, 1976. — [9],226p ; 18cm. — (Moore, John, b.1907. Brensham trilogy)
Originally published: London : Collins, 1945.
Pbk : £0.70
ISBN 0-330-02868-5
(B77-02603)

Moore, Nina Louise. A summer to remember / by Nina Louise Moore. — London : Hale, 1977. — 160p ; 20cm.
ISBN 0-7091-6282-0 : £3.20
(B77-28173)

Moore, Robin. The family man / [by] Robin Moore with Milt Machlin. — St Albans : Panther, 1977. — 496p ; 18cm.
Originally published: New York : Pyramid, 1974.
ISBN 0-586-04212-1 Pbk : £0.80
(B77-08081)

Moore, Robin. The set up / [by] Robin Moore with Milt Machlin. — [Sevenoaks] : Coronet, 1977. — 288p ; 18cm.
Originally published: New York : Pyramid Publications, 1975.
ISBN 0-340-21525-9 Pbk : £0.90
(B77-15527)

Moore, William, *b.1930.* The soldiers, storm of steel / [by] William Moore. — London : Sphere, 1975. — 190p : plans ; 18cm.
ISBN 0-7221-6154-9 Pbk : £0.50
(B77-08082)

Morant, Alexander. The princess and the parvenu / by Alexander Morant. — London : Hale, 1977. — 224p ; 21cm.
ISBN 0-7091-6260-x : £3.80
(B77-34151)

Moray, Helga. Caviar or crusts / [by] Helga Moray. — London : Hale, 1977. — 3-247p ; 21cm.
ISBN 0-7091-5863-7 : £3.75
(B77-13897)

Moray, Helga. Footsteps in the night / [by] Helga Moray. — London : Corgi, 1976. — 286p ; 18cm.
Originally published: London : Hale, 1975.
ISBN 0-552-10298-9 Pbk : £0.70
(B77-02604)

Moray, Helga. The ruby fleet / [by] Helga Moray. — London : Corgi, 1977. — 221p ; 18cm.
Originally published: London : Hale, 1976.
ISBN 0-552-10452-3 Pbk : £0.75
(B77-30682)

Morgan, Dave. Adverse camber / [by] Dave Morgan. — London : Hale, 1977. — 190p ; 21cm. — (Hale SF)
ISBN 0-7091-6023-2 : £3.50
(B77-16608)

Morgan, Stanley. A blow for Gabriel Horn / [by] Stanley Morgan. — London : W.H. Allen, 1977. — 190p ; 23cm.
ISBN 0-491-01868-1 : £3.50
(B77-14417)

Morgan, Stanley. The rise of Randy Comfort / [by] Stanley Morgan. — London : Futura Publications, 1976. — 186p ; 18cm.
ISBN 0-86007-347-5 Pbk : £0.60
(B77-08594)

Morgan, Stanley. Tobin in Tahiti / [by] Stanley Morgan. — London : Futura Publications, 1976. — 192p ; 18cm.
ISBN 0-86007-284-3 Pbk : £0.60
(B77-08595)

Morice, Anne. Murder in mimicry / [by] Anne Morice. — London [etc.] : Macmillan, 1977. — 192p ; 21cm.
ISBN 0-333-19901-4 : £3.25
(B77-11414)

Morice, Anne. Scared to death / [by] Anne Morice. — London [etc.] : Macmillan, 1977. — 192p ; 20cm.
ISBN 0-333-22768-9 : £3.25
(B77-30683)

Morrell, David. Testament / [by] David Morrell. — London [etc.] : Pan Books, 1977. — 237p ; 18cm.
Originally published: New York : M. Evans, 1975 ; London : Chatto and Windus, 1976.
ISBN 0-330-25379-4 Pbk : £0.75
(B77-28938)

Morris, Janet E. High couch of Silistra : (returning creation) / by Janet E. Morris. — Toronto ; London [etc.] : Bantam, 1977. — [7], 246p : map ; 18cm.
ISBN 0-552-60522-0 Pbk : £0.75
(B77-25915)

Morris, Wright. The man who was there / by Wright Morris. — Lincoln, [Neb.] ; London : University of Nebraska Press, 1977. — [9], 236p ; 21cm.
Originally published: New York : Scribner, 1947.
ISBN 0-8032-0881-2 : £8.20
ISBN 0-8032-5813-5 Pbk : £2.45
(B77-25916)

Morris, Wright. One day / [by] Wright Morris. — Lincoln [Neb.] ; London : University of Nebraska Press, 1976. — [7],433p ; 21cm.
'A Bison book'. — Originally published: New York : Atheneum, 1965.
ISBN 0-8032-0879-0 : £10.45
ISBN 0-8032-5841-0 Pbk : £3.75
(B77-00983)

Morrison, Emmeline. Wintersmount / by Emmeline Morrison. — London : Remploy, 1976. — 256p ; 20cm.
Originally published: London : Hutchinson, 1955.
ISBN 0-7066-0667-1 : £2.75
(B77-03228)

Mortimer, John, *b.1923.* Will Shakespeare / [by] John Mortimer. — [London] : Coronet, 1977. — 256p ; 18cm.
Also published: London : Hodder and Stoughton, 1977.
ISBN 0-340-21979-3 Pbk : £0.85
(B77-27416)

Mortimer, Penelope. Long distance / [by] Penelope Mortimer. — Harmondsworth [etc.] : Penguin, 1977. — 173p ; 18cm.
Originally published: London : Allen Lane, 1974.
ISBN 0-14-004294-6 Pbk : £0.70
(B77-29724)

Morton, Anthony. The Baron, king-maker / [by] John Creasey as Anthony Morton. — Sevenoaks : Coronet, 1977. — 192p ; 18cm.
Originally published: London : Hodder and Stoughton, 1975.
ISBN 0-340-21246-2 Pbk : £0.65
(B77-14937)

Morton, Stella. The unchanging shore / [by] Stella Morton. — London : Remploy, 1976. — 287p ; 19cm.
Originally published: London : Hodder and Stoughton, 1971.
ISBN 0-7066-0689-2 : £2.75
(B77-10581)

Moyes, Patricia. Black widower / [by] Patricia Moyes. — Harmondsworth [etc.] : Penguin, 1977. — 222p ; 19cm. — (Penguin crime fiction)
Originally published: London : Collins, 1975.
ISBN 0-14-004334-9 Pbk : £0.70
(B77-25207)

Moyes, Patricia. To kill a coconut / [by] Patricia Moyes. — London : Collins [for] the Crime Club, 1977. — 222,[1]p ; 21cm.
ISBN 0-00-231836-9 : £2.95
(B77-05692)

Muir, James A. Breed, cry for vengeance / [by] James A. Muir. — London : Sphere, 1977. — 139p ; 18cm.
ISBN 0-7221-8958-3 Pbk : £0.50
(B77-16062)

Muir, James A. Breed, death stage / [by] James A. Muir. — London : Sphere, 1977. — 143p ; 18cm.
ISBN 0-7221-6263-4 Pbk : £0.65
(B77-28939)

Muir, James A. Breed, the lonely hunt / [by] James A. Muir. — London : Sphere, 1976. — 126p ; 18cm.
ISBN 0-7221-8956-7 Pbk : £0.45
(B77-06300)

Muir, James A. Breed, the silent kill / [by] James A. Muir. — London : Sphere, 1977. — 141p ; 18cm.
ISBN 0-7221-8957-5 Pbk : £0.50
(B77-06888)

Mullally, Frederic. Hitler has won / [by] Frederic Mullally. — London : Pan Books, 1977. — [9],293p ; 18cm.
Originally published: London : Macmillan, 1975.
ISBN 0-330-24883-9 Pbk : £0.80
(B77-06301)

Munro, Hugh. The brain robbers : a Clutha tale / by Hugh Munro. — London : Hale, 1977. — 159p ; 20cm.
ISBN 0-7091-5883-1 : £3.15
(B77-08083)

Munro, Mary. Shadow across the desert / by Mary Munro. — London : Hale, 1977. — 156p ; 20cm.
ISBN 0-7091-5973-0 : £3.10
(B77-15528)

Munthe, Adam John. A note that breaks the silence : the story of Peire Carcasse and Little Beast / [by] Adam John Munthe. — London [etc.] : Bodley Head, 1977. — 240p : map ; 21cm.
ISBN 0-370-30035-1 : £4.95
(B77-29725)

Murdoch, Iris. Bruno's dream / [by] Iris Murdoch. — Harmondsworth [etc.] : Penguin, 1976. — [5],311p ; 18cm.
Originally published: London : Chatto and Windus, 1969.
Pbk : Unpriced
ISBN 0-14-003176-6
(B77-01825)

Murdoch, Iris. Bruno's dream / [by] Iris Murdoch. — St Albans : Triad, 1977. — 269p ; 18cm.
Originally published: London : Chatto and Windus, 1969.
ISBN 0-586-04485-x Pbk : £0.85
(B77-24502)

Murdoch, Iris. Henry and Cato / [by] Iris Murdoch. — London : Chatto and Windus, 1976. — [7],340p ; 21cm.
ISBN 0-7011-2195-5 : £4.00
(B77-14418)

Murdoch, Iris. A severed head / [by] Iris Murdoch. — Harmondsworth [etc.] : Penguin, 1976. — 205p ; 18cm.
Originally published: London : Chatto and Windus, 1961.
ISBN 0-14-002003-9 Pbk : Unpriced
(B77-01826)

Murphy, John, *b.1921.* Pay on the way out / [by] John Murphy. — London : Hale, 1977. — [7],275p ; 20cm.
Originally published: New York : Scribner, 1975.
ISBN 0-7091-5982-x : £3.50
(B77-12692)

Murphy, Nonie Carol. Mutual arrangements / [by] Nonie Carol Murphy. — London [etc.] : Hodder and Stoughton, 1977. — 316p ; 23cm.
Originally published: New York : Simon and Schuster, 1976.
ISBN 0-340-22079-1 : £4.50
(B77-26560)

Murray, Jill. Autumn at Andersgate / by Jill Murray. — London : Hale, 1976. — 192p ; 20cm.
ISBN 0-7091-5853-x : £2.95
(B77-00441)

Murray, Jill. Sweet tyranny / by Jill Murray. — London : Hale, 1977. — 191p ; 20cm.
ISBN 0-7091-6299-5 : £3.20
(B77-28940)

Murray, Julia. A gentleman of honour / by Julia Murray. — London : Hale, 1977. — 189p ; 21cm.
ISBN 0-7091-5735-5 : £3.50
(B77-05693)

Murray, Julia. The notorious Lady May / [by] Julia Murray. — London : Hale, 1977. — 173p ; 21cm.
ISBN 0-7091-5914-5 : £3.25
(B77-17757)

Murray, Julia. Wed for a wager / by Julia Murray. — London : Hale, 1977. — 3-188p ; 21cm.
ISBN 0-7091-6287-1 : £3.85
(B77-32864)

Muskett, Netta. Give back yesterday / [by] Netta Muskett. — London : Arrow Books, 1976. — 190p ; 18cm.
Originally published: London : Hutchinson, 1955.
ISBN 0-09-913530-2 Pbk : £0.50
(B77-05075)

Muskett, Netta. The long road / [by] Netta Muskett. — London : Sphere, 1977. — 304p ; 18cm.
Originally published: London : Hale, 1951.
ISBN 0-7221-6275-8 Pbk : £0.75
(B77-19738)

Muskett, Netta. Love in amber / [by] Netta Muskett. — London : Arrow Books, 1977. — 192p ; 18cm.
Originally published: London : Hutchinson, 1942.
Pbk : £0.50
ISBN 0-09-9-6110-4
(B77-09963)

Muskett, Netta. Rock pine / [by] Netta Muskett. — London : Sphere, 1977. — 269p ; 18cm.
Originally published: London : Hale, 1952.
ISBN 0-7221-6276-6 Pbk : £0.75
(B77-19739)

Muskett, Netta. Safari for seven / [by] Netta Muskett. — London : Sphere, 1977. — 319p ; 18cm.
Originally published: London : Hale, 1952.
ISBN 0-7221-6273-1 Pbk : £0.75
(B77-19740)

Muskett, Netta. The touchstone / [by] Netta Muskett. — London : Arrow Books, 1976. — 224p ; 18cm.
Originally published: London : Hutchinson, 1962.
ISBN 0-09-913490-x Pbk : £0.60
(B77-04415)

Muskett, Netta. The Weir House / [by] Netta Muskett. — London : Arrow Books, 1977. — 252p ; 18cm.
Originally published: London : Hutchinson, 1962.
ISBN 0-09-914430-1 Pbk : £0.55
(B77-12693)

Mydans, Shelley. Thomas / [by] Shelley Mydans. — [London] ([14 St James's Place, S.W.1]) : Fount Paperbacks, 1977. — 510p ; 18cm.
Originally published: London : Collins, 1965.
ISBN 0-00-624813-6 Pbk : £0.95
(B77-30684)

Myers, Robert John. The cross of Frankenstein / [by] Robert J. Myers. — London : Sphere, 1977. — 156p ; 18cm.
Originally published: Philadelphia : Lippincott ; London : Hamilton, 1975.
ISBN 0-7221-6297-9 Pbk : £0.65
(B77-32865)

Myers, Robert John. The slave of Frankenstein / [by] Robert J. Myers. — London : Sphere, 1977. — 160p ; 18cm.
Originally published: Philadelphia : Lippincott, 1976.
ISBN 0-7221-6298-7 Pbk : £0.65
(B77-22890)

Nace, Pierce. Eat them alive / [by] Pierce Nace. — London : New English Library, 1977. — 158p ; 18cm.
Also published: United States : Manor Books, 1977.
ISBN 0-450-03871-8 Pbk : £0.75
(B77-34152)

Nahal, Chaman. Azadi / [by] Chaman Nahal. — London : Deutsch, 1976[i.e.1977]. — 371p ; 23cm.
Originally published: Boston, Mass. : Houghton Mifflin, 1975.
ISBN 0-233-96549-1 : £4.25
(B77-09301)

Naipaul, Vidiadhar Surajprasad. Guerrillas / [by] V.S. Naipaul. — Harmondsworth [etc.] : Penguin, 1977. — 253p ; 19cm.
Originally published: London : Deutsch, 1975.
ISBN 0-14-004323-3 Pbk : £0.80
(B77-20651)

Naipaul, Vidiadhar Surajprasad. In a free state / [by] V.S. Naipaul. — Harmondsworth [etc.] : Penguin, 1977. — 246p ; 18cm.
Originally published: London : Deutsch, 1971.
Pbk : £0.80
ISBN 0-14-003711-x
(B77-20652)

Naipaul, Vidiadhar Surajprasad. Mr Stone and the Knights Companion / [by] V.S. Naipaul. — Harmondsworth [etc.] : Penguin, 1977. — 126p ; 18cm.
Originally published: London : Deutsch, 1963.
Pbk : £0.55
ISBN 0-14-003712-8
(B77-20653)

Naipaul, Vidiadhar Surajprasad. The mystic masseur / [by] V.S. Naipaul. — Harmondsworth [etc.] : Penguin, 1977. — 220p ; 18cm.
Originally published: London : Deutsch, 1957.
Pbk : £0.70
ISBN 0-14-002156-6
(B77-20654)

Narayan, Rasipuram Krishnaswamy. The painter of signs / [by] R.K. Narayan. — London : Heinemann, 1977. — [6],183p ; 23cm.
Originally published: New York : Viking Press, 1976.
ISBN 0-434-49602-2 : £3.50
(B77-12694)

Narayan, Rasipuram Krishnaswamy. The Ramayana : a shortened modern prose version of the Indian epic / [retold] by R.K. Narayan (suggested by the Tamil version of Kamban). — Harmondsworth [etc.] : Penguin, 1977. — xv, 172p : ill ; 20cm.
'... by no means a translation nor a scholarly study, but may be called a resultant literary product out of the impact of Kamban on my mind as a writer' - Introduction. — This version originally published: New York : Viking Press, 1972 ; London : Chatto and Windus, 1973.
ISBN 0-14-004428-0 Pbk : £1.25
(B77-33437)

Nash, Nathaniel Richard. East wind, rain / [by] N. Richard Nash. — London : W.H. Allen, 1977. — [4],373p ; 23cm.
Also published: New York : Atheneum, 1977.
ISBN 0-491-02181-x : £4.95
(B77-28174)

Nassauer, Rudolf. Midlife feasts / [by] Rudolf Nassauer. — London : Cape, 1977. — 208p ; 21cm.
ISBN 0-224-01389-0 : £4.50 : CIP rev.
(B77-12126)

Nathan, Robert. Heaven and hell and the Megas factor / [by] Robert Nathan. — Large print [ed.]. — London : Prior [etc.], 1976. — [9], 159p ; 24cm.
Originally published: New York : Delacorte Press, 1975.
ISBN 0-86043-016-2 : £4.25
(B77-07629)

Nation, Terry. Survivors / [by] Terry Nation. — London : Futura Publications, 1976. — 205p ; 18cm.
Also published: London : Weidenfeld and Nicolson, 1976.
ISBN 0-86007-170-7 Pbk : £0.60
(B77-09302)

Neels, Betty. The fifth day of Christmas / by Betty Neels. — London : Mills and Boon, 1976. — 188p ; 17cm.
Originally published: 1971.
ISBN 0-263-72335-6 Pbk : £0.30
(B77-00442)

Neels, Betty. Gem of a girl / by Betty Neels. — London : Mills and Boon, 1976. — 188p ; 17cm.
ISBN 0-263-72327-5 Pbk : £0.30
(B77-05694)

Neeper, Cary. A place beyond man / by Cary Neeper. — London [etc.] : Millington, 1976. — [10],270p : plan ; 23cm.
Originally published: New York : Scribner, 1975.
ISBN 0-86000-066-4 : £3.50
(B77-14938)

Neilan, Sarah. An air of glory / by Sarah Neilan. — London [etc.] : Hodder and Stoughton, 1977. — 192p ; 23cm.
ISBN 0-340-21334-5 : £3.95
(B77-10953)

Neilan, Sarah. The Braganza pursuit / [by] Sarah Neilan. — London : Sphere, 1977. — 204p ; 18cm.
Originally published: London : Hodder and Stoughton, 1976.
ISBN 0-7221-6333-9 Pbk : £0.85
(B77-23742)

Neill, Robert. Witchfire at Lammas / [by] Robert Neill. — London : Hutchinson, 1977. — 232p ; 23cm.
ISBN 0-09-129690-0 : £3.95
(B77-28941)

Neve, Rosemary. My name is Celin / by Rosemary Neve. — Evesham : James, 1978. — 7-126p ; 20cm.
ISBN 0-85305-197-6 Pbk : £2.75
(B77-32216)

Neville, Anne. Gold in her hair / by Anne Neville. — London : Hale, 1977. — 159p ; 20cm.
ISBN 0-7091-6266-9 : £3.40
(B77-32217)

Neville, Anne. Second time of loving / by Anne Neville. — London : Hale, 1977. — 153p ; 20cm.
ISBN 0-7091-6125-5 : £3.20
(B77-22167)

Nevins, Francis M. Publish and perish / by Francis M. Nevins, Jr. — London : Hale, 1977. — [7],182p ; 20cm.
Originally published: New York : Putnam, 1975.
ISBN 0-7091-6077-1 : £3.15
(B77-17117)

Newby, Percy Howard. Kith / [by] P.H. Newby. — London : Faber, 1977. — [4],124p ; 21cm.
ISBN 0-571-11042-8 : £3.95
(B77-13328)

Newby, Percy Howard. The young May moon / [by] P.H. Newby. — Large print ed. — Bath : Chivers, 1977. — [5],424p ; 22cm.
Originally published: London : Cape, 1950.
ISBN 0-85997-270-4 : £6.00(£4.50 to members of the Library Association)
(B77-34153)

Newman, Andrea. An evil streak / [by] Andrea Newman. — London : Joseph, 1977. — 224p ; 23cm.
ISBN 0-7181-1569-4 : £4.25
(B77-14419)

Newman, Gordon F. A detective's tale / [by] G.F. Newman. — London : Sphere, 1977. — 174p ; 18cm. — (Newman, Gordon F. Law and order)
ISBN 0-7221-6362-2 Pbk : £0.65
(B77-23743)

Newman, Gordon F. The Guvnor / [by] G.F. Newman. — London : Hart-Davis MacGibbon, 1977. — 334p ; 23cm.
ISBN 0-246-10885-1 : £4.25
(B77-05076)

Newman, Gordon F. A prisoner's tale / by G.F. Newman. — London : Sphere, 1977. — 190p ; 18cm. — (Newman, Gordon F. Law and order)
ISBN 0-7221-6364-9 Pbk : £0.65
(B77-30685)

Newman, Kevin. Dislocated : an American carnival / [by] Kevin Newman. — Urbana ; York (27 Hawthorn Spinney, York) : Ex Aedibus, 1977. — [5],165p ; 21cm.
£3.25
(B77-28942)

Ngugi wa Thiong'o. Petals of blood / [by] Ngugi wa Thiong'o. — London [etc.] : Heinemann Educational, 1977. — [6],345p ; 23cm.
ISBN 0-435-90646-1 : £3.95
ISBN 0-435-90188-5 Pbk : £1.25
(B77-32218)

Nichols, John, *b.1940.* The Milagro beanfield war / by John Nichols ; illustrations by Rini Templeton. — London : Deutsch, 1977. — [7], 445p : ill ; 24cm.
Originally published: New York : Holt, Rinehart and Winston, 1974.
ISBN 0-233-96629-3 : £4.95
(B77-08596)

Nichols, Peter, *b.1928.* Ruffo in Calabria : a true novel / by Peter Nichols. — London : Constable, 1977. — 222p ; 23cm.
Based on the life of Fabrizio Ruffo.
ISBN 0-09-461680-9 : £4.50
(B77-30686)

Nicholson, Christina. The power and the passion / [by] Christina Nicholson. — London : Corgi, 1977. — 366p ; 18cm.
ISBN 0-552-10470-1 Pbk : £0.85
(B77-25917)

Nicole, Christopher. Black dawn / [by] Christopher Nicole. — London : Cassell, 1977. — [7],373p : geneal table ; 21cm.
ISBN 0-304-29784-4 : £4.95
(B77-19741)

Niland, D'Arcy. The shiralee / [by] D'Arcy Niland. — Large print ed. — Bath : Chivers, 1977. — [5],346p ; 23cm.
Originally published: London : Angus and Robertson, 1955.
ISBN 0-85997-253-4 : £5.20(£3.90 to members of the Library Association)
(B77-22168)

Niven, Larry. Inferno / [by] Larry Niven and Jerry Pournelle. — London : Wingate, 1977. — 192p : map ; 23cm.
Originally published: United States : s.n., 1976.
ISBN 0-85523-271-4 : £3.95
(B77-14420)

Niven, Larry. A world out of time : a novel / by Larry Niven. — London : Macdonald and Jane's, 1977. — [7],243p ; 21cm.
Originally published: New York : Holt, Rinehart and Winston, 1976.
ISBN 0-354-04143-6 : £3.95
(B77-13329)

Nobbs, David. The return of Reginald Perrin / [by] David Nobbs. — Harmondsworth [etc.] : Penguin, 1977. — 271p ; 18cm.
ISBN 0-14-004668-2 Pbk : £0.75
(B77-27417)

Nobbs, David. The return of Reginald Perrin : a novel / by David Nobbs. — London : Gollancz, 1977. — 271p ; 21cm.
ISBN 0-575-02374-0 : £4.20
(B77-27418)

Noel, Jeffrey. Johnny Perfect, the trouble with crime / [by] Jeffrey Noel. — London : Sphere, 1976. — 144p ; 18cm.
Spine title: The trouble with crime.
ISBN 0-7221-6399-1 Pbk : £0.65
(B77-02605)

Nolan, Christopher. Journal of a navvy / [by] Tom Goane ; edited [i.e. written] by Christopher Nolan. — Sevenoaks : Coronet, 1977. — 143p ; 18cm. — (Nolan, Christopher. Diaries of Tom Goane ; vol.2)
ISBN 0-340-21791-x Pbk : £0.60
(B77-28943)

Nolan, Christopher. Journal of a young rake / [by] Tom Goane ; edited [i.e. written] by Christopher Nolan. — London : Coronet, 1977. — 144p ; 18cm. — (Nolan, Christopher. Diaries of Tom Goane ; vol.1)
ISBN 0-340-21569-0 Pbk : £0.60
(B77-13330)

Nolan, Frederick. The Mittenwald syndicate / [by] Frederick Nolan. — London : Sphere, 1977. — 302p ; 18cm.
Originally published: New York : Morrow ; London : Cassell, 1976.
ISBN 0-7221-6427-0 Pbk : £0.95
(B77-28944)

Nolan, Frederick. The Ritter double-cross / [by] Frederick Nolan. — London : Futura Publications, 1976. — [5],169p ; 18cm. — (A contact book)
Originally published: London : Barker, 1974.
ISBN 0-86007-332-7 Pbk : £0.55
(B77-08597)

Noone, Carl. Even the rainbow's bent / [by] Carl Noone. — London : New English Library, 1977. — 188p ; 18cm.
ISBN 0-450-03401-1 Pbk : £0.95
(B77-30687)

Norman, Barry. A series of defeats / [by] Barry Norman. — London : Quartet Books, 1977. — [6],170p ; 23cm.
ISBN 0-7043-2124-6 : £4.25
(B77-12127)

North, Anne. Strictly no males / [by] Anne North. — London : New English Library, 1977. — 126p.
ISBN 0-450-03291-4 Pbk : £0.60
(B77-28175)

North, Elizabeth. Enough blue sky / by Elizabeth North. — London : Gollancz, 1977. — 190p ; 21cm.
ISBN 0-575-02251-5 : £4.20
(B77-13898)

Norton, André. Sorceress of the witch world / [by] Andre Norton. — London : Prior [etc.], 1977. — [2],221p : 2 maps(on lining papers) ; 21cm. — (Norton, André. Witch world novels of Andre Norton)
Originally published: New York : Ace Books, 1968 ; London : Tandem, 1970.
ISBN 0-86043-073-1 : £4.95
(B77-21482)

Norton, André. Spell of the witch world / [by] Andre Norton. — London : Prior [etc.], 1977. — [2],159p : 2 maps(on lining papers) ; 21cm. — (Norton, André. Witch world novels of Andre Norton)
Originally published: New York : Daw Books, 1972.
ISBN 0-86043-075-8 : £4.95
(B77-21483)

Norton, André. Three against the witch world / [by] Andre Norton. — London : Prior [etc.], 1977. — [2],189p : 2 maps(on lining papers) ; 21cm. — (Norton, André. Witch world novels of Andre Norton)
Originally published: New York : Ace Books, 1965 ; London : Tandem, 1970.
ISBN 0-86043-071-5 : £4.95
(B77-21484)

Norton, André. Warlock of the witch world / [by] Andre Norton. — London : Prior [etc.], 1977. — [2],222p : 2 maps(on lining papers) ; 21cm. — (Norton, André. Witch world novels of Andre Norton)
Originally published: New York : Ace Books, 1967 ; London : Tandem, 1970.
ISBN 0-86043-072-3 : £4.95
(B77-21485)

Norton, André. Web of the witch world / [by] Andre Norton. — London : Prior [etc.], 1977. — [2],192p : 2 maps(on lining papers) ; 21cm. — (Norton, André. Witch world novels of Andre Norton)
Originally published: New York : Ace Books, 1964 ; London : Tandem, 1970.
ISBN 0-86043-070-7 : £4.95
(B77-21486)

Norton, André. Witch world / [by] Andre Norton. — [1st ed. reprinted] ; [with a new introduction by Sarah Miesel]. — London : Prior [etc.], 1977. — xxix,3-222p : 2 maps(on lining papers) ; 21cm. — (Norton, André. Witch world novels of Andre Norton)
Originally published: New York : Ace Books, 1963 ; London : Tandem, 1970.
ISBN 0-86043-069-3 : £4.95
(B77-21487)

Norton, André. Wolfshead / by André Norton. — London : Hale, 1977. — 157p ; 21cm. — (Hale SF)
Originally published: as 'Secret of the lost race'. New York : Ace Books, 1959.
ISBN 0-7091-6181-6 : £3.60
(B77-30688)

Norton, André. Wraiths of time / [by] André Norton. — London : Gollancz, 1977. — [5], 210p ; 21cm.
Originally published: New York : Atheneum, 1976.
ISBN 0-575-02276-0 : £3.20
(B77-13331)

Norton, André. Year of the unicorn / [by] Andre Norton. — London : Prior [etc.], 1977. — [2], 224p : 2 ill, 2 maps(on lining papers) ; 21cm. — (Norton, André. Witch world novels of Andre Norton)
Originally published: New York : Ace Books, 1965 ; London : Tandem, 1970.
ISBN 0-86043-074-x : £4.95
(B77-21488)

Nova, Craig. Turkey hash / [by] Craig Nova. — Henley-on-Thames : A. Ellis, [1977]. — [5], 197p ; 23cm.
Originally published: New York : Harper and Row, 1972.
ISBN 0-85628-037-2 : £4.50 : CIP rev.
(B77-18381)

Nowra, Louis. The misery of beauty : the loves of Frogman / [by] Louis Nowra. — London [etc.] : Angus and Robertson, 1976. — [5], 203p ; 22cm.
Originally published: in Australia. 1976.
ISBN 0-207-13365-4 : £3.80
(B77-30689)

Nye, Nelson Coral. Strawberry Roan / [by] Nelson Nye. — London : Jenkins, 1976. — 140p ; 21cm.
Originally published: / under the name Clem Colt. New York : Dodd, Mead ; London : Ward Lock, 1953.
ISBN 0-214-20243-7 : £2.25
(B77-05695)

Nye, Nelson Coral. The Texas gun / [by] Nelson Nye. — London : Jenkins, 1976. — 158p ; 21cm.
Originally published: United States : s.n., 1970.
ISBN 0-214-20248-8 : £2.25
(B77-05696)

Oates, Joyce Carol. Childwold / [by] Joyce Carol Oates. — London : Gollancz, 1977. — [7],295p ; 21cm.
Originally published: New York : Vanguard Press, 1976.
ISBN 0-575-02348-1 : £4.95
(B77-28176)

O'Brian, Patrick. The Mauritius command / [by] Patrick O'Brian. — London : Collins, 1977. — [9],268p : maps ; 22cm.
ISBN 0-00-222383-x : £3.95
(B77-24503)

O'Brien, Darcy. A way of life like any other / [by] Darcy O'Brien. — London : Martin Brian and O'Keeffe, 1977. — viii,149p ; 21cm.
ISBN 0-85616-480-1 : £4.00
(B77-28177)

O'Brien, Edna. Girl with green eyes / [by] Edna O'Brien. — Harmondsworth [etc.] : Penguin, 1977. — 213p ; 18cm. — (Peacock books)
Originally published: as 'The lonely girl'. London : Cape, 1962.
ISBN 0-14-047102-2 Pbk : £0.65
(B77-33438)

O'Brien, Edna. Johnny I hardly knew you : a novel / by Edna O'Brien. — London : Weidenfeld and Nicolson, 1977. — 143p ; 23cm.
ISBN 0-297-77284-8 : £3.65
(B77-19742)

O'Brien, Kate. Mary Lavelle / [by] Kate O'Brien. — Large print ed. — Bath : Chivers, 1977. — xi,446p ; 23cm.
Originally published: London : Heinemann, 1936.
ISBN 0-85997-209-7 : £5.60(£4.20 to members of the Library Association)
(B77-09964)

O'Brien, Robert C. Z for Zachariah / [by] Robert C. O'Brien. — London : Collins, 1976. — 188p ; 18cm. — (Lions)
Originally published: New York : Atheneum, 1974 ; London : Gollancz, 1975.
ISBN 0-00-671081-6 Pbk : £0.50
(B77-10954)

Odell, Kathleen. Mission to Circassia / [by] Kathleen Odell. — London [etc.] : Heinemann, 1977. — [4],250p : map(on lining papers) ; 23cm.
ISBN 0-434-01950-x : £4.50
(B77-20655)

O'Doherty, Malachi. Belfast story / by Malachi O'Doherty. — Whitley Bay (10 Greenhaugh Rd, South Wellfield, Whitley Bay, Tyne & Wear NE25 9HF) : Erdesdun Pomes [for] 'Ostrich', 1976. — [1],56p ; 21cm.
ISBN 0-905274-02-4 Sd : £0.30
(B77-04417)

O'Donnell, Lillian. The baby merchants / [by] Lillian O'Donnell. — Toronto [etc.] ; London : Bantam, 1976. — [5],217,[1]p ; 18cm. — (O'Donnell, Lillian. Norah Mulcahaney detective novels)
Originally published: New York : Putnam, 1975.
ISBN 0-552-62511-6 Pbk : £0.60
(B77-15529)

O'Donnell, Peter. Last day in Limbo / [by] Peter O'Donnell. — London [etc.] : Pan Books, 1977. — 236p ; 18cm.
Originally published: London : Souvenir Press, 1976.
ISBN 0-330-25142-2 Pbk : £0.75
(B77-21489)

Offutt, Andrew J. Cormac Mac Art, sword of the Gael / [by] Andrew J. Offutt. — London : Sphere, 1977. — 220p ; 18cm.
ISBN 0-7221-6512-9 Pbk : £0.75
(B77-32219)

O'Flaherty, Liam. Skerrett / [by] Liam O'Flaherty. — Portmarnock : Wolfhound Press, 1977. — 287p : port ; 21cm.
Originally published: London : Gollancz, 1932.
ISBN 0-905473-10-8 : £4.50
ISBN 0-905473-11-6 Pbk : Unpriced
(B77-24504)

O'Grady, Anne. Operation Midas / [by] Anne O'Grady. — London : Corgi, 1977. — 188p ; 18cm.
Originally published: London : P. Davies, 1973.
ISBN 0-552-10377-2 Pbk : £0.70
(B77-19013)

O'Hara, John. Appointment in Samarra / [by] John O'Hara. — Large print ed. — Bath : Lythway Press, 1977. — ix,370p ; 22cm.
Originally published: London : Faber, 1935.
ISBN 0-85046-708-x : £4.85
(B77-22169)

O'Hara, Patrick. The Yangtze run / [by] Patrick O'Hara. — London : Arlington Books, 1977. — 238p ; 23cm.
ISBN 0-85140-248-8 : £3.75
(B77-19014)

Okpi, Kalu. The smugglers / [by] Kalu Okpi. — London [etc.] : Macmillan, 1977. — [2],141p ; 18cm. — (Pacesetters)
For adolescents.
ISBN 0-333-23082-5 Pbk : £0.59
(B77-31490)

Oliver, Marina. Campaign for a bride / by Marina Oliver. — London : Hale, 1977. — 181p ; 21cm.
ISBN 0-7091-5631-6 : £3.50
(B77-09303)

Oliver, Marina. Charms of a witch / [by] Marina Oliver. — London : Hale, 1977. — 175p ; 21cm.
ISBN 0-7091-5889-0 : £3.50
(B77-20656)

Oliver, Marina. Strife beyond Tamar / by Marina Oliver. — London : Hale, 1977. — 176p ; 21cm.
ISBN 0-7091-6250-2 : £3.70
(B77-28945)

Olsen, Theodore V. Day of the buzzard / [by] T.V. Olsen. — London : Coronet, 1977. — 175p ; 18cm.
Originally published: New York : Fawcett, 1976.
ISBN 0-340-21816-9 Pbk : £0.50
(B77-23744)

Olsen, Theodore V. High lawless / [by] T.V. Olsen. — Large print ed. — Leicester : Ulverscroft, 1977. — [5],244p ; 23cm. — (Ulverscroft large print series : [Western])
Originally published: New York : Fawcett, 1960 ; London : Muller, 1961.
ISBN 0-85456-515-9 : £2.65
(B77-08084)

Olsen, Theodore V. Mission to the West / [by] T.V. Olsen. — London : Sphere, 1977. — 187p ; 18cm.
Originally published: Garden City, N.Y. : Doubleday, 1973.
ISBN 0-7221-6526-9 Pbk : £0.65
(B77-22891)

Olsen, Theodore V. Soldier blue / [by] T.V. Olsen. — London : Sphere, 1976. — 187p ; 18cm.
Originally published: as 'Arrow in the sun', Garden City, N.Y. : Doubleday, 1969 ; and as 'Soldier blue', London : Sphere, 1971.
ISBN 0-7221-6527-7 Pbk : £0.65
(B77-02606)

O'Nair, Mairi. Four winds meet / by Mairi O'Nair. — London : Mills and Boon, 1976. — 189p ; 19cm.
ISBN 0-263-09057-4 : £1.95
(B77-14421)

O'Neill, Edward Aloysius. The Rotterdam delivery / [by] Edward O'Neill. — London : Sphere, 1977. — 253p ; 18cm.
Originally published: London : Gollancz, 1976.
ISBN 0-7221-6542-0 Pbk : £0.85
(B77-25918)

Onyeama, Dillibe. Juju : a novel / by Dillibe Onyeama. — London : Satellite Books, 1977. — 143p ; 23cm.
ISBN 0-905186-57-5 : £4.00
(B77-20657)

Orczy, Emmuska, *Baroness.* By the gods beloved / by Baroness Orczy. — London [etc.] : White Lion Publishers, 1977. — 255p ; 21cm.
Facsimile reprint of: 1st ed. London : Greening and Co., 1905.
ISBN 0-7274-0271-4 : £3.50
(B77-06302)

Ordway, Peter. Object of the exercise / [by] Peter Ordway. — London : Hale, 1977. — 190p ; 21cm.
ISBN 0-7091-6010-0 : £3.25
(B77-08085)

Orgill, Douglas. The Astrid factor / by Douglas Orgill. — Hornchurch : I. Henry, 1977. — [4], 186p ; 21cm.
Originally published: London : P. Davies, 1968.
ISBN 0-86025-108-x : £3.25
(B77-25208)

Ormerod, Roger. This murder come to mind / by Roger Ormerod. — London : Hale, 1977. — 192p ; 20cm.
ISBN 0-7091-6230-8 : £3.25
(B77-22892)

Ormerod, Roger. Too late for the funeral : a Mallin & Coe story / by Roger Ormerod. — London : Hale, 1977. — 184p ; 20cm.
ISBN 0-7091-5983-8 : £3.15
(B77-14939)

O'Rourke, Frank. Gun hand / [by] Frank O'Rourke. — London : Corgi, 1977. — 141p ; 18cm.
Originally published: New York : Ballantine, 1953 ; London : Hamilton, 1961.
ISBN 0-552-10461-2 Pbk : £0.50
(B77-31491)

O'Rourke, Frank. Latigo / [by] Frank O'Rourke. — London : Corgi, 1977. — 128p ; 18cm.
Originally published: New York : Random House, 1953.
ISBN 0-552-10407-8 Pbk : £0.50
(B77-16063)

O'Rourke, Frank. Violence at sundown / [by] Frank O'Rourke. — London : Corgi, 1977. — 190p ; 18cm.
Originally published: New York : Random House, 1953.
ISBN 0-552-10430-2 Pbk : £0.50
(B77-20658)

Orr, Mary. Rich girl, poor girl / [by] Mary Orr. — London : W.H. Allen, 1977. — [7],294p ; 23cm.
Originally published: New York : Dial Press, 1975.
ISBN 0-491-02280-8 : £4.95
(B77-19743)

Osborne, Beresford. The disciples of Nemesis / by Beresford Osborne. — London : Hale, 1977. — 192p ; 20cm. — ([Hale crime])
ISBN 0-7091-6097-6 : £3.15
(B77-15530)

Osborne, Beresford. The receivers / by Beresford Osborne. — London : Hale, 1977. — 184p ; 20cm.
ISBN 0-7091-6329-0 : £3.50
(B77-30690)

Osbourne, Ivor. The mercenary / [by] Ivor Osbourne. — London : Collings, 1977. — viii, 136p ; 23cm.
ISBN 0-86036-021-0 : £4.50
(B77-18382)

Osmond, Andrew. Saladin! / [by] Andrew Osmond. — London : Arrow Books, 1977. — 320p : maps ; 18cm.
Originally published: London : Hutchinson, 1975.
ISBN 0-09-914240-6 Pbk : £0.80
(B77-28178)

Ottum, Bob. The Tuesday blade : a novel / by Bob Ottum. — London : Heinemann, 1977. — 3-226p ; 23cm.
Originally published: New York : Simon and Schuster, 1976.
ISBN 0-434-56100-2 : £3.90
(B77-09965)

Packer, Bernard. Doctor Caro / [by] Bernard Packer. — London : Heinemann, 1977. — [5], 309p ; 23cm.
Originally published: as 'Caro'. New York : Dutton, 1975.
ISBN 0-434-57500-3 : £3.90
(B77-05697)

Packer, Joy, *Lady.* Leopard in the fold / [by] Joy Packer. — London : Corgi, 1977. — 191p ; 18cm.
Originally published: London : Eyre and Spottiswoode, 1969.
ISBN 0-552-10443-4 Pbk : £0.65
(B77-20659)

Packer, Joy, *Lady.* Valley of the Vines / [by] Joy Packer. — London : Corgi, 1977. — 284p ; 18cm.
Originally published: London : Eyre and Spottiswoode, 1955.
ISBN 0-552-10442-6 Pbk : £0.80
(B77-20660)

Packer, Joy, *Lady.* Veronica / [by] Joy Packer. — London : Corgi, 1977. — 172p ; 18cm.
Originally published: London : Eyre and Spottiswoode, 1970.
ISBN 0-552-10444-2 Pbk : £0.65
(B77-21490)

Page, Vicki. The house of Harron / [by] Vicki Page. — London : Hale, 1977. — 172p ; 21cm.
ISBN 0-7091-5932-3 : £3.50
(B77-20661)

Pargeter, Edith. Afterglow and nightfall / [by] Edith Pargeter. — London [etc.] : Macmillan, 1977. — [9],342p : map(on lining papers), geneal table ; 21cm. — (Pargeter, Edith. Brothers of Gwynedd ; book 4)
ISBN 0-333-21786-1 : £4.95
(B77-27419)

Parker, John, *b.1926.* The village cricket match / [by] John Parker. — London : Weidenfeld and Nicolson, 1977. — [5],145p ; 23cm.
ISBN 0-297-77317-8 : £3.65
(B77-19744)

Parker, Robert Brown. God save the child / [by] Robert B. Parker. — Harmondsworth [etc.] : Penguin, 1977. — 169p ; 18cm. — (Penguin crime fiction)
Originally published: Boston, Mass. : Houghton Mifflin, 1974 ; London : Deutsch, 1975.
ISBN 0-14-004471-x Pbk : £0.70
(B77-31492)

Parker, Robert Brown. Mortal stakes / [by] Robert B. Parker. — Harmondsworth [etc.] : Penguin, 1977. — 176p ; 18cm. — (Penguin crime fiction)
Originally published: Boston, Mass. : Houghton Mifflin, 1975 ; London : Deutsch, 1976.
ISBN 0-14-004399-3 Pbk : £0.70
(B77-31493)

Parker, Robert Brown. Promised land / [by] Robert B. Parker. — London : Deutsch, 1977. — [5],182p ; 21cm.
Originally published: Boston, Mass. : Houghton Mifflin, 1976.
ISBN 0-233-96922-5 : £3.50
(B77-30691)

Parker, Robert Brown. Promised land / [by] Robert B. Parker. — Large print [ed.]. — London : Prior [etc.], 1977. — [5],347p ; 25cm.
Originally published: Boston, Mass. : Houghton Mifflin, 1976.
ISBN 0-86043-077-4 : £4.95
(B77-26561)

Parkin, Molly. Write up / [by] Molly Parkin. — London : Joseph, 1977. — 237p ; 23cm.
ISBN 0-7181-1597-x : £4.50
(B77-22170)

Parkinson, Cyril Northcote. Devil to pay / [by] C. Northcote Parkinson. — London : Methuen, 1977. — 273p,[4]p of plates : maps ; 18cm.
Originally published: London : J. Murray, 1973.
ISBN 0-413-36910-2 Pbk : £0.75
(B77-09966)

Parkinson, Cyril Northcote. The fireship / [by] C. Northcote Parkinson. — London ([11 New Fetter La., EC4P 4EE]) : Magnum Books, 1977. — 191p : maps ; 18cm.
'The second Richard Delancey novel' - p.1. — Originally published: London : J. Murray, 1975.
ISBN 0-413-36920-x Pbk : £0.70
(B77-09304)

Parkinson, Cyril Northcote. Touch and go / [by] C. Northcote Parkinson. — London : J. Murray, 1977. — 230,[5]p : maps ; 22cm.
ISBN 0-7195-3371-6 : £3.95
(B77-22893)

Parris, Barney. Big night at Mrs Maria's : a novel / by Barney Parris. — London [etc.] : Mews Books ; London : Distributed by New English Library, 1977. — 126p ; 19cm.
ISBN 0-452-00064-5 Pbk : £0.50
(B77-05077)

Passes, Alan. Big step / [by] Alan Passes. — London : Allison and Busby, 1977. — 166p ; 23cm.
ISBN 0-85031-204-3 : £4.50
ISBN 0-85031-205-1 Pbk : £1.95
(B77-30692)

Paton, Alan. Cry, the beloved country : a story of comfort in desolation / [by] Alan Paton. — Large print ed. — Bath : Lythway Press, 1977. — vi,441p ; 23cm.
Originally published: London : Cape, 1948.
ISBN 0-85046-705-5 : £4.85
(B77-17118)

Paton, Alan. Too late the Phalarope / [by] Alan Paton. — Harmondsworth [etc.] : Penguin, 1977. — 200p ; 19cm.
Originally published: London : Cape, 1953.
Pbk : £0.70
ISBN 0-14-003216-9
(B77-24505)

Patterson, James. The Thomas Berryman number / by James Patterson. — London : Secker and Warburg, 1977. — [4],256p ; 23cm.
Originally published: Boston, Mass. : Little, Brown, 1976.
ISBN 0-436-36360-7 : £3.90
(B77-00984)

Pattinson, James. Final run / [by] James Pattinson. — London : Hale, 1977. — 189p ; 21cm.
ISBN 0-7091-5268-x : £3.70
(B77-28946)

Pattinson, James. The no-risk operation / [by] James Pattinson. — London : Hale, 1977. — 191p ; 21cm.
ISBN 0-7091-5019-9 : £3.50
(B77-09967)

Pattinson, James. The Spanish Hawk / [by] James Pattinson. — London : Hale, 1977. — 192p ; 21cm.
ISBN 0-7091-5119-5 : £3.70
(B77-19745)

Pattinson, James. Special delivery / by James Pattinson. — London : Hale, 1976. — 189p ; 21cm.
ISBN 0-7091-4893-3 : £3.25
(B77-01827)

Paul, Barbara. The seventeenth stair / [by] Barbara Paul. — London (110 Warner Rd, S.E.5) : Troubadour, 1976. — [4],240p ; 18cm.
Originally published: London : Macdonald and Jane's, 1975.
ISBN 0-86007-186-3 Pbk : £0.60
(B77-08598)

Paul, Charlotte. Phoenix Island / [by] Charlotte Paul. — St Albans : Mayflower, 1977. — 430p : map ; 18cm.
Originally published: New York : New American Library, 1976.
ISBN 0-583-12751-7 Pbk : £0.75
(B77-22171)

Peake, Lilian. A bitter loving / by Lilian Peake. — London : Mills and Boon, 1976. — 186p ; 18cm.
ISBN 0-263-72329-1 Pbk : £0.30
(B77-05698)

Peake, Lilian. Somewhere to lay my head / by Lilian Peake. — London : Mills and Boon, 1977. — 188p ; 17cm.
ISBN 0-263-72387-9 Pbk : £0.35
(B77-21491)

Pearce, Brenda. Worlds for the grabbing / [by] Brenda Pearce. — London : Dobson, 1977. — 3-222p ; 21cm. — ([Dobson science fiction])
ISBN 0-234-72040-9 : £3.95
(B77-29726)

Pearce, Mary Emily. Apple tree lean down / [by] Mary E. Pearce. — St Albans : Mayflower, 1977. — 254p ; 18cm.
Originally published: London : Macdonald and Co., 1973.
ISBN 0-583-12739-8 Pbk : £0.75
(B77-24506)

Pearce, Mary Emily. Apple tree saga / [by] Mary E. Pearce. — London : Macdonald and Jane's, 1977. — [9],494p ; 24cm.
This collected edition originally published: as 'Apple tree lean down'. New York : St Martin's Press, 1976. — Contents: Apple tree lean down. Originally published: London : Macdonald and Co., 1973 - Jack Mercybright. Originally published: 1974 - The sorrowing wind. Originally published: 1975.
ISBN 0-354-04099-5 : £4.95
(B77-15531)

Pearce, Mary Emily. Cast a long shadow / [by] Mary E. Pearce. — London : Macdonald and Jane's, 1977. — [5],246p ; 23cm.
ISBN 0-354-04098-7 : £3.95
(B77-14940)

Pearce, Mary Emily. Jack Mercybright / [by] Mary E. Pearce. — St Albans : Mayflower, 1977. — 176p ; 18cm.
Originally published: London : Macdonald and Jane's, 1974.
ISBN 0-583-12741-x Pbk : £0.75
(B77-27420)

Pearson, Diane. Csardas / [by] Diane Pearson. — London : Corgi, 1977. — 680p ; 18cm.
Originally published: London : Macmillan, 1975. — Bibl.: p.679-680.
ISBN 0-552-10375-6 Pbk : £1.25
(B77-13332)

Peel, Colin Dudley. Flameout / by Colin D. Peel. — London : Hale, 1976. — 191p ; 20cm.
ISBN 0-7091-5855-6 : £2.95
(B77-01828)

Pegus, Rae Palmer. A family of strangers / by Rae Palmer Pegus. — London : Hale, 1977. — 192p ; 20cm.
ISBN 0-7091-6036-4 : £3.20
(B77-30693)

Pemberton, Margaret. Rendezvous with danger / [by] Margaret Pemberton ; edited by Lesley Saxby. — London (110 Warner Rd, S.E.5) : Troubadour, 1976. — [4],164p ; 18cm.
Originally published: London : Macdonald and Jane's, 1974.
ISBN 0-86007-185-5 Pbk : £0.50
(B77-08086)

Pendleton, Don. Executioner 22, Hawaiian hellground / [by] Don Pendleton. — London : Corgi, 1976. — [7],177p ; 18cm.
Originally published: New York : Pinnacle Books, 1975.
ISBN 0-552-10302-0 Pbk : £0.60
(B77-02607)

Pendleton, Don. Executioner 23, St Louis showdown / [by] Don Pendleton. — London : Corgi, 1977. — [7],181p ; 18cm.
Also published: New York : Pinnacle Books, 1977.
ISBN 0-552-10382-9 Pbk : £0.60
(B77-11415)

Pendleton, Don. Executioner 24, Canadian crisis / [by] Don Pendleton. — London : Corgi, 1977. — ix,181p ; 18cm.
Originally published: New York : Pinnacle Books, 1975.
ISBN 0-552-10457-4 Pbk : £0.60
(B77-31494)

Pendleton, Don. Executioner 25, Colorado Kill-Zone / [by] Don Pendleton. — London : Corgi, 1977. — [11],180p ; 18cm.
Originally published: New York : Pinnacle Books, 1976.
ISBN 0-552-10501-5 Pbk : £0.60
(B77-24507)

Pendry, Eric Douglas. The way to go home / [by] Eric Pendry. — London : Secker and Warburg, 1977. — [5],185p ; 23cm.
ISBN 0-436-36628-2 : £3.90
(B77-28947)

Pentecost, Hugh. Die after dark / [by] Hugh Pentecost. — London : Hale, 1977. — [4], 186p ; 20cm.
Originally published: New York : Dodd, Mead, 1976.
ISBN 0-7091-6294-4 : £3.50
(B77-30694)

Pentecost, Hugh. The fourteen dilemma / [by] Hugh Pentecost. — London : Hale, 1977. — [4] ,184p ; 20cm.
Originally published: under the name Judson Philips. New York : Dodd, Mead, 1976.
ISBN 0-7091-5918-8 : £3.15
(B77-05699)

Percy, Walker. Lancelot / [by] Walker Percy. — London : Secker and Warburg, 1977. — [7], 257p ; 23cm.
ISBN 0-436-56111-5 : £4.50
(B77-28179)

Percy, Walker. The moviegoer / [by] Walker Percy. — London : Secker and Warburg, 1977. — [9],242p ; 23cm.
Originally published: New York : Knopf, 1961 ; London : Eyre and Spottiswoode, 1963.
ISBN 0-436-36662-2 : £4.10
(B77-26562)

Pereira, Wilfred Dennis. Contact / [by] W.D. Pereira. — London : Hale, 1977. — 192p ; 21cm. — (Hale SF)
ISBN 0-7091-5934-x : £3.25
(B77-09968)

Perrault, Ernest G. Spoil! / [by] E.G. Perrault. — [London] : Fontana, 1977. — 220p ; 18cm.
Originally published: Toronto : Doubleday Canada, 1975 ; London : Collins, 1976.
ISBN 0-00-614995-2 Pbk : £0.70
(B77-25209)

Perrin, Robert. Jewels / [by] Robert Perrin. — London [etc.] : Routledge and Kegan Paul, 1977. — [8],272p,[4]p of plates : ill, ports ; 22cm.
Bibl.: p.271-272.
ISBN 0-7100-8700-4 : £4.95 : CIP rev.
(B77-17758)

Perrot, Irene. River of revelation / [by] Irene Perrot. — Ilfracombe : Stockwell, 1977. — 182p ; 22cm.
ISBN 0-7223-0991-0 : £3.00
(B77-31495)

Perry, Ritchie. Dead end / [by] Ritchie Perry. — London : Collins [for] the Crime Club, 1977. — 195p ; 21cm.
ISBN 0-00-231088-0 : £3.25
(B77-21492)

Peters, Elizabeth. The Camelot caper / [by] Elizabeth Peters. — [London] : Coronet, 1977. — 190p ; 18cm.
Originally published: New York : Meredith Press, 1969 ; London : Cassell, 1976.
ISBN 0-340-20023-5 Pbk : £0.75
(B77-27421)

Peters, Elizabeth. Crocodile on the sandbank / [by] Elizabeth Peters. — London : Cassell, 1976. — xi,273p ; 21cm.
Originally published: New York : Dodd, Mead, 1975.
ISBN 0-304-29728-3 : £3.50
(B77-08087)

Peters, Elizabeth. Ghost in green velvet / [by] Elizabeth Peters. — London : Cassell and Collier Macmillan, 1977. — [9],241p ; 21cm.
Originally published: as 'Legend in green velvet'. New York : Dodd, Mead, 1976.
ISBN 0-304-29825-5 : £3.95
(B77-18383)

Peters, Ellis. The grass widow's tale / by Ellis Peters. — Hornchurch : I. Henry, 1977. — 192p ; 21cm.
Originally published: London : Collins, 1968.
ISBN 0-86025-085-7 : £3.35
(B77-21493)

Peters, Ellis. A morbid taste for bones : a mediaeval whodunnit / [by] Ellis Peters. — London [etc.] : Macmillan, 1977. — 192p ; 21cm.
ISBN 0-333-22324-1 : £3.50
(B77-21494)

Peters, Ellis. The piper on the mountain / by Ellis Peters. — Hornchurch : I. Henry, 1976. — 192p ; 21cm.
Originally published: London : Collins, 1966.
ISBN 0-86025-071-7 : £2.95
(B77-04418)

Peters, L T. The eleventh plague / [by] L.T. Peters. — St Albans : Mayflower, 1976. — 160p ; 18cm.
Originally published: New York : Simon and Schuster, 1973 ; London : Secker and Warburg, 1974.
ISBN 0-583-12540-9 Pbk : £0.60
(B77-04419)

Peters, Maureen. The crystal and the cloud / [by] Maureen Peters. — London : Hale, 1977. — 192p ; 21cm.
Based on the life of Saint Bernadette of Lourdes.
ISBN 0-7091-6170-0 : £3.70
(B77-27422)

Peters, Maureen. The gallows herd / [by] Maureen Peters. — [London] : Fontana, 1976. — 160p ; 18cm.
Originally published: London : Hale, 1973.
ISBN 0-00-614038-6 Pbk : £0.60
(B77-06889)

Peters, Maureen. The Rose of Hever / [by] Maureen Peters. — London [etc.] : White Lion Publishers, 1976. — 221,[1]p ; 21cm.
Originally published: London : Hale, 1969. — Based on the life of Anne Boleyn.
ISBN 0-7274-0205-6 : £3.50
(B77-03765)

Petrie, Glen. Mariamne / [by] Glen Petrie. — London : Macmillan, 1977. — 405p ; 23cm.
ISBN 0-333-19617-1 : £4.50
(B77-10955)

Petrocelli, Orlando R. Olympia's inheritance / [by] Orlando R. Petrocelli. — London : New English Library, 1977. — 224p ; 18cm.
Originally published: New York : Dodd, Mead, 1974 ; London : New English Library, 1975.
ISBN 0-450-02810-0 Pbk : £0.95
(B77-24508)

Petron, Angela. Prelude to happiness / by Angela Petron. — London : Hale, 1977. — 191p ; 20cm.
ISBN 0-7091-6236-7 : £3.10
(B77-20662)

Peyton, K.M. The right-hand man / [by] K.M. Peyton ; illustrated by Victor Ambrus. — Oxford [etc.] : Oxford University Press, 1977. — [6],218p : ill ; 23cm.
For adolescents.
ISBN 0-19-271391-4 : £3.25 : CIP rev.
(B77-04443)

Philips, Judson. Backlash / [by] Judson Philips. — London : Gollancz, 1977. — [4],183p ; 21cm. — ([Gollancz thriller])
ISBN 0-575-02187-x : £3.60
(B77-04420)

Phillips, David Graham. Susan Lenox : her fall and rise / David Graham Phillips. — [1st ed. reprinted] ; afterword by Elizabeth Janeway. — Carbondale [etc.] : South Illinois University Press ; London [etc.] : Feffer and Simons, 1977. — v-xix[i.e. xxiii],490p ; 20cm. — (Lost American fiction)
Facsimile reprint of: 1st ed., originally published in 2 vols. New York : D. Appleton, 1917.
ISBN 0-8093-0773-1 : £9.70
(B77-13899)

Picton, Bernard. The expert / [by] Bernard Picton. — London : Hale, 1977. — 192p ; 21cm.
'Based on the BBC television series' - jacket. — Originally published: London : Sphere, 1976.
ISBN 0-7091-5959-5 : £3.50
(B77-08088)

Pike, Charles R. Days of blood / [by] Charles R. Pike. — St Albans : Mayflower, 1977. — 125p ; 18cm. — (Pike, Charles R. Jubal Cade ; 9)
ISBN 0-583-12619-7 Pbk : £0.50
(B77-26563)

Pike, Charles R. The killing ground / [by] Charles R. Pike. — St Albans : Mayflower, 1977. — 144p ; 18cm. — (Pike, Charles R. Jubal Cade ; 10)
ISBN 0-583-12620-0 Pbk : £0.50
(B77-25919)

Pike, Geoff. Golightly adrift / [by] Geoff Pike. — London [etc.] : Angus and Robertson, 1977. — [6],250p ; 22cm.
ISBN 0-207-95769-x : £4.20
(B77-24509)

Pike, Geoff. Henry Golightly : a novel of the sea / [by] Geoff Pike. — London [etc.] : Pan Books, 1977. — 255p ; 18cm.
Originally published: London : Angus and Robertson, 1974.
ISBN 0-330-25119-8 Pbk : £0.70
(B77-26564)

Pike, Robert L. Deadline 2 a.m. : a Lieutenant Reardon novel / by Robert L. Pike. — London : Hale, 1977. — [7],183p ; 20cm.
Originally published: Garden City, N.Y. : Doubleday, 1976.
ISBN 0-7091-5896-3 : £3.15
(B77-08089)

Pilcher, Rosamunde. Sleeping tiger / [by] Rosamunde Pilcher. — Large print ed. — Leicester : Ulverscroft, 1977. — [5],303p ; 23cm. — (Ulverscroft large print series : [romance])
Originally published: London : Collins, 1967.
ISBN 0-7089-0022-4 : £2.95
(B77-19746)

Pilcher, Rosamunde. Under Gemini / by Rosamunde Pilcher. — London : Collins, 1977. — [5],282p ; 22cm.
Originally published: New York : St Martin's Press, 1976.
ISBN 0-00-222488-7 : £3.75
(B77-32866)

Piserchia, Doris. A billion days of earth / by Doris Piserchia. — Toronto [etc.] ; London : Bantam, 1976. — [8],210,[1]p ; 18cm.
'A Frederik Pohl Selection' - cover.
ISBN 0-552-68805-3 Pbk : £0.65
(B77-16064)

Piserchia, Doris. Mister Justice / [by] Doris Piserchia. — London : Dobson, 1977. — 176p ; 21cm. — (Dobson science fiction)
Originally published: New York : Ace Books, 1973.
ISBN 0-234-77144-5 : £3.95
(B77-29727)

Plaidy, Jean. The bastard king / [by] Jean Plaidy. — London [etc.] : Pan Books, 1977. — 333p : ill, geneal table ; 18cm. — (Plaidy, Jean. Norman trilogy ; 1)
Originally published: London : Hale, 1974. — Bibl.: p.7. — Based on the life of William the Conqueror.
ISBN 0-330-25077-9 Pbk : £0.80
(B77-20663)

Plaidy, Jean. Caroline, the Queen / by Jean Plaidy ; [text decorations by B.S. Biro]. — London [etc.] : Pan Books, 1976. — 381p ; 18cm. — (Plaidy, Jean. Georgian saga ; 3)
Originally published: London : Hale, 1968. — Bibl.: p.6. — Based on the life of Queen Caroline, consort of George II.
ISBN 0-330-24550-3 Pbk : £0.80
(B77-08599)

Plaidy, Jean. The heart of the lion / [by] Jean Plaidy. — London : Hale, 1977. — 331p : geneal table ; 23cm. — (Plaidy, Jean. Plantagenet saga ; 3)
Bibl.: p.7-8. — Based on the life of Richard the Lionheart.
ISBN 0-7091-5283-3 : £3.95
(B77-28948)

Plaidy, Jean. The last of the Stuarts / [by] Jean Plaidy. — London : Hale, 1977. — 319,7-317, 7-428p ; 21cm.
Bibl.: p.428. — Contents: The three crowns. Originally published: 1965 - The haunted sisters. Originally published: 1966 - The Queen's favourites. Originally published: 1966.
ISBN 0-7091-6197-2 : £4.95
(B77-22172)

Plaidy, Jean. The lion of justice / [by] Jean Plaidy. — London [etc.] : Pan Books, 1977. — 286p : geneal table ; 18cm. — (Plaidy, Jean. Norman trilogy ; 2)
Originally published: London : Hale, 1975. — Bibl.: p.7. — Based on the life of Henry I, King of England.
ISBN 0-330-25175-9 Pbk : £0.80
(B77-32220)

Plaidy, Jean. Perdita's prince / [by] Jean Plaidy. — London [etc.] : Pan Books, 1976. — 333p : ill ; 18cm. — (Plaidy, Jean. Georgian saga ; 6)
Originally published: London : Hale, 1969. — Bibl.: p.7.
ISBN 0-330-24842-1 Pbk : £0.70
(B77-02609)

Plaidy, Jean. The revolt of the eaglets / [by] Jean Plaidy. — London : Hale, 1977. — 330p : coats of arms, geneal tables ; 23cm.
Bibl.: p.9.
ISBN 0-7091-4698-1 : £3.75
(B77-13333)

Plante, David. The darkness of the body / [by] David Plante. — Harmondsworth [etc.] : Penguin, 1977. — 154p ; 19cm.
Originally published: London : Cape, 1974.
ISBN 0-14-004268-7 Pbk : £0.75
(B77-30695)

Platt, Kin. The body beautiful murder / [by] Kin Platt. — London : Hale, 1977. — [4],177p ; 20cm.
Originally published: New York : Random House, 1976.
ISBN 0-7091-6229-4 : £3.50
(B77-30696)

Platt, Kin. The Princess Stakes murder / [by] Kin Platt. — London : Hale, 1977. — [7], 211p ; 20cm.
Originally published: New York : Random House, 1973.
ISBN 0-7091-5945-5 : £3.25
(B77-12695)

Platts-Mills, Barney. Double trouble : a story for a horror film / [by] Barney Platts-Mills. — London : Duckworth, 1977. — 112p ; 23cm.
ISBN 0-7156-1207-7 : £3.95
(B77-26565)

Player, Robert. Let's talk of graves, of worms, and epitaphs / [by] Robert Player. — Harmondsworth [etc.] : Penguin, 1977. — 206p ; 18cm. — (Penguin crime fiction)
Originally published: London : Gollancz, 1975. — Bibl.: p.206.
ISBN 0-14-004329-2 Pbk : £0.60
(B77-24510)

Player, Robert. The month of the mangled models / by Robert Player. — London : Gollancz, 1977. — 160p ; 21cm. — ([Gollancz thriller])
ISBN 0-575-02379-1 : £3.75
(B77-31496)

Pleydell, Susan. Brighouse Hotel / [by] Susan Pleydell. — London : Collins, 1977. — 221p ; 21cm.
ISBN 0-00-222043-1 : £3.95
(B77-27423)

Pollitz, Edward Alan. The 2000% rule / [by] Edward A. Pollitz, Jr. — London : New English Library, 1977. — [4],299p ; 19cm.
Originally published: Indianapolis : Bobbs-Merrill, 1974 ; London : New English Library, 1975.
ISBN 0-450-03357-0 Pbk : £1.00
(B77-28949)

Pollitz, Edward Alan. The forty-first thief / [by] Edward A. Pollitz. — St Albans : Panther, 1977. — 367p ; 18cm.
Cover title: The 41st thief. — Originally published: New York : Delacorte Press ; London : Hart-Davis MacGibbon, 1975.
ISBN 0-586-04309-8 Pbk : £0.75
(B77-21495)

Ponsonby, Doris Almon. Kaye's Walk / [by] D.A. Ponsonby. — London : Hurst and Blackett, 1977. — 184p ; 20cm.
ISBN 0-09-129670-6 : £3.50
(B77-30697)

Pook, Peter. Pook's china doll / [by] Peter Pook. — London : Hale, 1977. — 188p ; 21cm.
ISBN 0-7091-5799-1 : £3.25
(B77-07630)

Pook, Peter. Pook's curiosity shop / [by] Peter Pook. — London : Hale, 1977. — 188p ; 21cm.
ISBN 0-7091-6122-0 : £3.70
(B77-34154)

Pope, Dudley. Ramage's mutiny : a novel / by Dudley Pope. — London : Alison Press, 1977. — [8],232p : map ; 23cm.
ISBN 0-436-37734-9 : £3.90
(B77-13334)

Porteous, Crichton. The battle mound / by Crichton Porteous. — London : Remploy, 1976. — 190p ; 20cm.
Originally published: London : Hale, 1955.
ISBN 0-7066-0680-9 : £2.75
(B77-03766)

Porter, Alvin. Die-hard lawman / by Alvin Porter. — London : Hale, 1977. — 156p ; 20cm.
ISBN 0-7091-6038-0 : £2.95
(B77-14941)

Porter, Joyce. Dover and the claret tappers : a novel / by Joyce Porter. — London : Weidenfeld and Nicolson, 1976. — 203p ; 20cm.
ISBN 0-297-77154-x : £3.75
(B77-05700)

Porter, Joyce. Who the heck is Sylvia? : a novel / by Joyce Porter. — London : Weidenfeld and Nicolson, 1977. — 176p ; 23cm.
ISBN 0-297-77322-4 : £3.95
(B77-19747)

Portis, Charles. True grit / [by] Charles Portis. — Harmondsworth [etc.] : Penguin, 1977. — 155p ; 18cm. — (Peacock books)
Originally published: New York : Simon and Schuster, 1968 ; London : Cape, 1969.
ISBN 0-14-047093-x Pbk : £0.50
(B77-12128)

Portus, Martin. What did you pinch today? / [by] Martin Portus and Jane Sharman. — Sydney [etc.] ; London : Holt, Rinehart and Winston, 1976. — 72p : ill ; 19cm. — (Flashpoint series)
For adolescents.
ISBN 0-03-900097-4 Pbk : Unpriced
(B77-28180)

Potok, Chaim. In the beginning / [by] Chaim Potok. — Harmondsworth [etc.] : Penguin, 1977. — [5],454p ; 19cm.
Originally published: New York : Knopf, 1975 ; London : Heinemann, 1976.
ISBN 0-14-004349-7 Pbk : £1.10
(B77-27424)

Potter, Jeremy. Death in the forest / [by] Jeremy Potter. — London : Constable, 1977. — 191p ; 23cm.
Based on the life of Edith, Rose of Romsey.
ISBN 0-09-461860-7 : £4.25
(B77-23745)

Powell, Anthony, *b.1905.* A dance to the music of time / [by] Anthony Powell. — [London] : Fontana.
In 12 vols.
[1] : A question of upbringing : a novel. — 1977. — 223p ; 18cm.
Originally published: London : Heinemann, 1951.
ISBN 0-00-614538-8 Pbk : £0.85
(B77-34155)

[2] : A buyer's market : a novel. — 1977. — 286p ; 18cm.
Originally published: London : Heinemann, 1952.
ISBN 0-00-614539-6 Pbk : £0.95
(B77-34156)

[3] : The acceptance world : a novel. — 1977. — 223p ; 18cm.
Originally published: London : Heinemann, 1955.
ISBN 0-00-614540-x Pbk : £0.85
(B77-34157)

[4] : At Lady Molly's : a novel. — 1977. — 237p ; 18cm.
Originally published: London : Heinemann, 1957.
ISBN 0-00-614541-8 Pbk : £0.85
(B77-34158)

[5] : Casanova's Chinese restaurant : a novel. — 1977. — 221p ; 18cm.
Originally published: London : Heinemann, 1960.
ISBN 0-00-614542-6 Pbk : £0.85
(B77-34159)

[6] : The kindly ones : a novel. — 1977. — 256p ; 18cm.
Originally published: London : Heinemann, 1962.
ISBN 0-00-614543-4 Pbk : £0.95
(B77-34160)

[7] : The valley of bones : a novel. — 1977. — 254p ; 18cm.
Originally published: London : Heinemann, 1964.
ISBN 0-00-614544-2 Pbk : £0.95
(B77-34161)

[8] : The soldier's art : a novel. — 1977. — 221p ; 18cm.
Originally published: London : Heinemann, 1966.
ISBN 0-00-614545-0 Pbk : £0.85
(B77-34162)

[9] : The military philosophers : a novel. — 1977. — 250p ; 18cm.
Originally published: London : Heinemann, 1968.
ISBN 0-00-614546-9 Pbk : £0.95
(B77-34163)

[10] : Books do furnish a room : a novel. — 1977. — 255p ; 18cm.
Originally published: London : Heinemann, 1971.
ISBN 0-00-614547-7 Pbk : £0.95
(B77-34164)

[11] : Temporary kings : a novel. — 1977. — 284p ; 18cm.
Originally published: London : Heinemann, 1973.
ISBN 0-00-614548-5 Pbk : £0.95
(B77-34165)

[12] : Hearing secret harmonies : a novel. — 1977. — 252p ; 18cm.
Originally published: London : Heinemann, 1975.
ISBN 0-00-614271-0 Pbk : £0.95
(B77-34166)

Powell, Margaret. Beryl's lot / [by] Margaret Powell with Lee Mackenzie ; from characters originally created by Kevin Laffan. — London : Sphere.
Book 3. — 1977. — 141p ; 18cm.
'Based on a series originated by Kevin Laffan and transmitted by Yorkshire Television'. — Book 3 has author statement: Margaret Powell and Lee Mackenzie.
ISBN 0-7221-6977-9 Pbk : £0.65
(B77-07631)

Powers, Anne. The four queens / by Anne Powers. — London : Hale, 1977. — 224p ; 21cm.
Based on the lives of Marguerite d'Anjou, Elizabeth Woodville, Anne Neville and Elizabeth Plantagenet.
ISBN 0-7091-6313-4 : £3.95
(B77-29728)

Pownall, David. African horse / [by] David Pownall. — Harmondsworth [etc.] : Penguin, 1977. — 272p ; 19cm.
Originally published: London : Faber, 1975.
ISBN 0-14-004362-4 Pbk : £0.90
(B77-32867)

Pownall, David. God Perkins / [by] David Pownall. — London : Faber, 1977. — [5],142p ; 21cm.
ISBN 0-571-10947-0 : £3.95
(B77-12129)

Pownall, David. The raining tree war / [by] David Pownall. — Harmondsworth [etc.] : Penguin, 1977. — 222p ; 19cm.
Originally published: London : Faber, 1974.
ISBN 0-14-004361-6 Pbk : £0.90
(B77-32868)

Powys, John Cowper. Morwyn : the vengeance of God / [by] John Cowper Powys. — London : Sphere, 1977. — 271p ; 18cm. — (The Dennis Wheatley library of the occult)
Originally published: London : Cassell, 1937.
ISBN 0-7221-6980-9 Pbk : £0.95
(B77-06890)

Powys, Theodore Francis. Mr Weston's good wine / [by] T.F. Powys. — Large print ed. — Bath : Lythway Press, 1977. — [5],414p ; 23cm.
Originally published: London : Chatto and Windus, 1927.
ISBN 0-85046-706-3 : £4.85
(B77-17119)

Poyer, Joe. The day of reckoning / [by] Joe Poyer. — London : Sphere, 1977. — 271p ; 18cm.
Originally published: London : Weidenfeld and Nicolson, 1976.
ISBN 0-7221-6981-7 Pbk : £0.75
(B77-19748)

Preston, Ivy. Sunlit seas / by Ivy Preston. — London : Hale, 1977. — 159p ; 20cm.
ISBN 0-7091-6028-3 : £3.10
(B77-19749)

Preston, Jane. Tawny river / by Jane Preston. — London : Hale, 1977. — 176p ; 20cm.
ISBN 0-7091-5987-0 : £3.10
(B77-14942)

Price, Anthony. Our man in Camelot / [by] Anthony Price. — Sevenoaks : Coronet, 1977. — 224p ; 18cm.
Originally published: London : Gollancz, 1975.
ISBN 0-340-21987-4 Pbk : £0.95
(B77-34167)

Price, Emerson. Inn of that journey / by Emerson Price. — [1st ed. reprinted] ; [with an] afterword by the author. — Carbondale [etc.] : Southern Illinois University Press ; London [etc.] : Feffer and Simons, 1977. — 3-276p ; 22cm. — (Lost American fiction)
Facsimile reprint of: 1st ed. Caldwell, Idaho : Caxton Printers, 1939.
ISBN 0-8093-0812-6 : £5.95
(B77-30698)

Price, Eugenia. New moon rising / [by] Eugenia Price. — London [etc.] : Hodder and Stoughton, 1976. — 3-281p ; 23cm.
Originally published: Philadelphia : Lippincott, 1969 ; London : Collins, 1970.
ISBN 0-340-20891-0 : £3.95
(B77-00985)

Price, Richard, *b.1949.* The wanderers / [by] Richard Price. — London [etc.] : Pan Books, 1977. — 218p ; 18cm.
Originally published: Boston, Mass. : Houghton Mifflin, 1974 ; London : Chatto and Windus, 1975.
ISBN 0-330-25105-8 Pbk : £0.70
(B77-19750)

Priest, Christopher. A dream of Wessex / [by] Christopher Priest. — London : Faber, 1977. — [6],199p ; 21cm.
ISBN 0-571-11118-1 : £4.25 : CIP rev.
(B77-22894)

Priestley, Brian. Makariri gold / [by] Brian Priestley. — London [etc.] : Macmillan, 1977. — 192p ; 21cm.
ISBN 0-333-21621-0 : £3.50
(B77-20664)

Priestley, John Boynton. Angel pavement / [by] J.B. Priestley. — Harmondsworth [etc.] : Penguin, 1977. — 3-500p ; 18cm. — (Penguin modern classics)
Originally published: London : Heinemann, 1930.
ISBN 0-14-000650-8 Pbk : £1.25
(B77-14943)

Priestley, John Boynton. Black-out in Gretley / [by] J.B. Priestley. — Large print ed. — Bath : Chivers, 1977. — [7],340p ; 22cm.
Originally published: London : Heinemann, 1942.
ISBN 0-85997-271-2 : £5.40(£4.05 to members of the Library Association)
(B77-34168)

Priestley, John Boynton. Found, lost, found, or, The English way of life / [by] J.B. Priestley. — Large print [ed.]. — London : Prior [etc.], 1977. — [5],197p ; 24cm.
Originally published: London : Heinemann, 1976.
ISBN 0-86043-036-7 : £3.95
(B77-13335)

Priestley, John Boynton. Three men in new suits / [by] J.B. Priestley. — Large print ed. — Bath : Chivers, 1977. — [5],242p ; 22cm.
Originally published: London : Heinemann, 1945.
ISBN 0-85997-261-5 : £4.80(£3.60 to members of the Library Association)
(B77-34169)

Prince, Alison. The doubting kind / [by] Alison Prince. — Basingstoke [etc.] : Macmillan. — (Topliner redstars)
In 2 vols. — Originally published: in 1 vol. London : Methuen, 1975. — For adolescents.
Part 1 : A friend in need. — 1977. — 144p ; 18cm.
ISBN 0-333-21750-0 Pbk : £0.50 : CIP rev.
(B77-06339)

Part 2 : All who love us. — 1977. — 127p ; 18cm.
ISBN 0-333-22321-7 Pbk : £0.50 : CIP rev.
(B77-06340)

Prince, Peter. Agents of foreign power / by Peter Prince. — London : Gollancz, 1977. — 126p ; 21cm.
ISBN 0-575-02228-0 : £3.80
(B77-07632)

Prior, Allan. The interrogators / [by] Allan Prior. — London [etc.] : White Lion Publishers, 1977. — [4],335p ; 23cm.
Originally published: London : Cassell, 1965.
ISBN 0-7274-0292-7 : £3.50
(B77-10582)

Prior, Allan. The operators / [by] Allan Prior. — London [etc.] : White Lion Publishers, 1977. — [4],276p ; 21cm.
Originally published: London : Cassell, 1966.
ISBN 0-7274-0297-8 : £4.50
(B77-25920)

Pronzini, Bill. The stalker / [by] Bill Pronzini. — London : Sphere, 1976. — 188p ; 18cm.
Originally published: New York : Random House, 1971 ; London : Hale, 1974.
ISBN 0-7221-7016-5 Pbk : £0.60
(B77-06303)

Pronzini, Bill. Undercurrent / [by] Bill Pronzini. — London : Sphere, 1977. — 187p ; 18cm.
Originally published: New York : Random House, 1973 ; London : Hale, 1975.
ISBN 0-7221-7020-3 Pbk : £0.65
(B77-06892)

Proud, Franklin M. The golden triangle / [by] Franklin M. Proud. — London : Sphere, 1976. — 267p ; 18cm.
ISBN 0-7221-7032-7 Pbk : £0.75
(B77-02610)

Purdom, Tom. The barons of behaviour / [by] Tom Purdom. — London : Dobson, 1977. — 189p ; 21cm. — (Dobson science fiction)
Originally published: New York : Ace Books, 1972.
ISBN 0-234-77543-2 : £3.95
(B77-32221)

Pym, Barbara. Quartet in autumn / [by] Barbara Pym. — London [etc.] : Macmillan, 1977. — [4],218p ; 21cm.
ISBN 0-333-22778-6 : £3.95
(B77-26566)

Pynchon, Thomas. Mortality and mercy in Vienna / [by] Thomas Pynchon. — [London] ([18 Hayes Court, New Park Rd, SW2 4EX]) : [Aloes Books], [1976]. — [24]p ; 21cm.
'First published by EPOCH in Spring 1959 Vol. ix, No.4' - p.[24].
ISBN 0-85652-023-3 Sd : Unpriced
(B77-04421)

Quantrill, Malcolm. On the Home Front / [by] Malcolm Quantrill. — London [etc.] : Quartet Books, 1977. — [7],182p ; 23cm.
ISBN 0-7043-2137-8 : £4.95
(B77-26567)

Queen, Ellery. And on the eighth day / [by] Ellery Queen. — London : Gollancz, 1977. — [5],191p ; 21cm. — ([The complete crime novels of Ellery Queen ; vol.28]) ([Gollancz vintage detection])
Originally published: New York : Random House ; London : Gollancz, 1964.
ISBN 0-575-02243-4 : £3.30
(B77-05078)

Queen, Ellery. Dead man's tale / by Ellery Queen. — London : Gollancz, 1977. — 159p ; 21cm. — ([Gollancz thrillers])
Originally published: New York : Pocket Books, 1961 ; London : New English Library, 1967.
ISBN 0-575-02256-6 : £3.50
(B77-16065)

Queen, Ellery. The fourth side of the triangle / [by] Ellery Queen. — London : Gollancz, 1977. — [5],183p ; 21cm. — ([Complete crime novels of Ellery Queen; vol.29]) ([Gollancz vintage detection])
Originally published: New York : Random House ; London : Gollancz, 1965.
ISBN 0-575-02244-2 : £3.30
(B77-04422)

Quentin, Dorothy. Bright horizon / [by] Dorothy Quentin. — Large print ed. — Bath : Lythway Press, 1977. — [5],328p ; 23cm.
Originally published: New York : Arcadia, 1946 ; London : Ward Lock, 1947.
ISBN 0-85046-711-x : £4.65
(B77-21496)

Quentin, Patrick. Shadow of guilt : a mystery novel / by Patrick Quentin. — London : Gollancz, 1977. — 208p ; 20cm. — ([Gollancz vintage detection])
Originally published: 1959.
ISBN 0-575-02262-0 : £3.30
(B77-15532)

Quentin, Patrick. Suspicious circumstances / by Patrick Quentin. — London : Gollancz, 1977. — 224p ; 20cm. — ([Gollancz vintage detection])
Originally published: 1957.
ISBN 0-575-02261-2 : £3.30
(B77-16066)

Quigley, John. King's Royal / [by] John Quigley. — London [etc.] : Pan Books, 1977. — 415p ; 18cm.
Originally published: London : Hamilton, 1975.
ISBN 0-330-25005-1 Pbk : £0.75
(B77-09969)

Quigley, John. Queen's Royal / [by] John Quigley. — London : Hamilton, 1977. — 436p ; 23cm.
ISBN 0-241-89621-5 : £4.95
(B77-22173)

Quiller, Andrew. Blood on the sand / [by] Andrew Quiller. — St Albans : Mayflower, 1977. — 127p ; 18cm. — (Quiller, Andrew. Eagles)
ISBN 0-583-12667-7 Pbk : £0.50
(B77-16067)

Quiller, Andrew. City of fire / [by] Andrew Quiller. — St Albans : Mayflower, 1976. — 142p ; 18cm. — (Quiller, Andrew. Eagles)
ISBN 0-583-12666-9 Pbk : £0.50
(B77-03767)

Quin, Ann. Berg / by Ann Quin ; afterword by Dulan Barber. — London : Quartet Books, 1977. — [6],177p ; 20cm.
Originally published: London : Calder, 1964.
ISBN 0-7043-3110-1 Pbk : £1.50
(B77-10583)

Quinn, Derry. The solstice man / [by] Derry Quinn. — London : Harrap, 1977. — 205p ; 23cm.
ISBN 0-245-53073-8 : £3.75
(B77-30699)

Rae, Doris. Sing a quiet tune / by Doris Rae. — London : Hale, 1977. — 191p ; 20cm.
ISBN 0-7091-6272-3 : £3.20
(B77-26568)

Rae, Doris. Spring song / by Doris Rae. — London : Hale, 1977. — 192p ; 20cm.
ISBN 0-7091-5921-8 : £3.10
(B77-13336)

Rae, Hugh Crauford. Harkfast! : the making of the King / [by] Hugh C. Rae. — London : Sphere, 1977. — 223p ; 18cm.
Originally published: London : Constable, 1976.
ISBN 0-7221-7212-5 Pbk : £0.95
(B77-31497)

Rae, Hugh Crauford. The Rookery : a novel of the Victorian underworld / [by] Hugh C. Rae. — London : Sphere, 1976. — 189p ; 18cm.
Originally published: London : Constable, 1974. — Bibl.: p.188-189.
ISBN 0-7221-7208-7 Pbk : £0.60
(B77-06304)

Ramsay, Diana. You can't call it murder / [by] Diana Ramsay. — London : Collins [for] the Crime Club, 1977. — 193p ; 21cm.
ISBN 0-00-231955-1 : £3.25
(B77-19751)

Ramsay, Jack. The golden lady / [by] Jack Ramsay ; based on an original idea by Keith Cavele and Chris Hutchins. — London : New English Library, 1977. — 160p ; 18cm.
ISBN 0-450-03515-8 Pbk : £0.75
(B77-28181)

Ramsay, Jack. The rage / [by] Jack Ramsay. — London : Sphere, 1977. — 155p ; 18cm.
ISBN 0-7221-5915-3 Pbk : £0.65
(B77-19752)

Randall, Bob. The fan / [by] Bob Randall. — London : Secker and Warburg, 1977. — [7], 242p ; 23cm.
Also published: New York : Random House, 1977.
ISBN 0-436-40250-5 : £3.90
(B77-20665)

Randall, Rona. Knight's Keep / [by] Rona Randall. — [London] : Fontana, 1977. — 192p ; 18cm.
Originally published: London : Collins, 1967.
ISBN 0-00-614387-3 Pbk : £0.65
(B77-09305)

Randall, Rona. Lyonhurst / [by] Rona Randall. — Revised ed. — [London] : Fontana, 1977. — 220p ; 18cm.
Previous ed.: published as 'Walk into my parlour'. London : Collins, 1962.
ISBN 0-00-614284-2 Pbk : £0.65
(B77-18386)

Randall, Rona. The watchman's stone / [by] Rona Randall. — [London] : Fontana, 1976. — 221p ; 18cm.
Originally published: London : Collins, 1975.
ISBN 0-00-614279-6 Pbk : £0.60
(B77-10956)

Rankine, John. The Thorburn enterprise / [by] John Rankine. — London : Dobson, 1977. — 184p ; 20cm. — ([Dobson science fiction])
ISBN 0-234-72051-4 : £3.95
(B77-31498)

Raphael, Frederic. The graduate wife / by Frederic Raphael. — Hornchurch : I. Henry, 1976. — [120]p ; 21cm.
Originally published: London : Cassell, 1962.
ISBN 0-86025-094-6 : £2.60
(B77-02611)

Raphael, Frederic. The trouble with England / by Frederic Raphael. — Hornchurch : I. Henry, 1977. — 106p ; 21cm.
Originally published: London : Cassell, 1962.
ISBN 0-86025-093-8 : £2.85
(B77-20666)

Rathbone, Julian. A raving monarchist / [by] Julian Rathbone. — London : Joseph, 1977. — 220p ; 21cm.
ISBN 0-7181-1641-0 : £4.50
(B77-27425)

Rauch, Earl Mac. New York, New York / [by] Earl Mac Rauch. — [London] : Coronet, 1977. — 173p ; 18cm.
Also published: New York : Simon and Schuster, 1977.
ISBN 0-340-22033-3 Pbk : £0.60
(B77-27426)

Raven, Simon. The survivors / [by] Simon Raven. — London [etc.] : Panther, 1977. — 282p ; 18cm. — (Raven, Simon. Alms for oblivion ; 10)
Originally published: London : Blond and Briggs, 1976.
ISBN 0-586-03713-6 Pbk : £0.95
(B77-32222)

Ray, Robert. Metamorphosis / by Robert Ray. — London : Hale, 1976. — 190p ; 21cm. — (Hale SF)
ISBN 0-7091-5872-6 : £3.25
(B77-00443)

Raymond, Diana. Horseman, pass by / [by] Diana Raymond. — London : Cassell, 1977. — [6],180p ; 21cm.
ISBN 0-304-29775-5 : £3.95
(B77-12696)

Raymond, Ernest. The Kilburn tale / [by] Earnest [i.e. Ernest] Raymond. — London [etc.] : White Lion Publishers, 1976. — [5], 282p ; 21cm.
Originally published: London : Cassell, 1947.
ISBN 0-7274-0231-5 : £3.95
(B77-05701)

Raymond, Ernest. Mr Olim / [by] Ernest Raymond. — London [etc.] : White Lion Publishers, 1977. — [7],216p ; 21cm.
Originally published: London : Cassell, 1961.
ISBN 0-7274-0296-x : £3.75
(B77-18387)

Raymond, Patrick. A matter of assassination / [by] Patrick Raymond. — London : Cassell, 1977. — [4],261p ; 21cm.
ISBN 0-304-29794-1 : £3.95
(B77-20667)

Rayner, Claire. Bedford Row / [by] Claire Rayner. — London : Cassell, 1977. — [8], 279p : geneal table ; 21cm. — (Rayner, Claire. Performers ; book 5)
ISBN 0-304-29851-4 : £4.25
(B77-22895)

Rayner, Claire. Paddington Green / [by] Claire Rayner. — London : Corgi, 1976. — 317p ; 18cm. — (Rayner, Claire. Performers ; book 3)
Originally published: London : Cassell, 1975.
ISBN 0-552-10398-5 Pbk : £0.85
(B77-10957)

Rayner, Claire. Soho Square / [by] Claire Rayner. — London : Corgi, 1977. — 348p : geneal tables ; 18cm. — (Rayner, Claire. Performers ; book 4)
Originally published: London : Cassell, 1976.
ISBN 0-552-10571-6 Pbk : £0.85
(B77-31499)

Rayner, William. Eating the big fish / [by] William Rayner. — London : Collins, 1977. — 195p ; 22cm.
ISBN 0-00-222208-6 : £3.50
(B77-23746)

Read, Lesley-Anne. Better to have loved / by Lesley-Anne Read. — London : Hale, 1977. — 188p ; 20cm.
ISBN 0-7091-6056-9 : £3.20
(B77-19753)

Redwood, Alec. The day of the redeemer / [by] Alec Redwood. — London : Hale, 1977. — 192p ; 21cm.
ISBN 0-7091-6168-9 : £3.70
(B77-25921)

Reeman, Douglas. Go in and sink / [by] Douglas Reeman. — London : Arrow Books, 1977. — 400p ; 18cm.
Originally published: London : Hutchinson, 1973.
Pbk : £0.80
ISBN 0-09-909760-5
(B77-05702)

Reeman, Douglas. HMS Saracen / [by] Douglas Reeman. — Large print ed. — Leicester : Ulverscroft, 1977. — [7],612p ; 23cm. — (Ulverscroft large print series : [fiction])
Originally published: London : Jarrolds, 1965.
ISBN 0-85456-513-2 : £2.65
(B77-08090)

Reeman, Douglas. A prayer for the ship / [by] Douglas Reeman. — London : Arrow Books, 1976. — 255p ; 18cm.
Originally published: London : Jarrolds, 1958.
Pbk : £0.70
ISBN 0-09-907890-2
(B77-05703)

Reeman, Douglas. The pride and the anguish / [by] Douglas Reeman. — London : Arrow Books, 1976. — 320p ; 18cm.
Originally published: London : Hutchinson, 1968.
ISBN 0-09-907940-2 Pbk : £0.75
(B77-03229)

Reeman, Douglas. Rendezvous, south Atlantic / [by] Douglas Reeman. — London : Arrow Books, 1976. — 384p ; 18cm.
Originally published: London : Hutchinson, 1972.
Pbk : £0.75
ISBN 0-09-907820-1
(B77-04423)

Reeman, Douglas. Winged escort / [by] Douglas Reeman. — London : Arrow Books, 1977. — 286p ; 18cm.
Originally published: London : Hutchinson, 1975.
ISBN 0-09-913380-6 Pbk : £0.75
(B77-12130)

Rees, David, *b.1936.* Risks / [by] David Rees. — London : Heinemann, 1977. — 92p ; 21cm. — (Pyramid books)
For adolescents.
ISBN 0-434-95819-0 : £2.20
(B77-34170)

Reeves, Lynette Pamela. Harlow's dimension / [by] L.P. Reeves. — London : Hale, 1977. — 158p ; 21cm. — (Hale SF)
ISBN 0-7091-5981-1 : £3.25
(B77-14944)

Reeves, Lynette Pamela. The stone age venture / by L.P. Reeves. — London : Hale, 1977. — 155p ; 21cm. — (Hale SF)
ISBN 0-7091-6281-2 : £3.60
(B77-28950)

Reid, Henrietta. The tartan ribbon / by Henrietta Reid. — London : Mills and Boon, 1976. — 189p ; 19cm.
ISBN 0-263-09055-8 : £1.95
(B77-14422)

Reid, Sheila. Perfumes of the East / by Sheila Reid. — London : Hale, 1977. — 156p ; 20cm.
ISBN 0-7091-6080-1 : £3.20
(B77-19754)

Rendell, Ruth. A demon in my view / [by] Ruth Rendell. — London : Arrow Books, 1977. — 184p ; 18cm.
Originally published: London : Hutchinson, 1976.
ISBN 0-09-914860-9 Pbk : £0.65
(B77-30700)

Rendell, Ruth. A judgement in stone / [by] Ruth Rendell. — London : Hutchinson, 1977. — 191p ; 23cm.
ISBN 0-09-129070-8 : £3.75
(B77-20668)

Reynolds, Mack. Tomorrow might be different / [by] Mack Reynolds. — London : Sphere, 1976. — 140p ; 18cm. — (Sphere science fiction)
'A shorter version of this novel was published in "The Magazine of Fantasy and Science Fiction" under the title "Russkies go home!" ...' - title page verso.
ISBN 0-7221-7317-2 Pbk : £0.65
(B77-02612)

Rhode, John. Dr Priestley's quest / [by] John Rhode. — Large print ed. — Bath : Lythway Press, 1977. — [5],312p ; 23cm. — (Lythway classics of crime and detection)
Originally published: London : Bles, 1926.
ISBN 0-85046-743-8 : £4.75
(B77-30701)

Rice, William. Doctor, no! / [by] William Rice. — St Albans : Mayflower, 1976. — 156p ; 18cm.
ISBN 0-583-12586-7 Pbk : £0.50
(B77-10584)

Richard, Adrienne. Into the road / by Adrienne Richard. — London : Gollancz, 1977. — [9], 206p ; 21cm.
Originally published: Boston, Mass. : Little, Brown, 1976. — For adolescents.
ISBN 0-575-02343-0 : £3.25
(B77-21497)

Richards, Alun. Ennal's Point / [by] Alun Richards. — London : Joseph, 1977. — 239p ; 23cm.
ISBN 0-7181-1507-4 : £4.25
(B77-16068)

Richmond, Grace. Testament of love / by Grace Richmond. — London : Hale, 1977. — 156p ; 20cm.
ISBN 0-7091-5939-0 : £3.10
(B77-13337)

Richmond, Grace. Two Doctor Greys / by Grace Richmond. — London : Hale, 1977. — 185p ; 20cm.
ISBN 0-7091-6157-3 : £3.20
(B77-22896)

Riefe, Alan. The conspirators : a Cage novel / by Alan Riefe. — London [etc.] : Mews Books ; London : Distributed by New English Library, 1977. — 141p ; 18cm. — (Riefe, Alan. Cage ; 2)
Originally published: New York : Popular Library, 1975.
ISBN 0-452-00073-4 Pbk : £0.60
(B77-12131)

Riley, Madeleine. An ideal friend / [by] Madeleine Riley. — London : Cape, 1977. — 183p ; 21cm.
ISBN 0-224-01354-8 : £3.50 : CIP rev.
(B77-08091)

Rimmer, Robert H. The Premar experiments / [by] Robert Rimmer. — London : New English Library, 1976. — 380p : 1 ill ; 18cm.
Originally published: New York : Crown, 1975. — Bibl.: p.370-380.
ISBN 0-450-03117-9 Pbk : £1.10
(B77-12132)

Ritchie, Claire. Master of Trelona / by Claire Ritchie. — London : Hale, 1977. — 153p ; 20cm.
Originally published: as 'Nurse on Castle Island' under the name Sharon Heath. United States : s.n., 1968?.
ISBN 0-7091-5905-6 : £3.10
(B77-09306)

Robbins, Harold. The lonely lady / [by] Harold Robbins. — London : New English Library, 1977. — 400p ; 18cm.
Originally published: New York : Simon and Schuster ; London : New English Library, 1976.
ISBN 0-450-03159-4 Pbk : £1.25
(B77-13900)

Robbins, Tom. Even cowgirls get the blues / [by] Tom Robbins. — London : Corgi, 1977. — [13] ,417p ; 18cm.
Originally published: Boston, Mass. : Houghton Mifflin, 1976.
ISBN 0-552-10513-9 Pbk : £0.95
(B77-22174)

Roberts, Cecil. Victoria four-thirty / by Cecil Roberts. — London [etc.] : Hodder and Stoughton, 1977. — 256p ; 23cm.
Originally published: 1937.
ISBN 0-340-21749-9 : £4.25
(B77-20669)

Roberts, Eleanor. But one queen / [by] Eleanor Roberts. — London : New English Library, 1977. — 175p ; 18cm.
Originally published: 1976. — Based on the life of Lettice Knollys.
ISBN 0-450-03247-7 Pbk : £0.90
(B77-30702)

Roberts, Irene. Stars above Raffael / by Irene Roberts. — London : Hale, 1977. — 189p ; 20cm.
ISBN 0-7091-6283-9 : £3.20
(B77-29729)

Roberts, Jan. The Judas sheep / [by] Jan Roberts. — Sevenoaks : Coronet, 1977. — 189p ; 18cm.
Originally published: London : Souvenir Press, 1974.
ISBN 0-340-21309-4 Pbk : £0.75
(B77-09307)

Roberts, Keith, *b.1935.* Anita / [by] Keith Roberts. — London [etc.] : Millington, 1976. — 221p ; 23cm.
ISBN 0-86000-070-2 : £3.50
(B77-15533)

Roberts, N M. The wine of courage : Polly's story : book one of an Australian trilogy / by N.M. Roberts. — Ilfracombe : Stockwell, 1977. — 227p : port ; 22cm.
ISBN 0-7223-1003-x : £3.75
(B77-34171)

Robertson, Frank Chester. Greener grows the grass / [by] Frank C. Robertson. — [London] : Fontana, 1977. — 160p ; 18cm.
Originally published: London : Collins, 1942.
ISBN 0-00-614661-9 Pbk : £0.50
(B77-18388)

Robertson, Frank Chester. The noose hangs high / [by] Frank C. Robertson. — [London] : Fontana, 1976. — 160p ; 18cm.
Originally published: London : Collins, 1944.
ISBN 0-00-613948-5 Pbk : £0.40
(B77-01829)

Robertson, Frank Chester. Rawhide / [by] Frank C. Robertson. — [London] : Fontana, 1977. — 160p ; 18cm. — (A Fontana western)
Originally published: London : Collins, 1963.
ISBN 0-00-614425-x Pbk : £0.50
(B77-05704)

Robeson, Kenneth. The angry ghost : a Doc Savage adventure / by Kenneth Robeson. — Toronto ; London [etc.] : Bantam, 1977. — [5], 120p ; 18cm. — (Robeson, Kenneth. Fantastic adventures of Doc Savage ; 86)
Originally published: in 'Doc Savage Magazine', 1940.
ISBN 0-553-02862-6 Pbk : £0.50
(B77-25922)

Robins, Denise. Come back, yesterday / [by] Denise Robins. — London [etc.] : Hodder and Stoughton, 1976. — 223p ; 20cm.
ISBN 0-340-21368-x : £3.25
(B77-02613)

Robins, Denise. The dark corridor / [by] Denise Robins. — London : Coronet, 1977. — 252p ; 18cm.
Originally published: London : Hodder and Stoughton, 1974.
ISBN 0-340-20809-0 Pbk : £0.60
(B77-23747)

Robins, Denise. Dust of dreams / [by] Denise Robins. — London : Arrow Books, 1976. — 160p ; 18cm.
Originally published: London : Hutchinson, 1943.
ISBN 0-09-913550-7 Pbk : £0.45
(B77-03230)

Robins, Denise. The feast is finished / [by] Denise Robins. — London [etc.] : Arrow Books, 1977. — 192p ; 18cm.
Originally published: London : Hutchinson, 1950.
ISBN 0-09-909350-2 Pbk : £0.50
(B77-31500)

Robins, Denise. The feast is finished / [by] Denise Robins. — London [etc.] : Arrow Books, 1977. — 192p ; 18cm.
Originally published: London : Hutchinson, 1950.
Pbk : £0.50
ISBN 0-09-909350-2
(B77-32869)

Robins, Denise. Heart of Paris / [by] Denise Robins. — London : Severn House : [Distributed by Hutchinson], 1977. — 192p ; 21cm.
Originally published: London : Hutchinson, 1951.
ISBN 0-7278-0227-5 : £3.15
(B77-17120)

Robins, Denise. Lovers of Janine / [by] Denise Robins. — Large print ed. — Bath : Lythway Press, 1977. — [5],168p ; 23cm.
Originally published: London : Mills and Boon, 1931.
ISBN 0-85046-712-8 : £3.95
(B77-21498)

Robins, Denise. The noble one / [by] Denise Robins. — London : Severn House : [Distributed by Hutchinson], 1977. — 255p ; 21cm.
Originally published: London : Hodder and Stoughton, 1957.
ISBN 0-7278-0318-2 : £3.50
(B77-28951)

Robins, Denise. Since we love / [by] Denise Robins. — London : Severn House : [Distributed by Hutchinson], 1977. — 256p ; 21cm.
Originally published: London : Hutchinson, 1953.
ISBN 0-7278-0234-8 : £3.25
(B77-22175)

Robins, Denise. Something to love / [by] Denise Robins. — London [etc.] : Arrow Books, 1977. — 192p ; 18cm.
Originally published: London : Hutchinson, 1951.
ISBN 0-09-915230-4 Pbk : £0.50
(B77-31501)

Robinson, Derek, *b.1932 (Apr.).* Kramer's war / [by] Derek Robinson. — London : Hamilton, 1977. — [5],346p ; 21cm.
ISBN 0-241-89578-2 : £3.95
(B77-13338)

Roddick, Barbara. All the proud rebels / by Barbara Roddick. — London : Hale, 1977. — 205p ; 21cm.
ISBN 0-7091-5778-9 : £3.70
(B77-34172)

Roddick, Barbara. The gold and the fever / by Barbara Roddick. — London : Hale, 1977. — 3-205p ; 21cm.
Bibl.: p.7-8.
ISBN 0-7091-6064-x : £3.85
(B77-29730)

Roddick, Barbara. The shadow of honour / [by] Barbara Roddick. — London : Hale, 1977. — 223p ; 21cm.
ISBN 0-7091-5643-x : £3.60
(B77-13339)

Roddick, Barbara. Thieves of mercy / [by] Barbara Roddick. — London : Hale, 1976. — 206p ; 21cm.
ISBN 0-7091-5481-x : £3.25
(B77-00444)

Rodman, Maia. Tuned out / [by] Maia Rodman. — Basingstoke [etc.] : Macmillan, 1976. — 125p ; 18cm. — (Topliners)
Originally published: New York : Dell, 1969. — For adolescents.
ISBN 0-333-19963-4 Pbk : £0.40
(B77-00479)

Rodowsky, Colby F. What about me? : a novel / by Colby F. Rodowsky. — New York ; London : F. Watts, 1976. — [5],137p ; 22cm.
ISBN 0-531-01209-3 : £2.50
(B77-21499)

Rogers, Ray Mount. The negotiator / [by] Ray Mount Rogers. — London : Hale, 1977. — [5], 302p ; 21cm.
Originally published: New York : D. McKay, 1975.
ISBN 0-7091-5648-0 : £3.95
(B77-05705)

Rohmer, Sax. Brood of the Witch Queen / [by] Sax Rohmer. — London : Sphere, 1976. — 188p ; 18cm. — (The Dennis Wheatley library of the occult ; vol.41)
Originally published: London : Pearson, 1918.
ISBN 0-7221-7440-3 Pbk : £0.60
(B77-15534)

Roiphe, Anne Richardson. Torch song / [by] Anne Roiphe. — London : Secker and Warburg, 1977. — [5],226p ; 23cm.
Also published: New York : Simon and Schuster, 1977.
ISBN 0-436-42452-5 : £3.90
(B77-10958)

Roland, Betty. No ordinary man / [by] Betty Roland. — [London] : Fontana, 1977. — 192p ; 18cm.
Originally published: London : Collins, 1974.
ISBN 0-00-614478-0 Pbk : £0.65
(B77-05706)

Rome, Margaret. Bride of Zarco / by Margaret Rome. — London : Mills and Boon, 1976. — 187p ; 19cm.
ISBN 0-263-09052-3 : £1.95
(B77-14945)

Rome, Margaret. Bride of Zarco / by Margaret Rome. — London : Mills and Boon, 1977. — 187p ; 17cm.
Originally published: 1976.
ISBN 0-263-72338-0 Pbk : £0.35
(B77-07633)

Ronder, Jack. Mouse code / [by] Jack Ronder. — London : Heinemann, 1977. — 87p ; 21cm. — (Pyramid books)
For adolescents.
ISBN 0-434-95817-4 : £2.10
(B77-13340)

Roscoe, Charles. Trail of no return / by Charles Roscoe. — London : Hale, 1977. — 175p ; 20cm.
ISBN 0-7091-5990-0 : £2.95
(B77-14423)

Roscoe, Janet. Someone to turn to / by Janet Roscoe. — London : Hale, 1977. — 157p ; 20cm.
ISBN 0-7091-6126-3 : £3.20
(B77-22897)

Roscoe, Janet. The time of the rowans / by Janet Roscoe. — London : Hale, 1977. — 192p ; 20cm.
ISBN 0-7091-5974-9 : £3.10
(B77-14946)

Rosenthal, Andrew. The extra man / [by] Andrew Rosenthal. — London : W.H. Allen, 1977. — 3-140p ; 23cm.
ISBN 0-491-02120-8 : £3.00
(B77-19755)

Ross, Angus, *b.1927.* The Aberdeen conundrum / [by] Angus Ross. — London : Long, 1977. — 185p ; 20cm.
ISBN 0-09-131510-7 : £3.50
(B77-28182)

Ross, Frank, *b.1938.* Dead runner / [by] Frank Ross. — London [etc.] : Macmillan, 1977. — 224p ; 23cm.
ISBN 0-333-21848-5 : £3.95
(B77-25210)

Ross, Regina. Falls the shadow / [by] Regina Ross. — London (110 Warner Rd, S.E.5) : Troubadour, 1976. — x,250p ; 18cm. — (A contact book)
Originally published: New York : Delacorte Press ; London : Barker, 1974.
ISBN 0-86007-184-7 Pbk : £0.65
(B77-08092)

Ross, Sheila. The tower of Monte Rado / [by] Sheila Ross. — [London] : Fontana, 1976. — 254p ; 18cm.
Originally published: London : Collins, 1974.
ISBN 0-00-614389-x Pbk : £0.60
(B77-10959)

Ross, William Edward Daniel. House in Lime Street / by W.E.D. Ross. — London : Hale, 1977. — 158p ; 20cm.
ISBN 0-7091-5835-1 : £3.10
(B77-12697)

Rossiter, Clare. Anne of Summer Ho / [by] Clare Rossiter. — New York : St Martin's Press ; London : Hale, 1977. — 160p ; 21cm.
ISBN 0-7091-5890-4 : £3.25
(B77-17121)

Rossiter, Clare. Orphanage miss / [by] Clare Rossiter. — London : Hale, 1976. — 188p ; 21cm.
ISBN 0-7091-5267-1 : £3.10
(B77-11416)

Rossiter, Clare. Three seasons at Askrigg / by Clare Rossiter. — New York : St Martin's Press ; London : Hale, 1977. — 3-191p ; 21cm.
ISBN 0-7091-6108-5 : £3.70
(B77-23748)

Rossiter, Oscar. Tetrasomy two / [by] Oscar Rossiter. — London : Corgi, 1976. — [7],196p ; 18cm. — (Corgi science fiction).
Originally published: Garden City, N.Y. : Doubleday, 1974 ; London : Hale, 1975.
ISBN 0-552-10280-6 Pbk : £0.60
(B77-04424)

Rossner, Judith. Any minute I can split / [by] Judith Rossner. — London : Weidenfeld and Nicolson, 1977. — [5],222p ; 23cm.
Originally published: New York : McGraw-Hill, 1972.
ISBN 0-297-77273-2 : £4.25
(B77-13341)

Rossner, Judith. Attachments / [by] Judith Rossner. — London : Cape, 1977. — 392p ; 21cm.
ISBN 0-224-01564-8 : £4.50 : CIP rev.
(B77-24511)

Rossner, Judith. Looking for Mr Goodbar / [by] Judith Rossner. — London : Coronet, 1976. — 287p ; 18cm.
Originally published: New York : Simon and Schuster ; London : Cape, 1975.
ISBN 0-340-20818-x Pbk : £0.90
(B77-19756)

Rossner, Judith. Nine months in the life of an old maid / by Judith Rossner. — London : Weidenfeld and Nicolson, 1977. — [5],183p ; 22cm.
Originally published: New York : Dial Press, 1969.
ISBN 0-297-77274-0 : £3.95
(B77-12698)

Rostand, Robert. The D'Artagnan signature / [by] Robert Rostand. — London [etc.] : Arrow Books, 1977. — [10],246p ; 18cm.
Originally published: New York : Putnam, 1975 ; London : Hutchinson, 1976.
ISBN 0-09-914870-6 Pbk : £0.75
(B77-29731)

Rostand, Robert. Viper's game / [by] Robert Rostand. — London : Arrow Books, 1977. — [4],267,[1]p ; 18cm.
Originally published: New York : Delacorte Press, 1974 ; London : Hodder and Stoughton, 1975.
ISBN 0-09-914010-1 Pbk : £0.75
(B77-10585)

Roth, Henry. Call it sleep / [by] Henry Roth. — Harmondsworth [etc.] : Penguin, 1976. — 440p ; 18cm. — (Penguin modern classics)
Originally published: New York : R.O. Ballou, 1934 ; London : Joseph, 1963.
ISBN 0-14-003893-0 Pbk : £1.25
(B77-12133)

Roth, Philip. My life as a man / [by] Philip Roth. — London : Corgi, 1976. — 331p ; 18cm.
Originally published: New York : Holt, Rinehart and Winston ; London : Cape, 1974.
ISBN 0-552-10247-4 Pbk : £0.75
(B77-01830)

Roth, Robert. Sand in the wind / [by] Robert Roth. — London : Corgi, 1976. — 573p : map ; 18cm.
Originally published: Boston, Mass. : Little, Brown, 1973 ; London : Joseph, 1974.
ISBN 0-552-10225-3 Pbk : £0.95
(B77-00445)

Rothwell, Hilda. Laces for a lady / by Hilda Rothwell. — London : Hale, 1977. — 160p ; 20cm.
ISBN 0-7091-6003-8 : £3.10
(B77-17759)

Rowan, Hester. The linden tree / [by] Hester Rowan. — London : Collins, 1977. — 157p ; 19cm.
ISBN 0-00-233449-6 : £2.95
(B77-22176)

Rowland, Alison. Light my candle / [by] Alison Rowland. — Ilfracombe : Stockwell, 1977. — 207p : port ; 23cm.
ISBN 0-7223-0990-2 : £1.50
(B77-20670)

Rowland, Iris. Hunter's dawn / by Iris Rowland. — London : Hale, 1977. — 155p ; 20cm.
ISBN 0-7091-6081-x : £3.20
(B77-30703)

Royce, Kenneth. The woodcutter operation / [by] Kenneth Royce. — London : Coronet, 1976. — 221p ; 18cm.
Originally published: London : Hodder and Stoughton, 1975.
ISBN 0-340-20816-3 Pbk : £0.60
(B77-02614)

Rubens, Bernice. The Ponsonby post / [by] Bernice Rubens. — London : W.H. Allen, 1977. — [5],186p ; 23cm.
ISBN 0-491-02110-0 : £3.95
(B77-20671)

Rudorff, Raymond. The house of the Brandersons : a novel of possession / by Raymond Rudorff. — London : Barrie and Jenkins, 1976[i.e.1977]. — 307p ; 21cm.
Originally published: New York : Arbor House, 1973.
ISBN 0-214-20244-5 : £3.95
(B77-08600)

Rudorff, Raymond. The Venice plot / [by] Raymond Rudorff. — London : Secker and Warburg, 1977. — [6],281p ; 23cm.
ISBN 0-436-43720-1 : £3.90
(B77-19757)

Rundle, Anne. Amberwood / [by] Anne Rundle. — St Albans : Mayflower, 1976. — 236p ; 18cm.
Originally published: London : Hale, 1972.
ISBN 0-583-12714-2 Pbk : £0.65
(B77-08093)

Rundle, Anne. Heronbrook / [by] Anne Rundle. — St Albans : Mayflower, 1977. — 205p ; 18cm.
Originally published: London : Hale, 1975.
ISBN 0-583-12715-0 Pbk : £0.60
(B77-12699)

Rundle, Anne. Judith Lammeter / [by] Anne Rundle. — St Albans : Mayflower, 1977. — 203p : geneal table ; 18cm.
Originally published: London : Hale, 1976.
ISBN 0-583-12716-9 Pbk : £0.65
(B77-22177)

Ruse, Gary Alan. A game of Titans : a novel / by Gary Alan Ruse. — Englewood Cliffs ; London [etc.] : Prentice-Hall, 1976. — xii, 288p : 1 ill, maps, plans ; 22cm.
Bibl.: p.284-288.
ISBN 0-13-346080-0 : £7.20
(B77-03768)

Rushdie, Salman. Grimus / [by] Salman Rushdie. — St Albans : Panther, 1977. — 271p ; 18cm.
Originally published: London : Gollancz, 1975.
ISBN 0-586-04289-x Pbk : £0.85
(B77-25211)

Russell, A J. The Devalino caper / [by] A.J. Russell. — London : Collins [for] the Crime Club, 1977. — 251p ; 21cm.
Originally published: New York : Random House, 1975.
ISBN 0-00-231094-5 : £2.95
(B77-22898)

Russell, Agnes. Larksong at dawn / [by] Agnes Russell. — London : Hale, 1977. — 187p ; 21cm.
ISBN 0-7091-6149-2 : £3.50
(B77-09970)

Russell, Martin. Dial death / [by] Martin Russell. — London : Collins [for] the Crime Club, 1977. — 195p ; 21cm.
ISBN 0-00-231093-7 : £3.25
(B77-30704)

Russell, Ray. Incubus / [by] Ray Russell. — London : Sphere, 1977. — 236p ; 18cm.
Originally published: New York : Morrow, 1976.
ISBN 0-7221-7550-7 Pbk : £0.75
(B77-12700)

Rutherford, Douglas. Return load / [by] Douglas Rutherford. — London : Collins for the Crime Club, 1977. — 250p ; 21cm.
ISBN 0-00-231838-5 : £2.95
(B77-08094)

Ryder, James. Vicious spiral / by James Ryder. — London : Hale, 1976. — 3-189p ; 21cm. — (Hale SF)
ISBN 0-7091-5795-9 : £3.25
(B77-00446)

Ryder, Jonathan. Trevayne / [by] Jonathan Ryder. — London : Futura Publications, 1976. — 446p ; 18cm.
Originally published: New York : Delacorte Press, 1973 ; London : Weidenfeld and Nicolson, 1974.
ISBN 0-86007-260-6 Pbk : £0.75
(B77-08601)

Ryman, Ras. Day of the Ultramind / by Ras Ryman. — London : Hale, 1977. — 3-188p ; 21cm. — (Hale SF)
ISBN 0-7091-6226-x : £3.60
(B77-34174)

St George, Geoffrey. The Proteus pact / [by] Geoffrey St George. — London : Sphere, 1977. — [4],291p ; 18cm.
Originally published: Boston, Mass. : Little, Brown, 1975 ; London : Gollancz, 1976.
ISBN 0-7221-7612-0 Pbk : £0.95
(B77-31502)

Salinger, Jerome David. The catcher in the rye / [by] J.D. Salinger. — Harmondsworth [etc.] : Penguin, 1977. — 220p ; 19cm. — (Peacock books)
Originally published: Boston, Mass. : Little, Brown ; London : Hamilton, 1951.
ISBN 0-14-047092-1 Pbk : £0.60
(B77-22899)

Salisbury, Carola. Dark inheritance / [by] Carola Salisbury. — London : Pan Books, 1977. — 268p ; 18cm.
Originally published: Garden City, N.Y. : Doubleday, 1975 ; London : Collins, 1976.
ISBN 0-330-25103-1 Pbk : £0.75
(B77-19758)

Salisbury, Carola. Mallion's pride / [by] Carola Salisbury. — Large print ed. — Leicester : Ulverscroft, 1977. — [6],516p ; 23cm. — (Ulverscroft large print series : [romance])
Originally published: Garden City, N.Y. : Doubleday ; London : Collins, 1975.
ISBN 0-85456-528-0 : £2.65
(B77-13901)

Salt, Jonathan. Avenger at large / by Jonathan Salt. — London : Hale, 1977. — 192p ; 20cm.
ISBN 0-7091-5966-8 : £3.15
(B77-12701)

Sams, Gideon. The punk : a novel / [by] Gideon Sams. — London (159 Wardour St., W.1) : Polytantric Press, 1977. — 62p ; 21cm.
For adolescents.
ISBN 0-905150-07-4 Pbk : £1.50
(B77-30705)

Samson, Joan. The auctioneer / [by] Joan Samson. — London [etc.] : Hodder and Stoughton, 1976. — 239p ; 21cm.
Originally published: New York : Simon and Schuster, 1975.
ISBN 0-340-21268-3 : £3.75
(B77-00986)

Samuels, Gertrude. Mottele : a partisan odyssey / by Gertrude Samuels. — New York [etc.] ; London : Harper and Row, 1976. — ix,179,[1] p ; 21cm.
'A Joan Kahn book' - half title page.
ISBN 0-06-013759-2 : £6.70
(B77-16069)

Sanchez, Thomas. Rabbit boss / [by] Thomas Sanchez. — Harmondsworth [etc.] : Penguin, 1977. — 519p ; 18cm.
Originally published: New York : Knopf, 1973 ; London : Secker and Warburg, 1974.
ISBN 0-14-004137-0 Pbk : £1.50
(B77-20672)

Sandberg, Peter Lars. Wolf Mountain / [by] Peter Lars Sandberg. — London : Barker, 1975. — [8],311p : map ; 23cm.
ISBN 0-213-16562-7 : £3.75
(B77-07634)

Sanders, Lawrence. The tangent objective / [by] Lawrence Sanders. — London : Hart-Davis MacGibbon, 1977. — 301p ; 23cm.
Originally published: New York : Putnam, 1976.
ISBN 0-246-10978-5 : £3.95
(B77-20673)

Sanders, Lawrence. The tangent objective / [by] Lawrence Sanders. — London [etc.] : Panther, 1977. — 301p ; 18cm.
Originally published: New York : Putnam, 1976 ; London : Hart-Davis MacGibbon, 1977.
ISBN 0-586-04723-9 Pbk : £0.80
(B77-32223)

Sanders, Lawrence. The tomorrow file / [by] Lawrence Sanders. — London : Corgi, 1977. — [7],551p ; 18cm.
Originally published: New York : Putnam, 1975.
ISBN 0-552-10493-0 Pbk : £0.95
(B77-28183)

Sanders, Leonard. The Hamlet warning / by Leonard Sanders. — London : W.H. Allen, 1977. — [7],280p ; 23cm.
Originally published: New York : Scribner, 1976.
ISBN 0-491-02090-2 : £4.50
(B77-20674)

Sandoz, Mari. Son of the gamblin' man : the youth of an artist : a novel / by Mari Sandoz. — Lincoln [Neb.] ; London : University of Nebraska Press, 1976. — x,333p ; 21cm.
Originally published: New York : Potter, 1960. — Based on the lives of John J. Cozad and Robert Henri.
ISBN 0-8032-0895-2 : £11.25
ISBN 0-8032-5833-x Pbk : £3.00
(B77-16070)

Sandstrom, Flora. The midwife of Pont Clery / [by] Flora Sandstrom. — Large print ed. — Bath : Chivers, 1977. — [5],360p ; 22cm.
Originally published: London : A. Barker, 1954.
ISBN 0-85997-262-3 : £5.60(£4.20 to members of the Library Association)
(B77-33439)

Sangster, Paul. The day of dog / [by] Paul Sangster. — Tadworth : World's Work, 1977. — 159p ; 23cm.
ISBN 0-437-73079-4 : £2.90
(B77-31503)

Santee, Ross. Cowboy / by Ross Santee ; illustrated by the author. — Lincoln [Neb.] ; London : University of Nebraska Press, 1977. — [9],257p : ill ; 21cm.
Facsimile reprint of: 1st ed. New York : Grosset and Dunlap, 1928.
ISBN 0-8032-0931-2 : £9.00
ISBN 0-8032-5867-4 Pbk : £2.60
(B77-33440)

Sapir, Richard. The destroyer, oil slick / [by] Richard Sapir and Warren Murphy. — London : Corgi, 1977. — [5],179p ; 18cm.
Originally published: as 'Oil slick'. New York : Pinnacle Books, 1974.
ISBN 0-552-10478-7 Pbk : £0.60
(B77-26569)

Saul, John Ralston. The birds of prey / [by] John Ralston Saul. — London [etc.] : Macmillan, 1977. — 247p ; 23cm.
ISBN 0-333-22599-6 : £3.95
(B77-32870)

Saunders, Anne. Beware this stranger / by Anne Saunders. — London : Hale, 1977. — 174p ; 20cm.
ISBN 0-7091-6187-5 : £3.20
(B77-22178)

Saunders, Jean. Nightmare / [by] Jean Saunders. — London : Heinemann, 1977. — 92p ; 21cm. — (Pyramid books)
For adolescents.
ISBN 0-434-95808-5 : £2.10
(B77-11417)

Saunders, John Monk. Single lady / [by] John Monk Saunders. — [1st ed. reprinted] ; afterword by Stephen Longstreet. — Carbondale [Ill.] [etc.] : Southern Illinois University Press ; London [etc.] : Feffer and Simons, 1976. — [7],395p,3 leaves of plates : ill ; 20cm. — (Lost American fiction)
Originally published: New York : Brewer and Warren, 1931.
ISBN 0-8093-0761-8 : £8.95
(B77-09971)

Sava, George. Mary Mary quite contrary / [by] George Sava. — London : Hale, 1977. — 192p ; 21cm.
ISBN 0-7091-5864-5 : £3.50
(B77-14424)

Savage, Elizabeth. The girls from the five great valleys / [by] Elizabeth Savage. — Large print [ed.]. — London : Prior [etc.], 1977. — [3], 369p ; 25cm.
Also published: Boston, Mass. : Little, Brown, 1977.
ISBN 0-86043-102-9 : £4.95
(B77-34175)

Savage, Jenny. The nemesis club / [by] Jenny Savage. — London [etc.] : Macmillan, 1977. — 191p ; 21cm.
ISBN 0-333-21219-3 : £3.25
(B77-17122)

Savarin, Julian Jay. The archives of haven / [by] Julian Jay Savarin. — London : Corgi, 1977. — 206p ; 18cm. — (Savarin, Julian Jay. Lemmus : a time odyssey ; 3) (Corgi science fiction)
ISBN 0-552-10408-6 Pbk : £0.70
(B77-16071)

Saxton, Judith. The Winter Queen / [by] Judith Saxton. — London : Constable, 1977. — 192p ; 23cm.
Based on the life of Elizabeth of Bohemia.
ISBN 0-09-461790-2 : £4.25
(B77-20675)

Scheff, Michael. Airport '77 : a novel / by Michael Scheff and David Spector based upon their screenplay ; story by H.A.L. Craig and Charles Kuenstle ... — London [etc.] : Pan Books, 1977. — 188p ; 18cm.
ISBN 0-330-25277-1 Pbk : £0.75
(B77-18389)

Schiddel, Edmund. The swing / [by] Edmund Schiddel. — Toronto [etc.] ; London : Bantam, [1977?]. — [9],468p ; 18cm.
Originally published: New York : Simon and Schuster, 1975 ; London : W.H. Allen, 1976.
ISBN 0-552-62224-9 Pbk : £0.95
(B77-26570)

Schoell, Yvonne. The argonauts / [by] Yvonne Schoell. — Toronto [etc.] ; London : Bantam, 1976. — [15],491p ; 18cm.
Originally published: Englewood Cliffs : Prentice-Hall, 1972.
ISBN 0-553-08889-0 Pbk : £0.75
(B77-09308)

Scholefield, Alan. Venom / [by] Alan Scholefield. — London : Heinemann, 1977. — [5],232p ; 23cm.
ISBN 0-434-67859-7 : £4.50
(B77-21500)

Science fiction special. — London : Sidgwick and Jackson.
20. — 1977. — [2],158,176,278p ; 20cm.
Contents: Orbit unlimited : science fiction / by Poul Anderson. Originally published: USA : Almat Publishing, 1961 ; London : Sidgwick and Jackson, 1974 - Singularity Station : science fiction / by Brian N. Ball. Originally published: New York : Daw Books, 1973 ; London : Sidgwick and Jackson, 1974 - The best of John W. Campbell. Originally published: London : Sidgwick and Jackson, 1973.
ISBN 0-283-98375-2 : £4.95
(B77-32871)

Science fiction special. — London : Sidgwick and Jackson.
21. — 1977. — [7],218,204,159p ; 20cm.
Contents: Enchanted pilgrimage / by Clifford D. Simak. Originally published: New York : Berkeley Publishing Corporation, 1975 ; London : Sidgwick and Jackson, 1976 - The portals / by Edward Andrew Mann. Originally published: New York : Simon and Schuster, 1974 ; London : Sidgwick and Jackson, 1975 - The man with a thousand names / by A.E. van Vogt. Originally published: New York : Daw Books, 1974 ; London : Sidgwick and Jackson, 1975.
ISBN 0-283-98404-x : £4.95
(B77-27427)

Science fiction special. — London : Sidgwick and Jackson.
22. — 1977. — [9],231,191,[5],184p ; 20cm.
Contents: To live again / by Robert Silverberg. Originally published: Garden City, N.Y. : Doubleday, 1969 ; London : Sidgwick and Jackson, 1975 - Cemetery world / by Clifford D. Simak. Originally published: New York : Putnam, 1973 ; London : Sidgwick and Jackson, 1975 - Multiface / by Mark Adlard. Originally published: London : Sidgwick and Jackson, 1975.
ISBN 0-283-98405-8 : £4.95
(B77-27428)

Scortia, Thomas Nicholas. The Prometheus crisis / [by] Thomas N. Scortia and Frank M. Robinson. — London [etc.] : Pan Books, 1977. — 318p ; 18cm.
Originally published: Garden City, N.Y. : Doubleday, 1975 ; London : Hodder and Stoughton, 1976.
ISBN 0-330-25330-1 Pbk : £0.80
(B77-34176)

Scott, Douglas, *b.1926.* The spoils of war / [by] Douglas Scott. — London : Secker and Warburg, 1977. — 287p ; 23cm.
ISBN 0-436-47526-x : £4.50
(B77-32224)

Scott, Gavin. Hot pursuit / [by] Gavin Scott. — London : Collins [for] the Crime Club, 1977. — 193p ; 21cm.
ISBN 0-00-231318-9 : £2.95
(B77-18390)

Scott, Mary, *b.1888.* Away from it all / [by] Mary Scott. — London : Hurst and Blackett, 1977. — 191p ; 21cm.
ISBN 0-09-128980-7 : £3.25
(B77-30706)

Scott, Norford. Smoke of the .45 / by Norford Scott. — London : Hale, 1977. — 160p ; 20cm.
ISBN 0-7091-6106-9 : £3.10
(B77-19759)

Scott, Paul. A division of the spoils / [by] Paul Scott. — St Albans : Panther, 1977. — [7], 599p ; 18cm.
Originally published: London : Heinemann, 1975.
ISBN 0-586-04306-3 Pbk : £1.50
(B77-22179)

Scott, Paul. The Raj quartet / [by] Paul Scott. — London : Heinemann, 1976. — 1925p in various pagings ; 24cm.
Contents: The jewel in the crown - The day of the scorpion - The towers of silence - A division of the spoils.
ISBN 0-434-68112-1 : £7.50
(B77-07635)

Scott, Paul. Staying on : a novel / [by] Paul Scott. — London [etc.] : Heinemann, 1977. — [5],216p ; 23cm.
ISBN 0-434-68113-x : £3.90
(B77-08602)

Scott, Virgil. Walk-in / [by] Virgil Scott, Dominic Koski. — London [etc.] : Hodder and Stoughton, 1977. — 253p ; 21cm.
Originally published: New York : Simon and Schuster, 1976.
ISBN 0-340-22048-1 : £3.95
(B77-28184)

Seale, Sara. These delights / [by] Sara Seale. — London [etc.] : Mills and Boon, 1976. — 186p ; 18cm. — (Mills and Boon classics)
Originally published: 1949.
ISBN 0-263-72228-7 Pbk : £0.35
(B77-14947)

Seale, Sara. To catch a unicorn / [by] Sara Seale. — Large print ed. — Leicester : Ulverscroft, 1977. — [6],359p ; 23cm. — (Ulverscroft large print series : [romance])
Originally published: London : Mills and Boon, 1964.
ISBN 0-7089-0000-3 : Unpriced
(B77-32225)

Seaman, Donald. The committee : a novel / by Donald Seaman. — London : Hamilton, 1977. — 192p ; 21cm.
ISBN 0-241-89633-9 : £3.95
(B77-22180)

Searls, Hank. Overboard : a novel / by Hank Searls. — London : Raven Books, 1977. — 283p : map ; 23cm.
ISBN 0-354-04181-9 : £3.95
(B77-19760)

Segal, Erich. Love story / by Erich Segal. — London [etc.] : Hodder and Stoughton, 1977. — [7],131p ; 22cm.
Originally published: New York : Harper and Row ; London : Hodder and Stoughton, 1970.
£2.95
ISBN 0-340-12735-x
(B77-30707)

Segal, Erich. Oliver's story / [by] Erich Segal. — London [etc.] : Granada, 1977. — [6],202p ; 23cm.
Also published: New York : Harper and Row, 1977.
ISBN 0-246-11007-4 : £2.95
(B77-15535)

Seifert, Elizabeth. A call for Dr Barton / by Elizabeth Seifert. — London : Severn House : [Distributed by Hutchinson], 1977. — [6],275p ; 21cm.
Originally published: New York : Dodd, Mead, 1956 ; London : Collins, 1957.
ISBN 0-7278-0210-0 : £3.75
(B77-06305)

Seifert, Elizabeth. The case of Dr Carlisle / [by] Elizabeth Seifert. — London [etc.] : White Lion Publishers, 1976. — 256p ; 21cm.
Originally published: London : Collins, 1953.
ISBN 0-85617-234-0 : £3.25
(B77-03769)

Seifert, Elizabeth. The doctor's affair / [by] Elizabeth Seifert. — London : Collins, 1977. — [5],245p ; 21cm.
Originally published: New York : Dodd, Mead, 1975.
ISBN 0-00-222152-7 : £3.25
(B77-09972)

Seifert, Elizabeth. The doctor's desperate hour / [by] Elizabeth Seifert. — London : Collins, 1977. — [4],244p ; 21cm.
Originally published: Boston, Mass. : Hall, 1976.
ISBN 0-00-222170-5 : £3.95
(B77-22181)

Seifert, Elizabeth. The doctor's desperate hour / [by] Elizabeth Seifert. — Large print ed. — London : Prior [etc.], 1977. — [5],321p ; 24cm.
Originally published: New York : Dodd, Mead, 1976 ; London : Collins, 1977.
ISBN 0-86043-043-x : £5.95
(B77-22900)

Seifert, Elizabeth. The doctor's strange secret / by Elizabeth Seifert. — London : Severn House : [Distributed by Hutchinson], 1977. — [9],271p ; 21cm.
Originally published: New York : Dodd, 1962 ; London : Collins, 1964.
ISBN 0-7278-0279-8 : £3.50
(B77-22182)

Seifert, Elizabeth. The honour of Doctor Shelton / [by] Elizabeth Seifert. — London : Severn House : [Distributed by Hutchinson], 1977. — 3-255p ; 21cm.
Originally published: New York : Dodd, Mead, 1962 ; London : Collins, 1963.
ISBN 0-7278-0219-4 : £3.50
(B77-27429)

Sela, Owen. The Bengali inheritance / [by] Owen Sela. — Sevenoaks : Coronet, 1976. — 206p ; 18cm.
Originally published: London : Hodder and Stoughton, 1975.
ISBN 0-340-20760-4 Pbk : £0.70
(B77-00987)

Sela, Owen. An exchange of eagles / by Owen Sela. — London [etc.] : Hodder and Stoughton, 1977. — 304p ; 21cm.
ISBN 0-340-20719-1 : £3.95
(B77-24512)

Selby, Hubert. The demon / [by] Hubert Selby, Jr. — London : Boyars : Distributed by Calder and Boyars, 1977. — [8],312p ; 23cm.
Originally published: New York : Playboy Press, 1976.
ISBN 0-7145-2598-7 : £4.95
(B77-15536)

Selwyn, Francis. Sergeant Verity presents his compliments / [by] Francis Selwyn. — London : Deutsch, 1977. — 267p ; 21cm.
ISBN 0-233-96806-7 : £3.95
(B77-13342)

Seton, Anya. Devil water / [by] Anya Seton ; a condensation by the editors of Reader's Digest Condensed Books. — Large print ed. — Leicester : Ulverscroft, 1977. — [4],515p ; 23cm. — (Ulverscroft large print series : [fiction])
This condensation originally published: Pleasantville, N.Y. ; London : Reader's Digest Association, 196-?.
ISBN 0-85456-554-x : £2.65
(B77-08603)

Seton, Cynthia Propper. A fine romance / [by] Cynthia Propper Seton. — London : Heinemann, 1977. — 192p ; 23cm.
Originally published: New York : Norton, 1976.
ISBN 0-434-60425-9 : £3.90
(B77-20676)

Seymour, Arabella, *b.1948.* Flesh and the devil / [by] Arabella Seymour. — London : Hale, 1977. — 208p : geneal tables ; 21cm.
ISBN 0-7091-6069-0 : £3.80
(B77-30708)

Seymour, Gerald. The glory boys / [by] Gerald Seymour. — [London] : Fontana, 1977. — 286p ; 18cm.
Originally published: London : Collins, 1976.
ISBN 0-00-614667-8 Pbk : £0.75
(B77-31504)

Seymour, Gerald. The glory boys / [by] Gerald Seymour. Majesty : Elizabeth II and the House of Windsor / [by] Robert Lacey. Ordinary people / [by] Judith Guest. A bag of marbles / [by] Joseph Joffo. — Collector's library ed. — London : Reader's Digest Association [etc.], 1977. — 512p : col ill, ports(some col) ; 21cm. — ('Reader's digest' condensed books)
ISBN 0-340-21949-1 : £2.95
Also classified at 941.085'092'4; 940.53'44
(B77-12702)

Seymour, Gerald. Harry's game / [by] Gerald Seymour. — [London] : Fontana, 1977. — 256p ; 18cm.
Originally published: London : Collins, 1975.
ISBN 0-00-614409-8 Pbk : £0.70
(B77-05707)

Seymour, Gerald. Kingfisher / [by] Gerald Seymour. — London : Collins, 1977. — 286p ; 21cm.
ISBN 0-00-222353-8 : £4.50
(B77-31505)

Seymour, Miranda. Daughter of darkness / [by] Miranda Seymour. — London : Hutchinson, 1977. — 256p ; 23cm.
ISBN 0-09-128530-5 : £3.95
(B77-26571)

Shaara, Michael. The killer angels : a novel / [by] Michael Shaara. — London : W.H. Allen, 1977. — xix,374p : maps, music ; 23cm.
Originally published: New York : McKay, 1974.
ISBN 0-491-02300-6 : £4.95
(B77-19761)

Shackleford, Jack D. The eve of midsummer / [by] Jack D. Shackleford. — London : Corgi, 1977. — 189p ; 18cm.
ISBN 0-552-10360-8 Pbk : £0.65
(B77-09309)

Shackleford, Jack D. The Strickland demon / [by] Jack D. Shackleford. — London : Corgi, 1977. — 142p ; 18cm.
ISBN 0-552-10464-7 Pbk : £0.60
(B77-30709)

Shackleford, Jack D. Tanith / [by] Jack D. Shackleford. — London : Corgi, 1977. — 188p : 1 ill ; 18cm. — (Corgi occult)
ISBN 0-552-10552-x : £0.80
(B77-28185)

Shann, Renée. The beauty of embers / [by] Renée Shann. — London : Hale, 1977. — 158p ; 20cm.
Originally published: London : Collins, 1966.
ISBN 0-7091-5811-4 : £3.20
(B77-34177)

Shann, Renée. Everyone needs a rainbow / [by] Renée Shann. — London : Collins, 1976. — 156p ; 20cm.
ISBN 0-00-233213-2 : £2.75
(B77-00447)

Shann, Renée. Never again / [by] Renée Shann. — Large print ed. — Bath : Lythway Press, 1977. — [5],275p ; 22cm.
Originally published: London : Collins, 1967.
ISBN 0-85046-694-6 : £4.30
(B77-11418)

Shann, Renée. Only time will tell / [by] Renée Shann. — London : Collins, 1977. — 158p ; 19cm.
ISBN 0-00-233615-4 : £2.75
(B77-19762)

Shann, Renée. Stay with me / [by] Renée Shann. — London : Collins, 1975. — 157p ; 20cm.
ISBN 0-00-233753-3 : £1.25
(B77-06306)

Shannon, Dell. Extra kill / by Dell Shannon. — London : Gollancz, 1977. — 288p ; 20cm. — ([Gollancz vintage detection])
Originally published: London : 'Daily express' Book Department, 1962.
ISBN 0-575-02267-1 : £3.75
(B77-19763)

Shannon, Dell. Knave of hearts / by Dell Shannon. — London : Gollancz, 1977. — 284p ; 20cm. — ([Gollancz vintage detection])
Originally published: New York : W. Morrow, 1962 ; London : 'Daily express' Book Department, 1963.
ISBN 0-575-02268-x : £3.75
(B77-19764)

Shannon, Dell. Murder with love / [by] Dell Shannon. — London : Sphere, 1976. — 207p ; 18cm.
Originally published: New York : Morrow, 1971 ; London : Gollancz, 1972.
ISBN 0-7221-7740-2 Pbk : £0.65
(B77-06893)

Shannon, Dell. Streets of death / by Dell Shannon. — London : Gollancz, 1977. — 222p ; 21cm. — ([Gollancz thriller])
Originally published: New York : Morrow, 1976.
ISBN 0-575-02185-3 : £3.75
(B77-20677)

Sharman, Nick. The cats / [by] Nick Sharman. — London : New English Library, 1977. — 160p ; 18cm.
ISBN 0-450-03711-8 Pbk : £0.75
(B77-34178)

Sharp, Margery. Summer visits / [by] Margery Sharp. — London : Heinemann, 1977. — 221p ; 23cm.
ISBN 0-434-69516-5 : £4.10
(B77-28952)

Sharpe, Tom. Blott on the landscape / [by] Tom Sharpe. — London : Pan Books, 1977. — 238p ; 18cm.
Originally published: London : Secker and Warburg, 1975.
ISBN 0-330-25080-9 : £0.75
(B77-22183)

Sharpe, Tom. Indecent exposure / [by] Tom Sharpe. — London : Secker and Warburg, 1977. — [4],248p ; 23cm.
Originally published: 1973.
£3.90
ISBN 0-436-45801-2
(B77-06307)

Sharpe, Tom. Porterhouse blue / [by] Tom Sharpe. — London : Secker and Warburg, 1977. — [4],220p ; 23cm.
Originally published: 1974.
£3.90
ISBN 0-436-45802-0
(B77-06308)

Sharpe, Tom. Riotous assembly / [by] Tom Sharpe. — London : Secker and Warburg, 1977. — [5],249p ; 23cm.
Originally published: 1971.
£3.90
ISBN 0-436-45800-4
(B77-05079)

Shatte, Phyllis. Ninety days to nine-o / [by] Phyllis Shatte. — Ilfracombe : Stockwell, 1976. — 187p ; 22cm.
ISBN 0-7223-0968-6 : £3.60
(B77-20678)

Shaw, Bob. Medusa's children / by Bob Shaw. — London : Gollancz, 1977. — 184p ; 21cm. — ([Gollancz SF])
ISBN 0-575-02249-3 : £4.20
(B77-10960)

Shaw, Bob. Night walk / [by] Bob Shaw. — London : Corgi, 1977. — 172p ; 18cm. — (Corgi science fiction)
Originally published: New York : Banner Books, 1967 ; London : New English Library, 1970.
ISBN 0-552-10507-4 Pbk : £0.70
(B77-24513)

Shaw, Bob. Orbitsville / [by] Bob Shaw. — London [etc.] : Pan Books, 1977. — 187p ; 18cm. — (Pan science fiction)
Originally published: London : Gollancz, 1975.
ISBN 0-330-25013-2 Pbk : £0.60
(B77-10586)

Shaw, Bob. Who goes here? / by Bob Shaw. — London : Gollancz, 1977. — 160p ; 21cm. — ([Gollancz SF])
ISBN 0-575-02347-3 : £3.95
(B77-27430)

Shaw, Catherine. The Casuarina tree / by Catherine Shaw. — London : Mills and Boon, 1976. — 188p ; 19cm.
ISBN 0-263-09018-3 : £1.95
(B77-10587)

Shaw, Irwin. Beggarman, thief / [by] Irwin Shaw. — London : Weidenfeld and Nicolson, 1977. — [7],372p ; 22cm.
ISBN 0-297-77425-5 : £4.95
(B77-30710)

Shaw, Irwin. Lucy Crown / [by] Irwin Shaw. — London : New English Library, 1977. — 253p ; 18cm.
Originally published: New York : Random House ; London : Cape, 1956.
ISBN 0-450-03246-9 Pbk : £0.85
(B77-31506)

Shaw, Irwin. Nightwork / [by] Irwin Shaw. — London [etc.] : Pan Books, 1976. — 335p ; 18cm.
Originally published: New York : Delacorte Press ; London : Weidenfeld and Nicolson, 1975.
ISBN 0-330-24833-2 Pbk : £0.75
(B77-06309)

Shaw, Irwin. Two weeks in another town / [by] Irwin Shaw. — London : New English Library, 1977. — 384p ; 18cm.
Originally published: New York : Random House ; London : Cape, 1960.
ISBN 0-450-03310-4 Pbk : £1.00
(B77-19765)

Shaw, Irwin. Voices of a summer day / [by] Irwin Shaw. — London : New English Library, 1977. — 191p ; 18cm.
Originally published: New York : Dial Press ; London : Weidenfeld and Nicolson, 1965.
ISBN 0-450-03355-4 Pbk : £0.70
(B77-19766)

Shaw, Ralph. Sin city / [by] Ralph Shaw. — London : Everest, 1976. — 288p ; 18cm.
Originally published: as 'Sweet and sour'. 1973.
ISBN 0-905018-08-7 Pbk : £0.75
(B77-12703)

Shea, Robert. Illuminatus! / [by] Robert Shea and Robert Anton Wilson. — London : Sphere.

In 3 vols.
Part 1 : The eye in the pyramid. — 1977. — 311p ; 18cm.
Originally published: New York : Dell, 1975 ; London : Sphere, 1976.
Pbk : £0.95
(B77-32226)

Part 1 : The eye in the pyramid. — 1976. — 311p ; 18cm.
Originally published: New York : Dell, 1975.
ISBN 0-7221-9208-8 Pbk : £0.75
(B77-00448)

Part 2 : The golden apple. — 1977. — 250p ; 18cm.
Spine title: The golden apple. — Originally published: New York : Dell, 1975.
ISBN 0-7221-9209-6 Pbk : £0.75
(B77-06310)

Part 3 : Leviathan. — 1977. — 253p : ill ; 18cm.
Spine title: Leviathan. — Originally published: New York : Dell, 1975.
ISBN 0-7221-9211-8 Pbk : £0.75
(B77-13343)

Shears, Sarah. Courage in parting / [by] Sarah Shears. — London : Elek, 1977. — [4],164p ; 21cm.
ISBN 0-236-40098-3 : £3.95
(B77-33441)

Shears, Sarah. Louise's inheritance / [by] Sarah Shears. — London [etc.] : Elek, 1977. — [5], 254p ; 21cm.
ISBN 0-236-40068-1 : £3.95
(B77-09973)

Sheckley, Robert. Options / [by] Robert Sheckley. — London [etc.] : Pan Books, 1977. — 156p ; 18cm. — (Pan science fiction)
Originally published: New York : Pyramid Publications, 1975.
ISBN 0-330-24885-5 Pbk : £0.60
(B77-06311)

Sheridan, Teresa. Malburne Scar / [by] Teresa Sheridan. — London : Macdonald and Jane's, 1977. — [4],186p ; 21cm. — (A troubadour)
ISBN 0-356-08257-1 : £3.75
(B77-19767)

Sherwood, John. Honesty will get you nowhere / by John Sherwood. — London : Gollancz, 1977. — 191p ; 21cm. — ([Gollancz thriller])
ISBN 0-575-02233-7 : £3.80
(B77-04425)

Sherwood, Martin. Maxwell's demon / [by] Martin Sherwood. — London : New English Library, 1977. — 160p ; 18cm.
Originally published: 1976.
ISBN 0-450-03300-7 Pbk : £0.75
(B77-28953)

Sherwood, Martin. Survival / [by] Martin Sherwood. — London : New English Library, 1977. — 128p ; 18cm.
Originally published: 1975.
ISBN 0-450-03036-9 Pbk : £0.60
(B77-13902)

Shimer, R H. The cricket cage / [by] R.H. Shimer. — Large print [ed.]. — London : Prior [etc.], 1977. — [5],623p ; 24cm.
Originally published: New York : Harper and Row, 1975.
ISBN 0-86043-029-4 : £5.95
(B77-12134)

Shipway, George. The Chilian Club : a diversion / [by] George Shipway. — St Albans : Mayflower, 1977. — 192p ; 18cm.
Originally published: London : P. Davies, 1971.

Pbk : £0.75
ISBN 0-583-12062-8
(B77-24514)

Shipway, George. Free lance / [by] George Shipway. — St Albans : Mayflower, 1977. — 288p ; 18cm.
Originally published: London : P. Davies, 1975.

ISBN 0-583-12576-x Pbk : £0.75
(B77-08604)

Shipway, George. Warrior in bronze / [by] George Shipway. — London : P. Davies, 1977. — [10],277p : geneal table, 2 maps ; 23cm.
Based on the life of Agamemnon.
ISBN 0-432-14757-8 : £4.50
(B77-34179)

Shoesmith, Kathleen Anne. The miser's ward / [by] Kathleen A. Shoesmith. — London : Hale, 1977. — 160p ; 21cm.
ISBN 0-7091-6165-4 : £3.50
(B77-22184)

Short, Agnes. The heritors / [by] Agnes Short. — London : Constable, 1977. — 256p : map ; 22cm.
ISBN 0-09-461610-8 : £4.50
(B77-12704)

Short, Frederick W. The ploughman : a novel / by Frederick W. Short. — London : Mitre Press, 1977. — 247p ; 22cm.
ISBN 0-7051-0255-6 : £3.00
(B77-34180)

Short, Luke. Hardcase / [by] Luke Short. — Toronto [etc.] ; London : Bantam, 1977. — [4], 169p ; 18cm.
Originally published: New York : Doubleday, 1942 ; London : Collins, 1965.
ISBN 0-552-60232-9 Pbk : £0.60
(B77-26572)

Short, Luke. High vermilion / [by] Luke Short. — [London] : Fontana, 1977. — 160p ; 18cm.
Originally published: London : Collins, 1948.
ISBN 0-00-614891-3 Pbk : £0.50
(B77-25212)

Short, Luke. Station West / [by] Luke Short. — Toronto [etc.] ; London : Bantam, 1976. — [4], 170p ; 18cm.
Originally published: Boston, Mass. : Houghton Mifflin ; London : Collins, 1947.
ISBN 0-553-02848-0 Pbk : £0.50
(B77-19015)

Shulman, Milton. Kill 3 / [by] Milton Shulman. — London [etc.] : White Lion Publishers, [1976]. — 192p ; 21cm.
Originally published: London : Collins, 1967.
ISBN 0-7274-0226-9 : £3.25
(B77-04426)

Shute, Nevil. A town like Alice ; [and], Pied piper ; [and], The far country ; [and], The chequer board ; [and], No highway / [by] Nevil Shute. — London : Heinemann : Octopus Books, 1976. — 924p ; 25cm.
ISBN 0-7064-0574-9 : £3.95
(B77-00449)

Siegler, Alan. Comrades / by Alan Siegler. — New York : St Martin's Press ; London : St James Press, 1976. — [7],152p ; 22cm.
£3.50
(B77-11419)

Sillitoe, Alan. Saturday night and Sunday morning / by Alan Sillitoe ; with an introduction by the author, commentary and notes by David Craig, a sequence of Nottingham photographs, and stills from the film. — Harlow : Longman, 1976. — xi,244,[3] p,[10]p of plates : ill ; 20cm. — (Longman imprint books)
This ed. originally published: without ill.: 1968. — Bibl.: p.[3].
ISBN 0-582-23342-9 Pbk : £1.10
(B77-06894)

Silverberg, Robert. Across a billion years / [by] Robert Silverberg. — London : Gollancz, 1977. — [4],249p ; 21cm.
Originally published: New York : Dial Press, 1969.
ISBN 0-575-02355-4 : £3.50
(B77-22185)

Silverberg, Robert. Downward to the earth / by Robert Silverberg. — London : Gollancz, 1977. — 190p ; 21cm. — ([Gollancz SF])
Originally published: Garden City, N.Y. : Doubleday, 1970.
ISBN 0-575-02298-1 : £3.95
(B77-21501)

Silverberg, Robert. Invaders from earth : science fiction / by Robert Silverberg. — London : Sidgwick and Jackson, 1977. — 142p ; 20cm.
Originally published: New York : Ace Books, 1958 ; and in 'A Robert Silverberg omnibus', London : Sidgwick and Jackson, 1970.
ISBN 0-283-98371-x : £3.50
(B77-16072)

Silverberg, Robert. Master of life and death : science fiction / by Robert Silverberg. — London : Sidgwick and Jackson, 1977. — 144p ; 20cm.
Originally published: New York : A.A. Wyn, 1957 ; and in 'A Robert Silverberg omnibus', London : Sidgwick and Jackson, 1970.
ISBN 0-283-98370-1 : £3.50
(B77-16609)

Silverberg, Robert. Shadrach in the furnace / by Robert Silverberg. — London : Gollancz, 1977. — [7],245p ; 21cm. — ([Gollancz SF])
Originally published: New York : Bobbs-Merrill, 1976.
ISBN 0-575-02191-8 : £3.80
(B77-10588)

Silverberg, Robert. Those who watch / [by] Robert Silverberg. — London : New English Library, 1977. — 176p ; 18cm.
Originally published: New York : New American Library, 1967.
ISBN 0-450-03260-4 Pbk : £0.75
(B77-26573)

Silverberg, Robert. To live again / [by] Robert Silverberg. — [London] : Fontana, 1977. — [7], 231p ; 18cm. — (Fontana science fiction)
Originally published: Garden City, N.Y. : Doubleday, 1969 ; London : Sidgwick and Jackson, 1975.
ISBN 0-00-614609-0 Pbk : £0.75
(B77-30711)

Silverberg, Robert. To open the sky / [by] Robert Silverberg. — London : Sphere, 1977. — 203p ; 18cm. — (Sphere science fiction)
Originally published: New York : Ballantine, 1967 ; London : Sphere, 1970.
ISBN 0-7221-7827-1 Pbk : £0.85
(B77-28954)

Silverberg, Robert. Up the line : [by] Robert Silverberg. — London : Sphere, 1975. — 207p ; 18cm.
Originally published: New York : Ballantine Books, 1969.
ISBN 0-7221-7835-2 Pbk : £0.50
(B77-12705)

Simak, Clifford Donald. Cemetery world / [by] Clifford D. Simak. — London (11 New Fetter La., EC4P 4EE) : Magnum Books, 1977. — 191p ; 18cm.
Originally published: New York : Putnam, 1973 ; London : Sidgwick and Jackson, 1975.
ISBN 0-417-02040-6 Pbk : £0.70
(B77-15537)

Simak, Clifford Donald. Enchanted pilgrimage / [by] Clifford D. Simak. — [London] : Fontana, 1977. — [4],218p ; 18cm. — (Fontana science fiction)
Originally published: New York : Berkley Publishing Corporation, 1975 ; London : Sidgwick and Jackson, 1976.
ISBN 0-00-614827-1 Pbk : £0.75
(B77-30712)

Simak, Clifford Donald. Ring around the sun / [by] Clifford D. Simak ; introduction by Harry Harrison. — London : New English Library, 1977. — 205p ; 22cm. — (SF master series)
Originally published: New York : Simon and Schuster, 1953 ; London : New English Library, 1967.
ISBN 0-450-03203-5 : £5.95
(B77-32227)

Simak, Clifford Donald. Shakespeare's Planet : science fiction / by Clifford D. Simak. — London : Sidgwick and Jackson, 1977. — [4], 188p ; 20cm.
Originally published: New York : Berkley Publishing Corporation, 1976.
ISBN 0-283-98373-6 : £3.50
(B77-19016)

Simak, Clifford Donald. Time and again / [by] Clifford D. Simak. — London : Magnum Books, 1977. — 255p ; 19cm.
Originally published: New York : Simon and Schuster, 1951 ; London : Heinemann, 1956.
ISBN 0-413-37670-2 : £2.75
ISBN 0-413-37680-x Pbk : £0.75
(B77-25213)

Simak, Clifford Donald. Way station / [by] Clifford Simak. — London [etc.] : White Lion Publishers, 1976. — [5],210p ; 21cm.
Originally published: Garden City, N.Y. : Doubleday, 1963 ; London : Gollancz, 1964.
ISBN 0-85617-848-9 : £3.25
(B77-03770)

Simpson, Dorothy, *b.1933.* Harbingers of fear / [by] Dorothy Simpson. — London : Macdonald and Jane's, 1977. — [5],184p ; 21cm. — (A Troubadour)
ISBN 0-354-04131-2 : £3.50
(B77-15538)

Simpson, George E. Ghostboat / [by] George E. Simpson and Neal R. Burger. — London : New English Library, 1977. — 287p,plate : 2 ill(1 col) ; 18cm.
Originally published: New York : Dell Publishing Co. ; London : New English Library, 1976.
ISBN 0-450-03141-1 Pbk : £0.75
(B77-09310)

Simpson, Margaret, *b.1913.* Love from a star / by Margaret Simpson. — London : Hale, 1977. — 187p ; 20cm.
ISBN 0-7091-6439-4 : £3.20
(B77-28955)

Sims, George, *b.1923.* Hunters Point / [by] George Sims. — Harmondsworth [etc.] : Penguin, 1976. — 159p ; 18cm. — (Penguin crime fiction)
Originally published: London : Gollancz, 1973.
ISBN 0-14-004142-7 Pbk : £0.60
(B77-01831)

Sinclair, Andrew. Cat / [by] Andrew Sinclair. — London : Sphere, 1977. — 158p ; 18cm.
Originally published: as 'The Surrey cat'. London : Joseph, 1976.
ISBN 0-7221-0418-9 Pbk : £0.85
(B77-28956)

Sinclair, Dennis. The blood brothers / [by] Dennis Sinclair. — London : Corgi, 1977. — 175p ; 18cm.
ISBN 0-552-10353-5 Pbk : £0.60
(B77-09311)

Sinclair, Dennis. The friends of Lucifer / [by] Dennis Sinclair. — London : Corgi, 1977. — 172p ; 18cm.
ISBN 0-552-10500-7 Pbk : £0.65
(B77-23749)

Sinclair, Dennis. The third force / [by] Dennis Sinclair. — London : Corgi, 1976. — 156p ; 18cm.
ISBN 0-552-10303-9 Pbk : £0.50
(B77-04427)

Sinclair, James. Warrior queen / [by] James Sinclair. — London : Souvenir Press, 1977. — 352p : map ; 21cm.
Based on the life of Queen Boadicea.
ISBN 0-285-62297-8 : £4.25 : CIP rev.
(B77-16610)

Sinclair, Michael. A long time sleeping / [by] Michael Sinclair. — St Albans : Panther, 1977. — 204p ; 18cm.
Originally published: London : Gollancz, 1975.
ISBN 0-586-04379-9 Pbk : £0.75
(B77-07636)

Sinclair, Olga. My dear fugitive / by Olga Sinclair. — London : Hale, 1976. — 176p ; 21cm.
ISBN 0-7091-5414-3 : £3.00
(B77-11420)

Sithole, Ndabaningi. Roots of a revolution : scenes from Zimbabwe's struggle / [by] Ndabaningi Sithole. — Oxford [etc.] : Oxford University Press, 1977. — [7],142p ; 21cm.
ISBN 0-19-215672-1 : £3.50 : CIP rev.
(B77-24515)

Size, Nicholas. The secret valley : the real romance of unconquered Lakeland ; with a foreword by Sir Hugh Walpole ; together with, Shelagh of Eskdale ; or, The Stone of Shame / by Nicholas Size. — Beckermet (Beckermet Bookshop, Beckermet, Cumbria) : Michael Moon, [1977]. — x,86,iii-xiv,82p,[13]leaves of plates : ill, maps ; 21cm.
Facsimile reprints. — 'The secret valley' originally published: Kendal : T. Wilson, 1929. — 'Shelagh of Eskdale' originally published: London : F. Warne, 1932.
ISBN 0-904131-16-5 : £3.00
(B77-33442)

Skelton, Clement Lister. Hardacre : a novel / by C.L. Skelton. — London : Hart-Davis MacGibbon, 1977. — 432p : geneal table ; 23cm.
ISBN 0-246-10977-7 : £4.95
(B77-14948)

Slade, Jack. Apache junction / [by] Jack Slade. — London : Jenkins, 1976. — 186p ; 21cm.
Originally published: New York : Tower Publications, 1975.
ISBN 0-214-20238-0 : £2.25
(B77-05708)

Slade, Jack. Durango kill / [by] Jack Slade. — London : Jenkins, 1976. — 158p ; 21cm.
Originally published: United States: s.n., 1975.
ISBN 0-214-20233-x : £2.25
(B77-06312)

Sladek, John. Invisible Green : a Thackeray Phin mystery / by John Sladek. — London : Gollancz, 1977. — [5],186p ; 21cm. — ([Gollancz detection])
ISBN 0-575-02315-5 : £3.95
(B77-19768)

Sladek, John. The Reproductive System / [by] John Sladek. — St Albans : Panther, 1977. — 188p ; 18cm. — (Panther science fiction)
Originally published: London : Gollancz, 1968.
ISBN 0-586-04287-3 Pbk : £0.60
(B77-13344)

Slater, Nigel. Crossfire : a novel of an African coup d'état / [by] Nigel Slater. — London : Collins, 1977. — 193p ; 22cm.
ISBN 0-00-222478-x : £3.95
(B77-34181)

Slaughter, Carolyn. Columba / [by] Carolyn Slaughter. — London : Hart-Davis MacGibbon, 1977. — 188p ; 21cm.
ISBN 0-246-10980-7 : £3.50
(B77-19769)

Slaughter, Frank Gill. East Side General / [by] Frank G. Slaughter. — London : Arrow Books, 1977. — 288p ; 18cm.
Originally published: Garden City, N.Y. : Doubleday, 1952 ; London : Jarrolds, 1953.
Pbk : £0.75
ISBN 0-09-909360-x
(B77-21502)

Slaughter, Frank Gill. The healer / [by] Frank G. Slaughter. — Large print ed. — Leicester : Ulverscroft, 1977. — [7],477p ; 23cm. — (Ulverscroft large print series : [general fiction])
Originally published: New York : Doubleday ; London : Jarrolds, 1955.
ISBN 0-7089-0047-x : £2.95
(B77-28186)

Slaughter, Jim. Blue star range / [by] Jim Slaughter. — London : Hale, 1977. — 160p ; 20cm.
ISBN 0-7091-4627-2 : £2.95
(B77-10589)

Slaughter, Jim. The guns of summer / [by] Jim Slaughter. — London : Hale, 1977. — 160p ; 20cm.
'A Boon Helm Western'.
ISBN 0-7091-4628-0 : £3.10
(B77-19770)

Slaughter, Jim. The hangtree / [by] Jim Slaughter. — London : Hale, 1977. — 158p ; 20cm.
'A Boone Helm Western'.
ISBN 0-7091-4629-9 : £3.10
(B77-32872)

Smalley, Peter. Trove / [by] Peter Smalley. — London : Collins, 1977. — 220p ; 22cm.
ISBN 0-00-222481-x : £4.25
(B77-21503)

Smart, Elizabeth. By Grand Central Station I sat down and wept / [by] Elizabeth Smart. — [1st ed. reprinted] ; foreword by Brigid Brophy. — London (21 Formosa St., W.9) : Polytantric Press, 1977. — 128p ; 20cm.
First ed. originally published: London : Editions Poetry, 1945.
ISBN 0-905150-03-1 : £2.95
(B77-32873)

Smedley, Agnes. Daughter of earth / [by] Agnes Smedley ; afterword by Rosalind Delmar. — London : Virago, 1977. — [6],279p ; 21cm.
Originally published: New York : Coward-McCann, 1929.
ISBN 0-86068-003-7 : £5.50
ISBN 0-86068-004-5 Pbk : £1.95
(B77-20679)

Smith, Edward Elmer. Strangler's moon / [by] E.E. 'Doc' Smith with Stephen Goldin. — St Albans : Panther, 1977. — 158p ; 18cm. — (Smith, Edward Elmer. Family d'Alembert series ; vol.2) (Panther science fiction)
Originally published: s.l. : s.n., 1976.
ISBN 0-586-04335-7 Pbk : £0.50
(B77-08095)

Smith, Eleanor, *Lady.* Caravan / [by] Eleanor Smith. — Large print ed. — Bath : Chivers, 1976. — [9],530p ; 22cm.
Originally published: London : Hutchinson, 1943.
ISBN 0-85997-201-1 : £5.60(£4.20 to members of the Library Association)
(B77-03231)

Smith, Frederick Escreet. 633 Squadron, Operation Crucible / [by] Frederick E. Smith. — London : Cassell and Collier Macmillan, 1977. — 206p ; 21cm.
ISBN 0-304-29828-x : £3.75
(B77-19017)

Smith, Frederick Escreet. 633 Squadron, Operation Rhine Maiden / [by] Frederick E. Smith. — London : Corgi, 1976. — 286p ; 18cm.
Originally published: London : Cassell, 1975.
ISBN 0-552-10155-9 Pbk : £0.75
(B77-06313)

Smith, Frederick Escreet. The persuaders at large / by Frederick E. Smith. — Brighton : Henry Publications, 1976. — 158p ; 21cm.
'Based on screenplays by Val Guest, Terence Feely and Brian Clemens'. — This collection originally published: as book 3 of 'The persuaders'. London : Pan Books, 1973.
ISBN 0-86025-012-1 : £2.85
(B77-07637)

Smith, Frederick Escreet. Saffron's army / [by] Frederick E. Smith. — London [etc.] : White Lion Publishers, 1977. — 255p ; 21cm.
Originally published: London : Futura Publications, 1976.
ISBN 0-7274-0274-9 : £3.50
(B77-12135)

Smith, Guy Newman. Bamboo guerillas / [by] Guy N. Smith. — London : New English Library, 1977. — 141p ; 18cm.
ISBN 0-450-03412-7 Pbk : £0.70
(B77-28957)

Smith, Guy Newman. The black knights : a truckers novel / by Guy Smith. — London [etc.] : Mews Books ; London : Distributed by New English Library, 1977. — 112p ; 18cm. — (Smith, Guy Newman. The truckers ; no.1)
ISBN 0-452-00072-6 Pbk : £0.55
(B77-08096)

Smith, Guy Newman. Hi-jack! : a truckers novel / by Guy Smith. — London [etc.] : Mews Books ; London : Distributed by New English Library, 1977. — 112p ; 18cm. — (Smith, Guy Newman. The truckers ; no.2)
ISBN 0-452-00076-9 Pbk : £0.55
(B77-12706)

Smith, Harriet. Holiday village / by Harriet Smith. — London : Hale, 1977. — 159p ; 20cm.
ISBN 0-7091-5940-4 : £3.10
(B77-13903)

Smith, Jonathan. The English lover / [by] Jonathan Smith. — London : Hutchinson, 1977. — 192p ; 21cm.
ISBN 0-09-129410-x : £3.95
(B77-20680)

Smith, Martin Cruz. Nightwing / [by] Martin Cruz Smith. — London : Deutsch, 1977. — 254p ; 21cm.
Also published: New York : Norton, 1977.
ISBN 0-233-96948-9 : £3.95
(B77-28187)

Smith, Paul, *b.1925.* Come trailing blood / [by] Paul Smith. — [Revised ed.]. — London [etc.] : Quartet Books, 1977. — [11],244p ; 23cm.
Previous ed.: published as 'Esther's altar'. New York ; London : Abelard-Schuman, 1959.
ISBN 0-7043-2138-6 : £3.95
(B77-17123)

Smith, Robert A. The Kramer project / [by] Robert A. Smith. — London : Hale, 1977. — [13],203p ; 21cm.
Originally published: Toronto : Doubleday Canada, 1975.
ISBN 0-7091-5654-5 : £3.75
(B77-07638)

Smith, Vern E. The Jones men / [by] Vern E. Smith. — London : Futura Publications, 1976. — 283p ; 18cm.
Originally published: Chicago : Regnery, 1974 ; London : Weidenfeld and Nicolson, 1975.
ISBN 0-86007-289-4 Pbk : £0.75
(B77-08097)

Smith, Wilbur. Cry wolf / [by] Wilbur Smith. — London : Pan Books, 1977. — 413p ; 18cm.
Originally published: London : Heinemann, 1976.
ISBN 0-330-25097-3 Pbk : £0.80
(B77-26574)

Smith, Wilbur. A sparrow falls / [by] Wilbur Smith. — London : Heinemann, 1977. — 539p ; 23cm.
ISBN 0-434-71410-0 : £4.75
(B77-19771)

Smith, Wilbur. The sunbird / [by] Wilbur Smith ; a condensation by the editors of Reader's Digest Condensed Books. — Large print ed. — Leicester : Ulverscroft, 1977. — [4],333p ; 23cm. — (Ulverscroft large print series : [fiction])
Full ed. originally published: London : Heinemann, 1972.
ISBN 0-85456-556-6 : £2.65
(B77-13904)

Snow, Charles Percy, *Baron Snow.* In their wisdom / [by] C.P. Snow. — Harmondsworth [etc.] : Penguin, 1977. — 334p ; 19cm.
Originally published: London : Macmillan, 1974.
ISBN 0-14-004470-1 Pbk : £0.95
(B77-33443)

Snow, Lyndon. Honey for the bee / [by] Lyndon Snow. — Large print ed. — Bath : Lythway Press, 1977. — [5],303p ; 23cm.
Originally published: London : Collins, 1969.
ISBN 0-85046-701-2 : £4.60
(B77-17124)

Snow, Lyndon. I am Melinda / [by] Lyndon Snow. — London : Collins, 1977. — 158p ; 20cm.
Originally published: 1960.
ISBN 0-00-233351-1 : £2.75
(B77-14949)

Snow, Lyndon. Many a human heart / [by] Lyndon Snow. — London : Collins, 1976. — 159p ; 19cm.
Originally published: / under the name Vicky Lancaster. London : Hale, 1954.
ISBN 0-00-233528-x : £2.75
(B77-03232)

Snow, Lyndon. None can return / [by] Lyndon Snow. — Revised ed., large print ed. — Bath : Lythway Press, 1977. — [5],310p ; 22cm.
Revised ed. originally published: London : Collins, 1970.
ISBN 0-85046-751-9 : £4.70
(B77-33444)

Somerville-Large, Peter. Eagles near the carcase / by Peter Somerville-Large. — London : Gollancz, 1977. — 176p ; 21cm. — ([Gollancz thriller])
ISBN 0-575-02246-9 : £3.95
(B77-10961)

Spark, Muriel. The Abbess of Crewe / [by] Muriel Spark. — Harmondsworth [etc.] : Penguin, 1977. — 107p ; 19cm.
Originally published: London : Macmillan, 1974.
Pbk : £0.50
ISBN 0-14-004074-9
(B77-18391)

Sparks, Christine. More of the good life / by John Esmonde and Bob Larbey ; adapted from the television series by Christine Sparks. — Harmondsworth [etc.] : Penguin, 1977. — 190p ; 19cm.
ISBN 0-14-004628-3 Pbk : £0.65
(B77-30713)

Sparks, Christine. More of the good life / [by] John Esmonde and Bob Larbey ; adapted from the television series by Christine Sparks. — London : Severn House : [Distributed by Hutchinson], 1977. — 190p ; 21cm.
Also published: Harmondsworth : Penguin, 1977.
ISBN 0-7278-0312-3 : £3.25
(B77-28123)

Spring, Howard. All the day long / [by] Howard Spring. — [London] : Fontana, 1977. — 574p ; 18cm.
Originally published: London : Collins, 1959.
ISBN 0-00-614772-0 Pbk : £1.25
(B77-30714)

Spring, Howard. Fame is the spur / [by] Howard Spring. — [London] : Fontana, 1977. — 640p ; 18cm.
Originally published: London : Collins, 1940.
ISBN 0-00-614771-2 Pbk : £1.25
(B77-32228)

Spring, Howard. Rachel Rosing / [by] Howard Spring. — [London] : Fontana, 1977. — 255p ; 18cm.
Originally published: London : Collins, 1935.
ISBN 0-00-614776-3 Pbk : £0.75
(B77-22186)

Spring, Howard. Shabby tiger / [by] Howard Spring. — [London] : Fontana, 1977. — 254p ; 18cm.
Originally published: London : Collins, 1934.
ISBN 0-00-614775-5 Pbk : £0.75
(B77-22187)

Spring, Howard. Shabby tiger / [by] Howard Spring. — Fairwater ed. — London : Collins, 1976. — 3-254p ; 21cm.
Originally published: 1934.
ISBN 0-00-221765-1 : £3.00
(B77-14950)

Spruill, Steven G. Keepers of the gate / [by] Steven G. Spruill. — London : Hale, 1977. — [7],181p ; 21cm. — ([Hale SF])
ISBN 0-7091-6341-x : £3.75
(B77-30715)

Spurr, Clinton. Hell tracks / by Clinton Spurr. — London : Hale, 1976. — 156p ; 20cm.
ISBN 0-7091-5803-3 : £2.70
(B77-00450)

Squire, Lilian Stella. Lark song / by Lilian Stella Squire. — London : Hale, 1977. — 183p ; 20cm.
ISBN 0-7091-5952-8 : £3.10
(B77-13345)

Stableford, Brian. The paradise game / [by] Brian Stableford. — London : Dent, 1976. — 158p ; 21cm.
Originally published: New York : Daw Books, 1974.
ISBN 0-460-04308-0 : £3.25
(B77-06314)

Stables, Mira. High Garth / by Mira Stables. — London : Hale, 1977. — 184p ; 21cm.
ISBN 0-7091-5736-3 : £3.50
(B77-12136)

Stables, Mira. Honey-pot / [by] Mira Stables. — London : Hale, 1977. — 173p ; 21cm.
ISBN 0-7091-6259-6 : £3.50
(B77-28958)

Stables, Mira. Summer at Dorne / [by] Mira Stables. — London : Hale, 1977. — 157p ; 21cm.
ISBN 0-7091-5979-x : £3.50
(B77-19772)

Stafford, Caroline. The house by Exmoor / [by] Caroline Stafford. — London [etc.] : Millington, 1976. — 2-255p ; 23cm.
ISBN 0-86000-053-2 : £3.50
(B77-09312)

Stagg, Delano. Bloody beaches : a novel / by Delano Stagg. — London [etc.] : Mews Books : Distributed by New English Library, 1977. — 126p ; 19cm.
Originally published: Derby, Conn. : Monarch Books, 1961.
ISBN 0-452-00063-7 Pbk : £0.55
(B77-05709)

Stander, Siegfried. Flight from the hunter : a novel / by Siegfried Stander. — London : Gollancz, 1977. — 208p ; 21cm.
ISBN 0-575-02225-6 : £4.75
(B77-07639)

Standish, Buck. The land of buffalo grass / by Buck Standish. — London : Hale, 1977. — 157p ; 20cm.
ISBN 0-7091-6255-3 : £3.10
(B77-26575)

Standish, Buck. Riders of the law / by Buck Standish. — London : Hale, 1977. — 155p ; 20cm.
ISBN 0-7091-6017-8 : £2.95
(B77-16611)

Standish, Robert. Autumn cuckoo / [by] Robert Standish. — London : P. Davies, 1977. — [5], 201p ; 21cm.
ISBN 0-432-15728-x : £3.50
(B77-10962)

Standish, Robert. Bonin / [by] Robert Standish. — London : P. Davies, 1977. — viii,288p ; 20cm.
Originally published: 1943.
ISBN 0-432-15703-4 : £3.90
(B77-12137)

Standish, Robert. The cruise of the 'Three Brothers' / [by] Robert Standish. — London : P. Davies, 1976. — 208p ; 20cm.
Originally published: 1962.
ISBN 0-432-15704-2 : £3.50
(B77-02615)

Standish, Robert. The gulf of time / [by] Robert Standish. — London : P. Davies, 1976. — [4], 269p ; 20cm.
Originally published: 1947.
ISBN 0-432-15708-5 : £3.90
(B77-02616)

Standish, Robert. A worthy man / [by] Robert Standish. — London : P. Davies, 1977. — [4], 279p ; 20cm.
Originally published: 1952.
ISBN 0-432-15715-8 : £3.90
(B77-12138)

Stanley, Michael. The Swiss conspiracy / [by] Michael Stanley. — London : Futura Publications, 1976. — [4],299p ; 18cm.
ISBN 0-86007-364-5 Pbk : £0.75
(B77-12139)

Stapledon, Olaf. Nebula maker / [by] Olaf Stapledon. — Hayes, Middx (91 Wimborne Ave., Hayes, Middx) : Bran's Head Books Ltd, 1976. — x,126p ; 22cm.
ISBN 0-905220-06-4 : £3.50
(B77-08098)

Stark, Richard. Butcher's moon / [by] Richard Stark. — London : Coronet, 1977. — 297,[1]p ; 18cm.
Originally published: New York : Random House, 1974.
ISBN 0-340-21968-8 Pbk : £0.95
(B77-22188)

Stebel, Sidney Leo. The Vorovich affair / [by] S.L. Stebel. — Harmondsworth [etc.] : Penguin, 1977. — [7],248p ; 18cm. — (Penguin crime fiction)
Originally published: New York : Viking Press, 1975.
ISBN 0-14-004380-2 Pbk : Unpriced
(B77-12707)

Steele, William Owen. The man with the silver eyes / [by] William O. Steele. — New York ; London : Harcourt Brace Jovanovich, 1976. — [7],147p ; 21cm.
ISBN 0-15-251720-0 : Unpriced
(B77-22189)

Stegner, Wallace. The spectator bird / [by] Wallace Stegner. — Large print [ed.]. — London : Prior [etc.], 1977. — [2],409p ; 25cm.

Originally published: Garden City, N.Y. : Doubleday, 1976.
ISBN 0-86043-062-6 : £4.95
(B77-22190)

Stein, Aaron Marc. Coffin country / [by] Aaron Marc Stein. — London : Hale, 1976. — [7], 181p ; 20cm.
Also published: Garden City, N.Y. : Doubleday, 1976.
ISBN 0-7091-5850-5 : £2.95
(B77-00451)

Steinbeck, John. The short reign of Pippin IV : a fabrication / by John Steinbeck. — Harmondsworth [etc.] : Penguin, 1977. — [5], 151p ; 18cm.
Originally published: New York : Viking Press ; London : Heinemann, 1957.
ISBN 0-14-004290-3 Pbk : £0.70
(B77-24516)

Steinbeck, John. Tortilla Flat / [by] John Steinbeck. — Harmondsworth [etc.] : Penguin, 1977. — viii,151p ; 19cm.
Originally published: New York : Covici, Friede ; London : Heinemann, 1935.
ISBN 0-14-004240-7 Pbk : Unpriced
(B77-09313)

Stephens, Kay. Master of Masterton / [by] Kay Stephens. — London : Collins, 1977. — 192p ; 20cm.
ISBN 0-00-233514-x : £2.95
(B77-05710)

Stern, Richard Martin. Power / [by] Richard Martin Stern. — London [etc.] : Pan Books, 1977. — 288p ; 18cm.
Originally published: London : Secker and Warburg, 1975.
ISBN 0-330-25194-5 Pbk : £0.80
(B77-28959)

Stevens, Robert Tyler. Flight from Bucharest / by Robert Tyler Stevens. — London : Souvenir Press, 1977. — 319p : map ; 21cm.
ISBN 0-285-62275-7 : £3.95
(B77-18392)

Stevenson, Anne. Ralph Dacre / [by] Anne Stevenson. — Large print ed. — Leicester : Ulverscroft, 1977. — [7],463p ; 23cm. — (Ulverscroft large print series : [romance])
Originally published: London : Collins, 1967.
ISBN 0-85456-510-8 : £2.65
(B77-08605)

Stevenson, Dorothy Emily. The baker's daughter / [by] D.E. Stevenson. — Large print [ed.]. — London : Prior [etc.], 1977. — [6], 415p ; 24cm.
Originally published: New York : Farrar and Rinehart ; London : Collins, 1938.
ISBN 0-86043-040-5 : £4.95
(B77-12140)

Stevenson, Dorothy Emily. Charlotte Fairlie / [by] D.E. Stevenson. — [London] : Fontana, 1977. — 252p ; 18cm.
Originally published: London : Collins, 1954.
ISBN 0-00-614643-0 Pbk : £0.65
(B77-09314)

Stevenson, Dorothy Emily. Gerald and Elizabeth / [by] D.E. Stevenson. — Large print ed. — Leicester : Ulverscroft, 1977. — [6], 434p ; 23cm. — (Ulverscroft large print series : [romance])
Originally published: London : Collins, 1969.
ISBN 0-85456-518-3 : £2.65
(B77-13905)

Stevenson, Dorothy Emily. The house on the cliff / [by] D.E. Stevenson. — Large print ed. — Leicester : Ulverscroft, 1977. — [9],480p ; 23cm. — (Ulverscroft large print series : [romance])
Originally published: London : Collins, 1966.
ISBN 0-85456-537-x : Unpriced
(B77-19773)

Stevenson, Dorothy Emily. Miss Buncle's book / [by] D.E. Stevenson. — London : Collins, 1976. — 3-310p ; 21cm.
Originally published: London : Herbert Jenkins, 1934.
ISBN 0-00-222375-9 : £2.75
(B77-18393)

Stevenson, Dorothy Emily. Vittoria Cottage / [by] D.E. Stevenson. — Large print ed. — Leicester : Ulverscroft, 1977. — [4],411p ; 23cm. — (Ulverscroft large print series : [romance])
Originally published: London : Collins, 1949.
ISBN 0-7089-0057-7 : £2.95
(B77-32229)

Stevenson, J V. The dotty : a novel / by J.V. Stevenson. — London (21 Formosa St., W.9) : Polyantric Press, 1977. — 220p ; 23cm.
ISBN 0-905150-06-6 : £3.95
(B77-27431)

Steward, Dwight. The acupuncture murders / [by] Dwight Steward. — Harmondsworth [etc.] : Penguin, 1977. — 172p ; 18cm. — (Penguin crime fiction)
Originally published: New York : Harper and Row ; London : Barker, 1973.
ISBN 0-14-004332-2 Pbk : £0.60
(B77-25214)

Stewart, Dan. Savage gun / [by] Dan Stewart. — London : Jenkins, 1976. — 136p ; 21cm.
ISBN 0-214-20214-3 : £2.95
(B77-08606)

Stewart, Dan. Talman's war / [by] Dan Stewart. — London : Jenkins, 1976. — 160p ; 21cm.
ISBN 0-214-20219-4 : £2.95
(B77-09315)

Stewart, Fred Mustard. Six weeks : a novel / by Fred Mustard Stewart. — London : W.H. Allen, 1977. — [6],202p ; 21cm.
Originally published: New York : Arbor House, 1976.
ISBN 0-491-01838-x : £3.95
(B77-14425)

Stewart, George Rippey. Earth abides / [by] George R. Stewart. — London : Gollancz, 1977. — 334p ; 21cm. — ([Gollancz SF])
Originally published: 1950.
ISBN 0-575-02273-6 : £3.95
(B77-08099)

Stewart, Isobel. Man from yesterday / by Isobel Stewart. — London : Hale, 1977. — 154p ; 20cm.
ISBN 0-7091-5418-6 : £3.10
(B77-05711)

Stewart, Isobel. Sing no sad songs / by Isobel Stewart. — London : Hale, 1977. — 174p ; 19cm.
ISBN 0-7091-5689-8 : £3.20
(B77-28188)

Stewart, Isobel. Storm over yesterday / by Isobel Stewart. — London : Hale, 1977. — 159p ; 20cm.
ISBN 0-7091-5597-2 : £3.20
(B77-20681)

Stewart, John Innes Mackintosh. The 'Madonna of the Astrolabe' : a novel / [by] J.I.M. Stewart. — London : Gollancz, 1977. — 304p ; 20cm. — (Stewart, John Innes Mackintosh. Staircase in Surrey)
ISBN 0-575-02250-7 : £4.75
(B77-13906)

Stewart, Mary, *b.1916.* The Gabriel Hounds / [by] Mary Stewart. — Sevenoaks : Coronet, 1977. — 256p ; 18cm.
Originally published: London : Hodder and Stoughton, 1967. — Based on the life of Lady Hester Stanhope.
Pbk : £0.85
ISBN 0-340-04353-9
(B77-29732)

Stewart, Mary, *b.1916.* Madam, will you talk? / [by] Mary Stewart. — Sevenoaks : Coronet, 1977. — 191p ; 18cm.
Originally published: London : Hodder and Stoughton, 1955.
ISBN 0-340-01262-5 Pbk : £0.75
(B77-29733)

Stewart, Mary, *b.1916.* Touch not the cat / [by] Mary Stewart. — London [etc.] : Hodder and Stoughton, 1976. — 302p ; 23cm.
ISBN 0-340-20157-6 : £3.50
(B77-03771)

Stewart, Mary, *b.1916.* Touch not the cat / [by] Mary Stewart. — Sevenoaks : Coronet, 1977. — 285p ; 18cm.
Originally published: London : Hodder and Stoughton, 1976.
ISBN 0-340-21984-x Pbk : £0.95
(B77-29734)

Stewart, Mary, *b.1916.* Touch not the cat / [by] Mary Stewart. — Large print ed. — Leicester : Ulverscroft, 1977. — [8],516p ; 23cm. — (Ulverscroft large print series : [romantic suspense])
Originally published: London : Hodder and Stoughton, 1976.
ISBN 0-7089-0026-7 : £2.95
(B77-20682)

Stewart, Mary, *b.1916.* Wildfire at midnight / [by] Mary Stewart. — Sevenoaks : Coronet, 1977. — 224p : map ; 18cm.
Originally published: London : Hodder and Stoughton, 1956.
ISBN 0-340-01945-x Pbk : £0.75
(B77-29735)

Stewart, Sam. Fun with Dick and Jane : a novel / by Sam Stewart ; based on an original screenplay by Gerald Gaiser. — London : Sphere, 1977. — 239p : ill ; 18cm.
Also published: New York : Dell Publishing Co., 1977.
ISBN 0-7221-8164-7 Pbk : £0.75
(B77-16612)

Stiff, Peter. The Rain Goddess / [by] Peter Stiff. — London : New English Library, 1977. — 283p ; 18cm.
Originally published: Salisbury, Rhodesia : Jacaranda Press, 1973 ; London : New English Library, 1976.
ISBN 0-450-03118-7 Pbk : £0.90
(B77-09316)

Stirling, Jessica. The spoiled earth / [by] Jessica Stirling. — London [etc.] : Pan Books, 1977. — 478p ; 18cm.
Originally published: London : Hodder and Stoughton, 1974.
ISBN 0-330-25053-1 Pbk : £0.95
(B77-26576)

Stockholm, Marjorie. What happened to Virginia / [by] Marjorie Stockholm. — London : Hale, 1977. — 172p ; 20cm.
ISBN 0-7091-5906-4 : £3.10
(B77-09317)

Stone, Irving. The Greek treasure : a biographical novel of Henry and Sophia Schliemann / [by] Irving Stone. — London : Corgi, 1976. — 590p : map ; 18cm.
Originally published: Garden City, N.Y. : Doubleday ; London : Cassell, 1975. — Bibl.: p.585-590.
ISBN 0-552-10346-2 Pbk : £0.95
(B77-07640)

Stone, Zachary. The Modigliani scandal / [by] Zachary Stone. — [London] : Fontana, 1977. — 192p ; 19cm.
Originally published: London : Collins for the Crime Club, 1976.
ISBN 0-00-614521-3 Pbk : £0.70
(B77-17760)

Stone, Zachary. Paper money / [by] Zachary Stone. — London : Collins [for] the Crime Club, 1977. — 193p ; 21cm.
ISBN 0-00-231615-3 : £2.95
(B77-15539)

Storey, David. Flight into Camden / [by] David Storey. — Harmondsworth [etc.] : Penguin, 1976. — 234p ; 19cm.
Originally published: London : Longmans, 1960.
ISBN 0-14-001843-3 Pbk : £0.70
(B77-07641)

Storey, David. Pasmore / [by] David Storey. — Harmondsworth [etc.] : Penguin, 1976. — 171p ; 19cm.
Originally published: Harlow : Longman, 1972.
ISBN 0-14-004060-9 Pbk : £0.70
(B77-01832)

Storey, David. Radcliffe / [by] David Storey. — Harmondsworth [etc.] : Penguin, 1977. — 350p ; 18cm.
Originally published: London : Longman, 1963.
ISBN 0-14-002355-0 Pbk : £0.85
(B77-33445)

Storey, David. This sporting life / [by] David Storey. — Harmondsworth [etc.] : Penguin, 1976. — 253p ; 18cm.
Originally published: London : Longman, 1960.
ISBN 0-14-001674-0 Pbk : £0.75
(B77-01833)

Storr, Catherine. Who's Bill? / [by] Catherine Storr. — Basingstoke [etc.] : Macmillan, 1976. — 128p ; 18cm. — (Topliners)
'Based on the ATV series "Starting out"' - cover. — For adolescents.
ISBN 0-333-21464-1 Pbk : £0.40
(B77-00988)

Straker, John Foster. A gun to play with / [by] J.F. Straker. — Large print ed. — Bath : Lythway Press, 1977. — [5],341p ; 23cm.
Originally published: London : Harrap, 1956.
ISBN 0-85046-704-7 : £4.60
(B77-17125)

Straker, John Foster. Swallow them up / by J.F. Straker. — London : Hale, 1977. — 190p ; 20cm.
ISBN 0-7091-6153-0 : £3.25
(B77-31507)

Strange, Nora Kathleen. The silent grove / [by] Nora K. Strange. — Large print ed. — Bath : Lythway Press, 1977. — [4],380p ; 22cm.
Originally published: London : Hutchinson, 1954.
ISBN 0-85046-725-x : £4.85
(B77-34182)

Stranger, Joyce. Khazan : the horse that came out of the sea / [by] Joyce Stranger. — London : Collins : Harvill Press, 1977. — 196p ; 20cm.
ISBN 0-00-261415-4 : £3.25
(B77-34183)

Stranger, Joyce. Never tell a secret / [by] Joyce Stranger. — London : Corgi, 1977. — 143p ; 18cm.
Originally published: London : Collins : Harvill Press, 1975.
ISBN 0-552-10397-7 Pbk : £0.50
(B77-16073)

Stranger, Joyce. Rex / [by] Joyce Stranger. — London : Corgi, 1976. — 175p ; 18cm.
Originally published: London : Harvill Press, 1967.
ISBN 0-552-10311-x Pbk : £0.50
(B77-00452)

Stranger, Joyce. The running foxes / [by] Joyce Stranger ; illustrated by David Rook. — London : Corgi, 1976. — 142p ; 18cm.
Originally published: London : Hammond, 1965.
ISBN 0-552-10312-8 Pbk : £0.50
(B77-00453)

Strathern, Christine. Love in the limelight / [by] Christine Strathern. — Large print ed. — Bath : Lythway Press, 1976. — [4],267p ; 23cm.
Originally published: London : Collins, 1954.
ISBN 0-85046-686-5 : £4.15
(B77-06895)

Strathern, Christine. Love in the mist / [by] Christine Strathern. — Large print ed. — Bath : Lythway Press, 1977. — [4],283p ; 23cm.
Originally published: London : Collins, 1955.
ISBN 0-85046-713-6 : £4.50
(B77-21504)

Stratton, Rebecca. Fairwinds / [by] Rebecca Stratton. — Large print ed. — Leicester : Ulverscroft, 1977. — [7],254p ; 22cm. — (Ulverscroft large print series : [romance])
Originally published: London : Mills and Boon, 1974.
ISBN 0-7089-0033-x : Unpriced
(B77-34184)

Stratton, Rebecca. Gemini child / by Rebecca Stratton. — London : Mills and Boon, 1976. — 187p ; 19cm.
ISBN 0-263-09053-1 : £1.95
(B77-14951)

Stratton, Rebecca. Gemini child / by Rebecca Stratton. — London : Mills and Boon, 1977. — 186p ; 18cm.
Originally published: 1976.
ISBN 0-263-72339-9 Pbk : £0.35
(B77-06896)

Stratton, Rebecca. Girl in a white hat / by Rebecca Stratton. — London : Mills and Boon, 1977. — 188p ; 17cm.
ISBN 0-263-72386-0 Pbk : £0.35
(B77-21505)

Stratton, Ted. Tourist trap / [by] Ted Stratton. — London : Hale, 1977. — [4],187p ; 20cm.
Originally published: New York : Putnam, 1975.
ISBN 0-7091-6212-x : £3.25
(B77-20683)

Straub, Peter. Full circle / [by] Peter Straub. — London : Corgi, 1977. — 254p ; 18cm.
Originally published: as 'Julia'. New York : Coward, McCann, 1975 ; London : Cape, 1976.
ISBN 0-552-10471-x Pbk : £0.85
(B77-25923)

Straub, Peter. If you could see me now / [by] Peter Straub. — London : Cape, 1977. — 3-287p ; 23cm.
ISBN 0-224-01345-9 : £3.95 : CIP rev.
(B77-06315)

Street, Mary. The Gemini girl / by Mary Street. — London : Hale, 1977. — 157p ; 20cm.
ISBN 0-7091-6189-1 : £3.20
(B77-22901)

Strong, Susan, *b.1927.* Error of judgement / [by] Susan Strong. — London : Hale, 1977. — 191p ; 20cm.
ISBN 0-7091-6300-2 : £3.20
(B77-26577)

Stroud, John, *b.1923.* The shorn lamb / [by] John Stroud. — Large print ed. — Bath : Chivers, 1977. — [7],391p ; 23cm.
Originally published: London : Longmans, Green, 1960.
ISBN 0-85997-255-0 : £5.80(£4.35 to members of the Library Association)
(B77-21506)

Stuart, Alex. Doctor in the tropics / [by] Alex Stuart. — London : Corgi, 1976. — 173p ; 18cm. — (A Corgi romance)
Originally published: / under the name Vivian Stuart, as 'Pilgrim heart'. London : Jenkins, 1955.
ISBN 0-552-10160-5 Pbk : £0.45
(B77-05712)

Stuart, Anthony. Snap judgement / [by] Anthony Stuart. — London : Macdonald and Jane's, 1977. — [10],206p ; 23cm.
ISBN 0-354-04134-7 : £3.95
(B77-17126)

Stuart, Francis, *b.1902.* A hole in the head / [by] Francis Stuart. — London : Martin Brian and O'Keeffe, 1977. — 215p ; 21cm.
ISBN 0-85616-470-4 : £4.00
(B77-33446)

Stuart, Ian, *b.1922.* Flood tide / by Ian Stuart. — London : Hale, 1977. — 157p ; 20cm.
ISBN 0-7091-6047-x : £3.15
(B77-13907)

Stuart, Ian, *b.1922.* Sand trap / by Ian Stuart. — London : Hale, 1977. — 160p ; 20cm.
ISBN 0-7091-6307-x : £3.25
(B77-32874)

Stuart, Vivian. Sailors on horseback / [by] Vivian Stuart. — London : Hale, 1977. — 223p ; 21cm.
Originally published: as 'Escape from hell'. United States: s.n., 1976. — Bibl.: p.223.
ISBN 0-7091-5748-7 : £3.60
(B77-12708)

Stubbs, Jean. The golden crucible / [by] Jean Stubbs. — London [etc.] : Macmillan, 1977. — 287p : facsim ; 23cm.
ISBN 0-333-17989-7 : £3.95
(B77-12709)

Stubbs, Jean. The golden crucible / [by] Jean Stubbs. — Large print [ed.]. — London : Prior [etc.], 1977. — [8],494p ; 25cm.
Originally published: New York : Stein and Day, 1976 ; London : Macmillan, 1977.
ISBN 0-86043-099-5 : £5.95
(B77-34185)

Stubbs, Jean. The painted face : an Edwardian mystery / [by] Jean Stubbs. — Harmondsworth [etc.] : Penguin, 1976. — 240p ; 19cm. — ([An Inspector Lintott mystery])
Originally published: London, etc. : Macmillan, 1974.
ISBN 0-14-004173-7 Pbk : £0.65
(B77-01834)

Styles, Showell. Mr Fitton's commission / [by] Showell Styles. — London : Faber, 1977. — 3-190p : map ; 20cm.
ISBN 0-571-11071-1 : £3.95 : CIP rev.
(B77-23750)

Styles, Showell. Sea road to Camperdown / [by] Showell Styles. — London : Sphere, 1976. — 157p : map ; 18cm.
Originally published: London : Faber, 1968. — Based on the life of Lord Duncan of Camperdown.
ISBN 0-7221-8232-5 Pbk : £0.65
(B77-02617)

Styles, Showell. A sword for Mr Fitton / [by] Showell Styles. — London : Sphere, 1977. — 159p : map ; 18cm.
Originally published: London : Faber, 1975.
ISBN 0-7221-8236-8 Pbk : £0.65
(B77-12710)

Sudworth, Gwynedd. The game of kings / by Gwynedd Sudworth. — London : Hale, 1977. — 5-188p ; 21cm.
Based on the life of Richard Neville, Earl of Warwick.
ISBN 0-7091-5870-x : £3.50
(B77-14952)

Sudworth, Gwynedd. Richard Whittington, London's mayor / [by] Gwynedd Sudworth. — Large print ed. — Leicester : Ulverscroft, 1977. — [11],363p : geneal table ; 23cm. — (Ulverscroft large print series : [non-fiction])
Originally published: London : Hale, 1975. — Based on Richard Whittington's life.
ISBN 0-85456-514-0 : £2.65
(B77-08607)

Sule, Mohammed. The undesirable element / [by] Muhammed Sule. — London [etc.] : Macmillan, 1977. — [4],121p ; 18cm. — (Pacesetters)
For adolescents.
ISBN 0-333-23083-3 Pbk : £0.59
(B77-31508)

Summers, Dennis. Master of ghosts / by Dennis Summers. — London : Hale, 1977. — 3-188p ; 21cm. — (Hale SF)
ISBN 0-7091-5915-3 : £3.60
(B77-34186)

Summers, Dennis. Robot in the glass / [by] Dennis Summers. — London : Hale, 1977. — 190p ; 21cm. — (Hale SF)
ISBN 0-7091-5725-8 : £3.25
(B77-13346)

Summers, Essie. The kindled fire / [by] Essie Summers. — Large print ed. — Leicester : Ulverscroft, 1977. — [7],365p ; 23cm. — (Ulverscroft large print series : [romance])
Originally published: London : Mills and Boon, 1969.
ISBN 0-7089-0013-5 : £2.95
(B77-19774)

Summers, Essie. The smoke and the fire / [by] Essie Summers. — Large print ed. — Leicester : Ulverscroft, 1977. — [8],381p ; 23cm. — (Ulverscroft large print series : [romance])
Originally published: London : Mills and Boon, 1964.
ISBN 0-85456-520-5 : £2.65
(B77-13908)

Summers, Essie. Through all the years / by Essie Summers. — London : Mills and Boon, 1976. — 188p ; 17cm.
Originally published: 1974.
ISBN 0-263-72347-x Pbk : £0.30
(B77-05713)

Sumner, Richard. Mistress of the boards : the further adventures of Nell Gwynne / [by] Richard Sumner. — London : Coronet, 1977. — 284p ; 18cm.
ISBN 0-340-21300-0 Pbk : £0.75
(B77-09318)

Sumner, Richard. Mistress of the boards / [by] Richard Sumner. — London : Hale, 1977. — 284p ; 21cm.
Also published: London : Coronet, 1977. — Based on the life of Nell Gwyn.
ISBN 0-7091-6133-6 : £4.15
(B77-20684)

Susann, Jacqueline. Dolores / [by] Jacqueline Susann. — London : Corgi, 1977. — 187p ; 18cm.
Originally published: as 'Jacqueline Susann's Dolorès'. London : W.H. Allen, 1975.
ISBN 0-552-10538-4 Pbk : £0.75
(B77-32875)

Sutherland, Elizabeth. The eye of God / [by] Elizabeth Sutherland. — London : Constable, 1977. — 230p ; 23cm.
ISBN 0-09-461660-4 : £3.95
(B77-21507)

Sutton, Graham. Smoke across the fell / [by] Graham Sutton. — Large print ed. — Bath : Chivers, 1976. — [7],452p ; 23cm.
Originally published: London : Collins, 1947.
ISBN 0-85997-157-0 : £5.00(£3.75 to members of the Library Association)
(B77-04428)

Swann, Thomas Burnett. Will-o-the-wisp / [by] Thomas Burnett Swann. — London : Corgi, 1976. — 160p ; 18cm.
ISBN 0-552-10358-6 Pbk : £0.60
(B77-09319)

Swarthout, Glendon. The eagle and the Iron Cross / [by] Glendon Swarthout. — London [etc.] : Pan Books, 1977. — 224p ; 18cm.
Originally published: New York : New American Library, 1966 ; London : Heinemann, 1967.
ISBN 0-330-24882-0 Pbk : £0.60
(B77-06316)

Swarthout, Glendon. They came to Cordura / [by] Glendon Swarthout. — London [etc.] : Pan Books, 1977. — 187p ; 18cm.
Originally published: New York : Random House ; London : Heinemann, 1958.
ISBN 0-330-24860-x Pbk : £0.60
(B77-06897)

Sweetman, Rosita. Fathers come first / [by] Rosita Sweetman. — London [etc.] : Pan Books, 1977. — 189p ; 18cm.
Originally published: London : Joseph, 1974.
ISBN 0-330-24891-x Pbk : £0.70
(B77-12141)

Swindells, Robert Edward. When darkness comes / [by] Robert E. Swindells. — London [etc.] : Beaver Books, 1977. — 3-157p ; 20cm.
Originally published: Leicester : Brockhampton Press, 1973. — For adolescents.
ISBN 0-600-39374-7 Pbk : £0.60
(B77-13347)

Swinnerton, Frank. Some achieve greatness / [by] Frank Swinnerton. — Large print [ed.]. — London : Prior [etc.], 1977. — [5],509p ; 25cm.

Originally published: London : Hamilton, 1976.

ISBN 0-86043-060-x : £5.50
(B77-22191)

Symonds, John. A Christmas story / [by] John Symonds. — North Walsham (12 New Rd, North Walsham, Norfolk NR28 9DF) : Warren House Press, 1977. — [5],28p ; 21cm.
Limited ed. of 250 copies.
Pbk : £3.00
(B77-34187)

Symons, Julian. The gigantic shadow / [by] Julian Symons. — London : Severn House : [Distributed by Hutchinson], 1977. — 192p ; 21cm.
Originally published: London : Collins, 1958.
ISBN 0-7278-0231-3 : £3.25
(B77-20685)

Symons, Julian. The killing of Francie Lake / by Julian Symons. — London : Severn House : [Distributed by Hutchinson], 1977. — 256p ; 21cm.
Originally published: London : Collins, 1962.
ISBN 0-7278-0236-4 : £3.25
(B77-08608)

Symons, Julian. The man who killed himself / [by] Julian Symons. — Harmondsworth [etc.] : Penguin, 1977. — 167p ; 18cm. — (Penguin crime fiction)
Originally published: London : Collins, 1967.
ISBN 0-14-004143-5 Pbk : £0.70
(B77-20686)

Symons, Julian. The man who lost his wife / [by] Julian Symons. — Harmondsworth [etc.] : Penguin, 1977. — 204p ; 19cm. — (Penguin crime fiction)
Originally published: London : Collins for the Crime Club, 1970.
ISBN 0-14-004348-9 Pbk : £0.75
(B77-20687)

Symons, Julian. The man whose dreams came true / [by] Julian Symons. — Harmondsworth [etc.] : Penguin, 1977. — 237p ; 19cm. — (Penguin crime fiction)
Originally published: London : Collins, 1968.
ISBN 0-14-004347-0 Pbk : £0.75
(B77-20688)

Symons, Julian. The paper chase / by Julian Symons. — London : Severn House : [Distributed by Hutchinson], 1977. — 256p ; 21cm.
Originally published: London : Collins, 1956.
ISBN 0-7278-0303-4 : £3.75
(B77-34188)

Symons, Julian. The progress of a crime / by Julian Symons. — London : Collins [for] the Crime Club, 1977. — [2],256p ; 21cm.
Originally published: 1960.
ISBN 0-00-231642-0 : £2.95
(B77-26578)

Symons, Julian. A three pipe problem / [by] Julian Symons. — Harmondsworth [etc.] : Penguin, 1977. — 192p ; 19cm. — (Penguin crime fiction)
Originally published: London : Collins, 1975.
ISBN 0-14-004330-6 Pbk : £0.60
(B77-25215)

Tanous, Peter. The petrodollar takeover / [by] Peter Tanous & Paul Rubinstein. — London : Arrow Books, 1977. — 254p ; 18cm.
Originally published: New York : Putnam, 1975 ; London : Deutsch, 1976.
ISBN 0-09-915150-2 Pbk : £0.75
(B77-21508)

Tarkington, Booth. The magnificent Ambersons / [by] Booth Tarkington. — Bath : Chivers, 1976. — [4],516p ; 19cm.
Facsimile reprint of: 1st ed. Garden City, N.Y. : Doubleday, Page and Co., 1918.
ISBN 0-85997-229-1 : £5.80(£4.35 to members of the Library Association)
(B77-06317)

Tarrant, John, *b.1927.* The Rommel plot / [by] John Tarrant. — London : Raven Books, 1977. — 250p ; 23cm.
ISBN 0-354-04185-1 : £4.25
(B77-28189)

Tatford, Grace D. Doctor's dilemma / by Grace D. Tatford. — Eastbourne (Upperton House, The Avenue, Eastbourne, E. Sussex BN21 3YB) : Upperton Press, 1976. — [3],82p ; 19cm.
ISBN 0-900725-52-4 Pbk : £0.40
(B77-09320)

Taylor, Bernard, *b.1934.* Sweetheart, sweetheart / by Bernard Taylor. — London : Souvenir Press, 1977. — 335p ; 21cm.
ISBN 0-285-62243-9 : £4.25
(B77-30716)

Taylor, Margaret Stewart. A dream reborn / [by] Margaret Stewart Taylor. — London : Hale, 1977. — 221p ; 21cm.
ISBN 0-7091-5924-2 : £3.60
(B77-17127)

Taylor, May. Deeper waters : a novel / by May Taylor. — London : Mitre Press, 1977. — 187p ; 27cm.
ISBN 0-7051-0254-8 : £2.60
(B77-34189)

Tenn, William. Of men and monsters / by William Tenn. — London : Gollancz, 1977. — 251p ; 21cm. — ([Gollancz SF])
Originally published: New York : Walker, 1968 ; London : Ballantine Books, 1971.
ISBN 0-575-02377-5 : £3.95
(B77-28960)

Tey, Josephine. The singing sands / [by] Josephine Tey. — Harmondsworth [etc.] : Penguin, 1977. — 202p ; 19cm. — (Penguin crime fiction)
Originally published: London : P. Davies, 1952.

ISBN 0-14-004257-1 Pbk : £0.65
(B77-08100)

Theroux, Paul. The consul's file / [by] Paul Theroux. — London : Hamilton, 1977. — 192p : 1 ill ; 21cm.
ISBN 0-241-89657-6 : £3.95
(B77-19775)

Theroux, Paul. Saint Jack / [by] Paul Theroux. — Uniform ed. — London : Hamilton, 1977. — 251p ; 21cm.
Originally published: London : Bodley Head, 1973.
ISBN 0-241-89822-6 : £3.95
(B77-31509)

Thomas, Barry. Wings / [by] Barry Thomas. — London : Pan Books : British Broadcasting Corporation, 1977. — 174p : ill ; 18cm.
Based on the BBC television series 'Wings' created by the author.
ISBN 0-330-25043-4 Pbk : £0.50
ISBN 0-563-17169-3 (British Broadcasting Corporation) Pbk : £0.50
(B77-06898)

Thomas, Barry. Wings / [by] Barry Thomas. — London : British Broadcasting Corporation, 1977. — 174p ; 22cm.
Based on the BBC television series 'Wings' created by the author. — Originally published: London : Pan Books : British Broadcasting Corporation, 1977.
ISBN 0-563-17260-6 : £3.00
(B77-13348)

Thomas, Craig. Firefox / [by] Craig Thomas. — London : Joseph, 1977. — 288p : map(on lining papers) ; 23cm.
ISBN 0-7181-1570-8 : £4.25
(B77-20689)

Thomas, Craig. Rat trap / [by] Craig Thomas. — London : Joseph, 1976. — 237p ; 21cm.
ISBN 0-7181-1497-3 : £3.95
(B77-06318)

Thomas, Jack William. 'Reds' / by Jack W. Thomas. — Toronto [etc.] ; London : Bantam, 1976. — [5],202p ; 18cm.
Originally published: 1970. — For adolescents.
ISBN 0-552-68739-1 Pbk : £0.50
(B77-02618)

Thomas, Leslie, *b.1931.* Bare Nell / [by] Leslie Thomas. — London : Eyre Methuen, 1977. — [5],330p ; 21cm.
ISBN 0-413-34690-0 : £4.50
(B77-29736)

Thomas, Leslie, *b.1931.* Dangerous Davies : the last detective / [by] Leslie Thomas. — London [etc.] : Pan Books, 1977. — 239p ; 18cm.
Originally published: London : Eyre Methuen, 1976.
ISBN 0-330-25173-2 Pbk : £0.80
(B77-32230)

Thomas, Leslie, *b.1931.* Stand up virgin soldiers / [by] Leslie Thomas. — London [etc.] : Pan Books, 1976. — 251p ; 18cm.
Originally published: London : Eyre Methuen, 1975.
ISBN 0-330-24776-x Pbk : £0.75
(B77-01835)

Thomas, Ross. The money harvest / [by] Ross Thomas. — London [etc.] : Pan Books, 1977. — 220p ; 18cm.
Originally published: New York : Morrow ; London : Hamilton, 1975.
ISBN 0-330-25058-2 Pbk : £0.70
(B77-13909)

Thomas, Ross. Yellow-dog contract / [by] Ross Thomas. — London : Hamilton, 1977. — 264p ; 21cm.
ISBN 0-241-89580-4 : £3.95
(B77-12711)

Thompson, Anne Armstrong. Message from Absalom / [by] Anne Armstrong Thompson. — Large print ed. — Leicester : Ulverscroft, 1977. — [5],383p ; 23cm. — (Ulverscroft large print series : [adventure, suspense])
Originally published: New York : Simon and Schuster, 1975 ; London : Hodder and Stoughton, 1976.
ISBN 0-7089-0016-x : £2.95
(B77-22192)

Thompson, Brian, *b.1935.* Buddy boy : a novel / by Brian Thompson. — London : Gollancz, 1977. — 160p ; 21cm.
ISBN 0-575-02319-8 : £4.20
(B77-22193)

Thompson, E V. Chase the wind / [by] E.V. Thompson. — London [etc.] : Macmillan, 1977. — 416p ; 23cm.
ISBN 0-333-21469-2 : £4.95
(B77-22902)

Thompson, Earl. Tattoo / [by] Earl Thompson. — London [etc.] : Pan Books, 1977. — [6], 687p ; 18cm.
Originally published: New York : Putnam, 1974.
ISBN 0-330-24856-1 Pbk : £1.00
(B77-21509)

Thompson, Russ. The iron mountains / by Russ Thompson. — London : Hale, 1977. — 160p ; 20cm.
ISBN 0-7091-5341-4 : £2.95
(B77-10590)

Thomson, Daisy Hicks. Myrtle for my love / by D.H. Thomson. — London : Hale, 1977. — 182p ; 20cm.
ISBN 0-7091-5859-9 : £3.10
(B77-18394)

Thomson, Daisy Hicks. A time for love / by D.H. Thomson. — London : Hale, 1977. — 187p ; 20cm.
ISBN 0-7091-6014-3 : £3.20
(B77-26579)

Thomson, Daisy Hicks. The voice of love / by D.H. Thomson. — London : Hale, 1977. — 184p ; 20cm.
ISBN 0-7091-5713-4 : £3.10
(B77-05714)

Thomson, June. Case closed / [by] June Thomson. — London : Constable, 1977. — 207p ; 21cm. — (Constable crime)
ISBN 0-09-461580-2 : £3.50
(B77-07642)

Thornburg, Newton. Cutter and Bone / [by] Newton Thornburg. — London : Heinemann, 1977. — [5],313p ; 23cm.
Originally published: Boston, Mass. : Little, Brown, 1976.
ISBN 0-434-77895-8 : £3.90
(B77-05715)

Thornton, Adele. Practise to deceive / by Adele Thornton. — London : Mills and Boon, 1976. — 186p ; 19cm.
ISBN 0-263-09031-0 : £1.95
(B77-10591)

Thorpe, Kay. Safari south / by Kay Thorpe. — London : Mills and Boon, 1976. — 187p ; 17cm.
ISBN 0-263-72330-5 Pbk : £0.30
(B77-05716)

Thorpe, Sylvia. The reluctant adventuress / [by] Sylvia Thorpe. — London : Corgi, 1977. — 222p ; 18cm. — (Corgi Georgian romance series)
Originally published: London : Hurst and Blackett, 1963.
ISBN 0-552-10480-9 Pbk : £0.50
(B77-26580)

Thorpe, Sylvia. Romantic lady / [by] Sylvia Thorpe. — London : Corgi, 1977. — 224p ; 18cm.
Originally published: London : Hurst and Blackett, 1960.
ISBN 0-552-10525-2 Pbk : £0.60
(B77-32876)

Thorpe, Sylvia. The scapegrace / [by] Sylvia Thorpe. — London : Corgi, 1977. — 176p ; 18cm. — (Corgi Georgian romance series)
Originally published: London : Hurst and Blackett, 1971.
ISBN 0-552-10479-5 Pbk : £0.50
(B77-26581)

Thorpe, Sylvia. The silver nightingale / [by] Sylvia Thorpe. — London : Corgi, 1977. — 222p ; 18cm. — (Corgi Georgian romance series)
Originally published: London : Hurst and Blackett, 1974.
ISBN 0-552-10577-5 Pbk : £0.50
(B77-31510)

Thubron, Colin. The God in the mountain : a novel / [by] Colin Thubron. — London : Heinemann, 1977. — [4],379p ; 23cm.
ISBN 0-434-77985-7 : £4.90
(B77-21510)

Thurley, Geoffrey. The house in Astrakhan / [by] Geoffrey Thurley. — Sydney ; London [etc.] : Hodder and Stoughton, 1977. — 163p ; 22cm.
ISBN 0-340-22161-5 : £3.60
(B77-27432)

Thurlow, David. Incubus / by David Thurlow & Ross Peers. — London : Hale, 1977. — 184p ; 20cm.
ISBN 0-7091-6231-6 : £3.25
(B77-22903)

Thurlow, David. Schade / [by] David Thurlow and Ross Peers. — London : Hale, 1977. — 188p ; 21cm.
ISBN 0-7091-6102-6 : £3.25
(B77-21511)

Tibble, Anne. The God Spigo / [by] Anne Tibble. — London : Duckworth, 1976. — 105p ; 23cm.
ISBN 0-7156-1092-9 : £3.25
(B77-09974)

Tidy, Bill. The great Eric Ackroyd disaster / [by] Bill Tidy. — London : Arrow Books, 1977. — 96p : chiefly ill ; 18cm.
Originally published: London : Hutchinson, 1976.
ISBN 0-09-915980-5 Pbk : £0.65
(B77-30717)

Tidyman, Ernest. The last Shaft / [by] Ernest Tidyman. — London : Corgi, 1976. — 159p ; 18cm.
Originally published: London : Weidenfeld and Nicolson, 1975.
ISBN 0-552-10354-3 Pbk : £0.60
(B77-04429)

Tilley, Patrick. Fade-out / [by] Patrick Tilley. — London : Sphere, 1977. — 416p : ill, map ; 18cm.
Originally published: London : Hodder and Stoughton, 1975.
ISBN 0-7221-8514-6 Pbk : £0.95
(B77-16074)

Tilsley, Frank. Mutiny / [by] Frank Tilsley ; foreword by Vincent Tilsley. — Large print ed. — Bath : Chivers, 1977. — ix,438p ; 22cm.
Originally published: London : Eyre and Spottiswoode, 1958.
ISBN 0-85997-237-2 : £5.60(£4.20 to members of the Library Association)
(B77-22194)

Timlett, Peter Valentine. The power of the serpent / [by] Peter Valentine Timlett. — London : Corgi, 1976. — [5],246p : ill ; 18cm.
ISBN 0-552-10314-4 Pbk : £0.75
(B77-01836)

Timlett, Peter Valentine. The twilight of the serpent / [by] Peter Valentine Timlett. — London : Corgi, 1977. — [4],ix,210p : 2 maps ; 18cm.
ISBN 0-552-10434-5 Pbk : £0.70
(B77-19018)

Timperley, Rosemary. The devil of the lake / [by] Rosemary Timperley. — London : Hale, 1977. — 191p ; 21cm.
ISBN 0-7091-5800-9 : £3.70
(B77-19776)

Timperley, Rosemary. The man with the beard / [by] Rosemary Timperley. — London : Hale, 1977. — 192p ; 21cm.
ISBN 0-7091-5678-2 : £3.50
(B77-09975)

Timperley, Rosemary. The phantom husband / [by] Rosemary Timperley. — London : Hale, 1977. — 188p ; 21cm.
ISBN 0-7091-5960-9 : £3.80
(B77-28961)

Tippette, Giles. The mercenaries / [by] Giles Tippette. — London : Sphere, 1977. — 272p ; 18cm.
Originally published: New York : Delacorte Press, 1976.
ISBN 0-7221-8537-5 Pbk : £0.95
(B77-28962)

Tolkien, John Ronald Reuel. The silmarillion / [by] J.R.R. Tolkien ; edited by Christopher Tolkien. — London [etc.] : Allen and Unwin, 1977. — 3-365p,[2]leaves of plates(1 fold) : 5 geneal tables, 2 col maps ; 23cm.
Index.
ISBN 0-04-823139-8 : £4.95
(B77-28963)

Townsend, John Rowe. Good-night, Prof, love / [by] John Rowe Townsend. — Harmondsworth [etc.] : Penguin, 1977. — 145p ; 18cm. — (Peacock books)
Originally published: London : Oxford University Press, 1970. — For adolescents.
ISBN 0-14-047107-3 Pbk : £0.60
(B77-27433)

Townsend, John Rowe. The Xanadu manuscript / [by] John Rowe Townsend ; illustration by Paul Ritchie. — Oxford [etc.] : Oxford University Press, 1977. — [5],170p : 1 ill ; 23cm.
For adolescents.
ISBN 0-19-271406-6 : £2.95
(B77-19019)

Tracy, Honor. The man from next door : a novel / by Honor Tracy. — London : Hamilton, 1977. — [5],186p ; 21cm.
ISBN 0-241-89585-5 : £3.75
(B77-14953)

Tranter, Nigel. Chain of destiny / [by] Nigel Tranter. — Sevenoaks : Coronet, 1977. — 445p : map ; 18cm.
Originally published: London : Hodder and Stoughton, 1964. — Based on the life of King James the 4th of Scotland.
ISBN 0-340-21238-1 Pbk : £1.25
(B77-12712)

Tranter, Nigel. Fast and loose / [by] Nigel Tranter. — London [etc.] : White Lion Publishers, 1977. — 250p ; 21cm.
Originally published: London : Ward Lock, 1951.
ISBN 0-85617-207-3 : £3.75
(B77-14954)

Tranter, Nigel. A folly of princes : the second of a trilogy of novels on the rise of the house of Stewart / by Nigel Tranter. — London [etc.] : Hodder and Stoughton, 1977. — 384p : geneal tables ; 23cm.
ISBN 0-340-20864-3 : £4.95
(B77-11421)

Tranter, Nigel. Man's estate / [by] Nigel Tranter. — Large print ed. — Leicester : Ulverscroft, 1977. — [4],349p ; 22cm. — (Ulverscroft large print series : [general fiction])
Originally published: London : Ward Lock, 1946.
ISBN 0-7089-0037-2 : Unpriced
(B77-34190)

Tranter, Nigel. The Wallace / [by] Nigel Tranter. — Sevenoaks : Coronet, 1977. — 442p ; 18cm.
Originally published: London : Hodder and Stoughton, 1975. — Based on the life of William Wallace.
ISBN 0-340-21237-3 Pbk : £1.25
(B77-12713)

Travers, Ben. A cuckoo in the nest / [by Ben Travers]. — London : W.H. Allen, 1977. — 283p ; 21cm.
Originally published: London : J. Lane, 1922.
ISBN 0-491-02102-x : £4.50
(B77-34191)

Travers, Ben. Mischief / [by] Ben Travers. — London : W.H. Allen, 1977. — 255p ; 21cm.
Originally published: London : J. Lane, 1925.
ISBN 0-491-02112-7 : £3.95
(B77-34192)

Travers, Ben. Rookery Nook / [by] Ben Travers. — London : W.H. Allen, 1977. — 253p ; 21cm.
Originally published: London : J. Lane, 1923.
ISBN 0-491-02122-4 : £3.95
(B77-34193)

Tremayne, Peter. Dracula unborn / [by] Peter Tremayne. — Folkestone : Bailey and Swinfen, 1977. — 3-222p : geneal table ; 23cm. — (Ghost hunters' library)
ISBN 0-561-00299-1 : £3.95
(B77-31511)

Tresillian, Richard. The bondmaster / by Richard Tresillian. — London : Arlington Books, 1977. — 382p ; 23cm. — (Tresillian, Richard. Bondmaster saga ; book 1)
ISBN 0-85140-246-1 : £4.50
(B77-31512)

Trevanian. The main / [by] Trevanian. — London [etc.] : Granada, 1977. — 283p ; 23cm.
Originally published: New York : Harcourt Brace Jovanovich, 1976.
ISBN 0-246-10993-9 : £3.95
(B77-30718)

Trevaskis, Eve. King's wake / by Eve Trevaskis. — London : Hale, 1977. — 190p : geneal table ; 21cm.
ISBN 0-7091-6118-2 : £3.70
(B77-34194)

Trevelyan, Robert. Pendragon : late of Prince Albert's Own / [by] Robert Trevelyan. — London : Coronet, 1976. — 191p ; 18cm.
Originally published: London : Hodder and Stoughton, 1975.
ISBN 0-340-20812-0 Pbk : £0.60
(B77-00989)

Trevor, Elleston. Blue jay summer / [by] Elleston Trevor. — London : New English Library, 1977. — 191p ; 18cm.
ISBN 0-450-03152-7 Pbk : £0.75
(B77-08609)

Trevor, Elleston. The Theta syndrome / [by] Elleston Trevor. — London : New English Library, 1977. — 205p ; 22cm.
ISBN 0-450-03227-2 : £3.95
(B77-32877)

Trevor, Meriol. The civil prisoners / [by] Meriol Trevor. — London [etc.] : Hodder and Stoughton, 1977. — 190p : geneal table ; 21cm.
ISBN 0-340-21751-0 : £3.95
(B77-28190)

Trevor, William. Elizabeth alone / [by] William Trevor. — St Albans : Triad, 1977. — 288p ; 18cm.
Originally published: London : Bodley Head, 1973.
ISBN 0-586-04489-2 Pbk : £0.95
(B77-14955)

Trew, Antony. Kleber's convoy / [by] Antony Trew. — [London] : Fontana, 1976. — 191p ; 18cm.
Originally published: New York : St Martin's Press, 1973 ; London : Collins, 1974.
ISBN 0-00-613986-8 Pbk : £0.60
(B77-06899)

Trew, Antony. The Soukour deadline / [by] Antony Trew. — [London] : Fontana, 1977. — 188p ; 18cm.
Originally published: as 'Ultimatum'. London : Collins, 1976.
ISBN 0-00-615031-4 Pbk : £0.70
(B77-31513)

Trilling, Lionel. The middle of the journey / [by] Lionel Trilling. — Harmondsworth [etc.] : Penguin, 1977. — xxiii,7-315p ; 18cm. — (Penguin modern classics)
Originally published: New York : Viking Press, 1947 ; London : Secker and Warburg, 1948.
ISBN 0-14-001923-5 Pbk : £0.95
(B77-24517)

Tripp, Miles. The once a year man / [by] Miles Tripp. — London [etc.] : Macmillan, 1977. — 189p ; 21cm.
ISBN 0-333-19902-2 : £3.50
(B77-11422)

Trouncer, Margaret. The lady of my delight : the love story of an abbess / [by] Margaret Trouncer. — London : Hale, 1977. — 188p ; 21cm.
Bibl.: p.182-183. — Based on the life of Louis de Bourbon-Condé.
ISBN 0-7091-5794-0 : £3.50
(B77-09321)

Troy, Una. Caught in the furze / [by] Una Troy. — London : Hale, 1977. — 174p ; 21cm.
ISBN 0-7091-6289-8 : £3.85
(B77-32231)

Tryon, Thomas. The other / [by] Thomas Tryon. — Sevenoaks : Coronet, 1977. — [5],230p ; 18cm.
Originally published: New York : Knopf ; London : Cape, 1971.
ISBN 0-340-21806-1 Pbk : £0.80
(B77-29737)

Tubb, Edwin Charles. The jester at Scar / [by] E.C. Tubb. — London [etc.] : Arrow Books, 1977. — 126p ; 18cm. — (Tubb, Edwin Charles. Dumarest saga ; 5)
Originally published: with 'To Venus! To Venus!' / by David Grinnell. New York : Ace Books, 1970.
ISBN 0-09-913970-7 Pbk : £0.50
(B77-10592)

Tubb, Edwin Charles. Jondelle / by E.C. Tubb. — London : Arrow Books, 1977. — 159p ; 18cm. — (Tubb, Edwin Charles. Dumarest saga ; 10)
Originally published: New York : DAW Books, 1973.
ISBN 0-09-914490-5 Pbk : £0.50
(B77-23751)

Tubb, Edwin Charles. Lallia / [by] E.C. Tubb. — London [etc.] : Arrow Books, 1977. — 116p ; 18cm. — (Tubb, Edwin Charles. Dumarest saga ; 6)
ISBN 0-09-914050-0 Pbk : £0.50
(B77-10593)

Tubb, Edwin Charles. Mayenne / [by] E.C. Tubb. — London : Arrow Books, 1977. — 159p ; 18cm. — (Tubb, Edwin Charles. Dumarest saga ; 9)
Originally published: New York : DAW Books, 1973.
ISBN 0-09-914480-8 Pbk : £0.50
(B77-30719)

Tubb, Edwin Charles. Rogue planet / [by] E.C. Tubb. — London : Barker, 1977. — 143p ; 23cm. — (Space 1999)
Based on television play scripts of the Incorporated Television Company Limited, 1975.
ISBN 0-213-16632-1 : £3.75
(B77-12714)

Tubb, Edwin Charles. Technos / by E.C. Tubb. — London [etc.] : Arrow Books, 1977. — 136p ; 18cm. — (Tubb, Edwin Charles. Dumarest saga ; 7)
Originally published: New York : Ace Books, 1972.
ISBN 0-09-913950-2 Pbk : £0.50
(B77-17128)

Tubb, Edwin Charles. Veruchia / [by] E.C. Tubb. — London [etc.] : Arrow Books, 1977. — 190p ; 18cm. — (Tubb, Edwin Charles. Dumarest saga ; 8)
Originally published: New York : Ace Books, 1973.
ISBN 0-09-913960-x Pbk : £0.50
(B77-17129)

Tucker, Wilson. Ice and iron / [by] Wilson Tucker. — London : Arrow Books, 1977. — [7],181p ; 18cm. — (Arrow science fiction)
Originally published: Garden City, N.Y. : Doubleday, 1974 ; London : Gollancz, 1975.
ISBN 0-09-913910-3 Pbk : £0.60
(B77-12715)

Tucker, Wilson. The Lincoln hunters / by Wilson Tucker. — London : Gollancz, 1977. — 159p ; 21cm. — ([Gollancz SF])
Originally published: New York : Rinehart, 1958.
ISBN 0-575-02297-3 : £3.95
(B77-22904)

Turk, Frances. The rectory at Hay / [by] Frances Turk. — Large print ed. — Bath : Lythway Press, 1977. — [7],293p ; 23cm.
Originally published: London : Wright and Brown, 1966.
ISBN 0-85046-714-4 : £4.55
(B77-21512)

Turk, Frances. A visit to Marchmont / [by] Frances Turk. — Large print ed. — Leicester : Ulverscroft, 1977. — [5],330p ; 23cm. — (Ulverscroft large print series : [romance])
Originally published: London : Wright and Brown, 1964.
ISBN 0-7089-0046-1 : Unpriced
(B77-28191)

Turland, Eileen. Desert quest / by Eileen Turland. — London : Hale, 1977. — 192p ; 20cm.
ISBN 0-7091-6127-1 : £3.20
(B77-19777)

Turpin, Allan. The little medicine bottle / [by] Allan Turpin. — London : Hamilton, 1977. — [4],182p ; 21cm.
ISBN 0-241-89615-0 : £3.95
(B77-14956)

Tute, Warren. The Cairo sleeper / [by] Warren Tute. — London : Constable, 1977. — 208p ; 20cm.
ISBN 0-09-461330-3 : £3.95
(B77-31514)

Tuttle, Wilbur Coleman. Greenhorn trail / [by] W.C. Tuttle. — [London] : Fontana, 1976. — 125p ; 18cm. — (A Fontana western)
ISBN 0-00-614385-7 Pbk : £0.45
(B77-17761)

Tuttle, Wilbur Coleman. The king of Blue Grass Valley / [by] W.C. Tuttle. — [London] : Fontana, 1977. — 127p ; 18cm.
ISBN 0-00-614839-5 Pbk : £0.50
(B77-13349)

Tuttle, Wilbur Coleman. The lone wolf / [by] W.C. Tuttle. — [London] : Fontana, 1977. — 128p ; 18cm.
Originally published: London : Collins, 1967.
ISBN 0-00-614795-x Pbk : £0.50
(B77-30720)

Tuttle, Wilbur Coleman. Vanishing brands / by W.C. Tuttle. — London : Hale, 1977. — 173p ; 20cm.
ISBN 0-7091-6158-1 : £3.10
(B77-26582)

Tyler, Anne. Earthly possessions / [by] Anne Tyler. — London : Chatto and Windus, 1977. — 200p ; 21cm.
Also published: New York : Knopf, 1977.
ISBN 0-7011-2234-x : £4.50 : CIP rev.
(B77-25216)

Uhlman, Fred. Reunion / [by] Fred Uhlman ; with an introduction by Arthur Koestler. — London : Collins : Harvill Press, 1977. — 112p ; 22cm.
Originally published: London : Adam Books, 1971.
ISBN 0-00-261708-0 : £2.50
(B77-11423)

Underwood, Michael, *b.1916.* The fatal trip / [by] Michael Underwood. — London [etc.] : Macmillan, 1977. — 191p ; 20cm.
ISBN 0-333-21975-9 : £3.25
(B77-30721)

Underwood, Michael, *b.1916.* Murder with malice / [by] Michael Underwood. — London [etc.] : Macmillan, 1977. — 223p ; 21cm.
ISBN 0-333-21136-7 : £3.25
(B77-06900)

Unst, Alexander. Operation Doringa / [by] Alexander Unst. — Ilfracombe : Stockwell, 1976. — 271p : map ; 22cm.
ISBN 0-7223-0917-1 : £4.00
(B77-10594)

Unsworth, Barry. Mooncranker's gift / [by] Barry Unsworth. — Harmondsworth [etc.] : Penguin, 1977. — 272p ; 19cm.
Originally published: London : Allen Lane, 1973.
ISBN 0-14-004310-1 Pbk : £0.90
(B77-24518)

Upfield, Arthur. Madman's Bend / [by] Arthur Upfield. — Large print ed. — Leicester : Ulverscroft, 1977. — [4],337p ; 23cm. — (Ulverscroft large print series : [mystery])
Originally published: London : Heinemann, 1963.
ISBN 0-7089-0032-1 : Unpriced
(B77-34195)

Upfield, Arthur. The mountains have a secret / [by] Arthur Upfield. — London : Heinemann, 1977. — v,209p ; 20cm.
Originally published: 1952.
£3.10
ISBN 0-434-81159-9
(B77-19020)

Upfield, Arthur. Venom House / [by] Arthur Upfield. — London : Pan Books, 1977. — 201p ; 18cm.
'An Inspector Napoleon Bonaparte mystery' - cover. — Originally published: New York : Doubleday, 1952 ; London : Heinemann, 1953.
ISBN 0-330-25124-4 Pbk : £0.60
(B77-26583)

Upfield, Arthur. Winds of evil / [by] Arthur W. Upfield. — Large print ed. — Leicester : Ulverscroft, 1977. — [4],433p ; 23cm. — (Ulverscroft large print series : [mystery])
Originally published: Sydney ; London : Angus and Robertson, 1937.
ISBN 0-7089-0054-2 : £2.95
(B77-32232)

Upfield, Arthur. Wings above the Diamantina / [by] Arthur W. Upfield. — Large print ed. — Leicester : Ulverscroft, 1977. — [5],462p ; 23cm. — (Ulverscroft large print series : [mystery])
'Television title: Boney and the Claypan Mystery'. — Originally published: Sydney : Angus and Robertson ; London : Hamilton, 1936.
ISBN 0-7089-0009-7 : £2.95
(B77-22195)

Upshall, Helen. Tears won't set you free / by Helen Upshall. — London : Hale, 1977. — 192p ; 20cm.
ISBN 0-7091-6421-1 : £3.40
(B77-32233)

Upward, Edward. The spiral ascent : a trilogy of novels / [by] Edward Upward. — London : Heinemann, 1977. — [5],788p ; 21cm.
Contents: In the thirties. Originally published: 1962 - The rotten elements. Originally published: 1969 - No home but the struggle.
ISBN 0-434-81172-6 : £6.50
(B77-20690)

Ure, Jean. All in a summer season / [by] Jean Ure. — London : Corgi, 1977. — 160p ; 18cm. — (Ure, Jean. Riverside Theatre romance series ; no.2)
ISBN 0-552-10384-5 Pbk : £0.50
(B77-12716)

Ure, Jean. Early stages / [by] Jean Ure. — London : Corgi, 1977. — 173p ; 18cm. — (Ure, Jean. Riverside Theatre romance series ; no.1)
ISBN 0-552-10383-7 Pbk : £0.50
(B77-13350)

Uren, Rhona. The nun walked at night / by Rhona Uren. — London : Hale, 1977. — 184p ; 21cm.
ISBN 0-7091-6315-0 : £3.85
(B77-32234)

Uris, Leon. Trinity / [by] Leon Uris. — London : Corgi, 1977. — 890p : 2 maps ; 18cm.
Originally published: London : Deutsch, 1976.
ISBN 0-552-10565-1 Pbk : £1.60
(B77-28964)

Urquhart, Colin. My Father is the gardener / [by] Colin Urquhart. — London [etc.] : Hodder and Stoughton, 1977. — 221p ; 18cm. — (Hodder Christian paperbacks)
ISBN 0-340-21327-2 Pbk : £0.95
(B77-30722)

Vallance, Douglas. The Milngavie connection / by Douglas Vallance. — London : Hale, 1977. — 207p ; 20cm.
ISBN 0-7091-6199-9 : £3.25
(B77-28965)

Van der Post, Laurens. A far-off place / [by] Laurens van der Post. — Harmondsworth [etc.] : Penguin, 1976. — 414p ; 18cm.
Originally published: London : Hogarth Press, 1974.
ISBN 0-14-004164-8 Pbk : £0.95
(B77-01837)

Van Every, Dale. Bridal journey / [by] Dale Van Every. — Toronto [etc.] ; London : Bantam, 1976. — [5],312,[1]p ; 18cm.
Originally published: New York : Messner, 1950 ; London : Heinemann, 1952.
ISBN 0-552-62139-0 Pbk : £0.65
(B77-02619)

Van Greenaway, Peter. The destiny man / by Peter van Greenaway. — London : Gollancz, 1977. — 222p ; 21cm. — ([Gollancz suspense])
ISBN 0-575-02301-5 : £4.25
(B77-30723)

Van Greenaway, Peter. Doppelganger / [by] Peter Van Greenaway. — St Albans : Panther, 1977. — 223p ; 18cm.
Originally published: London : Gollancz, 1975.
ISBN 0-586-04414-0 Pbk : £0.60
(B77-12717)

Van Rjndt, Philippe. The Tetramachus collection / [by] Philippe van Rjndt. — London : Macdonald and Jane's, 1977. — 287p ; 23cm.
Originally published: New York : Putnam, 1976.
ISBN 0-354-04121-5 : £3.95
(B77-09976)

Van Slyke, Helen. The best place to be / by Helen Van Slyke. — London : New English Library, 1976. — [5],354p ; 24cm.
Also published: Garden City, N.Y. : Doubleday, 1976.
ISBN 0-450-03221-3 : £4.95
(B77-03233)

Van Stockum, Hilda. The borrowed house / [by] Hilda Van Stockum. — London : Collins, 1977. — 190p ; 18cm.
Originally published: New York : Farrar, Straus and Giroux, 1975. — For adolescents.
ISBN 0-00-671211-8 Pbk : £0.50
(B77-31515)

Van Vogt, Alfred Elton. Earth's last fortress ; and, The three eyes of evil / [by] A.E. Van Vogt. — London : Sphere, 1977. — 173p ; 18cm. — (Sphere science fiction)
'Earth's last fortress ; and, The three eyes of evil' originally published: in 1 vol. as 'The three eyes of evil ; and, Earth's last fortress', London : Sidgwick and Jackson, 1973. 'Earth's last fortress' originally published: New York : Ace Books, 1960. — 'Three eyes of evil' originally published: as 'Siege of the unseen', New York : Ace Books, 1959.
ISBN 0-7221-8732-7 Pbk : £0.85
(B77-34196)

Van Vogt, Alfred Elton. The secret galactics / [by] A.E. Van Vogt. — London : Sphere, 1977. — 189p ; 18cm. — (Sphere science fiction)
Originally published: Englewood Cliffs : Prentice-Hall, 1974 ; London : Sidgwick and Jackson, 1975.
ISBN 0-7221-8735-1 Pbk : £0.75
(B77-19778)

Van Vogt, Alfred Elton. Tyranopolis / [by] A.E. Van Vogt. — London : Sphere, 1977. — 170p ; 18cm. — (Sphere science fiction)
Originally published: as 'Future glitter'. New York : Ace Books, 1973 ; London : Sidgwick and Jackson, 1976.
ISBN 0-7221-8734-3 Pbk : £0.85
(B77-28966)

Van Vogt, Alfred Elton. The universe maker ; [and, The proxy intelligence] / [by] A.E. Van Vogt. — London : Sphere, [1977]. — 189p ; 18cm. — (Sphere science fiction)
Originally published: London : Sidgwick and Jackson, 1976. — 'The universe maker' originally published: New York : Ace Books, 1953? - 'The proxy intelligence' originally published: in 'If' magazine, October 1968.
ISBN 0-7221-8733-5 Pbk : £0.75
(B77-22905)

Vance, Jack. Big Planet / [by] Jack Vance. — Sevenoaks : Coronet, 1977. — 158p ; 18cm.
Originally published: New York : Avalon Books, 1957.
ISBN 0-340-21251-9 Pbk : £0.65
(B77-19779)

Vance, Jack. Showboat world / [by] Jack Vance. — Sevenoaks : Coronet, 1977. — 171p : map ; 18cm.
Originally published: New York : Pyramid, 1975.
ISBN 0-340-21252-7 Pbk : £0.65
(B77-21513)

Vance, Jack. To live forever / [by] Jack Vance. — London : Sphere, 1976. — 189p ; 18cm. — (Sphere science fiction)
Originally published: New York : Ballantine Books, 1956.
ISBN 0-7221-8730-0 Pbk : £0.60
(B77-14957)

Vaughan, Gary. East zone snatch / by Gary Vaughan. — London : Hale, 1977. — 186p ; 20cm.
ISBN 0-7091-6112-3 : £3.15
(B77-17762)

Vaughan, Helen. The briar rose / [by] Helen Vaughan. — London : Collins, 1977. — 158p ; 19cm.
ISBN 0-00-233060-1 : £2.95
(B77-27434)

Vaughan, Helen. The stepping-stone / [by] Helen Vaughan. — London [etc.] : Collins, 1977. — 160p ; 19cm.
ISBN 0-00-233914-5 : £2.75
(B77-09322)

Vaughan, Matthew. Chalky / [by] Matthew Vaughan. — London [etc.] : Pan Books, 1977. — 204p ; 18cm.
Originally published: London : Secker and Warburg, 1975.
ISBN 0-330-25057-4 Pbk : £0.70
(B77-13910)

Vern, Sarah. Beloved image / by Sarah Vern. — London : Hale, 1977. — 207p ; 20cm.
ISBN 0-7091-6218-9 : £3.20
(B77-21514)

Vern, Sarah. Woman of ice / by Sarah Vern. — London : Hale, 1977. — [4],188p ; 20cm.
ISBN 0-7091-5975-7 : £3.10
(B77-15540)

Vernon, Claire. The doctor was a guest / [by] Claire Vernon. — London : Hale, 1976. — 156p ; 20cm.
ISBN 0-7091-5714-2 : £2.95
(B77-00454)

Vernon, Claire. The doctor was hijacked / by Claire Vernon. — London : Hale, 1977. — 174p ; 20cm.
ISBN 0-7091-5988-9 : £3.10
(B77-21515)

Vernon, Kay R. The phantom of Fonthill Park / [by] Kay R. Vernon. — London : Hale, 1977. — [5],184p ; 21cm.
Originally published: Garden City, N.Y. : Doubleday, 1976.
ISBN 0-7091-6336-3 : £3.85
(B77-30724)

Vidal, Gore. 1876 / [by] Gore Vidal. — St Albans : Panther, 1977. — 359p ; 18cm.
Originally published: New York : Random House ; London : Heinemann, 1976.
ISBN 0-586-04703-4 Pbk : £1.00
(B77-20691)

Vidal, Gore. Myron / [by] Gore Vidal. — St Albans : Panther, 1977. — 204p ; 18cm.
Originally published: New York : Random House, 1974 ; London : Heinemann, 1975.
ISBN 0-586-04300-4 Pbk : £0.60
(B77-12718)

Viney, Jayne. The last Saxon / [by] Jayne Viney. — London : Hale, 1976. — 222p ; 21cm.
Based on the life of Harold II.
ISBN 0-7091-5594-8 : £3.50
(B77-01838)

Vinton, Anne. The hospital in Buwambo / [by] Anne Vinton. — Large print ed. — Leicester : Ulverscroft, 1977. — [7],396p ; 23cm. — (Ulverscroft large print series : [romance])
Originally published: London : Mills and Boon, 1957.
ISBN 0-7089-0055-0 : £2.95
(B77-32235)

Vinton, Anne. The time of enchantment / [by] Anne Vinton. — London [etc.] : Mills and Boon, 1976. — 187p ; 18cm. — (Mills and Boon classics)
Originally published: 1956.
ISBN 0-263-72216-3 Pbk : £0.35
(B77-11424)

Vizard, Bronwen. Mist on the hills / by Bronwen Vizard. — London : Hale, 1977. — 190p 20cm.
ISBN 0-7091-6297-9 : £3.20
(B77-28192)

Vonnegut, Kurt. Slapstick, or, Lonesome no more! / [by] Kurt Vonnegut. — St Albans : Panther, 1977. — 186p : ill ; 18cm.
Originally published: New York : Delacorte Press/S. Lawrence ; London : Cape, 1976.
ISBN 0-586-04012-9 Pbk : £0.75
(B77-15541)

Waddell, Helen. Peter Abelard : a novel / [by] Helen Waddell. — [London] ([14 St James's Place, S.W.1]) : Fount Paperbacks, 1977. — 253p ; 18cm.
Originally published: London : Constable, 1933.
ISBN 0-00-624812-8 Pbk : £0.95
(B77-30725)

Wade, Stephen. In search of Jasper Mc.Doom / [by Stephen Wade]. — Breakish : Aquila, 1976. — [17]p ; 23cm.
Also available in a limited ed. of 26 copies, signed and lettered by the author.
ISBN 0-7275-0127-5 Sd : £0.40
ISBN 0-7275-0128-3 Signed ed. : £1.50
(B77-15542)

Wagner, Karl Edward. Bloodstone / [by] Karl Edward Wagner. — Sevenoaks : Coronet, 1977. — 303p ; 18cm.
Originally published: New York : Warner Paperbacks, 1975.
ISBN 0-340-21812-6 Pbk : £0.85
(B77-25217)

Wainwright, John, *b.1921.* The day of the peppercorn kill / [by] John Wainwright. — London [etc.] : Macmillan, 1977. — 192p ; 20cm.
ISBN 0-333-21759-4 : £3.50
(B77-31516)

Wainwright, John, *b.1921.* Do nothin' till you hear from me / [by] John Wainwright. — London [etc.] : Macmillan, 1977. — 224p ; 21cm.
ISBN 0-333-21400-5 : £3.50
(B77-22196)

Wainwright, John, *b.1921.* A nest of rats / [by] John Wainwright. — London [etc.] : Macmillan, 1977. — 223p ; 21cm.
ISBN 0-333-21161-8 : £3.25
(B77-19780)

Wainwright, John, *b.1921.* Pool of tears / [by] John Wainwright. — London [etc.] : Macmillan, 1977. — 221p ; 21cm.
ISBN 0-333-19809-3 : £3.25
(B77-06901)

Wakefield, Dan. Home free : a novel / by Dan Wakefield. — London [etc.] : Hart-Davis MacGibbon, 1977. — 237p ; 21cm.
ISBN 0-246-11012-0 : £4.50
(B77-22906)

Wakefield, Tom. Trixie Trash, star ascending / [by] Tom Wakefield. — London [etc.] : Routledge and Kegan Paul, 1977. — [6],178p ; 23cm.
ISBN 0-7100-8574-5 : £3.95 : CIP rev.
(B77-08101)

Waldman, Frank. The pink panther strikes again / [by] Frank Waldman. — London : Barker, 1977. — 144p ; 23cm.
' ... based on the film "The pink panther strikes again" ... ' - jacket.
ISBN 0-213-16638-0 : £3.75
(B77-12719)

Waldman, Frank. The return of the pink panther / [by] Frank Waldman. — London : Barker, 1977. — 5-141p ; 23cm.
' ... based on the film "The return of the pink panther" ... ' - jacket.
ISBN 0-213-16639-9 : £3.75
(B77-12720)

Walker, Alice. Meridian / by Alice Walker. — London : Deutsch, 1976. — [11],228p ; 22cm.
Also published: New York : Harcourt Brace Jovanovich, 1976.
ISBN 0-233-96837-7 : £3.50
(B77-12721)

Walker, David, *b.1911.* Pot of gold / [by] David Walker. — Toronto ; London : Collins, 1977. — 182p : 1 ill ; 21cm.
ISBN 0-00-221669-8 : £3.95
(B77-22197)

Walker, Frank. Vipers & Co / [by] Frank Walker ; illustrated by Trevor Stubley. — London [etc.] : Macmillan, 1976. — 147p : ill ; 21cm.
ISBN 0-333-19430-6 : £2.95
(B77-03234)

Walker, Frank, *b.1930.* Banjo / [by] Frank Walker ; illustrations by David Hughes. — London : Joseph, 1977. — 192p : ill ; 23cm.
ISBN 0-7181-1593-7 : £4.25
(B77-19781)

Walker, Frank, *b.1930.* Jack / [by] Frank Walker. — London : Sphere, 1977. — 184p : ill ; 18cm.
Originally published: London : Joseph, 1976.
ISBN 0-7221-8878-1 Pbk : £0.75
(B77-24519)

Walker, Lucy. The call of the pines / [by] Lucy Walker. — [London] : Fontana, 1977. — 189p ; 18cm.
Originally published: London : Collins, 1963.
ISBN 0-00-614786-0 Pbk : £0.50
(B77-14426)

Walker, Lucy. Gamma's girl / [by] Lucy Walker. — London : Collins, 1977. — 220p ; 21cm.
ISBN 0-00-222260-4 : £3.50
(B77-21516)

Walker, Lucy. Heaven is here / [by] Lucy Walker. — Large print ed. — Leicester : Ulverscroft, 1977. — [5],356p ; 23cm. — (Ulverscroft large print series : [romance])
Originally published: London : Collins, 1957.
ISBN 0-7089-0024-0 : £2.95
(B77-19782)

Walker, Lucy. A man called Masters / [by] Lucy Walker. — [London] : Fontana, 1977. — 192p ; 18cm.
Originally published: London : Collins, 1965.
ISBN 0-00-615028-4 Pbk : £0.60
(B77-27435)

Walker, Lucy. The mountain that went to the sea / [by] Lucy Walker. — [London] : Fontana, 1977. — 160p ; 18cm.
Originally published: London : Collins, 1971.
ISBN 0-00-614479-9 Pbk : £0.50
(B77-13911)

Walker, Lucy. The one who kisses / [by] Lucy Walker. — [London] : Fontana, 1977. — 190p ; 18cm.
Originally published: London : Collins, 1954.
ISBN 0-00-615027-6 Pbk : £0.60
(B77-27436)

Walker, Lucy. The runaway girl / [by] Lucy Walker. — [London] : Fontana, 1977. — 156p ; 18cm.
Originally published: London : Collins, 1975.
ISBN 0-00-614530-2 Pbk : £0.50
(B77-13912)

Walker, Peter Norman. The MacIntyre plot / by Peter N. Walker. — London : Hale, 1977. — 207p ; 20cm.
ISBN 0-7091-5967-6 : £3.15
(B77-12722)

Walker, Peter Norman. Missing from home / by Peter N. Walker. — London : Hale, 1977. — 183p ; 20cm.
ISBN 0-7091-6211-1 : £3.25
(B77-34197)

Wallace, Doreen. Ashbury people / [by] Doreen Wallace. — Large print ed. — Leicester : Ulverscroft, 1976. — [7],316p ; 23cm. — (Ulverscroft large print series : [romance])
Originally published: London : Collins, 1968.
ISBN 0-85456-500-0 : £2.65
(B77-08610)

Wallace, Edgar. The people of the river / [by] Edgar Wallace. — London [etc.] : White Lion Publishers, 1976. — 256p ; 21cm.
Originally published: London : Ward Lock, 1912.
ISBN 0-7274-0232-3 : £3.25
(B77-03772)

Wallace, Edgar. Sanders / [by] Edgar Wallace. — London [etc.] : White Lion Publishers, 1977. — 191p ; 21cm.
Originally published: London : Hodder and Stoughton, 1926.
ISBN 0-7274-0237-4 : £3.50
(B77-12723)

Wallace, Irving. The man / [by] Irving Wallace. — London [etc.] : White Lion Publishers, 1977. — [7],760p ; 22cm.
Originally published: New York : Simon and Schuster, 1964 ; London : Cassell, 1965.
ISBN 0-7274-0277-3 : £6.25
(B77-09977)

Wallace, Irving. The man / by Irving Wallace ; a condensation by the editors of Reader's Digest Condensed Books. — Large print ed. — Leicester : Ulverscroft, 1977. — [4],361p ; 23cm. — (Ulverscroft large print series : [fiction])
This condensation originally published: Pleasantville, N.Y. ; London : Reader's Digest Association, 196-?.
ISBN 0-85456-558-2 : £2.65
(B77-13913)

Wallace, Irving. The R document / [by] Irving Wallace. — London : Corgi, 1977. — 320p ; 18cm.
Originally published: New York : Simon and Schuster ; London : Cassell, 1976.
ISBN 0-552-10495-7 Pbk : £0.85
(B77-31517)

Wallace, Irving. The R document / [by] Irving Wallace. — Large print ed. — London : Prior [etc.], 1977. — [5],634p ; 25cm.
Originally published: London : Cassell, 1976.
ISBN 0-86043-038-3 : £5.95
(B77-12142)

Wallace, James. The guardian of Krandor / [by] James Wallace. — London : Hale, 1977. — 192p ; 21cm. — (Hale SF)
ISBN 0-7091-5817-3 : £3.50
(B77-15543)

Wallace, James. The plague of the golden rat / by James Wallace. — London : Hale, 1976. — 183p ; 21cm. — (Hale SF)
ISBN 0-7091-5655-3 : £3.25
(B77-01839)

Wallace, Jane. The hidden Venus / [by] Jane Wallace. — London : Hurst and Blackett, 1977. — 183p ; 20cm.
ISBN 0-09-129660-9 : £3.50
(B77-30726)

Walsh, Sheila Frances. Madalena / [by] Sheila Walsh. — London : Hurst and Blackett, 1976. — 185p ; 20cm.
ISBN 0-09-126580-0 : £3.25
(B77-05080)

Walsh, Sheila Frances. The sergeant major's daughter / [by] Sheila Walsh. — London : Hurst and Blackett, 1977. — 185p ; 19cm.
ISBN 0-09-131210-8 : £3.50
(B77-30727)

Walters, Hugh. The Caves of Drach / [by] Hugh Walters. — London : Faber, 1977. — 3-136p ; 21cm.
ISBN 0-571-11037-1 : £2.95
(B77-17130)

Walthew, Kenneth. A queen for royal George / by Kenneth Walthew. — London : Hale, 1977. — 174p ; 21cm.
Based on the life of George III.
ISBN 0-7091-6177-8 : £3.50
(B77-22907)

Warby, Marjorie. Desmond's daughters / [by] Marjorie Warby. — London : Collins, 1977. — 159p ; 20cm.
ISBN 0-00-233185-3 : £2.75
(B77-19783)

Ward, Jonas. Buchanan calls the shots / [by] Jonas Ward. — London : Coronet, 1977. — 144p ; 18cm.
Originally published: New York : Fawcett, 1975.
ISBN 0-340-21244-6 Pbk : £0.50
(B77-19784)

Warde, Joan. Fran for short / by Joan Warde. — London : Hale, 1977. — 192p ; 20cm.
ISBN 0-7091-6029-1 : £3.10
(B77-17763)

Warner, Douglas. Death of a dreamer / [by] Douglas Warner. — London [etc.] : White Lion Publishers, 1977. — 174p ; 21cm.
Originally published: London : Cassell, 1964.
ISBN 0-85617-013-5 : £3.75
(B77-32879)

Warner, Marina. In a dark wood / [by] Marina Warner. — London : Weidenfeld and Nicolson, 1977. — [5],250p ; 23cm.
Bibl.: p.249-250.
ISBN 0-297-77266-x : £4.50
(B77-20692)

Warner, Mignon. Grave error / by Mignon Warner. — London : Hale, 1977. — 184p ; 20cm.
ISBN 0-7091-6025-9 : £3.15
(B77-13351)

Warner, Sylvia Townsend. Kingdoms of Elfin / by Sylvia Townsend Warner. — London : Chatto and Windus, 1977. — [7],222p ; 21cm.
ISBN 0-7011-2202-1 : £4.50
(B77-04430)

Warren, Patricia Nell. The fancy dancer / by Patricia Nell Warren. — Toronto [etc.] ; London : Bantam, 1977. — [4],250p ; 18cm.
Originally published: New York : Morrow, 1976.
ISBN 0-552-60387-2 Pbk : £0.85
(B77-31518)

Warren, Patricia Nell. The front runner / [by] Patricia Nell Warren. — Toronto [etc.] ; London : Bantam, 1975[i.e.1976]. — [4],314,[1] p ; 18cm.
Originally published: New York : Morrow, 1974.
ISBN 0-552-10286-5 Pbk : £0.65
(B77-02620)

Warren, Robert Penn. A place to come to : a novel / by Robert Penn Warren. — London : Secker and Warburg, 1977. — [7],401p ; 23cm.
ISBN 0-436-56317-7 : £4.50
(B77-16075)

Warren, Tony. Rising damp / by Eric Chappell ; adapted from the Yorkshire Television series by Tony Warren. — London : Sphere, 1977. — 160p ; 18cm.
ISBN 0-7221-8912-5 Pbk : £0.65
(B77-13352)

Warren, Tony. Rising damp / [by] Eric Chappell ; adapted from the Yorkshire Television series by Tony Warren. — London : Severn House : [Distributed by Hutchinson], 1977. — 160p ; 21cm.
Also published: London : Sphere, 1977.
ISBN 0-7278-0243-7 : £3.25
(B77-34198)

Waterhouse, Keith. Billy Liar on the moon / [by] Keith Waterhouse. — Harmondsworth [etc.] : Penguin, 1977. — 202p ; 18cm.
Originally published: London : Joseph, 1975.
ISBN 0-14-004283-0 Pbk : £0.60
(B77-20693)

Watkins, Leslie. The killing of Idi Amin / [by] Leslie Watkins. — London : Everest, 1976. — 208p ; 23cm.
ISBN 0-905018-21-4 : £3.50
(B77-12724)

Watson, Colin, *b.1920.* Coffin scarcely used / [by] Colin Watson. — London : Eyre Methuen, 1977. — 173p ; 19cm. — (Watson, Colin, b.1920. Flaxborough chronicles)
Originally published: London : Eyre and Spottiswoode, 1958.
ISBN 0-413-37870-5 : £2.95
(B77-28967)

Watson, Colin, *b.1920.* The Flaxborough crab / [by] Colin Watson. — London : Eyre Methuen, 1977. — 175p ; 19cm. — (Watson, Colin, b.1920. Flaxborough chronicles)
Originally published: London : Eyre and Spottiswoode, 1969.
ISBN 0-413-37900-0 : £2.95
(B77-28968)

Watson, Colin, *b.1920.* Hopjoy was here / [by] Colin Watson. — London : Magnum Books, 1977. — 157p ; 18cm. — (Watson, Colin. Flaxborough chronicles)
'Murder most English' - cover. — Originally published: London : Eyre and Spottiswoode, 1962.
ISBN 0-417-01810-x Pbk : £0.70
(B77-25924)

Watson, Colin, *b.1920.* Lonelyheart 4122 / [by] Colin Watson. — London : Magnum Books, 1977. — 160p ; 18cm. — (Watson, Colin. Flaxborough chronicles)
'Murder most English' - cover. — Originally published: London : Eyre and Spottiswoode, 1967.
ISBN 0-417-01880-0 Pbk : £0.70
(B77-25925)

Watson, Colin, *b.1920.* One man's meat / [by] Colin Watson. — London : Eyre Methuen, 1977. — 192p ; 21cm.
ISBN 0-413-34780-x : £3.50
(B77-17131)

Watson, Ian. Alien embassy / by Ian Watson. — London : Gollancz, 1977. — 208p ; 21cm. — ([Gollancz SF])
ISBN 0-575-02336-8 : £4.20
(B77-31519)

Watson, Ian. The Jonah kit / [by] Ian Watson. — St Albans : Panther, 1977. — 192p ; 18cm. — (Panther science fiction)
Originally published: London : Gollancz, 1975.
ISBN 0-586-04385-3 Pbk : £0.60
(B77-14958)

Watson, Ian. The Martian Inca / by Ian Watson. — London : Gollancz, 1977. — 207p ; 21cm. — ([Gollancz SF])
ISBN 0-575-02218-3 : £3.95
(B77-08102)

Watson, Simon. No man's land / [by] Simon Watson. — Harmondsworth [etc.] : Puffin Books, 1977. — 207p : map ; 19cm. — (Puffin books)
Originally published: London : Gollancz, 1975.
ISBN 0-14-030951-9 Pbk : £0.50
(B77-29738)

Waugh, Alec. Love in conflict / by Alec Waugh. — London : Severn House : [Distributed by Hutchinson], 1977. — [6],247p ; 21cm.
Originally published: as '"- 'Sir', she said"', London : Chapman and Hall, 1930.
ISBN 0-7278-0212-7 : £3.50
(B77-25926)

Waugh, Evelyn. Decline and fall ; [and], Black mischief ; [and], A handful of dust ; [and], Scoop ; [and], Put out more flags ; [and], Brideshead revisited / [by] Evelyn Waugh. — London : Heinemann : Secker and Warburg : Octopus Books, 1977. — 3-864p ; 25cm.
ISBN 0-905712-15-3 : £4.95
(B77-30728)

Waugh, Hillary. Born victim / [by] Hillary Waugh. — London : Gollancz, 1977. — [5], 184p ; 21cm. — ([Gollancz vintage thriller])
Originally published: Garden City, N.Y. : Doubleday, 1962 ; London : Gollancz, 1963.
ISBN 0-575-02295-7 : £3.75
(B77-20694)

Waugh, Hillary. Death and circumstance / [by] Hillary Waugh. — London : Gollancz, 1977. — 3-216p ; 21cm. — ([Gollancz vintage thriller])
Originally published: Garden City, N.Y. : Doubleday ; London : Gollancz, 1963.
ISBN 0-575-02296-5 : £3.75
(B77-20695)

Waugh, Hillary. The late Mrs D / [by] Hillary Waugh. — London : Gollancz, 1977. — 3-192p ; 21cm. — ([Gollancz vintage thriller])
Originally published: Garden City, N.Y. : Doubleday ; London : Gollancz, 1962.
ISBN 0-575-02242-6 : £3.30
(B77-08103)

Waugh, Hillary. Seaview Manor / by Hillary Waugh. — London : Gollancz, 1977. — [4], 276p ; 21cm. — ([Gollancz thriller])
Originally published: Garden City, N.Y. : Doubleday, 1976.
ISBN 0-575-02205-1 : £3.80
(B77-10963)

Waugh, Hillary. That night it rained / by Hillary Waugh. — London : Gollancz, 1977. — 3-186p ; 21cm. — ([Gollancz vintage thriller])
Originally published: Garden City, N.Y. : Doubleday ; London : Gollancz, 1961.
ISBN 0-575-02241-8 : £3.30
(B77-08104)

Weale, Anne. The lonely shore / [by] Anne Weale. — Large print ed. — Leicester : Ulverscroft, 1977. — [9],303p ; 23cm. — (Ulverscroft large print series : [romance])
Originally published: London : Mills and Boon, 1956.
ISBN 0-85456-511-6 : £2.65
(B77-08611)

Weale, Anne. The sea waif / [by] Anne Weale. — Large print ed. — Leicester : Ulverscroft, 1977. — [7],317p ; 23cm. — (Ulverscroft large print series : [romance])
Originally published: London : Mills and Boon, 1967.
ISBN 0-7089-0012-7 : £2.95
(B77-22198)

Weale, Anne. Terrace in the sun / [by] Anne Weale. — Large print ed. — Bath : Lythway Press, 1977. — [5],361p ; 22cm.
Originally published: London : Mills and Boon, 1966.
ISBN 0-85046-702-0 : £4.80
(B77-17764)

Weatherby, William John. Death of an informer / [by] W.J. Weatherby. — London : Robson, 1977. — 188p ; 21cm.
ISBN 0-903895-88-9 : £2.95
(B77-13353)

Weatherby, William John. Home in the dark / [by] W.J. Weatherby. — London : Robson Books, 1977. — 156p ; 21cm.
ISBN 0-86051-006-9 : £3.25 : CIP rev.
(B77-16613)

Weatherby, William John. Murder at the UN / [by] W.J. Weatherby. — London : Robson, 1977. — [5],185p ; 23cm.
ISBN 0-86051-003-4 : £3.25
(B77-13354)

Webb, Charles. Elsinor : a novel / by Charles Webb. — London : Gollancz, 1977. — [4], 212p ; 21cm.
Originally published: New York : McGraw-Hill, 1976.
ISBN 0-575-02255-8 : £4.20
(B77-16076)

Webb, Forrest. Go for out / [by] Forrest Webb. — London : W.H. Allen, 1977. — [4],188p ; 23cm.
ISBN 0-491-02270-0 : £3.95
(B77-19785)

Webb, Neil. Gun handy / [by] Neil Webb. — London : Hale, 1977. — 156p ; 20cm.
ISBN 0-7091-5885-8 : £2.80
(B77-05717)

Webb, William Thomas. After the inferno / by William Thomas Webb. — London : Hale, 1977. — 3-190p ; 21cm. — (Hale SF)
ISBN 0-7091-6052-6 : £3.25
(B77-21517)

Webb, William Thomas. The eye of Hollerl-Ra / by William Thomas Webb. — London : Hale, 1977. — 190p ; 21cm. — (Hale SF)
ISBN 0-7091-6182-4 : £3.60
(B77-26584)

Webster, Jan. Colliers Row / [by] Jan Webster. — London : Collins, 1977. — [1],276p ; 22cm.
ISBN 0-00-222491-7 : £3.95
(B77-06319)

Weir, Jonnet. Shadow on yesterday / by Jonnet Weir. — London : Hale, 1977. — 153p ; 20cm.
ISBN 0-7091-6463-7 : £3.20
(B77-28193)

Weir, Rosemary. Uncle Barney and the shrink-drink / [by] Rosemary Weir ; illustrated by Carolyn Dinan. — London : Abelard-Schuman : Sadler, 1977. — 64p : ill ; 21cm. — (A grasshopper book)
ISBN 0-200-72383-9 : £1.75
ISBN 0-200-72384-7 Pbk : £0.50
(B77-17132)

Weiss, David. The Venetian : a novel / by David Weiss. — London : W.H. Allen, 1977. — 367p ; 25cm.
Originally published: New York : Morrow, 1976.
ISBN 0-491-02101-1 : £4.95
(B77-26585)

Welcome, John. Grand National : a novel / by John Welcome. — London : Sphere, 1977. — 335p ; 18cm.
Originally published: London : Hamilton, 1976.
ISBN 0-7221-8981-8 Pbk : £0.95
(B77-13355)

Weldon, David. The chaos contract / [by] David Weldon. — London : New English Library, 1977. — 174p ; 18cm.
ISBN 0-450-03346-5 Pbk : £0.70
(B77-28194)

Weldon, Fay. Female friends / [by] Fay Weldon. — London : Pan Books, 1977. — 237p ; 20cm. — (Picador)
Originally published: London : Heinemann, 1975.
ISBN 0-330-25060-4 Pbk : £1.00
(B77-19786)

Wells, Herbert George. The food of the gods / [by] H.G. Wells. — London : Sphere, 1977. — 223p ; 18cm. — (Sphere science fiction)
Originally published: London : Collins, 1904.
ISBN 0-7221-8987-7 Pbk : £0.75
(B77-28969)

Wells, Herbert George. The sleeper awakes / [by] H.G. Wells. — London : Sphere, 1976. — 204p ; 18cm. — (Sphere science fiction)
ISBN 0-7221-8979-6 Pbk : £0.60
(B77-13356)

Wells, Herbert George. The time machine ; [and], The island of Dr Moreau ; [and], The invisible man ; [and], The first men in the moon ; [and], The food of the gods ; [and], In the days of the comet ; [and], The war of the worlds / [by] H.G. Wells. — London : Heinemann : Octopus Books, [1977]. — 3-828p ; 25cm.
ISBN 0-905712-00-5 : £3.95
(B77-13357)

Wells, Hondo. Prairie raiders / [by] Hondo Wells. — London : New English Library, 1977. — 112p ; 18cm.
Originally published: New York : Ace Books, 1963.
ISBN 0-450-03435-6 Pbk : £0.60
(B77-25927)

Wells, Hondo. Shadow at noon : a novel / by Hondo Wells. — London [etc.] : Mews Books ; London : Distributed by New English Library, 1977. — 109p ; 18cm.
Originally published: New York : Pyramid Books, 1955.
ISBN 0-452-00075-0 Pbk : £0.55
(B77-12725)

Wentworth, Patricia. The catherine-wheel / [by] Patricia Wentworth. — Large print ed. — Leicester : Ulverscroft, 1977. — [7],492p : geneal table ; 23cm. — (Ulverscroft large print series : [mystery])
Originally published: London : Hodder and Stoughton, 1951.
ISBN 0-85456-534-5 : £2.95
(B77-19787)

Wentworth, Patricia. Fool errant / [by] Patricia Wentworth. — London [etc.] : White Lion Publishers, 1977. — 310p ; 21cm.
Originally published: London : Hodder and Stoughton, 1929.
ISBN 0-7274-0311-7 : £3.95
(B77-33447)

Wentworth, Patricia. The gazebo / by Patricia Wentworth. — London : Remploy, 1976. — 255p ; 19cm.
Originally published: London : Hodder and Stoughton, 1958.
ISBN 0-7066-0691-4 : £2.75
(B77-10595)

Wentworth, Patricia. The ivory dagger / [by] Patricia Wentworth. — Large print ed. — Leicester : Ulverscroft, 1977. — [5],473p ; 23cm. — (Ulverscroft large print series : [mystery])
Originally published: London : Hodder and Stoughton, 1953.
ISBN 0-85456-525-6 : £2.65
(B77-13914)

Wentworth, Patricia. The listening eye / [by] Patricia Wentworth. — Sevenoaks : Coronet, 1977. — 224p ; 18cm. — (A Miss Silver thriller)
Originally published: London : Hodder and Stoughton, 1957.
ISBN 0-340-21794-4 Pbk : £0.70
(B77-26586)

Wentworth, Patricia. Poison in the pen / [by] Patricia Wentworth. — Sevenoaks : Coronet, 1977. — 220p ; 18cm. — (A Miss Silver thriller)
Originally published: London : Hodder and Stoughton, 1957.
ISBN 0-340-21792-8 Pbk : £0.70
(B77-26587)

West, Jessamyn. The massacre at Fall Creek / [by] Jessamyn West. — London : Pan Books, 1976. — 349p ; 18cm.
Originally published: New York : Harcourt Brace Jovanovich ; London : Macmillan, 1975.
ISBN 0-330-24738-7 Pbk : £0.75
(B77-06902)

West, Mae. Pleasure man / [by] Mae West. — London : Corgi, 1976. — 253p ; 18cm.
Originally published: New York : Dell, 1975.
ISBN 0-552-10299-7 Pbk : £0.70
(B77-02621)

West, Morris. The big story / [by] Morris West. — [London] : Fontana, 1976. — 156p ; 18cm.
Originally published: London : Heinemann, 1957.
ISBN 0-00-614315-6 Pbk : £0.65
(B77-13915)

West, Morris. Daughter of silence / [by] Morris West. — [London] : Fontana, 1976. — 224p ; 18cm.
Originally published: London : Heinemann, 1961.
ISBN 0-00-614316-4 Pbk : £0.65
(B77-06320)

West, Morris. The devil's advocate / [by] Morris West. — [London] : Fontana, 1977. — 287p ; 18cm.
Originally published: London : Heinemann, 1959.
ISBN 0-00-614460-8 Pbk : £0.75
(B77-14959)

West, Morris. The devil's advocate ; [and], The second victory ; [and], Daughter of silence ; [and], The salamander ; [and], The shoes of the fisherman / [by] Morris West. — London : Heinemann : Octopus Books, 1977. — 3-861p : ill ; 25cm.
ISBN 0-905712-17-x : £4.95
(B77-25928)

West, Morris. The Salamander / [by] Morris West ; a condensation by the editors of Reader's Digest Condensed Books. — Large print ed. — Leicester : Ulverscroft, 1977. — [4] ,326p ; 23cm. — (Ulverscroft large print series : [fiction])
This condensation originally published: Pleasantville, N.Y. : Reader's Digest Association, 197-?.
ISBN 0-85456-559-0 : £2.65
(B77-15544)

West, Morris. The second victory / [by] Morris West. — [London] : Fontana, 1977. — 218p ; 18cm.
Originally published: London : Heinemann, 1958.
ISBN 0-00-614308-3 Pbk : £0.70
(B77-30729)

West, Morris. The shoes of the Fisherman / [by] Morris West. — [London] : Fontana, 1976. — 256p ; 18cm.
Originally published: London : Heinemann, 1963.
ISBN 0-00-614314-8 Pbk : £0.65
(B77-06321)

Westall, Robert. The machine-gunners / [by] Robert Westall. — Harmondsworth [etc.] : Puffin Books, 1977. — 186p ; 18cm.
Originally published: London : Macmillan, 1975. — For adolescents.
ISBN 0-14-030973-x Pbk : £0.60
(B77-27437)

Westall, Robert. The Watch House / [by] Robert Westall. — London [etc.] : Macmillan, 1977. — 228p ; 21cm.
For adolescents.
ISBN 0-333-23237-2 : £3.50
(B77-31520)

Westall, Sheila. The Galmart affair / [by] Sheila Westall. — Large print ed. — Leicester : Ulverscroft, 1977. — [5],322p ; 23cm. — (Ulverscroft large print series : [mystery])
Originally published: London : Hale, 1975.
ISBN 0-85456-526-4 : £2.65
(B77-13916)

Westheimer, David. Over the edge / [by] David Westheimer. — London [etc.] : Pan Books, 1977. — 176p ; 18cm.
Originally published: Boston, Mass. : Little, Brown, 1972 ; London : Joseph, 1974.
ISBN 0-330-25083-3 Pbk : £0.70
(B77-23752)

Westlake, Donald E. Brothers keepers / [by] Donald E. Westlake. — London [etc.] : Hodder and Stoughton, 1977. — [7],254p : plan ; 22cm.
Originally published: New York : M. Evans, 1975.
ISBN 0-340-21594-1 : £3.95
(B77-10596)

Westlake, Donald E. Jimmy the Kid / [by] Donald E. Westlake. — London : Coronet, 1977. — 174p ; 18cm.
Originally published: New York : M. Evans, 1974 ; London : Hodder and Stoughton, 1975.
ISBN 0-340-21823-1 Pbk : £0.75
(B77-24520)

Weston, Carolyn. Rouse the demon / [by] Carolyn Weston. — London : Gollancz, 1977. — [4],155p ; 21cm. — ([Gollancz detection])
Originally published: New York : Random House, 1976.
ISBN 0-575-02245-0 : £3.50
(B77-11425)

Wetering, Janwillem van de. The corpse on the dike / [by] Janwillem van de Wetering. — London : Heinemann, 1977. — [7],182p ; 23cm.
Originally published: Boston, Mass. : Houghton Mifflin, 1976.
ISBN 0-434-85922-2 : £3.50
(B77-08105)

Wetering, Janwillem van de. Death of a hawker / [by] Janwillem van de Wetering. — London : Heinemann, 1977. — [5],185p ; 23cm.
ISBN 0-434-85923-0 : £3.90
(B77-28195)

Weverka, Robert. The Waltons / [by] Robert Weverka. — London : Corgi, 1977. — [4],155, [1]p ; 18cm.
'Based on the television series created by Earl Hamner, Jr'. — Originally published: Toronto ; London : Bantam, 1974.
ISBN 0-552-10592-9 Pbk : £0.65
(B77-28970)

Weverka, Robert. The Waltons, the Easter story / [by] Robert Weverka. — London : Corgi, 1977. — [4],184,[1]p ; 18cm.
'Based on the television series created by Earl Hamner, Jr'. — Originally published: Toronto ; London : Bantam, 1976.
ISBN 0-552-10594-5 Pbk : £0.70
(B77-28971)

Wheatley, Dennis. The Devil rides out ; [and], The haunting of Toby Jugg ; [and], Gateway to hell ; [and], To the Devil - a daughter / [by] Dennis Wheatley. — London : Heinemann : Octopus Books, 1977. — 3-864p ; 25cm.
ISBN 0-905712-18-8 : £4.95
(B77-24521)

White, Alan, *b.1924.* The long hand of death / [by] Alan White. — London : Barrie and Jenkins, 1977. — 192p ; 21cm.
ISBN 0-214-20204-6 : £3.95
(B77-17765)

White, Antonia. The lost traveller / [by] Antonia White. — Bath : Chivers, 1977. — [5],314p ; 21cm.
Originally published: London : Eyre and Spottiswoode, 1950.
ISBN 0-85997-241-0 : £5.80(£4.35 to members of the Library Association)
(B77-14960)

White, Christopher, *b.1924.* Panzertrap / [by] Christopher White. — London : Futura Publications, 1976. — 172p ; 18cm. — (White, Christopher, b.1924. Commandos ; 1)
ISBN 0-86007-288-6 Pbk : £0.50
(B77-08612)

White, Eric Walter. Images of H.D. / [by] Eric W. White. From 'The mystery' / [by] H.D. — London : Enitharmon Press, 1976. — 3-58p,[2] p of plates,leaf of plate : ports ; 25cm.
Limited ed. of 400 copies of which 50 are signed by Eric W. White.
ISBN 0-901111-89-9 : £4.20
(B77-10964)

White, James Dillon. A spread of sail / [by] James Dillon White. — London : New English Library, 1977. — 175p ; 18cm. — (White, James Dillon. Kelso ; no.5)
Originally published: London : Hutchinson, 1975.
ISBN 0-450-03194-2 Pbk : £0.85
(B77-25218)

White, James Dillon. A wind in the rigging / [by] James Dillon White. — London : New English Library, 1977. — 176p ; 18cm. — (White, James Dillon. Kelso ; no.4)
Originally published: London : Hutchinson, 1973.
ISBN 0-450-03097-0 Pbk : £0.70
(B77-12143)

White, John Morgan. Snowy Mountains saga ; and, Tropicana / [by] John Morgan White. — Ilfracombe : Stockwell, 1977. — 201p,[8]p of plates : ill, maps ; 22cm.
ISBN 0-7223-0978-3 : £3.75
(B77-32236)

White, Jonathan. Double act / [by] Jonathan White. — Sevenoaks : Coronet, 1977. — 143p ; 18cm.
ISBN 0-340-21991-2 Pbk : £0.75
(B77-29739)

White, Jonothan. Double up / [by] Jonothan White. — Sevenoaks : Coronet, 1977. — 144p ; 18cm.
ISBN 0-340-21811-8 Pbk : £0.60
(B77-26588)

White, Simon. The English captain / by Simon White. — New York : St Martin's Press ; London : Hale, 1977. — 3-203p ; 21cm.
ISBN 0-7091-5944-7 : £3.60
(B77-28972)

White, Terence Hanbury. The book of Merlyn : the unpublished conclusion to 'The once and future king' / [by] T.H. White ; prologue by Sylvia Townsend Warner ; illustrations by Trevor Stubley. — Austin ; London : University of Texas Press, 1977. — xxi,137p : ill ; 26cm.
ISBN 0-292-70718-5 : £5.25
(B77-34199)

Whitehead, Barbara, *b.1930.* The caretaker wife / [by] Barbara Whitehead. — London : Heinemann, 1977. — [6],167p ; 22cm.
ISBN 0-434-86440-4 : £3.50
(B77-06322)

Whitelaw, Stella. Another word for love / by Stella Whitelaw. — London : Hale, 1977. — 183p ; 19cm.
ISBN 0-7091-5989-7 : £3.10
(B77-20696)

Whiting, Charles. The destroyers, Operation Kill Ike / by Charles Whiting. — London : Sphere, 1975. — 157p ; 18cm.
Also published: London : Seeley, 1975.
ISBN 0-7221-9080-8 Pbk : £0.65
(B77-25929)

Whiting, Charles. The destroyers, Operation Werewolf / [by] Charles Whiting. — London : Sphere, 1975. — 140p : map ; 17cm.
ISBN 0-7221-9088-3 Pbk : £0.65
(B77-19021)

Whiting, Charles. T-Force, massacre at Metz / [by] Charles Whiting. — London : Sphere, 1976. — 157p : 2 plans ; 18cm.
ISBN 0-7221-9092-1 Pbk : £0.55
(B77-06903)

Whiting, Charles. T-Force, the last mission / [by] Charles Whiting. — London : Sphere, 1976. — 169p : plan ; 18cm.
ISBN 0-7221-9095-6 Pbk : £0.65
(B77-06904)

Whiting, Charles. Wolf hunt / [by] Charles Whiting. — London : Futura Publications, 1976. — 189p : 2 ill ; 18cm. — (Whiting, Charles. Spymaster ; 1)
ISBN 0-86007-318-1 Pbk : £0.60
(B77-09323)

Whitney, Phyllis Ayame. Columbella / [by] Phyllis A. Whitney. — Large print ed. — Leicester : Ulverscroft, 1977. — [7],455p ; 23cm. — (Ulverscroft large print series : [romantic suspense])
Originally published: Garden City, N.Y. : Doubleday, 1966 ; London : Hale, 1967.
ISBN 0-7089-0001-1 : £2.95
(B77-31521)

Whitney, Phyllis Ayame. The golden unicorn / [by] Phyllis A. Whitney. — London : Heinemann, 1977. — [5],279p ; 23cm.
Originally published: Garden City, N.Y. : Doubleday, 1976.
ISBN 0-434-86475-7 : £3.90
(B77-06323)

Whitney, Phyllis Ayame. The golden unicorn / [by] Phyllis A. Whitney. — Large print [ed.]. — London : Prior [etc.], 1977. — [5],610p ; 24cm.
Originally published: Garden City, N.Y. : Doubleday, 1976 ; London : Heinemann, 1977.
ISBN 0-86043-056-1 : £5.95
(B77-22908)

Whitney, Phyllis Ayame. Hunter's Green / [by] Phyllis Whitney. — London : Pan Books, 1977. — 223p ; 18cm.
Originally published: New York : Doubleday, 1968 ; London : Heinemann, 1969.
ISBN 0-330-24898-7 Pbk : £0.70
(B77-09978)

Whitney, Phyllis Ayame. Spindrift / [by] Phyllis Whitney. — London : Pan Books, 1977. — 283p ; 18cm.
Originally published: Garden City, N.Y. : Doubleday ; London : Heinemann, 1975.
ISBN 0-330-24739-5 Pbk : £0.70
(B77-28973)

Whitney, Phyllis Ayame. The stone bull / [by] Phyllis A. Whitney. — London : Heinemann, 1977. — [7],304p ; 23cm.
Also published: Garden City, N.Y. : Doubleday, 1977.
ISBN 0-434-86478-1 : £4.50
(B77-28974)

Whitney, Phyllis Ayame. The turquoise mask / [by] Phyllis Whitney. — London : Pan Books, 1977. — 268p ; 18cm.
Originally published: Garden City, N.Y. : Doubleday, 1974 : London : Heinemann, 1975.
ISBN 0-330-24897-9 Pbk : £0.70
(B77-09979)

Wiat, Philippa. The atheling / [by] Philippa Wiat. — London : Hale, 1977. — 190p : geneal table ; 21cm. — (Wiat, Philippa. Wyatt saga)
ISBN 0-7091-5879-3 : £3.70
(B77-22909)

Wiat, Philippa. My lute be still / by Philippa Wiat. — London : Hale, 1977. — 207p : geneal table ; 21cm.
Bibl.: p.8.
ISBN 0-7091-5632-4 : £3.60
(B77-14427)

Wilcox, Collin. The third victim / [by] Collin Wilcox. — London : Hale, 1977. — 221p ; 20cm.
ISBN 0-7091-6321-5 : £3.25
(B77-28975)

Wiles, Domini. Death flight / [by] Domini Wiles. — London [etc.] : Collins, 1977. — 196p ; 22cm.
ISBN 0-00-222157-8 : £3.75
(B77-17766)

Wilhelm, Kate. The Clewiston test / [by] Kate Wilhelm. — London [etc.] : Hutchinson, 1977. — [7],244p ; 21cm.
Originally published: New York : Farrar Straus Giroux, 1976.
ISBN 0-09-128810-x : £3.75
(B77-09980)

Wilkins, Eric. The flesh peddlers / [by] Eric Wilkins. — London : Futura Publications, 1976. — 157p ; 18cm.
ISBN 0-86007-279-7 Pbk : £0.50
(B77-08613)

Willard, Anne. The wind of fate / [by] Anne Willard. — London : Macdonald and Jane's, 1977. — [4],220p ; 21cm. — (A troubadour)
ISBN 0-354-04117-7 : £3.50
(B77-13358)

Williams, Alan, *b.1935.* Shah-Mak / [by] Alan Williams. — St Albans : Panther, 1977. — 318p ; 18cm.
Originally published: London : Blond and Briggs, 1976.
ISBN 0-586-04640-2 Pbk : £0.75
(B77-24522)

Williams, Andrew, *b.1944.* Origins of the Mafia / [by] Andrew Williams. — London : Futura Publications, 1976. — 176p ; 18cm.
ISBN 0-86007-372-6 Pbk : £0.60
(B77-12726)

Williams, Charles, *b.1886.* War in heaven / [by] Charles Williams. — London : Sphere, 1976. — 205p ; 18cm. — (The Dennis Wheatley library of the occult)
Originally published: London : Gollancz, 1930.
ISBN 0-7221-9156-1 Pbk : £0.75
(B77-02622)

Williams, David. Tank / [by] David Williams. — London : Corgi, 1977. — 205p ; 18cm.
ISBN 0-552-10454-x Pbk : £0.75
(B77-30730)

Williams, David, *b.1926.* Treasure by degrees / [by] David Williams. — London : Collins [for] the Crime Club, 1977. — 195p ; 21cm.
ISBN 0-00-231839-3 : £2.95
(B77-22910)

Williams, David, *b.1926.* Unholy writ / [by] David Williams. — London : Collins [for] the Crime Club, 1976. — 192p ; 21cm.
ISBN 0-00-231851-2 : £2.95
(B77-18395)

Williams, David, *b.1926.* Unholy writ / [by] David Williams. — London : New English Library, 1977. — 156p ; 18cm.
Originally published: London : Collins, 1976.
ISBN 0-450-03726-6 Pbk : £0.70
(B77-34200)

Williams, Eric Cyril. The drop in / by Eric C. Williams. — Morley : Elmfield Press, 1977. — 166p ; 22cm.
ISBN 0-7057-0064-x : £3.95
(B77-31522)

Williams, Jeanne. A lady bought with rifles / [by] Jeanne Williams. — London : W.H. Allen, 1977. — 352p ; 23cm.
Originally published: New York : Coward, McCann and Geoghegan, 1976.
ISBN 0-491-02002-3 : £4.95
(B77-28196)

Williams, Nigel. My life closed twice / [by] Nigel Williams. — London : Secker and Warburg, 1977. — [5],197p ; 23cm.
ISBN 0-436-57154-4 : £3.90
(B77-21518)

Williams, T Jeff. The glory hole / [by] T. Jeff Williams. — London : Corgi, 1977. — 286p ; 18cm.
ISBN 0-552-10499-x Pbk : £0.85
(B77-26589)

Williams, Tennessee. The Roman spring of Mrs Stone / [by] Tennessee Williams. — St Albans : Panther, 1977. — 111p ; 18cm.
Originally published: New York : New Directions ; London : Lehmann, 1950.
ISBN 0-586-04405-1 Pbk : £0.60
(B77-08106)

Williams, Wirt. The far side / [by] Wirt Williams. — Toronto [etc.] ; London : Bantam, 1976. — 347,[1]p ; 18cm.
Originally published: New York : Horizon Press, 1972.
ISBN 0-553-07798-8 Pbk : £0.75
(B77-04431)

Williamson, Jack. The Cometeers / [by] Jack Williamson. — London : Sphere, 1977. — 186p ; 18cm. — (Williamson, Jack. Legion of space series ; 2) (Sphere science fiction)
Originally published: Reading, Pa : Fantasy Press, 1950.
ISBN 0-7221-9173-1 Pbk : £0.65
(B77-25930)

Williamson, Jack. The humanoids / [by] Jack Williamson. — London : Sphere, 1977. — 189p ; 18cm. — (Sphere science fiction)
Originally published: New York : Simon and Schuster, 1949 ; London : Museum Press, 1953.
ISBN 0-7221-9176-6 Pbk : £0.85
(B77-32237)

Williamson, Jack. The legion of space / [by] Jack Williamson. — London : Sphere, 1977. — 189p ; 18cm. — (Williamson, Jack. Legion of space series ; 1) (Sphere science fiction)
Originally published: Reading, Pa : Fantasy Press, 1947.
ISBN 0-7221-9171-5 Pbk : £0.85
(B77-12727)

Williamson, Jack. The legion of time ; [and, After world's end] / [by] Jack Williamson. — London : Sphere, 1977. — 203p ; 18cm. — (Sphere science fiction)
This collection originally published: Reading, Pa. : Fantasy Press, 1952.
ISBN 0-7221-9175-8 Pbk : £0.75
(B77-30731)

Williamson, Sherman. The glory trap / [by] Sherman Williamson. — London : New English Library, 1977. — 189p ; 22cm.
ISBN 0-450-03183-7 : £4.75
(B77-27438)

Williamson, Tony. The connector / [by] Tony Williamson. — [London] : Fontana, 1977. — 192p ; 18cm.
Originally published: London : Collins, 1976.
ISBN 0-00-614487-x Pbk : £0.70
(B77-18396)

Williamson, Tony. Doomsday contract / [by] Tony Williamson. — London : Collins, 1977. — 192p ; 22cm.
ISBN 0-00-222153-5 : £3.50
(B77-14428)

Willingham, Calder. The big nickel / [by] Calder Willingham. — St Albans : Mayflower, 1977. — 286p ; 18cm.
Originally published: New York : Dial Press, 1975 ; London : Hart-Davis, MacGibbon, 1976.
ISBN 0-583-12551-4 Pbk : £0.75
(B77-14961)

Willis, Ted, *Baron Willis.* The Churchill Commando / [by] Ted Willis. — London [etc.] : Macmillan, 1977. — 224p ; 21cm.
ISBN 0-333-21815-9 : £3.75
(B77-25219)

Willis, Ted, *Baron Willis.* The left-handed sleeper / [by] Ted Willis. — London : Pan Books, 1977. — 240p ; 18cm.
Originally published: London : Macmillan, 1975.
ISBN 0-330-25025-6 Pbk : £0.70
(B77-12144)

Willis, Ted, *Baron Willis.* Man-eater / [by] Ted Willis. — London : Pan Books, 1977. — 190p ; 18cm.
Originally published: London : Macmillan, 1976.
ISBN 0-330-25174-0 Pbk : £0.70
(B77-32238)

Willock, Colin. Gorilla / [by] Colin Willock. — London [etc.] : Macmillan, 1977. — 383p ; 23cm.
ISBN 0-333-21181-2 : £4.95
(B77-34201)

Willock, Ruth. The twisted key / [by] Ruth Willock. — London : Collins, 1977. — 180p ; 22cm.
ISBN 0-00-222485-2 : £3.95
(B77-23753)

Wilson, A N. The sweets of Pimlico / [by] A.N. Wilson. — London : Secker and Warburg, 1977. — [5],179p ; 23cm.
ISBN 0-436-57600-7 : £3.50
(B77-19788)

Wilson, Christine, *b.1930.* A garland of whispers / [by] Christine Wilson. — London : Hale, 1977. — 157p ; 20cm.
ISBN 0-7091-6301-0 : £3.20
(B77-28976)

Wilson, Colin. The black room / [by] Colin Wilson. — London : Sphere, 1977. — 298p ; 18cm.
Originally published: London : Weidenfeld and Nicolson, 1971.
ISBN 0-7221-9205-3 Pbk : £0.95
(B77-19022)

Wilson, Colin. The killer / [by] Colin Wilson. — St Albans : Panther, 1977. — 221p ; 18cm.
Originally published: London : New English Library, 1970.
ISBN 0-586-04631-3 Pbk : £0.60
(B77-14962)

Wilson, Colin. The space vampires / [by] Colin Wilson. — London [etc.] : Panther, 1977. — [7],214p ; 18cm. — (Panther science fiction)
Originally published: London : Hart-Davis MacGibbon, 1976.
ISBN 0-586-04333-0 Pbk : £0.75
(B77-32239)

Wilson, F Paul. Healer : science fiction / by F. Paul Wilson. — London : Sidgwick and Jackson, 1977. — [4],183p ; 20cm.
Originally published: Garden City, N.Y. : Doubleday, 1976.
ISBN 0-283-98376-0 : £3.50
(B77-21519)

Wilson, Gertrude Mary. Death on a broomstick / by G.M. Wilson. — London : Hale, 1977. — 183p ; 20cm.
ISBN 0-7091-5968-4 : £3.15
(B77-12145)

Wilson, Jacqueline. Making hate / [by] Jacqueline Wilson. — London [etc.] : Macmillan, 1977. — 189p ; 21cm.
ISBN 0-333-21969-4 : £3.25
(B77-21520)

Wilson, Jeanne. Troubled heritage / [by] Jeanne Wilson. — London [etc.] : Macmillan, 1977. — 271p : geneal tables ; 21cm.
ISBN 0-333-21177-4 : £3.95
(B77-06324)

Wilson, Phillip. Kiwi strike / [by] Phillip Wilson. — London : New English Library, 1977. — 159p ; 18cm.
Originally published: as 'Pacific Star'. Wellington, N.Z. : Alister Taylor ; London : Hale, 1976.
ISBN 0-450-03410-0 Pbk : £0.75
(B77-32240)

Wilson, Robert Hendrie. A blank card / by Robert Hendrie Wilson. — London : Hale, 1977. — 189p ; 21cm. — (Hale SF)
ISBN 0-7091-5964-1 : £3.25
(B77-12728)

Wilson, Sandra. The Penrich dragon / [by] Sandra Wilson. — London : Hale, 1977. — 192p ; 21cm.
ISBN 0-7091-5925-0 : £3.70
(B77-28197)

Wilson, Steve. The Post traveller : a motorcycle Grail quest epic and science fiction Western / [by] Steve Wilson. — London : Pan Books, 1977. — [9],245p : map ; 18cm. — (Pan science fiction)
Originally published: London : Macmillan, 1976.
ISBN 0-330-25225-9 Pbk : £0.70
(B77-31523)

Wilson, Trevor Edward. The newcomers / [by] T.E. Wilson. — New Zealand : Dunmore Press ; London : Hale, 1977. — 174p ; 21cm.
ISBN 0-7091-6100-x : £3.50
(B77-20697)

Winchester, Kay. Staddlecombe / by Kay Winchester. — London : Hale, 1977. — 188p ; 20cm.
ISBN 0-7091-5907-2 : £3.10
(B77-09324)

Wingate, John. Avalanche / [by] John Wingate. — London : Weidenfeld and Nicolson, 1977. — [7],153p : map ; 23cm.
ISBN 0-297-77243-0 : £3.95
(B77-10597)

Wingate, John. Black tide / [by] John Wingate. — London : Weidenfeld and Nicolson, 1977. — xvi,171p : map ; 23cm.
ISBN 0-297-77320-8 : £3.95
(B77-19789)

Wingate, William. Fireplay / [by] William Wingate. — London : Hutchinson, 1977. — 239p ; 23cm.
ISBN 0-09-129480-0 : £3.50
(B77-20698)

Winslow, Pauline Glen. The Witch Hill murder / [by] Pauline Glen Winslow. — London : Collins [for] the Crime Club, 1977. — 286p ; 21cm.
Originally published: New York : St Martin's Press, 1976.
ISBN 0-00-231916-0 : £3.25
(B77-27439)

Winspear, Violet. The burning sands / by Violet Winspear. — London : Mills and Boon, 1976. — 185p ; 19cm.
ISBN 0-263-09024-8 : £1.95
(B77-09981)

Winspear, Violet. Dragon Bay / [by] Violet Winspear. — London [etc.] : Mills and Boon, 1976. — 188p ; 18cm. — (Mills and Boon classics)
Originally published: 1969.
ISBN 0-263-72231-7 Pbk : £0.35
(B77-14963)

Winspear, Violet. Palace of the peacocks / [by] Violet Winspear. — Large print ed. — Bath : Lythway Press, 1977. — [5],275p ; 23cm.
Originally published: London : Mills and Boon, 1969.
ISBN 0-85046-703-9 : £4.60
(B77-17133)

Winspear, Violet. The sun tower / by Violet Winspear. — London : Mills and Boon, 1976. — 186p ; 17cm.
ISBN 0-263-72328-3 Pbk : £0.30
(B77-05718)

Winton, John. Good enough for Nelson / [by] John Winton. — London : Joseph, 1977. — 239p ; 23cm.
ISBN 0-7181-1643-7 : £4.50
(B77-27440)

Winton, John. One of our warships / [by] John Winton. — London : Sphere, 1977. — 188p ; 18cm.
Originally published: London : Joseph, 1975.
ISBN 0-7221-0401-4 Pbk : £0.65
(B77-19023)

Winward, Walter. The conscripts / [by] Walter Winward. — London : Futura Publications, 1976. — 302p ; 18cm. — (A contact book)
Originally published: London : Cassell, 1968.
ISBN 0-86007-239-8 Pbk : £0.75
(B77-12729)

Winward, Walter. Rough deal / [by] Walter Winward. — London : Weidenfeld and Nicolson, 1977. — [5],200p ; 23cm.
ISBN 0-297-77286-4 : £3.95
(B77-19790)

Wise, Leonard. The Big Biazarro : a novel / by Leonard Wise. — London [etc.] : Hart-Davis MacGibbon, 1977. — 256p ; 23cm.
Also published: Garden City, N.Y. : Doubleday, 1977.
ISBN 0-246-10995-5 : £3.95
(B77-19791)

Wiseman, Thomas. The day before sunrise / [by] Thomas Wiseman. — London [etc.] : Pan Books, 1977. — 300p : maps ; 18cm.
Originally published: London : Cape, 1976.
ISBN 0-330-25075-2 Pbk : £0.80
(B77-19792)

Wittman, George. A matter of intelligence / by George Wittman. — London : Hale, 1977. — xii,238p ; 21cm.
Originally published: New York : Macmillan, 1975.
ISBN 0-7091-5888-2 : £3.75
(B77-17767)

Wodehouse, Pelham Grenville. Aunts aren't gentlemen / [by] P.G. Wodehouse. — Harmondsworth [etc.] : Penguin, 1977. — 3-153p ; 18cm.
Originally published: London : Barrie and Jenkins, 1974.
ISBN 0-14-004192-3 Pbk : £0.65
(B77-12146)

Wodehouse, Pelham Grenville. The cat-nappers : a Jeeves and Bertie story / [by] P.G. Wodehouse. — Large print [ed.]. — London : Prior [etc.], 1977. — [5],276p ; 24cm.
Originally published: as 'Aunts aren't gentlemen'. London : Barrie and Jenkins, 1974.
ISBN 0-904000-63-x : £4.50
(B77-12147)

Wodehouse, Pelham Grenville. The coming of Bill / [by] P.G. Wodehouse. — London : Barrie and Jenkins, 1976. — 252p ; 20cm.
Originally published: London : Jenkins, 1920.
ISBN 0-257-65715-0 : £3.95
(B77-00990)

Wodehouse, Pelham Grenville. French leave / [by] P.G. Wodehouse. — London : Barrie and Jenkins, 1976. — 206p ; 20cm.
Originally published: London : Jenkins, 1955.
£3.95
ISBN 0-257-65831-9
(B77-00991)

Wodehouse, Pelham Grenville. Frozen assets / [by] P.G. Wodehouse. — London : Barrie and Jenkins, 1976. — 219p ; 20cm.
Originally published: London : Jenkins, 1964.
ISBN 0-257-65835-1 : £3.95
(B77-00992)

Wodehouse, Pelham Grenville. If I were you / [by] P.G. Wodehouse. — London : Barrie and Jenkins, 1976. — 160p ; 20cm.
Originally published: London : Herbert Jenkins, 1931.
ISBN 0-257-65949-8 : £3.95
(B77-00993)

Wodehouse, Pelham Grenville. Jeeves and the feudal spirit / [by] P.G. Wodehouse. — Sevenoaks : Coronet, 1977. — 176p ; 18cm.
Originally published: London : Jenkins, 1954.
ISBN 0-340-21789-8 Pbk : £0.60
(B77-28977)

Wodehouse, Pelham Grenville. Joy in the morning / [by] P.G. Wodehouse. — London : Coronet, 1977. — 221p ; 18cm.
Originally published: New York : Doubleday, 1946 ; London : Jenkins, 1947.
ISBN 0-340-21788-x Pbk : £0.70
(B77-30732)

Wodehouse, Pelham Grenville. Leave it to Psmith / [by] P.G. Wodehouse. — London : Barrie and Jenkins, 1976. — 240p ; 20cm.
Originally published: London : Jenkins, 1923.
ISBN 0-257-65999-4 : £3.95
(B77-00994)

Wodehouse, Pelham Grenville. Money for nothing / [by] P.G. Wodehouse. — London : Barrie and Jenkins, 1976. — 240p ; 20cm.
Originally published: London : Jenkins, 1928.
ISBN 0-257-66073-9 : £3.95
(B77-00995)

Wodehouse, Pelham Grenville. Much obliged, Jeeves / [by] P.G. Wodehouse. — London : Sphere, 1977. — 192p ; 18cm.
Originally published: London : Barrie and Jenkins, 1971.
ISBN 0-7221-9270-3 Pbk : £0.65
(B77-18397)

Wodehouse, Pelham Grenville. Ring for Jeeves / [by] P.G. Wodehouse. — London : Sphere, 1977. — 187p ; 18cm.
Originally published: London : Jenkins, 1953.
ISBN 0-7221-9268-1 Pbk : £0.65
(B77-19024)

Wodehouse, Pelham Grenville. Spring fever / [by] P.G. Wodehouse. — London : Barrie and Jenkins, 1976. — 256p ; 20cm.
Originally published: London : Jenkins, 1948.
ISBN 0-257-66290-1 : £3.95
(B77-00996)

Wodehouse, Pelham Grenville. Summer moonshine / [by] P.G. Wodehouse. — Harmondsworth [etc.] : Penguin, 1976. — 237p ; 19cm.
Originally published: New York : Doubleday Dorran, 1937 ; London : Jenkins, 1938.
Pbk : £0.65
ISBN 0-14-002547-2
(B77-03235)

Wodehouse, Pelham Grenville. Sunset at Blandings / [by] P.G. Wodehouse ; with notes and appendices by Richard Usborne ; illustrations by Ionicus. — London : Chatto and Windus, 1977. — 213p : ill, facsims, plans ; 21cm.
'... runs in Wodehouse's text to the end of the sixteenth chapter of a planned twenty-two chapters ... [and] ... contains a selection of the author's own working notes, of his first hand-written draft for the book, and of his detailed notes on the final stages of the plot' - publisher's note. — Ill. on lining papers.
ISBN 0-7011-2237-4 : £3.95 : CIP rev.
(B77-20699)

Wodehouse, Pelham Grenville. Thank you, Jeeves / [by] P.G. Wodehouse. — London : Coronet, 1977. — 192p ; 18cm.
Originally published: London : Jenkins, 1934.
ISBN 0-340-21790-1 Pbk : £0.60
(B77-31524)

Wohl, Burton. Rollercoaster / [by] Burton Wohl ; based on a screen play by Richard Levinson & William Link. — London [etc.] : Mayflower, 1977. — 144p ; 18cm.
ISBN 0-583-12829-7 Pbk : £0.75
(B77-27441)

Wolf, Gary K. Killerbowl / [by] Gary K. Wolf. — London : Sphere, 1976. — 155p : 1 ill ; 18cm.
Originally published: Garden City, N.Y. : Doubleday, 1975.
ISBN 0-7221-9271-1 Pbk : £0.60
(B77-06325)

Wolfe, Gene. Operation Ares / by Gene Wolfe. — London : Dobson, 1977. — 208p ; 21cm.
Originally published: United States : s.n., 1970.
ISBN 0-234-72050-6 : £3.95
(B77-32241)

'Woman's own' fiction for leisure. — London : IPC Magazines.
No.1-. — 1977-. — 19cm.
Monthly. — 192p. in 1st issue.
Pbk : £0.30
ISSN 0140-5055
(B77-29740)

Wood, Bari. The killing gift / [by] Bari Wood. — London : Pan Books, 1977. — 284p ; 18cm.
Originally published: New York : Putnam, 1975 ; London : Heinemann, 1976.
ISBN 0-330-25102-3 Pbk : £0.75
(B77-20700)

Wood, Bari. Twins : a novel / by Bari Wood and Jack Geasland. — London : Heinemann, 1977. — 316p ; 23cm.
ISBN 0-434-87785-9 : £4.50
(B77-19793)

Wood, Christopher, *b.1935.* The further adventures of Barry Lyndon by himself. — London : Futura Publications, 1976. — 222p ; 18cm.
Author: Christopher Wood.
ISBN 0-86007-309-2 Pbk : £0.60
(B77-08614)

Wood, Christopher, *b.1935.* James Bond, the spy who loved me / [by] Christopher Wood. — London : Cape, 1977. — 222p ; 20cm.
ISBN 0-224-01497-8 : £3.50 : CIP rev.
(B77-11426)

Wood, Flora Maitland. Lady of the night / by Flora Maitland Wood. — London : Hale, 1977. — 183p ; 20cm.
ISBN 0-7091-6239-1 : £3.20
(B77-30733)

Wood, Kenneth, *b.1922.* A period of violence / by Kenneth Wood. — London : Dobson, 1977. — 3-158p ; 21cm.
For adolescents.
ISBN 0-234-72025-5 : £2.95
(B77-28198)

Woodhouse, Emma. Romany magic / [by] Emma Woodhouse. — St Albans : Mayflower, 1977. — 158p ; 18cm. — (A Mayflower romance)
ISBN 0-583-12451-8 Pbk : £0.50
(B77-03773)

Woodhouse, Martin. The Medici guns / [by] Martin Woodhouse and Robert Ross. — Sevenoaks : Coronet, 1977. — 256p : map ; 18cm.
Originally published: London : Dent, 1974.
ISBN 0-340-21970-x Pbk : £0.95
(B77-26590)

Woods, Sara. The law's delay / [by] Sara Woods. — London [etc.] : Macmillan, 1977. — 223p ; 21cm.
ISBN 0-333-19895-6 : £3.25
(B77-06905)

Woodward, Lilian. That man in her life / by Lilian Woodward. — London : Hale, 1977. — 157p ; 20cm.
ISBN 0-7091-6030-5 : £3.10
(B77-17768)

Woodward, Lilian. A very special love / by Lilian Woodward. — London : Hale, 1976. — 154p ; 20cm.
ISBN 0-7091-5797-5 : £2.95
(B77-01840)

Woolf, Virginia. Flush : a biography / [by] Virginia Woolf. — Harmondsworth [etc.] : Penguin, 1977. — 111p ; 18cm.
Originally published: London : L. & V. Woolf, 1933. — Bibl.: p.103.
ISBN 0-14-004453-1 Pbk : £0.65
(B77-33448)

Woolf, Virginia. Jacob's room / [by] Virginia Woolf. — St Albans : Triad, 1976. — 173p ; 18cm.
Originally published: London : L. and V. Woolf, 1922.
ISBN 0-586-04445-0 Pbk : £0.90
(B77-03236)

Woolf, Virginia. Orlando : a biography / [by] Virginia Woolf. — St Albans : Triad, 1977. — 208p ; 18cm.
Originally published: London : L. and V. Woolf, 1928. — Index.
ISBN 0-586-04448-5 Pbk : £0.85
(B77-08615)

Woolf, Virginia. The Pargiters : the novel-essay portion of 'The Years' / by Virginia Woolf ; edited with an introduction by Mitchell A. Leaska. — London : Hogarth Press, 1978. — xliv,167p : facsim, geneal table ; 23cm.
ISBN 0-7012-0435-4 : £6.50 : CIP rev.
(B77-21521)

Woolf, Virginia. To the lighthouse / [by] Virginia Woolf. — St Albans : Triad, 1977. — 192p ; 18cm.
Originally published: London : Hogarth Press, 1927.
ISBN 0-586-04450-7 Pbk : £0.75
(B77-22911)

Woolf, Virginia. The waves / [by] Virginia Woolf. — London [etc.] : Triad, 1977. — 200p ; 18cm.
Originally published: London : Hogarth Press, 1931.
ISBN 0-586-04452-3 Pbk : £0.80
(B77-27442)

Woolf, Virginia. The waves, the two holograph drafts / [by] Virginia Woolf ; transcribed and edited by J.W. Graham. — London : Hogarth Press, 1976. — 843p in various pagings : facsims ; 26cm.
Index.
ISBN 0-7012-0406-0 : £20.00
(B77-25220)

Worboys, Anne. The Barrancourt destiny / by Anne Worboys. — London [etc.] : Hodder and Stoughton, 1977. — 251p ; 21cm.
ISBN 0-340-21748-0 : £3.95
(B77-22912)

Worboys, Anne. The lion of Delos / [by] Anne Worboys. — St Albans : Mayflower, 1977. — 223p ; 18cm.
Originally published: London : Hodder and Stoughton, 1975.
ISBN 0-583-12737-1 Pbk : £0.75
(B77-25931)

Wright, Grahame. Jog Rummage / [by] Grahame Wright. — London : Pan Books, 1977. — 205p ; 18cm.
Originally published: London : Heinemann, 1974.
ISBN 0-330-25182-1 Pbk : £0.70
(B77-32242)

Wright, Patricia. Journey into fire / [by] Patricia Wright. — London : Collins, 1977. — [7], 391p : 2 maps ; 22cm.
ISBN 0-00-222111-x : £4.95
(B77-21522)

Wright, Richard, *b.1908.* Native son / [by] Richard Wright ; with an introduction by the author. — Harmondsworth [etc.] : Penguin, 1977. — 462p ; 19cm. — (Penguin modern classics)
Originally published: New York : Harper ; London : Gollancz, 1940.
Pbk : £1.00
ISBN 0-14-003481-1
(B77-15545)

Wrightson, Patricia. The ice is coming / [by] Patricia Wrightson. — London : Hutchinson, 1977. — 223p : map(on lining papers) ; 23cm.
ISBN 0-09-129150-x : £2.95
(B77-20701)

Wyckoff, James. Slater's book / [by] James Wyckoff. — Large print [ed.]. — London : Prior [etc.], 1977. — [3],202p ; 25cm.
Originally published: Garden City, N.Y. : Doubleday, 1976.
ISBN 0-86043-100-2 : £4.50
(B77-34202)

Wykham, Helen. Cavan : an episode among figurines / [by] Helen Wykham. — London : Boyars, 1977. — 3-138p ; 23cm.
ISBN 0-7145-2593-6 : £4.95
(B77-30734)

Wyllie, John. The butterfly flood / [by] John Wyllie. — London : Barrie and Jenkins, 1977. — [7],180p ; 23cm.
Originally published: Garden City, N.Y. : Doubleday, 1975.
ISBN 0-214-20347-6 : £3.95
(B77-13917)

Wynd, Oswald. The ginger tree / [by] Oswald Wynd. — London : Collins, 1977. — 294p ; 22cm.
ISBN 0-00-222261-2 : £4.50
(B77-22199)

Wyndham, John, *b.1903.* The seeds of time / [by] John Wyndham ; with an introduction by the author ; illustrated by Kathy Wyatt. — Exeter : Wheaton, 1976. — ii-viii,155p : 1 ill ; 21cm. — (Literature for life series)
Originally published: London : Joseph, 1956.
ISBN 0-08-021100-3 Pbk : £1.05
(B77-07643)

Wynne, Pamela. Carols by candlelight / [by] Pamela Wynne. — Large print ed. — Bath : Lythway Press, 1977. — [4],300p ; 22cm.
Originally published: London : Collins, 1958.
ISBN 0-85046-695-4 : £4.40
(B77-11427)

Wynne, Pamela. Climbing to happiness / [by] Pamela Wynne. — Large print ed. — Bath : Lythway Press, 1977. — [6],313p ; 22cm.
Originally published: London : Collins, 1958.
ISBN 0-85046-726-8 : £4.55
(B77-27443)

Wyse, Lois. Kiss, inc. / [by] Lois Wyse. — London : New English Library, 1977. — [7], 255p ; 22cm.
Also published: Garden City, N.Y. : Doubleday, 1977.
ISBN 0-450-03456-9 : £4.95
(B77-27444)

Yerby, Frank. Captain rebel / [by] Frank Yerby. — Large print ed. — Leicester : Ulverscroft, 1977. — [4],487p ; 23cm. — (Ulverscroft large print series : [historical romance])
Originally published: New York : Dial Press, 1957 ; London : Heinemann, 1958.
ISBN 0-85456-521-3 : £2.65
(B77-13918)

Yerby, Frank. Griffin's Way / [by] Frank Yerby. — London : Pan Books, 1975. — 251p ; 18cm.
Originally published: New York : Dial Press, 1962 ; London : Heinemann, 1963.
ISBN 0-330-24601-1 Pbk : £0.60
(B77-08107)

Yerby, Frank. An odour of sanctity : a novel of Moorish Spain / [by] Frank Yerby. — London : Pan Books, 1977. — 637p ; 18cm.
Originally published: New York : Dial Press, 1965 ; London : Heinemann, 1966.
ISBN 0-330-25147-3 Pbk : £1.00
(B77-21523)

Yerby, Frank. The old gods laugh : a modern romance / [by] Frank Yerby. — London : Pan Books, 1977. — 335p ; 18cm.
Originally published: New York : Dial Press ; London : Heinemann, 1964.
ISBN 0-330-25082-5 Pbk : £0.80
(B77-20702)

Yerby, Frank. A rose for Ana María / [by] Frank Yerby. — London : Heinemann, 1976. — 219p ; 23cm.
ISBN 0-434-89038-3 : £3.50
(B77-05081)

Yerby, Frank. Tobias and the Angel / [by] Frank Yerby. — London : Pan Books, 1977. — 317p ; 18cm.
Originally published: New York : Dial Press ; London : Heinemann, 1975.
ISBN 0-330-25054-x Pbk : £0.80
(B77-14429)

Yglesias, Helen. Family feeling / [by] Helen Yglesias. — London [etc.] : Hodder and Stoughton, 1977. — [9],309p ; 23cm.
Originally published: New York : Dial Press, 1976.
ISBN 0-340-21718-9 : £4.50
(B77-24523)

York, Andrew. The fascinator / [by] Andrew York. — London : Arrow Books, 1977. — 191p ; 18cm.
Originally published: London : Hutchinson, 1975.
ISBN 0-09-914500-6 Pbk : £0.60
(B77-31525)

York, Andrew. The predator / [by] Andrew York. — London : Arrow Books, 1977. — 192p ; 18cm.
Originally published: London : Hutchinson, 1968.
ISBN 0-09-915220-7 Pbk : £0.60
(B77-26591)

York, Andrew. Tallant for trouble / [by] Andrew York. — London : Hutchinson, 1977. — 184p ; 21cm.
ISBN 0-09-128370-1 : £3.50
(B77-09325)

York, Elizabeth. The heir of Berkwell / [by] Elizabeth York. — London : Hale, 1977. — 204p ; 21cm.
ISBN 0-7091-5693-6 : £3.60
(B77-17134)

York, Elizabeth. The house of the enchantress / [by] Elizabeth York. — London : Hale, 1977. — 176p ; 21cm.
ISBN 0-7091-6068-2 : £3.50
(B77-22913)

Yorke, Margaret. The cost of silence / [by] Margaret Yorke. — London : Hutchinson, 1977. — 184p ; 21cm.
ISBN 0-09-128660-3 : £3.75
(B77-19794)

Yount, John. The trapper's last shot / [by] John Yount. — Sevenoaks : Coronet, 1977. — 240p ; 18cm.
Originally published: New York : Random House, 1973 ; London : Deutsch, 1974.
ISBN 0-340-21299-3 Pbk : £0.80
(B77-09326)

Yuill, P.B. Hazell and the menacing jester / [by] P.B. Yuill. — Harmondsworth [etc.] : Penguin, 1977. — 189p ; 19cm. — (Penguin crime fiction)
Originally published: London : Macmillan, 1976.
ISBN 0-14-004400-0 Pbk : £0.60
(B77-24524)

Yuill, P.B. Hazell and the three-card trick / [by] P.B. Yuill. — Harmondsworth [etc.] : Penguin, 1977. — 204p ; 19cm. — (Penguin crime fiction)
Originally published: London : Macmillan, 1975.
ISBN 0-14-004278-4 Pbk : £0.60
(B77-24525)

Zelazny, Roger. Damnation Alley / [by] Roger Zelazny. — London : Sphere, 1976. — 157p ; 18cm. — (Sphere science fiction)
Originally published: New York : Putnam, 1969 ; London : Faber, 1971.
ISBN 0-7221-9425-0 Pbk : £0.60
(B77-02623)

Zelazny, Roger. Doorways in the sand / [by] Roger Zelazny. — London : W.H. Allen, 1977. — [5],185p ; 22cm.
Originally published: New York : Harper and Row, 1976.
ISBN 0-491-02022-8 : £3.95
(B77-32243)

Zelazny, Roger. Sign of the unicorn / [by] Roger Zelazny. — London : Faber, 1977. — [5],186p ; 21cm.
Originally published: Garden City, N.Y. : Doubleday, 1975.
ISBN 0-571-11013-4 : £3.95
(B77-19025)

Zelazny, Roger. To die in Italbar / [by] Roger Zelazny. — London : Corgi, 1977. — 174p ; 18cm.
Originally published: Garden City, N.Y. : Doubleday, 1973 ; London : Faber, 1975.
ISBN 0-552-10463-9 Pbk : £0.70
(B77-32880)

Zelazny, Roger. Today we choose faces / [by] Roger Zelazny. — London : Futura Publications, 1976. — 3-174p ; 18cm. — (An orbit book)
Originally published: New York : New American Library, 1973 ; London : Millington, 1974.
ISBN 0-86007-838-8 Pbk : £0.60
(B77-08616)

Zindel, Paul. I never loved your mind / [by] Paul Zindel. — [London] : Fontana, 1977. — 128p ; 18cm. — (Lions)
Originally published: New York : Harper and Row, 1970 ; London : Bodley Head, 1971.
ISBN 0-00-671208-8 Pbk : £0.50
(B77-09327)

Zindel, Paul. The pigman / [by] Paul Zindel. — London : Collins, 1976. — 124p : ill ; 18cm. — (Lions)
Originally published: New York : Harper and Row, 1968 ; London : Bodley Head, 1969.
ISBN 0-00-671111-1 Pbk : £0.50
(B77-06906)

Zuckerman, George. The potato peelers / [by] George Zuckerman. — London : Futura Publications, 1976. — [5],250p ; 18cm.
Originally published: New York : Dodd, Mead, 1974.
ISBN 0-86007-316-5 Pbk : £0.70
(B77-09328)

823.91FS — ENGLISH FICTION, 1900-. SHORT STORIES

Again, dangerous visions : 46 original stories / edited by Harlan Ellison ; illustrations by Ed Emshwiller. — London [etc.] : Millington, 1976. — xxvii,760p : ill, port ; 23cm.
This collection originally published: Garden City, N.Y. : Doubleday, 1972.
ISBN 0-86000-062-1 : £6.00
(B77-15546)

Again, dangerous visions / edited by Harlan Ellison ; illustrations by Ed Emshwiller. — London [etc.] : Pan Books. — (Pan science fiction)
In 2 vols. — This collection originally published: in 1 vol. Garden City, N.Y. : Doubleday, 1972 ; London : Millington, 1976.
Vol.1. — 1977. — xxvii,450p : ill ; 18cm.
ISBN 0-330-25068-x Pbk : £0.80
(B77-13919)

Vol.2. — 1977. — xxvii,448p : ill ; 18cm.
ISBN 0-330-25096-5 Pbk : £0.80
(B77-13920)

Aickman, Robert. Tales of love and death / by Robert Aickman. — London : Gollancz, 1977. — 192p ; 21cm. — ([Gollancz fantasy & macabre])
ISBN 0-575-02335-x : £4.75
(B77-26592)

Aldiss, Brian Wilson. Last orders, and other stories / [by] Brian W. Aldiss. — London : Cape, 1977. — 223p ; 21cm.
ISBN 0-224-01487-0 : £3.95 : CIP rev.
(B77-14964)

Alfred Hitchcock presents, Murder racquet. — St Albans : Mayflower, 1977. — 159p ; 18cm.
ISBN 0-583-12643-x Pbk : £0.60
(B77-25932)

Alfred Hitchcock presents stories to be read with the lights on. — London [etc.] : Pan Books.
This collection originally published in 1 vol. : New York : Random House, 1973 ; London : Reinhardt, 1974.
Book 1. — 1976. — 250p ; 18cm.
ISBN 0-330-24597-x Pbk : £0.60
(B77-03237)

Book 2. — 1977. — 188p ; 18cm.
This collection originally published: in 1 vol. New York : Random House, 1973 ; London : Reinhardt, 1974.
ISBN 0-330-25248-8 Pbk : £0.70
(B77-34203)

Analog. — London : Dobson. — ([Dobson science fiction])
9 / edited by Ben Bova. — 1977. — xiii,249p ; 23cm.
ISBN 0-234-72014-x : £3.95
(B77-34204)

Anderson, Poul. Agent of the Terran Empire / [by] Poul Anderson. — [Sevenoaks] : Coronet, 1977. — 187p ; 18cm.
This collection originally published: Philadelphia : Chilton Books, 1965.
ISBN 0-340-21245-4 Pbk : £0.70
(B77-15547)

Anderson, Poul. The Queen of Air and Darkness, and other stories / [by] Poul Anderson. — London : New English Library, 1977. — 144p ; 18cm.
This collection originally published: New York : New American Library, 1973.
ISBN 0-450-03161-6 Pbk : £0.60
(B77-19795)

Andromeda : an original SF anthology. — London : Futura Publications.
1 / edited by Peter Weston. — 1976. — 206p ; 18cm. — (An orbit book)
ISBN 0-86007-891-4 Pbk : £0.65
(B77-08617)

Archives of evil / presented by Christopher Lee and Michel Parry. — London : W.H. Allen, 1977. — 172p ; 23cm.
ISBN 0-491-02042-2 : £3.95
(B77-32244)

Asimov, Isaac. The best of Isaac Asimov / [edited by Angus Wells]. — London : Sphere. — (Sphere science fiction)
In 2 vols. — This collection originally published: in 1 vol. London : Sidgwick and Jackson, 1973.
1954-1972. — 1977. — 172p ; 18cm.
Bibl.: p.167-172.
ISBN 0-7221-1257-2 Pbk : £0.65
(B77-13359)

Asimov, Isaac. The bicentennial man, and other stories / [by] Isaac Asimov. — London : Gollancz, 1977. — [9],211p ; 23cm.
ISBN 0-575-02240-x : £3.50
(B77-08108)

Asimov, Isaac. More tales of the Black Widowers / [by] Isaac Asimov. — London : Gollancz, 1977. — ix,180p ; 21cm. — ([Gollancz detection])
This collection originally published: Garden City, N.Y. : Doubleday, 1976.
ISBN 0-575-02271-x : £3.60
(B77-14430)

Asimov, Isaac. Through a glass, clearly / by Isaac Asimov. — Hornchurch : I. Henry, 1977. — 124p ; 21cm.
This collection published: London : New English Library, 1967.
ISBN 0-86025-124-1 : £3.25
(B77-22914)

Baldwin, James. Going to meet the man / [by] James Baldwin. — London : Corgi, 1976. — 221p ; 18cm.
This collection originally published: New York : Dial Press, 1964 ; London : Joseph, 1965.
ISBN 0-552-10292-x Pbk : £0.65
(B77-00455)

Ballard, James. Rolling all the time : stories / by James Ballard. — Urbana [etc.] ; London : University of Illinois Press, 1976. — [7],168p ; 21cm. — (Illinois short fiction)
ISBN 0-252-00613-5 : £5.60
ISBN 0-252-00614-3 Pbk : £2.40
(B77-00997)

Ballard, James Graham. The four-dimensional nightmare / [by] J.G. Ballard. — Harmondsworth [etc.] : Penguin, 1977. — 211p ; 18cm. — (Penguin science fiction)
'Reprinted, with the two stories "Prima belladonna" and "Studio 5, the stars" replaced by "The overloaded man" and "Thirteen to Centaurus" - title page verso. — This collection originally published: London : Gollancz, 1963.
ISBN 0-14-002345-3 Pbk : £0.55
(B77-30735)

Ballard, James Graham. Low-flying aircraft, and other stories / [by] J.G. Ballard. — London : Cape, 1976. — 191p ; 21cm.
ISBN 0-224-01311-4 : £3.50
(B77-01841)

Barstow, Stan. The desperadoes, and other stories / [by] Stan Barstow. — London : Corgi, 1977. — 187p ; 18cm.
This collection originally published: London : Joseph, 1961.
ISBN 0-552-10556-2 Pbk : £0.75
(B77-27445)

Barstow, Stan. A season with Eros / [by] Stan Barstow. — London : Corgi, 1977. — 190p ; 18cm.
This collection originally published: London : Joseph, 1971.
ISBN 0-552-10557-0 Pbk : £0.75
(B77-27446)

Barthelme, Donald. Amateurs / [by] Donald Barthelme. — London [etc.] : Routledge and Kegan Paul, 1977. — viii,184p ; 23cm.
This collection originally published: New York : Farrar, Straus and Giroux, 1976.
ISBN 0-7100-8742-x : £3.95 : CIP rev.
(B77-23754)

Bates, Herbert Ernest. Now sleeps the crimson petal, and other stories / [by] H.E. Bates. — Large print ed. — Bath : Chivers, 1976. — [7], 285p ; 22cm.
This collection originally published: London : Joseph, 1961.
ISBN 0-85997-197-x : £5.60(£4.20 to members of the Library Association)
(B77-02624)

Beckett, Samuel. Four novellas / [by] Samuel Beckett ; [translated by the author and Richard Seaver]. — London : J. Calder : [Distributed by Calder and Boyars], 1977. — 95p ; 21cm.
Contents: First love - The expelled - The calmative - The end.
ISBN 0-7145-3612-1 : £3.50
(B77-09329)

Before the golden age : a science fiction anthology of the 1930's / edited by Isaac Asimov. — London : Futura Publications.
In 4 vols. — This collection originally published: in 1 vol. Garden City, N.Y. : Doubleday ; London : Robson Books, 1974.
Vol.1. — 1975. — [13],223p ; 18cm. — (An orbit book)
ISBN 0-86007-803-5 Pbk : £0.50
(B77-09330)

Bentley, Phyllis. Kith and kin : nine tales of family life / [by] Phyllis Bentley. — Large print ed. — Bath : Chivers, 1977. — [7],308p ; 22cm.
This collection originally published: London : Gollancz, 1960.
ISBN 0-85997-204-6 : £5.60(£4.20 to members of the Library Association)
(B77-09982)

The **best** crime stories / introduction by Michael Stapleton. — London [etc.] : Hamlyn, 1977. — 749p ; 21cm.
ISBN 0-600-38241-9 : £2.95
(B77-30736)

The **best** horror stories / introduction by Lynn Picknett. — London [etc.] : Hamlyn, 1977. — 751p ; 21cm.
ISBN 0-600-38244-3 : £2.95
(B77-30737)

The **best** science-fiction stories / introduction by Michael Stapleton. — London [etc.] : Hamlyn, 1977. — 750p ; 21cm.
ISBN 0-600-38243-5 : £2.95
(B77-25933)

Bester, Alfred. The great short fiction of Alfred Bester. — London : Gollancz.
Vol.1 : The light fantastic. — 1977. — 254p ; 21cm. — ([Gollancz SF])
This collection originally published: New York : Berkley Publishing, 1976.
ISBN 0-575-02294-9 : £4.25
(B77-22200)

Bester, Alfred. Starburst / [by] Alfred Bester. — London [etc.] : Pan Books, 1977. — 156p ; 18cm. — (Pan science fiction)
Originally published: New York : New American Library, 1958 ; London : Sphere, 1968.
ISBN 0-330-25111-2 Pbk : £0.60
(B77-19796)

Beynon, John, *b.1903.* Sleepers of Mars / [by] John Wyndham writing as John Beynon Harris [i.e. John Beynon] ; introduction by Walter Gillings. — [London] : Coronet, 1977. — 155p ; 18cm.
Cover has author statement: / John Wyndham. — This collection originally published: 1973. — Previous control number ISBN 0-340-17326-2.
Pbk : £0.60
ISBN 0-340-17326-2
(B77-27447)

Beynon, John, *b.1903.* Wanderers of time / [by] John Wyndham writing as John Beynon Harris [i.e. John Beynon] ; introduction by Walter Gillings. — [London] : Coronet, 1977. — 158p ; 18cm.
Cover has author statement: / John Wyndham. — This collection originally published: 1973. — Previous control number ISBN 0-340-17306-8.
Pbk : £0.60
ISBN 0-340-17306-8
(B77-27448)

Blackwood, Algernon. Tales of terror and darkness / [by] Algernon Blackwood. — London [etc.] : Spring Books, 1977. — [5], 793p ; 21cm.
ISBN 0-600-30347-0 : £2.50
(B77-32245)

Blakiston, Noel. The collected stories of Noel Blakiston. — London : Constable, 1977. — 3-332p ; 23cm.
ISBN 0-09-461540-3 : £4.95
(B77-10598)

Blish, James. Star Trek / adapted by James Blish. — London : Severn House : [Distributed by Hutchinson].
4. — 1977. — ix,134p ; 21cm.
'Based on the famous television series created by Gene Roddenberry' - jacket. — Originally published: Toronto ; London : Bantam, 1971.
ISBN 0-7278-0263-1 : £3.15
(B77-23755)

5. — 1977. — viii,136p ; 21cm.
'Based on the famous television series created by Gene Roddenberry' - jacket. — Originally published: Toronto ; London : Bantam, 1972.
ISBN 0-7278-0271-2 : £3.15
(B77-23756)

Blish, James. The testament of Andros / [by] James Blish. — London [etc.] : Arrow Books, 1977. — 216p ; 18cm.
This ed. of this collection originally published: as 'Best science fiction stories of James Blish'. London : Faber, 1973.
ISBN 0-09-914840-4 Pbk : £0.60
(B77-28199)

Bloch, Robert. Atoms and evil / [by] Robert Bloch. — London : Corgi, 1977. — 172p ; 18cm.
This collection originally published: New York : Fawcett Publications, 1962 ; London : Hale, 1976.
ISBN 0-552-10486-8 Pbk : £0.65
(B77-26593)

A **book** of contemporary nightmares / edited by Giles Gordon. — London : Joseph, 1977. — 192p ; 23cm.
ISBN 0-7181-1571-6 : £4.25
(B77-08618)

The **book** of Mars : tales of Mars, men and Martians / edited by Jane Hipolito and Willis E. McNelly ; with an introduction by Isaac Asimov. — London : Futura Publications, 1976. — xix,332p ; 18cm. — (An orbit book)
This collection originally published: as 'Mars, we love you'. Garden City, N.Y. : Doubleday, 1971.
ISBN 0-86007-893-0 Pbk : £0.85
(B77-09331)

Bradbury, Ray. The golden apples of the sun / [by] Ray Bradbury. — St Albans : Panther, 1977. — [6],169p ; 18cm.
This collection originally published: London : Hart-Davis, 1953.
ISBN 0-586-04358-6 Pbk : £0.60
(B77-14431)

Bradbury, Ray. The illustrated man / [by] Ray Bradbury. — St Albans : Panther, 1977. — 204p ; 18cm.
Originally published: Garden City, N.Y. : Doubleday, 1951 ; London : Hart-Davis, 1952.
ISBN 0-586-04359-4 Pbk : £0.60
(B77-07644)

Bradbury, Ray. Long after midnight / [by] Ray Bradbury. — London : Hart-Davis MacGibbon, 1977. — 256p ; 21cm.
This collection originally published: New York : Knopf, 1976.
ISBN 0-246-10986-6 : £3.95
(B77-17135)

Brown, George Mackay. Witch, and other stories / [by] George Mackay Brown ; with an introduction [by the author] ; with commentary and notes by D.M. Budge. — London : Longman, 1977. — xviii,158p ; 19cm. — (The heritage of literature series)
'Text ... from the volumes "A Calendar of Love", "A Time to Keep" and "Hawkfall"' - title page verso.
ISBN 0-582-34916-8 Pbk : £0.95
(B77-25221)

Cairncross, George. Red windsor / by George Cairncross, Brian Moses and Louis Trifon. — Corby (10 Minden Close, Danesholme, Corby, [Northants.] NN18 9EW) : Excello and Bollard, [1977]. — [19]p ; 30cm.
ISBN 0-904339-42-4 Sd : £0.20
(B77-11428)

Carter, Graeme. Drakula meets Hardcastle! / [by] Graeme Carter. — Corby (10 Minden Close, Danesholme, Corby, Northants. NN18 9EW) : Excello and Bollard, [1977]. — [34]p ; 33cm.
Contents: Great excavations - Drakula - The adventures of Josiah Hardcastle.
ISBN 0-904339-20-3 Sd : Unpriced
(B77-11429)

A **century** of short stories / collected and introduced by Aidan Higgins. — London : Cape, 1977. — 414p ; 23cm.
Also published: London : Book Club Associates, 1977.
ISBN 0-224-01551-6 : £3.95 : CIP rev.
(B77-24526)

Chesterton, Gilbert Keith. The innocence of Father Brown / [by] G.K. Chesterton. — Large print ed. — Bath : Lythway Press, 1976. — xi, 372p ; 23cm. — (Lythway classics of crime and detection)
This collection originally published: London : Cassell, 1911.
ISBN 0-85046-689-x : £4.50
(B77-02625)

Chetwynd-Hayes, Ronald. Tales of fear and fantasy / [by] R. Chetwynd-Hayes. — [London] : Fontana, 1977. — 160p ; 18cm.
ISBN 0-00-614678-3 Pbk : £0.60
(B77-09332)

Clarke, Arthur Charles. The best of Arthur C. Clarke / [edited by Angus Wells]. — London : Sphere.
This collection originally published: in 1 vol. London : Sidgwick and Jackson : Sphere, 1973.
1937-1955. — 1976. — 152p ; 18cm.
Bibl.: p.149-152.
ISBN 0-7221-2410-4 Pbk : £0.65
(B77-07645)

1956-1972. — 1977. — 200p ; 18cm. — (Sphere science fiction)
Bibl.: p.197-200.
ISBN 0-7221-2454-6 Pbk : £0.75
(B77-16077)

Clarke, Arthur Charles. The best of Arthur C. Clarke / edited by Angus Wells. — London : Sidgwick and Jackson.
This collection originally published: in 1 vol. London : Sidgwick and Jackson : Sphere, 1973.
Vol.1 : 1937-1955. — 1977. — 151p ; 20cm.
ISBN 0-283-98402-3 : £3.95
(B77-32881)

Vol.2 : 1956-1972. — 1977. — 191p ; 20cm.
ISBN 0-283-98403-1 : £3.95
(B77-32882)

Clifford, Francis. Ten minutes on a June morning, and other stories / by Francis Clifford. — London [etc.] : Hodder and Stoughton, 1977. — 188p ; 23cm.
ISBN 0-340-21742-1 : £3.95
(B77-27449)

Cloete, Stuart. Canary pie / [by] Stuart Cloete. — London : Collins, 1976. — 237p ; 22cm.
ISBN 0-00-222103-9 : £3.75
(B77-18398)

Cloete, Stuart. More nights of Jean Macaque / [by] Stuart Cloete. — [London] : Fontana, 1977. — 221p ; 18cm.
This collection originally published: London : Collins, 1975.
ISBN 0-00-614482-9 Pbk : £0.70
(B77-09333)

Cold fear : new tales of terror / selected by Hugh Lamb. — London : W.H. Allen, 1977. — 175p ; 23cm.
ISBN 0-491-02082-1 : £3.95
(B77-32246)

Conrad, Joseph. Tales of unrest / [by] Joseph Conrad. — Harmondsworth [etc.] : Penguin, 1977. — 185p ; 19cm. — (Penguin modern classics)
Originally published: London : T. Fisher Unwin, 1898.
ISBN 0-14-003885-x Pbk : £0.60
(B77-15548)

Costie, C M. The collected Orkney dialect tales of C.M. Costie. — Kirkwall ('The Orcadian' Office, Kirkwall, Orkney) : Kirkwall Press, 1976. — 190,[2]p ; 23cm.
ISBN 0-9500612-8-x : £3.60
(B77-05719)

Cronin, Archibald Joseph. Adventures of a black bag / [by] A.J. Cronin. — London : New English Library, 1976. — 158p ; 18cm.
This collection originally published: 1969.
ISBN 0-450-03238-8 Pbk : £0.60
(B77-01842)

Cthulhu : tales of the Cthulhu Mythos / edited by Jon M. Harvey ; illustrations by Jim Pitts. — [Burton-on-Trent] ([37 Hawkins La., Burton-on-Trent, Staffordshire]) : Spectre Press, [1976]. — 24p : ill ; 21cm.
Contents: Harold's blues / by Glen Singer - Baptism of fire / by Andrew Darlington.
ISBN 0-905416-00-7 Sd : £0.50
(B77-06326)

Curley, Daniel. Love in the winter : stories / by Daniel Curley. — Urbana [etc.] ; London : University of Illinois Press, 1976. — [5],118p ; 21cm. — (Illinois short fiction)
ISBN 0-252-00551-1 : £5.60
ISBN 0-252-00578-3 Pbk : £2.40
(B77-00998)

Decade, the 1940s / edited by Brian W. Aldiss and Harry Harrison. — London : Pan Books, 1977. — 223p ; 18cm. — (Pan science fiction)
This collection originally published: London : Macmillan, 1975.
ISBN 0-330-25033-7 Pbk : £0.70
(B77-12148)

Decade, the 1950s / edited by Brian W. Aldiss and Harry Harrison. — London : Pan Books, 1977. — 219p ; 18cm. — (Pan science fiction)
This collection originally published: London : Macmillan, 1976.
ISBN 0-330-25034-5 Pbk : £0.70
(B77-12149)

Decade, the 1960s / edited by Brian W. Aldiss and Harry Harrison. — London [etc.] : Macmillan, 1977. — 287p ; 21cm.
ISBN 0-333-19002-5 : £3.95
(B77-06327)

Deep space / edited by Robert Silverberg. — London : Corgi, 1977. — 172p ; 18cm. — (Corgi science fiction)
This collection originally published: New York : Nelson, 1973 ; London : Abelard-Schuman, 1976.
ISBN 0-552-10551-1 Pbk : £0.70
(B77-28200)

Derleth, August. Regarding Sherlock Holmes : the adventures of Solar Pons / [by] August Derleth. — London : Futura Publications, 1976. — [5],vii,233p ; 18cm.
Cover title: The adventures of Solar Pons. — This collection originally published: as 'In re : Sherlock Holmes'. Sauk City : Mycroft and Moran, 1945.
ISBN 0-86007-280-0 Pbk : £0.60
(B77-08619)

Dick, Philip Kindred. The preserving machine, and other stories / [by] Philip K. Dick. — London [etc.] : Pan Books, 1977. — 286p ; 18cm. — (Pan science fiction)
This collection originally published: New York : Ace Books, 1969 ; London : Gollancz, 1971.
Pbk : £0.70
ISBN 0-330-23363-7
(B77-28978)

Dick, Philip Kindred. The variable man, and other stories / [by] Philip K. Dick. — London : Sphere, 1977. — 220p ; 18cm. — (Sphere science fiction)
This collection originally published: New York : Ace Books, 1957 ; London : Sphere, 1969.
Pbk : £0.75
ISBN 0-7221-2958-0
(B77-32247)

Doyle, Lynn. Ballygullion / [by] Lynn Doyle. — Belfast : Blackstaff Press, [1976]. — [5],110p ; 22cm.
This collection originally published: Dublin : Maunsel, 1908.
ISBN 0-85640-109-9 Pbk : £1.80
(B77-05720)

Doyle, *Sir* Arthur Conan. The exploits of Brigadier Gerard / [by] Sir Arthur Conan Doyle. — [1st ed. reprinted] ; with an introduction by Fitzroy Maclean. — London [etc.] : Pan Books, 1977. — 221p ; 18cm.
This collection originally published: London : G. Newnes, 1896.
ISBN 0-330-24845-6 Pbk : £0.70
(B77-09983)

Du Maurier, *Dame* Daphne. The birds, and other stories / [by] Daphne du Maurier. — London [etc.] : Pan Books, 1977. — 237p ; 18cm.
This collection originally published: as 'The apple tree'. London : Gollancz, 1952.
ISBN 0-330-25081-7 Pbk : £0.75
(B77-23757)

Eden, Dorothy. The house on Hay Hill, and other stories / [by] Dorothy Eden. — London : Severn House : [Distributed by Hutchinson], 1977. — 224p ; 21cm.
This collection originally published: New York : Fawcett Publications ; London : Coronet, 1976.
ISBN 0-7278-0237-2 : £3.50
(B77-08620)

Eden, Dorothy. Yellow is for fear, and other stories / by Dorothy Eden. — London : Severn House : [Distributed by Hutchinson], 1977. — 224p ; 20cm.
This collection originally published: New York : Ace Books, 1968.
ISBN 0-7278-0273-9 : £3.75
(B77-30739)

The **Edward** De Bono science fiction collection / edited by George Hay. — Leeds : Elmfield Press, 1976. — 217p ; 23cm.
ISBN 0-7057-0068-2 : £4.95
(B77-04432)

Eerie, weird and wicked : an anthology / chosen by Helen Hoke ; illustrated by Alex Brychta. — London : Dent, 1977. — [5],151p : ill ; 24cm.
ISBN 0-460-06704-4 : £3.95 : CIP rev.
(B77-07646)

Eight American stories : short stories / by Sherwood Anderson ... [et al.] ; selected and edited by D.L. James ; with a collection of American photographs. — London : Longman, 1977. — vi,186p : ill, map ; 19cm. — (Longman imprint books)
Bibl.: p.185.
ISBN 0-582-23327-5 Pbk : Unpriced
(B77-13360)

Ellery Queen's masters of mystery : stories from the 'Mystery magazine' / edited by Ellery Queen. — London : Gollancz, 1977. — 318p : ill ; 21cm. — ([Gollancz thriller])
ISBN 0-575-02265-5 : £4.75
(B77-24527)

Ellison, Harlan. Approaching oblivion / [by] Harlan Ellison. — London [etc.] : Pan Books, 1977. — [9],164p ; 18cm. — (Pan science fiction)
This collection originally published: New York : Walker, 1974 ; London : Millington, 1976.
ISBN 0-330-25197-x Pbk : £0.60
(B77-28979)

Ellison, Harlan. The beast that shouted love at the heart of the world / [by] Harlan Ellison. — London [etc.] : Millington, 1976. — [8],215p ; 23cm.
Originally published: New York : Avon, 1969.
ISBN 0-86000-065-6 : £3.50
(B77-15549)

English short stories of today. — London [etc.] : Oxford University Press for the English Association.
4th series / selected by Roger Sharrock. — 1976. — xii,295p ; 19cm.
ISBN 0-19-217415-0 Pbk : £2.50
(B77-07647)

Ferreira, Rick. The darling fishes, and other tales of fantasy, horror and the supernatural / [by] Rick Ferreira. — London : Kimber, 1977. — 204p ; 23cm.
ISBN 0-7183-0065-3 : £3.25
(B77-19797)

Fetler, Andrew. To Byzantium : stories / by Andrew Fetler. — Urbana [etc.] ; London : University of Illinois Press, 1976. — [7],112p ; 21cm. — (Illinois short fiction)
ISBN 0-252-00583-x : £5.60
ISBN 0-252-00584-8 Pbk : £3.40
(B77-01843)

The **fifth** Fontana book of great horror stories / edited by Mary Danby. — [London] : Fontana, 1977. — 189p ; 18cm.
This collection originally published: 1970.
Pbk : £0.50
(B77-32248)

The **first** Fontana book of great horror stories / selected by Christine Bernard. — [London] : Fontana, 1977. — 221p ; 18cm.
This collection originally published: 1966.
ISBN 0-00-614767-4 Pbk : £0.50
(B77-18399)

First love : stories / compiled by John L. Foster. — London : Heinemann, 1977. — 94p ; 21cm. — (Pyramid books)
For adolescents.
ISBN 0-434-95821-2 : £2.20
(B77-34205)

Fletcher, David, *b.1940.* Raffles / [by] David Fletcher. — London : Pan Books, 1977. — [4], 217p ; 18cm.
'Adapted from the Yorkshire Television series written by Philip Mackie, based upon the stories of E.W. Hornung' - cover.
ISBN 0-330-25141-4 Pbk : £0.60
(B77-06907)

Fontana book of great ghost stories. — [London] : Fontana.
12th / selected by R. Chetwynd-Hayes. — 1976. — 190p ; 18cm.
ISBN 0-00-614448-9 Pbk : £0.50
(B77-01844)

Forester, Cecil Scott. The man in the yellow raft, and other short stories / [by] C.S. Forester. — London [etc.] : Pan Books, 1977. — 189p ; 18cm.
This collection originally published: London : Joseph, 1969.
Pbk : £0.70
ISBN 0-330-02742-5
(B77-25934)

Foster, Alan Dean. Star Trek log / by Alan Dean Foster ; based on the popular animated series created by Gene Roddenberry. — London : Corgi.
5. — 1976. — [9],195p ; 18cm.
This collection originally published: New York : Ballantine Books, 1975. — Contents: The Ambergris element / adapted from a script by Margaret Armen - The pirates of Orion / adapted from a script by Howard Weinstein - Jihad / adapted from a script by Stephen Kandel.
ISBN 0-552-10315-2 Pbk : £0.60
(B77-02626)

Four modern story-tellers / edited by M.T. Fain. — London : Heinemann Educational, 1977. — iv,188p ; 19cm.
Bibl. — Stories by Scott Fitzgerald, Somerset Maugham, William Sansom, Doris Lessing.
ISBN 0-435-13200-8 Pbk : £0.95
(B77-12730)

The **fourth** Fontana book of great horror stories / selected by Christine Bernard. — [London] : Fontana, 1977. — 190p ; 18cm.
This collection originally published: 1969.
ISBN 0-00-614768-2 Pbk : £0.50
(B77-18401)

Frights : new stories of suspense and supernatural terror / edited by Kirby McCauley. — London : Gollancz, 1977. — [9],293p ; 21cm. — (Gollancz fantasy and macabre)
This collection originally published: New York : St Martin's Press, 1976.
ISBN 0-575-02260-4 : £4.25
(B77-15550)

Futrelle, Jacques. Great cases of The Thinking Machine / by Jacques Futrelle ; with an introduction by E.F. Bleiler. — New York : Dover Publications [etc.] ; London : Constable, 1976. — [2],ix,170p : port ; 22cm.
ISBN 0-486-23335-9 Pbk : £2.10
(B77-15551)

Future city / edited by Roger Elwood. — London : Sphere, 1976. — 236p ; 18cm. — (Sphere science fiction)
This collection originally published: New York : Trident Press, 1973.
ISBN 0-7221-3315-4 Pbk : £0.75
(B77-02627)

Future love : a science fiction anthology / compiled by Victoria Williams. — Basingstoke [etc.] : Macmillan, 1977. — 125p ; 18cm. — (Topliners)
For adolescents.
ISBN 0-333-21859-0 Pbk : £0.45 : CIP rev.
(B77-05721)

Gadd, Jeremy. Molls to maidens : tales of suspense & suspenders, from seedy, sepia bedsitdom through the cold light of day to James Bond / [by Jeremy Gadd, Brian Moses, Val Segal]. — Corby : Excello and Bollard, [1977]. — [20]p ; 30cm.
ISBN 0-904339-49-1 Sd : Unpriced
(B77-17769)

The **ghost** book. — London : Barrie and Jenkins.
12th. — 1976. — 192p ; 21cm.
ISBN 0-214-20216-x : £2.95
(B77-10965)

Gilliatt, Penelope. Splendid lives : stories / by Penelope Gilliatt. — London : Secker and Warburg, 1977. — [7],147p ; 23cm.
ISBN 0-436-17956-3 : £3.50
(B77-19798)

Glanville, Brian. A bad lot / [by] Brian Glanville. — London : Severn House : [Distributed by Hutchinson], 1977. — 144p ; 20cm.
Also published: Harmondsworth : Penguin, 1977.
ISBN 0-7278-0309-3 : £3.25 : CIP rev.
(B77-22201)

Glanville, Brian. A bad lot, and other stories / [by] Brian Glanville. — Harmondsworth [etc.] : Penguin, 1977. — 144p ; 18cm. — (Peacock books)
ISBN 0-14-047090-5 Pbk : £0.50
(B77-25222)

Glyn, Caroline. A mountain at the end of night : stories of dream and vision / by Caroline Glyn. — London : Gollancz, 1977. — 216p ; 21cm.
ISBN 0-575-02300-7 : £4.95
(B77-22915)

Godwin, Gail. Dream children : stories / by Gail Godwin. — London : Gollancz, 1977. — [7], 242p ; 21cm.
This collection originally published: New York : Knopf, 1976.
ISBN 0-575-02212-4 : £4.50
(B77-05082)

The **gourmet** crook book / edited by Tony Wilmot. — London : Everest, 1976. — 236p ; 18cm.
ISBN 0-905018-02-8 Pbk : £0.75
(B77-12150)

Hammett, Dashiell. The big knockover, and other stories / [by Dashiell Hammett] ; edited and with an introduction by Lillian Hellman. — Harmondsworth [etc.] : Penguin, 1977. — 414p ; 18cm. — (Penguin crime fiction)
This collection originally published: as 'The big knockover', New York : Random House ; and as 'The Dashiell Hammett story omnibus', London : Cassell, 1966.
Pbk : £0.95
ISBN 0-14-002941-9
(B77-25223)

Hammett, Dashiell. The continental op / [by] Dashiell Hammett ; selected and with an introduction by Steven Marcus. — London : Pan Books, 1977. — 255p ; 18cm.
This collection originally published: New York : Random House, 1974 ; London : Macmillan, 1975.
ISBN 0-330-25112-0 Pbk : £0.80
(B77-19799)

Harrison, Harry. The best of Harry Harrison. — London : Sidgwick and Jackson, 1976 [i.e. 1977]. — 315p ; 20cm.
ISBN 0-283-98340-x : £4.95
(B77-09334)

The **haunted** and the haunters : tales of ghosts and other apparitions / chosen by Kathleen Lines. — Abridged [ed.]. — London : Heinemann Educational, 1976. — [6],154p ; 20cm. — (The new windmill series ; 209)
Full ed.: London : Bodley Head, 1975.
ISBN 0-435-12209-6 : £0.80
(B77-04433)

Head, Bessie. The collector of treasures, and other Botswana village tales / [by] Bessie Head. — London [etc.] : Heinemann Educational, 1977. — x,109p ; 19cm. — (African writers series ; 182)
ISBN 0-435-90182-6 Pbk : £0.95
(B77-28201)

Heinlein, Robert Anson. The best of Robert Heinlein / [edited by Angus Wells]. — London : Sphere.
In 2 vols. — This collection originally published: in 1 vol. London : Sidgwick and Jackson : Sphere, 1973.
1939-1942. — 1975. — 212p ; 18cm.
Bibl.: p.209-212.
ISBN 0-7221-4467-9 Pbk : £0.55
(B77-13361)

1939-1942. — 1977. — 212p ; 18cm.
Bibl.: p.209-312.
ISBN 0-7221-4469-5 Pbk : £0.65
(B77-32249)

1947-1959. — 1977. — 154p ; 18cm.
Bibl.: p.151-154.
ISBN 0-7221-4468-7 Pbk : £0.45
(B77-32250)

Hemingway, Ernest. Men without women / [by] Ernest Hemingway. — St Albans : Triad, 1977. — 132p ; 18cm.
This collection originally published: New York : Scribner, 1927 ; London : Cape, 1928.
ISBN 0-586-04472-8 Pbk : £0.75
(B77-22916)

Hemingway, Ernest. The snows of Kilimanjaro, and other stories / [by] Ernest Hemingway. — St Albans : Triad, 1977. — 143p ; 18cm.
ISBN 0-586-04461-2 Pbk : £0.60
(B77-12731)

Herbert, Frank. The best of Frank Herbert / [edited by Angus Wells]. — London : Sphere.
In 2 vols. — This collection originally published: in 1 vol. London : Sidgwick and Jackson, 1975.
1952-1964. — 1976. — 155p ; 18cm.
Bibl.: p.154-155.
ISBN 0-7221-4523-3 Pbk : £0.55
(B77-08109)

1952-1964. — 1977. — 155p ; 18cm.
Bibl.: p.154-155.
ISBN 0-7221-4534-9 Pbk : £0.75
(B77-31526)

1965-1970. — 1976. — 170p ; 18cm.
Bibl.: p.169-170.
ISBN 0-7221-4528-4 Pbk : £0.55
(B77-08110)

1965-1970. — 1977. — 170p ; 18cm.
Bibl.: p.169-170.
ISBN 0-7221-4535-7 Pbk : £0.75
(B77-31527)

Highsmith, Patricia. Little tales of misogyny / [by] Patricia Highsmith. — London : Heinemann, 1977. — [5],144p ; 21cm.
ISBN 0-434-33517-7 : £3.90
(B77-28980)

Howard, Robert Ervia. Tigers of the sea / [by] Robert E. Howard ; edited by Richard L. Tierney. — London : Sphere, 1977. — 159p ; 18cm.
This collection originally published: s.l. : Zebra Books, 1974?.
ISBN 0-7221-4726-0 Pbk : £0.65
(B77-25224)

Howard, Robert Ervin. King Kull / [by] Robert E. Howard ; edited by Glenn Lord. — London : Sphere, 1976. — 187p : map ; 18cm.
ISBN 0-7221-4716-3 Pbk : £0.60
(B77-14965)

Howard, Robert Ervin. The lost valley of Iskander / [by] Robert E. Howard. — London : Futura Publications, 1976. — [12], 194p : ill ; 18cm. — (An orbit book)
Originally published: s.l. : s.n., 1974?.
ISBN 0-86007-880-9 Pbk : £0.60
(B77-08621)

Howard, Robert Ervin. Marchers of Valhalla / [by] Robert E. Howard. — London : Sphere, 1977. — 156p ; 18cm.
ISBN 0-7221-4728-7 Pbk : £0.65
(B77-15552)

Howard, Robert Ervin. Worms of the earth / [by] Robert E. Howard. — London : Futura Publications, 1976. — 3-188p ; 18cm. — (An orbit book)
This collection originally published: s.l. : s.n., 1969?.
ISBN 0-86007-879-5 Pbk : £0.60
(B77-08622)

Human-machines : an anthology of stories about cyborgs / edited, with an introduction and notes by Thomas N. Scortia and George Zebrowski. — London : Hale, 1977. — xxv, 244p ; 21cm. — (Hale SF)
This collection originally published: New York : Vintage Books, 1975.
ISBN 0-7091-5926-9 : £3.75
(B77-08111)

Huxley, Aldous. Brief candles : four stories / [by] Aldous Huxley. — St Albans : Triad, 1977. — 224p ; 18cm.
This collection originally published: New York : Fountain Press ; London : Chatto and Windus, 1930.
ISBN 0-586-04435-3 Pbk : £0.95
(B77-07648)

Introduction : stories by new writers. — London : Faber.
6. — 1977. — 3-224p ; 21cm.
ISBN 0-571-11035-5 : £3.95
(B77-07649)

Irish ghost stories / written by Robert Bernen ... [et al.] ; edited by Joseph Hone. — London : Hamilton, 1977. — [5],169p ; 20cm.
ISBN 0-241-89680-0 : £4.25
(B77-30740)

Jacobson, Dan. Through the wilderness : selected stories / [by] Dan Jacobson. — Harmondsworth [etc.] : Penguin, 1977. — [5], 197p ; 19cm.
This collection originally published: as 'Inklings'. London : Weidenfeld and Nicolson, 1973.
ISBN 0-14-004078-1 Pbk : £0.80
(B77-07650)

John Creasey's crime collection : an anthology / by members of the Crime Writers' Association. — London : Gollancz.
1977 / edited by Herbert Harris. — 1977. — 200p ; 21cm. — ([Gollancz thriller])
ISBN 0-575-02313-9 : £4.25
(B77-23758)

Johnson, Dorothy Marie. The man who knew the Buckskin Kid / [by] Dorothy M. Johnson. — London : Corgi, 1976. — 93p ; 18cm.
ISBN 0-552-10309-8 Pbk : £0.45
(B77-02628)

Jones, Elwyn, *b.1923.* Dick Barton, special agent / [by] Elwyn Jones. — London : Barker, 1977. — 256p ; 23cm.
'By arrangement with the British Broadcasting Corporation'. — Three complete stories rewritten from the original scripts by Edward J. Mason and Geoffrey Webb.
ISBN 0-213-16619-4 : £3.95
(B77-08623)

Jordan, John. Yams / by John Jordan. — Dublin ([Knocksedan House, Swords, Co. Dublin]) : Poolbeg Press, 1977. — 109p ; 19cm.
ISBN 0-905169-05-0 Pbk : £1.50
(B77-31528)

Josipovici, Gabriel. Four stories / [by] Gabriel Josipovici. — London (23 Fitzwarren Gardens, N19 [3TR]) : The Menard Press, 1977. — 47p ; 22cm.
ISBN 0-903400-22-7 Pbk : £1.50
(B77-11430)

Joyce, James, *b.1882.* Dubliners / by James Joyce ; text, criticism and notes edited by Robert Scholes and A. Walton Litz. — Harmondsworth [etc.] : Penguin, 1976. — vi, 504p : facsims, maps ; 20cm. — (The Viking critical library)
Originally published: New York : Viking Press, 1969. — Bibl.: p.453-461.
ISBN 0-14-015505-8 Pbk : Unpriced
(B77-03238)

Joyce, James, *b.1882.* Dubliners / [by] James Joyce ; the corrected text with an explanatory note by Robert Scholes and fifteen drawing[s] by Robin Jacques. — St Albans : Triad, 1977. — 207p : ill ; 18cm.
This corrected text originally published: London : Cape, 1967.
ISBN 0-586-04476-0 Pbk : £0.75
(B77-12732)

Kaufman, Sue. The master, and other stories / [by] Sue Kaufman. — London : Hamilton, 1977. — [7],228p ; 21cm.
Originally published: Garden City, N.Y. : Doubleday, 1976.
ISBN 0-241-89603-7 : £3.95
(B77-16078)

Kelly, Maeve. A life of her own, and other stories / by Maeve Kelly. — Dublin (Knocksedan House, Swords, Co. Dublin) : Poolbeg Press, 1976. — 144p ; 19cm.
ISBN 0-905169-04-2 Pbk : £1.20
(B77-25935)

King, Francis, *b.1923.* Hard feelings, and other stories / [by] Francis King. — London : Hutchinson, 1976. — 206p ; 21cm.
ISBN 0-09-127620-9 : £3.95
(B77-17136)

Lanier, Sterling Edmund. The peculiar exploits of Brigadier Ffellowes / [by] Sterling E. Lanier ; introduction by Arthur C. Clarke. — London : Sidgwick and Jackson, 1977. — [13],159p ; 20cm.
This collection originally published: New York : Walker, 1971.
ISBN 0-283-98372-8 : £3.95
(B77-19026)

Lavin, Mary. The shrine, and other stories / by Mary Lavin. — London : Constable, 1977. — 156p ; 21cm.
ISBN 0-09-461640-x : £2.95
(B77-22917)

Lawrence, David Herbert. The complete short stories [of] D.H. Lawrence. — Harmondsworth [etc.] : Penguin.
In 3 vols. — This collection originally published: New York : Viking Press, 1961.
Vol.3. — 1977. — [6]p,p587-853 ; 19cm.
ISBN 0-14-004383-7 Pbk : Unpriced
(B77-24528)

Le Guin, Ursula Kroeber. Orsinian tales / [by] Ursula K. Le Guin. — London : Gollancz, 1977. — [7],179p ; 21cm.
This collection originally published: New York : Harper and Row, 1976.
ISBN 0-575-02286-8 : £3.75
(B77-22918)

Leiber, Fritz. Night's black agents / [by] Fritz Leiber. — London : Sphere, 1977. — 240p ; 18cm.
This collection originally published: Sauk City : Arkham House, 1947 ; Jersey : Neville Spearman, 1975.
ISBN 0-7221-5476-3 Pbk : £0.85
(B77-25936)

Leinster, Murray. The best of Murray Leinster / edited by Brian Davis. — London : Corgi, 1976. — 174p ; 18cm.
ISBN 0-552-10333-0 Pbk : £0.60
(B77-05722)

Lewis, Clive Staples. The dark tower, and other stories / [by] C.S. Lewis ; edited by Walter Hooper. — London : Collins, 1977. — 158p ; 22cm.
ISBN 0-00-222155-1 : £3.95
(B77-06328)

Lloyd, Jeremy. Are you being served? / based on the BBC TV series from an original idea by Jeremy Lloyd and written by Jeremy Lloyd and David Croft. — London [etc.] : White Lion Publishers, 1977. — 189p ; 21cm.
This collection originally published: St Albans : Mayflower, 1976.
ISBN 0-7274-0214-5 : £3.25
(B77-16079)

Long, Frank Belknap. The early Long / [by] Frank Belknap Long. — London : Hale, 1977. — xxviii,211p ; 21cm. — (Hale SF)
This collection originally published: Garden City, N.Y. : Doubleday, 1975.
ISBN 0-7091-5854-8 : £3.50
(B77-00456)

Lovecraft, Howard Phillips. The haunter of the dark, and other tales of horror / by H.P. Lovecraft ; edited, and with an introduction by August Derleth. — London : Gollancz, 1977. — 303p ; 20cm. — ([Gollancz fantasy & macabre])
This collection originally published: 1951.
ISBN 0-575-00339-1 : £3.95
(B77-13362)

Lovecraft, Howard Phillips. The horror in the museum, and other tales / [by] H.P. Lovecraft and others. — St Albans : Panther, 1975. — 206p ; 18cm.
This collection originally published: in the collection 'The horror in the museum'. Sauk City, Wis. : Arkham House, 1970.
ISBN 0-586-04230-x Pbk : £0.50
(B77-10599)

Lutyens, Mary. Forthcoming marriages / [by] Mary Lutyens. — London [etc.] : White Lion Publishers, 1977. — 320p ; 21cm.
This collection originally published: London : Murray, 1933.
ISBN 0-85617-075-5 : £3.95
(B77-32883)

McAlmon, Robert. A hasty bunch : short stories / by Robert McAlmon. — [1st ed. reprinted] ; afterword by Kay Boyle. — Carbondale [etc.] : Southern Illinois University Press ; London [etc.] : Feffer and Simons, 1977. — ix,300p ; 20cm. — (Lost American fiction)
Facsimile reprint: 1st ed. Paris : Contact Editions, 1922.
ISBN 0-8093-0798-7 : £6.70
(B77-13921)

MacLaverty, Bernard. Secrets, and other stories / [by] Bernard MacLaverty. — Belfast : Blackstaff Press, 1977. — 130,[1]p ; 22cm.
ISBN 0-85640-101-3 : £3.95
(B77-21524)

Maclean, Norman, *b.1902.* A river runs through it, and other stories / [by] Norman Maclean. — Large print ed. — London : Prior [etc.], 1977. — xviii,422p ; 22cm.
This collection originally published: Chicago ; London : University of Chicago Press, 1976.
ISBN 0-86043-033-2 : £4.95
(B77-12733)

MacMahon, Bryan. The end of the world, and other stories / by Bryan MacMahon. — Dublin ([Knocksedan House, Swords, Co. Dublin]) : Poolbeg Press, 1976. — 156p ; 19cm.
ISBN 0-905169-03-4 Pbk : £1.20
(B77-25937)

Mankowitz, Wolf. The day of the women and the night of the men : fables / by Wolf Mankowitz ; illustrated by Charles Raymond. — London : Robson, 1977. — 112,[2]p : ill ; 23cm.
ISBN 0-903895-61-7 : £5.25
(B77-22202)

Maugham, Robin. Lovers in exile / [by] Robin Maugham. — London : W.H. Allen, 1977. — [7],264p ; 24cm.
ISBN 0-491-02130-5 : £4.95
(B77-22919)

Maugham, William Somerset. Collected short stories [of] W. Somerset Maugham. — London : Pan Books.
In 4 vols. — This collection originally published: in 3 vols, as 'The complete short stories'. London : Heinemann, 1951.
Vol.1. — 1976. — 476p ; 18cm.
ISBN 0-330-24489-2 Pbk : £0.95
(B77-08112)

Vol.2. — 1976. — 478p ; 18cm.
ISBN 0-330-24490-6 Pbk : £0.95
(B77-08113)

Modern African stories / edited by Ellis Ayitey Komey and Ezekiel Mphahlele. — London : Faber, 1977. — 227p ; 19cm.
This collection originally published: 1964.
ISBN 0-571-11217-x Pbk : £1.25
(B77-31529)

Moorhouse, Frank. Tales of mystery and romance / [by] Frank Moorhouse. — London [etc.] : Angus and Robertson, 1977. — [8], 162p : ill ; 23cm.
ISBN 0-207-95700-2 : £4.80
(B77-09335)

More Devil's kisses / edited by Linda Lovecraft. — London : Corgi, 1977. — 188p ; 18cm. — (A Corgi original)
ISBN 0-552-10508-2 Pbk : £0.70
(B77-22203)

Morgan, Speer. Frog gig, and other stories / by Speer Morgan. — Columbia [Miss.] ; London : University of Missouri Press, 1976. — [9], 109p ; 22cm. — (A breakthrough book)
ISBN 0-8262-0206-3 : £4.50
(B77-15553)

Morland, Nigel. Mrs Pym, and other stories / [by] Nigel Morland ; introduced by Eric Ambler. — Henley-on-Thames : A. Ellis, 1976. — [6],218p ; 23cm.
ISBN 0-85628-031-3 : £3.95
(B77-03774)

Mortimer, Penelope. Saturday lunch with the Brownings : stories / by Penelope Mortimer. — Harmondsworth [etc.] : Penguin, 1977. — 190p ; 18cm.
This collection originally published: London : Hutchinson, 1960.
ISBN 0-14-003955-4 Pbk : £0.75
(B77-29741)

Murphy, Michael Joseph. Mountainy crack : tales of Slieve Gullioners / [by] Michael J. Murphy. — Belfast : Blackstaff Press, 1976. — 158p ; 21cm.
ISBN 0-85640-119-6 Pbk : £2.65
(B77-06329)

Mutants : eleven stories of science fiction / edited by Robert Silverberg. — London : Corgi, 1977. — 204p ; 18cm. — (Corgi science fiction)

This collection originally published: Nashville : Nelson, 1974 ; London : Abelard-Schuman, 1976.
ISBN 0-552-10387-x Pbk : £0.65
(B77-13363)

My favourite story : an anthology / edited by Denys Val Baker. — London : Kimber, 1977. — 240p ; 23cm.
ISBN 0-7183-0025-4 : £3.25
(B77-19800)

Nebula award stories. — London : Corgi.
9 / edited by Kate Wilhelm. — 1976. — 253p ; 18cm.
'This series of books, compiled by the Science Fiction Writers of America ...' - cover. — This collection originally published: New York : Harper and Row ; London : Gollancz, 1974.
ISBN 0-552-10307-1 Pbk : £0.75
(B77-03239)

10 / edited by James Gunn. — 1977. — 255p ; 18cm.
'... Nebula Award Volumes ... contain the stories the writers [i.e. the Science Fiction Writers of America] consider the best science fiction stories of the year' - Introduction. — This collection originally published: London : Gollancz, 1975.
ISBN 0-552-10485-x Pbk : £0.85
(B77-25938)

New dimensions : science fiction. — London : Gollancz.
No.7 / edited by Robert Silverberg. — 1977. — vii,229p : 1 ill, plans ; 21cm. — ([Gollancz SF])
ISBN 0-575-02324-4 : £4.75
(B77-20704)

The **new** improved sun : an anthology of Utopian science fiction / edited by Thomas M. Disch. — London : Hutchinson, 1976. — 192p ; 21cm.

ISBN 0-09-124200-2 : £3.95
(B77-05723)

Niven, Larry. Inconstant moon / [by] Larry Niven. — London : Sphere, 1977. — 200p ; 18cm. — (Sphere science fiction)
'The original edition of this book contained twelve stories. The Sphere edition contains seven' - title page verso. — This collection originally published: London : Gollancz, 1973.
ISBN 0-7221-6381-9 Pbk : £0.85
(B77-28981)

Nolan, William Francis. Wonderworlds / by William F. Nolan. — London : Gollancz, 1977. — 192p ; 21cm. — ([Gollancz SF])
ISBN 0-575-02248-5 : £4.50
(B77-13365)

Noonan, Gillman. A sexual relationship, and other stories / by Gillman Noonan. — Dublin (Knocksedan House, Swords, Co. Dublin) : Poolbeg Press, 1976. — 147p ; 19cm.
ISBN 0-905169-01-8 Pbk : £0.90
(B77-25939)

Nova / edited by Harry Harrison. — London : Hale.
3. — 1977. — ix,243p ; 22cm. — (Hale SF)
This collection originally published: New York : Walker, 1973.
ISBN 0-7091-5704-5 : £3.50
(B77-08114)

Nova. — London : Sphere.
3 / edited by Harry Harrison. — 1975. — 192p ; 18cm.
This collection originally published: New York : Walker, 1973.
ISBN 0-7221-4321-4 Pbk : £0.55
(B77-09336)

Nova / edited by Harry Harrison. — London : Hale. — (Hale SF)
This collection originally published: New York : Walker, 1974 ; London : Sphere, 1976.
4. — 1977. — [7],216p ; 21cm.
ISBN 0-7091-5540-9 : £3.50
(B77-13366)

O'Brien, Edna. The love object / [by] Edna O'Brien. — Harmondsworth [etc.] : Penguin, 1976. — 168p ; 19cm.
This collection originally published: London : Cape, 1968.
Pbk : £0.60
(B77-07651)

O'Faoláin, Seán. Stories of Sean O'Faolain. — Harmondsworth [etc.] : Penguin, 1977. — 349p ; 18cm.
This collection originally published: as 'Midsummer night madnews, and other stories', New York : Viking Press, 1932 ; and as 'Stories of Sean O'Faolain', Harmondsworth : Penguin, 1970. — Previous control number ISBN 0-14-003195-2.
Pbk : £0.90
ISBN 0-14-003195-2
(B77-15554)

O'Hara, John. The time element, and other stories / [by] John O'Hara. — London : Coronet, 1976. — 224p ; 18cm.
This collection originally published: New York : Random House, 1972 ; London : Hodder and Stoughton, 1973.
ISBN 0-340-21015-x Pbk : £0.80
(B77-02629)

One hundred years of science fiction / edited by Damon Knight. — London [etc.] : Pan Books. — (Pan science fiction)
Cover title: 100 years of science fiction. — This collection originally published: in 1 vol. New York : Simon and Schuster, 1968 ; London : Gollancz, 1969.
Book 1. — 1977. — x,226p : ill, facsims ; 18cm.
Pbk : £0.70
ISBN 0-330-02982-7
(B77-23759)

Book 2. — 1977. — x,179p ; 18cm.
Pbk : £0.70
ISBN 0-330-02983-5
(B77-23760)

Packer, Nancy Huddleston. Small moments : stories / by Nancy Huddleston Packer. — Urbana [etc.] ; London : University of Illinois Press, 1976. — [7],155p ; 21cm. — (Illinois short fiction)
ISBN 0-252-00615-1 : £5.60
ISBN 0-252-00616-x Pbk : £2.40
(B77-00999)

Parsons, Stephen. Routine convoy ; and, By royal appointment / [by] Stephen Parsons ; illustrated by Kate Parsons. — Ilfracombe : Stockwell, 1977. — 46p : ill ; 18cm.
ISBN 0-7223-1005-6 Pbk : £1.50
(B77-25940)

Paton, Alan. Debbie go home / [by] Alan Paton. — Harmondsworth [etc.] : Penguin, 1977. — 127p ; 18cm.
Originally published: London : Cape, 1961.
ISBN 0-14-002298-8 Pbk : £0.60
(B77-24529)

Pearce, Philippa. The shadow-cage, and other tales of the supernatural / [by] Philippa Pearce ; illustrated by Janet Archer. — Harmondsworth : Kestrel Books, 1977. — 142p ; 23cm.
ISBN 0-7226-5243-7 : £2.75
(B77-15555)

The **Penguin** book of Scottish short stories / compiled with an introduction by J.F. Hendry. — Harmondsworth [etc.] : Penguin, 1977. — 247,[1]p ; 19cm.
This collection originally published: 1970.
Pbk : £0.80
ISBN 0-14-003128-6
(B77-19027)

The **Penguin** book of sea stories / edited by Alun Richards. — Harmondsworth [etc.] : Penguin, 1977. — 437p ; 19cm.
ISBN 0-14-004211-3 Pbk : £1.10
Also classified at 910'.45
(B77-27450)

'People's friend' annual. — Dundee [etc.] : D.C. Thomson.
[1978] / scenic views J. Campbell Kerr. — 1977. — 5-188p : ill(some col) ; 22cm.
Col. ill. on lining papers.
£0.70
(B77-31530)

Personal choice / edited by Denys Val Baker. — London : Kimber, 1977. — 224p ; 22cm.
ISBN 0-7183-0255-9 : £3.75
(B77-30741)

The **pirate** of the round pond, & other strange adventure stories / edited and introduced by Hugh Greene. — London [etc.] : Bodley Head, 1977. — 220p ; 23cm. — ([A book for new adults])
ISBN 0-370-30013-0 : £3.75
(B77-16614)

Podgórecki, Adam. Short stories of Si-tien / [by] Adam Podgórecki. — London : Poets' and Painters' Press, 1977. — 40p ; 22cm.
Pbk : Unpriced
(B77-32884)

Pohl, Frederik. The best of Frederik Pohl / introduction by Lester del Rey. — London : Sidgwick and Jackson, 1976[i.e.1977]. — xvi, 363p ; 20cm.
This collection originally published: Garden City, N.Y. : Doubleday, 1975.
ISBN 0-283-98341-8 : £4.95
(B77-08624)

Race, John. Tales from the computer room / by John Race. — [Uxbridge] ([c/o The Computer Science Department, Brunel University, Uxbridge, Middx UB8 3PH]) : The author, [1977]. — [4],42p : 1 ill ; 21cm.
ISBN 0-9505975-0-3 Sd : £0.65
(B77-30742)

The **real** thing : seven stories of love / edited by Peggy Woodford. — London [etc.] : Bodley Head, 1977. — 173p ; 23cm.
ISBN 0-370-30018-1 : £2.95
(B77-26594)

Rippier, Joseph Storey. Goodnight, morning / [by] Jo Rippier. — Gerrards Cross : Smythe, 1977. — 126p ; 23cm.
ISBN 0-901072-54-0 : Unpriced
(B77-26595)

Roberts, Keith, *b.1935.* The grain kings / [by] Keith Roberts. — London [etc.] : Panther, 1977. — 208p ; 18cm. — (Panther science fiction)
This collection originally published: London : Hutchinson, 1976.
ISBN 0-586-04313-6 Pbk : £0.65
(B77-32251)

Saki. The best of Saki (H.H. Munro) / selected and with an introduction by Graham Greene. — Harmondsworth [etc.] : Penguin, 1977. — xi,179p ; 20cm.
This collection originally published: New York : Viking Press, 1961.
ISBN 0-14-004484-1 Pbk : Unpriced
(B77-22920)

Science fiction discoveries / edited by Carol and Frederick [i.e. Frederik] Pohl. — Toronto [etc.] ; London : Bantam, 1976. — xi,272,[1]p ; 18cm.
ISBN 0-553-08635-9 Pbk : £0.65
(B77-04434)

Science fiction, the great years / edited by Carol and Frederik Pohl. — London : Sphere, 1977. — 287p ; 18cm. — (Sphere science fiction)
This collection originally published: New York : Ace Books, 1973 ; London : Gollancz, 1974.
ISBN 0-7221-6924-8 Pbk : £0.75
(B77-06908)

Scortia, Thomas Nicholas. Caution! inflammable! / [by] Thomas N. Scortia ; introduction by Theodore Sturgeon. — Toronto [etc.] ; London : Bantam, 1976 [i.e. 1977]. — xv,270p ; 18cm.
Originally published: Garden City, N.Y. : Doubleday, 1975.
ISBN 0-553-02580-5 Pbk : £0.60
(B77-09337)

Scottish short stories. — London : Collins.
1977 / preface by James Allan Ford. — 1977. — 192p ; 22cm.
ISBN 0-00-222476-3 : £3.75
(B77-22921)

Searle, Chris. The black man of Shadwell : four stories / by Chris Searle. — London (14, Talacre Rd, London NW5 3PE) : Writers and Readers Publishing Cooperative, 1976. — 103p ; 21cm.
ISBN 0-904613-15-1 : £2.25
(B77-03240)

The **second** bedside book of great detective stories / edited by Herbert van Thal. — London : A. Barker, 1977. — 256p : map ; 23cm.
ISBN 0-213-16627-5 : £4.95
(B77-20705)

The **second** Mayflower book of black magic stories / edited by Michel Parry. — St Albans : Mayflower, 1974. — 205p ; 18cm.
ISBN 0-583-12333-3 Pbk : £0.40
(B77-19801)

Shaw, Bernard. The black girl in search of God, and some lesser tales / [by] Bernard Shaw ; wood engravings by John Farleigh ; definitive text under the editorial supervision of Dan H. Laurence. — Harmondsworth [etc.] : Penguin, 1977. — 340p : ill ; 19cm.
This collection originally published: London : Constable, 1934.
ISBN 0-14-000567-6 Pbk : £1.50
(B77-19028)

Shaw, Irwin. God was here but He left early / [by] Irwin Shaw. — London [etc.] : Pan Books, 1977. — 219p ; 18cm.
Contents: Whispers in Bedlam - Small Saturday - The Mannichon solution - Where all things wise and fair descend.
ISBN 0-330-24343-8 Pbk : £0.70
(B77-26596)

Shaw, Irwin. Mixed company / [by] Irwin Shaw. — London : New English Library, 1977. — 416p ; 18cm.
This collection originally published: New York : Random House, 1950 ; London : Cape, 1952.
ISBN 0-450-03344-9 Pbk : £1.25
(B77-30743)

Shaw, Irwin. Tip on a dead jockey, and other stories / [by] Irwin Shaw. — London [etc.] : Pan Books, 1977. — 192p ; 18cm.
This collection originally published: London : Cape, 1957.
ISBN 0-330-25184-8 Pbk : £0.70
(B77-26597)

Short stories. — Huddersfield : Schofield and Sims.
2 / compiled by Roger Mansfield ; illustrated by Neville Swaine. — 1977. — 127p : col ill, col ports ; 20cm.
ISBN 0-7217-0331-3 Pbk : Unpriced
(B77-29742)

Sillitoe, Alan. The loneliness of the long-distance runner / [by] Alan Sillitoe. — Large print ed. — Bath : Lythway Press, 1977. — [5],246p ; 23cm.
This collection originally published: London : W.H. Allen, 1959.
ISBN 0-85046-720-9 : £4.40
(B77-26598)

Silverberg, Robert. The best of Robert Silverberg. — London : Sidgwick and Jackson, 1977. — xiv,258p ; 19cm.
This collection originally published: New York : Pocket Books, 1976.
ISBN 0-283-98400-7 : £4.95
(B77-32252)

Silverberg, Robert. Born with the dead / [by] Robert Silverberg. — London : Coronet, 1977. — 219p ; 18cm.
This collection originally published: New York : Random House, 1974 ; London : Gollancz, 1975. — Contents: Born with the dead - Thomas the proclaimer - Going.
ISBN 0-340-21297-7 Pbk : £0.80
(B77-09338)

Simak, Clifford Donald. The best of Clifford D. Simak / edited by Angus Wells. — London : Sphere, 1975. — 253p ; 18cm.
This collection originally published: London : Sidgwick and Jackson, 1975. — Bibl.: p.251-253.
ISBN 0-7221-7836-0 Pbk : £0.60
(B77-13367)

Smith, Clark Ashton. Other dimensions / [by] Clark Ashton Smith. — St Albans : Panther.
This collection originally published: Sauk City : Arkham House, 1970.
Vol.1. — 1977. — 187p ; 18cm.
ISBN 0-586-04350-0 Pbk : £0.60
(B77-08115)

Smith, Clark Ashton. Other dimensions. — St Albans : Panther.
This collection originally published: in 1 vol. Sauk City : Arkham House, 1970.
Vol.2 / [by] Clark Ashton Smith. — 1977. — 191p ; 18cm.
ISBN 0-586-04351-9 Pbk : £0.60
(B77-08625)

Smith, Clark Ashton. Tales of science and sorcery / [by] Clark Ashton Smith. — St Albans : Panther, 1976. — 223p ; 18cm.
This collection originally published: Sauk City : Arkham House, 1964.
ISBN 0-586-04352-7 Pbk : £0.60
(B77-03776)

Smith, George Oliver. Venus equilateral / [by] George O. Smith. — London : Futura Publications.
Originally published: in 1 vol. Philadelphia : Prime Press, 1947.
Vol.1. — 1975. — 240p ; 18cm. — (An orbit book)
ISBN 0-86007-860-4 Pbk : £0.75
(B77-08626)

Smith, Ian Crichton. The hermit, and other stories / by Ian Crichton Smith. — London : Gollancz, 1977. — 160p ; 21cm.
ISBN 0-575-02340-6 : £4.20
(B77-27451)

Souls in metal : an anthology of robot futures / compiled by Mike Ashley. — New York : St Martin's Press ; London : Hale, 1977. — 207p ; 21cm. — ([Hale SF])
ISBN 0-7091-5891-2 : £3.50
(B77-12734)

Space : a collection of science fiction stories. — London : Abelard-Schuman.
4 / [edited by Richard Davis]. — 1977. — x, 132p ; 23cm.
ISBN 0-200-72512-2 : £3.50
(B77-28202)

Spaced out / edited by Michel Parry ; (with illustrations by Jim Pitts). — London : Panther, 1977. — 192p : ill ; 18cm.
ISBN 0-586-04167-2 Pbk : £0.75
(B77-32885)

Spectre : a collection of ghost stories. — London : Abelard-Schuman.
4 / [edited by Richard Davis]. — 1977. — [11], 145p ; 23cm.
ISBN 0-200-72513-0 : £3.50
(B77-28203)

Spence, Alan. Its colours they are fine / [by] Alan Spence. — London : Collins, 1977. — 222p ; 21cm.
ISBN 0-00-222286-8 : £3.95
(B77-19802)

Spinrad, Norman. No direction home : an anthology of science fiction stories / by Norman Spinrad. — [London] : Fontana, 1977. — 190p ; 18cm. — (Fontana science fiction)
This collection originally published: s.l. : s.n., 1975 ; London : Millington, 1976.
ISBN 0-00-614811-5 Pbk : £0.75
(B77-31531)

Stories of horror and suspense : an anthology / edited by Denys Val Baker. — London : Kimber, 1977. — 192p ; 23cm.
ISBN 0-7183-0395-4 : £3.75
(B77-32253)

Storr, Catherine. Tales from a psychiatrist's couch / [by] Catherine Storr. — London [etc.] : Quartet Books, 1977. — [7],152p ; 23cm.
ISBN 0-7043-2139-4 : £4.25
(B77-17137)

Strange planets : an anthology of science fiction / edited by Amabel Williams-Ellis and Michael Pearson. — Glasgow [etc.] : Blackie, 1977. — 176p ; 23cm.
ISBN 0-216-90233-9 : £3.00
(B77-13368)

Sturgeon, Theodore. Case and the dreamer, and other stories / [by] Theodore Sturgeon. — London [etc.] : Pan Books, 1974. — 155p ; 18cm. — (Pan science fiction)
ISBN 0-330-24884-7 Pbk : £0.60
(B77-06330)

The **supernatural** solution / edited by Michael [i.e. Michel] Parry. — London [etc.] : White Lion Publishers, 1977. — 222p ; 21cm.
This collection originally published: New York : Topliner ; St Albans : Panther, 1976.
ISBN 0-7274-0252-8 : £3.25
(B77-08116)

Supernova. — London : Faber.
1 : SF introduction. — 1976. — iii-xii,225p ; 20cm.
ISBN 0-571-10984-5 : £3.95
(B77-00458)

Sutherland, Margaret. Getting through, and other stories / [by] Margaret Sutherland. — London : Heinemann, 1977. — [7],179p ; 23cm.
ISBN 0-434-75242-8 : £3.90
(B77-20706)

Tangent. — Loch Katrine (c/o I. Garbutt, Editor, Brenachoile Lodge, Loch Katrine, Callander, Perthshire) : British Science Fiction Association.
1 - ; [Feb. 1977]-. — 1977-. — ill ; 30cm.
Published at irregular intervals. — 28p. in 1st issue.
Sd : £0.30
(B77-14966)

The **taste** of fear / edited by Hugh Lamb. — Sevenoaks : Coronet, 1977. — 237p ; 18cm.
This collection originally published: London : W.H. Allen, 1976.
ISBN 0-340-22005-8 Pbk : £0.85
(B77-34206)

The **tenth** Fontana book of great horror stories / edited by Mary Danby. — [London] : Fontana, 1977. — 192p ; 18cm.
ISBN 0-00-614272-9 Pbk : £0.60
(B77-18402)

The **third** Fontana book of great horror stories / edited by Christine Bernard. — [London] : Fontana, 1977. — 188p ; 18cm.
This collection originally published: 1968.
ISBN 0-00-614655-4 Pbk : £0.50
(B77-18400)

'The **times**' anthology of ghost stories. — London : Corgi, 1977. — 190p ; 18cm.
'... selected from ... [stories] entered in a ghost story competition organized in the spring of 1975 by Jonathan Cape in conjunction with "The Times" newspaper'. Publisher's note. — This collection originally published: London : Cape, 1975.
ISBN 0-552-10474-4 Pbk : £0.70
(B77-25941)

Tiptree, James. Ten thousand light-years from home / [by] James Tiptree, Jr ; with an introduction by Harry Harrison. — London [etc.] : Pan Books, 1977. — 255p ; 18cm. — (Pan science fiction)
Spine title: 10,000 light-years from home. — This collection originally published: United States? : s.n., 1973? ; London : Eyre Methuen, 1975.
ISBN 0-330-24895-2 Pbk : £0.60
(B77-09984)

Tomorrow, Inc. : SF stories about big business / edited by Martin Harry Greenberg and Joseph D. Olander. — London : Robson, 1977. — 256p ; 23cm.
This collection also published: New York : Taplinger, 1977.
ISBN 0-903895-97-8 : £3.75
(B77-13922)

Undesirable properties : thirteen haunted houses / edited by Peter C. Smith. — London : Kimber, 1977. — 216p ; 23cm.
ISBN 0-7183-0275-3 : £3.95
(B77-28982)

Universe. — London : Dobson. — (Dobson science fiction)
This collection originally published: New York : Random House, 1973.
3 / edited by Terry Carr. — 1977. — iii-xi, 3-209p ; 21cm.
ISBN 0-234-72016-6 : £3.95
(B77-32886)

4 / edited by Terry Carr. — 1977. — [5],241, [1]p ; 21cm. — (Dobson science fiction)
This collection originally published: New York : Random House, 1974.
ISBN 0-234-72055-7 : £3.95
(B77-34207)

Val Baker, Denys. The secret place, and other Cornish stories / [by] Denys Val Baker. — London : Kimber, 1977. — 207p ; 23cm.
ISBN 0-7183-0285-0 : £3.75
(B77-30744)

Vance, Jack. The many worlds of Magnus Ridolph / [by] Jack Vance. — London : Dobson, 1977. — 3-146p : ill ; 21cm.
This collection originally published: New York : Ace, 1966.
ISBN 0-234-77917-9 : £3.95
(B77-32887)

Victor, Paul. A further stir of porridge / [by] Dick Clement and Ian La Frenais ; adapted from the TV series by Paul Victor. — London : British Broadcasting Corporation, 1977. — 191p ; 18cm.
ISBN 0-563-17214-2 Pbk : £0.70
(B77-31532)

Victor, Paul. A further stir of porridge / [by] Dick Clement and Ian la Frenais ; adapted from the TV series by Paul Victor. — London : British Broadcasting Corporation, 1977. — 191p ; 21cm.
ISBN 0-563-17393-9 : £3.00
(B77-28983)

Wallace, Edgar. Again Sanders / [by] Edgar Wallace. — London [etc.] : White Lion Publishers, 1977. — 159p ; 21cm.
This collection originally published: London : Hodder and Stoughton, 1928.
ISBN 0-7274-0227-7 : £3.75
(B77-34208)

Wallace, Edgar. The mind of Mr J.G. Reeder / [by] Edgar Wallace. — Large print ed. — Bath : Lythway Press, 1977. — [5],234p ; 22cm. — (Lythway classics of crime and detection)
Originally published: London : Hodder and Stoughton, 1925.
ISBN 0-85046-730-6 : £4.30
(B77-24530)

Weinbaum, Stanley Grauman. A Martian odyssey, and other stories / [by] Stanley G. Weinbaum ; introduction by Isaac Asimov ; afterword by Robert Bloch. — London : Sphere, 1977. — 316p ; 18cm. — (Sphere science fiction)
This collection originally published: as 'The best of Stanley G. Weinbaum'. New York : Ballantine Books, 1974.
ISBN 0-7221-8960-5 Pbk : £0.95
(B77-28984)

When evil wakes : an anthology of the macabre / edited by August Derleth. — London : Sphere, 1977. — 255p ; 18cm.
This collection originally published: London : Souvenir Press, 1963.
ISBN 0-7221-2918-1 Pbk : £0.85
(B77-31533)

White, James, *b.1928.* Monsters and medics / [by] James White. — London : Corgi, 1977. — 189p ; 18cm.
Also published: New York : Ballantine Books, 1977.
ISBN 0-552-10462-0 Pbk : £0.75
(B77-32254)

White, Terence de Vere. Chimes at midnight : twelve stories / by Terence de Vere White. — London : Gollancz, 1977. — 158p ; 21cm.
ISBN 0-575-02290-6 : £4.25
(B77-22204)

Williams, Mary. Unseen footsteps : ghost stories / [by] Mary Williams. — London : Kimber, 1977. — 190p ; 23cm.
ISBN 0-7183-0305-9 : £3.75
(B77-28985)

Williams, Mary. The walk at twilight : stories of ghosts and the occult / [by] Mary Williams. — London : Kimber, 1977. — 192p ; 23cm.
ISBN 0-7183-0035-1 : £3.25
(B77-20707)

Wilson, Angus, *b.1913.* A bit off the map, and other stories / [by] Angus Wilson. — Harmondsworth [etc.] : Penguin, 1976. — 173p ; 18cm.
This collection originally published: London : Secker and Warburg, 1957.
ISBN 0-14-002375-5 Pbk : £0.60
(B77-07652)

Wilson, Angus, *b.1913.* The wrong set, and other stories / [by] Angus Wilson. — Harmondsworth [etc.] : Penguin, 1976. — 201p ; 18cm.
This collection originally published: London : Secker and Warburg, 1949.
ISBN 0-14-001355-5 Pbk : £0.65
(B77-07653)

Winter's crimes. — London [etc.] : Macmillan.
8 / edited by Hilary Watson. — 1976. — 256p ; 21cm.
ISBN 0-333-18545-5 : £3.25
(B77-00459)

Winter's tales. — London [etc.] : Macmillan.
23 / edited by Peter Collenette. — 1977. — 200p ; 21cm.
ISBN 0-333-19823-9 : £3.95
(B77-32888)

Wodehouse, Pelham Grenville. Lord Emsworth and others / [by] P.G. Wodehouse. — London : Barrie and Jenkins, 1976. — 208p ; 20cm.
Originally published: London : Jenkins, 1937.
ISBN 0-257-66024-0 : £3.95
(B77-01000)

Wolfe, Tom. Mauve gloves & madmen, clutter & vine, and other stories, sketches, and essays / [by Tom Wolfe] ; illustrated by the author. — New York : Farrar, Straus and Giroux ; [Leicester] ([Euston St., Freemen's Common, Aylestone Rd, Leicester LE2 7SS]) : Distributed by WHS Distributors, 1976. — [9],243p : ill ; 22cm.
ISBN 0-374-20424-1 : £3.50
(B77-24531)

Wollheim, Donald Allen. Two dozen dragon eggs / [by] Donald A. Wollheim. — London : Dobson, 1977. — 192p ; 21cm. — ([Dobson science fiction])
This collection originally published: United States : Daw Books, 1969.
ISBN 0-234-72054-9 : £3.95
(B77-24532)

Wyndham, John, *b.1903.* The best of John Wyndham / [edited by Angus Wells]. — London : Sphere. — (Sphere science fiction)
Originally published: in 1 vol. 1973.
1951-1960. — 1977. — 160p ; 18cm.
Bibl.: p.158-159.
ISBN 0-7221-9374-2 Pbk : £0.65
(B77-10600)

The **year's** best science fiction. — London : Sphere.
No.2 / edited by Harry Harrison & Brian Aldiss. — 1970. — 207p ; 18cm.
This collection originally published: 1969.
Pbk : £0.25
(B77-08117)

No.8 / edited by Harry Harrison and Brian Aldiss. — 1976. — 253p ; 18cm. — (Sphere SF)
ISBN 0-7221-4398-2 Pbk : £0.65
(B77-07654)

The **year's** best science fiction. — London : Futura Publications. — (An orbit book)
No.9 / edited by Harry Harrison and Brian Aldiss. — 1976. — 206p ; 18cm.
ISBN 0-86007-894-9 Pbk : £0.65
(B77-08627)

The **zeitgeist** machine : a new anthology of science fiction / selected by Damien Broderick. — London [etc.] : Angus and Robertson, 1977. — [7],200p ; 20cm.
ISBN 0-207-13474-x : £3.95
(B77-31534)

823.91J — ENGLISH FICTION, 1900-. CHILDREN'S STORIES

2000 AD annual. — London : IPC Magazines. 1978. — 1977. — 3-127p : chiefly ill(some col) ; 28cm. — (A Fleetway annual)
ISBN 0-85037-376-x : £1.00
ISSN 0140-7155
(B77-33449)

'**Action**' annual. — London : IPC Magazines. 1978. — 1977. — 2-143p : chiefly ill(some col) ; 28cm. — (A Fleetway annual)
ISBN 0-85037-321-2 : £1.00
(B77-32255)

Adams, Christopher. Murder, London - New York / adapted by Christopher Adams from 'Murder, London - New York' by John Creasey. — London : Hutchinson, 1976. — 128p ; 19cm. — (A bulls-eye book)
'Murder, London - New York' originally published: London : Hodder and Stoughton, 1958.
ISBN 0-09-127831-7 Pbk : £0.65
(B77-04435)

Adamson, Jean. Topsy and Tim at the circus / [by] Jean and Gareth Adamson. — Glasgow [etc.] : Blackie, 1977. — [22]p : col ill ; 19cm. — (Adamson, Jean. Topsy and Tim handy books)
ISBN 0-216-90402-1 : £1.25
ISBN 0-216-90403-x Pbk : £0.45
(B77-28204)

Adamson, Jean. Topsy and Tim go camping / [by] Jean and Gareth Adamson. — Glasgow [etc.] : Blackie, 1977. — [24]p : col ill ; 18cm. — (Adamson, Jean. Topsy and Tim handy books)
ISBN 0-216-90404-8 : £1.25
ISBN 0-216-90405-6 Pbk : £0.45
(B77-29743)

Adamson, Jean. Topsy and Tim go shopping / [by] Jean and Gareth Adamson. — Glasgow [etc.] : Blackie, 1977. — [24]p : col ill ; 19cm. — (Adamson, Jean. Topsy and Tim handy books)
ISBN 0-216-90408-0 : £1.25
ISBN 0-216-90409-9 Pbk : £0.45
(B77-28205)

Adamson, Jean. Topsy and Tim on the farm / [by] Jean and Gareth Adamson. — Glasgow [etc.] : Blackie, 1977. — [24]p : col ill ; 19cm. — (Adamson, Jean. Topsy and Tim handy books)
Originally published: 1970.
ISBN 0-216-90299-1 : £1.25
ISBN 0-216-90300-9 Pbk : £0.45
(B77-23761)

Adamson, Jean. Topsy and Tim's Friday book / [by] Jean and Gareth Adamson. — Glasgow [etc.] : Blackie, 1977. — [24]p : col ill ; 19cm. — (Adamson, Jean. Topsy and Tim handy books)
Originally published: 1961.
ISBN 0-216-90311-4 : £1.25
ISBN 0-216-90312-2 Pbk : £0.45
(B77-23762)

Adamson, Jean. Topsy and Tim's Monday book / [by] Jean and Gareth Adamson. — Glasgow [etc.] : Blackie, 1977. — [24]p : col ill ; 19cm. — (Adamson, Jean. Topsy and Tim handy books)
Originally published: 1960.
ISBN 0-216-90303-3 : £1.25
ISBN 0-216-90304-1 Pbk : £0.45
(B77-23763)

Adamson, Jean. Topsy and Tim's Saturday book / [by] Jean and Gareth Adamson. — Glasgow [etc.] : Blackie, 1977. — [24]p : col ill ; 19cm. — (Adamson, Jean. Topsy and Tim handy books)
Originally published: 1961.
ISBN 0-216-90313-0 : £1.25
ISBN 0-216-90314-9 Pbk : £0.45
(B77-23764)

Adamson, Jean. Topsy and Tim's Thursday book / [by] Jean and Gareth Adamson. — Glasgow [etc.] : Blackie, 1977. — [24]p : col ill ; 19cm. — (Adamson, Jean. Topsy and Tim handy books)
Originally published: 1961.
ISBN 0-216-90309-2 : £1.25
ISBN 0-216-90310-6 Pbk : £0.45
(B77-23765)

Adamson, Jean. Topsy and Tim's Tuesday book / [by] Jean and Gareth Adamson. — Glasgow [etc.] : Blackie, 1977. — [24]p : col ill ; 19cm. — (Adamson, Jean. Topsy and Tim handy books)
Originally published: 1960.
ISBN 0-216-90305-x : £1.25
ISBN 0-216-90306-8 Pbk : £0.45
(B77-23766)

Adamson, Jean. Topsy and Tim's Wednesday book / [by] Jean and Gareth Adamson. — Glasgow [etc.] : Blackie, 1977. — [24]p : col ill ; 19cm. — (Adamson, Jean. Topsy and Tim handy books)
Originally published: 1961.
ISBN 0-216-90307-6 : £1.25
ISBN 0-216-90308-4 Pbk : £0.45
(B77-23767)

Ahlberg, Allan. Fred's dream / [text by] Allan Ahlberg ; pictures by Janet Ahlberg. — Glasgow [etc.] : Collins, 1976. — [32]p : col ill ; 21cm. — (Ahlberg, Allan. Brick Street boys)
ISBN 0-00-138061-3 : £1.50
(B77-00460)

Ahlberg, Allan. The great marathon football match / [text by] Allan Ahlberg ; pictures by Janet Ahlberg. — Glasgow [etc.] : Collins, 1976. — [32]p : col ill ; 21cm. — (Ahlberg, Allan. Brick Street boys)
ISBN 0-00-138058-3 : £1.50
(B77-00461)

Ahlberg, Allan. Here are the Brick Street boys / [text by] Allan Ahlberg ; pictures by Janet Ahlberg. — London : Collins, 1976. — [33]p : col ill ; 21cm. — (Ahlberg, Allan. Brick Street boys) (Picture lions)
Originally published: Glasgow : Collins, 1975.
ISBN 0-00-660870-1 Sd : £0.50
(B77-10966)

Ahlberg, Allan. A place to play / [text by] Allan Ahlberg ; pictures by Janet Ahlberg. — London : Collins, 1976. — [33]p : chiefly col ill ; 21cm. — (Ahlberg, Allan. Brick Street boys) (Picture lions)
Originally published: Glasgow : Collins, 1975.
ISBN 0-00-660871-x Sd : £0.50
(B77-10967)

Ahlberg, Janet. Burglar Bill / [by] Janet & Allan Ahlberg. — London : Heinemann, 1977. — [32]p : col ill ; 21cm.
ISBN 0-434-92500-4 : £2.40
(B77-08118)

Ahlberg, Janet. Jeremiah in the dark woods / [by] Janet and Allan Ahlberg. — Harmondsworth : Kestrel Books, 1977. — 48p : ill(some col) ; 23cm.
ISBN 0-7226-5357-3 : £2.75
(B77-30745)

Aiken, Joan. The faithless lollybird, and other stories / [by] Joan Aiken ; illustrated by Pat Marriott. — London : Cape, 1977. — 223p : ill ; 21cm.
ISBN 0-224-01332-7 : £3.50 : CIP rev.
(B77-08119)

Ainsworth, Ruth. Beauty and the beast / [adapted by] Ruth Ainsworth. — Maidenhead : Purnell, 1977. — [20]p : col ill ; 21cm.
Based on the story by Perrault. — This adaptation originally published: 1969.
ISBN 0-361-03943-3 Sd : £0.30
(B77-27452)

Ainsworth, Ruth. Jack and the beanstalk / [adapted by] Ruth Ainsworth. — Maidenhead : Purnell, 1977. — [20]p : col ill ; 21cm.
Based on the story by Perrault. — This adaptation originally published: 1969.
ISBN 0-361-03944-1 Sd : £0.30
(B77-27453)

Ainsworth, Ruth. Little Red Riding Hood / [adapted by] Ruth Ainsworth. — Maidenhead : Purnell, 1977. — [20]p : col ill ; 21cm.
Based on the story by Perrault. — This adaptation originally published: 1968.
ISBN 0-361-03942-5 Sd : £0.30
(B77-28206)

Ainsworth, Ruth. The phantom roundabout, and other ghostly tales / [by] Ruth Ainsworth ; illustrated by Shirley Hughes. — London : Deutsch, 1977. — 173p : ill ; 21cm.
ISBN 0-233-96788-5 : £3.25
(B77-28207)

Ainsworth, Ruth. Puss in boots / [adapted by] Ruth Ainsworth. — Maidenhead : Purnell, 1977. — [20]p : col ill ; 21cm.
Based on the story by Perrault. — This adaptation originally published: 1969.
ISBN 0-361-03946-8 Sd : £0.30
(B77-28208)

Ainsworth, Ruth. The sleeping beauty / [adapted by] Ruth Ainsworth. — Maidenhead : Purnell, 1977. — [20]p : col ill ; 21cm.
Based on the story by Perrault. — This adaptation originally published: 1967.
ISBN 0-361-03941-7 Sd : £0.30
(B77-28209)

Ainsworth, Ruth. Snow White / [adapted by] Ruth Ainsworth. — Maidenhead : Purnell, 1977. — [20]p : col ill ; 21cm.
Based on the story of the Brothers Grimm. — This adaptation originally published: 1969.
ISBN 0-361-03945-x Sd : £0.30
(B77-27454)

Ainsworth, Ruth. Up the airy mountain : stories of magic / by Ruth Ainsworth ; illustrated by Eileen Browne. — London : Heinemann, 1977. — 133p : ill(some col) ; 25cm.
ISBN 0-434-92588-8 : £3.90
(B77-30746)

Alexander, Lloyd. The Castle of Llyr / [by] Lloyd Alexander. — London : Fontana, 1977. — 160p ; 18cm. — (Lions)
Originally published: New York : Holt, Rinehart and Winston, 1966 ; London : Heinemann, 1968.
ISBN 0-00-671128-6 Pbk : £0.50
(B77-09339)

Alexander, Marc. The mist lizard / [by] Marc Alexander. — London : Muller, 1977. — [6], 154p ; 23cm.
ISBN 0-584-62054-3 : £3.50 : CIP rev.
(B77-17770)

Alington, Gabriel. Willow's luck / [by] Gabriel Alington. — London : Heinemann, 1977. — [4] ,121p ; 23cm.
ISBN 0-434-92670-1 : £2.90
(B77-16080)

Allan, Mabel Esther. An island in a green sea / [by] Mabel Esther Allan. — London [etc.] : Dent, 1977. — [4],187p ; 18cm. — (Dent dolphins)
Originally published: New York : Atheneum, 1972 ; London : Dent, 1973.
ISBN 0-460-02758-1 Pbk : £0.65
(B77-33450)

Allan, Mabel Esther. My family's not forever / [by] Mabel Esther Allan. — London : Abelard, 1977. — 127p ; 21cm.
ISBN 0-200-72479-7 : £2.95
(B77-19803)

Allan, Mabel Esther. A school in danger / [by] Mabel Esther Allan ; illustrated by Eric Winter. — London [etc.] : White Lion Publishers, 1976. — 223p,[3]p of plates : ill ; 21cm.
Originally published: London : Blackie, 1952.
ISBN 0-85686-134-0 : £2.75
(B77-04436)

Allan, Ted. Willie the squowse / [by] Ted Allan ; illustrated by Quentin Blake. — London : Cape, 1977. — 57p : ill ; 24cm.
'... first published in 'The Times Saturday Review' in 1973 ; subsequently it was included in 'The Times anthology of children's stories'. Cape, 1974'.
ISBN 0-224-01396-3 : £1.95 : CIP rev.
(B77-08628)

Allen, A J. Master Shrew, and other stories / [by] A.J. Allen ; [illustrated by Cora E.M. Paterson]. — Ilfracombe : Stockwell, 1976. — 16p : ill ; 18cm.
ISBN 0-7223-0971-6 Pbk : £0.30
(B77-10968)

Allen, Joy. Teeth for Charlie / [by] Joy Allen ; illustrated by Janet Duchesne. — London : Hamilton, 1976. — 48p : col ill ; 19cm. — (Gazelle books)
ISBN 0-241-89421-2 : £0.95
(B77-00462)

Allen, Judy. The spring on the mountain / [by] Judy Allen ; illustrated by John Hurford. — Harmondsworth [etc.] : Puffin Books, 1977. — 143p : ill, map ; 18cm. — (Puffin books)
Originally published: London : Cape, 1973.
ISBN 0-14-030906-3 Pbk : £0.45
(B77-25942)

Allen, Linda. Flight of fancy / [by] Linda Allen ; illustrated by Gerald Rose. — London : Abelard, 1977. — 96p : ill ; 21cm. — ([A grasshopper book])
ISBN 0-200-72497-5 : £1.95
ISBN 0-200-72498-3 Pbk : £0.60
(B77-20708)

Althea. Desmond and the stranger / by Althea ; illustrated by the author. — Cambridge : Dinosaur Publications, 1976. — [24]p : col ill ; 15x18cm. — (Althea's dinosaur books)
ISBN 0-85122-123-8 Sd : £0.35
(B77-00463)

Althea. Desmond goes boating / by Althea ; illustrated by the author. — London : Evans Bros, 1977. — [24]p : col ill ; 24x27cm.
ISBN 0-237-44884-x : £1.75
(B77-13369)

Althea. Desmond goes boating / by Althea ; illustrated by the author. — Cambridge : Dinosaur Publications, 1977. — [24]p : col ill ; 15x18cm. — (Althea's dinosaur books)
ISBN 0-85122-129-7 Sd : £0.35
(B77-13370)

Althea. Desmond goes to Scotland / by Althea ; illustrated by the author. — London : Evans Bros, 1977. — [24]p : chiefly col ill ; 24x26cm.
Originally published: Cambridge : Polyprint, 1969.
ISBN 0-237-44890-4 : £1.75
(B77-29744)

Althea. Smith the lonely hedgehog / by Althea ; illustrated by the author, based on a story by Helena Moore. — 2nd ed. — Cambridge : Dinosaur Publications, 1977. — 24p : col ill ; 15x18cm. — (Althea's dinosaur books)
Previous ed.: 1970.
ISBN 0-85122-137-8 Sd : £0.40
(B77-28210)

Amanda doll dressing book. — Maidenhead : Purnell, 1977. — [20]p : ill(some col) ; 26cm.
Sd : £0.15
ISBN 0-361-03794-5
Also classified at 745.59'22
(B77-12151)

Anderson, Verily. The Brownies and the christening / [by] Verily Anderson ; illustrated by Lesley Smith. — London [etc.] : Hodder and Stoughton Children's Books, 1977. — 121p : ill ; 20cm.
ISBN 0-340-20216-5 : £2.20
(B77-22922)

Andrews, Stephen. Cubs at play / [by] Stephen Andrews ; illustrated by Val Biro. — London [etc.] : Hodder and Stoughton, 1977. — 120p : ill ; 20cm.
ISBN 0-340-20482-6 : £2.20
(B77-20709)

Andy Pandy's annual. — Maidenhead : Purnell. [1977] / illustrated by Phil Gascoine. — 1977. — 2-47p : col ill ; 27cm.
Text, col. ill. on lining papers.
ISBN 0-361-03892-5 : £1.25
(B77-34209)

Anglund, Joan Walsh. What colour is love? / [by] Joan Walsh Anglund. — London : Collins, 1967 [i.e. 1977]. — [32]p : ill(some col) ; 17cm.

Originally published: New York : Harcourt, Brace and World, 1966 ; London : Collins, 1967.
ISBN 0-00-193380-9 : £0.95
(B77-32256)

Animal storytime. — Glasgow [etc.] : Collins, 1975. — 4-93p : col ill ; 27cm.
ISBN 0-00-138179-2 : £1.95
(B77-06909)

Annett, Cora. How the witch got Alf / by Cora Annett ; illustrated by Steven Kellogg. — New York ; London : F. Watts, [1977]. — 48p : ill ; 24cm.
Originally published: New York : F. Watts, 1975.
ISBN 0-85166-649-3 : £1.95
(B77-28986)

Appiah, Peggy. Why the hyena does not care for fish, and other tales from the Ashanti gold weights / [by] Peggy Appiah ; illustrated by Joanna Stubbs. — London : Deutsch, 1977. — 77p : ill ; 23cm.
ISBN 0-233-96903-9 : £2.95
(B77-23768)

The **archery** contest. — Maidenhead : Purnell, 1974. — [16]p : col ill ; 12cm. — ([Minikins])
Cover title: Robin Hood, the archery contest.
Sd : £0.06
(B77-19804)

Arden, William. Alfred Hitchcock and the Three Investigators in the mystery of the dancing devil / text by William Arden ; based on characters created by Robert Arthur ; illustrated by Roger Hall. — London [etc.] : Collins, 1977. — 159p : ill ; 22cm. — (Alfred Hitchcock mystery series ; 25)
Originally published: New York : Random House, 1976.
ISBN 0-00-160025-7 : £1.95
(B77-25226)

Arden, William. Alfred Hitchcock and the Three Investigators in the mystery of the shrinking house / text by William Arden based on characters created by Robert Arthur. — London : Armada, 1976. — 157p ; 18cm. — (Alfred Hitchcock mystery series ; 18)
Spine title: The mystery of the shrinking house. — Originally published: New York : Random House, 1972 ; London : Collins, 1973.
ISBN 0-00-691191-9 Pbk : £0.40
(B77-11432)

Arden, William. Alfred Hitchcock and the Three Investigators in the secret of Phantom Lake / text by William Arden based on characters created by Robert Arthur. — London : Armada Paperbacks, 1976. — 158p ; 18cm. — (Alfred Hitchcock mystery series ; 19)
Originally published: New York : Random House, 1973 ; London : Collins, 1974.
ISBN 0-00-691217-6 Pbk : £0.40
(B77-05724)

Ardizzone, Edward. Little Tim and the brave sea captain / by Edward Ardizzone. — [2nd ed.]. — Harmondsworth [etc.] : Puffin Books, 1977. — [48]p : ill(some col) ; 20cm. — (Picture puffins)
This ed. originally published: London : Oxford University Press, 1955.
ISBN 0-14-050175-4 Sd : £0.60
(B77-15556)

Ardizzone, Edward. Ship's cook Ginger : another Tim story / by Edward Ardizzone. — London [etc.] : Bodley Head, 1977. — 48p : ill(some col) ; 26cm.
ISBN 0-370-30004-1 : £2.50
(B77-23769)

The **aristocats** and O'Malley. — Maidenhead : Purnell, 1974. — [16]p : col ill ; 12cm. — ([Minikins])
Sd : £0.06
(B77-19805)

The **aristocats** and the inheritance. — Maidenhead : Purnell, 1974. — [16]p : col ill ; 12cm. — ([Minikins])
Sd : £0.06
(B77-19806)

The **aristocats** are rescued. — Maidenhead : Purnell, 1974. — [16]p : col ill ; 12cm. — ([Minikins])
Sd : £0.06
(B77-19807)

The **aristocats** come home. — Maidenhead : Purnell, 1974. — [16]p : col ill ; 12cm. — ([Minikins])
Sd : £0.06
(B77-19808)

The **aristocats** get lost. — Maidenhead : Purnell, 1974. — [16]p : col ill ; 12cm. — ([Minikins])
Sd : £0.06
(B77-19809)

The **Armada** ghost book. — London : Armada.
9th / edited by Mary Danby ; illustrated by Peter Archer. — 1977. — 125p : ill ; 18cm.
ISBN 0-00-691263-x Pbk : £0.40
(B77-13371)

The **Armada** monster book. — London : Armada.
3rd / edited by R. Chetwynd-Hayes ; illustrated by Peter Archer. — 1977. — 125p : ill ; 18cm. — (Armada spinechiller series)
ISBN 0-00-691256-7 Pbk : £0.40
(B77-13372)

Armada sci fi. — London : Armada Books.
1 / edited by Richard Davis ; illustrated by Jim Cawthorne. — 1975. — 127p : ill ; 18cm.
ISBN 0-00-690903-5 Pbk : £0.35
(B77-06910)

2 / edited by Richard Davis ; illustrated by Jim Cawthorne. — 1975. — 126p : ill ; 18cm.
ISBN 0-00-691044-0 Pbk : £0.35
(B77-06911)

Armitage, Ronda. The lighthouse keeper's lunch / [by] Ronda and David Armitage. — London : Deutsch, 1977. — [32]p : col ill ; 26cm.
ISBN 0-233-96868-7 : £2.75
(B77-25943)

Armstrong, Richard. The mutineers / [by] Richard Armstrong ; illustrated by Gareth Floyd. — London : Dent, 1977. — 175p : ill ; 18cm. — (Dent dolphins)
Originally published: 1968.
ISBN 0-460-02749-2 Pbk : £0.60
(B77-25944)

Armstrong, Richard. Sabotage at the forge / [by] Richard Armstrong ; illustrated by L.F. Lupton. — London [etc.] : White Lion Publishers, 1977. — 192p : ill ; 21cm.
Originally published: London : Dent, 1946.
ISBN 0-85686-296-7 : £2.95
(B77-08120)

An **Arthur** Rackham story book. — London : Harrap, 1977. — [42]p : ill ; 19cm. — (Reading with mother)
ISBN 0-245-53176-9 : £0.95
(B77-34210)

Ashley, Bernard. All my men / [by] Bernard Ashley. — Oxford [etc.] : Oxford University Press, 1977. — 159p ; 23cm.
ISBN 0-19-271390-6 : £2.95 : CIP rev.
(B77-07655)

Ashley, Bernard. The trouble with Donovan Croft / [by] Bernard Ashley ; illustrated by Fermin Rocker. — Harmondsworth : Puffin Books, 1977. — 192p : ill ; 18cm. — (Puffin books)
Originally published: London : Oxford University Press, 1974.
ISBN 0-14-030974-8 Pbk : £0.50
(B77-26599)

At the zoo. — Maidenhead : Purnell, 1977. — [8]p : chiefly col ill ; 19cm. — (My first book) (A Purnell board book)
Cover title.
Pbd : £0.20
(B77-10601)

Atwater, Richard. Mr Popper's penguins / [by] Richard and Florence Atwater ; illustrated by Robert Lawson. — London : Collins, 1976. — 93p : ill ; 20cm. — (Lions)
Originally published: Boston, Mass. : Little, Brown, 1938 ; London : Harrap, 1939.
ISBN 0-00-671121-9 Pbk : £0.45
(B77-10969)

Auerill, Esther. Jenny's birthday book / by Esther Auerill. — New York [etc.] ; London : Harper and Row, 1977. — [38]p : ill(some col) ; 19x27cm.
Originally published: 1954.
£3.75
(B77-31535)

Avery, Gillian. Huck & her time machine / [by] Gillian Avery. — London : Collins, 1977. — 192p ; 22cm.
ISBN 0-00-184775-9 : £3.50
(B77-13373)

Babbitt, Natalie. The search for delicious / [by] Natalie Babbitt. — [London] : Fontana, 1977. — 128p : ill ; 18cm. — (Lions)
Originally published: New York : Farrar, Straus and Giroux, 1969 ; London : Chatto and Windus, 1975.
ISBN 0-00-671205-3 Pbk : £0.50
(B77-30747)

Babbitt, Natalie. Tuck everlasting / [by] Natalie Babbitt. — London : Chatto and Windus, 1977. — [4],139p ; 21cm.
Originally published: New York : Farrar, Straus and Giroux, 1975.
ISBN 0-7011-5095-5 : £2.95 : CIP rev.
(B77-05725)

Baby's own colour annual. — London : IPC Magazines.
1978. — 1977. — 47p : chiefly col ill ; 30cm. — (A Fleetway annual)
Cover title.
ISBN 0-85037-323-9 : £1.65
(B77-32889)

Bagnall, Jill. Crayfishing with Grandmother / written by Jill Bagnall ; illustrated by Barbara Strathdee ; Maori text by Hapi Potae. — Auckland ; London : Collins, 1975. — [31]p : ill(chiefly col) ; 26cm.
Originally published: Auckland : Collins, 1973.
ISBN 0-00-185087-3 : Unpriced
(B77-31536)

Baker, Alan, *b.1951.* Benjamin and the box / story and pictures by Alan Baker. — London : Deutsch, 1977. — [32]p : chiefly col ill ; 18x22cm.
ISBN 0-233-96895-4 : £1.95
(B77-34211)

Baker, Jeannie. Grandfather / story and pictures by Jeannie Baker. — London : Deutsch, 1977. — [28]p : col ill ; 28cm.
ISBN 0-233-96864-4 : £2.95
(B77-26600)

Baker, Margaret Joyce. The birds of Thimblepins / [by] Margaret J. Baker ; illustrated by Elizabeth Grant. — London [etc.] : White Lion Publishers, 1976. — [7], 128p : ill ; 21cm.
Originally published: London : Harrap, 1960.
ISBN 0-85686-220-7 : £2.75
(B77-01001)

Baker, Margaret Joyce. Castaway Christmas / [by] Margaret J. Baker ; illustrated by Richard Kennedy. — Harmondsworth [etc.] : Puffin Books, 1977. — 140p : ill ; 18cm. — (Puffin books)
Originally published: London : Methuen, 1963.
ISBN 0-14-030325-1 Pbk : £0.40
(B77-03777)

Baker, Margaret Joyce. Cut off from crumpets / [by] Margaret J. Baker ; illustrated by Richard Kennedy. — London [etc.] : White Lion Publishers, 1977. — 176p : ill ; 21cm.
Originally published : London : Methuen, 1964.
ISBN 0-85686-225-8 : £3.15
(B77-15557)

Baker's dozen : a collection of stories / edited by Leon Garfield. — London : Ward Lock, 1976. — 144p : ill ; 24cm.
This collection originally published: 1973.
£2.95
ISBN 0-7063-1408-5
(B77-01845)

Ball, Brian. Jackson's holiday / [by] Brian Ball ; based on an idea by Amanda Ball ; illustrated by Carolyn Harrison. — London : Hamilton, 1977. — 95p : ill ; 19cm. — (Antelope books)
ISBN 0-241-89540-5 : £1.25
(B77-06912)

Bambi's big day. — Maidenhead : Purnell, 1977. — Fold leaf : col ill ; 15cm. — (A mini pop-up book)
Cover title: Walt Disney's Bambi's big day. — Leaf folded and cut to create three dimensional effect ; six pictures in all.
ISBN 0-361-03613-2 : £0.65
(B77-14967)

Barber, John, *b.1944.* Panthers' moon / adapted by John Barber from 'Panthers' moon' by Victor Canning. — London : Hutchinson, 1977. — 127p ; 19cm. — (A bulls-eye book)
'Panthers' moon' originally published: London : Hodder and Stoughton, 1948.
ISBN 0-09-131611-1 Pbk : Unpriced
(B77-32890)

Barker, Cicely Mary. The fairy's gift / written and illustrated by Cicely Mary Barker. — Glasgow : Blackie [etc.], 1977. — [32]p : ill(chiefly col) ; 18cm.
Originally published: as 'Groundsel and necklaces'. London : Blackie, 1946.
ISBN 0-216-90385-8 : £1.10
ISBN 0-216-90386-6 Pbk : £0.50
(B77-25945)

Barling, Tom. 20,000 leagues under the sea / retold [and illustrated] by Tom Barling ; from the original by Jules Verne. — London : Pan Books, 1977. — 125p : ill ; 20cm. — (Piccolo adventure library)
ISBN 0-330-25130-9 Pbk : £0.50
(B77-27455)

Barling, Tom. Treasure Island / retold by Tom Barling ; from the original by Robert Louis Stevenson ; ... illustrations by Tom Barling. — London : Pan Books, 1977. — 157p : ill ; 20cm. — (Piccolo adventure library)
ISBN 0-330-25131-7 Pbk : £0.50
(B77-26601)

Barrie, Alexander, *b.1923.* Fly for three lives / [by] Alexander Barrie ; cover illustration by C.L. Doughty, text illustrations by Paul Wright. — Abridged ed. — London [etc.] : Pan Books, 1977. — 141p : ill ; 18cm. — (Barrie, Alexander, b.1923. Jonathan Kane adventures ; 1) (Piccolo)
Full ed.: London : Muller, 1975.
ISBN 0-330-25072-8 Pbk : £0.45
(B77-13923)

Barrie, Alexander, *b.1923.* Jonathan Kane's jungle run / [by] Alexander Barrie ; illustrated by Paul Wright. — London : Muller, 1977. — [8],179p : ill ; 23cm. — (Barrie, Alexander, b.1923. Jonathan Kane adventures)
ISBN 0-584-63038-7 : £3.50 : CIP rev.
(B77-10970)

Barrie, Alexander, *b.1923.* Let them all starve / [by] Alexander Barrie ; cover illustration by C.L. Doughty, text illustrations by Paul Wright. — Abridged ed. — London [etc.] : Pan Books, 1977. — 142p : ill ; 18cm. — (Barrie, Alexander, b.1923. Jonathan Kane adventures ; 3) (Piccolo)
Full ed.: London : Muller, 1975.
ISBN 0-330-25073-6 Pbk : £0.45
(B77-13924)

Barrie, Alexander, *b.1923.* Operation Midnight / [by] Alexander Barrie ; cover illustration by C.L. Doughty, text illustrations by Paul Wright. — Abridged ed. — London [etc.] : Pan Books, 1977. — [2],139p : ill ; 18cm. — (Barrie, Alexander, b.1923. Jonathan Kane adventures ; 2) (Piccolo)
Full ed.: London : Muller, 1975.
ISBN 0-330-25071-x Pbk : £0.45
(B77-13925)

Barry, Margaret Stuart. The monster in Woozy garden / written by Margaret Stuart Barry ; the artist is Andrea Smith ... — London : Harrap, 1977. — [25]p : ill(chiefly col) ; 18cm.
ISBN 0-245-52832-6 Sd : £0.40
(B77-14968)

Barry, Margaret Stuart. Tommy Mac / [by] Margaret Stuart Barry ; illustrated by Dinah Dryhurst. — Harmondsworth [etc.] : Puffin Books, 1977. — 169,[1]p : ill ; 19cm. — (Puffin books)
Originally published: London : Longman Young, 1972.
Pbk : £0.45
ISBN 0-14-030664-1
(B77-30748)

Barry, Margaret Stuart. The Woozies go visiting / written by Margaret Stuart Barry ; the artist is Andrea Smith ... — London : Harrap, 1977. — [25]p : ill(chiefly col) ; 18cm.
ISBN 0-245-52833-4 Sd : £0.40
(B77-14969)

Barry, Margaret Stuart. Woozies hold a frubarb week / written by Margaret Stuart Barry ; the artist is Andrea Smith ... — London : Harrap, 1977. — [25]p : ill(chiefly col) ; 18cm.
ISBN 0-245-52831-8 Sd : £0.40
(B77-14970)

Barry, Margaret Stuart. Woozy and the weight watchers / written by Margaret Stuart Barry ; the artist is Andrea Smith ... — London : Harrap, 1977. — [25]p : ill(chiefly col) ; 18cm.
ISBN 0-245-52830-x Sd : £0.40
(B77-14971)

Barton, Pat. Waiting for the Jubilee / [by] Pat Barton. — Glasgow [etc.] : Blackie, 1976. — 141p ; 21cm.
ISBN 0-216-90196-0 : £3.25
(B77-00464)

Batchelor, Mary. Peg and James and the new baby / by Mary Batchelor ; illustrated by Jolyne Knox. — London [etc.] : Pickering and Inglis, 1977. — [20]p : col ill ; 22cm.
Text, col. ill. on lining papers.
ISBN 0-7208-2251-3 : £0.70
(B77-26602)

Batchelor, Mary. Peg and James go to market / by Mary Batchelor ; illustrated by Jolyne Knox. — London [etc.] : Pickering and Inglis, 1977. — [20]p : col ill ; 22cm.
Text, col. ill. on lining papers.
ISBN 0-7208-2250-5 : £0.70
(B77-26603)

Batchelor, Mary. Peg and James go to the park / by Mary Batchelor ; illustrated by Jolyne Knox. — London [etc.] : Pickering and Inglis, 1977. — [20]p : col ill ; 22cm.
Text, col. ill. on lining papers.
ISBN 0-7208-2253-x : £0.70
(B77-26604)

Batchelor, Mary. Peg and James plant some bulbs / by Mary Batchelor ; illustrated by Jolyne Knox. — London [etc.] : Pickering and Inglis, 1977. — [20]p : col ill ; 22cm.
Text, col. ill. on lining papers.
ISBN 0-7208-2252-1 : £0.70
(B77-26605)

'Battle picture weekly' annual. — London : IPC Magazines.
1978. — 1977. — 143p : chiefly ill(some col), ports ; 28cm. — (A Fleetway annual)
Cover title.
ISBN 0-85037-324-7 : £1.00
(B77-32891)

Baum, Lyman Frank. The marvellous land of Oz / by L. Frank Baum ; illustrated by Biro. — London : Dent, 1977. — xii,164p : ill ; 18cm. — (A Dent dolphin)
Originally published: Chicago : Reilly and Briton ; London : Revell, 1904.
ISBN 0-460-02750-6 Pbk : £0.60
(B77-25227)

Baum, Lyman Frank. The master key : an electrical fairy tale / by L. Frank Baum ; illustrations by F.Y. Cory. — New York : Dover Publications [etc.] ; London : Constable, 1976. — [16],245p,[11]leaves of plates : ill ; 21cm.
Facsimile reprint of: 1st ed. Indianapolis : Bowen-Merrill, 1901.
ISBN 0-486-23382-0 Pbk : £2.15
(B77-25228)

Baum, Thomas. Hugo the hippo / by Thomas Baum. — New York ; London : Harcourt Brace Jovanovich, 1976. — 64p : col ill ; 19x22cm.
Based on the film 'Hugo the hippo'.
ISBN 0-15-237300-4 : £3.85
(B77-24533)

Baum, Willi. The golden mountain : the adventures of Jack and Pete / [by] Willi Baum ; based on the text by Ernst A. Ekker. — London : Dent, 1977. — [32]p : chiefly col ill ; 26cm.
Translation and adaptation of: 'Fred und Tom und der goldene Berg'. Ravensburg : Otto Maier, 1977.
ISBN 0-460-06793-1 : £2.50 : CIP rev.
(B77-06331)

Bawden, Nina. The peppermint pig / [by] Nina Bawden. — Harmondsworth [etc.] : Puffin Books, 1977. — 155p ; 18cm. — (Puffin books)
Originally published: London : Gollancz, 1975.
ISBN 0-14-030944-6 Pbk : £0.50
(B77-14972)

Baxter, Alida. Emmie and the witch's button / [by] Alida Baxter. — London : Wingate, 1977. — 119p : ill ; 21cm. — (A longbow book)
ISBN 0-85523-441-5 : £2.95
(B77-31537)

Baxter, Gillian. Pantomime ponies / [by] Gillian Baxter ; illustrated by Elisabeth Grant. — London : Methuen, 1977. — 141p : ill ; 18cm.
Originally published: 1969.
ISBN 0-416-57120-4 Pbk : £0.55
(B77-28211)

Baxter, Gillian. Ponies in harness / [by] Gillian Baxter ; illustrated by Elisabeth Grant. — London : Methuen, 1977. — 127p : ill ; 19cm. — (A pied piper book)
ISBN 0-416-56380-5 : £1.85
(B77-22924)

Baxter, Gillian. Ponies in harness / [by] Gillian Baxter ; illustrated by Elisabeth Grant. — London : Methuen, 1977. — 127p : ill ; 18cm.
ISBN 0-416-58210-9 Pbk : £0.60
(B77-28212)

Baxter, Gillian. Special delivery / [by] Gillian Baxter ; illustrated by Elisabeth Grant. — London : Methuen, 1977. — 128p : ill ; 18cm.
Originally published: 1967.
ISBN 0-416-57130-1 Pbk : £0.55
(B77-21526)

Bayley, Viola. Caribbean adventure / [by] Viola Bayley. — London [etc.] : White Lion Publishers, 1977. — 142p : ill ; 21cm.
Originally published: London : Dent, 1971.
ISBN 0-85686-281-9 : £2.95
(B77-07656)

'BB'. The little grey men go down the bright stream / [by] 'BB' ; illustrated by Denys Watkins-Pitchford. — [New ed.]. — London : Methuen, 1977. — 256p : ill ; 18cm.
This ed.: i.e. 2nd ed. published as 'Down the bright stream'. 1969.
ISBN 0-416-56440-2 Pbk : £0.75
(B77-09986)

'BB'. The wizard of Boland / [by] 'BB' ; illustrated by D.J. Watkins-Pitchford. — Leicester : Knight Books, 1977. — 154p : ill ; 18cm.
Originally published: London : Edmund Ward, 1959.
Pbk : £0.60
ISBN 0-340-04183-8
(B77-17771)

Beachcroft, Nina. A visit to Folly Castle / [by] Nina Beachcroft. — London : Heinemann, 1977. — [4],140p ; 23cm.
ISBN 0-434-92854-2 : £2.90
(B77-33451)

Beal, George. A hundred fables of Aesop / retold by George Beal ; illustrated by Percy J. Billinghurst. — London [etc.] : Angus and Robertson, 1977. — 207p : ill ; 24cm.
ISBN 0-207-95754-1 : £3.50
(B77-31538)

Beames, Margaret. The greenstone summer / [by] Margaret Beames. — London : Stanmore Press, 1977. — 101p ; 23cm.
ISBN 0-900707-41-0 : £2.00
(B77-30749)

The **'Beano'** book. — London : D.C. Thomson.
1978. — 1977. — [137]p : chiefly col ill ; 28cm.

Col. ill. on lining papers.
£1.00
(B77-31539)

Beckett, J. One for the road / [by] J. Beckett. — Ilfracombe : Stockwell, 1976. — 142p ; 19cm.
ISBN 0-7223-0969-4 : £2.50
(B77-19810)

Beckwith, Lillian. The Spuddy / [by] Lillian Beckwith ; decorations by Victor Ambrus. — London : Arrow Books, 1976. — 96p : ill ; 18cm.
Originally published: London : Hutchinson, 1974.
ISBN 0-09-913330-x Pbk : £0.50
(B77-03241)

Bedtime tales. — London : Dean, 1977. — 4-61p : ill ; 21cm. — (Dean's 'little ones' reader' series)
Not the same as B74-25597.
ISBN 0-603-04268-6 : £0.30
(B77-30750)

The **'Beezer'** book. — London : D.C. Thomson.
[1978]. — 1977. — [90]p : chiefly col ill ; 28cm.
Col. ill., text on lining papers.
£0.95
(B77-31540)

Bell, Glenys. Our own riding stables / [by] Glenys Bell ; illustrated by Garrick Tremain. — Wellington [N.Z.] [etc.] ; London : A.H. and A.W. Reed, 1975. — [7],168p : ill ; 22cm.
ISBN 0-589-00943-5 : £4.30
(B77-22925)

Bemelmans, Ludwig. Madeline / story & pictures by Ludwig Bemelmans. — Harmondsworth [etc.] : Puffin Books, 1977. — [46]p : chiefly col ill ; 23cm. — (Picture puffin)
Originally published: New York : Simon and Schuster, 1939 ; London : Verschoyle, 1952.
ISBN 0-14-050198-3 Pbk : Unpriced
(B77-24534)

Bemelmans, Ludwig. Madeline in London / by Ludwig Bemelmans. — Harmondsworth [etc.] : Puffin Books, 1977. — [56]p : chiefly col ill ; 23cm. — (Picture puffin)
Originally published: New York : Viking Press, 1961 ; London : Deutsch, 1962.
ISBN 0-14-050199-1 Pbk : Unpriced
(B77-24535)

Benabo, Brian. Ace of diamonds in New York / [by] Brian Benabo. — London [etc.] : White Lion Publishers, 1977. — [6],73p : ill ; 24cm.
ISBN 0-85686-280-0 : £2.50
(B77-22926)

Benchley, Nathaniel. Sam the Minuteman / by Nathaniel Benchley ; pictures by Arnold Lobel. — Tadworth : World's Work, 1976. — 2-62p : ill(chiefly col) ; 22cm. — (An I can read history book ; no.105)
Originally published: New York : Harper and Row, 1969.
ISBN 0-437-90105-x : £1.90
(B77-01002)

Berends, Polly Berrien. Jack Kent's book of nursery tales / with text adapted by Polly Berrien. — Abridged ed. — London : Fontana, 1977. — [32]p : col ill ; 22cm. — (Picture lions)
Full ed. originally published: New York : Random House, 1970 ; Glasgow : Collins, 1973.

ISBN 0-00-660876-0 Sd : £0.50
(B77-18403)

Berenstain, Stan. The bear detectives : the case of the missing pumpkin / by Stan and Jan Berenstain. — [London] : Collins, 1976. — [42] p : chiefly col ill ; 24cm. — (I can read it all by myself) (Beginner books)
Originally published: New York : Beginner Books, 1975.
ISBN 0-00-171162-8 : £0.95
(B77-14432)

Beresford, Elisabeth. The island bus / [by] Elisabeth Beresford ; illustrated by Gavin Rowe. — London : Methuen, 1977. — 141p : ill ; 18cm.
Originally published: 1968.
ISBN 0-416-84750-1 Pbk : £0.60
(B77-21527)

Beresford, Elisabeth. The Wombles to the rescue / [by] Elisabeth Beresford ; illustrations drawn from Ivor Wood's original film puppets by Margaret Gordon. — Harmondsworth [etc.] : Puffin Books, 1977. — 123,[1]p : ill ; 19cm. — (Puffin books)
Originally published: London : E. Benn, 1974.
ISBN 0-14-030981-0 Pbk : £0.45
(B77-33452)

Berrisford, Judith Mary. A colt in the family / [by] Judith M. Berrisford ; illustrated by Anne Gordon. — Leicester : Knight Books, 1977. — [1],120p : ill ; 18cm.
Originally published: Leicester : Brockhampton Press, 1962.
ISBN 0-340-21658-1 Pbk : £0.60
(B77-21528)

Berrisford, Judith Mary. Jackie and the misfit pony / [by] Judith M. Berrisford ; illustrated by Geoffrey Whittam. — London : Armada Paperbacks, 1977. — 128p : ill ; 18cm.
Originally published: London : Hodder and Stoughton, 1975.
ISBN 0-00-691139-0 Pbk : £0.40
(B77-05726)

Berrisford, Judith Mary. Jackie on Pony Island / [by] Judith M. Berrisford ; illustrated by Geoffrey Whittam. — London [etc.] : Hodder and Stoughton, 1977. — 120p : ill ; 19cm.
ISBN 0-340-20589-x : £2.20
(B77-25229)

Berrisford, Judith Mary. Pony forest adventure / [by] Judith M. Berrisford ; illustrations by Geoffrey Whittam. — London [etc.] : Dragon Books, 1977. — 108p : ill ; 18cm.
Originally published: London : University of London Press, 1957.
ISBN 0-583-30247-5 Pbk : £0.50
(B77-32257)

Berrisford, Judith Mary. Skipper to the rescue! / [by] Judith M. Berrisford ; illustrated by Grace Lodge. — London [etc.] : White Lion Publishers, 1977. — 120p : ill ; 21cm.
Originally published: as 'Skipper and the Headland four'. Leicester : Brockhampton Press, 1957.
ISBN 0-85686-223-1 : £2.75
(B77-33453)

Berrisford, Judith Mary. Sue's circus horse / [by] Judith M. Berrisford ; illustrated by Leslie Atkinson. — St Albans : Dragon Books, 1977. — 141p : ill ; 18cm.
Originally published: London : University of London Press, 1951.
ISBN 0-583-30246-7 Pbk : £0.50
(B77-27456)

Beshlie. Snailsleap Lane / by Beshlie. — St Albans : Hart-Davis Educational ; London : Gallery Five, 1977. — 5-60p : ill(some col) ; 26cm.
ISBN 0-247-12838-4 : £3.50
(B77-32258)

Betjeman, *Sir* **John.** Archie and the Strict Baptists / [by] John Betjeman ; illustrated by Phillida Gili. — London : J. Murray, 1977. — [32]p : col ill ; 26cm.
ISBN 0-7195-3429-1 : £2.50
(B77-32259)

Bibby, Violet. Tinner's quest / [by] Violet Bibby. — London : Faber, 1977. — 3-154p ; 21cm.
ISBN 0-571-11029-0 : £2.95
(B77-13926)

Bicknell, Sally. The midwinter violins / [by] Sally Bicknell. — Harmondsworth [etc.] : Puffin Books, 1976. — 169p ; 19cm. — (Puffin books)
Originally published: London : Chatto and Windus, 1973.
ISBN 0-14-030879-2 Pbk : £0.50
(B77-03242)

Bigelow, Robert. Stubborn bear / by Robert Bigelow ; illustrated by Wallace Tripp. — Tadworth : World's Work, 1977. — [32]p : col ill ; 16x24cm.
Originally published: Boston, Mass. : Little, Brown, 1970.
ISBN 0-437-27410-1 : £2.40
(B77-20711)

The **'Bimbo'** book. — Dundee [etc.] : D.C. Thomson.
1978. — [1977]. — [58]p : chiefly col ill ; 25cm.
Col. ill., text on lining papers.
£0.80
(B77-31541)

Bird, Maria. Andy Pandy and the woolly lamb / by Maria Bird ; illustrated by Matvyn Wright. — [New ed.]. — Maidenhead : Purnell, 1977. — [13]p : col ill ; 21cm.
Previous ed.: 1972.
ISBN 0-361-03846-1 : £0.25
(B77-15558)

Biro, Val. Gumdrop has a birthday / story and pictures by Val Biro. — London [etc.] : Hodder and Stoughton, 1977. — [27]p : chiefly col ill ; 25cm.
ISBN 0-340-21940-8 : £2.80
(B77-22927)

The **birthday** present. — Maidenhead : Purnell, 1974. — [16]p : col ill ; 12cm. — ([Minikins])
Sd : £0.06
(B77-19811)

Bisset, Donald. Beginning to read storybook / [by] Donald Bisset, Elisabeth Beresford, Elizabeth Rose. — London [etc.] : E. Benn, 1977. — 116p in various pagings : col ill ; 21cm.
Contents: Benjie, the circus dog / by Donald Bisset ; illustrated by Val Biro - Peter climbs a tree / by Elisabeth Beresford ; illustrated by Margery Gill - Tim's giant marrow / by Elizabeth Rose ; illustrated by Gerald Rose - Little Bear's pony / by Donald Bisset ; illustrated by Shirley Hughes.
ISBN 0-510-08105-3 : £1.75
(B77-15559)

Bisset, Donald. The story of Smokey Horse / [by] Donald Bisset ; illustrated by the author. — London : Methuen, 1977. — 96p : ill ; 21cm. — ([A read aloud book])
ISBN 0-416-56020-2 : £1.80
(B77-20712)

Bisset, Donald. This is ridiculous / [by] Donald Bisset. — London [etc.] : Beaver Books, 1977. — 79p : ill ; 20cm.
ISBN 0-600-38757-7 Pbk : £0.45
(B77-13374)

Blake, Quentin. Snuff / written and illustrated by Quentin Blake. — Harmondsworth [etc.] : Puffin Books, 1977. — [33]p : col ill ; 20cm. — (Picture puffins)
Originally published: London : Cape, 1973.
ISBN 0-14-050167-3 Sd : £0.50
(B77-15560)

Blance, Ellen. The big monster book / [by] Ellen Blance and Ann Cook ; illustrated by Quentin Blake. — London : Longman. — (Longman tadpole books)
This collection originally published: as 'Monster series'. 1973.
1st. — 1976. — 110p in various pagings : col ill ; 22cm.
Contents: 1 : Monster comes to the city - 2 : Monster looks for a house - 3 : Monster cleans his house - 4 : Monster looks for a friend - 5 : Monster meets lady monster 6 : Monster and the magic umbrella.
ISBN 0-582-18611-0 : £2.25
(B77-09340)

2nd. — 1976. — [2],24,24,24p : col ill ; 22cm.
Contents: 7 : Monster goes to the museum. Originally published: 1976 - 8 : Monster on the bus. Originally published : 1976 - 9 : Monster goes to school. Originally published : 1976.
ISBN 0-582-18612-9 : £1.75
(B77-09341)

3rd. — 1976. — [2],24,24,24p : col ill ; 22cm.
Contents: 10 : Monster at school. Originally published: 1976 - 11 : Monster has a party. Originally published: 1976 - 12 : Monster goes to the zoo. Originally published: 1976.
ISBN 0-582-18613-7 : £1.75
(B77-09342)

Bloom, Freddy. The boy who couldn't hear / text by Freddy Bloom ; illustrations by Michael Charlton. — London [etc.] : Bodley Head, 1977. — 3-30p : chiefly col ill ; 16x17cm.
Col. ill. on lining papers.
ISBN 0-370-01811-7 : £1.75
(B77-31542)

Blue Peter. — London : British Broadcasting Corporation.
14th book / [Biddy Baxter, Edward Barnes and Rosemary Gill devised and wrote the Blue Peter book]. — 1977. — 3-78p : ill(some col), facsims, ports(some col) ; 28cm.
Cover title. — Ill. on lining papers. — With solutions to puzzles.
ISBN 0-563-17287-8 : £1.25
(B77-24536)

Blyton, Enid. The big Enid Blyton book. — Revised ed. — London [etc.] : Hamlyn, 1976. — 5-141p : col ill ; 28cm.
Col. ill. on lining papers. — Previous ed.: 1961.
ISBN 0-600-33143-1 : £1.95
(B77-00465)

Blyton, Enid. The big Enid Blyton story annual. — [Maidenhead] : Purnell.
[1977]. — [1977]. — 4-93p : col ill ; 27cm.
Col. ill. on lining papers. — Originally published: 1972.
ISBN 0-361-03898-4 : £1.50
(B77-13375)

Blyton, Enid. Big Noddy book / by Enid Blyton. — London : Sampson Low, Marston : Dobson : [Distributed by] Purnell.
[1977]. — 1977. — [60]p : ill(chiefly col) ; 25cm.
Col. ill. on lining papers. — Originally published: as 'Noddy's big new book'. 1957.
ISBN 0-361-03893-3 : £1.00
(B77-11433)

Blyton, Enid. Brer Rabbit and the Wattle Weasel / [by] Enid Blyton ; illustrated by Val Biro. — Leicester : Knight Books, 1977. — 96p : ill ; 18cm.
Originally published: London : Latimer House, 1952.
ISBN 0-340-21956-4 Pbk : £0.45
(B77-17772)

Blyton, Enid. Enid Blyton's happy story book / illustrations by Eileen Soper. — London [etc.] : White Lion Publishers, 1977. — 160p : ill ; 21cm.
This collection originally published: London : Hodder and Stoughton, 1942.
ISBN 0-85686-262-2 : £2.75
(B77-33454)

Blyton, Enid. Fun for the Secret Seven / [by] Enid Blyton ; illustrated by Derek Lucas. — Leicester : Knight Books, 1977. — 96p : ill ; 18cm. — (Blyton, Enid. Secret Seven ; 15)
Originally published: Leicester : Brockhampton Press, 1963.
ISBN 0-340-18241-5 Pbk : £0.45
(B77-17773)

Blyton, Enid. Hurrah for the circus! / [by] Enid Blyton. — [Abridged] ed. — London : Armada, [1977]. — 157p : ill ; 18cm.
This ed. originally published: 1972. — Previous control number ISBN 0-00-690501-3.
Pbk : £0.40
ISBN 0-00-690501-3
(B77-16616)

Blyton, Enid. Merry Mister Meddle / [by] Enid Blyton ; illustrated by Rene Cloke. — St Albans : Dragon, 1976. — 144p : ill ; 18cm. — (Blue dragon)
Originally published: London : Newnes, 1954.
ISBN 0-583-30192-4 Pbk : £0.35
(B77-11434)

Blyton, Enid. Noddy gives a tea party / [by Enid Blyton]. — Maidenhead : Purnell, 1977. — [12] p : chiefly col ill ; 21cm.
Col. ill. on lining papers.
ISBN 0-361-03844-5 : £0.25
(B77-14973)

Blyton, Enid. Noddy's busy day ; and, Bad luck for Noddy / by Enid Blyton. — Maidenhead : Purnell, 1977. — [20]p : col ill ; 25cm.
Text, col. ill. on lining papers. — Originally published: 1973.
ISBN 0-361-03860-7 : £0.45
(B77-27457)

Blyton, Enid. The Secret Seven / [by] Enid Blyton ; illustrated by Derek Lucas. — Leicester : Knight Books, 1977. — 96p : ill ; 18cm. — (Blyton, Enid. Secret Seven ; 1)
Originally published: Leicester : Brockhampton Press, 1949.
Pbk : £0.45
ISBN 0-340-04156-0
(B77-17774)

Blyton, Enid. Story party at Green Hedges / [by] Enid Blyton ; illustrated by Grace Lodge. — London : Armada Paperbacks, 1976. — 96p : ill ; 20cm.
Originally published: London : Hodder and Stoughton, 1949.
ISBN 0-00-691143-9 Pbk : £0.40
(B77-04437)

Bock, Valerie. Teng's story : a tale of modern Thailand / by Valerie Bock. — London : Leprosy Mission, [1976]. — [2],34p : ill ; 21cm.
Sd : £0.35
(B77-03243)

Bock, Valerie. The umbrella girl : a painting book from Thailand / [text by Valerie Bock ; drawings by Jeanette Taylor]. — London : Leprosy Mission, 1976. — [16]p : ill ; 22cm.
Sd : £0.20
Also classified at 741
(B77-03778)

Bond, Michael. Paddington at the station / [by] Michael Bond ; illustrated by Barry Wilkinson. — [London] : [Collins], 1976. — [48]p : col ill ; 15cm. — (Collins colour cubs)
'This story comes from "A bear called Paddington" and is based on the television film. It has been specially written ... for younger children' - note.
ISBN 0-00-123339-4 : £0.95
ISBN 0-00-123334-3 Pbk : £0.30
(B77-17775)

Bond, Michael. Paddington carpenter / [by] Michael Bond. — [London] : Collins, 1977. — [19]p : chiefly ill(some col) ; 28cm. — (Bond, Michael. Paddington's colouring books)
ISBN 0-00-143179-x Sd : £0.30
Also classified at 741
(B77-34213)

Bond, Michael. Paddington conjurer / [by] Michael Bond. — [London] : Collins, 1977. — [19]p : ill(some col) ; 28cm. — (Bond, Michael. Paddington's colouring books)
ISBN 0-00-143176-5 Sd : £0.30
Also classified at 741
(B77-33455)

Bond, Michael. Paddington cook / [by] Michael Bond. — [London] : Collins, 1977. — [19]p : chiefly ill(some col) ; 28cm. — (Bond, Michael. Paddington's colouring books)
ISBN 0-00-143178-1 Sd : £0.25
Also classified at 741
(B77-33456)

Bond, Michael. Paddington goes to the sales / [by] Michael Bond ; illustrated by Barry Wilkinson. — [London] : [Collins], 1976. — [48]p : col ill ; 15cm. — (Collins colour cubs)
'This story is based on the television film and has been specially written ... for younger children' - note.
ISBN 0-00-123341-6 : £0.95
ISBN 0-00-123336-x Pbk : £0.30
(B77-17776)

Bond, Michael. Paddington golfer / [by] Michael Bond. — [London] : Collins, 1977. — [19]p : ill(some col) ; 28cm. — (Bond, Michael. Paddington's colouring books)
ISBN 0-00-143177-3 Sd : £0.30
Also classified at 741
(B77-33457)

Bond, Michael. Paddington on top / [by] Michael Bond ; illustrated by Peggy Fortnum. — London : Collins, 1977. — 132p : ill ; 20cm. — (Lions)
Originally published: 1974.
ISBN 0-00-671227-4 Pbk : £0.60
(B77-13376)

Bond, Michael. Paddington takes a bath / [by] Michael Bond ; illustrated by Barry Wilkinson. — [London] : [Collins], 1976. — [48]p : col ill ; 15cm. — (Collins colour cubs)
'This story comes from "A bear called Paddington" and is based on the television film. It has been specially written ... for younger children' - note.
ISBN 0-00-123340-8 : £0.95
ISBN 0-00-123335-1 Pbk : £0.30
(B77-17777)

Bond, Michael. Paddington's new room / [by] Michael Bond ; illustrated by Barry Wilkinson. — [London] : [Collins], 1976. — [48]p : col ill ; 15cm. — (Collins colour cubs)
'This story comes from "More about Paddington" and is based on the television film. It has been specially written ... for younger children' - note.
ISBN 0-00-123342-4 : £0.95
ISBN 0-00-123337-8 Pbk : £0.30
(B77-17778)

Bond, Michael. Paddington's pop-up book / [by] Michael Bond ; pictures by Ivor Wood. — London : Collins, 1977. — Fold leaf : col ill ; 28cm.
Cover title. — Leaf folded and cut to create three-dimensional effect, 10 pictures in all.
ISBN 0-00-182157-1 : £2.50
(B77-29745)

Bonsall, Crosby. The case of the hungry stranger / by Crosby Bonsall. — Tadworth : World's Work, 1977. — 64p : col ill ; 22cm. — (An I can read mystery book)
Originally published: New York : Harper, 1963 ; Tadworth : World's Work, 1964.
ISBN 0-437-96012-9 Sd : £0.60
(B77-34214)

Bonsall, Crosby. The case of the scaredy cats / by Crosby Bonsall. — Tadworth : World's Work, 1977. — 64p : col ill ; 22cm. — (An I can read book) (An I can read mystery)
Originally published: New York : Harper, 1971 ; Tadworth : World's Work, 1973.
ISBN 0-437-96005-6 Sd : £0.60
(B77-16617)

A **book** of elephants / compiled by Katie Wales ; illustrated by David McKee. — London : Kaye and Ward, 1977. — 64p : ill(chiefly col) ; 25cm.
ISBN 0-7182-1147-2 : £2.25
(B77-18404)

A **book** of magicians / edited by Roger Lancelyn Green ; illustrated by Victor Ambrus. — Harmondsworth [etc.] : Puffin Books, 1977. — 268p : ill ; 19cm. — (Puffin books)
Originally published: as 'The Hamish Hamilton book of magicians'. London : Hamilton, 1973.
ISBN 0-14-030939-x Pbk : £0.65
(B77-22928)

Boshell, Gordon. Captain Cobwebb / [by] Gordon Boshell ; illustrated by Graham Thompson. — London : Armada, [1977]. — 127p : ill, maps ; 19cm.
Originally published: London : Chatto and Windus, 1967.
ISBN 0-00-691126-9 Pbk : £0.40
(B77-18405)

Boshell, Gordon. Captain Cobwebb and the mischief man / [by] Gordon Boshell ; illustrated by Trevor Stubley. — London : Macdonald and Jane's, 1977. — [5],130p : ill ; 23cm.
ISBN 0-354-08009-1 : £3.00
(B77-06332)

Boshell, Gordon. Captain Cobwebb's adventurers / [by] Gordon Boshell ; illustrated by Graham Thompson. — London : Armada, 1977. — 128p : ill ; 18cm.
Originally published: London : Macdonald and Co., 1973.
ISBN 0-00-691110-2 Pbk : £0.45
(B77-19812)

Boshell, Gordon. Captain Cobwebb's cobra / [by] Gordon Boshell ; illustrated by Graham Thompson. — London : Armada, 1977. — 128p : ill ; 18cm.
Originally published: London : Chatto and Windus, 1971.
ISBN 0-00-691125-0 Pbk : £0.45
(B77-19813)

Boshell, Gordon. Captain Cobwebb's cowboys / [by] Gordon Boshell ; illustrated by Graham Thompson. — London : Armada, [1977]. — 128p : ill, map ; 19cm.
Originally published: London : Chatto and Windus, 1969.
ISBN 0-00-691127-7 Pbk : £0.40
(B77-18406)

Boshell, Gordon. The Mendip money-makers / [by] Gordon Boshell. — London : Target Books, 1977. — [6],132p : 1 ill ; 19cm. — (Boshell, Gordon. Secret Guardians series)
Originally published: Folkestone : Bailey and Swinfen, 1976.
ISBN 0-426-11746-8 Pbk : £0.60
(B77-24537)

Boshell, Gordon. The Mendip money-makers / [by] Gordon Boshell. — Folkestone : Bailey and Swinfen, 1976. — [6],132p : 1 ill ; 23cm. — (Boshell, Gordon. Secret Guardians series)
ISBN 0-561-00287-8 : £2.95
(B77-02631)

Boston, Lucy Maria. An enemy at Green Knowe / [by] Lucy M. Boston ; illustrated by Peter Boston. — Harmondsworth [etc.] : Puffin Books, 1977. — 140,[1]p : ill ; 19cm. — (Puffin books)
Originally published: London : Faber, 1964.
ISBN 0-14-030910-1 Pbk : £0.40
(B77-14974)

Boston, Lucy Maria. A stranger at Green Knowe / [by] Lucy M. Boston ; illustrated by Peter Boston. — Harmondsworth : Puffin Books, 1977. — 171,[2]p : ill ; 19cm. — (Puffin books)
Originally published: London : Faber, 1961.
ISBN 0-14-030871-7 Pbk : £0.50
(B77-07657)

Brandenberg, Franz. I don't feel well! / by Franz Brandenberg ; illustrated by Aliki. — London : Hamilton, 1977. — [32]p : chiefly col ill ; 24cm.
Originally published: as 'I wish I was sick, too!'. New York : Greenwillow, 1976.
ISBN 0-241-89576-6 : £2.50
(B77-10602)

Breinburg, Petronella. Sally-Ann in the snow / [by] Petronella Breinburg ; with illustrations by Ossie Murray. — London [etc.] : Bodley Head, 1977. — [26]p : chiefly col ill ; 24cm.
ISBN 0-370-01809-5 : £2.50
(B77-17779)

Brent-Dyer, Elinor Mary. Carola storms the Chalet School / [by] Elinor M. Brent-Dyer. — London : Armada, 1977. — 159p ; 18cm.
Originally published: London : W. and R. Chambers, 1951.
ISBN 0-00-691310-5 Pbk : £0.45
(B77-30751)

Brent-Dyer, Elinor Mary. A genius at the Chalet School / [by] Elinor M. Brent-Dyer. — Abridged ed. — [London] : Armada, 1977. — 125p ; 18cm.
This ed. originally published: 1969.
ISBN 0-00-691412-8 Pbk : £0.45
(B77-34215)

Briggs, Raymond. The strange house / written and illustrated by Raymond Briggs. — London [etc.] : Beaver Books, 1977. — 78p : ill ; 20cm.
Originally published: London : Hamilton, 1961.
ISBN 0-600-38230-3 Pbk : £0.50
(B77-12735)

Brogan, Mike. Counter attack! / [by] Mike Brogan. — [Henley-on-Thames] : A. Ellis, 1977. — 3-118p : ill ; 20cm. — (Brogan, Mike. Action man)
ISBN 0-85628-065-8 : £2.25 : CIP rev.
(B77-30752)

Brogan, Mike. Hold the bridge / [by] Mike Brogan. — [Henley-on-Thames] : A. Ellis, 1977. — 3-126p : ill ; 20cm. — (Brogan, Mike. Action man)
ISBN 0-85628-060-7 : £2.25 : CIP rev.
(B77-15561)

Brogan, Mike. Operation sky-drop / [by] Mike Brogan. — [Henley-on-Thames] : A. Ellis, 1977. — 3-123p : ill ; 20cm. — (Brogan, Mike. Action man)
ISBN 0-85628-062-3 : £2.25 : CIP rev.
(B77-15562)

Brogan, Mike. Snow, ice and bullets / [by] Mike Brogan. — London : Carousel Books, 1977. — 128p : ill ; 18cm. — (Brogan, Mike. Action man) (Carousel books)
Also published: Henley-on-Thames : A. Ellis, 1977.
ISBN 0-552-52074-8 Pbk : £0.50
(B77-27458)

Brogan, Mike. Snow, ice and bullets / [by] Mike Brogan. — [Henley-on-Thames] : A. Ellis, 1977. — 3-128p : ill ; 20cm. — (Brogan, Mike. Action man)
ISBN 0-85628-063-1 : £2.25 : CIP rev.
(B77-15563)

Brogan, Mike. The taking of Monte Carrillo / [by] Mike Brogan. — London : Carousel Books, 1977. — 121p : ill ; 18cm. — (Brogan, Mike. Action man) (Carousel books)
Also published: Henley-on-Thames : A. Ellis, 1977.
ISBN 0-552-52075-6 Pbk : £0.50
(B77-27459)

Brogan, Mike. The taking of Monte Carrillo / [by] Mike Brogan. — [Henley-on-Thames] : A. Ellis, 1977. — 3-121p : ill ; 20cm. — (Brogan, Mike. Action man)
ISBN 0-85628-061-5 : £2.25 : CIP rev.
(B77-15564)

Brogan, Mike. The tough way out / [by] Mike Brogan. — [Henley-on-Thames] : A. Ellis, 1977. — 3-124p : ill ; 20cm. — (Brogan, Mike. Action man)
ISBN 0-85628-064-x : £2.25 : CIP rev.
(B77-30753)

Bronin, Andrew. Gus and Buster work things out / story by Andrew Bronin ; illustrated by Cyndy Szekeres. — Tadworth : World's Work, 1977. — 63p : ill(some col) ; 22cm.
Originally published: New York : Coward, McCann & Geoghegan, 1975.
ISBN 0-437-29150-2 : £2.40
(B77-24538)

Brook, Judy. Belinda / [by] Judy Brook. — Tadworth : World's Work, 1976. — [32]p : col ill ; 30cm.
ISBN 0-437-29207-x : £2.50
(B77-00466)

Brown, George Mackay. Pictures in the cave / by George Mackay Brown ; illustrated by Ian MacInnes. — London : Chatto and Windus, 1977. — 136p : ill ; 22cm.
ISBN 0-7011-5081-5 : £3.25
(B77-11435)

Brown, Pamela. Every day is market day / [by] Pamela Brown. — London [etc.] : Hodder and Stoughton, 1977. — 120p ; 22cm.
ISBN 0-340-21777-4 : £2.80
(B77-26606)

Brown, Roy, *b.1921.* Chubb to the rescue / [by] Roy Brown ; illustrated by Margaret Belsky. — London : Abelard-Schuman, 1977. — 126p : ill ; 21cm. — (A grasshopper book)
ISBN 0-200-72499-1 : £2.25
ISBN 0-200-72500-9 Pbk : £0.60
(B77-24539)

Brown, Roy, *b.1921.* Flight of sparrows / [by] Roy Brown. — Leicester : Knight Books, 1977. — 120p ; 18cm.
Originally published: London : Abelard-Schuman, 1972.
ISBN 0-340-18739-5 Pbk : £0.60
(B77-24540)

Browne, Anthony. A walk in the park / [by] Anthony Browne. — London : Hamilton, 1977. — [32]p : chiefly col ill ; 26cm.
ISBN 0-241-89397-6 : £2.75
(B77-19814)

Browne, Caroline. Mrs Christie's farmhouse / [by] Caroline Brown. — London : E. Benn, 1977. — [32]p : chiefly col ill ; 28cm.
ISBN 0-510-09802-9 : £2.50
(B77-19815)

The **Brownie** annual. — Maidenhead : Purnell [for] the Girl Guides Association.
1978 / edited by Robert Moss. — 1977. — 3-94p : ill(some col) ; 27cm.
Ill. on lining papers.
ISBN 0-361-03894-1 : £1.50
(B77-32260)

Buckeridge, Anthony. Jennings at large / [by] Anthony Buckeridge. — London : Armada, 1977. — 157p ; 18cm.
ISBN 0-00-691248-6 Pbk : £0.45
(B77-30754)

Buckeridge, Anthony. Jennings in particular / [by] Anthony Buckeridge. — New (revised) ed. — London : Armada Paperbacks, 1976. — 3-192p ; 18cm.
This ed. originally published: London : Collins, 1972.
ISBN 0-00-691215-x Pbk : £0.40
(B77-01846)

Bull, Angela. Griselda / [by] Angela Bull. — London : Collins, 1977. — 181p ; 22cm.
ISBN 0-00-183723-0 : £3.50
(B77-27460)

Bunting, Eve. Winter's coming / by Eve Bunting ; pictures by Howard Knotts. — New York ; London : Harcourt Brace Jovanovich, 1977. — [32]p : chiefly ill ; 22cm. — (Let me read books)
ISBN 0-15-298036-9 : £3.20
ISBN 0-15-298037-7 Pbk : £1.05
(B77-34218)

'**Bunty**' for girls. — London : D.C. Thomson.
[1978]. — 1977. — 4-125p : chiefly col ill ; 28cm.
Col. ill. on lining papers.
£0.95
(B77-31543)

Burke, David. Come midnight Monday / [by] David Burke ; illustrated by Janet Mare. — London : Methuen [etc.], 1977. — [4],224p : ill, map(on lining papers) ; 21cm.
Originally published: Sydney : Methuen, 1976.
ISBN 0-416-56530-1 : £3.25
(B77-22205)

Burnham, Jeremy. Children of the stones / [by] Jeremy Burnham and Trevor Ray. — London : Carousel Books, 1977. — 189p : ill ; 20cm. — (Carousel books)
ISBN 0-552-52067-5 Pbk : £0.50
(B77-16081)

Burningham, John. Come away from the water, Shirley / [by] John Burningham. — London : Cape, 1977. — [28]p : chiefly col ill ; 20x28cm.
ISBN 0-224-01373-4 : £2.50
(B77-34219)

Burton, Hester. A Grenville goes to sea / [by] Hester Burton ; illustrated by Colin McNaughton. — London : Heinemann, 1977. — 46,[1]p : ill ; 21cm. — (Long ago children books)
ISBN 0-434-94926-4 : £2.10
(B77-19029)

Burton, Hester. Tim at the fur fort / [by] Hester Burton ; illustrated by Victor Ambrus. — London : Hamilton, 1977. — 88p : ill ; 19cm. — (Antelope books)
ISBN 0-241-89571-5 : £1.25
(B77-19816)

'**Buster**' book. — London : IPC Magazines.
1978. — [1977]. — 128p : of ill ; 28cm. — (A Fleetway annual)
Cover title.
ISBN 0-85037-325-5 Pbk : £0.85
(B77-32892)

Butterworth, Ben. Danger in the mountains / [by] Ben Butterworth and Bill Stockdale ; illustrated by Maureen and Gordon Gray. — London : Methuen, 1977. — 64p : ill, map ; 18cm. — (Butterworth, Ben. Jim Hunter books)
ISBN 0-423-50400-2 Pbk : £0.55
(B77-28213)

Butterworth, Ben. The diamond smugglers / [by] Ben Butterworth and Bill Stockdale ; illustrated by Maureen and Gordon Gray. — London : Methuen, 1977. — 64p : ill ; 18cm. — (Butterworth, Ben. Jim Hunter books)
ISBN 0-423-50410-x Pbk : £0.55
(B77-28987)

Butterworth, Jenny. The bird whistle / [by] Jenny Butterworth ; illustrated by Babette Cole. — London : Kaye and Ward, 1977. — 122p : ill ; 23cm.
ISBN 0-7182-1162-6 : £2.75
(B77-22929)

Byars, Betsy. The house of wings / [by] Betsy Byars. — Harmondsworth [etc.] : Puffin Books, 1977. — 110p ; 19cm. — (Puffin books)
Originally published: New York : Viking Press, 1972 ; London : Bodley Head, 1973.
ISBN 0-14-030887-3 Pbk : £0.45
(B77-12152)

Cannan, Joanna. I wrote a pony book / [by] Joanna Cannan. — London [etc.] : Hodder and Stoughton, 1977. — 152p ; 21cm.
Originally published: London : Collins, 1950.
ISBN 0-340-19640-8 : £3.20
(B77-27461)

Carey, M V. Alfred Hitchcock and the Three Investigators in the mystery of Death Trap Mine / text by M.V. Carey ; based on characters created by Robert Arthur. — London [etc.] : Collins, 1977. — 158p ; 22cm. — (Alfred Hitchcock mystery series ; 24)
Originally published: New York : Random House, 1976.
ISBN 0-00-160026-5 : £1.95
(B77-25230)

Carey, M V. Alfred Hitchcock and the Three Investigators in the mystery of the invisible dog / text by M.V. Carey ; based on characters created by Robert Arthur. — London [etc.] : Collins, 1976. — 160p ; 22cm. — (Alfred Hitchcock mystery series ; 23)
Originally published: New York : Random House, 1975.
ISBN 0-00-160024-9 : £1.95
(B77-14975)

Carlson, Dale. The plant people / by Dale Carlson ; photographs by Chuck Freedman. — New York ; London : F. Watts, 1977. — [2], 94p : ill ; 22cm.
ISBN 0-531-00380-9 : £2.25
(B77-32261)

Carlyon, Richard. The dark lord of Pengersick / by Richard Carlyon ; illustrated by Pauline Ellison. — London : G. Whizzard Publications Ltd : [Distributed by] Deutsch, 1976. — [2], 131p,[9]p of plates : ill, map ; 24cm.
Ill. on lining papers.
ISBN 0-233-96773-7 : £3.25
(B77-16618)

Carpenter, Humphrey. The Joshers, or, London to Birmingham with 'Albert' and 'Victoria' : a story of the canals / by Humphrey Carpenter ; with illustrations by Robert J. Wilson. — London [etc.] : Allen and Unwin, 1977. — 120p : ill ; 23cm.
ISBN 0-04-823142-8 : £3.50
(B77-27462)

Carruth, Jane. Johann Wyss's 'Swiss family Robinson' / retold by Jane Carruth ; [illustrations by Gordon King]. — Maidenhead : Purnell, 1977. — [60]p : col ill, port ; 30cm. — (Purnell colour classics)
Spine title: Swiss family Robinson. — Col. ill. on lining papers.
ISBN 0-361-03872-0 : £1.50
(B77-12153)

Carruth, Jane. Mark Twain's 'Tom Sawyer' / retold by Jane Carruth ; [illustrated by John Worsley]. — Maidenhead : Purnell, 1977. — [60]p : col ill, port ; 30cm. — (Purnell colour classics)
Spine title: Tom Sawyer. — Col. ill. on lining papers.
ISBN 0-361-03873-9 : £1.50
(B77-12154)

Carryl, Charles Edward. A capital ship, or, The walloping window-blind / [text by] Charles Edward Carryl ; pictures by Paul Galdone. — Tadworth : World's Work, 1976 [i.e. 1977]. — [35]p : chiefly col ill, music ; 19x25cm.
Originally published: New York : McGraw-Hill, 1963 ; London : Bodley Head, 1964.
ISBN 0-437-30898-7 : £2.50
(B77-08629)

Carter, Bruce. Speed Six! / [by] Bruce Carter. — Harmondsworth [etc.] : Puffin Books, 1977. — 155,[1]p ; 18cm. — (Puffin books)
Originally published: London : J. Lane, 1953.
Pbk : £0.50
ISBN 0-14-030271-9
(B77-19817)

Carter, Diana. Zozu the robot / [by] Diana Carter ; illustrations by Mike Rose. — Harmondsworth [etc.] : Puffin Books, 1976. — 111p : ill ; 19cm. — (Puffin books)
Originally published: London : Sidgwick and Jackson, 1974.
ISBN 0-14-030767-2 Pbk : £0.40
(B77-03779)

Catherall, Arthur. The last run, and other stories / [by] Arthur Catherall. — London [etc.] : Dent, 1977. — 128p ; 20cm.
ISBN 0-460-06837-7 : £3.50 : CIP rev.
(B77-22930)

Catherall, Arthur. Twelve minutes to disaster, and other stories / [by] Arthur Catherall. — London : Dent, 1977. — 123p : ill ; 21cm.
ISBN 0-460-06783-4 : £2.95
(B77-06333)

Caveney, Sylvia. Little Zip's dressing-up book / by Sylvia Caveney ; pictures by Simon Stern. — London : Pelham, 1977. — [24]p : col ill ; 24x25cm.
ISBN 0-7207-0949-0 : £2.50
(B77-28214)

Caveney, Sylvia. Little Zip's zoo counting book / by Sylvia Caveney ; pictures by Simon Stern. — London : Pelham, 1977. — [24]p : col ill ; 24x25cm.
ISBN 0-7207-0950-4 : £2.50
(B77-28215)

Cedar, Sally. The magnificent uniform / written by Sally Cedar ; illustrated by Rita van Bilsen. — London : Macdonald and Jane's, 1977. — [26]p : col ill ; 30cm.
Originally published: in German translation as 'Die verflixte Uniform'. Zürich : Bohem, 1976.
ISBN 0-354-08007-5 : £2.95
(B77-09987)

Chance, Stephen. Septimus and the Danedyke mystery / [by] Stephen Chance. — Harmondsworth [etc.] : Puffin Books, 1977. — 156p ; 18cm. — (Puffin books)
Originally published: London : Bodley Head, 1971.
Pbk : £0.50
ISBN 0-14-030627-7
(B77-12155)

Chapman, Elizabeth. Marmaduke and Joe / by Elizabeth Chapman ; pictures by Eccles Williams. — London [etc.] : Hodder and Stoughton, 1977. — 89p : ill ; 20cm.
Originally published: Leicester : Brockhampton Press, 1954.
£2.20
ISBN 0-340-03625-7
(B77-28988)

Chapman, Elizabeth. Marmaduke goes to Switzerland / [by] Elizabeth Chapman ; pictures by Eccles Williams. — London [etc.] : Hodder and Stoughton, 1977. — 88p : ill ; 20cm.
ISBN 0-340-20270-x : £1.80
(B77-03780)

Charles, Frank. Beyond the midnight mountains / [by] Frank Charles ; illustrations by Lynn Smith. — London (3 Fitzroy Sq., W1P 6JD) : Andersen Press, 1977. — 160p : ill ; 20cm. — (Andersen young readers library)
ISBN 0-905478-20-7 : £2.50
(B77-30755)

The **Charles** Hamilton companion. — Maidstone (30 Tonbridge Rd, Maidstone, Kent) : Museum Press.
Vol.3 : A new anthology from the works of Charles Hamilton / with contributions from Una Hamilton-Wright, Roger Jenkins, Les Rowley ; compiled, edited and arranged by John Wernham. — [1977]. — xvi,304p : ill, facsims, ports ; 22cm.
Pbk : Unpriced
Primary classification 823'.9'12
(B77-26637)

Chatfield, Keith. Issi's magic tonic / [by] Keith Chatfield ; illustrated by Edward C. Standon. — London : Pan Books, 1976. — 143p : ill ; 18cm. — (A piccolo book)
'As featured on Thames Television' - cover. — Also published: London : Heinemann, 1976.
ISBN 0-330-24843-x Pbk : £0.40
(B77-02632)

Chenery, Janet. Pickles and Jake / [by] Janet Chenery ; illustrated by Lilian Obligado. — Tadworth : World's Work, 1977. — [56]p : col ill ; 24cm.
Originally published: New York : Viking Press, 1975.
ISBN 0-437-31400-6 : £2.60
(B77-20713)

Chesher, Kim. The Carnford inheritance / [by] Kim Chesher. — London : Hamilton, 1977. — 140p ; 23cm.
ISBN 0-241-89542-1 : £3.25
(B77-14433)

Chia Hearn-chek. The bird hunter : an Indonesian folktale / retold by Chia Hearn Chek ; illustrated by Kwan Shan Mei. — London : Macdonald and Jane's, 1977. — [34] p : chiefly col ill ; 20x26cm. — (Folktales from the Orient) (Moongate collection)
Originally published: Singapore : Alpha Press, 1972.
ISBN 0-354-08026-1 : £1.95
(B77-28216)

Chia Hearn-chek. The dragon of Kinabalu : a Borneo folktale / retold by Chia Hearn Chek ; illustrated by Kwan Shan Mei. — London : Macdonald and Jane's, 1977. — [34]p : chiefly col ill ; 20x26cm. — (Folktales from the Orient) (Moongate collection)
Originally published: Singapore : Alpha Press, 1975.
ISBN 0-354-08027-x : £1.95
(B77-28217)

Chigbo, Thomas. Odenigbo / [by] Thomas Chigbo. — London : Evans Bros, 1976. — [4], 76p : ill ; 22cm. — (Evans Africa library)
ISBN 0-237-50067-1 Sd : £0.80
(B77-02633)

Chilton, Irma. The magic cauldron, and other folktales / [by] Irma Chilton ; illustrated by Rosemary Thomas. — Swansea : C. Davies, 1976. — 144p : ill ; 22cm.
ISBN 0-7154-0300-1 : £2.25
(B77-01847)

Chipperfield, Joseph Eugene. Dark Fury : stallion of Lost River Valley / [by] Joseph E. Chipperfield. — London [etc.] : Beaver Books, 1977. — 206p ; 20cm.
Originally published: London : Hutchinson, 1956.
ISBN 0-600-32952-6 Pbk : £0.60
(B77-31544)

Christopher, John, *b.1922.* Beyond the burning lands / [by] John Christopher. — Harmondsworth [etc.] : Puffin Books, 1977. — 153p ; 18cm. — (Puffin books)
Originally published: London : Hamilton, 1971.
Pbk : £0.50
ISBN 0-14-030625-0
(B77-07659)

Christopher, John, *b.1922.* The city of gold and lead / [by] John Christopher. — London [etc.] : Beaver Books, 1977. — 159p ; 20cm.
Originally published: London : Hamilton, 1967.
ISBN 0-600-31931-8 Pbk : £0.60
(B77-13377)

Christopher, John, *b.1922.* The pool of fire / [by] John Christopher. — London [etc.] : Beaver Books, 1977. — 156p,[1]p ; 20cm.
Originally published: London : Hamilton, 1968.
ISBN 0-600-37134-4 Pbk : £0.60
(B77-12736)

Christopher, John, *b.1922.* The Prince in Waiting / [by] John Christopher. — Harmondsworth [etc.] : Puffin Books, 1977. — 155p ; 19cm. — (Puffin books)
Originally published: London : Hamilton, 1970.
Pbk : £0.50
ISBN 0-14-030617-x
(B77-07660)

Christopher, John, *b.1922.* The sword of the spirits / [by] John Christopher. — Harmondsworth [etc.] : Puffin Books, 1977. — 153p ; 18cm. — (Puffin books)
Originally published: London : Hamilton, 1972.
Pbk : £0.50
ISBN 0-14-030630-7
(B77-07661)

Christopher, John, *b.1922.* The White Mountains / [by] John Christopher. — London [etc.] : Beaver Books, 1976. — 3-153,[3]p ; 20cm.
Originally published: London : Hamilton, 1967.

ISBN 0-600-39367-4 Pbk : £0.60
(B77-12737)

Clark, Ann Nolan. Secret of the Andes / by Ann Nolan Clark ; with drawings by Jean Charlot. — Harmondsworth [etc.] : Puffin Books, 1976. — [7],120p : 2 ill ; 20cm. — (A puffin book)
Originally published: New York : Viking Press, 1952.
ISBN 0-14-030926-8 Pbk : Unpriced
(B77-03781)

Clark, Elizabeth. Stories to tell / [by] Elizabeth Clark ; text illustrations by Cara Lockhart-Smith ; cover illustration by Julie Marshall. — London : Pan Books, 1977. — 90p : ill ; 20cm. — (Piccolo)
This collection originally published: Leicester : Brockhampton Press, 1974.
ISBN 0-330-25271-2 Pbk : £0.50
(B77-28989)

Clark, Mavis Thorpe. Pony from Tarella / [by] Mavis Thorpe Clark. — Leicester : Knight Books, 1977. — 190p ; 18cm.
Originally published: Melbourne : Heinemann, 1959.
ISBN 0-340-20079-0 Pbk : £0.60
(B77-08630)

Clarke, Pauline. The twelve and the Genii / [by] Pauline Clarke ; illustrated by Cecil Leslie. — Harmondsworth [etc.] : Puffin Books, 1977. — 206p : ill ; 19cm. — (Puffin books)
Originally published: London : Faber, 1962.
ISBN 0-14-030916-0 Pbk : £0.60
(B77-17780)

Claydon, Graham. Jonathan's dream / [by] Graham Claydon ; illustrated by Malcolm King. — London : Falcon Books, 1976. — 63p : ill ; 21x22cm.
ISBN 0-85491-843-4 : £1.75
ISBN 0-85491-536-2 Pbk : £0.80
(B77-01848)

Cleary, Beverly. The mouse and the motorcycle / [by] Beverly Cleary ; illustrated by Louis Darling. — Harmondsworth [etc.] : Puffin Books, 1977. — 142p : ill ; 18cm. — (Puffin books)
Originally published: New York : Morrow, 1965 ; London : Hamilton, 1974.
ISBN 0-14-030970-5 Pbk : £0.45
(B77-24541)

Cleaver, Vera. Dust of the earth / [by] Vera and Bill Cleaver. — Oxford [etc.] : Oxford University Press, 1977. — [5],134p ; 23cm.
Originally published: Philadelphia : Lippincott, 1975.
ISBN 0-19-271400-7 : £2.50 : CIP rev.
(B77-04402)

Cleaver, Vera. The mimosa tree / [by] Vera and Bill Cleaver. — Oxford [etc.] : Oxford University Press, 1977. — 109p ; 23cm.
Originally published: Philadelphia : Lippincott, 1970.
ISBN 0-19-271404-x : £2.50 : CIP rev.
(B77-07662)

Clewes, Dorothy. The lost Tower treasure / [by] Dorothy Clewes ; illustrated by Shirley Hughes. — London [etc.] : White Lion Publishers, 1976. — 191p : ill ; 21cm.
Originally published: London : Collins, 1960.
ISBN 0-85686-251-7 : £2.75
(B77-03782)

Clewes, Dorothy. The singing strings / [by] Dorothy Clewes ; with drawings by Shirley Hughes. — London [etc.] : White Lion Publishers, 1977. — 192p : ill ; 21cm.
Originally published: London : Collins, 1961.
ISBN 0-85686-256-8 : £2.95
(B77-12738)

Clive, *Lady* **Mary.** Christmas with the savages / by Mary Clive ; decorated by Philip Gough. — London : Macmillan, 1977. — vii,177p : ill ; 23cm.
Originally published: 1955.
ISBN 0-333-05280-3 : £3.95
(B77-26607)

Coatsworth, Elizabeth. Sword of the wilderness / [by] Elizabeth Coatsworth ; illustrated by Roger Payne. — London [etc.] : Beaver Books, 1977. — 125p : ill ; 20cm.
Originally published: New York : Macmillan, 1936 ; London : Blackie, 1972.
ISBN 0-600-38232-x Pbk : £0.55
(B77-13378)

Codd, Carol. Chooki and the ptarmigan / [by] Carol Codd ; illustrated by Michael Codd. — London : Robson Books, 1976. — [32]p : ill(chiefly col) ; 24cm.
ISBN 0-903895-96-x : £1.95
(B77-03244)

Cole, Babette. Promise solves the problem / [by] Babette Cole ; bubble calligraphy by Monica Gripaios. — London : Kaye and Ward, 1977. — [26]p : chiefly col ill ; 28cm. — (Cole, Babette. Amazing adventures of Promise)
Col. ill. on lining papers.
ISBN 0-7182-1163-4 : £2.50
(B77-23770)

Cole, Michael, *b.1933.* Bod and breakfast / [by] Michael and Joanne Cole. — London : Methuen, 1977. — [32]p : chiefly col ill ; 13x14cm.
ISBN 0-416-56110-1 Sd : £0.35
(B77-14434)

Cole, Michael, *b.1933.* Bod and the cake / [by] Michael and Joanne Cole. — London : Methuen, 1977. — [32]p : chiefly col ill ; 13x14cm.
ISBN 0-416-56130-6 Sd : £0.35
(B77-14435)

Cole, Michael, *b.1933.* Bod and the dog / [by] Michael and Joanne Cole. — London : Methuen, 1977. — [32]p : chiefly col ill ; 13x14cm.
ISBN 0-416-56140-3 Sd : £0.35
(B77-14436)

Cole, Michael, *b.1933.* Bod and the grasshopper / [by] Michael and Joanne Cole. — London : Methuen, 1977. — [32]p : chiefly col ill ; 13x14cm.
ISBN 0-416-81070-5 Sd : £0.35
(B77-14437)

Cole, Michael, *b.1933.* Bod and the kite / [by] Michael and Joanne Cole. — London : Methuen, 1977. — [32]p : chiefly col ill ; 13x14cm.
ISBN 0-416-81080-2 Sd : £0.35
(B77-14438)

Cole, Michael, *b.1933.* Bod on the beach / [by] Michael and Joanne Cole. — London : Methuen, 1977. — [32]p : chiefly col ill ; 13x14cm.
ISBN 0-416-56120-9 Sd : £0.35
(B77-14439)

Cole, Michael, *b.1933.* A lot of Bod : six complete stories about Bod and his friends / [by] Michael and Joanne Cole. — London : Methuen, 1977. — [194]p : chiefly col ill ; 14x15cm.
Contents: Bod and breakfast - Bod on the beach - Bod and the cake - Bod and the dog - Bod and the grasshopper - Bod and the kite.
ISBN 0-416-58790-9 : £1.95
(B77-28218)

Cole, Tamasin. Magnum Mouse / [pictures by] Tamasin Cole ; story by James Cressey. — London : A. and C. Black, 1977. — [42]p : chiefly col ill ; 16cm.
ISBN 0-7136-1714-4 : £0.95
ISBN 0-7136-1735-7 Schools pack : £3.00
(B77-20714)

Cole, Tamasin. Palava parrot / [pictures by] Tamasin Cole ; story by James Cressey. — London : A. and C. Black, 1977. — [42]p : chiefly col ill ; 16cm.
ISBN 0-7136-1715-2 : £0.95
ISBN 0-7136-1735-7 Schools pack : £3.00
(B77-20715)

Cole, Tasmin. The dragon and George / [pictures by] Tasmin Cole ; story by James Cressey. — London : A. and C. Black, 1977. — [26]p : chiefly col ill ; 27cm.
ISBN 0-7136-1760-8 : £2.50
(B77-34220)

Coleman, Leslie. Fort Wilberforce / [by] Leslie Coleman ; illustrated by John Laing. — Glasgow [etc.] : Blackie, 1977. — 3-90p : ill ; 24cm.
ISBN 0-216-90215-0 : £2.95
(B77-11436)

Coleman, Leslie. Wilberforce and the blue cave / [by] Leslie Coleman ; illustrations by John Laing. — London [etc.] : Beaver Books, 1977. — 95p : ill ; 20cm.
Originally published: Glasgow : Blackie, 1974.
ISBN 0-600-39386-0 Pbk : £0.45
(B77-26608)

Coleman, Leslie. Wilberforce the whale / [by] Leslie Coleman. — London [etc.] : Beaver Books, 1976. — 94p : ill ; 20cm.
Originally published: Glasgow : Blackie, 1973.
ISBN 0-600-39370-4 Pbk : £0.45
(B77-12739)

Coleman, Olive K. The pixie who got lost and Marian's dream / [by] Olive K. Coleman ; illustrated by Cora E.M. Paterson. — Ilfracombe : Stockwell, 1977. — 48p : ill ; 18cm.
ISBN 0-7223-1081-1 Pbk : £0.50
(B77-34221)

Collin, Paul Ries. Calling Bridge / [by] Paul Ries Collin ; illustrated by Harold Jones. — London : Oxford University Press, 1976. — [7], 86p : ill ; 23cm.
ISBN 0-19-271395-7 : £2.95
(B77-01003)

Cookson, Catherine. Go tell it to Mrs Golightly / [by] Catherine Cookson ; illustrated by Margery Gill. — London : Macdonald and Jane's, 1977. — [5],149p ; 21cm.
ISBN 0-354-08029-6 : £2.75
(B77-22931)

Coombs, Patricia. Dorrie and the amazing magic elixir / [written and illustrated by] Patricia Coombs. — Tadworth : World's Work, 1977. — [48]p : ill(some col) ; 26cm.
Originally published: New York : Lothrop, Lee and Shepard, 1974.
ISBN 0-437-32798-1 : £2.60
(B77-32893)

Coombs, Patricia. Dorrie and the witch doctor / by Patricia Coombs. — Tadworth : World's Work, 1977. — [48]p : chiefly ill(some col) ; 26cm.
Originally published: New York : Lothrop, Lee and Shepard, 1967.
ISBN 0-437-32793-0 : £2.50
(B77-08631)

Coombs, Patricia. Dorrie and the witch's imp / by Patricia Coombs. — Tadworth : World's Work, 1977. — [47]p : ill(some col) ; 26cm.
Originally published: New York : Lothrop, Lee and Shepard, 1975.
ISBN 0-437-32795-7 : £2.60
(B77-17138)

Coombs, Patricia. Dorrie's magic / written and illustrated by Patricia Coombs. — Tadworth : World's Work, 1977. — 48p : ill(some col) ; 26cm.
Originally published: New York : Lothrop, Lee and Shepard, 1962.
ISBN 0-437-32797-3 : £2.50
(B77-32894)

Coombs, Patricia. Dorrie's play / written and illustrated by Patricia Coombs. — Tadworth : World's Work, 1976. — [48]p : chiefly ill(some col) ; 26cm.
Originally published: New York : Lothrop, Lee and Shepard, 1965.
ISBN 0-437-32796-5 : £2.40
(B77-08632)

Coombs, Patricia. Molly Mullett / by Patricia Coombs. — Tadworth : World's Work, 1977. — [38]p : col ill ; 26cm.
Originally published: New York : Lothrop, Lee and Shepard, 1975.
ISBN 0-437-32794-9 : £2.50
(B77-22206)

Cooper, Lettice. Parkin / [by] Lettice Cooper ; illustrated by Rosie Evans. — London : Harrap, 1977. — [42]p : ill(chiefly col) ; 19cm. — (Reading with mother)
ISBN 0-245-53174-2 : £0.95
(B77-26609)

Cooper, Susan. Greenwitch / [by] Susan Cooper. — Harmondsworth [etc.] : Puffin Books, 1977. — 153,[1]p ; 18cm. — (Puffin books)
Originally published: London : Chatto and Windus, 1974.
ISBN 0-14-030901-2 Pbk : £0.50
(B77-08121)

Cooper, Susan. The grey king / [by] Susan Cooper. — Harmondsworth [etc.] : Puffin Books, 1977. — 190p ; 19cm. — (Puffin books)
Originally published: London : Chatto and Windus, 1975.
ISBN 0-14-030952-7 Pbk : £0.50
(B77-22932)

Cope, Kenneth. Striker, second leg / [by] Kenneth Cope. — London : British Broadcasting Corporation, 1977. — 96p ; 20cm.
ISBN 0-563-17288-6 Pbk : £0.60
(B77-19818)

'**Cor!!**' comic annual. — London : IPC Magazines.
1978. — [1977]. — 143p : chiefly ill(some col) ; 28cm. — (A Fleetway annual)
Cover title.
ISBN 0-85037-326-3 : £1.00
(B77-32895)

Coudrille, Jonathon. Farmer Fisher's ... [R]ussian Christmas / words, pictures and music by Jonathon Coudrille. — London : G. Whizzard : Deutsch, 1976. — [36]p : chiefly col ill ; 20x30cm & phonodisc (2s. 18cm. 45 r.p.m).
ISBN 0-233-96774-5 Sd : £2.25
(B77-15565)

Cox-Chapman, Mally. Baggywrinkle / [by] Mally Cox-Chapman ; illustrated by Peter Wingham. — London : Heinemann, 1977. — [8],143p : ill ; 21cm.
ISBN 0-434-93171-3 : £2.90
(B77-25946)

Cresswell, Helen. Donkey days / by Helen Cresswell ; illustrated by Shirley Hughes. — London [etc.] : E. Benn, 1977. — 28p : col ill ; 21cm. — (Beginning to read books)
ISBN 0-510-08505-9 : £1.25
ISBN 0-510-08506-7 Pbk : £0.95
(B77-21529)

Cresswell, Helen. Ordinary Jack / [by] Helen Cresswell ; illustrated by Jill Bennett. — London : Faber, 1977. — 3-191p : ill ; 21cm. — (Cresswell, Helen. Bagthorpe saga)
ISBN 0-571-11114-9 : £3.25 : CIP rev.
(B77-19819)

Cresswell, Helen. Two Hoots and the King / by Helen Cresswell ; illustrated by Martine Blanc. — London [etc.] : E. Benn, 1977. — 28p : col ill ; 18cm. — (First steps in reading)
ISBN 0-510-11800-3 : £0.95
(B77-17139)

Cresswell, Helen. Two Hoots play hide and seek / by Helen Cresswell ; illustrated by Martine Blanc. — London [etc.] : E. Benn, 1977. — 28p : col ill ; 18cm. — (First steps in reading)
ISBN 0-510-11803-8 : £0.95
(B77-17140)

Cresswell, Helen. Up the pier / [by] Helen Cresswell ; illustrated by Gareth Floyd. — Harmondsworth [etc.] : Puffin Books, 1977. — 141p : ill ; 18cm. — (Puffin books)
Originally published: London : Faber, 1971.
ISBN 0-14-030971-3 Pbk : £0.45
(B77-24542)

Crompton, Richmal. Just William, and other stories / [by] Richmal Crompton. — London [etc.] : Collins, 1977. — 3-310p ; 21cm.
This collection originally published: in 2 vols as 'Just William', London : Newnes, 1922 ; and 'William's bad resolution', London : Newnes, 1956.
ISBN 0-00-162014-2 : £2.95
(B77-16619)

Crompton, Richmal. Sweet William / [by] Richmal Crompton ; illustrated by Thomas Henry. — London : Armada, 1977. — 126p : ill ; 19cm.
Originally published: London : Newnes, 1936.
ISBN 0-00-691296-6 Pbk : £0.45
(B77-16620)

Crompton, Richmal. William - the bold / [by] Richmal Crompton ; illustrated by Thomas Henry. — Abridged ed. — London : Armada Books, 1977. — 159p : ill ; 18cm.
This ed. originally published: London : Newnes, 1963.
ISBN 0-00-691015-7 Pbk : £0.45
(B77-10603)

Crompton, Richmal. William - the rebel / [by] Richmal Crompton ; illustrated by Thomas Henry. — Abridged ed. — London : Armada, 1977. — 156p : ill ; 19cm.
This ed. originally published: London : Newnes, 1966.
ISBN 0-00-691391-1 Pbk : £0.45
(B77-29746)

Crompton, Richmal. William again / [by] Richmal Crompton ; illustrated by Thomas Henry. — Abridged ed. — London : Armada, 1977. — 159p : ill ; 18cm.
This ed. originally published: London : Newnes, 1967.
ISBN 0-00-691392-x Pbk : £0.45
(B77-29747)

Crompton, Richmal. William carries on / [by] Richmal Crompton ; illustrated by Thomas Henry. — Abridged ed. — London : Armada, 1977. — 128p : ill ; 19cm.
This ed. originally published: London : Newnes, 1963.
ISBN 0-00-691329-6 Pbk : £0.45
(B77-16621)

Crompton, Richmal. William, the gangster / [by] Richmal Crompton. — [1st ed. reprinted] ; with new illustrations by Patrick Gavin, in the style of Thomas Henry. — London : Armada, 1977. — 127p : ill ; 18cm.
Originally published: London : Newnes, 1934.
ISBN 0-00-691331-8 Pbk : £0.45
(B77-16622)

Crompton, Richmal. William, the outlaw / [by] Richmal Crompton ; illustrated by Thomas Henry. — Abridged ed. — London : Armada, 1977. — 159p : ill ; 18cm.
This ed. originally published: London : Newnes, 1963.
ISBN 0-00-691330-x Pbk : £0.45
(B77-16623)

Crompton, Richmal. William's happy days / [by] Richmal Crompton ; illustrated by Thomas Henry. — Abridged ed. — London : Armada Books, 1977. — 157p : ill ; 18cm.
This ed. originally published: London : Newnes, 1964.
ISBN 0-00-691292-3 Pbk : £0.45
(B77-10604)

Cumberlege, Vera Gladys. Trapped by the tide, and other stories / [by] Vera Cumberlege ; illustrated by Gavin Rowe. — London : Deutsch, 1977. — 112p : ill ; 21cm.
Includes: 'Shipwreck'. Originally published: 1972.
ISBN 0-233-96899-7 : £2.95
(B77-26610)

Cunliffe, John. Farmer Barnes fells a tree / story by John Cunliffe ; pictures by Joan Hickson. — London : Deutsch, 1977. — [32]p : ill(some col) ; 26cm.
ISBN 0-233-96852-0 : £2.25
(B77-09988)

Cunliffe, John. Giant Kippernose and other stories / [by] John Cunliffe ; illustrated by Fritz Wegner. — London : Pan Books, 1977. — 111p : ill ; 18cm. — (Piccolo)
This collection originally published: London : Deutsch, 1972.
ISBN 0-330-25038-8 Pbk : £0.45
(B77-09989)

Cunliffe, John. The great dragon competition and other stories / [by] John Cunliffe ; illustrated by Alexy Pendle. — London : Pan Books, 1977. — 120p : ill ; 18cm. — (Piccolo)
This collection originally published: London : Deutsch, 1973.
ISBN 0-330-25039-6 Pbk : £0.45
(B77-09990)

Cunliffe, John. Small Monkey tales / [by] John Cunliffe ; illustrated by Gerry Downes. — Harmondsworth [etc.] : Puffin Books, 1977. — 72,[1]p : ill ; 20cm. — (A young puffin)
Originally published: London : Deutsch, 1974.
ISBN 0-14-030982-9 Pbk : £0.50
(B77-33464)

Curry, Jane Louise. Poor Tom's ghost / [by] Jane Curry. — Harmondsworth : Kestrel Books, 1977. — [6],178p : 2 ill, plan ; 23cm.
Originally published: New York : Atheneum, 1977.
ISBN 0-7226-5306-9 : £3.25
(B77-26611)

Cutler, Ivor. The animal house / story by Ivor Cutler ; pictures by Helen Oxenbury. — London : Heinemann, 1976. — [32]p : col ill ; 26cm.
Col. ill. on lining papers.
ISBN 0-434-93353-8 : £2.50
(B77-01004)

Cutler, Ivor. Meal one / [by] Ivor Cutler ; pictures by Helen Oxenbury. — London : Pan Books, 1976. — [32]p : col ill ; 22cm. — (Piccolo picture books)
Originally published: London : Heinemann, 1971.
ISBN 0-330-24752-2 Sd : £0.50
(B77-01005)

Dahl, Norman. Oscar / [by] Norman Dahl ; illustrated by Mary Edwards. — London : Harrap, 1977. — [42]p : ill(some col) ; 19cm. — (Reading with mother)
£0.95
(B77-26612)

Dahl, Roald. Danny the champion of the world / [by] Roald Dahl ; illustrated by Jill Bennett. — Harmondsworth [etc.] : Puffin Books, 1977. — 175p : ill ; 20cm. — (Puffin books)
Originally published: London : Cape, 1975.
ISBN 0-14-030912-8 Pbk : £0.50
(B77-14976)

Dahl, Roald. The wonderful story of Henry Sugar and six more / [by] Roald Dahl. — London : Cape, 1977. — 249p : ill ; 25cm.
ISBN 0-224-01547-8 : £3.50 : CIP rev.
(B77-20716)

'The **Dandy**' book. — London : D.C. Thomson. [1978]. — 1977. — [135]p : chiefly col ill ; 28cm.
Col.ill., text on lining papers.
£1.00
(B77-31545)

Darke, Marjorie. My uncle Charlie / by Marjorie Darke ; with pictures by Jannat Houston. — Harmondsworth : Kestrel Books, 1977. — 26p : col ill ; 21cm. — (A minnow book)
Also published: Harmondsworth : Puffin Books, 1977.
ISBN 0-7226-5272-0 : £1.30
(B77-22933)

Darke, Marjorie. The star trap / [by] Marjorie Darke ; decorations by Michael Jackson. — London : Collins, 1976. — 189p : ill ; 18cm. — (Lions)
Originally published: Harmondsworth : Longman Young Books, 1974.
ISBN 0-00-671109-x Pbk : £0.50
(B77-06913)

Davies, Evelyn, *b.1920.* Joseph's bear / [by] Evelyn Davies ; illustrated by Jane Paton. — Harmondsworth [etc.] : Puffin Books, 1977. — 76p : ill ; 20cm. — (A young puffin)
Originally published: London : Hamilton, 1975.
ISBN 0-14-030979-9 Pbk : £0.50
(B77-29748)

Davies, Evelyn, *b.1920.* The little foxes / [by] Evelyn Davies ; illustrated by Jane Paton. — London : Hamilton, 1977. — 88p : ill ; 19cm. — (Antelope books)
ISBN 0-241-89749-1 : £1.25
(B77-30756)

Davis, Daphne. Walt Disney's the Donald Duck book / by Daphne Davis ; illustrated by Hawley Pratt and Al White. — Maidenhead : Purnell, 1977. — [16]p : chiefly col ill ; 21cm. — (A Purnell shape book)
Originally published: United States? : s.n., 1971.
Sd : Unpriced
(B77-07663)

De Bono, Edward. The case of the disappearing elephant : a 3G mystery / [by] Edward de Bono ; illustrated by George Craig. — London [etc.] : Dent, 1977. — 109p : ill ; 20cm.
ISBN 0-460-06797-4 : £3.50 : CIP rev.
(B77-22934)

De Hamel, Joan. X marks the spot / [by] Joan de Hamel. — Harmondsworth [etc.] : Puffin Books, 1976. — 171p : ill, map ; 19cm. — (Puffin books)
Originally published: Guildford : Lutterworth Press, 1973.
ISBN 0-14-030864-4 Pbk : £0.50
(B77-12740)

De la Mare, Walter. Collected stories for children / [by] Walter de la Mare ; illustrated by Robin Jacques. — Harmondsworth [etc.] : Puffin Books, 1977. — 476p : ill ; 19cm. — (Puffin books)
In slip-case. — This collection originally published: London : Faber, 1947.
ISBN 0-14-030934-9 Pbk : £1.50
(B77-27463)

De Roo, Anne. Mick's country cousins / [by] Anne de Roo ; cover illustration by Tina Murray. — London : Pan Books, 1977. — 157p ; 18cm. — (Piccolo)
Originally published: London : Macmillan, 1974.
ISBN 0-330-25151-1 Pbk : £0.50
(B77-26613)

De Roo, Anne. Scrub fire / [by] Anne de Roo. — London : Heinemann, 1977. — v,106p ; 23cm.
ISBN 0-434-96100-0 : £2.90
(B77-31546)

DeJong, Meindert. The almost all-white rabbity cat / [by] Meindert DeJong ; illustrated by Gioia Fiammenghi. — Harmondsworth : Puffin Books, 1977. — 96p : ill ; 18cm. — (Puffin books)
Originally published: Guildford : Lutterworth Press, 1972.
ISBN 0-14-030674-9 Pbk : £0.45
(B77-08122)

Delgado, Alan. The very hot water-bottle / [by] Alan Delgado ; illustrated by Edward Lewis. — London [etc.] : Hodder and Stoughton, 1977. — 119p : ill ; 19cm.
Originally published: Leicester : Brockhampton Press, 1962.
ISBN 0-340-21580-1 : £2.00
(B77-06914)

Denison, Mary. Ballet in Romilly Street / [by] Mary Denison. — London : Dobson, 1977. — 144p ; 21cm.
ISBN 0-234-77325-1 : £2.75
(B77-23771)

Dennis, Wesley. Flip / story and pictures by Wesley Dennis. — Harmondsworth [etc.] : Puffin Books, 1977. — [64]p : chiefly ill ; 23cm. — (Picture puffin)
Originally published: New York : Viking Press, 1941.
ISBN 0-14-050203-3 Pbk : Unpriced
(B77-33465)

Dennis, Wesley. Flip and the morning / story and pictures by Wesley Dennis. — Harmondsworth [etc.] : Puffin Books, 1977. — [63]p : chiefly ill ; 23cm. — (Picture puffin)
Originally published: New York : Viking Press, 1951.
ISBN 0-14-050204-1 Pbk : Unpriced
(B77-33466)

Dennis the Menace. — London : D.C. Thomson.
1978. — 1977. — [90]p : chiefly col ill ; 28cm.
Col. ill on lining papers.
£0.80
(B77-31547)

Derwent, Lavinia. The boy from Sula / [by] Lavinia Derwent ; cover illustration by Prudence Seward ; text illustrations by Felicity Lowe. — London : Pan Books, 1977. — 143p : ill ; 18cm. — ([Piccolo books])
Originally published: London : Gollancz, 1973.
ISBN 0-330-24888-x Pbk : £0.45
(B77-07664)

Derwent, Lavinia. Macpherson's lighthouse adventure / [by] Lavinia Derwent ; illustrated by Leslie Smith. — Glasgow [etc.] : Blackie, 1977. — 128p : ill ; 21cm.
ISBN 0-216-90154-5 : £2.95
(B77-22207)

Derwent, Lavinia. Song of Sula / [by] Lavinia Derwent ; text and cover illustrations by Prudence Seward. — London : Pan Books, 1977. — 127p : ill ; 18cm. — (Piccolo)
Originally published: London : Gollancz, 1976.
ISBN 0-330-25203-8 Pbk : £0.50
(B77-28990)

Devine, Pauline. King Longbeard : a fairy story / by Pauline Devine ; illustrations by Pat Walsh. — Dublin (11 Clare St., Dublin 2) : O'Brien Press Ltd, 1977. — [31]p : ill(chiefly col) ; 21x22cm.
Ill. on lining papers.
ISBN 0-905140-10-9 : £2.70
(B77-34222)

Diana for girls. — Dundee [etc.] : D.C. Thomson.
[1978]. — 1977. — [122]p : chiefly ill(chiefly col), ports(chiefly col) ; 28cm.
Col. ill., text on lining papers.
£1.00
(B77-31548)

Dickens, Monica. The horses of Follyfoot / [by] Monica Dickens. — London : Pan Books, 1977. — 142p ; 20cm. — (Piccolo books)
'The latest Follyfoot adventure based on the Yorkshire Television series' - cover. — Originally published: London : Heinemann, 1975.
ISBN 0-330-25216-x Pbk : £0.50
(B77-31549)

Dickinson, Peter. Annerton pit / Peter Dickinson. — London : Gollancz, 1977. — 175p ; 21cm.
ISBN 0-575-02239-6 : £3.25
(B77-13379)

Dickinson, Peter. The dancing bear / [by] Peter Dickinson ; illustrated by David Smee. — Harmondsworth [etc.] : Puffin Books, 1977. — 239p : ill, map ; 19cm. — (Puffin books)
Originally published: London : Gollancz, 1972.
Pbk : £0.55
ISBN 0-14-030678-1
(B77-21530)

Dicks, Terrance. Doctor Who and the claws of Axos / [by] Terrance Dicks. — London : Wingate, 1977. — 141p ; 21cm. — (A longbow book)
'Based on the BBC television serial "The claws of Axos" by Bob Baker and Dave Martin ...'.
ISBN 0-85523-181-5 : £2.50
(B77-17781)

Dicks, Terrance. Doctor Who and the Dalek invasion of earth ... / [by] Terrance Dicks. — London : Wingate, 1977. — 142p ; 21cm. — (A Longbow book)
'Based on the BBC television serial "Doctor Who and the World's End" by Terry Nation ...'.
ISBN 0-85523-171-8 : £2.50
(B77-14440)

Dicks, Terrance. Doctor Who and the Mutants / [by] Terrance Dicks. — London : Target Books, 1977. — 127p ; 18cm.
'Based on the BBC television serial "The Mutants" by Bob Baker and Dave Martin ...'. — Also published: London : Wingate, 1977.
ISBN 0-426-11690-9 Pbk : £0.60
(B77-22935)

Dicks, Terrance. Doctor Who and the planet of evil / [by] Terrance Dicks. — London : Target Books, 1977. — 126p ; 19cm.
'Based on the BBC television serial "The planet of evil" by Louis Marks ...'.
ISBN 0-426-11682-8 Pbk : £0.60
(B77-22208)

Dicks, Terrance. Doctor Who and the planet of evil / [by] Terrance Dicks. — London : Wingate, 1977. — 126p ; 21cm. — (A longbow book)
'Based on the BBC television serial "The planet of evil" by Louis Marks ...'.
ISBN 0-85523-231-5 : £2.95
(B77-22209)

Dicks, Terrance. Doctor Who and the pyramids of Mars / [by] Terrance Dicks. — London : Wingate, 1977. — 125p ; 21cm.
'Based on the BBC television serial "Pyramids of Mars" by Stephen Harris ...'.
ISBN 0-85523-141-6 : £2.50
(B77-06915)

Dillon, Eilís. A family of foxes / [by] Eilís Dillon ; illustrated by Richard Kennedy. — Harmondsworth [etc.] : Puffin Books, 1977. — 124,[1]p : ill ; 19cm. — (Puffin books)
Originally published: London : Faber, 1964.
ISBN 0-14-030949-7 Pbk : £0.40
(B77-27464)

Dillon, Eilís. The house on the shore / [by] Eilís Dillon ; illustrated by Peter Archer. — London [etc.] : Beaver Books, 1977. — 189p : ill ; 18cm.
Originally published: / illustrated by Richard Kennedy. London : Faber, 1955.
ISBN 0-600-34540-8 Pbk : £0.50
(B77-22936)

Dillon, Eilís. The king's room / [by] Eilís Dillon ; illustrated by Richard Kennedy. — London : Hamilton, 1977. — 120p : ill ; 23cm.
Originally published: 1970.
ISBN 0-241-89666-5 : £1.95
(B77-19820)

Dillon, Eilís. The lost island / [by] Eilís Dillon. — London [etc.] : Beaver Books, 1976. — 188p ; 20cm.
Originally published: London : Faber, 1952.
ISBN 0-600-35517-9 Pbk : £0.60
(B77-12741)

Disney, Walt. Walt Disney's Bambi and Thumper. — Maidenhead : Purnell, 1977. — [8]p : chiefly col ill ; 19cm.
ISBN 0-361-03834-8 Pbd : Unpriced
(B77-27465)

Disney time annual. — London : IPC Magazines.
1978. — 1977. — 3-79p : ill(chiefly col) ; 28cm. — (A Fleetway annual)
Cover title: Walt Disney's Disney time annual.
ISBN 0-85037-329-8 : £1.45
ISSN 0140-7171
(B77-33467)

Disneyland annual. — London : IPC Magazines.
1978. — [1977]. — 71p : ill(chiefly col) ; 31cm. — (A Fleetway annual)
Cover title.
ISBN 0-85037-328-x : £1.45
(B77-32896)

Dixon, Franklin W. The clue of the broken blade / by Franklin W. Dixon. — London [etc.] : Collins, 1977. — 157p : 1 ill ; 19cm. — (Dixon, Franklin W. Hardy boys mystery stories ; 37)
Originally published: New York : Grosset and Dunlap, 1942 ; London : Sampson Low, 1953.
ISBN 0-00-160538-0 : £1.25
(B77-33468)

Dixon, Franklin W. The crisscross shadow / [by] Franklin W. Dixon. — London : Armada Books, 1976. — 156p : 1 ill ; 18cm. — (Dixon, Franklin W. Hardy boys mystery stories ; 23)
Originally published: New York : Grosset and Dunlap, 1953 ; London : Sampson Low, Marston, 1965.
ISBN 0-00-691145-5 Pbk : £0.40
(B77-00467)

Dixon, Franklin W. Danger on Vampire Trail / by Franklin W. Dixon. — London [etc.] : Collins, 1977. — 158p : 1 ill ; 19cm. — (Dixon, Franklin W. Hardy boys mystery stories ; 42)
Originally published: New York : Grosset and Dunlap, 1971.
ISBN 0-00-160543-7 : £1.25
(B77-33469)

Dixon, Franklin W. Footprints under the window / [by] Franklin W. Dixon. — London : Armada Books, 1976. — 157p : 1 ill ; 18cm. — (Dixon, Franklin W. Hardy boys mystery stories ; 24)
Originally published: New York : Grosset and Dunlap, 1933 ; Newcastle upon Tyne : H. Hill, 1957.
ISBN 0-00-691144-7 Pbk : £0.40
(B77-00468)

Dixon, Franklin W. The mark on the door / [by] Franklin W. Dixon. — London : Armada, 1977. — 160p : ill ; 18cm. — (Dixon, Franklin W. Hardy boys mystery stories ; 27)
Originally published: New York : Grosset and Dunlap, 1934 ; Newcastle upon Tyne : H. Hill, 1957.
ISBN 0-00-691297-4 Pbk : £0.40
(B77-13380)

Dixon, Franklin W. The mysterious caravan / by Franklin W. Dixon. — London [etc.] : Collins, 1977. — 160p : 1 ill ; 19cm. — (Dixon, Franklin W. Hardy boys mystery stories ; 41)
Originally published: New York : Grosset and Dunlap, 1975.
ISBN 0-00-160542-9 : £1.25
(B77-33470)

Dixon, Franklin W. The secret of Skull Mountain / by Franklin W. Dixon. — London [etc.] : Collins, 1977. — 157p : 1 ill ; 19cm. — (Dixon, Franklin W. Hardy boys mystery stories ; 40)
Originally published: New York : Grosset and Dunlap, 1948 ; London : Sampson Low, 1966.
ISBN 0-00-160541-0 : £1.25
(B77-33471)

Dixon, Franklin W. The secret of Wildcat Swamp / by Franklin W. Dixon. — London [etc.] : Collins, 1977. — 160p : 1 ill ; 19cm. — (Dixon, Franklin W. Hardy boys mystery stories ; 38)
Originally published: New York : Grosset and Dunlap, 1952 ; London : Sampson Low, 1966.
ISBN 0-00-160539-9 : £1.25
(B77-33472)

Dixon, Franklin W. The yellow feather mystery / [by] Franklin W. Dixon. — London : Armada, 1977. — 159p : 1 ill ; 18cm. — (Dixon, Franklin W. Hardy boys mystery stories ; 28)
Originally published: New York : Grosset and Dunlap, 1953 ; London : Low, Marston, 1965.
ISBN 0-00-691298-2 Pbk : £0.40
(B77-13381)

Dobson, Julia. The smallest man in England / [by] Julia Dobson ; illustrated by Joanna Troughton. — London : Heinemann, 1977. — 43,[1]p : ill ; 21cm. — (Long ago children books)
Based on the life of Jeffrey Hudson.
ISBN 0-434-94921-3 : £1.90
(B77-05727)

Donald and his guard dog. — Maidenhead : Purnell, 1974. — [16]p : col ill ; 12cm. — ([Minikins])
Sd : £0.06
(B77-19821)

Donnison, Polly. More stories of William the dragon / [by] Polly Donnison. — London [etc.] : Pan Books, 1977. — [1],24p : col ill ; 16x22cm. — (Piccolo picture books)
These stories originally published: in 'William the dragon'. London : Sidgwick and Jackson, 1972.
ISBN 0-330-25220-8 Sd : £0.50
(B77-13927)

Donnison, Polly. Stories of William the dragon / [by] Polly Donnison. — London [etc.] : Pan Books, 1977. — [1],24p : ill(chiefly col) ; 16x22cm. — (Piccolo picture books)
These stories originally published: in 'William the dragon'. London : Sidgwick and Jackson, 1972.
ISBN 0-330-25219-4 Sd : £0.50
(B77-13928)

Dove, Anthea. At home for Christmas / by Anthea Dove. — London : Catholic Truth Society, [1977]. — [15]p : col ill ; 19cm.
Sd : Unpriced
(B77-24543)

Drake, Joan. Mr Bubbus and the apple-green engine / [by] Joan Drake ; illustrated by Val Biro. — London [etc.] : Beaver Books, 1977. — 3-77p : ill ; 20cm.
Originally published: Leicester : Brockhampton Press, 1971.
ISBN 0-600-36275-2 Pbk : £0.45
(B77-32262)

Drake, Joan. Mr Grimpwinkle buys a bus / [by] Joan Drake ; drawings by Gordon Burrell. — London [etc.] : Hodder and Stoughton, 1977. — 88p : ill ; 20cm.
Originally published: Leicester : Brockhampton Press, 1961.
£2.20
ISBN 0-340-17176-6
(B77-28991)

Drew, Patricia. Caramelia / written and illustrated by Patricia Drew. — London [etc.] : E.Benn, 1977. — 28p : chiefly col ill ; 21cm. — (Beginning to read books)
ISBN 0-510-08507-5 : £1.25
ISBN 0-510-08508-3 Pbk : £0.95
(B77-21531)

Duncan, Ronald. Mr and Mrs Mouse / by Ronald Duncan ; drawings by Rose Marie Duncan. — Welcombe (Welcombe, Bideford, Devon) : Rebel Press, 1977. — 16p,plate : ill(incl 1 col) ; 20cm.
Unpriced
(B77-32897)

Durrell, Gerald. The donkey rustlers / [by] Gerald Durrell ; illustrated by Anne Mieke van Ogtrop. — [London] : Fontana, 1977. — 125p : ill ; 18cm. — (Lions)
Originally published: London : Collins, 1968.
ISBN 0-00-671360-2 Pbk : £0.50
(B77-27466)

Durrell, Gerald. The talking parcel / [by] Gerald Durrell. — London : Collins, 1976. — 190p ; 18cm. — (Lions)
Originally published: 1974.
ISBN 0-00-671218-5 Pbk : £0.50
(B77-01849)

Duvoisin, Roger. Crocus / [by] Roger Duvoisin. — London [etc.] : Bodley Head, 1977. — 2-32p : chiefly col ill ; 26cm.
ISBN 0-370-30001-7 : £2.85
(B77-30757)

Duvoisin, Roger. Petunia's treasure / [by] Roger Duvoisin. — London [etc.] : Bodley Head, 1977. — [32]p : chiefly col ill ; 26cm.
Originally published: New York : Knopf, 1975.
ISBN 0-370-01812-5 : £2.50
(B77-06916)

Eadington, Joan. Jonny Briggs / [by] Joan Eadington ; as told in 'Jackanory' by Bernard Holley ; illustrated by William Marshall. — London : British Broadcasting Corporation, 1977. — 80p : ill ; 20cm.
ISBN 0-563-17268-1 Pbk : £0.60
(B77-13382)

Earnshaw, Brian. Dragonfall 5 and the super horse / [by] Brian Earnshaw ; illustrated by Simon Stern. — London : Methuen, 1977. — [5],148p : ill ; 20cm. — (A Pied Piper book)
ISBN 0-416-56520-4 : £2.25
(B77-28219)

Eden, Terry. Animal Kwackers Popland story book / written & illustrated by Terry Eden. — Esher (Royal Mills, Esher, Surrey) : Redwood International : Bookmark Ltd, 1977. — 3-61p : col ill ; 31cm.
ISBN 0-86102-000-6 : Unpriced
(B77-33473)

Edwards, Dorothy. My Naughty Little Sister and Bad Harry / [by] Dorothy Edwards ; illustrated by Shirley Hughes. — Harmondsworth [etc.] : Puffin Books, 1976. — 79p : ill ; 20cm. — (A young puffin)
Originally published: London : Methuen, 1974.
ISBN 0-14-030878-4 Pbk : £0.40
(B77-01850)

Edwards, Dorothy. My naughty little sister and Bad Harry's rabbit / [by] Dorothy Edwards & Shirley Hughes. — London : Methuen, 1977. — [24]p : ill(chiefly col) ; 22cm.
ISBN 0-416-56410-0 : £1.95
(B77-30758)

Edwards, Hazel. General store / [by] Hazel Edwards. — Sydney ; London [etc.] : Hodder and Stoughton, 1977. — [5],131p ; 22cm.
ISBN 0-340-21917-3 : £3.60
(B77-21532)

Edwards, Hugh. Sea Lion Island / by Hugh Edwards ; illustrations by John Richards. — London [etc.] : Angus and Robertson, 1977. — [5],79p : ill ; 24cm. — (Edwards, Hugh. Sea Witch series)
ISBN 0-207-13340-9 : £3.20
(B77-28992)

Edwards, John Emlyn. The adventures of Little Mookra / [by] John Emlyn Edwards ; illustrated by Keith Waite. — London : Methuen, 1977. — 3-93p : ill, music ; 21cm. — ([A read aloud book])
ISBN 0-416-86150-4 : £2.35
(B77-29749)

Edwards, John Emlyn. Yard-arm for a gallows / [by] John E. Edwards ; with drawings by B.S. Biro. — London : Dent, 1977. — 3-176p : ill ; 18cm. — (Dent dolphins)
Originally published: 1966.
ISBN 0-460-02745-x Pbk : £0.60
(B77-25947)

Edwards, Lynne. The dodo is a solitary bird / [by] Lynne and Brian Edwards. — Tadworth : World's Work, 1977. — [40]p : chiefly col ill ; 24cm.
ISBN 0-437-36401-1 : £3.50
(B77-27467)

Elliot, Margaret. When the night crow flies / [by] Margaret Elliot ; illustrated by Colin Dunbar. — London : Abelard, 1977. — 125p : ill ; 21cm. — (A grasshopper book)
ISBN 0-200-72493-2 : £2.25
ISBN 0-200-72494-0 Pbk : £0.60
(B77-28993)

Elliott, Janice. The birthday unicorn / [by] Janice Elliott ; illustrated by Michael Foreman. — Harmondsworth [etc.] : Puffin Books, 1977. — 103p : ill ; 19cm. — (Puffin books)
Originally published: London : Gollancz, 1970. — Previous control number ISBN 0-14-030576-9.
Pbk : £0.45
ISBN 0-14-030576-9
(B77-25948)

Elson, Diane, *b.1953.* Cheryl the baby cheetah / by Diane Elson. — London [etc.] : Beaver Books, 1977. — [32]p : chiefly col ill ; 21cm.
'A junglies story' - cover.
ISBN 0-600-35251-x Sd : £0.40
(B77-34223)

Elson, Diane, *b.1953.* The junglies go to Australia / by Diane Elson. — London [etc.] : Beaver Books, 1977. — [32]p : col ill ; 21cm.
'A junglies story' - cover.
ISBN 0-600-35253-6 Sd : £0.40
(B77-34224)

Elson, Diane, *b.1953.* Olivia the ostrich has a special day / [by] Diane Elson. — London [etc.] : Beaver Books, 1977. — [32]p : chiefly col ill ; 21cm.
'A junglies story' - cover.
ISBN 0-600-35254-4 Sd : £0.40
(B77-34225)

Elson, Diane, *b.1953.* The short-sighted hippopotamus / by Diane Elson. — London [etc.] : Beaver Books, 1977. — [32]p : col ill ; 21cm.
'A junglies story' - cover.
ISBN 0-600-35252-8 Sd : £0.40
(B77-34226)

Emu stew : an illustrated collection of stories and poems for children / edited by Patricia Wrightson. — Harmondsworth [etc.] : Kestrel Books, 1976. — 256p : ill(some col) ; 23cm.
ISBN 0-7226-5169-4 : £3.95
(B77-08123)

Escott, John. A walk down the pier / [by] John Escott ; illustrated by Frances Phillips. — London : Hamilton, 1977. — 88p : ill ; 19cm. — (Antelope books)
ISBN 0-241-89361-5 : £1.25
(B77-06917)

Estes, Eleanor. The coat-hanger Christmas tree / [by] Eleanor Estes ; illustrated by Susanne Suba. — Oxford : Oxford University Press, 1976. — [6],77p : ill ; 21cm.
Originally published: New York : Atheneum, 1973.
ISBN 0-19-271396-5 : £2.50
(B77-05085)

Evans, Alan, *b.1930.* Running scared / [by] Alan Evans ; illustrated by Robert Geary. — London [etc.] : Beaver Books, 1977. — 95p : ill ; 18cm.
Originally published: Leicester : Brockhampton Press, 1975.
ISBN 0-600-37597-8 Pbk : £0.40
(B77-25231)

Exciting stories from the past / selected and edited by Leonard Matthews. — London [etc.] : Hamlyn, 1977. — 188p : ill ; 22cm. — (Hamlyn story library)
ISBN 0-600-35246-3 : £1.00
(B77-19030)

Fair, Sylvia. The ivory anvil / [by] Sylvia Fair. — Harmondsworth [etc.] : Puffin Books, 1977. — 140p,[1]p ; 19cm. — (Puffin books)
Originally published: London : Gollancz, 1974.
ISBN 0-14-030917-9 Pbk : £0.50
(B77-17782)

Fantastic adventure stories for boys / selected and edited by Leonard Matthews. — London [etc.] : Hamlyn, 1977. — 189p : ill ; 22cm. — (Hamlyn story library)
ISBN 0-600-35245-5 : £1.00
(B77-19031)

Fantasy tales / edited by Barbara Ireson. — London : Faber, 1977. — 3-218p ; 23cm.
ISBN 0-571-10922-5 : £3.50 : CIP rev.
(B77-19032)

Farjeon, Annabel. The cock of Round Hill / [by] Annabel Farjeon ; illustrated by Charlotte Firmin. — London : Kaye and Ward, 1977. — 85p : ill ; 20cm. — (Early bird series ; [no.33])
ISBN 0-7182-1027-1 : £1.50
(B77-15566)

Farmer, Penelope. The coal train / [by] Penelope Farmer ; illustrated by William Bird. — London : Heinemann, 1977. — 46p : ill ; 21cm. — (Long ago children books)
ISBN 0-434-94929-9 : £2.50
(B77-31550)

Farmer, Penelope. William and Mary / [by] Penelope Farmer ; cover illustration by Peter Richardson ; text illustrations by Nancy Petley-Jones. — London : Pan Books, 1977. — 156p : ill ; 18cm. — (Piccolo)
Originally published: London : Chatto and Windus, 1974.
ISBN 0-330-25100-7 Pbk : £0.50
(B77-20717)

Farrell, Anne. The gift-wrapped pony / [by] Anne Farrell. — London : Knight Books, 1977. — 158p ; 18cm.
Originally published: Sydney : Hodder and Stoughton, Australia ; Leicester : Brockhampton Press, 1974.
ISBN 0-340-21622-0 Pbk : £0.60
(B77-05728)

Farrell, Sally. Her kingdom for a pony / [by] Sally Farrell ; illustrated by Noela Young. — Sydney ; London [etc.] : Hodder and Stoughton, 1977. — 151p : ill ; 22cm.
ISBN 0-340-21424-4 : £3.60
(B77-19033)

Fatio, Louise. Marc and Pixie and the walls in Mrs Jones's garden / by Louise Fatio and Roger Duvoisin. — Sydney ; London [etc.] : Hodder and Stoughton, 1977. — [32]p : chiefly col ill ; 26x21cm.
Originally published: New York : McGraw-Hill, 1975.
ISBN 0-340-21961-0 : £2.80
(B77-20718)

Feil, Hila. The ghost garden / [by] Hila Feil. — London [etc.] : Macmillan, 1977. — [5],230p ; 21cm.
Originally published: New York : Atheneum, 1975.
ISBN 0-333-21137-5 : £2.95
(B77-11437)

Fidler, Kathleen. The railway runaways / [by] Kathleen Fidler ; illustrated by Terry Gabbey. — Glasgow [etc.] : Blackie, 1977. — 93p : ill ; 21cm.
ISBN 0-216-90296-7 : £2.95
(B77-14977)

Finkel, George. The Loyal Virginian / [by] George Finkel. — London [etc.] : White Lion Publishers, 1976. — [6],189p : maps ; 23cm.
Originally published: London : Angus and Robertson, 1968.
ISBN 0-85686-255-x : £2.75
(B77-05729)

The **first** 'St Michael' book of Andy Pandy favourites. — Maidenhead : Purnell [for Marks and Spencer Limited], 1977. — [76]p : col ill ; 29cm.
ISBN 0-361-04007-5 : £1.25
(B77-32898)

The **first** 'St Michael' book of Disney favourites. — Maidenhead : Purnell [for Marks and Spencer Limited], 1977. — [76]p : col ill ; 29cm.
ISBN 0-361-04006-7 : £1.25
(B77-32899)

The **first** 'St Michael' book of Noddy favourites. — Maidenhead : Purnell, 1977. — [76]p : col ill ; 29cm.
ISBN 0-361-04004-0 : Unpriced
(B77-25949)

Fitzgerald, John Dennis. More adventures of the Great Brain / by John D. Fitzgerald ; illustrated by Fritz Wegner. — London : Dent, 1977. — [2],142p : ill ; 18cm. — (Dent dolphins)
Originally published: New York : Dial Press, 1969 ; London : Dent, 1972.
ISBN 0-460-02727-1 Pbk : £0.50
(B77-06918)

Fleischman, Sid. Kate's secret riddle book / by Sid Fleischman ; illustrated by Barbara Bottner. — New York ; London : F. Watts, 1977. — [30]p : col ill ; 22cm. — (An easy-read story book)
ISBN 0-531-00377-9 : £1.95
(B77-32900)

Foreman, Michael, *b.1938.* Panda's puzzle, and his voyage of discovery / [by] Michael Foreman. — London : Hamilton, 1977. — [32] p : chiefly col ill ; 29cm.
ISBN 0-241-89651-7 : £2.95
(B77-28994)

Forest, Antonia. Autumn term / [by] Antonia Forest. — Harmondsworth [etc.] : Puffin Books, 1977. — 285p ; 18cm. — (Puffin books)
Originally published: London : Faber, 1948.
ISBN 0-14-030954-3 Pbk : £0.65
(B77-27468)

Fox, Paula. A likely place / [by] Paula Fox ; text illustrations by Trevor Stubley ; cover illustration by Tina Murray. — London : Pan Books, 1977. — 62p : ill ; 18cm. — (Piccolo)
Originally published: New York : Macmillan, 1967 ; London : Macmillan, 1968.
ISBN 0-330-25098-1 Pbk : £0.40
(B77-20719)

Fox, Paula. The slave dancer : a novel / by Paula Fox ; text illustrations by Chris Mowlan ; cover illustration by Nancy Petley-Jones. — London : Pan Books, 1977. — 143p : ill ; 18cm. — (Piccolo)
Originally published: Scarsdale, N.Y. : Bradbury Press, 1973 ; London : Macmillan, 1974.
ISBN 0-330-25018-3 Pbk : £0.45
(B77-10605)

Fraser, *Lady* **Antonia.** Robin Hood / [by] Antonia Fraser ; illustrated by Victor Ambrus. — London : Sidgwick and Jackson, 1977. — 192p : ill ; 23cm.
Originally published: / illustrated by Geoffrey Whittam. London : Weidenfeld and Nicolson, 1955.
ISBN 0-283-98411-2 : £3.95
(B77-31551)

Freeman, Barbara Constance. A pocket of silence / [by] Barbara C. Freeman ; with decorations by the author. — London [etc.] : Macmillan, 1977. — 171p : ill ; 21cm.
ISBN 0-333-21733-0 : £2.95
(B77-20720)

Freeman, Don. Beady Bear / story and pictures by Don Freeman. — Harmondsworth [etc.] : Puffin Books, 1977. — [48]p : chiefly ill ; 19x23cm. — (Picture puffin)
Originally published: New York : Viking Press, 1955.
ISBN 0-14-050197-5 Pbk : Unpriced
(B77-22937)

Freeman, Don. Dandelion / story and pictures by Don Freeman. — Harmondsworth [etc.] : Puffin Books, 1977. — [48]p : chiefly col ill ; 20x23cm. — (Picture puffin)
Originally published: New York : Viking Press, 1964 ; Kingswood : World's Work, 1965.
ISBN 0-14-050218-1 Pbk : Unpriced
(B77-31552)

Freeman, Don. The paper party / story and pictures by Don Freeman. — Tadworth : World's Work, 1977. — [40]p : chiefly col ill ; 21x26cm.
Originally published: New York : Viking Press, 1974.
ISBN 0-437-41005-6 : £2.60
(B77-08633)

Fremlin, Robert. Three friends / by Robert Fremlin ; illustrated by Wallace Tripp. — Tadworth : World's Work, 1977. — 64p : ill ; 21cm.
Originally published: Boston, Mass. : Little, Brown, 1975.
ISBN 0-437-41041-2 : £1.90
(B77-06919)

Freschet, Berniece. Grizzly bear / by Berniece Freschet ; drawings by Donald Carrick. — Tadworth : World's Work, 1977. — [40]p : col ill ; 26cm.
Originally published: New York : Scribner, 1975.
ISBN 0-437-26550-1 : £2.90
(B77-06920)

Frewer, Glyn. The trackers / [by] Glyn Frewer ; illustrated by Richard Kennedy. — London : Abelard-Schuman ; [Chalfont St Giles] : Sadler, 1976. — 64p : ill ; 20cm. — (A grasshopper book)
ISBN 0-200-72414-2 : £1.55
ISBN 0-200-72415-0 Pbk : £0.45
(B77-03245)

Front, Sheila. The golden goose / adapted from the folk tale by Sheila Front ; illustrated by Charles Front. — London [etc.] : E. Benn, 1977. — 28p : col ill ; 21cm. — (Beginning to read books)
ISBN 0-510-08503-2 : £1.25
ISBN 0-510-08504-0 Pbk : £0.95
(B77-21533)

Fry, Rosalie Kingsmill. Gypsy princess / [by] Rosalie K. Fry ; illustrated by Philip Gough. — London [etc.] : White Lion Publishers, 1977. — [4],90p : ill ; 21cm.
Originally published: New York : Dutton ; London : Dent, 1969.
ISBN 0-85686-286-x : £2.25
(B77-07665)

Funny folk : a book of comic tales / [compiled by] Aidan Chambers ; illustrated by Trevor Stubley. — London : Heinemann, 1976. — [6], 130p : ill(some col) ; 25cm.
ISBN 0-434-93161-6 : £3.50
(B77-01006)

Furchgott, Terry. Phoebe and the hot water bottles / story by Terry Furchgott and Linda Dawson ; pictures by Terry Furchgott. — London : Deutsch, 1977. — [32]p : col ill ; 26cm.
ISBN 0-233-96860-1 : £2.75
(B77-12742)

Furminger, Jo. Blackbirds' pony trek / [by] Jo Furminger ; illustrations by Susan Hunter. — London [etc.] : Hodder and Stoughton, 1977. — 120p : ill ; 21cm.
ISBN 0-340-20953-4 : £3.00
(B77-32854)

Gág, Wanda. Millions of cats / by Wanda Gág. — Harmondsworth [etc.] : Puffin Books, 1976. — [33]p : ill ; 16x20cm. — (Picture puffin)
Originally published: New York : Coward-McCann, 1928 ; London : Faber, 1929.
ISBN 0-14-050168-1 Sd : £0.50
(B77-13383)

Galdone, Paul. The frog prince / adapted from the retelling by the Brothers Grimm by Paul Galdone. — Tadworth : World's Work, 1977. — [39]p : col ill ; 21x26cm.
This adaptation originally published: New York : McGraw-Hill, 1974.
ISBN 0-437-42523-1 : £2.80
(B77-22210)

Galdone, Paul. Little Red Riding Hood / adapted from the retelling by the Brothers Grimm [by] Paul Galdone. — Tadworth : World's Work, 1977. — [32]p : chiefly col ill ; 21x26cm.
This adaptation originally published: New York : McGraw-Hill, 1974.
ISBN 0-437-42524-x : £2.60
(B77-22211)

Gallico, Paul. The adventures of Jean-Pierre / [by] Paul Gallico ; illustrated by Gioia Fiammenghi. — London [etc.] : Pan Books, 1975. — 94p : ill ; 18cm. — (A piccolo book)
Contents: The day the guinea pig talked. Originally published: London : Heinemann, 1963 - The day Jean-Pierre was pignapped. Originally published: London : Heinemann, 1964.
ISBN 0-330-24358-6 Pbk : £0.35
(B77-08124)

Gannett, Ruth Stiles. My father's dragon / story by Ruth Stiles Gannett ; illustrations by Ruth Chrisman Gannett. — London : Collins, 1976. — 93p : ill, map ; 20cm. — (Lions)
Originally published: New York : Random House, 1948 ; London : Macmillan, 1957.
ISBN 0-00-671118-9 Pbk : £0.50
(B77-01851)

Garfield, Leon. The dumb cake / [by] Leon Garfield ; illustrated by Faith Jaques. — London : Heinemann, 1977. — 47p : ill ; 23cm. — (Garfield, Leon. Garfield's apprentices)
ISBN 0-434-94040-2 : £2.40
(B77-31553)

Garfield, Leon. Labour in vain / [by] Leon Garfield ; illustrated by Faith Jaques. — London : Heinemann, 1977. — 47p : ill ; 23cm. — (Garfield, Leon. Garfield's apprentices ; 6)
ISBN 0-434-94035-6 : £2.10
(B77-14441)

Garfield, Leon. The sound of coaches / [by] Leon Garfield ; with engravings by John Lawrence. — Harmondsworth [etc.] : Puffin Books, 1977. — 236p : ill ; 19cm. — (Puffin books)
Originally published: Harmondsworth : Kestrel Books, 1974.
ISBN 0-14-030961-6 Pbk : £0.60
(B77-21534)

Garfield, Leon. Tom Titmarsh's devil / [by] Leon Garfield ; illustrated by Faith Jaques. — London : Heinemann, 1977. — 47p : ill ; 23cm. — (Garfield, Leon. Garfield's apprentices)
ISBN 0-434-94039-9 : £2.40
(B77-31554)

Garfield, Leon. The valentine / [by] Leon Garfield ; illustrated by Faith Jaques. — London : Heinemann, 1977. — 47p : ill ; 23cm. — (Garfield, Leon. Garfield's apprentices ; 5)
ISBN 0-434-94036-4 : £2.10
(B77-13384)

Garner, Alan. Granny Reardun / [by] Alan Garner ; etchings by Michael Foreman. — London : Collins, 1977. — 58p : ill ; 21cm.
ISBN 0-00-184288-9 : £2.50
(B77-30759)

Garner, Alan. Tom Fobble's day / [by] Alan Garner ; etchings by Michael Foreman. — London : Collins, 1977. — 3-72p : ill ; 21cm.
ISBN 0-00-184832-1 : £2.50
(B77-10606)

Gelman, Rita Golden. Hey, kid! / by Rita Golden Gelman ; illustrated by Carol Nicklaus. — New York ; London : F. Watts, 1977. — [32]p : col ill ; 22cm. — (An easy-read story book)
ISBN 0-531-00376-0 : £1.95
(B77-32901)

Gentle, Mary. A hawk in silver / [by] Mary Gentle. — London : Gollancz, 1977. — 192p ; 21cm.
ISBN 0-575-02386-4 : £3.75
(B77-29750)

Geras, Adèle. Apricots at midnight, and other stories from a patchwork quilt / [by] Adèle Geras ; illustrated by Doreen Caldwell. — London : Hamilton, 1977. — 142p : ill ; 24cm.
ISBN 0-241-89479-4 : £3.50
(B77-14442)

Gervaise, Mary. The secret of Pony Pass / [by] Mary Gervaise. — London : Armada Books, 1974. — 126p : ill ; 19cm.
Originally published: London : Lutterworth Press, 1965.
ISBN 0-00-691017-3 Pbk : £0.35
(B77-03246)

Ghostly and ghastly / edited by Barbara Ireson ; illustrated by William Geldart. — London [etc.] : Beaver Books, 1977. — 222p : ill ; 18cm.
ISBN 0-600-34065-1 Pbk : £0.55
(B77-30760)

Gibb, Eileen, *b.1911.* Sammy the shunter bumper book / by Eileen Gibb ; illustrated by Jack Atkins. — London : Allan, [1976]. — 64p : col ill ; 25cm.
ISBN 0-7110-0745-4 : £1.25
(B77-00469)

Gibbs, May. Bib and Bub / based on May Gibbs' original strip cartoons ; illustrated by Dan Russell. — London [etc.] : Angus and Robertson, 1977. — [27]p : chiefly col ill ; 30cm.
Text, col. ill. on lining paper.
ISBN 0-207-13469-3 : £0.95
(B77-30761)

The **Girl** Guide annual. — Maidenhead : Purnell [for] the Girl Guides Association.
1978 / edited by Robert Moss. — 1977. — 3-94p : ill(some col), map, ports(1 col) ; 27cm.
Ill. on lining papers.
ISBN 0-361-03896-8 : £1.50
(B77-32263)

Godden, Rumer. The dolls' house / [by] Rumer Godden ; illustrated by Joanna Jamieson. — Harmondsworth : Puffin Books, 1976. — 139, [1]p : ill ; 20cm. — (A young puffin)
Originally published: London : Joseph, 1947.
Pbk : £0.45
(B77-07666)

Graham, Harriet. The Lucifer stone / [by] Harriet Graham. — London : Collins, 1976. — 158p ; 18cm. — (Lions)
Originally published: London : Abelard-Schuman, 1973.
ISBN 0-00-671117-0 Pbk : £0.50
(B77-10971)

Graham, Harriet. The year they stopped Christmas / [by] Harriet Graham ; illustrated by Geoffrey Bargery. — London : Hamilton, 1977. — 87p : ill ; 19cm. — (Antelope books)
ISBN 0-241-89703-3 : £1.25
(B77-26614)

Graham, John. I love you, mouse / [by] John Graham ; pictures by Tomie de Paola. — New York ; London : Harcourt Brace Jovanovich, 1976. — [32]p : ill ; 22cm.
ISBN 0-15-238005-1 : £3.25
(B77-17783)

Graham, Margaret Bloy. Benjy's dog house / [by] Margaret Bloy Graham. — Harmondsworth [etc.] : Puffin Books, 1977. — [31]p : col ill ; 20cm. — (Picture puffins)
Originally published: New York : Harper and Row, 1973 ; London : Bodley Head, 1974.
ISBN 0-14-050219-x Sd : £0.50
(B77-24544)

Graham, Nielson. Fred Basset and the spaghetti / by Nielson Graham ; illustrated by Alex Graham. — London : Associated Newspapers Group, 1977. — [30]p : col ill ; 31cm. — (A 'Daily mail' publication)
£1.50
(B77-27469)

Gramatky, Hardie. Little Toot through the Golden Gate / [by] Hardie Gramatky. — Tadworth : World's Work, 1977. — 88p : ill(some col) ; 20cm.
Originally published: New York : Putnam, 1975.
ISBN 0-437-44012-5 : £2.70
(B77-17784)

Grant, Gwen. Matthew and his magic kite / written by Gwen Grant ; illustrated by Daniel Strodl. — London (3 Fitzroy Sq., W.1) : Andersen Press [etc.], 1977. — [29]p : col ill ; 24cm.
ISBN 0-905478-14-2 : £2.50
(B77-31555)

Great adventure stories for boys / selected and edited by Leonard Matthews. — London [etc.] : Hamlyn, 1977. — 188p : ill ; 22cm. — (Hamlyn story library)
ISBN 0-600-35244-7 : £1.00
(B77-19034)

Green, Christina. Beetle boy / [by] Christina Green ; illustrated by Laszlo Acs. — London : Hamilton, 1977. — 86p : ill ; 19cm. — (Antelope books)
ISBN 0-241-89565-0 : £1.25
(B77-14443)

Green, Cliff. The incredible steam-driven adventures of Riverboat Bill / [by] Cliff Green ; illustrated by Stephen Axelsen. — Sydney [etc.] ; London : Hodder and Stoughton, 1975. — 146p : ill, map(on lining papers) ; 22cm.
ISBN 0-340-19723-4 : Unpriced
(B77-32264)

Green, Marion. The magician who lived on the mountain / [by] Marion Green ; pictures John Dyke. — London [etc.] : Hodder and Stoughton, 1977. — [32]p : chiefly col ill ; 25cm.
ISBN 0-340-20586-5 : £2.80
(B77-21535)

Green, Roger Lancelyn. The tale of Thebes / [by] Roger Lancelyn Green ; illustrated by Jael Jordan. — Cambridge [etc.] : Cambridge University Press, 1977. — iii-xix,102p : ill, geneal table, 2 maps ; 23cm.
ISBN 0-521-21410-6 : £3.00
ISBN 0-521-21411-4 Pbk : £1.50
(B77-31556)

Greene, Bette. Summer of my German soldier / [by] Bette Greene. — Harmondsworth : Puffin Books, 1977. — 206p ; 18cm. — (Puffin books)

Originally published: New York : Dial Press, 1973 ; London : Hamilton, 1974.
ISBN 0-14-030985-3 Pbk : £0.60
(B77-26615)

Greene, Graham. The little fire engine / by Graham Greene. — [New ed.] / illustrated by Edward Ardizzone. — Harmondsworth [etc.] : Puffin Books, 1977. — 3-48p : col ill ; 15x20cm. — (Picture puffins)
This ed. originally published: London : Bodley Head, 1973.
ISBN 0-14-050210-6 Sd : £0.60
(B77-24545)

Greene, Graham. The little train / by Graham Greene. — [New ed.] / illustrated by Edward Ardizzone. — Harmondsworth [etc.] : Puffin Books, 1977. — [48]p : col ill ; 15x20cm. — (Picture puffins)
This ed. originally published: London : Bodley Head, 1973.
ISBN 0-14-050194-0 Sd : £0.60
(B77-27470)

Gregor, Arthur Stephen. Does Poppy live here? / by Arthur S. Gregor ; illustrated by Roger Duvoisin. — [Abridged ed.]. — Tadworth : World's Work, 1976. — [32]p : ill(some col) ; 26cm.
Col. ill. on lining papers. — Previous ed.: i.e. 1st ed., New York : Lothrop, Lee and Shepard, 1957 ; Tadworth : World's Work, 1967.
ISBN 0-437-44400-7 : £2.10
(B77-07667)

Gregson, Maureen. The feathered serpent / [by] Maureen Gregson. — London : Carousel, 1977. — 143p : ill ; 18cm.
'... adapted from the Thames Television series, "The Feathered Serpent", written by John Kane' - backcover.
ISBN 0-552-52079-9 Pbk : £0.50
(B77-28220)

Grey, Peter. The phantom horse / [by] Peter Grey. — London [etc.] : White Lion Publishers, 1977. — 182p ; 21cm.
Originally published: London : World Distributors, 1960.
ISBN 0-85686-233-9 : £2.95
(B77-32902)

The **Greyfriars** holiday annual. — London : H. Baker.
1976 / [edited by W. Howard Baker]. — 1976. — 243p in various pagings : ill(some col) ; 28cm.
Facsimile reprints of stories originally published in 'The Magnet', 'The "Magnet" Library', 'The Penny Popular', 'The Gem' between the years 1916-1936 and 'Charles Hamilton, Greyfriars and myself', presidential address to the 'Private Libraries Association' by Raymond Lister, 9th April 1974.
ISBN 0-7030-0075-6 : £3.90
(B77-00470)

Griffiths, Brian. Shoni and Isath : a folk story from Pakistan / retold by Brian Griffiths ; illustrated by Trevor Stubley. — [Rochdale] ([Teacher's Centre, Baillie St., Rochdale OL16 1MW]) : Rochdale M.B.C. Education Department, [1977]. — [1],8,[1]p,plate : ill ; 21cm.
Sd : £0.35
(B77-29751)

Griffiths, Helen. Pablo / [by] Helen Griffiths ; illustrated by Victor Ambrus. — London : Hutchinson, 1977. — 192p : ill ; 21cm.
ISBN 0-09-129110-0 : £3.25
(B77-28995)

Groom, Olive Lilian. The Landon quest / by Olive L. Groom. — London : Pickering and Inglis, 1976. — [1],149p ; 19cm.
ISBN 0-7208-2228-9 : £1.00
(B77-03783)

Grumpy the dwarf. — Maidenhead : Purnell, 1974. — [16]p : col ill ; 12cm. — ([Minikins])
Sd : £0.06
(B77-19822)

Hall, Martin. Nobody's house / by Martin Hall. — London : Armada Books, 1976. — 125p ; 18cm. — (Armada spinechiller series)
ISBN 0-00-691194-3 Pbk : £0.40
(B77-10607)

Hall, Willis. The summer of the dinosaur / [by] Willis Hall ; illustrated by John Griffiths. — London [etc.] : Bodley Head, 1977. — 189p : ill ; 23cm.
ISBN 0-370-30003-3 : £2.95
(B77-14978)

Hallett, Phyllis. Jumping cats / [by] Phyllis Hallett. — London : Dobson, 1977. — [2], 166p : ill ; 21cm.
Ill. on lining papers.
ISBN 0-234-72030-1 : £2.95
(B77-23772)

Halls, Mary. Willie the Russell / [by] Mary Halls ; illustrated by Cora E.M. Paterson. — Ilfracombe : Stockwell, 1977. — 21p : ill ; 18cm.
ISBN 0-7223-1009-9 Pbk : £0.40
(B77-23773)

Hansel and Gretel / [illustrated by Mary McClain]. — London : Chatto and Windus [etc.], 1975. — 3 fold leaves : chiefly col ill ; 18cm. — (A peepshow book)
Fold. leaves superimposed one on the other to create a three-dimensional effect ; five pictures in all. — Based on the story by the Brothers Grimm.
ISBN 0-7011-2141-6 : £1.50
(B77-06334)

Hardcastle, Michael. On the ball : a Mark Fox story / [by] Michael Hardcastle. — London : Armada Books, 1977. — 125p ; 19cm. — (Hardcastle, Michael. Mark Fox books ; 3)
ISBN 0-00-691151-x Pbk : £0.45
(B77-28221)

Hardcastle, Michael. The Saturday horse / [by] Michael Hardcastle ; illustrated by Trevor Stubley. — London : Methuen, 1977. — 126p : ill ; 19cm. — (A pied piper book)
ISBN 0-416-56470-4 : £1.85
(B77-22938)

Hardcastle, Michael. The Saturday horse / [by] Michael Hardcastle ; illustrated by Trevor Stubley. — London : Methuen, 1977. — 126p : ill ; 18cm.
ISBN 0-416-58240-0 Pbk : £0.60
(B77-29752)

Hardcastle, Michael. Shooting star : a Mark Fox story / [by] Michael Hardcastle. — London : Armada Books, 1977. — 127p ; 19cm. — (Hardcastle, Michael. Mark Fox books ; 4)
ISBN 0-00-691152-8 Pbk : £0.45
(B77-28222)

Hargreaves, Georgina. 20,000 leagues under the sea / [by] Jules Verne ; retold and illustrated by Georgina Hargreaves. — London : Dean, 1977. — [44]p : col ill ; 27cm.
ISBN 0-603-06260-1 : £0.75
(B77-29753)

Hargreaves, Georgina. Gulliver's travels / [by] Jonathan Swift ; retold and illustrated by Georgina Hargreaves. — London : Dent, 1977. — [44]p : col ill ; 27cm.
ISBN 0-603-06262-8 : £0.75
(B77-29754)

Hargreaves, Georgina. The man in the iron mask / [by] Alexandre Dumas ; retold and illustrated by Georgina Hargreaves. — London : Dean, 1977. — [44]p : col ill ; 27cm.
ISBN 0-603-06261-x : £0.75
(B77-29755)

Hargreaves, Georgina. The three musketeers / [by] Alexandre Dumas ; retold and illustrated by Georgina Hargreaves. — London : Dean, 1977. — [44]p : col ill ; 27cm.
ISBN 0-603-06259-8 : £0.75
(B77-29756)

Hargreaves, Roger. Grandfather clock / story and pictures by Roger Hargreaves. — Leicester : Hodder and Stoughton Children's Books, 1977. — [29]p : chiefly col ill ; 25cm.
ISBN 0-340-21500-3 : £2.60
(B77-19823)

Hargreaves, Roger. The Mr Men on holiday / by Roger Hargreaves. — London : Thurman, 1976. — [38]p : ill(chiefly col) ; 21x24cm.
ISBN 0-85985-055-2 Sd : £0.85
(B77-11438)

Harper, Anita. Ella climbs a mountain / by Anita Harper ; with pictures by Michael Jackson. — Harmondsworth : Kestrel Books, 1977. — 25p : col ill ; 21cm. — (A Minnow book)
ISBN 0-7226-5251-8 : £1.30
(B77-22939)

Harris, Hazel P. On the trail of te kakaha / [by] Hazel P. Harris ; illustrations by Jean Oates. — Christchurch, N.Z. [etc.] ; London : Whitcoulls, 1977. — 130p : ill, map ; 21cm. — ([Kairangi series])
ISBN 0-7233-0521-8 : Unpriced
(B77-19824)

Harris, Rosemary, *b.1923.* I want to be a fish / by Rosemary Harris ; with pictures by Jill Bennett. — Harmondsworth : Kestrel Books, 1977. — 25p : ill(chiefly col) ; 21cm. — (A Minnow book)
Also published: Harmondsworth : Puffin Books, 1977.
ISBN 0-7226-5302-6 : £1.30
(B77-22940)

Harris, Rosemary, *b.1923.* The moon in the cloud / [by] Rosemary Harris. — Harmondsworth [etc.] : Puffin Books, 1977. — 171p ; 19cm. — (Puffin books)
Originally published: London : Faber, 1968.
ISBN 0-14-030911-x Pbk : £0.50
(B77-14979)

Harris, Rosemary, *b.1923.* The shadow on the sun / [by] Rosemary Harris. — Harmondsworth [etc.] : Puffin Books, 1977. — 175p ; 18cm. — (Puffin books)
Originally published: London : Faber, 1970.
ISBN 0-14-030980-2 Pbk : £0.50
(B77-32903)

Hart, James. Roy of the Rovers / [by] James Hart. — London : New English Library, 1977. — 128p : ill ; 18cm.
ISBN 0-450-03323-6 Pbk : £0.60
(B77-23774)

Having fun. — Maidenhead : Purnell, 1977. — [8]p : chiefly col ill ; 19cm. — (My first book) (A Purnell board book)
Cover title.
Pbd : £0.20
(B77-10608)

Hayes, Geoffrey. The alligator and his Uncle Tooth : a novel of the sea / by Geoffrey Hayes. — London : Andersen Press : Hutchinson, 1977. — [5],85p : ill ; 21cm. — (Andersen young readers library)
Also published: New York : Harper and Row, 1977.
ISBN 0-905478-25-8 : £2.25
(B77-28223)

Hayes, Geoffrey. Bear by himself / by Geoffrey Hayes. — New York [etc.] ; London : Harper and Row, [1976]. — 32p : col ill ; 20cm.
ISBN 0-06-022262-x : £2.95
(B77-25950)

Hayes, Richard. The secret army / [by] Richard Hayes. — London [etc.] : Macmillan, 1977. — 210p ; 21cm.
ISBN 0-333-21425-0 : £2.95
(B77-14980)

Heffron, Dorris. Crusty crossed / [by] Dorris Heffron. — London [etc.] : Macmillan, 1976. — 177p ; 21cm.
ISBN 0-333-19735-6 : £2.95
(B77-03247)

Heilbroner, Joan. This is the house where Jack lives / by Joan Heilbroner ; illustrated by Aliki. — Tadworth : World's Work, 1977. — 63p : col ill ; 22cm. — (An I can read book)
Originally published: New York : Harper and Row, 1962 ; Tadworth : World's Work, 1963.
ISBN 0-437-96011-0 Pbk : £0.60
(B77-34227)

Heins, Paul. Snow White / by the Brothers Grimm ; freely translated from the German by Paul Heins ; with illustrations by Trina Schart Hyman. — Tadworth : World's Work, 1977. — [48]p : chiefly col ill ; 23cm.
ISBN 0-437-45095-3 : £2.50
(B77-33474)

Henderson, Jennifer. The snowman / [by] Jennifer Henderson. — London [etc.] : Macmillan, 1977. — 194p ; 21cm.
ISBN 0-333-21503-6 : £2.95
(B77-14981)

Henry, Marguerite. Misty of Chincoteague / by Marguerite Henry ; illustrated by Wesley Dennis. — Glasgow [etc.] : Collins, 1977. — 4-173p : ill(some col), 2 maps ; 24cm.
Originally published: Chicago : Rand McNally, 1947 ; London : Collins, 1961.
ISBN 0-00-138124-5 : £2.95
(B77-14444)

Henry, Marguerite. Mustang : wild spirit of the West / by Marguerite Henry ; illustrated by Robert Lougheed. — Glasgow [etc.] : Collins, 1977. — 3-222p : ill(some col) ; 24cm.
Col. ill. on lining papers. — Originally published: Chicago : Rand-McNally, 1966 ; London : Collins, 1968.
ISBN 0-00-138202-0 : £2.95
(B77-14445)

Henry, Marguerite. Palio : the wildest horse race in the world / [by] Marguerite Henry ; illustrated by Lynd Ward. — [London] : Fontana, 1976. — 213,[2]p : ill ; 20cm. — (Lions)
Originally published: as 'Gaudenzia, pride of the Palio'. Chicago : Rand McNally, 1960.
ISBN 0-00-670802-1 Pbk : £0.60
(B77-16083)

Henry, Marguerite. San Domingo : the Medicine Hat stallion / by Marguerite Henry ; illustrated by Robert Lougheed. — Glasgow [etc.] : Collins, 1977. — 233p : ill(some col), map ; 24cm.
Originally published: Chicago : Rand McNally, 1972 ; Glasgow : Collins, 1975. — Bibl.: p.233.
£2.95
ISBN 0-00-138119-9
(B77-21536)

Hersom, Kathleen. Johnny Oswaldtwistle / [by] Kathleen Hersom ; illustrated by Lesley Smith. — London : Methuen, 1977. — 91p : ill ; 21cm. — ([A read aloud book])
ISBN 0-416-85040-5 : £1.90
(B77-27471)

Hildick, Edmund Wallace. A cat called Amnesia / [by] E.W. Hildick ; illustrated by Val Biro. — London : Deutsch, 1977. — [7], 152p : ill ; 23cm.
Originally published: New York : White, 1976.
ISBN 0-233-96867-9 : £2.95
(B77-19035)

Hildick, Edmund Wallace. Lemon Kelly and the home-made boy / [by] E.W. Hildick ; illustrated by Iris Schweitzer. — London [etc.] : White Lion Publishers, 1977. — 173p : ill ; 21cm.
Originally published: London : Dobson, 1968.
ISBN 0-85686-266-5 : £3.15
(B77-14982)

Hildick, Edmund Wallace. Lemon Kelly digs deep / [by] E.W. Hildick ; illustrated by Margery Gill. — London [etc.] : White Lion Publishers, 1977. — 158p : ill ; 21cm.
Originally published: London : Cape, 1964.
ISBN 0-85686-271-1 : £2.50
(B77-33475)

Hildick, Edmund Wallace. Meet Lemon Kelly / [by] E.W. Hildick ; illustrated by Margery Gill. — London [etc.] : White Lion Publishers, 1976. — 157p : ill ; 21cm.
Originally published: London : Cape, 1963.
ISBN 0-85686-276-2 : £2.50
(B77-03248)

Hildick, Edmund Wallace. My kid sister / [by] E.W. Hildick ; illustrated by Iris Schweitzer. — London [etc.] : Hodder and Stoughton, 1977. — 57p : ill ; 19cm.
Originally published: Cleveland : World Publishing, 1971 ; Leicester : Brockhampton, Press, 1973.
£2.20
ISBN 0-340-16942-7
(B77-32904)

Hill, Denise. William and the Mutt / [by] Denise Hill ; illustrated by Janet Paton. — London : Hamilton, 1977. — 87p : ill ; 19cm. — (Antelope books)
ISBN 0-241-89541-3 : £1.25
(B77-06921)

Hinchcliffe, Philip. Doctor Who and the seeds of doom / [by] Philip Hinchcliffe. — London : Wingate, 1977. — 128p ; 21cm. — (A longbow book)
'Based on the BBC television serial "Doctor Who and the Seeds of Doom" by Robert Banks Stewart ...'.
ISBN 0-85523-161-0 : £2.50
(B77-14983)

Hoban, Lillian. Arthur's pen pal / story and pictures by Lillian Hoban. — Tadworth : World's Work, 1977. — 64p : col ill ; 22cm. — (An I can read book ; no.108)
Originally published: New York : Harper and Row, 1976.
ISBN 0-437-90108-4 : £2.10
(B77-23775)

Hoban, Russell. A baby sister for Frances / by Russell Hoban ; pictures by Lillian Hoban. — Harmondsworth : Puffin Books, 1977. — 31p : col ill ; 20cm. — (Picture puffins)
Originally published: London : Faber, 1964.
ISBN 0-14-050154-1 Sd : £0.50
(B77-07668)

Hoban, Russell. A bargain for Frances / by Russell Hoban ; pictures by Lillian Hoban. — Tadworth : World's Work, 1977. — 63p : col ill ; 22cm. — (An I can read book)
Originally published: New York : Harper and Row, 1970 ; Tadworth : World's Work, 1971.
ISBN 0-437-96003-x Sd : £0.60
(B77-16624)

Hoban, Russell. A birthday for Frances / by Russell Hoban ; pictures by Lillian Hoban. — Harmondsworth [etc.] : Puffin Books, 1977. — 32,[1]p : col ill ; 20cm. — (Picture puffins)
Originally published: New York : Harper, 1968 ; London : Faber, 1970.
ISBN 0-14-050223-8 Sd : £0.50
(B77-30762)

Hoban, Russell. Bread and jam for Frances / [text] by Russell Hoban ; pictures by Lillian Hoban. — Harmondsworth [etc.] : Puffin Books, 1977. — 31,[1]p : col ill ; 20cm. — (Picture puffins)
Originally published: New York : Harper and Row, 1964 ; London : Faber, 1966.
ISBN 0-14-050176-2 Sd : £0.50
(B77-15567)

Hoban, Russell. Dinner at Alberta's / by Russell Hoban ; pictures by James Marshall. — London : Cape, 1977. — [40]p : ill ; 21cm.
Originally published: New York : Crowell, 1975.
ISBN 0-224-01393-9 : £2.50 : CIP rev.
(B77-07670)

Hoban, Russell. Harvey's hideout / by Russell Hoban ; pictures by Lillian Hoban. — Harmondsworth [etc.] : Puffin Books, 1976. — [41]p : col ill ; 20cm. — (Picture puffins)
Originally published: New York : Parents Magazine Press, 1969 ; London : Cape, 1973.
ISBN 0-14-050159-2 Sd : £0.60
(B77-01852)

Hoban, Russell. Tom and the two handles / by Russell Hoban ; pictures by Lillian Hoban. — Tadworth : World's Work, 1977. — 64p : col ill ; 22cm. — (I can read book)
Originally published: New York : Harper, 1965 ; Tadworth : World's Work, 1966.
ISBN 0-437-96010-2 Sd : £0.60
(B77-34228)

Hoff, Syd. Julius / story and pictures by Syd Hoff. — Tadworth : World's Work, 1977. — 64p : col ill ; 22cm. — (An I can read book)
Originally published: New York : Harper, 1959 ; Tadworth : World's Work, 1960.
ISBN 0-437-96001-3 Sd : £0.60
(B77-16625)

Hoff, Syd. Sammy the seal / story and pictures by Syd Hoff. — Tadworth : World's Work, 1977. — 2-64p : col ill ; 22cm. — (An I can read book)
Originally published: New York : Harper, 1959 ; Tadworth : World's Work, 1960.
ISBN 0-437-96009-9 Sd : £0.60
(B77-34229)

Hogrogian, Nonny. The contest / adapted and illustrated by Nonny Hogrogian. — London : Hamilton, 1977. — [32]p : ill(chiefly col) ; 26cm.
Col. ill. on lining papers. — Originally published: New York : Greenwillow Books, 1976.
ISBN 0-241-89577-4 : £2.80
(B77-10609)

Holiday, Jane. The bus boggart / [by] Jane Holiday ; illustrated by Trevor Stubley. — London : Hamilton, 1977. — 88p : ill ; 19cm. — (Antelope books)
ISBN 0-241-89613-4 : £1.25
(B77-19825)

Holyoak, Christina. Pascal and the lioness / [by] René Guillot ; translated and adapted by Christina Holyoak ; illustrated by Barry Wilkinson ; &, Tipiti, the robin / [by] René Guillot ; translated by Gwen Marsh ; illustrated by Charles Keeping. — London [etc.] : Bodley Head, 1976. — 100p : ill ; 21cm. — (New acorn library)
'Pascal and the lioness' originally published: 1965. Adaptation of: 'Grichka et les loups'. Paris : Hachette, 1960. — 'Tipiti, the robin' originally published: 1962.
ISBN 0-370-10900-7 : £2.25
(B77-00471)

Hoover, Roseanna. The fireflies : a story / by Max Bolliger ; translated [from the German] and adapted by Roseanna Hoover ; with pictures by Jiří Trnka. — London : Evans Bros, 1977. — [43]p : col ill ; 33cm.
This translation and adaptation originally published: New York : Atheneum, 1970. — Translation and adaptation of: 'Leuchtkäferchen'. Zürich : Artemis, 1969.
ISBN 0-237-44874-2 : £3.50
(B77-34230)

'Hotspur' book for boys. — London : D.C. Thomson.
1978. — 1977. — 4-125p : chiefly col ill ; 28cm.
Col. ill. on lining papers.
£0.95
(B77-31557)

Hough, Charlotte. The holiday story book / written and illustrated by Charlotte Hough. — London [etc.] : Beaver Books, 1976. — 174p : ill ; 20cm.
This collection originally published: as 'Charlotte Hough's holiday book'. London : Heinemann, 1975.
ISBN 0-600-34525-4 Pbk : £0.60
(B77-12743)

Hubley, Faith. The hat / written and illustrated by Faith and John Hubley. — New York ; London : Harcourt Brace Jovanovich, 1974. — [48]p : chiefly ill ; 21x27cm.
'Adapted from the film "The Hat" by John and Faith Hubley' - title page verso.
ISBN 0-15-233611-7 : £1.65
(B77-21537)

Huddy, Delia. Gold top Tigger / [by] Delia Huddy ; illustrated by Nicole Goodwin. — London : Hamilton, 1977. — 48p : col ill ; 20cm. — (Gazelle books)
ISBN 0-241-89648-7 : £0.95
(B77-23776)

Huddy, Delia. Sandwich Street safari / [by] Delia Huddy ; illustrated by Nicole Goodwin. — London : Hamilton, 1977. — 88p : ill ; 19cm. — (Antelope books)
ISBN 0-241-89566-9 : £1.25
(B77-19036)

Hughes, Monica. Earthdark / [by] Monica Hughes. — London : Hamilton, 1977. — [6], 122p ; 23cm.
ISBN 0-241-89544-8 : £2.75
(B77-14984)

Hughes, Richard, *b.1900.* The wonder-dog : the collected children's stories of Richard Hughes / illustrations by Anthony Maitland. — London : Chatto and Windus, 1977. — 180p : ill ; 23cm.
ISBN 0-7011-5091-2 : £3.95 : CIP rev.
(B77-14446)

Hughes, Shirley. Dogger / [by] Shirley Hughes. — London [etc.] : Bodley Head, 1977. — [32] p : col ill ; 27cm.
ISBN 0-370-30006-8 : £2.50
(B77-29757)

Hughes, Shirley. It's too frightening for me! / written and drawn by Shirley Hughes. — London [etc.] : Hodder and Stoughton, 1977. — 48p : ill ; 23cm.
ISBN 0-340-21656-5 : £1.95
(B77-22212)

Hunt, Roderick. Chutney and the fossil / by Roderick Hunt ; illustrated by Joan Beales. — Exeter : Wheaton, 1977. — 32p : col ill ; 22cm.

ISBN 0-08-019825-2 : £1.25
ISBN 0-08-019819-8 Sd : £0.55(non-net)
(B77-17141)

Hunt, Roderick. Chutney and the new boy / by Roderick Hunt ; illustrated by Joan Beales. — Exeter : Wheaton, 1977. — 32p : col ill ; 22cm.

ISBN 0-08-019828-7 : £1.25
ISBN 0-08-019822-8 Sd : £0.55(non-net)
(B77-17142)

Hunt, Roderick. Chutney at the circus / by Roderick Hunt ; illustrated by Joan Beales. — Exeter : Wheaton, 1977. — 32p : col ill ; 22cm.

ISBN 0-08-019827-9 : £1.25
ISBN 0-08-019821-x Sd : £0.55(non-net)
(B77-20721)

Hunt, Roderick. Chutney in the snow / by Roderick Hunt ; illustrated by Joan Beales. — Exeter : Wheaton, 1977. — 32p : col ill ; 22cm.

ISBN 0-08-019830-9 : £1.25
ISBN 0-08-019824-4 Sd : £0.55(non-net)
(B77-17143)

Hunt, Roderick. Chutney on the beach / by Roderick Hunt ; illustrated by Joan Beales. — Exeter : Wheaton, 1977. — 32p : col ill ; 22cm.

ISBN 0-08-019829-5 : £1.25
ISBN 0-08-019823-6 Sd : £0.55(non-net)
(B77-20722)

Hunt, Roderick. Chutney on the river / by Roderick Hunt ; illustrated by Joan Beales. — Exeter : Wheaton, 1977. — 32p : col ill ; 22cm.

ISBN 0-08-019826-0 : £1.25
ISBN 0-08-019820-1 Sd : £0.55(non-net)
(B77-17144)

Hunter, Mollie. The wicked one / [by] Mollie Hunter. — London : Hamilton, 1977. — 136p ; 23cm.
ISBN 0-241-89570-7 : £2.80
(B77-26616)

Hunter, Norman. Professor Branestawm's great revolution, and other incredible adventures / [by] Norman Hunter ; illustrated by George Adamson. — Harmondsworth [etc.] : Puffin Books, 1977. — 136p : ill ; 19cm. — (Puffin books)
This collection originally published: London : Bodley Head, 1974.
ISBN 0-14-030919-5 Pbk : £0.45
(B77-18407)

Hynds, Marie. Strange stories from the Land of Grass / [by] Marie Hynds ; illustrations by Anna Dzierzek. — Glasgow [etc.] : Blackie, 1977. — 32p : col ill ; 23cm. — (Blackie's fun to read books)
Cover title.
ISBN 0-216-90378-5 : £1.95
(B77-34231)

Hynds, Marie. Swansdown / [by] Marie Hynds ; illustrations by Shirley Tourret. — Glasgow [etc.] : Blackie, 1977. — 32p : col ill ; 24cm. — (Blackie's fun to read books)
Cover title.
ISBN 0-216-90375-0 : £1.95
(B77-34232)

If I had a bus. — [Swindon] ([Restrop Manor, Purton, Swindon, Wilts.]) : Child's Play (International) Ltd, 1976. — Fold board book ([1],16p) : chiefly col ill ; 81mm. — (A Child's Play stretch book)
Cover title.
ISBN 0-85953-061-2 : Unpriced
(B77-29758)

If I had a dog. — [Swindon] ([Restrop Manor, Purton, Swindon, Wilts.]) : Child's Play (International) Ltd, 1976. — Fold board book ([1],16p) : chiefly col ill ; 81mm. — (A Child's Play stretch book)
Cover title.
ISBN 0-85953-063-9 : Unpriced
(B77-29759)

If I had a farm. — [Swindon] ([Restrop Manor, Purton, Swindon, Wilts.]) : Child's Play (International) Ltd, 1976. — Fold board book ([1],16p) : chiefly col ill ; 81mm. — (A Child's Play stretch book)
Cover title.
ISBN 0-85953-064-7 : Unpriced
(B77-29760)

If I had a house. — [Swindon] ([Restrop Manor, Purton, Swindon, Wilts.]) : Child's Play (International) Ltd, 1976. — Fold board book ([1],16p) : chiefly col ill ; 81mm. — (A Child's Play stretch book)
Cover title.
ISBN 0-85953-062-0 : Unpriced
(B77-29761)

In the country. — Maidenhead : Purnell, 1977. — [8]p : chiefly col ill ; 19cm. — (My first book) (A Purnell board book)
Cover title.
Pbd : £0.20
(B77-10610)

In the garden. — Maidenhead : Purnell, 1977. — [8]p : chiefly col ill ; 19cm. — (My first book) (A Purnell board book)
Cover title.
Pbd : £0.20
(B77-10611)

Ingram, Tom. The outcasts / [by] Tom Ingram. — London : Hutchinson, 1977. — 158p ; 21cm.

ISBN 0-09-131650-2 : £3.25
(B77-28996)

Ireland, Kenneth. The fogou / by Kenneth Ireland. — London : Dobson, 1977. — 152p ; 21cm.
ISBN 0-234-72028-x : £2.95
(B77-31558)

'Jack and Jill' book. — London : IPC Magazines.
1978. — 1977. — 79p : chiefly ill(some col) ; 28cm. — (A Fleetway annual)
Cover title.
ISBN 0-85037-331-x : £1.15
(B77-32905)

Jack and the beanstalk / [illustrated by Irana Shepherd]. — London : Chatto and Windus [etc.], 1977. — 3 fold leaves : chiefly col ill ; 18cm. — (A peepshow book)
Fold. leaves superimposed one on the other to create a three-dimensional effect ; five pictures in all.
ISBN 0-7011-2223-4 : £1.50
(B77-25951)

'Jackie'. — London : D.C. Thompson.
1978. — 1977. — 3-94p : ill(some col), ports(some col) ; 28cm.
Cover title. — Col. ill., text on lining papers.
£1.05
(B77-31559)

Jaeger, Karel. The little banditta / by Karel Jaeger ; with illustrations by Cam. — London [etc.] : White Lion Publishers, 1977. — [112]p : ill ; 23cm.
Originally published: London : Putnam, 1957.
ISBN 0-85686-248-7 : £2.50
(B77-33476)

Jarrell, Randall. The bat-poet / by Randall Jarrell ; pictures by Maurice Sendak. — Harmondsworth : Kestrel Books, 1977. — [4], 43p : ill ; 24cm.
Originally published: New York : Macmillan, 1964.
ISBN 0-7226-5358-1 : £2.50
(B77-26617)

Jarrell, Randall. The gingerbread rabbit / by Randall Jarrell ; pictures by Garth Williams. — [London] : Fontana, 1977. — [6],55p : ill ; 20cm. — (Lions)
Originally published: New York : Macmillan, 1964 ; London : Collier Macmillan, 1967.
ISBN 0-00-671230-4 Pbk : £0.45
(B77-16084)

Jean, Beverley. Lofty stories / by Beverley Jean. — London ([171 Edward St.], SE3 7LX) : Swanglade Ltd, [1977]. — 23p : ill ; 16cm.
Sd : £0.35
(B77-17785)

Jeffers, Susan. Three jovial huntsmen / adapted and illustrated by Susan Jeffers. — Harmondsworth [etc.] : Puffin Books, 1977. — [31]p : chiefly col ill ; 23cm. — (Picture puffin)

Originally published: Scarsdale, N.Y. : Bradbury Press, 1973 ; London : Hamilton, 1974. — 'A "Mother Goose" rhyme' - cover.
ISBN 0-14-050226-2 Pbk : Unpriced
(B77-34233)

Jeffries, Roderic. The boy who knew too much / [by] Roderic Jeffries. — London [etc.] : Hodder and Stoughton, 1977. — 90p : 1 ill ; 23cm.
ISBN 0-340-20712-4 : £2.60
(B77-19826)

Jeffries, Roderic. The riddle in the parchment / [by] Roderic Jeffries ; frontispiece and map by Gavin Rowe. — London [etc.] : Hodder and Stoughton, 1976. — 152p : 1 ill, map(on lining papers) ; 21cm.
ISBN 0-340-19638-6 : £2.40
(B77-06922)

Jellinek, Joanna. Georgina and the dragon / [by] Joanna Jellinek, Agnes Molnar. — London : F. Warne, 1977. — [25]p : chiefly col ill ; 25cm.
ISBN 0-7232-2020-4 : £2.95
(B77-24546)

Jemima Puddle-Duck's painting book / from the original designs by Beatrix Potter. — London [etc.] : F. Warne, [1976]. — [16]p : ill ; 22cm. — ([Potter painting books])
ISBN 0-7232-1995-8 Sd : £0.40
Also classified at 741
(B77-04438)

Jenkins, Alan Charles. The winter-sleeper / [by] Alan C. Jenkins ; illustrated by Graham Humphreys. — London : Hamilton, 1977. — 88p : ill ; 19cm. — (Antelope books)
ISBN 0-241-89568-5 : £1.25
(B77-10612)

Jennings, Eve. The mine kid kidnap / [by] Eve Jennings. — London : Hamilton, 1977. — [7], 115p ; 23cm.
ISBN 0-241-89649-5 : £2.75
(B77-23777)

Jeremy Fisher's painting book / from the original designs by Beatrix Potter. — London [etc.] : F. Warne, [1976]. — [16]p : ill ; 22cm. — ([Potter painting books])
ISBN 0-7232-1994-x Sd : £0.40
Also classified at 741
(B77-04439)

Jermieson, Allan. The house with no windows / [by] Allan Jermieson. — Glasgow [etc.] : Blackie, 1977. — 3-123p ; 23cm.
ISBN 0-216-90168-5 : £3.25
(B77-13386)

Jezard, Alison. Albert's circus / by Alison Jezard ; illustrated by Margaret Gordon. — London : Gollancz, 1977. — 63p : ill ; 24cm.
ISBN 0-575-02280-9 : £2.20
(B77-17786)

Jiminy Cricket. — Maidenhead : Purnell, 1974. — [16]p : col ill ; 12cm. — ([Minikins])
Sd : £0.06
(B77-19827)

'Jinty' annual. — London : IPC Magazines.
1978. — [1977]. — 3-142p : chiefly ill(some col), col ports ; 28cm. — (A Fleetway annual)
Cover title. — Ill., text on lining papers.
ISBN 0-85037-333-6 : £1.15
(B77-32906)

Joanna doll dressing book. — Maidenhead : Purnell, 1977. — [20]p : ill(some col) ; 26cm.
Sd : £0.15
ISBN 0-361-03794-5
Also classified at 745.59'22
(B77-12156)

Johns, William Earl. Biggles, air detective / by W.E. Johns. — London : Dean, 1952 [i.e. 1977]. — 151p ; 20cm.
Originally published: London : Latimer House, 1952.
ISBN 0-603-03410-1 : £0.40
(B77-30763)

Johns, William Earl. Biggles and the black peril / by W.E. Johns. — London : Dean, [1977]. — 184p ; 20cm.
Originally published: London : Thames Publishing Co., 1953.
ISBN 0-603-03403-9 : £0.40
(B77-30764)

Johns, William Earl. Biggles flies again / by W.E. Johns. — London : Dean, [1977]. — 183p ; 20cm.
Originally published: London : J. Hamilton, 1934.
ISBN 0-603-03402-0 : £0.40
(B77-30765)

Johns, William Earl. Biggles of 266 / by W.E. Johns. — London : Dean, [1977]. — 183p ; 20cm.
Originally published: London : Thames Publishing Co., 1956.
ISBN 0-603-03407-1 : £0.40
(B77-30766)

Johns, William Earl. Biggles of the Camel Squadron / by W.E. Johns. — London : Dean, [1977]. — 182p ; 20cm.
Originally published: London : J. Hamilton, 1934.
ISBN 0-603-03404-7 : £0.40
(B77-30767)

Johns, William Earl. Biggles of the Special Air Police / by W.E. Johns. — London : Dean, [1977]. — 183p ; 20cm.
Originally published: London : Thames Publishing Co., 1953.
ISBN 0-603-03408-x : £0.40
(B77-30768)

Johns, William Earl. Biggles, pioneer air fighter / by W.E. Johns. — London : Dean, [1977]. — 184p ; 20cm.
Originally published: London : Thames Publishing Co., 1954.
ISBN 0-603-03405-5 : £0.40
(B77-30769)

Johns, William Earl. The boy Biggles / by W.E. Johns. — London : Dean, 1968 [i.e. 1977]. — 182p ; 20cm.
Originally published: 1968.
£0.40
ISBN 0-603-03401-2
(B77-30770)

Johnston, Johanna. Sugarplum & Snowball / [by] Johanna Jonnston ; illustrated by Idelette Bordigoni. — Tadworth : World's Work, 1976. — [40]p : ill(some col) ; 21x26cm.
Originally published: New York : Knopf, 1968.
ISBN 0-437-51103-0 : £2.40
(B77-01853)

Jones, Diana Wynne. Charmed life / [by] Diana Wynne Jones. — London [etc.] : Macmillan, 1977. — [5],209p ; 21cm.
ISBN 0-333-21426-9 : £2.95
(B77-11439)

Jones, Diana Wynne. Eight days of Luke / [by] Diana Wynne Jones. — Harmondsworth [etc.] : Puffin Books, 1977. — 174p ; 18cm. — (Puffin books)
Originally published: London : Macmillan, 1975.
ISBN 0-14-030969-1 Pbk : £0.50
(B77-24547)

Jones, Diana Wynne. The ogre downstairs / [by] Diana Wynne Jones. — Harmondsworth : Puffin Books, 1977. — 189p ; 18cm. — (Puffin books)
Originally published: London : Macmillan, 1974.
ISBN 0-14-030898-9 Pbk : £0.55
(B77-08126)

Jones, Gwyneth A. Water in the air / [by] Gwyneth A. Jones. — London [etc.] : Macmillan, 1977. — 179p ; 21cm.
ISBN 0-333-22757-3 : £3.50
(B77-27472)

Jones, Harold. There & back again / [by] Harold Jones. — Oxford [etc.] : Oxford University Press, 1977. — [32]p : col ill ; 20cm.
ISBN 0-19-279715-8 : £1.75
(B77-30771)

'Judy' for girls annual. — London : D.C. Thomson.
1978. — 1977. — [124]p : chiefly col ill, 2 maps(1 col), ports(some col) ; 28cm.
Col. ill., text on lining papers.
£0.95
(B77-31560)

'June' book. — London : IPC Magazines.
[1978]. — [1977]. — 95p : chiefly ill(some col) ; 28cm. — (A Fleetway annual)
Cover title.
ISBN 0-85037-334-4 : £1.45
(B77-32907)

Kahl, Virginia. The duchess bakes a cake / written and illustrated by Virginia Kahl. — London : Collins, 1977. — [33p] : col ill ; 22cm. — (Picture lions)
Originally published: New York : Scribner, 1955.
ISBN 0-00-660866-3 Sd : £0.50
(B77-25232)

Kantrowitz, Mildred. Willy Bear / by Mildred Kantrowitz ; illustrated by Nancy Winslow Parker. — London [etc.] : Bodley Head, 1977. — [31]p : col ill ; 18cm.
Originally published: New York : Parents Magazine Press, 1976.
ISBN 0-370-30045-9 : £1.95
(B77-32908)

Karp, Naomi J. The turning point / [by] Naomi J. Karp. — New York ; London : Harcourt Brace Jovanovich, 1976. — [4],154p ; 21cm.
ISBN 0-15-291238-x : Unpriced
(B77-17787)

Katy doll dressing book. — Maidenhead : Purnell, 1977. — [20]p : ill(some col) ; 26cm.
Sd : £0.15
ISBN 0-361-03794-5
Also classified at 745.59'22
(B77-12157)

Kaye, Geraldine. Children of the turnpike / [by] Geraldine Kaye ; illustrated by Gareth Floyd. — London [etc.] : Hodder and Stoughton, 1976. — 152p ; 22cm.
ISBN 0-340-19544-4 : £2.40
(B77-06335)

Kaye, Geraldine. A nail, a stick and a lid / [by] Geraldine Kaye ; illustrated by Linda Birch. — Leicester : Brockhampton Press : Knight Books, 1975. — [24]p : col ill ; 21cm. — (Stepping stones)
ISBN 0-340-19645-9 : £0.60
ISBN 0-340-19642-4 Pbk : £0.35
(B77-02634)

Kaye-Smith, Sheila. The children's summer / [by] Sheila Kaye-Smith. — Large print ed. — Bath : Chivers, 1977. — [9],374p ; 22cm.
Originally published: London : Cassell, 1932.
ISBN 0-85997-263-1 : £5.80(£4.35 to members of the Library Association)
(B77-34234)

Keats, Ezra Jack. Pssst! Doggie - / by Ezra Jack Keats. — New York ; London : F. Watts, 1973. — [32]p : of col ill ; 26cm.
ISBN 0-531-02598-5 : £1.95
(B77-32909)

Keats, Ezra Jack. The snowy day / [by] Ezra Jack Keats. — Harmondsworth [etc.] : Puffin Books, 1976. — 35p : chiefly col ill ; 19x23cm. — ([Picture puffin])
Originally published: New York : Viking Press, 1962 ; London : Bodley Head, 1967.
ISBN 0-14-050182-7 Pbk : Unpriced
(B77-01854)

Keats, Ezra Jack. Whistle for Willie / [by] Ezra Jack Keats. — Harmondsworth [etc.] : Penguin, 1977. — 31,[1]p : chiefly col ill ; 17x20cm. — ([Picture puffin])
Originally published: New York : Viking Press, 1964 ; London : Bodley Head, 1966.
ISBN 0-14-050011-1 Sd : £0.50
(B77-22941)

Keene, Carolyn. The bungalow mystery / [by] Carolyn Keene. — London : Armada, 1976. — 160p : 1 ill ; 18cm. — (Keene, Carolyn. Nancy Drew mystery stories)
Originally published: New York : Grosset and Dunlap, 1960 ; London : Collins, 1972.
ISBN 0-00-691216-8 Pbk : £0.40
(B77-11440)

Keene, Carolyn. Password to Larkspur Lane / [by] Carolyn Keene. — London : Armada Paperbacks, 1976. — 160p : ill ; 18cm. — (Keene, Carolyn. Nancy Drew mystery stories ; 12)
Originally published: New York : Grosset and Dunlap, 1966 ; London : Collins, 1972.
ISBN 0-00-691161-7 Pbk : £0.40
(B77-10972)

Keeping, Charles. Inter-city / [by] Charles Keeping. — Oxford [etc.] : Oxford University Press, 1977. — [32]p : of ill(chiefly col) ; 29cm.
ISBN 0-19-279716-6 : £2.95
(B77-32910)

Kellogg, Steven. Much bigger than Martin / story and pictures by Steven Kellogg. — [London] : F. Warne, 1977. — [32]p : col ill ; 29cm.
Originally published: New York : Dial Press, 1976.
ISBN 0-7232-2054-9 : £2.95
(B77-32265)

Kellogg, Steven. The mystery beast of Ostergeest / [by] Steven Kellogg. — [London] : F. Warne, 1977. — [32]p : chiefly col ill ; 29cm.
Originally published: New York : Dial Press, 1971.
ISBN 0-7232-2028-x : £2.95
(B77-15568)

Kemp, Gene. Christmas with Tamworth Pig / [by] Gene Kemp ; illustrated by Carolyn Dinan. — London : Faber, 1977. — 93p : ill ; 21cm.
ISBN 0-571-11117-3 : £2.50 : CIP rev.
(B77-22942)

Kemp, Gene. The turbulent term of Tyke Tiler / [by] Gene Kemp ; illustrated by Carolyn Dinan. — London : Faber, 1977. — 3-118p : ill ; 21cm.
ISBN 0-571-10966-7 : £2.75
(B77-08127)

Kendall, Lace. Rain boat / [by] Lace Kendall ; illustrated by Charles Keeping. — London : Hamilton, 1977. — 136p : ill ; 23cm.
Originally published: New York : Coward-McCann, 1965 ; London : Hamilton, 1966.
ISBN 0-241-89787-4 : £1.95
(B77-28997)

Kennedy, Richard. The porcelain man / by Richard Kennedy ; illustrated by Marcia Sewall. — London : Hamilton, 1977. — 31p : col ill ; 20x25cm.
Originally published: Boston, Mass. : Little, Brown, 1976.
ISBN 0-241-89754-8 : £2.75
(B77-28224)

Kennett, John. King Solomon's mines / [by] H. Rider Haggard ; retold by John Kennett ; illustrated by Fred Vaughn. — Glasgow [etc.] : Blackie, 1977. — [7],136p : ill, map ; 19cm. — (The Kennett library : long series)
ISBN 0-216-90355-6 : £1.30
(B77-15569)

Kent, Jack. There's no such thing as a dragon / story and pictures by Jack Kent. — London : Abelard, 1977. — [32]p : chiefly col ill ; 21cm.
Originally published: New York : Golden Press, 1975.
ISBN 0-200-72465-7 : £3.25
ISBN 0-200-72466-5 Pbk : £0.75
(B77-34235)

Kerr, Judith. The other way round / [by] Judith Kerr. — London : Fontana, 1977. — 220p ; 18cm. — (Lions)
Originally published: London : Collins, 1975.
ISBN 0-00-671234-7 Pbk : £0.65
(B77-25952)

Kerr, Judith. When Willy went to the wedding / written and illustrated by Judith Kerr. — London : Fontana, 1977. — [33]p : chiefly col ill ; 22cm. — (Picture lions)
Originally published: London : Collins, 1972.
ISBN 0-00-661340-3 Sd : £0.60
(B77-28225)

Kesteven, G.R. The awakening water / [by] G.R. Kesteven. — London : Chatto and Windus, 1977. — 160p ; 21cm.
ISBN 0-7011-2229-3 : £3.25 : CIP rev.
(B77-09343)

King, Clive. The night the water came / [by] Clive King ; illustrated by Mark Peppé. — Harmondsworth [etc.] : Puffin Books, 1976. — 138p : ill ; 19cm. — (Puffin books)
Originally published: Harmondsworth : Longman Young Books, 1973.
ISBN 0-14-030769-9 Pbk : £0.45
(B77-01855)

King, Eve. Prince Peter of Siam ; and, Sally Sheepdog's adventure / [by] Eve King ; illustrated by Cora E.M. Paterson. — Ilfracombe : Stockwell, 1976. — 23p : ill ; 18cm.
ISBN 0-7223-0961-9 Pbk : £0.40
(B77-10973)

King, Kathleen. Katie and the bicycle! : (with a view to road safety) / by Kathleen King ; illustrations by Janet Vendrell. — [Coleraine] ([Bungalow 18, Drumadraw, Coleraine, Co. Londonderry]) : [The author], [1976]. — [18]p : ill ; 29cm.
ISBN 0-9504087-1-9 Sd : £0.50
(B77-06923)

'Knockout' annual. — London : IPC Magazines. 1978. — [1977]. — 143p : chiefly ill(chiefly col) ; 28cm. — (A Fleetway annual)
Cover title.
ISBN 0-85037-335-2 : £1.15
(B77-32911)

Koenig, Marion. The tale of Fancy Nancy : a Spanish folk tale / adapted by Marion Koenig ; illustrated by Klaus Ensikat. — London : Chatto and Windus, 1977. — [26]p : chiefly col ill ; 25cm.
Translation and adaptation of: 'Kieselchen' / written and illustrated by Klaus Ensikat. Berlin : Altberliner Verlag Lucie Groszer, 1976.
ISBN 0-7011-5100-5 : £2.25
(B77-27473)

Kraus, Robert. The gondolier of Venice / by Robert Kraus ; illustrated by Robert Byrd. — London : Andersen Press : Hutchinson, 1977. — [32]p : chiefly ill ; 26cm.
Originally published: New York : Windmills Books, 1976.
ISBN 0-905478-16-9 : £1.75
(B77-28226)

Kraus, Robert. Herman the helper / by Robert Kraus ; pictures by Jose Aruego & Ariane Dewey. — Harmondsworth : Kestrel Books, 1977. — [32]p : chiefly col ill ; 31cm.
Originally published: New York : Windmill Books, 1974.
ISBN 0-7226-5296-8 : £2.25
(B77-11441)

Krauss, Ruth. Charlotte and the white horse / [text] by Ruth Krauss ; pictures by Maurice Sendak. — London : Bodley Head, 1977. — [24]p : chiefly col ill ; 17cm.
Originally published: New York : Harper, 1955.
ISBN 0-370-30012-2 : £1.75
(B77-12744)

Krazy annual. — London : IPC Magazines. [1978]. — 1977. — 2-143p : chiefly ill(some col) ; 28cm. — (A Fleetway annual)
ISBN 0-85037-373-5 : £1.00
ISSN 0140-718x
(B77-33477)

Kyle, Elisabeth. The reivers' road / [by] Elisabeth Kyle ; illustrated by A.R. Watson. — London [etc.] : White Lion Publishers, 1977. — vi,250p : ill ; 21cm.
Originally published: London : Nelson, 1953.
ISBN 0-85686-291-6 : £3.00
(B77-08128)

Lambert the lion cub. — Maidenhead : Purnell, 1974. — [16]p : col ill ; 12cm. — ([Minikins])
Sd : £0.06
(B77-19828)

Lanier, Sterling Edmund. The war for The Lot / [by] Sterling E. Lanier. — London : Sidgwick and Jackson, 1977. — 256p : map ; 21cm.
Originally published: Chicago : Follett, 1969.
ISBN 0-283-98377-9 : £3.50
(B77-20723)

Lavelle, Sheila. Ursula Bear / [by] Sheila Lavelle ; illustrated by Thelma Lambert. — London : Hamilton, 1977. — 48p : col ill ; 20cm. — (Gazelle books)
ISBN 0-241-89647-9 : £0.95
(B77-23778)

Lawrence, Ann. Between the forest and the hills / [by] Ann Lawrence ; decorations by Chris Molan. — Harmondsworth : Kestrel Books, 1977. — 221p : ill, maps ; 23cm.
ISBN 0-7226-5282-8 : £3.50
(B77-10974)

Lawrence, Ann. The conjuror's box / [by] Ann Lawrence ; cover illustration by Gwen Fulton ; text illustrations by Brian Alldridge. — London : Pan Books, 1977. — 190p : ill ; 18cm. — (Piccolo)
Originally published: London : Kestrel Books, 1974.
ISBN 0-330-25101-5 Pbk : £0.50
(B77-25233)

Lawrence, Ann. Oggy at home / by Ann Lawrence ; illustrated by Hans Helweg. — London : Gollancz, 1977. — 112p : ill ; 21cm.
ISBN 0-575-02366-x : £2.95
(B77-33478)

Le Guin, Ursula Kroeber. Earthsea / by Ursula Le Guin. — London : Gollancz, 1977. — 191, 160,207p : maps ; 21cm.
Map on lining papers. — Contents: A wizard of Earthsea. Originally published: Berkeley : Parnassus Press, 1968 ; Harmondsworth : Penguin, 1971 - The tombs of Atuan. Originally published: New York : Atheneum, 1971 ; London : Gollancz, 1972 - The farthest shore. Originally published: New York : Atheneum, 1972 ; London : Gollancz, 1973.
ISBN 0-575-02274-4 : £4.25
(B77-10975)

Leach, Christopher, *b.1925.* Searching for skylights / by Christopher Leach. — London : Dent, 1977. — 122p ; 21cm.
ISBN 0-460-06745-1 : £2.95
(B77-06336)

Leaf, Munro. The story of Ferdinand / [by] Munro Leaf ; illustrated by Robert Lawson. — Harmondsworth [etc.] : Puffin Books, 1977. — [73]p : ill ; 20cm. — (A young puffin)
Originally published: New York : Viking Press, 1936 ; London : Hamilton, 1937.
ISBN 0-14-030328-6 Pbk : £0.45
(B77-34236)

Leaf, Munro. The story of Ferdinand / by Munro Leaf ; illustrated by Robert Lawson. — Harmondsworth [etc.] : Puffin Books, 1977. — [72]p : ill ; 23cm. — (Picture puffin)
Originally published: New York : Viking Press, 1936 ; London : Hamilton, 1937.
ISBN 0-14-050234-3 Pbk : Unpriced
(B77-34237)

Lee, Josephine. The fabulous manticora / [by] Josephine Lee. — Leicester : Knight Books, 1977. — 3-193p : 1 ill ; 18cm.
Originally published: London : Cape, 1973.
ISBN 0-340-18432-9 Pbk : £0.60
(B77-21538)

Lee, Tanith. East of midnight / [by] Tanith Lee. — London [etc.] : Macmillan, 1977. — 175p ; 21cm.
ISBN 0-333-23069-8 : £3.50
(B77-27474)

Leeson, Robert. The demon bike rider / [by] Robert Leeson ; illustrated by Jim Russell. — London : Fontana, 1977. — 94p : ill ; 20cm. — (Lions)
Originally published: London : Collins, 1976.
ISBN 0-00-671320-3 Pbk : £0.50
(B77-25953)

Lefebure, Molly. The hunting of Wilberforce Pike / [by] Molly Lefebure ; illustrated by A. Wainwright. — London : Collins, 1975. — 128p : ill ; 18cm. — (Lions)
Originally published: London : Gollancz, 1970.
ISBN 0-00-670945-1 Pbk : £0.35
(B77-03249)

Leigh, Bill. Sink-hole / [by] Bill Leigh. — London : Gollancz, 1977. — 142p ; 21cm.
ISBN 0-575-02275-2 : £3.40
(B77-13387)

Leigh, Heather Elsie. Fernando and his foreign friends / [by] Heather Leigh ; illustrated by A. Atterbury. — Ilfracombe : Stockwell, 1976. — 24p : ill(some col), map ; 18cm.
ISBN 0-7223-0962-7 Pbk : £0.30
(B77-10976)

Leitch, Patricia. A devil to ride / [by] Patricia Leitch. — London : Armada, 1976. — 127p : 1 ill ; 18cm. — (Leitch, Patricia. Jinny at Finmory)
ISBN 0-00-691171-4 Pbk : £0.40
(B77-11442)

Leitch, Patricia. For love of a horse / [by] Patricia Leitch. — London : Armada, 1976. — 125p ; 18cm. — (Leitch, Patricia. Jinny at Finmory)
ISBN 0-00-691170-6 Pbk : £0.40
(B77-11443)

Leo Leggins and the Flodolopos. — [London] : Collins, 1976. — [48]p : chiefly col ill ; 15cm. — (Collins colour cubs)
ISBN 0-00-123307-6 : £0.95
ISBN 0-00-123302-5 Pbk : £0.30
(B77-18408)

Leo Leggins and the gigantic giant. — [London] : Collins, 1976. — [48]p : chiefly col ill ; 15cm. — (Collins colour cubs)
ISBN 0-00-123306-8 : £0.95
ISBN 0-00-123301-7 Pbk : £0.30
(B77-18409)

Leo Leggins and the Viking dragon. — [London] : Collins, 1976. — [48]p : chiefly col ill ; 15cm. — (Collins colour cubs)
ISBN 0-00-123308-4 : £0.95
ISBN 0-00-123303-3 Pbk : £0.30
(B77-18410)

Leo Leggins and the witch's pool. — [London] : Collins, 1976. — [48]p : chiefly col ill ; 15cm. — (Collins colour cubs)
ISBN 0-00-123309-2 : £0.95
ISBN 0-00-123304-1 Pbk : £0.30
(B77-18411)

LeSieg, Theo. Hooper Humperdink - ? Not him! / by Theo. LeSieg ; illustrated by Charles E. Martin. — [London] : Collins, 1977. — [40] p : chiefly col ill ; 24cm. — (A beginning beginner book) (A bright and early book)
Originally published: New York : Beginner Books, 1976.
ISBN 0-00-171228-4 : £0.95
(B77-14985)

LeSieg, Theo. Would you rather be a bullfrog? / by Theo. LeSieg ; illustrated by Roy McKie. — London [etc.] : Collins : Harvill Press, 1976. — [28]p : chiefly col ill ; 24cm. — (A beginning behinner book) (A bright and early book)
Originally published: New York : Random House, 1975.
ISBN 0-00-171290-x : £0.95
(B77-04440)

Leslie, Stephen. Three men in a maze / [devised by] Stephen Leslie ; illustrated by Alf Bates. — London : Transworld, 1977. — [93]p : chiefly ill ; 13x20cm. — (A tracker action book)
'The text which accompanies the illustrations, is from Jerome K. Jerome's immortal "Three Men in a Boat"' - p.[1].
ISBN 0-552-56007-3 Pbk : £0.45
(B77-32266)

Lester, Julius. Long journey home / [by] Julius Lester. — Harmondsworth [etc.] : Puffin Books, 1977. — 160p ; 18cm. — (Puffin books)

This collection originally published: New York : Dial Press, 1972 ; Harmondsworth : Longman Young Books, 1973.
ISBN 0-14-030903-9 Pbk : £0.50
(B77-12745)

Lindsay, Norman. The magic pudding : being the adventures of Bunyip Bluegum and his friends Bill Barnacle and Sam Sawnoff / by Norman Lindsay. — Sydney ; London [etc.] : Angus and Robertson. — (The young Australia series)
In 4 vols. — Originally published: in 1 vol. Sydney : Angus and Robertson, 1918 ; London : Hamilton, 1936.
[1] : First slice. — 1977. — [29]p : ill(chiefly col) ; 30cm.
Text on lining papers.
ISBN 0-207-12244-x : £0.95
(B77-24548)

[2] : Second slice. — 1977. — [30]p : ill(chiefly col) ; 30cm.
Text on lining papers.
ISBN 0-207-12290-3 : £0.95
(B77-24549)

[3] : Third slice. — 1977. — [30]p : ill(chiefly col) ; 30cm.
Text on lining papers.
ISBN 0-207-12420-5 : £0.95
(B77-24550)

[4] : Fourth slice. — 1977. — [29]p : ill(chiefly col) ; 30cm.
Text on lining paper.
ISBN 0-207-12959-2 : £0.95
(B77-24551)

Line, David. Mike and me / [by] David Line. — London : Heinemann Educational, 1977. — 156p ; 20cm. — (The new windmill series ; 218)
Originally published: London : Cape, 1974.
ISBN 0-435-12218-5 : £0.85
(B77-32267)

Linfield, Esther. The lion of the Kalahari / [by] Sam B. Hobson and George Carey Hobson ; translated and adapted from the Afrikaans by Esther Linfield. — London : Gollancz, 1977. — x,118p : ill, 2 maps ; 21cm.
Translation and adaptation of: 'Shankwan van die dvine'. Pretoria : J.L. van Schaik, 1930.
ISBN 0-575-02278-7 : £2.95
(B77-13929)

Lingard, Joan. Snake among the sunflowers / [by] Joan Lingard. — London : Hamilton, 1977. — [6],122p ; 23cm.
ISBN 0-241-89547-2 : £2.50
(B77-19037)

'Lion' annual. — London : IPC Magazines. [1978]. — 1977. — 128p : chiefly ill ; 28cm. — (A Fleetway annual)
ISBN 0-85037-336-0 Pbk : £0.85
(B77-32912)

Lionni, Leo. A colour of his own / [by] Leo Lionni. — London : Fontana, 1977. — [34]p : col ill ; 21cm. — (Picture lions)
Originally published: London : Abelard-Schuman, 1975.
ISBN 0-00-660873-6 Sd : £0.60
(B77-27475)

Lionni, Leo. The greentail mouse / by Leo Lionni. — London : Collins, 1976. — [33]p : col ill ; 22cm. — (Picture lions)
Originally published: New York : Pantheon Books, 1973 ; London : Abelard-Schuman, 1974.
ISBN 0-00-660848-5 Sd : £0.45
(B77-10977)

Lionni, Leo. Pezzettino / [by] Leo Lionni. — London (3 Fitzroy Sq., W.1) : Andersen Press Ltd [etc.], 1977. — [34]p : chiefly col ill ; 26cm.
Originally published: New York : Pantheon Books, 1975.
ISBN 0-905478-08-8 : £2.75
(B77-22213)

Lisker, Sonia O. Two special cards / by Sonia O. Lisker and Leigh Dean ; pictures by Sonia O. Lisker. — New York ; London : Harcourt Brace Jovanovich, 1976. — [48]p : ill ; 21cm.
ISBN 0-15-292222-9 : £3.50
(B77-17788)

'Little star'. — Dundee [etc.] : D.C. Thomson. 1978. — [1977]. — [58]p : chiefly col ill ; 25cm.
Col. ill., text on lining papers.
£0.80
(B77-31561)

Lively, Penelope. Fanny's sister / [by] Penelope Lively ; illustrated by John Lawrence. — London : Heinemann, 1976. — 43p : ill ; 21cm. — (Long ago children books)
ISBN 0-434-94924-8 : £2.10
(B77-19038)

Lively, Penelope. Going back / [by] Penelope Lively ; cover illustration by Nancy Pettey-Jones. — London : Pan Books, 1977. — 110p ; 18cm. — (Piccolo)
Originally published: London : Heinemann, 1975.
ISBN 0-330-25253-4 Pbk : £0.50
(B77-34238)

Lobel, Arnold. How the rooster saved the day / [text by] Arnold Lobel ; pictures by Anita Lobel. — London : Hamilton, 1977. — [32]p : col ill ; 21x26cm.
Originally published: New York : Greenwillow Books, 1977.
ISBN 0-241-89696-7 : £2.75
(B77-28998)

Lobel, Arnold. Mouse tales / [story and pictures] by Arnold Lobel. — Tadworth : World's Work, 1977. — 64p : col ill ; 22cm. — (An I can read book)
Originally published: New York : Harper and Row, 1972 ; Tadworth : World's Work, 1973.
ISBN 0-437-96006-4 Sd : £0.60
(B77-16626)

Locke, Elsie. The boy with the snowgrass hair / [by] Elsie Locke and Ken Dawson ; illustrations by Jean Oates, maps by Cath Brown. — Christchurch, N.Z. [etc.] ; London : Whitcoulls, 1976. — 183p : ill, maps ; 21cm. — ([Kairangi series])
ISBN 0-7233-0468-8 : Unpriced
(B77-09344)

Locke, Elsie. Ugly little Paua ; [and], Moko's hideout ; [and], To fly to Siberia ; [and], Tricky Kelly / [by] Elsie Locke. — Christchurch, N.Z. [etc.] ; London : Whitcoulls, 1976. — 52p : col ill(on lining papers) ; 25cm.
Cover title: Moko's hideout.
ISBN 0-7233-0466-1 : Unpriced
(B77-09345)

Lofting, Hugh. Introducing Doctor Dolittle / [by] Hugh Lofting ; compiled by Olga Fricker. — Harmondsworth [etc.] : Puffin Books, 1977. — 268p : ill ; 19cm. — (Puffin books)
Originally published: as 'Doctor Dolittle, a treasury'. Philadelphia : Lippincott, 1967 ; London : Cape, 1968.
ISBN 0-14-030880-6 Pbk : £0.70
(B77-07671)

Long, short and tall tales / ... stories and verses ... by Janet Barber ... [et al.] ; ... illustrations ... by Joan Beales ... [et al.]. — London [etc.] : Hamlyn, 1977. — 5-157p : ill(some col) ; 28cm.

Col. ill., text on lining papers.
ISBN 0-600-35524-1 : £2.50
(B77-23779)

Lynch, Patricia. The turf-cutter's donkey : an Irish story of mystery and adventure / [by] Patricia Lynch ; illustrated by Jack B. Yeats. — London [etc.] : White Lion Publishers, 1977. — viii,237p,[5] leaves of plates : ill ; 21cm.
Facsimile reprint of: 1st ed. London : Dent, 1934.
ISBN 0-85686-295-9 : £2.95
(B77-12746)

McCann, Sean. The golden goal / [by] Sean McCann ; illustrated by Barry Raynor. — London [etc.] : Hodder and Stoughton, 1977. — 88p : ill ; 21cm.
ISBN 0-340-20626-8 : £2.80
(B77-16627)

McCloskey, Robert. Homer Price / by Robert McCloskey. — Harmondsworth [etc.] : Puffin Books, 1976. — 149,[3]p : ill ; 20cm. — (A puffin book)
Originally published: New York : Viking Press, 1943.
ISBN 0-14-030927-6 Pbk : Unpriced
(B77-03784)

McCloskey, Robert. Time of wonder / by Robert McCloskey. — Harmondsworth [etc.] : Puffin Books, 1977. — 63p : col ill ; 23cm. — (Picture puffin)
Originally published: New York : Viking Press, 1957.
ISBN 0-14-050201-7 Pbk : Unpriced
(B77-26618)

McCullagh, Sheila Kathleen. The dancers from the Land of Mor / [by] Sheila McCullagh ; drawings by Peter Rush. — St Albans : Hart-Davis Educational, 1977. — [1],48p : ill(some col) ; 22cm. — (McCullagh, Sheila Kathleen. Hummingbirds)
ISBN 0-247-12642-x Sd : £0.85
(B77-19829)

McCullagh, Sheila Kathleen. The giant owls of the high hills / [by] Sheila McCullagh ; drawings by Eccles. — St Albans : Hart-Davis Educational, 1977. — [1],48p : ill(some col) ; 22cm. — (McCullagh, Sheila Kathleen. Hummingbirds)
ISBN 0-247-12643-8 : £0.85
(B77-19830)

McCullagh, Sheila Kathleen. The green man and the golden bird / [by] Sheila McCullagh ; drawings by Peter Rush. — St Albans : Hart-Davis Educational, 1976. — [1],48p : ill(some col) ; 22cm. — (McCullagh, Sheila Kathleen. Hummingbirds)
ISBN 0-247-12637-3 Sd : £0.85
(B77-01007)

McCullagh, Sheila Kathleen. The horses of the moonlight / [by] Sheila McCullagh ; drawings by Tony Morris. — St Albans : Hart-Davis Educational, 1976. — [1],48p : ill(some col) ; 22cm. — (McCullagh, Sheila Kathleen. Hummingbirds)
ISBN 0-247-12640-3 Sd : £0.85
(B77-01008)

McCullagh, Sheila Kathleen. Jacca and the talking dog / [by] Sheila McCullagh ; drawings by Arthur Hall. — St Albans : Hart-Davis Educational, 1977. — [1],48p : ill(some col) ; 22cm. — (McCullagh, Sheila Kathleen. Hummingbirds)
ISBN 0-247-12641-1 Sd : £0.85
(B77-19831)

McCullagh, Sheila Kathleen. The magic cloak / [by] Sheila McCullagh ; drawings by Eccles. — St Albans : Hart-Davis Educational, 1976. — [1],48p : ill(some col) ; 22cm. — (McCullagh, Sheila Kathleen. Hummingbirds)
ISBN 0-247-12639-x Sd : £0.85
(B77-01009)

McCullagh, Sheila Kathleen. Mrs Blue-hat is very cross / [by] Sheila McCullagh ; drawings by Eccles. — St Albans : Hart-Davis Educational, 1976. — [1],48p : ill(some col) ; 22cm. — (McCullagh, Sheila Kathleen. Hummingbirds)
ISBN 0-247-12638-1 Sd : £0.85
(B77-01010)

McCullagh, Sheila Kathleen. Peter and the little fox / [by] Sheila McCullagh ; drawings by Tony Morris. — St Albans : Hart-Davis Educational, 1977. — [1],48p : ill(some col) ; 22cm. — (McCullagh, Sheila Kathleen. Hummingbirds)
ISBN 0-247-12644-6 Sd : £0.85
(B77-19832)

McDermott, Gerald. Arrow to the sun : a Pueblo Indian tale / adapted and illustrated by Gerald McDermott. — Harmondsworth : Kestrel Books, 1977. — [46]p : chiefly col ill ; 25x28cm.
Originally published: New York : Viking Press, 1974.
ISBN 0-7226-5406-5 : £2.95
(B77-19039)

Macdonald, David. Vulpina : the story of a fox / [by] David Macdonald ; illustrated by David and Thea Nockles. — London : Collins, 1977. — 77p : ill ; 24cm.
ISBN 0-00-195229-3 : £2.50
(B77-24552)

MacDonald, Elizabeth. The incredible magic plant / [by] Elizabeth MacDonald ; with illustrations by David Knight. — Tadworth : World's Work, 1976. — [48]p : ill(chiefly col) ; 22cm.
ISBN 0-437-57001-0 : £2.50
(B77-00474)

Macdonald, Fiona. The duke who had too many giraffes, and other stories / by Fiona Macdonald ; pictures by Jill Murphy. — London : Allison and Busby, 1977. — 46p : ill ; 22cm.
ISBN 0-85031-169-1 : £1.95
(B77-25954)

Mace, Elisabeth. The ghost diviners / [by] Elisabeth Mace. — London : Deutsch, 1977. — 144p ; 21cm.
ISBN 0-233-96869-5 : £2.50
(B77-19040)

Macfarlane, Iris. The month of the night / [by] Iris Macfarlane. — Harmondsworth [etc.] : Puffin Books, 1977. — 154p : ill ; 19cm. — (Puffin books)
These translations originally published: London : Chatto and Windus, 1973. — New translations of 14 stories originally collected and translated by J.F. Campbell in his 'Popular tales of the West Highlands'. Edinburgh : Edmonston and Douglas, 1860-62.
ISBN 0-14-030881-4 Pbk : £0.50
(B77-12158)

McGough, Roger. Mr Noselighter / by Roger McGouch ; illustrated by André François. — London : G. Whizzard Publications Ltd : [Distributed by] Deutsch, 1976. — [42]p : chiefly ill(chiefly col) ; 21x25cm.
Col. ill. on lining papers.
ISBN 0-233-96822-9 : £2.50
(B77-07672)

McGovern, Ann. Half a kingdom : an Icelandic folktale / by Ann McGovern ; pictures by Nola Langner. — New York ; London : F. Warne, 1977. — [44]p : ill ; 22x27cm.
'... based on an Icelandic folktale published in the European folklore series "European Folk Tales, Volume 1" ...' - title page verso.
ISBN 0-7232-6137-7 : £2.50
(B77-34239)

Machon, Roy. Cranmer the crocodile / written and drawn by Roy Machon. — Cobham : Starfish Books, [1976]. — [78]p : ill ; 18cm.
ISBN 0-900708-96-4 Pbk : £0.30
(B77-05730)

McKee, David. The magician and the petnapping / story and pictures by David McKee. — London : Abelard-Schuman, 1976. — [28]p : col ill ; 28cm.
Col. ill. on lining papers.
ISBN 0-200-72451-7 : £2.65
(B77-01856)

McKee, David. Two admirals / [by] David McKee. — London (3 Fitzroy Sq., W.1) : Andersen Press Ltd [etc.], 1977. — [32]p : chiefly col ill ; 29cm.
ISBN 0-905478-06-1 : £2.50
(B77-19833)

McLachlan, Edward. Simon and the dinosaur / [by] Edward McLachlan. — Leicester : Knight Books, 1977. — [32]p : ill(chiefly col) ; 21cm. — (Colour knight)
Originally published: Leicester : Brockhampton Press, 1973.
ISBN 0-340-21953-x Pbk : £0.60
(B77-14986)

McLachlan, Edward. Simon and the moon rocket / [by] Edward McLachlan. — Leicester : Knight Books, 1977. — [22]p : ill(chiefly col) ; 21cm. — (Colour knight)
Originally published: Leicester : Brockhampton Press, 1972.
ISBN 0-340-21952-1 Pbk : £0.60
(B77-14987)

McLeish, Kenneth. The peace players / [by] Kenneth McLeish ; illustrated by Jeroo Roy. — London : Heinemann, 1977. — 47,[1]p : ill ; 21cm. — (Long ago children books)
Based on the lives of Aristophanes, Apollodoros and Hermon.
ISBN 0-434-94923-x : £1.90
(B77-05731)

McMurtry, Stan. The Bunjee venture / by Stan McMurtry. — Henley-on-Thames (Kestrels House, Peppard Common, Henley-on-Thames) : Cressrelles Publishing Co., 1977. — 128p : ill ; 21cm.
ISBN 0-85956-026-0 : £2.50
(B77-23780)

McNaughton, Colin. Walk rabbit walk / story by Colin McNaughton and Elizabeth Attenborough ; pictures by Colin McNaughton. — London : Heinemann, 1977. — [32]p : chiefly col ill ; 21cm.
ISBN 0-434-94988-4 : £2.40
(B77-19041)

McNeill, Janet. The three crowns of King Hullabaloo / [by] Janet McNeill ; illustrated by Mike Cole. — Leicester : Brockhampton Press : Knight Books, 1975. — [24]p : col ill ; 21cm. — (Stepping stones)
ISBN 0-340-19527-4 : £0.80
ISBN 0-340-19529-0 Pbk : £0.35
(B77-02635)

The **Magic** Roundabout annual. — London : IPC Magazines.
[1978]. — [1977]. — [44]p : chiefly ill(chiefly col) ; 31cm. — (A Fleetway annual)
'Based on the popular BBC television series'. — Cover title. — Ill. (incl. 1 col.), text on lining papers.
ISBN 0-85037-339-5 : £1.65
(B77-32913)

['The **magnet**'. Vol.45, no.1374-1376 ; June 16th-June 30th, 1934. Vol.46, no.1377-1382 ; July 7th-August 4th, 1934]. The Popper Island rebels / by Frank Richards. — London : H. Baker, 1976. — 260p in various pagings : ill(some col), port ; 28cm. — ([Howard Baker 'Magnet' ; vol.46])
Facsimile reprints. — Includes original pagings.
ISBN 0-7030-0103-5 : £4.50
(B77-13388)

['The **magnet**'. Vol.46, no.1398-1400 ; December 1st-December 15th, 1934. Vol.52, no.1541-1544 ; August 28th-September 18th, 1937]. The dictator of Greyfriars / by Frank Richards. — London : H. Baker, 1976. — 203p in various pagings : ill(some col), port ; 28cm. — ([Howard Baker 'Magnet' ; vol.43])
Facsimile reprints. — Includes original pagings.
ISBN 0-7030-0086-1 : £3.90
(B77-05732)

['The **magnet**'. Vol.49, no.1461-1468 ; February 15th-April 4th, 1936]. Billy Bunter in Brazil / by Frank Richards. — London : H. Baker, 1976. — 230p in various pagings : ill(some col), port ; 28cm. — ([Howard Baker 'Magnet' ; vol.44])
Facsimile reprints. — Includes original pagings.
ISBN 0-7030-0087-x : £3.90
(B77-05733)

['The **magnet**'. Vol.49, no.1471-1478 ; April 25th-June 13th, 1936]. Gunmen at Greyfriars / by Frank Richards. — London : H. Baker, 1976. — 230p in various pagings : ill(some col), port ; 28cm. — ([Howard Baker 'Magnet' ; vol.45])
Facsimile reprints. — Includes original pagings.
ISBN 0-7030-0089-6 : £3.90
(B77-13389)

[The **magnet.** Vol.50, no.1493-1497 ; September 26th-October 24th, 1936, no.1499-1501 ; November 7th-November 21st, 1936]. The schoolboy smuggler / [by] Frank Richards. — London : H. Baker, 1976. — 231p in various pagings : ill(some col), port ; 28cm. — ([Howard Baker 'Magnet' ; vol.47])
Facsimile reprints. — Includes original pagings.
ISBN 0-7030-0105-1 : £4.50
(B77-25234)

[The **magnet.** Vol.50, no.1502-1506 ; November 28th-December 26th, 1936. Vol.51, no.1507-1509 ; January 2nd-January 16th, 1937]. Bunter's Christmas party / by Frank Richards. — London : H. Baker, 1976. — 235p in various pagings : ill(some col), port ; 28cm. — ([Howard Baker 'Magnet' ; vol.48])
Facsimile reprints. — Includes original pagings.
ISBN 0-7030-0106-x : £4.50
(B77-25235)

[The **magnet.** Vol.55, no.1615-1622 ; January 28th-March 18th, 1939]. The mystery man of Greyfriars / by Frank Richards. — London : H. Baker, 1977. — 231p in various pagings : ill, port ; 28cm. — ([Howard Baker 'Magnet' ; vol.49])
Facsimile reprints. — Includes original pagings.
ISBN 0-7030-0111-6 : £4.50
(B77-25236)

['The **Magnet**'. Vol.56, no.1660-1663 ; December 9th-December 30th, 1939. Vol.57, no.1664-1667 ; January 6th-January 28th, 1940]. The mystery of the moat house / by Frank Richards. — London : H. Baker, 1974. — 199p in various pagings : ill, port ; 28cm. — ([Howard Baker 'Magnet' ; vol.29])
Facsimile reprints. — Includes original pagings.
ISBN 0-7030-0059-4 : £3.20
(B77-19834)

Maguire, Michael. Mylor : the most powerful horse in the world / [by] Michael Maguire ; illustrated by Nicholas Armstrong. — London : Target Books, 1977. — 192p : ill ; 18cm.
ISBN 0-426-11877-4 Pbk : £0.60
(B77-23781)

Mahood. Why are there more questions than answers, Grandad? / [by] Kenneth Mahood. — Harmondsworth [etc.] : Puffin Books, 1977. — [33]p : col ill ; 20cm. — (Picture puffins)
Originally published: London : Macmillan, 1974.
ISBN 0-14-050166-5 Sd : £0.50
(B77-11444)

Mahy, Margaret. The boy who was followed home / [text] by Margaret Mahy ; pictures by Steven Kellogg. — London : Dent, 1977. — [31]p : chiefly col ill ; 27cm.
Originally published: New York : F. Watts, 1975.
ISBN 0-460-06723-0 : £2.50 : CIP rev.
(B77-08129)

Mahy, Margaret. Nonstop nonsense / [by] Margaret Mahy ; with pictures by Quentin Blake. — London [etc.] : Dent, 1977. — 128p : ill ; 24cm.
ISBN 0-460-06806-7 : £3.50 : CIP rev.
(B77-19835)

Mahy, Margaret. The pirate uncle / [by] Margaret Mahy ; illustrated by Mary Dinsdale. — London [etc.] : Dent, 1977. — 125p : ill ; 21cm.
ISBN 0-460-06795-8 : £3.50 : CIP rev.
(B77-17145)

'**Mandy**' stories for girls. — London : D.C. Thomson.
1978. — 1977. — 3-126p : chiefly ill(chiefly col) ; 28cm.
Col. ill., text on lining papers.
£0.95
(B77-31562)

Manning-Sanders, Ruth. A book of dragons / [by] Ruth Manning-Sanders ; illustrated by Robin Jacques. — London : Methuen, 1977. — 3-130p : ill ; 20cm.
This collection originally published: 1964.
ISBN 0-416-58110-2 Pbk : £0.60
(B77-28227)

Manning-Sanders, Ruth. A book of kings and queens / [by] Ruth Manning-Sanders ; illustrated by Robin Jacques. — London : Methuen, 1977. — 126p,plate : ill(incl 1 col) ; 24cm.
ISBN 0-416-57610-9 : £3.50
(B77-29762)

Manning-Sanders, Ruth. A book of magic animals / [by] Ruth Manning-Sanders ; illustrated by Robin Jacques. — London : Methuen, 1977. — 127p : ill ; 20cm.
This collection originally published: 1974.
ISBN 0-416-58030-0 Pbk : £0.60
(B77-21539)

Manning-Sanders, Ruth. A book of monsters / [by] Ruth Manning-Sanders ; illustrated by Robin Jacques. — London : Methuen, 1977. — 128p : ill ; 20cm.
This collection originally published: 1975.
ISBN 0-416-58100-5 Pbk : £0.60
(B77-21540)

Manning-Sanders, Ruth. A book of sorcerers and spells / [by] Ruth Manning-Sanders ; illustrated by Robin Jacques. — London : Methuen, 1977. — 125p : ill ; 30cm.
Originally published: 1973.
ISBN 0-416-58120-x Pbk : £0.60
(B77-28228)

Manning-Sanders, Ruth. The Spaniards are coming! / [by] Ruth Manning-Sanders ; illustrated by Joel Jordan. — London : Heinemann, 1977. — 48p : ill ; 21cm. — (Long ago children books)
Originally published: 1969.
£1.90
ISBN 0-434-94902-7
(B77-05086)

Manning-Sanders, Ruth. The three witch maidens / [by] Ruth Manning-Sanders ; illustrated by William Geldart. — London : Beaver Books, 1977. — 174p : ill ; 20cm.
This collection originally published: London : Methuen, 1972.
ISBN 0-600-38755-0 Pbk : £0.60
(B77-30772)

Manning-Sanders, Ruth. Tortoise tales / [by] Ruth Manning-Sanders ; illustrated by Donald Chaffin. — London : Methuen, 1976. — 96p : ill ; 20cm. — ([A read aloud book])
Originally published: 1972. — Includes an additional story.
ISBN 0-416-58360-1 : £1.75
(B77-28999)

Manning-Sanders, Ruth. The town mouse and the country mouse / Aesop's fable retold by Ruth Manning-Sanders ; illustrated by Harold Jones. — London [etc.] : Angus and Robertson, 1977. — [26]p : col ill ; 25cm.
ISBN 0-207-95749-5 : £2.80
(B77-30773)

Margolis, Richard Jules. Big bear to the rescue / by Richard J. Margolis ; pictures by Robert Lopshire. — Tadworth : World's Work, 1977. — 40p : col ill ; 22cm.
Originally published: New York : Greenwillow Books, 1975.
ISBN 0-437-57122-x : £2.40
(B77-26619)

Mark, Jan. Under the autumn garden / by Jan Mark ; illustrated by Colin Twinn. — Harmondsworth : Kestrel Books, 1977. — 176p : ill ; 23cm.
ISBN 0-7226-5347-6 : £2.95
(B77-34240)

Marks, James Macdonald. Hijacked! / [by] J.M. Marks ; illustrated by Fermin Rocker. — Harmondsworth [etc.] : Puffin Books, 1977. — 190p : ill, map ; 18cm. — (Puffin books)
Originally published: as 'Jason'. London : Oxford University Press, 1973.
ISBN 0-14-030962-4 Pbk : £0.55
(B77-20724)

Marris, Ruth. The Virgin and the angel / [by] Ruth Marris ; illustrated by Ann Dalton. — London : Heinemann, 1977. — 43p : ill ; 21cm. — (Long ago children books)
ISBN 0-434-95036-x : £2.10
(B77-19042)

Marsden, John, *b.1946.* The adventures of Ulysses / retold by John Marsden ; from Homer's Odyssey ; ... illustrations by Tom Barling. — London : Pan Books, 1977. — 91p : ill, map ; 20cm. — (Piccolo adventure library)
ISBN 0-330-25134-1 Pbk : £0.50
(B77-26620)

Marshall, Sybil. Nicholas and Finnegan / [by] Sybil Marshall ; pictures by Peter Edwards. — Harmondsworth [etc.] : Puffin Books, 1977. — 32p : ill(some col) ; 20cm. — (A young puffin original)
ISBN 0-14-030907-1 Sd : £0.50
(B77-29763)

Marter, Ian. Doctor Who and the ark in space / [by] Ian Marter. — London : Wingate, 1977. — 140p ; 21cm. — (A Longbow book)
'Based on the BBC television serial "The Ark in Space" by Robert Holmes ...'.
ISBN 0-85523-191-2 : £2.50
(B77-17789)

Martin, David, *b.1915.* The cabby's daughter / [by] David Martin. — London : Heinemann Educational, 1976. — [4],136p ; 20cm. — (The new windmill series ; 213)
Originally published: Hornsby : Hodder and Stoughton, Australia ; Leicester : Brockhampton Press, 1974.
ISBN 0-435-12213-4 : £0.85
(B77-03250)

Martin, Reginald. The wild woods of Wyoming / [by] Reginald Martin ; illustrated by Ross. — London : Abelard-Schuman, 1976. — 91p : ill ; 21cm. — (A grasshopper book)
ISBN 0-200-72443-6 : £1.75
ISBN 0-200-72444-4 Pbk : £0.50
(B77-05734)

Maskery, R P. Land of dreams / [by] R.P. Maskery ; illustrated by Cora E.M. Paterson. — Ilfracombe : Stockwell, 1976. — 32p : ill ; 18cm.
ISBN 0-7223-0996-1 Pbk : £0.45
(B77-10978)

Mattingley, Christobel. New patches for old / [by] Christobel Mattingley. — London [etc.] : Hodder and Stoughton, 1977. — 256p ; 23cm.
ISBN 0-340-20593-8 : £3.50
(B77-17146)

Mattingley, Christobel. The picnic dog ; with, The surprise mouse ; and, Worm weather / [by] Christobel Mattingley ; illustrated by Carolyn Dinan. — Leicester : Knight Books, 1977. — 96p : ill ; 18cm.
'The picnic dog' originally published: London : Hamilton, 1970. — 'The surprise mouse' originally published: London : Hamilton, 1974. — 'Worm weather' originally published: London : Hamilton, 1971.
ISBN 0-340-19531-2 Pbk : £0.45
(B77-09991)

Mattingley, Christobel. The special present / [by] Christobel Mattingley ; illustrated by Noela Young. — Sydney ; London : Collins, 1977. — 96p : col ill ; 25cm.
ISBN 0-00-185022-9 : £3.50
(B77-19836)

May, Catherine M. Josef's house of dreams / [by] Catherine M. May. — London : Pickering and Inglis, 1976. — 79p ; 19cm.
ISBN 0-7208-2233-5 : £0.80
(B77-03251)

May, Jean. Patches / [by] Jean May. — Leeds : E.J. Arnold.
In 4 vols.
Ken's crazy Saturday ; [and], The bomb. — 1977. — 48p : ill ; 23cm.
ISBN 0-560-03032-0 Sd : Unpriced
(B77-30774)

Mr Smith has his chips ; [and], A horse called Jeffrey. — 1977. — 48p : ill ; 23cm.
ISBN 0-560-03030-4 Sd : Unpriced
(B77-30775)

Mrs Spinks ; [and], Flood. — 1977. — 48p : ill ; 23cm.
ISBN 0-560-03033-9 Sd : Unpriced
(B77-30776)

The diggers ; [and], Jane's story. — 1977. — 48p : ill ; 23cm.
ISBN 0-560-03031-2 Sd : Unpriced
(B77-30777)

Mayer, Mercer. You're the scaredy-cat / [by] Mercer Mayer. — Tadworth : World's Work, 1977. — [40]p : chiefly col ill ; 24cm.
Originally published: New York : Parents' Magazine Press, 1974.
ISBN 0-437-57315-x : £2.70
(B77-31563)

Mayne, William. It / [by] William Mayne. — London : Hamilton, 1977. — 189p ; 23cm.
ISBN 0-241-89695-9 : £3.50
(B77-29000)

Mayne, William. Max's dream / [by] William Mayne ; illustrated by Laszlo Acs. — London : Hamilton, 1977. — 88p : ill ; 24cm.
ISBN 0-241-89546-4 : £2.95
(B77-19043)

Mayne, William. Party pants / [by] William Mayne ; illustrated by Joanna Stubbs. — Leicester : Knight Books, 1977. — [24]p : col ill ; 21cm. — (A stepping stones book)
ISBN 0-340-21212-8 : £1.20
ISBN 0-340-21211-x Sd : £0.60
(B77-17791)

Mayne, William. Plot night / [by] William Mayne ; illustrated by Janet Duchesne. — London : Hamilton, 1977. — 120p : ill ; 23cm.
Originally published: 1963.
ISBN 0-241-89669-x : £1.95
(B77-23782)

Mayne, William. Skiffy / [by] William Mayne ; illustrated by Nicholas Fisk. — London : Hamilton, 1977. — 120p : ill ; 23cm.
Originally published: 1972.
ISBN 0-241-89670-3 : £1.95
(B77-26621)

Mickey and Wamba-Wu. — Maidenhead : Purnell, 1974. — [16]p : col ill ; 12cm. — ([Minikins])
Sd : £0.06
(B77-19837)

Mickey the sheriff. — Maidenhead : Purnell, 1974. — [16]p : col ill ; 12cm. — ([Minikins])
Sd : £0.06
(B77-19838)

Mickey's circus. — Maidenhead : Purnell, 1974. — [16]p : col ill ; 12cm. — ([Minikins])
Sd : £0.06
(B77-19839)

Mickey's circus adventure. — Maidenhead : Purnell, 1977. — Fold leaf : col ill ; 15cm. — (A mini pop-up book)
Cover title: Walt Disney's Mickey's circus adventure. — Leaf folded and cut to create three dimensional effect ; six pictures in all.
ISBN 0-361-03612-4 : £0.65
(B77-14988)

Micklethwaite, Mavis. The enchanted birds : legendary tales from Ireland and Wales / re-told by Mavis Micklethwaite ; illustrated by Anne Mieke. — London : Macdonald and Jane's, 1977. — [5],87p : ill ; 23cm.
Bibl.: p.82.
ISBN 0-354-08022-9 : £2.95
(B77-13390)

Micklethwaite, Mavis. The miraculous cow : legends of British saints / re-told by Mavis Micklethwaite ; illustrated by Maggie Scott. — London : Macdonald and Jane's, 1977. — [5], 87p : ill ; 23cm.
ISBN 0-354-08025-3 : £2.95
(B77-23783)

Miller, Carey. The lost world / retold by Carey Miller ; from the original by Sir Arthur Conan Doyle ; ... illustrations by Tom Barling. — London : Pan Books, 1977. — 123p : ill ; 20cm. — (Piccolo adventure library)
ISBN 0-330-25132-5 Pbk : £0.50
(B77-26622)

Miller, Margaret Jessy. The fearsome tide / [by] Margaret Miller ; illustrated by Carol Tarrant. — London : Abelard-Schuman ; [Chalfont St Giles] : Sadler, 1976. — 64p : ill ; 20cm. — (A grasshopper book)
ISBN 0-200-72385-5 : £1.55
ISBN 0-200-72386-3 Pbk : £0.45
(B77-03252)

Milne, Alan Alexander. Eeyore finds the Wolery / [by] A.A. Milne ; illustrated by E.H. Shepard. — London : Methuen, 1977. — [28] p : col ill ; 20cm. — (Milne, Alan Alexander. Piglet books)
Originally published: in 'The house at Pooh Corner'. 1928. — These illustrations originally published: in 'The house at Pooh Corner', 1974 and 'Winnie-the-Pooh', 1973.
ISBN 0-416-58330-x : £0.85
(B77-13930)

Milne, Alan Alexander. Piglet does a very grand thing / [by] A.A. Milne ; illustrated by E.H. Shepard. — London : Methuen, 1977. — [28] p : col ill ; 20cm. — (Milne, Alan Alexander. Piglet books)
Originally published: in 'The house at Pooh Corner'. 1928. — These illustrations originally published: in 'The house at Pooh Corner', 1974 and 'Winnie-the-Pooh', 1973.
ISBN 0-416-58290-7 : £0.85
(B77-13931)

Milne, Alan Alexander. Tiggers don't climb trees / [by] A.A. Milne ; illustrated by E.H. Shepard. — London : Methuen, 1977. — [28] p : col ill ; 20cm. — (Milne, Alan Alexander. Piglet books)
Originally published: in 'The house at Pooh Corner'. 1928. — These illustrations originally published: in 'The house at Pooh Corner', 1974 and 'Winnie-the-Pooh', 1973.
ISBN 0-416-58320-2 : £0.85
(B77-13932)

Minarik, Else Holmelund. Little Bear / by Else Holmelund Minarik ; pictures by Maurice Sendak. — Tadworth : World's Work, 1977. — 63p : col ill ; 22cm. — (An I can read book)
Originally published: New York : Harper, 1957 ; Tadworth : World's Work, 1958.
ISBN 0-437-96008-0 Sd : £0.60
(B77-34241)

Mintoft, Jean. The man from the moors / by Jean Mintoft. — London : Pickering and Inglis, 1976. — 160p ; 19cm.
ISBN 0-7208-2229-7 : £1.00
(B77-03785)

Mitchell, Elyne. Son of the whirlwind / [by] Elyne Mitchell ; illustrated by Victor Ambrus. — London : Hutchinson, 1976. — 144p : ill ; 23cm.
ISBN 0-09-130120-3 : £2.75
(B77-09992)

A **mixed** bag : ten more famous tales / illustrated by Peter Dennis. — London [etc.] : Beaver Books, 1977. — 111p : ill ; 20cm.
ISBN 0-600-36274-4 Pbk : £0.55
(B77-12747)

Moeri, Louise. Star Mother's youngest child / [by] Louise Moeri ; illustrated by Trina Schart Hyman. — London : Macdonald and Jane's, 1977. — [48]p : ill ; 18cm.
Originally published: Boston, Mass. : Houghton Mifflin, 1975.
ISBN 0-354-08028-8 : £2.50
(B77-22214)

Moffatt, Derry. Treasure Island / adapted from Walt Disney Productions' screen presentation by Derry Moffatt ; illustrated by Tony Masero. — London : New English Library, 1977. — 125p,[8]p of plates : ill(some col) ; 18cm.
ISBN 0-450-03309-0 Pbk : £0.60
(B77-14447)

Monster fun annual. — London : IPC Magazines.
1978. — 1977. — 3-142p : chiefly ill(some col) ; 28cm. — (A Fleetway annual)
Cover title. — Col. ill. on lining papers.
ISBN 0-85037-342-5 : £1.15
(B77-32914)

Montgomery, Lucy Maud. Chronicles of Avonlea / [by] L.M. Montgomery. — London [etc.] : Angus and Robertson, 1975. — 5-236p ; 20cm.
Originally published: Boston, Mass : Page ; London : Sampson and Low, 1912.
ISBN 0-207-12353-5 : Unpriced
(B77-20725)

Moore, Patrick. Planet of fear / [by] Patrick Moore. — London : Armada, 1977. — 128p ; 18cm. — (Moore, Patrick. Scott Saunders space adventure series)
ISBN 0-00-691308-3 Pbk : £0.45
(B77-28229)

Moore, Patrick. Spy in space : a Scott Saunders space adventure / [by] Patrick Moore. — London : Armada, 1977. — 127p ; 19cm. — (Moore, Patrick. Scott Saunders space adventure series ; 1)
ISBN 0-00-691309-1 Pbk : £0.45
(B77-30778)

More reading with mother : a collection of stories and verse / selected by Frank Waters. — London : Harrap, 1976. — 192p : ill ; 23cm.
ISBN 0-245-53008-8 : £2.50
(B77-01011)

Morey, Walt. Year of the black pony / [by] Walt Morey. — London : Collins, 1977. — [5],152p ; 22cm.
Originally published: New York : Dutton, 1976.
ISBN 0-00-184947-6 : £2.95
(B77-28230)

Morgan, Alison. At Willie Tucker's place / [by] Alison Morgan ; illustrated by Trevor Stubley. — Harmondsworth [etc.] : Puffin Books, 1977. — 111p : ill, map ; 19cm. — (Puffin books)
Originally published: London : Chatto and Windus, 1975.
ISBN 0-14-030988-8 Pbk : £0.45
(B77-20726)

Morgan, Geoffrey. Lame duck / [by] Geoffrey Morgan ; illustrated by Joanna Shibbs. — London : Abelard, 1977. — 61p : ill ; 21cm. — (A grasshopper book)
ISBN 0-200-72340-5 : £1.75
ISBN 0-200-72341-3 Pbk : £0.50
(B77-29764)

Morgan, Helen, *b.1921.* Mary Kate and the school bus, and other stories / [by] Helen Morgan ; illustrated by Shirley Hughes. — Harmondsworth [etc.] : Puffin Books, 1977. — 80p : ill ; 20cm. — (A young puffin)
Originally published: London : Faber, 1970.
ISBN 0-14-030972-1 Pbk : £0.40
(B77-24553)

Morgan, Helen, *b.1921.* Two in the garden / [by] Helen Morgan ; illustrated by Jillian Willett. — London [etc.] : White Lion Publishers, 1977. — 88p : ill ; 21cm.
Originally published: Leicester : Brockhampton Press, 1964.
ISBN 0-85686-238-x : £2.50
(B77-33479)

Morris, Johnny. Goodnight tales / by Johnny Morris ; illustrated by Gwen Green, Douglas Hall and Terry Rogers ; heading drawings by Meg Rutherford. — London [etc.] : Hamlyn, 1977. — 5-157p : ill(some col) ; 28cm.
ISBN 0-600-31405-7 : £2.50
(B77-30779)

Moss, Elaine. Polar / story by Elaine Moss ; pictures by Jeannie Baker. — Harmondsworth [etc.] : Puffin Books, 1977. — [33]p : col ill ; 20cm. — (Picture puffins)
Originally published: London : Deutsch, 1975.
ISBN 0-14-050195-9 Sd : £0.60
(B77-24554)

Mowgli and Bagheera the panther. — Maidenhead : Purnell, 1974. — [16]p : col ill ; 12cm. — ([Minikins])
Sd : £0.06
(B77-19840)

Mowgli and Baloo the bear. — Maidenhead : Purnell, 1974. — [16]p : col ill ; 12cm. — ([Minikins])
Sd : £0.06
(B77-19841)

Mowgli and Shere Khan the tiger. — Maidenhead : Purnell, 1974. — [16]p : col ill ; 12cm. — ([Minikins])
Sd : £0.06
(B77-19842)

Mowgli and the apes. — Maidenhead : Purnell, 1974. — [16]p : col ill ; 12cm. — ([Minikins])
Sd : £0.06
(B77-19843)

Mowgli and the elephants. — Maidenhead : Purnell, 1974. — [16]p : col ill ; 12cm. — ([Minikins])
Sd : £0.06
(B77-19844)

My animal storybook / stories were specially written for this book by Georgina Adams ... [et al.] ; the illustrations are by Grahame Corbett ... [et al.]. — London [etc.] : Hamlyn, 1976. — 4-157p : ill(chiefly col) ; 28cm.
Col. ill. on lining papers.
ISBN 0-600-30313-6 : £1.95
(B77-00475)

My first annual. — Maidenhead : Purnell.
[1977] / illustrated by Sabine Price. — 1977. — [15]p : chiefly col ill ; 29cm.
ISBN 0-361-03903-4 : £1.35
(B77-32915)

Nation, Terry. Rebecca's world : journey to the forbidden planet / [by] Terry Nation ; illustrated by Larry Learmonth. — London [etc.] : Beaver Books, 1976. — 127p : ill ; 20cm.
Originally published: London : G. Whizzard Publications, 1975.
ISBN 0-600-37583-8 Pbk : £0.55
(B77-12748)

Naughton, Bill. My pal Spadger / [by] Bill Naughton ; illustrated by Charles Mozley. — London : Dent, 1977. — 3-130p : ill ; 21cm.
ISBN 0-460-06733-8 : £2.95
(B77-06337)

Needle, Jan. Albeson and the Germans / by Jan Needle. — London : Deutsch, 1977. — 127p ; 21cm.
ISBN 0-233-96900-4 : £2.75
(B77-26623)

Neve, Margaret. More and better / [by] Margaret Neve. — London : Macmillan, 1977. — [31]p : col ill ; 26cm.
ISBN 0-333-21588-5 : £2.95
(B77-30780)

Neville, Malcolm. The sandmen and the smugglers / [by] Malcolm Neville ; illustrated by John Harrold. — Glasgow [etc.] : Blackie, 1977. — 143p : ill ; 24cm.
ISBN 0-216-90336-x : £3.50
(B77-19845)

Newell, Ellen. Aunt Hannah's companion / [by] Ellen Newell ; illustrated by Cora E.M. Paterson. — West Moors : The author ; Ilfracombe : [Distributed by] Stockwell, 1977. — 47p : ill ; 18cm.
ISBN 0-7223-0558-3 Pbk : Unpriced
(B77-23784)

Newman, Robert, *b.1909.* Merlin's mistake / [by] Robert Newman. — London [etc.] : Beaver Books, 1977. — 173p ; 20cm.
Originally published: New York : Atheneum, 1970 ; London : Hutchinson, 1971.
ISBN 0-600-36267-1 Pbk : £0.60
(B77-12749)

Newton, Paul. The amazing weathercock / [by] Paul Newton. — Tadworth : World's Work, 1977. — 103p ; 23cm.
ISBN 0-437-62710-1 : £2.50
(B77-26624)

Neyland, Bertram. In the hands of the enemy / [by] Bertram Neyland. — London : Pickering and Inglis, 1976. — 160p ; 19cm.
ISBN 0-7208-2226-2 : £1.00
(B77-03253)

Nichols, Beverley. The wickedest witch in the world / [by] Beverley Nichols. — Leicester : Knight Books, 1977. — 184p ; 18cm.
Originally published: London : W.H. Allen, 1971.
ISBN 0-340-19785-4 Pbk : £0.60
(B77-09346)

Nicoll, Helen. Meg's veg / by Helen Nicoll and Jan Pieńkowski. — London [etc.] : Heinemann, 1976. — [30]p : col ill ; 21cm.
ISBN 0-434-95639-2 : £2.10
(B77-17792)

Nicoll, Helen. Mog's mumps / by Helen Nicoll and Jan Pieńkowski. — London [etc.] : Heinemann, 1976. — [30]p : col ill ; 21cm.
ISBN 0-434-95640-6 : £2.10
(B77-17793)

Niland, Deborah. ABC of monsters / [by] Deborah Niland. — Sydney ; London [etc.] : Hodder and Stoughton, 1976. — [32]p : chiefly col ill ; 15x23cm.
ISBN 0-340-20985-2 : £1.75
(B77-12750)

Nobes, Patrick. Diamonds are forever / adapted by Patrick Nobes ; from 'Diamonds are forever' by Ian Fleming. — London : Hutchinson, 1977. — 128p ; 19cm. — (A bulls-eye book)
ISBN 0-09-129941-1 Pbk : £0.65
(B77-34242)

Nobes, Patrick. Jaws / adapted by Patrick Nobes ; from 'Jaws' by Peter Benchley. — London : Hutchinson, 1977. — 128p ; 19cm. — (Bulls-eye book)
'Jaws' originally published: Garden City, N.Y. : Doubleday ; London : Deutsch, 1974.
ISBN 0-09-131001-6 Pbk : £0.70
(B77-32268)

Nobes, Patrick. The man with the golden gun / adapted by Patrick Nobes from 'The man with the golden gun' by Ian Fleming. — London : Hutchinson, 1976. — 124p ; 19cm. — (A bulls-eye book)
'The man with the golden gun' originally published: London : Cape, 1965.
ISBN 0-09-127821-x Pbk : £0.65
(B77-04441)

Noddy catches a thief. — [Maidenhead] : Purnell, 1977. — [4]p : chiefly col ill ; 19cm.
Cover title. — Col. ill. on lining papers.
Pbd : £0.35
(B77-12159)

Noddy's day out. — [Maidenhead] : Purnell, 1977. — [4]p : chiefly col ill ; 19cm.
Cover title. — Col. ill. on lining papers.
Pbd : £0.35
(B77-12160)

The **Noel** Streatfeild weekend story book : an anthology. — London [etc.] : Dent, 1977. — 153p : ill ; 25cm.
ISBN 0-460-06766-4 : £3.50 : CIP rev.
(B77-17147)

Norman, Hilda. Guitar Golly / by Hilda Norman. — [Hove] ([4 Brunswick Sq., Hove, Sussex, BN3 1EG]) : James Publishing House, [1976]. — [14]p : 1 ill ; 22cm.
Sd : £0.15
(B77-25955)

Norton, André. Red Hart magic / by André Norton ; illustrated by Donna Diamond. — London : Hamilton, 1977. — [9],179p : ill ; 23cm.
Originally published: New York : Crowell, 1976.
ISBN 0-241-89730-0 : £3.25
(B77-28231)

Norton, André. Star Ka'at / [by] André Norton and Dorothy Madlee ; illustrated by Bernard Colonna. — Glasgow [etc.] : Blackie, 1977. — 142p : ill ; 21cm.
Originally published: New York : Walker, 1976.
ISBN 0-216-90297-5 : £3.25
(B77-20727)

Norton, André. Steel magic / [by] Andre Norton ; illustrated by Robin Jacques. — London : Hamilton, 1977. — 155p : ill ; 23cm.
Originally published: Cleveland, Ohio : World Publishing Co., 1965 ; London : Hamilton, 1967.
ISBN 0-241-89786-6 : £1.95
(B77-29001)

Norton, André. The zero stone / [by] Andre Norton. — London [etc.] : Beaver Books, 1977. — 236p ; 18cm.
Originally published: New York : Viking Press, 1968 ; London : Gollancz, 1974.
ISBN 0-600-39534-0 Pbk : £0.45
(B77-22215)

Nwakoby, Awele. Ten in the family / [by] Awele Nwakoby. — London [etc.] : Evans Bros, 1977. — [4],67p : ill ; 22cm. — (Evans Africa library)
ISBN 0-237-50070-1 Sd : £0.90
(B77-25238)

Nye, Robert. Out of the world and back again / [by] Robert Nye ; illustrated by Joanna Troughton. — London [etc.] : Collins, 1977. — 93p : ill ; 21cm. — (Collins young fiction)
ISBN 0-00-184626-4 : £2.25
(B77-29765)

Oakley, Graham. The church mice adrift / [by] Graham Oakley. — London [etc.] : Macmillan, 1976. — [36]p : chiefly col ill ; 21x26cm.
ISBN 0-333-19760-7 : £2.50
(B77-00476)

O'Dell, Scott. The '290' / [by] Scott O'Dell. — Oxford [etc.] : Oxford University Press, 1977. — [8],104p : ill ; 23cm.
Originally published: Boston, Mass. : Houghton Mifflin, 1976.
ISBN 0-19-271412-0 : £2.75 : CIP rev.
(B77-22943)

O'Dell, Scott. Zia / [by] Scott O'Dell ; illustration by Sage Reynolds. — Oxford [etc.] : Oxford University Press, 1977. — 127p : 1 ill ; 23cm.
Originally published: Boston : Houghton Mifflin, 1976.
ISBN 0-19-271402-3 : £2.95 : CIP rev.
(B77-04416)

O'Flaherty, Liam. All things come of age : a rabbit story / by Liam O'Flaherty ; illustrations by Terence O'Connell. — Portmarnock : Wolfhound Press, 1977. — 2-15p : ill ; 22cm.
ISBN 0-905473-08-6 : £1.50
(B77-25956)

O'Flaherty, Liam. The test of courage / [by] Liam O'Flaherty ; illustrations by Terence O'Connell. — Portmarnock : Wolfhound Press, 1977. — 3-27p : ill ; 22cm.
ISBN 0-905473-06-x : £1.50
(B77-27476)

Ogilvie, Annabel. The woolly rhino finds a friend / Annabel Ogilvie wrote the story ; T.A.B. Renton drew the pictures. — London : Jupiter Books, 1976. — [28]p : ill(chiefly col) ; 25cm.
Col. ill. on lining papers.
ISBN 0-904041-50-6 : £1.25
(B77-14989)

Ogilvie, Annabel. The Woolly Rhino finds a new home / Annabel Ogilvie wrote the story, T.A.B. Renton drew the pictures. — London : Jupiter Books, 1976. — [26]p : ill(some col) ; 25cm.
ISBN 0-904041-51-4 : £1.25
(B77-15570)

Ogilvie, Annabel. The woolly rhino meets the woolly mammoth / Annabel Ogilvie wrote the story ; T.A.B. Renton drew the pictures. — London : Jupiter Books, 1976. — [28]p : ill(chiefly col) ; 25cm.
Col. ill. on lining papers.
ISBN 0-904041-52-2 : £1.25
(B77-14990)

Ogilvie, Annabel. The woolly rhino takes a holiday / Annabel Ogilvie wrote the story ; T.A.B. Renton drew the pictures. — London : Jupiter Books, 1976. — [28]p : ill(chiefly col) ; 25cm.
Col. ill. on lining papers.
ISBN 0-904041-53-0 : £1.25
(B77-14991)

O'Harris, Pixie. Marmaduke the possum in the cave of the gnomes / written and illustrated by Pixie O'Harris ; adapted by Daniel Hargreaves. — London [etc.] : Angus and Robertson, 1977. — [28]p : col ill ; 30cm.
Text, col. ill. on lining papers.
ISBN 0-207-13468-5 : £0.95
(B77-29766)

Oldfield, Pamela. The terribly plain princess, and other stories / [by] Pamela Oldfield ; with pictures by Glenys Ambrus. — London [etc.] : Hodder and Stoughton, 1977. — 88p : ill ; 20cm.
ISBN 0-340-20713-2 : £2.40
(B77-00477)

Oldham, June. Wraggle taggle war / [by] June Oldham ; illustrated by Sally Holmes. — London : Abelard, 1977. — [4],118p : ill ; 23cm.
ISBN 0-200-72514-9 : £3.25
(B77-19044)

Oman, Carola. Robin Hood, the prince of outlaws : a tale of the fourteenth century from the 'Lytell geste' / by Carola Oman ; illustrated with line drawings and 8 colour plates by S. Van Abbé. — London : Dent [etc.], [1976]. — xii,242p,[8]leaves of plates : ill(some col) ; 23cm. — ([Children's illustrated classics; no.7])
Originally published: / with illustrations by Jack Matthew. 1937.
ISBN 0-460-05007-9 : £2.10
(B77-02636)

Once, twice, thrice and then again / edited by Dorothy Edwards ; illustrated by Juliette Palmer. — Guildford [etc.] : Lutterworth Press, 1976. — 64p : ill ; 26cm.
Text, ill. on lining papers.
ISBN 0-7188-2238-2 : £2.60
(B77-01857)

Once, twice, thrice upon a time / edited by Dorothy Edwards ; illustrated by Juliette Palmer. — Guildford [etc.] : Lutterworth Press, 1976. — 64p : ill ; 26cm.
Text, ill. on lining papers.
ISBN 0-7188-2237-4 : £2.60
(B77-01858)

Orbach, Ruth. Apple pigs / written and illustrated by Ruth Orbach. — London [etc.] : Collins, 1976. — [32]p : ill(chiefly col) ; 27cm.
ISBN 0-00-183707-9 : £2.95
(B77-17794)

Orbach, Ruth. One-eighth of a muffin and that was that / [by] Ruth Orbach. — Revised ed. — London : Collins, 1976. — [33]p : col ill ; 21cm. — (Picture lions)
Previous ed.: London : Cape, 1974.
ISBN 0-00-660860-4 Sd : £0.50
(B77-10979)

Orrom, Mary. The secret pony / story and pictures by Mary and Michael Orrom. — London : Pelham, 1977. — [48]p : chiefly col ill ; 24cm.
ISBN 0-7207-0962-8 : £2.95
(B77-23785)

Osborne, Maureen. Twice upon a time / [by] Maureen Osborne ; illustrated by Eileen Brown. — London : Heinemann, 1977. — [4],156p : ill ; 23cm.
ISBN 0-434-95580-9 : £2.90
(B77-26625)

Overton, Jenny. The thirteen days of Christmas / [by] Jenny Overton ; illustrated by Shirley Hughes. — Harmondsworth [etc.] : Puffin Books, 1977. — 140p : ill ; 19cm. — (Puffin books)
Originally published: London : Faber, 1972.
ISBN 0-14-030870-9 Pbk : £0.50
(B77-29767)

Pacholek, E. Murphy and the appletree / written by E. Pacholek ; illustrated by J. Pead. — London : Thurman, 1975. — [24]p : col ill ; 13x14cm.
ISBN 0-85985-024-2 Sd : £0.25
(B77-03786)

Pacholek, E. Murphy and the runaway sock / written by E. Pacholek ; illustrated by J. Pead. — London : Thurman, 1975. — [23]p : col ill ; 13x14cm.
ISBN 0-85985-025-0 Sd : £0.25
(B77-03787)

Pacholek, E. Murphy in the snow / written by E. Pacholek ; illustrated by J. Pead. — London : Thurman, 1975. — [23]p : col ill ; 13x14cm.
ISBN 0-85985-026-9 Sd : £0.25
(B77-03788)

Paley, Claudia. Benjamin the true / by Claudia Paley ; illustrated by Trina Schart Hyman. — London : Stanmore Press, 1975. — [5],90p : ill(chiefly col) ; 24cm.
ISBN 0-900707-36-4 : £1.50
(B77-19045)

Palmer, C Everard. The cloud with the silver lining / [by] C. Everard Palmer ; illustrated by Laszlo Acs. — Harmondsworth [etc.] : Puffin Books, 1976. — 157p : ill ; 19cm. — (Puffin books)
Originally published: London : Deutsch, 1966.
Pbk : £0.50
ISBN 0-14-030613-7
(B77-01859)

Palmer, Geoffrey, *b.1912 (Aug.).* Stories of Robin Hood / [by] Geoffrey Palmer and Noel Lloyd ; illustrated by Derek Stenberg. — London [etc.] : Pan Books, 1976. — 159p : ill ; 18cm. — (A piccolo original)
ISBN 0-330-24641-0 Pbk : £0.40
(B77-02637)

Palmer, Geoffrey, *b.1912 (Aug.).* Stories of Robin Hood / [by] Geoffrey Palmer and Noel Lloyd ; illustrated by Derek Stenberg. — London : Severn House : [Distributed by Hutchinson], 1977. — 159p : ill ; 21cm.
Originally published: London : Pan Books, 1976.
ISBN 0-7278-0260-7 : £2.75
(B77-13391)

Parish, Peggy. Amelia Bedelia and the surprise shower / by Peggy Parish ; pictures by Fritz Siebel. — Tadworth : World's Work, 1977. — 64p : col ill ; 22cm. — (An I can read book)
Originally published: New York : Harper and Row, 1966 ; Tadworth : World's Work, 1967.
ISBN 0-437-96007-2 Sd : £0.60
(B77-34243)

Parish, Peggy. Come back, Amelia Bedelia / by Peggy Parish ; pictures by Wallace Tripp. — Tadworth : World's Work, 1977. — 64p : col ill ; 22cm. — (An I can read book)
Originally published: New York : Harper, 1971 ; Tadworth : World's Work, 1973.
ISBN 0-437-96004-8 Sd : £0.60
(B77-16628)

Parish, Peggy. Good work, Amelia Bedelia / by Peggy Parish ; pictures by Lynn Sweat. — Tadworth : World's Work, 1977. — 56p : col ill ; 22cm.
Originally published: New York : Greenwillow Books, 1976.
ISBN 0-437-66105-9 : £2.50
(B77-20728)

Park, Ruth. The muddle-headed wombat in the springtime / [by] Ruth Park ; illustrated by Noela Young. — London [etc.] : Angus and Robertson, 1976. — 67p : ill ; 25cm.
Originally published: Sydney : Educational Press ; London : Angus and Robertson, 1970.
ISBN 0-207-13082-5 : £1.50
(B77-25239)

Park, Ruth. The muddle-headed wombat in the treetops / [by] Ruth Park ; illustrated by Noela Young. — London [etc.] : Angus and Robertson, 1976. — 67p : ill ; 25cm.
Originally published: Sydney : Educational Press ; London : Angus and Robertson, 1965.
ISBN 0-207-94505-5 : £1.50
(B77-25240)

Park, Ruth. The muddle-headed wombat on a rainy day / [by] Ruth Park ; illustrated by Noela Young. — London [etc.] : Angus and Robertson, 1976. — 67p : ill ; 25cm.
Originally published: Sydney : Educational Press, 1969 ; London : Angus and Robertson, 1970.
£1.50
ISBN 0-207-95211-6
(B77-25957)

Park, Ruth. The muddle-headed wombat on holiday / [by] Ruth Park ; illustrated by Noela Young. — London [etc.] : Angus and Robertson, 1976. — 67p : ill ; 25cm.
Originally published: 1964.
ISBN 0-207-13074-4 : £1.50
(B77-26626)

Parker, Alan, *b.1944.* Bugsy Malone / [by] Alan Parker. — London : Armada, 1976. — 126p,[8] p of plates : ill ; 18cm.
ISBN 0-00-691198-6 Pbk : £0.50
(B77-15571)

Parker, Alan, *b.1944.* Puddles in the lane / by Alan Parker. — London : G. Whizzard Publications Ltd : [Distributed by] Deutsch, 1977. — [3],231p : ill ; 21cm.
Ill., ports on lining papers.
ISBN 0-233-96937-3 : £3.25
(B77-29768)

Parker, Richard. More snakes than ladders / [by] Richard Parker ; drawings by Jillian Willett. — London [etc.] : White Lion Publishers, 1976. — 120p : ill ; 21cm.
Originally published: Leicester : Brockhampton Press, 1960.
ISBN 0-85686-240-1 : £2.75
(B77-01012)

Parker, Richard. Snatched / [by] Richard Parker ; illustrated by Peter Kesteren [i.e. Kesteven]. — Harmondsworth [etc.] : Puffin Books, 1977. — 126p : ill ; 19cm. — (Puffin books)
Originally published: Newton Abbot : David and Charles, 1974.
ISBN 0-14-030977-2 Pbk : £0.50
(B77-29769)

Parsons, Virginia. The bears' adventure / [by] Virginia Parsons. — [London] : Collins, 1977. — [48]p : col ill ; 16cm. — (Collins colour cubs)
ISBN 0-00-123385-8 : £0.95
ISBN 0-00-123380-7 Pbk : £0.30
(B77-28232)

Parsons, Virginia. Fred the whistling postman / [by] Virginia Parsons. — [London] : Collins, 1977. — [48]p : col ill ; 16cm. — (Collins colour cubs)
ISBN 0-00-123386-6 : £0.95
ISBN 0-00-123381-5 Pbk : £0.30
(B77-27477)

Parsons, Virginia. The little goat family / [by] Virginia Parsons. — [London] : Collins, 1977. — [48]p : col ill ; 16cm. — (Collins colour cubs)
ISBN 0-00-123387-4 : £0.95
ISBN 0-00-23382-3 Pbk : £0.30
(B77-27478)

Parsons, Virginia. Mr Gootch and the pennyfarthings / [by] Virginia Parsons. — [London] : Collins, 1977. — [48]p : col ill ; 16cm. — (Collins colour cubs)
ISBN 0-00-123384-x : £0.95
ISBN 0-00-123379-3 Pbk : £0.30
(B77-28233)

Patchett, Mary Elwyn. The proud eagles / [by] Mary Patchett ; illustrated by Maurice Wilson. — London [etc.] : White Lion Publishers, 1977. — [5],215p : ill ; 23cm.
Originally published: London : Heinemann, 1960.
ISBN 0-7274-0221-8 : £4.95
(B77-06338)

Patten, Brian. Jumping mouse / retold by Brian Patten ; illustrated by Mary Moore. — Harmondsworth : Puffin Books, 1977. — 46p : ill(some col) ; 20cm. — (Picture puffins)
Originally published: London : Allen and Unwin, 1972.
ISBN 0-14-050115-0 Sd : £0.60
(B77-07673)

Paulden, Sydney. Yan and the battle for Bergania / [by] Sydney Paulden ; illustrated by David McKee. — London : Abelard-Schuman, 1977. — 111p : ill ; 21cm. — (A grasshopper book)
ISBN 0-200-72495-9 : £2.25
ISBN 0-200-72496-7 Pbk : £0.60
(B77-20729)

Paulsen, Gary. Winterkill / by Gary Paulsen. — London : Abelard, 1977. — 142p ; 21cm.
Originally published: Nashville : Nelson, 1976.
ISBN 0-200-72520-3 : £3.50
(B77-13933)

Paws annual. — Maidenhead : Purnell.
[1977] / [written by Michael Sullivan and Sally Gordon ; illustrated by Hutchings]. — 1977. — 2-47p : chiefly col ill ; 27cm.
Col. ill., text, on lining papers.
ISBN 0-361-03907-7 : £1.25
(B77-25958)

Paws at the seaside. — Maidenhead : Purnell, 1977. — [4]p : chiefly col ill ; 19cm.
Cover title. — Col. ill., text on lining papers.
ISBN 0-361-03837-2 Pbd : £0.35
(B77-11445)

Paws goes shopping. — Maidenhead : Purnell, 1977. — [4]p : chiefly col ill ; 19cm.
Cover title. — Col. ill., text on lining papers.
Pbd : £0.35
ISBN 0-361-03837-3
(B77-11446)

Peake, Mervyn. Letters from a lost uncle / [by] Mervyn Peake. — London : Pan Books, 1977. — [128]p : ill ; 20cm. — (Picador)
Originally published: London : Eyre and Spottiswoode, 1948.
ISBN 0-330-25037-x Pbk : Unpriced
(B77-19846)

Pearce, Cherry. The nervous dragon, and other stories / [by] Cherry Pearce. — London : Kaye and Ward, 1977. — 89p : ill ; 21cm.
ISBN 0-7182-1143-x : £1.90
(B77-10980)

Pearce, Philippa. What the neighbours did and other stories / [by] Philippa Pearce ; illustrated by Faith Jaques. — London : Longman, 1977. — 120p : ill ; 21cm. — (Pleasure in reading)
This collection originally published: London : Longman Young Books, 1972.
ISBN 0-582-18038-4 : £1.00
(B77-14992)

Peet, Bill. Cyrus the unsinkable sea serpent / [by] Bill Peet. — London : Deutsch, 1977. — [2],46p : col ill ; 26cm.
Originally published: Boston, Mass. : Houghton Mifflin, 1975.
ISBN 0-233-96776-1 : £2.75
(B77-20730)

Peet, Bill. The gnats of Knotty Pine / [by] Bill Peet. — London : Deutsch, 1977. — [2],46p : chiefly col ill ; 26cm.
Originally published: Boston, Mass. : Houghton Mifflin, 1975.
ISBN 0-233-96896-2 : £2.75
(B77-33480)

Perkins, Janet. Haffertee finds a place of his own / by Janet and John Perkins ; illustrations by Gillian Gaze. — Berkhamsted : Lion Publishing, 1977. — 5-61p : col ill ; 22cm.
ISBN 0-85648-066-5 : £1.50
(B77-26627)

Perkins, Janet. Haffertee goes exploring / by Janet and John Perkins ; illustrations by Gillian Gaze. — Berkhamsted : Lion Publishing, 1977. — 5-61p : ill(chiefly col) ; 22cm.
ISBN 0-85648-067-3 : £1.50
(B77-26628)

Perkins, Janet. Haffertee Hamster Diamond / by Janet and John Perkins ; illustrations by Gillian Gaze. — Berkhamsted : Lion Publishing, 1977. — 5-60p : col ill ; 22cm.
ISBN 0-85648-065-7 : £1.50
(B77-26629)

Perkins, Janet. Haffertee's first Christmas / by Janet and John Perkins ; illustrations by Gillian Gaze. — Berkhamsted : Lion Publishing, 1977. — 5-61p : ill(chiefly col) ; 22cm.
ISBN 0-85648-068-1 : £1.50
(B77-26630)

Peter Rabbit's painting book / from the original designs by Beatrix Potter. — London [etc.] : F. Warne, [1976]. — [16]p : ill ; 22cm. — ([Potter painting books])
ISBN 0-7232-1993-1 Sd : £0.40
Also classified at 741
(B77-04442)

Peyton, K.M. The edge of the cloud / [by] K.M. Peyton ; illustrated by Victor G. Ambrus. — Harmondsworth [etc.] : Puffin Books, 1977. — 192p : ill ; 18cm. — (Puffin books)
Originally published: London : Oxford University Press, 1969.
ISBN 0-14-030905-5 Pbk : £0.50
(B77-12161)

Peyton, K.M. Prove yourself a hero / [by] K.M. Peyton. — Oxford [etc.] : Oxford University Press, 1977. — [5],137p ; 23cm.
ISBN 0-19-271409-0 : £2.95 : CIP rev.
(B77-17148)

Phipson, Joan. Hide till daytime / [by] Joan Phipson ; illustrated by Mary Dinsdale. — London : Hamilton, 1977. — 88p ; 19cm. — (Antelope books)
ISBN 0-241-89612-6 : £1.25
(B77-19046)

Phipson, Joan. The way home / [by] Joan Phipson. — Leicester : Knight Books, 1977. — 188p ; 18cm.
Originally published: London : Macmillan, 1973.
ISBN 0-340-20080-4 Pbk : £0.60
(B77-09993)

Picton, Jo. Molly of St Christopher's Ward / by Jo Picton. — London : Pickering and Inglis, 1976. — 106p ; 19cm.
ISBN 0-7208-2232-7 : £0.90
(B77-03789)

Pinkwater, Manus. Blue moose / written and illustrated by Manus Pinkwater. — Glasgow [etc.] : Blackie, 1977. — 47p : ill ; 24cm.
Originally published: New York : Dodd, Mead, 1975.
ISBN 0-216-90426-9 : £2.50
(B77-28234)

Pinky and Perky annual. — Maidenhead : Purnell.
[1978]. — 1977. — 3-47p : col ill ; 27cm.
ISBN 0-361-03890-9 : £1.25
(B77-23786)

Pinocchio. — Maidenhead : Purnell, 1974. — [16]p : col ill ; 12cm. — ([Minikins])
Sd : £0.06
(B77-19847)

Pinocchio and the puppet theatre. — Maidenhead : Purnell, 1977. — Fold leaf : col ill ; 15cm. — (A mini pop-up book)
Cover title: Walt Disney's Pinocchio and the puppet theatre. — Leaf folded and cut to create three dimensional effect ; six pictures in all.
ISBN 0-361-03615-9 : £0.65
(B77-14993)

Pistorius, Carol. Karmenka / [by] Carol Pistorius ; illustrated by Carol Marais. — London [etc.] : Macmillan, 1977. — 208p : ill, map ; 21cm.
ISBN 0-333-21428-5 : £3.25
(B77-19848)

'Playhour' annual. — London : IPC Magazines.
1978. — 1977. — 2-79p : chiefly ill(chiefly col) ; 28cm. — (A Fleetway annual)
ISBN 0-85037-345-x : £1.15
(B77-32916)

Playland annual. — London : Polystyle Publications ; London (12 Paul St., EC2A 4JS) : Distributed by Argus Distribution Ltd.
[1977]. — 1976. — 3-62p : chiefly col ill ; 29cm.
Cover title. — Col. ill. on lining papers.
ISBN 0-85096-059-2 : £0.99
(B77-11447)

Pleasence, Donald. Scouse the mouse / by Donald Pleasance. — London : New English Library, 1977. — 48p : col ill ; 30cm.
ISBN 0-450-03216-7 Pbk : £2.50
(B77-32269)

Pluto goes hunting. — Maidenhead : Purnell, 1974. — [16]p : col ill ; 12cm. — ([Minikins])
Sd : £0.06
(B77-19849)

Pluto in the circus. — Maidenhead : Purnell, 1974. — [16]p : col ill ; 12cm. — ([Minikins])
Sd : £0.06
(B77-19850)

Poignant, Axel. Children of Oropiro / [by] Axel & Roslyn Poignant. — London [etc.] : Angus and Robertson, 1976. — [40]p : chiefly ill(chiefly col), col maps on lining papers ; 26cm.
ISBN 0-207-95582-4 : £3.20
(B77-06924)

Pomerantz, Charlotte. The piggy in the puddle / [by] Charlotte Pomerantz ; illustrated by James Marshall. — London : Methuen, 1977. — [31] p : col ill ; 19cm.
Originally published: New York : Macmillan, 1974.
ISBN 0-416-55440-7 : £2.45
(B77-30781)

Poole, Josephine. Touch and go / [by] Josephine Poole. — London : Hutchinson, 1976. — 157p ; 21cm.
ISBN 0-09-127330-7 : £2.95
(B77-22944)

Pope, Ray. Telford tells the truth : a 'Model-railway men' adventure / [by] Ray Pope ; illustrated by Gareth Floyd. — London : Macdonald and Jane's, 1977. — 94p : ill, map ; 23cm.
ISBN 0-354-08023-7 : £2.95
(B77-22216)

Porter, James. The Swiftlet Isles / [by] James Porter ; illustrated by Tony Oliver. — Sydney ; London [etc.] : Hodder and Stoughton, 1977. — 3-122p : ill, map(on lining papers) ; 22cm.
ISBN 0-340-21918-1 : £3.60
(B77-19047)

Postgate, Oliver. Ivor the engine, snowdrifts / story by Oliver Postgate ; pictures by Peter Firmin. — London : Fontana, 1977. — [33]p : col ill ; 22cm. — (Picture lions)
ISBN 0-00-660875-2 Sd : £0.50
(B77-15572)

Postgate, Oliver. Ivor the engine, the first story / story of Oliver Postgate ; pictures by Peter Firmin. — London : Fontana, 1977. — [33]p : col ill ; 22cm. — (Picture lions)
Originally published: as 'Ivor the engine'. London : Abelard-Schuman, 1962.
ISBN 0-00-660874-4 Sd : £0.50
(B77-15573)

Postgate, Oliver. Mr Rumbletum's gumboot / story by Oliver Postgate ; pictures by Peter Firmin. — London : Carousel Books, 1977. — [27]p : col ill ; 19cm. — (Carousel books)
'A Bagpuss story'. — Originally published: London : Pelham, 1975.
ISBN 0-552-52066-7 Sd : £0.40
(B77-08634)

Postgate, Oliver. Nogmania / by Oliver Postgate and Peter Firmin. — London : Kaye and Ward, 1977. — [48]p : ill ; 25cm. — (Postgate, Oliver. Sage of Noggin the Nog)
ISBN 0-7182-1180-4 Pbk : £0.95
(B77-31564)

Postgate, Oliver. Silly old Uncle Feedle / story by Oliver Postgate ; pictures by Peter Firmin. — London : Carousel Books, 1977. — [27]p : col ill ; 19cm. — (Carousel books)
'A Bagpuss story'. — Originally published: London : Pelham, 1975.
ISBN 0-552-52064-0 Sd : £0.40
(B77-08635)

Postgate, Oliver. The song of the Pongo / story by Oliver Postgate ; pictures by Peter Firmin. — London : Carousel Books, 1977. — [27]p : col ill ; 19cm. — (Carousel books)
'A Bagpuss story'. — Originally published: London : Pelham, 1975.
ISBN 0-552-52065-9 Sd : £0.40
(B77-08636)

Potter, Margaret, *b.1926.* Tony's special place / [by] Margaret Potter ; illustrated by Trevor Stubley. — London [etc.] : Bodley Head, 1977. — 126p : ill ; 21cm. — (New acorn library)
ISBN 0-370-30008-4 : £2.35
(B77-15574)

Preston, Edna Mitchell. The temper tantrum book / [by] Edna Mitchell Preston ; illustrated by Rainey Bennett. — Harmondsworth [etc.] : Puffin Books, 1976. — [36]p : chiefly col ill ; 23cm. — (Picture puffin)
Originally published: New York : Viking Press, 1969.
ISBN 0-14-050181-9 Pbk : Unpriced
(B77-01860)

Price, Susan. Home from home / [by] Susan Price. — London : Faber, 1977. — 3-123p ; 21cm.
ISBN 0-571-11022-3 : £2.95
(B77-12162)

'Princess Tina' annual. — [London] : [IPC Magazines].
[1978]. — [1977]. — 3-78p : chiefly col ill ; 28cm. — (A Fleetway annual)
Cover title. — Text, ill. on lining papers.
ISBN 0-85037-346-8 : £1.65
(B77-32917)

Pullein-Thompson, Christine. I carried the horn / [by] Christine Pullein-Thompson ; illustrated by Charlotte Hough. — London [etc.] : White Lion Publishers, 1977. — 254p : ill ; 21cm.
Originally published: London : Collins, 1951.
ISBN 0-85686-236-3 : £2.75
(B77-19851)

Pullein-Thompson, Christine. Pony Patrol SOS / [by] Christine Pullein-Thompson. — St Albans : Dragon Books, 1977. — 94p ; 18cm.
ISBN 0-583-30241-6 Pbk : £0.40
(B77-27479)

Pullein-Thompson, Christine. Riders from afar / [by] Christine Pullein-Thompson ; with drawings by Charlotte Hough. — London [etc.] : White Lion Publishers, 1976. — 192p : ill ; 21cm.
Originally published: London : Collins, 1954.
ISBN 0-85686-241-x : £2.75
(B77-03254)

Pullein-Thompson, Diana. Ponies in the valley / [by] Diana Pullein-Thompson. — London : Collins, 1976. — 128p ; 18cm.
ISBN 0-00-691079-3 Pbk : £0.40
(B77-06925)

Pullein-Thompson, Diana. Three ponies and Shannan / [by] Diana Pullein-Thompson. — London : Armada Books, 1977. — 126p : ill ; 19cm. — (An Armada pony book)
Originally published: London : Collins, 1947.
ISBN 0-00-691332-6 Pbk : £0.45
(B77-22217)

Pullein-Thompson, Diana. Three ponies and Shannan / [by] Diana Pullein-Thompson ; illustrated by Anne Bullen. — London [etc.] : White Lion Publishers, 1977. — 160p : ill ; 21cm.
Originally published: London : Collins, 1947.
ISBN 0-85686-231-2 : £3.15
(B77-16085)

Pullein-Thompson, Josephine. Plenty of ponies / [by] Josephine Pullein-Thompson. — London [etc.] : White Lion Publishers, 1977. — 159p : ill ; 21cm.
Originally published: London : Collins, 1949.
ISBN 0-85686-226-6 : £2.95
(B77-12751)

Pullein-Thompson, Josephine. Pony Club team / [by] Josephine Pullein-Thompson. — London : Armada, 1977. — 158p ; 18cm. — (An Armada pony book)
Originally published: London : Collins, 1950.
ISBN 0-00-691299-0 Pbk : £0.45
(B77-30782)

Pullein-Thompson, Josephine. Race horse holiday / [by] Josephine Pullein-Thompson. — London : Armada, 1977. — 127p : ill ; 19cm. — (An Armada pony book)
Originally published: 1971.
ISBN 0-00-691356-3 Pbk : £0.45
(B77-34244)

Raoul-Duval, François. Hum-Hum and Gurigoo, or, How the rivers and the oceans were created : based on legends of the South-American Indians / [by] François Raoul-Duval ; illustrated by Agnes Molnar. — London : Robson Books, 1976. — [34]p : ill(chiefly col) ; 20x27cm.
ISBN 0-903895-67-6 : £1.95
(B77-03790)

Rayner, Mary. Garth Pig and the ice cream lady / [by] Mary Rayner. — London [etc.] : Macmillan, 1977. — [32]p : chiefly col ill ; 27cm.
ISBN 0-333-22040-4 : £3.25
(B77-32918)

Read, Beryl J. Pip's mountain / [by] Beryl J. Read. — London : Pickering and Inglis, 1976. — 87p : ill ; 19cm.
ISBN 0-7208-2235-1 : £0.80
(B77-03255)

Read, Beryl J. The runaway girl / by Beryl J. Read. — London : Pickering and Inglis, 1976. — 88p ; 19cm.
ISBN 0-7208-2236-x : £0.80
(B77-03256)

Read to me : a story for every day of the week. — London (382 Edgware Rd, W2 1EP) : Polystyle Publications Ltd.
No.1- ; 27th Jan. to 2nd Feb. 1977-. — 1977-. — ill(chiefly col) ; 29cm.
Weekly. — 15p. in 1st issue.
Sd : £0.08
(B77-10981)

Rees, David, *b.1936.* The ferryman / [by] David Rees. — London : Dobson, 1977. — [2],167p : ill, map(on lining papers) ; 20cm.
ISBN 0-234-72027-1 : £2.95
(B77-30783)

Rees, David, *b.1936.* Landslip / [by] David Rees ; illustrated by Gavin Rowe. — London : Hamilton, 1977. — 128p : ill ; 24cm.
ISBN 0-241-89539-1 : £3.50
(B77-19048)

Rees, David, *b.1936.* The missing German / [by] David Rees. — London : Dobson, 1976. — 119p ; 21cm.
ISBN 0-234-77696-x : £2.50
(B77-01013)

Rees, David, *b.1936.* The spectrum / [by] David Rees. — London : Dobson, 1977. — 152p ; 21cm.
ISBN 0-234-72020-4 : £2.95
(B77-23787)

Reeves, James. Exploits of Don Quixote / retold by James Reeves ; illustrated by Edward Ardizzone. — London [etc.] : Blackie, 1977. — 7-219p : ill ; 23cm.
This adaptation originally published: 1959.
ISBN 0-216-90467-6 : £3.95
ISBN 0-216-90466-8 Pbk : £1.75
(B77-34245)

Reid, Meta Mayne. The Noguls and the horse / [by] Meta Mayne Reid ; illustrated by Tony Morris. — London : Abelard-Schuman ; [Chalfont St Giles] : Sadler, 1976. — 63p : ill ; 21cm. — (A grasshopper book)
ISBN 0-200-72348-0 : £1.55
ISBN 0-200-72349-9 Pbk : £0.45
(B77-09994)

Reiss, Johanna. The journey back / [by] Johanna Reiss ; illustration by Fermin Rocker. — Oxford [etc.] : Oxford University Press, 1977. — vi,122p : 1 ill ; 23cm.
Originally published: New York : Crowell, 1976.
ISBN 0-19-271403-1 : £2.95 : CIP rev.
(B77-07674)

Remington, Barbara. Boat / written and illustrated by Barbara Remington. — London : Macdonald and Jane's, 1977. — [48]p : ill ; 23cm.
Originally published: Garden City, N.Y. : Doubleday, 1975.
ISBN 0-354-08024-5 : £2.60
(B77-22218)

The **rescue.** — Maidenhead : Purnell, 1974. — [16]p : col ill ; 12cm. — ([Minikins])
Cover title: The rescue, Robin Hood.
Sd : £0.06
(B77-19852)

Rice, Eve. New blue shoes / story and pictures by Eve Rice. — London [etc.] : Bodley Head, 1977. — [32]p : col ill ; 22cm.
Originally published: New York : Macmillan, 1975.
ISBN 0-370-01803-6 : £1.95
(B77-06926)

Rice, Eve. What Sadie sang / story and pictures by Eve Rice. — London [etc.] : Bodley Head, 1977. — [32]p : col ill ; 14x17cm.
Originally published: New York : Greenwillow Books, 1976.
ISBN 0-370-30052-1 : £1.75
(B77-29770)

Richards, Frank, *b.1875.* Yarooh! : a feast of Frank Richards / presented by Gyles Brandreth. — London : Eyre Methuen, 1976. — 176p : ill, facsims, ports ; 26cm.
Ill. on lining papers.
ISBN 0-413-34410-x : £4.50
(B77-02638)

Richardson, Henry Handel. The getting of wisdom / [by] Henry Handel Richardson. — London : Heinemann, 1977. — [6],233p ; 20cm.
Originally published: 1910.
ISBN 0-434-95950-2 : £2.90
(B77-20731)

Riddell, James. Animal lore and disorder / by James Riddell. — London : Atrium Press Ltd : [Distributed by] Cape, 1976 [i.e. 1977]. — [32] p : col ill ; 21cm.
Pages in 2 separated horizontal segments. — Originally published: London : Riddle Books, 1947.
ISBN 0-224-01333-5 : £1.50 : CIP rev.
(B77-05735)

Riddell, James. Hit or myth / by James Riddell. — London : Atrium Press : Cape, 1977. — [32] p : col ill ; 21x23cm.
Pages in 2 separated horizontal segments. — Originally published: London : Riddle Books, 1949.
ISBN 0-224-01334-3 : £1.50
(B77-30784)

Roach, Marilynne K. Two Roman mice / by Horace (Quintus Horatius Flaccus) ; retold and illustrated by Marilynne K. Roach. — London : Kaye and Ward, 1977. — 48p : ill ; 14x17cm.
Includes original Latin text. — This translation and adaptation originally published: New York : Crowell, 1975. — '... a fairly literal translation of Horace's 'Satire' II, vi, somewhat adapted for non-Romans' - Notes.
ISBN 0-7182-1160-x : £1.25
(B77-26631)

Robbins, Maria. Six in a box / retold by Maria Robbins ; illustrated by Diane Dawson. — London : Pelham, [1976]. — Box : col ill ; 80mm.
Contents: The big radish - Lazy Jack - Henry Penny - The princess and the pea - The mouse and the lion - The runaway pancake.
ISBN 0-7207-0939-3 : £2.25
(B77-00478)

Roberts, Doreen. The other side of the day / [by] Doreen Roberts. — London [etc.] : Oxford University Press, 1976. — [32]p : chiefly col ill ; 29cm.
ISBN 0-19-279712-3 : £3.25
(B77-03257)

Robertshaw, Alan. King Solomon's mines / retold by Alan Robertshaw ; from the original by Rider Haggard ; ... illustrations by Tom Barling. — London : Pan Books, 1977. — 107p : ill ; 20cm. — (Piccolo adventure library)
ISBN 0-330-25133-3 Pbk : £0.50
(B77-26632)

Robertshaw, Alan. The last of the Mohicans / retold by Alan Robertshaw ; from the original by James Fenimore Cooper ; ... illustrations by Tom Barling. — London : Pan Books, 1977. — 107p : ill ; 20cm. — (Piccolo adventure library)
ISBN 0-330-25135-x Pbk : £0.50
(B77-26633)

Robin Hood. — Maidenhead : Purnell, 1977. — 120p : 1 ill ; 21cm. — (A Purnell classic)
Cover title: The adventures of Robin Hood. — Originally published: London : Bancroft, 1968.
ISBN 0-361-03563-2 : Unpriced
(B77-22219)

Robinson, Barbara. The worst kids in the world / [by] Barbara Robinson ; illustrated by Judith Gwyn Brown. — London [etc.] : Beaver Books, 1976. — 3-77p : ill ; 20cm.
Originally published: as 'The best Christmas pageant ever'. New York : Harper and Row, 1972 ; London : Faber, 1974.
ISBN 0-600-34526-2 Pbk : £0.50
(B77-12752)

Robinson, Joan Gale. The summer surprise / [by] Joan G. Robinson ; illustrated by Glenys Ambrus. — London : Collins, 1977. — 110p : ill ; 21cm. — ([Collins young fiction])
ISBN 0-00-184350-8 : £1.95
(B77-10613)

Robinson, William Heath. The adventures of Uncle Lubin / told and illustrated by W. Heath Robinson. — London ([Russell Chambers, WC2E 8AD]) : Minerva Press, 1972. — [16], 117p : chiefly ill ; 22cm.
Cover title: Uncle Lubin. — Facsimile reprint of: 1st ed. London : Grant Richards, 1902.
ISBN 0-85636-004-x : £2.50
(B77-27480)

Rockwell, Anne. Big boss / [by] Anne Rockwell. — Tadworth : World's Work, 1977. — 64p : col ill ; 22cm.
Originally published: New York : Macmillan, 1975.
ISBN 0-437-71652-x : £2.20
(B77-20732)

Rockwell, Anne. The gollywhopper egg / [by] Anne Rockwell. — Tadworth : World's Work, 1977. — [5],57p : col ill ; 22cm.
Originally published: New York : Macmillan, 1974.
ISBN 0-437-71601-5 : £2.40
(B77-20733)

Rockwell, Anne. The story snail / [by] Anne Rockwell. — Tadworth : World's Work, 1977. — [5],57p : col ill ; 22cm.
Originally published: New York : Macmillan, 1974.
ISBN 0-437-71600-7 : £2.30
(B77-06927)

Roose-Evans, James. The lost treasure of Wales : an Odd & Elsewhere story / [by] James Roose-Evans ; pictures by Brian Robb. — London : Deutsch, 1977. — 96p : ill ; 22cm.
ISBN 0-233-96784-2 : £2.50
(B77-09995)

Rose, Anne. Hamid and the Sultan's son / [by] Anne Rose ; illustrated by Charles Robinson. — New York ; London : Harcourt Brace Jovanovich, [1976]. — 48p : col ill ; 21cm.
Published in the United States: 1975.
ISBN 0-15-270101-x : £3.80
(B77-05736)

Rose, Charles. From our garden / by Charles Rose ; illustrations by Leon Olin and Sylvia Gainsford. — Canterbury ([79 Northgate, Canterbury, Kent]) : Hawthorn Publications, [1977]. — [2],75p : ill(some col) ; 21cm.
Pbk : £0.70
(B77-32270)

Rose, Gerald, *b.1935.* 'Ahhh!' said stork / [by] Gerald Rose. — London : Faber, 1977. — [28] p : chiefly col ill ; 26cm.
Text, col. ill. on lining papers.
ISBN 0-571-11097-5 : £2.50 : CIP rev.
(B77-19853)

Rose, Gerald, *b.1935.* Ironhead / [by] Gerald Rose. — Harmondsworth [etc.] : Puffin Books, 1977. — [33]p : chiefly col ill ; 20cm. — (Picture puffins)
Originally published: London : Faber, 1973.
ISBN 0-14-050224-6 Sd : £0.50
(B77-34246)

Ross, Diana. The story of the little red engine / story by Diana Ross ; pictures by Leslie Wood. — Harmondsworth [etc.] : Puffin Books, 1976. — [33]p : ill(some col) ; 15x20cm. — (Picture puffins)
Originally published: London : Faber, 1945.
ISBN 0-14-050161-4 Sd : £0.50
(B77-01861)

Ross, Tony. Hugo and the man who stole colours / [by] Tony Ross. — London (3 Fitzroy Sq., W.1) : Andersen Press Ltd [etc.], 1977. — [24]p : col ill ; 24cm.
ISBN 0-905478-07-x : £2.50
(B77-19854)

Ross, Tony. Hugo and the wicked winter / [by] Tony Ross. — London : Sidgwick and Jackson, 1977. — 45p : ill(some col) ; 23cm.
ISBN 0-283-98218-7 : £2.60
(B77-25959)

Ruffell, Ann. A piece of earth / [by] Ann Ruffell ; drawings by Beryl Sanders. — London : Dobson, 1977. — 137p : ill ; 21cm.
ISBN 0-234-72021-2 : £2.50
(B77-34247)

Rupert and the lonely bird / illustrated by Colin Petty ; based on an original story by Frederick Chaplain. — Maidenhead : Purnell, 1977. — 4-45p : col ill ; 19cm. — (Rupert colour library)
ISBN 0-361-03858-5 : £0.60
(B77-24555)

Rupert and the muddled magic / illustrated by John Harrold ; based on an original story by Frederick Chaplain. — Maidenhead : Purnell, 1977. — 4-45p : col ill ; 19cm. — (Rupert colour library)
Col. ill. on lining papers.
ISBN 0-361-03853-4 : £0.60
(B77-22945)

Rupert and the strange kingdom / illustrated by Paula Cox ; based on an original story by Frederick Chaplain. — Maidenhead : Purnell, 1977. — 4-45p : col ill ; 19cm. — (Rupert colour library)
Col. ill. on lining papers.
ISBN 0-361-03857-7 : £0.60
(B77-23788)

Rupert and the swift journey / illustrated by Paula Cox ; based on an original story by Frederick Chaplain. — Maidenhead : Purnell, 1977. — 4-45p : col ill ; 19cm. — (Rupert colour library)
ISBN 0-361-03856-9 : £0.60
(B77-19049)

Rupert goes fishing. — Maidenhead : Purnell, 1977. — [8]p : of col ill ; 19cm.
Pbd : £0.35
(B77-12753)

Rupert the postman. — Maidenhead : Purnell, 1977. — [8]p : of col ill ; 19cm.
Pbd : £0.35
(B77-12754)

Rush, Philip. Death to the strangers! / [by] Philip Rush ; illustrated by Val Biro. — London [etc.] : Hodder and Stoughton, 1977. — 120p : ill ; 20cm.
Ill., text on lining papers.
ISBN 0-340-20590-3 : £2.20
(B77-06928)

Ryan, John, *b.1921.* Captain Pugwash and the elephant. — [London] : Collins, 1976. — [48] p : col ill ; 16cm. — (Collins colour cubs)
Author: John Ryan. — 'Based on the BBC tv series "Captain Pugwash" ' - p.[48].
ISBN 0-00-123371-8 : £0.95
ISBN 0-00-123351-3 Pbk : £0.30
(B77-18412)

Ryan, John, *b.1921.* Captain Pugwash and the new ship. — [London] : Collins, 1976. — [48] p : col ill ; 15cm. — (Collins colour cubs)
Author: John Ryan. — 'Based on the BBC tv series "Captain Pugwash"' - p.[48].
ISBN 0-00-123372-6 : £0.95
ISBN 0-00-123352-1 Pbk : £0.30
(B77-18413)

Ryan, John, *b.1921.* Captain Pugwash and the ruby. — [London] : Collins, 1976. — [48]p : col ill ; 16cm. — (Collins colour cubs)
Author: John Ryan. — 'Based on the BBC tv series "Captain Pugwash"' - p.[48].
ISBN 0-00-123373-4 : £0.95
ISBN 0-00-123353-x Pbk : £0.30
(B77-18414)

Ryan, John, *b.1921.* Captain Pugwash and the treasure chest. — [London] : Collins, 1976. — [48]p : col ill ; 15cm. — (Collins colour cubs)
Author: John Ryan. — 'Based on the BBC tv series "Captain Pugwash"' - p.[48].
ISBN 0-00-123374-2 : £0.95
ISBN 0-00-123354-8 Pbk : £0.30
(B77-18415)

Ryan, John, *b.1921.* Dodo's delight, or, Doodle and the state secrets / story and pictures by John Ryan. — London : Deutsch [for] Book Club Associates, 1977. — [32]p : chiefly col ill ; 26cm.
ISBN 0-233-96893-8 : £2.95
(B77-34248)

Ryan, Lawrie. A boy called Tully / [by] Lawrie Ryan ; illustrated by Genevieve Rees. — London : Hutchinson, 1977. — 190p : ill ; 22cm.
ISBN 0-09-130240-4 : £3.50
(B77-30785)

Sage, Alison. Tom Cat / [by] Susi Bohdal ; [translated from the German] ; adapted by Alison Sage. — London [etc.] : E. Benn, 1977. — [25]p : ill ; 31cm.
Originally published: in German. Zürich : Nord-Süd Verlag, 1977.
ISBN 0-510-09807-x : £2.25
(B77-27481)

Salkey, Andrew. Hurricane / [by] Andrew Salkey ; illustrated by William Papas. — Harmondsworth [etc.] : Puffin Books, 1977. — 153p : ill ; 19cm. — (Puffin books)
Originally published: London : Oxford University Press, 1964.
ISBN 0-14-030963-2 Pbk : £0.50
(B77-25960)

Salvesen, Joan. Uprooted! / [by] Joan Salvesen ; illustrated by Jo Worth. — London : Abelard-Schuman, 1977. — [5],153p : ill ; 23cm.
ISBN 0-200-72475-4 : £3.10
(B77-13392)

Sampson, Derek. Grump and the hairy mammoth / [by] Derek Sampson ; illustrated by Simon Stern. — London : Methuen, 1977. — 90p : ill ; 20cm.
Originally published: London : Methuen Children's Books, 1971.
ISBN 0-416-58020-3 Pbk : £0.50
(B77-15575)

Sanders, Martha. Alexander and the magic mouse / story by Martha Sanders ; pictures by Philippe Fix. — London [etc.] : Pan Books, 1977. — [1],32p : col ill ; 22cm. — (Piccolo picture books)
Originally published: New York : American Heritage Publishing Co., 1969 ; London : Cape, 1971.
ISBN 0-330-25020-5 Sd : £0.60
(B77-33481)

Saunders, Ken F. Wanganui adventure / [by] Ken F. Saunders ; illustrations by Jean Oates. — Christchurch, N.Z. [etc.] ; London : Whitcoulls, 1977. — 116p : ill, 2 maps ; 21cm. — ([Kairangi series])
ISBN 0-7233-0498-x : Unpriced
(B77-19050)

Saville, Malcolm. Good dog Dandy / [by] Malcolm Saville. — London [etc.] : White Lion Publishers, 1977. — 157p ; 21cm.
Originally published: London : Collins, 1971.
ISBN 0-85686-243-6 : £2.75
(B77-33482)

Saville, Malcolm. Saucers over the moor / [by] Malcolm Saville. — Revised ed. — London : Armada Books, 1976. — 159p : map ; 18cm. — (Saville, Malcolm. Lone Pine adventures)
This ed. originally published: London : Collins, 1972.
ISBN 0-00-691160-9 Pbk : £0.40
(B77-10982)

Saville, Malcolm. Saucers over the moor / [by] Malcolm Saville. — Revised ed. — London [etc.] : Collins, 1976. — 159p : map ; 21cm. — (Saville, Malcolm. Lone Pine adventures)
This ed. originally published: 1972.
£2.95
ISBN 0-00-160211-x
(B77-10983)

Saville, Malcolm. The secret of the gorge / [by] Malcolm Saville. — Revised ed. — London : Armada, 1977. — 159p : map ; 18cm. — (Saville, Malcolm. Lone Pine adventures)
This ed. originally published: London : Collins, 1972.
ISBN 0-00-691328-8 Pbk : £0.45
(B77-17795)

Saville, Malcolm. The sign of the alpine rose / [by] Malcolm Saville. — London [etc.] : White Lion Publishers, 1976. — 224p : ill, map on lining papers ; 21cm.
Originally published: London : Lutterworth Press, 1950.
ISBN 0-85686-189-8 : £2.75
(B77-03791)

Saville, Malcolm. Susan, Bill and the golden clock / [by] Malcolm Saville. — Leicester : Knight Books, 1976. — 127p ; 18cm.
Originally published: London : Nelson, 1955.
ISBN 0-340-20500-8 Pbk : £0.45
(B77-10984)

Saville, Malcolm. Susan, Bill and the vanishing boy / [by] Malcolm Saville ; illustrated by Ernest Shepard. — London [etc.] : White Lion Publishers, 1977. — vi,120p : ill ; 21cm.
Originally published: London : Nelson, 1955.
ISBN 0-85686-104-9 : £2.95
(B77-12755)

Saville, Malcolm. Two fair plaits / [by] Malcolm Saville ; illustrated by Lunt Roberts. — London [etc.] : White Lion Publishers, 1977. — 192p : ill, map(on lining paper) ; 21cm.
Originally published: London : Lutterworth Press, 1948.
ISBN 0-85686-184-7 : £2.50
(B77-19051)

Saville, Malcolm. Where's my girl? / [by] Malcolm Saville. — London [etc.] : Collins, 1976. — 160p : map ; 21cm. — (Saville, Malcolm. Lone Pine adventures)
Originally published: 1972.
£2.95
ISBN 0-00-160210-1
(B77-12756)

Sawyer, Ruth. The way of the storyteller / [by] Ruth Sawyer. — Revised ed. — Harmondsworth [etc.] : Penguin, 1976. — 5-356p : music ; 18cm.
This ed. originally published: New York : Viking Press, 1962. — Bibl.: p.334-348. — Index.
ISBN 0-14-004436-1 Pbk : Unpriced
Primary classification 372.6'4
(B77-16305)

Scarry, Richard. The great pie robbery / written and illustrated by Richard Scarry. — London : Fontana, 1977. — 32,[1]p : chiefly col ill ; 16x22cm. — (Picture lions)
'A Richard Scarry mystery' - p.1. — Originally published: New York : Random House ; London : Collins, 1969.
ISBN 0-00-661314-4 Sd : £0.60
(B77-20734)

Scarry, Richard. The supermarket mystery / written and illustrated by Richard Scarry. — London : Fontana, 1977. — 32,[1]p : chiefly col ill ; 16x22cm. — (Picture lions)
'A Richard Scarry mystery' - p.1. — Originally published: New York : Random House ; London : Collins, 1969.
ISBN 0-00-661313-6 Sd : £0.60
(B77-20735)

Schlee, Ann. Desert drum / [by] Ann Schlee ; illustrated by John Sewell. — London : Heinemann, 1977. — 44p : ill ; 21cm. — (Long ago children books)
ISBN 0-434-94932-9 : £2.50
(B77-31565)

Schneider, Myra. Marigold's monster / [by] Myra Schneider ; illustrated by Thelma Lambert. — London : Heinemann, 1977. — [4], 145p : ill ; 21cm.
ISBN 0-434-96217-1 : £2.90
(B77-20736)

School friend annual. — London : IPC Magazines.
1978. — 1977. — 3-94p : ill(some col), plans ; 28cm. — (A Fleetway annual)
ISBN 0-85037-350-6 : £1.45
(B77-32271)

Schulman, Janet. The big hello / by Janet Schulman ; illustrated by Lillian Hoban. — Tadworth : World's Work, 1977. — 32p : col ill ; 22cm.
Originally published: New York : Greenwillow Books, 1976.
ISBN 0-437-73575-3 : £2.40
(B77-20737)

'**Scorcher**' annual. — London : IPC Magazines.
1978. — 1977. — 2-127p : chiefly ill(some col), ports(some col) ; 28cm. — (A Fleetway annual)
ISBN 0-85037-351-4 : £1.25
(B77-32919)

'**Score**' annual. — London : IPC Magazines.
1978. — 1977. — 3-127p : chiefly ill(some col), ports(some col) ; 28cm. — (A Fleetway annual)
With answers.
ISBN 0-85037-352-2 : £1.35
(B77-32920)

Scott, Erin. Stories of Timothy John / [by] Erin Scott ; illustrated by Cora E.M. Paterson. — Ilfracombe : Stockwell, 1977. — 34p : ill ; 18cm.
ISBN 0-7223-1027-7 Pbk : £0.60
(B77-25961)

The **scout's** pathfinder annual. — Maidenhead : Purnell.
1978. — 1977. — 3-94p : ill(some col), map, music, ports ; 27cm.
'Published in conjunction with the Scout Assoc.' - inside front cover. — Ill. on lining papers.
ISBN 0-361-03895-x : £1.50
(B77-32272)

The **second** book of pony stories / edited by Christine Pullein-Thompson ; cover illustration by Christine Molan ; text illustrations by Ron Stenberg. — London : Pan Books, 1977. — 125p : ill ; 18cm. — (Piccolo original)
ISBN 0-330-24889-8 Pbk : £0.45
(B77-06341)

Sellers, Lucy. Ben Badger tales / [by] Lucy Sellers ; illustrated by Brian Duggan. — Ilfracombe : Stockwell, 1977. — 68p : ill ; 19cm.
ISBN 0-7223-0965-1 : £1.95
(B77-21541)

Sharmat, Marjorie Weinman. Nate the great and the lost list / by Marjorie Weinman Sharmat ; illustrations by Marc Simont. — Tadworth : World's Work, 1977. — 48p : ill(some col) ; 22cm.
Originally published: New York : Coward, McCann & Geoghegan, 1975.
ISBN 0-437-74202-4 : £2.40
(B77-24556)

Shepherd, Jo. Puff to the rescue / written by Jo Shepherd ; illustrated by William Oakey. — Tadworth : World's Work, 1977. — [32]p : chiefly ill(some col) ; 19x26cm.
ISBN 0-437-64440-5 : £2.50
(B77-33484)

Sherry, Sylvia. Mat, the little monkey / [by] Sylvia Sherry ; illustrated by Grabianski. — London : Dent, 1977. — 5-44p : ill(some col) ; 25cm.
ISBN 0-460-06673-0 : £2.95 : CIP rev.
(B77-10614)

'**Shiver** and shake' annual. — London : IPC Magazines.
1978. — [1977]. — 143p : chiefly ill(chiefly col) ; 28cm. — (A Fleetway annual)
Cover title.
ISBN 0-85037-353-0 : £1.00
(B77-32921)

Sillitoe, Alan. Big John and the stars / [by] Alan Sillitoe ; illustrated by Agnes Molnar. — London : Robson, 1977. — [28]p : col ill ; 25cm.
ISBN 0-86051-016-6 : £2.25 : CIP rev.
(B77-23789)

Sillitoe, Alan. The city adventures of Marmalade Jim / [by] Alan Sillitoe. — Newly illustrated and revised ed. / illustrated by Shelagh McGee. — London : Robson, 1977. — [28]p : ill(chiefly col) ; 25cm.
Previous ed.: / illustrated by Dorothy Rice. London : Macmillan, 1967.
ISBN 0-86051-017-4 : £2.25 : CIP rev.
(B77-23790)

Silvester, Rose-Mary. Ship in the moonlight / by Rose-Mary Silvester. — London : Pickering and Inglis, 1976. — 160p ; 19cm.
ISBN 0-7208-2227-0 : £1.00
(B77-03792)

Six little ducklings. — Maidenhead : Purnell, 1974. — [16]p : col ill ; 12cm. — ([Minikins])
Sd : £0.06
(B77-19855)

Skorpen, Liesel Moak. Michael / by Liesel Moak Skorpen ; pictures by Joan Sandin. — Tadworth : World's Work, 1977. — 41p : chiefly col ill ; 23cm.
Originally published: New York : Harper and Row, 1975.
ISBN 0-437-74674-7 : £2.50
(B77-23791)

Sleep tight, sweet dreams : stories for bedtime / selected by Wendy Craig. — [London] : [Spectator Publications for Glaxo-Farley Foods Ltd], [1977]. — 61p : col ill ; 25cm.
Cover title.
ISBN 0-900869-30-5 : Unpriced
(B77-04444)

Sleigh, Barbara. Charlie Chumbles / [by] Barbara Sleigh ; illustrated by Frank Francis. — Leicester : Knight Books, 1977. — [24]p : col ill ; 21cm. — (A stepping stones book)
ISBN 0-340-20840-6 : Unpriced
ISBN 0-340-20839-2 Sd : £0.60
(B77-17149)

Sleigh, Barbara. Ninety-nine dragons / [by] Barbara Sleigh ; illustrated by Gunvor Edwards. — Harmondsworth [etc.] : Puffin Books, 1977. — 71,[1]p : ill ; 20cm. — (A young puffin)
Originally published: Leicester : Brockhampton Press, 1974.
ISBN 0-14-030921-7 Pbk : £0.40
(B77-17796)

Smith, Jim. The frog band and Durrington Dormouse / [by] Jim Smith. — Tadworth : World's Work, 1977. — [32]p : chiefly col ill ; 30cm.
ISBN 0-437-75905-9 : £2.75
(B77-29002)

Smith, Joan. November and the truffle pig / [by] Joan Smith ; illustrated by Janet Duchesne. — London : Hamilton, 1977. — 88p : ill ; 19cm. — (Antelope books)
ISBN 0-241-89567-7 : £1.25
(B77-10615)

Smith, Ray. The long slide / by Mr and Mrs Smith. — London : Cape, 1977. — [25]p : chiefly col ill ; 23x28cm.
ISBN 0-224-01347-5 : £2.50 : CIP rev.
(B77-05737)

Snow White's party. — Maidenhead : Purnell, 1977. — Fold leaf : col ill ; 15cm. — (A mini pop-up book)
Cover title: Walt Disney's Snow White's party. — Leaf folded and cut to create three dimensional effect ; six pictures in all.
ISBN 0-361-03614-0 : £0.65
(B77-14994)

Snyder, Zilpha Keatley. A witch in the family / [by] Zilpha Keatley Snyder. — London [etc.] : Beaver Books, 1977. — 172p ; 18cm.
Originally published: Guildford : Lutterworth Press, 1973.
ISBN 0-600-39384-4 Pbk : £0.50
(B77-26634)

Softly, Barbara. Place Mill / [by] Barbara Softly ; illustrated by Shirley Hughes. — London : Collins, 1976. — 158p : ill, map ; 18cm. — (Lions)
Originally published: London : Macmillan, 1962.
ISBN 0-00-671028-x Pbk : £0.50
(B77-10985)

Softly, Barbara. Ponder and William at home / [by] Barbara Softly ; with drawings by Diana John. — Harmondsworth [etc.] : Puffin Books, 1977. — 94,[1]p : ill ; 20cm. — (A young puffin)
Originally published: London : Longman Young Books, 1972.
ISBN 0-14-030902-0 Pbk : £0.40
(B77-07675)

Sooty's annual, with all his TV friends. — Maidenhead : Purnell.
[1977]. — 1977. — 3-45p : ill(chiefly col) ; 27cm.
Col. ill. on lining papers.
ISBN 0-361-03891-7 : £1.25
(B77-24557)

Southall, Ivan. What about tomorrow / [by] Ivan Southall. — London [etc.] : Angus and Robertson, 1977. — 139p ; 23cm.
ISBN 0-207-13379-4 : £3.20
(B77-14448)

Sowter, Nita. Maisie Middleton / [by] Nita Sowter. — London : A. and C. Black, 1977. — [25]p : chiefly col ill ; 19cm.
ISBN 0-7136-1716-0 : £1.95
(B77-19856)

Spano, Ann. Alice in Wonderland : based on Walt Disney Productions' cartoon feature film / this adaptation by Ann Spano. — London : New English Library, 1977. — 128p : ill(some col) ; 20cm. — (A read and colour book)
ISBN 0-450-03278-7 Pbk : £0.80
Also classified at 741
(B77-09996)

'Sparky' book. — London : D.C. Thomson.
1978. — 1977. — [122]p : chiefly col ill ; 28cm.

Col. ill. on lining papers.
£0.95
(B77-31566)

Spectres, spooks and shuddery shades / selected by Helen Hoke ; illustrations Charles Keeping. — London [etc.] : F. Watts, 1977. — 191p : ill ; 24cm.
ISBN 0-85166-620-5 : £3.50
(B77-20738)

Spence, Eleanor. A candle for Saint Antony / [by] Eleanor Spence. — Oxford : Oxford University Press, 1977. — [4],140p ; 23cm.
ISBN 0-19-271415-5 : £2.95
(B77-29771)

Spier, Peter. Tin Lizzie / written and illustrated by Peter Spier. — Tadworth : World's Work, 1976. — [46]p : col ill ; 21x27cm.
Originally published: Garden City, N.Y. : Doubleday, 1975.
ISBN 0-437-76511-3 : £2.90
(B77-01014)

Spooner, Alan. The Singers of the field / [by] Alan Spooner ; illustrated by Peter Rush. — Harmondsworth : Kestrel Books, 1977. — 160p : ill ; 21cm.
ISBN 0-7226-5301-8 : £2.95
(B77-19052)

Standen, Michael. Over the wet lawn / [by] Michael Standen. — Oxford [etc.] : Oxford University Press, 1977. — [6],168p : map ; 23cm.
ISBN 0-19-271410-4 : £2.95 : CIP rev.
(B77-17150)

Steig, William. Abel's island / [by] William Steig. — London : Hamilton, 1977. — [5], 119p : ill ; 23cm.
Originally published: New York : Farrar, Straus and Giroux, 1976.
ISBN 0-241-89477-8 : £3.00
(B77-22220)

Stein, Nora. World famous stories / [adapted by Nora Stein ; illustrators Toni Goffe, Frank Huffman]. — London : Macdonald Educational, 1977. — 4-125p : chiefly col ill ; 27cm.
'Adapted from "Starkers Legends" ...' - preliminaries.
ISBN 0-356-05548-5 : £1.95
(B77-27482)

Steinbeck, John. The red pony / [by] John Steinbeck ; cover illustration by Brian Sanders. — London : Pan Books, 1975. — 90p ; 18cm. — (A piccolo book)
Originally published: New York : Covici-Friede, 1937 ; London : Heinemann, 1938.
ISBN 0-330-24565-1 Pbk : £0.40
(B77-08130)

Stern, Simon. The Hobyahs : an old story / told & illustrated by Simon Stern. — London : Methuen, 1977. — [32]p : chiefly col ill ; 19cm.

'Adapted from a story of the same name in Joseph Jacobs' "More English fairy tales". [London : D. Nutt], 1894'.
ISBN 0-416-85020-0 : £1.60
(B77-14995)

Stewart, Agnes Charlotte. Silas and Con / [by] A.C. Stewart. — Glasgow [etc.] : Blackie, 1977. — [8],120p ; 23cm.
ISBN 0-216-90335-1 : £3.25
(B77-06929)

Stobbs, William. A mini called Zak : a picture book / by William Stobbs. — Harmondsworth : Puffin Books, 1975. — [32]p : chiefly col ill ; 20cm. — (Picture puffins)
Originally published: London : Bodley Head, 1973.
ISBN 0-14-050122-3 Sd : £0.50
(B77-07676)

Stone, Colin. The legend of the gnomes / [by] Colin Stone with Jane Sherwin ; illustrated by Nicola Smee. — London [etc.] : Chappell ; [London] : [Distributed by] Deutsch, 1976. — [32]p : ill(some col) ; 30cm.
ISBN 0-903443-15-5 Sd : £1.50
(B77-06930)

Stories and poems for the young / selected and with a commentary by Bryna and Louis Untermeyer. — London [etc.] : Hamlyn, 1977. — 252p : ill(some col) ; 27cm.
This collection originally published: as 'Stories and poems for the very young'. New York : Golden Press, 1973.
ISBN 0-600-38210-9 : £2.50
(B77-19857)

Stories for children : chosen by parents for reading aloud / selected by members of the Federation of Children's Book Groups ; edited by Anne Wood. — London [etc.] : Hodder and Stoughton, 1977. — 160p : ill ; 23cm.
ISBN 0-340-21386-8 : £2.95
ISBN 0-340-22137-2 Pbk : £1.50
(B77-23792)

Stories for seven-year-olds and other young readers / edited by Sara & Stephen Corrin ; illustrated by Shirley Hughes. — Harmondsworth [etc.] : Puffin Books, 1976. — 188p : ill ; 20cm. — (A young puffin)
This collection originally published: London : Faber, 1964.
ISBN 0-14-030882-2 Pbk : £0.60
(B77-03793)

Stories of the city / selected by Veronica Harvey. — London : Evans Bros, 1977. — 126p : ill ; 23cm.
ISBN 0-237-44877-7 : £3.75
(B77-30786)

Storr, Catherine. Hugo and his grandma / by Catherine Storr ; illustrated by Nita Sowter. — Cambridge : Dinosaur Publications, 1977. — [24]p : chiefly col ill ; 15x18cm. — (Althea's dinosaur books)
ISBN 0-85122-136-x Sd : £0.40
(B77-27483)

Stoutenburg, Adrien. American tall tales / [by] Adrien Stoutenburg ; illustrated by Richard M. Powers. — Harmondsworth [etc.] : Puffin Books, 1976. — 112p : ill ; 20cm. — (A puffin book)
This collection originally published: New York : Viking Press, 1966.
ISBN 0-14-030928-4 Pbk : Unpriced
(B77-05087)

Streatfeild, Noel. Ballet shoes : a story of three children on the stage / [by] Noel Streatfield ; illustrated by Ruth Gervis. — New ed. — London : Dent, 1977. — [6],184p : ill ; 23cm.
Previous ed.: 1959.
ISBN 0-460-06821-0 : £3.50 : CIP rev.
(B77-22946)

Streatfeild, Noel. Ballet shoes for Anna / [by] Noel Streatfeild ; illustrated by Mary Dinsdale. — [London] : Fontana, 1977. — 160p : ill ; 18cm. — (Lions)
Originally published: London : Collins, 1972.
Pbk : £0.50
ISBN 0-00-671114-6
(B77-16086)

Streatfeild, Noel. Curtain up / [by] Noel Streatfeild ; illustrations by D.L. Mays. — London : Dent, [1977]. — 288p : ill ; 18cm. — (Pennant books ; no.23) (A Dent dolphin)
Originally published: 1944.
ISBN 0-460-02743-3 Pbk : £0.70
(B77-06342)

Streatfeild, Noel. Tennis shoes / [by] Noel Streatfeild ; illustrated by D.L. Mays. — Revised ed. — London : Dent, 1977. — vii, 215p : ill ; 19cm. — (Pennant books ; no.46) (A Dent dolphin)
This ed. originally published: 1952.
ISBN 0-460-02744-1 Pbk : £0.70
(B77-22947)

Streatfeild, Noel. When the siren wailed / [by] Noel Streatfeild ; illustrated by Margery Gill. — London : Fontana, 1977. — 157p : ill ; 18cm. — (Lions)
Originally published: London : Collins, 1974.
ISBN 0-00-671238-x Pbk : £0.50
(B77-16629)

Stuart, Forbes. The magic horns : folk tales from Africa / retold by Forbes Stuart ; illustrated by Charles Keeping. — London : Abelard-Schuman, 1974. — 5-93p : ill ; 22cm.
ISBN 0-200-72176-3 : £2.25
(B77-05088)

Stuart, Marie. Aladdin ; [and], Ali Baba / retold by Marie Stuart ; with illustrations by Robert Ayton. — Loughborough : Ladybird Books, 1976. — [1],89p : col ill ; 25cm. — (A Ladybird special)
Adaptations of: 'Aladdin and his wonderful lamp' ; and 'Ali Baba and the forty thieves', 1975.
ISBN 0-7214-7501-9 : £1.00
(B77-15576)

Sudbery, Rodie. Long way round / [by] Rodie Sudbery ; illustrated by Sally Long. — London : Deutsch, 1977. — 110p : ill ; 23cm.
ISBN 0-233-96872-5 : £2.95
(B77-19858)

Sutcliff, Rosemary. Blood feud / [by] Rosemary Sutcliff ; illustrated by Charles Keeping. — London : Oxford University Press, 1976 [i.e. 1977]. — ix,144p : ill, map(on lining paper), plan(on lining paper) ; 23cm.
ISBN 0-19-271392-2 : £2.95
(B77-02639)

Sutcliff, Rosemary. The Eagle of the Ninth / [by] Rosemary Sutcliff ; illustrated by C. Walter Hodges. — Harmondsworth [etc.] : Puffin Books, 1977. — 300p : ill, map, port ; 18cm. — (Puffin books)
Originally published: London : Oxford University Press, 1954.
ISBN 0-14-030890-3 Pbk : £0.65
(B77-14996)

Sutcliff, Rosemary. Shifting sands / [by] Rosemary Sutcliff ; illustrated by Laszlo Acs. — London : Hamilton, 1977. — 92p : ill ; 19cm. — (Antelope books)
ISBN 0-241-89549-9 : £1.25
(B77-20739)

Sutcliff, Rosemary. Sun horse, moon horse / [by] Rosemary Sutcliff ; decorations by Shirley Felts. — London [etc.] : Bodley Head, 1977. — 112p : ill ; 23cm.
ISBN 0-370-30048-3 : £2.75
(B77-29772)

Sutcliff, Rosemary. Warrior Scarlet : [by] Rosemary Sutcliff / illustrated by Charles Keeping. — Harmondsworth [etc.] : Puffin Books, 1976. — 233p : ill ; 18cm. — (Puffin books)
Originally published: London : Oxford University Press, 1958.
ISBN 0-14-030895-4 Pbk : £0.55
(B77-01862)

Sutton, Eve. Johnny Sweep / [by] Eve Sutton ; illustrated by Paul Wright. — London : Hamilton, 1977. — 88p : ill ; 19cm. — (Antelope books)
ISBN 0-241-89750-5 : £1.25
(B77-30787)

Sutton, Eve. Tuppenny Brown / [by] Eve Sutton ; illustrated by Paul Wright. — London : Hamilton, 1977. — 87p : ill ; 19cm. — (Antelope books)
ISBN 0-241-89319-4 : £1.25
(B77-06931)

Swindello, Robert Edward. Voyage to Valhalla / [by] Robert Swindello ; illustrated by Victor G. Ambrus. — London : Heinemann Educational, 1977. — 120p : ill ; 20cm. — (New windmill series ; 217)
Originally published: London : Hodder and Stoughton, 1976.
ISBN 0-435-12217-7 : £0.75
(B77-34249)

Swindells, Robert. The ice palace / [by] Robert Swindells ; illustrated by June Jackson. — London : Hamilton, 1977. — 91p : ill ; 19cm. — (Antelope books)
ISBN 0-241-89614-2 : £1.25
(B77-22221)

Swindells, Robert Edward. The very special baby / [by] Robert Swindells ; pictures by Victor Ambrus. — London [etc.] : Hodder and Stoughton, 1977. — 48p : ill ; 23cm.
ISBN 0-340-21623-9 : £1.95
(B77-20740)

Symons, Geraldine. Now and then / [by] Geraldine Symons. — London : Faber, 1977. — 3-147p ; 21cm.
ISBN 0-571-11024-x : £2.95
(B77-13934)

Synge, Ursula. Kalevala : heroic tales from Finland / [retold by] Ursula Synge. — London [etc.] : Bodley Head, 1977. — 222p ; 23cm.
ISBN 0-370-30054-8 : £3.50
(B77-30788)

Talbot, Toby. The rescue / [by] Toby Talbot ; illustrated by Jeroo Roy. — London : Abelard-Schuman, 1976. — 63p : ill ; 20cm. — (A grasshopper book)
Originally published: New York : Putnam, 1973.
ISBN 0-200-72437-1 : £1.55
ISBN 0-200-72438-x Pbk : £0.45
(B77-03258)

'**Tammy**' annual. — London : IPC Magazines.
1978. — [1977]. — 2-143p : chiefly ill(some col) ; 28cm. — (A Fleetway annual)
With answers.
ISBN 0-85037-357-3 : £1.00
(B77-32922)

Tapio, Pat Decker. The lady who saw the good side of everything / by Pat Decker Tapio ; illustrated by Paul Galdone. — Tadworth : World's Work, 1977. — [32]p : col ill ; 20x26cm.
Originally published: New York : Seabury Press, 1975.
ISBN 0-437-78160-7 : £2.40
(B77-17151)

Tate, Joan. Luke's garden / [by] Joan Tate ; illustrated by Trevor Stubley. — [New ed.]. — London [etc.] : Hodder and Stoughton, 1977. — 88p : ill ; 19cm.
'A shorter version of "Luke's Garden" was published by Heinemann Educational Books in 1967' - title page verso.
ISBN 0-340-20851-1 : £2.00
(B77-06343)

Tate, Joan. You can't explain everything / [by] Joan Tate. — London : Longman, 1976. — 63p : ill ; 20cm. — (Knockouts)
Contents: The wooden man - The bubbles.
ISBN 0-582-23133-7 Pbk : £0.40
(B77-05738)

Taylor, Don, *b.1935.* Breadcrumbs and clay / [by] Don Taylor ; illustrated by Lesley Smith. — London : Hamilton, 1976. — 48p : col ill ; 19cm. — (Gazelle books)
ISBN 0-241-89422-0 : £0.95
(B77-14449)

Taylor, Elisabeth Russell. The gifts of the tarns / [by] Elisabeth Russell Taylor ; illustrated by Mairi Hedderwick. — London : Collins, 1977. — 3-77p : ill ; 21cm. — ([Collins young fiction])
ISBN 0-00-184269-2 : £2.25
(B77-20741)

Taylor, Mildred. Roll of thunder, hear my cry / [by] Mildred Taylor. — London : Gollancz, 1977. — [8],276p ; 21cm.
Originally published: New York : Dial Press, 1976.
ISBN 0-575-02384-8 : £3.50
(B77-29003)

Taylor, Theodore. The cay / [by] Theodore Taylor. — Harmondsworth : Puffin Books, 1977. — 105p ; 19cm. — (Puffin books)
Originally published: Garden City, N.Y. : Doubleday, 1969 ; London : Bodley Head, 1970.
Pbk : £0.45
ISBN 0-14-030595-5
(B77-18416)

'**Teddy** Bear' annual. — London : IPC Magazines.
1978. — 1977. — 5-79p : chiefly ill(some col) ; 28cm. — (A Fleetway annual)
ISBN 0-85037-358-1 : £1.45
(B77-32273)

Testa, Fulvio. The emperor's new clothes / [by] Fulvio Testa ; adapted from the tale by Hans Christian Andersen. — London : Abelard-Schuman, 1976. — [24]p : col ill ; 30cm.
This adaptation originally published: Zürich : Bohem Press, 1974.
ISBN 0-200-72481-9 : £2.95
(B77-07677)

Thaler, Mike. What can a hippotamus be? / words by Mike Thaler ; pictures by Robert Grossman. — Tadworth : World's Work, 1977. — [32]p : chiefly col ill ; 26cm.
Originally published: New York : Parents' Magazine Press, 1975.
ISBN 0-437-78300-6 : £2.60
(B77-20742)

Thatcher, Dora. Tommy and the island / [by] Dora Thatcher ; drawings by Biro. — London [etc.] : Hodder and Stoughton, 1977. — 88p : ill ; 20cm.
ISBN 0-340-21539-9 : £2.00
(B77-32274)

Thody, Philip. A true life reader of children and parents / [by] Philip Thody. — London : Wildwood House, 1977. — [6],130p : ill ; 24cm.

ISBN 0-7045-0311-5 : £2.95
(B77-32275)

Thomas, Michael, *b.1937.* The golden keel / adapted by Michael Thomas from 'The golden keel' by Desmond Bagley. — London : Hutchinson, 1977. — 127p ; 19cm. — (A bulls-eye book)
ISBN 0-09-131591-3 Pbk : £0.70
(B77-32276)

The **three** in the blue balloon : the story of the first balloon flight / adapted from Hans Baumann's original text ; pictures by Antoni Boratynski. — London : Angus and Robertson, 1976. — [25]p : col ill ; 24cm.
Col. ill. on lining papers. — Adaptation of: 'Die Drie im Blauen Ballon'. Stuttgart : Thienemanns, 1976.
ISBN 0-207-95725-8 : £2.80
(B77-07678)

The **three** little pigs / [illustrated by Karen Acosta]. — London : Chatto and Windus [etc.], 1977. — 3 fold leaves : chiefly col ill ; 18cm. — (A peepshow book)
Fold. leaves superimposed one on the other to create a three-dimensional effect ; five pictures in all.
ISBN 0-7011-2224-2 : £1.50
(B77-25962)

The **three** little pigs build a house. — Maidenhead : Purnell, 1974. — [16]p : col ill ; 12cm. — ([Minikins])
Sd : £0.06
(B77-19859)

Thrilling detection & mystery stories / selected and edited by Leonard Matthews. — London [etc.] : Hamlyn, 1977. — 192p : ill ; 22cm. — (Hamlyn story library)
ISBN 0-600-35243-9 : £1.00
(B77-19053)

Thurber, James. The great Quillow / by James Thurber ; illustrated by Doris Lee. — New York ; London : Harcourt Brace Jovanovich, 1975. — [4],54,[1]p : col ill ; 22cm. — (Voyager picture books)
Originally published: New York : Harcourt Brace, 1944.
ISBN 0-15-636490-5 Pbk : £1.05
(B77-06344)

Thurber, James. The white deer / [by] James Thurber ; with drawings by the author. — Harmondsworth [etc.] : Puffin Books, 1976. — 93p : ill ; 18cm. — (Puffin books)
Originally published: New York : Harcourt Brace, 1945 ; London : Hamilton, 1946.
ISBN 0-14-030897-0 Pbk : £0.35
(B77-08637)

'Tiger' annual. — London : IPC Magazines. 1978. — 1977. — 2-127p : chiefly ill(some col), ports(some col) ; 28cm. — (A Fleetway annual)
ISBN 0-85037-360-3 : £1.15
(B77-32923)

Time for play / illustrated by 'Fel'. — Maidenhead : Purnell, 1977. — [20]p : chiefly col ill ; 25cm. — (A Purnell fireside tale)
Col. ill. on lining papers.
ISBN 0-361-03861-5 : Unpriced
(B77-12757)

Time to play tales. — London : Dean, 1977. — 4-61p : ill ; 21cm. — (Dean's 'little ones' reader' series)
ISBN 0-603-04265-1 : £0.30
(B77-30789)

Tison, Annette. Barbapapa's ark / [by] Annette Tison & Talus Taylor. — London [etc.] : Pan Books, 1977. — [32]p : chiefly col ill ; 16x22cm. — (Piccolo picture books)
Originally published: London : F. Warne, 1974.
ISBN 0-330-25019-1 Sd : £0.50
(B77-09347)

Titus, Eve. Basil and the pygmy cats : a Basil of Baker Street mystery / by Eve Titus ; illustrated by Paul Galdone. — Sydney ; London [etc.] : Hodder and Stoughton, 1977. — 96p : ill, map ; 21cm.
Originally published: New York : McGraw-Hill, 1971.
ISBN 0-340-19803-6 : £2.80
(B77-19860)

'Toby' annual. — London : IPC Magazines. 1978. — 1977. — 4-77p : ill(chiefly col) ; 28cm. — (A Fleetway annual)
ISBN 0-85037-361-1 : £1.45
(B77-32924)

Todd, Herbert Eatton. Bobby Brewster's bee / [by] H.E. Todd ; illustrated by Lilian Buchanan. — London [etc.] : Hodder and Stoughton, 1977. — 87p : ill ; 19cm.
This collection originally published: Brockhampton Press, 1972.
ISBN 0-340-22167-4 : £2.20
(B77-32925)

Todd, Herbert Eatton. Bobby Brewster's wishbone / [by] H.E. Todd ; illustrated by Lilian Buchanan. — 2nd ed. [i.e. 1st ed. reprinted]. — London [etc.] : Hodder and Stoughton, 1977. — 87p : ill ; 19cm.
Originally published: Leicester : Brockhampton Press, 1974.
ISBN 0-340-21400-7 : £1.80
(B77-05089)

'Toddler's own' colour annual. — [London] : [IPC Magazines].
1978. — [1977]. — [44]p : chiefly ill(chiefly col) ; 30cm. — (A Fleetway annual)
Cover title.
ISBN 0-85037-362-x : £1.65
(B77-33485)

Tom Kitten's painting book / from the original designs by Beatrix Potter. — London [etc.] : F. Warne, [1976]. — [16]p : ill ; 22cm. — ([Potter painting books])
ISBN 0-7232-1996-6 Sd : £0.40
Also classified at 741
(B77-04445)

Tomlinson, Jill. The gorilla who wanted to grow up / [by] Jill Tomlinson ; illustrated by Joanne Cole. — London : Methuen, 1977. — 78p : ill ; 21cm. — ([A read aloud book])
ISBN 0-416-57240-5 : £1.80
(B77-27484)

Tomlinson, Jill. The hen who wouldn't give up / [by] Jill Tomlinson ; illustrated by Joanne Cole. — London : Methuen, 1977. — 96p : ill ; 21cm. — ([A read aloud book])
Originally published: as 'Hilda the hen'. 1967.
ISBN 0-416-56390-2 : £1.75
(B77-27485)

Tourtel, Mary. The first 'St Michael' book of Rupert favourites / [by] Mary Tourtel. — Maidenhead : Purnell [for Marks and Spencer Limited], 1977. — [76]p : col ill ; 29cm.
ISBN 0-361-04005-9 : £1.25
(B77-33486)

Townsend, John Rowe. The intruder / [by] John Rowe Townsend ; illustrated by Graham Humphreys. — Harmondsworth [etc.] : Penguin, 1977. — 191p : ill, map ; 18cm. — (Peacock books)
Originally published: Oxford : Oxford University Press, 1969.
ISBN 0-14-047101-4 Pbk : £0.60
(B77-25963)

Townsend, John Rowe. Top of the world / [by] John Rowe Townsend ; illustrated by Nikki Jones. — London : Oxford University Press, 1976. — [5],72p : ill ; 23cm.
ISBN 0-19-271388-4 : £2.50
(B77-01015)

Townsend, John Rowe. Widdershins Crescent / [by] John Rowe Townsend. — London : Hutchinson, 1977. — 192p : map ; 20cm.
Originally published: 1965.
ISBN 0-09-075360-7 : £2.95
(B77-32926)

Townson, Hazel. The jam spell / [by] Hazel Townson ; illustrated by Geoffrey Bargery. — London : Hamilton, 1977. — 87p : ill ; 19cm. — (Antelope books)
ISBN 0-241-89569-3 : £1.25
(B77-14450)

Toytime tales. — London : Dean, 1977. — 4-60p : ill ; 21cm. — (Dean's 'little ones' reader' series)
ISBN 0-603-04267-8 : £0.30
(B77-30790)

Tozer, Katharine. Mumfie's magic box / [by] Katharine Tozer ; with illustrations by the author. — London : Carousel Books, 1977. — 189p : ill ; 20cm.
Originally published: London : J. Murray, 1938.
ISBN 0-552-52068-3 Pbk : £0.50
(B77-16087)

Tracy doll dressing book. — Maidenhead : Purnell, 1977. — [20]p : ill(some col) ; 26cm.
Sd : £0.15
ISBN 0-361-03794-5
Also classified at 745.59'22
(B77-12163)

Tranter, Nigel. Border riding / by Nigel Tranter ; illustrated by Richard Kennedy. — London [etc.] : White Lion Publishers, 1977. — 120p : ill ; 21cm.
Originally published: Leicester : Brockhampton Press, 1959.
ISBN 0-85686-242-8 : £2.75
(B77-25964)

Tranter, Nigel. Spaniard's Isle / [by] Nigel Tranter ; illustrated by Richard Kennedy. — London [etc.] : White Lion Publishers, 1977. — 128p : ill ; 21cm.
Originally published: Leicester : Brockhampton Press, 1958.
ISBN 0-85686-247-9 : £2.25
(B77-19861)

Trease, Geoffrey. The claws of the eagle / [by] Geoffrey Trease ; illustrated by Ionicus. — London : Heinemann, 1977. — 44p : ill ; 21cm. — (Long ago children books)
ISBN 0-434-94930-2 : £2.50
(B77-31567)

Trease, Geoffrey. The Field of the Forty Footsteps / [by] Geoffrey Trease. — London [etc.] : Macmillan, 1977. — [6],183p ; 21cm.
ISBN 0-333-23070-1 : £3.25
(B77-31568)

Trease, Geoffrey. Violet for Bonaparte / [by] Geoffrey Trease. — London [etc.] : Macmillan, 1976. — 175p ; 21cm.
ISBN 0-333-21186-3 : £2.95
(B77-00480)

Treece, Henry. Vinland the good / [by] Henry Treece ; decorations by William Stobbs ; map by Richard Treece. — Harmondsworth [etc.] : Puffin Books, 1977. — 144p : ill, map ; 19cm. — (Puffin books)
Originally published: London : Bodley Head, 1967.
Pbk : £0.50
ISBN 0-14-030475-4
(B77-18417)

Treece, Henry. War dog / [by] Henry Treece ; illustrated by C.L. Doughty. — London [etc.] : Beaver Books, 1977. — 111p : ill ; 20cm.
Originally published: / illustrated by Roger Payne. Leicester : Brockhampton Press, 1962.
ISBN 0-600-39379-8 Pbk : £0.50
(B77-12758)

Treece, Henry. The windswept city / [by] Henry Treece ; illustrated by Faith Jaques. — London : Hamilton, 1977. — 121p : ill, maps ; 23cm.
Originally published: 1967.
ISBN 0-241-89672-x : £1.95
(B77-22222)

Tresselt, Alvin. It's time now! / [text by] Alvin Tresselt ; illustrated by Roger Duvoisin. — Tadworth : World's Work, 1976. — [33]p : col ill ; 26cm.
Ill. on lining papers. — Originally published: New York : Lothrop, Lee and Shepard, 1969 ; Tadworth : World's Work, 1971.
£2.50
ISBN 0-437-81206-5
(B77-11448)

Troughton, Joanna. What made Tiddalik laugh / retold and illustrated by Joanna Troughton. — Glasgow [etc.] : Blackie, 1977. — [32]p : chiefly col ill ; 26cm.
ISBN 0-216-90431-5 : £2.95
(B77-34250)

Tully, John. The crocodile / [by] John Tully ; illustrated by Clifford Bayly. — London [etc.] : Beaver Books, 1977. — 127p : ill, map ; 20cm.
Originally published: London : British Broadcasting Corporation, 1972.
ISBN 0-600-31958-x Pbk : £0.55
(B77-30791)

Twilight tales. — London : Dean, 1977. — 4-61p : ill ; 21cm. — (Dean's 'little ones' reader' series)
ISBN 0-603-04266-x : £0.30
(B77-30792)

Twinkle. — Dundee [etc.] : D.C. Thomson. 1978. — [1977]. — [58]p : chiefly col ill ; 25cm.
Col. ill., text on lining papers.
£0.80
(B77-31569)

Udry, Janice May. A tree is nice / by Janice May Udry ; pictures by Marc Simont. — Tadworth : World's Work, 1977. — [32]p : chiefly ill(some col) ; 29cm.
Originally published: New York : Harper, 1956 ; Tadworth : World's Work, 1971.
£2.50
ISBN 0-437-82180-3
(B77-24558)

Ungerer, Tomi. The 3 robbers / [by] Tomi Ungerer. — London : Methuen, 1977. — [40] p : col ill ; 19cm.
Originally published: 1962.
ISBN 0-416-80600-7 Sd : £0.60
(B77-29004)

Uttley, Alison. Little Grey Rabbit's storybook / by Alison Uttley ; pictures by Margaret Tempest. — London : Collins, 1977. — 160p : ill(chiefly col) ; 25cm.
Ill. on lining papers. — Contents: Little Grey Rabbit's party - Wise Owl's story - Little Grey Rabbit's washing day - Moldy Warp the Mole - Fuzzypeg goes to school - Little Grey Rabbit's Christmas.
ISBN 0-00-194162-3 : £3.50
(B77-28235)

Uttley, Alison. Stories for Christmas / [by] Alison Uttley ; chosen by Kathleen Lines ; illustrated by Gavin Rowe. — London : Faber, 1977. — 128p : ill ; 23cm.
ISBN 0-571-11074-6 : £2.95 : CIP rev.
(B77-19862)

Uttley, Alison. A traveller in time / [by] Alison Uttley ; illustrated by Faith Jaques. — Harmondsworth [etc.] : Puffin Books, 1977. — 286p : ill ; 18cm. — (Puffin books)
Originally published: London : Faber, 1939.
ISBN 0-14-030931-4 Pbk : £0.65
(B77-25241)

Uttley, Alison. Yours ever, Sam Pig / [by] Alison Uttley ; with drawings by A.E. Kennedy. — Harmondsworth [etc.] : Puffin Books, 1977. — 185,[1]p : ill ; 20cm. — (A young puffin)
Originally published: London : Faber, 1951.
ISBN 0-14-030914-4 Pbk : £0.55
(B77-15577)

'**Valiant**' annual. — London : IPC Magazines.
1978. — [1977]. — 2-143p : chiefly ill(some col), ports ; 28cm. — (A Fleetway annual)
ISBN 0-85037-363-8 : £1.25
(B77-32927)

Van Woerkom, Dorothy. The queen who couldn't bake gingerbread : an adaptation of a German folk tale / by Dorothy van Woerkom ; illustrated by Paul Galdone. — Tadworth : World's Work, 1977. — [32]p : col ill ; 21x27cm.
ISBN 0-437-86015-9 : £2.90
(B77-34251)

Vaughan, Carol. Missing Matilda / [by] Carol Vaughan. — Leicester : Knight Books, 1977. — 96p ; 18cm.
Originally published: London : Blackie, 1964.
ISBN 0-340-19171-6 Pbk : £0.60
(B77-32277)

Vaughan, Carol. Trekkers' trail / [by] Carol Vaughan ; illustrated by Constance Marshall. — London [etc.] : White Lion Publishers, 1977. — 3-125p : ill ; 21cm.
Originally published: London : Blackie, 1967.
ISBN 0-85686-261-4 : £2.75
(B77-07679)

Vaughan, Carol. Two foals for Matilda / [by] Carol Vaughan ; illustrated by Constance Marshall. — London [etc.] : White Lion Publishers, 1976. — 124p : ill ; 21cm.
Originally published: London : Blackie, 1965.
ISBN 0-85686-246-0 : £2.50
(B77-03259)

Vavra, Robert. Romany free / [text] by Robert Vavra ; paintings by Fleur Cowles. — London : Collins, 1977. — 45p : col ill ; 22x30cm.
ISBN 0-00-216725-5 : £3.50
(B77-28236)

The '**Victor**' book for boys. — London : D.C. Thomson.
1978. — 1977. — 4-125p : chiefly col ill ; 28cm.
Ill. on lining papers.
£0.95
(B77-31570)

Virin, Anna. Elsa tidies her house / [by] Anna Virin. — London : Coventure, 1976. — [24]p : chiefly ill(chiefly col) ; 16cm.
Originally published: s.l. : s.n., 1973 ; Leicester : Brockhampton Press, 1974.
ISBN 0-904576-12-4 : £0.75
(B77-06932)

Waber, Bernard. Good night Ben / by Bernard Waber. — Hornsby, N.S.W. : Hodder and Stoughton (Australia) ; Leicester : Brockhampton Press, 1974. — 48p : col ill ; 27cm.
Originally published: as 'Ira sleeps over'. Boston, Mass. : Houghton Mifflin, 1972.
ISBN 0-340-19123-6 : £2.20
(B77-01863)

Wahl, Jan. The Clumpets go sailing / story by Jan Wahl ; illustrated by Cyndy Szekeres. — Tadworth : World's Work, 1977. — [40]p : col ill ; 19x25cm.
Originally published: New York : Parents Magazine Press, 1975.
ISBN 0-437-84177-4 : £2.50
(B77-08638)

Wahl, Jan. SOS Bobomobile, or, The further adventures of Melvin Spitznagle and Professor Mickimecki / [by] Jan Wahl ; pictures by Fernando Krahn. — Harmondsworth [etc.] : Puffin Books, 1977. — 121p : ill ; 18cm. — (Puffin books)
Originally published: New York : Delacorte Press, 1973 ; Harmondsworth : Kestrel Books, 1975.
ISBN 0-14-030953-5 Pbk : £0.40
(B77-34252)

Walker, Barbara Kerlin. Teeny-Tiny and the witch-woman / by Barbara K. Walker ; illustrated by Michael Foreman. — London (3 Fitzroy Sq., W.1) : Andersen Press Ltd [etc.], 1977. — [30]p : col ill ; 26cm.
Originally published: New York : Pantheon Books, 1975.
ISBN 0-905478-09-6 : £2.75
(B77-22949)

Walsh, Jill Paton. The butty boy / [by] Jill Paton Walsh ; text illustrations by Juliette Palmer ; cover illustration by Carolyn Scrace. — London : Pan Books, 1977. — 93p : ill ; 18cm. — (Piccolo)
Originally published: London : Macmillan, 1975.
ISBN 0-330-25099-x Pbk : £0.45
(B77-29005)

Walsh, Jill Paton. Crossing to Salamis / [by] Jill Paton Walsh ; illustrated by David Smee. — London : Heinemann, 1977. — 43p : ill ; 21cm. — (Long ago children books)
ISBN 0-434-94925-6 : £2.10
(B77-19054)

Walsh, Jill Paton. The walls of Athens / [by] Jill Paton Walsh ; illustrated by David Smee. — London : Heinemann, 1977. — 39p : ill ; 21cm. — (Long ago children books)
ISBN 0-434-94931-0 : £2.50
(B77-31571)

Walt Disney presents the Bambi book / illustrations by the Walt Disney Studio ; adapted by Mel Crawford. — Maidenhead : Purnell, 1977. — [16]p : chiefly col ill ; 21cm. — (A Purnell shape book)
Originally published: United States? : s.n., 1971.

Sd : Unpriced
(B77-07680)

Walt Disney presents the Winnie-the-Pooh book / pictures by the Walt Disney Studio ; adapted by Al White. — Maidenhead : Purnell, 1977. — [16]p : chiefly col ill ; 21cm. — (A Purnell shape book)
Originally published: United States? : s.n., 1971.

Sd : Unpriced
(B77-07681)

Walt Disney presents Winnie the Pooh. — Maidenhead : Purnell, 1977. — [13]p : col ill ; 21cm.
Originally published: United States? : s.n., 1974.

ISBN 0-361-03845-3 : £0.25
(B77-15578)

Walt Disney's Cinderella doll dressing book. — Maidenhead : Purnell, 1977. — [20]p : ill(some col) ; 26cm.
Sd : £0.30
ISBN 0-361-03804-6
Also classified at 745.59'22
(B77-12164)

Walt Disney's Donald on a picnic. — Maidenhead : Purnell, 1977. — [12]p : col ill ; 27cm.
Pbd : £0.75
ISBN 0-361-03839-9
(B77-14997)

Walt Disney's greatest stories. — [Maidenhead] : [Purnell for Marks and Spencer Limited].
Bambi ; Lady and the tramp ; Jungle book. — [1977]. — [76]p : col ill ; 29cm.
Cover title. — This collection originally published: 1976.
£1.25
ISBN 0-361-03909-3
(B77-32928)

Winnie the Pooh / [adapted from the Winnie-the-Pooh books by A.A. Milne]. — [1977]. — [76]p : col ill ; 29cm.
Cover title. — Originally published: 1976.
£1.25
ISBN 0-361-03910-7
(B77-32929)

Walt Disney's Mickey Mouse annual. — London : IPC Magazines.
1978. — [1977]. — 3-78p : chiefly ill(chiefly col), ports ; 28cm. — (A Fleetway annual)
Cover title. — Col. ill., text on lining papers. — Spine title: Mickey Mouse annual.
ISBN 0-85037-341-7 : £1.45
(B77-32930)

Walt Disney's Mickey Mouse book / illustrated by Al White. — Maidenhead : Purnell, 1977. — [16]p : chiefly col ill ; 21cm. — (A Purnell shape book)
Originally published: United States? : s.n., 1971.

Sd : Unpriced
(B77-07682)

Walt Disney's Snow White doll dressing book. — Maidenhead : Purnell, 1977. — [20]p : ill(some col) ; 26cm.
Sd : £0.30
ISBN 0-361-03804-6
Also classified at 745.59'22
(B77-12165)

Walt Disney's story of Mickey and the beanstalk. — Maidenhead : Purnell, 1977. — [12]p : col ill ; 21cm.
ISBN 0-361-03843-7 : £0.75
(B77-14998)

Walt Disney's the ugly duckling. — Maidenhead : Purnell, 1977. — [12]p : col ill ; 27cm.
ISBN 0-361-03839-9 Pbd : £0.75
(B77-14999)

Walters, Hugh. Boy astronaut / [by] Hugh Walters ; illustrated by Trevor Ridley. — London : Abelard, 1977. — 61p : ill ; 21cm. — (A grasshopper book)
ISBN 0-200-72491-6 : £1.75
ISBN 0-200-72492-4 Pbk : £0.50
(B77-32931)

The '**War** picture library' annual. — London : IPC Magazines.
[1978]. — 1977. — 128p : chiefly ill ; 28cm. — (A Fleetway annual)
Cover title.
ISBN 0-85037-365-4 Pbk : £0.85
(B77-32932)

Wardell, Phyl. Hazard Island / [by] Phyl Wardell ; illustrations by Albert Wagenvoort ; [map by Jean Oates]. — Christchurch, N.Z. [etc.] ; London : Whitcoulls, 1976. — 160p : ill, map ; 21cm. — ([Kairangi series])
ISBN 0-7233-0489-0 : Unpriced
(B77-09348)

Warlord for boys : all-action, all-picture war stories. — [London] : [D.C. Thomson].
1978. — [1977]. — 3-126p : chiefly ill(chiefly col) ; 28cm.
Cover title. — Ill. on lining papers.
£0.95
(B77-31573)

Waters, Frank, *b.1909.* The day the village blushed / [by] Frank Waters ; illustrated by George Adamson. — London : Harrap, 1977. — [42]p : ill(chiefly col) ; 19cm. — (Reading with mother)
ISBN 0-245-53175-0 : £0.95
(B77-34253)

Watkins, Eleanor. A kid from the city / [by] Eleanor Watkins. — London : Pickering and Inglis, 1976. — 88p ; 19cm.
ISBN 0-7208-2234-3 : £0.80
(B77-03260)

Watkins-Pitchford, Denys James. Wild lone : the story of a Pytchley fox / written and illustrated by D.J. Watkins-Pitchford ('BB'). — New ed. — London [etc.] : Beaver Books, 1977. — 191p : ill ; 18cm.
This ed. originally published: under the name BB. London : Methuen, 1970.
ISBN 0-600-39388-7 Pbk : £0.55
(B77-30793)

Watson, Simon. The partisan / [by] Simon Watson. — Harmondsworth [etc.] : Puffin Books, 1976. — 124p ; 18cm. — (Puffin books)

Originally published: London : Gollancz, 1973.
ISBN 0-14-030867-9 Pbk : £0.45
(B77-03794)

Watts, Marjorie-Ann. Crocodile medicine / [by] Marjorie-Ann Watts. — London : Deutsch, 1977. — [32]p : col ill ; 25cm.
ISBN 0-233-96863-6 : £2.50
(B77-13935)

Way, Irene. Armada quest / by Irene Way. — London : Pickering and Inglis, 1976. — 119p ; 19cm.
ISBN 0-7208-2230-0 : £0.90
(B77-03795)

Wayne, Jenifer. The smoke in Albert's garden / [by] Jenifer Wayne ; illustrated by Margaret Palmer. — Harmondsworth [etc.] : Puffin Books, 1977. — 175p : ill ; 18cm. — (Puffin books)
Originally published: London : Heinemann, 1974.
ISBN 0-14-030899-7 Pbk : £0.50
(B77-08131)

Webb, Marcia. Mumfie the elephant / [by] Marcia Webb. — Ealing : Carousel Books, 1977. — 127p : ill ; 20cm. — (Carousel books)
'Based on the television show "Here comes Mumfie"' - cover. — Also published: London : J. Murray, 1977.
ISBN 0-552-52072-1 Pbk : £0.50
(B77-33487)

Webb, Marcia. Mumfie the elephant / [by] Marcia Webb. — London : J. Murray, 1977. — 128p : ill ; 21cm.
'Based on the characters in Katharine Tozer's stories'.
ISBN 0-7195-3372-4 : £1.95
(B77-22950)

Weir, Rosemary. Albert and the dragonettes / [by] Rosemary Weir ; illustrated by Gerald Rose. — London : Abelard-Schuman, 1977. — 120p : ill ; 21cm. — (A grasshopper book)
ISBN 0-200-72487-8 : £2.25
ISBN0-200-72488-6 Pbk : £0.60
(B77-28237)

Weiss, Leatie. Heather's feathers / by Leatie Weiss ; illustrated by Ellen Weiss. — New York ; London : F. Watts, 1976. — [32]p : col ill ; 22cm.
ISBN 0-85166-617-5 : £2.50
(B77-20743)

Welch, Ronald. Captain of dragoons / [by] Ronald Welch ; illustrated by William Stobbs. — Harmondsworth [etc.] : Puffin Books, 1977. — 251,[1]p : ill, map ; 18cm. — (Puffin books)
Originally published: London : Oxford University Press, 1956.
ISBN 0-14-030978-0 Pbk : £0.60
(B77-29773)

Welch, Ronald. Knight crusader / [by] Ronald Welch ; illustrated by William Stobbs. — Harmondsworth [etc.] : Puffin Books, 1977. — 272p : ill, 2 maps ; 18cm. — (Puffin books)
Originally published: London : Oxford University Press, 1954.
ISBN 0-14-030920-9 Pbk : £0.60
(B77-18418)

Weldrick, Valerie. Time sweep / [by] Valerie Weldrick ; illustrated by Ron Brooks. — London : Hutchinson, 1976. — 131p : ill ; 23cm.
ISBN 0-09-130100-9 : £2.75
(B77-09997)

Wells, Rosemary. Benjamin & Tulip / by Rosemary Wells. — Harmondsworth [etc.] : Puffin Books, 1977. — [33]p : chiefly col ill ; 11x20cm. — (Picture puffins)
Originally published: New York : Dial Press, 1973.
ISBN 0-14-050177-0 Sd : £0.50
(B77-18419)

Wells, Rosemary. Benjamin and Tulip / by Rosemary Wells. — Harmondsworth : Kestrel Books, 1977. — [32]p : chiefly col ill ; 12x21cm.
Also published: Harmondsworth : Puffin Books, 1977. — Originally published: New York : Dial Press, 1973.
ISBN 0-7226-5253-4 : £1.50
(B77-19055)

Wells, Rosemary. Morris's disappearing bag : a Christmas story / by Rosemary Wells. — Harmondsworth : Kestrel Books, 1977. — [40] p : chiefly col ill ; 21cm.
Originally published: New York : Dial Press, 1975.
ISBN 0-7226-5413-8 : £1.75
(B77-26635)

Wensell, Ulises. David / [by] Ulises Wensell. — London : Evans Bros, 1977. — 32p : chiefly col ill ; 32cm. — (Wensell, Ulises. Jackson family)
Text, col. ill. on lining papers.
ISBN 0-237-44880-7 : £1.95
(B77-25242)

Wensell, Ulises. Jenny and Steve / [by] Ulises Wensell. — London : Evans Bros, 1977. — 32p : chiefly col ill ; 25cm. — (Wensell, Ulises. Jackson family)
Text, col. ill. on lining papers.
ISBN 0-237-44878-5 : £1.95
(B77-25243)

Wensell, Ulises. Mum and dad / [by] Ulises Wensell. — London : Evans Bros, 1977. — 32p : chiefly col ill ; 25cm. — (Wensell, Ulises. Jackson family)
Text, col. ill. on lining papers.
ISBN 0-237-44879-3 : £1.95
(B77-25244)

Wensell, Ulises. Smudge / [by] Ulises Wensell. — London : Evans Bros, 1977. — 32p : chiefly col ill ; 25cm. — (Wensell, Ulises. Jackson family)
Text, col. ill. on lining papers.
ISBN 0-237-44881-5 : £1.95
(B77-25245)

Whitbread, Peter. The Flockton Flyer / [by] Peter Whitbread ; illustrated by Denis Manton. — London : Independent Television Books Ltd : Arrow Books, 1977. — 95p : ill, music ; 20cm. — (Look-in books)
'From the Southern Television series' - cover.
ISBN 0-09-915460-9 Pbk : £0.65
(B77-31574)

White, Terence Hanbury. The sword in the stone / [by] T.H. White. — London : Collins, 1976. — 286p : 2 ill ; 22cm.
Originally published: 1938.
ISBN 0-00-184780-5 : £2.25
(B77-15000)

White, Terence Hanbury. The sword in the stone / [by] T.H. White. — London : Collins, 1977. — 286p ; 18cm. — (Lions)
Originally published: 1938.
ISBN 0-00-671305-x Pbk : £0.65
(B77-16088)

Whiteley, John. The city is a web / by John Whiteley. — London : Pickering and Inglis, 1976. — [1],118p ; 19cm.
ISBN 0-7208-2231-9 : £0.90
(B77-03261)

'Whizzer' and 'Chips' annual. — London : IPC Magazines.
1978. — 1977. — 153p : of col ill ; 28cm. — (A Fleetway annual)
Cover title.
ISBN 0-85037-366-2 : £1.00
(B77-32933)

'Whoopee!' annual. — London : IPC Magazines.
1978. — [1977]. — 143p : chiefly ill(some col) ; 28cm. — (A Fleetway annual)
Cover title.
ISBN 0-85037-367-0 : £1.00
(B77-32934)

Wiggin, Kate Douglas. Rebecca of Sunnybrook Farm / [by] Kate Douglas Wiggin. — London : New English Library, 1977. — 208p ; 18cm.
Originally published: Boston, Mass. : Houghton Mifflin ; London : Gay and Bird, 1903.
ISBN 0-450-03544-1 Pbk : £0.85
(B77-29006)

Wild, Robin. The bears' ABC book / [by] Robin and Jocelyn Wild. — London : Heinemann, 1977. — [32]p : col ill ; 25cm.
ISBN 0-434-97263-0 : £2.50
(B77-19863)

Wildsmith, Brian. Maurice Maeterlinck's 'Blue bird' / [adapted and illustrated by] Brian Wildsmith. — Oxford [etc.] : Oxford University Press, 1976 [i.e. 1977]. — 4-37p : chiefly col ill ; 29cm.
Translation and adaptation of: 'L'oiseau bleu'. Paris : L'Illustration, 1909.
ISBN 0-19-279714-x : £2.95
(B77-08132)

Willard, Barbara. The eldest son / [by] Barbara Willard. — Harmondsworth : Kestrel Books, 1977. — 206p ; 23cm. — (Willard, Barbara. Mantlemass novels)
ISBN 0-7226-5257-7 : £3.25
(B77-13393)

Willard, Barbara. Harrow and harvest / [by] Barbara Willard. — Harmondsworth [etc.] : Puffin Books, 1977. — 203p ; 19cm. — (Willard, Barbara. Mantlemass novels) (Puffin books)
Originally published: Harmondsworth: Kestrel Books, 1974.
ISBN 0-14-030923-3 Pbk : £0.55
(B77-12759)

Willard, Barbara. Priscilla Pentecost / [by] Barbara Willard ; illustrated by Doreen Roberts. — New ed. — London : Hamilton, 1977. — 120p : ill ; 23cm.
Previous ed.: 1970.
ISBN 0-241-89676-2 : £1.95
(B77-26636)

Willard, Barbara. The suddenly gang / [by] Barbara Willard ; illustrated by Lynette Hemmant. — London : Hamilton, 1977. — 120p : ill ; 23cm.
Originally published: 1963.
ISBN 0-241-89677-0 : £1.95
(B77-19864)

Williams, Dorian. Kingdom for a horse / [by] Dorian Williams ; illustrated by Val Biro. — London : Dent, 1977. — 140p : ill ; 18cm. — (A Dent dolphin)
Originally published: 1971.
ISBN 0-460-02746-8 Pbk : £0.60
(B77-25246)

Williams, Hilda. She promised she would write / by Hilda Williams ; illustrated by Tony Williams. — London (22 Greenwich Church St., S.E.10) : Andrew Lissack, [1977]. — [3], 50p : ill ; 22cm.
Sd : £0.90
(B77-34254)

Williams, Jay. Danny Dunn and the homework machine / [by] Jay Williams and Raymond Abrashkin ; illustrated by Anne Mieke. — London : Macdonald and Jane's, 1977. — 119p : ill ; 23cm.
Originally published: as 'Danny Dunn and the homework machine', New York : Whittlesey House, 1958 ; and as 'The homework machine', Leicester : Brockhampton Press, 1960.
ISBN 0-354-08011-3 : £2.75
(B77-06933)

Williams, Jay. Danny Dunn on a desert island / [by] Jay Williams and Raymond Abrashkin ; illustrated by Anne Mieke. — Harmondsworth [etc.] : Puffin Books, 1976. — 112p : ill ; 18cm. — (Puffin books)
Originally published: New York : Whittlesey House, 1957 ; London : Macdonald, 1968.
ISBN 0-14-030877-6 Pbk : £0.40
(B77-03796)

Williams, Jay. Daylight robbery / [by] Jay Williams. — Harmondsworth : Kestrel Books, 1977. — 120p ; 21cm.
Originally published: as 'The burglar next door'. New York : Four Winds Press, 1976.
ISBN 0-7226-5247-x : £2.25
(B77-08133)

Williams, Jenny. Favourite fairy tales / [illustrations by] Jenny Williams ; [text by David Grant]. — Glasgow [etc.] : Collins, 1976. — 3-78p : col ill ; 29cm.
Col. ill. on lining papers.
ISBN 0-00-138104-0 : £2.95
(B77-15001)

Williams, Ursula Moray. Malkin's mountain / [by] Ursula Moray Williams ; illustrated by Shirley Hughes. — [Revised ed.]. — London : Hamilton, 1976. — 124p : ill ; 23cm.
Revised ed. originally published: 1970.
£1.80
(B77-01016)

Williams, Ursula Moray. The three toymakers / [by] Ursula Moray Williams ; illustrated by Shirley Hughes. — Revised ed. — London : Hamilton, 1976. — 128p : ill ; 23cm.
This ed. originally published: 1970.
£1.80
ISBN 0-241-01792-0
(B77-01017)

Williams, Ursula Moray. The toymaker's daughter / [by] Ursula Moray Williams ; illustrated by Shirley Hughes. — London : Hamilton, 1976. — 127p : ill ; 23cm.
Originally published: 1968.
ISBN 0-241-91407-8 : £1.80
(B77-01018)

Williams-Ellis, Amabel, *Lady.* The Arabian Nights / stories retold by Amabel Williams-Ellis ; illustrated by Pauline Diana Baynes. — London [etc.] : Blackie, 1976. — 348p : ill ; 23cm.
This collection originally published: 1957.
ISBN 0-216-90318-1 : £3.25
(B77-34255)

Williams-Ellis, Amabel, *Lady.* Fairy tales from East and West / retold by Amabel Williams-Ellis ; illustrated by William Stobbs. — Glasgow [etc.] : Blackie, 1977. — 128p : ill ; 23cm.
ISBN 0-216-90253-3 : £1.95
ISBN 0-216-90252-5 Pbk : £0.95
(B77-11449)

Williams-Ellis, Amabel, *Lady.* Fairy tales from everywhere / retold by Amabel Williams-Ellis ; illustrated by William Stobbs. — Glasgow [etc.] : Blackie, 1977. — 128p : ill ; 23cm.
ISBN 0-216-90257-6 : £1.95
ISBN 0-216-90256-8 Pbk : £0.95
(B77-11450)

Williams-Ellis, Amabel, *Lady.* Fairy tales from here and there / retold by Amabel Williams-Ellis ; illustrated by William Stobbs. — Glasgow [etc.] : Blackie, 1977. — 124p : ill ; 23cm.
ISBN 0-216-90255-x : £1.95
ISBN 0-216-90254-1 Pbk : £0.95
(B77-11451)

Williams-Ellis, Amabel, *Lady.* Fairy tales from near and far / retold by Amabel Williams-Ellis ; illustrated by William Stobbs. — Glasgow [etc.] : Blackie, 1977. — 128p : ill ; 23cm.
ISBN 0-216-90251-7 : £1.95
ISBN 0-216-90250-9 Pbk : £0.95
(B77-11452)

Williams-Ellis, Amabel, *Lady.* Fairy tales from the British Isles / retold by Amabel Williams-Ellis ; illustrated by Pauline Diana Baynes. — Glasgow [etc.] : Blackie, 1976. — 328p : ill ; 23cm.
This collection originally published: 1960.
ISBN 0-216-90288-6 : £3.95
(B77-03262)

Williams-Ellis, Amabel, *Lady.* [Fairy tales from the British Isles. Selections]. British fairy tales / retold by Amabel Williams-Ellis ; illustrated by Pauline Diana Baynes. — Glasgow [etc.] : Blackie, 1976. — 168p : ill ; 22cm.
'British fairy tales' originally published: 1965 - 'Fairy tales from the British Isles' originally published: 1960.
ISBN 0-216-90290-8 : Unpriced
ISBN 0-216-90230-4 Pbk : £0.95
(B77-03263)

Williams-Ellis, Amabel, *Lady.* [Fairy tales from the British Isles. Selections]. More British fairy tales / retold by Amabel Williams-Ellis ; illustrated by Pauline Diana Baynes. — Glasgow [etc.] : Blackie, 1976. — [8],169-328p : ill ; 22cm.
'More British fairy tales' originally published: 1965 - 'Fairy tales from the British Isles' originally published: 1960.
ISBN 0-216-90289-4 : Unpriced
ISGN 0-216-90231-2 Pbk : £0.95
(B77-03264)

Williams-Ellis, Amabel, *Lady.* The rain-god's daughter, and other African fairy-tales / retold by Amabel Williams-Ellis ; illustrated by Tom Brooks. — Glasgow [etc.] : Blackie, 1977. — 94p : ill ; 23cm.
ISBN 0-216-90324-6 : £2.95
(B77-30794)

Willis, Anne-Marie. Blinky Bill and the pelicans / adapted by Anne-Marie Willis ; illustrated by Stephen Axelsen. — London [etc.] : Angus and Robertson, 1976. — [20]p : col ill ; 30cm.
'Based on "The complete adventures of Blinky Bill" by Dorothy Wall'.
ISBN 0-207-13288-7 : £0.95
(B77-06934)

Wills, Jonathan. Linda and the lighthouse / written and illustrated by Jonathan Wills. — Edinburgh : Canongate Publishing, 1976. — [34]p : col ill ; 21x27cm.
ISBN 0-903937-22-0 : £2.50
(B77-13936)

Wilson, David Henry. Elephants don't sit on cars / by David Henry Wilson ; illustrated by Patricia Drew. — London : Chatto and Windus, 1977. — 95p : ill ; 21cm.
ISBN 0-7011-2273-0 : £2.50 : CIP rev.
(B77-21542)

Wise, Cicely. Cindy the canal-boat cat / [by] Cicely Wise ; illustrated by Cora E.M. Paterson. — Ilfracombe : Stockwell, 1977. — 40p : ill ; 18cm.
ISBN 0-7223-1034-x Pbk : £0.40
(B77-23793)

Wodehouse, Pelham Grenville. Mike at Wrykyn / [by] P.G. Wodehouse. — London : Barrie and Jenkins, 1976. — 189p ; 20cm.
Originally published: London : Jenkins, 1953.
ISBN 0-257-66066-6 : £3.95
(B77-01864)

The **Wombles** special. — [London] : [IPC Magazines].
'Based on the BBC Television series "The Wombles"'.
[1976]. — [1976]. — 40p : ill(some col) ; 28cm.

Sd : £0.25
(B77-19056)

[1977]. — [1977]. — 40p : ill(some col) ; 28cm.

Sd : £0.30
(B77-19057)

The **wonderful** world of Disney annual. — London : IPC Magazines.
1978. — [1977]. — 4-77p : chiefly ill(chiefly col) ; 28cm. — (A Fleetway annual)
Col. ill. on lining papers.
ISBN 0-85037-368-9 : £1.65
(B77-32935)

Wood, Lorna. Hags by starlight / [by] Lorna Wood ; with drawings by Kiddell-Monroe. — London [etc.] : White Lion Publishers, 1977. — [5],100p : ill ; 21cm.
Originally published: London : Dent, 1970.
ISBN 0-85686-237-1 : £2.95
(B77-12760)

Wood, M A. The year the raiders came / [by] M.A. Wood ; illustrated by Victor Ambrus. — London : Andersen Press : Hutchinson, 1977. — vi,120p : ill ; 20cm. — (The Andersen young readers library)
ISBN 0-905478-10-x : £2.50
(B77-20744)

Wrightson, Patricia. The Rocks of Honey / [by] Patricia Wrightson ; illustrated by Margaret Horder. — Harmondsworth [etc.] : Puffin Books, 1977. — 176p : ill ; 18cm. — (Puffin books)
Originally published: Sydney : Angus and Robertson, 1960 ; London : Angus and Robertson, 1961.
Pbk : £0.45
ISBN 0-14-030269-7
(B77-30795)

Wyatt, Woodrow. The further exploits of Mr Saucy Squirrel / [by] Woodrow Wyatt ; illustrated by Gareth Floyd. — London [etc.] : Allen and Unwin, 1977. — 95p : ill ; 25cm.
ISBN 0-04-823143-6 : £3.25
(B77-27486)

Yeoman, John. The boy who sprouted antlers / [text by] John Yeoman ; [illustrated by] Quentin Blake. — Revised ed. — London : Collins, 1976. — 61p : ill ; 20cm. — (Lions)
Previous ed.: London : Faber, 1961.
ISBN 0-00-671116-2 Pbk : £0.40
(B77-07683)

Yeoman, John. Sixes and sevens / text by John Yeoman ; pictures by Quentin Blake. — Harmondsworth [etc.] : Puffin Books, 1976. — [29]p : col ill ; 17x20cm. — (Picture puffins)
Originally published: London : Blackie, 1971.
ISBN 0-14-050158-4 Sd : £0.50
(B77-01865)

Yeoman, John. The young performing horse / story by John Yeoman ; pictures by Quentin Blake. — London : Hamilton, 1977. — [32]p : col ill ; 26cm.
ISBN 0-241-89693-2 : £2.95
(B77-29774)

Yolen, Jane. The moon ribbon, and other tales / by Jane Yolen ; illustrated by David Palladini. — London [etc.] : Dent, 1977. — [8],54p : ill ; 23cm.
This collection originally published: New York : Crowell, 1976.
ISBN 0-460-06836-9 : £2.50 : CIP rev.
(B77-19865)

Young, Helen, *b.1938.* A throne for Sesame / [by] Helen Young ; illustrated by Shirley Hughes. — London : Deutsch, 1977. — [32]p : col ill ; 26cm.
ISBN 0-233-96871-7 : £2.75
(B77-19866)

Young winter's tales. — London [etc.] : Macmillan.
7 / edited by M.R. Hodgkin. — 1976. — 240p ; 21cm.
ISBN 0-333-18547-1 : £3.25
(B77-03265)

Zabel, Jennifer. The toymaker's loaves / written by Jennifer Zabel ; illustrated by Christopher Masters. — London : F. Warne, 1977. — [32] p : col ill ; 20x28cm.
ISBN 0-7232-2046-8 : £2.95
(B77-34256)

Zalben, Jane Breskin. Basil and Hillary / [by] Jane Breskin Zalben. — Tadworth : World's Work, 1977. — [32]p : chiefly col ill ; 24cm.
Originally published: New York : Macmillan, 1975.
ISBN 0-437-89262-x : £2.60
(B77-20745)

Zion, Gene. Harry and the lady next door / by Gene Zion ; pictures by Margaret Bloy Graham. — Tadworth : World's Work, 1977. — 62p : col ill ; 22cm. — (An I can read book)

Originally published: New York : Harper, 1960 ; Tadworth : World's Work, 1962.
ISBN 0-437-96002-1 Sd : £0.60
(B77-16630)

Zolotow, Charlotte. May I visit? / [by] Charlotte Zolotow ; with illustrations by Erik Blegvad. — Tadworth : World's Work, 1977. — 32p : col ill ; 21cm.
Originally published: New York : Harper and Row, 1976.
ISBN 0-437-89511-4 : £2.10
(B77-21543)

Zolotow, Charlotte. When the wind stops / by Charlotte Zolotow ; pictures by Howard Knotts. — Tadworth : World's Work, 1977. — 32p : chiefly ill ; 24cm.
Originally published: New York : Abelard-Schuman, 1962 ; London : Abelard-Schuman, 1964.
ISBN 0-437-89510-6 : £2.10
(B77-09349)

823.912 — ENGLISH FICTION, 1900-1945

823'.9'12 — Books. Organisations. *Great Britain. National Book League. Exhibits: Items associated with Potter, Beatrix. Catalogues*

Clark, Keith, *b.1947.* Peter Rabbit's 75th birthday exhibition : a souvenir catalogue / [prepared by Keith Clark]. — London : National Book League, 1976. — 40p : ill ; 25cm.
'Catalogue of the exhibition held at the National Book League 16th December-14th January 1977' - title page verso.
ISBN 0-85353-254-0 Sd : £0.40
(B77-09998)

823'.9'12 — Children's stories in English. Potter, Beatrix. Tale of Peter Rabbit. *Textual criticisms*

The **history** of 'The tale of Peter Rabbit' : taken mainly from Leslie Linder's 'A history of the writings of Beatrix Potter' together with the text and illustrations from the first privately printed edition / [edited by Anne Emerson]. — London [etc.] : F. Warne, 1976. — 63p,8p of plates : ill(some col), facsims ; 24cm.
Includes the text of the first privately printed edition of Beatrix Potter's 'The tale of Peter Rabbit'.
ISBN 0-7232-1988-5 : £2.25
(B77-05090)

823'.9'12 — Children's stories in English. Richards, Frank, b.1875. *Critical studies*

The **Charles** Hamilton companion. — Maidstone (30 Tonbridge Rd, Maidstone, Kent) : Museum Press.
Vol.3 : A new anthology from the works of Charles Hamilton / with contributions from Una Hamilton-Wright, Roger Jenkins, Les Rowley ; compiled, edited and arranged by John Wernham. — [1977]. — xvi,304p : ill, facsims, ports ; 22cm.
Pbk : Unpriced
Also classified at 823'.9'1J
(B77-26637)

823'.9'12 — Children's stories in English. Streatfeild, Noel. *Autobiographies*

Streatfeild, Noel. A vicarage family / by Noel Streatfeild. — [London] : Fontana, 1977. — 224p ; 18cm. — (Lions)
Originally published: London : Collins, 1963.
ISBN 0-00-671229-0 Pbk : £0.65
(B77-18420)

823'.9'12 — Fiction in English. Bloom, Ursula. *Autobiographies*

Bloom, Ursula. Life is no fairy tale / [by] Ursula Bloom. — Large print ed. — Bath : Firecrest, 1977. — [8],296p,[12]p of plates : ill, facsim, ports ; 23cm.
Originally published: London : Hale, 1976.
ISBN 0-85119-010-3 : £4.60
(B77-20746)

823'.9'12 — Fiction in English. Bowen, Elizabeth. *Biographies*

Glendinning, Victoria. Elizabeth Bowen : portrait of a writer / [by] Victoria Glendinning. — London : Weidenfeld and Nicolson, 1977. — x, 261p,[8]p of plates : ill, ports ; 23cm.
Bibl.: p.247-249. — Index.
ISBN 0-297-77369-0 : £6.50
(B77-27487)

823'.9'12 — Fiction in English. Chesterton, Gilbert Keith. *Critical studies*
Boyd, Ian. The novels of G.K. Chesterton : a study in art and propaganda / [by] Ian Boyd. — London : Elek, 1975. — iii-xii,241p ; 23cm.
Index.
ISBN 0-236-31028-3 : £4.95
(B77-01866)

823'.9'12 — Fiction in English. Christie, Dame Agatha. *Autobiographies*
Christie, *Dame* Agatha. An autobiography / [by] Agatha Christie. — London : Collins, 1977. — 542p,[20]p of plates : ill, ports(some col) ; 23cm.
Index.
ISBN 0-00-216012-9 : £7.95
(B77-32936)

823'.9'12 — Fiction in English. Christie, Dame Agatha. *Critical studies*
Agatha Christie : first lady of crime / edited by H.R.F. Keating. — London : Weidenfeld and Nicolson, 1977. — 224p : ill, facsims, ports ; 26cm.
Bibl.: p.217-219. — Index.
ISBN 0-297-77295-3 : £5.00
(B77-18421)

823'.9'12 — Fiction in English. Conrad, Joseph. *Conference proceedings*
International Conference on Conrad, *Canterbury, 1974.* Joseph Conrad : a commemoration : papers from the 1974 International Conference on Conrad / edited by Norman Sherry. — London [etc.] : Macmillan, 1976. — xvi,224p ; 23cm.
Index.
ISBN 0-333-19109-9 : £7.95
(B77-08639)

823'.9'12 — Fiction in English. Conrad, Joseph. Special themes: Seafaring. *Critical studies*
Burgess, C F. The fellowship of the craft : Conrad on ships and seamen and the sea / by C.F. Burgess. — Port Washington ; London : Kennikat Press, 1976. — xii,160p ; 23cm. — (Kennikat Press national university publications : literary criticism series)
Bibl.: p.2. — Index.
Unpriced
(B77-18422)

823'.9'12 — Fiction in English. Conrad, Joseph. Special themes: Self-possession
Daleski, Hillel Matthew. Joseph Conrad : the way of dispossession / [by] H.M. Daleski. — London : Faber, 1977. — 3-234p ; 23cm.
Index.
ISBN 0-571-10816-4 : £5.95
(B77-09999)

823'.9'12 — Fiction in English. Croft-Cooke, Rupert, 1973-1976. *Autobiographies*
Croft-Cooke, Rupert. The green, green grass : being the twenty-fourth and final book in the sequence 'The sensual world' / by Rupert Croft-Cooke. — London : W.H. Allen, 1977. — 192p ; 23cm.
ISBN 0-491-01836-3 : £4.95
(B77-20747)

823'.9'12 — Fiction in English. Dell, Ethel May. *Biographies*
Dell, Penelope. Nettie and Sissie : the biography of Ethel M. Dell and her sister Ella / by Penelope Dell. — London : Hamilton, 1977. — xv,175p,[4]p of plates : facsim, ports ; 23cm.
Index.
ISBN 0-241-89663-0 : £5.50
(B77-22951)

823'.9'12 — Fiction in English. Doyle, Sir Arthur Conan. *Biographies*
Higham, Charles, *b.1931.* The adventures of Conan Doyle : the life of the creator of Sherlock Holmes / by Charles Higham. — London : Hamilton, 1976. — 368,[2]p,[14]p of plates : ill, ports ; 23cm.
Also published: New York : Norton, 1976. — Bibl.: p.347-354. — Index.
ISBN 0-241-89498-0 : £4.95
(B77-00481)

Pearsall, Ronald. Conan Doyle : a biographical solution / [by] Ronald Pearsall. — London : Weidenfeld and Nicolson, 1977. — vii,208p,[8]p of plates : ill, ports ; 23cm.
Bibl.: p.196-200. — Index.
ISBN 0-297-77272-4 : £5.95
(B77-13937)

Pearson, Hesketh. Conan Doyle : his life and art / by Hesketh Pearson. — London : Macdonald and Jane's, 1977. — xiii,193p,[8]p of plates : ports ; 23cm.
Originally published: London : Methuen, 1943. — Index.
ISBN 0-354-04216-5 : £4.95
(B77-29007)

823'.9'12 — Fiction in English. Du Maurier, Dame Daphne. *Autobiographies*
Du Maurier, *Dame* Daphne. Growing pains : the shaping of a writer / by Daphne du Maurier. — London : Gollancz, 1977. — 173p,leaf of plate,[22]p of plates : ill, ports ; 23cm.
ISBN 0-575-02284-1 : £4.95
(B77-18423)

823'.9'12 — Fiction in English. Forester, Cecil Scott. Hornblower stories. *Critical studies*
Forester, Cecil Scott. The Hornblower companion / [by] C.S. Forester ; with maps and drawings by Samuel H. Bryant. — London : Joseph, 1977. — 140p : ill, facsim, maps ; 27cm.
Originally published: 1964.
ISBN 0-7181-0187-1 : £5.50
(B77-18424)

823'.9'12 — Fiction in English. Forster, Edward Morgan. *Biographies*
Furbank, Philip Nicholas. E.M. Forster : a life / [by] P.N. Furbank. — London : Secker and Warburg.
Vol.1 : The growth of the novelist (1879-1914). — 1977. — xvi,272p,[8]p of plates : ill, geneal tables, map, ports ; 25cm.
Index.
ISBN 0-436-16755-7 : £6.50
(B77-21544)

823'.9'12 — Fiction in English. Forster, Edward Morgan. Howards End. *Critical studies*
Widdowson, Peter. E.M. Forster's 'Howards End' : fiction as history / [by] Peter Widdowson. — London : Chatto and Windus for Sussex University Press [etc.], 1977. — 124p ; 20cm. — (Text and context)
Bibl.: p.122-124.
ISBN 0-85621-067-6 : £3.50 : CIP rev.
ISBN 0-85621-068-4 Pbk : £1.75
(B77-06935)

823'.9'12 — Fiction in English. Greene, Graham. Power and the glory. *Study outlines*
Handley, Graham. Brodie's notes on Graham Greene's 'The power and the glory' / [by] Graham Handley. — London [etc.] : Pan Books, 1977. — 62p ; 20cm. — (Pan revision aids)
ISBN 0-330-50071-6 Pbk : £0.60
(B77-34257)

823'.9'12 — Fiction in English. Greene, Graham. Quiet American. *Study outlines*
Burton, Harry McGuire. Notes on Graham Greene's 'The quiet American' / compiled by H.M. Burton. — London [etc.] : Methuen, 1976. — [2],30p ; 22cm. — (Study-aid series)
Bibl.: p.30.
ISBN 0-413-34860-1 Sd : £0.60
(B77-13394)

823'.9'12 — Fiction in English. Hartley, Leslie Poles. Go-between, The. *Study outlines*
Altena, I. Notes on L.P. Hartley's 'The go-between' / compiled by I. Altena. — London [etc.] : Methuen, 1976. — [7],39p ; 22cm. — (Study-aid series)
Bibl.: p.39.
ISBN 0-413-37030-5 Sd : £0.60
(B77-13395)

823'.9'12 — Fiction in English. Isherwood, Christopher. *Biographies*
Fryer, Jonathan. Isherwood : a biography of Christopher Isherwood / [by] Jonathan Fryer. — London : New English Library, 1977. — [7], 300p,[16]p of plates : ill, ports ; 22cm.
Bibl.: p.289-290. — Index.
ISBN 0-450-03205-1 : £7.50
(B77-25247)

823'.9'12 — Fiction in English. Isherwood, Christopher, 1929-1939. *Autobiographies*
Isherwood, Christopher. Christopher and his kind, 1929-1939 / [by] Christopher Isherwood. — London : Eyre Methuen, 1977. — 252p ; 24cm.
ISBN 0-413-37130-1 : £4.95
(B77-16089)

823'.9'12 — Fiction in English. Joyce, James, b.1882. *Biographies*
Davies, Stan Gébler. James Joyce : a portrait of the artist / [by] Stan Gébler Davies. — London : Abacus, 1977. — 287p,[8]p of plates : ill, ports ; 20cm.
Originally published: London : Davis-Poynter, 1975. — Bibl.: p.275-277. — Index.
ISBN 0-349-10740-8 Pbk : £1.95
(B77-19868)

823'.9'12 — Fiction in English. Joyce, James, b.1882. *Critical studies*
Peake, C H. James Joyce : the citizen and the artist / [by] C.H. Peake. — London : Edward Arnold, 1977. — x,369p ; 24cm.
Bibl.: p.ix-x. — Index.
ISBN 0-7131-5900-6 : £9.95
(B77-19058)

823'.9'12 — Fiction in English. Joyce, James, b.1882. Finnegans wake. *Critical studies*
Begnal, Michael Henry. Narrator and character in 'Finnegans wake' / [by] Michael H. Begnal and Grace Eckley. — Lewisburg : Bucknell University Press ; London (108 New Bond St., W1Y 0QX) : Associated University Presses, [1976]. — 241p ; 22cm.
Published in the United States: 1975. — Bibl. — Index.
ISBN 0-8387-1337-8 : £5.00
(B77-01019)

823'.9'12 — Fiction in English. Joyce, James, b.1882. Finnegans wake. Characters. *Encyclopaedias*
Glasheen, Adaline. Third census of 'Finnegans wake' : an index of the characters and their roles / revised and expanded from the second census by Adaline Glasheen. — Berkeley [etc.] ; London : University of California Press, 1977. — lxxxiv,314p ; 24cm.
Bibl.: p.xvii-xix.
ISBN 0-520-02980-1 : £13.90
(B77-27488)

823'.9'12 — Fiction in English. Joyce, James, b.1882. Finnegans wake. Semiotic aspects
McHugh, Roland. The sigla of 'Finnegans wake' / [by] Roland McHugh. — London : Edward Arnold, 1976. — vii,150p : ill, maps ; 23cm.
Bibl.: p.139-145. — Index.
ISBN 0-7131-5903-0 : £7.50
(B77-05739)

823'.9'12 — Fiction in English. Joyce, James, b.1882. Influence of Homer & Shakespeare, William
Ellmann, Richard. The consciousness of Joyce / [by] Richard Ellmann. — London : Faber, 1977. — ix,150p ; 23cm.
Bibl.: p.96-134. — Index.
ISBN 0-571-10849-0 : £5.50
(B77-09350)

823'.9'12 — Fiction in English. Joyce, James, b.1882. Portrait of the artist as a young man. *Critical studies*
Approaches to Joyce's 'Portrait' : ten essays / Thomas F. Staley and Bernard Benstock, editors. — [Pittsburgh] : University of Pittsburgh Press ; London : Feffer and Simons, 1976. — xii,241p ; 22cm.
ISBN 0-8229-3331-4 : £8.96
(B77-33488)

823'.9'12 — Fiction in English. Kingsmill, Hugh. Interpersonal relationships with Muggeridge, Malcolm & Pearson, Hesketh
Ingrams, Richard. God's apology : a chronicle of three friends / [by] Richard Ingrams. — London : Deutsch, 1977. — 256p,[4]p of plates : ill, ports ; 23cm.
Bibl.: p.253. — Index.
ISBN 0-233-96888-1 : £5.50
Also classified at 070'.92'4; 828'.9'1208
(B77-25248)

823'.9'12 — Fiction in English. Lawrence, David Herbert. *Critical studies*
Littlewood, J C F. D.H. Lawrence / by J.C.F. Littlewood ; edited by Ian Scott-Kilvert. — Harlow : Longman for the British Council.
1 : 1885-1914. — 1976. — 2-60p : port ; 22cm. — (Writers and their work ; 254)
Bibl.: p.50-55.
ISBN 0-582-01254-6 Sd : £0.40
(B77-25249)

823'.9'12 — Fiction in English. Lowry, Malcolm. *Critical studies*

Miller, David, *b.1950.* Malcolm Lowry and the voyage that never ends / [by] David Miller. — London : Enitharmon Press, 1976. — 3-55,[1]p, [2]leaves of plates : facsim, port ; 22cm.
Also available in a limited ed. of 50 copies signed by the author.
ISBN 0-901111-77-5 : £2.70
ISBN 0-901111-78-3 Pbk : £1.80
(B77-13396)

823'.9'12 — Fiction in English. Mannin, Ethel. *Autobiographies*

Mannin, Ethel. Sunset over Dartmoor / [by] Ethel Mannin ; photographs by F.W. Ziemsen. — London : Hutchinson, 1977. — 200p,[8]p of plates : ill ; 23cm.
Index.
ISBN 0-09-128010-9 : £4.95
(B77-20749)

823'.9'12 — Fiction in English. Maugham, William Somerset. *Biographies*

Curtis, Anthony. Somerset Maugham / [by] Anthony Curtis. — London : Weidenfeld and Nicolson, [1977]. — 216p : ill, facsims, ports ; 26cm.
Facsim. on lining papers. — Bibl.: p.208-209. — Index.
ISBN 0-297-77367-4 : £6.50
(B77-26638)

Raphael, Frederic. W. Somerset Maugham and his world / [by] Frederic Raphael. — London : Thames and Hudson, 1976. — 128p : ill, facsims, ports ; 24cm.
Bibl.: p.120-121. — Index.
ISBN 0-500-13059-0 : £3.95
(B77-09351)

823'.9'12 — Fiction in English. Peake, Mervyn. *Periodicals*

Mervyn Peake review. — Ipswich (c/o Administrative Secretary, Central Library, Northgate St., Ipswich, Suffolk) : Mervyn Peake Society.
Continues: The Mervyn Peake Society newsletter.
No.3- ; Autumn 1976-. — 1976-. — ill, facsims ; 21cm.
Two issues a year. — 36p. in 3rd issue.
Sd : Free to members
ISSN 0309-1309
Primary classification 741'.092'4
(B77-05555)

823'.9'12 — Fiction in English. Powell, Anthony, b.1905. Music of time. Characters. *Dictionaries*

Spurling, Hilary. Handbook to Anthony Powell's 'Music of time' / [by] Hilary Spurling. — London : Heinemann, 1977. — xx,330p ; 23cm.
ISBN 0-434-72410-6 : £7.50
(B77-30796)

823'.9'12 — Fiction in English. Priestley, John Boynton. *Autobiographies*

Priestley, John Boynton. Instead of the trees : a final chapter of autobiography / [by] J.B. Priestley. — London : Heinemann, 1977. — [5], 152p ; 23cm.
ISBN 0-434-60368-6 : £3.50
(B77-11453)

823'.9'12 — Fiction in English. Thirkell, Angela. *Biographies*

Strickland, Margot. Angela Thirkell : portrait of a lady novelist / [by] Margot Strickland. — London : Duckworth, 1977. — x,182p,leaf of plate,[8]p of plate : ill, facsims, 2 geneal tables, ports ; 23cm.
Ill. on lining papers. — Bibl.: p.174-175. — Index.
ISBN 0-7156-1124-0 : £5.95
(B77-32278)

823'.9'12 — Fiction in English. Tolkien, John Ronald Reuel. *Biographies*

Carpenter, Humphrey. J.R.R. Tolkien : a biography / by Humphrey Carpenter. — London : Allen and Unwin, 1977. — [11],287p, 16p of plates : ill, facsim, geneal table, ports ; 24cm.
Bibl.: p.268-275. — Index.
ISBN 0-04-928037-6 : £4.95
(B77-19869)

823'.9'12 — Fiction in English. Tolkien, John Ronald Reuel. *Critical studies*

Kilby, Clyde Samuel. Tolkien and 'The Silmarillion' / [by] Clyde Kilby. — Berkhamsted : Lion Publishing, 1977. — 89p, plate : port ; 20cm. — (An Aslan book)
Originally published: Wheaton : H. Shaw, 1976. — Index.
ISBN 0-85648-078-9 Pbk : £0.95
(B77-27489)

Noad, Charles E. The trees, the jewels and the rings : a discursive enquiry into things little known on middle-earth / by Charles E. Noad. — Harrow (11 Regal Way, Harrow, Middx HA3 0RZ) : Tolkien Society, 1977. — [1],44p ; 21cm.
Bibl.: p.41-42.
ISBN 0-905520-01-7 Sd : £1.00
(B77-17152)

823'.9'12 — Fiction in English. Tolkien, John Ronald Reuel. *Encyclopaedias*

Tyler, J E A. The Tolkien companion / [by] J.E.A. Tyler ; edited by S.A. Tyler ; illustrated by Kevin Reilly. — London : Pan Books, 1977. — [11],531p : ill, geneal tables, maps ; 20cm. — (Picador)
Originally published: London : Macmillan, 1976.
ISBN 0-330-24593-7 Pbk : £1.50
(B77-15002)

823'.9'12 — Fiction in English. Tolkien, John Ronald Reuel. Compared with Teutonic myths

Noel, Ruth S. The mythology of Middle-earth / [by] Ruth S. Noel. — London : Thames and Hudson, 1977. — x,198p ; 22cm.
Bibl.: p.192-193. — Index.
ISBN 0-500-01187-7 : £4.50
Also classified at 293'.1'3
(B77-27490)

823'.9'12 — Fiction in English. Webb, Mary. *Biographies*

Steff, Bernard. My dearest acquaintance : a biographical sketch of Mary and Henry Webb / by Bernard Steff ; foreword by the Viscount Bridgeman. — Ludlow ([139 Corve St.], Ludlow, Shropshire) : Kings' Bookshop, 1977. — 22,[1]p : map ; 22cm.
ISBN 0-9505777-0-7 Sd : £0.60
(B77-23794)

823'.9'12 — Fiction in English. Wheatley, Dennis. *Autobiographies*

Wheatley, Dennis. The time has come - : the memoirs of Dennis Wheatley. — London : Hutchinson.
The young man said : 1897-1914. — 1977. — 255p,leaf of plate,[12]p of plates : ill, ports ; 23cm.
Index.
ISBN 0-09-127890-2 : £4.95
(B77-06346)

823'.9'12 — Fiction in English. Wodehouse, Pelham Grenville. *Critical studies*

Edwards, Owen Dudley. P.G. Wodehouse : a critical and historical essay / [by] Owen Dudley Edwards. — London : Martin Brian and O'Keeffe, 1977. — 232p ; 21cm.
Index.
ISBN 0-85616-420-8 : £4.00
(B77-28242)

Usborne, Richard. Wodehouse at work to the end / [by] Richard Usborne. — Revised ed. — London : Barrie and Jenkins, 1976 [i.e. 1977]. — 255p ; 23cm.
Previous ed.: published as 'Wodehouse at work'. London : Jenkins, 1961. — Index.
ISBN 0-214-20211-9 : £5.95
(B77-11454)

823'.9'12 — Fiction in English. Woolf, Virginia. *Biographies*

Spater, George. A marriage of true minds : an intimate portrait of Leonard and Virginia Woolf / [by] George Spater and Ian Parsons. — London : Cape : Hogarth Press, 1977. — xiv,210p : ill, facsims, ports ; 25cm.
Index.
ISBN 0-224-01407-2 : £5.95 : CIP rev.
ISBN 0-7012-0436-2 (Hogarth) : £5.95 CIP rev.
Also classified at 070.5'092'4
(B77-18425)

823'.9'12 — Fiction in English. Woolf, Virginia. *Critical studies*

Lee, Hermione. The novels of Virginia Woolf / [by] Hermione Lee. — London : Methuen, 1977. — xiii,237p ; 20cm.
Bibl.: p.226-229. — Index.
ISBN 0-416-82860-4 : £5.50
ISBN 0-416-82870-1 Pbk : £2.95
(B77-21545)

823'.9'12 — Fiction in English. Woolf, Virginia. *Diaries*

Woolf, Virginia. The diary of Virginia Woolf. — London : Hogarth Press.
Bibl.: p.328. — Index.
Vol.1 : 1915-1919 / introduced by Quentin Bell ; edited by Anne Olivier Bell. — 1977. — xxviii,356p : geneal table ; 24cm.
ISBN 0-7012-0424-9 : £8.50 : CIP rev.
(B77-07684)

823'.9'12 — Short stories in English. O'Flaherty, Liam. *Critical studies*

Kelly, Angeline A. Liam O'Flaherty the storyteller / [by] A.A. Kelly. — London [etc.] : Macmillan, 1976. — xiii,154p : port ; 23cm.
Bibl.: p.138-149. — Index.
ISBN 0-333-19768-2 : £7.95
(B77-05740)

823'.9'1209 — Fiction in English, 1900-1975. *Critical studies. Readings*

The **novel** today : contemporary writers on modern fiction / edited by Malcolm Bradbury. — [London] : Fontana, 1977. — 256p ; 18cm.
Also published: Manchester : Manchester University Press, 1977. — Bibl.: p.250-253.
ISBN 0-00-633371-0 Pbk : £1.25
(B77-17797)

The **novel** today : contemporary writers on modern fiction / edited by Malcolm Bradbury. — Manchester : Manchester University Press [etc.], 1977. — 256p ; 23cm.
Also published: London : Fontana, 1977. — Bibl.: p.250-253.
ISBN 0-7190-0677-5 : £4.95
(B77-19870)

823'.9'1209 — Fiction in English, 1900-1976. *Critical studies*

Lodge, David. The modes of modern writing : metaphor, metonymy, and the typology of modern literature / [by] David Lodge. — London : Edward Arnold, 1977. — xvi,279p ; 24cm.
Index.
ISBN 0-7131-5949-9 : £9.50
(B77-34258)

823'.9'1209 — Fiction in English. Huxley, Aldous. Brave new world & Orwell, George. Nineteen eighty-four. *Critical studies*

Calder, Jenni. Huxley and Orwell, 'Brave new world' and 'Nineteen eighty-four' / by Jenni Calder. — London : Edward Arnold, 1976. — 61p ; 19cm. — (Studies in English literature ; no.63)
Bibl.: p.60. — Index.
ISBN 0-7131-5919-7 : £3.30
ISBN 0-7131-5920-0 Pbk : £1.60
(B77-10616)

823'.9'12093 — Fiction in English, 1900-1975. Special themes: Colonialism. *Critical studies*

Mahood, Molly Maureen. The colonial encounter : a reading of six novels / [by] M.M. Mahood. — London : Collings, 1977. — [9], 211p ; 23cm.
Index.
ISBN 0-86036-016-4 : £4.75
(B77-06936)

823'.9'120932 — Fiction in English, 1900-1945. Special subjects: Rural regions. Social life. *Critical studies*

Cavaliero, Glen. The rural tradition in the English novels, 1900-1939 / [by] Glen Cavaliero. — London [etc.] : Macmillan, 1977. — xiii,240p ; 23cm.
Bibl.: p.227-233. — Index.
ISBN 0-333-21800-0 : £8.95
(B77-22952)

823'.9'120932 — Fiction in English, 1900-1970. Special subjects: England. Social conditions, 1920-1970. *Critical studies*

Atkins, John, *b.1916.* Six novelists look at society : an enquiry into the social views of Elizabeth Bowen, L.P. Hartley, Rosamund Lehman[n], Christopher Isherwood, Nancy Mitford, C.P. Snow / by John Atkins. — London : J. Calder : [Distributed by Calder and Boyars], 1977. — 284p ; 23cm.
Index.
ISBN 0-7145-3535-4 : £6.95
(B77-30797)

823'.9'1209351 — Fiction in English, 1900-1976. Special subjects: Frankenstein. *Critical studies*

The **Frankenstein** file / [edited by] Peter Haining. — London : New English Library, 1977. — 128p : ill, facsims, ports ; 27cm.
List of films: p.125-126.
ISBN 0-450-03305-8 Pbk : £3.50
Primary classification 791.43'0909'351
(B77-29615)

823.914 — ENGLISH FICTION, 1945-
823'.9'14 — Children's stories in English. White, Paul. *Autobiographies*

White, Paul. Alias Jungle Doctor : an autobiography / by Paul White. — Exeter : Paternoster Press, 1977. — [10],224p,[18]p of plates : ill, ports ; 22cm.
ISBN 0-85364-205-2 Pbk : £2.25 : CIP rev.
(B77-18426)

823'.9'14 — Fiction in English. Clarke, Arthur Charles. *Critical studies*
Arthur C. Clarke / edited by Joseph D. Olander and Martin Harry Greenberg. — Edinburgh : P. Harris, 1977. — 254p ; 22cm. — (Writers of the 21st century)
Also published: New York : Taplinger Publishing Co., 1977. — Bibl.: p.237-244. — Index.
ISBN 0-904505-41-3 : £6.00
(B77-30798)

823'.9'14 — Fiction in English. Cronin, Archibald Joseph. *Autobiographies*
Cronin, Archibald Joseph. Adventures in two worlds / [by] A.J. Cronin. — London : New English Library, 1977. — 284p ; 18cm.
Originally published: London : Gollancz, 1952.
ISBN 0-450-03195-0 Pbk : £0.95
(B77-21546)

823'.9'14 — Fiction in English. FitzGibbon, Constantine. *Autobiographies*
FitzGibbon, Constantine. Man in aspic / [by] Constantine FitzGibbon. — London : Hart-Davis MacGibbon, 1977. — viii,184p ; 23cm.
ISBN 0-246-10945-9 : £5.25
(B77-20750)

823'.9'14 — Fiction in English. Murdoch, Iris. *Critical studies*
Byatt, Antonia Susan. Iris Murdoch / by A.S. Byatt ; edited by Ian Scott-Kilvert. — Harlow : Longman for the British Council, 1976. — 3-42p,plate : port ; 22cm. — (Writers and their work ; 251)
Bibl.: p.39-42.
ISBN 0-582-01252-x : £0.40
(B77-06937)

824.7 — ENGLISH ESSAYS, 1800-1837
824'.7 — Essays in English. Smith, Sydney, b.1771. *Biographies*
Pearson, Hesketh. The Smith of Smiths : being the life, wit and humour of Sydney Smith / by Hesketh Pearson. — [1st ed. reprinted] ; with an introduction by Malcolm Muggeridge. — London : Folio Society, 1977. — 299p,[14] leaves of plates : ill, facsim, ports ; 23cm.
In slip case. — Originally published: London : Hamish Hamilton, 1934. — Bibl.: p.297-299.
ISBN 0-85067-107-8 : £6.25(to members only)
(B77-11455)

824.912 — ENGLISH ESSAYS, 1900-1945
824'.9'12 — Essays in English, 1900-1945. *Texts*
Churchill, *Sir* **Winston Spencer,** *b.1874.* The collected essays of Sir Winston Churchill / general editor Michael Wolff. — Centenary limited ed. — [London] ([44 Museum St., WC1A 1LY]) : Library of Imperial History.
'The collection ... is issued [in full vellum] as a limited edition restricted to owners of the Collected Works ...' - half title page. — Also available in buckram for sale to members of the public.
Vol.3 : Churchill and people. — 1976. — xi, 347p ; 25cm.
In slip case.
ISBN 0-903988-44-5 : £180.00 the set
Buckram ed. : £72.00 the set
(B77-12166)

Greene, Graham. Collected essays / [by] Graham Greene. — Harmondsworth [etc.] : Penguin, 1977. — 345p ; 18cm.
This collection originally published: London : Bodley Head, 1969.
Pbk : £0.95
(B77-08134)

Priestley, John Boynton. The happy dream : an essay / by J.B. Priestley. — Andoversford (Manor Farm, Andoversford, Glos.) : Whittington Press, 1976. — [7],35,[1]p ; 21cm.
Limited ed. of 400 signed, numbered copies. — In slip case.
ISBN 0-904845-08-7 : £12.00
(B77-01867)

825.914 — ENGLISH SPEECHES, 1945-
825'.9'14 — Speeches in English, 1945-. *Texts*
Muir, Frank. The Rectorial address of Mr Frank Muir, delivered at the University of St Andrews on 28th April 1977. — [St Andrews] ([University of St Andrews Students' Representative Council, Students' Union, College Gate, St Andrews, Fife KY16 9AG]) : [University of St Andrews], [1977]. — [8]p ; 21cm. — (University of St Andrews. Rectorial addresses)
Sd : £0.10
(B77-27491)

826.912 — ENGLISH LETTERS, 1900-1945
826'.9'12 — Letters in English, 1900-1945. *Texts*
Stark, Freya. Letters [of] Freya Stark / edited by Lucy Moorehead. — Tisbury : Compton Russell.
Vol.3 : The growth of danger, 1935-39. — 1976. — [9],302p : maps(on lining papers) ; 24cm.
Index.
ISBN 0-85955-038-9 : £7.95
(B77-24559)

827 — ENGLISH SATIRE AND HUMOUR
827 — Humour in English. Australian writers, 1945-. *Texts*
Everage, *Dame* **Edna.** Dame Edna's coffee table book : a guide to gracious living and the finer things of life by one of the first ladies of world theatre / by Dame Edna Everage. — London : Harrap, 1976. — 112p : ill(some col), facsims, geneal table, ports(some col) ; 24cm.
Also available in limited ed. of 250 copies signed by the authoress.
ISBN 0-245-53046-0 Pbk : £3.95
ISBN 0-245-53077-0 Signed ed. : £25.00
(B77-03797)

Everage, *Dame* **Edna.** Dame Edna's coffee table book : a guide to gracious living and the finer things of life by one of the first ladies of world theatre / by Dame Edna Everage. — London : Sphere, 1977. — 112p : ill(some col), coat of arms, facsims, geneal table, ports(some col) ; 24cm.
Originally published: London : Harrap, 1976.
ISBN 0-7221-3382-0 Pbk : £1.95
(B77-27492)

827'.008 — Children's humour in English. *Anthologies*
Hoke, Helen. Laughs, laughs, laughs / selected and told by Helen Hoke ; illustrated by Richard Erdoes. — London [etc.] : F. Watts, 1977. — 224p : ill ; 24cm.
Originally published: as 'More jokes, jokes, jokes'. New York : F. Watts, 1965.
ISBN 0-85166-665-5 : £3.50
(B77-33489)

827'.008 — Humour in English, to 1976. *Anthologies*
The **book** of nonsense : an anthology / edited by Paul Jennings. — London : Raven Books, 1977. — [20],424p ; 24cm.
ISBN 0-354-04037-5 : £6.95
(B77-33490)

827.4 — ENGLISH SATIRE AND HUMOUR, 1625-1702
827'.4 — Humour in English, 1625-1702. *Texts. Facsimiles*
The **man** in the moon : discovering a world of knavery under the sun, with a perfect nocturnal containing several strange wonders out of the Antipodes Magyland, Faryland, Greenland, Tenebrie and other parts adjacent. — St Peter Port : Toucan Press, 1977. — 8p ; 21cm.
Attributed to S.S., a satirist. — Facsimile reprint of: 1663 ed. s.l. : s.n., 1663.
Sd : Unpriced
(B77-31575)

827.8 — ENGLISH SATIRE AND HUMOUR, 1837-1900
827'.8'080352 — Humour in English, 1837-1976. Special subjects: Great Britain. Royal families. *Anthologies*
'Punch' and the monarchy / edited by William Davis. — London : Hutchinson, [1977]. — 184p : ill(some col), ports ; 29cm.
Index.
ISBN 0-09-129370-7 : £4.95
(B77-25965)

827.912 — ENGLISH SATIRE AND HUMOUR, 1900-1945
827'.9'12 — Humour in English, 1900-1945. *Texts*
Potter, Stephen. One-upmanship : being some account of the activities and teaching of the lifemanship correspondence college of one-upness and gameslifemastery / [by] Stephen Potter ; illustrated by Frank Wilson. — Harmondsworth [etc.] : Penguin, 1977. — 151p : ill ; 18cm.
Originally published: London : Hart-Davis, 1952.
ISBN 0-14-001828-x Pbk : £0.50
(B77-27493)

Potter, Stephen. Some notes on lifemanship : with a summary of recent researches in gamesmanship / by Stephen Potter ; ... illustrated by Frank Wilson. — Harmondsworth [etc.] : Penguin, 1977. — 117p : ill, facsim, maps ; 18cm.
Cover title: Lifemanship. — Originally published: London : Hart-Davis, 1950.
ISBN 0-14-001827-1 Pbk : £0.50
(B77-27494)

Potter, Stephen. The theory and practice of gamesmanship, or, The art of winning games without actually cheating / by Stephen Potter ; illustrated by Frank Wilson. — Harmondsworth [etc.] : Penguin, 1978 [i.e. 1977]. — 103p : ill, map, port ; 19cm.
Cover title: Gamesmanship. — Originally published: London : Hart-Davis, 1947.
ISBN 0-14-001826-3 Pbk : £0.50
(B77-27495)

Potter, Stephen. The theory & practice of gamesmanship, or, The art of winning games without actually cheating / by Stephen Potter ; illustrated by Frank Wilson. — London [etc.] : Hart-Davis MacGibbon, 1977. — 128p : ill, map, port ; 20cm.
Spine title: Gamesmanship. — Originally published: London : Hart-Davis, 1947. — Index.
ISBN 0-246-63590-8 : £1.95
(B77-32937)

827.914 — ENGLISH SATIRE AND HUMOUR, 1945-
827'.9'14 — Humour in English, 1945-. *Texts*
Briggs, Raymond. Fungus the bogeyman / [by] Raymond Briggs. — London : Hamilton, 1977. — 41p : chiefly col ill ; 31cm.
ISBN 0-241-89553-7 : £2.75
(B77-24560)

Brooke-Taylor, Tim. The Goodies file / [by Tim Brooke-Taylor, Bill Oddie, Graeme Garden]. — London : Sphere, [1977]. — [96]p : ill(chiefly col), ports ; 28cm.
Originally published: London : Weidenfeld and Nicolson, 1974.
ISBN 0-7221-1881-3 Pbk : £1.75
(B77-27496)

Brooke-Taylor, Tim. The Goodies file / [by Tim Brooke-Taylor, Bill Oddie, Graeme Garden]. — London : Sphere, 1974. — [96]p : ill(some col), ports ; 28cm.
Also published: London : Weidenfeld and Nicolson, 1974.
ISBN 0-7221-1886-4 Pbk : £1.25
(B77-19871)

Coren, Alan. The peanut papers, in which Miz Lillian writes / [by] Alan Coren ; illustrations by Chic Jacob and Glyn Rees. — London : Robson, 1977. — 95p : ill, port ; 20cm.
ISBN 0-86051-019-0 Pbk : £0.70 : CIP rev.
(B77-23795)

Dodd, Maurice. The Perishers dotty dictionary / written by Maurice Dodd ; drawn by Dennis Collins. — London : Mirror Group Books, 1977. — 96p : ill ; 20cm.
ISBN 0-85939-097-7 Pbk : £0.70
(B77-31576)

Gifford, Denis. Stewpot's fun book / [by] Denis Gifford ; comic strips by Trevor Metcalfe ; other drawings by Denis Gifford. — London : Independent Television Books : Arrow Books, 1977. — 96p : ill ; 20cm. — (Look-in books)
ISBN 0-09-915490-0 Pbk : £0.65
(B77-24561)

The **making** of the Goodies' disaster movie. — London : Weidenfeld and Nicolson, 1977. — [92]p : ill(chiefly col), col maps, ports ; 29cm.
Cover title. — Text on lining papers.
ISBN 0-297-77338-0 : £3.25
(B77-29775)

Morecambe, Eric. The Morecambe & Wise special. — [London] : [Weidenfeld and Nicolson], 1977. — [78]p,(2 fold) : chiefly ill(some col), facsims(some col), ports(some col) ; 29cm.
Cover title. — Col. ill., col. ports on lining papers.
ISBN 0-297-77306-2 : £3.25
(B77-26639)

Pilgrim, Anne, *b.1947.* Pertaining to the horse : poems & pictures / by Anne Pilgrim ; with a foreword by Dorian Williams. — [Scarborough] ([48a Ranshill Rd, Scarborough, N. Yorkshire]) : [The author], [1976]. — [5],26 leaves : chiefly ill ; 30cm.
ISBN 0-9505471-0-7 Pbk : £1.50
(B77-04446)

827'.9'1408 — Humour in English, 1945-. *Anthologies*
The **2nd** Armada book of fun / selected by Mary Danby. — London : Armada, 1977. — 128p : ill ; 18cm.
Originally published: London : Collins, 1972.
ISBN 0-00-691165-x Pbk : £0.40
(B77-16090)

The 3rd Armada book of fun / chosen by Mary Danby. — [London] : Armada, 1977. — 3-128p : ill ; 18cm.
Originally published: London : Collins, 1975.
ISBN 0-00-691291-5 Pbk : £0.40
(B77-16091)

The Armada book of fun / selected by Mary Danby. — London : Armada, 1977. — 3-128p : ill ; 18cm.
Originally published: 1970.
ISBN 0-00-691164-1 Pbk : £0.40
(B77-16092)

Laughing matter / [edited by] Kay Batchelor ; book illustrations by George Robinson. — Great Missenden (67 High St., Great Missenden, Bucks.) : Topaz Records Ltd, 1976. — [144]p : ill(some col), ports ; 28cm.
ISBN 0-905553-00-4 Pbk : £1.75
(B77-16093)

Pass the port : the best after-dinner stories of the famous. — Cirencester ([Phoenix Way], Cirencester, [Glos.]) : Christian Brann Ltd, 1976. — 238p : ill, facsim ; 23cm.
Index.
ISBN 0-9504923-0-2 : £3.95
(B77-07685)

827'.9'1408 — Humour in English, 1945-. *Anthologies. For entertainers*
Stone, Sol. Patter punches / by Sol Stone. — Bideford (64 High St., Bideford, Devon) : Supreme Magic Company, 1976?. — 31p ; 20cm.
ISBN 0-901127-20-5 Sd : £0.85
(B77-04447)

827'.9'1408 — Humour in English, 1945-. *Anthologies. Serials*
Pick of 'Punch'. — London : Hutchinson. [1977] / edited by William Davis. — 1977. — 192p : ill, ports ; 29cm.
Index.
ISBN 0-09-131400-3 : £4.50
(B77-29776)

827'.9'1408032 — Humour in English, 1945- . Special subjects: Ireland (Republic). Social conditions. *Anthologies*
Dublin opinion : an entertainment for 1977 / editor James D. O'Donnell ; art director Raymond Dyne. — Dublin (31 Killiney Hill Rd, Killiney, Co. Dublin) : Louis O'Sullivan, Dublin Opinion (1969) Ltd, 1976. — 127p : ill, ports ; 30cm.
ISBN 0-9505300-0-x Pbk : £3.00
(B77-12167)

827'.9'1408032 — Humour in English, 1945-. Special subjects: Scotland. *Anthologies*
'Punch' on Scotland / edited by Miles Kington. — [London] : Punch Publications : Distributed by Robson, 1977. — 160p : ill, ports ; 23cm.
ISBN 0-86051-002-6 Pbk : £1.50
(B77-19059)

827'.9'14080355 — Humour in English, 1945- . Special subjects: Health. *Anthologies*
The **'Punch'** book of health / edited by William Davis. — [Sevenoaks] : Coronet, 1976. — 144p : ill ; 21cm.
Originally published: London : Punch Publications, 1975.
ISBN 0-340-20999-2 Pbk : £0.80
(B77-02640)

828 — ENGLISH MISCELLANY
828 — Prose in English. Australian writers, 1945- . Special subjects: Livestock: Dogs. *Texts*
Stevens, Lyla. A dog called Debbie / [by] Lyla Stevens ; illustrated by Jean Elder. — Leicester : Knight Books, 1977. — 126p : ill ; 18cm.
Originally published: Hornsby, N.S.W. : Hodder and Stoughton, Australia ; Leicester : Brockhampton Press, 1973.
ISBN 0-340-21888-6 Pbk : £0.60
(B77-26640)

828 — Prose in English. New Zealand writers, 1945-. Special subjects: Pets: Keas. *Texts*
Falla, Molly, *Lady.* A kea on my bed / [by] Molly Falla. — Auckland ; London : Collins, 1975 [i.e. 1976]. — 40p : ill(some col), port ; 26cm.
Ill. on lining paper. — Originally published: Auckland : Collins, 1974.
ISBN 0-00-216915-0 : £2.75
(B77-07686)

828'.08 — Biographical prose in English, 1558-1976. *Critical studies*
Shelston, Alan. Biography / [by] Alan Shelston. — London : Methuen, 1977. — ix,82p ; 20cm. — (The critical idiom ; 34)
Bibl.: p.75-77. — Index.
ISBN 0-416-83680-1 : £2.35
ISBN 0-416-83690-9 Pbk : £1.20
(B77-12168)

828.3 — ENGLISH MISCELLANY, 1558-1625
828'.3'08 — Prose in English. Burton, Robert, b.1577. Anatomy of melancholy. *Critical studies*
Fox, Ruth A. The tangled chain : the structure of disorder in 'The anatomy of melancholy' / [by] Ruth A. Fox. — Berkeley [etc.] ; London : University of California Press, 1976. — xiii, 282p : facsim ; 21cm.
Bibl.: p.xii-xiii. — Index.
ISBN 0-520-03085-0 : £8.00
(B77-13938)

828.4 — ENGLISH MISCELLANY, 1625-1702
828'.4'08 — Prose in English. Bunyan, John. *Critical studies*
Baird, Charles William. John Bunyan : a study in narrative technique / [by] Charles W. Baird. — Port Washington, N.Y. ; London : Kennikat Press, 1977. — [7],160p ; 23cm. — (Kennikat Press national university publications : literary criticism series)
Bibl.: p.152-155. — Index.
ISBN 0-8046-9162-2 : £8.45
(B77-28244)

828.5 — ENGLISH MISCELLANY, 1702-1745
828'.5'09 — English literature, 1702-1745. *Texts*
Swift, Jonathan. [Selected works]. Gulliver's travels, and other writings / [by] Jonathan Swift ; edited by Louis A. Landa. — London [etc.] : Oxford University Press, 1976. — xxviii, 564p : 1 ill, maps ; 21cm.
This collection originally published: Boston, Mass. : Houghton Mifflin, 1960. — Bibl.: p.563-564.
ISBN 0-19-281206-8 Pbk : £2.75
(B77-01020)

Wortley Montagu, *Lady* **Mary.** Essays and poems ; and, Simplicity : a comedy / [by] Lady Mary Wortley Montagu ; edited by Robert Halsband and Isobel Grundy. — Oxford : Clarendon Press, 1977. — xi,412p,leaf of plate,6p of plates : facsims, port ; 22cm.
Includes 2 poems in French. — Index.
ISBN 0-19-812444-9 : £14.50
(B77-15003)

828.6 — ENGLISH MISCELLANY, 1745-1800
828'.6'08 — Satirical prose in English, 1745-1800. *Texts. Facsimiles*
Beckford, William. Biographical memoirs of extraordinary painters (1780) / [by] William Beckford. — [1st ed. reprinted] ; with a new introduction by Philip Ward. — Cambridge [etc.] : Oleander Press, 1977. — [17],158p : ports ; 21cm.
Facsimile reprint of: 1st ed. London : J. Robson, 1780.
ISBN 0-900891-13-0 Pbk : £4.00
(B77-06938)

828'.6'0809 — Autobiographical prose in English, 1745-1800. Compared with autobiographical fiction in English, 1745-1800
Spacks, Patricia Meyer. Imagining a self : autobiography and novel in eighteenth-century England / [by] Patricia Meyer Spacks. — Cambridge, Mass. ; London : Harvard University Press, 1976. — [9],342p ; 25cm.
Index.
ISBN 0-674-44005-6 : £11.25
Primary classification 823'.6'09
(B77-09241)

828'.6'09 — English literature. Godwin, William. *Correspondence with Wollstonecraft, Mary*
Godwin, William. Godwin & Mary : letters of William Godwin and Mary Wollstonecraft / edited by Ralph M. Wardle. — Lincoln, Neb. ; London : University of Nebraska Press, 1977. — x,125p : ill, ports ; 21cm.
'A Bison book'. — This collection originally published: Lawrence, Kan. : University of Kansas Press, 1966 ; London : Constable, 1967. — Index.
ISBN 0-8032-0901-0 : £6.00
ISBN 0-8032-5852-6 Pbk : Unpriced
Also classified at 301.41'2'0924
(B77-31577)

828'.6'09 — English literature. Goldsmith, Oliver. *Biographies*
Ginger, John. The notable man : the life and times of Oliver Goldsmith / [by] John Ginger. — London : Hamilton, 1977. — xv,408p,12p of plates : ill, ports ; 23cm.
Bibl.: p.395-400. — Index.
ISBN 0-241-89626-6 : £7.95
(B77-21547)

828.7 — ENGLISH MISCELLANY, 1800-1837
828'.7'08 — Satirical prose in English, 1800-1837. *Texts*
Lockhart, John Gibson. Peter's letters to his kinfolk / [by] John Gibson Lockhart ; edited by William Ruddick. — Edinburgh : Scottish Academic Press, 1977. — xxiii,204p ; 23cm.
At head of title: The Association for Scottish Literary Studies.
ISBN 0-7073-0135-1 : £3.95
(B77-32279)

828'.7'09 — English literature. Scott, Sir Walter, bart, 1831-1832. *Biographies*
Sultana, Donald. 'The siege of Malta' rediscovered : an account of Sir Walter Scott's Mediterranean journey and his last novel / [by] Donald E. Sultana. — Edinburgh : Scottish Academic Press, 1977. — xii,215p,leaf of plate,[8]p of plates : ill, facsims(on lining paper), maps, ports ; 24cm.
Ill. on lining paper. — Bibl.: p.196-199. — Index.
ISBN 0-7073-0131-9 : £7.50
Also classified at 823'.7
(B77-29777)

828.8 — ENGLISH MISCELLANY, 1837-1900
828'.8'08 — Prose in English. Carlyle, Jane Welsh. *Correspondence*
Carlyle, Jane Welsh. I too am here : selections from the letters of Jane Welsh Carlyle / [edited] with an introduction and notes by Alan and Mary McQueen Simpson. — Cambridge [etc.] : Cambridge University Press, 1977. — xx,307p,8p of plates : ill, facsim, geneal table, map, ports ; 24cm.
Bibl.: p.297-300. — Index.
ISBN 0-521-21304-5 : £6.50
(B77-23796)

828'.8'08 — Prose in English. Carlyle, Thomas. Correspondence with Browning, Robert, b.1812. *Critical studies*
Sanders, Charles Richard. The Carlyle-Browning correspondence and relationship / by Charles Richard Sanders. — Manchester (Manchester M3 3EH) : John Rylands University Library of Manchester, 1975. — [1],67p ; 25cm.
'Reprinted from the "Bulletin of the John Rylands University Library of Manchester", Vol.57, No.1, Autumn, 1974 and Vol.57, No.2, Spring, 1975'.
ISBN 0-905578-02-3 Sd : £1.50
Also classified at 821'.8
(B77-04448)

828'.8'0808 — Prose in English, 1837-1900. *Anthologies*
The **portable** Victorian reader / edited with an introduction by Gordon S. Haight. — Harmondsworth [etc.] : Penguin Books, 1976. — xlvi,658p : ill ; 19cm. — (The Viking portable library)
Spine title: Victorian reader. — Originally published: New York : Viking Press, 1972. — Bibl.: p.xlvi.
ISBN 0-14-015069-2 Pbk : Unpriced
(B77-01021)

828'.8'09 — English literature, 1837-1900. *Texts*
Wilde, Oscar. [Works]. The works of Oscar Wilde. — London : Spring Books, 1977. — ix, 957p ; 21cm.
This collection originally published: 1963.
ISBN 0-600-39372-0 : £2.75
(B77-31578)

Wilde, Oscar. The portable Oscar Wilde / selected and edited by Richard Aldington. — Harmondsworth [etc.] : Penguin, 1977. — viii, 690p ; 18cm. — (The Viking portable library)
This collection originally published: New York : Viking Press, 1946. — Includes: The critic as artist - The picture of Dorian Gray - Salomé - The importance of being earnest - De profundis - The ballad of Reading gaol.
ISBN 0-14-015016-1 Pbk : £1.95
(B77-27497)

828'.8'09 — English literature. Carroll, Lewis. *Critical studies*
Huxley, Francis. The raven and the writing desk / [by] Francis Huxley. — London : Thames and Hudson, 1976. — 191p : ill, facsims, geneal tables, map, ports ; 23cm.
Index.
ISBN 0-500-01155-9 : £3.95
(B77-01868)

828'.8'09 — English literature. Kipling, Rudyard. *Autobiographies*

Kipling, Rudyard. Something of myself : for my friends, known and unknown / [by] Rudyard Kipling. — Harmondsworth [etc.] : Penguin, 1977. — 176p ; 18cm. — (Penguin modern classics)
Originally published: London : Macmillan, 1937. — Index.
ISBN 0-14-004207-5 Pbk : £0.70
(B77-19872)

828'.8'09 — English literature. Kipling, Rudyard. *Biographies*

Wilson, Angus, *b.1913.* The strange ride of Rudyard Kipling : his life and works / [by] Angus Wilson. — London : Secker and Warburg, 1977. — xiv,370p,[56]p of plates : ill, facsims, ports ; 25cm.
Index.
ISBN 0-436-57516-7 : £6.90
(B77-29778)

828'.8'09 — English literature. Kipling, Rudyard. *Critical studies*

Kipling / [translated from the Italian]. — Maidenhead : Sampson Low, 1977. — 136p : ill(chiefly col), facsims, ports(some col) ; 22cm. — (Giants of literature)
Originally published: in Italian. Milan : Arnoldo Mondadori, 1968?. — Bibl.: p.135.
ISBN 0-562-00050-x : £2.75
(B77-12169)

828'.8'09 — English literature. Macaulay, Thomas Babington, Baron Macaulay. *Correspondence*

Macaulay, Thomas Babington, *Baron Macaulay.* The letters of Thomas Babington Macaulay / edited by Thomas Pinney. — Cambridge [etc.] : Cambridge University Press.
Vol.4 : September 1841-December 1848. — 1977. — xii,407p,plate : coat of arms, ports ; 24cm.
Spine title: The letters of Macaulay. — Index.
ISBN 0-521-21126-3 : £16.00
(B77-08135)

828'.8'09 — English literature. Macaulay, Thomas Babington, Baron Macaulay. *Critical studies*

Young, Kenneth. Macaulay / by Kenneth Young ; edited by Ian Scott-Kilvert. — Harlow : Longman for the British Council, 1976. — 2-59p,plate : port ; 22cm. — (Writers and their work ; 225)
Bibl.: p.56-59.
ISBN 0-582-01263-5 Sd : £0.40
(B77-26641)

828.91 — ENGLISH MISCELLANY, 1900-
828'.91'140808023 — Spoken prose in English. Narratives, 1945-. *Anthologies*

Talkshop : a selection of tape transcripts collected by members of the Role of Language in Education Course, 1975-76 / foreword by Harold Rosen. — [London] : University of London Institute of Education, [1976]. — [3], 85[i.e. 103]p : ill ; 30cm.
ISBN 0-85473-075-3 Sp : £0.50
(B77-16632)

828.912 — ENGLISH MISCELLANY, 1900-1945
828'.9'1208 — Humorous prose in English, 1900-1945. *Texts*

Lancaster, *Sir* **Osbert.** The Littlehampton bequest / [by] Osbert Lancaster ; foreword by Roy Strong. — London (11 New Fetter La., EC4P 4EE) : Magnum Books, 1977. — 95p : ill ; 18cm.
Originally published: London : J. Murray, 1973.
ISBN 0-417-02030-9 Pbk : £0.65
(B77-16094)

Strong, Patience. Homes and gardens / [by] Patience Strong. — [New ed.]. — London : Muller, 1976. — [5],58p : chiefly ill(some col) ; 22cm.
Cover title: Patience Strong's book of homes and gardens. — Previous ed.: published as 'Book of homes and gardens'. 1953.
ISBN 0-584-10624-6 : £1.95
(B77-03266)

Wodehouse, Pelham Grenville. Louder and funnier / [by] P.G. Wodehouse. — London : Barrie and Jenkins, 1976. — 152p ; 20cm.
This collection originally published: London : Faber, 1932.
ISBN 0-257-66025-9 : £3.95
(B77-01869)

828'.9'1208 — Prose in English, 1900-1945. *Texts*

Sellar, Walter Carruthers. Garden rubbish and other country bumps / by W.C. Sellar and R.J. Yeatman ; with affrontispiece and numerous insulting illustrations by Stephen Dowling. — London : Magnum Books, 1977. — xii,125p : ill ; 18cm.
Originally published: London : Methuen, 1936.
ISBN 0-417-02050-3 Pbk : £0.65
(B77-25966)

Yeatman, Robert Julian. Horse nonsense / ... consisting of pictures by John Reynolds and text by R.J. Yeatman in collaboration with W.C. Sellar. — London : Magnum Books, 1977. — [9],127p : ill ; 18cm.
Originally published: London : Methuen, 1933.
ISBN 0-417-02000-7 Pbk : £0.65
(B77-25967)

828'.9'1208 — Prose in English. Pearson, Hesketh. Interpersonal relationships with Kingsmill, Hugh & Muggeridge, Malcolm

Ingrams, Richard. God's apology : a chronicle of three friends / [by] Richard Ingrams. — London : Deutsch, 1977. — 256p,[4]p of plates : ill, ports ; 23cm.
Bibl.: p.253. — Index.
ISBN 0-233-96888-1 : £5.50
Primary classification 823'.9'12
(B77-25248)

828'.9'1208 — Prose in English. Sommerfield, John. *Autobiographies*

Sommerfield, John. The imprinted : recollections of then, now and later on / [by] John Sommerfield. — [London] : London Magazine Editions, 1977. — 176p ; 23cm.
ISBN 0-904388-26-3 : £5.00
(B77-25968)

828'.9'1209 — English literature, 1900-1945. *Texts*

Auden, Wystan Hugh. The English Auden : poems, essays and dramatic writings, 1927-1939 / edited by Edward Mendelson. — London : Faber, 1977. — iii-xxv,469p : port ; 24cm.
Index.
ISBN 0-571-10832-6 : £8.95 : CIP rev.
(B77-22953)

Webb, Mary. Collected prose and poems : a selection of Mary Webb's hitherto uncollected and unpublished work / edited with an introduction by Gladys Mary Coles. — Shrewsbury : Wildings, 1977. — xv,130p,[2] leaves of plates : ill, 2 ports ; 23cm.
Bibl.: p.129-130.
ISBN 0-85489-015-7 : £5.50
(B77-24562)

828'.9'1209 — English literature. Beckett, Samuel. *Periodicals*

Journal of Beckett studies. — London : J. Calder : Beckett Archive, University of Reading : [Distributed by Calder and Boyars]. [No.1]- ; [Winter 1976]-. — 1976-. — ill, plans ; 21cm.
Two issues a year. — [3],112p.,[8]p. of plates in 1st issue. — Bibl.
Pbk : £2.20(£3.75 yearly)
ISSN 0309-5207
Also classified at 848'.9'1409
(B77-13939)

828'.9'1209 — English literature. Duncan, Ronald. *Autobiographies*

Duncan, Ronald. Obsessed : a third volume of autobiography / [by] Ronald Duncan. — London : Joseph, 1977. — 166p ; 23cm.
Index.
ISBN 0-7181-1592-9 : £4.95
(B77-23797)

828'.9'1209 — English literature. Lewis, Clive Staples. *Biographies. Juvenile literature*

Arnott, Anne. The secret country of C.S. Lewis / by Ann Arnott ; illustrations by Patricia Frost. — London [etc.] : Hodder and Stoughton, 1976. — 127p : ill ; 18cm. — (Hodder Christian paperbacks)
Originally published: 1974. — Bibl.: p.125-127.
ISBN 0-340-20686-1 Pbk : £0.65
(B77-19060)

828'.9'1209 — English literature. Lewis, Clive Staples. *Critical studies*

Holmer, Paul L. C.S. Lewis : the shape of his faith and thought / [by] Paul L. Holmer. — London : Sheldon Press, 1977. — xii,116p ; 22cm.
Originally published: New York : Harper and Row, 1976.
ISBN 0-85969-115-2 Pbk : £2.25
(B77-22223)

828'.9'1209 — English literature. O'Connor, Frank. *Critical studies*

Wohlgelernter, Maurice. Frank O'Connor : an introduction / by Maurice Wohlgelernter. — New York ; Guildford : Columbia University Press, 1977. — xxiv,222p : port ; 24cm.
Bibl.: p.207-213. — Index.
ISBN 0-231-04194-2 : Unpriced
(B77-19061)

828'.9'1209 — English literature. Sitwell, Constance. *Autobiographies*

Sitwell, Constance. Bounteous days / [by] Constance Sitwell ; with an introduction by James Pope Hennessy. — London (Kingly Court, 10 Kingly St., W1A 4ES) : Cecil Woolf, 1976. — [5],73p,plate : port ; 22cm.
ISBN 0-900821-32-9 : £2.50
(B77-18427)

828'.9'1209 — English literature. Sitwell, Sir Osbert, bart. *Autobiographies*

Sitwell, *Sir* **Osbert,** *bart.* Left hand, right hand! : an autobiography / [by] Osbert Sitwell. — London [etc.] : Quartet Books.
In 4 vols.
Vol.1 : The cruel month. — 1977. — xv,272p ; 20cm.
Originally published: London : Macmillan, 1945. — Index.
ISBN 0-7043-3155-1 Pbk : £2.50
(B77-25969)

Vol.2 : The scarlet tree. — 1977. — vii,319p ; 20cm.
Originally published: London : Macmillan, 1946. — Index.
ISBN 0-7043-3157-8 Pbk : £2.50
(B77-25970)

Vol.3 : Great morning. — 1977. — vii,324p.
Originally published: London : Macmillan, 1948. — Index.
ISBN 0-7043-3156-x Pbk : £2.50
(B77-27498)

Vol.4 : Laughter in the next room. — 1977. — vii,381p ; 20cm.
Originally published: London : Macmillan, 1949. — Index.
ISBN 0-7043-3162-4 Pbk : £2.50
(B77-27499)

828.914 — ENGLISH MISCELLANY, 1945-
828'.9'140208 — Children's humorous quotations in English, 1945-. *Anthologies*

Knight book of howlers / collected and illustrated by Richard E. Gregory. — Leicester : Knight Books, 1977. — 91p : ill ; 18cm.
ISBN 0-340-20227-0 Pbk : £0.50
(B77-24563)

828'.9'140208 — Quotations in English, 1945-. *Anthologies*

'Private eye's' psecond book of pseuds / drawings by John Glashan ; [selected and introduced by Richard Ingrams]. — London : Private Eye Productions : Deutsch, 1977. — 96p : ill ; 19cm.
Ill. on lining papers.
ISBN 0-233-96945-4 : £1.95
(B77-29008)

828'.9'1407 — Experimental writing in English, 1945-. *Texts*

Ank, Elbo. Treasured chest / by Elbo Ank. — Corby : Excello and Bollard, 1977. — [27]p ; 15cm.
ISBN 0-904339-55-6 Sd : Unpriced
(B77-32280)

Breakwell, Ian. Diary extracts, 1968-1976 / [by] Ian Breakwell. — [Nottingham] ([11 East Circus St., Nottingham NG1 5AF]) : Midland Group Nottingham, 1977. — [3],45p : ill, facsims ; 21cm.
'Published ... for an exhibition of the "Continuous Diary" at: Arnolfini, Narrow Quay, Bristol, 11-1-1977 to 19-2-1977, Institute of Contemporary Arts, The Mall, London S.W.1, 2-3-1977 to 12-4-1977, Midland Group, Carlton Street, Nottingham, 31-5-1977 to 3-7-1977' - title page verso.
ISBN 0-9504911-1-x Sd : £1.50
(B77-09352)

Buck, Paul, *b.1946.* Lust / [by] Paul Buck ; with drawings by Alejandro. — Hebden Bridge (12 Foster Clough, Hebden Bridge, W. Yorkshire HX7 5QZ) : Pressed Curtains, 1976. — 58p,[3] leaves of plates : ill ; 30cm.
Also available in limited ed. of 30 copies signed by the author and artist, 26 of which are lettered and offered for sale.
ISBN 0-9504368-2-8 Sd : £1.20
(B77-01022)

Coffey, Brian. The big laugh / [by] Brian Coffey. — Dublin (Highbury, Sandycove Rd, Glenageary, Co. Dublin) : Sugar Loaf, 1976. — 29,[1]p : ill(some col) ; 25cm.
Limited ed. of 500 numbered copies.
ISBN 0-904105-01-6 Pbk : £3.00
(B77-10617)

Finlay, Ian Hamilton. Imitations, variations, reflections, copies / by Ian Hamilton Finlay. — [Lanark] ([Stonypath, Dunsyre, Lanark]) : Wild Hawthorn Press, 1976. — [14]leaves : 2 ill ; 12cm.
Limited ed. of 350 signed and numbered copies. — 4 cards ([7] sides) as inserts.
ISBN 0-900805-52-8 Pbk : £2.00
(B77-09353)

Griffiths, Bill. War w. Windsor / [by] Bill Griffiths ; visual texts Sean O'Huigin. — [New ed.]. — London (262 Randolph Ave., W.9) : Writers Forum ; London : Private Press, 1976. — [20]p : ill ; 21cm.
Previous ed.: 1974.
ISBN 0-905194-04-7 Sd : Unpriced
(B77-10618)

Ward, Tony. Prorata / [by Tony Ward]. — Todmorden : Arc Publications, [1976]. — [10] leaves : col ill ; 18cm.
Limited ed. of 150 numbered copies of which 10 are signed by the author.
ISBN 0-902771-63-9 Sd : £0.45
ISBN 0-902771-64-7 Signed ed. : £1.00
(B77-00482)

828'.9'1408 — Humorous prose in English, 1945-. *Texts*

Austen, Stan. Peek-a-boob too / [by] Stan Austen. — London : Jupiter Books, 1976. — [60]p : of col ill ; 20cm.
ISBN 0-904041-63-8 Pbk : £1.25
(B77-15579)

Boston, Richard. Baldness be my friend / [by] Richard Boston. — London : Elm Tree Books, 1977. — [5],152p ; 23cm.
ISBN 0-241-89732-7 : £4.95
(B77-29009)

Corbett, Ronnie. Ronnie Corbett's small man's guide / edited and compiled by Spike Mullins ; with illustrations by Bill Tidy. — London : Sphere, 1977. — 124p : ill ; 18cm.
Originally published: London : Joseph ; Walton-on-Thames : M. and J. Hobbs Ltd, 1976.
ISBN 0-7221-2504-6 Pbk : £0.95
(B77-26642)

Coren, Alan. All except the Bastard / [by] Alan Coren. — London : Robson Books, 1976. — 192p ; 23cm.
Originally published: London : Gollancz, 1969.
ISBN 0-903895-79-x : £3.25
(B77-00483)

Coren, Alan. The dog it was that died / [by] Alan Coren. — London : Robson Books, 1976. — 192p ; 23cm.
Originally published: London : Hutchinson, 1965.
ISBN 0-903895-80-3 : £3.25
(B77-00484)

Coren, Alan. Golfing for cats / [by] Alan Coren. — London : Coronet, 1976. — [6],154p : ill ; 30cm.
Originally published: London : Robson Books, 1975.
ISBN 0-340-20998-4 Pbk : £0.60
(B77-01870)

Coren, Alan. The lady from Stalingrad Mansions / [by] Alan Coren. — London : Robson, 1977. — 160p ; 23cm.
ISBN 0-86051-007-7 : £3.25 : CIP rev.
(B77-18428)

Goldstein-Jackson, Kevin. Joke, after joke, after joke, after joke - / by Kevin Goldstein-Jackson. — Kingswood : Elliot Right Way Books, 1977. — 125p ; 19cm. — (Paperfronts)
Index.
Pbk : £0.50
(B77-32938)

Grenfell, Joyce. George, don't do that - : six nursery school sketches and 'Writer of children's books' / by Joyce Grenfell ; illustrated by John Ward. — London [etc.] : Macmillan, 1977. — 72p : ill ; 23cm.
Ill. on lining papers.
ISBN 0-333-22080-3 : £1.95
(B77-25971)

Irwin, Dick. The Geordie laff inn / by Dick Irwin ; illustrated by R. Thompson. — Newcastle upon Tyne : Graham, 1976. — 38p : ill ; 22cm.
ISBN 0-85983-029-2 Sd : £0.50
(B77-06939)

Jennings, Paul. I must have imagined it / [by] Paul Jennings. — London : Joseph, 1977. — 219p ; 21cm.
ISBN 0-7181-1651-8 : £4.50
(B77-28245)

Marshall, Arthur. I say! / [by] Arthur Marshall. — London : Hamilton, 1977. — [9],180p ; 23cm.
ISBN 0-241-89682-7 : £4.95
(B77-22954)

Myles na gCopaleen. The best of Myles : a selection from 'Cruiskeen lawn' / [by] Myles na Gopaleen (Flann O'Brien) ; edited and with a preface by Kevin O Nolan. — London [etc.] : Pan Books, 1977. — 400p : ill ; 20cm.
This collection originally published: London : MacGibbon and Kee, 1968.
ISBN 0-330-24855-3 Pbk : £1.00
(B77-07687)

Myles na gCopaleen. Further cuttings from 'Cruiskeen lawn' / [by] Myles na Gopaleen (Flann O'Brien) ; edited and with a preface by Kevin O'Nolan. — London [etc.] : Hart-Davis MacGibbon, 1976. — 189p : port ; 23cm.
'... selections from "Cruiskeen lawn", Myles na Gopaleen's column in "The Irish Times" ...' - Preface.
ISBN 0-246-10875-4 : £5.00
(B77-13940)

O'Gorman, Erroll. To amuse and confuse / [by] Erroll O'Gorman. — Ilfracombe : Stockwell, 1977. — 47p ; 19cm.
ISBN 0-7223-0806-x : £1.50
(B77-31579)

Waugh, Auberon. Four crowded years : the diaries of Auberon Waugh, 1972-1976 / edited by N.R. Galli ; Nicolas Bentley drew the pictures. — London : Private Eye Productions Ltd : Deutsch, 1976. — [158]p : ill ; 22cm.
ISBN 0-233-96825-3 : £2.75
(B77-01023)

828'.9'1408 — Prose in English, 1945- . Special subjects: Animals. *Texts*

Tovey, Doreen. The coming of Saska / [by] Doreen Tovey ; illustrated by Maurice Wilson. — London : Joseph, 1977. — 168p : ill ; 23cm.
ISBN 0-7181-1559-7 : £3.95
(B77-12761)

828'.9'1408 — Prose in English, 1945- . Special subjects: Badgers. *Texts*

Clarkson, Ewan. The badgers of Summercombe / [by] Ewan Clarkson ; illustrated by David Murray. — London : Hutchinson, 1977. — 159p : ill ; 23cm.
ISBN 0-09-129920-9 : £3.95
(B77-29010)

828'.9'1408 — Prose in English, 1945- . Special subjects: Jack Russell terriers. *Texts*

Willock, Colin. Dudley : the worst dog in the world : an account / by Colin Willock ; illustrated by William Garfit. — London : Deutsch, 1977. — 80p : ill ; 23cm.
ISBN 0-233-96926-8 : £2.95
(B77-29011)

828'.9'1408 — Prose in English, 1945- . Special subjects: Livestock: Dogs. *Texts*

Stranger, Joyce. Two's company / [by] Joyce Stranger. — London : Joseph, 1977. — 191p,[8] p of plates : ill, ports ; 23cm.
ISBN 0-7181-1610-0 : £4.50
(B77-27500)

828'.9'1408 — Prose in English, 1945- . Special subjects: Livestock: Horses. *Texts*

Mullen, C J J. Life on a slightly used horse / [by] C.J.J. Mullen ; illustrated by Al Ostervich. — South Brunswick [etc.] : Barnes ; London : Yoseloff, 1975. — 173p : ill ; 22cm.
ISBN 0-498-01405-3 : £2.75
(B77-28246)

828'.9'1408 — Prose in English, 1945- . Special subjects: Wildcats. *Texts*

Brown, Philip, *b.1913.* Uncle Whiskers / [by] Philip Brown. — [London] : Fontana, 1977. — 95p ; 18cm.
Originally published: London : Deutsch, 1974.
ISBN 0-00-634739-8 Pbk : £0.50
(B77-32281)

Dudley, Ernest. Scrap / [by] Ernest Dudley. — Sevenoaks : Coronet, 1977. — 142,[1]p,[4]p of plates : col ill, col ports ; 18cm.
Originally published: London : Muller, 1974.
ISBN 0-340-21311-6 Pbk : £0.85
(B77-27501)

828'.9'1408 — Prose in English, 1945-. *Texts*

Arnold, Jeannette. Willow seeds and wild roses : prose and poetry / by Jeannette Arnold. — London : Mitre Press, 1977. — 62p,plate : 1 ill ; 20cm.
ISBN 0-7051-0256-4 : £1.60
Primary classification 821'.9'14
(B77-20540)

Chamberlain, Michael. Promenades / [by] Michael Chamberlain. — [Pensnett] : Grosseteste Press, 1976. — 44p ; 22cm.
Limited ed. of 300 copies, of which the first 30 were signed by the author. — '... also issued as a part of "Grosseteste Review", Vol.9, no.1' - colophon.
ISBN 0-901597-47-3 Sd : £0.40
ISBN 0-901597-48-1 Signed ed. : £1.50
(B77-00485)

De Freyne, Leo. Trailer / [by Leo de Freyne]. — Dublin : Dolmen Press for the author, 1977. — Folder([3]p) : 1 ill ; 22cm.
Limited ed. of 200 copies signed and numbered by the author.
Unpriced
(B77-22224)

Lee, Laurie. I can't stay long / [by] Laurie Lee. — Harmondsworth [etc.] : Penguin, 1977. — 230p ; 19cm.
This collection originally published: London : Deutsch, 1975.
ISBN 0-14-004327-6 Pbk : £0.60
(B77-24564)

Lubbock, Joseph Guy. Perceptions of the earth / original prints and text by J.G. Lubbock. — London (30 Long Acre, WC2E 9LT) : Bertram Rota (Publishing) Ltd, 1977. — [43]p : col ill ; 34cm.
Full leather. — In slip case.
Unpriced
Also classified at 769'.92'4
(B77-31580)

Middleton, Christopher. Pataxandu, & other prose / [by] Christopher Middleton. — Manchester : Carcanet New Press, 1977. — 107p ; 23cm.
ISBN 0-85635-172-5 : £2.90
(B77-17799)

Prather, Hugh. Notes to myself : my struggle to become a person / [by] Hugh Prather. — Toronto [etc.] ; London : Bantam, 1976. — [160]p ; 18cm.
Originally published: Lafayette : Real People Press, 1970.
ISBN 0-553-08629-4 Pbk : £0.65
(B77-06347)

Richards, C J. Born under Pisces, and other stories / [by] C.J. Richards. — Alresford ([c/o Arthur H. Stockwell Ltd, Elms Court, Ilfracombe, Devon]) : The author, 1976. — 81p ; 21cm.
ISBN 0-7223-0890-6 Pbk : Unpriced
(B77-11456)

828'.9'1408 — Prose in English, 1945-. Special subjects: Pets: Cats & dogs. *Texts*

Pluckwell, George. It's raining cats and dogs / by George E. Pluckwell. — Colchester (Rowhedge, Colchester, Essex) : Modern Poets, 1977. — [30]p ; 30cm.
Sd : Unpriced
(B77-22955)

828'.9'1408 — Prose in English. Paul, Leslie. *Autobiographies*

Paul, Leslie. First love : a journey / [by] Leslie Paul. — London : S.P.C.K., 1977. — viii,215p ; 23cm.
ISBN 0-281-02975-x : £4.95
(B77-25250)

828'.9'1409 — English literature, 1945-. *Texts*

Curtis, Tony, *b.1946.* Out of the dark wood : prose, poems, stories / [by] Tony Curtis. — Barry (47 Glen Mavis Way, Barry, [S. Glam.]) : Edge Press, 1977. — [1],37p : port ; 21cm.
ISBN 0-906040-00-0 Sd : £0.40
(B77-24565)

Draper, John Kerrison. Miscellany and diversity / by John Kerrison Draper. — London [etc.] : Regency Press, 1976. — 237p ; 23cm.
Includes 'Barchester towers'. Originally published: London : Draper, 1953 as an adaptation of : 'Barchester towers' / by Anthony Trollope.
ISBN 0-7212-0477-5 : £2.50
(B77-10986)

Kennedy, Andrew. Perspectives : poetry and prose / by Andrew Kennedy. — [London] ([11 Crystal Palace Rd, S.E.22]) : The author, 1977. — [36]p : 1 col ill ; 21cm.
Limited ed. of 200 copies.
ISBN 0-9505902-0-7 Sd : Unpriced
(B77-30799)

Lyre, Larry. The gilded youth of pantomime / by Larry Lyre. — London [etc.] : Regency Press, 1976. — 213p ; 23cm.
ISBN 0-7212-0479-1 : £2.40
(B77-10000)

828'.9'1409 — English literature. Scriven, Ronald Charles. *Autobiographies*
Scriven, Ronald Charles. Edge of darkness, edge of light / by R.C. Scriven. — London : Souvenir Press, 1977. — 224p ; 23cm.
ISBN 0-285-62287-0 : £3.50 : CIP rev.
(B77-13397)

829 — OLD ENGLISH LITERATURE
829'.3 — Poetry in Old English. Beowulf. *English texts*
Beowulf / translated [from the Anglo-Saxon] by Kevin Crossley-Holland and introduced by Bruce Mitchell, with drawings by Brigitte Hanf. — Cambridge [etc.] : Brewer, 1977. — xiv, 150p : ill, geneal tables, map ; 23cm.
This translation originally published: London : Macmillan, 1968. — Bibl.: p.147-150.
£3.50
(B77-29012)

830.9 — GERMAN LITERATURE. HISTORY AND CRITICAL STUDIES
830'.9 — German literature. Influence of French literature, 1770-1895
Furst, Lilian Renée. Counterparts : the dynamics of Franco-German literary relationships, 1770-1895 / [by] Lilian R. Furst. — London : Methuen, 1977. — xi,201p ; 23cm.
Bibl.: p.185-191. — Index.
ISBN 0-416-67360-0 : Unpriced
Also classified at 840'.9
(B77-28247)

830'.9 — German literature. Literary periods, 1600-1976. Definition
Periods in German literature / edited by J.M. Ritchie. — London : Wolff, 1977. — viii,320p ; 22cm.
Originally published: 1966. — Bibl. — Index.
ISBN 0-85496-032-5 Pbk : £3.95
(B77-20751)

830'.9 — German literature, to 1976. *Critical studies*
Garland, Henry Burnand. A concise survey of German literature / [by] H.B. Garland. — 2nd ed. — London [etc.] : Macmillan, 1976. — 140p : map ; 23cm.
Previous ed.: 1971. — Bibl.: p.130-131. — Index.
ISBN 0-333-21362-9 : £5.95
ISBN 0-333-21363-7 Pbk : £2.95
(B77-23798)

830'.9'001 — German literature, to 1150. *Critical studies*
Bostock, John Knight. A handbook on Old High German literature / by J. Knight Bostock. — 2nd ed. / revised by K.C. King and D.R. McLintock. — Oxford : Clarendon Press, 1976. — xv,344p,fold plate : geneal tables, maps ; 22cm.
Previous ed.: 1955. — Bibl.: p.332-336. — Index.
ISBN 0-19-815392-9 : £15.00
(B77-04449)

830'.9'005 — German literature, 1625-1830. *Critical studies*
Radandt, Friedhelm. From Baroque to Storm and Stress, 1720-1775 / [by] Friedhelm Radandt. — London : Croom Helm [etc.], 1977. — 3-209p ; 23cm. — ([The literary history of Germany ; 4])
Bibl.: p.186-202. — Index.
ISBN 0-85664-351-3 : £7.95
(B77-08640)

830'.9'007 — German literature. Influence of Russian literature, 1830-1920
Kostka, Edmund Karl. Glimpses of Germanic-Slavic relations from Pushkin to Heinrich Mann / [by] Edmund Kostka. — Lewisburg : Bucknell University Press ; London (108 New Bond St., W1Y 0QX) : Associated University Presses, [1976]. — 3-162p ; 22cm.
Published in the United States: 1975. — Bibl.: p.144-154. — Index.
ISBN 0-8387-1371-8 : £3.75
Also classified at 891.7'09'003
(B77-03798)

830'.9'00912 — German literature, 1900-1945. Political aspects
Williams, Cedric Ellis. Writers and politics in modern Germany (1918-1945) / [by] C.E. Williams. — London [etc.] : Hodder and Stoughton, 1977. — vii,94p ; 22cm.
Bibl.: p.vi-vii.
ISBN 0-340-18442-6 Pbk : £1.75
(B77-16633)

831.6 — GERMAN POETRY, 1750-1830
831'.6 — Poetry in German, 1750-1830. *German-English parallel texts*
Goethe, Johann Wolfgang von. Goethe's Roman elegies / translated with an introduction and notes by David Luke. — London : Chatto and Windus, 1977. — 101p ; 23cm.
Parallel German and English text, English introduction and notes.
ISBN 0-7011-2219-6 : £3.95 : CIP rev.
(B77-21548)

831'.6 — Poetry in German. Gessner, Salomon. *Critical studies*
Hibberd, John. Salomon Gessner : his creative achievement and influence / [by] John Hibberd. — Cambridge [etc.] : Cambridge University Press, 1976. — vii,183p,8p of plates : ill, facsims, port ; 23cm. — (Anglica Germanica series ; 2)
Bibl.: p.171-180. — Index.
ISBN 0-521-21234-0 : £5.90
(B77-04450)

831.912 — GERMAN POETRY, 1900-1945
831'.91'2 — Poetry in German, 1900-1945. *English texts*
Hesse, Hermann. Poems / [by] Hermann Hesse ; selected and translated from the German by James Wright. — London : Cape, 1977. — 79p ; 22cm.
Parallel German text and English translation. — These translations originally published: New York : Farrar, Straus and Giroux, 1970 ; London : Cape, 1971.
ISBN 0-224-01548-6 Pbk : £0.95 : CIP rev.
(B77-24566)

Rilke, Rainer Maria. The voices / [by] Rainer Maria Rilke ; translated [from the German] by Robert Bly. — Denver : Ally Press ; [Bedford] : Sceptre Press, 1977. — [16]p ; 19cm.
Also available in a cased ed. signed by the translator. — Translation of: a selection from 'Buch der Bilder'. 2. sehr verm. Ausg. Berlin : A. Juncker, 1906.
ISBN 0-915408-15-5 Sd : Unpriced
ISBN 0-915408-16-3 Signed ed.: Unpriced
(B77-30800)

831'.9'12 — Poetry in German, 1900-1945. *German-English parallel texts*
Ausländer, Rose. Selected poems [of] Rose Ausländer / translated from the German by Ewald Osers. — London : London Magazine Editions, 1977. — 72p ; 22cm.
Parallel German text and English translation. — Bibl.: p.71.
ISBN 0-904388-27-1 Pbk : £2.75
(B77-20752)

831'.9'12 — Poetry in German. Usinger, Fritz. *Critical studies*
Barker, Christine R. The poetic vision of Fritz Usinger / by Christine R. Barker. — [Hull] (German Department, Hull University, [Hull HU6 7RX]) : 'New German Studies', 1977. — [5],114p,[4]p of plates : 1 ill, ports ; 21cm. — ('New German studies' monographs ; vol.1 ISSN 0309-5959)
Bibl.: p.112-114.
ISBN 0-85958-501-8 Pbk : Unpriced
(B77-18429)

832 — GERMAN DRAMA
832'.051 — Drama in German. Tragedies, 1517-1750. *Critical studies*
Benjamin, Walter. The origin of German tragic drama / [by] Walter Benjamin ; translated [from the German] by John Osborne. — London : NLB, 1977. — [1],256p ; 22cm.
Translation of: 'Ursprung des deutschen Trauerspiels'. Revidierte Ausg. Frankfurt am Main : Suhrkamp, 1963. — Index.
ISBN 0-902308-13-0 : £7.25
(B77-27502)

832.6 — GERMAN DRAMA, 1750-1830
832'.6 — Drama in German, 1750-1830. *English texts*
Goethe, Johann Wolfgang von. [Faust. Part 1. English]. Faust / [by] Johann Wolfgang von Goethe ; with eighteen lithographs by Eugène Delacroix ; with a new introduction by Michael Marqusee. — [London] : Paddington Press, 1977. — 174p : ill, port ; 28cm. — (Masterpieces of the illustrated book)
These illustrations originally published: with French translation. Paris : C. Motte, 1828.
ISBN 0-448-22184-5 Pbk : £2.95
Also classified at 769'.92'4
(B77-16634)

Kleist, Heinrich von. [Der zerbrochene Krug. English]. The broken jug / [by] Heinrich von Kleist ; translated by Roger Jones. — Manchester : Manchester University Press, 1977. — xii,83p : 1 ill ; 19cm. — (Classics of drama in English translation)
'Der zerbrochene Krug' originally published: Berlin : s.n., 1811.
ISBN 0-7190-0667-8 Pbk : £1.80
(B77-17153)

832'.6 — Drama in German, 1750-1830. *Texts*
Schiller, Friedrich. Wilhelm Tell / by Schiller ; edited with an introduction and notes by H.B. Garland. — London : Harrap, 1976. — xxiv, 143p : ill, map, port ; 17cm. — (Harrap's German classics)
German text, English introduction and notes. — Originally published: 1950. — Bibl.: p.xxiii.
ISBN 0-245-53019-3 Pbk : £1.80
(B77-12170)

832.912 — GERMAN DRAMA, 1900-1945
832'.9'12 — Drama in German, 1900-1945. *English texts*
Brecht, Bertolt. Collected plays [of] Bertolt Brecht / edited by John Willett and Ralph Manheim. — London : Eyre Methuen. — (Brecht, Bertolt. Plays, poetry and prose)
Vol.7 : [1942-1946]. — 1976. — xxvii,443p ; 23cm.
Contents: The visions of Simone Machard - Schweyk in the Second World War - The Caucasian chalk circle - The Duchess of Malfi.
ISBN 0-413-36840-8 : £12.00
ISBN 0-413-37040-2 Pbk : £3.95
(B77-10001)

Brecht, Bertolt. Mr Puntila and his man Matti / [by] Bertolt Brecht ; translated by John Willett. — London : Eyre Methuen, 1977. — 95p ; 19cm.
Translation of: 'Herr Puntila und sein Knecht Matti'. Berlin : Suhrkamp, 1950.
ISBN 0-413-37290-1 Pbk : £1.50
(B77-17154)

Horváth, Ödön von. Tales from the Vienna Woods / [by] Ödön von Horváth ; translated by Christopher Hampton. — London : Faber, 1977. — [8],111,[5]p ; 20cm.
Eleven men, 11 women. — Translation of: 'Geschichten aus dem Wiener Wald'. s.l. : s.n., 193- ?.
ISBN 0-571-11063-0 Pbk : £1.75
(B77-09354)

832'.9'12 — Drama in German. Brecht, Bertolt. *Critical studies*
Morley, Michael. Brecht : a study / by Michael Morley. — London : Heinemann Educational [etc.], 1977. — vii,135p ; 21cm.
Bibl.: p.134-135.
ISBN 0-435-38594-1 : £3.00
(B77-14451)

Willett, John. The theatre of Bertolt Brecht : a study from eight aspects / [by] John Willett. — Revised ed. [i.e. 3rd ed.] ; [with a revised bibliography]. — London : Eyre Methuen, 1977. — 240p : ill, facsim, ports ; 20cm. — (An Eyre Methuen dramabook)
This ed. originally published: London : Methuen, 1967. — Bibl.: p.226-232. — Index.
ISBN 0-413-34360-x Pbk : £2.50
(B77-28248)

832'.9'12 — National theatres. *Great Britain. National Theatre. Exhibits: British items associated with Brecht, Bertolt. Catalogues*

Jacobs, Nicholas. Bertolt Brecht in Britain / compiled and edited by Nicholas Jacobs and Prudence Ohlsen to accompany an exhibition at the National Theatre, London ; introduction by John Willett. — [London] ([30 Prince of Wales Cres., N.W.1]) : Irat Services Ltd/TQ Publications, 1977. — 2-100p : ill, facsims, ports ; 25cm.
Bibl.: p.93-98. — Index.
ISBN 0-904844-11-0 Pbk : £2.50
(B77-14452)

832.914 — GERMAN DRAMA, 1945-
832'.9'14 — Drama in German, 1945-. *English texts*

Bernhard, Thomas. The force of habit : a comedy / by Thomas Bernhard ; translated by Neville and Stephen Plaice. — London : Heinemann Educational [for] the National Theatre, 1976. — x,94p ; 19cm. — (National Theatre. Plays)
Translation of: 'Die Macht der Gewohnheit'. Frankfurt am Main : Suhrkamp, 1974.
ISBN 0-435-23120-0 Pbk : £1.25
(B77-06940)

832'.9'14 — Drama in German, 1945-. *Welsh texts*

Dürrenmatt, Friedrich. Ymweliad yr hen foneddiges : comedi drasig mewn tair act / [gan] Friedrich Dürrenmatt ; cyfieithiad gan John Gwilym Jones a G.L. Jones ; y golygu gan Gwyn Thomas. — [Cardiff] : Gwasg Prifysgol Cymru ar ran Cyngor Celfyddydau Cymru, 1976. — ii-xii,110p ; 19cm. — (Dramâu'r byd)
Translation of: 'Der Besuch der alten Dame'. Zürich : Verlag der Arche, 1963.
ISBN 0-7083-0630-6 Pbk : £0.70
(B77-01871)

832'.9'14 — Drama in German. Hochhuth, Rolf. *Critical studies*

Taëni, Rainer. Rolf Hochhuth / by Rainer Taëni ; translated from the German by R.W. Last. — London : Wolff, 1977. — 152p ; 20cm. — (Modern German authors : new series ; vol.5)
Translation of: 'Rolf Hochhuth'. Munich : Beck, 1977. — Bibl.: p.151-152.
ISBN 0-85496-057-0 : £3.50
ISBN 0-85496-058-9 Pbk : £2.50
(B77-23799)

832'.9'14 — Universities. Colleges. Libraries. *Dyfed. Aberystwyth. University College of Wales. Library. Exhibits: Items associated with Dürrenmatt, Friedrich. Catalogues*

University College of Wales. *Library.* Friedrich Dürrenmatt : [catalogue of] an exhibition illustrating his work, prepared in conjunction with his visit to this College as holder of the Welsh Arts Council international writers' prize / [produced by members of the University College of Wales Library staff]. — [Aberystwyth] ([Hugh Owen Building, Penglais, Aberystwyth, Dyfed SY23 3DZ]) : [The Library], 1976. — [1],14p ; 21cm.
Bibl.: p.12-14.
ISBN 0-904222-03-9 Sd : Unpriced
(B77-04451)

832'.9'1408 — Drama in German, 1945-. *Anthologies. English texts*

Bauer, Wolfgang. Shakespeare the sadist / [by] Wolfgang Bauer ; [translated from the German by] Renata and Martin Esslin. Bremen coffee / [by] Rainer Werner Fassbinder ; [translated from the German by] Anthony Vivis. My foot my tutor / [by] Peter Handke ; [translated from the German by] Michael Roloff. Stallerhof / [by] Franz Xaver Kroetz ; [translated from the German by] Katharina Helm. — London : Eyre Methuen, 1977. — 96p ; 20cm. — ([Methuen's modern plays])
ISBN 0-413-34380-4 : £3.95
ISBN 0-413-34390-1 Pbk : £1.50
(B77-29013)

833 — GERMAN FICTION
833'.02 — Novellen in German, 1795-1890. *Critical studies*

Swales, Martin. The German novelle / by Martin Swales. — Princeton ; Guildford : Princeton University Press, 1977. — xi,229p ; 23cm.
Bibl.: p.215-226. — Index.
ISBN 0-691-06331-1 : £11.30
(B77-29014)

833.6 — GERMAN FICTION, 1750-1830
833'.6 — Fiction in German, 1750-1830. *English texts*

Wyss, Johann David. [Schweizerischer Robinson. English]. The Swiss family Robinson / [by] Johann R. [i.e. Johann David] Wyss. — Abridged [ed.]. — Maidenhead : Purnell, 1976. — 139p : 1 ill ; 21cm. — (A Purnell classic)
ISBN 0-361-03548-9 : £0.50
(B77-10619)

833'.6 — Short stories in German. Kleist, Heinrich von. *Critical studies*

Dyer, Denys. The stories of Kleist : a critical study / [by] Denys Dyer. — London : Duckworth, 1977. — viii,205p ; 23cm.
Bibl.: p.195-202. — Index.
ISBN 0-7156-0995-5 : £7.95
(B77-33492)

833.8 — GERMAN FICTION, 1856-1900
833'.8 — Fiction in German, 1856-1900. *English texts*

Mörike, Eduard. [Mozart auf der Reise nach Prag. English]. Mozart's journey to Prague / by Eduard Mörike ; translated by Leopold von Loewenstein-Wertheim. — London : J. Calder : [Distributed by Calder and Boyars], 1976. — 3-93p ; 21cm. — (European classics editions)
This translation originally published: 1957.
ISBN 0-7145-0388-6 : £3.50
ISBN 0-7145-0389-4 Pbk : £1.25
(B77-10620)

Spyri, Johanna. Heidi / [by] Johanna Spyri. — Abridged [ed.]. — Maidenhead : Purnell, 1977. — 126p ; 21cm. — (A Purnell classic)
ISBN 0-361-03557-8 : £0.50
(B77-15004)

833.91F — GERMAN FICTION, 1900-. NOVELS (INCLUDING TRANSLATIONS)
833'.9'1F — Fiction in German, 1900-. *Texts (including translations)*

Becker, Jurek. Jacob the liar / [by] Jurek Becker ; translated and with a preface by Melvin Kornfeld. — New York ; London : Harcourt Brace Jovanovich, [1976]. — ix,266p ; 21cm.
'A Helen and Kurt Wolff book'. — This translation published in the United States: 1975. — Translation of: 'Jakob der Lügner'. Berlin : Aufbau-Verlag, 1969.
ISBN 0-15-145975-4 : £5.35
(B77-05741)

Bienek, Horst. Bakunin, an invention / [by] Horst Bienek ; translated from the German by Ralph R. Read. — London : Gollancz, 1977. — 119p ; 21cm.
Translation of: 'Bakunin, eine Invention'. München : C. Hauser, 1970.
ISBN 0-575-02236-1 : £3.95
(B77-13398)

Böll, Heinrich. The bread of those early years / [by] Heinrich Böll ; translated from the German by Leila Vennewitz. — London : Secker and Warburg, 1976. — 124p ; 23cm.
Translation of: 'Das Brot der frühen Jahre'. Cologne : Kiepenheuer und Witsch, 1955.
ISBN 0-436-05450-7 : £2.90
(B77-10621)

Broch, Hermann. The death of Virgil / [by] Hermann Broch ; translated [from the German] by Jean Starr Untermeyer. — London [etc.] : Routledge and Kegan Paul, 1977. — [1],493,[1] p ; 23cm.
This translation originally published: New York : Pantheon Books, 1945 ; London : Routledge, 1946. — Translation of: 'Der Tod des Vergil'. New York : Pantheon Books, 1945.

ISBN 0-7100-8763-2 : £6.50 : CIP rev.
(B77-25251)

Darlton, Clark. Escape to Venus / [by] Clark Darlton ; [translated by Wendayne Ackerman ; edited by Forrest J. Ackerman and Frederik Pohl]. — London : Futura Publications, 1976. — 116p ; 18cm. — (Perry Rhodan series ; 15) (An orbit book)
This translation originally published: New York : Ace Books, 1972. — 'Originally published in magazine form in Germany ...' - p.1.
ISBN 0-86007-895-7 Pbk : £0.50
(B77-08641)

Ernsting, Walter. The day the gods died / [by] Walter Ernsting ; translated by Wendayne Ackerman ; introduction by Erich von Däniken. — London : Corgi, 1977. — [10],240p ; 18cm.
This translation originally published: New York : Bantam, 1976. — Translation of: 'Der Tag, an dem die Götter starben'. W. Germany : s.n., 1976.
ISBN 0-552-10361-6 Pbk : £0.65
(B77-13399)

Habe, Hans. Palazzo : a novel / by Hans Habe ; translated by Salomé Hangartner. — London : W.H. Allen, 1977. — [7],343p ; 23cm.
Translation of: 'Palazzo'. Olten ; Freiburg i. Br : Walter, 1975.
ISBN 0-491-01746-4 : £3.95
(B77-17155)

Handke, Peter. The goalie's anxiety at the penalty kick / [by] Peter Handke ; translated by Michael Roloff. — London : Eyre Methuen, 1977. — 92p ; 21cm.
This translation originally published: New York : Farrar, Straus and Giroux, 1972. — Translation of: 'Die Angst des Tormanns beim Elfmeter'. Frankfurt am Main : Suhrkamp, 1970.
ISBN 0-413-45080-5 : £3.50
(B77-22956)

Handke, Peter. Short letter, long farewell / [by] Peter Handke ; translated by Ralph Manheim. — London : Eyre Methuen, 1977. — [5],167p : map(on lining papers) ; 21cm.
This translation originally published: New York : Farrar, Straus and Giroux, 1974. — Translation of: 'Der kurze Brief zum langen Abschied'. Frankfurt am Main : Suhrkamp, 1972.
ISBN 0-413-33710-3 : £3.95
(B77-22957)

Heinrich, Willi. Cross of iron / [by] Willi Heinrich ; translated from the German by Richard and Clara Winston. — Abridged ed. — London : Corgi, 1977. — 285p ; 18cm.
Full ed. of this translation originally published: as 'The willing flesh'. London : Weidenfeld and Nicolson, 1956. — Translation and revision of: 'Das geduldige fleisch'. Stuttgart : Deutsche Verlags-Anstalt, 1955.
ISBN 0-552-10343-8 Pbk : £0.75
(B77-08642)

Herlin, Hans. The reckoning / [by] Hans Herlin ; translated from the German by Eric Mosbacher. — London : Pan Books, 1977. — 255p ; 18cm.
This translation originally published: as 'Commemorations'. London : Heinemann, 1975. — Translation of: 'Freunde'. München ; Zürich : Dromer Knaur, 1974.
ISBN 0-330-24858-8 Pbk : £0.75
(B77-06941)

Heym, Stefan. Five days in June : a novel / by Stefan Heym. — London [etc.] : Hodder and Stoughton, 1977. — 352p ; 23cm.
Spine title: 5 days in June. — Translation of: '5 Tage im Juni'. München : Bertelsmann, 1974.
ISBN 0-340-21205-5 : £4.95
(B77-10622)

Kafka, Franz. The trial / [by] Franz Kafka ; a new translation by Douglas Scott and Chris Waller ; with an introduction by J.P. Stern. — London : Pan Books, 1977. — 254p ; 20cm. — (Picador)
Translation of: 'Der Prozess'. Berlin : Die Schmiede, 1925.
ISBN 0-330-24468-x Pbk : £0.80
(B77-22958)

Kirst, Hans Hellmut. The revolt of Gunner Asch / [by] Hans Hellmut Kirst ; translated from the German by Robert Kee. — Bath : Chivers, 1977. — 254p ; 19cm.
This translation originally published: as 'The revolt of Gunner Asch', Boston, Mass. : Little, Brown, 1955 ; and as 'Zero eight fifteen', London : Weidenfeld and Nicolson, 1956. — Translation of: 'Null-acht fünfzehn', Bd 1. Wien : Desch, 1954.
ISBN 0-85997-276-3 : £5.20(£3.90 to members of the Library Association)
(B77-29779)

Kirst, Hans Hellmut. A time for payment / [by] Hans Hellmut Kirst ; translated by J. Maxwell Brownjohn. — [London] : Fontana, 1977. — 288p ; 18cm.
This translation originally published: London : Collins, 1976. — Translation of: 'Alles hat seinen Preis'. Hamburg : Hoffmann und Campe, 1974.
ISBN 0-00-614522-1 Pbk : £0.80
(B77-15580)

Konsalik, Heinz Günther. Battalion 999 / [by] Heinz G. Konsalik ; translated by Oliver Coburn. — Henley-on-Thames : A. Ellis, 1976. — [5],238p ; 23cm.
Translation of: 'Strafbataillon 999'. München : Lichtenberg, 1963.
ISBN 0-85628-033-x : £4.25
(B77-09355)

Konsalik, Heinz Günther. Highway to hell / [by] Heinz G. Konsalik ; translated by Robert Vacha. — Henley-on-Thames : A. Ellis, 1976. — [5],237p ; 23cm.
Translation of: 'Die Rollbahn'. Munich : Heyne, 19--?.
ISBN 0-85628-034-8 : £4.25
(B77-09356)

Mahr, Kurt. The ghosts of Gol / [by] Kurt Mahr ; [translated by Wendayne Ackerman ; edited by Donald A. Wollheim]. — London : Futura Publications, 1976. — 126p ; 18cm. — (Perry Rhodan series ; 10) (An orbit book)
This translation originally published: New York : Ace Books, 1971. — 'Originally published in magazine form in Germany ... ' - p.1.
ISBN 0-86007-869-8 Pbk : £0.45
(B77-09357)

Mahr, Kurt. Menace of the mutant master / [by] Kurt Mahr. — London : Futura Publications, 1976. — 124p ; 18cm. — (Perry Rhodan series ; 18) (An orbit book)
This translation originally published: New York : Ace Books, 1972?. — 'Originally published in magazine form in Germany ...' - p.1.
ISBN 0-86007-917-1 Pbk : £0.50
(B77-12762)

Mahr, Kurt. Venus in danger / [by] Kurt Mahr ; [translated by Wendayne Ackerman]. — London : Futura Publications, 1976. — 127p ; 18cm. — (Perry Rhodan series ; 14) (An orbit book)
This translation originally published: New York : Ace, 1972.
ISBN 0-86007-892-2 Pbk : £0.50
(B77-09358)

Mann, Thomas. Confessions of Felix Krull, confidence man : memoirs, part 1 / [by] Thomas Mann ; translated from the German by Denver Lindley. — London : Secker and Warburg, 1977. — 408p ; 21cm.
This translation originally published: 1955. — Translation of: 'Bekenntnisse des Hochstaplers Felix Krull'. Frankfurt am Main : Fischer, 1954.
ISBN 0-436-27231-8 : £4.90
(B77-03799)

Mann, Thomas. Lotte in Weimar / [by] Thomas Mann ; translated from the German by H.T. Lowe-Porter. — Harmondsworth [etc.] : Penguin, 1976. — 331p ; 19cm. — (Penguin modern classics)
This translation originally published: London : Secker and Warburg, 1940. — Translation of: 'Lotte in Weimar'. Stockholm : Bermann-Fischer, 1940.
ISBN 0-14-002850-1 Pbk : £0.80
(B77-01872)

Ott, Wolfgang. Sharks and little fish / [by] Wolfgang Ott ; translated by Oliver Coburn. — London : Corgi, 1977. — 448p ; 18cm.
This translation originally published: London : Hutchinson, 1957. — Translation of: 'Haie und kleine Fische'. Munich : Langen-Müller, 1956.
ISBN 0-552-10425-6 Pbk : £0.95
(B77-21549)

Roth, Joseph. Flight without end / [by] Joseph Roth ; translated by David Le Vay, in collaboration with Beatrice Musgrave. — London : Owen, 1977. — 144p ; 19cm.
Translation of: 'Die Flucht ohne Ende'. München : K. Wolff, 1927.
ISBN 0-7206-0324-2 : £4.25
(B77-13400)

Scheer, Karl Herbert. Enterprise stardust / [by] K-H. Scheer and Walter Ernsting ; introduction by Forrest J. Ackerman ; [translated and edited by Wendayne Ackerman]. — London : Severn House : [Distributed by Hutchinson], 1977. — 189p ; 21cm. — (Perry Rhodan ; 1)
This translation originally published: New York : Ace Books, 1969 ; London : Futura Publications, 1974. — Originally published in magazine form in Germany.
ISBN 0-7278-0255-0 : £2.95
(B77-15005)

Scheer, Karl Herbert. Enterprise stardust / [by] K-H. Scheer and Walter Ernsting ; introduction by Forrest J. Ackerman ; [translated and edited by Wendayne Ackerman]. — London : Futura Publications, 1974. — 189p ; 18cm. — (Perry Rhodan series ; 1) (An orbit book)
This translation originally published: New York : Ace Books, 1969. — 'Originally published in magazine form in Germany ...' - p.1.
ISBN 0-86007-819-1 Pbk : £0.35
(B77-08643)

Scheer, Karl Herbert. The immortal unknown / [by] K.H. Scheer ; [translated by Wendayne Ackerman ; edited by Forrest J. Ackerman and Frederik Pohl]. — London : Futura Publications, 1976. — 127p ; 18cm. — (Perry Rhodan series ; 13) (An orbit book)
This translation originally published: New York : Ace Books, 1972. — 'Originally published in magazine form in Germany ...' - p.1.
ISBN 0-86007-888-4 Pbk : £0.45
(B77-08644)

Scheer, Karl Herbert. The radiant dome / [by] K-H. Scheer and Walter Ernsting ; [translated and edited by Wendayne Ackerman]. — London : Severn House : [Distributed by Hutchinson], 1977. — 188p ; 21cm. — (Perry Rhodan series ; 2)
This translation originally published: New York : Ace Books, 1969 ; London : Futura Publications, 1974. — Originally published: in German. Germany : s.n., 196-?.
ISBN 0-7278-0281-x : £2.95
(B77-17156)

Selinko, Annemarie. Désirée / [by] Annemarie Selinko ; translated by Arnold Bender and E.W. Dickes. — [London] : Fontana, 1977. — 512p ; 18cm.
This translation originally published: London : Heinemann, 1953. — Translation of: 'Désirée'. Cologne : Kiepenheuer und Witsch, 1951.
ISBN 0-00-614589-2 Pbk : £0.95
(B77-16095)

Werfel, Franz. The song of Bernadette / [by] Franz Werfel ; translated by Ludwig Lewisohn. — St Albans : Mayflower, 1977. — 446p ; 18cm.
This translation originally published: New York : Viking Press ; London : Hamilton, 1942. — Translation of: 'Das Lied von Bernadette'. Stockholm : Bermann-Fischer, 1941. — Based on the life of Bernadette Soubirous.
ISBN 0-583-12756-8 Pbk : £0.95
(B77-20753)

833.91J — GERMAN FICTION, 1900-. CHILDREN'S STORIES (INCLUDING TRANSLATIONS)

833'.9'1J — Children's stories in German, 1900-. *Texts (including translations)*

Beisner, Monika. Ramses in Rio Moto / pictures by Monika Beisner ; story by Hans Dörflinger ; [translated from the German by the authors]. — London [etc.] : Dent, 1977. — [28]p : col ill ; 25cm.
Translation of: 'Ramses in Rio Moto'. Munich : K. Thienemanns, 1977.
ISBN 0-460-06850-4 : £3.50
(B77-29015)

Brychta, Jan. Katzimir the greatest / a picture book by Jan Brychta ; words by Hans Baumann ; translated [from the German] by Gwen Marsh. — London : Dent, 1977. — [26] p : chiefly col ill ; 27cm.
Translation of: 'Katzimir der Grosste'. Ravensburg : Maier, 1977.
ISBN 0-460-06828-8 : £2.95 : CIP rev.
(B77-19873)

Damjan, Mischa. Francesco and his donkeys / [by] Mischa Damjan ; illustrated by Mona Ineichen ; translated [from the German] by Patricia Crampton. — London : Andersen Press : Hutchinson, 1977. — 80p : ill ; 21cm. — (The Andersen young readers library)
Translation of: 'Francesco und seine Eselchen'. Stuttgart : Thienemanns, 197-?.
ISBN 0-905478-12-6 : £1.95
(B77-29016)

Fuchshuber, Annegert. Henry and the bombardon / [by] Annegert Fuchshuber ; translated [from the German] by Gwen Marsh. — London [etc.] : Dent, 1977. — [28]p : col ill, port ; 24cm.
Translation of: 'Vom Bombardon'. Stuttgart : Thienemanns, 1977.
ISBN 0-460-06845-8 : £2.95
(B77-28249)

Heuck, Sigrid. The pony, the bear and the stolen apples / [by] Sigrid Heuck ; translated [from the German] by Gwen Marsh. — London [etc.] : Dent, 1977. — [28]p : col ill, port ; 24cm.
Translation of: 'Die Pony-Bären-Apfel-Geschichte'. Stuttgart : Thienemanns, 1977.
ISBN 0-460-06844-x : £2.95
(B77-29017)

Horna, Luis de. The prince who learned how to make bread / [by] Luis de Horna ; translated by Anthea Bell. — London ([3 Fitzroy Sq., W.1]) : Andersen Press Ltd, 1977. — [26]p : col ill ; 31cm.
Translation of: 'Soll ich dir zeigen wie man Brot bäckt'. Zurich : Bohem Press, 1975.
ISBN 0-905478-04-5 : £2.75
(B77-10002)

Hüttner, Doralies. Come on, David, jump / [by] Doralies Hüttner ; translated from the German by Gertrud Mander ; illustrated by Michael Charlton. — London [etc.] : Angus and Robertson, 1977. — [5],121p : ill ; 20cm.
Translation of: 'Los, Jürgen, spring'. Reinbek bei Hamburg : Rowohlt Taschenbuch Verlag, 1974.
ISBN 0-207-95687-1 : £3.20
(B77-30801)

Janosch. Hey presto! you're a bear! / [written and illustrated by] Janosch ; translated [from the German] by Klaus Flugge. — London (3 Fitzroy Sq., W.1) : Andersen Press Ltd [etc.], 1977. — [28]p : chiefly col ill ; 25x28cm.
Translation of: 'Ich sag, du bist ein Bär!'. s.l. : Beltz & Gelberg, 1977.
ISBN 0-905478-18-5 : £2.95
(B77-32282)

Janosch. Luke Caraway : master magician or Indian chief / written and illustrated by Janosch ; translated [from the German] by Anthea Bell. — London : Andersen Press : Hutchinson, 1977. — 94p : ill ; 21cm. — (The Andersen young readers library)
Translation of: 'Lukas Kümmel Zauberkünstler oder Indianerhäuptling'. Recklinghausen : Paulus, 1968.
ISBN 0-905478-05-3 : £1.95
(B77-34260)

Kästner, Erich. Lottie and Lisa : a novel for children / by Erich Kästner ; translated from the German by Cyrus Brooks ; illustrated from drawings by Walter Trier. — London : Heinemann Educational, 1977. — 155p : ill ; 20cm. — (The windmill series ; 219)
This translation originally published: London : Cape, 1950. — Translation of: 'Das doppelte Lottchen'. Zürich : Atrium Verlag, 1949.
ISBN 0-435-12219-3 : £0.85
(B77-32940)

Könner, Alfred. Olrik : a day in the life of a penguin / by Alfred Könner ; illustrated by Karl-Heinz Appelmann ; translated from the German by Richard Sadler. — Barton-under-Needwood ([c/o W.J. Williams and Sons (Books) Ltd, Ashcroft, Small Meadow La., Barton-under-Needwood, Staffs. DE13 8BA]) : Wrens Park Publishing, 1977. — [25] p : col ill ; 25cm.
Col. ill on lining papers. — Originally published: in German. Berlin : Altberliner Verlag Lucie Groszer, 1976.
ISBN 0-905778-00-6 : £2.00
(B77-34261)

Könner, Alfred. Silko : a day in the life of a heron / by Alfred Könner ; illustrated by Gerhard Lahr ; translated from the German by Richard Sadler. — Barton-under-Needwood ([c/o W.J. Williams and Sons (Books) Ltd, Ashcroft, Small Meadow La., Barton-under-Needwood, Staffs. DE13 8BA]) : Wrens Park Publishing, 1977. — [25]p : col ill ; 25cm.
Col. ill. on lining papers. — Originally published: in German. Berlin : Altberliner Verlag Lucie Groszer, 1975.
ISBN 0-905778-01-4 : £2.00
(B77-34262)

Konopka, Ursula. George the dragon / [pictures by] Ursula Konopka ; text by Joseph Guggenmos ; [translated from the German]. — London [etc.] : Dent, 1977. — [26]p : col ill ; 21x27cm.
Translator: Gwen Marsh. — Translation of: 'Franz der Drache'. Munich : Verlag Heinrich Ellerman, 1976.
ISBN 0-460-06815-6 : £3.25 : CIP rev.
(B77-19874)

Lobe, Mira. 'Hoppelpop!' / [by] Mira Lobe ; pictures by Angelika Kaufmann ; translated [from the German] by Gwen Marsh. — London [etc.] : Dent, 1977. — [26]p : ill(some col) ; 29cm.
Translation of: 'Dann rufen alle Hoppelpopp'. Wien : Jugend und Volk, 1977.
ISBN 0-460-06848-2 : £3.50
(B77-28250)

Murschetz, Luis. Mole / [by] Luis Murschetz ; [translated from the German]. — London : Methuen, 1977. — [30]p : chiefly col ill ; 19cm. — (A Methuen picture paperback)
This translation originally published: 1973. — Translation of: 'Der Maulwurf Grabowski'. Zürich : Diogenes, 1972.
ISBN 0-416-58150-1 Sd : £0.60
(B77-27503)

Nöstlinger, Christine. Four days in the life of Lisa / [by] Christine Nöstlinger ; translated by Anthea Bell. — London : Abelard, 1977. — 135p ; 23cm.
Translation of: 'Studenplan'. Weinheim : Beltz, 1975?.
ISBN 0-200-72480-0 : £3.15
(B77-24567)

Press, Hans Jürgen. The adventures of the Black Hand Gang / [by] H.J. Press ; [translated from the German by Barbara Littlewood]. — London : Methuen, 1977. — 128p : ill ; 18cm.
This translation originally published: 1976. — Translation of: 'Die Abenteur des Schwarzen Hand'. Ravensburg : O. Maier, 1965.
ISBN 0-416-58160-9 Pbk : £0.50
(B77-28251)

Preussler, Otfried. The final adventures of the robber Hotzenplotz / [by] Otfried Preussler ; illustrated by F.J. Tripp ; translated [from the German] by Anthea Bell. — Leicester : Knight Books, 1977. — 96p : ill ; 18cm.
This translation originally published: London : Abelard-Schuman, 1974. — Translation of: 'Hotzenplotz 3'. Stuttgart : K. Thienemann, 1973.
ISBN 0-340-19532-0 Pbk : £0.60
(B77-25252)

Preussler, Otfried. The green bronze bell / [by] Otfried Preussler ; illustrated by Herbert Holzing ; translated by Caroline Gueritz. — London : Hamilton, 1977. — [25]p : chiefly col ill ; 30cm.
Translation of: 'Die Glocke von grünem Erz'. Stuttgart : Thienemanns, 1976.
ISBN 0-241-89543-x : £2.75
(B77-06942)

Resch, Barbara. The singing bird / [by] Barbara Resch ; [translated from the German by Peggy Blakeley]. — London : A. and C. Black, 1977. — [32]p : col ill ; 28cm.
Translation of: 'Der Vogel singt der König springt'. Vienna : Jungbrunnen, 1976.
ISBN 0-7136-1768-3 : £2.25
(B77-27504)

Sendak, Maurice. Seven little monsters / [by] Maurice Sendak. — London [etc.] : Bodley Head, 1977. — [9]leaves(1 fold) : chiefly col ill ; 13x23cm.
One leaf printed on both sides. — Fold. plate tipped in. — These illustrations originally published: with German text. Zurich : Diogenes Verlag, 1975.
ISBN 0-370-30024-6 : £1.95
(B77-24568)

Steger, H V. Nuair a thagann Crúbach / [le] H.V. Steger ; Clodagh Uí Riagáin a chuir an leagan Gaeilge in oiriúint do leanaí 7-9 mbliana d'aois. — Baile Átha Claith [i.e. Dublin] ([Bothar an Phoirt Thoir, Baile Átha Cliath 3]) : Oifig an tSoláthair, 1976. — [42]p : col ill ; 22x30cm.
Translation of: 'Wenn Kubaki kommt'. Zürich : Diogenes, 1976.
ISBN 0-905621-13-1 : Unpriced
(B77-06943)

Stoye, Rüdiger. Toots bites back / written and illustrated by Rüdiger Stoye ; English translation by Geoffrey Strachan. — London : Methuen, 1977. — [27]p : col ill ; 30cm.
Translation of: 'Wie der Hund Putzi seinem Herrchen in den Hintern biss'. Ravensburg : Otto Maier Verlag, 1975.
ISBN 0-416-84320-4 : £2.95
(B77-13941)

Velthuijs, Max. The little boy and the big fish / written and illustrated by Max Velthuijs ; [translated from the German]. — London : Abelard-Schuman, 1977. — [31]p : col ill ; 29cm.
This translation originally published: 1969. — Translation of: 'Der Junge und der Fisch'. Zurich : Nord-Süd-Verlag, 1969.
£3.25
ISBN 0-200-71610-7
(B77-25253)

Zimnik, Reiner. Little owl / [by] Reiner Zimnik & Hanne Axmann ; English version [i.e. translated] by Leila Berg. — London : Methuen, 1977. — [32]p : col ill ; 19cm. — (A Methuen picture paperback)
This translation originally published: 1960. — Translation of: 'Die Geschichte vom Käuzchen'. s.l. : s.n., 196-?.
ISBN 0-416-58140-4 Sd : £0.60
(B77-27505)

833.912 — GERMAN FICTION, 1900-1945
833'.9'12 — Fiction in German. Kafka, Franz. Prozess, Der. *Critical studies. Readings*

Twentieth century interpretations of 'The trial' : a collection of critical essays / edited by James Rolleston. — Englewood Cliffs ; London [etc.] : Prentice-Hall, [1977]. — ix,112p : 1 ill ; 22cm.
Published in the United States: 1976. — Bibl.: p.108-112.
ISBN 0-13-926345-4 : £5.55
ISBN 0-13-926337-3 Pbk : £2.05
(B77-12763)

833'.9'12 — Fiction in German. Kafka, Franz. Schloss, Das. *Critical studies*

Robert, Marthe. The old and the new : from Don Quixote to Kafka / [by] Marthe Robert ; translated [from the French] by Carol Cosman ; foreword by Robert Alter. — Berkeley [etc.] ; London : University of California Press, 1977. — xiii,322p ; 21cm.
Translation of: 'L'ancien et le nouveau'. Paris : Payot, 1967.
ISBN 0-520-02509-1 : £8.75
Also classified at 863'.3
(B77-25254)

833'.9'12 — Fiction in German. Mann, Thomas. *Critical studies*

Reed, Terence James. Thomas Mann : the uses of tradition / [by] T.J. Reed. — Oxford : Clarendon Press, 1976. — xv,433p,[4]p of plates : ill, ports ; 23cm.
Originally published: 1974. — Bibl.: p.415-424. — Index.
£9.50
ISBN 0-19-815742-8
ISBN 0-19-815747-9 Pbk : £3.15
(B77-14453)

833.914 — GERMAN FICTION, 1945-
833'.9'140932 — Fiction in German. East German writers, 1945-1970. Special themes: Germany. Partition. *Critical studies*

Hutchinson, Peter, *b.1944.* Literary presentations of divided Germany : the development of a central theme in East German fiction, 1945-1970 / [by] Peter Hutchinson. — Cambridge [etc.] : Cambridge University Press, 1977. — vii,204p ; 23cm. — (Anglica Germanica series ; 2)
Bibl.: p.184-199. — Index.
ISBN 0-521-21609-5 : £7.50
(B77-29780)

838.912 — GERMAN MISCELLANY, 1900-1945
838'.9'1208 — Prose in German, 1900-1945. *English texts*

Frisch, Max. Sketchbook, 1946-1949 / [by] Max Frisch ; translated [from the German] by Geoffrey Skelton. — New York ; London : Harcourt Brace Jovanovich, 1977. — xiii,301p ; 22cm.
'A Helen and Kurt Wolff book'. — Translation of: 'Tagebuch 1946-1949'. Frankfurt am Main : Suhrkamp, 1950.
ISBN 0-15-182893-8 : £8.40
(B77-34263)

838.914 — GERMAN MISCELLANY, 1945-
838'.9'1407 — Experimental writing in German, 1945-. *English texts*

Heissenbüttel, Helmut. Texts / [by] Helmut Heissenbüttel ; selected and translated by Michael Hamburger. — London : Boyars : Distributed by Calder and Boyars, 1977. — 119p ; 25cm.
'This selection taken from "Gelegenheitsgedichte und Klappentexte" (1973) and "Das Durchhauen des Kohlhaupts" (1974) published by Hermann Luchterhand Verlag [Berlin], and from six "Textbücher" (1960-1967). Vols.1-5 published by Walter-Verlag [Freiburg (Breisgau)], Vol.6 ... by Herman Luchterhand Verlag [Berlin]' - title page verso.
ISBN 0-7145-2589-8 : £7.50
ISBN 0-7145-2590-1 Pbk : £3.50
(B77-12171)

839.09 — YIDDISH LITERATURE
839'.09'301 — Short stories in Yiddish, to ca 1950. *Anthologies. English texts*

Great works of Jewish fantasy : Yenne Velt / compiled, translated [from the Yiddish] and introduced by Joachim Neugroschel. — London : Cassell, 1976. — xiii,713p ; 23cm.
ISBN 0-304-29767-4 : £6.95
(B77-10003)

839'.09'33F — Fiction in Yiddish, 1860-. *Texts (including translations)*

Singer, Isaac Bashevis. A crown of feathers, and other stories / [by] Isaac Bashevis Singer. — Harmondsworth [etc.] : Penguin, 1977. — 303p ; 18cm.
This collection originally published: New York : Farrar, Straus and Giroux, 1973 ; London : Cape, 1974.
ISBN 0-14-004325-x Pbk : £0.95
(B77-25255)

Singer, Isaac Bashevis. Enemies : a love story / by Isaac Bashevis Singer ; [translated by Aliza Shevrin and Elizabeth Shub]. — Harmondsworth [etc.] : Penguin, 1977. — 220p ; 19cm.
This translation originally published: London : Cape, 1972. — '... first published in the "Jewish Daily Forward" in 1966 under the title 'Sonim, di Geschichte fun a Liebe"' - Author's note.
ISBN 0-14-004326-8 Pbk : £0.80
(B77-23800)

Singer, Isaac Bashevis. Naftali the storyteller and his horse, Sus, and other stories / [by] Isaac Bashevis Singer ; illustrated by Margot Zemach ; [translated from the Yiddish by Joseph Singer, Ruth Schachner Finkel and the author]. — Oxford [etc.] : Oxford University Press, 1977. — [8],83p : ill ; 23cm.
This collection originally published: New York : Farrar, Straus, Giroux, 1976.
ISBN 0-19-271413-9 : £2.25 : CIP rev.
(B77-16615)

839.31 — DUTCH LITERATURE
839.3'1'164 — Poetry in Dutch, 1945-. *English texts*

Verhagen, Hans. Stars over Bombay / [by] Hans Verhagen ; translated by Peter Nijmeijer. — Deal (11 Duke St., Deal, Kent) : Transgravity Press, 1976. — 3-83p ; 22cm.
Also available in a signed ed.
ISBN 0-85682-028-8 Pbk : £1.50
ISBN 0-85682-029-6 Signed ed. : £7.50
(B77-10004)

839.3'1'16408 — Poetry in Dutch, 1945-. *Anthologies. English texts*

Four Dutch poets : Lucebert, Gerrit Kouwenaar, Sybren Polet, Bert Schierbeck / edited by Peter Nijmeijer. — [Deal] ([11 Duke St., Deal, Kent]) : Transgravity Press, 1976. — 3-62p ; 22cm.
ISBN 0-85682-036-9 Pbk : £2.00
ISBN 0-85682-037-7 Signed ed. : Unpriced
(B77-10005)

839.3'1'36J — Children's stories in Dutch, 1900-. *Texts (including translations)*

Biegel, Paul. The elephant party, and other stories / [by] Paul Biegel ; translated from the Dutch by Patricia Crampton ; illustrated by Babs van Wely. — Harmondsworth [etc.] : Puffin Books, 1977. — 90p : ill ; 20cm. — (A young puffin original)
This collection also published: Harmondsworth : Kestrel Books, 1977. — Translation of: 'Het olifantenfeest'. Haarlem : Uitgeversmaatschappij Holland, 1973.
ISBN 0-14-030950-0 Pbk : £0.40
(B77-21551)

Biegel, Paul. The elephant party, and other stories / [by] Paul Biegel ; translated from the Dutch by Patricia Crampton ; illustrated by Babs van Wely. — Harmondsworth : Kestrel Books, 1977. — 90p : ill ; 21cm.
This collection also published: Harmondsworth : Puffin Books, 1977. — Translation of: 'Het olifantenfeest'. Haarlem : Uitgeversmaatschappij Holland, 1973.
ISBN 0-7226-5289-5 : £2.25
(B77-22225)

Biegel, Paul. Far beyond and back again / [by] Paul Biegel ; translated by Patricia Crampton ; illustrated by Cherry Calnan. — London : Dent, 1977. — 92p : ill ; 21cm.
Translation of: 'Het stenen beeld'. Haarlem : U.M. Holland, 1974.
ISBN 0-460-06737-0 : £2.75
(B77-06944)

Biegel, Paul. The king of the copper mountains / [by] Paul Biegel ; English version by Gillian Hume and Paul Biegel ; illustrations by Babs van Wely. — London : Dent, 1977. — vi,176p : ill ; 19cm. — (Dent dolphins)
This translation originally published: 1969. — Translation of: 'Het sleutelkruid'. Haarlem : Uitgeversmaatschappij, 1965.
ISBN 0-460-02742-5 Pbk : £0.55
(B77-06348)

Bruna, Dick. Miffi yn y parc chwarae / [gan] Dick Bruna. — Abertawe [i.e. Swansea] : C. Davies, 1976. — 26p : col ill ; 16cm.
Originally published: in Dutch. 1975.
Unpriced
(B77-18430)

Bruna, Dick. Miffi yn yr ysbyty / [gan] Dick Bruna. — Abertawe [i.e. Swansea] : C. Davies, 1976. — 26p : col ill ; 16cm.
Originally published: in Dutch. 1975.
Unpriced
(B77-18431)

Heymans, Margriet. Cait agus Bábóga / Margriet Heymans a scríobh agus a léirigh ; Eibhlín Ní Mhuircheartaigh a d'aistrigh do leanaí 6-8 mbliana d'aois. — [Baile Átha Cliath, i.e. Dublin] ([Baile Átha Cliath 4]) : [Oifig an tSoláthair], 1975. — 24p : col ill ; 22cm.
Translation of: 'Kattekwaad en Popperommel'. Rotterdam : Lemniscaat, 1975.
£0.45
(B77-03267)

Schmidt, Annie Maria Geertruida. Dusty and Smudge and the bride / [by] Annie M.G. Schmidt ; translated [from the Dutch] by Lance Salway ; illustrated by Fiep Westendorp. — London : Methuen, 1977. — [20]p : col ill ; 15x21cm. — (A Methuen starting book)
Translation of: 'Floddertje en de bruid' published in 'Floddertje'. Amsterdam : Querido, 1973.
ISBN 0-416-55210-2 : £1.00
ISBN 0-416-55220-x Pbk : Unpriced
(B77-29781)

Schmidt, Annie Maria Geertruida. Dusty and Smudge and the soap suds / [by] Annie M.G. Schmidt ; translated [from the Dutch] by Lance Salway ; illustrated by Fiep Westendorp. — London : Methuen, 1977. — [19]p : col ill ; 15x21cm. — (A Methuen starting book)
Translation of: 'Schuim' published in 'Floddertje'. Amsterdam : Querido, 1973.
ISBN 0-416-55170-x : £1.00
ISBN 0-416-55180-7 Pbk : £0.45
(B77-27506)

Schmidt, Annie Maria Geertruida. Dusty and Smudge keep cool / [by] Annie M.G. Schmidt ; translated [from the Dutch] by Lance Salway ; illustrated by Fiep Westendorp. — London : Methuen, 1977. — [20]p : col ill ; 15x21cm. — (A Methuen starting book)
Translation of: 'Allemaal kaal' published in 'Floddertje'. Amsterdam : Querido, 1973.
ISBN 0-416-55190-4 : £1.00
ISBN 0-416-55200-5 Pbk : £0.45
(B77-27507)

Schmidt, Annie Maria Geertruida. Dusty and Smudge spill the paint / [by] Annie M.G. Schmidt ; translated [from the Dutch] by Lance Salway ; illustrated by Fiep Westendorp. — London : Methuen, 1977. — [20]p : col ill ; 15x21cm. — (A Methuen starting book)
Translation of: 'Opgesloten' published in 'Floddertje'. Amsterdam : Querido, 1973.
ISBN 0-416-55150-5 : £1.00
ISBN 0-416-55160-2 Pbk : £0.45
(B77-27508)

Schouten, Alet. The sea lord / [by] Alet Schouten ; translated from the Dutch by Patricia Crampton ; illustrated by Rien Poortvliet. — London : Methuen, 1977. — 142p : ill ; 21cm.
Translation of: 'De zeeridder'. Bussum : Van Holkema & Warendorf, 1970.
ISBN 0-416-56030-x : £2.95
(B77-26644)

Verburg, Jan Marinus. The Island of Nose / [by] Jan Marinus Verburg, Annie M.G. Schmidt ; translated [from the Dutch] by Lance Salway. — London [etc.] : Methuen, 1977. — 5-48p : col ill ; 36cm.
Translation of: 'Tom Tippelaar'. Amsterdam : Querido's Uitgeverij, 1977?.
ISBN 0-416-86210-1 : Unpriced
(B77-30802)

839.3'1'8208 — Prose in Dutch, 1450-1600. *English texts. Facsimiles*

[**Reynard** the Fox]. The historye of Reynart the Foxe / [translated from the Dutch by William Caxton]. — London (32 Davies St., W.1) : David Paradine Developments Ltd, 1976. — [150]p : port ; 24cm.
Spine title: Reynart the Foxe. — Facsimile reprint of: 1489 ed. Westminster : W. Caxton, 1489.
£7.45
(B77-16096)

839.32 — FLEMISH LITERATURE

839.3'2'164 — Poetry in Flemish, 1945-. *English texts*

Snoek, Paul. In the sleep trap : poems / by Paul Snoek ; translated by Peter Nijmeijer. — London (58 Blakes La., New Malden, Surrey KT3 6NX) : Tangent Books, 1976. — 17p ; 21cm.
ISBN 0-904945-03-0 Sd : £0.30
(B77-04452)

839.3'2'16408 — Poetry in Flemish, 1945-. *Anthologies. English texts*

Four Flemish poets : Hugo Claus, Gust Gils, Paul Snoek, Hugues C. Penarth / edited by Peter Nijmeijer. — [Deal] ([11 Duke St., Deal, Kent]) : Transgravity Press, 1976. — 3-47p : ports ; 22cm.
ISBN 0-85682-034-2 Pbk : £1.90
ISBN 0-85682-035-0 Signed ed. : Unpriced
(B77-10006)

839.5 — SCANDINAVIAN LITERATURES

839'.6'8 — Prose in Old Norse. *English texts*

[**Egils** saga Skallgrímssonar. *English*]. Egil's saga / translated with an introduction by Hermann Pálsson and Paul Edwards. — Harmondsworth [etc.] : Penguin, 1976. — 254p : geneal tables, maps ; 18cm. — (The Penguin classics)
Sometimes attributed to Snorri Sturluson.
ISBN 0-14-044321-5 Pbk : £0.75
(B77-03268)

Orkneyinga saga : the history of the Earls of Orkney / translated from the Icelandic and introduced by Hermann Pálsson and Paul Edwards. — London : Hogarth Press, 1978. — 223p,[4]p of plates : ill, facsim, geneal table, maps ; 23cm.
ISBN 0-7012-0431-1 : £7.50 : CIP rev.
(B77-17157)

839.7 — SWEDISH LITERATURE

839.7'1'72 — Poetry in Swedish, 1900-1945. *Swedish-English parallel texts*

Lagerkvist, Pär. Evening land = Aftonland / by Pär Lagerkvist ; translated by W.H. Auden and Leif Sjöberg ; with an introduction by Leif Sjöberg. — London : Souvenir Press, 1977. — 193,[1]p ; 22cm. — (A condor book)
Parallel Swedish text and English translation, English introduction. — This translation originally published: Detroit : Wayne State University Press, 1975. — Swedish text originally published: Stockholm : Bonnier, 1953. — Bibl.: p.42.
ISBN 0-285-64812-8 : £4.00
ISBN 0-285-64813-6 Pbk : £2.50
(B77-13942)

839.7'2'74 — Drama in Swedish, 1945-. *English texts*

Bergman, Ingmar. Scenes from a marriage / [by] Ingmar Bergman ; translated from the Swedish by Alan Blair. — Toronto [etc.] ; London : Bantam, 1977. — viii,213p,[8]p of plates : ill, port ; 18cm.
This translation originally published: London : Calder and Boyars, 1974. — Translation of: 'Scener ur ett äktenskap'. Stockholm : Norstedt, 1973.
ISBN 0-552-68725-1 Pbk : £0.75
(B77-34264)

839.7'3'7F — Fiction in Swedish, 1900-. *Texts (including translations)*

Beckman, Gunnel. Mia alone / [by] Gunnel Beckman ; translated from the Swedish by Joan Tate. — [1st ed. reprinted] / [with editorial material prepared by Josie Levine]. — London : Longman, 1977. — 126,[18]p : ill, port ; 20cm. — (Knockouts)
This translation originally published: as 'The loneliness of Mia'. London : Bodley Head, 1975. — Translation of: 'Varen da allting hände'. Stockholm : Bonnier, 1974. — For adolescents.
ISBN 0-582-22274-5 Pbk : £0.60
(B77-31581)

Bergman, Ingmar. Four stories / by Ingmar Bergman ; translated from the Swedish by Alan Blair. — London : Boyars : Distributed by Calder and Boyars, 1977. — 168p ; 23cm.
'... the origins of four of Bergman's greatest movies' - jacket. — These translations originally published: Garden City, N.Y. : Doubleday, 1976. — Contents: The touch - Cries and whispers - The hour of the wolf - A passion.
ISBN 0-7145-2602-9 : £4.95
(B77-19062)

Jansson, Tove. Sun city / by Tove Jansson ; translated from the Swedish by Thomas Teal. — London : Hutchinson, 1977. — 160p ; 21cm.
This translation originally published: New York : Pantheon Books, 1976. — Translation of: 'Solstaden'. Stockholm : Bonnier, 1974.
ISBN 0-09-128390-6 : £3.50
(B77-16635)

Lundgren, Max. For the love of Lisa / [by] Max Lundgren ; translated by Joan Tate. — Basingstoke [etc.] : Macmillan, 1977. — 111p ; 18cm. — (Topliner redstars)
Translation of: 'Ole kallar mej Lise'. Stockholm : Bonnier, 1969. — For adolescents.
ISBN 0-333-21858-2 Pbk : £0.50 : CIP rev.
(B77-05679)

Sjöwall, Maj. The locked room : the story of a crime / [by] Maj Sjöwall and Per Wahlöö ; translated from the Swedish by Paul Britten Austin. — Harmondsworth [etc.] : Penguin, 1977. — 265p ; 18cm. — (Penguin crime fiction)
This translation originally published: New York : Pantheon Books, 1973 ; London : Gollancz, 1974. — Translation of: 'Det slutna rummet'. Stockholm : Norstedt, 1972.
ISBN 0-14-004247-4 Pbk : £0.80
(B77-12172)

Sjöwall, Maj. The terrorists / [by] Maj Sjöwall and Per Wahlöö ; translated from the Swedish by Joan Tate. — London : Gollancz, 1977. — [4],280p ; 21cm. — ([Gollancz detection])
This translation originally published: New York : Pantheon Books, 1976. — Translation of: 'Terroristerna'. Stockholm : P.A. Norstedt, 1975.
ISBN 0-575-02231-0 : £4.20
(B77-13943)

Wästberg, Per. Love's gravity / by Per Wästberg ; translated by Ann Henning. — London : Souvenir Press, 1977. — 359p ; 23cm.
Translation of: 'Jordmanen'. Stockholm ; Wahlström och Widstrand, 1972.
ISBN 0-285-62270-6 : £4.95
(B77-15006)

Winberg, Anna-Greta. When someone splits. — Basingstoke : Macmillan Education, Jan. 1978. — 1v. — (Topliner tridents)
Translation of: 'När nagon bara sticker'. Stockholm : Rabén och Sjögren, 1972. — Previous control number ISBN 0-333-22733-6. — For adolescents.
ISBN 0-333-23635-1 : CIP entry
(B77-32941)

839.7'3'7J — Children's stories in Swedish, 1900-. *Texts (including translations)*

Beckman, Gunnel. A room of his own / [by] Gunnel Beckman ; translated from the Swedish by Joan Tate. — Basingstoke [etc.] : Macmillan, 1976. — 108p ; 18cm. — (Topliner redstars)
This translation originally published: London : Bodley Head, 1973. — Translation of: 'Försök att första'. Stockholm : Bonnier, 1971. — For adolescents.
ISBN 0-333-19967-7 Pbk : £0.45
(B77-03269)

Gripe, Maria. Elvis and his secret / [by] Maria Gripe ; with drawings by Harald Gripe ; translated from the Swedish by Sheila La Farge. — London : Chatto and Windus, 1977. — [4], 153p : ill ; 21cm.
This translation originally published: New York : Delacorte Press, 1976. — Translation of: 'Elvis Karlsson'. Stockholm : Bonnier, 1972.
ISBN 0-7011-5098-x : £3.25 : CIP rev.
(B77-09359)

Gydal, Monica. Olly sees it through / by Monica Gydal & Thomas Danielsson ; pictures by Mats Andersson ; English text by Charles Ellis. — London [etc.] : Hodder and Stoughton.
In 6 vols.
5 : When Olly saw an accident. — 1977. — 3-30p : ill(chiefly col) ; 27cm.
Translation of: 'Sa var det när Ola sag en olycka'. Sweden : Sveriges Radios Forlag, 1975.
ISBN 0-340-21684-0 : £2.20
(B77-11457)

6 : When Olly moved house. — 1977. — 3-30p : col ill ; 27cm.
Translation of: 'Sa var det när Ola flyttade'. Sweden : Sveriges Radios Forlag, 1975.
ISBN 0-340-21683-2 : £2.20
(B77-11458)

Hellberg, Hans-Eric. Follow my leader / [by] Hans-Eric Hellberg ; translated by Joan Tate. — Basingstoke [etc.] : Macmillan, 1977. — 126p ; 18cm. — (Topliners)
Translation of: 'J & J'. Stockholm : Albert Bonniers Förlag, 1972.
ISBN 0-333-22749-2 Pbk : £0.45 : CIP rev.
(B77-19875)

Lagercrantz, Rose. Tulla's summer / [by] Rose Lagercrantz ; translated from the Swedish by George Blecher and Lone Thygesen-Blecher ; illustrated by Lady McCrady. — New York ; London : Harcourt Brace Jovanovich, 1977. — [6],121p : ill ; 21cm.
Translation of: 'Tullesommar'. Stockholm : Rabén och Sjögren, 1973.
ISBN 0-15-291095-6 : £4.50
(B77-32942)

Larsson, Carl. Our farm / [pictures by] Carl Larsson ; English version [i.e. translation from the Swedish] by Olive Jones. — London : Methuen, 1977. — [34]p : chiefly col ill ; 24x32cm.
Translation of: 'Spadarvet'. Stockholm : Bonniers, 1966.
ISBN 0-416-57190-5 : £3.50
(B77-10007)

Lindgren, Astrid. Emil in the soup tureen / [by] Astrid Lindgren ; translated from the Swedish by Lilian Seaton ; illustrated by Björn Berg. — London [etc.] : Beaver Books, 1977. — 94p : ill ; 20cm.
This translation originally published: Leicester : Brockhampton Press, 1970. — Translation of: 'Emil i Lönneberga'. Stockholm : Rabén och Sjögren, 1963.
ISBN 0-600-33160-1 Pbk : £0.45
(B77-31582)

Lindgren, Astrid. Karlson flies again / [by] Astrid Lindgren ; translated from the Swedish by Patricia Crampton ; illustrated by Ilon Wikland. — London : Methuen, 1977. — [5], 138p : ill ; 21cm.
Translation of: 'Karlsson pa taket flyger igen'. Stockholm : Rabén och Sjögren, 1962.
ISBN 0-416-58390-3 : £2.95
(B77-29782)

Lindgren, Astrid. Karlson on the roof / [by] Astrid Lindgren ; translated from the Swedish by Patricia Crampton ; illustrated by Ilon Wikland. — London : Methuen, 1977. — [5], 120p : ill ; 18cm.
This translation originally published: 1975. — Translation of: 'Lillebror och Karlsson pa taket'. Stockholm : Rabén och Sjögren, 1955.
ISBN 0-416-58010-6 Pbk : £0.60
(B77-10623)

Lindgren, Astrid. Pippi goes abroad / [by] Astrid Lindgren ; translated by Marianne Turner ; newly illustrated by Richard Kennedy. — Harmondsworth [etc.] : Puffin Books, 1977. — 173p : ill ; 19cm. — (Puffin books)
This translation originally published: London : Oxford University Press, 1956. — Translation of: 'Pippi Langstrump gar ombord'. Stockholm : Rabén och Sjögren, 1948.
ISBN 0-14-030913-6 Pbk : £0.50
(B77-15581)

Lindgren, Astrid. Pippi goes on board / [by] Astrid Lindgren ; translated [from the Swedish] by Florence Lamborn ; illustrated by Louis S. Glanzman. — Harmondsworth [etc.] : Puffin Books, 1977. — 140p : ill ; 20cm. — (Puffin books)
This translation originally published: New York : Viking Press, 1957. — Originally published: in Swedish. Stockholm : S.A., 1957.
Pbk : Unpriced
(B77-28252)

Lindgren, Astrid. Pippi in the South Seas / [by] Astrid Lindgren ; translated by Gerry Bothmer ; illustrated by Louis S. Glanzman. — Harmondsworth [etc.] : Puffin Books, 1977. — 125,[1]p : ill ; 20cm. — (Puffin books)
This translation originally published: New York : Viking Press, 1959. — Translation of: 'Pippi Langstrump i Söderhavet'. Stockholm : Rabén och Sjögren, 1955.
ISBN 0-14-030958-6 Pbk : Unpriced
(B77-24569)

Lindgren, Astrid. Pippi Longstocking / [by] Astrid Lindgren ; translated [from the Swedish] by Florence Lamborn ; illustrated by Louis S. Glanzman. — Harmondsworth [etc.] : Puffin Books, 1977. — 3-160p : ill ; 20cm. — (Puffin books)
This translation originally published: New York : Viking Press, 1950. — Translation of: 'Pippi Langstrump'. Stockholm : Rabén och Sjögren, 1945.
ISBN 0-14-030957-8 Pbk : £0.50
(B77-33493)

Löfgren, Ulf. Albin is never afraid / written and illustrated by Ulf Löfgren. — London : Macdonald and Jane's, 1975. — [26]p : col ill ; 24x28cm.
Translation of : 'Albin är aldrig rädd'. Stockholm : Almqvist och Wiksell, 1975.
ISBN 0-356-08155-9 : £1.00
(B77-19063)

Löfgren, Ulf. Albin lends a hand / written and illustrated by Ulf Löfgren. — London : Macdonald and Jane's, 1975. — [25]p : col ill ; 24x28cm.
Translation of: 'Albin hjälper till'. Stockholm : Almqvist och Wiksell, 1975.
ISBN 0-356-08156-7 : £1.00
(B77-19064)

Wolde, Gunilla. Emma and the doctor / [illustrated by] Gunilla Wolde ; English text Alison Winn. — London [etc.] : Hodder and Stoughton, 1977. — [24]p : chiefly col ill ; 17cm.
These illustrations originally published: with Swedish text. Stockholm : Almqvist och Wiksell, 1976.
ISBN 0-340-21546-1 : £0.85
(B77-11459)

Wolde, Gunilla. Emma's workshop / [illustrated by] Gunilla Wolde ; English text Alison Winn. — London [etc.] : Hodder and Stoughton, 1977. — [24]p : chiefly col ill ; 17cm.
These illustrations originally published: with Swedish text. Stockholm : Almqvist och Wiksell, 1976.
ISBN 0-340-21545-3 : £0.85
(B77-11460)

839.81 — DANISH LITERATURE
839.8'1'16 — Poetry in Danish, 1800-1900. *Danish-English parallel texts*

Andersen, Hans Christian. The Snow Queen, and other poems / [by] Hans Christian Andersen ; translated for the first time into English verse by Anne Born. — [Richmond, Surrey] : Keepsake Press, 1977. — 16p ; 23cm.
Parallel Danish text and English translation, English introduction. — Limited ed. of 185 copies.
ISBN 0-901924-42-3 Sd : £0.45
(B77-19065)

Hatzfeld-Rea, Maud Eleanor. Lone journey through yesterday / [by] M.E. Hatzfeld-Rea. — Ilfracombe : Stockwell, 1976. — 119p,[8]p of plates ; 18cm.
ISBN 0-7223-0945-7 Pbk : £1.75
(B77-12788)

839.8'1'36 — Fiction in Danish, 1800-1900. *English texts*

Andersen, Hans Christian. [Fairy tales. English]. Hans Andersen's fairy tales : a selection. — Maidenhead : Purnell, 1977. — 138p : 1 ill ; 21cm. — (A Purnell classic)
This collection originally published: London : Bancroft, 1966.
ISBN 0-361-03559-4 : £0.50
(B77-22959)

Andersen, Hans Christian. [Fairy tales. English]. Hans Christian Andersen's fairy tales / illustrations by Jenny Thorne. — Maidenhead : Purnell, 1977. — 188p,[8] leaves of plates : ill(some col) ; 21cm. — (A Purnell de luxe classic)
ISBN 0-361-03870-4 : £1.50
(B77-25972)

839.8'1'37F — Fiction in Danish, 1900-. *Texts (including translations)*

Hassel, Sven. Assignment Gestapo / [by] Sven Hassel ; translated [from the French] by Jean Ure. — London : Allison and Busby, 1976. — 347p ; 23cm.
This translation originally published: London : Corgi, 1971. — Translation of: 'Camarades de front'. Paris : Presses de la Cité, 1965. — Originally published: in Danish as 'Gestapo'. Kobenhaven : Grafisk, 1963.
ISBN 0-85031-197-7 : £3.95
(B77-29018)

Hassel, Sven. The bloody road to death / [by] Sven Hassel ; [translated from the Danish by Tim Bowie]. — London : Corgi, 1977. — 317p ; 18cm.
Originally published: in Danish. Denmark : s.n., 1977?.
ISBN 0-552-10400-0 Pbk : £0.85
(B77-17158)

839.8'1'37J — Children's stories in Danish, 1900-. *Texts (including translations)*

Bodker, Cecil. Leopard / [by] Cecil Bodker ; translated [from the Danish] by Solomon Deressa and Gunnar Poulsen. — Oxford [etc.] : Oxford University Press, 1977. — [4],138p ; 23cm.
This translation originally published: New York : Atheneum, 1975. — Translation of: 'Leoparden'. Kobenhavn : Branner og Korch, 1970.
ISBN 0-19-271414-7 : £2.95 : CIP rev.
(B77-20754)

S., Svend Otto. Jasper the taxi dog / [by] Svend Otto S. ; translated by Joan Tate. — London : Pelham, 1977. — [26]p : col ill ; 26cm.
Col. ill., text on lining paper. — Translation of: 'Taxa-hunden Jesper'. Copenhagen : Gyldendalske Boghandel, 1977.
ISBN 0-7207-0965-2 : £2.50
(B77-22226)

S., Svend Otto. Tim and Trisha / [by] Svend Otto S. ; translated by Joan Tate. — London : Pelham, 1977. — [24]p : col ill ; 22x27cm.
Col. ill., text on lining papers. — Translation of: 'Tim og Trine'. Copenhagen : Gyldendalske Boghandel, 1976.
ISBN 0-7207-0930-x : £2.50
(B77-12764)

839.82 — NORWEGIAN LITERATURE
839.8'2'26 — Drama in Norwegian, 1800-1900. *English texts*

Ibsen, Henrik. The Oxford Ibsen. — Oxford [etc.] : Oxford University Press.
In 8 vols.
Vol.8 : Little Eyolf, John Gabriel Borkman, When we dead awaken / edited and translated [from the Norwegian] by James Walter McFarlane. — 1977. — xiii,390p ; 23cm.
Bibl.: p.383-390.
ISBN 0-19-211387-9 : £10.50 : CIP rev.
(B77-17159)

839.8'2'36 — Fiction in Norwegian, 1800-1900. *English texts*

Hamsun, Knut. Victoria : a love story / by Knut Hamsun ; newly translated from the Norwegian by Oliver Stallybrass. — London : Pan Books, 1977. — 128p ; 20cm. — (Picador)
This translation originally published: New York : Farrar, Straus and Giroux, 1969 ; London : Souvenir Press, 1974.
ISBN 0-330-24887-1 Pbk : £0.75
(B77-06945)

Hamsun, Knut. The wanderer / [by] Knut Hamsun ; translated from the Norwegian by Oliver and Gunnvor Stallybrass. — London : Pan Books, 1977. — 253p ; 20cm. — (Picador)
This translation originally published: New York : Farrar, Straus and Giroux ; London : Souvenir Press, 1975. — Contents: Under the autumn star. Translation of: 'Under hoststjernen. 1906 - On muted strings. Translation of: 'En vandrer spiller med sordin'. Kristiania og Kobenhavn : Gyldendalske boghandel, Nordisk forlag, 1909.
ISBN 0-330-25150-3 Pbk : £0.95
(B77-22227)

839.8'2'37F — Fiction in Norwegian, 1900-. *Texts (including translations)*

Masterson, Louis. The demon from Nicaragua / [by] Louis Masterson. — London : Corgi, 1976. — 126p ; 18cm.
Originally published: in Norwegian. Oslo : Bladkompaniet, 1970.
ISBN 0-552-10331-4 Pbk : £0.45
(B77-04453)

Undset, Sigrid. Kristin Lavransdatter / [by] Sigrid Undset ; translated from the Norwegian by Charles Archer and J.S. Scott. — London : Pan Books, 1977. — 3-956p : 1 ill, plans ; 20cm. — (Picador)
This translation originally published: New York : Knopf, 1929 ; London : Cassell, 1930. — Translation of: 'Kristin Lavransdatter'. Oslo : H. Aschehoug, 1920-22. — Contents: The garland / translated by Charles Archer and J.S. Scott. This translation originally published: London : Gyldendal, 1922. Translation of: 'Kransen'. Oslo : H. Aschehoug, 1920 - The mistress of Husaby / translated by Charles Archer. This translation originally published: New York : Knopf ; London : Gyldendal, 1925. Translation of: 'Husfrue'. Oslo : H. Aschehoug, 1922 - The cross / translated by Charles Archer. This translation originally published : New York ; London : Knopf, 1927. Translation of: 'Korset'. Oslo : H. Aschehoug, 1922.
ISBN 0-330-25202-x Pbk : £2.50
(B77-26645)

839.8'2'37J — Children's stories in Norwegian, 1900-. *Texts (including translations)*

Vestly, Anne-Catharina. Eight children and a truck / [by] Anne-Cath. Vestly ; translated from the Norwegian by Patricia Crampton ; illustrated by John Dyke. — London : Methuen, 1977. — 188p : ill ; 18cm.
This translation originally published: 1973. — Translation of: 'Atte sma, to store og en lastebil'. Oslo : Tiden Norsk, 1957.
ISBN 0-416-58170-6 Pbk : £0.60
(B77-21552)

Vestly, Anne-Catharina. Eight children and Rosie / [by] Anne-Cath. Vestly ; translated from the Norwegian by Patricia Crampton ; illustrated by John Dyke. — London : Methuen, 1977. — 127p : ill ; 21cm.
Translation of: 'En liten takk fra Anton'. Oslo : Tiden Norsk Forlag, 1960.
ISBN 0-416-55130-0 : £2.25
(B77-17160)

Vestly, Anne-Catharina. Hallo Aurora! / [by] Anne-Cath. Vestly ; translated from the Norwegian by Eileen Amos ; illustrated by Gunvor Edwards. — Harmondsworth [etc.] : Puffin Books, 1977. — 160p : ill ; 19cm. — (A young puffin)
This translation originally published: Harmondsworth : Longman Young Books, 1973. — Translation of: 'Aurora i blokk Z'. Oslo : Tiden Norsk, 1966.
ISBN 0-14-030935-7 Pbk : £0.50
(B77-24570)

840 — ROMANCE LITERATURES

840 — Poetry in Romance languages, 1327-1625. Special subjects: Love. *Anthologies*

Fifty Renascence love-poems / translated by Edwin Morgan ; [selected by Ian Fletcher]. — Reading ([c/o Department of Typography and Graphic Communication, University of Reading, 2 Earley Gate, Whiteknights, Reading RG6 2AU]) : Whiteknights Press, 1975. — 80p ; 19cm.
Limited ed. of 200 copies. — Parallel Italian, French and Spanish texts and English translations.
ISBN 0-7049-0104-8 Pbk : Unpriced
(B77-19876)

840'.3 — French literature. *Encyclopaedias*

The **concise** Oxford dictionary of French literature / edited by Joyce M.H. Reid. — [Abridged ed.]. — Oxford : Clarendon Press, 1976. — [6],670p : map ; 21cm.
Full ed. originally published as: 'The Oxford companion to French literature' / compiled and edited by Sir Paul Harvey and J.E. Heseltine. 1959.
ISBN 0-19-866118-5 : £5.95
ISBN 0-19-281200-9 Pbk : £2.95
(B77-01873)

840.9 — FRENCH LITERATURE. HISTORY AND CRITICAL STUDIES

840'.9 — French literature, 1100-1945. Classicism. *Festschriften*

The **classical** tradition in French literature : essays presented to R.C. Knight by colleagues, pupils and friends / edited by H.T. Barnwell ... [et al.]. — London : Grant and Cutler, 1977. — [4],256p ; 23cm.
Bibl.: p.5-8.
ISBN 0-7293-0052-8 Pbk : £8.00
(B77-31583)

840'.9 — French literature. Criticism. Barthes, Roland. *Autobiographies*

Barthes, Roland. Roland Barthes / translated [from the French] by Richard Howard. — London [etc.] : Macmillan, 1977. — [4],188p : ill, facsims, ports ; 21cm.
Translation of: 'Roland Barthes'. Paris : Seuil, 1975.
ISBN 0-333-22665-8 : £7.95
(B77-25973)

840'.9 — French literature. Criticism. Barthes, Roland. *Critical studies*

Thody, Philip. Roland Barthes : a conservative estimate / [by] Philip Thody. — London [etc.] : Macmillan, 1977. — x,180p ; 23cm.
Bibl.: p.158-159. — Index.
ISBN 0-333-21926-0 : £8.95
(B77-31584)

840'.9 — French literature. Influence of German literature, 1770-1895

Furst, Lilian Renée. Counterparts : the dynamics of Franco-German literary relationships, 1770-1895 / [by] Lilian R. Furst. — London : Methuen, 1977. — xi,201p ; 23cm.
Bibl.: p.185-191. — Index.
ISBN 0-416-67360-0 : Unpriced
Primary classification 830'.9
(B77-28247)

840'.9'007 — French literature, 1815-1900. Compared with English literature, 1800-1900

Sabin, Margery. English Romanticism and the French tradition / [by] Margery Sabin. — Cambridge, Mass. ; London : Harvard University Press, 1976. — xv,294p ; 24cm.
Index.
ISBN 0-674-25686-7 : £11.25
Primary classification 820'.9'007
(B77-05599)

840'.9'00912 — French literature, 1900-1961. Political aspects

Flower, John Ernest. Writers and politics in modern France (1909-1961) / [by] J.E. Flower. — London [etc.] : Hodder and Stoughton, 1977. — vii,78p ; 22cm.
Bibl.: p.vi-vii.
ISBN 0-340-18439-6 Pbk : £1.50
(B77-16636)

840'.9'96 — French literature. African writers, to 1975. *Critical studies*

Blair, Dorothy Sara. African literature in French : a history of creative writing in French from West and Equatorial Africa / [by] Dorothy S. Blair. — Cambridge [etc.] : Cambridge University Press, 1976. — xx,348p : map, port ; 24cm.
Bibl.: p.324-339. — Index.
ISBN 0-521-21195-6 : £12.50
(B77-01874)

841 — FRENCH POETRY

841 — Poetry in French. Belgian writers. Michaux, Henri. *Critical studies*

Broome, Peter. Henri Michaux / by Peter Broome. — London : Athlone Press, 1977. — [6],153p ; 21cm. — (Athlone French poets)
Bibl.: p.150-151. — Index.
ISBN 0-485-14605-3 : £5.75
ISBN 0-485-12205-7 Pbk : £2.50
(B77-25974)

841'.008 — Poetry in French, ca 1600-1900. *Anthologies*

Selected poems of Théophile de Viau, André Chénier, Victor Hugo / edited with notes by S.A. Warman, M.J. O'Regan, T.D. Hemming. — Bristol ([Wills Memorial Building, Queen's Rd, Bristol BS8 1RJ]) : University of Bristol, Department of French, 1976. — 142p ; 21cm.
French text, English introductory material and notes. — Bibl.: p.5-6.
ISBN 0-905580-00-1 Pbk : £1.85
(B77-09360)

841.1 — FRENCH POETRY, TO 1400

841'.1 — Poetry in Anglo-Norman, to 1400. *Texts*

Thomas of Kent. [Le roman de toute chevalerie]. The Anglo-Norman 'Alexander' : (Le roman de toute chevalerie) / by Thomas of Kent ; edited by Brian Foster with the assistance of Ian Short. — London (c/o Westfield College, NW3 7ST) : Anglo-Norman Text Society. — (Anglo-Norman Text Society. Publications ; nos. 29-31) (Anglo-Norman texts)
Vol.1 : Texts and variants. — 1976. — [5], 300p,plate : facsim ; 23cm.
ISBN 0-905474-01-5 : £9.00
(B77-26646)

La **vie** de Saint Laurent : an Anglo-Norman poem of the twelfth century / edited by D.W. Russell. — London (c/o Westfield College, NW3 7ST) : Anglo-Norman Text Society, 1976. — x,78p,plate : facsim ; 23cm. — (Anglo-Norman Text Society. Publications ; no.34) (Anglo-Norman texts)
A critical text based on the two extant MSS. in the Bibliothèque nationale and the British Library. — Bibl.: p.v. — Index.
ISBN 0-905474-00-7 : £4.00
(B77-23801)

841'.1 — Poetry in Old French. *Texts*

Renart, Jehan. Le lay de l'ombre / [by] Jean Renart ; edited from Ms B.N. Nouvelles Acquisitions 1104 ; text and glossary established by B.J. Levy, A. Hindley ; notes by F.W. Langley ; introduction by C.E. Pickford. — [Hull] ([Hull HU6 7RX]) : University of Hull, Department of French, 1976. — [2],xvi,80p ; 21cm.
Old French text, English introduction and notes. — Bibl.: p.xii-xiii.
ISBN 0-85958-520-4 Sp : £1.00
(B77-17800)

841'.1'08023 — Poetry in Old French. Fabliaux. *Anthologies*

Selected fabliaux / edited from B.N. Fonds Français 837, Fonds Français 19152 and Berlin Hamilton 257 by B.J. Levy ; with notes by C.E. Pickford. — [Hull] ([Hull HU6 7RX]) : [University of Hull, Department of French], 1976. — [1],xvii,154p : ill ; 21cm.
Middle French text, English introduction and notes. — Bibl.: p.xiii-xv. — Index.
Sp : £1.00
ISBN 0-85958-515-8
(B77-01875)

841.3 — FRENCH POETRY, 1500-1600

841'.3 — Poetry in French, 1500-1600. *Texts*

Ronsard, Pierre de. Ronsard / selected and edited by Grahame Castor and Terence Cave. — Manchester : Manchester University Press. In 2 vols.
2 : Odes, hymns and other poems. — 1977. — xiii,289p ; 22cm.
French text, English preface and notes. — Index.
ISBN 0-7190-0673-2 Pbk : £4.50
(B77-22960)

841'.3 — Poetry in French. La Ceppède, Jean de. *Critical studies*

Chilton, Paul A. The poetry of Jean de La Ceppède : a study in text and context / by Paul A. Chilton. — Oxford [etc.] : Oxford University Press, 1977. — ix,240p ; 22cm. — (Oxford modern languages and literature monographs)
Bibl.: p.224-236. — Index.
ISBN 0-19-815529-8 : £10.00 : CIP rev.
(B77-08645)

841'.3'08 — Poetry in French, 1500-1600. *Anthologies*

Chanson verse of the early Renaissance / edited by Brian Jeffery. — London (Preachers' Court, Charterhouse, EC1M 6AS) : Tecla Editions. Vol.2. — 1976. — 3-374p ; 21cm.
Index.
ISBN 0-9502241-1-1 Pbk : £8.00
ISBN 84-399-5991-5
(B77-07688)

841'.3'09354 — Poetry in French, 1500-1600. Special themes: Love. *Critical studies*

Minta, Stephen. Love poetry in sixteenth-century France : a study in themes and traditions / [by] Stephen Minta. — Manchester : Manchester University Press, 1977. — vii,173p ; 23cm.
Bibl.: p.167-173.
ISBN 0-7190-0676-7 : £8.50 : CIP rev.
(B77-22228)

841.7 — FRENCH POETRY, 1815-1848
841'.7 — Poetry in French. Hugo, Victor. Contemplations, Les. *Critical studies*
Nash, Suzanne. 'Les contemplations' of Victor Hugo : an allegory of the creative process / by Suzanne Nash. — Princeton ; Guildford : Princeton University Press, [1977]. — xi,229p : 1 ill ; 23cm.
Published in the United States: 1976. — Bibl.: p.209-221. — Index. — Includes extracts in French from 'Les contemplations'.
ISBN 0-691-06313-3 : £10.60
(B77-12765)

841.8 — FRENCH POETRY, 1848-1900
841'.8 — Poetry in French, 1848-1900. *French-English parallel texts*
Mallarmé, Stéphane. The poems [of] Mallarmé. — Bilingual ed. / translated [from the French] with an introduction by Keith Bosley. — Harmondsworth [etc.] : Penguin, 1977. — 303p ; 19cm. — (Penguin poets)
Index.
ISBN 0-14-042203-x Pbk : £1.50
(B77-26647)

Rimbaud, Arthur. Complete works, selected letters [of] Rimbaud / translation, introduction and notes by Wallace Fowlie. — Chicago ; London : University of Chicago Press, 1975. — xi,370p : port ; 21cm.
Parallel French text and English translation. — These translations originally published: 1966. — Index.
ISBN 0-226-71972-3 : Unpriced
ISBN 0-226-71973-1 Pbk : Unpriced
(B77-00486)

841'.8 — Poetry in French, 1848-1900. *Texts*
Laforgue, Jules. Les complaintes / [par] Jules Laforgue ; edited by Michael Collie. — London : Athlone Press, 1977. — viii,184p ; 21cm. — (Athlone French poets)
French text, English introduction and commentaries. — Bibl.: p.182-184.
ISBN 0-485-14713-0 : £6.50
ISBN 0-485-12713-x Pbk : £2.50
(B77-22961)

841'.8 — Poetry in French. Baudelaire, Charles. *Biographies*
De Jonge, Alex. Baudelaire, prince of clouds : a biography / by Alex de Jonge. — New York ; London : Paddington Press, 1976. — 240p : port ; 25cm.
Bibl.: p.236. — Index.
ISBN 0-8467-0137-5 : £5.95
(B77-18432)

841'.8 — Poetry in French. Laforgue, Jules. *Critical studies*
Collie, Michael. Jules Laforgue / by Michael Collie. — London : Athlone Press, 1977. — [10],134p ; 21cm. — (Athlone French poets)
Bibl.: p.129-132. — Index.
ISBN 0-485-14606-1 : £5.75
ISBN 0-485-12206-5 Pbk : £2.50
(B77-25975)

841'.8 — Poetry in French. Rimbaud, Arthur. *Biographies*
Bonnefoy, Yves. Rimbaud / [by] Yves Bonnefoy ; translated [from the French] by Paul Schmidt. — New York [etc.] ; London : Harper and Row, 1973. — [5],145p : port ; 21cm. — (Harper colophon books)
Translation of: 'Rimbaud par lui-même'. Paris : Éditions du Seuil, 1961.
ISBN 0-06-090297-3 Pbk : Unpriced
(B77-20755)

841.912 — FRENCH POETRY, 1900-1945
841'.9'12 — National libraries. *Scotland. National Library of Scotland. Exhibits: Items associated with Valéry, Paul. Catalogues*
National Library of Scotland. Paul Valéry / National Library of Scotland. — Edinburgh ([George IV Bridge, Edinburgh EH1 1EW]) : [The Library], 1976. — [1],10,[18] leaves ; 30cm.
Catalogue of an exhibition.
ISBN 0-902220-19-5 Sd : £0.30
(B77-16637)

841'.9'12 — Poetry in French, 1900-1945. *English texts*
Frénaud, André. A round O : eighteen poems / [by] André Frénaud ; selected and translated [from the French] by Keith Bosley. — Egham (4 Northcroft Villas, Northcroft Rd, Englefield Green, Egham, Surrey TW20 0DZ) : Interim Press, 1977. — 29,[1]p ; 22cm.
Limited ed. of 250 copies.
ISBN 0-904675-08-4 Sd : £0.40
(B77-28253)

841'.9'12 — Poetry in French, 1900-1945. *French-English parallel texts*
Cendrars, Blaise. Complete postcards from the Americas : poems of road and sea / [by] Blaise Cendrars ; translated, with an introduction, by Monique Chefdor. — Berkeley [etc.] ; London : University of California Press, 1976. — viii, 251p,[8]p of plates : ill, facsim, ports ; 22cm.
Parallel French text and English translation. — Bibl.: p.247-251. — Contents include: Documentaires. Originally published: as 'Kodak (documentaire)'. Paris : Stock, 1924.
ISBN 0-520-02716-7 : £8.00
(B77-12766)

Char, René. Poems of René Char / translated and annotated by Mary Ann Caws and Jonathan Griffin. — Princeton ; Guildford : Princeton University Press, 1976. — xxxii,292[i. e.294],[4]p of plates : ill, facsims, ports ; 23cm. — (The Lockert library of poetry in translation)
Parallel French text and English translation.
ISBN 0-691-06297-8 : £10.50
ISBN 0-691-01325-x Pbk : £3.45
(B77-03800)

Saint-John Perse. Song for an equinox / [by] St-John Perse ; translated from the French by Richard Howard. — Princeton ; Guildford : Princeton University Press, 1977. — [5],32p ; 21cm. — (Bollingen series ; 69, 2)
Parallel French text and English translation. — French text originally published: as 'Chant pour un équinoxe'. Paris : Gallimard, 1975.
ISBN 0-691-09938-3 : £3.80
(B77-28254)

841'.9'12 — Poetry in French, 1900-1945. *Texts*
Michaux, Henri. Au pays de la magie / [by] Henri Michaux ; edited by Peter Broome. — London : Athlone Press, 1977. — [9],146p ; 21cm. — (Athlone French poets)
French text, English introduction and commentaries. — Bibl.: p.145-146.
ISBN 0-485-14711-4 : £6.00
ISBN 0-485-12711-3 Pbk : £2.75
(B77-20756)

841'.9'12 — Poetry in French. American writers. Barney, Natalie Clifford. *Biographies*
Wickes, George. The Amazon of letters : the life and loves of Natalie Barney / by George Wickes. — London : W.H. Allen, 1977. — 286p,[16]p of plates : ill, ports ; 22cm.
Also published: New York : Putnam, 1977. — Bibl.: p.273-278. — Index.
ISBN 0-491-01608-5 : £5.95
(B77-09361)

841'.9'12 — Poetry in French. Apollinaire, Guillaume. *Critical studies*
Little, Roger. Guillaume Apollinaire / by Roger Little. — London : Athlone Press, 1976. — x, 145p ; 21cm. — (Athlone French poets)
Bibl.: p.137-139. — Index.
ISBN 0-485-14608-8 : £5.50
ISBN 0-485-12208-1 Pbk : £2.50
(B77-03801)

841'.9'12 — Poetry in French. Char, René. *Critical studies*
Caws, Mary Ann. The presence of René Char / [by] Mary Ann Caws. — Princeton ; Guildford : Princeton University Press, 1976. — xii,336,[1]p : facsims, port ; 23cm.
Index.
ISBN 0-691-06305-2 : £11.50
(B77-05091)

841'.9'1209 — Poetry in French, 1900- . Poets. Sensibility. Expounded by imagery
Sensibility and creation : studies in twentieth-century French poetry / edited by Roger Cardinal. — London : Croom Helm [etc.], 1977. — [4],252p ; 23cm.
Bibl.: p.241-250.
ISBN 0-85664-339-4 : £7.95
(B77-07689)

841.914 — FRENCH POETRY, 1945-
841'.9'14 — Poetry in French, 1945-. *Texts*
Beckett, Samuel. Collected poems in English and French / [by] Samuel Beckett. — London : J. Calder : [Distributed by Calder and Boyars], 1977. — xi,147p ; 21cm.
ISBN 0-7145-3608-3 : £4.50
ISBN 0-7145-3613-x Pbk : Unpriced
Primary classification 821'.9'12
(B77-16566)

842 — FRENCH DRAMA
842 — Drama in French. Belgian writers, 1848-1900. *Texts*
Quillard, Pierre. La fille aux mains coupees / [par] Pierre Quillard ; et, Les flaireurs / [par] Charles van Lerberghe ; textes établis et présentés par Jeremy Whistle. — [Exeter] : University of Exeter, 1976. — xxiv,36,[1]p ; 21cm. — (Textes littéraires ; 22)
Cover title: Deux pièces symbolistes. — 'La fille aux mains coupees' originally published: Paris : s.n., 1886. — 'Les flaireurs' originally published: Bruxelles : Lacomblez, 1894. — Bibl. : p.33-36.
ISBN 0-85989-086-4 Pbk : £0.60
Primary classification 842'.8
(B77-16097)

842'.052 — Drama in French. Comedies, 1552-1784. *Critical studies*
Brereton, Geoffrey. French comic drama : from the sixteenth to the eighteenth century / [by] Geoffrey Brereton. — London : Methuen, 1977. — x,290p ; 23cm.
Bibl.: p.277-284. — Index.
ISBN 0-416-78220-5 : £6.00
ISBN 0-416-80710-0 Pbk : £3.00
(B77-16638)

842.3 — FRENCH DRAMA, 1500-1600
842'.3 — Drama in French, 1500-1600. *Texts*
Garnier, Robert. Les Juifves / [par] Robert Garnier ; text presented by Keith Cameron. — Exeter (24 Velwell Rd, Exeter) : Elm Bank Publications, 1977. — [1],x,92p : 1 ill ; 21cm.
French text, English introduction. — 'Appendix A provides the English translation of a passage from the "Jewish Antiquities" ... [of Josephus]. Appendix B ... gives a translation of the dedicatory poem in Latin to "Les Juifves" and also a commentary ...' - Introduction. — Bibl.: p.x.
Sd : £1.00
(B77-16639)

842.4 — FRENCH DRAMA, 1600-1715
842'.4 — Drama in French, 1600-1715. *Texts*
Corneille, Pierre. Horace / [by] Corneille ; edited with an introduction and notes by Peter H. Nurse. — London : Harrap, 1976. — 159p,[3] leaves of plates : ill, facsim ; 17cm. — (Harrap's French classics)
French text, English introduction and notes. — Originally published: 1963. — Bibl.: p.62-63.
ISBN 0-245-53041-x Pbk : £1.40
(B77-10987)

842'.4 — Drama in French. Molière. *Critical studies*
McBride, Robert. The sceptical vision of Molière : a study in paradox / [by] Robert McBride. — London [etc.] : Macmillan, 1977. — xii,250p ; 23cm.
Bibl.: p.242-247. — Index.
ISBN 0-333-21180-4 : £10.00
(B77-21553)

842.5 — FRENCH DRAMA, 1715-1789
842'.5 — Drama in French, 1715-1789. *Texts*
Beaumarchais, Pierre Augustin Caron de. Le mariage de Figaro / [by] Beaumarchais ; edited with an introduction and notes by Louis Allen. — London : Harrap, 1976. — lxii,168p : ill, port ; 17cm. — (Harrap's French classics)
French text, English introduction and notes. — Originally published: 1952. — Bibl.: p.lx-lxii.
ISBN 0-245-53024-x Pbk : £1.50
(B77-10988)

842'.5 — Drama in French. Beaumarchais, Pierre Augustin Caron de. *Biographies*
Grendel, Frédéric. Beaumarchais : the man who was Figaro / [by] Frédéric Grendel ; translated from the French by Roger Greaves. — London : Macdonald and Jane's, 1977. — viii, 305p,[8]p of plates : ill, plan, ports ; 25cm.
Translation of: 'Beaumarchais, ou, La calomnie'. Paris : Flammarion, 1973. — Bibl.: p.299-300. — Index.
ISBN 0-354-04021-9 : £6.95
(B77-22962)

842.8 — FRENCH DRAMA, 1848-1900
842'.8 — Drama in French, 1848-1900. *Texts*
Quillard, Pierre. La fille aux mains coupees / [par] Pierre Quillard ; et, Les flaireurs / [par] Charles van Lerberghe ; textes établis et présentés par Jeremy Whistle. — [Exeter] : University of Exeter, 1976. — xxiv,36,[1]p ; 21cm. — (Textes littéraires ; 22)
Cover title: Deux pièces symbolistes. — 'La fille aux mains coupees' originally published: Paris : s.n., 1886. — 'Les flaireurs' originally published: Bruxelles : Lacomblez, 1894. — Bibl. : p.33-36.
ISBN 0-85989-086-4 Pbk : £0.60
Also classified at 842
(B77-16097)

842.912 — FRENCH DRAMA, 1900-1945
842'.9'12 — Drama in French, 1900-1945. *Texts*
Camus, Albert. Les justes / by Albert Camus ; edited by Edward O. Marsh. — London : Harrap, 1976. — 108p : port ; 19cm.
French text, English introduction and notes. — Originally published: 1960. — Bibl.: p.33-34.
ISBN 0-245-53036-3 Pbk : £1.25
(B77-10989)

Cocteau, Jean. Orphée : the play and the film / [by] Jean Cocteau ; edited with an introduction and selection of film-stills by E. Freeman. — Oxford : Blackwell, 1976. — xliii,129p,16p of plates : ill, plan, ports ; 19cm. — (Blackwell's French texts)
French texts, English introduction and notes. — Bibl.: p.xliii. — Contents: Orphée. Originally published: Paris : s.n., 1927 - Orphée, film. Originally published: Paris : Editions de la Parade, 1951.
ISBN 0-631-00720-2 Pbk : £3.25
Also classified at 791.43'7
(B77-05742)

Montherlant, Henry de. Port-Royal / [by] Henry de Montherlant. — Critical ed. / by Richard Griffiths. — Oxford : Blackwell, 1976. — lxv, 97p ; 19cm. — (Blackwell's French texts)
French text, English introduction and notes. — 'Port Royal' originally published: Paris : Gallimard, 1954. — Bibl.: p.lxii-lxv.
ISBN 0-631-00730-x Pbk : £3.00
(B77-05743)

843 — FRENCH FICTION
843 — Fiction in French. African writers, 1945-. *Critical studies*
Gakwandi, Shatto Arthur. The novel and contemporary experience in Africa / [by] Shatto Arthur Gakwandi. — London [etc.] : Heinemann Educational, 1977. — [6],136p ; 23cm.
Bibl.: p.131-132. — Index.
ISBN 0-435-91320-4 : £5.00
ISBN 0-435-91321-2 Pbk : £1.90
Primary classification 823
(B77-34058)

843'.01 — Short stories in French. Anthologie de contes et nouvelles modernes. Comprehension. *Exercises, worked examples. For Irish students. Secondary school texts*
Hogan, Denise. Conlon's 'Anthologie de contes et nouvelles modernes' : questions and vocabulary / [par] Denise Hogan. — [Tallaght] : Folens, [1977]. — 42p ; 22cm.
French text, English introduction.
Sd : £0.45
(B77-22229)

843.1 — FRENCH FICTION, TO 1400
843'.1 — Fiction in Old French. *Middle French texts. Facsimiles*
Gyron le courtoys / introductory note by C.E. Pickford. — London : Scolar Press, 1977. — ca 500p : ill ; 36cm. — (Arthurian romances ; 4)
'... a reproduction of the copy of "Gyron le Courtoys" now in the National Library of Wales' - Introductory note. — Facsimile reprint of: the edition published Paris : Verard, ca 1501.
ISBN 0-85967-353-7 : £35.00
(B77-30803)

843.4 — FRENCH FICTION, 1600-1715
843'.4 — Fiction in French, 1600-1715. *English texts*
Perrault, Charles. The fairy tales of Charles Perrault / translated [from the French] and with a foreword by Angela Carter ; illustrated with etchings by Martin Ware. — London : Gollancz, 1977. — 159p : ill ; 24cm.
Ill. on lining papers. — Bibl.: p.159.
ISBN 0-575-02279-5 : £3.50
(B77-26648)

843'.4 — Fiction in French, 1600-1715. *Texts*
Dufresny, Charles. Amusemens sérieux et comiques / [par] Charles Dufresny ; texte présenté et annoté par John Dunkley. — [Exeter] : University of Exeter, 1976. — xxxiv, 98p : 1 ill, facsims ; 21cm. — (Textes littéraires ; 23)
Originally published: Paris : Chez Claude Barbin, 1699. — Bibl.: p.92-97.
ISBN 0-85989-091-0 Sd : £1.00
(B77-17161)

Horry, Nicolas. Rabelais ressuscité / [par] Nicolas Horry. — [1. éd., réimprimée] / texte présenté et annoté par Neil Goodley. — [Exeter] : University of Exeter, 1976. — xlix, 50p : facsim ; 21cm. — (Textes littéraires)
Originally published: Rouen : Jean Petit ; Paris : A. du Brueil, 1611. — This reprint is based on the A. du Brueil edition.
ISBN 0-85989-006-6 Pbk : £1.00
(B77-04454)

843.5 — FRENCH FICTION, 1715-1789
843'.5 — Fiction in French, 1715-1789. *English texts*
Diderot, Denis. [La religieuse. English]. The nun / [by] Denis Diderot ; translated from the French with an introduction by Leonard Tancock. — Harmondsworth [etc.] : Penguin, 1977. — 189p ; 19cm. — (The Penguin classics)

This translation originally published: London : Folio Society, 1972.
Pbk : £0.55
ISBN 0-14-044300-2
(B77-26649)

Laclos, Pierre Ambroise François Choderlos de. [Les liaisons dangereuses. English]. Les liaisons dangereuses / [by] Choderlos de Laclos ; translated [from the French] and with an introduction by P.W.K. Stone. — Harmondsworth [etc.] : Penguin, 1977. — 396p ; 18cm. — (The Penguin classics)
This translation originally published: 1961.
Pbk : £0.85
ISBN 0-14-044116-6
(B77-28255)

Montesquieu, Charles Louis de Secondat, *baron de.* [Lettres persanes. English]. Persian letters / [by] Montesquieu ; translated [from the French] with an introduction and notes by C.J. Betts. — Harmondsworth [etc.] : Penguin, 1977. — 342p ; 18cm. — (The Penguin classics)
This translation originally published: 1973. — Bibl.: p.35-36.
Pbk : £0.95
ISBN 0-14-044281-2
(B77-29019)

843.6 — FRENCH FICTION, 1789-1815
843'.6 — Fiction in French. Sade, Donatien Alphonse François, Marquis de. *Biographies*
Thomas, Donald. The Marquis de Sade / [by] Donald Thomas. — London : Weidenfeld and Nicolson, 1976. — x,214p : ill, facsim, ports ; 26cm.
Bibl.: p.208-210. — Index.
ISBN 0-297-77140-x : £5.95
(B77-12767)

843.7 — FRENCH FICTION, 1815-1848
843'.7 — Fiction in French, 1815-1848. *English texts*
Balzac, Honoré de. [La peau de chagrin. English] . The wild ass's skin : (La peau de chagrin) / [by] Honoré de Balzac ; translated and with an introduction by Herbert J. Hunt. — Harmondsworth [etc.] : Penguin, 1977. — 285p ; 19cm. — (The Penguin classics)
Bibl.: p.17.
ISBN 0-14-044330-4 Pbk : £1.00
(B77-19877)

Balzac, Honoré de. Selected short stories [of] Honoré de Balzac / selected and translated with an introduction by Sylvia Raphael. — Harmondsworth [etc.] : Penguin, 1977. — 271p ; 18cm. — (The Penguin classics)
ISBN 0-14-044325-8 Pbk : £1.00
(B77-12173)

Hugo, Victor. [Les Misérables. English]. Les Misérables / [by] Victor Hugo ; translated and with an introduction by Norman Denny ; lithographs by Charles Keeping. — London : Folio Press, 1976. — 2v.(xiii,629p,[24] leaves of plates;v,471p,[24] leaves of plates) : ill(chiefly col) ; 26cm.
In slip case.
ISBN 0-85067-106-x : £22.50
(B77-10624)

Hugo, Victor. [Notre-Dame de Paris. English]. The hunchback of Notre Dame / [by] Victor Hugo. — Abridged [ed.]. — London : New English Library, 1976. — 176p ; 18cm.
ISBN 0-450-03234-5 Pbk : £0.75
(B77-02641)

Stendhal. [La Chartreuse de Parma. English]. The Charterhouse of Parma / [by] Stendhal ; translated by C.K. Scott Moncrieff ; wood-engravings by Zelma Blakely. — London : Folio Society, 1977. — 498p : ill ; 23cm.
This translation originally published: New York : Boni and Liveright, 1925 ; London : Chatto and Windus, 1951.
£7.95
(B77-22230)

843.8 — FRENCH FICTION, 1848-1900
843'.8 — Fiction in French, 1848-1900. *English texts*
Flaubert, Gustave. [Salammbo. English]. Salammbo / [by] Gustave Flaubert ; translated with an introduction by A.J. Krailsheimer. — Harmondsworth [etc.] : Penguin, 1977. — 282p ; 18cm. — (The Penguin classics)
ISBN 0-14-044328-2 Pbk : £1.00
(B77-18433)

Maupassant, Guy de. Tales of supernatural terror / [by] Guy de Maupassant ; selected and translated [from the French] by Arnold Kellett. — London [etc.] : Pan Books, 1977. — xi, 160p ; 18cm.
These translations originally published: 1972.
Pbk : £0.50
ISBN 0-330-23397-1
(B77-29020)

Maupassant, Guy de. [Une vie. English]. A woman's life / [by] Guy de Maupassant ; translated [from the French] with an introduction by H.N.P. Sloman. — Harmondsworth [etc.] : Penguin, 1977. — 202p ; 18cm. — (Penguin classics)
This translation originally published: 1965.
ISBN 0-14-044161-1 Pbk : £0.65
(B77-30805)

Sand, George. [François le champi. English]. The country waif / [by] George Sand ; translated by Eirene Collis ; introduction by Dorothy Wynne Zimmerman. — Lincoln [Neb.] ; London : University of Nebraska Press, 1977. — xxviii, 181p : port ; 22cm.
'The text of this edition of "The Country Waif" is reproduced from the original volume in the collections of the Memorial Library, University of Wisconsin. Published in 1930 by the Scholartis Press ... London, it also included George Sand's "The Castle of Pictordu" ...' - A Note on the Edition. — Bibl.: p.xxvii-xxviii.
ISBN 0-8032-0888-x : £8.65
ISBN 0-8032-5850-x Pbk : £3.00
(B77-19066)

843'.8 — Fiction in French, 1848-1900. *Texts*
Flaubert, Gustave. Trois contes / by Gustave Flaubert ; edited with an introduction, notes and commentary by Colin Duckworth. — London : Harrap, 1976. — 244p,leaf of plate,[4]p of plates : ill, map, port ; 19cm.
French text, English introduction, notes and commentary. — Originally published: 1959. — Bibl.: p.244.
ISBN 0-245-53048-7 Pbk : £1.40
(B77-12174)

843'.8 — Fiction in French. Dujardin, Édouard. Lauriers sont coupés. *Critical studies*
McKilligan, Kathleen M. Edouard Dujardin, 'Les lauriers sont coupés' and the interior monologue / [by] Kathleen M. McKilligan. — Hull : University of Hull, 1977. — xi,108p ; 22cm. — (Occasional papers in modern languages)
Bibl.: p.104-108.
ISBN 0-85958-413-5 Pbk : £3.15
(B77-29783)

843'.8 — Fiction in French. Flaubert, Gustave. Education sentimentale. *Critical studies*
Kettle, Arnold. Flaubert's 'Sentimental education' / prepared by Arnold Kettle ; for the [Open University] Course Team. — Milton Keynes : Open University Press, 1976. — 43p : ill ; 30cm. — (Arts, a third level course : the revolutions of 1848 ; unit 13) (A321 ; 13)
ISBN 0-335-05056-5 Pbk : £0.95
(B77-27509)

843'.8 — Fiction in French. Sand, George. *Biographies*
Maurois, André. Lélia : the life of George Sand / [by] André Maurois ; translated from the French by Gerard Hopkins. — Harmondsworth [etc.] : Penguin, 1977. — 592p,[8]p of plates : ill, facsim, ports ; 19cm.
This translation originally published: London : Cape, 1953. — Translation of: 'Lélia, ou, La vie de George Sand'. Paris : Hachette, 1952. — Bibl.: p.575-585. — Index.
ISBN 0-14-004354-3 Pbk : Unpriced
(B77-13944)

843'.8 — Fiction in French. Zola, Émile.
Biographies
Hemmings, Frederick William John. The life and times of Emile Zola / [by] F.W.J. Hemmings. — London : Elek, 1977. — 192p : ill, facsims, geneal table, ports ; 25cm.
Index.
ISBN 0-236-40055-x : £7.50
(B77-26650)

843'.8 — Short stories in French, 1848-1900.
English texts
Maupassant, Guy de. The diary of a madman, and other tales of horror / [by] Guy de Maupassant ; selected and translated by Arnold Kellett. — London [etc.] : Pan Books, 1976. — 170p ; 18cm.
ISBN 0-330-24849-9 Pbk : £0.60
(B77-04455)

843.91F — FRENCH FICTION, 1900-. NOVELS (INCLUDING TRANSLATIONS)
843'.9'1F — Fiction in French, 1900-. *Texts (including translations)*
Arsan, Emmanuelle. Laure / [by] Emmanuelle Arsan ; translated from the French by Celeste Piano. — London [etc.] : Mayflower, 1977. — 176p ; 18cm.
Translation of: 'Laure'. Paris : Bedfond, 1976.
ISBN 0-583-13029-1 Pbk : £0.80
(B77-27510)

Benzoni, Juliette. A snare for Catherine / [by] Juliette Benzoni ; translated by Anne Carter. — London : Pan Books, 1977. — 364p ; 18cm.
This translation originally published: London : Heinemann, 1974. — Translation of: 'Piège pour Catherine'. Paris : Trévise, 1973.
ISBN 0-330-25000-0 Pbk : £0.80
(B77-12175)

Bernanos, Georges. The diary of a country priest / [by] Georges Bernanos ; translated from the French by Pamela Morris. — [London] ([14 St James's Place, S.W.1]) : Fount Paperbacks, 1977. — 253p ; 18cm.
This translation originally published: London : Boriswood, 1937. — Translation of: 'Journal d'un curé de campagne'. Paris : Plon, 1936.
ISBN 0-00-624463-7 Pbk : £0.95
(B77-30806)

Bodard, Lucien. The French Consul / [by] Lucien Bodard ; translated from the French by Barbara Bray. — London : W.H. Allen, 1977. — [5],406p : map ; 23cm.
Translation of: 'Monsieur le consul'. Paris : Grasset et Fasquelle, 1973.
ISBN 0-491-02131-3 : £4.95
(B77-26651)

Bonnecarrère, Paul. The golden triangle / [by] Paul Bonnecarrère ; translated by Oliver Coburn. — Henley-on-Thames : A. Ellis, 1977. — 3-250p ; 23cm.
Translation of: 'Le triangle d'or'. Paris : Fayard, 1976.
ISBN 0-85628-054-2 : £3.95 : CIP rev.
(B77-13401)

Camus, Albert. The fall ; and, The outsider / [by] Albert Camus ; translated from the French by Stuart Gilbert. — Large print ed. — Bath : Lythway Press, 1977. — [5],306p ; 22cm.
This translation of 'The fall', originally published: London : Hamilton, 1957. Translation of: 'La chute'. Paris : Gallimard, 1956. — This translation of 'The outsider', originally published: London : Hamilton, 1946. Translation of: 'L'étranger'. Paris : Gallimard, 1942.
ISBN 0-85046-744-6 : £4.60
(B77-33494)

Cauvin, Patrick. Blind love / [by] Patrick Cauvin ; translated from the French by Elaine P. Halperin. — Large print [ed.]. — London : Prior [etc.], 1976. — [3],355p ; 24cm.
This translation originally published: London : Joseph, 1975. — Translation of: 'L'Amour aveugle'. Paris : J.C. Lattes : Edition spéciale, 1974.
ISBN 0-904000-47-8 : £4.95
(B77-07690)

Céline, Louis Ferdinand. Castle to castle / [by] Louis-Ferdinand Céline ; translated by Ralph Manheim. — [1st English ed. reprinted] ; with a new introduction by Kurt Vonnegut, Jr. — Harmondsworth [etc.] : Penguin, 1976. — xxix, 359p ; 18cm.
This translation originally published: New York : Delacorte, 1968 ; London : Blond, 1969. — Translation of: 'D'un château l'autre'. Paris : Gallimard, 1957.
ISBN 0-14-004341-1 Pbk : Unpriced
(B77-05744)

Céline, Louis Ferdinand. North / [by] Louis-Ferdinand Céline ; translated by Ralph Manheim. — [1st English ed. reprinted] ; with a new introduction by Kurt Vonnegut, Jr. — Harmondsworth [etc.] : Penguin, 1976. — xv, 454p ; 18cm.
This translation originally published: London : Bodley Head, 1972. — Translation of: 'Nord'. Paris : Gallimard, 1960.
ISBN 0-14-004342-x Pbk : Unpriced
(B77-05745)

Chez nous en France : nouvelles d'écrivains contemporains / edited with notes, vocabulary and biographical introductions by R.P.L. Ledésert and D.M. Ledésert. — London : Harrap, 1976. — 128p ; 18cm.
French text and introductions, English notes. — This collection originally published: 1960.
ISBN 0-245-53014-2 Pbk : £1.25
(B77-10990)

Constantine, Eddie. The God player / [by] Eddie Constantine ; [translated by Abigail Israel]. — [Henley-on-Thames] : A. Ellis, 1976. — [4], 328p ; 23cm.
This translation also published: New York : Random House, 1976. — Translation of: 'Le propriétaire'. Paris : J.C. Lattès, 1975.
ISBN 0-85628-032-1 : £3.95
(B77-01024)

Divomlikoff, Lavr. The traitor / [by] Lavr Divomlikoff ; translated from the French by J.F. Bernard. — London : Corgi, 1977. — 236p ; 18cm.
This translation originally published: Garden City, N.Y. : Doubleday, 1973 ; London : Heinemann, 1974. — Translation of 'Le trêtre'. Paris : Robert Morel, 1972.
ISBN 0-552-10519-8 Pbk : £0.75
(B77-26652)

Duras, Marguerite. The square ; [and], Ten-thirty on a summer night ; [and], The afternoon of Monsieur Andesmas / [by] Marguerite Duras. — London : J. Calder, 1977. — 288p ; 21cm.
The square / translated by Sonia Pitt-Rivers and Irina Morduch. This translation originally published: 1959. Translation of: 'Le Square'. Paris : Gallimard, 1955. — Ten-thirty on a summer night / translated by Anne Borchardt. This translation originally published: 1962. Translation of: 'Dix heures et demie du soir en été'. Paris : Gallimard, 1960. — The afternoon of Monsieur Andesmas / translated by Anne Borchardt. This translation originally published: 1964. Translation of: 'L'Après-midi de Monsieur Andesmas'. Paris : Gallimard, 1962.
ISBN 0-7145-3601-6 : £5.50
ISBN 0-7145-3602-4 Pbk : Unpriced
(B77-09362)

Gary, Romain. The colours of the day / [by] Romain Gary ; translated from the French by Stephen Becker. — London [etc.] : White Lion Publishers, 1976. — 271p ; 21cm.
'The opportunity has been taken by the author to add certain passages to the translation of the original French text and to make some rearrangements and changes which will be incorporated into future French editions' - Author's note. — Translation and revision of: 'Les couleurs du jour'. Paris : Gallimard, 1952.
ISBN 0-85617-882-9 : £3.75
(B77-05092)

Gary, Romain. The way out / [by] Romain Gary ; translated from the French by Sophie Wilkins. — London : Joseph, 1977. — [4], 201p ; 21cm.
This translation also published: as 'Your ticket is no longer valid'. New York : Braziller, 1977. — Translation of: 'Au-delà de cette limite votre ticket n'est plus valable'. Paris : Gallimard, 1975.
ISBN 0-7181-1599-6 : £4.25
(B77-25976)

Gobineau, Marceline. Stephanie / [by] Marceline Gobineau. — London : Wingate.
[Vol.5] : The savage land / translated from the French by Jocasta Innes. — 1976. — 221p ; 23cm.
Translation of: 'Stéphanie : le prix de la liberté'. Part 1. Paris : Editions de Trévise, 1973.
ISBN 0-85523-121-1 : £3.50
(B77-01876)

[Vol.6] : The price of freedom / translated from the French by Jocasta Innes. — 1977. — 253p ; 23cm.
Translation of: 'Stéphanie : le prix de la liberté'. Part 2. Paris : Éditions de Trévise, 1973.
ISBN 0-85523-281-1 : £3.95
(B77-22963)

Hébrard, Frédérique. A husband's a husband / [by] Frédérique Hébrard ; translated from the French by Irene Ash. — London : J. Murray, 1977. — 202p ; 22cm.
Translation of: 'Un mari c'est un mari'. Paris : Flammarion, 1976.
ISBN 0-7195-3441-0 : £3.95
(B77-27511)

Ionesco, Eugene. Le solitaire / [by] Eugene Ionesco ; edited with an introduction and notes by H.F. Brookes and C.E. Fraenkel. — London : Heinemann Educational, 1977. — xxxi,7-225p ; 20cm. — (Heinemann French texts)
French text, English introduction and notes. — 'Le solitaire' originally published: Paris : Mercure de France, 1973. — Bibl.: p.207-208.
ISBN 0-435-37103-7 Pbk : £1.80
(B77-22964)

Marsay, Pierre. Leaving standing still / [by] Pierre Marsay ; translated [from the French] by David Pryce-Jones. — London [etc.] : Quartet Books, 1977. — 3-122p ; 23cm.
Translation of: 'Les départs immobiles'. Paris : Gallimard, 1972.
ISBN 0-7043-2122-x : £3.95
(B77-32944)

Mauriac, François. Le mystère Frontenac / [par] François Mauriac ; edited with an introduction and notes by Anthony M.C. Wilcox. — London : Harrap, 1976. — 223p : map, port ; 19cm.
French text, English introduction and notes. — Originally published: 1964. — Bibl.: p.39-41.
ISBN 0-245-53017-7 Pbk : £1.65
(B77-10991)

Merle, Robert. The virility factor : a novel / by Robert Merle ; translated from the French by Martin Sokolinsky. — London : Weidenfeld and Nicolson, 1977. — [5],344p ; 23cm.
Translation of: 'Les hommes protégés'. Paris : Gallimard, 1974.
ISBN 0-297-77431-x : £4.95
(B77-26653)

Modiano, Patrick. Villa triste / by Patrick Modiano ; translated from the French by Caroline Hillier. — London : Gollancz, 1977. — 128p ; 21cm.
Translation of: 'Villa triste'. Paris : Gallimard, 1975.
ISBN 0-575-02234-5 : £4.50
(B77-10992)

Raspail, Jean. The camp of the saints / [by] Jean Raspail ; translated by Norman Shapiro. — London : Sphere, 1977. — 327p ; 18cm.
This translation originally published: New York : Scribner, 1975. — Translation of: 'Le camp des saints'. Paris : Laffont, 1973.
ISBN 0-7221-7222-2 Pbk : £0.95
(B77-19878)

Rivoyre, Christine de. Boy / [by] Christine de Rivoyre ; translated by Eileen Ellenbogen. — Harmondsworth [etc.] : Penguin, 1976. — 285p ; 19cm.
This translation originally published: London : Hamilton, 1974. — Translation of: 'Boy'. Paris : Grasset et Fasquelle, 1973.
ISBN 0-14-004124-9 Pbk : £0.75
(B77-01877)

Robbe-Grillet, Alain. Project for a revolution in New York : a novel / by Alain Robbe-Grillet ; translated from the French by Richard Howard. — London : Calder and Boyars, 1973. — [5],183p ; 21cm.
This translation originally published: New York : Grove Press, 1972. — Translation of: 'Projet pour une révolution à New York'. Paris : Editions de Minuit, 1970.
ISBN 0-7145-0956-6 : £2.50
(B77-19067)

Sagan, Françoise. Scars on the soul / [by] Françoise Sagan ; translated from the French by Joanna Kilmartin. — Harmondsworth [etc.] : Penguin, 1977. — 124p ; 19cm.
This translation originally published: London : Deutsch, 1974. — Translation of: 'Des bleus à l'âme'. Paris : Flammarion, 1972.
ISBN 0-14-004357-8 Pbk : £0.65
(B77-30807)

Sagan, Françoise. Silken eyes / [by] Françoise Sagan ; translated from the French by Joanna Kilmartin. — London : Deutsch, 1977. — 160p ; 21cm.
Translation of: 'Des yeux de soie'. Paris : Flammarion, 1975.
ISBN 0-233-96859-8 : £3.25
(B77-28256)

Sajer, Guy. The forgotten soldier / [by] Guy Sajer. — London : Sphere, 1977. — 560p : maps ; 18cm.
Translator: Lily Emmet. — This translation originally published: New York : Harper and Row ; London : Weidenfeld and Nicolson, 1971. — Translation of: 'Le Soldat oublié'. Paris : R. Laffont, 1967.
ISBN 0-7221-7580-9 Pbk : £1.25
(B77-10008)

Sarraute, Nathalie. Fools say : a novel / by Nathalie Sarraute ; translated by Maria Jolas. — London : J. Calder : [Distributed by Calder and Boyars], 1977. — [1],152p ; 21cm.
This translation originally published: New York : G. Braziller, 1977. — Translation of: 'Disent les imbéciles'. Paris : Gallimard, 1976.
ISBN 0-7145-3631-8 : £5.25
(B77-23802)

Schoendoerffer, Pierre. The paths of the sea / [by] Pierre Schoendoerffer ; translated [from the French] by Patrick O'Brian. — London : Collins, 1977. — 3-266p ; 22cm.
Translation of: 'Le crabe tambour'. Paris : Grasset et Fasquelle, 1976.
ISBN 0-00-222136-5 : £4.50
(B77-27512)

Schwarz-Bart, André. The last of the just / [by] André Schwarz-Bart ; translated [from the French] by Stephen Becker. — Harmondsworth [etc.] : Penguin, 1977. — 383p ; 18cm. — (Penguin modern classics)
This translation originally published: London : Secker and Warburg, 1961. — Translation of: 'Le dernier des justes' Paris : Editions du Seuil, 1959.
ISBN 0-14-004292-x Pbk : £1.25
(B77-27513)

Simenon, Georges. The bottom of the bottle / [by] Georges Simenon ; translated from the French by Cornelia Schaeffer. — London : Hamilton, 1977. — 157p ; 20cm.
Translation of: 'Le fond de la bouteille'. Paris : Presses de la Cité, 1949.
ISBN 0-241-89681-9 : £3.50
(B77-19879)

Simenon, Georges. Complete Maigret short stories / [by] Georges Simenon. — London : Hamilton.
Vol.2 : Maigret's pipe / translated from the French by Jean Stewart. — 1977. — [5],330p ; 23cm.
ISBN 0-241-89707-6 : £5.50
(B77-28257)

Simenon, Georges. The disappearance of Odile / [by] Georges Simenon ; translated [from the French] by Lyn Moir. — Harmondsworth [etc.] : Penguin, 1977. — 123p ; 19cm. — (Peacock books)
This translation originally published: London : Hamilton, 1972. — Translation of: 'La disparation d'Odile'. Paris : Presses de la Cité, 1971.
ISBN 0-14-047115-4 Pbk : £0.60
(B77-33495)

Simenon, Georges. The eleventh Simenon omnibus / [by] Georges Simenon. — Harmondsworth [etc.] : Penguin, 1977. — 382p ; 19cm. — (Penguin crime fiction)
Contents: The Venice train / translated by Alastair Hamilton. This translation originally published: London : Hamilton, 1974. Translation of 'Le train de Venise'. Paris : Presses de la Cité, 1965 - Maigret and the millionaires / translated by Jean Stewart. This translation originally published: London : Hamilton, 1974. Translation of 'Maigret voyage'. Paris : Presses de la Cité, 1958 - The innocents / translated by Eileen Ellenbogen. This translation originally published: London : Hamilton, 1973. Translation of 'Les innocents'. Paris : Presses de la Cité, 1972.
ISBN 0-14-004248-2 Pbk : £0.95
(B77-12176)

Simenon, Georges. Four days in a lifetime / [by] Georges Simenon ; translated from the French by Louise Varèse. — London : Hamilton, 1977. — [4],219p ; 20cm.
This translation originally published: s.l. : s.n., 1953. — Translation of: 'Les quatre jours du pauvre homme'. Paris : Presses de la Cité, 1949.
ISBN 0-241-89535-9 : £3.50
(B77-08136)

Simenon, Georges. Maigret and the Hotel Majestic / [by] Georges Simenon ; translated from the French by Caroline Hillier. — London : Hamilton, 1977. — 155p ; 20cm.
Translation of: 'Maigret et les Caves du Majestic'. France : s.n., 1942.
ISBN 0-241-89728-9 : £3.50
(B77-19880)

Simenon, Georges. Maigret and the spinster / [by] Georges Simenon ; translated from the French by Eileen Ellenbogen. — London : Hamilton, 1977. — [4],155p ; 20cm.
Translation of: 'Cécile est morte'. Originally published: in 'Maigret revient'. Paris : Gallimard, 1942.
ISBN 0-241-89586-3 : £3.25
(B77-08137)

Simon, Claude. Triptych / [by] Claude Simon ; translated from the French by Helen R. Lane ; with an introduction by John Fletcher. — London : J. Calder, 1977. — xv,171p ; 22cm.
Translation of: 'Triptyque'. Paris : Les Editions de Minuit, 1973.
ISBN 0-7145-3609-1 : £5.50
(B77-26654)

Travelling towards Epsilon : an anthology of French science fiction / edited by Maxim Jakubowski ; translations by Beth Blish and Maxim Jakubowski. — London : New English Library, 1977. — 288p ; 22cm.
ISBN 0-450-03068-7 : £4.95
(B77-13402)

843.91J — FRENCH FICTION, 1900-. CHILDREN'S STORIES (INCLUDING TRANSLATIONS)
843'.9'1J — Children's stories in French, 1900-. *Texts (including translations)*

366 dreamtime stories / translated by Elizabeth Cooper and John Orpen ; [illustrations by Kerstin Buisson et al.]. — London [etc.] : Hamlyn, 1976. — 4-237p : col ill ; 28cm.
Col. ill. on lining papers. — 'Most of the stories in this book have been taken from "365 rêves d'or, un conte chaque soir'. Other stories and poems by Georgina Adams and Rosemary Garland' - note.
ISBN 0-600-32926-7 : £2.75
(B77-06946)

Berna, Paul. The last dawn / [by] Paul Berna ; [translated from the French]. — London : Angus and Robertson, 1977. — 172p ; 21cm.
Translation of: 'La dernière aube'. Paris : Editions G.P., 1974.
ISBN 0-207-95707-x : £3.20
(B77-30808)

Berna, Paul. The mystery of the cross-eyed man / [by] Paul Berna ; translated from the French by John Buchanan-Brown ; illustrated by Barry Wilkinson. — Harmondsworth [etc.] : Puffin Books, 1977. — 171,[1]p : ill, map ; 18cm. — (Puffin books)
This translation originally published: London : Bodley Head, 1965. — Translation of: 'Les pèlerins de Chiberta'. Paris : Générale Publicité, 1958.
ISBN 0-14-030373-1 Pbk : £0.50
(B77-24571)

Brunhoff, Jean de. The story of Babar the little elephant / [by] Jean de Brunhoff ; [translated from the French]. — London : Methuen, 1977. — 48p : chiefly col ill ; 19cm. — (A Methuen picture paperback)
Translator: Merle Haas. — This translation originally published: New York : H. Smith and R. Haas, 1933 ; London : Methuen, 1934. — Translation of: 'Histoire de Babar, le petit éléphant'. Paris : Editions du Jardin des modes, 1931.
ISBN 0-416-80550-7 Sd : £0.65
(B77-27514)

Dumas, Philippe. Lucy, Edward's daughter / [by] Philippe Dumas ; [translated from the French by Gwen Marsh]. — London : Dent, 1977. — 48p : ill(some col) ; 16x23cm.
Translation of: 'Lucie, la fille d'Edouard'. Paris : Flammarion, 1977.
ISBN 0-460-06841-5 : £1.95 : CIP rev.
(B77-23803)

Dumas, Philippe. The story of Edward / [by] Philippe Dumas ; [translated by Gwen Marsh]. — London : Dent, 1977. — 48p : ill(some col) ; 16x23cm.
Translation of: 'Histoire d'Edouard'. Paris : Flammarion, 1976.
ISBN 0-460-06792-3 : £1.50 : CIP rev.
(B77-06349)

Fix, Philippe. Arabella, the pink and gold spotted elephant / [by] Philippe & Réjane Fix. — [London] : [Cape], [1977]. — 4-29p : col ill ; 33cm.
Cover title. — This translation originally published: Manchester : World Distributions, 1971. — Translation of 'L'éléphant rose à point d'or'. Paris : Editions des Deux Coqs d'Or, 1970.
ISBN 0-224-01302-5 : £1.95
(B77-06947)

Fix, Philippe. The kangaroo with a hole in her pocket / [by] Philippe & Réjane Fix. — [London] : [Cape], [1977]. — 4-29p : col ill ; 33cm.
Cover title. — This translation originally published: Manchester : World Distributions, 1971. — Translation of: 'Le kangourou à la poche percée'. Paris : Editions des Deux Coqs d'Or, 1970.
ISBN 0-224-01301-7 : £1.95
(B77-06948)

Fix, Philippe. Popcorn the hipporhino / [by] Philippe & Réjane Fix. — [London] : [Cape], [1977]. — 4-29p : col ill ; 33cm.
Cover title. — Translation of: 'Popcorn, l'hippoporhinos'. Paris : Editions des Deux Coqs d'Or, 1973.
ISBN 0-224-01303-3 : £1.95
(B77-06949)

Goscinny. Nicholas and the gang again / Goscinny & Sempé ; translated by Anthea Bell ; illustrated by Sempé. — London : Abelard, 1977. — 111p : ill ; 21cm.
ISBN 0-200-72463-0 : £2.50
(B77-19068)

Goscinny. Nicholas and the gang at school / [by] Goscinny & Sempé ; translated by Anthea Bell ; illustrated by Sempé. — London : Abelard-Schuman, 1976. — 3-143p : ill ; 21cm.
ISBN 0-200-72462-2 : £2.50
(B77-12768)

Rabier, Benjamin. Gideon in the forest / [by] Benjamin Rabier ; [translated from the French by Olive Jones]. — London : Methuen, 1977. — [48]p : chiefly col ill ; 32cm.
Translation of: 'Gédéon dans la forêt'. Paris : Librairie Garnier Frères, 1930.
ISBN 0-416-11950-6 : £4.95
(B77-30809)

843.912 — FRENCH FICTION, 1900-1945
843'.9'12 — Fiction in French. Beauvoir, Simone de. Special themes: Feminism

Leighton, Jean. Simone de Beauvoir on woman / [by] Jean Leighton ; foreword by Henri Peyre. — Rutherford [etc.] : Fairleigh Dickinson University Press ; London (108 New Bond St., W1Y 0QX) : Associated University Presses, [1976]. — 230p ; 22cm.
Published in the United States: 1975. — Bibl.: p.224-225. — Index.
ISBN 0-8386-1504-x : £4.50
(B77-07691)

843'.9'12 — Fiction in French. Bernanos, Georges. Monsieur Ouine & Sous le soleil de Satan. Characters: Satan

Kemp, Marie Ann. Manifestations of Satan in two novels of Georges Bernanos / [by] Marie Ann Kemp. — Hemel Hempstead (Hemel Hempstead, Herts. HP1 1HD) : Academic Board of Dacorum College, 1976. — [2],24p ; 21cm. — (Dacorum College of Further Education. Occasional papers ; no.5)
Bibl.: p.24.
ISBN 0-903978-05-9 Sd : £0.30
(B77-06950)

843'.9'12 — Fiction in French. Céline, Louis Ferdinand. *Biographies*

McCarthy, Patrick. Céline / [by] Patrick McCarthy. — Harmondsworth [etc.] : Penguin, 1977. — 352p ; 20cm.
Originally published: London : Allen Lane, 1975. — Bibl.: p.341-344. — Index.
ISBN 0-14-004534-1 Pbk : £1.60
(B77-29021)

843'.9'12 — Fiction in French. Malraux, André. *Biographies*

Madsen, Axel. Malraux : a biography / by Axel Madsen. — London : W.H. Allen, 1977. — 383p : ill, ports ; 24cm.
Originally published: New York : Morrow, 1976. — Bibl.: p.365-368. — List of works: p.363-364. — Index.
ISBN 0-491-02070-8 : £7.50
(B77-19069)

843'.9'12 — Fiction in French. Proust, Marcel. *Biographies*

Painter, George Duncan. Marcel Proust : a biography / [by] George D. Painter. — Harmondsworth [etc.] : Penguin. — (Peregrine books)
In 2 vols.
Vol.1. — 1977. — xv,334p : maps ; 20cm.
Originally published: London : Chatto and Windus, 1959. — Index.
ISBN 0-14-055131-x Pbk : £2.50
(B77-31585)

Vol.2. — 1977. — [11],435p : map ; 20cm.
Originally published: London : Chatto and Windus, 1965. — Bibl.: p.359-373. — Index.
ISBN 0-14-055132-8 Pbk : £2.50
(B77-31586)

843'.9'12 — Fiction in French. Ramuz, Charles Ferdinand. *Critical studies*

Bevan, D G. The art and poetry of Ramuz : reflections on immobility and movement in the novels / [by] D.G. Bevan. — New York ; Cambridge : Oleander Press, 1977. — [6],v, 186p,[8]p of plates : 1 ill, facsim, ports ; 22cm.
Bibl.: p.184-186. — List of works: p.181-183.
ISBN 0-902675-47-8 : £1.20
(B77-13403)

848.5 — FRENCH MISCELLANY, 1715-1789

848'.5'09 — French literature. Voltaire. *Correspondence*

Voltaire. Correspondence and related documents [of Voltaire]. — Definitive ed. / by Theodore Besterman. — Oxford ([c/o Taylor Institution, St Giles, Oxford OX1 3NA]) : Voltaire Foundation.
51 : Bibliography of the printed letters, list of printed works cited in the notes, key to pseudonyms and nicknames, index of annotated works and phrases, index of quotations, list of appendixes, classified index of illustrations in Voltaire's correspondence, 1953-1964. — 1977. — [10]p,21-1142 columns ; 23cm. — (The complete works of Voltaire ; 135)
ISBN 0-7294-0052-2 : £28.50
(B77-08646)

848.6 — FRENCH MISCELLANY, 1789-1815

848'.6'09 — French literature. Chateaubriand, François René de, vicomte. *Biographies*

Painter, George Duncan. Chateaubriand : a biography / [by] George D. Painter. — London : Chatto and Windus.
In 3 vols.
Vol.1 : (1768-93) : The longed-for tempests. — 1977. — [10],321p,[8]p of plates : ill, facsims, music, ports ; 24cm.
Maps on lining papers. — Bibl.: p.285-294. — Index.
ISBN 0-7011-2184-x : £7.95 : CIP rev.
(B77-17162)

848.7 — FRENCH MISCELLANY, 1815-1848

848'.7'09 — French literature. Hugo, Victor. *Biographies*

Richardson, Joanna. Victor Hugo / [by] Joanna Richardson. — London : Weidenfeld and Nicolson, 1976. — x,334p,[8]p of plates : ports ; 23cm.
Bibl.: p.312-326. — Index.
ISBN 0-297-77127-2 : £10.00
(B77-01025)

848.912 — FRENCH MISCELLANY, 1900-1945

848'.9'1208 — Prose in French, 1900-1945. *English texts*

Beckett, Samuel. For to end yet again, and other fizzles / [by] Samuel Beckett. — London : J. Calder, 1976. — 54p ; 21cm.
'Still' was originally written in English ; the other stories have been translated from the original French by the author. — Translation of: 'Pour finir encore et autres foirades'. Paris : Editions de Minuit, 1976. — 'Still' originally published: Milan : M'Arte Edizioni, 1974.
ISBN 0-7145-3599-0 : £3.50
ISBN 0-7145-3600-8 Pbk : Unpriced
(B77-01878)

Rougemont, Denis de. The growl of deeper waters : essays / by Denis de Rougemont ; translated from the French by Samuel Hazo with Beth Luey. — [Pittsburgh] : University of Pittsburgh Press ; London : Feffer and Simons ; [London] : [Distributed by Transatlantic Book Service], 1976. — xi,84p ; 21cm.
'The Swiss selection of the International Poetry Forum'. — Translation of: 'Doctrine fabuleuse'. Neuchâtel, Paris : Ides et Calends, 1947. — Includes one additional essay.
ISBN 0-8229-3315-2 : £4.46
(B77-05746)

Viallaneix, Paul. The first Camus : an introductory essay / by Paul Viallaneix. Youthful writings / by Albert Camus ; translated from the French by Ellen Conroy Kennedy. — London : Hamilton, 1977. — [7], 279,[1]p ; 21cm. — ([Cahiers Albert Camus ; 2])
This translation originally published: New York : Knopf, 1976. — Translation of 'Le Premier Camus, suivi de écrits de jeunesse d'Albert Camus'. Paris : Gallimard, 1973. — Bibl.: p.103-104.
ISBN 0-241-89521-9 : £5.50
(B77-06951)

848'.9'1209 — French literature, 1900-1945. *English texts*

Valéry, Paul. Paul Valéry : an anthology / selected with an introduction by James R. Lawler. — London [etc.] : Routledge and Kegan Paul, 1977. — xxiii,355,[1]p : 1 ill ; 21cm.
'... from The Collected Works of Paul Valéry edited by Jackson Mathews'. — Includes some poems in French with parallel English translations.
ISBN 0-7100-8806-x : £6.95 : CIP rev.
ISBN 0-7100-8764-0 Pbk : £3.50
(B77-25256)

848'.9'1209 — French literature. Artaud, Antonin. *Critical studies*

Hayman, Ronald. Artaud and after / [by] Ronald Hayman. — Oxford [etc.] : Oxford University Press, 1977. — xvi,189p,[16]p of plates : ill, ports ; 21cm.
Bibl.: p.163-166. — Index.
ISBN 0-19-211744-0 : £6.00 : CIP rev.
ISBN 0-19-281208-4 Pbk : £2.25
(B77-20757)

848'.9'1209 — French literature. Gide, André. *Critical studies*

Bettinson, Christopher David. Gide : a study / by Christopher Bettinson. — London : Heinemann Educational [etc.], 1977. — [8], 104p ; 21cm.
Spine title: André Gide : a study. — Bibl.: p.102-104.
ISBN 0-435-37586-5 : £2.80
(B77-15008)

848'.9'1209 — French literature. Gide, André, to 1900. *Autobiographies*

Gide, André. If it die - / [by] André Gide ; translated [from the French] by Dorothy Bussy. — Harmondsworth [etc.] : Penguin, 1977. — 305p ; 18cm. — (Penguin modern classics)
This translation originally published: London : Secker and Warburg, 1950. — Translation of: 'Si le grain ne meurt'. s.l. : s.n., 1920.
ISBN 0-14-001234-6 Pbk : £0.95
(B77-31587)

848.914 — FRENCH MISCELLANY, 1945-

848'.9'1409 — French literature. Beckett, Samuel. *Periodicals*

Journal of Beckett studies. — London : J. Calder : Beckett Archive, University of Reading : [Distributed by Calder and Boyars]. [No.1]- ; [Winter 1976]-. — 1976-. — ill, plans ; 21cm.
Two issues a year. — [3],112p.,[8]p. of plates in 1st issue. — Bibl.
Pbk : £2.20(£3.75 yearly)
ISSN 0309-5207
Primary classification 828'.9'1209
(B77-13939)

849 — PROVENCAL LITERATURE

849'.1'2 — Poetry in Old Provençal, 1100-1300. *Texts*

Rogier, Peire. The poems of the troubadour Peire Rogier / [edited by] Derek E.T. Nicholson. — Manchester : Manchester University Press [etc.], 1976. — ix,171p ; 23cm.
Old French text, English introduction and notes. — Bibl.: p.165-171.
ISBN 0-7190-0614-7 : £5.95
(B77-07692)

849.9 — CATALAN LITERATURE

849'.9'12 — Poetry in Catalan, 1350-1450. *Catalan-English parallel texts*

March, Ausias. Selected poems [of] Ausias March / edited and translated by Arthur Terry. — Edinburgh : Edinburgh University Press, 1976. — [7],144p ; 21cm. — (Edinburgh bilingual library ; 12)
Parallel Catalan text and English translations. — Bibl.: p.142-143.
ISBN 0-85224-309-x : £4.00
ISBN 0-85224-296-4 Pbk : £2.50
(B77-17163)

850.9 — ITALIAN LITERATURE. HISTORY AND CRITICAL STUDIES

850'.9 — Italian literature, to 1976. *Critical studies*

Cairns, Christopher. Italian literature : the dominant themes / [by] Christopher Cairns. — Newton Abbot [etc.] : David and Charles [etc.], 1977. — 189p ; 23cm. — (Comparative literature)
Bibl.: p.178-186. — Index.
ISBN 0-7153-7391-9 : £6.50
(B77-22231)

851.1 — ITALIAN POETRY, TO 1375

851'.1 — Poetry in Italian. Guittone d'Arezzo. *Critical studies*

Moleta, Vincent. The early poetry of Guittone d'Arezzo / [by] Vincent Moleta. — London (Hon. Treasurer, MHRA, King's College, Strand, WC2R 2LS) : Modern Humanities Research Association, 1976. — viii,147p ; 24cm. — (Modern Humanities Research Association. Dissertation series ; vol.9)
Bibl.: p.144-145. — Index.
ISBN 0-900547-41-3 : £6.00
(B77-00487)

851'.1 — Poetry in Italian, to 1375. *English texts*

Botticelli, Sandro. The drawings by Sandro Botticelli for Dante's 'Divine Comedy' : after the originals in the Berlin museums and the Vatican / [introductory text by] Kenneth Clark ; [commentaries compiled and written by George Robinson]. — London : Thames and Hudson, 1976. — 218p : ill(some col), facsim(on lining papers) ; 37cm.
'Extracts from Dante's "Divine Comedy" "The Inferno" "The Purgatorio" "The Paradiso" translated by John Ciardi' - title page verso.
ISBN 0-500-23256-3 : £35.00
Primary classification 741.9'45
(B77-04972)

851'.1 — Poetry in Italian, to 1375. *Italian-English parallel texts*

Petrarch. Petrarch's lyric poems : the 'Rime sparse', and other lyrics / translated and edited by Robert M. Durling. — Cambridge, Mass. ; London : Harvard University Press, 1976. — xiii,657p : facsim ; 24cm.
Parallel Italian text and English translation, English introduction. — Bibl.: p.637-646. — Index.
ISBN 0-674-66345-4 : £14.95
(B77-04456)

851.3 — ITALIAN POETRY, 1492-1542

851'.3 — Poetry in Italian, 1492-1542. *English texts*

Ariosto, Lodovico. [Orlando furioso. English]. Orlando furioso = The frenzy of Orlando : a romantic epic / by Ludovico Ariosto ; translated [from the Italian] with an introduction by Barbara Reynolds. — Harmondsworth [etc.] : Penguin. — (The Penguin classics)
In 2 vols.
Part 1. — 1977. — 827p : ill, geneal tables, maps, ; 18cm.
This translation originally published: 1975. — Index.
Pbk : £2.50
ISBN 0-14-044311-8
(B77-28258)

Part 2. — 1977. — 794p : ill, map ; 19cm.
Index.
ISBN 0-14-044310-x Pbk : £2.50
(B77-28259)

851.6 — ITALIAN POETRY, 1748-1814

851'.6 — Poetry in Italian. Foscolo, Ugo, 1816-1827. *Biographies*

Franzero, Carlo Maria. A life in exile : Ugo Foscolo in London, 1816-1827 / [by] Carlo Maria Franzero. — London : W.H. Allen, 1977. — xiii,127p,[8]p of plates : ill, facsims, ports ; 23cm.
Translation of: 'Ugo Foscolo a Londra'. Parma : Guanda, 1971.
ISBN 0-491-02281-6 : £3.50
(B77-28260)

851.7 — ITALIAN POETRY, 1814-1859

851'.7 — Poetry in Italian, 1814-1859. *English texts*

Burgess, Anthony. Abba Abba / [by] Anthony Burgess. — London : Faber, 1977. — 127p ; 21cm.
Contains poems by Giuseppe Gioacchino Belli translated into English.
ISBN 0-571-11125-4 : £3.95 : CIP rev
Primary classification 823'.9'1F
(B77-07590)

851.914 — ITALIAN POETRY, 1945-
851'.9'14 — Poetry in Italian, 1945-. *English texts*
Levi, Primo. Shema : collected poems of Primo Levi / translated from the Italian by Ruth Feldman & Brian Swann ; introduction by Edouard Roditi ; afterword, self-interview by Primo Levi translated by Ruth Feldman. — London (23 Fitzwarren Gardens, N.19) : Menard Press, 1976. — 56p ; 22cm.
Bibl.: p.55-56.
ISBN 0-903400-26-x Pbk : £1.80
(B77-12769)

852.5 — ITALIAN DRAMA, 1585-1748
852'.5 — Drama in Italian, 1585-1748. *Italian-English parallel texts*
Guarini, Giovanni Battista. [Il pastor fido. English & Italian]. Il pastor fido = The faithful shepherd / [by] Battista Guarini ; translated (1647) by Richard Fanshawe ; edited with introduction by J.H. Whitfield. — Edinburgh : Edinburgh University Press, 1976. — x,413p ; 21cm. — (Edinburgh bilingual library ; 11)
Parallel Italian text and English translation. — Bibl.: p.412-413.
ISBN 0-85224-310-3 : £5.00
ISBN 0-85224-291-3 Pbk : £2.50
(B77-17164)

852.6 — ITALIAN DRAMA, 1748-1814
852'.6 — Drama in Italian. Goldoni, Carlo. *Biographies*
Holme, Timothy. A servant of many masters : the life and times of Carlo Goldoni / [by] Timothy Holme. — London : Jupiter Books, 1976. — 200p,[16]p of plates : ill(some col), port ; 26cm.
Bibl.: p.195-196. — List of works: p.189-194. — Index.
ISBN 0-904041-61-1 : £5.50
(B77-17801)

853.1 — ITALIAN FICTION, TO 1375
853'.1 — Short stories in Italian. Boccaccio, Giovanni. Decamerone. *Critical studies. Readings*
Critical perspectives on the 'Decameron' / edited by Robert S. Dombroski. — London [etc.] : Hodder and Stoughton, 1976. — [7],148p ; 23cm.
Bibl.: p.145-146.
ISBN 0-340-16151-5 : £4.90
ISBN 0-340-21473-2 Pbk : £2.50
(B77-01879)

853.2 — ITALIAN FICTION, 1375-1492
853'.2 — Fiction in Italian, 1375-1492. *English texts*
Leonardo da Vinci. Leonardo da Vinci's fantastic animals / interpreted and transcribed by Bruno Nardini ; English language text by David Grant ; illustrated by Adriana Saviozzi Mazza ; introduction by Isabel Quigly. — Glasgow [etc.] : Collins, 1976. — 4-93p : ill(chiefly col), facsim, map, col port ; 29cm.
Facsim. on lining papers. — Originally published: in Italian. Florence : Centro Internazionale del Libro, 1974.
ISBN 0-00-138137-7 : £3.95
(B77-15009)

853.8 — ITALIAN FICTION, 1859-1900
853'.8 — Fiction in Italian, 1859-1900. *English texts*
Collodi, Carlo. [Pinocchio. English]. The adventures of Pinocchio / [by] Carlo Collodi. — London : Armada Paperbacks, 1977. — 156p ; 18cm.
ISBN 0-00-690314-2 Pbk : £0.40
(B77-05747)

Svevo, Italo. As a man grows older / [by] Italo Svevo ; translated from the Italian by Beryl de Zoete. — Harmondsworth [etc.] : Penguin, 1977. — 224p ; 19cm. — (Penguin modern classics)
This translation originally published: London : Putnam, 1932. — Translation of: 'Senilità'. s.l. : s.n., 1898.
ISBN 0-14-002319-4 Pbk : £0.75
(B77-12177)

853.91F — ITALIAN FICTION, 1900-. NOVELS (INCLUDING TRANSLATIONS)
853'.9'1F — Fiction in Italian, 1900-. *Texts (including translations)*
Calvino, Italo. The castle of crossed destinies / [by] Italo Calvino ; translated from the Italian by William Weaver. — London : Secker and Warburg, 1977. — [9],129p,[8]p of plates : ill(some col) ; 25cm.
This translation originally published: New York : Harcourt Brace Jovanovich, 1976. — Translation of: 'Il castello dei destini incrociati'. Torino : Einaudi, 1973. — 'Pages 3 to 48 originally appeared in Italo Calvino's "Tarots : The Visconti Pack in Bergamo and New York", published by Franco Maria Ricci editore' - title page verso.
ISBN 0-436-08221-7 : £4.50
(B77-16098)

Giovene, Andrea. The book of Guiliano Sansevero / [by] Andrea Giovene. — Harmondsworth [etc.] : Penguin.
In 4 vols.
Vol.2 : The dilemma of love / translated by Bernard Wall. — 1977. — 220p ; 18cm.
This translation originally published: London : Collins, 1973. — Translation of: 'L'Autobiografia di Giuliano di Sansevero', vol.3. Milano : Rizzoli, 1967?.
ISBN 0-14-004113-3 Pbk : £0.75
(B77-08647)

Magnani, Luigi. Beethoven's nephew / by Luigi Magnani ; translated by Isabel Quigly. — London : W.H. Allen, 1977. — viii,120p ; 23cm.
Translation of: 'Il nipote di Beethoven'. Torino : Einaudi, 1972. — Based on the life of Karl van Beethoven.
ISBN 0-491-01688-3 : £3.50
(B77-10625)

Moravia, Alberto. Bitter honeymoon, and other stories / [by] Alberto Moravia ; [translated by Bernard Wall, Baptista Gilliat Smith and Frances Frenaye]. — St Albans : Panther, 1977. — 221p ; 18cm.
These translations originally published: London : Secker and Warburg, 1954.
ISBN 0-586-04242-3 Pbk : £0.75
(B77-07693)

Silone, Ignazio. Fontamara / [di] Ignazio Silone ; edited, with introduction, notes and vocabulary, by Judy Rawson. — Manchester : Manchester University Press, 1977. — vi,290p : maps, port ; 19cm. — (Italian texts)
Italian text, English introduction and notes. — This text of 'Fontamara' originally published: Milano : Mondadori, 1949. — Bibl.: p.11-13.
ISBN 0-7190-0662-7 Pbk : £2.60
(B77-22965)

859 — ROMANIAN LITERATURE
859'.1'32 — Poetry in Romanian, 1900-1945. *Romanian-English parallel texts*
Arghezi, Tudor. Selected poems of Tudor Arghezi / translated by Michael Impey and Brian Swann. — Princeton ; Guildford : Princeton University Press, 1976. — xxvi,223p : ill ; 23cm. — (The Lockert library of poetry in translation)
Parallel Romanian text and English translation, English introduction and preface.
ISBN 0-691-06298-6 : £11.50
ISBN 0-691-01328-4 Pbk : £4.15
(B77-05093)

860.9 — SPANISH LITERATURE. HISTORY AND CRITICAL STUDIES
860'.9'005 — Spanish literature, 1800-1900. Role of historical determinism
Ramsden, Herbert. The 1898 movement in Spain : towards a reinterpretation with special reference to 'En torno al caticismo' and 'Idearium español' / by H. Ramsden. — Manchester : Manchester University Press [etc.], 1974. — vii,212p ; 23cm.
Bibl.: p.211-212.
ISBN 0-7190-0565-5 : £4.95
(B77-19881)

861 — SPANISH POETRY
861 — Poetry in Spanish. Chilean writers, 1910-1945. *Spanish-English parallel texts*
Parra, Nicanor. Emergency poems / [by] Nicanor Parra ; translated by Miller Williams. — London : Boyars : Distributed by Calder and Boyars, 1977. — vi,154p ; 21cm.
Parallel Spanish text and English translation. — These translations originally published: New York : New Directions, 1972. — Spanish text originally published: in 'Obra gruesa'. Santiago de Chile : Editorial Universitaria, 1969. — Index.
ISBN 0-7145-2508-1 : £5.95
ISBN 0-7145-2526-x Pbk : £2.50
(B77-05748)

861 — Poetry in Spanish. Chilean writers. Neruda, Pablo. *Autobiographies*
Neruda, Pablo. Memoirs / [by] Pablo Neruda ; translated from the Spanish by Hardie St Martin. — London : Souvenir Press, 1977. — [5],370p ; 22cm. — (A condor book)
This translation also published: New York : Farrar, Straus and Giroux, 1977. — Translation of: 'Confieso que he vivido ; memorias'. Barcelona : Editorial Seix Barral, 1974. — Index.
ISBN 0-285-64810-1 : £6.50
ISBN 0-285-64811-x Pbk : £3.95
(B77-15583)

861 — Poetry in Spanish. Peruvian writers. Vallejo, César. Trilce. *Critical studies. Spanish texts*
Neale-Silva, Eduardo. César Vallejo en su fase trílcica / [por] Eduardo Neale-Silva. — Madison ; London : University of Wisconsin Press, 1975 [i.e. 1976]. — 663p : 1 ill ; 22cm.
Published in the United States: 1975. — Index.
ISBN 0-299-06774-2 Pbk : £16.00
(B77-06952)

861 — Poetry in Spanish. Venezuelan writers. Bello, Andrés. *Biographies*
Caldera, Rafael. Andrés Bello : philosopher, poet, philologist, educator, legislator, statesman / by Rafael Caldera ; translated [from the Spanish] by John Street. — London : Allen and Unwin, 1977. — 3-165p,4p of plates : ill, port ; 23cm.
Translation of: 'Andrés Bello'. 5. ed. Caracas? : s.n., 1973. — Bibl.: p.161-165.
ISBN 0-04-920049-6 : £8.50
(B77-21554)

861'.04 — Lyric poetry in Spanish, to 1976. *Anthologies*
The **Spanish** traditional lyric / edited by John G. Cummins. — Oxford [etc.] : Pergamon, 1977. — xi,179p ; 22cm. — (Pergamon Oxford Spanish series)
Spanish text, English introduction and notes. — Bibl.: p.37-39. — Index.
ISBN 0-08-018117-1 : £6.25
ISBN 0-08-018116-3 Pbk : £3.25
(B77-25977)

861.2 — SPANISH POETRY, 1369-1516
861'.2 — Poetry in Spanish, 1369-1516. *Texts*
Martínez de Burgos, Juan. The 'Cancionero de Martínez de Burgos' : a description of its contents, with an edition of the prose and poetry of Juan Martínez de Burgos / [edited by] Dorothy Sherman Severin. — [Exeter] : University of Exeter, 1976. — xxxii,75p ; 21cm. — (Exeter Hispanic texts ; 12 ISSN 0305-8700)

Spanish text, English introduction and notes. — Cover title : Martínez de Burgos. — Bibl.: p.66-74.
ISBN 0-85989-065-1 Pbk : £1.00
(B77-03802)

861.3 — SPANISH POETRY, 1516-1700
861'.3 — Poetry in Spanish, 1516-1700. *Spanish-English parallel texts*
Góngora y Argote, Luis de. [La fábula de Polifemo y Galatea. English]. Polyphemus and Galatea / [by] Luis de Góngora ; with verse translation [from the Spanish] by Gilbert F. Cunningham. — Edinburgh : Edinburgh University Press, 1977. — ix,172p ; 22cm.
Parallel Spanish text and English translation. — Index. — Includes: 'A study in the interpretation of a baroque poem' / by Alexander A. Parker ; and, 'The Ovidian source' (Metamorphoses XIII, 738-897), parallel Latin text and English translation by David West.
ISBN 0-85224-264-6 : £4.50
(B77-33496)

861.62 — SPANISH POETRY, 1900-1945
861'.6'2 — Poetry in Spanish. Alberti, Rafael. *Autobiographies*
Alberti, Rafael. The lost grove / [by] Rafael Alberti ; translated [from the Spanish] and edited by Gabriel Berns. — Berkeley [etc.] ; London : University of California Press, 1976. — [7],323p : ill, facsim, ports ; 23cm.
Translation of: 'La arboleda perdida'. Buenos Aires : Campañía General Fabril, 1959.
ISBN 0-520-02786-8 : £8.95
(B77-23804)

861′.6′208 — Poetry in Spanish, 1900-1975. *Anthologies. Spanish-English parallel texts*

Roots and wings : poetry from Spain, 1900-1975 : a bilingual anthology / Hardie St Martin, editor. — New York [etc.] ; London : Harper and Row, 1976. — xxv,528p ; 24cm.
Parallel Spanish text with English translation. — Bibl.: p.511-525. — Index.
ISBN 0-06-013976-5 : £10.00
ISBN 0-06-013981-1 Pbk : Unpriced
(B77-29022)

861.64 — SPANISH POETRY, 1945-
861′.6′4 — Poetry in Spanish, 1945-. *Spanish-English parallel texts*

González, Angel. Harsh world and other poems / [by] Angel González ; translated by Donald D. Walsh. — Princeton ; Guildford : Princeton University Press, 1977. — ix,172p ; 23cm. — (The Lockert library of poetry in translation)
Parallel Spanish text and English translation.
ISBN 0-691-06326-5 : £9.40
ISBN 0-691-01333-0 Pbk : £2.95
(B77-19070)

862.3 — SPANISH DRAMA, 1516-1700
862′.3 — Drama in Spanish, 1516-1700. *English texts*

Calderón de la Barca, Pedro. [El gran teatro del mundo. English]. The great stage of the world : an allegorical auto sacramental / [by] Don Pedro Calderón de la Barca ; translated by George W. Brandt. — Manchester : Manchester University Press, 1976. — xxiv,48p : 2 ill ; 19cm. — (Classics of drama in English translation)
Bibl.: p.xxii.
ISBN 0-7190-0571-x Pbk : £1.80
(B77-03803)

862′.3 — Drama in Spanish, 1516-1700. *Texts*

Two Jesuit Ahab dramas ... / edited by Nigel Griffin. — [Exeter] : University of Exeter, 1976. — xxv,171p ; 21cm. — (Exeter Hispanic texts ; 13 ISSN 0305-8700)
Latin and Spanish text, English introduction and notes. — Contents: Tragoedia cui nomen inditum Achabus / by Miguel Venegas - Tragaedia Jezabelis.
ISBN 0-85989-007-4 Pbk : £1.00
Primary classification 872′.04
(B77-17802)

862.62 — SPANISH DRAMA, 1900-1945
862′.6′2 — Drama in Spanish, 1900-1945. *English texts*

García Lorca, Federico. Three tragedies [of] Federico García Lorca / translated by James Graham-Luján and Richard L. O'Connell ; introduction by Francisco García Lorca. — Harmondsworth [etc.] : Penguin, 1976. — 203p ; 19cm. — (Penguin plays)
This collection of translations originally published: New York : New Directions, 1947 ; London : Secker and Warburg, 1959. — Contents: Blood wedding. Translation of: 'Bodas de sangre'. 1933 - Yerma. Translation of: 'Yerma'. 1935 - The house of Bernarda Alba. Translation of: 'La casa de Bernarda Alba. 1940.
ISBN 0-14-048020-x Pbk : £0.65
(B77-02642)

Valle-Inclán, Ramón Mariá del. Divinas palabras = Divine words : a village tragi-comedy / by Ramón del Valle-Inclán ; English version by Trader Faulkner. — London : Heinemann Educational [for] the National Theatre, 1977. — iv,79p ; 19cm. — (National Theatre. Plays)
'Acting edition'. — Nine men, 7 women, supers. — Translation of: 'Divinas palabras'. Madrid : Imprenta Yagües, 1920.
ISBN 0-435-23425-0 Pbk : £1.75
(B77-24572)

862′.6′2 — Drama in Spanish, 1900-1945. *Welsh texts*

García Lorca, Federico. Priodas waed / [gan] Federico García Lorca ; cyfieithiad ... gan R. Bryn Williams a John Rowlands ; y golygu gan Gwyn Thomas. — [Cardiff] : Gwasg Prifysgol Cymru ar ran Cyngor Celfyddydau Cymru, 1977. — ii-xi,68p ; 19cm. — (Dramâu'r byd)
Translation of: 'Bodas de sangre'. Madrid : Ediciones del árbol, 1935.
ISBN 0-7083-0638-1 Pbk : £0.70
(B77-25257)

862′.6′2 — Drama in Spanish. Alberti, Rafael. *Critical studies*

Popkin, Louise B. The theatre of Rafael Alberti / [by] Louise B. Popkin. — London : Tamesis, 1975. — iii-xv,2-183p ; 24cm. — (Colección Támesis : serie A, monografías ; 47)
Bibl.: p.178-183.
ISBN 0-7293-0004-8 : £12.50
(B77-30810)

863 — SPANISH FICTION
863 — Fiction in Spanish. Cuban writers. Carpentier, Alejo. *Critical studies*

González Echevarría, Roberto. Alejo Carpentier, the pilgrim at home / [by] Roberto González Echevarría. — Ithaca ; London : Cornell University Press, 1977. — 307,[1]p ; 23cm.
Bibl.: p.275-299. — Index.
ISBN 0-8014-1029-0 : £10.00
(B77-24573)

863 — Fiction in Spanish. Cuban writers. Carpentier, Alejo; Lezama Lima, José & Cabrera Infante, Guillermo. *Critical studies*

Souza, Raymond D. Major Cuban novelists : innovation and tradition / [by] Raymond D. Souza. — Columbia ; London : University of Missouri Press, 1976. — xi,120p ; 23cm.
Bibl.: p.109-120.
ISBN 0-8262-0210-1 : £7.50
(B77-18434)

863 — Fiction in Spanish. Latin American writers, 1910-. *Critical studies*

Brotherston, Gordon. The emergence of the Latin American novel / [by] Gordon Brotherston. — Cambridge [etc.] : Cambridge University Press, 1977. — viii,164p ; 23cm.
Bibl.: p.150-160. — Index.
ISBN 0-521-21478-5 : £6.50
(B77-28261)

Donoso, José. The boom in Spanish American literature : a personal history / by José Donoso ; translated [from the Spanish] by Gregory Kolovakos. — New York ; Guildford : Columbia University Press [for] the Center for Inter-American Relations, 1977. — xiv,122p ; 22cm.
Translation of: 'Historia personal del "boom"' Barcelona : Editorial Anagraima, 1972. — Index.
ISBN 0-231-04164-0 : £6.45
ISBN 0-231-04165-9 Pbk : Unpriced
(B77-19072)

863 — Short stories in Spanish. Uruguayan writers, 1888-1910. *English texts*

Quiroga, Horacio. The decapitated chicken, and other stories / by Horacio Quiroga ; selected & translated by Margaret Sayers Peden ; introduction by George D. Schade ; illustrations by Ed Lindlof. — Austin ; London : University of Texas Press, 1976. — xviii,195p : ill ; 21cm. — (The Texas pan American Series)
ISBN 0-292-77514-8 : £6.30
(B77-06953)

863.3 — SPANISH FICTION, 1516-1700
863′.3 — Fiction in Spanish, 1516-1700. *English texts*

Cervantes Saavedra, Miguel de. The portable Cervantes / translated and edited, with an introduction and notes, by Samuel Putnam. — Harmondsworth [etc.] : Penguin, 1976. — ix, 854p ; 18cm. — (The Viking portable library)
This collection of translations originally published: New York : Viking Press, 1951. — Bibl.: p.35-38. — Includes 'Don Quixote'.
ISBN 0-14-015057-9 Pbk : Unpriced
(B77-06954)

863′.3 — Fiction in Spanish, 1516-1700. *Texts*

Quevedo y Villegas, Francisco Gómez de. La vida del buscón Llamado don Pablos / [por] Francisco de Quevedo ; edited with an introduction and notes by B.W. Ife. — Oxford [etc.] : Pergamon, 1977. — vii,286p ; 22cm. — (Pergamon international library) (Pergamon Oxford Spanish series)
Spanish text, English introduction and notes. — Bibl.: p.35-36.
ISBN 0-08-021855-5 : £9.00
(B77-32945)

863′.3 — Fiction in Spanish. Cervantes Saavedra, Miguel de. Don Quixote. *Critical studies*

Robert, Marthe. The old and the new : from Don Quixote to Kafka / [by] Marthe Robert ; translated [from the French] by Carol Cosman ; foreword by Robert Alter. — Berkeley [etc.] ; London : University of California Press, 1977. — xiii,322p ; 21cm.
Translation of: 'L'ancien et le nouveau'. Paris : Payot, 1967.
ISBN 0-520-02509-1 : £8.75
Primary classification 833′.9′12
(B77-25254)

863′.3 — Fiction in Spanish. Gracián y Morales, Baltasar. Criticón. Allegory. Structure

Kassier, Theodore L. The truth disguised : allegorical structure and technique in Gracian's 'Criticon' / [by] Theodore L. Kassier. — London : Tamesis, 1976. — iii-viii,150p ; 24cm. — (Colección Támesis ; serie A : monografías ; 53)
Index.
ISBN 0-7293-0006-4 : £11.00
(B77-07694)

863.6F — SPANISH FICTION, 1900-. NOVELS (INCLUDING TRANSLATIONS)
863′.6F — Fiction in Spanish, 1900-. *Texts (including translations)*

Arreola, Juan José. The fair / [by] Juan José Arreola ; translated by John Upton ; illustrations by Barbara Whitehead. — Austin ; London : University of Texas Press, 1977. — [1],ix,154p : ill ; 24cm. — (The Texas pan American series)
Translation of: 'La feria'. México : Mortiz, 1963.
ISBN 0-292-72417-9 : £7.50
(B77-24574)

Borges, Jorge Luis. Doctor Brodie's report / [by] Jorge Luis Borges ; translated by Norman Thomas di Giovanni in collaboration with the author. — Harmondsworth [etc.] : Penguin, 1976. — 106p ; 19cm.
This translated collection originally published: New York : Dutton, 1972 ; London : Allen Lane, 1974. — Translation of: 'El informe de Brodie'. Buenos Aires : Emece Editores, 1970.
ISBN 0-14-004057-9 Pbk : £0.60
(B77-15584)

Borges, Jorge Luis. Fictions / [by] Jorge Luis Borges ; edited and with an introduction by Anthony Kerrigan ; [translated by Anthony Kerrigan and others]. — London : Calder and Boyars, 1974. — 159p ; 19cm.
This translated collection originally published: as 'Ficciones', New York : Grove Press ; London : Weidenfeld and Nicolson, 1962 ; and as 'Fictions', London : Calder, 1965. — Translation of: 'Ficciones'. Buenos Aires : Emecé Editores, 1956.
ISBN 0-7145-0957-4 : £3.50
(B77-01880)

Cuentos americanos de nuestros días : ten Spanish American short stories / edited with a general introduction, biographical introductions, notes and vocabulary by Jean Franco. — London : Harrap, 1976. — 179p : maps ; 20cm.

Spanish text, English introductions and notes. — This collection originally published: 1965. — Bibl.: p.16.
ISBN 0-245-53037-1 Pbk : £1.70
(B77-11461)

Delibes, Miguel. Cinco horas con Mario / [por] Miguel Delibes ; edited by Leo Hickey. — London : Harrap, 1977. — xli,382p : port ; 19cm. — (Modern world literature series)
Spanish text, English introduction and notes. — Originally published: Barcelona : Ediciones Destino, 1966. — Bibl.: p.2-4.
ISBN 0-245-50401-x Pbk : £3.65
(B77-30811)

Fuentes, Carlos. The death of Artemio Cruz / [by] Carlos Fuentes ; translated from the Spanish by Sam Hileman. — London : Secker and Warburg, 1977. — [5],306p ; 23cm.
This translation originally published: London : Collins, 1964. — Translation of: 'La muerte de Artemio Cruz'. México : Fondo de Cultura Económica, 1962.
ISBN 0-436-16761-1 : £3.90
(B77-34266)

García Márquez, Gabriel. The autumn of the patriarch / [by] Gabriel García Márquez ; translated from the Spanish by Gregory Rabassa. — London : Cape, 1977. — [5],229p ; 23cm.
This translation originally published: New York : Harper and Row, 1976. — Translation of: 'El otoño del patriarca'. Esplugas de Llobregat : Plaza and Janés, 1975.
ISBN 0-224-01394-7 : £4.50 : CIP rev.
(B77-06350)

Gonzalez Aller, Faustino. Niña Huanca / [by] Faustino Gonzalez-Aller ; translated from the Spanish by Margaret Sayers Peden. — London : Secker and Warburg, 1977. — [7], 243p ; 23cm.
Translation of: 'Niña Huanca'. Barcelona : Seix Barral, 1974. — Previous control number ISBN 0-436-18330-7.
£3.90
ISBN 0-436-18330-7
(B77-20758)

Scorza, Manuel. Drums for Rancas / [by] Manuel Scorza ; translated from the Spanish by Edith Grossman. — London : Secker and Warburg, 1977. — x,214p ; 23cm.
This translation also published: New York : Harper and Row, 1977. — Translation of: 'Redoble por Rancas'. Barcelona : Editorial Planeta, 1970.
ISBN 0-436-44421-6 : £3.90
(B77-21555)

Vazquez-Figueroa, Alberto. Ebano / [by] Alberto Vazquez-Figueroa. — London : Hale, 1977. — 254p ; 21cm.
Translation of: 'Ebano'. Esplugas de Llobregat : Plaza and Janés, 1974?.
ISBN 0-7091-6065-8 : £3.95
(B77-22967)

868.3 — SPANISH MISCELLANY, 1516-1700
868'.3'08 — Humorous prose in Spanish, 1516-1700. *Texts*
Soons, Alan. Haz y envés del cuento risible en el Siglo de Oro : estudio y antología / [por] Alan C. Soons. — London : Tamesis, 1976. — [6], 106p ; 24cm. — (Colección Támesis ; serie A : monografías ; 49)
Bibl.
ISBN 0-7293-0005-6 : £5.00
(B77-07695)

868.62 — SPANISH MISCELLANY, 1900-1945
868'.6'209 — Spanish literature, 1900-1945. *Texts with facsimiles*
García Lorca, Federico. Autógrafos / [de] Federico García Lorca ; prólogo, transcripción y notas por Rafael Martínez Nadal. — Oxford : Dolphin Book Co., 1975-76. — 2v.(xxxvi,263p; lvii,145p) : 1 ill ; 28cm.
In slip case. — Includes facsimiles.
Pbk : £25.00
ISBN 0-85215-052-0 Vol.1
ISBN 0-85215-053-9 Vol.2
(B77-13945)

869.1 — PORTUGUESE POETRY
869'.1'2 — Poetry in Portuguese, 1500-1800. *English texts*
Camões, Luiz de. Some poems [of] Camões / translated from the Portuguese by Jonathan Griffin. — London (23 Fitzwarren Gardens, N19 3TR) : The Menard Press, 1976. — 41,[2] p ; 22cm.
Includes 2 essays by Jorge de Sena and Helder Macedo.
ISBN 0-903400-20-0 Sd : £0.75
(B77-06955)

869'.1'41 — Poetry in Portuguese, 1900-1945. *English texts*
Pessoa, Fernando. Stations of the cross / by Fernando Pessoa ; translated by J.C.R. Green. — Breakish : Aquila, 1976. — [23]p ; 21cm.
Also available in limited ed. of 26 copies, signed and lettered by the translator.
ISBN 0-7275-0176-3 Sd : £0.25
ISBN 0-7275-0177-1 Signed ed. : £1.25
(B77-15585)

Reis, Ricardo. The ancient rhythm / [by] Ricardo Reis ; translated by J.C.R. Green. — Breakish : Aquila, 1976. — [23]p ; 21cm.
Also available in a limited ed. of 26 copies, signed and lettered by the translator.
ISBN 0-7275-0178-x Sd : £0.25
ISBN 0-7275-0179-8 Signed ed. : £1.25
(B77-15586)

869.3 — PORTUGUESE FICTION
869'.3'4J — Children's stories in Portuguese, 1900-. *Texts (including translations)*
Ostrovsky, Vivian. Mumps / story by Vivian Ostrovsky ; illustrated by Rose Ostrovsky. — Harmondsworth : Kestrel Books, 1977. — [26] p : col ill ; 23cm.
Col. ill. on lining papers. — Translation of: 'Caxumba!'. Rio de Janeiro? : Gráficia Editora Primor, 1976.
ISBN 0-7226-5300-x : £1.95
(B77-15587)

870 — ITALIC LITERATURES
870'.8'001 — Latin literature, to ca 500. *Anthologies. English texts*
The **portable** Roman reader / edited, and with an introduction, by Basil Davenport. — Harmondsworth [etc.] : Penguin, 1977. — xiii, 656p ; 18cm. — (The Viking portable library)
Spine title: Roman reader. — This collection of translations originally published: New York : Viking Press, 1951.
ISBN 0-14-015056-0 Pbk : £1.95
(B77-14454)

871 — LATIN POETRY
871'.01 — Poetry in Latin. Lucretius Carus, Titus. De rerum natura. Special themes: Politics
Nichols, James Hunt. Epicurean political philosophy : the 'De rerum natura' of Lucretius / [by] James H. Nichols, Jr. — Ithaca ; London : Cornell University Press, 1976. — 214p ; 23cm.
Index.
ISBN 0-8014-0993-4 : £8.05
(B77-09363)

871'.01 — Poetry in Latin, to ca 500. *Texts*
Virgil. Eclogues [of] Vergil / edited by Robert Coleman. — Cambridge [etc.] : Cambridge University Press, 1977. — viii,303p ; 19cm. — (Cambridge Greek and Latin classics)
Latin text, English introduction and commentary. — Bibl.: p.298-300. — Index.
ISBN 0-521-20082-2 : £10.50
ISBN 0-521-29107-0 Pbk : £3.95
(B77-21556)

871'.01 — Poetry in Latin. Virgil. Compared with Shakespeare, William
Knight, George Wilson. Vergil and Shakespeare / by G. Wilson Knight. — Exeter : University of Exeter, 1977. — [1],26,[1]p ; 21cm. — (Jackson Knight memorial lecture ; 9th)
'Delivered at the University of Exeter 27th February 1976'.
ISBN 0-85989-037-6 Sd : £0.50
Primary classification 822.3'3
(B77-15472)

872 — LATIN DRAMATIC POETRY AND DRAMA
872'.01 — Drama in Latin, to ca 500. *English texts*
Terence. The comedies [of] Terence / translated with an introduction by Betty Radice. — Revised ed. — Harmondsworth [etc.] : Penguin, 1976. — 398p ; 18cm. — (The Penguin classics)

Previous ed. of these translations: published in 2 vols, 'The brothers and other plays', 1965 ; and 'Phormio and other plays', 1967. — Bibl.: p.396-398.
ISBN 0-14-044324-x Pbk : £1.25
(B77-03804)

872'.01 — Drama in Latin, to ca 500. *Texts*
Seneca, Lucius Annaeus, *b. 5 B.C.?.*
Agamemnon / [by] Seneca ; edited with a commentary by R.J. Tarrant. — Cambridge [etc.] : Cambridge University Press, 1976. — viii,409p : 1 ill ; 23cm. — (Cambridge classical texts and commentaries ; 18)
Latin text, English introduction and commentary. — Bibl.: p.382-391. — Index.
ISBN 0-521-20807-6 : £15.00
(B77-06352)

872'.04 — Drama in Latin, 1350-. *Texts*
Two Jesuit Ahab dramas ... / edited by Nigel Griffin. — [Exeter] : University of Exeter, 1976. — xxv,171p ; 21cm. — (Exeter Hispanic texts ; 13 ISSN 0305-8700)
Latin and Spanish text, English introduction and notes. — Contents: Tragoedia cui nomen inditum Achabus / by Miguel Venegas - Tragaedia Jezabelis.
ISBN 0-85989-007-4 Pbk : £1.00
Also classified at 862'.3
(B77-17802)

873 — LATIN EPIC POETRY AND FICTION
873'.01 — Epic poetry in Latin, to ca 500. *Texts*
Virgil. [Aeneid. Book 4. English & Latin]. Selections from 'Aeneid' IV / [by] Virgil ; with a further selection from the English translation of C. Day Lewis ; [edited by] J.V. Muir. — Cambridge [etc.] ; Cambridge University Press, 1977. — [6],68p : map ; 22cm. — (Cambridge Latin texts)
The whole of 'Aeneid' 4 made up of selected Latin and English passages. — Latin and English text, English notes and vocabulary.
ISBN 0-521-21581-1 Sd : £0.85
(B77-20759)

Virgil. [Aeneid. Book 4. English & Latin]. Selections from 'Aeneid' IV / [by] Virgil ; with a further selection from the English translation of C. Day Lewis ; [edited by] J.V. Muir. — Cambridge [etc.] ; Cambridge University Press. — (Cambridge Latin texts)
Handbook. — 1977. — vi[i.e.vii],68p ; 22cm.
Bibl.: p.4.
ISBN 0-521-21645-1 Sd : £1.95
(B77-25978)

Virgil. [Aeneid. Book 6]. P. Vergili Maronis Aeneidos, Liber sextus / with a commentary by R.G. Austin. — Oxford : Clarendon Press, 1977. — xii,303p : ill, maps, plan ; 20cm.
Latin text, English notes. — Bibl.: p.ix-x. — Index.
ISBN 0-19-872077-7 : £5.00 : CIP rev.
(B77-09364)

873'.01 — Fiction in Latin, to ca 500. *English texts*
Petronius Arbiter. [Satyricon. English]. The Satyricon / [by] Petronius. The apocolocyntosis / [by] Seneca / translated [from the Latin] with introductions and notes by J.P. Sullivan. — Harmondsworth [etc.] : Penguin, 1977. — 3-228p ; 18cm. — (Penguin classics)
This translation of 'The Satyricon' originally published: in 'The Satyricon ; and, The fragments'. 1965. — This translation of 'The apocolocyntosis' originally published: in 'Arion'. Austin : University of Texas Press, 1966.
ISBN 0-14-044313-4 Pbk : £0.85
(B77-32283)

874 — LATIN LYRIC POETRY
874'.008 — Lyric poetry in Latin, B.C.70-A.D.1674. *Anthologies. Latin-English parallel texts*
More Latin lyrics from Virgil to Milton / translated by Helen Waddell ; edited & with an introduction by Dame Felicitas Corrigan. — London : Gollancz, 1976. — 392p,[4]p of plates : facsims, ports ; 23cm.
Parallel Latin text and English translation. — Bibl.: p.34. — Index.
ISBN 0-575-02177-2 : £7.50
(B77-01026)

874'.01 — Lyric poetry in Latin, to ca 500. *Texts*
Ovid. [Ars amatoria. Book 1]. Ars amatoria, Book 1 / [by] Ovid ; edited with an introduction and commentary by A.S. Hollis. — Oxford : Clarendon Press, 1977. — xxiv, 171p : ill, map ; 19cm.
Latin text, English introduction and commentary. — Bibl.: p.156-158. — Index.
ISBN 0-19-814441-5 : £5.00
(B77-19882)

875 — LATIN SPEECHES
875'.01 — Speeches in Latin, to ca 500. *English texts*
Cicero, Marcus Tullius. [Orationes. English. *Selections].* Selected political speeches of Cicero / translated [from the Latin and] with an introduction by Michael Grant. — Harmondsworth [etc.] : Penguin, 1977. — 335p : maps ; 18cm. — (The Penguin classics)
These translations originally published: 1969. — Bibl.: p.323-324. — Index.
Pbk : £0.80
ISBN 0-14-044214-6
(B77-24575)

876 — LATIN LETTERS
876'.01 — Letters in Latin, to ca 500. *Texts*
Cicero, Marcus Tullius. Epistulae ad familiares / Cicero ; edited by D.R. Shackleton Bailey. — Cambridge [etc.] : Cambridge University Press. In 2 vols.
Vol.1 : 62-47 BC. — 1977. — xii,541p : 2 ill ; 23cm. — (Cambridge classical texts and commentaries ; 16)
Latin text, English commentary and introduction. — Bibl.: p.ix-xii. — Index.
ISBN 0-521-21152-2 : £22.50
(B77-25258)

Vol.2 : 47-43 BC. — 1977. — x,630p ; 23cm. — (Cambridge classical texts and commentaries ; 17)
Latin text, English commentary. — Bibl.: p.vii-x. — Index.
ISBN 0-521-21151-4 : £22.50
(B77-25259)

877 — LATIN SATIRE AND HUMOUR
877'.01'09 — Satire in Latin, to ca 500. *Critical studies*
Coffey, Michael. Roman satire / [by] Michael Coffey. — London : Methuen [etc.], 1976. — xvi,289p ; 23cm.
Index.
ISBN 0-416-85120-7 : £7.50
ISBN 0-416-85130-4 Pbk : £4.90
(B77-01881)

880 — CLASSICAL AND MODERN GREEK LITERATURES
880'.07'1241 — Secondary schools. Curriculum subjects: Classics. Teaching. *Great Britain*
Sharwood Smith, John. On teaching classics / [by] J.E. Sharwood Smith. — London [etc.] : Routledge and Kegan Paul, 1977. — viii,93p ; 22cm. — (Students library of education)
Bibl.: p.82-93.
ISBN 0-7100-8580-x : £3.25 : CIP rev.
(B77-07696)

880'.07'1242 — Comprehensive schools. Curriculum subjects: Classics. *England, 1972-1974. Inquiry reports*
Great Britain. *Department of Education and Science. HM Inspectorate (England).* Classics in comprehensive schools : a discussion paper / by some members of HM Inspectorate of Schools. — London : H.M.S.O., 1977. — v,71p : forms ; 25cm. — (Matters for discussion ; 2 ISSN 0309-5746)
ISBN 0-11-270442-5 Pbk : £1.50
(B77-11462)

880'.09 — Classical literatures. *Critical studies. Essays*
Yale classical studies. — Cambridge [etc.] : Cambridge University Press.
Vol.25 : Greek tragedy / edited for the Department of Classics by T.F. Gould and C.J. Herington. — 1977. — ix,350p ; 24cm.
ISBN 0-521-21112-3 : £10.50
(B77-25979)

880'.8'001 — Greek literature, to ca 500. *Anthologies. English texts*
Greek literature : an anthology : translations from Greek prose and poetry / chosen by Michael Grant. — Harmondsworth [etc.] : Penguin, 1976. — 491p : map ; 18cm. — (The Penguin classics)
This collection of translations originally published: as 'Greek literature in translation'. 1973. — Bibl.: p.487-488. — Index.
ISBN 0-14-044323-1 Pbk : £1.00
(B77-09365)

882 — CLASSICAL GREEK DRAMATIC POETRY AND DRAMA

882'.01 — Drama in Greek. Aeschylus. *Critical studies*
Gagarin, Michael. Aeschylean drama / [by] Michael Gagarin. — Berkeley [etc.] ; London : University of California Press, 1976. — xi, 239p ; 23cm.
Bibl.: p.219-228. — Index.
ISBN 0-520-02943-7 : £10.20
(B77-13946)

882'.01 — Drama in Greek. Aeschylus. Prometheus bound. Authenticity
Griffith, Mark. The authenticity of 'Prometheus bound' / [by] Mark Griffith. — Cambridge [etc.] : Cambridge University Press, 1977. — xii,419p ; 23cm. — (Cambridge classical studies)
Bibl.: p.366-379. — Index.
ISBN 0-521-21099-2 : £12.50
(B77-29023)

882'.01 — Drama in Greek, to ca 500. *English texts*
Aeschylus. The complete plays of Aeschylus / translated into English rhyming verse with commentaries and notes by Gilbert Murray. — London : Allen and Unwin, [1976]. — [2], 266p ; 19cm.
Originally published: 1952.
ISBN 0-04-882055-5 Pbk : £2.95
(B77-01027)

Aeschylus. [Oresteia. English]. The Oresteia / [by] Aeschylus ; translated [from the Greek] by Robert Fagles ; introductory essay, notes and glossary by Robert Fagles and W.B. Stanford. — Harmondsworth [etc.] : Penguin, 1977. — 335p : ill, geneal table ; 18cm. — (The Penguin classics)
This translation originally published: London : Wildwood House, 1976. — Bibl.: p.281-283. — Contents: Agamemnon - The libation bearers - The Eumenides.
ISBN 0-14-044333-9 Pbk : £1.00
(B77-27516)

882'.01 — Drama in Greek, to ca 500. *Greek-English parallel texts*
Sophocles. [Antigone. English & Greek (Classical Greek). *Selections].* Bilingual selections from Sophocles' 'Antigone' : an introduction to the text for the Greekless reader / [by] Joan V. O'Brien. — Carbondale [etc.] : Southern Illinois University Press ; London [etc.] : Feffer and Simons, 1977. — xxxvi,100p ; 25cm.
Parallel Greek and English text, English introduction and notes.
ISBN 0-8093-0826-6 : £3.71
(B77-30812)

882'.01 — Drama in Greek, to ca 500. *Texts*
Euripides. Medea / [by] Euripides ; edited by Alan Elliott. — London [etc.] : Oxford University Press, [1977]. — viii,165p,plate : 1 ill ; 19cm.
Greek text, English introduction and notes. — This ed. originally published: 1969.
Pbk : £1.95
ISBN 0-19-912006-4
(B77-13404)

882'.01 — Drama in Greek, to ca 500. Asides. *Critical studies*
Bain, David. Actors & audience : a study of asides and related conventions in Greek drama / [by] David Bain. — Oxford [etc.] : Oxford University Press, 1977. — x,230p ; 22cm. — (Oxford classical and philosophical monographs)
Index.
ISBN 0-19-814714-7 : £9.75
(B77-15588)

882'.01'09 — Drama in classical languages. Comedies, to ca 500. *Critical studies*
Sandbach, Francis Henry. The comic theatre of Greece and Rome / [by] F.H. Sandbach. — London : Chatto and Windus, 1977. — 168p,4p of plates : ill, plans ; 21cm. — (Ancient culture and society)
Bibl.: p.159-163. — Index.
ISBN 0-7011-2193-9 : £4.50
ISBN 0-7011-2194-7 Pbk : £2.25
(B77-14455)

883 — CLASSICAL GREEK EPIC POETRY AND FICTION

883'.01 — Epic poetry in Greek. Hesiod. *Critical studies*
Pucci, Pietro. Hesiod and the language of poetry / [by] Pietro Pucci. — Baltimore ; London : Johns Hopkins University Press, 1977. — vii,152p ; 24cm.
Bibl.: p.143-145. — Index.
ISBN 0-8018-1787-0 : Unpriced
(B77-23805)

883'.01 — Epic poetry in Greek. Homer. *Critical studies*
Trypanis, Constantine Athanasius. The Homeric epics / [by] C.A. Trypanis ; [translated from the Greek by William Phelps]. — Warminster : Aris and Phillips, 1977. — xi,114p ; 22cm.
Bibl.: p.vi-x. — Index.
ISBN 0-85668-085-0 : £6.00
ISBN 0-85668-086-9 Pbk : £2.75
(B77-23806)

883'.01 — Epic poetry in Greek. Homer. Related to orally transmitted poetry. *Essays*
Kirk, Geoffrey Stephen. Homer and the oral tradition / [by] G.S. Kirk. — Cambridge [etc.] : Cambridge University Press, 1976. — viii,223p ; 23cm.
Index.
ISBN 0-521-21309-6 : £7.50
Also classified at 809.1
(B77-05749)

883'.01 — Epic poetry in Greek, to ca 500. *English texts*
The **Homeric** hymns / translation, introduction and notes [by] Apostolos N. Athanassakis. — Baltimore ; London : Johns Hopkins University Press, 1976. — xv,107,[2]p ; 26cm.
ISBN 0-8018-1791-9 : £6.80
ISBN 0-8018-1792-7 Pbk : £1.70
(B77-12770)

884 — CLASSICAL GREEK LYRIC POETRY

884'.01 — Lyric poetry in Greek, to ca 500. *English texts*
Archilochos. Archilochos / introduced, translated and illustrated by Michael Ayrton ; with an essay by G.S. Kirk. — London : Secker and Warburg, 1977. — [9],47p : ill ; 30cm.
Ill. on lining papers. — Bibl.: p.47.
ISBN 0-436-02853-0 : £9.50
(B77-26655)

885 — CLASSICAL GREEK SPEECHES

885'.01 — Speeches in Greek, to ca 500. *Greek-English parallel texts*
Libanius. Selected works [of] Libanius / with an English translation, introduction and notes by A.F. Norman. — Cambridge, Mass. : Harvard University Press ; London : Heinemann. — (The Loeb classical library ; 452)
In 3 vols.
2 : Selected orations. — 1977. — xiv,542p ; 17cm.
Parallel Greek text and English translation. — Bibl.: p.ix-xiv. — Index.
ISBN 0-434-99452-9 : £3.40
(B77-25260)

888 — CLASSICAL GREEK MISCELLANY

888'.01'08 — Prose in Greek, to ca 500. *English texts. Facsimiles*
Aesop. [Fables. English]. The history and fables of Aesop / translated [from the French] ... by William Caxton. — London : Scolar Press, 1976. — [8]p,cxlii fol : ill ; 29cm.
Spine title: The fables of Aesop. — Limited ed. of 500 numbered copies. — 'Reproduced in facsimile from the copy in the Royal Library, Windsor Castle, with an introduction by Edward Hodnett'.
ISBN 0-85967-304-9 : £25.00
(B77-02643)

889 — MODERN GREEK LITERATURE

889'.1'32 — Poetry in modern Greek. Cavafy, Constantine Petrou. Special themes: Egypt. Alexandria. *Critical studies*
Keeley, Edmund. Cavafy's Alexandria : study of a myth in progress / [by] Edmund Keeley. — London : Hogarth Press, 1977. — ix,196p : map ; 24cm.
Originally published: Cambridge, Mass. : Harvard University Press, 1976. — Bibl.: p.171-172. — Index.
ISBN 0-7012-0415-x : £7.50
(B77-15010)

889'.1'34 — Poetry in modern Greek, 1945-. *English texts*
Mitropoulos, Mona. From 'Yellow' to 'Nostos' / [by] Mona Mitropoulos ; [translated by David Phillips]. — London (18 Carlisle St., W.1) : Narcis, 1974. — 3-46p ; 22cm.
ISBN 0-903136-03-1 Pbk : £1.00
(B77-01028)

889'.1'34 — Poetry in Modern Greek, 1945-. *Modern Greek-English parallel texts*
Alexiou, Georgia. Thorn = Agkathi / [by] Georgia Alexiou ; with an English rendering [from the Greek] by Reginald Witt. — London (6 Denmark St., WC2H 8LP) : Zeno Booksellers and Publishers, 1977. — 2-86p ; 24cm.
Parallel Greek text and English translation.
ISBN 0-7228-0015-0 Pbk : £1.50
(B77-29024)

891.2/4 — INDIC LITERATURES

891'.2'1 — Poetry in Sanskrit. *English texts*
Jayadeva. [G-itagovinda. English]. Love song of the Dark Lord : Jayadeva's G-itagovinda / edited and translated [from the Sanskrit] by Barbara Stoler Miller. — New York ; Guildford : Columbia University Press, 1977. — xx,125p : ill ; 23cm. — (Columbia College. Program of translations from the oriental classics) (Unesco. Collection of representative works : Indian series)
English text only.
ISBN 0-231-04029-6 Pbk : £3.70
(B77-29784)

Jayadeva. [G-itagovinda. English & Sanskrit]. Love song of the Dark Lord : Jayadeva's G-itagovinda / edited and translated [from the Sanskrit] by Barbara Stoler Miller. — New York ; Guildford : Columbia University Press, 1977. — xx,225p : ill ; 24cm. — (Columbia College. Program of translations from the oriental classics) (Unesco. Collection of representative works : Indian series)
English and Sanskrit texts.
ISBN 0-231-04028-8 : £11.00
(B77-29785)

891'.2'1008 — Poetry in Sanskrit. *Anthologies. English texts*
Poems from the Sanskrit / translated with an introduction by John Brough. — Harmondsworth [etc.] : Penguin, 1977. — 151p ; 18cm. — (Penguin classics)
These translations originally published: 1968.
ISBN 0-14-044198-0 Pbk : Unpriced
(B77-22968)

891'.4 — Indian literatures, 1947-1974. *Critical studies*
Aspects of Indian literature : the changing pattern / edited by Suresh Kohli. — Delhi [etc.] : Vikas ; Hemel Hempstead (66 Wood Lane End, Hemel Hempstead, Herts.) : Distributed by International Book Distributors Ltd, 1975. — ix,179p ; 22cm.
Index.
ISBN 0-7069-0376-5 : Unpriced
(B77-10626)

891'.43'12 — Poetry in Hindi, 1345-1645. *English texts*
Kab-ir. Try to live to see this! / [by] Kabir ; versions by Robert Bly. — Denver : The Ally Press ; [Knotting] : Sceptre Press, 1976. — [16] p ; 18cm.
ISBN 0-915408-12-0 Sd : £1.00
(B77-01882)

891'.43'15 — Poetry in Hindi, 1895-1920. *English texts*
Nirala. [Poems. Selections. English]. A season on the earth : selected poems of Nirala / translated by David Rubin. — New York ; Guildford : Columbia University Press, 1976 [i.e. 1977]. — 152p ; 24cm. — (Unesco. Collections of representative works : Indian series)
ISBN 0-231-04160-8 : £9.50
ISBN 0-231-04161-6 Pbk : £3.00
(B77-11463)

891'.44'15 — Poetry in Bengali, 1895-1920. *English texts*
Tagore, *Sir* **Rabindranath.** Lipika : prose poems / [by] Rabindranath Tagore ; translated [from the Bengali] and with an introduction by Aurobindo Bose. — London : Owen, 1977. — 140p ; 22cm.
'... [27 poems] from the original "Lipika", with ... other prose poems, a personal letter from Tagore, and a group of poems ... written ... in 1941' - jacket.
ISBN 0-7206-0505-9 : £4.50
(B77-32284)

891'.479'12 — Poetry in Rajasthani, 1345-1645. *Rajasthani-English parallel texts*
The V¯isaladevar¯asa / a restoration of the text [by] John D. Smith. — Cambridge [etc.] : Cambridge University Press, 1976 [i.e. 1977]. — viii,335p : 2 ill ; 23cm. — (University of Cambridge. Oriental publications ; no.26)
Parallel text and English translation. — 'The closest similarity is to be found between the language of our text and Middle M¯arw¯ar¯i ... Old Gujar¯at¯i is older in overall structure ... in certain grammatical details ... [it] resembles neither ... but bears a close similarity to the Central and Western dialects of Modern M¯arw¯ar¯i' - p.45. — Bibl.: p.3-5.
ISBN 0-521-20815-7 : £14.00
(B77-08648)

891.5 — IRANIAN LITERATURES
891'.55'1008 — Poetry in Persian, to ca 1930. *Anthologies. English texts*
The **collected** Persian poems / [translated by] J.C.E. Bowen. — Warminster : Aris and Phillips, 1976. — 3v. : ill ; 21cm.
Cover title. — Contents: A new selection from 'The rubaiyat of Omar Khayyam / rendered into English verse by John Charles Edward Bowen. These translated selections originally published: London : Unicorn Press, 1961 - Poems from the Persian / translated by John Charles Edward Bowen. This translated collection originally published: Oxford : Blackwell, 1948 - The golden pomegranate / rendered into English verse by John Charles Edward Bowen. This translated collection originally published : Bombay : Thacker, 1957.
ISBN 0-85668-038-9 Pbk : £5.50
(B77-02644)

891'.55'11 — Poetry in Persian, 1000-1389. *English texts*
Omar Khayyam. [Rubaiyat. English]. The rubaiyat of Omar Khayyam (who wrote the original stanzas) and Edward FitzGerald (whose "translation" made the poem widely popular among English-speaking people) and Ernest Ludwig Gabrielson (who has ventured to alter the order of FitzGerald's stanzas slightly, and also the number thereof : in addition, he has added his own interpretation). — Caernarfon (2 Bryn Hyfryd, Penisarwaen, Caernarfon [LL55 4BU]) : Rainbow Publications, [1977]. — [5],109,[1]p ; 21cm.
ISBN 0-9505555-0-9 Pbk : £1.86
(B77-09366)

891'.55'13 — Poetry in Persian, 1900-. *English texts*
Baraheni, Reza. God's shadow : prison poems / [by] Reza Baraheni ; [translated by the poet]. — Bloomington ; London : Indiana University Press, 1976. — 103p ; 25cm.
Also published: in Persian. New York : Abjad Publications, 1976.
ISBN 0-253-13218-5 : £7.15
(B77-05750)

891.62 — IRISH LITERATURE
891.6'2'0994174 — Irish literature. Galway (County) writers. *Biographical dictionaries*
Maher, Helen. Galway authors : a contribution towards a biographical and bibliographical index, with an essay on the history and literature in Galway / by Helen Maher. — Galway ([County Library Headquarters, Courthouse, Galway]) : Galway County Libraries, 1976. — [8],vi,116p ; 22cm.
Index.
ISBN 0-9505595-0-4 : £3.75
Primary classification 820'.9'94174
(B77-17051)

891.6'2'1008 — Poetry in Irish, to 1974. *Anthologies*
Éigse : duanaire nua na hArdteistiméireachta / [eagarthóir] Breandán Ó Conaire. — Baile Átha Cliath [i.e. Dublin] : Mac Goill agus Macmillan, 1974. — xvi,587p : ill, facsims, ports ; 25cm.
ISBN 0-7171-0709-4 Pbk : Unpriced
(B77-05094)

891.6'2'13 — Poetry in Irish. Translations into English language. Ferguson, Sir Samuel. *Critical studies*
O'Driscoll, Robert. An ascendancy of the heart : Ferguson and the beginnings of modern Irish literature in English / [by] Robert O'Driscoll ; with an introduction by Máire Cruise O'Brien. — Dublin : Dolmen Press, 1976. — 84p : music ; 23cm.
ISBN 0-85105-317-3 : £4.50
(B77-02645)

891.6'2'14 — Poetry in Irish, 1850-. *Texts*
Ó Fiannachta, Pádraig. Donn Bó agus dánta eile / [le] Pádraig Ó Fiannachta. — Má Nuad [i.e. Maynooth] ([St Patrick's College, Maynooth, Co. Kildare]) : 'An Sagart', 1977. — 56p ; 22cm.
Index. — Includes 3 poems with English translations.
£1.00
Pbk : £0.50
(B77-17166)

Ó Floinn, Críostóir. Aisling dhá abhainn / [le] Críostóir Ó Floinn. — Baile Átha Cliath [i.e. Dublin] (29 Lower O'Connell St., Dublin 1) : Foilseacháin Náisiúnta Tta, 1977. — 80p ; 19cm.
£1.50
(B77-31588)

891.6'2'34F — Fiction in Irish, 1850-. *Texts (including translations)*
Ó Cadhain, Máirtín. An tSraith tógtha / [le] Máirtín Ó Cadhain. — Baile Átha Cliath [i.e. Dublin] : Sáirséal agus Dill, 1977. — 158p : port ; 19cm.
ISBN 0-902563-62-9 : £3.00
(B77-28262)

891.63 — GAELIC LITERATURE
891.6'3'13 — Poetry in Gaelic, 1830-. *Gaelic-English parallel texts*
Maclean, Sorley. Reothairt is contraigh = Spring tide and neap tide : taghadh de dhàin, 1937-72 = selected poems, 1932-72 / [le] Somhairle MacGill-Eain = Sorley Maclean. — Dùn Eideann [i.e. Edinburgh] : Canongate Publishing, 1977. — ix,182p ; 23cm.
Parallel Gaelic and English text.
ISBN 0-903937-15-8 : £5.00
ISBN 0-903937-16-6 Pbk : Unpriced
(B77-25980)

891.6'3'13 — Poetry in Gaelic, 1830-. *Texts*
Mac a'Ghobhainn, Iain. Rabhdan is rudan / le Iain Mac a'Ghobhainn ; na deilbh le Calum Fearghastan. — Glaschu [i.e. Glasgow] (29 Sràid Waterloo, Glaschu C.2) : Gairm, 1973. — [2],21p : ill ; 21cm. — (Clo-bhualaidhean Gairm ; aireamh 36)
ISBN 0-901771-42-2 Sd : Unpriced
(B77-20760)

891.6'3'1308 — Poetry in Gaelic, 1830-. *Anthologies. Gaelic-English parallel texts*
Modern Scottish Gaelic poems = Nua-bhàrdachd Ghàidhlig : a bilingual anthology = duanaire da-theangach / by Sorley Maclean ... [et al.] = le Somhairle MacGill-Eain ... [et al.] ; edited and introduced by Donald MacAulay = deasaichte le roimh-radha aig Domhnall MacAmhlaigh. — Edinburgh : Southside (Publishers), 1976. — 3-220p : 1 ill ; 22cm.
Parallel Gaelic text and English translations.
ISBN 0-900025-20-4 : £4.95
(B77-15011)

891.6'3'33F — Fiction in Gaelic, 1830-. *Texts (including translations)*
Mac A'Ghobhainn, Iain. An t-aonaran / [le] Iain Mac a'Ghobhainn. — Glaschu [i.e. Glasgow] (Glasgow G12) : Roinn nan Cànan Ceilteach, Oilthigh Ghlaschu [Department of Celtic, Glasgow University], 1976. — [4],80p ; 18cm. — (University of Glasgow. Department of Celtic. Leabhraichean ùra Gàidhlig ; aireamh 9)
ISBN 0-903204-07-x Pbk : Unpriced
(B77-10993)

891.6'3'33J — Children's stories in Gaelic, 1830-. *Texts (including translations)*
Mac-a-Phì, Aonghas. Aisling Thorcuill / le Aonghas Mac-a-phì agus Sheila Denoon. — Glaschu [i.e. Glasgow] ([29 Waterloo St., Glasgow G2 6BZ]) : Gairm, 1975. — 48p : ill ; 18x21cm. — (Clo-bhualaidhean Gairm ; leabhar 41)
ISBN 0-901771-50-3 Pbk : £0.60
(B77-09367)

MacLeoid, Fionnlagh. Tugainn cuairt / [le] Fionnlagh MacLeoid ; dealbhan le Jewel B. Nic a'Ghobhainn. — Inbhirnis [i.e. Inverness] (Tigh Obar-Thairbh, Inbhirnis IV1 1EU) : An Comunn Gaidhealach, 1976. — [2],46p : ill ; 22cm.
ISBN 0-9502727-2-8 Sd : £0.65
(B77-09368)

891.66 — WELSH LITERATURE
891.6'6'08002 — Welsh literature. Pembrokeshire dialect literature, 1600-. *Anthologies*
Wês wês : cerddi, straeon ac ysgrifau yn y Ddyfedeg / golygwyd gan John Phillips a Gwyn Griffiths. — Llandysul : Gwasg Gomer, 1976. — 95p ; 19cm.
ISBN 0-85088-380-6 Pbk : £0.75
(B77-10627)

891.6'6'09002 — Welsh literature, 1600-1976. *Critical studies. Essays. Welsh texts*
Jones, John Gwilym. Swyddogaeth beirniadaeth ac ysgrifau eraill / [gan] John Gwilym Jones. — Dinbych [i.e. Denbigh] : Gwasg Gee, 1977. — 329p,plate : port ; 23cm.
£4.50
(B77-21557)

891.6'6'1008 — Poetry in Welsh, to 1971. *Anthologies. English texts*
The **Oxford** book of Welsh verse in English / chosen by Gwyn Jones. — Oxford [etc.] : Oxford University Press, 1977. — xxxvii,313p ; 19cm.
Includes some poems translated from the Welsh. — Index.
ISBN 0-19-211858-7 : £3.95
Also classified at 821'.008
(B77-13947)

891.6'6'1008 — Poetry in Welsh, to ca 1970. *Anthologies. English texts*
To look for a word : collected translations from Welsh poetry / by Gwyn Williams. — Llandysul : Gomer Press, 1976. — xv,278p ; 22cm.
ISBN 0-85088-356-3 Pbk : £3.00
(B77-02646)

891.6'6'105 — Christian poetry in Welsh, 1600-. *Anthologies*
Ffenestri agored : llawlyfr o weddïan cyfoes / golygyddion Harri Parri a William Williams. — Caernarfon : Llyfrfa'r Methodistiaid Calfinaidd, 1976. — 188p ; 22cm.
Index.
Pbk : £1.00
(B77-17803)

891.6'6'11 — Poetry in Welsh, to 1600. *Texts*
Rhys Brydydd. Gwaith Rhys Brydydd a Rhisiart ap Rhys / casglwyd gan John Morgan Williams ; golygwyd gan Eurys I. Rowlands. — Caerdydd [i.e. Cardiff] : Gwasg Prifysgol Cymru ar ran Bwrdd Gwybodau Celtaidd Prifysgol Cymru, 1976. — [1],xi,92p ; 23cm.
Bibl.: p.x-xi. — Index.
ISBN 0-7083-0621-7 : £2.50
(B77-05095)

891.6'6'1108 — Poetry in Welsh, to 1600. Triads. *Anthologies. English texts*
Iolo Morganwg. The triads of Britain / compiled by Iolo Morganwg ; translated [from the Welsh] by W. Probert ; with an introduction and glossary by Malcolm Smith. — London : Wildwood House, 1977. — 112p : ill ; 21cm.
Bibl.: p.112.
ISBN 0-7045-0290-9 Pbk : £2.95
(B77-28263)

891.6'6'1109 — Poetry in Welsh, to 1600. *Critical studies. Welsh texts*
Lloyd, David Myrddin. Rhai agweddau ar ddysg y Gogynfeirdd : darlith goffa G.J. Williams a draddodwyd yng Ngholeg y Brifysgol, Caerdydd, Tachwedd 12, 1976 / gan D. Myrddin Lloyd. — Caerdydd [i.e. Cardiff] : Gwasg Prifysgol Cymru, 1977. — 29p ; 21cm. — (G.J. Williams memorial lectures)
ISBN 0-7083-0658-6 Sd : Unpriced
(B77-32285)

Thomas, Gwyn, *b.1936.* Y traddodiad barddol / [gan] Gwyn Thomas. — Caerdydd [i.e. Cardiff] : Gwasg Prifysgol Cymru, 1976. — 240p ; 22cm.
ISBN 0-7083-0623-3 Pbk : £2.75
(B77-09369)

891.6'6'12 — Poetry in Welsh, 1600-. *Texts*
Alun Cilie. Cerddi Pentalar / [gan] Alun Cilie ; golygydd T. Llew Jones. — Llandysul : Gwasg Gomer, 1976. — 94p,leaf of plate,[2]fold p of plates : geneal table, map, port ; 22cm.
ISBN 0-85088-373-3 Pbk : £1.00
(B77-00488)

Bowen, Euros. Cynullion / [gan] Euros Bowen. — Llandysul : Gwasg Gomer, 1976. — 113p ; 23cm.
Previous control number ISBN 0-85088-345-8.
ISBN 0-85088-346-6 : £1.75
(B77-10010)

Bowen, Euros. O'r corn aur / [gan] Euros Bowen. — Dinbych [i.e. Denbigh] : Gwasg Gee, 1977. — 45p ; 23cm.
Unpriced
(B77-29025)

Culpitt, David Henry. O'r gadair freichiau : cyfrol & farddoniaeth yn cynnwys adroddiadau i blant, telynegion, sonedau a phenillion telyn / gan D.H. Culpitt. — Llandysul : Gwasg Gomer, 1976. — 67p ; 19cm.
ISBN 0-85088-348-2 Pbk : £0.75
(B77-10628)

Davies, Bryan Martin. Y golau caeth / [gan] Bryan Martin Davies. — Llandysul : Gwasg Gomer, 1972. — 76p ; 22cm.
ISBN 0-85088-147-1 : £0.75
(B77-29786)

Davies, Thomas James. Munud o edrych / [gan] T.J. Davies. — Llandysul : Gwasg Gomer, 1976. — 92p : ill ; 19cm. — (Llyfrau poced Gomer)
ISBN 0-85088-352-0 Pbk : £0.75
Primary classification 242
(B77-10151)

Eckley, Geraint. Cerddi hoe a hamdden / [gan] Geraint Eckley. — Abertawe [i.e. Swansea] : C. Davies, 1977. — 34p ; 22cm. — (Cyfres cerddi'r plant ; 1)
ISBN 0-7154-0415-6 Sd : £0.40
(B77-23807)

Elfyn, Menna. Mwyara : cerddi / [gan] Menna Elfyn. — Llandysul : Gwasg Gomer, 1976. — 52p ; 22cm.
ISBN 0-85088-369-5 Pbk : £0.75
(B77-01029)

Evans, Donald. Egin / [gan] Donald Evans. — Llandysul : Gwasg Gomer, 1976. — 82p ; 22cm.
£1.75
Pbk : £1.00
(B77-10629)

Evans, Einion. Cerddi'r parlwr / gan Einion Evans. — Llandysul : Gwasg Gomer, 1977. — 71p ; 22cm.
ISBN 0-85088-446-2 Pbk : £1.00
(B77-29026)

Gwynn Ap Gwilym. Y winllan werdd / [gan] Gwynn ap Gwilym. — Abertawe [i.e. Swansea] : C. Davies, 1977. — 66p ; 21cm.
Includes some poems translated from the Irish.
ISBN 0-7154-0426-1 Pbk : £1.25
(B77-30813)

Jones, Bobi. Gwlad Llun / [gan] Bobi Jones. — Abertawe [i.e. Swansea] : C. Davies, 1976. — 111p ; 22cm.
Index.
ISBN 0-7154-0330-3 : £2.75
(B77-18435)

Jones, Charles. Charles Jones, Mynytho. — Abertawe [i.e. Swansea] : C. Davies, 1977. — [1],43p ; 19cm. — (Cyfres beirdd bro ; 6)
ISBN 0-7154-0401-6 Pbk : £1.25
(B77-34267)

Jones, David Samuel. Hud yr Hydref : cerddi D.S. Jones / wedi eu golygu gan T. Llew Jones. — Llandysul : Gwasg Gomer, 1976. — 101p ; 22cm.
ISBN 0-85088-374-1 Pbk : £1.00
(B77-00489)

Jones, Medwyn. Medwyn Jones, Llangwm. — Abertawe [i.e. Swansea] : C. Davies, 1977. — 64p ; 19cm. — (Cyfres beirdd bro ; 5)
ISBN 0-7154-0400-8 Pbk : £1.25
(B77-33497)

Jones, Moses Glyn. Mae'n ddigon buan / [gan] Moses Glyn Jones. — Abertawe [i.e. Swansea] : C. Davies, 1977. — 63p ; 21cm.
ISBN 0-7154-0421-0 Pbk : £1.25
(B77-30814)

Lewis, Gwyneth. Llwybrau bywyd / [gan] Gwyneth Lewis. — [Aberystwyth] : Urdd Gobaith Cymru, [1977]. — [1],50p : port ; 22cm.
'Cyfrol arobryn Cystadleuaeth y Fedal Lenyddiaeth yn Eisteddfod Genedlaethol Urdd Gobaith Cymru, Y Barri a'r Fro, 1977'. — Note.
Sd : £0.50
Also classified at 891.6'6'8208
(B77-22232)

Lloyd, Islwyn. Emynau a cherddi / gan Islwyn Lloyd. — Abertawe [i.e. Swansea] ([11 St Helen's Rd, Swansea]) : Tŷ John Penry, 1977. — 69p ; 19cm.
ISBN 0-903701-07-3 Pbk : £0.80
(B77-12771)

Morgan, Derec Llwyd. Iliad Homer : cyfaddasiad radio ynghyd ag ysgrif ar 'Apêl Homer' / gan Derec Llwyd Morgan. — Llandysul : Gwasg Gomer, 1976. — 75p,[3]leaves of plates : ill ; 22cm.
ISBN 0-85088-350-4 : £1.25
(B77-05096)

Owain, Owain. Cerddi ddoe a fory / gan Owain Owain. — Llandysul : Gwasg Gomer, 1977. — 54p : ill ; 22cm.
ISBN 0-85088-433-0 Pbk : £0.85
(B77-33498)

Owen, Dafydd. Crist croes / [gan] Dafydd Owen. — Abertawe [i.e. Swansea] ([11 St Helen's Rd, Swansea]) : Tŷ John Penry, 1977. — 65p ; 19cm.
ISBN 0-903701-09-x Pbk : £1.00
(B77-16099)

Owen, Dafydd. Sôn am sbri! / [gan] Dafydd Owen. — Dinbych [i.e. Denbigh] : Gwasg Gee, 1976. — 29p : ill ; 25cm.
ISBN 0-7074-0096-1 : £1.40
(B77-08138)

Rees, George, *b.1873.* 'O! Fab y Dyn' : emynau a cherddi caeth George Rees / detholiad gan Brynley F. Roberts. — Caernarfon : Llyfrfa'r Methodistiaid Calfinaidd, 1976. — 64p ; 19cm.
Pbk : £0.60
(B77-05097)

Roberts, Emrys. Rhys y craen a cherddi eraill i blant / [gan] Emrys Roberts. — Abertawe [i.e. Swansea] : C. Davies, 1977. — 43p ; 22cm. — (Cyfres cerddi'r plant ; 2)
ISBN 0-7154-0416-4 Sd : £0.40
(B77-23808)

Saunders, Tim. Teithiau / [gan] Tim Saunders. — Talybont, Dyfed (Talybont, Dyfed SY24 5ER) : Y Lolfa, 1977. — [2],40,[1]p : ill, facsims, ports ; 25cm. — (Cyfres y beirdd answyddogol ; 2)
ISBN 0-904864-26-x Sd : £0.75
(B77-15589)

Williams, Rhydwen. Ystlumod / [gan] Rhydwen Williams. — Abertawe [i.e. Swansea] : C. Davies, 1975. — 35p : ill ; 21cm.
ISBN 0-7154-0267-6 Pbk : £0.90
(B77-00490)

891.6'6'12 — Poetry in Welsh. Gwilym Cowlyd. *Biographies. Welsh texts*
Davies, Glynne Gerallt. Gwilym Cowlyd, 1828-1904 / gan G. Gerallt Davies. — Caernarfon : Llyfrfa'r Methodistiaid Calfinaidd, 1976. — 205p ; 19cm.
Index.
ISBN 0-901330-69-8 : £1.50
(B77-06353)

891.6'6'12 — Poetry in Welsh. Hopcyn, Wil. Interpersonal relationships with Maddocks, Ann. *Welsh texts*
Richards, Brinley. Wil Hopcyn a'r ferch o Gefn Ydfa / [gan] Brinley Richards. — Abertawe [i.e. Swansea] ([11 St Helen's Rd, Swansea]) : Tŷ John Penry, 1977. — 94p ; 19cm.
Pbk : £1.25
Also classified at 942.9'07'20924
(B77-17804)

891.6'6'12 — Poetry in Welsh. Williams, Waldo. *Festschriften. Welsh texts*
Waldo : cyfrol deyrnged i Waldo Williams / wedi'i golygu gan James Nicholas. — Llandysul : Gwasg Gomer, 1977. — 275p : geneal tables ; 22cm.
Bibl.: p.230-252. — Includes one chapter in English.
ISBN 0-85088-436-5 : £3.50
(B77-31589)

891.6'6'1208 — Poetry in Welsh, 1600-. *Anthologies*
Awen ysgafn 'Y Cilie' / golygydd Gerallt Jones. — Llandysul : Gwasg Gomer, 1976. — 74p, plate : 1 ill ; 22cm.
ISBN 0-85088-366-0 Pbk : £0.90
(B77-02647)

891.6'6'1208 — Poetry in Welsh, 1600-. *Anthologies. Secondary school texts*
Dragon's hoard : an anthology of modern poetry for Welsh secondary schools / edited by Sam Adams and Gwilym Rees Hughes. — Llandysul : Gwasg Gomer, 1976. — 133p ; 22cm.
Poems in Welsh and English. — 'The poems in the Welsh language are accompanied by translations' - Foreword. — Index.
ISBN 0-85088-322-9 Pbk : £1.50
Primary classification 821'.9'1208
(B77-03197)

891.6'6'1208 — Poetry in Welsh, 1600-. *Anthologies. Serials*
Cerddi. — Llandysul : Gwasg Gomer.
'77 / golygydd W. Rhys Nicholas. — 1977. — 118p ; 21cm.
ISBN 0-85088-397-0 Pbk : £1.50
(B77-27517)

Cerddi Prifeirdd. — Abertawe [i.e. Swansea] : C. Davies.
Cyf. 1 / casglwyd a golygwyd gan Alan Llwyd. — 1977. — 74p ; 22cm.
ISBN 0-7154-0422-9 : £2.50
(B77-27518)

891.6'6'1208 — Poetry in Welsh. Glamorgan writers. Tribannau, 1600-. *Anthologies*
Tribannau Morgannwg / [caegliwyd gan] Tegwyn Jones ; gyda nodiadau ar rai ceinciau triban gan Daniel Huws. — Llandysul : Gwasg Gomer, 1976. — 3-242p : music ; 19cm.
Index.
ISBN 0-85088-364-4 Pbk : £1.50
(B77-01883)

891.6'6'120938 — Poetry in Welsh, 1600-. Special subjects: Christianity. *Critical studies. Welsh texts*
Tilsley, Gwilym R. Crefydd y beirdd : darlith D.J. James 1977 / gan Gwilym R. Tilsley. — Abertawe [i.e. Swansea] ([11 St Helen's Rd, Swansea]) : Tŷ John Penry, 1977. — 38p ; 19cm. — (Darlith D.J. James ; 1977)
'Traddodwyd yng Ngholeg y Brifysgol, Aberystwyth'.
Sd : £0.40
(B77-20761)

891.6'6'22 — Drama in Welsh, 1600-. *Texts*
Edwards, Huw Lloyd. Y lefiathan : ffantasi mewn pum golygfa / gan Huw Lloyd Edwards. — Dinbych [i.e. Denbigh] : Gwasg Gee, 1977. — 71p ; 22cm.
Pbk : £1.80
(B77-26657)

Jones, John Gwilym. Ac eto nid myfi : drama dair act / gan John Gwilym Jones. — Dinbych [i.e. Denbigh] : Gwasg Gee, 1976. — 86p,plate : 1 ill ; 22cm.
ISBN 0-7074-0097-x Pbk : £1.50
(B77-08139)

Jones, John Gwilym. Rhyfedd y'n gwnaed : tair drama / gan John Gwilym Jones. — Dinbych [i.e. Denbigh] : Gwasg Gee, 1976. — 72p ; 22cm.
Contents: Tri chyfaill - Dwy ystafell - Un briodas.
ISBN 0-7074-0098-8 Pbk : £1.50
(B77-08140)

Lewis, Saunders. Blodeuwedd : drama mewn pedair act / [gan] Saunders Lewis. — [Denbigh] : Gwasg Gee, [1977]. — 98p ; 22cm.
Originally published: 1948.
Pbk : £1.00
(B77-33499)

Roberts, Eigra Lewis. Byd o amser : drama wedi ei seilio ar hanes Ann Thomas (Griffiths), Dolwar Fechan / gan Eigra Lewis Roberts. — Llandysul : Gwasg Gomer, 1976. — 93p ; 19cm.
ISBN 0-85088-355-5 Pbk : £1.10
(B77-05098)

Williams, Gwyn, *b.1904.* Troelus a Chresyd : trasiedi / wedi ei olygu a'i ddiweddaru gan Gwyn Williams. — Llandysul : Gwasg Gomer, 1976. — 110p ; 22cm.
Based on a play written in Peniarth MS. 106, held at the National Library of Wales.
ISBN 0-85088-367-9 Pbk : £1.25
(B77-10011)

891.6'6'31 — Fiction in Welsh. Mabinogion. *Critical studies*

MacCana, Proinsias. The mabinogi / [by] Proinsias MacCana. — [Cardiff] : University of Wales Press [for] the Welsh Arts Council, 1977. — [3],140p,plate : facsim ; 25cm. — (Writers of Wales)
Limited ed. of 1000 numbered copies.
ISBN 0-7083-0655-1 Pbk : £1.50
(B77-31590)

891.6'6'31 — Fiction in Welsh, to 1600. *English texts*

The **mabinogi** and other medieval Welsh tales / translated [from the Welsh] with an introduction by Patrick K. Ford. — Berkeley [etc.] ; London : University of California Press, 1977. — xii,205p : 2 maps ; 23cm.
Bibl.: p.30-32. — Index.
ISBN 0-520-03205-5 : £1.85
(B77-30815)

891.6'6'31 — Fiction in Welsh, to 1600. *Texts*

[Peredur]. Historia Peredur vab Efrawc / golygwyd gyda rhagymadrodd, nodiadau testunol a geirfa gan Glenys Witchard Goetinck. — Caerdydd [i.e. Cardiff] : Gwasg Prifysgol Cymru ar ran Bwrdd Gwybodan Celtaidd Prifysgol Cymru, 1976. — xxixp, p7-190 ; 19cm.
Bibl.
ISBN 0-7083-0440-0 : £3.50
(B77-03805)

891.6'6'32F — Fiction in Welsh, 1600-. *Texts (including translations)*

Aled Islwyn. Lleuwen / gan Aled Islwyn. — Y Bala : Llyfrau'r Faner, 1977. — [3],276p ; 20cm.
£2.50
(B77-24576)

Charles-Evans, Hazel. Eluned Caer Madog / gan Hazel Charles Evans. — Llandysul : Gwasg Gomer, 1976. — 225p ; 19cm. — (Llyfrau poced Gomer)
ISBN 0-85088-401-2 Pbk : £1.25
(B77-05099)

Dewi Emlyn. Llythyrau Anna Beynon / [gan Dewi Emlyn] ; golygydd D. Elwyn Davies. — Llandysul : Gwasg Gomer, 1976. — 96p ; 19cm.
Originally published: in 'Yr Haul', Carmarthen, 1870.
ISBN 0-85088-480-2 Pbk : £0.75
(B77-06956)

Edwards, Jane. Dros fryniau Bro Afallon / gan Jane Edwards. — Llandysul : Gwasg Gomer, 1976. — 162p ; 22cm.
ISBN 0-85088-391-1 : £1.75
(B77-10012)

Evans, Bernard. Cyrch Ednyfed : nofel / gan Bernard Evans. — Llandysul : Gwasg Gomer, 1977. — 122p ; 19cm.
ISBN 0-85088-493-4 Pbk : £0.80
(B77-33500)

Evans, Tudor Wilson. Cilfach Lamorna / [gan] T. Wilson Evans. — Abertawe [i.e. Swansea] : C. Davies, 1977. — 142p ; 19cm.
ISBN 0-7154-0386-9 Pbk : £1.50
(B77-29787)

Griffith, Stephen. Mab y trofannau / [gan] Stephen Griffith. — Abertawe [i.e. Swansea] : C. Davies, 1977. — 132p ; 22cm.
ISBN 0-7154-0428-8 Pbk : Unpriced
(B77-29788)

Hughes, Richard Cyril. Dinas ddihenydd / [gan] Richard Cyril Hughes. — Llandysul : Gwasg Gomer, 1976. — 221p : geneal table, map ; 22cm.
ISBN 0-85088-471-3 : £2.75
(B77-10013)

Jones, Idwal. Mr Saceus a'i short : storïau pregethwr / [gan] Idwal Jones. — Llanrwst (Llanrwst, Gwynedd) : Llyfrau Tryfan, 1976. — 97p ; 19cm.
Pbk : Unpriced
(B77-27519)

Jones, Rhiannon Davies. Llys Aberffraw / gan Rhiannon Davies Jones. — Llandysul : Gwasg Gomer, 1977. — 204p ; 19cm.
ISBN 0-85088-496-9 Pbk : £1.25
(B77-29789)

Jones, Tom, *b.1950.* Brain yn y brwyn / [gan] Tom Jones. — Dinbych [i.e. Denbigh] : Gwasg Gee, 1976. — 89p ; 19cm.
ISBN 0-7074-0095-3 Pbk : £1.00
(B77-05100)

Lloyd, John Selwyn. Breuddwyd yw ddoe : nofel garu fer / gan J. Selwyn Lloyd. — Llandysul : Gwasg Gomer, 1976. — 66p ; 19cm. — (Llyfrau poced Gomer)
ISBN 0-85088-470-5 Pbk : £0.75
(B77-05101)

Lloyd, John Selwyn. Esgyrn sychion / [gan] J. Selwyn Lloyd. — Llandysul : Gwasg Gomer, 1977. — 110p ; 19cm. — (Llyfrau poced Gomer)
ISBN 0-85088-483-7 Pbk : £0.90
(B77-27520)

Owain, Owain. Mical, 1780-1849 : cofiant dychmygus / gan Owain Owain. — Llandysul : Gwasg Gomer, 1976. — 131p : map ; 19cm. — (Llyfrau poced Gomer)
Based on the life of the Rev. Michael Roberts.
ISBN 0-85088-411-x Pbk : £0.75
(B77-05102)

Parri, Dafydd. Un nos Lun a storïau eraill : cyfrol o storïau byrion / [gan] Dafydd Parri. — Llandysul : Gwasg Gomer, 1976. — 135p ; 19cm. — (Llyfrau poced Gomer)
ISBN 0-85088-381-4 Pbk : £0.75
(B77-10014)

Parri-Jones, Tom. Y ddau bren : nofel / gan Tom Parri Jones. — Llandysul : Gwasg Gomer, 1976. — 137p ; 19cm.
ISBN 0-85088-421-7 Pbk : £0.75
(B77-05751)

Parri-Jones, Tom. Y felltith a storïau eraill / [gan] Tom Parri Jones. — [Denbigh] : Gwasg Gee, 1977. — 92p ; 19cm.
Pbk : £1.00
(B77-23809)

Parry, Geraint W. Trechu'r eryr / [gan] Geraint W. Parry. — Llandysul : Gwasg Gomer, 1977. — 172p : map ; 19cm.
ISBN 0-85088-444-6 Pbk : £1.10
(B77-27521)

Pritchard, Marged. Nid mudan mo'r môr / [gan] Marged Pritchard. — Llandysul : Gwasg Gomer [ar ran] Llys yr Eisteddfod Genedlaethol, 1976. — 244p ; 19cm. — (Eisteddfod Genedlaethol Frenhinol Cymru. Medal ryddiaith ; 1976)
ISBN 0-85088-375-x Pbk : £1.50
(B77-10015)

Richards, Tom. Pobol y Cwm / cyfaddaswyd gan Tom Richards. — Llandysul : Gwasg Gomer, 1976. — 126p : ill ; 21cm.
'Seiliedig ar ddrama-gyfres deledu BBC Cymru'. — 'Pobol y Cwm cyfres 1' - cover.
ISBN 0-85088-422-5 Pbk : £0.90
(B77-05103)

Roberts, Kate. Feet in chains : a novel / by Kate Roberts ; translated from the original Welsh by Idwal Walters and John Idris Jones. — Cardiff (41 Lochaber St., Cardiff CF2 3LS) : John Jones Cardiff Ltd, 1977. — 133p ; 23cm.
Translation of: 'Traed mewn cyffion'. Aberystwyth : Gwasg Aberystwyth, 1936.
ISBN 0-902375-23-7 : £3.25
(B77-30816)

Roberts, Kate. The living sleep : a novel / by Kate Roberts ; translated from the Welsh by Wyn Griffith. — Cardiff (41 Lochaber St., Cardiff CF2 3LS) : John Jones Cardiff Ltd, 1976. — 3-195p ; 22cm.
Translation of: Y byw sy'n cysgu'. Dinbych : Gwasg Gee, 1956.
ISBN 0-902375-14-8 : £3.95
(B77-03806)

Williams, Emlyn, *b.1915.* Blagur o'r llwch / gan Emlyn Williams. — Bala : Llyfrau'r Faner, 1976. — [2],164p ; 20cm.
ISBN 0-901695-32-7 : £2.00
(B77-16640)

Williams, John Roberts. Arch Noa a rhai o'r creaduriaid / [gan] John Roberts Williams. — Nant Peris (Nant Peris, Gwynedd) : Gwasg Gwynedd, 1977. — 84p ; 18cm.
Pbk : £0.80
(B77-27522)

891.6'6'32J — Children's stories in Welsh, 1600-. *Texts (including translations)*

Chilton, Irma. Breichled Modlen : nofel arobryn yn Eisteddfod Powys 1975 / [gan] Irma Chilton. — Abertawe [i.e. Swansea] : C. Davies, 1977. — 55p ; 22cm.
ISBN 0-7154-0414-8 Pbk : £0.75
(B77-23810)

Cooke, Catherine. Roli a Samson / [gan] Catherine Cooke. — Llanelli ([Llanelli, Dyfed]) : Gwasg Dyfed, 1977. — [31]p : ill ; 20cm.
Pbk : Unpriced
(B77-33501)

Hughes, Emily. Y Tomosiaid ar y mynydd / [gan] Emily Hughes ; arluniwyd gan Thomas Charles Williams. — Llandysul : Gwasg Gomer, 1976. — 73p : ill ; 21cm.
ISBN 0-85088-451-9 Pbk : £0.90
(B77-05104)

Jones, Janet. Eli yr eliffant bach a storïau eraill / [gan] Janet Jones ; arluniwyd gan Penny Walton. — Dinbych [i.e. Denbigh] : Gwasg Gee, 1977. — 124p : col ill ; 20cm.
ISBN 0-7074-0099-6 Pbk : £1.50
(B77-10016)

Jones, Mary, *b.1908.* Ysgub gymysg / [gan] Mary Jones ; lluniau gan Jac Jones. — Llandysul : Gwasg Gomer, 1976. — 64p : ill ; 21cm.
With answers. — Previous control number B7710630.
ISBN 0-85088-345-8 Pbk : £0.95
(B77-10630)

Jones, Stephen. Y sŵn / gan Stephen Jones. — Llandysul : Gwasg Gomer, 1976. — 133p ; 21cm.
ISBN 0-85088-349-0 Pbk : £1.25
(B77-10631)

Parri, Dafydd. Y Llewod yn colli menig / [gan] Dafydd Parri ; y lluniau a'r clawr [gan] Elwyn Ioan. — Talybont, Dyfed (Talybont, Dyfed SY24 5ER) : Y Lolfa, 1977. — 95p : ill, ports ; 19cm. — (Cyfres y Llewod ; 9)
ISBN 0-904864-40-5 Pbk : £0.75
(B77-19074)

Parri, Dafydd. Pum cyfrinach y Llewod / [gan] Dafydd Parri ; y clawr a'r lluniau [gan] Elwyn Ioan. — Talybont, Dyfed (Talybont, Dyfed SY24 5ER) : Y Lolfa, 1977. — 95p : ill ; 19cm. — (Cyfres y Llewod ; 10)
ISBN 0-904864-41-3 : Unpriced
ISBN 0-904864-42-1 Pbk : £0.75
(B77-19075)

Phillips, Juli. Hwyl cyn noswylio / [gan] Juli Phillips ; lluniau gan Bernadette Watts. — Caerdydd [i.e. Cardiff] : Gwasg y Dref Wen, 1977. — 63p : ill ; 19cm. — (Cyfres y wiwer)
Pbk : £1.10
(B77-22233)

Roberts, Emrys. Siarc! / [gan] Emrys Roberts. — [Abersoch] ([Creigle, Abersoch, Pwllheli, Gwynedd]) : Gwasg Tŷ ar y Graig, 1976. — 87p : ill ; 20cm.
Pbk : £1.25
(B77-33502)

Strange, Morfudd. Y llyfr mawr difyr / [gan] Morfudd Strange. — Abertawe [i.e. Swansea] : Hughes a'i Fab, 1977. — 212p,[8]p of plates : ill(some col) ; 26cm.
£2.50
(B77-27523)

Thomas, David John, *b.1903.* Storïau natur i blant / [gan] D.J. Thomas ; lluniau gan Rob Phillips. — Llandysul : Gwasg Gomer, 1976. — 24p : col ill ; 21cm.
ISBN 0-85088-340-7 Sd : £0.45
(B77-10632)

Walters, Olwen Llewelyn. Prydwen yn dysgu bod yn nyrs / [gan] O. Ll. Walters. — Llanelli ([Llanelli, Dyfed]) : Gwasg Dyfed, 1976. — 125p : ill ; 19cm.
Unpriced
(B77-33503)

Williams, Anwen P. Antur Elin a Gwenno : stori i blant 9-11 oed / [gan] Anwen P. Williams ; lluniau gan Alan Howard. — Llandysul : Gwasg Gomer, 1976. — 49p : ill ; 22cm.
ISBN 0-85088-343-1 Pbk : £0.60
(B77-10633)

891.6'6'32 — Fiction in Welsh. Owen, Daniel. *Critical studies. Welsh-English parallel texts*
Jones, John Gwilym. The novelist from Mold / by John Gwilym Jones ; [translated from the Welsh by the author]. — [Mold] ([Mold, Clwyd]) : Daniel Owen Memorial Room Committee, 1976. — 18,20p ; 21cm. — (Daniel Owen memorial lecture ; 1)
'... the lecturer's own translation ... of the public discourse given at Bethesda Chapel, Mold, on the evening of 29 October 1975' - Introduction. — Includes the original Welsh text, printed tête-bêche, under the title 'Nofelydd yr Wyddgrug.
ISBN 0-9505597-0-9 Sd : £0.50
(B77-12179)

891.6'6'32 — Fiction in Welsh. Roberts, Kate. *Critical studies. Welsh texts*
Emyr, John. Enaid clwyfus : golwg ar waith Kate Roberts / [gan] John Emyr. — Dinbych [i.e. Denbigh] : Gwasg Gee, 1976. — 256p ; 23cm.
Index.
ISBN 0-7074-0094-5 : £3.50
(B77-05752)

891.6'6'8208 — Humorous prose in Welsh, 1600-. *Texts*
Ap Lewys, Edgar. Hiwmor y glöwr / [gan] Edgar ap Lewys ; cartŵnau Elwyn Ioan. — Talybont, Dyfed (Talybont, Dyfed SY24 5ER) : Y Lolfa, 1977. — 96p : ill ; 19cm. — (Pocedlyfrau'r Lolfa)
ISBN 0-904864-34-0 Pbk : £0.85
(B77-16100)

891.6'6'8208 — Prose in Welsh, 1600-. *Texts*
Lewis, Gwyneth. Llwybrau bywyd / [gan] Gwyneth Lewis. — [Aberystwyth] : Urdd Gobaith Cymru, [1977]. — [1],50p : port ; 22cm.
'Cyfrol arobryn Cystadleuaeth y Fedal Lenyddiaeth yn Eisteddfod Genedlaethol Urdd Gobaith Cymru, Y Barri a'r Fro, 1977'. — Note.
Sd : £0.50
Primary classification 891.6'6'12
(B77-22232)

891.6'6'8208 — Prose in Welsh. Jenkins, Robert Thomas. *Critical studies*
Llywelyn-Williams, Alun. R.T. Jenkins / [by] Alun Llywelyn-Williams. — [Cardiff] : University of Wales Press [for] the Welsh Arts Council, 1977. — [3],70p,plate : port ; 25cm. — (Writers of Wales)
Limited ed. of 1000 numbered copies. — Bibl.: p.63-65.
ISBN 0-7083-0653-5 Pbk : £1.50
(B77-34268)

891.6'6'820809 — Prose in Welsh, 1600-1972. *Critical studies. Welsh texts*
Y **traddodiad** rhyddiaith yn yr ugeinfed ganrif : (darlithiau Dewi Sant) / golygydd Geraint Bowen. — Llandysul : Gwasg Gomer, 1976. — 397p ; 22cm.
Index.
ISBN 0-85088-328-8 : £5.00
(B77-10634)

891.6'6'8209 — Welsh literature. Gruffydd, William John, b.1881. *Autobiographies*
Gruffydd, William John, *b.1881.* The years of the locust / by W.J. Gruffydd ; a translation from the Welsh by D. Myrddin Lloyd. — Llandysul : Gomer Press, 1976. — [1],207p ; 23cm.
Translation of: 'Hen atgofion : blynyddoedd y locust'. Aberystwyth : Gwasg Aberystwyth, 1936. — Index.
ISBN 0-85088-342-3 : £2.75
(B77-06957)

891.7 — RUSSIAN LITERATURE

891.7'08'0042 — Russian literature, 1917-. *Anthologies. English texts*
Russian writing today / edited by Robin Milner-Gulland and Martin Dewhirst. — Harmondsworth [etc.] : Penguin, 1977. — 495p ; 19cm.
ISBN 0-14-004174-5 Pbk : £1.25
(B77-13948)

891.7'08'0044 — Russian literature. Expatriate writers, 1945-. *Anthologies. English texts. Serials*
Kontinent : the alternative voice of Russia and Eastern Europe. — Sevenoaks : Coronet.
[1] / editorial advisers ... Nicholas Bethell and Barry Rubin. — 1977. — 180p ; 18cm.
'... contents [largely] ... selected from Volumes I & II of the original Russian language edition'. — Originally published: London : Deutsch, 1976.
ISBN 0-340-21317-5 Pbk : £0.90
(B77-21558)

891.7'09'002 — Russian literature, 1700-1800. *Critical studies*
Russian literature in the age of Catherine the Great : a collection of essays / edited by A.G. Cross. — Oxford ([Wightwick, Boars Hill, Oxford OX1 5DR]) : Willem A. Meeuws, 1976. — [2],229p : facsim, ports ; 22cm.
Bibl.: p.197-217. — Index.
ISBN 0-902672-29-0 Pbk : £4.50
(B77-20762)

891.7'09'003 — Russian literature, 1800-1917. *Critical studies. Readings. Russian texts*
Ars poetica. — Letchworth : Prideaux Press. — (Russian titles for the specialist ; no.97 ISSN 0305-3741)
1 / [pod redaktsieĭ M.A. Petrovskogo]. — 1976. — [4],143p ; 21cm.
Facsimile reprint of: 1st ed. : Moskva : Gosudarstvennaia Akademiia Khudozhestvennykh Nauk, 1927.
ISBN 0-85536-092-5 Pbk : £6.60(the set)
(B77-04457)

2 / [pod redaktsieĭ M.A. Petrovskogo i B.I. Iarkho]. — 1976. — [2],211p,[2]leaves of plates ; 21cm.
Facsimile reprint of: 1st ed. Moskva : Gosudarstvennaia Akademiia Khudozhestvennykh Nauk, 1928.
ISBN 0-85536-093-3 Pbk : £6.60(the set)
(B77-04458)

891.7'09'003 — Russian literature. Influence of German literature, 1830-1920
Kostka, Edmund Karl. Glimpses of Germanic-Slavic relations from Pushkin to Heinrich Mann / [by] Edmund Kostka. — Lewisburg : Bucknell University Press ; London (108 New Bond St., W1Y 0QX) : Associated University Presses, [1976]. — 3-162p ; 22cm.
Published in the United States: 1975. — Bibl.: p.144-154. — Index.
ISBN 0-8387-1371-8 : £3.75
Primary classification 830'.9'007
(B77-03798)

891.7'1'009 — Poetry in Russian. Prosody. *Critical studies*
Unbegaun, Boris Ottokar. Russian versification / by B.O. Unbegaun. — Letchworth : Prideaux Press, 1977. — iii-xiii,164p : ill ; 21cm. — (Russian texts for students ; 4)
Originally published: Oxford : Clarendon Press, 1956. — Bibl.: p.156-160. — Index.
Pbk : £2.40
(B77-29790)

891.7'1'1 — Poetry in Russian, to 1700. *English texts*
[Slovo o polku Igoreve. *English].* The song of Igor's campaign : an epic of the twelfth century / translated from Old Russian [with a foreword and commentary] by Vladimir Nabokov. — New York [etc.] ; London : McGraw-Hill, 1975 [i.e. 1976]. — [4],135p : geneal table, map ; 20cm.
Published in the United States: 1975. — This translation originally published: New York : Vintage, 1960.
ISBN 0-07-045719-0 Pbk : £2.45
(B77-02648)

891.7'1'208 — Poetry in Russian, 1700-1917. *Anthologies. Russian-English parallel texts*
Selections from Russian poetry / translated [and selected] by Eugene Citovich ; with an historical outline plus biographical notes by Enid Baldry ; and a foreword by Elizabeth Manners. — London : Mitre Press, 1976. — 62p ; 19cm.
Parallel Russian text and English translations.
ISBN 0-7051-0248-3 : £2.00
(B77-09370)

891.7'1'3 — Poetry in Russian, 1800-1917. *English texts*
Mandelstam, Osip. Selected poems [of] Osip Mandelstam / translated [from the Russian] by Clarence Brown and W.S. Merwin ; with an introduction by Clarence Brown. — Harmondsworth [etc.] : Penguin, 1977. — 139p ; 20cm. — (Penguin modern European poets)
These translations originally published: London : Oxford University Press, 1973. — Index.
ISBN 0-14-042191-2 Pbk : £0.95
(B77-26658)

891.7'1'3 — Poetry in Russian, 1800-1917. *Texts*
Minskiĭ, N M. Stikhotvoren"iia = Selected poems / N.M. Minskiĭ = N.M. Minsky. — Letchworth : Prideaux Press, 1977. — [6],246, [2]p ; 21cm. — (Russian titles for the specialist ; no.111 ISSN 0305-3741)
Russian title transliterated. — Russian text. — 2nd title page in Russian.
Pbk : £2.40
(B77-23811)

Sologub, Fedor. Fimiamy = Incense / F. Sologub. — Letchworth : Prideaux Press, 1977. — [2],110p ; 20cm. — (Russian titles for the specialist ; no.43)
Russian title transliterated. — Russian text. — 2nd title page in Russian. — Facsimile reprint of: 1st ed., Peterburg : Stranstvuiushchiĭ entuziast, 1920.
Pbk : £0.90
(B77-29791)

891.7'1'3 — Poetry in Russian. Blok, Aleksandr Aleksandrovich. Special subjects: Russia. *Critical studies. Russian texts. Facsimiles*
Babenchikov, M V. Al. Blok i Rossiia = A. Blok and Russia / M. Babenchikov. — Letchworth : Prideaux Press, 1977. — [2],92p ; 21cm. — (Russian titles for the specialist ; no.110 ISSN 0305-3741)
Russian title transliterated. — Russian text. — Second title page in Russian. — Facsimile reprint of: 1st ed. Moskva : Gosudarstvennoe izdatel'stvo, 1923.
Pbk : £1.80
(B77-25261)

891.7'1'3 — Poetry in Russian. Lermontov, Mikhail Iur'evich. *Biographies*
Kelly, Laurence. Lermontov : tragedy in the Caucasus / [by] Laurence Kelly. — London : Constable, 1977. — 259p,leaf of plate,[24]p of plates : ill, ports(2 col) ; 23cm.
Bibl.: p.243-250. — Index. — Includes poems by Lermontov in English translation.
ISBN 0-09-461710-4 : £6.50
(B77-31591)

891.7'1'3 — Poetry in Russian. Lermontov, Mikhail Iur'evich. *Critical studies. Russian texts*
Eĭkhenbaum, B M. Lermontov / B. Eĭkhenbaum. — Letchworth : Prideaux Press, 1977. — [2], 167p ; 21cm. — (Russian titles for the specialist ; no.14 ISSN 0305-3741)
Russian title transliterated. — Russian text. — Second title page in Russian. — Facsimile reprint of: 1st ed. Leningrad : Gos. izd-vo, 1924.
Pbk : £1.80
(B77-32946)

891.7'1'3 — Poetry in Russian. Mandelstam, Osip. *Biographies*
Mandelstam, Nadezhda. Hope abandoned : a memoir / [by] Nadezhda Mandelstam ; translated [from the Russian] by Max Hayward. — Harmondsworth [etc.] : Penguin, 1976. — 767p ; 18cm.
This translation originally published: New York : Atheneum, 1973 ; London : Collins : Harvill Press, 1974. — Translation of: 'Vtoraia kniga'. Paris : YMCA Press, 1972. — Index.
ISBN 0-14-004186-9 Pbk : £1.95
Primary classification 947.084'2'0924
(B77-08156)

891.7'1'3 — Poetry in Russian. Mandelstam, Osip. *Critical studies*
Baines, Jennifer. Mandelstam : the later poetry / [by] Jennifer Baines. — Cambridge [etc.] : Cambridge University Press, 1976. — xv,253p ; 22cm.
Bibl.: p.245-246. — Index.
ISBN 0-521-21273-1 : £8.00
(B77-09371)

891.7'1'3 — Poetry in Russian. Pushkin, Alexander. *Critical studies. Russian texts*
Tertz, Abram. Progulki s Pushkinym / Abram Terts. — London : Overseas Publications Interchange : Collins, 1975. — 178p ; 19cm.
Russian title transliterated, Russian text. — Second title page has English title 'Strolling with Pushkin'.
ISBN 0-00-216860-x : £5.00
(B77-19076)

891.7'1'3 — Poetry in Russian. Pushkin, Alexander. *Russian viewpoints. Readings*
Russian views of Pushkin / edited and translated by D.J. Richards and C.R.S. Cockrell. — Oxford ([Wightwick, Boars Hill, Oxford OX1 5DR]) : William A. Meeuws, 1976. — [7],xxv, 263p : port ; 23cm.
Index.
ISBN 0-902672-18-5 : £8.50
ISBN 0-902672-19-3 Pbk : £3.50
(B77-21559)

891.7'1'3 — Poetry in Russian. Pushkin, Alexander. Correspondence to Gnedich, Nikolaĭ Ivanovich. *Critical studies*
Bel'chikov, N F. Pushkin i Gnedich = Pushkin and Gnedich / [by] N.F. Bel'chikov = N.F. Belchikov. — Letchworth : Prideaux Press, 1976. — 39p : facsims ; 21cm. — (Russian titles for the specialist ; no.93 ISSN 0305-3741)
Russian text. — Russian title transliterated. — Originally published: USSR : s.n., 1924.
ISBN 0-85536-097-6 Pbk : £0.75
(B77-10635)

891.7'1'42 — Poetry in Russian, 1917-1945. *Texts*
TSvetaeva, Marina Ivanovna. Molodets : poems / [by] Marina TSvetaeva. — Letchworth : Prideaux Press, 1977. — 3-105p ; 21cm. — (Russian titles for the specialist ; no.18 ISSN 0305-3741)
Originally published: Praga : Plamia, 1924.
Pbk : £1.20
(B77-19077)

TSvetaeva, Marina Ivanovna. TSar' devitsa = The king maiden / Marina Tsvetaeva. — Letchworth : Prideaux Press, 1977. — 159p ; 21cm. — (Russian titles for the specialist ; no.19 ISSN 0305-3741)
Russian title transliterated. — Russian text. — Second title page in Russian. — Facsimile reprint of: 1st ed. Moskva : Gosudarstvennoe Izdatel'stvo, 1922.
Pbk : £1.50
(B77-27524)

891.7'1'42 — Poetry in Russian. Pasternak, Boris. *Critical studies*
Gifford, Henry. Pasternak : a critical study / by Henry Gifford. — Cambridge [etc.] : Cambridge University Press, 1977. — xiii,280p ; 23cm. — (Major European authors)
Bibl.: p.271-274. — Index.
ISBN 0-521-21288-x : £8.00
(B77-10017)

891.7'1'44 — Poetry in Russian, 1945-. *English texts*
Yevtushenko, Yevgeny. Love poems / [by] Yevgeny Yevtushenko ; [translated from the Russian]. — London : Gollancz, 1977. — xv, 126p ; 21cm. — ([Gollancz poets])
This collection of translations originally published: as 'From desire to desire'. Garden City, N.Y. : Doubleday, 1976.
ISBN 0-575-02393-7 : £2.50
ISBN 0-575-02397-x Pbk : £1.50
(B77-32286)

891.7'1'44 — Poetry in Russian, 1945-. *Texts*
Berger, IAkov. Kogda ukhodit parokhod - / IAkov Berger. — London ([35 Bradbury Court, St John's Park, S.E.3]) : [The author], 1977. — 96p ; 21cm.
Russian title transliterated. — Russian text.
Pbk : £2.00
(B77-17805)

891.7'2'3 — Drama in Russian, 1800-1917. *Texts*
Andreev, Leonid Nikolaevich. Anfisa = Anfisa / [by] Leonid Andreev = L. Andreev. — Letchworth : Prideaux Press, 1976. — 111p ; 21cm. — (Russian titles for the specialist ; no.88 ISSN 0305-3741)
First title transliterated. — Russian text. — Facsimile reprint of: 1st ed. Berlin : J. Ladyschnikow, 1909.
ISBN 0-85536-089-5 Pbk : £1.50
(B77-01030)

Andreev, Leonid Nikolaevich. Prekrasnyia sabinianki = The beautiful Sabine women / Leonid" Andreev". — Letchworth : Prideaux Press, 1977. — 38p ; 21cm. — (Russian titles for the specialist ; no.103 ISSN 0305-3741)
Russian title transliterated. — Russian text. — Facsimile reprint of: 1st ed. Berlin : J. Ladyschnikow, 1912.
ISBN 0-85536-101-8 Pbk : £0.90
(B77-15012)

Artsybashev, Mikhail Petrovich. D'iavol = The devil / M. Artsybashev. — Letchworth : Prideaux Press, 1977. — [2],125p ; 23cm. — (Russian titles for the specialist ; no.102 ISSN 0305-3741)
Russian title transliterated. — Russian text. — Second title page in Russian. — Facsimile reprint of: 1st ed. Varshava : Izdan'ie Knizhnago Sklada 'Za Svoboda', 1925.
Pbk : £2.40
(B77-25262)

Chekhov, Anton Pavlovich. [Diadia Vania. English]. Uncle Vanya = Diadia Vania / [by] Anton Chekhov ; edited with an introduction, notes and a select vocabulary by David Magarshack. — Letchworth : Bradda Books, 1976. — 104p ; 21cm. — (The library of Russian classics)
Russian text, English introduction and notes. — Russian title transliterated. — This ed. originally published: London : Harrap, 1962.
Pbk : £1.50
(B77-16641)

Griboedov, Aleksandr Sergeevich. Gore ot uma : : comedy in four acts in verse / [by] A.S. Griboyedov ; introduction and notes by D.P. Costello. — Letchworth : Prideaux Press, 1977. — iii-xxvii,202 [i.e. 204]p ; 21cm. — (Russian texts for students ; 3)
Russian title transliterated. — Russian text, English introduction and notes. — Originally published: Oxford : Clarendon Press, 1951.
ISBN 0-85536-103-4 Pbk : £2.40
(B77-15013)

Sologub, Fedor. Zalozhniki zhizni = Hostages of life / Fedor Sologub = F. Sologub. — Letchworth : Prideaux Press, 1976. — 104p ; 21cm. — (Russian titles for the specialist ; no.90 ISSN 0305-3741)
First title transliterated. — Facsimile reprint of: 1st ed., originally published: USSR : s.n., 1912.
ISBN 0-85536-091-7 Pbk : £1.50
(B77-03807)

891.7'2'3 — Drama in Russian. Chekhov, Anton Pavlovich. *Critical studies*
Hahn, Beverly. Chekhov : a study of the major stories and plays / [by] Beverly Hahn. — Cambridge [etc.] : Cambridge University Press, 1977. — xiii,351p ; 23cm. — (Major European authors)
Bibl.: p.343-345. — Index.
ISBN 0-521-20951-x : £9.90
(B77-16642)

891.7'2'42 — Drama in Russian, 1917-1945. *Texts*
Kazakov, IUriĭ Pavlovich. Pervoe svidanie = The first meeting : a play / IU. Kazakov = Yu. Kazakov. — Letchworth : Prideaux Press, 1977. — 17p ; 21cm. — (Russian titles for the specialist ; no.105 ISSN 0305-3741)
Russian text. — Russian title transliterated. — Originally published: USSR : s.n., 1955.
Pbk : Unpriced
(B77-13949)

891.7'2'42 — Drama in Russian. Babel, Isaac. *Critical studies. Russian texts*
I. Babel', stat'i i materialy = I. Babel, articles, bibliography. — Letchworth : Prideaux Press, 1977. — 102p ; 21cm. — (Mastera sovremennoĭ literatury) (Russian titles for the specialist ; no.47 ISSN 0305-3741)
Russian title transliterated. — Russian text. — Second title page in Russian. — Facsimile reprint of: 1st ed., Leningrad : Academia, 1928. — Bibl.: p.100-101.
Pbk : £1.50
Primary classification 891.7'3'42
(B77-25264)

891.7'2'44 — Drama in Russian, 1945-. *English texts*
Amal'rik, Andreĭ. East-West ; &, Is uncle Jack a conformist : two plays / by Andrey Amalrik ; [translated by Daniel Weissbort]. — London : Eyre Methuen, 1976. — xii,34p ; 21cm. — (Methuen's new theatrescripts ; no.4)
These translations originally published: in 'Nose! nose? no-se! and other plays'. New York : Harcourt Brace Jovanovich, 1973. — Originally published: in 'P'esy'. Amsterdam : Alexander Herjen Foundation, 1970.
ISBN 0-413-29390-4 Sd : £1.00
(B77-04459)

Arbuzov, Alekseĭ Nikolaevich. Old-world : a play in two parts / by Aleksei Arbuzov ; translated by Ariadne Nicolaeff. — London [etc.] : French, 1977. — 43p ; 19cm. — (French's theatre scripts)
'"Old-world" is a fairly free translation of "Staromodnaia Komediia" by Aleksei Arbuzov. It contains alterations made during rehearsals without reference to the Russian text' - Translator's note. — 1 man, 1 woman.
ISBN 0-573-01708-5 Sd : £1.00 : CIP rev.
(B77-20763)

891.7'2'44 — Drama in Russian, 1945-. *Texts*
Bulgakov, Mikhail Afanas'evich. Beg = Flight : a play / Mikhail Bulgakov = by M. Bulgakov. — Letchworth : Prideaux Press, 1977. — 3-96p : 1 ill ; 20cm. — (Russian titles for the specialist ; no.7 ISSN 0305-3741)
Russian text. — Russian title transliterated. — Originally published: 1970 ; and in : 'Dramy i komedii'. Moskva : Iskusstvo, 1965.
Pbk : £0.90
(B77-22969)

Bulgakov, Mikhail Afanas'evich. Don Kikhot = Don Quixote : a play / Mikhail Bulgakov = by M. Bulgakov. — Letchworth : Prideaux Press, 1974. — [2],102p : port ; 20cm. — (Russian titles for the specialist ; no.23 ISSN 0305-3741)
Originally published: 1971 ; and in 'Dramy i komedii'. Moskva : Iskusstvo, 1965.
£0.90
(B77-22970)

891.7'3'3 — Fiction in Russian, 1800-1917. *English texts*
Dostoevskiĭ, Fedor Mikhaĭlovich. [The brothers Karamazov]. The notebooks for 'The brothers Karamazov' / [by] Fyodor Dostoevsky ; edited and translated by Edward Wasiolek. — Chicago ; London : University of Chicago Press, 1971 [i.e. 1976]. — vi,279p : facsims, port ; 23cm.
This translation originally published: 1971. — 'Based upon the Russian edition of the notebooks for "The brothers Karamazov" as contained in "F.M. Dostoevsky materialy i issledovaniia" / edited by A.S. Dolinin (Leningrad, 1935)' - title page verso. — Index.
ISBN 0-226-15969-8 Pbk : £3.05
(B77-01884)

Gogol', Nikolaĭ Vasil'evich. [Nevskiĭ Prospekt. English]. The Nevsky Prospect / [by] N.V. Gogol ; [translated by Rosa Portnova]. — Letchworth : Bradda Books, 1976. — 35p ; 21cm.
This translation originally published: in 'Tales from Gogol'. London : Sylvan Press, 1945.
ISBN 0-904679-09-8 Pbk : £0.96
(B77-07697)

Tolstoy, Leo, *Count.* [Anna Karenina. English]. Anna Karenin / [by] L.N. Tolstoy ; translated and with an introduction by Rosemary Edmonds. — Harmondsworth [etc.] : Penguin, 1977. — 853p ; 19cm.
This translation originally published: London : Penguin, 1954.
ISBN 0-14-004498-1 Pbk : £1.50
(B77-26659)

Tolstoy, Leo, *Count.* [Anna Karenina. English]. Anna Karenina / [by] Leo Tolstoy ; translated from the Russian by Constance Garnett. — London : Pan Books, 1977. — 784p ; 20cm.
This translation originally published: as 'Anna Karenin'. London : Heinemann, 1901.
ISBN 0-330-24802-2 Pbk : £1.50
(B77-22234)

Turgenev, Ivan Sergeevich. [Pervaia liubov'. English]. First love / [by] Ivan Turgenev ; translated from the Russian by Isaiah Berlin. — Harmondsworth [etc.] : Penguin, 1977. — 93p ; 19cm. — (Peacock books)
This translation originally published: in 'First love, and, Rudin'. London : Hamilton, 1950. — Translation of 'Pervaia liubov''.
ISBN 0-14-047095-6 Pbk : £0.45
(B77-12180)

891.7'3'3 — Fiction in Russian. 1800-1917. *Texts*
Andreev, Leonid Nikolaevich. V tumane = In the fog / L. Andreev. — Letchworth : Prideaux Press, 1977. — 44p ; 21cm. — (Russian titles for the specialist ; no.99 ISSN 0305-3741)
Russian title transliterated. — Originally published: Moskva : Molodaia gvardiia, 1928.
Pbk : £0.60
(B77-17167)

Andreev, Leonid Nikolaevich. Zhili-byli = Once upon a time / L. Andreev. — Letchworth : Prideaux Press, 1977. — 26p ; 21cm. — (Russian titles for the specialist ; no.100 ISSN 0305-3741)
Russian title transliterated. — Originally published: in 'Zhizn" 1901, March, no.3.
Pbk : £0.60
(B77-17168)

Artsybashev, Mikhail Petrovich. Krov' = Blood / M. Artsybashev. — Letchworth : Prideaux Press, 1977. — 37p ; 21cm. — (Russian titles for the specialist ; no.101 ISSN 0305-3741)
Russian text, Russian title transliterated. — Originally published: USSR : s.n., 1908.
ISBN 0-85536-098-4 Pbk : £0.90
(B77-13405)

Dostoevskiĭ, Fedor Mikhaĭlovich. Dvoĭnik = The double / F.M. Dostoevskiĭ = F.M. Dostoevsky. — Letchworth : Prideaux Press, 1976. — 123p ; 21cm. — (Russian titles for the specialist ; no.92 ISSN 0305-3741)
Russian text. — Russian title transliterated.
ISBN 0-85536-094-1 Pbk : £0.90
(B77-07698)

891.7'3'3 — Fiction in Russian. Dostoevskiĭ, Fedor Mikhaĭlovich. *Biographies*
Frank, Joseph, *b.1918.* Dostoevsky / [by] Joseph Frank. — Princeton ; Guildford : Princeton University Press.
[Vol.1] : The seeds of revolt, 1821-1849. — 1976. — xvi,401,[1]p : ill, ports ; 25cm.
Index.
ISBN 0-691-06260-9 : £11.50
(B77-01031)

891.7'3'3 — Fiction in Russian. Dostoevskiĭ, Fedor Mikhaĭlovich. *Critical studies*
Frank, Joseph, *b.1918.* Dostoevsky / [by] Joseph Frank. — London : Robson.
In 4 vols. — Index.
[Vol.1] : The seeds of revolt, 1821-1849. — 1977. — xiv,401p : ill, ports ; 24cm.
Originally published: Princeton ; Guildford : Princeton University Press, 1976.
ISBN 0-86051-015-8 : £8.95 : CIP rev.
(B77-18436)

Holquist, Michael. Dostoevsky and the novel / [by] Michael Holquist. — Princeton ; Guildford : Princeton University Press, 1977. — xiii,202p ; 23cm.
Index.
ISBN 0-691-06342-7 : £9.40
(B77-28264)

891.7'3'3 — Fiction in Russian. Dostoevskiĭ, Fedor Mikhaĭlovich. Brothers Karamazov. Special themes: Atheism
Sutherland, Stewart R. Atheism and the rejection of God : contemporary philosophy and 'The Brothers Karamazov' / [by] Stewart R. Sutherland. — Oxford : Blackwell, 1977. — viii,152p ; 23cm. — (Values and philosophical inquiry)
Bibl.: p.146-150. — Index.
ISBN 0-631-17500-8 : £6.75
(B77-27525)

891.7'3'3 — Fiction in Russian. Tolstoy, Leo, Count. *Critical studies*
Cain, T G S. Tolstoy / [by] T.G.S. Cain. — London : Elek, 1977. — xiii,210p ; 22cm. — (Novelists and their world)
Bibl.: p.205-208. — Index.
ISBN 0-236-40073-8 : £5.95
(B77-10994)

891.7'3'3 — Fiction in Russian. Turgenev, Ivan Sergeevich
Pritchett, Victor Sawdon. The gentle barbarian : the life and work of Turgenev / [by] V.S. Pritchett. — London : Chatto and Windus, 1977. — [9],243p,8p of plates : ill, ports ; 23cm.
ISBN 0-7011-2208-0 : £5.95 : CIP rev.
(B77-09372)

891.7'3'3 — Short stories in Russian, 1800-1917. *English texts*
Tolstoy, Leo, *Count.* Master and man, and other stories / [by] Leo Tolstoy ; translated [from the Russian] and with an introduction by Paul Foote. — Harmondsworth [etc.] : Penguin, 1977. — 271p ; 18cm. — (Penguin classics)
Contents: Father Sergius - Master and man. Translation of: 'Khoziain i rabotnik'. Leningrad : s.n., 1895 - Hadji Murat. Translation of: 'Khadzhi Murat'. Leningrad : s.n., 1912.
ISBN 0-14-044331-2 Pbk : £0.90
(B77-32947)

891.7'3'3 — Short stories in Russian, 1800-1917. *Texts*
Chekhov, Anton Pavlovich. Selected short stories [of] Anton Chekhov / edited by G.A. Birkett and Gleb Struve. — Letchworth : Prideaux Press, 1977. — [2],235p ; 21cm. — (Oxford Russian readers) (Russian texts for students ; 5)
Russian text, English introduction, notes and vocabulary. — This selection originally published: Oxford : Clarendon Press, 1951.
Pbk : £2.40
(B77-20764)

891.7'3'30924 — Fiction in Russian, 1800-1917. *Plot outlines*
Berry, Thomas Edwin. Plots and characters in major Russian fiction / [compiled by] Thomas E. Berry. — Hamden : Archon Books ; Folkestone : Dawson. — (The plots and characters series)
Vol.1 : Pushkin, Lermontov, Turgenev, Tolstoi. — 1977. — xvi,226p ; 23cm.
ISBN 0-7129-0759-9 : £8.50
Also classified at 891.7'3'30927
(B77-31592)

891.7'3'30927 — Fiction in Russian, 1800-1917. Characters. *Dictionaries*
Berry, Thomas Edwin. Plots and characters in major Russian fiction / [compiled by] Thomas E. Berry. — Hamden : Archon Books ; Folkestone : Dawson. — (The plots and characters series)
Vol.1 : Pushkin, Lermontov, Turgenev, Tolstoi. — 1977. — xvi,226p ; 23cm.
ISBN 0-7129-0759-9 : £8.50
Primary classification 891.7'3'30924
(B77-31592)

891.7'3'4F — Fiction in Russian, 1917-. *Texts (including translations)*
Andreev, Leonid Nikolaevich. Gubernator = The governor / L. Andreev = Leonid Andreev. — Letchworth : Prideaux Press, 1977. — 56p ; 20cm. — (Russian titles for the specialist ; no.98 ISSN 0305-3741)
Russian title transliterated. — Russian text. — Originally published: Berlin, J. Ladyschnikow, 1922.
ISBN 0-85536-099-2 Pbk : £0.75
(B77-12181)

Belyĭ, Andreĭ. Vozvrashchen'e na rodinu = Returning home / Andreĭ Belyĭ = A. Bely. — Letchworth : Prideaux Press, 1977. — 88p ; 23cm. — (Russian titles for the specialist ; no.104 ISSN 0305-3741)
Russian title transliterated. — Russian text. — Second title page in Russian. — Facsimile reprint of: 1st ed. Moskva : Knigoizdatel'stvo Pisateleĭ v Moskve, 1922.
Pbk : £1.80
(B77-26660)

Bulgakov, Mikhail Afanas'evich. A country doctor's notebook / [by] Mikhail Bulgakov ; translated from the Russian by Michael Glenny. — [London] : Fontana, 1976. — 158p ; 18cm.
This collection of translations originally published: London : Collins, 1975. — Originally published: in Russian in 'Krasnaia panorama' and 'Meditsinskiĭ rabotnik' between 1925 and 1927.
ISBN 0-00-614423-3 Pbk : £0.70
(B77-03270)

Bulgakov, Mikhail Afanas'evich. Teatral'nyĭ roman = A theatrical novel / M. Bulgakov. — Letchworth : Prideaux Press, 1977. — 140p : ill ; 20cm. — (Russian titles for the specialist ; no.37 ISSN 0305-3741)
Russian title transliterated. — Russian text. — Originally published: 1971.
Pbk : £1.25
(B77-22971)

Karamzin, Nikolaĭ Mikhaĭlovich. Natal'ia, boiarskaia doch' = Natalie, the boyar's daughter / [by] N.M. Karamzin. — Letchworth : Prideaux Press, 1976. — 42p ; 21cm. — (Russian titles for the specialist ; no.93 ISSN 0305-3741)
Russian text. — Russian title transliterated.
ISBN 0-85536-095-x Pbk : £0.60
(B77-07700)

Karamzin, Nikolaĭ Mikhaĭlovich. Rytsar' nashego vremeni = A knight of our times / [by] N.M. Karamzin. — Letchworth : Prideaux Press, 1977. — 32p ; 21cm. — (Russian titles for the specialist ; no.94 ISSN 0305-3741)
Russian text. — Russian title transliterated.
ISBN 0-85536-096-8 Pbk : £0.60
(B77-07701)

Kataev, Valentin Petrovich. Time, forward! / [by] Valentine Kataev ; authorized translation from the Russian by Charles Malamuth. — Bloomington ; London : Indiana University Press, 1976 [i.e. 1977]. — [6],345p ; 22cm. — (A midland book)
This translation originally published: New York : Farrar and Rinehart, 1933 ; London : Gollancz, 1934. — Translation of: Vremia, vpered! Moskva : s.n., 1932.
ISBN 0-253-36018-8 : £9.75
ISBN 0-253-20204-3 Pbk : £3.00
(B77-12772)

Kollontaĭ, Aleksandra Mikhaĭlovna. Love of worker bees / [by] Alexandra Kollontai ; translated [from the Russian] by Cathy Porter ; afterword by Sheila Rowbotham. — London : Virago, 1977. — 232p ; 21cm.
Translation of: 'Liubov' pchel trudovykh'. Moskva : s.n., 1923. — Contents: Vasilisa Malygina - Three generations - Sisters.
ISBN 0-86068-005-3 : £6.95
ISBN 0-86068-006-1 Pbk : £2.50
(B77-31593)

Selected readings in Soviet literature / prepared [i.e. compiled] by Michael Glenny ; for the [Open University] course team. — Milton Keynes : Open University, 1976. — 132p ; 21x30cm. — (Social sciences, a third level course : Soviet government and politics ; block 2, option 3) (D333 ; option 3, SR)
Pbk : Unpriced
(B77-04460)

Suslov, Il'ia P. Here's to your health, Comrade Shifrin! / [by] Ilya Suslov ; translated [from the Russian] by Maxine Bronstein ; foreword by Maurice Friedberg. — Bloomington ; London : Indiana University Press, 1977. — xviii,204p ; 22cm.
Originally published: in Russian. USSR : s.n., 197-.
ISBN 0-253-13710-1 : £6.75
(B77-25263)

Tertz, Abram. The Makepeace experiment : Lyubimov / [by] Abram Tertz ; translated [from the Russian] by Manya Harari. — [London] : Fontana, 1977. — 128p ; 18cm.
This translation originally published: London : Collins ; Harvill Press, 1965. — Translation of: 'Liubimov'. Vashington : s.n., 1964. Originally published: in Polish translation as 'Lubimow'. Paryz : Instytut Literacki, 1963.
ISBN 0-00-613686-9 Pbk : £0.75
(B77-30817)

Tertz, Abram. The trial begins / [by] Abram Tertz ; translated from the Russian by Max Hayward. — [London] : Fontana, 1977. — 95p ; 18cm.
This translation originally published: London : Collins, 1960. — 'First published [in Russian] by the monthly review "Kultura" [Paris] : Maisons Lafitte, 196-?' - title page verso.
ISBN 0-00-613688-5 Pbk : £0.70
(B77-30818)

Zamiatin, Evgeniĭ Ivanovich. We / [by] Yevgeny Zamyatin ; translated by Bernard Guilbert Guerney ; introduction by Michael Glenny. — Harmondsworth [etc.] : Penguin, 1977. — 223p ; 19cm. — (Penguin modern classics)
This translation originally published: London : Cape, 1970.
Pbk : £0.75
ISBN 0-14-003510-9
(B77-15590)

891.7'3'4J — Children's stories in Russian, 1917-. *Texts (including translations)*
Chukovskiĭ, Korneĭ Ivanovich. The silver crest : a Russian boyhood / [by] Kornei Chukovsky ; translated by Beatrice Stillman. — Oxford [etc.] : Oxford University Press, 1977. — [5], 136p ; 23cm.
This translation originally published: New York : Holt, Rinehart and Winston, 1976. — Translation of: 'Serebrianyĭ gerb'. Moskva : Gos. izd-vo detskoĭ lit-ry, 1961.
ISBN 0-19-271399-x : £2.95 : CIP rev.
(B77-07699)

Korinets, Iuriĭ Iosifovich. In the middle of the world / by Juri Korinetz ; translated from the German by Anthea Bell. — London [etc.] : Hodder and Stoughton Children's Books, 1977. — 160p : 1 ill ; 23cm.
Based on the authorized German translation by Hans Baumann, 197- . — Originally published: in Russian. Moskva? : Detskaia lit-ra?, 1973.
ISBN 0-340-18963-0 : £3.10
(B77-12773)

891.7'3'42 — Fiction in Russian. Nabokov, Vladimir. Adaptations in English by Nabokov, Vladimir. Compared with originals
Grayson, Jane. Nabokov translated : a comparison of Nabokov's Russian and English prose / by Jane Grayson. — Oxford [etc.] : Oxford University Press, 1977. — xi,257p ; 23cm. — (Oxford modern languages and literature monographs)
Bibl.: p.232-251. — Index.
ISBN 0-19-815527-1 : £9.50
Also classified at 813'.5'4
(B77-12182)

891.7'3'42 — Fiction in Russian. Pasternak, Boris. *Biographies*
Gladkov, Aleksandr Konstantinovich. Meetings with Pasternak : a memoir / by Alexander Gladkov ; translated from the Russian and edited with notes and introduction by Max Hayward. — London : Collins : Harvill Press, 1977. — 223p ; 22cm.
Translation of: 'Vstrechi s Pasternakom'. Paris : Y.M.C.A. Press, 1973.
ISBN 0-00-262507-5 : £4.95
(B77-26661)

891.7'3'42 — Fiction in Russian. Sholokhov, Mikhail. And quiet flows the Don & Don flows home to the sea. Authorship. *Critical studies*
Medvedev, Roĭ Aleksandrovich. Problems in the literary biography of Mikhail Sholokhov / [by] Roy A. Medvedev ; translated from the Russian [MS.] by A.D.P. Briggs. — Cambridge [etc.] : Cambridge University Press, 1977. — vii,227p ; 23cm.
Index.
ISBN 0-521-21333-9 : £6.90
(B77-22235)

891.7'3'42 — Short stories in Russian. Babel, Isaac. *Critical studies. Russian texts*
I. Babel', stat'i i materialy = I. Babel, articles, bibliography. — Letchworth : Prideaux Press, 1977. — 102p ; 21cm. — (Mastera sovremennoĭ literatury) (Russian titles for the specialist ; no.47 ISSN 0305-3741)
Russian title transliterated. — Russian text. — Second title page in Russian. — Facsimile reprint of: 1st ed., Leningrad : Academia, 1928. — Bibl.: p.100-101.
Pbk : £1.50
Also classified at 891.7'2'42
(B77-25264)

891.7'3'42 — Short stories in Russian. Zoshchenko, Mikhail. *Critical studies. Russian texts*
M. Zoshchenko, stat'i i materialy = M. Zoshchenko, articles, bibliography. — Letchworth : Prideaux Press, 1977. — [2],95p ; 20cm. — (Mastera sovremennoĭ literatury) (Russian titles for the specialist ; no.48 ISSN 0305-3741)
Russian title transliterated. — Russian text. — Second title page in Russian. — Facsimile reprint of: 1st ed., Leningrad : Academia, 1928. — Bibl.: p.93-94.
Pbk : £1.50
(B77-25265)

891.7'3'44 — Fiction in Russian. Solzhenitsyn, Aleksandr Isaevich. *Critical studies*
Clément, Olivier. The spirit of Solzhenitsyn / [by] Olivier Clément ; [translated from the French by Sarah Facett and Paul Burns]. — London : Search Press [etc.], 1976. — 234,[1]p ; 23cm.
'Published originally in French under the title "L'esprit de Soljenitsyne" by Editions Stock of Paris [1974] (with the exception of Part six, which is published here for the first time' - title page verso.
ISBN 0-85532-372-8 : £5.95
(B77-08649)

891.7'3'44 — Fiction in Russian. Solzhenitsyn, Aleksandr Isaevich, 1940-1964. *Biographies*
Reshetovskaia, Natal'ia A. Sanya : my husband Aleksandr Solzhenitsyn / by Natalya Reshetovskaya ; translated from the Russian [MS?] by Elena Ivanoff. — London : Hart-Davis, MacGibbon, 1977. — [9],284p,[16] p of plates : ports ; 23cm.
This translation originally published: Indianapolis : Bobbs-Merrill Co., 1975. — Index.
ISBN 0-246-10972-6 : £4.95
(B77-15591)

891.7'3'44 — Fiction in Russian. Solzhenitsyn, Alexsandr Isaevich. Political beliefs. *Critical studies*
Carter, Stephen. The politics of Solzhenitsyn / [by] Stephen Carter. — London [etc.] : Macmillan, 1977. — xii,162p ; 23cm.
Bibl.: p.153-156. — Index.
ISBN 0-333-19560-4 : £5.95
(B77-29027)

891.7'4'42 — Essays in Russian, 1917-1945. *English texts*
Mandelstam, Osip. Osip Mandelstam : selected essays / [selected and] translated by Sidney Monas. — Austin ; London : University of Texas Press, 1977. — xxvi,245p ; 24cm. — (Dan Danciger publications series)
Index.
ISBN 0-292-76006-x : £12.00
(B77-26662)

891.7'4'44 — Essays in Russian, 1945-. *English texts*
Tertz, Abram. A voice from the chorus / [by] Abram Tertz (Andrey Sinyavsky) ; translated from the Russian by Kyril Fitzlyon and Max Hayward ; with an introduction by Max Hayward. — [London] : Fontana, 1977. — xxiii,328p ; 18cm.
This translation originally published: London : Collins : Harvill Press, 1976. — Translation of: 'Golos iz khora'. London : Stenvalli, 1973.
ISBN 0-00-634849-1 Pbk : £1.25
(B77-32287)

891.7'6'309 — Letters in Russian, 1800-1917. *Critical studies*
Todd, William Mills. The familiar letter as a literary genre in the age of Pushkin / [by] William Mills Todd, III. — Princeton ; Guildford : Princeton University Press, 1976. — xii,230p ; 23cm. — (Columbia University. Russian Institute. Studies)
Bibl.: p.209-221. — Index.
ISBN 0-691-06319-2 : £10.50
(B77-06355)

891.7'8'308 — Satirical prose in Russian, 1800-1917. *Texts*
Saltykov-Shchedrin, Mikhail Evgrafovich. M.E. Saltykov-Shchedrin : selected satirical writings / edited by I.P. Foote. — Oxford : Clarendon Press, 1977. — [6],284p ; 23cm.
Russian text, English introduction and notes. — Bibl.: p.283-284.
ISBN 0-19-815641-3 : £9.50 : CIP rev.
(B77-11464)

891.7'8'309 — Russian literature. Gogol', Nikolaĭ Vasil'evich. Sexuality
Karlinsky, Simon. The sexual labyrinth of Nikolai Gogol / [by] Simon Karlinsky. — Cambridge, Mass. ; London : Harvard University Press, 1976. — xi,333p : ill, ports ; 24cm.
Bibl.: p.317-323. — Index.
ISBN 0-674-80281-0 : £10.50
(B77-10018)

891.7'8'309 — Russian literature. Gogol', Nikolaĭ Vasil'evich. Special themes: Supernatural. *Russian texts*
Merezhkovskiĭ, Dmitriĭ Sergeevich. Gogol' i chort" = Gogol and the devil / D.S. Merezhkovsk ii. — Letchworth : Prideaux Press, 1976. — [5],219p ; 20cm. — (Russian titles for the specialist ; no.96 ISSN 0305-3741)
Russian title transliterated. — Russian text. — Originally published: Moskva : Knigoizdatel'stvo 'Skorpion"', 1906.
ISBN 0-85536-088-7 Pbk : £3.60
(B77-05105)

891.7'8'309 — Russian literature. Rozanov, Vasiliĭ Vasil'evich. *Critical studies. Early works. Russian texts*
Shklovskiĭ, Viktor Borisovich. Rozanov / Viktor Shklovskiĭ. — Letchworth : Prideaux Press, 1977. — [2],56p ; 20cm. — (Russian titles for the specialist ; no.60 ISSN 0305-3741)
Title transliterated. — Facsimile reprint of: 1st ed. Petrograd : Opoiaz, 1921.
Pbk : £0.90
(B77-15592)

891.7'8'4208 — Prose in Russian, 1917-1945. *Texts*
Belyĭ, Andreĭ. Odna iz obiteleĭ tsarstva teneĭ = In the kingdom of shadows / Andreĭ Belyĭ = Andrey Bely. — Letchworth : Prideaux Press, 1977. — [2],75p ; 20cm. — (Russian titles for the specialist ; no.14 ISSN 0305-3741)
Russian title transliterated. — Russian text. — Second title page in Russian. — Facsimile reprint of: 1st ed. Leningrad : Gosudarstvennoe Izdatel'stvo, 1924.
Pbk : £0.90
(B77-32288)

891.7'8'4408 — Prose in Russian, 1945-. *Polish texts*
Erofeev, Venedikt. Moskwa-Pietuszki : poemat / Wieniedikt Jerofiejew ; tlumaczyli z rosyjskiego Nina Karsov i Szymon Szechter ; slowo wstępne napisal ; przypisy opracowal Nikita Stavisky. — Londyn (London) (3 Ashness Rd, SW11 6RY) : Kontra, 1976. — 139p ; 22cm.
Published in the original Russian in 'Ami', no.3, 1973.
ISBN 0-9502324-6-7 Pbk : £3.00
(B77-00491)

891.79 — UKRAINIAN LITERATURE
891.7'9'13 — Poetry in Ukrainian, 1917-. *Polish texts*
Kostets'kyĭ, Ihor. Surowe sonety / Igor Kostecki ; przelozyl i szkic o poecie napisal Jerzy Neimojowski. — Londyn [i.e. London] : Oficyna Poetów i Malarzy, 1976. — 3-94p : port tipped in ; 22cm.
ISBN 0-902571-94-x Pbk : £2.00
Primary classification 891.7'9'13
(B77-13950)

891.7'9'13 — Poetry in Ukrainian, 1917-. *Texts*
Franko, Ivan Iakovlevich. Vybrani poeziï / Ivan Franko. — London (28 Minster Rd, N.W.2) : Ukrainian Students' Union in Great Britain, 1976. — 104p ; 22cm.
Title transliterated.
Sd : Unpriced
(B77-32289)

891.7'9'13 — Poetry in Ukrainian. Kostets'kyĭ, Ihor. *Critical studies. Polish texts*
Kostets'kyĭ, Ihor. Surowe sonety / Igor Kostecki ; przelozyl i szkic o poecie napisal Jerzy Neimojowski. — Londyn [i.e. London] : Oficyna Poetów i Malarzy, 1976. — 3-94p : port tipped in ; 22cm.
ISBN 0-902571-94-x Pbk : £2.00
Also classified at 891.7'9'13
(B77-13950)

891.8 — SLAVIC LITERATURES
891.8 — Poetry in Slavonic languages. *Critical studies*
Morgan, Edwin. East European poets / prepared for the [Open University] Course Team by Edwin Morgan. Poetry in public / prepared for the [Open University] Course Team by Alasdair Clayre. — Milton Keynes : Open University Press, 1976. — 54p : ports ; 30cm. — (Arts, a third level course : twentieth century poetry ; unit 32) (A306 ; 32)
Bibl.
ISBN 0-335-05123-5 Pbk : £0.95
Also classified at 821'.9'1409
(B77-04461)

891.8 — Slavonic literatures, 1800-1970. *Essays*
Milosz, Czeslaw. Emperor of the earth : modes of eccentric vision / [by] Czeslaw Milosz. — Berkeley [etc.] ; London : University of California Press, 1977. — x,253p ; 23cm.
ISBN 0-520-03302-7 : £6.70
(B77-25981)

891.82 — SERBO-CROATIAN LITERATURE
891.8'2'35F — Fiction in Serbo-Croatian, 1900-. *Texts (including translations)*
Kiš, Danilo. Garden, ashes / [by] Danilo Kiš ; translated by William J. Hannaher. — New York ; London : Harcourt Brace Jovanovich, [1976]. — [4],170p ; 21cm.
Published in the United States: 1975. — Translation of: 'Bašta, pepeo'. Belgrade : Prosveta, 1965.
ISBN 0-15-134287-3 : £5.35
(B77-07702)

891.85 — POLISH LITERATURE
891.8'5'17 — Poetry in Polish, 1919-. *English texts*
Herbert, Zbigniew. Selected poems [of] Zbigniew Herbert / translated [from the Polish] with an introduction and notes by John Carpenter and Bogdana Carpenter. — Oxford [etc.] : Oxford University Press, 1977. — xiv,82p ; 22cm.
ISBN 0-19-211861-7 Pbk : £2.75 : CIP rev.
(B77-24577)

891.8'5'17 — Poetry in Polish, 1919-. *Polish-English parallel texts*
Różewicz, Tadeusz. The survivor, and other poems / by Tadeusz Różewicz ; translated and introduced by Magnus J. Krynski and Robert A. Maguire. — Princeton ; Guildford : Princeton University Press, [1977]. — xix, 160p ; 23cm. — (The Lockert library of poetry in translation)
Parallel Polish text and English translation, English introduction. — This collection published in the United States: 1976.
ISBN 0-691-06315-x : £10.50
ISBN 0-691-01332-2 Pbk : £2.95
(B77-10995)

Taborski, Boleslaw. Duet / [by] Boleslaw Taborski. — London : Oficyna Poetow i Malarzy, 1975. — 8p ; 23cm.
Parallel English and Polish text.
Sd : £1.00
(B77-07703)

891.8'5'17 — Poetry in Polish, 1919-. *Texts*
Kobrzyński, Boleslaw. Pańskie oko pegaza tuczy : wybór twórczości / Boleslaw Kobrzyński. — Londyn [i.e. London] : Oficyna Poetów i Malarzy, 1976. — 143p ; 22cm.
ISBN 0-902571-95-8 Pbk : £2.00
(B77-13406)

Libert, Antoni. Cybulski / Antoni Libert. — Londyn [i.e. London] : Poets' and Painters' Press, 1976. — 99p ; 22cm.
ISBN 0-902571-87-7 Pbk : £1.80
(B77-03808)

Polanowski, Tadeusz. Fraszka, wazka, niewazka / Tadeusz Polanowski. — Londyn [i.e. London] : Oficyna Poetów i Malarzy, 1977. — 63p ; 22cm.
Pbk : £1.60
(B77-25982)

Wit-Wyrostkiewicz, Boguslaw. Wolanie o slowo / Boguslaw Wit-Wyrostkiewicz. — Londyn [i.e. London] : Oficyna Poetów i Malarzy, 1977. — 45,[1]p ; 22cm.
Pbk : Unpriced
(B77-30819)

891.8'5'2708 — Avant garde drama in Polish, 1919-1976. *Anthologies. English texts*

Twentieth-century Polish avant-garde drama : plays, scenarios, critical documents / by Stanislaw Ignacy Witkiewicz ... [et al.] ; edited, with an introduction, by Daniel Gerould ; translated by Daniel Gerould in collaboration with Eleanor Gerould. — Ithaca ; London : Cornell University Press, 1977. — 288p : ill ; 23cm.
Bibl.: p.281-287.
ISBN 0-8014-0952-7 : £12.00
(B77-27526)

891.8'5'36 — Fiction in Polish, 1795-1919. *Texts*

Mniszek, Helena. Ordynat Michorowski : powieść / Helena Mniszek. — Londyn [i.e. London] : Orbis Books, 1977. — 146p ; 22cm.
Originally published: Toronto : Polish Alliance Press, 1969.
ISBN 0-901149-11-x Pbk : £3.00
(B77-29792)

Mniszek, Helena. Trędowata : powieść / Helena Mniszek. — Londyn [i.e. London] : Orbis Books, 1977. — 404p ; 22cm.
Originally published: Warszawa : s.n., 1909.
ISBN 0-901149-10-1 Pbk : £5.70
(B77-28265)

891.8'5'37F — Fiction in Polish, 1919-. *Texts (including translations)*

Andrzejewski, Jerzy. Lludw a diemwnt = Popiól i diament / gan Jerzy Andrzejewski ; cyfieithiad o'r Bwyleg gan John Elwyn Jones. — Llandysul : Gwasg Gomer, [1976]. — 180p ; 23cm.
Translation of: 'Popiól i diament'. Warsaw : Czytelnik, 1948.
ISBN 0-85088-323-7 : £3.00
(B77-01032)

Emill, Ewa. Goście : powieść / Ewa Emill. — Londyn [i.e. London] : Oficyna Poetów i Malarzy, 1977. — 303p ; 22cm.
Pbk : Unpriced
(B77-31594)

Kisielewski, Stefan. Przygoda w Warszawie : powieść / Stefan Kisielewski. — Londyn [i.e. London] : Polska Fundacja Kulturalna, 1976. — 136p ; 19cm.
ISBN 0-85065-115-8 Pbk : £1.20
(B77-12774)

Panas, Henryk. The gospel according to Judas / [by] Henryk Panas ; translated [from the Polish] by Marc E. Heine. — London : Hutchinson, 1977. — 254p ; 23cm.
Translation of: 'Wedlug Judasza'. Olsztyn : Pojezierze, 1973.
ISBN 0-09-131140-3 : £4.50
(B77-28266)

Paporisz, Romuald. Strefa Dejaniry : opowiadanie fantastyczne / Romuald Paporisz. — Hove (23 Coleridge St., Hove, E. Sussex BN3 5AB) : Caldra House Publishers, [1977?]. — 127p ; 19cm.
Pbk : £0.85
(B77-26663)

Romanowiczowa, Zofia. Sono felice / Zofia Romanowiczowa. — Londyn [i.e. London] : Polska Fundacja Kulturalna, 1977. — 182p ; 19cm.
ISBN 0-85065-111-5 Pbk : £1.20
(B77-13407)

Schulz, Bruno. The street of crocodiles / [by] Bruno Schulz ; translated by Celina Wieniewska ; introduction by Jerzy Ficowski ; introduction translated by Michael Kandel. — Harmondsworth [etc.] : Penguin, 1977. — 160p ; 18cm. — (Writers from the other Europe)
This translation originally published: as 'The street of crocodiles', New York : Walker, 1963 ; and as 'Cinnamon shops'. London : MacGibbon and Kee, 1963. — Translation of: Sklepy cynamonowe'. Krakow : s.n., 1934.
ISBN 0-14-004227-x Pbk : Unpriced
(B77-12183)

Szechter, Szymon. Bridge on ice / [by] Szymon Szechter ; translated by Frances Carroll & Nina Karsov. — London : Boyars : Distributed by Calder and Boyars, 1977. — 104p ; 21cm. — (Signature series ; 26)
Originally published: in Polish. London : Kontra, 1975.
ISBN 0-7145-2596-0 : £3.50
ISBN 0-7145-2597-9 Pbk : Unpriced
(B77-25267)

Tarnawski, Wit. Ksiądz Antoni : powieść / Wit Tarnawski. — Londyn [i.e. London] : Polska Fundacja Kulturalna, 1977. — 208p ; 19cm.
ISBN 0-85065-114-x Pbk : £1.20
(B77-12184)

Witkiewicz, Stanislaw Ignacy. Insatiability : a novel in two parts / by Stanislaw Ignacy Witkiewicz ; translated [from the Polish] with an introduction and commentary by Louis Iribarne. — Urbana [etc.] ; London : University of Illinois Press, 1977. — [1],xlv,447p ; 24cm.
'Russian and East European Center, published in conjunction with the Office of International Programs and Studies' - half-title page verso. — Translation of: 'Nienasycenie'. Warsaw : Panstwowy Instytut Wydawn., 1957. — Bibl.: p.445-447.
ISBN 0-252-00572-4 : £11.25
(B77-25983)

Wyrwa, Józef. Krystyna : opowieść z dziejów Armii Krajowej / Józef Wyrwa. — Londyn [i.e. London] : Officyna Poetów i Malarzy, [1977]. — 207p ; 22cm.
ISBN 0-902571-93-1 Pbk : £3.50
(B77-13408)

891.8'5'37J — Children's stories in Polish, 1919-. *Texts (including translations)*

Konwicki, Tadeusz. The anthropos-spectre-beast / [by] Tadeusz Konwicki ; translated [from the Polish] by George and Audrey Korwin Rodziszewski ; illustrated by Julek Heller. — Oxford [etc.] : Oxford University Press, 1977. — [2],189p ; 23cm.
Translation of: 'Zwierzoczlekoupiór'. Warsaw : Czytelnik, 1972.
ISBN 0-19-271407-4 : £3.25 : CIP rev.
(B77-16643)

891.8'5'37 — Fiction in Polish. Wasilewska, Wanda. *Biographies. Polish texts*

Ciolkosz, Adam. Wanda Wasilewska : dwa szkice biograficzne / Adam Ciolkosz. — Londyn [i.e. London] (10, Queen Anne's Gardens W4 1TU) : Polonia Book Fund Ltd, 1977. — 62p : ill, ports ; 21cm.
Pbk : £1.50
(B77-19078)

891.8'5'6 — Poetry in Polish. Leśmian, Boleslaw. *Critical studies*

Stone, Rochelle Heller. Boleslaw Leśmian : the poet and his poetry / by Rochelle Heller Stone. — Berkeley [etc.] ; London : University of California Press, 1976. — xi,364p ; 23cm.
Bibl.: p.338-353. — Index.
ISBN 0-520-02549-0 : £12.75
(B77-13951)

891.86 — CZECH LITERATURE

891.8'6'25 — Drama in Czech, 1900-. *English texts*

Kohout, Pavel. Poor murderer : a play in two acts / translated from the Czech play of Pavel Kohout and the German version of G. and A. Baumrucker by Herbert Berghof and Laurence Luckinbill. — New York ; London [etc.] : French, [1977]. — 102p : plan ; 19cm.
'The work is based on the Leonid N. Andreev short story "Mysl'" (Thought) 1902'. — Translation of: 'Ubohy vrah'. Prague? : s.n., 1971.
ISBN 0-573-61442-3 Sd : £1.65
(B77-24578)

891.8'6'35F — Fiction in Czech, 1900-. *Texts (including translations)*

Kundera, Milan. The farewell party / [by] Milan Kundera ; translated from the Czech [MS.] by Peter Kussi. — London : J. Murray, 1977. — [5],209p ; 22cm.
This translation originally published: New York : Knopf, 1976.
ISBN 0-7195-3442-9 : £3.95
(B77-30820)

891.87 — SLOVAK LITERATURE

891.8'7 — Poetry in Slovak. Orszagh, Pavol. *Biographies*

Lubran, Alfred. A man of the stars : the Slovakian poet Hviesdoslav : an illustrated summary / by Alfred Lubran. — London : Narbulla Agency Press, 1974. — 52p : ill(some col), ports ; 89mmx21cm.
Limited ed. of 90 copies printed in black and brown, 75 copies on Glastonbury pure white paper, and 15 copies on Glastonbury book antique laid paper. — 'Based on ... a book by Stanislav Smatlak, published by Obzor Publishing House, Bratislava, 1969 and translated by M. Hunnigenova ...' - p.3. — Previous control number ISBN 0-905014-05-7.
ISBN 0-905014-03-0 Pbk : £5.00
ISBN 0-905014-05-7 Glastonbury antique laid paper. ISBN 0-905014-04-9 Glastonbury pure white paper
(B77-03809)

891.92 — LITHUANIAN LITERATURE

891'.92'33F — Fiction in Lithuanian, 1900-. *Texts (including translations)*

B¯udavas, Stasys. Europiete / Stasys B¯udavas. — [London] : Nida Press, 1976. — 173p ; 19cm. — (Nidos Knygu Klubo leidinys ; nr.98)
ISBN 0-901941-25-5 : £2.00
(B77-07704)

892.4 — HEBREW LITERATURE

892.4'08'006 — Hebrew literature. Israeli writers, 1947-. *Anthologies. English texts*

New writing from Israel 1976 : stories, poems, essays / selected and edited by Jacob Sonntag. — London : Corgi, 1976. — 256p ; 18cm.
ISBN 0-552-10284-9 Pbk : £0.95
(B77-05106)

892.4'1'5 — Poetry in Hebrew, 1885-1947. *English texts*

Goldberg, Leah. Selected poems [of] Leah Goldberg / translated and introduced by Robert Friend ; foreword by Yehuda Amichai ; afterword by Gershom Scholem. — London (23 Fitzwarren Gardens, N19 3TR) : Menard Press [etc.], 1976. — 64p ; 22cm.
ISBN 0-903400-25-1 Pbk : £1.80
(B77-12775)

Vogel, David. The dark gate : selected poems of David Vogel / translated from the Hebrew by A.C. Jacobs. — London (23 Fitzwarren Gardens, N.19) : Menard Press, 1976. — 35p, [4]p of plates : ports ; 22cm.
ISBN 0-903400-23-5 Pbk : £1.20
(B77-12776)

892.4'1'6 — Poetry in Hebrew, 1947-. *English texts*

Ravikovitch, Dahlia. A dress of fire / [by] Dahlia Ravikovitch ; poems translated from the Hebrew by Chana Block. — London (23 Fitzwarren Gardens, N19 [3TR]) : The Menard Press, 1976. — 47p ; 22cm.
ISBN 0-903400-28-6 Pbk : £1.20
(B77-12185)

Vinner, Shlomo. For a few hours only : selected poems of Shlomo Vinner / edited by Howard Schwartz ; translated from the Hebrew by Laya Firestone ... [et al.]. — St Louis [Mo.] : Singing Bone Books ; London (23 Fitzwarren Gardens, N19 3TR) : Menard Press, 1976. — [5],36p ; 22cm.
Includes 3 poems in Hebrew with parallel English translations. — Translation of: 'Rak-leshaot-sfurot'. Jerusalem : s.n., 1972.
ISBN 0-903400-21-9 Pbk : £0.75
(B77-11465)

892.4'3'6F — Fiction in Hebrew, 1947-. *Texts (including translations)*

Ka-Tzetnik 135633. Sunrise over hell / by Ka-tzetnik 135633 ; translated from the Hebrew by Nina de-Nur. — London : W.H. Allen, 1977. — [7],215p ; 23cm.
Translation of: 'Salamandra'. Tel-Aviv : Dvir Publishing Co., 197-.
ISBN 0-491-01707-3 : £3.95
(B77-07705)

Oz, Amos. Unto death / [by] Amos Oz ; translated from the Hebrew by Nicholas de Lange in collaboration with the author. — [London] : Fontana, 1977. — 125p ; 18cm.
This translated collection originally published: New York : Harcourt Brace Jovanovich, 1975 ; London : Chatto and Windus, 1976. — Translation of: 'Ahavah' me 'uheret'. s.l. : s.n., 1971. — Contents: Crusade - Late love.
ISBN 0-00-614597-3 Pbk : £0.75
(B77-28267)

892.7 — ARABIC LITERATURE
892'.7'132 — Poetry in Arabic, 661-750. *Arabic & English texts*

Bašš̄ar. Selections from the poetry of Bašš̄ar / edited with translation and commentary and an introductory sketch of Arabic poetic structures by A.F.L. Beeston. — Cambridge [etc.] : Cambridge University Press, 1977. — [5],72,[18]p ; 26cm.
Arabic text, English translation, commentary and introduction.
ISBN 0-521-21664-8 : £6.50
ISBN 0-521-29223-9 Pbk : £2.40
(B77-25268)

892'.7'1608 — Poetry in Arabic, 1945-. *Anthologies. English texts*

Modern Arab poets, 1950-1975 / translated and edited by Issa J. Boullata. — London : Heinemann Educational, 1976. — xii,148p ; 19cm. — (Arab authors ; 6)
This collection also published: Washington, D.C. : Three Continents Press, 1976.
ISBN 0-435-99406-9 Pbk : £1.80
(B77-12186)

892'.7'35 — Fiction in Arabic, 1800-1945. Lebanese writers. *English texts*

Awwad, Tawfiq Yusuf. Death in Beirut : a novel / by Tawfig Yusuf Awwad ; translated [from the Arabic] by Leslie McLoughlin. — London : Heinemann Educational, 1976. — xiv, 190p : map, plan ; 19cm. — (Arab authors ; 5)
Translation of: 'Taw ah in Bayrut'. Beirut : Dar el Adab, 1972.
ISBN 0-435-99405-0 Pbk : £1.95
(B77-01033)

893 — HAMITIC AND CHAD LITERATURES
893'.1 — Egyptian literature. *Anthologies. English texts*

Ancient Egyptian literature : a book of readings / [selected] by Miriam Lichtheim. — Berkeley [etc.] ; London : University of California Press.
Vol.1 : The Old and Middle Kingdoms. — [1976]. — xxi,245p ; 24cm.
Published in the United States: 1973. — Index.
ISBN 0-520-09443-3 : £7.15
(B77-06356)

894 — URAL-ALTAIC, PALAEOSIBERIAN, DRAVIDIAN LITERATURES
894'.3'533F — Fiction in Turkish, 1850-. *Texts (including translations)*

Bilbasar, Kemal. Gemmo : a novel / [by] Kemal Bilbasar ; translated from the Turkish by Esin B. Rey with Marianna Fitzpatrick. — London : Owen, 1976. — 223p ; 19cm. — (Unesco. Collection of representative works : Turkish series)
Translation of: 'Cemo'. Istanbul : Evren yayinlari, 1966.
ISBN 0-7206-0424-9 : £4.75
(B77-06357)

Kemal, Yashar. The undying grass / [by] Yashar Kemal ; translated from the Turkish by Thilda Kemal. — London : Collins : Harvill Press, 1977. — 322p ; 22cm.
Translation of: 'Olmez otu'. Istanbul : Ant Yayinlari, 1968.
ISBN 0-00-261820-6 : £4.25
(B77-17169)

894'.511'13 — Poetry in Hungarian, 1900-. *English texts*

Radnóti, Miklós. The witness : selected poems / by Miklós Radnóti ; translated from the Hungarian by Thomas Orszag-Land ; woodcuts by Nicholas Parry. — Market Drayton ([Market Drayton, Salop]) : Tern Press, 1977. — 3-59p : ill ; 21cm.
ISBN 0-906057-02-7 Pbk : £0.75
(B77-25984)

894'.511'1308 — Poetry in Hungarian, 1900-. *Anthologies. English texts*

Modern Hungarian poetry / edited, with an introduction, by Miklós Vajda ; [translated from the Hungarian] ; foreword by William Jay Smith. — New York ; Guildford : Columbia University Press, 1977. — xxxv,289p,[12]p of plates : ports ; 24cm.
Index.
ISBN 0-231-04022-9 : £8.80
(B77-29028)

894'.511'23 — Drama in Hungarian, 1900-. *English texts*

Heimler, Eugene. The storm (the tragedy of Sinai) / by Eugene Heimler ; English version (after the Hungarian) and introduction by Anthony Rudolf. — London (23 Fitzwarren Gardens N19 3TR) : Menard Press, 1976. — [6],41,[4]p ; 21cm.
ISBN 0-903400-19-7 Pbk : £0.90
(B77-03810)

894'.511'33F — Fiction in Hungarian, 1900-. *Texts (including translations)*

Konrad, George. The case worker / [by] George Konrad ; translated [from the Hungarian] by Paul Aston. — London : Hutchinson, 1977. — [4],172p ; 20cm. — (Open University. Set books)
This translation originally published: New York : Harcourt Brace Jovanovich, 1974 ; London : Hutchinson, 1975. — Translation of: 'A látogató'. Budapest : Magvetö, 1969.
ISBN 0-09-131701-0 Pbk : £2.25
(B77-29029)

Lajossy, Sándor. A fehér asszony : társadalmi regény / Lajossy Sándor. — London (21 Palliser Rd, Barons Court, W14 9EB) : Turul Nyomda, 1976. — 150p ; 20cm.
ISBN 0-9505542-0-0 Pbk : Unpriced
(B77-06958)

894'.541'1008 — Orally transmitted poetry in Finnish, to 1976. *Anthologies. Finnish-English parallel texts*

Finnish folk poetry, epic : an anthology in Finnish and English / edited and translated by Matti Kuusi, Keith Bosley, Michael Branch. — Helsinki : Finnish Literature Society ; London : C. Hurst [etc.], 1977. — 607p,[28]p of plates : ill, map, music, ports ; 24cm. — (Suomalaisen Kirjallisuuden Seura. Publications ; 329)
English introduction, parallel Finnish text and English translations. — Bibl.: p.603-606. — Index.
ISBN 0-903983-82-6 : £18.50
(B77-22236)

894.8 — DRAVIDIAN LITERATURES
894'.814'3'7F — Fiction in Kannada, 1940-. *Texts (including translations)*

Anantha Murthy, U R. Samskara : a rite for a dead man : a translation of U.R. Anantha Murthy's Kannada novel / by A.K. Ramanujan. — Delhi ; Oxford [etc.] : Oxford University Press, 1976. — xi,153p ; 18cm. — (A three crowns book)
Translation of: 'Samsk ara'. Dharwar : Man ohara Grantham al a, 1966.
ISBN 0-19-560687-6 Pbk : £1.95
(B77-16101)

895.1 — CHINESE LITERATURE
895.1'08 — Chinese literature. Japanese writers, 700-. *Anthologies. English texts*

Japanese literature in Chinese. — New York ; London : Columbia University Press. — (Columbia College. Program of translations from the Oriental classics, publications)
Vol.2 : Poetry & prose in Chinese by Japanese writers of the later period / translated by Burton Watson. — 1976. — [9],191p ; 22cm.
Bibl.: p.20-22. — Index.
ISBN 0-231-04146-2 : £7.63
(B77-09373)

895.1'08'005 — Chinese literature. Taiwan writers, 1912-1974. *Anthologies. English texts*

An **anthology** of contemporary Chinese literature : Taiwan, 1949-1974 / edited and compiled by Chi Pang-yuan ... [et al.]. — Taipei : National Institute for Compilation and Translation ; Seattle ; London : Distributed by University of Washington Press, 1975. — 2v. ([2],xxi,556,[1];[2],xii,470p) ; 23cm.
£18.90
(B77-13409)

895.1'09'375 — Chinese literature, ca 700-ca 1000. Special subjects: Fertility goddesses: Water women. *Critical studies*

Schafer, Edward Hetzel. The divine woman : dragon ladies and rain maidens in T'ang literature / by Edward H. Schafer. — Berkeley [etc.] ; London : University of California Press, 1973. — viii,191p ; 23cm.
Bibl.: p.117-175. — Index.
ISBN 0-520-02465-6 : £8.00
(B77-27527)

895.1'1'008 — Poetry in Chinese, ca B.C. 600-ca A.D. 1800. *Anthologies. Chinese-English parallel texts*

A **golden** treasury of Chinese poetry : 121 classical poems / translated by John A. Turner ; with notes and Chinese texts compiled and edited by John J. Deeney with the assistance of Kenneth K.B. Li. — [Hong Kong] : Chinese University of Hong Kong ; Seattle ; London : Distributed by the University of Washington Press, 1976. — [5],345p ; 20cm. — ('Renditions' books)
Parallel Chinese text and English translations. — Index.
ISBN 0-295-95506-6 : £8.00
(B77-03811)

895.1'1'00803538 — Erotic poetry in Chinese, ca B.C.200-ca A.D.1350. *Anthologies. English texts*

Booth, Martin. Stalks of jade : renderings from the Chinese / by Martin Booth. — London (23 Fitzwarren Gardens, N19 3TR) : The Menard Press, 1976. — 21,[1]p ; 23cm.
ISBN 0-903400-14-6 Sd : £0.65
(B77-08650)

895.1'1'2 — Poetry in Chinese. Juan Chi. *Critical studies*

Holzman, Donald. Poetry and politics : the life and works of Juan Chi, AD 210-263 / [by] Donald Holzman. — Cambridge [etc.] : Cambridge University Press, 1976. — xi,316p : facsims ; 24cm. — ([Cambridge studies in Chinese history, literature and institutions])
Bibl.: p.286-302. — Index.
ISBN 0-521-20855-6 : £9.50
(B77-09374)

895.1'1'308 — Poetry in Chinese, 700-1000. *Anthologies. English texts*

Poems of the late T'ang / translated [from the Chinese] with an introduction by A.C.Graham. — [1st ed.] reprinted ; with additional preface. — Harmondsworth [etc.] : Penguin, 1977. — 175p ; 19cm. — (Unesco. Collection of representative works : Chinese series) (The Penguin classics)
This translated collection originally published: 1965.
ISBN 0-14-044157-3 Pbk : £0.60
(B77-27528)

895.1'2'408 — Drama in Chinese, ca 1000-1912. *Anthologies. English texts*

Six Yüan plays / translated [from the Chinese] with an introduction by Liu Jung-en. — Harmondsworth [etc.] : Penguin, 1977. — 285p ; 19cm. — (Penguin classics)
These translations originally published: 1972. — Bibl.: p.37.
Pbk : £0.85
ISBN 0-14-044262-6
(B77-30821)

895.1'3'4 — Fiction in Chinese, ca 1000-1912. *English texts*

Ts'ao Chan Hsüeh-ch'in. The story of the stone : a Chinese novel / by Cao Xueqin ; translated by David Hawkes. — Harmondsworth [etc.] : Penguin. — (The Penguin classics)
In 5 vols.
Vol.1 : The golden days. — 1976. — 540,[2]p : geneal tables ; 19cm.
This translation originally published: 1973.
Pbk : £1.00
ISBN 0-14-044293-6
(B77-05107)

Vol.2 : The Crab-flower Club. — 1977. — 603p : ill, geneal tables ; 19cm.
ISBN 0-14-044326-6 Pbk : £1.95
(B77-19079)

895.1'3'5 — Short stories in Chinese. Lu Xun. *Critical studies*

Lyell, William A. Lu Hsün's vision of reality / [by] William A. Lyell, Jr. — Berkeley [etc.] ; London : University of California Press, 1976. — x,355p : ill, ports ; 25cm.
Bibl.: p.334-347. — Index.
ISBN 0-520-02940-2 : £11.65
(B77-15014)

895.6 — JAPANESE LITERATURE
895.6'09 — Japanese literature, to 1898. *Critical studies*

Aston, W G. A history of Japanese literature / by W.G. Aston. — [New ed.] ; with an introduction by Terence Barrow. — Rutland, Vt [etc.] : Tuttle ; London : Prentice-Hall, 1972. — xviii,408p ; 19cm.
Previous ed.: London : Heinemann, 1899. — Bibl.: p.400-403. — Index.
ISBN 0-8048-0997-6 Pbk : £2.80
(B77-26664)

895.6'09'003 — Japanese literature, 1603-1868. *Critical studies*
Keene, Donald. World within walls : Japanese literature of the pre-modern era, 1600-1867 / [by] Donald Keene. — London : Secker and Warburg, 1976. — xv,606,[1]p ; 24cm.
Also published: New York : Holt, Rinehart and Winston, 1976. — Bibl. — Index.
ISBN 0-436-23266-9 : £11.75
(B77-05108)

895.6'1'108 — Poetry in Japanese, to 1185. *Anthologies. Transliterated Japanese-English parallel texts*
Japanese poetry : the 'Uta' / [compiled and translated by] Arthur Waley. — New ed. [i.e. 1st ed. reprinted] ; introduction by Carmen Blacker. — London : Allen and Unwin, 1976. — 2-112p : facsim ; 21cm.
Parallel transliterated Japanese text and English translation, introduction, vocabulary and notes in English. — This collection originally published: Oxford : Clarendon Press, 1919.
ISBN 0-04-895022-x : £2.95
(B77-01885)

895.6'1'3 — Poetry in Japanese, 1603-1868. *English texts*
Issa. The year of my life : a translation of Issa's 'Oraga Haru' / by Nobuyuki Yuasa. — 2nd ed. — Berkeley ; London : University of California Press, 1972. — [8],142p : ill ; 20cm.
Previous ed. of this translation: Berkeley : University of California Press ; London : Cambridge University Press, 1960.
ISBN 0-520-02328-5 : Unpriced
ISBN 0-520-02160-6 Pbk : Unpriced
(B77-20765)

895.6'3'1 — Fiction in Japanese, to 1185. *English texts*
Murasaki Shikibu. The tale of Genji / [by] Murasaki Shikibu ; translated with an introduction by Edward G. Seidensticker. — London : Secker and Warburg, 1976. — 2v. (xix,100,xii p,[2]leaves) : ill ; 25cm.
In slip case.
ISBN 0-436-45950-7 : £15.00
(B77-01034)

895.6'3'4 — Fiction in Japanese. S¯oseki, Natsume. Characters. Psychology. *Critical studies*
Doi, Takeo. The psychological world of Natsume S¯oseki / by Doi Takeo ; translated from the Japanese with an introduction and synopses by William Jefferson Tyler. — [Cambridge, Mass.] : East Asian Research Center, Harvard University ; Cambridge, Mass. ; London : Distributed by Harvard University Press, 1976. — xii,161p ; 24cm. — (Harvard East Asian monographs ; 68)
Translation of: 'S¯oseki non shinteki sekai'. Tokyo : Shibund¯o, 1969. — Index.
ISBN 0-674-72116-0 : £11.25
(B77-06358)

895.6'3'409 — Fiction in Japanese, 1868-1973. *Critical studies*
Miyoshi, Masao. Accomplices of silence : the modern Japanese novel / [by] Masao Miyoshi. — Berkeley [etc.] ; London : University of California Press, 1974. — xx,194p ; 24cm.
Index.
ISBN 0-520-02540-7 : Unpriced
(B77-20766)

895.6'3'5F — Fiction in Japanese, 1945-. *Texts (including translations)*
Kawabata, Yasunari. The lake / [by] Yasunari Kawabata ; translated by Reiko Tsukimura. — London : Owen, 1977. — 160p ; 19cm. — (Unesco. Collection of representative works : Japanese series)
This translation originally published: New York : Kodansha International, 1974. — Translation of: 'Mizuumi'. Japan : s.n., 1954.
ISBN 0-7206-2000-7 : £3.95
(B77-10019)

Komatsu, Sakyo. Japan sinks / [by] Sakyo Komatsu ; translated from the Japanese by Michael Gallagher. — London : New English Library, 1977. — 192p ; 22cm.
This translation originally published: New York : Harper and Row, 1976. — Translation of: 'Nippon chinbotsu'. Tokyo : K¯obunsha, 1973.
ISBN 0-450-03209-4 : £4.25
(B77-22237)

Mishima, Yukio. Confessions of a mask / [by] Yukio Mishima ; translated by Meredith Weatherby. — London : Panther, 1977. — 206p ; 18cm.
This translation originally published: Norfolk, Conn. : New Directions, 1958 ; London : Owen, 1960. — Translation of: 'Kamen no kokuhaku'. Japan : s.n., 1949.
Pbk : £0.75
ISBN 0-586-03724-1
(B77-24579)

Mishima, Yukio. Death in midsummer, and other stories / [by] Yukio Mishima. — Harmondsworth [etc.] : Penguin, 1977. — 186p ; 19cm.
These translations originally published: New York : New Directions, 1966 ; London : Secker and Warburg, 1967.
Pbk : £0.60
ISBN 0-14-003322-x
(B77-15593)

Mishima, Yukio. The decay of the angel / [by] Yukio Mishima ; translated from the Japanese by Edward G. Seidensticker. — Harmondsworth [etc.] : Penguin, 1977. — 205p ; 18cm. — (Mishima, Yukio. Sea of fertility ; [4])
This translation originally published: New York : Knopf, 1974 ; London : Secker and Warburg, 1975. — Translation of: 'Tennin gosui'. Tokyo : Shinchosha, 1971.
ISBN 0-14-004246-6 Pbk : £0.90
(B77-32948)

Mishima, Yukio. Runaway horses / [by] Yukio Mishima ; translated from the Japanese by Michael Gallagher. — Harmondsworth [etc.] : Penguin, 1977. — 395p ; 19cm.
This translation originally published: London : Secker and Warburg, 1973. — Translation of: 'Homba'. Tokyo : Shinchosha, 1969.
ISBN 0-14-004167-2 Pbk : £1.00
(B77-15594)

Mishima, Yukio. The temple of dawn / [by] Yukio Mishima ; translated from the Japanese by E. Dale Saunders and Cecilia Segawa Seigle. — Harmondsworth [etc.] : Penguin, 1977. — 285p ; 18cm. — (Mishima, Yukio. Sea of fertility ; 3)
This translation originally published: New York : Knopf, 1973 ; London : Secker and Warburg, 1974. — Translation of: 'Akatsuki no Tera'. Tokyo : Shinchosha, 1970.
ISBN 0-14-004198-2 Pbk : £0.90
(B77-32949)

895.6'3'5J — Children's stories in Japanese, 1945-. *Texts (including translations)*
Kasuya, Masahiro. The beginning of the rainbow / pictures by Masahiro Kasuya ; story by Shona McKellar. — London : Evans Bros, 1977. — [25]p : chiefly col ill ; 22x31cm.
These illustrations originally published: with Japanese text. Japan : Shiko-sha, 1976.
ISBN 0-237-44872-6 : £2.95
(B77-26665)

Kimura, Yasuko. Cuthbert and the sea monster / pictures by Yasuko Kimura ; story by Kim Chesher. — London : Evans Bros, 1977. — [33] p : chiefly col ill ; 20x27cm.
These illustrations originally published: with Japanese text. Japan : Shiko-sha, 1977.
ISBN 0-237-44876-9 : £2.95
(B77-30822)

895.9 — THAI AND OTHER LITERATURES OF SOUTHEAST ASIA
895.9'1'13 — Poetry in Thai, 1900-. *Thai-English parallel texts*
Thongyoyworakawinto, *Phra Maha.* A village ordination = Baphachapawatkamklawn / Phra Maha Thongyoy Worakawinto Taeng ; [translated from the Thai with English text by] Thomas Silcock. — Lund : Studentlitteratur ; London : Curzon Press, 1976. — [7],xxiii p,93 leaves,xxi p of plates : ill ; 23cm. — (Nordiska Asieninstitutet. Monograph series ; no.25 ISSN 0069-1712)
Parallel title and primary author statement transliterated. — Leaves printed on both sides. — Parallel Thai text and English translation.
ISBN 0-7007-0092-7 Pbk : £3.50 : CIP rev.
(B77-09375)

896 — AFRICAN LITERATURES
896 — Orally transmitted literature in African languages, to 1969. *Critical studies*
Finnegan, Ruth Hilary. Oral literature in Africa / [by] Ruth Finnegan. — Nairobi ; Oxford [etc.] : Oxford University Press, 1976. — xix,558p,fold plate : map ; 22cm. — (Oxford library of African literature)
Originally published: London : Clarendon Press, 1970. — Bibl.: p.522-536. — Index.
ISBN 0-19-572413-5 Pbk : £13.50
(B77-24580)

896'.392'09 — Swahili literature. Style. Linguistic aspects
Maw, Joan. Swahili style : a study / [by] Joan Maw. — London : University of London, School of Oriental and African Studies, 1974. — vii,77p ; 26cm.
ISBN 0-7286-0000-5 Pbk : Unpriced
Primary classification 808
(B77-19593)

896'.5 — Poetry in Acholi. Okot p'Bitek. *Critical studies*
Heron, G A. The poetry of Okot p'Bitek / [by] G.A. Heron. — London : Heinemann Educational [etc.], 1976. — ix,163p ; 23cm. — (Studies in African literature)
Bibl.: p.157-159. — Index.
ISBN 0-435-91600-9 : £5.00
ISBN 0-435-91601-7 Pbk : £2.00
(B77-03812)

901 — HISTORY. PHILOSOPHY AND THEORY
901 — Historiology. *Philosophical perspectives*
Mandelbaum, Maurice. The anatomy of historical knowledge / [by] Maurice Mandelbaum. — Baltimore ; London : Johns Hopkins University Press, 1977. — viii,232p ; 24cm.
Index.
ISBN 0-8018-1929-6 : £10.50
(B77-24581)

Martin, Rex. Historical explanation : re-enactment and practical inference / [by] Rex Martin. — Ithaca ; London : Cornell University Press, 1977. — 267,[1]p ; 23cm. — (Contemporary philosophy)
Bibl.: p.255-262. — Index.
ISBN 0-8014-1084-3 : Unpriced
(B77-34269)

Walsh, William Henry. An introduction to philosophy of history / [by] W.H. Walsh. — 3rd (revised) ed. reprinted / with an addenda to the bibliographical section. — [Hassocks] : Harvester Press, 1976. — 215p ; 23cm.
Third revised ed. originally published: London : Hutchinson, 1967. — Bibl.: p.207-209. — Index.
ISBN 0-85527-289-9 : £5.50
(B77-06959)

902 — HISTORY. MISCELLANY
902'.02 — World events, B.C.5000-A.D.1975. *Chronologies. Juvenile literature*
1,000 great events / edited by Lynne Sabel and Philip Steele. — London [etc.] : Hamlyn, 1977. — 2-352p : ill(some col), facsims, 2 maps(1 col), col plan, ports(some col) ; 25cm.
Index.
ISBN 0-600-38743-7 : £2.95
(B77-34270)

903 — HISTORY. DICTIONARIES, ENCYCLOPAEDIAS, CONCORDANCES
903 — World, to 1975. *Encyclopaedias*
Encyclopedia of the nations : a practical guide to the geographic, historical, political, social & economic status of all nations, their international relationships and the United Nations system / [editor and publisher Moshe Y. Sachs]. — 5th ed. — [New York] : Worldmark Press ; London ([150 Southampton Row, W.C.1]) : Distributed by the New Caxton Library Service Ltd, 1976. — 5v. : ill, maps ; 29cm.
Col. maps on lining papers. — 'Issued in the United States of America and Canada as "Worldmark encyclopedia of the nations"' - title page verso. — Previous ed.: s.l. : Otevel Ltd, 1971. — Bibl. — Indexes.
ISBN 0-903322-18-8 : £69.00
(B77-29030)

Longman illustrated companion to world history / edited by Grant Uden. — London [etc.] : Longman ; [Harmondsworth] : Kestrel Books, 1976. — 2v.([16],1040p,64p of plates) : ill(some col), facsims, geneal table, maps, plans, ports(some col) ; 24cm.
Col. maps on lining papers. — Bibl. — Index.
ISBN 0-582-20520-4 : £12.50
(B77-01035)

904 — HISTORY. COLLECTED ACCOUNTS OF SPECIAL KINDS OF EVENTS

904'.7 — Battles, to 1976. *Dictionaries*

Young, Peter, *b.1915.* A dictionary of battles / [by] Peter Young with Michael Calvert. — London : New English Library.
In 4 vols.
[Vol.1] : 1816-1976. — 1977. — x,606p : ill(on lining papers), maps ; 26cm.
Bibl.: p.605-606.
ISBN 0-450-02842-9 : £9.95
(B77-10020)

905 — HISTORY. PERIODICALS

905 — Historical events. *Socialist viewpoints. Periodicals*

History workshop : a journal of socialist historians. — Oxford (P.O. Box 69, Oxford OX2 7XA) : History Workshop Journal ; London : Distributed by Pluto Press.
Issue 1- ; Spring 1976-. — [1976]-. — ill, facsims, maps ; 24cm.
Two issues a year. — [2],287p.,[4]p . of plates in 1st issue.
Pbk : £5.00 yearly
ISSN 0309-2984
(B77-10636)

907 — HISTORY. STUDY AND TEACHING

907'.12 — Secondary schools. Curriculum subjects: History. Teaching

Garvey, Brian. Models of history teaching in the secondary school / [by] Brian Garvey, Mary Krug. — Oxford [etc.] : Oxford University Press, 1977. — [8],192p : ill, maps ; 20cm. — (Oxford studies in education ; 13)
Bibl.
ISBN 0-19-919061-5 Pbk : £2.50
(B77-24582)

907'.12'41 — Secondary schools. Curriculum subjects: History. Projects. *Great Britain. Schools Council History 13-16 Project. Reports, surveys*

Schools Council History 13-16 Project. A new look at history / Schools Council History 13-16 Project. — Edinburgh : Holmes-McDougall, 1976. — 88p : ill, forms, map, ports ; 25cm.
ISBN 0-7157-1553-4 Pbk : £1.40
(B77-16644)

907'.2 — Historiography

Gilbert, Felix. History : choice and commitment / [by] Felix Gilbert. — Cambridge, Mass. ; London : Belknap Press of Harvard University Press, 1977. — ix,549p ; 24cm.
Index.
ISBN 0-674-39656-1 : £12.65
Primary classification 320.9'45
(B77-33083)

Lewis, Bernard, *b.1916.* History : remembered, recovered, invented / [by] Bernard Lewis. — Princeton ; Guildford : Princeton University Press, 1976[i.e.1977]. — ix,111p ; 21cm.
'Originally presented as the Benjamin Gottesman lectures, Yeshiva University, 1974' - Library of Congress Cataloguing in Publication data. — Originally published: 1975. — Index.
ISBN 0-691-03547-4 : £5.55
ISBN 0-691-00211-8 Pbk : £2.05
(B77-10637)

907'.2 — Historiography. *Essays*

Momigliano, Arnaldo. Essays in ancient and modern historiography / [by] Arnaldo Momigliano. — Oxford : Blackwell, 1977. — x, 387p ; 23cm. — (Blackwell's classical studies)
Index.
ISBN 0-631-17900-3 : £12.00
(B77-19081)

907'.2 — Historiography. Related to mythopoeic aspects of literature. *Conference proceedings*

English Institute, *Columbia University.* The literature of fact : selected papers from the English Institute / edited with a foreword by Angus Fletcher. — New York ; Guildford : Columbia University Press, 1976. — xxvii, 172p ; 21cm.
'The "Literature of fact" occupied the attention of the English Institute during two sessions of its meetings, in 1974 and 1975' - Foreword.
ISBN 0-231-04144-6 : £5.90
Primary classification 809
(B77-06234)

907'.2 — Historiology. Related to social sciences

Bullock, Alan, *Baron Bullock.* Is history becoming a social science? : the case of contemporary history / [by] Alan Bullock. — Cambridge [etc.] : Cambridge University Press, 1977. — [1],23,[1]p ; 19cm. — (The Leslie Stephen lecture ; 1976)
'... delivered in the University of Cambridge on 5 March 1976' - p.23.
ISBN 0-521-29222-0 Sd : £0.60
Also classified at 300
(B77-34271)

907'.2'024 — Historiography. Ranke, Leopold von

Krieger, Leonard. Ranke : the meaning of history / [by] Leonard Krieger. — Chicago ; London : University of Chicago Press, 1977. — xiii,402p ; 24cm.
Bibl.: p.388-392. — Index.
ISBN 0-226-45349-9 : £16.10
(B77-28268)

907'.2'041 — Historiology. Organisations: Historical Association. *Periodicals*

Kennington news. — London : Historical Association.
No.1- ; Feb. 1977-. — [1977]-. — 30cm.
6p. in 1st issue.
Sd : Free to members of the Association
(B77-19883)

907'.2'0439 — Hungarian historiography, 1000-1956

Vardy, Steven Bela. Modern Hungarian historiography / [by] Steven Bela Vardy. — Boulder : 'East European quarterly' ; New York ; Guildford : Distributed by Columbia University Press, 1976. — xii,333p ; 23cm. — (East European monographs ; no.17 [i.e. no.16])
Bibl.: p.289-309. — Index.
ISBN 0-914710-08-7 : Unpriced
(B77-02649)

907'.6 — Secondary schools. Examinations. Development. *Ireland (Republic). Study examples: History. Reports, surveys*

Public Examinations Evaluation Project. The Public Examinations Evaluation Project : a progress report / by J. Heywood, S. McGuinness, D. Murphy. — Dublin (School of Education, Trinity College, Dublin 2) : The Project, 1977. — ii,32,10 leaves ; 30cm. — (Public Examinations Evaluation Project. Reports ; vol. 1, no.3)
Sd : Unpriced
Primary classification 510'.76
(B77-31162)

907'.6 — World, to 1966. *Questions & answers. For Irish students. Secondary school texts*

O'Donnell, Seán. History workbook / [by] Seán O'Donnell. — Tallaght : Folens, [1977]. — 151p ; 25cm. — (Folens student aids) (Intermediate Certificate)
Fill-in book.
Pbk : Unpriced
(B77-31595)

O'Donnell, Seán. History workbook / [by] Seán O'Donnell. — Tallaght : Folens. — (Intermediate Certificate)
Key. — [1977]. — 130p ; 25cm.
Pbk : Unpriced
(B77-31596)

909 — WORLD HISTORY

909 — Castles. *Juvenile literature*

Unstead, Robert John. See inside a castle / [author R.J. Unstead] ; [illustrations Dan Escott, Brian Lewis, Richard Hook]. — London : Hutchinson, 1977. — 4-29p : col ill, plans ; 29cm. — (See inside)
Bibl.: p.28. — Index.
ISBN 0-09-128690-5 : £1.50
(B77-31597)

909 — Civilization. *Forecasts*

Kahn, Herman. The next 200 years : a scenario for America and the world / by Herman Kahn, William Brown and Leon Martel, with the assistance of the staff of the Hudson Institute. — London : Associated Business Programmes, 1977. — xxi,241p : ill ; 23cm.
Originally published: New York : Morrow, 1976. — Bibl.: p.229-231. — Index.
ISBN 0-85227-071-2 : £5.95
(B77-25269)

909 — Civilization. *Transcripts of discussions*

Toynbee, Arnold, *b.1889.* Choose life : a dialogue / [by] Arnold Toynbee and Daisaku Ikeda ; edited by Richard L. Gage. — London [etc.] : Oxford University Press, 1976. — 348p ; 24cm.
Also published: as 'Man himself must choose'. Tokyo : Kodansha, 1976. — Index.
ISBN 0-19-215258-0 : £9.50
(B77-02650)

909 — Civilization, to 1976

Bowle, John. Man through the ages / [by] John Bowle. — [New ed.]. — London : Weidenfeld and Nicolson, 1977. — viii,312p : maps ; 25cm.
Previous ed.: published as 'A new outline of world history', London : Allen and Unwin ; and as 'Man through the ages', Boston, Mass. : Little, Brown, 1963. — Index.
ISBN 0-297-77207-4 : £10.00
(B77-23812)

909 — Human geography

Bradford, M G. Human geography : theories and their applications / [by] M.G. Bradford and W.A. Kent. — Oxford [etc.] : Oxford University Press, 1977. — [4],180p : ill, maps ; 24cm. — (Science in geography ; 5)
Bibl. — Index.
ISBN 0-19-913227-5 Pbk : £2.50
(B77-25985)

De Blij, Harm Jan. Human geography : culture, society, and space / [by] Harm J. de Blij. — New York ; London [etc.] : Wiley, 1977. — xvi,444p : ill(chiefly col), col maps, ports ; 25cm.
Bibl. — Index.
ISBN 0-471-20047-6 : £10.00
(B77-17806)

Kolars, John F. Human geography : spatial design in world society / [by] John F. Kolars, John D. Nystuen ; drawings by Derwin Bell. — New York ; London [etc.] : McGraw-Hill, 1974. — xvii,281p : ill(chiefly col), maps(chiefly col), plan ; 25cm. — (McGraw-Hill series in geography)
Index.
ISBN 0-07-035327-1 : Unpriced
(B77-21562)

Perpillou, Aimé Vincent. Human geography / [by] Aimé Vincent Perpillou. — 2nd ed. / translated [from the French MS.] by the late E.D. Laborde and S.H. Beaver. — London [etc.] : Longman, 1977. — xxi,570p,[16]p of plates : ill, chart, maps ; 22cm. — (Geographies for advanced study)
Previous ed.: London : Longmans, 1966. — Bibl.: p.553-563. — Index.
ISBN 0-582-48571-1 : £8.95
ISBN 0-582-48572-x Pbk : £5,50
(B77-22972)

Tidswell, William Vincent. Pattern and process in human geography / [by] Vincent Tidswell. — London : University Tutorial Press, 1976. — [5],314p : ill, charts, maps ; 22cm.
Bibl. — Index.
ISBN 0-7231-0719-x Pbk : £2.40
(B77-02651)

909 — Human geography. *For Caribbean students. Secondary school texts*

Lewis, Gerwyn Elidor David. Peoples of other lands / [by] G.E.D. Lewis ; edited by Joyce Matadeen. — New ed. — [Port of Spain] : Longman Caribbean : Longman, 1977. — [4], 132p : ill(chiefly col), col maps, col port ; 25cm. — (Caribbean colour geography)
Col. maps on inside covers. — Previous ed.: 1967.
ISBN 0-582-76540-4 Pbk : £1.70
(B77-28269)

909 — Human geography. *Great Britain & France. Conference proceedings*

Franco-British Conference in Human Geography, *London, 1975.* Human geography in France & Britain : papers presented to the Franco-British Conference in Human Geography held at the Royal Geographical Society, London, 8-10 April, 1975 / edited by John I. Clarke & Ph. Pinchemel. — London : Social Science Research Council, 1976. — 77p ; 30cm.
Contributions in English and French. — Bibl.
ISBN 0-900296-39-9 Pbk : £1.00
(B77-16645)

909 — Human geography. *Reviews of research*

Progress in human geography : an international review of geographical work in the social sciences and humanities. — [London] : [Edward Arnold].
With 'Progress in physical geography' supersedes: Progress in geography.
Vol.1, no.1- ; Mar. 1977-. — 1977-. — ill, maps ; 24cm.
Three issues a year. — iv,176p. in 1st issue. — Bibl.
Pbk : £12.50 yearly
ISSN 0309-1325
(B77-32950)

909 — Human geography. *Secondary school texts*
Robinson, Harry, *b.1915.* Human geography / [by] H. Robinson. — 2nd ed. — Plymouth : Macdonald and Evans, 1976. — viii,216p : ill, maps ; 19cm. — (The M. & E. handbook series)
Previous ed.: London : Macdonald and Evans, 1969. — Index.
ISBN 0-7121-0810-6 Pbk : £1.35
(B77-21563)

909 — World, to 1974
Concise encyclopedia of world history / [edited by] Lionel Munby. — Maidenhead : Purnell, 1977. — 2-256p : ill(some col), col facsims, col geneal tables, maps(some col), ports(some col) ; 31cm.
Cover title: Purnell's concise encyclopedia of world history. — Index.
ISBN 0-361-03502-0 : £3.50
(B77-23813)

909 — World, to 1975
Roberts, John Morris. The Hutchinson history of the world / [by] J.M. Roberts. — London : Hutchinson, 1976. — 1127p : ill, facsims, maps, plans, ports ; 26cm.
Index.
ISBN 0-09-126970-9 : £9.95
(B77-01036)

909 — World, to 1975. *For Kenyan students. Secondary school texts*
Wilson, Derek Alan. KJSE world history : a revision scheme for students preparing for the Kenya Junior Secondary Examination / [by] D.A. Wilson. — London [etc.] : Evans Bros, 1976. — 64p ; 19cm. — (Evans pocket facts)
ISBN 0-237-49921-5 Sd : Unpriced
(B77-19082)

909'.04'91411 — Indian emigrants, to 1975
Tinker, Hugh. The banyan tree : overseas emigrants from India, Pakistan, and Bangladesh / [by] Hugh Tinker. — Oxford [etc.] : Oxford University Press, 1977. — x, 204p ; 23cm.
Index.
ISBN 0-19-215946-1 : £5.00
(B77-15595)

909'.04'918 — Slavonic culture. *Serials*
California Slavic studies. — Berkeley [etc.] ; London : University of California Press.
Vol.8 / editors Nicholas V. Riasanovsky, Gleb Struve, Thomas Eekman. — 1975. — [5],166p ; 24cm.
ISBN 0-520-09519-7 : Unpriced
(B77-10021)

909'.04'9185082 — Polish emigrants. Social life, 1932-1975. *Personal observations. Polish texts*
Arciszewska, Zofia. Po obu stronach oceanu : wspomnienia / Zofia Arciszewska. — [London] : Polska Fundacja Kulturalna, 1976. — 238p, [16]p of plates : ill, facsims, ports ; 21cm.
ISBN 0-85065-109-3 Pbk : £2.70
(B77-08651)

909'.04'924 — Jews. *Essays. Polish texts*
Vincenz, Stanislaw. Tematy zydowskie / Stanislaw Vincenz ; wstęp Jeanne Hersch. — Londyn [i.e. London] : Oficyna Poetów i Malarzy, 1977. — 219p ; 21cm.
Pbk : £2.00
(B77-30823)

909'.04'924 — Jews, 1096-1974. *Chronologies*
Fraenkel, Josef. Every day in Jewish history / by Josef Fraenkel. — London (55 New Cavendish St., W.1) : Cultural Department of the World Jewish Congress, [1977]. — [1],64p ; 22cm.
Index.
Sd : £0.50
(B77-24583)

909'.04'924 — Jews. Jewish historiography, to 1923
Kochan, Lionel. The Jew and his history / [by] Lionel Kochan. — London [etc.] : Macmillan, 1977. — x,164p ; 23cm.
Bibl.: p.147-158. — Index.
ISBN 0-333-19227-3 : £7.95
(B77-23815)

909'.04'9240821 — Jews, 1914-1919
Abramsky, Chimen. War, revolution and the Jewish dilemma / by C. Abramsky. — London : H.K. Lewis for [University] College, 1975. — 33p ; 26cm. — (University College, London. Inaugural lectures)
'... delivered ... 28 April 1975'.
ISBN 0-7186-0433-4 Sd : £0.65
(B77-14456)

909'.04'927 — Arab Islamic civilization, to 1976. *Festschriften*
Arabic and Islamic garland : historical, educational and literary papers presented to Abdul-Latif Tibawi / by colleagues, friends and students. — London ([146 Park Rd, N.W.8]) : Islamic Cultural Centre, 1977. — 239p,[2] leaves of plates : 1 ill, col port ; 26cm.
Includes one paper in German. — Bibl.
£8.00
(B77-30824)

909'.04'927 — Arabs. Attitudes of Britons, to 1976
Nasir, Sari J. The Arabs and the English / [by] Sari J. Nasir. — London : Longman, 1976. — xii,175p,[16]p of plates : ill, facsims, ports ; 23cm.
Index.
ISBN 0-582-78046-2 : £7.50
(B77-29793)

909'.04'96 — African migrants, to ca 1970
The **African** diaspora : interpretive essays / edited by Martin L. Kilson, Robert I. Rotberg. — Cambridge, Mass. ; London : Harvard University Press, 1976. — xv,510p : maps ; 25cm.
Index.
ISBN 0-674-00779-4 : £13.90
(B77-05753)

909'.04'96 — Negroes, to 1900. *Readings from contemporary sources*
Africans abroad : a documentary history of the black diaspora in Asia, Latin America, and the Caribbean during the age of slavery / [edited by] Graham W. Irwin. — New York ; Guildford : Columbia University Press, 1977. — xvi,408p ; 24cm.
Bibl.: p.391-399. — Index.
ISBN 0-231-03936-0 : £14.70
ISBN 0-231-03937-9 Pbk : £5.30
(B77-23814)

909.07 — Civilization, 43-1492. *Secondary school texts*
The **way** it was / series editor Brian Chaplin. — Edinburgh : W. and R. Chambers.
[End of the Roman Empire and the new invaders]. The kingdom of the Picts / [by] Anna Ritchie. — 1977. — [1],49p : ill, maps ; 25cm.
Bibl.: p.49. — Index.
ISBN 0-550-75534-9 Sd : £1.10
(B77-19884)

[The Viking age]. Charlemagne / [by] John Gillingham. — 1977. — [1],49p : ill, facsims, maps ; 25cm.
Bibl.: p.49. — Index.
ISBN 0-550-75515-2 Sd : £1.10
(B77-16646)

[The Viking age]. Cnut and Edward the Confessor / [by] Jane Sayers. — 1977. — [1], 49p : ill, facsims, geneal tables, maps ; 25cm.
Bibl.: p.49. — Index.
ISBN 0-550-75516-0 Sd : £1.10
(B77-19885)

[The Viking age]. Fury of the Vikings / [by] Mark Roberts. — 1977. — [1],49p : ill, facsims, maps, plans ; 25cm.
Bibl.: p.49. — Index.
ISBN 0-550-75517-9 Sd : £1.10
(B77-16647)

[The Viking age]. King Alfred the Saxon leader / [by] Joan Blyth. — 1977. — [1],49p : ill, facsims, geneal tables, maps, plan ; 25cm.
Bibl.: p.49. — Index.
ISBN 0-550-75514-4 Sd : £1.10
(B77-16648)

[The Viking age]. The Vikings in Scotland : stories from the sagas / [by] Eric Simpson. — 1977. — [1],49p : ill, geneal table, maps ; 25cm.
Bibl.: p.49. — Index.
ISBN 0-550-75535-7 Sd : £1.10
(B77-19886)

909.07'06'21 — Antiquities, ca 400-ca 1500. Organisations: Society for Medieval Archaeology. *Directories*
Society for Medieval Archaeology. List of members, corrected to 30 April / Society for Medieval Archaeology. — [London] ([c/o University College, Gower St., W.C.1]) : [The Society].
1976. — [1976]. — [1],40p ; 25cm.
Sd : £0.50
(B77-19083)

909.08 — Escapes, 1597-1945
My favourite escape stories / edited by P.R. Reid. — London [etc.] : Beaver Books, 1977. — 220p ; 18cm.
This collection originally published: Guildford : Lutterworth Press, 1975.
ISBN 0-600-36281-7 Pbk : £0.55
(B77-30825)

909.08 — Sea battles by Great Britain. Royal Navy, 1588-1807 & 1916
Warner, Oliver. Great naval actions of the British navy 1588-1807 and 1916 / [by] Oliver Warner. — Newton Abbot [etc.] : David and Charles, 1976. — 159p : ill, maps, plans, ports ; 25cm.
Cover title: Great naval actions. — Bibl.: p.154-155. — Index.
ISBN 0-7153-7266-1 : £5.95
(B77-04462)

909'.09'1712492 — Dutch colonies, 1600-1800
Boxer, Charles Ralph. The Dutch seaborne empire, 1600-1800 / [by] C.R. Boxer. — [1st ed. reprinted] ; [with an augmented bibliography]. — London : Hutchinson, 1977. — xxvi,326p,leaf of plate,16p of plates : ill, maps, ports ; 24cm. — (The history of human society)
Originally published: 1965. — Bibl.: p.307-314. — Index.
ISBN 0-09-131051-2 Pbk : £3.75
(B77-30826)

909'.09'1823082 — Pacific region. Historical events. Periodicals: Pacific Historical Review, 1932-1974. *Indexes*
'The **Pacific** historical review', a cumulative index to volumes I-XLIII, 1932-1974 / compiled by Anna Marie and Everett Gordon Hager. — Berkeley [etc.] ; London : University of California Press, 1976[i.e.1977]. — [4],579p ; 24cm.
Published in the United States: 1976.
ISBN 0-520-03035-4 : £20.00
(B77-15015)

909'.09'71241 — Commonwealth Secretariat
Commonwealth Secretariat. The Commonwealth Secretariat. — [New ed.]. — London : The Secretariat, [1977]. — [4],18p ; 21cm.
Sd : Unpriced
(B77-21564)

909'.09'71241 — Commonwealth Secretariat. *Reports, surveys. Serials*
Commonwealth Secretary-General. Report to heads of Government / by the Commonwealth Secretary-General. — London : Commonwealth Secretariat.
6th : covering the period April 1975 to April 1977. — [1977]. — vii,87p ; 24cm.
Cover title: Report of the Commonwealth Secretary-General. 1977. — Bibl.: p.75-78.
Pbk : Unpriced
ISSN 0306-4360
(B77-21565)

909'.09'71241 — Commonwealth, to 1973
Bowle, John. The imperial achievement : the rise and transformation of the British Empire / [by] John Bowle. — Harmondsworth [etc.] : Penguin, 1977. — 592p,[16]p of plates : ill, maps, ports ; 18cm. — (Pelican books)
Originally published: London : Secker and Warburg, 1974. — Index.
ISBN 0-14-021960-9 Pbk : £1.95
(B77-08652)

909'.09'712410826 — Commonwealth, 1965-1976
Ingram, Derek. The imperfect Commonwealth / [by] Derek Ingram. — London : Collings, 1977. — x,165p ; 23cm.
Bibl.: p.146-147. — Index.
ISBN 0-86036-049-0 : £3.95
(B77-22239)

909'.09'712410827 — Commonwealth
Great Britain. *Central Office of Information. Reference Division.* Britain and the Commonwealth / [prepared by Reference Division, Central Office of Information]. — 2nd ed. — London : H.M.S.O., 1977. — [3],47p ; 21cm.
Previous ed.: London : Central Office of Information, 1973.
ISBN 0-11-700923-7 Sd : £0.90
(B77-22238)

909'.09'712410827 — Commonwealth. *Questions & answers. Juvenile literature*
McKenzie, John, *b.1925.* The Commonwealth, well what do you know / [written and drawn by] John McKenzie. — London : Commonwealth Institute, [1977]. — [36p] : ill, map ; 30cm.
With answers.
ISBN 0-900906-45-6 Sd : £0.20
(B77-11466)

909'.09'712410827 — Commonwealth countries. *Yearbooks*
A **year** book of the Commonwealth / Foreign and Commonwealth Office. — London : H.M.S.O.
1976. — 1977. — ix,755p,fold plate : col map ; 22cm.
Index.
ISBN 0-11-580186-3 Pbk : £10.00
(B77-09376)

909'.09'712469 — Portuguese colonies, 1415-1825
Boxer, Charles Ralph. The Portuguese seaborne empire, 1415-1825 / [by] C.R. Boxer. — London : Hutchinson, 1977. — xxvi,426p,16p of plates : ill, facsim, maps, ports ; 24cm. — (The history of human society)
Originally published: 1969. — Bibl.: p.392-414. — Index.
ISBN 0-09-131071-7 Pbk : £3.95
(B77-27529)

909'.09'724082 — Developing countries. Political events. Influence of China & Soviet Union, 1949-1974
Soviet and Chinese influence in the Third World / edited by Alvin Z. Rubinstein. — New York [etc.] ; London : Praeger ; [London] : [Distributed by Martin Robertson], 1976. — xi, 232p ; 24cm. — (Praeger special studies in international politics and government)
'This book is an outgrowth of a Conference on Soviet and Chinese Influence in the Third World that was held in Philadelphia on October 25 and 26, 1973' - Preface. — Originally published: 1975. — Index.
ISBN 0-275-64690-4 Pbk : £3.50
(B77-03813)

909'.09'732 — Towns. *Middle school texts*
Howard, Joanna. How a town works / [by] Joanna Howard ; [illustrators Nick Skelton, Gary Rees]. — London : Macdonald Educational, 1977. — 2-46p : ill(some col) ; 25cm. — (Macdonald new reference library ; 4)

Text on lining paper. — Bibl.: p.44. — Index.
ISBN 0-356-05803-4 : £1.50
(B77-22973)

909'.09'732 — Urban regions. *History. Reviews of research*
Urban history yearbook. — [Leicester] : Leicester University Press.
1977 / editor H.J. Dyos. — 1977. — 224p : ill, maps ; 25cm.
Bibl.: p.145-183. — Index.
ISBN 0-7185-6077-9 Pbk : Unpriced
ISSN 0306-0845
(B77-24584)

909'.09'749270827 — Arab countries. *Periodicals*
The **Arab** dimension in world affairs. — London (Lake View, Vale of Health, NW3 1AN) : Europ-Oil Prices (London).
[Vol.] 1, [no.] 01- ; 16th-31st Dec. 1976-. — [1977]-. — 30cm.
Twenty-four issues a year. — 8 leaves in 1st issue.
Sd : £180.00 yearly
ISSN 0309-4952
(B77-15016)

909'.09'812 — Western civilisation, to 2000
Johnson, Paul. Enemies of society / [by] Paul Johnson. — London : Weidenfeld and Nicolson, 1977. — [9],278p ; 25cm.
Bibl.: p.261-267. — Index.
ISBN 0-297-77294-5 : £5.95
(B77-29031)

909'.09'812 — Western world, 1558-1895. *Secondary school texts*
Schools Council History 13-16 Project. Enquiry in depth / Schools Council History 13-16 Project ; [team, David Sylvester et al.]. — Edinburgh : Holmes-McDougall.
Britain 1815-51. — 1977. — 168p : ill, facsims, maps, music, ports ; 19x25cm.
Bibl.: p.166-167.
ISBN 0-7157-1567-4 Pbk : Unpriced
(B77-26666)

Schools Council History 13-16 Project. Enquiry in depth / Schools Council History 13-16 Project ; [team, David Sylvester et al.]. — Edinburgh : Holmes-McDougall.
Elizabethan England. — 1977. — 176p : ill, chart, coat of arms, facsims, geneal tables, maps, plan, ports ; 19x25cm.
Bibl.: p.174-175.
ISBN 0-7157-1563-1 Pbk : Unpriced
(B77-26667)

Schools Council History 13-16 Project. Enquiry in depth / Schools Council History 13-16 Project ; [team David Sylvester et al.]. — Edinburgh : Holmes McDougall.
The American West, 1840-95. — 1977. — 184p : ill, facsims, maps, ports ; 19x25cm.
ISBN 0-7157-1565-8 Pbk : Unpriced
(B77-30827)

909'.09'812082 — Western culture, 1900-1935. *Marxist viewpoints. Early works*
Caudwell, Christopher. The concept of freedom / by Christopher Caudwell. — London : Lawrence and Wishart, 1977. — 260p ; 22cm.
This collection originally published: 1965. — Index.
ISBN 0-85315-393-0 Pbk : £2.00
Also classified at 530'.09
(B77-28270)

909'.09'8120827 — Western civilization. *Islamic viewpoints*
Lari, Sayid Mujtaba Rukni Musawi. Western civilisation through Muslim eyes / by Sayid Mujtaba Rukni Musawi Lari ; translated [from the Persian] by F.J. Goulding. — Guildford : F.J. Goulding ; Worthing (Montague Place, Worthing, Sussex BN11 3BG) : [Distributed by] Optimus Books, 1977. — xii,146p ; 23cm.
Translation of: 'Seema-yi-Tamaddun-i-Gharb'. Tehran : Sadr Publishing House, 1970.
Pbk : £1.00
(B77-15017)

909.8 — Civilization, 1750-1975
Browne, Harry. World history / [by] Harry Browne. — 2nd ed. — Cambridge [etc.] : Cambridge University Press.
2 : 1900-1975. — 1977. — [8],296p : ill, maps, ports ; 22cm.
Previous ed.: published as 'World history. 2 : 1900-1968'. London : Cambridge University Press, 1970. — Index.
ISBN 0-521-21196-4 Pbk : £2.75
(B77-10638)

909.8 — Political events, 1860-1975
Jones, Barry, *b.1932.* Age of apocalypse : compendium of history, 1860 to the present day / [by] Barry Jones. — South Melbourne ; London [etc.] : Macmillan, 1975. — viii,336p : ill, maps, ports ; 24cm.
Index.
ISBN 0-333-17585-9 Pbk : £3.95
(B77-21566)

909.8'08 — World, 1870-1975. *Documents. Secondary school texts*
Documents on world history / [compiled by] John Wroughton, Denys Cook. — Basingstoke [etc.] : Macmillan.
Book 1 : 1870-1918. — 1976. — 128p : ill, facsim, ports ; 22cm.
ISBN 0-333-19105-6 Pbk : £1.45
(B77-08653)

Book 2 : 1919 to the present day. — 1976. — 128p : ill, ports ; 22cm.
ISBN 0-333-19106-4 Pbk : £1.45
(B77-08654)

909.81 — World, 1860-1880
Wynn Jones, Michael. The world 100 years ago / [by] Michael Wynn Jones. — London [etc.] : Macmillan, 1977. — 224p : ill, ports ; 23cm.
Originally published: 1976. — Bibl.: p.219. — Index.
ISBN 0-333-21192-8 Pbk : £2.95
(B77-29032)

909.82 — Disasters, 1871-1976. Historical sources: Newspapers
Wynn Jones, Michael. Deadline disaster : a newspaper history / [by] Michael Wynn Jones. — Newton Abbot [etc.] : David and Charles, 1976. — 192p : ill, facsims ; 34cm.
Ill. on lining papers. — Index.
ISBN 0-7153-7291-2 : £7.50
(B77-07707)

909.82 — Disasters, 1878-1963
Prideaux, Michael. World disasters / [compiled by Michael Prideaux]. — London [etc.] : Spring Books, 1976. — 128p : ill, facsims, ports ; 31cm.
'This material first appeared in "Disaster"' - Introduction. — Ill. on lining papers.
ISBN 0-600-39375-5 : £1.95
(B77-01887)

909.82 — Disasters, 1902-1976
Great disasters : catastrophes of the twentieth century / edited by John Canning. — [London] : Octopus Books, [1976]. — 5-124p : ill(some col), col facsim, ports ; 29cm.
Col. ill. on lining papers. — Index.
ISBN 0-7064-0546-3 : £2.50
(B77-03814)

909.82 — Political events, 1891-1975. *Secondary school texts. For New Zealand students*
Perspectives in modern history / general editor J.H. Jensen. — Wellington [N.Z.] ; London [etc.] : Reed Education.
2 : [cultural interaction] : Black and white in South Africa, 1919-61 : a study in cultural interaction / [by] Geoffrey Rice. — 1976. — vi, 50p : ill, maps, ports ; 20x22cm.
Originally published: 1975. — Bibl.: p.48.
ISBN 0-589-04570-9 Pbk : £1.65
Primary classification 309.1'04
(B77-24020)

Perspectives in modern history / general editor J.H. Jensen. — London [etc.] : Reed Educational.
6 : Leadership. — 1976. — vi,98p : ill, coat of arms, maps, music, ports ; 20x22cm.
Bibl. — Contents: China, 1921-49 / by W. Rushbrook - Leadership in Indonesia since 1945 / by J.S. Hoadley.
ISBN 0-589-04566-0 Pbk : £3.05
Primary classification 309.1'04
(B77-02063)

909.82 — Political events, 1900-1976. *For Irish students. Secondary school texts*
Jennings, A. Intermediate Certificate history, the modern world / [by] A. Jennings. — Dublin : Helicon : Distributed by Educational Company of Ireland, 1977. — [1],96p : ill, facsims, maps, ports ; 21cm. — (Study assessment series)
ISBN 0-904916-63-4 Sd : £1.10
(B77-16649)

909.82 — Political events, 1945-1976. *Secondary school texts*
Booth, M B. Our world today - political / by M.B. Booth ; illustrations by Trevor Stubley. — Huddersfield : Schofield and Sims, 1977. — 253p : ill(some col), facsim, col maps, ports ; 26cm. — (Britain and the world ; 5)
Bibl.: p.248-249. — Index.
ISBN 0-7217-1560-5 : £1.95
(B77-23816)

909.82 — Political events, ca 1910-1975
Mowat, Robert Case. Four papers on contemporary history / by R.C. Mowat. — Oxford (Department of Design, Oxford Polytechnic, Headington, Oxford OX3 0BP) : Oxford Polytechnic, 1976 [i.e. 1977]. — 58p in various pagings ; 21cm. — (Oxford Polytechnic. Papers)
Sd : £0.75
(B77-12187)

909.82 — World events, 1945-1970
Taylor, Duncan. A short history of the post war world, 1945-1970 / [by] Duncan Taylor. — London : Dobson, 1977. — 240p ; 23cm.
Index.
ISBN 0-234-77667-6 : £3.95
ISBN 0-234-77856-3 Pbk : £2.50
(B77-22974)

909.82'022'2 — Social life, 1900-1950. *Illustrations. Secondary school texts. Cards*
History in photographs, 1900-1950. — Sydney ; London [etc.] : Reed Education.
1. — 1975 [i.e. 1976]. — 1v. : chiefly ill, ports ; 25cm.
Sixty one sheets (122 sides) in folder. — In plastic wallet. — Published in Australia: 1975.
ISBN 0-589-09157-3 : Unpriced
(B77-02652)

909.82'08 — Political events, 1912-1972. *Essays*
Wilson, Edmund. Letters on literature and politics, 1912-1972 / [by] Edmund Wilson ; edited by Elena Wilson ; introduction by Daniel Aaron ; foreword by Leon Edel. — London [etc.] : Routledge and Kegan Paul, 1977. — xxxvii,768p : ill, facsims, ports ; 24cm.
Also published: New York : Farrar, Straus and Giroux, 1977. — Index.
ISBN 0-7100-8761-6 : £12.50 : CIP rev.
Primary classification 809
(B77-25156)

909.82'092'2 — Social life, 1900-1945. *Personal observations. Collections. Secondary school texts*
I can remember- / compiled by Nicci Crowther. — London : Edward Arnold, 1976. — 48p : ill, facsims, ports ; 24cm.
ISBN 0-7131-0077-x Sd : £1.00
(B77-03815)

909.82'2 — Social life, 1920-1930
Anglo, Michael. Nostalgia, spotlight on the twenties / [by] Michael Anglo. — London : Jupiter Books, 1976. — 144p,[16]p of plates : ill(some col), facsims, ports ; 30cm. — ([Nostalgia series])
ISBN 0-904041-47-6 : £4.95
(B77-16102)

909.82'3 — Social life, 1930-1939
Anglo, Michael. Nostalgia, spotlight on the thirties / [by] Michael Anglo. — London : Jupiter Books, 1976. — [2],144p,[12]p of plates : ill(some col), ports ; 31cm. — ([Nostalgia series])
ISBN 0-904041-48-4 : £4.95
(B77-16103)

909.82'5 — World, 1952
Macksey, Kenneth. The Guinness book of 1952 / [by] Kenneth Macksey. — Enfield : Guinness Superlatives, 1976. — 5-124p : ill, ports ; 29cm. — ([Guinness silver anniversary series])
ISBN 0-900424-40-0 : £2.95
(B77-12188)

909.82'5'0924 — Army operations by Great Britain. Army, 1953-1970. *Officers' personal observations*
Kitson, Frank. Bunch of five / [by] Frank Kitson. — London : Faber, 1977. — iii-xiii, 306p,[8]p of plates : ill, maps, ports ; 23cm.
Index.
ISBN 0-571-11050-9 : £5.95
(B77-10022)

909.82'7 — Civilization, 1970-
Camilleri, Joseph. Civilization in crisis : human prospects in a changing world / [by] Joseph A. Camilleri. — Cambridge [etc.] : Cambridge University Press, 1976. — viii,303p : 1 ill ; 22cm.
Index.
ISBN 0-521-21248-0 : £7.50
ISBN 0-521-29078-3 Pbk : £2.50
(B77-18438)

Wilhelm, Donald. Creative alternatives to communism : guidelines for tomorrow's world / [by] Donald Wilhelm. — London [etc.] : Macmillan, 1977. — xii,173p ; 23cm.
Index.
ISBN 0-333-21852-3 : £4.95
ISBN 0-333-21856-6 Pbk : £1.50
(B77-17807)

909.82'7'05 — World. *Yearbooks*
The **Europa** year book : a world survey. — London : Europa.
1977. Vol.1 : International organizations. Europe. — 1977. — xxiii,1457p : col maps(on lining papers) ; 26cm.
Index.
ISBN 0-905118-07-3 : £15.00
(B77-25986)

1977. Vol.2 : Africa, the Americas, Asia, Australasia. — 1977. — xiv,1894p : col map(on lining papers) ; 26cm.
Index.
ISBN 0-905118-08-1 : £19.00
(B77-25987)

909.82'7'05 — World events. *Yearbooks*
The **annual** register : world events. — London : Longman.
1976 / edited by H.V. Hodson, assisted by Bishakha Bose. — 1977. — xvi,541p,leaf of plate,[8]p of plates : ill, maps, ports ; 23cm.
Index.
ISBN 0-582-50113-x : £16.00
(B77-22240)

910 — GEOGRAPHY, TRAVEL
910 — Geographical features
English, Paul Ward. World regional geography : a question of place / [by] Paul Ward English ; with the assistance of James Andrew Miller. — New York [etc.] ; London : Harper's College Press, 1977. — xvi,591,[48]p : ill(some col), col maps, ports ; 29cm. — (Harper & Row series in geography)
Bibl. — Index.
ISBN 0-06-167401-x : £11.95
(B77-15596)

The **new** encyclopedia of the world / foreword by Emrys Jones ; edited by Robin Kerrod. — London : Octopus Books, 1976. — 252p : ill(chiefly col), col charts, maps(chiefly col) ; 31cm.
Col. ill. on lining papers. — Index.
ISBN 0-7064-0536-6 : £3.95
(B77-01037)

910 — Geographical features. *For East African students. Secondary school texts*
Taylor, P F. Geography : a revision scheme for students preparing for the East African Certificate of Education and the Cambridge Overseas School Certificate / [by] P.F. Taylor. — [New ed.]. — London [etc.] : Evans Bros, 1976. — 64p : ill, maps ; 19cm. — (Evans pocket facts)
Previous ed.: s.l. : Progress Publications, 1970.
ISBN 0-237-49972-x Sd : £0.50
(B77-09377)

910 — Geographical features. *For Irish students. Secondary school texts*
MacNamara, William. Intermediate Certificate geography / [by] William MacNamara. — Dublin : Helicon, 1976. — [1],72p : ill, maps ; 26cm. — (Study assessment series)
Four fold. sheets ([4] sides ; col. maps) in pocket.
ISBN 0-904916-59-6 Sd : £1.43
(B77-04463)

910 — Geographical features. *For Kenyan students. Secondary school texts*
Taylor, P F. KJSE geography : a revision scheme for students preparing for the Kenya Junior Secondary Examination / [by] P.F. Taylor. — [New ed.]. — London [etc.] : Evans Bros, 1976. — 64p : ill, maps ; 19cm. — (Evans pocket facts)
Previous ed.: s.l. : Progress Publications, 1971.
ISBN 0-237-49974-6 Sd : £0.50
(B77-09378)

910 — Geographical features. *Juvenile literature*
Tyler, Jenny. The children's encyclopedia of our world / [by Jenny Tyler, Lisa Watts and Tessa Campbell ; illustrated by Bob Hersey and Peter Mousedale]. — London : Usborne, 1976. — [1], 98p : chiefly ill(chiefly col), col maps ; 29cm.
Text, col. ill. on lining papers. — Index.
ISBN 0-86020-065-5 : Unpriced
(B77-31599)

910 — Geographical features. *Secondary school texts*
Bunnett, R B. General geography in diagrams / [by] R.B. Bunnett. — 3rd ed. — London : Longman, 1976. — xiii,375p : ill, charts, maps ; 25cm.
Previous ed.: i.e. 1st ed., 1975. — Index. — '... comprises the full text of the metric edition of the author's "Physical geography in diagrams" with a complete section on human geography' - cover. — Metric ed. of 'Physical geography in diagrams' originally published: Harlow : Longman, 1973.
ISBN 0-582-69969-x Pbk : £2.15
(B77-14457)

Israel, Saul. World geography today / [by] Saul Israel, Norma H. Roemer, Loyal Durand, Jr. — [New ed.]. — New York ; London [etc.] : Holt, Rinehart and Winston, [1977]. — [8], 568p,[8]p of plates : ill(some col), col maps ; 26cm.
This ed. originally published: New York : Holt, Rinehart and Winston, 1971?. — Bibl. — Index.
ISBN 0-03-084298-0 : £8.00
(B77-09379)

Lamb, Maureen. A revision course in 'O' Level geography / by Maureen Lamb. — 2nd (metric) ed. — London : Allman.
In 2 vols.
Vol.2 : World structure and relief, climate, natural regions, etc. — 1975. — 191p : ill, charts, maps ; 25cm.
Previous ed.: 1970. — Bibl.: p.191.
ISBN 0-204-74694-9 Pbk : £1.95(non-net)
(B77-01888)

Long, Molly. World problems : a topic geography / [by] M. Long, B.S. Roberson. — 2nd ed. — London [etc.] : Hodder and Stoughton, 1977. — vii,216p : ill, maps, plans ; 17x24cm. — (Secondary school series)
Previous ed.: London : English Universities Press, 1969. — Index.
ISBN 0-340-22177-1 Pbk : £1.75
(B77-24585)

Poxon, Eileen Margaret. Visual geographies / [by] E.M. Poxon and J.D. Poxon. — Oxford [etc.] : Pergamon.
In 8 vols.
Unit 1 : Great Britain / line illustrations by Jacqueline Apthorpe and Gordon O. Bell. — New ed. — 1977. — 63p : ill(some col), col maps, col plans ; 30cm.
Previous ed.: 1972.
ISBN 0-08-021900-4 Pbk : £1.50
(B77-21567)

Poxon, Eileen Margaret. Visual geographies / [by] E.M. Poxon and J.D. Poxon. — Oxford [etc.] : Pergamon.
In 8 vols.
Unit 8 : Our world. — 1977. — 47p : ill(some col), maps(chiefly col) ; 30cm.
ISBN 0-08-020903-3 Pbk : £1.05
(B77-21568)

Young, Eric William. A course in world geography / [by] Young & Lowry. — London : Edward Arnold.
Book 7 : North America, including Central America and the Caribbean Islands / by E.W. Young ; maps and diagrams by Peter Jackson and Roy Mole. — 3rd ed. — 1976. — 256p : ill, maps, ports ; 22cm.
Previous ed.: 1970. — Index.
ISBN 0-7131-0061-3 Pbk : £1.80
(B77-00492)

Young, Eric William. A course in world geography / [by] Young & Lowry. — London : Edward Arnold.
Book 8 : East Africa, physical, regional and human / by E.W. Young, B.H. Mottram. — 3rd ed. / with the assistance of T.S. Kamwela, W.F. Minns ; maps and diagrams by Cartographic Enterprises. — 1977. — 232p : ill, charts, maps ; 22cm.
Previous ed.: / by E.W. Young and M.A. Esmail. 1971. — Index.
ISBN 0-7131-0172-5 Pbk : £1.80 : CIP rev.
(B77-26668)

910 — Geography
Kolars, John F. Geography : the study of location, culture and environment / [by] John F. Kolars, John D. Nystuen ; drawings by Derwin Bell. — New York ; London [etc.] : McGraw-Hill, 1974. — xix,448p : ill(chiefly col), maps(chiefly col), plan ; 25cm. — (McGraw-Hill series in geography)
Bibl. — Index.
ISBN 0-07-035309-3 : Unpriced
(B77-21569)

910 — Geography. *Essays*
Sauer, Carl Ortwin. Land and life : a selection from the writings of Carl Ortwin Sauer / edited by John Leighly. — Berkeley [etc.] ; London : University of California Press, [1976]. — vi, 435p : ill, maps, port ; 21cm.
Originally published: 1963. — Bibl.: p.407-413. — Index.
ISBN 0-520-02633-0 : £12.60
ISBN 0-520-01124-4 Pbk : £3.15
(B77-04464)

910 — Geography. *For Irish students. Secondary school texts*
Hannon, Michael. Geography / [by] Michael Hannon. — Dublin : Helicon : Distributed by the Educational Company of Ireland, 1977. — iv,104p : ill, charts, maps ; 26cm. — (Leaving Certificate) (Study assessment series)
Eight fold. sheets ([8] sides: col. maps) in pocket. — Bibl.: p.104.
Sd : £2.75
(B77-18439)

910 — Geography. *For Kenyan students. Primary school texts*
Kenya primary geography / [by H.A. Curtis et al.]. — London [etc.] : Evans Bros.
[Standard 3] : A geography picture book / [photographs by Vincent Oliver ; illustrated by Stuart Edwards]. — 1977. — [2],24,[2]p : ill(chiefly col), plans, maps ; 28cm.
ISBN 0-237-50100-7 Sd : £0.75
(B77-29794)

910 — Geography. *For Nigerian students. Secondary school texts*
Quinn-Young, Charles Theodore. Geography for Nigerian schools / [by] C.T. Quinn-Young, J.E.H. White. — Ibadan : Evans Brothers (Nigeria Publishers) Ltd ; London : Evans Bros.

Book 1 : Introductory. — 2nd ed. / artwork by Stan Martin. — 1976. — [4],60p : ill, charts, maps, plans ; 25cm.
This ed. originally published: 1974.
ISBN 0-237-49881-2 Sd : £0.78
(B77-01038)

Quinn-Young, Charles Theodore. Geography for Nigerian schools / [by] C.T. Quinn-Young, J.E.H. White. — Ibadan : Evans Brothers (Nigeria Publishers) Ltd ; London : Evans Bros.

Book 2 : Nigeria. — 3rd ed. — 1976. — 64p : ill, charts, maps ; 25cm.
Previous ed.: 1973.
ISBN 0-237-50107-4 Sd : £0.78
(B77-01039)

Quinn-Young, Charles Theodore. Geography for Nigerian schools / [by] C.T. Quinn-Young, J.E.H. White. — Ibadan : Evans Brothers (Nigeria Publishers) Ltd ; London : Evans Bros.

Book 3 : Africa. — 3rd ed. / illustrations by Ray Martin. — 1976. — 93p : ill, charts, maps ; 25cm.
Previous ed.: 1973.
ISBN 0-237-50108-2 Sd : £0.80
(B77-01040)

910 — Geography. *Secondary school texts*
Buchanan, Ronald Hull. The world of man / [by] Ronald H. Buchanan. — [1st ed. reprinted] ; [with a few modifications]. — London : Longman, 1976. — viii,304p : ill, maps, plans, ports ; 23cm. — (Geographies, an intermediate series)
Originally published: Dublin : Educational Company of Ireland, 1976. — Bibl.: p.304.
ISBN 0-582-35151-0 Pbk : £3.50
(B77-05754)

Goh Cheng Leong. Elements of geography / [by] Goh Cheng Leong. — Kuala Lumpur ; Oxford [etc.] : Oxford University Press, 1976. — iv, 222p : ill, maps ; 25cm. — (Modern certificate guides)
With answers.
ISBN 0-19-581024-4 Pbk : £1.95
(B77-19887)

Israel, Saul. World geography today. — [New ed.] / [by] Saul Israel, Douglas L. Johnson, Denis Wood. — New York ; London [etc.] : Holt, Rinehart and Winston, [1977]. — x,566p, [8]p of plates : ill(some col), col charts, col maps ; 26cm.
This ed. published in the United States: 1976. — Previous ed.: / by Saul Israel, Norma H. Roemer, Loyal Durand. 1971. — Index.
ISBN 0-03-089521-9 : £8.75
(B77-10023)

Lamb, Maureen. A revision course in 'O' Level geography / by Maureen Lamb. — 2nd (metric) ed. — London : Allman.
In 2 vols.
Vol.1 : British Isles, weather and map-reading. — 1976. — 127p : ill, charts, maps ; 25cm.
Previous ed.: 1966.
ISBN 0-204-74696-5 Pbk : £1.50
(B77-12189)

Oxford geography project. — London : Oxford University Press.
Worksheets / [by John Rolfe et al.]. — [1977]. — [32] leaves : ill, chiefly maps ; 28cm.
Cover title. — Spirit masters.
ISBN 0-19-833432-x Pbk : £6.50
(B77-13410)

Stone, W G. Geographic fundamentals / [by] W.G. Stone, R. Spencer Inch, David C.P. Lee. — 2nd ed. — London : Heinemann Educational, 1975. — 264p : ill(chiefly col), col maps ; 23cm.
Previous ed.: Jurong (Singapore) : McGraw-Hill Far Eastern Publishers, 1970 ; London : Heinemann, 1972. — Index.
ISBN 0-435-34851-5 Pbk : £1.80
(B77-00493)

Sutherland, Euan. Colour encyclopedia of the world / [by] Euan & Kate Sutherland. — Revised [ed.] / by Antony Kamm. — London : Ward Lock, 1976. — 195p : col ill, col maps ; 29cm.
Previous ed.: published as 'Our world in colour', 1968. — Index.
ISBN 0-7063-5187-8 : £2.95
(B77-04465)

910 — Travel by businessmen. *Periodicals*
Business traveller : an insider's guide to cheaper travel. — London (60 Fleet St., EC4Y 1LA) : 'Business Traveller'.
No.1- ; Winter 1976-. — 1976-. — ill, forms, plans, ports ; 28cm.
Quarterly. — 'An "Export Times" publication' - cover. — 52p. in 1st issue.
Sd : £0.90
ISSN 0309-9334
(B77-32951)

910 — Underground features. *Juvenile literature*
Ramsbottom, Edward. Under the ground / [by] Edward Ramsbottom and Joan Redmayne ; illustrated by Martin Caulkin. — London [etc.] : Macmillan, 1977. — 16p : col ill, col map ; 30cm. — (Bright ideas)
ISBN 0-333-19640-6 Sd : £0.48
(B77-23817)

910 — World. Geographical features. *Juvenile literature*
Ward Lock's pictorial atlas / edited by Jane Olliver. — London : Ward Lock, 1977. — 4-61p : col ill, col maps ; 33cm.
Col. map on lining papers. — Index.
ISBN 0-7063-5333-1 : £2.50
(B77-25988)

910'.01'519537 — Geography. Causal analysis. Variables. Correlation
Davidson, Norman, *b.1940.* Causal inferences from dichotomous variables / by Norman Davidson. — Norwich (University of East Anglia, Norwich NR4 7TJ) : Geo Abstracts Ltd, 1976. — [1],37,[1]p : ill ; 21cm. — (Concepts and techniques in modern geography ; no.9 ISSN 0306-6142)
Bibl.: p.36-37.
ISBN 0-902246-59-3 Sd : £0.50
(B77-12190)

910'.01'8 — Geography. Quantitative methods
Smith, David Marshall. Patterns in human geography / [by] David M. Smith. — Harmondsworth [etc.] : Penguin, 1977. — 373p : ill, maps ; 20cm. — (Penguin education)

Originally published: Newton Abbot : David and Charles, 1975. — Bibl.: p.352-368. — Index.
ISBN 0-14-080926-0 Pbk : £2.00
(B77-16104)

910'.01'82 — Geography. Statistics. Diagrams
Perry, Allen Howard. Statistical diagrams in geography : a workbook for Leaving Certificate / by Allen H. Perry, Vivien C. Perry ; diagrams and maps by G.B. Lewis. — Dublin : Educational Company of Ireland, 1977. — 96p : ill, charts, maps ; 21cm.
Sd : £0.99
(B77-30828)

910'.01'84 — Geography. Mathematical models. Time factors
Thrift, Nigel. An introduction to time geography / by Nigel Thrift. — Norwich (University of East Anglia, Norwich NR4 7TJ) : Geo Abstracts Ltd, 1977. — [1],37,[1]p : ill ; 21cm. — (Concepts and techniques in modern geography ; no.13 ISSN 0306-6142)
Bibl.: p.34-37.
ISBN 0-902246-67-4 Sd : £0.50
(B77-11467)

910'.01'84 — Geography. Statistical models
Wrigley, Neil. An introduction to the use of logit models in geography / by Neil Wrigley. — Norwich (University of East Anglia, Norwich NR4 7TJ) : Geo Abstracts Ltd, 1976. — [1],33, [1]p : ill, map ; 21cm. — (Concepts and techniques in modern geography ; no.10 ISSN 0306-6142)
Bibl.: p.31-33.
ISBN 0-902246-62-3 Sd : £0.50
(B77-11468)

910'.02 — Natural barriers. *Juvenile literature*
Barriers / planned and edited by Beverley Birch. — London : Macdonald Educational, 1977. — 47p : ill(chiefly col) ; 29cm. — (Conquests of nature)
Index.
ISBN 0-356-05556-6 : £2.00
(B77-27530)

910'.02 — Physical geographical features
Bradshaw, Michael John. Earth, the living planet / [by] Michael J. Bradshaw. — London [etc.] : Hodder and Stoughton, 1977. — 302p : ill(some col), charts, maps ; 28cm.
Bibl.: p.291-293. — Index.
ISBN 0-340-12375-3 Pbk : £4.95
(B77-17808)

Greenland, David. The earth in profile : a physical geography / [by] David Greenland, Harm J. de Blij. — San Francisco : Canfield Press ; New York [etc.] ; London : Harper and Row, 1977. — xii,468p : ill(some col), col charts, col maps, 2 ports ; 29cm.
Bibl. — Index.
ISBN 0-06-383615-7 : Unpriced
(B77-21570)

910'.02 — Physical geographical features. *Juvenile literature*
Purnell's illustrated nature atlas / edited by Norman Barrett. — Maidenhead : Purnell, 1977. — 4-61p : col ill, col maps ; 33cm.
Col. ill., text on lining papers. — Index.
ISBN 0-361-03874-7 : £1.95
(B77-23818)

910'.02 — Physical geographical features. *Middle school texts*
Money, David Charles. Basic geography / [by] D.C. Money. — 3rd ed. — London : University Tutorial Press, 1976. — 160,[3]p : ill(chiefly col), col charts, col maps ; 25cm.
Previous ed.: 1972. — Index.
ISBN 0-7231-0730-0 Pbk : £2.05
(B77-00494)

910'.02 — Physical geography
Gardner, James S. Physical geography / [by] James S. Gardner. — New York [etc.] ; London ([28 Tavistock St., WC2E 7PN]) : Harper's College Press, 1977. — [17],571p ill(some col), maps(chiefly col) ; 29cm.
Col. ill. on lining paper. — Bibl. — Index.
ISBN 0-06-167411-7 : £11.20
(B77-29033)

Kolars, John F. Physical geography : environment and man / [by] John F. Kolars, John D. Nystuen ; drawings by Derwin Bell. — New York ; London [etc.] : McGraw-Hill, [1976]. — xvi,344p : ill(chiefly col), charts, facsims, maps(chiefly col) ; 25cm. — (McGraw-Hill series in geography)
Published in the United States: 1975. 'Together with the companion vol., "Human geography", comprised a divided and expanded version of the original work, "Geography". [New York: McGraw-Hill, 1974]' - Library of Congress Cataloging in Publication data.
ISBN 0-07-035290-9 : £11.60
(B77-05109)

Strahler, Arthur Newell. Geography and man's environment / [by] Arthur N. Strahler, Alan H. Strahler. — New York ; London [etc.] : Wiley, 1977. — xiii,525p : ill(some col), charts, maps(chiefly col) ; 29cm.
Bibl.: p.493-509. — Index.
ISBN 0-471-01870-8 : £11.20
(B77-23819)

910'.02 — Physical geography. *Reviews of research*
Progress in physical geography : an international review of geographical work in the natural and environmental sciences. — London : Edward Arnold.
With 'Progress in human geography', supersedes : 'Progress in geography'.
Vol.1, no.1- ; Mar. 1977-. — 1977-. — ill ; 24cm.
Three issues a year. — iv,184p. in 1st issue. — Bibl.
ISBN 0-7131-7109-x Pbk : £12.50 yearly
ISSN 0309-1333
(B77-17809)

910'.02'13 — Tropical regions. Physical geographical features. *For South-east Asian students. Secondary school texts*
Lockwood, John George. The physical geography of the tropics : an introduction / [by] John G. Lockwood. — Kuala Lumpur ; London [etc.] : Oxford University Press, 1976. — viii,162p : ill, charts, maps ; 26cm. — (Oxford in Asia college texts)
Bibl. — Index.
ISBN 0-19-580319-1 Pbk : £8.50
(B77-26669)

910'.02'154 — Deserts
Goudie, Andrew. The warm desert environment / [by] Andrew Goudie and John Wilkinson. — Cambridge [etc.] : Cambridge University Press, 1977. — vii,88p : ill, 2 charts, maps ; 26cm. — (Cambridge topics in geography series)
Bibl.: p.83-84. — Index.
ISBN 0-521-21330-4 : £4.00
ISBN 0-521-29105-4 Pbk : £1.95
(B77-22241)

Petrov, M P. Deserts of the world / [by] M.P. Petrov ; translated from Russian by IPST [i.e. Israel Program for Scientific Translations] staff. — New York [etc.] : Wiley [etc.] ; Chichester : Distributed by Wiley, 1976. — viii,447p : ill, maps ; 25cm.
'A Halsted Press book'. — [6] fold sheets (maps) in pocket. — Translation of: 'Pustyni zemnogo shara'. Leningrad : Nauka, 1973. — Bibl.: p.411-429. — Index.
ISBN 0-470-68447-x : £33.50
(B77-19084)

910'.02'1693 — Rivers & streams. Geographical aspects. *Primary school texts*
Ramsbottom, Edward. Streams and rivers / [by] Edward Ramsbottom and Joan Redmayne ; illustrated by Roy Spencer. — London [etc.] : Macmillan, 1977. — 16p : chiefly col ill ; 30cm. — (Bright ideas)
ISBN 0-333-19641-4 Sd : £0.48
(B77-24586)

910'.09'11 — Cold regions. Geographical features. *Secondary school texts*
Marchington, Trevor. Cold and temperate lands / by Trevor Marchington. — Metric ed. — London : Macdonald Educational, 1977. — [1], 24p : ill(chiefly col), col charts, col maps ; 27cm. — (Macdonald colour units : geography)
ISBN 0-356-05417-9 Sd : £0.75
Primary classification 910'.09'12
(B77-29034)

910'.09'12 — Temperate regions. Geographical features. *Secondary school texts*
Marchington, Trevor. Cold and temperate lands / by Trevor Marchington. — Metric ed. — London : Macdonald Educational, 1977. — [1], 24p : ill(chiefly col), col charts, col maps ; 27cm. — (Macdonald colour units : geography)
ISBN 0-356-05417-9 Sd : £0.75
Also classified at 910'.09'11
(B77-29034)

910'.09'13 — Tropical regions. Geographical features
Jarrett, Harold Reginald. Tropical geography : an introductory study of the humid tropics / [by] H.R. Jarrett. — Plymouth : Macdonald and Evans, 1977. — xv,222p : ill, maps ; 22cm. — (Aspect geographies)
Bibl.: p.213-216. — Index.
ISBN 0-7121-2018-1 Pbk : £3.50
(B77-10639)

910'.09'13 — Tropical regions. Geographical features. *Secondary school texts*
Marchington, Trevor. Tropical lands / by Trevor Marchington. — Metric ed. — London : Macdonald Educational, 1977. — [2],24p : ill(chiefly col), col charts, col maps ; 27cm. — (Macdonald colour units : geography)
ISBN 0-356-05418-7 Sd : £0.75
(B77-26670)

910'.09'15 — Jungles. Geographical aspects. *Juvenile literature*
Stein, Nora. Jungles / [written and planned by Nora Stein]. — London : Macdonald Educational, 1977. — 2-47p : ill(chiefly col), col map, col ports ; 29cm. — (Topic books)
Index.
ISBN 0-356-05447-0 : £1.60
(B77-13953)

910'.09'154 — Desert caravans, to 1976
Wellard, James. Samarkand and beyond : a history of desert caravans / [by] James Wellard. — London : Constable, 1977. — 205p,leaf of plate,[12]p of plates : ill, maps, ports ; 23cm.
Bibl.: p.189-197. — Index.
ISBN 0-09-461410-5 : £5.95
(B77-32290)

910'.09'1631 — Voyages by dinghies: Wanderer (Boat). *North Atlantic Ocean. Personal observations*
Dye, Frank. Ocean-crossing Wayfarer : to Iceland and Norway in an open boat / [by] Frank and Margaret Dye ; foreword by Ian Proctor. — Newton Abbot [etc.] : David and Charles, 1977. — 144p : ill,charts, plans, port ; 23cm.
ISBN 0-7153-7371-4 : £4.50
(B77-27531)

910'.09'1631 — Voyages by liners: Uganda (Ship). *North Atlantic Ocean, 1970. Personal observations. Welsh texts*
Ifans, Glyn. Gwynt yr ynysoedd bach / [gan] Glyn Ifans. — Llandysul : Gwasg Gomer, 1975. — 97p,[2]leaves of plates,[8]p of plates : ill ; 19cm. — (Llyfrau poced Gomer)
ISBN 0-85088-319-9 Pbk : £0.50
(B77-01889)

910'.09'16363 — Mysteries. *North Atlantic Ocean. Bahama waters*
Berlitz, Charles. Without a trace / [by] Charles Berlitz, with the collaboration of J. Manson Valentine. — London : Souvenir Press, 1977. — xi,180p,[24]p of plates : ill, facsims, ports ; 23cm.
Also published: Garden City, N.Y. : Doubleday, 1977. — Bibl.: p.179-180.
ISBN 0-285-62286-2 : £3.95 : CIP rev.
(B77-15597)

910'.09'16381 — Voyages by yachts: Sylvia (Ship). *Western Mediterranean Sea, 1971-1973. Personal observations*
Hoare, Mike. Three years with 'Sylvia' / [by] Mike Hoare. — London : Hale, 1977. — 188p, [12]p of plates : ill, map, plan, ports ; 23cm.
ISBN 0-7091-6194-8 : £4.50
(B77-30829)

910'.09'1641 — Voyages. *Gulf of California, 1941. Personal observations*
Steinbeck, John. [Sea of Cortez. *Selections]*. The log from the 'Sea of Cortez' : the narrative portion of the book 'Sea of Cortez' / by John Steinbeck ; ... reissued with a profile 'About Ed Ricketts'. — Harmondsworth [etc.] : Penguin, 1976. — lxvi,286p : map ; 18cm.
Originally published: New York : Viking Press, 1951 ; London : Heinemann, 1958. — Index.
ISBN 0-14-004261-x Pbk : Unpriced
(B77-02653)

910'.09'167 — Voyages by yachts: Ice Bird (Ship). *Antarctic Ocean, 1972-1974. Personal observations*
Lewis, David, *b.1917.* 'Ice Bird' : the first single-handed voyage to Antarctica / [by] David Lewis. — [London] : Fontana, 1977. — 224p,[8]p of plates : ill, map, ports ; 18cm.
Originally published: London : Collins, 1975. — Bibl.: p.219.
ISBN 0-00-634669-3 Pbk : £0.80
(B77-08655)

910'.09'1673 — Antarctic Ocean. Exploration. Shipwrecks: Endurance (Ship). Crew. Rescue
Worsley, F A. The great Antarctic rescue : Shackleton's boat journey / [by] F.A. Worsley. — [1st ed. reprinted] ; [with a new] introduction by Sir Edmund Hillary. — London : Times Books, 1977. — 220p : ill, map, ports ; 22cm.
Map on lining papers. — Originally published: as 'Shackleton's boat journey'. London : P. Allan, 1933.
ISBN 0-7230-0162-6 : £5.50
(B77-18440)

910'.09'171241 — Commonwealth countries. *Practical information. For British immigrants*
Cooper, John Christopher. The emigrants guide / by J.C. Cooper. — London (14 Poland St., W.1) : Demographic Research Associates, 1975. — 302p,[10]leaves : ill, forms, maps ; 30cm.
ISBN 0-9505380-0-0 Pbk : Unpriced
Also classified at 916.8'04'6
(B77-02654)

910'.09'173 — Human settlements. Geographical aspects. *Secondary school texts*
Dinkele, Geoffrey William. Settlement and services / [by] Geoff Dinkele, Stephen Cotterell, Ian Thorn. — London : Harrap, 1976. — 86p : ill, maps, plans ; 28cm. — (Harrap's course in reformed geography)
ISBN 0-245-52383-9 Sd : £1.75
(B77-07708)

Hudson, Fred Stansfield. A geography of settlements / [by] F.S. Hudson. — 2nd ed. — Plymouth : Macdonald and Evans, 1976. — xviii,364p : ill, maps, plans ; 22cm. — (Aspect geographies)
Previous ed.: 1970. — Bibl.: p.339-345. — Index.
ISBN 0-7121-0726-6 Pbk : £3.50
(B77-07709)

910'.09'1732 — Urban regions. Geographical features. *Secondary school texts*
Briggs, Kenneth. Introducing urban structure / [by] K. Briggs. — London [etc.] : Hodder and Stoughton, 1977. — 60p : ill, maps ; 19x25cm. — (Introducing the new geography)
Bibl.: p.3.
ISBN 0-340-20254-8 Sd : £0.80
(B77-15598)

Briggs, Kenneth. Introducing urban structure / [by] K. Briggs. — London [etc.] : Hodder and Stoughton. — (Introducing the new geography)
Workbook. — 1977. — 32p : ill, maps ; 19x25cm.
With answers. — Fill-in book.
ISBN 0-340-20255-6 Sd : £0.35
(B77-15599)

910'.28 — Geography. Applications of aerial photography
Lo, C P. Geographical applications of aerial photography / [by] C.P. Lo. — New York : Crane, Russak ; Newton Abbot [etc.] : David and Charles, 1976. — 330p,[16]p of plates : ill, maps ; 23cm.
Index.
ISBN 0-7153-7199-1 : £6.95
(B77-01890)

910'.28'5424 — Geographical features. Spatial analysis. Applications of digital computer systems. Programming languages: Fortran IV language
MacDougall, E Bruce. Computer programming for spatial problems / [by] E. Bruce MacDougall. — London : Edward Arnold, 1976. — vii,160p : ill, form ; 25cm.
Bibl.: p.154-155. — Index.
ISBN 0-7131-5865-4 Pbk : £5.50
(B77-12191)

910'.3 — World. *Gazetteers*
De Sola, Ralph. Worldwide what & where : geographic glossary & traveller's guide / [compiled and edited by] Ralph De Sola. — Santa Barbara : ABC-Clio ; Oxford : EBC-Clio, [1976]. — ix,720p ; 26cm.
Published in the United States: 1975.
ISBN 0-87436-147-8 : £13.50
(B77-01041)

910'.4 — Commonwealth expeditions, 1945-1975
Cranfield, Ingrid. The challengers : British & Commonwealth adventure since 1945 / [by] Ingrid Cranfield. — London : Weidenfeld and Nicolson, 1976. — xvii,298p,[12]p of plates : ill, ports ; 23cm.
Index.
ISBN 0-297-77239-2 : £5.95
(B77-02655)

910'.4 — Expeditions. *Manuals*
Expeditions : the experts' way / edited by John Blashford-Snell and Alistair Ballantine. — London : Faber, 1977. — 256p : ill, port ; 21cm.
Bibl.: p.246-251.
ISBN 0-571-11021-5 : £4.95 : CIP rev.
ISBN 0-571-11116-5 Pbk : £2.60
(B77-07710)

World Expeditionary Association. Off the beaten track : an expedition & travel handbook / [World Expeditionary Association]. — London (45 Brompton Rd, Knightsbridge, S.W.3) : World Expeditionary Association, UK and International Office, [1976]. — 62p : ill, port ; 21cm.
ISBN 0-905802-00-4 Sd : Free to Association subscribers
(B77-03816)

910'.4 — Expeditions. Brathay Exploration Group. *Reports, surveys. Serials*
Brathay Exploration Group. Account of expeditions / Brathay Exploration Group. — Ambleside ([Brathay Hall], Ambleside, Cumbria) : Brathay Hall Trust.
1976. — 1976. — [6],62[i.e. 63]p,[5] leaves of plates,[4]p of plates : ill, maps ; 30cm.
ISBN 0-906015-00-6 Sp : Unpriced
(B77-16105)

910'.4 — Expeditions by school parties. Equipment
Young Explorers' Trust. Expedition equipment guide / The Young Explorers' Trust. — Stockport (238 Wellington Rd South, Stockport, Cheshire SK2 6NW) : The Trust, 1976. — 62p ; 21cm.
ISBN 0-905965-02-7 Pbk : £1.00
(B77-13411)

910'.4 — Ruins. *Description & travel*
Beny, Roloff. Roloff Beny interprets in photographs 'Pleasure of ruins' by Rose Macaulay / text selected and edited by Constance Babington Smith. — London : Thames and Hudson, 1977. — [1],240,[1]p : ill(some col), plans ; 26cm.
Ill. on lining papers. — '... a revised edition of "Pleasure of Ruins" by Rose Macaulay, interpreted in photographs by Roloff Beny, which was first published in 1964 [i.e. 1965]' - title page verso. — Index.
ISBN 0-500-54048-9 : £7.95
(B77-29035)

910'.4 — Universities. *Oxfordshire. Oxford. University of Oxford. Clubs: Oxford University Exploration Club. Expeditions. Periodicals*
Oxford University Exploration Club. Bulletin of the Oxford University Exploration Club. — Oxford (13 Bevington Rd, Oxford) : The Club. New series : Vol.1- ; [1976]-. — 1976-. — ill, maps ; 30cm.
Annual. — [4],31p. in new series, vol.1. — Bibl.
£1.00
ISSN 0309-5983
(B77-19888)

910'.41 — Voyages round the world by Drake, Sir Francis, 1577-1580
Wilson, Derek. The world encompassed : Drake's great voyages 1577-1580 / by Derek Wilson. — London : Hamilton, 1977. — xiii,240p : ill, charts, coat of arms, facsim, maps, ports ; 24cm.
Bibl.: p.232-236. — Index.
ISBN 0-241-89624-x : £5.95
(B77-32291)

910'.45 — Exploration. Voyages, to 1818. *Juvenile literature*
Biland, Karla. Voyages of discovery / by Karla Biland ; [translated from the German by Neil Jones]. — London : Robson Books, 1976. — 60p : ill(some col), maps, ports ; 25cm. — (Through artists' eyes)
Originally published: in German. Leipzig : Edition Leipzig, 1976.
ISBN 0-903895-41-2 : £1.60
(B77-01891)

910'.45 — Oceans. Bed. Exploration, to 1975. *Juvenile literature*
Kolář, Bohumil. Explorers of the deep : from the oldest divers to the inhabitants of underwater cities / [by] Bohumil Kolář and Oldřich Unger ; illustrated by Karel Havlíček and Pavel Dvorský ; [translated from the Czech by Paul Wilson]. — London [etc.] : Hamlyn, 1976. — 166p : ill(some col), map, port ; 25cm.
ISBN 0-600-36726-6 : £2.25
(B77-21571)

910'.45 — Seafaring, 1870-1930
The **Penguin** book of sea stories / edited by Alun Richards. — Harmondsworth [etc.] : Penguin, 1977. — 437p ; 19cm.
ISBN 0-14-004211-3 Pbk : £1.10
Primary classification 823'.9'1FS
(B77-27450)

910'.45 — Seafaring, ca 1950
Hartog, Jan de. A sailor's life / [by] Jan de Hartog. — London [etc.] : White Lion Publishers, 1976. — 162p ; 23cm.
Originally published: New York : Harper ; London : Hamilton, 1956.
ISBN 0-7274-0246-3 : £2.95
(B77-02656)

910'.45 — Voyages by Galleon Leicester (Ship), 1582-1583. *Diaries*
Madox, Richard. An Elizabethan in 1582 : the diary of Richard Madox, Fellow of All Souls / [edited] by Elizabeth Story Donno. — London (c/o Map Library, The British Library, Reference Division, Great Russell St., WC1B 3DG) : The Hakluyt Society, 1976. — xvi,365p, [2]leaves of plates(1 fold),[16]p of plates : ill, facsims, maps ; 23cm. — (Hakluyt Society. Second series ; no.147)
Index.
ISBN 0-904180-04-2 : £8.00(free to members of the Society)
(B77-22975)

910'.45 — Voyages by Providence (Ship). Logs, 1791-1793. *Texts. Facsimiles*
Providence *(Ship).* The log of HMS 'Providence', 1791-1793 / by W. Bligh. — Guildford (33 Cline Rd, Guildford, Surrey GU1 3ND) : Genesis Publications Ltd, 1976. — 951p,[6] leaves of plates(5 fold) : ill(incl 1 col), charts(some col), chiefly facsims, maps, plans, port ; 35cm.
In slip case. — Limited ed. of 500 numbered copies. — 'The reproduction has been made from the documents referenced ADM 55/152 and ADM 55/153 which are kept in two volumes at the Public Record Office, London' - note. — Bibl.: p.19. — Includes facsimile reprint of: A description of the mangostan and the bread-fruit / by John Ellis. Originally published: London : Edward and Charles Dilly, 1775.
ISBN 0-904351-01-7 : £168.00
Special leather bound ed. : Unpriced
(B77-10640)

910'.45 — Voyages from Great Britain to New Zealand by sailing ships, 1875-1876. *Diaries*
Grayson, John, *fl.1875.* Life at sea : a nineteenth century voyage to New Zealand : the diary of John Grayson / edited with an introduction by John Fines. — Old Woking (The Gresham Press, Old Woking, Surrey GU22 9LH) : Unwin Brothers Ltd, 1976. — xviii,50p : ill, port ; 21cm. — (Looking back ; vol.3)
ISBN 0-9502121-9-9 Pbk : £1.55
(B77-02657)

910'.453 — English pirates, 1603-1620
Senior, C M. A nation of pirates : English piracy in its heyday / [by] C.M. Senior. — Newton Abbot [etc.] : David and Charles [etc.], 1976. — 166p : ill, facsims ; 23cm.
Bibl.: p.158-159. — Index.
ISBN 0-7153-7264-5 : £3.95
(B77-05110)

910'.453 — Pirates. *Juvenile literature*
Law, Felicia. Pirates / written by Felicia Law ; illustrated by Gary Rees. — Glasgow [etc.] : Collins, 1977. — 32p : chiefly col ill, col maps ; 22cm. — (Dandelions)
ISBN 0-00-106002-3 : £0.50
(B77-32292)

910'.453 — Pirates, to ca 1700
Grant, Neil, *b.1938.* Buccaneers / [by] Neil Grant. — London [etc.] : Angus and Robertson, 1976. — 128p : ill, facsim, maps, ports ; 23cm.
ISBN 0-207-95583-2 : £3.20
(B77-03271)

910'.5 — Geography. *Serials*
Reading geographer. — Reading (Whiteknights, Reading RG6 2AB) : Department of Geography, University of Reading.
Vol.4 : 1975, March / editor Peter Clark. — 1975. — [2],104p : ill, maps ; 21cm. — (Geographical papers ISSN 0305-5914)
Bibl.
ISBN 0-7049-0450-0 Sd : £0.50
ISSN 0309-3263
(B77-10641)

910'.5 — Periodicals on geography: Periodicals with London imprints. *Texts*
The **Londoner** : journal of the Geography Section, City of London Polytechnic. — [London] ([Calcutta House Precinct, Old Castle St., E1 7NT]) : [City of London Polytechnic, Geography Section].
No.1- ; 1972-. — [1972]-. — maps ; 30cm.
Published at irregular intervals. — [1],28p. in 3rd issue.
Sd : Unpriced
ISSN 0309-2348
(B77-07711)

910'.7'1041 — Schools. Curriculum subjects: Geography. Teaching. *Great Britain*
Boden, Philip. Developments in geography teaching / [by] Philip Boden. — London : Open Books, 1976. — xii,127p : ill ; 21cm. — (The changing classroom)
Bibl.: p.123-125. — Index.
ISBN 0-7291-0038-3 : £3.90
ISBN 0-7291-0033-2 Pbk : £1.75
(B77-01042)

910'.7'1041 — Schools. Curriculum subjects: Geography. Teaching. Special themes: Geographical aspects of association football. *Great Britain*
Bale, John, *b.1940.* Geography and football : the use of ideas from football in the teaching of geography / by J. Bale and D. Gowing. — Sheffield (343 Fulwood Rd, Sheffield S10 3BP) : Geographical Association, 1976. — [4], 29p : ill, maps ; 26cm. — (Teaching geography occasional papers ; no.28 ISSN 0305-9464)
Bibl.: p.29.
ISBN 0-900395-57-5 Sd : £0.60(£0.50 to members)
(B77-16650)

910'.7'11 — Higher education institutions. Curriculum subjects: Geography. Teaching. *Periodicals*
Journal of geography in higher education. — Oxford (Headington, Oxford OX3 0BP) : Faculty of Modern Studies, Oxford Polytechnic.

Vol.1, no.1- ; Spring 1977-. — 1977-. — ill, maps ; 21cm.
96p. in 1st issue.
Sd : £3.00
ISSN 0309-8265
(B77-27532)

910'.7'1241 — Secondary schools. Curriculum subjects: Geography. *Great Britain. For teaching*
Environmental geography : a handbook for teachers / edited by Keith Wheeler and Bryan Waites. — St Albans : Hart-Davis Educational, 1976. — 272p : ill, facsims, forms, maps ; 24cm.
Bibl. — Index.
ISBN 0-247-12724-8 Pbk : £7.50
(B77-01892)

910'.7'24 — Geography. Field studies. *Secondary school texts*
Haddon, John, *b.1919.* Fieldwork in geography / [by] John Haddon. — Exeter : Wheaton.
In 3 vols.
Book 1 : Mapwork for local studies / illustrated by Tony Alleway. — 1974. — 72p,2p of plates : ill(some col), maps(some col), col plan ; 20x21cm.
ISBN 0-08-016769-1 Pbk : £0.95
(B77-33504)

Book 2 : The human element / illustrated by Tony Alleway. — 1974. — 83p : ill(some col), forms, maps(some col), col plan ; 20x21cm.
ISBN 0-08-016770-5 Pbk : £0.95
(B77-33505)

910'.76 — Geographical features. *Exercises, worked examples. Secondary school texts*
Lyth, Mike. Man and environment / [by] Mike Lyth ; [illustrations by Alex Fung]. — St Albans : Hart-Davis Educational, 1976. — [1], 56p : ill, charts, facsims, map ; 25cm. — (Science testers)
ISBN 0-247-12606-3 Sd : £1.10
(B77-06359)

910'.76 — Geographical features. *Questions & answers. Secondary school texts*
Corps, Norman D. A [question] guide to CSE geography / [by] Norman D. Corps. — London : Cassell, 1977. — 64p : ill, maps ; 25cm.
Title from publisher's information. — With answers. — Bibl.: p.7.
ISBN 0-304-29868-9 Sd : £1.20
(B77-30830)

Hamilton, John Sutherland. Multiple choice geography : questions for first examinations and revision / by J.S. Hamilton. — 2nd ed. — London : Edward Arnold, 1977. — xii,145p : ill, maps ; 22cm.
Previous ed.: 1973.
ISBN 0-7131-0141-5 Pbk : £1.60 : CIP rev.
(B77-09380)

910'.7'8 — Schools. Curriculum subjects: Geography. Use of landscape drawings. *For teaching*
Simmons, Roy Laurence. Landscape drawing : a neglected aspect of graphicacy / by R.L. Simmons and J.K. Mears. — Sheffield : Geographical Association, 1977. — [4],19p : ill, plan ; 26cm. — (Teaching geography occasional papers ; no.29 ISSN 0305-9464)
Bibl.: p.16-17.
Sd : Unpriced
(B77-17810)

910'.8 — Travel. *Essays*
Napier, Malcolm. Some further thoughts / by Malcolm Napier. — London [etc.] : Regency Press, 1977. — 46p ; 20cm.
£1.20
(B77-34272)

910'.92'2 — Geographers. *Biographies. Serials*
Geographers : bibliographical studies. — London : Mansell Information Publishing.
Vol.1 / edited by T.W. Freeman, Marguerita Oughton and Philippe Pinchemel ; on behalf of the International Geographical Union Commission on the History of Geographical Thought. — 1977. — xii,125p : ports ; 28cm. — (Studies in the history of geography)
Bibl. — Index.
ISBN 0-7201-0637-0 Pbk : £12.50 : CIP rev.
ISSN 0308-6992
(B77-07712)

910'.92'4 — Exploration. Cook, James, b.1728. *Biographies*
Skelton, Raleigh Ashlin. Captain James Cook after two hundred years / [by] R.A. Skelton. — London : British Museum Publications for the British Library, 1976. — 32p,A-B leaves of plates,xxiv p of plates : ill(incl 1 col), charts, facsim, map, 2 ports(1 col) ; 23cm.
'... address was delivered before the Hakluyt Society in the Beveridge Hall, University of London, on 18 July 1968...' - note. — Originally published: London : British Museum, 1969.
ISBN 0-7141-0382-9 : £2.50
ISBN 0-7141-0285-6 Pbk : £1.50
(B77-30831)

910'.92'4 — Privateering. Morgan, Sir Henry, b.ca 1635. *Biographies*
Pope, Dudley. Harry Morgan's way : the biography of Sir Henry Morgan, 1635-1684 / [by] Dudley Pope. — London : Secker and Warburg, 1977. — xx,379p,[16]p of plates : ill, facsims, geneal table, maps, ports ; 24cm.
'An Alison Press Book'. — Bibl.: p.366-368. — Index.
ISBN 0-436-37735-7 : £6.90
(B77-32952)

910'.92'4 — Voyages. Chichester, Sir Francis. *Autobiographies*
Chichester, *Sir* Francis. The lonely sea and the sky / [by] Francis Chichester. — London [etc.] : Pan Books, 1977. — 399p,[8]p of plates : ill, maps, plans, ports ; 18cm.
Originally published: London : Hodder and Stoughton, 1964. — Index.
ISBN 0-330-30021-0 Pbk : £0.95
(B77-23820)

910'.942 — English exploration, 1558-1603. *Secondary school texts*
Reeves, Marjorie. Explorers of the Elizabethan age / [by] Marjorie Reeves ; illustrated from contemporary sources. — London : Longman, 1977. — 96p : ill, facsim, maps, ports ; 20cm. — (Then and there series)
Text, map on inside covers.
ISBN 0-582-21728-8 Pbk : Unpriced
(B77-27533)

911 — HISTORICAL GEOGRAPHY
911'.17'4924 — Jews, to 1975. *Atlases*
Gilbert, Martin. Jewish history atlas / [by] Martin Gilbert. — 2nd ed. / cartography by Arthur Banks and T.A. Bicknell. — London : Weidenfeld and Nicolson, 1976. — [9]p,121[i.e. 136]p of maps,[4]p ; 26cm.
Previous ed.: 1969. — Bibl.: (4p.).
ISBN 0-297-77258-9 : £4.25
ISBN 0-297-77259-7 Pbk : £3.00
(B77-02658)

911'.4 — Europe. Geographical features, B.C. 450-A.D. 1330
Pounds, Norman John Greville. An historical geography of Europe, 450 B.C.-A.D.1330 / [by] Norman J.G. Pounds. — Cambridge [etc.] : Cambridge University Press, 1976. — xiv,475p : ill, maps ; 23cm.
Originally published: 1973. — Index.
ISBN 0-521-29126-7 Pbk : £6.90
(B77-05755)

911'.41 — Great Britain. Geographical features, to 1974
Hyams, Edward. The changing face of Britain / [by] Edward Hyams. — St Albans : Paladin, 1977. — 256p : ill, maps, plans, ports ; 20cm.
Originally published: as 'The changing face of England'. Harmondsworth : Kestrel Books, 1974. — Bibl.: p.248-249. — Index.
ISBN 0-586-08258-1 Pbk : £1.50
(B77-10024)

911'.41 — Great Britain. Geographical features, to 1976
Millward, Roy. Landscapes of Britain / [by] Roy Millward and Adrian Robinson. — Newton Abbot [etc.] : David and Charles, 1977. — 112p : ill, maps, plans ; 25cm.
Bibl.
ISBN 0-7153-7181-9 : £4.95
(B77-20767)

911'.42 — England. Geographical features, 1086
Darby, Henry Clifford. Domesday England / by H.C. Darby. — Cambridge [etc.] : Cambridge University Press, 1977. — xiv,416p,plate : col facsim, maps ; 24cm. — ([The Domesday geography of England])
Index.
ISBN 0-521-21307-x : £20.00
(B77-10025)

911'.42 — England. Geographical features, to 1955
Hoskins, William George. The making of the English landscape / by W.G. Hoskins. — [1st ed. reprinted] ; [with a new introduction by the author]. — London [etc.] : Hodder and Stoughton, 1977. — 326p : ill, maps, plans ; 23cm.
Originally published: London : Hodder and Stoughton, 1955. — Bibl.: p.304-312. — Index.
ISBN 0-340-21916-5 : £4.50
(B77-23821)

911'.422'74 — Hampshire. Greatham. Geographical features, ca 1485-ca 1603
Yates, Edward Marshall. Tudor Greatham : a social geography of a Hampshire village / [by] E.M. Yates. — [London] ([Strand, WC2R 2LS]) : [University of London King's College, Department of Geography], 1977. — [1],60p,[3] leaves of plates : 1 ill, facsim, geneal tables, maps ; 30cm. — (King's College, London. Geography Department. Occasional papers ; no.4 ISSN 0309-2178)
Sp : £1.00
(B77-34273)

911'.423'75 — Antiquities. Sites. *Cornwall. Penwith (District). Atlases*
Maxwell, I S. Historical atlas of West Penwith / compiled by I.S. Maxwell. — Sheffield (Sheffield S10 2TN) : Department of Geography, University of Sheffield, 1976. — vii, 20p,20 leaves of plates : ill, col maps ; 29x34cm.
Transparent overlay (map) as insert.
Sp : Unpriced
(B77-20768)

911'.424'6 — Staffordshire. Geographical features, to 1975
Palliser, David Michael. The Staffordshire landscape / by D.M. Palliser ; editor, Roy Millward. — London [etc.] : Hodder and Stoughton, 1976. — 283p,[32]p of plates : ill, maps, plans ; 22cm. — (The making of the English landscape)
Map on lining papers. — Bibl.: p.11. — Index.
ISBN 0-340-12994-8 : £5.95
(B77-10026)

911'.425'8 — Hertfordshire. Geographical features, to 1976
Munby, Lionel M. The Hertfordshire landscape / by Lionel M. Munby. — London [etc.] : Hodder and Stoughton, 1977. — 267p,[32]p of plates : ill, maps ; 23cm. — (The making of the English landscape)
Map on lining papers. — Bibl. — Index.
ISBN 0-340-04459-4 : £5.95
(B77-32953)

911'.428'3 — Yorkshire. East Riding. Geographical features, to 1975
Allison, Keith John. The East Riding of Yorkshire landscape / by K.J. Allison. — London [etc.] : Hodder and Stoughton, 1976. — 272p,[32]p of plates : ill, maps, plans ; 22cm. — (The making of the English landscape)
Map on lining papers. — Bibl. — Index.
ISBN 0-340-15821-2 : £5.95
(B77-10027)

911'.44 — France. Geographical features, to 1976
Themes in the historical geography of France / edited by Hugh D. Clout. — London [etc.] : Academic Press, 1977. — xxviii,594p : ill, maps, plans ; 24cm.
Bibl.: p.565-583. — Index.
ISBN 0-12-175850-8 : £18.00
(B77-33506)

911'.496 — Balkan Peninsula. Geographical features, to 1976
An **historical** geography of the Balkans / edited by Francis W. Carter. — London [etc.] : Academic Press, 1977. — xxvii,599p,fold leaf, fold plate : ill, maps, plans ; 24cm.
Bibl.: p.581-589. — Index.
ISBN 0-12-161750-5 : £22.00
(B77-29037)

911'.56 — Middle East. Political events, 1917-1974. *Atlases*
Gilbert, Martin. The Arab-Israeli conflict : its history in maps / [by] Martin Gilbert. — 2nd ed. — London : Weidenfeld and Nicolson, 1976. — [6],109[i.e. 114]p : of maps ; 26cm.
Previous ed.: 1974.
ISBN 0-297-77240-6 : £4.25
ISBN 0-297-77241-4 Pbk : 2.50
(B77-02659)

911'.6 — Africa, to 1975. *Atlases*
Freeman-Grenville, Greville Stewart Parker. A modern atlas of African history / [by] G.S.P. Freeman-Grenville ; cartography E. Hausman. — London : Collings, 1976. — 63p : of col maps ; 25cm.
Bibl.: p.52. — Index.
ISBN 0-86036-011-3 : £3.00
ISBN 0-86036-009-1 Pbk : £1.50
(B77-03817)

911'.68 — Southern Africa. Geographical features, ca 1800-1975
Christopher, A J. Southern Africa / [by] A.J. Christopher. — Folkestone : Dawson [etc.], 1976. — 292p : ill, facsim, maps, plans ; 23cm. — (Studies in historical geography ISSN 0308-6607)
Ill. on lining papers. — Bibl.: p.270-285. — Index.
ISBN 0-7129-0694-0 : £8.00
(B77-06960)

912 — ATLASES AND MAPS
912 — World. *Atlases*
The **atlas** of world geography / consultant editor Emrys Jones ; introduction by Magnus Magnusson. — [London] ([59 Grosvenor Street, W.1]) : Sundial, [1977]. — 80,112,64p : ill(chiefly col), col maps, port ; 29cm.
Spine title: The St Michael atlas of world geography. — Col. ill. on lining paper. — Index.
ISBN 0-904230-34-1 : £2.99
(B77-29038)

The **Hamlyn** pictorial atlas of the world / [geographical consultant John Salt ; authors Jack Tresidder et al.]. — London [etc.] : Hamlyn, 1976. — 176p : col ill, col maps ; 38cm.
'A Philip/Salamander book'. — Col. ill. on lining papers. — Index.
ISBN 0-600-39363-1 : £5.95
(B77-00495)

The **international** atlas = Der internationale Atlas = El atlas international = L'atlas international. — [3rd revised ed.]. — London : G. Philip, 1977. — xvi,312,222p : col maps, col ill ; 38cm.
English, German, Spanish and French text. — Also published: Chicago : Rand McNally, 1977. — Previous ed.: Chicago : Rand McNally ; London : G. Philip, 1972. — Index.
ISBN 0-540-05321-x : £25.00
(B77-17811)

Mini atlas. — [New ed.]. — Edinburgh : J. Bartholomew, 1976. — [4],128,32p : chiefly col maps ; 14cm.
Cover title: Mini pocket atlas. — Previous ed.: 1975. — Index.
ISBN 0-85152-759-0 Pbk : £0.95
(B77-04466)

Philips' Jubilee atlas : published to commemorate the Silver Jubilee of Her Majesty Queen Elizabeth II, 1952-1977 / [edited by Harold Fullard]. — London : G. Philip, 1977. — 375p in various pagings : ill(chiefly col), col charts, chiefly col maps, col ports ; 29cm.
In slip case. — Index.
£13.50
(B77-22976)

Philips new world atlas / edited by Harold Fullard. — London : G. Philip, 1976. — 268p in various pagings : ill(chiefly col), charts, chiefly col maps ; 29cm.
Index.
ISBN 0-540-05316-3 : £4.75
(B77-12192)

Philips universal atlas / edited by Harold Fullard. — London : G. Philip, 1976. — 367p in various pagings : ill(chiefly col), charts, chiefly col maps ; 29cm.
In slip case. — Col. ill. on lining papers. — Spine title: Universal atlas. — Index.
ISBN 0-540-05315-5 : £8.50
(B77-12193)

Reader's Digest Association. The 'Reader's digest' great world atlas / [Reader's Digest Association]. — 3rd ed. — London [etc.] : The Association, 1977. — 184p : ill(chiefly col), col chart, col maps ; 40cm.
Previous ed.: i.e. 2nd ed., 6th revise. 1975. — Index.
£7.95
(B77-22243)

'The **Times**' atlas of the world. — Comprehensive ed. 5th ed. reprinted with revision / maps prepared by John Bartholomew & Son ... — London : Times Books, 1977. — xl,224p,123[i.e. 244]p of plates : col ill, col charts, col maps ; 46cm.
Col. maps on lining papers. — Guide to conventional signs and abbreviations as insert. — This ed. originally published: 1975. — Index.
ISBN 0-7230-0165-0 : £29.50
(B77-19085)

World atlas. — [London] : Collins, 1977. — [2], 49p : col ill, col charts, chiefly col maps ; 27cm.
Index.
ISBN 0-00-447047-8 Sd : £0.90
(B77-27534)

912 — World. *Atlases. Juvenile literature*
Campbell, Tessa. The children's picture atlas / [by] Tessa Campbell ; illustrated by Peter Mousdale ; edited by Jenny Tyler and Lisa Watts. — London : Usborne, 1976. — 32p : col ill, col maps ; 28cm. — (Children's guides)
Index.
ISBN 0-86020-060-4 Pbk : £0.75
(B77-12194)

Thornford, Charles. Our world / compiled by Charles Thornford ; designed by Ideogram. — Huddersfield : Schofield and Sims.
Checkpoint. — 1976. — [46]p : ill(some col), col maps ; 30cm.
ISBN 0-7217-1036-0 Sd : £0.30
(B77-06360)

912 — World. *Atlases. Secondary school texts*
New junior atlas. — [London] : Collins, 1976. — [2],49p : chiefly col maps, col ill ; 27cm.
Index.
ISBN 0-00-447005-2 Sd : £0.75
(B77-17812)

Philips' new school atlas. — 60th ed. / edited by Harold Fullard. — London : G. Philip, 1976. — viii,64,24p : ill(some col), chiefly maps(chiefly col) ; 28cm.
Index.
Pbk : £1.20
ISBN 0-540-05305-8
(B77-02660)

912'.014 — Map reading. *For Caribbean students. Secondary school texts*
Dwarika, N J. Certificate level map reading for the Caribbean / [by] N.J. Dwarika. — London [etc.] : Macmillan, 1977. — iv,36p : ill(some col), col maps ; 28cm.
ISBN 0-333-19492-6 Sd : £0.95
(B77-25270)

912'.014 — Map reading. *For West African students. Secondary school texts*
Nimako, D Annor. Map reading for West Africa / by D. Annor Nimako. — New ed. — London : Longman, 1977. — iv,60p : ill(some col), maps(some col) ; 28cm.
Previous ed.: 1969.
ISBN 0-582-60347-1 Sd : £1.30
(B77-33507)

912'.014 — Map reading. *Manuals*
Map reading. — [New ed.]. — Wakefield : EP Publishing, 1976. — 40p : ill(some col), maps(some col), plan ; 14x21cm. — (Know the game)
With answers. — Previous ed.: 1965.
ISBN 0-7158-0442-1 Sd : £0.45
(B77-04467)

912'.014 — Map reading. *Secondary school texts*
Hawkes, Leslie Roy. A course in mapwork / [by] L.R. Hawkes. — Exeter [etc.] : Wheaton, 1977. — 52p : ill(some col), charts, maps(some col), plan ; 30cm.
Index.
ISBN 0-08-021761-3 Pbk : £0.95
(B77-27535)

912'.014 — Ordnance Survey maps of Great Britain. Map reading. *Manuals. For walking*
Brown, Terence Henry Charles. The Spur book of map and compass / [by] Terry Brown and Rob Hunter. — Bourne End : Spurbooks, 1977. — 62p : ill, maps ; 19cm. — (A Spurbooks venture guide)
Originally published: 1975.
Pbk : £0.90
ISBN 0-902875-99-x
(B77-31601)

912'.0148 — Shipping. Navigational aids: British Admiralty charts. Symbols. *Lists*
Great Britain. *Hydrographic Department.*
Symbols and abbreviations used on Admiralty charts / [Hydrographic Department]. — Ed. 3. — Taunton : Hydrographer of the Navy, 1976. — [32]p : ill(chiefly col) ; 30cm. — (Chart 5011)
Previous ed.: i.e. Book ed. 2. 1973. — Index.
ISBN 0-7077-0106-6 Sd : £0.60
(B77-09381)

912'.0942 — English maps, to ca 1860
Hodgkiss, Alan Geoffrey. Discovering antique maps / [by] Alan G. Hodgkiss. — [New ed.]. — Aylesbury : Shire Publications, 1977. — 71p : ill, facsim, maps ; 18cm. — (Discovering series ; no.98)
Previous ed.: 1975. — Bibl.: p.67. — Index.
ISBN 0-85263-389-0 Pbk : £0.60
(B77-32293)

912'.1309'14276 — Central Lancashire. Social conditions. *Atlases*
Central Lancashire Development Corporation. A social atlas of Central Lancashire / [Central Lancashire Development Corporation]. — Preston (Cuerdon Pavilion, Bamber Bridge, Preston PR5 6AZ) : The Corporation, 1976. — 2-71p(2 fold) : chiefly maps(chiefly col) ; 43x22cm.
Twenty eight sheets of col. maps printed on transparent acetate in pocket. — Bibl.: p.66. — Index.
ISBN 0-904335-02-x : £14.80
(B77-18441)

912'.1338'10942 — Agricultural industries. Farms. Types. Distribution. *England. Atlases*
Great Britain. *Ministry of Agriculture, Fisheries and Food. Statistics Division II.* Type of farming maps for England and Wales / [Ministry of Agriculture, Fisheries and Food, Statistics Division II]. — Guildford (Government Buildings, Epsom Rd, Guildford, Surrey GU1 2LD) : The Division, [1977]. — [1],viii leaves,13 leaves of plates : chiefly maps ; 30cm.
ISBN 0-904243-02-8 Sd : £0.50
(B77-09382)

912'.1427'9411 — English language. Scottish dialect. Words. Distribution. *Atlases*
Linguistic Survey of Scotland. The linguistic atlas of Scotland / [Linguistic Survey of Scotland]. — London : Croom Helm.
Scots section. Vol.1 / edited with an introduction by J.Y. Mather and H.H. Speitel ; cartography by G.W. Leslie ; editorial assistant I.E. Mather. — 1975. — [8],429p : facsim, form, maps ; 28cm.
ISBN 0-85664-160-x : £29.50
Also classified at 912'.1491'63
(B77-03818)

912'.1491'63 — Gaelic language. Words. Distribution. *Atlases*
Linguistic Survey of Scotland. The linguistic atlas of Scotland / [Linguistic Survey of Scotland]. — London : Croom Helm.
Scots section. Vol.1 / edited with an introduction by J.Y. Mather and H.H. Speitel ; cartography by G.W. Leslie ; editorial assistant I.E. Mather. — 1975. — [8],429p : facsim, form, maps ; 28cm.
ISBN 0-85664-160-x : £29.50
Primary classification 912'.1427'9411
(B77-03818)

912'.1551'13 — Continental drift. *Atlases*
Smith, Alan Gilbert. Mesozoic and Cenozoic paleocontinental maps / [by] A.G. Smith, J.C. Briden. — Cambridge [etc.] : Cambridge University Press, 1977. — 63p : chiefly maps ; 25cm. — (Cambridge earth science series)
ISBN 0-521-29117-8 Sd : £1.95
(B77-27536)

912'.15514'7136 — North Sea. Tidal streams. *Charts*
Great Britain. *Hydrographic Department.* Tidal stream atlas, North Sea, southern portion / [Hydrographic Department]. — Ed. 3. — Taunton : Hydrographer of the Navy, 1976. — [16]p : chiefly col charts ; 30cm. — (NP ; 251)
Cover title: Admiralty tidal stream atlas, North Sea, southern portion.
ISBN 0-7077-0102-3 Sd : £0.60
(B77-01043)

912'.1589'394223 — Seaweeds. Distribution. *Kent. Atlases*
Tittley, Ian. An atlas of the seaweeds of Kent / by Ian Tittley and James H. Price. — Maidstone ([c/o] F.H. Brightman, 59 Rosendale Rd, London S.E.21) : [Kent Field Club], 1977. — [1],80p : chiefly maps ; 21cm. — (Kent Field Club. Transactions ; vol.7)
Bibl.: p.6-8. — Index.
Sd : Unpriced
(B77-33508)

912'.1595'1820941 — Roundworms. Distribution. *Great Britain. Atlases*
Provisional atlas of the nematodes of the British Isles / general editors J. Heath, D.J.F. Brown and B. Boag. — Dundee (Invergowrie, Dundee [DD2 5DA]) : Scottish Horticultural Research Institute ; Abbots Ripton : Institute of Terrestrial Ecology, Biological Records Centre, 1977. — [76]p : chiefly maps ; 28cm. — (European invertebrate survey)
English text, English, French and German preface. — Index. — Contents: Part 1: Longidoridae / edited by D.J.F. Brown and C.E. Taylor - Part 2: Trichodoridae / edited by B. Boag and T.J.W. Alphey - Part 3: Criconematidae / edited by B. Boag and K.J. Orton Williams.
ISBN 0-904282-04-x Sp : £2.00
(B77-15018)

912'.1595'30941 — Crustacea. Distribution. *Great Britain. Atlases*
Provisional atlas of the Crustacea of the British Isles / general editor John Heath. — Huntingdon (Abbots Ripton, Huntingdon [PE17 2LS]) : Natural Environment Research Council, Institute of Terrestrial Ecology, Monks Wood Experimental Station. — (European invertebrate survey)
Part 1 : Isopoda, Oniscoidea : woodlice / edited for the British Isopoda Study Group by Paul T. Harding ; [prepared from records received by the Biological Records Centre]. — 1976. — [15] p,32p of plates : maps ; 28cm.
Bibl.: p.[13]-[14].
ISBN 0-904282-03-1 Sp : Unpriced
(B77-15600)

912'.1595'78094246 — Lepidoptera. Distribution. *Staffordshire. Atlases*
Atlas of the lepidoptera of Staffordshire. — Stoke-on-Trent (Broad St., Hanley, Stoke-on-Trent, Staffs.) : Stoke-on-Trent City Museum and Art Gallery.
Part 2 : Moths : Lasicoampidae-Geometridae (Larentiinae) / author R.G. Warren ; editor G. Halfpenny. — [1976]. — [2],66p : maps ; 21cm. — (Staffordshire Biological Recording Scheme publication ; no.2 ISSN 0309-2100)
Bibl.: p.1.
Sd : £0.50
(B77-03272)

912'.1598'2941 — Birds. Distribution. *Great Britain. Atlases*
The **atlas** of breeding birds in Britain and Ireland / compiled by J.T.R. Sharrock. — [Berkhamsted] : Poyser [for the] British Trust for Ornithology [and the] Irish Wildbird Conservancy, 1976. — 477p : ill, maps(chiefly col) ; 27cm.
Bibl. — Index.
ISBN 0-85661-018-6 : £9.00
(B77-07713)

912'.4 — Europe. *Atlases. For motoring*
John Bartholomew and Son Limited. Road atlas Europe / Bartholomew. — [1976 ed.]. — Edinburgh : J. Bartholomew, 1976. — 136p : chiefly col maps ; 30cm.
Col. map and text on lining papers. — Index.
ISBN 0-85152-749-3 : £2.75
(B77-04468)

912'.41 — Great Britain. *Atlases. For motoring*
Automobile Association. AA Great Britain road atlas. — 5th revised ed. — London : Geographia ; Basingstoke : Automobile Association, 1976. — xvi,192,95p : col ill, chiefly col maps ; 31cm.
Spine title: Great Britain road atlas. — Col. map on lining paper. — Previous ed.: 1975. — Index.
£5.95
ISBN 0-09-211500-4
(B77-07714)

Esso road atlas [of] Great Britain & Ireland. — London : Stanford.
[1975] / [cartographic editor Harold Fullard]. — 1975. — [2],259p : col ill, chiefly col maps ; 29cm.
Index.
ISBN 0-540-05301-5 : £3.75
(B77-05111)

'Reader's digest' AA new book of the road / [edited and designed by the Reader's Digest Association]. — 2nd ed., 2nd revise. — London : Reader's Digest Association with the Automobile Association, 1977. — 416p,(128 fold) : ill(chiefly col), chart, col maps ; 29cm.
Spine title: New book of the road. — Previous ed.: i.e. 2nd ed, 1st revise. 1976.
£8.95
(B77-32294)

Road atlas Britain / Bartholomew. — [Edinburgh] : Bartholomew.
[1976 ed.]. — 1976. — 120p : of col maps ; 30cm.
Col. ill., col. map on lining papers. — Index.
ISBN 0-85152-727-2 : £2.25
(B77-06961)

912'.41 — Towns. *Great Britain. Atlases*
Automobile Association. AA town plans / editor Gail Harada. — [Basingstoke] : Automobile Association, 1976. — 224p : ill(some col), col maps ; 20x21cm.
ISBN 0-09-128191-1 Pbk : £2.50
(B77-05112)

912'.418'35 — Dublin region. *Atlases*
The **Hennessy** brandy Dublin street finder. — [Dublin?] : Jas. Hennessy and Co., [1977]. — ix,80p : chiefly maps ; 22cm.
Index.
Pbk : Unpriced
(B77-30832)

912'.421 — London. *Atlases*
Automobile Association. AA Greater London street atlas. — London : Geographia ; Basingstoke : A.A., 1977. — 402p in various pagings : ill, chiefly col maps ; 31cm.
Spine title: Greater London street atlas. — Col. maps on lining papers. — Index.
ISBN 0-09-211490-3 : £8.95
(B77-14458)

Nicholson London street finder. — [New ed.]. — London : R. Nicholson, [1977]. — [2],160,[117] p : ill, chiefly maps(chiefly col) ; 20cm.
Scale of maps : ca 5 inches to 1 mile or ca 3 inches to 1 mile. — Previous ed.: published as 'Nicholson's London street finder'. 1974. — Index.
ISBN 0-900568-98-4 Pbk : £0.75
(B77-32295)

912'.421'2 — London (City), 1676. Maps. Facsimiles
Ogilby, John. A large and accurate map of the City of London : ichnographically describing all the streets, lanes, alleys, courts, yards, churches, halls and houses, etc. / actually surveyed and delineated by John Ogilby ; introductory notes by Ralph Hyde. — Lympe Castle (Lympe Castle, Kent) : Harry Margary [for] Guildhall Library, London, 1976. — [5],21 leaves : coat of arms, facsims, plan, 2 ports ; 45x57cm.
Facsimile reprint. — Originally published: London : The author, 1676. — Bibl.: leaf [5].
£18.00
Pbk : £9.00
(B77-10028)

912'.422'1 — Surrey, 1579-1823. *Maps. Facsimiles. Collections*
Two hundred and fifty years of map-making in the County of Surrey : a collection of reproductions of printed maps published between the years 1579-1823 / with introductory notes by William Ravenhill. — Lympne Castle (Lympne Castle, Kent) : Harry Margary, 1974. — [1],29leaves : ill, coats of arms, chiefly maps ; 60x84cm.
ISBN 0-903541-27-0 Pbk : Unpriced
(B77-15601)

912'.422'5 — East & West Sussex. *Atlases*
Sussex : with 48 town centre street maps, road maps with index, population gazetteer, administrative districts, postcode districts, index to streets. — 2nd revision. — Ashford (Rushton, Smarden, Ashford, Kent) : Estate Publications, [1977]. — [1],64p : of col maps ; 21cm. — (Estate Publications county atlases)
Index.
ISBN 0-86084-036-0 Sd : £0.95
(B77-29795)

912'.422'5 — East Sussex. Brighton (District), Hove (District) & Lewes (District). *Atlases*
Brighton : Lewes, Newhaven, Seaford. — 3rd revision. — Ashford (Rushton, Smarden, Ashford, Kent) : Estate Publications, [1977]. — [4],33,[1]p : col maps ; 22cm. — (Estate Publications street atlases)
Index.
ISBN 0-86084-038-7 Sd : £0.50
Also classified at 912'.422'69
(B77-31602)

912'.422'6 — West Sussex. Crawley, Horsham (District) & Mid Sussex (District). *Atlases*
Crawley and Mid Sussex : Horley, Horsham, Burgess Hill, Haywards Heath, East Grinstead, Hassocks, Hurstpierpoint. — 2nd revision. — Ashford (Rushton, Smarden, Ashford, Kent) : Estate Publications, [1977]. — [1],33p : col maps ; 22cm. — (Estate Publications street atlases)
Index.
ISBN 0-86084-037-9 Sd : £0.50
(B77-31603)

912'.422'6 — Western West Sussex. *Atlases. For walking*
Rammell, J C. A ramblers atlas of Western Sussex / [by J.C. Rammell, L.H.H. Rush ; based upon the Ordnance Survey maps]. — Chichester (45 South St., Chichester, Sussex) : Collins and French Ltd.
Vol.1 : North. — [1976]. — [2],33p : chiefly maps(chiefly col) ; 15x21cm.
Index.
ISBN 0-905813-00-6 Sd : £1.20
(B77-03819)

Vol.2 : South. — [1976]. — [2],31,[1]p : chiefly maps(chiefly col) ; 15x21cm.
Index.
ISBN 0-905813-01-4 Sd : £1.20
(B77-03820)

Vol.3 : East. — Chichester (42 North St., Chichester, Sussex) : E.M. French, [1977]. — [2],36,[1]p : of col maps ; 15x21cm.
Index.
Sd : £1.20
(B77-29039)

912'.422'69 — West Sussex. Adur (District). *Atlases*
Brighton : Lewes, Newhaven, Seaford. — 3rd revision. — Ashford (Rushton, Smarden, Ashford, Kent) : Estate Publications, [1977]. — [4],33,[1]p : col maps ; 22cm. — (Estate Publications street atlases)
Index.
ISBN 0-86084-038-7 Sd : £0.50
Primary classification 912'.422'5
(B77-31602)

912'.422'93 — Berkshire. Reading. *Atlases*
Reading and district map book. — Carshalton : Forward Publicity, [1976]. — 60p : ill, maps ; 24cm.
Index.
ISBN 0-7174-0721-7 Sd : Unpriced
(B77-08141)

912'.423'5 — Devon. *Atlases*
Devon : street maps of 37 towns with index, road map with index, population gazetteer, administrative districts and postcode districts. — Ashford (Rushton, Smarden, Ashford, Kent) : Estate Publications, [1977]. — 64p : of col maps ; 21cm. — (Estate Publications county atlases)
Index.
ISBN 0-86084-022-0 Sd : £0.95
(B77-29796)

912'.424'65 — Staffordshire. Burton upon Trent, 1679-1850. *Maps. Collections*
Burton upon Trent and district in maps before 1850 / [compiled by Staffordshire County Council Education Department]. — [Stafford] ([Tipping St., Stafford]) : [The Department], [1977]. — [1],vi p,[1],27 leaves : ill, maps ; 30cm. — (Local history source book ; L.29 ISSN 0306-5820)
Sd : £0.40
(B77-30833)

912'.424'65 — Staffordshire. Burton upon Trent, 1865-1882. *Maps. Collections*
Burton-upon-Trent maps, 1865 & 1882 / [compiled by Staffordshire County Education Department]. — [Stafford] ([Tipping St., Stafford]) : [The Department], 1977. — [1]p,36 leaves of plates : maps ; 30cm. — (Local history source book ; no.L.30 ISSN 0306-5820)
'This booklet reproduces two maps of the latter half of the nineteenth century ... The first map was originally surveyed by Thomas Spooner ... first published in 1857 and revised in 1865 ... [as] "A Plan of the Town of Burton-upon-Trent in the County of Stafford, 1865" ... The second map is the first edition of the 25 inches to a mile Ordnance Survey map ... published in 1884'.
Sd : Unpriced
(B77-30834)

912'.424'96 — West Midlands (Metropolitan County). Birmingham, to 1975. *Maps. Collections*
Jones, John Morris. Maps of Birmingham : with notes providing an introduction to the historical geography of the Manor, Borough, City and Metropolitan District of Birmingham / [by] John Morris Jones. — Birmingham (Margaret St., Birmingham B3 3BU) : City of Birmingham Education Department, 1976. — 70,[1]p : maps, plans ; 31cm.
Bibl.: p.3.
Sd : £1.00
(B77-07715)

912'.425'6 — Bedfordshire, 1607-1852. *Maps. Facsimiles. Collections*
Hopkinson, M F. Old county maps of Bedfordshire / text by M.F. Hopkinson. — [Luton] ([Wardown Park, Luton LU2 3HA]) : Luton Museum and Art Gallery, 1976. — [3], 50p : coats of arms, facsims, maps ; 29cm.
Bibl.: p.45.
ISBN 0-9501232-9-3 Sd : £1.00
(B77-13412)

912'.427'31 — Greater Manchester (Metropolitan County). Trafford (District). *Atlases*
Metropolitan Borough of Trafford official street plan. — Carshalton : Forward Publicity, [1977]. — [1],80,[1]p : ill, maps ; 24cm.
Index.
Sd : £0.60
(B77-33509)

912'.427'54 — Merseyside (Metropolitan County). Knowsley (District). *Atlases*
Metropolitan borough of Knowsley, official street and area plan. — Carshalton : Forward Publicity, [1976]. — 40p : maps ; 25cm.
Index.
ISBN 0-7174-0713-6 Sd : £0.27
(B77-03273)

912'.428'1 — Yorkshire, 1767-1770. *Maps. Facsimiles*
Jefferys, Thomas. The County of York, surveyed in MDCCLXVII, VIII, IX and MDCCLXX / engraved by Thomas Jefferys, MDCCLXXI. — [1st ed., reprinted] ; introductory notes by J.B. Harley and J.C. Harvey. — Lympne Castle (Lympne Castle, Kent) : Harry Margary, 1973. — [3],20leaves : ill, facsim, chiefly maps ; 64,72cm.
Facsimile reprint of: 1st ed., London : Robert Sayer and John Bennett, 1775.
ISBN 0-903541-26-2 Pbk : Unpriced
(B77-15602)

912'.428'25 — South Yorkshire (Metropolitan County). Barnsley (District). *Atlases*
Official street and area plan, Metropolitan Borough of Barnsley. — Carshalton : Forward Publicity, [1976]. — 76,[1]p : coat of arms, maps ; 25cm.
Index.
ISBN 0-7174-0725-x Sd : Unpriced
(B77-09383)

912'.429 — Wales, 1573-1848. *Maps. Facsimiles*
Booth, John, *b.1926.* Antique maps of Wales / [by] John Booth. — Montacute (Montacute, Somerset) : Montacute Bookshop, 1977. — [1], xiii,132p : ill, coats of arms, maps ; 26cm.
Silver Jubilee Appeal ed. limited to 1000 copies. — Bibl.: p.127. — Index.
Unpriced
(B77-22977)

912'.7 — North America, 1770-1776. *Maps. Facsimiles. Collections*
North America at the time of the Revolution : a collection of eighteenth century maps / with introductory notes by William P. Cumming and Douglas W. Marshall. — Lympne Castle (Lympne Castle, Kent) : Harry Margary.
Part 3. — 1975. — [24]leaves : chiefly maps ; 58x77cm.
ISBN 0-903541-25-4 Pbk : Unpriced
(B77-15603)

913 — ANCIENT WORLD
913.3'04 — Ancient Palestine. Description & travel. *School texts*
Parsons, Coralie. Getting to know about the countryside in the lands of the Bible / [by] Coralie Parsons ; artist - Anne Farncombe. — Redhill : Denholm House Press, 1976. — 32p : ill(chiefly col), col maps ; 25cm. — (Getting to know about ; book 8)
Index.
ISBN 0-85213-149-6 Sd : £0.75
(B77-09384)

913.8′8 — Mycenaean civilization. Geographical aspects. *Conference proceedings*
Mycenaean geography : proceedings of the Cambridge colloquium, September 1976 / edited by John Bintliff. — Cambridge (Laundress Lane Faculty Rooms, Cambridge CB2 1SD) : British Association for Mycenaean Studies, 1977. — [4],119[i.e.127]p,[32]p of plates : ill, maps ; 30cm.
Cover title. — '... colloquium held in Cambridge at Leckhampton and Corpus Christi College on September 27th and 28th 1976' - Preface. — Bibl.
Pbk : £2.50
(B77-29797)

913.9′7′04 — Exploration. Hanno. Periplus. *North Africa. Critical studies. French-English parallel texts*
Ramin, Jacques. Le Périple d'Hannon = The periplus of Hanno / [by] Jacques Ramin. — Oxford : British Archaeological Reports, 1976. — [6],121,4p : col maps ; 29cm. — (British archaeological reports : supplementary series ; 3)
French and English text.
ISBN 0-904531-35-x Sd : £2.40
(B77-00496)

914 — EUROPE
914 — Western Europe. Geographical features. *Secondary school texts*
Bealt, Allan. Western Europe : a systematic geography / [by] Allan Bealt. — London [etc.] : Pitman, 1977. — viii,201p : ill, maps ; 25cm.
Index.
ISBN 0-273-25267-4 Pbk : £2.50 : CIP rev.
(B77-10029)

Randle, Thomas William. Geographical studies in Western Europe / [by] T.W. Randle. — 3rd ed. — Edinburgh : Oliver and Boyd, 1977. — [6], 201,[1]p : ill, maps ; 25cm.
Previous ed.: 1975.
ISBN 0-05-003067-1 Pbk : £1.95
(B77-34274)

Robinson, Harry, *b.1915.* Western Europe / by Harry Robinson. — 5th ed. — London : University Tutorial Press, 1977. — ii-x,579p : ill, maps ; 22cm. — (Advanced Level geography series)
Previous ed.: 1974. — Index.
ISBN 0-7231-0734-3 Pbk : £2.85
(B77-12195)

914′.04′52 — Europe. Description & travel, 1933-1935. *Personal observations*
Fermor, Patrick Leigh. A time of gifts : on foot to Constantinople : from the Hook of Holland to the Middle Danube / [by] Patrick Leigh Fermor. — London : J. Murray, 1977. — [7], 291p,[3]leaves of plates : map, port ; 23cm.
Index.
ISBN 0-7195-3348-1 : £6.50
(B77-29798)

914′.04′55 — Europe. *Guidebooks. For hitch-hiking*
Welsh, Ken. Hitch-hiker's guide to Europe : how to see Europe by the skin of your teeth / [by] Ken Welsh. — London [etc.] : Pan Books. 1977-78 : revised and updated. — 1977. — 268p : maps ; 20cm.
ISBN 0-330-25186-4 Pbk : £0.80
(B77-13413)

914′.04′55 — Europe. *Guidebooks. For youth hostelling*
Youth Hostels Association (England and Wales). Youth hosteller's guide to Europe / [Youth Hostels Association (England and Wales)]. — 8th ed. / [edited by Richard Quilter]. — London : Y.H.A. Services, 1977. — 492p : maps ; 19cm.
Previous ed.: 1975. — Index.
ISBN 0-900833-12-2 Pbk : £2.00(£1.75 to members of the Association)
(B77-21572)

914′.04′55 — Europe. Description & travel
Troll, Thaddäus. A mosaic of Europe / [by] Thaddäus Troll. — London ([24 Friern Park, North Finchley, N.12]) : Ferndale Publications, [1977]. — 203p : col ill ; 27x31cm.
Parallel German, English and French text. — Originally published: Kunzelsau-Thalwill : Sigloch Service Edition, 1976.
ISBN 0-905746-00-7 : £12.00
(B77-10996)

914′.04′55 — Western Europe. Description & travel, 1961-1963. *Personal observations*
Hitner, John. Two for the road : Ph D European plan / [by] John and Elizabeth Hitner. — Ilfracombe : Stockwell, 1977. — 195p,[2]leaves of plates,[8]p of plates : ill(incl 1 col), facsims ; 22cm.
Index.
ISBN 0-7223-0997-x : £4.25
Also classified at 378.1′553′0924
(B77-29799)

914.1 — GREAT BRITAIN
914.1 — Ancient monuments in guardianship of Great Britain. Department of the Environment. *Great Britain. Directories*
Great Britain. *Department of the Environment.* List and map of historic monuments in the care of the state open to the public / Department of the Environment, Scottish Development Department, Welsh Office. — 7th ed. — [London] : H.M.S.O., 1976. — [2],31,[2]p(2 fold) ; col maps ; 21cm.
Previous ed.: published as 'List and map of historic monuments open to the public'. 1972.
ISBN 0-11-670782-8 Sd : £0.25
(B77-07716)

914.1 — Great Britain. Geographical features. *Secondary school texts*
Graves, Norman John. Geography of the British Isles / [by] Norman J. Graves, John Talbot White. — 4th ed. — London : Heinemann Educational, 1976. — [6],314p : ill, maps, plans ; 24cm.
Previous ed.: 1974. — Index.
ISBN 0-435-34275-4 Pbk : £2.15
(B77-02661)

Preece, Dorothy Mary. The British Isles / [by] D.M. Preece and H.R.B. Wood. — 19th ed. — London : University Tutorial Press, 1977. — viii,292p,leaf of plate,[24]p of plates : ill, charts, maps ; 20cm. — (Modern geography series)
Previous ed.: 1974. — Index.
ISBN 0-7231-0750-5 Pbk : £1.35
(B77-22244)

Simmons, Winifred Margaret. The British Isles : excluding Eire / [by] W.M. Simmons assisted by R.T. Way. — 3rd ed. — Plymouth : Macdonald and Evans, 1976. — xii,282p : ill, charts, maps ; 22cm. — (The New Certificate geography series)
Index.
ISBN 0-7121-0248-5 Pbk : £2.50
(B77-06361)

914.1′003 — Great Britain. *Gazetteers*
John Bartholomew and Son Limited. Bartholomew gazetteer of Britain / compiled by Oliver Mason. — Edinburgh : J. Bartholomew, 1977. — xlviii,271p,128p of plates : ill, col charts, maps(chiefly col) ; 30cm.
Col. map on lining papers.
ISBN 0-85152-771-x : £9.50
(B77-22245)

914.1′04′730924 — Great Britain. Visits by Omai, 1774-1776
Alexander, Michael, *b.1920.* Omai, noble savage / [by] Michael Alexander. — London : Collins : Harvill Press, 1977. — 223p,[12]p : ill, ports ; 22cm.
Ill. on lining papers. — Bibl.: p.213-215. — Index.
ISBN 0-00-262610-1 : £5.95
(B77-16107)

914.1′04′857 — Ancient Roman antiquities. *Great Britain. Guidebooks*
English Tourist Board. Discover Roman Britain / a promotion by the English, Wales and Scottish Tourist Boards. — London : English Tourist Board, 1977. — [2],16,[1]p : ill(chiefly col), col maps, plan ; 21cm.
Bibl.: (1p.).
Sd : £0.25
(B77-23823)

914.1′04′857 — Gardens. *Great Britain. Guidebooks*
Coats, Peter. Great gardens of Britain / [by] Peter Coats. — London (11 St John's Hill, SW11) : Artus Publishing Co. [for Marks and Spencer Ltd], 1977. — 185p : col ill ; 31cm.
Not the same as B67-18621. — Jacket title: St Michael book of great gardens of Britain. — Col. ill. on lining papers. — Index.
£2.99
(B77-34275)

914.1′04′857 — Gardens open to the public. *Great Britain. Guidebooks*
Hellyer, Arthur George Lee. The Shell guide to gardens : the finest British and Irish gardens open to the public / described and introduced by Arthur Hellyer. — London : Heinemann, 1977. — [8],280p,[16]p of plates : ill(some col), maps ; 23cm.
Bibl.: p.68-69. — Index.
ISBN 0-434-32627-5 : £2.95
(B77-11469)

914.1′04′857 — Great Britain. *Guidebooks*
Automobile Association. AA guide to stately homes, castles and gardens. — Basingstoke : A.A. ; London : Distributed by Hutchinson. [1977] : over 2,000 places to visit / [editor Gail Harada ; compiler Pamela Stagg]. — 1976. — 284p,52p of plates : ill, facsim, col maps, ports ; 23cm.
Cover title. — Index.
ISBN 0-09-128171-7 Pbk : £1.95
(B77-06962)

Automobile Association. Royal Britain / [produced by the Publications Division of the Automobile Association ; editor Michael Buttler]. — [Basingstoke] : [AA], [1976]. — 216p : ill(some col), maps(chiefly col), ports(chiefly col) ; 21x22cm.
Index.
ISBN 0-09-128200-4 Pbk : £3.50
(B77-03821)

914.1′04′857 — Great Britain. *Guidebooks. For motoring*
Automobile Association. AA hand-picked tours in Britain : day drives along quiet roads through all parts of the countryside, with halts in historic villages and towns and visits to castles, gardens, follies and other selected places of interest / [edited and designed by the Reader's Digest Association]. — London : Drive Publications for the Automobile Association, 1977. — 424p : ill(chiefly col), col maps, ports(some col) ; 29cm.
Text, col. map on fold. lining paper. — Index.
£8.95
(B77-23824)

Automobile Association. AA illustrated guide to Britain. — 2nd ed., 3rd revise. — London : Drive Publications, 1976. — 544p : ill(chiefly col), facsims, maps(chiefly col), ports(chiefly col) ; 27cm.
Second ed. originally published: 1974. — Index.
ISBN 0-903356-20-1 : £7.95
(B77-06362)

Automobile Association. AA illustrated guide to Britain / edited by Drive Publications Limited for the Automobile Association. — 3rd ed. — Basingstoke : Drive Publications for the A.A., 1977. — 544p : ill(chiefly col), facsim, col maps, ports(some col) ; 26cm.
Previous ed.: i.e. 2nd ed., 3rd revise. 1976. — Index.
£8.95
(B77-32296)

Royal Automobile Club. Guide and handbook / Royal Automobile Club. — London : R.A.C. [1977]. — 1977. — 542,48p : ill, col maps ; 21cm.
Text on lining papers. — Index.
ISBN 0-902628-15-1 : £3.50(£2.00 to members of the R.A.C.)
(B77-15604)

914.1′04′857 — Great Britain. *Practical information. For tourists*
British Tourist Authority. Britain : a traveller's guide / British Tourist Authority. — London : B.T.A., 1977. — 24p : col ill ; 22cm.
ISBN 0-85630-356-9 Sd : Unpriced
(B77-13414)

914.1′04′857 — Great Britain. Description & travel
Rowse, Alfred Leslie. Heritage of Britain / [by] A.L. Rowse. — London (11 St John's Hill, S.W.11) : Artus Publishing Co. Ltd [for Marks and Spencer Ltd], 1977. — 184p : col ill, col ports ; 31cm.
Jacket title: St Michael heritage of Britain. — Col. ill. on lining papers. — Index.
£2.99
(B77-34276)

914.1′04′857 — Great Britain. Description & travel. *Juvenile literature*
Weimar, Stig. Great Britain is like this / [by] Stig Weimar ; [translated from the Danish]. — London : Kaye and Ward, 1977. — [29]p : col ill, maps(some col) ; 26cm.
Originally published: in Danish. Copenhagen : Gyldendalske Boghandel, 1977.
ISBN 0-7182-1167-7 : £2.25
(B77-31604)

914.1'04'857 — Great Britain. Places with occult associations. Description & travel
Wilcock, John. A guide to occult Britain : the quest for magic in pagan Britain / [by] John Wilcock. — London : Sphere, 1977. — 314p,[2] leaves of plates : 2 maps ; 18cm.
Originally published: London : Sidgwick and Jackson, 1976. — Bibl.: p.310-311. — Index.
ISBN 0-7221-9140-5 Pbk : £1.25
(B77-31605)

914.1'04'857 — Great Britain. Rural regions. *Walkers' guides*
No through road : the AA book of country walks / [edited and designed by the Reader's Digest Association]. — 1st ed., 1st revise. — London : Drive Publications for the Automobile Association, 1976. — 1v. : ill(chiefly col), facsim, maps(chiefly col), ports(some col) ; 30cm.
1. 'Walking in Britain' (152p.: Pbk) 2.'Selected walks' ([415]p.: Ls.) 3. 'Walker's handbook' (64p.: 12x19cm: Sd in notebook format), plastic wallet all in binder. — First ed. originally published: 1975. — Bibl. — Index.
ISBN 0-903356-19-8 : £9.95
(B77-01044)

914.1'04'857 — Inland waterways. *Great Britain. Practical information*
Waterway users' companion / British Waterways Board. — London : British Waterways Board, Amenity Services Division.
1976. — [1976]. — [1],64,[2]p,fold plate : ill, maps(chiefly col) ; 21cm.
ISBN 0-903218-12-7 Sd : £0.60
(B77-09385)

1977. — [1977]. — [2],64,[1]p : ill, map ; 21cm.

ISBN 0-903218-15-1 Sd : £0.60
(B77-09386)

914.1'04'8570240313 — Great Britain. *Guidebooks. For American tourists*
Winks, Robin William. An American's guide to Britain / [by] Robin W. Winks. — London : A. and C. Black, 1977. — xi,382p : ill, maps ; 23cm.
Maps on lining papers. — Bibl. — Index.
ISBN 0-7136-1660-1 : £6.95 : CIP rev.
(B77-06363)

914.1'04'8570247966 — Great Britain. *Practical information. For cycling & motorcycling*
Britain, Britain on two wheels / [British Tourist Authority]. — London : B.T.A.
1977-78. — 1977. — [2],35p : maps ; 21cm. — (British Tourist Authority. Information sheets ; no. 369/77/153)
ISBN 0-85630-587-1 Sd : £0.20
(B77-27537)

914.1'04'85703 — Great Britain. Description & travel. *Encyclopaedias*
Treasures of Britain and treasures of Ireland. — 3rd ed., 1st revise. — London : Drive Publications for the Automobile Association, 1977. — 680p(56 fold) : ill(chiefly col), facsims(chiefly col), col maps, music, plans, ports(chiefly col) ; 29cm.
Col. ill. on lining papers. — This ed. originally published: 1976.
£8.95
(B77-32954)

914.1'09'73 — Human settlements. Geographical aspects. *Great Britain. Secondary school texts*
Scudamore, C N J. Settlement problems / [by] C.N.J. Scudamore. — Exeter : Wheaton, 1977. — [5],73p : ill, maps, plans ; 30cm. — (Pergamon topic geographies)
ISBN 0-08-020994-7 Pbk : £1.45
(B77-32297)

914.1'09'732 — Great Britain. Urban regions. Geographical features. *Secondary school texts*
Thomas, Spencer. Urban land use / [by] Spencer Thomas. — Bognor Regis (16 Inglewood Drive, Bognor Regis, Sussex) : Dome Education.
In 3 vols.
1 : Downtown. — 1977. — [2],29,[1]p : ill, maps, plans ; 22cm. — (Geographical models made easy)
ISBN 0-9505499-0-8 Sd : £0.50
(B77-18442)

914.1'09'734 — Great Britain. Rural regions. Geographical features
Turner, James. The countryside of Britain / [by] James Turner ; photographs by Edwin Smith. — London : Ward Lock, 1977. — 200p : ill(some col) ; 27cm.
Index.
ISBN 0-7063-5020-0 : £5.95
(B77-22246)

914.11 — SCOTLAND

914.11 — Scotland. Geographical features
Lea, K J. A geography of Scotland / [by] K.J. Lea with contributions from G. Gordon and I.R. Bowler. — Newton Abbot [etc.] : David and Charles, 1977. — 261p,16p of plates : ill, maps ; 23cm.
Bibl.: p.239-253. — Index.
ISBN 0-7153-7422-2 : £7.50
(B77-25271)

McIntosh, Ian Graham. The face of Scotland / by I.G. McIntosh and C.B. Marshall. — 3rd ed. — Oxford [etc.] : Pergamon, 1977. — xiv, 230p : ill, maps ; 24cm. — (Pergamon international library)
Previous ed.: 1970. — Bibl.: p.218-219. — Index.
ISBN 0-08-021321-9 : £7.00
ISBN 0-08-021320-0 Pbk : £4.00
(B77-23825)

914.11 — Scotland. Geographical features. *Secondary school texts*
Resources for Scottish geography / general editor Derek Keatch. — London [etc.] : Heinemann Educational.
Pupils book 3 : Forth studies / [by] Andrew Baird ... [et al.] ; edited by Derek Keatch. — 1977. — [6],72p : ill, maps ; 25cm.
ISBN 0-435-34475-7 Sd : £1.25
(B77-15019)

914.11'001'4 — Scotland. Place names
Nicolaisen, William Fritz Hermann. Scottish place-names : their study and significance / [by] W.F.H. Nicolaisen. — London : Batsford, 1976. — xxviii,210p : maps ; 23cm.
Bibl.: p.xiv-xxi. — Index.
ISBN 0-7134-3253-5 : £4.95
(B77-00497)

914.11'04 — Scotland. State visits by British monarchs, 1086-1976
Cadell, Patrick. Royal visits to Scotland / [by] Patrick Cadell ; [for the] National Library of Scotland. — Edinburgh : H.M.S.O., 1977. — 29p : ill, facsim ; 19cm.
ISBN 0-11-491481-8 Sd : £1.50
(B77-17170)

914.11'04'73 — Scotland. Description & travel, ca 1780
Heron, R. Scotland delineated / [by] R. Heron. — Edinburgh : Thin, 1975. — 398,[9]p,[9]leaves of plates(1 fold) : maps ; 22cm.
Limited ed. of 500 copies. — Facsimile reprint of: 2nd ed. Edinburgh : Bell and Bradfute ; London : G.G. and J. Robinson, 1799. — Index.
£5.75
(B77-09387)

914.11'04'857 — Castles. *Scotland. Guidebooks*
Fenwick, Hubert. Scotland's castles / [by] Hubert Fenwick ; photographs by the author. — London : Hale, 1976. — 350p : ill, coat of arms, plans ; 23cm.
Index.
ISBN 0-7091-5731-2 : £6.50
(B77-01045)

914.11'04'857 — Scotland. *Guidebooks*
Brooks, John Attwood. Scotland in colour / text by John Brooks. — Norwich : Jarrold and Sons, 1977. — 27p(2 fold) : chiefly col ill, col map ; 25cm. — (A Jarrold 'Sandringham' book)

English text, French and German captions.
ISBN 0-85306-673-6 Sd : £0.40
(B77-30835)

The **new** Shell guide to Scotland. — New [ed.] / edited by Donald Lamond Macnie from the original Shell guide edited by Moray McLaren, retaining his historical introduction and essays and arranged in 12 gazetteers under the new Regions and Island areas. — London : Ebury Press, 1977. — 479p,16,[16]p of plates : ill(some col), facsims, col maps, ports ; 25cm.
Ill. on lining papers. — Previous ed.: i.e. 2nd ed., published as 'The Shell guide to Scotland' / by Moray McLaren. 1972. — Bibl.: p.462-464. — Index.
£6.50
ISBN 0-7181-3036-7
(B77-10997)

Scottish Tourist Board. Enjoy Scotland, 1977 : a world of a difference / [Scottish Tourist Board]. — [Edinburgh] : The Board, [1977]. — 30p : col ill, col map ; 30cm.
Sd : Unpriced
(B77-18443)

914.11'04'857 — Scotland. *Guidebooks. For motoring*
Keating, Leslie. Scotland by car / [by] Leslie Keating. — [Havant] : K. Mason, [1977]. — 143p : ill, maps ; 15cm.
ISBN 0-85937-058-5 Pbk : £0.95
(B77-17171)

Scottish Tourist Board. Scotland for the motorist / [Scottish Tourist Board]. — Edinburgh : S.T.B., [1977]. — 43p : ill, maps(some col) ; 26x11cm.
Sd : £0.60
(B77-19086)

914.11'04'857 — Scotland. Description & travel
Brooks, John Attwood. Look at Scotland / written by John Brooks. — Norwich : Jarrold and Sons, 1977. — [32]p : col ill, col map ; 25cm. — (Jarrold Cotman house book series)
English text, French and German captions.
ISBN 0-85306-716-3 Sd : £0.60
(B77-20769)

Morton, Henry Vollam. The splendour of Scotland / [by] H.V. Morton. — London : Eyre Methuen, 1976. — 160p : ill(chiefly col), map ; 26cm.
'Based on extracts taken from "In search of Scotland" (Methuen, 1929) and "In Scotland again" (Methuen, 1933)' - title page verso. — Ill. on lining papers. — Bibl.: p.160.
ISBN 0-413-34720-6 : £4.95
(B77-02662)

914.11'04'857 — Scotland. Rural regions. *Guidebooks*
Countryside Commission for Scotland. Scotland's countryside : the official guide / [Countryside Commission for Scotland]. — [Revised ed.]. — Perth (Battleby, Redgorton, Perth [PH1 3EW]) : The Commission, 1977. — 87p,4,16p of plates : ill(some col), col maps ; 20cm.
Cover title: The official guide to Scotland's countryside. — Previous ed.: 1974.
ISBN 0-902226-40-1 Pbk : £0.75
(B77-17813)

914.11'09'73 — Human settlements. Geographical aspects. *Scotland. Secondary school texts*
Homescapes / authors Allan C. Ayers ... [et al.] ; general editor T.H. Masterton ; illustrated by Barry Adamson and Tim Smith. — Edinburgh : Oliver and Boyd, 1977. — [2],126p : ill(chiefly col), maps(chiefly col), 2 plans(1 col) ; 26cm. — (Outlook geography)
ISBN 0-05-002948-7 Pbk : Unpriced
(B77-33510)

914.111'04'73 — Scotland. Highlands & Islands. Description & travel, 1786. *Facsimiles*
Knox, John, *b.1720.* A tour through the Highlands of Scotland and the Hebride Isles in 1786 / [by] John Knox. — Edinburgh : Thin, 1975. — [4],vi,276,50p ; 22cm.
Spine title: The Highlands and Hebrides in 1786. — Facsimile reprint of: 1st ed. London : J. Walter, 1787.
ISBN 0-901824-38-0 : £5.75
(B77-06364)

914.111'04'857 — Scotland. Highlands & Islands. Description & travel. *Personal observations*
Cooper, Derek. Hebridean connection : a view of the Highlands and Islands / [by] Derek Cooper ; with photographs by Gus Wylie. — London [etc.] : Routledge and Kegan Paul, 1977. — xviii,184p,[16]p of plates : ill, maps ; 24cm.
Ill. on lining papers. — Index.
ISBN 0-7100-8484-6 : £4.95
(B77-16651)

914.114'04'857 — Scotland. Western Isles. *Guidebooks*
Brooks, John Attwood. The Western Isles / with text by J.A. Brooks. — [New ed.]. — Norwich : Jarrold and Sons, [1977]. — [34]p : col ill, col map ; 20cm. — (A Cotman color book)
English text, English, French and German captions.
Sd : £0.40
(B77-34277)

914.114'04'857 — Scotland. Western Isles. Description & travel. *Personal observations*
Duxbury, Ken. Lugworm island hopping / [by] Ken Duxbury ; with drawings, maps and photographs by the author. — London : Pelham, 1976. — 135p,[8]p of plates : ill, maps, ports ; 23cm.
ISBN 0-7207-0940-7 : £4.75
Also classified at 914.23'7'04857
(B77-06963)

914.115 — Scotland. Moray Firth region. Description & travel
Graham, Cuthbert. Portrait of the Moray Firth / by Cuthbert Graham. — London : Hale, 1977. — 3-242p,[24]p of plates : ill, map, ports ; 23cm. — ([Portrait books])
Bibl.: p.232-233. — Index.
ISBN 0-7091-6018-6 : £3.95
(B77-16652)

914.115'04'857 — Scotland. Highlands. *Guidebooks*
Murray, William Hutchison. The Scottish Highlands / [by] W.H. Murray. — Edinburgh : Scottish Mountaineering Trust ; Reading : [Distributed by] West Col Productions, 1976. — 301p,[40]p of plates : ill, maps ; 22cm. — (Scottish Mountaineering Club. District guide books : new series)
Map on lining papers. — Bibl.: p.237-243. — Index.
ISBN 0-901516-83-x : £6.50
(B77-05756)

914.116'2'04857 — Ancient monuments. *Scotland. Highland Region. Caithness (District). Guidebooks*
Visits to ancient Caithness / written for Caithness Field Club by John Bramman ... [et al.]. — Wick (c/o Mrs M. Gladstone, 11 Miller Ave., Wick) : Caithness Field Club, 1976. — 32p : ill, plans ; 21cm.
ISBN 0-9505550-0-2 Sd : £0.45
(B77-09388)

914.117'5 — Scotland. Highland Region. Inverness (District). Loch Ness region. *Guidebooks. For motoring*
Gunn, Douglas Maxwell. Loch Ness country by car / compiled [and written] by Douglas Gunn ; photography by Douglas Gunn and Alan Titchmarsh. — Norwich : Jarrold and Sons, [1977]. — [1],33p : ill, maps(1 col) ; 21cm. — (The Jarrold 'White Horse' series)
Index.
ISBN 0-85306-693-0 Sd : £0.45
(B77-18444)

914.118'5'04857 — Scotland. Highland Region. Lochaber (District). *Guidebooks*
Gant, Frank. Fort William, Glencoe & Lochaber / text by Frank Gant. — Newport, Isle of Wight : Dixon, 1977. — [32]p : col ill, col map ; 21cm.
Sd : Unpriced
(B77-20770)

914.12'23 — Scotland. Grampian Region. Elgin. *Guidebooks*
Moray Society. Elgin : a short illustrated guide to the ancient city and royal burgh / compiled by the Moray Society ; with illustrations by A.M. Brown. — [Elgin] ([County Buildings, Elgin, Morayshire IV30 1BX]) : Department of Recreation, Moray District Council, [1977]. — [7]p : ill, map ; 30cm.
Sd : £0.15
(B77-32298)

914.12'35 — Castles. *Scotland. Grampian Region. Peterculter. Drum Castle. Guidebooks*
National Trust for Scotland. Drum Castle, Aberdeenshire / the National Trust for Scotland ; historical text written by Cuthbert Graham ; tour text by David Learmont ... ; colour photography by Martin Johnston. — Edinburgh : The Trust, 1977. — [28]p : ill(chiefly col), coat of arms ; 21cm.
Bibl.: p.[27].
Sd : £0.50
(B77-25989)

914.12'35'0025 — Scotland. Grampian Region. Aberdeen. *Directories*
Post Office Aberdeen directory. — [Aberdeen] ([21 Adelphi, Aberdeen AB1 2BL]) : [Post Office Aberdeen Directory Ltd].
1976-1977. — [1976]. — xvi,475p : ill ; 22cm.
Index.
ISBN 0-900018-07-0 : £2.50
(B77-01893)

914.12'8 — Scotland. Tayside Region. Perth. *Guidebooks*
Perth, the heart of Scotland : official guide book. — [Perth] ([The Round House, Marshall Place, Perth]) : [Perth Tourist Association].
[1977]. — [1977]. — [52]p : ill(some col), col maps ; 21cm.
ISBN 0-905363-02-7 Sd : £0.20
(B77-14459)

914.13'04'857 — South-east Scotland. *Guidebooks*
Munro, Robert William. Edinburgh and the Borders / [by] R.W. Munro. — Glasgow [etc.] : Collins, 1977. — 96p : ill(some col), col maps ; 17cm. — (Collins holiday guides to Britain)
Index.
ISBN 0-00-435743-4 Pbk : £0.50
(B77-16108)

914.13'04'857 — Southern Scotland. Description & travel
Lindsay, Maurice. The Lowlands of Scotland, Edinburgh and the South / by Maurice Lindsay. — Revised ed. — London : Hale, 1977. — xii,308p,[16]p of plates : ill, map ; 23cm.
Previous ed.: 1956. — Bibl.: p.295-297. — Index.
ISBN 0-7091-5718-5 : £4.50
(B77-16653)

914.13'1'04857 — Scotland. Central Region. *Practical information. For businessmen*
Central Region. *Industrial Development Department.* Scotland's Central Region / [prepared by Industrial Development Department, Central Regional Council]. — Stirling (Viewforth, Stirling FK8 2ET) : [The Department], [1977]. — [12]p : col ill, col maps ; 21x30cm.
Col. map tipped in.
Sd : Unpriced
(B77-20771)

914.13'12 — Scotland. Central Region. Trossachs. *Guidebooks*
Guide to Callander, Trossachs and the Rob Roy country. — [2nd ed.]. — Callander ([Cross Street Printing Works, Callander, Perthshire FK17 8EA]) : James Fleming and Co., [1976]. — 69p : ill(some col), map ; 20cm.
Previous ed.: 1973.
Sd : £0.30
(B77-30836)

914.13'12 — Scotland. Central Region. Trossachs. Geographical features. *Reports, surveys*
Evans, F J. The Trossachs report / [by] F.J. Evans. — Redgorton (Battleby, Redgorton, Perth PH1 3EW) : Countryside Commission for Scotland, 1972. — [3],vi,148p,[11]leaves of plates(10 fold) : maps ; 30cm. — (Trossachs study)
ISBN 0-902226-11-8 Sp : £1.00
(B77-04469)

914.13'85 — Scotland. Borders Region. Yarrow Water valley. *Walkers' guides*
Cameron, Alex. By Yarrow's stream : walking in the historic Scottish borderland / [by] Alex Cameron ; foreword by David Steel ; illustrated with photographs by the author. — Edinburgh : Albyn Press, [1977]. — 79p,[8]p of plates : ill, maps(on lining papers), port ; 22cm.
ISBN 0-284-40012-2 : £2.75
(B77-32299)

914.14'23'04857 — Scotland. South-western Highlands. Description & travel
Thomson, Unity. History, people and places in the Western Highlands / [by] Unity Thomson. — Bourne End : Spurbooks, 1977. — 144p : ill, facsim, map(on lining papers), ports ; 23cm.
Spine title: The Western Highlands. — Bibl.: p.12. — Index.
ISBN 0-904978-22-2 : £5.00
(B77-21573)

914.14'23'04857 — Scotland. South-western Highlands. Description & travel. *Personal observations*
Mitchell, William Reginald. Highland autumn / [by] W.R. Mitchell. — London : Hale, 1977. — 191p,[24]p of plates : ill, 2 maps ; 23cm.
Index.
ISBN 0-7091-6062-3 : £4.25
(B77-22978)

914.14'23'04857 — Scotland. Strathclyde Region. Argyll and Bute (District). *Description & travel*
Tranter, Nigel. Argyll and Bute / by Nigel Tranter. — London [etc.] : Hodder and Stoughton, 1977. — 396p,[32]p of plates : ill, maps ; 23cm. — (The Queen's Scotland)
Bibl.: p.371-372. — Index.
ISBN 0-340-21031-1 : £5.95
(B77-21574)

914.14'25 — Scotland. Strathclyde Region. Dumbarton. *Guidebooks*
Dumbarton District Council, the official guide. — London : Burrow, [1977]. — 24p : ill ; 19cm.
Sd : £0.40
(B77-26671)

914.14'54'04857 — Scotland. Strathclyde Region. East Kilbride (District). *Guidebooks*
The **official** guide to East Kilbride. — 4th ed. — London : Burrow, [1977]. — 88p,fold plate : ill, maps ; 21cm.
ISBN 0-85026-649-1 Pbk : Unpriced
(B77-12196)

914.14'61 — Ancient monuments. *Scotland. Strathclyde Region. Arran. Guidebooks*
McLellan, Robert. Ancient monuments of Arran : official guide / by Robert McLellan ; [for the] Department of the Environment. — Edinburgh : H.M.S.O., 1977. — 2-52p : ill, plans ; 21cm.
Bibl.: p.51-52.
ISBN 0-11-491447-8 Sd : £1.00
(B77-29800)

914.14'64 — Castles. *Scotland. Strathclyde Region. Kyle and Carrick (District). Culzean Castle. Guidebooks*
National Trust for Scotland. A tour of Culzean Castle : a concise guide to the house and contents / National Trust for Scotland. — Edinburgh : National Trust for Scotland, 1977. — Folder([8]p) : ill, plan ; 22cm.
Includes 'Tour of the house' / by David Learmont.
£0.15
(B77-22247)

914.14'64 — Scotland. Strathclyde Region. Ayr. *Walkers' guides*
Brash, Ronald William. Round old Ayr : a guided walk / [by] Ronald W. Brash and Allan Leach ; illustrated by G.S. Copeland. — [Mauchline] ([c/o Dr J. Strawhorn, 12 Eastpark Ave., Mauchline, Ayrshire KA5 5BS]) : Ayrshire Archaeological and Natural History Society, 1977. — [21]p : ill, 2 maps ; 21cm.
Originally published: 1972. — Bibl.: p.[21].
Sd : £0.30
(B77-25990)

914.14'92 — Scotland. Dumfries and Galloway Region. Castle Douglas. *Walkers' guides*
Gibson, Jean Craig. Foot forward in Castle Douglas / by Jean C. Gibson. — Castle Douglas (104 King St., Castle Douglas, Kirkcudbrightshire) : Barry Smart, 1976. — 72p : ill, coat of arms, map, port ; 22cm.
ISBN 0-905785-00-2 Sd : £0.50
(B77-00498)

914.14'92'04857 — Scotland. Dumfries and Galloway Region. Stewartry (District). *Guidebooks. For motoring*
Gibson, Jean Craig. Round about Castle Douglas / [by] Jean C. Gibson. — Castle Douglas (104 King St., Castle Douglas, Kirkcudbrightshire) : Barry Smart, [1976]. — 96p : ill ; 22cm.
ISBN 0-905785-01-0 Sd : £0.60
(B77-01894)

914.15 — IRELAND

914.15 — Ireland. Geographical features. *Secondary school texts*
British Broadcasting Corporation. Irish geography : BBC Radio for Schools, Autumn. — London : British Broadcasting Corporation [for] the School Broadcasting Council for the United Kingdom, 1977. — 32p : chiefly ill, maps ; 30cm.
ISBN 0-563-30049-3 Sd : Unpriced
(B77-31606)

914.15'04'824 — Gardens. *Ireland. Guidebooks*
Malins, Edward. Irish gardens / by Edward Malins and the Knight of Glin. — Dublin : Eason and Son Ltd ; [Norwich] : [Jarrold and Sons], 1977. — [25]p : ill(chiefly col) ; 25cm. — (The Irish heritage series ; 11)
Fold. cover.
ISBN 0-85306-681-7 Sd : £0.70
(B77-17814)

914.15'04'824 — Inland waterways. Description & travel. *Ireland. Personal observations*
Gardner, Raymond. Land of time enough / by Raymond Gardner. — London [etc.] : Hodder and Stoughton, 1977. — 224p,[16]p of plates : ill, facsim, map(on lining papers), ports ; 23cm.

Bibl.: p.223-224.
ISBN 0-340-21745-6 : £4.95
(B77-32955)

914.15'04'824 — Ireland. *Guidebooks*
Fodor's Ireland / Eugene Fodor, Robert C. Fisher editors. — London : Hodder and Stoughton.
1977 : excluding Northern Ireland / Richard Moore European editor. — 1977. — 316,[3]p, [12]p of plates : ill(some col), maps ; 19cm.
Index.
ISBN 0-340-21414-7 : £4.50
(B77-06365)

914.15'04'824 — Ireland. Mountainous regions. Description & travel
Mould, Daphne Desirée Charlotte Pochin. The mountains of Ireland / [by] D.D.C. Pochin Mould. — 2nd ed. — Dublin : Gill and Macmillan, 1976. — 160p : ill, map ; 23cm.
Previous ed.: London : Batsford, 1955. — Bibl.: p.13. — Index.
ISBN 0-7171-0815-5 : £6.95
(B77-01895)

914.15'04'824 — Round towers. *Ireland. Guidebooks*
Barrow, Lennox. Irish round towers / text by Lennox Barrow. — Dublin : Eason and Son Ltd ; [Norwich] : [Jarrold and Sons], 1976. — [25]p : ill(some col), col map ; 25cm. — (The Irish heritage series ; 8)
Fold. cover.
ISBN 0-85306-679-5 Sd : £0.70
(B77-17815)

914.16'0025 — Northern Ireland. *Directories*
Belfast and Northern Ireland directory. — Belfast (51 Donegall St., Belfast BT1 2GB) : Century Services Ltd.
1976 : ninety-sixth ed. — [1976]. — [8],664, 310a p : ill ; 26cm.
Index.
ISBN 0-903152-11-8 : £9.75
(B77-12777)

914.17'007'24 — Geography. Field studies. *Ireland (Republic). Secondary school texts*
Perry, Allen Howard. Geographical field studies in Ireland / [by] Allen H. Perry and Vivien C. Perry. — Dublin : Educational Company of Ireland.
In 2 vols.
[1] : A course to Intermediate Certificate / maps and illustrations G. Lewis. — 1977. — viii,128p : ill, maps, plans ; 19x21cm.
Bibl.: p.128.
Pbk : £1.65
(B77-17172)

914.17'04'824 — Ireland (Republic). Description & travel
Clarke, Harold, *b.1932.* The splendour of Ireland / written by Harold Clarke. — [Norwich] : [Jarrold and Sons], [1977]. — [64] p : col ill, 5 ports(4 col) ; 29cm.
ISBN 0-85306-683-3 : £2.90
(B77-12778)

914.18 — Ireland (Republic). Leinster. Barrow River. *Guidebooks. For boating*
Delany, Ruth. Guide to tbe Barrow : Lowtown to St Mullins / [compiled by Ruth Delany, Jeremy Addis ; maps by Vincent Delany]. — [Dublin] ([Kingston House, Ballinteer, Dublin 14]) : Inland Waterways Association of Ireland, 1977. — [2],50p : ill, maps ; 23cm.
Bibl.: p.47.
Sp : Unpriced
(B77-17816)

914.18'22 — Meath (County). Slane. *Guidebooks*
Trench, C E F. Slane / by C.E.F. Trench ; with drawings by Bea Orpen. — Dublin (126 Lr Baggot St., Dublin 2) : National Trust for Ireland, 1976. — [2],48,[2]p : ill, col map ; 21cm.
ISBN 0-903693-03-8 Sd : £0.90
(B77-04470)

914.18'35 — Cathedrals. *Dublin. St Patrick's Cathedral, Dublin. Guidebooks*
Jackson, Victor. St Patrick's Cathedral, Dublin / [by] Victor Jackson. — Norwich : Jarrold and Sons, 1976. — [28]p(2 fold) : ill(some col), plan, ports ; 25cm. — (The Irish heritage series ; 9)
ISBN 0-900346-07-8 Sd : £0.70
(B77-01896)

914.19'2 — Antiquities. *Tipperary (County). Roscrea region. Guidebooks*
Cunningham, George, *b.1940.* Roscrea and district : monuments and antiquities : illustrated guide / [by] George Cunningham. — Roscrea (Roscrea, [Co. Tipperary]) : Parkmore Press, 1976. — 100p : ill, facsim, maps, plan, ports ; 21x27cm.
'An abbreviated form of some chapters appeared in "Roscrea People", 1974-1976' - title page verso. — Bibl.: p.96-98. — Index.
ISBN 0-9505368-0-6 Sd : £1.50
(B77-01046)

914.19'5'04824 — Cork (County). Description & travel
Jennett, Seán. Cork and Kerry / [by] Seán Jennett ; with 23 photographs by the author. — London : Batsford, 1977. — 175p : ill, map ; 23cm.
Index.
ISBN 0-7134-0437-x : £4.50
Also classified at 914.19'6'04824
(B77-20772)

914.19'6'04824 — Kerry (County). Description & travel
Jennett, Seán. Cork and Kerry / [by] Seán Jennett ; with 23 photographs by the author. — London : Batsford, 1977. — 175p : ill, map ; 23cm.
Index.
ISBN 0-7134-0437-x : £4.50
Primary classification 914.19'5'04824
(B77-20772)

914.2 — ENGLAND
914.2'04'83 — England. Description & travel, 1933. *Personal observations*
Priestley, John Boynton. English journey : being a rambling but truthful account of what one man saw and heard and felt and thought during a journey through England during the autumn of the year 1933 / [by] J.B. Priestley. — Harmondsworth [etc.] : Penguin, 1977. — 395p ; 18cm.
Originally published: London : Heinemann : Gollancz, 1934. — Index.
ISBN 0-14-004274-1 Pbk : £0.95
(B77-17173)

914.2'04'857 — Cathedrals. *England. Guidebooks*
Pepin, David. Discovering cathedrals / [by] David Pepin ; with drawings by the author. — 2nd ed. — Aylesbury : Shire Publications, 1974. — 79p,[16]p of plates : ill, plans ; 18cm. — (Discovering series ; no.112)
Previous ed.: 1971. — Bibl.: p.78. — Index.
ISBN 0-85263-279-7 Pbk : £0.35
(B77-19087)

914.2'04'857 — England. *Guidebooks*
Leeds, Christopher Anthony. Historical guide to England : (journey into history) / [by] Christopher A. Leeds ; illustrations by John Penny. — Swanage (39 Rabling Rd, Swanage, Dorset BH19 1ED) : Croxton Press, 1976. — [4],212p : ill ; 21cm.
Index.
ISBN 0-9504027-1-0 Pbk : £1.80
(B77-12197)

Look at England / with text by Lisa Newcombe. — Norwich : Jarrold and Sons, 1977. — [33]p : col ill ; 25cm. — (Jarrold Cotman house book series)
ISBN 0-85306-703-1 Sd : £0.60
(B77-25991)

914.2'04'857 — England. Description & travel. *Personal observations*
Peel, John Hugh Brignall. Peel's England / [by] J.H.B. Peel ; with photographs by Kenneth Scowen. — Newton Abbot [etc.] : David and Charles, 1977. — 192p : ill ; 25cm.
Index.
ISBN 0-7153-7380-3 : £4.95
(B77-34278)

914.2'04'857 — Inland waterways. Description & travel. *England. Personal observations*
Burton, Anthony. Back door Britain / [by] Anthony Burton. — London : Deutsch, 1977. — 189p,[12]p of plates : ill, maps(on lining papers) ; 23cm.
Index.
ISBN 0-233-96876-8 : £4.95
(B77-22248)

914.2'04'857 — Long-distance footpaths. Description & travel. *England*
Millar, T G. Long distance paths of England and Wales / [by] T.G. Millar. — Newton Abbot [etc.] : David and Charles, 1977. — 160p : ill, maps ; 24cm.
Bibl.: p.150-151. — Index.
ISBN 0-7153-7332-3 : £4.95
(B77-20773)

914.2'04'857 — National Trust properties. *England. Guidebooks*
National Trust. The National Trust guide / compiled and edited by Robin and Rosemary Joekes. — 2nd ed. — London : Cape, 1977. — 608p,[16]p of plates : ill(some col), col maps, ports ; 24cm.
Previous ed.: 1973. — Index.
ISBN 0-224-01486-2 : £7.95 : CIP rev.
(B77-24587)

914.2'04'857 — Prehistoric antiquities. *England. Guidebooks*
Thomas, Nicholas, *b.1928.* A guide to prehistoric England / [by] Nicholas Thomas. — 2nd ed. — London : Batsford, 1976. — 270p : ill, maps, plans ; 23cm.
Previous ed.: 1960. — Bibl.: p.258-264. — Index.
ISBN 0-7134-3267-5 : £5.95
ISBN 0-7134-3268-3 Pbk : £2.50
(B77-27538)

914.2'04'8570222 — England. Description & travel. *Illustrations*
Preston, Eileen, *b.1929.* Curious England / [text and photographs by] Eileen Preston. — Aylesbury : Shire Publications, 1977. — 32p : chiefly ill ; 21cm. — (Shire album ; 22)
ISBN 0-85263-360-2 Sd : £0.50
(B77-31607)

914.21 — Buildings of historical importance. *Central London. Walkers' guides. Middle school texts*
London, the making of a city. — [London] : [Thames Television] ; [London] ([47a Grayling Rd, N16 0BT]) : [Modus Operandi Ltd], [1976]. — 67p : ill, coat of arms, maps(some col), plans, port ; 22cm.
Published to accompany a series of programmes originally made for evening transmission and now specially edited for schools. — Bibl.: p.65-67.
Sd : Unpriced
(B77-10642)

914.21 — England. Thames River. Port of London Authority reaches. Description & travel. *Personal observations*
Shrapnel, Norman. A view of the Thames / [by] Norman Shrapnel ; with line drawings by George Murray. — London [etc.] : Collins, 1977. — 2-253p : ill, maps ; 23cm.
Bibl.: p.243-244. — Index.
ISBN 0-00-216551-1 : £5.95
(B77-22979)

914.21 — Trails. *London. Thames River region. Silver Jubilee Walkway. Walkers' guides*
Civic Trust. The Silver Jubilee Walkway / [Civic Trust]. — London : Civic Trust for the London Celebrations Committee for the Queen's Silver Jubilee, 1977. — 72p : ill, maps, ports ; 21cm.
'Official map/guide' (fold. ([2] sides): ill., col. maps) as insert. — Bibl.: p.71-72.
ISBN 0-900849-86-x Pbk : £1.50
ISBN 0-900849-85-1 Official map/guide : £0.25
(B77-27539)

914.21'001'4 — London. Street names. *Lists*
Wittich, John. Discovering London street names / [by] John Wittich. — Aylesbury : Shire Publications, 1977. — 96p ; 18cm. — (Discovering series ; no.225)
Index.
ISBN 0-85263-366-1 Pbk : £0.70
(B77-32956)

914.21'0025 — London. *Directories*
Kelly's Post Office London directory. — Kingston upon Thames : Kelly's Directories.
1977 : 178th ed. — 1977. — 64,2333,[16]p : ill, col maps ; 29cm.
Tab indexed. — 'including street atlas'. — Index.
ISBN 0-610-00491-3 : £13.00
(B77-15605)

914.21'04'81 — Canals. Description & travel. *London, 1885. Early works*
Through London by canal, 1885 / introduced by Arthur Lowe. — [London] : British Waterways Board, 1977. — 24,[1]p : ill ; 15x21cm.
Extracts from an article originally published in 'Harper's new monthly magazine', 1885. — Bibl.: p.24.
ISBN 0-903218-17-8 Sd : £0.45
(B77-25992)

914.21'04'857 — Ancient Roman antiquities. *London. Guidebooks*
Alcock, Joan Pilsbury. Londinium : a practical guide to the visible remains of Roman London. — Completely revised and rewritten ed. / prepared [by] Joan P. Alcock ; for the London Branch of the Classical Association ; introduction by Margaret Roxan. — London (c/o Miss J. Cook, 132 Woodwarde Rd, SE22 8UR) : London Branch of the Classical Association, 1977. — 40p : ill, 2 maps, plan ; 21cm.
Previous ed.: / prepared by the London Branch of the Classical Association. Twickenham : The Branch, 1971. — Bibl.: p.37-39.
Sd : Unpriced
(B77-26672)

914.21'04'857 — London. *Guidebooks*
Banks, Francis Richard. The Penguin guide to London / [by] F.R. Banks. — 7th ed. — Harmondsworth [etc.] : Penguin, 1977. — 590p, fold plate : maps(1 col), plans ; 18cm.
Col. map tipped in. — Previous ed.: 1973. — Index.
Pbk : £1.50
ISBN 0-14-070417-5
(B77-21575)

Britain, quick guide to London / British Tourist Authority. — London : B.T.A.
[1976] [editor Cyril Palmer]. — 1976. — [1], 44p : ill, map ; 21cm.
Index.
ISBN 0-85630-283-x Sd : Unpriced
(B77-01897)

Colour guide to London. — London : Pitkin Pictorials, 1977. — 128p : col ill, col maps, col ports ; 18cm.
Text, ill. on inside covers.
ISBN 0-85372-232-3 Pbk : £1.30
(B77-26673)

Gant, Frank. A guide to London / text by Frank Gant. — Newport, Isle of Wight : Dixon, 1976. — [1],33p : col ill, col map ; 21cm.
English, French and German text.
ISBN 0-900336-39-0 Sd : £0.39
(B77-07717)

Michelin et Cie. London / Michelin. — London (81 Fulham Rd, SW3 6RD) : Michelin Tyre Co., 1977. — 3-192p[i.e.184]p : ill, col maps, col plans, ports ; 26x12cm. — (Michelin green guides)
Cover title. — Index.
Pbk : Unpriced
ISBN 2-06-015430-8
(B77-27540)

Newcombe, Lisa. Look at London / with text by Lisa Newcombe. — Norwich : Jarrold and Sons, 1977. — [32]p : col ill, maps ; 25cm. — (Jarrold Cotman house book series)
'A Jarrold colour publication'. — English text, French, German, Spanish and Italian lists of photographs.
ISBN 0-85306-696-5 Sd : £0.60
(B77-13415)

Nicholson's London guide : a comprehensive pocket guide to London's sights, pleasures and services with new maps and street index. — [4th ed.] / editor Gail Rebuck ; researcher Helen Benedict. — London : R. Nicholson, [1977]. — 157p : ill(some col), col maps ; 18cm.
Previous ed.: 1971. — Index.
ISBN 0-900568-99-2 Pbk : £0.75
(B77-25993)

Piper, David. The companion guide to London / [by] David Piper. — 6th ed. — London : Collins, 1977. — 3-520p,[24]p of plates : ill, maps, plans, port ; 22cm.
Previous ed.: 1974. — Bibl.: p.483-485. — Index.
£6.50
ISBN 0-00-211125-x
ISBN 0-00-211478-x Pbk : £3.50
(B77-19889)

Tingey, Frederick. Letts visit London / [by] Frederick Tingey. — London [etc.] : Letts, 1977. — 80p,16p of plates : ill, col maps ; 17cm. — (Letts guides)
ISBN 0-85097-198-5 Pbk : £0.75
(B77-17817)

914.21'04'857 — London. *Guidebooks. For students*
Nicholson's students' London. — London : R. Nicholson, 1977. — 96p : col ill, col maps ; 18cm.
Index.
ISBN 0-905522-06-0 Pbk : £0.75
(B77-28271)

914.21'04'857 — London. *Walkers' guides*
Edwards, Dennis F. Walks around London town / by Dennis F. Edwards ; illustrations Pamela Tumath. — Ilford (884 Eastern Ave., Ilford, Essex) : Circle Publications, 1976. — [2], 81p,10p of plates : ill, col maps ; 16cm.
ISBN 0-9502012-4-3 Pbk : £0.65
(B77-22249)

Wittich, John. Off-beat walks in London / [by] John Wittich and Ron Phillips. — [3rd ed.]. — [Aylesbury] : Shire Publications, [1977]. — 55p : maps ; 18cm. — (Discovering series ; 63) (A discovering guide)
Previous ed.: 1973. — Index.
ISBN 0-85263-378-5 Pbk : £0.50
(B77-30837)

914.21'04'857 — London. Description & travel
Plimmer, Charlotte. London : a visitor's companion / [by] Charlotte and Denis Plimmer. — London : Batsford, 1977. — 208p : maps, plan ; 23cm.
Index.
ISBN 0-7134-0443-4 : £3.95
(B77-28272)

914.21'2 — Cathedrals. *London (City). St Paul's Cathedral. Guidebooks*
Ewin, *Sir* **David Floyd.** St Paul's Cathedral / [by] Sir David Floyd Ewin. — London : Pitkin Pictorials, 1976. — [1],24p : chiefly col ill, col port, plan ; 18cm.
ISBN 0-85372-218-8 Sd : £0.40
(B77-06964)

914.21'2'0025 — London (City). *Directories*
City of London directory & livery companies guide : a comprehensive guide to the business markets of the City of London and a complete list of livery companies and their members. — London (4 Moorfields, EC2Y 9AB) : City Press.
1977 : 113th year. — [1977]. — [1],311p : ill ; 23cm.
Previously published: as 'City of London directory with livery companies guide'. — Index.
ISBN 0-901129-11-9 : £9.50
(B77-10998)

914.21'2'04857 — London (City). *Guidebooks*
The **City** of London. — [New ed.]. — London : Burrow, [1976]. — 199,[2]p(2 fold) : ill(some col), col coat of arms, col map ; 19x25cm.
Bibl.: p.87-89. — Index.
ISBN 0-85026-642-4 Pbk : Unpriced
(B77-05113)

914.21'32 — Collegiate churches. *London. Westminster (London Borough). Westminster Abbey. Guidebooks*
Baker, John Austin. The living splendour of Westminster Abbey / [by] John Austin Baker. — Norwich : Jarrold for the Dean and Chapter of Westminster, 1977. — 64p : col ill, col ports ; 27cm. — ([Jarrold Brancaster book series])
English text, English, French and German captions.
ISBN 0-85306-704-x : Unpriced
(B77-34279)

914.21'32 — Collegiate churches. *London. Westminster (London Borough). Westminster Abbey. Guidebooks. French texts*
Fox, Adam. L'Abbaye de Westminster / [par Adam Fox] ; [traduit de l'anglais]. — London : Pitkin Pictorials, 1977. — 24,[1]p : col ill, plan ; 23cm. — (Livres 'Pride of Britain')
Translation of: 'The pictorial history of Westminster Abbey'. New ed. 1971.
ISBN 0-85372-221-8 Pbk : £0.50
(B77-25994)

914.21'32 — Collegiate churches. *London. Westminster (London Borough). Westminster Abbey. Guidebooks. German texts*
Fox, Adam. Die Westminster-Abtei / [von Adam Fox] ; [aus dem Englischen übersetzt]. — London : Pitkin Pictorials, 1977. — 24,[1]p : col ill, plan ; 23cm. — ('Pride of Britain' Bücher)
Translation of: 'The pictorial history of Westminster Abbey'. New ed. 1971.
ISBN 0-85372-224-2 Sd : £0.50
(B77-25995)

914.21'32 — Collegiate churches. *London. Westminster (London Borough). Westminster Abbey. Guidebooks. Italian texts*
Fox, Adam. L'Abbazia di Westminster / [di Adam Fox] ; [tradotto dall' inglese]. — London : Pitkin Pictorials, 1977. — 24,[1]p : col ill, plan ; 23cm. — (Libretti 'Pride of Britain')
Translation of: 'The pictorial history of Westminster Abbey'. New ed. 1971.
ISBN 0-85372-222-6 Sd : £0.50
(B77-25996)

914.21'32 — Collegiate churches. *London. Westminster (London Borough). Westminster Abbey. Guidebooks. Spanish texts*
Fox, Adam. La Abadia de Westminster / [por Adam Fox] ; [traducido del inglés]. — London : Pitkin Pictorials, 1977. — 24,[1]p : col ill, plan ; 23cm. — (Libros 'Pride of Britain')
Translation of: 'The pictorial history of Westminster Abbey'. New ed. 1971.
ISBN 0-85372-223-4 Sd : £0.50
(B77-29041)

914.21'32 — Government buildings. *London. Westminster (London Borough). Palace of Westminster. Guidebooks*
Mackenzie, Kenneth Roderick. The Palace of Westminster / [by] Kenneth Mackenzie. — Norwich : Jarrold and Sons, 1977. — [64]p : ill(chiefly col), ports(some col) ; 27cm. — ([Jarrold Brancaster book series])
£2.50
(B77-30838)

914.21'34'04857 — London. Kensington and Chelsea (London Borough). *Guidebooks*
The **Royal** Borough of Kensington and Chelsea, official guide. — [London] : Burrow.
1977-1978. — [1977]. — 72p : ill, col coat of arms, map, port ; 21cm.
Pbk : Unpriced
(B77-25272)

914.21'42 — London. Camden (London Borough). Hampstead & Highgate. *Guidebooks*
Norrie, Ian. Hampstead, Highgate Village and Kenwood : a short guide, with suggested walks / by Ian Norrie ; drawings by Ronald Saxby, photographs by Philip Greenall. — [London] ([6A Hampstead High St., N.W.3]) : High Hill Press, 1977. — 65p : ill, map ; 19x24cm.
'... based on "Hampstead : a short guide" and "Highgate and Kenwood : a short guide"' - title page verso. — Bibl.: p.65.
ISBN 0-900462-14-0 Sd : £1.20
(B77-16109)

914.21'42'04857 — London. Camden (London Borough). *Guidebooks*
London Borough of Camden. — [New ed.]. — London : Burrow, [1976]. — 88p : ill, map ; 25cm.
Index.
ISBN 0-85026-631-9 Pbk : Unpriced
(B77-01047)

London Borough of Camden. — [New ed.]. — London : Burrow, [1977]. — 88p : ill, map ; 25cm.
ISBN 0-85026-645-9 Pbk : Unpriced
(B77-10643)

914.21'43'04857 — London. Islington (London Borough). *Guidebooks*
Islington, the London Borough official guide. — [New ed.]. — London : Burrow, [1977]. — 100p : ill, col coat of arms, map, ports ; 25cm.
Bibl.: p.18.
Pbk : Unpriced
(B77-26674)

914.21'5 — Castles. *London. Tower Hamlets (London Borough). Tower of London. Guidebooks. French texts*
Hedley, Olwen. La Tour de Londres de sa Majesté / [texte par Olwen Hedley] ; [traduit de l'anglais]. — London : Pitkin Pictorials, 1977. — 24,[1]p : col ill, plan ; 23cm. — (Livres 'Pride of Britain')
Translation of: 'Her Majesty's Tower of London'. 1976. — Includes: 'Les armes et armures' / par A.R. Dufty.
ISBN 0-85372-225-0 Sd : £0.50
(B77-25273)

914.21'5 — Castles. *London. Tower Hamlets (London Borough). Tower of London. Guidebooks. German texts*
Hedley, Oliver. Der königliche Tower von London / [von Oliver Hedley] ; [aus dem Englischen übersetzt]. — London : Pitkin Pictorials, 1977. — 24,[1]p : col ill, plan ; 23cm. — ('Pride of Britain' Bücher)
Translation of: 'Her Majesty's Tower of London'. 1976. — Includes 'Die Waffen und Rüstungun' / von A.R. Duffy.
ISBN 0-85372-226-9 Sd : £0.50
(B77-26675)

914.21'62'04857 — London. Greenwich (London Borough). *Guidebooks*
London Borough of Greenwich official guide. — [New ed.]. — London : Burrow, [1977]. — 88p : ill(some col), col coat of arms, map ; 25cm.
ISBN 0-85026-647-5 Pbk : Unpriced
(B77-10030)

914.21'64 — London. Southwark (London Borough). Herne Hill. *Guidebooks*
Herne Hill record. — [Sutton] ([74 Mulgrave Rd, Sutton, Surrey]) : J. Wright.
2. — 1976. — [2],24,[1]p : ill, facsim ; 26cm.
ISBN 0-905137-04-3 Sd : £0.35
ISSN 0308-3292
Also classified at 914.21'65
(B77-01048)

914.21'65 — London. Lambeth (London Borough). Herne Hill. *Guidebooks*
Herne Hill record. — [Sutton] ([74 Mulgrave Rd, Sutton, Surrey]) : J. Wright.
2. — 1976. — [2],24,[1]p : ill, facsim ; 26cm.
ISBN 0-905137-04-3 Sd : £0.35
ISSN 0308-3292
Primary classification 914.21'64
(B77-01048)

914.21'73 — Parks. *London. Redbridge (London Borough). Wanstead Park. Guidebooks*
Addison, *Sir* William, *b.1905*. Wanstead Park / [by] William Addison. — [London] : Corporation of London, [1977?]. — 24p : ill(some col), col map, plan ; 22cm.
Originally published: 1973.
Sd : £0.25
(B77-32300)

914.21'78'04857 — London. Bromley (London Borough). *Walkers' guides*
Daniell, Philip A. Country walks around Bromley, Downe, Biggin Hill / by Philip A. Daniell ; jacket design and illustrations by Kathleen Freeth. — Ilford (884 Eastern Ave., Ilford, Essex) : Circle Publications, 1976. — 47p : ill, maps ; 16cm.
ISBN 0-9502012-2-7 Pbk : £0.50
(B77-22980)

914.21'83 — London. Hillingdon (London Borough). Northwood & Ruislip. *Directories*
Kemp's official directory of the districts of Ruislip, Northwood and Eastcote in the London Borough of Hillingdon, also includes Moor Park. — London : Kemps.
1976. — [1976]. — 2-188,[2]p(2 fold) : ill, map ; 21cm.
ISBN 0-905255-09-7 Pbk : £0.80
(B77-13954)

914.21'83 — London. Hillingdon (London Borough). Uxbridge. *Directories*
Kemp's Uxbridge & district local directory : incorporating Cowley, Hillingdon and Ickenham. — London : Kemp's.
1977 : [23rd ed.]. — 1977. — 156p,fold plate : map ; 21cm.
Cover title: Kemp's local directory of Uxbridge and district.
ISBN 0-905255-12-7 Pbk : £0.80
(B77-13955)

914.21'86 — Railways. Accidents. *London. Harrow (London Borough), 1952*
Coombs, L F E. The Harrow railway disaster 1952 : twenty-five years / [by] L.F.E. Coombs. — Newton Abbot [etc.] : David and Charles, 1977. — 164p : ill, maps ; 23cm.
Bibl.: p.156-158. — Index.
ISBN 0-7153-7409-5 : £4.95
(B77-29801)

914.21'88'04857 — London. Haringey (London Borough). *Guidebooks*
Haringey official guide. — [New ed.]. — London : Burrow, [1976]. — 40p : ill ; 25cm.
Previous control number B7700499.
ISBN 0-85026-641-6 Sd : Unpriced
(B77-00499)

914.21'93 — London. Merton (London Borough). Merton Park. *Walkers' guides*
Merton Park conservation area / illustrations by Peter Harris. — [London] ([c/o E.F. Waugh, 24 Mostyn Rd, S.W.19]) : Merton Town Trails Association, 1976. — Folder ([6]p) : ill, map ; 21x10cm. — (Merton town trails ; 3)
£0.05
(B77-01898)

914.21'94'04857 — London. Kingston upon Thames (London Borough). *Guidebooks*
Royal Borough of Kingston upon Thames official guide. — [New ed.]. — Carshalton : Home Publishing Co., [1976]. — 116p : ill, col coat of arms, map, ports ; 21cm.
ISBN 0-7174-0728-4 Pbk : Unpriced
(B77-09389)

914.22 — Central Southern England. *Guidebooks*
Elliott, Ronald London. Where to go, what to do in the South : 500 places to visit in the wet and dry / by R.L. & M.J. Elliott. — 5th revised ed. — Tavistock (Merchants House, Barley Market St., Tavistock, Devon) : Heritage Publications ; [London] : New English Library, 1977. — 175p : ill, maps ; 18cm.
Previous ed.: 1976. — Index.
ISBN 0-903975-46-7 Pbk : £0.60
(B77-15020)

914.22 — Long-distance footpaths. *Southern England. Ridgeway. Walkers' guides*
Jennett, Seán. The Ridgeway Path / [by] Seán Jennett. — London : H.M.S.O. for the Countryside Commission, 1976. — viii,112p : ill(some col), col maps ; 21cm. — (Long-distance footpath guides ; no.6)
'Prepared for the Countryside Commission by the Central Office of Information' - title page verso. — Bibl.: p.109.
ISBN 0-11-700743-9 Pbk : £2.50
(B77-12198)

914.22'04'8570242 — South-east England. *Guidebooks. For Christians*
Pepin, David. Pilgrims guide to the South East / by David Pepin. — London [etc.] : Mowbrays, 1977. — 64p : ill, maps, ports ; 21cm.
Bibl. — Index.
ISBN 0-264-66388-8 Pbk : £0.95
(B77-25274)

914.22'1 — Surrey. Countryside adjacent to Wey and Arun Canal. *Walkers' guides*
Mackintosh, Aeneas. Wey-South Path : from Guildford to the South Downs / by Aeneas Mackintosh. — [Horsham] ([Hon. Treasurer, 12 Station Rd, Horsham, W. Sussex RH13 5EY]) : Wey and Arun Canal Trust, [1976]. — [20]p : ill, maps ; 21cm.
ISBN 0-9505475-0-6 Sd : £0.25
Also classified at 914.22'6
(B77-07718)

914.22'1'04857 — Surrey. *Guidebooks*
Watkin, Bruce. Surrey / by Bruce Watkin. — London : Faber, 1977. — 192p,plate : ill, col map ; 24cm. — (A Shell guide)
Ill. on lining papers. — Index.
ISBN 0-571-09609-3 : £3.75
(B77-12779)

914.22'12'04857 — Surrey. Spelthorne (District). *Guidebooks*
The **Borough** of Spelthorne official guide. — [New ed.]. — Carshalton : Home Publishing Co., [1977]. — 80,[2]p(2 fold) : ill(incl 1 col), col coat of arms, maps ; 21cm.
Pbk : £0.72
(B77-31608)

914.22'142'04857 — Surrey. Woking. *Guidebooks*
Woking, the official guide and directory of services. — London : G.W. May, [1976]. — 136p,[2]fold p of plates : ill, coat of arms, maps ; 25cm.
Index.
ISBN 0-904455-44-0 Pbk : £0.35
(B77-01049)

914.22'15'04857 — Surrey. Epsom and Ewell (District). *Guidebooks*
Epsom & Ewell Borough official guide. — Gloucester : British Publishing Co., [1977]. — 56,[2]p(2 fold) : ill(some col), maps(1 col) ; 21cm.
ISBN 0-7140-1502-4 Sd : £0.30
(B77-17818)

914.22'3'04857 — Kent. *Guidebooks*
Kent leisure guide. — London : Pyramid Press, [1976]. — 56p : ill ; 21cm.
ISBN 0-902824-31-7 Sd : Unpriced
(B77-01899)

914.22'3'04857 — Parks. *Kent. Guidebooks*
White, John Talbot. The parklands of Kent / [by] John Talbot White. — Sheerness (31 Broadway, Sheerness, Kent) : A.J. Cassell, [1976]. — 176p : ill, maps ; 19cm.
Bibl.: p.174-176.
ISBN 0-903253-06-2 Pbk : £1.30
(B77-00500)

914.22'315'04857 — Kent. Gravesham (District). *Guidebooks*
Gravesham Borough official handbook. — [New ed.]. — Carshalton : Home Publishing Co., [1977]. — 52p : ill, map ; 21cm.
Pbk : £0.30
(B77-18445)

914.22'352 — Shipwrecks. *Kent. Coastal waters. Goodwin Sands, 1298-1975*
Larn, Richard. Goodwin Sands shipwrecks / [by] Richard Larn. — Newton Abbot [etc.] : David and Charles, 1977. — 176p : ill, charts, maps ; 23cm.
Bibl.: p.162-164. — Index.
ISBN 0-7153-7202-5 : £4.50
(B77-25275)

914.22'36 — Kent. Westerham. *Guidebooks*
Westerham and Crockham Hill, Kent, official guide. — [New ed.]. — Carshalton : Forward Publicity, [1977]. — 20,[3]p(2 fold) : ill, 2 maps(1 col) ; 19cm.
Sd : £0.24
(B77-31609)

914.22'372 — Kent. Borough Green & Wrotham. *Guidebooks*
Wrotham, Borough Green and district official guide. — [New ed.]. — Carshalton : Forward Publicity, [1977]. — 24,[1]p : ill, map ; 19cm.
ISBN 0-7174-0737-3 Sd : Unpriced
(B77-11470)

914.22'38 — Kent. Southborough. *Guidebooks*
Southborough official guide. — [New ed.]. — London : Burrow, [1977]. — 24p : ill, map ; 19cm.
Sd : £0.40
(B77-34280)

914.22'5 — Footpaths. *East & West Sussex. Forest Way. Walkers' guides*
East Sussex *(County). Planning Department.* Forest Way / [East Sussex County Planning Department]. — Lewes (Southover House, Southover Rd, Lewes) : The Department, [1976]. — Folder ([16]p) : ill, col map ; 19cm.
ISBN 0-900348-48-8 : £0.15
(B77-02663)

914.22'5 — Heritage coasts. *East Sussex. Coastal regions. Sussex Heritage Coast. Guidebooks*
East Sussex *(County). Council.* The Sussex heritage coast : a pictorial guide and map to the paths and places of interest / [East Sussex County Council]. — [Lewes] ([County Hall, St Anne's Cres., Lewes, E. Sussex BN7 1SW]) : The Council, 1977. — Sheet(13p) : ill, col maps ; 69x45cm fold to 23x12cm.
£0.50
(B77-19088)

914.22'5 — Windmills. *East & West Sussex. Guidebooks*
Austen, Brian H. Seven Sussex windmills / [by] Brian H. Austen. — Special souvenir ed. — [Hove] ([22 St Leonards Gardens, Hove, E. Sussex BN3 4QB]) : [The author], 1977. — [1], 26 leaves : ill, maps ; 26cm.
Bibl.: p.25.
Sd : £0.50
(B77-26676)

914.22'5'04857 — Buildings of historical importance. *East & West Sussex. Guidebooks*
Holmes, Fiona. Sussex, castles, gardens & ancient houses / by F. Holmes. — St Ives, Cornwall : Pike, 1976. — 32p : ill, map ; 21cm. — (Viewing Sussex series)
ISBN 0-85932-166-5 Sd : £0.50
(B77-34281)

914.22'5'04857 — East Sussex. *Walkers' guides*
Eastbourne Rambling Club. On foot in East Sussex / Eastbourne Rambling Club. — 6th ed. — Eastbourne (c/o H. Comber, 28 Kinfauns Ave., Eastbourne, [E. Sussex] BN22 8SS) : The Club, 1977. — [1],56,[2]p(2 fold) : ill, maps ; 19cm.
Previous ed.: 1975.
Sd : £0.50
(B77-17174)

914.22'51 — East Sussex. Pevensey. *Guidebooks*
Pevensey and Pevensey Bay official guide. — [New ed.]. — Carshalton : Forward Publicity, [1977]. — 24,[1]p : ill, 2 maps ; 19cm.
Sd : £0.24
(B77-19089)

914.22'51 — East Sussex. Polegate. *Guidebooks*
Polegate, Sussex, official guide. — [New ed.]. — Carshalton : Forward Publicity, [1977]. — 20, [3]p(2 fold) : ill, map ; 19cm.
Sd : Unpriced
(B77-25276)

914.22'52 — Buildings of historical importance. *East Sussex. Battle. Walkers' guides*
East Sussex *(County). Council.* Battle town and abbey walk / [East Sussex County Council] ; [prepared by Michael Barnard]. — [Lewes] ([County Hall, St Anne's Cres., Lewes, E. Sussex BN7 1SW]) : The Council, 1977. — [2], 14p : ill, map ; 22x30cm.
ISBN 0-900348-55-0 Sd : £0.25
(B77-15606)

914.22'52 — East Sussex. Rye. *Guidebooks*
Saville, Malcolm. Portrait of Rye : with some sketches of places worth visiting within easy reach of the ancient town / by Malcolm Saville ; with woodcuts by Michael Renton ; with a new poem by Patric Dickinson. — East Grinstead (5 West St., East Grinstead, Sussex) : Henry Goulden Ltd, 1976. — 93p : ill ; 22cm.
Bibl.: p.91. — Index.
ISBN 0-904822-05-2 : £5.00
ISBN 0-904822-06-0 Pbk : £3.50
(B77-04471)

914.22'56 — Royal residences. *East Sussex. Brighton. Royal Pavilion, Art Gallery and Museums, Brighton. Guidebooks*
Royal Pavilion, Art Gallery and Museums, Brighton. Illustrated guide and introduction to the collections in the Art Gallery and Museum, Brighton / [photography by John Barrow]. — [Brighton] ([Royal Pavilion, Art Gallery and Museums, Brighton BN1 1UE]) : Brighton Borough Council Amenities Committee, 1975. — [24]p,[4]p of plates : ill(some col), ports(1 col) ; 24cm.
Sd : £0.50
Also classified at 708'.22'56
(B77-06965)

Royal Pavilion, Art Gallery and Museums, Brighton. The Royal Pavilion, Brighton / [Royal Pavilion, Museums and Art Gallery ; photographs by Eric de Maré et al. ; text by David Higginbottom in consultation with the Director]. — Brighton (c/o The Royal Pavilion, Museums and Art Gallery, Brighton BN1 1UE) : Amenities Committee of the Brighton Borough Council, [1977]. — [55]p : ill(chiefly col), facsims, ports ; 30cm.
Sd : £0.50
(B77-24588)

914.22'56 — Royal residences. *East Sussex. Brighton. Royal Pavilion, Art Gallery and Museums, Brighton. Guidebooks. French texts*
Royal Pavilion, Art Gallery and Museums, Brighton. Le Pavillon Royal de Brighton / [Royal Pavilion, Art Gallery and Museums, Brighton] ; [photographies par Eric de Maré, Louis Klemantaski, John Barrow ; texte de David Higginbottom en collaboration avec le Directeur du Pavillon]. — [Brighton] ([The Royal Pavilion, Art Gallery and Museums, Brighton BN1 1UE]) : Brighton Borough Council Amenities Committee, [1976]. — [55] p : ill(chiefly col), facsims, ports ; 30cm.
Also available in English without catalogue pages.
ISBN 0-9502372-4-8 Sd : £0.45
Also classified at 708'.22'56
(B77-01900)

914.22'57 — East Sussex. Seaford. *Guidebooks*
Seaford. — [New ed.]. — Gloucester : British Publishing Co., [1977]. — 64,[2]p(2 fold) : ill, 2 maps ; 12x19cm.
Bibl.: p.39.
ISBN 0-7140-1631-4 Sd : £0.20
(B77-25997)

914.22'6 — West Sussex. Countryside adjacent to Wey and Arun Canal. *Walkers' guides*
Mackintosh, Aeneas. Wey-South Path : from Guildford to the South Downs / by Aeneas Mackintosh. — [Horsham] ([Hon. Treasurer, 12 Station Rd, Horsham, W. Sussex RH13 5EY]) : Wey and Arun Canal Trust, [1976]. — [20]p : ill, maps ; 21cm.
ISBN 0-9505475-0-6 Sd : £0.25
Primary classification 914.22'1
(B77-07718)

914.22'62 — West Sussex. Petworth region. *Guidebooks*
Petworth parish and surrounding district, Sussex, official guide. — [New ed.]. — Carshalton : Forward Publicity, [1977]. — 34,[2]p (2 fold) : ill, maps ; 19cm.
ISBN 0-7174-0740-3 Sd : Unpriced
(B77-15021)

914.22'65 — West Sussex. Burgess Hill. *Guidebooks*
Burgess Hill official guide. — [New ed.]. — Carshalton : Home Publishing Co., [1977]. — 28p,[2]fold p of plates : ill, col coat of arms, map ; 21cm.
Colophon has publisher: Forward Publicity.
ISBN 0-7174-0734-9 Sd : Unpriced
(B77-09390)

914.22'67 — West Sussex. East Preston. *Guidebooks*
East Preston, including Angmering on Sea Estate, official guide. — 5th ed. — Carshalton : Forward Publicity, [1977]. — 16,[4]p(2 fold) : ill, map ; 19cm.
ISBN 0-7174-0735-7 Sd : Unpriced
(B77-12199)

914.22'67 — West Sussex. Rustington. *Guidebooks*
Rustington, West Sussex, official guide. — [New ed.]. — Carshalton : Forward Publicity, [1977]. — 30p : ill ; 21cm.
ISBN 0-7174-0726-8 Sd : Unpriced
(B77-10644)

914.22'732 — Hampshire. Romsey. *Guidebooks*
The **town** of Romsey, Hampshire, illustrated official guide. — [New ed.]. — Gloucester : British Publishing Co., [1977]. — 48,[2]p(2 fold) : ill, map, ports ; 19cm.
ISBN 0-7140-1590-3 Sd : £0.30
(B77-20774)

914.22'735 — Cathedrals. *Hampshire. Winchester. Winchester Cathedral. Guidebooks*
Sykes, Norman. Winchester Cathedral / [by N. Sykes]. — [New ed.]. — London : Pitkin Pictorials, 1976. — [1],25p : col ill, plan ; 23cm. — (Pride of Britain books)
Previous ed.: 1971.
ISBN 0-85372-216-1 Sd : £0.40
(B77-17175)

914.22'735 — Cathedrals. *Hampshire. Winchester. Winchester Cathedral. Guidebooks. French texts*
Sykes, Norman. La Cathédrale de Winchester / [par N. Sykes] ; [traduit de l'anglais]. — London : Pitkin Pictorials, 1976. — [1],25p : col ill, plan ; 23cm. — (Livres 'Pride of Britain')
Translation of: 'Winchester Cathedral'. New ed. 1976.
ISBN 0-85372-214-5 Sd : £0.50
(B77-17176)

914.22'735 — Cathedrals. *Hampshire. Winchester. Winchester Cathedral. Guidebooks. German texts*
Sykes, Norman. Die Kathedral von Winchester / [von N. Sykes] ; [aus den Englischen übersetzt]. — London : Pitkin Pictorials, 1976. — [1],25p : col ill, plan ; 23cm. — ('Pride of Britain' Bücher)
Translation of: 'Winchester Cathedral'. New ed. 1976.
ISBN 0-85372-215-3 Sd : £0.50
(B77-17177)

914.22'74'04857 — Hampshire. East Hampshire (District). *Guidebooks*
East Hampshire district official guide. — Carshalton : Home Publishing Co., [1976]. — 52p : ill, map ; 21cm.
ISBN 0-7174-0718-7 Sd : Unpriced
(B77-06966)

914.22'75 — Castles. *Hampshire. New Forest (District). Hurst Castle. Guidebooks*
Craster, Oswin Edmund. Hurst Castle, Hampshire / [by] O.E. Craster. — [London] : Department of the Environment, 1976. — 8p : plan ; 22cm. — (Ancient monuments and historic buildings)
Originally published: 1949.
Sd : £0.04
(B77-17178)

914.22'75 — Hampshire. Totton & Eling. *Guidebooks*
Totton and Eling official town guide and information book. — Gloucester : British Publishing Co., [1977]. — 28,[2]p(2 fold) : ill, 2 maps ; 21cm.
ISBN 0-7140-1552-0 Sd : £0.25
(B77-26677)

914.22'75'04857 — Hampshire. New Forest. *Walkers' guides*
Evening, Peter. Walks in the New Forest / by Peter Evening. — [Dorchester] ([County Hall, Dorchester, Dorset DT1 1XJ]) : Dorset County Council, Education Committee.
Part 3 : The southern area. — 1976. — [2], 50p : ill, maps ; 21cm.
Cover title: New Forest walks.
ISBN 0-85216-121-2 Sd : Unpriced
(B77-03822)

Hatts, Leigh. Country walks around the New Forest / by Leigh Hatts ; illustrations by Kenneth Hatts. — Ilford (884 Eastern Ave., Ilford, Essex) : Circle Publications, 1976. — 55p : ill, maps ; 15cm.
ISBN 0-9502012-3-5 Pbk : £0.50
(B77-21576)

914.22'75'04857 — Hampshire. New Forest. Description & travel
Vesey-Fitzgerald, Brian. Portrait of the New Forest / [by] Brian Vesey-Fitzgerald. — 2nd ed. — London : Hale, 1977. — 208p,[24]p of plates : ill, map ; 23cm. — ([Portrait books])
Previous ed.: 1966. — Index.
ISBN 0-7091-6400-9 : £3.95
(B77-29802)

914.22'75'04857 — Hampshire. New Forest (District). *Guidebooks*
New Forest District Council official guide. — Gloucester : British Publishing Co., [1977]. — 152p,[2]fold p of plates : ill(some col), maps(1 col) ; 21cm.
ISBN 0-7140-1599-7 Pbk : £0.60
(B77-29042)

914.22'792'04857 — Hampshire. Portsmouth. *Guidebooks*
City of Portsmouth official handbook. — Carshalton : Home Publishing Co., [1977]. — 96p : ill(some col), map ; 24cm.
Pbk : Unpriced
(B77-26678)

914.22'8'04857 — Isle of Wight. Description & travel
Sibley, Patricia. Discovering the Isle of Wight / [by] Patricia Sibley. — London : Hale, 1977. — 207p,[24]p of plates : ill, map ; 23cm.
Index.
ISBN 0-7091-6063-1 : £4.50
(B77-29803)

914.22'82 — Castles. *Isle of Wight. Carisbrooke. Carisbrooke Castle. Guidebooks*
Great Britain. *Department of the Environment.* Carisbrooke Castle, Isle of Wight / [Department of the Environment]. — [London] : The Department, [1977]. — Folder ([4]p) : col ill, plan ; 16cm.
£0.04
(B77-23826)

914.22'82 — Country houses. *Isle of Wight. East Cowes. Osborne House. Visits by Victoria, Queen of Great Britain, 1831-1901*
Florance, Arnold. Queen Victoria at Osborne / by Arnold Florance ; foreword by Earl Mountbatten. — [Newport, Isle of Wight] ([60 Clatterford Rd, Carisbrooke, Newport, Isle of Wight]) : [The author], 1977. — viii,90p : ill, facsims, geneal table, map, ports ; 21cm.
Bibl.: p.88-89.
Pbk : Unpriced
(B77-33511)

914.22'9'04857 — Berkshire. Description & travel
Higham, Roger. Berkshire and the Vale of White Horse / [by] Roger Higham. — London : Batsford, 1977. — 182p : ill, map ; 23cm.
Index.
ISBN 0-7134-0681-x : £4.50
Also classified at 914.25'76'04857
(B77-25277)

914.22'93'04857 — Berkshire. Reading. *Walkers' guides*
Reading Museum and Art Gallery. Reading, walk-about guide / [Reading Museum and Art Gallery]. — Reading (Blagrave St., Reading [Berks.]) : The Museum and Art Gallery, [1976]. — Fold sheet : ill, col map ; 30x42cm fold to 30x11cm.
£0.05
(B77-20775)

914.22'96 — Castles. *Berkshire. Windsor. Windsor Castle. Guidebooks*
The **official** guide to Windsor Castle. — 23rd ed. — Windsor ([Windsor Castle, Windsor, Berks.]) : Superintendent of the Castle, 1977. — 48,[1]p : ill, plan ; 22cm.
Previous ed.: 1973. — Bibl.: (1p.).
Sd : £0.15
(B77-29804)

914.22'96 — Castles. *Berkshire. Windsor. Windsor Castle. Precincts. Guidebooks*
Mackworth-Young, *Sir* **Robin.** Walk-round guide to the precincts of Windsor Castle / [by] Sir Robin Mackworth-Young. — London : Pitkin Pictorials, 1977. — [2],25p(2 fold) : col ill, plan ; 18cm.
ISBN 0-85372-220-x Sd : Unpriced
(B77-23827)

914.22'96 — Castles. Collegiate churches. *Berkshire. Windsor. Windsor Castle. St George's Chapel. Guidebooks*
Blackburne, Harry William. The romance of St George's Chapel, Windsor Castle / by Harry Blackburne and Maurice Bond. — 10th ed. (revised). — Windsor (2 Victoria St., Windsor) : Oxley and Son (Windsor) Ltd for the Society of the Friends of St George's Chapel, 1976. — [2],86,[1]p : ill, plan, ports ; 22cm.
Previous ed.: 1973. — Bibl.: p.84-86.
ISBN 0-902187-19-8 Sd : Unpriced
(B77-11471)

914.22'96'04857 — Berkshire. Windsor and Maidenhead (District). *Guidebooks*
Windsor and Maidenhead official guide. — Carshalton : Home Publishing Co., [1977]. — 136p : ill(some col), maps ; 21cm.
Pbk : Unpriced
(B77-19090)

914.22'97'04857 — Berkshire. Slough. *Guidebooks*
The **Borough** of Slough official guide. — [9th ed.]. — London : Burrow, [1976]. — 104,[2]p(2 fold) : ill, coat of arms, map ; 21cm.
ISBN 0-85026-628-9 Pbk : Unpriced
(B77-01050)

914.23 — Antiquities associated with Arthur, King. *South-west England. Guidebooks. For motoring*
West Country Tourist Board. King Arthur's country / West Country Tourist Board. — Exeter (Trinity Court, Southernhay East, Exeter EX1 1QS) : The Board, [1976]. — Folder([8]p) : ill, col map ; 21cm.
ISBN 0-903774-17-8 : Unpriced
(B77-04472)

914.23 — South-west England. Geographical features. *Secondary school texts*
Waterhouse, Cyril. The South West / [by] Cyril Waterhouse. — London [etc.] : Hodder and Stoughton, 1977. — [4],44p : ill, maps ; 19x25cm. — (A regional geography of the British Isles)
ISBN 0-340-18795-6 Sd : £0.95
(B77-29805)

914.23'04'857 — Long-distance footpaths. *South-west England. Coastal regions. South-west Peninsula Coast Path. Walkers' guides*
Ward, Ken, *b.1926.* The South-west Peninsula Coast Path / by Ken Ward and John H.N. Mason. — London : Letts. — (Coastal walks)
In 3 vols.
1 : Minehead to St Ives. — 1977. — 96p : col maps ; 22x11cm.
Bibl.: p.96.
ISBN 0-85097-258-2 Pbk : £0.95
(B77-19091)

2 : St Ives to Plymouth. — 1977. — 96p : col maps ; 22x11cm.
Bibl.: p.96.
ISBN 0-85097-259-0 Pbk : £0.95
(B77-19092)

3 : Plymouth to Poole. — 1977. — 96p : col maps ; 22x11cm.
Bibl.: p.96.
ISBN 0-85097-260-4 Pbk : £0.95
(B77-19093)

914.23'04'857 — South-west England. *Guidebooks*
West country holidays : a comprehensive tourist guide for country and seaside. — Gloucester : British Publishing Co.
[1977]. — [1977]. — 152p : ill, maps ; 22cm.
ISBN 0-7140-1564-4 Pbk : £0.30
(B77-13416)

West Country Tourist Board. Touring England's West Country / West Country Tourist Board. — [New ed.]. — Exeter : The Board, [1977]. — 16p : col ill, col maps ; 21cm.
Previous ed.: 1975.
ISBN 0-903774-19-4 Sd : £0.15
(B77-15022)

914.23'12 — Wiltshire. Corsham. *Guidebooks*
Corsham, Wiltshire, the official guide. — Gloucester : British Publishing Co., [1977]. — 28,[2]p(2 fold) : ill, map ; 19cm.
ISBN 0-7140-1561-x Sd : £0.25
(B77-17819)

914.23'12'04857 — Wiltshire. North Wiltshire (District). *Guidebooks*
North Wiltshire district official guide. — Carshalton : Home Publishing Co., [1976]. — 104p(2 fold) : ill(1 col), maps ; 21cm.
ISBN 0-7174-0719-5 Pbk : £0.25
(B77-06366)

914.23'13'04857 — Wiltshire. Thamesdown (District). *Guidebooks*
Borough of Thamesdown official guide. — [New ed.]. — London : Burrow, [1977]. — 108p : ill(some col), col coat of arms ; 21cm.
ISBN 0-85026-651-3 Pbk : Unpriced
(B77-10645)

914.23'15 — Parish churches. *Wiltshire. Edington. Priory Church of St Mary, St Katharine and All Saints, Edington. Illustrations*
A **pictorial** guide to the Priory Church of St Mary, St Katharine & All Saints, Edington, near Westbury, Wilts. / [compiled by R.E.H. Dudley]. — 3rd ed. — [Westbury] ([Edington Vicarage, Westbury, Wilts.]) : [R.E.H. Dudley], 1976. — 23p : chiefly ill, map ; 32cm.
Previous ed.: 197-?.
Sd : £0.35
(B77-17820)

914.23'15 — Tithe barns. *Wiltshire. Bradford-on-Avon. Guidebooks*
Great Britain. *Department of the Environment.* The medieval tithe barn, Bradford-on-Avon, Wiltshire / Department of the Environment. — [London] : [The Department], 1977. — Folder (4p) : ill, plan ; 22cm. — (Ancient monuments and historic buildings)
£0.05
(B77-21577)

914.23'15'04857 — Wiltshire. West Wiltshire (District). *Guidebooks*
The **District** of West Wiltshire official guide. — Carshalton : Home Publishing Co., [1976]. — 92,[1]p : ill ; 21cm.
ISBN 0-7174-0731-4 Sd : Unpriced
(B77-09391)

914.23'19 — Cathedrals. *Wiltshire. Salisbury. Salisbury Cathedral. Guidebooks*
Smethurst, Arthur Frederick. Salisbury Cathedral / by the late A.F. Smethurst. — London : Pitkin Pictorials, 1976. — 24,[1]p : col ill, plan ; 23cm. — (Pitkin 'pride of Britain' books)
ISBN 0-85372-217-x Sd : £0.40
(B77-16654)

914.23'19 — Cathedrals. *Wiltshire. Salisbury. Salisbury Cathedral. Guidebooks. French texts*
Smethurst, Arthur Frederick. La Cathédrale de Salisbury / par A.F. Smethurst ; [traduit de l'anglais]. — London : Pitkin Pictorials, 1976. — 24,[1]p : col ill, plan ; 23cm. — (Pitkin 'pride of Britain' books)
Translation of: 'Salisbury Cathedral'. 1976.
ISBN 0-85372-212-9 Sd : £0.40
(B77-16655)

914.23'19 — Cathedrals. *Wiltshire. Salisbury. Salisbury Cathedral. Guidebooks. German texts*
Smethurst, Arthur Frederick. Die Kathedrale von Salisbury / [von] A.F. Smethurst ; [aus dem Englischen übersetzt]. — London : Pitkin Pictorials, 1976. — 24,[1]p : col ill, plan ; 23cm. — (Pitkin 'pride of Britain' books)
Translation of: 'Salisbury Cathedral'. 1976.
ISBN 0-85372-213-7 Sd : £0.40
(B77-16656)

914.23'19 — Wiltshire. Wilton. *Guidebooks*
Borough of Wilton official guide. — [New ed.]. — London : G.W. May for the Town Council, [1976]. — 44,[2]p(2 fold) : ill, facsim, maps ; 19cm.
ISBN 0-904455-46-7 Sd : £0.20
(B77-00501)

914.23'3 — Long-distance footpaths. *Dorset. Coastal regions. Dorset Coast Path. Walkers' guides*
Countryside Commission. Dorset Coast Path / [prepared by the Countryside Commission and the Central Office of Information]. — Cheltenham : The Commission, 1977. — Fold sheet : ill, col map ; 32x30cm fold to 21x10cm.
Unpriced
(B77-21578)

914.23'3'0014 — Dorset. Place names
Mills, Anthony David. The place-names of Dorset / by A.D. Mills. — Nottingham (School of English Studies, The University, Nottingham NG7 2RD) : English Place-Name Society.
In 5 vols.
Part 1 : The Isle of Purbeck, the Hundreds of Rowbarrow, Hasler, Winfrith, Culliford Tree, Bere Regis, Barrow, Puddletown, St George. — 1977. — xxxvii,384p : maps ; 23cm. — (English Place-Name Society. Publications ; vol.52)
Index.
ISBN 0-904889-02-5 : £8.50
(B77-27541)

914.23'3'04857 — Dorset. *Guidebooks*
Dorset, official guide to the county. — 11th ed. — Gloucester : British Publishing Co., 1977. — 112,[2]p(2 fold), ill(some col), col coat of arms, col map, ports ; 25cm.
ISBN 0-7140-1629-2 Pbk : £0.30
(B77-25278)

914.23'3'04857 — Dorset. Description & travel
Wightman, Ralph. Portrait of Dorset / by Ralph Wightman. — 3rd ed. / edited by Geoffrey N. Wright. — London : Hale, 1977. — 192p,[24]p of plates : ill, map ; 23cm. — ([Portrait books])
Previous ed.: 1968. — Index.
ISBN 0-7091-6446-7 : £4.50
(B77-28273)

914.23'3'04857 — Dorset. Description & travel. *For environmental studies*
From Bournemouth into Dorset : notes. — [Dorchester] ([County Hall, Dorchester, Dorset DT1 1XJ]) : Dorset County Council, Education Committee. — (Environmental studies)
Beaminster. — 1976. — [1],8p ; 21cm.
'Tutor: J.F. Parsons'.
Sd : £0.05
(B77-05757)

Forde Abbey. — 1976. — [1],8p ; 21cm.
'Tutor: J.F. Parsons'.
Sd : £0.05
(B77-05758)

914.23'32'04857 — Dorset. North Dorset (District). *Guidebooks*
North Dorset District, official guide. — Carshalton : Home Publishing Co., 1977. — 68,[1]p : ill, map ; 21cm.
Sd : Unpriced
(B77-25998)

914.23'34 — Dorset. Ferndown. *Guidebooks*
Ferndown and district official guide / photographs by S.F. James. — [New ed.]. — Gloucester : British Publishing Co., [1977]. — 40,[2]p(2 fold) : ill, map ; 19cm.
ISBN 0-7140-1525-3 Sd : £0.20
(B77-14460)

914.23'35'04857 — Dorset. Weymouth and Portland (District). *Guidebooks*
Weymouth and Portland. — St Ives, Cambs. : Photo Precision, [1977]. — [1],32p : chiefly col ill, 2 col maps ; 19cm.
Cover title: Colourmaster Weymouth and Portland.
ISBN 0-85933-169-5 Sd : £0.40
(B77-23828)

914.23'36 — Cottages. *Dorset. Purbeck (District). Clouds Hill. Guidebooks*
National Trust. Clouds Hill, Dorset / [National Trust]. — [New ed.]. — [London] : The Trust, 1977. — 22p,[4]p of plates : ill, port ; 22cm.
Previous ed.: 1970.
Sd : £0.35
Primary classification 940.4'15'0924
(B77-33528)

914.23'39'04857 — Buildings of historical importance. *Dorset. Christchurch. Walkers' guides*
Dear, G D. Christchurch walk / by G.D. Dear. — [Dorchester] ([County Hall, Dorchester, Dorset DT1 1XJ]) : Dorset County Council, Education Committee. — (Environmental studies)
No.1. — [1976]. — [3],9[i.e.11]p : ill, map ; 21cm.
Sd : Unpriced
(B77-05759)

914.23'4'04857 — Channel Islands. *Guidebooks*
Mead, Robin. Letts go to the Channel Islands and the Isles of Scilly / by Robin Mead and Lois Calvert. — London : Letts, 1977. — 94p : ill, 2 col maps ; 19cm. — (Letts guides)
ISBN 0-85097-223-x Pbk : £0.75
(B77-12200)

914.23'41'04857 — Jersey. *Guidebooks*
Know Jersey : a complete book of reference for everyone living in or interested in the beautiful Isle of Jersey. — St Helier (5 Burlington House, St Saviour's Rd, St Helier, Jersey) : Ashton and Denton Publishing Co. (C.I.) Ltd. 1977. — [1977]. — [2],294[i.e.290]p(6 fold) : ill, map ; 22cm.
Pbk : £0.40
(B77-29043)

914.23'41'04857 — Jersey. *Guidebooks. French texts*
Connaître Jersey : le guide pour faire aussi agréable que possible votre séjour à Jersey : Jersey, 'la Reine de la Manche'. — St Helier (5 Burlington House, St Saviour's Rd, St Helier, Jersey) : Ashton and Denton Publishing Co. (C.I.) Ltd.
1977. — [1977]. — 166[i.e.162]p(4 fold) : ill, 2 col maps ; 23cm.
Pbk : Unpriced
(B77-31610)

914.23'41'04857 — Jersey. *Guidebooks. French-English parallel texts*
Jersey. — Norwich : Jarrold and Sons, 1972. — [36]p : col ill, col map ; 25cm.
Parallel French and English text.
ISBN 0-85306-556-x Sd : Unpriced
(B77-19890)

914.23'41'04857 — Jersey. Description & travel
The island of Jersey. — Norwich : Jarrold and Sons, 1972. — [36]p : col ill, col map ; 25cm. — (Jarrold Cotman house book series)
Parallel French and English text.
ISBN 0-85306-710-4 Sd : £0.60
(B77-21579)

914.23'42'04857 — Guernsey. *Guidebooks*
Know Guernsey : including Alderney, Sark and Herm : a book of reference for everyone living in or interested in the Bailiwick of Guernsey. — [11th ed.]. — St Helier (5 Burlington House, St Saviour's Rd, St Helier, Jersey) : Ashton and Denton Publishing Co. (C.I.) Ltd, [1977?]. — 262[i.e.250]p(10 fold) : ill, maps ; 22cm.
Pbk : £0.40
(B77-30839)

914.23'47 — Cornwall. Calstock region. *Guidebooks*
The heart of the Tamar Valley, Calstock and Gunnislake official guide. — [New ed.]. — Gloucester : British Publishing Co., [1977]. — 48p : ill, maps ; 19cm.
ISBN 0-7140-1584-9 Sd : £0.20
(B77-11472)

914.23'5 — Devon. Plymouth region. *Guidebooks. For motoring*
Titchmarsh, Peter. Plymouth country by car / compiled [and written] by Peter and Helen Titchmarsh ; photography by Alan and Peter Titchmarsh. — Norwich : Jarrold and Sons, [1977]. — [1],32,[1]p : ill, maps(1 col) ; 21cm. — (The Jarrold 'White Horse' series)
Index.
ISBN 0-85306-692-2 Sd : £0.40
(B77-12201)

914.23'5 — Long-distance footpaths. *South Devon. Coastal regions. South Devon Coast Path. Walkers' guides*
Countryside Commission. South Devon coast path / [prepared by the Countryside Commission and the Central Office of Information]. — Cheltenham : The Commission, 1976. — Folder([10]p) : ill, col map ; 21x10cm.
ISBN 0-902590-54-5 : Unpriced
(B77-15607)

914.23'5 — Shipwrecks. *Devon. Coastal waters, to 1973*
Larn, Richard. Devon shipwrecks / [by] Richard Larn. — London [etc.] : Pan Books, 1977. — 223p,[16]p of plates : ill, maps ; 20cm.
Originally published: Newton Abbot : David and Charles, 1974. — Bibl.: p.188-190. — Index.
ISBN 0-330-25167-8 Pbk : £1.25
(B77-22250)

914.23'5 — South Devon. *Guidebooks*
Elliott, Ronald London. Sam's guide to South Devon / by R.L. Elliott & S.P. Farley. — [s.l.] : Elliott Publications ; Tavistock (Merchants House, Barley Market St., Tavistock, Devon) : Heritage Publications, 1977. — [1],30p : ill, maps ; 21cm.
Cover title: Follow Sam through - South Devon.
ISBN 0-903975-86-6 Sd : £0.30
(B77-29806)

914.23'5'04857 — Devon. *Walkers' guides*
Green, Christina. Walks in Devon / [by] Christina Green. — Bourne End : Spurbooks, 1977. — 64p : maps ; 19cm. — (A Spurbooks footpath guide)
ISBN 0-904978-12-5 Pbk : £0.75
(B77-30840)

914.23'5'04857 — Devon. Description & travel
St Leger-Gordon, Douglas. Devon / [by] D. St Leger-Gordon. — Revised ed. [i.e. 3rd ed.]. — London : Hale, 1977. — 192p,[24]p of plates : ill, map ; 19cm. — (Hale's topographical paperbacks)
This ed. originally published: as 'Portrait of Devon'. 1970. — Bibl.: p.8. — Index.
ISBN 0-7091-6224-3 Pbk : £1.50
(B77-15023)

Westlake, Roy J. View of Devon / described and photographed by Roy J. Westlake. — London : Hale, 1977. — 224p : ill, map ; 23cm.
Index.
ISBN 0-7091-6196-4 : £4.50
(B77-29807)

914.23'52'04857 — Devon. North Devon (District). Description & travel. *Personal observations*
Farson, Daniel. A window on the sea / [by] Daniel Farson ; illustrated by John Dyke. — London : Joseph, 1977. — 191,[1]p : ill, map(on lining papers) ; 23cm.
Ill. on lining papers.
ISBN 0-7181-1594-5 : £5.25
(B77-25999)

914.23'53 — Castles. *Devon. Lydford. Lydford Castle. Guidebooks*
Great Britain. *Department of the Environment.* Lydford Castle, Devonshire / Department of the Environment. — [London] : [The Department], 1977. — 8p : plan ; 22cm. — (Ancient monuments and historic buildings)
Originally published: 1947.
Sd : £0.04
(B77-17179)

914.23'53'04857 — Devon. Dartmoor. *Guidebooks*
Green, Christina. Dartmoor / by Christina Green ; illustrations by Eve. — Newton Abbot (Thatchers Cottage, Ideford, Newton Abbot [Devon]) : Ideford Publications, [1976]. — [2], 14p : ill ; 16cm. — (Evergreen project book ; no.1)
Bibl.: p.14.
ISBN 0-905006-03-8 Sd : £0.30
(B77-02664)

914.23'55 — Devon. Newton Abbot. *Guidebooks*
Official guide to Newton Abbot, the ideal centre. — [New ed.]. — Gloucester : British Publishing Co., [1976]. — 128p : ill(some col) ; 17cm.
ISBN 0-7140-1554-7 Pbk : £0.10
(B77-10646)

914.23'55'04857 — Devon. Teignbridge (District). *Guidebooks*
Teignbridge, from Dartmoor to the sea at Teignmouth and Dawlish, South Devon. — Norwich : Jarrold and Sons.
[1977]. — 1977. — [1],106p : ill(chiefly col), 2 col maps ; 23cm.
Cover title. — 'Street map of Teignmouth' (fold. sheet) ; and, 'Classified list of accommodation, 1977' / Teignbridge District Council (fold. sheet ([3]p.)) as inserts.
ISBN 0-9500068-7-4 Pbk : Unpriced
(B77-12202)

914.23'57 — Devon. Ottery St Mary. *Guidebooks*
Ottery St Mary *(Parish). Council.* Ottery St Mary, Devon, the official guide of the Town Council / by F. Burns, Town Clerk. — [New ed.]. — London : Burrow, [1976]. — 28p : ill, col map ; 19cm.
ISBN 0-85026-633-5 Sd : Unpriced
(B77-01051)

914.23'592 — Castles. *Devon. Totnes. Totnes Castle. Guidebooks*
Rigold, Stuart Eborall. Totnes Castle, Devon / [by] S.E. Rigold. — [London] : Department of the Environment, 1977. — 8p : plan ; 22cm. — (Ancient monuments and historic buildings)
Originally published: 1952.
Sd : £0.04
(B77-17180)

914.23'595 — Devon. Torquay. *Walker's guides*
A walk around and above Torquay Harbour. — [Torquay] ([1 Hesketh Cres., Torquay, Devon]) : Meadfoot-Wellswood and Area Residents' Association, [1976]. — 2v. (Folders([1],5p ;6p) : ill ; 21cm.
ISBN 0-905854-02-0 : £0.05
(B77-03823)

914.23'7'04857 — Cornwall. *Guidebooks*
Hammond, Reginald James William. Complete Cornwall / [by] Reginald J.W. Hammond and Kenneth E. Lowther. — London : Ward Lock, 1977. — 160p : ill, maps, plan ; 20cm. — (Red guide)
Index.
ISBN 0-7063-5355-2 : £3.95
(B77-22981)

914.23'7'04857 — Cornwall & Isles of Scilly. Description & travel. *Personal observations*
Duxbury, Ken. Lugworm island hopping / [by] Ken Duxbury ; with drawings, maps and photographs by the author. — London : Pelham, 1976. — 135p,[8]p of plates : ill, maps, ports ; 23cm.
ISBN 0-7207-0940-7 : £4.75
Primary classification 914.114'04'857
(B77-06963)

914.23'7'04857 — Long-distance footpaths. *Cornwall. Coastal regions. Cornwall Coast Path. Walkers' guides*
Pyatt, Edward Charles. Cornwall coast path : Section 3 of the South-west peninsula coast path / [by] Edward C. Pyatt. — London : H.M.S.O. for the Countryside Commission, 1976. — vii,112p : ill(some col), col maps ; 21cm. — (Long-distance footpath guide ; no.5)
Bibl.: p.112.
ISBN 0-11-700740-4 Pbk : £2.50
(B77-12780)

914.23'71 — Cornwall. Bodmin. *Guidebooks*
Munn, Pat. The Cornish capital : introducing Bodmin / [by] Pat Munn ; with a foreword by L.E. Long. — Revised ed. — Bodmin (45 Fore St., Bodmin, Cornwall PL31 2JA) : Bodmin Books Ltd, 1977. — [13],94p,[12]p of plates : ill, facsims, maps ; 21cm.
Previous ed.: 1973. — Bibl.: p.88-90. — Index.
ISBN 0-9501732-8-2 : Unpriced
ISBN 0-904534-02-2 Sd : £0.70
(B77-15024)

914.23'72 — Castles. *Cornwall. Lostwithiel. Restormel Castle. Guidebooks*
Radford, Courtenay Arthur Ralegh. Restormel Castle / [by] C.A. Ralegh Radford. — [London] : Department of the Environment, 1977. — 8p : plan ; 22cm. — (Ancient monuments and historic buildings)
Originally published: 1947.
Sd : £0.04
(B77-17181)

914.23'72 — Cornwall. Newquay. *Guidebooks*
Newquay. — Newquay (Municipal Offices, Marcus Hill, Newquay, Cornwall) : Borough of Restormel, Tourism and Publicity Department. [1977]. — [1976]. — 168p : ill(some col), col maps ; 23cm.
Fold. col. map as insert.
Pbk : Unpriced
(B77-07719)

914.23'76 — Shipwrecks. *Cornwall. Lizard Peninsula. Coastal waters, 1808-1898*
Tangye, Nigel. From rock and tempest / [by] Nigel Tangye. — London : Kimber, 1977. — 191p : map ; 23cm.
Bibl.: p.190-191.
ISBN 0-7183-0315-6 : £3.75
(B77-30841)

914.23'78 — Castles. *Cornwall. St Mawes. St Mawes Castle. Guidebooks*
Great Britain. *Department of the Environment.* St Mawes Castle, Cornwall / Department of the Environment. — [London] : [The Department], 1977. — Folder(6p) : plan ; 22cm. — (Ancient monuments and historic buildings)
Originally published: 1948.
£0.02
(B77-17182)

914.23'78 — Cornwall. Falmouth. *Guidebooks*
Trevena, Nigel. Falmouth mini guide / [text and drawings by Nigel Trevena]. — Falmouth (Minnie Place, Falmouth, Cornwall) : Bantam, [1977]. — [2],48,[1]p : ill, 2 maps ; 15cm.
Sd : Unpriced
(B77-20776)

914.23'78 — Cornwall. Penryn. *Guidebooks*
Penryn official guide. — [New ed.]. — Carshalton : Forward Publicity, [1977]. — 24, [1]p : ill, map ; 19cm.
Sd : £0.18
(B77-30842)

914.23'78 — Cornwall. Truro. *Guidebooks*
City of Truro and district official guide. — [New ed.]. — Gloucester : British Publishing Co., [1977]. — 136,[2]p(2 fold) : ill(some col), col coat of arms, maps(1 col) ; 19cm.
ISBN 0-7140-1610-1 Pbk : £0.50
(B77-18446)

914.23'79'04857 — Isles of Scilly. Description & travel
Grigson, Geoffrey. The Scilly Isles / [by] Geoffrey Grigson ; with illustrations by Fred Uhlman. — Revised re-set ed. — London : Duckworth, 1977. — 62p : ill, map ; 24cm.
Previous ed.: London : Elek, 1948. — Bibl.: p.59-62.
ISBN 0-7156-1103-8 : £4.95
ISBN 0-7156-1104-6 Pbk : £1.95
(B77-21580)

914.23'8'04857 — Somerset. *Guidebooks*
Somerset and parts of Avon. — St Ives, Huntingdon : Photo Precision Ltd, [1976]. — [2],32p : col ill, col map ; 19cm. — (Colourmaster tourist guide ; 5)
ISBN 0-85933-079-6 Sd : £0.40
Also classified at 914.23'9'04857
(B77-01901)

914.23'85'04857 — Somerset. Quantocks. *Guidebooks*
Lawrence, Berta. Discovering the Quantocks / [by] Berta Lawrence. — Revised [ed.]. — Aylesbury : Shire Publications, 1977. — 48p : ill, map ; 18cm. — (Discovering series ; no.195)
Previous ed.: 1974. — Bibl.: p.47. — Index.
ISBN 0-85263-364-5 Sd : £0.50
(B77-09392)

914.23'89 — Abbeys. *Somerset. Yeovil (District). Muchelney Abbey. Guidebooks*
Great Britain. *Department of the Environment.* Muchelney Abbey, Somerset / [Department of the Environment]. — [London] : The Department, 1977. — Folder ([4]p) : 2 col ill, 2 col plans ; 16cm. — (Ancient monuments and historic buildings)
£0.04
(B77-33513)

914.23'89 — Country houses. *Somerset. Yeovil. Montacute House. Guidebooks*
National Trust. Montacute House, Somerset / [National Trust]. — [New ed.]. — [London] : The Trust, 1977. — 48p : ill, geneal table, plans, ports ; 25cm.
Previous ed.: 1971. — Bibl.: p.44.
Sd : £0.50
(B77-32301)

914.23'89'04857 — Somerset. Yeovil (District). *Guidebooks*
Yeovil District Council official handbook. — Carshalton : Home Publishing Co., [1976]. — 136p : ill, maps ; 21cm.
ISBN 0-7174-0730-6 Pbk : Unpriced
(B77-09393)

914.23'9'04857 — Avon. *Guidebooks*
Somerset and parts of Avon. — St Ives, Huntingdon : Photo Precision Ltd, [1976]. — [2],32p : col ill, col map ; 19cm. — (Colourmaster tourist guide ; 5)
ISBN 0-85933-079-6 Sd : £0.40
Primary classification 914.23'8'04857
(B77-01901)

914.23'93 — Cathedrals. *Avon. Bristol. Bristol Cathedral. Guidebooks*
Harrison, Douglas Ernest William. A walk round Bristol Cathedral : a guide to the main points of interest ... / written by the late D.E.W. Harrison. — [Bristol] ([The Cathedral, Bristol]) : Friends of Bristol Cathedral, 1976. — [4],18,[1]p(2fold) : ill, col plan ; 19cm.
Originally published: 196-?.
Sd : £0.15
(B77-17821)

914.23'93 — Town houses. *Avon. Bristol. Georgian House. Guidebooks*
Georgian House. The Georgian House guide book. — [Bristol] ([Queen's Rd, Bristol BS8 1RL]) : City of Bristol Museum and Art Gallery, [1976]. — [1],20p : ill, coat of arms ; 22cm.
Bibl.: p.18-19.
ISBN 0-900199-07-5 Sd : £0.25
(B77-03824)

914.23'93'0025 — Avon. Bristol, 1775. *Directories. Facsimiles*
Sketchley, James. Sketchley's Bristol directory, 1775 / with an introduction by Bryan Little. — Bath : Kingsmead Reprints, 1971. — [20], 128p : 1 ill ; 20cm.
Facsimile reprint of: 1775 ed. Bristol : J. Sketchley, 1775.
ISBN 0-901571-59-8 : £1.50
(B77-05760)

914.23'93'04857 — Avon. Bristol. *Guidebooks*
The **city** of Bristol : the official handbook of the Corporation of the city of Bristol ... — London : Burrow, [1977]. — 144p : ill, coat of arms ; 25cm.
Cover title: Bristol.
Pbk : £2.00
(B77-34282)

914.23'96 — Avon. Nailsea. *Guidebooks*
Nailsea official guide. — [3rd ed.]. — Gloucester : British Publishing Co., [1977]. — 32,[2]p(2 fold) : ill, maps ; 19cm.
ISBN 0-7140-1547-4 Sd : £0.15
(B77-26000)

914.23'96 — Avon. Portishead. *Guidebooks*
Portishead official guide. — [New ed.]. — Carshalton : Forward Publicity, [1977]. — 24, [1]p : ill, map ; 21cm.
Sd : £0.24
(B77-20777)

914.23'96 — Avon. Winscombe. *Guidebooks*
Winscombe and district, Somerset, official guide. — [New ed.]. — Gloucester : British Publishing Co., [1977]. — 24p : ill, map ; 19cm.
ISBN 0-7140-1568-7 Sd : £0.20
(B77-18447)

914.23'96 — Avon. Yatton. *Guidebooks*
Yatton Parish Council official guide. — [New ed.]. — Gloucester : British Publishing Co., [1977]. — 16,[2]p(2 fold) : ill, maps(1 col) ; 21cm.
ISBN 0-7140-1457-5 Sd : £0.20
(B77-10999)

914.23'98'048570222 — Avon. Bath. Description & travel. *Illustrations*
Tompkins, John. Portraits of Bath / by John Tompkins ; drawings by Grace D. Bratton. — Bath : Kingsmead, 1976. — 48p : ill ; 26cm.
ISBN 0-901571-78-4 : £1.75
ISBN 0-901571-80-6 Pbk : £0.95
Primary classification 821'.9'14
(B77-03204)

914.24 — Long-distance footpaths. *Welsh Marches. Offa's Dyke Path. Walkers' guides*
Jones, John B. Offa's Dyke path / [by] John B. Jones. — London : H.M.S.O. for the Countryside Commission, 1976. — x,114p : ill, col maps ; 21cm. — (Long-distance footpath guide ; no.4)
Bibl.: p.114.
ISBN 0-11-700350-6 Pbk : £2.50
(B77-12781)

Richards, Mark. Through Welsh border country following Offa's Dyke path / [by] Mark Richards. — Gloucester : Thornhill Press, 1976. — xvi,209p : ill, maps ; 19cm.
Index.
ISBN 0-904110-29-x : Unpriced
ISBN 0-904110-53-2 Pbk : £1.95
(B77-23829)

914.24'04'81 — Canals. *England. Midlands. Grand Union Canal. Description & travel, 1858*
Hollingshead, John. On the canal : a narrative of a voyage from London to Birmingham in 1858 / [by] John Hollingshead ; introduced by Ronald Russell. — Stoke Bruerne (Stoke Bruerne, Towcester, Northants.) : Waterways Museum, 1973. — 48p : ill ; 15x22cm.
Reprinted from: 'Household words' / edited by Charles Dickens. London : Bradbury and Evans, 1850-1859.
Sd : £0.40
(B77-26001)

914.24'04'857 — England. Midlands. *Guidebooks*
Places to visit from Leicester. — Leicester (12 Bishop St., Leicester LE1 6AA) : Information Bureau, Leicester City Council Recreational and Cultural Services Department.
1977. — [1977]. — [1],63p ; 22cm.
Index.
Sd : £0.35
(B77-17822)

914.24'04'857 — England. West Midlands. Description & travel
Bird, Vivian. Exploring the West Midlands / [by] Vivian Bird. — London : Batsford, 1977. — 200p : ill, map ; 23cm.
Index.
ISBN 0-7134-0435-3 : £4.25
(B77-20778)

914.24'1'04857 — Gloucestershire. *Guidebooks*
Gloucestershire county guide. — Gloucester : British Publishing Co., [1977]. — 136,[2]p(2 fold) : ill(some col), col coat of arms, maps(chiefly col) ; 21cm.
ISBN 0-7140-1630-6 Pbk : £0.60
(B77-25279)

914.24'12 — Gloucestershire. Bishop's Cleeve. *Guidebooks*
Bishop's Cleeve, Gloucestershire, official guide. — [New ed.]. — Gloucester : British Publishing Co., [1976]. — 23p : ill, map ; 19cm.
ISBN 0-7140-1577-6 Sd : £0.15
(B77-10647)

914.24'12 — Gloucestershire. Winchcombe. *Guidebooks*
Winchcombe and district official guide. — [New ed.]. — Gloucester : British Publishing Co., [1977]. — 48,[2]p(2 fold) : ill, maps ; 19cm.
ISBN 0-7140-1533-4 Sd : £0.25
(B77-18448)

914.24'13 — Forest parks. *Gloucestershire. Forest of Dean (District). Dean Forest Park. Guidebooks*
Clarke, Arthur. Wye Valley and the Royal Forest of Dean ... : the official guide of the Wyedean Tourist Board / original text by Arthur Clarke. — 26th ed. / revised by A.G.R. Cross. — Gloucester : British Publishing Co. for the Board, [1977]. — 124,[2]p(2 fold) : ill, maps ; 21cm.
Index.
ISBN 0-7140-1607-1 Pbk : £0.35
Primary classification 914.29'5
(B77-12206)

914.24'13 — Gloucestershire. Newent. *Guidebooks*
Newent, Gloucestershire, official guide. — [New ed.]. — Carshalton : Forward Publicity, [1977]. — 20,[1]p : ill, map ; 19cm.
Sd : £0.18
(B77-31611)

914.24'17 — Gloucestershire. Northleach. *Guidebooks*
The **official** guide to Northleach with Eastington (Gloucestershire). — [New ed.]. — Gloucester : British Publishing Co., [1977]. — 25p : ill, maps ; 19cm.
ISBN 0-7140-1573-3 Sd : £0.10
(B77-14461)

914.24'17 — Parish churches. *Gloucestershire. Lechlade. Parish Church of St Lawrence, Lechlade. Guidebooks*
Radcliffe-Cox, Henry Richard Radcliffe. The Parish Church of St Lawrence, Lechlade-on-Thames, Gloucestershire : a short guide and history / [by H.R.R. Radcliffe-Cox]. — [Revised ed.]. — Gloucester : British Publishing Co., [1976]. — 3-24p : ill ; 19cm.
ISBN 0-7140-1566-0 Sd : £0.12
(B77-10648)

914.24'17'04857 — England. Cotswolds. Description & travel
Cash, James Allan. History, people and places in the Cotswolds / [by] J. Allan Cash. — Revised ed. — Bourne End, Bucks : Spurbooks, 1975. — 160p : ill, map ; 21cm.
Previous ed.: 1974. — Bibl.: p.10. — Index.
ISBN 0-902875-45-0 : £2.25
(B77-01052)

Crosher, Geoffrey Robins. Along the Cotswold ways / [by] G.R. Crosher. — London [etc.] : Pan Books, 1977. — 224p,[8]p of plates : ill, map ; 20cm.
Originally published: London : Cassell, 1976. — Bibl.: p.215-216. — Index.
ISBN 0-330-25143-0 Pbk : £1.25
(B77-20779)

914.24'17'04857 — Gloucestershire. Cotswolds. Description & travel
Wright, Louise. Cotswold heritage / by Louise Wright ; with drawings by James Priddey. — London : Hale, 1977. — 240p : ill, maps ; 17x24cm.
Index.
ISBN 0-7091-6223-5 : £5.95
(B77-29808)

914.24'19 — Gloucestershire. Painswick. *Guidebooks*
The **official** guide to Painswick, the queen of the Cotswolds. — [New ed.]. — Gloucester : British Publishing Co., [1977]. — 60p : ill, maps ; 19cm.
ISBN 0-7140-1589-x Sd : £0.20
(B77-20780)

914.24'4'04857 — Hereford and Worcester. *Guidebooks*
The **county** of Hereford and Worcester, the official guide. — Gloucester : British Publishing Co., [1977]. — 144p : ill(some col), col coat of arms, col map, port ; 25cm.
ISBN 0-7140-1549-0 Pbk : £1.00
(B77-20781)

Hereford and Worcester. — St Ives, Cambs. : Photo Precision, [1977]. — [2],32p : chiefly col ill, col map ; 19cm.
Cover title: Colourmaster Hereford and Worcester.
ISBN 0-85933-167-9 Sd : £0.40
(B77-23830)

914.24'41 — Hereford and Worcester. Bewdley. *Guidebooks*
Bewdley official guide. — [Silver Jubilee ed.]. — Gloucester : British Publishing Co., [1977]. — 36p : ill, maps ; 19cm.
ISBN 0-7140-1671-3 Sd : Unpriced
(B77-30843)

914.24'41'04857 — Hereford and Worcester. Wyre Forest (District). *Guidebooks*
Wyre Forest District official guide. — Carshalton : Home Publishing Co., [1977]. — 96,[2]p(2 fold) : ill, maps ; 21cm.
Pbk : £0.60
(B77-19094)

914.24'42'04857 — Hereford and Worcester. Bromsgrove (District). *Guidebooks*
District of Bromsgrove official guide. — Carshalton : Home Publishing Co., [1977]. — 96p : ill, coat of arms, map, port ; 21cm.
Pbk : Unpriced
(B77-25280)

914.24'45 — Castles. *Hereford and Worcester. Goodrich. Goodrich Castle. Guidebooks*
Great Britain. *Department of the Environment.* Goodrich Castle, Herefordshire / [Department of the Environment]. — [London] : The Department, [1977]. — Folder ([4]p) : ill, plan ; 16cm.
£0.04
(B77-23831)

914.24'46 — Cathedrals. *Hereford and Worcester. Hereford. Hereford Cathedral. Guidebooks*
Morgan, Frederick Charles. A walk round Hereford Cathedral. — [New enlarged ed.] / [by F.C. and P.E. Morgan]. — [Hereford] ([Hereford Cathedral, Hereford]) : Friends of Hereford Cathedral Publications Committee, 1976. — [1],16,[1]p : ill, plan ; 22cm.
Previous ed.: 1930.
Sd : Unpriced
(B77-29044)

914.24'48'04857 — Hereford and Worcester. Worcester. *Guidebooks*
The **City** of Worcester. — Gloucester : British Publishing Co., [1977]. — 128,[2]p(2 fold) : ill(some col), facsim, col map ; 22cm.
ISBN 0-7140-1615-2 Pbk : £0.90
(B77-24589)

914.24'49 — Hereford and Worcester. Broadway. *Guidebooks*
Broadway, Worcestershire, the official guide. — [New ed.]. — Carshalton : Forward Publicity, [1977]. — 24,[1]p : ill, map ; 21cm.
ISBN 0-7174-0736-5 Sd : Unpriced
(B77-13417)

914.24'5'0025 — Towns. Streets. *Salop. Directories*
Shropshire street guide. — Denton [Manchester] (2 Victoria St., Denton [Manchester]) : Ashton and Denton Publishing Co.
1977 ed. — [1977]. — 133p ; 22cm.
Pbk : £0.55
ISSN 0140-2552
(B77-28274)

914.24'53 — Salop. Market Drayton. *Guidebooks*
Market Drayton, Shropshire, official guide. — [New ed.]. — Carshalton : Forward Publicity, 1977. — 32,[1]p : ill, map ; 19cm.
Sd : Unpriced
(B77-24590)

914.24'53'04857 — Salop. North Shropshire (District). *Guidebooks*
North Shropshire official guide. — London : Burrow, [1977]. — 44p : ill ; 19cm.
Sd : £0.40
(B77-26679)

914.24'54 — Abbeys. *Salop. Buildwas. Buildwas Abbey. Guidebooks*
Great Britain. *Department of the Environment.* Buildwas Abbey, Shropshire / Department of the Environment. — [London] : [The Department], 1976. — 7,[1]p : plan ; 22cm. — (Ancient monuments and historic buildings)
Originally published: 1952.
Sd : £0.025
(B77-17183)

914.24'54 — Abbeys. *Salop. Shrewsbury. Haughmond Abbey. Guidebooks*
Great Britain. *Department of the Environment.* Haughmond Abbey, Shropshire / [Department of the Environment]. — [London] : The Department, [1977]. — Folder([4]p) : ill, plan ; 16cm.
£0.04
(B77-24591)

914.24'54 — Salop. Pontesbury. *Guidebooks*
Pontesbury, Shropshire, official guide. — [New ed.]. — Carshalton : Forward Publicity, [1976]. — 24p : ill, map ; 19cm.
ISBN 0-7174-0714-4 Sd : £0.12
(B77-00502)

914.24'56 — Buildings of historical importance. *Salop. Coalbrookdale. Walkers' guides*
Ironbridge Gorge Museum Trust. Coalbrookdale : a walk through Coalbrookdale, to explore its historic buildings and sites / Ironbridge Gorge Museum Trust ; [text by Barrie Trinder]. — [Ironbridge] ([Ironbridge, Telford, Salop TF8 7AW]) : The Trust, 1977. — 8p : ill(incl 1 col), facsim, map ; 25cm.
Sd : £0.15
(B77-29809)

914.24'56 — Parish churches. *Salop. Newport. St Nicolas Church, Newport. Guidebooks*
Barrow, Charles Clement. A short history of the S. Nicolas Church, Newport, Salop / by C.C. Barrow. — 12th ed. — Gloucester : British Publishing Co., [1977]. — 3-24p : ill ; 19cm.
Cover title: The story of S. Nicolas Church, Newport.
ISBN 0-7140-1587-3 Sd : £0.05
(B77-11000)

914.24'56 — Salop. Ironbridge Gorge region. Description & travel, 1754-1955. *Readings from contemporary sources*
'The **most** extraordinary district in the world' : Ironbridge and Coalbrookdale : an anthology of visitors' impressions of Ironbridge, Coalbrookdale and the Shropshire coalfield / edited with an introduction by Barrie Trinder. — London [etc.] : Phillimore [for] Ironbridge Gorge Museum Trust, 1977. — x,125p : ill, 2 maps, plans, ports ; 26cm.
Spine title: Ironbridge and Coalbrookdale. — Bibl.: p.122. — Index.
ISBN 0-85033-244-3 : £4.95
(B77-32957)

914.24'56 — Salop. Newport. *Guidebooks*
Newport official guide. — [New ed.]. — Gloucester : British Publishing Co., [1977]. — 36p : ill, 2 maps ; 19cm.
ISBN 0-7140-1531-8 Sd : £0.20
(B77-26002)

914.24'57 — Salop. Ludlow, 1878. *Guidebooks. Facsimiles*
The **tourist's** guide to Ludlow, and handbook to Ludlow Castle and Church. — Illustrated ed. — [Shrewsbury] ([7 London Rd, Shrewsbury, Salop]) : Shropshire County Library, 1977. — [4],36[i.e.46]p : ill ; 18cm.
Facsimile reprint of: Illustrated ed. Ludlow : Josiah Smith, 1879.
ISBN 0-903802-04-x Sd : £0.50
(B77-19095)

914.24'59 — Salop. Bridgnorth. *Guidebooks*
Bridgnorth official guide. — [New ed.]. — Carshalton : Forward Publicity, [1977]. — 36,[3]p(2 fold) : ill, coat of arms, map ; 21cm.
Sd : £0.30
(B77-33514)

914.24'61 — Staffordshire. Churnet Valley. Description & travel
Porter, Lindsey. The Churnet Valley and Alton Towers / [by] Lindsey Porter & Laurie Landon. — Hartington (The Market Place, Hartington, Buxton, Derbyshire SK17 0AL) : Moorland Publishing Co., 1977. — 48p : ill, maps ; 21cm.
Pbk : £0.80
(B77-32958)

914.24'64 — Staffordshire. Stone. *Guidebooks*
Stone town, official guide and handbook. — [New ed.]. — [Gloucester] : [British Publishing Co.], [1977]. — [1],36p : ill, coat of arms, maps ; 19cm.
ISBN 0-7140-1596-2 Sd : £0.15
(B77-25281)

914.24'65'04857 — Staffordshire. East Staffordshire (District). *Guidebooks*
East Staffordshire official guide. — Carshalton : Home Publishing Co., [1977]. — 80p : ill(some col), col coat of arms, maps ; 24cm.
Pbk : Unpriced
(B77-22251)

914.24'66 — Parish churches. *Staffordshire. Kinver. St Peter's Church, Kinver. Guidebooks*
The **Parish** Church of St Peter, Kinver. — [New ed.]. — Gloucester : British Publishing Co., [1977]. — 16,[1]p : ill ; 19cm.
ISBN 0-7140-1604-7 Sd : £0.10
(B77-11001)

914.24'66'04857 — Staffordshire. South Staffordshire (District). *Guidebooks*
South Staffordshire official guide. — London : Burrow, [1977]. — 56p : ill ; 19cm.
ISBN 0-85026-643-2 Sd : Unpriced
(B77-11473)

914.24'67'04857 — Staffordshire. Cannock Chase (District). *Guidebooks*
Cannock Chase, the official guide. — Gloucester : British Publishing Co., 1976. — 59p,[2]fold p of plates : ill(some col), maps ; 22cm.
ISBN 0-7140-1430-3 Pbk : Unpriced
(B77-11474)

914.24'85 — Parish churches. *Warwickshire. Dunchurch. Parish Church of St Peter, Dunchurch. Guidebooks*
A **guide** to the Parish Church of St Peter, Dunchurch with St Edmund, Thurlaston. — [New ed.]. — Gloucester : British Publishing Co., [1977]. — 20,[1]p : ill ; 19cm.
ISBN 0-7140-1591-1 Sd : £0.10
(B77-11002)

914.24'87 — Castles. *Warwickshire. Kenilworth. Kenilworth Castle. Guidebooks*
Great Britain. *Department of the Environment.* Kenilworth Castle, Warwickshire / Department of the Environment. — London : H.M.S.O., [1977]. — Folder ([4]p) : ill(some col), col plan ; 16cm.
£0.04
(B77-32959)

Thompson, Michael Welman. Kenilworth Castle, Warwickshire / [by] M.W. Thompson. — London : H.M.S.O., 1977. — 28p,fold plate : ill, map, plans ; 21cm. — (Great Britain. Department of the Environment. Official handbooks) (Ancient monuments and historic buildings)
Bibl.: p.28.
ISBN 0-11-670785-2 Sd : £0.40
(B77-08656)

914.24'87 — Footpaths. *Warwickshire. Kenilworth. Walkers' guides*
Kenilworth Footpath Preservation Group. Kenilworth footpaths / Kenilworth Footpath Preservation Group. — Kenilworth (c/o 69 John O'Grant Rd, Kenilworth, Warwickshire CV8 1DY) : The Group, 1977. — [2],36p : 1 ill, maps ; 21cm.
Sd : £0.50
(B77-29045)

914.24'89 — Buildings associated with Shakespeare, William. *Warwickshire. Stratford-upon-Avon. Guidebooks. Spanish, Swedish & Japanese texts*
Fox, Levi. Stratford-upon-Avon : nueva guía ilustrada en color = ny guide med färgillustrationer = Shin kar̄a gaidobukku Sh̄ekusupia Seitan-chi Shintaku Ky̆okaī / con texto descriptivo por = och beskrivande text av Levi Fox. — Norwich : Jarrold and Sons [for] the Shakespeare Birthplace Trust, [1976]. — [34]p : ill(chiefly col), coats of arms, col maps ; 19cm.
Spanish, Swedish and Japanese text.
ISBN 0-85306-661-2 Sd : £0.40
(B77-04473)

914.24'89 — Parish churches. *Warwickshire. Southam. Southam Parish Church. Guidebooks*
Southam Parish Church ... : a history and guide book. — Revised [ed.]. — Gloucester : British Publishing Co., 1977. — 22p : ill, facsim ; 19cm.
ISBN 0-7140-1605-5 Sd : £0.10
(B77-14462)

914.24'91'04810922 — West Midlands (Metropolitan County). Wolverhampton. Visits by British royal families, 1866-1971. *Illustrations*
Royal visits to Wolverhampton / compiled by Ann Humphreys. — [Wolverhampton] ([Central Library, Snow Hill, Wolverhampton WV1 3AX]) : Wolverhampton Public Libraries, 1977. — [59]p : chiefly ill, facsims, ports ; 21cm.
ISBN 0-905654-01-3 Sd : £0.90
(B77-25282)

914.24'93 — Parish churches. *West Midlands (Metropolitan County). Halesowen. Parish Church of St John the Baptist, Halesowen. Guidebooks*
Lay, Walter Edwin. Halesowen Parish Church St John Baptist : a guide and historical sketch / by W.E. Lay. — 6th ed. ; frontispiece photograph by J. Campbell. — Gloucester : British Publishing Co., [1977]. — 24p : ill ; 19cm.
ISBN 0-7140-1601-2 Sd : Unpriced
(B77-12782)

914.24'94'04857 — West Midlands (Metropolitan County). Sandwell (District). *Guidebooks*
Sandwell Metropolitan Borough official guide. — Gloucester : British Publishing Co., [1977]. — 160p : ill(some col), coats of arms(1 col), maps(1 col) ; 24cm.
ISBN 0-7140-1456-7 Pbk : £0.60
(B77-18449)

914.24'96'0025 — West Midlands (Metropolitan County). Birmingham. *Directories*
The '**Birmingham** post' year book and who's who. — Birmingham (Colmore Circus, Queensway, Birmingham B4 6AX) : Birmingham Post and Mail Ltd.
1976-77 : twenty-eighth annual issue. — [1976]. — 636,[260]p,plate : ill, coats of arms, maps, plans, ports ; 19cm.
'Supplement to the 'Birmingham Post' year book and who's who 1976-77' ([3]p.), train timetable ([2]p.), and fold. map in pocket. — Index.
ISBN 0-901883-09-3 : £4.50
(B77-03274)

914.24'96'04857 — West Midlands (Metropolitan County). Birmingham. *Guidebooks*
Birmingham *(City). Publicity Section.*
Birmingham, the magic city : a handbook to the City of Birmingham / designed and prepared by the City of Birmingham Publicity Section. — London : Burrow, [1977]. — 93p : ill(some col), col maps, col plan ; 30cm.
ISBN 0-7093-0001-8 Pbk : Unpriced
(B77-24592)

Birmingham Centrum / [prepared for the Birmingham Branch of the International Police Association]. — Gloucester : British Publishing Co., [1977]. — [2],34p : ill, port ; 25cm.
'Rackhams Department Store' (Folder [12]p.) in pocket.
ISBN 0-7140-1583-0 Sd : Unpriced
(B77-11475)

914.24'96'04857 — West Midlands (Metropolitan County). Birmingham. *Walkers' guides*
Brumtrails. — Birmingham (c/o Ian Laughton, Central Institute, Brasshouse Passage, Birmingham B1 2HR) : Birmingham Urban Studies Centres Committee.
4 / [compiled by Peter Sword]. — 1976. — [16]p(2 fold) : map ; 21cm.
'... researched and compiled ... as part of the Scouts Saturday Event, 3rd July 1976' - p.[16].
Sd : Unpriced
(B77-05114)

914.24'97'04857 — West Midlands (Metropolitan County). Solihull (District). *Guidebooks*
Solihull Metropolitan Borough, official guide. — [New ed.]. — Carshalton : Home Publishing Co., [1977]. — 92,[2]p(2 fold) : ill, maps ; 21cm.
Pbk : £0.48
(B77-30844)

914.24'98'0025 — West Midlands (Metropolitan County). Coventry. *Directories*
'**Coventry** evening telegraph' year book and who's who : a reference book for Coventry and Warwickshire including Warwick, Leamington Spa, Kenilworth, Rugby, Nuneaton, Bedworth and Stratford-on-Avon. — Coventry (Corporation St., Coventry, CV1 1FP) : Coventry Newspapers Ltd.
1977. — [1976]. — 320,[217],xxiii p,[2]leaves of plate : ill, coat of arms, maps(on lining papers), ports ; 19cm.
Index.
ISBN 0-902464-10-8 : £2.50
(B77-03825)

914.24'98'04857 — West Midlands (Metropolitan County). Coventry. *Guidebooks*
City of Coventry official guide. — London : G.W. May, [1976]. — 108p : ill, maps ; 25cm.
Cover title.
ISBN 0-904455-45-9 Pbk : £0.45
(B77-00503)

914.25 — England. Countryside adjacent to London-Derby railway line. *Guidebooks*
Palmer, John, *b.1948.* The Midland line to London / [by] John Palmer. — Brampton (34 Glenthorne Close, Brampton, Chesterfield S40 3AR) : Grayson Publications, 1976. — [1],53p : ill, map ; 21cm. — (A 'read as you go' guide)
ISBN 0-900709-07-3 Pbk : £1.20
Primary classification 385'.0942
(B77-06010)

914.25 — England. Northern East Midlands. *Guidebooks*
Out and about : 300 ideas for outings within 40 miles of Derby / [Derby and District Consumer Group]. — Derby ([c/o] Mrs J. Steer, 478 Duffield Rd, Allestree, Derby) : The Group.
1977 : 3rd ed. / [compiled by Ann Hutchinson, Jane Steer]. — 1977. — [2],32,[1]p ; 21cm.
Previously published: as 'Out and about : 250 ideas for outings within 40 miles of Derby'.
Sd : £0.30
(B77-33515)

914.25'1'04857 — Derbyshire. *Guidebooks*
Derbyshire guide. — Derby (Lodge La., Derby DE1 3HE) : Derbyshire Countryside Ltd.
1977 ed. — 1977. — [1],257p,fold plate tipped in : ill, coat of arms, maps(1 col) ; 22cm.
Index.
ISBN 0-85100-046-0 Pbk : £0.55
(B77-13956)

914.25'1'04857 — Derbyshire. *Guidebooks. For motoring*
Merrill, John Nigel. Explore Derbyshire by car / by John N. Merrill. — 2nd ed. — Clapham, N. Yorkshire : Dalesman, 1976. — 62,[1]p : ill, maps ; 14x22cm.
Previous ed.: 1974. — Index.
ISBN 0-85206-347-4 Pbk : £0.60
(B77-14463)

914.25'1'04857 — Derbyshire. Description & travel
Porteous, Crichton. Pictorial Derbyshire / by Crichton Porteous. — Derby (Lodge La., Derby) : Derbyshire Countryside Ltd, 1977. — 24p : col ill, col map ; 24cm.
Sd : £0.40
(B77-21581)

914.25'11 — Derbyshire. Castleton. *Guidebooks*
Innes-Smith, Robert. Castleton and its caves / by Robert Innes-Smith. — Derby (Lodge La., Derby [DE1 3HE]) : Derbyshire Countryside Ltd, 1976. — [2],16,[1]p : ill(some col), maps ; 24cm.
ISBN 0-85100-045-2 Sd : £0.30
(B77-04474)

914.25'11'04857 — England. Peak District. *Guidebooks*
Exploring the Peak District / edited by Peter Grayson ; based on original material by Margaret Hides. — Chesterfield (34 Glenthorne Close, Brampton, Chesterfield, Derbyshire S40 3AR) : Grayson Publications, 1977. — 56p : ill ; 19cm.
Index.
ISBN 0-900709-06-5 Pbk : £0.75
(B77-13957)

914.25'13 — Derbyshire. Bakewell. *Guidebooks*
Innes-Smith, Robert. Bakewell / by Robert Innes-Smith. — Derby (Lodge La., Derby) : Derbyshire Countryside Ltd, 1977. — [2],16p : ill(some col), map ; 24cm.
Sd : £0.30
(B77-29810)

914.25'16 — Country houses. *Derbyshire. Kedleston. Kedleston Hall. Guidebooks*
Scarsdale, Richard Nathaniel Curzon, *Viscount.*
Kedleston Hall : the historic home of the Curzon family / [by the 2nd Viscount Scarsdale]. — [New ed.]. — Derby ([Lodge La., Derby]) : Derbyshire Countryside Ltd, 1977. — 24,[1]p : ill(some col), coat of arms, geneal table, ports ; 24cm.
Previous ed.: 1973.
Sd : £0.30
(B77-24593)

914.25'17 — Derbyshire. Derby region. *Guidebooks*
Derby official guide. — [New ed.]. — London : Burrow, [1977]. — 120p : ill(some col), col coat of arms, maps(1 col) ; 25cm.
Pbk : £2.00
(B77-20782)

In and around Derby. — [2nd enlarged ed.]. — Derby (Britannic House, 5 St Mary's Gate, Derby) : Derby and Derbyshire Junior Chamber of Commerce, [1976]. — 128p : ill, maps, plan ; 21cm.
Previous ed.: 1975.
ISBN 0-9502840-2-5 Sd : £0.30
(B77-01053)

914.25'32 — Parish churches. *Lincolnshire. Holton le Clay. Holton le Clay Church. Guidebooks*
Holton le Clay church guide / [research and drawings by John Sills and David Redman]. — [Holton le Clay] ([Church Walk, Holton le Clay, Grimsby, S. Humberside]) : [The Church], [1974]. — [8]p : ill, plan ; 21cm.
ISBN 0-9505770-0-6 Sd : £0.10
(B77-18454)

914.25'35'04857 — Lincolnshire. North Kesteven (District). *Guidebooks*
North Kesteven official guide. — [New ed.]. — Carshalton : Home Publishing Co., [1977]. — 92,[3]p(2 fold) : ill, map ; 21cm.
Sd : £0.48
(B77-32302)

914.25'37'04857 — Lincolnshire. Boston (District). *Guidebooks*
Boston official guide. — [New ed.]. — London : Burrow, [1977]. — 40p : ill ; 21cm.
ISBN 0-85026-650-5 Sd : Unpriced
(B77-10649)

914.25'4'04857 — Canals. *Leicestershire. Walkers' guides*
Anderson, John. Waterside walks in Leicestershire / [by] John Anderson ; cover and sketches by William T. Adams. — Blaby (29 The Fairway, Blaby, Leicester) : The author, 1977. — 2-63p : ill, coat of arms, maps ; 20cm.
ISBN 0-9504777-1-0 Sd : Unpriced
(B77-32961)

914.25'4'04857 — Leicestershire. Description & travel
Bailey, Brian John. Portrait of Leicestershire / by Brian J. Bailey. — London : Hale, 1977. — 224p,[24]p of plates : ill, map ; 23cm.
Bibl.: p.214-216. — Index.
ISBN 0-7091-6005-4 : £3.95
(B77-18450)

914.25'44 — Country houses. *Leicestershire. Hungarton. Quenby Hall. Guidebooks*
De Lisle, G. Quenby Hall, Hungarton, Leicestershire / [text by the Squire de Lisle and Robert Innes-Smith]. — Derby : English Life Publications, 1977. — [12]p,[4]p of plates : ill(incl 1 col), coat of arms ; 14x21cm.
Sd : £0.30
(B77-19096)

914.25'44 — Country houses. *Leicestershire. West Langton. Langton Hall. Guidebooks*
Langton Hall near Market Harborough, Leicestershire / [photography by Sydney W. Newbery]. — Derby : English Life Publications, 1977. — [8]p,[4]p of plates : ill, map ; 14x21cm.
Sd : £0.30
(B77-19097)

914.25'44'04857 — Leicestershire. Harborough (District). *Guidebooks*
Harborough District Council official guide. — Gloucester : British Publishing Co., [1977]. — 72p,[2]p of plates(2 fold) : ill(some col), maps(1 col) ; 21cm.
Cover title: District of Harborough official guide.
Pbk : £0.50
(B77-26003)

914.25'49'04857 — Leicestershire. Hinckley and Bosworth (District). *Guidebooks*
Residents' and visitors' guide to the Charter Borough of Hinckley and Bosworth. — Gloucester : British Publishing Co., [1977]. — 72,[2]p(2 fold) : ill(some col), maps(1 col) ; 21cm.
ISBN 0-7140-1556-3 Pbk : £0.30
(B77-26680)

914.25'5'04857 — Northamptonshire. *Guidebooks*
Gould, Jack. Discovering Northamptonshire / [by] Jack Gould. — 2nd ed. — Aylesbury : Shire Publications, 1977. — 64p : ill, maps ; 18cm.
Previous ed.: 1969. — Index.
ISBN 0-85263-341-6 Sd : £0.60
(B77-29046)

914.25'5'04857 — Northamptonshire. Description & travel
Webb, Peter Gorham. Portrait of Northamptonshire / [by] Peter Gorham Webb. — London : Hale, 1977. — [1],206p,[24]p of plates : ill, map ; 23cm.
Index.
ISBN 0-7091-6061-5 : £4.50
(B77-20783)

914.25'52'04857 — Northamptonshire. Kettering (District). *Guidebooks*
Kettering borough official guide. — Carshalton : Home Publishing Co., [1977]. — 80,[2]p(2 fold) : ill, coat of arms, maps ; 21cm.
Index.
Pbk : Unpriced
(B77-22982)

914.25'54 — Northamptonshire. Higham Ferrers. *Guidebooks*
Higham Ferrers, Northamptonshire, the official guide. — [New ed.]. — Gloucester : British Publishing Co., [1977]. — 24p : ill, map ; 19cm.
ISBN 0-7140-1546-6 Sd : £0.15
(B77-11476)

914.25'56'04857 — Northamptonshire. Daventry (District). *Guidebooks*
Daventry District official guide. — Carshalton : Home Publishing Co., [1976]. — 64,[1]p : ill, map ; 21cm.
ISBN 0-7174-0727-6 Sd : Unpriced
(B77-09394)

914.25'59 — Parish churches. *Northamptonshire. Slapton. Saint Botolph's Church, Slapton. Guidebooks*
Chapman, Reginald. Saint Botolph's Church, Slapton, and its wallpaintings. — Towcester (Abthorpe, Towcester, Northants.) : The author, 1976. — [18]p : ill, facsims ; 21x30cm.
Author: R. Chapman. — Limited ed. of 750 copies. — Fold. facsim. tipped in.
Sd : £1.00
(B77-20784)

914.25'61 — Bedfordshire. Bedford. *Directories*
Kelly's directory of Bedford and Kempston. — Kingston upon Thames : Kelly's Directories.
1976 : 19th ed. : complete with street plan. — 1976. — iv,580p,fold plate : ill, map ; 19cm.
Index.
ISBN 0-610-00479-4 Pbk : £2.30
ISSN 0305-9502
(B77-10031)

914.25'71 — Oxfordshire. Chipping Norton. *Guidebooks*
Chipping Norton, Oxfordshire, the official guide. — [New ed.]. — Gloucester : British Publishing Co., [1977]. — 36p : ill, map ; 19cm.
ISBN 0-7140-1576-8 Sd : £0.20
(B77-13958)

914.25'73 — Parish churches. *Oxfordshire. Bicester. Parish Church of St Edburg, Bicester. Guidebooks*
The **Parish** Church of St Edburg, Bicester. — [New ed.]. — Gloucester : British Publishing Co., [1977]. — 3-19p : ill ; 19cm.
Cover title: Guide to the parish church of St Edburg, Bicester.
ISBN 0-7140-1598-9 Sd : Unpriced
(B77-13959)

914.25'73'04857 — Oxfordshire. Cherwell (District). *Guidebooks*
Cherwell District, official guide. — Carshalton : Home Publishing Co., [1977]. — 124p : ill, fold maps tipped in ; 21cm.
Pbk : £0.75
(B77-32303)

914.25'74'04857 — Oxfordshire. Oxford. *Guidebooks*
The **Oxford** guide : maps, shops, trains, hotels, museums, restaurants : factual information for visitors and residents. — [Oxford] ([10 Kingston Rd, Oxford]) : ['Daily information'].
1976-7 : 6th ed. — [1976]. — [2],44,[1]p : ill, maps ; 28cm.
Bibl.: p.11. — Index.
Sd : £0.60
(B77-22252)

914.25'76 — Oxfordshire. Abingdon. *Directories*
Abingdon who's who and directory. — [Abingdon] : Abingdon Town Council : Abbey Press.
1977-78. — [1977]. — 352p,fold plate : ill, coats of arms, map ; 19cm.
Cover title. — Index.
ISBN 0-900012-39-0 Pbk : £0.55
(B77-15025)

914.25'76 — Oxfordshire. Abingdon. *Guidebooks*
A **guide** to Abingdon on Thames. — [New ed.]. — Abingdon : Abbey Press (Oxon.), [1976]. — [1],64p,fold plate : ill, map ; 19cm.
Bibl.: p.64.
ISBN 0-900012-40-4 Sd : £0.45
(B77-16657)

914.25'76'04857 — Oxfordshire. Vale of White Horse (District). Description & travel
Higham, Roger. Berkshire and the Vale of White Horse / [by] Roger Higham. — London : Batsford, 1977. — 182p : ill, map ; 23cm.
Index.
ISBN 0-7134-0681-x : £4.50
Primary classification 914.22'9'04857
(B77-25277)

914.25'83 — Hertfordshire. Ware. *Guidebooks*
Ware, Hertfordshire, the official guide. — [New ed.]. — Gloucester : British Publishing Co., [1977]. — 56,[2]p(2 fold) : ill, maps ; 19cm.
ISBN 0-7140-1351-x Sd : £0.30
(B77-26004)

914.25'83'04857 — Hertfordshire. East Hertfordshire (District). *Guidebooks*
East Hertfordshire official guide. — London : Burrow, [1977]. — 40p : ill ; 21cm.
Sd : £0.60
(B77-24594)

914.25'84 — Castles. *Hertfordshire. Berkhamsted. Berkhamsted Castle. Guidebooks*
Peers, *Sir* **Charles.** Berkhamsted Castle, Hertfordshire / by the late Sir Charles Peers. — [London] : Department of the Environment, [1977]. — Folder (6p) : plan ; 22cm. — (Ancient monuments and historic buildings)
£0.05
(B77-33516)

914.25'84 — Parish churches. *Hertfordshire. King's Langley. Parish Church of All Saints, King's Langley. Guidebooks*
Hicks, William Charles Reginald. The Parish Church of All Saints, King's Langley ; [and], The tomb of Edmund of Langley and Isabel of Castile / [by W.C.R. Hicks]. — [King's Langley] ([The Vicarage, King's Langley, Herts.]) : [All Saints' Parochial Church Council, [1976]. — 24p : ill, plan ; 21cm.
ISBN 0-9505346-0-9 Sd : £0.35
(B77-00504)

914.25'892'04857 — Hertfordshire. Watford. *Guidebooks*
Watford, an official guide ... — [New ed.]. — [London] : Burrow, [1977]. — 92p,[2]p(2 fold) : ill, coat of arms, map ; 25cm.
Pbk : £1.50
(B77-22983)

914.25'895'04857 — Hertfordshire. Hertsmere (District). *Guidebooks*
Borough of Hertsmere official guide. — Gloucester : British Publishing Co., [1977]. — 64p : ill, 2 maps(1 col) ; 21cm.
Sd : £0.30
(B77-26005)

914.25'97 — Buckinghamshire. Chesham. *Guidebooks*
Chesham, Buckinghamshire, the official town guide. — Gloucester : British Publishing Co., [1977]. — 32,[2]p(2 fold) : ill, maps ; 19cm.
ISBN 0-7140-1420-6 Sd : £0.15
(B77-13960)

914.25'97'04857 — Buckinghamshire. Chilterns. *Walkers' guides*
Pigram, Ronald James. Country walks around Buckinghamshire Chilterns / by Ron Pigram ; illustrated by the author. — [Ilford] ([884 Eastern Ave., Ilford, Essex]) : [Circle Publications], [1976]. — [1],50p : ill, maps ; 16cm.
ISBN 0-9502012-1-9 Pbk : £0.50
(B77-22984)

914.25'98 — Buckinghamshire. Burnham Beeches. *Guidebooks*
Le Sueur, Arthur Denis Carrington. Burnham Beeches and the manor of Allerds-in-Burnham / [by] A.D.C. Le Sueur. — [New ed.]. — [London] : Corporation of London, [1977?]. — 32p : ill(incl 2 col), 2 maps(1 col) ; 22cm.
This ed. originally published: 1972.
Sd : £0.22
(B77-32962)

914.25'98 — Buckinghamshire. Denham. *Guidebooks*
Le Messurier, Colin. A guide to Denham, Buckinghamshire / by Colin Le Messurier. — [Chalfont St Giles] ([c/o D.K. Trafford, 2 Bayesville Cottages, Deanway, Chalfont St Giles, Bucks.]) : Denham Parish Council, [1976]. — [25]p : ill, map ; 22cm.
ISBN 0-9505365-0-4 Sd : £0.20
(B77-00505)

914.26'04'857 — East Anglia. Fens. *Guidebooks*
The **Fenland** guide. — St Ives, Cambs. (8 Market Hill, St Ives, Cambs.) : Adtour Publications Ltd.
1976. — [1976]. — 64p : ill, col map ; 21cm.
Sd : Unpriced
(B77-26006)

914.26'1'04857 — Norfolk. Description & travel
Yaxley, David. Portrait of Norfolk / [by] David Yaxley. — London : Hale, 1977. — 208p,[24]p of plates : ill, maps ; 23cm.
Index.
ISBN 0-7091-6267-7 : £4.50
(B77-26681)

914.26'12 — Norfolk. Walsingham. *Guidebooks. For Roman Catholics*
Connelly, Roland William. Walsingham pilgrim book : a guide to the shrine / by Roland Connelly. — Great Wakering : Mayhew-McCrimmon [for] the Pilgrim Bureau, 1975. — 31p : ill, map ; 15cm.
Sd : £0.20
(B77-10650)

914.26'12'04857 — Norfolk. North Norfolk (District). *Guidebooks*
Court, Alexander Norman. North Norfolk : an official guide / text by A.N. Court. — [Revised ed.]. — [Cromer] ([P.O. Box 3, Cromer, Norfolk]) : North Norfolk District Council, [1977]. — 2-31p : col ill, col map ; 21cm.
Index.
Sd : Unpriced
(B77-33517)

914.26'13 — Norfolk. Downham Market. *Guidebooks*
Downham Market official guide. — [New ed.]. — Carshalton : Forward Publicity, [1977]. — 32,[2]p(2 fold) : ill, map ; 19cm.
Sd : Unpriced
(B77-21582)

914.26'13'04857 — Norfolk. West Norfolk (District). *Guidebooks*
West Norfolk District Council official guide. — Gloucester : British Publishing Co., [1977]. — 80p : ill(some col), col map ; 21cm.
ISBN 0-7140-1560-1 Pbk : Unpriced
(B77-30845)

914.26'14 — Norfolk. Swaffham. *Guidebooks*
Swaffham, Norfolk, official guide. — [New ed.]. — Gloucester : British Publishing Co., [1977]. — 36,[2]p(2 fold) : ill, 2 maps, ports ; 19cm.
ISBN 0-7140-1621-7 Sd : £0.20
(B77-26007)

914.26'14 — Replicas of Icenic villages. *Norfolk. Cockley Cley. Guidebooks*
Roberts, *Sir* **Peter,** *bart, b.1912.* Replica of an Iceni village (as it was in 60 A.D.) at Cockley Cley, nr. Swaffham, Norfolk / commentary by Sir Peter Roberts. — [Swaffham] ([c/o Estate Office, Cockley Cley, Swaffham, Norfolk]) : [The author], [1976]. — [1],8p ; 22cm.
ISBN 0-9505326-0-6 Sd : £0.10
(B77-00506)

914.26'15 — Cathedrals. *Norfolk. Norwich. Norwich Cathedral. Guidebooks*
Webster, Alan. Norwich Cathedral / by Alan Webster. — Norwich : Jarrold and Sons, 1977. — [17]p : chiefly col ill, plan ; 25cm. — (Jarrold Cotman house book series)
ISBN 0-85306-705-8 Sd : Unpriced
(B77-22985)

914.26'15'04857 — Norfolk. Norwich. Description & travel
Historic Norwich. — Norwich : Jarrold and Sons, 1976. — [36]p : ill(some col), col map, ports ; 25cm.
English text, English, French and German introduction and captions.
ISBN 0-85306-667-1 Sd : £0.60
(B77-32963)

914.26'17 — Norfolk. Aylsham. *Guidebooks*
Guide to - Aylsham, Norfolk. — Carshalton : Forward Publicity, [1977]. — 24,[1]p : ill, map ; 19cm.
ISBN 0-7174-0742-x Sd : Unpriced
(B77-15026)

914.26'17 — Water pumping windmills. *Norfolk. Reedham. Berney Arms Mill. Guidebooks*
Wailes, Rex. Berney Arms Mill, Reedham, Norfolk / by Rex Wailes. — [London] : Department of the Environment, 1976. — Folder(6p) : 1 ill ; 22cm. — (Ancient monuments and historic buildings)
Originally published: 1957.
£0.02
(B77-17184)

914.26'17'04857 — Norfolk. Broadland (District). *Guidebooks*
Broadland in colour. — Norwich : Jarrold and Sons, 1977. — [33]p : col ill, map ; 20cm. — (A Cotman-color book)
English text, French and German captions.
ISBN 0-85306-708-2 Sd : £0.40
(B77-25283)

914.26'17'04857 — Norfolk Broads. *Guidebooks. For boating*
What to do on the Norfolk Broads : the complete guide to the Broads. — Norwich : Jarrold and Sons.
1977 / editor Joanna Halpin. — 1977. — 96p : ill, maps(chiefly col) ; 20x25cm.
Index.
ISBN 0-85306-664-7 Pbk : £0.75
(B77-06367)

914.26'18'04857 — Norfolk. Great Yarmouth (District). *Guidebooks*
Great Yarmouth official holiday guide. — Great Yarmouth (14 Regent St., Great Yarmouth NR30 1RW) : [Great Yarmouth District Council], Department of Publicity and Amenities.
1977. — [1977]. — 208p : ill(some col), col maps, ports ; 23cm.
ISBN 0-9500096-8-7 Pbk : Unpriced
(B77-10032)

914.26'19'04857 — Norfolk. South Norfolk (District). *Guidebooks*
District of South Norfolk official guide. — [New ed.]. — Carshalton : Home Publishing Co., [1977]. — 56,[2]p(2 fold) : ill, map ; 21cm.
Sd : Unpriced
(B77-26008)

914.26'4 — South-western Suffolk. Description & travel
Pawsey, James Thomas. Constable country / text by James T. Pawsey. — Ipswich ([Dales Rd, Ipswich, Suffolk]) : F.W. Pawsey and Sons, 1973. — 18p(1 fold) : chiefly ill(chiefly col), col map, port ; 19cm.
English text, English, French and German captions. — Originally published: 1970.
ISBN 0-9500785-1-4 Sd : £0.50
Also classified at 914.26'7
(B77-10651)

914.26'4'0455 — Suffolk. Description & travel, ca 1600. *Early works*
The chorography of Suffolk / edited by Diarmaid MacCulloch. — Ipswich : Boydell Press [for the] Suffolk Records Society, 1976. — x,170p, [4]p of plates : facsims ; 24cm.
Index.
ISBN 0-85115-069-1 : £6.00
(B77-22253)

914.26'4'04857 — Suffolk. *Guidebooks. For motoring*
Rotheroe, John. Discovering Suffolk / [by] John Rotheroe ; with contributions from W.G. Arnott, R.A. Campbell. — 4th ed. — Aylesbury : Shire Publications, 1977. — 63p : ill, map ; 18cm.
Previous ed.: 1975. — Index.
ISBN 0-85263-372-6 Sd : £0.60
(B77-29048)

914.26'41 — Suffolk. Beccles. *Guidebooks*
Beccles official guide. — [New ed.]. — London : Burrow, [1977]. — 32,[2]p(2 fold) : ill, map ; 19cm.
ISBN 0-85026-644-0 Sd : Unpriced
(B77-10652)

914.26'43'04857 — Suffolk. Forest Heath (District). *Guidebooks*
Forest Heath District official street and area map. — Carshalton : Forward Publicity, [1977]. — [1],28,[1]p,[2] fold p of plates : ill, maps ; 21cm.
Sd : Unpriced
(B77-25284)

914.26'44 — Buildings of historical importance. *Suffolk. Bury St Edmunds. Walkers' guides*
Place, Monica. A walk round historic Bury St Edmunds / compiled by Monica Place, Martin J. Lightfoot ; edited by Eileen F. Morris ; illustrated by Roy V. Morris. — [Bury St Edmunds] ([c/o Record Office, Bury St Edmunds, Suffolk]) : Bury St Edmunds Society, 1975. — [18]p : ill, map ; 15x21cm.
ISBN 0-905791-00-2 Sd : £0.20
(B77-01054)

914.26'44'04857 — Suffolk. St Edmundsbury (District). *Guidebooks*
Borough of St Edmundsbury / [compiled and edited by Harry R. Marsh]. — [Bury St Edmunds] ([c/o Information Officer, Thingoe House, Bury St Edmunds, Suffolk IP33 1HH]) : St Edmundsbury Borough Council, 1976. — 200p : ill(some col), coat of arms, maps(some col), plan ; 24cm.
ISBN 0-905953-00-2 : £0.75
(B77-10653)

914.26'45'04857 — Suffolk. Mid Suffolk (District). *Guidebooks*
Mid Suffolk District official guide. — [New ed.]. — Carshalton : Home Publishing Co., [1977]. — 88,[1]p : ill, map ; 21cm.
Sd : Unpriced
(B77-10033)

914.26'46 — Suffolk. Felixstowe. *Guidebooks*
Felixstowe and the Suffolk coast. — [Woodbridge] ([Council Offices, Melton Hill, Woodbridge, Suffolk]) : [Suffolk Coastal District Council], [1977]. — 92p : ill(chiefly col), col map ; 21cm.
Cover title.
Pbk : Unpriced
(B77-26682)

914.26'46'04857 — Suffolk. Coastal regions. Description & travel
White, Archie. Tideways & byways in Essex & Suffolk / by Archie White ; illustrated by the author. — Hornchurch : I. Henry, 1977. — 216p : ill, maps ; 21cm.
Originally published: London : Edward Arnold, 1948. — Index.
ISBN 0-86025-814-9 : £4.55
Primary classification 914.26'7
(B77-23832)

914.26'48 — Suffolk. East Bergholt region. *Guidebooks. For motoring*
Kenyon, Lionel Frederick Robert. As John Constable saw it / [by L.F.R. Kenyon]. — Dedham (Duchy Barn, Dedham, Essex) : Council for the Protection of Rural England, Countryside Centre, [1976]. — [11]p : ill ; 30cm.
ISBN 0-9505348-0-3 Sd : £0.25
Also classified at 741.9'42
(B77-00507)

914.26'48 — Suffolk. Stour Valley. *Guidebooks. For motoring*
Titchmarsh, Peter. The Stour Valley by car : a tour of John Constable's countryside and beyond / compiled [and written] by Peter and Helen Titchmarsh ; photography by Alan and Peter Titchmarsh. — Norwich : Jarrold and Sons, [1977]. — [1],32,[1]p : ill, maps(1 col) ; 21cm. — (The Jarrold 'White Horse' series)
Index.
ISBN 0-85306-689-2 Sd : £0.45
Also classified at 914.26'71
(B77-19098)

914.26'49'04857 — Suffolk. Ipswich. *Guidebooks*
Borough of Ipswich official guide. — Carshalton : Home Publishing Co., [1976]. — 140p : ill(some col), col coat of arms, maps ; 21cm.
English text, Dutch, French and German note. — Index.
ISBN 0-7174-0733-0 Pbk : Unpriced
(B77-09395)

914.26'5'04857 — Cambridgeshire. *Guidebooks*
Cambridgeshire county handbook. — Carshalton : Home Publishing Co., [1977]. — 112p : ill, col coat of arms, maps ; 24cm.
ISBN 0-7174-0744-6 Pbk : Unpriced
(B77-16110)

914.26'5'04857 — Cambridgeshire. Rural regions. Description & travel
Jeevar, Peter. Curiosities of rural Cambridgeshire / [by] Peter Jeevar. — Cambridge : Oleander Press, 1977. — 48p : ill, map ; 21cm. — (Cambridgetown, gown, and county ; 16)
Bibl.: p.47. — Index.
ISBN 0-900891-12-2 Sd : £1.30
(B77-26708)

914.26'57'04857 — Villages. *Cambridgeshire. South Cambridgeshire (District). Walkers' guides*
South Cambridgeshire *(District). Council.* Gt Shelford to Ickleton : nine villages in the Cam Valley / [South Cambridgeshire District Council]. — [Cambridge] ([South Cambridgeshire Hall, 9 Hills Rd, Cambridge CB2 1PB]) : The Council, 1976. — [36]p : ill, maps ; 21cm.
Sd : £0.25
(B77-04475)

914.26'59 — Dovecots. *Cambridgeshire. Guidebooks*
Jeevar, Peter. Dovecots of Cambridgeshire / [text and illustrations by] Peter Jeevar. — Cambridge : Oleander Press, 1977. — 48p : ill, map ; 21cm.
ISBN 0-900891-06-8 Sd : £1.20
(B77-03275)

914.26'59 — Universities. Colleges. *Cambridgeshire. Cambridge. St John's College. Guidebooks*
St John's College. Saint John's College, Cambridge : a guide for visitors / [text by John Pritchard]. — Cambridge ([c/o College Office, St John's College, Cambridge]) : St John's College, 1976. — [2],32,[2]p(2 fold) : ill, coats of arms, facsim, plan, ports ; 21cm.
ISBN 0-9501085-1-0 Sd : £0.40
(B77-06967)

914.26'59'04857 — Cambridgeshire. Cambridge. *Guidebooks*
Cyclists' Touring Club. *Cambridge District Association.* Show yourself round Cambridge / [Cambridge District Association of the Cyclists' Touring Club]. — [Cambridge] ([c/o Mr G.B. Rich, 26 Springfield Rd, Cambridge]) : The Club, [1977]. — [2],24p : ill, map ; 22cm.
Previous ed.: 1970.
Sd : £0.20
(B77-10034)

914.26'59'04857 — Cambridgeshire. Cambridge. Description & travel
Graham-Cameron, Malcolm. The Cambridge scene / by M.G. Graham-Cameron ; illustrations by Colin King. — Cambridge : Dinosaur Publications for Cambridge City Council, 1977. — 32p : col ill ; 23cm.
ISBN 0-85122-141-6 Sd : £0.50
(B77-34283)

Reeve, Frank Albert. The Cambridge nobody knows / [by] F.A. Reeve. — Cambridge : Oleander Press, 1977. — 48p : ill, map ; 22cm. — (Cambridge town, gown and county ; vol.14)

ISBN 0-900891-10-6 Sd : £1.20 : CIP rev.
(B77-08142)

914.26'7 — Essex. Coastal regions. Description & travel
White, Archie. Tideways & byways in Essex & Suffolk / by Archie White ; illustrated by the author. — Hornchurch : I. Henry, 1977. — 216p : ill, maps ; 21cm.
Originally published: London : Edward Arnold, 1948. — Index.
ISBN 0-86025-814-9 : £4.55
Also classified at 914.26'46'04857
(B77-23832)

914.26'7 — Essex. Colne River region. *Guidebooks*
Clarke, J V C. The Essex Colne / [by] J.V.C. Clarke. — Colne Engaine (The Lodge, Mill La., Colne Engaine, Essex) : The author, 1976. — [2],20p : ill, maps ; 21cm.
Sd : £0.20
(B77-25285)

914.26'7 — Footpaths. *Essex. Three Forests Way. Walkers' guides*
Matthews, Fred. The Three Forests Way : a long distance circular walk linking the three Essex forests of Epping, Hatfield and Hainault / by Fred Matthews and Harry Bitten. — [Abridge] (['Glen View', London Rd, Abridge, Essex]) : [West Essex Ramblers Association], [1977]. — [2],25p : maps ; 21cm.
Sd : £0.45
(B77-30846)

914.26'7 — Long-distance footpaths. *Essex. Essex Way. Walkers' guides*
Clarke, J V C. The Essex Way / [by] J.V.C. Clarke. — Colne Engaine (The Lodge, Mill La., Colne Engaine, Essex) : The author, 1977. — [2],25p : ill, map ; 21cm.
Sd : £0.30
(B77-25286)

914.26'7 — North Essex. Description & travel
Salmon, John. The Suffolk-Essex border / [by] John Salmon ; illustrated by Michael Norman. — Ipswich : Boydell Press, 1977. — [8]p,120p : ill, map ; 23cm.
Index.
ISBN 0-85115-074-8 : £3.50
Primary classification 322.4'4'0973
(B77-12203)

914.26'7 — North-eastern Essex. Description & travel
Pawsey, James Thomas. Constable country / text by James T. Pawsey. — Ipswich ([Dales Rd, Ipswich, Suffolk]) : F.W. Pawsey and Sons, 1973. — 18p(1 fold) : chiefly ill(chiefly col), col map, port ; 19cm.
English text, English, French and German captions. — Originally published: 1970.
ISBN 0-9500785-1-4 Sd : £0.50
Primary classification 914.26'4
(B77-10651)

914.26'7'04857 — Essex. *Guidebooks*
Essex County Council, county handbook. — [London] : Burrow, [1976]. — 180p : ill(some col), col coat of arms, maps(some col) ; 25cm.
ISBN 0-85026-636-x Pbk : Unpriced
(B77-01902)

914.26'7'04857 — Essex. *Guidebooks. For motoring*
Jarvis, Stanley Melville. Discovering Essex / [by] S.M. Jarvis. — 2nd ed. — Aylesbury : Shire Publications, 1977. — 68p : ill, maps ; 18cm. — (Discovering series ; no.105)
Previous ed.: Tring : Shire Publications, 1971. — Index.
ISBN 0-85263-370-x Sd : £0.60
(B77-32964)

914.26'7'04857 — Essex. Description & travel
Manning, Stanley Arthur. Portrait of Essex / [by] S.A. Manning ; photographs by Richard Jemmett. — London : Hale, 1977. — 191p,[24] p of plates : ill, map ; 23cm.
Index.
ISBN 0-7091-6388-6 : £4.50
(B77-34284)

914.26'71 — Essex. Stour Valley. *Guidebooks. For motoring*
Titchmarsh, Peter. The Stour Valley by car : a tour of John Constable's countryside and beyond / compiled [and written] by Peter and Helen Titchmarsh ; photography by Alan and Peter Titchmarsh. — Norwich : Jarrold and Sons, [1977]. — [1],32,[1]p : ill, maps(1 col) ; 21cm. — (The Jarrold 'White Horse' series)
Index.
ISBN 0-85306-689-2 Sd : £0.45
Primary classification 914.26'48
(B77-19098)

914.26'712'04857 — Essex. Uttlesford (District). *Guidebooks*
The **District** of Uttlesford official guide. — Carshalton : Home Publishing Co., [1977]. — 88,[2]p(2 fold) : ill, map ; 21cm.
Pbk : £0.60
(B77-19099)

914.26'74 — Essex. Epping. *Guidebooks*
Epping town official guide. — Carshalton : Forward Publicity, [1977]. — 48,[1]p : ill, map ; 21cm.
Sd : £0.24
(B77-19891)

914.26'756 — Essex. Dengie region. Description & travel
Maldon *(District). Council.* Dengie coastal walks / produced by Maldon District Council. — [Maldon] ([Council Offices, Maldon, Essex]) : The Council, [1977]. — Folder([6]p) : ill, map ; 31cm.
Unpriced
(B77-14464)

914.26'756 — Essex. Maldon. Description & travel
Maldon *(District). Council.* Maldon trail / produced by the Maldon District Council. — [Maldon] ([Council Offices, Maldon, Essex]) : [The Council], [1977]. — Folder([6]p) : ill, map ; 31cm.
Unpriced
(B77-14465)

914.26'76 — Parish churches. *Essex. East Horndon. All Saints Church, East Horndon. Guidebooks*
Starr, Christopher. East Horndon Church : a history and guide / by Christopher Starr. — London (St Andrew-by-the-Wardrobe, Queen Victoria St., EC4V 5DE) : Redundant Churches Fund, [1977]. — [1],15p,[4]p of plates : ill, geneal table, plan ; 24cm.
Bibl.: p.15.
ISBN 0-9502402-4-9 Sd : £0.30
(B77-13961)

914.26'772'04857 — Essex. Basildon. *Guidebooks*
Basildon, a comprehensive guide to the district. — [New ed.]. — Gloucester : British Publishing Co., [1977]. — 128,[2]p(2 fold) : ill, maps ; 22cm.
ISBN 0-7140-1520-2 Pbk : £0.30
(B77-10654)

914.26'775 — Offshore pirate radio services. Radio ships: Mi Amigo (Ship). Grounding on Long Sand, Thames Estuary, 1975. *Personal observations*
Barrett, Simon. SOS, 10 days in the life of a lady / [by] Simon Barrett. — London (77 New Bond St., W.1) : Music Radio Promotions, 1976. — [6],vi,105p : ill, map, plan, ports ; 23cm.
ISBN 0-905590-00-7 : £4.50
(B77-28275)

914.27'1'04857 — Cheshire. Description & travel
Dore, Robert Norman. Cheshire / [by] R.N. Dore. — London : Batsford, 1977[i.e.1976]. — 192p : ill, map ; 23cm.
Index.
ISBN 0-7134-3187-3 : £3.95
(B77-00508)

914.27'14 — Cathedrals. *Cheshire. Chester. Chester Cathedral. Guidebooks*
Addleshaw, George William Outram. Chester Cathedral : the stained glass windows, mosaics, monuments and some of its other treasures / by G.W.O. Addleshaw. — 5th ed. — Gloucester : British Publishing Co., 1977. — 40p : ill, plan, port ; 19cm.
ISBN 0-7140-1638-1 Sd : £0.10
(B77-34285)

914.27'14 — Cheshire. Chester. *Guidebooks*
Jarman, Cyril Edgar. Chester, cathedral and city / described by C.E. Jarman ; and photographed by R.H. Tilbrook. — Norwich : Jarrold and Sons, [1977]. — [28]p(2 fold) : ill(some col), map, plan ; 25cm.
Originally published: 1972.
Sd : £0.50
ISBN 0-85306-579-9
(B77-31612)

Mason, Edward Harold. The city of Chester : the ancient Roman fortress of Deva / [by E.H. Mason]. — [Revised ed.] / [revised by Joan Houghton ; photographs by Gerald Newbery]. — London : Pitkin Pictorials, 1977. — [2],24,[1]p : ill(some col) ; 23cm. — (Pitkin 'pride of Britain' books)
Previous ed.: London : Pitkin, 196-?.
ISBN 0-85372-229-3 Sd : £0.50
(B77-22254)

914.27'17'04857 — Cheshire. Ellesmere Port and Neston (District). *Guidebooks*
Borough of Ellesmere Port and Neston official guide. — [Carshalton] : Home Publishing Co., [1976]. — 80p : ill, map ; 24cm.
ISBN 0-7174-0745-4 Pbk : Unpriced
(B77-15608)

914.27'32'0025 — Greater Manchester (Metropolitan County). Salford (District). *Directories*
Salford City Libraries. *Salford Central Area Library.* Salford area, some useful addresses / [Salford Central Area Library, Salford City Libraries]. — [Salford] ([Peel Park, Salford M5 4WU]) : Salford Central Area Library, Cultural Services Department, 1977. — [2],48p ; 26cm.
Index.
Sd : £0.20
(B77-34286)

914.27'32'04857 — Greater Manchester (Metropolitan County). Salford (District). *Guidebooks*
City of Salford official guide. — Gloucester : British Publishing Co., [1977]. — 136p : ill(some col), maps(1 col) ; 24cm.
ISBN 0-7140-1254-8 Pbk : £0.60
(B77-18451)

914.27'35'0025 — Towns. Streets. *Greater Manchester (Metropolitan County). Tameside (District). Directories*
Tameside street guide. — Denton [Manchester] (2 Victoria St., Denton, [Manchester]) : Ashton and Denton Publishing Co.
1977 ed. — [1977]. — 170p ; 22cm.
Pbk : £0.55
ISSN 0140-2544
(B77-28276)

914.27'36'04857 — Greater Manchester (Metropolitan County). Wigan (District). *Guidebooks*
The **Metropolitan** Borough of Wigan, official handbook. — [New ed.]. — London : Burrow, [1976]. — 128p : ill(some col), maps ; 25cm.
ISBN 0-85026-630-0 Pbk : Unpriced
(B77-01055)

The **Metropolitan** Borough of Wigan official handbook. — [New ed.]. — London : Burrow, [1977]. — 128p : ill(some col), map ; 25cm.
ISBN 0-85026-646-7 Pbk : Unpriced
(B77-10655)

914.27'5'04857 — Merseyside (Metropolitan County). *Guidebooks*
Brack, Alan. The new Merseyside / by Alan Brack ; [photography Ron Jones et al.]. — Liverpool (P.O. Box 95, Metropolitan House, Old Hall St., Liverpool L69 3EL) : Public Relations Office, Merseyside County Council, [1976]. — 51,[1]p : col ill, maps(incl 1 col), ports(chiefly col) ; 30cm.
ISBN 0-905161-01-7 Sd : £0.75
(B77-00509)

Discover Merseyside : city, coast, countryside / English Tourist Board. — [London] : The Board.
1977. — [1977]. — [2],26p : ill, col maps, ports ; 21cm.
ISBN 0-903265-90-7 Sd : Unpriced
(B77-15609)

914.27'6'04857 — Lancashire. *Guidebooks. For motoring*
Alcock, Joan Pilsbury. Discovering Lancashire / [by] Joan P. Alcock. — Aylesbury : Shire Publications, 1977. — 55p,[8]p of plates : ill, maps ; 18cm. — (Discovering series ; no.171)
Index.
ISBN 0-85263-218-5 Sd : £0.60
(B77-34287)

914.27'6'04857 — Lancashire. Description & travel
Eyre, Kathleen. Lancashire landmarks / by Kathleen Eyre ; illustrated by Gordon Ashton & A. Turner. — Clapham, N. Yorkshire : Dalesman, 1976. — 80p : ill ; 21cm.
Index.
ISBN 0-85206-370-9 Pbk : £0.90
(B77-34288)

Lofthouse, Jessica. Portrait of Lancashire / [by] Jessica Lofthouse. — 3rd ed. — London : Hale, 1977. — 239p,[24]p of plates : ill, map ; 24cm.
Previous ed.: 1973. — Index.
ISBN 0-7091-6359-2 : £4.20
(B77-29049)

914.27'615'04857 — Lancashire. Chorley (District). *Guidebooks*
Chorley official guide. — [New ed.]. — Carshalton : Home Publishing Co., [1977]. — 44,[3]p(2 fold) : ill, 2 maps ; 21cm.
Sd : £0.40
(B77-19100)

914.27'642'04857 — Lancashire. Burnley (District). *Guidebooks*
Burnley official guide, 1977. — London : Pyramid Press, [1977]. — 120p : ill(some col), col plan ; 25cm.
Pbk : Unpriced
(B77-18452)

914.27'685 — Lancashire. Clitheroe. *Walkers' guides*
A **walk** through Clitheroe. — [Clitheroe] ([Planning Department, Princess Ave., Clitheroe, Lancs. BB7 2AL]) : Ribble Valley Borough Council ; [Clitheroe] : Clitheroe Civic Society, 1976. — [15]p(2 fold) : ill, col map ; 22cm.
Sd : £0.20
(B77-05115)

914.27'685 — Lancashire. Forest of Bowland. *Guidebooks. For motoring*
Mitchell, William Reginald. Bowland & Pendle Hill : a tourist's guide / by W.R. Mitchell. — [Clapham, N. Yorkshire] : Dalesman, 1977. — 72p : ill, coats of arms, maps ; 21cm.
Originally published: 1971.
ISBN 0-85206-376-8 Pbk : £0.75
(B77-15027)

914.27'69 — Lancashire. Silverdale. *Guidebooks*
Arnside and Silverdale : a practical guide for visitors / compiled by 'Cumbria' ; illustrated by J.J. Thomlinson. — Clapham, N. Yorkshire : Dalesman, 1976. — 32p : ill, map ; 19cm. — (A Dalesman mini-book)
ISBN 0-85206-355-5 Sd : £0.35
Also classified at 914.27'83
(B77-17185)

914.27'8'0025 — Cumbria, 1829. *Directories*
Parson, William. [History, directory, and gazetteer of the counties of Cumberland and Westmorland]. A history, directory and gazetteer of Cumberland and Westmorland : with that part of the Lake District in Lancashire, forming the Lordships of Furness and Cartmel / by William Parson and William White. — Beckermet (Beckermet Bookshop, Beckermet, Cumbria) : Michael Moon, 1976. — [2],732,xxxvi p : map ; 23cm.
Spine title: Directory of Cumberland and Westmorland with Furness and Cartmel. — Facsimile reprint. — 'History, directory and gazetteer of the counties of Cumberland and Westmorland' originally published: Leeds : W. White, 1829. — Index.
ISBN 0-904131-12-2 : £10.00
(B77-06968)

914.27'8'0475 — Cumbria. Lake District, 1835. *Guidebooks. Early works*
Wordsworth, William. [A guide through the district of the lakes in the North of England]. Wordsworth's guide to the Lakes. — 5th ed. / with an introduction, appendices, and notes textual and illustrative by Ernest de Sélincourt. — Oxford [etc.] : Oxford University Press, 1977. — xxxii,212p,[6]leaves of plates,[8]p of plates : ill, map ; 20cm.
Facsimile reprint of 5th ed. with de Sélincourt introduction and notes, London : Henry Frowde, 1906. — 5th ed. originally published: as 'A guide through the district of the lakes in the North of England'. Kendal : Hudson and Nicholson, 1835. — Index.
ISBN 0-19-281219-x Pbk : £1.50
(B77-23833)

914.27'8'0483 — Cumbria. Lake District. Description & travel, 1913. *Personal observations. Manuscripts. Facsimiles*
Valentine, Herbert. Tales of a tent : a remarkable diary of camping holidays in Lakeland in the halcyon days before the First World War / written and illustrated by Herbert and Agnes W. Valentine. — Beckermet (Beckermet, Cumbria) : Michael Moon at the Beckermet Bookshop, 1977. — [59]p : ill ; 25cm.
'... originally compiled in 1913' - title page verso.
ISBN 0-904131-14-9 Pbk : £2.00
(B77-23834)

914.27'8'04857 — Cumbria. Description & travel
Lefebure, Molly. Cumbrian discovery / by Molly Lefebure. — London : Gollancz, 1977. — 352p, [16]p of plates : ill, map ; 24cm.
Bibl.: p.342-343. — Index.
ISBN 0-575-02235-3 : £7.95
(B77-23835)

914.27'8'04857 — Cumbria. Lake District. Description & travel
Nicholson, Norman. The lakes / [by] Norman Nicholson. — Revised ed. — London : Hale, 1977. — 190p,[24]p of plates : ill, map ; 19cm. — (Hale's topographical paperbacks)
This ed. originally published: as 'Portrait of the lakes'. 1972. — Index.
ISBN 0-7091-6246-4 Pbk : £1.50
(B77-15028)

914.27'8'04857 — Cumbria. Lake District. Description & travel. *Personal observations*
Griffin, Arthur Harold. A year in the Fells : pages from a country diary / [by] A.H. Griffin ; photographs by Geoffrey Berry. — London : Hale, 1976. — 206p,[24]p of plates : ill ; 23cm.
Index.
ISBN 0-7091-5814-9 : £4.50
(B77-00510)

914.27'83 — Cumbria. Arnside. *Guidebooks*
Arnside and Silverdale : a practical guide for visitors / compiled by 'Cumbria' ; illustrated by J.J. Thomlinson. — Clapham, N. Yorkshire : Dalesman, 1976. — 32p : ill, map ; 19cm. — (A Dalesman mini-book)
ISBN 0-85206-355-5 Sd : £0.35
Primary classification 914.27'69
(B77-17185)

914.27'86 — Castles. *Cumbria. Brougham. Brougham Castle. Guidebooks*
Charlton, John. Brougham Castle, Westmorland / by John Charlton. — [London] : Department of the Environment, 1977. — 11p : plan ; 22cm. — (Ancient monuments and historic buildings)
Originally published: 1950.
Sd : £0.04
(B77-17186)

914.27'86 — Country houses. *Cumbria. Dacre. Dalemain. Guidebooks*
Dalemain. — Derby : English Life Publications, 1977. — 16,[1]p : ill(some col), coat of arms, geneal table, ports ; 24cm.
Sd : Unpriced
(B77-23836)

914.27'89 — Cumbria. Carlisle. *Guidebooks*
Lakescene guide to Carlisle, the border city. — [New ed.]. — Carlisle (12 Lonsdale St., Carlisle [CA1 1DD]) : Lakescene Publications, [1977]. — [2],50p : ill, map ; 21cm.
Sd : £0.35
(B77-28277)

914.27'9'04857 — Isle of Man. *Guidebooks*
Isle of Man = Ellan Vannin Veg Veen. — London : Geographia, [1977]. — 95p,[8]p of plates,fold leaf of plate : ill, maps(1 col) ; 19cm. — (A Geographia guide)
Col. coat of arms on back cover. — Index.
Pbk : £0.60
(B77-29811)

914.28'04'857 — Christian church. Buildings. *Northeast England. Guidebooks*
Northumbria Christian pilgrimage / by Graham Trasler ... [et al.]. — Newcastle upon Tyne : F. Graham, 1977. — 63p : ill, facsims, plans ; 22cm.
'... published in connection with the Northumbria Tourist Board's Christian Pilgrimage Achievement Holiday'.
ISBN 0-85983-059-4 Sd : £0.85
(B77-29812)

914.28'1'04857 — Churches. *Yorkshire. Guidebooks*
Carter, Robert Alistair. A visitor's guide to Yorkshire churches / compiled by Robert A. Carter ; with an introduction by Derek Linstrum. — Bradford (Idle, Bradford, W. Yorkshire BD10 8NL) : Watmoughs Ltd [for] the Yorkshire Arts Association, 1976. — viii, 124p,fold plate : ill, coat of arms, facsim, map, ports ; 15x21cm.
Bibl.: p.121. — Index.
ISBN 0-903775-02-6 Pbk : £1.40
(B77-05761)

914.28'1'04857 — Structures of historical importance. *Yorkshire. Guidebooks*
Willis, Ronald. Yorkshire scene / by Ronald Willis ; photography by Thelma Willis. — Nelson : Hendon Publishing Co., 1977. — 48p : ill ; 14x22cm.
ISBN 0-86067-018-x Sd : £0.90
(B77-23837)

914.28'1'04857 — West Yorkshire (Metropolitan County). *Guidebooks*
West Yorkshire official county guide. — Carshalton : Home Publishing Co., [1977]. — 156p,[2]fold p of plates : ill(some col), col coat of arms, maps, ports ; 24cm.
ISBN 0-7174-0724-1 Pbk : £0.60
(B77-10656)

914.28'1'04857 — Yorkshire. Description & travel
Scott, Harry John. Yorkshire / [by] Harry J. Scott. — Revised ed. — London : Hale, 1977. — 207p,[16]p of plates : ill, map ; 19cm. — (Hale's topographical paperbacks)
This ed. originally published: as 'Portrait of Yorkshire'. 1970. — Index.
ISBN 0-7091-6245-6 Pbk : £1.50
(B77-15029)

914.28'15 — West Yorkshire. Ackworth. *Walkers' guides*
Camplin, C E. Ackworth Trail / devised by C.E. Camplin. — [Pontefract] ([Stepaside, Stonegate La., Ackworth, Pontefract, W. Yorkshire WF7 7AB]) : [The author], [1976]. — [2],17 leaves,fold plate : maps ; 22cm.
ISBN 0-9505679-0-6 Sd : £0.05
(B77-13962)

914.28'15 — West Yorkshire (Metropolitan County). Hemsworth. *Guidebooks*
Hemsworth official guide. — [New ed.]. — Carshalton : Forward Publicity, [1977]. — 24, [3]p(2 fold) : ill, map ; 19cm.
Sd : £0.24
(B77-31613)

914.28'17 — West Yorkshire (Metropolitan County). Bingley. *Walkers' guides*
Firth, Gary. Bingley historical trail / by Gary Firth. — Nelson : Hendon Publishing Co., 1977. — 32p,[4]p of plates : ill, map ; 17x24cm.
ISBN 0-86067-014-7 Sd : £1.00
(B77-19101)

914.28'3 — Shipwrecks. *Humberside. Coastal waters, to 1972*
Godfrey, Arthur, *b.1941.* Shipwrecks of the Yorkshire coast / by Arthur Godfrey and Peter J. Lassey. — Clapham, N. Yorkshire : Dalesman, 1976. — 168p : ill, maps ; 22cm.
Originally published: 1974. — Bibl.: p.165-166.
Pbk : £2.00
ISBN 0-85206-227-3
Primary classification 914.28'4
(B77-00511)

914.28'3'04857 — Humberside. *Guidebooks*
Humberside official guide. — Carshalton : Home Publishing Co., [1976]. — 208p(2 fold) : ill(some col), coat of arms, map ; 24cm.
ISBN 0-7174-0729-2 Pbk : Unpriced
(B77-09396)

914.28'31'04857 — Humberside. Scunthorpe. *Guidebooks*
Borough of Scunthorpe official guide. — Carshalton : Home Publishing Co., [1977]. — 80,[2]p(2 fold) : ill, 2 maps ; 21cm.
Index.
Pbk : £0.48
(B77-18453)

914.28'32'04857 — Humberside. Glanford (District). *Guidebooks*
Glanford Borough official guide. — Carshalton : Home Publishing Co., [1977]. — 44,[2]p(2 fold) : ill, map ; 21cm.
ISBN 0-7174-0723-3 Sd : Unpriced
(B77-10657)

914.28'35'04857 — Humberside. Boothferry (District). *Guidebooks*
Boothferry District Council, official guide & handbook. — London : Burrow, [1976]. — 52p : ill, map ; 21cm.
ISBN 0-85026-638-6 Sd : Unpriced
(B77-01903)

914.28'4 — North Yorkshire. Vale of York. *Walkers' guides*
Ramblers' Association. *York Group.* Walks in the Vale of York / compiled by the Ramblers' Association, York Group ; maps prepared by John Mills ; illustrations drawn by Kitty Price. — York (c/o David Nunns, 26 Fir Tree Close, York) : The Group, 1977. — 64p : ill, maps ; 19cm.
Fold. cover.
Sd : £0.85
(B77-27542)

914.28'4 — Shipwrecks. *North Yorkshire. Coastal waters, to 1972*

Godfrey, Arthur, *b.1941.* Shipwrecks of the Yorkshire coast / by Arthur Godfrey and Peter J. Lassey. — Clapham, N. Yorkshire : Dalesman, 1976. — 168p : ill, maps ; 22cm.
Originally published: 1974. — Bibl.: p.165-166.
Pbk : £2.00
ISBN 0-85206-227-3
Also classified at 914.28'3
(B77-00511)

914.28'4'04857 — Yorkshire. North Riding. Description & travel

Barker, Malcolm G. Yorkshire, the North Riding / [by] Malcolm G. Barker. — London : Batsford, 1977. — 198p : ill, map ; 23cm.
Index.
ISBN 0-7134-3189-x : £3.95
(B77-24595)

914.28'4'048570222 — North Yorkshire. Dales. Description & travel. *Illustrations*

Wainwright, Alfred. A Dales sketchbook / [by] A. Wainwright. — Kendal ([22 Strictlandgate, Kendal, Cumbria]) : 'Westmorland Gazette', [1977]. — [161]p : ill, maps ; 19x24cm.
£2.00
(B77-27543)

914.28'41 — North Yorkshire. Malham region. Description & travel

Raistrick, Arthur. Malham and Malham Moor / by Arthur Raistrick. — [New ed.]. — Clapham, N. Yorkshire : Dalesman, 1976. — x, 126p,[8]p of plates : ill, maps ; 21cm. — (The Yorkshire Dales library ; 2)
This ed. originally published: 1971. — Bibl.: p.123-124. — Index.
ISBN 0-85206-322-9 Pbk : £1.00
(B77-00512)

914.28'41'04857 — North Yorkshire. Craven (District). *Walkers' guides*

Speakman, Colin. Walking in the Craven Dales / by Colin Speakman. — 3rd ed. — Clapham, N. Yorkshire : Dalesman, 1976. — 64p : ill, maps ; 19cm. — (A Dalesman mini-book)
Previous ed.: 1973. — Bibl.: p.64.
ISBN 0-85206-338-5 Pbk : £0.50
(B77-17187)

914.28'42 — Abbeys. *North Yorkshire. Ripon. Fountains Abbey. Guidebooks*

Great Britain. *Department of the Environment.* Fountains Abbey, Yorkshire / [Department of the Environment]. — [London] : The Department, [1977]. — Folder ([4]p) : 3 col ill, col plan ; 16cm. — (Ancient monuments and historic buildings)
£0.04
(B77-33518)

914.28'46 — Castles. *North Yorkshire. Helmsley. Helmsley Castle. Guidebooks*

Great Britain. *Department of the Environment.* Helmsley Castle, Yorkshire / [Department of the Environment]. — [London] : The Department, [1977]. — Folder([4]p) : ill, plan ; 16cm.
£0.04
(B77-23838)

914.28'46 — North Yorkshire. Countryside adjacent to Whitby and Pickering Railway. Description & travel, 1836

Belcher, Henry. A tour of the Whitby & Pickering Railway in 1836 / by Henry Belcher ; with notes and introduction by John Cranfield. — Pinner (85 Cecil Park, Pinner, Middx) : Cranfield and Bonfiel Books, 1977. — vi,44p, [12]p of plates : ill ; 22cm.
Originally published: in 'Illustrations of the scenery on the line of the Whitby and Pickering Railway in the north eastern part of Yorkshire' / from drawings by G. Dodgson. London : Longman, 1863. — Index.
ISBN 0-904071-03-0 Sd : £1.05
(B77-12204)

914.28'46 — North Yorkshire. Malton & Norton. *Guidebooks*

Malton and Norton-on-Derwent official guide. — Carshalton : Forward Publicity, [1976]. — 64, [1]p : ill, 2 maps ; 21cm.
ISBN 0-7174-0720-9 Sd : Unpriced
(B77-07720)

914.28'46'04857 — North Yorkshire. Ryedale (District). *Guidebooks*

Rushton, John. The Ryedale story : a Yorkshire countryside handbook / by John Rushton ; [illustrated by Norman Appleton]. — [Malton] ([Administrative Centre, Welham Rd, Norton, Malton, N. Yorkshire YO17 9DT]) : Ryedale District Council, [1976]. — [2],146,[3]p of plates : ill, maps ; 25cm.
Index.
Pbk : £1.25
(B77-10035)

Ryedale *(District). Council.* The Ryedale District of North Yorkshire : official guide book / issued by the Ryedale District Council ; text ... [and] ... line drawings ... by Norman Appleton. — Malton (Administrative Centre, 21 Welham Rd, Norton, Malton, N. Yorkshire YO17 9DT) : The Council, [1977]. — [1],65p : ill, maps(1 col) ; 24cm.
Index.
Sd : £0.20
(B77-11477)

Ryedale in North Yorkshire. — Malton (21 Welham Rd, Norton, Malton, N. Yorkshire) : Ryedale District Council, [1977]. — Folder ([7]p) : ill, col map ; 23cm.
£0.20
(B77-09397)

914.28'47 — Castles. *North Yorkshire. Scarborough. Scarborough Castle. Guidebooks*

Great Britain. *Department of the Environment.* Scarborough Castle, Yorkshire / Department of the Environment. — [London] : [The Department], [1977]. — Folder([4]p) : col ill, col plan ; 16cm. — (Ancient monuments and historic buildings)
£0.04
(B77-24596)

Great Britain. *Department of the Environment.* Scarborough Castle, Yorkshire / Department of the Environment. — [London] : [The Department], 1977. — 8p : plan ; 22cm. — (Ancient monuments and historic buildings)
Originally published: 1955.
Sd : £0.04
(B77-17188)

914.28'47 — Parish churches. *North Yorkshire. Scarborough. St Martin-on-the-Hill, Scarborough. Guidebooks*

Winpenny, David. St Martin-on-the-Hill : a guide / by David Winpenny. — [Halifax] ([36 Tewit Green, Bradshaw, Halifax, W. Yorkshire]) : [The author], [1977]. — 20p : ill ; 21cm.
Sd : £0.25
(B77-28279)

914.28'48 — Castles. *North Yorkshire. Richmond. Richmond Castle. Guidebooks*

Great Britain. *Department of the Environment.* Richmond Castle, Yorkshire / [Department of the Environment]. — [London] : The Department, [1977]. — Folder([4]p) : ill, plan ; 16cm.
£0.04
(B77-21583)

914.28'49 — Country houses. *North Yorkshire. Hambleton (District). Beningbrough Hall. Guidebooks*

National Trust. Beningbrough Hall, North Yorkshire / [the National Trust]. — London : National Trust, 1977. — 36p : ill, geneal table, plan ; 22cm.
Bibl.: p.34.
Sd : Unpriced
(B77-32965)

914.28'49 — Priories. *North Yorkshire. Osmotherley. Mount Grace Priory. Guidebooks*

Great Britain. *Department of the Environment.* Mount Grace Priory, Yorkshire / Department of the Environment. — [London] : [The Department], 1977. — 10,[1]p : plan ; 22cm. — (Ancient monuments and historic buildings)
Originally published: 1959.
Sd : £0.04
(B77-17189)

914.28'49'04857 — North Yorkshire. Hambleton (District). *Guidebooks*

Hambleton District official guide. — Carshalton : Home Publishing Co., [1977]. — 72,[4]p(2 fold) : ill, map ; 21cm.
ISBN 0-7174-0739-x Sd : Unpriced
(B77-12205)

914.28'51'04857 — Cleveland. Stockton-on-Tees (District). *Guidebooks*

Borough of Stockton-on-Tees official guide. — Gloucester : British Home Publishing Co., [1977]. — 100p : ill(some col) ; 21cm.
Pbk : Unpriced
(B77-27544)

914.28'54 — Cleveland. Guisborough. *Guidebooks*

Guisborough official guide. — [New ed.]. — Carshalton : Forward Publicity, [1977]. — 37, [1]p,[2] fold p of plates : ill, maps ; 21cm.
Sd : Unpriced
(B77-25287)

914.28'68'04857 — Durham (County). Derwentside (District). *Guidebooks*

Derwentside District, official guide. — Carshalton : Home Publishing Co., [1976]. — 68p : ill, map ; 21cm.
ISBN 0-7174-0716-0 Sd : Free
(B77-03826)

914.28'71 — Tyne & Wear (Metropolitan County). Hetton. *Guidebooks*

Hetton town official guide. — Carshalton : Forward Publicity, [1977]. — 34p : ill, map, plan ; 21cm.
ISBN 0-7174-0741-1 Sd : Unpriced
(B77-15610)

914.28'71'04857 — Tyne and Wear (Metropolitan County). Sunderland (District). *Guidebooks*

Borough of Sunderland official guide. — [New ed.]. — Carshalton : Home Publishing Co., [1977]. — 84p : ill, coat of arms, map, ports ; 24cm.
Pbk : £0.48
(B77-31614)

914.28'8'0014 — Fields. Names. *Northumberland*

Beckensall, Stan. Northumberland field names / by Stan Beckensall ; maps by Richard Parkin ; photographs by Terry White. — Newcastle upon Tyne : F. Graham, [1977]. — 72p : 1 ill, facsim, maps(1 col) ; 28cm.
Sd : £3.00
(B77-27545)

914.28'8'04857 — Northumberland. *Guidebooks*

Northumberland county handbook. — [New ed.]. — London : Burrow, [1977]. — 100p : ill, col coat of arms, map, port ; 25cm.
Pbk : £1.50
(B77-23839)

914.28'81'04857 — Ancient Roman fortifications. *Northern England. Hadrian's Wall. Walkers' guides*

Mizon, Graham. A guide to walking Hadrian's Wall / by Graham Mizon. — Nelson : Hendon Publishing Co., 1977. — 48p : ill, maps ; 14x22cm.
Bibl.: p.47-48.
ISBN 0-86067-012-0 Sd : £0.80
(B77-21584)

914.28'81'04857 — Ancient Roman fortifications. *Northern England. Hadrian's Wall. Walkers' guides. French texts*

Great Britain. *Department of the Environment.* Le mur d'Hadrian : petit guide / préparé par le Department of the Environment. — [London] : H.M.S.O., 1969. — Folder ([12]p) : ill(incl 1 col), col map, col plans ; 22cm.
ISBN 0-11-670121-8 : £0.12
(B77-29813)

914.28'87 — Hermitages. *Northumberland. Warkworth. Warkworth Hermitage. Guidebooks*

Blair, Charles Henry Hunter. Warkworth Hermitage, Northumberland / history by the late C.H. Hunter Blair ; [description by the late H.L. Honeyman]. — [London] : Department of the Environment, 1977. — Folder (6p) : plan ; 22cm. — (Ancient monuments and historic buildings)
Originally published: 1954.
£0.02
(B77-17190)

914.28'87 — Priories. *Northumberland. Pauperhaugh. Brinkburn Priory. Guidebooks*

Great Britain. *Department of the Environment.* Brinkburn Priory, Northumberland / Department of the Environment. — [London] : [The Department], 1976. — Sheet([2]p) : 1 ill ; 21cm. — (Ancient monuments and historic buildings)
Originally published: 1967.
£0.02
(B77-17191)

914.28'89 — Northumberland. Farne Islands. *Guidebooks*
Graham, Frank, *b.1913.* The Farne Islands : Seahouses, Beadnell, Embleton, Dunstanburgh Castle and Craster / by Frank Graham ; drawings by Susan Martin. — Newcastle upon Tyne : Graham, 1976. — 32p : ill, maps, plan ; 22cm. — (Northern history booklet ; no.69 ISSN 0550-855x)
ISBN 0-85983-068-3 Sd : £0.30
(B77-14466)

914.29 — WALES
914.29 — Wales. Geographical features. *Secondary school texts*
Davies, Margaret, *b.1914.* Looking at Wales / [by] Margaret Davies. — 3rd ed. — London : A. and C. Black, 1977. — 64p : ill, maps(some col) ; 25cm. — (Looking at geography ; 6)
Previous ed.: 1969. — Index.
ISBN 0-7136-1748-9 Pbk : £0.95
(B77-22986)

914.29 — Wales. Geographical features. *Welsh texts*
Price, Mary, *b.1920.* Daearyddiaeth Cymru heddiw / [gan] Mary Price ; addasiad Cymraeg B.L. Davies. — Abertawe [i.e. Swansea] : C. Davies, 1977. — [10],186p : ill, maps(1 col) ; 22cm.
Translation of: 'A modern geography of Wales'. 1974. — Index.
ISBN 0-7154-0393-1 : £2.50
(B77-18455)

914.29'008 — Wales. Geographical features. *Essays*
Bowen, Emrys George. Geography, culture and habitat : selected essays (1925-1975) of E.G. Bowen / selected and introduced by Harold Carter, Wayne K.D. Davies. — Llandysul : Gomer Press, 1976. — xxxiii,275p,[2]leaves of plates : ill, maps, port ; 23cm.
Bibl.: p.x-xxi.
ISBN 0-85088-351-2 : £6.00
(B77-08657)

914.29'04'81 — Wales. Description & travel, 1854. *Personal observations*
Borrow, George. Wild Wales : its people, language and scenery / [by] George Borrow ; with an introduction by Cecil Price. — [London] : Fontana, 1977. — 544p : map, port ; 18cm.
Originally published: London : Murray, 1862. — Bibl.: p.543-544. — Index.
ISBN 0-00-634909-9 Pbk : £1.25
(B77-32304)

Borrow, George. Wild Wales : its people, language and scenery / by George Borrow. — Souvenir ed. / [photographs by R. Cecil Hughes] ; with an introduction by Cecil Price. — London [etc.] : Collins, 1977. — 544p,[64]p of plates : ill, map, port ; 19cm.
Souvenir ed. originally published: 1955. — Bibl. : p.543-544. — Index.
ISBN 0-00-420208-2 : £3.50
(B77-19892)

914.29'04'81 — Wales. Description & travel, ca 1890
[Welsh pictures drawn with pen and pencil. *Selections].* Welsh pictures from Victorian times / edited by Brian John ... — Newport, Dyfed (Brian S. John, Trefelin, Cilgwyn, Newport, Dyfed) : Greencroft Books, 1977. — 100p : ill ; 21cm.
'Welsh pictures drawn with pen and pencil' originally published: / edited by Richard Lovett. London : Religious Tract Society, 1892. — Index.
ISBN 0-905559-00-2 Pbk : £1.50
(B77-25288)

914.29'04'857 — Rivers. Description & travel. *Wales. Welsh texts*
Dilyn afon / golygydd Ifor Rees. — Abertawe [i.e. Swansea] : C. Davies, 1977. — 116p,[4] leaves of plates : ill, 4 maps, 2 ports ; 22cm.
ISBN 0-7154-0334-6 Pbk : £1.75
(B77-26683)

914.29'04'857 — Roads used for cattle droving. *Wales. Walkers' guides*
Toulson, Shirley. The drovers' roads of Wales / photographs by Fay Godwin ; written by Shirley Toulson. — London : Wildwood House, 1977. — 240p : ill, maps ; 21cm.
Bibl.: p.236-237. — Index.
ISBN 0-7045-0251-8 : £5.95
ISBN 0-7045-0252-6 Pbk : Unpriced
(B77-29050)

914.29'04'857 — Wales. *Guidebooks*
The **complete** Wales : a survey of the main holiday areas and places of interest. — 3rd ed. / edited by Reginald J.W. Hammond. — London : Ward Lock, 1976. — 318p,[14]leaves of plates,[16]p of plates : ill, maps(some col) ; 19cm. — (The red guides)
Previous ed.: 1972. — Index.
ISBN 0-7063-1712-2 : £3.95
(B77-11478)

Llewellyn, Alun. The Shell guide to Wales / introduction by Wynford Vaughan-Thomas ; gazetteer by Alun Llewellyn. — London : Joseph, 1977. — 360p : ill(some col), col maps ; 26cm.
Ill. on lining papers. — Originally published: 1969. — Bibl.: p.353-354. — Index.
£6.50
ISBN 0-7181-4019-2
(B77-14467)

Wales / [Wales Tourist Board]. — Cardiff : The Board.
[1976] / [produced by the Wales Tourist Board and the British Tourist Authority]. — 1977. — 16p : ill(chiefly col), maps(1 col) ; 30cm.
ISBN 0-85630-415-8 Sd : Unpriced
(B77-14468)

914.29'04'857 — Wales. *Guidebooks. For motoring*
Keating, Leslie. Wales by car / [by] Leslie Keating. — Havant : K. Mason, 1977. — 143p : ill, maps ; 15cm.
ISBN 0-85937-057-7 Pbk : £0.95
(B77-16111)

914.29'1'0474 — North Wales. Description & travel, 1830. *Early works*
Gastineau, Henry. [Wales illustrated. Vol.1]. North Wales illustrated : in a series of views, comprising the picturesque scenery, towns, castles, seats of the nobility & gentry, antiquities &c. / engraved on steel from original drawings by Henry Gastineau ; accompanied by historical and topographical descriptions. — Wakefield : EP Publishing, 1977. — [168]p : chiefly ill ; 26cm.
Facsimile reprint of: 1st ed., originally published as vol.1 of 'Wales illustrated'. London : Jones, 1830.
ISBN 0-7158-1217-3 : £5.25
(B77-15030)

914.29'1'04857 — North Wales. Caves. *Guidebooks. For exploration*
Oldham, Tony. The caves of North Wales / by Tony Oldham. — Crymmych (Rhychydwr, Crymmych, Dyfed SA41 3RB) : Anne Oldham, 1977. — [3],x,63p : ill ; 26cm.
Bibl.
Sd : £1.50
(B77-27546)

914.29'2'04857 — Gwynedd. *Guidebooks. For motoring. Welsh texts*
Owen, Emyr. Moduro Gwynedd / [gan] Emyr Owen. — Talybont, Dyfed (Talybont, Dyfed ST24 5ER) : Y Lolfa, 1977. — 96p : ill, maps ; 19cm. — (Pocedlyfrau'r Lolfa)
Previous control number ISBN 0-904864-30-8.
ISBN 0-904864-31-6 : Unpriced
ISBN 0-904864-30-8 Pbk : £0.85
(B77-27547)

914.29'21 — Castles. *Gwynedd. Ynys Môn. Beaumaris. Beaumaris Castle. Guidebooks*
Great Britain. *Department of the Environment.* Beaumaris Castle, Anglesey, Gwynedd / produced by the Department of the Environment ; on behalf of the Secretary of State for Wales. — [London] : [The Department], [1976]. — Folder([4]p) : ill, 2 plans(1 col) ; 16cm.
£0.04
(B77-21585)

914.29'21 — Megalithic tombs. *Gwynedd. Ynys Môn. Barclodiad y Gawres Chambered Cairn. Guidebooks*
Powell, Thomas George Eyre. Barclodiad y Gawres chambered cairn, Anglesey / [by] T.G.E. Powell ; prepared by the Department of the Environment on behalf of the Secretary of State for Wales = paratowyd gan Adran yr Amgylchedd ar ran Ysgrifennydd Gwladol Cymru. — [London] : H.M.S.O., 1976. — 5, [2[p : ill, plan ; 22cm.
English text, Welsh note. — Originally published: 1964.
Sd : £0.04
(B77-17192)

914.29'21 — Shipwrecks: Royal Charter (Ship). *Gwynedd. Ynys Môn. Coastal waters, 1859*
McKee, Alexander. The golden wreck / [by] Alexander McKee. — London : New English Library, 1977. — 191p ; 18cm.
Originally published: London : Souvenir Press, 1961.
ISBN 0-450-03471-2 Pbk : £0.70
(B77-26684)

914.29'23 — Gwynedd. Lleyn Peninsula. *Guidebooks*
The **Lleyn** peninsula. — St Ives, Cambs. : Photo Precision, [1977]. — [2],32p : chiefly col ill, col map ; 19cm.
Cover title: Colourmaster the Lleyn Peninsula.
ISBN 0-85933-171-7 Sd : Unpriced
(B77-25289)

914.29'23 — Gwynedd. Lleyn Peninsula. *Guidebooks. For motoring*
Titchmarsh, Jim. Lleyn Peninsula by car / compiled [and written] by Jim Titchmarsh ; photography by Alan and Jim Titchmarsh. — Norwich : Jarrold and Sons, [1977]. — [1],32, [1]p : ill, maps(1 col) ; 21cm. — (The Jarrold 'White Horse' series)
Index.
ISBN 0-85306-690-6 Sd : £0.45
(B77-18456)

914.29'25 — Castles. *Gwynedd. Caernarvon. Caernarvon Castle. Guidebooks*
Great Britain. *Department of the Environment.* Caernarfon Castle / prepared by the Department of the Environment ; on behalf of the Secretary of State for Wales. — [London] : [The Department], [1976]. — Folder([4]p) : ill, col plan ; 16cm.
£0.04
(B77-21586)

914.29'25 — Cathedrals. *Gwynedd. Bangor. Bangor Cathedral. Guidebooks*
Dowse, Ivor Roy. The Cathedral Church of St Deiniol, Bangor, Gwynedd, Wales / [by Ivor R. Dowse]. — [Bangor] : [Bangor Cathedral], [1977]. — [2],24p : ill, coats of arms, plans ; 25cm.
ISBN 0-905229-03-7 Sd : £0.30
(B77-15031)

914.29'25 — Country houses. *Gwynedd. Bangor. Penrhyn Castle. Guidebooks*
National Trust. Penrhyn Castle, Gwynedd / [National Trust]. — [New ed.]. — [London] : The Trust, 1977. — 16p,leaf of plate,[6]p of plates : ill, plan ; 25cm.
Previous ed.: 1975.
Sd : £0.30
(B77-33519)

914.29'27 — Castles. *Gwynedd. Conway. Conway Castle. Guidebooks. French texts*
Great Britain. *Welsh Office.* Le Château de Conwy, Gwynedd / Secrétaire d'Etat pour le Pays de Galles. — [London] : [Department of the Environment], [1977]. — Folder([4]p) : ill, plan ; 16cm.
£0.04
(B77-23840)

914.29'27 — Gwynedd. Llanrwst. *Guidebooks*
Llanrwst, the official guide. — [New ed.]. — Gloucester : British Publishing Co., [1977]. — 32,[2]p(2 fold) : ill, 2 maps, port ; 19cm.
ISBN 0-7140-1656-x Sd : Unpriced
(B77-26009)

914.29'27 — Private chapels. *Gwynedd. Llanrwst. Gwydir Uchaf Chapel. Guidebooks*
Hague, Douglas Bland. Gwydir Uchaf Chapel, Gwynedd / [by] D.B. Hague ; prepared by the Department of the Environment on behalf of the Welsh Office. — [London] : [The Department], 1976. — 8p : plan ; 22cm.
Originally published: 1953.
Sd : £0.04
(B77-17193)

914.29'29 — Castles. *Gwynedd. Harlech. Harlech Castle. Guidebooks. French texts*
Great Britain. *Welsh Office.* Le château de Harlech, Gwynedd / Secrétaire d'état pour le Pays de Galles. — [London] : [Department of the Environment], [1976]. — Folder([4]p) : col ill, col plan ; 16cm.
£0.04
(B77-22255)

914.29'3'04857 — Clwyd. *Guidebooks*
Clwyd official guide. — London : Burrow, [1977]. — 80,[2]p(2 fold) : ill(some col), coat of arms, maps(1 col), ports ; 21cm.
ISBN 0-85026-648-3 Pbk : Unpriced
(B77-10658)

914.29'33 — Clwyd. Holywell. *Guidebooks*
Holywell official guide. — Carshalton : Forward Publicity, [1976]. — 24,[2]p(2 fold) : ill, map ; 19cm.
ISBN 0-7174-0722-5 Sd : Unpriced
(B77-07721)

914.29'33'04857 — Clwyd. Delyn (District). *Guidebooks*
Borough of Delyn official guide. — Carshalton : Home Publishing Co., [1977]. — 32,[1]p : ill, map ; 21cm.
ISBN 0-7174-0743-8 Sd : Unpriced
(B77-15032)

914.29'37 — Clwyd. Denbigh. *Guidebooks*
Denbigh = Dinbych : official town guide. — [New ed.]. — Gloucester : British Publishing Co., [1977]. — 24p : ill, maps ; 19cm.
Includes Welsh text.
ISBN 0-7140-1555-5 Sd : £0.15
(B77-27548)

914.29'37 — Clwyd. Ruthin. *Guidebooks*
Ruthin, Clwyd, town guide. — Gloucester : British Publishing Co., [1976]. — 44p,[2]fold p of plates : ill, maps ; 19cm.
ISBN 0-7140-1343-9 Sd : £0.25
(B77-11479)

914.29'4'0474 — South Wales. Description & travel, 1830. *Early works*
Gastineau, Henry. [Wales illustrated. Vol.2]. South Wales illustrated : in a series of views, comprising the picturesque scenery, towns, castles, seats of the nobility & gentry, antiquities, &c. / engraved on steel from original drawings by Henry Gastineau ; accompanied by historical and topographical descriptions. — Wakefield : EP Publishing, 1977. — [189]p : chiefly ill ; 26cm.
Facsimile reprint of: 1st ed., originally published as vol.2 of 'Wales illustrated'. London : Jones, 1830.
ISBN 0-7158-1163-0 : £4.75
(B77-15033)

914.29'4'04857 — South Wales. *Guidebooks*
Howell, Peter. The companion guide to South Wales / [by] Peter Howell and Elisabeth Beazley. — London : Collins, 1977. — 351p, [16]p of plates : ill, maps, plans ; 22cm.
Col. map on lining papers. — Bibl.: p.333-336. — Index.
ISBN 0-00-216772-7 : £6.95
ISBN 0-00-216774-3 Pbk : £3.50
(B77-16112)

914.29'4'04857 — South Wales. *Walkers' guides*
Styles, Showell. Welsh walks & legends, South Wales / [by] Showell Styles. — Cardiff (41 Lochaber St., Cardiff CF2 3LS) : John Jones Cardiff Ltd, 1977. — 63p : ill, map ; 22cm.
ISBN 0-902375-06-7 : Unpriced
ISBN 0-902375-07-5 Pbk : £1.25
Also classified at 398.2'09429'4
(B77-23841)

914.29'5 — England. Wye Valley. *Guidebooks*
Brooks, John Attwood. The Wye Valley / text by John Brooks. — Norwich : Jarrold and Sons, 1977. — [33]p : col ill, col map ; 20cm. — (A Cotman color book)
English text, French and German captions.
ISBN 0-85306-719-8 Sd : £0.40
(B77-26011)

Clarke, Arthur. Wye Valley and the Royal Forest of Dean ... : the official guide of the Wyedean Tourist Board / original text by Arthur Clarke. — 26th ed. / revised by A.G.R. Cross. — Gloucester : British Publishing Co. for the Board, [1977]. — 124,[2]p(2 fold) : ill, maps ; 21cm.
Index.
ISBN 0-7140-1607-1 Pbk : £0.35
Also classified at 914.24'13
(B77-12206)

914.29'5'04857 — Mid Wales. *Guidebooks*
Mid Wales. — St Ives, Cambs. : Photo Precision, [1977]. — [1],32p : col ill, col map ; 19cm. — (Colourmaster guide)
ISBN 0-85933-164-4 Sd : Unpriced
(B77-22256)

914.29'5'04857 — Powys. *Guidebooks*
Powys official county guide. — Gloucester : British Publishing Co., [1977]. — 88p : ill(2 col), 2 maps(1 col) ; 21cm.
ISBN 0-7140-1585-7 Pbk : Unpriced
(B77-30847)

914.29'61 — Abbeys. *Dyfed. Pontrhydfendigaid. Strata Florida Abbey. Guidebooks. Welsh texts*
Smith, Jenkyn Beverley. Abaty Ystrad Fflur, Dyfed / [gan] J. Beverley Smith, W.G. Thomas. — Llundain [i.e. London] : H.M.S.O., 1977. — 32p,fold plate : ill, plan(tipped in) ; 21cm. — (Great Britain. Department of the Environment. Official handbooks)
At head of title: Paratowyd gan Adran yr Amgylchedd ar ran Ysgrifennydd Gwladol Cymru. — Bibl.: p.32.
ISBN 0-11-670341-5 Sd : £0.50
(B77-32966)

914.29'61'04 — Dyfed. Ceredigion (District). Description & travel, 1188-1971. *Readings from contemporary sources*
A literary excursion northwards from Lampeter / compiled by Belinda Humfrey ; [for the] Conference of University Teachers of English ; with a map by Tony Watson. — Lampeter ([Lampeter, Dyfed SA48 7ED]) : St David's University College, [1976]. — [4],33[i.e. 35]p,[4]p of plates : ill, 2 maps ; 21cm.
Sd : Unpriced
(B77-20785)

914.29'61'04857 — Dyfed. Ceredigion (District). *Guidebooks*
Ceredigion *(District). Council.* Aberystwyth and the coast and countryside of Ceredigion / [Ceredigion District Council]. — [New ed.]. — [Aberystwyth] ([6 Park Ave., Aberystwyth]) : The Council, [1977]. — 103p : col ill, maps(1 col) ; 21cm.
Cover title. — Text on inside covers.
Pbk : Unpriced
(B77-28280)

914.29'62 — Churches. *Dyfed. St Davids. St Non's Chapel. Guidebooks. Welsh-English parallel texts*
Evans, John Wyn. St Non's Chapel, St Davids, Dyfed = Capel S Non, Tyddewi, [Dyfed] / [by J.W. Evans] ; prepared by the Department of the Environment on behalf of the Secretary of State for Wales = paratowyd gan Adran yr Amgylchedd ar van Ysgrifennydd Gwladol Cymru. — [London] : [The Department], 1976. — Folder(6p) : 1 ill ; 22cm.
English and Welsh text. — Bibl.: p.3.
£0.02
(B77-17194)

914.29'62'04857 — Dyfed. Preseli (District). *Guidebooks*
Preseli District Council, official handbook. — London : Burrow, [1976]. — 44p : ill ; 19cm.
ISBN 0-85026-639-4 Sd : Unpriced
(B77-03276)

914.29'65'04857 — Dyfed. Carmarthenshire. *Guidebooks. For motoring*
Titchmarsh, Jim. Gower coast & Carmarthen country by car / compiled [and written] by Jim Titchmarsh ; photography by Alan and Jim Titchmarsh. — Norwich : Jarrold and Sons, [1977]. — [1],32,[1]p : ill, maps(1 col) ; 21cm. — (The Jarrold 'White Horse' series)
Index.
ISBN 0-85306-691-4 Sd : £0.45
Also classified at 914.29'82
(B77-18457)

914.29'71 — Castles. *Mid Glamorgan. Coity. Coity Castle. Guidebooks*
Radford, Courtenay Arthur Ralegh. Coity Castle, Glamorgan / [by] C.A. Ralegh Radford ; produced by the Department of the Environment on behalf of the Welsh Office. — [London] : [The Department], 1976. — Folder(4p) : plan ; 22cm.
Originally published: 1946.
£0.02
(B77-17195)

914.29'75'04857 — Mid Glamorgan. Merthyr Tydfil (District). *Guidebooks*
Merthyr Tydfil official guide. — [New ed.]. — Carshalton : Home Publishing Co., [1976]. — 56,[2]p(2 fold) : ill, maps ; 21cm.
ISBN 0-7174-0715-2 Sd : Unpriced
(B77-02665)

914.29'78'04857 — Mid Glamorgan. Taff-Ely (District). *Guidebooks*
Borough of Taff-Ely official guide. — Carshalton : Home Publishing Co., [1976]. — 48,[3]p(2 fold) : ill, map ; 21cm.
ISBN 0-7174-0732-2 Sd : Unpriced
(B77-09398)

914.29'82 — West Glamorgan. Gower. *Guidebooks. For motoring*
Titchmarsh, Jim. Gower coast & Carmarthen country by car / compiled [and written] by Jim Titchmarsh ; photography by Alan and Jim Titchmarsh. — Norwich : Jarrold and Sons, [1977]. — [1],32,[1]p : ill, maps(1 col) ; 21cm. — (The Jarrold 'White Horse' series)
Index.
ISBN 0-85306-691-4 Sd : £0.45
Primary classification 914.29'65'04857
(B77-18457)

914.29'84 — Abbeys. *West Glamorgan. Neath. Neath Abbey. Guidebooks*
Butler, Lawrence. Neath Abbey, West Glamorgan = Abaty Nedd, Gorllewin Morgannwg / [by] L.A.S. Butler ; prepared by the Department of the Environment on behalf of the Secretary of State for Wales. — London : H.M.S.O., 1976. — 31p,fold plate : ill, plan ; 22cm. — (Great Britain. Department of the Environment. Official handbooks)
Text in English, summary in English and Welsh. — Bibl.: p.28.
ISBN 0-11-670338-5 Sd : £0.40
(B77-06969)

914.29'85'04857 — West Glamorgan. Afan (District). *Guidebooks*
Borough of Afan official guide. — Carshalton : Home Publishing Co., [1977]. — 32,[1]p : ill, coat of arms ; 21cm.
Sd : £0.24
(B77-32967)

914.29'86 — Megalithic tombs. *South Glamorgan. St Lythans. St Lythan Long Cairn & Tinkinswood Long Cairn. Guidebooks*
Savory, Hubert Newman. Tinkinswood and St Lythan long cairns, Glamorgan / [by] H.N. Savory ; prepared by the Department of the Environment on behalf of the Secretary of State for Wales. — [London] : [The Department], 1977. — 10,[1]p : ill, plans ; 22cm.
Originally published: 1950. — Bibl.: p.9.
Sd : £0.04
(B77-17196)

914.29'89'04857 — South Glamorgan. Vale of Glamorgan (District). Description & travel. *Welsh texts*
Davies, Aneirin Talfan. Crwudro Bro Morgannwg / [gan] Aneirin Talfan Davies. — Abertawe [i.e. Swansea] : C. Davies.
Cyfrol 2. — 1976. — [10],244p : ill, facsim, ports ; 23cm.
Index.
ISBN 0-7154-0283-8 : £4.95
(B77-29814)

Sutton, Glyn. Bro Morgannwg / [gan] Glyn Sutton. — Abertawe [i.e. Swansea] : C. Davies, 1977. — 80p : ill, port ; 22cm. — (Cyfres crwydro bröydd Cymru ; 1)
ISBN 0-7154-0410-5 Pbk : £1.25
(B77-20786)

914.29'98 — Castles. *Gwent. Chepstow. Chepstow Castle. Guidebooks*
Great Britain. *Department of the Environment.* Chepstow Castle, Gwent / Department of the Environment. — [London] : [The Department], [1976]. — Folder([4]p) : ill, plan ; 16cm. — (Ancient monuments and historic buildings)
£0.04
(B77-24597)

914.29'98 — Castles. *Gwent. Grosmont. Grosmont Castle. Guidebooks*
Radford, Courtenay Arthur Ralegh. Grosmont Castle, Gwent / [by] C.A. Ralegh Radford ; produced by the Department of the Environment on behalf of the Welsh Office. — [London] : [The Department], 1976. — 5,[1]p : plan ; 22cm.
Originally published: 1946.
Sd : £0.02
(B77-17197)

914.3 — CENTRAL EUROPE, GERMANY
914.3'04'87 — Germany. *Guidebooks*
Fodor's Germany, West and East / Eugene Fodor editor. — London : Hodder and Stoughton.
1977 / Robert C. Fisher executive editor ; Richard Moore, Betty Glauert associate editors ... ; drawings by Beryl Sanders ; introduction by George Bailey. — 1977. — 501p,[36]p of plates : ill(some col), maps(chiefly col), ports ; 19cm.
Index.
ISBN 0-340-21408-2 : £4.50
(B77-23842)

914.3′1′0487 — East Germany. *Practical information. For British businessmen*
British Overseas Trade Board. The German Democratic Republic / [British Overseas Trade Board]. — [New ed.]. — [London] : The Board, 1977. — 53p : map ; 21cm. — (Hints to business men)
Previous ed.: 1976. — Bibl.: p.46-48.
ISBN 0-85605-281-7 Sd : Unpriced
(B77-11480)

914.3′4 — West Germany. Rhineland. Geographical features. *Secondary school texts*
Wightman, Margaret. The Rhine valley / by Margaret Wightman. — London : Harrap, 1977. — 32p : ill, facsim, maps, music ; 14x22cm. — (Discovering Germany)
ISBN 0-245-52896-2 Sd : £0.60
(B77-12783)

914.3′52 — West Germany. Bremen (Land). Geographical features. *Secondary school texts*
Leggott, Martin. Lower Saxony and Bremen / by Martin Leggott. — London : Harrap, 1977. — 32p : ill, maps ; 14x22cm. — (Discovering Germany)
ISBN 0-245-52898-9 Sd : £0.60
Primary classification 914.3′59
(B77-12784)

914.3′59 — West Germany. Lower Saxony. Geographical features. *Secondary school texts*
Leggott, Martin. Lower Saxony and Bremen / by Martin Leggott. — London : Harrap, 1977. — 32p : ill, maps ; 14x22cm. — (Discovering Germany)
ISBN 0-245-52898-9 Sd : £0.60
Also classified at 914.3′52
(B77-12784)

914.36 — AUSTRIA
914.36′04′5 — Austria. *Guidebooks*
Letts go to Austria. — Completely revised [ed.]. — London : Letts, 1977. — 96p : ill, col map ; 19cm. — (Letts guides)
Includes English-German vocabulary. — Previous ed.: 1974.
ISBN 0-85097-216-7 Pbk : £0.75
(B77-12207)

914.36′13′045 — Austria. Vienna. Description & travel
Moore, Charles. Vienna, city of melodies / by Charles Moore. — Melksham : Venton, 1977. — 112p,8p of plates : ill, map(on lining papers) ; 22cm. — (Travalogs series) (White Horse library)
Index.
ISBN 0-85475-135-1 : £3.50
(B77-20787)

914.39 — HUNGARY
914.39′04′5 — Hungary. Description & travel
McNair-Wilson, Diana. Hungary / [by] Diana McNair-Wilson. — London : Batsford, 1976. — 192p,[16]p of plates : ill, map ; 23cm.
Index.
ISBN 0-7134-3199-7 : £4.50
(B77-01056)

914.4 — FRANCE
914.4 — France. Geographical features. *Secondary school texts*
Hawkes, Leslie Roy. France, our nearest neighbour / [by] L.R. Hawkes ; illustrated by Jacqueline Apthorpe. — 2nd ed. — Exeter : Wheaton, 1977. — [8],135p : ill, maps ; 25cm. — (Regional geographies)
Previous ed.: Oxford : Pergamon, 1972. — Index.
ISBN 0-08-016263-0 Pbk : £1.50
(B77-22257)

914.4′04′83 — France. *Guidebooks*
Dennis-Jones, Harold. Letts go to France / by Harold Dennis-Jones. — 2nd ed. — London : Letts, 1977. — 96p : ill, col map ; 19cm. — (Letts guides)
Includes English-French vocabulary. — Previous ed.: 1975.
ISBN 0-85097-220-5 Pbk : £0.75
(B77-12208)

Fodor's France / Eugene Fodor, editor. — [London] : Hodder and Stoughton.
1977 / Robert C. Fisher, executive editor, Richard Moore, European editor, Betty Glauert, associate editor ... ; drawings by Graham Byfield. — 1977. — xii,543p,[12]p of plates : ill(incl 4 col), maps ; 19cm.
Index.
ISBN 0-340-21407-4 : £4.50
(B77-21587)

914.4′04′83 — France. *Guidebooks. For camping*
Deschamps, Marion. Camping in France / [by] Marion Deschamps. — London : Hale, 1977. — 189p,[8]p of plates : ill, maps ; 21cm.
Index.
ISBN 0-7091-6089-5 : £3.95
(B77-30848)

914.4′04′83 — France. *Practical information. For British businessmen*
British Overseas Trade Board. France / [British Overseas Trade Board]. — [New ed.]. — London : The Board, 1977. — 84p : ill ; 21cm. — (Hints to business men)
Previous ed.: 1976. — Bibl.: p.69-71.
Sd : Unpriced
(B77-23843)

914.4′04′83 — France. Description & travel
Gougaud, Henri. France observed / text by Henri Gougaud and Colette Gouvion ; translated from the French by Genevieve Westham. — London : Kaye and Ward [etc.], 1977. — 182p : ill(chiefly col), col map ; 27cm. — ([The réalités series])
Translation of: 'Voir la France'. Paris : Librairie Hachette, 1976.
ISBN 0-7182-1170-7 : £7.95
(B77-28281)

Roberts, Nesta. The face of France / by Nesta Roberts. — London [etc.] : Hodder and Stoughton, 1976. — 254p : ill, maps(on lining papers), music ; 23cm.
ISBN 0-340-20118-5 : £4.50
(B77-01057)

914.4′04′83 — France. Wine-growing regions. *Guidebooks. For motoring*
Tingey, Frederick. Wine roads of France / [by] Frederick Tingey. — London [etc.] : Letts, 1977. — 96p : ill, maps ; 22cm. — (Letts guides)
ISBN 0-85097-176-4 Pbk : £0.85
(B77-18458)

914.4′04′830207 — France. Description & travel. *Personal observations. Humorous texts*
Reid, Colin, *b.1923.* I kiss your little hand, madame - and more disasters abroad / [by] Colin Reid ; drawings by Colin Reid Jnr. — [Henley on Thames] : Kestrels House, Peppard Common, Henley on Thames, Oxon. : Cressrelles Publishing Co. Ltd, 1977. — 3-162p : ill ; 23cm.
ISBN 0-85956-017-1 : £2.75
Also classified at 914.6′04′830207
(B77-34289)

914.4′1 — France. Britanny. Geographical features. *Secondary school texts*
Morris, Elisabeth. Brittany / by Elisabeth Morris. — London : Harrap, 1976. — 32p : ill, facsim, maps ; 14x22cm. — (The regions of France)
Originally published: 1974.
Sd : £0.50
ISBN 0-245-52440-1
(B77-25290)

914.4′1 — France. Brittany. Geographical features. *Secondary school texts*
Morris, Elisabeth. Brittany / by Elisabeth Morris. — London : Harrap, 1974. — 32p : ill, maps, ports ; 14x22cm. — (Destination France : the regions of France)
ISBN 0-245-52440-1 Sd : Unpriced
(B77-19102)

914.4′36′0483 — France. Paris. *Guidebooks*
Cronin, Vincent. The companion guide to Paris / [by] Vincent Cronin. — 3rd revised ed. — [London] : Fontana, 1975. — 256p,[16]p of plates : ill, maps, plans, 2 ports ; 18cm.
This ed. originally published: London : Collins, 1973. — Bibl.: p.249-250. — Index.
ISBN 0-00-613765-2 Pbk : £0.95
(B77-01904)

Kadish, Ferne. Paris on ... 500 [dollars] a day / [by] Ferne Kadish, Kathleen Kirtland. — New York : Collier Books ; London : Collier Macmillan, 1977. — xi,208p ; 21cm.
ISBN 0-02-097780-8 Pbk : £3.75
(B77-34290)

Michelin et Cie. Paris / Michelin. — English ed., 2nd ed. — London (81 Fulham Rd, SW3 6RD) : Michelin Tyre Co. Ltd, 1976. — 178p : ill(some col), col maps, col plans ; 26x12cm. — (Michelin green guide)
Previous ed.: i.e. New ed., 1972. — Index.
Pbk : £2.05
ISBN 2-06-111550-0
(B77-17198)

Paris and environs. — 1st ed. (in this form) / edited by Ian Robertson. — London : E. Benn [etc.], 1977. — 288p,24p of plates : maps(chiefly col), plans(1 col) ; 20cm. — (The blue guides)
Previous ed. i.e. 3rd ed.: published as 'Paris' / edited by Stuart Rossiter. 1968. — Index.
ISBN 0-510-01000-8 : £7.00
ISBN 0-510-01003-2 Pbk : Unpriced
(B77-32305)

914.4′36′0483 — France. Paris. Description & travel
Deslandres, Yvonne. Paris observed / translated from the French by Patrick Greene. — London : Kaye and Ward [etc.], 1977. — 155, [1]p : ill(chiefly col), 2 maps(1 col), plan, ports ; 27cm. — ([The réalités series])
Author: Yvonne Deslandres. — Translation of: 'Voir Paris'. Paris : Librairie Hachette, 1973. — Index.
ISBN 0-7182-1179-0 : £7.95
(B77-21588)

914.4′36′0483 — France. Paris. Description & travel. *Personal observations*
Shaw, Irwin. Paris! Paris! / [text] by Irwin Shaw and [illustrations by] Ronald Searle. — London : Weidenfeld and Nicolson, 1977. — [11],211p : ill ; 24cm.
ISBN 0-297-77275-9 : £4.95
Also classified at 741.5′942
(B77-19103)

914.4′36′0483 — France. Paris. Description & travel. *Secondary school texts*
Savage, Roger. In the shadow of the Eiffel Tower / [by] Roger Savage. — London : Edward Arnold, 1977. — 112p : ill, facsims, maps ; 25cm.
ISBN 0-7131-0089-3 Sd : £2.25
(B77-29815)

914.4′4′0483 — France. Burgundy. Description & travel
Lands, Neil. History, people and places in Burgundy / [by] Neil Lands. — Bourne End : Spurbooks, 1977. — 160p : ill, map(on lining papers) ; 23cm.
Spine title: Burgundy. — Bibl.: p.158. — Index.
ISBN 0-904978-30-3 : £5.00
(B77-29816)

914.4′7′0483 — France. Aquitaine. Description & travel
Macdonald, Lyn. Bordeaux and Aquitaine / [by] Lyn Macdonald. — London : Batsford, 1976. — 191p : ill, map ; 23cm.
Index.
ISBN 0-7134-3183-0 : £4.50
(B77-01058)

914.4′7′0483 — South-west France. *Guidebooks*
Barber, Richard, *b.1941.* The companion guide to South-West France : Bordeaux and the Dordogne / [by] Richard Barber. — London : Collins, 1977. — 288p,[24]p of plates : ill, facsim, maps, plan ; 22cm.
Bibl.: p.280-281. — Index.
ISBN 0-00-211149-7 : £6.95
ISBN 0-00-216773-5 Pbk : £4.25
(B77-20788)

914.5 — ITALY
914.5 — Italy. Adriatic coastal regions. *Guidebooks. For sailing*
Denham, Henry Mangles. The Adriatic : a sea-guide to the Dalmatian coast and islands, Venice and Eastern Italy / [by] H.M. Denham. — 2nd ed. — London : J. Murray, 1977. — xii, 259p,[12]p of plates : ill, maps ; 25cm. — (Denham, Henry Mangles. Sea guides)
Previous ed.: 1967. — Index.
ISBN 0-7195-3359-7 : £10.00
Primary classification 914.97
(B77-28282)

914.5′04′92 — Italy. *Guidebooks*
Letts go to Italy. — Completely revised [ed.]. — London : Letts, 1977. — 96p : ill, col map ; 19cm. — (Letts guides)
Previous ed.: i.e. 2nd ed., 1974.
ISBN 0-85097-215-9 Pbk : £0.75
(B77-13418)

914.5′04′92 — Italy. *Guidebooks. For youth hostelling*
Youth Hostels Association (England and Wales). Youth hosteller's guide to Europe - Italy / [Youth Hostels Association (England and Wales)] ; [written by R.M. Stuttard]. — 9th ed. — London : Y.H.A. Services, 1977. — 32,[1]p : maps ; 19cm.
Previous ed.: 1974. — Index.
ISBN 0-900833-42-4 Sd : £0.30
(B77-13419)

914.5'04'92 — Italy. *Practical information. For British businessmen*
British Overseas Trade Board. Italy / [British Overseas Trade Board]. — [New ed.]. — London : The Board, 1976. — 52p : ill ; 21cm. — (Hints to business men)
Previous ed.: 1975. — Bibl.: p.45-47.
Sd : Unpriced
(B77-09399)

914.5'04'92 — Italy. Wine-growing regions. *Guidebooks. For motoring*
Tingey, Nancy. Wine roads of Italy / [by] Nancy Tingey. — London [etc.] : Letts, 1977. — 96p : ill, maps ; 22cm. — (Letts guides)
ISBN 0-85097-177-2 Pbk : £0.85
(B77-18459)

914.5'18'0492 — Ligurian Sea region. Description & travel. *Personal observations*
Deane, Shirley. The expectant mariner / [by] Shirley Deane. — [London] : Fontana, 1975. — 222p : map ; 18cm.
Originally published: London : J. Murray, 1962.
ISBN 0-00-633842-9 Pbk : £0.65
(B77-01905)

914.5'31 — Italy. Venice. *Guidebooks*
Inglis, William. Letts visit Venice / [by] William Inglis. — London [etc.] : Letts, 1977. — 70p, [10]p of plates : ill, col maps ; 18cm. — (Letts guides)
ISBN 0-85097-210-8 Pbk : £0.75
(B77-17823)

914.5'31 — Italy. Venice. Description & travel. *Juvenile literature*
Barnes, Edward. 'Blue Peter' special assignment - Venice and Brussels / [by] Edward Barnes and Dorothy Smith ; with fourteen full colour photographs and with line drawings by Sara Silcock. — London : Severn House : [Distributed by Hutchinson], 1976. — 92p,leaf of plate,[6]p of plate : ill(some col), ports ; 20cm.
'... based on the Blue Peter Special Assignment programme on BBC television' - cover. — Originally published: London : Pan Books, 1974.
ISBN 0-7278-0185-6 : £2.50
Also classified at 914.93'3
(B77-00513)

914.5'53 — Italy. Lucca. Description & travel, ca 1960. *Personal observations*
Bartlett, Vernon. Tuscan retreat / [by] Vernon Bartlett ; with illustrations by Maurice Bartlett. — Large print ed. — Leicester : Ulverscroft, 1976. — [9],338p : ill ; 23cm. — (Ulverscroft large print series : [non-fiction])
Originally published: London : Chatto and Windus, 1964.
ISBN 0-85456-505-1 : £2.65
(B77-10036)

914.5'7'0492 — Southern Italy. Description & travel
Pereira, Anthony. Pompeii, Naples and Southern Italy / [by] Anthony Pereira. — London : Batsford, 1977. — ix,213p,[16]p of plates : ill, map ; 24cm.
Bibl.: p.206-207. — Index.
ISBN 0-7134-0815-4 : £5.95
(B77-22258)

914.58'04'92 — Antiquities. *Italy. Sicily. Guidebooks*
Guido, Margaret. Sicily : an archaeological guide : the prehistoric and Roman remains and the Greek cities / [by] Margaret Guido. — [2nd ed.]. — London : Faber, 1977. — 3-223p : ill, maps, plans ; 20cm. — (Archaeological guides)
Previous ed.: 1967. — Bibl.: p.212-214. — Index.
ISBN 0-571-10881-4 Pbk : £2.60
(B77-22259)

914.58'04'92 — Italy. Sicily. Description & travel. *Personal observations*
Durrell, Lawrence. Sicilian carousel / [by] Lawrence Durrell. — London : Faber, 1977. — 3-223p,[4] leaves of plates : ill ; 23cm.
Index. — '... includes several poems ... not previously published' - jacket.
ISBN 0-571-11062-2 : £5.25 : CIP rev.
(B77-10037)

914.59 — SARDINIA
914.59'04'92 — Italy. Sardinia. *Guidebooks*
Holme, Timothy. Sardinia / by T. and B. Holme and B. Ghirardelli ; with 16 photographs by Janet March-Penny. — Revised ed. — London : Cape, 1977. — 3-188p : ill, maps ; 18cm. — (Travellers' guides)
Col. maps on lining papers. — Previous ed.: 1967. — Bibl.: p.181. — Index.
ISBN 0-224-61133-x : £3.95
(B77-06368)

914.59'04'92 — Italy. Sardinia. Description & travel
Waite, Virginia. Sardinia / [by] Virginia Waite. — London : Batsford, 1977. — 168p,[16]p of plates : ill, map ; 23cm.
Index.
ISBN 0-7134-0039-0 : £4.50
(B77-31615)

914.6 — IBERIAN PENINSULA, SPAIN
914.6 — Northern Spain. *Guidebooks*
Dennis-Jones, Harold. Letts go to Northern Spain / by Harold Dennis-Jones. — London : Letts, 1977. — 96p : ill, col map ; 19cm. — (Letts guides)
Includes English-Spanish vocabulary.
ISBN 0-85097-173-x Pbk : £0.75
(B77-13420)

914.6'04'83 — Spain. *Guidebooks*
Downie, Robert Angus. Letts roadbook of Spain / [by] R. Angus Downie. — London [etc.] : Letts, 1977. — 128p,16p of plates : ill, col maps ; 27cm. — (Letts guides)
ISBN 0-85097-233-7 : £2.95
(B77-23844)

914.6'04'83 — Spain. *Practical information. For British businessmen*
British Overseas Trade Board. Spain (including the Canary Islands) / [British Overseas Trade Board]. — [New ed.]. — London : The Board, 1976. — 60p : ill ; 21cm. — (Hints to business men)
Previous ed.: 1975. — Bibl.: p.48-50.
ISBN 0-85605-260-4 Sd : Unpriced
(B77-05762)

914.6'04'83 — Spain. Description & travel
Moore, Charles. Contrasting Spain / by Charles Moore. — Melksham : Venton, 1977. — 173p, 8p of plates : ill, map(on lining papers) ; 22cm. — (Travelogs series) (White Horse library)
Index.
ISBN 0-85475-128-9 : £3.95
(B77-24598)

914.6'04'830207 — Spain. Description & travel. *Personal observations. Humorous texts*
Reid, Colin, *b.1923.* I kiss your little hand, madame - and more disasters abroad / [by] Colin Reid ; drawings by Colin Reid Jnr. — [Henley on Thames] : Kestrels House, Peppard Common, Henley on Thames, Oxon. : Cressrelles Publishing Co. Ltd, 1977. — 3-162p : ill ; 23cm.
ISBN 0-85956-017-1 : £2.75
Primary classification 914.4'04'830207
(B77-34289)

914.6'7 — Spain. Costa Brava & Costa Dorada. *Guidebooks*
Dennis-Jones, Harold. Letts go to Costa Brava and the Costa Dorada / by Harold Dennis-Jones. — Completely revised [ed.]. — London : Letts, 1977. — 96p : ill, col map ; 19cm. — (Letts guides)
Includes English-Spanish vocabulary. — Previous ed.: i.e. 1st ed., 1974.
ISBN 0-85097-211-6 Pbk : £0.75
(B77-13421)

914.6'75'0482 — Spain. Balearic Islands, 1974. *Guidebooks*
Jerome, Philip. Majorca : Minorca, Ibiza, Formentera / by Philip Jerome and Ian McIntosh. — [London] : [Collins], 1975. — 96p : ill, col maps ; 17cm. — (Collins holiday guides)
Index.
ISBN 0-00-435740-x Pbk : £0.60
(B77-04476)

914.6'75'0483 — Spain. Balearic Islands. *Guidebooks*
Dennis-Jones, Harold. Letts go to Majorca, Menorca, Ibiza, and Formentera / by Harold Dennis-Jones. — Completely revised [ed.]. — London : Letts, 1977. — 96p : ill, col maps ; 19cm. — (Letts guides)
Includes English-Spanish vocabulary. — Previous ed.: i.e. 1st ed., 1974.
Pbk : £0.75
ISBN 0-85097-103-9
(B77-13963)

914.6'8 — Spain. Costa del Sol. *Guidebooks*
Dennis-Jones, Harold. Letts go to Costa del Sol and the South of Spain / by Harold Dennis-Jones. — Completely revised [ed.]. — London : Letts, 1977. — 96p : ill, col map ; 19cm. — (Letts guides)
Includes English-Spanish vocabulary. — Previous ed.: i.e. 1st ed., 1974.
ISBN 0-85097-212-4 Pbk : £0.75
(B77-13964)

914.69 — PORTUGAL
914.69'04'42 — Portugal. *Guidebooks*
Dennis-Jones, Harold. Letts go to Portugal / by Harold Dennis-Jones. — Revised [ed.]. — London : Letts, 1977. — 96p : ill ; 19cm. — (Letts guides)
Previous ed.: i.e. 1st ed., 1974.
Pbk : £0.75
ISBN 0-85097-106-3
(B77-12785)

Fodor's Portugal / Eugene Fodor, William Curtis editors. — [London] : Hodder and Stoughton. 1977 / Robert C. Fisher executive editor, Richard Moore European editor ; drawings by Kolos. — 1977. — x,310p,[12]p of plates : ill(incl 4 col), maps ; 19cm.
Index.
ISBN 0-340-21579-8 : £4.50
(B77-21589)

914.69'04'42 — Portugal. *Practical information. For British businessmen*
British Overseas Trade Board. Portugal, Madeira and the Azores / [British Overseas Trade Board]. — [New ed.]. — London : The Board, 1976. — [1],68p : ill, map ; 21cm. — (Hints to business men)
Previous ed.: 1975. — Bibl.: p.61-62.
ISBN 0-85605-263-9 Sd : Unpriced
(B77-05763)

914.69'42 — Portugal. Lisbon. *Guidebooks*
Wright, Carol. Lisbon / [by] Carol Wright. — London : Dent, 1975. — vii,88p : ill, 2 maps ; 19cm.
Originally published: 1971. — Index.
ISBN 0-460-02178-8 Pbk : £0.65
(B77-08658)

914.7 — EASTERN EUROPE, SOVIET UNION
914.7 — Soviet Union. Geographical features
Lydolph, Paul Edward. Geography of the USSR / [by] Paul E. Lydolph ; cartographers Don and Denise Temple. — 3rd ed. — New York ; London [etc.] : Wiley, 1977. — xvi, 495p : ill, charts, maps(chiefly col) ; 26cm.
Map on lining paper. — Previous ed.: 1970. — Bibl. — Index.
ISBN 0-471-55724-2 : £12.70
(B77-19893)

914.7'04'85 — Soviet Union. *Guidebooks*
Fodor's Soviet Union. — [London] : Hodder and Stoughton.
1976-1977 / Eugene Fodor, Robert C. Fisher, editors ... — 1976. — 543p,[12]p of plates : ill(some col), maps(some col), plans ; 21cm.
Fold. sheet (2 sides) (col. maps) in pocket. — Index.
ISBN 0-340-20322-6 : £5.25
(B77-06970)

Gross, Eugenie. The Soviet Union : a guide for travellers / [by] Eugenie and Jeffrey Gross. — London : J. Murray, 1977. — x,436p : maps ; 21cm.
Index.
ISBN 0-7195-3361-9 : £5.95
(B77-19894)

914.7'04'85 — Soviet Union. *Practical information. For British businessmen*
British Overseas Trade Board. Union of Soviet Socialist Republics / [British Overseas Trade Board]. — London : The Board, 1976. — 88p : ill, map ; 21cm. — (Hints to business men)
Bibl.: p.75-77.
ISBN 0-85605-261-2 Sd : Unpriced
(B77-05764)

914.71 — FINLAND
914.71'04'3 — Finland. *Guidebooks*
Nickels, Sylvie. Finland / by Sylvie Nickels ; with 15 photographs by Sylvie Nickels and Penny Tweedie. — Revised ed. — London : Cape, 1977. — 240p : ill, map ; 18cm. — (Travellers' guides)
Col. maps on lining papers. — Previous ed.: 1965. — Bibl.: p.229-233. — Index.
ISBN 0-224-01281-9 : £4.95
(B77-05765)

914.71'04'3 — Finland. *Practical information. For British businessmen*
British Overseas Trade Board. Finland / [British Overseas Trade Board]. — [New ed.]. — London : The Board, [1976]. — 51p : map ; 21cm. — (Hints to business men)
Previous ed.: 1975. — Bibl.: p.44-46.
ISBN 0-85605-280-9 Sd : Unpriced
(B77-11481)

914.72/9 — SOVIET UNION. SPECIAL LOCALITIES
914.7'31 — Russia (RSFSR). Moscow. *Guidebooks*
Smith, Desmond. Smith's guide to Moscow. — London : Cape, 1976. — xiv,335,xii,[3]p : ill, maps ; 19cm.
Map on lining papers. — Originally published: as 'Smith's Moscow'. New York : Knopf, 1974. — Bibl..: p.330-335. — Index.
ISBN 0-224-01265-7 : £4.95
(B77-01906)

914.8 — SCANDINAVIA
914.8'04'8 — Scandinavia. *Guidebooks*
Fodor's Scandinavia / Eugene Fodor editor. — [London] : Hodder and Stoughton.
1977 / Robert C. Fisher executive editor, Richard Moore European editor ; drawings by H. Dunkergod. — Illustrated ed. ; with atlas and city plans. — 1977. — 528p,[8]p of plates : ill, maps, plans, ports ; 21cm.
Index.
ISBN 0-340-21420-1 : £5.95
(B77-30849)

914.81 — NORWAY
914.81'04'4 — Norway. *Practical information. For British businessmen*
British Overseas Trade Board. Norway / [British Overseas Trade Board]. — London : The Board, 1977. — 41p ; 21cm. — (Hints to business men)
Bibl.: p.34-36.
Sd : Unpriced
(B77-07723)

914.85 — SWEDEN
914.85'04'5 — Sweden. *Practical information. For British businessmen*
British Overseas Trade Board. Sweden / [British Overseas Trade Board]. — [New ed.]. — London : The Board, 1977. — 49p : ill ; 21cm. — (Hints to business men)
Previous ed.: 1976. — Bibl.: p.40-42.
Sd : Unpriced
(B77-20789)

914.89 — DENMARK
914.89 — Denmark. Geographical features. *Juvenile literature*
Weimar, Stig. Denmark is like this / [by] Stig Weimar ; translated [from the Danish] by Joan Tate. — London : Kaye and Ward, [1977]. — [29]p : ill(chiefly col), col maps, port ; 26cm.
Text on lining paper. — This translation originally published: Copenhagen : Gyldendal, 1976. — Translation of: 'Kender du Danmark'. Copenhagen : Gyldendalske Boghandel, 1976.
ISBN 0-7182-1142-1 : £1.95
(B77-10659)

914.89'04'5 — Denmark. *Guidebooks*
Dennis-Jones, Harold. Letts go to Denmark / by Harold Dennis-Jones. — Complete revised [ed.]. — London : Letts, 1977. — 96p : ill, col map ; 19cm. — (Letts guides)
Includes English-Danish vocabulary. — Previous ed.: i.e. 1st ed., 1975.
ISBN 0-85097-221-3 Pbk : £0.75
(B77-13422)

914.89'04'5 — Denmark. *Practical information. For British businessmen*
British Overseas Trade Board. Denmark / [British Overseas Trade Board]. — [New ed.]. — London : The Board, 1977. — 52p : ill ; 21cm. — (Hints to business men)
Previous ed.: 1976. — Bibl.: p.44-46.
Sd : Unpriced
(B77-20790)

914.912 — ICELAND
914.91'2'044 — Iceland. *Practical information. For British businessmen*
British Overseas Trade Board. Iceland / [British Overseas Trade Board]. — [New ed.]. — London : The Board, 1977. — [1],40p : ill, map ; 21cm. — (Hints to business men)
Previous ed.: 1975. — Bibl.: p.31-32.
Sd : Unpriced
(B77-34291)

914.92 — NETHERLANDS
914.92'04'7 — Inland waterways. Description & travel. *Netherlands*
Pilkington, Roger. Small boat through Holland / by Roger Pilkington ; illustrated by David Knight. — Hornchurch : I. Henry, 1976. — vi, 217p : ill, maps ; 21cm.
Originally published: London : Macmillan, 1958.
ISBN 0-86025-807-6 : £3.95
(B77-10660)

914.92'04'7 — Netherlands. *Guidebooks*
Chester, Carole. Holland / [by] Carole Chester. — Glasgow [etc.] : Collins, 1977. — 96p : ill(some col), col maps ; 17cm. — (Collins holiday guides)
Index.
ISBN 0-00-435748-5 Pbk : £0.60
(B77-16113)

Dennis-Jones, Harold. Letts go to Holland / by Harold Dennis-Jones. — Completely revised [ed.]. — London : Letts, 1977. — 96p : ill, col map ; 19cm. — (Letts guides)
Previous ed.: 1975. — Includes English-Dutch vocabulary.
ISBN 0-85097-222-1 Pbk : £0.75
(B77-12209)

914.92'04'7 — Netherlands. Description & travel
Cowie, Donald. Holland : the land and the people / [by] Donald Cowie. — South Brunswick [etc.] : Barnes ; London : Yoseloff, 1974. — 245p,[4]p of plates : ill(some col), 2 maps, ports ; 26cm.
Index.
ISBN 0-498-01414-2 : £4.00
(B77-19895)

914.92'3 — Netherlands. Amsterdam. *Guidebooks*
Dennis-Jones, Harold. Letts visit Amsterdam / [by] Harold Dennis-Jones. — London [etc.] : Letts, 1977. — 71p,[7]p of plates,leaf of plate : ill, col maps ; 18cm. — (Letts guides)
ISBN 0-85097-209-4 Pbk : £0.75
(B77-17199)

914.93 — BELGIUM
914.93'04'4 — Belgium. *Guidebooks*
Belgium and Luxembourg. — 5th ed. / edited by John Tomes. — London : E. Benn [etc.], 1977. — 336p,8p of plates : maps(chiefly col), col plan ; 20cm. — (The blue guides)
Previous ed.: / edited by Litellus Russell Muirhead. 1963. — Index.
ISBN 0-510-01002-4 : £7.50
ISBN 0-510-01004-0 Pbk : £5.00
Also classified at 914.93'5'044
(B77-20791)

Fodor's Belgium and Luxembourg / Eugene Fodor, editor. — [London] : Hodder and Stoughton.
1976-77 / Robert C. Fisher, executive editor, Betty Glauert, Richard Moore, associate editors ... ; drawings by Keith West. — 1976. — 312p, [12]p of plates : ill(some col), maps ; 19cm.
Index.
ISBN 0-340-20334-x : £3.95
(B77-06369)

914.93'3 — Belgium. Brussels. Description & travel. *Juvenile literature*
Barnes, Edward. 'Blue Peter' special assignment - Venice and Brussels / [by] Edward Barnes and Dorothy Smith ; with fourteen full colour photographs and with line drawings by Sara Silcock. — London : Severn House : [Distributed by Hutchinson], 1976. — 92p,leaf of plate,[6]p of plate : ill(some col), ports ; 20cm.
'... based on the Blue Peter Special Assignment programme on BBC television' - cover. — Originally published: London : Pan Books, 1974.
ISBN 0-7278-0185-6 : £2.50
Primary classification 914.5'31
(B77-00513)

914.935 — LUXEMBOURG
914.93'5'044 — Luxembourg. *Guidebooks*
Belgium and Luxembourg. — 5th ed. / edited by John Tomes. — London : E. Benn [etc.], 1977. — 336p,8p of plates : maps(chiefly col), col plan ; 20cm. — (The blue guides)
Previous ed.: / edited by Litellus Russell Muirhead. 1963. — Index.
ISBN 0-510-01002-4 : £7.50
ISBN 0-510-01004-0 Pbk : £5.00
Primary classification 914.93'04'4
(B77-20791)

914.94 — SWITZERLAND
914.94'04'7 — Switzerland. *Guidebooks*
Hawkes, John, *b.1910.* Letts go to Switzerland and Liechtenstein / by John and Moira Hawkes. — London : Letts, 1977. — 96p : ill, col map ; 19cm. — (Letts guides)
Includes English-French-German-Italian vocabulary.
ISBN 0-85097-174-8 Pbk : £0.75
(B77-12786)

914.95 — GREECE
914.95'04'7 — Greece. *Guidebooks*
Sidgwick, Christopher. Letts go to Greece / by Christopher Sidgwick. — Completely revised [ed.]. — London : Letts, 1977. —.94p : ill ; 19cm. — (Letts guides)
Previous ed.: 1974.
ISBN 0-85097-219-1 Pbk : £0.75
(B77-12210)

914.95'04'7 — Greece. *Practical information. For British businessmen*
British Overseas Trade Board. Greece / [British Overseas Trade Board]. — [New ed.]. — London : The Board, 1977. — 48p : ill ; 21cm. — (Hints to business men)
Previous ed.: 1976. — Bibl.: p.40-41.
Sd : Unpriced
(B77-23845)

914.95'04'7 — Greece. Description & travel. *Personal observations*
Val Baker, Denys. A long way to Land's End / [by] Denys Val Baker. — London : Kimber, 1977. — 208p ; 23cm.
ISBN 0-7183-0105-6 : £3.25
(B77-21590)

914.95'5'047 — Greece. Ionian Islands. *Guidebooks*
Mead, Robin. Letts go to the Greek Islands / by Robin Mead. — London : Letts, 1977. — 94p : ill, col maps ; 19cm. — (Letts guides)
ISBN 0-85097-199-3 Pbk : £0.75
(B77-12787)

Young, Martin. Corfu and the other Ionian islands / by Martin Young ; with 16 photographs by Cora Pongracz. — Revised ed. — London : Cape, 1976. — 357p : ill, maps ; 18cm. — (Travellers' guide)
Col. maps on lining papers. — Previous ed.: 1971. — Bibl.: p.342-345. — Index.
ISBN 0-224-01307-6 : £3.95
(B77-06370)

914.97 — YUGOSLAVIA
914.97 — Yugoslavia. Coastal regions. *Guidebooks. For sailing*
Denham, Henry Mangles. The Adriatic : a sea-guide to the Dalmatian coast and islands, Venice and Eastern Italy / [by] H.M. Denham. — 2nd ed. — London : J. Murray, 1977. — xii, 259p,[12]p of plates : ill, maps ; 25cm. — (Denham, Henry Mangles. Sea guides)
Previous ed.: 1967. — Index.
ISBN 0-7195-3359-7 : £10.00
Also classified at 914.5
(B77-28282)

914.97'04'2 — Yugoslavia. *Guidebooks*
Mason, John, *b.1914.* Letts go to Yugoslavia / by John and Anne Mason. — Completely revised [ed.]. — London : Letts, 1977. — 96p : ill ; 19cm. — (Letts guides)
Previous ed.: i.e. 2nd ed., 1974.
ISBN 0-85097-267-1 Pbk : £0.75
(B77-12211)

914.97'04'2 — Yugoslavia. Description & travel, 1930-1937. *Personal observations*
West, Rebecca. Black lamb and grey falcon : a journey through Yugoslavia / by Rebecca West. — [Revised ed.]. — London [etc.] : Macmillan, 1977. — [9],1181p : ill, 2 maps(1 col)(on lining papers) ; 23cm.
This ed. originally published: 1955. — Bibl.: p.1153-1158. — Index.
ISBN 0-333-00418-3 : £9.95
Also classified at 949.7
(B77-30850)

914.998 — CRETE
914.998'04'4 — Greece. Crete. *Guidebooks*
Rossiter, Stuart. Crete / [by] Stuart Rossiter. — 2nd ed. — London : E. Benn [etc.], 1977. — 119p : maps(some col), plans ; 20cm. — (The blue guides)
Previous ed.: 1974. — Index.
ISBN 0-510-01122-5 : £4.00
ISBN 0-510-01123-3 Pbk : £2.50
(B77-12212)

915 — EURASIA, ASIA

915 — Asia. Geographical features. *Secondary school texts. Welsh texts*
Davies, Aled Lloyd. Asia / [gan] Aled Lloyd Davies. — [Cardiff] : Gwasg Prifysgol Cymru, 1977. — [12],93p : ill(some col), col maps, ports ; 27cm.
Bibl.: p.90. — Index.
ISBN 0-7083-0643-8 : £2.50
(B77-26012)

915'.04'42 — Asia. *Guidebooks*
Moss, Chris. Guide to Asia, 77 / [by Chris Moss and Mike Young]. — [2nd ed.]. — London (15 Athelstone Rd, N.4) : Strawberry Jam Publications, 1977. — [1],60p : maps ; 30cm.
Sd : £1.20
(B77-31616)

On your own : Air Siam's student guide to Asia / edited by Richard Rawson. — Stanford, Calif. : Volunteers in Asia [etc.] ; London : [Distributed by] Prentice-Hall, 1976. — 239p : ill, maps, plan ; 18cm.
ISBN 0-8048-1176-8 Pbk : £1.75
(B77-00514)

915'.04'42 — Asia. *Practical information. For motoring*
McElduff, Colin. Trans-Asia motoring / [by] Colin McElduff. — London (Wilton House, Hobart Place, S.W.1) : Wilton House Gentry Ltd, 1976. — 254p : ill, maps, port ; 25cm.
Bibl.: p.26. — Index.
ISBN 0-905064-01-1 : £5.40
(B77-06971)

915.1 — CHINA AND ADJACENT AREAS

915.1'04'250924 — China. Description & travel, ca 1270-1295. Polo, Marco. *Secondary school texts*
Latham, Ronald Edward. Marco Polo : traveller to the East / [written by Ronald Latham] ; illustrated by Brian Lewis ... — London : Macdonald Educational, 1977. — 2-47p : col ill, col maps ; 29cm. — (Macdonald famous people)
Text on lining papers. — Index.
ISBN 0-356-05166-8 : £1.60
(B77-06972)

915.1'04'5 — China. *Practical information. For British businessmen*
British Overseas Trade Board. The People's Republic of China / [British Overseas Trade Board]. — [New ed.]. — London : The Board, 1977. — 49p : ill, map ; 21cm. — (Hints to business men)
Previous ed.: 1975. — Bibl.: p.42-44.
Sd : Unpriced
(B77-27549)

915.1'25'04 — Hong Kong. *Guidebooks*
Papineau's guide to Hong Kong and spotlight on Macau. — Singapore : André Publications ; Tunbridge Wells ([Abacus House, Speldhurst Rd, Tunbridge Wells, Kent TN4 0HU]) : [Distributed by] Abacus-Kent Ltd.
8th ed. / editor Aristide J.G. Papineau. — 1976 [i.e. 1977]. — 200p,[2]fold leaves of plates : ill(some col), maps(some col), port ; 19cm.
This ed. published in Singapore : 1976.
ISBN 0-85626-115-7 Pbk : £1.95
(B77-08659)

9th ed. / editor Aristide J.G. Papineau. — 1977. — 216p,[2]fold leaves of plates : ill(some col), 2 col maps, port ; 19cm.
ISBN 0-85626-134-3 Pbk : £2.10
(B77-27550)

915.1'25'04 — Hong Kong. *Practical information. For British businessmen*
British Overseas Trade Board. Hong Kong and Macao / [British Overseas Trade Board]. — [New ed.]. — London : The Board, 1976. — [1] ,70p : ill, map ; 21cm. — (Hints to business men)
Previous ed.: 1975. — Bibl.: p.63-65.
ISBN 0-85605-264-7 Sd : Unpriced
Also classified at 915.1'26'045
(B77-05766)

915.1'26'045 — Macau. *Practical information. For British businessmen*
British Overseas Trade Board. Hong Kong and Macao / [British Overseas Trade Board]. — [New ed.]. — London : The Board, 1976. — [1] ,70p : ill, map ; 21cm. — (Hints to business men)
Previous ed.: 1975. — Bibl.: p.63-65.
ISBN 0-85605-264-7 Sd : Unpriced
Primary classification 915.1'25'04
(B77-05766)

915.1'5'043 — Tibet. Exploration by women, 1872-1911
Miller, Luree. On top of the world : five women explorers in Tibet / [by] Luree Miller. — [London] : Paddington Press, 1976. — 222p : ill, maps, ports ; 24cm.
Map on lining papers. — Bibl.: p.210-214. — Index.
ISBN 0-8467-0138-3 : £5.95
(B77-32306)

915.19'5'0443 — South Korea. *Practical information. For British businessmen*
British Overseas Trade Board. The Republic of Korea / [British Overseas Trade Board]. — London : The Board, 1977. — 47p : ill, maps ; 21cm. — (Hints to business men)
Bibl.: p.39-41.
ISBN 0-85605-268-x Sd : Unpriced
(B77-10038)

915.2 — JAPAN

915.2'04'4 — Japan. *Guidebooks*
Fodor's Japan and Korea / Eugene Fodor, Robert C. Fisher, editors. — [London] : Hodder and Stoughton.
1977 / Richard Moore, associate editor. — 1977. — 512p,[16]p of plates : ill(some col), maps ; 21cm.
Index.
ISBN 0-340-21417-1 : £5.95
(B77-06371)

915.2'04'4 — Japan. *Practical information. For British businessmen*
British Overseas Trade Board. Japan / [British Overseas Trade Board]. — [New ed.]. — London : The Board, 1976. — 64p : ill, map ; 21cm. — (Hints to business men)
Previous ed.: 1975. — Bibl.: p.53-56.
ISBN 0-85605-277-9 Sd : Unpriced
(B77-09400)

915.3 — ARABIA

915.3'04 — Arabia. Exploration, to ca 1950
Brent, Peter. Far Arabia : explorers of the myth / [by] Peter Brent. — London : Weidenfeld and Nicolson, 1977. — xi,239p,[8]p of plates : ill, map, ports ; 23cm.
Bibl.: p.229-230. — Index.
ISBN 0-297-77344-5 : £6.95
(B77-22987)

915.3'04'4 — Arabia. Exploration, 1819. *Diaries*
Sadleir, George Forster. Diary of a journey across Arabia (1819) / [by] George Forster Sadleir. — [1st ed. reprinted] ; with a new introduction by F.M. Edwards. — Naples : Falcon Press ; New York ; Cambridge : Oleander Press, 1977. — 161p : map ; 22cm. — (Arabia past and present ; 5)
Spine title: A journey across Arabia (1819). — First ed. originally published: Bombay : Byculla, 1866.
ISBN 0-902675-59-1 : £8.00 : CIP rev.
(B77-07724)

915.3'5'045 — Oman & United Arab Emirates. *Practical information. For British businessmen*
British Overseas Trade Board. United Arab Emirates and the Sultanate of Oman / [British Overseas Trade Board]. — [New ed.]. — [London] : The Board, 1976. — [1],112p : ill, maps ; 21cm. — (Hints to business men)
Previous ed.: 1975. — Bibl.: p.89-92.
ISBN 0-85605-266-3 Pbk : Unpriced
(B77-10039)

915.3'63'045 — Qatar. *Practical information. For British businessmen*
British Overseas Trade Board. Bahrain and Qatar / [British Overseas Trade Board]. — [New ed.]. — London : The Board, 1977. — 96p : ill, 3 maps ; 21cm. — (Hints to business men)
Previous ed.: 1976.
Sd : Unpriced
Also classified at 915.3'65'045
(B77-33520)

915.3'65'045 — Bahrain. *Practical information. For British businessmen*
British Overseas Trade Board. Bahrain and Qatar / [British Overseas Trade Board]. — [New ed.]. — London : The Board, 1977. — 96p : ill, 3 maps ; 21cm. — (Hints to business men)
Previous ed.: 1976.
Sd : Unpriced
Primary classification 915.3'63'045
(B77-33520)

915.3'67'045 — Kuwait. *Practical information. For British businessmen*
British Overseas Trade Board. Kuwait / [British Overseas Trade Board]. — [New ed.]. — London : The Board, 1977. — 47p : ill, 2 maps ; 21cm. — (Hints to business men)
Previous ed.: 1976. — Bibl.: p.40-42.
Sd : Unpriced
(B77-20792)

915.3'8'045 — Saudi Arabia. *Practical information. For British businessmen*
British Overseas Trade Board. Saudi Arabia / [British Overseas Trade Board]. — [New ed.]. — [London] : The Board, 1976. — [1],68p : ill, maps ; 21cm. — (Hints to business men)
Previous ed.: 1975. — Bibl.: p.45-47.
ISBN 0-85605-267-1 Sd : Unpriced
(B77-09401)

The **businessman's** guide to Saudi Arabia / edited by Anthony Purdy. — London : Arlington Books, 1976. — [7],330p : ill, form, maps ; 23cm.
ISBN 0-85140-252-6 : £7.50
(B77-27551)

915.4 — SOUTH ASIA, INDIA

915.4 — Mountaineering expeditions. *Western Himalayas, 1820-1875*
Keay, John. When men and mountains meet : the explorers of the Western Himalayas, 1820-75 / [by] John Keay. — London : J. Murray, 1977. — x,277p,[16]p of plates : ill, maps, ports ; 23cm.
Bibl.: p.263-270. — Index.
ISBN 0-7195-3334-1 : £6.50
(B77-16658)

915.4 — South Asia. Indus River. Description & travel, 1836-1837. *Personal observations*
Wood, John, *b.1811.* A journey to the source of the River Oxus / by John Wood ; with an essay on the geography of the Valley of the Oxus by Henry Yule ... — [New ed. reprinted] ; [with] an introduction by G.E. Wheeler. — Karachi ; London [etc.] : Oxford University Press, 1976. — cv,[2],280p,[3]fold leaves of plates : 1 ill, maps ; 23cm. — (Oxford in Asia historical reprints from Pakistan)
Facsimile reprint of: New ed. London : J. Murray, 1872.
ISBN 0-19-577215-6 : £11.00
(B77-10661)

915.4'04'4 — India (Republic). *Guidebooks*
Fodor's India / Eugene Fodor, William Curtis, editors. — [London] : Hodder and Stoughton.
1976-77 / Robert C. Fisher, executive editor ... — 1976. — 600p,[20]p of plates, fold leaf of plate : ill(some col), maps(1 col), plans ; 21cm.
Col. map tipped in. — Index.
ISBN 0-340-20329-3 : £4.95
(B77-06372)

915.4'04'5 — India (Republic). *Practical information. For British businessmen*
British Overseas Trade Board. India / [British Overseas Trade Board]. — [New ed.]. — London : The Board, 1977. — 68p : ill, map ; 21cm. — (Hints to business men)
Previous ed.: 1975. — Bibl.: p.57-59.
ISBN 0-85605-291-4 Sd : Unpriced
(B77-15034)

915.4'04'5 — India (Republic). Description & travel
Elliott, James, *b.1898.* India / [by] James Elliott. — London : Batsford, 1977. — 238p : ill, map ; 23cm.
Bibl.: p.230. — Index.
ISBN 0-7134-0234-2 : £4.95
(B77-27552)

915.4'04'5 — South Asia. Description & travel. *Personal observations*
Beard, J A. Lhasas and lamas / [by] J.A. Beard. — Ilfracombe : Stockwell, 1977. — 153p,[4]p of plates : ill, map, port ; 18cm.
ISBN 0-7223-0972-4 Pbk : £1.75
(B77-22988)

915.4'6 — Mountaineering expeditions. *Himalayas. Hidden Peak, 1975. Personal observations*
Messner, Reinhold. The challenge / [by] Reinhold Messner ; translated [from the German] by Noel Bowman and Audrey Salkeld. — London : Kaye and Ward [etc.], 1977. — 205p : ill(some col), 2 facsims, 2 maps, ports ; 24cm.
Translation of: 'Die Herausforderung'. Munich : BLV Verlagsgesellschaft, 1976.
ISBN 0-7182-1159-6 : £4.75
Also classified at 915.49'6
(B77-26013)

915.4'6 — Mountaineering expeditions. *Karakoram Range. K2, 1902-1975*
Rowell, Galen. In the throne room of the mountain gods / [by] Galen Rowell. — London : Allen and Unwin, 1977. — x,326p : ill(some col), map, ports(some col) ; 29cm.
Also published: San Francisco : Sierra Club Books, 1977. — Bibl.: p.323-324. — Index.
ISBN 0-04-910060-2 : £10.00
(B77-30851)

915.491 — PAKISTAN
915.49'13 — Kashmir. Baltistan. Description & travel, 1975. *Personal observations*
Murphy, Dervla. Where the Indus is young : a winter in Baltistan / [by] Dervla Murphy. — London : J. Murray, 1977. — [10],266p,[2] leaves of plates,[8]p of plates : ill, 2 maps, ports ; 23cm.
Bibl.: p.264. — Index.
ISBN 0-7195-3335-x : £4.95
(B77-17200)

915.492 — BANGLADESH
915.49'2'045 — Bangladesh. *Practical information. For British businessmen*
British Overseas Trade Board. Bangladesh / [British Overseas Trade Board]. — [New ed.]. — London : The Board, 1977. — 43p : ill, map ; 21cm. — (Hints to business men)
Previous ed.: 1975. — Bibl.: p.36-37.
ISBN 0-85605-284-1 Sd : Unpriced
(B77-13423)

915.496 — NEPAL
915.49'6 — Expeditions. *Himalayas. Everest, 1974. Personal observations*
Donaldson, Jean. Innocents to Everest : a family journey to Everest / [by] Jean Donaldson. — St Ives, Cornwall : United Writers Publications, 1976. — 211p,leaf of plate,[12]p of plates : ill, maps, ports ; 22cm.
ISBN 0-901976-35-0 : £4.95
(B77-16659)

915.49'6 — Mountaineering expeditions. *Himalayas. Everest. South-west face, 1975*
Bonington, Chris. Everest the hard way / [by] Chris Bonington. — London : Arrow Books, 1977. — 352p,[40]p of plates : ill(chiefly col), maps, col ports ; 18cm.
Includes contributions from other members of the British Everest Expedition. — Originally published: London : Hodder and Stoughton, 1976. — Bibl.: p.343-344. — Index.
ISBN 0-09-915940-6 Pbk : £1.25
(B77-30852)

915.49'6 — Mountaineering expeditions. *Himalayas. Jannu. North face, 1975. Personal observations*
Dingle, Graeme. Wall of shadows : Jannu, the New Zealand adventure / [by] Graeme Dingle. — Auckland ; London [etc.] : Hodder and Stoughton, 1976. — 177p,[24]p of plates : ill(chiefly col), maps(on lining papers), col ports ; 24cm.
ISBN 0-340-21450-3 : £6.95
(B77-25291)

915.49'6 — Mountaineering expeditions. *Himalayas. Lhotse, 1975. Personal observations*
Messner, Reinhold. The challenge / [by] Reinhold Messner ; translated [from the German] by Noel Bowman and Audrey Salkeld. — London : Kaye and Ward [etc.], 1977. — 205p : ill(some col), 2 facsims, 2 maps, ports ; 24cm.
Translation of: 'Die Herausforderung'. Munich : BLV Verlagsgesellschaft, 1976.
ISBN 0-7182-1159-6 : £4.75
Primary classification 915.4'6
(B77-26013)

915.49'6 — Mountaineering expeditions by Army Mountaineering Association. *Himalayas. Everest, 1976*
Fleming, Jon. Soldiers on Everest : the joint Army Mountaineering Association, Royal Nepalese Army Mount Everest expedition, 1976 / [by] Jon Fleming & Ronald Faux. — London : H.M.S.O., 1977. — xvi,239p,[24]p of plates : ill(some col), maps, ports ; 19cm.
At head of title: Ministry of Defence.
ISBN 0-11-772130-1 Pbk : £2.00
(B77-19896)

915.5 — IRAN
915.5'04'5 — Iran. *Practical information. For British businessmen*
British Overseas Trade Board. Iran / [British Overseas Trade Board]. — [New ed.]. — London : The Board, 1976. — 64p : map ; 21cm. — (Hints to business men)
Previous ed.: 1975. — Bibl.: p.47-49.
ISBN 0-85605-265-5 Sd : Unpriced
(B77-05767)

915.6 — MIDDLE EAST
915.6'04'4 — Middle East. Description & travel, 1953-1974. *Personal observations*
Bennett, John Godolphin. Journeys in Islamic countries / [by] John G. Bennett. — Sherborne, Glos. : Coombe Springs Press.
In 2 vols.
Vol.1. — 1976. — [4],123p,[6]leaves of plates,[2]p of plates : ill, maps, port ; 21cm.
ISBN 0-900306-24-6 Pbk : £1.50
(B77-11482)

Vol.2. — 1977. — [5],173p,[12]leaves of plates : ill, maps, ports ; 21cm.
ISBN 0-900306-38-6 Pbk : £1.75
(B77-29051)

915.61'04'3 — Turkey. *Practical information. For British businessmen*
British Overseas Trade Board. Turkey / [British Overseas Trade Board]. — [New ed.]. — London : B.O.T.B., 1976. — 58p,fold plate : ill, map ; 21cm. — (Hints to business men)
Previous ed.: 1975. — Bibl.: p.43-44. — Previous control number B7700515.
ISBN 0-85605-262-0 Sd : Unpriced
(B77-00515)

915.64'5'044 — Cyprus. *Practical information. For British businessmen*
British Overseas Trade Board. Cyprus / [British Overseas Trade Board]. — [London] : The Board, 1976. — [1],51p : ill, map ; 21cm. — (Hints to business men)
Bibl.: p.42-43.
ISBN 0-85605-272-8 Sd : Unpriced
(B77-10040)

915.67'5 — Southern Iraq. Marshes. Description & travel. *Personal observations*
Young, Gavin. Return to the marshes : life with the Marsh Arabs of Iraq / [text] by Gavin Young ; photography by Nik Wheeler. — London : Collins, 1977. — 224p : col ill, col map(on lining papers) ; 27cm.
Bibl.: p.222. — Index.
ISBN 0-00-216713-1 : £6.95
(B77-20793)

915.67'5 — Southern Iraq. Marshes. Description & travel, 1951-1958. *Personal observations*
Thesiger, Wilfred. The marsh Arabs / [by] Wilfred Thesiger. — London : Allen Lane, 1977. — 233p,[48]p of plates : ill, maps, ports ; 23cm.
Originally published: London : Longmans, 1964. — Index.
ISBN 0-7139-1049-6 : £6.00
(B77-29052)

915.691'04'4 — Syria. *Practical informtion. For British businessmen*
British Overseas Trade Board. Syrian Arab Republic / [British Overseas Trade Board]. — [New ed.]. — [London] : The Board, 1977. — 43p : map ; 21cm. — (Hints to business men)
Previous ed.: 1975. — Bibl.: p.36-38.
ISBN 0-85605-282-5 Sd : Unpriced
(B77-11483)

915.695'04'4 — Jordan. *Practical information. For British businessmen*
British Overseas Trade Board. Jordan / [British Overseas Trade Board]. — [New ed.]. — London : The Board, 1977. — 50p : ill, 2 maps ; 21cm. — (Hints to business men)
Previous ed.: 1975. — Bibl.: p.42-44.
Sd : Unpriced
(B77-29817)

915.8 — CENTRAL ASIA
915.8'04 — Central Asia. Description & travel, 1845-1846. *Personal observations*
Ferrier, Joseph Pierre. Caravan journeys and wanderings in Persia, Afghanistan, Turkistan and Beloochistan with historical notices of the countries lying between Russia and India / by J.P. Ferrier ; translated from the original unpublished [French] manuscript by William Jesse. — [1st ed.] reprinted / edited by H.D. Seymour. — Karachi ; London [etc.] : Oxford University Press, 1976. — xlviii,534p,fold plate : 1 ill, map, port ; 23cm. — (Oxford in Asia historical reprints from Pakistan)
Facsimile reprint of: 1st ed. London : J. Murray, 1856.
ISBN 0-19-577214-8 : £13.00
(B77-27553)

915.8'5'047 — Turkmenistan. Description & travel, 1819-1820. *Diaries*
Murav'ev, Nikolaĭ N. [Puteshestv‿ie v″ Turkmen‿iiu i Khivu v″ 1819 i 1820 godakh. English]. Journey to Khiva through the Turkoman country / by Nikolay Murav'yov ; [translated from the German by W.S.A. Lockhart]. — London (P.O. Box 127, N.W.8) : Oguz Press, 1977. — [5],xvii,177p,[14] leaves of plates(2 fold),[2]p of plates : ill, facsim, maps, plan, ports ; 25cm.
Facsimile reprint. — This translation originally published: Calcutta : Foreign Department Press, 1871. — Translated from a German version of Murav'ev's 'Puteshestv‿ie ...'. Berlin : Reimer, 1824. — Originally published: in Russian. Moscow : August Semyon Printing House, 1822.
ISBN 0-905820-00-2 : £9.75
(B77-13965)

915.8'5'04808 — Turkmenistan. Description & travel, 1835-1882. *Readings from contemporary sources. Facsimiles*
The **country** of the Turkomans : an anthology of exploration from the Royal Geographical Society / with an introduction by Sir Duncan Cumming. — London (P.O. Box 127, N.W.8) : Oguz Press [for] the Society, 1977. — xli, 3-263p,[6]p of plates,[2] leaves of plates(1 fold) : ill, maps, ports ; 25cm.
'... articles ... taken from the early Journals and Proceedings of the Royal Geographical Society, London' - title page verso. — Facsimile reprints.
ISBN 0-905820-01-0 : £12.50
(B77-21591)

915.9 — SOUTH-EAST ASIA
915.9'04 — Association of South-east Asian Nations countries. *Guidebooks*
Papineau's guide to Asean lands of tropical beauty. — Singapore : André Publications ; Tunbridge Wells ([Abacus House, Speldhurst Rd], Tunbridge Wells, Kent TN4 0HU) : [Distributed by] Abacus-Kent Ltd.
6th ed. / editor Aristide J.G. Papineau. — 1975 [i.e. 1977]. — 420p : ill(some col), maps(some col), ports ; 19cm.
Published in Singapore: 1975.
ISBN 0-85626-110-6 Pbk : £2.25
(B77-07725)

7th ed. / editor Aristide J.G. Papineau. — 1977. — 416p,fold plate : ill(some col), col maps, ports ; 19cm.
ISBN 0-85626-131-9 Pbk : £2.60
(B77-27554)

915.9'04 — South-east Asia. *Guidebooks*
Taylor, Maurice. Island hopping through the Indonesian Archipelago / [by] Maurice Taylor ; with Trail Finders. — London : Wilton House, Hobart Place, S.W.1 : Wilton House Gentry Ltd, 1976. — 256p : ill, maps ; 24cm.
Bibl.: p.189-190. — Index.
ISBN 0-905064-10-0 : £5.40
(B77-08660)

915.93 — THAILAND
915.93 — Thailand. Bangkok. *Guidebooks*
Papineau's guide to Bangkok : city of enchantment. — Singapore : André Publications ; Tunbridge Wells ([Abacus House, Speldhurst Rd], Tunbridge Wells, Kent TN4 0HU) : [Distributed by] Abacus-Kent Ltd.
9th ed. / editor Aristide J.G. Papineau. — 1976 [i.e. 1977]. — 156,[2]p(2fold) : ill(some col), col map, col port ; 19cm.
Published in Singapore: 1976.
ISBN 0-85626-114-9 Pbk : £1.75
(B77-08661)

10th ed. / editor Aristide J.G. Papineau. — 1977. — 148p,fold plate : ill(some col), col map, col port ; 19cm.
ISBN 0-85626-135-1 Pbk : £1.95
(B77-28283)

915.93 — Thailand. Geographical features
Sternstein, Larry. Thailand : the environment of modernisation / [by] Larry Sternstein ; maps and diagrams by Peter Daniell. — Sydney ; London [etc.] : McGraw-Hill, 1976. — xiii, 200p : ill(some col), maps(some col) ; 28cm.
Bibl.: p.189-200.
ISBN 0-07-093321-9 : £16.65
(B77-03277)

915.93'04'4 — Thailand. *Guidebooks*
Duncan, William, *b.1944.* Thailand : a complete guide / [by] William Duncan ; sketches by Ikuko Duncan. — Rutland, Vt [etc.] : Tuttle ; London : [Distributed by] Prentice-Hall, 1976. — 384p,[16]p of plates,fold leaf of plate : ill, maps(some col), plan ; 20cm.
Index.
ISBN 0-8048-1158-x : £5.30
(B77-05768)

915.95 — MALAYSIA
915.95'04'5 — Malaysia. *Guidebooks*
Papineau's guide to Malaysia : land of exotic splendour. — Singapore : André Publications ; Tunbridge Wells ([Abacus House, Speldhurst Rd], Tunbridge Wells, Kent TN4 0HU) : [Distributed by] Abacus-Kent Ltd.
4th ed. / editor Aristide J.G. Papineau. — 1975 [i.e. 1977]. — 256,[2]p(2 fold) : ill(some col), maps(chiefly col), 2 ports ; 19cm.
Published in Singapore: 1975.
ISBN 0-85626-098-3 Pbk : £1.95
(B77-08662)

5th ed. / editor Aristide J.G. Papineau. — [1977]. — 260p,fold plate : ill(some col), 3 maps(2 col) ; 19cm.
ISBN 0-85626-129-7 Pbk : Unpriced
(B77-32968)

915.95'2 — Singapore (City). *Guidebooks*
Papineau's guide to Singapore and spotlight on Malaysia. — Singapore : André Publications ; Tunbridge Wells ([Abacus House, Speldhurst Rd, Tunbridge Wells, Kent TN4 0HU]) : [Distributed by] Abacus-Kent Ltd.
28th ed. / editor Aristide J.G. Papineau. — 1975 [i.e. 1977]. — 270p,[2]fold p of plates : ill(some col), col maps, ports ; 19cm.
This ed. published in Singapore : 1975.
ISBN 0-85626-111-4 Pbk : £1.95
(B77-08663)

29th ed. / editor Aristide J.G. Papineau. — 1977. — 286p,fold plate : ill(some col), col maps, ports ; 19cm.
ISBN 0-85626-132-7 Pbk : £2.10
(B77-27555)

915.95'2'045 — Singapore. *Practical information. For British businessmen*
British Overseas Trade Board. Singapore / [British Overseas Trade Board]. — [New ed.]. — London : The Board, 1977. — 47p : ill, map ; 21cm. — (Hints to business men)
Previous ed.: 1975. — Bibl.: p.40-42.
Sd : Unpriced
(B77-20794)

915.98 — INDONESIA
915.98'04'3 — Indonesia. *Practical information. For British businessmen*
British Overseas Trade Board. Indonesia / [British Overseas Trade Board]. — [New ed.]. — London : The Board, 1977. — 44p : ill, map ; 21cm. — (Hints to business men)
Previous ed.: 1975. — Bibl.: p.32-34.
Sd : Unpriced
(B77-18460)

915.98'2 — Indonesia. Java. Djakarta. *Guidebooks*
Papineau's guide to Jakarta : city of beautiful happenings. — Singapore : André Publications ; Tunbridge Wells ([Abacus House, Speldhurst Rd], Tunbridge Wells, Kent TN4 0HU) : [Distributed by] Abacus-Kent Ltd.
3rd ed. / editor Aristide J.G. Papineau. — 1976 [i.e. 1977]. — 242p,fold plate : ill(some col), map, 2 ports(1 col) ; 19cm.
Published in Singapore : 1976.
ISBN 0-85626-112-2 Pbk : £1.75
(B77-08664)

4th ed. / editor Aristide J.G. Papineau. — 1977. — 236p,fold plate : ill(some col), map, 2 ports(1 col) ; 19cm.
ISBN 0-85626-136-x Pbk : £1.95
(B77-27556)

915.98'6 — Indonesia. Bali. *Guidebooks. French-German-English parallel texts*
Papineau's guide to Bali : island paradise / editor Aristide J.G. Papineau. — Singapore : André Publications ; Tunbridge Wells ([Abacus House, Speldhurst Rd], Tunbridge Wells, Kent TN4 9HU) : [Distributed by] Abacus-Kent Ltd, [1977]. — 144p, fold plate : ill(some col), col map ; 19cm.
Text in English, German and French. — Published in Singapore: 1975.
ISBN 0-85626-113-0 Pbk : £1.95
(B77-08665)

915.99 — PHILIPPINES
915.99'04'4 — Philippines. *Practical information. For British businessmen*
British Overseas Trade Board. Philippines / [British Overseas Trade Board]. — [New ed.]. — London : The Board, 1977. — 45p : ill, map ; 21cm. — (Hints to business men)
Previous ed.: 1975. — Bibl.: p.38-40.
Sd : Unpriced
(B77-30853)

916 — AFRICA
916 — Africa. Geographical features
Best, Alan C G. African survey / [by] Alan C.G. Best, Harm J. de Blij. — New York ; London [etc.] : Wiley, 1977. — xiii,626p : ill, maps ; 26cm.
Bibl. — Index.
ISBN 0-471-20063-8 : £12.00
(B77-18461)

916 — Africa. Geographical features. *Secondary school texts*
Africa and the islands / by R.J. Harrison Church ... [et al.]. — 4th ed. — London [etc.] : Longman, 1977. — xvii,542p : ill, maps ; 22cm. — (Geographies, an intermediate series)
Previous ed.: 1971. — Bibl. — Index.
ISBN 0-582-35197-9 Pbk : £4.50
(B77-22260)

Hickman, Gladys Minnie. The new Africa / [by] Gladys Hickman. — 2nd ed. — London [etc.] : Hodder and Stoughton, 1976. — 179p,[4]p of plates : ill, maps(some col), plans ; 25cm.
Previous ed.: London : University of London Press, 1973. — Index.
ISBN 0-340-20959-3 Pbk : £2.20
(B77-05769)

916'.04 — Africa. Exploration, to 1877
Mountfield, David. A history of African exploration / [by] David Mountfield. — London [etc.] : Hamlyn, 1976. — 160p : ill(some col), maps, plan, ports ; 31cm.
Maps on lining papers. — Bibl.: p.158. — Index.
ISBN 0-600-01131-3 : £4.95
(B77-01907)

916'.04'30924 — Africa. Exploration by Alexander, Boyd, b.1873
Alexander, Joan. Whom the gods love : Boyd Alexander's expedition from the Niger to the Nile 1904-7, and his last journey, 1908-10 / [by] Joan Alexander ; [maps drawn by Reginald Piggott]. — London : Heinemann, 1977. — [10] ,310p,[16]p of plates : ill, maps, ports ; 23cm.
Bibl.: p.299-301. — Index.
ISBN 0-434-01814-7 : £4.90
(B77-05116)

916.11 — TUNISIA
916.1'1'045 — Tunisia. *Guidebooks*
Dennis-Jones, Harold. Letts go to Morocco & Tunisia / by Harold Dennis-Jones. — Completely revised [ed.]. — London : Letts, 1977. — 96p : ill, col maps ; 19cm. — (Letts guides)
Includes English-French vocabulary. — Previous ed.: 1974.
ISBN 0-85097-214-0 Pbk : £0.75
Primary classification 916.4'04'5
(B77-12213)

916.12 — LIBYA
916.1'2'044 — Libya. *Practical information. For British businessmen*
British Overseas Trade Board. Libyan Arab Republic / [British Overseas Trade Board]. — London : The Board, 1977. — 50p : 2 maps ; 21cm. — (Hints to business men)
Bibl.: p.41-43.
Pbk : Unpriced
(B77-07726)

916.2 — EGYPT
916.2'04'5 — Egypt. Description & travel
Fedden, Robin. Egypt : land of the valley / [by] Robin Fedden. — [New ed.]. — London : J. Murray, 1977. — 158p,[2] leaves of plates,32p of plates : ill, 2 maps ; 23cm.
Previous ed.: i.e. 1st ed., published as 'The land of Egypt'. London : Batsford, 1939. — Bibl.: p.151-153. — Index.
ISBN 0-7195-3342-2 : £5.50
(B77-15611)

916.24 — SUDAN
916.24'04'4 — Sudan. *Practical information. For British businessmen*
British Overseas Trade Board. Sudan / [British Overseas Trade Board]. — London : The Board, 1977. — 58,[1]p : map ; 21cm. — (Hints to business men)
Bibl.: p.51-53.
Sd : Unpriced
(B77-07727)

916.3 — ETHIOPIA
916.3'04'6 — Ethiopia. *Practical information. For British businessmen*
British Overseas Trade Board. Ethiopia, Somalia and the French Territory of the Afars and Issas / [British Overseas Trade Board]. — [New ed.]. — London : The Board, 1977. — 84p : ill, maps ; 21cm. — (Hints to business men)
Previous ed.: 1975. — Bibl.: p.78-80.
Sd : Unpriced
Also classified at 916.7'73'045
(B77-23846)

916.4 — MOROCCO
916.4'04'5 — Morocco. *Guidebooks*
Dennis-Jones, Harold. Letts go to Morocco & Tunisia / by Harold Dennis-Jones. — Completely revised [ed.]. — London : Letts, 1977. — 96p : ill, col maps ; 19cm. — (Letts guides)
Includes English-French vocabulary. — Previous ed.: 1974.
ISBN 0-85097-214-0 Pbk : £0.75
Also classified at 916.1'1'045
(B77-12213)

Fodor's Morocco / Eugene Fodor, William Curtis editors. — London : Hodder and Stoughton.
1977 / Robert C. Fisher executive editor ; Richard Moore associate editor ; main texts written by Pierre Guillemot ; maps by Raymond Xhardez ; drawings by W. Rondas ; introduction by Harold Dennis-Jones. — 1977. — 366p,[12]p of plates : ill(some col), maps ; 19cm.
Index.
ISBN 0-340-21419-8 : £4.50
(B77-24599)

916.5 — ALGERIA
916.5'04'5 — Algeria. *Practical information. For British businessmen*
British Overseas Trade Board. Algeria / [British Overseas Trade Board]. — [New ed.]. — London : The Board, 1977. — 44p : 2 maps ; 21cm. — (Hints to business men)
Previous ed.: 1975. — Bibl.: p.37-39.
Sd : Unpriced
(B77-18462)

916.6 — WEST AFRICA
916.6 — West Africa. Geographical features. *Secondary school texts*
Iloeje, Nwadilibe P. A new geography of West Africa / [by] N.P. Iloeje. — Metricated ed. — London : Longman, 1977. — iv,172p : ill, maps ; 25cm.
With answers to the objective tests. — Previous ed.: 1972. — Bibl.: p.169. — Index.
ISBN 0-582-60344-7 Pbk : £1.70
(B77-28284)

916.6'04 — West Africa. Exploration. Park, Mungo
Brent, Peter. Black Nile : Mungo Park and the search for the Niger / by Peter Brent. — London [etc.] : Gordon and Cremonesi, 1977. — [2],200p,[16]p of plates : ill, ports ; 27cm.
Bibl.: p.193-194. — Index.
ISBN 0-86033-017-6 : £7.90 : CIP rev.
(B77-12789)

916.61 — MAURITANIA
916.6'1 — Shipwrecks: Medusa (Ship). *Mauritania. Coastal waters, 1816*
McKee, Alexander. Death raft / [by] Alexander McKee. — [London] : Fontana, 1976. — 268p, [8]p of plates : ill, chart, map, plan, port ; 18cm.
Originally published: London : Souvenir Press, 1975. — Index.
ISBN 0-00-634133-0 Pbk : £0.85
(B77-13424)

916.6'1'045 — Mauritania. *Practical information. For British businessmen*
British Overseas Trade Board. Senegal and Mauritania / [British Overseas Trade Board]. — [New ed.]. — London : B.O.T.B., 1976. — 48p : ill, map ; 21cm. — (Hints to business men)
Previous ed.: 1974. — Bibl.: p.37-39.
ISBN 0-85605-257-4 Sd : Unpriced
Also classified at 916.6'3'045
(B77-00516)

916.62 — MALI, UPPER VOLTA, NIGER
916.6'2'04 — Niger & Upper Volta. *Practical information. For British businessmen*
British Overseas Trade Board. Ivory Coast, Niger and Upper Volta / [British Overseas Trade Board]. — [New ed.]. — [London] : The Board, 1977. — 58p : 2 maps ; 21cm. — (Hints to business men)
Previous ed.: 1975. — Bibl.: p.50-54.
Sd : Unpriced
Also classified at 916.66'8'045
(B77-33521)

916.63 — SENEGAL
916.6'3'045 — Senegal. *Practical information. For British businessmen*
British Overseas Trade Board. Senegal and Mauritania / [British Overseas Trade Board]. — [New ed.]. — London : B.O.T.B., 1976. — 48p : ill, map ; 21cm. — (Hints to business men)
Previous ed.: 1974. — Bibl.: p.37-39.
ISBN 0-85605-257-4 Sd : Unpriced
Primary classification 916.6'1'045
(B77-00516)

916.64 — SIERRA LEONE
916.6'4'044 — Sierra Leone. *Practical information. For British businessmen*
British Overseas Trade Board. Sierra Leone / [British Overseas Trade Board]. — London : B.O.T.B., 1976. — 44p : ill, map ; 21cm. — (Hints to business men)
Bibl.: p.34-36.
ISBN 0-85605-258-2 Sd : Unpriced
(B77-00517)

916.651 — GAMBIA
916.6'51'043 — Gambia. *Practical information. For British businessmen*
British Overseas Trade Board. The Gambia / [British Overseas Trade Board]. — [New ed.]. — London : The Board, 1977. — 38p : maps ; 21cm. — (Hints to business men)
Previous ed.: 1975. — Bibl.: p.32-33.
Sd : Unpriced
(B77-20795)

916.668 — IVORY COAST
916.66'8'045 — Ivory Coast. *Practical information. For British businessmen*
British Overseas Trade Board. Ivory Coast, Niger and Upper Volta / [British Overseas Trade Board]. — [New ed.]. — [London] : The Board, 1977. — 58p : 2 maps ; 21cm. — (Hints to business men)
Previous ed.: 1975. — Bibl.: p.50-54.
Sd : Unpriced
Primary classification 916.6'2'04
(B77-33521)

916.67 — GHANA
916.67 — Ghana. Geographical features. *For West African students. Secondary school texts*
Dickson, Kwamina Busumafi. A new geography of Ghana / [by] Kwamina B. Dickson, George Benneh. — Metricated ed. — London : Longman, 1977. — 173p : ill, charts, maps ; 25cm.
Previous ed.: 1970. — Index.
ISBN 0-582-60343-9 Pbk : £1.75
(B77-20796)

916.67'04'5 — Ghana. *Practical information. For British businessmen*
British Overseas Trade Board. Ghana / [British Overseas Trade Board]. — [New ed.]. — London : The Board, 1976. — 50p,fold plate : ill, maps ; 21cm. — (Hints to business men)
Previous ed.: 1975. — Bibl.: p.39-41.
Sd : Unpriced
(B77-09402)

916.69 — NIGERIA
916.69'04'5 — Nigeria. *Practical information. For British businessmen*
British Overseas Trade Board. Nigeria / [British Overseas Trade Board]. — [New ed.]. — London : The Board, 1977. — 60p : ill, map ; 21cm. — (Hints to business men)
Previous ed.: 1976. — Bibl.: p.48-50.
Sd : Unpriced
(B77-23847)

916.7 — CENTRAL AFRICA
916.7'0076 — East Africa. Geographical features. *Exercises, worked examples. Secondary school texts*
Brittain, Herbert, *b.1922.* East Africa atlas notebook / [by] H. Brittain. — 5th ed. — London : University of London Press, 1975. — 63p : ill, maps ; 28cm.
Previous ed.: 1966.
ISBN 0-340-16790-4 Sd : £0.80
(B77-05117)

916.724 — CONGO
916.7'24'045 — Congo. Practical information. *For British businessmen*
British Overseas Trade Board. The People's Republic of the Congo / [British Overseas Trade Board]. — [London] : The Board, 1976. — [1],35p : map ; 21cm. — (Hints to business men)
Bibl.: p.27-29.
ISBN 0-85605-269-8 Sd : Unpriced
(B77-10662)

916.751 — ZAIRE
916.75'1'043 — Expeditions. *Zaire. Zaire River Expedition, 1974-1975*
Snailham, Richard. A giant among rivers : the story of the Zaire River Expedition, 1974-75 / [by] Richard Snailham. — London [etc.] : Hutchinson, 1976. — xxv,294p,[24]p of plates : ill, maps, ports ; 23cm.
Maps on lining papers. — Bibl.: p.283-284. — Index.
ISBN 0-09-127610-1 : £5.95
(B77-14469)

916.762 — KENYA
916.76'2 — Kenya. Geographical features. *For Kenyan students. Primary school texts*
Kenya primary geography / [by H.A. Curtis et al.]. — London [etc.] : Evans Bros.
Standard 4 : People and their work. Pupils' book. — 1977. — [4],60p : col ill ; 28cm.
ISBN 0-237-50103-1 Sd : £0.75
(B77-32969)

916.76'2'044 — Kenya. *Practical information. For British businessmen*
British Overseas Trade Board. Kenya / [British Overseas Trade Board]. — [New ed.]. — London : The Board, 1977. — 50p : ill, maps ; 21cm. — (Hints to business men)
Previous ed.: 1975. — Bibl.: p.43-45.
Sd : Unpriced
(B77-23848)

916.77 — SOMALIA, SOCOTRA, DJIBOUTI (REPUBLIC)
916.7'73'045 — Somalia. *Practical information. For British businessmen*
British Overseas Trade Board. Ethiopia, Somalia and the French Territory of the Afars and Issas / [British Overseas Trade Board]. — [New ed.]. — London : The Board, 1977. — 84p : ill, maps ; 21cm. — (Hints to business men)
Previous ed.: 1975. — Bibl.: p.78-80.
Sd : Unpriced
Primary classification 916.3'04'6
(B77-23846)

916.79 — MOZAMBIQUE
916.7'9'043 — Mozambique. *Practical information. For British businessmen*
British Overseas Trade Board. Mozambique / [British Overseas Trade Board]. — London : The Board, 1977. — 40p : map ; 21cm. — (Hints to business men)
Bibl.: p.33-34.
Sd : Unpriced
(B77-07728)

916.8 — SOUTHERN AFRICA
916.8'04'6 — South Africa. *Practical information. For British immigrants*
Cooper, John Christopher. The emigrants guide / by J.C. Cooper. — London (14 Poland St., W.1) : Demographic Research Associates, 1975. — 302p,[10]leaves : ill, forms, maps ; 30cm.
ISBN 0-9505380-0-0 Pbk : Unpriced
Primary classification 910'.09'171241
(B77-02654)

916.8'04'6 — Southern Africa. *Practical information. For British businessmen*
British Overseas Trade Board. Southern Africa : (South Africa, SW Africa (Namibia), Botswana, Swaziland, Lesotho) / [British Overseas Trade Board]. — [New ed.]. — London : The Board, 1977. — 108p : ill, 2 maps ; 21cm. — (Hints to business men)
Previous ed.: 1976. — Bibl.: p.84-89.
Sd : Unpriced
(B77-20797)

916.8'4 — South Africa. Natal. Drakensberg Mountains. Description & travel
Dodds, David A. A cradle of rivers : the Natal Drakensberg / [by] David A. Dodds. — Cape Town ; London [etc.] : Purnell, 1975. — viii, 128p,[40]p of plates : ill(some col), map, ports ; 32cm.
Bibl.: p.vi. — Index.
ISBN 0-360-00292-7 : £17.50
Also classified at 916.8'6
(B77-15612)

916.8'6 — Lesotho. Drakensberg Mountains. Description & travel
Dodds, David A. A cradle of rivers : the Natal Drakensberg / [by] David A. Dodds. — Cape Town ; London [etc.] : Purnell, 1975. — viii, 128p,[40]p of plates : ill(some col), map, ports ; 32cm.
Bibl.: p.vi. — Index.
ISBN 0-360-00292-7 : £17.50
Primary classification 916.8'4
(B77-15612)

916.891 — RHODESIA
916.89'1 — Rhodesia. Salisbury. Geographical features
Salisbury : a geographical survey of the capital of Rhodesia / edited by George Kay and Michael Smout. — London [etc.] : Hodder and Stoughton, 1977. — viii,119p : ill, maps ; 25cm.
ISBN 0-340-19905-9 Pbk : £3.50
(B77-18463)

916.9 — INDIAN OCEAN ISLANDS
916.9'1'045 — Malagasy Republic. *Practical information. For British businessmen*
British Overseas Trade Board. The Democratic Republic of Madagascar / [British Overseas Trade Board]. — London : B.O.T.B., 1976. — 44p : ill, map ; 21cm. — (Hints to business men)
Bibl.: p.36-37.
ISBN 0-85605-256-6 Sd : Unpriced
(B77-01908)

916.9'8 — Mauritius & Réunion (Island). *Practical information. For British businessmen*
British Overseas Trade Board. Mauritius and Réunion / [British Overseas Trade Board]. — [London] : The Board, 1976. — 63p : ill, maps ; 21cm. — (Hints to business men)
Bibl.: p.47-50.
ISBN 0-85605-270-1 Sd : Unpriced
(B77-10041)

917 — NORTH AMERICA
917 — North America. Geographical features
Dury, George Harry. The United States and Canada / [by] G.H. Dury and R.S. Mathieson. — 2nd ed. — London : Heinemann Educational, 1976. — xii,327p : ill, maps ; 26cm.
Previous ed.: 1970. — Bibl.: p.299-304. — Index.
ISBN 0-435-34271-1 : £6.50
(B77-03827)

917 — North America. Geographical features. *Secondary school texts*
Knowles, Richard, *b.1936.* North America in maps : topographical map studies of Canada and the USA / [by] R. Knowles, P.W.E. Stowe. — London [etc.] : Longman, 1976. — 95,[1]p : ill(some col), col charts, col maps ; 21x33cm.
Bibl.
ISBN 0-582-31017-2 Pbk : £3.95
(B77-00518)

Russell, David Frederick Ernest. North America : the USA and Canada / [by] D.F.E. Russell. — Exeter : Wheaton, 1977. — xi, 105p : ill, maps ; 23x25cm. — (Pergamon regional geographies)
'Answers to: Tasks for students' (sheet ([2]p.)) as insert. — Index.
ISBN 0-08-020372-8 Pbk : £1.60
(B77-23849)

917 — North America. Great Lakes region. Geographical features. *Secondary school texts*
Jones, Sheila, *b.1929.* Atlantic to the Great Lakes / [by Sheila Jones]. — London : Longman, 1977. — [1],49p : ill(chiefly col), facsim, col maps, ports ; 23cm. — (Longman revised colour geographies)
Bibl.: p.49.
ISBN 0-582-20132-2 Sd : £0.85
(B77-30854)

917'.04'4 — North America. Description & travel, 1845. *Diaries*
Dunlop, Alexander Graham. The New World journal of Alexander Graham Dunlop, 1845 / edited by David Sinclair and Germaine Warkentin. — Edinburgh : P. Harris, 1976. — xxxii,121p,[6]p of plates : ill, facsims, map, ports ; 23cm.
Index.
ISBN 0-904505-17-0 : £4.50
(B77-05118)

917'.04'53 — North America. Description & travel. *Personal observations*
Langley, Robert. Lobo / [by] Bob Langley. — London : Hale, 1977. — 175p,[8]p of plates : ill, ports ; 23cm.
ISBN 0-7091-6335-5 : £4.25
(B77-32970)

917.1 — CANADA
917.1'04'644 — Canada. *Practical information. For British businessmen*
British Overseas Trade Board. Canada / [British Overseas Trade Board]. — [New ed.]. — [London] : The Board, 1977. — 80p : ill, map ; 21cm. — (Hints to business men)
Previous ed.: 1976. — Bibl.: p.67-70.
Sd : Unpriced
(B77-21592)

917.11'04'4 — British Columbia. *Practical information. For British businessmen*
British Overseas Trade Board. Canada West, your opportunity / [British Overseas Trade Board]. — London : The Board, 1976. — [1], 36p : col ill, col maps ; 30cm.
Booklet ([2],33p.; 15x21cm; Sd) in pocket.
ISBN 0-85605-248-5 Sd : Unpriced
Primary classification 917.123'04'3
(B77-01909)

917.12 — Canada. Prairie provinces. Geographical features. *Secondary school texts*
Dunlop, Stewart. The prairies / [by Stewart Dunlop]. — London : Longman, 1976. — 49p : ill(chiefly col), facsim, col maps ; 23cm. — (Longman revised colour geographies)
Bibl.: p.49.
ISBN 0-582-20133-0 Sd : £0.85
(B77-09403)

917.123'04'3 — Alberta. *Practical information. For British businessmen*
British Overseas Trade Board. Canada West, your opportunity / [British Overseas Trade Board]. — London : The Board, 1976. — [1], 36p : col ill, col maps ; 30cm.
Booklet ([2],33p.; 15x21cm; Sd) in pocket.
ISBN 0-85605-248-5 Sd : Unpriced
Also classified at 917.11'04'4
(B77-01909)

917.16'23 — Treasure hunting. *Nova Scotia. Oak Island*
Furneaux, Rupert. Money pit : the mystery of Oak Island / [by] Rupert Furneaux. — [London] : Fontana, 1976. — 158p,[8]p of plates : ill, facsim, maps ; 18cm.
Originally published: as 'The money pit mystery'. London : Tom Stacey Ltd, 1972.
ISBN 0-00-634189-6 Pbk : £0.65
(B77-04477)

917.19'5 — Expeditions. *Northwest Territories. Baffin Island. Oxford University Baffin Expedition (1976)*
Oxford University Baffin Expedition (1976). Oxford University Baffin Expedition / [edited by Steve Parr]. — [Oxford] (Trinity College, Oxford]) : [The editor], [1977]. — [1],40p : ill, ports ; 30cm.
Sd : Unpriced
(B77-33522)

917.2 — MEXICO, MIDDLE AMERICA
917.2'04'82 — Mexico. *Practical information. For British businessmen*
British Overseas Trade Board. Mexico / [British Overseas Trade Board]. — [New ed.]. — London : The Board, 1977. — 56p : ill, map ; 21cm. — (Hints to business men)
Previous ed.: 1975. — Bibl.: p.50-52.
Sd : Unpriced
(B77-23850)

917.282 — BELIZE
917.282'04'5 — Belize. *Practical information. For British businessmen*
British Overseas Trade Board. Jamaica, Belize and the Cayman Islands / [British Overseas Trade Board]. — [New ed.]. — London : The Board, 1977. — 68p : maps ; 21cm. — (Hints to business men)
Previous ed.: 1975. — Bibl.: p.60-63.
Sd : Unpriced
Primary classification 917.292'04'6
(B77-18464)

917.29 — WEST INDIES
917.29'04'5 — West Indies. Description & travel
Hannau, Hans Walter. The West Indian islands / [by] Hans W. Hannau. — London : Hale, 1977. — 135p : ill(chiefly col), maps, port ; 22cm.
Maps on lining papers. — Adaptation of: 'The Caribbean islands in full colour', Munich : Andermann, 1963 ; London : Hale, 1974 ; and 'The islands of the Caribbean', Miami : Argos, 1969. — Index.
ISBN 0-7091-6491-2 : £4.50
(B77-32971)

917.291'04'64 — Cuba. *Practical information. For British businessmen*
British Overseas Trade Board. Cuba / [British Overseas Trade Board]. — London : The Board, 1976. — 38p : 2 maps ; 21cm. — (Hints to business men)
Bibl.: p.33-34.
Sd : Unpriced
(B77-09404)

917.292'04'6 — Jamaica & Cayman Islands. *Practical information. For British businessmen*
British Overseas Trade Board. Jamaica, Belize and the Cayman Islands / [British Overseas Trade Board]. — [New ed.]. — London : The Board, 1977. — 68p : maps ; 21cm. — (Hints to business men)
Previous ed.: 1975. — Bibl.: p.60-63.
Sd : Unpriced
Also classified at 917.282'04'5
(B77-18464)

917.294'04'6 — Haiti. *Practical information. For British businessmen*
British Overseas Trade Board. Haiti / [British Overseas Trade Board]. — [New ed.]. — London : The Board, 1977. — 39p : map ; 21cm. — (Hints to business men)
Previous ed.: 1975. — Bibl.: p.33-34.
Sd : Unpriced
(B77-29818)

917.29'6 — Bahamas. Geographical features. *For West Indian students. Secondary school texts*
Evans, Frederick Colin. The Bahamas / [by] F.C. Evans, R.N. Young. — Cambridge [etc.] : Cambridge University Press [etc.], 1976 [i.e. 1977]. — [2],64p : ill, maps, plans ; 25cm.
ISBN 0-521-21292-8 Sd : £1.05
(B77-13966)

917.29'83'044 — Trinidad and Tobago. *Practical information. For British businessmen*
British Overseas Trade Board. Trinidad and Tobago / [British Overseas Trade Board]. — [New ed.]. — London : The Board, 1977. — 45p : ill ; 21cm. — (Hints to business men)
Previous ed.: 1975. — Bibl.: p.37-39.
Sd : Unpriced
(B77-30855)

917.3 — UNITED STATES
917.3'04'56 — United States. Description & travel, 1829-1830. *Personal observations*
Tuckett, Francis. A journey in the United States in the years 1829 and 1830 / by Francis Tuckett ; edited by Hubert C. Fox ... — Plymouth ([23 New St.], The Barbican, Plymouth [Devon]) : St Nicholas Books, 1976. — x,103p,fold plate : facsim, map, 2 ports tipped in ; 25cm.
Limited ed. of 400 numbered copies signed by the editor.
£6.00
(B77-19104)

917.3'04'610924 — Long-distance overland travel. *United States, 1849. Personal observations*
Royce, Sarah. A frontier lady : recollections of the Gold Rush and early California / by Sarah Royce ; with a foreword by Katharine Royce ; edited by Ralph Henry Gabriel. — Lincoln, [Neb.] ; London : University of Nebraska Press, 1977. — xv,144p,plate : map ; 21cm.
Facsimile reprint of: 1st ed. New Haven : Yale University Press, 1932.
ISBN 0-8032-0909-6 : £6.75
ISBN 0-8032-5856-9 Pbk : £1.80
Primary classification 979.4'04'0924
(B77-28321)

917.3'04'926 — United States. Description & travel
Hannau, Hans Walter. The USA book / [by] Hans W. Hannau. — Abridged and revised ed. — London : Hale, 1977. — 191p : col ill, col maps(on lining papers) ; 22cm.
Full ed.: published as 'USA in full colour'. Springfield, Mass. : Merriam, 1972 ; London : Hale, 1973.
ISBN 0-7091-6116-6 : £4.50
(B77-19897)

917.4 — UNITED STATES. NORTH-EASTERN STATES
917.41'45 — Maine. Mount Desert Island. Description & travel
Butcher, Russell D. Maine paradise : Mount Desert Island and Acadia National Park / by Russell D. Butcher ; drawings by Marie Ivey Menzietti ; photographs by the author and the artist ; prelude by Carl W. Buchheister. — Harmondsworth [etc.] : Penguin, 1976. — 96p : ill(chiefly col), map ; 22x25cm.
Originally published: New York : Viking Press, 1973. — Bibl.: p.95-96.
ISBN 0-14-004316-0 Pbk : Unpriced
(B77-00519)

917.47'1'044 — New York (City). *Guidebooks*
Chester, Carole. New York / [by] Carole Chester. — London : Batsford, 1977. — 168p : ill, map ; 23cm.
Index.
ISBN 0-7134-0183-4 : £4.50
(B77-25292)

917.5 — UNITED STATES. SOUTH-EASTERN STATES
917.52'04'4 — Maryland. *Guidebooks*
Maryland : a new guide to the Old Line State. — [Revised ed.] / compiled and edited by Edward C. Papenfuse ... [et al.]. — Baltimore ; London : Johns Hopkins University Press, 1976. — xxi,463,[2]p : ill, maps ; 24cm. — (Studies in Maryland history and culture)
Previous ed.: published as 'Maryland, a guide to the Old Line State' / compiled by staff of the Maryland Writers' Project. New York : Oxford University Press, 1940. — Index.
ISBN 0-8018-1874-5 : £12.80
ISBN 0-8018-1871-0 Pbk : £3.95
(B77-14470)

917.6 — UNITED STATES. SOUTH CENTRAL STATES
917.64'351'046 — Texas. San Antonio. Description & travel
Ramsdell, Charles. San Antonio : a historical and pictorial guide / by Charles Ramsdell. — Revised ed. / by Carmen Perry. — Austin ; London : University of Texas Press, 1976. — xx,291p : ill, maps, ports ; 13x21cm.
Previous ed.: Austin : University of Texas Press, 1959. — Index.
ISBN 0-292-77525-3 Pbk : £3.75
(B77-03278)

917.8 — UNITED STATES. WESTERN STATES
917.86'04'2 — Montana. Description & travel, 1878-1879. *Personal observations*
Garcia, Andrew. Tough trip through paradise, 1878-1879 / [by] Andrew Garcia ; edited by Bennett H. Stein ; introduction by Richard Cupidi. — London : Abacus, 1977. — 302p,[12] p of plates : ill, maps, ports ; 20cm.
Originally published: Boston, Mass. : Houghton Mifflin, 1967.
ISBN 0-349-11422-6 Pbk : £1.75
(B77-19105)

917.9 — UNITED STATES. PACIFIC COAST STATES
917.94'61'045 — California. San Francisco. Description & travel, 1915. *Correspondence*
Wilder, Laura Ingalls. West from home : letters of Laura Ingalls Wilder to Almanzo Wilder, San Francisco 1915 / edited by Roger Lea MacBride ; historical setting by Margot Patterson Doss. — Guildford [etc.] : Lutterworth Press, 1976. — xviii,124p,[24]p of plates : ill, map, ports ; 21cm.
Originally published: New York : Harper and Row, 1974.
ISBN 0-7188-2270-6 : £3.50
(B77-04478)

917.97'003 — Washington (State). Place names. *Dictionaries*
Phillips, James W. Washington State place names / [by] James W. Phillips. — [New ed.] / with corrections and additions. — Seattle ; London : University of Washington Press, 1976. — xvii,167p : col maps(on lining papers) ; 23cm.
Previous ed.: i.e. 1st ed., Seattle : University of Washington Press, 1971. — Bibl.: p.165-167.
ISBN 0-295-95158-3 : £8.00
ISBN 0-295-95498-1 Pbk : £4.00
(B77-04479)

917.97'98'044 — National parks. *Washington (State). Olympic National Park. Guidebooks*
Leissler, Frederick. Roads and trails of Olympic National Park / by Frederick Leissler. — 3rd revised ed. — Seattle ; London : University of Washington Press [for] the Pacific Northwest National Parks Association, 1976. — xii,84,16p of plates,fold leaf of plate : ill, col maps ; 21cm.

Previous ed.: i.e. 2nd revised ed., 1971. — Index.
ISBN 0-295-95143-5 Pbk : £3.20
(B77-05770)

918 — SOUTH AMERICA
918 — Latin America. Geographical features. *Secondary school texts*
Robinson, Harry, *b.1915.* Latin America / [by] H. Robinson. — 4th ed. — Plymouth : Macdonald and Evans, 1977. — xv,523p : ill, charts, maps, 2 plans ; 22cm. — (The new Certificate geography series : Advanced Level)
Previous ed.: 1970. — Bibl.: p.511-513. — Index.
ISBN 0-7121-1235-9 Pbk : £4.50
(B77-26014)

918'.04'3 — South America. *Guidebooks*
The **South** American handbook. — Bath : Trade and Travel Publications.
1977 : fifty-third annual ed. / editor John Brooks ; associate editor Joyce Candy ; assistant editor Philippa Hughes. — 1976. — 1032p,8p of plates : ill, maps(some col) ; 18cm.
Bibl.: p.1000-1002. — Index.
ISBN 0-900751-08-8 : £6.00
(B77-03828)

918'.04'3 — South America. Description & travel. *Personal observations*
Snow, Sebastian. The rucksack man / [by] Sebastian Snow ; foreword by Eric Newby. — London : Sphere, 1977. — 244p,[8]p of plates : ill, maps ; 18cm.
Originally published: London : Hodder and Stoughton, 1976.
ISBN 0-7221-7978-2 Pbk : £1.25
(B77-32307)

918.1 — BRAZIL
918.1'04'6 — Brazil. *Practical information. For British businessmen*
British Overseas Trade Board. Brazil / [British Overseas Trade Board]. — [New ed.]. — London : The Board, 1977. — 71p : map ; 21cm. — (Hints to business men)
Previous ed.: 1976. — Bibl.: p.63-66.
Sd : Unpriced
(B77-18465)

918.2 — ARGENTINA
918.2'04'6 — Argentina. *Practical information. For British businessmen*
British Overseas Trade Board. Argentina / [British Overseas Trade Board]. — [New ed.]. — London : The Board, 1977. — 54p : map ; 21cm. — (Hints to business men)
Previous ed.: 1975. — Bibl.: p.47-49.
Sd : Unpriced
(B77-18466)

918.2'7'046 — Argentina. Patagonia. Description & travel. *Personal observations*
Chatwin, Bruce. In Patagonia / [by] Bruce Chatwin. — London : Cape, 1977. — [4],204p, [8]p of plates : ill, map ; 23cm.
Map on lining papers. — Bibl.: p.201-203.
ISBN 0-224-01419-6 : £4.95 : CIP rev.
(B77-17201)

918.4 — BOLIVIA
918.4'04'5 — Bolivia. *Practical information. For British businessmen*
British Overseas Trade Board. Bolivia / [British Overseas Trade Board]. — [London] : The Board, 1976. — 47p : ill, map ; 21cm. — (Hints to business men)
Bibl.: p.38-40.
ISBN 0-85605-273-6 Sd : Unpriced
(B77-10042)

918.61 — COLOMBIA
918.61'04'63 — Colombia. *Practical information. For British businessmen*
British Overseas Trade Board. Colombia / [British Overseas Trade Board]. — [New ed.]. — London : The Board, 1977. — 51p : ill, map ; 21cm. — (Hints to business men)
Previous ed.: 1975. — Bibl.: p.42-44.
Sd : Unpriced
(B77-20798)

918.61'04'63 — Colombia. Jungles. Description & travel. *Personal observations*
Reed, Robert. Amazon dream : escape to the unknown / by Robert Reed. — London : Gollancz, 1977. — 288p : maps ; 23cm.
ISBN 0-575-02232-9 : £5.95
(B77-22261)

918.92 — PARAGUAY
918.92'04'7 — Paraguay. *Practical information. For British businessmen*
British Overseas Trade Board. Paraguay / [British Overseas Trade Board]. — [London] : The Board, [1976]. — 45p : map ; 21cm. — (Hints to business men)
Bibl.: p.37-39.
ISBN 0-85605-283-3 Sd : Unpriced
(B77-12214)

919.3 — MELANESIA, NEW ZEALAND
919.31'003 — New Zealand. Place names. *Dictionaries*
Reed, Alexander Wyclif. Place names of New Zealand / [by] A.W. Reed. — Wellington, N.Z. [etc.] ; London : A.H. and A.W. Reed, 1975. — xvi,510p ; 22cm.
ISBN 0-589-00933-8 : £9.10
(B77-19898)

919.312'2 — National parks. *New Zealand. Urewera National Park. Long-distance footpaths: Waikaremoana Track. Walkers' guides*
Temple, Philip. The Shell guide to the Waikaremoana Track / by Philip Temple. — Christchurch, N.Z. [etc.] ; London : Whitcoulls, 1977. — 40p : ill, form, col map, port ; 18cm.
ISBN 0-7233-0497-1 Sd : £1.50
(B77-23851)

919.312'2 — New Zealand. Auckland. Geographical features. *Secondary school texts*
Hutson, Anthony Brian Austin. Auckland / [by] A.B.A. Hutson. — Wellington [N.Z.] ; London [etc.] : A.H. and A.W. Reed, 1975. — Portfolio : ill, facsims, maps, plan, ports ; 28cm.

Four booklets (32p.;24p.;24p.;32p.) in portfolio.
£3.90
(B77-03829)

919.312'7 — National parks. *New Zealand. Tongariro National Park. Long-distance footpaths: Tongariro Track. Walkers' guides*
Temple, Philip. The Shell guide to the Tongariro Track / by Philip Temple. — Christchurch, N.Z. [etc.] ; London : Whitcoulls, 1976 [i.e. 1977]. — 40p : ill, form, col map, 2 ports ; 18cm.
Published in New Zealand: 1976.
ISBN 0-7233-0487-4 Sd : £1.55
(B77-13967)

919.315'04'3 — New Zealand. South Island. Description & travel
McCaskill, Lance W. Unspoiled New Zealand, South Island / text by L.W. McCaskill. — Wellington [N.Z.] [etc.] ; London : A.H. and A.W. Reed, 1977. — [112]p : col ill, map ; 29cm.
ISBN 0-589-00961-3 : £7.35
(B77-21593)

919.315'3 — Long-distance footpaths. *New Zealand. Heaphy River region. Heaphy Track. Walkers' guides*
Temple, Philip. The Shell guide to the Heaphy Track / by Philip Temple. — Christchurch, N.Z. [etc.] ; London : Whitcoulls, 1976 [i.e. 1977]. — 40p : ill, form, col map, ports ; 18cm.

Published in New Zealand: 1976.
ISBN 0-7233-0486-6 Sd : £1.55
(B77-13425)

919.315'4 — National parks. *New Zealand. Mount Cook National Park & Westland National Park. Long-distance footpaths: Copland Track. Walkers' guides*
Temple, Philip. The Shell guide to the Copland Track / by Philip Temple. — Christchurch, N.Z. [etc.] ; London : Whitcoulls, 1977. — 40p : ill, form, col map, ports ; 18cm.
ISBN 0-7233-0496-3 Sd : £1.50
(B77-24600)

919.315'7 — Long-distance footpaths. *New Zealand. Humboldt Mountains region. Routeburn Track. Walkers' guides*
Temple, Philip. The Shell guide to the Routeburn Track / by Philip Temple. — Christchurch, N.Z. [etc.] ; London : Whitcoulls, 1976 [i.e. 1977]. — 40p : ill, form, col map, port ; 18cm.
Published in New Zealand: 1976.
ISBN 0-7233-0485-8 Sd : £1.55
(B77-13426)

919.315'7 — National parks. *New Zealand. Fiordland National Park. Long-distance footpaths: Hollyford Track. Walkers' guides*
Temple, Philip. The Shell guide to the Hollyford Track / by Philip Temple. — Christchurch, N.Z. [etc.] ; London : Whitcoulls, 1977. — 40p : ill, form, col map, port ; 18cm.
ISBN 0-7233-0495-5 Sd : £1.50
(B77-23852)

919.315'7 — National parks. *New Zealand. Fiordland National Park. Long-distance footpaths: Milford Track. Walkers' guides*
Temple, Philip. The Shell guide to the Milford Track / by Philip Temple. — Christchurch, N.Z. [etc.] ; London : Whitcoulls, 1976 [i.e. 1977]. — 40p : ill, form, col map, ports ; 18cm.

Published in New Zealand: 1976.
ISBN 0-7233-0484-x Sd : £1.55
(B77-13968)

919.315'7 — New Zealand. Fiordland. Exploration, 1770-1904
Hall-Jones, John. Fiordland explored : an illustrated history / [by] John Hall-Jones. — Wellington [N.Z.] [etc.] ; London : A.H. and A.W. Reed, 1976. — xii,148p : ill, maps, ports ; 26cm.
Maps on lining papers. — Bibl.: p.144-145. — Index.
ISBN 0-589-00973-7 : £9.50
(B77-21594)

919.4 — AUSTRALIA
919.4'04'1 — Australia. Discovery. Role of Portuguese explorers, 1500-1600
McIntyre, Kenneth Gordon. The secret discovery of Australia : Portuguese ventures 200 years before Captain Cook / [by] Kenneth Gordon McIntyre. — Medindie ; London : Souvenir Press, 1977. — xxi,427p : ill, maps ; 23cm.
Map on lining papers. — Bibl.: p.403-413. — Index.
ISBN 0-285-62303-6 : £6.50
(B77-34292)

919.4'04'6 — Australia. *Practical information. For British businessmen*
British Overseas Trade Board. Australia / [British Overseas Trade Board]. — [New ed.]. — [London] : The Board, 1976. — 84p : ill, map ; 21cm. — (Hints to business men)
Previous ed.: 1975. — Bibl.: p.67-69.
ISBN 0-85605-259-0 Sd : Unpriced
(B77-00520)

919.4'04'6 — Australia. Description & travel. *Personal observations*
Powell, Margaret. Margaret Powell down under. — London : Sphere, 1977. — 188p ; 18cm.
Originally published: London : Joseph, 1976.
ISBN 0-7221-0421-9 Pbk : £0.85
(B77-32308)

919.6 — POLYNESIA
919.6'31 — Marquesas Islands. Fatu-Hiva. Exploration, 1936-1938. *Personal observations*
Heyerdahl, Thor. Fatu-Hiva : back to nature / [by] Thor Heyerdahl. — Harmondsworth [etc.] : Penguin, 1976. — 303p,[16]p of plates : ill, maps, ports ; 19cm.
Originally published: London : Allen and Unwin, 1974.
ISBN 0-14-004188-5 Pbk : £0.95
(B77-05119)

919.69'04'4 — Hawaii. *Guidebooks*
Davenport, William Wyatt. Fodor's Hawaii / by William W. Davenport and others. — [London] : Hodder and Stoughton.
1977 / Eugene Fodor, Robert C. Fisher, editors ... ; foreword by James A. Michener. — 1977. — 352p,[12]p of plates : ill(some col), maps ; 19cm.
Index.
ISBN 0-340-21411-2 : £4.50
(B77-07729)

919.8 — POLAR REGIONS
919.8'1'04 — Norway. Spitzbergen. Description & travel. *Personal observations*
Maxwell, A.E. The year-long day : one man's Arctic / by A.E. Maxwell and Ivar Ruud ; photographs by Ivar Ruud. — London : Gollancz, 1977. — 3-240p : ill, ports ; 23cm.
Originally published: Philadelphia : Lippincott, 1976.
ISBN 0-575-02306-6 : £6.95
(B77-27557)

919.8'2 — Voyages by canoes. *Greenland. Narssarssuaq region. Coastal waters. Personal observations*
Simpson, Myrtle, *b.1930.* Vikings, Scots and Scraelings / by Myrtle Simpson. — London : Gollancz, 1977. — 189p,[16]p of plates : ill, 2 maps, ports ; 23cm.
ISBN 0-575-02208-6 : £5.50
(B77-22989)

919.8'9 — Antarctic. Ross Sea region. Description & travel. *Personal observations*
Conly, Maurice. Ice on my palette / [paintings and sketches by] Maurice Conly ; text by Neville Peat. — Christchurch, N.Z. [etc.] ; London : Whitcoulls, 1977. — 64p : ill(chiefly col), 2 col maps ; 27x35cm.
ISBN 0-7233-0500-5 : £11.45
Primary classification 759.9931
(B77-23613)

919.8'9'04 — Antarctic. Exploration by Mawson, Sir Douglas, 1911-1913
Bickel, Lennard. This accursed land / [by] Lennard Bickel. — London [etc.] : Macmillan, 1977. — x,210p,[12]p of plates : ill, facsim, maps(on lining papers), ports ; 23cm.
Includes 'An appreciation' by Eric Norman Webb.
ISBN 0-333-22939-8 : £4.95
(B77-24601)

919.8'9'04 — Expeditions. *Antarctic. Svenska sydpolar-expeditionem, 1901-1903. Personal observations*
Nordenskjöld, Otto. Antarctica, or, Two years amongst the ice of the South Pole / by Otto Nordenskjöld and Joh. Gunnar Andersson ; [translated from the Swedish]. — [1st ed.], new impression ; with a foreword by Sir Vivian Fuchs and a biographical note. — London : C. Hurst, 1977. — vii,v-xviii,608p,[2]p of plates,[3] leaves of plates(2 fold) : ill, maps, plan, ports ; 23cm.
Facsimile reprint. — First ed. of this translation originally published: London : Hurst and Blackett, 1905. — Translation of: 'Antarctic, tva ar bland sydpolens isar'. Stockholm : Bonniers Forlag, 1904. — Index.
ISBN 0-903983-71-0 : £12.00
(B77-17824)

920 — BIOGRAPHY
920'.009'03 — Persons, 1700-1965. *Biographies. Juvenile literature*
They amazed the world / illustrated by Peter Dennis and Carlo Tora. — London : Beaver Books, 1977. — 125p : ill ; 20cm.
'The articles in this collection were originally published in the magazine "Look and learn" between 1962 and 1975' - title page verso.
ISBN 0-600-30331-4 Pbk : £0.50
(B77-31617)

920'.009'034 — Heroes. *Western world, ca 1810-1976*
Calder, Jenni. Heroes : from Byron to Guevara / [by] Jenni Calder. — London : Hamilton, 1977. — xii,211p,8p of plates : ill, ports ; 23cm.
Index.
ISBN 0-241-89536-7 : £6.95
Primary classification 809'.933'52
(B77-12609)

920'.02 — Eccentrics, to 1976. *Encyclopaedias*
Garrett, Richard. They must have been crazy : an encyclopedia of eccentricity / [by] Richard Garrett ; illustrated by Peter Clark. — London [etc.] : Pan Books, 1977. — 144p : ill ; 18cm. — (Piccolo true adventures)
Index.
ISBN 0-330-25126-0 Pbk : £0.50
(B77-29053)

920'.02 — Persons, to ca 1970. *Biographies. Primary school texts. Welsh texts*
Bundock, D Watkin. Camrau'r cewri / y gwersi a'r arlunio gan D. Watkin Bundock. — [Aberdare] ([22 Stuart St., Aberdare, M. Glam. CF44 7LY]) : [Gwasg y Fflam ar ran] y Gymdeithas Undodaidd, 1972. — 44p : ill, facsim, ports ; 18x25cm.
Sd : Unpriced
(B77-16661)

920'.02'05 — Persons. *Biographical dictionaries. Serials*
Dictionary of international biography : a biographical record of contemporary achievement. — Cambridge ([Market Hill, Cambridge CB2 3QP]) : International Biographical Centre.
1977 : Vol.13 / editorial director Ernest Kay. — 1977. — 2v.([54],999p) ; 26cm.
ISBN 0-900332-41-7 : Unpriced
(B77-14471)

920'.038 — Ancient Greeks, B.C.444-B.C.272. *Biographies. Early works*
Plutarch. [Lives. English. *Selections].* The age of Alexander : nine Greek lives / by Plutarch ; translated [from the Greek] and annotated by Ian Scott-Kilvert ; introduction by G.T. Griffith. — Harmondsworth [etc.] : Penguin, 1977. — 443p : maps ; 18cm. — (The Penguin classics)
This translation originally published: 1973.
Pbk : £0.95
ISBN 0-14-044286-3
(B77-26015)

920'.041 — Britons. *Biographical dictionaries. Serials*
Kelly's handbook. — Kingston upon Thames : Kelly's Directories.
1977 : 101st ed. — 1977. — 1653p : ill ; 23cm.
ISBN 0-610-00493-x : £18.00
(B77-26016)

Who's who : an annual biographical dictionary. — London : A. and C. Black.
1977 : one hundred and twenty-ninth year of issue. — 1977. — 31,8,2688p ; 24cm.
ISBN 0-7136-1710-1 : £20.00
(B77-20799)

920'.041 — Britons, 1485-1603. *Biographical dictionaries*
Hoffmann, Ann. Lives of the Tudor age, 1485-1603 / by Ann Hoffmann. — London : Osprey Publishing, 1977. — xi,500p : ports ; 24cm.
Bibl.: p.v-vi. — Index.
ISBN 0-85045-092-6 : £12.50
(B77-24602)

920'.041 — Country houses. *Derbyshire. North East Derbyshire (District). Hardwick Hall. Portrait paintings. Subjects. Biographies*
National Trust. Hardwick Hall, Derbyshire : biographical notes on the portraits at Hardwick / [National Trust]. — [London] : The Trust, 1977. — 19p ; 22cm.
Sd : £0.25
(B77-32972)

920'.0411 — Scottish graduates, to 1410. *Biographical dictionaries*
Watt, Donald Elmslie Robertson. A biographical dictionary of Scottish graduates to AD 1410 / by D.E.R. Watt. — Oxford : Clarendon Press, 1977. — xliii,607p ; 24cm.
Bibl.: p.xxxi-xlii. — Index.
ISBN 0-19-822447-8 : £30.00 : CIP rev.
(B77-06373)

920'.0423'7 — Cornish persons, 1400-1966. *Biographies*
Coulson-Thomas, Colin J. Great Cornish men and women / by Colin J. Coulson-Thomas. — Tavistock (c/o Heritage Publications, Merchants House, Barley Market St., Tavistock, Devon) : Elliott Publications, 1977. — [1],28p : 1 ill, map, ports ; 15x22cm.
ISBN 0-903975-81-5 Sd : £0.50
(B77-27558)

920'.0425'1 — Derbyshire persons, ca 1520-1975. *Biographies*
Derbyshire characters : some famous men and women of the county / [edited by Robert Innes-Smith]. — [Derby] ([Lodge La., Derby DE1 3HE]) : [Derbyshire Countryside Ltd], [1977]. — 56p : ill, facsim, ports ; 22cm.
Cover title.
Pbk : £0.80
(B77-26685)

920'.0429 — Welsh persons, 1500-1800. *Biographies. Welsh texts*
Williams, Ellis Wynne. Portreadau o enwogion / [gan] Ellis Wynne Williams. — Llandysul : Gwasg Gomer, 1976. — 96p : 1 ill, maps, ports ; 22cm.
ISBN 0-85088-337-7 Pbk : £1.10
(B77-12215)

920'.0429'3 — Clwyd persons, ca 400-ca 1860. *Biographies. Welsh texts*
Lewis, Brenda, *b.1923.* Enwogion Clwyd / [gan] Brenda Lewis. — Llandysul : Gwasg Gomer, 1976. — 75p : ill, map, ports ; 21cm.
ISBN 0-85088-341-5 Pbk : £0.80
(B77-12216)

920'.06 — Africans. *Biographical dictionaries*
Africa year book and who's who. — London (54A Tottenham Court Rd, W1P 0BT) : Africa Journal Ltd.
1977 / [editor-in-chief Raph Uwechue]. — 1976. — xlvii,1364p,[8]p of plates : ill(some col), forms, maps, ports ; 25cm.
ISBN 0-903274-05-1 : £20.00
Primary classification 960'.3'05
(B77-05153)

920'.073 — Americans. *Biographical dictionaries. Serials*
Who was who in America : with world notables. — Chicago : Marquis Who's Who ; London : Distributed by Prior.
Vol.6 : 1974-1976 : with index to all 'Who was who' volumes. — 1976. — xii,673p ; 26cm.
Index.
ISBN 0-8379-0207-x : £32.65
(B77-15613)

920'.073 — Americans, to 1974. *Biographical dictionaries*
Encyclopedia of American biography / John A. Garraty, editor ; Jerome L. Sternstein, associate editor. — New York [etc.] ; London : Harper and Row, [1976]. — xv,1241p ; 24cm.
Published in the United States: 1974.
ISBN 0-06-011438-x : £16.85
(B77-06374)

920'.075 — Persons. *United States. Southern states. Biographical dictionaries*
Who's who in the South and Southwest. — Chicago : Marquis Who's Who ; London : Distributed by Prior.
1975-1976 : 14th ed. : including Alabama, Arkansas, the District of Columbia, Florida, Georgia, Kentucky, Louisiana, Mississippi, North Carolina, Oklahoma, South Carolina, Tennessee, Texas, Virginia, Puerto Rico and the Virgin Islands. — 1975. — xiv,789p ; 31cm.
ISBN 0-8379-0814-0 : £35.00
(B77-03279)

920'.0773'994 — Illinois persons. Carbondale persons, 1852-1905. *Biographical dictionaries*
Wright, John W D. A history of early Carbondale, Illinois, 1852-1905 / [by] John W.D. Wright. — Carbondale [etc.] : Southern Illinois University Press for the Jackson County Historical Society ; London [etc.] : Feffer and Simons, 1977. — x,368p : ill, facsims, maps, ports ; 25cm.
Bibl.: p.353-354. — Index.
ISBN 0-8093-0789-8 : £8.80
Primary classification 977.3'994
(B77-21647)

920'.097 — Persons. *North America. Mid-West region. Biographical dictionaries*
Who's who in the Midwest. — Chicago : Marquis Who's Who ; London : Distributed by Prior.
1976-1977 : 15th ed. : including Illinois, Indiana, Iowa, Kansas, Michigan, Minnesota, Missouri, Nebraska, North Dakota, Ohio, South Dakota and Wisconsin and in Canada, Manitoba and Western Ontario. — 1976. — xiv,823p ; 31cm.
ISBN 0-8379-0715-2 : £35.00
(B77-03280)

920.71'05 — Men. *Biographical dictionaries. Serials*
Men of achievement. — Cambridge ([Cambridge CB2 3QP]) : International Biographical Centre.
Vol.4 : 1977 / editorial director Ernest Kay. — 1977. — x,708p : ports ; 26cm.
ISBN 0-900332-43-3 : Unpriced
ISSN 0306-3666
(B77-34293)

920.71'09'034 — Men, ca 1850-1973. *Biographies*
Walshe, Robert Daniel. Power and persuasion : biographies of twenty great men of the 19th and 20th centuries / [by] R.D. Walshe, J.J Cosgrove, E.B. McKillop. — Sydney [etc.] ; London : Reed Education, 1974 [i.e. 1976]. — 296p : ill, maps, ports ; 22cm.
Text on lining papers. — Published in Australia: 1974. — Index.
ISBN 0-589-09135-2 : £6.50
ISBN 0-589-09141-7 Pbk : Unpriced
(B77-03830)

920.71'09'04 — Men, 1900-1975. *Personal observations*
Cooke, Alistair. Six men / [by] Alistair Cooke. — London [etc.] : Bodley Head, 1977. — 207p : ports ; 22cm.
ISBN 0-370-30056-4 : £4.95
(B77-30856)

920.72 — Women. *Biographical dictionaries*
The **world** who's who of women. — Cambridge : International Biographical Centre.
3rd ed. : [1976] / editorial director Ernest Kay. — 1976. — xii,935p : ports ; 26cm.
ISBN 0-900332-40-9 : £24.00
(B77-03281)

920.72'02'07 — Women, to 1945. *Biographies. Humorous texts*
Armour, Richard. It all started with Eve / [by] Richard Armour ; suitably illustrated by Campbell Grant. — Large print [ed.]. — London : Prior [etc.], 1977. — xv,235p : ill ; 24cm.
Originally published: New York : McGraw-Hill, 1956 ; London : Hammond, Hammond, 1957.
ISBN 0-86043-027-8 : £4.50
(B77-13970)

920.72'09'034 — Women, 1861-1964. *Biographies*
Sorell, Walter. Three women : lives of sex and genius / [by] Walter Sorell. — London : Wolff, 1977. — xx,234p : 1 ill, ports ; 23cm.
Originally published: Indianapolis : Bobbs-Merrill, 1975. — Bibl.: p.225-228. — Index.
ISBN 0-85496-258-1 : £5.95
(B77-30857)

920.72'09429 — Women. *Wales, ca 1535-1896. Biographies. Welsh texts*
Roberts, Eigra Lewis. Siwgwr a sbeis / [gan] Eigra Lewis Roberts. — Llandysul : Gwasg Gomer, 1975. — 121p : geneal table, ports ; 19cm.
ISBN 0-85088-336-9 Pbk : £0.50
(B77-01911)

920.72'0973 — Negro women. *United States, 1800-1900. Autobiographies*
Black women in nineteenth-century American life : their words, their thoughts, their feelings / edited with an introduction by Bert James Loewenberg and Ruth Bogin. — University Park ; London : Pennsylvania State University Press, 1976. — xi,355p ; 24cm.
Bibl.: p.333-346. — Index.
ISBN 0-271-01207-2 : £12.75
(B77-32973)

929 — GENEALOGY AND HERALDRY
929'.09417 — Genealogy. *Ireland (Republic). Readings*
Burke's introduction to Irish ancestry / [edited by Hugh Montgomery-Massingberd]. — London : Burke's Peerage, 1976. — viii,64p : geneal table ; 25cm.
'... first appeared as a special introductory section in the American edition of Burke's Irish Family Records, published 1976' - title page verso.
ISBN 0-85011-021-1 Pbk : £1.25
(B77-12217)

929'.09425'7 — Genealogy. *Oxfordshire. Periodicals*
The **Oxfordshire** family historian : the journal of the Oxfordshire Family History Society. — Chichester (c/o Hon. Editor, J.S.W. Gibson, 11 Westgate, Chichester, Sussex PO19 3ET) : The Society.
Vol.1-, no.1- ; Spring 1977-. — 1977-. — 21cm.

Quarterly. — 25p. in 1st issue.
Sd : £0.75
ISSN 0309-2275
(B77-13971)

929.1 — GENEALOGY
929'.1'06241 — Genealogy. Organisations. *Great Britain. Association of Genealogists and Record Agents. Directories*
Association of Genealogists and Record Agents. List of members / the Association of Genealogists and Record Agents. — Ruislip (c/o The Hon. Secretary, 123 West End Rd, Ruislip, Middx HA4 6JS) : [The Association]. 1977. — [1977]. — [11]p ; 21cm.
Sd : Unpriced
(B77-32309)

929'.1'0941 — Genealogy. *Great Britain. Amateurs' manuals*
Matthews, Constance Mary. Your family history : and how to discover it / [by] C.M. Matthews ; with decorations by Chevron. — Guildford [etc.] : Lutterworth Press, 1976. — 144p,8p of plates : ill, coats of arms, facsims, geneal tables, map ; 25cm.
Bibl.: p.117-120. — Index.
ISBN 0-7188-2179-3 : £3.95
(B77-03282)

Willis, Arthur James. Genealogy for beginners / [by] Arthur J. Willis. — 3rd ed. — Chichester : Phillimore, 1976. — [6],191,[4]leaves of plates(4 fold),[4]p of plates : ill, coat of arms, facsims, geneal tables, map ; 23cm.
Previous ed.: 1970. — Index.
£2.95
ISBN 0-900592-31-1
(B77-27559)

929'.1'0942 — English persons, 1500-1977. *Genealogies*
Franklyn, Charles Aubrey Hamilton. The genealogy of Anne the Quene (Anne Bullen) and other English families including Broughton of Impens, N. Petherton, Bridgwater, Co. Somerset, Pontifex of West Wycombe, Co. Buckingham, Waddington of Mexborough, Co. York, Walwyn of Kilmersdon and Frome, Co. Somerset, and of Bognor Regis, Co. Sussex, together with a supplement to 'A short genealogical and heraldic history of four families' ... / by Charles A.H. Franklyn. — [Hassocks] ([Wickham Hill House, Hassocks, E. Sussex]) : [The author], 1977. — 101p : coats of arms, geneal table ; 25cm.
Spine title: Anne the Quene. — Limited ed. of 70 numbered copies. — Bibl.: p.11.
£5.00
(B77-22262)

929.1'0942 — Parish registers. *England, to 1862. Early works*
Burn, John Southerden. Registrum ecclesiae parochialis : the history of parish registers in England : also of the registers of Scotland, Ireland, the East and West Indies, the Dissenters, and the Episcopal Chapels in and about London, with observations on Bishops' transcripts, and the provisions of the Act of the 52nd George III Cap.146 / by John Southerden Burn. — 2nd ed. — Wakefield : EP Publishing, 1976. — [1],viii,296p ; 23cm.
Cover title: The history of parish registers in England. — Facsimile reprint of: 2nd ed. London : Russell Smith, 1862. — Index.
ISBN 0-7158-1202-5 : £5.95
(B77-26017)

929.2 — FAMILY HISTORIES
929'.2 — Families included in publications by Burke's Peerage Limited, to 1976. *Lists*
Burke's family index. — London : Burke's Peerage, 1976. — xxxii,171p : port ; 22cm.
Bibl.: p.xiii-xxx.
ISBN 0-85011-022-x : £6.50
(B77-25294)

929'.2'06241 — Families. Historiology. Organisations. *Great Britain. Federation of Family History Societies. Periodicals*
Federation of Family History Societies. Federation news : official journal of the Federation of Family History Societies. — [Tollerton] ([c/o Mrs E. Simpson, 2 Stella Grove, Tollerton, Notts. NG12 4EY]) : [The Federation].
Vol.1, no.1- ; Feb. 1975-. — [1975]-. — 30cm.
Published at irregular intervals. — Sheet (2 sides) as 1st issue.
Unpriced
(B77-16662)

929'.2'0941 — Families. Genealogical aspects. *Great Britain. Periodicals*
Family history news and digest. — Tollerton (General Secretary, Peapkin's End, 2 Stella Grove, Tollerton, Notts. NG12 4EY) : Federation of Family History Societies.
Vol.1, no.1- ; Summer 1977-. — [1977]. — 30cm.
Quarterly. — [2],30p. in 1st issue.
Sd : £0.75
ISSN 0309-8559
(B77-29055)

929'.2'0941 — Knox family. *Great Britain, 1881-1971. Biographies*
Fitzgerald, Penelope. The Knox brothers : Edmund ('Evoe'), 1881-1971, Dillwyn, 1883-1943, Wilfred, 1886-1950, Ronald, 1888-1957 / [by] Penelope Fitzgerald. — London [etc.] : Macmillan, 1977. — 294p,[8]p of plates : ill, facsims, geneal table, ports ; 23cm.
Bibl.: p.277-279. — Index.
ISBN 0-333-19426-8 : £4.95 : CIP rev.
(B77-17202)

929'.2'0941 — Ross family. *Great Britain, 1694-ca 1900*
Race, Mary. Family tree / [by] Mary Race. — Ilfracombe : Stockwell, 1977. — 47p ; 19cm.
ISBN 0-7223-1024-2 Pbk : £0.75
(B77-26018)

929'.2'09411 — Benzies family. *Scotland, 1260-1695*
A **Benzies** inheritance, 1260-1695 / [compiled by] Frank Benzies. — Coupar Angus : Culross, [1977]. — iii-xiv,128p,[9]leaves of plates : ill(chiefly col), ports(chiefly col) ; 22cm.
ISBN 0-900323-26-4 : £1.50
(B77-27560)

929'.2'09411 — Cameron clan. *Scotland. Highland Region. Lochaber (District), to 1971*
Stewart, John. The Camerons : a history of Clan Cameron / by John Stewart of Ardvorlich. — [Glasgow] ([c/o 40 Upper Craigs, Stirling, Scotland]) : Clan Cameron Association, 1974. — xx,344p,leaf of plate,xxiv p of plates : ill(some col), col coat of arms, facsims, geneal tables, maps, ports(1 col) ; 24cm.
Fold. sheet(1 side) (col. map, col. ill., and col. coat of arms) as insert. — Bibl.: p.317-318. — Index.
ISBN 0-9505551-0-x : £3.20
(B77-06375)

929'.2'09411 — Clans. *Scotland. Highlands & Islands, to 1976*
Munro, Robert William. Highland clans and tartans / [by] R.W. Munro. — [London] : Octopus Books, [1977]. — 128p : ill(chiefly col), col coats of arms, facsims(some col), maps(chiefly col), ports(chiefly col) ; 29cm.
Index.
ISBN 0-7064-0498-x : £2.95
(B77-22263)

929'.2'09411 — Clans. Tartans. *Scotland*
Bain, Robert. The clans and tartans of Scotland / [by Robert Bain]. — 5th ed. / enlarged and re-edited by Margaret O. MacDougall ; heraldic adviser P.E. Stewart-Blacker ; with a foreword by the Countess of Erroll. — Glasgow [etc.] : Collins, 1976. — 320p : col ill, coats of arms, col maps(on lining papers) ; 19cm.
Previous ed.: / enlarged and re-edited by Margaret O. MacDougall. 1959. — Bibl.: p.318-319.
ISBN 0-00-411117-6 : £1.95
ISBN 0-00-411118-4 Silk tartan ed. : £3.50
(B77-22264)

Bain, Robert. The clans and tartans of Scotland / [by Robert Bain]. — 6th ed. / enlarged and re-edited by Margaret O. MacDougall ; heraldic adviser P.E. Stewart-Blacker ; with a foreword by the countess of Erroll. — Glasgow [etc.] : Collins, 1977. — 320p : col ill, coats of arms, col maps(on lining papers), col port ; 19cm.
Previous ed.: 1976. — Bibl.: p.318-319.
£1.95
ISBN 0-00-411117-6
ISBN 0-00-411118-4 Silk tartan ed. : £3.50
(B77-34294)

Grimble, Ian. Scottish clans & tartans / [by] Ian Grimble. — London [etc.] : Hamlyn, 1977. — 272p : col ill, map ; 20cm.
Originally published: 1973. — Index.
ISBN 0-600-31935-0 Pbk : £1.95
(B77-22265)

Scottish Tartans Society. The guide to Scottish tartans : tartans and histories of Scotland's clans and families : with a unique Scottish-English dictionary and an index relating family and clan names to the tartans / prepared and authenticated by the Scottish Tartans Society ; foreword by Sir Iain Moncreiffe of that Ilk. — London : Shepheard-Walwyn, 1977. — [64]p : col ill ; 26x11cm.
Index.
ISBN 0-85683-034-8 Pbk : £1.35
(B77-26686)

929'.2'09411 — Lockhart family. *Scotland, to 1976*
Lockhart, Simon Macdonald. Seven centuries : a history of the Lockharts of Lee and Carnwath / by Simon Macdonald Lockhart. — Carnwath (Estate Office, Carnwath, Lanark) : The author, [1977]. — x,317p,[12]p of plates,fold leaf of plate : ill, geneal tables, map, ports ; 23cm.
Index.
£6.00
(B77-19899)

929'.2'09411 — MacDougall clan. *Scotland. Strathclyde Region. Argyll and Bute (District), to 1976*
Starforth, D M H. A short history of the Clan MacDougall / [by] Michael Starforth. — [Oban] ([c/o Madam MacDougall of MacDougall, Dunollie Castle, Oban, Argyll]) : [Clan MacDougall], [1977]. — [2],50p,[6]p of plates : ill(incl 1 col), col coat of arms, geneal table, map, port ; 19cm.
Cover title: An official short history of the Clan MacDougall. — Spine title: Clan MacDougall.
Pbk : £1.00
(B77-24603)

929'.2'09411 — Mackay clan, to 1976
Mackay, R L. The history of the Clan Mackay : its origin, history and dispersal / by R.L. Mackay. — [Wolverhampton] ([5 Parklands, Finchfield, Wolverhampton WV3 9DG]) : The author], [1977]. — [4],30p : map ; 21cm.
Sd : £1.25
(B77-23854)

929'.2'09415 — Families. *Ireland, to 1975. Biographies*
Burke's Irish family records. — [5th ed.] / [editor Hugh Montgomery-Massingberd]. — London : Burke's Peerage, 1976. — xxxii, 1237p ; 26cm.
Also available in a limited ed. of 350 autographed copies. — Previous ed.: published as 'Burke's genealogical and heraldic history of the landed gentry of Ireland' / edited by L.G. Pine. 1958.
ISBN 0-85011-018-1 : £38.00
Signed ed. : £78.00
(B77-05120)

929'.2'09415 — Shaw family. *Dublin, 1852-1876*
Harris, Nathaniel. The Shaws : the family of George Bernard Shaw / [by] Nathaniel Harris ; illustrated by Andrew Farmer. — London : Dent, 1977. — 63p : ill, ports ; 23cm. — (Harris, Nathaniel. Families in history)
Bibl.: p.63.
ISBN 0-460-06735-4 : £2.75
(B77-09405)

929'.2'0942 — Benson family & Strachey family. *England, ca 1850-ca 1930*
Askwith, Betty. Two Victorian families / by Betty Askwith. — London : Chatto and Windus, 1973. — 263p,8p of plates : geneal tables, ports ; 23cm.
Originally published: 1971. — Bibl.: p.350-251. — Index.
£3.15
(B77-10663)

929'.2'0942 — Booty family. *England, ca 1500-1975*
Booty, Harold. Some Bootys and their forebears : a family history / compiled by Harold Booty ; based on his own researches as well as those commissioned from Charles A. Bernau and L.H. Haydon Whitehead. — [London] ([26 Rothesay Court, SE11 5SX]) : The author, 1976. — [4],xviii,217p : ill, coat of arms, facsims, geneal tables, map, plan, ports ; 22cm.
Limited ed. of 300 copies. — Bibl.: p.194. — Index.
ISBN 0-9505419-0-7 : £4.00
(B77-05121)

929'.2'0942 — Cecil family. *England, 1520-1972*
Cecil, *Lord* **David.** The Cecils of Hatfield House : a portrait of an English ruling family / [by] David Cecil. — London : Cardinal, 1975. — 320p : ill(some col), col coat of arms, facsims, geneal table, maps, ports(some col) ; 25cm.
Originally published: London : Constable, 1973. — Bibl.: p.312. — Index.
ISBN 0-351-15516-3 Pbk : £2.95
(B77-19106)

929'.2'0942 — Cecil family. *England. Documents*
Cecil family. Calendar of the manuscripts of the Most Honourable the Marquess of Salisbury preserved at Hatfield House, Hertfordshire. — London : H.M.S.O. — (Historical Manuscripts Commission. Publications ; 9)
Cover title: Salisbury (Cecil) manuscripts.
Part 24 : Addenda 1605-1668 / edited by G. Dyfnallt Owen. — 1976. — xvi,401p ; 25cm.
Index.
ISBN 0-11-440062-8 : £20.00
(B77-01059)

929'.2'0942 — Fairhead family. *England, to 1975*
Fairhead, Albert Edward. The Fairhead series, I to X / [by] A.E. Fairhead. — [Norwich] ([506 Earlham Rd, Norwich NOR 11G]) : [The author], [1976?]. — 435p in various pagings : ill, geneal tables, ports ; 22cm.
Spine title.
ISBN 0-9505167-1-6 : £10.00
(B77-04480)

929'.2'0942 — Hamley family, to 1976. Genealogical aspects
Hamley, Douglas W. The Hamley, Hambly, Hamlyn group of families : historical and genealogical notes / compiled by Douglas W. Hamley. — Norwich (21 New St., Cawston, Norwich) : D.W. and J.C. Hamley, [1977]. — [24],288p : coat of arms, maps ; 21cm.
Bibl.: p.[24].
Pbk : £6.00
(B77-17825)

929'.2'0942 — Marfleet family. *History. Periodicals*
Marfleet Society. The Marfleet Society newsletter. — Leicester (c/o J.K. Marfleet, 4 Robotham Close, Huncote, Leicester LE9 6BB) : Marfleet Society.
Vol.1, no.1 - ; July 1976-. — 1976-. — 30cm.
Quarterly. — 6p. in 1st issue.
Sd : £1.50 yearly
ISSN 0308-6380
(B77-04481)

929'.2'0942 — Nelson family. *England, 1749-1805*
Harris, Nathaniel. The Nelsons : the family of Horatio Nelson / [by] Nathaniel Harris ; illustrated by Andrew Farmer. — London : Dent, 1977. — 64p : ill, map, ports ; 23cm. — (Harris, Nathaniel. Families in history)
Bibl.: p.64.
ISBN 0-460-06736-2 : £2.75
(B77-09406)

929'.2'0942 — Palgrave family. *Norfolk, 1667-1922. Documents*
Archives of Flegg relating to the Palgraves / [compiled by Derek A. Palgrave]. — Doncaster (c/o D.A. Palgrave, 210 Bawtry Rd, Doncaster, S. Yorkshire DN4 7BZ) : Palgrave Society, [1975]. — [4],20p : 2 facsims, map ; 30cm.
Index.
ISBN 0-9505335-3-x Sp : £0.50
(B77-04482)

929'.2'0942 — Poulett family. *Somerset. Hinton St George, to 1968*
Winn, Colin G. The Pouletts of Hinton St George / [by] Colin G. Winn. — London : Research Publishing Co., 1976. — 202p,[6] leaves of plates(1 fold),[16]p of plates : ill, col coat of arms, geneal table, ports(some col), plans(on lining papers) ; 26cm.
Bibl.: p.187-189. — Index.
ISBN 0-7050-0032-x : £7.00
Also classified at 942.3'89
(B77-08143)

929'.2'0942 — Savill family. *Essex, to 1976*
Watson, John Arthur Fergus. Savills : a family and a firm, 1652-1977 / [by] John A.F. Watson. — London : Hutchinson, 1977. — 173p,leaf of plate,[8]p of plates : geneal table, ports ; 23cm.
Index.
ISBN 0-09-129590-4 : £4.50
(B77-28285)

929'.2'0942 — Swinnerton family. *Periodicals*
Swinnerton family. Swinnerton family history : heraldic and genealogical studies of the Swinnerton family. — [Stourbridge] ([Beech Tree House, Norton Rd, Stourbridge, Worcs.]) : [I.S. Swinnerton].
Vol.1, no.1- ; May 1974-. — [1974]-. — ill, coats of arms, facsims, geneal tables, ports ; 30cm.
Published at irregular intervals. — Sheet ([2]p.) as 1st issue.
£2.50
ISSN 0308-6755
(B77-34295)

929'.2'0942 — Towneley family. *Lancashire, to 1976. Biographies*
Chapples, Leslie. The Towneleys of Towneley : a chronicle of the life and times of the later Towneleys / [by] Leslie Chapples. — [Burnley] ([7 Thornton Rd, Pike Hill, Burnley, Lancs.]) : [The author], [1976]. — [49]p : ill, ports ; 22cm.
Bibl.: p.[49].
ISBN 0-9505491-0-x Sd : £0.55
(B77-07730)

929'.2'094235 — Families. Genealogical aspects. *Devon. Periodicals*
The **Devon** family historian. — Plymouth (c/o The Hon. Secretary, 96 Beaumont St., Plymouth PL2 4AN) : Devon Family History Society.
No.1- ; Jan. 1977-. — [1977]-. — 22cm.
Quarterly. — [2],32p. in 1st issue.
Sd : £2.00 yearly
ISSN 0309-3735
(B77-12790)

929'.2'094251 — Families. *Central Derbyshire. History. Periodicals*
Mid-Derbyshire Family History Society. Branch news / Mid-Derbyshire Family History Society. — [Ripley] ([c/o Hon. Secretary, 147 Lowes Hill, Ripley, Derby]) : [The Society].
[Issue no.1]- ; [Aug. 1976]-. — [1976]-. — 30cm.
Annual. — [1],8p. in 1st issue. — Bibl.
Sd : Unpriced
ISSN 0140-637x
(B77-33523)

929'.2'094259 — Families. Genealogical aspects. *Buckinghamshire. Periodicals*
Origins : the bulletin of the Buckinghamshire Family History Society. — Aylesbury (The Editor, 2 Winchester House, Bishops Walk, Aylesbury, Bucks. HP21 7LD) : The Society.
Vol.1, no.1- ; Winter 1976-. — 1976-. — 30cm.
Quarterly. — 13p. in 1st issue.
Sd : Unpriced
ISSN 0140-1920
(B77-26019)

929'.2'094261 — Families. *Norfolk. Genealogies*
Palgrave-Moore, Patrick. A selection of revised and unpublished Norfolk pedigrees / compiled by Patrick T.R. Palgrave-Moore and Michael J. Sayer. — [Hethersett] (c/o P.T.R. Palgrave-Moore, Grove House, Hethersett, Norfolk) : Norfolk and Norwich Genealogical Society.
Part 2. — 1976. — [7],177p : of ill, coats of arms, geneal tables ; 26cm. — (Norfolk genealogy ; vol.8)
Cover title: Norfolk pedigrees. — Chiefly notebook format. — Index.
ISBN 0-905641-09-4 : Unpriced
(B77-08666)

929'.2'094265 — Families. Genealogical aspects. *Cambridgeshire. Periodicals*
Cambridgeshire Family History Society. Journal of the Cambridgeshire Family History Society. — Cambridge (c/o Hon. Editor, 12 Berrylands, Milton Rd, Cambridge CB4 1XW) : The Society.
Vol.1, no.1- ; Feb. 1977-. — [1977]-. — 30cm.
Quarterly. — 7p. in 1st issue.
Sd : £0.50(free to members)
ISSN 0309-5800
(B77-17826)

929'.2'0943 — Hartburg family. *Germany. Bavaria, to 1933. Biographies*
Orléans, Marion, *princesse d'.* A castle in Bavaria / [by] Marion and Thibaut d'Orléans ; translated [from the French] by Helen Weaver. — London : Heinemann, 1977. — 286p : geneal table ; 23cm.
Translation of: 'Un château en Bavière'. Paris : Balland, 1973.
ISBN 0-434-20150-2 : £4.50
(B77-27561)

929'.2'0972981 — Austin family. *Barbados, 1685-1900*
Burslem, Dora P. An old colonial family, 1685-1900 / by Dora P. Burslem and Audrie D. Manning. — [Evesham] ([The Old Farm House, Ashton-under-Hill, Evesham, Worcs.]) : [A.M.I. Austin], [1973]. — [2],55p : geneal tables, ports ; 21cm.
Sd : £1.00
(B77-29056)

929'.2'0973 — Lewis family. *United States, ca 1770-ca 1830*
Merrill, Boynton. Jefferson's nephews : a frontier tragedy / [by] Boynton Merrill, Jr. — Princeton ; Guildford : Princeton University Press, 1976. — xv,462,[1]p : ill, facsims, geneal tables, maps, ports ; 25cm.
Bibl.: p.425-440. — Index.
ISBN 0-691-04640-9 : £11.50
(B77-06973)

929'.2'0973 — MacRae clan. *South-eastern United States, to ca 1900*
MacRae, Donald, *b.1910.* From Kintail to Carolina / by Donald MacRae. — [Glasgow] ([37 Cranworth St., Glasgow G12 8AF]) : [The author], [1976]. — [5],95p : ill, geneal tables, map ; 20cm.
Bibl.: p.93-94.
ISBN 0-9502730-1-5 Pbk : £1.50
(B77-06376)

929.3 — GENEALOGICAL SOURCES

929'.3422'5 — British military forces. Personnel. Marriages. *East & West Sussex, 1750-1812. Lists*
Burchall, Michael John. Sussex military marriages, 1750-1812 / compiled and edited by Michael J. Burchall. — Brighton (2 Sussex Sq., Brighton BN2 5AB) : MS 'Manuscripts of Sussex' for the Sussex Family History Group.
Part 1. — 1975. — [64]p ; 26cm.
Limited ed. of 150 copies. — Bibl.: p.[3]. — Index.
ISBN 0-9504657-2-0 Sd : £1.00
(B77-02667)

929'.3424'6 — Families. *Staffordshire, 1532-1533. Lists*
A **list** of families in the Archdeaconry of Stafford, 1532-3 / edited by Ann J. Kettle. — [Stafford] ([Staffordshire County Record Office, County Buildings, Eastgate St., Stafford]) : Staffordshire Record Society, 1976. — xxvi, 216p ; 23cm. — (Collections for a history of Staffordshire : 4th series ; vol.8)
'The manuscript ... is now in the Joint Record Office at Lichfield (B/A/27ii) ...' - Introduction. — Index.
Pbk : Unpriced
(B77-20800)

929'.3424'92 — Parish registers. *West Midlands (Metropolitan County). Walsall. Texts*
Walsall *(Parish).* Deanery of Walsall, Walsall parish register. — [Dudley] ([c/o John S. Roper, 133 Tipton Rd, Woodsetton, Dudley, Worcs.]) : Staffordshire Parish Registers Society.
Walsall bapt[isms] 1646-1675, marr[iages] 1662-1754. — 1975. — 155p ; 23cm.
Cover title.
£2.00
(B77-25295)

929'.3425'93 — Church of England. Buckingham (Archdeaconry). Ecclesiastical courts. Probate records, 1483-1523. *Latin texts*
Buckingham *(Archdeaconry).* The courts of the Archdeaconry of Buckingham, 1483-1523 / edited, with an introduction, by E.M. Elvey. — [Aylesbury] ([c/o H.A. Hanley, Record Office, County Hall, Aylesbury, Bucks. HP20 1UA]) : Buckinghamshire Record Society, 1975. — xxx, 449p : map ; 25cm. — (Buckinghamshire Record Society. Publications ; no.19)
'The archives of the archdeaconry of Buckingham were deposited at the Buckinghamshire Record Office in 1959. The records for the period 1483-1523 ... are contained in four MSS.: D/A/We/1, D/A/V/1, D/A/C/1, and D/A/Wf/1' - Introduction. — English and Latin text. — Index.
ISBN 0-901198-15-3 : £15.00
(B77-10043)

929.4 — PERSONAL NAMES
929.4 — Pseudonyms. *Dictionaries*
Clarke, Joseph Francis. Pseudonyms / [by] Joseph F. Clarke. — London : Elm Tree Books, 1977. — xiv,252p ; 23cm.
Bibl.: p.251-252.
ISBN 0-241-89588-x : £5.50
(B77-12218)

929.4'0942 — English forenames. *Dictionaries*
Withycombe, Elizabeth Gidley. The Oxford dictionary of English Christian names / by E.G. Withycombe. — 3rd ed. — Oxford : Clarendon Press, 1977. — xlvii,310p ; 21cm.
Previous ed.: London : Oxford University Press, 1950.
ISBN 0-19-869124-6 : £4.50
(B77-26687)

929.4'0942 — English forenames. Related to signs of the zodiac
Parker, Derek. Derek & Julia Parker's compleat zodiac name book : the guide to your name and naming your child. — London : Luscombe, 1976. — 96p : ill ; 5cm.
Index on lining papers.
ISBN 0-86002-079-7 : £2.95
Also classified at 133.5'2
(B77-01060)

929.4'0942 — English forenames, to 1976
Dunkling, Leslie. First names first / [by] Leslie Alan Dunkling. — London : Dent, 1977. — 285p : ill, 2 facsims ; 24cm.
Bibl.: p.271-272. — Index.
ISBN 0-460-12025-5 : £4.50 : CIP rev.
(B77-08667)

929.5 — EPITAPHS
929'.5 — Epitaphs in English. *Anthologies*
Drinkwater, P. Fine fruit from death's orchard / gathered by Mr P. Drinkwater of Shipston-on-Stour in the county of Warwick. — Shipston-on-Stour (56 Church St., Shipston-on-Stour, Warwickshire) : [The author], 1976. — [21]p ; 15cm.
Sd : £0.07
(B77-17203)

929'.5 — Graveyards. Monumental inscriptions. Recording. *Manuals*
Jones, Jeremy. How to record graveyards / by Jeremy Jones ; edited by Philip Rahtz. — London (7 Marylebone Rd, NW1 5HA) : Council for British Archaeology : Rescue, 1976. — vi,40p : ill, forms, plans ; 22cm.
Bibl.: p.38-40.
ISBN 0-900312-30-0 Sd : £0.75
(B77-01061)

929'.5'09416 — Monumental inscriptions. *Northern Ireland. Collections*
Clarke, Richard Samuel Jessop. Gravestone inscriptions / compiled by R.S.J. Clarke. — Belfast ([66 Balmoral Ave., Belfast BT9 6NY]) : Ulster Historical Foundation. — (Ulster-Scot genealogical series ISSN 0305-5825)
Vol.16 : County Down, barony of Ards. — [1976]. — x,181p : ill, port ; 24cm.
Pbk : £2.00
(B77-14472)

929'.5'09422 — Churchyards. Monumental inscriptions. Recording. *Southern England. Manuals*
White, Henry Leslie. Monuments and their inscriptions : a practical guide / by H. Leslie White ; incorporating recommendations by John L. Rayment on behalf of the Federation of Family History Societies. — London (37 Harrington Gardens, SW7 4JX) : Society of Genealogists, 1977. — [4],60p : ill, plan ; 21cm.

Bibl.: p.57-60.
ISBN 0-901878-20-0 Sd : £1.00
(B77-15614)

929'.5'0942234 — Nonconformist churches. Cemeteries. *Kent. Canterbury. Wincheap cemetery. Monumental inscriptions, 1849-1938*
The **memorial** inscriptions of the Nonconformist Burial Ground in Wincheap, Canterbury / containing a plan of the burial ground by Richard A. Jones ; and an exact copy of every legible inscription on every gravestone, 1849-1938, transcribed by Duncan W. Harrington. — [Sheldwich?] ([c/o Alan Neame, Fisher St., Sheldwich, Kent]) : Kent Family History Society, 1976. — 36p : ill, plan ; 30cm. — (Kent Family History Society. Record publications ; no.1 ISSN 0308-9037)
Index.
ISBN 0-9505375-0-0 Sd : £1.00
(B77-09407)

929'.5'0942619 — Parish churches. *Norfolk. Stockton. St Michael's Church, Stockton. Churchyards. Monumental inscriptions. Texts*
Stockton's stone charters : a survey of the epitaphs in the churchyard of Saint Michael's Church at Stockton in the county of Norfolk / [compiled by] by Simon E. Pronk. — [Stockton, Norfolk] ([Pronk's Place, Stockton, Norfolk]) : [The author], [1976]. — [14]leaves ; 30cm.
Index.
Sd : Unpriced
(B77-29819)

929.6 — HERALDRY
Neubecker, Ottfried. Heraldry : sources, symbols and meaning / [by] Ottfried Neubecker, with contribution by J.P. Brooke-Little ; designed by Robert Tobler ; [translated from the German MS. by Nicholas Fry]. — London : Macdonald and Jane's, 1977. — 288p(8 fold) : ill(chiefly col), coat of arms(chiefly col), facsims(chiefly col), col map, ports(chiefly col) ; 29cm.
This translation originally published: New York : McGraw-Hill, 1976. — Bibl.: p.273-275. — Index.
ISBN 0-354-04157-6 : £22.50
(B77-32974)

929.6 — Heraldry. *British Israel Movement viewpoints*
Bennett, William Howard. Symbols of our Celto-Saxon heritage / by W.H. Bennett. — London (6 Buckingham Gate, SW1E 6JP) : Covenant Books, 1976. — xxi,210p : ill(chiefly col), coats of arms(chiefly col), geneal tables, maps, port ; 24cm.
£5.50
(B77-29820)

929.6'0941 — Heraldry. *Great Britain. Juvenile literature*
Patrick, Benjamin. The how and why wonder book of heraldry / written by Benjamin Patrick ; illustrated by George Cropper. — London : Transworld, 1976. — 48p : ill(some col), coats of arms(some col) ; 28cm.
Bibl.: p.47. — Index.
ISBN 0-552-86583-4 Pbk : £0.50
(B77-05771)

929.7 — ROYAL HOUSES, PEERAGE, LANDED GENTRY
929.7 — Monarchs, to 1975. *Biographical dictionaries*
Rowland-Entwistle, Theodore. Famous kings and emperors / [by] Theodore Rowland-Entwistle and Jean Cooke. — Newton Abbot [etc.] : David and Charles, 1976. — 124p ; 23cm. — (Brief biographies)
ISBN 0-7153-7240-8 : £3.50
(B77-03283)

929.7'025 — Aristocracy. *Directories*
The **royalty,** peerage and nobility of the world / compiled and edited from official sources. — London (Observatory House, Observatory Gardens, W8 7NS) : Annuaire de France.
91st vol. — International ed. — [1976]. — xvi, 869p,[2]p of plates,leaf of plate : ill, col coat of arms, ports ; 19cm.
'... new, enlarged edition in English of the "Annuaire de la noblesse de France et d'Europe" [France? : s.n., 197-?]' - Preface.
ISBN 0-9503480-1-5 : £16.80
(B77-00521)

929.7'2 — Baronetage. *Great Britain, to 1977*
Lindsay, *Sir* **Martin,** *bart.* The baronetage / [by] Sir Martin Lindsay of Dowhill, Bt. — Woking (Old Vicarage, Send, Woking, Surrey) : The author, 1977. — 32p ; 22cm.
Bibl.: p.28.
ISBN 0-9505673-0-2 Sd : £2.25
(B77-13972)

929.7'2 — England. Royal families, ca 1130-1216. *Biographies*
Duggan, Alfred. Devil's brood : the Angevin family / [by] Alfred Duggan. — Bath : Chivers, 1976. — 3-278p,fold leaf : geneal table ; 22cm.
Originally published: London : Faber, 1957. — Bibl.: p.270. — Index.
ISBN 0-85997-226-7 : £5.20(£3.90 to members of the Library Association)
(B77-05772)

929.7'2 — Great Britain. Princesses Royal, to 1965. *Biographies*
Cathcart, Helen. Anne and the Princesses Royal / [by] Helen Cathcart. — London : Star Books, 1975. — viii,208p,[8]p of plates : ports ; 19cm.
Originally published: London : W.H. Allen, 1973. — Bibl.: p.207-208.
ISBN 0-352-30048-5 Pbk : £0.75
Also classified at 941.085'0924
(B77-19107)

929.7'2 — Great Britain. Royal families, 495-1977. *Genealogies*
Freeman-Grenville, Greville Stewart Parker. The Queen's lineage : from AD 495 to the Silver Jubilee of Her Majesty Queen Elizabeth II / [by] G.S.P. Freeman-Grenville. — London : Collings, 1977. — [7],2-42p : ill, chiefly geneal tables ; 25cm.
Text on lining paper. — Index.
ISBN 0-86036-037-7 : £2.95
ISBN 0-86086-041-5 Pbk : £0.95
(B77-29057)

929.7'2 — Stuart family. *Scotland. Genealogies*
Addington, Arthur Charles. The Royal House of Stuart : the descendants of King James VI of Scotland, James I of England / [by] A.C. Addington. — London : Skilton.
Vol.3. — 1976. — viii,215p : geneal tables ; 33cm.
Bibl.: p.121-123. — Index.
ISBN 0-284-40006-8 : £12.60
(B77-02668)

929.7'2 — Titled classes & honours system. *Great Britain*
Great Britain. *Central Office of Information.* Honours and titles in Britain / prepared for British Information Services by the Central Office of Information. — [London] : [Central Office of Information], 1976. — [2],22p : geneal table ; 24cm.
Bibl.: p.22.
Sd : Unpriced
(B77-10044)

929.8 — ARMORIAL BEARINGS
929.8'0941 — British royal coats of arms, to 1976
Brooke-Little, John Philip. Royal heraldry : beasts and badges of Britain / by J.P. Brooke-Little. — Derby : Pilgrim, 1977. — [1], 24p : ill(some col), coats of arms(chiefly col), port ; 24cm.
Sd : £0.50
(B77-21595)

Petchey, William John. Armorial bearings of the sovereigns of England : a short account. — 2nd ed. revised / by W.J. Petchey ; shields of arms drawn by Royman Browne. — London : Bedford Square Press [for the] Standing Conference for Local History, 1977. — iv,31p : 1 ill, coats of arms, geneal table ; 25cm.
Previous ed.: i.e. Revised ed., published as 'A short account of the armorial bearings of the sovereigns of England'. London : National Council of Social Service, 1967. — Bibl.: p.29-31.
ISBN 0-7199-0926-0 Sd : £1.25
(B77-29058)

929.8'09411 — Scottish coats of arms, to 1973. Ordinaries of arms. *Texts*
Balfour Paul, *Sir* **James.** An ordinary of arms. — Edinburgh ([Court of the Lord Lyon, H.M. New Register House, Edinburgh EH1 3YT]) : [Lyon Office].
Vol.2 : contained in the Public register of all arms and bearings in Scotland, 1902-1973 (Vol.16/68, Vols 16/70-53/11 inclusive, Vols 54/1-55/67 inc., and Vols 56/1-76 and 57/1-46 inc.) / compiled in Lyon Office [by the late David Reid of Robertland and Vivien Wilson]. — 1977. — xvi,3-525p : coat of arms ; 24cm.
In slip case. — De-luxe ed. in slip case also available. — Index. — Previous control number ISBN 0-9505299-1-5.
ISBN 0-9505299-0-7 : £40.00
ISBN 0-9505299-1-5 De-luxe ed.: £40.00
(B77-19900)

929.8'09421 — Churches. Royal coats of arms. *Central London*
Pardoe, Rosemary Anne. Royal arms in the churches of Central London / [by R.A. Pardoe]. — Hartford (24 Othello Close, Hartford, Huntingdon PE18 7SU) : The author, 1976. — 8p ; 21cm.
Sd : £0.25
(B77-12219)

929.8'09424'89 — Memorials. Family coats of arms. *Warwickshire. Little Wolford*
Drinkwater, Peter, *b.1947.* Lapide loquente, or, The speaking stone : being a heraldic analysis of certain carved armorials at present set up at Little Wolford in the county of Warwick, and touching upon the histories of the Sheldon, Willington, Greville, Catesby, & Hyckes families in that shire ... / [by P. Drinkwater]. — Shipston-on-Stour ([56] Church St., Shipston-on-Stour [Warwickshire]) : The author, 1977. — [4],18p : coats of arms ; 13cm.
Limited ed of 300 copies.
Sd : £0.15
(B77-18467)

929.8'09426'12 — Parish churches. *Norfolk. North Barningham. North Barningham Church. Coats of arms*
Palgrave, Derek Aubrey. Heraldry at North Barningham Church / [by D.A. Palgrave]. — Doncaster (c/o D.A. Palgrave, 210 Bawtry Rd, Doncaster, S. Yorkshire [DN4 7BZ]) : Palgrave Society, 1976. — [2],14p : coats of arms(1 col), geneal table ; 30cm.
ISBN 0-9505335-2-1 Sp : £0.50
(B77-04483)

929.8'09427'1 — Cheshire family coats of arms, ca 1585. *Illustrations*
Family name and arms of the county of Chester / editor P. Timmis Smith. — [Astbury] ([St Mary's Cottage, Astbury, Congleton, Cheshire]) : The editor, [1977]. — [2]p,[19] leaves : 1 ill, coats of arms, facsims, map ; 28cm.
'... plates of arms reprinted from "The Vale-royal[l] of England", published by Daniel King [i.e. London : J. Streater], 1656 [and] compiled ... by William Smith [and William Webb]' - title page verso.
ISBN 0-9505693-0-5 : £2.75
(B77-15615)

929.9 — FLAGS
929.9'05 — Flags. *Periodicals*
Flag Institute. Bulletin / Flag Institute. — Chester (8 Newton La., Chester CH2 3RB) : The Institute.
Supersedes: Flagmaster.
Serial 001- ; 01.02.77-. — [1977]-. — ill, coats of arms ; 26cm.
Published at irregular intervals. — [10] leaves in 1st issue.
Sd : £0.25
ISSN 0309-085x
(B77-16663)

930 — ANCIENT HISTORY, TO CA. 500 AD.
930 — Ancient civilizations
Hollister, Charles Warren. Roots of the Western tradition : a short history of the ancient world / [by] C. Warren Hollister. — 3rd ed. — New York ; London [etc.] : Wiley, 1977. — xii, 234p : ill, maps ; 22cm.
Previous ed.: 1972. — Bibl. — Index.
ISBN 0-471-40720-8 Pbk : £4.65
(B77-19108)

Landsburg, Alan. In search of lost civilisations / [by] Alan Landsburg. — London : Corgi, 1977. — xv,206p,[32]p of plates : ill ; 18cm.
Originally published: New York : Bantam Books, 1976. — Bibl.: p.203-205.
ISBN 0-552-10413-2 Pbk : £0.85
(B77-20801)

930 — Ancient civilizations. Expounded by etymology
Cohane, John Philip. The key / [by] John Philip Cohane ; preface by Cyrus H. Gordon. — [London] : Fontana, 1975. — 224p,8p of plates : ill ; 18cm.
Originally published: New York : Crown Publishers, 1969 ; London : Turnstone Books, 1973. — Bibl.: p.201-207. — Index.
ISBN 0-00-633724-4 Pbk : £0.80
Primary classification 412
(B77-06618)

930 — Ancient world
The **Cambridge** ancient history. — Cambridge [etc.] : Cambridge University Press.
Vols 1 and 2. Plates. — New ed. / edited by I.E.S. Edwards ... [et al.]. — 1977. — xlii, 181p : of ill ; 24cm.
'In the first edition of this History, the initial volume of plates consisted of illustrations to the text of volumes I-IV' - Preface.
ISBN 0-521-20571-9 : £7.50
(B77-28286)

930 — Civilization, to ca 500
Hawkes, Jacquetta. The atlas of early man / [by] Jacquetta Hawkes, assisted by David Trump. — London [etc.] : Macmillan, 1976. — 256p : ill(chiefly col), col maps, col ports ; 29cm.
Index.
ISBN 0-333-19897-2 : £10.00
(B77-02669)

The **rise** of man / [editor Frances M. Clapham ; assistant editor Abigail Frost ; contributors Peter Andrews et al. ; illustrators John Barber et al.]. — Maidenhead : Sampson Low, 1976. — 160p : ill(chiefly col), facsims, maps ; 29cm. — ([The Sampson Low visual world library])
Index.
ISBN 0-562-00043-7 : £4.50
Also classified at 573.2
(B77-06974)

930'.02'02 — World events, B.C.10000-A.D.799. *Chronologies*
Mellersh, Harold Edward Leslie. Chronology of the ancient world, 10,000 BC to AD799 / [by] H.E.L. Mellersh. — London : Barrie and Jenkins, 1976. — ix,500p ; 26cm.
Index.
ISBN 0-214-20088-4 : £9.50
(B77-02670)

930'.022'2 — Ancient civilizations. *Illustrations. For Irish students. Primary school texts*
Dreaper, E. Pictorial history / [by] E. Dreaper, A. Collins. — Dublin : Helicon : Distributed by the Educational Company of Ireland.
No.1 : Early man. — 1977. — 16p : ill, maps ; 30cm.
Sd : £0.26
(B77-23855)

No.2 : The Egyptians. — 1977. — 16p : ill, maps ; 30cm.
Sd : £0.26
(B77-23856)

930.1 — ARCHAEOLOGY
Fowler, Peter Jon. Approaches to archaeology / [by] Peter J. Fowler. — London : A. and C. Black, 1977. — 203p : ill, facsim, form, maps, plans ; 26cm.
Bibl. — Index.
ISBN 0-7136-1747-0 : £6.50 : CIP rev.
(B77-17827)

Hester, James J. Introduction to archaeology / [by] James J. Hester. — New York ; London [etc.] : Holt, Rinehart and Winston, 1976. — xiii,479p : ill, maps, plans ; 25cm.
Text, ill. on lining papers. — Bibl. — Index.
ISBN 0-03-080179-6 : £8.00
(B77-01912)

930'.1 — Antiquities
Hawkins, Gerald Stanley. Beyond Stonehenge / [by] Gerald S. Hawkins. — London : Arrow Books, 1977. — xv,319p : ill, map, plans, ports ; 21cm.
Originally published: New York : Harper and Row ; London : Hutchinson, 1973. — Bibl.: p.307-310. — Index.
ISBN 0-09-914070-5 Pbk : £2.50
(B77-17204)

930'.1 — Antiquities. *Festschriften*
Problems in economic and social archaeology / edited by G. de G. Sieveking, I.H. Longworth and K.E. Wilson. — London : Duckworth, 1976. — xxvi,626p : ill, facsims, maps, plans ; 28cm.
' ... in honour of Grahame Clark ... ' - p.v. — Bibl. — Index.
ISBN 0-7156-0942-4 : £24.00
(B77-06377)

930'.1 — Archaeology. *Juvenile literature*
Laing, Lloyd Robert. All about archaeology / [by] Lloyd and Jennifer Laing. — London [etc.] : W.H. Allen, 1977. — 159p : ill ; 23cm.
Bibl.: p.153-154. — Index.
ISBN 0-491-02440-1 : £3.25
(B77-20802)

930'.1 — Archaeology. Related to anthropology
Archaeology and anthropology : areas of mutual interest / edited by Matthew Spriggs. — Oxford : British Archaeological Reports, 1977. — [8],176p : ill, plans ; 30cm. — (British archaeological reports : supplementary series ; 19)
Bibl.
ISBN 0-904531-63-5 Pbk : £3.30
Primary classification 301.2
(B77-20909)

930'.1 — Prehistoric man
Waechter, John. Prehistoric man : the fascinating story of man's evolution / [by] John Waechter. — London : Octopus Books, 1977. — 96p : ill(chiefly col), col map ; 33cm.
Col. ill. on lining papers. — Index.
ISBN 0-7064-0605-2 : £2.95
(B77-30858)

930'.1 — Prehistoric man. *Juvenile literature*
Hinde, Cecilia. Wonder why book of the first men on earth / [by] Cecilia Hinde ; illustrated by John Sibbick. — London : Transworld, 1977. — [2],32p : col ill, col map ; 29cm.
Index. — Previous control number ISBN 0-552-57001-x.
ISBN 0-552-98035-8 : £1.35
ISBN 0-552-57001-x
(B77-12791)

McCord, Anne. The children's picture prehistory / [by] Anne McCord ; illustrated by Bob Hersey ; designed by Graham Round. — London : Usborne.
Early man. — 1977. — 32p : ill(chiefly col), col map ; 28cm.
Bibl.: p.32. — Index.
ISBN 0-86020-131-7 : £1.95
ISBN 0-86020-130-9 Pbk : £0.95
(B77-29059)

McGowen, Tom. Collins book of prehistoric people / [by] Tom McGowen ; illustrated by Rod Ruth. — Glasgow [etc.] : Collins, 1977. — 3-60p : ill(some col) ; 29cm.
Originally published: as 'Album of prehistoric man'. Chicago : Rand McNally, 1975. — Index.
ISBN 0-00-104107-x : £1.95
(B77-17205)

930'.1'018 — Archaeology. Methodology
For theory building in archaeology : essays on faunal remains, aquatic resources, spatial analysis and systemic modeling / edited by Lewis R. Binford. — New York [etc.] ; London : Academic Press, 1977. — xvii,419p : ill, maps ; 24cm. — (Studies in archeology)
'Most of the papers grew out of an advanced seminar ... conducted with graduate students and colleagues [by the editor at the University of New Mexico] ...' - General introduction. — Bibl. — Index.
ISBN 0-12-100050-8 : £17.40
(B77-22266)

930'.1'018 — Archaeology. Methodology. *Essays*
Binford, Lewis R. An archaeological perspective / [by] Lewis R. Binford ; with a contribution by George I. Quimby. — New York [etc.] ; London : Seminar Press, 1972 [i.e. 1976]. — xii,464p : ill ; 24cm. — (Studies in archaeology)
Originally published: 1972. — Bibl. — Index.
ISBN 0-12-785053-8 Pbk : £4.90
(B77-08668)

930'.1'018 — Archaeology. Spatial analysis
Spatial archaeology / edited by David L. Clarke. — London [etc.] : Academic Press, 1977. — xi, 386p : ill, maps, plans ; 24cm.
Bibl. — Index.
ISBN 0-12-175750-1 : £9.50
(B77-30859)

930'.1'025 — Archaeology. *Directories*
The **archaeologists'** year book : an international directory of archaeology and anthropology. — Poole : Dolphin Press.
1977 / [edited by Michael Ridley]. — 1976. — 312p : ill ; 23cm.
Index.
ISBN 0-85642-061-1 : £8.00
(B77-01063)

930'.1028 — Archaeological investigation. Applications of earth sciences. *Conference proceedings*
Sediments in Archaeology *(Conference), University of Southampton, 1973.*
Georarchaeology : earth science and the past / edited by D.A. Davidson and M.L. Shackley. — London : Duckworth, 1976. — x,408p : ill, forms, maps ; 26cm.
'The papers in this volume were presented at a symposium on the theme "Sediments in archaeology" [held in the University of Southampton on 15-16 December 1973]' - Preface. — Bibl. — Index.
ISBN 0-7156-0925-4 : £16.00
(B77-03831)

930'.10283 — Antiquities. Excavation of remains. *Juvenile literature. Welsh texts*
Archaeoleg. — London : Macdonald Educational [etc.], 1976. — 48p : ill(chiefly col), col map, ports(1 col) ; 29cm.
At head of title: Hyn o fyd. — Adaptation of: 'Archaeology' / by Clare Goff. London : Macdonald and Co., 1973. — Bibl.: p.48. — Index.
ISBN 0-356-05469-1 : £1.60
(B77-03284)

930'.10285 — Antiquities. Dating. Scientific techniques
Fleming, Stuart James. Dating in archaeology : a guide to scientific techniques / [by] Stuart Fleming. — London : Dent, 1976. — 272p : ill, maps ; 26cm.
Bibl.: p.263-267. — Index.
ISBN 0-460-04241-6 : £8.95
(B77-06975)

930'.1'09 — Archaeology, to 1976
Ward, Anne. Adventures in archaeology / [by] Anne Ward. — London [etc.] : Hamlyn, 1977. — 160p : ill(some col), facsim, ports ; 31cm.
Ill. on lining papers. — Bibl.: p.158-159. — Index.
ISBN 0-600-30232-6 : £4.95
(B77-24604)

930'.1'0924 — Archaeology. Mallowan, Sir Max Edgar Lucien. *Autobiographies*
Mallowan, *Sir* **Max Edgar Lucien.** Mallowan's memoirs / [by] Max Mallowan. — London : Collins, 1977. — 320p,[16]p of plates : ill, map, plan, ports ; 24cm.
Facsim., map on lining papers. — Index.
ISBN 0-00-216506-6 : £6.95
(B77-27562)

930'.1'0924 — Archaeology. Pitt-Rivers, Augustus Henry. *Biographies*
Thompson, Michael Welman. General Pitt-Rivers : evolution and archaeology in the nineteenth century / by M.W. Thompson. — Bradford-on-Avon : Moonraker Press, 1977. — 164p : ill, facsims, plan, port ; 22cm.
Index.
ISBN 0-239-00162-1 : £4.95
(B77-17206)

932 — ANCIENT HISTORY. EGYPT
932 — Ancient Egypt. Akhetaten. Social life. *Juvenile literature*
Unstead, Robert John. See inside an Egyptian town / series editor [and author] R.J. Unstead ; [illustrations Bill Stallion et al.]. — London : Hutchinson, 1977. — 4-29p : col ill, col map, col plan ; 29cm. — (See inside)
Bibl.: p.28. — Index.
ISBN 0-09-131500-x : £1.50
(B77-32310)

932 — Ancient Egypt. Archaeological sources
Ruffle, John. Heritage of the pharaohs : an introduction to Egyptian archaeology / [by] John Ruffle. — Oxford : Phaidon, 1977. — 224p : ill(some col), facsims, maps, plans ; 25cm.
Bibl.: p.212-215. — Index.
ISBN 0-7148-1657-4 : £7.95
ISBN 0-7148-1726-0 Pbk : £5.95
(B77-34296)

932 — Ancient Egypt. Social life
Kamil, Jill. The ancient Egyptians / [by] Jill Kamil ; maps and drawings by Elizabeth Rodenbeck. — Newton Abbot [etc.] : David and Charles, 1976. — 152p : ill, maps, plan ; 23cm. — (How they lived and worked)
Bibl.: p.147. — Index.
ISBN 0-7153-7260-2 : £3.95
(B77-07731)

932 — Ancient Egypt, to B.C.30. *Juvenile literature*
Boase, Wendy. A closer look at ancient Egypt / [by] Wendy Boase ; illustrated by Angus McBride, Eric Thomas. — London : Hamilton, [1977]. — 3-30p : ill(chiefly col), col map, col plan ; 27cm. — (A closer look book ; 13)
Text, col. ill. on lining paper.
ISBN 0-241-89560-x : £1.75
(B77-19109)

932 — Ancient Egyptian antiquities. *Egypt. Luxor*
Kamil, Jill. Luxor : a guide to ancient Thebes / [by] Jill Kamil ; photographs by Alistair Duncan and George Allen ; plans by Hassan Ibrahim. — 2nd ed. — London [etc.] : Longman, 1976. — [1],181,[1]p : ill, maps(incl 1 col), plans ; 19cm.
Previous ed.: Harlow : Longman, 1973.
ISBN 0-582-78065-9 Pbk : £1.40
(B77-00522)

932 — Ancient Egyptian antiquities. Excavation of remains. *Egypt, to ca 1920*
Fagan, Brian Murray. The rape of the Nile : tomb robbers, tourists, and archaeologists in Egypt / [by] Brian M. Fagan. — London : Macdonald and Jane's, 1977. — xiv,399p : ill, facsims, maps, ports ; 24cm.
Originally published: New York : Scribner, 1975. — Bibl.: p.377-381. — Index.
ISBN 0-354-04091-x : £6.95
(B77-22990)

932 — Ancient Egyptian civilization
Cottrell, Leonard. The lost pharaohs / [by] Leonard Cottrell. — London [etc.] : Pan Books, 1977. — 220p,[16]p of plates : ill ; 18cm.
Originally published: London : Evans Bros, 1950.
ISBN 0-330-02303-9 Pbk : £0.80
Also classified at 932'.007'2
(B77-34297)

Jordan, Paul. Egypt : the black land / [by] Paul Jordan. — Oxford : Phaidon Press, 1976. — 207p : ill(some col), facsim, maps, ports ; 25cm.
Index.
ISBN 0-7148-1677-9 : £6.00
ISBN 0-7148-1722-8 Pbk : £3.50
(B77-09408)

932 — Ancient Egyptian civilization. *Nile Valley*
Butzer, Karl Wilhelm. Early hydraulic civilization in Egypt : a study in cultural ecology / [by] Karl W. Butzer. — Chicago ; London : University of Chicago Press, 1976. — xv,134p : ill, maps ; 24cm. — (Prehistoric archaeology and ecology)
Bibl.: p.113-134.
ISBN 0-226-08634-8 : £6.00
ISBN 0-226-08635-6 Pbk : £1.90
(B77-06378)

932 — Ancient Egyptian pyramids. *Egypt*
Mendelssohn, Kurt. The riddle of the pyramids / [by] Kurt Mendelssohn. — London : Sphere, 1977. — 208p,[32]p of plates : ill, geneal table, map, plans, ports ; 18cm.
Originally published: London : Thames and Hudson, 1974. — Bibl.: p.201-204. — Index.
ISBN 0-7221-6030-5 Pbk : £1.75
(B77-29060)

Sykes, Egerton. Predynastic Egypt and the Great Pyramids / [by] Egerton Sykes. — Brighton (58 West St., Brighton, E. Sussex) : Markham House Press Ltd, 1977. — 28p : ill ; 21cm.
Bibl.: p.28.
Sd : £2.00
(B77-33524)

932 — Ancient Egyptian pyramids. *Egypt. Giza. Great Pyramid. Theories*
Valentine, Tom. The great pyramid : man's monument to man / [by] Tom Valentine. — St Albans : Panther, 1977. — 144,[16]p of plates : ill, maps, ports ; 18cm.
Originally published: New York : Pinnacle Books, 1975.
ISBN 0-586-04645-3 Pbk : £0.60
(B77-27563)

932 — Ancient Egyptian pyramids. Egypt. Giza. Great Pyramid. Dimensions. Related to astronomical data about Mars
Saunders, Michael William. Pyramid-Mars connection : true or false?. — 2nd ed. — Caterham (Caterham, Surrey) : Downs Books, 1977. — 14 columns : ill, plan ; 21x30cm.
Author: M.W. Saunders. — Previous ed.: 1976. — Previous control number ISBN 0-9502260-6-8.
Sd : £0.40
ISBN 0-9502260-6-8
Primary classification 523.4'3
(B77-15268)

932 — Ancient Egyptian temples. Excavation of remains. Research projects. *Egypt. Tel el Amarna. Reports, surveys*
Akhenaten Temple Project. The Akhenaten Temple Project. — Warminster : Aris and Phillips.
Vol.1 : Initial discoveries / [by] Ray Winfield Smith and Donald B. Redford with contributions by ... [others] ; (with the editorial assistance of Diane Marie Sot). — 1976. — xvii,181p,[74]p of plates,[21]leaves of plates(9 fold) : ill ; 31cm.
Ill. on lining papers. — Bibl.: p.159-170. — Index.
ISBN 0-85668-034-6 : £12.50
(B77-27564)

932 — Deaths associated with excavation of remains of royal tombs in Egypt, to 1972
Vandenberg, Philipp. The curse of the pharaohs / [by] Philipp Vandenberg ; translated [from the German] by Thomas Weyr. — Sevenoaks : Coronet, 1977. — 235p : ill, geneal table, maps, plan ; 18cm.
This translation originally published: Philadelphia : Lippincott ; London : Hodder and Stoughton, 1975. — Translation of: 'Der Fluch der Pharaonen'. Bern : Scherz, 1973. — Bibl.: p.221-226. — Index.
ISBN 0-340-21310-8 Pbk : £0.70
Primary classification 133.4'0932
(B77-16161)

932 — Museums. *London. Camden (London Borough). British Museum. Exhibits: Antiquities from tomb of Tutankhamun, Pharaoh of Egypt. Catalogues*
British Museum. The treasures of Tutankhamun : [catalogue of an exhibition held at the British Museum, 1972] / [text by] I.E.S. Edwards [Keeper of Egyptian Antiquities] ; foreword by Lord Trevelyan. — Harmondsworth [etc.] : Penguin, 1976. — 48,[96]p,[16]p of plates : ill(some col), map, plan ; 25cm.
Originally published: London : British Museum, 1972. — Bibl.: p.[95].
ISBN 0-14-004287-3 Pbk : Unpriced
(B77-07732)

932'.0022'2 — Ancient Egyptian civilization. *Illustrations. Juvenile literature*
Allan, Tony. The Time Traveller book of pharaohs and pyramids / [by] Tony Allan assisted by Vivienne Henry ; illustrated by Toni Goffe ; designed by John Jamieson. — London : Usborne, 1977. — 32p : col ill, col map ; 28cm.
Spine title: Pharaohs and pyramids. — Bibl.: p.32. — Index.
£1.95
ISBN 0-86020-084-1 Pbk : £0.95
(B77-29061)

932'.007'2 — Egyptology, to 1950
Cottrell, Leonard. The lost pharaohs / [by] Leonard Cottrell. — London [etc.] : Pan Books, 1977. — 220p,[16]p of plates : ill ; 18cm.
Originally published: London : Evans Bros, 1950.
ISBN 0-330-02303-9 Pbk : £0.80
Primary classification 932
(B77-34297)

932'.007'2024 — Egyptology. Breasted, James Henry. *Biographies*
Breasted, Charles. Pioneer to the past : the story of James Henry Breasted, archaeologist / told by his son Charles Breasted. — Chicago ; London : University of Chicago Press, 1977. — xii,436p : map, ports ; 23cm. — (A phoenix book)
Originally published: New York : C. Scribner's Sons, 1943. — Index.
ISBN 0-226-07186-3 Pbk : £4.10
(B77-32311)

932'.0074'02142 — Museums. *London. Camden (London Borough). British Museum. Stock: Ancient Egyptian antiquities. Catalogues*
British Museum. Catalogue of Egyptian antiquities in the British Museum. — London : British Museum Publications Ltd for the Trustees.
4 : Glass / by John D. Cooney. — 1976. — xvi,180p,viii p of plates : ill(some col) ; 37cm.
Bibl. — Index.
ISBN 0-7141-0918-5 : £35.00
(B77-00523)

932'.0074'02142 — Museums. *London. Camden (London Borough). Petrie Museum. Guidebooks*
Petrie Museum. Guide to the Petrie Museum of Egyptian Archaeology. — London ([Gower St., WC1N 1AX]) : Department of Egyptology, University College, London, [1977]. — [2],18, [1]p : 2 maps, plan ; 30cm.
Sd : £0.20
(B77-32975)

932'.01 — Ancient Egypt. Social life, ca B.C.1560-ca B.C.1085. *Juvenile literature*
Unstead, Robert John. Living in ancient Egypt, the New Kingdom / [by] R.J. Unstead ; illustrated by Ron Stenberg. — London : A. and C. Black, 1977. — 43p : ill(some col) ; 23cm.
Ill. on lining papers. — Bibl.: p.43. — Index.
ISBN 0-7136-1713-6 : £1.45
(B77-09409)

932'.01 — Ancient Egyptian civilization, to ca B.C.600
Hawkes, Jacquetta. The first great civilizations : life in Mesopotamia, the Indus Valley and Egypt / [by] Jacquetta Hawkes. — Harmondsworth [etc.] : Penguin, 1977. — 512p, [16]p of plates : ill, maps, ports ; 19cm. — (The history of human society) (Pelican books)
Originally published: London : Hutchinson, 1973. — Bibl.: p.490-492. — Index.
ISBN 0-14-021973-0 Pbk : £2.25
Primary classification 935
(B77-24605)

933 — ANCIENT HISTORY. PALESTINE, TO 70 A. D.
933 — Antiquities. Excavation of remains. *Israel. Jerusalem, 1968-1974*
Jerusalem revealed : archaeology in the Holy City, 1968-1974 / edited by Yigael Yadin ; [English translation from the Hebrew and abridgement by R. Grafman]. — New Haven ; London : Yale University Press [for] the Israel Exploration Society, 1976. — viii,140p,iv p of plates : ill(some col), maps, plans ; 28cm.
'... articles adapted from "Qadmoniot"' - half title verso. — Originally published: Jerusalem : Israel Exploration Society, 1975. — Bibl.: p.137. — Index.
ISBN 0-300-01965-3 : £9.30
(B77-16114)

934 — ANCIENT HISTORY. INDIA
934 — Ancient Indian civilization, to 1200
Rawson, Philip. Indian Asia / by Philip Rawson. — Oxford : Elsevier-Phaidon, 1977. — 152p : ill(chiefly col), col maps, plans(2 col), ports ; 29cm. — (The making of the past)
Bibl.: p.137. — Index.
ISBN 0-7290-0046-x : £4.50
(B77-29821)

935 — ANCIENT HISTORY. NEAR EAST
935 — Ancient Iranian civilization
Herrmann, Georgina. The Iranian revival / by Georgina Herrmann. — Oxford : Elsevier-Phaidon, 1977. — 150p : ill(chiefly col), col maps, col plans ; 29cm. — (The making of the past)
Bibl.: p.137. — Index.
ISBN 0-7290-0045-1 : £4.50
(B77-28287)

935 — Ancient Iranian civilization, B.C.600-A.D.1100
Frye, Richard Nelson. The heritage of Persia / [by] Richard N. Frye. — 2nd ed. — London : Cardinal, 1976. — xii,330p,[8]p of plates : ill, geneal tables, maps ; 20cm. — (History of civilisation)
Previous ed.: London : Weidenfeld and Nicolson, 1963. — Bibl.: p.303-310. — Index.
ISBN 0-351-16340-9 Pbk : £1.50
(B77-14473)

935 — Ancient Mesopotamian civilization
Moorey, Peter Roger Stuart. Ancient Iraq : (Assyria and Babylonia) / by P.R.S. Moorey. — Oxford ([University of Oxford, Oxford OX1 2PH]) : Ashmolean Museum, 1976. — x,57p : ill, maps ; 23cm.
Bibl.: p.53-54. — Index.
ISBN 0-900090-36-7 Pbk : £1.50
(B77-08144)

Postgate, Nicholas, *b.1945.* The first empires / by Nicholas Postgate. — Oxford : Elsevier-Phaidon, 1977. — 152p : ill(chiefly col), maps(chiefly col), plans(some col), ports(some col) ; 29cm. — (The making of the past)
Bibl.: p.137. — Index.
ISBN 0-7290-0042-7 : £4.50
(B77-22991)

935 — Ancient Mesopotamian civilization, to ca B.C.600
Hawkes, Jacquetta. The first great civilizations : life in Mesopotamia, the Indus Valley and Egypt / [by] Jacquetta Hawkes. — Harmondsworth [etc.] : Penguin, 1977. — 512p, [16]p of plates : ill, maps, ports ; 19cm. — (The history of human society) (Pelican books)
Originally published: London : Hutchinson, 1973. — Bibl.: p.490-492. — Index.
ISBN 0-14-021973-0 Pbk : £2.25
Also classified at 932'.01
(B77-24605)

935 — Antiquities. Excavation of remains. *Iraq. Ur. Reports, surveys*
Woolley, *Sir* Leonard. Ur excavations / by Sir Leonard Woolley. — London : British Museum Publications Ltd.
Vol.7 : The Old Babylonian period / by Sir Leonard Woolley and Sir Max Mallowan ; edited by T.C. Mitchell. — 1976. — xviii,260p, 129p of plates : ill, plans ; 33cm.
'Publications of the Joint Expedition of the British Museum and of the Museum of the University of Pennsylvania to Mesopotamia'. — Index.
ISBN 0-7141-1087-6 : £45.00
(B77-30860)

935'.01 — Sumerian civilization. *Festschriften*
Sumerological studies in honor of Thorkild Jacobsen on his seventieth birthday, June 7, 1974 / [edited by Stephen J. Lieberman]. — Chicago ; London : University of Chicago Press, 1976 [i.e. 1977]. — xiv,316p : ill, maps, port ; 25cm. — (Assyriological studies ; no.20)
Includes 3 contributions in German. — Published in the United States: 1976. — Bibl.
ISBN 0-226-62282-7 Pbk : £9.90
(B77-11484)

936 — ANCIENT HISTORY. EUROPE NORTH AND WEST OF ITALIAN PENINSULA
936 — La Tène oppida. *Western Europe, B.C. 100-B.C. 10*
Collis, John. Defended sites of the late La Tène in Central and Western Europe / [by] John Collis. — Oxford : British Archaeological Reports, 1975. — [13],267p : ill, maps, plans ; 30cm. — (British archaeological reports : supplementary series ; 2)
Spine title: Late La Tène sites. — Bibl.: p.236-267.
ISBN 0-904531-34-1 Sd : £5.50
Also classified at 936.3
(B77-02671)

936 — Megalithic monuments. Astronomical aspects. *Europe, to 1976*
Michell, John. A little history of astro-archaeology : stages in the transformation of a heresy / [by] John Michell. — London : Thames and Hudson, 1977. — 96p : ill, facsims, maps, plans, ports ; 22cm.
Bibl.: p.90-91. — Index.
ISBN 0-500-01183-4 : £3.50
(B77-19110)

Michell, John. Secrets of the stones : the story of astro-archaeology / [by] John Michell. — Harmondsworth [etc.] : Penguin, 1977. — 96p : ill, facsims, maps, ports ; 21cm.
Originally published: as 'A little history of astro-archaeology'. London : Thames and Hudson, 1977. — Bibl.: p.90-91. — Index.
ISBN 0-14-004491-4 Pbk : Unpriced
(B77-20803)

936 — North-western European Iron Age civilization
Glob, Peter Vilhelm. The bog people : Iron-Age man preserved / [by] P.V. Glob ; translated from the Danish by Rupert Bruce-Mitford. — London : Faber, 1977. — 200p : ill, 2 maps ; 20cm.
This translation originally published: 1969. — Translation of: 'Mosefolket'. Kobenhavn : Gyldendal, 1966. — Bibl.: p.193-197. — Index.
ISBN 0-571-11079-7 Pbk : £1.95 : CIP rev.
(B77-23857)

936'.004'916 — Celtic civilization, to ca 500. *Juvenile literature*
Place, Robin. The Celts / [by] Robin Place. — London : Macdonald Educational, 1977. — 4-61p : ill(chiefly col), col maps ; 27cm. — (Peoples of the past)
Index.
ISBN 0-356-05470-5 : £1.75
(B77-19901)

936'.004'916 — Celtic peoples, to ca 500
Herm, Gerhard. The Celts : the people who came out of the darkness / [by] Gerhard Herm ; [translated from the German]. — London : Weidenfeld and Nicolson, 1976. — [7],312p,[16] p of plates : ill, maps, plan ; 23cm.
Translation of: 'Die Kelten'. Düsseldorf ; Wien : Econ, 1975. — Bibl.: p.297-298. — Index.
ISBN 0-297-77165-5 : £6.50
(B77-01886)

936.1 — Antiquities. *Great Britain. Juvenile literature*
Vince, John. History all around you / [by] John Vince ; illustrated by Peter Kesteven. — New ed. — Exeter : Wheaton, 1977. — vii,74p : ill, coats of arms ; 22cm.
Previous ed.: 1964. — Index.
ISBN 0-08-021364-2 : £1.95
(B77-30861)

936.1 — Archaeology. *Great Britain, to ca 1850. Essays*
Piggott, Stuart. Ruins in a landscape : essays in antiquarianism / [by] Stuart Piggott. — Edinburgh : Edinburgh University Press, 1976. — viii,212p : ill, facsims, plan, port ; 21cm.
Index.
ISBN 0-85224-303-0 : £4.00
ISBN 0-85224-311-1 Pbk : £1.75
(B77-05123)

936.1'0023 — Archaeology. *Great Britain. Career guides*
Bishop, John. Opportunities for archaeologists / by John Bishop ; edited by Philip Rahtz and Susan Hirst. — Hertford (15a Bull Plain, Hertford, Herts.) : RESCUE, 1975. — 48p ; 21cm. — (RESCUE. Publications ; no.5)
Bibl.: p.44-45.
Sd : £0.90(£0.70 to members of RESCUE)
(B77-05773)

936.1'005 — Archaeology. *Great Britain. Periodicals*
Current research in archaeology. — [London] ([31 Gordon Sq., WC1H 0PY]) : [University of London, Institute of Archaeology].
Supersedes: Newsletter for archaeologists.
No.1- ; May 1977-. — 1977-. — 30cm.
8p. in 1st issue. — Bibl.
Sd : Unpriced
ISSN 0140-3060
(B77-34298)

Newsletter for archaeologists. — London (31 Gordon Sq., WC1H 0PY) : Institute of Archaeology.
No.1-. — [1977]-. — 30cm.
Three issues a year. — [4]p. in 1st issue.
Sd : Unpriced
(B77-16115)

936.1'01 — Ancient British civilization. *Stories for children*
Morris, Margery. Stories of the Ancient Britons / [by] Margery Morris ; cover illustration by Richard Hook ; text illustrated by Juliet Stanwell-Smith ; stories illustrated by Michael Whittlesea. — London : Pan Books, 1977. — 143p : ill, maps, plans ; 20cm. — (Piccolo original)
'Before each adventure is a factual birds-eye-view of the period ...' - cover. — Also published: London : Severn House, 1977.
ISBN 0-330-24075-7 Pbk : £0.50
(B77-09410)

Morris, Margery. Stories of the ancient Britons / [by] Margery Morris ; text illustrations by Juliet Stanwell-Smith, stories illustrated by Michael Whittlesea. — London : Severn House : [Distributed by Hutchinson], 1977. — 143p : ill, maps ; 21cm.
'Before each adventure is a factual birds-eye view of the period ...' - jacket. — Also published: London : Pan Books, 1977.
ISBN 0-7278-0292-5 : £2.75
(B77-22993)

936.1'01 — Iron Age hill forts. *Great Britain*
Hillforts : later prehistoric earthworks in Britain and Ireland / edited by D.W. Harding. — London [etc.] : Academic Press, 1976. — xiv, 579p,[4]fold leaves of plates : ill, maps, plans ; 27cm.
Bibl.: p.541-564. — Index.
ISBN 0-12-324750-0 : £24.00
(B77-01064)

936.1'01 — Neolithic British civilization
MacKie, Euan Wallace. Science and society in prehistoric Britain / [by] Euan W. MacKie. — London : Elek, 1977. — xii,252p,[8]p of plates : ill, 2 charts, maps, plans ; 25cm. — (Elek archaeology and anthropology)
Bibl.: p.240-247. — Index.
ISBN 0-236-40041-x : £12.50
(B77-23858)

936.1'04 — Ancient Roman antiquities. *Great Britain*
Laing, Jennifer. Finding Roman Britain / [by] Jennifer Laing. — Newton Abbot [etc.] : David and Charles, 1977. — 136p : ill ; 22cm.
Bibl.: p.119. — Index.
ISBN 0-7153-7406-0 : £3.95
(B77-29822)

936.1'1'005 — Antiquities. Excavation of remains. *Scotland. Serials*
Discovery and excavation in Scotland / [Scottish Group, Council for British Archaeology]. — Edinburgh ([c/o National Museum of Antiquities, Queen St., Edinburgh EH2 1JD]) : The Group.
1976. — [1976]. — [1],106p ; 22cm.
Bibl.: p.89-102.
ISBN 0-901352-08-x Sd : £1.35
ISSN 0419-411x
(B77-11003)

936.11'005 — Archaeology. *Scotland. Serials*
Barrow : Glasgow University Archaeological Society magazine. — [Glasgow] ([c/o the Editor, Archaeology Department, 9 Lilybank Gardens, Glasgow]) : [The Society].
Vol.1- ; 1974-1975-. — [1975]-. — ill, maps, plans ; 26cm.
Annual. — 32p., fold. plate in 1st issue.
Sd : £0.30
ISSN 0309-5282
(B77-16116)

936.1'1'0061411 — Antiquities. Organisations. *Scotland. Ancient Monuments Board for Scotland. Reports, surveys. Serials*
Ancient Monuments Board for Scotland. Annual report ... / Ancient Monuments Board for Scotland. — Edinburgh : H.M.S.O.
23rd : 1976. — [1977]. — 9p,[4]p of plates : ill ; 25cm. — ([1976-77 H.C.]409)
ISBN 0-10-240977-3 Sd : £0.45
ISSN 0306-591x
(B77-19111)

936.1'1'01 — Prehistoric antiquities. *Scotland*
Feachem, Richard, *b.1914.* Guide to prehistoric Scotland / [by] Richard Feachem. — 2nd ed. — London : Batsford, 1977. — 223p : ill, maps, plans ; 23cm.
Previous ed.: 1963. — Bibl.: p.202-203. — Index.
ISBN 0-7134-3263-2 : £5.50
ISBN 0-7134-3264-0 Pbk : £2.95
(B77-10045)

936.1'5 — Burial places: Barrows. *Ireland. Early works*
Coffey, George. New Grange and other incised tumuli in Ireland / [by] George Coffey. — [New ed.]. — Poole : Dolphin Press, 1977. — 127p : ill, maps, plans ; 24cm. — (Dolphin archaeologies)
Previous ed.: published as 'New Grange, Brugh na Boinne, and other incised tumuli in Ireland'. Dublin : Hodges, Figgis and Co. ; London : Williams and Norgate, 1912. — Index.
ISBN 0-85642-041-7 : £4.75
Primary classification 936.1'8'22
(B77-16664)

936.1'5'01 — Prehistoric antiquities. *Ireland*
Herity, Michael. Ireland in prehistory / [by] Michael Herity and George Eogan. — London [etc.] : Routledge and Kegan Paul, 1977. — xvi,302p : ill, maps, plans, ports ; 25cm.
Bibl.: p.256-282. — Index.
ISBN 0-7100-8413-7 : £8.95
(B77-09411)

936.16 — Antiquities. *Northern Ireland. Reports, surveys. Serials*
Historic monuments : report by the Department of the Environment for Northern Ireland on the discharge of the historic monuments functions laid down in the Historic Monuments Act (Northern Ireland) 1971 during the period 1 April to 31 March. — Belfast : H.M.S.O.
1974-1975. — [1976]. — [1],11p ; 25cm.
Previously issued by the Northern Ireland Department of Finance.
ISBN 0-337-08077-1 Sd : £0.28
(B77-04484)

1975-1976. — [1977]. — 11p ; 25cm.
ISBN 0-337-08095-x Sd : £0.25
(B77-20804)

936.1'8'22 — Burial places: Barrows. *Meath (County). Newgrange. Early works*
Coffey, George. New Grange and other incised tumuli in Ireland / [by] George Coffey. — [New ed.]. — Poole : Dolphin Press, 1977. — 127p : ill, maps, plans ; 24cm. — (Dolphin archaeologies)
Previous ed.: published as 'New Grange, Brugh na Boinne, and other incised tumuli in Ireland'. Dublin : Hodges, Figgis and Co. ; London : Williams and Norgate, 1912. — Index.
ISBN 0-85642-041-7 : £4.75
Also classified at 936.1'5
(B77-16664)

936.1'9'3 — Antiquities. *Southern Clare (County)*
Shannon Archaeological and Historical Society. The other Clare : between unknown and well known : stages in the history of South Clare / produced by the Shannon Archaeological and Historical Society. — [Shannon Town] ([c/o Comprehensive School, Shannon Town, Co. Clare, Eire]) : [The Society], [1977]. — [1],34p : ill, maps, plans ; 30cm.
Sd : £0.55
(B77-30862)

936.2 — Antiquities. England. Expounded by signs of the zodiac
Terrestrial zodiac in Britain. — Cambridge ([142 Pheasant Rise], Bar Hill, Cambridge [CB3 8SD]) : Institute of Geomantic Research, 1976. — 91p(2 fold) : ill, maps ; 29cm.
Cover title: Terrestrial zodiacs in Britain. — Index. — Contents: The Nuthampstead zodiac / by Nigel Pennick (Not the same as B73-23702) - The Pendle zodiac / by Robert Lord.
ISBN 0-905376-03-x Pbk : £2.65
(B77-23859)

936.2 — Archaeological investigation. *England*
Dyer, James. Discovering archaeology in England and Wales / [by] James Dyer. — 4th ed. — Aylesbury : Shire Publications, 1976. — 85p : ill, plans ; 18cm. — (Discovering series ; no.46)
Previous ed.: 1973. — Bibl.: p.80. — Index.
ISBN 0-85263-340-8 Pbk : £0.65
(B77-10665)

936.2'006'142 — Antiquities. Organisations. *England. Ancient Monuments Board for England. Reports, surveys. Serials*
Ancient Monuments Board for England. Annual report ... / Ancient Monuments Board for England. — London : H.M.S.O.
23rd : 1976. — [1977]. — [1],17p : ill ; 25cm. — ([1976-77 H.C.]411)
ISBN 0-10-241177-8 Sd : £0.60
ISSN 0306-5901
(B77-19112)

936.2'0074'02651 — Museums. *Cambridgeshire. Peterborough. Peterborough Museum and Art Gallery. Stock: English antiquities, to 43. Catalogues*
Peterborough Museum and Art Gallery. A guide catalogue to the prehistoric archaeological collections in the Peterborough City Museum / by Miranda J. Green. — [Peterborough] ([Priestgate, Peterborough, Cambs.]) : [Peterborough Museum and Art Gallery], 1977. — [1],ii,19,[12]p : ill ; 30cm.
Cover title: Prehistoric Peterborough. — Bibl.: p.17-19.
ISBN 0-905952-00-6 Sd : £1.20
(B77-10664)

936.2'00992 — England. Kings, B.C. 1115-A.D. 689. *Early works*
Geoffrey of Monmouth, *Bp of St Asaph.* [Historia regum Britanniae. English]. The history of the kings of Britain / [by] Geoffrey of Monmouth ; translated [from the Latin] with an introduction by Lewis Thorpe. — Harmondsworth [etc.] : Penguin, 1976. — 373p : map ; 18cm. — (Penguin classics)
This translation originally published: 1966. — Bibl.: p.46-47. — Index.
Pbk : £0.95
ISBN 0-14-044170-0
(B77-03832)

936.2'04 — Ancient Roman towns. *England*
Sorrell, Alan. Roman towns in Britain / [by] Alan Sorrell ; foreword by Graham Webster. — London : Batsford, 1976. — 80p : ill, map, ports ; 23x30cm.
Index.
ISBN 0-7134-3237-3 : £3.95
(B77-02672)

936.2'2'01 — Mesolithic antiquities. *Southern England*
Palmer, Susann. Mesolithic cultures of Britain / [by] Susann Palmer. — Poole : Dolphin Press, 1977. — 230p : ill, 3 maps ; 25cm.
Bibl.: p.220-225. — Index.
ISBN 0-85642-062-x : £7.00
(B77-34299)

936.22'11 — Antiquities. Sites. *Surrey. Countryside adjacent to proposed Egham-Lyne Crossing Section of Motorway M25*
Johnson, Bernard, *b.1946.* Archaeology and the M25, 1971-1975 / by Bernard Johnson ; with contributions by John Barrett and David Bird ; illustrations by Jennie Scripps. — Aldershot (134c North La., Aldershot, Hants.) : Archaeological Publications Service for Surrey Archaeological Society, 1975. — [1],41p : ill, form, maps, plans ; 22cm.
Bibl.: p.38-39.
Sd : Unpriced
(B77-29062)

936.2'2'795 — Ancient Roman temples. Excavation of remains. *Hampshire. Hayling Island, to 1976. Reports, surveys*
Downey, Robert. The Roman temple on Hayling Island, first interim report on excavations, 1976 / [by] Robert Downey, Anthony King, Grahame Soffe. — London (Flat 4, 18 Delancey St., N.W.1) : Robert Downey, 1977. — [3],14p,6 leaves of plates : ill, map, plans ; 30cm.
Bibl.: p.13-14.
Sd : £0.30
(B77-23860)

936.2'2'91 — Mesolithic settlements. *Berkshire. Halfway. Wawcott 3. Excavation of remains, to 1970. Reports, surveys*
Froom, F R. Wawcott III : a stratified mesolithic succession / [by] F.R. Froom. — Oxford : British Archaeological Reports, 1976. — [12], 209p : ill, maps ; 30cm. — (British archaeological reports ; 27 ISSN 0306-1205)
Bibl.: p.208-209.
ISBN 0-904531-30-9 Sd : £3.90
(B77-00524)

936.2'2'98 — Iron Age hill forts: Caesar's Camp. *Berkshire. Bracknell (District)*
Green, T K. Iron age Bracknell : Caesar's Camp / by T.K. Green. — Bracknell ([c/o 3 Lynwood Chase, Bracknell, Berks.]) : Bracknell and District Historical Society, 1977. — ii,14p : maps, plan ; 21cm. — (Bracknell and District Historical Society. Booklets ; no.1 ISSN 0140-203x)
Bibl.: p.14.
Sd : £0.30
(B77-25296)

936.23 — Ancient Roman villas. *South-west England, to 407*
Branigan, Keith. The Roman villa in South-West England / [by] Keith Branigan. — Bradford-on-Avon : Moonraker Press, 1977. — 127p : ill, maps, plans ; 20x22cm.
Bibl.: p.118-124. — Index.
ISBN 0-239-00164-8 : £4.25
(B77-12792)

936.2'3'1009732 — Towns. Archaeological investigation. *Wiltshire. Proposals*
Haslam, Jeremy. Wiltshire towns : the archaeological potential / by Jeremy Haslam with Annette Edwards ; illustrations by Claudia R. White Haslam ; cover photography by David Nicholson. — Devizes (Devizes Museum, 41 Long St., Devizes, Wilts. [SN10 1NS]) : Wiltshire Archaeological and Natural History Society, [1976]. — [6],111p : maps ; 30cm.
Bibl.
ISBN 0-9501965-3-3 Sp : £2.50
(B77-00525)

936.2'3'17 — Neolithic monuments. *Wiltshire. Avebury. Expounded by worship of Great Goddess*
Dames, Michael. The Avebury cycle / [by] Michael Dames. — London : Thames and Hudson, 1977. — 240p : ill, facsims, maps, plans ; 25cm.
Bibl.: p.233-235. — Index.
ISBN 0-500-05030-9 : £6.50
(B77-34301)

936.2'3'3 — Antiquities. *Dorset*
Osborn, George Howard. Exploring ancient Dorset / [by] George Osborn. — Sherborne (Milborne Port, Sherborne, Dorset DT9 5HJ) : Dorset Publishing Co., 1976. — [1],48p : ill, maps ; 19x25cm.
Bibl.: p.48.
ISBN 0-902129-25-2 Sd : £0.90
(B77-05774)

936.2'3'5 — Antiquities. Registration. *Devon. Manuals*
Devon Committee for Rescue Archaeology. The sites and monuments register and parish check-lists / Devon Committee for Rescue Archaeology, sub-committee of the Devon Archaeological Society ; edited by Henrietta Miles. — Exeter (c/o Hon. Secretary, Department of Extra-mural Studies, Exeter University, Gandy St., Exeter [Devon]) : The Committee, [1977]. — [2],39,[2]p : ill, facsims, forms ; 25cm. — (DAS/DCRA publications ; no.1)
Bibl.
ISBN 0-9505690-0-3 Sd : £0.70
(B77-15616)

936.2'3'74 — Megalithic circles. *Cornwall. Minions. Hurlers. Early works. Facsimiles*
Dymond, C W. The Hurlers : Cornish stone circles / by C.W. Dymond. — Cambridge (142 Pheasant Rise, Bar Hill, Cambridge CB3 8SD) : Institute of Geomantic Research, 1977. — [2], 14p : 1 ill ; 21cm. — (Institute of Geomantic Research. Occasional papers ; 8 ISSN 0308-1966)
Facsimile reprint of: 1879 ed. Great Britain : s.n., 1879.
Sd : £0.60
(B77-29823)

936.2'3'85 — Prehistoric antiquities. *England. Exmoor. White Ladder*
Eardley-Wilmot, H. White Ladder : an early site on Exmoor : interim report to November 1976 / [by H. Eardley-Wilmot]. — North Molton (Wilson's, North Molton [Devon]) : The author, 1977. — [2],24p,[5]leaves of plates : maps, plans ; 30cm.
Sd : Unpriced
(B77-17207)

936.2'4'1 — Antiquities. *Gloucestershire*
Royal Commission on Historical Monuments (England). Ancient and historical monuments in the County of Gloucester / Royal Commission on Historical Monuments (England). — London : H.M.S.O.
Vol.1 : Iron Age and Romano-British monuments in the Gloucestershire Cotswolds. — 1976. — lvi,157p,68p of plates,[14] leaves of plates(13 fold) : ill(some col), maps(some col), plans ; 29cm.
Four fold. sheets(4p.) in pocket. — Index.
ISBN 0-11-700713-7 : £25.00
(B77-11485)

936.2'4'12 — Iron Age hill forts: Crickley Hill. Excavation of remains. *Gloucestershire, 1969- . Reports, surveys. Serials*
Dixon, Philip Willis. Crickley Hill : preliminary notes / [by Philip Dixon]. — [Cheltenham] ([Pittville, Cheltenham, Glos. GL52 3JG]) : [Gloucestershire College of Art and Design]. 1969. — [1970]. — 5p,[4] leaves : ill, plans ; 30cm.
Sd : £0.25
(B77-16665)

Dixon, Philip Willis. Crickley Hill report / [by] Philip Dixon. — Cheltenham (Pittville, Cheltenham, Glos. GL52 3JG) : Gloucestershire College of Art and Design.
3rd : 1971. — [1972]. — [2]p,14,9 leaves : ill, plans ; 30cm.
Bibl.: leaf 14.
Sd : £0.55
(B77-16666)

4th : 1972. — [1973]. — [2] leaves,9p,7 leaves(1 fold) : ill, maps, plans ; 30cm.
Bibl.: p.9.
£0.40
(B77-16667)

5th : 1973. — [1974]. — 12p,17 leaves(3 fold) : ill, maps, plans ; 30cm.
Bibl.: p.12.
£0.70
(B77-16668)

936.2'4'68 — Excavation of remains. *Staffordshire. Fisherwick, 1973. Reports, surveys*
Smith, Christopher. Second report of excavations at Fisherwick, Staffs., 1973 : ice-wedge casts and a Middle Bronze Age settlement / by Christopher A. Smith. — Walsall (c/o J.W. Whiston, 58 Wednesbury Rd, Walsall WS1 3RS) : South Staffordshire Archaeological and Historical Society, [1976]. — [1],17p,plate : ill, maps ; 24cm.
'Extract from "Transactions" 1974-1975 volume 16'.
ISBN 0-904689-98-0 Sd : £0.45
(B77-00526)

936.2'5'301 — Prehistoric antiquities. *Lincolnshire*
May, Jeffrey. Prehistoric Lincolnshire / by Jeffrey May. — Lincoln (86 Newland, Lincoln) : History of Lincolnshire Committee, 1976. — xix,251p,leaf of plate,2-9p of plates : ill, maps, plans ; 24cm. — (History of Lincolnshire ; vol.1)
Bibl.: p.216-236. — Index.
ISBN 0-902668-00-5 : £4.50
(B77-15617)

936.2'5'65 — Human settlements. Excavation of remains. *Bedfordshire. Dunstable region, to 1976. Reports, surveys*
Matthews, Charles Leslie. Occupation sites on a Chiltern ridge : excavations at Puddlehill and sites near Dunstable, Bedfordshire / [by] C.L. Matthews for the Manshead Archaeological Society of Dunstable. — Oxford : British Archaeological Reports.
Part 1 : Neolithic, Bronze Age and Early Iron Age / with foreword & summary by C.F.C. Hawkes. — 1976. — [11],xvi,209p : ill, map, plans(1 col) ; 30cm. — (British archaeological reports ; 29 ISSN 0306-1205)
ISBN 0-904531-32-5 Pbk : £3.90
(B77-00527)

936.2'5'76 — Bronze Age enclosures. Excavation of remains. *Oxfordshire. Rams Hill, 1972-1973. Reports, surveys*
Bradley, Richard, *b.1946.* Rams Hill, a Bronze Age defended enclosure and its landscape / [by] Richard Bradley & Ann Ellison with ... [others]. — Oxford : British Archaeological Reports, 1975. — [12],264p,[22]p of plates : ill, maps, plans ; 30cm. — (British archaeological reports ; 19 ISSN 0306-1205)
Bibl.: p.244-264.
ISBN 0-904531-22-8 Pbk : £5.50
(B77-00528)

936.2'6 — Antiquities. Archaeological investigation. *East Anglia. Reports, surveys. Serials*
East Anglian archaeology.
Report no.4 : Norfolk / [editor Peter Wade-Martins]. — Gressenhall [Union House, Gressenhall, Dereham, Norfolk NR20 4DR] : Norfolk Archaeological Unit [for the Scole Committee for Archaeology in East Anglia], 1976. — Gressenhall [Union House, Gressenhall, Dereham, Norfolk NR20 4DR] : Norfolk Archaeological Unit [for the Scole Committee for Archaeology in East Anglia], 1976. — x,21p,[3]fold leaves of plates,[2]p of plates : ill, maps ; 30cm.
Bibl.: p.19-21.
Pbk : £1.00
ISSN 0307-2460
(B77-29824)

East Anglian archaeology. — Gressenhall (Union House, Gressenhall, Dereham, Norfolk NR20 4DR) : Norfolk Archaeological Unit [for] the Scole Committee for Archaeology in East Anglia.
Report no.5 : Norfolk / [editor Peter Wade-Martins]. — 1977. — xv,247p,[9] leaves of plates(5 fold),[20]p of plates : ill, maps, plans ; 30cm.
Bibl.: p.239-246.
Pbk : Unpriced
ISSN 0307-2460
(B77-28288)

936.2'6 — Prehistoric antiquities. Wandlebury-Hatfield Forest alignment. Astronomical aspects. *East Anglia*
O'Brien, C A E. An integrated astronomical complex of earthworks at Wandlebury and Hatfield Forest from the third millenium B.C. : for the establishment of solar and lunar calendars and for an apparent attempt at measuring the circumference of the earth / [by] C.A.E. O'Brien. — Thaxted (Claypitts, Thaxted, Essex) : [The author], 1976. — v[i.e. viii],80p : ill ; 30cm.
ISBN 0-9505426-0-1 Pbk : Unpriced
(B77-05124)

936.2'6'5 — Cambridgeshire, to 43
Taylor, Alison, *b.1947.* Prehistoric Cambridgeshire / [by] Alison Taylor. — Cambridge : Oleander Press, 1977. — 48p : ill, map, plan ; 21cm. — (Cambridge town, gown and county ; 9)
Bibl.: p.48.
ISBN 0-900891-05-x Sd : £1.30
(B77-25297)

936.2'6'504 — Ancient Roman antiquities. *Cambridgeshire*
Browne, David M. Roman Cambridgeshire / [by] David M. Browne. — Cambridge : Oleander Press, 1977. — 48p : ill, 2 maps, 2 plans ; 21cm.
Bibl.: p.48.
ISBN 0-900891-09-2 Sd : £1.30
(B77-32976)

936.2'6'51 — Archaeological investigation. *Cambridgeshire. Peterborough (District). Reports, surveys. Serials*
Durobrivae : a review of Nene Valley archaeology / [Nene Valley Research Committee]. — Peterborough (Mrs C. Mackreth, 32 Hall La., Werrington, Peterborough PE4 6RA) : The Committee.
5 : 1977 / [edited by John Peter Wild]. — [1977]. — 35p : ill, maps, plans ; 21x30cm.
Bibl.
Sd : Unpriced
ISSN 0307-7756
(B77-30863)

936.2'7 — Antiquities. Archaeological investigation. *Northern England, ca B.C.1000-ca A.D.100. State-of-the-art reviews*
Challis, Aidan John. Later prehistory from the Trent to the Tyne / [by] A.J. Challis & D.W. Harding. — Oxford : British Archaeological Reports, 1975. — 2v.([15],247p;[11],179p) : ill, maps ; 30cm. — (British archaeological reports ; 20 ISSN 0306-1205)
Bibl.: p.192-223 (Part 1). — Index.
ISBN 0-904531-23-6 Pbk : £6.50
(B77-00529)

936.2'7 — Antiquities. Sites. *Northern England. Reports, surveys*
Northern Archaeological Survey. Archaeology in the north : report of the Northern Archaeological Survey / [written] by P.A.G. Clack and P.F. Gosling with contributions by ... [others] ; illustrations by B.H. Gill ; edited by D.W. Harding. — [Durham] ([46 Saddler St., Durham DH1 3NU]) : The Survey, 1976. — xiii,304p(42 fold) : ill, maps(some col) ; 30cm.
Bibl.
ISBN 0-905096-00-2 Pbk : £8.50
(B77-01913)

936.2'8'13 — Iron Age enclosures. Excavation of remains. *West Yorkshire (Metropolitan County). Oldfield Hill, 1960-1967. Reports, surveys*
Toomey, James Patrick. An Iron Age enclosure at Oldfield Hill, Meltham / by J.P. Toomey. — Honley (c/o The Editor, Hall Ing House, Honley, Huddersfield, [W. Yorkshire]) : 'The Brigantian', 1976. — 16p : ill, 2 maps, plans ; 26cm.
ISBN 0-905747-00-3 Sd : £0.75
(B77-00530)

936.2'8'3 — Antiquities. Archaeological investigation. *Humberside. Proposed site of Motorway M180. Reports, surveys*
M180 Joint Archaeological Committee. Archaeology on the M180 / M180 Joint Archaeological Committee ; [written by John R. Samuels]. — [Kingston upon Hull] ([Central Library, Albion St., Kingston upon Hull HU1 3TF]) : Humberside County Leisure Services, [1977]. — [4],13p : ill, map, plans ; 30cm.
ISBN 0-904451-07-0 Sd : £0.50
(B77-21596)

936.2'8'32 — Ancient Roman villas. *Humberside. Winterton. Roman Villa, Winterton. Excavation of remains, 1958-1967. Reports, surveys*
Stead, Ian Mathieson. Excavations at Winterton Roman villa, and other Roman sites in North Lincolnshire, 1958-1967 / by I.M. Stead, with contributions by D. Charlesworth ... [et al.]. — London : H.M.S.O., 1976. — xviii,325p,[4] leaves of plates,42p of plates(4 fold) : ill, maps(1 col), plans ; 29cm. — (Great Britain. Department of the Environment. Archaeological reports ; no.9)
Index.
ISBN 0-11-670570-1 : £25.00
(B77-10666)

936.2'8'43 — Antiquities. Archaeological investigation. *North Yorkshire. York*
Excavations in York / [York Archaeological Trust]. — [London] ([7 Marylebone Rd, NW1 5HA]) : [Council for British Archaeology].
1973-1974 : 2nd interim report / by P.V. Addyman, with contributions by ... [others]. — [1976]. — [2],32p,[2],viii p of plates(2 fold) : ill, maps, plans ; 24cm.
Summaries in English, French and German. — Bibl.: p.32.
ISBN 0-900312-39-4 Pbk : £2.00
(B77-10046)

York Archaeological Trust. The archaeology of York / [York Archaeological Trust] ; [general editor P.V. Addyman]. — London (7 Marylebone Rd, NW1 5HA) : Council for British Archaeology.
[Vol.] 3 : The legionary fortress. [Fascicule] 1 : The Church Street sewer and an adjacent building / [by] J.B. Whitwell. — 1976. — 55p, [4],xvi p of plates,(4 fold),fold leaf of plate : ill, map, plans ; 24cm.
Cover title. — English text, English , French and German summary. — Bibl.: p.53-55.
ISBN 0-900312-40-8 Pbk : £2.60
(B77-10047)

[Vol.] 14 : The past environment of York. [Fascicule] 1 : The environmental evidence from Church Street Roman sewer system / [by] P.C. Buckland. — 1976. — 44p : ill, map, plans ; 24cm.
Cover title. — English text, English, French and German summary. — Bibl.: p.42-44.
ISBN 0-900312-41-6 Pbk : £2.00
(B77-10048)

[Vol.] 17 : The small finds. [Fascicule] 1 : Finds from a Roman sewer system and an adjacent building in Church Street / [by] Arthur MacGregor. — 1976. — 30p,plate : ill ; 24cm.
Cover title. — English text, English, French and German summary. — Bibl.: p.28-30.
ISBN 0-900312-31-9 Pbk : £1.35
(B77-10049)

936.2'8'46 — Ancient Roman antiquities. *North Yorkshire. Malton*
Malton Museum. Roman Malton and the Malton Museum / [written by Alwyn Taylor et al.]. — [York] ([Museum Gardens, York YO1 2DR]) : [Yorkshire Museum], [1976]. — [2],14p : ill, maps ; 21cm.
ISBN 0-905807-00-6 Sd : £0.10
(B77-03285)

936.2'8'47 — Burial places: Barrows. *North Yorkshire. Gristhorpe. Gristhorpe Tumulus. Excavation of remains, 1834. Reports, surveys. Facsimiles*
Williamson, W C. Description of the tumulus opened at Gristhorpe, near Scarborough, with engravings of the coffin, weapons, &c. / by W.C. Williamson. — 3rd ed., revised and re-written. — Leeds : Prehistory Research Section, Yorkshire Archaeological Society, 1976. — [1],17p : ill ; 25cm.
Cover title: The Bronze Age tree trunk coffin burial found at Gristhorpe near Scarborough. — Facsimile reprint of: 3rd ed., revised and re-written. Scarborough : S.W. Theakston, 1872. — '... 1872 discussion has been omitted' - Introduction.
ISBN 0-902122-22-3 Sd : Unpriced
(B77-15036)

936.2'8'81 — Ancient Roman antiquities. Excavation of remains. *Northumberland. Chesterholm*
Birley, Robin. Vindolanda : a Roman frontier post on Hadrian's Wall / [by] Robin Birley. — London : Thames and Hudson, 1977. — 184p : ill(some col), maps, plans ; 26cm. — (New aspects of antiquity)
Bibl.: p.177. — Index.
ISBN 0-500-39014-2 : £9.50
(B77-34302)

936.2'8'81 — Ancient Roman fortifications. *Northumberland. Hadrian's Wall. Forts & watermills. Excavation of remains, 1907-1913*
Simpson, F Gerald. Watermills and military works on Hadrian's Wall : excavations in Northumberland, 1907-1913 / by F. Gerald Simpson [et al.] ; edited by Grace Simpson ; with a contribution on watermills by Lord Wilson of High Wray. — Kendal : Titus Wilson, 1976. — xvi,198p,[51]leaves of plates(17 fold) : ill, maps, plans ; 26cm.
Limited ed. of 400 copies. — Index.
ISBN 0-9504685-0-9 : £10.50
(B77-21597)

936.2'9'005 — Antiquities. *Wales. Periodicals*
'**Archaeologia** Cambrensis'. — Cardiff ([c/o National Library of Wales, Aberystwyth, Dyfed]) : Cambrian Archaeological Association.

Index to 'Archaeologia Cambrensis', 1901-1960 / compiled by T. Rowland Powel, with lists and notes by Donald Moore. — 1976. — xxi,313p : map ; 25cm.
ISBN 0-9500251-9-4 : Unpriced
(B77-12221)

936.2'9'89 — Ringworks. Excavation of remains. *South Glamorgan. Llantrithyd, 1960-1969. Reports, surveys*
Cardiff Archaeological Society. Llantrithyd : a ringwork in South Glamorgan / Cardiff Archaeological Society. — Cardiff (c/o Staff Tutor in Archaeology, Department of Extra-Mural Studies, University College Cardiff, 38 Park Place, Cardiff CF1 3BB) : The Society, 1977. — [5],81[i.e.88]p,[3]leaves,[2]leaves of plates,[22]p of plates : ill, maps, plans ; 30cm.
Bibl.
ISBN 0-9505846-0-6 Sp : Unpriced
(B77-28289)

936.3 — La Tène oppida. *Central Europe, B.C.100-B.C.10*
Collis, John. Defended sites of the late La Tène in Central and Western Europe / [by] John Collis. — Oxford : British Archaeological Reports, 1975. — [13],267p : ill, maps, plans ; 30cm. — (British archaeological reports : supplementary series ; 2)
Spine title: Late La Tène sites. — Bibl.: p.236-267.
ISBN 0-904531-34-1 Sd : £5.50
Primary classification 936
(B77-02671)

936.6 — Asturian antiquities. *Portugal. Minho (Province). Reports, surveys. French-English parallel texts*
Maury, Jean. Typologie et préhistoire de l'Asturien du Portugal = The Asturian in Portugal, typology and chronology / [by] Jean Maury ; translated from the French by Elisabeth Weeks. — Oxford : British Archaeological Reports, 1977. — [5],105p : ill, 2 maps ; 30cm. — (British archaeological reports : supplementary series ; 21)
Spine title: L'Asturien du Portugal. — French text with English translation. — Bibl.: p.28-29.
ISBN 0-904531-67-8 Pbk : £2.10
(B77-21598)

937 — ANCIENT HISTORY. ROME
937 — Ancient Roman antiquities
Vickers, Michael. The Roman world / by Michael Vickers. — Oxford : Elsevier-Phaidon, 1977. — 149p : ill(chiefly col), facsims(1 col), maps(chiefly col), col plans, ports(chiefly col) ; 29cm. — (The making of the past)
Bibl.: p.137. — Index.
ISBN 0-7290-0044-3 : £4.50
(B77-22994)

937 — Ancient Roman civilisation. *Secondary school texts*
Amey, Peter. Pax Romana / by Peter Amey. — London : Harrap, 1976. — [1],32p : ill, 2 maps, port ; 24cm. — (Harrap world history programme : set 10)
ISBN 0-245-52193-3 Sd : £0.60
(B77-26688)

937 — Ancient Roman civilization. *Juvenile literature*
Ramondt, Sophie. The Romans / [by] Sophie Ramondt ; [translated from the Dutch by Marian Powell]. — Guildford [etc.] : Lutterworth Press, 1976. — 122p : ill ; 23cm. — (New horizons in history series ; [5])
Originally published: in Dutch. Bussum : Uniboek, 1973. — Index.
ISBN 0-7188-2284-6 : £2.60
(B77-03286)

937 — Ancient Roman villas. Social life, to ca 500
Percival, John, *b.1937.* The Roman villa : an historical introduction / [by] John Percival. — London : Batsford, 1976. — 230p : ill, maps, plans ; 26cm. — (Batsford studies in archaeology)
Bibl.: p.219-221. — Index.
ISBN 0-7134-3238-1 : £10.00
(B77-01914)

937 — Ancient Rome, B.C.285-. *Secondary school texts*
Freebairn-Smith, S J. From trial to triumph / [by] S.J. Freebairn-Smith, G.N. Littlejohn ; illustrated by D.S. McGibbon. — London : Heinemann Educational.
In 3 vols.
1 : Winner take all. — 1977. — x,110p : ill, maps, plans, ports ; 25cm.
Bibl.: p.107. — Index.
ISBN 0-435-36320-4 Pbk : £1.50
(B77-19113)

2 : Chief factors for the gods. — 1977. — viii, 140p : ill, 2 geneal tables, maps, plans, ports ; 25cm.
Bibl.: p.136. — Index.
ISBN 0-435-36321-2 Pbk : £1.75
(B77-23861)

937 — Ancient Rome, to 565
Sinnigen, William Gurnee. A history of Rome to A.D.565. — 6th ed. / [by] William G. Sinnigen, Arthur E.R. Boak. — New York : Macmillan ; London : Collier Macmillan, 1977. — xviii,557p : ill, geneal tables, maps, ports ; 24cm.
Maps on lining papers. — Previous ed.: / by Arthur E.R. Boak, William G. Sinnigen. 1965. — Bibl.: p.520-532. — Index.
ISBN 0-02-410800-6 : £11.25
(B77-23862)

937'.0022'2 — Ancient Roman civilization. *Illustrations. Juvenile literature*
Amery, Heather. The Time Traveller book of Rome and Romans / [by] Heather Amery and Patricia Vanags ; illustrated by Stephen Cartwright and designed by John Jamieson. — London : Usborne, 1976. — 32p : chiefly col ill, col map ; 28cm.
Bibl.: p.32. — Index.
ISBN 0-86020-070-1 Pbk : £0.75
(B77-10667)

Ancient Romans / general editor Boswell Taylor ; consultant historian John D. Bareham ; illustrator John Pittaway ; further research by Antony Kamm. — Leicester : Knight Books, 1977. — 32p : of ill, maps, plans, ports ; 21cm. — (Picture teach yourself : project books)
Originally published: as 'Picture reference book of the ancient Romans'. Leicester : Brockhampton Press, 1970.
ISBN 0-340-21433-3 Pbk : £0.50
(B77-06976)

937'.00973'2 — Towns. *Ancient Rome. Secondary school texts*
Hodge, Peter, *b.1940.* Roman towns / [by] Peter Hodge. — Revised ed. — London : Longman, 1977. — 49p : ill, maps, plans ; 16x21cm. — (Aspects of Roman life)
Previous ed.: 1972. — Bibl.: p.49.
ISBN 0-582-20301-5 Sd : £0.70
(B77-32977)

937'.01 — Ancient Rome, B.C.625-B.C.390
Ogilvie, Robert Maxwell. Early Rome and the Etruscans / [by] R.M. Ogilvie. — [London] : Fontana, 1976. — 190p,[8]p of plates : ill, maps ; 18cm. — (Fontana history of the ancient world)
Also published: Hassocks : Harvester Press, 1976. — Bibl.: p.177-184. — Index.
ISBN 0-00-633349-4 Pbk : £1.00
(B77-13427)

Ogilvie, Robert Maxwell. Early Rome and the Etruscans / [by] R.M. Ogilvie. — Hassocks : Harvester Press, 1976. — 190p,[8]p of plates : ill, maps ; 23cm. — (Fontana history of the ancient world ; vol.1)
Bibl.: p.177-184. — Index.
ISBN 0-85527-086-1 : £6.50
(B77-03287)

937'.02 — Ancient Rome, B.C.510-B.C.50. *Essays*
Gabba, Emilio. Republican Rome, the army and the allies / [by] Emilio Gabba ; translated [from the Italian] by P.J. Cuff. — Oxford : Blackwell, 1976. — xi,272p ; 24cm.
'Gabba's articles have recently been collected in "Esercito e Società nella tarda repubblica romana" (Florence [: Nuova Italia editrice,] 1973) and I [the translator] have selected the most important of them for translation ... The text ... used is that in "Esercito e Società", which has incorporated some useful amendments and additions to the original articles' - Preface. — Index.
ISBN 0-631-17150-9 : £12.00
Primary classification 355'.00937
(B77-07862)

937'.05'0924 — Ancient Rome. Cicero, Marcus Tullius. Works. *Latin-English parallel texts*
Cicero, Marcus Tullius. [Works. English and Latin]. Cicero. — Cambridge, Mass. : Harvard University Press ; London : Heinemann.
In 28 vols.
10 : In Catilinam, I-IV. Pro Murena. Pro Sulla. Pro Flacco. — New ed. / with an English translation by C. Macdonald. — 1977. — xxxix,596p ; 17cm. — (The Loeb classical library ; 324)
Parallel Latin text and English translation, English introduction and notes. — Previous ed.: / by Louis E. Lord. 1937. — Bibl.: p.575-583. — Index.
ISBN 0-434-99324-7 : £3.40
(B77-13973)

937'.06 — Ancient Rome, 138-476. Gibbon, Edward. Decline and fall of the Roman Empire. *Conference proceedings*
Edward Gibbon and the decline and fall of the Roman Empire / edited by G.W. Bowersock, John Clive, Stephen R. Graubard. — Cambridge, Mass. ; London : Harvard University Press, 1977. — xiii,257p : facsim, ports ; 25cm.
'... a conference under the auspices of the American Academy of Arts and Sciences ... [was held] in Rome on January 7, 1976 ... for three days ...' - Introduction. — Index.
ISBN 0-674-23940-7 : £7.70
(B77-25298)

937'.07 — Ancient Rome. Social life, ca 45-200
Liversidge, Joan. Everyday life in the Roman Empire / [by] Joan Liversidge ; drawings by Eva Wilson. — London : Batsford [etc.], 1976. — 239p : ill, maps, plans, ports ; 23cm.
Bibl.: p.227-231. — Index.
ISBN 0-7134-3239-x : £3.50
(B77-01915)

937'.07'0924 — Ancient Rome. Tiberius, Emperor of Rome. *Latin texts. Early works*
Velleius Paterculus. [Historiae Romanae. Liber 2. Ch. 94-131]. The Tiberian narrative (2.94-131) / [by] Velleius Paterculus ; edited with an introduction and commentary by A.J. Woodman. — Cambridge [etc.] : Cambridge University Press, 1977. — xix,292p ; 23cm. — (Cambridge classical texts and commentaries ; 19)
Latin text, English introduction and notes. — Bibl.: p.xii-xix. — Index.
ISBN 0-521-21397-5 : £12.50
(B77-29825)

937'.08 — Ancient Rome, 306-337. *Secondary school texts*
Killingray, Margaret. Constantine / by Margaret Killingray. — London : Harrap, 1976. — [1], 32p : ill, maps ; 24cm. — (Harrap world history programme : set 10)
ISBN 0-245-52194-1 Sd : £0.60
(B77-26689)

937'.6 — Forum. *Ancient Rome. Rome. Secondary school texts*
Mulryne, T W. The Roman Forum / [by] T.W. Mulryne. — London : Bell, 1977. — 32p : ill, map ; 21cm. — (The ancient world in action)
ISBN 0-7135-1959-2 Sd : £1.00
(B77-24607)

937'.7 — Antiquities. Excavation of remains. *Italy. Monte Irsi, 1971-1972. Reports, surveys*
Monte Irsi, Southern Italy : the Canadian excavations in the Iron Age and Roman sites, 1971-1972 / edited by Alastair Small ; with contributions by Graeme Barker ... [et al.]. — Oxford : British Archaeological Reports, 1977. — [8],296p(4 fold) : ill, maps, plans ; 30cm. — (British archaeological reports : supplementary series ; 20)
Bibl. — Index.
ISBN 0-904531-66-x Pbk : £5.50
(B77-23863)

937'.7 — Archaeological investigation. *Italy. Herculaneum & Pompeii, to ca 1970*
Trevelyan, Raleigh. The shadow of Vesuvius : Pompeii AD 79 / [by] Raleigh Trevelyan. — London : Joseph, 1976. — 128p : ill(some col), ports(chiefly col) ; 26cm.
Ill. on lining papers.
ISBN 0-7181-1557-0 : £4.50
(B77-03288)

Trevelyan, Raleigh. The shadow of Vesuvius : Pompeii AD 79 / [by] Raleigh Trevelyan. — London : Folio Society, 1976. — 128p : ill(some col), facsims, ports ; 26cm.
Ill. on lining papers. — Also published: London : Joseph, 1976.
ISBN 0-85067-102-7 : £4.50
(B77-03833)

937'.7 — Italy. Pompeii. Social life, 1-79. *Juvenile literature*
Unstead, Robert John. Living in Pompeii / [by] R.J. Unstead ; illustrated by Laszlo Acs. — London : A. and C. Black, 1976. — 43p : ill(some col), map(on lining papers), col plan ; 23cm. — (The 'Living in' series)
Index.
ISBN 0-7136-1707-1 : £1.45
(B77-01065)

937'.8 — Antiquities. *Malta*
Lewis, Harrison. Ancient Malta : a study of its antiquities / [by] Harrison Lewis ; illustrated by Hilda Bruhm Lewis. — Gerrards Cross : Smythe, 1977. — 168p : ill ; 21cm.
Bibl.: p.168.
ISBN 0-901072-25-7 Pbk : £4.00
(B77-19902)

938 — ANCIENT HISTORY. GREECE
938 — Ancient Greece. City states, B.C.700-B.C.338
Sealey, Raphael. A history of the Greek city states, ca 700-338 BC / [by] Raphael Sealey. — Berkeley [etc.] ; London : University of California Press, 1976. — xxi,516p : ill, maps, ports ; 24cm.
Bibl.: p.xv-xix. — Index.
ISBN 0-520-03125-3 : £12.00
(B77-13974)

938 — Ancient Greece. Social life, to B.C.323. *Secondary school texts*
Discovering the Greeks / [by] P. Kenneth Corsar ... [et al.] ; drawings by Philip M.L. Page. — London : Edward Arnold, 1977. — vi,170p : ill, maps, plan, ports ; 24cm. — (Classical studies)
ISBN 0-7131-0033-8 Pbk : £2.95
(B77-15037)

938 — Ancient Greek civilization, to ca 200
Finley, Moses I. The ancient Greeks / [by] M.I. Finley. — [1st ed.] reprinted with revisions. — Harmondsworth [etc.] : Penguin, 1977. — 204p, 24p of plates : ill, facsim, map ; 18cm. — (Pelican books)
First ed. originally published: London : Chatto and Windus, 1963. — Bibl.: p.193-198. — Index.
Pbk : £1.20
ISBN 0-14-020812-7
(B77-34303)

938 — Classical antiquities, B.C.1000-B.C.476
Atlas of classical archaeology / edited by M.I. Finley ; maps and plans by John Flower. — London : Chatto and Windus, 1977. — 256p : ill(some col), col maps, plans(some col) ; 29cm.
Bibl. — Index.
ISBN 0-7011-2199-8 : £8.50
(B77-13428)

938'.0022'2 — Ancient Greek civilization. *Illustrations. Juvenile literature*
Ancient Greeks / general editor Boswell Taylor ; illustrator John Pittaway ; further research by Antony Kamm. — [Leicester] : Knight Books, [1977]. — 32p : ill, facsim, maps, plans, ports ; 21cm. — (Picture teach yourself : project books)
Originally published: as 'Picture reference book of the ancient Greeks'. Leicester : Brockhampton Press, 1974.
ISBN 0-340-21754-5 Pbk : £0.50
(B77-19903)

938'.005 — Ancient Greek antiquities. *Serials*
British School of Archaeology at Athens. The annual of the British School at Athens. — London (31 Gordon Sq., WC1H 0PY) : The School.
No.70 : 1975. — [1975]. — [5],209p,30p of plates : ill, maps, plans ; 26cm.
Bibl.: p.177-182. — Index.
ISBN 0-904887-00-6 : £20.00
(B77-03289)

938'.005 — Classical antiquity. *Serials*
California studies in classical antiquity. — Berkeley [etc.] ; London : University of California Press.
Vol.8. — [1977]. — viii,295p,[42]p of plates, leaf of plate : ill, facsims, map, port ; 26cm.
'The Editors are pleased to dedicate this volume ... to W. Kendrick Pritchett ...' - p.ii. — Published in the United States: 1976.
ISBN 0-520-09547-2 : £10.00
(B77-14475)

Illinois classical studies. — Urbana [etc.] ; London : University of Illinois Press [for the Classics Department, University of Illinois].
Vol.2 : 1977 / Miroslav Marcovich, editor. — 1977. — viii,332p : ill, facsims ; 24cm.
ISBN 0-252-00629-1 : £6.75
(B77-25299)

938'.007 — Classical studies. *Periodicals*
Liverpool classical monthly. — Liverpool (Dept of Greek, The University, P.O. Box 147, Liverpool L69 3BX) : John Pinsent.
Vol.1, no.1- ; Jan. 1976-. — 1976-. — 30cm.
Ten issues a year. — 10p. in 1st issue.
Sd : £3.00 yearly
ISSN 0309-3700
(B77-10668)

938'.007'2024 — Ancient Greek culture. Historiology. Dodds, Eric Robertson. *Autobiographies*
Dodds, Eric Robertson. Missing persons : an autobiography / [by] E.R. Dodds. — Oxford : Clarendon Press, 1977. — x,202p,[8]p of plates : ill, ports ; 23cm.
Index.
ISBN 0-19-812086-9 : £5.95 : CIP rev.
(B77-22267)

938'.007'2024 — Classical studies. Henry, James, b.1798. *Ireland. Biographies*
Richmond, John, *b.1925.* James Henry of Dublin : physician, versifier, pamphleteer, wanderer, and classical scholar / by John Richmond. — Blackrock (8 Beaumont Gardens, Blackrock, Co. Dublin) : The author, 1976. — 64p : geneal table, maps, port ; 22cm.
ISBN 0-9505342-0-x Sd : Unpriced
(B77-23865)

938'.01 — Ancient Greece, B.C.1650-B.C.1050
Hooker, J T. Mycenaean Greece / [by] J.T. Hooker. — London [etc.] : Routledge and Kegan Paul, 1976 [i.e. 1977]. — xiii,316p : ill, maps, plans ; 23cm. — (States and cities of Ancient Greece)
Bibl.: p.256-308. — Index.
ISBN 0-7100-8379-3 : £6.50
(B77-05125)

938'.01 — Ancient Greece. City states, to B.C.700. Archaeological sources
Snodgrass, Anthony McElrea. Archaeology and the rise of the Greek state / [by] A.M. Snodgrass. — Cambridge [etc.] : Cambridge University Press, 1977. — [1],37,[1]p : maps ; 19cm. — (University of Cambridge. Inaugural lectures)
'... delivered ... on 1 March 1977' - p.35.
ISBN 0-521-29244-1 Sd : £0.70
(B77-34304)

938'.01 — Ancient Greek civilization, ca B.C.800-ca B.C.700
Finley, Moses I. The world of Odysseus / by M.I. Finley. — 2nd ed. (revised and reset). — London : Chatto and Windus, 1977. — 192p : map ; 23cm.
Previous ed.: i.e. Revised ed., 1956. — Bibl.: p.178-185. — Index.
ISBN 0-7011-2244-7 : £4.95 : CIP rev.
(B77-19904)

938'.09 — Classical civilization, 1-ca 100
Lohse, Eduard. The New Testament environment / [by] Eduard Lohse ; [translated from the German by John E. Steely]. — London : S.C.M. Press, 1976. — 300p : geneal tables, maps ; 23cm. — (New Testament library)
This translation also published: Nashville : Abingdon Press, 1976. — Translation of: 'Umwelt des Neuen Testaments'. 2., durchges. u. erg. Aufl. Gottingen : Vandenhoeck und Ruprecht, 1974. — Bibl.: p.281-285. — Index.
ISBN 0-334-02213-4 : £6.00
Primary classification 296'.09'01
(B77-01169)

938'.5 — Ancient Greece. Athens. Social life, B.C.484-B.C.406. *Sources of data: Drama in Greek. Euripides. Bacchae*
Rankin, Herbert David. Pentheus and Plato : a study in social disintegration / by H.D. Rankin. — [Southampton] ([Highfield, Southampton SO9 5NH]) : University of Southampton, 1975. — 32p ; 21cm. — (University of Southampton. Inaugural lectures)
'... delivered at the University 20 November, 1975'. — Bibl.: p.30.
ISBN 0-85432-154-3 Sd : £0.40
Also classified at 938'.5
(B77-03834)

938'.5 — Ancient Greece. Athens. Social life, B.C.484-B.C.406. *Sources of data: Plato. Republic*
Rankin, Herbert David. Pentheus and Plato : a study in social disintegration / by H.D. Rankin. — [Southampton] ([Highfield, Southampton SO9 5NH]) : University of Southampton, 1975. — 32p ; 21cm. — (University of Southampton. Inaugural lectures)
'... delivered at the University 20 November, 1975'. — Bibl.: p.30.
ISBN 0-85432-154-3 Sd : £0.40
Primary classification 938'.5
(B77-03834)

938'.5'030924 — Athenian Empire. Themistocles. *Biographies*
Podlecki, Anthony Joseph. The life of Themistocles : a critical survey of the literary and archaeological evidence / [by] A.J. Podlecki. — Montreal ; London : McGill-Queen's University Press, 1975. — xv, 250p,8p of plates : ill, maps ; 26cm.
Bibl.: p.209-224. — Index.
ISBN 0-7735-0185-1 : Unpriced
(B77-18468)

939 — ANCIENT HISTORY. SOUTHEASTERN EUROPE
939 — Ancient Middle East
Velikovsky, Immanuel. Ages in chaos / [by] Immanuel Velikovsky. — London : Sidgwick and Jackson.
Vol.4 : Peoples of the sea. — 1977. — xviii, 261p,leaf of plate,[14]p of plates : ill ; 23cm.
Also published: New York : Doubleday, 1977. — Index.
ISBN 0-283-98246-2 : £5.95
(B77-10669)

939 — Ancient Middle Eastern civilisation, to B.C.612. Archaeological sources
Burney, Charles. From village to empire : an introduction to Near Eastern archaeology / [by] Charles Burney. — Oxford : Phaidon, 1977. — 224p : ill(some col), maps, plans ; 26cm.
Bibl.: p.205-212. — Index.
ISBN 0-7148-1730-9 : £7.95
ISBN 0-7148-1731-7 Pbk : £5.95
(B77-33525)

939 — Ancient Middle Eastern civilization, to ca B.C.2000
Whitehouse, Ruth. The first cities / [by] Ruth Whitehouse. — Oxford : Phaidon, 1977. — 207p : ill(some col), maps, plans ; 25cm.
Bibl.: p.199. — Index.
ISBN 0-7148-1678-7 : £6.95
ISBN 0-7148-1724-4 Pbk : £4.95
(B77-30864)

939 — Ancient Middle Eastern Neolithic antiquities
Singh, Purushottam. Neolithic cultures of Western Asia / [by] Purushottam Singh. — London [etc.] : Seminar Press, 1974. — xii, 240p,[3] leaves of plates(2 fold) : ill(incl 1 col), maps, plans ; 24cm.
Bibl. — Index.
ISBN 0-12-785795-8 : £4.00
(B77-19905)

939 — Antiquities. *Middle East*
Magnusson, Magnus. BC, the archaeology of the Bible lands / [by] Magnus Magnusson ; drawings and maps by Shirley Felts. — London [etc.] : Bodley Head : British Broadcasting Corporation, 1977. — 239p,[32]p of plates : ill(some col), maps(some col), plans, ports(1 col) ; 26cm.
'... [based on] the television documentary series ... first transmitted on BBC2 in the late winter and spring of 1977' - Dedication. — Bibl.: p.234-235. — Index.
ISBN 0-370-30015-7 : £6.50
ISBN 0-563-17209-6 (British Broadcasting Corporation) : £6.50
(B77-16669)

939 — Antiquities. *Middle East. Illustrations*
Bell, Gertrude. Gertrude Bell (1868-1926) : a selection from the photographic archive of an archaeologist and traveller / [compiled] by Stephen Hill. — [Newcastle upon Tyne] (Newcastle upon Tyne NE1 7RU) : Department of Archaeology, the University of Newcastle upon Tyne, 1976. — 24p : chiefly ill, map, port ; 25cm.
ISBN 0-905423-00-3 Sd : £0.30
(B77-03835)

939.2 — ANCIENT HISTORY. ASIA MINOR
939.2 — Hittite civilization
Lehmann, Johannes. The Hittites : people of a thousand gods / [by] Johannes Lehmann ; translated [from the German] by J. Maxwell Brownjohn. — London : Collins, 1977. — 317p,[20]p of plates : ill, map, plan ; 23cm.
Col. map on lining papers. — Translation of: 'Die Hethiter'. Munich : Bertelsmann, 1975. — Bibl.: p.309-312. — Index.
ISBN 0-00-216314-4 : £5.75
(B77-10050)

939.7 — ANCIENT HISTORY. NORTH AFRICA
939'.73 — Ancient Carthage, to B.C.146
Lloyd, Alan. Destroy Carthage! : the death throes of an ancient culture / by Alan Lloyd. — London : Souvenir Press, 1977. — 186p,[8]p of plates : ill, maps ; 23cm.
Bibl.: p.184-186.
ISBN 0-285-62235-8 : £3.95 : CIP rev.
(B77-20805)

939.8 — ANCIENT HISTORY. SOUTHEAST EUROPE
939'.8 — Ancient Roman villas. *Bulgaria. Chatalka. Roman Villa, Chatalka. Excavation of remains, 1963-1964. Reports, surveys*
Nikolov, Dimitur. The Thraco-Roman Villa Rustica near Chatalka, Stara Zagora, Bulgaria / [by] Dimitur Nikolov ; translated from the Bulgarian by Michael Holman. — Oxford : British Archaeological Reports, 1976. — [6], 169p(2 fold) : ill, map, plans ; 30cm. — (British archaeological reports : supplementary series ; 17)
Half title: Thraco-Roman villa at Chatalka. — Cover title: The Roman villa at Chatalka, Bulgaria. — Spine title: Roman villa, Chatalka, Bulgaria.
ISBN 0-904531-60-0 Pbk : £3.60
(B77-24608)

939'.8 — Carpi antiquities. *Romania. Moldavia, 100-400. Reports, surveys*
Bichir, Gh. The archaeology and history of the Carpi from the second to the fourth century AD / [by] Gh Bichir ; revised by the author ; translated from the Romanian by Nubar Hampartumian. — Oxford : British Archaeological Reports, 1976. — 2v.([11],211p; [4],iii-clxxxviii p of plates) : ill, maps, plans ; 30cm. — (British archaeological reports : supplementary series ; 16)
Spine title: Archaeology of the Carpi. — Translation and revision of: 'Cultura carpică'. Bucharest : Editura Academiei, 1973. — Bibl.: p.[7]-[10].
ISBN 0-904531-55-4 Pbk : £8.90
(B77-21599)

940 — HISTORY. EUROPE
940 — Churches. Archaeological investigation. *Europe, to 1975. Reports, surveys*
The **archaeological** study of churches / edited by Peter Addyman, Richard Morris. — London (7 Marylebone Rd, NW1 5HA) : Council for British Archaeology, 1976. — vii,79p,[8]plates : ill, plans ; 30cm. — (Council for British Archaeology. Research reports ; no.13)
Bibl.
ISBN 0-900312-35-1 Pbk : £4.50
(B77-01066)

940 — Europe, to 1976. *Festschriften*
Tribute to an antiquary : essays presented to Marc Fitch by some of his friends / edited by Frederick Emmison and Roy Stephens. — London (69 Aldwych, WC2B 4DY) : Leopard's Head Press, 1976. — xvi,332p,[12]leaves of plates,[18]p of plates : ill, facsims, geneal table, map, plan, port ; 25cm.
ISBN 0-904920-00-3 : £10.00
(B77-12222)

940 — European Community countries. *Periodicals. For women*
Women & Europe : news and views on European affairs of special interest to women and their organisations. — London (1a Whitehall Place, SW1A 2HA) : European Movement.
Vol.1, no.1- ; May-June 1976-. — 1976-. — ill, ports ; 30cm.
Six issues a year. — Folder ([4]p.) as 7th issue.
Unpriced
ISSN 0309-9199
(B77-33526)

940'.04'41 — Norman civilization, 911-ca 1150. *Juvenile literature*
Rooke, Patrick John. The Normans / [by] Patrick Rooke. — London : Macdonald Educational, 1977. — 4-61p : ill(chiefly col), facsim, col maps, col plans ; 27cm. — (Peoples of the past)
Index.
ISBN 0-356-05471-3 : £1.75
(B77-26020)

940'.04'41 — Normans. *Western Europe, 911-ca 1150*
Le Patourel, John. The Norman Empire / by John Le Patourel. — Oxford : Clarendon Press, 1976. — ix,416p(2 fold) : geneal table, 2 maps ; 23cm.
Bibl.: p.355-381. — Index.
ISBN 0-19-822525-3 : £15.00
(B77-07733)

940'.04'916 — Celtic civilization. *For Irish students. Secondary school texts*
Curriculum Development Unit. The Celtic way of life / [Curriculum Development Unit] ; [editor Agnes McMahon]. — Dublin (11 Clare St., Dublin 2) : O'Brien Press, 1976. — 136p : ill, maps ; 22cm.
Includes portions from 'The Ulster cycle' with one story in Irish.
ISBN 0-905140-19-2 : £3.95
Also classified at 398.2'2'09415
(B77-09412)

940'.04'916 — Universities. Celtic studies teachers. *Great Britain. Directories*
Mruck, Martin L. Handbook of university teachers of English language and literature, linguistics and Celtic studies in Great Britain and Ireland / [compiled and] edited by Martin L. Mruck. — London (11 Arlington St., S.W.1) : Deutscher Akademischer Austauschdienst, 1975. — vii,235p ; 24cm.
Index.
Pbk : Unpriced
Primary classification 420'.7'1141
(B77-22523)

940'.07 — European studies. Information sources. *Manuals*
Freeman, Peggotty. European studies handbook / compiled by Peggotty Freeman & Heather Nicholas. — London : Longman [for the Centre for Contemporary European Studies, University of Sussex], 1977. — 239p ; 24cm.
ISBN 0-582-36305-5 Pbk : £3.75
(B77-32978)

940.1 — HISTORY. EUROPE, 476-1453
940.1 — European civilization, to ca 1500
Peters, Edward, *b.1936.* Europe : the world of the Middle Ages / [by] Edward Peters. — Englewood Cliffs ; London [etc.] : Prentice-Hall, 1977. — xvii,620p : ill, maps, ports ; 24cm.
Bibl.: p.587-615. — Index.
ISBN 0-13-291898-6 : £13.55
(B77-15618)

940.1 — Western European civilization, 1000-1400. *Festschriften*
Order and innovation in the Middle Ages : essays in honor of Joseph R. Strayer / edited by William C. Jordan, Bruce McNab, Teofilo F. Ruiz. — Princeton ; Guildford : Princeton University Press, 1976. — xii,582p : ill, geneal tables, maps, port ; 25cm.
Bibl. — Index.
£13.90
ISBN 0-691-05231-x
(B77-01067)

940.1 — Western European civilization. Related to Byzantine civilization, 330-1600
Geanakoplos, Deno John. Interaction of the 'sibling' Byzantine and western cultures in the Middle Ages and Italian Renaissance (330-1600) / [by] Deno John Geanakoplos. — New Haven ; London : Yale University Press, 1976. — xxiii,416p : ill, maps, ports ; 24cm.
Bibl.: p.377-403. — Index.
ISBN 0-300-01831-2 : £18.15
Primary classification 949.5
(B77-10075)

940.1'05 — Europe, ca 1- ca 1600. *Serials*
Viator : medieval and Renaissance studies. — Berkeley [etc.] ; London : University of California Press [for] the Center for Medieval and Renaissance Studies, University of California, Los Angeles.
Vol.6 : 1975 / [editor Lynn White, Jr ; assistant editors Henry Ansgar Kelly, Richard H. Rouse]. — 1975. — vi,390,[1]p,[60]p of plates(2 fold),[2]leaves of plates : ill, facsims, music, plans(some col) ; 26cm.
Includes a contribution in German.
ISBN 0-520-02870-8 : £12.60
(B77-12793)

Vol.8 : 1977 / [editors Henrik Birnbaum et al.]. — 1977. — vi,462p,[33]p of plates : ill, facsims, geneal table, maps, ports ; 26cm.
ISBN 0-520-03363-9 : £12.00
(B77-30865)

940.1'05 — European culture, 300-1600. *Serials*
Medievalia et humanistica : studies in medieval & Renaissance culture. — Cleveland ; London : Press of Case Western Reserve University ; [Cambridge] : [Cambridge University Press].
New series, no.1 : in honour of S. Harrison Thomson / edited by Paul Maurice Clogan. — 1970. — xii,251p : ill, music, ports ; 24cm.
ISBN 0-521-21032-1 : £9.00
(B77-06977)

New series, no.2 : Medieval and Renaissance studies in review / edited by Paul Maurice Clogan. — 1971. — xii,223p,[12]p of plates : ill, facsims ; 24cm.
ISBN 0-521-21033-x : £9.00
(B77-06978)

Medievalia et humanistica : studies in medieval & Renaissance culture. — Cambridge [etc.] : Cambridge University Press.
New series, no.7 : Medieval poetics / edited by Paul Maurice Clogan. — 1976. — xii,209p : ill, music ; 24cm.
ISBN 0-521-21331-2 : £9.50
(B77-11486)

940.1'7 — Europe, 1077-1380. *Secondary school texts*
Clifford, Alan. Canossa / by Alan Clifford. — London : Harrap, 1976. — [1],32p : ill, map, ports ; 24cm. — (Harrap world history programme : set 10)
ISBN 0-245-52195-x Sd : £0.60
(B77-26690)

940.1'7 — European civilization, 1100-1500
Matthew, Donald. The medieval European community / [by] Donald Matthew. — London : Batsford, 1977. — 6,11-515p ; 24cm.
Index.
ISBN 0-7134-3254-3 : £12.50
(B77-10051)

940.1'7'0222 — Europe. Social life, ca 1240. *Illustrations. Juvenile literature*
Hindley, Judy. The Time Traveller book of knights and castles / [by] Judy Hindley ; illustrated by Toni Goffe ; designed by John Jamieson. — London : Usborne, 1976. — 32p : chiefly col ill, col maps ; 28cm.
Bibl.: p.32. — Index.
ISBN 0-86020-068-x Pbk : £0.75
(B77-12223)

940.1'8 — Crusades
Riley-Smith, Jonathan Simon Christopher. What were the crusades? / [by] Jonathan Riley-Smith. — London [etc.] : Macmillan, 1977. — 92p ; 23cm.
Bibl.: p.77-84. — Index.
ISBN 0-333-21372-6 : £4.95
ISBN 0-333-21373-4 Pbk : Unpriced
(B77-22995)

940.2 — HISTORY. EUROPE, 1453-
940.2 — Europe, ca 1500-ca 1700. *Transcripts of discussions*
European history, 1500-1700 / [edited by Peter Wells]. — London (85 Linden Gardens, W2 4EU) : Sussex Books, 1976. — 232p : ill, facsim, map, port ; 21cm. — (Questions in history)
Bibl.: p.225-232.
ISBN 0-905272-06-4 : £3.85
ISBN 0-905272-07-2 Pbk : £1.85
(B77-08670)

940.2 — Royal courts. *Europe, 1400-1800*
The **courts** of Europe : politics, patronage and royalty, 1400-1800 / edited by A.G. Dickens ; with texts by A.G. Dickens ... [et al.]. — London : Thames and Hudson, [1977]. — 335p : ill(some col), coats of arms, facsims, geneal tables, plans, ports(some col) ; 28cm.
Bibl.: p.328-331. — Index.
ISBN 0-500-25050-2 : £16.00
(B77-28290)

940.2'076 — Europe, 1760-1848. *Questions & answers. Secondary school texts*
Rayner, Edgar Geoffrey. New objective tests in history, 1760-1848, British and European / [by] E.G. Rayner, R.F. Stapley, J.B. Watson. — London [etc.] : Hodder and Stoughton, 1977. — xi,113p : ill, maps ; 22cm. — (New objective tests series)
With answers. — Bibl.: p.105-108.
ISBN 0-340-19423-5 Pbk : £1.50
(B77-19114)

940.2'076 — Europe, 1763-1914. *Exercises, worked examples. Secondary school texts*
Tucker, Elizabeth M M. Europe, 1763-1914 / [by] Elizabeth M.M. Tucker. — London : Edward Arnold, 1977. — iv,68p : ill, maps, port ; 25cm. — (History stimulus questions)
ISBN 0-7131-0105-9 Sd : £1.50
(B77-21600)

940.2'08 — Europe, 1450-1789. *Readings from contemporary sources. Secondary school texts*
European history, 1450-1789 / [compiled by] M.M. Reese. — London : Edward Arnold, 1977. — [6],58p ; 22cm. — (Documents for history revision)
ISBN 0-7131-0134-2 Sd : £1.20
(B77-21601)

940.2'08 — Europe, ca 1500-ca 1950. *Readings from contemporary sources*
Modern Europe and America / edited by William H. McNeill and Schuyler Owen Houser. — New York ; London [etc.] : Oxford University Press, 1973 [i.e. 1976]. — xi,312p : ill, music ; 21cm. — (Readings in world history ; vol.10)
Originally published: New York : Oxford University Press, 1973.
ISBN 0-19-501631-9 Pbk : £2.75
Also classified at 973'.08
(B77-06379)

940.21 — HISTORY. EUROPE, 1453-1517
940.2'1 — Europe, 1360-1600
New, John Frederick Hamilton. The Renaissance and Reformation : a short history / [by] John F.H. New. — 2nd ed. — New York ; London [etc.] : Wiley, 1977. — xi,201p : ill, facsims, maps, port ; 22cm.
Previous ed.: 1969. — Index.
ISBN 0-471-63342-9 Pbk : £4.00
(B77-22996)

940.23 — HISTORY. EUROPE, 1517-1648
940.2'32 — Europe, 1500-1600
Cowie, Leonard Wallace. Sixteenth-century Europe / [by] Leonard W. Cowie. — Edinburgh : Oliver and Boyd, 1977. — 340p : geneal tables, maps ; 23cm.
Bibl.: p.327-330. — Index.
ISBN 0-05-002829-4 : £5.00
ISBN 0-05-002828-6 Pbk : £3.50
(B77-15619)

940.25 — HISTORY. EUROPE, 1648-1789
940.2'53 — Europe, 1713-1783
Anderson, Matthew Smith. Europe in the eighteenth century, 1713-1783 / [by] M.S. Anderson. — 2nd ed. — London : Longman, 1976. — xi,447p : maps ; 23cm. — (A general history of Europe)
Previous ed.: 1961. — Bibl.: p.418-420. — Index.
ISBN 0-582-48671-8 : £7.95
ISBN 0-582-48672-6 Pbk : £3.75
(B77-05775)

940.2'53'0924 — Europe. Social life. Casanova, Giovanni Giacomo. *Biographies*
Masters, John. Casanova / [by] John Masters. — London : Futura Publications, 1976. — 256p ; 18cm.
Originally published: London : Joseph, 1969. — Bibl.: p.249-250. — Index.
ISBN 0-86007-368-8 Pbk : £0.75
(B77-14476)

940.27 — HISTORY. EUROPE, 1789-1815
940.2'7 — British prisoners of war. *France, 1809-1814. Personal observations*
Casse, George Richard. A prisoner of France (1809-1814) : a narrative of the Napoleonic wars / by George Richard Casse. — [2nd ed. reprinted] ; [with preface to the 1828 ed. and a new appendix and glossary]. — London : H. Baker, 1976. — [10],170p : ill ; 20cm.
Facsimile reprint of: 2nd ed. London : s.n., 1841.
ISBN 0-7030-0096-9 : £2.50
(B77-09413)

940.2'7 — Napoleonic Wars. Allied armies
Napoleon's enemies / edited by Richard Warner ; with a foreword by David Chandler. — London : Osprey Publishing, 1977. — 192p : ill(some col), facsim, 2 maps, ports ; 26cm.
'Much factual information, some half-tones, and many colour plates have been taken from books in the Men-at-Arms series ...' - Acknowledgement. — Index.
ISBN 0-85045-172-8 : £5.95
(B77-26021)

940.2'7 — Napoleonic Wars. Army campaigns by France. Armée, 1813-1815
Lawford, James Philip. Napoleon : the last campaigns, 1813-15 / [by] James Lawford, [with Peter Young]. — Maidenhead : Sampson Low, 1977. — 160p : ill(some col), col plans, col maps, ports ; 32cm.
Ill. on lining papers. — Index.
ISBN 0-562-00065-8 : £6.95
(B77-30866)

940.2'7 — Napoleonic Wars. Army operations by Great Britain. Army, 1800-1815. Light cavalry
Pimlott, John, *b.1948.* British light cavalry / by John Pimlott ; illustrated by Emir Bukhari. — London : Almark Publishing, 1977. — 48p : ill(some col), maps, plans ; 21x22cm. — (Nations in arms, 1800-1815)
Bibl.: p.45,48.
ISBN 0-85524-271-x : £2.25
(B77-18469)

940.2'7 — Napoleonic Wars. Army operations by Portugal. Exercito
Pivka, Otto von. The Portuguese army of the Napoleonic Wars / text by Otto von Pivka ; colour plates by Michael Roffe. — London : Osprey Publishing, 1977. — 40p,[8]p of plates : ill(some col) ; 25cm. — (Men-at-arms series)
ISBN 0-85045-251-1 Pbk : £1.95
(B77-14477)

940.2'7 — Napoleonic Wars. Army operations by Scandinavian armies, 1807-1814
Cassin-Scott, Jack. Scandinavian armies in the Napoleonic wars / text by Jack Cassin-Scott ; colour plates by Michael Roffe. — London : Osprey Publishing, 1976. — 40p,A-Hp of plates : ill(some col), maps, plan, ports ; 25cm. — (Men-at-arms series)
ISBN 0-85045-252-x Pbk : £1.95
(B77-01068)

940.2'7 — Napoleonic Wars. Battle of Austerlitz
Duffy, Christopher. Austerlitz, 1805 / [by] Christopher Duffy. — London : Seeley Service, 1977. — xiii,194p,[12]p of plates : ill, plans, ports ; 23cm.
Bibl.: p.176-178. — Index.
ISBN 0-85422-128-x : £5.95
(B77-13975)

940.2'7 — Napoleonic Wars. Franco-Austrian campaign, 1809
Petre, Francis Loraine. Napoleon & the Archduke Charles : a history of the Franco-Austrian campaign in the valley of the Danube in 1809 / by F. Loraine Petre. — 1st ed. [reprinted] ; introduction by David G. Chandler. — London : Arms and Armour Press [etc.], 1976. — [9],v-ix,413p,[12]p of plates(4 fold) : ill, maps, plans, ports ; 23cm.
Facsimile reprint of: 1st ed. London : J. Lane, 1909. — Index.
ISBN 0-85368-221-6 : £5.95
(B77-03290)

940.2'7 — Napoleonic wars. Naval operations by Great Britain. Royal Navy
Parkinson, Cyril Northcote. Britannia rules : the classic age of naval history, 1793-1815 / [by] C. Northcote Parkinson. — London : Weidenfeld and Nicolson, 1977. — viii,199p,[16]p of plates : ill, plans, ports ; 24cm.
Index.
ISBN 0-297-77287-2 : £5.95
(B77-16670)

940.2'7 — Napoleonic Wars. Peninsular campaign
Read, Jan. War in the Peninsula / by Jan Read. — London : Faber, 1977. — 256p,[8]p of plates : ill, map, ports ; 23cm.
Bibl.: p.243-247. — Index.
ISBN 0-571-10645-5 : £6.95 : CIP rev.
(B77-08671)

940.2'7'0924 — Napoleonic Wars. Peninsular campaign. Army operations by Great Britain. Army. 95th (Rifle) Regiment, 1808-1809. *Other ranks' personal observations*
Harris, John, *fl.1802-1814.* Recollections of Rifleman Harris / as told to Henry Curling. — [New ed.] / edited and introduced by Christopher Hibbert. — London : Cooper [for the] Military Book Society, 1977. — xi,128p ; 23cm.
This ed. originally published: London : Cooper, 1970. — Index.
£3.95
ISBN 0-85052-005-3
(B77-26692)

940.28 — HISTORY. EUROPE, 1815-1914
940.2'8 — Europe, 1789-1974. *Secondary school texts*
Richards, Denis. An illustrated history of modern Europe, 1789-1974 / [by] Denis Richards. — 6th ed. — London : Longman, 1977. — [10], 374p : ill, facsim, maps, ports ; 24cm.
Previous ed.: published as 'An illustrated history of modern Europe, 1789-1945'. London : Longmans, Green, 1950. — Index.
ISBN 0-582-34106-x Pbk : £2.95
(B77-19906)

940.2'8 — Europe, 1814-ca 1950. *Secondary school texts*
The **European** experience : topics in modern history / general editor John H. Jensen. — Wellington ; London [etc.] : Reed Education.
Vol.1 : Forces of change / [contributors John H. Jensen et al.]. — Revised ed. — 1975. — ii-xii,263p : ill, facsim, maps, ports ; 24cm.
Previous ed.: 1971. — Bibl.
ISBN 0-589-04063-4 Pbk : £5.65
(B77-01916)

940.2'8 — Europe, 1870-1975
Joll, James. Europe since 1870 : an international history / [by] James Joll. — 2nd ed. — Harmondsworth [etc.] : Penguin, 1976. — xiii, 543p : maps ; 20cm. — (A pelican book)
Previous ed.: London : Weidenfeld and Nicolson, 1973. — Bibl.: p.501-506. — Index.
ISBN 0-14-021918-8 Pbk : £1.75
(B77-06979)

940.2'8 — Europe. Dynasties, 1848-1918
Sulzberger, Cyrus Leo. The fall of eagles / [by] C.L. Sulzberger. — London : Hodder and Stoughton, 1977. — 408p : ill(some col), col coats of arms, maps, ports(some col) ; 25cm.
Index.
ISBN 0-340-21641-7 : £9.95
Also classified at 943'.07; 943.6'04; 947.08
(B77-32312)

940.2'8 — Europe. Political events, 1848-1878
Grenville, John Ashley Soames. Europe reshaped, 1848-1878 / [by] J.A.S. Grenville. — [London] : Fontana, 1976. — 412p : maps ; 18cm. — (Fontana history of Europe)
Also published: Hassocks : Harvester Press, 1976. — Bibl.: p.393-402. — Index.
ISBN 0-00-634237-x Pbk : £1.25
(B77-13976)

940.2'8 — Europe. Revolutions, 1760-1975
Essays on modern European revolutionary history / by Stanley H. Palmer ... [et al.] ; introduction by Charles Tilly ; edited by Bede K. Lackner and Kenneth Roy Philp. — Austin ; London : University of Texas Press, 1977. — xxiii,132p ; 23cm. — (The Walter Prescott Webb memorial lectures ; 11 ISSN 0083-713x)
Bibl.: p.87-88.
ISBN 0-292-72021-1 : £6.00
(B77-23866)

940.2'8 — Western Europe, 1800-1900. *Transcripts of discussions*
Nineteenth century Europe / [edited by Andrew Hardman]. — London (85 Linden Gardens, W2 4EU) : Sussex Books, 1976. — 3-171p : ill ; 21cm. — (Questions in history)
Bibl.: p.167-171.
ISBN 0-905272-10-2 : Unpriced
ISBN 0-905272-11-0 Pbk : Unpriced
(B77-08672)

940.2'8'0222 — Europe. Social life, 1850-1914. *Illustrations*
The last of old Europe : a grand tour with A.J.P. Taylor. — London : Sidgwick and Jackson, 1976. — 225p : chiefly ill, ports ; 26cm.
Ill. on lining papers.
ISBN 0-283-98254-3 : £5.95
(B77-01917)

940.2'8'0924 — Western Europe. Social life, 1812-1862. *Personal observations*
Gronow, Rees Howell. [The reminiscences of Captain Gronow. *Selections]*. Selections from 'The reminiscences of Captain Gronow' / edited and introduced by Nicolas Bentley. — London : Folio Society, 1977. — 271p,[12] leaves of plates : ill, map(on lining papers), ports ; 26cm.
'... it is from the first three volumes [published 1861-1865] that the greater part of this selection has been made' - Introduction. — Index.
£6.95
(B77-24609)

940.2'84 — Europe. Revolutions, 1848
Surveys and themes / [prepared by John Breuilly et al. for the Open University Course Team]. — Milton Keynes : Open University Press, 1976. — 46p ; 30cm. — (Arts, a third level course : the revolutions of 1848 ; unit 16) (A321 ; 16)
ISBN 0-335-05058-1 Pbk : £1.00
(B77-03291)

940.3 — HISTORY. WORLD WAR 1, 1914-1918
940.3 — World War 1. *For slow learning adolescents*
Healey, Tim. The First World War / [text by Tim Healey] ; [edited by Dale Gunthorp]. — London : Macdonald Educational, 1977. — 3-46p : ill(some col), facsims, col map, music, ports ; 25cm. — (Action world)
Text on lining papers. — Index.
ISBN 0-356-05566-3 : £1.50
(B77-29063)

940.3 — World War 1. *Secondary school texts. Teaching kits*
World War One / edited by Peter Liddle. — London : Longman.
Teacher's pack. — 1977. — Case : ill, facsims, forms, maps, plans, ports ; 52x41cm.
Seventeen booklets, 5 maps (5 sheets (5 sides)), [16]p. of facsimile newspapers. — Bibl.: p.18-21 (Teacher's notes). — Index.
ISBN 0-582-20684-7 : £12.50
(B77-22997)

940.3'1504'2 — World War 1. Role of British women
Marwick, Arthur. Women at war, 1914-1918 / [by] Arthur Marwick. — [London] : Fontana [for the] Imperial War Museum, 1977. — 176p : ill, facsims, ports ; 25cm.
Bibl.: p.172. — Index.
ISBN 0-00-634496-8 Pbk : £2.50
(B77-16671)

Marwick, Arthur. Women at war, 1914-1918 / [by] Arthur Marwick. — London : Croom Helm [for] the Imperial War Museum, 1977. — 176p : ill, facsims, ports ; 26cm.
Bibl.: p.172. — Index.
ISBN 0-85664-424-2 : £6.95
(B77-16672)

940.3'162'0941 — Peace movements. *Great Britain, 1914-1919*
Robbins, Keith. The abolition of war : the 'Peace Movement' in Britain, 1914-1919 / [by] Keith Robbins. — Cardiff : University of Wales Press, 1976. — 255p ; 23cm.
Bibl.: p.237-246. — Index.
ISBN 0-7083-0622-5 : £5.00
(B77-01069)

940.3'22'73 — United States. Foreign relations. Role of trade unions, 1914-1918
Larson, Simeon. Labor and foreign policy : Gompers, the AFL and the First World War, 1914-18 / [by] Simeon Larson. — Rutherford [etc.] : Fairleigh Dickinson University Press ; London (108 New Bond St., W1Y 0QX) : Associated University Presses, [1976]. — 176p ; 22cm.
Published in the United States: 1975. — Bibl.: p.162-170. — Index.
ISBN 0-8386-1290-3 : £4.25
(B77-01918)

940.4'01 — World War 1. Grand strategy
Military History Symposium, *3rd, Royal Military College of Canada, 1976.* War aims and strategic policy in the Great War, 1914-1918 / edited by Barry Hunt and Adrian Preston. — London : Croom Helm [etc.], 1977. — 131p ; 23cm.
'... the papers ... were originally presented ... to the Third Annual Military History Symposium held at the Royal Military College of Canada on 25 and 26 March, 1976 ...' - Preface. — Index.
ISBN 0-85664-597-4 : £6.95 : CIP rev.
(B77-17828)

940.4'12'47 — World War 1. Army operations by Russia. Armiía
Rutherford, Ward. The ally : the Russian army in World War I / [by] Ward Rutherford. — London : Gordon and Cremonesi, 1977. — [11] ,303p,[16]p of plates : ill, maps, plans, ports ; 24cm.
Originally published: as 'The Russian army in World War I'. 1975. — Bibl. — Index.
ISBN 0-86033-039-7 Pbk : £2.90
(B77-28291)

940.4'144 — World War 1. Western Front. Army operations
Ellis, John, *b.1945.* Eye-deep in hell / [by] John Ellis. — [London] : Fontana, 1977. — [5], 214p : ill, facsims, map, ports ; 24cm.
Originally published: London : Croom Helm, 1976. — Bibl.: p.207. — Index.
ISBN 0-00-633745-7 Pbk : £2.50
(B77-28292)

Ellis, John, *b.1945.* Eye-deep in hell / [by] John Ellis. — London : Croom Helm, 1976. — [5], 215p : ill, facsims, map, ports ; 25cm.
Bibl.: p.207. — Index.
ISBN 0-85664-382-3 : £5.95
(B77-01070)

940.4'144'0924 — World War 1. Western Front. Army operations by Great Britain. Army. Machine Gun Corps, 1915-1918. *Other ranks' personal observations*
Russell, Arthur, *b.1896.* The machine gunner / [by] Arthur Russell. — Kineton : Roundwood Press, 1977. — xi,172p,leaf of plate,[8]p of plates : ill, map, plans, port ; 23cm.
ISBN 0-900093-44-7 : £5.00
(B77-23867)

940.4'15'0924 — World War 1. Arabian campaign. *Personal observations*
Lawrence, Thomas Edward. Seven pillars of wisdom : a triumph / [by] T.E. Lawrence. — Harmondsworth [etc.] : Penguin, 1977. — 700p, 8p of plates : ill, maps, ports ; 20cm. — (Penguin modern classics)
Originally published: London : Cape, 1935. — Index.
ISBN 0-14-001696-1 Pbk : £1.75
(B77-17208)

940.4'15'0924 — World War 1. Arabian campaign. Lawrence, Thomas Edward. *Biographies*
Stewart, Desmond. T.E. Lawrence / by Desmond Stewart. — London : Hamilton, 1977. — iii-xii, 352p,12p of plates : ill, maps, ports ; 25cm.
Index.
ISBN 0-241-89644-4 : £7.50
(B77-21602)

940.4'15'0924 — World War 1. Arabian campaign. Lawrence, Thomas Edward. *Periodicals*
T.E. Lawrence studies. — London (5 West Hill, SW15 2UL) : 'T.E. Lawrence studies'.
Vol.1, no.1- ; Spring 1976-. — 1976-. — facsims, ports ; 21cm.
Two issues a year. — [1],85p.,[4]p. of plates in 1st issue. — Includes 1 article in French. — Bibl.
Pbk : Unpriced
ISSN 0308-4582
(B77-03836)

940.4'15'0924 — World War 1. Arabian campaign. Lawrence, Thomas Edward, 1918-1935. *Biographies*
Hyde, Harford Montgomery. Solitary in the ranks : Lawrence of Arabia as airman and private soldier / [by] H. Montgomery Hyde. — London : Constable, 1977. — 288p,leaf of plate,[24]p of plates : ill, facsims, ports ; 23cm.
Bibl.: p.273-277. — Index.
ISBN 0-09-462070-9 : £6.95
(B77-34305)

940.4'15'0924 — World War 1. Arabian campaign. Lawrence, Thomas Edward. Local associations: Dorset. Purbeck (District)
National Trust. Clouds Hill, Dorset / [National Trust]. — [New ed.]. — [London] : The Trust, 1977. — 22p,[4]p of plates : ill, port ; 22cm.
Previous ed.: 1970.
Sd : £0.35
Also classified at 914.23'36
(B77-33528)

940.4'21'0922 — World War 1. Western Front. Army operations by Great Britain. Army. Grenadier Guards. 2nd Battalion, 1914. *Diaries. Collections*
'Fifteen rounds a minute' : the Grenadiers at war, August to December 1914 / edited from the diaries and letters of Major 'Ma' Jeffreys and others by J.M. Craster. — London [etc.] : Macmillan, 1976. — x,186p,[8]p of plates : ill, facsim, maps, plans, ports ; 23cm.
Index.
ISBN 0-333-19689-9 : £4.50
(B77-05127)

940.4'24 — World War 1. Battle of Loos. *Personal observations. Collections*
Warner, Philip. The Battle of Loos / [by] Philip Warner. — London : Kimber, 1976. — x,245p : ill, facsims, maps, ports ; 24cm.
Index.
ISBN 0-7183-0424-1 : £5.75
(B77-03292)

940.4'272 — World War 1. Battle of the Somme. Battlefields, 1916-1918. Compared with battlefields, 1971-1976
Giles, John. The Somme : then and now / [by] John Giles. — Folkestone : Bailey and Swinfen, 1977. — [4],xiii,140p : ill, facsims, maps, ports ; 22x27cm.
Bibl.: p.139.
ISBN 0-561-00298-3 : £10.50
(B77-31618)

940.4'31'0924 — World War 1. Battle of Ypres, 1917. *Other ranks' personal observations*
Gladden, Edgar Norman. Ypres, 1917 : a personal account / [by] E. Norman Gladden. — New ed. — London : Kimber, 1977. — 192p : maps ; 24cm.
Originally published: 1967. — Index.
ISBN 0-7183-0235-4 : £3.95
(B77-28293)

940.4'4 — World War 1. Air operations
Batchelor, John. Fighting aircraft of World War One and Two / [illustrated by John Batchelor ; compiled by Susan Joiner]. — London : Phoebus, 1976. — 256p : ill(some col), maps(chiefly col), ports ; 31cm.
Ill. on lining papers. — Index.
ISBN 0-7026-0007-5 : £4.95
Also classified at 940.54'4
(B77-33529)

940.4'41 — World War 1. Air operations by fighter aeroplanes. Pilots
Jackson, Robert, *b.1941.* Fighter pilots of World War I / [by] Robert Jackson. — London : A. Barker, 1977. — vii,152p ; 23cm.
ISBN 0-213-16645-3 : £3.95
(B77-20806)

Reynolds, Quentin. They fought for the sky : the story of the First World War in the air / [by] Quentin Reynolds. — London [etc.] : Pan Books, 1977. — 285p,[16]p of plates : ill, ports ; 18cm.
Originally published: London : Cassell, 1958. — Bibl.: p.276-279. — Index.
Pbk : £0.75
ISBN 0-330-24011-0
(B77-20807)

940.4'49'410924 — World War 1. Air operations by Great Britain. Royal Flying Corps. Ball, Albert, b.1896
Bowyer, Chaz. Albert Ball, VC / [by] Chaz Bowyer. — London : Kimber, 1977. — 208p, [24]p of plates : ill, map, ports ; 25cm.
Bibl.: p.200-201. — Index.
ISBN 0-7183-0045-9 : £5.25
(B77-22998)

940.4'49'410924 — World War 1. Western Front. Air operations by Great Britain. Royal Air Force. Bristol F2B aeroplanes. *Officers' personal observations*
Noble, Walter. With a Bristol fighter squadron / [by] Walter Noble ; with an introduction by Winston S. Churchill. — Large print ed. — Bath : Chivers, 1977. — viii,198p,vii p of plates : ill, port ; 22cm.
Originally published: London : Andrew Melrose, 1920.
ISBN 0-85997-230-5 : £5.60(£4.20 to members of the Library Association)
(B77-23868)

940.4'49'410924 — World War 1. Western Front. Air operations by Great Britain. Royal Air Force. No.48 Squadron & Great Britain. Royal Air Force. No.88 Squadron, 1918. *Officers' personal observations*
Vee, Roger. Flying minnows : memoirs of a World War One fighter pilot, from training in Canada to the Front Line, 1917-1918 / [by] 'Roger Vee' (Vivian Voss). — [1st ed. reprinted] ; with appendices by Norman Franks. — London : Arms and Armour Press [etc.], 1977. — 318p,[12]p of plates : ill ; 23cm.

Facsimile reprint of: 1st ed. London : Hamilton, 1935.
ISBN 0-85368-121-x : £4.95
(B77-15620)

940.4'49'410924 — World War 1. Western Front. Air operations by Great Britain. Royal Flying Corps. *Officers' personal observations*
Lewis, Cecil. Sagittarius rising / [by] Cecil Lewis. — Harmondsworth [etc.] : Penguin, 1977. — 266p ; 18cm.
Originally published: London : Peter Davies, 1936.
ISBN 0-14-004367-5 Pbk : £0.80
(B77-17209)

940.4'49'430924 — World War 1. Air operations by Germany. Luftstreitkräfte. *Officers' personal observations*
Richthofen, Manfred, *Freiherr von.* The Red Baron / [by] Manfred, Freiherr von Richthofen ; translated [from the German] by Peter Kilduff ; edited by Stanley M. Ulanoff. — London : Sphere, 1976. — xiv,225p,[16]p of plates : ill, ports ; 18cm.
This translation originally published: Garden City, N.Y. : Doubleday, 1969 ; Folkestone : Bailey and Swinfen, 1974. — Translation of: 'Der Rote Kampfflieger'. Neue Aufl. Berlin : Ullstein, 1933.
ISBN 0-7221-8776-9 Pbk : £0.75
(B77-06980)

940.4'49'430924 — World War 1. Air operations by Germany. Luftstreitkräfte. Richthofen, Manfred, freiherr von. *Juvenile literature. Fill-in books*
Knight, Dennis. Baron Richthofen / [by Dennis Knight]. — London ([Dept. RWH], 100 Drayton Park, N5 1NA) : Royal Sovereign Group Ltd, 1976. — [2],16,[2]p,[2]leaves of plates : ill(chiefly col), col plans, ports(chiefly col) ; 15x21cm. — (Knight, Dennis. Activity books)
Contains Letraset instant pictures.
ISBN 0-900862-43-2 Sd : Unpriced
(B77-06380)

940.4'5 — British ships. Losses, 1914-1918. *Lists. Early works*
British vessels lost at sea, 1914-18. — Cambridge : Stephens, 1977. — vii,36,[1],ii, 184p ; 24cm.
'A [facsimile] reprint of the original official publications "Navy losses" and "Merchant shipping (losses)" which were first published in August 1919 by His Majesty's Stationery Office, London'. — Index.
ISBN 0-85059-291-7 : £3.95 : CIP rev.
(B77-22268)

940.4'5 — World War 1. Naval operations
Batchelor, John. Fighting ships of World War One and Two / [illustrated by John Batchelor ; compiled by Anne Maclean and Suzanne Poole]. — London : Phoebus, 1976. — 255p : ill(some col), facsim, maps(some col), ports(some col) ; 31cm.
Ill. on lining papers. — Index.
ISBN 0-7026-0006-7 : £4.95
Also classified at 940.54'5
(B77-32979)

940.4'54 — World War 1. South Atlantic campaigns. Naval operations by Great Britain. Royal Navy. Armed merchant cruisers: Carmania (Ship). Battle with Cap Trafalgar (Ship)
Simpson, Colin, *b.1931.* The ship that hunted itself / [by] Colin Simpson. — London : Weidenfeld and Nicolson, 1977. — 207p : ill, facsim, plan, ports ; 23cm.
ISBN 0-297-77337-2 : £5.25
(B77-32980)

940.4'81'41 — World War 1. Army operations by Great Britain. Army. 4th East Yorkshire Regiment. *Correspondence*
Slack, Cecil Moorhouse. Grandfather's adventures in the Great War, 1914-1918 ... / [by] Cecil Moorhouse Slack. — Ilfracombe : Stockwell, 1977. — 284p,[2]p of plates,[5]leaves of plates : ill, map(on lining paper), plan(on lining paper), ports ; 22cm.
ISBN 0-7223-0970-8 : £2.00
(B77-26022)

940.4'81'41 — World War 1. Army operations by Great Britain. Army. Gloucestershire Regiment, 1917-1918. *Other ranks' personal observations*
Marks, Thomas Penrose. The laughter goes from life : in the trenches of the First World War / [by] Thomas Penrose Marks. — London : Kimber, 1977. — 190p : map ; 24cm.
ISBN 0-7183-0055-6 : £4.50
(B77-30867)

940.4'81'41 — World War 1. Army operations by Great Britain. Army. Royal Regiment of Fusiliers. *Other ranks' personal observations*
Hiscock, Eric. The bells of Hell go ting-a-ling a-ling : an autobiographical fragment without maps / by Eric Hiscock. — London : Arlington Books, 1976. — [7],149p ; 23cm.
ISBN 0-85140-257-7 : £3.75
(B77-02673)

940.4'86 — World War 1. Secret service operations by Allied secret services
Cook, Graeme. Missions most secret / [by] Graeme Cook. — London : Harwood-Smart, 1976. — xi,186p ; 23cm.
Bibl.: p.186.
ISBN 0-904507-17-3 : £3.95
Primary classification 940.54'86
(B77-25303)

940.5 — HISTORY. EUROPE, 1918-
940.5 — Europe, 1914-1973. *Secondary school texts*
Europe / editor John Robottom. — London : Longman.
Workcards / [by] Tom Allan. — 1977. — 1v. ; 23cm. — (Making the modern world)
One card, 3 copies each of 5 cards ([12] sides) in plastic envelope.
ISBN 0-582-22081-5 : £0.95
(B77-19115)

940.51 — HISTORY. EUROPE, 1918-1930
940.5'1'0222 — Western Europe. Social life, 1920-1930. *Illustrations*
The **roaring** twenties / [compiled by] Sandy Wilson. — London : Eyre Methuen, 1976. — [128]p : of ill, facsims, ports ; 24cm. — (Picturefile)
ISBN 0-413-32980-1 Pbk : £1.95
(B77-12224)

940.53 — HISTORY. WORLD WAR 2, 1939-1945
940.53 — World War 2. *Juvenile literature*
Healey, Tim. The Second World War / [text by Tim Healey] ; [planned and edited by Dale Gunthorp]. — London : Macdonald Educational, 1977. — 3-47p : ill(some col), col map, ports(some col) ; 25cm. — (Action world)

Col. ill., index on lining papers.
ISBN 0-356-05562-0 : £1.25
(B77-18470)

940.53 — World War 2. *Secondary school texts. Teaching kits*
Ray, John, *b.1929.* The Second World War / [by] John Ray. — London : Heinemann Educational, 1977. — 1v. : ill(some col), col map, plans, ports ; 25cm. — (History broadsheets)
Seventeen folders ([80]p.), 2 sheets ([4]sides) in plastic envelope.
ISBN 0-435-31747-4 : £1.80
(B77-26693)

940.53 — World War 2. *Soviet viewpoints*
The **Russian** version of the Second World War : the history of the war as taught to Soviet schoolchildren / edited by Graham Lyons. — London : Cooper, 1976. — xvii,142p,[8]p of plates : ill, maps ; 23cm.
Map on lining papers. — Translated selections from: 'Istoriia SSSR' / I.V. Bekhin, M.I. Belenkiĭ, M.P. Kim. Moskva : Prosveshchenie, 1956? and 'Noveĭshaia istoriia' / P.M. Kuz'michev et al. Moskva : Prosveshchenie, 1956?. — Bibl. — Index.
ISBN 0-85052-221-8 : £3.95
(B77-03293)

940.53 — World War 2, 1939
Bethell, Nicholas, *Baron Bethell.* The war Hitler won : September 1939 / [by] Nicholas Bethell. — London : Futura Publications, 1976. — viii, 472p : ill, facsims, maps, plans ; 18cm.
Originally published: London : Allen Lane, 1972. — Bibl.: p.450-453. — Index.
ISBN 0-86007-310-6 Pbk : £1.50
(B77-10052)

940.53 — World War 2, 1939-1941
Lukacs, John. The last European war, September 1939-December 1941 / [by] John Lukacs. — London [etc.] : Routledge and Kegan Paul, 1976 [i.e. 1977]. — xi,562p,[16]p of plates : ill, ports ; 24cm.
Originally published: Garden City, N.Y. : Anchor Press, 1976. — Bibl.: p.539-551. — Index.
ISBN 0-7100-8510-9 : £7.95
(B77-09414)

940.53'1 — World War 2. Economic aspects
Milward, Alan Steele. War, economy and society, 1939-1945 / [by] Alan S. Milward. — London : Allen Lane, 1977. — xiv,395p : 1 ill ; 23cm. — (History of the world economy in the twentieth century ; 5)
Bibl.: p.366-388. — Index.
ISBN 0-7139-1022-4 : £7.00
(B77-22999)

940.53'1503'924 — Jews. Genocide, 1939-1945
Dawidowicz, Lucy S. The war against the Jews, 1933-45 / [by] Lucy Dawidowicz. — Harmondsworth [etc.] : Penguin, 1977. — 550p : 2 maps ; 18cm. — (Pelican books)
Originally published: London : Weidenfeld and Nicolson, 1975. — Bibl.: p.523-536. — Index.
ISBN 0-14-022007-0 Pbk : £1.95
Also classified at 323.1'19'24043
(B77-27565)

940.53'1503'924 — Jews. Genocide, 1939-1945. Theories
Butz, A R. The hoax of the twentieth century / by A.R. Butz. — Richmond, Surrey (23 Ellerker Gardens, Richmond, Surrey TW10 6AA) : Historical Review Press, [1976]. — 315p : ill, facsims, maps, plan ; 22cm.
Bibl.: p.300-304. — Index.
ISBN 0-9505505-0-7 : £3.50
(B77-06981)

940.53'162'0924 — Conscientious objection. Jägerstätter, Franz. *Austria, 1943. Biographies*
Kent, Bruce. Franz Jägerstätter : (the man who said 'no' to Hitler) / by Bruce Kent. — London : Catholic Truth Society, 1976. — [2], 9p ; 17cm.
Sd : £0.10
(B77-00531)

940.53'2'0924 — World War 2. Diplomacy, 1941-1944. *Personal observations. Serbo-Croatian texts*
Yovanovitch, Slobodan. Zapisi o problemima i ljudima, 1941-1944 / Slobodan Jovanović ; predgovor Radoja L. Kneževića. — London (200 Liverpool Rd, N1 1LF) : Izdanje Udruženja Srpskih Pisaca i Umetnika u Inostranstvu, 1976. — [2],84p,plate : facsims, ports ; 23cm.
ISBN 0-9505432-0-9 Pbk : £1.50
(B77-05776)

940.53'22 — World War 2. Roosevelt, Franklin Delano. *Correspondence with Churchill, Sir Winston Spencer, b.1874*
Lash, Joseph P. Roosevelt and Churchill, 1939-1941 : the partnership that saved the West / [by] Joseph P. Lash. — London : Deutsch, 1977. — 528p,[16]p of plates : ill, col maps(on lining papers), ports ; 25cm.
Originally published: New York : Norton, 1976. — Bibl.: p.494. — Index.
ISBN 0-233-96844-x : £6.95
(B77-23000)

940.53'22'41 — Great Britain. Foreign relations, 1939-1945
Woodward, *Sir* Llewellyn. British foreign policy in the Second World War / by Sir Llewellyn Woodward. — London : H.M.S.O. — (History of the Second World War : United Kingdom civil series)
In 5 vols.
Vol.5 / in collaboration with M.E. Lambert. — 1976. — xvii,542p ; 25cm.
Index.
ISBN 0-11-630191-0 : £10.00
(B77-03294)

940.53'22'73 — United States. Military policies, 1941-1943. Political aspects
Stoler, Mark A. The politics of the second front : American military planning and diplomacy in coalition warfare, 1941-1943 / [by] Mark A. Stoler. — Westport, Conn. ; London : Greenwood Press, 1977. — xiii,244,[1]p ; 22cm. — (Contributions in military history ; no.12)
Bibl.: p.217-229. — Index.
ISBN 0-8371-9438-5 : Unpriced
(B77-32981)

940.53'25'485 — Sweden. Foreign relations, 1939-1945
Carlgren, W M. Swedish foreign policy during the Second World War / [by] W.M. Carlgren ; translated [from the Swedish] by Arthur Spencer. — London [etc.] : E. Benn, 1977. — xi,257p : ill, maps, ports ; 23cm. — (A Benn study : history)
Translation of: 'Svensk utrikespolitik, 1939-1945'. Stockholm : Almänna förlaget, 1973. — Bibl.: p.230-234. — Index.
ISBN 0-510-00013-4 : £8.75
(B77-31722)

940.53'4 — Resistance movements. *Europe, 1940-1945*
Foot, Michael Richard Daniell. Resistance : an analysis of European resistance to Nazism, 1940-1945 / [by] M.R.D. Foot. — London : Eyre Methuen, 1976. — xix,346p : ill(on lining papers) ; 24cm.
Bibl.: p.321-322. — Index.
ISBN 0-413-34710-9 : £6.95
(B77-01071)

940.53'44 — France. Occupation by German military forces, 1940-1944. *Childhood reminiscences*
Joffo, Joseph. A bag of marbles / [by] Joseph Joffo ; translated from the French by Martin Sokolinsky and Judith Landry. — London : Corgi, 1976. — 206p ; 18cm.
This translation originally published: London : Joseph, 1975. — Translation of: 'Un sac de billes'. Paris : J.C. Lattès, 1973.
ISBN 0-552-10274-1 Pbk : £0.65
(B77-00532)

Seymour, Gerald. The glory boys / [by] Gerald Seymour. Majesty : Elizabeth II and the House of Windsor / [by] Robert Lacey. Ordinary people / [by] Judith Guest. A bag of marbles / [by] Joseph Joffo. — Collector's library ed. — London : Reader's Digest Association [etc.], 1977. — 512p : col ill, ports(some col) ; 21cm. — ('Reader's digest' condensed books)
ISBN 0-340-21949-1 : £2.95
Primary classification 823'.9'1F
(B77-12702)

940.53'44 — Resistance movements. *France, 1940-1944. Personal observations*
Frenay, Henri. The night will end / [by] Henri Frenay ; [translated from the French by Dan Hofstadter]. — Sevenoaks : Coronet, 1977. — 430p,[12]p of plates : ill, facsim, ports ; 18cm.
This translation originally published: London : Abelard-Schuman, 1976. — Translation of: 'La nuit finira'. Paris : Laffont, 1973. — Index.
ISBN 0-340-20000-6 Pbk : £1.00
(B77-15038)

940.53'47'65 — Resistance movements. *Belorussia. Novogrudok region. Armia Krajowa, 1940-1945. Polish texts*
Prawdzic-Szlaski, Janusz. Nowogródczyzna w Walce, 1940-1945 / Janusz Prawdzic-Szlaski. — Londyn [i.e. London] : Oficyna Poetów i Malarzy, 1976. — [2],283p,[28]p of plates : ill, maps(1 col), plan, ports ; 22cm.
Port. tipped in. — Index.
ISBN 0-902571-88-5 Pbk : £5.80
(B77-05128)

940.53'481 — Resistance movements. Baalsrud, Jan. Escapes. *Norway, 1943*
Howarth, David. Escape alone / [by] David Howarth. — [London] : Fontana, 1977. — 190p,[4]p of plates : ill, map, port ; 18cm.
Originally published: as 'We die alone'. London : Collins, 1955.
ISBN 0-00-634859-9 Pbk : £9.75
(B77-34306)

940.53'497 — Resistance movements. Partisans. *Yugoslavia, 1941-1945. Personal observations*
Djilas, Milovan. Wartime / [by] Milovan Djilas ; translated [from the Serbo-Croatian MS.] by Michael B. Petrovich. — London : Secker and Warburg, 1977. — x,470p,[16]p of plates : ill, col map(on lining papers), ports ; 25cm.
This translation also published: New York : Harcourt Brace Jovanovich, 1977. — Index.
ISBN 0-436-12970-1 : £7.95
(B77-27566)

940.54 — World War 2. Military campaigns, 1939-1941
Baldwin, Hanson Weightman. The crucial years, 1939-1941 : the world at war / [by] Hanson W. Baldwin. — London : Weidenfeld and Nicolson, 1976. — ix,499p,[16]p of plates : ill, col maps, plans ; 24cm.
Col. maps on lining papers. — Also published: New York : Harper and Row, 1976. — Index.
ISBN 0-297-77089-6 : £12.50
(B77-09415)

940.54'012 — World War 2. Grand strategy of Great Britain, 1940-1941
Barclay, Glen St John. Their finest hour / [by] Glen St J. Barclay. — London : Weidenfeld and Nicolson, 1977. — ix,192p ; 23cm.
Bibl.: p.173-182. — Index.
ISBN 0-297-77340-2 : £4.95
(B77-24610)

940.54'012 — World War 2. Strategy. Role of Great Britain. Cabinet. Joint Planning Staff. *Diaries*
Wheatley, Dennis. Stranger than fiction / [by] Dennis Wheatley. — London : Arrow Books, 1976. — 414p ; 18cm.
Originally published: London : Hutchinson, 1959.
ISBN 0-09-913590-6 Pbk : £0.95
(B77-06381)

940.54'05'094427 — Great Britain. Army. Atrocities by Nationalsozialistische Deutsche Arbeiter-Partei. Schutzstaffel. Leibstandarte 'Adolf Hitler'. *France. Wormhout, 1940*
Aitken, Leslie. Massacre on the road to Dunkirk : Wormhout, 1940 / by Leslie Aitken. — London : Kimber, 1977. — [1],189p,[8]p of plates : ill, plans, ports ; 24cm.
Bibl.: p.181-182. — Index.
ISBN 0-7183-0165-x : £4.75
(B77-26023)

940.54'05'094762 — Cemeteries. *London. Hounslow (London Borough). Gunnersbury. Gunnersbury Cemetery. Memorials: Katyn Memorial*
Fitzgibbon, Louis. The Katyn memorial / by Louis Fitzgibbon ; foreword by Prince Eugene Lubomirski. — London (23 Coleridge St., Hove, Sussex) : SPK-GRYF Publications Ltd, 1977. — 48p,[16]p of plates : ill, ports ; 22cm.
Bibl.: p.46-48.
Pbk : Unpriced
(B77-26694)

940.54'12'41 — World War 2. Army operations by Great Britain. Army. 51st Highland Division
Grant, Roderick. The 51st Highland Division at war / [by] Roderick Grant. — London : Allan, 1977. — 160p,[4]p of plates : ill(some col), maps(on lining papers), ports(some col) ; 30cm.
ISBN 0-7110-0735-7 : £4.95
(B77-02674)

940.54'12'41 — World War 2. Military operations by Great Britain. Army
Hay, Ian. Arms and the men / [by] Ian Hay. — London : H.M.S.O., 1977. — x,330p,[16]p of plates,fold leaf of plate : ill, maps ; 22cm. — (The Second World War, 1939-1945)
Originally published: 1950. — Index.
ISBN 0-11-772195-6 Pbk : £2.00
(B77-32982)

940.54'12'438 — World War 2. Military operations by Allied forces. Polish commandos. *Polish texts*
Monsior, Tadeusz A. Commando : zolnierze w zielonych beretach w Drugiej Wojnie Światowej z 1 - szej Samodzielnej Kompanii 'Commando' (No.10 IA Commando - 6 Troop) i 2 - go Banonu Komandosów Zmotoryzowanych / [Tadeusz A. Monsior]. — [London] ([8 Highfield Ave., Wembley]) : [The author], [1976?]. — 147p : ill, coat of arms, facsims, maps, plans, ports ; 24cm.
Cover title: Polscy Komandosi.
ISBN 0-9505554-0-1 Pbk : £2.70
(B77-10670)

940.54'13'43 — World War 2. Army operations by Germany. Heer. Generals, 1940-1945
Downing, David. The Devil's virtuosos : German generals at war, 1940-5 / [by] David Downing. — London : New English Library, 1977. — 256p,[8]p of plates : ill, maps, plans, ports ; 22cm.
Bibl.: p.249-251. — Index.
ISBN 0-450-03079-2 : £4.95
(B77-23917)

940.54'13'43 — World War 2. Army operations by Germany. Heer. Tank units
Warner, Philip. Panzer / [by] Philip Warner. — London : Weidenfeld and Nicolson, 1977. — 144p : ill(some col), facsim, maps(some col) ; 29cm.
Ill. on lining papers. — Index.
ISBN 0-297-77316-x : £4.95
(B77-27567)

940.54'2 — World War 2. Battles
Decisive battles of Hitler's war / edited by Antony Preston ; introduction by Laurence F. Orbach. — London [etc.] : Hamlyn, 1977. — 256p : ill(some col), col facsim, maps(some col), col plans, ports(some col) ; 31cm. — (A quarto book)
Ill. on lining papers. — Index.
ISBN 0-600-31403-0 : £4.95
(B77-21603)

940.54'21 — American ships. Air raids by Germany. Luftwaffe. *Italy. Bari, 1943*
Infield, Glenn Berton. Disaster at Bari / [by] Glenn B. Infield. — London : New English Library, 1976. — 256p : facsims, map, plans ; 18cm.
Originally published: New York : Macmillan, 1971 ; London : Hale, 1974.
ISBN 0-450-02659-0 Pbk : £0.85
(B77-07734)

940.54'21 — Combined operations by Great Britain. Royal Marines. *France. Bordeaux, 1942*
Phillips, Cecil Ernest Lucas. Cockleshell heroes / [by] C.E. Lucas Phillips ; with the co-operation of H.G. Hasler ; foreword by the Earl Mountbatten of Burma. — London [etc.] : Pan Books, 1977. — 255p,[8]p of plates : ill, maps, plan, ports ; 18cm.
Originally published: London : Heinemann, 1956.
ISBN 0-330-10458-6 Pbk : £0.75
(B77-27568)

940.54'21 — England. Air raids by Germany. Luftwaffe, 1939-1944
Price, Alfred. Blitz on Britain : the bomber attacks on the United Kingdom, 1939-1945 / [by] Alfred Price. — London : I. Allan, 1977. — 192p : ill, maps, plan, ports ; 25cm.
Index.
ISBN 0-7110-0723-3 : £4.95
(B77-20808)

940.54'21 — Heavy water. Production. Sabotage by Great Britain. Army. Special Operations Executive. Norwegian Section. *Norway. Vemork, 1942-1943*
Gallagher, Thomas. The Telemark raid : sabotaging the Nazi nuclear bomb / [by] Thomas Gallagher. — London : Corgi, 1976. — 238p : 2 maps ; 18cm.
Originally published: as 'Assault in Norway'. New York : Harcourt Brace Jovanovich ; London : Macdonald and Jane's, 1975. — Index.
ISBN 0-552-10327-6 Pbk : £0.65
(B77-05129)

940.54'21 — West Midlands (Metropolitan County). Coventry. Air raids by Germany. Luftwaffe, 1940 (November)
Longmate, Norman. Air raid : the bombing of Coventry, 1940 / [by] Norman Longmate. — London : Hutchinson, 1976. — [2],302p,[16]p of plates : ill, facsim, maps, ports ; 23cm.
Bibl.: p.272-276. — Index.
ISBN 0-09-127900-3 : £5.95
(B77-04485)

940.54'21 — World War 2. Atlantic campaign. Naval operations by Great Britain. Royal Navy. Battleships: Royal Oak (Ship). Sinking
Snyder, Gerald S. The 'Royal Oak' disaster / [by] Gerald S. Snyder. — London : Kimber, 1976. — 240p,[24]p of plates : ill, maps, plans, ports ; 25cm.
Bibl.: p.230-232. — Index.
ISBN 0-7183-0005-x : £5.75
(B77-05777)

940.54'21 — World War 2. Battle of Aachen, 1944
Whiting, Charles. Bloody Aachen / [by] Charles Whiting. — London : Cooper, 1976. — 159p : maps, plan ; 23cm.
Also published: London : Corgi, 1976.
ISBN 0-85052-213-7 : £4.95
(B77-21604)

940.54'21 — World War 2. Battle of Arnhem, 1944
Urquhart, Robert Elliott. Arnhem / [by] R.E. Urquhart. — London [etc.] : Pan Books, 1977. — 221p,[8]p of plates : ill, maps, plans, ports ; 18cm. — (British battles series)
Originally published: London : Cassell, 1958.
ISBN 0-330-23273-8 Pbk : £0.80
(B77-23869)

940.54'21 — World War 2. Battle of Britain
The **Battle** of Britain / editors Kenneth Munson, John W.R. Taylor. — London : New English Library, 1976. — 128p : ill(some col), facsim, ports ; 31cm.
ISBN 0-450-03077-6 : £3.25
(B77-23001)

Deighton, Len. Fighter : the true story of the Battle of Britain / [by] Len Deighton ; with an introduction by A.J.P. Taylor. — London : Cape, 1977. — 304p,[40]p of plates : ill(some col), col maps, ports ; 23cm.
Bibl.: p.295-296. — Index.
ISBN 0-224-01422-6 : £4.95 : CIP rev.
(B77-18471)

940.54'21 — World War 2. Battle of Caen
Maule, Henry. Caen : the brutal battle and break-out from Normandy / [by] Henry Maule. — Newton Abbot [etc.] : David and Charles, 1976. — 176p,16p of plates : ill, map, plans, ports ; 23cm.
Index.
ISBN 0-7153-7283-1 : £4.95
(B77-11004)

940.54'21 — World War 2. Battle of Stalingrad. Army operations by Germany. Heer. 6e Armee
Konsalik, Heinz Günther. The heart of the 6th Army / [by] Heinz G. Konsalik ; translated from the German by Oliver Coburn. — Henley-on-Thames : A. Ellis, 1977. — [6], 298p ; 23cm.
Translation of: 'Herz der 6. Armee'. Bayreuth : Hestia-Verlag, 197-?.
ISBN 0-85628-052-6 : £4.95 : CIP rev.
(B77-29827)

940.54'21 — World War 2. Battle of the Ardennes, 1944
Toland, John. Battle : the story of the Bulge / [by] John Toland. — London : Severn House : [Distributed by Hutchinson], 1977. — 7-413p : 5 plans ; 21cm.
Originally published: New York : Random House, 1959 ; London : Muller, 1960.
ISBN 0-7278-0247-x : £5.25
(B77-10053)

940.54'21 — World War 2. Dunkirk campaign. Evacuation of Great Britain. Army. British Expeditionary Force, 1940
Barker, Arthur J. Dunkirk : the great escape / [by] A.J. Barker. — London [etc.] : Dent, 1977. — 240p : ill, facsim, maps, ports ; 25cm.
Col. plan on lining papers. — Bibl.: p.237-238. — Index.
ISBN 0-460-12020-4 : £5.95 : CIP rev.
(B77-15621)

940.54'21 — World War 2. Greek & Cretan campaigns, 1941
Buckley, Christopher. Greece and Crete, 1941 / [by] Christopher Buckley. — London : H.M.S.O., 1977. — x,311p,[16]p of plates : ill, maps, 3 ports ; 22cm. — (The Second World War, 1939-1945)
Originally published: 1952. — Index.
ISBN 0-11-772193-x Pbk : £2.00
(B77-33531)

940.54'21 — World War 2. Italian campaign
Linklater, Eric. The campaign in Italy / [by] Eric Linklater. — London : H.M.S.O., 1977. — xi,480p,fold leaf of plate,[16]p of plates : ill, maps, ports ; 22cm. — (The Second World War, 1939-1945)
Originally published: 1951. — Index.
ISBN 0-11-772198-0 Pbk : £3.00
(B77-32983)

940.54'21 — World War 2. Normandy campaign. D-Day, 1944. Combined operations by Allied forces
Ryan, Cornelius. The longest day : June 6, 1944 / [by] Cornelius Ryan. — Large print ed. — Leicester : Ulverscroft, 1977. — [10],510p ; 23cm. — (Ulverscroft large print series : [non-fiction])
Originally published: New York : Simon & Schuster, 1959 ; London : Gollancz, 1960.
ISBN 0-85456-523-x : £2.65
(B77-17210)

940.54'21 — World War 2. Normandy campaign. D-Day, 1944. Combined operations by Allied forces. *Juvenile literature. Fill-in books*
Knight, Dennis. D-Day landings / [by Dennis Knight]. — London ([Dept. RWH], 100 Drayton Park, N5 1NA) : Royal Sovereign Group Ltd, 1976. — [2],16,[2]p,[2]leaves of plates : ill(chiefly col), col map, ports(some col) ; 15x21cm. — (Knight, Dennis. Activity books)
Contains Letraset instant pictures.
ISBN 0-900862-46-7 Sd : £0.50
(B77-06382)

940.54'21 — World War 2. Norwegian campaign. Naval operations by Great Britain. Royal Navy
Brookes, Ewart. Prologue to a war : the Navy's part in the Narvik Campaign / [by] Ewart Brookes. — London [etc.] : White Lion Publishers, 1977. — 192p,[8]p of plates : ill, maps, ports ; 23cm.
Originally published: London : Jarrolds, 1966. — Bibl.: p.187. — Index.
ISBN 0-7274-0240-4 : £5.75
(B77-21605)

940.54'21 — World War 2. Russian campaign. Army operations by Union of Soviet Socialist Republics. Armiía, 1941-1943. Armoured combat vehicles: Tanks
Grove, Eric. Russian armour, 1941-1943 / [by] Eric Grove ; with illustrations by The County Studios. — London : Almark Publishing, 1977. — 72p : ill(some col), col plans ; 21x22cm. — (The mechanics of war)
ISBN 0-85524-269-8 : £2.50
(B77-18472)

940.54'21 — World War 2. Sicilian campaign. Combined operations by Allied forces, 1943
Pack, Stanley Walter Croucher. Operation 'Husky' : the Allied invasion of Sicily / [by] S.W.C. Pack ; introduction by Lord Ashbourne. — Newton Abbot [etc.] : David and Charles, 1977. — 186p : ill, map, plans, ports ; 23cm.
Bibl.: p.180. — Index.
ISBN 0-7153-7382-x : £4.95
(B77-27569)

940.54'21 — World War 2. Western European campaigns
Buckley, Christopher. Norway. The commandos. Dieppe / [by] Christopher Buckley. — London : H.M.S.O., 1977. — x,276p,[16]p of plates : ill, maps ; 22cm. — (The Second World War, 1939-1945)
Originally published: 1952. — Index.
ISBN 0-11-772194-8 Pbk : £2.00
(B77-32984)

940.54'21 — World War 2. Western European campaigns, 1940 & Battle of Britain
Parkinson, Roger. Dawn on our darkness : the summer of 1940 / [by] Roger Parkinson. — London [etc.] : Granada, 1977. — ix,236p,[8]p of plates : ill, maps, ports ; 23cm.
Bibl.: p.221-222. — Index.
ISBN 0-246-10839-8 : £5.95
(B77-29826)

940.54'21 — World War 2. Western European campaigns. Air operations by Great Britain. Royal Air Force. Bomber Command. No 8 Group
Bowyer, Chaz. Path Finders at war / [by] Chaz Bowyer. — London : I. Allan, 1977. — 160p : ill, facsim, map, ports ; 30cm.
ISBN 0-7110-0757-8 : £5.50
(B77-19907)

Musgrove, Gordon. Pathfinder force : a history of 8 Group / [by] Gordon Musgrove. — London : Macdonald and Jane's, 1976. — x,302p,[32]p of plates : ill, facsim, maps, ports ; 25cm.
Index.
ISBN 0-354-01017-4 : £6.95
(B77-04486)

940.54'21 — World War 2. Western European campaigns. Army operations by Canada. Army, 1942: Dieppe Raid
Mellor, John. Forgotten heroes : the Canadians at Dieppe / [by] John Mellor. — Toronto ; London [etc.] : Methuen, 1975. — vii,163p,[16] p of plates : ill, facsims, map, ports ; 24cm.
ISBN 0-458-91180-1 : Unpriced
(B77-09417)

940.54'21 — World War 2. Western European campaigns. Army operations by Great Britain. Army. Eighth Army. Seventh Armoured Division, 1943-1945
Forty, George. Desert Rats at war / [by] George Forty. — London : Allan.
2 : Europe. — 1977. — 160p : ill, facsims, plans, ports ; 30cm.
Bibl.: p.160.
ISBN 0-7110-0733-0 : £5.25
Primary classification 940.54'23
(B77-17830)

940.54'21 — World War 2. Western European campaigns. Combined operations by Great Britain. Army. 1st Airborne Division, 1944: Arnhem Drop
Hagen, Louis. Arnhem lift / [by] Louis Hagen ; with a foreword by Sir Frederick A.M. Browning. — [2nd] ed. — London : Severn House : [Distributed by Hutchinson], 1977. — 128p : 2 maps ; 21cm.
This ed. originally published: London : Hammond, 1953.
ISBN 0-7278-0314-x : £3.50
(B77-28294)

940.54'21 — World War 2. Western European campaigns. Military operations by Great Britain. Army. 21st Army Group, 1944-1945
North, John. North-west Europe, 1944-5 : the achievement of 21st Army Group / [by] John North. — London : H.M.S.O., 1977. — xii, 270p,fold plate,[24]p of plates : ill, facsim, maps, ports ; 22cm. — (The Second World War, 1939-1945)
Originally published: 1953. — Index.
ISBN 0-11-772197-2 Pbk : £2.00
(B77-34308)

940.54'21'0924 — Great Britain. Army. 1st Airborne Division. Personnel. Escapes. *Netherlands. Arnhem, 1944-1945. Officers' personal observations*
Hackett, *Sir* **John,** *b.1910.* I was a stranger / by Sir John Hackett. — London : Chattoo and Windus, 1977. — 219p : map ; 23cm.
ISBN 0-7011-2211-0 : £4.95 : CIP rev.
(B77-19116)

940.54'21'0924 — World War 2. Battle of France. Air operations by Great Britain. Royal Air Force. No.1 Squadron, 1939-1940. *Officers' personal observations*
Richey, Paul. Fighter pilot : a personal record of the campaign in France, 1939-1940 / [by] Paul Richey. — Revised ed. / edited by Diana Richey. — London [etc.] : Pan Books, 1977. — xii,147p,[8]p of plates : ill, map, ports ; 18cm.
This ed. originally published: 1969.
Pbk : £0.60
ISBN 0-330-02405-1
(B77-26024)

940.54'21'0924 — World War 2. North Atlantic campaign. Naval operations by Great Britain. Royal Navy. Destroyers. *Officers' personal observations*
Macintyre, Donald, *b.1904.* U-boat killer / [by] Donald Macintyre ; foreword by Robert B. Carney. — [Revised and updated] ed. — London : Seeley Service, 1976. — 3-176p ; 23cm.
This ed. also published: London : Corgi, 1976. — Previous ed.: London : Weidenfeld and Nicolson, 1956.
ISBN 0-85422-131-x : £4.95
(B77-09416)

940.54'21'0924 — World War 2. Western European campaigns. Combined operations by Great Britain. Army. Parachute units: Arnhem Drop. *Officers' personal observations*
Angus, Tom. Men at Arnhem / by Tom Angus. — London : Cooper, 1976. — 208p : maps ; 23cm.
ISBN 0-85052-215-3 : £4.95
(B77-05130)

940.54'23 — World War 2. Middle Eastern campaigns, 1941 & Madagascan campaign, to 1942
Buckley, Christopher. Five ventures : Iraq, Syria, Persia, Madagascar, Dodecanese / [by] Christopher Buckley. — London : H.M.S.O., 1977. — xi,257p,[20]p of plates : ill, maps ; 22cm. — (The Second World War, 1939-1945)
Originally published: 1954. — Index.
ISBN 0-11-772196-4 Pbk : £2.00
(B77-33532)

940.54'23 — World War 2. North African campaign. Army operations by Germany. Heer. Afrikakorps
Lewin, Ronald. The life and death of the Afrika Korps : a biography / [by] Ronald Lewin. — London : Batsford, 1977. — 207p,16p of plates : ill, maps, plans ; 24cm.
Bibl.: p.198-199. — Index.
ISBN 0-7134-0685-2 : £5.50
(B77-25300)

Lucas, James. Panzer Army Africa / [by] James Lucas. — London : Macdonald and Jane's, 1977. — xii,211p,[32]p of plates : ill, map, plans, ports ; 25cm.
Bibl.: p.203-204. — Index.
ISBN 0-354-01056-5 : £6.95
(B77-21606)

940.54'23 — World War 2. North African campaign. Army operations by Great Britain. Army. Eighth Army
Wilkinson-Latham, John. Montgomery's desert army / text by John Wilkinson-Latham ; colour plates by Gerry Embleton. — London : Osprey Publishing, 1977. — 40p,[8]p of plates : ill(some col), map, ports ; 25cm. — (Men-at-arms series)

Text accompanying plates in English, French and German.
ISBN 0-85045-250-3 Pbk : £1.95
(B77-26695)

940.54'23 — World War 2. North African campaign. Army operations by Great Britain. Army. Eighth Army. Seventh Armoured Division, 1940-1943
Forty, George. Desert Rats at war / [by] George Forty. — London : Allan.
2 : Europe. — 1977. — 160p : ill, facsims, plans, ports ; 30cm.
Bibl.: p.160.
ISBN 0-7110-0733-0 : £5.25
Also classified at 940.54'21
(B77-17830)

940.54'23 — World War 2. North African campaign. Army operations by Great Britain. Army. First Army & Great Britain. Army. Eighth Army, 1941-1943
Blaxland, Gregory. The plain cook and the great showman : the First and Eighth Armies in North Africa / [by] Gregory Blaxland. — London : Kimber, 1977. — 303p,[24]p of plates : ill, maps, plans, ports ; 25cm.
Index.
ISBN 0-7183-0185-4 : £6.95
(B77-23870)

940.54'23 — World War 2. North African campaign. Army operations by Great Britain. Army. Long Range Desert Group. G (Foot Guards) Patrol
Crichton-Stuart, Michael. G patrol / by Michael Crichton Stuart ; introduction by Bernard Fergusson. — London : Kimber, 1976. — 206p, [12]p of plates : ill, maps(on lining papers), ports ; 25cm.
Originally published: 1958.
ISBN 0-7183-0454-3 : £4.50
(B77-26025)

940.54'23 — World War 2. North African campaign. Relief of Tobruk, 1941-1942
Sandars, John. Operation Crusader / by John Sandars ; colour illustrations by Allard. — London : Almark Publishing, 1976. — 48p : col ill, map, plans ; 24cm. — (Great battles)
Spine title: 'Crusader, the relief of Tobruk'.
ISBN 0-85524-246-9 : £2.50
ISBN 0-85524-245-0 Pbk : Unpriced
(B77-10671)

940.54'23'0924 — World War 2. North African campaign. Army operations by Great Britain. Army. Royal Irish Fusiliers. D Company, 1943. *Officers' personal observations*
Horsfall, John, *b.1915.* The wild geese are flighting / [by] John Horsfall. — Kineton : Roundwood Press, 1976. — xvi,182p,fold leaf of plate,12p of plates : ill(incl 1 col), maps, ports ; 25cm.
Index.
ISBN 0-9504905-0-4 : £2.30
(B77-08673)

940.54'25 — Singapore. Occupation by Japanese military forces, 1941-1945
Caffrey, Kate. Out in the midday sun : Singapore 1941-45 / [by] Kate Caffrey. — London : New English Library, 1977. — 320p : maps, plans ; 18cm.
Originally published: London : Deutsch, 1974. — Bibl.: p.318-320.
ISBN 0-450-03110-1 Pbk : £0.95
(B77-06383)

940.54'25 — World War 2. Battle of the Java Sea
Van Oosten, F C. The Battle of the Java Sea / [by] F.C. van Oosten. — London : Allan, 1976. — 128p,[32]p of plates : ill, maps, plans, ports ; 18cm. — (Sea battles in close-up ; 16)
Bibl.: p.121-123. — Index.
ISBN 0-7110-0615-6 : £3.50
(B77-04487)

940.54'25 — World War 2. Battle of the Sittang. Army operations by Japan. Army. 28 Army
Allen, Louis. Sittang : the last battle / [by] Louis Allen. — London : Arrow Books, 1976. — xx, 267p : maps ; 18cm.
Originally published: London : Macdonald and Co., 1973. — Bibl.: p.257-258. — Index.
ISBN 0-09-913560-4 Pbk : £0.70
(B77-01919)

940.54'25 — World War 2. Indian Ocean campaign. Naval operations, 1942 (April)
Tomlinson, Michael. The most dangerous moment / [by] Michael Tomlinson. — London : Kimber, 1976. — 205p,[12]p of plates : ill, map, ports ; 24cm.
Bibl.: p.195-196. — Index.
ISBN 0-7183-0434-9 : £5.25
(B77-01920)

940.54'25 — World War 2. Pacific campaigns. Naval operations by United States. Navy. Fifth Fleet. Flagships: Indianapolis (Ship). Sinking
Newcomb, Richard Fairchild. Abandon ship! : death of the 'USS Indianapolis' / [by] Richard F. Newcomb. — Revised ed. — London : Corgi, 1977. — 222p : map, plan ; 18cm.
This ed. originally published: Bloomington, London : Indiana University Press, 1976.
ISBN 0-552-10476-0 Pbk : £0.75
(B77-28295)

940.54'25 — World War 2. Singapore campaign
Allen, Louis. Singapore, 1941-1942 / [by] Louis Allen. — London : Davis-Poynter, 1977. — 343p : maps ; 23cm. — (The politics and strategy of the Second World War)
Bibl.: p.319-328. — Index.
ISBN 0-7067-0181-x : £6.50
(B77-23871)

940.54'25 — World War 2. Singapore campaign. Naval operations by Great Britain. Royal Navy. Battle cruisers: Prince of Wales (Ship). Sinking
Middlebrook, Martin. Battleship : the loss of the 'Prince of Wales' and the 'Repulse' / [by] Martin Middlebrook and Patrick Mahoney. — London : Allen Lane, 1977. — x,366p,[16]p of plates : ill, maps, plans, ports ; 23cm.
Bibl.: p.357. — Index.
ISBN 0-7139-1042-9 : £5.95
Primary classification 940.54'25
(B77-32985)

940.54'25 — World War 2. Singapore campaign. Naval operations by Great Britain. Royal Navy. Battleships: Repulse (Ship). Sinking
Middlebrook, Martin. Battleship : the loss of the 'Prince of Wales' and the 'Repulse' / [by] Martin Middlebrook and Patrick Mahoney. — London : Allen Lane, 1977. — x,366p,[16]p of plates : ill, maps, plans, ports ; 23cm.
Bibl.: p.357. — Index.
ISBN 0-7139-1042-9 : £5.95
Also classified at 940.54'25
(B77-32985)

940.54'25'0924 — World War 2. Burma campaign. Army operations by Great Britain. Army. South-east Asia Command. Special Force. Wingate, Orde
Tulloch, Derek. Wingate in peace and war / [by] Derek Tulloch ; edited by the late Arthur Swinson. — London : Futura Publications, 1976. — [4],300p ; 18cm.
Originally published: London : Macdonald, 1972. — Index.
ISBN 0-86007-293-2 Pbk : £0.90
(B77-10054)

940.54'25'0924 — World War 2. Malaya campaign. Military operations by native guerrilla groups. *British officers' personal observations*
Chapman, Frederick Spencer. The jungle is neutral / [by] F. Spencer Chapman ; with a foreword by Earl Wavell. — St Albans : Triad : Mayflower, 1977. — 382p,[4]p of plates : ill, maps ; 18cm.
Originally published: London : Chatto and Windus, 1949.
ISBN 0-583-12816-5 Pbk : £0.75
(B77-10672)

940.54'26 — World War 2. Battle of Buna
Mayo, Lida. Bloody Buna : the campaign that halted the Japanese invasion of Australia / [by] Lida Mayo. — London : New English Library, 1977. — 191p : maps, plans ; 18cm.
Originally published: Garden City, N.Y. : Doubleday, 1974 ; Newton Abbot : David and Charles, 1975.
ISBN 0-450-03192-6 Pbk : £0.75
(B77-20809)

940.54'4 — World War 2. Air operations
Batchelor, John. Fighting aircraft of World War One and Two / [illustrated by John Batchelor ; compiled by Susan Joiner]. — London : Phoebus, 1976. — 256p : ill(some col), maps(chiefly col), ports ; 31cm.
Ill. on lining papers. — Index.
ISBN 0-7026-0007-5 : £4.95
Primary classification 940.4'4
(B77-33529)

940.54'4'0922 — World War 2. Air operations by fighter aeroplanes. Pilots. *Personal observations. Collections*
Men at war / compiled by Aidan Chambers. — Basingstoke [etc.] : Macmillan, 1977. — [6], 106p ; 18cm. — (Topliners)
ISBN 0-333-22748-4 Pbk : £0.45 : CIP rev.
(B77-19910)

940.54'41 — World War 2. Air operations. Use of radar
Price, Alfred. Instruments of darkness : the history of electronic warfare / [by] Alfred Price. — New expanded and updated ed. — London : Macdonald and Jane's, 1977. — 284p, [32]p of plates : ill, maps, plans, ports ; 24cm.
Previous ed.: London : Kimber, 1967. — Index. — Includes two chapters on electronic warfare after World War 2.
ISBN 0-354-01062-x : £5.95
(B77-23002)

940.54'41 — World War 2. Ground attack
Chant, Christopher. Ground attack / by Christopher Chant ; with illustrations by Keith Moseley. — London : Almark Publishing, 1976. — 72p : ill(some col), plans, ports ; 21x22cm. — (The mechanics of war)
ISBN 0-85524-249-3 : £2.50
(B77-02675)

Shores, Christopher Francis. Ground attack aircraft of World War II / [by] Christopher Shores. — London : Macdonald and Jane's, 1977. — 3-191p : ill, ports ; 25cm. — (A Macdonald illustrated war study)
Bibl.: p.187. — Index.
ISBN 0-356-08338-1 : £4.95
(B77-13429)

940.54'49'41 — World War 2. Air operations by Great Britain. Royal Air Force. *Stories, anecdotes. Secondary school texts*
McHarrie, Dennis. Out of the blue : long, short and tall stories of the Royal Air Force / [by] Dennis McHarrie. — London : Edward Arnold, 1977. — 64p : ill ; 22cm.
ISBN 0-7131-0153-9 Pbk : £0.90
(B77-31619)

940.54'49'41 — World War 2. Air operations by Great Britain. Royal Air Force. Bomber Command, 1940-1944
Barker, Ralph. Strike hard, strike sure : epics of the bombers / [by] Ralph Barker. — London [etc.] : Pan Books, 1977. — 208p,[8]p of plates : ill, maps, ports ; 18cm.
This collection originally published: London : Chatto and Windus, 1963. — Index.
ISBN 0-330-02513-9 Pbk : £0.60
(B77-21607)

940.54'49'41 — World War 2. Air operations by Great Britain. Royal Air Force. Bristol Beaufighter aeroplanes
Bowyer, Chaz. Beaufighter at war / [by] Chaz Bowyer. — London : Allan, 1976. — 160p : ill, ports ; 30cm.
Bibl.: p.160.
ISBN 0-7110-0704-7 : £4.95
(B77-02676)

940.54'49'41 — World War 2. Air operations by Great Britain. Royal Air Force. No.617 Squadron
Brickhill, Paul. The dam busters / [by] Paul Brickhill ; with a foreword by Lord Tedder. — Revised ed. — London : Evans Bros, 1977. — x,238p,leaf of plate,[12]p of plates : ill, ports ; 21cm.
Previous ed.: 1951. — Index.
ISBN 0-237-44886-6 : £5.25
(B77-32313)

940.54'49'41 — World War 2. Naval air operations by Royal Navy. Fleet Air Arm. Fairey Swordfish aeroplanes
Harrison, William Alfred. Swordfish special / [by] W.A. Harrison. — London : I. Allan, 1977. — 80p : ill, ports ; 30cm.
ISBN 0-7110-0742-x : £2.75
(B77-23003)

940.54'49'410922 — World War 2. Air operations by Great Britain. Royal Air Force. Supermarine Spitfire aeroplanes, 1940. *Personal observations. Collections*
Spitfire squadron / edited by David Guthrie. — London : Corgi, 1976. — 142p ; 18cm.
ISBN 0-552-10326-8 Pbk : £0.50
(B77-06982)

940.54'49'410924 — World War 2. Air operations by Great Britain. Royal Air Force, 1940-1943. Avro Lancaster aeroplanes. *Officers' personal observations*
Raymond, Robert S. A Yank in Bomber Command / by Robert S. Raymond ; edited by Michael Moynihan ; preface by Noble Frankland. — Newton Abbot [etc.] : David and Charles [etc.], 1977. — 159p,[4]p of plates : map, ports ; 23cm.
ISBN 0-7153-7317-x : £4.50
(B77-17211)

940.54'49'410924 — World War 2. Air operations by Great Britain. Royal Air Force. Bomber Command. *Officers' personal observations*
Gibson, Guy. Enemy coast ahead / [by] Guy Gibson ; with an introduction by Sir Arthur Harris. — London [etc.] : Pan Books, 1977. — xvi,317p,[4]p of plates : 2 ill, ports ; 18cm.
Originally published: London : Joseph, 1946.
ISBN 0-330-02452-3 Pbk : £0.80
(B77-22269)

940.54'49'410924 — World War 2. Air operations by Great Britain. Royal Air Force. Bomber Command, 1943-1944. Avro Lancaster aeroplanes. *Officers' personal observations*
Currie, Jack. Lancaster target / [by] Jack Currie. — London : New English Library, 1977. — 175p ; 18cm.
ISBN 0-450-03280-9 Pbk : £0.70
(B77-25301)

940.54'49'410924 — World War 2. Air operations by Great Britain. Royal Air Force. Hawker Hurricane aeroplanes. *Diaries*
Barclay, George. Angels 22 : a self-portrait of a fighter pilot / [by] George Barclay ; edited by Humphrey Wynn ; with a foreword by Sir John Grandy. — Revised ed. — London : Arrow Books, 1977. — 224p,[12]p of plates : ill, facsims, ports ; 18cm.
Previous ed.: published as 'Fighter pilot'. London : Kimber, 1976. — Bibl.: p.212. — Index.
ISBN 0-09-916130-3 Pbk : £0.85
(B77-33533)

940.54'49'410924 — World War 2. Air operations by Great Britain. Royal Air Force. Supermarine Spitfire aeroplanes, 1940. *Diaries*
Johnstone, Sandy. Enemy in the sky : my 1940 diary / [by] Sandy Johnstone. — London : Kimber, 1976. — 191p,[12]p of plates : ill, ports ; 24cm.
Index.
ISBN 0-7183-0474-8 : £4.75
(B77-02677)

940.54'49'410924 — World War 2. Naval air operations by Great Britain. Royal Navy. Fleet Air Arm. Fairey Swordfish aeroplanes. *Officers' personal observations*
Lamb, Charles, *b.1914.* War in a stringbag / [by] Charles Lamb ; foreword by Sir Charles Evans. — London [etc.] : Cassell and Collier Macmillan, 1977. — [12],340p,[16]p of plates : ill, map, ports ; 23cm.
Map on lining papers. — Index.
ISBN 0-304-29778-x : £5.75
(B77-26026)

940.54'49'410924 — World War 2. Night air operations by Great Britain. Royal Air Force. Fighter aeroplanes. *Officers' personal observations*
Rawnsley, Cecil Frederick. Night fighter / [by] C.F. Rawnsley and Robert Wright ; foreword by John Cunningham. — Morley : Elmfield Press, 1976. — 3-382p : map ; 22cm.
Originally published: London : Collins, 1957.
ISBN 0-7057-0077-1 : £4.95
(B77-23872)

940.54'49'43 — World War 2. Air operations by Germany. Luftwaffe. Ground attack units
Pegg, Martin. Luftwaffe ground attack units, 1939-45 / by Martin Pegg ; colour plates by Terry Hadler and Gerry Embleton. — London : Osprey Publishing, 1977. — 48p : ill(some col), ports ; 25cm. — (Airwar series ; 4) (Aircam)
Text accompanying illustrations in English, French and German.
ISBN 0-85045-137-x Pbk : £1.95
(B77-27570)

940.54'49'43 — World War 2. Air operations by Germany. Luftwaffe. Junkers JU87 aeroplanes
Robertson, Bruce. JU87 Stuka / [by] Bruce Robertson and Gerald Scarborough. — Cambridge : Stephens [for] Airfix Products Ltd, 1977. — 96p : ill ; 26cm. — (Classic aircraft ; no.5)
ISBN 0-85059-193-7 : £2.95
Also classified at 623.74'63
(B77-23873)

940.54'49'73 — World War 2. Air operations by United States. Army Air Force. 15th Air Force
Rust, Kenn C. Fifteenth Air Force story : - in World War II / [by] Kenn C. Rust. — Temple City : Historical Aviation Album ; London : [Distributed by] Hersant, 1976. — 64p : ill, maps ; 28cm.
ISBN 0-911852-79-4 Pbk : £4.45
(B77-08145)

940.54'49'73 — World War 2. Air operations by United States. Army Air Force. Boeing B17 aeroplanes
Freeman, Roger Anthony. B-17 Fortress at war / [by] Roger A. Freeman. — London : Allan, 1977. — 192p : ill(some col), ports ; 30cm.
ISBN 0-7110-0686-5 : £5.50
(B77-10055)

940.54'49'94 — World War 2. Air operations by Australia. Royal Australian Air Force. Mustang aeroplanes
Anderson, Peter N. Mustangs of the RAAF and RNZAF / [by] Peter N. Anderson. — Sydney [etc.] ; London : A.H. and A.W. Reed, 1975. — [4],103,[5]p : ill(some col), coats of arms, facsim, maps, ports ; 29cm.
Bibl.: p.[2] (first sequence). — Index.
ISBN 0-589-07130-0 : £9.10
Also classified at 951.9'042
(B77-19908)

940.54'5 — Soviet Union. Convoys from & to Iceland & Scotland, 1941-1945
Schofield, Brian Betham. The Arctic convoys / [by] B.B. Schofield. — London : Macdonald and Jane's, 1977. — x,198p,[32]p of plates : ill, maps, plans, ports ; 24cm.
Map on lining papers. — Bibl.: p.138. — Index.
ISBN 0-354-01112-x : £5.95
(B77-24612)

940.54'5 — World War 2. Naval operations
Batchelor, John. Fighting ships of World War One and Two / [illustrated by John Batchelor ; compiled by Anne Maclean and Suzanne Poole]. — London : Phoebus, 1976. — 255p : ill(some col), facsim, maps(some col), ports(some col) ; 31cm.
Ill. on lining papers. — Index.
ISBN 0-7026-0006-7 : £4.95
Primary classification 940.4'5
(B77-32979)

940.54'5 — World War 2. Naval operations by Allied navies. Escort ships
Elliott, Peter. Allied escort ships of World War II : a complete survey / [by] Peter Elliott. — London : Macdonald and Jane's, 1977. — 575p : ill ; 26cm.
Index.
ISBN 0-356-08401-9 : £15.00
(B77-21608)

940.54'5 — World War 2. Naval operations by boats
Cook, Graeme. Small boat raiders / [by] Graeme Cook. — London : Hart-Davis MacGibbon, 1977. — 131p ; 23cm.
Bibl.: p.131.
ISBN 0-246-10807-x : £3.50
(B77-20810)

940.54'5 — World War 2. Naval operations by motor torpedo boats
Cooper, Bryan. The E-boat threat / [by] Bryan Cooper. — London : Macdonald and Jane's, 1976. — 138p : ill, maps ; 25cm. — (A Macdonald illustrated war study)
Bibl.: p.134. — Index.
ISBN 0-356-08144-3 : £4.95
(B77-03837)

940.54'51'0924 — World War 2. Naval operations by Germany. Kriegsmarine. Submarines. Prien, Günther. *Biographies*
Frank, Wolfgang. Enemy submarine : the story of Gunther Prien, captain of U47 / [by] Wolfgang Frank ; [translated from the German by Lynton Hudson]. — London : New English Library, 1977. — 156p : map ; 18cm.
This translation originally published: London : Kimber, 1954. — Translation of: 'Prien greift an'. Hamburg : Köhler, 1942.
ISBN 0-450-02941-7 Pbk : £0.66
(B77-17831)

940.54'52 — German naval blockades. Penetration by ships carrying cargoes of steel. Binney, George. *North Sea, 1941-1945*
Barker, Ralph. The blockade busters / by Ralph Barker. — London : Chatto and Windus, 1976. — 224p,[12]p of plates : ill, map, ports ; 23cm.
Bibl.: p.213-215. — Index.
ISBN 0-7011-2189-0 : £5.00
(B77-01921)

940.54'59'41 — British ships. Losses, 1939-1945. *Lists. Early works*
British vessels lost at sea, 1939-45. — Cambridge : Stephens, 1976. — vi,70p;vi,103p ; 24cm.
Index. — Contents: Ships of the Royal Navy : statement of losses during the Second World War. London : H.M.S.O., 1947 - British merchant vessels lost or damaged by enemy action during Second World War. London : H.M.S.O., 1947.
ISBN 0-85059-267-4 : £3.95
(B77-05131)

940.54'59'41 — Great Britain. Convoys from United States, 1943: SC122 & HX229
Rohwer, Jürgen. The critical convoy battles of March 1943 : the battle for HX.229SC122 / [by] Jürgen Rohwer ; [translated from the German by Derek Masters]. — London : I. Allan, 1977. — 256p,[32]p of plates : ill, facsims, maps, plans, ports ; 23cm.
Translation and revision of: German text ; originally published: Germany : s.n., 1975. — Bibl.: p.245-253. — Index.
ISBN 0-7110-0749-7 : £5.95
(B77-28296)

940.54'59'41 — Soviet Union. Convoys from Scotland, 1942: PQ18
Smith, Peter Charles, *b.1940.* Convoy PQ18 : Arctic victory / [by] Peter C. Smith. — London : New English Library, 1977. — 237p : 1 ill, maps, plans ; 18cm.
Originally published: as 'Arctic victory : the story of convoy PQ18'. London : Kimber, 1975.
ISBN 0-450-03120-9 Pbk : £0.80
(B77-09418)

940.54'59'41 — World War 2. Naval operations by Great Britain. Royal Navy
Kemp, Peter Kemp. Victory at sea, 1939-1945 / written with the approval of the Admiralty by P.K. Kemp ; with a foreword by Viscount Cunningham of Hyndhope. — London [etc.] : White Lion Publishers, 1976. — 383p,[16]p of plates : ill, maps, ports ; 23cm.
Originally published: London : Muller, 1957. — Index.
ISBN 0-7274-0027-4 : £5.50
(B77-02678)

Roskill, Stephen Wentworth. The war at sea, 1939-1945 / by S.W. Roskill. — London : H.M.S.O. — (History of the Second World War : United Kingdom military series)
Vol.1 : The defensive. — 1976. — xxiii,718p, [39]leaves of plates(37 fold),[42]p of plates : ill, maps(chiefly col), plans(chiefly col), ports ; 25cm.
Originally published: 1954. — Index.
ISBN 0-11-630188-0 Pbk : £12.00
(B77-09419)

940.54'59'41 — World War 2. Naval operations by Great Britain. Royal Navy, 1939-1940. Dummy warships
Hampshire, Arthur Cecil. The phantom fleet / [by] A. Cecil Hampshire. — London [etc.] : White Lion Publishers, 1977. — 208p,[8]p of plates : ill, 2 ports ; 23cm.
Originally published: London : Kimber, 1960.
ISBN 0-7274-0263-3 : £5.25
(B77-18473)

940.54'59'41 — World War 2. Naval operations by Great Britain. Royal Navy. Destroyers: Petard (Ship)
Connell, G G. Fighting destroyer : the story of HMS 'Petard' / [by] G.G. Connell. — London : Kimber, 1976. — 271p,[16]p of plates : ill, 2 maps, ports ; 24cm.
Bibl.: p.263-264. — Index.
ISBN 0-7183-0444-6 : £5.75
(B77-03295)

940.54'59'410924 — World War 2. Naval operations by Great Britain. Royal Navy. *Officers' personal observations*
Bull, Peter. To sea in a sieve / [by] Peter Bull. — London : Corgi, 1977. — 205p ; 18cm.
Originally published: London : P. Davies, 1956.
ISBN 0-552-10380-2 Pbk : £0.65
(B77-14478)

940.54'59'410924 — World War 2. Naval operations by Great Britain. Royal Navy, 1940-1942. Destroyers: Electra (Ship). *Officers' personal observations*
Cain, T J. H.M.S. 'Electra' / [by] T.J. Cain ; as told to A.V. Sellwood. — London : Futura Publications, 1976. — vii,280p ; 18cm.
Originally published: London : Muller, 1959. — Index.
ISBN 0-86007-330-0 Pbk : £0.65
(B77-10056)

940.54'59'43 — World War 2. Naval operations by Germany. Kriegsmarine. Battleships: Graf Spee (Ship)
Powell, Michael. The last voyage of the 'Graf Spee' / [by] Michael Powell. — London [etc.] : White Lion Publishers, 1976. — 192p ; 21cm.
Originally published: as 'Graf Spee'. London : Hodder and Stoughton, 1956.
ISBN 0-7274-0256-0 : £4.95
(B77-10673)

940.54'72 — British Royal Air Force prisoners of war. Escapes, 1939-1945
Brickhill, Paul. Escape, or die : authentic stories of the RAF Escaping Society / [by] Paul Brickhill ; with introduction by H.E. Bates and foreword by Sir Basil Embry. — London [etc.] : Pan Books, 1977. — 190p ; 18cm.
Originally published: London : Evan Bros, 1952.
ISBN 0-330-02098-6 Pbk : £0.60
(B77-28297)

940.54'72 — Soviet prisoners of war. Forced repatriation by Allied forces, 1944-1947
Bethell, Nicholas, *Baron Bethell.* The last secret : forcible repatriation to Russia, 1944-7 / [by] Nicholas Bethell ; introduction by Hugh Trevor-Roper. — London : Futura Publications, 1976. — 287p,[8]p of plates : ill, ports ; 18cm.
Originally published: London : Deutsch, 1974. — Index.
ISBN 0-86007-273-8 Pbk : £0.90
(B77-10674)

940.54'72'430924 — British prisoners of war. *Germany, 1940-1945. Diaries*
Mansel, John. The Mansel diaries : the diaries of Captain John Mansel, prisoner-of-war, and camp forger, in Germany, 1940-45 / edited by E.G.C. Beckwith. — Blockley : The editor ; London : Distributed by Wildwood House, 1977. — xi,156p,16p of plates : ill, facsims, maps, ports ; 26cm.
Index.
£4.50
(B77-27571)

940.54'72'430924 — British prisoners of war: Day, Wings. Escapes. *Germany, 1939-1945*
Smith, Sydney, *b.1912.* 'Wings' Day : the man who led the RAF's epic battle in German captivity / [by] Sydney Smith. — London [etc.] : Pan Books, 1977. — 285p,[4]p of plates : ill, ports ; 18cm.
Originally published: London : Collins, 1968.
Pbk : £0.75
ISBN 0-330-02494-9
(B77-27572)

940.54'72'430924 — British prisoners of war. Escapes. *Germany, 1940-1944. Other ranks' personal observations*
Beeson, George. Five roads to freedom / [by] George Beeson. — London : Cooper, 1977. — xii,123p,[4]p of plates : ill, facsims, ports ; 23cm.
ISBN 0-85052-230-7 : £4.95
(B77-18474)

940.54'72'430924 — British prisoners of war. Escapes. *Germany, 1941-1944. Other ranks' personal observations*
Pape, Richard. Boldness be my friend / [by] Richard Pape ; with foreword by Lord Tedder and introduction by Sir Archibald McIndoe. — London [etc.] : Pan Books, 1977. — 254p,[4]p of plates : ill, maps, plan, ports ; 18cm.
Originally published: London : Elek, 1953.
ISBN 0-330-10393-8 Pbk : £0.75
(B77-31620)

940.54'72'430924 — British prisoners of war. Escapes. *Netherlands, 1944. Officers' personal observations*
Kessel, Lipmann. Surgeon at arms / [by] Lipmann Kessel ; with John St John. — London : Cooper, 1976. — 200p ; 22cm.
Originally published: London : Heinemann, 1958.
ISBN 0-85052-219-6 : £4.95
(B77-05132)

940.54'72'430924 — British prisoners of war. Escapes. *Netherlands, 1944. Personal observations*
Warrack, Graeme. Travel by dark : after Arnhem / [by] Graeme Warrack ; foreword by Prince Bernhard of the Netherlands. — [London] : Fontana, 1976. — 256p : map ; 19cm.
Originally published: London : Harvill Press, 1963.
ISBN 0-00-634552-2 Pbk : £0.75
(B77-03296)

940.54'72'430924 — English prisoners of war. Escapes. *Germany, 1944-1945. Personal observations*
Jones, Francis Stephen. Escape to nowhere / [by] Francis S. Jones. — St Albans : Triad, 1977. — 236p : map ; 18cm.
Originally published: London : Bodley Head, 1952.
ISBN 0-583-12817-3 Pbk : £0.75
Primary classification 940.54'72'430924
(B77-09420)

940.54'72'430924 — English prisoners of war. Escapes. *Greece, 1941-1944. Personal observations*
Jones, Francis Stephen. Escape to nowhere / [by] Francis S. Jones. — St Albans : Triad, 1977. — 236p : map ; 18cm.
Originally published: London : Bodley Head, 1952.
ISBN 0-583-12817-3 Pbk : £0.75
Also classified at 940.54'72'430924; 940.54'72'450924
(B77-09420)

940.54'72'430924 — New Zealand prisoners of war. Escapes. *Greece, 1941-1942. Personal observations*
Thomas, Walter Babington. Dare to be free / [by] W.B. Thomas. — London [etc.] : Pan Books, 1977. — 235p : map, plans ; 18cm.
Originally published: London : Wingate, 1951.
ISBN 0-330-10629-5 Pbk : £0.70
(B77-23874)

940.54'72'430924 — Prisoners of war: Prominente. *East Germany. Colditz, 1940-1945. Personal observations*
Romilly, Giles. Hostages at Colditz / [by] Giles Romilly and Michael Alexander. — London : Sphere, 1977. — 237p ; 18cm.
Originally published: as 'The privileged nightmare', London : Weidenfeld and Nicolson, 1954 ; and as 'Hostages at Colditz', 1972.
ISBN 0-7221-7465-9 Pbk : £0.75
(B77-11487)

940.54'72'450924 — English prisoners of war. Escapes. *Italy, 1940-1944. Other ranks' personal observations*
Bishop, Jack. In pursuit of freedom / by Jack Bishop. — London : Cooper, 1977. — 3-126p ; 23cm.
ISBN 0-85052-223-4 : £4.95
(B77-24613)

940.54'72'450924 — English prisoners of war. Escapes. *Italy, 1941-1944. Personal observations*
Jones, Francis Stephen. Escape to nowhere / [by] Francis S. Jones. — St Albans : Triad, 1977. — 236p : map ; 18cm.
Originally published: London : Bodley Head, 1952.
ISBN 0-583-12817-3 Pbk : £0.75
Primary classification 940.54'72'430924
(B77-09420)

940.54'72'450924 — Scottish prisoners of war. Escapes. *Italy, 1943-1945. Officers' personal observations*
Reid, Ian, *b.1915.* Prisoner at large : the story of five escapes / [by] Ian Reid. — London : Futura Publications, 1976. — 352p : map ; 18cm.
Originally published: London : Gollancz, 1947.
ISBN 0-86007-360-2 Pbk : £0.85
(B77-14479)

940.54'72'520924 — Allied prisoners of war. *Indonesia. Java. Bandung, 1942-1945. Officers' personal observations*
Van der Post, Laurens. The night of the new moon / [by] Laurens van der Post. — Harmondsworth [etc.] : Penguin, 1977. — 125p, [8]p of plates : ill, facsim, ports ; 18cm.
Originally published: London : Hogarth, 1970.
ISBN 0-14-004359-4 Pbk : £0.75
(B77-26027)

940.54'72'520924 — Australian prisoners of war. *South-east Asia, 1941-1944. Other ranks' personal observations*
Braddon, Russell. The naked island / [by] Russell Braddon. — [New] ed.. — London [etc.] : Pan Books, 1977. — 286p,[4]p of plates : 1 ill, ports ; 18cm.
This ed. originally published: 1955.
Pbk : £0.75
ISBN 0-330-02169-9
(B77-23875)

940.54'72'520924 — British prisoners of war. *South-east Asia, 1942-1945. Other ranks' personal observations*
Pounder, Thomas. Death camps of the River Kwai / [by] Thomas Pounder. — St Ives, Cornwall : United Writers Publications, 1977. — 262p : ill, map ; 22cm.
ISBN 0-901976-37-7 : £4.95
(B77-23876)

940.54'72'520924 — British prisoners of war. Escapes. *Singapore. Pasir Panjang, 1942. Personal observations*
McCormac, Charles. You'll die in Singapore / [by] Charles McCormac. — London [etc.] : Pan Books, 1977. — 192p : map ; 18cm.
Originally published: London : Hale, 1954.
ISBN 0-330-10452-7 Pbk : £0.60
(B77-28298)

940.54'72'520924 — Canadian prisoners of war. *Philippines. Santo Tomas, 1941-1945. Personal observations*
Prising, Robin. Manila, goodbye / [by] Robert [i.e. Robin] Prising. — London : Corgi, 1977. — 191p ; 18cm.
Originally published: Boston, Mass. : Houghton-Mifflin, 1975 ; London : Heinemann, 1976.
ISBN 0-552-10546-5 Pbk : £0.75
Primary classification 959.9'035'0924
(B77-29853)

940.54'7541 — World War 2. Burma campaign. Army operations by Great Britain. Army. Queen Alexandra's Royal Army Nursing Corps. *Officers' personal observations*
Beaumont, Winifred Hilda. A detail on the Burma front / [by] Winifred Beaumont. — London : British Broadcasting Corporation, 1977. — 160p : map ; 24cm.
ISBN 0-563-17193-6 : £3.50
(B77-19909)

940.54'7543 — World War 2. Army operations by Germany. Heer. Medical services, 1940-1945. *Other ranks' personal observations*
Häring, Bernard. Embattled witness : memories of a time of war / [by] Bernard Häring. — London : Burns and Oates, 1977. — ix,116p ; 22cm.
Originally published: New York : Seabury Press, 1976.
ISBN 0-86012-052-x Pbk : £2.25
(B77-32314)

940.54'8 — Great Britain. Royal Navy. Rendering Mines Safe Section, 1940-1945. Mould, John Stuart & Syme, Hugh Randall. *Stories, anecdotes. Juvenile literature*
Southall, Ivan. Seventeen seconds / [by] Ivan Southall. — Leicester : Knight Books, 1977. — 128p ; 18cm.
This adaptation originally published: Leicester : Brockhampton Press, 1974. — Adaptation of 'Softly tread the brave'. London : Angus and Robertson, 1961.
ISBN 0-340-20132-0 Pbk : £0.60
(B77-27573)

940.54'81'41 — World War 2. *British personal observations*
Hood, Stuart. Pebbles from my skull / [by] Stuart Hood. — Morley : Elmfield Press, 1977. — 153p ; 22cm.
Originally published: London : Hutchinson, 1963.
ISBN 0-7057-0074-7 : £4.50
(B77-31621)

940.54'81'41 — World War 2, 1940-1945. *British personal observations*
St Albans, Suzanne Marie Adèle Beauclerk, *Duchess of.* Uncertain wings / [by] the Duchess of St Albans. — London : W.H. Allen, 1977. — [7],216p,[8]p of plates : ill, ports ; 23cm.
ISBN 0-491-02250-6 : £4.95
(B77-20811)

940.54'81'41 — World War 2. Army operations by Great Britain. Army. XXX Corps, 1944-1945. *Officers' personal observations*
Horrocks, *Sir* **Brian.** Corps commander / [by] Sir Brian Horrocks with Eversley Belfield and H. Essame. — London : Sidgwick and Jackson, 1977. — xvi,256p : ill, map, plans, ports ; 24cm.
Index.
ISBN 0-283-98320-5 : £6.95
(B77-23877)

940.54'81'41 — World War 2. Military operations by Great Britain. Army. 2nd Queen's Own Cameron Highlanders. C Company, 1940-1944. *Officers' personal observations*
Cochrane, Peter. Charlie Company : in service with C Company 2nd Queen's Own Cameron Highlanders, 1940-44 / [by] Peter Cochrane. — London : Chatto and Windus, 1977. — xii, 179p,[8]p of plates : ill, maps, ports ; 23cm.
Index.
ISBN 0-7011-2280-3 : £4.95 : CIP rev.
(B77-21609)

940.54'81'73 — World War 2, 1941. *American personal observations*
Reynolds, Quentin. Only the stars are neutral / [by] Quentin Reynolds. — Bath : Chivers, 1977. — xi,299p ; 21cm.
Originally published: New York : Random House ; London : Cassell, 1942.
ISBN 0-85997-244-5 : £5.40(£4.05 to members of the Library Association)
(B77-25302)

940.54'81'73 — World War 2. Military operations by American military forces, 1943. *Personal observations*
Steinbeck, John. Once there was a war / [by] John Steinbeck. — Harmondsworth [etc.] : Penguin, 1977. — xiv,173p ; 18cm.
Originally published: New York : Viking Press, 1958 ; London : Heinemann, 1959.
ISBN 0-14-004291-1 Pbk : £0.70
(B77-26028)

940.54'82'43 — Germany. Heer. Afrikakorps. Desertion. *North Africa, 1941. Personal observations*
Bahnemann, Gunther. I deserted Rommel / [by] Gunther Bahnemann. — London : Arrow Books, 1976. — 256p ; 18cm.
Originally published: London : Jarrolds, 1961.
ISBN 0-09-913570-1 Pbk : £0.60
(B77-01072)

940.54'86 — World War 2. Secret service operations by Allied secret services
Cook, Graeme. Missions most secret / [by] Graeme Cook. — London : Harwood-Smart, 1976. — xi,186p ; 23cm.
Bibl.: p.186.
ISBN 0-904507-17-3 : £3.95
Also classified at 940.4'86
(B77-25303)

940.54'86'0924 — Uranium supplies. Rescue by Sautter, Paul. *Europe, 1944-1945*
Richardson, Cordell. Uranium trail East / [by] C. Richardson. — London : Bachman and Turner, 1977. — 144p : ill, facsim, maps, port ; 23cm.
Index.
ISBN 0-85974-054-4 : £3.95
(B77-34309)

940.54'86'41 — World War 2. Naval intelligence operations by Great Britain. Admiralty. Operational Intelligence Centre
Beesly, Patrick. Very special intelligence : the story of the Admiralty's Operational Intelligence Centre, 1939-1945 / [by] Patrick Beesly ; with a foreword by the Earl Mountbatten of Burma. — London : Hamilton, 1977. — xv,271p,[8]p of plates : ill, facsims, map(on lining papers), ports ; 23cm.
Bibl.: p.261-263. — Index.
ISBN 0-241-89606-1 : £5.95
(B77-13977)

940.54'86'410924 — Anti-German espionage. *Europe, 1931-1945. Personal observations*
Minshall, Merlin. Guilt-edged / [by] Merlin Minshall ; foreword by Len Deighton. — St Albans : Panther, 1977. — 256p : 1 ill, 2 maps, plan ; 18cm.
Originally published: London : Bachman and Turner, 1975. — Index.
ISBN 0-586-04421-3 Pbk : £0.75
(B77-10057)

940.54'86'410924 — British espionage. *Gibraltar, 1942-1943. Personal observations*
Darling, Donald. Sunday at large : assignments of a secret agent / [by] Donald Darling. — London : Kimber, 1977. — 174p,[12]p of plates : ill, ports ; 24cm.
Index.
ISBN 0-7183-0215-x : £4.75
(B77-22393)

940.54'86'440924 — Anti-German espionage. Katona, Edita. *Europe. Autobiographies*
Katona, Edita. Code-name Marianne : an autobiography / [by] Edita Katona ; with Patrick Macnaghten. — [London] : Fontana, 1977. — 212,[9]p,[4]p of plates : 1 ill, ports ; 18cm.
Originally published: London : Collins : Harvill Press, 1976.
ISBN 0-00-635041-0 Pbk : £0.85
(B77-32315)

940.54'86'470924 — World War 2. Anti-German espionage. Radó, Sándor
Radó, Sándor. Code name Dora / [by] Sándor Radó ; translated from the authorized German edition by J.A. Underwood. — London : Abelard, 1977. — xxiii,298p : plans ; 22cm.
Translation of: 'Deckname Dora'. Stuttgart : Deutsche Verlags-Anstalt, 1972. — Originally published: in Hungarian as 'Dóra jelenti'. Budapest : Kossuth Könyvkiadó, 1971.
ISBN 0-200-72339-1 : £4.95
(B77-16673)

940.54'86'470924 — World War 2. Anti-German espionage. Trepper, Leopold. *Autobiographies*
Trepper, Leopold. The great game : the story of the Red Orchestra / [by] Leopold Trepper ; [in collaboration with Patrick Rotman ; translated from the French by Helen Weaver]. — London : Joseph, 1977. — xi,442p : facsims ; 24cm.
This translation originally published: New York : McGraw-Hill, 1976. — Translation of: 'Le grand jeu'. Paris : Editions Albin Michel, 1975. — Index.
ISBN 0-7181-1533-3 : £6.95
(B77-21610)

940.54'86'4810924 — Anti-German espionage. Baalsrud, Jan. Escapes. *Norway, 1943*
Howarth, David. We die alone / [by] David Howarth. — London : Collins, 1976. — 5-255p : map ; 21cm.
Originally published: 1955.
£3.50
ISBN 0-00-211927-7
(B77-03297)

940.54'86'73 — World War 2. Espionage by United States. Office of Strategic Services, 1941-1945
Alcorn, Robert Hayden. No bugles for spies : tales of the OSS / [by] Robert Hayden Alcorn. — London [etc.] : White Lion Publishers, 1977. — ix, 209p ; 23cm.
Originally published: New York : McKay, 1962 ; London : Jarrolds, 1963.
ISBN 0-7274-0270-6 : £4.95
(B77-08674)

940.54'87'43 — German espionage. *Great Britain, 1939-1945*
Peis, Günter. The mirror of deception : how Britain turned the Nazi spy machine against itself / [by] Günter Peis ; [translated from the German by William Steedman]. — London : Weidenfeld and Nicolson, 1977. — 190p,[8]p of plates : ill, facsims, ports ; 23cm.
Translation of: 'So ging Deutschland in die Falle'. Düsseldorf : Econ Verlag, 1976. — Bibl.: p.182-183. — Index.
ISBN 0-297-77343-7 : £5.25
(B77-24614)

940.54'87'430924 — German espionage, 1937-1942. *Personal observations*
Eppler, John. Operation Condor : Rommel's spy / [by] John Eppler ; translated [from the French] by S. Seago. — London : Macdonald and Jane's, 1977. — [5],250p,[8]p of plates : ports ; 23cm.
Translation of: 'Condor : l'espion de Rommel'. Paris : Lafont, 1974. — Index.
ISBN 0-356-08419-1 : £5.95
(B77-25304)

940.54'87'430924 — Germany. Nationalsozialistische Deutsche Arbeiter-Partei. Schutzstaffel, 1939-1943. Schmidt, Kitty
Norden, Peter. Salon Kitty : a true story / by Peter Norden ; translated [from the German] by J. Maxwell Brownjohn. — Sevenoaks : Coronet, 1977. — 223p ; 18cm.
This translation originally published: as 'Madam Kitty'. London : Abelard-Schuman, 1973. — Translation of: 'Salon Kitty'. München : Südwest Verlag, 1972.
ISBN 0-340-22554-8 Pbk : £0.85
ISBN 0-340-18641-0
(B77-32316)

940.54'87'430924 — World War 2. Military operations by Germany. Heer. Special forces. Skorzeny, Otto
Foley, Charles. Commando extraordinary / by Charles Foley ; with a foreword by Sir Robert Laycock. — Morley : Elmfield Press, 1977. — x,232p ; 22cm. — ([Morley war classics series])
Originally published: London : Longmans, Green, 1954. — Index.
ISBN 0-7057-0075-5 : £4.95
(B77-31622)

940.54'886'41 — World War 2. British propaganda
Cruickshank, Charles Grieg. The fourth arm : psychological warfare 1938-1945 / [by] Charles Cruickshank. — London : Davis-Poynter, 1977. — 200p ; 23cm.
Bibl.: p.191. — Index.
ISBN 0-7067-0212-3 : £6.50
(B77-32317)

940.55 — Europe, 1945-1975. *Secondary school texts*
Cameron, Fraser. Europe since 1945 / [by] Fraser Cameron. — London : Edward Arnold, 1976. — viii,88p : ill, facsims, maps, ports ; 24cm.
ISBN 0-7131-0074-5 Sd : £1.50
(B77-02679)

940.55 — Europe. Social life, 1945
Longmate, Norman. When we won the war : the story of victory in Europe, 1945 / [by] Norman Longmate. — London : Hutchinson, 1977. — 192p,[16]p of plates : ill, map, ports ; 23cm.
Index.
ISBN 0-09-128510-0 : £4.95
(B77-23878)

940.55'092'4 — Europe. Political events, 1945-1974. *Personal observations*
Wheeler-Bennett, *Sir* John Wheeler. Friends, enemies and sovereigns / by Sir John Wheeler-Bennett ; with a foreword by Harold Macmillan. — London [etc.] : Macmillan, 1976. — 176p ; 23cm.
Index.
ISBN 0-333-18168-9 : £4.95
(B77-04488)

941 — HISTORY. GREAT BRITAIN

941 — Archives. Organisations. *Great Britain. Historical Manuscripts Commission. Reports, surveys. Serials*
Historical Manuscripts Commission. Secretary's report to the Commissioners / the Royal Commission on Historical Manuscripts. — London : H.M.S.O.
1976-1977. — 1977. — [5],24p ; 25cm.
Bibl.: p.17-20.
ISBN 0-11-440096-2 Sd : £0.70
(B77-31623)

941 — British civilization, to 1976
Healey, Tim. Great Britain : the land and its people / adapted by Tim Healey from the original text by Francis Coleman ; illustrations by John Shackell ... [et al.]. — Easy reading ed. — London : Macdonald Educational, 1977. — 4-61p : chiefly ill(chiefly col), col maps, ports(some col) ; 29cm. — (Macdonald countries)
Col. ill., col. maps on lining papers. — Index.
ISBN 0-356-05568-x : £2.25
(B77-24615)

941 — British civilization, to ca 1850
George, William. British heritage : in colour / [by] William George. — Poole : Blandford Press, 1976. — 222p : ill(some col), col coat of arms, facsims(some col), map, ports(some col) ; 20cm.
Ill. on lining paper.
ISBN 0-7137-8519-5 : £2.95
(B77-03838)

941 — Buildings of historical importance. Projects. *Great Britain. Juvenile literature*
Brandreth, Gyles. Project, castles and historic houses / [by] Gyles Brandreth ; illustrated by Rowan Barnes Murphy. — London : Carousel Books, 1977. — 158p : ill, geneal table, 2 maps, music, ports ; 20cm. — (Carousel books)
With answers.
ISBN 0-552-54121-4 Pbk : £0.50
(B77-26696)

941 — Castles. *Great Britain, to 1642. Secondary school texts*
Birt, David. Castles / [by] David Birt. — London : Edward Arnold, 1977. — 32p : ill, maps, plan ; 25cm. — (Yesterday today)
ISBN 0-7131-0139-3 Sd : Unpriced : CIP rev.
(B77-09421)

941 — Disasters caused by weather. *Great Britain, 1638-1972*
Holford, Ingrid. British weather disasters / [by] Ingrid Holford. — Newton Abbot [etc.] : David and Charles, 1976. — 127p : ill, charts, maps ; 26cm.
Index.
ISBN 0-7153-7276-9 : £4.95
(B77-05133)

941 — Great Britain, 1066-1485. *Secondary school texts*
Lane, Peter. The Middle Ages / [by] Peter Lane. — London : Batsford, 1977. — 96p : ill, coats of arms, facsims, maps, plans, ports ; 26cm. — (Visual sources series)
Index.
ISBN 0-7134-0033-1 : £2.95
(B77-27574)

941 — Great Britain. Battles, 1066-1746
Daniell, David Scott. Battles and battlefields / [by] David Scott Daniell ; illustrations and maps by William Stobbs. — London [etc.] : Beaver Books, 1976. — 191p : ill, geneal tables, plans ; 20cm.
Originally published: London : Batsford, 1961. — Index.
ISBN 0-600-31404-9 Pbk : £0.65
(B77-13430)

941 — Great Britain, B.C.55-. *Secondary school texts*
Ray, John, *b.1929*. Headline history / [by] John Ray. — London : Evans Bros.
In 5 vols.
55 BC to 1485. — 1976. — 96p : ill, facsims, maps, ports ; 25cm.
ISBN 0-237-29170-3 Pbk : £1.40
(B77-06387)

Tudor and Stuart times. — 1977. — 80p : ill, maps, ports ; 26cm.
ISBN 0-237-29171-1 Pbk : £1.50
(B77-32318)

941 — Great Britain, B.C.55-A.D.1950. *Juvenile literature*
Trease, Geoffrey. Days to remember : a garland of historic anniversaries / [by] Geoffrey Trease ; text and cover illustrations by Joanna Troughton. — London : Pan Books, 1977. — 190p : ill ; 20cm. — (Piccolo)
Originally published: London : Heinemann, 1973.
ISBN 0-330-25217-8 Pbk : £0.60
(B77-34310)

941 — Great Britain. Historical events, to 1973. Local associations
Johnson, Paul. A place in history / [by] Paul Johnson. — London : Omega, 1974. — 224p : ill(some col), facsims, map, plan, ports(some col) ; 25cm.
'... to accompany, in written and pictorial form, a series of documentary films presented by Thames Television' - Preface. — Also published: London : Weidenfeld and Nicolson, 1974. — Bibl.: p.223.
ISBN 0-86007-702-0 Pbk : £1.95
(B77-10675)

941 — Great Britain. Social life, 1660-. *Secondary school texts. Teaching kits*
Handling history kits. — London [etc.] : Hutchinson.
2 : Britain : the industrial age / [by] Robert Unwin. — 1976. — Case : ill, facsims, forms, maps ; 25cm.
Teacher's manual (64p.), 40 work cards ([80] sides) and 15 copies of archive booklet (32p.). — Bibl.: p.61-62 (teacher's manual). — List of films and filmstrips: p.63-64 (teacher's manual).
ISBN 0-09-126760-9 : £15.50
(B77-06983)

941 — Great Britain. Social life, B.C.75-A.D.1975
Fry, Plantagenet Somerset. 2,000 years of British life : a social history of England, Wales, Scotland and Ireland / [by] Plantagenet Somerset Fry. — Glasgow [etc.] : Collins, 1976. — 3-256p : ill, facsims, maps, plans, ports ; 25cm.
Bibl.: p.251-252. — Index.
ISBN 0-00-106172-0 : £4.95
(B77-23879)

941 — Great Britain, to 1603. *Primary school texts*
Sauvain, Philip Arthur. Imagining the past / [by] Philip Sauvain ; illustrated by David Bryant. — London [etc.] : Macmillan.
1 : Prehistoric Britain. — 1976. — 32p : ill, plan ; 25cm.
Index.
ISBN 0-333-15206-9 Sd : £0.45
(B77-01073)

2 : Roman Britain. — 1976. — 32p : ill, map, plan ; 25cm.
Index.
ISBN 0-333-15207-7 Sd : £0.45
(B77-01074)

3 : A castle. — 1976. — 32p : ill, plans ; 25cm.
Index.
ISBN 0-333-15208-5 Sd : £0.45
(B77-01075)

4 : An abbey. — 1976. — 32p : ill, facsim, plans ; 25cm.
Index.
ISBN 0-333-15209-3 Sd : £0.45
(B77-01076)

5 : A medieval town. — 1976. — 32p : ill ; 25cm.
Index.
ISBN 0-333-15210-7 Sd : £0.45
(B77-01077)

6 : A Tudor mansion. — 1976. — 32p : ill, plan ; 25cm.
Index.
ISBN 0-333-15211-5 Sd : £0.45
(B77-01078)

941 — Great Britain, to 1976. *Juvenile literature*
Grant, Neil, *b.1938*. Hamlyn children's history of Britain / [by] Neil Grant ; [illustrations by Colin Andrew et al.]. — London [etc.] : Hamlyn, 1977. — 321p : ill(some col), facsims(some col), col geneal tables, maps(chiefly col), ports(some col) ; 26cm.
Index.
ISBN 0-600-31398-0 : £3.95
(B77-31624)

941 — Great Britain, to 1978. *Juvenile literature*
Cochlin, René. Flashback / written and illustrated by R. Cochlin. — London : Hutchinson.
In 6 vols.
4 : From George III to the present day. — 1977. — 95p : ill, facsims, geneal table, maps, plans, ports ; 30cm.
ISBN 0-09-128001-x Sd : £1.25
(B77-14480)

941 — Ley systems. *Great Britain*
Bell, Harry, *b.1935*. Forgotten footsteps / [by] Harry Bell. — East Kilbride ([62 New Plymouth, Westwood, East Kilbride, Lanark]) : Ley-line Publications, 1977. — [24]p,fold plate : ill, maps ; 21cm.
Sd : £0.60
(B77-33534)

Screeton, Paul. Quicksilver heritage : the mystic leys : their legacy of ancient wisdom / [by] Paul Screeton. — London : Abacus, 1977. — 288p,[8]p of plates : ill, map ; 20cm.
Originally published: Wellingborough : Thorsons, 1974. — Bibl.: p.255-280. — Index.
ISBN 0-349-13142-2 Pbk : £1.95
(B77-08675)

941 — Parish churches. *Great Britain, to 1975. Secondary school texts*
Acland, Robin. Parish churches / [by] Robin Acland. — London : Edward Arnold, 1977. — 32p : ill, facsims, map, plans ; 25cm. — (Yesterday today)
ISBN 0-7131-0140-7 Sd : Unpriced : CIP rev.
(B77-09422)

941 — Piers. *Great Britain, to 1976*
Adamson, Simon H. Seaside piers / [by] Simon H. Adamson. — London : Batsford [for] the Victorian Society, 1977. — 116p : ill, map, plans ; 26cm.
Ill., plan on lining papers. — Index.
ISBN 0-7134-0242-3 : £3.95
(B77-23880)

941'.002'02 — Great Britain. Violent events, 1485-1976. *Chronologies*
Pennick, Nigel. Free England : being a chronology of uprisings, invasions, riots & disaffection in the British Isles (1485 to the present day) / compiled by Nigel Pennick, Rupert Pennick & John Nicholson. — [Revised ed.]. — [Cambridge] ([142 Pheasant Rise, Bar Hill, Cambridge CB3 8SD]) : [Nigel Pennick], [1976]. — [10]p ; 30cm.
Previous ed.: published as 'The primer of English violence'. Cambridge : Cokaygne Press, 1974.
ISBN 0-9505403-0-7 Sd : £0.20
(B77-03839)

941'.0022'2 — Great Britain, to 1975. *Illustrations*
Picture panorama of British history / prepared in consultation with John Shepherd. — London : Owlet Books, 1976. — 296p : chiefly ill, maps, ports ; 26cm.
ISBN 0-263-06247-3 : £4.95
(B77-16118)

941'.003 — Great Britain. Literary associations, to 1976. *Encyclopaedias*
Eagle, Dorothy. The Oxford literary guide to the British Isles / compiled and edited by Dorothy Eagle, Hilary Carnell. — Oxford : Clarendon Press, 1977. — xiii,415,[31]p : maps ; 21cm.
Bibl.: p.415. — Index.
ISBN 0-19-869123-8 : £3.95
Also classified at 820'.3
(B77-18475)

941'.004'91411 — Indians. Organisations. *Great Britain. Bharatiya Vidya Bhavan. UK Centre. Periodicals*
Bharatiya Vidya Bhavan. Bhavan's newsletter. — London (37 New Oxford St., W.C.1) : Bharatiya Vidya Bhavan, UK Centre.
Dec. 1976-. — [1976]-. — ill, ports ; 30cm.
Monthly. — 9p. in 1st issue.
Sd : Unpriced
(B77-11005)

941'.004'916 — Celtic culture. *Great Britain, to ca 1800. Conference proceedings*
Celtic Continuity *(Conference), Liverpool, 1976.* Studies in Celtic survival / edited by Lloyd Laing. — Oxford : British Archaeological Reports, 1977. — [5],123p : ill, maps ; 30cm. — (British archaeological reports ; 37 ISSN 0306-1205)
'With the exception of one paper (No.2) ... the papers here presented were all given at a Conference on the subject of "Celtic Continuity" held in Liverpool from the 20th to 22nd March, 1976' - Editor's Introduction. — Bibl.
ISBN 0-904531-65-1 Sd : £2.40
(B77-22270)

941'.004'916 — Celtic peoples. Celtic historiography. *Great Britain, to 1200*
Hughes, Kathleen. The early Celtic idea of history and the modern historian / [by] Kathleen Hughes. — Cambridge [etc.] : Cambridge University Press, 1977. — [1],24,[1] p ; 19cm. — (University of Cambridge. Inaugural lectures)
'... delivered in the University of Cambridge on 5 November 1976' - p.24.
ISBN 0-521-21675-3 Sd : £0.60
(B77-22992)

941'.00973'2 — Great Britain. Urban regions. Social life, 1837-1901
The **Victorian** city : images and realities / edited by H.J. Dyos and Michael Wolff. — London [etc.] : Routledge and Kegan Paul.
In 4 vols. — Originally published: in 2 vols. 1973.
Vol.1 : Past and present ; and, Numbers of people. — 1976 [i.e. 1977]. — xvi,224,xiv p,[50]p of plates : ill, facsims, maps ; 25cm.
Index.
ISBN 0-7100-8458-7 Pbk : £4.95
(B77-09423)

941'.00973'2 — Towns. *Great Britain. Illustrations. Juvenile literature*
Mills, Caroline. Henry discovers - the town / [by Caroline Mills]. — London (27 Chancery La., WC2A 1NF) : Foxwood Publishing Ltd, 1977. — [7]leaves,[2]p(1 fold) : of col ill ; 25x20cm. — (Turn-over picture books) (Foxcub books)
Leaves in 3 separated horizontal segments. — Notebook format.
ISBN 0-904897-46-x Sp : £1.25
(B77-29064)

941'.00973'4 — Countryside. *Great Britain. Illustrations. Juvenile literature*
Mills, Caroline. Henry discovers - the countryside / [by Caroline Mills]. — London (27 Chancery La., WC2A 1NF) : Foxwood Publishing Ltd, 1977. — [7]leaves,[2]p(1 fold) : of col ill ; 25x20cm. — (Turn-over picture books) (Foxcub books)
Leaves in 3 separated horizontal segments. — Notebook format.
ISBN 0-904897-47-8 Sp : £1.25
(B77-29065)

941'.00973'4 — Great Britain. Rural regions. *Periodicals*
Ruris. — Lincoln (Lincoln LN1 3DY) : Centre for the Study of Rural Society, Bishop Grosseteste College of Higher Education.
No.1- ; Summer 1977-. — [1977]-. — 30cm.
Three issues a year. — [3],28p. in 1st issue.
Sd : £1.50 yearly
ISSN 0140-0932
(B77-29828)

Vole. — London (20 Fitzroy Sq., W.1) : Wheatear Productions.
Monthly. — 64p. in 1st issue.
1- ; 1977-. — 1977-. — ill, facsims, maps, ports ; 27cm.
Sd : £0.60
ISSN 0140-4571
(B77-31625)

941'.00973'4 — Great Britain. Rural regions, ca 1920-1975
The **countryman's** Britain / edited by Crispin Gill. — Newton Abbot [etc.] : David and Charles, 1976. — 203p : ill, maps, ports ; 24cm.
Bibl.: p.197-199. — Index.
ISBN 0-7153-7284-x : £5.25
(B77-10058)

941'.00992 — Great Britain. Monarchs, 1042-1976. *Questions & answers. Juvenile literature*
Brandreth, Gyles. The royal quiz book / [by] Gyles Brandreth ; illustrated by Rowan Barnes Murphy. — London : Carousel Books, 1976. — 128p : ill ; 20cm. — (Carousel books)
With answers.
ISBN 0-552-54113-3 Pbk : £0.45
(B77-05134)

941'.00992 — Great Britain. Monarchs, 802-1975
Andrews, Allen. Kings & queens of England & Scotland / [by] Allen Andrews ; with an introduction by Dulcie M. Ashdown. — London [etc.] : Marshall Cavendish, 1976. — 184p : chiefly ill(some col), coats of arms(1 col), facsims, geneal table, map, ports(some col) ; 29cm.
Index.
ISBN 0-85685-136-1 : £3.95
(B77-11006)

941'.00992 — Great Britain. Monarchs. Local associations: London. Westminster (London Borough). Collegiate churches: Westminster Abbey
Bevan, Bryan. Royal Westminster Abbey / [by] Bryan Bevan. — London : Hale, 1976. — 192p, [12]p of plates : ill, ports ; 23cm.
Bibl. — Index.
ISBN 0-7091-5813-0 : £5.00
(B77-05135)

941'.00992 — Great Britain. Monarchs, to 1976
National Portrait Gallery. Royal faces : 900 years of British monarchy / National Portrait Gallery ; [text by Hugh Clayton ; picture selection and captions by Mary Pettman and Richard Ormond]. — London : H.M.S.O., 1977. — [1],56p : col geneal table, ports(some col) ; 28cm.
ISBN 0-11-290209-x Pbk : £1.95
(B77-12225)

941'.00992 — Great Britain. Monarchs, to 1977
Burke's guide to the British monarchy / [by] Mark Bence-Jones ... [et al.] ; edited by Hugh Montgomery-Massingberd. — London : Burke's Peerage : New English Library, 1977. — 143p : ill(chiefly col), coats of arms(some col), geneal tables, ports(some col) ; 30cm.
ISBN 0-85011-024-6 : £8.50
ISBN 0-85011-025-4 Pbk : £4.25
(B77-29066)

941'.00992 — Great Britain. Queens, to 1821
Alexander, Marc. The outrageous queens / [by] Marc Alexander. — London : Muller, 1977. — 200p,[32]p of plates : ill(some col), facsims, ports(some col) ; 21cm.
ISBN 0-584-97054-4 : £4.95
(B77-28299)

941'.00992 — Great Britain. Queens, to 1976
Lofts, Norah. Queens of Britain / [by] Norah Lofts. — London [etc.] : Hodder and Stoughton, 1977. — 192p,[8]p of plates : ill, facsim, ports(some col) ; 25cm.
ISBN 0-340-21587-9 : £5.95
(B77-20812)

941'.00992 — Great Britain. Royal families, 973-1976
Plumb, John Harold. Royal heritage : the story of Britain's royal builders and collectors / by J.H. Plumb. — London : British Broadcasting Corporation, 1977. — 360p : ill(some col), facsims, ports(some col) ; 30cm.
'Published in association with the television series written by Huw Wheldon and J.H. Plumb'. — Ill. on lining papers. — Index.
ISBN 0-563-17082-4 : £10.00
Also classified at 708'.9'41
(B77-19911)

941'.00992 — Great Britain. Royal families, to 1977. Local associations: Lancashire. Rossendale (District)
Elliott, Jon. Royalty and Rossendale : a survey of Rossendale connections with the Crown from the earliest times : including a catalogue of exhibits in the Royalty and Rossendale exhibition at the Rossendale Museum, June 4-July 10 1977 / by Jon Elliott. — Rossendale (Rawtenstall, Rossendale, Lancs. BB4 6QU) : The Museum, 1977. — [1],23p ; 16x22cm.
Sd : £0.25
(B77-29067)

941'.00992 — Museums. *East Sussex. Brighton. Royal Pavilion, Art Gallery and Museums, Brighton. Exhibits: Items associated with British royal children, 1199-1976. Catalogues*
Royal Pavilion, Art Gallery and Museums, Brighton. Royal children through the ages : [catalogue of a] jubilee exhibition, 5 July-25 Sept. / Royal Pavilion, Art Gallery and Museums, Brighton ... — [Brighton] ([Brighton, E. Sussex]) : [Royal Pavilion, Art Gallery and Museums], [1977]. — Portfolio : ill, facsim ; 23x32cm.
Sheet (1 side) and 4 booklets (31 leaves ; Sd).
£0.50
(B77-24616)

941.03 — Great Britain. Social life, 1272-1485. *Secondary school texts*
Jamieson, Jean Mary. Medieval Britain, 1272-1485 / [by] Jean M. Jamieson ; drawings by Philip Page. — London : Edward Arnold, 1977. — 48p : ill, facsims, maps, plan, ports ; 20x26cm.
Index.
ISBN 0-7131-0165-2 Sd : £1.25 : CIP rev.
(B77-22271)

941.05 — Great Britain, 1485-1603. *Secondary school texts*
Lane, Peter. Tudor England / [by] Peter Lane. — London : Batsford, 1977. — 96p : ill, coat of arms, facsim, maps, plans, ports ; 26cm. — (Visual sources series)
Index.
ISBN 0-7134-0035-8 : £2.95
(B77-27575)

941.05 — Great Britain, 1485-1688. *Transcripts of discussions*
The **Tudors** and Stuarts / [edited by William Lamont]. — London (85 Linden Gardens, W2 4EU) : Sussex Books, 1976. — 3-216p : ill, ports ; 21cm. — (Questions in history)
Bibl.: p.210-216.
ISBN 0-905272-04-8 : Unpriced
ISBN 0-905272-05-6 Pbk : £1.85
(B77-09424)

941.06 — Great Britain, 1603-1688. *Secondary school texts*
Lane, Peter. The Stuart age / [by] Peter Lane. — London : Batsford, 1977. — 96p : ill, coats of arms, facsims, maps, plans, ports ; 26cm. — (Visual sources series)
Index.
ISBN 0-7134-0037-4 : £2.95
(B77-27576)

941.06 — Great Britain. Social life, ca 1662-1778. *Study examples: Lloyd family. School texts*
Rowlands, Marie Bernadette. The Lloyds / [by] Marie Rowlands. — Sunbury-on-Thames [etc.] : Nelson, 1977. — 48,[1]p : ill, facsims, geneal tables, maps, ports ; 25cm. — (Family history patches)
Bibl.: p.48.
ISBN 0-17-426007-5 Sd : £0.70
(B77-19912)

941.06'092'2 — Great Britain. Statesmen, 1621-1718. *Biographies*
Chapman, Hester Wolferstan. Four fine gentlemen / [by] Hester Chapman. — London : Constable, 1977. — 301p,[4] leaves of plates : 4 ports ; 23cm.
Bibl.: p.289-291. — Index.
ISBN 0-09-461700-7 : £6.50
(B77-21611)

941.06'3'072 — Great Britain. Political events, 1640-1660. Historiography, to 1976
Richardson, Roger Charles. The debate on the English revolution / [by] R.C. Richardson. — London : Methuen, 1977. — xi,195p ; 23cm.
Bibl.: p.185-188. — Index.
ISBN 0-416-81750-5 : £6.75
ISBN 0-416-81760-2 Pbk : £2.95
(B77-23004)

941.06'6'0924 — Great Britain. Albemarle, George Monck, Duke of. *Biographies*
Ashley, Maurice. General Monck / [by] Maurice Ashley. — London : Cape, 1977. — viii,316p, plate : 2 maps, port ; 23cm.
Bibl.: p.255-258. — Index.
ISBN 0-224-01287-8 : £6.95 : CIP rev.
(B77-05778)

941.07 — Great Britain, 1800-1900. *Secondary school texts*
Nineteenth-century Britain / [editor John Robottom]. — London : Longman.
Workcards / [by] Tom Allan. — 1977. — 1v. ; 23cm. — (Making the modern world)
One card, 3 copies each of 5 cards ([12] sides) in plastic envelope.
ISBN 0-582-22086-6 : £0.95
(B77-19117)

941.07 — Great Britain, 1800-1900. *Transcripts of discussions*
Nineteenth century Britain / [edited by Andrew Hardman]. — London (85 Linden Gardens, W2 4EU) : Sussex Books, 1976. — 3-171p : ill ; 21cm. — (Questions in history)
Bibl.: p.166-171.
ISBN 0-905272-08-0 : Unpriced
ISBN 0-905272-09-9 Pbk : Unpriced
(B77-08679)

941.07 — Great Britain. Political events, 1784-1939. *Secondary school texts*
Miller, Stuart Tindale. British political history, 1784-1939 / [by] S.T. Miller. — Plymouth : Macdonald and Evans, 1977. — ix,228p ; 19cm.
Bibl.: p.211. — Index.
ISBN 0-7121-0256-6 Pbk : £2.25
(B77-32986)

941.07'076 — Great Britain, 1760-1914. *Exercises, worked examples. Secondary school texts*
Tucker, Elizabeth M M. Britain, 1760-1914 / [by] Elizabeth M.M. Tucker. — London : Edward Arnold, 1977. — vi,82p : ill, facsims, maps, plan, port ; 25cm. — (History stimulus questions)
ISBN 0-7131-0098-2 Sd : £1.50
(B77-21622)

941.07'092'2 — Great Britain. Prime ministers, to 1963. *Biographies*
Wilson, *Sir* Harold, *b.1916*. A Prime Minister on Prime Ministers / [by] Harold Wilson. — London : Weidenfeld and Nicolson : Joseph, 1977. — 334p : ill(some col), facsim, ports(some col) ; 26cm.
Ill. on lining papers. — Index.
ISBN 0-7181-1625-9 : £7.50
(B77-32319)

941.07'092'2 — Great Britain. Prime ministers, to 1974
The **Prime** Ministers / edited by Herbert Van Thal. — London : Allen and Unwin.
In 2 vols.
Vol.1 : Sir Robert Walpole to Sir Robert Peel / with an introduction by G.W. Jones. — 1974 [i.e. 1977?]. — 3-391p,24p of plates : ports ; 24cm.
Originally published: 1974. — Bibl.
ISBN 0-04-942152-2 Pbk : £3.50
(B77-26697)

Vol.2 : From Lord John Russell to Edward Heath / with an introduction by Robert Blake. — 1975 [i.e. 1977?]. — 3-419p,[23]p of plates : ports ; 24cm.
Originally published: 1975. — Bibl.
ISBN 0-04-942153-0 Pbk : £3.50
(B77-26698)

941.07'092'2 — Great Britain. Prime ministers. Wives, 1735-1941. *Biographies*
McLeod, Kirsty. The wives of Downing Street / [by] Kirsty McLeod. — London : Collins, 1976. — 223p,[8]p of plates : ports ; 23cm.
Bibl.: p.209-212. — Index.
ISBN 0-00-211953-6 : £4.95
(B77-08677)

941.07'092'4 — Great Britain. Trelawny, Edward John. *Biographies*
St Clair, William. Trelawny : the incurable romancer / [by] William St Clair. — London : J. Murray, 1977. — xii,235p,[20]p of plates : ill, facsim, ports ; 24cm.
Bibl.: p.201-205. — Index.
ISBN 0-7195-3424-0 : £7.50
(B77-29068)

941.07'2'08 — Great Britain. Jacobite Rebellion, 1745-1746. *Readings from contemporary sources. Secondary school texts*
Cameron, Alexander Durand. The Jacobites in the Forty-five / [by] A.D. Cameron. — Edinburgh : Oliver and Boyd, 1977. — 49p : ill, facsims, maps, plans, ports ; 19x25cm. — (Exploring history)
Bibl.: p.49.
ISBN 0-05-003012-4 Sd : £0.65
(B77-23883)

941.07'3 — Great Britain, 1811-1820
Low, Donald Alexander. That sunny dome : a portrait of Regency Britain / [by] Donald A. Low. — London [etc.] : Dent [etc.], 1977. — xv,208p,[16]p of plates : ill, ports ; 24cm.
Bibl.: p.202-203. — Index.
ISBN 0-460-12008-5 : £5.95 : CIP rev
(B77-15622)

941'.07'30924 — Great Britain. Charlotte Augusta, Princess. Death. Medical aspects
An **obstetric** tragedy : the case of Her Royal Highness the Princess Charlotte Augusta : some unpublished documents of 1817 / [compiled] by Franco Crainz. — London : Heinemann Medical, 1977. — vi,77p,[2]p of plates,[4]leaves of plates : facsims, ports ; 23cm.
Bibl.: p.48-61.
ISBN 0-433-06664-4 : £3.50
(B77-29069)

941.07'4'0924 — Great Britain. George IV, King of Great Britain. *Biographies*
Hibbert, Christopher. George IV / [by] Christopher Hibbert. — Harmondsworth [etc.] : Penguin, 1976. — 851p ; 19cm.
Originally published: in 2 vols as 'George IV, Prince of Wales, 1762-1811', Harlow : Longman, 1972 ; and 'George IV, Regent and King, 1811-1830', London : Allen Lane, 1973. — Bibl.: p.788-805. — Index.
ISBN 0-14-021966-8 Pbk : £3.50
(B77-03298)

941.07'4'0924 — Great Britain. Melbourne, William Lamb, Viscount. *Biographies*
Ziegler, Philip. Melbourne : a biography of William Lamb, 2nd Viscount Melbourne / [by] Philip Ziegler. — London : Collins, 1976. — 412p,[16]p of plates : ill, ports ; 24cm.
Index.
ISBN 0-00-216510-4 : £6.50
(B77-01922)

941.07'5'0924 — Great Britain. Political events, 1831-1840. *Diaries*
Holland, Henry Richard Vassall Fox, *Baron*. The Holland House diaries, 1831-1840 : the diary of Henry Richard Vassall Fox, third Lord Holland, with extracts from the diary of Dr John Allen / edited with introductory essay and notes by Abraham D. Kriegel. — London [etc.] : Routledge and Kegan Paul, 1977. — lxiv,513p ; 24cm.
Index.
ISBN 0-7100-8406-4 : £12.50
(B77-08678)

941.081 — Great Britain. Political events, ca 1830-1850
Donnachie, Ian Lowe. Britain and Ireland in the 1840s / prepared by Ian Donnachie, John Golby and Gillian Kay ; for the [Open University] Course Team. — Milton Keynes : Open University Press, 1976. — 83,[1]p : ill, facsims, maps, ports ; 30cm. — (Arts, a third level course : the revolutions of 1848 ; units 14-15) (A321 ; 14-15)
ISBN 0-335-05057-3 Pbk : £0.95
(B77-28300)

941.081 — Great Britain. Social life, 1837-1901
Wood, Christopher, *b.1941*. Victorian panorama : paintings of Victorian life / [by] Christopher Wood. — London : Faber, 1976. — 260p,[8] leaves of plates : ill(some col), ports ; 26cm.
Bibl.: p.248-251. — Index.
ISBN 0-571-10780-x : £12.50
Primary classification 756
(B77-01681)

941.081 — Great Britain. Social life, 1840-1935. *Correspondence*
Hughes family. Anglesey family letters, 1840-1935 / [Hughes family] ; edited by Elizabeth Grace Roberts. — Liverpool (25 [i.e. 22] Gressingham Rd, Liverpool L18 6JT) : The editor, 1976. — 126,14,xii p,[10]p of plates,[2]fold leaves of plates : ill, geneal tables, ports ; 23cm.
ISBN 0-9503153-1-1 : £3.00
Also classified at 973
(B77-01923)

941.081 — Great Britain. Social life, 1875. *Middle school texts*
Eddershaw, David. One hundred years ago : highways & byways / [by David Eddershaw, Mary Hodges, Martyn Heighton]. — Sunbury-on-Thames : Nelson, 1976. — 1v. : ill(chiefly col), music, plan ; 14x22cm.
Teacher's notes - 'Homes' / by David Eddershaw - 'Travel' / by David Eddershaw - 'Life on a farm' / by Mary Hodges - 'Shops and street traders' / by Martyn Heighton.
ISBN 0-17-422151-7 Sd : £1.50
(B77-14481)

941.081 — Royal weddings. *Great Britain, 1840-1973*
Argy, Josy. Britain's royal brides / [by] Josy Argy and Wendy Riches. — London : Sphere, 1977. — 100p,[32]p of plates : ill, facsim, ports ; 20cm.
Originally published: Newton Abbot : David and Charles, 1975. — Bibl.: p.100.
ISBN 0-7221-7340-7 Pbk : £1.50
(B77-20813)

941.081'022'2 — Great Britain. Social life, 1837-1901. *Illustrations. Juvenile literature*
Victorians / general editor Boswell Taylor ; consultant historian John West ; illustrator Leslie Marshall. — [Leicester] : Knight Books, 1977. — 32p : chiefly ill, facsims, ports ; 21cm. — (Picture teach yourself : project books)
Originally published: Leicester : Brockhampton Press, 1965.
ISBN 0-340-21753-7 Pbk : £0.50
(B77-32987)

941.081'05 — Great Britain, 1837-1901. *Periodicals*
1837 to 1901 : journal of the Loughborough Victorian Studies Group. — Loughborough : Loughborough University, Department of Economics.
No.1- ; Oct. 1976-. — 1976-. — 30cm.
Annual. — 45p. in 1st issue. — Bibl.
Pbk : Unpriced
ISSN 0309-3441
(B77-10676)

941.081'092'2 — Great Britain. Victoria, Queen of Great Britain. Interpersonal relationships with Albert, Prince Consort of Victoria, Queen of Great Britain
Richardson, Joanna. Victoria and Albert : a study of a marriage / [by] Joanna Richardson. — London : Dent, 1977. — 239p : ill, ports ; 25cm.
Bibl.: p.233. — Index.
ISBN 0-460-04301-3 : £5.95
(B77-18476)

941.081'092'2 — Great Britain. Victoria, Queen of Great Britain. Interpersonal relationships with Disraeli, Benjamin, Earl of Beaconsfield
Aronson, Theo. Victoria and Disraeli : the making of a romantic partnership / [by] Theo Aronson. — London : Cassell, 1977. — xii, 212p,[8]p of plates : ill, ports ; 23cm.
Bibl.: p.203-206. — Index.
ISBN 0-304-29789-5 : £5.50
(B77-19118)

941.081'092'2 — Great Britain. Victoria, Queen of Great Britain. Interpersonal relationships with Edward VII, King of Great Britain
Bloom, Ursula. Edward and Victoria / [by] Ursula Bloom. — London : Hale, 1977. — 173p,[12]p of plates : ports ; 23cm.
ISBN 0-7091-5909-9 : £4.50
(B77-15623)

941.081'092'2 — Royal families. *Great Britain, 1858-1865*
Maas, Jeremy. The Prince of Wales's wedding : the story of a picture / [by] Jeremy Maas. — London : Cameron and Tayleur ; Newton Abbot : Distributed by David and Charles, 1977. — 100p : ill, facsims, plan, ports(some col) ; 26cm.
Index.
ISBN 0-7153-7419-2 : £5.95
Primary classification 759.2
(B77-20475)

941.081'092'4 — Great Britain. Albert, Prince Consort of Victoria, Queen of Great Britain. *Biographies*
Bennett, Daphne. King without a crown : Albert, Prince Consort of England, 1819-1861 / [by] Daphne Bennett. — London : Heinemann, 1977. — xvii,430p,[16]p of plates : ill, geneal table, ports ; 24cm.
Bibl.: p.388-393. — Index.
ISBN 0-434-06115-8 : £7.50
(B77-26699)

941.081'092'4 — Great Britain. Churchill, Jennie. *Biographies*
Churchill, Peregrine. Jennie, Lady Randolph Churchill : a portrait with letters / [by] Peregrine Churchill and Julian Mitchell. — [London] : Fontana, 1976. — 288p,[8]p of plates : 2 geneal tables, ports ; 18cm.
Originally published: London : Collins, 1974. — Index.
ISBN 0-00-634418-6 Pbk : £0.95
(B77-13431)

941.081'092'4 — Great Britain. Digby, Jane. *Biographies*
Schmidt, Margaret Fox. Passion's child : the extraordinary life of Jane Digby / [by] Margaret Fox Schmidt. — London : Hamilton, 1977. — xvii,268p,16p of plates : ill, facsims, plan, ports ; 24cm.
Originally published: New York : Harper and Row, 1976. — Bibl.: p.259-262. — Index.
ISBN 0-241-89532-4 : £5.95
(B77-09425)

941.081'092'4 — Great Britain. Disraeli, Benjamin, Earl of Beaconsfield. *Biographies*
Davis, Richard Whitlock. Disraeli / [by] R.W. Davis. — London : Hutchinson, 1976. — [1], xiii,231p ; 23cm. — (The library of world biography)
Index.
ISBN 0-09-127690-x : £3.95
(B77-13978)

941.081'092'4 — Great Britain. Lincoln, Susan Clinton, Countess of, 1831-1889. *Biographies*
Surtees, Virginia. A Beckford inheritance : the Lady Lincoln scandal / [by] Virginia Surtees. — Salisbury (The Chantry, Wilton, Salisbury) : Michael Russell (Publishing) Ltd, 1977. — viii, 147p,[2]leaves of plates : 2 ports ; 24cm.
Index.
ISBN 0-85955-055-9 : £4.20
(B77-26029)

941.081'092'4 — Great Britain. Lloyd George, David Lloyd George, Earl, 1863-1914. *Biographies*
Cregier, Don M. Bounder from Wales : Lloyd George's career before the First World War / [by] Don M. Cregier. — Colombia ; London : University of Missouri Press ; [London] : [Distributed by American University Publishers], 1976. — ix,292p ; 25cm.
Bibl.: p.266-281. — Index.
ISBN 0-8262-0203-9 : £10.00
(B77-05779)

941.081'092'4 — Great Britain. Politics. Chamberlain, Joseph. *Biographies*
Judd, Denis. Radical Joe : a life of Joseph Chamberlain / [by] Denis Judd. — London : Hamilton, 1977. — xvi,310p,[8]p of plates : ill, ports ; 23cm.
Bibl.: p.285-290. — Index.
ISBN 0-241-89631-2 : £7.95
(B77-20814)

Powell, Enoch. Joseph Chamberlain / [by] J. Enoch Powell. — London : Thames and Hudson, 1977. — 160p : ill, facsims, ports ; 25cm.
Index.
ISBN 0-500-01185-0 : £4.95
(B77-32321)

941.081'092'4 — Great Britain. Politics. Macaulay, Thomas Babington, Baron Macaulay
Hamburger, Joseph. Macaulay and the Whig tradition / [by] Joseph Hamburger. — Chicago ; London : University of Chicago Press, 1976. — xiii,274p ; 21cm.
Bibl.: p.191-192. — Index.
ISBN 0-226-31472-3 : £13.15
(B77-06984)

941.081'092'4 — Great Britain. Victoria, Queen of Great Britain, 1855. *Diaries*
Victoria, *Queen of Great Britain.* Leaves from a journal / [by] Queen Victoria. — London [etc.] : White Lion Publishers, 1977. — 160p, leaf of plate,[8]p of plates : ill, ports ; 23cm.
Originally published: London : Deutsch, 1961. — Index.
ISBN 0-7274-0084-3 : £4.95
(B77-08680)

941.081'092'4 — Great Britain. Wellington, Arthur Wellesley, Duke of. *Correspondence, 1833-1846*
Wellington, Arthur Wellesley, *Duke of.* Wellington, political correspondence. — London : H.M.S.O. — (The Prime Ministers' papers)
1 : 1833-November 1834 / edited by John Brooke and Julia Gandy. — 1975 [i.e. 1976]. — v,776p,plate : port ; 26cm.
Index.
ISBN 0-11-440051-2 : £18.50
(B77-01924)

941'.081'0924 — Great Britain. Wyndham, George. Interpersonal relationships with Blunt, Wilfred Scawen
Egremont, Max. The cousins : the friendship, opinions and activities of Wilfrid Scawen Blunt and George Wyndham / [by] Max Egremont. — London : Collins, 1977. — 320p,[8]p of plates : ill, geneal table(on lining papers), ports ; 23cm.
Bibl.: p.305-309. — Index.
ISBN 0-00-216134-6 : £6.50
Primary classification 821'.8
(B77-07559)

941.082 — Great Britain, ca 1870-1968. *Secondary school texts*
Britain / [editor John Robottom]. — London : Longman. — (Making the modern world)
Workcards / [by] Tom Allan. — 1977. — 1v. ; 23cm.
One card, 3 copies each of 5 cards ([12] sides) in polythene bag.
ISBN 0-582-22080-7 : £0.95
(B77-19913)

941.082 — Great Britain. Political events, 1868-1976
Hardman, J K. Britain in the modern world / [by] J.K. Hardman. — [London] : Collins.
In 2 vols.
Book 1 : 1868-1918. — 1977. — 96p : ill, maps, ports ; 26cm.
Index.
ISBN 0-00-327218-4 Pbk : £1.25
(B77-32322)

941.082 — Great Britain. Political events, 1880-1939
James, Robert Rhodes. The British revolution : British politics, 1880-1939 / [by] Robert Rhodes James. — London : Hamilton.
In 2 vols.
Vol.2 : From Asquith to Chamberlain, 1914-1939. — 1977. — xii,363p,[16]p of plates : ill ; 24cm.
Bibl.: p.341-344. — Index.
ISBN 0-241-89460-3 : £8.50
(B77-18477)

941.082 — Great Britain. Political events, 1900-1951. Historical sources: Archives
Cook, Chris. Sources in British political history, 1900-1951 / compiled for the British Library of Political and Economic Science by Chris Cook with ... [others]. — London [etc.] : Macmillan.
Vol.3 : A guide to the private papers of Members of Parliament, A-K. — 1977. — xiv, 281p ; 25cm.
ISBN 0-333-15038-4 : £15.00
(B77-19914)

Vol.4 : A guide to the private papers of members of parliament, L-Z. — 1977. — xiv, 272p ; 24cm.
ISBN 0-333-19160-9 : £15.00
(B77-25305)

941.082 — Great Britain. Social life, 1874-1965. *Secondary school texts*
Fincham, Paul. At the time of Winston Churchill / [by] Paul Fincham. — London : Longman, 1977. — 64p : ill, facsims, map, ports ; 24cm. — (Focus on history)
Index.
ISBN 0-582-18257-3 Pbk : £0.85
(B77-32320)

941.082'022'2 — Great Britain. Social life, 1900-1971. *Illustrations. Juvenile literature*
Twentieth century Britain / general editor Boswell Taylor ; research and illustrations Roy M. Schofield. — Leicester : Knight Books, 1977. — [1],32p : of ill, 2 facsims, maps, ports ; 21cm. — (Picture teach yourself : project books)
Cover title: 20th century Britain. — Originally published: as 'Picture reference book of twentieth century Britain'. Leicester: Brockhampton Press, 1972.
ISBN 0-340-21432-5 Pbk : £0.50
(B77-06985)

941.082'092'2 — Great Britain. Prime ministers, 1902-
British Prime Ministers in the twentieth century / edited by John P. MacKintosh. — London : Weidenfeld and Nicolson.
In 2 vols.
Vol.1 : Balfour to Chamberlain. — 1977. — [6], 282p ; 23cm.
Index.
ISBN 0-297-77291-0 : £8.95
(B77-23006)

941.082'092'4 — Great Britain. Churchill, Sir Winston Spencer, b.1874. *Biographies*
Churchill, Randolph Spencer. Winston S. Churchill / by Randolph S. Churchill and Martin Gilbert. — London : Heinemann.
Vol.4 : 1917-1922. Companion documents / [edited] by Martin Gilbert. — 1977. — 3v. (xxiii,2165p) : maps ; 24cm.
Index.
ISBN 0-434-13013-3 : £36.00
(B77-29829)

Pelling, Henry. Winston Churchill / [by] Henry Pelling. — London : Pan Books, 1977. — 5-724p,[8]p of plates : ill, ports ; 20cm.
Originally published: London : Macmillan, 1974. — Bibl.: p.646-660. — Index.
ISBN 0-330-25092-2 Pbk : £1.95
(B77-21612)

941.082'092'4 — Great Britain. Churchill, Sir Winston Spencer, b.1874. *Personal observations. Correspondence*
Thompson, Reginald William. Churchill and Morton : the quest for insight in the correspondence of Major Sir Desmond Morton and the author / [by] R.W. Thompson. — London [etc.] : Hodder and Stoughton, 1976. — 223p ; 24cm.
Index.
ISBN 0-340-18127-3 : £5.25
(B77-12226)

941.082'092'4 — Great Britain. Churchill, Sir Winston Spencer, b.1874. Local associations: United States
Pilpel, Robert H. Churchill in America, 1895-1961 : an affectionate portrait / [by] Robert H. Pilpel. — London : New English Library, 1977. — xiii,318p,[8]p of plates : ill, facsims, ports ; 22cm.
Originally published: New York : Harcourt Brace Jovanovich, 1976. — Bibl.: p.305-309. — Index.
ISBN 0-450-03198-5 : £6.00
(B77-24617)

941.082'092'4 — Great Britain. Churchill, Sir Winston Spencer, b.1874. Works. *Texts*
Churchill, *Sir* **Winston Spencer,** *b.1874.* The collected essays of Sir Winston Churchill / general editor Michael Wolff. — Centenary limited ed. — [London] ([44 Museum St., WC1A 1LY]) : Library of Imperial History.
'The collection ... is issued [in full vellum] as a limited edition restricted to owners of the Collected Works ...' - half title page. — Also available in buckram for sale to members of the public.
Vol.1 : Churchill and war. — 1976. — xxviii, 492p ; 25cm.
In slip case.
ISBN 0-903988-42-9 : £180.00 the set
Buckram ed. : £72.00 the set
(B77-06986)

Vol.2 : Churchill and politics. — 1976. — xi, 477p ; 25cm.
In slip case.
ISBN 0-903988-43-7 : £180.00 the set
Buckram ed. : £72.00 the set
(B77-06987)

Vol.4 : Churchill at large. — 1976. — xi,511p ; 25cm.
In slip case.
ISBN 0-903988-45-3 : £180.00 the set
Buckram ed. : £72.00 the set
(B77-16119)

941.082'092'4 — Great Britain. Colville, John Rupert. *Autobiographies*
Colville, John Rupert. Footprints in time / [by] John Colville. — London : Collins, 1976. — 5-287p : ill, facsim, port ; 24cm.
Index.
ISBN 0-00-216248-2 : £4.95
(B77-02680)

941.082'092'4 — Great Britain. Mosley, Lady Diana. *Autobiographies*
Mosley, *Lady* Diana. A life of contrasts : the autobiography of Diana Mosley. — London : Hamilton, 1977. — vii,296p,[12]p of plates : ill, ports ; 23cm.
Index.
ISBN 0-241-89629-0 : £5.50
(B77-17212)

941.082'092'4 — Great Britain. O'Casey, Eileen. *Autobiographies*
O'Casey, Eileen. Eileen / [by] Eileen O'Casey ; edited with an introduction by J.C. Trewin. — London [etc.] : Macmillan, 1976. — 224p,[8]p of plates : ill, ports ; 23cm.
Index.
ISBN 0-333-13472-9 : £4.50
(B77-04489)

941.082'092'4 — Great Britain. Politics. Brockway, Fenner, Baron Brockway. *Autobiographies*
Brockway, Fenner, *Baron Brockway.* Towards tomorrow : the autobiography of Fenner Brockway. — London : Hart-Davis MacGibbon, 1977. — 280p,[16]p of plates : 1 ill, facsim, ports ; 25cm.
Index.
ISBN 0-246-10847-9 : £8.50
(B77-23007)

941.082'3'0222 — Great Britain. Social life, 1901-1910. *Illustrations*
Goodall, John Strickland. An Edwardian Christmas / by John S. Goodall. — London [etc.] : Macmillan, 1977. — [64]p : of col ill ; 14x19cm.
ISBN 0-333-22078-1 : £1.95
(B77-32323)

941.082'3'0924 — Great Britain. Politics. Burns, John, b.1858. *Biographies*
Brown, Kenneth Douglas. John Burns / [by] Kenneth D. Brown. — London : Royal Historical Society : [Distributed by] Swift Printers, 1977. — [6],217,[1]p ; 23cm. — (Royal Historical Society. Studies in history)
Bibl.: p.205-210. — Index.
ISBN 0-901050-34-2 : £5.85
(B77-23885)

941.083 — British civilization, 1900-1939. *Middle school texts*
Hobley, Leonard Frank. 1900-1939 / [by] L.F. Hobley ; illustrated by Leslie S. Haywood. — London : Evans Bros, 1976. — 48p : ill, facsims, maps, ports ; 25cm. — (Knowing British history ; 11)
Bibl.: p.48.
ISBN 0-237-29159-2 Sd : £0.80
(B77-03299)

941.083 — Great Britain. Social life, 1930-1940
Cutforth, René. Later than we thought : a portrait of the thirties / [by] René Cutforth. — Newton Abbot [etc.] : David and Charles, 1976. — 160p : ill, facsims, ports ; 22cm.
Bibl.: p.153. — Index.
ISBN 0-7153-7123-1 : £4.95
(B77-05136)

941.083'092'4 — Great Britain. Lloyd George, David Lloyd George, Earl, 1922-1945. *Biographies*
Campbell, John. Lloyd George : the goat in the wilderness, 1922-1931 / [by] John Campbell. — London : Cape, 1977. — xii,383p,[8]p of plates : ill, ports ; 23cm.
Bibl.: p.359-365. — Index.
ISBN 0-224-01296-7 : £10.00 : CIP rev.
(B77-11488)

941.083'092'4 — Great Britain. Macdonald, James Ramsay. *Biographies*
Marquand, David. Ramsay MacDonald / [by] David Marquand. — London : Cape, 1977. — xvi,903p,[40]p of plates : ill, facsim, ports ; 24cm.
Ill. on lining papers. — Bibl.: p.797-799. — Index.
ISBN 0-224-01295-9 : £12.50
(B77-08683)

941.083'092'4 — Great Britain. Murphy, Joe, to 1945. *Autobiographies*
Murphy, Joe. Look back with tears / by Joe Murphy. — Altrincham : Sherratt, 1976. — 163p ; 22cm.
ISBN 0-85427-048-5 : £2.95
(B77-16674)

941.083'092'4 — Great Britain. Politics. Hoare, Samuel John Gurney, Viscount Templewood. *Biographies*
Cross, John Arthur. Sir Samuel Hoare, a political biography / [by] J.A. Cross ; with a foreword by Lord Butler. — London : Cape, 1977. — xv, 414p,[8]p of plates : ill, ports ; 23cm.
Bibl.: p.356-357. — Index.
ISBN 0-224-01350-5 : £10.00 : CIP rev.
(B77-13433)

941.084 — American military forces. Social life. *Great Britain, 1942-1945*
Lancaster-Rennie, Jean. - And over here! / [by] Jean Lancaster-Rennie. — [Wymondham] ([Damgate, Wymondham, Norfolk NR18 0BD]) : [Geo. R. Reeve Ltd], [1976]. — [8], 96p : ill, ports ; 21cm.
Pbk : £1.25
(B77-28301)

941.084 — Great Britain. Political events, 1939-1945
Addison, Paul. The road to 1945 : British politics and the Second World War / [by] Paul Addison. — London [etc.] : Quartet Books, 1977. — 334p,[8]p of plates : ill, facsim, ports ; 20cm.
Originally published: London : Cape, 1975. — Bibl.: p.313-322. — Index.
ISBN 0-7043-3154-3 Pbk : £2.95
(B77-23008)

941.084 — Great Britain. Social life, 1939-1945
Longmate, Norman. How we lived then : a history of everyday life during the Second World War / [by] Norman Longmate. — London : Arrow Books, 1977. — xvi,568p,[32]p of plates : ill, facsims ; 24cm.
Originally published: London : Hutchinson, 1971. — Index. — Previous control number ISBN 0-09-908080-x.
Pbk : £3.95
ISBN 0-09-908080-x
(B77-29830)

Marwick, Arthur. The home front : the British and the Second World War / [by] Arthur Marwick ; photographic research by Harold Chapman. — London : Thames and Hudson, 1976. — 192p : ill, ports ; 25cm.
Bibl.: p.187-188. — Index.
ISBN 0-500-25053-7 : £6.00
(B77-01925)

941.084 — Great Britain. Social life, 1940-1950
Jenkins, Alan, *b.1914.* The forties / [by] Alan Jenkins. — London : Heinemann, 1977. — 232p : ill(some col), facsims, ports(1 col) ; 26cm.
Ill. on lining papers. — Index.
ISBN 0-434-37288-9 : £6.90
(B77-25306)

941.084'092'2 — Great Britain. George VI, King of Great Britain & Elizabeth, Queen, consort of George VI, King of Great Britain. *Biographies*
Donaldson, Frances. King George VI and Queen Elizabeth / [by] Frances Donaldson. — London : Weidenfeld and Nicolson, 1977. — 127p,[8]p of plates : ill(some col), ports(some col) ; 28cm.
Index.
ISBN 0-297-77351-8 : £4.95
(B77-24618)

941.084'092'4 — England. Social life, 1939-1940. *Childhood reminiscences*
Hannam, Charles. A boy in your situation / [by] Charles Hannam. — London : Deutsch, 1977. — 216p : geneal table ; 21cm.
ISBN 0-233-96862-8 : £3.25
Primary classification 943.086'092'4
(B77-17237)

941.084'092'4 — Great Britain. Elizabeth, Queen, consort of George VI, King of Great Britain. *Biographies*
Duff, David. Elizabeth of Glamis : the story of the Queen Mother / [by] David Duff. — Revised ed. — London : Magnum Books, 1977. — 416p,[16]p of plates : ill, ports ; 18cm.
Previous ed.: London : Muller, 1973. — Bibl.: p.413-416.
ISBN 0-417-02010-4 Pbk : £1.25
(B77-23886)

Liversidge, Douglas. The Queen Mother / [by] Douglas Liversidge. — London : A. Barker, 1977. — ix,173p : ill, coat of arms(on lining papers), geneal table, ports ; 26cm.
Bibl.: p.169. — Index.
ISBN 0-213-16655-0 : £4.50
(B77-30868)

941.084'092'4 — Great Britain. Mitford, Unity. *Biographies*
Pryce-Jones, David. Unity Mitford, a quest / [by] David Pryce-Jones. — London : Weidenfeld and Nicolson, 1976. — [11],276p, [16]p of plates : ill, ports ; 24cm.
Bibl.: p.266-267. — Index.
ISBN 0-297-77156-6 : £6.50
(B77-00533)

941.084'092'4 — Great Britain. Windsor, Edward, Duke of. *Biographies*
Donaldson, Frances. Edward VIII / [by] Frances Donaldson. — London : Omega, 1976. — xii, 448p,[8]p of plates : 1 ill, geneal table, ports ; 20cm.
Originally published: London : Weidenfeld and Nicolson, 1974. — Index.
ISBN 0-86007-735-7 Pbk : £1.50
(B77-08684)

941.085 — British civilisation, 1945-1976. *Middle school texts*
Hobley, Leonard Frank. Since 1945 / [by] L.F. Hobley ; illustrated by Leslie S. Haywood. — London : Evans Bros, 1977. — 48p : ill, maps, ports ; 25cm. — (Knowing British history ; 12)
Bibl.: p.48.
ISBN 0-237-29162-2 Sd : £0.80
(B77-25307)

941.085 — British culture. Compared with American culture, 1945-1975
Snowman, Daniel. Kissing cousins : an interpretation of British and American culture, 1945-1975 / [by] Daniel Snowman. — London : Temple Smith, 1977. — 342p ; 23cm. — ([Comparative history])
Index.
ISBN 0-85117-107-9 : £6.50
Also classified at 973.92
(B77-19915)

941.085 — Great Britain. Political events, 1945-1974
Bartlett, Christopher John. A history of postwar Britain, 1945-1974 / [by] C.J. Bartlett. — London : Longman, 1977. — viii,360p ; 22cm.
Bibl.: p.337-347. — Index.
ISBN 0-582-48319-0 : Unpriced
ISBN 0-582-48320-4 Pbk : £4.50
(B77-33536)

941.085'092'2 — Great Britain. Royal families, 1952-1977
Counihan, Daniel. Royal progress : Britain's changing monarchy / [by] Daniel Counihan. — London : Cassell, 1977. — xi,219p,[16]p of plates : ill, ports ; 24cm.
Bibl.: p.206-210. — Index.
ISBN 0-304-29793-3 : £5.95
(B77-23009)

Jubilee / [editor Douglas Keay]. — London : IPC Magazines, 1977. — 190p : ill(some col), facsims, geneal table, ports(some col) ; 28cm.
Cover title: Jubilee : a celebration of the Queen's Silver Jubilee, 1952-1977.
ISBN 0-85037-364-6 Pbk : £1.60
(B77-13439)

Montague-Smith, Patrick Wykeham. The 'Country life' book of the royal silver jubilee / [by] Patrick Montague-Smith. — [London etc.] : [Hamlyn for] Country Life Books, [1976]. — 176p : ill(some col), geneal table, ports(some col) ; 31cm.
ISBN 0-600-38200-1 : £4.95
(B77-22272)

941.085'092'2 — Great Britain. Royal families, 1971-1975. *Illustrations*
Lemoine, Serge. The Royal Family at home and abroad / photography and text by Serge Lemoine ; edited by David Gibbon ... — New Malden (80 Coombe Rd, New Malden, Surrey KT3 4QZ) : Colour Library International Ltd, 1976. — 144p : chiefly of ports(mainly col) ; 28cm.
ISBN 0-904681-14-9 : £5.95
(B77-07735)

941.085'0924 — Great Britain. Anne, Princess. *Biographies*
Cathcart, Helen. Anne and the Princesses Royal / [by] Helen Cathcart. — London : Star Books, 1975. — viii,208p,[8]p of plates : ports ; 19cm.
Originally published: London : W.H. Allen, 1973. — Bibl.: p.207-208.
ISBN 0-352-30048-5 Pbk : £0.75
Primary classification 929.7'2
(B77-19107)

941.085'092'4 — Great Britain. Charles, Prince of Wales. *Biographies*
Fisher, Graham. Charles : the man and the prince / [by] Graham & Heather Fisher. — London : Hale, 1977. — 191p,[16]p of plates : ill, ports ; 23cm.
Index.
ISBN 0-7091-6095-x : £4.95
(B77-21613)

941.085'092'4 — Great Britain. Charles, Prince of Wales. Humour
Regan, Simon. Charles, the clown prince / [by] Simon Regan. — London : Everest, 1977. — 192p,[8]p of plates : ill(chiefly col), facsims, ports ; 25cm.
ISBN 0-905018-50-8 : £5.95
(B77-28302)

941.085'092'4 — Great Britain. Elizabeth II, Queen of Great Britain. *Biographies*
Cathcart, Helen. The Queen in her circle / [by] Helen Cathcart. — London : W.H. Allen, 1977. — x,211p,[16]p of plates : ports ; 23cm.
Index.
ISBN 0-491-02311-1 : £4.95
(B77-29070)

Edgar, Donald. Happy and glorious : the Silver Jubilee 1977 / [by] Donald Edgar. — London : Barker, 1977. — [10],95p,[48]p of plates : ill, facsims, ports ; 26cm.
Index.
ISBN 0-213-16629-1 : £4.50
(B77-12794)

Lacey, Robert. Majesty : Elizabeth II and the House of Windsor / [by] Robert Lacey. — London : Hutchinson, 1977. — 382p,[32]p of plates : ill, facsims, geneal table(on lining papers), map, ports ; 24cm.
Bibl.: p.343-347. — Index.
ISBN 0-09-128770-7 : £5.45
(B77-13434)

Lacey, Robert. Majesty : Elizabeth II and the House of Windsor / [by] Robert Lacey. — Large print ed. — Leicester : Ulverscroft, 1977. — [7],606p ; 23cm. — (Ulverscroft large print series : [non-fiction])
Originally published: London : Hutchinson, 1977.
ISBN 0-7089-0061-5 : £2.95
(B77-32324)

Seymour, Gerald. The glory boys / [by] Gerald Seymour. Majesty : Elizabeth II and the House of Windsor / [by] Robert Lacey. Ordinary people / [by] Judith Guest. A bag of marbles / [by] Joseph Joffo. — Collector's library ed. — London : Reader's Digest Association [etc.], 1977. — 512p : col ill, ports(some col) ; 21cm. — ('Reader's digest' condensed books)
ISBN 0-340-21949-1 : £2.95
Primary classification 823'.9'1F
(B77-12702)

941.085'092'4 — Great Britain. Elizabeth II, Queen of Great Britain. *Biographies. Illustrations*
Queen Elizabeth II : the Silver Jubilee book 1952-1977 / [compiled by] Michèle Brown. — Newton Abbot [etc.] : David and Charles, 1976. — 104p : chiefly ill(some col), ports ; 26cm.
ISBN 0-7153-7270-x : £3.95
(B77-06988)

941.085'092'4 — Great Britain. Elizabeth II, Queen of Great Britain. *Readings*
The **Queen**. — Harmondsworth [etc.] : Penguin, 1977. — 186p,[32]p of plates : ill, ports ; 19cm. — (A Penguin special)
ISBN 0-14-004490-6 Pbk : £0.75
(B77-21614)

The **Queen**. — London : Allen Lane, 1977. — 186p,[32]p of plates : ill, ports ; 23cm.
ISBN 0-7139-1060-7 : £3.95
(B77-21615)

941.085'092'4 — Great Britain. Elizabeth II, Queen of Great Britain. Coronation. *Juvenile literature*
Rice, Jo. The day the Queen was crowned / [by] Jo Rice ; illustrated by David Knight. — Tadworth : World's Work, 1977. — 64p : ill ; 22cm.
ISBN 0-437-71553-1 Pbk : £1.00
(B77-32325)

941.085'092'4 — Great Britain. Gloucester, Prince William, of. *Biographies*
William of Gloucester : pioneer prince / edited by Giles St Aubyn. — London : Muller, 1977. — 190,[1]p,plate : ill, coat of arms, facsims, geneal table, map, ports ; 26cm.
ISBN 0-584-10243-7 : £7.95
(B77-13435)

941.085'092'4 — Great Britain. Margaret, Princess. *Biographies*
Frischauer, Willi. Margaret : princess without a cause / [by] Willi Frischauer. — London : Joseph, 1977. — 220p,[8]p of plates : ports ; 23cm.
Index.
ISBN 0-7181-1611-9 : £5.25
(B77-21616)

941.085'092'4 — Great Britain. Philip, Prince, consort of Elizabeth II, Queen of Great Britain. *Biographies*
Liversidge, Douglas. Prince Philip : first gentleman of the realm / [by] Douglas Liversidge. — St Albans [etc.] : Panther, 1977. — 192p,[16]p of plates : ill, geneal tables, ports ; 20cm.
Originally published: London : Barker, 1976. — Bibl.: p.184. — Index.
ISBN 0-586-04767-0 Pbk : £1.00
(B77-28303)

941.085'092'4 — Great Britain. Politics. Powell, Enoch, 1950-1977
Berkeley, Humphry. The odyssey of Enoch : a political memoir / [by] Humphry Berkeley. — London : Hamilton, 1977. — [11],146p,[4]p of plates : ports ; 23cm.
Index.
ISBN 0-241-89623-1 : £4.95
(B77-23887)

941.085'092'4 — Great Britain. Politics. Smith, Cyril, b.1928. *Autobiographies*
Smith, Cyril, *b.1928.* Big Cyril / [by] Cyril Smith. — London : W.H. Allen, 1977. — [9], 245p,[16]p of plates : ill, ports ; 23cm.
Index.
ISBN 0-491-02261-1 : £5.50
(B77-27577)

941.085'092'4 — Great Britain. Politics. Stutchbury, Oliver Piers, 1950-1976. *Autobiographies*
Stutchbury, Oliver Piers. Too much government? : a political Aeneid / [by] Oliver Stutchbury. — Ipswich : Boydell Press, 1977. — 128p ; 23cm.
ISBN 0-85115-081-0 : £3.50
(B77-23010)

941.085'5'0924 — Great Britain. Morrison, Edith, Baroness Morrison, 1955-1965. *Autobiographies*
Morrison, Edith, *Baroness Morrison.* Memories of a marriage / [by] Lady Morrison of Lambeth. — London : Muller, 1977. — 142p, [24]p of plates : ports ; 24cm.
ISBN 0-584-10337-9 : £4.95 : CIP rev.
(B77-08682)

941.085'6 — Great Britain. Social life, 1960-1970
Levin, Bernard. The pendulum years : Britain and the sixties / [by] Bernard Levin. — London [etc.] : Pan Books, 1977. — 447p ; 18cm.
Originally published: London : Cape, 1970.
Pbk : £1.00
ISBN 0-330-23391-2
(B77-29071)

941.085'6'0924 — Great Britain. Political events, 1964-1970. *Diaries*
Crossman, Richard Howard Stafford. The diaries of a Cabinet Minister / [by] Richard Crossman. — London : Hamilton : Cape.
Index.
Vol.3 : Secretary of State for Social Services, 1968-70. — 1977. — 1039p,[12]p of plates : 1 ill, ports ; 24cm.
ISBN 0-241-89482-4 : £12.50 : CIP rev.
ISBN 0-224-01492-7 (Cape) : £12.50
(B77-22273)

941.085'7 — British civilization. *For foreign students*
Musman, Richard. Britain today / [by] Richard Musman. — 2nd ed. — London : Longman, 1977. — 238p : ill, charts, facsims, maps, ports ; 21cm. — (Longman background books)
Previous ed.: 1974. — Bibl.
ISBN 0-582-55261-3 Pbk : £2.00
(B77-17833)

941.085'7 — British civilization. *Forecasts*
Laidlow, Wilfred. A fireside chat : political, religious, prophetic / by Wilfred Laidlow. — Carlisle (26 Lonsdale St., Carlisle) : Charles Thurnam and Sons Ltd, 1977. — [23]p ; 19cm.
Sd : Unpriced
(B77-23888)

941.085'7'0222 — Great Britain. Elizabeth II, Queen of Great Britain. Silver jubilee celebrations, 1977. *Illustrations*
The **'Sunday** times' book of Jubilee year / edited by Hunter Davies. — London : Joseph, 1977. — 160p : ill(chiefly col), geneal table, chiefly ports(chiefly col) ; 30cm.
ISBN 0-7181-1672-0 : £5.50
(B77-33537)

941.085'7'05 — Great Britain. *Periodicals. For tourists*
Hello Britain : news for the independent traveller. — London : British Tourist Authority.
16p. in 1st issue. — English and French text.
No.1- ; Summer 1977-. — [1977]-. — ill, ports ; 38cm.
Bibl.
Sd : Unpriced
ISBN 0-85630-474-3
ISSN 0309-8109
(B77-16675)

941.085'7'0922 — Great Britain. Anne, Princess & Phillips, Mark. *Illustrations*
Djukanovic, Srdja. Anne & Mark / photographs by Srdja Djukanovic ; text by Judith Campbell. — London : Sidgwick and Jackson, 1976. — 144p : chiefly ill(some col), ports(some col) ; 26cm.
Index.
ISBN 0-283-98330-2 : £5.50
(B77-01926)

941.085'7'0924 — Great Britain. Nicholson, Vivian. *Autobiographies*
Nicholson, Vivian. Spend, spend, spend / [by] Vivian Nicholson and Stephen Smith. — London : Cape, 1977. — 215p,[16]p of plates : ill, ports ; 23cm.
ISBN 0-224-01339-4 : £3.95
(B77-08685)

941.1 — HISTORY. SCOTLAND
941.1 — Scotland. Battles, 1297-1746
Kinross, John. Discovering battlefields of Scotland / [by] John Kinross. — Aylesbury : Shire Publications, 1976. — 48p : ill, plans ; 18cm. — (Discovering series ; no.174)
Index.
ISBN 0-85263-221-5 Pbk : £0.50
(B77-11489)

941.1 — Scotland, to 1603
Dickinson, William Croft. Scotland from the earliest times to 1603 / [by] W. Croft Dickinson. — 3rd ed. / revised and edited by Archibald A.M. Duncan. — Oxford : Clarendon Press, 1977. — xi,442p : geneal tables, maps ; 22cm.
Previous ed.: London : Nelson, 1965. — Bibl.: p.403-413. — Index.
ISBN 0-19-822453-2 : £9.75 : CIP rev.
ISBN 0-19-822465-6 Pbk : £4.95
(B77-09426)

941.1 — Scotland, to 1976
Glover, Janet Reaveley. The story of Scotland / by Janet R. Glover. — New and revised ed. — London : Faber, 1977. — 394p : maps ; 21cm.
Previous ed.: 1960. — Bibl.: p.373-382. — Index.
ISBN 0-571-04931-1 : £6.25 : CIP rev.
ISBN 0-571-04935-4 Pbk : £3.75
(B77-07736)

941.1 — Scotland, to 1976. *Fill-in books. Juvenile literature*
Scotland for children : lots of fun and games for you to enjoy. — Glasgow : John Horn Ltd [for] the Scottish Tourist Board, [1977]. — [1],48p, [2]leaves of plates : ill(some col), maps(chiefly col) ports ; 30cm.
Includes press-out model. — Leaves perforated at inside edge. — With answers.
Sd : Unpriced
(B77-17834)

941.1'008 — Scotland, to 1976. *Readings*
Andrew Cruickshank's Scottish bedside book. — London [etc.] : Johnston and Bacon, 1977. — 244p : ill, map, ports ; 20cm.
Bibl.: p.242-244.
ISBN 0-7179-4224-4 : £4.50
(B77-30869)

941.102 — Scotland, 1200-1400. *Secondary school texts*
Donnachie, Ian Lowe. The wars of independence and the Scottish nation / [by] Ian Donnachie and Alasdair Hogg. — Edinburgh : Holmes-McDougall, 1976. — 48p : ill, facsims, geneal table, maps, plan, ports ; 25cm. — (Scottish search series)
Bibl.: p.48.
ISBN 0-7157-1474-0 Sd : £1.05
(B77-11490)

941.102'092'4 — Scotland. Robert I, King of Scots. *Biographies*
Barrow, Geoffrey Wallis Steuart. Robert Bruce and the community of the realm of Scotland / [by] G.W.S. Barrow. — 2nd ed. — Edinburgh : Edinburgh University Press, 1976. — xx,502p, [1],15p of plates : ill, facsims, geneal tables, maps ; 18cm.
Previous ed.: London : Eyre and Spottiswoode, 1965. — Index.
ISBN 0-85224-307-3 Pbk : £2.00
(B77-05137)

941.104'092'4 — Scotland. Mary, Queen, consort of James V, King of Scotland. *Biographies*
Marshall, Rosalind Kay. Mary of Guise / [by] Rosalind K. Marshall. — London : Collins, 1977. — 288p,8p of plates : ill, facsim, geneal tables, map, ports ; 24cm.
Index.
ISBN 0-00-216508-2 : £6.00
(B77-19119)

941.105'092'4 — Scotland. Mary, Queen of Scots. *Biographies. Secondary school texts*
Bold, Alan. Mary, Queen of Scots / [by] Alan Bold. — Hove : Wayland, 1977. — 96p : ill, facsim, ports ; 22cm. — (Wayland kings and queens)
Bibl.: p.93-94. — Index.
ISBN 0-85340-419-4 : £3.50
(B77-30870)

941.106'2'0924 — Scotland. Montrose, James Graham, Marquis of. *Biographies*
Cowan, Edward J. Montrose, for covenant and king / [by] Edward J. Cowan. — London : Weidenfeld and Nicolson, 1977. — ix,326p : map ; 23cm.
Index.
ISBN 0-297-77209-0 : £8.50
(B77-20816)

Hastings, Max. Montrose : the king's champion / by Max Hastings. — London : Gollancz, 1977. — 384p,[4]p of plates : ill(on lining papers), maps, ports ; 23cm.
Bibl.: p.367-369. — Index.
ISBN 0-575-02226-4 : £7.50
(B77-10059)

941.107 — Scotland. Intellectual life, ca 1750-ca 1820
Chitnis, Anand C. The Scottish Enlightenment : a social history / [by] Anand C. Chitnis. — London : Croom Helm [etc.], 1976. — [7], 279p ; 23cm.
Bibl.: p.261-272. — Index.
ISBN 0-85664-349-1 : £8.50
(B77-08146)

941.107'3 — Scotland, 1791-1799. *Early works. Facsimiles*
The **statistical** account of Scotland, 1791-1799 / edited by Sir John Sinclair. — [New ed.] ; [regrouped according to county and arranged in alphabetical order under the general editorship of Donald J. Withrington and Ian R. Grant]. — Wakefield : EP Publishing.
In 20 vols. — Facsimile reprints. — Originally published: Edinburgh : W. Creech, 1791-99.
Vol.11 : South and East Perthshire, Kinross-shire / with a new introduction by Bruce Lenman. — 1976. — xli,685p,2 leaves of plates(1 fold) : ill, 2 maps ; 23cm.
Index.
ISBN 0-7158-1011-1 : £17.50(£300.00 for set of 20 vols)
(B77-06384)

Vol.12 : North and west Perthshire / with a new introduction by Bruce Lenman. — 1977. — 814,xliv p,[2]leaves of plates(1 fold) : map ; 23cm.
Index.
ISBN 0-7158-1012-x : £19.00(£300.00 for set of 20 vols) : CIP rev.
(B77-19120)

Vol.13 : Angus / with a new introduction by Bruce Lenman. — 1976. — xliii,675p,plate : 2 maps ; 23cm.
Index.
ISBN 0-7158-1013-8 : £17.50(£300.00 for set of 20 vols)
(B77-06385)

941.1082'092'4 — Scotland. Fraser, Amy Stewart. *Autobiographies*
Fraser, Amy Stewart. In memory long / [by] Amy Stewart Fraser. — London [etc.] : Routledge and Kegan Paul, 1977. — xi,305p : ill, maps(on lining papers) ; 23cm.
Bibl.: p.299-300. — Index.
ISBN 0-7100-8586-9 : £5.50 : CIP rev.
(B77-08147)

941.1082'092'4 — Scotland. MacVicar, Angus. *Autobiographies*
MacVicar, Angus. Heather in my ears : more confessions of a minister's son / [by] Angus MacVicar. — [London] : Fontana, 1977. — 191p,[4]p of plates : ill, ports ; 18cm.
Originally published: London : Hutchinson, 1974. — Index.
ISBN 0-00-634499-2 Pbk : £0.80
(B77-20817)

MacVicar, Angus. Rocks in my scotch : still more confessions of a minister's son / [by] Angus MacVicar. — London : Hutchinson, 1977. — [9],182p,[8]p of plates : ill, map(on lining paper), ports ; 23cm.
Index.
ISBN 0-09-128380-9 : £3.95
(B77-10677)

941.1'085'50922 — Scotland. Social life, 1950-1960. *Childhood reminiscences. Collections*
Jock Tamson's bairns : essays on a Scots childhood / edited by Trevor Royle. — London : Hamilton, 1977. — x,150p ; 23cm.
ISBN 0-241-89638-x : £5.50
(B77-27578)

941.1085'7 — Scotland. *Secondary school texts*
Carson, James Rawson. Scotland / by James R. Carson. — London : Harrap, 1977. — 48p : ill, maps, ports ; 19x22cm. — (The regions of Britain)
ISBN 0-245-53078-9 Sd : £0.95
(B77-33538)

941.11'00973'4 — Villages. *Scotland. Highlands & Islands, to 1975*
Grant, James Shaw. Highland villages / [by] James Shaw Grant. — London : Hale, 1977. — 192p,[32]p of plates : ill, 3 maps, port ; 23cm. — (The villages series)
Index.
ISBN 0-7091-5886-6 : £4.20
(B77-13979)

941.11'081'0222 — Scotland. Highlands & Islands. Social life, ca 1865-ca 1910. *Illustrations*
Victorian and Edwardian Highlands from old photographs / [introduction and commentaries by] Francis Thompson. — London : Batsford, 1976. — [120]p : chiefly ill, ports ; 26cm.
ISBN 0-7134-3224-1 : £2.95
(B77-01079)

941.13'2 — Scotland. Orkney. Sanday. Social life, 1904-1914. *Childhood reminiscences*
Cutt, William Towrie. Faraway world : an Orkney boyhood / [by] W. Towrie Cutt ; wood engravings by Joseph Sloan. — London : Deutsch, 1977. — 128p : ill, music ; 21cm.
ISBN 0-233-96866-0 : £2.95
(B77-22274)

941.14 — Scotland. Western Isles, to 1902. *Early works*
Mackenzie, William Cook. History of the Outer Hebrides : (Lewis, Harris, North and South Uist, Benbecula and Barra) / by W.C. Mackenzie. — Edinburgh : Thin, 1974. — [4], xiii-xl,623,[1],[2]leaves of plates,[2]p of plates : 4 ill ; 24cm.
Facsimile reprint of: 1903 ed. Paisley : Alexander Gardner, 1903. — Index.
ISBN 0-901824-31-3 : £9.45
(B77-00534)

941.14'085'60924 — Scotland. Hebrides. Social life, 1959-1964. *Personal observations*
Beckwith, Lillian. The Lillian Beckwith omnibus / decorations by Douglas Hall. — Omnibus ed. — London [etc.] : Hutchinson, 1976. — [5],207; 5-191; 5-203p : ill ; 23cm.
Contents: The hills is lonely. Originally published: 1959 - The sea for breakfast. Originally published: 1961 - The loud halo. Originally published: 1964.
ISBN 0-09-128320-5 : £4.95
(B77-01080)

Beckwith, Lillian. A rope - in case / [by] Lillian Beckwith ; decorations by Douglas Hall. — London : Arrow Books, 1977. — 192p : ill ; 18cm.
Originally published: London : Hutchinson, 1968.
ISBN 0-09-906640-8 : £0.60
(B77-18478)

941.14'085'70924 — Scotland. Hebrides. Social life. *Personal observations*
Beckwith, Lillian. Beautiful just! / [by] Lillian Beckwith ; decorations by Douglas Hall. — London : Arrow Books, 1977. — 173p : ill ; 18cm.
Originally published: London : Hutchinson, 1975.
ISBN 0-09-914110-8 Pbk : £0.60
(B77-17214)

Beckwith, Lillian. The hills is lonely / [by] Lillian Beckwith. — London : Arrow Books, 1977. — 256p : ill ; 18cm.
Originally published: London : Hutchinson, 1959.
ISBN 0-09-906620-3 Pbk : £0.65
(B77-16676)

Beckwith, Lillian. The loud halo / [by] Lillian Beckwith ; decorations by Douglas Hall. — London : Arrow Books, 1977. — 192p : ill ; 18cm.
Originally published: London : Hutchinson, 1964.
ISBN 0-09-906630-0 Pbk : £0.60
(B77-16677)

Beckwith, Lillian. The sea for breakfast / [by] Lillian Beckwith ; illustrated by Douglas Hall. — London : Arrow Books, 1977. — 191p : ill ; 18cm.
Originally published: London : Hutchinson, 1961.
ISBN 0-09-906650-5 Pbk : £0.60
(B77-17215)

941.15 — Scotland. Highlands. Social life, to ca 1815. *Early works*
Stewart, David, *b.1772.* Sketches of the character, manners and present state of the Highlanders of Scotland : with details of the military service of the Highland regiments / by David Stewart. — Edinburgh : Donald, 1977. — 2v.(xv,iv,595p, fold plate;viii,455,ci,[2]p(2 fold)) : col map ; 23cm. — ([Scottish reprint library ; vol.6])
Spine title: Sketches of the Highlanders of Scotland. — Facsimile reprint of: 2nd ed. Edinburgh : Constable, 1822. — Index.
ISBN 0-85976-023-5 : £35.00
(B77-29831)

941.17'2 — Country houses. *Scotland. Highland Region. Gairloch. Inverewe House. Gardens, to 1976. French texts*
National Trust for Scotland. Inverewe / [National Trust for Scotland]. — [Edinburgh] : The Trust, [1977]. — [5],p ; 21cm.
French text.
Sd : Unpriced
(B77-27579)

941.17'2 — Country houses. *Scotland. Highland Region. Gairloch. Inverewe House. Gardens, to 1976. German texts*
National Trust for Scotland. Inverewe / [National Trust for Scotland]. — [Edinburgh] : The Trust, [1977]. — [5]p ; 21cm.
German text.
Sd : Unpriced
(B77-27192)

941.17'2 — Scotland. Highland Region. Ross and Cromarty (District). Clachan. Social life, 1946-1947. *Personal observations*
Armstrong, Sybil. Clachan days / [by] Sybil Armstrong ; illustrated by the author. — London : Hutchinson, 1977. — 143p : ill ; 23cm.
ISBN 0-09-128850-9 : £3.45
(B77-23011)

941.18'2 — Scotland. Highland Region. Skye, to 1975
Gant, Frank. The Isle of Skye / text by Frank Gant. — Newport, Isle of Wight [etc.] : Dixon, 1976. — [32]p : col ill, col map ; 21cm.
ISBN 0-900336-38-2 Sd : £0.39
(B77-10060)

941.18'5 — Scotland. Highland Region. Small Isles, to 1976
Banks, Noel. Six Inner Hebrides : Eigg, Rum, Canna, Muck, Coll, Tiree / [by] Noel Banks. — Newton Abbot [etc.] : David and Charles, 1977. — 208p : ill, maps, ports ; 23cm. — (The islands series)
Bibl.: p.193-201. — Index.
ISBN 0-7153-7368-4 : £4.95
Also classified at 941.4'23
(B77-21617)

941.2'35'081 — Scotland. Grampian Region. Aberdeen. Social life, 1875-1910
Walkin' the mat : past impressions of Aberdeen / [compiled by Andrew Cluer]. — Aberdeen (P.O. Box 1, Aberdeen AB9 8PE) : Lantern Books, 1976. — [164]p : chiefly ill, facsims, music, ports ; 21x25cm.
Cover title.
ISBN 0-9502853-1-5 Pbk : £4.99
(B77-16120)

941.2'4 — Castles. *Scotland. Grampian Region. Crathes. Crathes Castle, to 1976. French texts*
National Trust for Scotland. Crathes / [National Trust for Scotland]. — [Edinburgh] : The Trust, [1977]. — [6]p ; 21cm.
Sd : Unpriced
(B77-27580)

941.2'8 — Scotland. Tayside Region. Blairgowrie, to 1975
Old Blairgowrie : tours, history, memories, tales. — [Blairgowrie] ([Leslie St., Blairgowrie, Perthshire]) : [Blairgowrie Branch Library], 1976. — [1],64p,[8]p of plates : ill, maps ; 21cm.
Bibl.: p.1.
ISBN 0-905452-01-1 Sd : £0.70
(B77-01927)

941.2'92 — Town houses. *Scotland. Fife Region. St Andrews. Queen Mary's House, to 1977*
Clark, Aylwin. 'Queen Mary's House' and those who lived in it / [by Aylwin Clark]. — St Andrews ([c/o The author, 18 Queen's Gardens, St Andrews, Fife KY16 9TA]) : The Council of St Leonards School, 1977. — 32p, ivp of plates : ill, plans, port ; 21cm.
ISBN 0-9505782-0-7 Sd : Unpriced
(B77-29072)

941.2'98 — Scotland. Fife Region. Culross, to 1976. *French texts*
National Trust for Scotland. Culross / [National Trust for Scotland]. — [Edinburgh] : The Trust, [1977]. — [6]p ; 21cm.
Sd : Unpriced
(B77-26700)

941.3'1 — Scotland. Forth River region. *History. Periodicals*
The Forth naturalist & historian. — Stirling ([c/o D.M. Dickie, Room 239, Viewforth, Stirling]) : Central Regional Council.
Vol.1- ; 1976-. — 1976-. — ill, maps ; 21cm.
Annual. — 173p. in 1976 issue. — Bibl.
Pbk : £1.00
ISSN 0309-7560
Primary classification 500.9'413'1
(B77-12999)

941.3'4 — Edinburgh, to 1975
Coutts, Herbert. Edinburgh : an illustrated history / [by] Herbert Coutts. — 2nd ed. — [Edinburgh] ([Huntly House Museum, 142 Canongate, Edinburgh EH8 8DD]) : City of Edinburgh Museums and Art Galleries, 1977. — [2],24p : ill, coats of arms, facsims, maps, ports ; 30cm.
Previous ed.: Edinburgh : Huntly House Museum, 1975.
Sd : Unpriced
(B77-29073)

941.3'4'0810222 — Edinburgh, 1860-1954. *Illustrations*
Edinburgh as it was / [compiled by] Norma Armstrong. — Nelson : Hendon Publishing Co.

Vol.2 : The people of Edinburgh. — 1977. — [1],45p : chiefly ill, facsim, ports ; 21x29cm.
ISBN 0-86067-021-x Sd : £1.60
(B77-23889)

941.3'92 — Scotland. Cheviot Hills. Social life. *Childhood reminiscences*
Derwent, Lavinia. Another breath of Border air / [by] Lavinia Derwent ; illustrated by Elizabeth Haines. — London : Hutchinson, 1977. — 156p : ill ; 23cm.
ISBN 0-09-129080-5 : £3.95
(B77-23890)

Derwent, Lavinia. A breath of Border air / [by] Lavinia Derwent ; illustrated by Elizabeth Haines. — London : Arrow Books, 1977. — 191p : ill ; 18cm.
Originally published: London : Hutchinson, 1975.
ISBN 0-09-914020-9 Pbk : £0.60
(B77-10678)

941.4'23 — Scotland. Strathclyde Region. Argyll and Bute (District). Inveraray, to 1971
Fraser, Alexander, *b.1912.* The Royal Burgh of Inveraray / [by] Alexander Fraser. — Edinburgh : St Andrew Press, 1977. — 224p, plate : 1 ill ; 22cm.
Bibl.
ISBN 0-7152-0354-1 Pbk : £1.75
(B77-23891)

941.4'23 — Scotland. Strathclyde Region. Argyll and Bute (District), to 1975
Campbell, Marion. Argyll : the enduring heartland / [by] Marion Campbell ; foreword by the Duke of Argyll ; illustrated by Frances Walker. — London : Turnstone Books, 1977. — xiv,267p : ill, geneal tables, col maps(on lining papers) ; 23cm.
Bibl.: p.253-257. — Index.
ISBN 0-85500-031-7 : £4.95
ISBN 0-85500-075-9 Limited ed. : £12.50
(B77-21618)

941.4'23 — Scotland. Strathclyde Region. Kintyre. *History. Periodicals*
Kintyre Antiquarian and Natural History Society. The magazine of the Kintyre Antiquarian & Natural History Society. — Campbeltown (c/o A. McNair, 47 Limecraigs, Campbeltown, Argyll) : The Society.
No.1- ; Spring 1977-. — [1977]-. — 21cm.
Two issues a year. — 28p. in 1st issue.
Sd : Unpriced
ISSN 0140-0762
(B77-23892)

941.4'23 — Scotland. Strathclyde Region. Tiree & Coll, to 1976
Banks, Noel. Six Inner Hebrides : Eigg, Rum, Canna, Muck, Coll, Tiree / [by] Noel Banks. — Newton Abbot [etc.] : David and Charles, 1977. — 208p : ill, maps, ports ; 23cm. — (The islands series)
Bibl.: p.193-201. — Index.
ISBN 0-7153-7368-4 : £4.95
Primary classification 941.18'5
(B77-21617)

941.4'43 — Scotland. Strathclyde Region. Glasgow. Social life, to 1976
Daiches, David. Glasgow / by David Daiches. — London : Deutsch, 1977. — xiv,243p,[16]p of plates : ill, facsims, maps, ports ; 24cm.
Map, ill. on lining papers. — Bibl.: p.230-232. — Index.
ISBN 0-233-96913-6 : £6.95 : CIP rev.
(B77-21619)

941.4'43 — Scotland. Strathclyde Region. Glasgow, to 1879. *Early works*
MacGeorge, Andrew. Old Glasgow : the place and the people : from the Roman occupation to the eighteenth century / by Andrew MacGeorge. — Wakefield : EP Publishing, 1976. — x,338p,[11] leaves of plates,[2]p of plates : ill, coats of arms, facsim, maps, plan ; 23cm.
Facsimile reprint of: 1st ed. Glasgow : Blackie, 1880. — Index.
ISBN 0-7158-1178-9 : £5.95
(B77-27581)

941.4'43'081 — Scotland. Strathclyde Region. Glasgow. Social life, 1858. *Early works*
Shadow. Midnight scenes and social photographs : being sketches of life in the streets, wynds and dens of the city of Glasgow / by Shadow. — [1st ed. reprinted] / with additional illustrations ; edited by Colin Harvey. — Glasgow (163 Mugdock Rd, Milngavie, Glasgow) : Heatherbank Press, 1976. — 142p,[24]p of plates : ill, facsims, port ; 20cm.
Facsimile reprint of: 1st ed. Glasgow : Murray, 1858.
ISBN 0-905192-01-x Pbk : £2.50
(B77-09427)

941.4'43'0810222 — Scotland. Strathclyde Region. Glasgow, 1855-ca 1930. *Illustrations*
Glasgow as it was / [compiled] by Michael Moss and John Hume. — Nelson : Hendon Publishing Co.
Vol.3 : Glasgow at work. — 1976. — [1],44,[1]p : chiefly ill, ports ; 22x29cm.
'This collection ... was made for an exhibition of the same name mounted by the University of Strathclyde'.
ISBN 0-902907-96-4 Sd : £1.40
(B77-01928)

941.4'57 — Palaces. *Scotland. Strathclyde Region. Hamilton. Hamilton Palace, to 1974*
Walker, Gavin. Hamilton Palace : a photographic record / compiled and written by G. Walker ; edited by C. Smith. — [Hamilton] ([Central Library, Cadzow St., Hamilton, Lanarkshire]) : Hamilton District Libraries and Museum Dept., [1977]. — [1],48,[1]p : ill, map, plans ; 21cm.
ISBN 0-9501983-2-3 Sd : £0.40
(B77-12227)

941.4'64 — Castles. *Scotland. Strathclyde Region. Kyle and Carrick (District). Culzean Castle, to 1976. French texts*
National Trust for Scotland. Culzean / [National Trust for Scotland]. — [Edinburgh] : The Trust, [1977]. — [5]p ; 21cm.
French text.
Sd : Unpriced
(B77-27582)

941.4'64 — Castles. *Scotland. Strathclyde Region. Kyle and Carrick (District). Culzean Castle, to 1976. German texts*
National Trust for Scotland. Culzean / [National Trust for Scotland]. — [Edinburgh] : The Trust, [1977]. — [5]p ; 21cm.
German text.
Sd : Unpriced
(B77-27583)

941.4'7'0810222 — Scotland. Dumfries and Galloway Region, ca 1860-ca 1940. *Illustrations*
Bygone Dumfries and Galloway from old photographs / [compilation and text] by Desmond Donaldson. — [New Abbey] ([Knockendoch, New Abbey, Dumfries]) : D. Donaldson.
Vol.1. — [1977]. — [74]p : of ill, ports ; 21x29cm.
Sd : £1.95
(B77-29074)

941.5 — HISTORY. IRELAND
941.5 — Castles. *Ireland, to 1970*
De Breffny, Brian. Castles of Ireland / [by] Brian de Breffny ; photographs by George Mott. — London : Thames and Hudson, 1977. — 208p : ill(some col), map, plans ; 26cm.
Index.
ISBN 0-500-24100-7 : £6.95
(B77-23012)

941.5 — Ireland. *History. Primary school texts. Irish texts*
McGillicuddy, Timothy Noel. An stair bheo / T.N. McGillicuddy a scríobh ; Doncha Ó Conchúir a d'aistrigh. — [Baile Átha Cliath i.e. Dublin] : Oifig an tSoláthair.
Cuid 1 / [léaráidí agus clúdach Jack Farrar i.e. Farrer]. — 1976. — [2],62p : ill(some col), maps ; 24cm.
Translation of: 'The living past. Part 1'. Dublin : Educational Company of Ireland, 1973.
ISBN 0-905621-15-8 Sd : £0.64
(B77-06989)

941.5 — Ireland. Historical events, to 1975. Attitudes of Irish
Harkness, David William. History and the Irish / [by] D.W. Harkness. — [Belfast] : Queen's University of Belfast, [1976]. — 15p ; 21cm. — (Queen's University of Belfast. New lecture series ; no.93)
'An inaugural lecture delivered before The Queen's University of Belfast on 5 May 1976'.
ISBN 0-85389-110-9 Sd : £0.40
(B77-02681)

941.5 — Ireland. Social life, to ca 1920. *Irish texts*
Cullen, Louis Michael. An saol in Éirinn / L.M. Ó Cuileáin (L.M. Cullen) a scríobh ; Tomás Ó Laoi a d'aistrigh. — Baile Átha Cliath [i.e. Dublin] (Oifig Dhíolta Foilseachán Rialtais, An Stuara, Ard-Oifig an Phoist, Baile Átha Cliath 1) : Oifig an tSoláthair, 1976. — xv,210p : ill, facsim, plans ; 23cm.
Translation of: 'Life in Ireland'. London : Batsford, 1968. — Bibl. — Index.
Unpriced
(B77-01930)

941.5 — Ireland, to 1975
Cowie, Donald. Ireland : the land and the people / [by] Donald Cowie. — South Brunswick ; New York : Barnes ; London : Yoseloff, 1976. — 248p,[4]p of plates : ill(some col), ports ; 26cm.
Index.
ISBN 0-498-01499-1 : £4.75
(B77-03300)

941.5 — Irish culture, to 1975. Influence of classical culture
Stanford, William Bedell. Ireland and the classical tradition / [by] W.B. Stanford. — Dublin : Allen Figgis [etc.], 1976. — x,261p ; 24cm.
Bibl.: p.251-254. — Index.
ISBN 0-900372-87-7 : £7.50
(B77-15039)

941.501 — Christian church. Buildings. *Ireland, 400-1200*
Hughes, Kathleen. The modern traveller to the early Irish church / [by] Kathleen Hughes and Ann Hamlin. — London : S.P.C.K., 1977. — x, 131p,[2]p of plates : ill ; 22cm.
Index.
ISBN 0-281-02944-x Pbk : £2.95
(B77-11491)

941.505 — Ireland, 1485-1603
Edwards, Robert Dudley. Ireland in the age of the Tudors : the destruction of Hiberno-Norman civilization / [by] R. Dudley Edwards. — London : Croom Helm [etc.], 1977. — 222p : 3 maps ; 23cm.
Bibl.: p.202-215. — Index.
ISBN 0-85664-454-4 : £7.95
(B77-15040)

941.507 — Ireland. Rebellions, 1798. *Teaching kits*
The '98 Rebellion / [with commentary] by Anthony Malcomson. — Belfast [etc.] : H.M.S.O. for the Public Record Office of Northern Ireland, 1976. — Portfolio : ill, facsims, maps, ports ; 31cm. — (Education facsimiles ; 81-100)
Twenty sheets (chiefly fold.) in folder, all in plastic envelope. — Originally published: 1971.
ISBN 0-337-23178-8 : £1.00
(B77-05780)

941.507'08 — Ireland. Social life, ca 1680- ca 1750. *Readings from contemporary sources*
Irish writings from the age of Swift / selected and introduced by Andrew Carpenter. — [1st ed. reprinted] ; with an introduction by J.G. Simms and an afterword by Denis Donoghue. — Dublin (6 Richmond Hill, Monkstown, Dublin) : Cadenus Press.
Vol.5 : The case of Ireland stated / by William Molyneux. — 1977. — 148,[1]p : facsim, port ; 23cm.
Limited ed. of 350 numbered copies of which no.1-200 are bound in quarter leather. — Originally published: as 'The case of Ireland's being bound by Acts of Parliament in England, stated', Dublin : Joseph Ray, 1698. — Bibl.: p.141-148.
Unpriced
(B77-22275)

Irish writings from the age of Swift / selected and introduced by Andrew Carpenter. — Dublin (6 Richmond Hill, Monkstown, Dublin) : Cadenus Press.
Vol.4 : Archbishop King's sermon on predestination. — [Corrected ed. reprinted] / introduced by David Berman and edited by Andrew Carpenter. — 1976. — 98p : facsim, port ; 23cm.
Limited ed. of 200 numbered copies. — Quarter leather, marbled boards. — This ed. originally published: as 'Divine predestination and fore-knowledge, consistent with the freedom of man's will'. Dublin : J. Gowan, 1727. — Bibl.: p.81-83.
ISBN 0-904375-04-8 : £7.50
(B77-07737)

Irish writings from the age of Swift / selected and introduced by Andrew Carpenter. — Dublin (6 Richmond Hill, Monkstown, Dublin) : Cadenus Press.
Vol.6 : A dialogue in Hybernian stile between A & B ; &, Irish eloquence / by Jonathan Swift ; edited by Alan Bliss. — 1977. — 102p : facsim, geneal table ; 23cm.
Limited ed. of 300 copies, of which 1-200 are bound in quarter calf. — Bibl.: p.7. — Index.
Unpriced
Quarter leather ed. : Unpriced
(B77-27585)

941.507'092'4 — Ireland. Tandy, Napper. *Biographies*
Coughlan, Rupert J. Napper Tandy / [by] Rupert J. Coughlan. — Dublin : Anvil Books, 1976. — xii,276p,[8]p of plates : ill, ports ; 23cm.
Bibl.: p.261-264. — Index.
ISBN 0-900068-34-5 : £6.50
(B77-19916)

941.508 — Ireland, 1800-1972
MacDonagh, Oliver. Ireland : the Union and its aftermath / [by] Oliver MacDonagh. — Revised and enlarged ed. — London : Allen and Unwin, 1977. — 176p ; 23cm.
Previous ed.: Englewood Cliffs : Prentice-Hall, 1968. — Bibl.: p.167-171. — Index.
ISBN 0-04-941004-0 : £6.50
ISBN 0-04-941005-9 Pbk : £3.50
(B77-27586)

941.5081 — Fighting by factions. *Ireland, 1800-1900*
O'Donnell, Patrick D. The Irish faction fighters of the 19th century / [by] Patrick D. O'Donnell. — Dublin : Anvil Books, 1975. — 192p : port ; 19cm.
ISBN 0-900068-36-1 Pbk : £1.00
(B77-01929)

941.5081'092'4 — Ireland. Lynch, Eliza Alicia. Interpersonal relationships with López, Francisco Solano
Brodsky, Alyn. Madame Lynch & friend : the true account of an Irish adventuress and the dictator of Paraguay who destroyed that American nation / [by] Alyn Brodsky. — London : Cassell, 1976. — xxi,312p ; 22cm.
Originally published: New York : Harper and Row, 1975. — Bibl.: p.297-301. — Index.
ISBN 0-304-29765-8 : £4.50
Primary classification 989.2'05'0924
(B77-10704)

941.5081'092'4 — Ireland. Parnell, Charles Stewart. *Biographies*
Foster, Robert Fitzroy. Charles Stewart Parnell : the man and his family / [by] R.F. Foster. — Hassocks : Harvester Press [etc.], 1976. — xx, 403p,[4]p of plates : 1 ill, geneal table, map, ports ; 23cm.
Index.
ISBN 0-85527-044-6 : £9.95
(B77-03301)

Lyons, Francis Stewart Leland. Charles Stewart Parnell / [by] F.S.L. Lyons. — London : Collins, 1977. — 704p,[8]p of plates : ill, ports ; 24cm.
Index.
ISBN 0-00-211682-0 : £8.50
(B77-20818)

941.5081'092'4 — Ireland. Political events. Role of Emmet, Robert, 1803
Robert Emmet, the insurrection of 1803 / [with commentary] by Geraldine Hume and Anthony Malcomson. — Belfast [etc.] : H.M.S.O. for the Public Record Office of Northern Ireland, 1976. — Portfolio : ill, facsims, map, ports ; 31cm. — (Education facsimiles ; 181-200)
Booklet (28p.), 20 sheets (chiefly fold.) in folder, all in plastic envelope. — Bibl.: p.24.
ISBN 0-337-23177-x : £1.00
(B77-06386)

941.5082'1'0922 — Ireland. Easter Rising, 1916. *Personal observations. Collections*
Dublin 1916 : an illustrated anthology / edited by Roger McHugh. — London : Arlington Books, 1976. — xxiii,399p,[64]p of plates : ill, facsims, ports ; 26cm.
Previous ed.: 1966.
ISBN 0-85140-247-x : £7.50
(B77-26031)

941.5082'1'0924 — Anglo-Irish War, 1920-1921. *Personal observations*
Barry, Tom. The reality of the Anglo-Irish war, 1920-21 in West Cork : refutations, corrections and comments on Liam Deasy's 'Towards Ireland free' / by Tom Barry. — Tralee [etc.] : Anvil Books, 1974. — 59p ; 19cm.
ISBN 0-900068-38-8 Sd : £0.40
(B77-05138)

941.5082'1'0924 — Ireland. Childers, Erskine, b.1870. *Biographies*
Boyle, Andrew. The riddle of Erskine Childers / [by] Andrew Boyle. — London [etc.] : Hutchinson, 1977. — 351p,[4]p of plates : ports ; 23cm.
Bibl.: p.333-336. — Index.
ISBN 0-09-128490-2 : £6.95
(B77-19121)

941.5082'1'0924 — Ireland. MacBride, Maud Gonne. *Biographies*
Levenson, Samuel. Maud Gonne / [by] Samuel Levenson. — London : Cassell, 1977. — xi, 436p,[8]p of plates : ports ; 23cm.
Originally published: New York : Reader's Digest Press, 1976. — Bibl.: p.423-428. — Index.
ISBN 0-304-29905-7 : £6.95
(B77-29832)

941.5082'1'0924 — Ireland. Politics. Griffith, Arthur. *Biographies*
Davis, Richard. Arthur Griffith / by Richard Davis. — Dundalk : Dundalgan Press for the Irish Historical Association, 1976. — 48p ; 22cm. — (Irish history series ; no.10)
Bibl.: p.45-48.
Sd : £0.50
(B77-01081)

941.5082'4 — Ireland. Social life
Uris, Jill. Ireland : a terrible beauty : the story of Ireland today / [photography by] Jill and [text by] Leon Uris. — London : Corgi, 1977. — 288 : ill(some col), maps, ports(some col) ; 24cm.
Originally published: Garden City, N.Y. : Doubleday ; London : Deutsch, 1976.
ISBN 0-552-98013-7 Pbk : £3.75
(B77-18479)

941.5082'4 — Parks. *Ireland. Secondary school texts*
Shannon, Denis. Irish parks / text Denis Shannon ; illustrations Michael McNamee. — [Tallaght] : Folens, [1977]. — [1],p.97-128 : col ill ; 25cm. — (Irish environmental library series ; no.24)
Sd : £0.60
(B77-19122)

941.5082'4'05 — Ireland. Political events. *Communist Party of Ireland viewpoints. Periodicals*
Irish socialist review : theoretical & discussion journal of the Communist Party of Ireland. — Dublin [etc.] (37 Pembroke La., Dublin) : Communist Party of Ireland.
No.1- ; 1977-. — [1977]-. — 25cm.
[1],23p. in 1st issue.
Sd : £0.30
(B77-13436)

941.5082'4'0924 — Ireland. Social life, 1972-1973. *Personal observations*
Brown, Richard Howard. The passion of Richard Brown. — London : Gordon and Cremonesi, 1977. — vii,167p ; 23cm.
Originally published: as 'I am of Ireland'. New York : Harper and Row, 1974.
ISBN 0-86033-054-0 : £5.90
(B77-26701)

941.6082 — Northern Ireland. Political events, 1918-1975
Farrell, Mike. Northern Ireland, the Orange state / [by] Michael Farrell. — London : Pluto Press, 1976. — 406p : maps ; 20cm.
Bibl.: p.385-395. — Index.
ISBN 0-902818-87-2 Pbk : £5.00
(B77-08686)

941.6082'3 — Northern Ireland. Political events, 1962-1975. *Sinn-Fein-The Workers' Party viewpoints*
Mac Giolla, Tomás. The struggle for democracy, peace & freedom / [by] Tomás Mac Giolla. — [Dublin] ([30 Gardiner Place, Dublin 1]) : [Repsol Publications], [1976]. — [4],9p ; 18cm.
'... speech ... delivered ... to the Boston Irish Forum, August 31st 1975' - Introduction. — Originally published: 1975.
ISBN 0-86064-001-9 Sd : £0.15
(B77-23893)

941.6082'4 — Northern Ireland. Political events. Influence of Irish in United States, 1969-1976
Clark, Dennis. Irish blood : Northern Ireland and the American conscience / [by] Dennis J. Clark. — Port Washington ; London : Kennikat Press, 1977. — x,97p ; 23cm. — (Kennikat Press national university publications)
Bibl.: p.91-93. — Index.
ISBN 0-8046-9163-0 : £6.75
(B77-23013)

941.6082'4'05 — Northern Ireland. Policies of British government. *Revolutionary Communist Group viewpoints. Periodicals*
Hands off Ireland! / Revolutionary Communist Group. — London (49 Railton Rd, SE24 0LN) : R.C.G Publications Ltd.
No.1- ; [Dec. 1976]-. — [1976]-. — 30cm.
Published at irregular intervals. — 16p. in 1st issue.
Sd : £0.20
ISSN 0309-2526
(B77-10061)

941.6082'4'0924 — Northern Ireland. Paisley, Ian Richard Kyle. *Biographies. Irish texts*
Ó Glaisne, Risteárd. Ian Paisley agus Tuaisceart Éireann / [le] Risteárd Ó Glaisne. — [Ireland] : Cló Morainn, 1971. — [5],231[i.e. 221]p ; 19cm.
Index.
Pbk : Unpriced
(B77-07739)

941.6'19 — Lisburn (District). Aghalee, 1677-1976
Brennan, S J. A brief history of Aghalee Parish to commemorate the three hundredth anniversary of the consecration of Aghalee Parish Church, 1st May, 1677-1st May, 1977 / by S.J. Brennan. — Newcastle, Co. Down ([Main St., Newcastle, Co. Down]) : Mourne Observer Press, 1977. — [5],30p : ill, ports ; 22cm.
Cover title: Aghalee Parish tercentenary, 1677-1977. — Bibl.: p.30.
Sd : Unpriced
(B77-23894)

941.6'58 — Newry and Mourne (District). Rostrevor, to 1971
Crowe, William Haughton. Village in seven hills : the story and stories of Rostrevor, Co. Down / by W. Haughton Crowe. — Dundalk : Dundalgan Press, 1973. — ix,106p,[2] leaves of plates,[22]p of plates : ill, map, ports ; 19cm.
Originally published: 1972. — Bibl.: p.102. — Index.
Pbk : Unpriced
Also classified at 398'.09416'58
(B77-05781)

941.6'7'0820222 — Belfast, 1870-ca 1970. *Illustrations*
D'ye mind the day- : pictures and memories from yesterday's 'Belfast telegraph' / [compiled by] John Pepper. — Belfast : Blackstaff Press, 1976. — 2-108p : of ill, facsims, ports ; 20x21cm.
ISBN 0-85640-114-5 Pbk : £1.95
(B77-03840)

941.7 — Ireland (Republic). Gaeltacht. *Secondary school texts*
Burns, Batt. The Gaeltacht / text Batt Burns ; illustrations Michael McNamee. — [Tallaght] : Folens, [1977]. — [1],p.33-64 : col ill, col maps ; 25cm. — (Irish environmental library series ; no.27)
Sd : £0.60
(B77-18480)

941.7'00973'4 — Ireland (Republic). Rural regions. Social life, to 1945
O'Neill, Timothy P. Life & tradition in rural Ireland / by Timothy P. O'Neill. — London : Dent, 1977. — xii,122p,[48]p of plates : ill, map, plan, port ; 25cm.
Index.
ISBN 0-460-04227-0 : £9.95 : CIP rev.
(B77-15624)

941.7082'1'0924 — Ireland (Republic). Pearse, Patrick Henry. *Biographies*
Edwards, Ruth Dudley. Patrick Pearse, the triumph of failure / by Ruth Dudley Edwards. — London : Gollancz, 1977. — xvii,384p,[8]p of plates : ill, facsims, ports ; 23cm.
Bibl.: p.362-372. — Index.
ISBN 0-575-02153-5 : £7.95
(B77-18481)

941.7082'2 — Ireland (Republic). Political events, 1932. *Communist viewpoints*
Gerhard. The Irish Free State and British imperialism / by Gerhard. — Cork (9 St Nicholas Church Place, Cove St., Cork, Republic of Ireland) : Cork Workers Club, 1976. — [2],19,[1]p : 1 ill ; 21cm. — (Cork Workers Club. Historical reprints ; no.18)
'First published in "The Communist International", May 1932' - title page verso.
Sd : £0.25
(B77-20819)

941.7082'4'0222 — Castles & cottages. *Ireland (Republic). Illustrations*
The **cottages** & castles of Ireland / commentary Sandy Lesberg. — New York ; London : Peebles Press International ; Freemen's Common (Euston St., Freemen's Common, Leics.) : Distributed by WHS Distributors, 1976. — 125p : chiefly ill(some col) ; 31cm.
Ill. on lining paper.
ISBN 0-672-52221-7 : £3.25
(B77-12228)

941.7082'4'05 — Ireland (Republic). *Yearbooks*
Administration yearbook and diary / [Institute of Public Administration]. — Dublin : The Institute.
1977 / edited by Daniel Sullivan. — 1976. — 328p : ill, maps, ports ; 26cm.
Unpaged diary between pages 264 and 265. — Index.
£5.00
ISBN 0-902173-69-3
(B77-10062)

941.73 — Museums. *Mayo (County). Knock. Knock Folk Museum. Guidebooks*
Knock Folk Museum. The light of other days : Knock Folk Museum, the golden treasury of Irish tradition / author and editor Tom Neary ; photography Seamus Mallee. — Knock, Co. Mayo ([Secretary, Inquiry Office, Knock Shrine, Claremorris, Co. Mayo]) : Custodians of Knock Shrine, 1974. — [88]p : ill, facsims, plan, ports ; 25cm.
Pbk : £0.50
(B77-20820)

941.73'082'405 — Mayo (County). *Newspapers*
The **western** journal. — [Ballina] ([Garden St., Ballina, Co. Mayo]) : ['The Western Journal'].
Vol.1, no.1- ; June 3rd 1977-. — 1977-. — ill, ports(some col) ; 58cm.
Weekly. — 24p. in 1st issue. — Includes a supplement, 'The Connacht farmer' (4p.).
Sd : £0.15
(B77-25308)

941.8 — Moated sites. *South-eastern Ireland, 1169-1513. Reports, surveys*
Barry, Terence B. The medieval moated sites of South-eastern Ireland : Counties Carlow, Kilkenny, Tipperary and Wexford / [by] Terence B. Barry. — Oxford : British Archaeological Reports, 1977. — [14],247p : ill, maps, plans ; 30cm. — (British archaeological reports ; 35 ISSN 0306-1205)
Spine title: Moated sites of SE Ireland. — Bibl.: p.232-247.
ISBN 0-904531-69-4 Pbk : £4.70
ISSN 0309-4863
(B77-23014)

941.8'02'0924 — Ireland (Republic). Leinster. Dermot MacMurrough, King of Leinster and the Foreigners. *Biographies*
Furlong, Nicholas. Dermot, king of Leinster and the foreigners / [by] Nicholas Furlong. — Tralee : Anvil Books, 1973. — 211p : port ; 19cm.
Bibl.: p.175-179. — Index.
ISBN 0-900068-37-x Pbk : £0.75
(B77-02682)

941.8'35 — Dublin, 1172-1976
The **Mansion** House. — [Dublin] : [Dublin Corporation], [1977]. — [10]p : ill, coat of arms ; 19cm.
Sd : Unpriced
(B77-24619)

941.8'35 — Dublin, to 1976
Clarke, Desmond. Dublin / [by] Desmond Clarke. — London : Batsford, 1977. — x,182p, [16]p of plates : ill, maps, ports ; 23cm.
Index.
ISBN 0-7134-0146-x : £5.50
(B77-25309)

941.8'35'08220924 — Dublin. Social life, ca 1930-ca 1940. *Childhood reminiscences*
MacThomáis, Éamonn. Gur cake & coal blocks / [by] Éamonn MacThomáis ; illustrations Liam Delaney and Michael O'Brien. — Dublin (11 Clare St., Dublin 2) : O'Brien Press, 1976. — 160p : ill ; 22cm.
ISBN 0-905140-08-7 : £4.20
(B77-03841)

941.8'38 — Dublin (County). Dún Laoghaire, to 1975. *Irish texts*
Ó Súilleabháin, Dónal. Ó Kingstown go Dún Laoghaire / [le] Dónal Ó Súilleabháin. — Baile Átha Cliath [i.e. Dublin] ([29 Sráid Uí Chonaill Íocht], Baile Átha Cliath) : Foilseacháin Náisiúnta Tta, 1976. — 158p,[8]p of plates : ill, plan ; 19cm.
Index.
£2.00
(B77-20821)

941.9'2 — Castles. *Tipperary (County). Nenagh. Nenagh Castle, to 1936*
Gleeson, D F. The castle and manor of Nenagh / [by] D.F. Gleeson and H.G. Leask. — Revised ed. — [Nenagh] ([c/o Mrs N. Murphy, Tyrone, Nenagh, Co. Tipperary]) : [Wordsnare Publications], 1976. — [1],iii p,p247-270,[4]p of plates : ill, geneal table, map, plans ; 22cm.
'A paper read to the Royal Society of Antiquaries of Ireland, 8 December 1936 ...'. — Previous ed.: / edited by Donal A. Murphy. Nenagh? : Nenagh Castle Restoration Working Party, 1971.
Sd : £0.70
(B77-20822)

941.9'2 — Tipperary (County). Nenagh, 1657-1914. *Early works. Facsimiles*
Sheehan, E H. Nenagh and its neighbourhood / by E.H. Sheehan. — Revised and enlarged ed. / [reprinted with additional photographs, captions and index ; edited by Noel Ryan and Donal A. Murphy]. — [Nenagh] ([c/o Mrs Nancy Murphy, 'Tyrone', Nenagh, Co. Tipperary]) : Wordsnare, 1976. — 98,[24]p,[14]p of plates : ill, map, plan, ports ; 21cm.
Limited ed. of 1000 copies. — Revised and enlarged ed. originally published: Nenagh? : The author, 1949. — Index.
Sd : £1.20
(B77-18482)

941.9'6 — Kerry (County). Blasket Islands. Social life, to 1976. *Irish texts*
Mac Tomáis, Seoirse. An Blascaod à bhí / [le] Seoirse Mac Tomáis. — Má Nuad [i.e. Maynooth] ([Maynooth College, Maynooth, Co. Kildare]) : 'An Sagart', 1977. — [1],27p ; 22cm.
Bibl.: p.27.
Sd : £0.30
(B77-23015)

941.9'6 — Kerry (County), to 1975
Barrington, Thomas Joseph. Discovering Kerry : its history, heritage & topography / by T.J. Barrington. — Dublin (31 Castle Park, Monkstown, County Dublin) : Blackwater Press, 1976. — 336p,[12]fold of plates : ill, facsims, geneal table, maps, plans, ports ; 26cm.
Maps on lining papers. — Bibl.: p.307-316. — Index.
ISBN 0-905471-00-8 : £10.00
(B77-30871)

942 — HISTORY. ENGLAND
942 — Castles. *England, to ca 1500*
Brown, Reginald Allen. English castles / [by] R. Allen Brown. — 3rd revised ed. — London : Batsford, 1976. — 240p : ill, facsims, maps, plans ; 26cm.
Previous ed.: 1962. — Index.
ISBN 0-7134-3119-9 : £6.95
(B77-01082)

942 — Castles. Social life. *England, 1000-1500. Juvenile literature*
Althea. Castle life / by Althea ; illustrated by Maureen Galvani. — London : Evans Bros, 1977. — [24]p : col ill ; 24x27cm.
ISBN 0-237-44885-8 : £1.75
(B77-14482)

Althea. Castle life / by Althea ; illustrated by Maureen Galvani. — Cambridge : Dinosaur Publications, 1976. — [24]p : col ill, port ; 15x18cm. — (Althea's dinosaur books)
ISBN 0-85122-124-6 Sd : £0.35
(B77-14483)

942 — Deneholes. *England*
Pennick, Ann. Dene-holes and subterranea / by Ann Pennick. — Cambridge (142 Pheasant Rise, Bar Hill, Cambridge CB2 8SD) : Fenris-Wolf, 1975. — [1],8p,plate : ill, plans ; 30cm. — (Megalithic visions antiquarian papers ; 9)
ISBN 0-905987-00-4 Sd : £0.30
(B77-14474)

942 — England, 1325-1625
Goodman, Anthony. A history of England from Edward II to James I / [by] Anthony Goodman. — London [etc.] : Longman, 1977. — xii,467p : ill, geneal tables, maps ; 22cm.
Bibl.: p.434-448. — Index.
ISBN 0-582-48281-x : Unpriced
ISBN 0-582-48282-8 Pbk : £4.95
(B77-30872)

942 — England. Local history
Rogers, Alan, *b.1933.* Approaches to local history / [by] Alan Rogers ; preface by W.G. Hoskins. — 2nd ed. — London [etc.] : Longman, 1977. — xvii,265p : ill, facsims, maps ; 25cm.
Previous ed.: published as 'This was their world'. London : British Broadcasting Corporation, 1972. — Index.
ISBN 0-582-48508-8 : £7.50
ISBN 0-582-48509-6 Pbk : £3.95
(B77-30873)

942 — England, to 1604. *Early works. Facsimiles*
Verstegan, Richard. A restitution of decayed intelligence / [by] Richard Verstegan. — Ilkley [etc.] : Scolar Press, 1976. — [29],338,[11]p, plate : ill, coat of arms ; 21cm. — (English recusant literature, 1558-1640 ; vol.323)
Facsimile reprint of: 1st ed., Antwerp : Printed by Robert Bruney, 1605. — Index.
ISBN 0-85967-340-5 : £10.00
(B77-06990)

942 — Structures of historical importance. *England*
Sturdy, David. Historic monuments of England and Wales / [by] David and Fiona Sturdy. — London : Dent, 1977. — 218p : ill, maps, plans ; 25cm.
Index.
ISBN 0-460-04158-4 : £6.50 : CIP rev.
(B77-08687)

942'.004'91412 — Pakistani immigrants. *England. Juvenile literature*
Blakeley, Madeleine. Nahda's family / [by] Madeleine Blakeley ; photographs by Jeremy Finlay. — London : A. and C. Black, 1977. — 25p : col ill, col ports ; 22cm.
ISBN 0-7136-1732-2 : £1.75
(B77-15625)

942'.004'9142 — Sikh immigrants. *England. Juvenile literature*
Lyle, Seán. Pavan is a Sikh / [by] Seán Lyle ; photographs by Jeremy Finlay. — London : A. and C. Black, 1977. — [26]p : ill(chiefly col), col map, ports(chiefly col) ; 22cm.
ISBN 0-7136-1721-7 : Unpriced
(B77-16121)

942'.007'1 — Schools. Curriculum subjects: Local history. *England. For teaching*
Stephens, William Brewer. Teaching local history / [by] W.B. Stephens. — Manchester : Manchester University Press, 1977. — x,182p : ill, facsim, plan ; 23cm.
Bibl.: p.163. — Index.
ISBN 0-7190-0660-0 : £5.95
(B77-12229)

942'.007'12 — English studies. Projects. *Secondary school texts*
Perks, Roger. English workshop / [by] Roger Perks. — Birmingham : Clearway Publishing Co.
[Level] 3 / editor R. Giles ; illustrations R. Fereday. — 1977. — [1],29p : ill ; 30cm. — (Clearway workshop series)
Pierced for binder. — Bibl.
ISBN 0-902336-63-0 Sd : £0.72
(B77-18483)

942'.008 — England. Social life, to 1837. *Readings from contemporary sources*
Every one a witness : commentaries of an era / [compiled] by A.F. Scott. — London [etc.] : White Lion Publishers.
The Roman age. — 1977. — xvi,351p : ill, map, ports ; 23cm.
Bibl.: p.327-329. — Index.
ISBN 0-7285-0043-4 : £5.95
ISBN 0-7285-0039-6 Pbk : £2.95
(B77-21620)

942'.00973'2 — Towns. Social life. *England, 400-1500*
Reynolds, Susan. An introduction to the history of English medieval towns / [by] Susan Reynolds. — Oxford : Clarendon Press, 1977. — xiv,234p,plate : maps ; 23cm.
Bibl.: p.202-223. — Index.
ISBN 0-19-822455-9 : £7.95 : CIP rev.
(B77-19123)

942'.00973'4 — England. Rural regions. *Periodicals*
['**Country** bizarre'. No.1-11]. The complete 'Country bizarre' : numbers 1-11 / edited by Andy Pittaway, Bernard Sc[h]ofield. — London ([9 Queen Anne's Gate, SW1H 9BY]) : Astragal Books, 1976. — [383]p : ill, maps, music ; 26cm.
Reprints issues of the magazine originally published 1970-74. — Bibl.
ISBN 0-85139-113-3 : £5.95
(B77-14484)

942'.00973'4 — England. Rural regions. Social life, 1900-1914
Thomas, Edward, *b.1878.* Edward Thomas on the countryside : a selection of his prose and verse / edited by Roland Gant. — London : Faber, 1977. — 183p ; 23cm.
Bibl.: p.181-183.
ISBN 0-571-10799-0 : £4.95
(B77-15041)

942'.00992 — England. Monarchs, 1377-1649. *Primary school texts*
Gregory, Olive Barnes. Kings and queens / [by] O.B. Gregory ; colour illustrations by Peter Kesteven ; line drawings by Susan Winters. — [Exeter] : Wheaton.
In 12 vols.
Charles I. — 1977. — 31p : ill(chiefly col), col geneal table ; 21cm.
ISBN 0-08-019815-5 Sd : £0.50(£5.70 the set)
(B77-17216)

Edward IV. — 1977. — 31p : ill(chiefly col), col geneal table ; 21cm.
ISBN 0-08-020432-5 Sd : £0.50(£5.70 the set)
(B77-17217)

Edward V and Richard III. — 1977. — 31p : ill(chiefly col), col geneal table, col plan ; 21cm.
ISBN 0-08-019809-0 Sd : £0.50(£5.70 the set)
(B77-17218)

Edward VI and Mary. — 1977. — 31p : ill(chiefly col), col geneal table ; 21cm.
ISBN 0-08-019812-0 Sd : £0.50(£5.70 the set)
(B77-17219)

Elizabeth. — 1977. — 31p : ill(chiefly col), col geneal table ; 21cm.
ISBN 0-08-019813-9 Sd : £0.50(£5.70 the set)
(B77-17220)

Henry IV. — 1977. — 31p : ill(chiefly col), col geneal table ; 21cm.
ISBN 0-08-019806-6 Sd : £0.50(£5.70 the set)
(B77-17221)

Henry V. — 1977. — 31p : ill(chiefly col), col geneal table ; 21cm.
ISBN 0-08-019807-4 Sd : £0.50(£5.70 the set)
(B77-17222)

Henry VI. — 1977. — 31p : ill(chiefly col), coat of arms, col geneal tables, col map ; 21cm.
ISBN 0-08-019808-2 Sd : £0.50(£5.70 the set)
(B77-17223)

Henry VII. — 1977. — 31p : ill(chiefly col), col geneal table, col map ; 21cm.
ISBN 0-08-019810-4 Sd : £0.50(£5.70 the set)
(B77-17224)

Henry VIII. — 1977. — 31p : ill(chiefly col), col geneal table ; 21cm.
ISBN 0-08-019811-2 Sd : £0.50(£5.70 the set)
(B77-17225)

James I. — 1977. — 31p : ill(chiefly col), col geneal table ; 21cm.
ISBN 0-08-019814-7 Sd : £0.50(£5.70 the set)
(B77-17226)

Richard II. — 1977. — 31p : ill(chiefly col), coat of arms, col geneal table ; 21cm.
ISBN 0-08-019805-8 Sd : £0.50(£5.70 the set)
(B77-17227)

942.01 — Anglo-Saxon antiquities. *England. Reviews of research*
The **archaeology** of Anglo-Saxon England / edited by David M. Wilson. — London : Methuen, 1976. — xvi,532p,xxi p of plates : ill, maps, plans ; 26cm.
Bibl.: p.463-511. — Index.
ISBN 0-416-15090-x : £30.00
(B77-05139)

942.01 — Antiquities. *England, 400-1189*
Helm, Peter James. Exploring Saxon and Norman England / [by] P.J. Helm. — London : Hale, 1976. — 187p,[16]p of plates : ill, map ; 23cm.
Bibl.: p.173-175. — Index.
ISBN 0-7091-5757-6 : £4.50
(B77-02683)

942.01 — England, 300-1066. *Secondary school texts*
Milliken, Ernest Kenneth. Saxon and Viking / by E.K. Milliken. — London : Harrap, 1976. — 112p : ill, maps, plans ; 20cm.
Originally published: 1944.
ISBN 0-245-53012-6 Pbk : £1.00
(B77-12230)

942.01 — England, 350-1066
Blair, Peter Hunter. An introduction to Anglo-Saxon England / [by] Peter Hunter Blair. — 2nd ed. — Cambridge [etc.] : Cambridge University Press, 1977. — xvi,380p, [2]leaves of plates,[14]p of plates : ill, facsims, maps, plans ; 23cm.
Previous ed.: 1956. — Bibl.: p.364-370. — Index.
ISBN 0-521-21650-8 : £12.50
ISBN 0-521-29219-0 Pbk : £3.95
(B77-24620)

942.01 — England, ca 400-1050
Fisher, Douglas John Vivian. The Anglo-Saxon age, c.400-1042 / by D.J.V. Fisher. — London : Longman, 1976. — x,374p : geneal tables, maps ; 22cm. — (A history of England)
Originally published: 1973. — Bibl.: p.353-357. — Index.
ISBN 0-582-48084-1 Pbk : £3.25
(B77-01083)

942.01'05 — England, 450-1066. *Essays. Serials*
Anglo-Saxon England. — Cambridge [etc.] : Cambridge University Press.
6 / edited by Peter Clemoes ; [contributors] Martin Biddle ... [et al.]. — 1977. — ix,316p, viii p of plates : ill, facsims, map ; 24cm.
Bibl.: p.267-316.
ISBN 0-521-21701-6 : £12.50
(B77-30874)

942.01'08 — Anglo-Saxon civilization, to 1066. *Extracts from periodicals*
Seo freolsungboc thaes teothan gemynddaeges thara Engliscra Gesitha MDXXVII = The book celebrating the tenth anniversary of the English companions 1976 AD. — Folkestone (51 Canterbury Rd, Folkestone, Kent) : English Companions, [1976]. — xxiv p ; 21cm.
Old English title transliterated. — '... contains articles that originally appeared in the first twenty "Withowinda"' - Preface.
ISBN 0-9505704-0-0 Sd : Unpriced
(B77-15626)

942.01'64 — England, 871-900. *Primary school texts*
Osborn, Jane R. At the time of King Alfred / [by] Jane R. Osborn. — London : Longman, 1977. — 64p : ill, facsims, maps, ports ; 24cm. — (Focus on history)
Index.
ISBN 0-582-18228-x Pbk : £0.85
(B77-32988)

942.01'64 — England. Social life, 871-899. *Middle school texts. Teaching kits*
Pelling, John. Alfred the Great / by John Pelling ; illustrated by Trevor Ridley. — Cambridge [etc.] : Cambridge University Press, 1977. — 1v. : ill(some col), maps(chiefly col), port ; 15x21cm. — (History first)
Four booklets, 12 folders ([36]p.) in plastic envelope. — Bibl.
ISBN 0-521-21322-3 : £2.75(non-net)
(B77-22276)

942.02 — England, 1066-1265. *Primary school texts*
Jamieson, Jean Mary. Normans and Crusaders / [by] Jean M. Jamieson ; drawings by Philip Page. — London : Edward Arnold, 1977. — 48p : ill, coats of arms, geneal table, maps, plans, ports ; 20x26cm.
Index.
ISBN 0-7131-0111-3 Sd : £1.25
(B77-23895)

942.02'1 — England. Norman Conquest
Howarth, David. 1066, the year of the conquest / [by] David Howarth ; illustrations to chapter headings by Gareth Floyd. — London : Collins, 1977. — 207p : ill, geneal table, map, plan ; 24cm.
Map on lining papers. — Index.
ISBN 0-00-211845-9 : £5.50
(B77-26032)

942.02'1'0924 — England. William I, King of England. *Biographies*
Douglas, David Charles. William the Conqueror : the Norman impact upon England / [by] David C. Douglas. — London : Eyre Methuen, 1977. — xii,476p,plate : geneal tables, maps, port ; 24cm. — ([English monarchs])
Originally published: London : Eyre and Spottiswoode, 1964. — Bibl.: p.427-447. — Index.
ISBN 0-413-24320-6 : £7.95
ISBN 0-413-38380-6 Pbk : £3.50
(B77-34311)

942.03'1'0924 — England. Henry II, King of England. *Biographies*
Warren, Wilfred Lewis. Henry II / [by] W.L. Warren. — London : Eyre Methuen, 1977. — xvi,693p,[34]p of plates : ill, facsims, geneal tables, maps ; 24cm. — ([English monarchs])
Originally published: 1973. — Bibl.: p.637-668. — Index.
£12.00
ISBN 0-413-25580-8
ISBN 0-413-38390-3 Pbk : £4.50
(B77-34312)

942.03 — England, 1216-1485
Wilkinson, Bertie. The later Middle Ages in England, 1216-1485 / by B. Wilkinson. — London : Longman, 1977. — xii,419p : geneal tables, maps ; 22cm. — (A history of England ; [3])
Originally published: 1969. — Bibl.: p.397-398. — Index.
ISBN 0-582-48032-9 Pbk : £4.50
(B77-31626)

942.03 — England. Social life, ca 1300-1400. *Secondary school texts*
Sayers, Jane Eleanor. At the time of Geoffrey Chaucer / [by] Jane Sayers. — London : Longman, 1977. — 64p : ill, coats of arms, facsim, geneal table, maps, plan, ports ; 24cm. — (Focus on history)
Index.
ISBN 0-582-18230-1 Pbk : £0.85
(B77-32326)

942.03'4 — England. Social life, ca 1250. *Juvenile literature*
Hadenius, Stig. How they lived in the age of knights / [by] Stig Hadenius and Birgit Janrup ; translated [from the Swedish] by Fred Thideman ; illustrated by Ulf Löfgren. — Guildford [etc.] : Lutterworth Press, 1976. — 32p : ill(chiefly col), col map(on lining papers) ; 23cm. — (How they lived ; 6)
Translation of: 'Roligt om historia, riddartiden'. Stockholm : Geber, 1969.
ISBN 0-7188-2200-5 : £1.10
(B77-05140)

942.03'5'0924 — England. Edward I, King of England. Itineraries, 1272-1307. *Texts*
Safford, E W. Itinerary of Edward I / [prepared by E.W. Safford ; for the Public Record Office]. — London : Swift.
'Compiled ... from the sources used for the "Itineraries" drawn up by H. Gough and T. Craib, with additions taken mainly from "Wardrobe Accounts" and "Chancery Warrants"'.
Part 3 : Index. — 1977. — [2],208p ; 33cm. — (List and Index Society. Publications ; vol.135)
ISBN 0-902573-56-x Pbd : £4.55
(B77-08688)

942.03'8 — England. Peasants' Revolt
Hilton, Rodney. Bond men made free : medieval peasant movements and the English rising of 1381 / [by] Rodney Hilton. — London : Methuen, 1977. — 240p ; 22cm. — (University paperbacks)
Originally published: London : Temple Smith, 1973. — Index.
ISBN 0-416-82520-6 Pbk : £2.40
Primary classification 322.4'2'094
(B77-16212)

942.03'8 — England. Peasants' Revolt. *Middle school texts*
Crowther, Nicci. The Peasants' Revolt / [by] Nicci Crowther and Roy Schofield. — London : Edward Arnold, 1977. — 32p : chiefly ill, map ; 25cm. — (Action history)
ISBN 0-7131-0178-4 Sd : £0.80 : CIP rev.
(B77-26033)

942.04 — England, 1400-1500
Lander, Jack Robert. Conflict and stability in fifteenth-century England / [by] J.R. Lander. — 3rd ed. — London : Hutchinson, 1977. — 222p ; 23cm. — ([Hutchinson university library])
Previous ed.: 1974. — Bibl.: p.189-200. — Index.
ISBN 0-09-129190-9 : £5.50
ISBN 0-09-129191-7 Pbk : £2.75
(B77-23016)

942.04'08 — England. Social life, 1400-1500. *Readings from contemporary sources*
Paston letters and papers of the fifteenth century / edited by Norman Davis. — Oxford : Clarendon Press.
In 3 parts.
Part 2. — 1976 [i.e. 1977]. — xxxiii,664p,[12]p of plates, leaf of plate : facsims ; 24cm.
Index.
ISBN 0-19-812555-0 : £25.00
(B77-06991)

942.04'6'0924 — England. Richard III, King of England. *Early works*
Cornwallis, *Sir* William. The economium of Richard III / by Sir William Cornwallis the younger ; edited by A.N. Kincaid ; with an introduction by J.A. Ramsden and A.N. Kincaid. — London ([24 Kent House, 87 Regent St., W1R 7HF]) : Turner and Devereux, 1977. — [2],xiv,33[i.e.65]p ; 30cm.
'The Chatsworth version [Hardwick MS.44] has been chosen as the basis of the text ...' - p.x. — Bibl.: p.viii-ix.
Pbk : £3.25
(B77-29075)

942.04'6'0924 — England. Richard III, King of England. Vindication. Organisations: Richard III Society, to 1975
Awdry, George. The Richard III Society : the first fifty years : a personal account / [by] George Awdry. — Upminster (65 Howard Rd, Upminster, Essex RM14 2UE) : The Society, [1977]. — [64]p,[4]p of plates,[2]leaves of plates : ill, ports ; 24cm.
ISBN 0-904893-01-4 Sd : £1.50
(B77-17228)

942.05 — England, 1450-1558
Davies, Clifford Stephen Lloyd. Peace, print and Protestantism / [by] C.S.L. Davies. — St Albans : Paladin, 1977. — 365p : ill, geneal tables ; 20cm. — (The Paladin history of England)
Originally published: London : Hart-Davis MacGibbon, 1976. — Bibl.: p.343-345. — Index.
ISBN 0-586-08266-2 Pbk : £1.25
(B77-13980)

942.05 — England, 1485-1603
Powell, Ken. English historical facts, 1485-1603 / [by] Ken Powell and Chris Cook. — London [etc.] : Macmillan, 1977. — vii,228p ; 24cm.
Bibl.: p.221-228.
ISBN 0-333-14888-6 : £10.00
(B77-28304)

942.05'1'0924 — England. Henry VII, King of England. *Biographies*
Chrimes, Stanley Bertram. Henry VII / [by] S.B. Chrimes. — London : Eyre Methuen, 1977. — xv,373p,leaf of plate,[16]p of plates : ill, facsims, geneal tables, maps, ports ; 24cm. — ([English monarchs])
Originally published: 1972. — Bibl.: p.345-354. — Index.
£7.95
ISBN 0-413-28590-1
ISBN 0-413-38400-4 Pbk : £3.50
(B77-34313)

942.05'1'0924 — England. Henry VIII, King of England, to 1509. *Biographies*
Bruce, Marie Louise. The making of Henry VIII / [by] Marie Louise Bruce. — London : Collins, 1977. — 254p,[8]p of plates : ill, geneal tables(on lining papers), ports ; 23cm.
Bibl.: p.233-237. — Index.
ISBN 0-00-211541-7 : £5.95
(B77-28305)

942.05'2 — England, 1509-1558
Elton, Geoffrey Rudolph. Reform and Reformation : England, 1509-1558 / [by] G.R. Elton. — London : Edward Arnold, 1977. — viii,423p ; 24cm. — (The new history of England ; 2)
Bibl.: p.397-410. — Index.
ISBN 0-7131-5952-9 : £9.95 : CIP rev.
ISBN 0-7131-5953-7 Pbk : £3.50
(B77-17835)

942.05'3 — England. Peasants' revolts, 1549
Cornwall, Julian. Revolt of the peasantry, 1549 / [by] Julian Cornwall. — London [etc.] : Routledge and Kegan Paul, 1977. — xi,254p : maps ; 23cm.
Bibl.: p.244-246. — Index.
ISBN 0-7100-8676-8 : £6.50 : CIP rev.
(B77-19124)

942.05'5 — England. War with Spain, 1568-1588. *Spanish texts. Secondary school texts*
Clarke, Robert Paul. Los ingleses y los españoles / by Robert P. Clarke. — Leeds : E.J. Arnold, 1976. — 48p : ill, maps, ports ; 22cm.
ISBN 0-560-02711-7 Sd : £0.75
Also classified at 946'.89
(B77-34314)

942.05'5 — England. War with Spain, 1587-1604
Graham, Winston. The Spanish armadas / [by] Winston Graham. — [London] : Fontana, 1976. — 256p,[8]p of plates : coats of arms, geneal tables, plan, ports ; 18cm.
Originally published: London : Collins, 1972. — Bibl.: p.244-247. — Index.
ISBN 0-00-634194-2 Pbk : £0.95
(B77-13437)

942.05'5'0924 — England. Drake, Sir Francis. *Biographies*
Thomson, George Malcolm. Sir Francis Drake / [by] George Malcolm Thomson. — London : Omega, 1976. — [10],358p,[8]p of plates : ill, maps, plans, ports ; 20cm.
Originally published: London : Secker and Warburg, 1972. — Bibl.: p.343-349. — Index.
ISBN 0-86007-736-5 Pbk : £1.60
(B77-08689)

942.05'5'0924 — England. Drake, Sir Francis. *Biographies. Juvenile literature*
Harper, Edyth. Sir Francis Drake / by Edyth Harper ; with illustrations by Frank Humphris. — Loughborough : Ladybird Books, 1977. — 52p : col ill, col map(on lining paper), col port ; 18cm. — (Ladybird history series ; 43)
Text on lining paper. — Index.
ISBN 0-7214-0465-0 : £0.24
(B77-18484)

942.05'5'0924 — England. Elizabeth I, Queen of England. *Biographies*
Johnson, Paul. Elizabeth I : a study in power and intellect / [by] Paul Johnson. — London : Omega, 1976. — [6],511p,[8]p of plates : ports ; 20cm.
Originally published: London : Weidenfeld and Nicolson, 1974. — Bibl.: p.487-492. — Index.
ISBN 0-86007-733-0 Pbk : £1.95
(B77-08690)

942.05'5'0924 — England. Elizabeth I, Queen of England. Interpersonal relations with suitors
Plowden, Alison. Marriage with my kingdom : the courtships of Elizabeth I / [by] Alison Plowden. — London [etc.] : Macmillan, 1977. — 216p,[8]p of plates : ports ; 22cm.
Bibl.: p.198-200. — Index.
ISBN 0-333-15792-3 : £4.95
(B77-23017)

942.05'5'0924 — England. Grenville, Sir Richard. *Biographies*
Rowse, Alfred Leslie. Sir Richard Grenville of the 'Revenge' / by A.L. Rowse. — London : Cape, 1977. — 367p ; 23cm.
Originally published: 1937. — Index.
ISBN 0-224-01356-4 : £6.50
(B77-09428)

942.05'5'0924 — England. Hickes, Sir Michael. *Biographies*
Smith, Alan Gordon Rae. Servant of the Cecils : the life of Sir Michael Hickes, 1543-1612 / [by] Alan G.R. Smith. — London : Cape, 1977. — 221p,8p of plates : ports ; 23cm.
Index.
ISBN 0-224-01154-5 : £7.50
(B77-15627)

942.05'5'0924 — England. Politics. Bacon, Sir Nicholas. *Biographies*
Tittler, Robert. Nicholas Bacon : the making of a Tudor statesman / [by] Robert Tittler. — London : Cape, 1976. — 256p,4p of plates : ill, coat of arms, geneal tables, port ; 23cm.
Bibl.: p.199. — Index.
ISBN 0-224-01286-x : £6.95
(B77-03842)

942.05'5'0924 — England. Raleigh, Sir Walter, b.1554. *Biographies*
Lacey, Robert. Sir Walter Ralegh / [by] Robert Lacey. — London : Cardinal, 1975. — 461p, [16]p of plates : ill, maps, ports ; 20cm.
Originally published: London : Weidenfeld and Nicolson, 1973. — Index.
ISBN 0-351-17129-0 Pbk : £2.00
(B77-08148)

942.05'5'0924 — England. Talbot, Elizabeth, Countess of Shrewsbury. *Biographies*
Durant, David N. Bess of Hardwick : portrait of an Elizabethan dynast / [by] David N. Durant. — London : Weidenfeld and Nicolson, 1977. — xiii,274p,[8]p of plates : ill, geneal tables, ports ; 23cm.
Bibl.: p.248-255. — Index.
ISBN 0-297-77305-4 : £6.95
(B77-23018)

Williams, Ethel Carleton. Bess of Hardwick / [by] E. Carleton Williams. — Bath : Chivers, 1977. — xi,312p,[8]p of plates : ill, geneal tables, ports ; 22cm.
Originally published: London : Longmans, Green, 1959. — Bibl.: p.296-303. — Index.
ISBN 0-85997-238-0 : £6.00(£4.50 to members of the Library Association)
(B77-16122)

942.06 — English civilization, 1603-1714. *Juvenile literature*
McLeod, Kirsty. Drums and trumpets : the House of Stuart / [by] Kirsty McLeod. — London : Deutsch, 1977. — 144p,[8]p of plates : ill(some col), facsim, maps(1 col), plan, ports(some col) ; 25cm. — (The mirror of Britain series)
Bibl.: p.138-140. — Index.
ISBN 0-233-96861-x : £3.95
(B77-29833)

942.06'092'2 — England. Monarchs, 1603-1714
Kenyon, John Philipps. The Stuarts : a study in English kingship / [by] J.P. Kenyon. — Revised ed. — London : Severn House : [Distributed by Hutchinson], 1977. — 223p,[24] p of plates : ill, geneal table, ports ; 21cm. — (British monarchy series)
Previous ed.: London : Batsford, 1958. — Bibl.: p.208-213. — Index.
ISBN 0-7278-0097-3 : £5.50
(B77-29076)

942.06'2 — English Civil War
Barbary, James. Puritan & Cavalier : the English civil war / [by] James Barbary. — London : Gollancz, 1977. — 192p : ill, facsims, maps, plans, ports ; 23cm.
Bibl.: p.182-183. — Index.
ISBN 0-575-02163-2 : £3.75
(B77-10679)

Ollard, Richard Lawrence. This war without an enemy : a history of the English civil wars / [by] Richard Ollard. — London : Hodder and Stoughton, 1976. — 224p,[16]p of plates : ill(some col), facsims, maps, plans, ports(some col) ; 26cm.
Facsims. on lining papers. — Index.
ISBN 0-340-20965-8 : £6.95
(B77-20823)

942.06'2 — English Civil War. *Juvenile literature*
Sutton, Harry Thomas. For king or commons : the inside story of Roundheads and Cavaliers / [by] Harry T. Sutton. — London (21 Little Russell St., W.C.1) : Heritage Books, 1977. — 48p : ill(some col), maps ; 21cm.
'A National Trust series for children'.
ISBN 0-906045-04-5 Pbk : £0.85
(B77-30875)

942.06'2 — English Civil War. Cotswolds campaign
Jennings, R W. The Cotswolds in the Civil War / [by] R.W. Jennings. — Cirencester (Park St., Cirencester, Glos. GL7 2BX) : Corinium Museum for Cotswold District Council, 1976. — [18]p : ill, plans ; 26cm.
Bibl.: p.17.
Sd : £0.75
(B77-19125)

942.06'2 — English Civil War. Role of Levellers
Brailsford, Henry Noel. The Levellers and the English Revolution / by H.N. Brailsford ; edited and prepared for publication by Christopher Hill. — Nottingham : Bertrand Russell Peace Foundation for Spokesman Books, 1976. — xvi,715p ; 19cm. — ('Spokesman' university paperbacks ; no.14)
Originally published: London : Cresset Press, 1961. — Bibl.: p.693-694. — Index.
ISBN 0-85124-154-9 Pbk : £2.95
(B77-13981)

942.06'2'0922 — Roundheads. *England, 1642-1660. Biographies*
Ridley, Jasper. The Roundheads / [by] Jasper Ridley. — London : Constable, 1976. — xi, 276p,leaf of plate,[16]p of plates : ill, map(on lining papers), ports(1 col) ; 23cm.
Bibl.: p.261-269. — Index.
ISBN 0-09-461230-7 : £5.50
(B77-01084)

942.06'2'0922 — Royalists. *England, ca 1630-ca 1660*
Bence-Jones, Mark. The Cavaliers / [by] Mark Bence-Jones. — London : Constable, 1976. — xi,206p,leaf of plate,[16]p of plates : ill, map(on lining papers), ports(1 col) ; 23cm.
Bibl.: p.196-200. — Index.
ISBN 0-09-461260-9 : £5.25
(B77-01085)

942.06'2'0924 — England. Charles I, King of England. *Serials*
The **Royal** Martyr annual. — [Edinburgh] ([c/o 15 Randolph Cres., Edinburgh 3]) : [Royal Martyr Church Union].
1977. — [1976]. — 31p : ill, ports ; 22cm.
ISBN 0-905798-00-7 Sd : £1.00(£0.50 to members)
(B77-02684)

942.06'2'0924 — England. Henrietta Maria, Queen, consort of Charles I, King of England. *Biographies*
Oman, Carola. Henrietta Maria / [by] Carola Oman. — London [etc.] : White Lion Publishers, 1976. — xv,366p,[8]p of plates : ports ; 23cm.
Originally published: London : Hodder and Stoughton, 1936. — Bibl.: p.xi-xv. — Index.
ISBN 0-7274-0154-8 : £6.50
(B77-01086)

942.06'2'0924 — England. Marten, Henry. *Biographies*
Waters, Ivor. Henry Marten and the Long Parliament / by Ivor Waters. — Chepstow ([41 Hardwick Ave.], Chepstow, Gwent) : Chepstow Society, 1976. — 79p : ill, ports ; 22cm.
Cover title: The prisoner of Chepstow Castle. — Originally published: 1973. — Bibl.: p.74-76. — Index.
ISBN 0-900278-36-6 Pbk : £1.00
(B77-10063)

942.06'2'0924 — England. Politics. Harington, John, b.1589, 1646-1653. *Diaries*
Harington, John, *b.1589.* The diary of John Harington, M.P., 1646-53 : with notes for his charges / edited by Margaret F. Stieg. — [Yeovil] ([c/o Mrs S.W. Rawlins, Newton Surmaville, Yeovil, Somerset]) : Somerset Record Society, 1977. — viii,121p ; 24cm. — (Somerset Record Society. Publications ; vol.74)

Bibl.
£1.50
(B77-31627)

942.06'3 — England, 1649-1666. *Secondary school texts*
Liversidge, Douglas. The Restoration / [by] Douglas Liversidge. — Hove : Wayland, 1977. — 128p : ill, ports ; 24cm. — (The documentary history series)
Bibl.: p.126. — Index.
ISBN 0-85340-428-3 : £3.50
(B77-21621)

942.06'4'0924 — England. Cromwell, Oliver. *Biographies*
Gardiner, Samuel Rawson. Oliver Cromwell / by Samuel Rawson Gardiner. — Wakefield : EP Publishing, 1976. — [5],319p,plate : port ; 20cm.
Facsimile reprint of: 1909 ed. London : Longmans, Green, 1909.
ISBN 0-7158-1181-9 : £4.95
(B77-30876)

Howell, Roger. Cromwell / by Roger Howell, Jr. — London : Hutchinson, 1977. — xii,269p ; 23cm. — (The library of world biography)
Bibl.: p.257-261. — Index.
ISBN 0-09-131410-0 : £4.50
(B77-26703)

942.06'4'0924 — England. Cromwell, Oliver. *Biographies. Secondary school texts*
Purves, Amanda. Cromwell / [by] Amanda Purves. — Hove : Wayland, 1977. — 96p : ill, ports ; 22cm. — (Wayland history makers)
Bibl.: p.94. — Index.
ISBN 0-85340-451-8 : £3.50
(B77-28306)

942.06'6 — England. Social life, 1666. *Middle school texts. Teaching kits*
Corfe, Tom. Samuel Pepys / by Tom Corfe ; illustrated by Valerie Bell. — Cambridge [etc.] : Cambridge University Press, 1976 [i.e. 1977]. — 1v. : ill(some col), facsim, 2 maps(1 col), ports(1 col) ; 15x21cm. — (History first)
Four booklets, 12 folders ([48]p.) in plastic envelope. — Bibl.
ISBN 0-521-21208-1 : £2.75
(B77-10064)

Corfe, Tom. Samuel Pepys / by Tom Corfe ; illustrated by Valerie Bell. — Cambridge [etc.] : Cambridge University Press. — (History first)
Spirit duplicator masters / drawings by Valerie Bell. — 1977. — [13]leaves : ill ; 28cm.
ISBN 0-521-21375-4 Sd : £3.00
(B77-13438)

942.06'6'0924 — England. Carteret, Sir George. *Biographies*
Balleine, George Reginald. All for the king : the life story of Sir George Carteret / by G.R. Balleine. — St Helier (The Jersey Museum, 9 Pier Rd, St Helier, Jersey, Channel Islands) : Société jersiaise, 1976. — xiv,188p,[2] leaves of plates,[6]p of plates : ill, facsim, geneal table, maps(on lining papers), ports ; 23cm.
Bibl.: p.167-170. — Index.
ISBN 0-901897-10-8 : £4.50
(B77-19917)

942.06'6'0924 — England. Charles II, King of England. *Biographies*
Falkus, Christopher. The life and times of Charles II / [by] Christopher Falkus ; introduction by Antonia Fraser. — London : Cardinal, 1975. — 127p,[40]p of plates : ill(incl 1 col), facsims, map, ports(some col) ; 20cm. — (Kings & Queens)
Cover title: Charles II. — Originally published: London : Weidenfeld and Nicolson, 1972. — Bibl.: p.121-122. — Index.
ISBN 0-351-16214-3 Pbk : £1.25
(B77-19918)

Wheatley, Dennis. 'Old Rowley' : a very private life of Charles II / [by] Dennis Wheatley. — London [etc.] : Arrow Books, 1977. — 192p ; 18cm.
Originally published: London : Hutchinson, 1933. — Index.
ISBN 0-09-913980-4 Pbk : £0.70
(B77-11007)

942.06'6'0924 — England. Charles II, King of England. *Biographies. Secondary school texts*
Gibson, Michael, *b.1936.* Charles II / [by] Michael Gibson. — Hove : Wayland, 1976. — 96p : ill, facsims, 2 maps, plans, ports ; 22cm. — (Wayland kings and queens)
Bibl.: p.94. — Index.
ISBN 0-85340-435-6 : £2.95
(B77-09429)

942.06'6'0924 — England. Pepys, Samuel. *Biographies*
Ollard, Richard Lawrence. Pepys : a biography / [by] Richard Ollard. — London [etc.] : Pan Books, 1977. — 368p : ill, facsims, maps ; 20cm.
Originally published: London : Hodder and Stoughton, 1974. — Index.
ISBN 0-330-25010-8 Pbk : £1.50
(B77-10680)

942.06'7'0924 — England. James II, King of England. *Biographies*
Ashley, Maurice. James II / [by] Maurice Ashley. — London [etc.] : Dent, 1977[i.e.1978]. — 342p,[16]p of plates : ill, maps, ports ; 24cm.

Bibl.: p.302-305. — Index.
ISBN 0-460-12021-2 : £7.50 : CIP rev.
(B77-32989)

942.07 — Children. Social life. *England, 1700-1800. Secondary school texts*
Harrison, Molly. The eighteenth century / [by] Molly Harrison ; illustrations by Sheila Maguire. — [New ed.]. — Amersham : Hulton, 1977. — [2],106p : ill, facsim ; 24cm. — (Children in history)
Previous ed.: published as 'Children in history. Book 3. 18th century'. 1961.
ISBN 0-7175-0766-1 Pbk : £1.35
(B77-28307)

942.07'092'4 — England. Nash, Beau. *Biographies*
Poole, Keith Baddeley. The two beaux / by Keith B. Poole. — Wakefield : EP Publishing, 1976. — viii,152p : ill, ports ; 21cm.
Bibl.: p.151-152.
ISBN 0-7158-1195-9 : £3.50
Also classified at 942.07'3'0924
(B77-17836)

942.07'2 — England. Political events, 1714-1760
Speck, William Arthur. Stability and strife : England, 1714-1760 / [by] W.A. Speck. — London : Edward Arnold, 1977. — viii,311p : 2 maps ; 24cm. — (The new history of England ; 6)
Bibl.: p.288-296. — Index.
ISBN 0-7131-5974-x : £9.95 : CIP rev.
ISBN 0-7131-5975-8 Pbk : £3.50
(B77-27587)

942.07'3'0924 — England. Brummell, George Bryan. *Biographies*
Cole, Hubert. Beau Brummell / [by] Hubert Cole. — London [etc.] : Granada, 1977. — 240p,leaf of plate,[16]p of plates : ill, facsim, ports ; 23cm.
Bibl.: p.226-228. — Index.
ISBN 0-246-10920-3 : £4.95
(B77-29077)

Poole, Keith Baddeley. The two beaux / by Keith B. Poole. — Wakefield : EP Publishing, 1976. — viii,152p : ill, ports ; 21cm.
Bibl.: p.151-152.
ISBN 0-7158-1195-9 : £3.50
Primary classification 942.07'092'4
(B77-17836)

942.07'3'0924 — England. Sussex, Augustus Frederick, Duke of. *Biographies*
Gillen, Mollie. Royal Duke : Augustus Frederick, Duke of Sussex (1773-1843) / by Mollie Gillen. — London : Sidgwick and Jackson, 1976 [i.e. 1977]. — 268p,[16]p of plates : ill, facsim, geneal table, ports ; 25cm.
Bibl.: p.246-250. — Index.
ISBN 0-283-98316-7 : £6.95
(B77-10681)

942.07'4 — England. Cato Street Conspiracy
Anand, Vidya Sagar. The Cato Street conspiracy / by V.S. Anand and F.A. Ridley. — London (25 Manchester Sq., W.1) : Medusa Press ; London : Distributed by Intercontex Marketing Company, 1977. — 120p : ill, ports ; 20cm.
Bibl.: p.116-117. — Index.
£2.75
(B77-18485)

942.081 — England. Social life, 1812-1870. Expounded by fiction in English. Dickens, Charles. *Primary school texts*
Favell, Christine. At the time of Charles Dickens / [by] Christine Favell. — London : Longman, 1977. — 64p : ill, facsims, plans, ports ; 24cm. — (Focus on history)
Index.
ISBN 0-582-18248-4 Pbk : £0.75
(B77-23897)

942.081 — England. Social life, 1837-1901
Compton, Piers. Victorian vortex : pleasures and peccadilloes of an age / [by] Piers Compton. — London : Hale, 1977. — 255p ; 23cm.
Bibl.: p.243-248. — Index.
ISBN 0-7091-6334-7 : £5.50
(B77-34315)

942.081'092'4 — England. Lovelace, Ada King, Countess of. *Biographies*
Moore, Doris Langley. Ada, Countess of Lovelace : Byron's legitimate daughter / [by] Doris Langley Moore. — London : J. Murray, 1977. — [13],5-397p,[12]p of plates : ill, ports ; 24cm.
Bibl.: p.387-388. — Index.
ISBN 0-7195-3384-8 : £9.50
(B77-29834)

942.081'092'4 — England. Rural regions. Social life, 1870-1879. *Diaries*
Kilvert, Francis. Journal of a country curate : selections from the diary of Francis Kilvert, 1870-79. — Abridged ed. / selected and with an introduction by Peter Wait ; photographic re-creations by Tim Stephens. — London : Folio Society, 1977. — 338p : ill, map(on lining papers), ports ; 23cm.
In slip case. — Full ed.: published in 3 vols. as 'Kilverts' diary'. London : Cape, 1938-1940.
£6.75
(B77-32327)

Kilvert, Francis. Kilvert's diary : selections from the diary of the Rev. Francis Kilvert / chosen, edited and introduced by William Plomer. — New and corrected ed. — London : Cape, 1977. — 3v.([4],396,[4]p of plates;448p,[8]p of plates,508p, [4]p of plates) : ill, facsims, col maps(on lining papers), ports ; 24cm.
In slip case. — This ed. originally published: 1960. — Index.
ISBN 0-224-01299-1 : £20.00
(B77-07060)

Kilvert, Francis. Kilvert's diary, 1870-1879 : selections from the diary of the Rev. Francis Kilvert / chosen, edited and introduced by William Plomer. — Harmondsworth [etc.] : Penguin, 1977. — 378p : 2 maps ; 18cm.
This selection originally published: London : Cape, 1944. — Index.
ISBN 0-14-004762-x Pbk : £1.25
(B77-32328)

942.082'092'4 — England. Ali, Beatrice. *Autobiographies*
Ali, Beatrice. The good deeds of a good woman / [by] Beatrice Ali ; recorded [and edited] between May and September 1975 [by Clive Murphy]. — London : Dobson, 1976. — 124p ; 23cm. — (Ordinary lives ; 1)
Sound disc (1s. ; 6in. 33 1/3 rpm) as insert.
ISBN 0-234-77891-1 : £4.95
(B77-04490)

942.082'092'4 — England. Carnarvon, Henry George Alfred Marius Victor Francis Herbert, Earl of. *Autobiographies*
Carnarvon, Henry George Alfred Marius Victor Francis Herbert, *Earl of.* No regrets / [by] the Earl of Carnarvon. — London : Weidenfeld and Nicolson, 1976. — vii,227p,[4]p of plates : ill, ports ; 23cm.
ISBN 0-297-77246-5 : £5.95
(B77-00535)

942.082'092'4 — England. Dolding, C. *Autobiographies*
Dolding, C. Blueprint for happiness here and in the hereafter / [by] C. Dolding. — Ashford, Kent : The author ; Ilfracombe : [Distributed by] Stockwell, 1977. — 35p ; 18cm.
ISBN 0-7223-1051-x Pbk : £1.00
(B77-27588)

942.082'092'4 — England. Ingram, Jim. *Autobiographies*
Ingram, Jim. The world's my university / [by] Jim Ingram. — Large print ed. — Leicester : Ulverscroft, 1977. — [8],470p ; 23cm. — (Ulverscroft large print series : [non-fiction])
Originally published: London : Harrap, 1965.
ISBN 0-7089-0050-x : Unpriced
(B77-29835)

942.082'092'4 — England. Powell, Albert. *Biographies*
Powell, Margaret. Albert, my consort / [by] Margaret Powell. — London : Sphere, 1976. — 188p ; 18cm.
Originally published: London : Joseph, 1975.
ISBN 0-7221-0422-7 Pbk : £0.75
(B77-32329)

942.082'092'4 — England. Sands, Ethel. *Biographies*
Baron, Wendy. Miss Ethel Sands and her circle / [by] Wendy Baron. — London : Owen, 1977. — xx,300p,[8]p of plates : ill, geneal tables, ports ; 23cm.
Bibl.: p.287-289. — Index.
ISBN 0-7206-0304-8 : £8.50
(B77-21623)

942.082'3'0222 — England. Social life, 1903-1913. *Illustrations*
The **golden** years, 1903-1913 : a pictorial survey of the most interesting decade in English history, recorded in contemporary photographs and drawings / [compiled by] Gordon Winter. — Harmondsworth [etc.] : Penguin, 1977. — 112p : of ill, facsims, ports ; 25cm.
Originally published: Newton Abbot : David and Charles, 1975.
ISBN 0-14-004366-7 Pbk : £1.25
(B77-31628)

942.083 — England. Intellectual life, 1919-1950
Green, Martin, *b.1927.* Children of the sun : a narrative of 'decadence' in England after 1918 / [by] Martin Green. — Revised, corrected [ed.]. — London : Constable, 1977. — 552p,[16]p of plates : ports ; 23cm.
Previous ed.: i.e. 1st ed. New York : Basic Books, 1976. — Index.
ISBN 0-09-461430-x : £7.50
(B77-29078)

942.083'092'4 — England. Gibney, Josephine. *Autobiographies*
Gibney, Josephine. Joe McGarrigle's daughter / [by] Josephine Gibney. — Kineton : Roundwood Press, 1977. — v,153p ; 23cm.
ISBN 0-900093-62-5 : £3.75
(B77-17229)

942.083'092'4 — England. Lane, Maxie, to 1939. *Autobiographies*
Lane, Maxie. Running! / [by] Maxie Lane. — London [etc.] : Macmillan, 1977. — [5],221p ; 23cm.
ISBN 0-333-21239-8 : £4.95
(B77-23898)

942.083'092'4 — England. Social life, 1910-1920. *Childhood reminiscences*
Maddocks, Margaret. An unlessoned girl / [by] Margaret Maddocks ; with drawings by Margaret Wetherbee. — London : Hutchinson, 1977. — 142p : ill ; 23cm.
Ill. on lining papers.
ISBN 0-09-128520-8 : £3.50
(B77-22278)

942.083'092'4 — England. Social life, 1926-1940. *Personal observations*
Fen, Elisaveta. A Russian's England : reminiscences of years 1926-1940 / [by] Elisaveta Fen. — Warwick (Warwick, CV35 0JA) : Paul Gordon Books, 1976. — x,467p,[8] p of plates : ill, ports ; 25cm.
ISBN 0-905576-00-4 : £5.50
(B77-10682)

942.084'092'4 — England. Morgan, Kay Summersby. Interpersonal relationships with Eisenhower, Dwight David, 1941-1945. *Personal observations*
Morgan, Kay Summersby. Past forgetting : my love affair with Dwight D. Eisenhower / [by] Kay Summersby Morgan. — London : Collins, 1977. — 220,[1]p,[16]p of plates : ill, facsims, ports ; 24cm.
Originally published: New York : Simon and Schuster, 1976.
ISBN 0-00-211645-6 : £4.95
Primary classification 973.917'092'4
(B77-05157)

942.085'092'4 — Polish refugees. Kruk, Zofia. *England, 1945-1968. Autobiographies*
Kruk, Zofia. The taste of hope / [by] Zofia Kruk. — London : Hutchinson, 1977. — [7], 197p ; 22cm.
ISBN 0-09-130230-7 : £4.50
(B77-26034)

942.085'4'0924 — England. Social life, 1942-1957. *Personal observations*
Murry, Colin. Shadows on the grass / by Colin Middleton Murry. — London : Gollancz, 1977. — 190p,[4]p of plates : ill, ports ; 23cm.
ISBN 0-575-02368-6 : £4.95
(B77-29079)

942.085'7 — England. Social life. *For foreign students*
Redlich, Monica. Everyday England / by Monica Redlich. — 4th revised ed. / revised by Irene Thornley. — London : Duckworth, 1977. — 5-179p : maps ; 23cm.
Previous ed.: 1968.
ISBN 0-7156-1232-8 : £5.95
ISBN 0-7156-1256-5 Pbk : £1.95
(B77-23899)

942.085'7'0924 — England. Rural regions. Social life. *Personal observations*
Peel, John Hugh Brignal. Country talk again / [by] J.H.B. Peel ; illustrated by Val Biro. — London : Hale, 1977. — 174p : ill ; 23cm.
ISBN 0-7091-6371-1 : £4.95
(B77-29080)

942.1/8 — HISTORY. ENGLAND. SPECIAL LOCALITIES
942.1 — Villages. *London, to 1976*
Shute, Nerina. London villages / [by] Nerina Shute. — London : Hale [etc.], 1977. — 208p, [12]p of plates : ill, maps, ports ; 23cm.
Bibl. — Index.
ISBN 0-7091-5812-2 : £4.50
(B77-13982)

942.1'00992 — Persons commemorated by blue plaques in Inner London. Local associations: Inner London. Residences
Mann, Christopher. Where the famous lived in London / [by] Christopher Mann ; photographs, Steve Lawrence ; drawings, Dacre Punt. — London (21 Conduit St., W1R 9TB) : Serpentine Press Ltd, 1974. — 96p : ill, maps ; 22cm.
ISBN 0-903961-01-6 Pbk : Unpriced
ISBN 0-903961-00-8 Pbk : £1.00
(B77-19919)

942.1'06 — London. Social life, 1603-1714. *Juvenile literature*
Miller, Peggy. Life in Stuart London / [by] Peggy Miller ; illustrated with photographs and with drawings by Gabrielle Stoddart. — London : Methuen, 1977. — 96p : ill, facsim, map, ports ; 26cm.
Bibl.: p.93. — Index.
ISBN 0-416-80190-0 : £3.60
(B77-31629)

942.1'07 — London. Political events, 1725-1848
London in the Age of Reform / edited by John Stevenson. — Oxford : Blackwell, 1977. — xxvi,214p : map ; 23cm.
Bibl.: p.213-214.
ISBN 0-631-17820-1 : £7.50 : CIP rev.
(B77-05782)

942.1'081'0924 — London. Social life, 1870-1879. *Childhood reminiscences*
Hughes, Mary Vivian. A London child of the 1870s / [by] M.V. Hughes. — Oxford [etc.] : Oxford University Press, 1977. — [5],141p ; 20cm.
Originally published: as 'A London child of the seventies'. London : Oxford University Press, 1934.
ISBN 0-19-281216-5 Pbk : £0.95 : CIP rev.
(B77-07740)

942.1'082'0922 — London. Social life, ca 1890-ca 1940. *Childhood reminiscences. Collections*
Where I was young : memories of London childhoods / [edited by] Valerie Jenkins ; with line drawings by George Murray. — London : Hart-Davis MacGibbon, 1976. — vi,161p : ill ; 25cm.
Ill. on lining papers. — Based on a series of interviews published in the 'Evening standard'.
ISBN 0-246-10873-8 : £4.95
(B77-06388)

942.1'082'30924 — London. Social life, ca 1900-ca 1910. *Childhood reminiscences*
Morgan, Verne. Yesterday's sunshine : reminiscences of an Edwardian childhood / [by] Verne Morgan. — [Sevenoaks] : Coronet, 1977. — [4],140p,[8]p of plates : ports ; 18cm.
Originally published: Folkestone : Bailey and Swinfen, 1974.
ISBN 0-340-19995-4 Pbk : £0.70
(B77-16678)

942.1'083'0924 — London. Social life, ca 1930-ca 1945. *Personal observations*
Henrey, *Mrs* **Robert.** Green leaves / [by] Mrs Robert Henrey. — Large print ed. — Bath : Firecrest, 1977. — [7],343p ; 22cm.
Originally published: London : Dent, 1976.
ISBN 0-85119-017-0 : £4.75
(B77-34316)

942.1'085'7 — London
Lawson, Andrew. Discover unexpected London / [by] Andrew Lawson. — Oxford : Elsevier-Phaidon, 1977. — 128p : col ill, col map, col ports ; 29cm.
Bibl.: p.128. — Index.
ISBN 0-7290-0066-4 : £4.95
(B77-26704)

942.1'085'7 — London. *Secondary school texts*
Mountfield, Anne. London / [by] Anne Mountfield. — London : Harrap, 1977. — 46p : ill, maps, ports ; 19x22cm. — (The regions of Britain)
ISBN 0-245-53079-7 Sd : £0.95
(B77-29081)

942.1'085'70222 — London. *Illustrations*
Canetti, Nicolai. The parks, squares & mews of London / principal photography Nicolai Canetti ; commentary Sandy Lesberg. — New York ; London : Peebles Press International ; Freemen's Common (Euston St., Freemen's Common, Leics.) : Distributed by WHS Distributors, 1976. — 125p : chiefly ill(some col) ; 31cm.
Ill. on lining papers.
ISBN 0-672-52222-5 : £3.25
(B77-11492)

Picture book of London / [compiled by] D.C. May ; preface by the Earl Grosvenor. — London [etc.] : Hamlyn, 1977. — 96p : chiefly col ill, col map ; 31cm.
Col. ill. on lining papers.
ISBN 0-600-37144-1 : £2.50
(B77-30878)

942.1'2 — Public libraries. *London (City). Guildhall Library. Exhibits: Items associated with London (City) & British monarchs, 1067-1977. Catalogues*
London *(City). Corporation.* The city and the crown. — [London] : [Corporation of London], [1977]. — [31]p : ill(some col), facsims(1 col), col ports ; 15x21cm.
'[Catalogue of an] exhibition, held in the Old Guildhall Library from June 20th to July 2nd 1977 ...' - p.[31]. '... organised by the Corporation of London ...' - p.[2].
Sd : Unpriced
(B77-32990)

942.1'2'066 — Fires. *London (City), 1666*
Ellis, Peter Berresford. The Great Fire of London : an illustrated account / [by] Peter Berresford Ellis. — London : New English Library, 1976. — 126p,[4]p of plates : ill(some col), coats of arms, facsims, maps, plans, ports(some col) ; 30cm.
Ill. on lining papers. — Bibl.: p.122. — Index.
ISBN 0-450-03228-0 : £8.50
(B77-32991)

942.1'2'0810222 — London (City), 1869-1958. Compared with London (City), ca 1975. *Illustrations*
City of London past & present : a pictorial record of the City of London / [compiled by] J.K. Fisher. — Oxford : Oxford Illustrated Press, 1976. — [64]p : chiefly ill ; 28cm.
ISBN 0-902280-34-1 : £3.25
(B77-01087)

942.1'32 — Government buildings. *London. Westminster (London Borough). Downing Street. No.10 Downing Street*
Charlton, John. No.10 Downing Street, SW1, City of Westminster / [by] John Charlton. — London : H.M.S.O., 1977. — [1],12,[1]p : col ill ; 16x21cm.
At head of title: Department of the Environment.
ISBN 0-11-670793-3 Sd : £0.50
(B77-16679)

942.1'32 — Government buildings. *London. Westminster (London Borough). Palace of Westminster, 1834-1976*
Cocks, *Sir* **Barnett.** Mid-Victorian masterpiece : the story of an institution unable to put its own house in order / [by] Barnett Cocks. — London [etc.] : Hutchinson, 1977. — 208p,[16]p of plates : ill, plan, ports ; 24cm.
Index.
ISBN 0-09-128260-8 : £6.95
(B77-19920)

942.1'34 — Town houses. *London. Kensington and Chelsea (London Borough). Pheasantry, The*
Macdonald, Nesta. The history of The Pheasantry, Chelsea, 1766-1977 / by Nesta Macdonald. — [London] ([Flat A, 247 Fulham Rd, SW3 6HY]) : [The author], 1977. — [4],23,[3]p : ill, facsims, map ; 21cm.
ISBN 0-9505605-0-2 Sd : £1.00
(B77-26035)

942.1'42 — London. Camden (London Borough). Kentish Town, to 1976
Tindall, Gillian. The fields beneath : the history of one London village / [by] Gillian Tindall. — London : Temple Smith, 1977. — 255p : ill, maps, plan ; 23cm.
Bibl.: p.240-243. — Index.
ISBN 0-85117-122-2 : £8.50
(B77-24621)

942.1'44 — Parks. *London. Hackney (London Borough). Victoria Park, to 1975*
Poulsen, Charles. Victoria Park : a study in the history of East London / by Charles Poulsen. — London (196 Cable St., E.1) : Stepney Books : Journeyman Press, 1976. — [8],120p : ill, plans ; 21cm.
Bibl.: p.119.
ISBN 0-904526-15-1 Pbk : £1.20
Primary classification 942.1'5
(B77-15628)

942.1'44'082 — London. Hackney (London Borough). Social life, 1933-1975
Barnes, Ron. Coronation cups and jam jars : a portrait of an East End family through three generations / [by] Ron Barnes. — London (136 Kingsland High St., E.8) : Centerprise, 1976. — 208p ; 22cm.
ISBN 0-903738-26-0 : £4.00
ISBN 0-903738-27-9 Pbk : £0.90
(B77-08691)

942.1'5 — Castles. *London. Tower Hamlets (London Borough). Tower of London, to 1977*
Rowse, Alfred Leslie. The Tower of London / [by] A.L. Rowse. — London : Joseph, 1977. — 48p : ill(some col), plan(on lining papers), col ports ; 19cm. — (Folio miniatures)
ISBN 0-7181-1544-9 : £1.95
(B77-29082)

942.1'5 — London. Tower Hamlets (London Borough). Bethnal Green. *Newspapers*
East ender, Bethnal Green. — [London] (High St., E15 2JB) : Wilson and Whitworth Publishing Ltd.
14th Apr. 1977-. — [1977]-. — ill, ports ; 42cm.
Weekly. — 32p. in 1st issue.
Sd : £0.07
ISSN 0140-5667
(B77-32992)

942.1'5 — London. Tower Hamlets (London Borough). Wapping. Social life, ca 1900-1920. *Childhood reminiscences*
Foakes, Grace. My part of the river / [by] Grace Foakes. — London : Futura Publications, 1976. — 192p ; 18cm.
Contents: Between high walls. Originally published: London : Shepheard-Walwyn, 1972 - My part of the river. Originally published: London : Shepheard-Walwyn, 1974.
ISBN 0-86007-350-5 Pbk : £0.65
(B77-10683)

942.1'5 — Parks. *London. Tower Hamlets (London Borough). Victoria Park, to 1975*
Poulsen, Charles. Victoria Park : a study in the history of East London / by Charles Poulsen. — London (196 Cable St., E.1) : Stepney Books : Journeyman Press, 1976. — [8],120p : ill, plans ; 21cm.
Bibl.: p.119.
ISBN 0-904526-15-1 Pbk : £1.20
Also classified at 942.1'44
(B77-15628)

942.1'5'08230924 — Working classes. Social life. *London. East End, 1902. Personal observations*
London, Jack. The people of the abyss / [by] Jack London. — [1st ed. reprinted] ; introduction by Jack Lindsay. — London (97 Ferme Park Rd, N8 9SA) : Journeyman Press, 1977. — [5],128p,8p of plates : ill ; 21cm.
First ed. originally published: New York : Macmillan ; London : Isbister, 1903.
ISBN 0-904526-17-8 Pbk : £1.20
(B77-23900)

942.1'5'0830924 — London. Tower Hamlets (London Borough). Social life, 1912-1933. *Personal observations*
Finn, Ralph Leslie. Spring in Aldgate / [by] Ralph L. Finn. — Large print ed. — Bath : Chivers, 1977. — [9],358p ; 22cm.
Originally published: London : Hale, 1968.
ISBN 0-85997-264-x : £5.60(£4.20 to members of the Library Association)
(B77-34317)

942.1'5'0840924 — London. Tower Hamlets (London Borough). Anna. *Biographies*
Fynn. Mister God, this is Anna / by Fynn ; illustrated by Papas. — [London] : Fontana, 1977. — 190p : ill ; 19cm.
Originally published: London : Collins, 1974.
ISBN 0-00-624563-3 Pbk : £0.60
(B77-11008)

942.1'5'0850924 — London. East End. Social life, 1945-1976. *Personal observations*
Scannell, Dorothy. Dolly's mixture / [by] Dorothy Scannell. — London [etc.] : Macmillan, 1977. — 206p ; 23cm.
ISBN 0-333-23236-4 : £3.95 : CIP rev.
(B77-23019)

942.1'62 — London. Greenwich (London Borough). Paragon, The & Paragon House, to 1976
Bonwitt, W. The history of the Paragon and Paragon House and their residents / by W. Bonwitt. — [London] ([74 Tranquil Vale, SE3 9BW]) : The Bookshop Blackheath Ltd, [1976]. — v,58p,[16]p of plates : ill, facsims, maps, ports ; 24cm.
Index.
ISBN 0-9505136-2-8 Pbk : £1.50
(B77-10684)

942.1'63 — London. Lewisham (London Borough). Blackheath, 1790-1970
Rhind, Neil. Blackheath village and environs, 1790-1970 / by Neil Rhind. — London ([74 Tranquil Vale, S.E.3]) : Bookshops Blackheath Ltd.
Also available in half leather binding.
Vol.1 : The village and Blackheath Vale. — 1976. — ii-xx,251p,[40]p of plates : ill, facsims, maps, plans, port ; 25cm.
Map on lining papers. — Bibl.: p.235-237. — Index.
ISBN 0-9505136-0-1 : £5.00
ISBN 0-9505136-1-x Half Leather ed. : £12.00
(B77-01088)

942.1'63 — London. Lewisham (London Borough). Sydenham, 1648-1975
Read, Joan. Read about Sydenham Wells / by Joan Read. — London (29 Ewhurst Rd, S.E.4) : The author, 1977. — [2],12p,plate : ill, map ; 25cm.
Sd : £0.35
(B77-19921)

942.1'63'0857 — London. Lewisham (London Borough). Social life. *Stories for children*
Read, Joan. Read about Lewisham / by Joan Read ; cartoons by Sam Morse. — London (29 Ewhurst Rd, S.E.4) : The author, 1976. — [6], 89p : ill, map ; 25cm.
Index.
ISBN 0-9505537-0-0 Sd : £1.25
(B77-08692)

942.1'64 — London. Southwark (London Borough). Bermondsey, to 1975
Gray, Geoffrey. A brief history and description of Bermondsey Parish Church, St Mary Magdalen, with St Olave, St John and St Luke / [by Geoffrey Gray]. — [New ed.] / [revised by Mervyn Wilson]. — [London] ([Bermondsey Rectory, 193 Bermondsey St., S.E.1]) : Bermondsey Parish Church, 1976. — 24p : ill, facsim, map, plan, port ; 15x21cm.
Previous ed.: published as 'The Parish Church of St Mary Magdalen, Bermondsey'. 1958. — Bibl.: p.24.
Sd : £0.50
(B77-23020)

942.1'64 — London. Southwark (London Borough). Camberwell, to 1875. *Early works. Facsimiles*
Blanch, William Harnett. [Ye parish of Camerwell]. The parish of Camberwell / [by] William Harnett Blanch. — London (50 Grove La., S.E.5) : Stephen Marks for the Camberwell Society, 1976. — [3],ii,xvi,486,[114]p,[15]leaves of plates,[70]p of plates : ill, facsims, maps, ports ; 25cm.
Facsimile reprint. — 'Ye parish of Camerwell' originally published: London : E.W. Allen, 1875. — Index.
£9.00
(B77-09430)

942.1'65 — Buildings of historical importance. *London. Lambeth (London Borough). Kennington. Lists*
Nicolson, Jim. A guide to some of the buildings of architectural and historic interest in the Kennington Conservation Area, London Borough of Lambeth / compiled by Jim Nicolson ; photographs by Jim Nicolson and Philip Vernon. — London (20 Albert Sq., SW8 1BS) : Vauxhall Society, 1975. — [12]p : ill, 2 maps ; 22cm.
Bibl.: p.[12].
Sd : Unpriced
(B77-21624)

942.1'65 — Palaces. *London. Lambeth (London Borough). Kennington Palace. Excavation of remains, 1965-1968. Reports, surveys*
Dawson, Graham John. The Black Prince's palace at Kennington, Surrey / [by] Graham J. Dawson. — Oxford : British Archaeological Reports, 1976. — [7],213p(8 fold) : ill, map, plans ; 30cm. — (British archaeological reports ; 26 ISSN 0306-1205)
ISBN 0-904531-29-5 Pbk : £3.90
(B77-00536)

942.1'72 — London. Waltham Forest (London Borough). Walthamstow. High Street. Social life, 1884-1929. *Childhood reminiscences*
Memories of High Street / compiled & edited by J.W. Howes. — [Walthamstow] ([Central Library, High St., E17 7JN]) : Libraries and the Arts Department, London Borough of Waltham Forest, 1977. — [2],ii,18p : ill ; 30cm.
ISBN 0-901974-06-4 Sd : £0.40
(B77-15629)

942.1'73 — London. Redbridge (London Borough). Wanstead, to 1946
Eastment, Winifred. Wanstead through the ages / by Winifred Eastment (Winifred V. Phillips) ; colour illustrations by Arthur Parsons ; black-and-white sketches by Arthur H. Barns. — 4th ed. — Wanstead (1 Spratt Hall Rd, E11 2RQ) : Dawn Press, 1976. — 180p,[20]p of plates, fold leaf of plate : ill(chiefly col), map ; 23cm.
Previous ed.: Letchworth : 'Essex countryside', 1969. — Index.
Pbk : £3.50
(B77-22280)

942.1'74'005 — London. Havering (London Borough). *History. Periodicals*
Havering history review : the journal of the Hornchurch & District Historical Society. — Cranham ([c/o The Hon. Sec., 1 Welbeck Drive, Langdon Hills, Laindon, Essex]) : The Society.
No.1- ; 1969-. — 1969-. — ill ; 21cm.
Annual. — ii,34p. in issue no.2.
Sd : £0.25
(B77-10065)

942.1'77 — London. Bexley (London Borough). Bexley, 1890-1977
A Bexley mosaic / edited by Joy Saynor. — [Bexleyheath] ([c/o F. Message, 104 Mayplace Road East, Bexleyheath, Kent]) : Workers' Educational Association, Bexley Branch, 1977. — viii,90p,[5]leaves of plates : ill, maps ; 30cm.
Pbk : £0.75
(B77-27589)

942.1'77 — London. Bexley (London Borough). Erith. *History*
Prichard, John A. A history of Erith / by John A. Prichard. — Bexley ([Hall Place, Bourne Rd, Bexley, Kent]) : London Borough of Bexley, Libraries and Museums Department.
Part 1 : From the earliest times to 1485. — 1976. — [2],17p,[4]p of plates : ill, facsim ; 22cm.
Index.
ISBN 0-902541-06-4 Sd : Unpriced
(B77-03843)

942.1'78 — London. Bromley (London Borough). Mottingham, to 1976
Parkinson, W H. Mottingham : from hamlet to urban village / [by] W.H. Parkinson. — [London] ([31 Mottingham Rd, S.E.9]) : Bromley Public Libraries, 1977. — [4],35p,[8]p of plates : ill, facsims, maps ; 30cm.
Bibl.: p.31-33. — Index.
Sd : £0.50
(B77-27590)

942.1'78'005 — London. Bromley (London Borough). *History. Periodicals*
Bromley local history. — Bromley ([c/o Hon. Secretary, 163 Tubbenden La., Orpington, Kent]) : Local History Society for the London Borough of Bromley.
No.1- ; 1976-. — 1976-. — ill, geneal tables, maps, plans, ports ; 21cm.
Annual. — [2],49p. in 1st issue. — Bibl.
Sd : £0.50
ISSN 0309-4782
(B77-13440)

942.1'82 — London. Hounslow (London Borough). Bedford Park. Social life, 1876-1975
Bolsterli, Margaret Jones. The early community at Bedford Park : 'corporate happiness' in the first garden suburb / by Margaret Jones Bolsterli. — London [etc.] : Routledge and Kegan Paul, 1977. — xii,136p : ill, facsim, plans, port ; 27cm.
Index.
ISBN 0-7100-8693-8 : £7.50 : CIP rev.
(B77-09431)

942.1'82 — London. Hounslow (London Borough). Hounslow, Cranford, Heston & Isleworth, 1875-1930. *Illustrations*
Hounslow as it was : a selection of photographs with captions of Hounslow, Cranford, Heston & Isleworth / [selected and written by Gillian Morris and Andrea Cameron et al.] ; for the Hounslow & District History Society. — Nelson : Hendon Publishing Co., 1977. — 48p : chiefly ill, ports ; 21x29cm.
ISBN 0-86067-013-9 Sd : £1.50
(B77-23901)

942.1'84 — London. Ealing (London Borough). Bedford Park. Social life, 1900-1910. *Childhood reminiscences*
Pearce, Sybil. The life of an Edwardian child in the first garden suburb of Bedford Park / by Sybil Pearce ; cover design by Joanne E. Walton. — [London] ([6 Bedford Rd, W.4]) : [The author], [1977]. — 18p : ill, ports ; 21cm.
Cover title: An Edwardian childhood in Bedford Park.
Sd : £0.85
(B77-19126)

942.1'84 — London. Ealing (London Borough). Brentham Garden Estate, to 1976
Johnson, Bernard, *b.1954.* Brentham : Ealing's garden suburb / compiled by Bernard Johnson ... — London (23 Neville Rd, W.5) : Brentham Society, [1977]. — 24p : ill, 2 maps ; 20cm.
ISBN 0-9505934-0-0 Sd : £0.90
(B77-34318)

942.1'87 — Farmhouses. *London. Barnet (London Borough). Wyldes, to 1968*
Venning, Philip. Wyldes : a new history / by Philip Venning. — [London] ([Wyldes, North End, N.W.3]) : [The author], 1977. — [1],15 leaves,plate : ill, facsim, map, 2 ports ; 30cm.
Bibl.: p.15.
Sp : Unpriced
(B77-23902)

942.1'87 — London. Barnet (London Borough). Hampstead Garden Suburb, to 1977
Grafton Green, Brigid. Hampstead Garden Suburb 1907-1977 / by Brigid Grafton Green. — London (c/o The Archivist, Hampstead Garden Suburb Institute, Central Sq., NW11 7BN) : Hampstead Garden Suburb Residents' Association, 1977. — 20p : ill, maps, ports ; 30cm.
ISBN 0-9505562-0-3 Sd : £0.50
(B77-27591)

942.1'88 — Flats: Southwood Park. Sites. *London. Haringey (London Borough), to 1976*
Pugh, Ralph Bernard. The site of Southwood Park / [by] Ralph B. Pugh. — [London] ([c/o Hon. Treasurer, 50 Collingwood Ave., N.10]) : Hornsey Historical Society, [1977]. — [1],13,[1] p : ill, maps ; 30cm.
'Reprinted from "Hornsey Historical Society Bulletin", No.12, December 1976'.
Sd : £0.48
(B77-17837)

942.1'88 — London. Haringey (London Borough). Hornsey. Social life, 1885-ca 1895. *Childhood reminiscences*
Monk, Edwin. Memories of Hornsey / [by] Edwin Monk ; with his further historical notes attached ; with illustrations by Brigid Peppin and introduction and notes by Joan Schwitzer. — [London] ([c/o Hon. Treasurer, 50 Collingwood Ave., N.10]) : Hornsey Historical Society, 1976. — 43p : ill, maps, port ; 21cm. — (Hornsey Historical Society. Occasional papers ; no.1)
ISBN 0-905794-00-1 Sd : £0.95
(B77-01089)

942.1'89 — London. Enfield (London Borough), to 1965
Pam, David Owen. The new Enfield : stories of Enfield, Edmonton and Southgate / by David Pam. — Enfield (Central Library, Cecil Rd, Enfield, Middx [EN2 6TW]) : London Borough of Enfield, Libraries, Arts and Entertainments Department, 1977. — [4],36p : ill, map, port ; 30cm.
Pbk : £0.75
(B77-19127)

942.1'89'062 — London. Enfield (London Borough), 1620-1660
Pam, David Owen. The rude multitude : Enfield and the Civil War / by D.O. Pam. — [Enfield] : Edmonton Hundreds [i.e. Hundred] Historical Society, 1977. — 17p,[2]p of plates : ill, maps, port ; 29cm. — (Edmonton Hundred Historical Society. Occasional papers : new series ; no.33 ISSN 0422-6240)
ISBN 0-902922-27-0 Pbk : £0.75
(B77-12231)

942.1'91 — London. Croydon (London Borough), to 1976
Croydon, the story of a hundred years / editor John B. Gent. — 4th ed. — Croydon (96A Brighton Rd, South Croydon, Surrey CR2 6AD) : Croydon Natural History and Scientific Society Ltd, 1977. — 61p : ill, facsims, map, ports ; 29cm.
Previous ed.: 1973. — Bibl.: p60.
ISBN 0-9501310-3-2 Pbk : £1.00
(B77-34319)

942.1'92'0810222 — London. Sutton (London Borough), 1855-1932. *Illustrations*
All our yesterdays : a pictorial record of the London Borough of Sutton over the last century / compiled by Ian Bradley, June Broughton, Douglas Cluett ; editor June Broughton ; design Shirley Edwards. — [Sutton] ([New Central Library, St Nicholas Way, Sutton, Surrey]) : Sutton Libraries and Arts Services, 1977. — [2],58p : of ill, ports ; 22x29cm.
ISBN 0-9503224-2-3 Sd : £0.95
(B77-24622)

942.1'93 — London. Merton (London Borough). Wimbledon, to 1837
Milward, Richard John. History of Wimbledon / by R.J. Milward. — [London] ([159 Coombe La., S.W.20]) : [The author].
Part 3 : Wimbledon in the time of the Civil War. — 1976. — 165,[3]p : ill, facsim, geneal table, maps, plans, ports ; 21cm.
Bibl.
ISBN 0-9501068-2-8 Pbk : £1.82
(B77-05783)

942.1'94 — Persons. *London. Kingston upon Thames (London Borough). Kingston, 1711-1939. Biographies*
Sampson, June. Characters of Kingston / by June Sampson. — Kingston upon Thames : Knapp, Drewett, [1976]. — 32p : ill, facsim, ports ; 21cm.
'Reprinted from the "Surrey Comet" May and June, 1974'.
ISBN 0-902042-06-8 Pbk : £0.70
(B77-02685)

942.1'95 — Art galleries. *London. Richmond upon Thames (London Borough). Orleans House Gallery. Exhibits: Items associated with Richmond Bridge. Catalogues*
Howard, Diana. Richmond Bridge and other Thames crossings between Hampton and Barnes : a short history ; together with the catalogue of the Richmond Bridge Bicentenary Exhibition, 2 October 1976 to 17 April 1977 [at the] Orleans House Gallery, Twickenham / [text and catalogue compiled by Diana Howard, Nicholas Lawrence]. — [Richmond, Surrey] ([The Retreat, Retreat Rd, Richmond, Surrey TW9 1PH]) : London Borough of Richmond upon Thames, Amenities Committee, 1976. — 47p,[8]p of plates : ill, maps ; 18x23cm.
Bibl.: p.36-37.
ISBN 0-903704-19-6 Pbk : £0.75
(B77-01090)

942.1'95 — Buildings associated with British royal families. *London. Richmond upon Thames (London Borough)*
The **heritage** of Richmond upon Thames in the year of Her Majesty's Jubilee, 1977. — [Richmond, Surrey] ([c/o Langton Bookshops Ltd, 4 Church St., Twickenham, Middx]) : London Borough of Richmond upon Thames, 1977. — [59]p : ill, coat of arms, ports ; 22cm.
Cover title: Richmond upon Thames in the year of Her Majesty's Jubilee, 1977.
Sd : £1.25
(B77-30879)

942.1'95 — Country houses. *London. Richmond upon Thames (London Borough). Bushy House, to 1975*
Foster, Peter. Bushy House / [by] Peter Foster and Edward Pyatt ; [line illustrations R.D. Treble]. — Teddington (Teddington, Middx [TW11 0LW]) : National Physical Laboratory, 1976. — [4],32p : ill, maps, plans, ports ; 30cm. — (National Physical Laboratory. Museum and Archives. Publications ; no.1 ISSN 0308-9843)
ISBN 0-9504496-1-x Pbk : £0.50
(B77-01931)

942.1'95 — London. Richmond upon Thames (London Borough). Richmond, to 1971
Dunbar, Janet. A prospect of Richmond / [by] Janet Dunbar. — Revised ed. — London [etc.] : White Lion Publishers, 1977. — xiii, 223p,[44]p of plates : ill(some col), facsims, maps, 2 ports(1 col) ; 23cm.
Revised ed. originally published: 1973. — Bibl.: p.217. — Index.
£5.75
ISBN 0-85617-995-7
(B77-18487)

942.1'95 — London. Richmond upon Thames (London Borough). Twickenham. Social life, 1702-1714
Simpson, Donald Herbert. Twickenham society in Queen Anne's reign from the letters of Isabella Wentworth / by D.H. Simpson. — [Twickenham] ([59 Park House Gardens, Twickenham, Middx TW1 2DF]) : Borough of Twickenham Local History Society, 1976. — [2],34p : 1 ill, map ; 20cm. — (Borough of Twickenham Local History Society. Papers ; no.35)
ISBN 0-903341-20-4 Sd : £0.40
(B77-06389)

942.2 — England. Middle Thames Valley, to 1977
Wilson, David Gordon, *b.1935.* The making of the Middle Thames / [by] David Gordon Wilson. — Bourne End, Bucks. : Spurbooks, 1977. — 3-159p : ill, facsim, maps, plan ; 23cm.
Index.
ISBN 0-904978-23-0 : £3.95
(B77-27592)

942.2 — South-east England, to 1976
White, John Talbot. The South-East, down and Weald : Kent, Surrey and Sussex / [by] John Talbot White. — London : Eyre Methuen, 1977. — 256p : ill, maps ; 23cm. — (The regions of Britain)
Bibl.: p.242-248. — Index.
ISBN 0-413-32090-1 : £6.95
ISBN 0-413-32100-2 Pbk : £2.95
(B77-22281)

942.2'084'0924 — South-east England. Social life, ca 1935-ca 1950. *Personal observations*
Scannell, Dorothy. Dolly's war / [by] Dorothy Scannell. — London : Pan Books, 1977. — 190p ; 18cm.
Originally published: London : Macmillan, 1975.
ISBN 0-330-24894-4 Pbk : £0.60
(B77-10685)

942.2'1 — Surrey, to 1900
Malden, Henry Elliot. A history of Surrey / by Henry Elliot Malden. — Wakefield : EP Publishing, 1977. — viii,321p ; 23cm.
Facsimile reprint of: Cheap ed. London : Elliot Stock, 1905. — Bibl.: p.310-318. — Index.
ISBN 0-7158-1228-9 : £5.25 : CIP rev.
(B77-13983)

942.2'1 — Surrey, to ca 1600. *Early works*
Camden, William. [Britannia. Surrey. English]. Camden's 'Britannia', Surrey & Sussex : from the edition of 1789 [translated from the Latin] by Richard Gough / annotated and edited by Gordon J. Copley. — London : Hutchinson, 1977. — iii-xxxii,80p : ill, maps, port ; 26cm.
Bibl. — Index.
ISBN 0-09-122000-9 : £7.50
Primary classification 942.2'5
(B77-20826)

942.2'12 — Personal property. Probate inventories. *Surrey. Sunbury-on-Thames, 1673-1724*
Heselton, Kenneth Yeaman. Sunbury household effects, 1673-1724 : (probate inventories) / [by] Kenneth Y. Heselton. — Sunbury-on-Thames (12 Heathcroft Ave., Sunbury-on-Thames, [Middx]) : Sunbury and Shepperton Local History Society, 1976. — [3],16p,plate : plans ; 30cm. — (Sunbury and Shepperton Local History Society. Occasional publications ; no.2 ISSN 0309-2070)
Bibl.: p.16.
ISBN 0-905178-01-7 Sd : £0.20
(B77-07741)

942.2'12 — Town houses. *Surrey. Sunbury-on-Thames. Green Street. Nos 39-41 Green Street, to 1975*
Freeman, George. History of 39-41 Green Street, Sunbury-on-Thames / [by] George Freeman. — Sunbury-on-Thames (12 Heathcroft Ave., Sunbury-on-Thames, [Middx]) : Sunbury and Shepperton Local History Society, 1977. — [2], 6p ; 26cm. — (Sunbury and Shepperton Local History Society. Occasional publications ; no.3 ISSN 0309-2070)
Sd : £0.10
(B77-16123)

942.2'13 — Surrey. Bagshot & Windlesham, to 1973
Eedle, Marie de Garis. A history of Bagshot and Windlesham / by Marie de G. Eedle. — London [etc.] : Phillimore, 1977. — x,262p,leaf of plate,[16]p of plates : ill, facsim, maps, ports ; 23cm.
Bibl.: p.245-249. — Index.
ISBN 0-85033-276-1 : £3.95
(B77-30880)

942.21'45 — Country houses. *Surrey. Walton-on-Thames. Ashley Park, ca 1550-ca 1925*
Blackman, Michael Ernest. History of Ashley Park, Walton-on-Thames / [by] Michael E. Blackman. — [Weybridge] ([c/o Hon. Secretary, Lobs Wood, Cedar Grove, Weybridge, Surrey]) : Walton and Weybridge Local History Society, 1976. — [4],31,[5]p : ill, geneal tables, map, plan ; 21cm. — (Walton and Weybridge Local History Society. Papers ; no.16 ISSN 0306-1248)
Cover title: Ashley Park.
ISBN 0-901524-20-4 Sd : £0.90
(B77-12232)

942.2'18 — Surrey. Blechingley, to 1976
Lambert, Uvedale H H. Blechingley : a short history / by Uvedale H.H. Lambert. — [2nd ed.]. — Guildford ([Castle Arch, Guildford, Surrey]) : Surrey Archaeological Society, 1949 [i.e. 1973]. — viii,44p,[4]p of plates,fold leaf of plate : ill, geneal tables, map, plans ; 22cm.
Previous ed.: 1949. — Bibl.: p.viii. — Index.
Sd : £0.50
(B77-26705)

942.2'18 — Surrey. Caterham & Warlingham, to 1976
Caterham and Warlingham : jubilee history / [by Jeoffry Spence et al.]. — [1st ed. reprinted with additions]. — [Caterham] ([17 Manor Ave., Caterham, Surrey]) : Bourne Society, 1977. — 40p : ill, coats of arms, facsim ; 19cm.
First ed. originally published: Caterham? : s.n., 1953. — Bibl.: p.38.
Sd : £0.30
(B77-23021)

942.2'18 — Surrey. Woldingham, to 1975
Greenwood, John, *b.1942.* History of Woldingham and Marden Park / by John Greenwood ; with illustrations by E.F. Bishop ... [et al.]. — [Caterham] ([17 Manor Ave., Caterham, Surrey]) : Bourne Society, 1976. — 4-44p : ill, coats of arms, geneal tables, maps ; 22cm.
ISBN 0-900992-19-0 Sd : £1.00
(B77-05141)

942.2'19 — Surrey. Bramley & Grafham, to 1977
Bramley Village Society. Bramley and Grafham : a short history / [Bramley Village Society]. — [Bramley] ([c/o The Well House, Bramley, Guildford, Surrey GU5 0BP]) : [The Society], [1977]. — [1],47p : ill, maps ; 21cm.
Sd : £0.75
(B77-26036)

942.2'19 — Surrey. Farnham. Social life, 1860-1870. *Childhood reminiscences*
Sturt, George. A small boy in the sixties / by George Sturt ; with a introduction by Arnold Bennett. — Hassocks : Harvester Press, 1977. — xvi,241p,[4]p of plates : ill ; 23cm.
Facsimile reprint of: 1st ed. Cambridge : Cambridge University Press, 1927. — Index.
ISBN 0-85527-244-9 : £4.95 : CIP rev.
(B77-13441)

942.2'3 — Buildings of historical importance. *Kent, to 1976*
Webb, William. Kent's historic buildings / [by] William Webb ; photographs by May Guest. — London : Hale, 1977. — 192p,[32]p of plates : ill, map ; 23cm.
Bibl.: p.185. — Index.
ISBN 0-7091-6147-6 : £4.50
(B77-32330)

942.2'3 — Kent, 1576-1972. *Early works. Facsimiles. Collections*
A **book** of Kent : made by the printers of Kent / edited by Marcus Crouch. — Tenterden (Caxton House, High St., Tenterden, Kent TN30 6BD) : Paul Norbury Publications, 1976. — [1],vii,56p : ill, facsim, map, ports ; 22cm.
Limited ed. of 1000 copies.
ISBN 0-904404-14-5 Pbk : £1.00
(B77-07742)

942.2'3 — Kent, to 1600. *Early works*
Camden, William. [Britannia. Kent. English]. Camden's 'Britannia', Kent : from the edition of 1789 [translated from the Latin] by Richard Gough / annotated and edited by Gordon J. Copley. — London : Hutchinson, 1977. — iii-xxxii,96p : ill, map, port ; 26cm.
Bibl. — Index.
ISBN 0-09-125240-7 : £7.50
(B77-20825)

942.2'3'05 — England. Provinces. Social life, 1500-1640. *Study regions: Kent*
Clark, Peter, *b.1944.* English provincial society from the Reformation to the Revolution : religion, politics and society in Kent, 1500-1640 / [by] Peter Clark. — Hassocks : Harvester Press, 1977. — xiii,504p : maps ; 24cm.
Index.
ISBN 0-85527-414-x : £17.95 : CIP rev.
(B77-05142)

942.2'315 — Kent. Gravesend, to 1975
Benson, James, *b.1878.* A history of Gravesend, or, A historical perambulation of Gravesend and Northfleet / by James Benson ; revised and edited by Robert Heath Hiscock. — London [etc.] : Phillimore, 1976. — xii,159p,[2]leaves of plates,[8]p of plates : ill, maps, port ; 23cm.
Index.
ISBN 0-85033-242-7 : £3.75
(B77-29836)

942.2'323 — Forts. *Kent. Chatham. Fort Pitt, to 1975*
Cooper, John, *b.1947.* Fort Pitt : some notes on the history of a Napoleonic fort, military hospital and technical school / [by] John Cooper. — Maidstone (Springfield, Maidstone, Kent) : Kent County Library, 1976. — [35]p : ill, maps, plans ; 20cm.
ISBN 0-905155-05-x Sd : £0.25
Primary classification 355.3'45
(B77-09619)

942.2'323 — Kent. Cuxton, to 1975
Church, Derek. Cuxton, a Kentish village / [by] Derek Church. — Sheerness (31 Broadway, Sheerness, Kent) : Arthur J. Cassell Ltd, 1976. — ix,177p : ill, maps, ports ; 23cm.
Maps on lining papers. — Bibl.: p.170-172. — Index.
ISBN 0-903253-12-7 : £3.30
(B77-09432)

942.2'33 — Kent. Upchurch. Social life, 1851-1856. *Diaries*
Woodruff, John. John Woodruff's journal, 1851-56. — [Upchurch] ([The Vicarage, 15 Oak La., Upchurch, Sittingbourne, Kent]) : [Keith Chave], [1976]. — [4],67p : ill, facsim ; 21cm.
Index.
ISBN 0-9505520-0-3 Sd : £0.30
(B77-07743)

942.2'34'0830924 — Kent. Canterbury (District). Rural regions. Social life, ca 1930-ca 1940. *Childhood reminiscences*
Kent, Joan. Wood smoke & pigeon pie / [by] Joan Kent. — Folkestone : Bailey and Swinfen, 1977. — [8],182p : ill ; 23cm.
ISBN 0-561-00297-5 : £3.90 : CIP rev.
(B77-17230)

942.2'352 — Kent. St Margaret's at Cliffe, 1086-1911. *Readings from contemporary sources*
Historical sketches of St Margaret's-at-Cliffe, 1086-1911 / edited by A.L. Macfie. — [St Margaret's Bay] ([Thalassa, Foreland Rd, St Margaret's Bay, Kent]) : [The editor], 1977. — 28p : ill, map ; 21cm.
Sd : Unpriced
(B77-26706)

942.2'372 — Kent. Tonbridge, to 1975
Chapman, Frank. The book of Tonbridge : the story of the town's past / by Frank Chapman. — Chesham ([Lee Farm House], Chesham, Bucks.) : Barracuda Books Ltd, 1976. — 3-148p : ill, coat of arms, facsims, maps, ports ; 31cm.
Map, ill. on lining papers. — Bibl.: p.148. — Index.
ISBN 0-86023-027-9 : £7.90
(B77-06390)

942.2'375 — Kent. Teston. *Reports, surveys*
Teston Village Appraisal Group. Teston : an appraisal. — [Teston] ([c/o The Secretary, Thackers, Malling Rd, Teston, Maidstone, Kent ME18 5AR]) : [The Group], [1976]. — [73]p : ill, maps ; 30cm.
Author: Teston Village Appraisal Group. — Cover title. — Limited ed. of 250 copies.
ISBN 0-9505433-0-6 Pbk : £1.50
(B77-04491)

942.2'375 — Kent. Teston, to 1974
Severn, Joan. The Teston story : Kent village life through the ages / by Joan Severn. — Teston (Woodlands Close, Teston, Kent ME18 5AL) : Rufus Fay Publications, [1976]. — [2],76p,[18]p of plates : ill, geneal tables, maps, ports ; 21cm.
Bibl.: p.70. — Index.
ISBN 0-9505522-0-8 Pbk : £1.75
(B77-05784)

942.2'38'0810222 — Kent. Tunbridge Wells, ca 1840-ca 1925. *Illustrations*
Tunbridge Wells as it was / [compiled] by Jean Mauldon. — Nelson : Hendon Publishing Co., 1977. — 44p : chiefly ill, ports ; 21x29cm.
ISBN 0-86067-017-1 Sd : £1.50
(B77-21625)

942.2'5 — East & West Sussex, to 1600. *Early works*
Camden, William. [Britannia. Surrey. English]. Camden's 'Britannia', Surrey & Sussex : from the edition of 1789 [translated from the Latin] by Richard Gough / annotated and edited by Gordon J. Copley. — London : Hutchinson, 1977. — iii-xxxii,80p : ill, maps, port ; 26cm.
Bibl. — Index.
ISBN 0-09-122000-9 : £7.50
Also classified at 942.2'1
(B77-20826)

942.2'5'009734 — Villages. *East & West Sussex, to 1976*
Baker, Michael Henry Chadwick. Sussex villages / [by] Michael H.C. Baker ; photographs by the author. — London : Hale, 1977. — 192p,[32]p of plates : ill, map ; 23cm. — (Village series)
Index.
ISBN 0-7091-5911-0 : £4.20
(B77-10686)

942.2'5'08570924 — East Sussex. Social life. *Personal observations*
Epton, Nina. Dora Bell's village cats / [by] Nina Epton. — London : Joseph, 1977. — [5],170p ; 23cm.
ISBN 0-7181-1584-8 : £3.95
(B77-22282)

942.2'51 — East Sussex. Ashdown Forest, to 1975
Christian, Garth. Ashdown Forest / [by] Garth Christian. — 3rd ed. — Forest Row : Society of the Friends of Ashdown Forest ; Bexhill-on-Sea (Providence Way, Eastwood Rd, Bexhill-on-Sea, Sussex) : Distributed by Gardners of Bexhill Ltd, 1976. — vii,78p,[8]p of plates : ill(incl 1 col) ; 23cm.
Previous ed.: 1968. — Index.
ISBN 0-9503664-1-2 Pbk : £2.00
(B77-33539)

942.2'54 — East Sussex. Hove. Cliftonville, 1850-1880
Cliftonville, Hove : a Victorian suburb / edited by John Lowerson. — Brighton (Brighton BN1 9RG) : Centre for Continuing Education, University of Sussex, 1977. — [2],25p : ill, facsim, maps ; 30cm. — (University of Sussex. Centre for Continuing Education. Occasional papers ; no.6 ISSN 0306-1108)
ISBN 0-904242-05-6 Sd : £0.35
(B77-29083)

942.2'56 — Chapels Royal. *East Sussex. Brighton. Chapel Royal, Brighton, to 1976*
Webb, M J. The history of the Chapel Royal, Brighton, 1793-1943 / by M.J. Webb. — [Barnet] ([13 Cedar Lawn Ave., Barnet, Herts.]) : [The author], 1977. — [2],40p,[2]p of plates : ill, map ; 30cm.
Bibl.: p.38-40.
Sd : £0.50
(B77-19922)

942.2'56 — East Sussex. Brighton region. Social life, 1500-1900
Brent, Colin Edward. A short economic and social history of Brighton, Lewes and the downland region between the Adur and the Ouse, 1500-1900 / by Colin E. Brent. — [Lewes] ([182 High St., Lewes, E. Sussex BN7 1YA]) : East Sussex County Council, [1976]. — iv,27p,plate : maps ; 30cm.
Bibl.: p.26-27.
Pbk : £0.20
(B77-11493)

942.2'56 — East Sussex. Rottingdean. Social life, 1915-ca 1930. *Childhood reminiscences*
Copper, Bob. Early to rise : a Sussex boyhood / [by] Bob Copper. — London : Heinemann, 1976. — [9],267p,[12]p of plates : ill, music, port ; 23cm.
Ill. on lining papers.
ISBN 0-434-14457-6 : £4.90
Also classified at 784.4'9422'5
(B77-01932)

942.2'57 — East Sussex. Lewes (District). Countryside adjacent to Ouse River, to 1975
McCarthy, Edna. Sussex river, journeys along the banks of the River Ouse, Newhaven to Lewes / by Edna & 'Mac' McCarthy. — Seaford (Elm Buildings, Croft La., Seaford, E. Sussex BN25 1SA) : Lindel Organization Limited, [1977]. — 2-68p : ill, maps ; 25cm.
Pbk : £1.00
(B77-24623)

942.2'6 — West Sussex, to 1977
Montgomery, John. History, people and places in West Sussex / [by] John Montgomery. — Bourne End : Spurbooks, 1977. — 159p : ill, map ; 22cm.
Index.
ISBN 0-902875-78-7 Pbk : £2.95
(B77-29084)

942.2'62 — West Sussex. Petworth, 1800-1850. *Personal observations*
Greenfield, John Osborn. Tales of old Petworth / [by John Osborn Greenfield]. — Petworth ([2 Station Cottages], The Old Station Yard, Petworth, Sussex) : The Window Press, 1976. — 2-112p : ill ; 19cm.
'The basic content consists of recollections by John Osborn Greenfield (1802-1869) ... expanded by a later unknown writer in the eighteen nineties' - Introduction.
ISBN 0-9504830-0-1 Pbk : £1.40
(B77-03844)

942.2'64 — West Sussex. Horsham, ca 1875-ca 1925. *Illustrations*
A picture of Horsham. — [Chichester] ([1A East Row, Chichester, W. Sussex PO19 1PD]) : West Sussex County Council, Library and Archives Service, 1976. — [30]p : of ill, facsim, ports ; 21cm.
ISBN 0-905139-02-x Sd : £0.50
(B77-04492)

942.2'67 — Country houses. *West Sussex. Bognor Regis. Hotham Park House, to 1975*
Allam, David P. A brief history of Hotham Park House, Bognor Regis / written and compiled by David P. Allam and Ronald Iden. — [Bognor Regis] (['Langley House', Willow Way, Aldwick Bay, Bognor Regis, Sussex]) : [The author], [1976]. — [4],12,[4]p,fold plate : ill, map, plans, port ; 21cm.
ISBN 0-9505465-0-x Sd : £0.50
(B77-03845)

942.2'68'070222 — West Sussex. Worthing, 1800-1960. *Illustrations*
Worthing : a pictorial history / [compiled] by D. Robert Elleray. — London [etc.] : Phillimore, 1977. — [126]p : chiefly ill, facsims, ports ; 25cm.
Ill. on lining papers. — Bibl.: p.[125]-[126].
ISBN 0-85033-263-x : £4.25
(B77-32993)

942.2'7 — Hampshire, to ca 1800. *Early works. Facsimiles*
Shore, Thomas William. A history of Hampshire, including the Isle of Wight / by T.W. Shore. — Wakefield : EP Publishing, 1976. — ix,286p ; 23cm.
Facsimile reprint of: 1st ed. London : Elliot Stock, 1892. — Index. — Includes a chapter on the Isle of Wight.
ISBN 0-7158-1177-0 : £5.50
(B77-17231)

942.2'732 — Hampshire. Andover, to 1976
Spaul, John Edward Houghton. Andover : an historical portrait / [by] John Spaul ; with drawings by Julia Whatley. — [Andover] ([c/o Public Library, Chantry Way, Andover, Hants.]) : Andover Local Archives Committee, 1977. — 160p : ill, facsims, maps, plan ; 23cm.
Maps on lining papers. — Index.
ISBN 0-903755-07-6 : £4.95
(B77-30881)

942.2'735 — Hampshire. Itchen Stoke, to 1971
Sanderson, Isabel. Itchen Stoke : a small parish in the Upper Itchen Valley, Hampshire / by I. Sanderson. — Alresford (Studio Bookshop, Alresford, Hants.) : Laurence Oxley, 1975. — vi,94p,[10]leaves of plates,[8]p of plates : ill, facsim, maps, plan, port ; 20cm.
ISBN 0-9501347-8-3 : £3.25
(B77-25311)

942.2'75 — Abbeys. *Hampshire. Beaulieu. Beaulieu Abbey, to 1538*
Hockey, Frederick. Beaulieu, King John's abbey : a history of Beaulieu Abbey, Hampshire, 1204-1538 / [by] Frederick Hockey. — [London] ([3 Wyndham Place, W.1]) : Pioneer Publications Ltd, 1976. — xiv,251p : ill, maps, plan(on lining paper) ; 23cm.
Ill. on lining paper. — Bibl.: p.234-240. — Index.
ISBN 0-9502786-1-0 : £4.95
(B77-10066)

942.2'75 — Hampshire. Lymington, to 1898. *Early works. Facsimiles*
King, Edward, *b.1821.* Old times re-visited in the borough and parish of Lymington / [by] Edward King. — 2nd ed. — Winchester : Shurlock, 1976. — [15],306p,[12]leaves of plates,[6]p of plates : ill, facsims, maps, music ; 23cm.
Facsimile reprint of: 2nd ed. London : Simpkin, Marshall, 1900.
ISBN 0-903330-22-9 : £5.50
(B77-12233)

942.2'75'0855 — Hampshire. New Forest. Social life, ca 1955
De Baïracli-Levy, Juliette. Wanderers in the New Forest / [by] Juliet de Baïracli-Levy ; with a foreword by Augustus John. — London : Faber, 1977. — 3-208p ; 20cm.
Originally published: 1958.
ISBN 0-571-11087-8 Pbk : £1.95
(B77-19128)

942.2'85 — Castles. *Isle of Wight. Yarmouth. Yarmouth Castle, to ca 1960*
Rigold, Stuart Eborall. Yarmouth Castle, Isle of Wight / by S.E. Rigold. — [London] : [H.M.S.O.], 1976. — 15,[1]p : plans ; 22cm. — (Ancient monuments and historic buildings)
Originally published: 1959.
ISBN 0-11-670042-4 Sd : £0.04
(B77-16124)

942.2'9'008 — Berkshire, to 1976. *Readings*
The **royal** county : a Berkshire miscellany to commemorate the silver jubilee of Her Majesty Queen Elizabeth II / edited by Michael Asser. — [Reading] ([Shire Hall, Reading, Berks.]) : Berkshire County Council, 1977. — [6],76,[2]p, [20]p of plates : ill(incl 1 col), coat of arms, facsims, col port ; 20x23cm.
ISBN 0-905538-36-6 : Unpriced
(B77-34320)

942.2'9'070222 — Berkshire, 1700-1800. *Illustrations*
A **prospect** of Berkshire : eight prints from the eighteenth century, selected from the local history collection at Reading Libraries. — [Reading] ([Blagrave St., Reading, Berks. RG1 1QL]) : Reading Libraries, 1976. — [10]leaves : of ill ; 24cm.
One leaf printed on both sides.
Sd : £2.25
ISBN 0-9501338-6-8
(B77-03846)

942.2'93'0855 — Berkshire. Reading, 1953
Phillips, Daphne. Coronation Reading : a portrait of the town as it was in 1953 / by Daphne Phillips. — [Reading] ([c/o Central Library, Blagrave St., Reading RG1 1QL]) : Reading Libraries, 1977. — [27]p : ill ; 20x21cm.
ISBN 0-9501338-8-4 Sd : £0.50
(B77-28308)

942.2'94 — Berkshire. Three Mile Cross. Social life, 1820-1830. *Personal observations*
Mitford, Mary Russell. Our village / by Mary Russell Mitford. — London [etc.] : White Lion Publishers, 1976. — 228p : ill ; 23cm.
This collection originally published: London : Harrap, 1947.
ISBN 0-85617-830-6 : £4.50
(B77-05785)

942.2'94 — Berkshire. Tilehurst, to 1975
Babbage, Terry. Tylehurst described / by Terry Babbage. — [Reading] ([c/o Central Library, Blagrave St., Reading RG1 1QL]) : Reading Libraries, 1976. — [2],22p : ill, facsim, map ; 30cm.
ISBN 0-9501338-7-6 Sd : £0.75
(B77-06391)

942.2'96 — Berkshire. Eton & Windsor, 1714-1837
Macnaghten, Angus. Windsor & Eton in Georgian times / [by] Angus Macnaghten. — [Ascot] ([New Mile Cottage, Ascot, Berks.]) : [The author], 1976. — 99p,[10]leaves of plates : ill ; 25cm.
Bibl.: p.91-92. — Index.
Pbk : £1.75
(B77-23022)

942.2'96 — Castles. *Berkshire. Windsor. Windsor Castle, to 1976*
Hibbert, Christopher. The court at Windsor : a domestic history / [by] Christopher Hibbert. — Revised ed. — London : Allen Lane, 1977. — 240p,[16]p of plates : ill(some col), coats of arms, col map, plan, ports(some col) ; 26cm.
Previous ed.: London : Longman, 1964. — Bibl. : p.232-235. — Index.
ISBN 0-7139-1019-4 : £5.95
(B77-17838)

942.2'98 — Berkshire. Bracknell, to 1965
Pooley, Lee. Bracknell before the new town / by Lee Pooley. — 2nd ed. — Bracknell : Allen Sharp ; [Bracknell] ([32 Makepiece Rd, Bracknell, Berks. RG12 2HJ]) : [Distributed by the author], [1977]. — [1],16p,fold plate : map ; 21cm.
Previous ed.: 1976.
Sd : £0.25
(B77-24624)

942.3'1 — Wiltshire, to 1975
Leete, J A. Wiltshire miscellany / by J.A. Leete. — Melksham : Venton, 1976. — 188p,[16]p of plates : ill ; 21cm. — (White Horse library)
Index.
ISBN 0-85475-127-0 : £4.95
(B77-05786)

942.3'1'0830222 — Wiltshire, 1914-1945. *Illustrations*
A **Wiltshire** camera, 1914-1945 / [compiled by] David Burnett. — Tisbury : Compton Russell, 1976. — [96]p : chiefly ill, facsims(on lining papers), ports ; 27cm.
ISBN 0-85955-045-1 : £4.25
(B77-23023)

942.3'12 — Country houses. *Wiltshire. Corsham. Corsham Court, to 1850*
Harcourt, Leslie. Corsham Court : a gothick dream / [by] Leslie Harcourt. — [London] ([232 Amesbury Ave., S.W.2]) : Gothick Dream, 1977. — 50p : ill, facsim, ports ; 15x21cm.
Bibl.: p.50.
Pbk : £1.50
(B77-27593)

942.3'12 — Wiltshire. Chippenham, to 1975
Chamberlain, Joseph Archibald. Chippenham : some notes on its history / compiled from various sources by Joseph A. Chamberlain. — Chippenham (32 Market Place, Chippenham, Wilts.) : Charter Trustees, 1976. — vii,199p,16p of plates : ill, coat of arms, geneal tables, map ; 23cm.
Map on lining-papers. — Bibl.: p.185-187. — Index.
ISBN 0-9505451-0-4 : £5.25
(B77-03302)

942.31'2 — Wiltshire. Minety, ca 1880-1970
Manners, Leonard J. An acre of England / [by] L.J. Manners ; illustrated by the author. — Old Woking (The Gresham Press, Old Woking, Surrey GU22 9LH) : Unwin Brothers Limited, 1977. — [14],138p,[8]p of plates : ill, geneal table, 2 maps, ports ; 24cm.
Originally published: as 'A countryman looks back'. Minety : Taylor and Sons, 1973.
ISBN 0-905418-07-7 : £7.80
ISBN 0-905418-06-9 Pbk : £3.50
(B77-21626)

942.3'13 — Wiltshire. Blunsdon St Andrew, to 1975
Levinge, E M. About Blunsdon : a north Wiltshire village / by E.M. Levinge & R.S. Radway. — [Blunsdon] ([Little Coster, Blunsdon, Swindon, Wilts.]) : [The authors], 1976. — 128p : ill, map ; 24cm.
ISBN 0-9505524-0-2 : £3.00
(B77-05787)

942.3'15 — Wiltshire. Bradford-on-Avon. Social Life, 1841
Langdon, Gee. The year of the map : portrait of a Wiltshire town in 1841 / [by] Gee Langdon. — Tisbury : Compton Russell, 1976. — 119p ; 26cm.
Fold. map in pocket.
ISBN 0-85955-040-0 : £6.00
(B77-05788)

942.3'19 — Buildings of historical importance. *Wiltshire. Salisbury. Reports, surveys*
Royal Commission on Historical Monuments (England). Ancient and historical monuments in the City of Salisbury (excluding the Cathedral Close) ... / the Royal Commission on the Ancient and Historical Monuments and Constructions of England. — London : H.M.S.O., [1977]. — 7p ; 25cm. — (Interim report ; 35th) (Cmnd.6679)
ISBN 0-10-166790-6 Sd : £0.20
(B77-11494)

942.3'19 — Wiltshire. Salisbury. Local history. *Periodicals*
The **Hatcher** review. — Salisbury (c/o The Editor, Chequers Cottage, Great Wishford, Wilts. SP2 0PQ) : Hatcher Society.
No.1- ; Spring 1976-. — 1976-. — ports ; 21cm.

Two issues a year. — [1],36p. in 1st issue.
Sd : £0.30
ISSN 0309-5118
(B77-14485)

942.3'3 — Dorset, 849-1935
Whaley, Peta. Dorset through history / by Peta Whaley. — Melksham : Venton, 1977. — 144p, 8p of plates : ill ; 23cm. — (White Horse library)
Bibl.: p.142. — Index.
ISBN 0-85475-113-0 : £5.25
(B77-23903)

942.3'3'0810222 — Dorset. Social life, 1857-1914. *Illustrations*
Victorian and Edwardian Dorset from old photographs / introduction and commentaries by Peter Irvine. — London : Batsford, 1977. — [120]p : chiefly ill, ports ; 26cm.
ISBN 0-7134-0148-6 : £3.95
(B77-31630)

942.3'3'085705 — Dorset. *Annuals*
The **Dorset** year book. — [Weymouth] ([79 St Mary St., Weymouth, Dorset DT4 8PL]) : Society of Dorset Men.
1977 : seventieth year of issue / edited by Nat. Byles. — [1977]. — 166p : ill, facsims, maps, plans, ports ; 25cm.
ISBN 0-901052-08-6 Pbk : £1.95
(B77-08693)

942.3'31 — Dorset. Dewlish. Social life, ca 1920-1930. *Childhood reminiscences*
Marsh, Bernard W. Memories of Dewlish / by Bernard W. Marsh ; drawings by Mrs R.J. Tennent. — [Dorchester] ([County Hall, Dorchester, Dorset]) : Dorset County Council Education Committee, [1977]. — [1],20p : ill, ports ; 21cm.
ISBN 0-85216-145-x Sd : Unpriced
(B77-10687)

942.3'38 — Dorset. Bournemouth. Southbourne, 1870-1901
Young, John Anthony. Southbourne on Sea, 1870-1901 / by J.A. Young. — [Dorchester] ([County Hall, Dorchester, Dorset DT1 1XJ]) : Dorset County Council, Education Committee, 1976. — [2],14p : facsims ; 21cm.
ISBN 0-85216-148-4 Sd : £0.15
(B77-03847)

942.3'38 — Dorset. Bournemouth. Talbot Village, to 1975
Gillett, Mildred. Wandering in Talbot Village : a study of philanthropy in the mid-nineteenth century / by Mildred Gillett. — [Dorchester] ([County Hall, Dorchester, Dorset DT1 1XJ]) : Dorset County Council, Education Committee, 1976. — [3],25p : maps ; 21cm.
ISBN 0-85216-149-2 Sd : £0.20
(B77-05143)

942.3'38 — Dorset. Bournemouth. Winton, to 1923
Lands, S J. The growth of Winton / by S.J. Lands. — [Dorchester] ([County Hall, Dorchester, Dorset DT1 1XJ]) : Dorset County Council, Education Committee, 1976. — [2], 38p : 2 maps ; 21cm.
ISBN 0-85216-151-4 Sd : £0.20
(B77-18488)

942.3'38 — Dorset. Wick, to 1976
Popplewell, Laurence. Wick : the last village on the Dorset Stour / [by] Laurence Popplewell. — [Dorchester] ([c/o Bournemouth Local Studies Publications, Teachers' Centre, 40 Lowther Rd, Bournemouth, Dorset]) : Dorset County Council, Education Committee, [1977]. — [2],24p : ill ; 21cm.
ISBN 0-85216-164-6 Sd : £0.30
(B77-34321)

942.3'4 — Channel Islands, to 1974
Lemprière, Raoul. The Channel Islands / [by] Raoul Lemprière. — Revised ed. — London : Hale, 1977. — 224p,[24]p of plates : ill, maps, ports ; 19cm. — (Hale's topographical paperbacks)
This ed. originally published: as 'Portrait of the Channel Islands'. 1975. — Bibl.: p.215. — Index.
ISBN 0-7091-6225-1 Pbk : £1.50
(B77-15042)

942.3'4 — Channel Islands, to 1976
The **Channel** Islands : a new study / edited by Victor Coysh ; contributors Victor Coysh ... [et al.]. — Newton Abbot [etc.] : David and Charles, 1977. — 255p : ill, maps, ports ; 26cm.

Bibl.: p.240-243. — Index.
ISBN 0-7153-7333-1 : £7.95
(B77-23904)

942.3'41 — Jersey. Parishes, to 1973
Ahier, Philip. A short parochial and commercial history of Jersey / by Philip Ahier and W.S. Ashworth. — [St Helier] ([5 Burlington House, St Saviour's Rd, St Helier, Jersey, C.I.]) : Ashton and Denton Publishing Co., [1977]. — 145p,[2]p of plates(2 fold) : ill, 2 geneal tables, map ; 22cm.
Sd : £1.75
Also classified at 338'.09423'41
(B77-23024)

942.3'41 — Parish churches. *Jersey. St Helier. St Saviour's Church, Jersey, to 1973*
Bois, F de L. The Parish Church of St Saviour, Jersey / [by] F. de L. Bois ; with a foreword by Falkner Allison. — London [etc.] : Phillimore, 1976. — xvi,168p,[18]p of plates : ill, plans, ports ; 25cm.
Bibl.: p.143-144. — Index.
ISBN 0-85033-237-0 : £12.00
(B77-27594)

942.3'42 — Guernsey, to 1976
Robinson, G W S. Guernsey / [by] G.W.S. Robinson. — Newton Abbot [etc.] : David and Charles, 1977. — 176p : ill, maps, ports ; 23cm. — (The islands series)
Bibl.: p.169-171. — Index.
ISBN 0-7153-7341-2 : £4.50
(B77-20827)

942.3'42'0720924 — Guernsey. Gosselin, Joshua. *Biographies*
McClintock, David. The life of Joshua Gosselin of Guernsey, 1739-1813 : greffier and soldier, antiquary and artist, plantsman and natural historian / by David McClintock. — [St Peter Port] : Toucan Press, 1976. — [1],2-32p : ill, facsim, geneal tables, plans, port ; 23cm.
ISBN 0-85694-086-0 Sd : £0.75
(B77-01091)

942.3'45 — Sark. to 1976
Hawkes, Ken. Sark / by Ken Hawkes. — Newton Abbot [etc.] : David and Charles, 1977. — 168p : ill, maps, ports ; 23cm. — (The islands series)
Bibl.: p.162-164. — Index.
ISBN 0-7153-7335-8 : £4.95
(B77-19129)

942.3'5 — Devon, to ca 1800. *Early works. Facsimiles*
Polwhele, Richard. The history of Devonshire / by Richard Polwhele. — [1st ed. reprinted] ; introduction by A.L. Rowse. — Dorking : Kohler and Coombes, 1977. — 3v.([7],xii,329, 3p,fold leaf;433p(in various pagings),15 leaves of plates;3p,p383-504,[32]p,9 leaves of plates) : ill, facsims, map ; 36cm.
Facsimile reprint of: 1st ed. London : Cadell, Johnson and Dilly, 1793-1806. — Index. — Includes a facsimile reprint of James Davidson's 'Manuscript index to Polwhele', from the original in the West Country Studies Library, Exeter.
ISBN 0-903967-04-9 : £60.00
(B77-27595)

942.3'5'003 — Devon, to 1976. *Encyclopaedias*
Kay-Robinson, Denys. Devon & Cornwall / [by] Denys Kay-Robinson. — Edinburgh [etc.] : J. Bartholomew, 1977. — x,229p,[4],8p of plates : ill(some cols), maps(some cols) ; 26cm.
Bibl.: p.205-207. — Index.
ISBN 0-7028-1014-2 : £4.95
Also classified at 942.3'7'003
(B77-21627)

942.3'52 — Devon. Ilfracombe, ca 1900-1975. *Personal observations*
Wilson, Lilian. Ilfracombe's yesterdays : a personal record of our local way of life and history, with a guide to some places of interest in other parts of North Devon / by Lilian Wilson. — Barnstaple : Adrienne and Peter Oldale ; Barnstaple ([Barbican Close, Barnstaple, North Devon]) : [Distributed by Surridge and Dawson], 1976. — 96p : ill, ports ; 20cm.
ISBN 0-9505401-0-2 Pbk : £1.25
(B77-01933)

942.3'53'083 — Devon. Dartmoor, 1930. *Early works*
Gordon, Douglas, *b.1888.* Dartmoor in all its moods / by Douglas Gordon. — Wakefield : EP Publishing, 1976. — viii,336p,[8]leaves of plates : ill ; 20cm.
Facsimile reprint of: 1st ed. London : J. Murray, 1931.
ISBN 0-7158-1153-3 : £4.95
(B77-17232)

942.3'55 — Devon. Dawlish, to 1850
Carter, Frederick James. Notes on old Dawlish, 1588-1850 / compiled by the late F.J. Carter, (1938) ; edited for the Dawlish Museum Society by H.G. Morgan. — [Dawlish] ([Dawlish, Devon]) : [The Society], 1976. — [1],40p : coat of arms ; 22cm. — (Dawlish Museum. Publications ; no.1)
Bibl.: p.40.
ISBN 0-905765-00-1 Sd : £0.35
(B77-00537)

942.3'56 — Buildings of historical importance. *Devon. Exeter. Illustrations*
Exeter, a city saved? / edited by R. Fortescue-Foulkes ; [for the] Exeter Civic Society. — [Exeter] ([c/o Hon. Secretary, Summercourt, Lodge Hill, Exeter EX4 4AB]) : The Society, 1977. — [21],44p : of ill, map(on cover) ; 22x30cm.
Bibl.: p.44.
Sd : Unpriced
(B77-29571)

942.3'56'0810222 — Devon. Exeter, ca 1880-ca 1935. *Illustrations*
ISCA Collection. Old Exeter : a portfolio of photographs [from the ISCA Collection] / [compiled] by Peter D. Thomas. — Plymouth (Faraday Rd, Prince Rock, Plymouth PL4 0ST) : Baron Jay Ltd, 1977. — [1],173p : chiefly ill, coats of arms, facsims, plan, ports ; 31cm.
ISBN 0-904593-04-5 : Unpriced
(B77-31631)

942.3'58 — Parish churches. *Devon. Plymouth. Parish Church of St Jude, Plymouth, to 1975*
Trethewey, Clifford. The master builders : a story of St Jude's Church, Plymouth / by Clifford Trethewey ; illustrated by Nelson R. Trethewey. — [Plymouth] : St Jude's Church ; [Plymouth] ([Faraday Rd, Prince Rock, Plymouth PL4 0ST]) : [Distributed by Baron Jay Ltd, Publishers], 1976. — 32p : ill, maps ; 26cm.
ISBN 0-9505384-0-x Sd : £0.45
(B77-01934)

942.3'7'003 — Cornwall, to 1976. *Encyclopaedias*
Kay-Robinson, Denys. Devon & Cornwall / [by] Denys Kay-Robinson. — Edinburgh [etc.] : J. Bartholomew, 1977. — x,229p,[4],8p of plates : ill(some cols), maps(some cols) ; 26cm.
Bibl.: p.205-207. — Index.
ISBN 0-7028-1014-2 : £4.95
Primary classification 942.3'5'003
(B77-21627)

942.3'7'0830924 — Cornwall. Social life, 1903-1922. *Childhood reminiscences*
Rowse, Alfred Leslie. A Cornish childhood : autobiography of a Cornishman / [by] A.L. Rowse. — [London] : Cardinal, [1975]. — [2], 282p ; 20cm.
Originally published: London : Cape, 1942. — Index.
ISBN 0-351-18069-9 Pbk : £1.10
(B77-19923)

942.3'7'0830924 — Cornwall. Social life, 1920-ca 1925. *Childhood reminiscences*
James, Erma Harvey. A grain of sand : memories of a Cornish childhood / [by] Erma Harvey James. — London : Kimber, 1976. — 188p ; 23cm.
ISBN 0-7183-0015-7 : £3.25
(B77-01935)

942.3'7'085705 — Cornwall. Social life. *Periodicals. Cornish texts*
An gannas. — [Liskeard] ([Trewyn, Lodge Hill, Liskeard, Cornwall]) : [G.M. Sandercock]. Nyver 1- ; mys Kevardhu 1976-. — [1976]-. — ill ; 30cm.
Monthly. — [6] leaves in 1st issue.
Sd : Unpriced
(B77-11495)

942.3'7'08570924 — Cornwall. Rural regions. Social life. *Personal observations*
Val Baker, Denys. The wind blows from the west / [by] Denys Val Baker. — London : Kimber, 1977. — 190p ; 23cm.
ISBN 0-7183-0265-6 : £3.75
(B77-29837)

942.3'71 — Cornwall. Launceston, to 1975
Venning, Arthur Bate. The book of Launceston : a portrait of the town / by Arthur Bate Venning. — Chesham ([Lee Farm House, Botley], Chesham, Bucks.) : Barracuda Books Ltd, 1976. — 3-148p : ill, coats of arms, facsims, maps, plans, ports ; 31cm.
Map, ill. on lining papers. — Bibl.: p.142-143. — Index.
ISBN 0-86023-024-4 : £8.25
(B77-06992)

942.3'75 — Cornwall. Mousehole, ca 1900-1910. *Childhood reminiscences*
Tregenza, Leo. Harbour village : yesterday in Cornwall / [by] Leo Tregenza. — London : Kimber, 1977. — 192p,[8]p of plates : ill ; 23cm.
ISBN 0-7183-0095-5 : £3.50
(B77-23905)

942.3'75 — Cornwall. St Ives, to 1977
Noall, Cyril. The book of St Ives : a portrait of the town / by Cyril Noall. — Chesham : Barracuda Books, 1977. — 3-148p : ill, facsims, maps, plans, ports ; 31cm.
Maps on lining papers. — Bibl.: p.143-144. — Index.
ISBN 0-86023-037-6 : £8.75
(B77-27596)

942.3'78 — Cornwall. St Agnes, to 1976
Pearce, Frank, *b.1909.* St Agnes : portrait of a Cornish village / [by] Frank Pearce. — Falmouth (Minnie Place, Falmouth, Cornwall) : Bantam, 1977. — [1],28p : ill ; 18x24cm.
Sd : Unpriced
(B77-20828)

942.3'78 — Cornwall. Truro, to 1914
Douch, Henry Leslie. The book of Truro : a portrait of the town / by H.L. Douch. — Chesham ([Lee Farm House, Botley], Chesham, Bucks.) : Barracuda Books Ltd, 1977. — 3-140p : ill, facsims, map, ports ; 31cm.
Ill., maps on lining papers. — Bibl.: p.135. — Index.
ISBN 0-86023-022-8 : £8.25
(B77-13442)

942.3'8'0810222 — Somerset. Social life, ca 1860-ca 1915. *Illustrations*
Victorian and Edwardian Somerset from old photographs / [introduction and commentaries by] David Bromwich & Robert Dunning. — London : Batsford, 1977. — ix,[111p] : chiefly ill, ports ; 26cm.
ISBN 0-7134-0405-1 : £3.95
(B77-08694)

942.3'83 — Somerset. Mendip region, to 1975
Mendip, a new study / edited by Robin Atthill ; contributors Robin Atthill ... [et al.]. — Newton Abbot [etc.] : David and Charles, 1976. — 287p,[24]p of plates : ill, maps, port ; 25cm.
Bibl.: p.263-277. — Index.
ISBN 0-7153-7297-1 : £7.50
(B77-08695)

942.3'83 — Somerset. Shepton Mallet, to 1872
Farbrother, John E. Shepton Mallet : notes on its history, ancient, descriptive, and natural / by John E. Farbrother. — Memorial ed. / with a biographical notice of the author by J.C. Earle, and supplementary chapters by E.H.F. Cosens. — Bridgwater ([County Library Headquarters] Mount St., Bridgwater, Somerset [TA6 3ES]) : Somerset County Library, 1977. — [4],xvi,249p, [10]leaves of plates : ill, ports ; 18cm.
Limited ed. of 400 copies. — Facsimile reprint of: Memorial ed. Shepton Mallet : Byrt, 1872. — Includes 'Cannard's grave', a poem.
ISBN 0-9503615-3-4 Pbk : £2.00
(B77-26037)

942.3'89 — Country houses. *Somerset. Hinton St George. Hinton House, to 1975*
Winn, Colin G. The Pouletts of Hinton St George / [by] Colin G. Winn. — London : Research Publishing Co., 1976. — 202p,[6] leaves of plates(1 fold),[16]p of plates : ill, col coat of arms, geneal table, ports(some col), plans(on lining papers) ; 26cm.
Bibl.: p.187-189. — Index.
ISBN 0-7050-0032-x : £7.00
Primary classification 929'.2'0942
(B77-08143)

942.3'9'085705 — Avon. *Periodicals*
Bristol and West Country illustrated. — Bristol (42 Baldwin St., Bristol BS1 1PN) : Brunel Press Ltd.
Vol.1, no.1- ; June 1977-. — 1977-. — ill, ports ; 30cm.
Monthly. — [2],65p. in 1st issue.
Sd : £0.40(£7.20 yearly)
ISSN 0140-4520
(B77-26038)

942.3'91 — Personal property. Probate inventories. *Avon. Frampton Cotterell region, 1539-1804. Texts*
The goods and chattels of our forefathers : Frampton Cotterell and District probate inventories, 1539-1804 / edited by John S. Moore. — London [etc.] : Phillimore, 1976. — xx,364p ; 23cm. — (Frampton Cotterell and District historical studies ; 1)
Index.
ISBN 0-85033-222-2 : £6.50
(B77-05144)

942.3'93'0830222 — Avon. Bristol, 1913-1921. *Illustrations*
Bristol as it was, 1913-1921 / the photographs collected by, and the book written, designed and published by Reece Winstone. — Bristol (23 Hyland Grove, Bristol 9) : R. Winstone, 1976. — 88p : chiefly ill, ports ; 26cm.
ISBN 0-900814-48-9 : £2.55
(B77-13984)

942.3'97 — Avon. Saltford, to 1975
Sims, Percy. A history of Saltford village / by Percy Sims ; edited by Lorna Leete-Hodge. — Saltford (5 The Batch, Saltford, Bristol, Avon) : P.T. Sims and R.W. Mawditt, 1976. — [5], 102p,fold leaf : ill, map, plan, ports ; 30cm.
ISBN 0-9505377-0-5 Pbk : £3.50
(B77-05789)

942.3'98 — Avon. Bath. Social life, to 1976
Hudson, Kenneth. Pleasures and people of Bath / [by] Kenneth Hudson. — London : Joseph, 1977. — 48p : ill(some col), map, ports(some col) ; 19cm. — (Folio miniatures)
Ill. on lining papers. — Bibl.: p.32.
ISBN 0-7181-1588-0 : £1.95
(B77-29085)

942.3'98 — Peasant houses, 1200-1400. Excavation of remains. *Avon. Bath. Barrow Mead, 1964. Reports, surveys*
Woodhouse, Jayne. Barrow Mead, Bath, 1964 : excavation of a medieval peasant house / [by] Jayne Woodhouse. — Oxford : British Archaeological Reports, 1976. — [7],73p : ill, maps, plans ; 30cm. — (British archaeological reports ; 28 ISSN 0306-1205)
Bibl.: p.62-64.
ISBN 0-904531-31-7 Sd : £1.30
(B77-00538)

942.4'07'3 — England. West Midlands, 1760-1800
Money, John, *b.1939.* Experience and identity : Birmingham and the West Midlands, 1760-1800 / [by] John Money. — Manchester : Manchester University Press, 1977. — viii, 312p ; 24cm.
Bibl.: p.295-306. — Index.
ISBN 0-7190-0672-4 : £9.95 : CIP rev.
(B77-11496)

942.4'1 — Gloucestershire. *History*
A history of the county of Gloucester. — Oxford [etc.] : Oxford University Press for the Institute of Historical Research. — (The Victoria history of the counties of England)
Vol.11 / edited by N.M. Herbert. — 1976. — xix,339p,leaf of plate,[20]p of plates : ill, maps, plans, ports ; 31cm.
Index.
ISBN 0-19-722745-7 : £30.00
(B77-04493)

942.4'1'08540924 — Gloucestershire. Rural regions. Social life, 1948. *Personal observations*
Phelps, Humphrey. Just over yonder / [by] Humphrey Phelps ; illustrated by Richard Reid. — London : Joseph, 1977. — 208p : ill ; 23cm.
ISBN 0-7181-1638-0 : £4.95
(B77-30882)

942.4'12 — Parish churches. *Gloucestershire. Deerhurst. St Mary's Church, Deerhurst. Antiquities. Excavation of remains, 1971-1973. Reports, surveys*
Rahtz, Philip Arthur. Excavations at St Mary's Church, Deerhurst, 1971-73 / [by] Philip Rahtz. — London (7 Marylebone Rd, NW1 5HA) : Council for British Archaeology, 1976. — iv,59p,xv p of plates : ill, plans, map ; 30cm. — (Council for British Archaeology. Research reports ; 15)
Bibl.: p.39-40.
ISBN 0-900312-34-3 Pbk : £4.50
(B77-02686)

942.4'13 — Gloucestershire. Beachley, to 1976
Waters, Ivor. Beachley : between the Wye and the Severn / [by] Ivor Waters. — Chepstow ([Chepstow, Gwent]) : Printing Club, Army Apprentices College, 1977. — [3],22,[1]p,[12]p of plates,[3]leaves of plates(1 fold) : ill, 2 maps, port ; 22cm.
Bibl.: p.21-22.
ISBN 0-9505799-0-4 Sd : £1.25
(B77-23906)

942.4'13'0830924 — Gloucestershire. Forest of Dean (District). Social life, ca 1910-ca 1920. *Childhood reminiscences*
Clark, Leonard, *b.1905.* A fool in the forest / [by] Leonard Clark ; illustrated by Richard Shirley Smith. — London : Dobson, 1977. — [2],158p : ill ; 22cm.
Originally published: 1965.
ISBN 0-234-77853-9 : Unpriced
ISBN 0-234-77462-2 Pbk : £0.80
(B77-32331)

942.4'17 — England. Cotswolds, to 1976
Finberg, Josceline. The Cotswolds / [by] Josceline Finberg. — London : Eyre Methuen, 1977. — 256p : ill, maps ; 23cm. — (The regions of Britain)
Bibl.: p.239-243. — Index.
ISBN 0-413-28500-6 : £6.95
ISBN 0-413-37330-4 Pbk : £2.95
(B77-21628)

942.4'17 — Gloucestershire. Blockley. Belcher, Richard Boswell. *Autobiographies*
Belcher, Richard Boswell. Autobiography of Richard Boswell Belcher of Banbury and Blockley, 1898 ; and, The riot at Blockley in 1878 / [edited and annotated on behalf of the Blockley Antiquarian Society by A.W. Exell and Norah M. Marshall. — [Moreton-in-Marsh] ([Church Gates, Blockley, Moreton-in-Marsh, Glos.]) : Blockley Antiquarian Society, 1976. — [4],38p : ill, geneal table, ports ; 21cm.
ISBN 0-9505393-0-9 Sd : £0.40
(B77-01936)

942.4'17 — Gloucestershire. Cirencester, to 1974. *Conference proceedings*
Studies in the archaeology and history of Cirencester : based on papers presented to a research seminar on the post-Roman development of Cirencester held at the Corinium Museum, November 1975 / edited by Alan McWhirr. — Oxford : British Archaeological Reports, 1976. — [10],100p : ill, facsims, maps, plans ; 30cm. — (British archaeological reports ; 30 ISSN 0306-1205)
ISBN 0-904531-43-0 Pbk : £3.90
(B77-00539)

942.4'17'0810222 — England. Cotswolds. Social life, ca 1900. *Illustrations*
Old Cotswold photographs / [compiled] by D.J. Viner. — Nelson : Hendon Publishing Co., 1977. — [48]p : chiefly ill, ports ; 14x22cm.
ISBN 0-86067-023-6 Sd : £1.00
(B77-22283)

942.4'17'0830924 — Gloucestershire. Cotswolds. Social life, 1918-ca 1930. *Childhood reminiscences*
Lee, Laurie. Cider with Rosie / [by] Laurie Lee ; with ten poems and an essay by Laurie Lee ; editor Chris Buckton. — Harlow : Longman, 1976. — viii,248p : ill, ports ; 19cm. — (Longman imprint books)
'Photographs include some from Laurie Lee's family album, and a collection taken in the Cotswolds, selected by the author'. — 'Cider with Rosie' originally published: London : Hogarth Press, 1959. — Bibl.: p.246-247.
ISBN 0-582-23359-3 Pbk : £1.10
(B77-00540)

Lee, Laurie. Cider with Rosie / [by] Laurie Lee. — Large print ed. — Bath : Chivers, 1977. — [11],321p ; 22cm.
Originally published: London : Hogarth Press, 1959.
ISBN 0-85997-265-8 : £5.40(£4.05 to members of the Library Association)
(B77-34322)

942.4'4 — Hereford and Worcester. Herefordshire, to 1974
Andere, Mary. Herefordshire : the enchanted land / [by] Mary Andere ; with illustrations by Peter Manders. — Revised ed. — [Hereford] ([Foley Estate, Hereford HR1 2SJ]) : Express Logic Ltd, 1976. — 127p : ill, maps ; 26cm.
Previous ed.: 1974. — Bibl.: p.119-120. — Index.
ISBN 0-904464-08-3 : £3.75
(B77-29838)

942.4'4 — Residences. *Hereford and Worcester. Herefordshire, to 1976*
Andere, Mary. Homes and houses of Herefordshire / by Mary Andere ; with an foreword by Roy Strong. — Hereford (Foley Estate, Hereford HR1 2SJ) : Express Logic Ltd, 1977. — 125p : ill, map ; 25cm.
Bibl.: p.122. — Index.
ISBN 0-904464-10-5 : £4.50 : CIP rev.
(B77-08149)

942.4'4'00216 — Places of historical importance. *Hereford and Worcester. Worcestershire. Lists*
Worcester *(County). Planning Department.* Register of countryside treasures / ... produced in the [Worcester] County Planning Department during 1970-73 ; research ... carried out entirely by J.H. Turner, who also wrote the text. — Worcester : [Worcester County Planning Department], 1973. [Supplement]. — [Worcester] [Farrier House, Farrier St., Worcester WR1 3EW] : [The County Council of Hereford and Worcester, Planning Department], 1976. — [1],12,[124]p : maps(chiefly col) ; 30cm.
ISBN 0-903987-08-2 Ls : £1.20
(B77-03848)

942.4'43 — Abbeys. *Hereford & Worcester. Redditch. Bordesley Abbey. Antiquities. Excavation of remains, to 1975. Reports, surveys*
Rahtz, Philip Arthur. Bordesley Abbey, Redditch, Hereford-Worcestershire : first report on excavations, 1969-1973 / [by] Philip Rahtz and Susan Hirst. — Oxford : British Archaeological Reports, 1976. — [4],277p,[3] leaves of plates,[17]p of plates : ill(incl 3 col), maps, plans ; 21x30cm. — (British archaeological reports ; 23 ISSN 0306-1205)
Twenty fold. sheets ([20] sides) (ill., maps, plans) in portfolio. — Bibl.: p.272-276.
ISBN 0-904531-26-0 Pbk : £5.90
(B77-01937)

942.4'48 — Buildings of historical importance. *Hereford and Worcester. Worcester. Commandery, to 1977*
Latta, Caroline. The Commandery : the Hospital of St Wulstan, Worcester / [by] Caroline Latta. — [Worcester] ([City Museum and Art Gallery, Foregate St., Worcester WR1 1DT]) : City of Worcester, 1977. — [2],32,[1]p,fold plate : ill(incl 3 col), facsims, map, plans, port ; 21cm.
Bibl.(1p.).
Sd : Unpriced
(B77-26707)

942.4'49 — Hereford and Worcester. Evesham, to 1976
Cox, Benjamin G. The book of Evesham : the story of the town's past / by Benjamin G. Cox. — Chesham : Barracuda Books, 1977. — 3-148p : ill, coats of arms, facsims, maps, ports ; 31cm.
Ill. on lining papers. — Bibl.: p.143-144. — Index.
ISBN 0-86023-043-0 : £8.75
(B77-22284)

942.4'6 — Southern Staffordshire, to 1800. *Early works. Facsimiles*
Shaw, Stebbing. The history and antiquities of Staffordshire / by Stebbing Shaw. — [1st ed. reprinted] ; introduction by M.W. Greenslade and G.C. Baugh. — Wakefield : EP Publishing [for] Staffordshire County Library. — (Classical county histories)
Vol.1. — 1976. — 714p in various pagings,[54] leaves of plates(3 fold) : ill, coats of arms, geneal tables, map, plans, ports ; 36cm.
Facsimile reprint of: 1st ed. London : J. Robson, 1798. — Index.
ISBN 0-85409-673-6 : £35.00
ISBN 0-85409-661-2 Set of 2 vols : £60.00
Also classified at 942.4'9
(B77-27597)

Vol.2. Part 1. — 1976. — 417p in various pagings,[48] leaves of plates(3 fold), 30p of plates : ill, coats of arms, geneal tables, map, ports ; 36cm.
Facsimile reprint of: 1st ed. London : J. Robson, 1801.
ISBN 0-85409-675-2 : £35.00
ISBN 0-85409-661-2 Set of 2 vols : £60.00
Also classified at 942.4'9
(B77-27598)

942.4'68 — Parish churches. *Staffordshire. Lichfield. St Michael's Church, Lichfield. Churchyards. Excavation of remains. Reports, surveys*
Gould, Dorothy. St Michael's churchyard, Lichfield, Staffs. / by Dorothy and Jim Gould. — [Walsall] ([c/o J.W. Whiston, 58 Wednesbury Rd, Walsall WS1 3RS]) : South Staffordshire Archaeological and Historical Society, [1976]. — [6]p : 1 ill, plan ; 25cm.
'Extract from "Transactions" 1974-1975 Volume XVI'.
ISBN 0-86061-000-4 Sd : £0.15
(B77-00541)

942.4'68 — Staffordshire. Lichfield. Social life, 1832-1900
Clayton, Howard. Cathedral city : a look at Victorian Lichfield / by Howard Clayton. — Lichfield (Rocklands, Wissage Rd, Lichfield, [Staffs.]) : The author, [1977]. — [5],171p,[20]p of plates : ill, facsims, 2 maps, ports ; 22cm.
Index.
ISBN 0-9503563-1-x : £3.60
(B77-29839)

942.4'8 — Warwickshire. Local history
Miscellany. — [Stratford-upon-Avon] ([The Hon. Secretary, c/o The Shakespeare Centre, Stratford-upon-Avon]) : Dugdale Society. — (Dugdale Society. Publications ; vol.31 ISSN 0307-6415)
1 / edited by Robert Bearman. — 1977. — [8], 212p,[2] leaves of plates : ill, geneal table, ports ; 25cm.
Includes two documents in Latin. — Index.
Unpriced
(B77-33540)

942.4′8 — Warwickshire, to 1975
Bird, Vivian. A short history of Warwickshire and Birmingham / [by] Vivian Bird. — London : Batsford, 1977. — 176p : ill, facsims, map, ports ; 23cm.
Bibl.: p.168-170. — Index.
ISBN 0-7134-0429-9 : £3.95
Also classified at 942.4′9
(B77-18489)

942.4′81 — Warwickshire. Hartshill & Oldbury. *History*
Allen, Joan, *b.1917.* Heardred's Hill : a history of the parishes of Hartshill and Oldbury, North Warwickshire / by Joan Allen ; illustrations by Lach. — Hartshill (78 Victoria Rd, Hartshill, Nuneaton [Warwickshire] CV10 0LR) : The author.
Part 1 : The prehistoric era, 10,000 BC to 43 AD. — 1977. — 36,[1]p : ill, maps ; 21cm.
Bibl. (1p.).
Sd : £0.45
(B77-24625)

Part 3 : Lords of the Manor : the Hardreshulles of Hardreshulle, 1125 AD to 1367 AD. — 1977. — 53p : ill, coats of arms, geneal table, maps, plan ; 21cm.
Bibl.: p.52.
Sd : £0.50
(B77-25313)

942.4′85 — Warwickshire. Rugby, to 1977
Rugby, further aspects of the past. — Rugby ([c/o] C. Steers, 150 Railway Terrace, Rugby) : Rugby Local History Group, [1977]. — [2],84,[1]p : ill, geneal tables, map ; 21cm.
'The articles contained in this symposium on Aspects of Rugby's History have been made possible by the activities of the Local History Group based at the Percival Guildhouse. The course was promoted by the Guildhouse and the West Midlands district of the Workers' Educational Association' - Acknowledgements.
Sd : £0.50
(B77-29086)

942.4′87 — Warwickshire. Leamington Spa. Social life, 1890-1953. *Personal observations. Collections*
The **Leamington** we used to know : a collection of memories of Leamington by members and friends of the Leamington Literary Society. — Kineton : Roundwood Press [for] the Leamington Literary Society, 1977. — x,141p,[16]p of plates : ill, music, ports ; 25cm.
ISBN 0-900093-65-x : £3.25
(B77-32332)

942.4′87 — Warwickshire persons: Stoneleigh persons, 1597-1650
Alcock, Nathaniel Warren. Stoneleigh villagers, 1597-1650 : based on the work of students in a University of Birmingham extramural class / [by] N.W. Alcock. — Coventry (Coventry CV4 7AL) : University of Warwick, Open Studies, 1975. — viii,58p,[2]p of plates : ill, geneal table, map, plans ; 30cm.
Index.
ISBN 0-902683-03-9 Sd : £0.70
(B77-19130)

942.4′9 — West Midlands (Metropolitan County). Black Country, to 1800. *Early works. Facsimiles*
Shaw, Stebbing. The history and antiquities of Staffordshire / by Stebbing Shaw. — [1st ed. reprinted] ; introduction by M.W. Greenslade and G.C. Baugh. — Wakefield : EP Publishing [for] Staffordshire County Library. — (Classical county histories)
Vol.1. — 1976. — 714p in various pagings,[54] leaves of plates(3 fold) : ill, coats of arms, geneal tables, map, plans, ports ; 36cm.
Facsimile reprint of: 1st ed. London : J. Robson, 1798. — Index.
ISBN 0-85409-673-6 : £35.00
ISBN 0-85409-661-2 Set of 2 vols : £60.00
Primary classification 942.4′6
(B77-27597)

Vol.2. Part 1. — 1976. — 417p in various pagings,[48] leaves of plates(3 fold), 30p of plates : ill, coats of arms, geneal tables, map, ports ; 36cm.
Facsimile reprint of: 1st ed. London : J. Robson, 1801.
ISBN 0-85409-675-2 : £35.00
ISBN 0-85409-661-2 Set of 2 vols : £60.00
Primary classification 942.4′6
(B77-27598)

942.4′9 — West Midlands (Metropolitan County), to 1975
Bird, Vivian. A short history of Warwickshire and Birmingham / [by] Vivian Bird. — London : Batsford, 1977. — 176p : ill, facsims, map, ports ; 23cm.
Bibl.: p.168-170. — Index.
ISBN 0-7134-0429-9 : £3.95
Primary classification 942.4′8
(B77-18489)

942.4′91′0810222 — West Midlands (Metropolitan County). Wolverhampton, 1840-. *Illustrations*
Wolverhampton as it was / [compiled] by John Roper. — Nelson : Hendon Publishing Co.
Vol.3. — 1976. — [1],44p : chiefly ill, ports ; 21x29cm.
'... based largely on the [Wolverhampton] Central Library collection ...' - Introduction.
ISBN 0-902907-98-0 Sd : £1.40
(B77-01092)

942.4′92 — Manor houses. Sites. *West Midlands (Metropolitan County). Walsall, to ca 1400. Moat Site. Excavation of remains, 1972-1974. Reports, surveys*
Wrathmell, Stuart. Excavations at the Moat Site, Walsall, Staffs., 1972-4 / [by] Stuart and Susan Wrathmell. — Walsall (c/o J.W. Whiston, 58 Wednesbury Rd, Walsall WS1 3RS) : [South Staffordshire Archaeological and Historical Society], [1976]. — p19-53,[3]leaves of plates(2 fold) : ill, maps, plans ; 24cm.
'Extract from "Transactions" 1974-1975 Volume XVI' - Cover.
ISBN 0-904608-97-2 Pbk : £1.00
(B77-01093)

942.4′93′0810222 — West Midlands (Metropolitan County). Dudley (District), 1850-1940. *Illustrations*
Dudley as it was / [compiled] by David F. Radmore. — Nelson : Hendon Publishing Co., 1977. — 44p : chiefly ill ; 21x29cm.
'This selection of pictures has been chosen from those in the Local Studies collection at Dudley Library' - Foreword.
ISBN 0-86067-010-4 Sd : £1.40
(B77-21629)

942.4′96 — West Midlands (Metropolitan County). Birmingham. Moorpool, 1910-1914. *Extracts from newspapers*
The **best** of 'The Moor Pool news' 1910-1914. — [Birmingham] ([c/o E. Lewis, 97 Ravenhurst Rd, Moorpool, Harborne, Birmingham B17 9DR]) : Harborne Tenants Silver Jubilee Committee, 1977. — [2],10p : ill ; 21cm.
Facsimile reprints.
Sd : £0.25
(B77-19131)

942.4′96 — West Midlands (Metropolitan County). Birmingham, to 1975
Whybrow, John. How Birmingham became a great city / by John Whybrow and Rachel Waterhouse. — [Birmingham] ([200 Stratford Rd, Birmingham B11 1AB]) : [John Whybrow Ltd], [1976]. — 120p : ill, maps, ports ; 26cm.
Text on lining paper. — Bibl.: p.119. — Index.
ISBN 0-9502459-1-7 : £8.95
(B77-15630)

942.4′96 — West Midlands (Metropolitan County). Sutton Coldfield, to 1972. *Juvenile literature*
Moss, Hilda. A royal town and its park : a history for junior citizens / by Hilda Moss ; illustrated by Sue Beeson. — [Birmingham] ([Central Libraries, Birmingham B3 3HQ]) : Birmingham Public Libraries, 1977. — 40p : ill ; 24cm.
Originally published: Sutton Coldfield : Sutton Coldfield Corporation, 1973. — Bibl.: p.8.
ISBN 0-7093-0000-x Sd : Unpriced
(B77-26039)

942.5′1′0810924 — Derbyshire. Social life, ca 1900. *Childhood reminiscences*
Ground, Hannah. New poems and true short stories / by Hannah Ground. — [Alfreton] ([172 Mansfield Rd, Alfreton, Derbyshire DE5 7JQ]) : [The author], [1977]. — [3],35p : ill, ports ; 19cm.
Sd : £1.25
Primary classification 821′.9′14
(B77-27328)

942.5′11 — Derbyshire. New Mills, to 1976
New Mills, a short history including an analysis of the census of 1851 / edited by J.H. Smith and J.V. Symonds. — [Manchester] ([13 Oxford Rd, Manchester]) : Manchester University Extra-Mural Department, [1977]. — 90p : ill, facsim, maps ; 22cm.
ISBN 0-902637-25-8 Sd : £1.50
(B77-34323)

942.5′12 — Derbyshire. Chesterfield, to 1976
Cooper, Roy. The book of Chesterfield : a portrait of the town / by Roy Cooper. — Chesham : Barracuda Books, 1977. — 3-148p : ill, coats of arms, facsims, maps, plans, ports ; 31cm.
Maps on lining papers. — Bibl.: p.143. — Index.
ISBN 0-86023-020-1 : £7.90
(B77-15631)

942.5′18 — Abbeys. *Derbyshire. Dale. Dale Abbey, to ca 1270. Early works*
De Musca, Thomas. The foundation of Dale Abbey in legend and chronicle : a new translation [from the Latin] and critical review of the chronicle [of Thomas de Musca] and legends concerning the foundation of Dale Abbey / by Richard Clark. — Ilkeston (c/o Mr. P. Stevenson, 16 Rigley Ave., Ilkeston, Derbyshire DE7 5LW) : Ilkeston and District Local History Society, 1977. — iv,44p,leaf of plate,[2]p of plates : ill, maps, plan ; 30cm. — (Ilkeston and District Local History Society. Occasional papers ; no.6 ISSN 0306-977x)
'... [a] new translation of Thomas de Musca's thirteenth century chronicle' - Foreword. — Index.
ISBN 0-902165-09-7 Sd : £0.60
(B77-17233)

942.5′24 — Nottinghamshire. Southwell. *Newspapers*
The **Bramley.** — Southwell ('The Ridge', Lower Kirklington Rd, Southwell, Notts. NG25 0DX) : Bramley Publications.
Continues: The Southwell Bramley.
No.25- ; May 1977-. — [1977]-. — ill(some col), facsims, ports ; 42cm.
Monthly. — 24p. in May 1977 issue.
Sd : Unpriced
ISSN 0309-9075
(B77-19132)

942.5′31 — Lincolnshire. South-eastern West Lindsey (District). *Newspapers*
Chronicle, Lincoln (North). — Lincoln (P.O. Box 10, Witham House, Pelham Bridge, Lincoln LN5 8XE) : Lincolnshire Standard Group.
Continues: Lincolnshire chronicle (Lincoln area).
No.7903- ; 27 Jan. 1977-. — 1977-. — ill, ports ; 42cm.
Weekly. — 40, 16p. in issue no.7903.
Sd : £0.07
ISSN 0309-6939
Primary classification 942.5′34
(B77-13986)

942.5′31 — Lincolnshire. Western West Lindsey (District). *Newspapers*
Chronicle, Lindsey (West). — Lincoln (P.O. Box 10, Witham House, Pelham Bridge, Lincoln LN5 8XE) : Lincolnshire Standard Group.
Continues: Lincolnshire chronicle (West Lindsey).
No.7903- ; Jan. 27 1977-. — 1977-. — ill, ports ; 42cm.
Weekly. — 40, 16p. in issue no.7903.
Sd : £0.07
ISSN 0309-7056
(B77-13985)

942.5′34 — Lincolnshire. Northern Lincoln. *Newspapers*
Chronicle, Lincoln (North). — Lincoln (P.O. Box 10, Witham House, Pelham Bridge, Lincoln LN5 8XE) : Lincolnshire Standard Group.
Continues: Lincolnshire chronicle (Lincoln area).
No.7903- ; 27 Jan. 1977-. — 1977-. — ill, ports ; 42cm.
Weekly. — 40, 16p. in issue no.7903.
Sd : £0.07
ISSN 0309-6939
Also classified at 942.5′31
(B77-13986)

942.5′35 — Lincolnshire. North-western North Kesteven (District). *Newspapers*
Chronicle, Kesteven (Fosse Way). — Lincoln (P.O. Box 10, Witham House, Pelham Bridge, Lincoln LN5 8XE) : Lincolnshire Standard Group.
Continues: Lincolnshire chronicle (North Kesteven).
No.7903- ; Jan. 27, 1977-. — 1977-. — ill, ports ; 42cm.
Weekly. — 40,16p. in issue no.7903.
Sd : £0.07
ISSN 0309-6912
(B77-13443)

942.5'37 — Lincolnshire. Boston. Social life. Effects of wars, 1899-1945
Middlebrook, Martin. Boston at war : being an account of Boston's involvement in the Boer War and the two World Wars / by Martin Middlebrook. — Boston, Lincs. (80 Sleaford Rd, Boston, Lincs. PE21 8EU) : Richard Kay Publications for the History of Boston Project, 1974. — vi,82p : ill, facsims, col map, ports ; 22cm. — (History of Boston series ; no.12 ISSN 0305-2079)
Index.
ISBN 0-902662-62-7 Sd : £1.20
(B77-20829)

942.5'38 — Anglo-Saxon cemeteries. Excavation of remains. *Lincolnshire. Baston, 1966. Reports, surveys*
Mayes, Philip. An Anglo-Saxon cemetery at Baston, Lincolnshire / [by] P. Mayes and the late M.J. Dean ; with a report on the pottery by J.N.L. Myres. — Sleaford (25 Westgate, Sleaford, [Lincs.]) : Society for Lincolnshire History and Archaeology, 1976. — 63p : ill, maps, plans ; 30cm. — (Occasional papers in Lincolnshire history and archaeology ; 3 ISSN 0307-2797)
ISBN 0-904680-05-3 Sd : £1.40(£1.00 to members)
(B77-01938)

942.5'38 — Lincolnshire. Harlaxton, to 1976
Murden, James. Harlaxton through the ages / [by] James Murden. — [Harlaxton] ([2 de Ligne Drive, Harlaxton, Grantham, Lincs.]) : [The author], [1976]. — [29]p ; 22cm.
ISBN 0-9505482-0-0 Sd : £0.50
(B77-04494)

942.5'4'0810222 — Leicestershire. Social life, 1860-1910. *Illustrations*
Victorian and Edwardian Leicestershire from old photographs / introduction and commentaries by Iona Cruickshank and Allen Chinnery. — London : Batsford, 1977. — [120]p : of ill, ports ; 26cm.
ISBN 0-7134-3190-3 : £3.95
(B77-09433)

942.5'42 — Castles. *Leicestershire. Leicester. Leicester Castle, to 1858. Early works*
Thompson, James, *b.1817.* An account of Leicester Castle / by James Thompson. — Melton Mowbray (Wymondham, Melton Mowbray, Leics.) : Sycamore Press Limited, 1977. — viii[i.e.10],54p,[4]leaves of plates : ill, map, plan ; 20cm.
Facsimile reprint of: 1st ed. Leicester : Crossley and Clarke, 1859.
£1.80
(B77-32333)

942.5'45 — Parish churches. *Leicestershire. Oakham. Oakham Parish Church, to 1930*
Haddelsey, Stephen Andrew. Oakham Parish Church / by Stephen Haddelsey. — 5th ed. — [Leicester] ([Saint Luke's Vicarage, 97 Halifax Drive, Stocking Farm, Leicester]) : The author, 1976. — 3-25p : ill ; 21cm.
Limited ed. of 1000 copies. — Previous ed.: 197-.
ISBN 0-9505504-0-x Sd : £0.25
(B77-05790)

942.5'46 — Leicestershire. Brooksby, to 1976
Hubbard, John R. Brooksby : the story of an estate and its people / written and illustrated by John R. Hubbard. — [Melton Mowbray] ([Brooksby, Melton Mowbray, Leics. LE14 2LJ]) : Brooksby Agricultural College, 1977. — [6],91p(5 fold),[3]leaves of plates : ill, coats of arms(some col), facsims, geneal tables, maps, plan, ports ; 30cm.
ISBN 0-85022-012-2 Sp : Unpriced
(B77-34324)

942.5'47 — Leicestershire. Charnwood (District). Soar River region. *Newspapers*
Soar Valley news. — [Barrow-upon-Soar] ([c/o The Editor, 3 South St., Barrow-upon-Soar, Leics. LE12 8LY]) : Soar Valley News.
No.1- ; Dec. 1975-. — 1975-. — ill, ports ; 31cm.
Monthly. — 12p. in 1st issue.
Sd : Free to residents
(B77-08150)

942.5'47 — Leicestershire. Charnwood (District), to 1976
Charnwood's heritage / edited by I.M. Evans. — [Leicester] ([96 New Walk, Leicester LE1 6TD]) : Leicestershire Museums, Art Galleries and Records Service, 1976. — [8],123p : ill, maps ; 22cm.
Bibl.: p.98-113. — Index.
ISBN 0-904671-21-6 Pbk : £1.45
(B77-15043)

942.5'5'0810222 — Northamptonshire. Social life, ca 1870-1914. *Illustrations*
Old Northamptonshire in photographs / compiled and edited by R.L. Greenall. — Northampton (27 Guildhall Rd, Northampton NN1 1EF) : Northamptonshire Libraries, 1976. — [160]p : of ill, ports ; 26cm.
ISBN 0-905391-02-0 : £3.25
(B77-03303)

942.5'63 — Bedfordshire. Langford, to 1975
Rutt, Michael. The people at the long ford : a social and economic history of Langford / by Michael Rutt ; edited by Paul Catcheside and Alan Threadgill. — [Bedford] ([c/o Biggleswade Area Library, Chestnut Ave., Biggleswade, Beds.]) : Bedfordshire County Library, [1976]. — [2],vi,77p : ill, maps ; 29cm.
Bibl.: p.75-77.
Pbk : £1.00
(B77-05791)

942.5'65 — Bedfordshire. Leighton Buzzard & Linslade, to 1976
Leighton Buzzard and District Preservation Society. Old Leighton Buzzard & Linslade / [Leighton Buzzard and District Preservation Society]. — Leighton Buzzard (c/o Hon. Secretary, 1 Woodland Ave., Leighton Buzzard, Beds. LU7 7JW) : The Society, 1976. — [2], 33p : ill, 2 maps ; 30cm.
Bibl.: p.33.
ISBN 0-9505424-0-7 Sd : £1.00
(B77-02687)

942.5'67'081 — Bedfordshire. Luton. Social life, ca 1855-1976
Luton, past and present : incorporating 'Old Luton' : a collection of 245 pictures / edited by Harold White. — Luton ([Crescent Rd, Luton LU2 0AG]) : White Crescent Press Ltd, 1977. — 152p : ill, coat of arms, facsims, maps, ports ; 23cm.
Bibl.: p.147. — Index.
ISBN 0-900804-20-3 : £3.00
(B77-10067)

942.5'7 — England. Middle Thames Valley. Local history. *Periodicals*
Time span : the journal of the Middle Thames Archaeological and Historical Society. — Slough (c/o The Editor, W.L.M. Nelmes, 26 Mildenhall Rd, Slough) : The Society.
Continues: News bulletin.
[No.21]- ; [Jan. 1977]-. — 1977-. — ill, coats of arms, maps ; 30cm.
Published at irregular intervals. — [2],24p. in issue no.21.
Sd : Unpriced
ISSN 0309-5169
(B77-16680)

942.5'71 — Oxfordshire. Ducklington, ca 1920-ca 1930. *Childhood reminiscences*
Harris, Mollie. The green years / [by] Mollie Harris. — London : Hale, 1976. — 159p,[8]p of plates : ill, ports ; 23cm.
ISBN 0-7091-5715-0 : £3.95
(B77-00542)

942.5'73 — Oxfordshire. Juniper Hill. Thompson, Flora. *Biographies*
Lane, Margaret, *b.1907.* Flora Thompson / by Margaret Lane. — London : J. Murray, 1976. — 28p : ill ; 22cm.
'... first published in "The Cornhill Magazine" (Spring 1957) ... later included in the author's volume of collected essays, Purely for Pleasure (Hamish Hamilton Ltd, London, and Alfred A. Knopf, New York) in 1967' - title page verso.
ISBN 0-7195-3322-8 Sd : £0.90
(B77-08696)

942.5'74'070222 — Oxfordshire. Oxford, 1772-1961. Compared with Oxford, 1976. *Illustrations*
Oxford old and new / [compiled by] Malcolm Graham ; [modern photographs by John Peacock]. — Wakefield : EP Publishing, 1976. — [5],98p : of ill ; 18x25cm.
ISBN 0-7158-1187-8 Pbk : £2.25
(B77-23907)

942.5'74'08230924 — Oxfordshire. Oxford. Lawrence, Thomas Edward, to 1910. *Biographies*
Marriott, Paul J. Oxford's legendary son, the young Lawrence of Arabia, 1888-1910 / by Paul J. Marriott. — [Oxford] ([41 Canning Cres., Oxford OX1 4XA]) : [The author], [1977]. — viii,100p,plate : ill, facsim, maps, plans, ports ; 21cm.
Cover title: The young Lawrence of Arabia, 1888-1910. — Index.
ISBN 0-9505730-0-0 Pbk : Unpriced
(B77-20830)

942.5'74'08230924 — Oxfordshire. Oxford. Social life, ca 1892-1914. *Childhood reminiscences*
Oman, Carola. An Oxford childhood / [by] Carola Oman. — London [etc.] : Hodder and Stoughton, 1976. — 192p,[8]p of plates : ill, geneal tables, ports ; 24cm.
Index.
ISBN 0-340-21265-9 : £5.25
(B77-02688)

942.5'76 — Personal property. Probate inventories. *Oxfordshire. Chilton, 1551-1725*
Denzey, Frank J. Chilton's chattels / [by] Frank J. Denzey. — [Didcot] ([Larkfield, Chapel Furlong, Upton, Didcot, Oxon. OX11 9JN]) : [The author], [1977]. — 68p : ill, facsim, map ; 21cm.
Bibl.: p.67-68. — Index.
Sd : £0.95
(B77-29087)

942.5'8'005 — Hertfordshire. *History. Periodicals*
Hertfordshire's past. — [Hatfield] (c/o H. Jones, 2 Chantry La., Hatfield, Herts. AL10 9HR) : Hertfordshire Archaeological Council : Hertfordshire Local History Council.
No.1- ; Autumn 1976-. — [1976]-. — ill, maps ; 21cm.
Six issues a year. — 20p. in 1st issue. — Bibl.: p.10.
Sd : £0.30
ISSN 0308-7719
(B77-10688)

942.5'8'0810222 — Hertfordshire. Social life, 1845-1913. *Illustrations*
Victorian and Edwardian Hertfordshire from old photographs / introduction and commentaries by Richard Whitmore. — London : Batsford, 1976. — [120]p : ill, ports ; 26cm.
ISBN 0-7134-3223-3 : £3.50
(B77-00543)

942.5'81 — Hertfordshire. Hitchin, 1854-1959
Poole, Helen. Old Hitchin : portrait of an English market town from the cameras of T.B. Latchmore and others / commentary by Helen Poole & Alan Fleck. — Hitchin (Bridge St., Hitchin, [Herts.]) : Eric T. Moore : North Hertfordshire Museums, 1976. — 128p : ill, maps, ports ; 26x27cm.
Index.
ISBN 0-9502391-2-7 : £7.50
(B77-33541)

942.5'83 — Hertfordshire. Ware, to 1976
Heath, Cyril. The book of Ware : a portrait of the town / by Cyril Heath. — Chesham : Barracuda Books, 1977. — 3-148p : ill, coats of arms, facsims, maps, plans, ports ; 27cm.
Plan, ill. on lining papers. — Bibl.: p.143. — Index.
ISBN 0-86023-035-x : £7.50
(B77-19924)

942.5'86 — Hertfordshire. Welwyn region, to 1976
Busby, Richard James. The book of Welwyn : the story of the five villages and the Garden City / by Richard J. Busby. — Chesham ([Lee Farm House, Botley], Chesham, Bucks.) : Barracuda Books Ltd, 1976. — 3-144p : ill, facsims, maps, ports ; 31cm.
Map on lining papers. — Bibl.: p.140. — Index.
ISBN 0-86023-023-6 : £7.90
(B77-06392)

942.5'892 — Hertfordshire. Watford, to 1883. *Early works*
Williams, Henry. History of Watford and trade directory / by Henry Williams. — [1st ed., reprinted] ; new introduction by Peter Taylor. — Watford ([The Open Book, 4 Ye Corner, Aldenham Rd, Watford, Herts.]) : Lesley Enstone, 1976. — [14],iii-viii,318[i.e. 300]p : ill, ports ; 19cm.
Limited ed. of 1,000 signed and numbered copies. — Facsimile reprint: of 1st ed. London : Pardon & Sons, 1884.
ISBN 0-9505675-1-5 : £5.00
(B77-13987)

942.5'892'00222 — Hertfordshire. Watford, to 1923. *Illustrations*
Illustrated companion to the 'History of Watford' (and district) / edited by Peter Taylor. — Watford ([The Open Book, 4 Ye Corner, Aldenham Rd, Watford, Herts.]) : Lesley Enstone, 1976. — 68p : of ill(some col), facsims, ports ; 24cm.
Limited ed. of 1,000 signed and numbered copies. — Bibl.: p.68.
ISBN 0-9505675-0-7 : £4.20
(B77-13988)

942.5'892'0840222 — Hertfordshire. Watford. Social life, 1939-1945. *Illustrations*
Watford at war, 1939-1945 / [compiled by G.I.J. Orton]. — [Watford] ([Central Library, Hempstead Rd, Watford, Herts.]) : [Hertfordshire Library Service], [1976]. — [62] p : of ill, ports ; 21cm.
Published in connection with an exhibition at the Central Library Exhibition Hall, January 1976.
ISBN 0-901354-09-0 Sd : £0.75
(B77-13989)

942.5'91 — Buckinghamshire. Olney region, to 1975
Osborn, Gordon. Cowper country : an introduction to the town of Olney and the immediate neighbourhood / by Gordon Osborn. — Olney (Pangea, West St., Olney, Bucks.) : The author, 1976. — ii-xii,96p : ill, facsims, map, ports ; 22cm.
ISBN 0-9505530-0-x : Unpriced
(B77-24626)

942.5'95 — Buckinghamshire. West Wycombe. Social life, 1700-1800. *Secondary school texts*
Green, Herbert, *b.1902.* Village life in the eighteenth century / [by] Herbert Green ; illustrated from contemporary sources. — London : Longman, 1976. — 96p : ill, facsims, map, plan, port ; 20cm. — (Then and there series)
ISBN 0-582-22122-6 Pbk : £0.50
(B77-05792)

942.5'95 — Country houses. *Buckinghamshire. Princes Risborough. Chequers, to 1977*
Fry, Plantagenet Somerset. Chequers : the country home of Britain's Prime Ministers / [by] Plantagenet Somerset Fry. — London : H.M.S.O., 1977. — xii,72p : col ill, col coat of arms, facsim, map, ports(chiefly col) ; 20x21cm.
Index.
ISBN 0-11-630230-5 Pbk : £2.95
(B77-32994)

942.5'97 — Buckinghamshire. Amersham, to 1976
Pike, Leslie Elgar. The book of Amersham : the story of a Chiltern town / by L. Elgar Pike and Clive Birch. — Chesham ([Lee Farm House, Botley, Chesham, Bucks.]) : Barracuda Books Ltd, 1976. — 3-144p : ill, facsims, maps, ports ; 31cm.
Ill. on lining papers. — Bibl.: p.140. — Index.
ISBN 0-86023-028-7 : £7.95
(B77-06993)

942.6 — East Anglia. Fens, to 1975
Parker, Anthony, *b.1925.* The Fenland / [by] Anthony Parker and Denis Pye. — Newton Abbot [etc.] : David and Charles, 1976. — 240p : ill, map ; 23cm. — (British topographical series)
Bibl.: p.232-237. — Index.
ISBN 0-7153-7296-3 : £4.95
(B77-06994)

942.6'081'0922 — East Anglia. Social life, 1800-1900. *Personal observations. Collections*
East Anglian reminiscences / chosen and edited by E.A. Goodwyn and J.C. Baxter. — Ipswich : Boydell Press, 1976. — [12],114p ; 23cm.
ISBN 0-85115-068-3 : £2.75
(B77-05793)

942.6'1'0810924 — Norfolk. Rural regions. Social life, ca 1900. *Childhood reminiscences*
Fenn, Ida. Tales of Norfolk / by Ida Fenn. — Wymondham (Wymondham, Norfolk) : Geo.R. Reeve Ltd, 1976. — [8],133p,[4]p of plates : ill, ports ; 22cm.
ISBN 0-900616-10-5 Pbk : £2.10
(B77-11497)

942.6'1'0830924 — Norfolk. Rural regions. Social life, ca 1915-ca 1935. *Personal observations*
Wigby, Frederick. Just a country boy / by Frederick C. Wigby. — Wymondham ([Damgate], Wymondham, Norfolk [NR18 0BD]) : Geo. R. Reeve Ltd, 1976. — [8],159p : ill, ports ; 22cm.
ISBN 0-900616-09-1 : £3.50
(B77-02689)

942.6'13 — Norfolk. King's Lynn, ca 1870-1945
Vintage King's Lynn / [compiled] by Michael Winton. — Nelson : Hendon Publishing Co., 1976. — 44p : chiefly ill, ports ; 21x29cm.
ISBN 0-86067-008-2 Sd : £1.40
(B77-05794)

942.6'14 — Norfolk. Caston. *History*
Barnes, John S. A history of Caston, Norfolk / by John S. Barnes. — Orpington ([56 Leamington Ave.,] Orpington, Kent [BR6 9QB]) : The author.
In 3 vols.
Part 3 ... — 1977. — x,131[i.e.133]p,fold plate : ill, coat of arms, facsim, maps, plans, ports ; 25cm.
Index.
Sd : Unpriced
(B77-18490)

942.6'14 — Norfolk. Thetford region, to ca 1900. *Essays*
Clover, R D. Tale of an area : a village study and history of Croxton, Kilverstone, and Barnham and the infancy of Thetford / [by] R.D. Clover ; illustrated with pen-and-ink drawings by the author. — Thetford (Thetford, Norfolk) : The author, 1975. — [22]p : ill ; 21cm.
ISBN 0-9505479-0-5 Sd : £0.50
(B77-05145)

942.6'15 — Norfolk. Norwich, to 1975
Day, James Wentworth. Norwich through the ages / by James Wentworth Day. — Ipswich (6 Great Colman St., Ipswich, Suffolk) : East Anglian Magazine Ltd, 1976. — [1],132p,[24]p of plates : ill, facsims, map, ports ; 22cm.
Bibl.: p.126. — Index.
ISBN 0-900227-23-0 : £4.50
(B77-02690)

942.6'19 — Norfolk. Starston region. Social life, to 1960
Riches, Roy. Oddments : an account of happenings in the Waveney Valley area / by Roy Riches. — [Harleston] ([4 Council Houses, Starston, Harleston, Norfolk]) : [The author], [1976]. — [50]p : ill, ports ; 22cm.
Sd : £1.00
(B77-25314)

942.6'4 — Suffolk, to 1976
Wilson, Derek. A short history of Suffolk / [by] Derek Wilson. — London : Batsford, 1977. — 176p,[16]p of plates : ill, map ; 23cm.
Bibl.: p.170-172. — Index.
ISBN 0-7134-0574-0 : £4.25
(B77-25315)

942.6'4'0820924 — Suffolk. Jobson, Allan. *Autobiographies*
Jobson, Allan. The creeping hours of time : an autobiography / by Allan Jobson. — London : Hale, 1977. — 156p,[12]p of plates : ill, ports ; 23cm.
ISBN 0-7091-5956-0 : £4.50
(B77-14486)

942.6'41 — Suffolk. Gunton, to 1976
Hedges, Alfred Alexander Charles. The Gunton story / by A.A.C. Hedges. — Lowestoft (Gunton Hall, Lowestoft, Suffolk) : Weathercock Press, 1977. — [3],26p : ill, maps ; 23cm.
Sd : £0.45
(B77-19133)

942.6'41 — Suffolk. Somerleyton, to 1976
Brooks, Edward Charles. A thousand years of village history / by Edward C. Brooks. — Somerleyton (Publications Secretary, Home Farm Somerleyton, [Suffolk]) : Trustees for the Parish Churches of Ashby, Herringfleet and Somerleyton, 1977. — [1],33p : ill, ports ; 25cm.
Sd : £0.50
(B77-27599)

942.6'43 — Personal property. Probate inventories. *Suffolk. Newmarket, 1662-1715. Texts*
Newmarket inventories, 1662-1715 / [edited] by Peter May. — Newmarket (10 Fitzroy St., Newmarket, [Suffolk] CB8 0JW) : The editor, 1976. — iv,44p ; 21cm.
ISBN 0-9503024-3-0 Sd : £0.50
(B77-04495)

942.6'45 — Suffolk. Debenham, to 1976
Heywood, Pauline. A short history of Debenham / compiled by Pauline Heywood. — [Debenham] ([Debenham, Stowmarket, Suffolk]) : [Debenham Heritage Committee], [1977]. — [18]p : ill, map, ports ; 30cm.
ISBN 0-9505626-0-2 Sd : Unpriced
(B77-11498)

942.6'48 — Suffolk. Hadleigh, to 1974
Jones, W A B. Hadleigh through the ages : a Viking royal town, medieval wool centre, chartered borough & archbishop's peculiar / by W.A.B. Jones. — Ipswich (6 Great Colman St., Ipswich, Suffolk) : East Anglian Magazine Ltd, 1977. — 136p : ill, coat of arms, 2 maps, ports ; 21cm.
Index.
ISBN 0-900227-25-7 Pbk : £2.95
(B77-22285)

942.6'5 — Cambridgeshire, 1086-1450
Darby, Henry Clifford. Medieval Cambridgeshire / [by] H.C. Darby. — Cambridge : Oleander Press, 1977. — 48p : ill, facsim, maps ; 21cm. — (Cambridge town, gown and county ; 15)
Bibl.: p.46.
ISBN 0-900891-11-4 Sd : £1.30
(B77-29089)

942.6'53 — Cambridgeshire. March, ca 1540 - ca 1650
Bevis, Trevor Allen. A journey back in time / [by] Trevor A. Bevis. — March (150 Burrowmoor Rd, March, Cambs. [PE15 9SS]) : The author.
In 4 vols.
March, beggars can't be choosers. — 1976. — [1]p;p65-102 : ill ; 21cm.
ISBN 0-901680-09-5 Pbk : £0.60
(B77-01939)

March, daily bread. — 1977. — [1]p,p103-138 : ill, map, plan ; 21cm.
Pbk : £0.60
(B77-23025)

942.6'53 — Castles. *Cambridgeshire. Wisbech. Wisbech Castle, to 1976*
Anniss, George. A history of Wisbech Castle / [by] George Anniss. — Ely (Back Hill, Ely, Cambs.) : E.A.R.O., Ely Resource and Technology Centre, 1977. — vii,37p : ill, 2 maps, plans ; 24cm.
'An EARO publication'.
ISBN 0-904463-15-x Sd : £1.00
(B77-24627)

942.6'54 — Cambridgeshire. Godmanchester, to 1976
Green, H J Michael. Godmanchester / [by] H.J.M. Green. — Cambridge : Oleander Press, 1977. — 49p : ill, maps, plans ; 22cm. — (Cambridge town, gown and county ; vol.18)
Bibl.: p.49.
ISBN 0-900891-18-1 Sd : £1.30 : CIP rev.
(B77-25316)

942.6'54 — Cambridgeshire. Huntingdon, to 1976
Dunn, Christopher. The book of Huntingdon : a portrait of the town / by Christopher Dunn ; additional photographs by George Arnot. — Chesham : Barracuda Books, 1977. — 3-148p : ill, coats of arms, facsims, maps, plan, ports ; 31cm.
Ill., map on lining papers. — Bibl.: p.144. — Index.
ISBN 0-86023-032-5 : £8.75
(B77-29840)

942.6'56 — Women. Social life. *Cambridgeshire. Isleham. Personal observations. Collections*
Chamberlain, Mary. Fenwomen : a portrait of women in an English village / [by] Mary Chamberlain. — London : Virago, 1977. — [4], 186p,[16]p of plates : ill ; 20cm.
Originally published: 1975.
ISBN 0-7043-3806-8 Pbk : £1.95
(B77-24628)

942.6'57 — Cambridgeshire. Sawston. Social life, 1886-1942. *Personal observations*
Teversham, Traviss Frederick. Reminiscence : a recording of some aspects of Sawston life between 1886 and 1942 / by an old inhabitant and Sawston's greatest historian Traviss Frederick Teversham. — Sawston ([The Vicarage, Sawston, Cambs.]) : [Ronald Bircham], 1976. — [4],29p ; 21cm.
Sd : £0.25
(B77-29090)

942.6'59 — Cambridgeshire. Cambridge, to 1975
Reeve, Frank Albert. Cambridge / [by] F.A. Reeve. — London : Batsford, 1976. — 184p, [12]p of plates : ill, maps, port ; 23cm.
Bibl.: p.178-179. — Index.
ISBN 0-7134-3225-x : £3.50
(B77-01094)

942.6'59 — Houses. *Cambridgeshire. Cambridge. Newnham Grange, to 1962*
Keynes, Margaret Elizabeth. A house by the river : Newnham Grange to Darwin College / by Margaret Elizabeth Keynes. — Cambridge (The Bursar, Darwin College, Cambridge CB3 9EU) : Darwin College, 1976. — xvii,259p,[4] leaves of plates,[12]p of plates : ill, maps, ports ; 22cm.
Ill. on lining papers. — Index.
ISBN 0-9505198-0-4 : £6.50
(B77-10689)

942.6'7'008 — Essex, to ca 1970. *Readings*
The **best** of 'Essex countryside' : a collection of sixty articles / compiled by E.V. Scott. — Letchworth (19 Baldock Rd, Letchworth, Herts. SG6 3JX) : County Guide Publications, 1976. — 127p : ill, coat of arms, facsim, maps, plans, ports ; 27cm.
A selection of articles taken from 'Essex countryside', 1952 to 1970.
ISBN 0-905858-00-x Pbk : £2.50
(B77-03849)

942.6'715 — Essex. Rayne, to 1976
Workers' Educational Association. *Rayne Branch.* Rayne : from early times to the present day / by the Rayne Branch of the Workers Educational Association. — Rayne (The Rectory, Shalford Rd, Rayne, Essex) : [Rayne WEA], 1977. — [1],80,[6]p of plates(2 fold) : ill, facsims, maps ; 21cm.
Bibl.: p.74.
Sd : Unpriced
(B77-23908)

942.6'715 — Houses. *Essex. Bocking. Old Deanery, Bocking, to 1975*
Hoffmann, Ann. Bocking Deanery : the story of an Essex peculiar / by Ann Hoffmann. — London [etc.] : Phillimore, 1976. — [16],136p, leaf of plate,[16]p of plates : ill, coat of arms, facsims, ports ; 23cm.
Bibl.: p.128-129. — Index.
ISBN 0-85033-226-5 : £3.75
(B77-03304)

942.6'723 — Essex. Rowhedge. Social life, 1890-1914. *Childhood reminiscences*
Leather, Margaret. Saltwater village / by Margaret Leather ; introduction by John Leather. — Lavenham : T. Dalton, 1977. — 140p : ill, map, ports ; 24cm.
Map on lining paper.
ISBN 0-900963-62-x : £4.80
(B77-25317)

942.6'74 — Essex. Epping, 1669-ca 1935. *Illustrations*
Bygone Epping : an album of views / compiled by Epping Forest District Council Museum Service. — Epping (323 High St., Epping, Essex) : The Council, 1976. — [4],45p : chiefly ill, ports ; 21cm. — (Epping Forest District Council Museum Service. Monographs ; no.1)
'Pictures from the collection of Sidney Hills (with additional photographs from the Museum Service)'.
ISBN 0-903930-04-8 Sd : £0.50
(B77-00544)

942.6'74 — Essex. Epping Forest, to 1976
Addison, ***Sir*** **William,** *b.1905.* Portrait of Epping Forest / [by] Sir William Addison. — London : Hale, 1977. — 191p,[24]p of plate : ill, map, ports ; 23cm.
Index.
ISBN 0-7091-6130-1 : £4.25
(B77-31633)

942.6'74 — Essex. Waltham Abbey, to 1974
Camp, John. King Harold's town / by John Camp and Dinah Dean ; for Waltham Abbey Historical Society. — 3rd ed. revised. — [Waltham Abbey] ([c/o Dr K. Bascombe, 25 Monkswood Ave., Walton Abbey, Essex]) : [The Society], 1975. — [1],12p ; 21cm.
Previous ed.: 1974?.
Sd : £0.25
(B77-18491)

942.6'752 — Essex. Chelmsford, to 1966
Torry, Gilbert. Chelmsford through the ages / by Gilbert Torry. — Ipswich (6 Great Colman St., Ipswich, Suffolk) : East Anglian Magazine Ltd, 1977. — 120p : ill, coats of arms, facsim, maps, ports ; 21cm.
Bibl.: p.117. — Index.
ISBN 0-900227-26-5 Pbk : £2.95
(B77-29841)

942.6'76 — Parish churches. *Essex. Great Warley. Church of St Mary the Virgin, Great Warley, to 1975*
The **Church** of St Mary the Virgin, Great Warley, Essex : history and guide. — [Great Warley] ([Tylers Croft, Great Warley, Brentwood, Essex CM13 3JA]) : [H.R. Wilkins], [1976]. — [1],44p : ill ; 21cm.
Contents: A digest of church and village history, 1247-1975 / by H.R. Wilkins - Illustrated guide / by A.W. Wellings.
Sd : £0.80
(B77-21630)

942.7'085'7 — Working class communities. Social life. *Northern England*
Nuttall, Jeff. Common factors, vulgar factions / [by] Jeff Nuttall and Rodick Carmichael. — London [etc.] : Routledge and Kegan Paul, 1977. — [7],152p : ill, facsims, ports ; 25cm.
ISBN 0-7100-8592-3 : £5.75 : CIP rev.
(B77-20866)

942.7'1'02 — Cheshire, 1066-1237
Husain, B M C. Cheshire under the Norman earls, 1066-1237 / by B.M.C. Husain ; cartography by A.G. Hodgkiss. — Chester (Watergate House, Watergate St., Chester) : Cheshire Community Council Publications Trust Ltd, 1973. — xi,142p,[4]p of plates : ill, facsims, geneal table, maps, plans ; 24cm. — (A history of Cheshire ; vol.4)
Map, text on lining papers. — Bibl.: p.133-134. — Index.
Unpriced
(B77-20831)

942.7'17 — Cheshire. Ellesmere Port, 1795-1921
Jarvis, Adrian. Ellesmere Port, canal town, 1795-1921 / by Adrian Jarvis. — Ellesmere Port (The Boat Museum, Ellesmere Port, Cheshire) : North Western Museum of Inland Navigation Ltd ; Bristol : Avon-Anglia Publications and Services, 1977. — 44p : ill, maps, plans ; 21cm.
Bibl.: p.43.
ISBN 0-905466-08-x Sd : Unpriced
(B77-27600)

942.7'3 — Greater Manchester (Metropolitan County), to 1975
Frangopulo, Nicholas Joseph. Tradition in action : the historical evolution of the Greater Manchester County / [by] N.J. Frangopulo. — Wakefield : EP Publishing, 1977. — xiv,306p, plate : ill, coats of arms(1 col), maps, ports ; 21cm.
Map on lining papers. — Bibl.: p.288-297. — Index.
ISBN 0-7158-1203-3 : £5.95
(B77-19925)

942.7'31 — Greater Manchester (Metropolitan County). Hale. Social life, 1890-1935. *Illustrations*
Hale and around : its past in pictures. — Altrincham : Sherratt for Hale Civic Society, 1976. — [90]p : chiefly ill, facsims, maps ; 18x21cm.
ISBN 0-85427-051-5 Pbk : £1.80
(B77-16125)

942.7'31 — Greater Manchester (Metropolitan County). Stretford, to 1975
Massey, S. A history of Stretford / by S. Massey. — Altrincham : Sherratt, 1976. — 238p,[18]p of plates : ill, coats of arms, maps, plan ; 23cm.
Bibl.: p.223. — Index.
ISBN 0-85427-046-9 : £3.60
(B77-16681)

942.7'32 — Greater Manchester (Metropolitan County). Irlam. Social life, 1896-1914. *Childhood reminiscences*
Goodier, James. Early days in Irlam village (1896-1914) / by James Goodier. — [Manchester] ([53 Sunningdale Drive, Irlam, Manchester]) : [Irlam, Cadishead and District Local History Society], [1977]. — [1],88p : ill ; 22cm.
Sd : Unpriced
(B77-25318)

942.7'32 — Greater Manchester (Metropolitan County). Worsley, to 1976. *Secondary school texts*
Pratt, Ian S. "Workedslegh" : a history of Worsley / by Ian S. Pratt. — [Manchester] ([160 Radcliffe New Rd, Whitefield, Manchester]) : The author, 1977. — [1],92p : ill, map, port ; 22cm.
Bibl.: p.90. — Index.
Pbk : £1.50
(B77-19926)

942.7'33 — Buildings of historical importance. *Greater Manchester (Metropolitan County). Manchester, 1825. Illustrations. Facsimiles*
Ralston, John. Views of the ancient buildings in Manchester / drawn from nature by John Ralston and on stone by A. Aglio ... [et al.]. — [1st ed. reprinted] ; with a new introduction [by Hugh Broadbent]. — Oldham (Aveyard, Broadbent and Co., [Spring La.], Lees, Oldham OL4 5AL) : Hugh Broadbent, 1975. — [12]p, [19] leaves of plates : ill, port ; 48cm.
Limited ed. of 500 numbered copies. — In case. — Also available in a de luxe ed. of 55 numbered copies, half-bound in leather. — Facsimile reprint of: 1st ed. Manchester : D. and P. Jackson, 1823-5. — Bibl.: p.[12].
ISBN 0-904848-00-0 Pbk : £18.00
ISBN 0-904848-01-9 De luxe ed.: £35.00
(B77-06393)

942.7'33 — Greater Manchester (Metropolitan County). Manchester. Victoria Park, 1820-1976
Spiers, Maurice. Victoria Park, Manchester : a nineteenth-century suburb in its social and administrative context / by Maurice Spiers. — Manchester : Manchester University Press for the Chetham Society, 1976. — xiv,104p,[3] leaves of plates(1 fold),12p of plates : ill, maps ; 23cm. — (Remains historical and literary connected with the Palatine counties of Lancaster and Chester : 3rd series ; vol.23)
Bibl.: p.xii-xiv. — Index.
ISBN 0-7190-1333-x : £7.60
(B77-08151)

942.7'33'0810222 — Greater Manchester (Metropolitan County). Manchester, ca 1850-. *Illustrations*
Manchester as it was / [compiled] by Chris Makepeace. — Nelson : Hendon Publishing Co.

Vol.5 : The inter war years, 1918-1938. — 1976. — [44]p : chiefly ill, ports ; 21x29cm.
ISBN 0-86067-006-6 Sd : £1.40
(B77-03850)

942.7'33'08230924 — Greater Manchester (Metropolitan County). Manchester. Social life, 1901-1935. *Personal observations*
Roberts, Robert. A ragged schooling : growing up in the classic slum / [by] Robert Roberts. — Manchester : Manchester University Press, 1976. — [8],224p : ill ; 21cm.
ISBN 0-7190-0652-x : £3.75
(B77-09434)

942.7'34 — Country houses. *Greater Manchester (Metropolitan County). Bramhall. Bramall Hall, to 1976*
Dean, E Barbara. Bramall Hall : the story of an Elizabethan manor house / by E. Barbara Dean. — [Stockport] ([Bibliographical Services Unit, Torkington Lodge, Hazel Grove, Stockport, Cheshire SK7 4RQ]) : Recreation and Culture Division, Metropolitan Borough of Stockport, 1977. — x,124p,[8]p of plates : ill, facsims, map, plan, ports ; 22cm.
Bibl.: p.115-116. — Index.
ISBN 0-905164-06-7 : £2.95
(B77-13990)

942.7'37 — Greater Manchester (Metropolitan County). Barrow Bridge, to ca 1900
O'Connor, Denis. Barrow Bridge, Bolton, Lancashire : a model industrial community of the 19th century / [by] Denis O'Connor. — [Bolton] ([4 Empire Rd, Breightmet, Bolton, Lancs.]) : [The author], [1972?]. — [6],38p : ill, map, ports ; 21cm.
Sd : £0.75
(B77-29842)

942.7'37 — Greater Manchester (Metropolitan County). Halliwell, 1640-1648
Billington, William D. Halliwell during the Civil War / [by Wm D. Billington]. — [Bolton] ([80 Crosby Rd, Bolton BL1 4FJ]) : [The author], [1976]. — [1],59p ; 21cm.
Index.
ISBN 0-9505392-0-1 Sd : £0.60
(B77-01940)

942.7'38 — Greater Manchester (Metropolitan County). Bury region. Social life, 1920-1950
Fullard, Florence. Open & see / by Florence Fullard. — Bury (8 St Paul's St., off Bell La., Bury, Lancs.) : The author, [1977]. — [64]p ; 30cm.
Pbk : Unpriced
(B77-27601)

942.7'51 — Merseyside (Metropolitan County). Tranmere, to ca 1965
Allison, J E. Sidelights on Tranmere / by J.E. Allison. — [Birkenhead] ([35 Balls Rd East, Birkenhead, Merseyside]) : Birkenhead History Society, 1976. — 99p : ill, maps, plans ; 21cm.
ISBN 0-9505671-0-8 Pbk : £1.15
(B77-13991)

942.7'53 — Parish churches. *Merseyside (Metropolitan County). Everton. St George's Church, Everton, 1814-1977*
Mould, Richard Francis. The iron church : a short history of Everton, its mother church, and one of its mid-Victorian churchwardens, including notes on how to start tracing a family tree / by R.F. Mould ; foreword by Neville Black. — Liverpool (9 St James' Close, West Derby, Liverpool L12 7JU) : Everton St George Press, 1977. — ix,79p : ill, facsims, form, geneal tables, maps, plans, ports ; 21cm.
Index.
ISBN 0-9505528-0-1 Sd : £1.00
(B77-27602)

942.7'57 — Working class communities. Social life. *Merseyside (Metropolitan County). St Helens, 1880-1900. Childhood reminiscences*
Stamper, Joseph. So long ago - / [by] Joseph Stamper. — Bath : Chivers, 1977. — 224p ; 21cm.
Originally published: London : Hutchinson, 1960.
ISBN 0-85997-272-0 : £5.20(£3.90 to members of the Library Association)
(B77-32995)

942.7'57'0810222 — Merseyside (Metropolitan County). St Helens (District), ca 1890-ca 1920. *Illustrations*
Vintage St Helens and district / [compiled] by Roger Hart. — Nelson : Hendon Publishing Co., 1976. — [44]p : of ill, ports ; 21x29cm.
ISBN 0-86067-007-4 Sd : £1.40
(B77-04496)

942.7'59 — Merseyside (Metropolitan County). Crosby, to 1976. *Illustrations*
Crosby in the past : a photographic record of the history of Crosby and district / [compiled by the Metropolitan Borough of Sefton, Libraries and Arts Services]. — [Litherland] ([Ford Library, Pendle Drive, Ford, Litherland L21 0HY]) : Metropolitan Borough of Sefton Libraries and Arts Services, 1977. — [2],30p : ill, maps ; 21cm.
Sd : £0.30
(B77-23026)

942.7'59 — Merseyside (Metropolitan County). Maghull, to 1976
Hordern, R. A history of Maghull / written by R. Hordern ; photography and presentation by I. Miller. — [Maghull] ([Maghull, Merseyside]) : R. Hordern and I. Miller, 1977. — 33p : ill, facsims, maps, plan ; 30cm.
Sd : £1.45
(B77-34325)

942.7'6 — Lancashire, to 1975
Bagley, John Joseph. A history of Lancashire / [by] J.J. Bagley ; cartography by D.H. Birch. — 6th ed. — London [etc.] : Phillimore, 1976. — 128p,leaf of plate,[24]p of plates : ill(some col), coats of arms, facsims, geneal table, maps, ports ; 26cm. — (The Darwen county history series)
Previous ed.: Henley-on-Thames : Darwen Finlayson, 1970. — Bibl.: p.120-123. — Index.
ISBN 0-85033-246-x : £4.95
(B77-29843)

942.7'6'0830222 — Lancashire. Social life, 1918-1939. *Illustrations*
Lancashire in the 20's and 30's from old photographs / [compiled by] C.E. Makepeace. — London : Batsford, 1977. — [88]p : chiefly ill, ports ; 26cm.
Ill. on lining papers.
ISBN 0-7134-0439-6 : £3.95
(B77-25319)

942.7'612'0840924 — Lancashire. West Lancashire (District). Rural regions. Social life, 1940-1945. *Personal observations*
Knappett, Rachel. A pullet on the midden / [by] Rachel Knappett. — Large print ed. — Bath : Chivers, 1977. — [11],321p ; 22cm.
Originally published: London : Joseph, 1946.
ISBN 0-85997-218-6 : £5.60(£4.20 to members of the Library Association)
(B77-15044)

942.7'615 — Lancashire. Chorley, 1939-1953
Birtill, George. The War and after / by George Birtill. — Chorley (32a Market St., Chorley, Lancs.) : Guardian Press, 1976. — 95p : ill ; 23cm.
ISBN 0-900421-22-3 Sd : £0.80
Also classified at 942.7'67
(B77-08152)

942.7'645 — Lancashire. Newchurch-in-Pendle. Social life, ca 1900-1976. *Personal observations*
Walton, Jean. Pendle Forest folk / [by] Jean Walton. — Nelson : Hendon Publishing Co., 1977. — 56p : ill, map ; 21cm.
ISBN 0-86067-005-8 Sd : £1.00
(B77-19927)

942.7'665 — Parish churches. *Lancashire. Preston. St Peter's Church, Preston, to 1973*
Makin, W. St Peter's Church, Preston / by W. Makin ; with photographs by John Brook. — Preston (Preston Polytechnic, Preston, Lancs.) : Harris Press, 1975. — [4],36p : ill, plan ; 21x22cm.
ISBN 0-905735-01-3 Sd : Unpriced
(B77-00545)

942.7'67 — Lancashire. Leyland, 1939-1953
Birtill, George. The War and after / by George Birtill. — Chorley (32a Market St., Chorley, Lancs.) : Guardian Press, 1976. — 95p : ill ; 23cm.
ISBN 0-900421-22-3 Sd : £0.80
Primary classification 942.7'615
(B77-08152)

942.7'8 — Castles. *Cumbria*
Hugill, Robert. Castles and peles of Cumberland and Westmorland : a guide to the strongholds of the Western English borderland together with an account of their development and their place in border history / [by] Robert Hugill ; illustrated with old prints and original drawings ; complete with glossary. — Newcastle upon Tyne : F. Graham, 1977. — vii,198p,[8]p of plates : ill, plans ; 23cm.
Jacket title: Castles of Cumberland and Westmorland.
ISBN 0-85983-069-1 : £5.00
(B77-31634)

942.7'8'003 — Cumbria, to 1976. *Encyclopaedias*
Parker, John, *b.1926.* Cumbria / [by] John Parker. — Edinburgh [etc.] : J. Bartholomew, 1977. — viii,193p,[4],7p of plates : ill(some col), maps(some col) ; 26cm.
Bibl.: p.178. — Index.
ISBN 0-7028-1004-5 : £4.95
(B77-20832)

942.7'8'008 — Cumbria. Lake District, to 1976. *Collections*
The **Lake** District : an anthology / compiled by Norman Nicholson. — London : Hale, 1977. — 288p ; 24cm.
Index.
ISBN 0-7091-5957-9 : £6.50
(B77-17234)

942.7'83 — Cumbria. Coniston. Ruskin, John, 1889-1899. *Personal observations*
Woolgar, Edward. No place like Coniston / [by] Edward Woolgar. — Bembridge (Bembridge School, Bembridge, Isle of Wight) : Yellowsands Press for the Ruskin Association, 1977. — [13]p,plate : port ; 23cm.
Limited ed. of 180 copies.
Sd : Unpriced
(B77-34326)

942.7'84 — Cumbria. Millom, to ca 1930
Warriner, Frank. Millom people and places / [by] Frank Warriner. — Beckermet (The Beckermet Bookshop, Beckermet, Cumbria) : Michael Moon, 1977. — [4],50p ; 23cm.
Limited ed. of 600 copies. — Facsimile reprint of: 1st ed. s.l. : s.n., 1937.
ISBN 0-904131-15-7 Pbk : £1.50
(B77-26709)

942.7'86 — Cumbria. Mardale, 1916-ca 1920. *Childhood reminiscences*
Hay, David. Mardale, the drowned village : being a Lakeland journey into yesterday / by David and Joan Hay. — [Kendal] ([c/o Geoffrey Berry, 27 Greenside, Kendal, Cumbria, LA9 5DX]) : Friends of the Lake District, 1976. — 80,[1]p,[12]p of plates : ill, maps, ports ; 22cm.
Bibl.: p.76-77.
ISBN 0-9504629-0-x Pbk : £1.50
(B77-00546)

942.7'87 — Society of Friends. Meeting houses. *Cumbria. Mosedale. Mosedale Meeting House, to 1974*
Grubb, Mollie. The Quakers of Mosedale / [by Mollie Grubb]. — London : Friends Home Service Committee, 1976. — [2],24p : ill, plan ; 13x19cm.
ISBN 0-85245-123-7 Sd : £0.30
(B77-05795)

942.7'89 — Cumbria. Carlisle, ca 1890-ca 1950. *Illustrations*
Carlisle : a photographic recollection / compiled by James P. Templeton. — Clapham, N. Yorkshire : Dalesman, 1976. — 80p : chiefly ill, ports ; 18x22cm.
ISBN 0-85206-360-1 Pbk : £1.50
(B77-00547)

942.7'9'01 — Irish settlements. Sources of evidence: Coins. Hoards. *Isle of Man, ca 1020-ca 1080*
Dolley, Michael. Some Irish dimensions to Manx history / [by] Michael Dolley. — [Belfast] : Queen's University of Belfast, [1976]. — 23p : coat of arms, maps ; 21cm. — (Queen's University of Belfast. New lecture series ; no.92)
'An inaugural lecture delivered before The Queen's University of Belfast on 28 January 1976'.
ISBN 0-85389-109-5 Sd : £0.40
(B77-03305)

942.8 — North-east England. Social life, to 1975
Atkinson, Frank, *b.1924.* Life & tradition in Northumberland and Durham / by Frank Atkinson. — London : Dent, 1977. — 168p, [48]p of plates : ill, facsim, maps, plans, ports ; 25cm.
Bibl.: p.153-155. — Index.
ISBN 0-460-04243-2 : £7.75 : CIP rev.
(B77-05146)

942.8'1 — Yorkshire. West Riding, to 1976
Pill, David Halton, *b.1940.* Yorkshire, the West Riding / [by] David H. Pill. — London : Batsford, 1977. — 207p : ill, map ; 23cm.
Index.
ISBN 0-7134-3188-1 : £3.95
(B77-08153)

942.8'1'003 — Yorkshire, to 1975. *Encyclopaedias*
Hewitt, John. Yorkshire alphabet / compiled by John Hewitt. — Clapham, N. Yorkshire : Dalesman, 1976. — 63p : ill, port ; 21cm.
ISBN 0-85206-372-5 Pbk : £0.60
(B77-17235)

942.8'1'081 — Yorkshire. Social life, ca 1850-1975. *Stories, anecdotes*
Boothroyd, Derrick. Nowt so queer as folk : a book of reminiscence about Yorkshire and Yorkshiremen / [by] Derrick Boothroyd. — Bradford (Idle, Bradford, W. Yorkshire BD10 8NL) : Watmoughs Limited, 1976. — [11], 211p ; 23cm.
ISBN 0-903775-03-4 : £3.95
(B77-03851)

942.8'15 — Cathedrals. *West Yorkshire (Metropolitan County). Wakefield. Wakefield Cathedral, to 1976*
Speak, Harold. 'For all the saints' : an outline history and guide [to] the Cathedral Church of All Saints, Wakefield / by Harold Speak and Jean Forrester. — Ossett (199 Kingsway, Ossett, W. Yorkshire WF5 8ED) : The authors, 1976. — 48p : ill, plans, ports ; 21cm.
ISBN 0-902829-05-x Sd : £0.45
(B77-01941)

942.8'15 — West Yorkshire (Metropolitan County). Wakefield. Local history. *Periodicals*
Wakefield Historical Society. Journal of the Wakefield Historical Society. — Wakefield (30 Newland Court, Sandal, Wakefield WF1 5AC) : Wakefield Historical Society.
[Vol.1]- ; [1974]-. — 1974-. — ill, facsims, maps, plans, ports ; 26cm.
Annual. — [6]p,[2] leaves of plate, 98 leaves of plate in vol.4. — Limited ed. of 1000 copies.
Pbk : Unpriced
ISSN 0305-5779
(B77-26710)

942.8′17 — Parish churches. *West Yorkshire (Metropolitan County). Bolton. Church of St James with St Chrysostom, to 1975*
Lister, Mary. The township of Bolton, Bradford and the Church of St James with St Chrysostom, 1877-1977 / [by] Mary Lister. — [Bolton, W. Yorkshire] ([15 Buttermere Rd, Bolton, Bradford, W. Yorkshire BD2 4JA]) : [The author], 1976. — [3],53,[1]p,[16]p of plates : ill, geneal table, map, plan, ports ; 22cm.
Bibl.: p.53.
Sd : £1.00
(B77-16126)

942.8′17 — Rectories. *West Yorkshire (Metropolitan County). Haworth. Haworth Parsonage, to 1976*
Kellett, Jocelyn. Haworth Parsonage : the home of the Brontës / by Jocelyn Kellett. — [Keighley] ([c/o The Brontë Museum, Haworth, Keighley, W. Yorkshire]) : The Brontë Society, 1977. — 80p,[4]leaves of plates : ill(some col), facsims, maps, plans ; 24cm.
ISBN 0-9505829-0-5 : £2.75
(B77-32334)

942.8′17 — West Yorkshire (Metropolitan County). Saltaire, to 1976
Titus of Salts / [edited by Roger W. Suddards ; photographs by Martin White ; illustrations and drawings by Barrie Birch and Trevor Skempton]. — Bradford ([High St.], Idle, Bradford, [W. Yorkshire BD10 8NL]) : Watmoughs Ltd, 1976. — 64p : ill, plan, port ; 22cm.
Bibl.: p.64.
ISBN 0-903775-05-0 Sd : £0.90
Primary classification 338.7′67′7310942817
(B77-05282)

942.8′19 — Parish churches. *West Yorkshire (Metropolitan County). Leeds. Holy Trinity Church, Leeds, to 1977*
Connor, W J. Holy Trinity Church, Leeds 250th Anniversary Exhibition : prepared by the Leeds Archives Department at Holy Trinity Church, Boar Lane, Leeds, 15-31 March 1977 / [notes compiled by W.J. Connor]. — [Leeds] ([Sheepcar, Leeds 7]) : [Leeds City Libraries, Archives Department], [1977]. — [1],10 leaves ; 30cm.
Bibl.: leaf 10.
Sd : Unpriced
(B77-19928)

942.8′19 — Parish churches. *West Yorkshire (Metropolitan County). Leeds. St Mary's Church, Garforth, to 1975*
Pickles, Walter. The history of St Mary's Church, Garforth / by W. Pickles. — [New ed.]. — [Garforth] ([24 Glebelands Close, Garforth, Leeds L525 1HY]) : The author, [1976]. — 24p ; 21cm.
Cover title: St Mary's Church, Garforth. — Previous ed.: published as 'The Parish Church of Garforth' / by G.E. Kirk. Leeds : J. Whitehead, 1934.
ISBN 0-9502870-1-6 Sd : £0.50
(B77-02691)

942.8′21 — South Yorkshire (Metropolitan County). Sheffield region. *Periodicals*
Sheffield and North Derbyshire topic. — [Sheffield] ([30 London Rd, Sheffield S2 4LN]) : [John Ball Publications Ltd].
July 1977-. — [1977]-. — ill, ports ; 29cm.
Cover title. — Monthly. — 106p. in 1st issue.
Pbk : £0.30
ISSN 0140-4989
(B77-24629)

942.8′23 — South Yorkshire (Metropolitan County). Rotherham, ca 1880-ca 1939. *Illustrations*
Rotherham as it was / [compiled by] Robert G. Neville & John Benson. — Nelson : Hendon Publishing Co., 1976. — 44p : chiefly ill, map, ports ; 21x29cm.
ISBN 0-902907-90-5 Sd : £1.40
(B77-03852)

942.8′4 — Buildings of historical importance. *North Yorkshire. Dales, to ca 1900*
Raistrick, Arthur. Buildings in the Yorkshire Dales : who built them, when and how? / by Arthur Raistrick. — Clapham, N. Yorkshire : Dalesman, 1976. — 88p : ill, plans ; 21cm. — (The Yorkshire Dales library ; 4)
Bibl.: p.88.
ISBN 0-85206-367-9 Pbk : £1.00
(B77-00548)

942.8′41 — North Yorkshire. Ingleton, 1860-1930. *Illustrations*
Old Ingleton / [compiled] by John Bentley. — Ingleton via Carnforth (c/o Broadwood Caravans, Ingleton via Carnforth [Lancs.]) : Ingleton Publications, 1976. — 48p : ill, facsim, ports ; 15x21cm.
ISBN 0-9502614-4-0 Sd : £0.50
(B77-11499)

942.8′41 — North Yorkshire. Skipton, ca 1830-ca 1930. *Illustrations*
Skipton : a pictorial recollection / compiled by J.K. Ellwood. — Clapham, N. Yorkshire : Dalesman, 1975. — 80p : of ill, facsims, ports ; 18x21cm.
ISBN 0-85206-310-5 Pbk : £1.50
(B77-05147)

942.8′41 — North Yorkshire. Thornton in Craven. Social life, 1880-1900
Mason, Roger. Granny's village / [by] Roger Mason. — London : P. Davies, 1977. — [10], 179p,[4]p of plates : ill, map, ports ; 23cm.
ISBN 0-432-09210-2 : £4.50
(B77-25320)

942.8′43 — North Yorkshire. York, to 1976
Willis, Ronald. Portrait of York / [by] Ronald Willis ; photography by Thelma Willis. — 2nd ed. — London : Hale, 1977. — 208p,[24]p of plates : ill, map ; 23cm.
Previous ed.: 1972. — Index.
ISBN 0-7091-5912-9 : £3.95
(B77-31635)

942.8′43′005 — North Yorkshire. York. Local history. *Periodicals*
York historian. — York (c/o The Secretary, Castle Museum, Tower St., York) : Yorkshire Architectural and York Archaeological Society.

Vol.1- ; 1976-. — [1976]-. — ill, maps, ports ; 25cm.
[1],56p. in 1st issue.
Sd : £2.00
ISSN 0309-3743
(B77-10068)

942.8′45 — West Yorkshire (Metropolitan County). Bowers Row. Social life, ca 1910-ca 1960. *Personal observations*
Bullock, Jim. Bowers Row : recollections of a mining village / [by] Jim Bullock. — Wakefield : EP Publishing, 1976. — x,230p : ill, map, plans, ports ; 21cm.
ISBN 0-7158-1197-5 : £4.95
(B77-06394)

942.8′46 — North Yorkshire. North York Moors, to 1976
Arnold, Denis Victor. The North York Moors : some glimpses of their history and a guide to further reading / [by] D.V. Arnold ; illustrated by C. Sparrow. — Northallerton (Foxton Mill, Osmotherley, Northallerton, [N.] Yorkshire) : The author, 1977. — [18]p : ill ; 22cm.
Bibl.: p.[10]-[18].
Sd : £0.25
(B77-19134)

942.8′47 — North Yorkshire. Scarborough. Social life, 1826-1914
Taylor, Alan Stuart. Scarborough Fair / by Alan S. Taylor. — Milnthorpe (1 Harmony Hill, Milnthorpe, Cumbria LA7 7QA) : The author, [1976]. — [12],59[i.e.75],[8]p,plate : 1 ill ; 30cm.
Bibl.: p.54C. — Index.
ISBN 0-9505617-0-3 Sp : £2.00
(B77-13444)

942.8′49 — North Yorkshire. Northallerton region. *Newspapers*
Northallerton, Thirsk & Bedale times. — Harrogate (Printing Works, Montpellier St., Harrogate, N. Yorkshire) : R. Ackrill Ltd.
Continues: Thirsk, Bedale & Northallerton times.
4 Feb. 1977-. — 1977-. — ill, ports ; 60cm.
Weekly. — 32p. in 4th Feb. 1977 issue.
Sd : £0.07
(B77-13992)

942.8′53 — Cleveland. Middlesbrough, to 1976
Carson, Robert. A short history of Middlesbrough / by Robert Carson. — [Middlesbrough] ([P.O. Box 99A, Municipal Buildings, Middlesbrough, Cleveland TS1 2QQ]) : Middlesbrough Borough Council, 1977. — 3-56p,[24]p of plates : ill ; 24cm.
ISBN 0-86083-000-4 : £0.65
ISBN 0-86083-001-2 Pbk : £0.65
(B77-23909)

942.8′54 — Cleveland. Marske-by-the-Sea, ca 1800-1975
Memories of Marske-by-the-Sea / researched and compiled by Peter Sotheran ; including memories collected around Marske during 1975 by Errington Junior School ; with photographs from the Local Photograph Library of the publisher. — Redcar (14 Queen St., Redcar, Cleveland [TS10 1AF]) : A.A. Sotheran Ltd, 1976. — [25]p,23 leaves of plates : ill, ports ; 21cm.
Bibl.: p.[25].
ISBN 0-905032-03-9 : £1.80
ISBN 0-905032-02-0 Sd : £0.90
(B77-13445)

942.8′54 — Cleveland. Redcar, to 1900
Cockcroft, Janet. Redcar and Coatham : a history to the end of the 19th century / by Janet Cockcroft ; edited by Peter Sotheran ; line drawings by M. John Halliwell. — Redcar (14 Queen St., Redcar, Cleveland) : A.A. Sotheran Ltd, 1976. — 3-85p,[8]p of plates : ill, coat of arms, facsims, maps ; 23cm.
Bibl.: p.83-85.
ISBN 0-905032-04-7 : £2.70
ISBN 0-905032-05-5 Pbk : £1.50
(B77-08697)

942.8′57′0810222 — Cleveland. Hartlepool, ca 1850-ca 1930. *Illustrations*
Hartlepool as it was / [compiled] by Douglas R.P. Ferriday. — Nelson : Hendon Publishing Co., 1977. — 44p : chiefly ill, facsims, ports ; 21x29cm.
ISBN 0-86067-009-0 Sd : £1.40
(B77-20833)

942.8′6 — Buildings. *Durham (County). Rural regions, ca 1700-1975*
Chapman, Vera. Rural Durham / by Vera Chapman. — Durham : Durham County Council, 1977. — [2],vi,75p : ill, maps, plans ; 30cm. — (Durham County Library. Local history publications ; no.11 ISSN 0306-0330)
Bibl.: p.73-75.
ISBN 0-903268-08-6 Pbk : £1.00
(B77-28309)

942.8′6 — Coal mining communities. Social life. *Durham (County), to 1976*
Mining and social change : Durham County in the twentieth century / edited by Martin Bulmer. — London : Croom Helm, 1978. — 318p : ill, maps ; 23cm.
Bibl.: p.285-296. — Index.
ISBN 0-85664-509-5 : £6.95 : CIP rev.
(B77-24630)

942.8′65 — Cathedrals. *Durham (County). Durham. Durham Cathedral. Teaching kits*
Durham County Joint Curriculum Study Group. Durham Cathedral / compiled by the Durham County Joint Curriculum Study Group. — Newcastle upon Tyne : Graham, [1977]. — Portfolio : ill(incl 2 col), coats of arms, facsims, maps, plans ; 25x39cm.
Ten booklets, 2 folders and 11 sheets (7 fold.). — Bibl.
ISBN 0-85983-054-3 : Unpriced
(B77-19929)

942.8′65 — Durham (County). Durham, to 1975
Historic Durham City. — Newcastle upon Tyne : Graham, 1976. — 24p : ill(some col), facsim, maps ; 28cm.
ISBN 0-85983-009-8 Sd : £1.00
(B77-02692)

942.8′76 — Tyne and Wear (Metropolitan County). Newcastle upon Tyne, to 1975
Hepple, Leslie W. A history of Northumberland and Newcastle upon Tyne / [by] Leslie W. Hepple ; drawings by Carolyn Lockwood. — London [etc.] : Phillimore, 1976. — 144p,leaf of plate,[20]p of plates : ill(incl 3 col), coats of arms, facsims, maps, ports ; 26cm. — (The Darwen county history series)
Bibl.: p.139-141. — Index.
ISBN 0-85033-245-1 : £4.95
Primary classification 942.8′8
(B77-27603)

942.8′79 — Tyne and Wear (Metropolitan County). Wallsend, ca 1900-1945. *Personal observations. Collections*
Where the Wall ends : recollections of a Tyneside town / written and illustrated by Wallsend-Willington Quay-Howdon residents ; [compiled and designed by Judith Rosalind Devons]. — Wallsend (67 Charlotte St., Wallsend, [Tyne and Wear] NE28 7PU) : Wallsend Arts Centre, 1977. — [2],96p,[36]p of plates : ill, coat of arms, ports ; 21cm.
ISBN 0-9505608-0-4 Pbk : £0.75
(B77-16127)

942.8'8 — Castles. *Northumberland, to 1975*
Graham, Frank, *b.1913.* The castle of Northumberland / by Frank Graham. — Newcastle upon Tyne : F. Graham, 1976. — 360p : ill, coats of arms, maps, plans ; 23cm.
ISBN 0-85983-019-5 : £6.00
(B77-23027)

942.8'8 — Northumberland, to 1975
Hepple, Leslie W. A history of Northumberland and Newcastle upon Tyne / [by] Leslie W. Hepple ; drawings by Carolyn Lockwood. — London [etc.] : Phillimore, 1976. — 144p,leaf of plate,[20]p of plates : ill(incl 3 col), coats of arms, facsims, maps, ports ; 26cm. — (The Darwen county history series)
Bibl.: p.139-141. — Index.
ISBN 0-85033-245-1 : £4.95
Also classified at 942.8'76
(B77-27603)

942.9 — HISTORY. WALES
942.9 — Wales, 1485-ca 1970
Williams, David, *b.1900.* A history of modern Wales / [by] David Williams. — 2nd ed. — London : J. Murray, 1977. — 318p,[2]leaves of plates,[14]p of plates : ill, facsims, map, ports ; 22cm.
Previous ed.: 1950. — Bibl.: p.305-306. — Index.
ISBN 0-7195-3357-0 : £5.25
ISBN 0-7195-3358-9 Pbk : £3.00
(B77-15632)

942.9 — Wales, to 1969
Miles, John, *b.1911.* Princes and people of Wales / [by] John Miles ; foreword by the late James Griffiths. — 2nd ed. — Risca : Starling Press, 1977. — 192p,[6]p of plates : geneal table, maps ; 22cm.
Previous ed.: published as 'Princes and people'. Llandysul : Gomerian Press, 1969.
ISBN 0-903434-28-8 : £3.00
(B77-28310)

942.9 — Wales, to 1976
Williams, Gwyn, *b.1904.* The land remembers : a view of Wales / by Gwyn Williams. — London : Faber, 1977. — 3-252p ; 23cm.
Bibl.: p.237-239. — Index.
ISBN 0-571-10323-5 : £5.95
(B77-15633)

942.9'007'2024 — Wales. Historiography. Giraldus Cambrensis. *Critical studies*
Richter, Michael. Giraldus Cambrensis : the growth of the Welsh nation / [by] Michael Richter. — Revised ed. — Aberystwyth : National Library of Wales, 1976. — x,148p ; 25cm.
Previous ed.: 1972. — Bibl.: p.136-143. — Index.
ISBN 0-901833-78-9 : £2.50
(B77-00549)

942.9'02 — Wales, 1066-1200
Walker, David, *b.1923.* The Norman conquerors / [by] David Walker. — Swansea : C. Davies, 1977. — 109p,[4]p of plates : ill, maps ; 22cm. — (A new history of Wales)
Bibl.: p.99-102. — Index.
ISBN 0-7154-0302-8 : £2.95
(B77-18492)

942.9'05 — Wales, 1485-1760. *Secondary school texts*
Fraser, David. The adventurers / by David Fraser. — Cardiff : University of Wales Press, 1976. — xiii,336p : ill, facsims, geneal tables, maps, plans, ports ; 21cm. — (Wales in history ; book 3, 1485-1760)
Bibl.: p.313-316. — Index.
ISBN 0-7083-0610-1 : £3.00
(B77-02693)

942.9'06 — Welsh civilization, 1660-1815
Evans, Evan David. A history of Wales, 1660-1815 / [by] E.D. Evans. — Cardiff : University of Wales Press, 1976. — x,267p : maps ; 23cm. — (Welsh history text books ; vol.2)
Bibl. — Index.
ISBN 0-7083-0624-1 : £3.00
(B77-01095)

942.9'07'20924 — Wales. Maddocks, Ann. Interpersonal relationships with Hopcyn, Wil. *Welsh texts*
Richards, Brinley. Wil Hopcyn a'r ferch o Gefn Ydfa / [gan] Brinley Richards. — Abertawe [i.e. Swansea] ([11 St Helen's Rd, Swansea]) : Tŷ John Penry, 1977. — 94p ; 19cm.
Pbk : £1.25
Primary classification 891.6'6'12
(B77-17804)

942.9'1'08560924 — North Wales. Rural regions. Social life, 1965-1974. *Personal observations*
West, Elizabeth. Hovel in the hills : an account of 'the simple life' / by Elizabeth West. — London : Faber, 1977. — 192p,[4],p of plates : ill ; 23cm.
ISBN 0-571-10994-2 : £3.95
(B77-10069)

942.9'2'00992 — Cathedrals. *Gwynedd. Bangor. Bangor Cathedral. Exhibits: Items associated with princes of Gwynedd, to 1283. Catalogues*
Walker, David, *b.1923.* Tywysogion Gwynedd = The princes of Gwynedd : Eglwys Gadeiriol Bangor, 28 Mai-30 Gorffennaf 1977 = Bangor Cathedral, 28 May-30 July 1977 ... / [text by David Walker and A.D. Carr]. — [Bangor, Gwynedd] ([Cathedral Chaplain's House, Glanrafon, Bangor, Gwynedd LL57 1LH]) : [Bangor Cathedral], [1977]. — 11p,[4]p of plates : ill, coats of arms ; 19x21cm.
'A commemorative booklet of the exhibition in the Cathedral Church of St Deiniol, Bangor ...' - cover. — Parallel Welsh and English texts.
Sd : £0.25
(B77-34327)

942.9'25 — Gwynedd. Nantlle Valley. Social life, ca 1920-1975. *Personal observations. Welsh texts*
Jones, Idwal. Codi mhac o'r Dyffryn / gan Idwal Jones. — Caernarfon ([Arfon-Dwyfor Library H.Q., Maesincla, Caernarfon, Gwynedd LL55 1LH]) : Cyngor Sir Gwynedd Gwasanaeth Llyfrgell, 1977. — 23p,plate : port ; 18cm. — (Gwynedd Library Service. Penygroes Library. Darlithiau blynyddol ; 1976-77)
Bibl.: p.23.
ISBN 0-9501551-3-6 Sd : Unpriced
(B77-19930)

942.9'25'08560924 — Gwynedd. Snowdonia. Rural regions. Social life, 1959-1966. *Personal observations*
Ruck, Ruth Janette. Hill farm story / [by] Ruth Janette Ruck. — London : Faber, 1976. — 239p,[12]p of plates : ill, ports ; 20cm.
Originally published: 1966.
ISBN 0-571-11081-9 Pbk : £2.25
(B77-25321)

942.9'29 — Gwynedd. Barmouth, to 1918
Abermaw = Barmouth / [compilation and text by] Ann Rhydderch. — [Caernarfon] ([County Offices, Caernarfon, Gwynedd]) : Gwynedd Archives Service, 1977. — [42]p : of ill, facsims, ports ; 21cm.
'... a selection of photographs deposited in the archives of the Area Record Office at Dolgellau'. — cover. — Parallel Welsh and English text.
ISBN 0-901337-20-x Sd : £1.25
(B77-27604)

942.9'32 — Clwyd. Mold. Riots, 1869
The **Mold** Riots. — Hawarden (The Old Rectory, Hawarden, Deeside CH5 3NR) : Clwyd Record Office, 1977. — [1],11p : ill ; 22cm.
Bibl.: p.11.
Sd : £0.15
(B77-27605)

942.9'32 — Clwyd. Rhyl, to 1974
Jones, Joseph William. Rhyl and round about / [by] J.W. Jones. — [Rhyl] ([21 Russell Rd, Rhyl, Clwyd LL18 3BS]) : [The author], 1976. — viii,116p : ill, facsims ; 21cm.
Pbk : £1.20
(B77-20834)

942.9'4'003 — South Wales, to 1976. *Encyclopaedias*
Thomas, Ruth, *b.1944.* South Wales / [by] Ruth Thomas. — Edinburgh [etc.] : J. Bartholomew, 1977. — ix,229p,[16]p of plates : ill(incl 3 col), maps(chiefly col), 2 ports(1 col) ; 26cm.
Bibl.: p.210-212. — Index.
ISBN 0-7028-1024-x : £4.95
(B77-23910)

942.9'51 — Country houses. *Powys. Newtown. Gregynog, to 1976*
Gregynog / edited by Glyn Tegai Hughes, Prys Morgan, J. Gareth Thomas. — Cardiff : University of Wales Press, 1977. — [7],146p,[5] leaves of plates : ill(incl 1 col), facsim, maps ; 26cm.
Includes a chapter in Welsh. — Bibl. — Index.
ISBN 0-7083-0634-9 : £5.50
(B77-26041)

942.9'51 — Powys. Kerry, to 1976
Jerman, H Noel. Kerry : the church and the village / by H. Noel Jerman ; line drawings by Kate Mellor. — [Kerry, Montgomeryshire] ([Dolforgan Gardens, Kerry, Newtown, Montgomeryshire SY16 4DN]) : [The author], [1976]. — [1],44,[1]p : ill, map ; 21cm.
ISBN 0-9505399-0-2 Sd : £0.50
(B77-02694)

942.9'6 — Dyfed, to 1976. *Welsh-English parallel texts*
Lewis, William John. Hanes darluniadol Dyfed = An illustrated history of Dyfed / [by W.J. Lewis]. — [Aberystwyth] ([Regional Library, Aberystwyth, Dyfed]) : Dyfed County Council, Library Department.
Cyfrol 1 = Vol.1 / Sir Aberteifi = Cardiganshire. — New ed. — [1976]. — 90,p, [26]p of plates : ill, facsims, maps, ports ; 19x25cm.
Parallel Welsh and English texts. — Previous ed.: published as 'Hanes darluniadol o Geredigion' = 'An illustrated history of Cardiganshire'. Aberystwyth : Cymdeithas Lyfrau Ceredigion, 1970.
ISBN 0-86075-000-0 Pbk : £1.95
(B77-11500)

942.9'61 — Dyfed. Llanfihangel Geneu'r-glyn. Social life, ca 1910. *Childhood reminiscences*
Macdonald, Tom. The white lanes of summer : a memoir / by Tom Macdonald. — Sevenoaks : Coronet, 1977. — 176p ; 18cm.
Originally published: London : Macmillan, 1975.
ISBN 0-340-21321-3 Pbk : £0.65
(B77-20835)

942.9'61 — Dyfed. Llangranog. Social life, ca 1880-ca 1900. *Childhood reminiscences. Welsh texts*
Jones, Fred. Hunangofiant gwas ffarm / [gan] Fred Jones ; golygwyd gan Gerallt Jones. — Abertawe [i.e. Swansea] ([11 St Helen's Rd, Swansea]) : Tŷ John Penry, 1977. — 90p ; 19cm.
£1.65
(B77-20836)

942.9'61 — Dyfed. Teifi River region. Social life. *Personal observations*
Macdonald, Tom. Where silver salmon leap / [by] Tom Macdonald. — Llandysul : Gwasg Gomer, 1976. — 116p : ill, map, ports ; 21cm.
Bibl.: p.116.
ISBN 0-85088-363-6 Pbk : £1.00
(B77-07744)

942.9'62'005 — Dyfed. Preseli (District) & South Pembrokeshire (District). Local history. *Periodicals*
Friends of the Pembrokeshire Museums. The journal / Friends of the Pembrokeshire Museums. — [Haverfordwest] ([c/o Peter F. Claughton, 1 Williamston Terrace, Llangwm, Haverfordwest, Pembrokeshire]) : [The Friends].
[No.1]- ; [1970]-. — [1970]-. — ill, facsims, maps ; 30cm.
Published at irregular intervals. — [1],40p. in 5th issue.
Sd : £0.75
ISSN 0309-4677
(B77-14487)

942.9'63 — Dyfed. Saundersfoot, 1800-1976
Howells, Roscoe. Old Saundersfoot from Monkstone to Marros / [by] Roscoe Howells. — Llandysul : Gomer Press, 1977. — [13], 133p : ill, facsim, map, ports ; 23cm.
Index.
ISBN 0-85088-423-3 : £4.50
(B77-31636)

942.9'65 — Dyfed. Whitland region. Social life, to 1975
Lewis, Ewart Thomas. Local heritage from Efailwen to Whitland : comprising the history of the parishes of Cilmaenllwyd, Henllanfallteg, Llanboidy, Llandysilio, Llanddewi Velfrey, Whitland / by E.T. Lewis ; with contributions by J. Towyn Jones and Haydn Lewis ; foreword by George Bancroft. — [Clunderwen] (Bryncleddau, Mynachlogddu, Clunderwen, Dyfed) : The author.
Vol.1 ; cover design by J. Towyn Jones ; line-illustrations by Stanley Williams ; photographs by Glan Harries [i.e. Harris], Stanley Williams and others. — 1975. — 290p, [60]p of plates : ill, facsims, maps, plan, ports ; 21cm.
ISBN 0-902126-04-0 Pbk : £1.20
(B77-01096)

Vol.2 ; cover design by J. Towyn Jones ; pen and ink illustrations by Wyn Owens and Towyn Jones ; photographs by Glan Harris, Stanley Williams and others. — 1976. — 235p,[48]p of plates,leaf of plate : ill, ports ; 21cm.
Index.
ISBN 0-902126-05-9 Pbk : £1.20
(B77-01097)

942.9'76 — Mid Glamorgan. Caerphilly. *History*
Jones, Glyndwr Goronwy. Cronicl Caerffili : a collection of notes relating to Caerphilly's past / [by] Glyndwr G. Jones. — Beckenham (Flat 1, 87 Copers Cope Rd, Beckenham, Kent) : G.G. Jones.
No.4. — [1977]. — [3],56[i.e.57] leaves,[8] leaves of plates : ill, col maps ; 30cm.
Fold. sheet (ill.,plan) in pocket.
Pbk : £2.00
(B77-21631)

Jones, Glyndwr Goronwy. Cronicl Caerffili : a collection of notes relating to Caerphilly's past / [by] Glyndwr G. Jones. — Beckenham (Flat 1, 87 Copers Cope Rd, Beckenham, Kent) : The author.
No.5. — [1977]. — [3],62 leaves,[13]leaves of plates(1 fold) : ill, maps, plans ; 30cm.
Pbk : £2.00
(B77-32996)

942.9'78 — Mid Glamorgan. Pontypridd region, ca 1900-1940. *Illustrations*
Old Pontypridd and district in photographs / foreword by Gwyn Thomas. — Barry : S. Williams, 1977. — [120]p : chiefly ill, ports ; 25cm.
'The illustrations in this book have been drawn entirely from the magnificent collection in Pontypridd Public Library' - Acknowledgements.
ISBN 0-900807-24-5 : £3.95
(B77-25322)

942.9'82 — Country houses. *West Glamorgan. Swansea. Clyne Castle, to 1976*
Griffiths, Ralph Alan. Clyne Castle, Swansea : a history of the building and its owners / [by] Ralph A. Griffiths. — Swansea (Publications Office, Singleton Park, Swansea SA2 8PP) : University College of Swansea, 1977. — 3-61p : ill(some col), col coat of arms, facsims, maps, ports(2 col) ; 20x21cm.
ISBN 0-86076-001-4 Pbk : £1.50
(B77-23028)

942.9'82 — Parish churches. *West Glamorgan. Pennard. St Mary's Parish Church, Pennard, to 1976*
Davies, Harold Richard John. The parish and church of St Mary, Pennard, Gower / by H.R.J. Davies and L.A. Toft. — 2nd ed. — [Pennard] ([c/o The Vicarage, 88 Pennard Rd, Pennard, Swansea SA3 2AD]) : Pennard Parochial Church Council, 1977. — 27p : ill, map, plan ; 22cm.
Previous ed.: 1971. — Bibl.: p.27.
Sd : £0.20
(B77-20837)

942.9'87 — Castles. *Cardiff. Cardiff Castle, to 1975*
Glenn, Charles. The lords of Cardiff Castle / [by] Charles Glenn. — Swansea : C. Davies, 1976. — 153p : ill, coats of arms, geneal tables, plans, ports ; 29cm.
Bibl.: p.153.
ISBN 0-7154-0301-x : £4.95
(B77-23029)

942.9'87'081 — Cardiff, 1870-1914
Daunton, M J. Coal metropolis, Cardiff 1870-1914 / [by] M.J. Daunton. — [Leicester] : Leicester University Press, 1977. — xi,260p,[16] p of plates : ill, maps, plans ; 24cm.
Index.
ISBN 0-7185-1139-5 : £12.00
(B77-14488)

942.9'89 — South Glamorgan. Barry, 1880-1935. *Illustrations*
Old Barry in photographs / with commentaries by Brian C. Luxton ; foreword by Gwyn Thomas. — Barry : S. Williams, 1977. — [120] p : of ill, ports ; 25cm.
ISBN 0-900807-25-3 : £3.95
(B77-30883)

942.9'9'005 — Gwent. *History. Periodicals*
Gwent local history : the journal of Gwent Local History Council. — [Newport] ([c/o 25 The Orchard, Ponthir, Newport, Gwent NP6 1GG]) : [Gwent Local History Council].
Continues: Presenting Monmouthshire.
No.41- ; [Nov. 1976]-. — [1976]-. — ill, facsims ; 22cm.
Quarterly. — 48p. in issue no.41.
Sd : £0.45
ISSN 0308-0374
(B77-04497)

942.9'9'008 — Gwent, to 1974. *Readings from contemporary sources*
Monmouthshire medley : a bedside book / compiled and edited by Reginald Nichols. — Pontypool ('Mentone', Sunlea Cres., Usk Rd, Pontypool, Gwent NP4 8AD) : Reginald Nichols.
Vol.2. — 1977. — 144p,fold leaf of plate,[14]p of plates : ill, facsims, map, ports ; 23cm.
ISBN 0-9505412-0-6 : £3.00
(B77-15045)

942.9'95 — Gwent. Tredegar. Social life, ca 1900-1975
Smith, William Clifford. Tredegar my town : the collected jottings of W.C. Smith / edited by F.E.A. Yates. — Risca : Starling Press, 1976. — 115p : ill, facsims, maps, ports ; 23cm.
ISBN 0-903434-25-3 : £3.00
(B77-15634)

942.9'97 — Gwent. Pontypool. Local history. *Periodicals*
The **Pontypool** recorder. — Pontypool (c/o The Secretary, Bracelands, Hillcrest Rd, New Inn, Pontypool, Gwent) : Pontypool Local History Society.
No.1- ; Autumn 1976-. — 1976-. — ill, plans ; 25cm.
[1],12p. in 1st issue.
Sd : £0.50 yearly
ISSN 0309-5266
(B77-13993)

942.9'98 — Gwent. Chepstow, to 1976. *Illustrations*
Waters, Mercedes. Changing Chepstow / [by] Mercedes Waters. — Revised [ed.]. — Chepstow (41 Hardwick Ave., Chepstow, Gwent NP6 5DS) : Chepstow Society, 1977. — 47p : chiefly ill, map ; 21cm. — (Chepstow Society. Pamphlet series ; no.6)
Previous ed.: 1970.
ISBN 0-900278-39-0 Sd : £0.60
(B77-24631)

943 — HISTORY. CENTRAL EUROPE, GERMANY
943 — Germany, to 1975
Detwiler, Donald Scaife. Germany : a short history / [by] Donald S. Detwiler. — Carbondale [etc.] : Southern Illinois University Press ; London [etc.] : Feffer and Simons, 1976. — xiii,273p : maps ; 24cm.
Bibl.: p.238-266. — Index.
ISBN 0-8093-0491-0 : Unpriced
ISBN 0-8093-0768-5 Pbk : Unpriced
(B77-00550)

943'.0005 — Central Europe. Political events. *Periodicals*
European bulletin & press : revue trimestrielle. — London (c/o A.J. Jez-Cydzik, 39 Stanwick Mansions, Stanwick Rd, W.14) : Central European Federalists.
Supersedes: European press.
[No.1]- ; 1976-. — [1976]-. — ill, ports ; 30cm.
Thirty two p. in Winter 1977 issue. — Contributions in English and Polish.
Sd : £0.40(£1.00 yearly)
ISSN 0309-474x
(B77-14489)

943'.004'924 — Jews. *Germany. Serials*
Leo Baeck Institute. Yearbook / Leo Baeck Institute. — London [etc.] : Secker and Warburg.
21 : 1976 / [editor Robert Weltsch]. — 1976. — xviii,379p,[4] leaves of plates,[10]p of plates : ill, facsims, ports ; 24cm.
Bibl.: p.297-349. — Index.
ISBN 0-436-24429-2 : £7.50
(B77-14490)

Leo Baeck Institute. Yearbook / Leo Baeck Institute. — London [etc.] : Secker and Warburg for the Institute.
22 : 1977 / [editor Robert Weltsch]. — 1977. — xix,361p,[12]p of plates,[5]leaves of plates : facsims, plans, ports ; 24cm.
Bibl.: p.273-328. — Index.
ISBN 0-436-24430-6 : £7.50
(B77-34328)

943'.031 — Germany. Peasants' War, 1525
The **German** Peasant War of 1525 / edited by Janos Bak. — London : Cass, 1976. — viii, 135p : ill, facsims, map ; 24cm. — (Library of peasant studies ; no.3)
'This group of studies first appeared in a Special Issue ... of "The Journal of Peasants Studies", Volume 3 No.1 ...' - title page verso. — Bibl.
ISBN 0-7146-3063-2 : £8.50
(B77-01942)

943'.044'0924 — Holy Roman Empire. Leopold I, Emperor of Germany. *Biographies*
Spielman, John P. Leopold I of Austria / [by] John P. Spielman. — London : Thames and Hudson, 1977. — 240p,[16]p of plates : ill, facsims, geneal tables, maps, music, ports ; 23cm. — (Men in office)
Bibl.: p.205-208. — Index.
ISBN 0-500-87005-5 : £6.50
(B77-12234)

943'.06 — Prussia. Political events, 1795-1815
Meinecke, Friedrich. The age of German liberation, 1795-1815 / [by] Friedrich Meinecke ; edited with an introduction by Peter Paret ; [translated from the German by Peter Paret and Helmuth Fischer]. — Berkeley [etc.] ; London : University of California Press, 1977. — xxiii,131p ; 23cm.
Translation of: 'Das Zeitalter der deutschen Erhebung (1797-1815)'. 6.Aufl. Göttingen : Vandenhoeck und Ruprecht, 1957. — Index.
ISBN 0-520-02792-2 : £8.75
(B77-23911)

943'.07 — Germany. Hohenzollern dynasty, 1848-1918
Sulzberger, Cyrus Leo. The fall of eagles / [by] C.L. Sulzberger. — London : Hodder and Stoughton, 1977. — 408p : ill(some col), col coats of arms, maps, ports(some col) ; 25cm.
Index.
ISBN 0-340-21641-7 : £9.95
Primary classification 940.2'8
(B77-32312)

943.08'092'2 — Germany. Political events. Role of Bismarck, Otto, fürst von & Bleichröder, Gerson von, 1859-1893
Stern, Fritz. Gold and iron : Bismarck, Bleichröder, and the building of the German Empire / [by] Fritz Stern. — London : Allen and Unwin, 1977. — [1],xxiv,620,[1]p,[16]p of plates : ill, facsims, ports ; 25cm.
Originally published: United States : s.n., 1977. — Bibl.: p.601-602. — Index.
ISBN 0-04-943021-1 : £11.50
(B77-19135)

943.08'4'0924 — Germany. Wilhelm II, Emperor of Germany. *Biographies*
Whittle, Tyler. The last Kaiser : a biography of William II, German Emperor and King of Prussia / [by] Tyler Whittle. — London : Heinemann, 1977. — [12],368p,[16]p of plates : ill, geneal table, map, ports ; 25cm.
Index.
ISBN 0-434-86491-9 : £6.50
(B77-23030)

943.08'4'0924 — Prussia. Viktoria Luise, Herzogin zu Braunschweig und Lüneberg. *Autobiographies*
Viktoria Luise, *Herzogin zu Braunschweig und Lüneburg.* The Kaiser's daughter : memoirs of HRH Viktoria Luise, Duchess of Brunswick and Lüneburg, Princess of Prussia / translated [from the German] and edited by Robert Vacha. — London : W.H. Allen, 1977. — xii, 276p,[24]p of plates : ill, geneal tables, ports ; 25cm.
Translation of: 'Ein Leben als Tochter des Kaisers', 'Im Glanz der Krone', and 'Im Strom der Zeit', Hanover : Göttingen, 1965-1974. — Index.
ISBN 0-491-01808-8 : £7.50
(B77-16682)

943.085 — Germany. Political events, 1918-1933
Larsen, Egon. Weimar eyewitness / [by] Egon Larsen. — London : Bachman and Turner, 1976. — 192p : ill, ports ; 23cm.
Bibl.: p.185-186. — Index.
ISBN 0-85974-051-x : £4.25
(B77-06995)

943.085 — Germany. Political events, 1923-1924. *Communist viewpoints*
Reissner, Larissa. Hamburg at the barricades, and other writings on Weimar Germany / [by] Larissa Reissner ; translated from the Russian and edited by Richard Chappell. — London : Pluto Press, 1977. — 209p : maps ; 22cm.
Bibl.: p.9-13. — Contents: Berlin, October 1923 - Hamburg at the barricades - In Hindenburg's country.
ISBN 0-904383-36-9 : £4.80
(B77-27606)

943.086 — Germany. Social life, 1933-1945
Grunberger, Richard. A social history of the Third Reich / [by] Richard Grunberger. — Harmondsworth [etc.] : Penguin, 1977. — 663p, [16]p of plates : ill, port ; 19cm. — (Pelican books)
Originally published: London : Weidenfeld and Nicolson, 1971. — Bibl.: p.593-594. — Index.
Pbk : £1.75
ISBN 0-14-021755-x
(B77-19931)

943.086'092'4 — Germany. Goebbels, Joseph. *Biographies*
Reimann, Viktor. The man who created Hitler : Joseph Goebbels / by Viktor Reimann ; translated from the German by Stephen Wendt. — London : Kimber, 1977. — [7],352p,[16]p of plates : ill, ports ; 24cm.
This translation originally published: Garden City, N.Y. : Doubleday, 1976. — Translation of: 'Dr Joseph Goebbels'. Wien : Molden, 1971. — Index.
ISBN 0-7183-0155-2 : £6.50
(B77-27607)

943.086'092'4 — Germany. Goering, Hermann. *Biographies*
Mosley, Leonard. The Reich Marshal : a biography of Hermann Goering / [by] Leonard Mosley. — London [etc.] : Pan Books, 1977. — 476p,[8]p of plates : ill, ports ; 18cm.
Originally published: London : Weidenfeld and Nicolson, 1974. — Index.
ISBN 0-330-24351-9 Pbk : £1.25
(B77-06996)

943.086'092'4 — Germany. Hess, Rudolf. *Biographies*
Bird, Eugene K. The loneliest man in the world : the inside story of the 30-year imprisonment of Rudolf Hess / [by] Eugene K. Bird. — London : Sphere, 1976. — 285p,[8]p of plates : ill, ports ; 18cm.
Originally published: New York : Viking ; London : Secker and Warburg, 1974.
ISBN 0-7221-1680-2 Pbk : £0.95
(B77-09435)

943.086'092'4 — Germany. Hitler, Adolf. *Biographies*
Fest, Joachim C. Hitler / [by] Joachim C. Fest ; translated [from the German] by Richard and Clara Winston. — Harmondsworth [etc.] : Penguin, 1977. — 1228p ; 18cm. — (Pelican biographies)
This translation originally published: New York : Harcourt Brace Jovanovich ; London : Weidenfeld and Nicolson, 1974. — Translation of: 'Hitler : e Biographie'. Berlin : Propyläen-Verlag, 1973. — Bibl.: p.1197-1212. — Index.
ISBN 0-14-021983-8 Pbk : £2.95
(B77-17236)

Snyder, Louis Leo. Hitler and Nazism / by Louis L. Snyder. — Toronto [etc.] ; London : Bantam, 1976. — [8],151p ; 18cm.
Originally published: New York : F. Watts, 1961 ; New York ; London : Bantam, 1967. — Index.
ISBN 0-552-68047-8 Pbk : £0.60
(B77-04498)

Toland, John. Adolf Hitler / by John Toland. — Garden City : Doubleday ; [Leicester] ([Euston St., Freemen's Common, Aylestone Rd, Leicester LE2 7SS]) : Distributed by WHS Distributors, 1976. — ii-xx,1035p,[64]p of plates : ill, facsims, geneal table, maps, ports ; 24cm.
Col. maps on lining papers. — Bibl.: p.909-923. — Index.
ISBN 0-385-03724-4 : £7.50
(B77-16128)

943.086'092'4 — Germany. Hitler, Adolf. *Correspondence*
Hitler, Adolf. Hitler's letters and notes / compiled and with commentary by Werner Maser ; translated from the German by Arnold Pomerans. — Toronto [etc.] ; London : Bantam, 1976. — xi,393p : ill, facsims, plan, ports ; 18cm.
This translation originally published: London : Heinemann, 1974. — Translation of: 'Hitlers Briefe und Notizen'. Düsseldorf : Econ, 1973. — Bibl.: p.386-7. — Index. — Includes facsimile reprints.
ISBN 0-552-66493-6 Pbk : £0.95
(B77-28311)

943.086'092'4 — Germany. Hitler, Adolf, 1939-1945
Irving, David. Hitler's war / [by] David Irving. — London [etc.] : Hodder and Stoughton, 1977. — xxxiii,926p : facsim, maps(on lining papers) ; 24cm.
Also published: New York : Viking Press, 1977. — Bibl.: p.824-828. — Index.
ISBN 0-340-16747-5 : £9.95
(B77-23912)

943.086'092'4 — Germany. Hitler, Adolf. Psychology
Binion, Rudolph. Hitler among the Germans / [by] Rudolph Binion. — New York ; Oxford [etc.] : Elsevier, 1976. — xv,207p : facsim ; 24cm.
Text on lining papers. — Bibl.: p.184-199. — Index.
ISBN 0-444-99033-x : £11.12
(B77-16683)

943.086'092'4 — Germany. Social life, 1943-1946. *Childhood reminiscences. Juvenile literature*
Francke, Gunhild. Last train west / [by] Gunhild Francke ; illustrated by Richard Kennedy. — Sydney ; London [etc.] : Hodder and Stoughton, 1977. — 102p : ill ; 22cm.
Ill. on lining papers. — Includes a poem in German with English translation.
ISBN 0-340-22160-7 : £3.60
(B77-29844)

943.086'092'4 — Germany. Social life, ca 1930-1939. *Childhood reminiscences*
Hannam, Charles. A boy in your situation / [by] Charles Hannam. — London : Deutsch, 1977. — 216p : geneal table ; 21cm.
ISBN 0-233-96862-8 : £3.25
Also classified at 941.084'092'4
(B77-17237)

943.086'092'4 — Germany. Zassenhaus, Hiltgunt, 1933-1945. *Autobiographies*
Zassenhaus, Hiltgunt. Walls / [by] Hiltgunt Zassenhaus. — Sevenoaks : Coronet, 1977. — 222p ; 18cm.
Originally published: Boston, Mass. : Beacon Press, 1974 ; London : Blond and Briggs, 1975.
ISBN 0-340-21298-5 Pbk : £0.80
(B77-10070)

943.087 — West Germany. Social life
Morey, George. West Germany / [by] George Morey. — London : Macdonald Educational, 1977. — 2-63p : ill(chiefly col), col chart, col maps, ports(some col) ; 29cm. — (Macdonald countries)
Originally published: London : Macdonald and Jane's, 1974. — Index.
£2.25
ISBN 0-356-04851-9
ISBN 0-356-05582-5 Pbk : £1.25
(B77-13994)

943.087 — West Germany. Social life. *Teaching kits. For German language teaching in secondary schools*
Boxford, Alan. Die Bundesrepublik Deutschland / written by Alan Boxford. — [London] : [Longman]. — (Longman German packs)
Pack 1. — [1976]. — 1v. : ill(some col), facsims, maps(some col), ports ; 30cm.
Teacher's book (19p.), 5 copies of each of 4 booklets, 13 sheets (12 fold.) (13 sides) in plastic bag. — Bibl.: p.19 (Teacher's book).
ISBN 0-582-21823-3 : £10.80
(B77-10071)

Pack 2 : Work sheets : 10 spirit masters. — [1976]. — [11]leaves : 2 ill, 2 maps ; 28cm.
Leaf [1] printed on both sides.
ISBN 0-582-21824-1 Sd : £1.85
(B77-10072)

Ferris, Tom. Das Leben in der BRD / written by Tom Ferris. — [London] : [Longman]. — (Longman German packs)
Pack 1. — [1976]. — 1v. : ill(some col), facsims, maps(some col), plan, port ; 30cm.
Teacher's book (12p.), 4 copies of each of 8 folders ([4]p), sheet ([1] side), sound disc (2s. 7in. 33 1/3 rpm) in plastic bag. — Bibl.: p.12 (Teacher's book).
ISBN 0-582-21821-7 : £8.50
(B77-10690)

Ferris, Tom. Das Leben in der BRD / written by Tom Ferris. — [London] : [Longman]. — (Longman German packs)
Pack 2 : Work sheets : 8 spirit masters. — [1976]. — [9]leaves : ill ; 28cm.
Leaf [1] printed on both sides.
ISBN 0-582-21822-5 Sd : £1.50
(B77-10073)

943'.32 — West Germany. Nuremberg, ca 1500-1600
Strauss, Gerald. Nuremberg in the sixteenth century : city politics and life between Middle Ages and modern times / [by] Gerald Strauss. — Revised ed. — Bloomington ; London : Indiana University Press, 1976. — ix,305p : ill, maps, port ; 22cm.
Previous ed.: New York ; London : Wiley, 1966. — Index.
ISBN 0-253-34149-3 : £9.35
ISBN 0-253-34150-7 Pbk : £3.75
(B77-21632)

943'.4'086 — Germany. Rhineland. Occupation by German military forces, 1936
Emmerson, James Thomas. The Rhineland crisis, 7 March 1936 : a study in multilateral diplomacy / [by] James Thomas Emmerson. — London : Temple Smith [for] the London School of Economics and Political Science, 1977. — 383p : 2 maps ; 23cm.
Bibl.: p.357-377. — Index.
ISBN 0-85117-096-x : £10.00
(B77-23913)

943'.512'080924 — West Germany. Schleswig-Holstein. Sternberg, Cecilia, Countess Sternberg. *Autobiographies*
Sternberg, Cecilia, *Countess Sternberg.* The journey / [by] Cecilia Sternberg. — London : Collins, 1977. — 576p,[8]p of plates : ill, ports ; 24cm.
Index.
ISBN 0-00-216380-2 : £8.00
(B77-25323)

943.6 — HISTORY. AUSTRIA
943.6'00973'2 — Towns. Social life. *Austria. Secondary school texts*
Sawers, Robin. Life in an Austrian town / written and illustrated by Robin Sawers. — London : Harrap, 1976. — 64p : ill, forms, map, ports ; 22cm.
ISBN 0-245-52802-4 Pbk : £1.55
(B77-03853)

943.6'04 — Austria. Habsburg dynasty, 1848-1918
Sulzberger, Cyrus Leo. The fall of eagles / [by] C.L. Sulzberger. — London : Hodder and Stoughton, 1977. — 408p : ill(some col), col coats of arms, maps, ports(some col) ; 25cm.
Index.
ISBN 0-340-21641-7 : £9.95
Primary classification 940.2'8
(B77-32312)

943.6'05 — Austria. *Juvenile literature*
Rothkopf, Carol Zeman. Austria / [by] Carol Zeman Rothkopf. — New York ; London : F. Watts, 1976. — [4],68p : ill, maps ; 23cm. — (A first book)
Index.
ISBN 0-85166-607-8 : £1.85
(B77-00551)

943.6'05'0924 — Austria. Hohenlohe, Stephanie, Fürstin. *Biographies*
Hohenlohe, Franz, *Fürst.* Steph, the fabulous princess / [by] Prince Franz Hohenlohe. — London : New English Library, 1976. — 205p, [16]p of plates : facsims, ports ; 22cm.
ISBN 0-450-02594-2 : £4.95
(B77-08154)

943.6'13'050222 — Austria. Vienna. *Illustrations*
The **coffee** houses & palaces of Vienna / commentary Sandy Lesberg. — New York ; London : Peebles Press International ; Leicester (Euston St., Freemen's Common, [Aylestone Rd], Leicester LE2 7SS) : [Distributed by] WHS Distributors, 1976. — 127p : chiefly ill(some col) ; 31cm.
Ill. on lining paper.
ISBN 0-672-52227-6 : £3.25
(B77-12235)

943.7 — HISTORY. CZECHOSLOVAKIA
943.7 — Czechoslovakia, 1949-1976
Wallace, William V. Czechoslovakia / by William V. Wallace. — London : E. Benn, 1977. — xv,374p,[16]p of plates : ill, maps, ports ; 23cm. — (Nations of the modern world)

Bibl.: p.357-364. — Index.
ISBN 0-510-39525-2 : £9.95
(B77-12236)

943.7'02 — Ancient Roman settlements: Gerulata. Cemeteries. Antiquities. Excavation of remains. *Czechoslovakia. Rusovce, 1965-1969. Reports, surveys*
Kraskovská, L'udmila. The Roman cemetery at Gerulata Rusovce, Czechoslovakia / [by] L'udmila Kraskovská ; revised by the author ; translated from the Slovak by Hana Schuck. — Oxford : British Archaeological Reports, 1976. — [8],108p,fold leaf of plate,vi p of plates : ill, map, plan ; 30cm. — (British archaeological reports : supplementary series ; 10)
Translation and revision of: 'Gerulata-Rusovce'. Martin : vyd. Osreta pre Slov. nar. múzeum v. Bratislave, 1974.
ISBN 0-904531-42-2 Pbk : £2.50
(B77-00552)

943.7'02'0924 — Czechoslovakia. Bohemia. Elizabeth, Queen of Bohemia. *Biographies*
Gorst-Williams, Jessica. Elizabeth the winter queen / [by] Jessica Gorst-Williams. — London : Abelard, 1977. — [9],198p,[4]p of plates : ill, ports ; 23cm.
Bibl.: p.191-196. — Index.
ISBN 0-200-72472-x : £4.50
(B77-17238)

943.8 — HISTORY. POLAND
943.8 — Poland. Political events, ca 1900-1976
Dziewanowski, Marian Kamil. Poland in the twentieth century / [by] M.K. Dziewanowski. — New York ; Guildford : Columbia University Press, 1977. — xv,309p,[16]p of plates : ill, maps, ports ; 24cm.
Bibl.: p.295-301. — Index.
ISBN 0-231-03577-2 : £11.00
(B77-27608)

943.8'005 — Poland, ca 1900-. *Serials. Polish texts*
Niepodległość : czasopismo poświęcone najnowszym dziejom polski. — Londyn [i.e. London] [etc.] (238 King St., W.6) : Instytut Józefa Pilsudskiego.
Tom dziesiąty. — 1976. — 269p ; 22cm.
ISBN 0-901215-67-8 Pbk : £6.00
(B77-07745)

943.8'04'0924 — Poland. Political events, 1914-1923. *Personal observations. Polish texts*
Zaniewicki, Zbigniew. Moje dwudziestolecie / Zbigniew Zaniewicki. — Londyn [i.e. London] : Polska Fundacja Kulturalna, 1976. — 192p : 1 ill, ports ; 19cm.
ISBN 0-85065-112-3 Pbk : £1.20
(B77-15635)

943.8'05 — Polish culture. *Polish texts*
Drobnik, Jerzy. Myśli przydrozne / Jerzy Drobnik. — Londyn [i.e. London] : Oficyna Poetów i Malarzy, 1977. — 337p : ill, facsim, port ; 21cm.
One ill., 1 port. tipped in. — Index.
ISBN 0-902571-92-3 Pbk : Unpriced
(B77-13995)

943.8'05'0924 — Poland. Political events, 1943-1956. *Personal observations. Polish texts*
Jurewicz, Leslaw. Niepotrzebny / Leslaw Jurewicz. — Londyn [i.e. London] : Polska Fundacja Kulturalna, 1977. — 223p : facsims ; 19cm.
ISBN 0-85065-113-1 Pbk : £1.20
(B77-15636)

943.8'05'0924 — Poland. Social life, ca 1930-1948. *Personal observations*
Uczen, W S. About my life / [by] W.S. Uczen ; [illustrated by Christine Wilkes]. — Bradford (Bradford College, Bolton Royd, Manningham La., Bradford 8) : Bradford Literacy Group, 1976. — [1],22,[1]p : ill ; 22cm.
ISBN 0-9505669-0-x Sd : £0.30
(B77-24632)

943.9 — HISTORY. HUNGARY
943.9'05 — Hungary. Political events, 1956
Lomax, Bill. Hungary 1956 / [by] Bill Lomax. — London : Allison and Busby, 1976. — 222p ; 23cm. — (Motive)
Bibl.: p.212-214. — Index.
ISBN 0-85031-188-8 : £5.25
ISBN 0-85031-189-6 Pbk : £2.95
(B77-02695)

944 — HISTORY. FRANCE
944'.007'2024 — France. Historiography. Michelet, Jules
Orr, Linda. Jules Michelet : nature, history and language / [by] Linda Orr. — Ithaca ; London : Cornell University Press, 1976. — xvi,215p ; 23cm.
Bibl.: p.207-210. — Index.
ISBN 0-8014-0976-4 : £10.00
(B77-13996)

944'.01 — France, ca 486-591. *Early works*
Gregory of Tours, *Saint.* [Historia Francorum. English]. The history of the Franks / [by] Gregory of Tours ; translated [from the Latin] with an introduction by Lewis Thorpe. — Harmondsworth [etc.] : Penguin, 1977. — 710p : geneal tables, map ; 19cm. — (Penguin classics)
This translation originally published: 1974. — Bibl.: p.56-58. — Index.
Pbk : £1.40
ISBN 0-14-044295-2
(B77-23031)

944'.025 — Hundred Years' War
Lloyd, Alan. The Hundred Years War / [by] Alan Lloyd. — London : Hart-Davis MacGibbon, 1977. — 176p : ill, map, plans, ports ; 26cm. — ([British at war])
Bibl.: p.171-172. — Index.
ISBN 0-246-10869-x : £5.95
(B77-23914)

944'.03 — France, 1560-1715
Briggs, Robin. Early modern France, 1560-1715 / [by] Robin Briggs. — Oxford [etc.] : Oxford University Press, 1977. — xi, 242p : 2 maps ; 21cm.
Bibl.: p.222-228. — Index.
ISBN 0-19-215815-5 : £4.25
ISBN 0-19-289040-9 Pbk : £2.25
(B77-25324)

944'.032 — France, 1620-1675
France in crisis, 1620-1675 / selected, translated and introduced by P.J. Coveney. — London [etc.] : Macmillan, 1977. — ix,273p ; 23cm.
Bibl.: p.255-261. — Index.
ISBN 0-333-10071-9 : £10.00
ISBN 0-333-21218-5 Pbk : £4.95
(B77-21633)

944'.032'0924 — France. Mazarin, Jules, to 1642. *Biographies*
Dethan, Georges. The young Mazarin / [by] Georges Dethan ; [translated from the French by Stanley Baron]. — London : Thames and Hudson, 1977. — 199p,[16]p of plates : ill, facsims, geneal table, map, ports ; 23cm. — (Men in office)
Translation and revision of: 'Mazarin et ses amis'. Paris : Berger-Levrault, 1968. — Bibl.: p.174-5. — Index.
ISBN 0-500-87004-7 : £7.50
(B77-27609)

944'.033 — France, 1643-ca 1685. *Secondary school texts*
Ritchie, William Kidd. The France of Louis XIV / [by] W.K. Ritchie. — London : Longman, 1977. — 96p : ill, geneal table, maps, plan, ports ; 20cm. — (Then and there series)
Text on inside back cover.
ISBN 0-582-20540-9 Pbk : £0.55
(B77-27610)

944.04 — France. Political events, 1787-1799
Soboul, Albert. The French Revolution, 1787-1799 : from the storming of the Bastille to Napoleon / [by] Albert Soboul ; translated from the French by Alan Forrest and Colin Jones. — London : NLB, 1974. — [8],638p ; 22cm.
Also published: in 2 vols. 1974. — Translation of: 'Précis d'histoire de la Révolution Française'. Paris : Éditions Sociales, 1962. — Index.
ISBN 0-902308-42-4 : £8.50
(B77-20838)

944.04 — France. Political events, 1789-1794. *Secondary school texts. Teaching kits*
Bearman, Graham William Leslie. The French Revolution / [by] Graham Bearman. — London : Heinemann Educational, 1977. — 1v. : ill(some col), maps, ports ; 25cm. — (History broadsheets)
Seventeen folders ([68]p.), 8 sheets ([16]sides) in plastic envelope.
ISBN 0-435-31749-0 : £1.80
(B77-26711)

944.04'08 — France. Political events, ca 1750-1815. Social aspects. *Essays*
French society and the Revolution / edited by Douglas Johnson. — Cambridge [etc.] : Cambridge University Press, 1976. — vi,321p ; 23cm. — ('Past and present' publications)
Articles originally published in the journal 'Past and present'. — Index.
ISBN 0-521-21275-8 : £5.00
(B77-02696)

944.04'092'4 — France. Politics. La Fayette, Marie Joseph du Motier, marquis de. *Biographies*
Buckman, Peter. Lafayette : a biography / by Peter Buckman. — New York ; London : Paddington Press, 1977. — 288p : port ; 25cm.
Bibl.: p.280-284. — Index.
ISBN 0-448-22060-1 : £5.95
(B77-15046)

944.04'092'4 — France. Talleyrand-Périgord, Charles Maurice de, prince de Bénévent. *Biographies*
Schumann, Maurice. Talleyrand, prophet of the Entente Cordiale / by Maurice Schumann. — Oxford : Clarendon Press, 1977. — 22p ; 22cm. — (The Zaharoff lecture ; 1976-7)
ISBN 0-19-952247-2 Sd : £0.90
(B77-29845)

944.04'1 — France. Peasants' revolt, 1789
Lefebvre, Georges, *b.1874.* The Great Fear of 1789 : rural panic in revolutionary France / [by] Georges Lefebvre ; translated from the French by Joan White ; introduction by George Rudé. — London : NLB, 1973[i.e. 1976]. — xvi,234p : 4 maps ; 21cm.
This translation originally published: 1973. — Translation of: 'La Grand Peur de 1789'. Paris : A. Colin, 1932. — Bibl.: p.217-224. — Index.
ISBN 0-902308-37-8 Pbk : £2.75
(B77-04499)

944.05 — France. Political events, 1814-1815. *Early works*
Macaulay, Thomas Babington, *Baron Macaulay.* Napoleon and the restoration of the Bourbons : the completed portion of Macaulay's projected 'History of France, from the restoration of the Bourbons to the accession of Louis Philippe' / edited by Joseph Hamburger. — London : Longman, 1977. — ix,117p : port ; 26cm.
ISBN 0-582-50827-4 : £5.50
(B77-34329)

944.05'092'2 — France. Political events. Role of Napoleon, Emperor of the French & Talleyrand-Périgord, Charles Maurice de, prince de Bénévent, 1814
Norman, Barbara, *b.1927.* Napoleon and Talleyrand : the last two weeks / [by] Barbara Norman. — London : Severn House : [Distributed by Hutchinson], 1977. — 299p : maps ; 23cm.
Originally published: New York : Stein and Day, 1976. — Bibl.: p.287-291. — Index.
ISBN 0-7278-0313-1 : £6.00
(B77-26712)

944.05'092'4 — France. Napoleon I, Emperor of the French. *Biographies*
Jones, Richard Benjamin. Napoleon : man and myth / [by] R. Ben Jones. — London [etc.] : Hodder and Stoughton, 1977. — 221p : maps, plans ; 22cm.
Bibl. — Index.
ISBN 0-340-17554-0 : £4.85
ISBN 0-340-17555-9 Pbk : £2.45
(B77-12795)

944.05'092'4 — France. Napoleon I, Emperor of the French. *Biographies. Secondary school texts*
Pratt, Stephen. Napoleon / [by] Stephen Pratt. — Hove : Wayland, 1976. — 96p : ill, facsims, maps, ports ; 22cm. — (Wayland kings and queens)
Bibl.: p.94. — Index.
ISBN 0-85340-389-9 : £2.95
(B77-06997)

944.05'092'4 — France. Napoleon I, Emperor of the French. *Secondary school texts*
MacIntyre, Duncan. Napoleon : the legend and the reality / [by] Duncan MacIntyre. — Glasgow [etc.] : Blackie, 1976. — [6],58p,[4]p of plates : ill, geneal tables, maps, plans, ports ; 22cm. — (Contrasts in history)
Text on lining papers. — Bibl.: p.58.
ISBN 0-216-90193-6 : £2.00
ISBN 0-216-90179-0 Educational ed. : £1.25
(B77-01098)

944.07 — French civilization, 1848-1945
Zeldin, Theodore. France, 1848-1945 / by Theodore Zeldin. — Oxford : Clarendon Press. — (Oxford history of modern Europe)
Vol.2 : Intellect, taste and anxiety. — 1977. — vii,1202p : 1 ill, maps ; 23cm.
Bibl.: p.1174-1180. — Index.
ISBN 0-19-822125-8 : £15.00 : CIP rev.
(B77-08698)

944.081 — France. Political events, 1870-1914
Anderson, Robert David. France 1870-1914 : politics and society / [by] R.D. Anderson. — London [etc.] : Routledge and Kegan Paul, 1977. — viii,215p : maps ; 23cm.
Bibl.: p.187-208. — Index.
ISBN 0-7100-8575-3 : £5.95
(B77-19932)

944.081'5 — France. Political events, 1936-1939
Adamthwaite, Anthony. France and the coming of the Second World War, 1936-1939 / [by] Anthony Adamthwaite. — London : Cass, 1977. — xxii,434p,4p of plates : ill, maps, ports ; 24cm.
Bibl.: p.414-426. — Index.
ISBN 0-7146-3035-7 : Unpriced
(B77-26713)

944.082 — France. Political events, 1940-1975. *Secondary school texts*
Tames, Richard. Modern France : state and society / [by] Richard Tames. — London : Harrap, 1977. — 95p : ill, ports ; 18x22cm.
Bibl.: p.94-95.
ISBN 0-245-52923-3 Pbk : £1.95
(B77-14491)

944.082 — French civilization, 1945-1977
Ardagh, John. The new France / [by] John Ardagh. — 3rd ed. — Harmondsworth [etc.] : Penguin, 1977. — 733p : map ; 18cm. — (Pelican books)
Previous ed.: 1973. — Bibl.: p.716-719. — Index.
Pbk : £1.95
ISBN 0-14-021171-3
(B77-28312)

944.083 — France. *French texts. Secondary school texts*
Roe, Claire Andrée. La France / [par] Claire Roe and Penrose Colyer. — [Harlow] : Longman, 1977. — 64p : ill, facsims, maps ; 25cm.
ISBN 0-582-33113-7 Sd : £0.95
(B77-26715)

944.083 — France. Social life
Carroll, Joseph Thomas. The French : how they live and work / [by] Joseph T. Carroll. — New, revised ed. — Newton Abbot [etc.] : David and Charles, 1977. — 159p : ill, map ; 23cm. — (How they live and work)
Previous ed.: i.e. 2nd revised ed. 1973. — Index.
ISBN 0-7153-7407-9 : £3.95
(B77-29091)

944.083 — France. Social life. *Secondary school texts*
Redstone, Sylvia Crofts. A visit to France / [by] Sylvia Redstone & Brendan Hearne. — London : Cassell.
Teacher's notes. — 1976. — [4],42p : 1 ill ; 25cm.
Originally published: as part of 'A visit to France'. 1975.
ISBN 0-304-29769-0 Sd : £1.45
(B77-01943)

944'.36 — Embassies. *France. Paris. Great Britain. Embassy (France), to 1975*
Gladwyn, Cynthia. The Paris embassy / [by] Cynthia Gladwyn. — London : Collins, 1976. — 255p,[16]p of plates : ill, plans(on lining papers), ports ; 22cm.
Bibl.: p.245-246. — Index.
ISBN 0-00-216640-2 : £6.00
(B77-02697)

944'.36'0815 — France. Paris. Night life, 1930-1939
Brassaï. The secret Paris of the 30's / [by] Brassaï ; translated from the French by Richard Miller. — London : Thames and Hudson, 1976. — [190]p : ill ; 28cm.
Originally published: in French. Paris : Gallimard, 1976.
ISBN 0-500-54040-3 : £10.50
(B77-04500)

944'.36'0830222 — France. Paris. *Illustrations*
Canetti, Nicolai. The rooftops of Paris / photography Nicolai Canetti ; commentary Sandy Lesberg. — New York ; London : Peebles Press International ; Leicester (Euston St., Freemen's Common, [Aylestone Rd], Leicester LE2 7SS) : [Distributed by] WHS Distributors, 1976. — 127p : chiefly ill(some col) ; 31cm.
Ill. on lining paper.
ISBN 0-672-52219-5 : £3.25
(B77-12237)

944'.9'00421 — British residents & visitors. *France. Riviera, to 1975*
Howarth, Patrick. When the Riviera was ours / [by] Patrick Howarth. — London [etc.] : Routledge and Kegan Paul, 1977. — xiii,232p, [32]p of plates : ill, map(on lining papers), ports ; 24cm.
Bibl.: p.216-222. — Index.
ISBN 0-7100-8465-x : £5.95
(B77-22290)

944'.9'083 — France. Provence. Social life. *Secondary school texts*
Ferguson, Ian. Provence / [by] Ian Ferguson and Don Groarke. — Basingstoke [etc.] : Macmillan, 1976. — 1v. : ill(chiefly col), col facsims, col maps ; 30cm. — (Discovering France)
Fold. sheet ([1] side), 2 booklets (18p.; 10 leaves), 8 copies of each of 5 folders ([4]p.) in plastic envelope.
ISBN 0-333-16796-1 : £8.50
(B77-07746)

945 — HISTORY. ITALY
945'.05 — Italian culture, 1300-1494
Hay, Denys. The Italian Renaissance in its historical background / [by] Denys Hay. — 2nd ed. — Cambridge [etc.] : Cambridge University Press, 1977. — xvi,228p,xxiv p of plates : ill, facsims, map ; 22cm. — (Wiles lectures)
'... given at the Queen's University of Belfast 1960' - half title page. — Previous ed.: published as 'The Italian Renaissance and its historical background'. 1961. — Bibl.: p.211-223. — Index.
ISBN 0-521-21321-5 : £5.00
ISBN 0-521-29104-6 Pbk : £1.25
(B77-07747)

945'.05 — Italy. Social life, 1490. *Middle school texts. Teaching kits*
Tynan, D M. Leonardo da Vinci / by D.M. Tynan ; illustrated by Valerie Bell. — Cambridge [etc.] : Cambridge University Press, 1977. — 1v. : ill(some col), facsims, maps(some col), ports(1 col) ; 15x21cm. — (History first)
Four booklets, 12 folders ([36]p.) in plastic envelope. — Bibl.
ISBN 0-521-21209-x : £2.75(non-net)
(B77-20839)

945'.05'0922 — Italy. Borgia dynasty. *Secondary school texts*
Sweetman, David. The Borgias / [by] David Sweetman. — Hove : Wayland, 1976. — 94p : ill, coats of arms, facsims, geneal tables, ports ; 22cm. — (Wayland history makers)
Bibl.: p.91. — Index.
ISBN 0-85340-395-3 : £3.50
(B77-09436)

945'.08'0924 — Italy. Garibaldi, Giuseppe. *Biographies. Secondary school texts*
Birch, Beverley. Garibaldi of the Red Shirts / [written and planned by Beverley Birch] ; illustrated by Clyde Pearson ... — London : Macdonald Educational, 1977. — 2-47p : ill(chiefly col), maps(chiefly col), col ports ; 29cm. — (Macdonald famous people)
Text on lining papers. — Index.
ISBN 0-356-05164-1 : £1.60
(B77-06395)

945.09'092'4 — Italy. Oberdank, Wilhelm. *Biographies*
Alexander, Alfred. The hanging of Wilhelm Oberdank / [by] Alfred Alexander. — [London] : London Magazine Editions, 1977. — 224p : ill, facsims, maps(on lining papers), music, ports ; 23cm.
Bibl.: p.217. — Index.
ISBN 0-904388-22-0 : £6.00
(B77-29092)

945.091'092'4 — Italy. Mussolini Ciano, Edda, contessa. *Autobiographies*
Mussolini Ciano, Edda, *contessa.* My truth / by Edda Mussolini Ciano ; as told to Albert Zarca ; translated from the French by Eileen Finletter. — London : Weidenfeld and Nicolson, 1977. — 256p : ill, facsims, ports ; 22cm.
This translation originally published: New York : Morrow, 1976. — Translation of: 'Témoignage pour un homme'. Paris : Stock, 1975. — Index.
ISBN 0-297-77302-x : £6.95
(B77-15637)

945.091'092'4 — Italy. Social life, 1929-1945. *Personal observations*
Agnelli, Susanna. We always wore sailor suits / [by] Susanna Agnelli ; [translated from the Italian]. — London : Corgi, 1977. — [5],217p ; 18cm.
This translation originally published: New York : Viking Press, 1975 ; London : Weidenfeld and Nicolson, 1976. — Translation of: 'Vestivamo alla marinara'. Milano : Mondadori, 1975.
ISBN 0-552-10530-9 Pbk : £0.75
(B77-29093)

945.092'092'4 — Italy. Political events. Role of De Lorenzo, Giovanni, 1956-1964
Collin, Richard. The De Lorenzo gambit : the Italian Coup Manqué of 1964 / [by] Richard Collin. — Beverly Hills ; London : Sage Publications, [1977]. — 65,[1]p ; 22cm. — (Sage research papers in the social sciences : contemporary European studies ; vol.5, no.90-034)
Published in the United States: 1976.
ISBN 0-8039-9942-9 Pbk : £1.75
(B77-12238)

945'.31 — Italy. Lagoon of Venice. Islands. Social life
Guiton, Shirley. A world by itself : tradition and change in the Venetian lagoon / [by] Shirley Guiton ; illustrations by John Lawrence. — London : Hamilton, 1977. — ix,202,[1]p : ill, map(on lining papers) ; 22cm.
ISBN 0-241-89434-4 : £4.95
(B77-09437)

945'.31 — Italy. Venice. Decay, 1966-1975
Fay, Stephen. The death of Venice / [by] Stephen Fay and Phillip Knightley. — London : Deutsch, 1976. — 190p,[8]p of plates : ill, col map(on lining paper), ports ; 22cm.
Ill. on lining paper. — Index.
ISBN 0-233-96835-0 : £4.25
(B77-09438)

945'.31 — Italy. Venice, to 1405
Norwich, John Julius Cooper, *Viscount.* Venice : the rise to empire / [by] John Julius Norwich. — London : Allen Lane, 1977. — 319p,[16]p of plates : ill, maps, ports ; 24cm.
Bibl.: p.303-307. — Index.
ISBN 0-7139-0742-8 : £7.50
(B77-33544)

945'.38'09 — Italy. Trentino-Alto Adige. Foreign relations between Austria & Italy, ca 1915-1969
Toscano, Mario. Alto Adige, South Tyrol : Italy's frontier with the German world / by Mario Toscano ; edited by George A. Carbone. — Baltimore ; London : Johns Hopkins University Press, [1976]. — xiv,283,[1]p : map ; 24cm.
Published in the United States: 1975. — Translation and revision of: 'Storia diplomatica della questione dell'Alto Adige'. 2.ed. Bari : Laterza, 1968. — Index.
ISBN 0-8018-1567-3 : £12.00
Also classified at 327.436'045; 327.45'0436
(B77-06998)

945'.393 — Italy. Trieste, to 1976
Powell, Nicolas. Travellers to Trieste : the history of a city / [by] Nicolas Powell. — London : Faber, 1977. — 3-172p,[12]p of plates : ill, map ; 23cm.
Bibl.: p.161-165. — Index.
ISBN 0-571-10792-3 : £6.95 : CIP rev.
(B77-24633)

945'.51 — Italy. Florence, 1527-1800
Cochrane, Eric. Florence in the forgotten centuries, 1527-1800 : a history of Florence and the Florentines in the age of the Grand Dukes / [by] Eric Cochrane. — Chicago ; London : University of Chicago Press, 1974. — xiv,594p : ill, map ; 24cm.
Originally published: 1973. — Bibl.: p.509-560. — Index.
Pbk : £6.00
ISBN 0-226-11150-4
(B77-01099)

945'.51 — Italy. Florence. Political events, 1378-1430
Brucker, Gene. The civic world of early Renaissance Florence / by Gene Brucker. — Princeton ; Guildford : Princeton University Press, 1977. — xii,526,[1]p ; 25cm.
Index.
ISBN 0-691-05244-1 : £18.80
(B77-23915)

945'.51 — Medici family. *Italy. Florence, 1360-1495*
Pottinger, George. The court of the Medici / [by] George Pottinger. — London : Croom Helm [etc.], 1978. — 141p : geneal table ; 23cm.
Bibl.: p.135-137. — Index.
ISBN 0-85664-605-9 : £5.95 : CIP rev.
(B77-26716)

945'.632'06 — Italy. Rome, 1500-1559
Partner, Peter. Renaissance Rome, 1500-1559 : a portrait of a society / [by] Peter Partner. — Berkeley [etc.] ; London : University of California Press, 1976. — xi,241p,[32]p of plates : ill, maps, ports ; 24cm.
Bibl.: p.227-231. — Index.
ISBN 0-520-03026-5 : £10.50
(B77-32335)

945'.73 — Italy. Naples (Kingdom), 1443-1458
Ryder, Alan Frederick Charles. The Kingdom of Naples under Alfonso the Magnanimous : the making of a modern state / by Alan Ryder. — Oxford : Clarendon Press, 1976. — x,409p, plate : 2 maps, port ; 23cm.
Bibl.: p.372-384. — Index.
ISBN 0-19-822535-0 : £12.50
(B77-05796)

945'.77'0910924 — Italy. Basilicata. Social life, 1935-1936. *Personal observations. Italian texts*
Levi, Carlo. Cristo si è fermato a Eboli / [di] Carlo Levi ; edited with an introduction, notes and a select vocabulary by Peter M. Brown. — London : Harrap, 1976. — 325p : map ; 19cm.
Italian text, English introduction and notes. — Originally published: 1965. — Bibl.: p.35-36.
ISBN 0-245-53018-5 Pbk : £2.75
(B77-12239)

945.8'04 — Italy. Sicily. Political events, 1130-1194
Norwich, John Julius Cooper, *Viscount.* The kingdom in the sun, 1130-1194 / [by] John Julius Norwich. — London : Faber, 1976. — xv,426p : 2 geneal tables, 3 maps ; 20cm.
Originally published: Harlow : Longmans, 1970. — Bibl.: p.405-415. — Index.
ISBN 0-571-10903-9 Pbk : £2.95
(B77-13997)

946 — HISTORY. IBERIAN PENINSULA, SPAIN

946 — Iberian Peninsula, to 1975
Payne, Stanley George. A history of Spain and Portugal / [by] Stanley G. Payne. — Madison, Wis. ; London : University of Wisconsin Press.
In 2 vols.
[Vol.] 1. — 1976. — xvii,349,[28]p,[16]p of plates : ill, geneal tables, maps, ports ; 22cm.
Originally published: Madison, Wis. : University of Wisconsin Press, 1973. — Bibl.: p.333-349. — Index.
ISBN 0-299-06274-0 Pbk : Unpriced
(B77-10691)

[Vol.] 2. — 1976. — xvp,p351-712,[28]p,[16]p of plates : ill, maps, ports ; 22cm.
Originally published: Madison, Wis. : University of Wisconsin Press, 1973. — Bibl.: p.701-712. — Index.
ISBN 0-299-06284-8 Pbk : Unpriced
(B77-10692)

946 — Spain, to 1975
Vilar, Pierre. Spain : a brief history / by Pierre Vilar ; translated [from the French] by Brian Tate. — 2nd ed. — Oxford [etc.] : Pergamon, 1977. — viii,140p : map ; 22cm. — (Pergamon international library) (Pergamon Oxford Spanish series)
Translation of: 'Histoire de l'Espagne'. 10.éd. Paris : Presses universitaires de France, 1976. — Previous ed. of this translation: 1967. — Index.
ISBN 0-08-021462-2 : Unpriced
ISBN 0-08-021461-4 Pbk : £2.25
(B77-30884)

946 — Spanish civilization, to 1974
Lowe, Alfonso. The culture and history of the Spanish / [by] Alfonso Lowe. — London : Gordon and Cremonesi, 1977. — 3-225p,[8]p of plates : ill(some col), map, ports ; 24cm.
Originally published: as 'The Spanish'. 1975. — Bibl.: p.216-218. — Index.
ISBN 0-86033-050-8 Pbk : £2.90
(B77-34330)

946'.007'2024 — Spanish civilisation. Historiography. Castro, Américo
Américo Castro and the meaning of Spanish civilization / edited by José Rubia Barcia, with the assistance of Selma Margaretten. — Berkeley [etc.] ; London : University of California Press, 1976. — xix,336p ; 23cm.
Folder ([3]p.: ports) as insert. — Bibl.: p.xv-xix. — Index.
ISBN 0-520-02920-8 : £10.90
(B77-34331)

946'.02 — Spain, 1000-1500
MacKay, Angus. Spain in the Middle Ages : from frontier to empire, 1000-1500 / [by] Angus MacKay. — London [etc.] : Macmillan, 1977. — xii,245p,6p of plates : 1 ill, maps ; 23cm. — (New studies in medieval history)
Bibl.: p.213-229. — Index.
ISBN 0-333-12816-8 : £8.95
ISBN 0-333-12817-6 Pbk : £2.95
(B77-21634)

946'.04 — Spain. Political events, 1560-1620
Thompson, I A A. War and government in Habsburg Spain, 1560-1620 / by I.A.A. Thompson. — London : Athlone Press, 1976. — ix,374p : 1 ill ; 23cm.
Bibl.: p.349-359. — Index.
ISBN 0-485-11166-7 : £9.00
(B77-04501)

946'.04'0924 — Spain. Pérez, Antonio, 1590-1611. *Correspondence*
A **Spaniard** in Elizabethan England : the correspondence of Antonio Pérez's exile / [compiled and edited by] Gustav Ungerer. — London : Tamesis. — (Colección Tamesis ; serie A : monografías ; 54)
Vol.2. — 1976. — [6],450p ; 24cm.
English introductions, documents in English, French, Spanish and Latin. — Bibl.: p.401-410. — Index.
ISBN 0-7293-0021-8 Pbk : £19.50
(B77-05148)

946.081 — Spain. Guernica. Air raids by Germany. Luftwaffe. Legion Kondor, 1937
Southworth, Herbert Rutledge. Guernica! Guernica! : a study of journalism, diplomacy, propaganda, and history / [by] Herbert Rutledge Southworth ; [translated from the French]. — Berkeley [etc.] ; London : University of California Press, 1977. — xxvii, 537p ; 25cm.
Translation of: 'La destruction de Guernica, 26 avril 1937'. Paris : Ruedo ibérico, 1974. — Bibl.: p.503-515. — Index.
ISBN 0-520-02830-9 : £15.00
(B77-31637)

946.08'1 — Spanish Civil War
Carr, Raymond. The Spanish tragedy : the Civil War in perspective / [by] Raymond Carr. — London : Weidenfeld and Nicolson, 1977. — xviii,336p : maps, plans ; 23cm.
Bibl.: p.312-322. — Index.
ISBN 0-297-77309-7 : £10.00
(B77-21635)

Thomas, Hugh, *b.1931.* The Spanish Civil War / [by] Hugh Thomas. — 3rd ed., revised and enlarged. — Harmondsworth [etc.] : Penguin, 1977. — xx,1115p : maps, plans ; 20cm. — (Pelican books)
Previous ed.: i.e. Revised ed., 1965. — Bibl.: p.1009-1041. — Index.
ISBN 0-14-020970-0 Pbk : £3.50
(B77-08155)

Thomas, Hugh, *b.1931.* The Spanish Civil War / [by] Hugh Thomas. — 3rd ed., revised and enlarged. — London : Hamilton, 1977. — xx, 1115,[16]p of plates : maps, plans, ports ; 23cm.

This ed. also published: Harmondsworth : Penguin, 1977. — Previous ed.: i.e. Revised ed. Harmondsworth : Penguin, 1965. — Bibl.: p.992-1041. — Index.
ISBN 0-241-89450-6 : £12.50
(B77-23916)

946.08'1 — Spanish Civil War. Air operations
Shores, Christopher Francis. Spanish Civil War air forces / by Christopher Shores ; colour plates by Tom Brittain and Gerry Embleton. — London : Osprey Publishing, 1977. — 48p : ill(some col), ports ; 25cm. — (Airwar series ; 3) (Aircam)
Text accompanying illustrations in English, French and German. — Bibl.: p.46.
ISBN 0-85045-135-3 Pbk : Unpriced
(B77-27611)

946.08'1 — Spanish Civil War. Madrid campaign
Hills, George. The Battle for Madrid / [by] George Hills. — London : Vantage Books [etc.] : Distributed by Hale, 1976. — 192p : ill, facsims, maps, plans, ports ; 26cm.
Ill. on lining papers. — Bibl.: p.187. — Index.
ISBN 0-904545-02-4 : £4.95
(B77-01100)

946.082 — Spain. Political events, 1939-1973
Hottinger, Arnold. Spain in transition : Franco's regime / [by] Arnold Hottinger. — Beverly Hills ; London : Sage Publications [for] the Center for Strategic and International Studies, 1974. — [6],62p ; 21cm. — (The Washington papers ; 18) (A Sage policy paper)
ISBN 0-8039-0204-2 Pbk : £1.00
(B77-20840)

946.082'092'4 — Spain. Franco Bahamonde, Francisco. *Biographies. Secondary school texts*
Kisch, Richard. Franco / [by] Richard Kisch. — Hove : Wayland, 1977. — 96p : ill, map, ports ; 22cm. — (Wayland history makers)
Bibl.: p.94. — Index.
ISBN 0-85340-302-3 : £3.50
(B77-12796)

946.083 — Spain. Social life. *Spanish texts. Secondary school texts*
Clarke, Robert Paul. España : impresiones de un pais / by Robert P. Clarke. — Leeds : E.J. Arnold, 1976. — 48p : ill, maps, ports ; 22cm.
Spanish text, English quizzes.
ISBN 0-560-02714-1 Sd : £0.75
(B77-32336)

946'.35 — Spain. Old Castile, to 1976. *Secondary school texts*
Jump, James Robert. Old Castile / [by] J.R. Jump. — London : Harrap, 1977. — 32p : ill, maps ; 14x22cm. — (Discovering Spain)
ISBN 0-245-53051-7 Sd : £0.70
(B77-18493)

946'.4 — Spain. New Castile, to 1976. *Secondary school texts*
Jump, James Robert. New Castile / [by] J.R. Jump. — London : Harrap, 1977. — 32p : ill, maps, music, port ; 14x22cm. — (Discovering Spain)
ISBN 0-245-53050-9 Sd : £0.70
(B77-17839)

946'.41 — Spain. Madrid, to 1976. *Spanish texts. Secondary school texts*
Clarke, Robert Paul. Madrid / by Robert P. Clarke. — Leeds : E.J. Arnold, 1976. — 46p : ill, 2 maps ; 22cm.
ISBN 0-560-02710-9 Sd : £0.75
(B77-32337)

946'.72 — Spain. Barcelona. Political events. Role of Spain. Ejército, 1905-1906
Romero-Maura, Joaquin. The Spanish army and Catalonia : the 'Cu-Cut! Incident' and the law of jurisdictions, 1905-1906 / [by] Joaquin Romero-Maura. — Beverly Hills ; London : Sage Publications, [1977]. — 31p ; 22cm. — (Sage research papers in the social sciences : contemporary European studies ; vol.5, no.90-033)
Published in the United States: 1976.
ISBN 0-8039-9941-0 Pbk : £1.75
(B77-10693)

946'.8'083 — Spain. Andalusia. *Secondary school texts*
Jump, James Robert. Andalusia / [by] J.R. Jump. — London : Harrap, 1977. — 32p : ill, maps ; 14x22cm. — (Discovering Spain)
ISBN 0-245-52978-0 Sd : £0.60
(B77-14492)

946'.89 — Gibraltar, to 1976
Clarke, Robert Paul. Los ingleses y los españoles / by Robert P. Clarke. — Leeds : E.J. Arnold, 1976. — 48p : ill, maps, ports ; 22cm.
ISBN 0-560-02711-7 Sd : £0.75
Primary classification 942.05'5
(B77-34314)

Dennis, Philip. Gibraltar / by Philip Dennis. — Newton Abbot [etc.] : David and Charles, 1977. — 152p : ill, map, plan ; 23cm. — (The islands series)
Bibl.: p.147-148. — Index.
ISBN 0-7153-7358-7 : £4.95
(B77-19137)

946.9 — Portugal, to 1975
Livermore, Harold Victor. A new history of Portugal / [by] H.V. Livermore. — 2nd ed. — Cambridge [etc.] : Cambridge University Press, 1976. — x,408p,xii p of plates : ill, maps, ports ; 23cm.
Previous ed.: 1966. — Index.
ISBN 0-521-21320-7 : £12.50
ISBN 0-521-29103-8 Pbk : £3.50
(B77-03854)

Oliveira Marques, Antonio Henrique de. History of Portugal / [by] A.H. de Oliveira Marques. — 2nd ed. — New York ; Guildford : Columbia University Press, 1976. — x,507,[3], 310p : ill, geneal tables, facsims, maps, ports ; 23cm.
Previous ed.: in 2 vols. 1972. — Bibl. — Index.
ISBN 0-231-08353-x Pbk : £6.90
(B77-08699)

946.9'02'0924 — Portugal. Henry, Prince of Portugal. *Biographies*
Ure, John. Prince Henry the Navigator / [by] John Ure. — London : Constable, 1977. — 207p,leaf of plate,[12]p of plates : ill, geneal table, maps, 2 ports(1 col) ; 23cm.
Ill. on lining papers. — Bibl.: p.193-195. — Index.
ISBN 0-09-461240-4 : £4.95
(B77-15047)

946.9'042 — Portugal. Political events, 1974-1975. *Communist viewpoints*
Mailer, Phil. Portugal, the impossible revolution? / by Phil Mailer. — London : Solidarity, 1977. — 2-399p : ill, facsims ; 22cm.
ISBN 0-900688-25-4 : £5.00
ISBN 0-900688-24-6 Pbk : £2.25
(B77-28313)

946.9'042 — Portugal. Political events. Role of military forces, 1974-1976
Porch, Douglas. The Portuguese armed forces and the revolution / [by] Douglas Porch. — London : Croom Helm [etc.], 1977. — [1], 273p : maps ; 23cm.
Bibl.: p.266-270. — Index.
ISBN 0-85664-391-2 : £7.95 : CIP rev.
(B77-12240)

946.9'042 — Portugal. Social life. *Juvenile literature*
Seth, Ronald. Let's visit Portugal / [by] Ronald Seth. — London [etc.] : Burke, 1976. — 96p : ill(some col), col maps ; 21cm.
Index.
ISBN 0-222-00499-1 : £1.35
ISBN 0-222-00497-5 Library ed. : £1.95
(B77-00553)

947 — HISTORY. EASTERN EUROPE, SOVIET UNION

947 — Eastern Europe. Political events. Foreign relations between Soviet Union & United States, 1945-1975
Kaufman, Edy. The superpowers and their spheres of influence / [by] Edy Kaufman. — London : Croom Helm, 1976. — 208p : ill ; 23cm.
Index.
ISBN 0-85664-389-0 : £7.95
Primary classification 980'.03
(B77-07754)

947 — Russian civilization, to 1976
Companion to Russian studies / edited by Robert Auty and Dimitri Obolensky, with the editorial assistance of Anthony Kingsford. — Cambridge [etc.] : Cambridge University Press.
In 3 vols.
2 : An introduction to Russian language and literature. — 1977. — xiii,300p ; 24cm.
Bibl. — Index.
ISBN 0-521-20894-7 : Unpriced
(B77-26043)

947 — Soviet Union, to 1975
Dmytryshyn, Basil. A history of Russia / [by] Basil Dmytryshyn. — Englewood Cliffs ; London [etc.] : Prentice-Hall, 1977. — xvii, 645p : ill, maps, ports ; 24cm.
Bibl. — Index.
ISBN 0-13-392134-4 : £11.95
(B77-27612)

947 — Soviet Union, to 1975. *Secondary school texts*
Reid, John David. A visual history of Russia / [by] J.D. Reid. — Revised ed. — London : Evans Bros, 1977. — 48p : ill, maps, ports ; 25cm.
Previous ed.: 1965.
ISBN 0-237-29201-7 Sd : £0.95
(B77-22291)

947'.0004'924 — Jews. Origins. *Eastern Europe*
Koestler, Arthur. The thirteenth tribe : the Khazar Empire and its heritage / [by] Arthur Koestler. — London : Pan Books, 1977. — 224p : ill, map ; 20cm. — (Picador)
Originally published: London : Hutchinson, 1976. — Bibl.: p.211-215. — Index.
ISBN 0-330-25069-8 Pbk : £0.95
Primary classification 947'.0004'943
(B77-30885)

947'.0004'943 — Eastern Europe. Khazar Empire, to ca 1000
Koestler, Arthur. The thirteenth tribe : the Khazar Empire and its heritage / [by] Arthur Koestler. — London : Pan Books, 1977. — 224p : ill, map ; 20cm. — (Picador)
Originally published: London : Hutchinson, 1976. — Bibl.: p.211-215. — Index.
ISBN 0-330-25069-8 Pbk : £0.95
Also classified at 947'.0004'924
(B77-30885)

947'.0006'21 — Eastern European culture. Organisations: International Committee for Soviet and East European Studies. *Periodicals*
International Committee for Soviet and East European Studies. International newsletter / International Committee for Soviet and East European Studies = Comité international d'études soviétiques et est-européennes = Internationales Komitee für Sowjet- und Osteuropastudien. — Glasgow (University of Glasgow, 15 Bute Gardens, Glasgow W.2) : International Information Centre for Soviet and East European Studies.
1- ; July 1976-. — [1976]-. — 23cm.
Three issues a year. — [1],37,x p. in 1st issue.
Sd : Unpriced
(B77-10074)

947'.0008 — Eastern Europe. *Essays*
Oxford Slavonic papers. New series. — Oxford : Clarendon Press.
Vol.9 / edited by Robert Auty, J.L.I. Fennell and I.P. Foote, general editor. — 1976. — [5], 116p,[4]p of plates : ill, facsim, ports ; 24cm.
ISBN 0-19-815650-2 : £6.50
ISSN 0078-7256
(B77-11501)

947'.007'2047 — Russia. Russian historiography, to 1917
Mazour, Anatole Grigorevich. Modern Russian historiography / [by] Anatole G. Mazour. — Revised ed. — Westport, Conn. ; London : Greenwood Press, 1975. — xiv,224,[1]p : 1 ill, facsims, port ; 22cm.
Previous ed.: i.e. 2nd ed. Princeton ; London : Van Nostrand, 1958. — Bibl.: p.211-217. — Index.
ISBN 0-8371-8285-9 : £10.45
(B77-16684)

947'.06'0922 — Russia. Elizabeth, Empress of Russia & Catherine II, Empress of Russia. *Biographies*
Coughlan, Robert. Elizabeth and Catherine : empresses of all the Russias / [by] Robert Coughlan ; edited by Jay Gold. — London : Millington [i.e. Omega], 1974 [i.e. 1976]. — 347p,[8]p of plates : ill, geneal table, ports ; 24cm.
Originally published: New York : Putnam ; London : Millington, 1974. — Bibl.: p.335-336. — Index.
ISBN 0-86007-743-8 Pbk : £1.50
(B77-13998)

947'.06'0924 — Russia. Catherine II, Empress of Russia. *Biographies*
Haslip, Joan. Catherine the Great / [by] Joan Haslip. — London : Weidenfeld and Nicolson, 1977. — x,404p,[16]p of plates : ill, map(on lining papers) ; 23cm.
Bibl.: p.387-390. — Index.
ISBN 0-297-77181-7 : £6.95
(B77-13999)

947'.07 — Crimean War. Army operations by Great Britain. Army. 5th Dragoon Guards. *Officers' personal observations*
Temple Godman, Richard. The fields of war : a young cavalryman's Crimea campaign / [by Richard Temple Godman] ; edited by Philip Warner. — London : J. Murray, 1977. — viii, 215p,[2]leaves of plates,[12]p of plates : ill, map, plan, ports ; 23cm.
Index.
ISBN 0-7195-3356-2 : £5.95
(B77-19933)

947'.07 — Crimean War. British medical services, 1854-1855. *Personal observations*
Terrot, Sarah Anne. Nurse Sarah Anne : with Florence Nightingale at Scutari / [by Sarah Anne Terrot] ; edited with an introduction and notes by Robert G. Richardson ; with a foreword by Charles Hugh Terrot. — London : J. Murray, 1977. — 183p,[8]p of plates : ill, map, ports ; 23cm.
Bibl.: p.179-180. — Index.
ISBN 0-7195-3385-6 : £4.95
(B77-25325)

947'.07'0924 — Russia. Bagrov, Stepan Mikhaĭlovich. *Biographies*
Aksakov, Sergeĭ Timofeevich. [Semeĭnaia khronika. English]. A Russian gentleman / [by] Serghei Aksakov ; translated [from the Russian] and with an introduction by J.D. Duff ; lithographs by Jane Johnson. — London : Folio Society, 1976. — 239p,[9]leaves of plates : col ill ; 23cm.
In slip case. — This translation originally published: London : Edward Arnold, 1917. Translation of: 'Semeĭnaia khronika'. Izd.2. Moskva : L. Stepanovoĭ, 1856.
ISBN 0-85067-104-3 : £5.50
(B77-03855)

947.08 — Russia. Romanov dynasty, 1848-1918
Sulzberger, Cyrus Leo. The fall of eagles / [by] C.L. Sulzberger. — London : Hodder and Stoughton, 1977. — 408p : ill(some col), col coats of arms, maps, ports(some col) ; 25cm.
Index.
ISBN 0-340-21641-7 : £9.95
Primary classification 940.2'8
(B77-32312)

947.08 — Russia. Social life, 1894-1917
Before the revolution : a view of Russia under the last tsar / [compiled by] Kyril FitzLyon and Tatiana Browning. — London : Allen Lane, 1977. — 3-205p : chiefly ill, ports ; 26cm.
Bibl.: p.69-70.
ISBN 0-7139-0894-7 : £6.95
(B77-34332)

947.08 — Soviet Union, 1879-1970. *Secondary school texts*
Russia / editor John Robottom. — London : Longman.
Workcards / [by] Tom Allan. — 1977. — 1v. ; 23cm. — (Making the modern world)
One card, 3 copies each of 5 cards ([12] sides) in plastic envelope.
ISBN 0-582-22083-1 : £0.95
(B77-19138)

947.08'022'2 — Soviet Union. Social life, 1860-1920. *Illustrations*
Russia in original photographs, 1860-1920 / [compiled by] Marvin Lyons ; edited by Andrew Wheatcroft. — London [etc.] : Routledge and Kegan Paul, 1977. — xii,212p : of ill, ports ; 30cm.
ISBN 0-7100-8653-9 : £9.50 : CIP rev.
(B77-25326)

947.08'05 — Soviet Union. Political events, ca 1900-ca 1920. *Serials*
Sbornik. — Leeds (c/o The editor, Department of Russian Studies, University of Leeds, Leeds LS2 9JT) : The Group.
No.2 : Papers of the second international conference of the Study Group on the Russian Revolution, held at the University of Keele, Staffordshire, England, January 1976 / [edited by David N. Collins]. — 1976. — 60,[17]p,4 leaves of plates : ill ; 30cm.
'Incorporating the Newsletter of the Study Group on the Russian Revolution'. — Includes facsimile reprint of: 'Vybornyia organizats͡ii v" arm͡ii / P.D. Burskiĭ. Moskva : I.K. Golubev, 1917.
Sd : Unpriced
ISSN 0308-1346
(B77-04502)

947.08'092'4 — Russia. Rasputin, Grigoriĭ Efimovich. *Biographies*
Rasputin, Maria. Rasputin : the man behind the myth : a personal memoir / [by] Maria Rasputin and Patte Barham. — London : W.H. Allen, 1977. — [5],266p,[8]p of plates : ill, ports ; 23cm.
Ill. on lining papers. — Also published: Englewood Cliffs : Prentice-Hall, 1977. — Index.
ISBN 0-491-02371-5 : £4.95
(B77-32997)

947.08'092'4 — Russia. Social life, 1914-1917. *Personal observations*
Dawe, Rosamond Ethel. A memoir of an English governess in Russia, 1914-1917 / by Rosamund E. Dawe. — Old Woking (The Gresham Press, Old Woking, Surrey) : Unwin Brothers Ltd, 1976. — x,45p,[8]p of plates : ill, facsim, ports ; 21cm. — (Looking back ; vol.1)
Originally published: Chichester : Bishop Otter College, 1973.
ISBN 0-9502121-7-2 Pbk : £1.55
(B77-02698)

947.08'092'4 — Soviet Union. Political events. Role of Lenin, Vladimir Il'ich, 1900-1924
Ginsborg, Paul. The politics of Lenin / [by] Paul Ginsborg. — [London] ([8 Cottons Gardens, E2 8DN]) : International Socialists, 1974. — 31p : ill, ports ; 21cm. — (International Socialists. Pamphlets)
ISBN 0-905998-03-0 Sd : £0.20
(B77-23918)

Ulam, Adam Bruno. Lenin and the Bolsheviks : the intellectual and political history of the triumph of Communism in Russia / [by] Adam B. Ulam. — [London] : Fontana, 1977. — ix, 785p ; 18cm. — (The Fontana library)
Originally published: as 'The Bolsheviks', New York : Macmillan, 1965 ; and as 'Lenin and the Bolsheviks', London : Secker and Warburg, 1966. — Index.
Pbk : £2.25
ISBN 0-00-631807-x
(B77-21636)

947.08'092'4 — Soviet Union. Political events. Role of Lenin, Vladimir Il'ich, ca 1900-1917
Shukman, Harold. Lenin and the Russian revolution / [by] Harold Shukman. — London : Longman, 1977. — 224p ; 20cm.
Originally published: London : Batsford, 1967. — Bibl.: p.210-212. — Index.
ISBN 0-582-48694-7 Pbk : £2.50
(B77-15638)

947'.08'0924 — Soviet Union. Tolstoy, Tatyana. *Autobiographies*
Tolstoy, Tatyana. Tolstoy remembered / [by] Tatyana Tolstoy ; translated from the French by Derek Coltman ; with an introduction by John Bayley. — London : Joseph, 1977. — 225p,[8]p of plates : ill, geneal table(on lining papers), ports ; 25cm.
Translation of: 'Avec Léon Tolstoï'. Paris : A. Michel, 1975.
ISBN 0-7181-1626-7 : £8.50
(B77-29094)

947.084'092'4 — Russia. Galitzine, Princess Nicholas. *Autobiographies*
Galitzine, *Princess* **Nicholas.** Spirit to survive : the memoirs of Princess Nicholas Galitzine. — London : Kimber, 1976. — 199p,[16]p of plates : ill, geneal table, ports ; 25cm.
ISBN 0-7183-0394-6 : £4.95
(B77-01101)

947.084'1 — Russia. Political events, 1917 (October-November)
Reed, John, *b.1887.* Ten days that shook the world / [by] John Reed. — [1st ed. reprinted] ; with an introduction by A.J.P. Taylor. — Harmondsworth [etc.] : Penguin, 1977. — xix, 7-351p ; 18cm. — (Penguin modern classics)
Originally published: New York : Boni and Liveright, 1919 ; London : Communist Party of Great Britain, 1926.
ISBN 0-14-002433-6 Pbk : £1.00
(B77-10694)

947.084'1 — Russia. Political events, 1917-1918
Keep, John Leslie Howard. The Russian revolution : a study in mass mobilization / [by] John L.H. Keep. — London : Weidenfeld and Nicolson, 1976. — xvii,614p : map ; 23cm. — (Revolutions in the modern world)
Bibl.: p.583-606. — Index.
ISBN 0-297-77210-4 : £12.50
(B77-01945)

947.084'1 — Soviet Union. Political events, 1917-1921
Berkman, Alexander. The Russian tragedy / by Alexander Berkman ; compiled and introduced by William G. Nowlin, Jr. — Sanday (Box A, Over the Water, Sanday, Orkney KW17 2BL) : Cienfuegos Press Ltd, 1976. — xviii,112p,[6]p of plates : ill, facsim, map, ports ; 22cm.
Contents: The Russian tragedy. Originally published: Berlin : Der Syndikalist, 1922 - The Russian Revolution and the Communist party. Originally published: Berlin : Der Syndikalist, 1922 - The Kronstadt rebellion. Originally published: Berlin : Der Syndikalist, 1922.
ISBN 0-904564-11-8 Pbk : Unpriced
(B77-03306)

947.084'1 — Soviet Union. Political events, 1917-1922. Cultural aspects
Claudin-Urondo, Carmen. Lenin and the cultural revolution / [by] Carmen Claudin-Urondo ; translated from the French by Brian Pearce. — Hassocks : Harvester Press [etc.], 1977. — [5], 134p ; 23cm. — (Marxist theory and contemporary capitalism)
Translation of: 'Lénine et la révolution culturelle'. Paris : Mouton, 1974. — Index.
ISBN 0-85527-800-5 : £4.95 : CIP rev.
(B77-23919)

947.084'1 — Soviet Union. Political events, 1917-1923
Carr, Edward Hallett. The Bolshevik Revolution, 1917-1923 / [by] Edward Hallett Carr. — Harmondsworth [etc.] : Penguin. — (Carr, Edward Hallett. History of Soviet Russia) (Pelican books)
Vol.3. — 1977. — 596p ; 19cm.
Originally published: London : Macmillan, 1953. — Bibl.: p.569-581. — Index.
ISBN 0-14-020751-1 Pbk : £1.75
(B77-30886)

947.084'1'0924 — Army operations by Poland. Wojsko. *Soviet Union, 1914-1920. Officers' personal observations. Polish texts*
Schally, Kazimierz. Wspomnienia Zolnierskie : z legionów i Rewolucji Bolszewickiej / Kazimierz Schally. — Londyn [i.e. London] : [Oficyna Poetów i Malarzy], 1977. — 88p : port ; 22cm.
Pbk : £2.00
(B77-11009)

947.084'1'0924 — Russia. Political events. 1917. *Personal observations. Polish texts*
Dąbrowski, Jan. Sluga gnuśny : fragment pamiętnika / Jan P. Dąbrowski ; do druku przygotowal i wstępem opatrzyl Leon Koczy. — Glasgow : Biblioteka Instytutu Polskiego i Muzeum Gen. Sikorskiego, 1976. — [15],68p : port ; 26cm.
ISBN 0-901504-05-x Pbk : Unpriced
(B77-16129)

947.084'2 — Soviet Union. Political events, 1924-1956. *Communist viewpoints*
Strong, Anna Louise. The Stalin era / [by] Anna Louise Strong. — [Belfast] : British and Irish Communist Organisation, 1976. — [1],77p ; 30cm.
'Athol books'. — Originally published: Altadema, Calif. : Today's Press, 1956.
ISBN 0-900988-54-1 Sd : £0.70
(B77-14000)

947.084'2'0924 — Russia. Social life, 1936-1941. *Personal observations*
Eeman, Harold. Inside Stalin's Russia : memories of a diplomat 1936-1941 / by Harold Eeman ; illustrated by the author. — London : Triton Books, 1977. — [6],202p : ill ; 23cm.
Ill. on lining papers.
ISBN 0-363-00100-x : £5.95
(B77-27613)

947.084'2'0924 — Soviet Union. Darel, Sylva, ca 1937-1953. *Autobiographies*
Darel, Sylva. A sparrow in the snow / [by] Sylva Darel ; translated from the Russian [MS.] by Barbara Norman. — Harmondsworth [etc.] : Penguin, 1977. — 186p ; 18cm.
This translation originally published: New York : Stein and Day, 1973 ; London : Souvenir Press, 1974.
ISBN 0-14-004155-9 Pbk : £0.70
(B77-09439)

947.084'2'0924 — Soviet Union. Mandelstam, Nadezhda. *Autobiographies*
Mandelstam, Nadezhda. Hope abandoned : a memoir / [by] Nadezhda Mandelstam ; translated [from the Russian] by Max Hayward. — Harmondsworth [etc.] : Penguin, 1976. — 767p ; 18cm.
This translation originally published: New York : Atheneum, 1973 ; London : Collins : Harvill Press, 1974. — Translation of: 'Vtoraia kniga'. Paris : YMCA Press, 1972. — Index.
ISBN 0-14-004186-9 Pbk : £1.95
Also classified at 891.7'1'3
(B77-08156)

947.084'2'0924 — Soviet Union. Stalin, Iosif Vissarionovich. *Biographies. Secondary school texts*
Hayes, David. Joseph Stalin / [by] David Hayes and F.H. Gregory. — Hove : Wayland, 1977. — 96p : ill, ports ; 22cm. — (Wayland history makers)
Bibl.: p.94. — Index.
ISBN 0-85340-276-0 : £3.50
(B77-20841)

947.084'2'0924 — Soviet Union. Trotsky, Leon, 1935. *Diaries*
Trotsky, Leon. Trotsky's diary in exile, 1935 / translated from the Russian [MS.] by Elena Zarudnaya. — [1st ed. reprinted] ; with a foreword by Jean van Heijenoort. — Cambridge, Mass. ; London : Harvard University Press, 1976. — xvii,218p,[10]p of plates : ill, facsims, port ; 22cm.
This translation originally published: Cambridge, Mass. : Harvard University Press, 1958 ; London : Faber, 1959. — Index.
ISBN 0-674-91006-0 : £7.50
(B77-05149)

947.085 — Soviet civilization
From under the rubble / by Alexander Solzhenitsyn ... [et al.] ; [edited by Alexander Solzhenitsyn] ; translated [from the Russian] by A.M. Brock ... [et al.] under the direction of Michael Scammell. — [London] : Fontana, 1976. — xii,308p ; 18cm.
This translated selection originally published: London : Collins ; Harvill Press, 1975. — Translation of: 'Iz-pod glyb'. Paris : YMCA Press, 1974. — Index.
ISBN 0-00-634158-6 Pbk : £0.95
(B77-25327)

947.085 — Soviet Union. *Juvenile literature*
Hewitt, Philip. Looking at Russia / [by] Philip Hewitt. — London : A. and C. Black [etc.], 1977. — 64p : ill(some col), facsim, col maps, ports(1 col) ; 24cm.
Index.
ISBN 0-7136-1706-3 : £1.95
(B77-32338)

947.085 — Soviet Union. Social life
Kaiser, Robert G. Russia : the people & the power / [by] Robert G. Kaiser. — London : Secker and Warburg, 1976. — xiii,499,[1]p,[2] leaves of plates : 2 ill, 2 maps ; 25cm.
Also published: New York : Atheneum, 1976. — Bibl.: p.485. — Index.
ISBN 0-436-23060-7 : £5.90
(B77-05797)

Kaiser, Robert G. Russia : the people and the power / [by] Robert G. Kaiser. — Abridged ed. — Harmondsworth : Penguin, 1977. — 469p : ill, maps ; 18cm. — (A pelican book)
Previous ed.: New York : Atheneum ; London : Secker and Warburg, 1976.
ISBN 0-14-022020-8 Pbk : £1.25
(B77-26718)

947.085'022'2 — Soviet Union. *Illustrations*
Russia / [text] by Marianne Sinclair ; with introductions by Heinrich Böll and Valentin Katayev. — London [etc.] : Marshall Cavendish, 1976. — [5],188p : chiefly ill(some col), maps, col ports ; 28cm.
Ill. on lining papers. — These illustrations and introductions originally published: in German. Stuttgart : Belser, 1970.
ISBN 0-85685-123-x : £6.95
(B77-14493)

947.085'08 — Soviet Union. *Essays*
Mihajlov, Mihajlo. Underground notes / by Mihajlo Mihajlov ; introduction by Vladimir Maximov ; translated by Maria Mihajlov Ivusic and Christopher W. Ivusic. — London [etc.] : Routledge and Kegan Paul, 1977. — xii,204p ; 23cm.
These translations originally published: Kansas : Sheed Andrews and McMeel, 1976. — Bibl.: p.201-202.
ISBN 0-7100-8762-4 : £5.25 : CIP rev.
(B77-23920)

947.085'092'4 — Soviet Union. Khrushchev, Nikita Sergeevich. *Autobiographies*
Khrushchev, Nikita Sergeevich. Khrushchev remembers / translated [from the Russian] and edited by Strobe Talbott. — Harmondsworth [etc.] : Penguin.
In 2 vols. — '... made up of material emanating from various sources at various times ... an authentic record of Nikita Khrushchev's words' - Publisher's note.
Vol.1 / with an introduction, commentary and notes by Edward Crankshaw. — 1977. — 669p, [8]p of plates : ports ; 18cm.
This translation originally published: Boston, Mass. : Little, Brown ; London : Deutsch, 1971. — Index.
ISBN 0-14-004194-x Pbk : £2.25
(B77-19934)

Vol.2 : The last testament / with a foreword by Edward Crankshaw and an introduction by Jerrold L. Schecter. — 1977. — 635p,[8]p of plates : 1 ill, ports ; 18cm.
This translation originally published: Boston, Mass. : Little, Brown ; London : Deutsch, 1974. — Index.
ISBN 0-14-004195-8 Pbk : £2.25
(B77-19935)

947.085'092'4 — Soviet Union. Khrushchev, Nikita Sergeevich, 1953-1964
Medvedev, Roĭ Aleksandrovich. Khrushchev : the years in power / [by] Roy A. Medvedev, Zhores A. Medvedev ; translated [from the Russian] by Andrew R. Durkin. — London [etc.] : Oxford University Press, 1977. — xiii, 198p : map, port ; 23cm.
This translation originally published: New York : Columbia University Press, 1976. — Translation of: 'N.S. Khrushchev, gody u vlasti'. Ann Arbor : Xerox University Microfilms, 1975. — Index.
ISBN 0-19-215835-x : £3.95
(B77-23921)

947.1 — HISTORY. FINLAND
947.1'03 — Russo-Finnish War. Role of Allied forces
Nevakivi, Jukka. The appeal that was never made : the Allies, Scandinavia and the Finnish Winter War, 1939-1940 / by Jukka Nevakivi ; [translated from the Finnish by Marjatta Nevakivi]. — London : C. Hurst, 1916. — xii, 225p : map ; 23cm.
Translation and revision of: 'Apu jota ei pyydetty'. Helsinki : Tammi, 1972. — Bibl.: p.213-218. — Index.
ISBN 0-903983-55-9 : £7.00
(B77-06396)

947.1'7 — Skolts. Social life. *Finland. Sevettijärvi region*
Ingold, Tim. The Skolt Lapps today / [by] Tim Ingold. — Cambridge [etc.] : Cambridge University Press, 1976. — xi,276p : ill, maps, plans ; 23cm. — (Changing cultures)
Bibl.: p.259-266. — Index.
ISBN 0-521-21299-5 : £7.00
ISBN 0-521-29090-2 Pbk : £2.95
(B77-05150)

947.2/9 — HISTORY. SOVIET UNION. SPECIAL LOCALITIES
947'.31 — Government buildings. *Russia (RSFSR). Moscow. Kremlin, to 1975*
Burian, Jiří. The kremlin of Moscow / text by Jiří Burian and Oleg A. Shvidkovsky ; photographs by Karel Neubert ; [translated from the Czech by Greta Mašková]. — London : Hale, 1977. — [131],xxxix p : ill(chiefly col), maps, col ports ; 31cm.
Col. ill. on lining papers. — Translation of: 'Moskevský Kreml'. Prague : Odeon, 1975. — Bibl.: p.xxxviii.
ISBN 0-7091-5436-4 : £12.50
(B77-16685)

948 — HISTORY. SCANDINAVIA
948'.02 — Vikings. Social life. *Juvenile literature*
Hadenius, Stig. How they lived in a Viking settlement / [by] Stig Hadenius and Birgit Janrup ; translated [from the Swedish] by Fred Thideman ; illustrated by Ulf Löfgren. — Guildford [etc.] : Lutterworth Press, 1976. — 32p : ill(chiefly col), col map ; 23cm. — (How they lived ; 5)
Ill. on lining papers. — Translation of: 'Roligt om historia, Vikingatiden'. Stockholm : Geber, 1968.
ISBN 0-7188-2199-8 : £1.10
(B77-05151)

948'.02 — Vikings, to ca 1100
Kirkby, Michael Hasloch. The Vikings / [by] Michael Hasloch Kirkby. — Oxford : Phaidon, 1977. — 207p : ill(some col), geneal tables, maps ; 25cm.
Index.
ISBN 0-7148-1718-x : £6.95
ISBN 0-7148-1727-9 Pbk : £4.95
(B77-30888)

948.1 — HISTORY. NORWAY
948.4'5'040924 — Norway. Lapland. Social life. *Personal observations*
Herbert, Marie. The reindeer people / by Marie Herbert. — London [etc.] : Hodder and Stoughton, 1976. — 187p,[8]p of plates : ill, map, ports ; 23cm.
Bibl.: p.185-187.
ISBN 0-340-21219-5 : £4.50
(B77-05798)

949.12 — HISTORY. ICELAND
949.1'2 — Iceland, to 1976
Magnússon, Sigurdur A. Northern sphinx : Iceland and the Icelanders from the settlement to the present / by Sigurdur A. Magnússon. — London : C. Hurst, 1977. — x,261p : map ; 23cm.
Bibl.: p.243-252. — Index.
ISBN 0-903983-59-1 : £7.50 : CIP rev.
(B77-07748)

949.2 — HISTORY. NETHERLANDS
949.2'03'0924 — Revolt of the Netherlands, 1572-1574. *Personal observations*
Morgan, Walter. The expedition in Holland, 1572-1574 : the revolt of the Netherlands, the early struggle for independence / [edited] from the manuscript by Walter Morgan by Duncan Caldecott-Baird. — London : Seeley Service, 1976. — [9],170p : ill, facsim, maps ; 25cm.
'Walter Morgan's manuscript (All Souls' College, M.S. 129) has been published in extenso ... ' - Preface. — Ill. on lining papers. — Bibl.: p.54-56. — Index.
ISBN 0-85422-071-2 : £15.00
(B77-09440)

949.2'04 — Netherlands. Political events, 1780-1813
Schama, Simon. Patriots and liberators : revolution in the Netherlands, 1780-1813 / [by] Simon Schama. — London [etc.] : Collins, 1977. — xx,745,[1]p : ill, maps ; 25cm.
Bibl.: p.707-716. — Index.
ISBN 0-00-216701-8 : £15.00
(B77-23032)

949.2'3 — Netherlands. Amsterdam. *Illustrations*
Pruis, Ab. The canals of Amsterdam / principal photography by Ab Pruis ; commentary Sandy Lesberg. — New York ; London : Peebles Press International ; Leicester (Euston St., Freemen's Common, [Aylestone Rd], Leicester LE2 7SS) : [Distributed by] WHS Distributors, 1976. — 127p : chiefly ill(some col) ; 31cm.
Ill. on lining paper.
ISBN 0-672-52218-7 : £3.25
(B77-12241)

949.4 — HISTORY. SWITZERLAND
949.4'07 — Switzerland
George Mikes introduces Switzerland / edited by Raffael Ganz. — London : Deutsch, 1977. — 168p,leaf of plate,[24]p of plates : col ill, map(on lining papers) ; 24cm.
ISBN 0-233-96757-5 : £4.50 : CIP rev.
(B77-20843)

949.5 — HISTORY. GREECE
949.5 — Byzantine civilization. Related to Western European civilization, 330-1600
Geanakoplos, Deno John. Interaction of the 'sibling' Byzantine and western cultures in the Middle Ages and Italian Renaissance (330-1600) / [by] Deno John Geanakoplos. — New Haven ; London : Yale University Press, 1976. — xxiii,416p : ill, maps, ports ; 24cm.
Bibl.: p.377-403. — Index.
ISBN 0-300-01831-2 : £18.15
Also classified at 940.1
(B77-10075)

949.5 — Byzantine civilization, to 1453
Foss, Clive. Rome and Byzantium / [by] Clive Foss and Paul Magdalino. — Oxford : Elsevier-Phaidon, 1977. — 149p : ill(chiefly col), facsims(chiefly col), col maps, plans(some col), ports(some col) ; 29cm. — (The making of the past)
Bibl.: p.137. — Index.
ISBN 0-7290-0012-5 : £4.50
(B77-29095)

949.5 — Greece. Political events, 324-1976
Woodhouse, Christopher Montague. Modern Greece : a short history / [by] C.M. Woodhouse. — [New ed.]. — London : Faber, 1977. — 3-332p : maps ; 20cm.
Previous ed.: published as 'The story of modern Greece'. 1968. — Bibl.: p.313-317. — Index.
ISBN 0-571-04936-2 Pbk : £2.95
(B77-31638)

949.5'03'0922 — Byzantine Empire. John II Comnenus, Emperor of the East & Manuel I Comnenus, Emperor of the East. *Biographies. Early works*
Cinnamus, Joannes. [Epitom¯e t¯on katorth¯omaton t¯o makarit¯e Vasilei kai porphyrogenn¯et¯o Kyr¯o I¯oann¯e t¯o Komn¯en¯o kai aph¯eg¯esis t¯on prachthent¯on t¯o aoidim¯o hyi¯o autou t¯o Vasilei kai porphyrogenn¯eto Kyr¯o Manou¯el t¯o Komn¯en¯o. English]. Deeds of John and Manuel Comnenus / by John Kinnamos ; translated [from the Greek] by Charles M. Brand. — New York ; Guildford : Columbia University Press, 1976. — xiii,274p : geneal table ; 24cm. — (Records of civilization, sources and studies ; no.95)
Index.
ISBN 0-231-04080-6 : £13.88
(B77-13446)

949.5'06 — Greece, 1821-1974
Greece in transition : essays in the history of modern Greece, 1821-1974 / edited by John T.A. Koumoulides with the assistance of Domna Visvizi-Dontas ; foreword by John Brademas. — London : Zeno, 1977. — xii, 334p ; 23cm.
Bibl. — Index.
ISBN 0-7228-0013-4 : £10.00
ISBN 0-7228-0014-2 Pbk : £8.00
(B77-34333)

949.5'07 — Greece. Political events, 1960-1975
Theodoracopulos, Taki. The Greek upheaval : kings, demagogues and bayonets / [by] Taki Theodoracopulos. — London (128 Kensington Church St., W8 4BH) : Stacey International, 1976. — 262p,viii p of plates : ill, ports ; 23cm.
Index.
ISBN 0-905743-00-8 : £4.90
(B77-26044)

949.5'5 — Greece. Corfu, to 1976
Dicks, Brian. Corfu / by Brian Dicks. — Newton Abbot [etc.] : David and Charles, 1977. — 190p : ill, charts, maps, ports ; 23cm. — (The islands series)
Bibl.: p.181-183. — Index.
ISBN 0-7153-7311-0 : £4.95
(B77-11502)

949.6 — HISTORY. BALKAN PENINSULA
949.6 — Ottoman Empire
Kinross, John Balfour, *Baron.* The Ottoman centuries : the rise and fall of the Turkish Empire / [by] Lord Kinross. — London : Cape, 1977. — 638p : ill, maps, ports ; 25cm.
Bibl.: p.623-624. — Index.
ISBN 0-224-01379-3 : £10.00
(B77-20844)

Shaw, Stanford Jay. History of the Ottoman Empire and modern Turkey / [by] Stanford Shaw [and Ezel Kural Shaw]. — Cambridge [etc.] : Cambridge University Press.
In 2 vols.
Vol.1 : Empire of the Gazis : the rise and decline of the Ottoman Empire, 1280-1808 / [by Stanford Shaw]. — 1976 [i.e. 1977]. — xv, 351p : 2 maps, plan ; 24cm.
Published in the United States: 1976. — Bibl.: p.ix-xii. — Index.
ISBN 0-521-21280-4 : £12.50
ISBN 0-521-29163-1 Pbk : £4.95
Primary classification 956.1
(B77-10696)

949.6'1 — Turkey. Istanbul. Social life, 1588. *Illustrations. Early works*
Life in Istanbul, 1588 : scenes from a traveller's picture book. — Oxford ([Broad St., Oxford]) : Bodleian Library, 1977. — 8p,24p of plates : ill, ports ; 22cm. — (Bodleian Library. Picture books ; no.15)
Bibl.: p.6.
Sd : £0.60
(B77-30889)

949.65'03 — Albania. Political events, 1944-1976
Logoreci, Anton. The Albanians : Europe's forgotten survivors / by Anton Logoreci. — London : Gollancz, 1977. — 230p,[8]p of plates : ill, map, ports ; 23cm.
Bibl.: p.216-221. — Index.
ISBN 0-575-02229-9 : £8.50
(B77-12797)

949.7 — HISTORY. YUGOSLAVIA
949.7 — Yugoslavia, ca 1800-1941
West, Rebecca. Black lamb and grey falcon : a journey through Yugoslavia / by Rebecca West. — [Revised ed.]. — London [etc.] : Macmillan, 1977. — [9],1181p : ill, 2 maps(1 col)(on lining papers) ; 23cm.
This ed. originally published: 1955. — Bibl.: p.1153-1158. — Index.
ISBN 0-333-00418-3 : £9.95
Primary classification 914.97'04'2
(B77-30850)

949.7'02'0924 — Yugoslavia. Ivanović, Vane. *Autobiographies*
Ivanović, Vane. LX : memoirs of a Jugoslav / by Vane Ivanović. — London : Weidenfeld and Nicolson, 1977. — xii,435p,[16]p of plates : ill, ports ; 24cm.
Index.
ISBN 0-297-77307-0 : £10.00
(B77-21637)

949.98 — HISTORY. CRETE
949.98 — Greece. Crete, to 1976
Hopkins, Adam. Crete : its past, present and people / by Adam Hopkins ; illustrated by Victor Shreeve. — London : Faber, 1977. — 249p : ill, maps, plans ; 20cm.
Bibl.: p.239-242. — Index.
ISBN 0-571-10411-8 : £5.50
(B77-14001)

949.98'04'0924 — Greece. Crete. Social life. *Personal observations*
Webb, Jackson. The last lemon grove / [by] Jackson Webb ; illustrations by Delia Delderfield. — London : Weidenfeld and Nicolson, 1977. — 185p : ill ; 23cm.
Ill. on lining papers.
ISBN 0-297-77374-7 : £4.95
(B77-27614)

950 — HISTORY. EURASIA, ASIA
950 — East Asia, South Asia & South-east Asia, 1824-1954. *For Malaysian students. Secondary school texts*
The **history** of South-east, South and East Asia : essays and documents / edited by Khoo Kay Kim. — Kuala Lumpur ; London [etc.] : Oxford University Press, 1977. — xvi,419p ; 22cm. — (Oxford in Asia college texts)
Bibl.: p.385-394. — Index.
ISBN 0-19-580359-0 Pbk : £7.50
(B77-28315)

950 — South-west Asia. Political events. Foreign relations between Great Britain & Russia, 1828-1914
Gillard, David. The struggle for Asia, 1828-1914 : a study in British and Russian imperialism / [by] David Gillard. — London : Methuen, 1977. — x,214p : maps ; 24cm.
Bibl.: p.186-197. — Index.
ISBN 0-416-13250-2 : £8.95
Also classified at 327.41'047; 327.47'041
(B77-31639)

950'.4 — Asia, 1900-1973. *Secondary school texts*
Asia / editor John Robottom. — London : Longman.
Workcards / [by] Tom Allan. — 1977. — 1v. ; 23cm. — (Making the modern world)
One card, 3 copies each of 5 cards ([12] sides) in plastic envelope.
ISBN 0-582-22082-3 : £0.95
(B77-19139)

950'.42 — Asia. Political events. Policies of government of United States, 1945-1953
Rose, Lisle A. Roots of tragedy : the United States and the struggle for Asia, 1945-1953 / [by] Lisle A. Rose. — Westport, Conn. ; London : Greenwood Press, 1976. — x,262p ; 22cm. — (Contributions in American history ; no.48)
Bibl.: p.255-256. — Index.
ISBN 0-8371-8592-0 : £12.75
(B77-17840)

950'.42'05 — Asia. *Serials*
Asian and African studies / Department of Oriental Studies of the Slovak Academy of Sciences, Bratislava. — Bratislava : Publishing House of the Slovak Academy of Sciences ; London : Curzon Press.
12 : 1976. — 1976. — 320p : facsims ; 25cm.
English, French, German text.
ISBN 0-7007-0101-x : £4.50
ISSN 0571-2742
Also classified at 960'.3'05
(B77-11010)

950'.42'05 — Asia. *Yearbooks*
The **Far** East and Australasia : a survey and directory of Asia and the Pacific. — London : Europa.
1976-77. — 1976. — xxiii,1331p : maps(chiefly col) ; 26cm.
Tab indexed. — Bibl.
ISBN 0-900362-95-2 : £22.00
(B77-01946)

Owen's commerce and travel and international register. — London (886 High Rd, N12 9SB) : Owen's Commerce and Travel Ltd.
1977 : 24th ed. — 1977. — [3],1211[i.e. 1229]p : ill, maps(1 col) ; 26cm.
Tab indexed.
ISBN 0-900576-08-1 : £9.00
ISSN 0078-7167
Primary classification 960'.3'05
(B77-18497)

951 — HISTORY. CHINA AND ADJACENT AREAS
951 — China, 1368-1976
Cotterell, Yong Yap. Chinese civilization : from the Ming revival to Chairman Mao / [by] Yong Yap & Arthur Cotterell. — London : Weidenfeld and Nicolson, 1977. — 256p : ill(some col), maps, plans, ports(some col) ; 26cm.
Ill. on lining papers. — Bibl.: p.247-249. — Index.
ISBN 0-297-77304-6 : £6.50
(B77-19936)

951 — China, to 1975. *Secondary school texts*
Catchpole, Brian. A map history of modern China / [by] Brian Catchpole ; maps and diagrams by Regmarad. — London : Heinemann Educational, 1976. — [5],145p : ill, maps, ports ; 26cm.
Bibl. — Index.
ISBN 0-435-31095-x Pbk : £1.90
(B77-03856)

951 — China, to 1976
Eberhard, Wolfram. A history of China / by Wolfram Eberhard. — 4th ed. / revised by the author. — London [etc.] : Routledge and Kegan Paul, 1977. — xix,388p,[16]p of plates : ill, maps, port ; 22cm.
Previous ed.: Berkeley : University of California Press, 1969. — Index.
ISBN 0-7100-8357-2 : £7.95
ISBN 0-7100-8358-0 Pbk : £3.95
(B77-06397)

951 — China, to 1976. *Secondary school texts*
Mitchell, Peter M. China : tradition and revolution / [by] Peter M. Mitchell ; study material prepared by Douglas M. Parker. — London : Edward Arnold, 1977. — vi,234p : ill, maps, ports ; 23cm.
Bibl. — Index.
ISBN 0-7131-0110-5 Pbk : £4.95
(B77-30890)

951 — Chinese civilization, 589-1793
Dawson, Raymond. Imperial China / [by] Raymond Dawson. — Harmondsworth [etc.] : Penguin, 1976. — 377p,[32]p of plates : ill, maps, port ; 18cm. — (The history of human society) (Pelican books)
Originally published: London : Hutchinson, 1972. — Index.
ISBN 0-14-021899-8 Pbk : £1.95
(B77-09441)

951'.007'2024 — China. Historiography. Backhouse, Sir Edmund
Trevor-Roper, Hugh. A hidden life : the enigma of Sir Edmund Backhouse / [by] Hugh Trevor-Roper. — London [etc.] : Macmillan, 1976. — viii,316p,[4]p of plates : facsim, ports ; 23cm.
Index.
ISBN 0-333-19883-2 : £4.95
(B77-02699)

951'.01 — Chinese civilization, to 1368
Capon, Edmund. Art and archaeology in China = Chung-kuo chih i-shu yü k'ao-ku / [by] Edmund Capon. — South Melbourne [etc.] : Macmillan Company of Australia ; Cambridge, Mass. ; London : Distributed by the M.I.T. Press, 1977. — 196p : ill(chiefly col), 2 maps ; 26cm.
Transliterated parallel title. — Ill. on lining papers. — Bibl. — Index.
ISBN 0-333-22937-1 : £15.00
(B77-23033)

951'.026 — China. Political events, 1368-1449
Farmer, Edward L. Early Ming government : the evolution of dual capitals / by Edward L. Farmer. — [Cambridge, Mass.] : East Asian Research Center, Harvard University ; Cambridge, Mass. ; London : Distributed by Harvard University Press, 1976. — xi,271p : maps ; 24cm. — (Harvard East Asian monographs ; 66)
Bibl.: p.229-251. — Index.
ISBN 0-674-22175-3 : £11.25
(B77-09442)

951'.03 — China, 1800-1900. *Conference proceedings*
Reform in nineteenth-century China / edited by Paul A. Cohen and John E. Schrecker. — [Cambridge, Mass.] : Harvard University, East Asian Research Center ; Cambridge, Mass. ; London : Distributed by Harvard University Press, 1976. — xii,415p ; 23cm. — (Harvard East Asian monographs ; 72)
'... the proceedings of a workshop held under the auspices of the East Asian Research Center ... July 7-18, 1975' - Preface. — Bibl.: p.339. — Index.
ISBN 0-674-75281-3 Pbk : £6.80
(B77-05152)

951'.03 — China, 1840-1911
Chesneaux, Jean. China from the Opium Wars to the 1911 revolution / by Jean Chesneaux, Marianne Bastid and Marie-Claire Bergère ; translated from the French by Anne Destenay. — Hassocks : Harvester Press, 1977. — vii, 413p : maps ; 25cm.
This translation also published: New York : Pantheon, 1977. — Translation of: 'Des guerres de l'opium à la guerre franco-chinoise, 1840-1885' and three chapters of 'De la guerre franco-chinoise à la fondation du parti communiste chinois, 1885-1921'. Paris : Hatier Université, 1972. — 'Volume 2 of this history, "China from the 1911 revolution to liberation" will be available in 1977' - jacket. — Bibl. — Index.
ISBN 0-85527-759-9 : £9.95
(B77-07749)

951'.03 — China, ca 1644-1912
Wakeman, Frederic, *b.1937.* The fall of Imperial China / [by] Frederic Wakeman, Jr. — New York : Free Press ; London : Collier Macmillan, 1977. — xi,276p : 1 ill, 2 maps ; 21cm. — (The transformation of modern China series)
Originally published: 1975. — Bibl.: p.257-266. — Index.
ISBN 0-02-933680-5 Pbk : £4.50
(B77-30891)

951'.03'0924 — China. K'ang-hsi, Emperor of China
Kessler, Lawrence Devlin. K'ang-hsi and the consolidation of Ch'ing rule, 1661-1684 / [by] Lawrence D. Kessler. — Chicago ; London : University of Chicago Press, 1976. — xi,251p ; 23cm.
Bibl.: p.229-241. — Index.
ISBN 0-226-43203-3 : £15.00
(B77-02700)

951'.03'0924 — China. K'ang-hsi, Emperor of China. *Autobiographies*
K'ang-hsi, *Emperor of China.* Emperor of China : self-portrait of K'ang-hsi / [compiled and translated from the Chinese] by Jonathan D. Spence. — Harmondsworth [etc.] : Penguin, 1977. — xxviii,218,ix p : ill, map ; 20cm. — (Peregrine books)
Originally published: New York : Knopf ; London : Cape, 1974. — Bibl.: p.208-218. — Index.
ISBN 0-14-055122-0 Pbk : £2.00
(B77-19937)

951'.03'0924 — China. Taiping Rebellion. *Personal observations*
Curwen, Charles Anthony. Taiping rebel : the deposition of Li Hsiu-ch'eng / [by] C.A. Curwen. — Cambridge [etc.] : Cambridge University Press, 1977. — viii,357p : col facsim ; 24cm. — (Cambridge studies in Chinese history, literature and institutions)
'This translation is from the Taiwan facsimile edition of the Deposition "Li Hsiu-ch'eng ch'in-kung shou-chi", Taipei 1961' - notes on the translation. — Bibl.: p.327-338. — Index.
ISBN 0-521-21082-8 : £12.50
(B77-09443)

951.04 — China, 1911-1975
Herdan, Innes. Introduction to China / [by] Innes Herdan. — London (152 Camden High St., N.W.1) : Anglo-Chinese Educational Institute, 1976. — [1],65p : ill, map ; 21cm. — (Modern China series ; no.7 ISSN 0309-0639)
Bibl.: p.62-63.
ISBN 0-903193-09-4 Sd : £0.45
(B77-02701)

951.04 — China, 1911-1975. *Secondary school texts*
Schools Council History 13-16 Project. The rise of Communist China / Schools Council History 13-16 Project ; [Project team David Sylvester et al.]. — Edinburgh : Holmes McDougall. — (Modern world studies)
[Student's book]. — 1977. — 88p : ill, col maps, ports ; 25cm.
ISBN 0-7157-1558-5 Pbk : £2.05
(B77-21638)

951.04 — China, 1912-1949
Sheridan, James E. China in disintegration : the Republican era in Chinese history, 1912-1949 / [by] James E. Sheridan. — New York : Free Press ; London : Collier Macmillan, 1977. — xii,338p : maps ; 21cm. — (The transformation of modern China series)
Originally published: 1975. — Bibl.: p.311-324. — Index.
ISBN 0-02-928650-6 Pbk : £4.50
(B77-30892)

951.04'1'0924 — China. Sun Yat-sen. *Biographies*
Wilbur, Clarence Martin. Sun Yat-sen : frustrated patriot / [by] C. Martin Wilbur. — New York ; Guildford : Columbia University Press, 1976. — xii,410p,8p of plates : ill, ports ; 24cm. — (Columbia University. East Asian Institute. Studies)
Bibl.: p.371-390. — Index.
ISBN 0-231-04036-9 : £10.41
(B77-09444)

951.04'2'0924 — China. Chiang Kai-shek. *Biographies*
Crozier, Brian, *b.1918.* The man who lost China : the first full biography of Chiang Kai-shek / by Brian Crozier ; with the collaboration of Eric Chou. — London [etc.] : Angus and Robertson, 1977. — xvii,430p,[16]p of plates : ill, maps, ports ; 24cm.
Originally published: New York : Scribner, 1976. — Index.
ISBN 0-207-95728-2 : £7.50
(B77-14494)

951.04'2'0924 — China. Social life, 1935-1945. *Personal observations*
Cliff, Norman. Courtyard of the happy way / by Norman Cliff. — Evesham : James, 1977. — 144p : map ; 20cm.
ISBN 0-85305-191-7 Pbk : £2.50
(B77-19140)

951.05 — China, 1949-1976
Bown, Colin. China, 1949-76 / [by] Colin Bown. — London : Heinemann Educational, 1977. — viii,192p : 1 ill, maps ; 23cm. — (Studies in modern history)
Index.
ISBN 0-435-32011-4 : £5.00
ISBN 0-435-32009-2 Pbk : £2.25
(B77-12798)

951.05 — China. Political events, 1942-1973
Brugger, William. Contemporary China / [by] Bill Brugger. — London : Croom Helm [etc.], 1977. — 5-451p : 2 maps ; 23cm.
Bibl.: p.425-439. — Index.
ISBN 0-85664-388-2 : £9.95
ISBN 0-85664-480-3 Pbk : £5.50
(B77-08700)

951.05 — China. Political events, ca 1945-1976
Chang, Yi-chun. Factional and coalition politics in China : the Cultural Revolution and its aftermath / [by] Y.C. Chang. — New York [etc.] ; London : Praeger, [1977]. — xiv,145p ; 25cm. — (Praeger special studies in international politics and government)
Published in the United States: 1976. — Index.
ISBN 0-275-00920-3 : £10.20
(B77-12799)

951.05 — China. Social life
Loescher, Gil. The Chinese way : life in the People's Republic of China / by Gil Loescher with Ann Dull Loescher. — New York ; London : Harcourt Brace Jovanovich, [1975]. — xv,206p : ill, maps, ports ; 24cm.
Published in the United States: 1974. — Bibl.: p.193-196. — Index.
ISBN 0-15-217507-5 : Unpriced
(B77-19938)

951.05'092'4 — China. Chiang Ch'ing. *Biographies*
Witke, Roxane. Comrade Chiang Ch'ing / [by] Roxane Witke. — London : Weidenfeld and Nicolson, 1977. — xxvi,549p,[34]p of plates : ill, facsims, map(on lining papers), ports ; 25cm.
Also published: Boston, Mass. : Little, Brown, 1977. — Index.
ISBN 0-297-77346-1 : £6.95
(B77-23034)

951.05'092'4 — China. Mao Tse-tung
FitzGerald, Charles Patrick. Mao Tse-Tung and China / [by] C.P. FitzGerald. — Revised ed. — Harmondsworth [etc.] : Penguin, 1977. — 197p : maps ; 18cm. — (Pelican books)
Previous ed.: London : Hodder and Stoughton, 1976. — Bibl.: p.191. — Index.
ISBN 0-14-021947-1 Pbk : £0.85
(B77-26045)

Mao Tse-tung in the scales of history : a preliminary assessment / organized by 'The China quarterly' and edited by Dick Wilson. — Cambridge [etc.] : Cambridge University Press, 1977. — xii,331p ; 23cm. — (Contemporary China Institute. Publications)
Bibl.: p.321-322. — Index.
ISBN 0-521-21583-8 : £10.50
ISBN 0-521-29190-9 Pbk : Unpriced
(B77-26720)

951.05'092'4 — China. Mao Tse-tung. *Biographies*
Carter, Peter, *b.1929.* Mao / [by] Peter Carter. — London : Oxford University Press, 1976. — [5],164p ; 23cm.
Bibl.: p.163-164.
ISBN 0-19-273140-8 : £3.25
(B77-01947)

951.05'092'4 — China. Mao Tse-tung. *Biographies. Secondary school texts*
Purcell, Hugh. Mao Tse-tung / [by] Hugh Purcell. — New York : St Martin's Press ; Hove : Wayland, 1977. — 96p : ill, maps, ports ; 22cm. — (Wayland history makers)
Bibl.: p.94-95. — Index.
ISBN 0-312-51399-2 : £3.50
(B77-23922)

951.05'092'4 — China. Mao Tse-tung. *Quotations. Chinese-Pinyin parallel texts*
Mao Tse-tung. Annotated quotations from Chairman Mao / [by] John DeFrancis. — New Haven ; London : Yale University Press, 1975. — xi,314p ; 26cm.
Text in parallel Chinese and Pinyin romanization, introduction and notes in English. — Index.
ISBN 0-300-01749-9 : £13.20
(B77-00554)

951.05'092'4 — China. Social life. *Personal observations*
Mason, Colin, *b.1926.* The view from Peking : an account of the Chinese people today / [by] Colin Mason. — London : Angus and Robertson, 1977. — [8],161p,[8]p of plates : col ill, map ; 23cm.
Index.
ISBN 0-207-95735-5 : £4.80
(B77-26046)

951'.215'03 — China. Hunan (Province). Political events, 1891-1907
Lewis, Charlton M. Prologue to the Chinese Revolution : the transformation of ideas and institutions in Hunan Province, 1891-1907 / by Charlton M. Lewis. — [Cambridge, Mass.] : East Asian Research Center, Harvard University ; Cambridge, Mass. ; London : Distributed by Harvard University Press, 1976. — xiv,317p : 2 maps ; 24cm. — (Harvard East Asian monographs ; 70)
Bibl.: p.277-295. — Index.
ISBN 0-674-71441-5 : £11.25
(B77-08701)

951'.35'0072 — China. Yunnan (Province), to 1900. Historiography
Ford, Joseph Francis. The local histories of Yünnan / [by] Joseph Francis Ford. — London (31B Torrington Sq., W.C.1) : China Society, [1977]. — 26p ; 21cm. — (China Society. Occasional papers ; no.19)
'... the revised version of a lecture delivered to the China Society in London on 25th November, 1974'.
Sd : Unpriced
(B77-19939)

951'.5'05 — Tibet. Social life, 1959-1976
Han Suyin. Lhasa, the open city : a journey to Tibet / [by] Han Suyin. — London : Cape, 1977. — xi,180p,[16]p of plates : ill, map, ports ; 23cm.
Bibl.: p.173-174. — Index.
ISBN 0-224-01329-7 : £4.95 : CIP rev.
(B77-06398)

951'.73'04 — Mongolia (People's Republic), 1921-1966
History of the Mongolian People's Republic / translated from the Mongolian and annotated by William A. Brown and Urgunge Onon. — [Cambridge, Mass.] : East Asian Research Center, Harvard University ; Cambridge, Mass. ; London : Distributed by Harvard University Press, 1976. — xv,910p : ill, facsims, maps, ports ; 26cm. — (Harvard East Asian monographs ; 65)
Translation of: 'Bugd naĭramdakh Mongol ard ulsyn tuukh'. Vol.3 / edited by Bagaryn Shirendyb et al. Ulan Bator : s.n., 1969?. — Bibl. — Index.
ISBN 0-674-39862-9 : £14.25
(B77-12242)

951.9'04 — Korea. Political events, 1945-1976. *Korea Committee viewpoints*
Korea Committee. Crisis in Korea / edited by Gavan McCormack & John Gittings ; produced by the Korea Committee, London and the Transnational Institute, Amsterdam. — Nottingham : Bertrand Russell Peace Foundation for Spokesman Books, 1977. — 190p ; 22cm.
Bibl.: p.186-188. — Index.
ISBN 0-85124-186-7 : £5.95
ISBN 0-85124-187-5 Pbk : Unpriced
(B77-29846)

951.9'042 — Korean War. Air operations by Australia. Royal Australian Air Force. Mustang aeroplanes
Anderson, Peter N. Mustangs of the RAAF and RNZAF / [by] Peter N. Anderson. — Sydney [etc.] ; London : A.H. and A.W. Reed, 1975. — [4],103,[5]p : ill(some col), coats of arms, facsim, maps, ports ; 29cm.
Bibl.: p.[2] (first sequence). — Index.
ISBN 0-589-07130-0 : £9.10
Primary classification 940.54'49'94
(B77-19908)

951.9'043 — Korea. Social life. *Colouring books*
Clarke, Rosemary. Let's look at Korea / drawings by Rosemary Clarke ; captions by Kathleen Wallis. — London : OMF Books, 1977. — [24]p : of ill, map ; 18x23cm. — (Overseas Missionary Fellowship. Painting books)
ISBN 0-85363-118-2 Sd : £0.30
(B77-20846)

952 — HISTORY. JAPAN
952'.005 — Japan. *History. Serials*
British Association for Japanese Studies. Proceedings of the British Association for Japanese Studies. — [Sheffield] ([Sheffield S10 2TN]) : University of Sheffield, Centre of Japanese Studies.
Vol.1 : 1976. Part 1 : History and international relations / edited by Peter Lowe. — [1976]. — vii,194p ; 29cm.
'The papers reproduced ... were delivered in the History and International Relations section of the second annual conference of the British Association for Japanese Studies, held at University College, Durham from 9 to 11 April ...' - Preface.
ISBN 0-904787-02-8 Pbk : £2.00
(B77-07751)

952'.008 — Japan, 1800-1975. *Readings*
The **Japan** reader / edited, annotated and with introductions by Jon Livingston, Joe Moore and Felicia Oldfather. — Harmondsworth [etc.] : Penguin. — (Pelican books)
In 2 vols. — Originally published: New York : Pantheon Books, 1973.
Vol.1 : Imperial Japan, 1800-1945. — 1976. — xix,517p : map ; 20cm.
Bibl.: p.497-498. — Index.
ISBN 0-14-021967-6 Pbk : £1.75
(B77-04503)

Vol.2 : Postwar Japan, 1945 to the present. — 1976. — xxi,600p : map ; 20cm.
Bibl.: p.581-582. — Index.
ISBN 0-14-021968-4 Pbk : £1.75
(B77-04504)

952'.01 — Japanese civilization, to 1185
Kidder, Jonathan Edward. Ancient Japan / by Edward Kidder. — Oxford : Elsevier-Phaidon, 1977. — 152p : ill(chiefly col), col maps, col plans ; 29cm. — (The making of the past)
Bibl.: p.137. — Index.
ISBN 0-7290-0047-8 : £4.50
(B77-29847)

952'.025 — Japanese civilization, 1600-1867. *Early works*
Dening, Walter. Japan in days of yore / [by Walter Dening]. — London (115 Bayham St, N.W.1) : Fine Books Ltd, 1976. — 346p in various pagings,[44]leaves of plates : col ill ; 21cm.
Facsimile reprint of: 1st ed., originally published in 4 vols. London : Griffith Farran, 1887-88.
£8.00
(B77-31640)

952.03'1'0924 — Japan. Social life, 1876-1905. *Diaries*
Baelz, Erwin. Awakening Japan : the diary of a German doctor / [by] Erwin Baelz ; edited by his son, Toku Baelz ; [translated from the German]. — [1st ed. reprinted] ; [with an] introduction by George Macklin Wilson. — Bloomington ; London : Indiana University Press, 1974. — xxx,406p,[4]p of plates,[3]leaves of plates : ill, ports ; 22cm.
This translation originally published: New York : Viking Press, 1932. — Translation of: 'Erwin Baelz, das Leben eines deutschen Arztes im erwachenden Japan'. Stuttgart : Engelhorns, 1931. — Index.
ISBN 0-253-31090-3 : £11.25
(B77-26047)

952.03'1'0924 — Japan. Social life, ca 1890-ca 1894. *Personal observations*
Hearn, Lafcadio. Glimpses of unfamiliar Japan / by Lafcadio Hearn. — Rutland, Vt [etc.] : Tuttle ; London : Prentice-Hall, 1976. — xvi, 699p ; 19cm.
Originally published: in 2 vols. Boston, Mass. : Houghton, Mifflin, 1894. — Index.
ISBN 0-8048-1145-8 Pbk : £3.50
(B77-06999)

952.04'08 — Japanese civilization. *Readings*
Introducing Japan : history, way of life, creative world, seen & heard, food & drink / edited by Paul Norbury. — Tenterden (Caxton House, High St., Tenterden, Kent) : Paul Norbury Publications, 1977. — xv,192p : ill(chiefly col), facsim, ports ; 23cm.
ISBN 0-904404-16-1 : £4.75
(B77-23923)

953 — HISTORY. ARABIA
953 — Arabian civilization, to 1973. *Conference proceedings*
Seminar for Arabian Studies, *8th, Oxford, 1974.* Proceedings of the eighth Seminar for Arabian Studies, held at the Oriental Institute, Oxford on 3rd-5th July, 1974. — London (c/o Institute of Archaeology, 31 Gordon Sq., WC1H 0PY) : Seminar for Arabian Studies, 1975. — [4],79p : ill, maps ; 25cm. — (Proceedings of the Seminar for Arabian Studies ; vol.5)
Bibl.
ISBN 0-903186-05-5 Pbk : £4.00
(B77-02702)

953'.32 — Yemen (Arab Republic). Political events, ca 1900-1976
Loring, Ulick. The Yemeni monarchy / compiled by Ulick Loring ; with a genealogy compiled by Jeffrey Finestone. — London (7 Bonchurch Rd, W10 5SD) : MPA Publications for the Hamid Ed-Din Order of the Crown of Yemen, [1977]. — 39p : ill, facsim, ports ; 19cm.
Sd : Unpriced
(B77-26048)

953'.5 — Oman. Political events. Role of British mercenaries, 1957-1976. *Socialist viewpoints*
Halliday, Fred. Mercenaries : 'counter-insurgency' in the Gulf / [by] Fred Halliday. — [Revised ed.]. — Nottingham : Bertrand Russell Peace Foundation for Spokesman Books, 1977. — 80p : ill, map ; 18cm.
'... first published by the Gulf Committee, London, in May 1976' - Acknowledgements.
ISBN 0-85124-197-2 Pbk : £0.95
(B77-32339)

953'.5 — Oman, to 1976
Townsend, John. Oman : the making of a modern state / [by] John Townsend. — London : Croom Helm, 1977. — 212p ; maps ; 23cm.
Bibl.: p.191. — Index.
ISBN 0-85664-446-3 : £7.95
(B77-14495)

953'.5 — United Arab Emirates. Zayed bin Sultan al Nahiyan. *Biographies*
Morris, Claud. The desert falcon : the story of H.H. Sheikh Zayed bin Sultan al Nahiyan, President of the United Arab Emirates / by Claud Morris. — London : Outline Series of Books : [Distributed by] Hale, 1976. — x,108p, plate : maps, port ; 23cm.
Index.
ISBN 0-904604-00-4 : £3.00
(B77-19940)

953'.6'0505 — Persian Gulf countries. *Yearbooks*
The **Gulf** handbook : a guide for businessmen and visitors. — Bath : Trade and Travel Publications ; London : Middle East Economic Digest Ltd.
1976-77 / joint editors Peter Kilner, Jonathan Wallace. — 1976. — xii,556,a-d p,8p of plates : maps(some col), ports ; 18cm.
Text on lining papers. — Bibl. — Index.
ISBN 0-900751-07-x : £7.75
ISSN 0309-197x
(B77-04505)

953'.65'050924 — Bahrain. Social life. *Personal observations*
Chappell, Herbert. Arabian fantasy / [by] Herbert Chappell ; photographs by Robin Constable. — London : Quartet Books, [1976]. — 144p,[32]p of plates : ill(some col), ports(some col) ; 31cm.
ISBN 0-7043-2129-7 : £8.50
(B77-09445)

953'.67'05 — Kuwait
Shaw, Ralph. Kuwait / [by] Ralph Shaw. — London [etc.] : Macmillan, 1976. — 192p : ill(some col), col map, col ports ; 28cm.
Index.
ISBN 0-333-21247-9 : £5.75 : CIP rev.
(B77-05799)

953'.8 — Saudi Arabia, to 1976
Long, David E. Saudi Arabia / [by] David E. Long. — Beverly Hills ; London : Sage Publications [for] the Center for Strategic and International Studies, Georgetown University, 1976. — 71p : geneal tables, map ; 22cm. — (The Washington papers ; 39) (A Sage policy paper)
Bibl.: p.63-64.
ISBN 0-8039-0660-9 Pbk : £1.95
(B77-14496)

954 — HISTORY. SOUTH ASIA, INDIA
954 — Europeans. Social life. *India, to 1947. Sources of data: Monumental inscriptions*
Wilkinson, Theon. Two monsoons / [by] Theon Wilkinson ; with drawings by Bill Smith. — London : Duckworth, 1976. — xvi,240p : ill, map ; 23cm.
Bibl.: p.228-230. — Index.
ISBN 0-7156-1015-5 : £5.95
(B77-01948)

954 — Indian civilization, to 1974. *Festschriften*
The **spirit** of India : volumes presented to Shrimati Indira Gandhi by the Indira Gandhi Abhinandan Samiti. — Bombay ; London [etc.] : Asia Publishing House, 1975. — 4v. : ill(some col), facsims, ports(some col) ; 30cm.
English, Hindi and Urdu text. — Includes a selection of the speeches and writings of Indira Gandhi.
Unpriced
(B77-34339)

954 — Military operations by European mercenaries. *North-western India, 1784-1803. Early works*
Compton, Herbert. A particular account of the European military adventures of Hindustan, from 1784 to 1803 / by Herbert Compton. — [1st ed.] reprinted ; with an introduction by John Pemble. — Karachi ; London [etc.] : Oxford University Press, 1976. — xvi,419p,[8] leaves of plates(1 fold) : ill, map, ports ; 23cm. — (Oxford in Asia historical reprints from Pakistan)
Facsimile reprint of: 1st ed. London : T. Fisher Unwin, 1892.
ISBN 0-19-577227-x : £12.50
(B77-27615)

954.02'9'0924 — India. Clive, Robert, Baron Clive, 1742-1774. *Biographies*
Edwardes, Michael. Clive, the Heaven-born general / [by] Michael Edwardes. — London : Hart-Davis MacGibbon, 1977. — ix,211p : ill, facsims, maps, plans, ports ; 24cm.
Bibl.: p.205. — Index.
ISBN 0-246-10623-9 : £5.95
(B77-10695)

954.03'17 — Indian Mutiny
Wilkinson-Latham, Christopher. The Indian Mutiny / text by Christopher Wilkinson-Latham ; colour plates by G.A. Embleton. — London : Osprey Publishing, 1977. — 40p,[8]p of plates : ill(some col), maps, ports ; 25cm. — (Men-at-arms series)
Text accompanying plates in English, French and German.
ISBN 0-85045-259-7 Pbk : £1.95
(B77-25329)

954.03'17 — Indian Mutiny. *Secondary school texts*
Rawding, Frederick William. The rebellion in India, 1857 / [by] F.W. Rawding. — Cambridge [etc.] : Cambridge University Press, 1977. — 48p : ill, maps, plans, ports ; 21x22cm. — (Cambridge introduction to the history of mankind : topic book)
ISBN 0-521-20683-9 Sd : £1.10
(B77-23035)

954.03'17 — Indian Mutiny. Siege of Delhi
Llewellyn, Alexander. The siege of Delhi / [by] Alexander Llewellyn. — London : Macdonald and Jane's, 1977. — vi,182p,[12]p of plates : ill, 2 maps, ports ; 23cm.
Bibl.: p.173-176. — Index.
ISBN 0-354-04092-8 : £5.95
(B77-25330)

954.03'5'0222 — India. Social life, 1857-1911. *Illustrations*
The **last** empire : photography in British India, 1855-1911 / preface by the Earl Mountbatten of Burma ; with texts by Clark Worswick and Ainslie Embree. — London : Gordon Fraser Gallery, 1976. — [7],149,[1]p : chiefly ill, ports ; 25x30cm.
'... accompanies an exhibition organized by the Asia House Gallery of the Asia Society for the summer of 1976' - title page verso. — Bibl.: p.148-149.
ISBN 0-900406-74-7 : £5.95
(B77-23924)

954.03'5'0222 — India. Social life, 1877-1947. *Illustrations*
Raj : a scrapbook of British India, 1877-1947 / [compiled by] Charles Allen. — London : Deutsch, 1977. — 142p : chiefly ill, facsims, ports ; 26cm.
Facsims. on lining papers.
ISBN 0-233-96921-7 : £5.95
(B77-33546)

954.03'5'0924 — India. Gandhi, Mohandas Karamchand, Mahatma. *Biographies*
Mehta, Ved. Mahatma Gandhi and his apostles / [by] Ved Mehta. — London : Deutsch, 1977. — xi,260p ; 25cm.
Also published: New York : Viking Press, 1977. — Index.
ISBN 0-233-96854-7 : £4.50
(B77-28316)

954.03'5'0924 — India. Gandhi, Mohandas Karamchand, Mahatma, 1928-1934
Brown, Judith Margaret. Gandhi and civil disobedience : the Mahatma in Indian politics, 1928-34 / [by] Judith M. Brown. — Cambridge [etc.] : Cambridge University Press, 1977. — xix,414p : 1 ill, port ; 23cm.
Bibl.: p.398-403. — Index.
ISBN 0-521-21279-0 : £15.50
(B77-11503)

954.03'5'0924 — India (Republic). Gayatri Devi, Maharani of Jaipur. *Autobiographies*
Gayatri Devi, *Maharani of Jaipur.* A princess remembers : the memoirs of the Maharani of Jaipur / by Gayatri Devi of Jaipur and Santha Rama Rau. — London : Weidenfeld and Nicolson, 1976. — 335p : ill, coat of arms(on lining papers), ports ; 24cm.
Index.
ISBN 0-297-77098-5 : £5.95
(B77-08702)

954.03'5'0924 — India (Republic). Mishra, D P. *Autobiographies*
Mishra, D P. Living an era / [by] D.P. Mishra. — Delhi [etc.] : Vikas ; Hemel Hempstead (66 Wood Lane End, Hemel Hempstead, Herts.) : [Distributed by] International Book Distributors.
Vol.1 : India's march to freedom. — 1975. — ix,625p : facsims ; 22cm.
Bibl.: p.599-602. — Index.
ISBN 0-7069-0355-2 : Unpriced
(B77-29848)

954.04 — India. Political events, 1947-1948
Collins, Larry. Freedom at midnight / [by] Larry Collins and Dominique Lapierre. — London : Pan Books, 1977. — vii,596p,[16]p of plates : ill, ports ; 18cm.
Originally published: London : Collins, 1975. — Bibl.: p.565-575. — Index.
ISBN 0-330-25145-7 Pbk : £1.50
(B77-24635)

954.04'092'4 — India (Republic). Nehru, Jawaharlal. *Biographies*
Pandey, Bishwa Nath. Nehru / [by] B.N. Pandey. — London [etc.] : Macmillan, 1976. — 499p,[8]p of plates : ill, 2 maps, ports ; 23cm.
Bibl.: p.464-470. — Index.
ISBN 0-333-10641-5 : £6.95
(B77-01949)

954.04'092'4 — South Asia. Stephens, Ian. *Autobiographies*
Stephens, Ian. Unmade journey / [by] Ian Stephens. — London : Stacey International : Distributed by Barrie and Jenkins, 1977. — xv, 448p,[16]p of plates : ill, ports ; 24cm.
Index.
ISBN 0-9503304-6-9 : £7.50
(B77-27616)

954.05 — India (Republic). Political events, 1975-1976
Selbourne, David. An eye to India : the unmasking of a tyranny / [by] David Selbourne. — Harmondsworth [etc.] : Penguin, 1977. — xiii,561p ; 19cm. — (A pelican original)
Bibl.: p.517-521. — Index.
ISBN 0-14-022026-7 Pbk : £1.50
(B77-29096)

954.05 — India (Republic). Political events, 1975-1977
Sinha, Sachchidanand. Emergency in perspective : reprieve and challenge / [by] Sachchidanand Sinha. — London (69 Great Russell St., WC1B 3BQ) : Books from India Ltd, 1977. — ix,122p ; 22cm.
Index.
£3.75
(B77-32999)

954.05 — India (Republic). Social life
Nentin, Maxine. Life in India / [by] Maxine Nentin, Manja Kaushalam, Balraj Khanna. — London : Commonwealth Institute, [1976]. — [3],15p : ill, map ; 30cm. — (Commonwealth topic ; no.12 ISSN 0306-3828)
Contents: Maharashtra / by Maxine Nentin - Uttar Pradesh / by Manja Kaushalam - Punjab / by Balraj Khanna.
Sd : £0.12
(B77-10076)

954.05'092'4 — India (Republic). Social life. *Personal observations*
Naipaul, Vidiadhar Surajprasad. India : a wounded civilization / [by] V.S. Naipaul. — London : Deutsch, 1977. — 174p ; 23cm.
ISBN 0-233-96936-5 : £3.95
(B77-29097)

954'.2 — India (Republic). Oudh, 1801-1859
Pemble, John. The Raj, the Indian Mutiny and the Kingdom of Oudh, 1801-1859 / [by] John Pemble. — Hassocks : Harvester Press, 1977. — xi,303p,[4]p of plates : ill, geneal table, maps, ports ; 23cm.
Bibl.: p.285-293. — Index.
ISBN 0-85527-109-4 : £10.95 : CIP rev.
(B77-07000)

954'.5 — India. Punjab, to 1845. *Early works*
Steinbach, Henry. The Punjaub : being a brief account of the country of the Sikhs / by Henry Steinbach. — [2nd ed. reprinted] ; with an introduction by W.H. McLeod. — Karachi ; London [etc.] : Oxford University Press, 1976. — xli,183p,fold leaf of plate : col map ; 19cm. — (Oxford in Asia historical reprints from Pakistan)
Facsimile reprint of: 2nd ed. London : Smith Elder and Co., 1846.
ISBN 0-19-577200-8 : £8.25
(B77-28317)

954'.6 — Kashmir culture: Ladakh district culture, to 1976
Snellgrove, David Llewellyn. The cultural heritage of Ladakh / [by] David L. Snellgrove and Tadeusz Skorupski. — Warminster : Aris and Phillips.
In 2 vols.
Vol.1 : Central Ladakh. — 1977. — xvi,144p, [5]leaves of plates,[8]p of plates : ill(some col), map(on lining papers), plan, ports ; 31cm.
1 col. ill. tipped in. — Bibl.: p.143. — Index.
ISBN 0-85668-058-3 : £12.50
(B77-25331)

954.8'02 — Southern India, to ca 1650
Nilakanta Sastri, Kallidaikurichi Aiyah. A history of South India from prehistoric times to the fall of Vijayanagar / [by] K.A. Nilakanta Sastri. — 4th ed. — Madras ; Oxford [etc.] : Oxford University Press, 1976. — xii,521p,leaf of plate,xx p of plates : ill(incl 2 col), geneal tables, maps ; 22cm.
Previous ed.: 1967. — Bibl. — Index.
ISBN 0-19-560686-8 Pbk : £5.25
(B77-02703)

954.91 — HISTORY. PAKISTAN
954.9'1 — Pakistan, to 1974
Kureishi, Rafiushan. The new Pakistan / [by] Rafiushan Kureishi. — London : Bell, 1977. — [6],146p : ill, port ; 22cm.
Index.
ISBN 0-7135-1996-7 Pbk : £3.25
(B77-23925)

954.9'1 — Pakistan, to 1976
Pakistan, past & present : a comprehensive study published in commemoration of the centenary of the birth of the founder of Pakistan / [editors Hamid Jalal et al.]. — London ([128 Kensington Church St., W8 4BH]) : Stacey International, [1977]. — 288p : ill(some col), facsims, geneal table, maps(chiefly col), ports(some col) ; 31cm.
Bibl.: p.283-284. — Index.
ISBN 0-9503304-9-3 : £18.00
(B77-32340)

954.9'1'0049159 — Pathans. *Pakistan, to 1957*
Caroe, *Sir* Olaf. The Pathans, 550 BC-AD 1957 / by Olaf Caroe. — Karachi ; London [etc.] : Oxford University Press, 1976 [i.e. 1977]. — xxii,521p,[16]leaves of plates(4 fold) : ill, maps(1 col), geneal tables, ports ; 23cm. — ([Oxford in Asia historical reprints from Pakistan])
Published in Pakistan: 1976. — Originally published: London : Macmillan, 1958. — Index.

ISBN 0-19-577221-0 : £16.50
Also classified at 958.1'004'9159
(B77-09446)

954.9'105 — Pakistan. Social life. *Juvenile literature*
Caldwell, John Cope. Let's visit Pakistan / [by] John C. Caldwell. — 2nd revised ed. — London [etc.] : Burke, 1974. — 96p : ill(some col), 2 col maps ; 21cm.
Previous ed.: i.e. 1st ed. 1966. — Index.
ISBN 0-222-00317-0 : £1.95
ISBN 0-222-00315-4 Library ed. : £1.95
(B77-29849)

954.9'18 — Pakistan. Sind, to ca 1930
Lambrick, Hugh Trevor. Sind : a general introduction / by H.T. Lambrick. — 2nd ed. — Hyderabad Sind : Sindhi Adabi Board ; Karachi ; London [etc.] : [Distributed by] Oxford University Press, 1975. — iii-xix,274p, [4]p of plates,[19]leaves of plates(15 fold) : ill, maps ; 23cm. — (History of Sind series ; vol.1)
Limited ed. of 1000 copies. — Previous ed.: Hyderabad: Sindhi Adabi Board, 1964. — Index.
ISBN 0-19-577220-2 : £6.25
(B77-10077)

954.92 — HISTORY. BANGLADESH
954.9'205 — Bangladesh. Political events. Role of foreign countries, 1975
Razzak, Abdur. Foreign powers & Bangladesh / [by] Abdur Razzak. — London (25 Balvernie Grove, SW18 5RR) : Bangladesh Krisak Sramik Awami League, UK Action Committee, 1977. — 7p : port ; 21cm. — (Bangladesh Krisak Sramik Awami League. BAKSAL pamphlets ; no.1 ISSN 0309-5142)
ISBN 0-9505703-0-3 Sd : £0.05
(B77-16687)

954.9'205'05 — Bangladesh. Political events. *Periodicals*
Bangladesh : current events. — Edgware (c/o 56 Methuen Rd, Edgware, Middx) : 'Banglar dak'.

[No.1]- ; July 1976-. — 1976-. — 30cm.
Monthly. — Sheet ([2])p. as 1st issue.
Unpriced
(B77-02704)

954.9'205'0924 — Bangladesh. Political events. Role of Mujib ur-Rahm̄an, Sheikh, 1971-1975. *Bengali texts*
Akht̄ar, M R. Mujiber rakta t̄al / M.R. Akhtar. — London (8 Plymton Ave., N.W.6) : The author, [1976]. — [64]p : ports ; 21cm.
In Bengali. — Transliterated title-page transcription.
ISBN 0-9505447-0-1 Sd : £1.00
(B77-04506)

954.93 — HISTORY. SRI LANKA
954.9'303 — Sri Lanka
Sri Lanka : a survey / K.M. de Silva, editor. — London : C. Hurst [for] the Institute of Asian Affairs, Hamburg, 1977. — xvi,496p : maps ; 23cm.
Bibl. — Index.
ISBN 0-903983-45-1 : £12.00 : CIP rev.
(B77-23036)

955 — HISTORY. IRAN
955 — Iran, to 1975
Wilber, Donald Newton. Iran, past and present / by Donald N. Wilber. — 8th ed. — Princeton ; Guildford : Princeton University Press, 1976. — ix,369p,[12]p of plates : ill, ports ; 23cm.
Previous ed.: 1975. — Bibl.: p.349-354. — Index.
ISBN 0-691-03108-8 : £14.10
ISBN 0-691-00021-2 Pbk : £3.95
(B77-07752)

955'.05 — Iran, 1900-1976
Twentieth century Iran / selected by Hossein Amirsadeghi ; assisted by R.W. Ferrier ; introduction by Sir Denis Wright. — London : Heinemann, 1977. — xv,299p,[8]p of plates : ill, maps, port ; 25cm.
Index.
ISBN 0-434-01984-4 : £7.50
(B77-21639)

955'.05 — Iran, 1975
Iran Financial and Commercial Service. Iran in perspective, 1975 : a report / by Iran Financial and Commercial Service. — Reading (8 Queen Victoria St., Reading RG1 1TG) : Paul R. Walter and Associates Inc., 1976. — [4],81 leaves : map ; 28cm.
Bibl.: p.80-81.
Sp : £7.00
(B77-29850)

955'.05 — Iran. Social life. *Juvenile literature*
Lyle, Garry. Let's visit Iran / [by] Garry Lyle. — London : Burke, 1977. — 96p : ill(some col), col map ; 21cm.
Index.
ISBN 0-222-00648-x : £1.35
ISBN 0-222-00647-1 Library ed. : £1.95
(B77-30894)

955'.05'0924 — Iran. Mohammed Reza Pahlavi, Shah of Iran. *Biographies*
Laing, Margaret. The Shah / [by] Margaret Laing. — London : Sidgwick and Jackson, 1977. — 263p,leaf of plate,[10]p of plates : ill, ports ; 24cm.
Bibl.: p.233. — Index.
ISBN 0-283-98336-1 : £6.95
(B77-11011)

Villiers, Gérard de. The imperial Shah : an informal biography / [by] Gérard de Villiers with Bernard Touchais and Annick de Villiers ; translated from the French by June P. Wilson and Walter B. Michaels. — English language ed. / [with additional material by June P. Wilson]. — London : Weidenfeld and Nicolson, 1976. — ix,305p : ill, ports ; 23cm.
This ed. also published: Boston, Mass. : Little, Brown, 1976. — Translation and revision of: 'L'Irréstible ascension de Mohammad Reza Shah d'Iran'. Paris : Plon, 1975.
ISBN 0-297-77263-5 : £6.00
(B77-10078)

955'.05'0924 — Iran. Mohammed Reza Pahlavi, Shah of Iran. *Transcripts of interviews*
Karanjia, R K. The mind of a monarch / [by] R.K. Karanjia. — London : Allen and Unwin, 1977. — 3-265p,[2]leaves of plates : ports(1 col) ; 24cm.
Transcriptions of interviews between the Shah of Iran and R.K. Karanjia.
ISBN 0-04-923069-7 : £6.95
(B77-23926)

956 — HISTORY. MIDDLE EAST
956 — Arab countries. Conflict with Israel, 1900-1976. *Secondary school texts*
Schools Council History 13-16 Project. Arab-Israeli conflict / Schools Council History 13-16 Project ; [team David Sylvester et al.]. — Edinburgh : Holmes-McDougall. — (Modern world studies)
[Student's book]. — 1977. — 96p : ill, col maps, ports ; 25cm.
ISBN 0-7157-1556-9 Pbk : £2.05
(B77-19941)

Teachers' guide. — 1977. — 15p ; 21cm.
ISBN 0-7157-1641-7 Sd : £0.75
(B77-19942)

956 — Middle East, 1900-1973. *Secondary school texts*
Africa and the Middle East / editor John Robottom. — London : Longman.
Workcards / [by] Tom Allan. — 1977. — 1v. ; 23cm. — (Making the modern world)
One card, 3 copies each of 5 cards ([12] sides) in plastic envelope.
ISBN 0-582-22085-8 : £0.95
Primary classification 960
(B77-19143)

956 — Middle East, 570-1974
Bacharach, Jere L. A Near East studies handbook / by Jere L. Bacharach. — Revised ed. — Seattle ; London : University of Washington Press, 1976. — xiii,158p : 1 ill, geneal tables, maps ; 28cm.
Previous ed.: 1974. — Bibl.: p.6-8. — Index.
ISBN 0-295-95514-7 : Unpriced
ISBN 0-295-95551-1 Pbk : Unpriced
(B77-30895)

956'.007 — Middle Eastern studies. *Reviews of research*
The **study** of the Middle East : research and scholarship in the humanities and the social sciences : a project of the Research and Training Committee of the Middle East Studies Association / edited by Leonard Binder. — New York ; London [etc.] : Wiley, [1977]. — vii,648p ; 24cm.
'A Wiley-Interscience publication'. — Published in the United States: 1976. — Bibl. — Index.
ISBN 0-471-07304-0 : £18.60
(B77-12800)

956'.04 — Arab-Israeli War, to 1976. *Christian viewpoints*
British Council of Churches. *Division of International Affairs.* Some reflections on the Arab-Israeli conflict : study paper / prepared by the Division of International Affairs of the British Council of Churches and the Conference of British Missionary Societies. — London : British Council of Churches, 1976. — [1],16p ; 21cm.
ISBN 0-85169-053-x Sd : £0.15
(B77-13447)

956'.04 — Middle East. Political events, 1967-1976. *Fabian viewpoints*
Klug, Tony. Middle East impasse : the only way out / [by] Tony Klug. — London : Fabian Society, 1977. — [2],38,[1]p : 2 maps(1 col) ; 22cm. — (Fabian research series ; 330 ISSN 0305-3555)
ISBN 0-7163-1330-8 Sd : £0.75
(B77-12243)

956'.04'05 — Books on Middle East. *Reviews. Periodicals*
Gazelle review of literature on the Middle East. — London : Ithaca Press.
No.1-. — 1976-. — 22cm.
Two issues a year. — [2],77p. in issue no.1. — Index.
Pbk : £1.80
ISSN 0308-7999
(B77-12244)

956'.04'05 — Middle East. Political events. *Extracts from newspapers. Periodicals*
Quote : what papers say about the Middle East. — London (1 Endsleigh St., WC1H 0DS) : Union of Jewish Students.
Vol.1, no.1- ; [Dec. 1975?]-. — [1975?]-. — ill, maps, ports ; 42cm.
Fortnightly. — Folder ([4]p.) as 1st issue. — Facsimile reprints.
Sd : Unpriced
ISSN 0140-363x
(B77-34340)

956'.04'05 — Middle East. Political events. *Periodicals*
Events : newsmagazine on the Middle East. — Beirut ; London (67 Southampton Row, WC1B 4ET) : Al-Hawadess.
No.1- ; Oct. 1st 1976-. — 1976-. — ill, ports ; 28cm.
Fortnightly. — 62p. in 1st issue.
Sd : £0.40
(B77-21640)

956'.046'0924 — Arab-Israeli War, 1967. Israeli military forces. Casualties. *Personal observations*
Haelyon, Yaacov. A doll's leg : the story of a war injury / [by] Yaacov Haelyon ; [translated from the Hebrew by Louis Williams]. — London : Dobson, 1975. — 221p ; 22cm.
This translation originally published: Cape Town : Malherbe, 1974. — Translation of: 'Regal shel bubah'. Tel Aviv : Am Oved Publishers, 1973.
ISBN 0-234-77527-0 : £3.95
(B77-20847)

956.1 — Turkey, to 1975
Shaw, Stanford Jay. History of the Ottoman Empire and modern Turkey / [by] Stanford Shaw [and Ezel Kural Shaw]. — Cambridge [etc.] : Cambridge University Press.
In 2 vols.
Vol.1 : Empire of the Gazis : the rise and decline of the Ottoman Empire, 1280-1808 / [by Stanford Shaw]. — 1976 [i.e. 1977]. — xv, 351p : 2 maps, plan ; 24cm.
Published in the United States: 1976. — Bibl.: p.ix-xii. — Index.
ISBN 0-521-21280-4 : £12.50
ISBN 0-521-29163-1 Pbk : £4.95
Also classified at 949.6
(B77-10696)

956.4'504 — Cyprus. Political events, 1959-1976
Vanezis, Procopios Nichola. Cyprus : the unfinished agony / [by] P.N. Vanezis. — London : Abelard-Schuman, 1977. — x,141p,[4] p of plates : ill, maps, ports ; 23cm.
Bibl.: p.112-115.
ISBN 0-200-72525-4 : £3.95
(B77-14497)

956.7'04 — Iraq. Policies of British government, 1914-1932
Sluglett, Peter. Britain in Iraq, 1914-1932 / [by] Peter Sluglett. — London : Ithaca Press for the Middle East Centre, St Antony's College, Oxford, 1976. — [13],360p : 2 maps ; 23cm. — (St Antony's College. Middle East Centre. Monographs ; no.4)
Bibl.: p.332-347. — Index.
ISBN 0-903729-16-4 : £6.50
(B77-01950)

956.7'4'03 — Ottoman Empire. Mesopotamia. Policies of British government, 1903-1914
Cohen, Stuart A. British policy in Mesopotamia, 1903-1914 / [by] Stuart A. Cohen. — London : Ithaca Press for the Middle East Centre, St Antony's College, Oxford, 1976. — [6],vii, 361p : 2 maps ; 23cm. — (St Antony's College. Middle East Centre. Monographs ; no.5)
Bibl.: p.323-346. — Index.
ISBN 0-903729-17-2 : £6.50
(B77-12245)

956.92'04 — Lebanon. Political events, 1975-1976
Bulloch, John. Death of a country : the Civil War in Lebanon / [by] John Bulloch. — London : Weidenfeld and Nicolson, 1977. — [6],202p,[8]p of plates : ill, maps, ports ; 23cm.
Index.
ISBN 0-297-77288-0 : £4.95
(B77-18494)

Kelidar, Abbas. Lebanon : the collapse of a state : regional dimensions of the struggle / by Abbas Kelidar and Michael Burrell ; [maps by Richard Natkiel]. — London : Institute for the Study of Conflict, 1976. — [2],19p : 2 maps ; 30cm. — (Conflict studies ; no.74 ISSN 0069-8792)
Bibl.: p.19.
ISBN 0-903366-50-9 Sd : £2.00
(B77-00555)

956.94 — Israel, ca 1850-1975
Sachar, Howard Morley. A history of Israel from the rise of Zionism to our time / [by] Howard M. Sachar. — Oxford : Blackwell, 1977. — [1], xix,883,xlix,[1]p : maps ; 25cm.
Originally published: New York : Knopf, 1976. — Bibl.: p.839-883. — Index.
ISBN 0-631-17870-8 : £14.00
(B77-19141)

956.94'001 — Zionism. Attitudes of Arabs, 1881-1914
Mandel, Neville J. The Arabs and Zionism before World War I / by Neville J. Mandel. — Berkeley [etc.] ; London : University of California Press, 1976. — xxiv,258p : facsim, 2 maps ; 25cm.
Bibl.: p.239-248. — Index.
ISBN 0-520-02466-4 : £10.50
(B77-31641)

956.94'001'0924 — Zionism. Weizmann, Chaim. *Biographies*
Litvinoff, Barnet. Weizmann : last of the patriarchs / by Barnet Litvinoff. — London [etc.] : Hodder and Stoughton, 1976. — 288p, [16]p of plates : ill, maps, ports ; 24cm.
Bibl.: p.269-270. — Index.
ISBN 0-340-20020-0 : £5.95
(B77-15639)

956.94'004'924 — Jewish settlements. Policies of German government. Influence of Zionist movements. *Palestine, 1897-1918*
Friedman, Isaiah. Germany, Turkey and Zionism, 1897-1918 / [by] Isaiah Friedman. — Oxford : Clarendon Press, 1977. — xv,461p ; 23cm.
Bibl.: p.429-451. — Index.
ISBN 0-19-822528-8 : £14.00 : CIP rev.
(B77-09447)

956.94'02 — Israel. Political events, 132-135
Applebaum, Shimon. Prolegomena to the study of the Second Jewish Revolt (AD 132-135) / [by] Shimon Applebaum. — Oxford : British Archaeological Reports, 1976. — [8],100p : 2 maps ; 30cm. — (British archaeological reports : supplementary series ; 7)
Bibl.: p.[7]-[8].
ISBN 0-904531-39-2 Sd : £1.95
(B77-00556)

956.94'04 — Israel. Political events, 1947-1948
Cameron, James. The making of Israel / [by] James Cameron. — London : Secker and Warburg, 1976. — [9],104p,plate : ill, map, ports ; 24cm.
Index.
ISBN 0-436-08230-6 : £3.90
(B77-02705)

956.94'05 — Israel. Social life
Zohar, Danah. Israel, the land and its people / [by] Danah Zohar. — London : Macdonald Educational, 1977. — 3-62p : ill(chiefly col), facsim, col maps, ports ; 29cm. — (Macdonald countries ; 19)
Col. ill. and col. maps on lining papers. — Index.
ISBN 0-356-05454-3 : £2.25
(B77-33547)

956.94'05'0924 — Israel. Rabin, Yitzhak. *Biographies*
Slater, Robert. Rabin of Israel : a biography / [by] Robert Slater. — London : Robson, 1977. — 304p,[8]p of plates : maps, ports ; 23cm.
Index.
ISBN 0-903895-90-0 : £6.50 : CIP rev.
(B77-23927)

956.94'4'050924 — Israel. Jerusalem. Social life. *Personal observations*
Bellow, Saul. To Jerusalem and back : a personal account / [by] Saul Bellow. — London : Alison Press : Secker and Warburg, 1976. — [4],182p ; 23cm.
Also published: New York : Viking Press, 1976.

ISBN 0-436-03951-6 : £3.90
(B77-05800)

957 — HISTORY. ASIATIC SOVIET UNION, SIBERIA
957'.3 — Prehistoric antiquities. *Russia (RSFSR). Ob region*
Chernetsov, Valeriĭ Nikolaevich. Prehistory of Western Siberia / [by] V.N. Chernetsov and W. Moszyńska ; edited by Henry N. Michael ; [translated from the Russian by David Kraus et al.]. — Montreal ; London : McGill-Queen's University Press [for the] Arctic Institute of North America, 1974. — xxvii,377p,[2]fold leaves of plates : ill, maps, plans ; 26cm. — (Anthropology of the north : translations from Russian sources ; no.9)
Index.
ISBN 0-7735-9074-9 : Unpriced
(B77-17841)

958 — HISTORY. CENTRAL ASIA
958.1'004'9159 — Pathans. *Afghanistan, to 1957*
Caroe, *Sir* **Olaf.** The Pathans, 550 BC-AD 1957 / by Olaf Caroe. — Karachi ; London [etc.] : Oxford University Press, 1976 [i.e. 1977]. — xxii,521p,[16]leaves of plates(4 fold) : ill, maps(1 col), geneal tables, ports ; 23cm. — ([Oxford in Asia historical reprints from Pakistan])
Published in Pakistan: 1976. — Originally published: London : Macmillan, 1958. — Index.

ISBN 0-19-577221-0 : £16.50
Primary classification 954.9'1'0049159
(B77-09446)

959 — HISTORY. SOUTH-EAST ASIA
959'.004'992 — Malays, Filipinos & Javanese. Attitudes of colonialists. *South-east Asia, ca 1600-ca 1945*
Alatas, Syed Hussein. The myth of the lazy native : a study of the image of the Malays, Filipinos and Javanese from the 16th to the 20th century and its function in the ideology of colonial capitalism / [by] Syed Hussein Alatas. — London : Cass, 1977. — vii,267p ; 23cm.
Bibl.: p.243-255. — Index.
ISBN 0-7146-3050-0 : £9.50
(B77-12246)

959.3 — HISTORY. THAILAND
959.3'02 — Thailand, 1300-1500
Charnvit Kasetsiri. The rise of Ayudhya : a history of Siam in the fourteenth and fifteenth centuries / [by] Charnvit Kasetsiri. — Kuala Lumpur ; London [etc.] : Oxford University Press, 1976 [i.e. 1977]. — xii,194p : map ; 23cm. — (East Asian historical monographs) (Oxford in Asia)
Published in Malaysia: 1976. — Bibl.: p.163-183. — Index.
ISBN 0-19-580313-2 : £14.25
(B77-12247)

959.3'03 — Thailand, ca 1850-1976
Caldwell, Malcolm. Thailand : towards the revolution / [by] Malcolm Caldwell. — London (Basement, 103 Gower St., WC1E 7HP) : Ad Hoc Group for Democracy in Thailand ; London : Institute of Race Relations, 1976. — [2],27,[1]p ; 21cm.
'... reproduced from "Race & Class", Vol.xviii, no.2, Autumn 1976' - title page verso.
ISBN 0-85001-017-9 Sd : £0.30
(B77-08703)

959.3'03'0924 — Thailand. Leonowens, Anna. *Biographies*
Landon, Margaret. Anna and the King of Siam / [by] Margaret Landon ; illustrated by Margaret Ayer. — Bath : Chivers, 1977. — 402p : ill, map ; 23cm.
Originally published: New York : Day, 1944 ; London : Harrap, 1945. — Based on the life of Anna Leonowens.
£5.20(£3.90 to members of the Library Association)
ISBN 0-85594-841-8
(B77-20848)

959.5 — HISTORY. MALAYSIA
959.5 — Malaysia & Singapore, to 1974
Ryan, Neil Joseph. A history of Malaysia and Singapore / [by] N.J. Ryan. — [5th ed.]. — Kuala Lumpur ; London [etc.] : Oxford University Press, 1976 [i.e. 1977]. — xiv,322p, [16]p of plates : ill, facsim, maps, ports ; 23cm.
Map on lining papers. — This ed. published in Malaysia: 1976. — Previous ed.: i.e. 4th ed. published as 'The making of modern Malaysia'. 1969. — Bibl.: p.306-310. — Index.
ISBN 0-19-580302-7 : £16.00
(B77-12248)

959.5'04'0924 — Malaysia & Singapore. Political events, 1941-1977. *Personal observations*
Thio Chan Bee. Extraordinary adventures of an ordinary man / [by] Thio Chan Bee. — London : Grosvenor Books, 1977. — iii-xiv, 125p : facsims ; 19cm. — (A Grosvenor biography)
ISBN 0-901269-28-x : Unpriced
ISBN 0-901269-27-1 Pbk : £1.25
(B77-26721)

959.5'05'0924 — Malaysia. Razak, Tun Abdul. *Biographies*
Shaw, William. Tun Razak : his life and times / [by] William Shaw. — London [etc.] : Longman, 1976. — [9],267p,16p of plates : ill, maps, ports ; 25cm.
Map on lining papers. — Bibl.: p.258-261. — Index.
ISBN 0-582-72414-7 : £5.95
(B77-26722)

959.5'1 — West Malaysia. Political events, 1874-1957
Malaya : the making of a neo-colony / edited by Mohamed Amin and Malcolm Caldwell. — Nottingham : Bertrand Russell Peace Foundation for Spokesman Books, 1977. — 265p ; 23cm.
ISBN 0-85124-189-1 : £7.50
ISBN 0-85124-190-5 Pbk : Unpriced
(B77-29098)

959.5'1'00421 — Britons. *West Malaysia, 1874-1903. Case studies*
Barr, Pat. Taming the jungle : the men who made British Malaya / [by] Pat Barr. — London : Secker and Warburg, 1977. — ix, 172p,[16]p of plates : ill, map, ports ; 23cm.
Bibl.: p.163-165. — Index.
ISBN 0-436-03365-8 : £4.90
(B77-32341)

959.5'2'05 — Singapore. Social life. *For Australian students & for New Zealand students*
Kennedy, Brian. Singapore : the lion city / [by] Brian Kennedy. — Sydney [etc.] ; London : Reed Education, 1976. — 24,[1]p : ill, coat of arms, facsim, 2 maps ; 25cm. — (Pageant of the Pacific : pageant of Asia ; 4)
Index.
ISBN 0-589-09186-7 Sd : £1.30
(B77-18495)

959.7 — HISTORY. VIETNAM
959.7 — Vietnam. Hanoi. Social life, 1974. *Diaries*
Raj, Kakkadan Nandanath. Hanoi diary / [by] K.N. Raj. — Bombay ; Oxford [etc.] : Oxford University Press, [1976]. — 60p ; 22cm.
Published in India: 1975. — Originally published: in serial form in 'Economic and political weekly'.
ISBN 0-19-560676-0 Sd : Unpriced
(B77-09448)

959.704 — Vietnam. Political events. Role of United States government, 1945-1975
Buttinger, Joseph. Vietnam : the unforgettable tragedy / [by] Joseph Buttinger. — London : Deutsch, 1977. — 191p : facsim, ports ; 25cm.
Also published: New York : Horizon Press, 1977. — Bibl.: p.181-185. — Index.
ISBN 0-233-96883-0 : £4.95
Also classified at 959.704'1
(B77-24636)

959.704 — Vietnamese wars, 1940-1975
Warner, Denis. Not with guns alone / [by] Denis Warner. — London : Hutchinson, 1977. — xv, 286p,[16]p of plates : ill, maps, plans, ports ; 22cm.
ISBN 0-09-130320-6 : £5.95
(B77-34342)

959.704'1 — Vietnam. Political events. Role of French government, 1945-1954
Buttinger, Joseph. Vietnam : the unforgettable tragedy / [by] Joseph Buttinger. — London : Deutsch, 1977. — 191p : facsim, ports ; 25cm.
Also published: New York : Horizon Press, 1977. — Bibl.: p.181-185. — Index.
ISBN 0-233-96883-0 : £4.95
Primary classification 959.704
(B77-24636)

959.704'3 — Vietnamese wars, 1954-1975. *Conference proceedings*
The **lessons** of Vietnam / edited by W. Scott Thompson & Donaldson D. Frizzell. — London : Macdonald and Jane's, 1977. — [7], xiii,288p,plate : maps ; 24cm.
Papers and discussions from a colloquium on 'The Military Lessons of the Vietnamese War' held at the Fletcher School of Law and Diplomacy in 1973-74 and a conference held in Cambridge and Medford, Mass., in May 1974. — Index.
ISBN 0-354-01092-1 : £10.50
(B77-19142)

959.704'32 — Vietnamese wars. Policies of United States government, 1963-1975
Brown, Weldon Amzy. The last chopper : the denouement of the American role in Vietnam, 1963-1975 / by Weldon A. Brown. — Port Washington ; London : Kennikat Press, 1976. — x,371p ; 24cm. — (National university publications)
Bibl.: p.355-359. — Index.
ISBN 0-8046-9121-5 : Unpriced
(B77-23037)

959.704'32 — Vietnamese wars. Policies of United States government. Influence of electorate, 1960-1975
Andrews, Bruce. Public constraint and American policy in Vietnam / [by] Bruce Andrews. — Beverly Hills ; London : Sage Publications, 1976. — 64p ; 22cm. — (Sage professional papers in international studies ; vol.4, no.02-042)
Bibl.: p.60-64.
ISBN 0-8039-0621-8 Pbk : £1.75
(B77-15048)

959.704'34 — American prisoners of war. Attempted rescue by United States. Army. *North Vietnam. Son Tay*
Schemmer, Benjamin F. The raid / [by] Benjamin F. Schemmer. — London : Macdonald and Jane's, 1977. — x,326p,[8]p of plates : ill, maps, ports ; 23cm.
Originally published: New York : Harper and Row, 1976. — Bibl.: p.315-318. — Index.
ISBN 0-354-01122-7 : £4.95
(B77-23928)

959.704'34 — Vietnamese Wars. Military operations by Communist military forces, 1975
Burchett, Wilfred Graham. Grasshoppers & elephants : why Viet Nam fell / by Wilfred Burchett. — New York : Urizen Books ; London : [Distributed by] Pluto Press, 1977. — [8],265p : maps ; 22cm.
ISBN 0-916354-65-2 : £7.50
ISBN 0-916354-66-0 Pbk : £2.95
(B77-29851)

959.704'342 — Vietnamese wars. My Lai massacre
United States. *Department of the Army.* The My Lai massacre and its cover-up : beyond the reach of law? : the Peers Commission [sic] report / with a supplement and introductory essay on the limits of law [by] Joseph Goldstein, Burke Marshall, Jack Schwartz. — New York : Free Press ; London : Collier Macmillan, 1976. — xiii,586p : facsims, maps, plans ; 18cm.
Chairman: William R. Peers. — 'Consists of ... "Report of the Department of the Army review of the preliminary investigations into the My Lai incident Vol.1 : The report of the investigation". [Washington, D.C. : The Department, 1974] ... includes texts of documents from World War II and Nuremberg and from the Vietnam War'.
ISBN 0-02-912240-6 Pbk : £2.25
(B77-14498)

959.704'38 — Vietnamese Wars. Military operations by United States. Marine Corps, 1965-1966. *Personal observations*
Caputo, Philip. A rumor of war / [by] Philip Caputo. — London [etc.] : Macmillan, 1977. — xix,346p : 2 maps ; 23cm.
Also published: New York : Holt, Rinehart and Winston, 1977.
ISBN 0-333-23066-3 : £5.50
(B77-29099)

959.8 — HISTORY. INDONESIA
959.8 — Indonesia, to 1950. *Juvenile literature*
Williams, Maslyn. The story of Indonesia / [by] Maslyn Williams ; illustrated by Elaine Haxton. — London [etc.] : Angus and Robertson, 1976. — 64p : ill(some col), col maps ; 20x26cm.
Col. ill. on lining papers. — Index.
ISBN 0-207-95605-7 : £3.20
(B77-09449)

959.8 — Indonesia, to 1976
Fryer, Donald Wilfred. Indonesia / by Donald W. Fryer and James C. Jackson. — London : E. Benn [etc.], 1977. — xxi,313p,[16]p of plates : ill, maps, ports ; 23cm. — (Nations of the modern world)
Bibl.: p.295-306. — Index.
ISBN 0-510-39003-x : £9.25
(B77-23038)

959.8'03 — Indonesia. Social life. *For Australian students & for New Zealand students*
Kennedy, Brian. Indonesia : a developing nation / [by] Brian Kennedy ; photographs by Lance Nelson. — Sydney [etc.] ; London : Reed Education, 1976. — 24,[1]p : ill, coat of arms, facsim, 2 maps ; 25cm. — (Pageant of the Pacific : pageant of Asia ; 2)
Index.
ISBN 0-589-09184-0 Sd : £1.30
(B77-18496)

959.8'03 — Indonesia. Social life, 1945-1975
Lee Khoon Choy. Indonesia, between myth and reality / [by] Lee Khoon Choy. — London (43 Dover St., W1X 3RE) : Nile and Mackenzie Ltd, 1976. — ix,222p,[8]p of plates : ill(some col), port ; 23cm.
Index.
ISBN 0-86031-019-1 : £4.95
(B77-15640)

959.8'1'01 — Indonesia. Sumatra, to 1810. *Early works*
Marsden, William. The history of Sumatra / by William Marsden. — 3rd ed. reprint[ed] ; introduced by John Bastin. — Kuala Lumpur ; London [etc.] : Oxford University Press, 1975. — xi,viii,479,[8]p,[29]leaves of plates(1 fold) : ill, map ; 29cm. — (Oxford in Asia historical reprints)
Facsimile reprint of: 3rd ed. London : J. M'Creedy, 1811. — Index.
£26.50
(B77-11504)

959.8'2'0220924 — Indonesia. Java. Social life, 1899-1904. *Correspondence*
Kartini, *Raden Adjeng.* Letters of a Javanese princess / [by] Raden Adjent Kartini ; translated from the original Dutch by Agnes Louise Symmers ; with a foreword by Louis Couperus. — [1st ed. reprinted] ; introduction by Sartono Kartodirdjo. — Kuala Lumpur ; Oxford [etc.] : Oxford University Press, 1976. — xviii[i.e.xxviii],310p ; 22cm. — (Oxford in Asia paperbacks)
This translation originally published: New York : Knopf, 1920 ; London : Duckworth, 1921. — Translation of: 'Door duisternis tot licht'. The Hague : s.n., 1911.
ISBN 0-19-580325-6 Pbk : £7.25
(B77-08704)

959.8'6 — Indonesia. Bali. Social life. *Juvenile literature*
Marks, Stan. Ketut lives in Bali / text [by] Stan Marks ; photographs [by] Rennie Ellis. — London : Methuen [etc.], 1977. — [48]p : ill, 2 maps ; 22cm. — (Children everywhere series)
Originally published: Sydney : Methuen of Australia, 1976.
ISBN 0-416-82370-x : £1.75
(B77-12249)

959.9 — HISTORY. PHILIPPINES
959.9 — Philippines, ca 1560-1945
Constantino, Renato. A history of the Philippines : from the Spanish Colonization to the Second World War / by Renato Constantino with the collaboration of Letizia R. Constantino. — New York ; London : Monthly Review Press, 1915 [i.e. 1976]. — xiii,459p ; 21cm.
Originally published: as 'The Philippines'. Philippines : s.n., 1975. — Index.
ISBN 0-85345-394-2 : £12.00
(B77-10697)

959.9'035'0924 — Philippines. Social life, 1941-1945. *Childhood reminiscences*
Prising, Robin. Manila, goodbye / [by] Robert [i.e. Robin] Prising. — London : Corgi, 1977. — 191p ; 18cm.
Originally published: Boston, Mass. : Houghton-Mifflin, 1975 ; London : Heinemann, 1976.
ISBN 0-552-10546-5 Pbk : £0.75
Also classified at 940.54'72'520924
(B77-29853)

959.9'7'0049921 — Tasaday. Social life. *Philippines. Mindanao. Personal observations*
Nance, John. The gentle Tasaday : a Stone Age people in the Philippine rain forest / [by] John Nance ; foreword by Charles A. Lindbergh. — New York ; London : Harcourt Brace Jovanovich, 1975. — iii-xiv,465p,[64]p of plates : ill, ports ; 18cm.
Also published: London : Gollancz, 1975. — Index.
ISBN 0-15-134990-8 : Unpriced
(B77-11505)

960 — HISTORY. AFRICA
960 — Africa. *History*
The **Cambridge** history of Africa. — Cambridge [etc.] : Cambridge University Press.
In 8 vols.
Vol.3 : from c.1050 to c.1600 / edited by Roland Oliver. — 1977. — xiii,803p : maps ; 24cm.
Bibl.: p.702-747. — Index.
ISBN 0-521-20981-1 : £20.00
(B77-06399)

Vol.5 : from c.1790 to c.1870 / edited by John E. Flint. — 1976. — xv,617p : maps ; 24cm.
Bibl.: p.539-580. — Index.
ISBN 0-521-20701-0 : £17.50
(B77-06400)

960 — Africa, 1800-1973. *Secondary school texts*
Africa and the Middle East / editor John Robottom. — London : Longman.
Workcards / [by] Tom Allan. — 1977. — 1v. ; 23cm. — (Making the modern world)
One card, 3 copies each of 5 cards ([12] sides) in plastic envelope.
ISBN 0-582-22085-8 : £0.95
Also classified at 956
(B77-19143)

960'.07 — African studies, 1945-1975. *Festschriften*
African studies since 1945 : a tribute to Basil Davidson : proceedings of a seminar in honour of Basil Davidson's sixtieth birthday [held] at the Centre of African Studies, University of Edinburgh, under the chairmanship of George Shepperson / edited by Christopher Fyfe ; [for the University of Edinburgh, Centre of African Studies]. — London : Longman, 1976. — vii, 255p ; 24cm.
Index.
ISBN 0-582-64207-8 : £7.00
ISBN 0-582-64208-6 Pbk : £3.50
(B77-04507)

960'.2 — Africa. Colonisation, 1870-1900
Strage, Mark. Cape to Cairo / [by] Mark Strage. — Harmondsworth [etc.] : Penguin, 1977. — 397p : maps ; 19cm.
Originally published: London : Cape, 1973. — Index.
ISBN 0-14-004182-6 Pbk : £1.25
(B77-14499)

960'.3 — Africa, 1950-1976. *Secondary school texts*
Clare, Roger. The new Africa / by Roger Clare. — London : Macdonald Educational, 1977. — [2],24,[1]p : ill(chiefly col), col maps, ports ; 28cm. — (Macdonald Educational colour units : world topics)
Bibl.(1p.).
ISBN 0-356-05420-9 Sd : £0.75
(B77-13448)

960'.3 — Africa. Political events, 1900-1975
Akintoye, Stephen Adebanji. Emergent African states : topics in twentieth century African history / by S.A. Akintoye. — London : Longman, 1976. — [5],250p : maps ; 22cm.
Index.
ISBN 0-582-60127-4 Pbk : £1.80
(B77-14002)

960'.3 — African civilization. *Teaching kits*
Life in Africa / compiled by Vivian Russell. — [New York] : [Grossman] ; London : Jackdaw [etc.], 1975. — Portfolio : ill, facsims, maps(1 col), music ports ; 23x35cm. — ([American] jackdaw : no.A24)
Introductory leaflet ([4]p.) and 20 items. — Bibl.
ISBN 0-305-62115-7 : £1.95
(B77-01951)

960'.3'05 — Africa. *Serials*
Asian and African studies / Department of Oriental Studies of the Slovak Academy of Sciences, Bratislava. — Bratislava : Publishing House of the Slovak Academy of Sciences ; London : Curzon Press.
12 : 1976. — 1976. — 320p : facsims ; 25cm.
English, French, German text.
ISBN 0-7007-0101-x : £4.50
ISSN 0571-2742
Primary classification 950'.42'05
(B77-11010)

960'.3'05 — Africa. *Yearbooks*
Africa guide : incorporating economic information from the Economist Intelligence Unit Ltd. — Saffron Walden (21 Gold St., Saffron Walden, Essex CB10 1EJ) : Africa Guide Company.
1977. — 1976. — 311p : ill, maps ; 27cm.
Index.
Pbk : Unpriced
ISSN 0308-678x
(B77-28318)

Africa year book and who's who. — London (54A Tottenham Court Rd, W1P 0BT) : Africa Journal Ltd.
1977 / [editor-in-chief Raph Uwechue]. — 1976. — xlvii,1364p,[8]p of plates : ill(some col), forms, maps, ports ; 25cm.
ISBN 0-903274-05-1 : £20.00
Also classified at 920'.06
(B77-05153)

Owen's commerce and travel and international register. — London (886 High Rd, N12 9SB) : Owen's Commerce and Travel Ltd.
1977 : 24th ed. — 1977. — [3],1211[i.e. 1229]p : ill, maps(1 col) ; 26cm.
Tab indexed.
ISBN 0-900576-08-1 : £9.00
ISSN 0078-7167
Also classified at 950'.42'05
(B77-18497)

960'.3'05 — Africa. Political events. *Marxist viewpoints. Periodicals*
Africa in struggle. — London (97 Caledonian Rd, N.1) : International Marxist Group 'Africa Commission'.
No.1- ; Oct. 1975-. — [1975]-. — ill, ports ; 30cm.
Three issues a year. — [2],28p. in 1st issue.
Sd : £0.30(£1.20 yearly)
(B77-01952)

961 — HISTORY. NORTH AFRICA
961 — Maghreb, to 1932
Laroui, Abdallah. The history of the Maghrib : an interpretive essay / [by] Abdallah Laroui ; translated from the French by Ralph Manheim. — Princeton ; Guildford : Princeton University Press, 1977. — viii,431,[1]p : geneal table, maps ; 23cm. — (Princeton studies on the Near East)
Translation of: 'L'histoire du Maghreb'. Paris : Maspero, 1970. — Bibl.: p.401-422. — Index.
ISBN 0-691-03109-6 : £16.90
(B77-29854)

961 — Maghreb, to 1975
North West Africa : a political and economic survey. — 3rd ed. / [edited by] Wilfrid Knapp. — Oxford [etc.] : Oxford University Press, 1977. — viii,453p : maps ; 23cm.
Map on lining papers. — Previous ed.: published as 'A survey of North West Africa (the Maghrib)' / edited by Nevill Barbour. London : Oxford University Press for the Royal Institute of International Affairs, 1962. — Bibl.: p.437-441. — Index.
ISBN 0-19-215635-7 : £12.50
(B77-15641)

961'.005 — Maghreb. *History. Periodicals*
The **Maghreb** review. — London (96 Marchmont St., WC1N 1AG) : 'Maghreb review'.
No.1- ; June-July 1976-. — 1976-. — ill ; 27cm.

Six issues a year. — 22p. in 1st issue. — Bibl.
Sd : £0.60(£5.00 yearly)
ISSN 0309-457x
(B77-10079)

961'.03'0924 — North Africa. Rābih Fadl Allāh. *Biographies*
Hallam, W K R. The life and times of Rabih Fadh Allah / [by] W.K.R. Hallam. — Ilfracombe : Stockwell, 1977. — 367p,[16]p of plates : ill, geneal table, maps, plan ; 22cm.
Bibl.: p.330-339. — Index.
ISBN 0-7223-0959-7 : £4.95
(B77-24637)

962 — HISTORY. EGYPT
962 — Egypt. Political events, 1798-1952
Richmond, *Sir* **J C B.** Egypt, 1798-1952 : her advance towards a modern identity / [by] J.C.B. Richmond. — London : Methuen, 1977. — xii,243p,[8]p of plates : ill, maps, ports ; 25cm.
Bibl.: p.232-234. — Index.
ISBN 0-416-14900-6 : £7.50
ISBN 0-416-85660-8 Pbk : £4.50
(B77-23929)

962'.05 — Egypt. Social life. *Juvenile literature*
Wilkins, Frances. Let's visit Egypt / [by] Frances Wilkins. — London : Burke, 1977. — 96p : ill(some col), col map ; 21cm.
Index.
ISBN 0-222-00650-1 : £1.35
ISBN 0-222-00616-1 Library ed. : £1.95
(B77-30896)

962.4 — HISTORY. SUDAN
962.4'04 — Sudan. Political events, 1969-1976
Sylvester, Anthony. Sudan under Nimeiri / by Anthony Sylvester. — London [etc.] : Bodley Head, 1977. — 224p,[16]p of plates : ill, maps, ports ; 23cm.
Index.
ISBN 0-370-11318-7 : £5.00
(B77-10080)

962.4'04 — Sudan. Social life
Ismail, Salah Khogali. The Sudan in pictures / by Salah Khogali Ismail. — New York : Sterling [etc.] ; London : Distributed by Ward Lock, 1976. — 64p : ill, map, ports ; 27cm. — (Visual geography series)
Index.
ISBN 0-7061-2176-7 : £1.95
(B77-03307)

962.5 — Nubia, to 1976
Adams, William Y. Nubia : corridor to Africa / [by] William Y. Adams. — London : Allen Lane, 1977. — xxv,797p,xxiv p of plates : ill, maps, plans ; 24cm.
Index.
ISBN 0-7139-0579-4 : £17.50
(B77-22292)

962.9'04 — Southern Sudan. Political events. Influence of guerrilla warfare, 1955-1972
O'Ballance, Edgar. The secret war in the Sudan, 1955-1972 / [by] Edgar O'Ballance. — London : Faber, 1977. — 174p : facsim, maps ; 23cm.
Index.
ISBN 0-571-10768-0 : £5.50 : CIP rev.
(B77-09450)

963 — HISTORY. ETHIOPIA
963'.06'05 — Ethiopia. Political events. *Ethiopian Democratic Union viewpoints. Periodicals*
Ethiopian Democratic Union. EDU advocate : newsletter of the Ethiopian Democratic Union. — [London] ([WC1V 6XX]) : [BM-EDU].
Vol.1, no.1- ; Dec. 1975-. — [1975]-. — 30cm.
Published at irregular intervals. — [8]p. in 1st issue.
Sd : £6.00 yearly
ISSN 0309-0094
(B77-03857)

964 — HISTORY. MOROCCO
964'.05 — Morocco. Social life. *Primary school texts. Irish texts*
Bas, Daniel. Hamad, an buachaill Múrach / [le] Daniel Bas ; [Eibhlín Ní Mhuircheartaigh a d'aistrigh do leanaí 7-10 mbliana d'aois]. — Baile Átha Cliath [i.e. Dublin] ([Baile Atha Cliath 4]) : Oifig an tSoláthair, 1976. — [15]p : chiefly col ill, col map ; 27cm. — (Sraith tíortha agus nósanna)
Ill. on lining papers. — Originally published: in Spanish. Barcelona : Betis, 1973.
ISBN 0-905621-12-3 : £0.48
(B77-07001)

964'.2 — Morocco. Tangier. Social life, 1961-1974. *Personal observations*
Stewart, Angus. Tangier : a writer's notebook / [by] Angus Stewart ; photographs by the author. — London : Hutchinson, 1977. — 240p,[8]p of plates : ill, map ; 23cm.
ISBN 0-09-128710-3 : £5.50
(B77-21641)

964'.5'03 — South-eastern Morocco. Political events, 1881-1912
Dunn, Ross E. Resistance in the desert : Moroccan responses to French imperialism 1881-1912 / [by] Ross E. Dunn ; illustrated by Jeanne Dunn. — London : Croom Helm [etc.], 1977. — 291p,5p of plates : ill, maps ; 23cm.
Bibl.: p.278-283. — Index.
ISBN 0-85664-453-6 : £12.50
(B77-22293)

965 — HISTORY. ALGERIA
965'.04 — War of Algerian Independence, 1954-1962
Horne, Alistair. A savage war of peace : Algeria, 1954-1962 / [by] Alistair Horne. — London [etc.] : Macmillan, 1977. — 604p,[16]p of plates : ill, maps, ports ; 24cm.
Bibl.: p.570-575. — Index.
ISBN 0-333-15515-7 : £8.95 : CIP rev.
(B77-16688)

966 — HISTORY. WEST AFRICA
966 — West Africa, 1000-1800. *For West African students. Secondary school texts*
Davidson, Basil. A history of West Africa, 1000-1800 / [by] Basil Davidson in collaboration with F.K. Buah and with the advice of J.F. Ade Ajayi. — New revised ed. — London : Longman, 1977. — xvi,318p : ill, facsim, maps, plans, port ; 22cm. — (The growth of African civilisation)
Previous ed.: i.e. New expanded ed. 1967. — Bibl.: p.295-296. — Index.
ISBN 0-582-60340-4 Pbk : £1.75
(B77-29855)

966 — West Africa, 1000-1972. *For West African students. Secondary school texts*
Buah, Francis Kwamina. West Africa since AD 1000 : history notes / [by] F.K. Buah. — London [etc.] : Macmillan.
In 2 vols.
Book 2 : The people and outsiders. — 1977. — vii,231p : maps ; 22cm.
Bibl.: p.218-220. — Index.
Pbk : £1.30
(B77-28319)

966 — West Africa. Colonisation by Western world, 1454-1578
Blake, John William. West Africa : quest for God and gold, 1454-1578 : a survey of the first century of white enterprise in West Africa, with particular reference to the achievement of the Portuguese and their rivalries with other European powers / [by] John W. Blake. — 2nd ed., revised and enlarged. — London : Curzon Press [etc.], 1977. — xxi,246p,leaves of plates : maps ; 23cm.
Previous ed.: published as 'European beginnings in West Africa, 1454-1578'. London : Longmans, 1937. — Bibl.: p.225-237. — Index.
ISBN 0-7007-0098-6 : £4.50 : CIP rev.
(B77-14003)

966 — West Africa. Decolonisation
Hargreaves, John Desmond. The end of colonial rule in West Africa / [by] John D. Hargreaves. — London : Historical Association, 1976. — 38p : ill, map ; 22cm. — (Historical Association. Pamphlets : general series ; 88)
Bibl.: p.37-38.
Sd : £0.75(£0.50 to members)
(B77-04508)

966 — West Africa, to 1977. *For East & West African students. Secondary school texts*
Crowder, Michael. West Africa : an introduction to its history / [by] Michael Crowder. — London : Longman, 1977. — [9],214p,[8]p of plates : ill(some col), facsims, geneal table, maps, plan, ports ; 25cm.
Bibl.: p.203-204. — Index.
ISBN 0-582-60003-0 Pbk : £2.00
(B77-23039)

966'.004'963 — Yoruba. *West Africa, to 1893*
Smith, Robert, *b.1919.* Kingdoms of the Yoruba / [by] Robert Smith. — 2nd ed. — [London] : Methuen, 1976. — xvi,266p : maps ; 19cm. — (Studies in African history ; 2)
Previous ed.: 1969. — Bibl.: p.245-256. — Index.
ISBN 0-416-84710-2 : £6.00
ISBN 0-416-84720-x Pbk : £3.60
(B77-05154)

966.62 — HISTORY. LIBERIA
966.6'203'0924 — Liberia. Tubman, William Vacanarat Shadrach, 1944-1971. *Biographies*
Wreh, Tuan. The love of liberty - : the rule of President William V.S. Tubman in Liberia, 1944-1971 / by Tuan Wreh. — London : C. Hurst, 1976. — xiv,138p : ill, coat of arms, maps, ports ; 23cm.
ISBN 0-903983-42-7 : £5.50
(B77-01953)

966.68 — HISTORY. IVORY COAST
966.6'8'05 — Ivory Coast. Social life
Rosellini, Albert. The Ivory Coast in pictures / by Albert Rosellini. — New York : Sterling [etc.] ; London : Distributed by Ward Lock, 1976. — 64p : ill, map, ports ; 27cm. — (Visual geography series)
Index.
ISBN 0-7061-2517-7 : £1.95
(B77-12801)

966.7 — HISTORY. GHANA
966.7 — Ghana. Ashanti. Osei Bonsu, Asantehene. *Middle school texts*
Segbawu, Kwami. Osei Bonsu, warrior King of Asante / [by] Kwami Segbawu. — London : Longman, 1977. — [3],59p : ill, map ; 20cm. — (Makers of African history)
ISBN 0-582-60927-5 Sd : £0.40
(B77-17239)

966.7 — Ghana. Ashanti. Osei Tutu, Asantehene. *Biographies*
Daaku, Kwame Yeboa. Osei Tutu of Asante / [by] K. Yeboa Daaku. — London [etc.] : Heinemann Educational, 1976. — 48p : ill, maps, ports ; 15x21cm. — (African historical biographies ; 6)
Bibl.: p.6.
ISBN 0-435-94470-3 Sd : £0.50
(B77-04509)

966.7 — Ghana. Social life, to 1975
Traditional life, culture and literature in Ghana / edited with an introduction by J.M. Assimeng. — Owerri [etc.] ; London : Conch Magazine Ltd (Publishers), 1976. — [4],184p ; 23cm. — (Africa in transition series ; 2)
Bibl.
ISBN 0-914970-26-7 : £13.03
(B77-23930)

966.7 — Ghana, to 1972. *For Ghanaian students. Secondary school texts*
Fynn, John Kofi. A junior history of Ghana / [by] J.K. Fynn. — London : Longman, 1975. — iv,91p : ill, facsims, maps, ports ; 19x22cm.
ISBN 0-582-60288-2 Sd : £0.75
(B77-11506)

966.7'05 — Ghana. Social life
Krampah, D E K. Life in Ghana / [by] D.E.K. Krampah. — [London] : Commonwealth Institute, [1977]. — [4],29p,[4]p of plates : ill, map ; 30cm. — (Commonwealth topic ; no.10
ISSN 0306-3828)
Sd : £0.25
(B77-21642)

966.9 — HISTORY. NIGERIA
966.9'03 — Nigeria. Colonisation by Great Britain, 1885-1914
Ikime, Obaro. The fall of Nigeria : the British conquest / [by] Obaro Ikime. — London [etc.] : Heinemann Educational, 1977. — xi,232p,[8]p of plates : ill, maps, ports ; 23cm.
Bibl.: p.224-226. — Index.
ISBN 0-435-94140-2 : £5.50
ISBN 0-435-94141-0 Pbk : £2.20
(B77-15642)

966.9'05 — Nigeria
Arnold, Guy. Modern Nigeria / [by] Guy Arnold. — London : Longman, 1977. — xiii, 192[i.e. 194]p,[16]p of plates : ill, maps, ports ; 25cm.
Index.
ISBN 0-582-64642-1 : £5.00
ISBN 0-582-64643-x Pbk : £2.75
(B77-11507)

966.9'05 — Nigeria. Social life. *Juvenile literature*
Freville, Nicholas. Let's visit Nigeria / [by] Nicholas Freville. — 2nd revised ed. — London [etc.] : Burke, 1974. — 95p : ill(some col), 2 col maps ; 21cm.
Previous ed.: i.e. 1st ed. 1968. — Index.
ISBN 0-222-00316-2 : £1.95
ISBN 0-222-00314-6 Library ed. : £1.95
(B77-29856)

966.9'05 — Nigerian Civil War
Nwankwo, Arthur Agwuncha. Nigeria : the challenge of Biafra / [by] Arthur A. Nwankwo. — London : Collings, 1972. — 117p ; 19cm.
ISBN 0-901720-33-x Pbk : £0.60
(B77-19943)

966.9'2 — Nigeria. Oyo (Kingdom), ca 1600-ca 1836
Law, Robin. The Oyo Empire, c.1600-c.1836 : a West African Imperialism in the era of the Atlantic slave trade / by Robin Law. — Oxford : Clarendon Press, 1977. — xiv,340p : maps ; 23cm. — (Oxford studies in African affairs)
Bibl.: p.313-325. — Index.
ISBN 0-19-822709-4 : £11.50 : CIP rev.
(B77-19144)

966.9'3'008 — Nigeria. Benin (Kingdom), ca 1485-ca 1957. *Essays*
Bradbury, R E. Benin studies / [by] R.E. Bradbury ; edited, with an introduction, by Peter Morton-Williams ; foreword by Daryll Forde. — London [etc.] : Oxford University Press for the International African Institute, 1973 [i.e. 1976]. — xxi,293p,iv p of plates : ill, geneal tables, map, ports ; 23cm.
Originally published: 1973. — Bibl.: p.283-288. — Index.
ISBN 0-19-724198-0 Pbk : £4.25
(B77-06401)

966.9'3'01 — Nigeria. Benin (Kingdom). Influence of Europeans, 1485-1897
Ryder, Alan Frederick Charles. Benin and the Europeans, 1485-1897 / [by] A.F.C. Ryder. — London : Longman, 1977. — xii,372p : map ; 22cm. — (Ibadan history series)
Originally published: Harlow : Longmans, 1969. — Bibl.: p.349-357. — Index.
ISBN 0-582-64639-1 Pbk : £3.25
(B77-19944)

966.9'4 — Antiquities. Excavation of remains. *Nigeria. Igbo-Ukwu, 1959-1964*
Shaw, Thurstan. Unearthing Igbo-Ukuru : archaeological discoveries in eastern Nigeria / [by] Thurstan Shaw. — Ibadan ; Glasgow [etc.] : Oxford University Press, 1977. — [11], 121p : ill, maps, plans, ports ; 24cm.
Index.
ISBN 0-19-575251-1 Pbk : £4.95
(B77-27617)

966.9'5 — Nigeria. Sokoto Caliphate, 1754-1903
Last, Murray. The Sokoto Caliphate / [by] Murray Last. — London : Longman, 1977. — lxxxii,280p : maps ; 22cm. — (Ibadan history series)
Originally published: 1967. — Bibl.: p.236-262. — Index.
ISBN 0-582-64637-5 Pbk : £3.00
(B77-16130)

966.9'5'01 — Nigeria. Northern states. Sokoto (Caliphate). Political events, 1804-1906
Adeleye, Rowland Adevemi. Power and diplomacy in Northern Nigeria, 1804-1906 : the Sokoto Caliphate and its enemies / [by] R.A. Adeleye. — London : Longman, 1977. — xvi, 387p : maps ; 22cm. — (Ibadan history series)
Originally published: Harlow : Longman, 1971.
ISBN 0-582-64640-5 Pbk : £3.00
(B77-17842)

967 — HISTORY. CENTRAL AFRICA
967 — East Africa, 1000-1970. *For East African students. Secondary school texts*
Wilson, Derek Alan. East African history, 1000-1970 : a revision scheme for students preparing for the East African Certificate of Education and the Cambridge Overseas School Certificate / [by] D.A. Wilson. — [New] ed. — London [etc.] : Evans Bros, 1976. — 64p ; 19cm. — (Evans pocket facts)
Previous ed.: s.l. : Progress Publications, 1969.
ISBN 0-237-49970-3 Sd : Unpriced
(B77-09451)

967 — East Africa, to 1963
History of East Africa. — Oxford : Clarendon Press.
In 3 vols.
Vol.2 / edited by Vincent Harlow and E.M. Chilver ; assisted by Alison Smith ; with an introduction by Margery Perham. — 1976. — lii,768p : maps ; 22cm.
Originally published: 1965. — Bibl.: p.700-736. — Index.
ISBN 0-19-822713-2 Pbk : £5.75
(B77-08705)

967 — Prehistoric Eastern African civilization
Phillipson, D W. The later prehistory of eastern and southern Africa / [by] D.W. Phillipson. — London [etc.] : Heinemann Educational, 1977. — xii,323p : ill, maps, plan ; 24cm.
Bibl.:p.294-316. — Index.
ISBN 0-435-94750-8 : £10.50
ISBN 0-435-94751-6 Pbk : £4.90
Also classified at 968.02
(B77-33548)

967'.005 — Africa south of the Sahara. *Yearbooks*
Africa south of the Sahara. — London : Europa.
1977-78 : 7th ed. — 1977. — xxiv,1183p : maps ; 26cm.
Col. maps on lining papers. — Bibl.
ISBN 0-905118-10-3 : Unpriced
(B77-29100)

967.3 — HISTORY. ANGOLA
967'.303 — Angola. Political events, 1955-1975. *Marxist viewpoints*
Gabriel, Claude. Angola in the whirlwind of permanent revolution / [by C. Gabriel]. — [London] ([97 Caledonian Rd, N1 9BT]) : ['Africa in struggle'], [1976]. — 39p : ill, maps, ports ; 30cm.
Includes one chapter by F. Cazals.
Sd : Unpriced
(B77-02706)

967.43 — HISTORY. CHAD
967'.43'004937 — Hausa. Settlement. Role of Muslim pilgrimages to Mecca. *Chad*
Works, John A. Pilgrims in a strange land : Hausa communities in Chad / [by] John A. Works, Jr. — New York ; Guildford : Columbia University Press, [1977]. — xxii, 280p : ill, maps ; 24cm.
Published in the United States: 1976. — Bibl.: p.261-273. — Index.
ISBN 0-231-03976-x : £11.35
(B77-11508)

967.62 — HISTORY. KENYA
967.6'2'008 — Kenya, 1500-1970. *Collections*
Kenya : the land, its art and its wildlife : an anthology / edited by Frederick Lumley ; photographs by Werner Forman ... [et al.]. — London : Studio Vista, 1976. — 4-124p : ill(some col), col map, col port ; 25cm.
Ill. on lining papers.
ISBN 0-289-70727-7 : £5.35
(B77-09452)

967.6'204'0222 — Kenya. *Illustrations*
Jones, David Keith. Faces of Kenya / [by] David Keith Jones. — London : Hamilton, 1977. — 215p,[32]p of plates : chiefly ill(some col), maps ; 33cm.
Ill. on lining papers.
ISBN 0-241-89748-3 : £10.00
(B77-32342)

967.8 — HISTORY. TANZANIA
967.8 — Tanzania. Mirambo, King of Urambo. *Biographies*
Unomah, A C. Mirambo of Tanzania / [by] A.C. Unomah. — London [etc.] : Heinemann Educational, 1977. — 47p : ill, maps, ports ; 15x21cm. — (African historical biographies)
ISBN 0-435-94374-x Sd : £0.65
(B77-26723)

967.8'2'004963 — Fipa. Historical sources: Oral traditions. *Tanzania. Structuralist perspectives*
Willis, Roy Geoffrey. On historical reconstruction from oral-traditional sources : a structuralist approach / by Roy G. Willis. — [Edinburgh] ([c/o Centre of African Studies, University of Edinburgh, Edinburgh EH8 9YL]) : [The author], [1977]. — [1],24p,plate : map ; 21cm. — (Melville J. Herskovits memorial lecture ; 12)
'... delivered under the auspices of the Program of African Studies, Northwestern University, on 16 February 1976'. — Bibl.: p.23.
Sd : Unpriced
(B77-34344)

967.8'2'004963 — Nyiha. Social life. *Tanzania. Personal observations*
Slater, Mariam K. African odyssey : an anthropological adventure / [by] Mariam K. Slater. — Bloomington ; London : Indiana University Press, [1977]. — [13],426p : ill, form, maps ; 22cm.
Published in the United States: 1976. — Bibl.: p.407-414. — Index.
ISBN 0-253-30269-2 : £9.40
(B77-11012)

968 — HISTORY. SOUTHERN AFRICA
968 — South Africa, to 1976
Davenport, Thomas Rodney Hope. South Africa : a modern history / [by] T.R.H. Davenport. — London [etc.] : Macmillan, 1977. — xvi,432p, [8]p of plates : ill, geneal tables, maps, ports ; 23cm. — (Cambridge Commonwealth series)
Bibl.: p.379-401. — Index.
ISBN 0-333-17961-7 : £10.00
ISBN 0-333-21182-0 Pbk : £4.95
(B77-21643)

Lacour-Gayet, Robert. A history of South Africa / [by] Robert Lacour-Gayet ; translated [from the French] by Stephen Hardman. — London : Cassell and Collier Macmillan, 1977. — xi,387p : maps ; 22cm.
Translation of: 'Histoire de l'Afrique du Sud'. Paris : Fayard, 1970. — Bibl.: p.353-365. — Index.
ISBN 0-304-29545-0 : £6.50
ISBN 0-304-29823-9 Pbk : £3.25
(B77-19145)

968 — Southern Africa, to 1975
Willcox, Alexander Robert. Southern land : the prehistory and history of Southern Africa / [by] A.R. Willcox. — Cape Town ; London [etc.] : Purnell, 1976. — xiii,274[i.e.282]p,[34]p of plates : ill(some col), maps, ports ; 26cm.
Map on lining papers. — Bibl.: p.258-260. — Index.
ISBN 0-360-00324-9 : £17.50
(B77-33549)

968'.007'2 — South Africa. Historiography
Wright, Harrison Morris. The burden of the present : liberal-radical controversy over southern African history / [by] Harrison M. Wright. — Cape Town : David Philip ; London : Collings, 1977. — vi,137p ; 19cm.
Bibl.: p.126-137.
ISBN 0-86036-052-0 : £4.25
ISBN 0-86036-053-9 Pbk : £2.75
(B77-16689)

968.02 — Prehistoric Southern African civilization
Phillipson, D W. The later prehistory of eastern and southern Africa / [by] D.W. Phillipson. — London [etc.] : Heinemann Educational, 1977. — xii,323p : ill, maps, plan ; 24cm.
Bibl.:p.294-316. — Index.
ISBN 0-435-94750-8 : £10.50
ISBN 0-435-94751-6 Pbk : £4.90
Primary classification 967
(B77-33548)

968.02 — Stone Age antiquities. *Southern Africa*
Sampson, C Garth. The Stone Age archaeology of Southern Africa / [by] C. Garth Sampson. — New York ; London : Academic Press, 1974. — xiv,518p : ill, maps ; 24cm. — (Studies in archaeology)
Text on lining papers. — Bibl.: p.451-485. — Index.
ISBN 0-12-785759-1 : Unpriced
(B77-19945)

968.04 — Zulu War, 1879. British soldiers. Correspondence
Emery, Frank. The red soldier : letters from the Zulu War, 1879 / by Frank Emery. — London [etc.] : Hodder and Stoughton, 1977. — 288p, [16]p of plates : ill, facsim, maps, plans, ports ; 24cm.
Facsim. on lining papers. — Bibl.: p.263-265. — Index.
ISBN 0-340-20672-1 : £6.25
(B77-26049)

968.05 — Southern Africa. Policies of British government, 1900-1945
Chanock, Martin. Unconsummated union : Britain, Rhodesia and South Africa, 1900-45 / [by] Martin Chanock. — Manchester : Manchester University Press, 1977. — xi,289p : maps ; 23cm.
Bibl.: p.277-284. — Index.
ISBN 0-7190-0634-1 : Unpriced
(B77-29101)

968.06 — South Africa. Political events, 1970-1976
Johnson, Richard William. How long will South Africa survive? / [by] R.W. Johnson. — London [etc.] : Macmillan, 1977. — viii,328p : 2 maps ; 23cm.
ISBN 0-333-22094-3 : £8.95 : CIP rev.
ISBN 0-333-22095-1 Pbk : £3.95
(B77-13449)

968.06 — Southern Africa. Influence of Soviet Union
Rees, David, *b.1928 (Oct.).* Soviet strategic penetration of Africa / by David Rees ; [map by Richard Natkiel]. — London : Institute for the Study of Conflict, 1976. — [2],20p : map ; 30cm. — (Conflict studies ; no.77 ISSN 0069-8792)
Two sheets ([3] sides) as insert.
ISBN 0-903366-52-5 Sd : £2.00
(B77-05801)

968.06 — Southern Africa. Policies of governments of Western world. *Bow Group viewpoints*
Blausten, Richard. Southern Africa, the need for a Western initiative / by Richard Blausten & Martyn Marriott. — London : Bow Publications, 1977. — 6[i.e.7]p ; 30cm. — (Bow Group. Memoranda)
Sd : £0.40
(B77-21644)

968.06 — Southern Africa. Political events, 1960-1976
Southern Africa in crisis / edited by Gwendolen M. Carter and Patrick O'Meara. — Bloomington ; London : Indiana University Press, 1977. — vii,279p : 1 ill, maps ; 25cm.
Bibl.: p.268-271. — Index.
ISBN 0-253-35399-8 : £9.35
(B77-23040)

968.06 — Southern Africa. Political events, 1974-1976
Callinicos, Alex. Southern Africa after Soweto / [by] Alex Callinicos and John Rogers. — London : Pluto Press, 1977. — viii,229p : maps ; 20cm.
Bibl.: p.214-220. — Index.
ISBN 0-904383-42-3 Pbk : £2.00
(B77-23932)

968.06 — Southern Africa. Political events, 1976-1977
Legum, Colin. Southern Africa, the year of the whirlwind / [by] Colin Legum. — London : Collings, 1977. — 72p ; 22cm. — (Current affairs series)
ISBN 0-86036-066-0 Pbk : £1.65
(B77-23931)

968'.1 — South Africa. Transvaal. Letaba region, to 1974
Cartwright, Alan Patrick. By the waters of the Letaba : a history of the Transvaal Lowveld - land of adventure / by A.P. Cartwright. — Cape Town [etc.] ; London : Purnell, 1974. — vii,184p,[32]p of plates : ill(some col), facsim, maps, ports ; 25cm.
Index.
ISBN 0-360-00279-x : Unpriced
(B77-26050)

968'.204 — Boer War
Farwell, Byron. The great Boer War / [by] Byron Farwell. — London : Allen Lane, 1977. — xiv,495p,[16]p of plates : ill, map, plans, ports ; 24cm.
Originally published: as 'The great Anglo-Boer War'. New York : Harper and Row, 1976. — Bibl.: p.470-477. — Index.
ISBN 0-7139-0820-3 : £7.50
(B77-10081)

Judd, Denis. The Boer War / [by] Denis Judd. — London : Hart-Davis MacGibbon, 1977. — 190p : ill, facsims, maps, ports ; 26cm. — ([The British at war])
Bibl.: p.187. — Index.
ISBN 0-246-10868-1 : £5.95
(B77-31642)

Wilkinson-Latham, Christopher. The Boer War / text by Christopher Wilkinson-Latham ; colour plates by Michael Roffe. — London : Osprey, 1977. — 40p,[8]p of plates : ill(some col), ports ; 25cm. — (Men-at-arms series)
ISBN 0-85045-257-0 Pbk : £1.95
(B77-12802)

968'.204'0924 — Boer War. Siege of Mafeking. *Diaries*
Plaatje, Solomon Tshekisho. The Boer War diary of Sol T. Plaatje : an African at Mafeking / edited by John L. Comaroff. — London : Cardinal, 1976. — 160p : map ; 20cm.
Originally published: London : Macmillan, 1973. — Bibl.: p.160.
ISBN 0-351-15548-1 Pbk : £0.90
(B77-10698)

968'.22 — South Africa. Soweto. Social life, 1950-1977. *Personal observations*
Sikakane, Joyce. A window on Soweto / by Joyce Sikakane. — London : International Defence and Aid Fund, 1977. — 80p,[8]p of plates : ill, plan, ports ; 21cm.
ISBN 0-904759-17-2 Pbk : £0.80
(B77-23041)

968'.4'04 — Zulu. *South Africa, ca 1820-1910*
Roberts, Brian, *b.1925.* The Zulu kings / [by] Brian Roberts. — London : Sphere, 1977. — 368p,[16]p of plates : ill, map, ports ; 18cm.
Originally published: London : Hamilton, 1974. — Bibl.: p.357-359. — Index.
ISBN 0-7221-7414-4 Pbk : £1.50
(B77-20849)

968'.4'050924 — Zulu. Buthelezi, Mangosuthu Gatsha. *South Africa. Biographies*
Temkin, Ben. Gatsha Buthelezi : Zulu statesman : a biography / by Ben Temkin. — Cape Town ; London [etc.] : Purnell, 1976. — xiv,413p,leaf of plate,[32]p of plates : 1 ill, 2 geneal tables, 2 maps, ports ; 24cm.
Index.
ISBN 0-360-00289-7 : £12.50
(B77-29857)

968'.7'004961 — Khoikhoi. *South Africa. Cape Province, to 1720*
Elphick, Richard. Kraal and castle : Khoikhoi and the founding of white South Africa / [by] Richard Elphick. — New Haven ; London : Yale University Press, 1977. — xxii,266p : 3 ill, 5 maps ; 25cm. — (Yale historical publications : miscellany ; 116)
Bibl.: p.241-255. — Index.
ISBN 0-300-02012-0 : £12.60
(B77-25333)

968'.8 — Namibia. Windhoek. *Illustrations*
Zur Strassen, Helmut. Windhoek / [by] Helmut Zur Strassen. — Cape Town ; London [etc.] : Purnell, 1975. — [48]p : chiefly ill(some col), map, port ; 22x24cm.
German, English and Afrikaans parallel text.
ISBN 0-360-00306-0 : £3.75
(B77-14500)

968.91 — HISTORY. RHODESIA

968.9'1 — Rhodesia. Lobengula, King of the Matabele. *Biographies*
Bhebe, Ngwabi. Lobengula of Zimbabwe / [by] Ngwabi Bhebe. — London [etc.] : Heinemann Educational, 1977. — 48p : ill, maps, ports ; 15x21cm. — (African historical biographies)
ISBN 0-435-94476-2 Sd : £0.65
(B77-26051)

968.9'1'010924 — Ndebele. Chiefs. *Rhodesia. Mzilikazi, Ndebele chief. Biographies*
Rasmussen, R Kent. Mzilikazi of the Ndebele / [by] R. Kent Rasmussen. — London [etc.] : Heinemann Educational, 1977. — 48p : ill, maps, ports ; 15x21cm. — (African historical biographies ; 13)
Bibl.: p.48.
ISBN 0-435-94475-4 Sd : £0.65
(B77-30897)

968.9'1'04 — Negroes. Atrocities by military forces. *Rhodesia. Reports, surveys*
Catholic Commission for Justice and Peace in Rhodesia. Civil war in Rhodesia : abduction, torture and death in the counter-insurgency campaign : a report / compiled by the Catholic Commission for Justice and Peace in Rhodesia. — London : Catholic Institute for International Relations ; Dublin : Trócaire-Catholic Agency for World Development : Irish Commission for Justice and Peace, 1976. — [7],102p : ill, facsims, map, ports ; 21cm.
Pbk : £1.00
(B77-32343)

968.94 — HISTORY. ZAMBIA

968.9'4 — Antiquities. *Eastern Zambia*
Phillipson, David Walter. The prehistory of Eastern Zambia / by D.W. Phillipson. — Nairobi ; London : British Institute in Eastern Africa ; [London] : [Distributed by Thames and Hudson], 1976. — xi,229p,[6]fold leaves,xxxi p of plates : ill, maps, plans ; 28cm. — (British Institute in Eastern Africa. Memoirs ; no.6)
Bibl.: p.221-226. — Index.
ISBN 0-500-97003-3 Pbk : £9.50
(B77-27618)

968.9'4 — Zambia, to 1975
Roberts, Andrew. A history of Zambia / [by] Andrew Roberts. — London [etc.] : Heinemann Educational, 1976. — xv,288p,vii p of plates : ill, maps, ports ; 23cm.
Bibl.: p.256-279. — Index.
ISBN 0-435-94245-x : £7.00
ISBN 0-435-94246-8 Pbk : £2.90
(B77-07753)

968.9'4'02 — Zambia. Political events, 1890-1964
Hall, Richard, *b.1925.* Zambia, 1890-1964 : the colonial period / [by] Richard Hall. — New ed. — London : Longman, 1976. — viii,225p, plate : 2 maps ; 22cm.
Previous ed.: published as 'Zambia'. London : Pall Mall Press, 1965. — Bibl.: p.197-202. — Index.
ISBN 0-582-64620-0 Pbk : £1.75
(B77-15049)

969 — HISTORY. INDIAN OCEAN ISLANDS

969 — South-western Indian Ocean. Islands. *Illustrations*
Cubitt, Gerald. Islands of the Indian Ocean = Iles de l'Océan Indien / [by] Gerald Cubitt ; [French translation by Charles Du Ry and Antoinette de Leon Silvestri]. — London : Cassell, 1977. — 176p : chiefly ill(some col), maps ; 29cm.
English and French parallel text. — Ill. on lining papers. — Originally published: Cape Town : Struik, 1975. — Index.
ISBN 0-304-29873-5 : £7.50
(B77-14501)

969'.82 — Mauritius, to 1972
Toussaint, Auguste. History of Mauritius / [by] Auguste Toussaint ; translated from the French by W.E.F. Ward. — London [etc.] : Macmillan, 1977. — vi,105p : ill, maps, ports ; 22cm.
Translation of: 'Histoire de l'Ile Maurice'. Paris : Presses Universitaires de France, 1971. — Bibl.: p.99-100. — Index.
ISBN 0-333-21628-8 Pbk : £1.25
(B77-23933)

970 — HISTORY. NORTH AMERICA

970 — Archaeology. Methodology. *Study regions: North America*
South, Stanley. Method and theory in historical archeology / [by] Stanley South. — New York [etc.] ; London : Academic Press, 1977. — xxiii,345p : ill, map, plans ; 24cm. — (Studies in archeology)
Bibl. — Index.
ISBN 0-12-655750-0 : £11.70
(B77-17843)

970'.004'97 — Aztecs. *Mexico, to ca 1600*
Davies, Nigel. The Aztecs : a history / [by] Nigel Davies. — London : Abacus, 1977. — xvii, 363p,[16]p of plates : ill, facsims, geneal table, maps ; 20cm.
Originally published: London : Macmillan, 1973. — Bibl.: p.348-354. — Index.
ISBN 0-349-10739-4 Pbk : £2.75
(B77-11509)

970'.004'97 — Eskimos. *Juvenile literature*
Hughes, Jill. A closer look at Eskimos / [by] Jill Hughes ; illustrated by Maurice Wilson. — London : Hamilton, [1977]. — 3-30p : ill(chiefly col), col map ; 27cm. — (A closer look book ; 14)
Text, col.ill. on lining papers.
ISBN 0-241-89562-6 : £1.75
(B77-19146)

970'.004'97 — Eskimos. Social life
Herbert, Wally. Eskimos / [by] Wally Herbert. — Glasgow [etc.] : Collins [etc.], 1976. — 128p : ill(chiefly col), maps(chiefly col), plan ; 26cm. — (International library)
Col. ill. on lining papers. — Bibl.: p.126. — Index.
ISBN 0-00-100177-9 : £2.95
(B77-23042)

Ritchie, Carson Irving Alexander. The Eskimo and his art / [by] Carson I.A. Ritchie. — London : Academy Editions [etc.], 1975. — 80p : ill, map ; 30cm.
ISBN 0-85670-014-2 : £4.95
Also classified at 709'.01'1097
(B77-13450)

970'.004'97 — Indians of North America. Social life, to ca 1930
Curtis, Edward Sheriff. [The North American Indian. Selections]. The vanishing race : selections from Edward S. Curtis' 'The North American Indian' / [compiled by] M. Gidley. — Newton Abbot [etc.] : David and Charles, 1976. — 192p : ill, map, ports ; 24cm.
'The North American Indian' originally published: in 20 vols. Seattle : E.S. Curtis, 1907-1930. — Index.
ISBN 0-7153-7364-1 : £4.95
(B77-05155)

970'.004'97 — Indians of North America, to 1972. *Readings from contemporary sources*
Vogel, Virgil J. This country was ours : a documentary history of the American Indian / by Virgil J. Vogel. — New York [etc.] ; London : Harper and Row, 1974 [i.e. 1976]. — xxxi,473p ; 21cm. — ([Series in urban and ethnic affairs]) (Torchbooks)
Published in the United States: 1974. — Originally published: New York : Harper and Row, 1972. — Bibl.: p.391-453. — Index.
ISBN 0-06-131735-7 Pbk : £4.45
(B77-02707)

970'.004'97 — Nahuas. Social life. *Mexico, ca 1550-ca 1750. Readings from contemporary sources. Nahuatl-English parallel texts*
Beyond the codices : the Nahua view of colonial Mexico / translated [from the Nahuatl] and edited by Arthur J.O. Anderson, Frances Berdan and James Lockhart ; with a linguistic essay by Ronald W. Langacker. — Berkeley [etc.] ; London : University of California Press, 1976. — ix,235p,[36]p of plates : facsims, geneal table ; 24cm. — (Latin American studies series ; vol.27)
Parallel Nahuatl text and English translation, Spanish appendix. — Bibl.: p.234-235.
ISBN 0-520-02974-7 : £9.60
(B77-15050)

970'.004'97 — Powhatan. Pocahontas. *Biographies*
Mossiker, Frances. Pocahontas : the life and the legend / [by] Frances Mossiker. — London : Gollancz, 1977. — xiii,383,xiii p,[8]p of plates : ill, ports ; 24cm.
Originally published: New York : Knopf, 1976. — Bibl.: p.371-383. — Index.
ISBN 0-575-02314-7 : £7.95
(B77-29858)

970'.004'97 — Quileutes, to 1975
Powell, Jay. Quileute : an introduction to the Indians of La Push / prepared for the Quileute Tribe by Jay Powell and Vickie Jensen. — Seattle ; London : University of Washington Press, 1976. — 80p : ill, facsims, maps, ports ; 29cm.
Bibl.: p.77, 79.
ISBN 0-295-95492-2 : £7.00
ISBN 0-295-95493-0 Pbk : £4.00
(B77-08158)

970'.004'97 — Teton Indians, ca 1760-ca 1930. *Stories, anecdotes*
White Bull, *Dakota chief.* The warrior who killed Custer : the personal narrative of Chief Joseph White Bull / translated [from the Dakota] and edited by James H. Howard. — Landmark ed. — Lincoln [Neb.] ; London : University of Nebraska Press, 1976 [i.e. 1977]. — xxi,84p,[24] p of plates : ill(some col) ; 24cm.
Dakota text with English translation, English commentary. — Originally published: Lincoln, Neb. : University of Nebraska Press, 1969. — Bibl.: p.83-84.
ISBN 0-8032-0080-3 : £10.50
(B77-12250)

970'.004'97 — Yahi. Ishi. *California. Biographies*
Kroeber, Theodora. Ishi in two worlds : a biography of the last wild Indian in North America / [by] Theodora Kroeber. — Berkeley [etc.] ; London : University of California Press, 1976. — [9],262p,[24]p of plates : ill(some col), facsims, maps, plan, ports ; 27cm.
Originally published: Berkeley : University of California Press ; London : Cambridge University Press, 1961. — Bibl.: p.253-259. — Index.
ISBN 0-520-00674-7 : £6.00
ISBN 0-520-00675-5 Pbk : £1.85
(B77-01102)

970.05 — America, 1900-1974. *Secondary school texts*
America / editor John Robottom. — London : Longman.
Workcards / [by] Tom Allan. — 1977. — 1v. ; 23cm. — (Making the modern world)
One card, 3 copies each of 5 cards ([12] sides) in plastic envelope.
ISBN 0-582-22084-x : £0.95
(B77-19147)

970.053 — North American culture, ca 1945-1972. *Essays*
Rosenberg, Harold. Discovering the present : three decades in art, culture and politics / [by] Harold Rosenberg. — Chicago ; London : University of Chicago Press, 1973[i.e.1976]. — xii,336p ; 22cm.
Originally published: 1973. — Index.
ISBN 0-226-72681-9 Pbk : £3.05
(B77-03308)

971 — HISTORY. CANADA
971'.003 — Canada, to 1975. *Encyclopaedias*
Colombo, John Robert. Colombo's Canadian references. — Toronto ; London [etc.] : Oxford University Press, 1976. — viii,576p ; 25cm.
ISBN 0-19-540253-7 : £11.50
(B77-15643)

971.06'44 — Canada. Social life
Nach, James. Canada in pictures / prepared by James Nach. — Revised ed. — New York : Sterling ; London : Distributed by Ward Lock, 1976. — 64p : ill, map, ports ; 26cm. — (Visual geography series)
Previous ed.: London : Oak Tree Press, 1966. — Index.
ISBN 0-7061-6006-1 : £1.95
(B77-01954)

Watson, Jessie. The Canadians : how they live and work / [by] Jessie and Wreford Watson. — Newton Abbot [etc.] : David and Charles [etc.], 1977. — 168p : ill, maps ; 23cm.
Bibl.: p.163-165. — Index.
ISBN 0-7153-7327-7 : £3.95
(B77-18498)

971.27'03'0924 — Manitoba. Social life, 1953-1967. *Personal observations*
Douglas, Molly. Going west with Annabelle / [by] Molly Douglas. — London : Hale [etc.], 1976. — 189p,[8]p of plates : ill, ports ; 23cm.
ISBN 0-7091-5771-1 : £4.50
(B77-02708)

971.4'281'030924 — Quebec (Province). Montreal. Social life, 1935-1947. *Personal observations*
Richler, Mordecai. The street / [by] Mordecai Richler. — Harmondsworth [etc.] : Penguin, 1977. — 128p ; 18cm.
This collection originally published: Toronto : McClelland and Stewart, 1969 ; London : Weidenfeld and Nicolson, 1972.
ISBN 0-14-004418-3 Pbk : Unpriced
(B77-15051)

971.8 — Newfoundland. Social life, 1800-1900
Moyles, R G. 'Complaints is many and various, but the odd divil likes it' : nineteenth century views of Newfoundland / [by] R.G. Moyles. — Toronto ; London [etc.] (17 Cockspur St., SW1Y 5BP) : Peter Martin Associates, 1975. — xiii,187p,[14]p of plates, [3]leaves of plates : ill, maps, ports ; 24cm.
Map on lining papers. — Bibl.: p.176-185.
ISBN 0-88778-098-9 : Unpriced
(B77-07002)

972 — HISTORY. MEXICO, MIDDLE AMERICA
972 — Aztec civilization. *Middle school texts. Teaching kits*
Lincoln, John Donald. Montezuma / by J.D. Lincoln ; illustrated by Joanna Troughton. — Cambridge [etc.] : Cambridge University Press, 1977. — 1v. : ill(some col), 3 maps(2 col), port ; 15x21cm. — (History first)
Four booklets, 12 folders ([48]p.) in plastic envelope. — Bibl.
ISBN 0-521-21302-9 : £2.75
(B77-10699)

972 — Maya civilization
Whitlock, Ralph. Everyday life of the Maya / [by] Ralph Whitlock ; drawings by Eva Wilson. — London : Batsford [etc.], 1976. — x,173p : ill, facsims, maps, port ; 23cm.
Bibl.: p.167. — Index.
ISBN 0-7134-3232-2 : £3.50
(B77-00557)

972'.02'0924 — Mexico. Conquest. Cortés, Hernándo. *Biographies*
Johnson, William Weber. Cortés / [by] William Weber Johnson. — London : Hutchinson, 1977. — iii-xviii,238p : maps(on lining papers), port ; 23cm. — (The library of world biography)
Originally published: Boston, Mass. : Little, Brown, 1975. — Bibl.: p.227-229. — Index.
ISBN 0-09-128480-5 : £4.25
(B77-12251)

972.08 — Mexico, 1910-1970. *Conference proceedings*
International Congress of Mexican History, *4th, Santa Monica, 1973.* Contemporary Mexico : papers of the IV International Congress of Mexican History / edited by James W. Wilkie, Michael C. Meyer, Edna Monzón de Wilkie. — Berkeley [etc.] ; London : University of California Press [etc.] [for U.C.L.A. Latin American Center], 1976. — xvii,858p : ill, maps ; 24cm. — (Latin American studies series ; vol.29)
English and Spanish text. — '"IV International Congress of Mexican History", October 17-21, 1973, Santa Monica, California' - p.iii. — Bibl. — Index.
ISBN 0-520-02798-1 : £22.05
ISBN 0-520-02871-6 Pbk : £9.60
(B77-26052)

972.9 — HISTORY. WEST INDIES
972.9'05'05 — Caribbean region. *Periodicals*
Caribbean insight magazine. — [London] ([c/o Image Enterprises Ltd, 35 Great Russell St., WC1B 3PP]) : [Raays London Publications]. Vol.1, no.1- ; [Oct. 1976]-. — [1976]-. — ill(some col), coats of arms, maps, ports(some col) ; 30cm.
Quarterly. — [2],64p. in 1st issue.
Sd : £0.75
ISSN 0308-7239
(B77-04510)

972.92'033'0924 — Jamaica. Cudjoe. *Biographies*
McFarlane, Milton. Cudjoe the Maroon / [by] Milton McFarlane. — London : Allison and Busby, 1977. — 144p : ill, 2 maps ; 23cm.
Index.
ISBN 0-85031-171-3 : £3.50
(B77-30898)

972.92'06'0924 — Jamaica. Social life, 1965-1967. *Personal observations*
Jones, Robert Gerallt. Jamaican interlude / [by] R. Gerallt Jones. — Swansea : C. Davies, 1977. — 196p : ill ; 22cm.
ISBN 0-7154-0340-0 : £5.25
(B77-33000)

972.9'72 — Virgin Islands, 1493-1974
Harrigan, Norwell. The Virgin Islands story / by Norwell Harrigan and Pearl Varlack. — [Kingston, Jamaica] : Caribbean Universities Press ; Epping : Bowker, 1975. — xix,214p : ill, 2 maps ; 24cm.
Bibl.: p.200-205. — Index.
ISBN 0-85935-027-4 : Unpriced
(B77-19946)

972.9'73 — St Christopher-Nevis-Anguilla. Anguilla, to 1923
Jones, S B. Annals of Anguilla, 1650-1923 / by S.B. Jones. — Belfast (2 Bristow Park, Belfast BT9 6TH) : Christian Journals Ltd, 1976. — 80p ; 18cm.
Originally published: s.l. : s.n., 1936.
ISBN 0-904302-26-1 Pbk : £1.04
(B77-01103)

973 — HISTORY. UNITED STATES
973 — American civilization, 1800-1975. *Conference proceedings*
Almost Chosen People *(Conference), University of Notre Dame, 1976.* An almost chosen people : the moral aspirations of Americans / editors Walter Nicgorski, Ronald Weber. — Notre Dame, Ind. ; London : University of Notre Dame Press, 1976. — x,160p ; 24cm.
'... conference held at the University of Notre Dame in the spring of 1976 and entitled "An Almost Chosen People : The Moral Aspirations of Americans"' - Foreword.
ISBN 0-268-00581-8 : £7.50
(B77-23934)

973 — American civilization. Influence of Calvin, Jean, to 1975
Kendall, R T. The influence of Calvin and Calvinism upon the American heritage / by R.T. Kendall. — London (c/o The Librarian, 78a Chiltern St., W1M 2HB) : Evangelical Library, 1976. — 24p ; 22cm. — (Evangelical Library. Annual lectures ; 1976)
ISBN 0-901891-04-5 Sd : £0.40
(B77-09453)

973 — American civilization, to 1976. *Juvenile literature*
McCarthy, M L. United States of America, the land and its people / [adapted by M.L. McCarthy from the original text by John Bear ; illustrators John Shackell ... et al.]. — Easy reading ed. — London : Macdonald Educational, 1977. — 4-61p : ill(chiefly col), col maps, ports(some col) ; 29cm. — (Macdonald countries)
Col. ill., col. maps on lining papers. — Adaptation of: 'United States of America, the land and its people' / by John Bear. London : Macdonald and Jane's, 1974. — Index.
ISBN 0-356-05569-8 : £2.25
(B77-27619)

973 — Archaeology. Methodology. *Study regions: United States*
Research strategies in historical archeology / edited by Stanley South. — New York [etc.] ; London : Academic Press, 1977. — xxix,345p : ill, facsim, form, maps ; 24cm. — (Studies in archeology)
Bibl. — Index.
ISBN 0-12-655760-8 : £13.85
(B77-23935)

973 — Eastern United States, 1936-ca 1955. *Childhood reminiscences*
Conroy, Frank. Stop-time / [by] Frank Conroy. — Harmondsworth [etc.] : Penguin, 1977. — 284p ; 18cm.
Originally published: New York : Viking Press, 1967 ; London : Bodley Head, 1968.
ISBN 0-14-004446-9 Pbk : Unpriced
(B77-17240)

973 — United States, 1844-1877
Brock, William Ranulf. Conflict and transformation : the United States, 1844-1877 / [by] William R. Brock. — Harmondsworth [etc.] : Penguin, 1976. — 488p ; 18cm. — (The pelican history of the United States ; vol.3) (A pelican original)
Originally published: Baltimore : Penguin, 1973 ; Harmondsworth : Penguin, 1975. — Bibl.: p.446-466. — Index.
Pbk : £1.50
ISBN 0-14-021242-6
(B77-22294)

Brock, William Ranulf. Conflict and transformation : the United States, 1844-1877 / [by] William R. Brock. — Harmondsworth [etc.] : Penguin, 1976. — 488p ; 18cm. — (The pelican history of the United States ; vol.3) (A pelican original)
Originally published: Baltimore : Penguin, 1973 ; Harmondsworth : Penguin, 1975. — Bibl.: p.446-466. — Index.
Pbk : £1.50
ISBN 0-14-021242-6
(B77-25335)

973 — United States. Places called Andover
Andovers here and there : (in England, America and 'way down under') / [compiled] by Ralph G. Chaffee. — Andover (c/o Public Library, Andover, Hants.) : Andover Local Archives Committee, 1976. — [4],35p : map ; 30cm.
ISBN 0-903755-06-8 Sd : Unpriced
(B77-08707)

973 — United States. Social life, 1856-1935. *Correspondence*
Hughes family. Anglesey family letters, 1840-1935 / [Hughes family] ; edited by Elizabeth Grace Roberts. — Liverpool (25 [i.e. 22] Gressingham Rd, Liverpool L18 6JT) : The editor, 1976. — 126,14,xii p,[10]p of plates,[2]fold leaves of plates : ill, geneal tables, ports ; 23cm.
ISBN 0-9503153-1-1 : £3.00
Primary classification 941.081
(B77-01923)

973 — United States, to 1973
Gardner, Lloyd Calvin. Looking backward : a reintroduction to American history / [by] Lloyd C. Gardner, William L. O'Neill. — New York ; London [etc.] : McGraw-Hill, [1976]. — xi, 529p : ill, facsims, maps, ports ; 24cm.
Published in the United States: 1974. — Bibl. — Index.
ISBN 0-07-022841-8 Pbk : £7.65
(B77-01104)

973 — United States, to 1974
Nevins, Allan. America : the story of a free people / [by] Allan Nevins and Henry Steele Commager. — 4th ed. / [revised by Henry Steele Commager, Milton Cantor]. — Oxford [etc.] : Oxford University Press, 1976. — xii, 643p : maps ; 18cm.
Previous ed.: Oxford : Clarendon Press, 1967. — Bibl.: p.595-610. — Index.
ISBN 0-19-873018-7 Pbk : £2.25
(B77-26053)

973 — United States, to 1975
Encyclopedia of American history / edited by Richard B. Morris. — Bicentennial ed. / associate editor Jeffrey B. Morris. — New York [etc.] ; London : Harper and Row, 1976. — xiv, 1245p : ill, facsims(on lining papers), maps, plans ; 24cm.
Previous ed.: [i.e. 4th ed.], 1970. — Index.
ISBN 0-06-013081-4 : £18.80
(B77-06402)

973 — United States, to 1975. *Secondary school texts*
Weisberger, Bernard Allen. The impact of our past : a history of the United States / [by] Bernard A. Weisberger ; inquiry and study aids Gerald Hardcastle ; consultants John W. Blassingame ... [et al.]. — 2nd ed., annotated teacher's ed. — New York ; London [etc.] : McGraw-Hill, 1976. — 31,832p : ill(some col), coats of arms, facsims, maps(chiefly col), plan, ports(some col) ; 26cm.
Previous ed.: New York : American Heritage Publishing Co., 1972. — Bibl. — Index.
ISBN 0-07-069087-1 : £12.05
ISBN 0-07-069086-3 Pupil's ed. : £9.95
(B77-05802)

973 — United States, to 1976
Garraty, John Arthur. A short history of the American nation / [by] John A. Garraty. — 2nd ed. — New York [etc.] ; London : Harper and Row, 1977. — xxi,547p : ill, facsims, maps, ports ; 24cm.
Previous ed.: 1974. — '... an abridgement of "The American Nation", Third Edition' - title page verso. — Bibl. — Index. — Includes the texts of the Declaration of Independence and the Constitution.
ISBN 0-06-042266-1 Pbk : £5.80
(B77-16131)

973 — United States, to 1976. *Secondary school texts*
Hall, David John, *b.1933.* A visual history of the United States / [by] D.J. Hall & S.L. Case. — 2nd revised ed. — London : Evans Bros, 1977. — 55p : ill, facsim, maps, ports ; 25cm.
Previous ed.: 1969.
ISBN 0-237-29200-9 Sd : £0.95
(B77-27620)

973'.008 — United States. Political events, 1821-1879. *Readings*
Beyond the Civil War synthesis : political essays of the Civil War era / Robert P. Swierenga editor. — Westport, Conn. ; London : Greenwood Press, 1975. — xx,348p : ill ; 22cm. — (Contributions in American history ; no.44)
Index.
ISBN 0-8371-7960-2 : £10.95
(B77-18499)

973'.04'6872 — Chicanos. *United States, to 1976*
Samora, Julian. A history of the Mexican-American people / [by] Julian Samora and Patricia Vandel Simon. — Notre Dame, Ind. ; London : University of Notre Dame Press, 1977. — xii,238p : ill, maps, ports ; 25cm.
Bibl. — Index.
ISBN 0-268-00545-1 : £7.50
ISBN 0-268-00546-x Pbk : £4.50
(B77-30899)

973'.04'91497 — Gypsies. *United States. Personal observations*
Maas, Peter. King of the gypsies / [by] Peter Maas. — London : Corgi, 1977. — xi,209,[1]p ; 18cm.
Originally published: New York : Viking Press, 1975 ; London : Cape, 1976.
ISBN 0-552-10412-4 Pbk : £0.75
(B77-16132)

973'.04'9185 — Polish immigrants. *United States. Polish texts*
Tyrmand, Leopold. Tu w Ameryce czyli dobre rady dla Polaków / Leopold Tyrmand. — Londyn [i.e. London] : Polska Fundacja Kulturalna, 1975. — 80p ; 21cm.
'Przedruk z tygodnika "Wiadomości" w Londynie' - cover.
ISBN 0-85065-108-5 Pbk : £1.00
(B77-09454)

973'.04'96073 — Negroes. *United States. History*
Foner, Philip Sheldon. History of black Americans / [by] Philip S. Foner. — Westport, Conn. ; London : Greenwood Press.
In 4 vols.
[Vol.1] : From Africa to the emergence of the cotton kingdom. — 1975. — 680[i.e.682]p : maps ; 24cm. — (Contributions in American history ; no.40)
Bibl.: p.595-662. — Index.
ISBN 0-8371-7529-1 : £19.95
(B77-17241)

973'.04'96073 — Negroes. *United States, to 1975. Readings*
Meier, August. Along the color line : explorations in the black experience / [by] August Meier and Elliott Rudwick. — Urbana [etc.] ; London : University of Illinois Press, 1976. — xvi,404p ; 24cm. — (Blacks in the New World)
ISBN 0-252-00636-4 : £11.25
(B77-29859)

973'.04'97 — Indians of North America. *United States, ca 1840-1890. Secondary school texts*
Beacroft, Bernard William. The last fighting Indians of the American West / [by] B.W. Beacroft ; illustrated from contemporary sources. — London : Longman, 1976. — 96p : ill, maps, ports ; 20cm. — (Then and there series)
Bibl.: p.92.
ISBN 0-582-20538-7 Pbk : £0.50
(B77-08708)

973'.07'2 — American studies. *Readings*
American studies : topics and sources / Robert H. Walker, editor. — Westport, Conn. ; London : Greenwood Press, 1976. — xi,393,[1] p : ports ; 25cm. — (Contributions in American studies ; no.24)
'These essays have appeared or will appear in "American Studies International" ...' - Introduction. — Bibl.: p.323-393. — Index.
ISBN 0-8371-8559-9 : £15.95
(B77-17844)

973'.07'2 — American studies. Research in foreign countries. *Readings*
American studies abroad / [edited by] Robert H. Walker. — Westport, Conn. ; London : Greenwood Press, 1975. — xi,160p : ports ; 22cm. — (Contributions in American studies ; no.22)
'Many of the ... essays have appeared in the pages of "American studies : an international newsletter" since the Spring issue of 1970' - Preface. — Index.
ISBN 0-8371-7951-3 : £9.75
(B77-17845)

973'.08 — United States, ca 1500-ca 1950. *Readings from contemporary sources*
Modern Europe and America / edited by William H. McNeill and Schuyler Owen Houser. — New York ; London [etc.] : Oxford University Press, 1973 [i.e. 1976]. — xi,312p : ill, music ; 21cm. — (Readings in world history ; vol.10)
Originally published: New York : Oxford University Press, 1973.
ISBN 0-19-501631-9 Pbk : £2.75
Primary classification 940.2'08
(B77-06379)

973'.08 — United States, to 1930. *Essays*
Turner, Frederick Jackson. Frederick Jackson Turner's legacy : unpublished writings in American history / edited with an introduction by Wilbur R. Jacobs. — Lincoln, Neb. ; London : University of Nebraska Press, 1977. — xv,217p : facsim, ports ; 21cm.
Originally published: San Marino, Calif. : Huntington Library, 1965. — Index.
ISBN 0-8032-0922-3 : £10.15
(B77-30900)

973'.08 — United States, to ca 1860. *Readings from contemporary sources*
Roots of America : an anthology of documents relating to American history in the West Sussex Record Office, Chichester, England / edited by Kim C. Leslie. — Chichester (County Hall, Chichester, [W. Sussex]) : West Sussex County Council, 1976. — vi,114p,iv p of plates : 2 ill, facsims, maps ; 26cm.
Index.
ISBN 0-900801-38-7 : £2.70
(B77-01105)

973.2 — HISTORY. UNITED STATES, 1607-1775
973.2 — United States, 1585-1776
Simmons, R C. The American colonies : from settlement to independence / [by] R.C. Simmons. — London : Longman, 1976. — ix, 438p : maps ; 24cm.
Also published: New York : D. McKay, 1976. — Bibl.: p.389-415. — Index.
ISBN 0-582-12779-3 : £8.95
(B77-10082)

973.2 — United States, 1607-1776
Bridenbaugh, Carl. The spirit of '76 : the growth of American patriotism before independence, 1607-1776 / [by] Carl Bridenbaugh. — London [etc.] : Oxford University Press, 1977. — xiii, 162p ; 21cm. — (A galaxy book)
Originally published: New York : Oxford University Press, 1975. — Index.
ISBN 0-19-502179-7 Pbk : £1.75
(B77-19148)

973.2'6'0924 — United States. Johnson, Sir William, b.1715. *Biographies*
Hamilton, Milton W. Sir William Johnson : colonial American, 1715-1763 / [by] Milton W. Hamilton. — Port Washington ; London : Kennikat Press, 1976. — xiv,402p,[16]p of plates : ill, facsims, maps, ports ; 24cm. — (Kennikat Press national university publications : series in American studies)
Index.
ISBN 0-8046-9134-7 : £14.85
(B77-23936)

973.2'7 — United States. Political events, 1760-1781
Griffith, Samuel B. In defense of the public liberty : Britain, America and the struggle for independence, 1760-81 / [by] Samuel B. Griffith. — London : Cape, 1977. — xvii,726p, [24]p of plates : ill, facsims, maps(1 col), ports ; 24cm.
Col. map on lining papers. — Originally published: Garden City, N.Y. : Doubleday, 1976. — Bibl.: p.698-709. — Index.
ISBN 0-224-01327-0 : £12.50 : CIP rev.
(B77-12252)

973.2'7 — United States. Political events. Role of working classes, 1760-1783
Foner, Philip Sheldon. Labor and the American Revolution / by Philip S. Foner. — Westport, Conn. ; London : Greenwood Press, 1976. — xi,256,[1]p ; 22cm.
Bibl.: p.234-246. — Index.
ISBN 0-8371-9003-7 : £11.95
(B77-19149)

973.2'7'0924 — United States. Boone, Daniel. *Biographies*
Elliott, Lawrence. Daniel Boone, the long hunter / by Lawrence Elliott. — London : Allen and Unwin, 1977. — xiv,242p,[4]p of plates : ill, map, ports ; 23cm.
Ill. on lining papers. — Originally published: as 'The long hunter'. New York : Reader's Digest Press, 1976. — Bibl.: p.228-236. — Index.
ISBN 0-04-920053-4 : £5.25
(B77-33001)

973.3 — HISTORY. UNITED STATES, 1775-1789
973.3 — War of American Independence
Interdisciplinary studies of the American Revolution / edited by Jack P. Greene and Pauline Maier. — Beverly Hills ; London : Sage Publications, 1976 [i.e. 1977]. — 164p : ill, map ; 22cm. — (Sage contemporary social science issues ; 31)
Spine title: The American Revolution. — Published in the United States: 1976. — '... originally appeared as a special issue of "The journal of interdisciplinary history" (Volume VI, Number 4, Spring 1976)' - title page verso.
ISBN 0-8039-0732-x Pbk : £2.50
(B77-09455)

Perspectives on the American Revolution : a bicentennial contribution / edited by George G. Suggs, Jr. — Carbondale [etc.] : Southern Illinois University Press for Southeast Missouri State University ; London [etc.] : Feffer and Simons, 1977. — xv,141p : 2 ill ; 22cm.
Index.
ISBN 0-8093-0827-4 : £5.95
(B77-34345)

973.3 — War of American Independence. *Conference proceedings*
Scottish Universities' American Bicentennial Conference, *Edinburgh, 1976.* Scotland, Europe and the American Revolution / edited by Owen Dudley Edwards & George Shepperson. — Edinburgh (1 Buccleuch Place, Edinburgh [8]) : Edinburgh University Student Publications, 1976. — [3],138p : maps, plan ; 30cm.
'... the product of the Scottish Universities' American Bicentennial Conference which took place at the Pollock Halls of Residence, Edinburgh University, 25-28 June 1976' - Editorial. — '... originally appeared as a series of essays forming Nos. 35 and 36 of the magazine "New Edinburgh Review" ...' - title page verso.
ISBN 0-904919-06-4 Pbk : £0.95
(B77-05803)

973.3'092'2 — United States. Adams, John, b.1735. Correspondence with Adams, Abigail Smith, 1762-1784. *Texts*
Adams family. The book of Abigail and John : selected letters of the Adams family, 1762-1784 / edited and with an introduction by L.H. Butterfield, Marc Friedlaender and Mary-Jo Kline. — Cambridge, Mass. ; London : Harvard University Press, 1976. — ix, 411p : ill, facsims, map, ports ; 21cm.
Originally published: 1975. — Index.
ISBN 0-674-07854-3 Pbk : £3.75
(B77-03858)

973.3'092'2 — War of American Independence. *Biographies*
Lynn, Kenneth Schuyler. A divided people / [by] Kenneth S. Lynn. — Westport, Conn. ; London : Greenwood Press, 1977. — xi,113,[1] p ; 22cm. — (Contributions in American studies ; no.30)
Index.
ISBN 0-8371-9271-4 : £9.50
(B77-31643)

973.3'15'03924 — War of American Independence. Role of Jews
Rezneck, Samuel. Unrecognized patriots : the Jews in the American Revolution / [by] Samuel Rezneck ; with a foreword by Jacob R. Marcus. — Westport, Conn. ; London : Greenwood Press, 1975. — xiv,299p : ill, facsim, ports ; 22cm.
Bibl.: p.281-288. — Index.
ISBN 0-8371-7803-7 : £11.50
(B77-16133)

973.3'3 — War of American Independence. Military operations by American military forces, 1775-1783. Strategy
Palmer, Dave Richard. The way of the fox : American strategy in the war for America, 1775-1783 / [by] Dave Richard Palmer. — Westport, Conn. ; London : Greenwood Press, 1975 [i.e. 1976]. — xx,229p : maps, port ; 22cm. — (Contributions in military history ; no.8)
Published in the United States: 1975. — Bibl.: p.219-222. — Index.
ISBN 0-8371-7531-3 : £10.25
(B77-02709)

973.3'4 — War of American Independence. Role of American military forces. Negro personnel
Davis, Burke. Black heroes of the American Revolution / [by] Burke Davis ; foreword by Senator Edward W. Brooke ; with prints and portraits of the period. — New York ; London : Harcourt Brace Jovanovich, 1976. — 80p : ill, facsims, ports ; 24cm.
Bibl.: p.78. — Index.
ISBN 0-15-208560-2 : £4.70
(B77-16134)

973.4 — HISTORY. UNITED STATES, 1789-1809
973.4'092'4 — United States. Hamilton, Alexander. *Correspondence*
Hamilton, Alexander, *b.1757.* The papers of Alexander Hamilton / Harold C. Syrett, editor. — New York ; Guildford : Columbia University Press.
Vol.23 : April 1799-October 1799 / associate editors Barbara A. Chernow, Joseph G. Henrich, Patricia Syrett. — 1976. — xiv,728p, [2]leaves of plate(1 fold) : map, port ; 24cm.
Index.
ISBN 0-231-08922-8 : £13.88
(B77-01955)

Vol.24 : November 1799-June 1800 / associate editors Barbara A. Chernow, Joseph G. Henrich, Patricia Syrett. — 1976. — xii,708p, plate : port ; 24cm.
Bibl.: p.vii-xi. — Index.
ISBN 0-231-08923-6 : £13.88
(B77-08159)

973.4'1'0924 — United States. Washington, George. *Biographies*
Emery, Noemie. Washington : a biography / [by] Noemie Emery. — London : Cassell, 1977. — 432p ; 22cm.
Originally published: New York : Pitman, 1976. — Bibl.: p.415-421. — Index.
ISBN 0-304-29900-6 : £7.95
(B77-28320)

973.7 — HISTORY. UNITED STATES, 1861-1865
973.7 — American Civil War
Schomaekers, G. The American Civil War / [by] G. Schomaekers ; [translated from the German by Anthony Kemp]. — Poole : Blandford Press, 1977. — 160p : ill, facsims, maps, plans, ports ; 26cm.
Translation of: 'Der amerikanische Bürgerkrieg'. Bussum : Unieboek, 1976. — Bibl.: p.158-159.
ISBN 0-7137-0872-7 : £4.75
(B77-29102)

973.7 — American Civil War. *Juvenile literature*
Katz, William Loren. An album of the Civil War / by William Loren Katz. — New York ; London : F. Watts, 1974 [i.e. 1977]. — [8],83, [1]p : ill, facsims, ports ; 29cm.
Originally published: New York : F. Watts, 1974. — Bibl.: p.80. — Index.
ISBN 0-531-01518-1 : £2.95
(B77-24638)

973.7'13'0922 — Confederate States of America. *Biographical dictionaries*
Wakelyn, Jon L. Biographical dictionary of the Confederacy / [by] Jon L. Wakelyn ; Frank E. Vandiver, advisory editor. — Westport, Conn. ; London : Greenwood Press, 1977. — xii,3-601, [1]p ; 25cm.
Bibl.: p.571-584. — Index.
ISBN 0-8371-6124-x : £23.50
(B77-31644)

973.7'13'0922 — Women. *Confederate States of America. Study examples: Chesnut, Mary Boykin; Clay, Virginia Tunstall & Davis, Varina Howell*
Wiley, Bell Irvin. Confederate women / [by] Bell Irvin Wiley. — Westport, Conn. ; London : Greenwood Press, 1975. — xiv,204p : ill, ports ; 22cm. — (Contributions in American history ; no.38)
Bibl.: p.195-198. — Index.
ISBN 0-8371-7534-8 : £8.95
(B77-17846)

973.7'2 — American Civil War. Role of Great Britain
Jenkins, Brian. Britain & the war for the Union / [by] Brian Jenkins. — Montreal ; London : McGill-Queen's University Press. Vol.1. — 1974. — x,315p ; 24cm.
Bibl.: p.289-305. — Index.
ISBN 0-7735-0184-3 : Unpriced
(B77-32344)

973.7'3 — American Civil War. Army operations
Battles lost and won : essays from Civil War history / edited by John T. Hubbell. — Westport, Conn. ; London : Greenwood Press, 1975. — xv,3-289,[1]p : ill ; 22cm. — (Contributions in American history ; no.45)
Index.
ISBN 0-8371-8166-6 : £11.25
(B77-33002)

973.7'3 — American Civil War. Battles
Johnson, Curt. Battles of the American Civil War / [by] Curt Johnson & Mark McLaughlin. — Maidenhead : Sampson Low, 1977. — 160p : ill(some col), col maps, col plans, ports ; 32cm.
Originally published: as 'Battles of the Civil War'. New York : Crown, 1977. — Index.
ISBN 0-562-00064-x : £6.95
(B77-31645)

973.7'34 — American Civil War. Army operations by United States. Army of the Potomac, 1863 (Summer)
Catton, Bruce. Glory road : the bloody route from Fredericksburg to Gettysburg / [by] Bruce Catton. — London [etc.] : White Lion Publishers, 1977. — x,389p : maps ; 23cm.
Spine title: The army of the Potomac, the glory road. — Map on lining papers. — Originally published: Garden City, N.Y. : Doubleday, 1952. — Bibl.: p.339-347. — Index. — '... the critical months between the autumn of 1862 and the following June ...' - jacket.
ISBN 0-7274-0335-4 : £5.95
(B77-17847)

973.7'57'0924 — American Civil War. Naval operations by Confederate States of America. Navy. Brain, John Clibbon
Hay, David. The last of the Confederate privateers / [by] David and Joan Hay. — Edinburgh : P. Harris, 1977. — x,178p : ill, facsims, geneal table, maps, ports ; 23cm.
Bibl.: p.173-174. — Index.
ISBN 0-904505-23-5 : £4.95
(B77-16135)

973.8 — HISTORY. UNITED STATES, 1865-1901
973.8 — United States, 1865-1900
Keller, Morton. Affairs of state : public life in late nineteenth century America / [by] Morton Keller. — Cambridge, Mass. ; London : Harvard University Press, 1977. — xiii,631p ; 24cm.
Index.
ISBN 0-674-00721-2 : £13.15
(B77-23937)

973.8 — United States. Wars with Indians of North America, 1860-1890
Katcher, Philip Royall Nibley. The American Indian Wars, 1860-1890 / text by Philip R.N. Katcher ; colour plates by G.A. Embleton. — London : Osprey Publishing, 1977. — 40p,[8]p of plates : ill(some col), ports ; 25cm. — (Men-at-arms series)
Bibl.: p.40.
ISBN 0-85045-049-7 Pbk : £1.95
(B77-14004)

973.8'08 — United States, 1881-1895. *Essays*
Martí, José. Inside the monster : writings on the United States and American imperialism / [by] José Martí ; translated [from the Spanish] by Elinor Randall with additional translations by ... [others] ; edited with an introduction and notes by Philip S. Foner. — New York ; London : Monthly Review Press, 1975. — 3-386p ; 22cm.
Index.
ISBN 0-85345-359-4 : £7.25
(B77-14502)

973.8'1 — United States. Reconstruction, to 1877
White, John, *b.1939.* Reconstruction after the American Civil War / [by] John White. — London : Longman, 1977. — vi,122p ; 20cm. — (Seminar studies in history)
Bibl.: p.111-119. — Index.
ISBN 0-582-31429-1 Pbk : £1.30
(B77-29103)

973.8'2'0924 — United States. Grant, Ulysses Simpson. *Correspondence*
Grant, Ulysses Simpson. The papers of Ulysses S. Grant / edited by John Y. Simon. — Carbondale [etc.] : Southern Illinois University Press ; London [etc.] : Feffer and Simons.
'... prepared under the auspices of the U.S. Grant Association' - jacket.
Vol.6 : September 1-December 8, 1862. — 1977. — xxiv,492p : map, ports ; 26cm.
Index.
ISBN 0-8093-0694-8 : £13.13
(B77-19150)

973.9 — HISTORY. UNITED STATES, 1901-
973.9 — United States, 1870-1976
Kolko, Gabriel. Main currents in modern American history / [by] Gabriel Kolko. — New York [etc.] ; London : Harper and Row, 1976. — xiii,433p ; 24cm.
Index.
ISBN 0-06-043757-x : £11.25
ISBN 0-06-012451-2 Pbk : £7.45
(B77-08709)

973.9'092'4 — United States. Mitford, Jessica. *Autobiographies*
Mitford, Jessica. A fine old conflict / [by] Jessica Mitford. — London : Joseph, 1977. — 270p,[8]p of plates : 1 ill, facsim, ports ; 24cm.
Index. — Includes 'Lifeitselfmanship, or, How to become a precisely-because man' as appendix. Originally published: under the name Decca Treuhaft, London : E. Marks, 1957.
ISBN 0-7181-1617-8 : £5.95
(B77-21645)

973.91 — United States. Political events, 1898-1928
Bates, J Leonard. The United States, 1898-1928 : progressivism and a society in transition / [by] J. Leonard Bates. — New York ; London [etc.] : McGraw-Hill, 1976. — xi,339p : ill, facsims, maps, ports ; 23cm. — (The modern America series)
Bibl. — Index.
ISBN 0-07-004050-8 Pbk : £5.75
(B77-04511)

973.91 — United States. Social life, 1920-1930
Carter, Paul Allen. Another part of the twenties / [by] Paul A. Carter. — New York ; Guildford : Columbia University Press, 1977. — xv,229p ; 24cm.
Bibl.: p.187-218. — Index.
ISBN 0-231-04134-9 : £5.70
(B77-19947)

973.91'2'0924 — United States. Taft, William Howard, 1908-1912. *Biographies*
Anderson, Donald F. William Howard Taft : a conservative's conception of the Presidency / [by] Donald F. Anderson. — Ithaca, N.Y. ; London : Cornell University Press, 1973. — xv, 355p,[8]p of plates : ill, ports ; 22cm.
Originally published: Ithaca, N.Y. : Cornell University, 1968. — Bibl.: p.341-346. — Index.
ISBN 0-8014-0786-9 : Unpriced
(B77-19948)

973.91'5'0924 — United States. Social life, 1925-1930. *Personal observations*
Barzini, Luigi, *b.1908.* O America : a memoir of the 1920s / [by] Luigi Barzini. — London : Hamilton, 1977. — [6],329p ; 23cm.
Also published: New York : Harper and Row, 1977.
ISBN 0-241-89584-7 : £5.50
(B77-22295)

973.91'6 — United States. Political events, 1929-1933
Rosen, Elliot A. Hoover, Roosevelt and the Brains Trust : from depression to New Deal / [by] Elliot A. Rosen. — New York ; Guildford : Columbia University Press, 1977. — xiii,446p,16p of plates : ill, ports ; 24cm.
Index.
ISBN 0-231-04172-1 : £12.50
(B77-26054)

973.917 — United States, 1940-1950
Phillips, Cabell. The 1940s : decade of triumph and trouble / by Cabell Phillips. — New York : Macmillan ; London : Collier Macmillan, 1975. — xi,414p,[32]p of plates : ill, ports ; 24cm. — (The 'New York times' chronicle of American life)
Index.
ISBN 0-02-596100-4 : £9.50
(B77-04512)

973.917 — United States. Social life. Influence of World War 2, 1939-1945
Blum, John Morton. V was for victory : politics and American culture during World War II / [by] John Morton Blum. — New York ; London : Harcourt Brace Jovanovich, 1976. — xii,372p ; 24cm.
Index.
ISBN 0-15-194080-0 : £7.90
(B77-16136)

973.917'022'2 — United States. Social life, 1935-1943. *Illustrations*
The **years** of bitterness and pride : Farm Security Administration, FSA photographs, 1935-1943 ... / [compiled by Jerry Kearns and Leroy Bellamy ; edited by Hiag Akmakjian]. — New York ; London [etc.] : McGraw-Hill, 1975 [i.e. 1977]. — [9],86p : of ill ; 18x26cm.
Published in the United States: 1975.
ISBN 0-07-019958-2 Pbk : £4.10
(B77-05156)

973.917'092'2 — United States. Roosevelt, Franklin Delano & Roosevelt, Eleanor. *Biographies*
Roosevelt, James. My parents : a differing view / by James Roosevelt ; with Bill Libby. — London : W.H. Allen, 1977. — xiii,369p,[16]p of plates : 1 ill, ports ; 24cm.
Originally published: Chicago : Playboy Press, 1976. — Index.
ISBN 0-491-02231-x : £6.95
(B77-26724)

973.917'092'2 — United States. Roosevelt, Franklin Delano & Roosevelt, Eleanor, 1933-1945. *Biographies*
Roosevelt, Elliott. A rendezvous with destiny : the Roosevelts of the White House / by Elliott Roosevelt and James Brough. — London : W.H. Allen, 1977. — 446p,[8]p of plates : 1 ill, ports ; 23cm.
Originally published: New York : Putnam, 1975. — Index.
ISBN 0-491-02080-5 : £5.95
(B77-26055)

973.917'092'4 — United States. Eisenhower, Dwight David. Interpersonal relationships with Morgan, Kay Summersby, 1941-1945. *Personal observations*
Morgan, Kay Summersby. Past forgetting : my love affair with Dwight D. Eisenhower / [by] Kay Summersby Morgan. — London : Collins, 1977. — 220,[1]p,[16]p of plates : ill, facsims, ports ; 24cm.
Originally published: New York : Simon and Schuster, 1976.
ISBN 0-00-211645-6 : £4.95
Also classified at 942.084'092'4
(B77-05157)

973.92 — American culture. Compared with British culture, 1945-1975
Snowman, Daniel. Kissing cousins : an interpretation of British and American culture, 1945-1975 / [by] Daniel Snowman. — London : Temple Smith, 1977. — 342p ; 23cm. — ([Comparative history])
Index.
ISBN 0-85117-107-9 : £6.50
Primary classification 941.085
(B77-19915)

973.92 — United States, 1945-1975
Grantham, Dewey Wesley. The United States since 1945 : the ordeal of power / [by] Dewey W. Grantham. — New York ; London [etc.] : McGraw-Hill, 1976. — x,310p : ill, maps, ports ; 23cm.
Bibl. — Index.
ISBN 0-07-024116-3 Pbk : £5.75
(B77-05158)

973.922'092'4 — United States. Onassis, Jacqueline. *Biographies*
Frischauer, Willi. Jackie / [by] Willi Frischauer. — London : Sphere, 1977. — 256p,[8]p of plates : ports ; 18cm.
Originally published: London : Joseph, 1976. — Bibl.: p.254-256.
ISBN 0-7221-0437-5 Pbk : £0.95
(B77-29104)

973.923'092'4 — United States. Politics. Humphrey, Hubert Horatio. *Autobiographies*
Humphrey, Hubert Horatio. The education of a public man : my life and politics / [by] Hubert H. Humphrey ; edited by Norman Sherman. — London : Weidenfeld and Nicolson, 1976. — xiii,513p,[24]p of plates : ill, ports ; 22cm.
Also published: Garden City, N.Y. : Doubleday, 1976. — Index.
ISBN 0-385-05603-6 : £10.00
(B77-08710)

973.924'092'4 — United States. Magruder, Gail. *Autobiographies*
Magruder, Gail. A gift of love / [by] Gail Magruder. — London : Oliphants, 1976. — 160p ; 23cm.
Also published: Philadelphia : A.J. Holman, 1976.
ISBN 0-551-00764-8 : £2.95
(B77-10700)

973.924'092'4 — United States. Nixon, Richard Milhous. Psychology
Abrahamsen, David. Nixon vs Nixon : an emotional tragedy / [by] David Abrahamsen. — New York : Farrar, Straus and Giroux ; [London] ([18 Old Compton St., W1V 6QT]) : Distributed by WHS Distributors, 1977. — xix, 267p : 1 ill, ports ; 22cm.
Index.
ISBN 0-374-22275-4 : £3.50
(B77-22296)

973.926'092'4 — United States. Carter, Jimmy. *Autobiographies*
Carter, Jimmy. Why not the best? / [by] Jimmy Carter. — Presidential ed. — Eastbourne : Kingsway, 1977. — 3-192p,[16]p of plates : ill(some col), ports(some col) ; 23cm.
Originally published: Nashville : Broadman Press, 1975.
ISBN 0-86065-000-6 : £4.50
(B77-30901)

973.926'092'4 — United States. Carter, Jimmy. Religious beliefs
Kucharsky, David. The man from Plains : a portrait of Jimmy Carter / [by] David Kucharsky. — London : Collins, 1977. — [12], 152p ; 21cm.
Originally published: New York : Harper and Row, 1976. — Index.
ISBN 0-00-216507-4 : £2.95
(B77-27621)

Nielsen, Niels Christian. The religion of President Carter / by Niels C. Nielsen. — London [etc.] : Mowbrays, 1977. — 162p ; 22cm.
Originally published: Nashville : Nelson, 1977.
ISBN 0-264-66464-7 Pbk : £2.95
(B77-27622)

973.9'83 — Trinidad and Tobago. Trinidad, 1592-1813
Naipaul, Vidiadhar Surajprasad. The loss of El Dorado : a history / [by] V.S. Naipaul. — [Revised ed.]. — Harmondsworth [etc.] : Penguin, 1977. — 394p : maps ; 19cm.
Revised ed. originally published: 1973. — Index.
Pbk : £0.95
ISBN 0-14-003641-5
(B77-23938)

974 — HISTORY. UNITED STATES. NORTH-EASTERN STATES

974.2'02 — New Hampshire, 1623-1741
Van Deventer, David Earl. The emergence of provincial New Hampshire, 1623-1741 / [by] David E. Van Deventer. — Baltimore ; London : Johns Hopkins University Press, 1976. — xviii,302p : maps ; 24cm.
Bibl.: p.284-291. — Index.
ISBN 0-8018-1730-7 : £10.15
(B77-01106)

974.4'3 — Massachusetts. Southbridge. Social life, 1878-1930. *Illustrations*
A **New** England town in early photographs : 149 illustrations of Southbridge, Massachusetts, 1878-1930 / selected and edited by Edmund V. Gillon, Jr ; introduction and captions by Arthur J. Kavanagh. — New York : Dover Publications [etc.] ; London : Constable, 1976 [i.e. 1977]. — [1],170p : ill, map, ports ; 24cm.
Published in the United States: 1976.
ISBN 0-486-23286-7 Pbk : £4.00
(B77-11510)

974.6'00973'4 — Connecticut. Rural regions. Social life
Morath, Inge. In the country / [photographs by] Inge Morath ; [text by] Arthur Miller. — London : Secker and Warburg, 1977. — 192p : ill(some col), ports ; 26cm. — (A studio book)
Ill. on lining papers. — Also published: New York : Viking Press, 1977.
ISBN 0-436-21778-3 : £7.50
(B77-15052)

Taber, Gladys. The best of Stillmeadow : a treasury of country living / [by] Gladys Taber ; edited and with an introduction by Constance Taber Colby ; drawings by Edward Shenton. — Large print [ed.]. — London : Prior [etc.], 1977. — [5],516p : ill ; 25cm.
This collection originally published: Philadelphia : Lippincott, 1976. — '... passages from ... [the author's] first seven books ...' - jacket.
ISBN 0-86043-053-7 : £5.95
(B77-22297)

974.7'1 — New York (City). Greenwich Village. *Illustrations*
Delaney, Edmund T. Greenwich Village : a photographic guide / by Edmund T. Delaney and Charles Lockwood ; with photographs by George Roos. — New York : Dover Publications [etc.] ; London : Constable, 1976. — [2],xvi,99p : ill, map, ports ; 24cm.
Index.
ISBN 0-486-23114-3 Pbk : £2.25
(B77-03859)

974.7'1'004924 — Jewish immigrants. Social life. *New York (City), 1881-1975*
Howe, Irving. The immigrant Jews of New York, 1881 to the present / [by] Irving Howe with the assistance of Kenneth Libo. — London [etc.] : Routledge and Kegan Paul, 1976. — xx, 714p,[48]p of plates : ill, ports ; 25cm. — (The Littmann library of Jewish civilization)
Originally published: as 'World of our fathers'. New York : Harcourt Brace Jovanovich, 1976. — Bibl.: p.685-693. — Index.
ISBN 0-7100-8333-5 : £8.00
(B77-02710)

974.7'1'004924 — Jews. Social life. *New York (City), ca 1900-1910. Childhood reminiscences*
Ruskay, Sophie. Horsecars and cobblestones / by Sophie Ruskay ; illustrations by Cecil B. Ruskay. — South Brunswick ; New York : Barnes ; London : Yoseloff, 1973. — 240p : ill ; 22cm.
Originally published: New York : Beechhurst Press, 1948.
ISBN 0-498-01301-4 : £2.00
(B77-19949)

974.7'1'02 — New York (City), 1664-1710
Archdeacon, Thomas J. New York City, 1664-1710 : conquest and change / [by] Thomas J. Archdeacon. — Ithaca ; London : Cornell University Press, 1976. — 197p : ill, maps ; 22cm.
Bibl.: p.170-189. — Index.
ISBN 0-8014-0944-6 : £7.85
(B77-05804)

974.7'1'040222 — New York (City). *Illustrations*
Canetti, Nicolai. The pavements of New York / photography Nicolai Canetti ; commentary Sandy Lesberg. — New York ; London : Peebles Press International ; Freemen's Common (Euston St., Freemen's Common, Leics.) : Distributed by WHS Distributors, 1976. — 125p : chiefly ill(some col) ; 31cm.
Ill. on lining paper.
ISBN 0-672-52220-9 : £3.25
(B77-11511)

974.7'1'040222 — New York (City), 1850-1915. *Illustrations*
New York, sunshine and shadow : a photographic record of the city and its people from 1850 to 1915 / [compiled by] Roger Whitehouse. — New York [etc.] ; London : Harper and Row, 1974. — [178],xvi p : ill, plan, ports ; 32cm.
Index.
ISBN 0-06-014616-8 : £11.25
(B77-25336)

974.7'1'040222 — New York (City), 1864-1938. Compared with New York (City), 1974-1975. *Illustrations*
New York then and now : 83 Manhattan sites photographed in the past and in the present / captions by Edward B. Watson ; contemporary photographs by Edmund V. Gillon, Jr. — New York : Dover Publications [etc.] ; London : Constable, 1976. — [3],171p : chiefly ill ; 26cm.
ISBN 0-486-23361-8 Pbk : £3.60
(B77-21646)

974.7'23 — New York (City). Brooklyn. New Lots, to 1887
Landesman, Alter F. A history of New Lots, Brooklyn to 1887 : including the villages of East New York, Cypress Hills and Brownsville / [by] Alter F. Landesman. — Port Washington ; London : Kennikat Press, 1977. — x,258p,[32]p of plates : ill, facsims, maps, plan, ports ; 24cm. — (Empire State historical publications series)
Map on lining papers. — Index.
ISBN 0-8046-9172-x : £7.60
(B77-22298)

974.7'25 — New York (State). Fire Island. Social life, ca 1975. *Personal observations*
Nichols, Jack. Welcome to Fire Island : visions of Cherry Grove and The Pines / [by] Jack Nichols ; photographs by Steve Yates. — New York : St Martin's Press ; London : St James Press, 1976. — [9],148p : ill, maps(on lining papers), ports ; 22cm.
ISBN 0-900997-81-8 : £4.50
(B77-16690)

974.8'004'31 — Pennsylvania Dutch culture, to 1972
Stoudt, John Joseph. Sunbonnets and shoofly pies : a Pennsylvania Dutch cultural history / [by] John Joseph Stoudt. — South Brunswick [etc.] : Barnes ; London : Yoseloff, 1973. — 272p,[12]p of plates : ill(some col), facsims(incl 2 col), maps, music, ports(some col) ; 32cm.
Index.
ISBN 0-498-01124-0 : £9.45
(B77-19950)

974.8'11'030222 — Pennsylvania. Philadelphia, 1839-1914. *Illustrations*
Free Library of Philadelphia. Old Philadelphia in early photographs, 1839-1914 : 215 prints from the collection of the Free Library of Philadelphia / [text by] Robert F. Looney. — New York : Dover Publications [for] the Library [etc.] ; London : Constable, 1976. — x, 228p : chiefly ill, 2 maps ; 30cm.
Index.
ISBN 0-486-23345-6 Pbk : £4.25
(B77-15053)

975 — HISTORY. UNITED STATES. SOUTH-EASTERN STATES
975.3 — Washington, D.C., 1800-1950
Green, Constance McLaughlin. Washington : a history of the capital, 1800-1950 / by Constance McLaughlin Green. — Princeton ; Guildford : Princeton University Press, 1976 [i.e. 1977]. — xix,445,xvii,558p,[48p] of plates : ill, maps, ports ; 24cm.
Originally published: in 2 vols as 'Washington: village and capital, 1800-1878' and 'Washington: capital city, 1879-1950'. Princeton: Princeton University Press, 1962-63. — Bibl. — Index.
ISBN 0-691-00585-0 Pbk : £6.05
(B77-12803)

975.7'71 — South Carolina. Columbia. Burning, 1865
Lucas, Marion Brunson. Sherman and the burning of Columbia / by Marion Brunson Lucas ; foreword by Bell I. Wiley. — College Station ; London ([c/o American University Publishers, 70 Great Russell St., WC1B 3BY]) : Texas A & M University Press, 1976. — 188p, [8]p of plates : 2 ill, maps ; 24cm.
Bibl.: p.175-182. — Index.
ISBN 0-89096-018-6 : £8.25
(B77-26056)

976 — HISTORY. UNITED STATES. SOUTH CENTRAL STATES
976.4'06'0922 — Texas. Smith, Clinton L & Smith, Jefferson D. Capture by Indians of North America, 1869-1874. *Personal observations*
Smith, Clinton L. The boy captives, (Clinton and Jeff Smith) / [as told to] J. Marvin Hunter. — New York ; London : Garland, 1977. — [4], 219p,plate : ports ; 23cm. — (The Garland library of narratives of North American Indian captivities ; vol.110)
Facsimile reprint of: 1st ed. Bandera, Tex. : Frontier times, 1927.
ISBN 0-8240-1734-x : £25.00
(B77-13451)

976.4'06'0924 — Texas. Krueger, Max Amadeus Paulus. *Autobiographies*
Krueger, Max Amadeus Paulus. Second fatherland : the life and fortunes of a German immigrant / by Max Amadeus Paulus Krueger ; edited with an introduction by Marilyn McAdams Sibley. — Revised ed. — College Station ; London ([c/o American University Publishers, 70 Great Russell St., WC1B 3BY]) : Texas A & M University Press, 1976. — xxii,161p,leaf of plate,[8]p of plates : ill, facsim, map, ports ; 24cm. — (Centennial series of the Association of Former Students, Texas A & M University ; no.4)
Previous ed.: published as 'Pioneer life in Texas'. San Antonio : Clegg, 1930. — Index.
ISBN 0-89096-017-8 : £7.50
(B77-23939)

976.9'754 — National parks. *Kentucky. Mammoth Cave National Park. Antiquities. Archaeological investigation*
Archeology of the Mammoth Cave area / edited by Patty Jo Watson. — New York ; London : Academic Press, 1974. — xxi,255p,fold plate : ill, maps ; 24cm. — (Studies in archeology)
Bibl.: p.243-252. — Index.
ISBN 0-12-785927-6 : Unpriced
(B77-20850)

977 — HISTORY. UNITED STATES. NORTH CENTRAL STATES
977.3'994 — Illinois. Carbondale. Social life, 1852-1905
Wright, John W D. A history of early Carbondale, Illinois, 1852-1905 / [by] John W.D. Wright. — Carbondale [etc.] : Southern Illinois University Press for the Jackson County Historical Society ; London [etc.] : Feffer and Simons, 1977. — x,368p : ill, facsims, maps, ports ; 25cm.
Bibl.: p.353-354. — Index.
ISBN 0-8093-0789-8 : £8.80
Also classified at 920'.0773'994
(B77-21647)

978 — HISTORY. UNITED STATES. WESTERN STATES
978 — United States. Western states, ca 1700-1975
Hassrick, Royal Brown. Cowboys and Indians : an illustrated history / [by] Royal B. Hassrick. — [London] : Octopus Books, [1976]. — 352p : ill(some col), facsims, 2 maps(1 col), ports(some col) ; 33cm.
Col. ill. on lining papers. — Bibl.: p.346. — Index.
ISBN 0-7064-0552-8 : £7.95
(B77-07003)

978'.003 — United States. Western states, to ca 1900. *Encyclopaedias*
McLoughlin, Denis. The encyclopedia of the old West / by Denis McLoughlin. — London [etc.] : Routledge and Kegan Paul, 1977. — 570p : ill ; 25cm.
Ill. on lining papers. — Originally published: as 'Wild and woolly'. Garden City, N.Y. : Doubleday, 1975. — Bibl.: p.565-570.
ISBN 0-7100-8628-8 : £8.50
(B77-33550)

978'.004'96073 — Negroes. *United States. Western states, 1830-1890*
Savage, W Sherman. Blacks in the West / [by] W. Sherman Savage. — Westport, Conn. ; London : Greenwood Press, 1976. — xvii,230p ; 22cm. — (Contributions in Afro-American and African studies ; no.23)
Bibl.: p.203-224. — Index.
ISBN 0-8371-8775-3 : £11.95
(B77-18500)

978'.007'2024 — United States. Great Plains. Historiography. Webb, Walter Prescott
Tobin, Gregory M. The making of a history : Walter Prescott Webb and 'The Great Plains' / [by] Gregory M. Tobin. — Austin ; London : University of Texas Press, 1976. — xx,184p : map, port ; 24cm.
Bibl.: p.159-176. — Index.
ISBN 0-292-75029-3 : £8.80
(B77-10701)

978'.02 — Mountain men. *North America. Rocky Mountains, ca 1800-ca 1850*
Blevins, Winfred. Give your heart to the hawks : a tribute to the mountain men / [by] Winfred Blevins. — London : Futura Publications, 1976. — 312p ; 18cm.
Originally published: Los Angeles : Nash, 1973. — Bibl.: p.299-302. — Index.
ISBN 0-86007-728-4 Pbk : £0.85
(B77-14503)

978'.02 — United States. Western states, 1780-1900
Rosa, Joseph George. Gunsmoke : a study of violence in the Wild West / [by] Joseph G. Rosa and Robin May. — London : New English Library, 1977. — 144p,[8]p of plates : ill(some col), facsims, ports ; 26cm.
Bibl.: p.141-142. — Index.
ISBN 0-450-03074-1 : Unpriced
(B77-26057)

978'.02 — United States. Western states. Social life, ca 1800-ca 1900. *Secondary school texts*
People of the West / [compiled by] John Foster and Rod Hunt. — Basingstoke [etc.] : Macmillan, 1977. — [1],32p : ill, facsim, map, ports ; 20x21cm. — (Investigations)
Bibl.
ISBN 0-333-19830-1 Sd : £0.55
(B77-29860)

978'.03 — United States. Western states, 1900-1976
Gressley, Gene M. The twentieth-century American West : a potpourri / [by] Gene M. Gressley. — Columbia ; London : University of Missouri Press, 1977. — xix,196p : ill, ports ; 21cm.
Index.
ISBN 0-8262-0218-7 : £9.00
(B77-33003)

978.2'02'0924 — Nebraska. Social life, 1857-1866. *Diaries*
Sanford, Mollie Dorsey. Mollie : the journal of Mollie Dorsey Sanford in Nebraska and Colorado Territories, 1857-1866 / with an introduction and notes by Donald F. Danker. — Lincoln [Neb.] ; London : University of Nebraska Press, 1976. — xii,199p ; 21cm.
'A Bison book'. — Originally published: Lincoln, Neb. : University of Nebraska Press, 1959.
ISBN 0-8032-5826-7 Pbk : £2.40
Also classified at 978.8'02'0924
(B77-08711)

978.8'02'0924 — Colorado. Social life, 1857-1866. *Diaries*
Sanford, Mollie Dorsey. Mollie : the journal of Mollie Dorsey Sanford in Nebraska and Colorado Territories, 1857-1866 / with an introduction and notes by Donald F. Danker. — Lincoln [Neb.] ; London : University of Nebraska Press, 1976. — xii,199p ; 21cm.
'A Bison book'. — Originally published: Lincoln, Neb. : University of Nebraska Press, 1959.
ISBN 0-8032-5826-7 Pbk : £2.40
Primary classification 978.2'02'0924
(B77-08711)

978.8'03 — Cowboys. Social life. *Colorado, 1930-1940. Personal observations*
Lavender, David. One man's West / by David Lavender ; line drawings by William Arthur Smith. — [3rd ed.]. — Lincoln [Neb.] ; London : University of Nebraska Press, 1977. — [4],316p : ill ; 21cm.
This ed. originally published: Garden City, N.Y. : Doubleday, 1965.
ISBN 0-8032-0908-8 : £10.00
ISBN 0-8032-5855-0 Pbk : £3.00
(B77-26058)

979 — HISTORY. UNITED STATES. PACIFIC COAST STATES
979 — South-western United States, to 1975
White, Jon Manchip. The great American desert : the life, history and landscape of the American southwest / [by] Jon Manchip White. — London : Allen and Unwin, 1977. — [15], 320p : ill, maps, ports ; 24cm.
Originally published: as 'A world elsewhere : one man's fascination with the American southwest'. New York : Crowell, 1975. — Index.
ISBN 0-04-917007-4 : £6.50
(B77-10702)

979'.004'97 — Apaches & Navaho. *South-western United States*
Dutton, Bertha Pauline. Navahos and Apaches : the Athabascan peoples / [by] Bertha P. Dutton. — Englewood Cliffs ; London [etc.] : Prentice-Hall, [1977]. — xiv,97p : ill, map ; 24cm.
'A Spectrum book'. — Published in the United States: 1976. — 'This book and its two companion volumes ... were originally published in one hardcover edition as "Indians of the American Southwest" (Prentice-Hall, 1975)' -p.vi. — Bibl.: p.84-97.
ISBN 0-13-610832-6 Pbk : £2.65
(B77-12804)

979'.004'97 — Civilization of Indians of North America. *North America. Pacific coastal regions*
Brown, Vinson. Peoples of the sea wind : the native Americans of the Pacific coast / [by] Vinson Brown. — New York : Collier Books ; London : Collier Macmillan, 1977. — xxi, 259p : ill, maps ; 26cm.
Bibl.: p.252-255. — Index.
ISBN 0-02-517300-6 : £10.50
ISBN 0-02-030700-4 Pbk : £6.00
(B77-30902)

979'.004'97 — Pueblo Indians. *South-western United States*
Dutton, Bertha Pauline. The Pueblos / [by] Bertha P. Dutton. — Englewood Cliffs ; London [etc.] : Prentice-Hall, [1977]. — xvii, 92p : ill, maps ; 24cm.
'A Spectrum book'. — Published in the United States: 1976. — 'This book and its two companion volumes ... were originally published in one hardcover edition as "Indians of the American Southwest" (Prentice-Hall, 1975)' - p.vi. — Bibl.: p.79-92.
ISBN 0-13-740159-0 Pbk : £2.65
(B77-13452)

979'.004'97 — Ranchería, Ute & Southern Paiute Indians. *South-western United States*
Dutton, Bertha Pauline. The Ranchería, Ute, and Southern Paiute peoples / [by] Bertha P. Dutton. — Englewood Cliffs ; London [etc.] : Prentice-Hall, [1977]. — xix,124p : ill, maps ; 24cm.
'A Spectrum book'. — Published in the United States: 1976. — 'This book and its two companion volumes ... were originally published in one hardcover edition as "Indians of the American Southwest" (Prentice-Hall, 1975)' - p.vi. — Bibl.: p.111-124.
ISBN 0-13-752923-6 Pbk : £3.20
(B77-13453)

979.1'35 — Prehistoric societies. Social change. Archaeological investigations. *Study regions: Arizona. Hay Hollow Valley*
Plog, Fred T. The study of prehistoric change / [by] Fred T. Plog. — New York ; London : Academic Press, 1974. — xii,199p : ill, maps ; 24cm. — (Studies in archaeology)
Bibl.: p.184-193. — Index.
ISBN 0-12-785645-5 : Unpriced
(B77-19951)

979.3'004'96073 — Negroes. *Nevada, 1860-ca 1900*
Rusco, Elmer Ritter. 'Good time coming?' : black Nevadans in the nineteenth century / [by] Elmer R. Rusco ; foreword by Kenneth W. Porter. — Westport, Conn. ; London : Greenwood Press, 1975. — xix,230,[1]p : ill, ports ; 22cm. — (Contributions in Afro-American and African studies ; no.15)
Bibl.: p.217-226. — Index.
ISBN 0-8371-8286-7 : Unpriced
(B77-03309)

979.4'004'97 — Indians of North America. *California*
Kroeber, Alfred Louis. Handbook of the Indians of California / [by] A.L. Kroeber. — New York : Dover Publications ; London : Constable, 1976. — [1],xviii,995p,[78]p of plates,[9]leaves of plates : ill, geneal table, maps, plans ; 22cm.
Col. maps on inside covers. — Facsimile reprint of: 1st ed. Washington, D.C. : Government Printing Office, 1925. — Bibl.: p.943-966. — Index.
ISBN 0-486-23368-5 Pbk : £7.10
(B77-27623)

979.4'04'0924 — California. Social life, 1849-ca 1855. *Personal observations*
Royce, Sarah. A frontier lady : recollections of the Gold Rush and early California / by Sarah Royce ; with a foreword by Katharine Royce ; edited by Ralph Henry Gabriel. — Lincoln, [Neb.] ; London : University of Nebraska Press, 1977. — xv,144p,plate : map ; 21cm.
Facsimile reprint of: 1st ed. New Haven : Yale University Press, 1932.
ISBN 0-8032-0909-6 : £6.75
ISBN 0-8032-5856-9 Pbk : £1.80
Also classified at 917.3'04'610924
(B77-28321)

979.4'05'0924 — Chinese immigrants. Social life. *California, ca 1940-ca 1955. Childhood reminiscences*
Kingston, Maxine Hong. The woman warrior : memoirs of a girlhood among ghosts / [by] Maxine Hong Kingston. — London : Allen Lane, 1977. — [7],209p ; 23cm.
Originally published: New York : Knopf, 1976.
ISBN 0-7139-1062-3 : £3.95
(B77-34347)

979.4'94'008 — California. Los Angeles, to 1975. *Readings*
Los Angeles : biography of a city / [compiled by] John & Laree Caughey. — Berkeley [etc.] ; London : University of California Press, [1977]. — xiv,509p : ill ; 24cm.
Published in the United States: 1976. — Bibl.: p.495-499. — Index.
ISBN 0-520-03079-6 : £11.95
(B77-13454)

979.7'94 — Washington (State). Olympic Peninsula, to 1954
Morgan, Murray. The last wilderness / by Murray Morgan. — Seattle ; London : University of Washington Press, 1976. — xi, 275p ; 21cm. — (Washington paperbacks ; 81)
Originally published: New York : Viking Press, 1955. — Index.
ISBN 0-295-95319-5 Pbk : £4.00
(B77-06403)

980 — HISTORY. SOUTH AMERICA
980 — Latin America, ca 1300-1977
Burns, Edward Bradford. Latin America : a concise interpretive history / [by] E. Bradford Burns. — 2nd ed. — Englewood Cliffs ; London [etc.] : Prentice-Hall, 1977. — xii, 307p : ill, maps, port ; 23cm.
Previous ed.: Englewood Cliffs : Hemel Hempstead : Prentice-Hall, 1972. — Bibl.: p.281-292. — Index.
ISBN 0-13-524314-9 Pbk : £6.35
(B77-16137)

980 — Latin America, to 1976
Fagg, John Edwin. Latin America : a general history / [by] John Edwin Fagg. — 3rd ed. — New York : Macmillan ; London : Collier Macmillan, 1977. — xiii,850p : maps ; 24cm.
Previous ed.: 1969. — Bibl.: p.808-832. — Index.
ISBN 0-02-334770-8 : £11.25
(B77-31646)

980'.003 — Latin America. *Encyclopaedias*
Encyclopedia of Latin America / edited by Helen Delpar. — New York ; London [etc.] : McGraw-Hill, [1976]. — xi,651p : ill, maps, ports ; 29cm.
Published in the United States: 1974. — Bibl.: p.649-651.
ISBN 0-07-016263-8 : £26.50
(B77-02711)

980'.004'98 — Inca culture. Effects of colonisation by Spain. *Peru, 1530-1580*
Wachtel, Nathan. The vision of the vanquished : the Spanish conquest of Peru through Indian eyes, 1530-1570 / [by] Nathan Wachtel ; translated [from the French] by Ben and Siân Reynolds. — Hassocks : Harvester Press, 1977. — vii,328p,[24]p of plates : ill, maps ; 22cm.
Translation of: 'La vision des vaincus : les Indiens du Pérou devant la conquête espagnol, 1530-1570'. Paris : Gallimard, 1971. — Bibl.: p.273-290. — Index.
ISBN 0-85527-119-1 : £10.50
(B77-20851)

980'.01 — Latin America. Spanish colonies, 1492-1806
Parry, John Horace. The Spanish seaborne empire / [by] J.H. Parry. — London : Hutchinson, 1977. — 416p,xvi p of plates : ill, chart, facsim, maps ; 24cm. — (The history of human society)
Originally published: 1966. — Bibl.: p.382-399. — Index.
ISBN 0-09-131061-x Pbk : £3.95
(B77-29105)

980'.01 — North-eastern South America. Spanish exploration, 1498-1505
Vigneras, Louis André. The discovery of South America and the Andalusian voyages / [by] Louis-André Vigneras. — Chicago ; London : University of Chicago Press for the Newberry Library, 1976. — ix,170p,11p of plates : maps ; 23cm. — (Studies in the history of discoveries)
Bibl.: p.157-160. — Index.
ISBN 0-226-85609-7 : £7.50
(B77-02666)

980'.02'0924 — South America. Bolívar, Simón. *Biographies*
Salcedo-Bastardo, José Luis. Bolivar : a continent and its destiny / by J.L. Salcedo-Bastardo ; edited and translated [from the Spanish] by Annella McDermott. — Richmond, Surrey : Richmond Publishing Co., 1977. — xv,191p,[2]p of plates,[6]leaves of plates : 1 ill, maps, ports ; 23cm.
Translation of: 'Bolívar'. Caracas : Academia Nacional de la Historia, 1972. — Bibl.: p.181-185. — Index.
ISBN 0-85546-199-3 : £6.25
(B77-24639)

980'.03 — Latin America. Political events. Foreign relations between Soviet Union & United States, 1945-1975
Kaufman, Edy. The superpowers and their spheres of influence / [by] Edy Kaufman. — London : Croom Helm, 1976. — 208p : ill ; 23cm.
Index.
ISBN 0-85664-389-0 : £7.95
Also classified at 947; 327.73'047; 327.47'073
(B77-07754)

980'.03 — Spanish America. Revolutions. Policies of United States government, 1910-1975
Blasier, Cole. The hovering giant : US responses to revolutionary change in Latin America / [by] Cole Blasier. — [Pittsburgh] : University of Pittsburgh Press ; London : Feffer and Simons : [Distributed by Transatlantic Book Service], 1976. — xix,315p,[16]p of plates : ill, ports ; 25cm. — (Pitt Latin American series)
Index.
ISBN 0-8229-3304-7 : £11.96
ISBN 0-8229-5264-5 Pbk : Unpriced
Primary classification 327.73'08
(B77-07109)

981 — HISTORY. BRAZIL
981'.004'98 — Indians of South America. Social life. *Brazil, 1934-1954. Personal observations*
Lévi-Strauss, Claude. Tristes tropiques / [by] Claude Lévi-Strauss ; translated [from the French] by John and Doreen Weightman. — Harmondsworth [etc.] : Penguin, 1976. — 544p : ill ; 19cm.
This translation originally published: London : Cape, 1973. — Translation of: 'Tristes tropiques'. Paris : Librairie Plon, 1955.
ISBN 0-14-004393-4 Pbk : £1.50
(B77-00558)

981'.06 — Brazil. Social life
Perry, Ritchie. Brazil, the land and its people / [by] Ritchie Perry. — London : Macdonald Educational, 1977. — 4-62p : ill(chiefly col), col maps, ports ; 29cm. — (Macdonald countries)
Col. ill., col. map on lining papers. — Index.
ISBN 0-356-05456-x : £2.25
(B77-28322)

982 — HISTORY. ARGENTINA

982 — Argentina. Political events, 1810-1973

Whitaker, Arthur Preston. The United States and the Southern Cone : Argentina, Chile and Uruguay / [by] Arthur P. Whitaker. — Cambridge, Mass. ; London : Harvard University Press, 1976 [i.e. 1977]. — xv,464p : maps(some col) ; 24cm. — (The American foreign policy library)
Col. maps on lining papers. — Published in the United States: 1976. — Bibl.: p.435-452. — Index.
ISBN 0-674-92841-5 : £14.95
Also classified at 983; 989.5
(B77-12805)

982′.2 — Argentina. Santa Fe (Province). Rebellions, 1893

Gallo, Ezequiel. Farmers in revolt : the revolutions of 1893 in the province of Santa Fe, Argentina / by Ezequiel Gallo. — London : Athlone Press for the University of London Institute of Latin American Studies, 1976. — [9],97p : map ; 23cm. — (University of London. Institute of Latin American Studies. Monographs ; 7)
Bibl.: p.91-93. — Index.
ISBN 0-485-17707-2 : £4.00
(B77-05805)

982′.7 — Welsh immigrants. Social life. *Argentina. Chubut, 1865-1905*

Owen, Geraint Dyfnallt. Crisis in Chubut : a chapter in the history of the Welsh colony in Patagonia / [by] Geraint Dyfnallt Owen. — Swansea : C. Davies, 1977. — [2],161p ; 22cm.
Bibl.: p.151-152. — Index.
ISBN 0-7154-0127-0 : £3.25
(B77-12806)

982′.7′0049166 — Welsh communities. *Argentina. Patagonia, to 1972. Welsh texts*

Davies, Gareth Alban. Tan tro nesaf : darlun o wladfa Gymreig Patagonia / gan Gareth Alban Davies ; lluniau gan Kyffin Williams. — Llandysul : Gwasg Gomer, 1976. — 2-157p : ill(incl 1 col on lining papers), 2 col maps, ports ; 22cm.
ISBN 0-85088-392-x : £2.75
(B77-10703)

983 — HISTORY. CHILE

983 — Chile. Political events, 1810-1973

Whitaker, Arthur Preston. The United States and the Southern Cone : Argentina, Chile and Uruguay / [by] Arthur P. Whitaker. — Cambridge, Mass. ; London : Harvard University Press, 1976 [i.e. 1977]. — xv,464p : maps(some col) ; 24cm. — (The American foreign policy library)
Col. maps on lining papers. — Published in the United States: 1976. — Bibl.: p.435-452. — Index.
ISBN 0-674-92841-5 : £14.95
Primary classification 982
(B77-12805)

983′.064 — Chile. Political events, 1970-1973

Roxborough, Ian. Chile : the state and revolution / [by] Ian Roxborough, Philip O'Brien, Jackie Roddick ; assisted by Michael Gonzalez. — London [etc.] : Macmillan, 1977. — x,304p ; 21cm.
Bibl.: p.293-300. — Index.
ISBN 0-333-19136-6 : £7.95
ISBN 0-333-19508-6 Pbk : £3.95
(B77-07004)

983′.064′0922 — Chile. Political events, 1970-1973. *Socialist viewpoints. Personal observations. Collections*

Henfrey, Colin. Chilean voices. — Hassocks : Harvester Press, 1977. — 1v.
Previous control number ISBN 0-85527-869-2.
ISBN 0-85527-879-x : CIP entry
ISBN 0-85527-879-x Pbk
(B77-07755)

985 — HISTORY. PERU

985 — Peru, to 1533

Bankes, George. Peru before Pizarro / [by] George Bankes. — Oxford : Phaidon, 1977. — 208p : ill(some col), facsims, map, plans, port ; 24cm.
Bibl.: p.200. — Index.
ISBN 0-7148-1784-8 : Unpriced
ISBN 0-7148-1785-6 Pbk : £4.95
(B77-29106)

985′.02′0924 — Peru. Conquest. Pizarro, Francisco. *Biographies. Juvenile literature*

Salentiny, Ferdinand. Pizarro : conqueror of Peru / by Ferdinand Salentiny ; illustrated by Louis Joos. — Edinburgh : W. and R. Chambers, 1977. — [28]p : col ill, map, col ports ; 19x20cm. — (History makers)
ISBN 0-550-31932-8 : £1.40
(B77-33004)

989.2 — HISTORY. PARAGUAY

989.2′05′0924 — Paraguay. López, Francisco Solano. Interpersonal relationships with Lynch, Eliza Alicia

Brodsky, Alyn. Madame Lynch & friend : the true account of an Irish adventuress and the dictator of Paraguay who destroyed that American nation / [by] Alyn Brodsky. — London : Cassell, 1976. — xxi,312p ; 22cm.
Originally published: New York : Harper and Row, 1975. — Bibl.: p.297-301. — Index.
ISBN 0-304-29765-8 : £4.50
Also classified at 941.5081′092′4
(B77-10704)

989.5 — HISTORY. URUGUAY

989.5 — Uruguay. Political events, 1810-1973

Whitaker, Arthur Preston. The United States and the Southern Cone : Argentina, Chile and Uruguay / [by] Arthur P. Whitaker. — Cambridge, Mass. ; London : Harvard University Press, 1976 [i.e. 1977]. — xv,464p : maps(some col) ; 24cm. — (The American foreign policy library)
Col. maps on lining papers. — Published in the United States: 1976. — Bibl.: p.435-452. — Index.
ISBN 0-674-92841-5 : £14.95
Primary classification 982
(B77-12805)

990 — HISTORY. OCEANIA, ATLANTIC OCEAN ISLANDS, POLAR REGIONS ETC

990 — Far East & Pacific islands. Role of Germany, 1870-1914

Germany in the Pacific and Far East, 1870-1914 / edited by John A. Moses, Paul M. Kennedy. — St Lucia, Queensland : University of Queensland Press ; Hemel Hempstead : Distributed by Prentice-Hall, 1977. — xx,417p : maps ; 23cm.
Bibl.: p.384-412. — Index.
ISBN 0-7022-1330-6 : £12.50
(B77-34348)

990 — Prehistoric civilisation. *South-western Pacific region. Conference proceedings*

Sunda and Sahul : prehistoric studies in Southeast Asia, Melanesia and Australia / edited by J. Allen, J. Golson, R. Jones. — London [etc.] : Academic Press, 1977. — xii, 647p : ill, maps ; 24cm.
'[Papers presented at] ... a symposium in the Social Sciences Section of the 13th Pacific Science Congress ... held in Vancouver, Canada in August 1975' - Preface. — Bibl. — Index.
ISBN 0-12-051250-5 : £12.50
(B77-30903)

993 — HISTORY. MELANESIA, NEW ZEALAND

993.102 — New Zealand. Social life, 1837-1901

Wood, June A. Victorian New Zealanders : an elegant family album descriptive of the lives and fortunes of New Zealanders who lived during the glorious reign of our late beloved Queen-Empress Victoria ... / by June A. Wood. — Wellington [N.Z.] [etc.] ; London : A.H. and A.W. Reed, 1974 [i.e. 1976]. — 80p : ill, facsims, ports ; 28cm.
Published in New Zealand: 1974.
ISBN 0-589-00844-7 Pbk : £2.55
(B77-05159)

993.102′3′0924 — New Zealand. Atkinson, Sir Harry. *Biographies*

Bassett, Judith. Sir Harry Atkinson, 1831-1892 / [by] Judith Bassett. — [Auckland] : Auckland University Press ; [London] : Oxford University Press, 1975. — xii,196p,[8]p of plates : ill, geneal tables, ports ; 23cm.
Bibl.: p.188-191. — Index.
ISBN 0-19-647934-7 : £8.75
(B77-01107)

993.103′092′4 — New Zealand. Politics. Nash, Sir Walter. *Biographies*

Sinclair, Keith. Walter Nash / [by] Keith Sinclair. — [Auckland] : Auckland University Press ; [London] : Oxford University Press, 1976. — xi,439p,[12]p of plates : ill, ports ; 26cm.
Bibl.: p.414-421. — Index.
ISBN 0-19-647949-5 : £12.50
(B77-14005)

993.103′092′4 — New Zealand. Social life, 1930-1935. *Personal observations*

Findlay, Mary. Tooth and nail : the story of a daughter of the Depression / [by] Mary Findlay. — Wellington [N.Z.] [etc.] ; London : A.H. and A.W. Reed, 1974. — [7],267p ; 23cm.
ISBN 0-589-00877-3 : £2.15
(B77-19952)

993.1′1 — New Zealand. Campbell Island, to 1975

Kerr, Ian S. Campbell Island : a history / [by] Ian S. Kerr. — Wellington [N.Z.] [etc.] ; London : A.H. and A.W. Reed, 1976. — xii, 182p,[16]p of plates : ill, facsims, maps, ports ; 23cm.
Two col. maps on lining papers. — Bibl.: p.169-173. — Index.
ISBN 0-589-00959-1 : £6.05
(B77-18501)

993.12′2 — New Zealand. Northland, to ca 1900

Reed, *Sir* Alfred Hamish. The story of Northland / by A.H. Reed. — Wellington [N.Z.] [etc.] ; London : A.H. and A.W. Reed, 1975 [i.e. 1976]. — 395p,[24]p of plates : ill, maps, plan, ports ; 22cm.
Map on lining papers. — Published in New Zealand: 1975. — Originally published: Wellington, N.Z. : A.H. and A.W. Reed, 1956. — Bibl.: p.375-6. — Index.
ISBN 0-589-00909-5 : £5.65
(B77-01108)

993.12′2 — New Zealand. Taupo region. *Illustrations*

Raymond, Val. Taupo / [by] Val Raymond. — Auckland ; London [etc.] : Hodder and Stoughton, 1976. — 59p : chiefly ill(some col) ; 22x29cm.
Ill. on lining papers.
ISBN 0-340-21453-8 : £6.95
(B77-33551)

993.12′7 — New Zealand. Palmerston North, to 1973

Petersen, George Conrad. Palmerston North : a centennial history / by George Conrad Petersen ; with an introduction on landforms in the Manawatu by Norman Whatman. — Wellington [N.Z.] ; London [etc.] : Reed [for the City Corporation of Palmerston North], 1973. — viii,254p,[48]p of plates : ill, coat of arms, facsims, maps, plan, ports ; 25cm.
Facsim. on lining papers. — Bibl.: p.244-245. — Index.
ISBN 0-589-00793-9 : £6.50
(B77-18502)

993.12′7 — New Zealand. Wellington, ca 1800-ca 1900. Compared with Wellington, 1974. *For New Zealand students. Middle school texts*

Barrington, Rosemary. The changing city, Wellington / by Rosemary Barrington. — Wellington [N.Z.] ; London [etc.] : Reed Education, 1975. — [1],24,[2]p : ill ; 25cm. — (People on earth)
Originally published: 1974.
ISBN 0-589-05001-x Sd : £1.05
(B77-20852)

993.12′7 — New Zealand. Wellington, to 1974

McIntyre, Peter. Peter McIntyre's Wellington. — Wellington [N.Z.] [etc.] ; London : A.H. and A.W. Reed, 1975. — [76]p : chiefly ill(some col), ports ; 28cm.
Col. ill. tipped in. — Ill. on lining papers.
ISBN 0-589-00936-2 : £12.60
Also classified at 759.9931; 741.9′931
(B77-01956)

993.15′4 — New Zealand. Jacksons Bay, to 1975

Roxburgh, Irvine. Jacksons Bay : a centennial history / [by] Irvine Roxburgh. — Wellington [N.Z.] [etc.] ; London : A.H. and A.W. Reed, 1976. — [9],198p,[16]p of plates : ill, maps(on lining papers), ports ; 23cm.
Bibl.: p.189-190. — Index.
ISBN 0-589-00919-2 : Unpriced
(B77-21648)

993.15′5′0220924 — New Zealand. Canterbury. Courage, Sarah Amelia, 1864-1890. *Autobiographies*

Courage, Sarah Amelia. Lights and shadows of colonial life : twenty-six years in Canterbury, New Zealand / by Sarah Amelia Courage. — 2nd annotated ed. — Christchurch, N.Z. [etc.] ; London : Whitcoulls, 1976. — 250p,[8]p of plates : ill, facsims, ports ; 22cm.
Previous ed.: Christchurch, N.Z. : Whitcombe and Tombs, 1896?.
ISBN 0-7233-0464-5 : Unpriced
(B77-10705)

993.15′7 — New Zealand. Cromwell region, to 1950

Parcell, James Crombie. Heart of the desert : a history of the Cromwell and Bannockburn Districts of Central Otago / [by] James Crombie Parcell. — Christchurch, N.Z. [etc.] ; London : Whitcoulls, 1976. — [10],370p,leaf of plate,xxviii p of plates : ill, facsim, maps, ports ; 22cm.
Originally published: Christchurch, N.Z. : Whitcombe and Tombs, 1951. — Index.
ISBN 0-7233-0465-3 : £7.30
(B77-22300)

994 — HISTORY. AUSTRALIA
994 — Australia, to 1973
Lacour-Gayet, Robert. A concise history of Australia / [by] Robert Lacour-Gayet ; translated [from the French] by James Grieve. — Harmondsworth [etc.] : Penguin, 1976. — xii,484p ; 19cm. — (Pelican books)
Translation of: 'Histoire de l'Australie'. Paris : Fayard, 1973. — Bibl.: p.435-459. — Index.
ISBN 0-14-021995-1 Pbk : £2.00
(B77-29107)

994.04'092'2 — Australia. Prime ministers, 1901-1972
Hughes, Colin Anfield. Mr Prime Minister : Australian prime ministers, 1901-1972 / [by] Colin A. Hughes. — Melbourne ; London [etc.] : Oxford University Press, 1976 [i.e. 1977]. — [7],208p : ports ; 22cm.
Published in Australia: 1976. — Index.
ISBN 0-19-550471-2 Pbk : £3.50
(B77-12253)

994.04'092'4 — Australia. Shaw, Sydney. *Autobiographies*
Shaw, Sydney. Over the fence / [by] Sydney Shaw. — Ilfracombe : Stockwell, 1977. — 161p ; 19cm.
ISBN 0-7223-0975-9 : £2.50
(B77-23940)

994.05 — Australia. Political events, 1939-1975
Griffiths, Tony. Contemporary Australia / [by] Tony Griffiths. — London : Croom Helm, 1977. — 165p ; 23cm.
Bibl.: p.153-155. — Index.
ISBN 0-85664-427-7 : £6.95
(B77-14504)

994.06 — Australia. *Juvenile literature*
Henderson, William Frederick. Looking at Australia / [by] W.F. & R.A. Henderson. — London : A. and C. Black [etc.], 1977. — 64p : ill(some col), col map ; 24cm. — (Looking at other countries)
Index.
ISBN 0-7136-1705-5 : £1.75
(B77-05806)

994.06 — Australia. Social life
Cornelia, Elizabeth. Australia : the land and its people / [by] Elizabeth Cornelia. — London : Macdonald Educational, 1977. — 4-61p : ill(chiefly col), facsims(some col), col maps, ports(some col) ; 29cm. — (Macdonald countries)
Col. ill., col. maps on lining papers. — Index.
ISBN 0-356-05455-1 : £2.25
(B77-27624)

994.3 — Queensland. Great Barrier Reef, to 1970
Holthouse, Hector. Ships in the coral / [by] Hector Holthouse. — Melbourne ; London [etc.] : Macmillan, 1976. — vi,146p,[8]p of plates : ill(some col), facsim, maps, ports ; 27cm.
Maps on lining papers. — Bibl.: p.142-143. — Index.
ISBN 0-333-21053-0 : £5.95
(B77-07756)

994.5'03'10924 — Australia. Victoria. Rural regions. Social life, 1869-1894. *Diaries*
Jenkins, Joseph, *b.1818.* Diary of a Welsh swagman, 1869-1894 / [by Joseph Jenkins] ; abridged and notated by William Evans. — South Melbourne [etc.] : Macmillan Co. of Australia ; London [etc.] : Macmillan, 1975. — xix,217p,plate : ill, facsims, map(on lining papers) ; 25cm.
'The line drawings appearing in this book are taken from "The picturesque atlas of Australia" ... published in 1886 by Picturesque Atlas Publishing Company, Limited, (U.K.)' - title page verso. — Ill. on lining papers.
ISBN 0-333-17555-7 : £5.50
(B77-01957)

996 — HISTORY. POLYNESIA
996'.8 — Banabans. Social life. *Ocean Island, to 1977*
Binder, Pearl. Treasure islands : the trials of the Ocean Islanders / [by] Pearl Binder. — London : Blond and Briggs, 1977. — 192p,[8]p of plates : ill, maps, ports ; 23cm.
Bibl.: p.192.
ISBN 0-85634-071-5 : £5.95
(B77-30904)

996.9'04 — Hawaii. Social life. *Primary school texts. Irish texts*
Bas, Daniel. Téanaí, an cailín Haváíoch / [le] Daniel Bas ; [Eibhlín Ní Mhuircheartaigh a d'aistrigh do leanaí 7-10 mbliana d'aois]. — Baile Atha Cliath [i.e. Dublin] ([Baile Atha Cliath 4]) : Oifig an tSoláthair, 1976. — [15]p : chiefly col ill, col map ; 27cm. — (Sraith tíortha agus nósanna)
Ill. on lining papers. — Originally published: in Spanish. Barcelona : Betis, 1973.
ISBN 0-905621-14-x : £0.48
(B77-07005)

998 — HISTORY. POLAR REGIONS
998 — Arctic & Antarctic. *Juvenile literature*
Connell, Stephanie. Lands of ice and snow / written by Stephanie Connell and Vivienne Driscoll. — London : Macdonald Educational, 1977. — [1],32p : col ill, col map ; 18cm. — (Readabout)
Adaptation of: 'Cold lands'. London : Macdonald and Co., 1970. — Index.
ISBN 0-356-05543-4 Sd : £0.35
(B77-13455)

998 — Polar regions. *Juvenile literature*
Armstrong, Patrick Hamilton. Polar regions / by P.H. Armstrong ; with illustrations by Gerald Witcomb. — Loughborough : Ladybird Books, 1977. — 52p : col ill, col maps, col ports ; 18cm. — (Ladybird leaders)
Text, col. ill. on lining papers. — Bibl.: p.[53]. — Index.
ISBN 0-7214-0476-6 : £0.24
(B77-26725)

998'.9 — Antarctic. Exploration. Scott, Robert Falcon. *Biographies*
Huxley, Elspeth. Scott of the Antarctic / [by] Elspeth Huxley. — London : Weidenfeld and Nicolson, 1977. — xiv,303p,[16]p of plates : ill, facsim, maps, ports ; 25cm.
Bibl.: p.289-290. — Index.
ISBN 0-297-77433-6 : £6.95
(B77-32345)